KYOHAKSA'S
Hyŏndae
KOREAN – ENGLISH DICTIONARY

교 학 사
현대한영사전

감수 : 연세대학교 명예교수
문학박사 조 성 규

KYOHAKSA

머 리 말

독해 중심의 수동적 영어 학습 활동을 흔히 수신형(受信型)이라 하고, 쓰고 말하는 발표력 중심의 능동적 학습 활동을 발신형(發信型)이라고 한다. 이런 관점에서 우리의 영어 교육은 수신형에 치우쳐 온 것이 사실이다. 그 결과 학습자는 발표력, 표현력이 독해력에 뒤지게 되었다. 그래서 영어를 읽고 듣기보다는 영어를 쓰고 말하기를 더 어려워하는 것이 현실이다.

독해력과 발표력이 고르게 균형을 이루지 못한 영어로써는 의사소통을 제대로 할 수가 없다. 양자 사이의 불균형을 바로잡는 길은 학습자가 발표력 훈련을 따로 쌓는 길 밖에 없다. 여기에 필수적으로 요구되는 것이 좋은 〈한영사전〉이다.

즉, 지금 우리에게 필요한 것은 뒤처진 영어 표현력이 독해력을 따라잡을 수 있도록 적극적으로 학습자를 이끌어 줄 수 있는 산 교재로서의 〈한영사전〉이다.

「현대한영사전」은 이러한 사명을 의식하고 편찬했다. 이러한 목표에 접근하기 위해서 우리는 특히 다음과 같은 점에 중점을 두었다.

1. **현대 생활에 필요한 10만 여어를 표제어로** 21세기에 대비할 풍부한 어휘와 참신한 표현을 고루 담았다. 세계 인명, 지명도 본문 표제어로 삼았고 예스러운 우리말도 가려 넣었다.
2. **활자를 크게** 인쇄 판면을 최대로 활용하여 활자를 키워서 가독성을 높였다.
3. **찾기 쉽고 보기 편리하게** 원하는 정보를 쉽게 찾아볼 수 있도록 요소별로 묶어 별행처리하여 입체적 편집을 꾀하였다. 이것이 친근감을 주어 자주 손이 가는 사전이 되어줄 것이다.
   ① 표제어의 풀이, 구(句)용례, 문장 예문, 뜻번호, ─○○하다, 복합어 등의 요소별로 구분하여 찾아 보기 쉽게 했다.
   ② 특히 문장 예문(full sentence)은 대부분 별행처리하여 찾기 쉽고 보기에 편리하게 했다.
4. **구어 중심의 참신한 역어(譯語)와 회화문을 많이** 역어는 대부분 일상 구어에서 많이 쓰는 참신한 영어 표현을 선택했다. 회화문 용례를 많이 넣어 곧바로 활용할 수 있게 했다.
5. **완전한 문장 예문을 더 많이** 구(句)로 된 용례보다 완전한 문장

으로 된 예문을 더 많이 수록하여 표현 사전의 기능을 높여서 이용에 도움이 되게 했다.

6. 표현사전다운 다양하고 구체적인 해설 작문에 도움이 되는 해설을 다양하고 폭넓게 넣었다. ① 유의어 해설 ② 테마 중심의 해설 ③ 2개 이상의 역어가 있을 때 선택 사용을 가능하기 위한 역어의 우리말 정의 ④ 본문 중간중간의 어법·용법·비교 해설

7. 2색도 인쇄에 많은 삽화 ① 본문의 각종 기호와 삽화의 일부를 색처리했다. ② 표제어의 이해를 돕기 위해 세밀한 학습적 삽화를 많이 실었다.

8. 충실한 기본어의 기술 일상 생활에서 가장 많이 쓰는 중요 기본어에는 많은 지면을 할애했다.

9. 우리말 속담을 표제어로 일상 생활에서 흔히 쓰는 주요한 우리말 속담을 대폭 표제어로 삼았다.

10. 알찬 부록 영어 표현 활동에 필수적인 학습·실무의 정보들을 알차게 수록했다.

이 「현대한영사전」은 정평이 나 있는 「현대영한사전」의 자매편이다. 이 사전이 21세기에 국내와 국제 사회에서 주역이 될 여러분의 영어 의사소통과 발표력 훈련에 조금이나마 도움이 되었으면 한다.

지난 5년 동안, 좋은 사전을 만들기 위하여 애쓰신 전문 집필진 여러분과 편집·생산 부서의 여러분께 깊은 사의를 표한다.

끝으로 감수를 맡아 주신 연세대학교 명예교수 조성규 박사님의 노고에 진심으로 감사 드린다.

1998년 1월

(주) **교학사 사서부**

이 사전의 사용법

1. 표제어

수록 어휘수	1. 이 사전의 수록 어휘수는 복합어를 포함하여 100,000어다.
글자체	2. 표제어는 고딕체로 표시하였다. 　　**가게　나라　마음씨** 　　**빠르다　살다　아름답다** 　　**탄자니아　클린턴**
한자어	3. 한자어는 우리말 뒤에 한자를 고딕체로 병기하였다. 　　**건설교통부 建設交通部** the Ministry of Construction and Transportation 　　**단문 單文** 〔文法〕a simple sentence
배열 순서	4. 어순은 가나다순으로 배열하였다. 된소리는 예사소리가 끝난 뒤에 일괄 처리했다. 　　**깊이**　　(ㄱ항의 예사 소리의 끝) 　　**까까머리** (ㄱ항의 된소리의 시작)
동음이의어 어깨 번호	5. 동음이의어는 순수 우리말, 한자어, 외래어, 접두어, 접미어의 순으로 배열하였다. 6. 글자는 같고 뜻이 다른 우리말·외래어 표제어에는 어깨 번호를 붙여 구별하였다. 　　**배**^{1}〈선박〉a ship; a boat (ship 보다 작은); a vessel (ship 보다 큰); 〈기선〉a steamer; 〈정기선〉a liner; 〈짐배〉a barge; **(총칭)** shipping; (water) craft 　　**배**^{2} 〈열매〉a pear ♦서양배 a (Western) pear 　　**배**^{3} **1**〔生〕the stomach (▶가장 일반적인 말. 배·위 등을 통틀어 말함); 〈복부〉the abdomen; (口) the belly; 〈장(腸)〉the bowels
「우리말＋한 자」의 합성 어	7. 표제어가 우리말과 한자의 합성어일 때는 우리말에 해당하는 부분을 —로 나타내고 한자를 병기하였다. 　　**가나다순 —順** the order of the Korean alphabet 　　**강기슭 江—** a riverside; the banks [shores] of a river 　　**강대하다 強大—** powerful; (big and) strong; mighty 　　**겉모양 —貌樣** outward appearance; outward show; look; front 　　**당일치기 當日—** ♦당일치기 여행 a day's trip
접두어·접미 어	8. 접두어·접미어에는 그 앞이나 뒤에 -을 붙였다. 　　**-가 -家 1**〈전문인 등〉a specialist; an expert; a veteran; a professional; a man **2**〈어떤 성질의 사람〉♦공상가 a daydreamer **3**〈많이 가진 사람〉♦수집가 a collector / 자본가 a capitalist **4**〈집안·가문〉a family 　　**날-** 〈익히지 않은〉raw; uncooked 《cabbage》; 〈자연 그대로의〉crude
우리말 속담 표제어	9. 친숙한 우리말 속담을 독립 표제어로 삼았다. 첫마디만 알면 바로 찾을 수 있다. 　　**가재는 게 편이라** (속담) Like attracts like. ⇌ Birds of a feather flock together.
세계 인명· 지명 등	10. 세계 인명·지명, 외래어, 약어를 광범위하게 표제어로 삼았다. 　　**가봉**〈나라 이름〉Gabon; 〈공식 명〉 the Gabonese Republic 　　**헤밍웨이**〈미국의 소설가〉Hemingway, Ernest (1899-1961)

2. 복합어

위치	1. 표제어에 준하는 복합어는 표제어 맨 뒤에, ■표를 붙여 수록하였다. 이 때 표제어 해당 부분은 —으로 대신한다.

이 사전의 사용법

순서	2. 「명사+표제어」로 된 복합어가 먼저 오고, 「표제어+명사」 형태가 뒤에 온다. 「표제어+명사」가 시작되는 자리에도 ■표를 다시 붙였다. **납부** 納付 〈세금・공과금 등의〉 payment; 〈물품의〉 delivery ■분할— divided payments; payment on an installment basis ■—금(액) the amount of payment —기한 the deadline for payment : 수업료 납부 기한은 언제냐? When is your tuition due [to be paid]? —자 a payer
용례	3. 복합어에 따른 용례는 해당 복합어 뒤에 : 기호를 붙여 제시하였다. **가스** gas; a gaseous matter; 〈연료용〉 (coal) gas; 〈장내의〉 gas; wind ■—난로 a gas heater [stove] : 가스 난로 좀 켜 주세요 Please turn on the gas stove.

3. 어의(語義)의 구분

어의 구분은 1, 2, 3,...으로	1. 한 표제어에 여러 가지 다른 뜻이 있는 항목은 어의를 1, 2, 3,... 등의 번호로 구분하였다. **건사하다** 1 〈일을 처리하다〉 supervise; manage; control; deal [cope] with ◆집안 일을 건사하다 manage [run] the household affairs; do housekeeping 2 〈보살피다〉 take care of; attend on [to]; look after ◆아기를 건사하다 take care of a baby 3 〈간수하다〉 keep (carefully); tuck away (in) ◆중요한 문서를 잘 건사하다 preserve important documents
어의의 정의	2. 한 표제어의 여러 가지 어의는 역어(譯語) 앞에 【 】, 〈 〉기호를 두어 그 속에 우리말로 정의를 달았다. 【 】는 대표적 정의에, 〈 〉는 개개의 역어의 정의에 썼다. 역어의 정의를 자세히 한 것은 역어를 골라 쓰는 데 도움이 되도록 하기 위해서다. **가지**¹ 【나무의】 a branch; 〈큰 가지〉 a bough; a limb; 〈잔 가지〉 a twig; 〈어린 가지〉 a shoot; 〈꽃・잎이 달린 채 자른〉 a wand; a sprig 《of jasmine》; a spray 《of peach blossoms》 **가지다** 1【지니다】〈손에〉 have; take; hold; 〈몸에〉 carry (with *one*); have (a thing) with *one*...

4. 역어(譯語)

역어	1. 역어란 표제어 또는 우리말 표현에 대응하는 영어 표현 또는 대역(對譯)을 말한다.
배열	2. 역어는 표준적이며 평이한 일상적 영어 표현을 골라 썼다. 역어의 배열은 일반적인 것을 먼저 놓고, 특수한 것을 뒤로 돌렸다.
구분	3. 역어와 역어 사이는 세미콜론(;)으로 구분하였다. **각오** 覺悟 〈결심〉 (a) resolution; 〈마음의 준비〉 readiness; preparedness; 〈체념〉 resignation **장 張** 〈책의〉 a leaf; 〈쪽〉 a page; 〈종이〉 a sheet
뉘앙스	4. 역어의 뜻의 차이나 뉘앙스의 차이는 역어 앞에 〈 〉에 우리말로 나타냈다. **가**¹ 〈모난 것의〉 an edge; 〈원형의 것, 그릇 등의〉 a brim; 〈끝〉 the end; the limits; 〈결・옆〉 side; -side; 〈경계〉 a border **무지 無知** 1〈모름〉 ignorance 《about》; 〈문맹〉 illiteracy; 〈어리석음〉 stupidity
관사	5. 명사 표제어의 경우에 가산명사에는 a, an 을 붙였고, 불가산명사에는 관사를 붙이지 않았다. 언제나 the 를 필요로 하는 명사에는 the 를, 주로 복수형으로 쓰이는 명사는 역어를 복수형으로 하기도 했다. **가위표** —標 a cross; an X

이 사전의 사용법

간 肝 〈간장〉 the liver; 〈담력·배짱·용기〉 courage; spirit; pluck; (口) guts
거적 a straw mat; (총칭) straw matting
유입 流入 (an) inflow; (an) influx; incoming
유적 遺跡 remains; ruins; vestiges; relics

철자	6. 철자는 미식을 위주로 했다. 역어가 (美), (英)에서 각각 차이가 있을 때는 다음과 같이 했다. 이층 二層 (美) the second floor; (英) the first floor
관련어	7. 역어와 밀접하게 결합되는 전치사, 부사(구), 부정사, 동사 등은 역어 뒤 또는 앞에 ( )에 넣어 제시했다. 또 역어에 대하여 목적어가 될 수 있는 말도 필요에 따라 ( )에 넣어 제시했다. 가당찮다 可當— 〈터무니 없다〉 wild (idea); absurd (project); preposterous (demand); exorbitant; 〈지나치다〉 awful; excessive; outrageous; 〈부당하다〉 unreasonable (price); unwarrantable; unjust (treatment); improper (conduct); undue; unsuitable 갈다³ 1 〈논밭을〉 plow; cultivate (land); till; get (the soil) turned over 갸웃하다 1 〈형용사적〉 somewhat slanted [inclined] ◆ 갸웃이 aslant; askew; obliquely 2 〈동사적〉 incline (*one's* head on one side); tilt (*one's* head); lean 거개 擧皆 most (of); the greater part (of); the vast majority (of); almost all
명사의 복수형	8. 필요에 따라 불규칙적으로 변화하는 명사의 복수형을 역어 뒤에 제시했다. 지침 指針 1 〈자석의〉 a compass needle; an index (*pl.* ~es, -dices)...
어원	9. 역어가 영어 이외의 외국어일 때는 [〈(프)] 식으로 어원을 밝혔다.
보충 설명	10. 역어의 보충 설명은 역어 뒤에 (▶)에 넣어 제시했다. ▶ 그는 그녀의 손을 잡았다 He took the girl by the hand. (▶보통 take the girl's hand 라고는 하지 않음)
형용사의 서술	11. 우리말 형용사의 서술적인 뜻을 나타내려면 "be 또는 동사+형용사"로 해야 하는 데 이 사전에서는 동사를 빼고 형용사만을 넣었다. 그러나 역어에 서술동사가 꼭 필요할 경우에는 그 앞에 〈서술적〉이라 명기하고 be 또는 다른 동사를 넣어 이를 단순 형용사와 구별하였다.
「표제어+하다」	12. 명사 표제어 풀이 뒤에 이어지는 —○○하다는 그 표제어의 형용사형이거나 동사형이다. 〈동사꼴〉 증명 證明 (a) proof; ... —증명하다 prove;... 〈형용사꼴〉 행복 幸福 happiness... —행복하다 happy...
「○○하다」의 독립 표제어화	13. 명사 표제어에 들어갈 역어가 마땅치 않을 때는 —○○하다가 바로 이어지며, 끝에 복합어가 따르지 않는 항목이면 —○○하다를 바로 표제어로 삼아 동사 또는 형용사로 만들어 풀이했다.
우리말의 음역	14. 우리말을 음역(音譯)한 역어는 이탤릭체로 표기하였다. 장구 (樂) a *changgu*
약어	15. 표제어가 약어(略語)인 경우에는 먼저 그 약어의 역어를 쓴 뒤에 완전한 철자들을 [<]에 넣어 어원을 밝혔다. 가트 GATT [<the *G*eneral *A*greement on *T*ariffs and *T*rade]
one, one's, oneself, sb, sb's, sth	16. 역어 및 용례 중에 나오는 *one, one's* 등 대표어는 이탤릭체로 하여 다음과 같이 표기하였다. ① *one, one's, oneself* 는 주어 자신 또는 일반 사람을 가리킨다. 이 말들은 문맥에 따라서 I, my, myself; you, your, yourself; he, his, himself; she, her, herself 등으로 바꿔 쓸 수 있음을 나타낸다. ② somebody 는 *sb* 로, somebody's 는 *sb's* 로 줄여 썼는데 이것은 주어 자신 이외의 인칭대명사 또는 인명으로 바꿔 쓸 수 있음을 나타낸다. ③ *sth* 은 something 을 줄여 쓴 말이다. ④ 「사항」은 a matter, 「장소」는 a place로 하여 《 》속에 넣었다.

거짓 1 〈명사적〉 a lie; a falsehood; 〈지어낸 일〉 fabrication; a fiction; 〈허위〉 a deceit; fraud ◆거짓 없는 대화 a sincere talk / 거짓 투성이 a pack of falsehoods / 거짓 웃음 a feigned smile / 거짓 눈물을 흘리다 shed sham tears; weep crocodile tears / 거짓임을 드러내다 prove *sth* to be false / 거짓으로 가르쳐 주다 give *sb* wrong information 《about》

걸머지다 1 〈짐을 등에 지다〉 carry 《a burden》 on *one's* back; strap 《a bundle》 on *one's* back; 〈책임 지다〉 shoulder [assume, take upon *oneself*] 《the responsibility of》, be burdened 《with》

解說 17. 주로 역어의 기본 풀이 뒤에 나오는 解說 란은 대부분 그 역어들의 동의어 해설이다.

가끔 1 〈이따금〉 sometimes; (every) now and then; from time to time; occasionally; once in a while; at times [moments]

> 解說 ***sometimes*** 가 가장 일반적인 말로서 넓은 뜻으로 쓰인다. ***(every) now and then, from time to time*** 은 일어나는 간격이 불규칙적이다. ***occasionally*** 는 「드물게」라는 느낌의 말로 sometimes 보다 일어나는 빈도가 낮다. 그 구어적인 표현이 ***(every) once in a while*** 이다.

반의어 18. 역어의 반의어는 (↔   )로 나타냈다.
발음 19. 발음이 까다로운 단어에는 발음 기호를 달았다.
가곡 歌曲 a song; 〈독일의〉 a lied [liːd] 《*pl*. lieder》; 〈프랑스의〉 a chanson [ʃǽnsən]

5. 용례와 예문

용례와 예문 1. 이 사전에서는 명사구·형용사구·부사구 등 구(phrase)로 된 예를 '용례'라 하고 완전한 문장(full sentence)으로 된 예를 '예문'이라고 구분하였다.

용례의 시작 2. 용례는 표제어의 풀이가 끝난 뒤에 제시했다.
간식 間食 a (between-meal) snack; eating between meals [snacks]
◆간식으로 감자 튀김을 먹다 eat potato chips between meals

용례의 순서 3. 용례의 순서는 명사구, 형용사구, 부사구, 동사구 등의 순이다.
용례의 구분 4. 한 용례에 2개 이상의 역어가 있을 때는 세미콜론(;)으로 구분하고, 용례와 용례 사이는 / 로 구분하였다.
달다⁴ 1 〈맛이〉 sweet; sugary; sweet-flavored
◆단것 sweet things; sweet-stuff; 〈과자〉 sweets; 〈美〉 candy / 너무 단 홍차 sugary tea / 설탕으로 달게 하다 sweeten 《coffee》 with sugar

예문의 시작 5. 완전한 문장인 예문은 용례가 끝난 다음에 제시했다.
건조 乾燥 dryness; aridity; 〈목재의〉 seasoning; drying; 〈탈수〉 dehydration
◆이상 건조 기후 abnormally dry weather
▶영동 지방에 건조 주의보가 발효 중이다 A dry weather warning [alert] is in force for the Yŏngdong District.

회화 6. 예문 중 회화문에는 ▶ 뒤에 會話 라는 약물을 넣어 제시했다.
▶ 會話 「차 한 잔 하러 오시겠어요?」「예, 곧 갈께요.」 "Would you like to come over for a cup of tea?" "OK. I'll be right over."
▶ 會話 「요즘 건강은 어떠십니까?」「덕분에 아주 좋습니다」 "How is your health of late [lately]?" "I am in [enjoying] excellent health, thank you."

⇌ 기호	7. 뜻이 비슷한 영문 예문이 2개 이상 나열될 때는 예문 사이에 ⇌를 넣었다. ▶ 그는 점차 건강이 나빠지고 있다 His health is failing [declining]. ⇌ He is failing [declining] in health. ▶ 어머니는 건강이 좋지 않으십니다 〈일시적으로〉 My mother is not very [quite] well. ⇌ 〈지속적으로〉 My mother is in poor [bad] health.
조사 중심의 일괄 처리	8. 용례·예문이 양적으로 많은 명사 표제어에서는 찾아보기 쉽도록 '명사+토씨'를 중심으로 분류하여 일괄 처리하였다. 이 때 토씨의 배열 순서는 소유격인 〈의〉, 주격인 〈은, 이, 가〉, 목적격인 〈을〉, 기타 〈에, 에서, 에게〉, 〈으로〉 등의 순서다. **마음** mind; heart; ... 〈**마음의**〉 마음의 벗 *one's* bosom friend; ... 〈**마음이[은]**〉 마음이 맞는 친구 a like-minded company; ... ▶ 그는 입은 험해도 마음은 착한 녀석이다 He has a foul tongue, but is, at heart, a good fellow. 〈**마음을**〉 마음을 합하여 with one accord; ... ▶ 그의 마음을 알 수가 없다 I can't understand [see through] him. 〈**마음에**〉 마음에 드는 그림 a picture which strikes *one's* fancy ▶ 이것이 가장 내 마음에 든다 This suits me [my taste] best.

6. 테마 해설

테마 해설	중요 표제어와 문법 항목 등에는 대형 테마 해설을 박스에 넣었다. 그 테마와 관련된 넓고 풍부한 표현들을 수록했다.

7. 유용한 부록

부 록	권말 부록에는 영문 작성에 도움이 되는 중요 동사의 유의어별 용법·문형, 전화 통화할 때의 영어, 국제 통화에서 잘 쓰는 표현, Writing의 기초지식, 영문일기 쓰는 법, 영문 이력서 쓰는 법, 영문 편지 쓰는 법, 수와 수식 읽는 법, 개수를 세는 법, 국어의 로마자 표기법(초록), 한국 행정 구역 로마자 표기, 대한민국 정부 기구명, 한국 전통 식품의 영어 표기, 명사·동사의 어형 변화 규칙, 세계의 주요 통화 일람, 도량형 환산표, 인권을 배려한 영어 표현, 불규칙 동사 변화표의 유용한 참고 자료를 풍성하게 실었다.

괄호와 기호의 용법

⟨ ⟩ ① 역어 앞에서 말뜻을 정의할 때 쓴다.
　　② ⟨명사적⟩ ⟨형용사적⟩ ⟨부사적⟩ ⟨동사적⟩ ⟨서술적⟩ 등의 용법을 지시할 때 쓴다.
; 　　역어와 역어 사이를 구분한다.
[ ] 　그 바로 앞의 어구와 바꿔 쓸 수 있는 어구를 나타낸다.
〖 〗 학술, 전문 용어를 나타낸다.
【 】 어의(語義) 중의 큰 구분을 나타낸다. 그 뒤에 ⟨ ⟩ 속에는 작은 뜻 구분이 따른다.
( ) ① 본문에 한자를 병기할 때 쓴다.
　　② 생략해도 되는 부분을 가리킨다.
《 》 문법상, 어법상, 구문상 특정한 관계를 보이기 위해 들어가는 전치사, 동사, 부정사, 동명사, 목적어 등을 나타낸다.
( ) 　(英) (美) (口) 등의 언어 용법 지시를 나타낸다.
　　(약어표 참조)
[ ] 　발음 기호를 나타낸다.
(↔) 　반대어·반의어를 나타낸다.
(▶) 역어·용례 뒤에 용법·어법상의 보충 설명을 할 때 쓴다.
[⟨] ① 외래어의 어원을 밝힐 때 쓴다.
　　② 약어의 원문을 밝힐 때 쓴다.
⇨ 　옛말의 현용어(現用語), 큰말과 작은말, 센말과 여린말, 약어와 본디말, 관련어 등을 참조할 것을 가리킨다.
= 　동의어인 표제어를 나타낼 때 쓴다.
解說 대부분 동의어 해설이다. 역어의 의미상의 차이나, 보다 구체적인 용법을 해설하여 역어 선택 사용의 지침이 된다.
♦ 　대부분 별행으로, 구(句)로 된 용례가 시작된다는 표시다.
/ 　구(句)로 된 용례와 용례 사이를 구분한다.
▶ 　완전한 문장으로 된 예문의 시작을 나타낸다. 원칙적으로 별행이다.
⇌ 　하나의 우리말 문장에 대하여 2개 이상의 완전한 영문으로 나타낼 수 있을 때 써서 그 앞뒤 문장의 뜻이 거의 같음을 가리킨다.
會話 예문이 대화체의 화화문임을 나타낸다.
■ 　복합어의 시작을 나타낸다.
— ① 명사·부사 표제어가 동사 또는 형용사의 기본형 —○○**하다**로 바뀌는 표시다. 원칙적으로 별행이다.
　　② 복합어에서 표제어 상당 부분을 대신한다. 이 사전에서는 복합어에서만 이 용법을 썼고 나머지는 표제어 상당 부분을 일일이 다 적었다.

약 어 표

1 외래어 관계

(그)················그리스어	(러)················러시아어	(일)················일본어
(네)················네덜란드어	(산)················산스크리트어	(중)················중국어
(뉴질)················뉴질랜드어	(스)················스페인어	(캐)················캐나다어
(독)················독일어	(오스)················오스트레일리아어	(포)················포르투갈어
(라)················라틴어	(이)················이탈리아어	(프)················프랑스어

2 용법 관계

(口)················구어	(美俗)················미국속어	(兒)················소아어
(文)················문어	(卑)················비어	(英)················영국용법
(美)················미국용법	(俗)················속어	(英口)················영국구어
(美口)················미국구어	(詩)················시어	(學俗)················학생속어

3 전문어 관계

〔建〕················건축(학)	〔放〕················방송	〔醫〕················의학
〔競〕················경기	〔紡〕················방적	〔印〕················인쇄
〔經〕················경제(학)	〔法〕················법률, 법학	〔電〕················전기
〔考古〕················고고학	〔保〕················보험	〔電算〕················컴퓨터
〔昆〕················곤충	〔服〕················복식	〔電子〕················전자공학
〔工〕················공학	〔簿〕················부기	〔占星〕················점성술
〔空〕················항공	〔史〕················역사, 사학	〔政〕················정치(학)
〔鑛〕················광물(학)	〔寫〕················사진	〔彫〕················조각
〔光〕················광학	〔社〕················사회학	〔鳥〕················조류(학)
〔敎〕················교육	〔商〕················상업	〔宗〕················종교
〔球〕················구기	〔生〕················생물(학)	〔證〕················증권, 주식
〔軍〕················군사	〔生化〕················생화학	〔地〕················지리
〔拳〕················권투	〔船〕················조선, 선박	〔地球物〕················지구물리학
〔菌〕················세균학	〔聖〕················성경	〔地質〕················지질학
〔그神〕················그리스신화	〔修〕················수사학	〔織〕················직물
〔劇〕················연극	〔數〕················수학	〔車〕················자동차
〔氣〕················기상	〔植〕················식물(학)	〔天〕················천문(학)
〔基〕················기독교	〔神〕················신화	〔哲〕················철학
〔機〕················기계	〔心〕················심리학	〔鐵〕················철도
〔勞〕················노동	〔樂〕················음악	〔蹴〕················축구
〔論〕················논리학	〔冶〕················야금	〔測〕················측량
〔籠〕················농구	〔野〕················야구	〔齒〕················치과(학)
〔農〕················농업	〔藥〕················약학	〔土〕················토목
〔代〕················대수학	〔魚〕················어류	〔統〕················통계학
〔動〕················동물(학)	〔言〕················언어학	〔TV〕················텔레비전
〔로神〕················로마신화	〔映〕················영화	〔貝〕················패류
〔로켓〕················로켓工學	〔藝〕················예술	〔韓醫〕················한의학
〔馬〕················마술, 승마	〔料〕················요리	〔海〕················항해, 해양
〔文〕················문학	〔郵〕················우편	〔解〕················해부
〔紋〕················문장(학)	〔遺〕················유전학	〔化〕················화학
〔物〕················물리학	〔倫〕················윤리학	〔畫〕················회화
〔博〕················박물	〔音聲〕················음성학	〔環境〕················환경공학

테마 해설 색인

가게를 나타내는 어휘 ······2	비행기 여행의 상식 ······1178
가능성의 표현 ······7	빈도의 표현 ······1180
가옥·방을 나타내는 어휘 ······27	빛깔의 이미지 ······1186
감사의 표현 ······61	사과의 표현 ······1201
감정의 표현 ······66	사역의 표현 ······1214
감탄사 ······69	상태와 상황의 표현 ······1252
게시·간판·광고의 주요 문례 ······133	소개의 표현 ······1318
결과의 표현 ······144	소망의 표현 ······1322
교통과 도로를 나타내는 어휘 ······275	쇼핑에 관한 표현 ······1354
구두점의 사용법 ······281	수와 양의 표현 ······1355
권유의 표현 ······315	스포츠 용어 ······1397
금전에 관한 표현 ······351	시각과 시간 ······1406
기후와 날씨 ······386	식사와 요리 ······1427
길안내 ······391	양보의 표현 ······1551
날짜·요일·연호 ······464	의도의 표현 ······1783
동등 비교의 표현 ······669	의뢰의 표현 ······1785
맛의 표현 ······822	자동차에 관한 표현 ······1878
맞장구치는 법 ······830	전화에 관한 표현 ······1963
명령의 표현 ······865	제안·요구·권유의 표현 ······1997
목적의 표현 ······888	지리 용어 ······2076
무게의 표현 ······906	철도 ······2156
배수의 표현 ······1036	최상급의 표현 ······2187
부엌과 조리기구 ······1117	추측의 표현 ······2195
부정의 표현 ······1121	크기의 표현 ······2245
비교의 표현 ······1163	

ㄱ

ㄱㄴ순 —順 the order of the Korean alphabet
♦ 색인 카드를 ㄱㄴ 순으로 정리하다 arrange index cards in alphabetical order [in the order of the Korean alphabet]
▶ 그들의 이름을 ㄱㄴ순으로 적으시오 Write down their names in alphabetical order.

ㄱ자 —字 the first letter of the Korean alphabet ♦ ㄱ자꼴 an L (shape) / ㄱ자꼴의 L-shaped

ㄱ자형 —字— 〈목수의 곱자〉 a L square; a carpenter's square

ㄱ자집 —字— an L-shaped house
♦ ㄱ자집은 전통 한옥 형태의 하나다 An L-shaped house is one of the traditional Korean house patterns.

가[1] 〈모난 것의〉 an edge; 〈원형의 것, 그릇 등의〉 a brim; 〈끝〉 the end; the limits; 〈곁·옆〉 side; -side; 〈경계〉 a border
▶ 나는 창가 자리를 잡았다 I took a window seat.
▶ 그녀는 입가에 미소를 띠고 나를 바라보았다 She looked at me with a smile on her lips.
▶ 난로가에 앉으십시오 Please sit by the fireside.
▶ 그는 벼랑가에 서서 바다를 내려다보았다 He looked over the edge of the cliff at the sea below.
▶ 길가에는 야생화가 많이 있었다 There were many wildflowers by the roadside.
▶ 그는 바닷가에서 자랐다 He was raised by the sea.
▶ 우리는 물가로 갔다 We went to the shore.

가[2] 〔樂〕 〈음계의 제 6음〉 la; A
■ 내림— A flat 올림— A sharp ■—음 la; A —장조〔단조〕 A major [minor]

가 可 1 〈좋음〉 good —가하다 ⇨ 가하다(可—)
2 〈표결에서〉 aye; yea; approval; OK **3** 〈성적의〉 a D; Passing; Average

가- 假- 1 〈임시의〉 temporary; provisional; interim; 〈비공식의〉 informal; 〈시험적인〉 tentative; 〈일시적인〉 transient; 〈임시 변통의〉 makeshift
2 〈가짜의〉 false; assumed

-가 -家 1 〈전문인 등〉 a specialist; an expert; a veteran; a professional; a man
♦ 미술가 an artist / 법률가 a lawyer / 소설가 a novelist
2 〈어떤 성질을 가진 사람〉 ♦ 공상가 a daydreamer / 낙천가 an optimist / 야심가 a man of ambition
3 〈많이 가진 사람〉 ♦ 수집가 a collector / 자본가 a capitalist
4 〈집안·가문〉 a family
♦ 케네디가 the Kennedy family

-가 -哥 〈성씨〉 the surname; the family name
▶ 제 성은 이가입니다 My name [surname] is Lee. ⇒ Lee is my family name.

-가 街 1 〈거리〉 a street; an avenue; a road; a drive
♦ 월가 the Wall Street
2 〈구역·지구〉 a district; a quarter; a center; an area
♦ 번화가 a downtown; busy quarters / 상점가 a shopping street [district, center] / 은행가 a banking area / 주택가 a residential quarters; an uptown / 한국인가 a Korean quarter; a Korea(n) town
3 〈행정구역〉 ga
♦ 종로 3가 Chongno 3-ga

-가 歌 〈노래〉 a song
♦ 농부가 a farmer's song / 응원가 a rooter's song; a fight song; (英) a supporter's song; cheers / 자장가 a lullaby; a nursery song; a cradle song

가가대소하다 呵呵大笑— roar with laughter; burst out laughing《at [over, about] *sth*》
▶ 그 사람은 내 농담을 듣고 가가대소했다 He laughed loudly at my joke. ⇒ He roared with laughter when he heard my joke. ⇒ He had a good [hearty] laugh over my joke.

가가호호 家家戶戶 〈집집마다〉 every [each] house; every door; house by house; from door to door; from house to house
♦ 가가호호 찾아다니다 make a house-to-house visit; visit from door to door
▶ 그 입후보자는 가가호호 찾아다녔다 The candidate made door-to-door visits.

가각 苛刻 —가각하다 heartless; cruel; brutal; severe

가각 街角 a street corner; the corner of an intersection

가감 加減 〈더하고 뺌〉 addition and subtraction; 〈증감〉 increase and decrease; 〈조절〉 adjustment; control
—가감하다 〈더하고 빼다〉 add and [or] subtract; 〈늘이고 줄이다〉 increase and decrease; 〈조절하다〉 adjust; control
■—법 〔數〕 a method of addition and subtraction —저항기 〔電〕 a rheostat

가갸 뒷자도 모른다 (속담) He is utterly [completely] illiterate. ⇒ He doesn't know A from B. ⇒ He can't say B to a battledore.

가게 a store; a shop; 〈노점 등〉 a stall; a stand; a kiosk
♦ 잘 되는 가게 a popular [prosperous] store / 가게 주인 a storekeeper; a shopkeeper
〈가게는〉 저 가게는 아주 싸다[비싸다] That store is very cheap [expensive].
▶ 저 가게는 일요일에 쉽니까[엽니까]? Is that store closed [open] on Sunday?
▶ 이 가게는 몇 시에 문을 엽니까[닫습니까]? What time is this store opened [closed]?
▶ 가게는 벌써 닫혀 있었다 I found the doors

가게를 나타내는 어휘

1. 가게
▶ 미국에서는 대체로 상품을 판매하는 가게는 store라 하고 전문점이나 공장, 작업장, 수리·가공을 하는 가게는 shop이라 한다. 영국에서는 대개 shop을 쓰지만 규모가 큰 가게는 store라고 한다.

보기	미국	영국
서점	a bookstore	a bookshop
약방	a drugstore	a chemist's (shop)
채소 가게	a vegetable store	a greengrocer's (shop)
애완동물 가게	a pet shop	a pet shop
구두 수리점	a shoe repair shop	a shoe repair shop
백화점	a department store	a department store

2. 가게의 간판
▶ 역사가 오래되어 널리 알려진 가게나 겉으로 보아 무엇을 취급하는지 뚜렷이 알 수 있는 가게는 대개 간판이나 창문에 store나 shop 등의 가게 이름만 써놓은 곳도 많다.
Macy's (뉴욕의 큰 백화점 메이시스)
Harrods (런던의 고급 백화점 해로즈)
Foyles (런던의 큰 서점 포일즈)
B. Dalton (미국의 대형 서적 체인점 돌턴)
그밖에 작은 가게 중에서도 서점이면 Bookstore, 구둣방이면 Shoe Store를 써놓기도 하지만 그냥 Books, Shoes라고 취급하는 품명만 써놓는 가게도 있다.

3. 가게의 종류
▶ 의류점 a clothing store / 신사 양품점 a men's shop; (英) (men's) outfitter; (美) a haberdashery (미국에서는 넥타이 등 장신구류를 팔며 영국에서는 단추·실·레이스·끈 등의 잡화 가게) / 양복점 (美) a tailor shop; (英) a tailor's shop / 양복점 a dressmaker's / 부티크 a boutique (소규모의 고급 여성복 전문점) / 모자점 a hat store; a milliner (여성 모자 가게) / 직물점 a clothier
▶ 식당 a restaurant; an eating house / 간이식당 a snack bar [counter]; a lunchroom; a coffee shop / 카페테리아 a cafeteria (셀프서비스 방식) / 대중 식당[밥집] a greasy spoon (흔히 "EAT"란 간판을 내건다) / 자동 판매식식당 (美) an automat (자동판매기 등을 통한 완전 셀프서비스의 간이식당) / 다방 a coffee shop; a tearoom; a café / 술집 a bar; (英) a pub (a public house의 약어); a tavern
▶ 식료품 가게 a grocery store; (英) grocer's (shop) / 빵집[제과점] a bakery; a bakeshop; a baker's (shop) / 정육점 (美) a butcher shop; (英) a butcher's (shop) / 어물전 a fish shop / 과자점 a candy store; (英) a sweetshop; a pastry shop; a confectionary / 유제품 판매점 dairy / 반찬 가게 (美) delicatessen (조리된 식품을 팔며 그 자리에서 먹을 수 있도록 카운터가 설치된 가게도 많다) / 쌀가게 a rice shop / 주류 판매점 a liquor shop
▶ 전기기구점 an electrical appliance store / 가구점 a furniture store / 철물점 a hardware store / 도자기 가게 a china store / 문방구점 a stationery store; stationer's / 헌책방 a secondhand bookstore / 책 대여점 a rental [lending] library / 귀금속[보석]상 a jewelry store
▶ 시계점 (美) a jewler's; watchmaker's / 안경점 an optical shop / 카메라 가게 a camera store / 스포츠 용품점 a sporting goods shop / 레코드 가게 a record shop / 악기점 a shop for musical instruments / 완구점 a toyshop / 우산 가게 an umbrella shop / 꽃가게 a flower shop; 〈꽃장수〉 a florist / 담배 가게 a tobacco shop; a tobacconist's (shop)
▶ 구둣방 a shoe store / 골동품 가게 a curio [antique] shop / 선물[토산품] 가게 a gift shop / 전당포 a pawnshop
▶ 세탁소 a dry cleaner's; a laundry / 동전 세탁소 (美) a launderette; a laundromat / 미용원 a beauty shop; a beauty parlor [salon] / 이발소 (美) a barbershop; a barber shop; (英) a barber's (shop) / 사진관 a photo studio
▶ 만물상〈잡화점〉 a variety store; a general store / 슈퍼마켓 a supermarket
▶ 할인점 a discount store (염가의 잡화를 파는 가게로서 a variety store, a dime store, five-and-ten cent store 등 여러 가지로 불린다. 규모가 작은 가게에서부터 Woolworth's와 같은 미국의 대형 체인점까지 여러 가지이다) / 중고품 판매점 (美) a thrift shop; (英) a secondhand shop (둘 다 주로 의류를 취급한다)

of the store closed.
〈가게를〉 그는 아침 9시에 가게를 연다 He opens his store at 9 in the morning.
▶ 그는 명동에 가게를 벌이고 있다 He has [runs, keeps] a store at Myŏng-dong.
▶ 그는 5시에 가게를 닫는다 He shuts up business at five.
〈가게에(서[는])〉 그 제품은 벌써 가게에 나와 있다 That product is already available in (the) stores [shops].
▶ 저 가게에는 물건이 많다 That store keeps a large variety of goods in store.
▶ 그는 저 가게에서 가방을 샀다 He bought a bag at that store.
▶ 저 가게에서 양말을 파는지 몰라 I wonder if they sell socks at that store.
▶ 저 가게에서는 담배를 팝니까? Do they sell cigarettes at that store?
▪ 구멍— a penny candy store; a dime [ten-cent] store 반찬— a grocery (store) 생선— a fish shop ■—채 the shop part of a house 가겟방 a shop [store] room 가게집 a store; a

house used as a store
가게 기둥에 입춘이라 〈속담〉 casting pearls before swine
가격 價格 〈값〉 a price; 〈값어치〉 (a) value ⇨ 값
■─견적─ an estimated value 공장도─ an ex factory price 도매[소매]─ a wholesale [retail] price 보급─ a sales promotion price 생산자[소비자]─ the producer('s) [consumer('s)] price 시장─ a market price [value] 액면─ a face value 적정─ the right price 정찰─ ⇨ 정찰(~가격) 침투─ penetration price ■─경기(景氣) inflationary expansion ─변동 fluctuation of price ─수준 a price level ─안정 price stability ─인상 a price advancement ─적정성 reasonableness of price ─조정 price adjustment ─차 a price margin ─체계 a price structure ─통제 price control ─표 a price list ─혁명 price revolution
가격협정 價格協定 an agreement on price; a price-maintenance agreement; a price agreement
♦ 가격 협정을 맺다 make [reach, conclude] an agreement on prices
가결 可決 〈승인〉 approval; 〈채택〉 adoption ─가결하다 〈승인하다〉 approve; 〈법안을 통과시키다〉 pass; 〈동의를 통과시키다〉 carry; 〈채택하다〉 adopt; 〈투표로〉 vote
▶ 그 법안은 압도적 다수로 가결되었다 The bill was passed [approved] by an overwhelming majority.
가결의 假決議 a temporary decision; a provisional resolution
가경 佳景 beautiful scenery; a beautiful scene [view]; a scenic place [spot]
▶ 이 지방은 가경이다 The scenery in this region is beautiful.
가경 佳境 〈재미있는 대목〉 the most interesting part; 〈최고조의 대목〉 climax
▶ 이야기는 가경으로 들어갔다 We reached the most interesting part of the story. ⇌ The story reached its climax.
가경지 可耕地 arable [cultivable] land
가계 家系 〈집안〉 a family; 〈혈통〉 a lineage
■─도 a family tree ─보(譜) a family pedigree
가계 家計 〈가정의 예산〉 a family [household] budget; 〈가정의 재정 상태〉 family finance; 〈생계비〉 housekeeping [household] expenses; living expenses
▶ 우리 집 가계는 적자[흑자]다 Our household budget is in the red [black].
▶ 그녀는 가계를 돕기 위해 아르바이트를 한다 She works part time to help (to) support her family.
■─부 household bookkeeping
가곡 歌曲 a song; 〈독일의〉 a lied [líːd] (*pl.* lieder); 〈프랑스의〉 a chanson [ʃǽnsən]
♦ 가곡집 a collection of 《Korean》 songs
가공 加工 〈식품·농산물의〉 processing; 〈기계에 의한〉 manufacturing ─가공하다 process; manufacture
▶ 우유는 버터와 치즈로 가공된다 Milk is made into butter and cheese.

■ 보세─ bonded processing ■─공장 processing plant ─비 processing expenses ─식품 processed foods ─업 processing; manufacturing; processing industries ─업자 a processor ─품 processed goods

가공 可恐 ♦ 가공할 전쟁의 실태 the terrifying [terrible] realities of war / 거대한 운석의 가공할 에너지 the awe-inspiring [enormous, tremendous] energy in gigantic meteorites / 가공할 만한 적 a terrible foe / 핵무기의 가공할 파괴력 the annihilating power of nuclear weapons

가공 架空 ♦ 가공의 〈상상의〉 imaginary; 〈소설 등의〉 fictional; 〈사실과 다른〉 fictitious; unreal / 가공의 인물 a fictitious person; 〈소설에 나오는〉 a fictional person

가공무역 加工貿易 improvement [processing] trade ■ 보세─ bonded processing trade 위탁─ processing deal trade

가관 可觀 1 〈볼만함〉 a sight; a spectacle; something to see
♦ 가관이다 be something to see; be well worth seeing; 〈경치가〉 command a fine view
▶ 한라산 꼭대기에서 바라본 해돋이는 가관이다 The sunrise seen from the top of Hallasan is a glorious spectacle.
2 〈꼴사나움〉 a sight
♦ 가관이다 be a sight; be unbecoming [unseemly, ungainly, unsightly]
▶ 네 꼴이 가관이구나 What a sight you are!
▶ 오후 내내 구멍을 파고 있던 그의 모습은 가관이었다 He was a sight after digging all afternoon.
▶ 그가 가발을 벗은 꼴은 가관이었다 Without a wig on, he was quite a sight.

가교 架橋 〈다리놓기〉 bridge-building; bridge construction; bridging

가교 假橋 〈임시의〉 a temporary [makeshift] bridge

가구 家口 〈집안 사람 전원〉 a household; a home; 〈식구〉 a family; 〈집〉 a house ♦ 새 가구 a new household
▶ 이 마을에는 20가구가 살고 있다 There are twenty families in the village.
■─수 the number of households [families] ─주(主) a householder; the head of a family [household]

가구 家具 furniture; furnishings

> 解説 *furniture*와 *furnishings*는 둘 다 집합적으로 가구들을 나타내는데 furniture는 식탁, 탁자, 의자, 찬장, 침대 등의 이동 가능한 것을 가리키며 셀 때는 a piece [an article] of furniture로 한다. furnishings는 furniture 보다 넓은 뜻으로 sink, bath, 또는 boiler 등의 설비도 포함된다.

♦ 가구 한 세트[일식] a set [a suite] of furniture / 가구 딸린 셋집 a furnished house for rent / 가구를 들이다 furnish [fit up] a room; put furniture into a room
▶ 그 방에는 많은 가구가 있었다 There was a lot of furniture in the room.
■─상 〈상인〉 a furniture dealer ─점 a furni-

가규 家規 〈집안의 규율〉 the rules [customs, principles] of a family

가극 歌劇 (an) opera; a musical drama ◆가극 구경을 가다 go to the opera / 가극에 출연하다 sing in an opera
■ 희(喜)— a comic opera ■ —가수 an opera singer —단 an opera company —장(場) an opera house

가금 家禽 a fowl; poultry; domestic fowls

가급적 可及的 〈될 수 있는 한〉 as ... as possible; as ... as one can; 〈할 수 있으면〉 if (it is) possible
▶ 가급적 일찍 오십시오 Please come as early as possible [you can].
▶ 가급적 여기에 있고 싶다 If possible, I'd like to stay here.
▶ 가급적 외식은 않기로 했다 I don't eat out if I can help it.

가긍하다 可矜— 〈불쌍하다〉 poor; miserable; pitiful (sight); piteous; wretched
◆가긍한 광경 a pitiful sight / 가긍한 모습 miserable [wretched] appearance / 가긍한 정상 a miserable condition; a sad plight / 가긍하게 여기다 take pity on sb

가까스로 〈겨우〉 barely; (only) just; 〈힘들게〉 with difficulty; 〈위태롭게〉 narrowly
◆가까스로 마지막 열차 시간에 대다 be just in time for the last train
▶ 그는 가까스로 분을 참았다 He withheld his anger with the greatest difficulty.
▶ 나는 가까스로 먹고 지낸다 I have barely [(only) just] enough money to live on. ⇒ All [The best] I can do is (to) support myself.
▶ 가까스로 5시까지 그 일을 마칠 수가 있었다 I barely finished [I (only) just finished] the job by 5 o'clock.
▶ 나는 가까스로 죽음을 면했다 I narrowly escaped death.

가까운 남이 먼 일가보다 낫다 (속담) A good neighbor is better than a far-dwelling kinsman.

가까워지다 1〈때·거리가〉 approach; draw [come] near; get near (a place); be near [close] at hand
◆봄이 가까워지면 with the approach of spring / 목적지에 가까워지다 approach [get closer to] one's destination / 완성에 가까워지다 be near [nearing] completion / 임종이 가까워지다 near one's end
▶ 그 배는 해안가에 가까워졌다 The ship approached [drew near] the shore.
▶ 시험이 가까워졌다 The examination is close at hand.
▶ 크리스마스가 가까워졌다 Christmas is just around the corner.
▶ 마감이 가까워졌다 The deadline is nigh.
2〈친해지다〉 become intimate with (each other); make friends with; become [get] acquainted with; come into close association
▶ 그들은 사이가 더욱 가까워졌다 Their relations have grown [gained] in intimacy.
▶ 그 둘 사이는 곧 가까워졌다 The two soon became intimate with each other.
▶ 그는 가까워지기 쉬운 사람이다 He is easy to approach [quite approachable].

가까이 1〈시간적으로〉 shortly ◆새벽녘 가까이 toward dawn
▶ 그는 1시 가까이 되어서 왔다 He came just [shortly] before one o'clock.
▶ 저녁 가까이 되어서 비가 오기 시작했다 It began to rain toward evening.
▶ 그는 1시간 가까이 늦었다 He was almost an hour late.
2〈공간적으로〉 close at hand; near [close] by; at a short distance
◆가까이 가다 approach; go [come] near / 가까이 가지 않다 keep [stay] away from sb / 학교 가까이에 살다 live near the school
▶ 이곳 가까이 우체국이 있습니까? Is there a post office around here?
▶ 좀더 가까이 오세요, 비밀 얘기니까 This is a secret, so come closer.
▶ 불을 휘발유에 가까이 대지 마라 Don't bring an open fire close to gasoline.
▶ 가까이서 보니까 그녀는 조금도 예쁘지 않다 Seen close up she is not at all pretty.
▶ 나는 책상을 창문 가까이로 옮겼다 I moved the desk near [close] to the window.
▶ 위험! 가까이 오지 마십시오 (게시) Danger! Keep away.
3〈거의〉 nearly; almost; 〈약〉 about
◆5만명 가까이 nearly fifty thousand people
▶ 아버지가 돌아가신지 10년 가까이 된다 It is nearly [almost] ten years since my father died.
▶ 우리는 거기서 한 시간 가까이 기다렸다 We waited there for almost [nearly, about] one hour.
4〈친하게〉 ▶ 우리는 여러 해 동안 가까이 지내 왔다 We've been close friends for years.
▶ 그들은 가까이 지내는 사이다 They are on friendly [good] terms with each other.

가까이하다 1〈친하게 사귀다〉 keep company with; make friends with; associate with; make one's acquaintance with
◆가까이하기 쉬운[어려운] 사람 a person who is easy [hard] to get along [on] with / 좋은 [나쁜] 친구와 가까이하다 keep good [bad] company / 가까이하지 않다 keep away from sb; avoid sb's company
▶ 그는 어딘지 모르게 가까이하기 어려운 데가 있다 There is something about him that discourages friendly advances.
▶ 가까이하는 친구를 보면 그 사람의 됨됨이를 알 수 있다 (속담) A man is known by the company he keeps.
▶ 가까이해 보면 그가 좋은 사람이라는 것을 알게 될 것이다 You will find him a good person if you get to know him better.
▶ 그런 패들을 가까이하지 마라 Keep aloof [away] from such company. ⇒ Don't mix in such company.
2〈좋아하다〉 like; be fond of; love; have a passion for; be hooked (on gambling [a girl])
◆책을 가까이하다 enjoy reading books; spend a lot of time reading books

▶학생들은 양서(良書)를 더욱 가까이해야 한다 Students must have more access to good books.
▶여색을 가까이하지 마라 Keep away from women. ⇌ Don't abandon yourself to the lusts of the flesh.
▶술을 가까이 하지 않는 것이 좋다 You'd better refrain [abstain] from drinking.

가깝다 1 〈거리가〉 close; near; nearby; short 《road》; close [near] by; (near, close) at hand; not far from 《one's house》
♦가까운 정거장 a nearby railway station / 가까운 곳에 somewhere near by / 가장 가까운 길을 택하다 take the nearest route
▶도서관은 공원과 가깝다 The library is near [close to] the park.
▶이제 목적지가 가깝다 Our destination is only a short way off. ⇌ We have nearly reached [arrived at] our destination.
▶버스 정거장은 여기서 가깝다 The bus stop is only a little way from here [is not far off].
▶학교는 이 길로 가는 것이 더 가깝다 This is the shorter way [shortcut] to the school.
2 〈시간이〉 near; close; early; immediate; short
♦가까운 장래에 in the near [immediate] future; pretty soon; in a short time; of these days; at an early date; before very long
▶이제 12시가 가깝다 It is nearly [almost] twelve. ⇌ It is getting on toward [(英) for] twelve.
▶봄이 아주 가깝다 Spring is just around the corner.
▶학년말이 가깝다 The end of the school year is not far away [nearly on us].
▶석유가 없어질 날이 가깝다 The time will soon come [The day is in sight] when we will run out of oil.
3 〈관계·사이가〉 near; close 《to》; akin to; friendly; intimate
♦가까운 친구 a close [bosom] friend; an intimate [old] friend / …와 가까운 사이다 be on intimate [friendly] terms with…
▶그녀는 우리 형과 가까운 사이다 She is on the intimate terms with my brother.
▶그 분은 내 가까운 친척 중의 한 사람이다 He is one of my close relatives.
4 〈수치·정도가〉 almost; nearly 《▶almost가 접근 정도가 강함》
▶그들이 하려고 하고 있는 일은 불가능에 가깝다 What they are attempting is almost [next to] impossible. (▶next to는 일반적으로 부정의 앞에 씀)
▶할머니는 연세가 90세에 가까우시다 Grandmother is nearly [almost] 90.
▶그의 회복은 기적에 가까웠다 His recovery was almost a miracle.
▶학급에는 40명에 가까운 학생이 있다 There are nearly [about] 40 students in the class.
5 〈비슷하다〉 near; almost; close [hard] upon; 〈서술적〉 be in the neighborhood 《of》; border [verge] on; approach to
▶원숭이는 인간에 가깝다 The ape is closely allied to man.
▶연민은 사랑에 가깝다 Pity is near to love.
▶그의 사상은 허무주의에 가깝다 His thought verges on nihilism.
6 〈비슷하다〉 familiar; well-known
♦가까운 예를 들면 to take [give] a familiar example

가꾸다 1 〈식물 등을 기르다〉 grow; cultivate; raise; rear
♦정원에 장미를 가꾸다 cultivate roses in the garden / 온실에서 토마토를 가꾸다 raise tomatoes in a hothouse [greenhouse]
2 〈치장하다〉 ornament; adorn; decorate
♦아름답게 가꾼 여자 a beautifully dressed lady / 호화롭게 가꾼 응접실 a gorgeously furnished drawing room / 몸을 가꾸다 tidy *oneself*; fit *oneself* out; (美) fix *oneself*; 〈화장하다〉 make up / 집을 가꾸다 decorate [pretty up] *one's* house

가꾸로 bottom up ⇨ 거꾸로

가끔 1 〈이따금〉 sometimes; (every) now and then; from time to time; occasionally; once in a while; at times [moments]

> 解說 *sometimes*가 가장 일반적인 말로서 넓은 뜻으로 쓰인다. (*every*) *now and then*, *from time to time*은 일어나는 간격이 불규칙적이다. *occasionally*는 「드물게」라는 느낌의 말로 sometimes보다 일어나는 빈도가 낮다. 그 구어적인 표현이 (*every*) *once in a while*이다.

▶그는 학교에 가끔 지각한다 He is sometimes late for school.
▶그는 가끔 전화만 걸어온다 He calls me [(英) gives me a ring] only occasionally.
▶나는 가끔 테니스를 한다 I play tennis once in a while.
▶내일은 가끔 소나기가 오겠습니다 〈일기 예보에서〉 We will have occasional rain showers tomorrow.
2 〈종종〉 often; frequently; several times 《to》 가끔 들르다 make frequent visits 《to》
▶그는 가끔 나를 방문한다 He often visits me.
▶나는 가끔 그런 생각이 들었다 That has often occurred to me.
▶이런 일은 가끔 일어난다 This sort of thing often happens. ⇌ Things like this are not uncommon.

가나 〈나라 이름〉 Ghana; 〈공식명〉 the Republic of Ghana
♦가나의 Ghan(a)ian
■―사람 a Ghan(a)ian

가나다순 ―順 the order of the Korean alphabet
♦가나다순의 좌석 배열 the seating arrangement in Korean alphabetical order / 가나다순으로 배열하다 arrange in Korean alphabetical order; alphabetize 《a list of words》
▶가나다순으로 목록을 작성해라 Make a list of them in Korean alphabetical order.

가나오나 〈어디서나〉 wherever *one* may go; 〈언제나〉 always

가난 1 〈빈곤〉 poverty; want; indigence; destitution; penury

♦가난 속에 죽다 die poor; die in poverty [penury] / 가난을 벗어나다 emerge from poverty / 모진 가난에 시달리다 be poverty-stricken; suffer abject [extreme, dire] poverty
▶가난은 범죄의 주된 요인이다 Poverty is a chief factor in crime.
▶그는 가난을 면할 날이 없다 His poverty is chronic.
▶가난 구제는 나라도 못 한다 (속담) There is no remedy for poverty.
―가난하다 poor(↔ rich); hard-up; indigent; destitute; 〈돈·생필품이 없다〉 needy; 〈극빈하다〉 poverty-stricken
♦가난한 사람 ⇨ 가난뱅이 / 찢어지게 가난하다 be poverty-stricken; be extremely poor; be as poor as a church mouse /가난한 농가에 태어나다 be born into a poor farmer's family / 가난한 사람들을 돕다 help the poor [needy people]/ 가난하게 살다 live in poverty; be badly off / 가난하게 자라다 be brought up in poverty; be raised in poverty
▶세계에는 아직도 가난한 사람들이 많다 There are still many needy people in the world.
▶그녀는 가난한 가족에게 음식을 좀 주었다 She gave some food to the poor [needy] family.
▶마음이 가난한 자는 복이 있나니 Blessed are the poor in spirit.
▶그는 가난해서 대학에 가지 못했다 He could not go to college because he was poor.
2 〈부족〉 scarcity; lack; want; shortage; scantiness; dearth
♦인재 가난 a dearth [shortage] of talented people

가난들다 〈부족하다〉 be short (of provision); be destitute (of money); run short; lack; want
♦인재에 가난들다 suffer from a shortage [dearth] of talented people [talent]

가난뱅이 a poor man; a pauper; (총칭) poor people; the poor [destitute, needy]; the have-nots

가납 假納 temporary payment (of a tax)
―가납하다 pay (a tax) temporarily; deliver (goods) temporarily

가납사니 〈수다쟁이〉 a talkative person; (口) a chatty person; (口) a chatterbox; 〈말다툼쟁이〉 a quarrelsome person; 〈말주변이 있는 사람〉 a glib speaker; a good talker

가내 家內 〈한 집안〉 a family; one's people [(美) folks]; 〈가정〉 a household; a home
♦가내 일동 the whole family; all the members of one's family / 가내의 family; domestic; household; home / 가내에서 in the home
▶가내 모두 건강합니다 My family are all well.
▶나는 가내의 안녕을 기원했다 I prayed (to the gods) for the safety of my family.
■―공업 a home [household, domestic] industry; home manufacturing ―공장 a domestic factory ―노동 homework ―문제 a family [household] affair ―부업 piecework done at home; homework ―제절(諸節) the whole family [household]; (all) the members of one's family: 가내 제절이 편안하십니까? How are your people? ⇒ How is your family?

가냘프다 1 〈목소리가〉 feeble; faint
▶아기가 가냘픈 목소리로 울었다 The baby cried with a feeble voice.
2 〈몸이〉 slim; slight; slender; 〈연약하다〉 feeble; weak; frail
♦가냘픈 여자 a woman with a slender figure / 가냘픈 팔 a thin and weak arm / 가냘픈 여자 손으로 with the weak hands of a woman / 몸매가 가냘프다 be of slender build
▶그녀는 가냘파 보이지만 건강하다 She looks slim but is healthy.

가누다 control; keep steady; keep under control
♦몸을 가누지 못하는 노인 a decrepit old man / 몸을 가누다 keep [preserve] one's balance; balance oneself; keep oneself steady/ 정신을 가누다 retain [keep] one's presence of mind [composure]; collect oneself / 정신을 가누지 못하다 lose one's head; lose one's presence of mind
▶노인은 몸을 가누지 못하고 그 자리에 넘어졌다 The old man lost his balance and fell down on the spot.
▶나는 서핑보드를 타고 몸을 가눌 수가 없다 I cannot keep my balance [balance myself] on a surfboard.

가느다랗다 very slender; very thin; lank(y); lean and long
♦가느다란 막대 a thin rod / 가느다란 팔[목] a slender arm [neck] / 가느다란 허리 a very slim waist / 가느다란 목소리로 in a weak [thin, feeble, faint] voice
▶그녀는 손가락이 가느다랗다 She has very slender fingers.

가느스름하다 somewhat thin; slightly slender
가늑골 假肋骨 [解] the false ribs
가는귀먹다 be a little hard of hearing; have poor hearing; be a little [slightly] deaf
▶그 환자는 가는귀먹었다 The patient is a little hard of hearing.

가늘다 1 〈둘레가 작다〉 thin(↔ thick); slender; 〈호리호리하다〉 slim; fine
♦가는 막대 a thin rod / 가는 붓 a slender writing brush / 가는 실 a fine thread / 가는 팔 [허리] a slender [slim] arm [waist] / 수족이 가늘다 have slender limbs
▶그는 대나무를 가늘게 깎았다 He whittled a piece of bamboo into a thin stick [untill it was very thin].
2 〈소리가 작다〉 weak; feeble; small; faint
♦가는 목소리로 말하다 speak in a small [weak] voice
3 〈너비가 좁다〉 narrow
♦눈을 가늘게 뜨고 보다 look at sth with a half-closed eyes
4 〈촘촘하다〉 fine; close; dense
♦가는 모시 fine ramie fabric
5 〈흔들림이 약하다〉 slight
▶그 여자는 손가락이 가늘게 떨리고 있었다 Her fingers were trembling slightly.

가늘어지다 get thin [fine]; become thin

가늠 1 ⇨ 겨냥

[thinnier, more slender]
♦ 끝이 점점 가늘어지다 taper to a point; taper off 《to the end》
▶ 깃대는 꼭대기 쪽으로 점점 가늘어진다 The flagpole tapers off to a point.

가늠 1
―**가늠하다** aim [take aim] 《at》; sight 《a target》; level [point] a gun 《at》
♦ 표적을 신중히 가늠하다 take careful aim at the target
2 〈판단·어림〉 judgment; discernment; sense of proportion
♦ 내 가늠으로는 in my estimation; according to my estimate / 가늠을 잡을 수가 없다 have no idea 《of》; be unable to figure 《it》 out
―**가늠하다** guess; make a guess; watch; estimate; weigh
♦ 눈으로 가늠하다 measure [estimate] 《the distance》 by the eye / 수를 가늠하다 guess the number 《of participants》 / 정세를 가늠하다 watch the development of a situation
▶ 그 일이 언제 끝날지 아직은 가늠할 수가 없다 The end of the task is not yet in sight.
■ ―쇠 the bead; the front sight ―자 〈총의〉 the sight(s); a gunsight; a backsight

가능 可能 possibility
―**가능하다** possible; practicable; within the range [bounds] of possibility
♦ 실행 가능한 계획 a feasible plan / 실행 가능한 방법 a practical method / 가능한 범위 내에서 as much [far] as possible; within the limits of possibility / 가능한 한 빨리 as soon as possible / 가능하다면 if (it is [be, were]) possible; if 《you》 can / 가능하게 하다 make 《a matter》 possible
▶ 가능한 범위 내에서 도와 드리겠습니다 I'll help you as far as possible.
▶ 그것은 얼마든지 가능한 일이다 That's quite possible.
▶ 불가능을 가능케 하려고 해도 소용없다 It's no use trying to make the impossible possible.

가능성 可能性 possibility; likelihood; 〈기회〉 chances; 〈잠재적인〉 potential; potentialities
♦ 가능성이 있는 possible; feasible / 가능성이 없는 impossible; not possible / 크게 매상을 올릴 가능성이 있는 《an invention》 with a big sales potential / 가능성이 전혀 없다 be absolutely impossible / 가능성을 개발하다 develop *one's* potential [potentialities]
▶ 그 회사는 파산할 가능성이 크다 The company is very likely to go bankrupt.
▶ 실험이 성공할 가능성은 있습니까? Is there a possibility that the experiment will succeed?
▶ 성공할 가능성은 반반이다 There is an even chance of success.
▶ 입학 시험에 합격할 가능성은 충분히 있다 There is a good [every] chance of passing the entrance examination.
▶ 한국은 커다란 가능성을 지닌 나라다 Korea is a country with great potentialities.

가다¹ 1 〈목적한 곳으로 움직이다〉 go (to); come; be bound [destined] for 《Pusan》 (탈것 등이); 〈방문하다〉 call 《on sb, at sb's house》; visit; pay sb a visit; 〈…을 향해 떠나다〉 leave for 《Cheju》; 〈출석하다〉 attend 《a meeting》; 〈길이 …로 통하다〉 lead to 《the station》; go

---

가능성의 표현

1. …일지도 모른다; …일 것이다
(1) may [might] do
▶ 저녁 무렵에 비가 올지도 모른다 It may rain toward evening. ⇌ It might rain toward evening.
▶ 그는 아마 정원에서 일을 하고 있을 것이다 He may be working in the garden.
▶ 그는 아마 당신이 결혼했다는 것을 모를 겁니다 He may not know that you are married. ⇌ He might not know that you are married. (▶ might는 약한 가능성을 나타내어 「어쩌면 …일도 있을지 모른다」는 등의 뜻이 있다)
(2) might do 〈간접화법에서〉
▶ 「오늘 밤에 비가 올지도 모른다」고 그는 말했다 He said, "It may [might] rain tonight." → He said that it may rain tonight.
▶ 「아버지는 정원에서 일을 하고 계실지도 모른다」고 나는 생각했다 I thought that father might be working in the garden. → I think that father may be working in the garden.
[어법]
가능성을 나타내는 may, might를 의문문에서 쓸 수는 없으므로 다른 어법으로 바꾼다.
May it rain tormorrow? (×) → Do you think it will rain tomorrow? (○)

2. …했을지도 모른다; …했을 것이다
(1) may have + 과거분사
▶ 그는 기차를 놓쳤을지도 모른다 He may have missed his train.
▶ 그들은 길을 잃었을지도 모른다 They may have lost their way.
▶ 그는 시험에 떨어졌을지도 모른다 He may not have passed the examination.
(2) might have + 과거분사 〈간접화법에서〉
▶ 「그는 기차를 놓쳤을지도 모른다」고 그녀는 말했다 She said, "He may have missed his train." → She said that he might have missed his train.
▶ 그들은 길을 잃었을지도 모른다고 우리는 생각했다 We thought that they might have lost their way. → We think that they may have lost their way. (▶ 시제의 일치에 따라 may가 might로 바뀐다)
(3) might have + 과거분사
▶ 그는 익사할 수도 있었는데 다행히 그 배에 타고 있지 않았다. Fortunately he was not in the boat. He might have been drowned. (▶ 가정법 문장과 비슷한 용법으로 「타고 있었더라면」의 뜻이 포함되어 있다)

가다¹

to 《Suwon》; 〈도달하다〉 get to; reach; arrive / 대전으로 가는 기차표 a ticket to Taejŏn / 부산에서 인천으로 가는 배 a ship bound from Pusan to Inch'ŏn / 걸어서 가다 go on foot 《to》; walk 《to》 / 타고 가다 go by 《train, plane, bus》; take 《a taxi to》 / 똑바로 가다 go straight on [ahead] / 스키 타러[낚시질] 가다 go skiing [fishing] / 여행을 가다 start [leave] on a journey [trip] / 유학을 가다 study abroad; go abroad for study / 하루 30마일을 가다 make [cover] thirty miles a day / 그 거리를 11시간에 가다 cover [make] the distance in eleven hours / 군대에 가다 enlist in [join] the army / 학교[교회]에 가다 go to school [church] / 시골로 가다 go down to the country / 언덕 쪽으로 가다 make [take one's way] toward the hill / 오른쪽으로 가다 turn to the right / 광주까지 가다 go as far as Kwangju / 가다가 되돌아오다 turn back halfway / 왔다 갔다 하다 come and go; shuttle 《between the two capitals》 / 가기는 배로, 돌아오기는 기차로 하다 go by boat and come back by train / 10분이면 갈 수 있다 《the place》 can be reached in ten minutes / 갈 데가 없다 have nowhere to go; be turned adrift 《in the world》

▶ 곧 가요 〈누가 부를 때〉 I'm coming.
▶ 나는 내일 인천에 갈 예정이다 I am going to Inch'ŏn tomorrow.
▶ 이 기차는 보스턴에 갑니까? Does this train go to Boston? ⇒ Is this train 《bound》 for Boston?
▶ 그 역에서 공원으로 가는 버스가 있습니다 There is a bus that runs to the park from the station.
▶ 언제 미국에 가니? When will you leave for America?
▶ 그는 비행기로 뉴욕에 갔다 He flew 《over》 to New York. ⇒ He went to New York by plane.
▶ 지난번 동창회에 갔었니? Did you go to [attend] the last class reunion?
▶ 口語 「어디 갔다 오셨습니까?」「경주에 갔다 왔읍니다」 "Where have you been?" "I have been to Kyŏngju."
▶ 아버지는 뉴욕에 가 계십니다 My father has gone to [is away in] New York.
▶ 거기 가거든 편지 주세요 Please write me a letter [drop a line] when you arrive there.
▶ 내일 당신 집에 가겠습니다 I'll come to your house tomorrow. ⇒ I'll come to see you [I'll call on you] tomorrow.
▶ 하와이에 가 보신 적이 있읍니까? Have you ever been in [to] Hawaii?
▶ 그 거리를 3시간에 가기는 어렵다 It is difficult to cover [make, do] the distance in three hours.
▶ 이 길로 가면 마포가 나온다 This street leads to Map'o.
▶ 이제 학교 갈 시간이다 It's time to go to school.
▶ 口語 「차 한 잔 하러 오시겠어요?」「예, 곧 갈게요」 "Would you like to come over for a cup of tea?" "OK. I'll be right over."

▶ 그 도시까지는 기차로 2시간이면 갈 수 있다 You can get to the city in two hours by train.

2 〈지탱·지속하다〉 last 《long》; keep [remain] good; hold 《up》; wear 《well》 (옷이); outlive; live 《out》; survive (목숨이)

♦ 오래 가는 천 serviceable cloth / 오래 가다 〈도구가〉 stand long use; last [keep] long; stand up well; be durable

▶ 나일론 밧줄은 목면 밧줄보다 오래 간다 Nylon ropes outlast cotton ones.
▶ 이 환자는 앞으로 오래 가지 못할 것 같다 I am afraid this patient will not live much longer.
▶ 그 건물은 앞으로 백 년은 더 갈 것이다 The building will stand another century.
▶ 이런 좋은 날씨는 2, 3일 갈 것이다 This fine weather will hold [last] for a few days.

3 〈죽다〉 pass away; die; depart 《from》 this life; be gone

♦ 나이 육십에 홀연히 가다 pass away [die] suddenly at the age of sixty

▶ 그는 젊어서 갔다 He died young.
▶ 그는 가고 없다 He is dead and gone. ⇒ He is no more.

4 〈연락이 닿다〉 reach; come to hand; be received

♦ 연락이 가다 get in touch 《with》; have connection 《with》

▶ 너한테 소식이 갔니? Have you heard the news?
▶ 2, 3일 있으면 통지가 갈 것이다 You'll receive a notice in a few days.

5 〈마음이 쏠리다〉 be inclined 《to, toward》; incline 《to》; tend 《to》

♦ 마음이 가다 become fond of; take a fancy to [for]; have a liking for [to] / 호감이 가다 be favorably disposed [inclined] toward sb

6 〈이해·짐작이 되다〉

♦ 이해가 가는 처사 an understandable [a comprehensible] measure / 납득이 가다 be convinced 《that》 / 이해가 가다 can understand [make out] / 호감이 가다 be favorably disposed [inclined] toward sb

▶ 나는 아직 납득이 안 간다 Still I am not open to conviction.
▶ 그렇다면 수긍이 간다 That makes sense (to me). ⇒ That explains it.
▶ 당신 시계를 누가 훔쳤는지 짐작이 갑니까? Have you any idea who stole your watch?
▶ 그녀는 납득이 안 가는 표정이다 She looks puzzled.
▶ 그 때는 그의 의도가 이해가 가지 않았다 I could not make out his intentions at that time.

7 〈생기다〉 be caused; come about

♦ 금이 간 찻잔 a cracked cup / 금이 가다 crack; have a crack / 손해가 가다 do not pay; suffer [sustain] a loss / 주름이 가다 get creased [wrinkled]

▶ 그 근거없는 소문 때문에 그들의 우정[사랑]에 금이 갔다 That groundless rumor has impaired [caused a crack in] their friendship [love].

8 〈소요되다〉 take; need; require

♦품이 많이 가다 require [need] much labor
► 이것을 만들려면 손이 많이 간다 It takes [requires] a lot of time and labor to make this.
9 〈값이 나가다〉 cost; be worth; be valued
♦시가로 천만원 가는 골동품 a curio worth of ten million won in today's money
► 그 꽃병은 시가로 2백만원 간다 The vase is valued at two million won in current prices.
► 쌀 한 가마에 15만원 간다 The (market) price of rice is 150,000 won a bag.
10 〈등급이 얼마 되다〉 rank 〈first, second〉; come 〈in an order, at a level〉
♦세계에서 으뜸가는 단거리 선수 a sprinter who ranks among the best in the world
► 영어에서는 그가 우리 반에서 첫째 간다 He leads the class in English.
► 부산은 한국에서 둘째 가는 대도시다 Pusan is the second largest city in Korea.
11 〈시간이 경과하다〉 pass 〈away〉; go by; elapse; pass by; roll by; fly〈빠르게〉
♦얼마 안 가서 in a short time; before long / 세월이 감에 따라 as time passes by [goes on]; with the lapse [passage] of time / 시간 가는 줄도 모르다 be unconscious of the flight of time
► 세월은 빨리도 간다 How quickly time flies!
► 이 달도 다 갔다 This month is up.
► 겨울이 가고 봄이 왔다 Winter is over and spring has come. ⇌ Winter is passed into spring.
► 나는 독서에 몰두해서 시간 가는 줄도 몰랐다 I was so much absorbed in reading that I was unconscious of the lapse of time.
12 〈어느 시기에 이르다〉 come 〈to〉; get 〈to〉; be brought 〈to〉
♦연말에 가서 toward the end [close] of the year / 결국에 가서는 in the long run; in the end; at last; after all / 갈 데까지 가다 go to the very limit; 〈口〉 go all the way
13 〈한창 때가 지나다〉
♦전성기가 가다 be past *one's* prime; be on the wane [decline] / 한물 가다 be out of season
14 〈전깃불이 꺼지다〉 go out; be out
► 전깃불이 갔다 The electric light has gone out.
15 〈음식이 상하다〉 go bad; spoil; turn sour [stale]
► 날씨가 더워지면 생선은 금방 간다 Fish go bad quickly in hot weather.
► 여름에 우유는 쉽게 간다 Milk easily goes bad [sour] in summer.
► 이 두부는 맛이 좀 갔다 This bean curd has turned a bit sour.
16 〈때가 빠지다〉 be taken out; be removed; come out [off]
♦옷의 때가 가다 dirt comes out of [comes off] clothes
가다² 〈동작·상태의 계속〉 ♦병이 나아 가다 be getting better
► 해가 점점 짧아져 간다 The days are shortening [getting shorter].
► 보리가 익어 가고 있다 The barley is ripening.
► 날씨가 나날이 더워져 가고 있다 It is getting warmer day by day.
► 인간 관계가 점점 냉혹해져 가는 것 같다 Human relationships seem to be getting colder.

가다가 **1** 〈때때로〉 sometimes; at times; occasionally; on [upon] occasion; 〈이따금〉 (every) now and then [again] ♦가다가 실수하다 make an occasional slip
► 가다가 일찍 일어날 때도 있다 Sometimes [At times] I get up early.
► 가다가 부모님께 편지를 쓴다 I write to my parents occasionally.
2 〈도중에〉 on *one's* way 〈to〉

가다듬다 **1** 〈정신을〉 tighten; straighten *oneself* up; brace [gather] *oneself* 〈up〉; brace 〈up〉 *one's* spirits; gird 〈up〉 *one's* loins; pull *oneself* together; collect *one's* scattered mind
♦기억을 가다듬다 bring back *one's* memory; refresh [awaken] *one's* memory / 마음을 가다듬다 gird *oneself* up (against)
► 나는 그 분을 만나기 전에 마음을 가다듬었다 I straightened myself up before meeting him.
► 정신을 가다듬고 더 열심히 일을 시작하자 Let's brace ourselves (up) and start working harder.
2 〈조절하다〉 tidy up; put 〈things〉 in order; set 〈things〉 in (good) order; adjust
♦(옷)매무시를 가다듬다 adjust *oneself* [*one's* dress] / 목소리[목청]를 가다듬다 clear *one's* throat; modulate *one's* voice

가다랑어 〈魚〉 a bonito 〈*pl.* ~ s〉; an oceanic bonito

가닥 **1** 〈낱낱의 줄〉 a ply; a strand 〈of a rope〉; a strip 〈of cloth〉
♦실 한 가닥 a piece of thread [string] / 두 가닥으로 꼰 실 two-ply thread [twine] / 세 가닥으로 꼰 밧줄 a three-ply rope; a three-strand rope; a rope of three strands / 두 가닥의 흰 줄이 쳐져 있다 be banded with two white stripes
► 이 밧줄은 50가닥의 실로 꼰 것이다 This rope is twined from fifty threads.
2 〈빛·희망 등의 줄기〉 ♦한 가닥의 희망[빛] a ray of hope [light]
► 그가 실패했기 때문에 한 가닥의 희망마저 사라졌다 His failure deprived me of my last hope.
► 성공할 한 가닥의 희망도 없다 There is not the faintest hope of success.

가단 歌壇 the world of songsters [singers, poets]
가단성 可鍛性 malleability [mæliəbíləti]
♦가단성이 있는 malleable [mǽliəbəl]
가단(주)철 可鍛(鑄)鐵 malleable iron
가담 加擔 **1** 〈원조〉 assistance; help; support; 〈관여〉 participation
―가담하다 〈편들다〉 take sides with; side with; stand by *sb's* side; 〈원조하다〉 assist; support; aid; 〈관여하다〉 participate [take part] in; be a party to; be involved in; join company with
♦서방측에 가담하다 be aligned with the West / 폭동에 가담하여 체포되다 be arrested

가당
for implication in a riot
▶ 나는 당분간 어느 편에도 가담하지 않겠다 I will be neutral for the time being.
▶ 그러한 계획에는 가담할 수 없다 I cannot support [lend myself to] such a project.
2 〈공모〉 conspiracy
―가담하다 be a party ((to)); conspire [fall in] with ((a matter))
▶ 그는 그 음모에 가담했다고 한다 They say he was a party to the plot.
■―자 an accomplice; a conspirator

가당 加糖 ◆ 가당한 sweetened ―분유 sugared powder [pulverized] milk ―연유 sweetened condensed milk

가당찮다 可當― 〈터무니 없다〉 wild ((idea)); absurd ((project)); preposterous ((demand)); exorbitant; 〈지나치다〉 awful; excessive; outrageous; 〈부당하다〉 unreasonable ((price)); unwarrantable; unjust ((treatment)) improper ((conduct)); undue; unsuitable
◆ 가당찮은 값 an outrageous price [bid]; a ridiculously high price / 가당찮은 요구 an excessive demand
▶ 네가 그런 일류 호텔에 묵는 것은 가당찮다 It is absurd of you to stay at such a prestigious hotel.
▶ 가당찮은 소리 마라 Don't talk nonsense.

가대 家垈 an estate; a homestead; house and lot; the site of a house; residence

가도 街道 a highway; a thoroughfare; a road
◆ 경춘 가도 the Kyŏng-Ch'un[Seoul-Ch'unch'ŏn] Highway / 상승 가도를 달리다 gain [win] successive victories; be ever-victorious / 출세 가도를 달리다 get ahead [on] in the world

가독 家督 〔法〕 a patrimony; the headship of a family
▶ 그는 가독을 상속했다 He succeeded to his father's house.
▶ 아버지는 가독을 넘겨주고 전원 생활을 누리고 계시다 My father has transferred the headship of his house and enjoys the charm of rural life.
■―상속 succession to ((the head position in)) a family ―상속권 the right of succession to a house; heirship ―상속인 the successor to a house; an heir(남자); an heiress(여자)

가돈 家豚 my son=가아(家兒)
가돌리늄 〔化〕 gadolinium
가동 可動 ◆ 가동의 movable; mobile
■―관절 diarthrosis ((*pl.* -ses)) ―교(橋) a movable bridge ―댐 a movable dam ―성 mobility; movability ―장치 movable equipment ―코일〔電〕a moving [movable] coil

가동 稼動 operation; work
◆ 가동 중이다 be in operation; be at work; be working; be operated / 가동을 중단하다 stop operation
―가동하다 operate; run; work; put into operation
▶ 발전소는 주야로 가동한다 Power plants operate night and day [round-the-clock].
■ 완전― full [full-scale] operation ―능력 the operating capacity ―률 the rate of operation; the working ratio ―시간 the hours of operation ―시설 available [operative, working] equipments ―인구 the man power; the work force ―일수 the number of workdays [days worked]

가동거리다 kick the legs; make the legs kick
◆ 어린아이 다리가 가동거리다 the legs of a baby kick in the air

가두 街頭 a street
◆ 가두에 (美) on the street; in open street / 가두에서 사람을 만나다 meet *sb* on [in] the street
▶ 그들은 가두에서 서명을 받고 있었다 They were collecting signatures on [in] the street.
■―검색 the on-the-street searching of a suspicious person ((by a policeman)) ―데모 (stage) a street demonstration ―사진 snapshot ―사진사 a pavement photographer ―판매 street peddling ―풍경 a streetscape [street scene] ―화가 a pavement artist

가두녹음 街頭錄音 a street-corner transcription; 〈라디오 프로그램의〉 a "Man on the Street" interview
■―반(班) a street-corner transcription service [unit]

가두다 shut *sb* in [up]; lock in [up]; cage in [up]; confine; imprison; pen
◆ 감방에 가두다 put *sb* into a cell [behind the bars]; throw *sb* into prison
▶ 유괴범은 아이를 방에 가두었다 The kidnapper shut the child up in [confined the child to] a room.
▶ 야생 새를 새장에 가두어 두는 것은 좋지 않다 It is not good to confine a wild bird in a bird cage.

가두리 〈모자·그릇 등의〉 a brim; 〈둥근 물건의〉 a rim; 〈옷 등의〉 a hem; 〈천의〉 selvage; selvedge ◆ 쟁반의 가두리 the edge [brim] of a tray
■―장식 edging; a frill

가두모금 街頭募金 collecting contributions on [in] the street; a street collection of subscriptions
◆ 가두 모금 운동을 벌이다 launch [start] an on-the-street campaign for raising funds ((for))
▶ 구세군이 가난한 사람들을 위해 가두 모금을 하고 있었다 The Salvation Army was making a street collection for the poor.

가두선전 街頭宣傳 street [wayside] propaganda [advertising] ◆ 가두 선전을 하다 propagandize [make propaganda] on [in] the street ■―반(班) a street propaganda squad ―원 a street propagandist ―차 a loudspeaker van

가두연설 街頭演說 street [(美) soapbox] oratory; a wayside [stump] speech
◆ 가두 연설을 하다 go on [take] the stump; soapbox ((at))
■―가 a street [stump, soapbox] orator

가동가동 swaying *one's* hips
가동거리다 sway *one's* hips
가드 〔球〕a guard; 〔拳〕 *one's* guard
가드레일 a guardrail; a crash barrier

가득 (to the) full; to capacity
♦돈이 가득 든 지갑 a wallet stuffed [filled] with money / 옷가지가 가득 든 트렁크 a trunk crammed with clothes / 가득 담아 stuff full / 한 잔 가득 따르다 fill a glass full [to the brim] / 가득 차다 become full; be filled up; be chock-full / 탱크에 물을 가득 채우다 fill a tank to the brim with water
▶그녀의 눈에는 눈물이 가득 괴어 있었다 Her eyes were filled with tears.
▶방에는 사람들이 가득 차 있었다 The room was packed [crammed] with people.

가득하다 full 《of》; chock-full; brimful; jam-packed 《with》; crammed 《crowded》 《with people》
♦책이 가득한 책장 a bookcase full of books / 가득해지다 become full; be filled up; fill (up)
♦정원에는 아름다운 꽃들이 가득하다 The garden is chock-full of beautiful flowers.
▶광에는 곡식이 가득했다 The barns were bursting with grain.
▶그의 마음은 근심으로 가득했다 Many anxieties occupied his mind.

가득히 full ⇨ 가득

가등기 假登記 provisional registration

가뜩이나 to make matters worse; (and) what is worse; over and above; besides; moreover
▶그는 가뜩이나 빚이 많은데 실직까지 했다 He was deeply in debt, and moreover he lost his job.
▶가뜩이나 어려운데 아버지마저 갑자기 돌아가셨다 To make matters worse, his father died suddenly.
▶가뜩이나 추운데 어떻게 냉차를 마시니? I am already so cold, how can I drink cold tea?

가뜬하다 1⟨짐·복장 등이⟩ (be) light; not heavy; casual
♦가뜬한 옷차림 《wear》 light dress; casual attire [wear]
2⟨심신이⟩ lighthearted; feel good; relieved
♦가뜬한 마음으로 with a light heart / 마음이 가뜬하다 feel lighthearted [relieved]; be light of heart
▶잠을 푹 자고나니 몸이 아주 가뜬하다 After a sound sleep I feel refreshed.

가뜬히 ⟨마음 등이 가볍게⟩ lightly; lightheartedly; ⟨손쉽게⟩ readily; easily; without difficulty [effort]
▶무거운 짐을 가뜬히 들어 올리다 lift up a heavy load without difficulty / 가뜬히 차려 입다 be lightly dressed [clothed]; wear a light suit
▶그것쯤 가뜬히 할 수 있다 It will be no effort to do it.

가라사대 say; as 《a saint [wiseman]》 says...
♦공자[예수] 가라사대 As Confucius [Jesus] says... / 성경에 가라사대 The bible says...

가라앉다 1⟨밑으로⟩ sink; be submerged; go under; go down 《to the bottom》; ⟨찌꺼기가⟩ settle
♦가라앉은 배 《the treasure of》 a sunken ship / 깊이 가라앉다 sink deep 《into the water》 / 바다 밑에 가라앉다 sink [dip] to the bottom of the sea 《under water》 / 배와 함께 가라앉다 go down [under] with the ship
▶폭풍으로 배가 가라앉았다 The ship sank by the violent wind.
▶그는 물속에 가라앉아 다시는 떠오르지 않았다 He sank under the water, never to appear above the surface.
▶찌꺼기가 가라앉아 포도주가 맑아졌다 The dregs settled and the wine was clear.
▶나무는 물에 가라앉지 않는다 Wood does not sink in water.
▶소나기가 한바탕 오면 먼지가 가라앉을 텐데 A shower will settle the dust.
2⟨잠잠해지다⟩ calm [quiet] down; go [die] down; abate; subside
▶마침내 바람이 가라앉았다 The wind has calmed [gone, died] down at last.
▶태풍이 가라앉기 시작했다 The typhoon began to subside.
3⟨진압되다⟩ be pacified; be put down; be repressed [suppressed]; be settled
▶이 소요도 곧 가라앉겠지 This disturbance will blow over in time.
▶폭동이 가라앉을 것 같지 않다 The riot is unlikely to be put down [suppressed].
4⟨진정되다⟩ calm down; become calm; cool down; recover *one's* composure; restore the presence of mind
♦가라앉은 마음으로 in a subdued mood
▶남편이 무사하다는 소식을 듣고 그녀는 불안한 마음이 가라앉았다 Her fears were allayed by the news of her husband's safety.
▶그의 분노는 아직 가라앉지 않았다 His anger hasn't cooled yet [lost its fire].
▶그들의 흥분은 곧 가라앉을 것이다 Their excitement will soon quiet down.
5⟨통증·부기가⟩ abate; subside; go down; be relieved 《a headache》; allay
▶부기가 가라앉았다 The swelling has gone down.
▶통증이 가라앉았다 The pain has gone [left me, abated].
▶아스피린을 먹었더니 통증이 가라앉았다 Aspirin relieved the pain.

가라앉히다 1⟨물속에⟩ sink; send to the bottom(전투 등에서); ⟨물에 담그다⟩ submerge
▶우리는 적함 3척을 가라앉혔다 We sank three enemy ships. ⇒ We sent three enemy ships to the bottom.
2⟨마음을⟩ calm (down); quiet (down); ⟨분노를⟩ soothe; appease; assuage
▶마음을 가라앉히게 Calm yourself, please. ⇒ Don't get excited.
▶나는 마음을 가라앉히려고 눈을 감았다 I closed my eyes to calm down [calm myself].
▶그는 마음을 가라앉히려고 애썼다 He tried to compose his mind [himself].
▶우리는 그의 분노를 가라앉히려고 애썼다 We tried to soothe his anger.
▶아무도 그의 노여움을 가라앉힐 수 없었다 Nobody could soothe [assuage] his anger.
3⟨고통 등을⟩ relieve; soothe; ease; assuage
▶치통을 가라앉히는 데는 이 약이 좋다 This medicine relieves toothache.
4⟨폭동 등을 진압하다⟩ suppress; put down

♦반란을 가라앉히다 put down [suppress] the rebellion

가락[1] **1** 〈음조〉 a tune; a key; a melody
♦가야금의 가락 a tune of a *kayagŭm* / 왈츠가락 waltz tune / 높은[낮은] 가락으로 in high [low] key / 가락에 맞게 노래[연주]하다 sing [play] in tune
▶그의 노래는 가락이 맞지 않는다 He sings out of tune [melody].
▶바이올린과 오케스트라가 가락이 맞지 않는다 The violin and the orchestra are not in tune.
2 〈일의 능률·기분〉 dexterity; skill; efficiency
♦일에 가락이 나다 get into the swing of *one's* work; warm up to *one's* work
▶이제야 제 가락이 나오는구나 You've got going at last.

가락[2] **1** 〈물레의〉 a spindle; a distaff
2 〈길쭉한 토막의 낱개〉 a stick; a bar
♦엿 한 가락 a stick of rice candy

가락국수 noodles; Korean noodle; wheat vermicelli

가락국숫집 a Korean noodle shop

가락지 a (finger) ring; a set of twin rings
♦가락지를 끼다[끼고 있다] put [wear] twin rings on (*one's* finger) / 가락지를 빼다 slip twin rings off (*one's* finger)

가람 伽藍 a Buddhist temple [monastery]; a cathedral

가랑눈 powdery snow; fine [light] snow ♦가랑눈이 내린다 A light powdery snow falls.

가랑니 a baby louse; a nit

가랑머리 a hairdo with two pigtails; hair braided in two plaits (hanging down the back)
♦가랑머리 소녀 a pigtailed girl / 가랑머리를 하다 wear *one's* hair in pigtails
▶소녀는 가랑머리를 하고 있었다 The girl wore [had] her hair in two plaits.

가랑무 a forked [furcated] radish

가랑비 a drizzle; a mizzle; fine rain; a light [drizzling] rain
♦가랑비가 온다 It is drizzling [mizzling]. ⇌ A light rain is falling.
▶일기예보에 따르면 오후에 가랑비가 내리겠다고 한다 According to the weather report, there will be [we will have] fine rain in the afternoon.

가랑비에 옷 젖는 줄 모른다 (속담) A small leak will sink a great ship. ⇌ Little strokes fell great oaks.

가랑이 a crotch [crutch]; 〈갈래진 것〉the fork
♦바짓가랑이 the crotch of (a pair of) trousers / 가랑이지다 branch off [away]; get [be] forked; bifurcate; ramify / 가랑이를 벌리다 spread *one's* legs apart / 가랑이를 벌리고 서다 stand with *one's* feet [legs] apart

가랑잎 1 〈낙엽〉 a fallen [dead] leaf; a dry leaf
2 (方) 〈떡갈잎〉 an oak leaf

가랑잎에 불붙기 (속담) flare [blaze] up like tinder; be quick to take offense

가랑잎이 솔잎더러 바스락거린다고 한다 (속담) The pot calls the kettle black.

가래[1] 〈긴 토막〉 a stick; a bar; a rod ■—떡 bar [stick] rice cake —엿 bar rice candy [taffy]

가래[2] phlegm [flém]; sputum (*pl.* ~s, -ta)
♦피가 섞인 가래 bloody phlegm / 가래가 끓다 have a hard, obstructive phlegm in *one's* throat / 가래가 많이 나오다 expectorate much; cough up much phlegm / 가래를 뱉다 cough out [bring up] phlegm; expectorate phlegm
▶목에 가래가 끓는다 The phlegm obstructs [sticks in] my throat.

가래[3] 〈농기구〉 a spade; a shovel (with a rope attached to each side of the blade) ♦가래도 파다 dig with a spade
■—꾼 a spader; a shoveler —질 spading; spadework; shoveling: 가래질하다 spade; plow

가래[4] 〈植〉〈열매〉 a wild walnut; 〈나무〉 a wild-walnut tree

가래침 spittle; expectoration; sputum ⇨ 가래
♦가래침을 뱉다 spit; expectorate ▶가래침을 뱉지 마시오 (게시) No spitting.

가래톳 a bubo (*pl.* ~es) ♦가래톳이 서다 have a bubo

가래날 the blade of a spade

가랫대 a spade hand

가랫밥 the clods of earth turned by a spade

가량 假量 1 〈어림 짐작〉 a guess;(a) conjecture;(an) estimate
—**가량하다** guess; conjecture; estimate (at); make [form] an estimate (of)
2 〈쯤〉 about; almost; some; more or less; or so; something like; approximately
♦3만원 가량 about 30,000 won / 5마일 가량 around five miles; five miles or so [thereabout(s)]/한 달 가량 about a month (or so) / 40세 가량의 남자 a man about 40 years of age
♦여기서 거리가 얼마 가량 됩니까? About how far is it from here?

가량없다 假量— 〈어림할 수 없다〉 immeasurable; inestimable; 〈어림 짐작도 못하다〉 be poor at guessing; have poor judgment
♦가량없는 사람 a man of very poor judgment / 가량없는 짓 outrageous conduct
▶비가 가량없이 왔다 We had a tremendous rain.
▶그 빌딩은 가량없이 높다 The building is an immeasurable height.

가려내다 〈분간하여 추리다〉 separate; single [pick] out; sort out; assort
♦나쁜 것에서 좋은 것을 가려내다 sort out [separate] the good ones from the bad / 쌀에서 뉘를 가려내다 separate [winnow] chaff from rice
▶코치는 우수 선수를 가려냈다 The coach picked out best players.

가려쓰다 use properly; make proper use of
♦말을 잘 가려 쓰다 pick *one's* words; be careful about the use of words

가려잡다 choose; select; pick out

가련하다 可憐— poor; piteous [pítiəs]; pitiful; pathetic; touching
♦가련한 고아 a poor orphan / 가련한 정경 a pitiful sight / 가련한 처지 a miserable condi-

tion; a sad plight / 가련히 여기다 feel pity for *sb*; take [have] pity [compassion] on *sb*
► 나는 그 우는 아이가 무척 가련했다 I felt a great pity [felt very sorry] for the sobbing child.
► 그들은 가련한 처지에 있었다 They were in a pitiable situation.
► 가련한 친구로군 What a poor fellow (he is)!
► 가련한 그 아이는 아버지의 죽음을 몰랐다 The poor child didn't know about his [her] father's death.
가렴 苛斂 extortion [exaction] of taxes
―가렴하다 exact heavy taxes 《from》; tax heavily
■**―주 구(誅求)** extortion [exaction] (of taxes): 가렴주구를 일삼다 extort heavy taxes 《from》; impose heavy [unjust] taxes 《on》
가렵다 itchy; itching; 〈서술적〉 feel itchy; be itchy
◆ 가려운 데를 긁다 scratch an itchy spot; scratch where *one* itches / 가려운 데를 긁어 주다 (비유) be very attentive [considerate]; attend to [on] *sb* with scrupulous care; leave nothing to desire [be desired] / 가려워 하다 complain of itching
► 귀가 가렵다 My ear itches.
► 등[전신]이 가렵다 I feel itchy in my back [all over].
► 모기에 물려서 가렵다 Mosquito bites itch.
► 가려우면 긁어라 Scratch yourself if you itch.
► 그녀는 내게 가려운 데를 긁어 주듯 친절하다 She attends to [on] me with utmost care.
가령 假令 1 〈이를테면〉 for example [instance]; let us say; say
◆ 가령 서울에서는 in Seoul, for example / 가령 한 권에 5천원이라고 치고 five thousand won per book, for example / 누군가가, 가령 네가 그런 짓을 했다면 if anyone, let me say you, had done so
► 가령 당신 같은 젊은이가 이 일에는 필요하다 Young men such as you are needed for this work.
2 〈가정하여〉 if; suppose (that); supposing [admitting, granting] that...; in case
◆ 가령 그렇다손 치더라도 admitting [granting] it is so; even if it were so
► 가령 자네가 내 입장이라면 어떻게 하겠나? Suppose you were in my position, what would you do?
► 가령 네 말이 사실이라 하더라도 그것은 구실이 안 된다 Granting that your statement is true, that makes no excuse.
가로 1 〈폭〉 width; breadth

> 解說 사각형의 경우 우리말에서는 그 방향에 따라 가로 또는 세로로 부르지만, 영어에서는 일반적으로 긴 쪽을 **length**, 짧은 쪽을 **width** 라고 한다.

► 이 그림은 가로가 2미터다 This picture is two meters wide [in width].
2 〈옆으로〉 across; crosswise; sideways; sidelong; transversely; horizontally

◆ 가로 건너다 go [walk, ride] across; traverse; cross / 줄을 가로 긋다 draw a line horizontally; draw a horizontal line / 물건을 가로 놓다 lay [put] a thing sideways / 가로 눕다 lie down 《on》; lay *oneself* down / 가로 쓰다 write from left to right / 고개를 가로 젓다 shake *one's* head
■**―대** 〈가로장〉 a crosspiece; 〈천칭의〉 the arm of the balance
가로 街路 a street; a road; **(美)** an avenue (시가지를 통과하는 길을 일반적으로 street라 하며 avenue와 street는 직각으로 교차함)
■**―등** a streetlight; a streetlamp [**(美)** road lamp] ―**청소원** a street cleaner [sweeper]; **(美)** a whitewing
가로놓이다 lie across; lie sideways; 〈방해되게〉 stand in the [*one's*] way
◆ 강에 가로놓인 다리 a bridge across [over] a river
► 그의 앞길에는 큰 난관이 가로놓여 있었다 A great difficulty was lying in wait for him [was lying ahead of him].
가로누이다 lay *sth* (down); place [put, lay] *sth* across
가로다지 〈방향〉 horizontal [transverse] direction; sideway; 〈물건〉 a thing placed [put] across
가로닫이 a sliding window [door]
가로되 as *sb* says...(⇨ 가라사대) ◆ 속담에 가로되 A proverb says [has it] that...
가로막다 interrupt *sb*; obstruct (the view); block [bar] (the way); intercept (light); cut in (a conversation); hinder (*one's* progress); prevent *sb* from (doing)
◆ 길을 가로막다 bar the passage; stand in *one's* way; block the way / 남의 말을 가로막다 cut *sb* short; interrrupt *sb*
► 그들은 굴의 입구를 큰 바위로 가로막았다 They blocked up the entrance to the cave with big rocks.
► 웬 낯선 사람이 대문을 가로막고 서 있었다 A stranger stood in the doorway.
가로막히다 be obstructed; be blocked (up); be barred [interrupted]
► 정원으로 통하는 길은 담장으로 가로막혀 있었다 The fence barred the way into the garden.
► 높은 건물들에 가로막혀 저쪽 경치가 보이지 않는다 The view is obstructed [shut out] by the tall buildings.
가로맡다 〈떠맡다〉 take over *sth*; take upon *oneself*; assume; 〈참견하다〉 interfere [meddle] (in); put [thrust] *one's* nose 《into》
◆ 남의 책임을 가로맡다 assume [undertake] another's responsibility
► 그는 남의 싸움을 가로맡았다 He made the fight his own.
► 남의 일에 이러쿵 저러쿵 가로맡고 나서지 마라 Don't meddle in other people's affairs.
가로새다 steal [slip] out of 《a room》; sneak [steal] away 《from company》; slip away [off]; get away [escape] stealthily
◆ 같이 가다가 도중에 가로새다 sneak away from company on the way

▶ 나는 그가 우리들에게서 가로새는 것을 보았다 I saw him sneak away from us.

가로세로 〈가로와 세로〉 length and breadth; 〈가로와 세로로〉 vertically and horizontally; lengthwise and breadthwise; 〈열 십 자로〉 crosswise; crossways
♦ 가로 세로 교차하는 도로 a crisscross of street / 가로 세로 8피트의 양탄자 an 8 × 8 foot carpet / 가로 세로 줄을 긋다 draw lines vertically and horizontally

가로수 街路樹 a roadside tree; a street tree ■—길 a tree-lined street [road]; a street [road] lined with trees; a boulevard; 〈산책길〉 an arbored walk

가로쓰기 writing in lateral line; horizontal writing
♦ 가로쓰기를 하다 write laterally [in lateral lines]; write from left to right

가로장 a crosspiece; a horizontal [cross] bar

가로줄 a horizontal [transverse] line ♦ 가로줄을 긋다 draw a line horizontally; draw a horizontal line

가로지르다 〈길을〉 cross (a street); traverse; go [cut] across; step across; 〈빗장 등을〉 put (a bar) across
♦ 대문을 빗장을 가로지르다 bar [bolt] a gate / 산과 들을 가로지르다 traverse hills and fields / 선로를 가로지르다 cross [go across] a track / 아무의 앞을 가로지르다 cross the path of sb
▶ 철도는 (유럽) 대륙을 동서로 가로지르고 있다 The railroad traverses the Continent from east to west.

가로채다 take [seige] a thing by force; steal; snatch; usurp (the throne); 〈말을〉 interrupt sb; cut sb short
♦ 공금을 가로채다 embezzle the public money / 남의 말을 가로채다 interrupt sb in his speech; interrupt sb's speech / 남의 재산을 가로채다 seize upon another's property

가로퍼지다 spread [widen] out; grow broad; 〈뚱뚱해지다〉 get pudgy [plump]; be stocky

가뢰 〈昆〉 a meloid; a tiger [an oil] beetle; a Spanish fly; a cantharis

가료 加療 medical treatment [care]
♦ 3주의 가료를 요하다 require three weeks' treatment
▶ 그녀는 성바울 병원에서 가료중이다 She is receiving [under] medical treatment in St. Paul's Hospital.
—**가료하다** treat (a patient); subject (a patient) to treatment

가루 powder; 〈금·석탄 등의〉 dust; 〈곡류의〉 flour (▶ 체로 치지 않은 거친 가루 또는 맷돌로 탄 가루는 meal이라고 함)
♦ 가루 모양의 powdery; powdered / 가루로 만들다[빻다] reduce to [grind into] powder; powder (corn); flour (wheat); pulverize
▶ 빵은 밀가루로 만든다 Bread is made from wheat flour.
■ **옥수수—** corn flour; (美) 〈맷돌로 탄〉 Indian meal ■—**받이**〔植〕⇨ 수분(受粉) —**붙이** 〈음식 재료〉 flour food ■—**비누** soap powder; washing powder ■—**약** powdered medicine; medicinal powder ■—**우유** powdered [dry] milk

가르다 1 〈분할하다〉 split; sever; separate; 〈쪼개다〉 divide; cut in two; 〈분류하다〉 classify; assort
♦ 머리카락을 가운데로[왼쪽으로] 가르다 part one's hair in the middle [on the left] / …을 다섯 조각으로 가르다 divide sth into five parts / 생선의 배를 가르다 cut open the abdomen of a fish; dress a fish 〈요리용으로〉 / 패를 가르다 split [divide] (the group) into (two) rival teams
2 〈분배하다〉 distribute [divide] (among); share (with)
♦ 이익을 반씩 가르다 split the profit half and half [fifty-fifty] / 음식을 갈라 먹다 share food with others
▶ 그는 재산을 세 아들에게 갈라 주었다 He divided [settled] his property among [on] his three sons.
3 〈이간하다〉 ⇨ 갈라놓다

가르마 a part (in one's hair); (英) a parting
♦ 가르마를 한가운데로[왼쪽으로] 타다 part one's hair in the middle [on the left]

가르치다 〈교수하다〉 teach (↔ learn); instruct (in); initiate (in, into); educate; give lessons (in); 〈알게 하다·알려 주다〉 show; inform (sb of); let...know; tell; 〈계몽하다〉 enlighten
♦ 장사의 비결을 가르치다 initiate sb in [into] the tricks of the trade / 컴퓨터의 사용법을 가르치다 train [instruct] sb in the use of a computer / 세상 일을 가르치다 school (his son) in the ways of the world / 시청각 교재로 영어를 가르치다 teach English with audio-visual aids [materials] / 피아노를 가르치다 give lessons in piano; give piano lessons
▶ 우리 아주머니께서는 고등학교에서 영어를 가르치신다 My aunt teaches English at a high school.
▶ 선생님은 학생들에게 거짓말을 해서는 안 된다고 가르치셨다 The teacher taught his students that they should not tell lies.
▶ 그는 곰에게 재주를 가르쳤다 He trained the bear to do tricks.
▶ 그는 젊은이들에게 애국심을 가르쳤다 He inculcated love of their country in the young people.
▶ 헤엄치는 법을 가르쳐 주십시오 Show me how to swim.
▶ 실례지만 잠실 운동장 가는 길 좀 가르쳐 주세요 Excuse me, but will you show me the way to the Chamshil Stadium?
▶ 어떻게 된 일입니까? 까닭을 가르쳐 주십시오 What is the matter? Tell me.
▶ 성함을 좀 가르쳐 주십시오 May I have your name, please?

가르침 〈교훈〉 teaching(s); an instruction; 〈훈계〉 a precept; a lesson; 〈교리〉 a doctrine; a dogma
♦ 공자와 맹자의 가르침 the teachings of Confucious and Mencius / 부처의 가르침 the doctrines [teachings] of Buddha; Buddhism / 가르침을 받다 receive sb's instruction; take [have] lessons (in English); be taught (by)

study ⟪under⟫; learn ⟪from⟫ / 가르침을 청하다 ask for *sb's* instruction
▶그것은 내게 좋은 가르침이 되었다 It was a valuable lesson to me.
▶그는 부모님의 가르침에 따랐다 He followed the lessons he learned from his parents. ⇌ He obeyed his parent's precepts.

가름 ⟨분할⟩ dividing; division; ⟨분리⟩ separation; ⟨분배⟩ distribution; sharing; ⟨분류⟩ classification **─가름하다** ⇨ 가르다 1, 2
■─대 ⟨수판의⟩ the middle bar of an abacus

가리¹ ⟨곡식더미⟩ a heap; a rick [stack] ⟪of hay⟫; a cock ♦가리를 가리다 cock; stack; make a pile; pile in ricks
■건초─ a haystack 노적─ an open-air stack of rice straw

가리² ⟨고기 잡는 기구⟩ a fish trap; a (fish) weir ♦가리를 놓다 set [lay] a weir [fish trap] ■─질 trap-fishing : 가리질하다 trap-fish

가리³ beef ribs ⇨ 갈비
가리가리 to pieces ⇨ 갈기갈기
가리개 ⟨가리는 물건⟩ a cover; a shade ⟪over the eye⟫; ⟨차양⟩ an awning; ⟨두 폭 병풍⟩ a two-fold screen
♦눈 가리개 a blindfold; ⟨말의⟩ blinders [blinkers] / 사람[말]에게 눈 가리개를 하다 blindfold *sb* ⟪put blinkers on a horse⟫

가리나무 ⟨솔가지 땔나무⟩ pine needles and twigs gathered for fuel

가리다¹ ⟨감추다⟩ hide; ⟨일부를⟩ overlap; ⟨덮어서⟩ shield; shelter; screen; veil; shroud; ⟨그늘지게⟩ shade ⟪one's eyes with one's hand⟫; cover (up); ⟨천으로⟩ drape
♦귀를 가리다 ⟨귀덮개로⟩ cover *one's* ears ⟪with earflaps⟫; ⟨손으로⟩ stop *one's* ears; place *one's* hands over *one's* ears / 눈을 가리다 blindfold; ⟨속이다⟩ hoodwink / 등불을 가리다 shade a lamp / 두 손으로 얼굴을 가리다 cover [hide] *one's* face with *one's* hands; ⟨슬퍼서⟩ bury *one's* face in *one's* hands / 손수건으로 입을 가리다 cover *one's* mouth with *one's* handkerchief / 햇빛을 가리다 screen [shade, protect] *sth* from the sun
▶그녀는 눈물이 앞을 가렸다 Her eyes were dimmed with tears. ⇌ Tears blurred her eyes.
▶그는 이마에 손을 얹어 햇빛을 가렸다 He shaded his eyes with his hand.
▶나무가 해를 가리고 있다 A tree keeps the sun off.
▶달[산 정상]이 구름에 가려서 보이지 않았다 The moon [summit of the mountain] was screened by the clouds.

가리다² 1 ⟨선택·구분하다⟩ choose; select; pick out; sort
♦때와 장소를 가리지 않고 disregarding the time and place / 밤낮을 가리지 않고 day and night; ⟪operate a factory⟫ around the clock / 수단을 가리지 않고 by fair means or foul; by hook or by crook; by any means / 둘 중에 하나를 가리다 choose between the two
▶너는 왜 그렇게 가리는 게 많니? Why do you have so many likes and dislikes?
▶친구는 잘 가려서 사귀어야 한다 You must be careful in choosing your friend.
▶나는 먹는 것은 그다지 가리지 않는다 I am not so particular about food [what I eat].
2 ⟨아이가 낯을⟩ bashful; be shy of ⟪strangers⟫
▶이 아이는 낯을 잘 가립니다 This child is often afraid of strangers.
▶그 아기는 엄마를 닮은 여자에게는 낯을 가리지 않는다 The baby takes familiar to a woman who resembles its mother.
3 ⟨분별·분간하다⟩ discern; distinguish ⟪between⟫; tell ⟪A from B⟫; discriminate
♦남녀노소를 가리지 않고 irrespective of age and sex / 선악을 가리다 distinguish [know the difference] between good and evil / 시비를 가리다 discriminate right and wrong; tell right from wrong; argue over who is right / 앞뒤를 가리다 weigh the consequences / 물불을 가리지 않다 go through fire and water; be willing to take any risk / 목적을 위해 수단을 가리지 않다 stick at nothing to gain [attain] *one's* end [object]
▶그는 언제나 공과 사를 분명히 가린다 He always draws a sharp line between public and private affairs.
▶그 두 권투 선수는 우열을 가리기 어려웠다 It was hard to tell which of the two boxers was better.
▶나는 그때 선악도 가릴 줄 모르는 어린애였다 I was then too young to know right from wrong.
4 ⟨셈을 따지다⟩ settle [clear] up ⟪one's debts⟫; settle [square] accounts ⟪with *sb*⟫; settle *one's* accounts
♦빚을 가리다 clear up *one's* debt / 아무와 셈을 가리다 square accounts with *sb*
5 ⟨머리를 다듬다⟩ untangle *one's* hair
♦머리를 가리다 run a comb through *one's* hair
▶그녀는 손가락으로 머리를 서둘러 가렸다 She hastily smoothed her hair back [down] with her fingers.

가리다³ ⟨쌓다⟩ pile up; rick; heap (up); stack
♦볏단을 가리다 stack the bundles of rice plants; pile rice plants in ricks / 장작을 높이 가리다 stack firewood high

가리마 a part ⇨ 가르마
가리맛 ⟨貝⟩ a kind of razor clam
■─살 razor-clam meat
가리비 ⟨貝⟩ a scallop; a scollop
가리사니 1 ⟨지각·분별(력)⟩ discretion; prudence; good sense; wisdom
♦가리사니 없는 여자 a senseless [foolish] woman
2 ⟨실마리⟩ a clue; the drift of an affair
♦가리사니를 잡을 수 없다 can't get what it is all about; be unable to figure it out
가리새¹ ⟨갈피⟩ the drift [thread, direction] of an affair; the thread of an argument; ⟨조리⟩ reason
▶가리새를 모르겠다 I can make nothing of it.
가리새² ⟨鳥⟩ a spoonbill
가리어지다 be [become] hidden [concealed];

get covered [buried]; be screened [cloaked, veiled]; be sheltered [obscured, obstructed]
▶ 해가 구름에 가리어졌다 The sun was obscured by the cloud.
▶ 그 범죄는 비밀에 가리어져 있다 The crime is shrouded in mystery.
▶ 도로 표지판이 잡초에 가리어져 있다 The road sign is hidden by [in] the weeds.

가리키다 〈지적하다〉 point to [at]; indicate; 〈나타내다〉 denote; signify; 〈눈금을〉 read; say; register; 〈지칭하다〉 mean; refer
♦길[방향]을 가리키다 point [indicate] the way [direction] / 지도상의 장소를 가리키다 point out [indicate] a place on a map / …을 손가락으로 가리키다 point (with) one's finger at (sb, sth)
▶ 기호 x는 미지수를 가리킨다 The sign x denotes an unknown quantity.
▶ 그 아이는 자기 집 쪽을 가리켰다 The child pointed in the direction of his home.
▶ 화살표는 동쪽을 가리키고 있다 The arrow points (to the) east.
▶ 바늘은 정북을 가리키고 있었다 The needle pointed right to the north.
▶ 시계 바늘은 9시를 가리키고 있었다 The hands of the clock stood at [indicated] nine.
▶ 온도계는 섭씨 35도를 가리키고 있었다 The thermometer read [indicated, stood at] 35 degrees centigrade.
▶ 「그」는 누구를 가리키는 것입니까? Who do you mean [refer to] by "he"?
▶ 사람을 손가락으로 가리키는 것은 실례다 It is rude to point at others.
▶ 그런 사람을 가리켜 노랭이라고 한다 We call a man like him a miser.

가마[1] 〈정수리의〉 the whirl [whorl] of hair on the vertex [crown of the head]; a hair whirl [whorl]

가마[2] 〈기와·질그릇〉 a kiln; 〈숯〉 a furnace
♦기와[질그릇] 가마 a tile [pottery] kiln / 도자기 가마 a porcelain kiln / 숯가마 a charcoal furnace / 벽돌을 가마에 굽다 bake bricks in a kiln

가마[3] 〈탈것〉 a palanquin; a sedan chair
♦가마를 메다 carry a palanquin on the shoulders / 가마를 타다 ride in a palanquin
■ —꾼 a palanquin bearer; a sedan chair carrier —채 the shafts [poles] of a sedan chair [palanquin]

가마니 a straw bag
♦가마니에 넣다 put in a straw bag
■ 쌀— a straw rice bag
■ —때기 a worn-out straw bag —틀 a bag-maker (machine)

가마 an object; a butt; a target
■ 걱정— a source of anxiety; a butt of scolding; a troublemaker 놀림— a butt of ridicule 맷— a butt of beatings 웃음— a laughing-stock

가마 밑이 노구솥 밑 검다 한다 (속담) The pot calls the kettle black.

가마솥 a caldron; a large kettle
가마우지 〔鳥〕 a cormorant
가막조개 〔貝〕 a corbicula

가만 ▶가만! Keep [Be] quiet [silent]!; Hush!; Hold on!; Wait!
▶가만! 누가 온다 Hush! Someone comes.
▶가만, 내 말도 좀 들어봐 OK, but listen to me.
▶그가 무슨 짓을 하든 가만 내버려 두시오 Leave him alone to do anything.

가만가만 quietly; softly
♦가만가만 걷다 walk softly; go with soft steps / 가만가만 이야기하다 talk in whispers

가만두다 1 〈그대로 두다〉 leave sb alone; let sb undisturbed; do not disturb sb; let sth as it is [stands]; leave sth intact
▶자는 애를 깨우지 말고 가만두어라 Don't disturb a sleeping child.
▶내 책상 위에 있는 것들을 가만두시오 Leave the things on my desk as they were.
2 〈참다〉 tolerate; endure; stand; 〈묵인하다〉 connive [kənáiv]
▶또 버릇없이 굴면 가만두지 않겠다 I won't tolerate [You'll pay dearly for] your further impudence.
▶그 녀석을 가만두지 않겠다 I'll teach him a lesson.
▶그런 행위는 가만둘 수 없다 I can't tolerate [suffer] such conduct.

가만있다 remain still [quiet]; keep silent; stay [be] motionless; sit still
♦하루 종일 방안[집안]에 가만있다 keep one's room [shut oneself up in the house] all day long
▶내가 돌아올 때까지 여기 가만있어라 Stick here till I get back.
▶그 아이는 잠시도 가만있지 않았다 The child was quite restless [always fidgety].

가만있자 well; just a minute; hold on; let me see
▶가만있자, 생각이 안 나네[그걸 어디다 두었더라?] Let me see, I can't remember (it) [where did I put it?].
▶가만있자, 네 생각이 옳을지도 모르겠다 Well, perhaps you are right.

가만히 1 〈조용히〉 calmly; quietly; still; silently; 〈조심스럽게〉 cautiously; carefully; 〈움직이지 않고〉 motionlessly; still; 〈부드럽게〉 softly; gently; tenderly
♦가만히 귀를 기울이다 listen closely / 가만히 기다리다 wait calmly ((for)) / 가만히 방을 나가다 leave the room in silence [without (saying) a word] / 가만히 놓다 put sth cautiously / 가만히 누워 있다 lie motionless / 가만히 말하다 speak in calm tone / 가만히 있다 keep [hold oneself] still
▶우리는 가만히 앉아 있었다 We sat silent [in silence].
▶그녀는 가만히 그의 손을 잡았다 She took his hand softly.
▶깨지지 않게 가만히 놓으세요 Put it down gently so that it doesn't break.
▶어째서 그 일을 내게 알리지 않고 가만히 있었지? What do you mean by keeping it from me? ⇌ Why have you kept it from me?
▶누가 그런 모욕을 받고 가만히 있을 수 있겠는가? Who can stomach such insults?

▶ 그렇게 많은 사람들이 고통 받고 있는데 가만히 보고만 있을 수는 없다 I can't remain indifferent when so many people are suffering.
2 〈몰래〉 stealthily; secretly; in secret; in private; on the sly
♦ 가만히 들어가다[나가다] enter [go out of] (a room) stealthily; steal into [out of] (a room) / 가만히 알려주다 tell sb in confidence [a whisper]; tip in confidence
▶ 그녀는 가만히 내 방에 들어섰다 She stole [slipped] into my room.
▶ 그는 아버지의 책상 서랍을 가만히 열었다 He stealthily opened the drawer in his father's desk.
3 〈그대로〉 ♦ 가만히 두다 leave *sth* as it is [stands]; leave *sth* untouched; leave [let] *sb* alone
▶ 그들은 그 일을 그냥 가만히 내버려 두었다 They left the work untouched.
▶ 그 문제는 가만히 내버려 두기로 했다 We have decided to let the matter rest [not to do anything about the problem].
4 〈곰곰이〉 seriously; carefully
▶ 그가 한 말을 가만히 생각해 보아라 Think over what he said.
가망 可望 〈희망〉 hope; promise; 〈가능성〉 possibility; probability; likelihood; (a) chance; 〈전망〉 prospect(s)

解說 *possibility*와 *chance*는 둘 다 「가능성이 있는 것」을 말하는데 chance가 보다 구어적이다. *prospect*는 「장래의 예측」이라는 뜻이 함축된 말이다.

♦ 회복될 가망이 없는 병 a desperate illness / 가망이 있는[없는] hopeful [hopeless]; promising [unpromising] (attempt) / 가망이 있다 be promising; be hopeful; 〈일이〉 have a bright prospect; 〈사람이〉 have a bright future for *one* / 성공할 가망이 충분하다 stand a fair [good] chance of success / 성공할 가망이 적다 have a poor [slim] chance of success
▶ 도저히 가망이 없다 There is not a dog's chance.
▶ 그녀가 회복될 가망이 있을까요? Is there any chance for her to recover?
▶ 그는 이제 가망이 없다 His chance is up. ⇒ (口) He is a goner.
▶ 그가 올 가망이 있습니까? Is there any probability of his coming?
▶ 그가 성공할 가망은 전혀 없다 There is no hope of his success.
▶ 그 의안이 통과될 가망은 전혀 없었다 There was no likelihood of the bill being passed. ⇒ There was no possibility that the bill would be passed.
가매장 假埋葬 temporary burial [interment]
—**가매장하다** bury temporarily
가맹 加盟 joining; affiliation; participation; alliance; entry (into)
—**가맹하다** join (in); associate *oneself* with; be affiliated [allied] with; become a member (of the league)
♦ 국제연합에 가맹시키다 seat (a newly independent country) in the United Nations
■ —국 a member nation 《of the United Nations》; 조약 가맹국 the signatory powers [nations] to a treaty —단체 a member [an affiliated] organization —자 a member; a participant —점 a member store 《of a chain store association》 —조합 an affiliated union
가면허 假免許 a temporary [provisional] license
가명 家名 〈이름〉 *one's* family name; 〈명성〉 the family honor; the good name of a family
♦ 가명을 날리다 raise the reputation [good name] of the family / 가명을 더럽히다 disgrace [dishonor, bring disgrace on] *one's* family [the family name] / 가명을 더럽히지 않도록 하다 keep up the credit of *one's* house / 가명을 잇다 succeed to *one's* family name
▶ 그의 위업은 크게 가명을 드높였다 His achievement greatly raised the reputation of his family.
가명 假名 an assumed name; a false name; a fictitious name; an alias; 〈저작자의〉 a pseudonym; 〈필명〉 a pen name
♦ 가명을 쓰다 assume a false name; use a pseudonym / 가명을 써서 under an alias / 가명으로 편지를 쓰다 write a letter under a fictitious [a false, an assumed] name
▶ 그는 김민호라는 가명으로 행세했다 He went by the alias [assumed name] of Kim Min-ho.
가명계좌 假名計座 a bogus name account; an account of bogus name
가무 歌舞 (enjoy) singing and dancing; all musical and other entertainments
▶ 정부는 가무 공연 행사를 일절 금지했다 The government ordered a suspension of all public performances in music and dancing.
■ —연(宴) a feast of singing and dancing
가무스름하다 blackish ⇨ 거무스름하다
가문 家門 *one's* family [clan]
♦ 한씨 가문 the Han family; the Hans and their clan / 가문의 명예 a credit [an honor] to *one's* family / 가문이 좋은 사람 a man of (good) family / 가문을 자랑으로 여기다 be proud of *one's* good birth / 좋은 가문에 태어나다 come of good stock [of a good family, parentage]; be wellborn; be of good lineage [birth, parentage, ancestry]
▶ 그는 우리 가문의 명예[수치]다 He is an honor [a dishonor] to our family.
▶ 지금은 가문을 따지는 시대가 아니다 We live in an age when birth and extraction are of little [no] account.
가문 家紋 〈문장〉 a family emblem [crest]; a coat armor; 〈방패 모양의〉 a coat of arms
가문비나무 【植】 a silver fir; a spruce
가물 a drought ⇨ 가뭄
가물가물 〈불빛이〉 flickeringly; shimmeringly; blinkingly; 〈먼 것이〉 vaguely; dimly; hazily; 〈의식이〉 faintly; dizzily —**가물가물하다** ⇨ 가물거리다
가물거리다 1 〈불빛이〉 flicker; glimmer; shimmer; blink
♦ 가물거리는 불빛 a flicker [glimmer] of

light; a flickering light
▶ 등불이 바람에 가물거리고 있었다 The lamp-light was flickering in the wind.
2 〈먼 데 것이〉 haze; become misty [hazy]; 〈눈이〉 grow dim; have dim sight; be blurred
♦ 멀리서 가물거리는 섬 an island dim in the distance / 눈이 가물거리다 one's eyes glaze over
▶ 눈이 가물거려서 잘 보이지 않았다 I was dazzled and could not see very well.
3 〈의식이〉 get fuzzy; have a dim consciousness [memory]
▶ 나는 그녀에 관해 가물거리는 기억밖에 없다 I have only dim [vague] memories of her.
가물다 1 〈날씨가〉 be droughty [rainless, dry]
▶ 오랫동안 날이 가물었다 We have been without rain for a long time.
▶ 날이 가물어서 농사를 망쳤다 The crops have failed because of dry weather.
2 〈인재가〉 lack; short; want
▶ 인재가 가물었다 We are short [suffer a shortage] of talented people.
가물들다 〈날씨가〉 become droughty; enter a long period of drought; 〈농작물이〉 suffer from a drought
가물철 the dry season
가물치 [魚] a snakehead; a snakehead mullet; a snakeheaded fish
가물타다 be easily affected [damaged] by a drought; be apt to suffer from [susceptible to] dry weather
▶ 이 신품종 벼는 쉽게 가물탄다 This new variety of rice is apt to suffer from droughts.
가뭄 a drought; dry weather; want of rain
♦ 오랜 가뭄 a long drought; a (long) spell of dry weather / 가뭄에 단비 a looked-for [welcome] rain during the dry season / 오랜 가뭄으로 생긴 피해 damage from [caused by] a prolonged drought
▶ 석 달 이상이나 가뭄이 들었다 We have a drought for over three months.
▶ 1년 동안 가뭄이 계속되었다 The drought lasted (for) a year.
가뭇가뭇하다 black-spotted; dotted [speckled] with black
♦ 가뭇가뭇한 수염이 나 있다 have a stubble of black beard
가뭇없다 〈눈에 띄지 않다〉 be out of sight; be nowhere to be seen; 〈소식이 없다〉 hear nothing from; 〈흔적이 없다〉 not found; leave no trace behind
♦ 가뭇없이 without (leaving any) trace
가뭇하다 blackish
가미 加味 1 〈음식 맛의〉 seasoning; flavoring —가미하다 flavor; tinge [season, lace] sth 《with》; put spices in
♦ 레몬향을 가미한 아이스크림 ice cream flavored with lemon / 쇠고기에 생강을 가미하다 season beef with ginger
▶ 그 여자는 커피에 브랜디를 가미해 마셨다 She took her coffee laced with brandy.
2 〈첨가〉 addition
♦ 위트를 가미한 대화 conversation seasoned with wit / 법에 인정을 가미하다 temper justice with mercy
▶ 이 과목의 성적은 시험 점수에 출석률을 가미해서 매긴다 The grade in this course will be your test score plus attendance.
3 〈다른 약재를 더 넣음〉 [韓醫] adding sth to a regular medical prescription
가발 假髮 a wig; false hair; 〈부분적 또는 미용상의〉 a hairpiece; a periwig; 〈남성용 또는 옛날 장식용의〉 a toupee [tupéi]; (총칭) wiggery
♦ 가발을 쓰다 wear [put on] a wig
■ —사 〈배우의〉 a wigmaker (for actors); a theatrical coiffeur —상(商) a wig maker
가방 a bag; a portfolio (pl. -lios)

> 解說 **bag**은 여러 가지 가방·가방류를 포괄해서 말하는 일반적인 말. 갈아입을 옷 등을 넣는 소형 여행 가방은 **suitcase**, 네모꼴의 대형 여행 가방은 **trunk**, 서류 가방은 일반적으로 **briefcase**라고 하는데, 같은 서류 가방이지만 직사각형이고 평평하며 견고한 것은 **attaché case**라고 한다. 흔히 말하는 007가방이다. 어깨에 메는 가방, 학생용 가방 등은 **satchel**이라고 한다.

♦ 가방을 들다 carry a bag / 가방에 넣다 put (things) in [into] a bag; 〈싸다〉 pack (up) a bag [trunk] / 가방에서 꺼내다 take [get] out of a bag
■ 책— 〈학생의〉 a satchel

가방 — 손잡이 handle — 플랩 flap — 멜빵 shoulder strap — 탭 tab — 사이드 포켓 exterior pocket

가법 加法 [數] addition ⇨ 덧셈
가법 家法 1 〈가정의 법도〉 family rules; a family code of regulations; a family constitution; 〈관습〉 family tradition [customs]
2 〈가전(家傳)의 방법〉 a technique [skill, art, formula] passed down in the family for generations(▶technique은 기법, skill은 기술, art는 기예, formula는 방식을 뜻함)
가벼워지다 be [become] lighter; 〈병세 등이〉 be less serious
♦ 마음이 가벼워지다 be relieved of one's worries; be lightened in heart (at the news)
▶ 이로써 마음의 짐이 가벼워졌다 This has relieved me of my burden. = This took the weight off my mind.
▶ 그 말을 들으니 마음이 가벼워지는군 I'm relieved [It's a relief] to hear that.
가벼이 lightly ⇨ 가볍게
가변 可變 variableness; variability; changeableness
♦ 가변적인 changeable; variable; controllable
■ —비용 [자본] variable cost [capital] —익 (翼) variable [adjustable] wings —저항기 a rheostat; a variable resistor —차선 a reversi-

ble lane / 전압 발전기 a variable voltage generator / 콘덴서 a variable condenser

가볍게 ⟨살짝⟩ lightly; softly; ⟨수월하게⟩ easily; without any effort [difficulty]; with ease; ⟨경미하게⟩ slightly; ⟨경솔하게⟩ rashly; indiscreetly; ⟨간단하게⟩ lightly; plainly; simply
♦문을 가볍게 두드리다 knock lightly at the door / 담을 가볍게 뛰어넘다 jump over the fence with ease / 가볍게 보아넘기다 overlook; pass over sth lightly / 인명을 가볍게 여기다 make light of human life / 가볍게 3승을 올리다 win three games lightly / 고통을 가볍게 하다 relieve [ease] suffering / 세금을 가볍게 하다 lighten [reduce] taxes / 6개월 금고형으로 가볍게 선고하다 reduce a sentence to six months' imprisonment
▶그는 큰 바위를 가볍게 들어 올렸다 He lifted (up) a huge rock easily [with ease].
▶그는 내 어깨[등]를 가볍게 두드렸다 He tapped me on the shoulder [back].
▶그는 가볍게 아침 식사를 마쳤다 He had a light breakfast.
▶나는 가볍게 일을 끝마쳤다 I finished the work with ease.
▶그 소년은 발걸음도 가볍게 집으로 돌아갔다 The boy went home on wings [with light steps].
▶쉬운 문제라도 가볍게 보아서는 안 된다 You must not make light of even an easy question.
▶입을 가볍게 놀리지 마라 Be careful what you say.

가볍다 1 ⟨무게가⟩ light; not heavy
♦가벼운 짐 a light load; light baggage [luggage] / 무게가 가볍다 be light in weight; weigh light / 체중이 가볍다 be lightweight; be light in weight
▶동생은 나보다 5킬로그램이 가볍다 My brother is five kilograms lighter than I.
▶이 짐은 내게는 가볍다 This baggage is light for me.
▶이 천은 솜털처럼 가볍다 This cloth is as light as a feather.
▶그는 몸이 가볍다 (비유) He is always willing to [ready for] work.
▶그 남자는 신장에 비해 체중이 좀 가벼운 편이다 For his height, the man is rather light.
2 ⟨경박하다⟩ rash; reckless; indiscreet; careless; hasty
♦입이 가볍다 ⟨잘 지껄이다⟩ be talkative; have a loose tongue; wag one's tongue too freely; ⟨잘 누설하다⟩ be a telltale; be given to talebearing
▶그 사람은 입이 가볍다 He can't keep a secret.
▶그녀는 궁둥이가 가볍다 She never sits still for long.
3 ⟨중요하지 않다⟩ light; insignificant; unimportant
♦책임이 가볍다 be not in a responsible position
▶너의 책임은 결코 가볍지 않다 Your responsibility is by no means light.
4 ⟨경미하다⟩ trifling; slight; not serious

♦가벼운 감기[두통] a slight [touch of] cold [headache] / 가벼운 범죄 a minor offense / 가벼운 우수를 띤 시 a poem with a touch of [tinged with] melancholy
▶우리측의 손해는 가볍다 The damage to us is minor.
▶내 상처는 가볍다 I am only slightly injured.
▶처벌은 예상했던 것보다 가벼웠다 The punishment was lighter than expected.
▶그의 병은 생각했던 것보다 가벼웠다 He was less serious than I had expected.
▶나는 가벼운 두통이 있다 I have a slight headache.
5 ⟨수월하다⟩ easy; simple; light
♦가벼운 일 an easy job; light work / 가벼운 읽을 거리 light [easy] reading / 가벼운 운동을 하다 take light exercises
6 ⟨홀가분하다⟩ light; lighthearted
♦가벼운 마음으로 with a light heart; without taking it too seriously; lightheartedly; cheerfully
▶가벼운 마음으로 와 주십시오 Please come lightheartedly.
7 ⟨담박하다⟩ not heavy; light; plain
♦가벼운 농담 a little [light] joke / 가벼운 식사 a light meal; a snack
▶저 음식점에서 가벼운 식사를 하는 게 어때요? Why don't we have a light meal [snack] at that restaurant?
8 ⟨경쾌하다⟩ light; nimble
♦몸놀림이 가벼운 사람 a nimble [an agile] person / 가벼운 발걸음으로 걷다 step lightly; go with light steps [on wings] / 가벼운 옷차림을 하다 be lightly dressed
▶그는 가벼운 옷차림으로 여행을 떠났다 Lightly dressed, he set forth on a trip.

가보 家譜 ⟨족보⟩ a genealogy; a lineage; a pedigree; a genealogical chart; a family tree

가보 家寶 ⟨보배⟩ a family [an ancestral] treasure; an heirloom
▶이 고려 청자는 우리 집안의 가보다 This Koryŏ celadon is our family heirloom.
▶그 향로는 대대로 내려오는 가보다 The incense burner is an heirloom of the family handed down for generations [from generation to generation].

가보 (일) ⟨노름의⟩ nine points in gambling; the lucky nine
♦가보를 잡다 draw nine-point hand / 가보로 먹다 win [get] the stakes with the number nine [nine-point hand]

가본 假本 a counterfeit copy; a spurious edition ⟨of books, pictures, calligraphy⟩

가봉 加俸 an additional [extra] allowance; a special allowance
♦연간 100만원의 가봉을 받다 get a special allowance of one million won per year (in addition to one's regular salary) / 가봉을 지급하다 grant an extra [additional] allowance ⟨of 300,000 won⟩
■연공— an allowance for long service; a long service allowance

가봉 假縫 basting; fitting; tacking
▶가봉은 언제 됩니까? When will it be ready

가봉

for a first fitting?
―가봉하다 baste; tack; have a (first) fitting
♦가봉하러 가다 go to a tailor's (shop) to be fitted [for a fitting]
▶나는 새 양복을 가봉했다 I had a new suit fitted on me.

가봉 〈나라 이름〉 Gabon; 〈공식명〉 the Gabonese Republic
♦가봉의 Gabonese ■―사람 a Gabonese; (총칭) the Gabonese

가부 可否 1 〈옳고 그름〉 right or wrong; good or bad; 〈적부〉 advisability; propriety 《of coeducation》
♦가부를 논하다 discuss [argue about] the advisability 《of a fund-raising campaign》
▶이제와서 가부를 논해도 어쩔 수 없다 It cannot be helped now even if we argue as to what is right and wrong.
2 〈찬부〉 ayes and nays; pros and cons; for and against
♦가부간(에) whether yes or no [right or wrong]; 〈어느 쪽이건간에〉 anyway; in either case / 가부를 의논하다 argue 《the question》 for and against [pro and con] / 투표로 가부를 정하다 decide sth by vote; put sth to vote; take a vote 《on》
▶남녀 공학에 대한 가부 논의가 활발해졌다 There are many views, pro and con on coeducation.
▶가부간 곧 좀 알려 주시오 Please let me know soon whether it is yes or no.
▶오늘은 가부간 그 일을 매듭짓겠다 At any rate I'll settle the matter today.
▶투표 결과는 가부 반반씩이었다 The votes were equally divided.
▶가부가 동수일 때는 의장의 결정에 따른다 In case of a tie, the presiding officer shall decide the issue.
▶우리는 그 계획 실행의 가부를 논의했다 We discussed all the pros and cons of the plan before carrying it out.
▶국회의원들은 법안의 가부를 투표에 부쳤다 The members of the national assembly voted for and against the bill.

가부장 家父長 a head of a family; a patriarch; [法] a paterfamilias (pl. patres-)
♦가부장제(도) patriarchy

가분수 假分數 [數] an improper fraction

가불 假拂 an advance (payment); payment in advance; 〈임시의〉 a suspense payment
―가불하다 advance; make an advance; pay in advance; pay 《money》 beforehand
♦봉급에서 30만원을 가불받다 get an advance of 300,000 won [have 300,000 won advanced] on one's salary
▶봉급에서 30만원만 가불해 주세요 Could you advance me 300,000 won on my salary?
■―계정 an advance account ―금 an advance ―액 an amount advanced

가붓하다 rather light

가빈에 사양처라 〈속담〉 When in poverty, a man wishes for a good wife.

가빈하다 家貧― be of a poor family; be in needy circumstances [poverty]

가뿐가뿐하다 《all things are》 light; 〈경쾌하다〉 airy; buoyant

가뿐하다 〈물건이〉 rather light; not heavy; 〈몸·행동이〉 airy; nimble; lightsome; buoyant; 〈마음이〉 light; without worry [anxiety]; carefree
♦몸이 가뿐하다 be in good condition; be [feel] well
▶내 서류 가방은 가뿐하다 My briefcase is light.
▶그 일이 해결되고 나니 마음이 가뿐하다 As the matter is settled, I am relieved of my worries [anxiety].
▶그 소식을 듣고 그녀는 마음이 가뿐해졌다 The news lightened her gloom.

가쁘다 〈숨이 차다〉 be out of breath; gasping [panting] 《for breath》; difficult in breathing; 〈힘에 겹다〉 burdensome; hard
♦가쁜 숨을 몰아 쉬며 gaspingly / 숨이 가쁘다 be short of breath; feel choky; can hardly breathe
▶나는 긴 계단을 오르면 숨이 가쁘다 I run [get] out of breath when I go up a long staircase.
▶숨이 가빠서 더는 못 뛰겠다 I am out of breath and can't run any farther.

가사 家事 housework (▶좁은 뜻으로는 집안 청소·정리의 뜻이며 취사는 포함되지 않음); housekeeping; household affairs; domestic work
♦가사 돕는 사람 a domestic helper / 가사를 도맡다 be in charge of the affairs of the household / 가사를 돕다 help 《one's mother》 with the housework / 가사를 배우다 learn housekeeping 《under sb》
▶그녀는 가사 때문에 내일 쉽니다 She will be absent tomorrow for family reasons.
▶그녀는 가사를 돌봐 줄 사람을 찾고 있다 She is looking for someone who will do housework.
▶아내가 죽은 후 조카딸이 쭉 우리(집) 가사를 돌봐 주고 있다 My niece has kept house for us ever since my wife died.
▶그녀는 가사에 쫓기고 있다 She is busy with her housework.
■―사건 [法] a legal case involving a family ―조정 [法] mediation of a family dispute

가사 假死 [醫] asphyxia; asphyxiation; suspended animation; apparent death
♦가사 상태에 빠지다 fall into a state of suspended animation / 가사 상태에 있다 be in a ashyxiation; be in a (temporary) state of suspended animation [apparent death] / 가사 상태에서 깨어나다 revive from apparent death 《by artificial respiration》
▶그녀는 지금 가사 상태다 She is now in a state of apparent death.

가사 袈裟 a Buddhist priest's stole

가사 歌詞 words 《of a song》; 〈가요〉 the lyrics; 〈오페라〉 the libretto
▶누가 이 노래의 가사를 지었습니까? Who wrote the words of this song?
▶이 노래의 곡조는 가사와 잘 맞지 않는다 The tune of this song does not quite fit the words

[lyrics].
가산 加算 add ⇨ 더하기
―가산하다 add 《to》; 〈산입하다〉 include 《interest》
◆ 이자를 가산하다 add [include] interest 《to principal》
▶ 가격에 소비세가 가산됩니다 A consumption tax will be added to the price.
▶ 이 5백만원에는 이자가 가산되어 있지 않다 Interest is not included in this five million won.
■ **―금** additional dues **―기** an summing amplifier **―세** an surtax **―연산 증폭기** adder
가산 家産 family property [estate]; one's fortune; one's means
◆ 가산을 탕진하다 [일으키다] squander [make] one's fortune
▶ 그는 가산이 기울었다 His fortune began to fall [ebb]. ⇌ He sank in fortune.
▶ 그는 당대에 막대한 가산을 일으켰다[모았다] He made a large fortune in his lifetime.
가산명사 可算名詞 〖文法〗 a countable(↔ uncountable) noun
가살 a hateful stuck-up attitude; snobbishly conceited airs
◆ 가살부리다[떨다, 빼다, 피우다] behave in a hateful stuck-up way / 가살스럽다 be stuck-up and hateful
■ **―(쟁)이** a hateful stuck-up person; a pert [saucy] person
가상 家相 the aspect [physiognomy] of a house
가상 假像 〈TV・레이더 등의〉a ghost (image); a false image; 〈광석 결정의〉a pseudomorph; 〈컴퓨터의〉 virtual ■ **―기억** 〖電算〗 virtual storage
가상 假想 imagination;(a) supposition
◆ 가상의 imaginary; hypothetical; supposed; assumed / 가상의 적과 싸우다 fight [tilt at] windmills
―가상하다 imagine; assume; suppose
◆ 적으로 가상하다 assume 《a country》 to be the enemy
■ **―원자전** a simulated atomic war **―적(국)** a hypothetical [an imaginary, a potential, a supposed] enemy 《country》
가상 嘉尙 applause; commendation; praise
―가상하다 admirable; commendable; laudable; praiseworthy
◆ 가상히 여기다 commend sb for 《his good act [deed]》
▶ 선생님은 내 선행을 가상히 여겨 칭찬해 주셨다 The teacher applauded me in appreciation of my good deeds.
가새지르다 lay 《two sticks》 across (each other); intersect; place [join] crosswise; crisscross ◆ 두 깃대를 가새지르다 set up two flagpoles across each other
가새표 ―標 a cross; an x ⇨ 가위표
가새풀 〖植〗 a milfoil; a yarrow
가석방 假釋放 parole; release on parole; conditional release [discharge]
▶ 그는 지금 가석방 중이다 He is on parole. ⇌ He is paroled.
―가석방하다 put [release] sb on parole
■ **―자** a criminal on parole; a parolee
가석하다 可惜― regrettable; deplorable; pitiful; sad; lamentable
▶ 그녀가 지금 서울에 없다니 가석하다 It's a pity (that) she is not in Seoul now.
▶ 그처럼 촉망되는 작가가 그렇게 젊은 나이에 죽다니 가석한 일이다 It is regrettable that a promising writer like him died so young.
▶ 그 사건은 그에게는 가석한 일이었다 The affair was lamentable business for him.
가선 ―線 1 〈의복 등의〉 a hem; a border; a fringe
◆ 저고리[에이프런]에 가선을 두르다 hem a jacket [put a border on an apron]
2 〈눈시울의〉 the wrinkles of a double eyelid fold
가선 架線 〈공사〉 overhead [aerial] wiring; 〈선〉 an overhead wire [line] ■ **―공(工)** a lineman **―공사** wiring work
가설 架設 〈전화 등의〉 installation; construction; erection; building
―가설하다 construct 《a railway》; build [construct] 《a bridge》; install 《a telephone》; lay 《a cable》; span 《a bridge》
◆ 가설 중이다 be under construction; be in process of being installed
▶ 집에 전화를 가설하고 싶은데요 I would like to install a telephone in my house.
▶ 저 산에 케이블을 가설하는 것은 난공사다 It is a hard job to build [construct] a cableway on that mountain.
■ **―공사** building [construction] work **―도** an erection diagram; an erection drawing **―주택** a temporary dwelling **―하중** erection load
가설 假設 1 〈임시 설치〉 temporary construction
◆ 가설한[된] temporary; provisional
―가설하다 construct [put up] temporarily; build [install] for the time being
▶ 강에 다리가 가설되었다 A temporary bridge was built across the river.
2 〈가정〉 supposition; 〖法〗 fiction
―가설하다 suppose; assume; presume
■ **―공사** false work; temporary work **―무대 (put up)** a makeshift stage
가설 假說 a hypothesis (pl. -ses)
◆ 가설의 hypothetic(al) / …이라는 가설에 입각하여 on the hypothesis that... / 가설을 세우다 set up [formulate] a hypothesis; hypothesize
▶ 그 가설은 증명되었다 The hypothesis was proved [verified].
■ **―검정** testing of statistical hypothesis
가설극장 假設劇場 a temporary theater
▶ 그곳에 가설 극장이 세워졌다 A temporary theater was built there.
가성 苛性 causticity ◆ 가성의 caustic
■ **―알코올** caustic alcohol
가성 假性 ◆ 가성의 false; temporary; pseud; pseudo ■ **―근시** false nearsightedness [shortsightedness]; 〖醫〗 pseudomyopia **―빈혈** pseudoanemia **―임신** false pregnancy

―콜레라 pseudocholera
가성 假聲 1 〔樂〕〈발성법〉falsetto
▶그는 지금 가성으로 노래를 부른다 He is singing in falsetto.
2 〈지어내는 목소리〉a false voice
♦가성을 내다 disguise *sb's* voice; make up the voice ((of))

가성대 假聲帶 〔解〕a false (vocal) cord

가세 苛稅 a heavy [high] tax [duty] ♦가세에 시달리다 suffer from heavy taxes

가세 加勢 〈거듦·도움〉help; assistance; support; backing; reinforcement
▶나는 친구의 가세를 구했다 I sought my friend's help.
―가세하다 help; aid; assist; back; give support to; line up with; 〈편들다〉take sides with; side with
♦약자 편에 가세하다 take sides with [stand by] the weaker / 적에게 가세하다 line up with the enemy
▶약자에게 가세하는 게 인정이다 It is humane to side [take sides] with the underdog.
▶내가 이제 가세하러 가겠다 I will come to your assistance.
▶어느 쪽에도 가세하지 마라 Don't take sides [commit yourself to either side].

가세 家勢 economic [financial] conditions of a family; family circumstances
♦가세가 기울다 sink in fortune / 가세가 넉넉하다 be well [comfortably] off; be in easy circumstances / 가세가 넉넉하지 못하다 be badly [poorly] off; be poorly [needily, narrowly] provided for
▶그 집은 가세가 기울고 있다 The fortunes of the family are on the wane [decline].

가소롭다 可笑― (be) laughable; ridiculous; ludicrous; absurd
▶그가 국민 경제를 논하다니 가소롭다 It is a ridicule that he should talk about national economy.
▶네가 그를 가르치겠다니 가소롭다 It is ridiculous to imagine you teaching him anything.
▶가소롭기 짝이 없다 It is utterly ridiculous.

가소성 可塑性 plasticity ⇨ 소성
♦열가소성의 thermoplastic / 가소성이 있는 plastic ■―소재 plastic materials ―점토 plastic clay

가소제 可塑劑 a plasticizer

가속 加速 acceleration(↔deceleration)
♦입자 가속기 a particle accelerator / 가속이 잘 되는 차 a car with good acceleration / 가속적인 accelerative; accelerating / 가속적으로 at an accelerating pace; with increasing speed / 가속이 붙다 gain speed; gather momentum
―가속하다 accelerate; pick up speed ♦가속되다 be accelerated
▶차는 가속했다 The car speeded up [accelerated, increased speed].
■―순간― 〈자동차의〉lightning acceleration
■―구간 acceleration area ―기 an accelerator ―력 accelerating [acceleration] force ―로켓 a booster (rocket) ―운동 〔物〕an accelerated motion ―장치 an accelerating system; an accelerator ―전압 acceleration voltage ―펌프[페달] an accelerator pump [pedal]

가속도 加速度 〔物〕acceleration
♦가속도로 with accelerated velocity; at increasing tempo
▶사태는 가속도로 악화되고 있었다 The situation was deteriorating with increasing speed.
■중력― gravitational acceleration ―계 an accelerometer ―계수 〔經〕the acceleration coefficiency ―곡선 an acceleration curve ―운동 an accelerated motion ―원리 〔經〕the acceleration principle ―지진계 an accelerograph

가솔린 (美) gasoline; **(英)** petrol; **(美口)** gas
▶가솔린이 떨어져 간다 We are [The car is] running out of gas.
▶이 차는 가솔린을 너무 많이 소비한다 This car uses [consumes] too much gasoline.
■―기관 a gasoline engine ―스탠드 a filling [service] station; **(美)** a gas station; **(英)** a petrol station ―차 a gasoline car

가송장 假送狀 〔商〕a pro forma [provisional] invoice

가쇄 枷鎖 1 〈족쇄〉a shackle; fetters; 〈수갑〉handcuffs; 〈항쇄〉a yoke
♦가쇄를 채우다 shackle [fetter] *sb* / 가쇄를 벗기다 unshackle [unfetter] *sb*
2 〈속박〉(비유) chains; bonds
▶아이들이 가쇄가 되어 그녀는 직장으로 복귀할 수 없었다 She was tied down by the children and wasn't able to return to work.

가수 假數 〔數〕a mantissa

가수 歌手 a singer; a vocalist
■여자― a woman [female] singer 오페라― an opera [operatic] singer 유행가― a pop [popular song] singer 재즈[샹송]― a jazz [chanson] singer

가수금 假受金 〔商〕a suspense receipt

가수분해 加水分解 〔化〕hydrolysis
―가수분해하다 hydrolyze; decompose in water

가수요 假需要 imaginary [disguised] demand; fictitious use; 〈투기성의〉speculative demand ♦가수요의 급증 a sudden [rapid] increase of imaginary demand

가스 gas; a gaseous matter; 〈연료용〉(coal) gas; 〈장내의〉gas; wind
♦가스 상태의 gaseous; gasiform / 가스 불을 약하게[세게] 하다 turn the gas down [up]
▶우리 집은 가스 시설이 되어 있다 We have gas laid on in the house.
▶그녀는 커피를 끓이기 위해 주전자를 가스 불에 올려놓았다 She put a kettle on the gas to make coffee.
〈가스의〉가스의 본관을 잠그는 것을 잊지 마라 Don't forget to turn off the gas at the main.
〈가스가〉장에 가스가 차다 have gas [wind] in the bowels
▶가스가 샌다 The gas escapes.
▶이 지역은 아직 가스가 들어오지 않는다 We don't have gas yet in this area.
▶가스가 새는 것 같다. 가스 냄새가 난다 There seems to be a gas leak. It smells gassy.

〈가스를〉 가스를 틀다[끄다] turn on [off] the gas; turn the gas on [out]
▶ 누구든지 가스를 튼 사람은 볼일을 마치면 반드시 꺼주십시오 Whoever turns on the gas, please be sure to turn it off when you are finished.
▶ 그 여자는 가스를 틀어 놓고 자살했다 She killed herself with gas. ⇒ She committed suicide by gassing herself.
〈가스에〉 가스에 중독되다 get poisoned by gas; be gassed
▶ 나는 공장에서 나오는 가스에 목이 상했다 My throat was damaged by the factory gas.
■ 가정용— household gas 도시— city gas 독— poison gas 배기— exhaust gas 액화— liquefied gas: 액화 천연[석유] 가스 liquefied natural [petroleum] gas 연료[조명용]— fuel [illuminating] gas 연탄— poisoning gas of coal briquette; carbon monoxide 유독— poisoning [poisonous] gas 재채기— sneezing gas 천연— natural gas 최루— tear gas 프로판— propane gas ■ —검침원 a gasman —경보기 a gas alarm —계량기 a gas meter —공급 사업 gas supply business —관 a gas pipe; 〈본관〉 a gas main —괴저(壞疽) 〔醫〕 gas gangrene —괴저균 a gas bacillus —기관[엔진] a gas motor [engine] —난로 a gas heater [stove]: 가스 난로 좀 켜 주세요 Please turn on the gas stove. —누출 a gas leak; an escape of gas —등 a gas lamp; a gaslight —라이터 a gas lighter —레인지 a gas range [cooker] —로(爐) a gas furnace —미터 (검침원) a gas meter (reader) —발생 the generation of gas —발전소 a gas power plant [station] —버너 a gas burner —설비 gas fittings [fixture] —성운(天) a gaseous nebula 《pl. ~s, -lae》 —실 a gas chamber —오븐 a gas oven —온수기 a gas water heater; 《英》 a geyser [gáizər] —요금 gas rate [charges]: 가스 요금 수금원 a gasman; a bill collector for gas —용접법(鎔接法) gas welding —전구 a gas-filled (light) bulb —정(井) natural gas well —조절기 a gas regulator —중독 《die from》 gas poisoning —총 〈최루탄용(用)〉 a gas gun —탄(彈) a gas shell [bomb] —탐지기 a gas detector —탱크 a gas tank; a gasholder —터빈 a gas turbine —폭발 a gas explosion —화(化) 《coal》 gasification —회사 a gas company

가스러지다 grow wild ⇨ 거스러지다
가스마스크 a gas mask; 〔軍〕 a gas helmet ♦ 가스 마스크를 쓰다 wear a gas mask [helmet]
가스체 —體 a gaseous body ♦ 가스체의 gaseous; gasiform
가스트로카메라 〈위(胃) 카메라〉 a gastrocamera
가슴 1 〈흉부〉 the chest; the breast; 〈품〉 the bosom; 〈여성의〉 the bust; 〔解〕 the thorax 《pl. ~es, -races》

解說 **chest**는 늑골 또는 흉골에 둘러싸인 부분으로, 심장·폐를 포함한 흉부 전체를 말한다. **breast**는 chest의 일부분으로, 어깨에서 부터 근육이 솟아오른 가슴 윗부분을 가리키는데 여성의 경우에는 유방을 가리키는 일이 많다. **bosom**은 사람의 가슴, 특히 여성의 가슴이나 의복의 가슴부분을 가리키지만, 비유적으로 감정·애정이 깃든 가슴·마음의 의미로도 쓰인다. **bust**는 특히 여성의 옷이나 신체의 가슴둘레를 말하지만 breast의 완곡어로 쓰이기도 한다.

♦ 넓은 가슴 a broad(↔narrow) chest / 가슴이 풍만한 여자 a full-bosomed [busty, bosomy] woman / 가슴을 드러낸 bare-bosomed 《waitress》 / 가슴이 납작하다 be flat-chested / 가슴이 답답하다 feel oppressed in the chest / 가슴을 쓸다[문지르다] pass one's hand over the breast / 주먹으로 가슴을 치다 beat one's chest with a fist / 가슴을 펴다 throw out [expand] one's chest
▶ 나는 가슴이 아프다 I have a pain in my chest.
▶ 그 여자는 가슴이 풍만하다 She has large breasts. ⇒ She is full-breasted.
▶ 그 소녀는 가슴이 나오고 있다 The girl's breasts are developing.
▶ 그는 가슴을 펴고 걸었다 He walked with his head held high.
▶ 가슴을 펴고 기운을 내라 Keep your chin up and be cheerful.
▶ 아기는 그녀의 가슴에 안겨 자고 있었다 The baby was sleeping in her breast [bosom].
2 〈폐·심장〉 the lung; the heart
♦ 가슴을 앓다 have lung [chest] trouble; suffer from tuberculosis
▶ 나는 흥분으로 가슴이 두근거렸다 My heart beat fast [rapidly] with excitement.
▶ 조금 달렸더니 가슴이 뛰었다 I felt my heart pound after running a little.
3 〈마음〉 the heart; the mind; feelings
♦ 가슴 깊이 간직한 생각 an idea cherished deep in one's heart / 가슴 아픈 heart-stricken; heartbroken; heartrending; brokenhearted; lamentable; regrettable / 가슴 아프게도 to one's sorrow [disappointment] / 가슴 아파하다 eat one's heart out 《over》; be heartsick of; grieve 《at, over》 / 가슴 깊이 묻어 두다 bury 《a secret》 within one's heart; keep 《a confidence》 within one's heart of hearts; hug 《a secret》 to one's bosom
▶ 아들을 잃는다는 것은 가슴 아픈 일이다 To lose one's son is a heartrending experience.
〈가슴이〉 가슴이 터지는 듯한 슬픔 heartbreaking [heartrending] grief / 가슴이 내려앉다 be greatly surprised; be startled / 가슴이 답답하다 have a pent-up feeling; feel frustrated / 가슴이 뭉클하다 have [feel] a lump in one's throat / 가슴이 미어지다 have one's heartbreak; be heartbroken [brokenhearted] / 가슴이 뿌듯하다 be satisfied 《with》; be gratified 《with, by》 / 가슴이 찢어지는 듯한 아픔을 느끼다 feel heartbroken / 가슴이 터질 것 같다 feel one's heart would break [rend]; feel as if one's heart would break [rend] / 가슴이 후련해지도록 울다 weep oneself out; weep one's fill

▶ 나는 그의 이야기를 듣고 가슴이 아팠다 It hurt me in my breast [It pained my heart] to hear his story.
▶ 그 고아를 생각하면 나는 가슴이 아프다 My heart aches for the orphan.
▶ 그는 편지를 읽으면서 가슴이 메었다[뭉클했다] He got all choked up [had a lump in his throat] as he read the letter.
▶ 나는 기대감으로 가슴이 벅찼다 My heart throbbed with expectation.
▶ 그는 가슴이 벅차서 말이 안 나왔다 He was too moved to speak ⇌ Words stuck in his heart with emotion.
▶ 나는 가슴이 뿌듯했다 It was a proud moment for me.
▶ 전화 벨이 울리자 나는 가슴이 철렁했다 When the telephone bell rang, my heart sank into my boots. ⇌ The telephone bell brought my heart into my mouth [boots].
▶ 하고 싶은 말을 다 하고 나니 가슴이 후련했다 After I had said my say, I felt as if a burden had been lifted off my mind.
〈가슴을〉 가슴을 설레게 하다 make *one's* heart flutter / 가슴을 울리다 touch *one's* heart-strings; strike *one's* bosom / 가슴을 죄다 be in great fear (of); feel anxious [uneasy] (about) / 가슴을 태우다 〈사람이〉 pine [sigh] (for); burn with passion; 〈사물이〉 burn *sb's* heart
▶ 그가 무사히 도착했다는 소식을 듣고 나는 가슴을 쓸어내렸다 I felt relieved [sighed with relief] to hear that he had arrived safely.
▶ 그 마지막 한 마디가 내 가슴을 찔렀다 The last word cut me to the heart [quick].
▶ 그녀는 애인이 보고 싶어 가슴을 태우고 있다 She is dying [yearning] to see her love.
▶ 그는 자식의 일로 가슴을 태우고 있다 He is very worried about his son.
〈가슴에〉 가슴에 간직하다 keep *sth* to *oneself* / 가슴에 사무치다 go to *one's* heart; sting *one* to the quick / 가슴에 와 닿다 come home to *one*; appeal to *one*
▶ 그녀는 그 비밀을 가슴에 묻어 두었다 She kept the secret to herself [in her bosom].
▶ 그의 충고가 내 가슴에 와 닿았다 His advice came home to me.
▶ 그들은 가슴에 희망을 가득 안고 이 학교에 입학했다 They entered this school with their hearts full of hope.

가슴걸이 〈말·소 등의〉 a martingale; a girth ♦가슴걸이식 마구 breast harness

가슴둘레 a chest size ⇨ 흉위(胸圍)

가슴속 *one's* heart; *one's* in(ner)most heart; the bottom of *one's* heart
♦가슴속 깊이 deep (down) in *one's* heart / 가슴속을 털어놓다 speak *one's* mind (to); unbosom *oneself* (to) / 가슴속에 간직하다 keep (a secret) to *one's* bosom; bury *sth* in *one's* bosom

가슴앓이 heartburn; a sour stomach; a chest trouble; 〔醫〕 pyrosis; cardialgia ♦가슴앓이를 앓다 have heartburn

가슴지느러미 〔魚〕 a pectoral (fin)

가슴츠레하다 sleepy ⇨ 거슴츠레하다

가슴털 hair on the chest; 〈새의〉 breast down ♦가슴털이 난 사나이 a man with hair on his chest [with a hairy chest]

가슴통 the breadth of the chest; chest expansion ♦가슴통이 넓다[좁다] be broad [narrow] of chest; have a broad [narrow] chest

가습 加濕 humidification ─**가습하다** humidify ■─**기** a humidifier

가시¹ **1** 〈장미 등의〉 a thorn; 〈선인장의〉 a spine; 〈밤송이·우엉 등의〉 a bur; 〈풀잎 등의〉 a prickle
♦가시가 있는[많은] thorny [spinous]; spiny (cactus); prickly / 잎에 가시가 있는 prickly-leafed / 가시에 손을 긁히다 scratch *one's* hand on a thorn
▶ 가시 없는 장미는 없다 (속담) Every rose has its thorn. ≒ No rose without a thorn.
▶ 가시에 내 손가락을 찔렸다 A thorn pricked my finger.
2 〈생선의〉 a fishbone; 〈지느러미의〉 a spine ♦가시가 많은 생선 a fish full of fine bones / 가시가 목에 걸리다 get [have] a bone stuck in *one's* throat
3 〈가는 조각〉 a splinter; a sliver ♦가시를 빼다 pull [draw, pick] out a splinter
▶ 내 손가락에 가시가 박혔다 I have a splinter in my finger.
4 (비유) ♦가시 돋친 농담 a jest with a sting in it; a spinous humor / 가시 돋친 말 a biting remark; stinging words / 가시 돋친 말을 하다 speak daggers (to *sb*); have a harsh tongue; say a biting thing
▶ 그 여자가 하는 말에는 가시가 돋쳐 있다 She has a biting tongue. ⇌ Her words carry a sting.
■눈엣— an eyesore; a hateful [detestable] person; an encumbrance ■—덤불 a thorny thicket [shrub]; a bramble ─면류관 a crown of thorns ─밭 a thornbush; brambles ─밭길 a thorny path; a brambly way : 가시밭길을 가다 follow [tread] a thorny path / 인생은 가시밭길이다 Life is full of troubles [worries]. ─섶 thorny firewood

가시² 〔구더기〕 a maggot; a worm

가시 可視 ♦가시적인 visible ■—거리 visibility range ─광선 a visible ray ─스펙트럼 a visible spectrum

가시나무 〈가시가 있는 나무〉 a thorny plant; a bramble; a brier; 〔植〕 a beech ♦가시나무 울타리 a thorn fence; a hedge of thorns

가시다 **1** 〈씻다·부시다〉 wash off [out]; rinse (off, out) 〈a bottle〉; 〈뒷맛을 없애다〉 take off [get rid of, kill] 〈an aftertaste〉
♦입안을 가시다 rinse [wash] out *one's* mouth / 약을 먹고 사탕으로 입을 가시다 take away the bitter taste of medicine with a candy
2 〈사라지다〉 disappear; be gone; fade away; leave (off); pass off
▶ 통증은 곧 가셨다 The pain soon left me [passed off]. ⇌ I was soon relieved of the pain.
▶ 내 얼굴의 흉터가 가셨다 The scar on my face disappeared [died away].

▶그녀의 얼굴에서 핏기가 싹 가셨다 The color fled [ebbed] from her face. ≒ Her face drained of color.
▶나는 아직 피로가 가시지 않았다 I have not quite recovered from the fatigue.

가시랭이 〈나무의〉 a thorn [splinter, sticker]; 〈풀의〉 a prickle

가시버시 husband and wife; man and wife [woman]; a (married) couple

가시세다 obstinate; tough and stubborn; unyielding; bullheaded

가시철 —鐵 a barb; a prickle
■—망 barbed-wire entanglements; 〔軍〕 a hedgehog —사 barbed wire; (英) barbwire; bob wire

가식 假植 tentative planting —**가식하다** plant (a tree) tentatively

가식 假飾 affectation; dissemblance; pretense; dissimulation; ostentation; hypocrisy
◆가식 없는 말[태도] words without trimmings [an unaffected attitude] / 가식 없는 문장 an unadorned [plain] style / 가식이 많은 사람 a showy [an ostentatious] person / 가식적인 hypocritical; affected; false
▶그는 아주 겸손하고 가식 없는 사람이다 He is quite a modest, plain person.
▶형은 그 여자의 가식 없는 아름다움에 마음을 빼앗겼다 My brother was fascinated with her simple [uncontrived] beauty.
▶그는 가식 없이 아주 솔직하게 말하는 사람이다 He is a very frank and straightforward person.
—**가식하다** make outward show; put a good face on *sth*; pretend, dissemble; dissimulate; play the hypocrite

가신 家臣 a vassal; a retainer

가심 〈부셔냄〉 rinsing; washing ⇨ 입가심
—**가심하다** wash (out); rinse; give 《a thing》 a rinse

가심끌 a finishing [reaming] chisel

가아 家兒 my son

가압 加壓 pressurization —**가압하다** apply [give] pressure 《to》; pressurize ■—솥 ⇨ 압력(~솥) —수형 원자로 a pressurized water reactor (略 PWR) —장치 a pressure device

가압류 假押留 〔法〕 provisional seizure [attachment]
—**가압류하다** put under provisional attachment; seize [attach] *sb's* property provisionally
—**결정** ruling of provisional attachment —**영장** a writ [warrant] of provisional attachment

가야금 伽倻琴 a *kayagŭm*; a (twelve-stringed) Korean harp
◆가야금을 뜯다 play a *kayagŭm*
—**연주자** a *kayagŭm* player

가약 佳約 1 〈만날 언약〉 a lover's rendezvous; an appointment [a date] 《with a girl》
2 〈혼약〉 a promise of marriage [to marry]; a marriage vow; an engagement
▶그들은 부부의 가약을 맺었다 They became man and wife. ≒ They got married.
■백년— a conjugal [matrimonial] tie: 백년가약을 맺다 exchange marriage vows; get married; become man and wife

가양주 家釀酒 home brew; home-brewed liquor

가언 假言 〔論〕 a hypothesis ◆가언적 hypothetical; conditional
■—(적)명제 a hypothetical proposition —적 삼단 논법 a hypothetical syllogism —적 추론 hypothetical reasoning —적 판단 hypothetical judgment

가업 家業 *one's* family business; *one's* father's occupation [trade]; 〈세업(世業)〉 a hereditary occupation [business]
◆가업을 계승하다[잇다] take over [succeed to] *one's* family [father's] business
▶우리 집의 가업은 대대로 포목상입니다 Our family business has been selling dry goods [(英) drapery] for generations.
▶나는 가업을 잇지 않으면 안 된다 I have to succeed to [carry on, take over] my father's occupation.
▶그는 가업을 이어 의사가 될 작정이다 He intends to be a physician, following in his father's footsteps [carrying on his father's practice].

가없다 boundless; unlimited; limitless; endless
◆가없는 바다 boundless ocean / 가없는 우주 unlimited space ▶우주는 가없다 There is no limit to the universe.

가역 可逆 〔物·化〕 ◆가역(성)의 reversible
■—기관 a reversible engine —반응[변화] 〔化〕 a reversible reaction [change] —성(性) reversibility —승압기 a reversible booster —전동기 a reversible motor —전지 a reversible cell

가연 可燃 ◆가연물 inflammables; combustibles

가연성 可燃性 (in)flammability; combustibility
◆가연성의 combustible; inflammable / 가연성 재료 a combustible [an inflammable] material
▶가연성 물질은 불에 가까이 하지 마라 Keep inflammables [combustibles] away from fire.
■—가스 inflammable [combustible] gas —시험 an inflammability test

가열 加熱 heating
◆가열 살균하다 sterilize by heating; heat-treat 《milk》
—**가열하다** heat 《water》; apply heat 《to》
▶이 쇠막대기가 빨갛게 달 때까지 가열하시오 Heat this iron bar until it becomes red-hot.
▶간호사는 수술 기구를 가열하여 소독한다 The nurse gives surgical instruments heat treatment.
■—가소물 thermoplastics —건조 〔藥〕 ustulation —곡선 a heating curve —기 a heater; a heating apparatus —분해 decomposition by heating —시험 a heating [heat] test —압착기 a hot-press —처리 heat treatment

가엾다 〈불쌍하다〉 poor; pitiable; pitiful; 〈애처롭다〉 pathetic; touching
◆가엾은 고아 a poor orphan / 가엾은 신세 a miserable [sad] state [plight] / 가엾은 이야기

a sad [pathetic] story / 가엾게도 sorry to say / 가엾어서 《spare sb》 out of pity / 가엾게 여기다[가엾어하다] feel pity [sorry] for; take pity on; pity sb; sympathize 《with》
► 가엾어라 What a pity! ⇌ Poor fellow! ⇌ Oh, poor thing!
► 그는 가엾은 녀석이다 He is a poor creature.
► 가엾게도 그 아이는 또 야단을 맞았다 The poor child was told off again.
► 가엾어서 볼 수가 없었다 It was too pitiful to watch.
► 가엾으니 살려 주어라 For pity's sake save the poor fellow.
► 그것을 보고 가엾이 여기지 않는 사람은 없었다 No one could look at it without pity.

가영수증 假領收證 a provisional [an interim] receipt

가오리 〔魚〕 a stingray; 《美》 a stingaree

가옥 家屋 a house; a building; (총칭) housing; 〔法〕 a messuage
■—대장 a house register [ledger] —매매 dealing in real estate —세 a house tax; 《英》 a house duty —소개업자[중개인] a house agent; a real estate agent —유지[관리]비 the upkeep [managing] expense of a house

가외 加外 〈특별한 것〉 an extra; 〈여분〉 an excess; what is left over; 〈잉여〉 a surplus
♦가외의 extra (payment); additional; too much; superfluous; excessive / 가외 비용[수입] extra expense [income] / 가외로 extra; in addition to / 가외로 일을 하다 work extra [overtime]; do extra work / 가외로 천원을 더 내다 pay 1,000 won extra
► 그에게는 가외의 수입이 있다 He has an additional source of income.
► 가외로 얼마 더 내면 됩니까? How much must I pay extra for it?

가요 歌謠 a song; a ballad
■대중— a pop(ular) song: 대중 가요계 the world of singers / 대중 가요 작사[작곡]가 a song-writer —계 the world of singers —곡 〈민요〉 a folk song; 〈대중 가요〉 a popular song: 가요곡 가수 a folk singer; a popular singer; a crooner —제 a song festival [fete]: 국제 가요제 an international song fete / 서울 국제 가요제 Seoul Song Festival

가요성 可撓性 flexibility ♦가요성의 flexible

가용 家用 1 〈살림 비용〉 living expenses; cost of living; housekeeping [family] expenses
♦가용의 for home [domestic] use / 가용을 절약하다 cut down [reduce] one's housekeeping expenses
2 〈집안의 소용〉 domestic [home] use
► 이것은 가용으로 남겨 둔 것이다 I have kept this for use at home.

가용물 可溶物 a soluble body
가용물 可鎔物 a fusible body
가용성 可溶性 solubility ♦가용성을 높이다 solubilize; increase the solubility ■—분말 (a) soluble powder —전분 (a) soluble starch
가용성 可鎔性 fusibility ■—금속 (a) fusible metal
가용합금 可鎔合金 a fusible alloy
가우스 〔電〕 a gauss

가운 家運 the fortunes of a family
♦가운을 회복하다 restore the (fallen) fortunes of one's family; retrieve the family fortunes
► 그 집의 가운이 기울고 있다 The fortunes of the family are on the wane [ebb, decline]. ⇌ His family is going downhill [beginning to ebb].

가운 a gown; 〈실내복〉 a dressing gown; 〈잠옷〉 a night gown ♦가운을 입은 (students) in gowns / 가운을 입다 wear (doctor's) gown

가운데 1 〈중앙·중간〉 the middle 《of》; the center 《of》
♦가운데의 middle; central / 가운데 토막 the center cut (of a fish) / 가운데 형 the middle brother / 가운데서 in the middle [center] of (the room) / 가운데를 싹둑 자르다 cut in two in the middle / 가운데를 잡다 hold sth in the middle; hold the middle of sth / 길 가운데로 걸어가다 walk in [keep to] the middle of the road
► 민 선생님이 가운데 들어 일을 결말지었다 The matter was settled through Mr. Min's mediation.
► 테이블 가운데 꽃병이 있다 There is a vase in the center of the table.
► 호수 한 가운데 쯤에 작은 섬이 있다 There is an islet about in the middle of the lake.
2 〈중에·속에〉 out of; of; between (둘 중에); among (셋 이상의); amongst (다수의)
► 너희들 가운데 among you; some of you / 두 사람 가운데 between the two / 이 가운데서 from among [out of] these
► 학생들 가운데는 우수한 사람도 있다 Some of the students are brilliant.
► 그들 가운데는 주디도 끼어 있었다 Among them was Judy.
► 나는 사계절 가운데서 여름을 가장 좋아한다 I like summer best of the four seasons.
► 그는 많은 후보자 가운데서 뽑혔다 He was selected out of [from among] many candidates.
► 이 손수건 가운데서 아무거나 마음에 드는 것을 골라라 You can choose any handkerchief you like out of these.
► 톰은 우리 다섯 명 가운데서 제일 키가 크다 Tom is the tallest (boy) of us five.
3 〈…하는[한] 중에〉 in the course of; while; amid(st); 〈참석하여〉 with sb in attendance; in the presence of sb
♦그럭저럭 하는 가운데 in the meantime [meanwhile] / 가난한 가운데 자라다 be raised in a poor home; be bred in poverty / 위험한 가운데 구출하다 rescue sb in the presence of danger
► 그는 박수가 울려퍼지는 가운데 홀을 떠났다 He left the hall amid a storm of applause.
► 개막식은 회장이 참석한 가운데 거행되었다 The opening ceremony was honored with the presence of the president.
► 바쁘신 가운데 와 주셔서 감사합니다 It's very kind of you to call on me in spite of your being pressed with work.

가운뎃손가락 the middle [second] finger

가옥·방을 나타내는 어휘

1. 집·주택
▶ **집** a house;《美》a home; a residence; a dwelling house (《英》에서는 home은 「안정을 위한 장소」를 가리키서 단순한 건물과 구별하는데《美》에서는 home을 house의 뜻으로 쓰는 일이 종종 있다. residence는 「당당하고 우아한 집」이고 dwelling house는 「가게나 사무실과 구별하여 주택」이란 뜻이다)

▶ **단독 주택** a detached house; a single family house / 산장식 독립 주택《英》a detached chalet house / 방갈로식 독립 주택《英》a detached bungalow / 두 세대용 연립주택《美》a duplex (house);《英》a semi-detached house / 두 세대용 산장식 연립주택《英》a semi-detached chalet house / 두 세대용 방갈로식 연립주택 a semi-detached bungalow / 단층집 a one-story [one-storied] house / 2층집 a tow-story [two-storied] house / 목조가옥 a wooden house / 목골조 가옥《英》a half-timbered house / 석[연와]조 가옥 a stone [brick] house / 조립식 주택 a prefab-ricated house / 셋집 a house for lent [《美》to let] / 농가 a farm house

▶ **한식 주택** a Korean-style house / 양식 주택 a Western-style house / 현대식 주택 an up-to-date house / 분양 주택 a house built for sale; (같은 형태로 지은) 규격형 소주택 a tract house / 이동식 주택 a mobile home [house] (a camper, a trailer house, a motor home 등)

2. 공동 주택
▶ **아파트** 〈건물 전체〉 an apartment house;《美》a block of flats; 〈한 세대용〉 an apartment;《英》a flat (영어의 an apartment house는 임대용·분양용 두 가지를 가리키는데 오토로크·엘리베이터·공용 세탁시설·오락실·휴게실 등을 비치하고 수영장이 있는 곳도 있어 한국의 아파트보다 고급이다. 「임대용」이라고 할 때는 a rented apartment house라 하고 「분양용 고급 맨션」은 a condominium, 약어로 a condo라고 한다) / 셋방식 아파트《英》a maisonette / 고층 아파트 a high-rise apartment building / 엘리베이터가 없는 아파트 a walk-up / 도시의 싸구려 아파트 a tenement (house) / 원룸 맨션[아파트]《美》a bed-sitter (모두가 욕실·부엌에 침실 하나) / 가구가 딸린[없는] 아파트 a furnished [an unfurnished] studio / 하숙 a bachelor's room (방만 빌림) / 청소·세탁·식사 제공 아파트《英》a service flat

▶ **단지(團地)** a housing development / 아파트 단지 an apartment complex / 주공 주택 public housing (엄밀히는 an apartment house built by the Korea Housing Corporation)

▶ **타운 하우스** a town house (몇집이 벽으로 이어져 있고 뜰을 같이 쓰는 저층 주택) / 테라스 하우스《英》a terraced house;《美》a row house (보통 1블록에 걸쳐서 여러 집이 벽으로 이어져 있다. 영국의 것은 앞쪽이 반지하고 뒤쪽에 뒷뜰이 붙어 있다. 미국의 것은 2층이 뒤로 물러나 있고 그 부분이 테라스로 되어 있다)

▶ **관리인** a superintendent;《古》a super; a custodian; janitor / 관리비 a maintenance cost [charge] / 공유 부분 a common area / 베란다 a veranda / 발코니 a balcony

▶ **집주인** 〈남자〉 a landlord; 〈여자〉 a landlady / 세든 사람 a tenant / 하숙[기숙]생 a boarder; a lodger / 집세 rent; rental / 1개월분 선불 집세 advance rent of one month / (집세) 보증금 a (security) deposit / 권리금 key money

3. 방
▶ **거실** a living room (일반 가정에서는 응접실을 겸함);《英》a sitting room / 객실, 응접실 a drawing room (일반 가정에서는 living room과 겸용); a parlor (큰 집의 응접실이라고 할 수 있는 말) / 레크리에이션 룸 a recreation room; a rec (미국에서는 대개 지하실에 있는데 거기서 가족이나 친구들과 게임을 즐기거나 한다) / 양실(洋室) a Western-style room / 한식 방 a Korean-style room / 침실 a bedroom / 아이들 방 a children's room / 육아실 a nursery / 서재 a study; a library / 벽장 a closet / 골방 a walk-in closet

▶ **식당** a dining room / 부엌 a kitchen (dining room과 겸용되는 가정이 많다)

▶ **욕실** a bathroom / 욕조 a bathtub / 샤워실 a shower room / 화장실 a bathroom (보통 변기(toilet bowl)도 bathroom에 설치되므로 이렇게 말한다)

▶ **천장** a ceiling / 벽 a wall / 마루 a floor

▶ **집을 신축하다** build a new house / 집을 증축하다 extend [enlarge] one's house / 집을 소유하다 own one's house / 집을 처분하다 sell one's house / 집을 빌리다 rent a house / 집세를 내다 pay the rent / 새 집으로 이사하다 move into a new house / 셋방을 찾다 look for a room to rent / 토지를 임대하다 lease land / 은행 융자로 집을 사다 buy [purchase] a house on a bank loan / 서재를 침실로 개조하다 convert a study into a bedroom

〈Dialog〉
A : 역 근처에 집을 하나 찾는 데요 I'm looking for a house in the neighborhood of the station.
B : 방은 몇개면 될까요? How many rooms would you like it to have?
A : 적어도 방이 셋은 있어야겠는데요 At least three rooms.
B : 좋은 집이 하나 있습니다 There is a good one.

가웃 〈반〉 and a half ◆넉 자 가웃 four feet and a half; four and a half feet / 서 말 가웃 three *mal* and a half

가위 《a pair of》 scissors; 〈큰 가위〉 shears; 〈양철 등을 자르는〉 snips; 〈털 등을 깎는〉 clippers; 〈차표 등을 찍는〉 a punch

가위
♦ 가위 한 자루 a pair of scissors / 가위로 깎다 clip ((the wool of a sheep)) / 가위로 자르다 cut *sth* with scissors; scissor; 〈가지 등을 치다〉 prune [trim] ((a tree)) / 가위로 표를 찍다 punch [clip] a ticket
▶ 가위는 물건을 자르는 데 쓰인다 A pair of scissors is used [Scissors are used] to cut things.
▶ 이 가위는 잘 든다[들지 않는다] These scissors cut [don't cut] well.

가위 可謂 1 〈이르자면〉 so to speak; the so-called; what is called; what you [they] (might) say [call]; what is well named [said]
▶ 이것은 가위 「일석이조」다 This is what you might call "killing two birds with one stone."
2 〈과연·참〉 really; truly; indeed; as can be said; literally; as may be expected
▶ 그는 가위 위인이다 He is indeed [truly] a great man.
▶ 그는 가위 학자다 He is a scholar worthy of the name.
▶ 그는 가위 당대의 영웅이다 He is really the greatest hero of the age.

가위눌리다 〈악몽에 시달리다〉 have a nightmare [a terrible dream, an incubus]; have a bad dream; be afflicted by [with] nightmare
▶ 나는 어젯밤에 가위눌렸다 I had a nightmare [bad dream] last night.
▶ 그는 가위눌려서 소리를 질렀다 Frightened by a nightmare, he cried out.

가위바위보 *kawi-pawi-po*; a kind of mora
♦ 가위바위보를 하다 play *kawi-pawi-po* [mora]; toss for *sth* / 가위바위보에서 「보」를 내다 show "*po*" at a mora / 가위바위보에서 이기다[지다] win [lose] the toss
▶ 가위바위보로 정하자 Let's toss (up) for it.

가위질 scissoring; 〈정원수의〉 trimming
―**가위질하다** cut ((a thing)) with scissors; scissor

가위춤 〈엿장수 등의〉 a scissors rattling; 〈헛가위질〉 idling a pair of scissors

가위표 ―標 a cross; an ×
♦ 가위표를 하다 mark with a cross / 가위표로 지우다 cross [×] (out) ((what one has written))

가윗날 Harvest Moon Day ⇨ 추석

가윗밥 waste pieces of cut cloth; cuttings; shreds [scraps]

가으내 throughout the autumn [(美) fall]; all through the autumn [(美) fall]

가을 1 〈계절〉 autumn; (美) fall
♦ 가을의 autumn(al); (美) fall / 늦[초]가을 late [early, the beginning of] autumn / 독서의 계절 가을 autumn, the best season for reading / 가을 꽃 an autumn flower / 가을 날 an autumn day / 맑은 가을 날씨 fine autumn weather / 가을 바람 an autumn(al) breeze [wind] / 가을 밤 an autumn night ;〈추석의〉 the harvest moon / 가을 보리 autumn-sown barley / 가을 비 an autumn rain / 가을철 the autumn season; (美) falltime / 가을 축제 an autumn festival / 가을 하늘 the autumn sky
▶ 오늘은 쾌청한 가을 날이다 Today is a fine autumn day.
▶ 낙엽 한 잎이 가을을 알린다 A single leaf falling is a sign of autumn coming.
▶ 가을도 깊어졌다 It is now well [deep] into (the) fall [autumn].
2 〈추수〉 harvest(ing); reaping
―**가을하다** harvest; reap ((a harvest)); gather in crops

가을갈이 autumn plowing; 〈파종〉 autumn planting ―**가을갈이하다** plow [plant] in autumn
■ ―씨 seeds for the autumn sowing

가을걷이 autumn [fall] harvesting; autumn [fall] reaping

가이거계수 ―計數 〔物〕 Geiger count ■ ―기 a Geiger counter

가이거·뮐러계수기 ―計數器 〔物〕 a Geiger-Müller counter

가이드 〈안내〉 guiding; 〈안내인〉 a (tour) guide; 〈안내서〉 a guidebook ♦ 가이드가 딸린 여행 a guided tour

가이사 〔聖〕 Caesar
▶ 가이사의 것은 가이사에게로 돌려라 Render to Caesar the things that are Caesar's(, and to God the things that are God's).

가이슬러관 ―管 〔物〕 a Geissler tube

가인 佳人 a beautiful woman; a beauty; a belle
■ 재자― the wits and beauties : 당대의 재자 가인 the wit and beauty of the age 절세― a woman of unsurpassed beauty

가인 家人 〈집안 사람〉 a member of *one's* family; *one's* family members

가인 歌人 a singer; a songster; a poet; a poetess (여자)

가인박명 佳人薄命 Beautiful flowers are soon picked. = Beauty and fortune are often bad friends. = Beauties die young.

가일층 加一層 even more; still [much] more; all the more
▶ 가일층 노력해라 You must make greater efforts.
▶ 건강에 가일층 유의하시오 Be more careful of your health.
▶ 그것이 사실이라면 가일층 좋다 If that is true, so much the better.

가입 加入 〈회·단체 등에 대한〉 joining; entry; admission; 〈전화 등에 대한〉 subscription; 〈조약 등에 대한〉 signing
▶ 회원 가입 절차는 어떻게 하면 됩니까? What procedure is necessary for obtaining the membership?
▶ 그는 가입을 신청했다 He applied for admission.
―**가입하다** enter (for); join ((an association)); affiliate *oneself* with ((a society)); become a member (of); subscribe (for); sign ((a treaty))
♦ 1억원의 생명 보험에 가입하다 insure *oneself* [*one's* life] for one hundred million won / 조합에 가입하다 become a member of a union / 클럽에 가입하다 join [become a member of] a club / 가입시키다 enlist *sb* in; initiate *sb* ((into a society))
▶ 그는 협회에 가입했다 He became a member of the society.

▶ 한국은 국제연합에 가입되어 있다 Korea is affiliated with the United Nations.
■—국 a member nation 《of the UN》; 〈조약의〉 a signatory (power) to a treaty; a treaty participant —금 an entrance fee
가입신청 加入申請 an application for admission;〈전화 등의〉 subscription
▶ 가입 신청은 3월 20일 오후 3시까지 입니다 Applications for admission may be sent in up to 3 p.m. March 20 [(英) 20 March].
■—자 an applicant for membership
가입자 加入者 〈단체의〉 a member;〈전화의〉 a (telephone) subscriber;〈보험의〉 a policy-holder
▶ 전화 가입자의 수가 해마다 늘고 있다 The number of the telephone subscribers has been on the increase year after year.
■ 신규— a new member [subscriber] ■ —명부 a subscriber list —선 a subscriber's line
가입학 假入學 entrance [admission] of a student on probation
♦ 가입학을 허가하다 admit 《a student to a college》 on probation
가자 〈팔레스타인의 항구도시〉 Gaza ■—지구 the Gaza Strip
가자미 〈魚〉 a flatfish; a flounder;〈작은 가자미〉 a dab
가작 佳作 〈잘된 작품〉 a fine [an excellent] work;〈입선작 외의〉 an unawarded good work; the next best work to the prizewinners
가장 (the) most; extremely; exceedingly
♦ 가장 북쪽의 항구 the northernmost port / 가장 심한 경우 an extreme case / 가장 인상적인 일 the most impressive thing / 가장 좋은 책 the best book / 가장 중요한 일 the most(↔ least) important thing; a matter of the greatest importance / 가장 친한 친구 one's best [closest, dearest] friend / 가장 힘이 덜 드는 방법 the least painful method / 가장 먼저 first of all / 가장 용감히 싸우다 fight most bravely
▶ 나는 그것이 가장 좋다 I like it best of all. ≒ I like it better than the others.
▶ 나는 봄을 가장 좋아한다 I like spring best.
▶ 건강이 가장 중요하다 Nothing is more important than health. ≒ Health is the most important thing [is everything].
▶ 그녀가 해준 말이 나를 가장 감동시켰다 What she had told me touched my heart most.
▶ 이 약은 두통에 가장 좋다 This medicine is best for headaches.
▶ 북유럽을 여행하기는 여름이 가장 좋다 Summer is the best season for travel to Northern Europe.
▶ 이것이 나를 가장 골치아프게 하는 문제다 This is the problem which puzzles me most.
▶ 자신에게 가장 잘 맞는 직업을 선택해야 한다 You should choose a job most suitable for you.
▶ 그 사람은 영국 역사상 가장 위대한 시인이다 He is the greatest poet that ever lived in England.
▶ 그는 반에서 가장 열심히 공부하는 학생이다 He is the most hardworking student in the class.
▶ 마지막 문제가 가장 어려웠다 The last question was the hardest.
▶ 그곳에 가는 데는 지하철이 가장 빠를 겁니다 The subway will be the fastest to get there by.
▶ 영어는 그가 우리 반에서 가장 잘 한다 He leads the class in English.
▶ 그 여자는 내가 가장 좋아하지 않는 타입이다 She is the type I like least.
▶ 삼촌이 나를 가장 잘 이해해 주신다 Nobody understands me better than my uncle.
▶ 내가 가장 애석하게 생각하는 것은 그를 볼 수가 없었다는 것이다 The thing I regret most is that I was not able to see him. ≒ I regret it most deeply that I couldn't see him.
가장 家長 the head [chief] of a family [household]; a patriarch;〈여자〉 a matriarch;〈남편〉 one's husband
■—권 the rights of a patriarch; patriarchal rights —정치 patriarchal government; patriarchalism —제도 patriarchy; a patriarchal system; patriarchism
가장 家藏 storing in one's own house ■—집물 household furnishings
가장 假裝 1【변장】 (a) disguise; (a) guise;〈무도회의〉 masquerade; (a) fancy dress
—**가장하다** disguise 《as a thief》; disguise oneself [be disguised] 《with [by wearing] a false mustache》; wear a disguise; dress up ♦ 가장하여 in disguise; in fancy dress
▶ 그녀는 신데렐라로 가장했다 She was disguised [disguised herself] as Cinderella.
▶ 그들은 가장한 왕을 보고 웃었다 They laughed at the King in disguise.
2〈거짓으로 꾸밈〉 pretense; feint; simulation; semblance; affectation; camouflage
—**가장하다** feign; pretend; affect; assume; simulate; make believe; put on a semblance of
♦ …을 가장하여 under pretense [the guise, the cloak, the semblance] of / 학자로[대학생으로] 가장하다 counterfeit [pretend to be] a scholar [a university student]
▶ 사실은 라디오를 듣고 있으면서 그 아이는 열심히 공부하는 것처럼 가장했다 The boy made a feint of studying hard, though actually he was listening to the radio.
▶ 그자는 우정을 가장하여 나를 속였다 He cheated me under pretense of friendship.
■—매매 (美)〔證〕 a wash sale —무도회 a costume [fancy dress, masked] ball; a masquerade —순양함 a converted [an auxiliary] cruiser —행렬 a costume procession; a fancy dress parade
가장귀 〈나뭇가지의 아귀〉 a fork [crotch] (of a tree) ♦ 가장귀지다 be forked; be furcate / 가장귀진 나뭇가지 a forked branch
가장자리 the edge 《of a desk》; the brink; the verge; the hem 《of a curtain》; the border; the fringe; the brim
♦ 테이블 가장자리 the edge of a table / 가장자리에 제비꽃을 심은 화단 a flowerbed bordered with violets

가재

■ —**감치기** overcasting —**뜨기** 〖裁縫〗 hemstitching; enlacement —**장식** a border; an edging; 〈술 장식〉 a fringe 《of a muffler》

가재 〖動〗 a crawfish; a crayfish

가재 家具 **1** 〈가구〉 household goods [effects, stuffs, belongings]; furniture; furnishings
◆ 가재 도구 goods and chattels / 가재를 정리하여 이사하다 pack up *one's* belongings and move 《to a new house》
▶ 화재로 가재 도구를 몽땅 잃었다 All my household effects were burned up [destroyed in the fire].
2 〈가산〉 family property; *one's* fortune

가재걸음 〈뒷걸음질〉 stepping back; drawing back; moving [walking] backward; 〈일의 지지부진〉 a snail's pace
◆ 가재걸음 치다 walk crayfish [crawfish]; move [walk] backward; make little progress; progress at a snail's pace
▶ 그의 일은 가재걸음 쳤다 His work made little [almost no] progress.

가재는 게 편이라 〈속담〉 Like attracts like. ⇒ Birds of a feather flock together.

가전 家傳 ◆ 가전의 handed down in a family; hereditary / 가전의 묘약 a secret remedy handed down from father to son / 가전의 보물 a family treasure [heirloom] / 가전의 비법 a hereditary secret; a secret recipe handed down in a family

가전제품 家電製品 electric household appliances; home electric(al) appliances

가절 佳節 **1** 〈명절〉 a fete day; an auspicious [a festive] occasion; a jubilee
◆ 중추 가절 the midautumn festival
2 〈계절〉 a beautiful season
◆ 양춘 가절 the pleasant springtime

가정 家政 housekeeping; homemaking; household [home] management
◆ 가정을 맡아보다 manage household affairs; keep house
■ —**과** a course in domestic science [economy]; the department of domestic science —**학** domestic science; home economics

가정 家庭 a home; a family; a household

> 〖解說〗 *home*은 사람이 보통 가족과 함께 사는 집을 말하며 따뜻한 가정적 분위기를 연상시킨다. *family*는 부부와 그 아이들, 때로는 아내와 아이들 또는 아이들만의 가정을 가리킨다. *household*는 가족보다 범위가 넓어져서 때로는 일하는 사람들이나 하숙인까지 포함하여 한 세대 전원을 의미한다.

◆ 모자[부자] 가정 a home of (a) mother [father] and child; a fatherless [motherless] home / 상류[중류] 가정 an upper-class [a middle-class] family / 유복한 가정 a well-to-do [wealthy] family / 좋은 가정 a good family / 즐거운 [단란한] 가정 a sweet [happy] home / 가정적인 남자 a family(-oriented) man / 가정적인 여자 a home-loving [home-minded] woman; a domestic woman / 가정적인 분위기 a homely [homelike] atmosphere / 가정풍(風)의 home-style 《meals》 / 가정의 행복 domestic happiness / 가정을 꾸미다[가지다] make [build, establish] a home; get married and settle down [have a family] / 가정을 파괴하다 break up a family / 가정에서 예절을 가르치다 teach good manners in the [at] home / 엄한 가정에서 자라다 be brought up in a strict family / 유복한 가정에서 태어나다 be born into a well-to-do family [with a silver spoon in *one's* mouth]
▶ 그녀는 대학을 졸업하면 결혼하여 가정을 갖겠다고 한다 She says she will get married and have a family when she graduates from college.
▶ 그 신혼 부부는 아파트에 가정을 꾸몄다 The newly-married couple have made their home in an apartment 《house》.
▶ 그녀는 가정적인 여성이다 She is a domestic type of a woman. ⇒ She is a good homemaker [housekeeper].
■ —**경제** household [domestic] economy —**란** 〈신문의〉 a domestic column [page]; the home-life section —**문제** home problems —**법원** a domestic (relations) court; the Court of Family Affairs; the Family Court —**불화** 〈가족 간의〉 family [domestic] trouble [discord]; 〈부부 간의〉 a quarrel [friction] between husband and wife —**사정** 《for》 *one's* family circumstances [reasons, matters]: 그녀는 가정 사정 때문에 회사를 그만둘 것이다 She will quit the company for her family matters. —**상비약** a household medicine; a domestic remedy 《for diarrhea》 —**생활** *one's* home [domestic, family] life —**소설** a domestic novel; a novel on family affairs —**요리** home cooking; a home-cooked meal —**요법** home treatment; a home [domestic] remedy —**용품** household utensils [articles, appliances] —**의학** home-doctoring —**쟁의** 《make》 a family dispute —**주부** a housewife —**파괴범** a criminal who destroyed family happiness 《by raping women after robbing》 —**평화** 《disturb》 the domestic peace —**폭력** violence in the home —**학 home economy [domestic science] —**학습** homework

가정 假定 (an) assumption; (a) supposition; (a) postulation; 〈가설〉 a hypothesis 《*pl.* -ses》
◆ 가정적(인) assumptive; hypothetic(al) / 이러한 가정 아래 on this assumption
▶ 우리는 연말까지는 그들이 귀국할 것이라는 가정하에 내년도 계획을 세우고 있다 We are planning for the next year on the assumption that they will come home by the end of the year.
—**가정하다** suppose; assume; presume; take 《this fact》 for granted
◆ …이라고 가정하고 on the assumption [supposition] that; supposing 《assuming, granted, granting》 that 《it is true》
▶ 그가 살아 있다고 가정하자 Let us suppose that he's living.
▶ A는 B와 같다고 가정하자 Let A be equal to B.
▶ 그 직을 제의받았다고 가정하고 당신은 그것을 수락하시겠습니까? Suppose [Supposing,

Assuming] (that) you're offered the job, will you accept it?

가정관 假定款 〚法〛 provisional articles 《of an incorporation》

가정교사 家庭教師 a private teacher; a (private) tutor; 〈여자〉 a governess
♦ 가정 교사를 두다 employ [hire] a tutor [private teacher] / 영어 가정 교사를 하다 teach 《a boy》 English at 《his》 home; tutor 《a boy》 in English / 가정 교사 자리를 찾다 look out for a tutor's position / 가정 교사 밑에서 공부하다 study under [with] a tutor / 가정 교사로 대학 등록금을 조달하다 meet one's university expenses by tutoring
▶ 아르바이트로 가정 교사를 하는 대학생들도 있다 Some college students work part-time as private tutors.

가정교육 家庭教育 home training [education, discipline] ▶ 학교 교육은 가정 교육에 바탕을 두고 있다 School education is based on training at home.

가정방문 家庭訪問 paying visits 《to homes》; a home visit; making a round of calls 《at homes》
—**가정방문하다** make a round of calls 《at one's pupil's homes》; pay visit 《to homes》

가정법 假定法 〚文法〛 the subjunctive mood
가정부 家政婦 a housekeeper; a housemaid
가정용 家庭用 ♦ 가정용의 for home [household, domestic] use; home-style / 가정용 전기 기구 [냉장고] household electric appliances [refrigerator]

가정의례 家庭儀禮 family rite [ritual] ♦ 가정 의례에 따라 in [according to] family rites —에 관한 법률 the Family Rite Law; the Family Ritual Code —준칙 the Simplified Family Rite [Ritual] Standards

가정환경 家庭環境 one's home [family] background [environment]
♦ 나쁜 가정 환경 a bad home environment / 가정 환경에 좌우되다 be influenced by one's home background
▶ 어린이 교육에는 가정 환경이 가장 중요하다 The home environment is the first consideration in the education of children.

가제 [〈獨〉 Gaze] (cotton, antiseptic) gauze ■ 소독— sterilized gauze

가제본 假製本 〚製本〛 a dummy; a sample binding; temporary binding

가져가다 〈지니고 가다〉 take sth along [with one]; carry; 〈가지고 가버리다〉 take off; take [carry] away; make off [away] 《with》
♦ 도로 가져가다 bring [take] back / 차로 가져가다 carry sth 《to a place》 by car
▶ 도둑이 사무실에서 금고를 가져갔다 The burglar carried the safe out of the office.
▶ 우산[도시락]을 가져가거라 Take your umbrella [lunch] with you.
▶ 누가 내 펜을 가져갔니? Who has taken [walked] off with my pen?
▶ 이 짐은 너무 무거워서 나 혼자서는 가져갈 수 없다 This baggage is too heavy for me to carry alone [by myself].

가져오다 1 〈가지고 오다〉 bring (over); fetch; get; bring [take, carry] sth with one
♦ 그가 가져온 정보에 따르면 according to the information received [obtained] from him / …에게 행운을 가져오다 bring sb good fortune / 가져오게 하다 get sb to bring; send 《to a shop》 for sth
▶ 나는 오늘 집에서 도시락을 가져왔다 I brought my lunch from home today.
▶ 물 한 컵 가져오너라 Get me a glass of water.
▶ 가서 내 모자를 가져오너라 Go and fetch my hat.
▶ 너 책[돈]은 얼마나 가져왔니? How many books [much money] have you brought with you?
2 〈초래하다〉 bring about [on, forth]; 〈원인이 되다〉 cause; produce; result [end] in
♦ 집안에 불행을 가져오다 bring misfortune on one's family / 실패를 가져오다 result in failure; cause a failure / 파멸을 가져오다 bring down ruin on sb
▶ 그 실험은 좋은 결과를 가져왔다 The experiment produced fine result.
▶ 과학의 진보는 우리의 생활에 많은 변혁을 가져왔다 The progress of science has brought about many changes in our lives.
▶ 작은 실수가 중대한 결과를 가져왔다 A little oversight led to [brought about] serious consequences.
▶ 폭풍우가 작물에 큰 피해를 가져왔다 The storm caused a great deal of damage to the crops.

가조약 假條約 a provisional treaty; an interim treaty ♦ 가조약을 맺다 conclude [enter into, make up] a provisional treaty 《with》

가조인 假調印 initialing; initial signing; an initial signature —**가조인하다** initial 《a treaty》 —식 an initialing ceremony

가족 家族 a family; a household; (口) one's people [〈美〉 folks]; 〈친척〉 kinsfolk

> 解説 **family**는 가족의 구성원을 가리키는데, 특히 아이들만을 뜻하기도 한다: 내게는 다섯 아이가 있다 I have a family of five. family는 단수 취급이 보통이지만 영국에서는 보통 가족 하나하나의 구성원을 의미할 경우에는 복수 취급한다: That family is popular around here. 그 가족은 이 근방에서는 평판이 좋다 / My family is [〈英〉 are] all early risers. ⇌ Everyone in my family is an early riser. 우리 가족은 모두 일찍 일어난다 다만 My whole family gets up early. 에서는 영미 모두 단수 취급한다.

♦ 가족의 familial 《organization》 / 가족의 수 the size of a family / 가족의 일원 a family member; one [a member] of the family / 가족에 적합한 음식점 a family restaurant / …의 가족의 일원이 되다 enter the family of 《Mr. Jones》 / 가족이 많다 [적다] have a large [small] family / 가족을 부양하다 support one's family / 가족처럼 대우하다 treat sb as a member of one's family; treat sb in a family way

▶ 우리 집은 가족이 적다 I have a small family.
▶ 가족이 외출한 사이에 우리 집에 도둑이 들었다 While we were out, our house was broken into.
▶ 〖會話〗「가족이 몇 분이십니까?」「우리 가족은 4명입니다」 "How large is your family?" "There are four (people) [four of us] in my family. ⇒ We are a family of four."
▶ 〖會話〗「가족들은 무고하십니까?」「덕분에 모두 건강합니다」 "How is your family?" "They are all very well [fine], thank you."
▶ 적은 수입으로 5인 가족을 부양하기는 쉽지 않다 It's not easy to support a family of five with a low income.
▶ 그는 가족을 데리고 유럽 여행을 갔다 He went on a trip to Europe with his family.
▶ 가족분들께 안부 전해 주십시오 Give my best regards [Say hello] to all your family.

■ ―대― a large family 복합― a composite family 부양― a dependent 소― a small family 핵― a nuclear family ■ ―구성 family structure [make-up] ―묘지 a family burial ground ―법 〖法〗 family law ―부양 의무 family responsibility ―석 a family box; family seats ―수당 family allowance ―여행 a family trip ―의식 a sense of family ―제도 the family system ―탕 a family bath ―회사 a family concern ―회의 《have, hold》 a family conference [council]

가족계획 家族計劃 family planning; family regulation
♦ 국제 가족 계획 연맹 International Planned Parenthood Federation / 한국 가족 계획 협회 the Planned Parenthood Federation of Korea
■ ―상담소 a family planning clinic

가주소 假住所 one's temporary address

가죽 〈피부〉 (a) skin; 〈말·소의〉 (a) hide; 〈무두질한〉 leather; 〈모피〉 (a) fur
♦ 생가죽 (a) rawhide; (a) raw skin; 〈양·염소 등의〉 (a) pelt / 여우 가죽 a fox fur / 호랑이 가죽 a tiger skin / 가죽을 댄 안락의자 a leather-covered armchair / 가죽으로 만든 leather-made; leather 《belt》 / 가죽을 대다[쓰우다] cover sth with leather / 가죽을 무두질하다 tan hide; dress leather / 가죽을 벗기다 skin [flay] 《a rabbit》
▶ 소는 가죽이 두껍다 The skin [hide] of a cow is thick.
▶ 사냥꾼은 자기가 쏜 사슴의 가죽을 벗겼다 The hunter skinned the deer he shot.
▶ 그는 사람의 가죽을 쓴 짐승이다 He is a brute in human guise [form].
▶ 그는 양의 가죽을 쓴 늑대다 He's a wolf in sheep's clothing.
▶ 그는 뼈와 가죽만 남았다 He's all skin and bones. ⇒ He is reduced to a mere skeleton [bag of bones].

■ ―가방 a leather bag ―구두 leather shoes; boots ―끈 a leather strap; a thong ―띠 a leather belt ―부대 a leather bag; 〈술을 담는〉 a wineskin; 〈물긷는〉 a waterskin ―세공 leatherwork; leathercraft ―숫돌 a razor strap; a strop ―옷 leather garments ―잠바 a leather jumper [jacket] ―장갑 《a pair of》 leather gloves ―장 정[제본] leather binding ―장정본 a leather-bound book; a book bound in leather ―제품 leather goods [products] ―채 a rawhide whip ―표지 a leather cover : 가죽 표지를 한 책 a book bound in leather

가죽나무 假― 〖植〗 a tree of heaven; an ailanthus

가중 加重 weighting; adding an extra weight; 〖法〗 aggravation
―가중하다 weight; 〖法〗 aggravate
■ ―과세 surcharge 《on》―절도죄 aggravated larceny ―처벌 an aggravated punishment ―치(値) 〖統〗 weight ―평균 a weighted average [mean] ―폭행 an aggravated assault ―형벌 an aggravated penalty

가중 苛重 〈가혹〉 harshness; severity; 〈무거움〉 heavy; excessiveness; onerousness
―가중하다 〈가혹하다〉 hard; harsh; 〈무겁다〉 heavy; excessive; onerous [ánərəs]
♦ …에게 가중한 세금을 매기다 impose heavy taxes [duties] on 《the people, imports and exports》
▶ 정부는 사치품에 가중한 세금을 매기려고 계획하고 있다 The government plans to impose heavier taxes on luxury items.

가증서 假證書 a provisional certificate; an interim bond

가증스럽다 可憎― hateful; abominable; detestable; spiteful
♦ 가증스러운 놈 a detestable fellow / 가증스러운 처사 spiteful conduct / 가증스러운 태도 hateful [provoking] behavior / 가증스럽기 이를 데 없는 죄 a most abominable crime / 가증스러운 말을 하다 say sth devastating; say provoking [spiteful] things 《to》
▶ 그가 이제 와서 나를 배반하다니 참으로 가증스러운 일이다 It is a despicable thing for him to betray me now.
▶ 그 여자는 가증스러울 정도로 침착해 보였다 She looked provokingly calm.

가지¹ 【나무의】 a branch; 〈큰 가지〉 a bough; a limb; 〈잔 가지〉 a twig; 〈어린 가지〉 a shoot; 〈꽃·잎이 달린 채 자른〉 a wand; a sprig 《of jasmine》; a spray 《of peach blossoms》
♦ 가지가 잘 뻗은 소나무 a pine tree with gracefully-shaped branches / 가지가 휘어지게 열린 감나무 a persimmon tree with branches heavily laden with fruit / 가지를 꺾다 break (off) a branch / 가지를 내다 branch off 《from》; shoot out branches; ramify / 가지를 뻗다 spread 《its》 branches (out) / 가지를 치다 [자르다] lop off [down] branches; take branches off 《a tree》; 〈전지하다〉 prune [trim] a tree
▶ 그 나무는 큰 가지들이 뻗어 나오고 있었다 The tree was spreading out its big boughs.
▶ 정원사는 죽은 가지를 잘라냈다 The gardener cut off dead branches.
■ ―꽃― a sprig; a spray

가지² 〖植〗 an eggplant; 〈열매〉 an egg [a mad] apple; a garden egg ■ ―색 aubergine purple

가지³ 〈종류〉 a kind; a sort; a variety

◆ 한 가지 a kind [sort] 《of》; 〈같은 종류〉 the same kind [sort] / 여러 가지 과일[스포츠] many kinds [sorts] of fruit [sports] / 여러 가지 꽃 various species [kinds] of flowers / 여러 가지로 생각해본 끝에 I thought a lot and finally...; After a great deal of thinking... / 세 가지로 나누다 divide [sort out] 《things》 into three classes
▶ 그녀는 여러 가지 종류의 책을 읽는다 She reads a lot of different (kinds of) books.
▶ 부탁이 한 가지 있습니다 I have a favor to ask of you.
▶ 나는 그 문제를 여러 가지 각도에서 생각해 보았다 I considered the matter from various angles.
▶ 이 귀절은 두 가지로 해석할 수 있다 This passage can be interpreted in two ways.
▶ 여러 가지로 정말 감사합니다 Thank you very much for everything [all you have done for me].
▶ 여러 가지로 폐를 끼쳐서 죄송합니다 I am sorry to have troubled you so much.
▶ 이 화단에는 꽃이 몇 가지나 심어져 있니? How many kinds of flowers are there in this flowerbed?

가지가지 various kinds of; a variety 《of》; all sorts 《of》; every sort and kind; various
◆ 가지가지 경험 《gain》 various experiences / 가지가지 물건 articles of every sort and kind; all sorts of things / 가지가지 용도 a variety of uses / 가지가지 크기의 상자 boxes of various sizes / 가지가지로 in many [different, various] ways; in every way / 가지가지 이유로 for various [many] reasons
▶ 차도 가지가지다 There are many kinds of cars.
▶ 뜰에는 가지가지 꽃이 활짝 피어 있었다 All kinds of flowers [Flowers of every sort and kind] were in full bloom in the garden.
▶ 가지가지 이유로 그는 그것을 인수하지 않았다 He didn't undertake it for various reasons.

가지각색 —各色 《of》 all sorts [kinds] 《of》 every description
◆ 가지각색의 various; different; varied / 가지각색의 사람들 all sorts (and conditions) of men / 가지각색의 생활상 diverse aspects of everyday life / 가지각색의 인생 경험 a variety of (human) experiences / 가지각색으로 variously; diversely; in various ways / 가지각색이다 be various; be all different
▶ 떠도는 소문이 가지각색이다 There are various rumors in the air.
▶ 그 문제에 관한 의견은 가지각색이었다 They were divided in opinion on the matter. ⇌ They all had different opinion on the matter.
▶ 미국 국민은 가지각색의 인종으로 구성되어 있다 The Americans comprise a medley of races.

가지고 1 〈…을[에게]〉 ▶ 고양이 가지고 그렇게 못살게 굴지 마라 Don't be so cruel to the cat.
▶ 그 여자 가지고 너무 그러지 마시오 Don't pick on her so.
▶ 가뜩이나 성난 사람 가지고 왜 그러니? Are you trying to make him still angrier?

2 〈…(으)로〉 ◆ 장난감을 가지고 놀다 play with a toy / 사소한 일을 가지고 화를 내다 get angry at trifles; take offense on the slightest provocation
▶ 그런 문제를 가지고 신경 쓰지 마라 Don't be worried over the matter.
▶ 무엇을 가지고 그렇게들 싸우니? What are you quarreling about?
▶ 한 달에 50만원 가지고 어떻게 삽니까? How can you live on five hundred thousand won a month?
▶ 이 사실만 가지고도 그가 얼마나 정직한지 충분히 알 수 있다 This fact alone is enough to show how honest he is.
3 〈상태〉 ▶ 그렇게 게을러 가지고 어떻게 시험에 합격하기를 바라겠니? Being so idle, how can you expect to pass the examination?
▶ 나는 그 사람의 여름 별장을 맡아 가지고 있다 I have charge of his summer cottage.

가지다 1 〈지니다〉 〈손에〉 have; take; hold; 〈몸에〉 carry 《with *one*》; have a thing with *one*
◆ 가진 돈 money on [in] hand; ready cash [money] / 가지러 가다 go for a thing; go to bring [fetch] / 가지러 보내다 send *sb* for a thing
▶ 그는 손에 책을 가지고 있다 He has a book in his hand.
▶ 신분 증명서를 가지고 있습니까? Do you have an identification card on [with] you?
▶ 그것을 단단히 가지고 가거라 Take firm hold of it.
▶ 할아버지는 항상 지팡이를 가지고 다니신다 My grandfather always carries a cane.
▶ 내가 가지고 있는 볼펜도 될니까? Will the ball-point pen I have on hand do?
▶ 지금 돈 가진 것 있니? Do you have any money with you [on hand]?
2 〈소유하다〉 own; have; possess; keep
◆ 어떤 뜻을 가지다 bear a meaning / 가진 자[나라]와 못 가진 자[나라] haves and have-nots
▶ 마음에 들면 무엇이든 가져라 Take whatever you like.
▶ 어머니는 조그만 가게를 가지고 계신다 My mother keeps [runs] a small shop.
▶ 그는 호텔을 세 개 가지고 있다 He owns [has] three hotels.
▶ 나는 차를 가지고 있지 않다 I don't have a car.
▶ 그는 막대한 재산을 가지고 있다 He has [possesses] great wealth.
▶ 사람은 이성을 가지고 있다 Man is endowed with reason.
▶ 그 나라에서는 여성은 투표권을 가지고 있지 않다 In that country women do not have the right to vote.
3 〈마음에 품다〉 have; hold 《an opinion》; entertain 《an idea》; harbor 《hatred》; cherish 《hopes》; bear 《a grudge against *sb*》
◆ 자본주의 사상을 가지다 embrace capitalism / 의심을 가지다 harbor suspicion 《against》 / 큰 뜻을 가지다 have [cherish] a great ambition / 희망을 가지다 cherish a hope 《that》

▶그는 내게 좋지 않은 감정을 가지고 있었다 He held [had] ill feelings toward me.
▶그는 그 방법에 대해 의문을 가지고 있었다 He had [entertained] doubts about that method.
▶그는 나에게 원한을 가지고 있는 것 같다 He seems to have [hold, bear, entertain] a grudge against me.
4 〈배다〉 conceive; be [become] pregnant
♦아기를 가지다 be pregnant; be (big) with child; be in the family way / 새끼를 가지다 be (big) with young; 〈소가〉 be in [with] calf; 〈개가〉 be in pup
▶그 여자는 아이를 가졌다 The woman is pregnant. ⇒ The woman is in the family way.
▶소가 새끼를 가졌다 The cow is heavy with calf.

가지런하다 even; uniform; equal; regular (teeth); be in order
♦높이가 가지런한 of the same [uniform] height / 가지런하지 않은 uneven; unequal; irregular / 높이가 가지런하지 않다 be of unequal height
▶이 끈들은 길이가 가지런하다 These strings are equal [the same] in length.

가지런히 uniformly; evenly; equally; regularly; trimly; in good order
♦신발을 가지런히 놓다 place one's shoes squarely [neatly, side by side] (on the doorstep); arrange shoes (in order) / 책을 가지런히 정돈하다 arrange books in the right order
▶당근을 크기가 가지런하게 잘라라 Cut a carrot into pieces of uniform [the same] size.

가지 많은 나무에 바람 잘 날 없다 《속담》 A mother with a large brood never has a peaceful day.

가지치기 trimming ⇨ 전지(剪枝)

가지치다 **1** 〈가지가 뻗다〉 branch out; spread [put out] branches **2** 〈가지를 자르다〉 take branches (off a tree); lop off [down] branches; prune [trim] a tree

가진급 假進級 passing on probation; conditional pass (of a student)
—**가진급하다** be passed on probation; be conditioned
♦가진급시키다 pass (a student) on probation; (美) condition (a student)
■—생 a conditioned student

가집행 假執行 〔法〕 provisional execution
—**가집행하다** execute provisionally; place (a house) under a temporary injunction

가짜 假— 〈위조·모조품〉 an imitation; a sham; a counterfeit; a fake; a bogus article; a forgery; a false article; 〈사람〉 a charlatan; a pretender; an imposter; a fraud

解説 *imitation*은 진짜와 비슷하게 만든 것, *sham*은 진짜이라고 믿을 만한 것을 말한다. 「위조품」의 뜻으로는 *counterfeit*가 일반적. *fake*는 속어에 가까운 구어.

♦가짜의 sham; bogus; fake(d); spurious [spjúəriəs]; imitation (amber); counterfeit; forged; false; mock / 정교한 가짜 an exquisite imitation / 가짜 진주 imitation pearls / 가짜를 진짜라고 속여 떠넘기다 pass [palm, fob] off a spurious article (upon sb) as genuine
▶이 그림[다이아몬드 반지]은 가짜다 This painting [diamond ring] is a fake.
▶이 서명은 가짜다 This signature is a forgery.
▶이 1만원권은 가짜다 This 10,000 won note is a forgery.
▶이 가게에는 가짜가 많다 There are so many fakes in this store.
▶추사(秋史)의 글씨에는 가짜가 많다 There are many imitation in the works with Ch'usa's signature.
▶나는 가짜 진주 목걸이를 속아서 샀다 I was palmed off with a fake pearl necklace.
■—다이아몬드 a faked [sham] diamond; a rhinestone —도장 a forged seal —돈 counterfeit [bogus, fake] money; a counterfeit [false, forged] coin [bank note] —모피 코트 a sham [fake] fur coat —보석 sham [flash] jewelry —여권 a forged passport —위스키 spurious whisky —의사 a quack (doctor); a (medical) charlatan —증서 a counterfeit [forged] bond —차량 번호판 a fraudulent car number plate —코 an artificial [a false] nose —편지 a forged letter : 가짜 편지를 쓰다 write a letter in a disguised hand —학생[형사] a bogus student [detective]

가차압 假差押 〔法〕 provisional seizure ⇨ 가압류(假押留)

가차없다 假借— merciless; relentless; ruthless ♦가차없는 비평가[재판관] an unsparing critic [judge]

가차 없이 假借— mercilessly; relentlessly; ruthlessly; unsparingly; without mercy
♦범법자를 가차없이 처벌하다 punish the offender ruthlessly [without the least consideration for the circumstances (involved)]; show [allow] no mercy toward the offender / 가차없이 철퇴를 내리다 mete out stringent punishment; crack down rigorously
▶속도 위반자는 가차없이 단속하겠다 We will punish speeders without mercy.
▶그는 나의 과실을 가차없이 비판했다 He criticized me mercilessly for my mistake.

가창력 歌唱力 singing ability; a skill as a singer ▶그 여자는 가창력이 있다 She has good singing ability. ⇒ She can sing well.

가창법 歌唱法 vocalism

가책 呵責 scolding; blame; censure
♦양심의 가책 the stings [pangs, pricks] of conscience; compunction / 양심의 가책을 받다 be conscience-stricken; feel the qualms [pricks] of conscience; have a guilty conscience
▶그는 그 돈을 받는 일에 약간의 가책을 느꼈다 He felt some qualms at receiving the money.
▶그는 양심의 가책을 못이겨 자기 죄를 자백했다 He was so conscience-stricken that he confessed to his crime.
▶당신은 양심의 가책을 느끼지 않습니까? Don't you feel the sting of conscience? ⇒

Doesn't your conscience bother [prick] you? ▶그 사람은 그 일 때문에 양심의 가책을 받는 것 같다 He seems to have a bad conscience about it.
가처분 假處分 〔法〕 provisional disposition ▶그는 사태를 수습하기 위해 가처분 신청을 했다 He applied for provisional disposition to settle the matter [case].
—**가처분하다** make provisional [arrange temporary] disposition 《of》; dispose of *sth* for the time being
가처분소득 可處分所得 〔經〕 a disposable income
가철 假綴 a temporary binding; paper binding —**가철하다** bind 《a book, the papers》 temporarily [in a temporary cover] ■—**본** a temporarily bound book; a book temporarily bound in paper
가청 可聽 ♦가청의 audible; audio ■—**거리** 《within》 earshot —**범위** the range of hearing; the audible range —**성** audibility —**신호** an audible signal —**역(閾)〔心〕** the threshold of audibility —**음** an audible sound —**한계** 〔物〕 the audible limit
가청주파(수) 可聽周波(數) 〔電〕 audio frequency (略 A.F.) ■—**증폭기** an audio frequency amplifier
가축 家畜 a domestic animal; 〈소〉 cattle; (총칭) livestock (▶cattle은 복수 취급, livestock은 단수·복수 동형임)
♦가축의 떼 a herd [〈줄지어가는〉 drove] of cattle / 반 가축화된 동물 a semi-domesticated animal / 가축을 치다 keep [raise] livestock; breed domestic animals
▶가축들이 풀밭에서 풀을 뜯고 있었다 Cattle were grazing in the pasture.
▶이 농장에서는 가축을 1천 두 사육하고 있다 On this farm they have a thousand head of cattle.
■—**개량** improvement of livestock —**병원** a veterinary hospital; 〈애완동물의〉 a pets' hospital —**사(舍)** a cattle stall —**사료** stock feed; feedstuff; 〈꼴〉 fodder —**사육** livestock husbandry —**시장** a livestock market —**위생시험소** a livestock experimental hygiene station —**인공수정** livestock artificial insemination —**차** a cattle car [truck, van]; 〈철도의〉 a stockcar; (美) a cow cage —**학** 〈축산학〉 animal husbandry
가출 家出 disappearance from home; 〈도망〉 abscondence; 〈애인과의〉 an elopement
♦가출 중이다 be missing from home
—**가출하다** run away from home; leave home; disappear [fly] from home; abscond; 〈애인과〉 elope
♦가출한 소녀를 보호하다 shelter runaway girls
▶요즘은 어린 소년 소녀들이 이유없이 많이 가출한다 Recently many young boys and girls run away from home for no reason.
■—**소년[소녀]** a runaway girl [boy]; a young runaway —**인(人)** a runaway
가출옥 假出獄 〔法〕 parole; release on parole; conditional release ⇨ 가석방

▶그는 가출옥 중이다 He is on parole.
—**가출옥하다** be released on parole [provisionally]; be paroled; (英) be released on a ticket-of-leave
♦죄수를 가출옥시키다 parole a prisoner; release [put] a prisoner on parole
■—**자** a person on parole; a parolee; (英) a ticket-of-leave man
가치 價値 value; worth; merit ⇨ 값어치

|解說| ***value***와 ***worth***는 둘 다 금전적 가치를 의미하지만 value는 사람의 평가에 따라 결정되는 가치, worth는 그 자체가 가지고 있는 가치다.

♦건강의 가치 the value of good health / 인간의 가치 man's worth / 전략적 가치 strategic value / 책의 가치 the merit of a book / 가치 있는 valuable; worthwhile; worthy / 매우 가치 있는 invaluable; priceless / 가치 없는 valueless; worthless; of no value
〈**가치가[는]**〉 100만원의 가치가 있는 물건 an article worth one million won / 거의[전혀] 가치가 없는 것 a thing of little [no] worth / 거론할 가치가 없는 not worth mentioning / 볼 만한 가치가 있다 be worth seeing
▶그 책은 읽을 가치가 있다 The book is worth reading. ⇌ It is worth while reading [to read] the book.
▶이것은 비싸지만 그만한 가치가 있습니다 This is expensive, but it's worth it [the money].
▶이 단지는 10만원의 가치가 있다 This pot is worth one hundred thousand won.
▶이 미술품들은 세월이 갈수록 확실히 가치가 높아질 것이다 These works of art will certainly increase in value over the years.
▶인간의 가치는 그 인격에 있다 Man's worth consists in what he is.
〈**가치를**〉 가치를 알다 know the value of; appreciate (the value of) *sth* / 가치를 떨어뜨리다 depreciate [detract] (the value of) *sth*
▶사람들은 그 그림의 높은 가치를 인정했다 People acknowledged the great value of the picture.
▶그는 시간의 가치를 모른다 He doesn't know the value of time.
〈**가치도**〉 한 푼의 가치도 없다 be not worth a penny [doit, (brass) farthing, (美口) red cent]
▶이것은 나에게는 아무런 가치도 없다 This is of no value to me.
▶그것은 서푼의 가치도 없다 It's mere trash.
▶그것은 비평할 가치도 없다 It is beneath criticism.
■**경제적—** commercial [economic] value **교환—** value in exchange; exchange [exchangeable] value **본질적—** intrinsic value 《of a coin》 **부가—** value added: 부가가치세 a value added tax **사용—** value in use **실질적—** practical [actual] value **이용[실용]—** utility value **화폐—** money value; the value of money **희소—** scarcity value ■—**관** a sense of values: 사람마다 가치관이 다르다 Everyone has his own (sense of) values. —**기준** a standard of

가치 value —론 〔哲〕 axiology; the study [theory] of values [worth] —척도 a measure of value —체계 a value system; a set of values —판단 (make) (a) value judgment; valuation

가친 家親 my father

가칭 假稱 1 〈임시 이름〉 a provisional [tentative, temporary] name
◆가칭「교학재단」 tentatively named "Kyohak Foundation"
▶그 도서관은 가칭「학생도서관」이라고 부르고 있다 The library is tentatively called "Students' Library."
—가칭하다 call [name] *sth*...tentatively [for the time being, provisionally]
2 ⇨ 사칭(詐稱)

가택 家宅 a house; a residence ■—방문 a house call; a visit to a house

가택수색 家宅搜索 house-searching; a search of *sb's* house; 〔法〕 a domiciliary visit [search]
◆가택 수색을 당하다 be subjected to a domiciliary search; have *one's* house searched
▶경찰이 가택 수색을 했다 The policemen searched the house.
—가택수색하다 search *sb's* house (for *sth*)
■—영장 a warrant to search the house; a search warrant

가택침입 家宅侵入 housebreaking; (a) trespass in *sb's* premises; unlawful entry; intrusion
—가택침입하다 trespass *sb's* premises; break and enter; 〔法〕 break a house
■—자 a housebreaker; a trespasser —죄 (the charge of) housebreaking; trespassing: 그 사람은 가택 침입죄로 고발당했다 The man was charged with housebreaking [trespass(ing)].

가토하다 加土— 〈뿌리에〉 cover roots with soil; earth up; hill; heap up 《some earth》; 〈무덤에〉 re-cover a grave with earth

가톨릭 〔宗〕 Catholicism; the (Roman) Catholic Church ◆가톨릭의 Catholic / 가톨릭을 믿다 believe in Catholicism ■—교회 the (Roman) Catholic Church

가톨릭교도 —教徒 a (Roman) Catholic ▶그는 가톨릭 교도가 되었다 He became a Roman Catholic. ⇒ He was converted to (Roman) Catholicism.

가트 GATT [*the General Agreement on Tariffs and Trade*]

가파르다 steep 《slope》; precipitous 《cliff》; sharp 《climb》
◆가파른 비탈길 a steep [rapid] ascent / 가파른 산길 a steep mountain path / 가파른 절벽 a precipitous cliff
▶계단이 아주 가파르다 The stairs are very steep.
▶그는 가파른 벼랑을 올라갔다 He climbed (up) the steep cliff.

가표 可票 an affirmative vote
◆가표를 던지다 vote for [in favor of]; cast an aye vote for 《a bill》
▶의안은 가표 206, 부표 178로 통과되었다 The bill was passed with 206 in favor to 178 against.

가풀막 a steep [sharp] slope; a steep ascent [descent] ◆가풀막지다 steep; precipitous

가풍 家風 a family tradition [custom]; the ways of a family; the way *one's* family does things
▶우리 며느리는 우리 집 가풍에 맞지 않는다 Our daughter-in-law is not in harmony with our family traditions [customs].
▶그녀는 시집의 가풍에 적응하지 못했다 She did not fit in with her husband's family customs.

가필 加筆 (a) correction; (a) retouch; revision
—가필하다 correct; retouch; revise; touch up
▶나는 그의 작품을 몇 군데 가필해 주었다 I made some improvements on his composition.
▶회의록이 몇 군데 가필되어 있었다 There were some corrections in the minutes of the meeting.

가하다 加— 1 〈더하다〉 add 《A to [and] B》; add [sum] up; 〈부가하다〉 supplement with; include
◆원금에 이자를 가하다 add interest to the principal / 2에 4를 가하다 add four to two; add two and four
▶3에 6을 가하면 9다 Three and six make [are] nine. ⇒ Six added to three makes [equals] nine.
▶숙박료를 가하여 10만원이 된다 It amounts to 100,000 won including hotel charges.
2 〈증가시키다〉 increase
▶차가 속도를 가했다 The car speeded up [increased speed].
3 〈주다〉 inflict; give
◆박차를 가하다 spur *one's* horse; (비유) spur [urge] *sb* 《to do》/ 비판을 가하다 criticize; pass judgment 《upon》/ 압력을 가하다 pressure [put pressure upon] *sb*; apply pressure 《to》/ 열을 가하다 apply heat; heat / 위해를 가하다 harm *sb*; do *sb* harm; inflict an injury 《on *sb*》/ 제재를 가하다 inflict punishment upon *sb*; punish; discipline
▶그녀는 그에게[그의 머리에] 일격을 가했다 She dealt the man a hard blow [gave a hard blow to his head, struck him on the head].
▶그 사람에게 벌을 가해야 한다 He should be punished.

가하다 可— 〈옳다〉 right; good; well; all right; 〈좋다〉 passable; fairly good
▶…라 해도 가하다 We may rightly say that…; It may safely be said that…
▶네 말이 가하다 What you say is right.
▶둘 중 어느 것을 택해도 가하다 You may choose either of the two.
▶둘 다[어느 쪽이든] 가하다 Either will do.

가학 加虐 cruel treatment; maltreatment; cruelty —가학하다 treat *sb* with cruelty; be curel to *sb* ■—성 성욕 이상[이상자] sadism [a sadist]

가해 加害 doing harm; inflicting injury; violence
◆가해를 당하다 sustain injuries 《from》/ 가해를 면하다 escape injury; be unhurt
—가해하다 do *sb* harm 《to》; inflict an injury

((on *sb*)); commit a violence ((on))
■ —행위 a harmful act; a violence
가해자 加害者 an injurer; an offender; an assaulter; an assailant; a wrongdoer; ⟨살해자⟩ a murderer
▶ 그 사람이 그 사고의 가해자다 He caused the accident.
▶ 가해자는 현장에서 체포되었다 The assailant was arrested on the spot.
가헌 家憲 a family constitution [dictum]; family rules
가호 加護 (divine) protection; guardianship; providence
◆ 신의 가호로 with the grace of God; by the protection of Heaven; thanks to God / 신의 가호를 빌다 pray to God for help; call upon God for protection; invoke divine aid
▶ 신의 가호가 있으시기를 May the grace of God be with you.
▶ 나는 신의 가호로 그 참사를 모면했다 I escaped the tragic accident through divine grace.
가혹 苛酷 severity; harshness; rigor; ⟨잔혹⟩ cruelty —**가혹하다** severe; hard; harsh; rigorous; cruel; brutal
◆ 가혹한 노동 조건 severe [hard] working conditions / 가혹한 법률 severe laws / 가혹한 비평 harsh [severe, scathing, sharp] criticism / 가혹한 사람 a severe person / 가혹한 취급[대우] cruel [severe] treatment / 가혹한 형벌 (inflict) a cruel [severe] punishment / 가혹하게 cruelly; severely; harshly; brutally / 가혹하게 취급하다 be hard ((on)); be harsh ((to, with)); deal cruelly [severely] ((with))
▶ 세상은 가혹하다 The world is stern.
▶ 그렇게 어린 아이를 매질하다니 가혹하구나 It is cruel of you to lash such a little child.
▶ 판사는 피고에게 매우 가혹했다 The judge was very hard on the defendant.
가황 加黃 〔化〕 vulcanization —**가황하다** vulcanize ■—**가마** a vulcanizing pan —**고무** vulcanized rubber —**기** a vulcanizer —**유** vulcanized oil
가효 佳肴 delicacies to be eaten with wine; a tasty side dish to go with wine
가훈 家訓 ((observe)) family precepts [mottoes]; the family code of conduct
가희 歌姬 a chantress; a songstress; a female singer
가히 可— ((may, might)) well; fairly well; ((can)) suitably [rightly]
▶ 그는 가히 당대의 석학이라고 할 수 있다 He is a man who might well be called the greatest scholar of the age.
▶ 그는 가히 그렇게 말할 수 있다 He may well say so.
▶ 그 사람의 슬픔은 가히 짐작할 만하다 We may well imagine how grieved he is.
▶ 선생님의 심정은 가히 짐작할 만하다 I can easily figure out how our teacher feels.
▶ 이로 보아 그가 얼마나 부지런한지 가히 알 수 있다 From this we can well imagine how diligent he is.
각 角 1 〈각도〉 an angle ◆ …와 30도의 각을 이루다 form [make] an angle of 30 degrees with…
2 〈4각〉 a square ◆ 여섯 치 각 짜리 기둥 a pillar six inches square
3 〈모퉁이〉 a corner ◆ 가각(街角) a street corner
4 〈뿔〉 a horn; an antler (사슴의) ◆ 각도장 a horn seal
■ **내[외]—** an interior [exterior] angle 둔— an obtuse angle 예— an acute angle 직— a right angle ■ **—가속도** angular acceleration **—대** 〔數〕 a prismoid **—화(化)** keratinization **—화증** keratosis

─ 각 ─

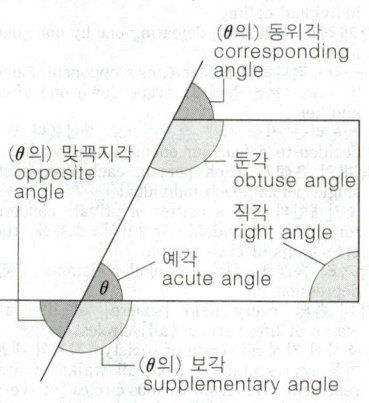

(θ의) 동위각
corresponding angle
(θ의) 맞꼭지각
opposite angle
둔각
obtuse angle
직각
right angle
예각
acute angle
θ
(θ의) 보각
supplementary angle

각 脚 〈다리〉 a leg; (口) pins; 〈짐승 고기의〉 a cut; one of parts into which a butchered animal is divided ◆ 각을 뜨다 cut up a butchered animal in several parts
각 各 each; every ⇨ **각각(各各)**
▶ 각 학교에서 식이 거행되었다 At each school, a ceremony was performed.
▶ 각 반에서 한 사람씩 나와 토론한다 One representative will come from each class for the discussion.
각가지 各— various kinds; all sorts [kinds]; every sort (and kind)
◆ 각가지 물건 various [many] kinds of things; all sorts [kinds] of things / 각가지 요리 도구 a variety of cooking utensils
▶ 우리는 각가지 새를 기르고 있습니다 We keep various sorts of birds.
각각 各各 each; every; all; individually; severally; separately
◆ 각각의 each; respective; individual; separate; several / 각각 살다 live separately
▶ 사람은 각각 생활 방식이 있다 Everyone has his own way of living.
▶ 선물은 각각 별도로 포장되어 있었다 Each gift was wrapped in a separate package.
▶ 소년들은 각각 개를 기르고 있다 Each boy [Each of the boys] keeps a dog.
▶ 우리는 각각 방이 따로 있다 We each have

our own room.
▶ 아이들은 각각 제자리에 앉았다 Each of the children took his (own) seat.
▶ 그 아이들은 각각 사과를 두 개씩 받았다 The children were given two apples each.
▶ 제 아들은 각각 18살, 15살, 12살입니다 My sons are 18, 15 and 12 years old respectively.
각각으로 刻刻— every moment [hour, minute]; from hour to hour; momentarily ◆ 각각으로 변하다 change every moment
각개 各個 each (one); every one ◆ 각개의 each; individual; respective
■—교련 individual drill —전투 individual battle —점호 an individual roll call —호출 individual calling
각개격파 各個擊破 defeating one by one [one after the other]
—각개격파하다 defeat 《one's opponents》 one by one; 〈토론 등에서〉 argue down one after another
▶ 우리는 적을 각개 격파하기로 결심했다 We decided to defeat our enemies one by one.
각개인 各個人 each person; each one; each single person; each individual
◆ 각개인의 문제 a matter of private concern for each individual / 각개인의 소유물 the belongings of each person
각거리 角距離 〔物〕 an angular distance; 〔天〕 depression
각계 各界 every field [sphere] of life; all walks of life; various [all] circles
◆ 사회 각계 all strata of society / 각계의 대표자들 representatives from all walks of life; representatives from various circles [of every sector of society] / 각계의 명사 notables [eminent people] from various fields / 각계 각층의 《people》 of all social standings [all levels of society]; all sorts and conditions of 《people》 / 각계의 의견을 듣다 listen to men of every social standing; collect opinions and comments from various walks of life
▶ 세상은 각계 각층의 사람들로 이루어져 있다 It takes all sorts of people to make the world.
▶ 각계를 대표하는 많은 명사들이 홀에 모였다 Many notables representing various departments of society met together in the hall.
각계수 角係數 〔數〕 an angularity coefficient
각고 刻苦 hard work; toil; untiring industry; arduous labor; close application
▶ 그의 성공은 여러 해에 걸친 각고의 산물이다 His success is the result of years of hard work.
▶ 그는 각고의 노력 끝에 대학자가 되었다 He worked hard and became a great scholar.
—각고하다 work hard [diligently]; apply oneself closely to 《one's studies》
각골난망 刻骨難忘 remembering forever; cherishing the memory of
▶ 은혜는 각골 난망입니다 I shall never forget what you have done for me.
—각골난망하다 be deeply impressed 《with》; (en)grave 《the words》 in the heart
각괄호 角括弧 square brackets

각광 脚光 〈극장의〉 footlights; spotlight
◆ 각광을 받다 〈세상에서〉 be highlighted; be spotlighted; be in the limelight; get into the spotlight; 〈무대에서〉 appear before the footlights
▶ 그는 베스트셀러 작가로서 각광을 받고 있다 As a best-selling author, he is in the limelight [spotlight].
▶ 그녀는 매스컴의 각광을 받고 있다 She is in the spotlight [limelight] of the mass communication.
▶ 이 연극은 마침내 각광을 받게 되었다 This drama has finally come to be staged [performed].
각국 各國 〈각 나라〉 every [each] country [nation]; 〈만국〉 the world; all countries; 〈여러 나라〉 various countries [states]
◆ 세계 각국 world nations; all countries of the world / 각국의 외교 사절 the foreign diplomatic representatives / 유럽 각국을 관광 여행하다 make a sightseeing tour of various European countries
▶ 그 파티에는 세계 각국의 주한 대사들이 참석했다 All foreign ambassadors to Korea were present at the party.
▶ 각국은 독자적인 전통을 가지고 있다 Each country has its own tradition.
▶ 대통령은 유럽 각국을 순방했다 The President made a tour of various European countries.
각군데 各— every [each] place; various [all] places; all sides
◆ 각군데의 in every [each] place; in various place; on all sides / 각군데에서 from various quarters
▶ 각군데 사람이 다 모였다 People from all parts of the country are gathered together.
각기 各其 〈명사적〉 each; every one; 〈부사적〉 each; severally; respectively; individually ⇨ 각각, 각자
▶ 사람은 각기 장점과 단점이 있다 Each man has his merits and his faults.
▶ 학생들은 각기 제 의견을 가지고 있다 The students each have their own opinions.
각기 脚氣 〔醫〕 beriberi ◆ 각기에 걸리다 get beriberi; suffer from [have an attack of] beriberi ■—충심(衝心) heart failure from beriberi
각기둥 角— 〔數〕 a prism
각내 閣內 각내의[에서] within [in, inside] the Cabinet / 각내의 분열을 초래하다 invite [cause] disunity within the Cabinet
각다귀 1 〔昆〕 a midge; a gnat; a striped mosquito 《pl.~ (e)s》
2 〈착취자〉 (비유) a bloodsucker; a vampire; an extortioner
■—판 a dog-eat-dog situation
각단 〈갈피〉 the turn 《of an event》; the drift; the point 《of an affair》; 〈실마리〉 a clue; a lead
▶ 일이 어떻게 돌아가는 건지 각단을 못 잡겠다 I cannot get the point [make head or tail] of the matter.
각도 角度 1 〈각(의 크기)〉 〔數〕 an angle

♦각도를 재다 measure the angle 《of》 / 사다리를 벽에 30도 각도로 기대 놓다 set a ladder at an angle of 30° [a 30° angle] to the wall
▶ 이것은 지면과 45°의 각도를 이룬다 This forms an angle of 45 degrees to the earth.
2 〈시각·관점〉 a viewpoint; a point of view; a standpoint; an angel (of vision)
♦이런 각도에서 보면 from this viewpoint / 모든 각도에서 검토하다 study 《a problem》 from all angles [every angle] / 다른 각도에서 보다 view *sth* from a different viewpoint
▶ 인생은 여러 각도에서 보아야 한다 We must view life from various angles.
▶ 그 문제를 다른 각도에서 검토해 봅시다 Let's examine the problem from a different viewpoint.
■ —게이지 an angle gauge —계 an angle meter; a goniometer [gòuniámətər] —측정 goniometry

각도기 角度器 a protractor; a graduator
■ 반원— a semicircular protractor 전원— a circular protractor

각등 角燈 a square hand-lantern; a bull's-eye (lantern)

각력 脚力 the strength of *one's* legs; *one's* walking and running ability
▶ 그는 각력이 전만 못한 것을 실감하고 있다 He realizes that his legs are not as strong as they used to be.

각령 閣令 〔法〕 a Cabinet order [decree, ordinance]

각로 脚爐 a foot warmer

각론 各論 discussion of details; an item-by-item discussion; the particulars
♦ 각론으로 들어가다 go into detail [particulars]
▶ 그것은 각론에 자세히 설명되어 있다 It is fully treated [explained] under each heading.
▶ 총론에는 찬성이나 각론에는 반대다 I'm not against the principle but I can't agree with each item.
▶ 총론은 그만하고 각론으로 들어갑시다 So much for the outline. Now let's go into detail [(the) details].

각료 閣僚 a member of the Cabinet; a Cabinet minister; **(총칭)** Ministry
♦ 한일 각료 회담 the Korea-Japan Ministerial Meeting / 각료의 일원이다 hold a portfolio; hold a seat in the Cabinet
▶ 각료들은 항의의 표시로 총사퇴하겠다고 말했다 The entire Ministry has threatened to resign in protest.
■ 경제— Cabinet ministers in charge of economic affairs; economic ministers: 경제 각료 회의를 소집하다 call a meeting of Cabinet ministers in charge of economic affairs 전— an ex-minister; a former minister ■ —급 회담 a conference at [on] ministerial level; a minister-level conference [talk] —회의 a Cabinet meeting

각루 刻漏 a water clock

각막 角膜 〔解〕 the cornea; the horny coat 《of the eye》 ■ —염 inflammation of the cornea; corneitis; keratitis —이식(술) a corneal transplant(ation) [graft(ing)]; keratoplasty: 각막 이식을 하다 perform a corneal transplant —혼탁 corneal opacity

각모 角帽 a square-shaped cap; 〈대학생의〉 a college [square] cap; 〈예복용의〉 a mortarboard; 〈학위 수여식 때의〉 a graduation cap

각목 角木 a square bar; a scantling; a balk; a baulk [bɔ́ːk]

각박 刻薄 〈몰인정〉 heartlessness; severity; cruelty; hardness of heart; 〈인색〉 stinginess; miserliness
—**각박하다** 〈박정하다〉 cold(hearted); heartless; hard(hearted); 〈세상살이가〉 exigent; hard to live; difficult for survival; 〈인색하다〉 niggardly
▶ 참으로 각박한 세상이로구나 What a hard world we are living in! ⇒ It's a hard [cold] world (we live in).
▶ 그는 각박한 사람이다 He is a coldhearted [heartless] man.
▶ 요즈음 (물가고로) 인심이 각박해지고 있다 People are getting hardhearted these days (of high prices).
▶ 너무 각박하게 그러지 마라 Be more generous.

각반 脚絆 leggings; gaiters ♦ 각반을 치고 with gaitered legs / 각반을 치다 wear leggings; put on gaiters

각방 各方 every direction; all directions; everywhere ♦ 각방으로 in every direction; in all quarters [directions] / 각방으로 사람을 보내다 send messengers in all directions

각방 各房 each [every] room ♦ 각방에 거처하다 live in separate rooms ▶ 그들은 각방을 쓴다 They live in separate rooms. ⇒ They each have their own rooms.

각방면 各方面 every direction [quarter]; all directions [quarters]; everywhere
♦ 사회 각 방면의 인사들 all classes of people; people in all walks of life / 각 방면에서 in every direction [quarter]; in all directions [quarters]/ 각 방면으로부터 from all quarters; from many sources
▶ 이 대학 졸업생들은 실업계의 각방면에서 활약하고 있다 The graduates of this university are taking an active part everywhere in the business world.

각배 各— **1** 〈짐승의〉 different litters from the same mother
2 〈이복(異腹)〉 having different mother
♦ 각배 형제[자매] brothers [sisters] born of different mothers; a half brother [sister]

각벌 各— 〈옷의〉 separate garments; 〈서류의〉 separate copies

각별하다 各別— **1** 〈특별하다〉 especial; particular; special; 〈평소와 다르다〉 unusual; extraordinary; exceptional; 〈두드러지다〉 noticeable; marked; remarkable
♦ 각별한 조심 special care / 각별한 호의 special favor
▶ 오늘 추위는 각별하다 Today's cold is exceptional [unusual].
▶ 월트는 그녀와 각별한 사이다 Walt is on intimate terms with her.
▶ 각별한 후원에 감사드립니다 Thank you

very much for your kind patronage.
2 〈깍듯하다〉 courteous; 〈정중하다〉 decorous; respectful; 〈예의 바르다〉 polite; civil
♦ 각별한 대접을 받다 be received with much courtesy

각별히 各別— **1** 〈특별하게〉 particularly; in particular; especially; exceptionally; remarkably; specially
♦ 각별히 더운 여름 an exceptionally hot summer / 각별히 조심하다 be extremely cautious [prudent]; take every precaution; take (special) precautions; take the best possible care; be most careful 《about》
▶ 나는 음악을 좋아하는데 클래식을 각별히 좋아한다 I like music, especially classical music.
▶ 그 여자들 중에서도 그녀가 각별히 아름답다 She is by far the most beautiful of them all.
▶ 건강에 각별히 유의하시기 바랍니다 I hope you will take special care of yourself.
2 〈깍듯이〉 courteously; politely; with due respect [courtesy]
♦ 각별히 대접하다 treat with (much) courtesy; give sb a warm reception

각본 脚本 〈연극의〉 a play; a drama; 〈영화의〉 a screenplay; 〈극·영화의 줄거리〉 a scenario (pl. ~s); 〈대본〉 a script ♦ 각본을 상연하다 stage a play / 텔레비전의 각본을 쓰다 write a play [script] for television
▶ 각본이 좋으냐 나쁘냐로 연극이 결정된다 Whether the scenario is done well or not decides the play.
■ **—가** 〈극작가〉 a playwright; a dramatist; 〈영화의〉 a scriptwriter; a scenario writer; a scenarist

각부 各部 **1** 〈각 부서〉 each [every] part [section, department]; 〈행정부의〉 each [every] ministry
♦ 각부 장관 the minister of each department
▶ 이 건에 관하여 관계 각부와 긴밀한 연락을 취하시기 바랍니다 You are requested to keep in close contact with all sections concerned with this matter.
2 〈각 부분〉 each [every] part; all [various] parts

각부 脚部 〈다리 부분〉 the leg
각부분 各部分 each [every] part ♦ 인체 각 부분의 구조 the structure of the parts of a body
각뿔 角— 〖幾〗 a pyramid —육— a six-sided pyramid 정— a regular pyramid 직— a right pyramid ■ —대《臺》a truncated pyramid

――――― **각뿔** ―――――

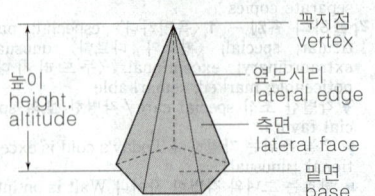

- 꼭지점 vertex
- 옆모서리 lateral edge
- 높이 height, altitude
- 측면 lateral face
- 밑면 base

각살림 各— living separately; living apart
—각살림하다 live separately [apart]
▶ 그들 형제는 각살림하고 있다 The brothers live each by himself.

각상 各床 〈독상〉 dinner tables laid [set] separately for each person; separate [individual] tables; 〈각각의 음식상〉 each dinner table
—각상하다 set individual tables
♦ 각상해서 먹다 dine at individual tables

각색 各色 **1** 〈각 빛깔〉 every [each] color; various [all] colors
2 〈각종〉 various kinds; every kind; all sorts [kinds] ♦ 각색 인종 people of various races; all races / 각양각색의 of every kind; of all sorts; all kinds of

각색 脚色 dramatization
—각색하다 dramatize 《a story》; arrange [adapt] 《a novel》 for the stage [screen]; make a stage [screen] version of 《a story》
♦ 텔레비전용으로 각색하다 arrange 《a story》 for TV
▶ 그것은 외국 소설을 각색한 것이다 That is a dramatization of [adapted from] a foreign novel.
■ **—가** a dramatizer; an adapter

각서 覺書 〈메모〉 a memorandum (pl. ~s, -da); (口) a memo (pl.~s); a memorial; 〈외교상의〉 a note; (프) a mémoire; 〈의정서〉 a protocol
♦ 각서의 교환 an exchange of notes [memoranda] / 각서를 보내다 send a note / 각서를 쓰다 write a memo; compose a memorandum
▶ 양국 정부 간에 각서를 교환했다 Notes have been exchanged between the two governments.

각선미 脚線美 a nice leg line; beautiful shape of legs
♦ 각선미가 있는 여성 a woman with attractive [shapely] legs
▶ 그녀는 각선미가 좋다 She has shapely legs.
▶ 그녀는 각선미가 자랑이다 She is proud of shapeliness of her legs.
■ **—대회** a leg-beauty contest [competition]
—대회 참가자 a leg-beauty contestant

각설 却說 〈화제를 돌릴 때〉 to return to our subject; now to resume our story; in the meanwhile; 〈이야기의 시작〉 (now) once upon a time; now
▶ 각설, 옛날에 예쁜 공주가 살았습니다 Now once upon a time there was a beautiful princess.
—각설하다 return to the subject; go back to the original topic [subject]; resume 《one's story》; get back [return] from a digression
▶ 각설하고 본제로 돌아갑시다 To resume our story, let's return to our topic.

각설이 却說— 〖民俗〗 a singing beggar
각설탕 角雪糖 lump sugar; cube sugar ♦ 각설탕 1개 a lump of sugar
각섬석 角閃石 〖鑛〗 amphibole; hornblende
각성 各姓 different surnames; people of [with] different surnames
■ **—바지** 〈성이 다른 사람들〉 men of different surnames; 〈이부(異父)형제〉 half [uterine]

brothers (with different surnames)

각성 覺醒 (an) awakening
—**각성하다** 〈잠·무지에서〉 wake up 《from》; awake; 〈잘못에서〉 awake to *one's* error; find out *one's* mistake; 〈미혹에서〉 be disillusioned; lose *one's* illusions; come to *one's* senses
♦ 각성시키다 awaken sb to sth; open sb's eyes; disabuse sb 《of his mistaken idea》; bring sb to 《his》 senses; disillusion; arouse
▶ 그 사고는 국민을 크게 각성시켰다 The accident was a great eye opener for the people.
■ —제 a stimulant; 《美俗》 a pep pill

각세공 角細工 hornwork ■ —품 a (piece of) hornwork

각속도 角速度 〔物〕 angular velocity

각시 1 〈인형〉 a maiden doll; a doll bride **2** 〈새색시〉 a bride; a newly-wedded woman ■ —놀음 playing with dolls: 각시놀음하다 play with dolls

각아비자식 各 — 子息 children by different fathers; half brothers [sisters] (with the same mother); uterine brothers [sisters]

각양각색 各樣各色 ♦ 각양각색의 various; all sorts of; of different [all] kinds [sorts]; various kinds; a variety of / 각양각색의 동물 various [different kinds of] animals / 각양각색의 사람들 all sorts (and conditions) of men; a motley of people / 각양각색으로 variously; in many [various, different] ways
▶ 각양각색의 차가 홀에 전시되어 있다 A variety of cars are displayed in the hall.
▶ 각양각색의 사람들이 모임에 나왔다 Various people attended the meeting.

각오 覺悟 〈결심〉 (a) resolution; 〈마음의 준비〉 readiness; preparedness; 〈체념〉 resignation
♦ 노여움을 살 각오를 하고 말하다 dare *sb's* anger and say
▶ 나는 최선을 다할 각오다 I am determined to do my best.
▶ 그는 목숨을 걸 각오다 He is ready to risk his life.
▶ 일이 아무리 어렵더라도 끝까지 해낼 각오가 되어 있나요? Are you resolved to carry through the work, however hard it may be?
—**각오하다** make up *one's* mind 《to sth, to do》; be ready [prepared] 《for》
♦ 죽음을 각오하다 be prepared for death / 각오하고 있다 〈할 먹고 있다〉 be resolved 《to do, that》; 〈마음의 준비가 되어 있다〉 be ready [prepared] 《for》; 〈체념하고 있다〉 be resigned 《to one's fate》
▶ 그는 죽음을 각오했었다 He was resigned to death.
▶ 비난은 각오하고 있다 I am prepared to be criticized [blamed].
▶ 그는 실패를 각오하고 새 사업에 착수했다 He was fully prepared for failure when he started a new enterprise.
▶ 그것이 각오한 바다 I expect nothing less than that.
▶ 그것은 각오할 수밖에 없네 You must make up your mind to that.

각외 閣外 ♦ 각외의 outside the Cabinet / 각외에서 《support the Government》 from outside the Cabinet

각운 脚韻 〔詩〕 a rhyme; an end rhyme ⇨ 운(韻)
♦ 각운을 밟다 rhyme lines

각운동 角運動 〔物〕 angular motion

각위 各位 every one of you; 〈편지에서〉 Gentlemen; Sirs; To whom it may concern
♦ 참석자 각위 all [those] present / 회원 각위 《to》 the members / 각위께서는 you all
▶ 내빈 각위의 건강을 위하여 축배를 올립니다 I drink to the health of all the guests present.
▶ 관계자 각위께는 추후 연락드리겠습니다 There will be an announcement to the members later.

각의 閣議 a Cabinet meeting [council, conference] ⇨ 국무회의
♦ 임시 각의 an extraordinary Cabinet meeting / 정례 각의 a regular [an ordinary] cabinet council / 각의를 소집하다[열다] call [hold] a Cabinet meeting / 각의를 주재하다 preside over a Cabinet council / 각의에 상정하다 put sth to the Cabinet [a Cabinet meeting]; submit sth to [lay sth before] a Cabinet meeting

각인 各人 〈각자〉 each (person); every one (of you); 〈모든 사람〉 everybody; all men
■ —각색 So many men, so many minds: 각인각색으로 in all their respective ways / 취미는 각인각색이다 Everybody has his own hobby.

각인 刻印 a (carved) stamp; a mark; a seal; a carved seal —**각인하다** carve a seal

각일각 刻一刻 every moment ⇨ 시시각각

각자 各自 each; each [every] one; everyone; 〈부사적〉 individually; respectively
♦ 각자의 each; respective; individual; several; *one's* own
▶ 각자의 의무를 다하다 Each of you fulfill your own duty.
▶ 그들은 각자의 집으로 돌아갔다 They return to their several homes.
▶ 그것은 각자의 자유다 Each person may do as he likes about it.
▶ 누구나 각자의 의견이 있다 Each (person) [Everyone] has his own opinion.
▶ 그들은 각자 자기 자리에 앉았다 They sat in their respective seats.
▶ 각자 공책을 가져올 것 Each of you [Everyone] has to bring your own notebook.
▶ 학생들은 각자 사전을 갖고 있다 Every student has a dictionary.
▶ 각자 더 노력하시오 I want every one of you to work harder.
▶ 우리는 각자 자기 의견을 말했다 We each expressed our ideas.

각재 角材 square lumber [《英》] timber ♦ 10인치의 각재 a ten-inch square lumber / 작은 각재 (a) scantling

각적 角笛 a horn; a bugle horn ♦ 각적을 불다 bugle; blast a horn

각종 各種 every [each] kind; various kinds; all kinds [sorts] 《of》; varieties
♦ 각종의 various; 《wines》 of every kind; all sorts [kinds, descriptions] of; wide variety

of / 각종 야외[실내] 경기 all sorts of outdoor [indoor] games / 각종 직업 occupations of various kinds
▶ 저희 점포에는 각종 악기가 두루 갖추어져 있습니다 We have musical instruments of all kinds. ≒ We have a wide variety of musical instruments.

각주 角柱 1 〈네모진 기둥〉 a square pillar 2 〈각기둥〉 [數] a prism

각주 脚註 a footnote ♦ 각주를 달다 add [give, put in] footnotes (to); give footnotes (to a book)

각지 各地 every [each] place [district, area]; all places; 〈여러 지방〉 various places; 〈전국〉 all parts of the country
♦ 전국 각지의 날씨 the weather of various parts of the country / 세계 각지에서 모은 진품들 rare articles collected from every corner [all parts] of the world / 세계 각지에(서) in various parts of the world
▶ 그 연극은 한국 각지에서 상연되었다 The play was staged in various Korean towns.
▶ 그 음악제에 전국 각지로부터 많은 젊은이들이 모여들었다 The music festival attracted a lot of young people from all parts [every corner] of the country.

각질 角質 〈뿔·손톱·발톱 등의〉 keratin; 〈절지 동물의〉 chitin [káitən] ♦ 각질의 horny; corneous / 각질화하다 keratinize
■ —섬유 〈해면류의〉 keratose —조직 corneous [horny] tissue —층 a horny layer

각처 各處 each [every] place; all [various] places [quarters]
♦ 각처에 everywhere; all over; in all [various] places; 〈여기 저기에〉 here and there / 각처에 경찰관을 배치하다 post policemen everywhere [all over the place]
▶ 각처의 사람들이 다 모였다 People from all over are here.

각추 角錐 [幾] a pyramid ⇨ 각뿔

각추렴 joint contribution; collecting from each; pooling; splitting; 〈회식 등의〉 Dutch treat [party]
—**각추렴하다** collect from each; contribute jointly; share the expenses; split the account; pool; go Dutch
▶ 그들은 비용을 각추렴했다 They split the expenses.
▶ 나도 함께 각추렴하게 해 주세요 Please let me take a share in the expenses.

각축 角逐 (a) competition; rivalry; struggle (for mastery) ♦ 각축을 벌이다 be at odds [variance] (with sb)
▶ 그들은 상을 타려고 서로 각축을 벌였다 They competed [vied] with each other for the prize.
—**각축하다** compete; vie (with); struggle (for); contend (against)
—**장** the arena of competition

각축전 角逐戰 a hot [sharp] contest; a keen competition ▶ 그들은 모두 그녀의 환심을 사려고 각축전을 벌였다 They all vied in paying her attention.

각층 各層 each [every] floor [story]

♦ 각층의 on [of] every floor / 각층에(서) at every floor / 각층에서는 엘리베이터 an elevator that stops at every floor

각테 角— a horn rim ■—**안경** horn-rimmed glasses [spectacles]

각통질 bloating an ox with fodder and water before selling it
—**각통질하다** force fodder and water down (an ox) ♦ 각통질한 소 a watered ox

각파 各派 〈정당〉 each party; 〈파벌〉 each faction; 〈유파〉 each school; 〈종파〉 each sect [denomination]

각피 角皮 [解] cuticle ■—소(素) cutin

각필하다 擱筆— lay down one's pen; stop [finish] writing; close (a letter)

각하 却下 (a) rejection, a turndown; [法] (a) dismissal
—**각하하다** reject; dismiss; turn down
♦ 상소를 각하하다 dismiss an appeal / 요청을 각하하다 turn down sb's request / 청원을 각하하다 reject [turn down] a petition
▶ 그의 제안[이의 신청]은 각하되었다 His proposal [objection] was rejected [overruled].

각하 閣下 〈2인칭〉 Your Excellency; 〈3인칭〉 His [Her] Excellency (pl. Their Excellencies); 〈미국의 판사·시장 등을 지칭하여〉 Your [His, Her] Honor

각혈 咯血 [醫] hemoptysis —**각혈하다** spit [cough] out blood; expectorate blood

간 〈짠 정도〉 a salty taste; saltiness; 〈조미〉 seasoning with salt
♦ 간이 맞다 be well seasoned with salt / 간이 싱겁다 be not well salted; be not salty enough / 간이 짜다 be too salty / 간을 보다 taste (a dish) to see how it is seasoned with salt
▶ 이것은 간이 좀 부족하다 This needs a touch of salt.
▶ 이 국은 간이 너무 짜다 This soup is too salty. ≒ There's too much salt in this soup.
—**간하다** season with salt; pickle (vegetables) with salt; salt [sauce] (fish)

간 肝 〈담장〉 the liver; 〈담력·배짱·용기〉 courage; spirit; pluck; (口) guts
♦ 간이 큰 사람 a man of pluck / 간이 크다 be bold; be daring; be plucky; have a lot of pluck [guts]/ 간이 콩알만해지다 be amazed; be astounded; be frightened out of one's wits / 간이 타다 be anxious (for); pine / 간을 녹이다 〈매혹시키다〉 charm; fascinate; enchant / 간을 졸이다 worry oneself / 간에 기별도 안 가다 have one's hunger [appetite] much unsatisfied; be hardly enough to be worth eating / 간에 붙었다 쓸개에 붙었다 하다 double deal; sit on the fence; turn one's coat readily

간 間 1 〈간살〉 a space ⇨ 칸살; 〈방〉 a room ⇨ 칸 ♦ 초가 삼간 a three-room thatched house; a shabby cottage
2 〈길이·너비의 단위〉 a kan ⇨ 칸

-간 -間 1 〈관계〉 relation; relationship
♦ 형제간 brotherly [fraternal] relation / 숙질간 the relationship of uncle and nephew
▶ 그들은 사제간이다 They are master and

disciple [pupil].
▶ 《會話》「너는 그와 무슨 관계냐?」「형제간입니다」 "What's your relationship [What relation are you] to him?" "We are brothers."
2 〈사이〉 between; among
♦ 부부간의 애정 affection [love] between man and wife / 세 나라간의 우호 관계 the friendly relations among the three countries / 형제간의 싸움 a quarrel between brothers / 친구간에 among *one's* friends / 양자간을 조정하다 mediate between the two parties
▶ 백화점간의 경쟁이 극심하다 The competition among the department stores is severe [serious, sharp].
▶ 김 교수는 학생들간에 인기가 있다 Professor Kim is popular among the students.
3 〈동안〉 for; during; in
♦ 10년간 사귀어 온 친구 a friend of ten years' standing / 10분간의 휴식 a ten minutes' recess / 과거 20년간 during [for] the past [last] twenty years / 3일간 계속하여 for three days running [on end] / 지난 1주일간에 in the past [last] week
▶ 요 며칠간 그를 만나지 못했다 I haven't seen him for some days past.
▶ 나는 그곳에 한 달간 묵었다 I stayed there for a month.
▶ 전국 소년체전은 5일부터 10일간 개최된다 The National Children's Sports Meet will be held for ten days beginning on the 5th.
▶ 그는 5일간에 그 일을 마쳤다 He finished the work in five days.
4 〈두 곳 사이〉 between
♦ 서울-일산간의 철도 the railway line between Seoul and Ilsan / 지호지간(指呼之間)에 있다 be within hail
▶ 이 기차는 서울-부산간을 약 4시간에 달린다 This train runs between Seoul and Pusan in about four hours.
5 〈막론하고〉 irrespective [regardless] of; whether or; either or
♦ 남자건 여자건간에 whether it is man or woman; irrespective of sex / 비가 오든 안 오든간에 rain or shine / 비용이 얼마가 들든간에 irrespective of cost / 어쨌든간에 at any rate / 좋든 나쁘든간에 whether for good or for evil
▶ 이것이든 저것이든간에 하나를 가져라 Take one of the two, either this one or that one.
▶ 결과가 어떻든간에 최선을 다하는 것이 중요하다 It's important to do your best no matter how the result turns out to be.
▶ 성공하든 실패하든간에 시도해 보겠다 I will try whether I shall succeed or not.

간간이¹ 間間— (in) each [every] room ⇨ 칸칸이]

간간이² 間間— **1** 〈이따금〉 sometimes; occasionally; now and then; from time to time; once in a while; at intervals
▶ 나는 길에서 간간이 그를 만난다 I sometimes see him on the street.
▶ 그런 일이 간간이 일어난다 It happens once in a while.
▶ 간간이 소나기가 오겠습니다 There will be showers from time to time.
2 〈듬성듬성〉 scatteringly; sparsely; thinly
▶ 그곳에는 농가가 간간이 있다 There are scattered farmhouses there. ⇌ The place is sparsely dotted with farmhouses.

간간짭짤하다 pleasantly salty; good and salty

간간하다¹ 〈맛이〉 saltish; pleasantly salty; nicely salted ▶ 음식이 간간하니 맛이 있다 This dish is nicely salty.

간간하다² 〈재미있다〉 tickling; fascinating; exciting; thrilling ♦ 이야기의 간간한 대목 the thrilling climax of a story

간거르다 間— alternate; leave an interval 《between》; skip *sth* every other ♦ 간걸러서 alternately

간격 間隔 1 〈공간적인〉 a space; an interval
♦ 일정한 간격을 두고 at regular intervals / 10미터 간격으로 at intervals of ten meters; ten meters apart 《from each other》 / 간격을 두다 [떼다] leave a space 《between》 / 간격을 좁히다 narrow the distance [space] 《between》
▶ 앞차와의 간격을 유지해야 한다 You have to keep a space between a car ahead and yours.
▶ 서로 간격을 좁히시오 Don't leave no space between yourselves.
▶ 우리는 3미터 간격으로 일정하게 기둥을 세웠다 We placed the posts at regular intervals of three meters.
2 〈시간적인〉 an interval
♦ 열차[선박]의 운행 간격 a headway / 15분 간격으로 운행하다 operate at an interval of fifteen minutes
▶ 버스는 몇분 간격으로 떠납니까? How often does the bus leave?
▶ 그 공항에서는 10분 간격으로 비행기가 이륙한다 Planes take off at intervals of ten minutes at the airport.
3 〈인간 관계의 소원함〉 an estrangement
▶ 그 일로 그는 가족과의 사이에 간격이 생겼다 The affair has estranged him from his family.

간결 簡潔 brevity; conciseness; terseness; compactness
♦ 전문(電文) 간결체 telegraphic brevity / 간결을 기하기 위해 for brevity
▶ 간결은 재치의 생명 Brevity is the soul of wit.
—간결하다 brief; concise; terse; compact

> 解說 ***concise***는 간단하고 명쾌하다는 뜻의 다소 격식을 차린 말. ***brief***는 말수가 적고 요령이 있다는 뜻.

♦ 간결한 문장 terse style / 간결한 설명 a concise explanation / 간결한 제목 terse headlines / 간결하게 briefly; concisely; tersely; compactly / 간결하게 대답[설명]하다 answer [explain] briefly
▶ 그의 설명은 간결하고 요령이 있었다 His explanation was brief [short, concise] and to the point.
▶ 그 저자는 문체가 간결하기로 유명하다 The author is famous for his concise style.
▶ 질문에 간결하게 답하시오 Answer briefly to

the question.
▶이 보고서는 장황한데 좀 간결하게 할 수 없겠나? This report is too wordy; can't you be more concise?

간경변 肝硬變 〔醫〕 cirrhosis (of the liver); hepatocirrhosis

간계 奸計 a trick; a dark [crafty] design [device]; a vicious plot; wiles
♦간계를 꾸미다 make a wicked design; devise [think out] an evil plot [a nasty trick] / 간계를 쓰다 use a dirty trick / 적의 간계에 빠지다 play into the enemy's hand / 간계로 속이다 deceive sb with a scheme

간곡하다 懇曲— cordial; hearty; kind; 〈간절하다〉 earnest; serious; eager ♦간곡한 충고 kind advice / 간곡한 편지 a kind letter

간곡히 懇曲— cordially; 〈열심히〉 earnestly; eagerly; 〈절실히〉 seriously; 〈거듭〉 repeatedly
♦간곡히 타이르다 admonish sb repeatedly (against, for); reason ((with sb)) earnestly; persuade sb earnestly
▶그는 흡연이 얼마나 해로운지를 간곡히 설명했다 He explained earnestly how bad it was to smoke.

간과 看過 〈못보고 넘김〉 failure to notice [grasp]; passing over; 〈묵인〉 connivance [kənáivəns] ((at wrongdoing)); overlooking
—**간과하다** fail to notice; miss; look over; pass sth over in silence; overlook ((a fault)); connive ((at))
▶당신은 문제의 핵심[본질]을 간과했다 You have failed to grasp the core [missed the true nature] of the problem.
▶사람들은 이 사실을 간과하는 수가 많다 People are apt to overlook this fact.
▶그는 그 사실을 간과하지 않았다 He didn't let the fact pass.= He didn't miss the fact.
▶물가 상승은 간과할 수 없는 중대한 문제다 The rise in (commodity) prices is a serious problem not to be overlooked.
▶그 일은 그냥 간과할 수 없다 I cannot let the matter pass (by) without making a protest.

간교 奸巧 craft; cunning; wiliness
—**간교하다** cunning; crafty; sly; wily
♦여우처럼 간교한 (as) wily [cunning] as a fox
▶그는 간교한 늙은 여우다 He is a cunning old fox.

간구 懇求 an earnest desire [request]; (an) entreaty; soliciting; begging
—**간구하다** earnestly request; beg; entreat; solicit
♦간구하옵건대… I earnestly desire that…; It is my earnest hope [wish] that…
▶그는 재판관에게 자비를 간구했다 He entreated the judge for mercy.
▶우리는 그의 조언을 간구했다 We solicited his advice [advice from him].

간국 salty liquids; a salt solution; brine ♦간국에 절이다 soak [steep] in brine

간균 桿菌 〔生〕 a bacillus ((pl. -li)); a bacterium ((pl. -ria))

간극 間隙 1〈벌어진 틈〉 a gap; an opening; a slit; a crevice; an aperture
▶그들은 그 간극을 메우려고 애썼다 They tried to bridge the gap.
2 〈불화〉 a difference; discord ((between)); a split; 〈친구간의〉 a breach of friendship

간기 刊記 a colophon; an imprint; a postscript (to a book)

간난 艱難 1 〈역경·고생〉 hardships; difficulties; adversity; trials; sufferings; tribulations
♦간난을 겪다 go through hardships; 〈口〉 have a rough time / 간난을 극복하다 get over difficulties / 간난을 참고 견디다 endure [bear, go through] hardships 2 ⇨ 가난

간난신고 艱難辛苦 ▶그는 간난 신고 끝에 겨우 일을 해냈다 He accomplished his task after a lot of difficulties.
—**간난신고하다** bear [undergo, go through] hardships
♦간난 신고하여 자식들을 키우다 manage to bring up one's children

간뇌 間腦 〔解〕 the diencephalon; the interbrain

간다라 〈고대 인도의 유적〉 Gandhara

간단 簡單 simplicity; 〈짧음·간명함〉 brevity; shortness
—**간단하다** simple; brief; short; straightforward; 〈평이하다〉 plain; 〈가볍다〉 light; 〈쉽다〉 easy
♦간단한 대답 a brief answer / 간단한 도구 simple tools / 간단한 문제 a simple problem [task] / 간단한 일 easy work / 간단한 편지 a brief [short] letter / 간단한 절차로 through a simple procedure / 간단한 식사를 하다 have a light [simple] meal
▶그를 속이기는 간단하다 It's very easy to take him in.
▶일은 간단했다 The job was easy [simple].
▶〔會話〕「어떻게 하면 되지?」「그건 간단해」 "How can I do it?" "It's very easy."

간단명료하다 簡單明瞭— simple and plain [clear]
♦간단명료하게 simply and clearly; tersely; concisely and plainly / 간단명료하게 말하다 speak briefly and to the point
▶우리는 간단 명료하게 말하도록 교육을 받았다 We were taught to speak briefly and to the point.

간단 間斷 〈끊임없다〉 incessant; ceaseless; continuous; continual
—**간단없이** incessantly; ceaselessly; continuously; unceasingly; without a break
♦간단없이 재잘거리다 chatter ceaselessly; talk without a pause
▶사람들이 간단없이 드나들었다 People were constantly coming in and out.
▶차가 간단없이 지나간다 There is a constant stream of cars.
▶비가 간단없이 내린다 It rains continuously.

간단히 簡單— simply; easily; briefly; in brief
♦간단히 말하면 to put it simply; in short; in brief; to be brief; simply put / 시험에 간단히 합격하다 pass one's exam easily [with ease]
▶간단히 말해서 네가 잘못이야 In short, you are in the wrong.
▶그는 그것을 아주 간단히 해치웠다 He fin-

ished it without the slightest difficulties.
▶ 간단히 해라 〈연설 등에서〉 Cut it short!
▶ 그는 상황[사건]을 간단히 설명했다 He explained the situation briefly [gave the brief account of the case].

간담 肝膽 1 〈간과 쓸개〉 liver and gall
2 〈속마음〉 one's inmost feelings; one's innermost heart
♦ 간담을 서늘하게 하는 광경 an appalling [a gruesome] sight / 간담이 내려앉다[떨어지다] be frightened out of one's wits / 간담이 서늘해지다 freeze in shock; be extremely frightened; be horrified / 간담을 서늘하게 하다 freeze sb's heart with terror; astound; take sb by surprise
▶ 호랑이의 포효 소리에 간담이 서늘했다 My blood ran cold [chill] as I heard the roar of a tiger.
▶ 그 사고는 그의 간담을 서늘하게 했다 The accident froze [curdled] his blood.

간담 懇談 a chat; a friendly talk
―**간담하다** have a familiar [friendly] talk ((with)); chat ((with)); have an informal talk ((with))
▶ 우리는 그를 중심으로 간담했다 We had a talk with him as the central figure.
■ ―회 a social gathering [meeting]; a round-table conference; 〈美口〉 a talk fest

간담상조 肝膽相照 ♦간담 상조하는 사이다 be inseparable [bosom, great] friends (like David and Jonathan [Damon and Pythias]) / 간담 상조하여 이야기를 나누다 have a heart-to-heart talk ((with))
▶ 그 두 사람은 간담 상조하는 사이다 The two are on very friendly terms with each other. ⇌ The two are great [close] friends.

간댕거리다 shake; dangle; tremble
♦ 그녀의 귀에 매달려 간댕거리는 귀고리 earrings dangling from her ears
▶ 아이들은 다리를 간댕거리며 담 위에 앉아 있었다 The children sat on the wall, (with) their legs dangling.

간데라 a metal hand lamp; a lantern

간데족족 everywhere [wherever] one goes
♦ 간데족족 말썽을 일으키다 make trouble wherever one goes

간동그리다 bundle up neatly; arrange neatly

간동맥 肝動脈 〖解〗a hepatic artery

간동하다 neatly bundled; neatly arranged

간두 竿頭 1 〈대막대기 끝〉 the tip of a rod
♦ 간두지세(之勢) the most critical situation
2 ⇨ 백척간두

간드랑거리다 swing gently; dangle; sway (to and fro); waver
▶ 초롱[풍경]이 바람에 간드랑거린다 A lantern dangles [The wind-bell is swinging] in the wind.
▶ 나뭇잎이 산들바람에 간드랑거리고 있었다 The leaves were trembling in the breeze.

간드러지다 coquettish; fascinating; bewitching; captivating; full of flirtation
♦ 간드러진 걸음걸이 a bewitching gait / 간드러진 목소리 a purring voice / 간드러지게 노래를 부르다 sing a song with a charming lilt / 간드러지게 웃다 laugh coquettishly
▶ 그 여자는 모습이 간드러진다 She looks enticing.

간들거리다 〈바람이〉 blow gently [softly]; 〈물체가〉 dangle; tremble; sway; waver; 〈태도 등이〉 act coquettishly; put on coquettish air; play the flirt
♦ 나무에서 간들거리는 나뭇잎 leaves swaying on a tree / 바람에 간들거리는 나뭇잎 trembling leaves in the air

간디스토마 肝― 〖動〗a liver fluke; 〈병〉 distomatosis; liver rot

간략 簡略 〈간단・간결〉 simplicity; brevity; terseness; 〈약식〉 informality
―**간략하다** simple; concise; brief; 〈약식의〉 informal
♦ 간략한 기사[보고] a short account [brief report] / 간략하게 하다 make brief; simplify
▶ 절차가 간략해졌다 The formalities have been simplified.
▶ 우리 결혼식은 가급적 간략하게 합시다 Let's make our wedding as simple as possible.

간막이 partitioning ⇨ 칸막이

간만 干滿 the ebb and flow ((of the tide)); flux and reflux; tide
▶ 황해는 간만의 차가 매우 크다 The tidal range is very great in the Yellow Sea.
▶ 조수에는 간만이 있다 The tide rises and falls. ⇌ The tide ebbs and flows.

간망 懇望 an entreaty; solicitation; an earnest request
♦ 간망에 의해 at sb's earnest request / 간망을 받아들이다 comply with [listen to] sb's earnest request [entreaty]
▶ 그녀의 간망에 못이겨 그는 마침내 승낙했다 He was unable to resist her entreaties, and finally consented.
―**간망하다** plead ((with sb to do)); entreat ((sb to do)); beg earnestly; implore; solicit
▶ 사람들은 그가 그 자리를 차지하기를 간망했다 He was earnestly requested to take up the post.

간맞다 well [properly] salted [seasoned]

간맞추다 season with salt; salt properly

간물 salty water; brine

간물 乾物 dried fish ⇨ 건물(乾物)

간밤 last night
▶ 간밤엔 몹시 추웠다 It was very cold last night.
▶ 간밤부터 내리는 비가 아직 그치지 않고 있다 It has been raining since last night.

간방 艮方 northeast; the northeastern quarter

간벌 間伐 thinning of a forest ―**간벌하다** thin out a forest

간병 看病 nursing; attendance; tending ((a sick person))
―**간병하다** nurse; tend; attend ((on)); look after; care for ♦ 헌신적으로 간병하다 attend on a sick person with devotion
■ ―인(人) a person tending the sick

간보다 taste; see how the food is salted [seasoned]

간부 姦夫 an adulterer; a paramour ♦ 간부를 두다 deceive one's husband; cuckold

간부 姦婦 an adulteress; a paramour ◆간부의 남편 a cuckold

간부 間夫 a paramour ⇨ 샛서방

간부 幹部 an executive; a leader; a leading [principal] member; (총칭) the (managing) staff;〈군대 등의〉a cadre [káːdri]
◆노동조합 간부 union leaders [officials] / 정당의 간부 the executive members [leaders] of a party / 중견 간부 mid-level [middle-ranking] executives / 회사의 간부 the executives [managing staff] of a company / 간부급에 있는 사람 (美) a person in an executive position [on the executive]; an executive
■최고― the top brass ■―직원 officials in responsible posts ―회의 an executive session [council]; a staff conference ―후보생 a military cadet

간빙기 間氷期 〔地〕 an interglacial period [epoch]; an interglacial

간사 奸詐 cunning; guile; wiles; craft
◆간사를 떨다[부리다] play a sly game
―**간사하다** cunning; crafty; guileful; sly; deceitful; wily; tricky

> 解說 *cunning*, *crafty*는 교활하다는 뜻. *tricky*는 꾀를 써서 상대방을 속이려고 하다, *dirty*는 비열하게 간사하다, *unfair*는 공정·공평하지 않다는 뜻.

◆간사한 인간 a cunning person; a crafty [foxy] fellow / 간사하게 cunningly; deceitfully; slyly; craftily

간사 幹事 a manager; a(n) (executive) secretary;〈회합 등의〉an organizer;〈공공 기관의〉 (英) a governor
◆단체 여행의 간사 a manager of a group trip / 동창회의 간사 a secretary of an alumni [a graduates'] association / 간사 회사〈사채 발행의〉a managing underwriter

간살 〈아첨〉 flattering; fawning; adulation; sycophancy; toadyism;〈아양〉coquetry
◆간살부리다 flatter; adulate; butter *sb* up; fawn on [upon] *sb*;〈여자가〉play the coquette; coquet 《with a man》
▶ 간살부리지 마라 Stop flattering.
▶ 그는 항상 사장에게 간살을 부린다 He is always making [playing] up to the president.
▶ 그 여자가 온갖 간살을 다 부려도 그는 말려들지 않았다 In spite of all her wiles, he was not attracted to her.
■―쟁이 a flatterer; a sycophant; a toadeater

간살 間― a space ⇨ 칸살

간상 奸商 a crooked dealer; a dishonest merchant; an illicit trader ■―배 (a gang of) dishonest merchants; (a group of) profiteers

간색 看色 〈보기〉sampling;〈물건〉a sample
―**간색하다** sample; test [judge] by a sample; assess by examining a small portion (of)
■―대 a trier

간색 間色 a compound [secondary] color; an intermediate [in-between] shade; demitint; halftone

간석지 干潟地 a tideland; a beach at ebb tide; a dry beach; a tidal [mud] flat ◆간석지를 개간하다 reclaim tidal land

간선 間選 indirect election ⇨ 간접(~선거)

간선 幹線 〈도로·철도 등의〉a trunk line; a main line; an artery
■―거(渠) a main sewer ―도로 a main [principal, trunk] road; (英) an arterial road; a highway; (美) a boulevard ―철도 an arterial railroad

간섭 干涉 1〈참견〉interference; meddling; 〈타국에 대한〉(an) intervention
◆무력에 의한 내정 간섭 armed intervention in the internal [domestic] affairs of another country / 외부의 간섭 outside intervention / 재판에 대한 정부의 간섭 governmental interference in a trial / 간섭을 받다 be interfered with / 외국의 간섭을 초래하다 invite [lead to] foreign intervention / 아무의 간섭도 받지 않다 be *one*'s own master
―**간섭하다** interfere (in *sb*'s affairs); intervene (in); meddle (in, with); (口) put [poke, thrust] *one*'s nose into; poke (into)

> 解說 *interfere*, *meddle*, *intervene*은 모두 사이에 끼어들어 쓸데없는 참견을 한다는 뜻인데, interfere에는 방해하여 망치게 한다는 뜻이 강하다.

◆간섭하기 좋아하는 interfering (neighbors); (people) in the habit of interfering in other people's affairs; meddlesome / 남의 일에 간섭하다 interfere in [meddle with] another's business / 내정에 간섭하다 intervene in the internal affairs (of a country) / 쓸데없이 간섭하다 make uncalled-for meddling / 간섭받다 be interfered (with)
▶ 어떤 나라가 그 나라의 외교 정책에 간섭하려고 했다 A certain country tried to intervene in [dictate] their diplomatic policies.
▶ 남의 일에 간섭하지 마라 Don't put [poke] your nose into other people's affairs.
▶ 아이들은 너무 간섭하지 않는 것이 좋다 Children ought to be left alone [to themselves] sometimes.
▶ 나는 간섭받는 것을 싫어한다 I hate to have people meddle in my affairs.
2〈광파·음파의〉interference ◆간섭성의 coherent (light) ―**간섭하다** interfere (in)
■공동(共同)― collective [joint] intervention 무력― armed intervention 선거[학원]― government interference in the election [in campus activities] ■―계(計) an interferometer ―굴절계 an interference refractometer ―권(圈)[상(像)][螺] an interference figure ―색 interference colors ―주의 interventionism; an interference policy: 불간섭주의 a nonintervention policy

간성 干城 a bulwark; a stronghold; a defender; a safeguard ◆국가의 간성 the bulwark of (security) to the state

간세 間稅 an indirect tax=간접(~세)

간소 簡素 simplicity; plainness
―**간소하다** simple; plain
◆간소한 생활 (lead) a simple life [plain living] / 간소한 식사 a homely [frugal, plain]

meal / 간소한 옷차림을 하다 be plainly dressed; be (dressed) in simple clothes
▶ 그녀의 복장은 간소한 것이 특징이다 Her clothes are characterized by their simplicity.
간소화 簡素化 simplification
♦ 생활 방식의 간소화 simplification of *one's* way of life
—**간소화하다** simplify; streamline
♦ 수속 절차를 간소화하다 streamline [simplify] official procedures; make the procedures simple / 정부[행정] 기구를 간소화하다 simplify government [administration] setup [structure]
간수 keeping; safekeeping; custody; storage; preserving; treasuring
—**간수하다** put aside [away] for future use; keep; preserve
♦ 소중히 간수하다 treasure (up); lock away / 가구를 창고 속에 간수하다 store the furniture in a warehouse
▶ 내 서류는 그녀가 간수하고 있다 She keeps my papers. ⇌ My papers are in her custody [keeping].
▶ 그것을 잘 간수해 두어라 Keep it in a safety place.
▶ 여름에는 음식을 잘 간수하지 않으면 상한다 In summer, food is easily spoiled by heat unless it is kept well.
간수 —水 bittern; brine
간수 看守 a (prison) guard ⇨ 교도관
간수 間數 the number of *kan* ⇨ 칸수
간식 間食 a (between-meal) snack; eating between meals [snacks]
♦ 간식으로 감자 튀김을 먹다 eat potato chips between meals
▶ 살을 빼고 싶으면 간식을 피해야 한다 If you want to lose weight, you will have to stop eating snacks.
—**간식하다** eat between meals; eat [have a snack] between meals
간신 奸臣 a treacherous subject; a villainous retainer
간신히 艱辛— barely; narrowly; hardly; by a (near) shave; with difficulty; just; only
♦ 간신히 도망치다 barely escape; have a narrow escape / 간신히 먹고 살다 make [earn] a bare living / 나오는 눈물을 간신히 억제하다 hold back tears with difficulty
▶ 나는 그것을 간신히 해치웠다 I was just able to manage it.
▶ 우리는 간신히 이겼다 We gained a narrow victory. ⇌ Victory was hardly won.
▶ 다저스는 양키스에게 간신히 이겼다 The Dodgers edged [nosed out] the Yankees.
▶ 그들은 간신히 위기를 넘겼다 They got through the crisis with difficulty.
▶ 길이 아주 좁아 소형차들도 간신히 지나갔다 The road was quite narrow and even small cars passed with difficulty.
▶ 그 아이는 발뒤꿈치를 들고 서면 간신히 창에 닿는다 The boy can just reach the window on tiptoe.
▶ 그는 간신히 막차를 잡아 탔다 He barely managed to catch the last train.

간악 奸惡 wickedness; treacherousness
—**간악하다** wicked; treacherous; villainous; knavish [néiviʃ]
♦ 간악한 무리 a gang of scoundrels; rogues; rascals / 간악한 인간 a wicked [treacherous] person
간암 肝癌 cancer of the liver; liver cancer
간언 諫言 remonstrance; admonition; expostulation; 〈충고〉 advice; counsel
♦ 간언을 듣다 listen [yield] to *one's* remonstrance
▶ 간언은 귀에 거슬린다 Admonitions are not sweet to the ear.
—**간언하다** remonstrate [expostulate] with *sb* 《on [about] his folly》; admonish *sb* 《against being impatient [not to do things like that]》
▶ 그는 주식[증권]에 손을 대지 말라고 상사에게 간언했다 He expostulated with his boss against speculating in stocks.
간염 肝炎 hepatitis; inflammation of the liver
♦ A [B, C]형 간염 hepatitis A [B, C] / 간염 예방 접종 the anti-hepatitis inoculation
■ **전염성—** infectious hepatitis **혈청—** serum hepatitis
간엽 肝葉 〔解〕 the lobe of the liver
간원 懇願 (an) entreaty; an earnest appeal; solicitation; 〈청원〉 a petition
▶ 그는 나의 간원을 들어 주려 하지 않았다 He wouldn't listen to my entreaties.
—**간원하다** entreat 《*sb* for *sth* [to do]》; implore; plead 《with *sb* to do [for *sth*]》; beg; make an earnest appeal 《to *sb* for *sth*》; solicit 《for》
▶ 그녀는 의사에게 아들의 생명을 구해 달라고 간원했다 She pleaded with [earnestly begged] the doctor to save her son's life.
간유 肝油 cod-liver oil 《당의(糖衣) 간유구 sugarcoated cod-liver oil pills
■ **무취(無臭)—** inodorous cod-liver oil ■ **—드롭스** cod-liver oil drops **—유제(乳劑)** emulsion of cod-liver oil
간음 姦淫 adultery; illicit intercourse; fornication; 〔法〕 criminal conversation
—**간음하다** commit adultery 《with》; misconduct *oneself* 《with》; have illicit relations 《with》
♦ 폭행 또는 협박으로 부녀자를 간음한 자 one who, by violence or threat, has obtained carnal knowledge of a woman
▶ 여자를 보고 음욕을 품는 자마다 마음에 이미 간음하였느니라 〈聖〉 Every one who looks at a woman lustfully has already committed adultery with her in his heart.
■ **—범[자]** 〈남자〉 an adulterer; 〈여자〉 an adulteress **—죄** adultery
간이 簡易 simplicity; easiness; handiness
—**간이하다** 〈간단하다〉 simple; 〈용이하다〉 facile [fǽsəl]; easy; plain
■ **—(생명)보험** postal life insurance; post office life insurance **—수도** a small water-supply system **—숙박소** 〈노동자용〉 day-laborers' lodgings; a common [public] lodging house; 〈싸구려 여인숙〉《美》 a flophouse **—식당** a quick-lunch; a lunchroom; a chop-

간작

house; (美) a snack bar; (英) cafeteria ━주택 a simple frame house; 〈조립식의〉 a prefabricated house; (美口) a prefab
간작 間作 〔農〕〈사이짓기〉 catch cropping; intercropping; 〈간접 소작〉 sharecropping
♦ 간작으로 무를 가꾸다 grow [raise] radishes as a catch crop
━간작하다 intercrop; grow (beans) between the rows of another crop
▶ 우리는 마마콩 사이에 감자를 간작했다 We grew potatoes between the rows of broad beans.
간잔지런하다 〈아주 가지런하다〉 even; uniform; 〈졸음이 오다〉 (*one's* eyelids are) heavy (with lack of sleep [drunkenness]); drowsy; slumberous
간장 ━醬 soy sauce; soy ♦ 간장통 a soy keg / 간장을 발라 굽다 broil with soy
간장 肝腸 the liver and intestines; 〈애〉 anxiety
♦ 간장이 타다 〈걱정하여〉 be deeply anxious [solicitous] (about); 〈사랑하여〉 burn (up) with love (for); be dying (for a woman) / 간장을 녹이다 charm; bewitch; captivate; fascinate / 간장을 태우게 하다 give *sb* trouble; cause anxiety to; worry
▶ 그녀는 간장이 녹는 듯이 울었다 She cried her heart out.
▶ 그녀의 미소는 뭇 남자들의 간장을 녹인다 Her smile captivates every man.
▶ 그는 늘 부모의 간장을 태운다 He keeps his parents worried sick all the time.
간장 肝臟 〔解〕 the liver ♦ 간장의[에 좋은] hepatic ▶ 그는 간장이 나쁘다 He has liver trouble.
■━경화 ⇨ 간경변(肝硬變) ━기능부전 hepatic insufficiency ━병[질환] (a) liver trouble [complaint, disorder] ━염 ⇨ 간염 ━이식 liver transplantation ━엑스트랙트 liver extract ━절개[절제술] hepatotomy [hepatectomy] ━종창(腫脹) swelling of the liver
간절하다 懇切━ earnest; eager; fervent; ardent; sincere
♦ 간절한 마음 an ardent passion [love]/ 간절한 부탁 an earnest request / 간절한 소원 an earnest [fervent] desire; an ardent hope / 간절한 충고 earnest advice / 간절한 호소 an ardent [emotional] appeal
▶ 한 잔 생각이 간절하다 I'm thirsty for a drink.
▶ 가고 싶은 생각은 간절하지만 갈 수가 없다 I really would like to go, but I can't.
간절히 懇切━ earnestly; eagerly; ardently; sincerely; wholeheartedly
♦ 간절히 부탁하다 entreat (*sb* to do) / 간절히 호소하다 appeal to *sb* with great emphasis
▶ 우리는 평화를 간절히 바라고 있다 We are eager for peace.
▶ 그들은 경기가 시작되기를 간절히 바라고 있었다 They were eager for the game to begin.
▶ 자중자애하시기를 간절히 빕니다 I sincerely hope you will take good care of yourself.
▶ 그녀는 그를 다시한번 보기를 간절히 원한다 She has an earnest wish to see him again.

간접 間接 indirectness
■━가열기 an indirect heater ━공임(工賃) indirect labor cost ━광(光) borrowed light ━국세 an indirect national tax ━난방 indirect heating ━목적어 an indirect object ━무역 indirect trade ━비 overhead [indirect] cost ━비료 indirect manure [fertilizer] ━선거 indirect election; 〈대통령의〉(美) voting for the presidential electors ━세 an indirect tax ━손해 consequential damage ━전염 infection ━조명 indirect illumination [lighting] ━증거 〔法〕 indirect [circumstantial, collateral] evidence ━촬영 〈X선의〉 fluoroscopy ━추리 mediate inference ━침략 an indirect invasion ━통제 indirect control ━화법 the indirect speech ━환(換) indirect exchange
간접적 間接的 indirect; mediate; secondhand; 〈우회적〉 roundabout; backhanded; oblique
♦ 간접적으로 indirectly; (at) secondhand; in a roundabout way / 간접적으로 듣다 have the news at second hand; learn (about *sth*) indirectly; learn by a side wind
▶ 그것은 우리에게 간접적인 영향을 줄 것이다 It will exert an indirect influence on us.
▶ 나는 그 소식을 간접적으로 들었다 I heard the news in a roundabout way [secondhand].
간조 干潮 (an) ebb [low] tide(↔high tide); low ebb ♦ 간조 때에 at low tide; at a low ebb
▶ 지금은 간조다 The tide is low [down] now. ⇌ It's low tide now.
▶ 오전 7시에 간조가 된다 The tide will be on the ebb at 7 a.m.
■━면[선] a low-water level [line] ━표(標) a low-water mark
간주곡 間奏曲 〔樂〕 an interlude; 〈막간의〉 an intermezzo (*pl*. ~s, -zi)
간주하다 看做━ regard (A as B); consider (A (to be) B); think of (A as B); deem; reckon; count (as, for); look on [upon] 《A as B》; take (for)
♦ 영웅으로 간주하다 regard [look upon] *sb* as a hero; consider *sb* (to be) a hero (▶ consider (that) *sb* is a hero라고 하는 것이 구어적임)
▶ 우리는 계약이 취소된 것으로 간주한다 We consider the contract cancelled.
▶ 경찰은 그를 요주의 인물로 간주했다 The police regarded him as a dangerous person.
▶ 침묵은 승낙으로 간주된다 Silence is regarded as consent.
▶ 그 사건은 해결된 것으로 간주된다 The case is looked upon as settled.
▶ 그는 그 일의 적임자로 간주된다 He is regarded [looked upon] as (being) fit for the job. ⇌ He is considered (to be) fit for the job. (▶ 수동태에서는 보통 to be를 생략함)
▶ 그는 권리를 포기한 것으로 간주되었다 He was considered to have renounced his right.
간지 干支 〈십간 십이지〉 the sexagenary cycle
간지럼 tickling (sensation); titillation
♦ 간지럼을 잘 타는 사람 a ticklish person / 간지럼을 타다 be ticklish; be sensitive to tickling / 간지럼을 태우다 tickle 《*sb* under the arm [a baby in the ribs]》; titillate

간지럽다 〈몸이〉《feel》 ticklish
♦간지러워하다 feel a tickle / 간지러워 못견디다 be tickled to death
▶나는 발바닥이 간지럽다 The sole of my foot tickles.
▶코가[등이] 간지럽다 My nose [back] tickles.

간직하다 1 〈물건을〉 keep; save; treasure (up); store (away); put aside; lay up; lock away
▶나는 그녀의 사진을 소중히 간직했다 I have kept her picture with care.
▶그들은 서류를 금고에 간직했다 They sealed the documents in a strongbox.
▶그것은 또 쓰게 될지 모르니 어디다 간직해 두시오 Please keep it somewhere, as we may (possibly) use it again.
2 〈마음에 품다〉 keep; hold; hoard; cherish
♦추억[비밀]을 간직하다 cherish *one's* memory [a secret] / 마음에 간직하다 lay *sth* up in *one's* mind; keep *sth* to *oneself*; bear in mind
▶그녀는 그것을 마음 속에 고이 간직했다 She treasured it in her mind.
▶가엾게도 소녀는 그 일을 혼자 가슴 속에 간직하고 있었다 The poor girl kept it all to herself.
▶그는 평생 그 추억을 가슴에 간직하고 있었다 He cherished the memory throughout his life.

간질 癎疾 [醫] epilepsy ♦경증(輕症) 간질 minor [masked] epilepsy / 중증(重症) 간질 major epilepsy / 간질(발작)을 일으키다 have an epileptic fit [seizure]
■—환자 an epileptic

간질간질하다 〈몸이〉 ticklish; tickling; 〈마음이〉 impatient 《for》; itchy 《for action》
♦발바닥[발가락]이 간질간질하다 feel ticklish on the sole of *one's* foot [feel a tickle on *one's* toe] / (말이 하고 싶어서) 입이 간질간질하다 have an itching tongue

간질거리다 1 feel ticklish 2 ⇨ 간질이다

간질이다 tickle; titillate ♦겨드랑이를 간질이다 tickle *sb* under the arm(s) [in the armpit]
▶그녀는 아기의 옆구리를 간질였다 She tickled the baby in the ribs.

간책 奸策 a shrewd [dirty] trick; a sinister scheme [design]; a sly artifice; a crafty design; wiles; machination
♦간책을 부리다 play [resort to] a dirty trick 《on》; use wiles / 간책에 말려[걸려]들다 fall victim to a scheme
▶그들은 그를 함정에 빠뜨리려고 간책을 부렸다 They schemed to trap him.

간척 干拓 land reclamation by drainage
—**간척하다** reclaim (land) by drainage
♦늪지대를 간척하다 drain off a marsh / 호수를 간척하다 reclaim land from a lake
■—공사 reclamation work —사업 a (land) reclamation project —지 reclaimed land: 해안의 간척지 land reclaimed along the shore

간첩 間諜 〈사람〉 a spy; a secret [an intelligence] agent; 〈행위〉 espionage
♦북한의 간첩 a secret agent for North Korea / 간첩을 보내다 send (out) a spy / 간첩을 색출하다 hunt [seek] out spies / 간첩을 잡다 capture a 《North Korean》 spy
■—고정 a residence espionage 무장— an armed espionage agent 이중— a double agent ■—단 a spy ring —망 a spy network; an espionage ring —비행 a spy flight —선[잠수함] a 《North Korean》 spy boat [submarine] —신고 a report on a suspect of espionage —영화 a spy movie —위성 a spy [an intelligence] satellite —죄 the crime of espionage —활동 espionage (activities)

간청 懇請 (an) entreaty; an earnest [eager] request; solicitation; supplication; adjuration
♦간청에 의해 at *sb's* earnest request; at *one's* solicitation / 간청을 거절하다 refuse [turn down] *sb's* earnest request
▶주인은 고맙게도 그의 간청을 들어 주었다 The master was kind enough to listen to [comply with] his entreaty.
—**간청하다** entreat 《*sb* to do [for *sth*]》; beg (earnestly); implore; beseech; solicit 《*sb* for》; supplicate; request earnestly
♦구명(救命)을 간청하다 supplicate *sb* to spare *one's* life / 도움을 간청하다 implore *sb* to give help [for help] / 허가를 간청하다 solicit *sb* for permission; request permission
▶그녀는 내게 협력을 간청했다 She entreated me for cooperation.

간추리다 summarize; sum up; condense; digest; epitomize; 《美》 brief ♦간추린 summarized; abridged
▶판사는 배심원에게 사건 전체를 간추려서 설명했다 The judge summed up the whole to the jury.

간취하다 看取— perceive; notice; detect; find
▶나는 그의 책략을 간취했다 I saw through his wiles.

간친회 懇親會 a social gathering [meeting]; a social [friendly] reunion
♦간친회를 열다 hold a social meeting; meet in reunion; 《美》 get together

간통 姦通 adultery; illicit intercourse; liaison [liéizan]; [法] criminal conversation
♦기혼자끼리의 간통 double adultery / 기혼자와 독신자간의 간통 single adultery
—**간통하다** commit adultery [misconduct] 《with》; have illicit intercourse 《with》
▶그의 아내는 그의 친구와 간통했다 His wife had an adulterous relationship with his friend.
■—자 〈남자〉 an adulterer; 〈여자〉 an adulteress —죄 criminal conversation; adultery: 간통죄로 고소하다 accuse *sb* of adultery; sue 《his wife and Mr. Paine》 on charges of adultery

간투사 間投詞 an interjection ⇨ 감탄사

간파하다 看破— read 《*sb's* thought》; see through [into] 《a fraud》; penetrate; pierce into
▶동기[속임수]를 간파하다 see through *sb's* motives [deceit] / 비밀을 간파하다 penetrate into the secret / 속셈을 간파하다 divine *sb's* thoughts
▶우리는 그의 위장[음모]을 간파했다 We penetrated his disguise [designs].
▶그의 본심은 간파하기가 어렵다 It is difficult

간판 看板 1 〈상점의〉 a signboard; a sign; 〈의사·변호사 사무실 등의〉(美口) a shingle
♦ 전당포[이발소]의 간판 a pawnbroker's [barber's] sign / 간판을 내걸다 put up [set up, hang out] a sign; 〈의사·변호사 등이〉(美) hang out *one's* shingle
▶ 저 음식점에는 간판이 걸려 있지 않다 That restaurant doesn't have a sign up.
▶ 그는 책방 간판을 내걸었다 He put up a bookstore's sign(board).
▶ 간판에는 「교과사」라고 쓰여 있었다 The sign read "Kyohaksa."
2 〈학벌〉 a school [an academic] career [background]
♦ 간판이 좋다 have a good [brilliant] academic career [background]
3 〈겉보기〉 appearance; show; look; 〈허울〉 false front; a front (man); a dummy; a figurehead
♦ 간판뿐인 이사 a dummy [figurehead] director / 자선이라는 간판 아래 under the cloak [in the disguise] of charity / 감세를 간판으로 삼아 under the banner of tax reduction / 간판 노릇을 하다 serve as a front man [figurehead]
▶ 저 연구소는 간판뿐이다 It is a reseach institute in name only.
4 〈인기 인물〉 a draw [(美) a draw girl]; a drawing card; an attraction; a beauty lure; 〈극단 등의〉 the leading actor; the prima donna
▶ 그녀는 이 극단의 유일한 간판이다 She is the only star [big] draw of this troupe.
■ 입─ a standing signboard ■ ─장이 a sign maker [painter]

간편하다 簡便 ─ 〈간단하다〉 simple; 〈편리하다〉 convenient; handy; portable 〈휴대에〉; 〈쉽다〉 easy
♦ 간편한 방법 an easy [a simple (and easy)] method [way] / 간편한 옷 casual wear [clothes] / 요리하기 간편한 음식 food easy to cook / 간편하게 simply; conveniently; easily / 간편한 생활을 하다 live a simple life / 짐을 간편하게 꾸리다 pack things conveniently [so that they will be handy]
▶ 수출 절차가 간편해졌다 The export procedure has been simplified.

간하다 salt; season with salt [soy]; apply salt (to)

간하다 諫─ remonstrate [expostulate] with; admonish; give (a king) candid [frank] advice; 〈하지 말라고〉 persuade *sb* (not to do); dissuade sb (from doing)
♦ 간하는 말을 듣지 않다 turn a deaf ear [give no ear] to *sb's* counsel [expostulation]
▶ 예언자는 왕에게 싸움을 그만두도록 간했다 The prophet remonstrated with the king against the battle.

간행 刊行 publication
─간행하다 publish; bring out; issue
♦ 신문을 간행하다 publish a newspaper / 간행되다 be published; come out; appear
▶ 회보는 연2회 간행된다 The bulletin is issued twice a year.
▶ 다도에 관한 책이 간행되었다 A book on tea ceremony has come out [has been brought out].
▶ 셰익스피어 전집이 간행되었다 The complete works of Shakespeare were published.
■ ─물 a publication : 정기 간행물 a periodical ─본 a (published) book ─일자 the date of publication

간헐 間歇 ♦ 간헐적인 intermittent (rain) / 간헐적으로 intermittently; by fits and starts; off and on
─열(熱) intermittent fever; chill and fever; 〈말라리아의〉 ague[éigjuː] ─운동 intermittent movement ─유전(遺傳) intermittent heredity ─전류 an intermittent current ─천(泉) a geyser; an intermittent fountain [spring]

간호 看護 nursing; care (of the sick); nursing care; tending (a sick person)
♦ 극진한 간호 careful nursing
▶ 내 헌신적인 간호에도 불구하고 여동생은 죽고 말았다 In spite of the devoted nursing I gave her, my sister died.
─간호하다 nurse; tend [attend on] (a sick person); look after; care for

> [解説] *nurse*는 특히 병원에서 환자를 간호하는 것을 말한다. *look after*, *tend* 는 환자에 국한하지 않고 넓은 뜻으로 돌보는 것, *attend*는 곁에서 시중드는 것을 말한다.

▶ 그녀는 밤새도록 병든 어머니를 간호했다 She nursed her sick mother all through the night. ⇌ She sat up all night with her sick mother.
▶ 우리에겐 간호해야 할 환자들이 있다 We have sick people to look after.
■ ─과장 a director of nursing (service) ─법 (the art of) nursing ─부장 a matron ─원 〈=간호사〉 ─조무사(助務士) a nurse's aide ─학 nursing science; the science of nursing ─학과 the department of nursing science ─학교 a school of nursing; a nurses' school [college]

간호사 看護師 a nurse; a sister; 〈남자〉 a male nurse [attendant]
■ 공인─ (美) a trained [graduate] nurse; a registered nurse (略 R.N.) 수(首)─ a chief [supervising] nurse 수습─ a probationer; a student nurse 파출─ a visiting nurse ■ ─양성소 a nurses' training school ─회 a nurses' agency

간혹 間或 1 〈이따금〉 occasionally; once in a while; now and then; at times [intervals]; sometimes; on occasion(s)
♦ 간혹 오는 손님 a casual visitor; 〈상점에〉 a stray customer / 간혹 들르다[찾아오다] drop [show up] once in a while [in a long while]
▶ 그에게서 간혹 편지가 온다 I hear from him once in a while [at intervals]. ⇌ I occasionally hear from him.
▶ 나는 그를 간혹 만난다 I see him once in a while.
2 〈띄엄띄엄〉 in places; at long intervals; sparsely; thinly
▶ 들판에는 간혹 가다 인가가 있다 There are a few straggling cottages in the fields.

▶ 바다에는 간혹 작은 섬들이 흩어져 있었다 The sea was sparsely dotted with islets.
간힘쓰다 endure [stand] pain with *one's* teeth clenched [set]; hold *one's* breath to withstand pain
갇히다 be shut up; be locked (up); be kept indoors; be confined; be imprisoned
◆ 감옥에 갇히다 be put in prison; be sent to jail / 방 안에 갇히다 be confined [locked (up)] in a room
▶ 열차는 눈에 갇혔다 The train was snowbound.
▶ 우리는 한 시간 가량이나 엘리베이터 안에 갇혀 있었다 We were shut up in the elevator for about an hour.
▶ 그는 이 보고서를 쓰느라고 사흘 동안 호텔에 갇혀 있었다 He was confined in a hotel for three days to write this report.
▶ 비 때문에 온종일 집안에 갇혀 있었다 The rain kept me indoors all day.
갈 〈…학(學)〉 science (of); study (of); -ics; -ology; 〈…론〉 a theory; a doctrine ■ 소리— phonetics; phonology 한글— the study of the Korean language; Koreanology
갈가리 to pieces ⇨ 가리가리
갈가마귀 〈鳥〉 a jackdaw
갈강거리다 ruckle ⇨ 갈그랑거리다
갈개 a shallow ditch; a gutter; a drain
갈겨쓰다 scrawl; scribble; dash off; write hurriedly [carelessly] ◆ 몇 줄 갈겨쓰다 scribble a few lines 《on a sheet of paper》/ 편지를 갈겨쓰다 dash off a letter
갈고랑막대기 a hooked [crooked] stick
갈고랑쇠 an iron hook; 〈사람〉 a cross-grained [perverse] person; an ill-natured person; (口) a screwball
갈고랑이, 갈고리 a hook; a crook; a gaff
◆ 갈고랑이 모양의 hook-shaped; hooked / 갈고랑이로 걸다 hook 《a box》
갈고쟁이, 갈고지 a wooden hook
갈구 渴求 an earnest [eager] desire 《for》; an ardent wish 《for》; craving [longing] 《for》
▶ 그의 지식에 대한 갈구는 채워질 수가 없었다 His thirst for knowledge could not be assuaged.
—갈구하다 crave [yearn, thirst] for; be thirsty after [for, of] 《knowledge》; desire eagerly [earnestly]
갈그랑거리다 make a gurgling sound; rattle; ruckle; 〈비둘기가〉 curr; 〈고양이가〉 purr
갈근거리다 be greedy＝걸근거리다
갈급증 渴急症 fret; impatience; irritation
◆ 갈급증이 나다 be in a fret; be impatient; be irritable; be in suspense
▶ 그녀는 갈급증이 나 안달하고 있었다 She was fretting with impatience.
갈기 a mane ◆ 갈기 있는 짐승 a maned beast; an animal with a mane
갈기갈기 to pieces; to [into] shreds
◆ 갈기갈기 찢다 tear [rend] *sth* to pieces; tear into strips; rip *sth* into tatters
▶ 내 옷이 갈기갈기 찢어졌다 My dress was torn to [into] shreds.
▶ 편지가 갈기갈기 찢어져 있었다 The letter was torn into pieces.
갈기다 1 〈때리다〉 beat; strike; knock; hit; thrash; (口) lick
◆ 따귀를 갈기다 slap *sb* on the ear; slap *one's* cheeks [face] / 머리를 갈기다 strike *sb* on the head / 콧등을 갈기다 punch *sb's* nose / 곤봉으로 갈기다 club; cudgel / 채찍으로 갈기다 flog; lash; whip / 녹초가 되게 갈기다 pommel [beat] *sb* to a jelly [mummy] / 호되게 갈기다 give *sb* a sound thrashing; hit hard
2 〈냅다 쏘다〉 fire 《a gun》 《by volleys》; let fly 《with a rifle》
◆ 소총으로 일제히 갈기다 fire off a volley of small arms
3 〈갈겨 쓰다〉 write hurriedly [hastily]; scrawl; scribble; dash off
4 〈쳐서 베다〉 cut; strike a blow 《with a sharp instrument》; slash
갈다¹ 〈바꾸다〉 change 《sth for a new one》; replace 《A by [with] B》; renew
◆ 구두창을 갈다 resole shoes / 물을 갈다 renew water 《in a tank》 / 이름을 갈다 change *one's* name
▶ 그녀는 더러운 수건을 깨끗한 것으로 갈았다 She changed the dirty towel for a clean one.
▶ 카펫을 새것으로 갈아야겠다 We have to renew the carpet.
갈다² 1 〈날이 서게 하다〉 whet; sharpen 《a knife》; grind 《an axe》; hone 《a razor》
◆ 낫을 숫돌에 갈다 whet a scythe[sáið] on the stone / 면도칼을 혁지에 갈다 strap [strop] a razor; sharpen a razor on a strap / 칼날을 갈다 sharpen a blade
2 〈문지르다〉 rub; file; polish; cut 《a diamond》; grind 《a lense》
◆ 먹을 갈다 grind [rub (down)] an ink stick / 보석을 갈다 cut [polish] a gem / 사과를 강판에 갈다 grate an apple / 줄로 손톱을 갈다 file *one's* fingernails
3 〈가루가 되게〉 grind; refine ◆ 밀을 갈다 grind wheat 《into flour》 / 곱게 갈다 grind 《wheat》 to fine powder
4 〈이를〉 gnash [grind, grate, grit] *one's* teeth ◆ 생각만 해도 이가 갈리다 gnash *one's* teeth at the thought
▶ 잠잘 때 이를 가는 사람들도 있다 Some people grind their teeth during their sleep.
▶ 그는 이를 갈며 분해했다 He gnashed his teeth in anger [with vexation].
갈다³ 1 〈논밭을〉 plow; cultivate 《land》; till; get 《the soil》 turned over

> 解說 *plow*는 쟁기, 괭이 등으로 흙을「파 일구고 잘게 하다」라는 구체적 동작에 중점이 있다. *cultivate*는 「경작하다」라는 뜻으로, 토지를 갈 뿐만 아니라 작물에 비료를 주거나 해서 기르는 것도 포함한다. *till*은 양쪽의 뜻으로 다 쓰인다.

◆ 논을 갈다 plow a rice field / 땅을 갈다 till [cultivate] land / 밭을 갈다 plow the field
2 〈심다·씨뿌리다〉 plant ◆ 밭에 밀을 갈다 plant the field to wheat; lay down a field in wheat

갈대 〚植〛 a reed
♦ 갈대가 무성한 늪 a marsh overgrown with reeds
▶ 인간은 생각하는 갈대다 Man is a thinking reed.
▶ 여자의 마음은 갈대와 같다 Woman is as fickle as a reed.
■ —꽃 the ears of a reed —발 a reed screen; a (hanging) screen made of reeds —밭 a field of reeds —피리 a reed (pipe)

갈등 葛藤 complications; trouble; discord; dissension; (a) conflict; 〈반목〉 feud
♦ 정신적인[감정적인] 갈등 mental [emotional] conflict / 마음의 갈등을 겪다 go through a psychological conflict / 갈등을 일으키다 cause trouble; breed discord / 가족의 정과 정의감 사이의 갈등으로 고민하다 be caught [torn] between family ties and *one's* sense of justice
▶ 그것 때문에 부자 간에 갈등이 생겼다 That caused complications [trouble] between the father and the son.
▶ 둘 사이에는 해묵은 갈등이 있다 There is a long-standing feud between the two.
▶ 두 사람의 결혼은 양가에 갈등을 야기시켰다 Their marriage caused difficulties [discord] between the two families.

갈라놓다 〈분리하다〉 divide; part; separate; 〈이간시키다〉 estrange (people); alienate (A from B); put a barrier (between)
♦ 갈라놓을 수 없는 indivisible; inseparable / 부부 사이를 갈라놓다 separate husband and wife / 어린 아이를 부모로부터 갈라놓다 take a little child away from its parents / 반[셋]으로 갈라놓다 divide *sth* into halves [three (parts)]
▶ 나는 싸우고 있는 두 사람을 갈라놓았다 I pulled apart the two men who were fighting.
▶ 그 사건이 그를 가족과 갈라놓았다 The affair estranged him from his family.

갈라디아서—書 〚聖〛 (the Letter of Paul to) the Galatians (略 Gal.)

갈라서다 〈따로 서다〉 stand apart; line up separately; 〈헤어지다·이혼하다〉 break up (with); split with; divorce *oneself* (from); be divorced (from); divorce
♦ 두 줄로 갈라 서다 stand apart in two rows; line up into two separate groups
▶ 그는 동업자와 갈라섰다 He broke with his partner.
▶ 그들은 결혼한 지 불과 석달만에 갈라서고 말았다 They broke up only after three months of married life.
▶ 그는 아내와 사이가 좋지 않았는데 결국 갈라섰다고 하더군 He was on bad terms with his wife and eventually divorced her, I hear.

갈라지다 1 〈쪼개지다〉 split; cleave; fissure; 〈금이 가다〉 crack
♦ 오랜 가뭄으로 갈라진 논바닥 a rice paddy cracked from a long drought
▶ 그 목재는 쉽게 갈라진다 The timber splits [cleaves] easily.
▶ 지진으로 땅이 갈라졌다 The ground was cracked by the earthquake. ⇌ The earthquake caused cracks in the ground.
▶ 그는 딛고 있던 얼음이 갈라져 연못에 빠졌다 The ice under him cracked and he fell into the pond.
2 〈분할되다〉 be divided; separate; 〈분열하다〉 split; break up; part; 〈분리되다〉 branch off (from); diverge (from); fork
♦ 남과 북으로 갈라지다 be divided into south and north / 두 조각으로 갈라지다 split into two pieces / 여러 패로 갈라지다 be divided into several groups / 본점에서 갈라져 나오다 be established as a branch of the head store
▶ 길은 여기서 세 갈래로 갈라진다 Here the road breaks [forks, branches] into three.
▶ 이 철도는 여기서 본선과 갈라진다 This railroad forks off from the main line here.
▶ 그 당은 여러 파로 갈라졌다 The party split into several factions.
▶ 그 문제에 관해 우리는 의견이 갈라졌다 We were divided in opinion on the subject.
▶ 경찰은 두 패로 갈라져 범인을 추적했다 The policemen separated into two groups to chase the criminal.
▶ 이들은 주류에서 갈라져 나온 일파다 This is a group that branched [broke] off from the main school.
▶ 그들은 좌우로 갈라져서 나를 통과시켜 주었다 They parted right and left to make way for me.
3 〈사람 사이가〉 part (from); be estranged (from); split with; separate from; part company with
▶ 그들은 돈 문제 때문에 갈라졌다 The problem of money parted them.

갈락토오스 galactose

갈래 〈갈라진 부분〉 a fork (of a road); 〈구분〉 a division; a section; a part; 〈분파〉 a branch; an offshoot; 〈종파〉 a sect; 〈당파〉 a faction
♦ 세 갈래 길 a three-forked [trifurcate(d)] road / 두 갈래가 되다 bifurcate; be divided into two branches / 여러 갈래로 나뉘다 be divided into several parts [sections]
▶ 길은 우리 앞에서 두 갈래로 갈라졌다 The road branched off [forked] in front of us.

갈륨 〚化〛 gallium

갈리다¹ 〈분할·분열되다〉 be divided [split] (into) ⇨ 갈라지다 2

갈리다² 〈목이 쉬다〉 become hoarse ♦ 목이 갈리게 고함을 지르다 shout *oneself* hoarse

갈리다³ 〈바뀌다〉 be changed (for); be replaced
▶ 담임 선생님이 갈렸다 A new teacher has taken over our class.
▶ 각료가 대폭 갈렸다 A sweeping change of Cabinet members has taken place.

갈리다⁴ 1 〚갈아지다〛 〈칼 등이〉 be whetted; be ground; be sharpened; 〈옥돌 등이〉 be polished; be filed; 〈곡물이〉 be ground
♦ 그것은 숫돌에 갈면 잘 갈린다 If it is whetted on a whetstone, it will become sharp.
▶ 이 밀은 잘[곱게] 갈리지 않는다 This wheat doesn't grind well [isn't ground fine].
2 〚갈게 하다〛 make [have] *sb* whet [grind, hone]; have [get] 《a knife》 sharpened; 〈옥돌

갈리다⁵ 1 〈논밭이 갈아지다〉 be plowed; get cultivated; be tilled
2 〈논밭을 갈게 하다〉 make *sb* plow; have *sb* cultivate; get *sb* to till
♦ 머슴에게 감자밭을 갈리다 have *one's* servant till the potato farm

갈림길 〈길〉 a forked [branch] road; 〈기로〉 a turning point (in *one's* career); a crossroad
♦ 갈림길에 이르다 come to the fork of a road / 생사의 갈림길에서 헤매다 hover between life and death
▶ 전쟁[경기]은 여기가 바로 승패의 갈림길이다 This is the turning point of the battle [in the game].
▶ 나는 이제 인생의 갈림길에 서게 된 것이다 I have now found myself standing at the crossroads of my life.

갈마들다 〈번갈아 들다〉 take turns; alternate 《with another》; rotate; come on by turns

갈마들이다 change turns; employ by turns

갈망 〈감당하여 처리함〉 control; dealing; management; settlement; conduct
▶ 네 빚 갈망은 네 스스로 해라 Settle your debts yourself.
▶ 그는 제 앞갈망도 못하면서 남의 일에 참견한다 Unable to handle his own business, he pokes his nose into another's.
─**갈망하다** control; manage; settle; deal [cope] with; set *sth* right; take care of
▶ 그 문제는 내가 갈망하겠다 I'll take care of the matter [problem]
▶ 나는 그 일을 갈망할 수 없다 I am not equal to the task.

갈망 渴望 a strong [an eager] desire 《for》; a craving 《for》; a longing 《for》; an ardent wish 《for》
♦ 지식에 대한 갈망을 충족시키다 satisfy *one's* hunger [thirst, craving] for knowledge
─**갈망하다** long [yearn, thirst] for; be anxious [eager] for; crave for; desire *sth* eagerly; have a strong desire for
▶ 그는 부를 갈망한다 He thirsts [crave] for wealth.
▶ 마을 사람들은 병원이 생기기를 갈망했다 The villagers were eager for [badly wanted] a hospital.
▶ 사람들은 위대한 지도자의 출현을 갈망하고 있다 People are yearning for the appearance of a great leader.

갈매 1 〈심녹색〉 deep green 2 〈열매〉 a fruit of the buckthorn ■ ─**나무** 〔植〕 a Dahurian buckthorn

갈매기 〔鳥〕 a sea gull; a sea mew

갈무리 〈간수〉 putting *sth* away in good order; 〈마무리〉 finishing; completion
─**갈무리하다** 〈간수하다〉 put *sth* away in good order; 〈마무리하다〉 finish (off, up); get *sth* finished [done]; put the finishing touches on

갈보 a prostitute; a harlot; a whore ♦ 갈보 노릇을 하다 live [go] on the streets; walk the streets; prostitute *oneself* ■ ─**집** a brothel; a whorehouse

갈분 葛粉 arrowroot starch ■ ─**떡** arrowroot cake

갈비 1 〈늑골〉 the ribs; 〔解〕 a costa (*pl*. -tae); 〈요리용의〉 a rib ♦ 돼지[쇠] 갈비 ribs of pork [beef] / 갈비를 굽다 roast [grill, broil] a rib
2 〈마른 사람〉 a skeleton; a skinny [lean, weedy, scrawny] person; a scarecrow
▶ 이봐, 갈비씨 Hey, skinny!
■ ─**불** a roast [grilled] rib ─**뼈** ⇨ 갈빗대 ─**새김** rib meat ─**찜** steamed short ribs ─**탕** beef-rib soup; short rib soup

갈빗대 a rib ♦ 갈빗대가 불거진 사람 a ribby man / 갈빗대가 부러지다 get a rib broken

갈색 褐色 brown
♦ 갈색의 brown / 엷은 황갈색 fawn color / 짙은[연한] 갈색 dark [light] brown / 갈색 피부 brown skin / 〈볕에 탄〉 tanned skin / 갈색을 띤 [갈색이 도는] 황색 brownish yellow
▶ 그녀는 머리카락이 갈색이다 She has brown hair.
■ ─**인종** the brown races ─**제비** a sand martin

갈색조류 褐色藻類 〔植〕 brown algae

갈수 渴水 (a) drought; (a) shortage of water; a water shortage
■ ─**기** the dry season; a period of water shortage [famine] ─**량** minimum flow ─**위**(位) the droughty water level

갈수록 as time goes by [on]
♦ 날이 갈수록 as days go by / 해가 갈수록 with the year
▶ 갈수록 추워진다 It is getting colder every day [from day to day].
▶ 갈수록 그 사람[고향]이 그리워진다 I miss him [long for home] more and more.
▶ 이야기는 갈수록 재미난다 The story becomes more and more interesting.
▶ 갈수록 해가 짧아진다 The days are getting shorter and shorter.
▶ 그는 날이 갈수록 병세가 악화되고 있다 He is getting worse day by [after] day.
▶ 올해의 매상은 후반으로 갈수록 늘어났다 The sales account this year has shown a rising tendency.

갈수록 태산이다 《속담》 Things go from bad to worse. ⇌ Things get worse and worse. ⇌ Out of the frying pan into the fire.

갈아내다 replace 《one thing by [with] another》; renew
♦ 탁한 공기를 갈아내다 let out the foul air; air out 《a room》; let 《fresh》 air in / 기와 [묵은 기왓장]를 갈아내다 get *one's* roof retiled [replace an old tile]

갈아대다 repaper 《a screen》; re-cover 《an umbrella》; renew 《a plaster》 ♦ 삿자리를 갈아댈 때가 되었다 Now it is time to renew the matting.

갈아들다 move in as a replacement; replace 《another》; take another's place; serve as a replacement [substitute, relief]
▶ 새 요리사가 갈아들었다 A new cook has replaced the old one.
▶ 애덤스 씨의 뒤를 이어 브라운 씨가 국무총리로 갈아들었다 Mr. Adams was replaced as

prime minister by Mr. Brown.

갈아들이다 replace *sb* with 《another》; change; substitute ♦매년 하인을 갈아들이다 change *one's* servant every year ▶그 집에서는 가정부를 새로 갈아들였다 The people in that family have taken on a new housekeeper.

갈아붙이다 renew; repaper 《a screen》; re-cover 《a book》 ♦고약을 갈아붙이다 renew a plaster / 표지를 갈아붙이다 re-cover [renew the cover of] a book

갈아주다 1 〈물건을 사다〉 buy; purchase ♦한 가게의 물건만 갈아주다 patronize [trade only at] a store
2 〈새것으로〉 change; renew ♦금붕어 어항의 물을 갈아주다 renew water in a goldfish bowl

갈아타다 change 《to,for》; transfer 《to》; 〈배를〉 transship ♦갈아타는 역 a station for changing 《cars》; a junction 《station》; a transfer point [stop] / 버스를 세 번 갈아타다 have three changes of bus / 다른 차를 갈아타다 switch to another car / 비행기 [기차]로 갈아타다 make plane [railway] connection ▶버스를 타고 가다가 지하철로 갈아탔다 I took a bus and transferred to the subway. ▶그는 익산에서 여수행 기차로 갈아탔다 He changed trains at Iksan for Yŏsu. ▶인천행 손님은 갈아타세요 《게시》 Change here for Inch'ŏn.

갈이¹ 〈경작〉 plowing; tillage; cultivation; 〈경지면적〉 the acreage to be covered by a day's plowing ♦밭갈이 plowing of a field / 이틀 갈이 the acreage that can be plowed by one person in two days

갈이² 〈갈아대기〉 changing; renewal; replacement ♦구두창[굽] 갈이 resoling [reheeling] 《of shoes》

갈조류 褐藻類 brown algae =갈색조류

갈증 渴症 thirst ♦갈증이 나다 feel thirsty / 갈증을 풀다 satisfy [relieve, quench] *one's* thirst 《with》

갈지자걸음 ―之字― a staggering [reeling] gait; a tipsy lurch; a reel ♦갈지자 걸음으로 걷다 stagger; reel; walk zigzag [in zigzags]; weave *one's* way ▶그 남자는 갈지자 걸음으로 비틀비틀 걸어갔다 The man went reeling along.

갈지자형 ―之字形 zigzag; a Z shape ♦갈지자형의 zigzag / 갈자자형으로 in zigzags ▶길이 갈지자형으로 구불구불하다 The road zigzags.

갈채 喝采 applause; 〈환호・박수〉 cheers; acclamation(s) ♦그칠 줄 모르는 갈채 round after round of [prolonged] cheers [applause] / 열광적인 [터져 나오는] 갈채 an enthusiastic [a burst of] applause / 갈채를 받다 draw a cheer 《from》; win applause; receive an ovation 《from》 / 갈채를 보내다 applaud 《a marvelous performance》 / 갈채에 답하다 acknowledge the cheers 《of the audience》 / 갈채 속에 등단하다 mount the platform amid cheers [applause] ▶우레와 같은 갈채가 터져나왔다 There broke out a storm [thunder] of applause. ▶그녀의 노래는 만장의 갈채를 받았다 Her song won the applause of the whole theater. ▶사람들은 그를 갈채로 맞이했다 People greeted [received] him with applause [acclamations].

―갈채하다 applaud; acclaim; cheer; give cheers ♦박수 갈채하다 clap *one's* hands in applause; give *sb* a clap and cheers / 일어나서 갈채하다 give *sb* a standing ovation ▶청중은 대통령의 연설에 박수 갈채했다 The audience applauded the President's address. ▶연주가 끝나자 청중은 열렬히 박수 갈채했다 The audience clapped their hands enthusiastically as a performance came to an end.

갈철광 褐鐵鑛 limonite; brown hematite

갈취 喝取 extortion [exaction] by threats; blackmail(ing); 《美俗》 racketeering
―갈취하다 extort 《by threats》; practice extortions; blackmail; 《美俗》 racketeer ♦돈을 갈취하다 blackmail *sb* of his money; extort money from [out of] *sb* / 돈을 갈취당하다 be blackmailed; be struck for money ▶그 협박범은 그에게서 막대한 금품을 갈취하려고 했다 The blackmailer tried to extort a large sum of money and other valuables from him.
■―자 a blackmailer; an extortionist; 《美俗》 a racketeer

갈치 〔魚〕 a hairtail; a scabbard [cutlass] fish

갈퀴 a 《bamboo》 rake ▶그는 갈퀴로 낙엽을 긁어 모았다 He raked up the fallen leaves.
■―나무 fallen leaves [dry herbs] for fuel
―질 raking 갈퀴발 tines of a rake

갈탄 褐炭 brown coal; lignite; wood coal

갈탕 葛湯 arrowroot gruel

갈파 喝破 〈꾸짖어 억누름〉 shouting down; 〈설파〉 proclamation; pronouncement 《of truth》
―갈파하다 shout down; declare; expound; proclaim; pronounce ♦진리를 갈파하다 give an expression to the truth ▶지구가 둥글다고 갈파한 사람은 누구인가? Who was it that proclaimed the earth was round?

갈팡질팡 in confusion; confusedly; at a loss ♦갈팡질팡 결단을 못 내리다 hover on the brink of a decision ▶그 문제에 대해 내 마음은 갈팡질팡이다 My mind is divided on the issue.
―갈팡질팡하다 get [be] confused; be upset; be embarrassed; do not know what to do; be at a loss; be flurried ♦갈팡질팡하는 대답 an incoherent reply ▶그는 어느 길로 가야 할지 갈팡질팡했다 He was at a loss which way to go. ▶외국인이 갑자기 말을 걸어오는 바람에 어떻게 말해야 좋을지 갈팡질팡했다 I was suddenly spoken to by a foreigner, and I did not know what to say. ▶우리가 갈팡질팡하는 통에 이런 일이 벌어졌다 This happened in the midst of all our

confusion and bewilderment.
▶ 나는 마음이 갈팡질팡하는 상태였기 때문에 질문의 뜻을 잘못 알아들었다 I was in a confused state of mind and misunderstood the question.
▶ 노인은 갈팡질팡하다가 차에 치었다 The old man got hit by a car while he was going around in a flurry.
▶ 그 사람은 이야기가 갈팡질팡하여 도무지 종잡을 수가 없었다 What he said was incoherent and I couldn't get the point at all.
▶ 갈팡질팡하지 말고 진정해라 Be calm. Don't be flurried.

갈포 葛布 kohemp cloth ■ —**벽지** kohemp wallpaper

갈피 1 〈책 등의〉 a space between layers [folds, leaves]
♦ 책갈피에 끼워 두다 put sth between the leaves of a book
▶ 책장을 넘기다가 책갈피에서 그 사진을 발견했다 I found that picture while I was turning over the leaves of a book.
2 〈요점〉 the point [sense, drift, the meaning]
♦ 갈피를 잡을 수 없다 cannot make head or tail 《of sth》; cannot grasp [catch, get] the point 《of a subject》
▶ 그는 어떻게 대답해야 할지 갈피를 못 잡았다 He was hazy about how to reply.
▶ 그 사람이 하는 말은 도무지 갈피를 못 잡겠다 I can make neither head nor tail of what he says.

갉다 1 〈이로〉 gnaw [nɔː]; nibble 《at》; crunch
▶ 쥐가 상자 모서리를 갉았다 The rats have gnawed the corner of the box off.
▶ 쥐가 판자벽을 갉아서 구멍을 냈다 Rats gnawed a hole through the panel.
2 ⇨ 긁다

갉아먹다 1 〈앞니로〉 gnaw at [on] 《a bone》; nibble 《at》; crunch; bite 《at》 ♦ 빵껍질을 갉아먹다 gnaw on a crust of bread / 잎을 갉아먹다 nibble away the leaves
▶ 토끼가 당근을 조금씩 갉아먹고 있었다 The rabbit is nibbling at the carrot.
2 〈남의 재물을〉 extort; squeeze; exploit ♦ 돈을 갉아먹다 extort [squeeze] money from sb; screw money out of sb

갉작거리다 1 〈앞니로〉 gnaw [crunch] successively; 〈펜촉 등으로〉 make a scratching sound
2 ⇨ 긁적거리다

감¹ 〈열매〉 a persimmon ♦ 곶감 a dried persimmon / 단감 a sweet persimmon / 떫은 감 an astringent persimmon / 익은 감 a ripe persimmon
■ —**씨** a persimmon stone

감² 1 〈재료〉 (a) material; stuff; 〈천〉 texture; weave; fabric
♦ 땔감 firewood; fuel / 서까랫감 raftering (material) / 양복감 suit material / 옷감 (dress) material; cloth / 좋은 감으로 옷을 짓다 tailor with good materials
▶ 그 감이 좋다 That is a good material.
2 〈알맞은 사람〉 a suitable person 《for》; a man fit [qualified] 《for》

♦ 대통령감 a presidential timber / 사윗감 a man who would make a good son-in-law; a likely son-in-law / 사장감 a man fit for presidency / 좋은 신랑[신부]감 a suitable marriage partner / 장군감 a man fit for a general
3 〈옷감의 단위〉 a pattern ♦ 모직 양복 한 감 a pattern of woolen cloth

감 減 〈줆〉 (a) decrease; (a) subtraction; (a) reduction
♦ 작년 대비 20% 감 a decrease of 20 percent compared with last year / 감1도 〔樂〕 the defective [diminished] first

감 感 1 〈느낌〉 (a) feeling; (a) sense; (a) sensation; 〈인상〉 an impression 《that》; 〈강한 감정〉 emotion
♦ 공포감 a sensation of fear / 만족감 a feeling of satisfaction / 열등[우월]감 inferiority [superiority] complex / 정의[죄악]감 a sense of justice [guilt] / …한 감이 있다 it gives the feeling that; it feels [seems] like… / 아무에게 …한 감을 주다 strike [impress] sb as…; give an impression of…
▶ 나는 마치 공중에 둥둥 뜬 듯한 감이 들었다 I felt as if I were floating in the air.
▶ 이미 때가 늦은[그것은 좀 큰] 감이 있다 It gives the feeling you came a day (too late) after the fair [it's rather big I'd say].
▶ 그 가죽은 거칠거칠한 감이 있었다 Its skin was rough to the touch.
▶ 그의 어조에는 좀 내려다보는 감이 있었다 There was a touch [smack] of condescension.
▶ 네가 그것을 내게 주다니 이상한 감이 든다 I feel it strange that you should give it to me.
▶ 그 여자는 행복감이 넘쳤다 She was filled with a feeling of happiness.
▶ 일반적으로 붉은색은 따뜻한 감을, 푸른색은 차가운 감을 준다 In general red gives a feeling of warmth and blue of cold.
▶ 그 여자는 공포감에 휩싸였다 A sensation of fear spread over her whole body.
2 〈감도〉 〔通信〕 sensitiveness; sensitivity; (radio) reception
♦ 감이 아주 좋다 be highly sensitive; be of high sensitivity; be hypersensitive
▶ 감이 어떻니? How do you hear?
▶ 감이 좋다[멀다] The voice is distinct [indistinct].

감가 減價 depreciation; reduction in price
—**감가하다** depreciate; reduce [mark down] the price
▶ 최근에 금이 대폭 감가되었다 Gold has greatly depreciated in value recently.

감가상각 減價償却 〔經〕 depreciation
♦ 기계의 감가 상각을 하다 depreciate a machine
■ **과소[과대]—** under [over] depreciation —**계정** depreciation account —**기금** a depreciation fund —**비** depreciation cost; 감가 상각비 보험 depreciation insurance —**액** depreciation amount —**자산** depreciable assets —**적립금[준비금]** depreciation reserve

감각 感覺 feeling; (a) sensation; a sense; sensibility 《of the skin》

감각적

[解說] *feeling*은 몸의 감각을 나타내는 일반적인 말로 특히 촉각을 나타낸다. *sensation*은 외부로부터의 자극에 대한 감각적 반응, *sense*는 시각·청각·후각·미각·촉각의 5감을 나타낸다. sense는 또한 「이해력·인식력」의 뜻으로, *sensibility*는 「감각력·감수성」의 뜻으로 쓰인다.

♦ 감각이 없는 insensible; senseless; devoid of sense; 〈손·발이 곱은〉 numb [nʌm] / 감각이 둔하다 have dull senses; be insensitive 《to》 / 감각이 예민하다 have a (keen) sense 《of distance》; have a (keen) feeling 《for color》; be sensitive / 감각이 시대에 뒤지다 be [*sb's* ideas are] behind the times / 감각을 잃다 become senseless; lose sensibility / 〈추위 등으로〉 go numb; lose all feeling [sensation] 《in *one's* toes》; be benumbed 《with cold》
▶ 추위로 발가락에 감각이 없다 My toes are senseless [numb] with cold.
▶ 이 시는 어쩐지 감각이 시대에 뒤떨어졌다 Somehow this poetry has the old sense.
▶ 그는 음악적[색채] 감각이 있다 He has an ear for music [eye for color].
▶ 화가는 예민한 색채 감각을 가지고 있어야 한다 An artist should have a color sense.
■—무— insensibility; insensitiveness; apathy 미적— *one's* sense of beauty; *one's* aesthetic sense 방향— a sense of direction 잔류— 〔心〕 aftersensation 평형— the sense of balance [equilibrium] 피부— cutaneous sensation —감정 sense-feeling —과민 hyperesthesia; hypersensitivity —권(圈) a sensory circle —기관 a sense [sensory] organ; a receptor; an exteroceptor —기능 a sense; a faculty of sensation —력 sensibility; sensitivity —론 sensationalism; sensualism; aesthetics —마비 sensory paralysis —모(毛) 〔動〕 a sensory hair; 〔植〕 a sensitive hair —묘사 〔藝〕 sensual description —세포 a sensory cell —식물 a sensitive plant —신경 a sensory nerve —이상 paresthesia —자료 〔心〕 a sense datum —중추 the sense center; the sensorium; the seat of sensation —착오 errors of sense —척도 (尺度) sensory scales

감각적 感覺的 sensible; 〈감각에 호소하는〉 sensuous; 〈육감적인〉 sensual ♦ 초감각적인 extrasensory 《perception》
■—기억 sentient memory —인상 a sensuous impression —쾌락 a pleasure of sense; sensual pleasures

감감(무)소식 no news [having heard nothing] for a long time
▶ 그는 2년 전부터 감감무소식이다 I haven't had any news from him for the past two years. ⇒ I haven't heard from him these two years.
▶ 동생은 언젠가 한번 다녀가고는 감감무소식이다 Nothing has been heard from my brother since he dropped in on me some time ago.

감감하다 1 〈소식이〉 hear nothing [have no news] from *sb*
▶ 그에게서는 오랫동안 소식이 감감하다 I have heard nothing from him for a long time.
2 〈거리·시간 등이〉 be far off [away]; be remote; be long before
▶ 이 일이 끝나려면 아직 감감하다 It will be long before this work is done.
▶ 우리가 그의 지식을 따라가려면 아직 감감하다 He is so far above us in his knowledge.
3 〈기억이〉 have entirely forgotten; 〈지식이〉 be completely ignorant [uninformed]
▶ 그 사람에 관해서는 감감하다 I don't know him at all [from Adam].
▶ 나는 그 일을 감감하게 잊고 있었다 I have entirely forgotten it. ⇒ It has entirely slipped from my mind.

감개 感慨 strong feeling; deep emotion
▶ 졸업을 맞이하니 감개 무량하다 My heart is full (of deep emotion) in leaving school.
▶ 지난날을 회상하니 감개 무량하다 A thousand emotions crowd on [well in] my mind, looking back upon the past.

감격 感激 strong [deep] emotion [feeling]; impression; 〈감사〉 (a) deep gratitude; a strong sense of gratitude
▶ 감격적인 장면 a moving [touching] scene; a soul-stirring scene / 감격이 되살아나다 recall with renewed emotion / 감격을 새로이 하다 renew *my* impression
▶ 그 책을 읽고 그는 감격의 눈물을 흘렸다 The book moved him to tears.
—감격하다 be deeply moved [touched, affected] 《by》; be very [deeply] impressed 《by, at, with》
♦ 감격하여 impelled by a strong sense of gratitude
▶ 나는 그녀의 친절에 감격했다 I was deeply moved [touched] by her kindness.
▶ 그가 성공했다는 소식에 가족은 모두 감격했다 All the family were moved [touched] at the news of his success.
▶ 우리는 그의 따뜻한 환영에 감격했다 We were very much impressed by his hearty welcome.
▶ 그는 감격하여 말을 못했다 His heart was too full for words.
▶ 핵실험 금지를 주장하는 그의 연설은 청중을 감격시켰다 His speech advocating nuclear test ban moved the hearts of the audience.

감광 減光 〔光·天〕 extinction

감광 感光 〔寫〕 exposure (to light); sensitization **—감광하다** 〈감광되다〉 be exposed to light ♦ 필름을 감광시키다 expose films to light
■—계 〈사진의〉 a sensitometer —기전 효과 photogalvanic effect —막[필름] a sensitive film —면 a photosensitive surface —색소 light sensitive [photosensitive] pigments —성 (photo)sensitivity : 감광성이 있는 photosensitive; sensitive to light —재료 (photo)sensitive [sensitized] materials —제[약] a sensitizer —지(紙) sensitized [photosensitive, light-sensitive] paper —처리 sensitizing —체 photoconductor; 〈눈의〉 a visual receptor —판 a sensitive plate

감광도 感光度 (photo)sensitivity 《of a film》

♦감광도가 높은 필름 (a) highly sensitive film / 감광도를 줄이다 desensitize ■—계 a sensitometer —측정 sensitometry
감국 甘菊 〔植〕 a mother chrysanthemum
감군 減軍 a cut in [reduction of] the armed forces; arms [armament] reduction; a cut-back in military strength
—**감군하다** cut [reduce] armed forces [military manpower]
♦주유럽 미군을 감군하다 reduce the American [U.S.] military presence in Europe
감귤 柑橘 a tangerine; a mandarin orange ■—농장 a tangerine orchard [plantation] —류 citrus fruits; oranges
감금 監禁 〈구속〉 confinement; 〈수감〉 imprisonment; 〈구류〉 detention (in custody) ♦엄중한 감금 close confinement
—**감금하다** imprison; confine; place sb in [under] confinement; put [keep] sb under lock and key; detain sb in custody; lock up
♦자택에 감금하다 place sb under house arrest / 감금당하다 be kept in confinement; be held prisoner
▶범인은 그 사람을 방에 감금했다 The criminal confined the man to his room.
▶그는 한 달간 감금되어 있었다 He was imprisoned for a month.
■독방— solitary confinement 불법— illegal detention; false imprisonment
감기 感氣 a cold; 〔醫〕 the common cold; 〈유행성 감기〉 influenza; (口) the flu
♦감기걸리다[들다] catch (a) cold; take (a) cold / 감기들어 있다 have a cold
〈감기가[는]〉 감기가 떨어지지 않다 cannot shake off [throw off, get rid of] one's cold
▶감기가 유행하고 있다 There's a lot of flu about. ⇒ Everybody's catching (bad) colds.
▶네게서 감기가 옮았다 You've given me your cold. ⇒ I've caught your cold.
▶내 감기는 보통 감기지 독감이 아니다 Mine is the common cold, not flu.
〈감기를〉 내게 감기를 옮기지 마라 Don't give me your cold.
〈감기에[로]〉 감기에 다시 걸리다 catch a fresh cold / 감기로 누워 있다 be in bed [be down, be laid up] with a cold
▶그는 감기에 잘 걸린다 He catches cold very easily. ⇒ He is susceptible [sensitive] to colds.
▶나는 지독한[가벼운] 감기에 걸렸다 I have (caught) a bad [slight] cold.
▶나는 감기에 걸려 학교에 결석했다 I was absent from school because of a cold.
▶감기에 걸릴 것 같다 I feel a cold coming on.
■기침— a cold on the chest [lungs] 유행성— influenza; the flu 코— a cold in the head [nose]; a head cold : 나는 코감기에 걸렸다 I have a cold in the head [nose]. —기운 a touch of cold : 감기 기운이 있다 have a slight [a touch of] cold —약 a remedy [medicine] for the cold, a cold remedy [tablet]
감기 고뿔도 남을 안 준다 (속담) be stingy; be closefisted; be niggardly
감기다¹ 〈씻어주다〉 give sb a bath [wash]; wash sb; (英) bath (a baby [patient]) ♦아기의 머리를 감기다 wash a baby's hair / 먹을 감기다 give a bath (to)

감기다² **1** 〔감아지다〕 〈실·끈 등이〉 be wound (up); be rolled (up); be coiled (around); 〈덩굴 등이〉 twine together; get twisted round; 〈스스로〉 wind itself round
▶이 시계는 태엽이 잘 감긴다 This clock winds easily.
▶밧줄이 내 발에 감겼다 My feet were caught in the rope.
▶실이 실패에 감겨 있다 Thread is wound on [to] a reel.
2 〈거치적거리다〉 cling [stick] to; hang on to; be [get] caught in (the wire)
♦젖은 옷이 몸에 감기다 wet clothes cling to one's body
▶치맛자락이 발에 감겨 걷기가 힘들다 I have trouble in walking with my skirt clinging to my legs.
3 〈감게 하다〉 make [let] sb wind [roll] ♦아들에게 시계의 태엽을 감기다 have one's son wind the clock

감기다³ **1** 〈눈이〉 (one's eyes) be shut [closed] of their own accord [of themselves]; 《one's eyes》 close
♦졸려서 눈이 감기다 be so sleepy (that) one's eyes are falling shut
▶그는 졸려서 눈이 감겼다 He felt his eyes heavy.
▶눈이 자꾸 감겨서 못 견디겠다 I cannot open my eyelids. They are glued together.
2 〈눈을〉 make sb's eyes fall shut; shut [close] sb's eyes ♦죽은 사람의 눈을 감기다 close the eyes of a dead person

감나무 〔植〕 a persimmon tree
감나무 밑에 누워도 삿갓 미사리를 대어라 (속담) No pains, no gains. ⇒ No mill, no meal.
감나무 밑에 누워 입안에 연시 떨어지기 바란다 (속담) One expects larks to fall ready roasted into his mouth.
감내 堪耐 enduring; endurance; perseverance
—**감내하다** endure; persevere; stand (up to)
♦감내할 수 없는 beyond [past] endurance / 많은 시련을 감내하다 stand [go through] many trials
▶우리는 많은 고통을 감내했다 We endured much pain.
▶감내할 수 없는 것을 참고 견디는 것이 진정한 인내다 True patience lies in bearing what is unbearable.

감다¹ **1** 〈실·끈 등을〉 wind [coil, twine, bind, tie] 《sth》 round 《another thing》; reel
♦나뭇가지에 밧줄을 감다 twine a cord around a branch / 실을 실패에 감다 wind thread on [to] a reel / 시계의 태엽을 감다 wind a clock / 털실을 둥글게 감다 roll [wind] wool into a ball / 필름을 감다 wind [advance] the film
▶그녀는 그의 팔에 붕대를 감았다 She bandaged his arm.
▶뱀은 나뭇가지를 친친 감았다 The snake wound around a branch.

감다² 2 〈입다〉 wear; put on; 〈몸을 싸다〉 wrap (in)
▶ 그 여자는 비단 옷만 몸에 감는다 She wears nothing but silk.
▶ 그는 몸은 비록 누더기를 감고 있어도 마음은 깨끗하다 He is (clad) in rags, but is pure in heart.

감다² 〈씻다〉 wash; bathe ◆미역감다 wash *oneself* [bathe] (in a river); have a swim / 머리를 감다 wash [shampoo] *one's* hair

감다³ 〈눈을〉 shut [close]
◆눈을 감다 shut [close] *one's* eyes; (비유) die; leave this world / 눈 감고 기도하다 give *one's* prayers with *one's* eyes shut
▶ 눈을 감고 있어도 네가 지금 무엇을 하고 있는지 알 수 있다 Even with my eyes closed I can tell what you are doing now.

감당하다 堪當— be equal to (the task); be capable of carrying out [performing]; be up to doing; be fit for [adequate to] 《*one's* post》; cope well; deal well with
◆적을 감당해내다 cope with the enemy / 감당하지 못하다 be beyond *one's* capacity; be unfit for; be too much for *one*
▶ 나는 이 일은 감당하기 어렵다 I find myself unequal to the task.
▶ 그는 워낙 기운이 센 놈이라 나로서는 감당하기 어렵다 He is so strong that he is more than a match for me.
▶ 그는 그 직책을 감당하기에는 너무 고령이다 He is too old for the post.
▶ 내 수입으로는 높은 생활 수준을 감당하지 못한다 My income does not take care of the high standard of living.
▶ 그는 그 직책을 충분히 감당할 수 있다 He is quite capable of filling the post [fully equal to the task].
▶ 그는 무슨 일이든 감당할 수 있다 He is equal to any task.

감도 感度 sensitiveness; sensibility; 〈필름·계기 등의〉 sensitivity; 〈라디오·텔레비전 등의〉 reception
◆고감도[저감도] 필름 a fast [slow] film / 감도가 좋다 be highly sensitive 《to》; be hypersensitive 《to》; 〈라디오가〉 have [get] good 《↔ poor》 reception / 감도가 나쁘다 be insensitive
▶ 산간 지역에서는 라디오의 감도가 좋지 않다 Radio reception is not good in mountainous district.
▶ 마이크로폰의 감도는 어떻습니까? How sensitive is the microphone?
■—시험 a sensitivity test —측정 sensitivity measurement; sensitometry

감독 監督 1 〈감독하는 일〉 supervision; control; superintendence; direction; management; 〈감시〉 surveillance
◆민 씨에게 공사의 감독을 맡기다 leave the work to the care of Mr. Min / 감독을 더욱 엄격히 하다 supervise more strictly; enforce a more strict control 《over》
▶ 그는 감독 소홀로 좌천[징계]당했다 He was relegated to a lesser position [reprimanded] for neglect of supervision [because of failure to supervise effectively].
▶ 그 사업은 정부의 감독 하에 수행되었다 The project was carried out under government control 《direction》.
▶ 그가 그렇게 한 것은 자네가 감독을 적절히 못한 탓이다 He did that because you didn't take proper care of him.
▶ 그가 시험 감독을 했다 He proctored the examination.
▶ 자네가 일을 할 필요는 없네. 직원들 감독만 해 주게 I don't want you to work. Only supervise [superintend, oversee] the workers.
—**감독하다** supervise; superintend; control; oversee; 〈팀 등을〉 manage; 〈영화를〉 direct; 〈보살피다〉 take [have] charge of; take care of; look after
◆스필버그가 감독한 영화 a film directed by Spielberg / 공사를 감독하다 oversee a construction work / 시험을 감독하다 supervise [美] proctor, [英] invigilate] an examination / 직원을 감독하다 oversee workers / 학생을 감독하다 look after [take charge of] *one's* pupils
▶ 그 그룹은 내가 감독했다 The group worked under my surveillance.
▶ 이 영화는 누가 감독했습니까? Who directed this film?
▶ 누가 이 일을 감독하고 있니? Who is bossing this job?
2 【감독자】 a superintendent; a supervisor; 〈시험의〉 [美] a proctor, [英] an invigilator; 〈인부 등의〉 a foreman; 〈스포츠의〉 a manager; 〈영화의〉 a director; 〈교회의〉 a bishop
■공사— a taskmaster : 그 사람이 공사 감독이다 He is the superintendent of [He is overseeing] the construction work. 공장— a factory inspector; an inspector of factories 대—〔宗〕 an archbishop 매장—〈백화점의〉 [英] a shopwalker; [美] a floorwalker 무대〔야구〕— a stage [baseball] manager 시험—〔美〕 a proctor, [英] an invigilator 시험장— a presiding officer 영화〔음악〕— a movie [music] director 조—〔映〕 an assistant director 총—〔野〕 a general manager 현장— a site [field] overseer; a foreman ■—관 an inspector; a superintendent —청 the competent authorities; the supervisory office —기관 the competent institutions —행정 supervisory administration

감독교회 監督敎會 the Episcopal [英] Anglican] Church ■—신도 an Episcopalian; [英] an Anglican

감돌다 1 〈둘레를〉 go [turn] round; turn about; circle round
2 〈길·물고기가〉 curve [bend] around; make a curve 《around》; meander [miǽndər]
▶ 강이 산 모퉁이를 감돌아 흐른다 The river curves around the bend of the mountain.
▶ 강이 만으로 감돌아 흘러 든다 The river winds to the bay.
▶ 오솔길이 계곡 위로 감돌아 이어진다 The path winds up the valley.
3 〈기운·분위기를 띠다〉 wear 《a sorrowful look》; have
◆입가에 감도는 미소 a smile on [playing about] *one's* lips

▶아련히 봄 향기가 감돌고 있다 There is a faint suggestion of spring in the air.
▶그 시인의 시에는 달콤한 우수가 감돌고 있다 His poems have a touch of sweet melancholy.
▶발칸 반도에 전운이 감돌고 있었다 War clouds hung low over the Balkan Peninsula.
▶그들 사이에 불안의 그림자가 감돌고 있다 A cloud of uneasiness is [hangs] upon them.

감동 感動 impression; emotion; excitement; a sensation (among the audience)
♦감동적인 moving 《words》; touching (music, speech); impressive 《scene》 / 관객에게 아무런 감동도 주지 못하다 fall flat on the audience
▶나는 그 책에서 많은 감동을 받았다 I am extremely impressed by the book.
▶그의 연설은 청중들에게 큰 감동을 주었다 His speech made a deep impression on the audience.
▶그 이야기는 내게 아무런 감동도 불러 일으키지 못했다 It called forth no response in my heart.
▶그들은 감동적인 재회를 했다 Their reunion was filled with emotion.
—**감동하다** be (deeply) impressed 《by》; be (deeply) moved [touched, affected] 《by》; feel emotion 《at》; be struck 《by, with》
♦감동하기 쉬운 사람[나이] an emotional [impressionable] man [age] / …을 보고 감동하다 be affected at the sight of... / 감동하여 눈물을 흘리다 be moved to tears / 감동시키다 move 《sb to tears》; impress; touch 《sb's heart》; cause profound emotion; appeal to sb
▶그녀의 정성에 그는 감동했다 Her sincerity touched his heart.
▶그의 말은 나를 깊이 감동시켰다 His words moved me deeply. ⇌ I was deeply impressed with his words.

감득하다 感得— realize; perceive; become aware [conscious] of; acquire a clear idea of; 〈영감으로〉 be inspired; 〈눈치채다〉 sense [sniff] 《a danger》; get wind of

감람 橄欖 〔植〕 an olive ■—나무 an olive tree —색 olive color [green] —암〔岩〕 peridotite
감람산 橄欖山 the Mount of Olives
감람석 橄欖石 〔鑛〕 olivine; 〈짙은 녹색의〉 peridot ■—고토— forsterite 귀〔貴〕— chrysolite

감량 減量 a loss in weight [quantity]; 〈운동선수의〉 reduction of one's weight
♦운송[보관] 상품의 감량 outage; 〈액체의 누손량〉 ullage / 체중 감량에 고생하다 have a hard time reducing one's weight
—**감량하다** 〈수량을〉 reduce the quantity 《of》; 〈체중을〉 reduce (↔ put on) one's weight
▶그는 5킬로그램을 감량해야 한다 He has to lose five kilograms.
■—경영 belt-tightening management

감로 甘露 1 〈단이슬〉 dew [refreshing] dew **2** 〈즙액〉 nectar; honeydew ♦감로 맛이 나다 be as sweet as nectar ■—수 sugared [sweet] water; nectar —주 sweet liquor

감루 感淚 tears of gratitude ♦그는 다만 감루를 흘릴 뿐이었다 He could only shed tears of gratitude.

감률 甘栗 〈단밤〉 a sweet chestnut; 〈군밤〉 a broiled [roasted] chestnut
감리교 監理教 the Methodist Church ■—교회 a Methodist church —도 a Methodist
감마 gamma ■—글로불린 gamma globulin —방사선 〔物〕 gamma radiation —선 외과 gamma surgery
감마선 —線 〔物〕 gamma rays; γ-rays
감마유 減摩油 〈윤활유〉 lubrication [lubricating] oil
감마제 減摩劑 〈윤활제〉a lubricant
감면 減免 reduction and exemption; 〈세금의〉 reduction of and exemption from 《taxes》; 〈형벌의〉 mitigation and remission
—**감면하다** 〈세금을〉 reduce and exempt; 〈형벌을〉 mitigate and remit
감명 感銘 (a deep) impression
♦감명 깊은 impressive 《speech [novel, performance]》 / 감명을 주다 〈사람이 주어〉 be (strongly) impressed 《with, by》; be moved [touched] 《by》; 〈사물이 주어〉 be (strongly) impressed on sb's mind; make impression on sb's mind; be engraved upon sb's heart
▶나는 그의 말에 깊은 감명을 받았다 I was deeply moved by [with, at] his words.
▶그의 연설은 청중에게 깊은 감명을 주었다 His speech had a great impression on the audience.
▶그 이야기는 우리에게 거의 감명을 주지 못했다 The story left little impression on us.
감모 減耗 〈감소〉 decrease; (a) diminution; a reduction —**감모하다** decrease; diminish; lessen
감물 persimmon tannin; the astringent [bitter] juice of a persimmon
감미 甘味 sweetness; a sweet taste
♦감미가 돌다 taste sweet
감미 甘美 sweetness ♦감미로운 목소리 honey-sweet voice / 감미로운 음악[선율] sweet music [an enchanting melody] / 감미로운 (honey) sweet; mellow; exquisite
감미료 甘味料 a sweetener; sweetening materials [agent]; sweetenings ■—인공— an artificial sweetener
감방 監房 a (prison) cell; a ward ♦감방 친구 a cellmate / 감방에 처넣다 throw [cast] sb into a cell
감배 減配 〈배당의〉 a reduction of [in] a dividend; 〈배급의〉 a reduction of [in] a ration
—**감배하다** reduce a dividend [ration] 《from...to...》
♦배당을 5%로 감배하다 cut dividends to 5 percent
▶전기에 회사는 불경기로 배당을 8% 감배했다 Last term the company reduced dividends by 8 percent because of business recession.
감법 減法 〔數〕 subtraction ⇨ 뺄셈
감별 鑑別 〈구별〉 discrimination; 〈판별〉 judgment; 〈식별〉 discernment
—**감별하다** distinguish [discriminate, differentiate] 《A from B》; judge; tell (between A and [from] B)
♦병아리 감별사 a chicken sexer / 병아리를 감별하다 sex a chicken; discern the sex of a

감복

fowl / 진위를 감별하다 distinguish between an imitation from [and] the original

감복 感服 admiration; wonder
—감복하다 admire; wonder 《at》; be struck with admiration; be deeply impressed 《by》
♦ 감복할 만한 행동 an admirable [a praise-worthy] deed / 용기에 감복하다 admire sb for [his] courage / 감복시키다 strike sb with admiration
▶ 우리는 그녀의 능력에 감복했다 We have been struck with [impressed by] her ability.
▶ 나는 그의 깊은 통찰력에 감복했다 I admired [was impressed by] the depth of his insight.

감복숭아 〔植〕 an almond

감봉 減俸 a salary reduction; a pay cut; a reduction in one's salary [pay]; a punitive wage cut
—감봉하다 reduce [cut down] one's salary 《from…to…》; dock
♦ 감봉당하다 have one's salary reduced 《by…percent》; have one's pay cut / 60만원에서 54만원으로 감봉되다 be reduced in pay from 600,000 won to 540,000 won
▶ 불황으로 종업원 모두가 10% 감봉되었다 The salaries [wages] of all employees were cut (down) by 10 percent because of business depression.

감비아 〈나라 이름〉 Gambia; 〈공식명〉 the Republic of The Gambia ♦ 감비아의 Gambian
■ —사람 a Gambian

감사 感謝 thanks; gratefulness; gratitude; appreciation; acknowledgment; 〈신에 대한〉 thanksgiving

解説 *thanks*가 일반적인 말. *gratitude*는 thanks 보다 감사의 마음이 강하고 격식을 차린 말. *appreciation*은 상대방의 행위를 충분히 평가하고 감사하는 것을 의미한다.

♦ 감사의 말 words [a speech] of thanks [gratitude] / 감사 기도를 올리다 〈식사 전[후]에〉 give thanks; say grace / 감사의 눈물을 흘리다 shed tears of gratitude / 감사의 뜻을 표하다 express one's (sense of) gratitude; express one's appreciation 《of》
▶ 도와 주셔서 뭐라고 감사의 말씀을 드려야 할지 모르겠습니다 I can never thank you enough [I don't know how to thank you] for your help.
▶ 일동을 대표하여 감사의 말씀을 드리고자 합니다 I'd like to say a few words of thanks on behalf of all present.
▶ 감사의 표시로 이것을 드립니다 I will give this to you as a token of my gratitude.
▶ 호의에 충심으로 감사를 드립니다 I thank you from the bottom of my heart [I am very grateful] for your favor. ⇌ I appreciate your favor.
—감사하다 〈동사적〉 thank sb (for his help); give one's thanks 《for》; express one's gratitude 《for》; express [show] one's appreciation 《of sb's services》; 〈형용사적〉 thankful; grateful (to sb for his sympathy)
♦ 신에게 감사하다 thank God; give thanks to God; bless God 《for》 / 행운에 감사하다 thank one's (lucky) stars / 감사하게 받다 accept 《a present》 thankfully [with thanks]
▶ (대단히) 감사합니다 Thank you (very much). (▶친한 사이에는 Many thanks. 또는 Thanks a lot. 등으로도 말하며 Thanks.는 무간한 사이에서 쓰는 구어체 표현임)
▶ 충심으로 감사합니다 I express my hearty [heartfelt] thanks to you.
▶會話 「커피 한 잔 하시겠습니까?」「예, 감사합니다」 "Will you have a cup of coffee?" "Thank you, please."
▶ 그는 감사하기는 커녕 항상 불평만 한다 He is always complaining and is never thankful.
■ —만찬회 a testimonial dinner —장(狀) a letter [note] of thanks [appreciation]; a citation; a thank-you card —절 a harvest thank offering; 〈美〉 Thanksgiving (Day)

감사 監事 an inspector; a supervisor; 〈회계의〉 an auditor; 〈회사의〉 a corporation controller
■ 상임— a standing auditor

감사 監査 inspection; superintendence; 〈회계의〉 an audit; auditing ♦ 엄밀한 감사 a strict inspection; 〈회계의〉 a strict [full] audit / 감사 보고 an audit report
—감사하다 inspect; superintend; 〈회계를〉 audit 《the company accounts》
■ 국정— parliamentary inspection of the administration 자체— a self-inspection ■ —원(院) the Board of Audit and Inspection —원장 the Chairman of the Board of Audit and Inspection —제도 an audit system

감산 減産 a drop [decrease] in production [output]; 〈인위적〉 curtailment [reduction] of production [output]
♦ 철강의 감산 a decrease in steel production; reduced steel output
—감산하다 cut [reduce, curtail] production (▶cut이 가장 구어적임)
▶ 이달에는 5% 감산되었다 Production decreased by five percent this month.

감산 減算 〈뺄셈〉 subtraction **—감산하다** 〈빼다〉 subtract

감상 感傷 sentimentality; sentiment
♦ 감상적인 sentimental (poem); emotional / 감상이 지나친 mawkish / 깊어 가는 가을을 보고 감상에 젖다 sentimentalize over the deepening of autumn
▶ 그녀는 그 책을 읽고 감상적인 기분이 되었다 She became sentimental reading the book.
▶ 나는 어린 시절을 생각하면 감상적이 된다 I get sentimental remembering my childhood.
■ —주의 sentimentalism —주의자 a sentimentalist

감상 感想 〈인상〉 one's impression(s); 〈생각 · 의견〉 one's thoughts [opinion]; one's sentiment(s); 〈논평〉 comment; 〈느낌〉 feelings

解説 *impression*은 보거나 듣거나 해서 마음에 받은 느낌을, *opinion*은 마음에 받은 느낌에 대한 자기의 의견을 말한다.

♦ 감상을 말하다 give one's impressions 《of》; comment 《on the poem》; give one's thoughts

감사의 표현

1. 대단히 고맙습니다
(1) thank를 써서
보통 가장 흔히 쓰이는 것으로는 Thanks. ⇌ Thanks a lot. ⇌ Many thanks. 등이 있다. 공손하게 말할 때는 Thank you very much.라고 한다.
▶ 会話 「수남아, 네 차례야」「응, 고마워」 "It's your turn, Su-nam." "Thanks."
▶ 会話 「자, 커피 들어요」「고맙습니다」 "Here's your coffee." "Oh, thanks a lot."
▶ 충심으로 감사드립니다 I thank you from the bottom of my heart.
▶ 전화 주셔서 고맙습니다 Thank you for calling.
(2) It is nice [kind] of you to...를 써서
▶ 알려 주셔서 대단히 고맙습니다 It's very kind of you to let me know (that).
▶ 어머니를 집까지 바래다 주셔서 고맙습니다 It's nice of you to see my mother home.
(3) appreciate, owe를 써서
▶ 협력해 주셔서 감사합니다 I appreciate your cooperation.
▶ 곧 회신 주시면 고맙겠습니다 I'd appreciate it if you would send your reply by return mail.
▶ 제게 오늘이 있음은 김 선생님 덕분입니다 I owe what I am to Mr. Kim.
(4) thankful, grateful 등을 써서
▶ 당신의 시의적절한 조언에 깊이 감사드립니다 I am most thankful for your timely advice.
▶ 그녀의 친절한 배려를 매우 감사하게 생각합니다 I'm very grateful to her for her kind attention.
▶ 선생께 깊이 감사하고 있습니다 I'm very much obliged to you. (▶약간 고풍인 공손한 말투)
(5) 기 타
▶ 우리들의 감사의 표시로 이것을 받아 주십시오 Please accept this as a token of our gratitude.
▶ 당신 덕분에 무사히 집에 돌아왔습니다 Thanks to you, I got home safely.

2. 천만의 말씀입니다
가장 일반적인 표현은 You are (quite) welcome.이고 그밖에 Not at all. ⇌ Don't mention it. 등이 있는데, 스스럼 없는 말로는 Any time. ⇌ (That's) O.K. ⇌ No problem. 등이 있다
▶ 会話 「태워다 주셔서 고맙습니다」「천만에요」 "Thank you for giving me a ride." "You're welcome."
▶ 会話 「멋진 선물을 주셔서 고맙습니다」「천만에요, 마음에 드신다니 기쁩니다」 "I appreciate your wonderful gift." "It's my pleasure. I'm glad you like it."
▶ 会話 「짐을 운반해 주시느라고 수고가 많으셨습니다」「아니오, 괜찮습니다」 "Thank you for carrying my luggage." "Oh no, not at all."

3. 남에게 권고를 받았을 때
무언가 권고를 받고 거절할 때라도 "No."라고만 하지 말고 반드시 "No, thank you."나 "Thanks just the same."(그렇지만 감사합니다) 등으로 호의에 감사하는 것이 에티켓이다.
▶ 会話 「커피를 한 잔 더 드시겠습니까?」「예, 고맙습니다」 "How about another cup of coffee?" "Yes, please." ⇌ "Thank you, I will."
(▶「아니오, 됐습니다」는 "Thank you, but I've had enough already.")
▶ 会話 「(변변치 않습니다만) 이것을 드리겠습니다」「이거 참, 고맙습니다」 "Here's a little something for you." "Oh, this is great!"

4. 칭찬을 받았을 때
영어권에서는 칭찬을 받았을 때는 대개 그 말을 그대로 받아들이고 고맙다는 인사를 하는 경우가 많다.
▶ 会話 「자네는 영어를 아주 잘 하는군」「그렇게 말씀하시니 기뻐요」 "You speak excellent English." "It's very kind of you to say so."
▶ 会話 「오늘 입으신 블라우스 멋진데요」「어머, 정말요? 감사합니다. 약간 화려하지 않을까 걱정했는데」 "You're wearing a lovely blouse today." "Oh, do you think so? Thanks a lot. I was wondering if it was a bit too loud."

5. 생일 선물을 받았을 때
⟨Dialog⟩
A : 주디, 생일 축하해 Happy birthday, Judy!
B : 오, 제인, 정말 고마워 Oh, Jane! How very thoughtful of you!
A : 천만에 Not at all.
B : 선물을 지금 열어봐도 될까? May I open it now?
A : 어서 열어봐 Go ahead.
B : 야아, 멋지다. 이러지 않아도 되는데 Oh, how lovely! You shouldn't have done it.
C : 이건 내 선물이야 This one is from me.
B : 톰! 정말 고마워. 진작부터 갖고 싶었던 가죽 장갑이야 Tom! How sweet of you. Just what I wanted: a pair of leather gloves!

(on); express *one's* sentiment(s) (on); remark (on); describe *one's* feelings (of) / 감상을 묻다 ask for *sb's* opinion (about)
▶ 방금 읽은 그 소설에 대한 감상을 말해보시오 State [Give] your impressions of the novel you've just read.
▶ 그는 그 문제에 대한 감상을 이야기했다 He expressed his opinion on the problem.
▶ 귀하의 의견과 감상을 보내주십시오 Please send your opinion and impressions to us.
■―록 a record of *one's* impressions ―문 a (written) description of *one's* impressions: 학생들은 독서 감상문을 썼다 The students wrote a book report.
감상 鑑賞 appreciation (of) ♦명화 감상회 a special show of noted films

▶ 제 취미는 회화 감상입니다 My hobby is looking at pictures.
—**감상하다** read 《poetry》; listen to 《music》; see [watch] 《a play》; 〈진가를 알다〉《can》 appreciate 《Shostakovich》; enjoy; savor 《a novel》
▶ 영어를 완전히 알지 못하면 영시를 감상할 수 없다 You can't appreciate English poetry [read English poetry appreciatively] without complete mastery of the English language.
■ 음악— listening to music
■ —가 an appreciator —비평 appreciative criticism

감상력 鑑賞力 an appreciative power
♦ 감상력이 있다[없다] have a keen [no] appreciation 《of art》; have an [no] eye 《for beauty [painting]》; have an [no] ear 《for music》
▶ 고전 음악에 대한 감상력을 길러야 한다 You must cultivate the appreciation of classical music.

감색 紺色 〈진남색〉 dark [deep, navy] blue
♦ 감색의 dark blue; navy blue / 감색 양복을 입다 wear [be dressed in] a navy-blue suit

감성 感性 sensitivity; sensibility; sense; 〈감수성〉 susceptibility ♦ 감성이 예민한 사람 a sensitive person
■ —계 〔哲〕 the material world; the world of sense —론 〔哲〕 aesthetics

감성돔 〔魚〕 a black porgy

감세 減稅 reduction of taxes; a tax reduction [cut] (↔increase)
♦ 소득세 감세 an income tax reduction / 대폭적인 감세 a drastic cut in taxes
—**감세하다** reduce [cut] taxes; lower taxes
▶ 이 품목들은 10% 감세되었다 The tax on these articles was reduced by ten percent.
■ —계획 a tax cut program —법안 a tax reduction bill; a bill for tax reduction —운동 an agitation for the reduction of taxes

감소 減少 〈수량의〉 (a) decrease(↔increase) 《in》; 〈정도의〉 reduction 《in》; (a) fall; drop; (a) diminution 《of》
♦ 인구[매출, 소득]의 감소 a decrease in population [sales, one's income] / 약간의[꾸준한] 감소를 나타내다 show a slight [steady] decrease [decline]
▶ 이것은 작년에 비해 5% 감소다 This is a decrease of five percent compared with last year.
—**감소하다** reduce; be reduced; diminish; lessen; drop; 〈서서히〉 dwindle
▶ 쌀 수요가 매년 감소하고 있다 The demand for rice has been decreasing [on the decrease] year by year.
▶ 출산율이 점차 감소해 왔다 The birthrate has decreased [dwindled] gradually.

감속 減速 speed reduction; deceleration(↔acceleration); slowdown
♦ 눈·비 올 때 감속 《게시》 Low gear when wet.
—**감속하다** reduce the speed 《of》; decelerate; slow down
♦ 차를 시속 20마일로 감속하다 reduce the speed of a car [slow a car down] to 20 miles an hour
▶ 교차로에 가까워지면 감속해야 한다 We should slow down before we reach the crossroads.
■ —경제 decelerated economy —장치[기어] a reduction gear —재(材) a moderator

감손 減損 〈줄어짐〉 decrease; diminution; 〈손실〉 loss; waste; 〈누출〉 leakage; 〔商〕 draft
—**감손하다** decrease; diminish; lessen; wear out ■ —액 depreciation

감쇄 減殺 diminution; decrease; reduction
—**감쇄하다** lessen 《the effect》; diminish 《the activity》; reduce

감쇠 減衰 decrease; decrement; 〔物〕 attenuation —**감쇠하다** be attenuated; become weak; damp ■ —기(器) an attenuator

감수 甘受 (willing) submission; readiness to suffer
—**감수하다** submit 《to sb's demand》; put up with; be resigned to 《one's fate》
♦ 고난을 감수하다 endure [put up with] hardship(s)/ 모욕을 감수하다 put up with [swallow] an insult; submit *oneself* to an insult / 비난을 감수하다 submit to reproach
▶ 그는 쓰라린 운명을 감수했다 He accepted his bitter fate.
▶ 나는 그런 가혹한 조건은 감수할 수 없다 I cannot submit to such severe terms.

감수 減水 the decrease [fall] of water
—**감수하다** 〈하천 등이〉 fall; subside; recede; sink
▶ 호수가 현저히 감수되었다 The lake has sunk considerably.
▶ 강물이 1미터 감수되었다 The water in the river has fallen one meter.
▶ 가뭄으로 저수지의 물이 반으로 감수되었다 The water level of the reservoir has fallen [dropped] by a half because of dry weather.

감수 減收 a fall [decrease] in yield [output, production, income]; 〈세입의〉 a revenue decrease
▶ 올해는 기후가 몹시 나빠서 밀 생산이 10% 감수다 The weather was very bad this year, so wheat production is down [shows a decrease of] ten percent.
—**감수하다** decrease; drop; fall off
▶ 올해 쌀농사는 예년보다 감수될 것 같다 This year's rice crop is likely to be below [under] the average year's crop.

감수 減壽 shortening *one's* life
—**감수하다** 《one's life》 be shortened; shorten *one's* life
▶ 그 사고를 당했을 때는 꼭 십년 감수하는 줄 알았다 I felt as if my life were shortened by ten years when I met with the accident.

감수 減數 〔數〕 a subtrahend
■ —분열 〔生〕 reduction [reducing] division; meiosis

감수 感受 impression; reception —**감수하다** be impressed 《with》; receive 《an impression》; be susceptible 《of, to》 ■ —기(器) 〔生理〕 a (sensory) receptor

감수 監修 (editorial) supervision

▶ 이 사전은 김 교수 감수 하에 편찬되었다 This dictionary was compiled under the supervision of [was supervised by] Professor Kim.
—**감수하다** supervise 《the compilation of a dictionary》; be chief editor of the compilation 《of》
◆ 한영 사전 편찬을 감수하다 supervise the compilation of an Korean-English dictionary
■ —**자** a chief editor; a supervisor

감수성 感受性 sensibility; receptivity; susceptibility; sensitiveness
◆ 감수성이 뛰어난 사람 a man of refined sensibilities / 감수성이 풍부한 시인 a sensitive poet / 감수성이 둔한 thick-skinned; dull; stolid
▶ 그녀는 색깔에 대한 감수성이 예민하다 She is sensitive to color. ⇒ She has a fine feeling [has fine sensibility] for color.
▶ 그는 감수성이 예민한 남자다 He is sensitive [has fine sensibility].
▶ 그는 나이가 들수록 감수성이 점점 무뎌졌다 As he grew older, he became more and more insensitive.

감숭감숭 ◆ 털이 감숭감숭 나다 be thinly covered with hair; short black curls sprout out; sprout dots of dark hair here and there
—**감숭감숭하다** sparsely dotted with black hair; thinly-haired
◆ 감숭감숭한 턱수염 a sparse beard; fuzz on the chin

감시 監視 1 〈지켜봄〉 (a) watch; watching; observation; 〈경계〉 lookout; vigil; 〈감독〉 supervision
◆ 감시를 게을리하다 neglect to watch / 감시를 두다 set a watch 《on》 / 감시를 받다 be subject to [be under] sb's superintendence
—**감시하다** watch; keep an eye on; keep (a) watch on [over]; observe; 〈출현을〉 watch (out) for
◆ 용의자를 감시하다 watch [keep (a) watch on] a suspect; keep a suspect under observation / 행동을 감시하다 watch [keep an eye on] sb's movement / 휴전[협정]의 이행을 감시하다 police a cease-fire [an agreement] / 엄중히 감시하다 watch closely; keep a close [strict] watch 《on, over》 / 엄중히 감시당하다 be closely watched; be (kept) under close observation
▶ 경찰은 그를 감시하고 있다 The police are keeping an eye on him.
▶ 그들은 포로를 엄중히 감시하라는 명령을 받았다 They were ordered to keep a close watch over the P.O.W.'s.
▶ 그의 행동은 감시받고 있다 His behavior bears watching.
2 〈형법상의〉 surveillance; police supervision
◆ 감시의 눈을 피하다 elude the vigilance 《of the police》
▶ 그의 동정은 경찰의 감시 하에 있다 His movements are placed under police surveillance.
—**감시하다** put [keep] sb under surveillance; exercise [conduct] surveillance 《over》
■ —**기구** a supervisory organization —**망** a surveillance network —**병** a guard —**선**(船) a guard [patrol] boat; (美) a cutter; 〈로켓에 대한〉 a monitoring vessel —**소**[**초소**] a guard box; a watchhouse; (美) a lookout; [軍] an observation post [point] —**인**[**원, 자**] a watchman; a guard; a guardian; a custodian; a keeper; a caretaker; a supervisor; an observer —**장치** surveillance equipment —**탑** a watchtower

감식 減食 reduction of one's diet [food intake]; a diet
▶ 그녀는 체중을 줄이려고 감식중이다 She is on a diet [dieting] to keep her weight down.
—**감식하다** eat less; reduce one's diet; cut down one's meals; be [go] on a diet (▶be는 상태, go는 동작을 나타냄)
■ —**요법** a reduced diet cure : 환자에게 감식 요법을 실시하다 reduce a patient's intake of food

감식 鑑識 〈식별〉 discernment; discrimination; 〈감정〉 judgment; 〈범죄의〉 (criminal) identification 《through fingerprints》
◆ 범죄 감식 자료 materials of criminal identification / 미술품 감식에 뛰어나다 be a good judge of [have an eye for] objects of art; be a connoisseur of works of art
▶ 감식 결과 용의자의 혈액형은 B형으로 판명되었다 The laboratory investigation made it clear that the suspect's blood type was B.
—**감식하다** judge; discern; discriminate
■ 범죄— criminal identification 지문— fingerprint identification —**가** a judge; a discerner; 〈미술품의〉 a connoisseur; 〈평가인〉 an appraiser —**과** 〈경찰의〉 the identification section —**력** ⇨ 감식안

감식안 鑑識眼 a critical [discerning] eye 《for》; discernment
◆ 감식안이 있는 사람 a discerning person; a good judge 《of》
▶ 그는 보석에 대한 감식안이 있다 He has an eye for jewelry. ⇒ He is a good judge of jewelry.

감실 龕室 an alcove; a shrine 《for a Buddhist image》; [가톨릭] a tabernacle

감실감실 ◆ 털이 감실감실 나다 be thinly haired; be covered with blackish fluff —**감실 감실하다** sparsely dotted with black hair

감실거리다 glimmer; gleam faintly; flicker at a dim distance ◆ 감실거리는 불빛 a faint gleam of light
▶ 먼 바다 위에 흰 돛이 감실거린다 A white sail is seen far out at sea.

감싸다 1 〈싸다〉 wrap 《in》; tuck up 《in》
◆ 머리를 감싸 쥐고 with one's head between one's hands / 몸을 감싸다 wrap oneself 《in a blanket》
▶ 그녀는 아기를 모포로 감쌌다 She wrapped her baby in a blanket [wrapped a blanket around her baby].
2 〈비호·보호하다〉 cover 《a guilty person》; shield [screen, shelter] sb; take sb under one's wing; protect 《the weak》; 〈변호하다〉 plead for sb
▶ 우리 형제가 싸울 때마다 어머니는 늘 동생을 감싸신다 Mother always screens my

감아올리다

younger brother whenever we brothers quarrel.
▶ 그녀는 나를 감쌌다 She stood up for me.
▶ 아버지는 항상 나를 감싸 주신다 My father always takes me under his wing.

감아올리다 wind up; roll up ♦돛을 감아올리다 furl [hoist] a sail / 밧줄을 감아올리다 roll up a screen ▶선원들은 닻을 감아올렸다 The sailors heaved (up) the anchor.

감안하다 勘案— take *sth* into consideration [account]
♦…이라는 사실을 감안하다 take into consideration the fact that… / 계획을 실행에 옮기기 전에 형편을 감안하다 take the circumstances into consideration before putting a plan into action
우리는 교통 체증을 감안하여 일찍 출발했다 We left early allowing for a traffic jam.
▶ 그녀가 어리다는 것을 감안해야 한다 You must take her youth into consideration [account].

감압 減壓 reduction of pressure; decompression —**감압하다** reduce the pressure (of); decompress
■—밸브 a reducing valve —장치 a decompression device —증류 distillation under reduced pressure

감액 減額 a reduction; a cut; a curtailment —**감액하다** reduce; make a reduction; cut down; curtail; diminish
▶ 그의 요구액이 절반 감액되었다 The amount of his claim was reduced by one-half.
▶ 손해 배상액은 100만원으로 감액되었다 The amount of compensation for damages was cut down to one million won.

감언 甘言 honeyed words; flattery; (美口) sweet talk (▶달콤한 말은 sweet [sugarcoated] words, 유혹은 주로 bait라고 함)
♦감언에 속아 넘어가다 be imposed upon by *sb's* honeyed words / 감언으로 구슬리다 use fair [sweet] words; coax; (美口) soft-soap / 감언으로 여자를 꾀다 allure [entice, seduce] a woman with honeyed words

감언이설 甘言利說 wheedling; soft and seductive language; glib talk; (口) slick talk
♦감언이설로 속여 …하게 하다 cajole *sb* into doing…
▶ 그의 감언이설에 속지 않도록 조심하시오 Be careful not to be taken in by his glib talk.
▶ 그녀는 악덕업자의 감언이설에 속아 황무지를 매입했다 She was cajoled [coaxed] into buying a piece of barren land by a dishonest dealer.
▶ 판매원은 감언이설로 꾀어 그에게 결함있는 차를 사게 했다 The salesman coaxed him into buying a defective car.
▶ 그 여자는 감언이설로 그에게서 돈을 우려냈다 She wheedled the money out of him.

감연히 敢然— 〈대담하게〉 daringly; boldly; 〈용감하게〉 bravely; 〈겁없이〉 fearlessly; dauntlessly
♦감연히 일어나다 stand up bravely [rise fearlessly] (against the enemy [oppressor])
▶ 그는 감연히 공직자 부패 일소에 나섰다 He determinedly set himself to wipe out corruption among public officials.
▶그들은 감연히 난국에 대처했다 They faced [met] the difficult situation bravely [resolutely].

감염 減鹽 —**감염하다** reduce [cut down] the amount of salt (in *one's* diet) ■—식 a low-salt diet

감염 感染 〈공기·물에 의한〉 infection; 〈접촉에 의한〉 contagion; 〈물듦〉 influence ♦감염성의 infectious; contagious
—**감염하다** be infected (with cholera); contract (a disease) by infection; catch (a disease from *sb*); get influenced
♦광견병에 감염된 개 a dog infected with rabies / 위험한 사상[나쁜 풍습]에 감염되다 be influenced by dangerous ideas [catch bad manners] / 감염되지 않다 〈면역이 되어〉 be immune (from)
▶ 이 병은 접촉에 의해 감염된다 This disease is contagious [spreads by contagion].
▶ 그는 콜레라에 감염되었다 He was infected with cholera.
■—공기— aerial [airborne] infection 원내— hospital [nosocomial] infection 이차— secondary infection (of) 재— reinfection —경로 an infection way [route] —원 the source of infection

감옥 監獄 a prison ⇨ 교도소

감원 減員 reduction of the staff; cutting down of the personnel; a personnel cut [reduction]; 〈일시적인〉 a layoff
—**감원하다** reduce [cut] the personnel (of an office); cut the number of employes
♦5퍼센트 감원하다 reduce the staff by 5 percent / 공무원[직원]을 대폭 감원하다 make a drastic cut in the number of public officials [the staff]; reduce the number of public officials [the staff, the personnel] drastically
■—바람 a sweeping reduction of the personnel

감음정 減音程 〔樂〕 a diminished interval

감읍하다 感泣— be moved to tears (by, with); shed tears of gratitude (for)
▶ 그는 재판관의 온정어린 말에 감읍했다 He was moved to tears by the judge's kind words.

감응 感應 1 〈신·부처의〉 response; answer; 〈공감〉 sympathy; 〈영감〉 inspiration
—**감응하다** 〈답하다〉 respond (to); 〈공감하다〉 sympathize (with); be inspired [affected, moved] (by); 〈신·부처가〉 hear (*sb's* prayer); answer; respond (to)
▶ 그의 정성에 신명도 감응한 것 같다 The gods seem to have responded to [have been moved by, have been touched by] his sincerity.
2 〈유도〉 induction; influence; action
—**감응하다** induce; be effective; act upon
■—도 sensitivity —도체 an induction conductor —반응 (an) induced reaction —방사선 induced radiation —시간 sensitive time —유전 (生) telegony —작용 inductivity; a responsive effect

감자 a (common) potato (*pl.* ~es); a white

[an Irish] potato
♦ 햇감자 a new potato / 감자밭 a potato field [patch, plot]/ 감자 껍질을 벗기다 peel [pare] potatoes
■ 씨— a seed potato ■ —튀김 a fried potato; a potato chip

감자 甘蔗 〈사탕수수〉 a sugarcane ■ —당(糖) cane sugar; 〔化〕 sucrose [súːkrous]

감자 減資 〔經〕 a capital reduction; a reduction of capital; a decrease in a company's normal capital
—감자하다 reduce [decrease] the capital 《of a company》
■ —잉여금 a reduction surplus ■—차익 gains from stock retirement; surplus from reduction of capital

감작 減作 〔農〕 a reduction of crop; a diminished yield; lessened [curtailed] crops

감전 感電 (receiving) a [an electric] shock
♦ 감전사하다 be killed by an electric shock; be [get] electrocuted
—감전하다 get [receive] a [an electric] shock; be struck by electricity
▶ 젖은 손으로 전선을 만지면 감전된다 You'll be get a [an electric] shock if you touch the wire with your wet hands.

감점 減點 points deducted; a demerit mark
—감점하다 subtract 《ten marks》 from sb's marks; give sb a demerit [bad] mark
▶ 영어 시험에서 10점 감점당했다 I had ten points taken off [deducted] on my English test.

감접이 the salvage; the selvedge; hems

감정 感情 feeling(s); (an) emotion; (a) sentiment; passion; 〈충동〉 (an) impulse; 〔心〕 affection

解說 *feeling*은 이성(理性)에 반대되는 감정을 뜻하는 가장 일반적인 말. *emotion*은 희로애락과 같은 강한 감정을, *sentiment*는 감정적 요소가 포함된 견해를, *passion*은 이성적 판단을 압도해 버릴 정도의 격한 애정이나 노여움을 나타낸다.

♦ 대일 감정 sentiment toward Japan / 강한 반일 감정 strong anti-Japanese sentiment(s) [feeling]
▶ 그는 감정대로 행동한다 He is a thrall to his passions.
〈감정의〉 감정(상)의 문제 a matter of sentiment [feeling]
▶ 인간은 감정의 동물이다 Man is an emotional creature. ⇌ All men have feelings. ⇌ Man is a creature of impulse.
〈감정이〉 감정이 복받치다[격해지다] one's feelings boil [run high]; get excited [worked up]/ 감정이 상하다 be offended 《by》; take offense 《at》
▶ 나는 그의 말에 감정이 상했다 His words offended me.
〈감정을〉 감정을 얼굴에 나타내다 show one's feelings [emotions] in one's face / 아무의 감정을 무시하다 do not consider [have no regard for] sb's feelings / 감정을 상하게 하다 hurt [wound] sb's feelings; offend sb / 감정을 숨기다 conceal [hide] one's feelings [emotions]/ 감정을 억누르다 control one's feelings; repress [suppress] one's emotions; contain oneself [one's passions]/ 감정을 표현하다 express one's feelings 《about nature in a poem》
▶ 그 사람은 좀처럼 감정을 드러내지 않는다 He seldom shows [betrays] his feelings [emotions].
▶ 친구들의 감정을 상하게 하지 않도록 주의해라 Be careful not to hurt the feelings of your friends.
〈감정에〉 일시적인 감정에 사로잡혀 on the impulse of the moment; impulsively / 감정에 치우치다 be carried away by [give way to] one's feelings / 이성보다 감정에 호소하다 appeal to one's emotions rather than to one's reason
▶ 그녀는 감정에 약하다 She is emotional [sentimental].
▶ 그는 감정에 치우치기 쉽다 He is apt to be swayed [influenced] by sentiment.
■ 국민— public feeling [sentiment]: 강한 국민 감정에 좌우되다 be influenced by strong public sentiment [feeling] 종교적— religious emotions [feelings] ■—감각 feeling sensation —교육 sentimental education —도착(倒錯) perversion of feelings —론 a sentimental argument; an argument charged with emotion; an impassioned debate —이입(移入)〔心〕 empathy —전이(轉移)〔精神分析〕 displacement

감정 憾情 an unpleasant [ill] feeling; ill [bad] blood; a grudge; displeasure; resentment
♦ 감정이 나다 get displeased; become angry / 감정이 있다 be ill [unfavorably] disposed 《toward》; feel resentment at sb; bear [have] a grudge against sb / 감정을 사다 court displeasure; earn sb's grudge; incur sb's grudge [ill will]
▶ 나는 그 사람에게 아무 감정도 없다 I bear [owe] him no grudge.

감정 鑑定 〈전문가의〉 an expert opinion; 〈판정〉 judgment; 〈평가〉 estimation; appraisal; 〈소송의〉 legal advice
♦ 미술품 감정 judgment of art objects / 필적 감정 handwriting analysis / 감정을 받다 have sth appraised 《by》; have an expert look at sth; seek an expert opinion
▶ 나는 골동품 감정을 전문가에게 의뢰했다 I asked to have the curios judged by a connoisseur.
▶ 그는 정신 감정이 필요하다 He needs a psychiatric test.
—감정하다 judge; give an (expert) opinion 《on》; 〈가격을〉 appraise; estimate; 〈필적을〉 identify
♦ 그림을 감정하다 judge a picture / 필적을 감정하다 identify [give an expert opinion on] sb's handwriting
▶ 전문가가 내 골동품의 가치를 감정했다 An expert appraised the value of my antiques.
▶ 우리는 그 그림을 전문가에게 감정받기로 결

감정의 표현

인간의 감정을 크게 「기쁨」 「노여움」 「슬픔」으로 나누어 그에 대한 영어 표현은 어떤 것이 있는지 살펴 보기로 한다.

1. 기쁨
(1) 가장 일반적인 표현

기뻐하고 있는 상태를 나타내는 가장 일반적인 형용사는 glad다. happy는 흔히 같은 뜻으로 쓰이지만 glad 쪽이 뜻이 강해서 실태를 믿났을 때의 기쁨을 나타내는 데는 happy 보다 glad 쪽이 기쁜 정도가 크다. 「만족감」에 중점을 두면 pleased라도 좋다. 기쁨의 정도가 더욱 클 때에는 delighted가 쓰인다. 또 갑자기 내방한 귀빈에 대해서는 pleasant surprise 등을 쓴다.

▶ 그녀가 돌아와 줘서 기쁩니다 I'm glad she has come back.
▶ 그 소식을 듣고 모두 대단히 기뻐하고 있습니다 We are very glad [happy] to hear the news.
▶ 자네가 와 줘서 기쁘네 I'm glad [happy] you are here with me.
▶ 네가 시험에 합격해서 우리는 모두 아주 기쁘다 We are all delighted that you've passed the examination.
▶ 이렇게 기쁠수가 What a pleasant surprise!

(2) 큰 기쁨의 표현

대단히 큰 기쁨은 jump [leap] for [with] joy, burst with joy 등으로 나타내는데 leap를 쓰는 것은 약간 구식 표현이다.

▶ 그는 아들의 성공 소식을 듣고 겅중겅중 뛰며 기뻐했다 He jumped for joy at his son's success.
▶ 그는 그 소식을 듣고 깡충깡충 뛰며 기뻐했다 He danced for [with] joy to hear the news.
▶ 사내아이는 기뻐서 미칠 지경이었다 The boy was bursting with joy.
▶ 그녀는 너무 기뻐서 넋을 잃었다 She was carried away with delight.

(3) 감탄사 등에 의한 기쁨의 표현
▶ 좋아 Bravo! (▶「멋지다」의 표현에도 해당함)
▶ 그거 멋있다 Wow! (▶강한 놀라움을 내포함)
▶ [회화]「금년 여름에는 미국에 데리고 갈게」「와아, 좋아라」 "I'll take you to America this summer." "Wow! [Gee!] That's great!" (▶ Gee!는 다소 속된 말)

2. 노여움
(1) 가장 일반적인 표현

화가 나있는 상태를 나타내는 가장 일반적인 형용사는 angry다. (美) 에서는 mad를 쓰기도 한다.

▶ 뭘 그렇게 화를 내니? What are you so angry about?
▶ 자네 나한테 화났나? Are you angry with me?
▶ 나한테 그렇게 화내지 말아요 Don't be so mad at me.
▶ 그것을 보고 그녀는 화가 나서 벌벌 떨었다 She trembled with anger at the sight.

(2) 심한 노여움의 표현

격노한 상태는 furious [fjúəriəs], 또는 burst into a fury [rage] 등으로 표현한다.

▶ 그는 딸이 외박을 했기 때문에 몹시 화가 났다 He was furious about his daughter's [with his daughter for] staying out all night.
▶ 내가 그의 신청을 거절했더니 그는 몹시 화를 냈다 He burst into a rage [fury] when I refused his offer.
▶ 그는 화가 나서 얼굴이 시뻘개졌다 He turned red with anger.

3. 슬픔
(1) 가장 일반적인 표현

슬퍼하는 상태를 표현하는 가장 일반적인 형용사는 sad다. 원인이 비교적 뚜렷한 지속적인 슬픔은 sorrow로 나타내는 수가 많다 (▶형용사형 sorrowful). 좀더 큰 슬픔에는 grief를 쓴다.

▶ 그녀는 슬퍼보였다 She looked sad.
▶ 우리는 헤어졌을 때 슬펐다 We parted in sorrow.
▶ 그녀는 첫아기를 잃고 비탄에 잠겼다 She suffered great grief at [over] the death of her first baby. ⇌ She grieved over [at] her first baby's death.

(2) 큰 슬픔의 표현

몹시 슬퍼하는 상태는 be filled with grief, be overwhelmed by grief 등으로 표현한다.

▶ 아들의 전사 통지에 접한 그녀는 비탄에 빠졌다 She was filled with [overwhelmed by] grief when she heard the news of her son's death in battle.
▶ 그 말을 듣고 그의 가슴은 터질 지경이었다 His heart nearly broke when he heard it.

(3) 감탄사 등에 의한 슬픔의 표현
▶ 아, 슬프도다 Ah! I'm sad.
▶ 아, 그녀는 이제 돌아오지 않는다 Alas! She has left me for good. (▶ Alas!는 문어적인 표현)

정했다 We decided to have the picture judged by a connoisseur.
━━**—가[인]** a judge; an identifier; 〈미술품의〉 a connoisseur; 〈골동품의〉 a virtuoso (*pl.* ~s, -si); 〈평가인〉 an appraiser; 〔法〕 an expert witness ━━**—가격** appraised [estimated] value; an appraisement ━━**—관** 〈세관의〉 a (customs) appraiser; (美) a supervisor ━━**—료** 〈미술품의〉 a fee for an expert opinion; 〈상품의〉 a surveying fee; 〔法〕 a fee for legal advice ━━**—서** 〈미술품의〉 a written statement of an expert opinion; 〈상품의〉 a surveyor's report; 〔法〕 an expert opinion in writing

감정적 感情的 emotional; sentimental; impulsive

◆감정적인 동기 sentimental motives / 감정적으로 되기 쉽다 be apt to be emotional / 감정적으로 말하다 speak ill-disposedly / 감정적으

감주 甘酒 a sweet drink made from rice (prepared with rice and malt)

감지 感知 perception; sensing ─**감지하다** perceive; be [become] aware of; sense [scent] 《danger, plot》
▶ 그는 즉시 그들의 음모를 감지했다 He immediately sensed their plot.
■─**기[장치]** 〔電子〕a sensor

감지덕지 感之德之 gratefully; very thankfully; with many [heartfelt] thanks
▶ 그는 내 제의를 감지덕지 받아들였다 He accepted my offer with thanks.
▶ 감지덕지 받을 것이지 무슨 불평이냐 You should accept it gratefully without grumbling.
─**감지덕지하다** be [feel] very thankful [grateful] 《for》
▶ 내가 준 몇푼 안 되는 돈에 그는 감지덕지했다 He was very grateful to me for the little money I offered him.

감질 疳疾 an insatiable [insatiate] appetite; a never satisfied desire
♦ 감질나다 feel eager to eat [have] more; feel insatiable; never feel satisfied; feel tantalized / 감질나 하다 (show that) one is eager to eat [have] more; (show that) one feels insatiable / 감질나게 하다 make sb feel insatiable; tantalize
▶ 한 잔으로는 감질만 난다. 한 잔 더 하자 One glass makes me all the more thirsty. Let's have another drink.
▶ 그 보급으로는 감질날 뿐이었다 The supply merely tantalized us.
▶ 비가 감질나게 왔다 It did not rain enough.

감쪽같다 1 〈고친 것이〉 as good as before; just as it was; just as before
♦ 감쪽같이 고치다 get sth all right again; mend sth just as it was
▶ 세탁을 하니 감쪽같았다 When washed, it was as good as before.
▶ 그는 부러진 파이프를 감쪽같이 고쳐놓았다 He has mended the pipe so you can't tell it was ever broken.
▶ 약을 먹었더니 치통이 감쪽같이 나았다 The toothache has completely gone by virtue of the remedy.
2 〈거짓·꾸민 일 등이〉 complete; perfect; fair; artful
♦ 감쪽같이 도망치다 make a perfect [clean] escape / 감쪽같이 사라지다 vanish completely / 감쪽같이 속다 be completely [fairly, nicely] taken in [deceived] / 감쪽같이 속이다 deceive [cheat, take in] nicely [fairly]
▶ 그 사람은 감쪽같이 속아 넘어갔다 He fell for it hook, line, and sinker.
▶ 그 모습은 감쪽같이 사라져 버렸다 The figure suddenly vanished like a phantom [dissolved into the air].
▶ 나는 감쪽같이 속아 가짜 피카소 그림을 샀다 I was palmed [fobbed] off with a counterfeit Picasso.

감찰 監察 inspection ─**감찰하다** inspect; supervise
■─**감** 〔軍〕the inspector general ─**관** an inspector

감찰 鑑札 a license; a certificate
♦ 감찰이 있는 licensed; registered / 감찰이 없는 without a license; unlicensed 《bars》/ 감찰 없이 《doing business》without a license / 감찰을 교부[갱신]하다 grant [renew] a license / 감찰을 받다 take [get, obtain] a license / 감찰을 취소[몰수]하다 revoke a license
▶ 그는 감찰이 아직 안 나와 영업을 못하고 있다 He cannot start business as the license has not yet been given.
■ 영업— a trade license: 음식점 영업 감찰 a trade license for a restaurant ■ ─료 a license fee

감채 減債 〔經〕partial payment of a debt ─**감채하다** sink 《a national debt》; pay a debt partially
■ ─기금 a sinking fund; an amortization fund: 감채 기금으로 분할 상환하다 amortize ─적립금 a sinking-fund reserve

감청 紺青 Prussian [deep] blue; ultramarine; navy blue

감초 甘草 〔植〕licorice; 〈뿌리〉a licorice root
♦ 감초 분말 licorice powder / 감초 즙 licorice extract

감촉 感觸 (the sense of) touch; feel
♦ 감촉이 좋다 be agreeable to touch / 감촉이 거칠다 feel rough
▶ 이 천은 감촉이 부드럽다[뻣뻣하다] This cloth is smooth [stiff] to the touch. ⇌ This cloth feels soft [stiff].
─**감촉하다** touch; feel; sense

감추다 〈숨기다〉hide; conceal 《one's identity》;〈덮어 가리다〉cover 《a face》; veil 《one's displeasure》;〈속이다〉disguise 《one's nationality》;〈비밀로 하다〉keep sth secret [back] 《from》;〈숨겨주다〉harbor 《fugitives》; shelter 《a criminal》
♦ 감추지 않고 without concealing; openly / 감정을 감추다 conceal one's feelings / 나이를 감추다 hide [conceal] one's age; make a secret of one's age / 마음의 동요를 감추다 cover one's confusion / 몸을 감추다 hide 《oneself》 《behind, under, in》; be in hiding / 불쾌을 감추다 veil one's displeasure / 사실을 감추다 suppress [cover up] a fact / 신분을 감추다 conceal one's identity / 자취[행방]를 감추다 disappear; go out of sight; vanish into thin air; cover one's tracks [traces]/ 종적을 감추다 go into hiding; hide out / 캐비닛 서랍 속에 감추다 put away sth in a cabinet drawer
▶ 고양이는 발톱을 감춘다 A cat retracts its claws.
▶ 그는 왼손으로 써서 필적을 감추었다 He disguised his handwriting by writing with his left hand.
▶ 그 사람은 빚을 갚지 않고 행방을 감추었다 He disappeared [hid himself] before he had paid his debt.

감축

▶나는 열쇠를 그들의 눈에 띄지 않는 곳에 감추었다 I put the key out of their sight.
▶그녀는 나에게 뭔가 감추고 있는 것 같다 It seems that she is keeping something from me.
▶그는 기쁨을 감추지 못했다 He could not conceal his joy.

감축 減縮 reduction; diminution; retrenchment; curtailment
♦주유럽 미군의 감축 the reduction of the U.S. Forces in Europe
—**감축하다** reduce; diminish; retrench; curtail; cut down
▶나는 비용을 감축하려고 애썼다 I tried to reduce my expenses.

감치다[1] 〈잊혀지지 않다〉 linger in *one's* mind
감치다[2] 〈꿰매다〉 hem; hemstitch; seam; sew up 〈an open seam〉
♦옷 가장자리를 감치다 hem the edge of a garment / 단춧구멍을 감치다 work buttonholes

감칠맛 1 〈음식의〉 savory taste; flavor; sapidity
♦감칠맛이 있다 be pleasant [mellow] to the taste; be palatable [tasty, sapid, savory]/ 감칠맛이 없다 be flat [insipid]
▶이건 감칠맛이 나는군요 It's got a good taste, hasn't it?
2 〈매력〉 attraction; magnetism
♦감칠맛 있는 말 magnetic words / 감칠맛 없는 글 a bald sentence
▶그 후보자의 연설에는 말로 형용하기 어려운 감칠맛 나는 뭔가가 있었다 There was something indescribably appealing in the candidate's speech.
▶청중은 시장의 감칠맛 없는 연설에 넌더리가 났다 The audience got sick and tired of the mayor's dull speech.

감탄 感歎 〈찬탄〉 admiration 《for, of》;〈경탄〉 wonder
—**감탄하다** admire; marvel 《at》; wonder 《at》; be struck [filled] with wonder [admiration]
♦감탄할 만한 admirable (performance); wonderful; marvelous; worthy of admiration / 감탄하여 admiringly; with [in] admiration / 감탄스럽게도 to *one's* admiration [credit]/ 감탄할 만큼 근면하게 with admirable diligence / 훌륭한 경치에 감탄하다 marvel at the fantastic sight / 감탄해 마지 않다 be lost in admiration; express great admiration / 감탄케 하다 evoke admiration from *sb*; impress *sb* favorably
▶나는 그의 노력에 매우 감탄했다 I was deeply impressed with his efforts.
▶그 쾌거에 모두가 감탄했다 Everybody expressed unstinted admiration for the great achievement.
▶우리는 그의 기억력에 감탄했다 We marveled at his good memory.
▶모두들 그 그림을 보고 감탄했다 All looked at the picture in wonder [with admiration].
▶그것은 감탄할 만한 행동이다 That is an admirable conduct.
▶그는 그 일을 해내서 모든 사람들을 감탄시켰다 He accomplished the task to the wonder and admiration of all.
▶감탄스럽게도 그 학생은 공부를 아주 열심히 했다 To our admiration the student worked very hard.
■—**문**〔文法〕 an exclamatory sentence —**부호** an exclamation mark [point] —**사**〔文法〕 an interjection; an exclamation

감탕 〈진흙탕〉 a muddy place [spot] 《in a road》; mire; quagmire
♦눈 녹은 감탕길 a muddy road [mud track] caused by the melting of snow / 감탕에 빠지다 fall into the mire

감퇴 減退 《a》 decline 《in energy》; ebb; failing 《of memory》; loss 《of appetite》
♦…의 감퇴를 보이다 show a decline of...
▶수요는 전반적으로 감퇴 상태에 있다 The demand remains generally in a slump.
—**감퇴하다** decline; decrease; fall off
♦식욕이 감퇴하다 lose *one's* appetite / 정력이 감퇴하다 decline in energy
▶나이를 먹으면 기억력이 감퇴한다 Our memory weakens [declines] as we grow older.
▶그는 체력이 감퇴하는 것 같다 His strength seems to ebb.
■—**기억력[시력]—** failing of memory [eyesight] : 시력감퇴를 느끼다 be aware that *one's* eyesight is weakening [failing] **식욕[정력]—** loss of appetite [in energy]

감투 1 〈머리에 쓰는〉 a horsehair cap (formerly worn by gentry [officials])
2 〈관직〉 a government [an official] post;〈좋은 자리〉 a distinguished [responsible] post [office]
♦감투를 노리다 hunt for a leading place / 감투를 쓰다 become a government official; assume office
■—**싸움** a struggle for an influential post

감투 敢鬪 a good fight; courageous fighting
—**감투하다** fight bravely [courageously, gallantly]; put up a good [manly] fight (▶bravely는 행동에, courageously는 정신면에 강조점을 둔 표현임)
■—**상** a fighting-spirit prize [award] —**정신** fighting spirit; fight : 감투정신이 투철하다 have plenty of fight in *one*

감표 減標 〔數〕 a minus sign ⇨ 뺄셈 (~표)

감하다 減— **1** 〈줄이다〉 decrease; lessen; reduce; 〈삭감하다〉 cut down; 〈경감하다〉 mitigate; commute (형벌 등을)
♦5분의 1을 감하다 reduce one-fifth / 5분의 1로 감하다 reduce *sth* to one-fifth / 가치를 감하다 detract from the value 《of》/ 형을 사형에서 무기 징역으로 감하다 commute a death sentence into [to] life imprisonment
▶현금 구매시 5% 감해 드립니다 We give [allow] a five percent discount on cash purchases.
2 〈빼다〉 subtract 《30 from 50》; deduct 《from》; take off
▶9에서 7을 감하면 2가 남는다 Seven from nine [Nine minus seven] leaves two.
3 〈줄다〉 lessen; decrease; grow less; be reduced; dwindle (점차)
♦가치가 감하다 decrease in value / 3분의 1로

감탄사

감탄사(interjection)는 글 중의 다른 말과 문법적인 관계없이 독립적으로 기쁨, 분노, 놀람, 슬픔 등을 나타낸다. 여기서는 감탄사뿐만 아니라 감탄문 등도 언급한다.

1. 놀람
▶이거 참 놀랍군 Boy, this is a surprise! ⇌ Wow! I'm surprised. ⇌ What a surprise!
▶어머나 My goodness! ⇌ Good gracious!
▶맙소사 [어머어머, 저런] Oh, my! ⇌ Oh dear! ⇌ Dear me! ⇌ My God!
▶음, 이전 어려운 문젠걸 Gee! This is a tough question. (▶Gee!는 Jesus (Christ)를 줄여서 완곡하게 쓰는 표현)
▶정말인가? 자네도 김군을 알고 있는가? Really? You know Mr. Kim, too?
▶[會話]「그 영화 벌써 봤어」「어, 정말?」"I saw that movie already." "Oh, yeah [jéə]?"
▶야, 이거 이런 곳에서 만나다니 기연이군 Well, well! What a coincidence seeing you here.
▶이크, 바퀴다 Eeek [í:k]! Cockroaches!

2. 기쁨
▶와아, 굉장하다 Wow [wáu]!
▶멋지다 [굉장하다, 좋다] Wonderful! ⇌ Great! ⇌ Bravo! ⇌ How wonderful!
▶맙소사 [이제 됐다] Thank God!
▶와아, 그거 굉장하군 Gee, that's terrific!
▶만세, 이제 시험은 모두 끝났다 Yippee [jípi]! I've finished all my exams.
▶잘했다 [수고했다] Well done! ⇌ Attaboy [ǽtəbɔ̀i]! (▶That's the boy!가 변한 말) ⇌ Attagirl!
▶이제 안심이다 Ah, I'm so relieved.
▶어머, 몰라보게 컸구나 My, you've grown (so big)!
▶참으로 운이 좋았구나 How lucky!
▶이걸 내게 준다고? 어머, 나 초콜릿 참 좋아하는데 Is this for me? Wow! I love chocolate.

3. 분노・매도・불쾌
「제기랄」「체」등에 해당하는 표현에 Oh my God!, Jesus (Christ)!, God damn it! 등 신을 남용하는 것이 있다. 이런 말들은 신앙심이 두터운 사람들에게는 혐오감을 주기 쉬우므로 주의할 필요가 있다.
▶제기랄, 속이 끓는다 Hang it! ⇌ Damn it!
▶뒈져 Go to hell! ⇌ Go jump in a lake!
▶부끄러운 줄 알아라 Shame on you!
▶구질구질하다 Nonsense! ⇌ (英) Rubbish!
▶아이구, 오늘은 고약하게 덥구나 Phew! It's awfully hot today.
▶이런, 수프에 머리칼이 들어 있네 Yuck! There's a hair in my soup.
▶네가 상관할 일이 아니야, 나가 (It's) None of your business! Get (the hell) out of here!
▶도대체 너는 누구한테 말하고 있다고 생각하는 거냐? Who (in the hell) do you think you're talking to?

4. 후회
▶참으로 아쉽다 What a shame! ⇌ What a pity!
▶어머, 우산을 안가지고 왔네 Oh dear! I forgot (to bring) my umbrella.
▶아차, 그와 도서관에서 만나기로 했었는데 Gosh! I was supposed to meet him in the library.
(▶gosh는 God의 완곡한 표현)

5. 슬픔・동정・고통
▶아아, 슬프다 How sad! ⇌ Oh dear! Alas! (▶Alas!는 문어로서 회화에서는 그다지 쓰이지 않음)
▶아아, 가엾은 소년 Ah, poor (little) boy!
▶[會話]「우리 개가 차에 치어 죽었습니다」「아이 끔찍해라」"Our dog was hit by the car and killed." "How terrible!" ⇌ "What a pity."
▶아야, 손가락이 문틈에 끼었어 Ouch! I got my finger caught in the door.

6. 기타
▶조용히 해. 이상한 소리가 들리지 않니? Hush! Don't you hear a strange sound?
▶그것 봐, 내가 말하지 않던? There now, didn't I tell you?
▶가만, 이 약품은 불붙기 쉬우니까 주의해야 해 Oops [wú(:)ps]! We've got to be very careful, as this chemical is inflammable.

감하다 be reduced to one-third
감행 敢行 decisive [resolute] action
―감행하다 dare [venture] ⟪to do⟫; take decisive [resolute] action; carry out resolutely
▶그들은 위험한 탐험을 감행했다 They ventured up(on) a dangerous expedition.
▶만일 파업이 감행되면 커다란 파문을 일으킬 것이다 The strike, if carried out, will have great repercussions.
감형 減刑 reduction [mitigation] of a penalty; commutation of a sentence ♦감형을 청원하다 ask for reduced sentence
―감형하다 mitigate a penalty [punishment]; commute a sentence; reduce a sentence to
▶판사는 정상을 참작하여 그를 감형해 주었다 The judge reduced his penalty in consideration of extenuating circumstances.
▶그 살인범은 사형에서 무기 징역으로 감형되었다 The murderer's death sentence was commuted to life imprisonment.
감호 減號 a minus sign ⇨ 뺄셈(~표)
감호 監護 〔法〕 care and custody
♦감호 조치를 취하다 take a measure for care and custody / 10년 징역에 5년 감호 처분을 선고하다 sentence ⟪a convict⟫ to 10 years in jail plus 5 years in prevention custody
감홍 甘汞 〈염화제일수은〉〔化〕 calomel
감화 感化 influence ⟪of one's teacher [a good man]⟫; (moral) reform
♦…의 감화를 받고 under the influence of / 쉽게 감화를 받다 be easily influenced / 좋은 감화를 주다 exercise [exert] a good influence

감화

〈upon〉
▶ 내가 영문학을 좋아하게 된 것은 김 교수님의 감화 때문이다 Prof. Kim inspired me with a love of English literature.
▶ 아이들은 부모에게서 감화를 잘 받는다 Children are easily influenced by their parents.
▶ 아버지는 불교의 감화를 받고 계셨다 My father was under the influence of Buddhism.
▶ 그 책은 많은 어린이들에게 감화를 주었다 The book had a good influence (up)on many children.
—**감화하다** influence; exert influence upon; inspire
♦ 감화되기 쉬운 easily influenced; susceptible to influence 《of *one's* friend》
■ —교육 reformatory instruction [training] —력 influence; power to influence —원 a (juvenile) reformatory; a correction [reformatory] school; 《美》 a reform school

감화 鹼化 〔化〕 saponification ⇨ 비누화(化)

감회 感懷 〈회포〉 sentiments; feelings; deep emotion; 〈회상〉 sentimental recollection; reminiscence; retrospection
♦ 감회에 젖어 있는 중년 남자 a middle-aged man full of emotion / 감회가 깊다 be deeply moved 《by》/ 감회에 젖다 be overcome by deep emotion; sentimentalize [become sentimental] 《over [about] the past》
▶ 그는 무량한 감회를 느끼며 추도사를 썼다 He wrote the memorial address from the fullness of his heart.
▶ 내 가슴은 깊은 감회로 벅찼다 My heart was filled with deep emotion.

감흥 感興 〈흥취〉 interest; fun; sport; pleasure
♦ 감흥이 이는 대로 as *one's* fancy dictates / 감흥이 일다 get [become] interested 《in》; be inspired 《by》; feel a sensation of pleasure / 감흥을 돋우다 arouse [stimulate, excite] *one's* interest 《in》; attract [capture] *one's* fancy
▶ 그의 이야기를 들어도 아무런 감흥이 일어나지 않았다 His speech did not appeal to me.
▶ 달 때문에 감흥이 솟아 그는 시를 한 편 지었다 Inspired by the moon, he composed a poem.
▶ 그의 멍청한 말이 사람들의 감흥을 모조리 깨버렸다 His silly remark spoiled everybody's fun completely.

감히 敢— daringly; boldly; fearlessly; without hesitation; 〈주제넘게〉 impertinently
♦ 감히 …하다 dare [venture] 《to do》;〈주제넘게〉 have the cheek [face] 《to do》; be impertinent enough 《to do》/ 감히 …이라고 말하다 venture to say… / 감히 목숨을 걸다 dare to risk *one's* life
▶ 감히 내 돈을 사기하다니 How dare you cheat me of my money?
▶ 감히 네가 그런 말을 하다니 How dare you say such a thing to me?
▶ 그들은 감히 오지[공격을 하지] 못했다 They did not dare to come [attack].

갑 甲 1 〈차례의〉 No. 1; the first; A
2 〈십간(十干)의〉 the first of the ten celestial stems [calendar signs]
3 〈등급〉 A one; the first [top] (grade); 〈성적〉 grade A; class "A"; 〈여럿 중의 하나〉 A; the former; the one
♦ 갑을 쌍방 both parties 《to a contract》/ 갑과 을 A and B;〈전자와 후자〉 the former and the latter; the one and the other / 갑을 쌍방 간에 between the two parties / 갑 지역에서 을 지역으로 from one place to the other [another] (▶ another는 셋 이상일 경우에 씀)
▶ 갑을의 차이는 거의 없다 There is little difference between A and B.
▶ 갑의 약은 을의 독 《속담》 One man's meat is another man's poison.
4 〔등딱지〕 〈게의〉 a shell; 〈거북의〉 a tortoise shell; 〈갑각류의〉 a carapace

갑 匣 a case; a box; a pack ♦ 담배 한 갑 a pack [package, 《英》 packet] of cigarettes
■ —성냥— a matchbox

갑 岬 〈곶〉 a cape; a promontory; a headland

갑각 甲殼 〔動〕 a shell; a crust; a carapace

갑각류 甲殼類 〔動〕 Crustacea [krʌstéiʃiə] ♦ 갑각류 동물 a crustacean ■ —학 crustaceology —학자 a crustaceologist

갑갑증 —症 boredom; tedium; tediousness; ennui

갑갑하다 〈답답하다〉 stifling; suffocating; stuffy; close; 〈좁다〉 uncomfortably narrow; confined; cramped; 〈가슴이나 배가〉 《feel》 heavy 《in the chest [stomach]》; 〈지겹다〉 boring; tedious; dull; tiresome
♦ 갑갑한 느낌이 들다 feel choky [suffocating]/ 갑갑해 죽겠다 be bored to death; be oppressed with tedium
▶ 진도가 더뎌서 갑갑하다 I am sick of my slow progress.
▶ 방이 갑갑해 못견디겠어요. 창문 좀 열어 주세요. Please open the window. I feel stifled in this room.
▶ 규칙에 묶인 일은 갑갑해서 싫다 Rigidly [Strictly] regulated work isn't in my line.
▶ 나는 한국 사회가 다소 갑갑하게 느껴졌다 I found Korean society a bit too confining [restricting].

갑골문자 甲骨文字 〔考古〕 inscriptions on animal bones and tortoise carapaces

갑근세 甲勤稅 the income tax of Grade A; the Grade A income tax
♦ 봉급에서 갑근세를 공제하다 deduct the income tax of Grade A from *one's* salary
■ —원천징수 imposition of the income tax of Grade A on the basic source of *one's* earning

갑론을박 甲論乙駁 the pros and cons; arguments pro and con
—**갑론을박하다** argue back and forth; discuss [argue] pro and con; argue for and against 《a matter》
▶ 우리는 그 문제를 둘러싸고 갑론을박했다 We argued the matter pro and con [debated for and against the matter].

갑문 閘門 〈물문〉 a sluice; a floodgate; 〈운하의〉 a lock (gate)

갑부 甲富 the richest [wealthiest] man (in a community); a magnate; a millionaire

갑사 甲紗 fine (silk) gauze [gossamer]

갑상선 甲狀腺 〔解〕 the thyroid gland

■―기능 항진 hyperthyroidism ―동맥[정맥] the thyroid artery [vein] ―비대(肥大) hypertrophied thyroid gland ―암 thyroid carcinoma [cancer] ―염 thyroiditis ―자극 호르몬 thyroid stimulating hormone (略 TSH) ―절제(술) thyroidectomy ―종(腫) a goiter; a struma 《*pl.* -mae》 ―호르몬 thyroid hormone; thyroxin(e)

갑옷 甲― (a suit of) armor; a coat of mail
◆갑옷을 입은 무사 an armored [armor-clad] warrior; a warrior (clad) in armor / 갑옷을 입다 put on *one's* armor
▶ 그는 갑옷을 입고 싸움터로 나갔다 He put on his armor and came forth to battle.
■―미늘 the scale of an armor

갑자기 〈별안간〉 suddenly; abruptly; on [all of] a sudden; all at once; 〈뜻밖에〉 unexpectedly; without warning [notice]; 〈불시에〉 out of the blue
◆갑자기 나타나다 burst upon the scene; appear suddenly / 갑자기 달려들다 spring at *sb* without any warning / 갑자기 들이닥치다 drop in without notice [unnoticed] / 갑자기 멎다 stop short; be brought to a sudden stop [halt] / 갑자기 방문하다 pay *sb* a surprise visit; call on *sb* without notice / 갑자기 시험을 보다 give an examination without notice / 갑자기 유명해지다 spring into fame
▶ 갑자기 날씨가 바뀌었다 The weather has made a sudden change.
▶ 그는 노크도 없이 갑자기 방으로 들어왔다 He came into the room suddenly without knocking.
▶ 앞차가 갑자기 서는 바람에 우리 차가 뒤에서 들이받았다 The car in front stopped without warning and we ran into it from behind.
▶ 기온이 갑자기 떨어졌다 The temperature dropped quickly.
▶ 저는 갑자기 일이 생겨서 참석을 못합니다 I cannot attend owing to an unexpected business.
▶ 아버지의 병세가 갑자기 악화되었다 My father's illness took a sudden turn for a worse.

갑작스럽다 abrupt; sudden; unexpected
◆갑작스러운 일 an unexpected thing [happening] / 갑작스러운 사태 변화 an unexpected turn of affairs / 갑작스러운 초대[방문] a surprise invitation [visit]
▶ 갑작스러운 질문이라서 나는 대답할 바를 몰랐다 Since it was an unexpected question, I was unable to answer it [at a loss for a reply to it].
▶ 우리는 그의 갑작스러운 죽음에 놀랐다 We were surprised at his sudden [unexpected] death.
▶ 그의 사임은 갑작스러운 일이었다 His resignation was very sudden.

갑절 1 〈2배〉 double; two times; twice; 〈몇 배〉 times; as much again
◆세 갑절 three times; treble / 백 갑절 centuple [séntəpəl] / 갑절 반 twice [double] and a half; two and a half times / 크기[길이]가 갑절이다 be twice as large [long] as; be twice the size [length] of; as large [long] again as / 값을 갑절로 받다 charge double prices / 거리를 갑절로 하다 double the distance; make the distance double
▶ 이것은 저것보다 갑절이나 좋다 This is twice as good as that.
▶ 그는 나이가 내 갑절이다 He is twice my age.
▶ 1등석 요금은 2등석 요금의 갑절이다 The first-class fare is double the second-class.
▶ 아기는 1년 동안에 체중이 갑절로 불었다 The baby doubled its weight in a year.
▶ 그 갑절만큼 가져라 Take as much again.
▶ 내 수입은 전보다 갑절이나 늘었다 My income is double what it was.
2 〈2배로〉 double; twice; twofold; as much again
◆갑절 비싸다 cost twice as much / 남보다 갑절 일하다 work twice as hard as others
▶ 그는 전보다 갑절 노력했다 He redoubled his efforts. ⇌ He worked twice as hard as before.
▶ 집세가 5년 전보다 갑절 비싸다 The house rent is twice as high as five years ago.

갑종 甲種 grade A; first [top] grade; A-1
◆신체검사에서 갑종 합격하다 pass as A on *one's* physical examination
■―근로 소득세 ⇨ 갑근세 ―합격자 a first-grade conscript; (美) a grade A selectee

갑주 甲冑 armor; a panoply
◆갑주 한 벌 a suit of armor / 갑주를 입은 무사 an armored warrior / 갑주로 몸을 감싸다 be clad in armor; be steel-clad
▶ 병사들은 갑주를 입고 있었다 The soldiers were (clad) in armor.

갑충 甲蟲 〈딱정벌레〉〔昆〕 a beetle; a coleopteron [kɑ̀liɑ́ptərən] 《*pl.* -ra》

갑판 甲板 〔海〕 a deck
◆갑판에 나가다 go [come] on deck; go topside; hit the deck / 갑판에서 바다로 떨어지다 fall overboard
▶ 파도가 갑판을 휩쓸었다 Waves washed [swept] the deck.
▶ 갑판에는 아무도 없다 There's nobody on deck.
▶ 전원 갑판에 집합 All hands on [above] deck!
■―뒷― the quarterdeck; the afterdeck 앞― the forward deck; the foredeck 주[상, 중, 하]― the main [upper, middle, lower] deck ■―사관 a deck officer ―선실 a deck cabin ―승강구 a hatchway ―실 a deckhouse ―여객 a deck passenger ―원 a deckhand; a deck-department seaman ―일지 a deck log ―장 a boatswain [bóusən]

갑피 甲皮 〈구두의〉 the uppers of leather shoes

값 1 〈가격〉 a price; a cost; a charge

> 解說 *price*는 상품의 가격으로 「값」이라고 하는 우리말에 해당하는 가장 일반적인 말. *cost*는 재료·수고·노력·품삯 등에 지급되는 돈을 뜻하며, *charge*는 부과되는 값, 즉 요금을 뜻한다.

값나가다

♦ …의 값 the price for… / 비싼[싼] 값 a high [low] price / 적당한 값 a moderate [reasonable] price
▶ 그 값이면 싸다[비싸다] It's cheap [dear] at that price.
▶ 손님들은 대개 값만 물어보고는 그냥 간다 Most of the people just ask the price and go away.
〈값이〉 값이 나가다 be valuable [of value, expensive] / 값이 닿다 〈흥정에서〉 reach a price *one* has in mind; 〈합당하다〉 be reasonable; be satisfactory / 값이 비싸다 be expensive; be high in price; be high-priced; be dear / 값이 싸다 be cheap; be low in price; be low-priced / 값이 오르다 the price rises [advances, goes up]; 〈물건이 주어〉 rise [advance, increase] in price / 값이 내리다 the price falls [goes down]; 〈물건이 주어〉 go down [fall, decline] in price / 값이 올랐을 때 팔아 치우다 sell out on the rise
▶ 값이 얼맙니까? How much (do you ask for it)? ⇌ What is the price?
▶ 값이 얼마면 쓰시겠습니까? About what price would you like, price?
▶ 값이 비싸다고 해서 반드시 품질이 좋은 것은 아니다 A high price is not necessarily an assurance of good quality.
▶ 값이 맞으면 팔겠소 I will sell it if you name a moderate price.
▶ 이 값이 제가 해드릴 수 있는 최저 가격입니다 This is the lowest (possible) price I can offer you.
▶ 값이 닿지 않아 사지 못했다 The price was too high and I couldn't buy it.
▶ 값이 맞지 않아 팔지 않았다 The price was not satisfactory and I didn't sell it.
▶ 값이 얼마든지 간에 사겠다 I will pay any price to obtain it.
〈값을〉 값을 깎다 beat [knock, whittle] down the price; haggle [bargain, dicker] 《with *sb*》 over the price / 값을 내리다 lower [reduce, put down] the price / 값을 매기다 price 《an article at 10,000 won》; mark the price on 《an article》; set a price on 《an article》 / 값을 보다 set [put] a price on 《an article》; appraise; evaluate; estimate / 값을 부르다[놓다] 〈살 사람이〉 make an offer 《of 5,000 won》 for 《an article》; name *one's* price; 〈팔 사람이〉 price 《an article at 5,000 won》; name [bid] a price 《for》 / 값을 올리다 raise [put up] the price; 〈경매에서〉 bid up the price / 값을 정하다 fix the price / 값을 치다 value 《an article at》; fix the price of 《an article》 / 값을 하다 be worth; deserve / 밥먹은 값을 하다 render a service for what *one* has eaten; sing for *one's* supper; earn *one's* bread [board]
▶ 물건 값을 지불해 주세요 I want you to pay for the goods.
▶ 그가 내 대신에 값을 치렀다 He paid the price for me.
▶ 그 사람의 집 값을 1억원으로 쳐서 내가 맡기로 했다 I have decided to take his house, valuing it at one hundred million won.
〈값에[으로]〉 좋은 값에 팔리다 sell at a good price; bring [fetch] a fair price; command a fair price
▶ 그 그림은 10억원이라는 엄청난 값에 팔렸다고 한다 I hear that the painting was sold at the staggering price of a billion won.
▶ 그 값으로는 본전도 안됩니다 Your figure is below the cost.
2 〈가치〉 value; worth; merit
♦ 값있다 be valuable [worthy] / 천금의 값이 있다 be worth its weight in gold; be priceless / 값(이) 없다 〈따질 수 없다〉 be priceless [invaluable]; 〈무가치하다〉 be worthless [valueless]
▶ 그는 대학 나온 값을 했다 He did not go to college for nothing.
▶ 그는 자기 가구를 값있는 것으로 생각하고 있다 He places a value on his furniture.
3 〔數〕 value
▶ x의 값을 구하라 Find the value of x.

값나가다 〈값지다〉 be valuable; be of value; be expensive
♦ 값나가는 물건 a valuable article; an expensive article; valuables
▶ 값나가는 물건[그림]은 몽땅 도둑맞았다[팔렸다] All the valuables [Valuable pictures] were stolen [all sold].

값싸다 cheap; inexpensive; low-priced; low in price
♦ 값싼 물건 a cheap [low-priced] article; a (good) bargain; 〈저질품〉 an inferior article / 값싼 감동 cheap emotion

값어치 value; worth (▶value는 주로 실제적인 유용성에서 본 가치를, worth는 정신적 가치를 가리키는 경우가 많음)
♦ 돈의 값어치 the value of money / 백만원의 값어치가 있다 be worth a million won / 읽을 만한 값어치가 있다 be worth reading; be worthy of reading / 한 푼의 값어치도 없다 be not worth a penny [farthing, cent, straw]; be trash
▶ 이 그림은 천만원을 주고 산다고 해도 충분히 그만한 값어치가 있다 This picture is well worth the price even if it costs you ten million won.
▶ 이 골동품은 5백만원의 값어치가 있다 This curio is worth five million won.
▶ 이 작품은 값어치가 크다[없다] This work is of great [no] value.
▶ 그것은 보기보다 값어치가 없다 It is not so good as it looks.
▶ 〔會話〕「이 반지의 값어치는 얼마나 됩니까?」「약 백만원쯤 됩니다」 "What's the value of this ring?" ⇌ "What's this ring worth?" "It is worth [valued at] about one million won."
▶ 그런 말을 하면 네 값어치가 떨어진다 I think you degrade yourself by saying that. ⇌ It is beneath your dignity to say such a thing.
▶ 사람의 값어치를 재산이나 사회적 지위로 매길 수는 없다 You cannot measure a man's worth [A man's worth cannot be measured] by his wealth or social status.

값지다 valuable; expensive; costly; of great value

♦값진 경험 a valuable experience / 값진 물건 a valuable article; a precious object; valuables / 값진 선물 an expensive [a costly] gift [present]
▶건강이 값지다는 것은 건강을 잃었을 때 가장 잘 알 수 있다 The value of good health is best known when it is lost.

갓¹ 〈머리에 쓰는〉 a *kat*; a traditional cylindrical Korean hat (made of horsehair); 〈버섯류의〉 a cap; a top; 〈전등의〉 a shade
■ 전등— a lampshade ■ —끈 the strings [chin straps] of a *kat*

갓² 〔植〕 leaf mustard ■ —김치 leaf mustard kimchi

갓³ 〈말림갓〉 a forest reserve; a reserved forest

갓⁴ 〈엮은 단위〉 a bundle [string] of ten (fish, etc.) tied together
♦고사리 한 갓 a bundle of dried ferns / 굴비 두 갓 two strings of dried yellow corbina

갓⁵ 〈방금〉 fresh [new, green] 《from》; just now; newly; recently
♦갓 결혼한 부부 a couple who have just married; a newly wedded couple; (美口) the newlyweds / 갓 구운 빵 bread fresh [hot] from the oven / 대학을 갓 나온 청년 a young man fresh from college; a new [fresh] graduate / 갓 낳은 달걀 a new-laid egg / 갓 지은 밥 rice hot from the pot / 갓 지은 집 a newly-built house; a new house / 시골에서 갓 올라온 처녀 a maiden fresh [new, green] from the country
▶그는 버스로 갓 도착했다 He has just arrived by bus.
▶그녀가 갓 다녀갔다 She has just been here.

갓- 〈수사 앞에서〉 just; exactly ▶그 의사는 나이가 갓서른이다 The doctor is barely [just] thirty years old.

갓나다 be just [newly] born; 〈싹이〉 have just started to sprout [grow] ♦갓난 송아지 a newly-born [newborn] calf

갓난아이 a newborn child; a baby; an infant

> 解說 ***baby***는 아직 걷거나 말하지 못하는 갓난아이를 가리키는 일반적인 말. 성별이 확실치 않거나 성별을 문제시하지 않는 경우는 it으로 받지만 성별이 확실할 때는 he나 she로 받는다. ***infant***는 baby의 딱딱한 말. (英)에서는 8살 이하의 어린이를 가리키는 수도 있다.

♦갓난아이 같은 babyish; babylike; infantile / 갓난아이 취급을 하다 treat *sb* as a baby

갓돌 〈성벽 등의〉 a copestone; a cope

강 江 a river

> 解說 「…강」은 the …River를 써서 the Han River(한강), the Naktong River(낙동강)처럼 쓰는데, 정관사가 붙을 때는 River를 생략해도 된다. (英)에서는 the River Han, the River Naktong의 어순이 많이 쓰인다.

♦폭이 100미터인 강 a river 100 meters wide [in width] / 흐름이 급한[느린] 강 a fast-flowing [slow-moving] river / 강을 따라[끼고] along a river / 강건너를 바라보다 look across a river / 강을 건너다 cross [go across] a river; 〈걸어서〉 wade across [ford] a stream
▶강 건너편에서 누군가 우리를 부르고 있다 Someone is calling us from the other side of the river.
▶강 한가운데서 말을 바꾸지 마라 (속담) Don't change horses in mid-stream.
▶강이 범람했다 The river overflowed.
▶대부분의 강은 바다로 흘러든다 Most rivers flow into the ocean.
▶우리는 한강을 거슬러 올라갔다[내려갔다] We went up [down] the Han (River).
▶우리는 강으로 낚시질 갔다 We went fishing in the river.

강 腔 〔解〕 a cavity
♦구강 the oral cavity / 복강 the abdominal cavity

강 綱 〔動〕 a class

강 鋼 steel
■ 경(硬)— hard [high] steel 니켈— nickel steel 연(軟)— mild [low] steel 탄소— carbon steel 특수— special steel

강- 强- 〈호된〉 severe; harsh; 〈억지의〉 forced, rough; trying; unreasonable; unjustifiable; 〈순전한〉 pure; straight; dry; unmitigated
■ —추위 (a spell of) dry cold weather —행군 a force march

-강 -强 odd a little more than [over]; something over 《ten pounds》
♦5미터 강 a little [bit] longer than five meters / 20% 강 a little over twenty percent
▶이것은 무게가 60킬로그램 강이다 This is sixty-odd kilograms in weight.

강가 江— a riverside; a riverbank
♦강가의 모래[자갈]밭 a river beach / 강가의 산책길 a riverside promenade / 강가의 풍경 the scenery along the river / 강가의 호텔 a hotel on a river; a riverside hotel / 강가에서 at the riverside / 강가에 살다 live on the banks of a river
▶그 아파트는 강가에 있다 The apartment building is situated on a river.

강간 强姦 rape; assault; violation ♦미성년자 강간 (美) statutory rape
—**강간하다** rape 《a woman》; assault; violate; commit a rape [an outrage] 《upon》 (▶ assault와 violate는 우회적인 완곡한 표현임)
■ —미수 an attempted rape [criminal assault] —범 a rapist —죄 rape; criminal assault

강강술래 *kanggangsullae*; a Korean circle [round] dance or the song for it

강건하다 剛健— vigorous; manly; virile ♦강건한 정신 a virile spirit / 강건한 기상을 기르다 cultivate the spirit of fortitude (and manliness)

강건하다 强健— 〈건강하다〉 healthy; 〈건장·튼튼하다〉 robust; 〈힘세다〉 strong, stout (▶ stout는 strong보다 의미가 강하고, 탄탄한 체격을 암시하는 표현임)
♦강건한 사람 a healthy person; a person of robust health / 강건한 신체 a strong [stout]

body; a robust constitution
▶ 그는 신체가 강건하다 He has a strong [robust] constitution.

강견 強肩 〈野〉 a strong arm ◆ 강견의 strong-armed; (a catcher) with a strong throwing arm
━외야수 an outfielder with a powerful throw; a strong-armed outfielder ━투수 a powerful [mighty] pitcher; a strong-armed pitcher

강경 強硬 ━강경하다 〈완고하다〉 strong; 〈단호하다〉 firm; resolute; unyielding; unbending; uncompromising
◆ 강경한 결의문 a strongly-worded resolution / 강경히 반대하다 oppose *sth* stubbornly; offer [raise, set up] a strong opposition / 강경하게 나오다 show a firm front
▶ 그들은 그 제안에 대해 강경한 태도를 취했다 They took a firm [tough] stand against the proposal.
▶ 나의 의견에 그는 강경히 반대했다 He was firmly opposed to my view. ⇌ He was dead (set) against my opinion.
━노선 a hard line ━수단 a drastic measure; a decisive step: 그는 강경 수단을 썼다 He took [resorted to] drastic [strong] measures. ━정책 a hard-line policy

강경파 強硬派 the hard-liners; the hard-line party [elements]; the tough elements; die-hards; 〈매파〉 the hawks ▶ 그는 강경파다 He is on the tough side.

강관 鋼管 a steel pipe [tube]
강구 江口 an estuary ⇨ 강어귀
강구 講究 consideration; contrivance
━강구하다 consider; provide 《a means》; contrive; devise 《a plan》; find [think, study] out
◆ 대책을 강구하다 take steps / 강력한 수단을 강구하다 take [adopt] hard [strong] measures
▶ 우리는 그런 사고에 대한 대응책을 강구해야 한다 We should take remedial measures to deal with such accident.
▶ 무엇을 해야 할지 모르기 때문에 아무런 대책도 강구하지 않기로 결정했다 Because we didn't know what to do, we have decided not to take any steps.

강국 強國 a great power; a strong [powerful] country [nation]; a leading country
◆ 경제[군사] 강국 an economic [a military] power (▶power에는 강국의 의미가 포함되어 있음)/ 세계 4대 강국 the four great powers of the world; the Big Four / 아시아의 강국 a strong [great] Asiatic power

강굽이 江━ a river bend; the crooks of a river

강권 強權 (the power of) authority; 〈법적인〉 legal authority; influence; 〈국가의〉 state power; the power of the state
◆ 강권적인 authoritarian / 강권을 발동하다 invoke the power of law 《against》; invoke legal authority [power] 《against》/ 강권을 발동하여 파업을 중지시키다 invoke the power of law to stop a strike
▶ 정부는 비상사태를 선포하고 강권을 발동했다 The government, declaring a state of emergency, took strong measures.
━발동 invocation of legal power ━정치 power [high-handed] politics ━주의 authoritarianism

강기 綱紀 official discipline ⇨ 기강(紀綱)
강기숙정 綱紀肅正 enforcement of official [government] discipline
▶ 강기숙정을 단행해야 한다 Official discipline should be enforced.

강기슭 江━ a riverside; the banks [shores] of a river
▶ 강기슭은 풀로 뒤덮여 있었다 The riverbank was overgrown with grass.

강낚시 江━ river fishing; fishing in a river
강남 江南 (the) south of a river; 〈서울의〉 south of the Han River; 〈양쯔강 남쪽〉 the south of the Yangtze
━지역 the area [district] south of a river; 〈서울의〉 the district south of the Han River

강낭콩 〈美〉 a kidney bean; 〈英〉 a French bean; a haricot (bean)

강다짐 1 〈맨밥을 먹음〉 forgoing the soup or other liquid *one* usually drinks while eating rice
━강다짐하다 eat boiled [cooked] rice without soup or water poured on it
2 〈까닭없이 나무람〉 scolding *sb* without listening to 〈his〉 side of the story
━강다짐하다 forcibly oppress and scold; scold [reprove] *sb* without reason
3 〈보수없이 부려먹음〉 forcing *sb* to work without pay ━강다짐하다 force *sb* to work without pay

강단 剛斷 〈결단력〉 decisiveness; determination; resolution; 〈끈기〉 tenacity; perseverance; toughness; stamina
◆ 강단지다 be quick in decision; be firm of purpose / 강단이 있다 have tenacity of purpose; be persevering; have the stamina (to keep on)

강단 講壇 a rostrum 《*pl*. ~s, -tra》; 〈학술의〉 a (lecture) platform; 〈설교의〉 a pulpit
◆ 강단에 서다 stand [appear] on a platform; take [occupy] the platform [rostrum]

강당 講堂 a lecture hall; 〈학교의〉 〈美〉 an auditorium 《*pl*. ~s, -ria》; 〈英〉 an assembly hall; 〈계단식〉 a lecture theater

강대국 強大國 a powerful country; a great [big] power ◆ 세계의 강대국들 the powers of the world

강대하다 強大━ powerful; (big and) strong; mighty
◆ 강대한 해군력 a mighty naval power / 강대해지다 become powerful

강도 剛度 〔物〕 (relative) stiffness
강도 強度 intensity; strength
◆ 지진의 강도 seismic intensity / 철사의 강도를 측정하다 measure the strength of wire
━시험 a strength test 《on a sample of steel》

강도 強盜 〈범인〉 a robber; a mugger; a burglar; a housebreaker; 〈행위〉 (a) robbery; (a) mugging; (a) burglary

[解説] **robbery**는 은행·상점·열차 등에서 강도질하는 것. **mugging**은 특히 거리·공원 등의 어둠 속에서 뒤에서 사람을 덮치는 것을 말하며 **burglary**는 야간에 남의 집에 무단 침입하여 강도질하는 것을 말한다.

♦ 흉기를 가진 강도 an armed robber / 노상 강도에게 털리다 be robbed by a highwayman ▶ 우리 집에 강도가 들었다 A burglar broke into my house. ⇌ My house was robbed. ▶ 그 좀도둑은 발각되자 위험한 강도로 변했다 The sneak thief turned into a dangerous robber when he was detected. ▶ 최근에 강도 사건이 종종 있다 There have been several robberies lately. ■권총— a holdup man; (美俗) a gunman; 〈행위〉 a holdup 무장— an armed robber 복면— a masked robber 은행— a bank burglar; 〈행위〉 bank robbery ■—단 a robber band —살인 burglary and murder

강도질 強盜— robbery; burglary ▶ 그들은 백주에 보석상에서 강도질을 했다 They robbed the jewelry store in broad daytime. ▶ 그것은 강도질이나 다름없다 It would be sheer robbery to do so. —**강도질하다** commit robbery; burglarize

강독 講讀 reading; translation ▶ 다음은 영어 강독 시간이다 We have English reading (class) next period. —**강독하다** read 《an English text》 ▶ 그는 대학에서 셰익스피어를 강독한다 He reads Shakespeare (with his class) at the university.

강둑 江— a riverbank; a river embankment; (美) a levee

강등 降等 demotion; downgrading; degradation —**강등하다** demote; degrade; downgrade ▶ 그는 술 때문에 사병으로 강등되었다 He was demoted to the rank of private for drunkenness.

강력 強力 great (physical) strength; power; might; 〈폭력〉 violence; force ♦ 초강력 수소 폭탄 a super-powerful hydrogen bomb [H-bomb] —**강력하다** strong; powerful; potent; 〈강대하다〉 mighty; 〈엔진 등이〉 high-power(ed) ♦ 강력한 반대 《meet with》 a stout [stubborn] opposition / 강력한 일격 a strong [crushing] blow / 강력한 팀 a strong team / 강력한 후원자 a powerful [a strong, an influential] supporter / 강력히 strongly; powerfully; 〈강경히〉 firmly; resolutely; stoutly ▶ 한국은 강력한 경제력을 갖게 되었다 Korea has had a mighty economy. ▶ 이 트럭은 엔진이 강력해서 산길에서도 안전하다 The engine of this truck is powerful enough to be quite safe on mountain roads. ▶ 그가 입후보를 선언했을 때 시민들은 강력히 지지했다 The citizens supported him strongly when he announced his candidacy. ■—계(係) 〈사람〉 an officer [official] in charge of crimes of violence; 〈부서〉 a section in charge of crimes of violence —범(犯) 〈사람〉 a criminal of violence; a major criminal; 〈죄〉 a crime of violence; a felony —비타민제 a high-potency vitamin preparation

강력분 強力粉 strong flour; extra-strength flour

강렬하다 強烈— intense; strong; powerful; severe ♦ 강렬한 색채 loud [hot] color / 강렬한 자극 a strong stimulus / 강렬하게 strongly; intensely ▶ 그 광경은 그에게 강렬한 인상을 주었다 The scene made a strong impression on him.

강령 綱領 〈기본 방침〉 general principles; 〈선언〉 declaration; 〈정강(政綱)〉 (美) a (party) platform; a plank 〈한 항목〉; (英) a party programme; 〈정책 방침〉 party lines ▶ 당 대회에서 새로운 강령이 채택되었다 A new platform was adopted at the party convention.

강론 講論 〈학술의〉 exposition; discussion; 〈교리의〉 preaching; teaching —**강론하다** expound; discuss; preach; teach

강림 降臨 descent; 〈그리스도의〉 the Advent ♦ 성령의 강림 the advent [descent] of the Holy Spirit [Ghost] —**강림하다** descend (to earth); come down ■—절 Advent

강마르다 dried-up; parched ♦ 강마른 논바닥 a dried-up paddy field

강매 強賣 aggressive peddling 《of goods》; coercive touting; (美) (the) hard sell ▶ 강매에 모두들 화가 났다 Everyone was angry at the hard sell. —**강매하다** force [press] sb to buy sth; force a sale on sb; push wares 《on》; tout ▶ 외판원은 그녀에게 화장품을 강매했다 The salesman forced her to buy cosmetics.

강멱 降冪 a descending power ⇨ 내림차

강모 剛毛 a bristle; a stiff hair; a seta 《pl. -tae》; a striga 《pl. -gae》 ♦ 강모가 많은 bristled; setose; bristly

강목 綱目 main points and details; an outline; 〈생물 분류의〉 class and order; divisions and subdivisions ♦ 강목을 나누다 classify; arrange in class

강물 江— river water ▶ 강물이 넘친다 The river overflows [is flooded]. ▶ 강물이 불었다 The river has risen [swollen].

강바닥 江— a riverbed [streambed]; the bottom of a river ♦ 강바닥에 가라앉다 sink to the bottom of a river

강바람 a strong, dry wind

강바람 江— a river breeze [wind]

강박 強迫 compulsion; coercion; duress ♦ 강박에 굴복하다 yield to coercion —**강박하다** coerce; compel; force 《sb to do》 ▶ 나는 자발적이라기 보다는 강박당해서 모금에 응했다 My donation was more forced than voluntary. ■—신경증 〔醫〕 obsessive [compulsive] neurosis

강박관념 強迫觀念 an obsession; a persistent idea [conception]
♦강박관념에 시달리다 suffer from an obsession
▶그는 누군가가 항상 자기를 보고 있지 않을까 하는 강박관념에 사로잡혀 있다 He is obsessed with [by] the idea that someone is always watching him.
▶그는 미행당하고 있다는 강박관념에 사로잡혀 있다 He is obsessed with the idea that he is being followed.

강반 江畔 bottomland; bottoms; 〈강가〉 a riverside; a riverbank; the bank [edge] of a river

강배 江— a riverboat; a rivercraft

강변 江邊 〈강가〉 a riverside
♦바다이 드러난 강변 a dry riverbed / 강변에 at the side of a river / 강변을 거닐다 walk along a river ■—도로 a riverside road [drive]

강변 強辯 a quibble; (a) sophistry
▶그런 식의 강변은 통하지 않는다 Such a far-fetched argument won't work.
—강변하다 quibble; reason against reason; insist obstinately 《on doing, that》; use a far-fetched argument
▶그는 그 시계가 자기 것이라고 강변했다 He insisted (obstinately) that the watch was his.
▶네가 아무리 강변해도 그 사실을 은폐할 수는 없다 You can argue as much as you like but you can't hide the facts.

강병 強兵 a strong soldier; 〈병력〉 a powerful [strong] army
■부국— enrichment and strengthening of a country : 부국 강병책 a measure to enrich and strengthen a country

강보 襁褓 a baby's quilt; swaddling clothes
♦갓난아이를 강보에 싸다 wrap a baby in swaddling clothes ■—유아 a baby [an infant] (in swaddling clothes)

강보합 強保合 ♦강보합의 〔證〕 (be) steady [firm] with an upward tendency

강북 江北 (the) north of a river; 〈서울의〉 north of the Han River ■—지역 the area [district] north of a river; 〈서울의〉 the district north of the Han River

강사 講師 〈강연회의〉 a speaker; a lecturer; 〈대학의〉 (美) an instructor; (英) a lecturer; 〈중·고교의〉 a part-time teacher; 〈심포지엄의〉 a panelist; the panel(강사단)
♦강사로 임명되다 be appointed a lecturer [to lectureship]
▶오늘은 강사가 누구입니까? Who is going to speak today?
■객원— a visiting lecturer 대학— a lecturer (on [in] English literature) at [of, in] a university; a college lecturer 시간— a part-time lecturer; 〈중·고교의〉 a part-time teacher 전임— a full-time lecturer

강삭 鋼索 a (steel) wire rope; a cable ♦강삭 철도 a funicular (railway)

강산 江山 rivers and mountains; 〈국토〉 a country; a land ♦삼천리 금수강산 the beautiful land of Korea, far and wide

강상 江上 〈물 위〉 (on) the surface of the river; 〈물가〉 (on) the riverbank ♦강상의 뗏목 rafts on the river

강샘 intense [unreasonable] jealousy
▶그 사람의 부인은 강샘이 있는 여자다 His wife is a jealous woman.
—강샘하다 feel a surge of unreasonable jealousy 《toward》; feel intense [burning] jealousy 《toward》; become intensely jealous

강선 鋼船 a steel vessel [ship, boat]
강선 鋼線 a steel wire
강설 降雪 snow; (a) snowfall
▶이것은 10년 이래 가장 큰 강설이다 This is the heaviest snowfall that we have ever had in the last ten years.
▶간밤에 100밀리미터의 강설이 내렸다 One hundred millimeters of snow fell last night.
▶영동지방 일대에 큰 강설이 있었다 There was a heavy snowfall throughout the Yŏngdong region.

강설량 降雪量 (the amount of) snowfall
▶올해는 강설량이 아주 적었다 We have had little snow this year.

강세 強勢 1 〔音聲〕 emphasis; (a) stress
♦강세가 있는[없는] 음절 a stressed [an unstressed] syllable / 강세를 두다 put [lay, place] emphasis 《on》; emphasize
▶3번째 음절에 강세를 두고 읽으시오 Read it with the stress on the third syllable.
2 〔樂〕 accent
3 〈시장·주식 시세의〉 a bull; a firm [high] tone; a bullish tendency [feeling, tone]; a strong feeling [market]
♦강세의 bullish; strong; firm; rising in price
▶오늘은 증권 시장이 강세다 Today a strong feeling prevails on the stock market.
▶시황은 오후에 강세로 돌아섰다 The market turned bullish in the afternoon.
■—시장 a bull market —주(株) bull shares

강속구 強速球 〔野〕 a fastball; a speedball; a smoke ball; (口) a fireball ♦강속구 투수 a strong-armed [speedball] pitcher; a smoke-ball hurler

강수 降水 rainfall; precipitation ■—밀도 rainfall density —시간 rainfall duration —확률 probability of precipitation —확률 예보 a rainfall probability forecast

강수량 降水量 〔氣〕 (the amount of) precipitation
▶한국은 연간 강수량이 많다 Korea has a high annual precipitation.
▶어젯밤에는 30밀리미터의 강수량을 보였다 There was precipitation of 30 millimeters last night.

강술 (have) a drink without any food; just liquor ♦강술을 마시다 have a drink without a relish

강술 講述 lecturing; expounding; an exposition —강술하다 lecture 《on》; give a lecture; 〈해설하다〉 expound

강습 強襲 a storm; an assault; 〔野〕 vehement attack ♦3루 강습 땅볼 a hot grounder to third baseman
▶그것은 3루를 지나는 강습 안타였다 It was a

sharply hit ball past third base.
―강습하다 storm; attack 《a castle》 by storm; 〈갑자기〉 assault
◆강습하여 점령하다 take [carry] 《a fort》 by storm [assault]
▶그 보병 중대는 적의 진지를 강습했다 The company of infantry made a raid [an assault] upon the enemy's camp.
강습 講習 a class; a (short) training course; studying
◆강습을 받다 attend a lecture class; take a course (of Korean); take lessons 《in swimming》; take classes 《in cookery》; join a seminar
▶여름에 수영 강습이 있다 A course in swimming is given in summer.
▶나는 하기 영어 강습을 받을 생각이다 I'm thinking of attending the summer course in English.
―강습하다 give a course (in, of)
■―생 a student; a trainee; (총칭) a lecture class ―소 a training school: 요리 강습소 a cooking school
강습회 講習會 a (short) course (of study); a (lecture) class; 〈전문적인〉 an institute; 〈실습회〉 a workshop
◆외국인을 위한 하계 한국어 강습회 a summer vacation course in Korean for foreigners / 강습회를 열다 offer courses 《in English》; hold an institute class
■ 교원― a teachers' institute 농업― (美) farmers' institute 동계[하계]― a winter [summer] school 영어― a course in English; an English class 프랑스 요리― the French cooking class
강신술 降神術 spiritualism; mediumism
■―사(士) a spiritualist ―회 a seance
강심 江心 the center [very middle] of a river
강심제 强心劑 a heart medicine [stimulant]; a cardiotonic (drug); (총칭) cardiotonics; a cardiac; a cordial
강아지 a little dog; (口) a pup; a puppy; a doggie
강아지풀 〔植〕 a foxtail
강안 江岸 a riverside; a riverbank ◆강안을 상류 쪽으로 걸어가다 walk up the riverbank
강안개 江― (a) river fog [mist]
강압 强壓 pressure; coercion; oppression
◆강압적인 high-handed; oppressive; 〈강제적인〉 coercive / 강압으로 유권자를 누르다 coerce voters with a high hand
▶그는 강압에 못이겨 그 일을 했다 He did it under pressure.
▶그의 태도는 매우 강압적이다 His attitude is very coercive.
―강압하다 put pressure [bring pressure to bear] on sb; coerce [(美) pressure] sb (into doing)
◆강압하여 복종시키다 coerce sb into submission
■―수단 high-handed [heavy-handed, coercive] measures; a strong-arm method ―정책 a high-handed [(美) big stick] policy
강약 强弱 〈힘의〉 strength and weakness; 〈음성의〉 (a) stress; (an) accent; 〈소리의〉 loudness
◆강약을 겨루다 contend for power [mastery]/ 강약을 넣어 읽다 read 《a sentence》 with the proper stress
▶이 시합에서 강약이 판명된다 This game will make it clear which side is (the) stronger.
■―격 (詩) trochee ―법 〔樂〕 dynamics ―부호 〔樂〕 an accent mark
강어귀 江― a river mouth; the mouth of a river; an estuary
강연 講演 a lecture; 〈연설〉 an address; a discourse
◆라디오 강연 a radio talk [lecture]/ 연속 강연 a series of lectures / 강연을 부탁하다 ask [invite] sb to give a lecture; ask sb to address [speak to] (students)
―강연하다 lecture [talk] 《on a subject》; give [deliver] a lecture 《on》; address 《a meeting》; make an address 《on》
◆라디오에서 강연하다 make a lecture over the radio 《on》
▶그는 역사학회에서 강연했다 He talked before the Historical Society.
▶그녀는 어제 텔레비전에서 강연했다 She gave a lecture on TV yesterday.
▶그는 미국의 역사에 대해 강연하기로 되어 있다 He is going to give [deliver] a lecture on American history.
■ 공개― a public lecture 시국― a lecture on the current topics ■―료 a lecturer's fee ―여행 a lecture tour ―자 a lecturer; a speaker ―회 a lecture meeting
강옥 鋼玉 corundum [kərʌ́ndəm] ⇨ 강옥석
강옥석 鋼玉石 〔鑛〕 corundum; ruby; sapphire
강온 强穩 toughness and moderateness
■―양면 정책 a carrot-and-stick policy ―양파 the tough elements [hardliners] and the moderates; the hawks and the doves
강요 强要 a forcible demand; coercion; exaction; extortion; compulsion
―강요하다 compel [force] 《sb to do》; 〈협박・압력 등으로〉 coerce [(口) high-pressure] 《sb into doing》; 〈지불・복종 등을〉 exact
◆기부를 강요하다 coerce sb into donating money / 노동을 강요하다 force labor 《upon sb》/ 복종을 강요하다 exact obedience from sb / 자백을 강요하다 extort [wring] a confession 《from sb》/ 강요당하다 be compelled [forced, driven] 《to do》
▶그는 나에게 뇌물을 강요했다 He exacted [extorted] bribes from me.
▶그는 그녀에게 즉시 지불[사직]하라고 강요했다 He demanded that she (should) pay for it [resign] immediately.
▶기부를 강요해서는 안 된다 We must not exact [demand] donations (from others).
강우 降雨 (a) rain; a rainfall; raining
◆많은[적은] 강우 an abundant [a scanty] rain(fall) / 심한 강우 heavy rain; (美) a downpour / 전국적인 강우 a general rainfall
▶금년에는 강우가 많았다[적었다] We have had much [little] rain this year.
▶강우로 경기가 중단되었다 The game was

강우량

interrupted because of rain.
■인공— artificial rain; rainmaking ■—대 a rain belt —도 a rainfall chart —분포 rainfall distribution —일 rain day —전선 a rain front

강우량 降雨量 the amount of rainfall; a rainfall (of 50 mm); (the record of) precipitation
◆중부 지방의 연간 강우량 the annual rainfall in the central districts
▶강우량이 적어서 저수지의 물이 줄었다 Lack of rain sank the reservoirs.
▶어제의 강우량은 30밀리였다 We had thirty millimeters of rain yesterday.

강음 強音 a strong sound; (詩) a beat; an ictus; 〔音聲〕 an accent; (a) stress

강의 講義 a lecture (on); a discourse; 〈해설〉(an) exposition; 〈설명〉 an explanation
◆현대 예술에 관한 강의 a lecture on modern art / 강의 준비를 하다 prepare one's lecture / 강의를 듣다 attend [be present at] a lecture / 강의를 빼먹다 cut [quit] a lecture; (美) play hooky / 강의를 시작하다 open one's course of lectures; start one's (series of) lectures / 강의를 필기하다 take notes on [of] a lecture
▶그녀는 학생들에게 영시에 관한 강의를 했다 She lectured [gave a lecture to] her students on English poetry.
▶나는 민 선생님 강의를 받고 있습니다 I am in Mr. Min's class.
▶그 학생들은 강의에 출석했다 The students attended the lecture.
—강의하다 lecture (on); expound; give a lecture (on); 〈연속으로〉 give a course (in German)
▶김 교수는 상대성 원리를 강의했다 Professor Kim expounded the theory of relativity.
▶그 교수는 대학에서 경제학을 강의하고 있다 That professor lectures [gives lectures] on economics at the university.
■공개— an open class; 〈대학의〉 an extension lecture [course] 문법— a lecture on grammar 한국사— lectures on Korean history ■—실 a lecture room

강의 強意 〈강조〉 emphasis ◆강의의 조사(助詞) a particle used for emphasis; an intensifying particle ■—어 〔文法〕 an intensifier; an intensive (word)

강의록 講義錄 a transcript of lectures; a lecture text; a correspondence course (in English)
◆강의록을 발행하다 offer [give] a correspondence course / 강의록으로 영어를 배우다 learn English by [through] correspondence; learn English on a correspondence [home-study] course

강인 強靭 toughness
—강인하다 tough; strong; tenacious; stiff; unyielding
◆강인한 의지 a tough spirit; a strong [an iron] will / 강인한 정신 a mind of steel / 강인한 신경을 가진 사람 a man of steely [iron] nerves / 강인하게 tenaciously; with toughness [tenacity]
▶그들은 강인하게 요새를 방어했다 They defended the fort tenaciously.
■—성 toughness, tenacity

강자 強者 a strong man; (총칭) the strong; the powerful ◆강자와 약자 the strong and the weak ▶강자가 언제나 승리하는 것은 아니다 The battle is not always to the strong.

강자성 強磁性 〔物〕 ferromagnetism ◆강자성의 ferromagnetic ■—체(體) a ferromagnetic body [substance]

강장 強壯 strong; lusty; robust; sturdy ◆그 분은 80세나 되었는데 아직도 강장하디 He is eighty years old but still in robust health.
■—음료 a tonic drink

강장동물 腔腸動物 〔生〕 a coelenterate [silént̬ərèit]

강장제 強壯劑 a tonic (medicine); a roborant; a cordial; (美俗) a pep pill ■—주사 a tonic shot : 강장제 주사를 맞다 have a tonic shot

강재 鋼材 steel (materials); 〈건축용〉 structural steel; 〈압연강〉 rolled steel ■ 반제품— semifinished steel products 재생— rerolled steel

강적 強敵 a powerful [formidable] enemy [adversary]; 〈경쟁의〉 a powerful [tough] rival [opponent, competitor]
◆강적과 싸우다 fight against a powerful enemy
▶준결승에서 한국 팀은 강적 독일 팀과 대전한다 In the semifinals, the Korean team faces tough opposition from the German team
▶그는 강적이었다 I found a formidable rival in him. ⇌ He was a strong opponent.
▶우리는 강적과 맞서지 않으면 안 된다 We have to confront a formidable enemy.

강점 強占 forcible occupation [possession] **—강점하다** occupy [possess] 《sb's house》 by force

강점 強點 a strong point; one's forte; one's strength; 〈이점〉 an advantage
◆강점과 약점 one's strong and weak points; one's forte and foible / …라는 강점이 있다 have the advantage of… / 남보다 강점을 갖고 있다 have an advantage over sb
▶그것이 그 사람의 최대 강점이다 That is where he is at his strongest.
▶그것은 무엇보다도 값이 싸다는 강점이 있다 Above all, it has the advantage of cheapness.
▶기억력이 뛰어나다는 데 그의 강점이 있다 His merit lies in his marvelous memory.
▶그의 강점은 재산이 막대하다는 것 뿐이다 His only strong point is his immense wealth.

강정 〈찹쌀 과자〉 a cake made of glutinous rice; a fried glutinous rice cake

강정제 強精劑 a tonic (medicine)

강제 強制 compulsion; coercion; constraint; enforcement
◆강제적(인) compulsory; coercive (measures); forced; mandatory; (口) pushy / 강제로 compulsorily; by compulsion; coercively; forcibly; 〈힘으로〉 by force; 〈고압적으로〉 overbearingly; high-handedly / 강제로 …시키다 coerce [force] sb into 《doing》; force [compel] sb to 《do》; exert coercion on sb to 《do》 /

강제로 결혼시키다 force sb into a marriage with 《another》 / 국회에서 법안을 강제로 통과시키다 ram a bill through the National Assembly
▶ 미국에서는 병역이 강제가 아니다 Military service is not compulsory in the United States.
▶ 그들은 그에게 강제로 서류에 서명하게 했다 They forced him to sign the paper.
▶ 나는 강제로 그의 명령에 따랐다 I obeyed his order under coercion.
—**강제하다** force; compel; coerce

解說 *force*는 「무리하게 무엇을 시키다」라는 뜻의 가장 일반적인 말. *compel*도 역시 무리하게 뭔가를 시킨다는 뜻이지만 force 보다는 강제의 정도가 약하다.

♦ 강제당해 on [under] compulsion; under pressure [duress]
■ —**가격** a forced price —**결혼** a forced marriage; a marriage by force —**경매** forced [compulsory] sale by auction —**공채** forced loan —**관리** compulsory administration —**력** compelling power [force]; 〈법적인〉 legal force —**매입** compulsory [forcible] purchase —**보험** compulsory insurance —**소개**(疏開) forced [compulsory] evacuation —**송환** enforced repatriation —**수색권** the official right to search —**이 행** compulsory performance —**접종** compulsory vaccination —**조정** compulsory mediation —**중재**〔勞〕 compulsory arbitration; legal intervention —**처분** disposition by legal force —**철거** forced demolition [dismantlement] —**통화**(通貨) forced currency; 〈법 화〉 legal tender —**해고** mandatory [forced] dismissal

강제노동 強制勞動 forced [compulsory] labor ♦ 강제노동을 과하다 impose forced labor 《on》 / 강제 노동을 시키다 force [compel] sb to work 《against his will》
■ —**수용소** a labor camp; a slave pen

강제수단 強制手段 a compulsory [coercive] measure; 〈소송 등의〉 a legal step ♦ 강제수단을 쓰다 appeal [resort] to compulsory measures

강제수용 強制收容 detention by legal force —**강제수용하다** put sb into custody; confine 《foreign nationals》 in a camp ■ —**소** a concentration camp

강제집행 強制執行 compulsory [forcible] execution; 〈압류〉 distraint; seizure; attachment —**강제집행하다** execute compulsorily; 〈압류하다〉 distrain
■ —**영장** a writ of execution; an execution; the final process —**정지** a stay of execution

강조 強調 (an) emphasis; (a) stress; accentuation
♦ 방화[방범] 강조 주간 Fire [Crime] Prevention Week
—**강조하다** emphasize; stress; accentuate; lay [place, put] emphasis [stress] 《upon》; underscore

♦ 평화를 강조한 연설 a speech stressing peace / 경제 개발의 필요성을 강조하다 stress [emphasize] the need of economic development / 국가 안보 문제를 강조하다 accentuate the idea of national security
▶ 선생님은 예습의 중요성을 강조하셨다 The teacher emphasized [stressed] the importance of making preparations for lessons.
▶ 작가는 작품의 그 부분을 특히 강조했다 The writer put a heavy stress on that part of the work.
▶ 이 책의 가치는 아무리 강조해도 지나치지 않다 You can't place too much stress on the value of this book.

강좌 講座 〈대학의〉 a (professor's [professorial]) chair; professorship; lectureship; 〈강습의〉 a lecture; a course
♦ 강좌를 개설하다 found [create, establish] a chair 《of》 / 국문학 강좌를 담당하다 hold [occupy] the chair of Korean Literature
▶ 박 교수는 미시간 대학에서 미 문학 강좌를 담당했다 Professor Park occupied the chair of American Literature at the University of Michigan.
■ —**가사[음악]**— lecture on housekeeping [music] **공개**— an extension course; an open lecture **라디오 영어**— a radio lecture [course] in English; a radio English course **성인**— an adult institute **특별**— a special course 《of English literature》 **현대 미술**— lecture on modern art

강주정 —酒酊 feigned drunkenness [intoxication]; an affected drunkenness
—**강주정하다** pretend to be drunk

강줄기 江— the course of a river ♦ 강줄기를 따라 걷다 walk along a river

강즙 薑汁 〈생강즙〉 ginger juice

강직 剛直 integrity; rectitude; probity; uprightness
—**강직하다** upright; unbending; incorruptible; staunch; have moral courage
♦ 강직한 사람 an upright man; a man of integrity [moral courage]
▶ 그는 강직하기로 유명했다 He was well-known for his integrity.

강직 強直 〈굳세고 정직함〉 integrity; uprightness; honesty; 〈시체 등의〉 rigidity; stiffness
♦ 사후 강직 cadaveric stiffness [rigidity]
—**강직하다** upright; honest; 〈시체 등이〉 stiffen; get stiff; become rigid
■ —**성 경련** tetanus

강진 強震 a very strong [severe, violent] earthquake; a severe shock [tremor] (of earthquake)
▶ 어젯밤 이곳에 강진이 있었다 We had a very strong earthquake here last night.
▶ 강진이 캘리포니아 지방을 심하게 뒤흔들었다 A severe earthquake jolted [rocked] the California District.
■ —**계**(計) a strong-motion seismograph

강짜 unreasonable [intense, burning] jealousy
♦ 강짜가 심한 여자 a jealous woman / 강짜를 부리다 show unreasonable jealousy

강철 鋼鐵 steel

강청

♦강철의 (made) of steel; steel / 강철제 선박 a steel-bound ship / 강철제 차 a steel-plated car / 강철 같은 마음 a heart of steel / 강철 같은 육체[의지] an iron physique [will] / 전부 강철로 된 all-steel (bridge) / 강철로 만들어지다 be made [built] of steel
■—관 a steel pipe [tube] —선(線) a steel wire —판 a steel plate [plank]

강청 強請 (make) an importunate [a persistent] demand (on sb)
—강청하다 demand persistently; importune ▶ 그는 나에게 기부금을 강청했다 He importuned me for contributions.

강체 剛體 〔物〕 a rigid body ■—역학 geostatics

강촌 江村 a riverside village

강추위 (a spell of) dry cold weather; a cold snap

강치 〔動〕 a sea lion; a hair seal

강타 強打 hard [power] hitting; a heavy [hard] blow; (美口) a slug; 〈크리켓·골프 등의〉 a swipe; 〈야구의〉 a heavy hit; a blast
♦강타를 퍼붓다 rain hard blows (on)
—강타하다 give sb a hard blow; hit hard; slog; swat (a ball)
♦어깨를 강타하다 strike sb a hard blow on the shoulder / 턱을 강타당하다 receive [get] a hard blow on the chin
■—자 〔野〕 a hard [power, long] hitter; (美口) a slugger

강탄 降誕 〈탄생〉 birth; nativity; 〈강림〉 advent; incarnation
♦예수의 강탄 the Nativity of Jesus Christ; the Advent / 그리스도 강탄절 Christmastide
—강탄하다 be born; be incarnated

강탈 強奪 extortion; 〈강도〉 robbery; 〈약탈〉 plunder; 〈선박·토지 등의〉 seizure; 〈수송 중의〉 (美口) hijacking; a hijack
—강탈하다 rob (sb of sth); seize (a ship); hijack (a plane); plunder
▶ 그들은 은행에서 3천만원을 강탈했다 They robbed the bank of thirty million won.
▶ 도둑들이 타이어 한 트럭을 강탈했다 The thieves hijacked a truckload of tires.
▶ 그는 10만원을 강탈당했다 He was robbed of one hundred thousand won.
■—물 plunder; spoil; booty —자 a mugger; 〈강도〉 a robber; a plunder; (美口) a hijacker

강태공 姜太公 〈낚시꾼〉 an angler; a Waltonian ♦강태공의 후예들 disciples of Sir Izaak Walton

강토 彊土 a territory; a realm; a domain

강판 鋼板 a steel sheet; sheet steel; 〈두꺼운〉 a steel plate

강판 薑板 a grater ♦강판에 갈다 grate (a radish)

강펄 江— bottomland; bottoms

강평 講評 (a) comment; (a) review; (a) criticism
▶ 나는 그의 연구에 대한 강평을 부탁받았다 I was asked to comment on his research.
—강평하다 comment [make comments] on; review

강포 強暴 ferocity; brutality; wildness —강포하다 hard and cruel; brutal; ferocious; fierce; ruthless

강폭 江幅 the width of a river ▶ 강폭이 100미터다 This river is a hundred meters across [wide, in width].

강풀 〈된풀〉 thick paste [starch] not tempered with water; undiluted paste [starch] ♦강풀치다 add a coat of paste [starch] to; overlay [coat] with thick paste [starch]

강풍 強風 a strong [high] wind; a violent wind; 〔氣〕 a gale
♦강풍을 만나다 encounter a gale / 강풍에 쓰러지다 be blown down in [by] a strong wind ▶ 강풍이 불고 있다 It is blowing hard. ⇌ The gail is blowing.
▶ 강풍에 담이 넘어졌다 The gail [strong wind] blew down the fence.
■—주의보 an advisory for gale; a strong-wind [gale] warning: 강풍 주의보를 내리다 issue a strong-wind warning

강하 降下 descent; a fall; a drop; 〈기압의〉 depression
♦급강하 sudden descent; a sudden fall; 〔空〕 nose diving / 기온의 강하 a drop in temperature
—강하하다 descend; 〈온도가〉 fall; drop; 〈착륙하다〉 land
▶ 어제 기온이 급강하했다 The temperature dropped sharply [fell suddenly] yesterday.
▶ 비행기가 고도 2천 피트로 강하했다 The airplane descended to a height [an altitude] of 2,000 feet.
■—각 an angle of descent —물질 fallout: 방사성 강하 물질 radioactive fallout (from a nuclear test) —지대 〈낙하산 부대의〉 a drop zone

강하다 強— 1 〈강력하다〉 strong; powerful; mighty; 〈튼튼하다〉 robust; stout; sturdy; 〈굳세다〉 firm
♦강한 나라 a strong [powerful] nation; a great power / 강한 신념 a firm belief / 강한 어조 an emphatic tone / 도덕심이 강한 사람 a person of strict morals [moral principles]; a virtuous person / 강하게 strongly; firmly / 심장이 강하다 have a strong [stout] heart / 책임감이 강하다 have a strong sense of responsibility / 강한 독일어 억양으로 말하다 speak with a strong [thick] German accent / 세력이 강해지다 increase in power / 강하게 나오다 show [assume] a firm [strong] attitude (toward); take a firm stand (against)
▶ 그는 의지가 강한 사람이다 He is a strong-willed man [man of strong will]. ⇌ He has a strong [an iron] will.
▶ 내 아이를 몸도 마음도 강한 아이로 키우고 싶다 I wish to bring up my child to be strong in mind and body.
▶ 그 나라에서는 정부가 민중의 강한 저항을 받고 있다 The government is strongly resisted in that country.
▶ 그는 정신력이 강한 사람이기 때문에 어떤 역경에도 굴하지 않을 것이다 Being strong-willed [strong-minded], he will not be subdued by any hardship.

▶운동을 하면 근육이 강해진다 Exercise strengthens muscles.
▶남자는 강하면서도 부드러운 맛이 있어야 한다 Strong manliness should be tempered with tender affection.
▶오늘 밤은 바람이 강하게 분다 It is very windy tonight. ⇌ The wind is blowing hard tonight.
2 〈…이 강점이다〉 ♦기계에 강하다 be good with machinery
▶그녀는 프랑스가[역사 과목이] 강하다 She is good at French [history].
▶그는 술이 강하다 He is a heavy drinker. ⇌ He drinks like a fish.
3 〈강력하다〉 strong; severe; intense
♦강한 감정 an intense feeling / 강한 빛 a strong [an intense] light / 강한 색채 a strong [an intense] color / 강한 술 hard [strong] liquor / 강한 인상 a deep [profound] impression
▶그는 내게 강한 인상을 심어 주었다 His image is deeply impressed on my mind.
4 〈저항력이 있다〉 resistant; tolerant
♦부식에 강한 금속 a metal that resists rust; a rust-resistant [rust-proof] metal / 추위에 강한 식물 a hardy plant / 질병에 강하다 be resistant [have resistance] to diseases / 추위에 강하다 have good resistance to cold
▶이 나무들은 공해에 강하다 These trees are tolerant of pollution.
▶이 건물은 지진에 강하다 This building is earthquake-proof.

강행 強行 enforcement; forcing
♦작업의 강행 rushing the work / 무리한 계획의 강행 the enforcement of an impractical plan
—**강행하다** force; enforce
♦폭우 속에서 경기를 강행하다 keep playing [start] a game in the downpour [in spite of the heavy rain] / 저물가 정책을 강행하다 enforce a low-price policy / 증세(增稅)를 강행하다 enforce a tax increase
▶우리의 반대에도 불구하고 그들은 그 정책을 강행했다 They enforced the policy in spite of our opposition.
▶그들은 위원회에서 표결을 강행했다 They forced a vote in the committee.

강행군 強行軍 (비유) an exhausting [a heavily-scheduled] trip [tour]
♦유럽을 일주하는 강행군 an exhausting tour around Europe
▶그것은 대단한 강행군이었다 It was a very rigorous schedule.
—**강행군하다** make [go on] a forced march
♦작업을 강행군하다 rush the work
▶강행군해서 걸으면 그 거리는 두 시간이면 갈 수 있을 것이다 If we walk as fast as we can, we may be able to cover the distance in two hours.

강호 江湖 〈강과 호수〉 rivers and lakes; 〈넓은 세상〉 the world; the (general) public; 〈은신처〉 a secluded place; 〈자연〉 nature

강호 強豪 〈선수〉 a powerful [an outstanding, an excellent] player; a veteran; an ace; 〈팀〉 a very strong team; (口) a powerhouse
♦전국에서 뽑힌 강호 팀 powerful teams selected from all over the country / 강호와 대전하다 compete with a powerful [an excellent] player; 〈강팀과〉 play against a strong [powerful] team

강호제현 江湖諸賢 the general public; people at large ♦강호 제현에게 호소하다 appeal to the public; call the attention of the general public to 《a fact》

강화 強化 strengthening; intensification; reinforcement; solidification; consolidation; 〈영양가의〉 enrichment; fortification
♦전력의 강화 buildup of war potential
—**강화하다** strengthen; 〈산업 등을〉 toughen; 〈단속 등을〉 enforce; tighten; 〈우호관계 등을〉 solidify 《friendly ties》; 〈구조·세력 등을〉 reinforce; 〈훈련 등을〉 intensify; 〈지위 등을〉 consolidate 《one's footing [position] in society》; fortify
♦국방을 강화하다 strengthen the national defenses / 군대를 강화하다 build up [reinforce] an army / 법률을 강화하다 tighten up the law / 불법 도박에 대한 단속을 강화하다 strengthen the enforcement of laws against illegal gambling / 체력을 강화하다 build up one's strength / 팀을 강화하다 strengthen a team; build up the strength of a team
▶그는 행정부 내에서의 발언권을 강화하려고 노력했다 He tried to strengthen his voice within the Administration.
■ —물 a fortifier —미[식품] enriched rice [food] —유리 tempered glass —제(劑)[化] a reinforcing agent

강화 講和 peace; (a) reconciliation
♦굴욕적인[명예로운] 강화 a humiliating [an honorable] peace / 강화를 맺다 conclude peace 《with》
▶양국간에 마침내 강화가 이루어졌다 The two countries finally made peace.
▶정부는 강화를 제의했다 The government made overtures of peace.
—**강화하다** make [conclude] peace 《with》; bury the hatchet; lay down one's arms; sheathe the sword
■ 단독— 《conclude》 a separate peace 전면— an overall peace
■ —조건 conditions of peace —협상 peace negotiations; negotiations for peace; a peace talk —회의 a peace conference

강화 講話 〈강의〉 a lecture; a talk; a discourse
♦논리학 강화 a lecture on logic
—**강화하다** lecture 《on》; give a lecture 《on》; address
♦국제 정세에 관하여 강화하다 lecture [give a lecture] on foreign affairs

강화사절 講和使節 a peace envoy [delegate]
■ —단 a peace mission [delegation]

강화조약 講和條約 《conclude》 a peace treaty [pact]; a treaty of peace
▶양국간에 마침내 강화 조약이 체결되었다 A peace treaty was finally concluded between the two countries.

강화훈련 強化訓練 intensified training

■ 합숙— intensified camp training : 대표선수들에게 합숙 강화 훈련을 실시하다 provide intensified camp training for the members of a (soccer) delegation

갖- 〈가죽〉 fur; leather ♦ 갖두루마기[저고리] a Korean overcoat (jacket) lined with fur

갖가지 a variety (of) ⇨ 가지가지

갖다¹ 1 ⇨ 가지다
2 〈가져다〉 ▶ 물 한 잔 갖다 다오 Get me a glass of water.

갖다² 〈구비하다〉 well [completely] equipped [furnished, provided]; have all sorts

갖바치 a maker of leather shoes; a shoemaker

갖바치 내일 모레 (속담) Don't count on the date that was promised.

갖신 〈가죽신〉 leather shoes

갖옷 clothes lined with fur; fur(-lined) clothes

갖은 〈모든〉 all; all sorts [kinds, manner] of; every possible; 〈빠짐없는〉 complete; perfect; 〈가지가지의〉 various; a variety of; 〈골고루 갖춘〉 (well-)assorted

♦ 갖은 고생을 하다 experience [go through] all kinds of hardships [troubles] / 갖은 수단을 다 쓰다 try every means available [conceivable]; try every possible method / 갖은 욕을 보다 suffer all sorts of humiliation / 갖은 죄를 범하다 have long list of criminal acts

▶ 그는 갖은 방법으로 그녀를 즐겁게 해 주었다 He entertained her in various ways.

▶ 갖은 방법으로 실험해 보았지만 나의 노력은 결실을 보지 못했다 I experimented in every possible way, but my efforts did not bear fruit.

—것 all sorts of things **—떡** 〈잘 만든〉 a well-made rice cake; 〈골고루 갖춘〉 assorted rice cakes **—소리** 〈온갖〉 unreasonable [unrealistic] words; 〈갖춘 척하는〉 self-conceited words **—양념** all sorts of spices; all-inclusive sauce

갖추 all; inclusively; completely; fully; with no omissions; leaving nothing (out)

♦ 세간살이를 갖추 들여놓다 get an assortment of household goods / 가게에 물건을 갖추 벌여 놓다 put out all kinds of goods in a store / 음식을 갖추 차리다 prepare a full-course dinner

갖추다 1 〈준비[구비]하다〉 get sth ready; arrange; prepare; furnish; equip; provide

♦ 형식을 갖추어 in accordance with formalities / 가구를 갖추다 get a complete suite of furniture / 도구 일습을 갖추다 get a complete set of tools / 무장을 갖추다 arm oneself; get under arms / 방어 태세를 갖추다 take a defensive attitude / 살림살이를 갖추다 furnish a house (with everything needed) / 갖가지 상품을 갖추다 keep a rich assortment of goods in stock / 필요한 서류를 갖추다 get all the necessary papers filled in / 근대적 설비를 갖추다 be equipped with modern conveniences / 떠날 준비를 갖추다 get ready to leave / 조건을 갖추다 meet [satisfy] requirements [conditions]

▶ 우리는 파티 준비를 모두 갖추었다 We got everything ready for the party.

▶ 우리는 야구 장비를 모두 갖추고 있다 We have got a complete set of baseball equipment.

▶ 나는 춘원의 작품을 빠짐없이 갖추고 있다 I have the complete works of Ch'unwon. ⇌ I have a complete set of Ch'unwon.

▶ 준비는 갖추어 있다 Our preparations are complete. ⇌ We are ready.

▶ 그 가게에는 각종 숙녀화가 갖추어져 있다 The store has a wide [large] choice of ladies' shoes. ⇌ They have various kinds of ladies' shoes in stock.

▶ 이 호텔에는 방마다 냉장고가 갖추어져 있다 Each room in this hotel is provided [furnished] with a refrigerator.

▶ 이 건물에는 소화기가 갖추어져 있지 않다 This building is not equipped with fire extinguishers.

2 〈지니다〉 possess; be blessed (with); be endowed (with talent)

♦ 풍부한[충분한] 지식을 갖추다 have a good [thorough] knowledge (of law)

▶ 그 사람은 문학적 재능[작곡의 재능]을 갖추고 있다 He is endowed with literary talent [the talent of composing music].

▶ 그는 훌륭한 지도자의 자질을 갖추고 있다 He possessed all the requirements of a good leader.

▶ 그는 미국인의 전형적인 장단점을 모두 갖추고 있다 He possesses both the typical strong and weak points of the American.

▶ 그들은 교사로서 충분한 자격을 갖추고 있다 They are well qualified as teachers.

▶ 그 여자는 아름다움과 지성, 그리고 건강을 모두 갖춘 여성이다 She is an all-round woman —beautiful, intelligent and healthy.

갖추쓰다 write (a Chinese character) in full stroke; omit nothing

갖풀 glue ⇨ 아교

같다 1 〈동일하다〉 the same; identical; one and the same; the selfsame

解說 the same은 같다는 뜻을 나타내는 일반적인 말. identical은 엄밀한 의미에서 외관이나 성질이 세부에 이르기까지 일치하고 있음을 말한다.

♦ 매년 같은 날에 on the same day every year / 거의 같다 be (very) much [almost] the same (as) / 꼭 같다 be the very same; be just the same / 같은 말을 몇 번이나 되풀이하다 say the same thing again and again; harp on the same string

▶ 내 경우도 같다 It is the same with me. ⇌ The same is the case with me.

▶ 그는 나이는 들었어도 마음은 젊었을 때와 같다 Though he is advanced in age, he remains the same in disposition as when he was young.

▶ 나는 그와 같은 학교에 다녔다 I attended the same school that [as] he did.

▶ 이 두 테이프에 들어 있는 목소리는 같은 목소리다 The voices on these two tapes are identical.

▶ 우리는 같은 잘못을 곧잘 저지른다 We are

apt to make the same kind of mistakes.
▶마크 트웨인과 사무엘 클레멘스는 같은 사람이었다 Mark Twain and Samuel Clemens were one and the same person.
▶나도 당신과 같은 생각입니다 I am of the same opinion as you (are).
▶[會話]「차 한 잔만 갖다 주세요」「나도 같은 것으로요」 "Please bring me a cup of tea." "The same for me [Same here], please."
▶그는 작년 여름에 입었던 것과 같은 재킷을 입고 있다 He is wearing the same jacket (that [as]) he wore last summer. ⇌ He is wearing the same jacket as last summer. (▶the same 다음에 절이 이어질 때 as는 같은 종류가, that은 동일물을 암시함)

2 〈동등하다〉 equal 《to》; uniform; equivalent 《to》
♦같은 금액 a like sum / 크기와 모양이 같은 꽃병 vases of uniform size and shape / 같은 입장에서 교섭하다 negotiate on equal terms
▶12펜스는 1실링과 같다 Twelve pence are equal to one shilling.
▶이런 경우 침묵은 승낙과 같다 Under these conditions silence amounts [is equivalent] to consent.
▶이 두 문장은 의미가 같다 These two sentences are equivalent in meaning.
▶그 두 공은 무게가 같다 The two balls are of equal [the same] weight.
▶그는 나와 키가 거의 같다 He is about as tall as I.

3 〈흡사하다〉 similar 《to》; like; alike
♦같은 생각을 가진 사람들 the like-minded (people) / 생김새가 같다 be exactly alike; be as like as two peas [eggs] / 새것과 같다 be as good as new / 성격이 같다 be of like disposition / 깨진 접시를 똑같은 것으로 대체하다 replace the broken dish with an identical one
▶형과 나는 식성이 같다 My brother and I have similar tastes in food.
▶그 사람은 거지나 같다 He is no better than a beggar.
▶이것은 내겐 사형 선고와 같다 This is as much as [tantamount to] a death sentence to me.
▶그것은 산에 가서 물고기를 찾는 것과 같다 You might as well go to a tree for fish.

4 〈동종이다〉 of the same kind [sort]; like; such...as
♦당신 같은 부자 such a rich man as he / 당신 같은 사람 a man like you; the likes of you / 떡 같은 것 something like a rice cake / 이와 같은 물건 an article of this kind [sort] / 장난감 같은 것 toys or the like / 서울 같은 대도시에 in a large city, such as Seoul
▶그는 그와 같은 말을 할 사람이 아니다 He is not the (sort of) man to say such a thing.
▶그는 네가 생각하는 것과 같은 대학자는 아니다 He is not such a great scholar as you think.
▶나는 연미복 같은 것은 없다 I don't have such a thing as a dress coat.
▶그는 일요일 같은 날에는 자주 찾아오곤 했다 He would call on me of a Sunday.
▶너는 학교 선생님 같은 사람이 될 수 있겠니? Can you be a teacher or anything like that?

5 〈추측〉 seem; appear; look; likely 《to do》
▶눈이 올 것 같다 It is likely to snow.
▶비가 온 것 같다 It looks as though it has rained.
▶그의 일이 무척 힘든 것 같다 His job seems to be very hard.
▶저건 북소리 같다 That sounds like a drum.
▶그는 아무리 보아도 공무원 같다 He is an officeholder to all appearance(s).
▶그는 이 사실을 모르는 것 같다 He seems [appears] to be ignorant of this fact.
▶내가 뭐 같으냐? What do you take me for?
▶나도 할 수 있을 것 같다 I feel I can do it.

6 〈공통〉 common
♦같은 마을 사람 a fellow townsman / 기원이 같다 have a common origin 《with》
▶자식을 사랑하는 마음은 어느 부모나 같다 Love for their own children is common to all parents.
▶그들은 국적은 다르지만 이해 관계는 같다 They differ in nationality, but their interests are common.

7 〈가정〉 if it were; in case
♦나 같으면 if it were me; if I were you / 옛날 같으면 if these were the old days
▶나 같으면 그런 짓은 안 한다 (If I were you,) I would not do such a thing.
▶그런 경우 너 같으면 어떻게 하겠니? What would you do in such a case?

8 〈…답다〉 like; worthy of; worth 《doing》
♦사람 같은 사람 a real man / 집 같은 집 a house worthy of the name; a house that is really [can really be called] a house
▶이 부근에는 공원 같은 공원이 없다 There is no park around here to speak of [worth mentioning].

9 〈비유〉 like; as
♦산더미 같은 파도 a mountain of a wave; a mountainous wave / 샛별 같은 눈 eyes like stars / 악마 같은 사내 a devil of a man / 어머니 같은 애정 motherly love / 천사 같은 소녀 an angel of a girl
▶아직 2월인데도 오늘은 정말 봄 같다 It's really springlike today, though it's still February.
▶도시 전체가 하나의 커다란 공원 같다 The whole city strikes us as one big park.
▶그것은 너무 꿈 같은 이야기여서 믿을 수가 없다 It's such a dreamlike story that I can't believe it.

같은 값이면 other things being equal; if it is all the same 《to》; preferably
▶같은 값이면 영어를 배우겠다 As long as the other things are equal, I would rather learn English.
▶같은 값이면 큰 것을 갖겠다 I will take the larger one, if I must take either.
▶같은 값이면 해변으로 가는 것이 좋겠지 You might as well go to the beach if you're going anywhere.
▶같은 값이면 다홍치마 《속담》 Other things being equal, choose the better one.

같이 1 〈같게〉 in the same way [manner]; likewise; like...; as...
▶그녀는 자기 어머니 같이 음식 솜씨가 좋다 She cooks well as [like] her mother does.
▶만약 내가 너 같이 행동하다가는 만인의 웃음거리가 될거다 If I were to behave like you, I would be laughed at by all.
▶그녀와 같이 그도 신앙심이 없었다 Like her, he had no religious feeling.
2 〈함께〉 ▶우리는 같이 여행했다 We traveled together.
▶會話「혼자 여행하십니까?」「아니오, 아들 내외랑 같이 다닙니다」 "Are you traveling on your own?" "No, my son and his wife are with me."
▶잠깐 기다려, 나하고 같이 가자 Wait a minute and I'll come with you.
▶같이 커피 한 잔 안 할래? Will you join us for a cup of coffee?
3 〈동시에〉 at the same time
▶두 가지 일을 같이 하지 마라 You must not do two things at a time.
▶우리는 같이 도착했다 We have arrived at the same time.
▶모자가 같이 건강하다 Mother and child are both doing well.
4 〈동등하게〉 equally; alike; 〈공평하게〉 impartially; 〈차별없이〉 indiscriminately
♦이익을 같이 나누다 divide profit equally [in equal part]
▶나를 그런 친구들과 같이 취급하면 섭섭하다 I don't like to be treated with such men.
5 〈…처럼〉 like; as; as...as; (not) so...as
▶그들은 개미같이 일하고 있다 They are working like (so many) ants.
▶그는 토끼같이 겁쟁이다 He is (as) timid as a rabbit.
▶그는 이제 전 같이 힘이 세지 않다 He is no longer as strong as he was. ⇒ He is not as [so] strong as he used to be.
6 〈그대로〉 like; as
♦아래와 같이 as (stated) below / 위와 같이 as (stated) above / 아시는[보시는] 바와 같이 as you know [see] / 여느때와 같이 as usual / 종전과 같이 as before

같이하다 share *sth* with; participate [take part] in; partake of
♦고락을 같이하다 share joys and sorrows [*one's* fortunes] with / 마음을 같이하다 be of one mind / 이해를 같이하다 have common interests (in *sth* with *sb*) / 일생을 같이하다 share *one's* life; be *one's* life companion [partner] / 때를 같이하여 at the same time [hour]; in the same instance
▶우리는 점심을 같이했다 We had lunch together.
▶그 둘은 의견을 같이하고 있다 The two of them have [are of] the same view [opinion].
▶나는 그와 운명을 같이 할 작정이다 I'm going to share my fate with him.

같잖다 〈주제넘다〉 impertinent; saucy; pert; 〈시시하다〉 trivial; insignificant; worthless; absurd; of no account
♦같잖은 물건 a no-good thing; a worthless

object; a trash / 같잖은 수작을 하다 talk nonsense; say silly [absurd] things / 같잖은 일로 화를 내다 get angry at trifles
▶그런 같잖은 녀석과는 사귀지 마라 Don't make friends with such a worthless [useless] fellow.
▶그는 같잖게도 그 사람들에게 말대꾸를 했다 He was impertinent enough to talk back to them.

갚다 1 〈빚 등을〉 pay back; repay; return; give back; refund
♦빚을 갚다 pay back [repay] *one's* debts / 빚을 다 갚다 clear off *one's* debts / 같은 물건으로 갚다 pay *sb* back in kind / 세 배로 쳐서 갚다 repay *sb* three-fold / 빚을 품으로 갚다 work out a debt
▶그는 내게 빚을 갚으라고 독촉했다 He urged me to pay back [repay] my debt.
▶꾸어간 돈을 갚으시오 Please repay me the money you borrowed.
▶빚을 갚을 기한이 되었다[지났다] The debt falls due [is overdue].
2 〈보답하다〉 repay 《another's kindness》; return; requite 《favors》; 〈보상하다〉 recompense *sb* for; compensate 《for》; repair; 〈보복하다〉 retaliate; revenge; avenge(▶revenge는 가해자에 대한 개인적 원한의 앙갚음을, avenge는 피해자를 대신한 당연 또는 정당한 보복을 의미함)
♦아버지의 원수를 갚다 avenge *one's* father's murder / 은혜를 갚다 repay *sb* for his kindness [favors]; return another's kindness / 똑같은 방법으로 갚다 return [requite] like for like / 받은 만큼 갚다 give as good as *one* gets / 주먹을 주먹으로 갚다 measure for measure; give blow for blow; meet force with force / 손해를 갚아주다 compensate for [recompense] the damage; repair [indemnify for] the loss
▶그들은 그 여자의 원수를 갚기로 결심했다 They decided to revenge [avenge] her death.
▶은혜를 원수로 갚으면 못쓴다 It is not good to return evil for good [bite the hand that feeds you].
▶그분의 은혜를 어떻게 갚으면 좋을까? How can I repay him for his kindness?

갚음 〈선행의〉 (a) reward; (a) return; (a) recompense; (a) compensation; 〈악행의〉 retribution; (a) punishment
▶그것은 당연한 갚음이다 That serves you right.
▶당신의 고운 마음씨에는 언젠가 갚음이 있을 것입니다 Your kindness will be someday rewarded fairly.

개[1] 〈포구〉 the tidal reaches 《of a river》; the mouth of a river; an inlet; an estuary; a cove; an embayment

개[2] [動] a dog; a canine [kéinain]; 〈암캐〉 a bitch; 〈사냥개〉 a hound; 〈똥개〉 a mongrel (dog); a cur; 〈애칭〉 a doggy; a doggie; 〈앞잡이〉 a tool; a cat's-paw; 〈밀고자〉 an informer
♦멍멍 bowwow; a doggie / 재주 부리는 개 a performing dog / 개돼지 같은 놈 a brute; an utter pig / 개의 canine / 개 같은 doggish;

doglike / 개에게 재주를 가르치다 teach a dog tricks
▶ 그는 나를 개 취급하듯 했다 He treated me like a dog.
▶ 그런 것은 개도 안 먹는다 Even a dog will turn up its nose at it.
▶ 그 놈은 개만도 못한 놈이다 He is worse than a beast.
▶ 개조심 (게시) Beware of the dog!; Beware — Fierce [Vicious] dog.
〈개가[는]〉 개가 짖는다 A dog is barking.
▶ 개는 반드시 매놓으시오 Be sure to keep your dogs on a leash [tied].
▶ 그 개는 낯선 사람을 보면 짖는다 The dog barks at strangers.
▶ 짖는 개는 물지 않는다 (속담) Barking dogs seldom bite.
〈개를〉개를 기르다 have [keep] a dog / 개를 풀어주다 let a dog loose / 쇼에 나갈 수 있도록 개를 훈련시키다 train a dog for a show
▶ 그는 개를 데리고 산책을 나갔다 He went out for a walk with a dog.
▶ 나는 매일 아침 저녁으로 개를 산책시킨다 I walk my dog every morning and evening.
━띠 (the year of) the Dog ━목걸이 a dog collar ━백장 a dog butcher [killer] ━싸움 a dogfight ━썰매 a dogsled ━애호가[사육가] a dog fancier; a kennelman; a dogman ━전시회 a dog [bench] show ━줄 a dog lead; a leash ━집 a kennel [kénl]; a doghouse

개

늘어진 귀 leather
귀 ear
허리 loin
코 nose
기갑 withers
등 back
엉덩이 rump, croup
코부분 muzzle
꼬리 tail
앞가슴 brisket
앞발 foreleg
뒷발 hind leg

개 個 a piece; a unit
♦ 비누 다섯개 five bars [cakes] of soap / 의자 다섯개 five chairs / 개당 가격 a unit price / 개당 50원 fifty won each [apiece]
■ 테이블에 사과가 세개 있다 There are three apples on the table.
▶〔會話〕「오렌지는 몇 개나 드릴까요?」「다섯 개만 주세요.」 "How many oranges do you want?" "Five, please."
▶ 이 복숭아는 한개에 천원이다 These peaches are one thousand won each.
개가 改嫁 〈재혼〉 remarriage 《of a woman》; deuterogamy [djùːtərágəmi]; digamy ♦ 개가를 권하다 advise 《a woman》 to remarry ━개가하다 remarry; marry again [second time]
개가 開架 open [free] access; open shelves; an open stack ■ ━식 도서관 an open-access [open-stack] library ━식 열람실 an open-shelf [open-stack] reading room
개가 凱歌 a triumphal [victory] song; a paean [píːən]
♦ 민주주의의 개가 a triumph for democracy / 개가를 부르다 sing in triumph; sing a triumphal tune / 개가를 올리다 win a victory 《over》; be victorious 《over》
▶ 그들은 개가를 올렸다 They raised [gave] a shout of triumph [victory].
개각 介殼 a shell; shells ━류 the shellfish; the Crustacea [krʌstéiʃiə] ━충 〔昆〕〈깍지벌레〉 a scale (insect); a coccid
개각 改閣 a cabinet reshuffle [shake-up]
♦ 일부 개각 a partial cabinet reshuffle / 전면 개각 a sweeping cabinet reshuffle / 개각을 단행하다 reshuffle [reorganize] cabinet portfolios
━개각하다 reshuffle the cabinet
개간 開墾 clearing; cultivation; reclamation 《of wasteland》
▶ 숲의 일부가 개간 중이다 A piece of land in a forest is being cleared for cultivation.
━개간하다 reclaim 《wasteland》; bring 《wasteland》 under cultivation; break up the soil
♦ 황무지를 개간하다 clear [reclaim] wasteland
■ ━계획 a development [reclamation] program ━사업 reclamation (work) ━지 a cultivated area; a reclaimed land
개감스럽다 ravenous; greedy; voracious ♦ 개감스럽게 먹다 devour; wolf *one's* food; gobble / 개감스럽게 다 먹어치우다 gobble up
개갑 介甲 1 〈거북 등의〉 a shell; a crust; a carapace [kǽrəpèis] 2 ⇨ 갑옷
개강 開講 beginning *one's* lectures; beginning school
▶ 3월 3일 개강 (게시) Lectures (will) begin on March 3rd.
━개강하다 begin 《a series of》 lectures 《on Western philosophy》; open a course 《in English》
▶ 월요일부터 개강한다 The classes will begin on Monday.
개개 箇箇 ♦ 개개의 individual; each; separate 《problem》; several / 개개로 one by one; separately; individually
▶ 개개의 문제에 관해 얘기할 시간이 없다 I don't have time to discuss each problem.
▶ 의사는 환자들을 개개로 진료했다 The doctor gave individual attention to each patient.
개개비 〔鳥〕 a reed warbler
개개인 箇箇人 individuals; each and every person
개거 開渠 an open channel [sewer, conduit]
개고기 1 〈개의 고기〉 dogmeat; dog flesh 2 〈막된 사람〉 a pest; a plague; a scoundrel; a hooligan; a blackguard
개골 unreasonable [unprovoked] anger; a

개골개골 nasty temper ◆개골내다 get into rage; get angry 《with *sb*》

개골개골 ▶개구리가 개골개골 울고 있었다 Frogs were croaking [singing, chirping].

개골창 〈배수로〉 a drain; a gutter; a sewer; 〈도랑〉 a ditch ◆개골창을 치다 clear (out) a ditch

개과 改過 reformation; 〈회개〉 repentance 《for *one's* sins》; contrition 《for》; remorse; penitence
◆개과 천선한 죄인 a reformed criminal / 개과 천선시키다 reform *sb*; reclaim 《a criminal》
▶개과 천선하면 죄를 용서받는다 Repentance wipes out sins.
―개과하다 〈잘못을 고치다〉 correct a fault; reform 《*oneself*》; 〈개회하다〉 feel remorse; repent 《of *one's* sins》; renounce 《*one's* former sins》; become [feel] penitent

개관 開館 the opening 《of a hall》
◆개관 첫날의 입장객 수 the number of people who entered the hall on the day of its opening / 개관 중이다 be open
▶개관 일시: 월요일부터 금요일, 오전 11시부터 오후 5시까지 Opening Hours : Monday through Friday, 11-5.
▶오전 9시 개관 (게시) Open at 9 a.m.
―개관하다 open 《a hall [building]》
▶도서관은 오전 9시에 개관한다 The library opens at 9 a.m.
■―시간 the opening hour ―식 the opening ceremony 《of a library》; (an) inauguration

개관 槪觀 〈개괄적 고찰〉 a general view [survey]; 〈윤곽·대요〉 an outline; a conspectus
◆역사적 개관 a historical survey
―개관하다 survey; take a general [bird's-eye] view 《of》; make a general survey 《of》; give a conspectus 《of》
▶우리는 국제 정세를 개관해 보았다 We surveyed the international situation.

개괄 槪括 a summary; a summing up; the generalization
◆개괄적인 general; generalized / 개괄적으로 in general; generally
―개괄하다 summarize; sum up; generalize
◆개괄해서 말하면 generally speaking; on the whole; to sum up; in short
▶현재의 상태는 몇마디로 개괄해서 말할 수 없다 The present situation cannot be summed up in a few words.

개교 開校 the foundation [opening] of a school ▶이 학교는 개교 50주년이 된다 This school has been open for fifty years.
―개교하다 open [found, inaugurate, start] a school
▶그 학교는 언제 개교합니까? When will the school be ready?
■―기념식 the opening ceremony of a school ―기념일 the anniversary of the foundation of a school

개구 開口 ―개구하다 〈입을 벌리다〉 open *one's* mouth; 〈말하기 시작하다〉 begin *one's* speech; open *one's* case
■―기(器) 〔外科〕 a mouth gag ―음 〔音聲〕 a broad

개구리 a frog; 〈식용의〉 a bullfrog ◆식용 개구리 an edible frog / 개구리 같은 froggy; frog-like ▶개구리가 울고 있다 A frog is croaking [chirping, singing].

개구리매 〔鳥〕 a marsh harrier

개구리밥 〔植〕 a duckweed

개구리 올챙이 적 생각 못한다 〈속담〉 An upstart will often forget his old pinching times. ⇌ Danger past, God forgotten.

개구리자리 〔植〕 a ditch [cursed] crowfoot

개구리참외 〔植〕 a spotted cantaloup(e)

개구리헤엄 the breaststroke ▶너 개구리헤엄 칠 줄 아니? Can you swim with the breast stroke [on your chest]?

개구멍 a doghole (in the wall [gate]) ■―바지 baby trousers with a slit in the bottom ―받이 a baby abandoned [deserted] by the doghole; a baby left at the doghole

개구쟁이 a brat; a naughty [an unruly] boy; a mischievous boy; an urchin; an imp
◆개구쟁이짓 naughtiness; brattiness / 개구쟁이짓을 하다 play pranks 《on *sb*》
▶사내 아이들은 대개 개구쟁이다 Most boys are rather mischievous.
▶우리 아이는 한창 개구쟁이 때라서 당해낼 수가 없어요 We cannot do anything with our boy now that he is at a mischievous age.
▶이 개구쟁이 녀석아 You little devil!

개국 開國 〈건국〉 the foundation of a state; 〈개방〉 the opening 《of Korea》
―개국하다 found [establish] a country [state]; 〈개방하다〉 open a country (to foreign intercourse [the world])
■―공신(功臣) a meritorious retainer at the founding of a dynasty ―주의 the open-door policy

개국하다 開局― open [set up, establish] a (new) post office [broadcasting station]

개그 〈익살〉 a gag ◆개그를 넣다 crack jokes; (put a) gag / 개그를 내뱉다 pull gags
▶그는 개그를 잘 한다 He is good at telling gags.
■―만화 comics full of gags ―맨 a gagman; a gagster

개근 皆勤 perfect attendance 《for three years》; non-absence
―개근하다 attend regularly (without missing a single day); be not absent a single day
▶나는 올해 학교를 개근했다 I have never been absent from school this year.
▶그는 지난 20년간 회사를 개근했다 He has not missed a single day of work for the past twenty years.
■―상[상장] a reward [certificate] for perfect attendance ―자 a person who has not missed a day 《at school [office]》

개기 皆旣 ―식(蝕) 〔天〕 a total eclipse; totality ―일식[월식] 〔天〕 a total solar [lunar] eclipse

개기 開基 1 〈터를 닦음〉 laying a foundation; groundbreaking ―개기하다 level [smooth] the ground; lay a foundation
2 〈절을 세움〉 ⇨ 개산(開山) ―개기하다 found a temple ▶이 절은 원효 대사가 개기했다 This

temple was founded by Saint Wonhyo.

개기름 (natural) grease on *one's* face; (skin) oil; oiliness
♦개기름이 흐르는 얼굴 an oily face [complexion]/개기름이 번질번질하고 뒤룩뒤룩 살찐 50대 남자 an oilyfaced fleshy man in his fifties

개 꼬리 삼년 두어도 황모 못 된다 《속담》 You can't make a silk purse out of a sow's ear.

개꼴 〈체면이〉 disgrace 《to》; dishonor; shame 《on》; a stain 《on》; 〈모양이〉 wretched condition; shabbiness
♦개꼴이 되다 be a disgrace to 《*one's* family》; be put to shame; bring disgrace upon *oneself*; bring shame on *oneself*

개꿈 an empty dream; a silly [wild] dream

개나리 〔植〕 a forsythia
▶개나리는 봄의 상징이다 The forsythia is the symbol of the spring.

개념 概念 a notion; a general idea; a conception; 〔哲〕 a concept; an idea
♦미(美)의 개념 notions of beauty / 사회라는 개념 the concept of society / 한국인의 행복의 개념 a Korean's idea of happiness / 개념적 사고 conceptual thinking / 개념적인 conceptional; notional / 개념상〔적으로〕 notionally; conceptually / 개념화하다 conceptualize / 문제를 개념적으로 파악하다 get a general idea of the matter
▶우리는 자유에 대한 명확한 개념을 가지고 있어야 한다 We should have a clear conception [concept] of freedom.
■기본— fundamental notions ■—론 conceptualism ■—론자 a conceptualist ■—실재론 realism ■—작용 conception

개다¹ 1 〈날씨가〉 become clear; clear up; 〈그치다〉 hold up; stop 《raining, snowing》
♦갠 날씨 clear weather / 어느 갠 날 아침 one fine morning / 구름 한 점 없이 맑게 갠 하늘 a cloudless [serene] sky
▶아침에는 비가 왔지만 그후 갰다 It rained in the morning but the sun came out later.
▶하늘이 맑게 개어 별이 총총하다 The sky is clear and the stars are out.
▶날씨가 갤 것같다 The weather looks [is] promising.
▶내일은 갤 것이다 It will be fine [nice] tomorrow. ⇒ It will clear up tomorrow.
2 〈기분이〉 be refreshed; cheer up
▶이것 때문에 기분이 갰다 This made me refreshed.
▶산책을 하면 기분이 갤 것이다 Taking a walk will cheer you up.

개다² 〈개키다〉 fold (up); turn down
♦옷을 개다 fold *one's* clothes / 이부자리를 개다 fold up [put away] the beddings / 다시 개다 refold
▶그는 담요를 반듯하게 갰다 He folded the blanket neatly.

개다³ 〈물에 풀어지게〉 knead [ní:d] 《with water》; 〈진흙 등을〉 work 《clay, mortar》; pug
♦진흙을 개다 knead [pug] clay / 페인트를 기름에 개다 dissolve paint in oil / 풀을 물에 개다 thin [temper] paste with water

개다래 a fruit of the silvervine ■—나무 〔植〕 a silvervine

개다리 a dog's leg ■—상제 an ill-mannered mourner ■—소반〔밥상〕 a small dining table with cabrioles ■—질 hateful kicking; mean and nasty conduct

개도국 開途國 〈개발 도상국〉 a developing country

개도 나갈 구멍을 보고 쫓아라 《속담》 Don't back him into a corner.

개떡 a pie-shaped cake made of coarse barley flour; a bran cake

개떡같다 ♦개떡 같은 녀석 a fellow of no account; a worthless fellow; 《美俗》 a punk / 개떡 같은 소리를 하다 talk nonsense [rubbish]/개떡 같이 여기다 make [think] nothing of; do not care a bit 《about》

개똥 〈개의 똥〉 dog dung [droppings]; a dog turd; 〈천한 것〉 trash; rubbish
♦개똥 같은 수작 nonsense; utter trash / 개똥 같다 be trash; be not worth a damn; be rubbishy
■—번역 crude [unidiomatic] translation ■—상놈 a vulgar [mean] fellow ■—참외 a wild melon ■—철학 a mockery of philosophy

개똥도 약에 쓰려면 없다 《속담》 Sometimes it is difficult to get something very common for emergency use. ⇌ When one comes to look for it, one finds it very hard to come at.

개똥밭 1 〈땅이 건 밭〉 a rich [fertile, fruitful] field 2 〈더러운 곳〉 a dirty place; a squalid place

개똥밭에 이슬 내릴 때가 있다 《속담》 Every dog has his day.

개똥밭에 인물 난다 《속담》 A great person may be born of perfectly ordinary parents.

개똥벌레 〔昆〕 a firefly; a glowfly; lightning beetle [bug]; 〈애벌레〉 a glowworm

개똥지빠귀 〔鳥〕 a thrush; a dusky ouzel [thrush]

개똥 참외도 먼저 맡는 이가 임자다 《속담》 Finding's keeping.

개략 概略 an outline; a summary; an epitome; 〈논문 등의〉 a résumé
♦개략적인 견적 (get) a rough estimate / 개략적인 rough 《copy》; broad 《outline》 / 개략적으로 말하면 roughly [generally] speaking
▶그는 그 사건의 개략을 말했다 He gave an outline of the event.
■—개략하다 give an outline 《of》; outline; summarize; epitomize

개량 改良 (an) improvement; amelioration; betterment
♦품종개량 〈가축의〉 improvement of a breed; 〈식물의〉 plant breeding
■—개량하다 improve; make *sth* better; ameliorate; reform 《a method》
♦품종을 개량하다 improve the breed 《of an animal》 / 종래의 방식을 개량하다 improve on [upon] the traditional method
▶그는 그 기계를 개량하려고 했다 He tried to improve the machine.
▶우리는 이 제도를 개량해야 한다 We must

make this system better.
▶ 개량할 여지가 있다[많다] There is some [much] room for further improvement.
▶ 이 타이프라이터는 많이 개량되었다 Great improvement has been made in this typewriter.
■ 사회— social reform 토양— soil amendment [enrichment] —농지 improved [reclaimed] farmland —종 an improved variety [breed]; a select breed —주의 reformism —형 an improved model

개런티 〈출연료〉 a guarantee; payment

기력 改曆 a reform [revision] of the calendar; 〈새해를 맞음〉 seeing the old year out and the new year in

개론 槪論 an outline (on); general remarks [considerations]; 〈개관〉 a survey (of); 〈입문〉 an introduction (to)
◆ 개론에서 각론으로 들어가다 descend from generalities to particulars
—개론하다 outline; give an outline [a survey, a summary account] (of)
■ 동물학[영문학]— an introduction to zoology [English literature]

개막 開幕 〈막을 올림〉 the raising of the curtain; the commencement of performance; 〈시작〉 the opening
◆ 스키 시즌의 개막 the opening of the ski season / 임시 국회의 개막 the opening of an extraordinary session of the National Assembly / 개막 중에 during the performance; while the performance is going on
—개막하다 raise [draw up] a curtain; begin [commence] the performance
▶ 오전 10시에 개막된다 The curtain rises [is raised] at 10 a.m.
▶ 주간 흥행은 3시, 야간 흥행은 6시에 개막된다 A matinee begins at 3 p.m. and a soiree from 6 p.m.
▶ 만국 박람회는 서울에서 3월 1일 개막된다 The International Exhibition will open on the 1st of March in Seoul.
—경기[전] a season opener; an opening game [match] —극 a curtain raiser [lifter] —시간 the time of the rising of the curtain —식 the opening ceremony [pageant] (of the Olympic Games) : 개막식 예행 연습 an opening ceremony rehearsal

개머루 〔植〕 a wild grape [vine]; an ampelopsis

개머리 〈총의〉 the gunstock; the stock ■—판 a butt plate [end]

개명 改名 changing one's name; rechristening
—개명하다 change one's name (to); rename (from A to B); be renamed
▶ 너는 언제 상호에서 민호로 개명했니? When did you change your name from Sang-ho to Min-ho?
■—신고 (send in) a report of one's changed name

개명 開明 civilization; enlightenment —개명하다 be [become] civilized; be enlightened
◆ 개명한 나라 a civilized country
■—시대 an enlightened age; the age of civilization

개무하다 皆無— ◆ 법률 지식이 개무하다 be utterly ignorant of law; have not the least knowledge of law
▶ 그들이 생존해 있을 희망은 개무하다 There is no hope of their being still alive.
▶ 나는 그 일에 관한 예비지식이 개무하다 I have no previous knowledge of the subject.
▶ 그가 승진할 가망은 개무하다 He has no chance whatever of being promoted.
▶ 시합에 이길 승산은 개무했다 We had no chance of gaining the game.

개문 開門 the opening of the gate —개문하다 open the gate [door] ▶ 오전 9시에 개문한다 The gate opens at 9 a.m.
■—발차 the starting (of a bus) with doors open

개미[1] 〈연줄에 먹이는〉 *gaemi*; powdered glass [porcelain] mixed with glue ◆ 개미 먹이다 strengthen [coat] (kite strings) with powdered glass [porcelain]

개미[2] 〔昆〕 an ant; a pismire
◆ 개미의 행렬 a line [trail] of ants / 개미의 formic / 개미처럼 일하다 work like an ant
▶ 회의장에는 개미 새끼 하나 얼씬거릴 수 없었다 The security in [around] the hall was very tight.
▶ 마을은 개미 새끼 하나 들어갈 틈도 없이 포위되었다 The town was closely besieged (by the enemy).
▶ 땅에는 개미가 득시글거리고 있었다 The ground was crawling with ants.
■ 병정— a dinergate; a soldier (ant) 여왕— a queen (ant) 일— a worker [slave] ant ■—구멍 an ant hole —굴 an ant tunnel —귀신 〔昆〕 an ant lion; a doodlebug —떼 a swarm [colony] of ants : 사람들이 그 여자 주위로 개미떼처럼 몰려들었다 People swarmed around her like ants. —마을 a colony of ragpickers —지옥 an ant lion's pit —집 an ant's nest —허리 (a beauty with) a wasp [slender] waist : 허리가 개미 허리 같은 여인 a wasp-waisted lady

개미 구멍으로 공든 탑 무너진다 (속담) A little leak will sink a great ship. ⇒ The burrowing of an ant can undermine an embankment.

개미 금탑 모으듯 한다 (속담) save up little by little

개미산 —酸 〔化〕 formic acid ＝의산(蟻酸), 포름산

개미 쳇바퀴 돌듯 한다 (속담) go [turn] round and round without getting anywhere
▶ 논의는 개미 쳇바퀴 돌듯 했다 The argument went round (and round) in circles without getting anywhere.

개미핥기 〔動〕 an anteater

개밋둑 an ant mound; an anthill; an ant heap; a formicary [fɔ́ːrməkèri]

개발 〈개의 발〉 a dog's paw

개발 開發 1 〈자원 등의〉 exploitation; 〈경지 등의〉 cultivation; 〈신제품의〉 development; 〈우주 등의〉 exploration
◆ 저개발국 an underdeveloped [a less developed] nation [country] / 개발을 촉진하다

facilitate development
—**개발하다** develop 《a new machine [backward region]》; open up 《a country》; exploit 《natural resources》; cultivate; tap 《a district》 ◆ 새로 개발한 기술 a newly-developed technique / 신제품[에너지 절약형 자동차]을 개발하다 develop new products [an energy-saving car]
▶ 해저 자원을 개발하기 위해 한층 더 노력해야 한다 We should redouble our efforts to develop our undersea resources.
▶ 우리는 천연 자원을 개발해야 한다 We have to exploit our natural resources.
2 〈계발〉 enlightenment; development —**개발하다** develop; enlighten ◆ 지능을 개발하다 develop the intellectual faculties
■ 경제— economic development : 경제개발 5개년 계획 a 5-year economic development plan 국토— land development 우주— space development : 우주 개발 계획 a space exploration [development] program 자원— resource development 전원(電源)— development of power resources —계획 a development project [program, plan] 《in Africa》 —교육 developmental education —금융 development credit —도상국 a developing country —비 development costs —사업 development works —수출 development export —원조 development aid —유보 지역 a reserved development district —융자 development loan —자 developer; an explorer —자금 a development fund —전략 development strategies —제한 구역 limited development district —차관 기금 development loan fund 《略 DLF》 —촉진 지역 development-promoted district

개발에 편자라 《속담》 Caviar(e) to the general. ≒ It is like casting pearls before swine.
개방 開放 opening; throwing open; 〈허용〉 lifting the ban
◆ 문호 개방주의[정책] the open-door principle [policy] / 성격이 개방적인 frank; open; candid; openhearted 《person》
—**개방하다** open; 〈열어 두다〉 leave 《the door》 open
◆ 문호를 개방하다 open doors 《to》 / 운동장을 개방하다 throw open a playground to the public
▶ 이 홀은 일반인에게 개방되어 있다 This hall is open to the public.
▶ 혁명 후 그 궁전은 미술관으로 국민에게 개방되었다 After the revolution, the palace was opened to the people as a museum.
■ —대학 an open college —도시 an open city —요법 open-air treatment —현 〔樂〕 an open string
개방성 開放性 openness; 〔醫〕 patency; persistence ■ —결핵 open tuberculosis
개버딘 〔織〕 gaberdine (fabrics)
개벽 開闢 〈천지 창조〉 the Creation; the beginning of the world; 〈천지가 뒤집힘〉 a convulsion of nature
◆ 천지 개벽 이래 since the beginning of the world; since the beginning of time; since the world began / 천지 개벽이 되어도 though the heavens fall
▶ 개벽 이래의 대 풍작이다 This is the best crop that has ever been.
—**개벽하다** 《the world》 be created; 〈천지가 뒤집힘〉 《nature》 be convulsed
개변 改變 (a) change; (an) alteration; (a) renovation; innovation; reformation —**개변하다** change [alter] 《a system》; renovate; make a change
개별 個別 ◆ 개별적(인) individual / 개별적으로 individually; severally; separately; 〈하나 하나〉 one by one / 개별 행동을 취하다 act independently [each for himself] / 개별적으로 말하다 talk *sth* over separately / 개별적으로 학생과 면담하다 meet and talk with the students individually
▶ 우리는 그 문제를 개별적으로 검토하기로 했다 We decided to consider those problems one by one [separately].
▶ 그들은 개별적으로 결정을 해야 했다 Each of them had to decide independently [for themselves].
■ —개념 〔哲〕 a distributive concept —심사 individual screening; polling 《by a jury》 —지도 individual guidance
개병 皆兵 universal conscription ◆ 국민 개병 제도 a universal conscription system
개복 開腹 —**개복하다** cut the abdomen open; 〔醫〕 perform a laparotomy
■ —수술 an abdominal operation : 개복수술을 받다 undergo an abdominal operation [a laparotomy]
개복치 〔魚〕 an ocean sunfish; a headfish
개봉 開封 1 〈편지의〉 opening [unsealing] 《a letter》
—**개봉하다** open 《a letter》; break the seal; unseal 《a letter》
◆ 편지를 개봉하지 않고 반송하다 send back [return] a letter unsealed [unopened]
▶ 크리스마스 카드를 개봉한 채로 보내도 된다 You can send a Christmas card unsealed.
2 〈영화의〉 a release; a first run; a premiere
—**개봉하다** release [premiere] 《a film》
◆ 아주 최근에 개봉된 한국 영화 a very recently released Korean film
▶ 이 영화는 세계 최초로 개봉되는 것이다 This is the world premiere of the film.
■ —관 a first-run movie house [theater]; a first-runner : 이곳은 개봉관으로 유명하다 This hall is noted for new releases. —영화 a first-run [newly-released] film [movie]; a release : 개봉 영화 시사회 a trade show
개불알꽃 〔植〕 a lady's slipper
개비 a piece of split wood [timber] ◆ 성냥개비 a matchstick / 장작 세 개비 three pieces of split firewood
개비 改備 a renewal; replacing
—**개비하다** renew; replace 《one thing by [with] another》; refixture; refurnish 《a room with a new wardrobe》
▶ 그들은 낡은 컴퓨터를 새것으로 개비했다 They have replaced their old computers with [by] new ones.
개산 開山 〔佛敎〕 〈절을 세움〉 founding [estab-

lishing] of a Buddhist temple
―개산하다 found [establish] a Buddhist temple
■―날 the dedication day of a Buddhist temple ―조사(祖師) the founder of a Buddhist temple; the originator

개산 概算 a rough calculation [estimation] ⇨ 어림(~셈)

개살구 a wild apricot

개새끼 1 〈개 새끼〉 a pup 《of a dog》; a puppy 2 ⇨ 개자식

개서 改書 1 〈고쳐 쓰기〉 rewriting; 〈고쳐 쓴 것〉 a rewrite
―개서하다 rewrite; write over again
2 〈어음·증서 등의〉 (a) renewal; 〈명의의〉 (a) transfer
◆ 〈주식의〉 명의 개서를 정지하다 close the transfer ledger
―개서하다 renew 《a bond [bill]》
▶ 그는 별장을 아들 앞으로 명의 개서했다 He transferred his cottage to his son.
―어음 a renewed bill

개선 改善 (an) improvement 《of service》; a change for the better; reformation; reform; (a) betterment
▶ 조금도 개선의 흔적이 보이지 않는다 It shows no sign of improvement.
―개선하다 improve; reform; (make sth) better
◆ 세제를 개선하다 improve the taxation system / 한·중 외교 관계를 개선하다 improve diplomatic relations between Korea and China
▶ 그는 체질을 개선하기 위해 노력했다 He tried to improve his constitution.
▶ 선거 방법은 좀더 개선할 여지가 많다 There is considerable room for improvement in the election process.
▶ 노인 복지가 개선되었다 The old men's welfare was improved.
■ 근로 조건― betterment [amelioration] of working conditions 생활― the improvement of living conditions 시설― improvement in accommodation 시정(市政)― civic betterment 처우― better treatment ■―책 a remedy; a reform measure

개선 改選 〈선거〉 reelection; 〈개편〉 reshuffle
◆ 임원 개선 the reshuffle of (the board of) directors / 반수 개선 reelection of half the members 《of the Senate》
―개선하다 reelect (the members)
▶ 우리는 의장을 개선하기로 결정했다 We decided to reelect the chairman.

개선 疥癬 〔醫〕 (have) the itch; (suffer from) scabies 〈단수 취급〉; 〈소·개 등의〉 mange [méindʒ]
■―충 an itch [a scab] mite

개선 凱旋 a triumphal return
―개선하다 return in triumph [with glory] 《to Seoul》; make a triumphal return 《to》; return from a victorious campaign
▶ 장군은 아일랜드에서 개선했다 The general made a triumphal return from Ireland.
■―가 a triumphal song; a paean ―군 returned troops [army]; victorious [victor] troops ―문 a triumphal arch; 〈파리의〉 the Arc de Triomphe ―식 a triumphal celebration ―열병식 a triumphal military review ―용사 a returned hero ―장군 a triumphant general : 개선 장군과 같은 환영을 받다 receive [return to] a hero's welcome ―행렬 a triumphal procession [parade]

개설 開設 establishment; 〈공식적인〉 inauguration; opening
―개설하다 establish; set up; inaugurate; open
◆ 사무실을 개설하다 set up an office / 신용장을 개설하다 open an L/C 《with a bank》 / 연구실을 개설하다 establish a laboratory
▶ 우리는 서울―모스크바간 신항로를 개설했다 We opened a new airline between Seoul and Moscow.
▶ 은행에 계좌를 개설해 주세요 Please open an account with the bank.
▶ 그 은행의 지점이 교외에 개설되었다 A branch of the bank was established in the suburbs.

개설 概說 〈대요〉 a general statement; an outline; a summary; 〈서설〉 an introduction 《to a subject》
―개설하다 give an outline [a summary account] 《of》; make a summary 《of》; treat 《a subject》 in outline
▶ 그 강좌는 1800년에서 1900년까지의 영문학을 개설한다 The course surveys English literature from 1800 to 1900.

개성 改姓 a change of one's family name [surname] ―개성하다 change one's family name [surname]

개성 個性 individual character; individuality; one's personality; idiosyncrasy; characteristic traits
◆ 개성이 강한 사람[뚜렷한 배우] a person [movie star] of strong individuality [distinct personal character] / 개성이 없는 사람 a man with no individuality / 개성적인 (a man) with a great deal of personality; (a work) marked by one's strong individuality / 개성을 기르다 [억누르다] develop [stifle] one's personality [individuality] / 개성을 발휘하다 show [display] one's originality / 개성을 존중하다 [무시하다] respect [disregard] sb's individuality
▶ 그는 개성이 있다 He has personality.
▶ 그는 개성이 뚜렷한 사람이다 He is a man of striking [remarkable] individuality.
▶ 그 작품 속에는 그녀의 개성이 뚜렷이 나타나 있다 The work is characterized by her personal taste [marked by her strong individuality].
▶ 옷은 그 사람의 개성을 나타낸다 Dress expresses the wearer's individuality.
■―교육 individual upbringing [education] ―주의 personalism

개소 個所 〈장소〉 a place; a spot; a site; 〈지점〉 a point; 〈부분〉 a part; a portion; a passage 《문장의》 ◆ 몇 개소에 물이 범람하다 be flooded in several places

개소리 silly [foolish] talk; nonsense; rubbish
▶ 무슨 개소리야 What arrant nonsense!
▶ 개소리 하는군 You talk nonsense.

▶개소리 하지 마라 Nonsense! ⇌ Don't talk nonsense [rubbish].
개수 一水 dishwater ⇨ 개숫물
개수 改修 〈수리〉 repair; mending; 〈개량〉 improvement 《of》
▶그 도로는 지금 개수 중이다 The road is now under repair.
―**개수하다** repair 《a building》; mend; improve 《a road》
▶그들은 막대한 비용을 들여 그 다리를 개수했다 They improved [repaired] the bridge at enormous [huge] cost.
■―공사 repair work
개수 個數 the number 《of articles》
▶개수가 얼마나 됩니까? How many (pieces) are there?
▶이 물품은 개수에 관계 없이 살 수 있습니다 You can buy as many of these articles as you like.
개수 槪數 round numbers ⇨ 어림(~수)
개수작 一酬酌 silly words; nonsense; rot ▶개수작 마라 Nonsense! ⇌ Stuff (and nonsense)!
개수통 一水桶 a dishpan; a dishwasher bucket
개술 槪述 giving an outline [a summary]; summarizing ―**개술하다** give an outline 《of》; summarize; sketch 《its》 outlines
개숫물 dishwater; dishwash; slops ♦개숫물을 버리다 empty a dishpan
개시 開市 1 〈시장을 엶〉 opening up a market; opening a fair
―**개시하다** open a fair; open up a market
2 〈마수걸이〉 the first sale of the day; an opening sale
▶오늘 아침에는 아직 개시도 못했다 We've sold nothing so far [We haven't made a sale yet] this morning.
―**개시하다** make the first sale of the day
■―손님 the first customer [buyer] of the day
개시 開始 beginning; start; commencement; 《口》 go-off; opening; inauguration ⇨ 시작
♦공격 개시일[시간] 〔軍〕 the D-day [zero hour]/시합 개시 the beginning [start, opening] of the game / 개시부터 from the outset / 개시가 좋다 make a good start
―**개시하다** open 《a game》; begin; commence; start 《business》; inaugurate 《bus service》
♦공격을 개시하다 open [launch, mount] an attack 《on, against》/ 시판을 개시하다 begin to sell / 작업을 개시하다 begin [start] work / 행동을 개시하다 go into action
▶그 노선은 15일부터 운행을 개시한다 The line will be opened to traffic on the 15th.
▶그 문제에 관해 우리는 미국과 교섭을 개시할 작정이다 We are going to open [enter into] negotiations with the U.S. over the matter.
▶그 회사는 머지 않아 영업을 개시할 것이다 The company will start business before long.
개식 開式 the opening of a ceremony ―**개식하다** open a ceremony ■―사(辭) an opening address (of a ceremony)
개신 改新 (a) renovation; (an) innovation; 《carry out》 (a) reform; (a) renewal ―**개신하다** renovate; innovate; renew; reform

개신교 改新敎 Protestantism
개심 改心 reform; amendment; 〈회개〉 repentance
―**개심하다** reform *oneself*; mend *one's* ways; turn over a new leaf
♦범인[비행 소년]을 개심시키다 reclaim [reform] a criminal [juvenile delinquent]
▶그녀는 완전히 개심했다 She has completely reformed herself.
▶그는 개심할 가망이 없다 He is incorrigible. ⇌ He is past praying for [beyond reclaim].
■―자 a reformed man; a penitent
개악 改惡 a change for the worse
♦세법의 개악 an undesirable [a detrimental] revision to [of] the tax law
―**개악하다** change *sth* for the worse; make *sth* worse
▶그 규정은 개악되었다 The regulations have been changed for the worse.
개안 開眼 1 〈눈을 뜸〉 opening *one's* eyes; 〈눈이 보이게 됨〉 gaining eyesight
―**개안하다** recover *one's* sight
2 〔佛敎〕 〈진리를 깨달음〉 spiritual awakening; enlightenment; 〈개안 공양〉 enshrinement of a newly-made Buddhist image; a ceremony to consecrate a newly-made Buddhist image
♦대불 개안 the consecration of a huge image of Buddha
―**개안하다** come enlightened; be awakened 《to a fact》; be (spiritually) enlightened; open *one's* eyes to 《the beauty of...》
■―수술 an eyesight recovery operation
개암 〔열매〕 a hazelnut; a filbert ―나무 〔植〕 a hazel (tree) ―사탕 hazelnut candy
개양귀비 一楊貴妃 〔植〕 a field [corn] poppy
개어귀 an estuary; the mouth of a river; an entry to a river
개업 開業 the opening [commencement] of (a) business [a trade]
♦개업 10주년 기념 대매출 a tenth anniversary sale / 개업 중이다 〈상점 등이〉 be open; 〈의사·변호사 등이〉 be in practice
▶그는 개업 내과의다 He is a physician in practice.
―**개업하다** start (a) business; establish *oneself* [set up] in business; open a store; 〈의사·변호사가〉 start [go into] practice
▶그 은행은 내일 개업합니다 The bank begins business tomorrow.
▶그는 변호사를 개업했다 He began a lawyer's practice. ⇌ He established himself as a lawyer.
▶그 병원은 언제 개업했습니까? When was the doctor's office opened?
■―비 the initial cost of business ―식 the opening ceremony ―안내 the announcement of opening a business ―의(醫) a medical practitioner; a practicing doctor [physician]
개역 改譯 retranslation; revision ―**개역하다** retranslate; revise [correct] a translation
■―성경 the Revised Version of the Bible ―자 a retranslator ―판 a revised version
개연성 蓋然性 probability ♦개연성이 높다 be highly [very] probable

개오 改悟 repentance; reformation ◆개오의 눈물 repentant tears ━개오하다 repent of *one's* sin; reform (*oneself*)

개오 開悟 〔佛教〕 prajna; spiritual awakening; (attainment of divine) enlightenment ━개오하다 be spiritually awakened 《to》; attain enlightenment

개오동나무 ━梧桐━ a catalpa; an Indian bean

개와 蓋瓦 1〈기와〉a tile 2〈지붕을 임〉roofing; tiling

개요 概要 〈개략·요약〉an outline; a summary; an epitome; a synopsis;〈논문 등의〉a resume [rézəmèi]
◆사건의 개요 (give *sb*) an outline [a summary] of the event / 세계사 개요 the outline of world history
▶이것이 그 사건의 개요입니다 This is the long and the short [the gist] of the matter.

개운 開運 opening up of good fortune [luck]; the betterment of *one's* fortune; improvement of *one's* lot [fortune]
━개운하다 bring good luck; have fortune on *one's* side

개운하다 1〈상쾌하다〉(feel) refreshed; feel well [fine]
▶이제 몸이 개운하다 Now I feel refreshed.
▶푹 자고 나니 머리가 개운해졌다 My mind was refreshed after a good sleep.
2〈마음이〉feel relieved; feel free and easy
▶일을 마치고 나니 개운하다 I feel easier [relieved] after I have finished my work.
3〈맛이〉simple; plain; refreshing

개울 a brook; a brooklet; a little stream; a streamlet;(美) a creek

개원 改元 the change of (the name of) an era [a dynasty] ━개원하다 change the name of an era; change a dynasty

개원 開院 1〈국회의〉the opening of the National Assembly [a National Assembly session]
━개원하다 open the National Assembly
2〈병원·학원의〉the opening (of a hospital)
━개원하다 open (a hospital)
▶그 자동차 [요리] 학원은 오늘 개원합니다 The drivers' [cooking] school opens today.
■━식 the opening ceremony (of the National Assembly)

-개월 -個月 ◆전치 3개월의 부상 a wound that will take 3 months to heal completely
▶1년은 12개월이다 There are twelve months in a year.
▶이 아이는 태어난 지 1년 6개월 되었습니다 It has been one year and six months since this child was born.

개의하다 介意━ mind; care [worry] about; be concerned about; trouble [concern] *oneself* about; pay attention to
◆비용을 개의치 않고 regardless of expense; without regard to cost / 남들이 어떻게 생각하든 개의치 않고 no matter what other people (may) think
▶나는 의복에는 개의치 않는다 I don't care about my clothes.
▶그는 칭찬이나 비난 따위에는 개의치 않는다 He is indifferent to praise or blame.
▶그 여자는 남들이 뭐라든 개의치 않았다 She didn't mind [care] what people said of her.
▶그는 우리가 아무리 조롱을 해도 전혀 개의치 않는 것 같았다 He never seemed to mind, no matter how much we kidded him.
▶성패에 개의치 말고 최선을 다해라 Do your best without worrying about the results.

개인 改印 a change of *one's* seal ━개인하다 change *sb's* (registered) seal ■━신고 a notice of the change of *one's* seal

개인 個人 an individual;〈사인(私人)〉a private person [citizen]
◆개인의〈개개의〉individual; personal;〈사적인〉private / 개인의 권리[자유] personal right [freedom] / 개인 또는 법인 〔法〕 a natural or juridical person / 개인적인 생각 a personal view / 개인적으로 individually; personally; in person / 개인 자격으로 in *one's* private capacity / 개인 면담을 하다 talk personally (with); have a personal interview (with)
▶이 타월들은 개인용이다 These towels are for individual use.
▶이것은 내 개인 재산이다 This is my personal property.
▶이것은 개인의 힘으로는 될 수 없다 This can not be done by individual effort.
▶개인의 권리를 침해하지 마라 Don't infringe on the rights of the individual [the individual's rights].
▶그것은 개인적 취향의 문제다 It's a matter of individual taste.
▶이것은 내 개인적인 문제다 This is my private affair.
▶나는 그녀와 개인적인 이야기를 하고 싶다 I'd like to have a personal talk with her.
▶나는 그와 개인적으로 관계가 없다 I have no personal relations [contact] with him.
▶우선 그녀를 개인적으로 만나 보겠습니다 First of all I'll meet her privately.
■━감정 personal feeling : 개인 감정에 지배되다 be affected by personal feeling [prejudice] ━경기 an individual sport [event] ━경영 private management ━관계 personal relations ━기(技)(be excellent in) individual skill ━기업 a private enterprise ━문제 a private affair; a personal matter ━사정 personal reasons : 그녀는 개인 사정으로 사직했다 She resigned from her post for personal reasons. ━소득 an individual [a personal] income ━소식란〈신문의〉personals; personal columns ━소지품 〔法〕 personal effects ━수표[어음] a personal check [bill] ━숭배 the personality cult ━심리학 individual psychology ━용 컴퓨터 a personal computer ━의견 personal opinion; private views : 내 개인 의견으로는 in my personal opinion ━전 (戰)〈경기의〉a game between individuals; a tournament series in single ━종목 an individual event ━종합 경기〈체조의〉individual combined exercises ━주택 a private house [residence]; an individual home ━차(差) differences among individuals; individual varia-

tions ━택시 an owner-driven [owner-operator] taxi : 개인 택시 운전 기사 an owner-operator cabby [cabman] ━통신망 personal communication network ━회사 a private firm [company] ━휴대 통신 personal communication service (略 PCS)

개인교수 個人教授 private lessons [instruction]; individual instruction [tuition]; tutoring (at *one's* own home) ▶나는 수학 개인 교수를 받고 있다 I'm taking private lessons [(英) tuition] in mathematics. ▶피아노 개인 교수 (게시) Piano lessons given. ━개인교수하다 give private lessons 《to》; coach; tutor
━료 a fee for separate lessons

개인전 個人展 a private [personal] exhibition; a one-man show [exhibition] ▶그는 남산화랑에서 개인전을 연다 He will have [give, hold] an exhibition of his pictures at Namsan Gallery.

개인주의 個人主義 individualism ◆개인주의적인 individualistic; 〈이기적인〉 egoistic; selfish ▶그 여자에게는 개인주의적인 데가 있다 There is something individualistic in her.
━자 an individualist

개인지도 個人指導 individual tuition; personal guidance ━개인지도하다 give personal guidance 《to》; tutor

개인플레이 個人━ a personal action ━개인플레이하다 act personally; 〈단체 경기에서〉 demonstrate *one's* personal skill

개입 介入 intervention; interference
━개입하다 intervene [interfere] 《in a dispute》; meddle 《in a matter》
◆내전에 개입하다 intervene in a civil war / 타국에 무력 개입하다 use military force to intervene in another country / 외환 시장에 개입하다 intervene on the foreign exchange market
▶다른 사람의 일에 개입하지 마라 Don't meddle [intervene] in other people's affairs.
━군사━ military [armed] intervention

개자리 〔植〕 a bur(r) clover; a snail clover; a medic

개자식 ━子息 〈욕으로서〉 a son of a bitch; an S.O.B.

개작 改作 (an) adaptation 《from, for》; recasting; rewriting
━개작하다 adapt 《*King Lear* for the Korean stage》; recast 《a story》; rewrite
◆소설을 방송용으로 개작하다 adapt a novel for broadcasting
▶그는 그 소설을 연극용으로 개작했다 He adapted the story for the stage.
▶이것은 세익스피어의 작품을 개작한 것이다 This is an adaptation from one of Shakespeare's works.
━자 an adapter

개잠 sleeping curled up (like a dog) ◆개잠자다 sleep curled up; curl (*oneself*) up (in a ball)

개잠 改━ a sleep [dozing off again] after waking up once in the morning ◆개잠들다 [자다] fall [sink] into a sleep [drop off to sleep] again after waking up once

개장 改葬 **1** 〈고쳐 다시 장사지냄〉 reinterment; reburial ━개장하다 reinter; rebury ◆유해를 개장하다 reinter [rebury] *sb's* remains **2** ⇨ 이장(移葬)

개장 改裝 **1** 〈새롭게 꾸밈〉 redecoration; (美) remodeling
━개장하다 redecorate; remodel; refurbish; 〈현대식으로〉 modernize
◆점포를 개장하다 redecorate [remodel] a store / 낡은 저택을 개장하여 호텔을 만들다 remodel an old mansion into a hotel
2 〈군함의〉 a refit; rearmament
▶그 군함은 개장을 위해 지금 독에 있다 The battleship is now in dock for a refit.
3 〈고쳐 포장함〉 a repackage; a repacking

개장 開場 opening; 〔證〕 the opening session; a call session; a call
◆개장 중이다 be open / 개장과 동시에 팔다[사다] sell [buy] at the opening session
▶오전 10시 개장 (게시) The doors open at 10:00 a.m.
━개장하다 open (the doors); 〈시장을〉 open a market; 〈증권 시장을〉 hold a session
▶스케이트장은 11월에 개장한다 The skating rink will open in November.
▶시세는 100달러에 개장했다 The market opened at 100 dollars.
▶경기장은 개장하자 마자 사람들이 몰려들었다 People surged into the stadium as soon as the gates were opened.
━가격 an opening price [quotation] ━시간 the opening hour; 〈시장의〉 market hours ━식 an opening [inauguration] ceremony

개재 介在 interposition; intervention
━개재하다 exist 《among》; lie [stand] between
▶두 사람 사이에는 무슨 복잡한 사정이 개재해 있는 것 같다 Some complicated circumstances seem to stand between the two.

개전 開戰 the opening [commencement] of hostilities; the outbreak of war
◆개전을 선포하다 declare war 《on, against》
━개전하다 open [commence] war [hostilities] 《against》; make [wage] war 《against》

개전 改悛 (a) repentance; penitence; 〈회개〉 contrition 《for》; 〈개심〉 reform
▶그는 개전의 정이 없다 He shows no signs of repentance.
▶그는 자기 행동에 대해 개전의 정이 뚜렷하다 He shows sincere repentance for what he has done.
━개전하다 reform *oneself*; repent 《of *one's* sins》

개점 開店 〈개업〉 the opening of a shop [store]; opening of business; 〈문을 염〉 opening the store (for the day)
◆개점을 축하하여 in celebration of the opening of a store
▶흡사 개점 휴업 상태다 We [They] are open for business, but are doing virtually none at all.
▶금일 개점 (게시) Opened today.
━개점하다 open [set up] a shop [store]

개정

▶그는 지난 달에 식료품점[서점]을 개점했다 He opened a grocery store [started a bookstore] last month. ⇌ He set up as a grocer [bookseller] last month.
━시간 the opening time [hour]

개정 改正 〈수정〉 (a) revision; (an) amendment; 〈변경〉 (an) alteration; 〈개선〉 (an) improvement
◆법률의 개정 an amendment to a law / 조약의 개정 a revision of a treaty / 전면 개정을 단행하다 make a full-scale revision ((of the civil law)
━개정하다 〈수정하다〉 revise; amend ((the constitution)); 〈변경하다〉 alter; change; 〈개선하다〉 improve
◆형법의 일부를 개정하다 make a partial amendment of the Criminal Code
▶낡은 제도를 개정하는 것이 필요하다 It is necessary to make improvement on (the) old system.
▶규칙이 개정되었다 The regulation was revised.
■헌법━ an amendment of the constitution; a constitutional amendment: 국민의 태반이 헌법 개정에 반대한다 Most of the people are against constitutional revision. ■━안 a revised bill [plan]; an amendment

개정 改定 (a) revision; a reform ━개정하다 revise ((the tariff)); reform ▶시간표가 이달부터 개정된다 The timetable will be altered starting this month.
━세율[요금] revised duties [rates] ━시간표 a revised [new] timetable: 개정 시간표는 3월 1일부터 시행된다 The revised timetable will be put into force on and after the 1st of March. ━가 the revised price

개정 改訂 ━개정하다 revise; edit ((a textbook)) anew ▶이 사전은 일부[전면] 개정되었다 This dictionary was partly [completely] revised.
■━증보 revision and enlargement ━증보판 a revised and enlarged edition ━판 a revised edition

개정 開廷 the opening [holding, sitting] of a court; 〈공판〉 a hearing; a trial
▶지금 개정 중이다 The court is now sitting [in session].
━개정하다 open the court; hold court [a trial]; sit
▶법정은 10시에 개정한다 The court will be opened at ten.
━일 a juridical [court] day

개제 改題 retitling ━개제하다 retitle; change the title ((of a book)) ◆…로 개제하여 재발행되다 be reissued under the new title of…

개조 改造 reconstruction; rebuilding; remodeling; alteration; reorganization
▶그 가게는 지금 개조 중이다 The store is now under reconstruction.
━개조하다 reconstruct; reorganize; remodel; alter; convert (▶remodel은 형태를, alter는 일부 변경을, convert는 어떤 것을 다른 것으로 변화시키는 것을 말함)
◆부엌을 개조하다 remodel a kitchen / 사회를 개조하다 reorganize a society
▶나는 집을 점포로 개조했다 I remodeled my house into a store.

개조 改組 (a) reshuffle ⇨ 개편(改編)

개조 個條 〈사항〉 an article; a clause; 〈항목〉 an item ◆8조의 요구 an eight-point demand
▶그 조약은 12개조로 이루어져 있다 The treaty consists of twelve articles.
■신앙━ articles of faith

개조 開祖 〈종파 등의〉 the founder ((of a sect [temple])); 〈시조〉 an originator; an initiator
▶본산(本山)의 개조는 원효 대사입니다 The founder of this temple was Saint Wonhyo.

개종 改宗 (a) conversion; proselytism
━개종하다 change one's religion; be converted to ((Catholicism))
◆개종시키다 convert sb ((to Christianity)); proselytize sb; make a convert of sb
▶그는 기독교로 개종했다 He turned Christian. ⇌ He was converted to Christianity.
▶그의 열렬한 설교는 많은 사람들을 개종시켰다 His fiery sermon made [won] many converts to his faith.
■━자 a convert ((to Buddhism)); a proselyte

개주 改鑄 〈화폐의〉 recoinage; 〈종·대포 등의〉 recasting; remolding ━개주 하 다 recoin ((money)); remold; recast ((a bell into guns))

개죽음 a useless death; an ignominious death
━개죽음하다 die in vain; die to no purpose [for nothing] (▶die like a dog는 「비참한 최후를 마치다」의 뜻임)
▶나는 개죽음하고 싶지 않다 I don't want to die in vain [a useless death].

개중 個中 〈여럿 가운데〉 among them [others]
◆개중에는 among them; some of them; of the number ▶개중에는 좋은 책도 있고 나쁜 책도 있다 Some books are good and some bad.

개진 開陳 statement
━개진하다 state; make a statement ((of)); set forth ((one's views)); express ((one's opinion))
▶그는 대중 앞에서 자기 의견을 개진했다 He stated his opinion in front of the public.

개집 a doghouse; a kennel

개차반 trash; a vulgar [mean] fellow; a churl

개착 開鑿 cutting; excavation; sinking ━개착하다 cut; 〈우물 을〉 sink; excavate; 〈운하 등을〉 build; construct ■━공사 excavation works ━기(機) an excavator

개찰 改札 the examination of tickets; 〈철도에서〉 punching ▶벌써 개찰이 시작되었다 The gate is already open. ━개찰하다 examine [punch] a ticket ((at the barrier))
━구 (a platform) wicket; a ticket barrier [gate]; a ticket inspector's gate ━원 a ticket examiner [clipper, puncher]

개척 開拓 〈토지의〉 clearing; reclamation; 〈자원의〉 exploitation; development; 〈삼림 지대의〉 deforestation; 〈식민지의〉 colonization; 〈신분야의〉 pathfinding
▶그것은 아직 미개척 분야이다 It belongs to an unexplored field.
▶그는 미개척 분야에 도전했다 He attempted to explore the untouched field.
━개척하다 reclaim ((the wilds)); put ((virgin

land) to the plow; clear (land of forests); bring (the wasteland) under cultivation; open up (a new field in science)
♦ 새 분야를 개척하다 break fresh ground / 수출 시장을 개척하다 find [seek, open up] an export market / 신천지를 개척하다 open up a new world / 운명을 개척하다 improve *one's* lot (by *one's* own efforts); carve out a career for *oneself*
▶ 스스로 운명을 개척해라 Seek your fortune on your own [for yourself].
▶ 우리는 황무지를 개척했다 We reclaimed the wasteland.
▶ 그들은 신제품 자동차의 시장을 개척했다 They have opened up a new market for the new cars.
▶ 언젠가 인간은 사막을 개척하여 농업에 이용하게 될 것이다 Someday man will reclaim the desert for agriculture.
■ ―사업 reclamation [exploitation] work ―자 〈식민〉 a colonist; 〈이민〉 a settler; 〈새 분야의〉 a pioneer; a trailblazer; a frontiersman ―정신 the pioneer [frontier] spirit ―지 reclaimed land; a settlement area

개천 開川 an open sewer [ditch]; 〈내〉 a streamlet; a brook; a brooklet

개천에 나도 제 날 탓이라 〈속담〉 Birth is much but breeding is more.

개천에서 용 난다 〈속담〉 A great person may be born of perfectly ordinary parents. ▶ 개천에서 용 났다 It is a case of a black hen laying white eggs. ⇒ He rose from rags to riches.

개천절 開天節 the National Foundation Day (of Korea); Anniversary of the Tangun's Accession

개체 個體 an [the] individual; an independent [individual] existence; a separate entity ♦ 개체를 식별하다 recognize (the monkeys) individually
■ ―개념[관념] 〔論〕 an individual concept ―군(群)〔動〕 population ―발생(학)〔生〕 ontogeny; ontogenesis ―변이 〔生〕 individual variation ―화(化) individuation

개초 蓋草 〈이엉〉 thatch(ing); 〈이엉으로 임〉 thatching; roofing with thatch ―**개초하다** thatch (a roof); roof (a house) with thatch
■ ―장이 a roofer; a (house) thatcher

개최 開催 holding; opening (a meeting)
♦ 개최 중이다 be open; 〈회의가〉 be in session; be sitting
▶ 경제 원조에 관한 국제 회의가 지금 제네바에서 개최 중이다 An international conference on economic aid is now under way in Geneva.
―**개최하다** hold; open (a meeting); give (a garden party); have (a farewell [welcome] meeting)
▶ 박람회는 내년에 개최된다 The exhibition [exposition] will open next year.
■ ―국 the host country ―기간 the period in which (an exhibition [a trade fair]) is held ―일 the day fixed for a meeting; 〈경기·경마 등의〉 a fixture ―지 the site (of an exposition [athletic meet]); the locale (of a conference)

개축 改築 rebuilding; reconstruction; alteration (to a building)
♦ 개축 중이다 be being rebuilt; be under [in course of] reconstruction [rebuilding]
▶ 우리 집[그 교량]은 지금 개축 중이다 Our house [The bridge] is now under reconstruction.
―**개축하다** rebuild (a house); remodel; reconstruct (a building); alter
■ ―공사 reconstruction works

개칠 改漆 〈칠의〉 repainting; recoating; 〈글씨의〉 correction; retouch
―**개칠하다** 〈칠을〉 repaint; recoat; revarnish; paint [plaster] afresh; 〈글씨를〉 correct [retouch] (a written letter)

개칭 改稱 renaming; the change of a name [designation, title]
―**개칭하다** rename; change the name [designation, title] (to); retitle
▶ 그 지역은 태백시로 개칭되었다 The name of the area was changed to T'aebaek City.

개키다 fold (up) (clothes [bedding]) elaborately ♦ 옷을 개키다 fold the clothes up neatly / 이부자리를 개키다 fold up beddings

개탄 慨嘆 deploring; regret; lamentation ♦ 개탄을 금할 수 없다 be most deplorable
―**개탄하다** deplore; lament (over); regret
♦ 개탄할 만한 deplorable; lamentable; regrettable / 사회의 병폐를 개탄하다 deplore the social evils
▶ 그의 행위[도덕의 몰락]는 실로 개탄하지 않을 수 없다 His behavior [The decline in public morals] is simply deplorable.
▶ 그것은 참으로 개탄할 만한 일이다 It is certainly regrettable.

개탕 開鐋 〈홈〉 a quirk; a fillister ♦ 개탕치다 groove; make [cut] a groove (in) ■ ―대패 a fillister (plane)

개통 開通 opening to traffic
―**개통하다** 〈신설〉 be opened to [for] traffic; go into operation; 〈복구〉 be reopened (for service)
▶ 최근에 두 도시 사이에 고속도로가 개통되었다 Recently, the highway was opened to traffic between the two cities.
▶ 불통 구간은 3시간 후에 개통되었다 The (train service in the) damaged section was reopened [restored] to traffic three hours later.
■ ―구간 a section of restored traffic

개통식 開通式 the formal opening (of a railway); the opening ceremony (of a new bridge)
▶ 어제 서강 대교의 개통식이 있었다 The Sŏgang Bridge was opened with due ceremony yesterday.

개판 utter [wild] confusion [disorder]; a mess; topsy-turvy ♦ 개판이 되다 fall into utter confusion

개판 改版 republishing; revision; 〔印〕 reset; 〈개판본〉 a revised edition ―**개판하다** revise (the current edition); issue a revised [new] edition; 〈조판을〉 reset

개패 ―牌 〈개 목의〉 a dog tag; (俗) 〈명찰〉 a name tag

개펄 tideland; a tidal flat; silt at an estuary; slime along the bank of an inlet

개편 改編 reorganization; (a) reshuffle
♦내각의 (일부) 개편 a (partial) Cabinet reshuffle / 당직[정부 기구]의 개편 reorganization of a party's hierarchy [government setups]
─개편하다 reorganize; reshuffle 《a Cabinet》
♦교과서를 개편하다 reedit [revise] a textbook / 회사의 조직을 개편하다 reorganize a company; undertake organizational changes within the company / 진용을 개편하다 rearrange the disposition of troops
▶새 사주는 회사를 완전히 개편했다 The new owner completely reorganized the firm.

개평 the winner's tip; a free handout
♦개평을 떼다 take away the winner's tip / 개평을 주다 give a cut [share of *one*'s winnings]
■─꾼 onlookers expecting some of the money given away by the gamblers

개평 槪評 a general [brief] comment 《on》; an overall criticism ─개평하다 make [give] a general comment 《on》; give an overall criticism 《of》

개폐 改廢 alteration and abolition 《of laws》
─개폐하다 reorganize; make a change 《in》

개폐 開閉 opening and [or] shutting
▶문의 개폐는 조용히 해 주십시오 Don't make a noise when you open and close the door.
─개폐하다 open and shut [close]; 〔電〕 make and break a circuit
▶이 문은 자동 개폐된다 This door opens and shuts automatically.
■─교(橋) a drawbridge; a balance [swing] bridge ─기〔전기의〕 a 《break and make》 switch; 〔사진기의〕 a shutter: 자동 개폐기 an automatic switch ─신호기 a switch signal ─장치 switchgear ─회로 a keying circuit

개표 開票 the counting [opening] of votes [ballots]; ballot counting
♦개표 결과를 공표하다 publish the results of vote counting [election results]
▶개표 결과 김 선생이 당선되었다 On opening the ballot, it was found that Mr. Kim was returned.
▶개표는 오후 7시부터 시작될 것이다 The votes will be counted beginning at 7 p.m.
▶그들은 개표를 시작했다 They have opened the ballot boxes.
▶나는 개표에 입회했다 I was among the witnesses when the votes were counted [when the ballot boxes were opened].
─개표하다 open the ballot boxes; count the votes
♦참관인 입회 하에 개표하다 count the votes with witness attending
■─관리인 a supervisor of a ballot counting office ─소 a ballot-counting office [place] ─율 the rate of vote counting: 현재 개표율은 20%다 Twenty percent of the ballots have been counted so far. ─참관인 a ballot-counting witness

개피떡 a rice-cake stuffed with adzuki bean jam

개학 開學 starting [reopening] of school 《after a vacation》 ─개학하다 open [begin] school; school begins ▶학교는 내일 개학한다 School opens tomorrow.
■─식[일] the opening ceremony [day] of the school year [term]

개함 開函 〈투표함의〉 opening of a ballot box ─개함하다 open the ballot boxes

개항 開港 the opening of a port ─개항하다 open a port 《to foreign trade》 ■─장(場) an open [a treaty] port

개헌 改憲 a constitutional amendment [revision]; a revision [an amendment] of the constitution
♦개헌을 제의[발의]하다 initiate [propose] a constitutional amendment
─개헌하다 amend [revise, reform] the constitution
■─안 《present [submit]》 a bill for amending the constitution ─운동 a movement for the constitutional amendment

개헤엄 the dog paddle ♦개헤엄치다 dog-paddle; do a dog paddle; swim with the dog paddle

개혁 改革 〈혁신〉 (a) reform; reformation; innovation; renovation; 〈개선〉 improvement
♦개혁의 기치를 높이 들다 hoist the banners of reform / 교육 개혁을 주창하다 advance an educational reform / 개혁에 착수하다 start a reform
▶정부는 세제에 대개혁을 단행했다 The Government made [carried out] drastic reforms in the taxation system.
─개혁하다 〈혁신하다〉 reform; make [carry out] reforms; renovate; innovate; 〈개선하다〉 improve
♦철두철미 개혁하다 reform from top to bottom
▶교육 제도를 근본적으로 개혁할 시기가 왔다 It is (high) time that drastic reforms were carried out in the educational system.
■─농지— an agrarian [a farmland] reform 사회— social reform 종교— religious reformation; 〔史〕 the Reformation 행정— 《carry out》 an administrative reform ■─안 a reform bill: 경제 개혁안 a plan of economic reform ─자 a reformer

개화 開化 civilization; enlightenment
─개화하다 be 《become, get》 civilized; be enlightened; be illuminated
♦개화된 국민 civilized people
▶그 나라는 이제 많이 개화되었다 It is now quite a civilized country.

개화 開花 blooming; flowering; bursting into bloom; efflorescence
♦문명의 개화 the flowering of civilization
─개화하다 flower; bloom; blossom; come into flower [bloom]; effloresce
▶문예 부흥은 레오나르도 다 빈치에 이르러 개화했다고 할 수 있다 The Renaissance can be said to have flowered in Leonardo da Vinci.
■─기 the flowering season

개활 開豁 ─개활하다 wide open ♦개활한 평야 a vastly open land / 조망이 개활하다 com-

mand extensive views ■—지(地) an open land
개황 概況 a general situation [condition]; an outlook; a survey ■경제— economic survey 일기— the general weather condition
개회 開會 the opening of a meeting [conference]; 〈의회의〉 the opening of a session
♦개회 중이다 be open; 〈국회가〉 be in session; be sitting / 개회를 선언하다 declare 《a meeting》 open; (美) call [announce] 《a meeting》 to order
▶의장이 개회를 선언하였다 The chairman called the meeting to order.
—개회하다 be opened; open the meeting; 〈국회가〉 begin its session; sit
▶국회는 내일부터 개회한다 The National Assembly opens [begins its session] tomorrow.
▶지금부터 개회합니다 〈개회 선언〉 I now declare this meeting open.
▶11시에 개회할 예정이다 The meeting will [is scheduled to] open at 11 o'clock.
■—사 (give [deliver]) an opening address [speech] —식 (hold) an opening ceremony [(美) exercise]; an inauguration
개회로 開回路 〔電〕 an open circuit
개흙 slime [mud] on the bank of an inlet; silt (at an estuary)
객 客 a caller; a visitor; a guest
객— 客— 1 〈가외의〉 extra; additional
2 〈쓸데 없는〉 needless; useless; uncalled-for
3 〈지난〉 last; latest
♦객년 last year / 객월 last month / 객춘 last spring
객고 客苦 sufferings [discomforts] of sb who is away from home; weariness from travel
♦객고를 풀다 relieve the tedium of a journey / 객고에 시달리다 be travel-worn; be wayworn
객관 客觀 〔哲〕 the object; 〈객관성〉 objectivity ♦객관화하다 objectify
■—가치 objective validity —묘사 (an) objective description —법 (an) objective method —식 시험 an objective test —정세 an objective situation —주의 objectivism —화(化) objectification
객관성 客觀性 objectivity (↔subjectivity)
▶그의 말에는 객관성이 거의 없다 His statement has little objectivity.
객관적 客觀的 objective
♦객관적인 비판을 하다 give objective criticism / 문제를 객관적으로 고찰하다 consider the problem objectively
▶기자는 객관적이어야 한다 Reporters should be objective.
▶그것을 좀더 객관적으로 보아야 한다 You should look at it more objectively.
▶객관적으로 말해서 그 실험은 성공하지 못할 것이다 Objectively (speaking), the experiment will not succeed.
객기 客氣 ill-advised bravery; rashness; blind daring
♦객기를 부리다 be carried away by a rash impulse
▶그가 그렇게 큰소리치는 것은 순전히 술마신

객기다 All his big talk is just Dutch courage.
객담 客談 (an) idle talk; empty talk; bosh
—객담하다 talk nonsense; waste words; say silly things
객담 喀痰 spitting; 〔醫〕 expectoration —객담하다 expectorate phlegm; spit (out) ■—검사 the examination of one's sputum
객사 客死 dying away from home
—객사하다 die in a strange [foreign] land; die away from home
▶그 남자는 뉴욕에서 객사했다 The man died while staying [during his stay] in New York.
객사 客舍 a hotel; an inn
객상 客商 a traveling merchant
객석 客席 〈극장 등의〉 a seat (in a theater); 〈택시의〉 a passenger seat
▶이 극장은 객석이 500석이다 This theater seats [has seats for] 500 people.
▶객석이 만원이다 All the seats are occupied.
■—안내인 an usher
객선 客船 a passenger boat [ship, steamer]; 〈대양 항로의 정기선〉 a (passenger) liner
객소리 客— (an) idle talk; bosh; prattle; twaddle; an uncalled-for remark
—객소리하다 talk idly [nonsense]; say useless things; tattle
▶객소리그만둬 Quit your idle talk. ⇌ Don't talk nonsense.
객스럽다 客— unnecessary; needless; uncalled-for ♦객스러운 짓 a useless [needless] behavior
객식구 客食口 a hanger-on (pl. hangers-on); a dependant not a member of one's own family; a sponger
객실 客室 〈호텔 등의〉 a guest room; 〈배·비행기의〉 a cabin; 〈열차의〉 a compartment; 〈특등실〉 a stateroom
■—당번[담당] 〈호텔의〉 a room clerk : 객실 담당에게 전화하다 call room service —승무원 a flight [cabin] attendant; (총칭) a cabin crew
객연 客演 guest appearance —객연하다 make a guest appearance 《in a show》; appear [perform, play] as a guest (on the stage)
객원 客員 an associate [honorary] member; (美) a guest member; a nonregular member
■—교수 a guest [visiting] professor —지휘자 a guest conductor
객주 客主 〈객줏집〉 an inn for merchants; a commission agency home; peddler's inn; 〈거간〉 commission agency
객지 客地 a strange land (where one is staying on a trip); a foreign land
♦객지 사람 a stranger; an outlander / 객지에 서 away from home; in a strange land; 〈여행 중에〉 during one's trip
▶그는 10년 동안 객지 생활을 했다 He was absent from home for ten years.
▶불행히도 그는 객지에서 병을 얻었다 Unfortunately he fell sick while he was away from home.
객쩍다 客— unnecessary; uncalled-for; be out of place; 〈실없다〉 idle; silly ♦객쩍은 소리 (an) idle talk

객차 客車 a passenger car [(英) carriage]; 〈열차〉 a passenger train
▶ 1등 객차는 앞쪽입니다 The first-class cars are in front.
객체 客體 **1** [哲] the object (↔subject)
♦ 범죄의 객체 the object of a crime / 개체화하다 objectify
▶ 영토와 국민은 국가의 객체다 The territory and people are the objects of the state.
2 〈객지에 있는 몸〉 a person (far) away from home; a person who is away on a journey
객초 客草 tobacco [cigarettes] for guests
객토 客土 earth brought from some other place (to improve the soil)
갤러리 〈골프・테니스의〉 a gallery
갤런 a gallon ♦ 1갤런으로 20마일 달리다 do twenty miles to the gallon
갤럽여론조사 the Gallup polls ■ —소 the American Institute of Public Opinion
갬대 〈나무칼〉 a wooden knife for weeding
갭 a gap
♦ 시간적인[세대간의] 갭 a time [generation] gap / 갭을 메우다 fill [bridge] a gap
▶ 그들의 의견에는 아직도 큰 갭이 있다 There is still a large gap between their opinions.
갭직하다 rather [a bit] light; lightish
갯 the shore of an estuary [inlet]; 〈물가〉 the waterside
갯가재 [動] a squilla (pl. ~s, -lae); a mantis prawn [crab, shrimp]
갯값 dog-cheap [dirt-cheap] price ♦ 갯값으로 팔다 sell sth cheap as dirt; sell (an article) for a mere song [the mud]
갯고랑 a small channel of tidewater on the shore of an inlet
갯나리 [動] a crinoid; a sea lily
갯바람 a sea breeze; briny [salt] air
갯벌 tideland ⇨ 개펄
갯솜 [動] a sponge ⇨ 해면(海綿)
갯지렁이 [動] a lugworm; a lobworm; a nereid
갱 坑 〈광갱(鑛坑)〉 a mine; 〈갱도〉 a pit; 〈사금광의〉 a drain 수(竪)— a shaft [pit] 탄— a coal mine 횡(橫)— a level; a drift [gallery]
갱 (美) a gangster; (美俗) a mobster; a gunman; 〈일당〉 a gang ■—영화 a gangster movie [film]
갱구 坑口 a minehead; a pithead [pit mouth]
갱내 坑內 the inside of a pit [shaft]
■—가스 mine gas —감독 an overman —케도 a pit line —부(夫) a pit [an underground] worker; a miner —사고 an accident in the pit —수(水) mine water —작업 inside [pit] labor; underground work —침수 mineflooding —화재 an underground [a pit] fire
갱년기 更年期 the critical age [time of life]; 〈완곡적〉 the turn [change] of one's life; 〈여성의〉 the menopause; [醫] the climacterium
♦ 갱년기의 변화 climacteric changes
■—장애 climacteric distress; 〈여성의〉 a menopausal disorder
갱도 坑道 **1** 〈광산의〉 a mining gallery; a drift; a level; a shaft [pit]
2 〈굴・지하도〉 a subterranean passage; a tunnel; [軍] a mine
▶ 갱도가 무너져버렸다 The tunnel roof has collapsed.
■—주— a gangway ■—작업 drift work —지주 timbering; pit props
갱목 坑木 mine timber; a mine pillar [support, post]; a pit prop
갱부 坑夫 a miner; a mine worker; 〈탄광의〉 a coal miner [pitman]
♦ 갱부로 일하다 work in a mine
■—병 miner's disease —십장 a foreman [reeve]
갱생 更生 revival; (a) rebirth; regeneration; rejuvenation; reform; 〈사회 복귀〉 rehabilitation
▶ 석방된 범죄자의 갱생을 촉진하는 것은 중요한 일이다 It is important to promote the rehabilitation of released prisoners.
—갱생하다 be reborn; be born again; turn over a new leaf; remake one's life; 〈범죄자가〉 be rehabilitated
♦ 갱생시키다 rehabilitate (a juvenile delinquent); get one back on the right track (again)
▶ 그는 한때는 비행 소년이었지만 갱생했다 He was once a juvenile delinquent, but he was reformed.
▶ 그는 나쁜 길에서 갱생했다 He has turned over a new leaf.
▶ 나는 그를 갱생시키려고 생각하고 있다 I am hoping to give him a fresh start (in life).
■—보호 시설 facilities for the relief and rehabilitation (of criminal offenders) —보호회 the Rehabilitation Guidance Association —사위 a chance [an opportunity] for revival after a narrow escape
갱소년 更少年 rejuvenation; restoration of youth —갱소년하다 be [become] rejuvenated; be restored to youth; become young again
갱신 更新 〈계약・기록 등의〉 (a) renewal —갱신하다 renew (a contract)
♦ 갱신할 수 있는 renewable / 기록을 갱신하다 break a record; make [establish] a new record; 〈자신의〉 better [improve on] one's own record
▶ 내 운전 면허를 갱신할 때가 되었다 It's time to renew my driver's license. ⇒ My driver's license has come up for renewal.
갱신못하다 cannot move at all; cannot move [stir, budge] an inch (from exhaustion)
갱외 坑外 ♦ 갱외의[에서] out of the pit / 석탄을 갱외로 운반하다 bring coal to the surface [grass]
■—부(夫) a surface worker; (美) a surfaceman; an out-of-pit worker —작업 surface work
갱지 更紙 pulp paper; rough (printing) paper; 〈신문 인쇄용의〉 newsprint
갱충맞다, 갱충쩍다 careless; heedless; slovenly; rash; hasty ♦ 갱충맞은 사람 a careless fellow / 갱충맞은 짓 (commit an) imprudent conduct [act]
갸기 a haughty attitude ⇨ 교기(驕氣)
갸륵하다 praiseworthy; admirable; commend-

able
♦갸륵한 마음씨 a commendable purpose / 갸륵한 젊은이 an admirable young man / 갸륵한 행실 exemplary behavior; good conduct / 갸륵하게도 admirably / 아무의 효성을 갸륵히 여겨 in reward for sb's filial heart / 갸륵한 일을 하다 do something good
▶그 게으른 아이가 밤 늦도록 열심히 공부한다는 것은 갸륵한 일이다 It is highly praiseworthy for the lazy boy to sit up studying hard till late at night.

갸름하다 somewhat long; (nicely) slender; pleasantly oval ♦갸름한 얼굴 an oval [a nicely tapered] face / 얼굴이 갸름한 예쁜 소녀 a girl with a sweet oval face

갸웃거리다 peep ⇨ 기웃거리다

갸웃하다 1〈형용사적〉somewhat slanted [inclined] ♦갸웃이 aslant; askew; obliquely
2〈동사적〉incline 《one's head on one side》; tilt 《one's head》; lean

갹금 醵金 raising of money [funds]; fundraising; a collection;〈기부〉contribution (▶「기부금」의 의미일 때는 countable noun이 됨)
—**갹금하다** take up a collection; raise money [a fund];〈기부하다〉contribute
♦유족을 위해 1천만원을 갹금하다 raise ten million won for a bereaved family

갹출 醵出 a contribution; sharing the expenses; chipping in
—**갹출하다** contribute money (to a fund); contribute each his own share; make contributions;《美口》chip in
♦구제 기금을 갹출하다 make a donation to a relief fund / 장학 기금을 갹출하다 contribute a scholarship fund 《for orphans》

갈쭉하다 longish ⇨ 길쭉하다

거 Well!; Why!; There!
▶거 참 좋다 Why, that's fine!
▶거 참 안됐다 Oh, that's too bad!
▶거 보라니까 There! Didn't I tell you?
▶거 누구요? Uh, who's there?

거간 居間〈일〉brokerage;〈사람〉a broker
—**거간하다** do (the) brokerage; broker

거간꾼 居間— a broker; a middleman; a commission agent [merchant] ♦집[토지] 거간꾼 a house [land] agent [broker]; a real-estate agent

거개 擧皆 most (of); the greater part (of); the vast majority 《of》; almost all
▶참석자는 거개가 대학생이었다 Those present were, for the most part, college students.
▶참석자의 거개가 그 계획에 찬성하였다 Most of the people present agreed to the plan.

거거익심하다 去去益甚—〈갈수록 더욱 심하다〉go from bad to worse; be worse and worse 《as time goes on》

거골 距骨〈解〉the anklebone ⇨ 복사뼈

거구 巨軀 a massive [huge] figure; a big [gigantic] frame [body]
♦신장 2미터 체중 150킬로그램의 거구 a massive figure of 2 meters in stature and 150 kilograms in weight / 거구의 사나이 a giant (of a man)
▶코끼리는 거구이면서도 동작이 빠르다 In spite of its bulk, the elephant can move fast.
▶그는 비대한 거구를 가지고 더위에 헐떡이고 있었다 He was gasping in hot weather with his massive, plump figure.

거국 擧國 the whole nation [country]
♦거국적인 nation-wide 《movement》 / 거국적으로 on a nation-wide scale; throughout [all over] the country
▶국민들은 거국적으로 국난에 대처했다[정부의 외교 정책을 지지했다] The whole nation faced the national crisis [supported the Government's foreign policy] as one solid body.
▶거국적으로 그 마라톤 선수를 환영했다 The whole nation welcomed the marathoner.
■—**일치** national unity; the whole nation in a body —**일치 내각** a government of national unity; a pan-national cabinet

거금 巨金 an enormous sum; a huge [large, big] sum 《of money》; a mint 《of》
♦거금을 들여서 at a great cost / 거금을 투입하다 spend [invest] an enormous sum [a great amount of money] 《on the construction of a building》
▶10억원이라면 거금이다 One billion won is a mint of money.

거금 距今 ago; back from today
▶거금 30년 전의 일이다 It dates back thirty years.
▶서울이 우리 나라의 도읍으로 정해진 것은 거금 6백여년 전의 일이다 It was about six hundred years ago that Seoul was chosen as the capital of our country.

거기 1〈장소〉that place; there
♦거기서부터 from there; thence / 여기서 거기까지 from here to that place [there]
▶이봐, 거기 있는 친구 Hi! You there!
▶[會話]「거기 누구세요?」「나예요」 "Who's there?" "It's me."
▶거기는 형편이 어떻습니까? How are things going on in your place?
▶거기는 벌써 눈이 왔겠지요 I suppose you have already had snow in your part of the country.
▶거기를 좀 긁어 다오 Please scratch there [that spot] for me.
▶거기에 서명하시오 Sign your name there.
▶거기에는 누군가가 있었다 There was someone there.

2〈그것[그 범위]〉
♦거기까지(는) so [that] far; to that extent / 거기에다 besides; moreover;〈설상가상으로〉(and) what is worse / 거기까지는 좋았는데 so far, so good, but...
▶거기가 바로 요점이다 That is just the point.
▶절약도 거기에 이르면 구두쇠가 된다 Economy carried to that extent is stinginess.
▶길을 잃었는데 거기에다 비마저 오기 시작했다 I lost my way and, what was worse, it began to rain.
▶거기까지는 알고 있다 I know that much.
▶거기까지는 인정한다 I admit so much.
▶거기까지는 생각 못했다 I never thought of that.

거꾸러뜨리다 1〈엎어뜨리다〉make fall flat

거꾸러지다

[headlong]; 〈때려눕히다〉 knock *sb* down; 〈발을 걸어 넘어뜨리다〉 trip *sb* up
▶ 그 남자는 강도를 일격에 거꾸러뜨렸다 The man knocked the robber down [floored the robber] with a single blow.
2 〈무너뜨리다〉 ruin; overthrow; 〈패배시키다〉 beat; defeat
♦ 강적을 거꾸러뜨리다 beat a strong opponent / 정부를 거꾸러뜨리다 overthrow [topple] the government
3 〈죽이다〉 kill; do away with; 〈俗〉 rub out; 〈美俗〉 blow out

거꾸러지다 1 〈엎어지나〉 fall (down); fall headlong; tumble down; be off *one's* feet
♦ 술에 취하여 거꾸러지다 fall down [collapse] dead-drunk / 앞으로 거꾸러지다 fall forward / 큰대자로 거꾸러지다 fall flat; fall full length; measure *one's* length on the ground
▶ 그 녀석은 돌에 채어 팍 거꾸러졌다 The fellow stumbled over a stone and fell.
2 〈죽다〉 die; succumb (to); 〈俗〉 kick the bucket
▶ 그 살인범은 총에 맞아 거꾸러졌다 The murderer was shot to death. ▶ 거꾸러져라 Go to hell! ⇒ Drop dead!
3 〈무너지다〉 go to ruin; collapse; fall; be overthrown; 〈패배하다〉 be defeated [beaten]

거꾸로 1 〈위아래로〉 bottom up [upward]; upside down
♦ 거꾸로 매달다 hang *sb* upside down; hang *sb* by (his) heels / 우표를 거꾸로 붙이다 put a stamp the wrong side up / 펜을 거꾸로 쥐다 hold a pen by the wrong end / 거꾸로 하다 invert; turn *sth* upside down; turn inside out
▶ 호수에서 백두산 모습이 거꾸로 비치고 있었다 Paektusan was reflected headforemost on the lake.
▶ 자네는 사진을 거꾸로 보고 있군 You're looking at the picture upside down.
2 〈곤두박질로〉 headlong; headfirst; head over heels; headforemost
▶ 그 도둑은 나무에서 거꾸로 떨어졌다 The thief fell from a tree head over heels.
▶ 비행기가 논바닥에 거꾸로 박혔다 An airplane made a nose dive [fell nose-first] into a paddy field.
3 〈역으로〉 the wrong way; the other way round; in the reverse order; reversely
♦ 거꾸로 말하면 conversely speaking / 나이를 거꾸로 먹다 age reversely / 숫자를 거꾸로 세다 count the figures backward / 일을 거꾸로 하다 put [set] the cart before the horse
▶ 그는 그 여자를 때려눕히려 했지만 거꾸로 그 여자가 그를 때려눕혔다 He was going to knock her down, but instead [on the contrary] he was knocked down by her.
▶ 그는 가끔 본심을 거꾸로 말한다 He sometimes says the opposite [reverse] of his real intention.
4 〈오히려〉 instead; on the contrary
▶ 나는 칭찬을 받기는 커녕 거꾸로 호되게 꾸지람을 들었다 Far from being praised, I was given a good scolding.

-거나 〈양보〉 whatever; whenever; however; 〈상반〉 whether...or...; 〈열거〉 and; or
▶ 비가 오거나 말거나 나는 외출하겠다 I will go out, whether it rains or not.
▶ 비가 오거나 눈이 내리거나 하면 오지 마라 Don't come, if it rains or snows.
▶ 그것은 있거나 없거나 마찬가지다 It doesn't matter [makes no difference] whether I have it or not.
▶ 네가 무슨 말을 하거나 나는 곧이듣지 않겠다 I won't believe you, whatever you may say.

거나하다 tipsy; mellow; hazy; 《be》 in a cheerful mood with drink
♦ 거나하게 취하다 be pleasantly drunk; be mellow [tipsy] from a drink
▶ 그는 자리를 뜰 때 이미 거나해 있었다 He was already warm with wine when he rose from the seat.
▶ 그 남자는 거나하여 노래를 흥얼거리고 있었다 Feeling a bit tipsy, the man was humming a tune.

거냉하다 去冷— take the chill off 《liquor》; warm [heat] up (a little)
▶ 거냉만 하시오 Just warm it up a little.

거년 去年 last year ⇨ 작년

거느리다 〈이끌다〉 lead; head 《a party》; 〈지휘하다〉 command 《an army》; 〈부양하다〉 have; take care of
♦ 종업원 천명을 거느리고 있는 회사 a firm with one thousand employees / 이순신 장군이 거느리는 수군 the naval forces under the command of Admiral Yi Sun-shin / 많은 가족을 거느리다 have a large family to support; have so many mouths to feed / 처자를 거느리다 support *one's* wife and children; have *one's* family
▶ 그녀는 다섯 자녀를 거느리고 있다 She has five children to feed [provide for].
▶ 그는 많은 부하를 거느리고 왔다 He came to us, followed by a lot of his subordinates.

-거늘 1 〈이미 …한데(도)〉 when; while
▶ 그들이 저렇게 어려움을 겪고 있거늘 어찌 버려둘 수 있겠는가? How can I leave them while [when] they are in such a trouble?
▶ 자네는 부자이거늘 왜 만족할 줄 모르니? Why not contented with all your riches?
▶ 동료들이 모두 일을 하거늘 나만 누워 있겠는가? How can I be confined to my bed while all my comrades are at work?
2 〈이미 …하니〉 now that; since; as
♦ 이미 그의 심중을 알았거늘 어찌할 작정이지? Now that you know his mind, what do you plan to do?

-거니 1 〈…한데〉 now that; since; as
▶ 나는 젊었거니 바위인들 무거우랴 Since I am youthful, can even a rock be heavy!
2 〈기대·예상〉 with the thought that...; I think [suppose, presume]
▶ 지금쯤 편지가 와 있겠거니 하고 빨리 돌아왔다 I have rushed home with the thought that the letter would surely be here by now.
▶ 나는 그가 이미 미국으로 떠났겠거니 생각했다 I thought that he had already left for America.

▶내일이면 그녀를 만날 수 있겠거니 생각하면 기쁘다 Assured of seeing her tomorrow, I am happy.
▶그가 죽었다는 소식은 들었지만 지금도 살아 있겠거니 싶다 I was informed of his death, but I still presume him to be alive.
3 〈동작의 되풀이〉 now...now; now...and then; what by [with]...and (what by [with]); by turns
◆인사를 주거니 받거니 하다 exchange greetings with
▶그녀와 나는 주거니 받거니 얘기가 끝이 없었다 What with my telling her and her telling me, there was no end to our talking.
▶그들은 술잔을 주거니 받거니 하며 실컷 마셨다 They drank their full, now offering, now accepting cups.

-거니와 as well (as); not only...but also; besides; what's more; but (even so)
▶그녀는 얼굴도 곱거니와 마음씨도 곱다 She has not only a pretty face but also a good nature.
▶그것은 건강에도 좋거니와 경제적이기도 하다 It is not only good for health but also economical.
▶나는 돈도 없거니와 시간도 없다 Not only do I lack money, but I don't have the time [leisure] (to spare).
▶나는 두번 다시 그를 만나지도 않았거니와 그걸 후회하지도 않았다 I never saw him again, nor did I regret it.
▶산도 높거니와 물도 맑다 The mountains are high and the waters are clear as well.
▶그 학생은 공부도 잘하거니와 운동도 잘한다 The student is a good athlete as well as a fine scholar.

거닐다 take a walk; stroll [ramble] about (the street); saunter about
◆공원을 거닐다 saunter about a park; take a walk in a park / 해변을 거닐다 take a stroll on the beach
▶사람들이 삼삼오오 숲속을 한가로이 거닐고 있다 People are walking leisurely by twos and threes in the woods.
▶나는 그녀와 함께 명동 거리를 즐겨 거닐곤 했다 I used to enjoy strolling with her along the Myŭng-dong (street).

거담 祛痰 the discharge of phlegm
■―제 an expectorant

거당 舉黨 the whole party
◆거당 일치하여 총선에 임하다 look toward the general election with a unified party determination
▶총재의 성명을 거당적으로 지지했다 The whole party supported the leader's statement.

거대 巨大 hugeness; enormousness
―**거대하다** 〈크기·정도가〉 huge; enormous; mammoth; gigantic; 〈규모가〉 colossal; 〈괴물적인〉 monstrous
◆거대한 대포 a big [monster] gun / 거대한 유조선 a huge tanker; a megatanker [supertanker] / 거대한 체구 a gigantic figure
▶수평선 위에 거대한 먹구름이 떠 있었다 There was a huge [an enormous] black mass of cloud over the horizon.
■―과학 Big Science ―기업 a conglomerate; a mammoth enterprise ―도시 a megalopolis ―세포[분자] a giant cell [molecule] ―적혈구 a macrocyte; a megalocyte ―종합대학교 a megavercity ―증 〔醫〕 gigantism

거덜거덜하다 unsteady; shaky; unstable; wavering
◆거덜거덜한 건물 a tottering building; a building ready to collapse / 거덜거덜한 살림 a precarious livelihood

거덜나다 〈결딴나다〉 collapse; crumble; fall down [off]; be ruined; 〈파산하다〉 go into bankruptcy; go [become] bankrupt; (口) go broke
◆거덜난 살림 an eliminated livelihood / 거덜날 지경이다 be on the verge of bankruptcy
▶은행이 거덜났다 The bank broke.
▶마침내 그의 사업도 거덜났다 At last his business was ruined.
▶불경기로 여러 회사가 거덜났다 Owing to the depression, many companies went bankrupt [down].
▶그 회사가 거덜난 것은 주로 운전 자본 부족 때문이었다 The failure of that company is chiefly attributed to the want of working capital.

거독 去毒 neutralization [removal] of poison (in medical herbs); detoxication ―**거독하다** detoxicate (in medical herbs)

거동 擧動 〈몸가짐〉 behavior; a manner; conduct; 〈행동〉 actions; doings; movement
◆수상한 거동 suspicious [strange] behavior / 거동이 수상한 사람 a man of suspicious behavior; a suspicious-looking man / 거동이 수상하다 act [behave] suspiciously
▶경찰은 거동이 수상한 남자를 체포했다 The police arrested a man acting strangely.
▶그는 거동이 수상해서 경찰의 조사를 받았다 The police called on him to account for his strange behavior.
▶그의 거동에는 침착성이 없다 His movements lack composure.
―**거동하다** behave [conduct, bear] *oneself*; act 〈like〉

거두 巨頭 a leader; a leading [a prominent, an eminent] figure; a big name
◆정계의 거두 a political leader; a leading statesman / 재계의 거두 a financial magnate; a leading businessman; a business tycoon
▶각계의 거두가 모였다 Leaders [Prominent figures] from a variety of fields assembled.
■―회담 summit talks; a top-level conference

거두다 **1** 〈모으다〉 collect; gather; get [bring] together; take in; 〈수확하다〉 harvest; reap (fields); gather in
◆기부금을 거두다 collect donations / 세금을 거두다 exact [collect, 〈부과하다〉 levy] taxes
▶정부는 세금을 거둔다 The government collects taxes.
▶빗방울이 떨어지기 전에 빨래를 거두어 주세요 Please take in the washings before it begins to rain.
▶농부들은 부지런히 곡식을 거두어 들이고 있

다 The farmers are busy harvesting [gathering in] their crops.
2 〈얻다〉 gain; obtain; achieve; get; win
▶우리는 만족할 만한[큰] 성과를 거두었다 We got [obtained] satisfactory [excellent] results.
▶타자 교체는 효과를 거두었다 The change of batters was effective.
▶우리는 그들에게 손쉬운 승리를 거두었다 We won [achieved, gained] (an) easy victory over them.
▶그들은 승리를 거두고 돌아왔다 They came home victorious.
3 〈돌보다〉 take care [charge] of; look after; care for
♦고아를 거두어 기르다 take an orphan and bring him up / 거두어 먹이다 feed with care
▶그의 막내동생은 삼촌이 거두었다 His uncle took care [charge] of his youngest brother.
▶아이들은 할머니가 거두기로 했다 The children were left in the care of their grandmother.
4 〈그치다〉 stop; end; cease; quit; 〈철회하다〉 withdraw; recall
♦눈물을 거두다 stop crying; dry *one's* tears / 명령을 거두다 withdraw a command [an order]
▶그녀는 숨을 거두었다 She breathed her last (breath) [passed away, gave up her breath].
5 〈모양을 내다〉 tidy (up) *oneself*; trim *oneself* up ▶그녀는 몸을 단정하게 거두었다 She trimmed herself up.
6 〈걷어치우다〉 shut up; wind up 《*one's* affairs》 ♦가게를 거두다 close down [up] *one's* store; give up *one's* business

거두절미하다 去頭截尾— 〈자르다〉 cut off the head and tail (of it); 〈요약하다〉 make a short story (of); summarize; brief
♦거두절미하면 to make [cut] a long story short
▶거두절미하고 요점만 말하겠습니다 I'll get straight to the point cutting off the head and tail of it.

거둠질 harvesting; gathering (in); reaping; collecting —**거둠질하다** harvest; reap in; gather in; collect

거둥 〈왕의 나들이〉 a royal visit [procession] —**거둥하다** pay a royal visit 《to》; proceed outside the palace

거드럭거드럭 swaggeringly; arrogantly; with a dignified air

거드럭거리다 put on (superior) airs; behave in a cocky way; hold *one's* head high
♦거드럭거리는 관리 a pompous [haughty, pretentious] official / 거드럭거리며 걷다 walk with a dignified air; swagger; strut about [along]
▶돈 좀 있다고 그렇게 거드럭거리지 마라 Don't be so stuck up because you are rich.
▶나는 그가 거드럭거리지 않아서 좋다 I like him for not being pompous.

거드름 a haughty [proud] attitude; haughtiness
♦거드름 부리다 have an air of importance; hold *one's* head high; ride the high horse
▶그는 항상 거드름 피우면서 말한다 He always speaks with an air of importance [in a lordly manner].
▶거드름 작작 부리고 빨리 말해 Tell me at once, and get off your high horse.

-**거든 1** 〈가정·조건〉 if; provided (that); when
▶그를 만나거든 이렇게 말하시오 If [Provided] you meet him, tell him like this.
▶바쁘지 않거든 놀러 오시오 Come and see me if you are free.
▶자라고 하거든 자라 Go on to bed when I tell you to.
▶그것을 찾거든 내게 알려다오 Let me know if [when] you find it.
2 〈더구나〉 how much more; still more; much [still] less
▶개도 주인의 은공을 알거든 하물며 사람이랴 If a dog is grateful to its master, how much more should a man be!
▶너도 잊지 않았거든 어찌 내가 잊을 수 있겠는가? Since you haven't forgotten it, how could I?
3 〈까닭〉 as; so; since
▶수다쟁이가 남아 있거든 방이 조용할 리 있는가? As far as the chatterbox is staying in the room, how can it be quiet?
4 〈경탄〉 sure(ly); certainly; indeed
▶비가 참 많이 왔거든 It certainly did rain!

거든그리다 wrap [pack] up lightly

거들 a girdle

거들다 help; assist; aid; lend [give] a (helping) hand 《to》

> [解說] *help*가 일반적인 말. *assist*는 특히 직무상 보좌하는 경우에 쓰인다. 또 뒤에 일을 가리키는 말이 올 때는 보통 with를, 장소를 가리키는 말이 올 때는 at을 쓴다.

♦말을 거들다 put in a (good) word for *sb* / 숙제를 거들다 help 《a child》 with 《his》 homework / 옷 입는 것을 거들다 help *sb* on with 《her》 clothes
▶그녀는 집안 일을 잘 거든다 She is helpful around the house.
▶이 짐 올리는[내리는] 것 좀 거들어 주세요 Would you please help me up [down] with this baggage?
▶좀 거들어 주지 않겠니? Won't you lend me a (helping) hand?
▶저녁식사 후 나는 어머니의 설거지를 거들었다 I helped mother (to) clear off the things after supper.
▶그는 나의 잡지 편집을 거들었다 He assisted me in editing the magazine.

거들떠보다 cast a glance 《at》; take notice 《of》; pay [give] attention 《to》
♦거들떠보지도 않고 without even [so much as] casting a glance 《at》
▶그는 자기 또래의 여자 아이들은 거들떠보지도 않는다 He takes no notice of [ignores] girls of his own age.
▶많은 사람이 지나갔지만 아무도 그녀를 거들떠보지 않았다 Many passed, but no one gave

her the slightest attention.
▶ 그는 돈 따위는 거들떠보지도 않았다 He did not care for [was not interested in] money at all.
▶ 나는 책을 거들떠볼 사이가 없었다 I hadn't time to glance over the book.

거들먹거리다 put on airs ⇨ 거드럭거리다

거듭 repeatedly; again; over again; over and over again; once more [again]
♦거듭 묻다 ask once more; ask the same question again / 거듭 사과하다 apologize 《to sb for one's negligence》 repeatedly
▶ 거듭 말하지만 이 일은 결코 잊지 않을 것이다 I repeat I will never forget this.
▶ 거듭 말하지만 이것이 당신의 마지막 기회입니다 Let me tell [remind] you once again that this is your last chance.
▶ 그는 실패했지만 거듭 시도했다 He failed but made another attempt.
▶ 거듭 충고를 했지만 그는 듣지 않았다 He turned a deaf ear to my repeated advice.

거듭거듭 over and over (again); again and again; many times

거듭나다 be born again; be reborn; resuscitate

거듭하다 repeat; do again (and again)
♦실패를 거듭한 끝에 after repeated failures / 회를 거듭할수록 as the game advances [progresses]/ 잔을 거듭하다 drink one cup [glass] of wine after another / 판(版)을 거듭하다 go through another edition [several editions] / 해를 거듭하다 spend many years
▶ 우리는 그 문제를 두고 회의를 거듭했다 We sat [met] in conference several times to discuss the matter.
▶ 그 회사는 발전을 거듭하고 있다 The firm is growing more and more prosperous.
▶ 그는 실수를 거듭하다가 해고되었다 He was fired [dismissed] because of (his) repeated errors [mistakes].
▶ 그녀의 연기는 회를 거듭할수록 향상되었다 Her performance improved with each repetition.
▶ 그는 거듭되는 불행에도 굴하지 않았다 He bore up under repeated [a series of] misfortunes.

거든하다 light; 〈심신이〉 feel light; feel good
♦거든한 마음으로 with a light heart / 몸이 다시 거든하다 be well [all right] again
▶ 그 약을 먹고 나니 몸이 거든하다 I feel [am] easy after taking that medicine.

거든히 lightly; 〈손쉽게〉 readily; easily; without difficulty [effort]
♦거든히 들어올리다 lift 《heavy baggage》 lightly / 거든히 이기다 win easily
▶ 그는 그 큰 돌을 거든히 들어올렸다 He lifted the big stone very easily [with great ease].
▶ 그는 강을 거든히 헤엄쳐 건넜다 He swam across the river with ease.
▶ 그는 밥 두 그릇을 거든히 비웠다 He made a short work of two bowls of boiled rice.
▶ 그것쯤 거든히 할 수 있다 It will be no effort to do it. ⇌ Nothing can be easier.

거래 去來 transactions; dealings; business; trade; 〈돈거래〉 lending and borrowing
♦술좌석에서 하는 거래 a Dutch [wet] bargain / 실속이 있는[없는] 거래 a good [poor] bargain / 주류의 부정 거래 illicit liquor traffic
〈거래가〉 은행과 거래가 있다 have a bank account; have an account at a bank
▶ 우리는 그 회사와 거래가 있다 We have business relations [dealings] with that company.
▶ 나는 그 은행과는 거래가 없다 I keep no account with that bank.
▶ 그들과는 거래가 끊어졌다 Our business connections with them were broken off.
〈거래를〉 거래를 계속하다 carry on transactions 《with》; keep an account 《with》 / 거래를 끊다 break off business relations [connections] / 거래를 맺다 strike [drive] a bargain with sb; enter into a connection [business relation] with 《a company》 / 거래를 신청하다 propose to open business 《with》 / 거래를 중지하다 suspend business / 거액의 농산물 거래를 하다 do a large (volume of) business in crops 《with》
▶ 우리는 그 회사와 직접 거래를 텄다 We have established direct trade relations with the firm.
▶ 수출입은행과 4월부터 거래를 개시할 예정이다 We are to open an account [correspondent relations] with the Export-Import Bank in April.
▶ 그와 유리한 거래를 했다 I drove a good [profitable] bargain with him.
〈거래에서[로]〉 이번 거래에서 그는 큰 손해를 보았다[큰 돈을 벌었다] He lost [made] a great deal of money on this deal.
▶ 그 거래로 나는 한 밑천 잡았다 The transaction afforded me a good profit.
—**거래하다** do business with; deal [have dealings] with; trade (in an article with sb)
▶ 당사는 그 회사와 20년이 넘게 거래하고 있다 We have been dealing [doing business] with the firm for more than twenty years.
▶ 그 회사와는 몇차례 양모 제품을 거래한 적이 있다 We have had several dealings with that firm regarding woolen products.
■ 공정— fair trade [transactions] 국내— domestic [home] trade 금전— lending and borrowing money 대량— a big [large-scale] transaction 부정[불법]— shady [illegal, unlawful] transactions 상— a business deal; business transactions; commercial dealings 신용— dealings on credit; credit transactions 암— black market 장내— transactions on exchanges 장외— off-board transactions 주식[증권]— dealings in stocks 현금— cash transactions 현물— spot transactions [sale] ■—가격 the market price; the price agreed on —관계 business connections [relations] —량[액] the volume [amount] of business; turnover : 뉴욕 증권거래소의 거래량 volume on the New York Stock Exchange —방법 the mode of dealing [transactions] —안내 a store bulletin —은행 one's bank; a correspondent bank —제한 restraint of trade —조건 terms and conditions of business

거래소 去來所 an exchange; 〈증권〉 a stock exchange [market]
♦ 거래소의 시세 an exchange quotation
■ 곡물[미곡]— a grain [rice] exchange 증권— a stock [securities] exchange

거래처 去來處 〈고객〉 a customer; a client; 〈거래관계자〉 a business acquaintance [connection] ♦ 거래처가 많다 have a large connection (in)

거론하다 擧論— make *sth* a subject of discussion; take a subject [problem] for discussion; touch (the point at issue)
▶ 이 책에서 그는 오늘날의 사회 문제를 거론하고 있다 In this book he discusses social problems of the day.

거루 a lighter ⇨ 거룻배

거룩하다 divine; heavenly; holy; sacred; sublime; noble
♦ 하느님의 거룩하신 은혜 divine grace / 거룩하신 하느님 holy God / 거룩한 가르침 holy teachings / 거룩한 자기 희생 sublime self-sacrifice

거룻배 a lighter; a barge; (총칭) lighterage
■ —사공 a lighterman; a bargeman

거류 居留 residence; residing
—거류하다 be a resident (of); reside (in); dwell [live] (at, in)
♦ 3년 이상 거류한 외국인 a foreigner of more than three years' residence
■ —외국인 foreign residents (in); resident aliens (in) —지 a settlement; a concession

거류민 居留民 (foreign) residents (in, at)
■ —재일— Korean residents in Japan —단 a settlement corporation : 재일 대한민국 거류민단 the Korean Residents Association in Japan

거르다¹ 〈여과하다〉 filter; strain (off [out]); percolate; leach
♦ 거른 물 filtered water / 〈체로〉 간장을 거르다 strain soy sauce (through a sieve) / 삶아낸 국물을 거르다 strain the stock / 모래로 물을 거르다 filter [percolate] water through sand / 차를 거르다 strain tea / 커피 찌꺼기를 걸러내다 strain out coffee grounds / 불순물을 걸러서 제거하다 filter out impurities

거르다² 〈건너뛰다〉 skip (over); omit
♦ 하루[이틀] 걸러 every other [third] day / 한 집 걸러 옆집 (the) nextdoor but one / 아침을 거르다 go without breakfast / 한 줄을 거르다 skip [omit] a line

거름 〈비료〉 manure; 〈화학 비료〉 fertilizer; 〈마소의 배설물〉 muck; dressing; 〈인분〉 night soil
♦ 거름을 주다 manure (the soil [field]); put fertilizer (on); fertilize (a plant [garden]); cover (the field) with manure [compost] / 거름을 푸다 dip out night soil
▶ 이 거름은 효과가 좋다 This manure works well.
—거름하다 manure (the field with dung); fertilize
■ —구덩이 a manure sink; 〈오물의〉 a cesspit [cesspool]; a night soil reservoir —통 a nightsoil [美俗] honey] bucket; a manure tub

거름종이 〔化〕 filter paper

거리¹ 〈길거리〉 a road; a street; 〈항간〉 the town
♦ 넓은[좁은] 거리 a broad [narrow] street / 번화한[쓸쓸한] 거리 a busy [deserted] street / 조용한[혼잡한] 거리 a quiet [crowded] street / 거리마다 on every street
〈거리의〉 거리의 불량배 street roughs; hooligans / 거리의 여론 the opinion of the man in the street / 거리의 천사 a homeless child; a street urchin [arab] / 거리의 화제가 되다 become the talk [gossip] of the town
▶ 거리의 소문을 모르고 계십니까? Aren't you aware of the gossip in the street?
〈거리는〉 저녁 무렵에 거리는 사람들로 붐비고 있었다 In the evening the streets were bustling with people.
〈거리를〉 거리를 지나가는 인파 the crowd passing along the street / 거리를 걷다 walk along [on] the street
▶ 거리를 지나다가 선생님을 만났다 I met my teacher as I was going along the street.
▶ 거리를 깨끗이 합시다 (게시) Keep the town tidy.
■ —네— a crossroads; a cross street 뒷— a back street 삼— a forked road; the fork of a road

거리² 〈재료〉 material; matter; stuff; makings; 〈원인〉 a cause; a source; 〈대상〉 a subject
▶ 그에게 말을 붙일 거리가 없다 I can't find any excuse [pretext] to approach him.
■ 걱정— a cause [source] of worry: 나에게는 걱정거리가 그칠 날이 없다 I never come to the end of my anxieties. 국— soup makings; soup stock 반찬— materials for making side dishes 불평— the cause of complaint 웃음— a laughingstock; a butt of ridicule 일— a piece of work; a job

거리 距離 (a) distance; 〈간격〉 an interval; a gap; 〈차이〉 (a) difference; 〈사정 거리〉 range
♦ 건너편까지의 거리 the distance across / 상당한 거리 a good [pretty long] distance / 지구와 태양간의 거리 the distance between the earth and the sun
〈거리가[는]〉 거리가 멀다 be distant; be far; 〈차이가 있다〉 be very different (from) / 상대방과의 거리가 벌어지다 lag behind *one's* opponent(s)
▶ 여기서 그 마을까지는 거리가 멀다 It's a long way [great distance] from here to the town.
▶ 〔會話〕「서울에서 수원까지는 거리가 얼마나 됩니까?」「약 40킬로미터입니다」 "How far is it [What is the distance] from Seoul to Suwon?" "It's about 40 kilometers."
▶ 우리는 아직도 의견에 상당한 거리가 있는 것 같다 There seems to be still a great difference of opinion between us.
▶ 나는 그 사람의 솜씨를 따라가려면 아직 거리가 멀다 I have a long way to go before I even approach his skill.
▶ 그것은 이상과는 거리가 먼 것이다 It is far removed from the ideal.
▶ 교통 수단이 발달함에 따라서 세계의 거리는 더욱 좁아진다 The world grow smaller as the means of transportation improve. ⇒

Advances in transportation shrink distances. 〈**거리를**〉 3미터의 거리를 두고 at intervals of 3 meters apart (from each other) / 거리를 벌려 놓다 〈이기다〉 get a good lead (on) / 거리를 재다 measure [calculate] the distance (of, between)
▶ 우리는 그 거리를 세 시간에 갔다 We covered [made, did] the distance in three hours.
▶ 그들과는 거리를 좀 두는 것이 좋다 You'd better keep them at a distance [keep a distance from them]. ⇌ You should stay clear of them.
▶ 앞차와는 안전 거리를 유지해라 Keep a safe distance from the car in front of you.
▶ 그는 선두 주자와의 거리를 점점 좁혀갔다 He gradually closed the gap [shortened the distance] between himself and the front-runner.
▶ 나는 2위 선수와의 거리를 더욱 넓혀 가고 있었다 I was widening my lead over the next runner.
〈**거리에**〉 같은 거리에 at equal distance (from the point) / 100미터 거리에 at 100-meters' [a 100-meter] distance / 일정한 거리에 at a certain distance
▶ 그곳은 엎어지면 코닿을 거리에 있다 It's within [at] a stone's throw.
▶ 야구장은 우리 학교에서 걸어서 갈 수 있는 거리에 있다 The ball park is within walking distance from our school.
▶ 요금은 거리에 따라서 다르다 The charge depends on [The fares vary with] the distance.
▶ 그 정거장은 걸어서[차로] 10분 거리에 있다 The station is ten minutes' walk [ride] from here.
■ 비행— fly; a flight 순항— a cruising distance 장(중, 단)— long [middle, short] distance 직선— distance in a straight line: 그 마을은 여기서 직선 거리로 10킬로미터쯤 된다 The village is about ten kilometers distant from here in a straight line. 착탄— the range (of a gun); (within) gunshot 활공— a gliding distance 활주— a taxiing distance ―감(感) the sense of distance ―경주 a distance race ―계 a range finder; a telemeter ―표 a distance mark [post]; 〈이정표〉 a milepost [milestone]

거리끼다 be afraid (of doing, to do); be shy (of [about] doing); weigh on *one's* mind; lie at *one's* heart; get on *one's* nerves; 〈망설이다〉 hesitate (to do)
▶ 나는 그 사실이 마음에 거리낀다 The fact weighs on my mind.
▶ 아무래도 마음에 거리낀다 It haunts me.
▶ 그것이 거리끼어 이 일까지 실패했다 That stood in the way of successful conclusion of this business.
▶ 그는 누구 앞에서든 거리끼지 않고 자기 의견을 말한다 He gives his opinion in anybody's presence.
▶ 경찰을 거리낄 이유가 전혀 없다 There is no reason to fear the police.
▶ 나는 아무것도 거리낄 것이 없다 I can look the world in the face.

거리낌 〈주저〉 hesitation; 〈가책〉 compunction; 〈사양〉 reserve
◆ 거리낌없는 비평 an unsparing criticism / 거리낌없는 친구 a friend on frank terms / 마음에 거리낌이 없다 do not weigh on one's mind
▶ 우리는 아무런 거리낌도 없었다 We were free from care [worry].

거리낌없이 without reserve [hesitation]; with no restraint; unreservedly; freely; 〈남에게 신경을 쓰지 않고〉 regardless of the others
◆ 거리낌없이 말하는 outspoken / 거리낌없이 말하다 speak without reserve; speak out / 남의 물건을 거리낌없이 쓰다 make free with another's possession
▶ 그는 그것이 자기 것이라고 거리낌없이 주장한다 He doesn't hesitate to claim it to be his possession.
▶ 그 남자는 아무 데서나 거리낌없이 담배를 피운다 The man smokes anywhere without the least compunction [quite unshamedly].

거마 車馬 horses and vehicles; traffic; transportation
■ ―비 traffic expenses; carfare

거만 巨萬 millions; a vast [fabulous] fortune
◆ 거만의 갑부다 be (as) rich as Croesus; be a multimillionaire
▶ 그는 거만의 부를 쌓았다 He has made a vast fortune [piled up vast wealth].

거만 倨慢 〈건방짐〉 haughtiness; 〈주제넘음〉 impertinence; self-importance
◆ 거만을 떨다 give *oneself* airs; ride the high horse
――**거만하다** arrogant; haughty; overbearing; domineering; lordly; pompous; high-hat
◆ 거만한 태도 a lofty air; a haughty bearing / 거만하게 haughtily; arrogantly; importantly / 거만한 사람의 콧대를 꺾다 humble *sb's* pride; knock *sb* off his high horse / 거만해 보이다 look self-important [haughty]; (口) look stuck-up; (口) look snooty / 거만하게 굴다 behave haughtily; assume an air of importance
▶ 그 사람은 태도가 거만하다 He has a high and mighty air about him. ⇌ He has a supercilious manner.
▶ 그는 누구에게나 거만하다 He is haughty to everybody.
▶ 그는 출세하더니 거만해졌다 He is stuck-up by his success.

거머들이다 rake [drive] in greedily; gather [collect] greedily

거머리 〔動〕 a leech; 〈성가신 사람〉 a bur; a nuisance; a pest
◆ 거머리같은 leechlike / 거머리처럼 달라붙다 stick like a leech / 거머리처럼 고혈을 빨다 leech *sb* (until his fortune is exhausted)

거머잡다 grab ⇨ 거머쥐다

거머쥐다 grab (at); grip; grasp; clutch [take hold of] greedily
◆ 멱살을 거머쥐다 grab *sb* by the collar / 실권을 거머쥐다 take [hold] the reins of (government) / 잔뜩 거머쥐다 take all that *one's* fist can hold

거멀못 a clamp; a cramp; a clincher

거목 巨木 a great [large, big] tree; a gigantic [towering] tree
거무스름하다 blackish; darkish; 〈얼굴이〉 swarthy
 ♦피부가 거무스름한 dark-skinned / 거무스름해지다 get [go, become] blackish [darkish]
 ▶천장은 연기에 그을어 거무스름했다 The ceiling was tinged black with smoke.
 ▶그는 거무스름한 옷을 입고 있었다 He was wearing a darkish [blackish] suit.
거문고 a *kŏmungo*; a Korean harp with six strings
거물 巨物 〈실력자〉 a big man; a magnate; (美口) a bigwig; a big shot; 〈요인〉 an important figure; a VIP; 〈물건〉 a big thing
 ♦당대의 거물 the lion of the day / 재계[정계]의 거물 a financial magnate [leading figure in the political world]; (口) a business mogul [big wheel in politics] / 거물 정치가 a politician of great caliber [of stature]; (口) a big-name [big-shot] politician
 ▶그는 이 업계의 거물이다 He is very important in this trade.
거뭇거뭇하다 black-spotted ⇨ 가뭇가뭇하다
거뭇하다 blackish ⇨ 가뭇하다
거미 a spider
 ▶거미가 집을 짓고 있는 것을 보았다 I saw a spider spinning its web.
 ■—발 〈보석의〉 a jewel support [chain] shaped like a spider's legs —집 a spider('s) web; cobwebs
거미도 줄을 쳐야 벌레를 잡는다 〈속담〉 No gains without pains.
거미줄 1 〈거미의 줄〉 a spider's thread; 〈거미집〉 a spider's web; a cobweb
 ♦거미줄 투성이의 cobwebby; full of cobwebs / 거미줄을 치다 spin [weave] a web / 거미줄을 털다 clear (the ceiling) of cobwebs / 입에 거미줄치다 starve; be starved [famished]; go hungry
 ▶전선이 거미줄 처럼 얽혀 있다 Telegraph wires are stretched like cobwebs.
 ▶낙엽 하나가 거미줄에 걸렸다 A fallen leaf was caught in a spider's web.
 2 〈수사망〉 a dragnet; a police cordon ♦거미줄을 치다 cast a dragnet (around the district); post [place] a cordon
거반 居牛 almost ⇨ 거지반
거베라 〔植〕 a gerbera; a Transvaal daisy
거병하다 擧兵— raise [muster] an army (against); take up arms (against) ▶반군이 남부에서 거병했다 A rebel army was raised in the south.
거보 巨步 a giant step; a mammoth stride; 〈공적〉 a brilliant achievement
 ♦거보를 내디디다 take a giant step (toward); make a mammoth stride (forward) (in); make long strides (in)
거봐라 Look!; See!; You see!; I told you so!
 ▶거봐라, 내 말이 맞잖아 There, I told you so! ⇌ Look! Didn't I tell you?
거부 巨富 a very wealthy [rich] person; a man of great wealth; a millionaire [billionaire]; a Croesus

거부 拒否 refusal; rejection; (a) denial; (a) veto 《*pl.* ~es》; disapproval

> 解說 **refusal**은 신중히 생각하여 불찬성의 태도를 취하기, **rejection**은 요구·제의 등을 딱 잘라서 거절하기, **denial**은 상대방의 권리 주장을 인정하지 않기, **veto**는 제안 등을 부인하는 것을 의미한다.

—**거부하다** deny; reject; refuse; turn down; veto (a proposal); boycott (a lecture)
 ♦딱 잘라 거부하다 refuse roundly; give *sb* a flat refusal / 법안을 거부하다 veto a bill / 제안을 거부하다 refuse [turn down, reject] a proposal
 ▶사장은 노조의 요구를 거부했다 The president rejected [turned down] the request of the union.
 ▶외국인 기자는 그 기자회견에 참가를 거부당했다 Foreign reporters were denied admission to the press conference.
 ■—반응 〔醫〕 rejection (symptoms): 그 환자는 이식된 장기에 거부 반응을 일으켰다 The patient rejected the transplanted organ.
거부권 拒否權 the veto right (of the Big Powers); a veto 《*pl.* ~es》
 ♦거부권이 없는 회원국 vetoless members / 거부권을 써서 부결시키다 veto (a proposal); block (a proposal) with a veto / 거부권을 행사하다 exercise *one's* veto (power) (over); veto
 ▶대통령은 그 의안에 거부권을 행사했다 The President vetoed the bill.
거북 〈육지·민물의〉 a tortoise; 〈바다의〉 a turtle
 ■—선 the "Turtle Ship [Boat]"; an ironclad warship shaped like a turtle
거북점 —占 divination by baked tortoise shells; 〈골패의〉 divination by using a set of dominoes of tortoise shapes
 ♦거북점을 치다 tell (*sb's*) fortune by baked [burning] tortoise shells
거북하다 1 〈몸이〉 unwell; out of condition [order]
 ♦뱃속이 거북하다 have something wrong with *one's* inside / 숨쉬기가 거북하다 breathe with difficulty; be out of breath
 ▶이 옷옷은 목께가 거북하다 I feel this coat tight about the neck.
 ▶속이 거북해요 I got my stomach out of order.
 2 〈마음이〉 awkward; embarrassing; ill at ease; uncomfortable
 ♦듣기 거북한 말 words offensive [disagreeable] to hear [to the ear] / 거북한 자리 an uncomfortable seat; an awkward meeting / 거북한 표현 an awkward [a clumsy] expression / 입장이 거북하다 find *oneself* in an awkward position / 거북하게 하다 make *sb* self-conscious; put *sb* out of countenance; abash
 ▶그 사람 앞에 가면 어쩐지 거북하다 I feel rather awkward in his presence.
 ▶그 사람이 빤히 쳐다봐서 나는 거북했다 He stared at me out of countenance.

▶ 낯선 집에 가면 거북한 법이다 One feels ill at ease in a stranger's house.
▶ 그들은 서로 만나기를 거북해 한다 They feel awkward about seeing each other.
▶ 그들은 사이가 거북해졌다 They don't get on so well as before.
▶ 나는 그곳에 있기가 몹시 거북해졌다 The place became too hot for me.

거붓하다 rather light ⇨ 가붓하다
거비 巨費 a great [huge] cost [outlay]; an enormous sum
거뿐하다 light ⇨ 가뿐하다
거뿟하다 (rather) light ⇨ 가붓하다
거사 居士 a retired scholar [official]; 〔佛教〕 a Buddhist devotee
거사 擧事 taking [initiating] an action; a revolt; an uprising **—거사하다** take [initiate] an action; undertake 《a revolt》; rise in revolt [rebellion] 《against》
■—일 the D-day 《for a military coup》
거상 巨商 a wealthy merchant; a merchant prince; a business magnate
거상 居喪 〈상중〉 being in mourning; 〈상복〉 a mourning attire [dress] **—거상하다** be in mourning
거상 巨像 a colossus 《pl. ~es, colossi》; a huge statue; a gigantic image
거석 巨石 a huge stone; 〔考古〕 a megalith
■—묘 a megalithic tomb **—문화** (a) megalithic culture
거선 巨船 a big [huge, mammoth] ship; a leviathan
거성 巨星 a big [giant] star; 〈인물〉 a great man; a prominent man; a luminary; (口) a big shot
▶ 문단의 거성 a great [leading] figure in the literary world; a great writer / 음악계의 거성 a musical superstar / 화단의 거성 a great painter
▶ 거성이 떨어졌다 A great man is lost [has died]. ⇌ A great star has fallen.
거세 去勢 1 〈가축 등의〉 castration; emasculation **—거세하다** castrate; emasculate; geld; 〈정신적으로〉 effeminate; enervate
▶ 이 소는 거세한 소다 This ox is castrated.
2 〈세력의 약화〉 weakening; 〈숙청〉 a purge; 〈축출〉 expulsion
—거세하다 purge 《disloyal elements》 from; destroy [undermine] sb's influence
▶ 그 나라의 사회주의 세력은 거세되었다 The socialist forces of the country were eradicated.
▶ 그의 사후 그 운동은 거세되었다 His death emasculated [enervated] the movement.
■—가축 a castrated animal; a neuter **—계** (鷄) a capon **—돈** (豚) a castrated pig **—마** (馬) a gelding **—술** castration; gelding **—양** a wether **—우** (牛) a bullock; a steer
거세다 violent; tough; coarse; wild; 〔晉聲〕 aspirated
♦ 거센 기질 a fiery temper; wild nature / 거센 바람 a strong [high, fierce] wind / 거센 소리 an aspirate; aspirated sounds / 거센 어조 a sharp [an excited] tone / 거센 여자 an unruly woman / 거센 폭풍우 a violent [furious] storm / 거센 세파에 시달리다 suffer the hardships of life; be buffeted about in the world / 거센 파도에 휩쓸리다 be tossed about by angry waves
▶ 배는 거센 파도를 헤치고 나아갔다 The ship plowed through the surging waves [high seas]. ⇌ The ship made her way into rough waters.
▶ 바람은 더욱더 거세어졌다 The wind became stronger and stronger [more and more furious].
▶ 불길이 거세어졌다 The fire gathered strength.

거소 居所 a dwelling place ⇨ 거처(居處)
거수 擧手 raising one's hand; 〈표결의〉 a show of hands
♦ 거수로 표결하다 vote 《on question》 by a show of hands
▶ 이 문제는 거수로 결정하겠습니다 We will decide this matter by a show of hands.
—거수하다 raise one's hand; 〈표결에서〉 show one's hand
▶ 찬성하는 분은 거수하여 주시기 바랍니다 Those in favor, please indicate by a show of hands.
▶ 질문이 있으면 거수해 주세요 Please raise your hand, if you have a question.
거수경례 擧手敬禮 a military [hand] salute
—거수경례하다 give [make] a military salute; raise one's hand in salute
거수기 擧手機 a rubber stamp
♦ 행정부의 정책에 거수기 노릇을 하다 rubber-stamp [be an amenable rubber stamp] for an administration policy
거스러미 〈손톱 뒤의〉 an agnail; a hangnail; 〈나무의〉 a fine split; a splinter ♦ 거스러미가 생기다 have [get] a hangnail
거스러지다 〈성질이〉 grow wild [stubborn, unruly]; become rough [rude]; become unmanageable [intractable]; 〈잔털이〉 bristle (up); get ruffled
▶ 그 아이가 아주 거스러졌다 The child has become intractably wild.
▶ 양탄자는 거스러져 있었다 The carpet was scuffed up.
거스르다 1 〈역행[거역]하다〉 run counter (to); go [act] against 《sb's will》; 〈반대하다〉 oppose; 〈따르지 않다〉 disobey; 〈반항하다〉 revolt [rebel] 《against》; defy
♦ …을 거슬러서 against…; in the face [teeth] of…; in defiance of… / 명령을 거스르다 act in defiance of orders / 시대의 조류를 거스르다 go against the tide [stream, current] of the times / 하늘의 뜻을 거스르다 fly in the face of Providence; give offense to the will of God / 바람을 거슬러서 나아가다 go in the teeth of the wind
▶ 그 남자는 물결을 거슬러 헤엄쳤다 He swam against the stream.
▶ 그는 남의 비위를 거스르지 않으려고 노력했다 He tried not to cause offense.
2 〈잔돈을〉 give [make] the change
♦ 거슬러 주다[받다] give back [get] the

거스름돈 change / 천원을 받고 2백원을 거슬러 주다 give two hundred won (in return) for one thousand won
▶만원짜리를 내시면 거슬러 드립니다 You will get change if you give a 10,000-won note.

거스름돈 change
♦만원짜리를 내고 받은 거스름돈 the change from a ten thousand-won note / 거스름돈을 속이는 상인[점원] a short-change artist / 거스름돈을 주다[받다] give (back) [get] the change / 거스름돈을 속이다 short-change / 거스름돈을 확인하다 examine *one's* change 《before leaving the counter》
▶거스름돈 여기 있습니다 Here's your change.
▶거스름돈이 백원입니다 That makes a hundred won change.
▶거스름돈은 그만 두세요 (You can [may]) Keep the change.
▶점원은 내게 거스름돈을 덜 주었다 The clerk gave me the wrong change.
▶거스름돈 없음 《게시》 No change given.

거슬거슬하다 〈성질이〉 rough; wild; disobedient; intractable; 〈피부가〉 rough; coarse
♦거슬거슬한 감촉[촉감] a rough [sandy] feel [texture] / 거슬거슬한 피부 rough [coarse] skin / 성질이 거슬거슬하다 have a rough disposition
▶그의 손은 터서 거슬거슬했다 His hands were chapped and rough.

거슬러올라가다 1 〈강을〉 go upstream [against the stream]; go [배로] sail, row] up 《a river》
▶연어는 알을 낳기 위해 강을 거슬러 올라간다 Salmon go upstream to spawn.
2 〈시대가〉 date [go] back 《to》; date from; trace back
♦기원을 거슬러 올라가다 trace *sth* back to its origin
▶이 축제는 중세까지 거슬러 올라간다 This festival dates back to the Middle Ages.
▶이야기는 내 어린 시절로 거슬러 올라간다 The story goes back to my childhood.
3 〈기한이〉 be retrospective 《to》; be retroactive 《to》
▶새로운 급여액[이 법률]은 5월 1일로 거슬러 올라가서 적용된다 The new pay scale [This law] is effective retroactive [retroactive] to May 1.

거슬리다 offend; be offensive; be against the grain; be in opposition to 《*one's* temper》
♦비위에 거슬리는 galling; provoking / 귀에 거슬리다 be [sound] harsh [grating, offensive] to the ear / 눈에 거슬리다 be unpleasant to the eye; be an eyesore / 뜻에 거슬리다 be not congenial; be not to *one's* taste [liking]
▶그 녀석이 하는 말, 하는 짓이 모두 내 비위에 거슬린다 Everything he does or says rubs me the wrong way.
▶그것은 내 성미에 거슬린다 It goes against the grain with me.
▶그의 빈정대는 듯한 웃음이 내 신경에 거슬렸다 His snide laugh jarred [got] on my nerves.
▶제가 감정에 거슬리는 말을 했다면 용서하십시오 Forgive me if my remark hurt your feelings [offended you].

거슴츠레하다 sleepy; drowsy; dull; heavy
♦거슴츠레한 눈으로 with sleepy [drowsy, dull, heavy] eyes / 눈이 거슴츠레하다 have heavy eyes; be dull-eyed [heavy-eyed]
▶너는 눈이 거슴츠레하구나 Your eyes look heavy.

거시기 〈대명사적〉 what-do-you-call-it; what-you-may-call-it; whatchamacallit; thingamabob; thingamajig; so-and-so; what's-his-name; 〈감탄사적〉 what was it [he] called that...
▶거시기 어디 갔지? Where is Mr. So-and-so [What's-his-name]?
▶내 거시기 어디 있지? Where is my whatchamacallit [thingumbob]?
▶거시기 그게 뭐더라? That—what was it called—that thingamajig?

거시적 巨視的 〔物·數·經〕 macroscopic; 〈견해가〉 comprehensive; all-inclusive
♦거시적인 견해 a broad point of view / 거시적인 세계 a macroscopic world / 사물을 거시적으로 보다 see *sth* in broad perspective; take a broad view of *sth*
■—경제학 macroeconomics —물리학 macrophysics —분석 〔經〕 macroscopic analysis; macroanalysis —이론 〔經〕 a macroscopic theory

거식하다 〈동사적〉 do something or other 《with》; 〈형용사적〉 hard 《to say》; awkward 《to say》
▶어쩐지 기분이 거식하다 Somehow I feel uneasy about it.
▶말하기 거식해서 아무 말도 하지 않았다 I was in some doubt whether I should bring it up, so I said nothing.
▶말하기 거식하지만 돈 좀 빌려 주세요 I hate to ask, but please lend me some money.

거식하다 擧式— hold a ceremony; 〈결혼의〉 celebrate [solemnize] the wedding 《of... and...》

거실 居室 a sitting room; a living room; a parlor
▶그를 거실로 안내하여라 Show him into the living room.

거액 巨額 an enormous [a huge] sum (of money); a lot [a great deal] of money
♦거액이 들다 cost an enormous sum of money / 거액을 벌다 make a lot of money / 거액에 달하다 reach [amount to] a huge [colossal] sum
▶1억원은 거액이다 One hundred million won is a mint of money.
▶그는 거액을 들여 20층짜리 빌딩을 지었다 He has built a 20-story building at great cost.

거목 〔植〕 a medic

거역 拒逆 disobedience; insubordination; objection; opposition
—거역하다 be disobedient [insubordinate] 《to》; disobey 《*one's* parents》; go [act] against 《*sb's* will》; object 《to》; oppose
♦상관의 명령을 거역하다 object to the order of *one's* superior; disobey [run counter to] commands of *one's* boss / 신의 뜻을 거역하다 give offense to the will of God

▶그는 부모님의 뜻을 거역하고 그 여자와 결혼했다 He married her against his parents' will [contrary to his parents' wishes].
▶명령을 절대 거역하지 않겠습니다 I will be all obedience to your commands.

거울 1 〈비춰보는〉 a mirror; a looking glass; [醫] a speculum ((*pl.* -la)
◆거울을 보고 넥타이를 매다 tie *one's* tie at a mirror / 거울에 자기 모습을 비춰 보다 look at [see] *oneself* in a mirror
▶신문[눈]은 사회[마음]의 거울이다 The press [eye] is the mirror of society [the soul].
▶그는 외출하기 전에 거울을 슬쩍 들여다보았다 Before going out, he had a quick look in the mirror.
▶그녀는 거울을 보면서 옷을 입고 있다 She is dressing in front of her mirror.
▶바다는 거울처럼 잔잔했다 The sea was as smooth as glass [like a mirror].
2 〈귀감〉 a pattern; a model; a paragon; an exemplar; a mirror
■-손— a hand mirror 편면(片面)— a one-way glass [mirror]

거울삼다 1 〈모범으로 삼다〉 follow the pattern [example, model] of *sb*; take *sb* for a model; learn from *sth*; pattern [model] after *sb*
◆부모님을 거울삼다 follow the pattern of *one's* parents / 현인의 덕행을 거울삼다 learn from the virtuous conducts of sages
2 〈경계하다〉 take warning [example] 《by》; take a lesson 《from》
◆과거의 실패를 거울삼아 in (the) light of the past failure
◆남의 실패를 거울삼아라 Take a lesson from [warning by] another's failure. ⇌ Learn wisdom from the follies of others.

거웃 pubic hair; pubes

거위¹ 〈鳥〉 a goose ((*pl.* geese); 〈수컷〉 a gander; a male goose; 〈兒〉 a goosey
■-새끼 a gosling

거위² 〈회충〉 an intestinal worm; a roundworm; an ascarid; a mawworm ■-배 stomach trouble caused by roundworms

거의 〈대체로〉 almost; nearly; practically; well-nigh; next to; 〈약〉 about; some; in the neighborhood of; 〈대부분〉 mostly; 〈부정적으로〉 little; few; hardly; scarcely
◆거의 전부 almost all; mostly; most 《of》 / 거의 한 시간 almost [nearly] one hour / 거의 불가능하다 be next to [nearly, virtually] impossible
▶그것은 거의 꿈 같았다 It was almost like a dream.
▶나는 그 일을 거의 잊어버렸다 I almost forgot about that.
▶도서관은 거의 완성되었다 The library is nearly [almost] completed.
▶[會話] 「다 끝났니?」「거의요」 "Are you through (with it)?" "Almost [Just about]."
▶나는 그것을 거의 공짜로 입수했다 I got it for next to nothing.
▶그녀는 거의 알몸이었다 She was all but nude.
▶나는 너와 체중이 거의 같다 I weigh about [almost] the same as you. (▶almost 나 nearly 는 약간 밑도는, about은 그 전후를 가리킴)
▶그 마을은 지금도 옛날과 거의 같다 The town is much [almost] the same now as it used to be.
▶협상은 거의 막바지 단계에 이르렀다 The negotiations have been brought well-nigh to a conclusion.
▶그가 성공한 것은 거의 기적이다 His success is little short of a miracle.
▶희망은 거의 없다 There is little hope.
▶그들에게는 먹을 것이 거의 없었다 They had scarcely [hardly] anything to eat.
▶그들은 내 설명을 거의 알아듣지 못했다 They understood (very) little of my explanation.
▶나는 그를 거의 못 만납니다 I hardly ever meet him.
▶그 사건은 아는 사람이 거의 없다 Hardly anyone knows [Very few people know] the incident.
▶나는 어젯밤 잠을 거의 못 잤다 I could hardly sleep last night.
▶[會話] 「여기 자주 오십니까?」「거의 안 옵니다」 "Do you come here often?" "Hardly ever."

거인 巨人 a giant; a Titan; a Goliath; 〈유력자〉 a leading figure; 〈거물〉 a great figure
◆여자 거인 a giantess / 재계의 거인 a leading figure in financial circles
■-국 a land of giants; 〈걸리버 여행기의〉 Brobdingnag -증 [醫] giantism; gigantism

거장 巨匠 a (great) master; 〈음악의〉 a maestro ((*pl.* ~s, -stri); a virtuoso
◆문단의 거장 a great [master] writer; a great man of letters / 미술의 거장 a great painter; a master artist / 악단(樂壇)의 거장 a celebrated [distinguished] musician

거재 巨財 a vast [an enormous] fortune; great [vast, colossal] wealth
◆거재를 쌓다 build up an enormous fortune / 거재를 투자하다 invest [sink] millions (of dollars) (in an enterprise)

거저 1 〈공짜로〉 free; free of charge; for nothing; by [of] free gift
◆남의 것을 거저 가져가다 take away another's belongings without paying for them
▶너한테는 그것을[한 부] 거저 주겠다 You shall have it for nothing [I'll give you a free copy].
▶거저 준대도 싫다 I would not have [take] it at [even as] a gift.
▶그 일을 거저 해 드리겠습니다 I will make no charge for the work.
▶거저 얻는 것만큼 비싼 것은 없다 Nothing is as costly as a free gift.
▶내가 너에게 이것을 주기는 주지만 거저는 아니다 This thing I'm handing you is not a handout.
▶나는 이 셔츠를 거저나 다름없이 샀다 I bought this shirt for practically nothing [at a giveaway price].
▶천원이라면 거저나 다름없습니다 At only one

thousand won, it is practically free. ⇌ It is 1,000 won and a present at that.
2 〈하는 일 없이〉 idly; lazily; without doing anything (in particular)
♦거저 세월만 보내다 idle [loaf] away *one's* time [days]; fool around [about]
▶나는 거저 앉아 있다 I am sitting down doing nothing.
▶거저 세월만 보내고 있지 마라 Don't stay fooling around [about].

거저먹기 an easy task [job]; an easy thing to do; a child's play
▶그것은 거저먹기다 That's quite an easy job [task]. ⇌ That's as easy as pie. ⇌ Nothing is easier. ⇌ That's cinch.

거적 a straw mat; (총칭) straw matting
♦거적을 덮다 cover *sth* with straw matting / 거적을 짜다 weave [make, plait] a straw mat / 거적에 싸다 wrap *sth* in straw matting
■—눈 eyes with the upper eyelids hanging down loosely; eyes with the drooping upper eyelids —때기 a piece of a straw mat —문 a door made of straw matting; a straw-mat door —송장 a corpse wrapped in straw matting —자리 a straw-mat seat

거적문에 돌쩌귀 (속담) Don't use a nail when string will do.

거절 拒絕 (a) rejection; (a) refusal; a turn-down; 〈퇴짜〉 a rebuff; (口) the brush-off
♦단호한 거절 a decided rejection / 거절 편지 a letter of refusal
—**거절하다** refuse; reject; turn down; decline; rebuff; deny; say no (to)

|解說| *refuse*는 신청·요구·초대 등을 분명하게 강한 어조로, *reject*는 제안·요구를 불필요·부적당하다고 단호히 거절하다란 뜻으로 reject가 refuse보다 강하다. *turn down*은 refuse, reject보다 완곡하고 스스럼없는 말투이고, *decline*은 신청·제안·초대 등을 정중하고 부드럽게 거절하다란 뜻이다.

♦면회를 거절하다 decline to see *sb*; deny *oneself* to a caller / 지급을 거절하다 refuse payment; decline to pay / 거절당하다 be rejected; get the brush-off
▶나는 그의 제의[요구]를 거절했다 I turned down [rejected] his offer [demand].
▶그는 나의 제의를 딱잘라서 거절했다 He refused [declined] my offer point-blank. ⇌ He gave a flat refusal [denial] to my offer.
▶오는 사람 거절하지 않고 가는 사람 쫓지 않는다 You are free to come and go.
▶그의 전근 요청은 거절당했다 His transfer request was rejected.
■인수[지급]— 〈어음의〉 nonacceptance [nonpayment] —증(症) (口) negativism —증서 a protest [for nonpayment [nonacceptance]]

거점 據點 〈근거지〉 a foothold; a base; 〈요새·진지〉 a stronghold; a position
♦성장 거점 도시 a nucleus city / 작전상의 거점을 확보하다 obtain [secure] a strategic foothold
▶이 회사는 유럽에 강력한 영업 거점을 보유하고 있다 This company has a strong business foothold in Europe.
■군사— a strategic point 방위— a strongpoint

거족적 舉族的 nationwide; national ♦거족적인 축제일 a day of national celebration / 거족적으로 on a national scale; throughout the nation

거주 居住 residence; dwelling; abode
♦거주 이전의 자유 the freedom of residence and change of residence / 거주가 일정치 않다 have no fixed abode [residence] / 거주를 확인하다 make certain of *sb's* address; ascertain *sb's* whereabouts
▶거주 불명 Address unknown. ⇌ Wrong address.
—**거주하다** live [dwell, reside] (at, in); be domiciled (at, in); inhabit (a place)
♦6개월 이상 거주한 외국인 a foreigner of more than six months' residence (in, at)
■—성 habitability; livability: 거주성이 좋은 집 a comfortable house to live in —시설 living accommodations; housing facilities —인구 the resident population —자격 residential qualifications —제한 residential restriction —증명서 a certificate of residence —지 *one's* place of residence —지역 the living [residential] district

거주권 居住權 the right of residence
♦거주권을 상실하다 lose *one's* claim to 《Korean》 domicile / 거주권을 침해하다 violate [infringe on] *sb's* right of residence

거주민 居住民 an inhabitant; a resident; 〈시민〉 a citizen; 〈토착민〉 a native

거주자 居住者 a resident; a dweller; an inhabitant
♦교외 거주자 a resident in the suburbs; a suburbanite / 불법 거주자 〈공유지·건물의〉 a squatter / 아파트 거주자 the inhabitants of an apartment house / 외국인 거주자 a foreign resident / 이 집의 전 거주자 the former occupants of this house

거죽 the surface; the face; 〈모피의〉 the grain side; 〈옷 등의〉 the right side

거중조정 居中調停 mediation; intermediation; intercession; arbitration; good offices
♦거중조정을 제의[부탁]하다 offer [ask] mediation / 거중조정에 나서다 undertake mediation; launch out for mediation; act as (a) peacemaker; 〈맡다〉 assume a mediation role
—**거중조정하다** mediate (between two countries); intermediate; arbitrate
♦분쟁을 거중 조정하다 mediate [arbitrate] a dispute (between contending nations)
▶회사와 노조를 거중 조정할 위원회가 지명되었다 A committee was appointed to arbitrate between the company and the union.
■—자 a mediator; an arbitrator; a peacemaker

거증 舉證 the establishment of a fact (by evidence); giving evidence —**거증하다** produce [present] evidence; establish a fact (by evidence)
■—책임 [法] the burden of proof

거지 a beggar; a mendicant; (美口) a panhandler
♦거지꼴 shabby look / 옷이 거지꼴이다 one's clothes get shabby / 거지 생활을 하다 go (about) begging; beg one's meals [bread]; live as a beggar / 거지 신세가 되다 be reduced to beggary; be brought to begging / 거지 (발싸개) 취급하다 treat sb as a beggar / 뱃속에 거지가 들어앉다 have a wolf in one's stomach / 거지로 죽다 die a beggar
▶한번 거지 생활에 맛들이면 평생 거지가 된다 Let a man be once a beggar and he will be a beggar all his life.
▶그 거지는 동냥을 별로 못 얻는다 The beggar gets little alms.

거지같다 good-for-nothing; trashy; wretched
♦거지같은 녀석[놈] a good-for-nothing; a wretched fellow; a worthless scamp / 거지같이 가난한 wretchedly poor
▶이 거지(발싸개) 같은 놈아 You filthy scum!
▶일이 거지 같이 되었다 Things took on an ugly look.

거지근성 ―根性 a mean [mercenary] spirit; the beggar
▶사람이 가난해지면 거지 근성이 나온다 When a man becomes poor, the beggar in him will come out.

거지반 居之半 almost; nearly; almost all
▶공사는 거지반 완성되었다 The work is nearly [almost] completed.
▶금년도 이제 거지반 갔다 This year is almost over now.
▶그는 평생을 거지반 해외에서 보냈다 He lived abroad for a great portion [the greater part] of his life.

거짓 1 〈명사적〉 a lie; a falsehood; 〈지어낸 일〉 fabrication; a fiction; 〈허위〉 a deceit; fraud
♦거짓 없는 대화 a sincere talk / 거짓 투성이 a pack of falsehoods / 거짓 웃음 a feigned smile / 거짓 눈물을 흘리다 shed sham tears; weep crocodile tears / 거짓임을 드러내다 prove sth to be false / 거짓으로 가르쳐 주다 give sb wrong information 《about》
▶그녀의 출생에 관한 이야기는 순전히 거짓이다 Her story of her birth is an out-and-out fabrication.
▶그의 말에는 거짓이 없다 All he says is true. ⇌ He always says the truth.
▶그는 법정에서 거짓 진술을 했다 He made a false statement in court.
2 〈부사적〉 falsely; deceitfully; fictitiously; dishonestly
♦거짓 친절한 체하다 feign kindness; pretend to be kind / 거짓 패주하다 pretend to be defeated and run away

거짓말 a lie; a falsehood; an untruth; (口) a story; 〈꾸며낸 이야기〉 a fabrication
♦계획적인 거짓말 a deliberate lie / 그럴 듯한 거짓말 a plausible [specious] lie / 빤히 들여다 보이는 거짓말 a transparent falsehood [lie] / 빤한 거짓말 a glaring lie / 새빨간 거짓말 a downright [barefaced] lie; a pure fabrication / 악의 없는[있는] 거짓말 a white [black] lie / 엄청난[터무니없는] 거짓말 a whopping lie / 거짓말 투성이 a pack [web, tissue] of lies / 거짓말 같은 사실 a case of fact being stranger than fiction / 거짓말 같은 이야기 an incredible story / 거짓말 잘하는 given to falsehood; mendacious / 거짓말을 늘어놓다 tell a pack [an array] of lies 《about》
▶거짓말 마라 You're a liar! ⇌ What a story! ⇌ You're just kidding me.
▶아무래도 거짓말 같다 That sounds incredible.
▶그가 아프다던 것은 새빨간 거짓말이었다 His illness was a perfect fake.
▶절대로 거짓말이 아니야 I mean everything I say.
▶그는 거짓말을 밥먹듯이 한다 He has no qualms about lying.
▶악의 없는 거짓말도 거짓말은 거짓말이다 A white lie is still a lie.
▶비가 두 시간이나 억수같이 쏟아지더니 갑자기 거짓말처럼 개었다 It had been raining hard for two hours, but it stopped suddenly as if by magic.

―거짓말하다 lie; tell a lie; tell an untruth; utter a falsehood
♦그럴 듯하게 거짓말하다 lie like the truth; lie as though telling the truth / 천연스럽게 거짓말하다 lie with a straight face / 태연히 거짓말하다 make no bones of telling a lie
▶그녀는 아프다고 거짓말하고 학교에 결석했다 She pretended to be ill and did not go to school.
▶거짓말하지 마라 Don't tell a lie!
▶그는 거짓말할 사람이 아니다 He is not a man to tell a lie.

거짓말쟁이 a liar; a fibber; a fibster; (口) a storyteller
♦거짓말쟁이라고 욕하다 call sb a liar; accuse sb of telling a lie
▶요 거짓말쟁이야 Oh, you story!
▶너는 순전히 거짓말쟁이구나 You're quite a fibber, aren't you?

거짓말탐지기 ―探知機 a lie detector; a polygraph ♦거짓말 탐지기로 조사하다 put sb under a lie detector; give sb a lie detector test

거참 Indeed!; O dear!; O my!; (O) Dear me!; Bless me!; Good gracious!
▶거참 묘하다 How odd [strange]!
▶거참 안됐군 Indeed, that was too bad!
▶거참 야단났는데 O dear! What shall I do?

거창하다 巨創― huge; enormous; gigantic
♦거창한 계획 a mammoth enterprise / 거창한 빌딩 a huge building / 거창한 직함 an ostentatious title / 사업을 거창하게 하다 carry on a business in a large way [on a large scale]
▶그 사람은 언제나 거창하게 말을 한다 He always talks in high-sounding terms.

거처 居處 〈거소〉 a dwelling place; one's abode [(place of) residence]; 〈거주〉 dwelling; living
▶거처를 옮기다 move [remove] 《to, into》; change one's address 《to》 / 거처를 정하다 take up one's abode 《at, in》; make one's home 《at, in》; settle down 《at, in》
▶그 분의 거처를 아십니까? Do you know

where he lives?
▶ 거처만이라도 알려 주시지요 Let me know at least where you are.
─거처하다 dwell [live, reside] (at, in)
거청숫돌 a rough whetstone [grindstone]
거초 裾礁 〔地質〕 a fringing reef
거추꾼 a caretaker; a protector; a sponsor
거추장스럽다 burdensome; troublesome; annoying; cumbersome; cumbrous
♦ 거추장스러운 것[존재] a burden; a nuisance; a drag (on) / 거추장스럽게 여기다 find [consider] *sth* troublesome; regard [look upon] *sth* as a nuisance
▶ 우산은 가지고 다니기 거추장스럽다 It is burdensome [It's a bother] to carry an umbrella.
▶ 그것은 내게는 거추장스러울 뿐이다 It is nothing but a white elephant to me.
▶ 그는 아이들을 데리고 다니는 것을 몹시 거추장스럽게 여긴다 He finds it such a burden to take the children around with him.
거추하다 〈보살피다〉 care for; take care [charge] of; stand by to help
거춤거춤 roughly; cursorily; in a cursory way [fashion] ♦ 방을 거춤거춤 치우다 clean a room roughly
거취 去就 〈태도〉 one's attitude; 〈진퇴〉 one's course of action
♦ 거취를 분명히 하다 make *one's* attitude [position] 《on a topic》 clear; make it clear where *one* stands; commit *oneself* (on) / 거취를 정하다 decide on *one's* attitude [*one's* course of action] / 거취를 결정하지 못하고 망설이다 do not know which course to take
▶ 그의 거취에 대해 사람들의 관심이 집중되었다 The attention of the people was centered [focused] on his moves.
거치 据置 〈지급 등의〉 deferment; 〈대출 등의〉 leaving (a loan) unredeemed
♦ 3년 거치 20년 상환 조건의 차관 a loan payable in twenty years following 3-year grace period / 3년 거치의 대출 a loan unredeemable for three years / 5년거치의 보험 insurance deferred for five years
─거치하다 leave (a loan) unredeemed; defer [delay, put off] (payment)
■─공채 deferred bonds ─연금[배당금] a deferred annuity [dividend] ─저금 deferred savings
거치 鋸齒 〈톱니〉 a sawtooth (*pl.* -teeth); 〈잎의〉 serration
♦ 거치 모양의 saw-tooth(ed); jagged; indented; serrate(d)
거치기간 据置期間 a period of deferment; a grace period
▶ 이 공채는 거치 기간이 얼마나 됩니까? How long will it be until this bond can be redeemed?
▶ 거치 기간이 끝나면 언제라도 예금을 인출할 수 있습니다 You can withdraw [draw out] your deposit anytime after the period of deferment.
거치다 pass [go] through; go by way of; go via (the Panama Canal); 〈들르다〉 drop in
♦ …의 손을 거쳐 through *sb's* hands / 시험을

거쳐 on [through an] examination / 시험을 거치지 않고 without examination / 많은 손을 거치다 pass through many hands / 세관을 거치다 pass a customhouse / 시련을 거치다 go through hardships / 수에즈 운하를 거쳐 아테네로 향해하다 sail to Athens via [by way of] the Suez Canal
▶ 나는 지금까지 많은 관문을 거쳤다 I have passed through many barriers.
▶ 그는 우리 집을 거쳐 갔다 He dropped into my house on his way.
▶ 허가를 얻으려면 정식 절차를 거쳐야 합니다 You must go through the formalities to get permission.
거치적거리다 be [stand] in *one's* way; get in the way; be an encumbrance [a nuisance] to; be a drag on; hamper; 〈옷 등이〉 cling to
♦ 거치적거리는 것이 없다 (비유) have no dependents; be [remain] single
▶ 통로에는 필요없는 상자들이 널려 있어 거치적거렸다 The passage was encumbered with useless boxes.
▶ 자네는 도움이 되기보다는 거치적거리기만 하는군 You are more of a hindrance than a help.
▶ 나는 치맛자락이 거치적거려서 걷는 데 애먹었다 I have trouble in walking with my skirt clinging to my legs.
거칠다 1 〈피부·결 등이〉 rough; coarse
♦ 거친 종이 coarse-grained paper / 거친 천 coarse cloth / 결이 거친 나무 timber of coarse grain / 거칠어지다 become rough; get chappy [chapped]
▶ 이 로션은 거친 피부에 좋다 This lotion is good for chapped [rough] skin.
2 〈파도 등이〉 rough; stormy; wild; raging; furious; turbulent
♦ 거친 파도 a heavy sea; a rough [wild, stormy] sea; raging waves [waters] / 거친 세파에 시달리다 be buffeted about in the world; be tossed about in the storms of life
▶ 바다가 온통 거칠어지고 있었다 The waves were rising high all over.
▶ 바람이 거칠게 불고 있다 It is blowing violently [hard].
3 〈성질·언행이〉 rough; rude; wild; violent

|解説| **rough**는 움직임이나 사람의 태도가 거칠다는 뜻. **rude**는 버릇없을 정도로 몹시 거칠다, **wild**는 난폭하여 감당할 수 없다, **violent**는 무서울 정도로 격렬하다는 뜻.

♦ 거친 말씨 harsh [violent] words [language] / 거친 목소리 a harsh voice / 거친 사내 a rude fellow / 성질이 거친 사람 a rough-natured [quick-tempered] person / 거친 생활을 하다 lead a rough life / 거칠게 다루다 handle *sth* roughly [in a rough manner]; treat *sb* roughly [rudely]
▶ 그는 성미가 거칠다 He has a violent temper.
▶ 그 사람은 말씨는 거칠지만 마음은 부드럽다 He is rough in speech, but warm in heart.
▶ 그는 거친 행동 때문에 종종 오해를 받았다

He was often misunderstood because of his rough behavior.
4 〈일솜씨가〉 rough 《workmanship》; slovenly
▶ 그 여자는 일을 거칠게 한다 She does her work carelessly [in a rough way]. ⇒ She works in a slovenly way.

거침없다 1 〈막힘이 없다〉 free from obstacles; unhindered; unobstructed; smooth
▶ 그는 질문에 거침없이 대답했다 He gave a ready answer to the question.
▶ 계획은 거침없이 진행되고 있다 The project is going ahead smoothly.
▶ 그녀는 프랑스어를 거침없이 구사한다 She speaks French fluently.
▶ 그녀는 그 난제를 거침없이 해결했다 She solved the hard problem easily [without (any) effort].
2 〈거리낌이 없다〉 unsparing; unreserved; unconstrained; free; straightforward
♦ 거침없는 비평 an unsparing [honest] criticism / 거침없이 without hesitation; unreservedly / 거침없이 거짓말을 하다 do not hesitate to tell a lie; tell lies without compunction [shame]
▶ 그의 태도는 아주 거침없었다 His manner was altogether free from constraint.
▶ 그는 거침없이 자기 생각을 이야기했다 He spoke out his thought. ⇒ He told (me) his idea without reserve.

거탈 〈겉〉 an appearance; (a) show; a look
▶ 거탈에 현혹되지 마라 Don't be misled by the mere appearance.

거트 〈장선(腸線)〉 a gut; a catgut

거포 巨砲 〈큰 대포〉 a big gun [cannon]; a huge [mammoth] gun; 〈야구의 강타자〉 a slugger

거푸 again and again; over (and over) again; time after time; repeatedly
♦ 담배 두 대를 거푸 피우다 smoke two cigarettes on end / 맥주 석 잔을 거푸 마시다 drink [take] three glasses of beer in quick succession
▶ 그들은 거푸 다섯 번을 패했다 They lost five times in a row [succession].

거푸집 〈주형〉 a mold; a cast; a matrix; 〈도배의 뜬 곳〉 a blister [an air bubble] left when pasting; 〈외관〉 one's figure
♦ 거푸집에 부어 주조하다 cast in a mold

거품 a bubble; foam; froth; 〈발효주의〉 barm; 〈곤충의〉 spit; spittle
♦ 맥주 거품 beer foam [suds] / 물거품 a water bubble; foam on water / 비누 거품 lather; soap suds [bubbles] / 거품이 이는 [투성이의] foamy; frothy; bubbly / 거품이 일다 (rise in) bubble / 거품처럼 사라지다 vanish like a bubble; come to nothing [naught]; end in smoke
▶ 맥주 거품이 잔 밖으로 넘쳐흘렀다 The foam on the beer bubbled up over the rim of the glass.
▶ 이 샴푸[비누]는 거품이 잘 인다 This shampoo [soap] lathers well [properly].
▶ 강물이 바위에 부딪혀 거품을 일으킨다 The river water foams against the rocks.
▶ 그는 말할 때 입에 거품을 문다 He foams [froths] at the mouth when talking.
▶ 강 표면이 거품으로 뒤덮여 있었다 The surface of the river was covered with foam.

거피하다 去皮— skin [flay] 《an animal》; rind|ráind| 《a melon》; peel 《an apple》; pare 《a potato》; bark 《a tree》

거한 巨漢 a giant (of a man); a big man [fellow]; a man of gigantic stature

거함 巨艦 a big [gigantic, mighty] warship; a leviathan [liváiəθən]

거해궁 巨蟹宮 〔天〕 the Crab; Cancer

거행 擧行 1 〈의식의〉 performance; celebration; solemnization **—거행하다** hold; give; perform; celebrate; solemnize
♦ 결혼식을 거행하다 celebrate [solemnize] a wedding / 졸업식을 거행하다 hold the graduation ceremony [〈美〉commencement]
▶ 그 행사는 언제 거행됩니까? When will the event take place?
▶ 개교 70주년 기념식은 다음달 초하루에 거행됩니다 The seventieth anniversary of our school will be held [celebrated] on the first of next month.
▶ 식은 예정대로 거행되었다 The ceremony went off [ahead] as planned.
2 〈명령의〉 carrying out an order **—거행하다** do 《as one is told》; act 《according to orders [commands]》; perform; carry out; put into practice
▶ 분부대로 거행하겠습니다 I will do as you tell me (to do). ⇒ I will carry out [execute] your order.

걱정 1 〈근심〉 worry; anxiety; care; concern; uneasiness; fear

> **解說** **worry**는 여러 가지로 생각하며 고민하는 것으로서 흔히 공연한 걱정을 뜻한다. **anxiety**는 장차 일어날 것 같은 일에 대해 또는 무슨 일이 일어날지 몰라서 막연히 불안하게 생각하는 것, **care**는 강한 관심과 책임감으로 마음에 걸리는 것인데, 앞의 두 단어보다 의미가 약하다. **concern**은 좀 격식을 차린 말로서 사람이나 사물에 관하여 걱정하는것. **uneasiness**는 불안하여 마음이 안정되지 않음을 나타낸다. **fear**는 나쁜 일이 생길까봐 걱정함을 의미한다.

♦ 나라 걱정 concern about state affairs / 돈 걱정 money troubles; worries about money; pecuniary anxiety [troubles] / 살림 걱정 cares [worries] about daily livelihood / 쓸데없는 걱정 idle cares; unnecessary [needless] anxiety / 집안 걱정 family [domestic] trouble(s) / 걱정으로 with [in] anxiety / 걱정 끝에 《die》 in an excess of anxiety / 걱정 없는 생활을 하다 lead a carefree life
▶ 그의 건강이 걱정이다 I am anxious about his health.
▶ 오늘밤 폭우가 내리지나 않을지 걱정이다 I'm afraid there will be a downpour tonight.
▶ 쓸데없는 걱정 마라 〈참견〉 Mind your own business. ⇒ It's none of your business.
▶ 그녀는 아무 걱정 없는 표정이다 She looks

free from worry.
▶ 너 걱정 있니? Do you have any trouble?
▶ 나는 아무 걱정 없이 일에 몰두할 수 있었다 I was able to devote myself to my work free from worries.
〈걱정이[은]〉 걱정이 되다 be anxious [worried] 《about》 / 걱정이 많다 be full of cares / 걱정이 없다 be carefree; be free from care [worry]
▶ 그는 걱정이 끊이지 않는다 He is never free from care [worry].
▶ 그 사람은 딸 때문에 걱정이 떠날 날이 없다 His daughter is a constant source of worry to him.
▶ 돈[내] 걱정은 마세요 You don't have to worry about money [me].
▶ 그녀의 가장 큰 걱정은 자식 교육이다 Her greatest worry is her child's education.
〈걱정을〉 걱정을 끼치다 cause anxiety to *sb*; give *sb* trouble; trouble *sb* / 세상 걱정을 잊다 forget all cares of life / 내일의 끼니 걱정을 하다 be anxious about *one's* bread for tomorrow / 쓸데없는 걱정을 하다 borrow trouble; be overanxious
▶ 나는 부모님께 많은 걱정을 끼쳐드렸다 I've caused [given] my parents much anxiety.
▶ 너무 걱정을 끼쳐 죄송합니다 I am sorry to have occasioned you (so) much anxiety.
〈걱정으로〉 그녀는 걱정으로 병이 났다 She got sick from anxiety.
〈걱정도〉 돈이 많으면 걱정도 많은 법 《속담》 Much coin, much care.
—걱정하다 worry (*oneself*) 《about》; be anxious [troubled] 《about》; concern *oneself* 《about》; feel uneasy 《about》
◆ 몹시 걱정하다 be oppressed with anxiety; be painfully anxious 《about》 / 지나치게 걱정하다 be overanxious; worry too much 《about》 / 하찮은 일로 걱정하다 worry about little things
▶ 어머니는 아들이 입학시험에 떨어질까봐 걱정했다 The mother feared [was afraid] (that) her son might fail the entrance exam.
▶ 걱정해 주셔서 고맙습니다 Thank you for being so concerned.
▶ 그는 자식의 장래를[그 일을 몹시] 걱정하고 있다 He is anxious about the future of his children [very much worried about it].
▶ 비용은 걱정하지 마라 Never mind (about) the expense!
▶ 만사가 잘 되어갈테니 걱정하지 마세요 Don't worry! Everything will be all right.
▶ 그것은 걱정할 일이 못된다 It's nothing to worry about.
▶ 걱정할 것 없다 There is nothing to worry about [fear]. ⇒ Never mind! ⇒ 《口》 No sweat.
▶ 나는 이 일이 몹시 걱정된다 This work is a great strain on my nerves.
▶ 그녀는 남편의 안부가 걱정되었다 She was anxious about her husband's safety.
▶ 자식을 혼자 여행 보내자니 걱정된다 It worries me to send my child alone on a journey.

▶ 때때로 나는 공부가 몹시 걱정되어 잠이 잘 오지 않는다 Sometimes I can't sleep well because study weighs heavily on my mind.
▶ 걱정되어 죽을 지경이었다 Worry was killing me.
2 〈꾸중〉 (a) scolding; (a) reproof; reproach; rebuke; reprimand; a lecture
▶ 나는 성적 때문에 아버지한테 걱정을 들었다 Father scolded [lectured] me for my poor grades.
—걱정하다 scold; reprove; reproach; rebuke; reprimand; chide; lecture
◆ 걱정 듣다 be scolded [rebuked]; get [catch] it 《from father》; get [have] a scolding

걱정거리 a source of concern [anxiety]; a cause for anxiety; a headache
▶ 걱정거리 없는 사람은 없다 There is nobody who is completely free from anxiety.
▶ 그것이 나의 유일한 걱정거리다 That is the only source of anxiety for me.
▶ 걱정거리가 많아서 큰일이군요 I am sorry that you have a lot of troubles.
▶ 걱정거리가 또 하나 생겼다 Now I have another weight on my mind.
▶ 그것으로 걱정거리를 하나 덜었다 It's a load off my mind.

걱정꾸러기 〈걱정하는 사람〉 a worrywart; a (natural) worrier; a worrier by nature; 〈걱정 끼치는 사람〉 (a person who is) a headache; a troublesome [worrisome] person [child]
▶ 너도 걱정꾸러기로구나 You worry too much. ⇒ You are of a worrying temperament.

걱정도 팔자 《속담》 〈남의 일에 참견함〉 Mind your own business. ⇒ It's none of your business. ⇒ 〈소심함〉 You're a natural worrier. ⇒ You always overworry yourself.

걱정스럽다 anxious; concerned 《air》; worried; uneasy
▶ 할머니의 건강이 걱정스럽다 I am anxious about my grandmother's health.
▶ 그는 걱정스러운 듯이 나를 쳐다보았다 He looked at me with an anxious look [a troubled face]. ⇒ He looked worriedly [anxiously] at me.
▶ 걱정스러워 보이는구나. 무슨 일이지? You look worried. What's the matter with you?

건 巾 a hood; a head-cover made of cloth; 〈두건〉 a mourner's hempen hood [cap]

건 腱 〖解〗 a tendon ■ 아킬레스— the Achilles(') tendon

건 鍵 〖樂〗 a key (of a piano) ◆ 흰[검은]건 a white [black] key / 88건 피아노 a piano with 88 keys

건 件 〈일·사건〉 a matter; an affair; a case; 〈문제〉 a subject
◆ 문제의 건 the case in question / 두 건의 절도[강도] 사건 two cases of theft [robbery]
▶ 그 건은 어떻게 되었습니까? What has become of that matter?
▶ 이 건에 관해 보다 상세히 이야기하고 싶습니다 We would like to talk about this subject more in detail.
▶ 서신에 언급하신 건에 대해서는 곧 회답드리

겠습니다 We will soon respond to the matter mentioned in your letter.
▶ 오늘은 교통 사고가 세 건밖에 없다 There are only three traffic accidents today.
건각 健脚 〈튼튼한 다리〉 strong [powerful, iron] legs; 〈잘 걷는 사람〉 a good walker
▶ 그는 건각이다 He is a good walker.
▶ 수백 명의 젊은 건각들이 그 마라톤 경주에 참가했다 Hundreds of iron-legged youths participated in the marathon race.
건강 健康 health; fitness
〈건강(상)의〉 건강의 고마움은 건강을 잃어 보지 않고는 모른다 You do not appreciate the blessing of good health until you lose it.
▶ 그는 건강상의 이유로 학장직을 사임했다 He resigned his post as dean for health reasons [because of ill health].
〈건강이[은]〉 건강이 허락하는 한 as far as health permits / 건강이 허락한다면 if one's health permits
▶ 그는 점차 건강이 나빠지고 있다 His health is failing [declining]. ⇌ He is failing [declining] in health.
▶ 어머니는 건강이 좋지 않으십니다 〈일시적으로〉 My mother is not very [quite] well. ⇌ 〈지속적으로〉 My mother is in poor [bad] health.
▶ 담배를 끊으면 건강이 좋아진다 If we stop smoking, our health will improve.
▶ 건강은 재산보다 낫다 Health is above [better than] wealth.
▶ 〖會話〗「요즘 건강은 어떻습니까?」「덕분에 아주 좋습니다」"How is your health of late [lately]?" "I am in [enjoying] excellent health, thank you."
〈건강을〉 건강을 위하여 (jog) for [to improve one's] health / 건강을 유지하다 keep [maintain, preserve] one's health; keep fit / 건강을 위해 건배하다 drink (to) sb's health; toast sb's health / 건강을 증진하다 promote [improve] one's health 《by swimming》
▶ 건강을 빕니다 I wish you good health.
▶ 그녀는 과로로 건강을 해쳤다 She injured herself from [ruined her health through] overwork.
▶ 아버지는 곧 건강을 회복하실 겁니다 My father will recover his health [get well] soon.
▶ 그녀는 건강을 유지하기 위해 적당한 운동을 한다 She takes moderate exercise to keep her health.
▶ 당신의 건강을 위해 건배! (Here's) To your health! ⇌ Your (very) good health!
〈건강에〉 건강에 좋다 be good for [beneficial to] health; do sb good / 건강에 나쁘다[해롭다] be bad for [injurious to] (the [one's]) health; do sb bad [harm]
▶ 이곳의 기후는 건강에 아주 좋다 The climate here is very healthful [healthy].
▶ 부디 건강에 주의하세요 You must [Please] take good care of yourself.
▶ 일찍 자고 일찍 일어나는 것은 건강에 좋다 It is good for health to keep early hours.
▶ 그는 항상 건강에 좋은 음식만 먹는다 He always eat wholesome food.

―**건강하다** healthy; fit; sound; 〈서술적〉 enjoy [be in] good health; be well

> 〖解說〗 ***healthy***는 평상시에 심신이 건강하여 불편한 데가 없음을, ***fit***는 특히 육체적으로 건강함을 의미하고 ***sound***는 몸과 마음이 더불어 불편한 데가 없는 상태를 말한다. ***well***은 일시적으로 건강하다는 뜻으로 보통 서술적으로 쓰인다.

♦ 건강해 보이는 노인 a healthy-looking old man / 건강해 보이다 look well
▶ 그 분은 건강하십니다 He is well [in good health].
▶ 나는 날 때부터 건강하다 I am naturally healthy. ⇌ I was born healthy.
■―**관리** health care; health management; management of one's health : 환절기의 건강관리 control of one's health [health care] at the change of season ―**법** how to keep fit [healthy]; hygiene : 이것이 나의 건강법이다 This is what I do to keep fit. ―**보험** health insurance : 건강 보험에 들어 있다 have health insurance; be on the health insurance list ―**보험증** a health insurance card ―**상담** 《go for》 a health consultation ―**상담소** a health consultation center; a health clinic ―**식** (be on) a health food diet ―**식품** health [wholesome] food ―**식품점** a health food store ―**아(兒)** a healthy child ―**증명서** a health certificate; a (medical) certificate of health; 〈선원의〉 a bill of health ―**증진** promotion of health ―**진단** a health [medical] examination; (美) a physical checkup : 건강진단을 받다 have [undergo] a physical checkup ―**진단서** a health certificate ―**체** a healthy body

건강미 健康美 healthy beauty; the glow of health
▶ 그녀는 건강미가 넘쳐흘렀다 She was in the lovely bloom of health. ⇌ She was the (very) picture of health.

건강상태 健康狀態 (the condition of) one's health; a hygienic [health] condition
♦ 건강 상태가 좋다[나쁘다] be in a good [bad] state of health / 건강 상태를 검사하다 check sb's physical condition

건껍찔하다 (be) a bit salty; quite brackish

건건하다 somewhat salty

건곤 乾坤 heaven and earth; the universe

건곤일척 乾坤一擲 playing a game of "all or nothing"; sink or swim; neck or nothing
♦ 건곤일척의 승부를 하다 stake everything one has [one's life] 《on》; play for all or nothing
▶ 그것은 그에게는 건곤일척의 대사업이었다 That was an ambitious undertaking he put everything he had into [he staked all his money on].

건과 乾果 dry [dried] fruits

건구온도계 乾球溫度計 a dry bulb thermometer

건국 建國 the founding of a country [nation, state]
♦ 건국의 대본(大本) the principles upon

which the state is established / 국가의 시조 the founder of a country [state]
▶그는 건국의 아버지 중 한 분으로 존경받고 있다 He is revered as one of the founding fathers of the nation.
—**건국하다** found a country [nation, state]
■—**기념일** National Foundation Day —**이념** the national ideal envisioned on the founding of a country; the spirit of the national foundation —**포장** the National Foundation Medal —**훈장** the Order of Merit for National Foundation

건군 建軍 the founding of the armed forces
♦건군 50돌을 맞다 mark the fiftieth anniversary of the founding of the Armed Forces
—**건군하다** found the armed forces

건기 乾期 the dry season

건깡깡이 (a man) doing with empty [bare] hands; (a man) working without technical skill
▶그는 거의 건깡깡이로 장사를 시작했다 He started the business with practically nothing.

건너 the opposite [other] side (of a river)
♦강 건너에 (live) across the river; on the opposite [other] side of the river / 길 건너에 over the road; across the street
▶저 건너 숲속은 대낮에도 어둡다 It is dark in the forest over there even during the daytime.
▶강 건너서 누가 우리를 부르고 있다 Someone was calling us from the other side of the river.

건너가다 go [walk] across; cross (over); 〈해외로〉 sail [go] over ♦미국으로 건너가다 go over to America
▶다리를 건너가면 바로 정거장이 나옵니다 Cross the bridge, and you will find the station.

건너긋다 draw (a line) across; write a horizontal stroke

건너다 1 〈넘다·가로지르다〉 go [pass] over; go [walk, run] across; cross (over); 〈나룻배로〉 ferry
♦길[다리]을 건너다 cross a road [bridge] / 바다를 건너다 sail [go] across the sea / 강을 헤엄쳐 건너다 swim across a river
▶우리는 다리를 건너서 저 마을로 간다 We go over the bridge to the town there.
▶신호등이 없는 곳에서 길을 건너지 마라 Don't cross the street at a place where there are no signal lamps.
2 〈전해지다〉 be conveyed [carried]
♦한 입 두 입 건너 퍼진 소문 a rumor whispered [past] from mouth to mouth
3 〈지나다〉 ♦한 집 건너 다음 집 the next door but one / 한 해 건너 한 번씩 (visit) at one year apart [one-year intervals]

건너다보다 〈저쪽을〉 look out across [over] (a river); look across (at); 〈탐내다〉 covet; hanker for [after]; cast a jealous eye (on)
♦남의 재산을 건너다보다 covet another's property

건너뛰다 〈뛰어 건너다〉 jump [leap] over (a ditch); 〈거르다〉 leave [cut] out; omit; skip
♦바위에서 바위로 건너뛰다 leap from rock to rock / 2학년을 건너뛰어 3학년이 되다 skip the second grade and enter the third / 몇 장(章) 건너뛰어 읽다 skip over some chapters
▶선생님은 출석을 부를 때 내 이름을 건너뛰셨다 The teacher skipped my name when he called the roll.
▶그 개울은 폭이 넓어 건너뛸 수가 없다 The stream is too broad to jump [leap] over.

건너오다 come across (a bridge); 〈도래하다〉 be introduced (from); be brought over (from abroad); 〈철새가〉 migrate
▶그들은 작은 배로 태평양을 건너왔다 They came across the Pacific by boat.
▶백조들이 우리 집에서 아주 가까운 호수로 건너왔다 Swans have migrated to a lake quite close to my house.

건너지르다 place [put, lay] sth across ♦도랑에 널빤지를 건너지르다 lay a plank across a ditch / 마당을 밧줄을 건너지르다 hang a rope across the yard

건너짚다 1 〈떠보다〉 ⇨ 넘겨짚다 2 〈팔을 뻗어〉 put one's hand(s) over [across]; reach across sth to touch another

건너편 —便 the opposite side; the other side
♦건너편의 opposite / 건너편 집 the house opposite [over the road, across the street] / 강 건너편에 on the other side of [across] the river
▶우체국은 영화관 바로 건너편이다 The post office is just opposite the movie theater.
▶부모님은 바로 길 건너편에 사신다 Our parents live right across the street from us.
▶길 건너편에 새 집이 하나 생겼다 A new house has been built on the opposite side of the street.
▶길 건너편에 우체통이 있다 There is a mailbox on the other side of the street.

건넌방 —房 the room opposite the main living room

건널목 〈철도의〉 a railroad crossing; 〈횡단보도〉 a pedestrian [road] crossing ♦건널목에서 정지하다 stop at a (railroad) crossing
■**무인—** (go over) an unattended crossing
■—**경보기** a crossing signal —**지기** a (crossing) gateman [guard]; a watchman; 〈美〉 a gate-tender; a flagman —**차단기** a crossing bar

건넛마을 a village on the other [at the opposite] side

건넛방 the room on the opposite side; the opposite room

건넛집 an opposite house; the house on the opposite [other] side

건네다 1 〈말을 걸다〉 speak [talk] to sb; address (oneself) to sb
▶나는 그 소녀에게 말을 건넸다 I addressed myself to the girl.
2 〈넘겨주다〉 hand over; deliver; give; pay
♦돈을 건네다 hand over [pay] money / 물건을 건네다 give [deliver] an article / 다음 사람에게 건네다 pass sth on to the next person / 편지를 살짝 건네다 slip a letter into sb's hand
▶민 선생님한테 이 편지를 건네고 곧장 돌아오너라 Come back soon after you have handed

this letter over to Mr. Min.
3 〈건너게 하다〉 ⇨ 건네주다
건네주다 〈건너게 하다〉 pass [put, set] *sb* over [across] 《a river》; carry across
♦나룻배로 건네주다 take *sb* over a river by ferryboat; ferry *sb* over the water
▶ 그는 배로 그들을 강 건너로 건네주었다 He carried [took] them across the river in a boat.
건달 乾達 a penniless rake; a jobless person; 〈불량배〉a sluggard; a scamp; a good-for-nothing (fellow)
▶ 그런 건달 녀석한테 내 딸을 줄 수는 없다 I can't give my daughter to such a good-for-nothing fellow.
■—패 a group of sluggards [scamps]
-건대 ♦내 경험에 비추어 보건대 judging from my experience / 생각하건대 on thinking
▶ 내가 보건대 그 책은 영 태작이다 In my opinion [view], that book is just trash.
▶ 잘은 모르지만 듣건대 그가 곧 사임한답니다 I don't know for certain, but they say he is going to resign.
▶ 내가 판단하건대 그는 아주 정직한 사람이다 I judge him to be a very honest man.
▶ 바라건대 꼭 성공하십시오 I wish you success.
▶ 비유하건대 인생이란 지나가는 나그네다 To speak figuratively, life is a passing stranger.
건대구 乾大口 a dried cod [codfish]
건더기 1〈국의〉solid stuff [ingredients]《in soup》;〈액체 속의〉solid matter in a mixture of liquid and solids
2〈내용〉substance ♦건더기 없는 이야기 an empty story / 말할 건더기가 없다 have no say (in the matter) / 변명할 건더기가 없다 have little excuse 《for》
건드리다 1〈손 등으로〉touch; jog; give *sth* a jog
▶ 젖은 손으로 전구를 건드리는 것은 위험하다 It is dangerous to touch an electric bulb with a wet hand.
▶ 건드리지 마시오 (게시) Hands off. ⇌ Don't touch this article.
2〈감정을〉provoke; vex; fret; irritate
♦남의 비위를 건드리다 offend [give offense to] *sb* / 남의 신경을 건드리다 irritate *sb's* nerves; get [jar] on *sb's* nerves
▶ 그의 무례한 대답이 상사의 비위를 건드렸다 His rude answer provoked the boss.
▶ 그녀는 항상 나의 아픈 곳을 건드린다 She always touches me on a sore spot [point].
3〈여자를〉make sport [fun] of; play [sport] with
건들거리다 1〈흔들리다〉wobble; shake; totter;〈매달린 것이〉dangle; swing; sway (to and fro)
▶ 바위가 건들거린다 The rocks shake.
▶ 테이블 위에 걸린 램프가 건들거리고 있다 The lamp above the table is swinging gently.
2〈바람이〉blow gently [softly]
3〈빈둥거리다〉idle [loiter, dawdle] *one's* time away; lead an idle life; fiddle about doing nothing

▶ 그는 대학을 나왔는데도 하는 일 없이 건들거리고 있다 Although he has finished college, he is at a loose end.
건들건들 in a tottering manner; idly **—건들건들하다** wobble ⇨ 건들거리다
건들바람 a cool [refreshing] breeze in early autumn
건듯건듯 〈대강〉in a rough-and-ready manner; roughly;〈빠르게〉in a hurry; in haste; hastily
♦신문을 건듯건듯 읽다 glance over [run *one's* eyes through] the papers / 일을 건듯건듯 해치우다 do a rough-and-ready job; make a quick job of it
건등 the part of an ore vein near the surface
건락 乾酪 cheese **—소**(素) casein
건량 乾量 dry measure
건류 乾溜 dry [destructive] distillation;〈석탄의〉carbonization
—건류하다 dry (up) by distillation; carbonize 《coal》
건립 建立 erection 《of》; building; construction ♦건립 중이다 be under [in course of] construction [erection]
—건립하다 erect (a bronze statue); build; raise; set up
▶ 이 기념비는 메리 여왕을 위해 건립되었다 This monument was erected [set up, put up] to Queen Mary.
-건마는 (even) though; although; still
♦최선을 다했건마는 though *one* did *one's* utmost / 내가 그렇게 충고를 했건마는 after all my advice
▶ 나는 그를 사랑하건마는 그는 나를 좋아하지 않는다 Although I love him, he does not care for me.
▶ 사람도 많건마는 왜 하필 내가 가야 하나? Why should I go of all persons?
▶ 품질은 좋건마는 값이 비싸다 I admit its fine quality. Still, it is too dear.
▶ 그는 전력을 다했건마는 실패했다 For all his utmost efforts, he failed.
-건만 though ⇨ -건마는
건망증 健忘症 forgetfulness; loss [slip] of memory;〔醫〕amnesia [æmníːʒə]
♦건망증이 심한 사람 a forgetful person; a person with a short memory
▶ 나는 요즘 건망증이 있다 I've been [become] forgetful these days.
▶ 나는 요즘 건망증이 심해졌다 My memory often fails me these days.
▶ 어쩌면 건망증이 이렇게 심할까 How forgetful I am!
▶ 나이를 먹으면 건망증이 생긴다 Age makes us forgetful. ⇌ One's memory fails with age.
건목 〈대강 만드는 일〉a rough [cursory, hasty] job;〈대강 만든 물건〉a rough-finished article **—건목치다** make a hasty job; do a rough job 《of》; rough-finish
건목 乾木 dried [seasoned] lumber [timber]
건몸달다 make vain [fruitless] efforts; get all heated up to no avail [for nothing]; fret *oneself* to no avail; be mad [crazy] about *sb* in vain; run madly about to no purpose; struggle in vain

♦건물닿다가 병나다 fret *oneself* ill
▶그는 한 여배우에게 건물닿아 있다 He makes a fool of himself over an actress. ⇒ He runs madly about an actress in vain.

건물 建物 a building; a structure; 〈큰 건조물〉 an edifice [édəfəs]
♦높은 건물 a tall building / 웅장한 건물 a magnificent [splendid] edifice
▶그것은 르네상스식 건물의 훌륭한 표본이다 It is a fine specimen of Renaissance structure. ■가(假)— a temporary building 고층— a high-rise building 목조[석조]— a wooden [stone] building 부속— an attached building 철근 콘크리트— a ferroconcrete [concrete steel] building; a reinforced [an armored] concrete building

건물 乾物 dried provisions; dried [jerked] fish [meat]; dry-cured foods ■—상 〈상인〉 a dry salter; 〈상점〉 a dried goods store; a drysaltery

건물로 乾— 〈쓸데없이〉 in vain; vainly; uselessly; with no particular reason; 〈까닭도 모르고〉 without knowing why; blindly; 〈힘 안 들이고〉 with ease; easily; without effort

건반 鍵盤 a keyboard; a fingerboard; a clavier ■—악기 a keyed [keyboard] instrument; a clavier

건방지다 impertinent; saucy; (self-)conceited; insolent; (美) smart-alecky; (美口) sassy; pert; cocky; cheeky; fresh
♦건방진 녀석 an impertinent [insolent] fellow; (美口) a smart-aleck / 건방진 말 impertinent [cheeky, saucy] remarks / 건방지게 굴다 behave impertinently; act fresh
▶그런 말을 하다니 건방지구나 You are impertinent [impudent] to say so.
▶그의 건방진 태도는 참을 수 없다 I can't stand his impudence [cocky attitude].
▶건방진 수작 마라 Don't say such cheeky things. ⇒ None of your cheek [impudence]
▶건방진 소리 같습니다만 그렇게 하지 않는 것이 좋지 않을까요? Excuse me for being forward, but wouldn't it be better not to do that?
▶나더러 술을 마시지 말라니 네가 어찌 그리 건방진 말을 할 수 있느냐? How dare you be so impudent as to say to me "Don't drink"?
▶그는 건방지게도 우리에게 지시를 했다 He had the insolence [was impudent enough] to give us directions.

건배 乾杯 a toast ♦건배를 제의하다 propose a toast 《to》
▶건배 Cheers! ⇒ Toast!
▶건강을 위해 건배 (To) your health!
—**건배하다** drink (a toast) to 《*sb's* health》; toast 《to》 *sb*; raise *one's* glass to
♦아무의 성공을 위해 건배하다 drink to *sb's* success
▶여러분, 건배합시다 Bottoms up, gentlemen.
▶신랑신부를 위해 건배합시다 Let's toast the bride and bridegroom.
▶김 교수의 건강을 위해 건배합시다 Let's drink to the health of Prof. Kim. ⇒ Allow me to propose the health of Prof. Kim.

건백 建白 a representation ⇨ 건의(建議)

건빵 乾— hardtack; (美) a cracker; (英) a dry [hard] biscuit

건사하다 1 〈일을 처리하다〉 supervise; manage; control; deal 〈cope〉 with
♦집안일을 건사하다 manage [run] the household affairs; do housekeeping
▶자기 일은 자기가 건사해야 한다 You must manage your own affairs.
2 〈보살피다〉 take care of; attend on [to]; look after ♦아기를 건사하다 take care of a baby / 환자를 건사하다 attend on a sick person
3 〈간수하다〉 keep (carefully); tuck away (in) ♦중요한 문서를 잘 건사하다 preserve important documents
▶계란은 잘 건사하지 않으면 썩기 쉽다 Eggs are apt to addle unless they are kept well.

건삼 乾蔘 (a) dried ginseng

건선 乾癬 〔醫〕 psoriasis [səráiəsəs]; scaly tetter

건선거 乾船渠 a dry [graving] dock ♦건선거에 넣다 drydock

건설 建設 construction; building; 〈설립〉 establishment; 〈창립〉 founding
♦건설적인 비판[의견] constructive criticism [opinion] / 건설적인 의견을 내다 present [express] a constructive idea [opinion]
▶그 자동차 도로는 현재 건설 중이다 That driveway is being constructed. ⇒ That driveway is now under construction.
▶그 다리 건설에 2년 걸렸다 It took two years to build [construct] the bridge.
—**건설하다** construct; build (up); erect; 〈설립하다〉 establish
♦댐[철도]을 건설하다 construct a dam [railway]
▶우리는 평화로운 나라[복지국가]를 건설하지 않으면 안 된다 We must build [establish] a peaceful nation [welfare state].
■—공사 construction [building] work : 도로 건설 공사 the road construction (work) —국(局) the Construction Bureau —기계 construction machinery [equipment] —분과위원회 the Construction Committee —비 construction cost [expenses]; the cost of construction —업 the construction industry [business] —업자 a builder; a building contractor —용지 a building lot —자 a builder; a constructor; 〈설립자〉 a founder —현장 a construction site —회사[업체] a building [construction] company

건설교통부 建設交通部 the Ministry of Construction and Transportation
■—장관 the Minister of the Construction and Transportation Ministry; the Construction and Transportation Minister

건성 inattentiveness; halfheartedness; lack of attention; absent-mindedness
♦건성으로 inattentively; absent-mindedly; vacantly; mechanically / 건성으로 듣다 listen to *sb* with only half *one's* mind; pay almost no attention to 《*sb's* talk》 / 건성으로 대답하다 answer in a halfhearted way

▶그는 그저 건성으로 대답했다 He gave only vague [evasive, vacant] answers.
▶내가 여기 건성으로 와 있는 줄 아니? Do you think I am here without any purpose?
▶너는 건성으로 듣고 있으니까 모른다 You cannot understand it, because you do not pay due attention (to it).
■—꾼 a rash person; a man who never thinks before he leaps

건성 乾性 dryness ◆건성의 dry(↔wet)
■—늑막염 dry pleurisy [plúərəsi] —수지(樹脂) element-convertible resin —유 drying oil

건성건성 in a casual [slovenly, superficial] way; in a rough-and-ready way [fashion]; loosely; carelessly
◆건성건성 가르치다 teach in a perfunctory manner / 일을 건성건성 하다 scamp one's work; do a slapdash job; get one's work done in a casual way

건수 件數 the number of cases
◆단속[취급] 건수 the number of cases of crackdown [handled] / 화재[교통 사고] 발생 건수 the number of fires [traffic accidents]
▶요즘 교통 사고 건수가 급증하고 있다 These days the number of car accidents are skyrocketing.

건습 乾濕 dryness and moisture [wetness]; humidity ■—구 습도계 a psychrometer; a wet and dry bulb hygrometer —도 the degree of humidity

건승 健勝 (being in) good health ▶건승을 빕니다 I wish you good health. —건승하다 enjoy [be in] good health ▶건승하시리라 믿습니다 I trust you are in the best of health.

건식 乾式 the dry process
■—방사(紡絲) dry spinning —변압기 a dry-type transformer —세탁법 dry cleaning —수량계 a dry-type water meter —염색 dry dyeing —정류기(整流器) a dry-type rectifier

건실 健實 steady; sound; stable; reliable; solid
◆건실한 견해 (have) sound views / 인생에 대한 건실한 생각 a sound philosophy for [of] life / 건실한 투자 a sound investment
▶그는 건실한 젊은이다 He is a reliable [steady, trustworthy] young man.
▶그는 노름꾼 생활에서 손을 씻고 건실한 생활을 하고 있다 He quit the life of a gambler and leads a sober hardworking life.
▶그는 건실하게 일하고 있다 He is steady at his work. ⇒ He works steadily.
▶그 사업은 아주 건실하게 운영되고 있다 The business is conducted on a perfectly sound basis.

건아 健兒 a stout boy; a vigorous [virile] youth; a strong [sturdy] young man ◆대한의 건아 a virile son of Korea

건어(물) 乾魚(物) a dried fish; 〈절이지 않은〉 a stockfish

건열멸균(법) 乾熱滅菌(法) dry sterilization

건울음 feigned weeping; make-believe crying; shedding unfelt tears ◆건울음을 울다 shed false [sham, crocodile] tears; pretend to weep; feign weeping

건위 健胃 making one's stomach strong; a strong stomach ■—정 a peptic tablet —제 a digestive; a peptic; a stomachic; a stomachal

건의 建議 〈제의〉 a proposal; a suggestion; 〈진언〉 a memorial; a representation
▶그 건의는 다수결로 채택되었다 The proposal was adopted by a large majority.
—건의하다 propose; suggest; make a proposal; 〈진언하다〉 present [submit] a memorial (to); make a representation (to)
▶그들은 시장에게 새 교량 건설을 건의했다 They memorialized [presented a memorial to] the Mayor for the construction of a new bridge.
■—서 a memorial; a representation; 〈(submit) a recommendation (to) —안 〈adopt〉 a proposition; a motion : 대정부 건의안 a recommendation to the government —자 a proposer —함 a suggestion box

건장하다 健壯— robust; sturdy; stout
◆건장한 청년 a youth of sturdy build / 건장한 체격 a robust constitution
▶그 청년은 체격이 건장하다 The youth has a strong constitution [robust build].
▶그들은 자녀를 건강하게 키웠다 They brought up their children to be strong [robust].

건재 建材 〈건축 재료〉 building [construction] materials ■—상 〈상점〉 a building [construction] materials shop; 〈상인〉 a building materials dealer [trader]

건재 [韓醫] dried medicinal herbs
■—약국 a wholesale medicinal-herb store; a herbalist's

건재하다 健在— be well; be in good health [condition]; be up and doing; (口) be going strong
▶양친은 건재하십니까? Are your parents still in good health [alive and well]?
▶그는 야구선수로서 여전히 건재하다 He is still a baseball player on the active list.
▶그 회사는 아직 건재하다 The company is still thriving.

건전 健全 —건전하다 healthy; sound; wholesome
◆건전한 독서 wholesome reading / 건전한 발달 sound development / 건전한 사상 wholesome [healthy] ideas / 건전한 상식 sturdy [hard] common sense / 건전한 오락 healthy amusement [recreations] / 건전한 텔레비전 프로그램 wholesome TV programs / 건전한 정신을 갖고 있다 be sound-minded
▶그는 몸과 마음이 다 건전하다 He is sound both in mind and in body.
▶그는 아주 건전한 생활을 하고 있다 He leads a very healthy life.
▶건전한 신체에 건전한 정신이 깃든다 (속담) A sound mind in a sound body. ⇒ Sound in body, sound in mind.
■—문학 healthy literature —예산 a balanced budget —재정 sound finance

건전지 乾電池 a dry cell; a dry battery

건조 建造 building; construction
◆건조 중이다 be being built; be under [in

건조 course of] construction
▶ 현재 대형 유조선을 건조 중이다 A mammoth tanker is now on the stocks [under construction].
▶ 이 조선소는 3만톤짜리 선박 건조 능력이 있다 This dockyard is capable of building a 30,000 ton ship.
—**건조하다** build; construct; lay down 《a warship》
■ —**물** a building; a structure; an edifice

건조 乾燥 dryness; aridity; 〈목재의〉 seasoning; drying; 〈탈수〉 dehydration ◆ 이상 건조 기후 abnormally dry weather
▶ 영동 지방에 건조 주의보가 발효 중이다 A dry weather warning [alert] is in force for the Yŏngdong District.
—**건조하다** 〈형용사적〉 dry; arid; seasoned 《wood》; 〈동사적〉 dry; season
▶ 공기가 매우 건조하니 화재를 조심하십시오 Look out for fire, as the air is exceedingly dry.
▶ 건조한 곳에 보관할 것 (표시) Keep [Must be kept] dry.
▶ 이 목재는 잘 건조되었다 This timber is well seasoned.
■ —**기**(期) the dry season —**기**(機) 〈세탁기 등의〉 a drier; a dryer; 〈공업용의〉 a drying machine; 〈음식물의〉 a desiccator —**기후** an arid climate —**냉동법** dehydrofreezing —**시간** the time of drying; drying time —**시험** a drying test —**식품** dehydrated food —**실** a drying room; a hothouse —**야채** dehydrated vegetables —**제**(劑) desiccant —**증** 〔醫〕 xerosis[ziərόusəs] —**지** dry ground [land] : 건조지 식물 plants of dry land; dry-land flora —**혈장** 〔醫〕 normal human plasma dried

건주정 乾酒酊 shammed [feigned] drunkenness —**건주정하다** sham [feign] drunkenness; pretend to be drunk

건지 a plumb [sounding] line (to test the depth of water)

건지다 1 〈물에서〉 take sth out of water; pick up; pull [draw] up
◆ 물에 빠뜨린 시계를 건지다 pick up a watch sunk in the water; take a watch out of water / 시체[익사체]를 건지다 bring a dead [drowned] body to the land / 금붕어를 몇 마리 건져내다 scoop up several goldfish
2 〈위험·죽음에서〉 rescue sb from 《danger》; save sb from 《death》; deliver sb from 《a difficulty》; help sb out of 《a difficulty》
◆ 파멸에서 건져 주다 retrieve sb from ruin / 물에 빠진 사람을 건져 주다 save a drowning man; save [rescue] sb from drowning
▶ 그녀는 간신히 목숨을 건졌다 She had a narrow escape [narrowly escaped] from death.
▶ 그는 나를 곤경에서 건져주었다 He helped me out of difficulties.
▶ 배가 가라앉을 때 그는 많은 아이들을 건져주었다 When the boat sank, he rescued many children.
3 〈손실을〉 take [get] back; regain; recover
◆ 손해본 것을 건지다 recover a loss

▶ 이것 가지고는 밑천도 못 건지겠다 This will not cover my original outlay.
▶ 이번 화재에서 건진 가구가 거의 없다 Very little of the furniture was saved in the recent fire.
▶ 하나도 건지지 못하고 몽땅 불타 버렸다 Nothing was saved from the fire. ⇌ All was lost in the fire.

건초 乾草 dried grass; hay ◆ 건초를 만들다 make hay ■ —**더미** a haycock; a haystack; a hayrick —**열** 〔醫〕 hay fever

건축 建築 construction; building; erection; 〈건축물〉 a building; a structure; 〈총칭〉 architecture
◆ 건축(상)의 architectural / 고딕 양식의 건축 architecture in Gothic style / 근대식 건축 modern architecture / 목조[콘크리트] 건축 a wooden [concrete] building
▶ 그는 전공이 건축이다 His field is architecture.
▶ 그의 집은 현재 건축 중이다 His house is now being built [under construction].
—**건축하다** build; construct; erect; put [set] up
▶ 그들은 여기에 100층짜리 고층 빌딩을 건축할 예정이다 They are going to build a 100 storied skyscraper here.
■ —**가** an architect —**공사** construction work —**공학** architectural engineering —**기사** an architect; a building engineer —**기술** building [construction] techniques —**면적** building area ▷ 건물 —**법규** the building law —**부지** a building site —**비** the cost of construction; building expenses —**사**(士) a registered [licensed] architect —**설계** architectural design —**양식** a style of building [architecture] : 르네상스 건축 양식의 교회 a church in the Renaissance style —**업** the building [construction] industry —**업자** a builder; a constructor; 〈도급[청부]업자〉 a building contractor —**자재** building [construction] materials —**청부업자** a (building) contractor —**학**[**술**] architecture; the science [art] of construction; architectonics —**허가** a building permit —**회사** a building [construction] company; an architectural [a construction] firm

건투 健鬪 a good fight; 〈노력〉 strenuous efforts
▶ 건투를 빕니다 Good luck (to you)! ⇌ I expect you to do your best.
—**건투하다** fight bravely; put up a good fight; 〈노력하다〉 make strenuous efforts
▶ 그는 건투한 보람도 없이 시험에 떨어졌다 He failed the examination, in spite of his strenuous efforts.

건판 乾板 〔寫〕 a dry (photographic) plate; 〔印〕 a gelatin dry plate ◆ 건판을 현상하다 develop a dry plate

건평 建坪 floor space; building area; floorage
◆ 건평 17평짜리 아파트 an apartment with a floor space of 17 p'yŏng
▶ 그의 집은 건평이 30평이다 His house has a floor space of 30 p'yŏng. ⇌ The floorage of his house covers an area of 30 p'yŏng.

건폐율 建蔽率 building coverage; the building-to-land ratio; percentage of ground area occupied by a building ♦ 건폐율 70%의 부지 a building site with a 70% coverage (ratio)

건포도 乾葡萄 raisins; 〈작고 씨 없는〉 currants; dried grapes; 〈과자에 든〉 plums ♦ 건포도가 든 케이크 a plum [raisin] cake

건포마찰 乾布摩擦 (have) a rubdown with a dry towel

건필 健筆 a ready [facile, powerful] pen ♦ 건필을 휘두르다 wield a powerful [facile] pen; be a prolific writer ■—가 a prolific [productive] writer

건함 建艦 building of warships; naval construction —건함하다 build [lay down] a warship

걷다¹ 〈안개 등이〉 clear off [away] ⇨ 걷히다 1

걷다² 1 〈말다〉 roll [turn] up 《one's sleeves》; tuck [turn, lift] up 《one's skirt》
♦ 바지를 무릎까지 걷고 with one's trousers pulled up to the knees / 셔츠의 소매를 걷어 올리다 hitch [roll] up the shirt sleeves / 커튼을 걷다 〈위로〉 gather up a curtain; 〈옆으로〉 draw aside a curtain (and fasten it)
▶ 여동생은 치맛자락을 걷어 올리고 해변가를 산책했다 My sister tucked up her skirt and strolled along the shore.
2 〈개키다〉 fold up; furl; 〈치우다〉 remove; take [put] away [off]; take [gather] in
♦ 그물을 걷다 haul in [draw up, pull in] a net / 명석을 걷다 roll up a mat / 무대장치를 걷다 strike a set / 빨래를 걷다 take [bring] in the washing / 기를 걷다 take [pull] down a flag; strike a flag
▶ 그 텐트는 걷기 쉽다 It is easy to strike the tent.
3 ⇨ 걷우다 1
4 〈일을 끝내다〉 finish [get through] 《one's work》; be through with 《one's work》; bring 《one's work》 to a close
▶ 오늘은 일을 이만 걷어야겠다 I'm going to call it a day.

걷다³ walk; go on foot; 〈성큼성큼〉 stride; 〈우쭐대며〉 prance; 〈한가롭게〉 saunter
♦ 걸어서 on foot / 길을 걷다 walk down [up, along] the road / 뚜벅뚜벅 걷다 strut; tramp; tread heavily / 비틀비틀 걷다 walk unsteadily [with unsteady steps]; totter; stagger / 사뿐사뿐 걷다 walk lightly; walk with light steps / 살금살금 걷다 walk with stealthy steps [foot]; walk on tiptoe / 아장아장 걷다 toddle [waddle] along / 연습 삼아 걷다 walk for practice / 절뚝절뚝 걷다 walk with a limp; walk lame / 천천히[빨리] 걷다 walk slowly [fast] / 터벅터벅 걷다 trudge along [one's (weary) way]; plod on / 한 걸음 한 걸음씩 걷다 go step by step / 걸어서 집에 가다 walk home / 걸어서 학교에 가다 walk to school; go to school on foot / 걸을 수 있게 되다 〈어린아이가〉 start walking [to walk]; become able to walk; 〈환자가〉 find [get back on] one's feet; start [be able] to walk again
▶ 그는 10킬로미터의 거리를 꼬박 걸었다 He walked a distance of ten kilometers.
▶ 오늘은 꽤 많이 걸었다 I have done a lot of walking today.
▶ 그는 너무 피곤해서 발을 질질 끌면서 걸었다 He was so tired (that) he dragged himself along.
▶ 경기장까지는 걸어서 10분 거리다 It takes ten minutes to get to the stadium on foot. ⇌ It is ten minutes' [a ten-minute] walk to the stadium.

걷어붙이다 tuck [roll] up 《one's sleeves》; bare [strip] 《one's arm》
♦ 팔을 걷어붙이고 with one's sleeves tucked up; with bare arms / 소매[팔]를 걷어붙이다 roll one's sleeves up (above one's elbows); roll [tuck] up one's sleeves; bare one's arms / 걷어붙인 소매를 내리다 roll down one's sleeves
▶ 그는 바지를 무릎까지 걷어붙였다 He turned up his trousers to the knees.

걷어차다 kick hard; give sb a hard kick
♦ 다리를 걷어차다 give a (hard) kick on the leg / 이불을 걷어차다 spurn off the bed clothes / 문을 걷어차다 kick the door open
▶ 그녀는 그 도둑의 정강이를 걷어찼다 She kicked the thief hard on the shin.
▶ 그 문은 걷어차야 열린다 The door will open if you give it a good kick.

걷어채다 be kicked (hard); get a (hard) kick
♦ 옆구리[배]를 걷어채다 get a kick in the side [belly]

걷어치우다 1 〈치우다〉 clear away; put [take] away ♦ 잡동사니를 걷어치우다 shift rubbish out of the way / 흩어진 물건들을 걷어치우다 clear away scattered things
2 〈그만두다〉 throw up; leave off; stop; give up; quit
♦ 가게를 걷어치우다 shut [close] up one's shop / 일을 걷어치우다 throw [give] up one's job; abandon [leave off] one's work / 장사를 걷어치우다 quit one's business
▶ 그녀는 사업을 걷어치우고 집안에 들어앉았다 She retired from the business and went into the home.

—걷이 a harvest; a collection; a gathering up
♦ 가을걷이 harvest; gathering

걷잡다 〈붙들다〉 hold; keep; stay; 〈참다〉 stop; keep back 《one's tears》; 〈막다〉 keep 《a danger [disease]》 at bay; control
♦ 걷잡을 새 없이 quickly; swiftly / 걷잡을 수 없는 혼란에 빠지다 fall into uncontrollable confusion
▶ 아무리 애써도 흘러내리는 눈물을 걷잡을 수가 없었다 Try as I might, I could not keep back my tears.

걷히다 1 〈구름·안개 등이〉 be lifted [dispelled]; clear [break] away
▶ 구름이 차츰 걷혔다 The clouds lifted by and by.
▶ 연기가 걷혔다 The smoke cleared away.
▶ 안개가 걷히자 붉은 꽃들이 보였다 When the mist cleared off [fog disappeared], we saw red flowers.
2 〈돈·곡식이〉 be collected; be gathered

▶ 세금이 잘 걷힌다 The tax has a good yield.
▶ 나락이 걷혔다 Crops were gathered.
▶ 의연금이 잘 걷히지 않는다 The collection of the subscriptions is far from satisfactory.

걸걸 covetously; voraciously; gluttonously; greedily ━**걸걸하다** be greedy; be ravenous (for); be gluttonous

걸걸하다 〈목소리가〉 guttural; husky ♦ 걸걸한 목소리 resonant voice; a husky

걸걸하다 傑傑— openhearted; free hearted; free and easy ▶ 그 친구는 성미가 걸걸하다 He is a free hearted fellow.

걸귀 乞鬼 〈새끼 낳은 뒤의 암퇘지〉 a mother pig; a littered sow; 〈식탐하는 사람〉 a glutton; a gormandizer
♦ 걸귀들린 voracious; gluttonous; ravenous / 걸귀처럼 먹다 eat greedily; eat like a hog / 걸귀들이 have a wolf in *one's* stomach

걸근거리다 1 〈탐내다〉 covet; be greedy 〈of, for〉 2 〈목구멍이 근지럽다〉 be tickled with phlegm ♦ 목구멍이 걸근거리다 have a scratchy throat; feel itching in throat

걸근걸근 〈탐하여〉 greedily; covetously; 〈목구멍이〉 scratchily; ticklishly ━**걸근걸근하다** ⇨ 걸근거리다

걸기대 乞期待 〈게시〉 Coming soon!; Please wait!

걸다¹ 1【달아매다】 hang (up); suspend; 〈고리에〉 hook; put up
♦ 천장에 램프를 걸다 suspend a lamp from the ceiling / 모자를 못에 걸다 hang [put] *one's* hat on a peg / 간판을 걸다 hang [put] up a signboard
▶ 외투는 옷걸이에 걸어 주십시오 Put your overcoat on the hanger.
▶ 누가 이 그림[달력, 거울]을 벽에 걸었이? Who hung this picture [calendar, mirror] on the wall?
2 〈내기를〉 bet (on, against); stake (on); wager; 〈계약금을〉 deposit money as security; 〈현상금을〉 offer a prize [reward] (for)
♦ 계약금 30만원을 걸다 make a deposit of three hundred thousand won (on a car) / 경마에 돈을 걸다 bet [stake, wager] money on a horse race / 짝수[홀수]에 걸다 stake *one's* money on the evens [odds] / 있는 돈을 몽땅 걸다 bet *one's* bottom dollar / 범인에게 현상금을 걸다 set [put] a price on a criminal / 돈을 걸고 화투를 하다 play flower cards for money
▶ 그는 인기마에 많은 돈을 걸었다 He staked [bet] a large sum of money on the favorite.
▶ 우리는 그가 이긴다는 쪽에 3대 1로 내기를 걸었다 We bet three to one that he would win.
▶ 어느 쪽이 이길지 돈을 걸자 Let's make [have] a bet as to which side will win.
▶ 얼마든지 걸겠다 The sky's the limit.
▶ 범인에게 10만 달러의 현상금이 걸려 있다 A reward of 100,000 dollars is being offered for the offender.
3 〈말·소송 등을〉 ♦ 농을 걸다 play [have] a joke on *sb* / 말을 걸다 speak [talk] to *sb*; address (*oneself* to) *sb*; accost / 영어로 말을 걸다 talk to [address] *sb* in English / 싸움[시비]을 걸다 provoke *sb* to a quarrel; pick up [seek] a quarrel with *sb*; trail [drag] *one's* coattails [coat] / 재판을 걸다 lay (a case) before the court; submit (a case) to the court; bring a suit (against *sb*); sue *sb* / 남을 걸고 넘어지다 involve [entangle] in (a crime)
▶ 그는 다리를 걸어서 나를 넘어뜨렸다 He tripped me with his foot.
▶ 어떤 여자가 시장에서 내게 말을 걸었다 A woman spoke [called] to me at the market.
4 〈전화하다〉 telephone; make a phone call
♦ 친구에게 전화를 걸다 call a friend (on the telephone); phone [telephone] a friend; (英) ring a friend up
▶ 오늘밤에 전화 걸어 주세요 Please call me [ring me (up)] tonight.
▶ 나중에 또 걸게요 I'll call again.
5 〈잠그다〉 lock (up); fasten (with a lock [latch])
♦ 문에 빗장을 걸다 bar a gate with a bolt / 문에 자물쇠를 걸다 fasten the door with a lock / 현관문[창문]을 걸다 fasten [lock, latch] the front door [a window]
6 〈목숨 등을〉 risk (*one's* life); stake (*one's* life on *sth*)
♦ 목숨을 건 사랑 love at the risk of *one's* life / 운명을 걸다 put the fate to a risk / 전재산을 걸다 risk *one's* fortune / 목숨을 걸고 싸우다 fight at the risk of *one's* life
▶ 그는 그 회담 결과에 정치 생명을 걸었다 He staked his political future on the outcome of the talks.
▶ 목숨을 걸고 비밀을 지킬 것을 맹세합니다 I swear on my life that I will keep the secret.
▶ 명예를 걸고 최선을 다하겠다 Upon [On] my honor I'll do my best.
7 〈작동시키다〉 ♦ 엔진의 시동을 걸다 start an engine; set an engine going
▶ 나는 브레이크를 걸어 차를 세웠다 I braked my car to a stop [halt].
▶ 네가 좋아하는 레코드판을 걸어 주마 Let me play your favorite record.
8 〈희망 등을〉 ♦ …에 기대를 걸다 place [set] *one's* hope on...; pin *one's* hope to
▶ 부모는 대개 자식들에게 큰 기대를 건다 Parents usually put much hope in their children.
▶ 그는 그 방법에 마지막 희망을 걸었다 He pinned [set] his last hopes on the method.
▶ 아들에게 너무 큰 기대를 걸지 마시오. Don't expect too much of [from] your son.
9 〈걸쳐 놓다〉 install; fix; put [place] into position ♦ 솥을 걸다 install a kettle (in a fireplace)
10 〈술법 등을〉 lay (on); exert; exercise; practice; play; apply; set (to)
♦ 마법을 걸다 lay *sb* under a spell; cast [lay] a spell (up)on *sb* / 최면술을 걸다 mesmerize [hypnotize] *sb*; practice hypnotism

걸다² 1 〈기름기가〉 rich (soil); fertile (land)
♦ 땅을 걸게 하다 make (barren) soil fertile
▶ 그곳은 땅이 걸다 The soil there is fertile.
2 〈음식 가짓수가 많다〉 rich; heavy; sumptuous (feast)
▶ 상차림이 걸다 The table is well loaded with

good things.
▶잔치가 걸다 It is a sumptuous feast.
3 〈식성이 좋다〉 omnivorous; gluttonous; not particular [fastidious]
▶그는 식성이 걸다 He is not particular [fastidious] about food. ⇒ He is not a fastidious eater.
4 〈말이 거리낌이 없다〉 foulmouthed; foul-tongued; abusive ▶그 사람은 입이 걸다 He is foulmouthed [foul-tongued].
5 〈솜씨있다〉 handy; dexterous (in, at); be a good hand (at); have a good hand (with)
6 〈걸쭉하다〉 thick; heavy ◆전 죽 thick [rich] gruel

걸대 a hooked pole (for hanging clothes, etc)
걸때 body dimension; the (size of) body ◆걸때가 큰 사람 a man of large build / 걸때가 크다 have a huge body
걸뜨다 float under the water; float below the surface of the water
걸러 after an interval; at intervals; skipping
◆5분 걸러 at 5-minute intervals / 하루 걸러 every other day / 한 집 걸러 다음 집 the next door but one
▶나는 이틀 걸러 목욕합니다 I take a bath every third day.
▶답은 한 줄 걸러 쓰시오 Write your answer on every other line.
걸러뛰다 skip; leave out; omit
◆3쪽을 걸러뛰다 skip (over) page three / 2, 3행 걸러뛰고 읽다 skip a few lines in reading
▶나는 재미없는 대목은 걸러뛰고 읽었다 I skipped the dull of a story.
걸레 1 【청소용】 a floorcloth; a dustcloth; a duster; 〈자루 걸레〉 a mop; a swab
◆마른[물] 걸레 a dry [wet, damp] duster / 걸레로 닦다 wipe (a pane) with a duster / 걸레로 마루를 훔치다 wipe the floor with a damp cloth / 걸레로 물을 훔쳐내다 swab up the water
2 (비유) rubbish; trash; worthless stuff; 〈너절한 사람〉 a good-for-nothing ◆걸레같은 worthless; good-for-nothing
■—받이 skirting　　—부정 rubbish; shabby [worthless] stuff; a good-for-nothing
걸레질 wiping with a damp cloth; mopping
—**걸레질하다[치다]** mop; wipe with a dust-cloth [damp cloth]
걸리다¹ 1 〈매달려 있다〉 hang (on, from); be suspended (on, from)
◆못에 걸려 있는 모자 a hat hanging on a peg [hook]
▶입구에 간판이 걸려 있다 A signboard was on the front door.
▶초승달이 서쪽 하늘에[무지개가 공중에] 걸려 있다 The new moon hangs low [A rainbow is hanging] in the western sky [in midair].
▶그림 한 점이 벽에 걸려 있었다 A picture was hanging on the wall.
2 〈병들다〉 become ill; get sick; fall [be taken] ill; be seized with [attacked by] (a disease); catch (flu)
◆감기에 걸리다 take [catch, get] (a) cold / 암에 걸리다 get cancer / 질병에 걸리기 쉽다 be susceptible to disease / 에이즈에 걸려 죽다 die of AIDS
▶그녀는 폐렴에 걸렸다 She was affected by pneumonia.
▶병에 걸리지 않도록 주의하시오 Take care not to fall ill [make yourself ill].
3 〈얽히다・얹히다〉 catch; be caught (in, by); hitch (on a nail)
◆먹은 것이 목에 걸리다 food sits [lies] heavy on one's stomach / 가래가 목에 걸리다 phlegm sticks to the throat / 바지가 철조망에 걸리다 get one's pants snagged on the barbed wires / 돌[밧줄]에 걸려 넘어지다 stumble [trip] over a stone [the rope]/ 못에 걸려 찢기다 have (one's coat) torn off at the nail
▶생선 가시가 목에 걸렸다 A fishbone stuck [got caught] in my throat.
▶낚싯바늘이 수초에 걸렸다 The hook got snagged on underwater weeds.
▶밧줄이 스크류에 걸렸다 The rope got entangled in the propeller.
▶연이 나무에 걸렸다 The kite lodged [got caught] in the tree.
▶내 셔츠가 못에 걸렸다 A nail caught my shirt.
4 〈걸려들다〉 be cheated; be tricked
◆사기에 걸리다 be swindled (by); fall a victim to (a) fraud / 적의 계략에 걸려들다 fall into enemy's trap; play into the enemy's hands; be a prey to enemy's plot
5 〈잡히다〉 be caught [entangled]; 〈덫 등에〉 be trapped; be entrapped ◆낚시에 걸리다 be hooked; take the hook
▶잠자리가 거미줄에 걸렸다 A dragonfly is [gets] entangled in a spider's web.
▶큰 물고기가 그물에 걸렸다 A big fish was caught in a net.
▶곰이 덫에 걸렸다 A bear was caught in a trap [trapped].
6 〈소요되다〉 take; require; need; cost
◆2년 걸리는 연구 a two-year study / 한 시간 걸리는 거리 an hour's distance
▶이 책을 쓰는 데 5년이나 걸렸다 It took me no less than five years to write this book.
▶나는 5분도 안 걸려서 그곳에 닿았다 I arrived there in less than five minutes.
▶이 일을 끝내는 데 1주일이 걸릴 것이다 It will take me a week to finish this work.
▶상처가 완전히 낫는 데는 한 달이 걸릴 것이다 It will be a month before the injury heals.
7 〈켕기다〉 weigh
▶시험이 항상 마음에 걸린다 The examination weighs heavily with me [upon my mind]. ⇒ The examination haunts me.
▶아버지의 병세가 마음에 걸린다 I am anxious about my father's condition.
▶그 문제가[그의 말이] 마음에 걸렸다 The matter hung [His words weighed] on my mind.
8 〈관계되다〉 be concerned in [with]; concern oneself in; have to do with; 〈달려있다〉 hang (on); rest
◆사활이 걸린 문제 a vital question / 큰 돈[목숨]이 걸리다 big money [one's life] is at

stake
▶이것은 국민의 복지가 걸린 문제다 It is of concern to the welfare of the people.
▶이 시합에 우승이 걸려 있다 Whether we win the championship depends upon this game.
9 〈위반되다〉 be against 《the law》; be contrary 《to the law》; 〈붙잡히다〉 be caught [taken]; **(俗)** be pinched
♦검열에 걸리다 fail to pass a censorship / 법망에 걸리다 fall into the meshes of the law; be picked up by the law
▶그는 교통 경찰에게[경찰의 검문에] 걸렸다 He was pinched by a traffic cop [caught in a police check].
▶그 악명높은 사기꾼도 마침내 법망에 걸렸다 At last the notorious swindler fell into the clutches of the law.
10 〈전화가 오다〉 put through 《a call》; get connected 《with》
▶네가 없는 사이에 친구에게서 전화가 걸려 왔었다 You had a call from a friend while you were away.
▶전화 잘못 걸렸습니다 You've got the wrong number.
11 〈상금이〉 hang 《on》
▶이 경주에 1천만원의 상금이 걸려 있다 There is a prize [purse] of ten million won riding [hanging] on this race.
12 〈혐의를 받다〉 fall on; be imposed on; be levied on
♦혐의가 걸리다 incur [invite] suspicious; fall under suspicion; be suspected 《of》
▶그는 수회[절도] 혐의에 걸려 있다 He is suspected of having accepted a bribe [of theft].
13 〈맞서다〉 play [fight] against; oppose; be up against ▶너는 그에게 걸리면 어린애나 다름없다 You are a baby in his hands.
14 〈작동되다〉 run; go; work; operate
▶소리를 내며 발동이 걸렸다 The motor caught with a roar.
▶시동이 걸렸다[잘 걸리지 않는다] The engine has started [won't start].
▶브레이크가 걸리지 않는다 The brake won't work.
15 〈문이 잠기다〉 be locked [fastened]; 〈빗장이〉 catch; be barred
▶대문이 걸려 있다 The front door is locked [fastened].
▶빗장이 잘 걸리지 않는다 The bolt does not catch properly.
16 〈말려들다〉 be involved 《in》; get entangled 《with》; be implicated 《in》
♦부정 사건에 걸리다 be implicated [involved] in a scandal / 도박꾼에게 걸리다 get entangled with [get into the clutches of] a gambler
▶그는 금전상의 의혹에 걸렸다 He was entangled in a financial scandal.
걸리다² 〈걷게 하다〉 make *sb* walk; walk 《a child》; make *sb* go on foot; 〔野〕 walk a batter 《on four balls》
걸맞다 〈어울리다〉 suitable; fitting; 〈비슷하다〉 well-balanced; well-matched; nicely-paired
♦걸맞은[걸맞지 않은] 부부 a well-assorted [ill-assorted] pair; a well-matched [an ill-matched] couple / 걸맞는 상대 a good match 《for *one*》/ 교육자에게 걸맞지 않은 행동 an act unbecoming to an educator / 수입에 걸맞은 생활을 하다 live up to *one's* income / 신분에 걸맞지 않은 생활을 하다 live above *one's* social standing
▶그들은 걸맞은 부부다 They are a well-matched couple.
걸머잡다 grasp; catch hold of; seize ♦머리채[멱살]를 걸머잡다 seize *sb* by the hair [collar]
걸머지다 1 〈짐을 등에 지다〉 carry 《a burden》 on *one's* back; strap 《a bundle》 on *one's* back; 〈책임지다〉 shoulder [assume, take upon *oneself*] 《the responsibility of》; be burdened 《with》
♦나라의 장래를 걸머진 젊은이 a young man on whose shoulders rest the destinies of the country / 중책을 걸머지다 be burdened with a grave duty / 책임을 걸머지다 take on [bear] (the) responsibility 《for, of》
▶아무도 책임을 걸머지고 그 일을 하려는 사람은 없을 것이다 No one will undertake the work on his own responsibility.
2 〈빚지다〉 get into debt; be in debt
♦남의 빚을 걸머지다 shoulder *sb's* debt(s) / 잔뜩 빚을 걸머지다 get heavily into debt; be deeply in debt
▶그는 아들의 빚을 걸머졌다 He shouldered [took responsibility for] his son's debt.
걸물 傑物 a great [remarkable] person; a master spirit; an extraordinary character
걸상 —床 a bench; 〈등받이가 없는〉 a form
걸쇠 a latch; 〈걸고리〉 a hasp ♦걸쇠를 걸다 latch; hasp / 걸쇠를 벗기다 unlatch; unhasp
걸스카우트 (총칭) the Girl Scouts; **(英)** the Girl Guides; 〈개인〉 a Girl Scout [Guide]
걸식 乞食 begging; mendicancy ━**걸식하다** beg for food [*one's* bread]; go 《about》 begging ♦문전 걸식하다 beg from door to door
걸신 乞神 a hungry demon; a hunger; a greed; voracity
♦걸신들린 사람 a voracious person; a man greedy for food / 걸신들리다 get greedy for food; get possessed by a hungry demon / 걸신들린 듯이 먹다 eat greedily [ravenously]; eat like a hog
▶ ━쟁이 a glutton; a gormandizer
걸어가다 go on foot; walk ♦산길[시골길]을 걸어가다 walk along [follow] a mountain path [country lane] ▶걸어가겠니, 아니면 차 타고 가겠니? Are you going to walk or ride?
걸어오다 come on foot ♦우리가 걸어온 길 the path we have followed
걸어 총 —銃 〔軍〕 a stack of arms ▶걸어 총 (口令) Stack [Pile] arms! ━**걸어총하다** stack [pile] arms
걸우다 fertilize the soil manure 《a field》; enrich
걸음 walking; stepping; 〈보조〉 step; 〈속도〉 pace
♦느린 걸음 a slow [poor] pace / 빠른 걸음 a quick [rapid] pace / 종종걸음 short and quick

steps; mincing steps / 한 걸음 한 걸음 step by step / 느린 걸음으로 at a snail's pace / 한 걸음 앞서다[뒤지다] be a step ahead [behind]/ 걸음이 빠르다[느리다] be quick [slow] of foot [on *one's* feet]; be a good [bad] walker / 걸음을 늦추다 slacken *one's* pace / 걸음을 빨리하다 quicken *one's* pace; walk more quickly
▶ 그녀는 걸음을 멈추었다 She came to a halt. ⇌ She stopped walking.
▶ 그 남자는 걸음아 날 살려라 하고 달아났다 The man ran away as fast as his legs could carry him.

걸음걸이 gait; walk; stride; 〈걸음새〉 *one's* manner of walking; the way *one* walks
♦ 무거운 걸음걸이 〈with〉 a heavy [leaden] step; a slow gait / 지친 듯한 걸음걸이 a weary walk / 걸음걸이가 묘하다 have a queer gait
▶ 그는 걸음걸이가 칠칠치 못하다 He walks with a slovenly gait.
▶ 그 여자는 걸음걸이가 묘하다 She has a strange way of walking.
▶ 걸음걸이로 그 사람인 줄 알았다 I recognized him by his walk.

걸음나비 a step; a pace; 〈큰〉 a stride
▶ 그는 걸음나비가 짧다 [길다] He walks with short [long] steps.

걸음마 ♦ 걸음마를 하다 toddle; find its feet
▶ 아기는 걸음마를 시작했다 The baby has begun to toddle. ▶ 걸음마 Steady! Steady! ⇌ Step firm.

걸음발타다 start to toddle; try [find] its feet

-걸이 a rack; a peg; a hanger ♦ 모자걸이 a hat rack / 수건걸이 a towel horse [rack]/ 옷걸이 a clothes hanger / 팔걸이 〈의자의〉 an arm rest; an elbow rest

걸인 乞人 a beggar

걸작 傑作 1 〈작품〉 a masterpiece; a great work
♦ 걸작 희곡집 a collection of dramatic masterpieces
▶ 이 그림은 세잔의 걸작이다 This picture is Cézanne's best work.
▶ 이것은 그의 일생일대의 걸작이다 This is the crown of his life's work.
▶ 그 소설은 한국 문학의 걸작이다 The novel is a masterpiece in Korean literature.
2 〈언행〉 a droll [funny] talk [behavior];〈사람〉 a funny fellow; a droll
▶ 그 친구 참 걸작이야 He is quite an eccentric [a jolly good] fellow. ⇌ He's quite a funny guy.
▶ 그 얘기는 정말 걸작이다 The story is quite interesting.

걸쭉하다 thick 〈soup〉; heavy; mushy

걸차다 〈기름지다〉 very fertile [productive, rich] ♦ 걸찬 땅 productive [fertile] soil

걸채 a pannier [dosser] rack; a saddle rack

걸쳐두다 hold *sth* in suspense; leave 〈an affair〉 unsettled; hang up; suspend ♦ 교섭을 걸쳐 두다 leave a negotiation in suspension

걸출 傑出 preeminence; prominence; excellence
─**걸출하다** prominent; outstanding; distinguished

♦ 걸출한 사람 an outstanding [a distinguished] person; a master spirit / 걸출한 작품 an outstanding work
▶ 그는 시인으로서 걸출하다 He stands out from [towers above] others as a poet.
▶ 그는 한국의 걸출한 작가 중 한 사람이다 He is one of the prominent writers in Korea.

걸치다 1 〈놓다〉 put 《a thing》 on [over]; 〈걸치다〉 lay over; place across
♦ 도랑에 널빤지를 걸치다 lay a plank across a ditch / 벽에 사다리를 걸치다 put up a ladder against the wall / 양다리를 걸치다 play (a) double (game); sit on the fence
2 〈계속되다 · 미치다〉 range 《from A to B》; extend over; stretch; spread over
♦ 다방면에 걸친 지식 《his》 multifarious learning / 3개월에 걸쳐 over a period of three months [three-month period]/ 월요일에서 토요일에 걸쳐 extending from Monday to Saturday; Monday through Saturday / 양대륙에 걸치다 stretch over two continents / 5킬로미터에 걸치다 extend [stretch] over five kilometers / 여러 번[장장 네 시간]에 걸쳐 강연하다 deliver a series of lectures [make a lecture (extending) over four hours]
▶ 그 사람은 다방면에 걸쳐 활동하고 있다 He is actively engaged in various fields.
▶ 그 평야는 3개 도에 걸쳐 있다 The plain stretches [extends] over three provinces.
3 〈입다〉 throw [slip] on; huddle on 《*one's* clothes》
♦ 잠옷을 급히 걸치다 slip on *one's* pajamas hurriedly / 몸에 실오라기 하나 걸치지 않다 be starknaked; have not a stitch on
▶ 그 남자는 급히 코트를 걸치고 나갔다 The man threw on his coat and went out.
4 〈술마시다〉 drink; take ♦ 한 잔 걸치다 have a drink / 맥주를 걸치다 take a pull at *one's* beer

걸태질하다 rake in money [property] shamelessly

걸듬다 grope [fumble] for *sth*

걸터앉다 bestride; sit astraddle [astride] ♦ 의자에 걸터앉다 perch on a stool

걸터타다 ride astride [astraddle, straddle] 《a horse》; 〈모로〉 ride 《a horse》 sideways

걸핏하면 too often; readily; habitually
♦ 걸핏하면 때리다 be ready to hit *sb* / 걸핏하면 울다 will cry over nothing / 걸핏하면 화를 내다[싸우다] get angry [pick a fight] at the slightest provocation
▶ 그는 걸핏하면 딸한테 간다 He goes to his daughter frequently on some pretext or other.
▶ 그 여자는 걸핏하면 그 사람 욕을 한다 She chooses every opportunity to insult him.
▶ 그녀는 걸핏하면 울었다 She was too ready to cry.

검 劍 a sword; 〈군도〉 a saber; 〈총검〉 a bayonet; 〈단검〉 a dagger
▶ 남자는 허리에 검을 차고 있었다 The man wore a sword at his side.
▶ 그는 재빨리 검을 뽑았다 He quickly drew his sword.

검객 劍客 a swordsman; a fencer

검거 檢擧 an arrest; 〈일제 검거〉 (口) nab; a roundup
—검거하다 arrest; take up; 〈일제히〉 (口) round up
♦ 일제[대량] 검거하다 make a wholesale [mass] arrest 《of》; round up 《narcotic traffickers》
▶ 그는 살인[강도] 혐의로 검거되었다 He was arrested on charges of murder [robbery].
▶ 그 간첩은 아직 검거되지 않고 있다 The spy is still at large.

검경 檢鏡 a microscopic examination [investigation]; 〈검사경〉 a speculum 《*pl.* -la》
■ **—판(板)** 〈현미경의〉 an object plate; a slide

검극 劍劇 a sword-fighting play; a sword (-rattling) play **—영화** an action film [movie] featuring sword fighting

검뇨 檢尿 〔醫〕 a urine analysis; uroscopy
—검뇨하다 examine *sb's* urine; 〈검사시키다〉 have *one's* urine examined ; **—기(器)** a urinometer

검누렇다 blackish yellow; dark yellow

검다¹ 〈긁어모으다〉 rake up; scrape [gather] up

검다² 1 〈먹빛 같다〉 black; dark
♦ 검은 머리 black hair / 검은 점 a black spot / 검은 눈동자의 여인 a darkeyed woman / 피부가 검은 darkskinned / 검디 검은 jet-black [coal-black]; black as coal [pitch] / 검은 것을 희다고 억지를 쓰다 swear black is white; talk black into white / 검어지다 become black / 검게 물들이다[칠하다] dye [paint] *sth* black / 볕에 검게 타다 be [get] tanned [sunburnt]/ 검게 하다 blacken; make *sth* black
▶ 그는 얼굴이 검다 He has a dark complexion.
▶ 그녀는 검은 옷을 입고 있다 She wears a black dress.(▶be (dressed) in black은 「상복을 입다」의 뜻)
2 〈엉큼하다〉 blackhearted; evil-minded; wicked ♦ 속이 검은 an evil-minded [a scheming] person; a schemer

검당계 檢糖計 〔化〕 a saccharimeter
검댕 soot
♦ 검댕 투성이의 얼굴 a sooty face / 검댕이 끼다[앉다] become sooty [sooted]; have soot (on it) / 검댕이 묻다 be smeared with soot
▶ 나는 석유 난로의 검댕을 털어냈다 I swept the soot out of my kerosine heater.
▶ 검댕으로 굴뚝이 막혔다 The chimney is choked (up) with soot.
▶ 부엌 천장이 검댕으로 뒤덮였다 The ceiling of the kitchen is covered with soot.

검덕귀신 —鬼神 a person with a dirty face; a person who is very dirty in his appearance

검도 劍道 (the art of) fencing; swordsmanship
♦ 검도를 하다[연마하다] practice fencing [take lessons in swordsmanship]
▶ 그는 검도의 달인이다 He is a master fencer [swordsman].
▶ 그 여자는 검도가 3단이다 She has a third grade in fencing [is a fencer of the third grade].
■ **—도장[사범]** a fencing school [master]

검둥개 a black dog

검둥개 먹 감듯 〈속담〉 be just as before; There is no improvement at all.

검둥이 1 〈개〉 a black dog; Blackie (부를 때) 2 〈흑인〉 a Negro 《*pl.* ~es》; Negroids; a colored man; (口) a darky; a blackie; (蔑) a nigger; 〈피부가 검은 사람〉 a dark-skinned person

검량 檢量 measuring; weighing; 〈공공기관에 의한〉 metage **—검량하다** measure; take measure of; 〈무게를〉 weigh **—기** a gauging rod; a gauger **—세** metage

검룡 劍龍 〔古生〕 a stegosaur; a stegosaurus

검루기 檢漏器 〔電〕 a ground detector

검류계 檢流計 〈전류의〉 a galvanometer

검류의 檢流儀 〈조류의〉 a current indicator

검무 劍舞 a sword dance ▷ 칼춤

검문 檢問 (an) inspection; a check
♦ 경찰에게 검문을 당하다 be questioned by a policeman / 검문을 통과하다 pass an inspection
▶ 우리는 건널목 바로 앞에서 검문을 받았다 Just before the crossing, we were ordered to stop for a check.
▶ 용의자의 차가 검문에 걸렸다 The suspect was caught at a traffic checkpoint [in a traffic check].
—검문하다 inspect; examine; check up 《a passerby [car]》
■ **—소** a checkpoint; a control point

검버섯 dark spots (on an old man's skin); a blotch ♦ 얼굴에 검버섯이 돋다 have blotches on *one's* face

검변 檢便 a stool test; feces examination; an examination of feces **—검변하다** make a stool test; examine *sb's* stool [feces]

검부러기 remnants [bits, odd ends] of dry grass [leaves]
♦ 짚 검부러기 bits of straw

검분 檢分 (an) inspection ▷ 검사(檢査)

검불 dry grass or leaves

검붉다 dark-red; blackish red

검사 劍士 a swordsman ▷ 검객

검사 檢事 a public prosecutor; a prosecuting attorney; (총칭) the prosecution
■ **고검—** a public prosecutor of a high public prosecutor's office **부장—** a chief public prosecutor **지방—** a district public prosecutor; (美) a district attorney **차장—** the assistant [deputy] prosecutor general
■ **—장** the director of the 《Seoul District》 prosecutor's office; a superintendent public prosecutor **—직무대리** a probational public prosecutor

검사 檢査 (an) inspection; (an) examination; a test; a check (up); 〈회계의〉 an audit; 〈기계 등의〉 an overhaul; 〈상품 품질의〉 conditioning

---

解説 ***test***는 기준에 맞는지의 여부를 검사하는 것. ***inspection***은 기준에 맞는지를 권한을 가지고 검사하는 것, ***examination***은 내용 등을 분명히 하기 위해 조사하는 것이다.

♦검사를 받다 go through [undergo] an examination; be examined [inspected] / 검사에 합격하다 pass the examination; stand the test; be O.K.'d / 검사에 불합격하다 fail to pass the examination; be rejected
▶나는 시력 검사를 받았다 I had my eyesight tested.
▶의사에게 정밀 검사를 받아 보세요 See a doctor for a complete physical examination.
▶입국시에는 세관 검사를 받아야 한다 We must undergo customs inspections when entering a country.
▶이 우물물은 수질 검사를 받지 않으면 안 된다 The water of this well must be examined.
▶검사필 (표시) Examined. ⇌ Inspected.
—검사하다 inspect; examine; check (up); test; audit (accounts); overhaul (a machine)
▶그는 철분함유 여부를 알아보려고 그 모래를 검사했다 He tested the sand for iron.
■ 방사능— a radiation test; a test for radiation 신체— a physical examination; (美) a physical checkup 안전— safety inspection [check] 위생— a sanitary inspection 적성— an aptitude test 정기— periodic inspection 지능— an intelligence [a mental, an I.Q.] test 차량— a (motor) vehicle inspection; a safety inspection 체력— an examination of physical strength; a test of strength 품질— a check on the quality (of the goods)
■ —관 an inspector; 〈세관의〉 an examiner; an examining officer; 〈회계의〉 an auditor —실 an inspecting room —증 a test certificate; 〈무역의〉 an inspection certificate

검사소 檢査所 an inspecting office [station]
♦국립 농산물 검사소 the National Agricultural Products Inspection Center / 국립 생사 검사소 the National Raw Silk Inspection Center

검산 檢算 verification of accounts; proving a calculation; checking —검산하다 verify [check, go over] the accounts; check one's figure; [數] prove (one's answer)

검색 檢索 〈세관원의〉 rummage; 〈컴퓨터의〉 a search; retrieval; access
—검색하다 search [look] (for); rummage
♦선박을 검색하다 rummage a ship (for contraband goods) / 컴퓨터에서 정보 [파일]를 검색하다 access information [files] from a computer
▶저장된 정보는 쉽게 검색할 수 있다 The stored information can be retrieved easily.

검소하다 儉素— frugal; thrifty; economical; simple; plain
♦검소한 생활을 하다 live [lead] a simple [frugal] life; live in a simple [small] way; live frugally [simply, plainly]
▶그녀는 옷차림이 검소하다 She is plainly dressed.
▶결혼식은 가까운 친척들만 초대한 검소한 것이었다 The wedding was a simple one, to which only the immediate family was invited.
▶그것은 검소하게 꾸며진 작은 방이었다 It was a small plainly furnished room.

검속 檢束 (an) arrest; custody; (a) restraint; detention
♦경찰의 일제 검속 a police roundup (of suspects)
—검속하다 arrest (for detention); detain; take sb into custody; place [put] sb under arrest
■ 보호— (a) protective arrest 예비— (a) preventive detention

검수 檢數 checking [collating] the quantity of goods —검수하다 check [collate] the quantity of goods ■ —원 a checker [collater] of goods quantity

검술 劍術 fencing; swordsmanship

검시 檢屍 a postmortem (examination); an autopsy; an [a coroner's] inquest

|解說| *postmortem*이나 *autopsy*는 사체를 해부하여 사인을 조사하는 것을 의미하며, *inquest*는 postmortem이나 autopsy의 결과에 기초하여 행해지는 사인의 심리로 재판의 일종이다.

▶검시 결과 그는 교살된 것으로 판명되었다 The autopsy revealed that he had been strangled to death.
—검시하다 examine (a corpse); hold an inquest over (a corpse); perform a postmortem [an autopsy] on (the body)
♦사인 규명을 위해 검시하다 examine a corpse to find out the cause of death
■ —관 a coroner; (美) a medical examiner

검실거리다 flicker at a dim distance ⇨ 감실거리다

검쓰다 〈몹시 쓰다〉 very bitter; (as) bitter as gall; 〈언짢고 섭섭하다〉 regretful

검안 檢案 (法) examination
—검안하다 examine ♦시체를 검안하다 carry out [conduct] a postmortem examination; make an autopsy (on)
■ —서 a death certificate; a certificate of death

검안 檢眼 an eye examination [test]; optometry; optometry —검안하다 examine sb's eyes; 〈시력을〉 test sb's eyesight
■ —경 (鏡) an ophthalmoscope —법 (法) ophthalmoscopy [ȧfθælmǽskəpi] —사 (士) an optometrist

검압기 檢壓器 a pressure gauge; a manometer

검약 儉約 economy; thrift; frugality
—검약하다 economize (on sth); save (oil); use (energy) carefully; be frugal [thrifty]
♦검약하게 지내다 live without waste [wasting anything]; lead a frugal life / 검약하여 돈을 모으다 save money by economizing (on)
▶불경기이기 때문에 우리는 검약하지 않으면 안 되었다 We had to economize on unnecessary expenditures because of the recession.
■ —가 a man of economy; a thrifty [frugal] person

검역 檢疫 quarantine; medical inspection
♦검역을 받다 be quarantined; be put in quarantine / 검역 중이다 be in quarantine
▶검역필 (표시) Passed Medical Inspection

—검역하다 quarantine; inspect ■—관 a quarantine officer [doctor]; a healthguard —기간 a quarantine period —선 a quarantine ship —소 a quarantine station; a lazaretto 《pl. ~s》 —항 a quarantine port [anchorage]

검열 檢閱 1 〈검사〉 inspection; examination ◆검열을 받다 be inspected ▶검열필 (표시) Passed inspection. —검열하다 inspect; examine ▶그들은 소지품을 엄중하게 검열했다 They strictly examined [checked] our personal effects [things, belongings]. 2 〈간행물·영화 등의〉 censorship ◆검열을 받다 be censored [submitted for censorship]/ 검열을 통과하다 pass censorship / 검열을 폐지[완화, 강화]하다 remove [ease, tighten] the censorship 《on》/ 검열에 걸리다 fail to pass censorship ▶검열(표시) Censored. ▶서적 및 정기 간행물은 검열을 받아야 한다 Books and periodicals shall have to be submitted for censorship. —검열하다 censor; put censorship 《on》 3 〈군대의〉 inspection; a review —검열하다 inspect; review ■사전[사후]— precensorship [post-censorship] 영화[신문]— film [press] censorship ■—관 a censor; 〈군대의〉 an inspector —규정 the code of censor —제도 the censorship system

검영법 檢影法 〈눈의〉 skiascopy; retinoscopy

검온 檢溫 〔醫〕 thermometry —검온하다 take *sb's* temperature ■—기 (clinical) thermometer

검유 檢乳 examination of milk ■—기 a lactoscope; a lactometer

검은자위 the black part of the eyeball; the iris

검은콩 a black soybean

검이경 檢耳鏡 an auriscope; an otoscope

검인 檢印 a seal [stamp] of approval; a proof mark; 〈저자의〉 the seal of the author ◆검인을 찍다 stamp; put *sb's* seal [stamp] (of approval) 《on》; affix a seal [stamp] (of approval) 《to》 ▶이 책에는 저자의 검인이 없다 This book does not have the auther's seal [imprint]. ▶검인필 (표시) Approved and sealed. ■—증 an approval certificate

검인정 檢認定 official approval [certification] and sanction; authorization ▶교육부 검인정필 (표시) Approved by the Ministry of Education. ■—교과서 an authorized textbook

검전기 檢電器 an electroscope; 〈누전의〉 a (voltage) detector

검정 black; black color ◆검정 물감 black dye / 검정 코트 《wear》 a black coat

검정 檢定 official sanction; authorization ◆교과서 검정 제도 the textbook authorization [screening] system —검정하다 give official sanction 《to》 ■시험[무시험]— license with [without] examination ■—교과서 an authorized textbook —료 an examination fee; a fee for official licensing

검정고시 檢定考試 a certificate [qualification, license] examination; the examination for the license ◆대학 입학 자격 검정고시에 합격하다 pass the qualifying [qualification] examination for college entrance ■교원 자격— an examination for the license of school teachers

검조의 檢潮儀 〔地〕 a tide gauge [register]

검증 檢證 〔法〕 〈검사〉 (an) inspection; (a) test; 〈유언의〉 probate; 〈실증〉 (a) verification —검증하다 inspect; test; probate; verify ◆가설을 검증하다 verify a hypothesis / 유언(장)을 검증하다 probate a will ■현장— an inspection of the scene; an on-the-spot inspection: 수사관이 살인 사건의 현장 검증을 했다 The investigator inspected the scene of the murder.

검진 檢診 (a) medical examination; a physical checkup ▶나는 해외 여행을 가기 전에 검진을 받았다 I got [had] a medical checkup [examination] before going abroad. —검진하다 examine; give a medical examination; check up 《on *sb's* health》 ■정기— a regular health checkup: 암의 정기 검진을 받다 have a periodic checkup for cancer 종합— a comprehensive medical testing 집단— a group [collective] medical examination

검질기다 tenacious; persevering; persistent ◆검질긴 남자 a patient man; a man of great tenacity [stamina]/ 검질기게 버티다 give stubborn resistence 《to》

검찰 檢札 examination of tickets ⇨ 검표

검찰 檢察 prosecution; investigation and prosecution ◆검찰측 증인 a witness for the prosecution / 검찰측과 변호인측 the prosecution and the defense / 검찰 당국에 따르면 according to the prosecutory authorities ■—관 a public prosecutor; (美) a prosecuting attorney —총장 the Public Prosecutor General; (英) the Director of Public Prosecutions

검찰청 檢察廳 the Public Prosecutor's Office; the Public Prosecutions Administration ■고등— the (Seoul) High Prosecutor's Office 대— the Supreme Public Prosecutor's Office 지방— the District Public Prosecutor's office

검출 檢出 〔化〕 detection; (chemical) search —검출하다 detect [find] (strontium 90) (by chemical analysis); analyze out ▶식수에서 독이 검출되었다 Some poison was detected [found] in the drinking water. ▶물고기에서 10ppm의 PCB가 검출되었다 Ten ppm of PCB was detected in the fish. ■—기[장치] a detector

검측측하다 〈빛깔이〉 dark; rough [dull] and black; 〈마음이〉 black-hearted

검침 檢針 the inspection of a meter; a gauge

examination ―검침하다 check [read] a 《gas》 meter ■―원 a 《water》 meterman; 〈가스의〉 a gas meter reader; a gasman

검토 檢討 (an) examination; (an) investigation; study; scrutiny
♦검토 중인 법안 the bill under investigation [examination]
▶그 계획은 아직 검토 중입니다 We are still considering [thinking about] the plan. ⇌ The plan is still under consideration.
―**검토하다** investigate; examine 《a theory》; inquire
♦《일을》 면밀히 검토하다 inquire into *sth* closely / 여러 모로 검토하다 consider 《the matter》 from all angles / 더 검토할 필요가 있다 require further examination
▶한 번만 더 검토해 주십시오 Would you think it over again?
■재― reexamination; restudying

검파 檢波 〔電〕 detection; demodulation
―**검파하다** detect; demodulate

검파기 檢波器 a 《wave》 detector; a cymoscope
■광석― a crystal detector 열전(熱電)― a thermoelectric detector 자기(磁氣)― a magnetic detector 전해(電解)― a electrolytic detector 진공관― a vacuum-tube detector

검표 檢票 examination of tickets
―**검표하다** examine [check, punch] tickets; 《美》 check up tickets
■―원 a ticket inspector; a ticket examiner

검푸르다 dark blue; pale and dark
♦검푸른 바다 a dark blue sea

검호 劍豪 a great swordsman; a master fencer

겁 怯 〈두려움〉 fear; fright; (a) terror
♦겁이 많은 cowardly; timid; chicken-hearted / 겁이 없는 fearless 《child》; bold; strong-hearted / 겁먹다 be frightened; be seized with fear; 《口》 get [have] cold feet 《at the last moment》/겁주다 terrify; inspire *sb* with awe

겁결 怯― 〈겁결에〉 driven by fear; from [out of] fear / 겁결에 비명을 지르다 scream in fear

겁나다 怯― be overcome with fright; be seized with fear [panic]; be intimidated
▶나는 지진이 겁난다 I dread earthquakes.
▶짖는 개는 누구나 겁난다 Anybody is scared by barking dogs.
▶나는 죽는 것이 겁난다 I am afraid of dying.
▶그 아이는 꾸중을 들을까봐 겁나서 잠자코 있었다 The boy did not say a word for fear of being scolded.

겁내다 怯― fear; be afraid of; dread; get into a funk; be in fear [terror]
♦겁내는 기색도 없이 without any 《sign of》 hesitation / 겁내지 않다 be fearless 《of》; be undaunted; be unawed
▶동물들은 불을 겁낸다 Animals dread fire.
▶그는 의무를 수행하기 위해서는 죽음도 겁내지 않았다 He faced death at the call of duty.
▶아무 것도 겁낼 것이 없다 You have nothing to fear.

겁보 怯― a coward ⇨ 겁쟁이

겁쟁이 怯― a coward; a faintheart; 《口》 a fraidy cat; a chicken; 《美俗》 a chicken
▶그는 아주 겁쟁이다 He is such a fraidy cat. ⇌ He is (as timid) as a hare.
▶그 친구 참 겁쟁이로군 How cowardly [What a coward] he is!

겁탈 劫奪 〈약탈〉 robbery; pillage; plunder; 〈강간〉 violation; rape
―**겁탈하다** 〈약탈하다〉 plunder; pillage; 〈강간하다〉 violate; rape
♦여자를 겁탈하다 violate a woman; commit a rape on a woman
■―자 〈약탈자〉 a plunderer; 〈강간자〉 a violator; a rapist

것 1 〈사물〉 things; a matter; 〈물체〉 a thing; an object; an article; a [the] one
♦이것 this; this one / 저것 that; that one / 그것 it / 어느 것 which one / 먹을 것 《look for》 something to eat / 본 것 the one that *sb* saw / 볼 것 the one to see / 싼[비싼] 것 a cheap [high-priced] one
▶이것이 저것보다 낫다 This is better than that.
▶뭔가 시커먼 것이 물에 떠 있었다 Something black was floating on the water.
▶이것은 마음에 안 드니 다른 것을 보여주시오 I don't like this one, show me another.
▶나는 단 것을 좋아하지 않는다 I don't like sweet things [stuff].
2 〈소유물〉 a possession; the one of; 's
♦네 것 yours / 내 것 mine / 남의 것 other people's possession; other's / 자기 것이 되다 come into *one's* possession
▶승리는 항상 강한 자의 것이다 Victory always goes to the strong.
▶이 책은 내 것이 아니라 네 것이다 This book is yours; not mine.
3 〈사실〉 a fact; 〈일〉 a thing; what
▶그가 정직하다는 것은 사실이다 It is true that he is honest.
▶시간을 지키는 것은 중요하다 Being [To be] punctual is important.
▶아침에 일찍 일어나는 것은 건강에 좋다 Early rising is good for the your health.
▶그가 말하는 것은 옳은 얘기다 What he says is right.
▶이상한 것은 아무 것도 없다 There is nothing strange.
4 〈사람·동물〉 a man; a person; a [the] one
▶너 같은 것 such a man as you ▶내게는 어린 것이 둘 있다 I have two young ones.
5 〈필요〉 ▶그녀가 흥분할 것은 하나도 없다 There is no occasion for her to get excited.
▶서두를[급할] 것은 없다 There is no need for haste.
▶올 것까지는 없다 You need not [don't have to] come.
6 〈가능성·추측〉 probable fact; the real likelihood
▶그는 아마 알 것이다 He may know it.
▶이것으로 충분할 것이다 This will probably be enough.
▶그녀는 30살 미만일 것이다 She is under thirty, I should think.

▶눈이 올 것 같다 It looks like snow.
7 〈예정〉 그는 내일 이쪽으로 올 것이다 He is (supposed) to come here tomorrow.
▶비행기는 오후 5시에 도착할 것이다 The plane is due at 5 p.m.
8 〈금지·의무〉 ▶학생들은 오전 8시에 등교할 것 The students are requested to school at 8 a.m.
▶여기서는 술마시는 것이 금지되어 있다 You are not supposed to [shouldn't] drink here.
▶잔디밭에 들어가지 말 것 (게시) Keep off the grass.

-것다 1 〈다짐〉 be; do; I assume [suppose, think]
▶너 이 집에 살것다 You must live in this house, (I assume).
▶네가 가기는 가겠다 You are going there, aren't you?
2 〈조건〉 given this and that
▶돈도 있것다 권력도 있것다 무슨 걱정이오? You've got both money and power, and what's the matter with you?
3 〈협박〉 surely be; certainly do
▶네가 그렇게 했것다 You certainly did [have done] so.
▶너 말 다 했것다 How dare you say such a thing to me?

겅중거리다 walk with bouncing; strides; stride

겉 1 【표면】 the surface; the face; 〈옷 등의〉 the right side
◆양탄자의 겉쪽 the right side of a carpet / …의 겉에 on the surface [face] of… / 겉만 보다 look only at the outside
▶어느 쪽이 겉입니까? Which side is the front?
▶고기를 겉이 갈색이 될 때까지 구워라 Broil the meat until the top side is brown.
2 〈외부〉 the outside; the exterior; 〈외관〉 the outward appearance
◆겉을 꾸미다 put a (surface) gloss on *sth*; make outward show / 사물의 겉만 보다 take a superficial view of things
▶그는 겉 다르고 속 다르다 His looks are deceptive. ⇒ He looks one thing and means another.
▶그녀는 겉으로는 어엿한 숙녀였다 Her outward appearance was that of a perfect lady.
▶그 사람은 겉으로는 사교적인 것 같지만 속으로는 고독하다 He seems outgoing on the surface, but inside he is lonely.
▶그는 그 소식에 충격을 받았지만 겉으로는 태연한 체했다 He was shocked by the news, but bore it with outward calm.
◆겉만 보고 사람을 판단하지 마라 Don't [You shouldn't] judge people only by their appearances.

겉가량 ―假量 a rough estimate (based on outward appearances); approximate figures; 〈눈대중〉 eye measurement
◆겉가량으로 at a rough estimate; by eye measure / 겉가량으로 1천만원 정도다 be roughly estimated at ten million won
―**겉가량하다** make a rough estimate; estimate roughly

겉겨 bran; chaff; outer hulls [husks] of grain
겉곡식 ―穀― unhulled grain
겉껍질 the outer cover; 〈과실 등의〉 a husk; 〈곡물의〉 a hull; 〈싹 등의〉 an envelope; 〈피부의〉 cuticle
겉꾸리다 keep up appearances; make outward show; put on a good face on *sth*; put up a good front
겉꾸림 keeping up appearances; putting on a good face; (a) pretense; a makeup
▶그의 친절은 순전히 겉꾸림이다 His kindness is a mere show [all pretense].
겉나깨 buckwheat chaff
겉날리다 scamp 《*one's* work》; do 《*one's* work》 in a careless [rough] manner
▶그는 절대로 일을 겉날리지 않는다 He never scamps his work. ⇒ He never does his work halfheartedly.
겉놀다 1 〈못·나사 등이〉 slip; do not fit
2 ⇨ 겉돌다
겉눈감다 pretend to close [shut] *one's* eyes
겉눈썹 an eyebrow
겉늙다 get old before *one's* time; look old for *one's* age; be prematurely gray
▶그는 겉늙어 보인다 He looks older than his age.
겉대 〈푸성귀의〉 an outer stalk [leaf]; 〈대나무의〉 the outer (hard) part of bamboo
겉대중 a rough estimate ⇨ 겉가량
겉더께 (surface) scum; scale
겉돌다 1 〈잘 어울리지 못하다〉 do not get along well; be out of keeping 《with》; do not mingle 《with》
2 〈잘 섞이지 않다〉 do not mix (together)
▶물과 기름은 서로 겉돈다 Oil and water don't mix. ⇒ Oil doesn't mix with water.
겉똑똑이 a superficially bright person
겉마르다 get dry on the surface; 〈곡식이〉 dry out before ripening; wither
겉말 mere words [talk]; lip service; honeyed words; shallow compliments ◆겉말로 좋게만 이야기하다 just talk fair words; be a little too ready with compliments
겉맞추다 show a surface friendliness 《to》; flatter; gloss [smooth] over
겉모양 ―貌樣 outward appearance; outward show; look; front ◆겉모양을 꾸미다 put a surface gloss on *sth*
▶겉모양은 믿을 것이 못된다 Appearances are deceptive [deceitful]. ⇒ Never judge by appearances.
▶사물은 반드시 겉모양과 같지는 않다 Things are not always what they seem.
▶그는 사물의 겉모양만 본다 He looks only at the surface of things.
▶겉모양보다는 마음이다 Handsome is that handsome does.
겉물 a liquid floating on another liquid; supernatant liquid [fluid]
◆겉물돌다 (a liquid) float on the surface without mixing
겉밤 an unhulled chestnut; chestnuts with their shells on

겉보기 the outward appearance; show; look

[解說] **appearance**는 의복 등을 포함한 겉보기를 나타내고 보통 단수형으로 쓴다. ***look***은 용모를 말하며 복수형으로 쓴다. 동사 look을 써서 표현하는 경우도 많다.

♦ 겉보기에는 outwardly; on the surface / 겉보기로 판단하다 judge by appearance / 겉보기보다 듬직하다 be heavier than (it) looks
▶ 그는 겉보기는 시골뜨기처럼 보인다 He has the appearance of a country bumpkin.
▶ 그는 겉보기에는 거칠지만 부드러운 남자다 He is a kind man with a rough exterior.
▶ 그 여자는 겉보기와는 딴판이다 She looks totally different from what she really is.
▶ 그는 겉보기처럼 겁쟁이가 아니다 He is not such a coward as he would appear to be.
겉보리 unhulled barley
겉봉 —封 an envelope; an outer envelop [wrapper]
♦ 겉봉에 on the front of an envelope / 겉봉을 뜯다 open an envelope; cut (a letter) open
▶ 나는 편지의 겉봉을 썼다 I wrote the address on the front of an envelope.
겉수수 unhulled African [Indian] millet
겉싸개 a cover [wrapper]; an outer wrapper [covering]
겉씨식물 —植物 a gymnosperm
겉약다 clever in a superficial way [only on the surface]; superficially smart [sharp]
겉여물다 be ripe only in appearance [on the surface]
겉옷 an outer garment
겉잎 the outer leaves
겉잠 〈선잠〉 a nap; a doze; a catnap; (口) a snooze; 〈자는 체하기〉 sham sleep; feigned sleep ♦ 겉잠(이) 들다 doze; catnap; snooze / 겉잠(을) 자다 pretend to be asleep
▶ 그는 책을 읽다가 겉잠이 들었다 He dozed off over a book.
겉잡다 1 〈걸가량하다〉 make a rough estimate; estimate roughly
▶ 이익은 겉잡아 2,000만원이었다 We roughly estimated the profit at twenty million won.
▶ 겉잡아 열흘이면 충분합니다 In my estimation ten days will be enough.
2 〈헤아리다〉 guess; (口) imagine; get a rough idea (of)
▶ 네 말은 통 겉잡을 수가 없다 I can't make head or tail of what you are saying
겉잣 pine nuts with their shells on
겉장 —張 〈표지〉 the cover of a book; 〈신문의 제 1 면〉 the front [first] page
겉저고리 a woman's outer jacket
겉절이 vegetables pickled [salted] right before eating; dish of salted vegetables
겉절이다 salt vegetables before seasoning elaborately; pickle vegetables right before eating
겉짐작 rough guess (based on appearances); a (mere) conjecture; a random guess
♦ 겉짐작으로 판단하다 judge by guess [guesswork]

▶ 그것은 단지 겉짐작에 불과하다 It's mere guesswork.
—**겉짐작하다** guess; make a rough estimate
겉치레 outward show; keeping up appearances; improving *one's* personal appearance
♦ 겉치레로 just for appearance's sake; for show; ostentatiously / 겉치레를 좋아하다 be fond of display
▶ 그 두 사람은 겉치레 인사를 나누었다 The two exchanged perfunctory greetings.
▶ 그가 화를 내는 것[그의 친절]은 겉치레에 불과하다 His anger [kindness] is only a pretense [a mere show].
—**겉치레하다** improve the appearance of; keep up appearances; put a varnish on 《a matter》
겉치마 an outer skirt
겉치장 —治粧 making outward show; dressing up [decorating] the outside; improving *one's* personal appearance; keeping up appearance
▶ 그녀는 겉치장에는 관심이 없다 She is unconcerned about her personal appearance.
—**겉치장하다** dress up [decorate] the outside; keep up appearances; make outward show
겉칠 the last [final] coating —**겉칠하다** give the last [final] coat (of paint)
겉핥기 a smattering; (a) superficial knowledge
♦ 겉 핥기(식)의 superficial [smattering] (knowledge); halfread / 겉핥기로 알다 have a smattering [superficial knowledge] 《of English》
▶ 그는 아는 것이 많지만 모두가 겉핥기다 He knows about a lot of things, but his knowledge is all superficial.
▶ 겉핥기로 알 바에는 차라리 모르는 게 낫다 One may as well know nothing than know things by halves.
▶ 나는 그리스어를 겉핥기로만 알고 있을 뿐이다 I have only a smattering of Greek.
게[1] 〔動〕 a crab
♦ 민물 게 a river crab / 게 가공선 a crab-cannery ship; a crab-packing vessel / 게잡이 crab fishing; crabbing / 게 통조림 tinned [(美) canned] crab; a tin [(美) can] of crab meat / 게의 등딱지 a carapace / 게의 집게발 (a pair of) claws [nippers]
▶ 게는 옆으로 긴다 Crabs crawl sideways.
▶ 아이가 게에게 손가락을 물렸다 The child had his fingers nipped by a crab.
■—눈 a crab's eye(s): 게눈 감추듯 하다 eat up in less than no time —**알젓** pickled crab eggs —**자리**〔天〕the Crab; Cancer
게[2] 〈거기〉 there ▶ 게 누구 없느냐? Is anybody there? ▶ 게 섰거라 Stop there! ⇒ Stop, you there! ▶ 게 좀 앉거라 Sit down there
게[3] 〈에게〉 for; to ♦ 내게 온 편지 a letter for me ▶ 그것은 내게 큰 도움이 되었다 It was of great help to me.
게[4] 〈것이·사람을 얕잡아서〉 ♦ 그까짓 게 a man like him / 네까짓 게 such a guy [fellow] as you
▶ 그게 누구 것이냐? Whose is that?

▶ 네까짓 게 뭘 하겠다구 You couldn't do anything.
▶ 저까짓 게 무슨 학자냐? How could a fellow [guy] like him be (called) a scholar?

게⁵ 〈사는 곳·집〉 one's place [hometown]; a part of one's country
▶ 우리게는 겨울에 몹시 춥다 In winter it is very cold in our part of the country.
▶ 우리게 친구들한테서 소식이 있니? Do you hear from our old friends back hometown?
▶ 우리게에서는 그렇게 하는 것이 풍습입니다 In my hometown it is customary to do so.

-게 1 〈친밀한 명령〉 do
▶ 들어오게 Come in.
▶ 앉게 Sit down.
▶ 우리 집에서 자게 You sleep at my house.
2 〈가정〉 may [might]; will [would]; then won't 〈it〉 turn out that…?
▶ 그랬다간 큰일 나게[매맞게]? If I do so, it would turn serious [I will get whipped, won't I]?
▶ 그런 돈이 있으면 좋게? It would be grand to have so much money, wouldn't it?
3 〈의문〉 ▶ 그 정도 돈을 가지고 무얼 사게? What can you afford to buy with such an amount of money?
4 〈사역〉 make sb do; cause sb to do
♦ 구두를 고치게 하다 have one's shoes mended / 불을 타오르게 하다 make the fire burn
▶ 그를 가게 했다 I made him go.
▶ 말에게 물을 마시게 했다 I made the horse drink water.
▶ 식사를 가져오게 할게요 I'll get your dinner sent in.
5 〈내용·정도의 제한〉 ♦ 쉽게 얘기하면 To put it simply / 똑똑하게 생기다 look smart / 우리의 생활을 넉넉하게 하다 enrich our lives / 이상하게 생각하다 think 〈it〉 strange / 재미있게 지내다 have fun; have a good time / 짧게 설명하다 explain sth briefly
▶ 감기들지 않게 조심해라 Be careful not to catch (a) cold.
▶ 그 소녀는 예쁘게 생겼다 The girl looks pretty.
6 〈상태의 조성〉 ▶ 이 대답이 그녀를 행복하게 [화나게] 했다 This answer made her happy [angry].
7 〈…하게 되다〉 come to 〈do〉; get to 〈do〉; grow into
♦ 담배를 피우게 되다 come to start smoking / 부모의 사랑을 알게 되다 come to appreciate one's parents' love / 음악을 좋아하게 되다 begin to be fond of music
▶ 어떻게 그 일을 알게 되었니? How did you come to hear of it?
▶ 언제 한국에 가시게 됩니까? When are you going to Korea?
▶ 그 외국인은 한국에 대해 관심을 갖게 되었다 The foreigner has come to have an interest in Korea.
▶ 내가 학교에 가게만 된다면 얼마나 좋을까 How nice it would be if only I could get to go to school!

게거품 〈게의〉 foam at the mouth of a crab; 〈사람·동물의〉 froth; foam ▶ 그 남자는 말할 때 입에서 게거품이 난다 The man foams at the mouth when talking.

게걸 greed for food; voracity ♦ 게걸들이다 become greedy for food; get an insatiable appetite / 게걸때다 eat one's fill

게걸거리다, 게걸대다 grumble; growl; (美口) grouch ♦ 술취해서 게걸거리다 babble [blather] drunkenly
▶ 그는 술만 취하면 게걸거린다 He always grumbles when he gets drunk.

게걸스럽다 greedy (for food); voracious; ravenous; gluttonous, 〈서술적〉 have an insatiable appetite; have a wolf in one's stomach
♦ 게걸스럽게 먹다 eat greedily [ravenously]; guzzle; eat like a hog [wolf]; wolf down 〈one's meal〉; shovel food into one's mouth

게걸음 a sidewise crawl [movement] of a crab ♦ 게걸음치다 walk [crawl] sideways; sidle; move sidewise ▶ 그는 군중 속을 게걸음으로 헤쳐나갔다 He sidled through the crowd.

게걸쟁이 a grumbler; a grouch

게검스럽다 greedy ⇨ 게걸스럽다

게꼬리 a dull fellow [clod]; a stupid [talentless] person

게꽁지만하다 shallow; short; superficial
▶ 게꽁지만한 학문 가지고 네가 무엇을 안다고 그래? What do you think you know with your two-bit worth of education?

-게끔 so as to 〈do〉; so that one [it] may 〈do〉 ⇨ -게¹ 4, 5, 6, 7
▶ 모두가 다 잘 알아듣게끔 똑똑히 말해라 Speak clearly so that everybody will understand you.
▶ 아무 뒤탈 없게끔 잘 처리하시오 Manage the matter carefully so that there will be no trouble in the future.

게놈 (遺) a genom(e) ■ —분석 genom(e) analysis

게다가 1 〈거기에 더하여〉 in addition to 〈it〉; added to this; what is more; 〈그리고 또한〉 besides; moreover; furthermore; 〈설상가상으로〉 to make matters worse; what is worse
▶ 그녀는 지적이고 게다가 미인이다 She is intelligent and good-looking besides.
▶ 그 집은 작고 게다가 너무 비싸기까지 했다 The house was small, and on top of that [moreover], it was too expensive.
▶ 그는 능력이 있고 게다가 돈도 많다 He has ability and plenty of money to go with it.
▶ 그녀는 산속에서 길을 잃었고 게다가 날까지 어두워지고 있었다 She lost herself in the mountain; what is worse, it began to grow dark.
▶ 비가 오고 게다가 바람마저 불었다 It rained and there was a wind to boot.
▶ 게다가 나는 상금 5백만원까지 받았다 In addition, I received a prize of five million won.
2 〈그곳에〉 there; over there; in that place
▶ 게다가 쓰레기를 버리지 마시오 Don't dump refuse over there.

게도 구럭도 다 잃었다 (속담) They ended up

falling between the two stools.

게딱지 the shell [crust] of a crab ♦게딱지 같다[만하다] 〈집이〉 very small; tiny; humble; shabby
▶ 나는 게딱지만한 집을 지었다 I built a very small house [humble cottage].
▶ 나는 게딱지만한 집에 살고 있다 I live in a tiny house [matchbox of a house].

게르마늄 〔化〕 germanium ■ —은광(銀鑛) argyrodite

게르만 the German (people) ♦게르만의 Germanic / 범(汎)게르만주의 Pan-Germanism ■ —말 the German language —민족 the Germanic race

게리맨더 〔美政〕 gerrymander

게릴라 〈전법〉 guerrilla; 〈사람〉 a guerrilla ♦대게릴라전 counterguerrilla warfare ■ 도시— guerrilla fighting in city streets; 〈사람〉 an urban guerrilla —병 a guerrilla —부대 a guerrilla band; a partisan unit —전(戰) guerrilla warfare [war]: 게릴라전을 펴다 conduct guerrilla operation; make guerrilla war —전술 (use) guerrilla tactics

게바라 〈쿠바의 혁명가〉 Guevara, Ernesto ['Che'] (1928-67)

게발 a crab's claws ♦글씨를 게발 그리듯 하다 write a scrawl; write a crabbed [very bad, clumsy] hand; scrawl; scribble

게슈타포 〈나치 독일의〉 the Gestapo

게스트 a guest; 〈텔레비전 등의〉 a guest performer ♦게스트로 출연하다 make a guest appearance 〈in a show〉 ■ —멤버 a guest member

게시 揭示 a notice; a bulletin
♦게시를 벽에 붙이다 〈압정으로〉 tack a notice to the wall; 〈핀으로〉 pin up a notice on the wall; 〈풀로〉 stick [fasten, fix] a sign on the wall / …라는 게시가 붙어 있다 There is a notice up saying [reporting] that…
▶ 상점 창문에「금일 휴업」이라는 게시가 나붙어 있었다 There was a notice up on the shopwindow saying "Closed Today."
—게시하다 put up a notice (on the wall); write up
■ —판 (美) a bulletin board; a billboard; (英) a notice board: 열차 발착 게시판 a railway station calendar

-게시리 so as to (do) ⇨ -게끔

게양 揭揚 hoisting; raising
—게양하다 put up; hoist; raise; fly
♦국기를 게양하다 hoist [put up] a national flag (in honor of the Independence Day)
▶ 집집마다 국기가 게양되어 있다 The national flag is hoisted over every door.

게염 〈탐욕〉 covetousness; avarice

♦게염나다[내다] become [get] covetous (of) / 게염부리다 covet; behave covetously / 게염스럽다 be covetous
▶ 넌 정말 게염스럽구나 How covetous you are!

게우다 1〈먹은 것을〉 vomit; bring [fetch] up; throw up
♦게울 것 같다 feel sick; feel like vomiting [throwing up]; retch
▶ 그는 먹은 것을 죄다 게우고 말았다 He threw up [vomited] all [everything] he had eaten.
2 〈부정 이익을〉 disgorge; replace [refund] 《ill-gotten money》
▶ 그는 횡령한 돈 100만원을 도로 게웠다 He has disgorged the embezzled one million won.

게으르다 idle; lazy; indolent
♦게으른 습관이 들다 form [fall into] an indolent [slothful] habit / 게을러지다 become lazy; get an indolent habit
▶ 그는 천성적으로 게으르다 He is idle by nature.
▶ 그는 게으른 생활을 하고 있다 He is leading an idle life [idling away his time].
▶ 너는 게을러 터져서 못쓰겠다 You are a good-for-nothing lazibones.
▶ 그녀는 게으르기 짝이 없다[게을러 빠졌다] She is laziness itself [is quite indolent].

게으름 laziness; idleness; indolence; 〈태만〉 neglect; negligence; inexertion ♦게으름 피우다[부리다] loaf; idle one's time away
■ —뱅이[쟁이] an idle person; a lazybones (▶단수·복수 동형); a lazy fellow; a dawdler [sluggard]; (口) a bum: 그는 타고난 게으름뱅이다 He is a born idler.

게을리 lazily; idly; indolently
—게을리하다 〈등한히 하다〉 neglect; be negligent [neglectful]; slight 《one's work》
♦문단속을 게을리하다 forget to lock the door / 의무를 게을리하다 neglect one's duties / 편지의 답장을 게을리하다 leave a letter unanswered; 〈상습적으로〉 be bad at answering letters
▶ 공부를 게을리해서는 안 된다 You shouldn't neglect your studies.
▶ 경계를 게을리하지 마라 Keep your eyes open.

게이지 a gauge; a gage ■ 표준— the standard gauge

게이트 〈문·탑승구〉 a gate; 〈경마의〉 a (starting) gate; (英) starting stalls
♦3번 게이트 〈공항의〉 Gate 3

게임 a game ♦게임을 하다 play [have] a game (of tennis)
■ 실내— a parlor [an indoor] game ■ —이론 game theory —차(差) 〔野〕 games behind;

게시·간판·광고의 주요 문례

1. 역·탈것에 관한 게시
▶ 발밑을 조심하시오 Watch [Mind] your step.
▶ 잔돈을 준비해 주십시오 Have exact fare, please.
▶ 승차권을 각자 가지고 계십시오 Please retain your ticket for collection.
▶ 초과 요금은 정산소로 와 주십시오 If you

have a fare to pay, please come to the excess fare window.
▶ 소매치기를 조심하시오 Beware of pickpockets.
▶ 선로횡단 금지 ― 벌금 5만원 Do not trespass on railway. ― Penalty 50 thousand won.
▶ 열차를 기다리시는 분은 플랫폼의 가장자리에 서지 마십시오 Stand clear of the edge of the platform when waiting for your train.
▶ 정차 중에는 사용을 금지하시고 사용 후에는 물을 틀어 놓으시오 Kindly flush toilet after each use except when train is standing in the station.
▶ 수화물은 검사를 받습니다 Carry-on baggage is subject to examination.
▶ 문 가까이에 서 있지 마십시오 Keep clear of doors.
▶ 열차에 뛰어 타거나 뛰어 내리지 마십시오 Do not attempt to enter or leave the carriage while the train is moving.
▶ 안내소 Information
▶ 입구 Entrance
▶ 출구 (美) Exit; (英) Way out
▶ 빈차 For Hire
▶ 코인로커 Coin(-operated) Lockers / 수화물 보관소 (美) Checkroom; (英) Left luggage Office

2. 도로표지・교통의 게시・표지
▶ 일방통행 One way.
▶ 돌아서 가시오 Detour.
▶ 우[좌]회전 금지 No right [left] turn.
▶ 우천시 미끄럼 주의 Warning ― Slippery when wet.
▶ 추월 금지 No passing.
▶ 횡단 금지 No crossing.
▶ 횡단 보도 Pedestrian Crossing; (美) Cross Walk; (英) Zebra Zone
▶ 경적을 울리시오 Sound your horn.
▶ 여기서부터 공사중 Men at work ahead.; Roadwork ahead.; Under Construction ahead.
▶ 어린이 조심 Check for children.; Drive with care ― Children playing.
▶ 제한속도 40킬로미터 Speed limit: 40k.p.h
▶ 자전거 통행 금지 No cycling allowed.
▶ 서행 하시오 Go slowly.
▶ 제차 통행 금지 Close to all vehicles.
▶ 머리 위를 조심하시오 Watch [Mind] your head.
▶ 무단 차량 주차 금지 No parking except for authorized vehicles.
▶ 위반시에 소유자 비용 부담으로 견인함 Cars illegally parked will be towed away at owner's expense.
▶ 통행 금지 No thoroughfare.
▶ U 턴 금지 No U-turn.
▶ 좌[우]측 통행 Keep to the left [right]
▶ 긴급전화 Phone for Aid / 주차장 (美) Parking Lot; (英) Car Park / 육교 Foot Bridge
▶ 보행자 전용 구역 Pedestrian Precinct
▶ 막다른 길 Dead End

3. 광장・공원・교외 등의 게시

▶ 주류 지참 금지 All alcoholic beverage prohibited (in this park).
▶ 쓰레기를 버리지 마십시오 No litter.
▶ 쓰레기는 가지고 가십시오 Take your litter home.
▶ 쓰레기는 쓰레기통에 넣어주십시오 Deposit litter in litterbin.
▶ 잔디밭에 들어가지 마십시오 (Please) Keep off the grass.
▶ 페인트[칠] 주의 Wet paint.; Fresh paint.
▶ 개는 입장 불가 Dogs are forbidden.
▶ 개는 쇠사슬로 매어둘 것 All dogs to be kept on a leash.
▶ 구기 금지 지역 Ball games are prohibited in this area.
▶ 산불 방지 Prevent forest fires.
▶ 화장실 (美) Rest Room; Comfort Station; (英) Toilet; Lavatory / 화재 경보기 Fire Alarm / 휴지통 (美) Trash Can; Litter; (英) Dustbin / 관광 전망대 Scenic Lookout / 소화전 Fire Hydrant

4. 상점・극장・공공시설 등의 게시물
▶ 주류 있습니다 Fully licensed.
▶〈음식을〉가지고 들어갈 수 있음 Take out [(英) away] service offered.
▶ 도매 전문 Wholesale only.
▶ 회원 외 출입금지 No admittance except for members; Members only.
▶〈병원의〉면회 사절 Don't disturb.
▶ 고서 고가 매입 High prices offered for used books.
▶ 담배는 재떨이가 있는 곳에서만 피우세요 Smoking allowed only where ashtrays are provided.
▶ 요리사 구함 Wanted a cook.
▶ 경비견 조심 ― 출입 금지 Guard dog on patrol. ― Keep out.
▶ 고장(수리)중 Out of order.
▶ 연말 대매출 Year-end Sale
▶〈거스름돈이 남지 않도록〉정확한 요금을 동전 투입구에 넣어 주시오 Put exact fare in coin slot.
▶〈엘리베이터 등의〉종업원 전용 Staff only.
▶ 전 좌석 예약 가능 All seats bookable in advance.
▶ 진열품에 손대지 마십시오 Don't touch exhibits.
▶ 벽보를 붙이지 마십시오 Post no bills.
▶ 금일 휴업 Closed today.
▶ 출입 금지 No trespassing.
▶ 난간을 잡으세요 Use handrail.
▶ 분실물에 대한 책임은 지지 않습니다 Please leave your hat, coat, etc. at your own risk.
▶ 매표소 (美) Ticket Office; (英) Booking Office
▶ 업자전용 입구 Tradesman's Entrance
▶ 계산대 Cashier
▶ 내부 전화 Housephone / 자동 판매기 Vendor; Automat; Vending Machine; Slot Machine
▶ 재고정리 대매출 (英) Clearance Sale
▶ 예약석 Reserved Seat
▶ 동전 교환 Coin Changer

game balance : 다저스는 메츠에게 두 게임차로 앞서 있다 The Dodgers have a 2-game lead over the Mets.

게장 —醬 crabs pickled in soy sauce; pickled crabs

게재 揭載 publication; putting into print ♦그 논문의 게재지 the magazine which carries the article / 다음 호에 게재 예정으로 appear in the next issue / 잡지에 게재중인 연재물 a serial running in a magazine; an article serially appearing in a magazine / 격일로 게재되는 appearing every other day
―**게재하다** publish; report; print; (美) run; carry (the news)
♦광고를 게재하다 insert [run] an advertisement / 소설을 게재하다 put [publish] a novel (in a magazine) / 신문에 게재되다 appear [be reported] in a newspaper
▶이 칼럼은 격일로[매주 월요일] 게재된다 This column appears every other day [every Monday].
▶내 논설이 「네이처」 10월호에 게재되었다 My article was printed in the October issue of "Nature."
■―**금지** a press ban; prohibition [suppression] of publication

게저분하다 dirty; unclean; laden with dirty things ♦포스터가 게저분하게 붙은 벽 a wall disorderly pasted with posters

게접스럽다 dirty; filthy; squalid; sordid

게젓 pickled crabs ⇨ 게장

게정 〈불평〉 a grumble; a complaint
♦게정내다[부리다] grumble / 게정스럽다 be grumbly
■―**꾼** a grumbler; (口) a crabber; (美俗) a griper

게트림 an arrogant belch; belching in a haughty manner ―**게트림하다** belch arrogantly; belch in a haughty manner

겔 【物·化】 gel ■―**화(化)** gelation : 겔화하다 gel; gelate

겔렌데 〈(獨) Gelände〉 〔스키〕 a slope

겨 chaff; hulls [husks] of grain; bran ♦겉겨 (outer) husks; hulls; chaff / 쌀겨 rice bran

겨냥 1 〈겨눔〉 aim; aiming
♦겨냥이 빗나가다 one's aim is off
▶그의 겨냥은 정확했다 His aim was true.
―**겨냥하다** aim (at); take aim (at); set one's sights (on)
♦바로[잘못] 겨냥하다 aim right(ly) [wrong(ly)]
▶그는 적을 겨냥하고 발사했다 He took aim and fired at the enemy.
2 〈치수〉 measure; size; dimension ♦겨냥내다 take the measure [dimensions] (of); measure; size
■―**대** a measuring rod; a yardstick

겨냥도 ―圖 a (rough) sketch; a sketch map [drawing] ♦겨냥도를 그리다 sketch; make a sketch of

겨누다 1 〈겨냥하다〉 aim (at); take aim (at); sight (a target); set one's sights (on)
♦정확히 겨누다 take accurate [sure] aim (at); draw a bead (on) / 총을 겨누다 take aim with one's gun (at); level [point] one's gun (at) / 겨누지 않고 쏘다 〈마구잡이로〉 shoot at random
2 〈대어보다〉 take the measure [dimensions] of; measure off the size; take the size of

겨드랑이 〈몸의〉 the armpit; 〈옷의〉 the armhole
▶겨드랑이에 끼다 carry [hold] a thing under one's arm / 겨드랑이에 땀이 나다 sweat under the arm
▶그는 영어 사전[우산]을 겨드랑이에 끼고 있었다 He was carrying an English dictionary [umbrella] under his arm.

겨레 〈민족〉 a nation; a race; a people; 〈동포〉 brothers; brethren; fellow countrymen; offspring of the same forefather ♦한 겨레 one and the same people
■―**붙이** members of a people [nation]

겨루다 emulate one another [each other] (in); compete [vie, contend, struggle] (with); strive (with another in doing)
♦용기[솜씨]를 겨루다 vie [compete] with sb in bravery [some art] / 힘을 겨루다 compete (with sb) in physical strength; measure one's strength (with, against)
▶다섯 학생이 콘테스트에서[상을 놓고] 겨루었다 Five students competed with each other in the contest [for the prize].
▶수학에 있어서는 우리 반에서 그와 겨룰 사람이 없다 He has no equal [is unrivaled] in mathematics in our class.

겨룸 (a) competition; a contest; emulation; measuring one's strength [talent] (with, against)
♦힘 겨룸 a contest of physical strength; a strength contest

겨를 leisure; spare [leisure] time; time to spare ⇨ 여가
♦겨를이 없다 have no leisure; have no time to spare; be (too) busy
▶나는 좀처럼 겨를이 없다 I am seldom at leisure.
▶그 사고는 너무 갑작스러워서 침착하게 숙고해 볼 겨를이 없었다 The accident was too sudden to allow time for calm deliberation.
▶나는 아침에 신문 읽을 겨를도 없다 I have no time for reading [to read] the paper in the morning.

겨리 a plow drawn by a yoke of oxen ■―**질** plowing with a two-ox plow

겨릿소 one of the oxen tethered to a two-ox plow

겨반지기 〈겨가 많이 섞인 쌀〉 chaffy rice; rice with husks in it

겨우 〈가까스로〉 hardly; barely; narrowly; 〈애써서〉 with diffculty [effort]; 〈고작〉 only; merely; no more than
♦겨우 도망치다 escape narrowly; have a narrow shave / 겨우 살아 가다 live barely; make a bare living / 겨우 이기다 win (a game) by a shave [narrow margin] / 겨우 20만원을 모으다 barely manage to collect two hundred thousand won / 겨우 시험에 합격하다 pass an examination with difficulty; (口) scrape

through the exam
▶ 그는 겨우 당선되었다 He was elected by a narrow majority.
▶ 그들은 적은 수입으로 겨우 살아 간다 They make out on a small income.
▶ 나는 겨우 목숨을 부지했다 I barely escaped death.
▶ 그는 겨우 시간에 대어 왔다 He barely managed to come in time.
▶ 출석자는 겨우 6명밖에 안 되었다 The number of attendants was no more than six.
▶ 그는 겨우 그녀를 설득했다 It took him a great deal of effort to persuade her.

겨우내 all through [throughout] the winter; all winter long
▶ 겨우내 눈이 펑펑 오면 좋겠다 I hope it snows thick and fast all winter through.
▶ 나는 겨우내 제주도에서 보냈다 I stayed in Chejudo all last winter.

겨우살이 1 〈겨울 옷〉 winter clothes; winter wear **2** ⇨ 월동(越冬) **3** 〖植〗 the mistletoe; a parasite

겨울 (a) winter
♦ 따뜻한 겨울 a mild [soft, green] winter / 추운 겨울 a cold [severe, hard] winter / 겨울옷 winter clothing / 겨울의 winter; wintry 《scene》/ 겨울용의 for winter use / 한겨울에 in midwinter; in the depths [midst] of winter / 겨울 준비를 하다 prepare for the (coming) winter / 겨울을 나다 pass the winter; winter (at, in)
▶ 날씨가 겨울다워졌다 The weather has a wintry nip in it. ≒ It has grown wintry.
▶ 겨울이 왔다 Winter has come.
▶ 겨울이 오면 봄도 멀지 않으리 If winter comes, can spring be far behind?
▶ 올 겨울은 몹시 춥다 It is very cold this winter.
■—날씨 wintry weather —방학 the winter vacation [holidays] —스포츠 (enjoy) winter sports —잠 wintering; hibernation —철 the winter (time)

겨워하다 feel *sth* to be more than *one* can manage; feel *sth* is beyond *one's* control; feel *sth* unmanageable [uncontrollable]
♦ 일을 힘에 겨워하다 feel the job is too much for *one*

겨이삭 〖植〗 a bent grass

겨자 〈양념〉 mustard; 〖植〗 a mustard ♦ 겨자를 친 음식 food dressed with mustard
▶ 겨자는 톡 쏘는 맛이 있다 Mustard stings.
■—씨 (a) mustard seed: 한 알의 겨자씨 a grain of mustard seed —채 vegetables with mustard dressing

격 格 1 〈품위〉 a manner; 〈격식〉 formality; a rule; 〈지위·등급〉 (a) standing; an order; status; a rank [class, grade]
♦ 격에 맞는 suitable [proportionate] to *one's* status [standing] / 격이 높다 be high in social standing; be of a distinguished style / 격이 떨어지다 fall in rank; be of lower grade / 격에 맞다 be regular; be in proper style [accordance with a rule]
▶ 저 호텔은 다른 호텔과는 격이 다르다 That hotel is in a different class from the rest.
▶ 그 사람은 너하고는 격이 다르다 He is on a different level from you [not in the same league as you are].
2 〈자격〉 capacity; character
♦ 격에 맞지 않는 짓을 하다 go out of *one's* character; do *sth* unbecoming / 대사 격으로 대우하다 treat as an ambassador; entertain in the capacity of an ambassador
▶ 이 일이 그의 격에 맞는다 This is just his job.
3 〖文法〗 a case ♦ 주[소유, 목적]격 the nominative [possessive, objective] case
4 〖論〗〈삼단논법의〉 a figure; a schema 《*pl.* -mata》
5 〈셈〉 ♦ 소 잃고 외양간 고치는 격이다 That is an instance of [That is, as it were,] shutting the stable door after the horse is stolen.

격 檄 a written appeal ⇨ 격문(檄文)

격감 激減 a sharp decrease; a marked decline —**격감하다** decrease [decline, fall off] sharply [remarkably]
▶ 수출이 격감했다 There was a big drop [a marked falling off] in exports.
▶ (전쟁으로) 인구가 격감했다 The population decreased sharply (as a result of the war).

격검 擊劍 fencing ⇨ 검도(劍道)

격나다 隔— 〈사이가 멀어지다〉 become estranged [alienated] 《from *sb*》; split with; break relations 《with》
▶ 그일 이후로 두 사람은 격났다 Since that event the two have become estranged.

격납고 格納庫 a hangar; an airplane [aviation] shed; an airshed
♦ 비행기를 격납고에 넣다 put an airplane in a hangar
■—이동— a portable hangar ■—갑판 〈항공모함의〉 a hangar deck

격년 隔年 every other [second] year; in alternate years
♦ 격년 간행의 biennial / 격년으로 to be held every other [second] year
▶ 그 보고서는 격년으로 간행되고 있다 The report is published once every two years. ≒ The report is a biennial publication.

격노 激怒 violent [great] anger; wild rage; fury; wrath
—**격노하다** get very angry; be [become] furious; burn with wrath; 《美》 get mad with anger
♦ 격노하여 in a rage; in the fury of *one's* passion / 격노케 하다 enrage; bring *sb* to a full fury
▶ 그는 그녀의 배신에 격노했다 He was furious at [about] her betrayal.

격돌 激突 a crash; a clash; 〈대결〉 a hot [sharp] contest
—**격돌하다** crash 《into》; clash 《against》; engage in a hot contest
▶ 양군은 넓은 평야에서 격돌했다 The armies clashed on the wide plain.
▶ 김 의원은 그 문제로 조의원과 격돌했다 Rep. Kim clashed with Rep. Cho about the matter.

격동 激動 〈진동〉 violent shaking; concussion; a severe shock; 〈사회·인심의 동요〉 excitement; agitation; upheaval; turbulence

—격동하다 be excited; be stirred up; be agitated
◆격동하는 사회 정세 turbulent social conditions / 문단을 격동시키다 stir up literary circles
▶ 온 나라[전세계]가 격동하였다 Immense excitement prevailed throughout the country [world].
▶ 세계는 지금 정치적으로 격동하고 있다 The world is now in the midst of a great political upheaval.

격랑 激浪 raging [angry] waves; heavy seas
◆격랑에 휩쓸리다 be swept away by the angry waves
▶ 격랑이 일었다 The waves ran high.
▶ 배는 격랑에 가랑잎처럼 흔들렸다 The ship was tossed about by the huge waves.

격려 激勵 (an) encouragement; urging; incitement; 〈자극〉 stimulation
◆격려의 말[편지] words [a letter] of encouragement
▶ 그는 많은 격려가 필요하다 He needs a lot of encouragement [encouraging].
—격려하다 encourage 《sb 《to do》; urge 《on》; spur on 《to some effort》; give encouragement to; cheer sb 《on》; stimulate
◆아무의 말에 격려되어 encouraged [spurred] by sb's words / 선수들을 격려하다 cheer the players
▶ 그는 나를 격려하여 연구를 계속하게 했다 He encouraged me [gave me encouragement] to continue my research.
■—사[연설] words [speech] of encouragement; stirring remarks; 《美口》 a chin-up sermon

격렬 激烈 violence; severity; intensity; vehemence
—격렬하다 violent; severe; intense; fiery; vehement; keen
◆격렬하게 violently; severely; intensely / 격렬한 어조로 in a fierce tone of voice; vehemently
▶ 논쟁[경쟁]은 격렬했다 The dispute [competition] was hot [fierce].
▶ 격렬한 통증이 등줄기를 따라 느껴졌다 I felt an acute [a terrible] pain shoot across my back.

격론 激論 a hot [cut-and-thrust] argument; a heated discussion
▶ 국회에서 격론이 벌어졌다 A very vehement debate took place in the National Assembly.
▶ 우리는 그 문제에 관해 오랫동안 격론을 벌였다 We had a long, heated discussion on the subject.
—격론하다 argue hotly 《with sb about sth》; have a heated discussion 《with sb about sth》

격류 激流 a torrent; a rapid stream [current]; a violent stream; rapids ◆격류를 건너다 go across a rushing stream
▶ 그는 격류에 휩쓸려 내려갔다 He was swept away by a torrent [rapid stream].

격리 隔離 isolation; insulation; segregation
—격리하다 isolate; separate; segregate; set sb apart 《from》

◆문명에서 격리되다 be isolated from civilization
▶ 환자들은 즉시 격리되었다 The patients were immediately quarantined.
▶ 흉악범은 사회에서 완전히 격리되어야 한다 The felon should be separated from society perfectly.
■—병실[병동] an isolation room [ward] —실 a quarantine room; 〈우주 비행사의〉 a mobile quarantine facility —환자 an isolated patient; patient in quarantine

격막 隔膜 〈횡격막〉 〔解〕 diaphragm; 〔生〕 〈격막〉 the septum 《pl. -ta》; the dissepiment ■—염 〔醫〕 inflammation of the diaphragm; diaphragmatitis

격멸 擊滅 destruction —격멸하다 destroy; exterminate ▶ 폭격으로 적이 격멸되었다 The bombing destroyed [annihilated] the enemy.

격무 激務 hard [strenuous] work; a busy office [post]; an arduous task
◆격무에 시달리다[쫓기다] be pressed with taxing work, be driven by arduous task / 격무로 쓰러지다 break down under [succumb to] the strain of the hard work; break down through overwork
▶ 그는 격무에 시달리고 있다 He is extremely busy with pressing duties.

격문 檄文 a written appeal; a manifesto 《pl. ~(e)s》; a (public) declaration
◆격문을 띄우다 issue a written appeal; send a manifesto [declaration] 《to》 / 전국에 격문을 띄우다 make a nationwide appeal in writing

격발 激發 an outburst (of temper); a sudden fit 《of passion》; explosion 《of anger》
◆감정의 격발 an outburst of emotion; an emotional outburst
—격발하다 burst out; explode
◆계급 의식을 격발시키다 awake sb suddenly to class consciousness
▶ 정부의 조치는 반대 운동을 격발시켰다 The government's action provoked a protest movement.
■—화약 a high explosive

격발 擊發 percussion ■—신관 a percussion fuse —장치 percussion lock: 권총에 격발 장치를 하다 make a revolver ready for firing

격벽 隔壁 〈건물의〉 a partition (wall); 〈배·광산의〉 a bulkhead; 〔法〕〈경계벽〉 a party wall; 〔生〕 the dissepiment

격변 激變 a sudden [violent] change
◆기후[환경]의 격변 rapid [sudden] changes in the weather [environment] / 사태의 격변 a sudden turn of events / 사회적 격변 an upheaval in society; rapid changes [a revolution] of society / 정치적 격변 a political upheaval; a violent change in politics
▶ 그 나라의 산업 구조는 지난 몇년간 격변을 겪었다 The industrial structure of the country underwent a drastic change in the last few years.
—격변하다 change suddenly [violently]; undergo a sudden [violent] change
◆격변하는 국제 정세에 대처하다 provide for rapid changes of the international situation

▶기후가 격변했다 The weather changed suddenly. ⇌ There was a sudden change in the weather.

격분 激忿 violent anger ⇨ 격노(激怒)

격분 激憤 rage; violent anger; wrath; fury ▶그들의 심한 냉대에 그의 격분은 극에 달했다 He was just beside himself with indignation over their coldest treatment.
—**격분하다** be enraged 《at, by》; fly into a rage [fury, passion]; burn with indignation ◆격분하여 in a rage [fury] / 격분시키다 enrage; infuriate
▶격분한 군중이 그 깡패들을 두들겨 팼다 The enraged crowd beat the racketeers [gangsters].
▶일본 수상의 망언이 한국 국민을 격분시켰다 The Japanese Premier's careless remark infuriated [enraged] the Korean people.

격상 格上 elevation in rank —**격상하다** raise; upgrade ▶그 과는 부로 격상되었다 The section was upgraded to (the rank of) a department.

격세유전 隔世遺傳 〈生〉 atavism; (a) reversion —**격세유전하다** revert 《to》; cast [throw] back 《to》

격세지감 隔世之感 impression of being poles apart [a different age]
▶격세지감이 있다 I feel as if I were living in quite a different age. ⇌ It seems as if it belonged to a different world [another age].
▶그는 격세지감을 느꼈다 He was deeply impressed by the change of times.

격식 格式 (a) formality; an established formality; a (fixed) rule; social rules; (a) status ◆격식상 for form's sake / 격식 차리지 않고 without formality; informally / 격식을 따지다 be particular about formalities / 격식을 차리다 stand on ceremony; stick to formalities
▶격식은 생략하도록 합시다 Let's dispense with formalities [ceremony].
▶그는 매사에 격식을 좋아한다 He likes to be ceremonious about everything.
◆할아버지는 격식을 중요시하신다 My grandfather sticks to formality.

격실 隔室 a compartment; 〈비행기의〉 a bay

격심하다 激甚— violent; fierce; vehement; intense; keen
◆격심한 경쟁 (a) keen competition / 격심한 더위[추위] intense [severe] heat [cold] / 격심한 불황 a severe economic depression / 격심한 타격을 입다 receive a terrible blow
▶그 나라는 빈부의 차가 격심하다 There is big cleavage between (the) rich and (the) poor in that country.
▶그 지진으로 그 나라는 격심한 피해를 입었다 That earthquake caused terrible damage in that country.

격앙하다 激昂— get [be] excited; be exasperated
◆격앙하기 쉬운 excitable; hot-tempered / 격앙시키다 excite; exasperate; provoke
▶그는 격앙된 어조로 우리를 비난했다 He reproached [blamed] us in a fiery [vehement] tone.

격야 隔夜 every other [second] night; a night's interval —**격야하다** have a night's interval 《between》

격양가 擊壤歌 a farmer's song [ballad] celebrating the good harvest and peaceful reigns [national prosperity]

격언 格言 a proverb; a saying; a maxim

> 解說 ***proverb***는 비유의 대상이 포함되어 있는 것: Even a worm will turn. 지렁이도 밟으면 꿈틀 한다. ***saying***은 진리를 꼭 알맞게 표현한 것: History repeats itself. 역사는 되풀이된다. ***maxim***은 처세훈이라고 일컬어지는 것: Early to bed and early to rise. 일찍 자고 일찍 일어나기.

◆격언에 이르기를 The proverb says that...; As the saying [proverb] goes [has it]...
▶격언에 이르듯이 「시간은 금이다」"Time is money," as the proverb goes.

격월 隔月 every other [second] month; (in) alternate months ◆격월로 발행하는 잡지 a bimonthly (magazine) / —**간** a bimonthly

격의 隔意 ◆격의 없는 unreserved; frank; confidential / 격의 없이 without reserve; unreservedly
▶나는 그녀와 격의 없이 이야기를 나누었다 I talked with her frankly [without reserve]. ⇌ I had a heart-to-heart talk with her.

격일 隔日 every other [second] day
◆격일로 every other [second] day; on alternate days / 격일로 일하다 shift once in two days
▶그는 격일 근무로 일한다 He works on one day and off the next.

격자 格子 1 〈창문의〉 a grille; a lattice; a grating ◆철격자 창 an iron bar; an iron-barred window / 격자로 된 of lattice; latticed 2 〈무늬〉 fretwork ◆격자 무늬의 checkered —**문** a lattice door —**세공** latticework; latticing —**창** a lattice(d) window; a grille

격전 激戰 a hot fight; a fierce [bloody] battle
◆격전을 치르다 fight a fierce battle 《with》
▶그곳에서 격전이 벌어지고 있었다 A fierce battle was going on there.
—**격전하다** fight hard [severely] 《against, with》; have a fierce battle; engage in hot fighting
—**지** 〈전투의〉 a hard-fought field; 〈선거의〉 a closely contested constituency: 여기는 제2차 세계대전의 격전지였다 A fierce battle was fought here during World War II.

격정 激情 a strong [violent] emotion; a passion; 〈분노〉 wild anger; fury
◆격정에 못 이겨 carried away by a fit of passion / 격정에 사로잡혀 in a fit of passion; out of temper / 격정을 누르다 hold the passion in check

격조 格調 a tone; a style ◆격조 높은 문장 writing in fine [noble, lofty] style / 격조 높은 연설 a high-toned speech

격조하다 隔阻— have no news 《from sb》; hear nothing; neglect to write
▶그간 격조했습니다 I haven't been to see you

for a long time. ⇌ I have been very remiss in writing to you.
▶ 격조하여 죄송합니다 Excuse me for not writing so long.

격주 隔週 every other [second] week
♦ 격주로 every other [second] week; (英) fortnightly
▶ 회의는 격주로 월요일에 열린다 A meeting is held on every other [alternate] Monday.
■ —간행물 a fortnightly; biweekly

격증 激增 a sudden [rapid] increase (in crime)
—**격증하다** increase suddenly [markedly]; 〈수량(水量)이〉 rise [swell] rapidly
▶ 수요가 격증했다 The demand (for it) showed a sharp [marked] increase.

격지 〈켜〉 (many) layers; manifold

격지 隔地 a distant [remote] place

격지 隔紙 a sheet of paper inserted between two layers

격지다 隔— get estranged [alienated]; (口) be at outs [odds] with; be on bad terms (with)

격진 激震 a severe earthquake; violent earthquake ▶ 어젯밤 이 지역에 격진이 있었다 A strong earthquake shook this area last night.

격차 格差 a gap; (a) difference
♦ 기업간의 격차 business disparity / 빈부의 격차 the gulf between rich and poor / 학교간 격차 the difference in quality of schools / 소득의 격차를 없애다 abolish earnings differentials / 임금 격차를 시정하다 set wage disparity right

격찬 激讚 high praise [tribute]; eulogy
▶ 그는 한국에서의 첫 연주에서 격찬을 받았다 He was highly praised for his first performance in Korea.
—**격찬하다** praise sb highly (for); speak highly of 〈his talent for music〉
▶ 그들은 그를 격찬했다 They praised him to the skies.

격철 擊鐵 the hammer (of a rifle) ⇨ 공이 (~치기)

격추하다 擊墜— shoot [bring] down (an enemy plane); (口) down (a plane)
▶ 그 비행기는 인천 상공에서 격추되었다 The plane was shot down [knocked out of the sky] over Inch'ŏn.

격침하다 擊沈— sink (a ship); send (a ship) to the bottom ▶ 배는 미사일에 맞아[잠수함에게] 격침되었다 The ship was hit [torpedoed] and sunk by a missile [submarine].

격통 激痛 an acute pain; a severe [sharp] pain; a pang ♦ 격통을 느끼다 feel a sharp [an acute] pain (in) / 격통을 꾹 참다 endure one's severe pain stoically

격퇴 擊退 a repulse —**격퇴하다** drive [beat] (the enemy) back; repulse (an enemy); repel (an attack) ▶ 그들은 침략자를 격퇴했다 They beat back the invaders.

격투 格鬪 a grapple; a (hand-to-hand) fight; fisticuffs
▶ 경찰관은 격투 끝에 강도를 붙잡았다 The policeman arrested the burglar after a scuffle.

—**격투하다** fight (hand to hand) 《with》; grapple 《with》
■ —**기(技)** (a) combative sport

격투 激鬪 a severe [fierce] fight; furious fisticuffs —**격투하다** fight fiercely [severely]

격파 擊破 beating out; destruction
—**격파하다** defeat 《the enemy》; crush; overthrow; 〈부수다〉 destroy 《an enemy warship》; smash up
♦ 적의 주력부대를 격파하다 smash the enemy's main force unit

격하 格下 degradation; (美) demotion; downgrading
—**격하하다** degrade; downgrade; lower the status (of); reduce sb to a lower position [rank]; (美) demote
♦ 외교 관계를 격하하다 downgrade diplomatic relations [ties] 《with》

격하다 隔— 〈사이를 두다〉 set apart; separate; part; 〈사이가 있다〉 be distant from; 〈칸막이하다〉 partition; block; screen; 〈시간을〉 make intervals (between)
♦ 벽을 격하여 with a wall between / 1시간을 격하여 after a one-hour interval / 벽을 격하고 있다 be separated by a wall
▶ 그 두 마을은 강 하나를 격하고 있다 The two villages lie facing each other across a river.
▶ 양국 대표는 테이블을 격하고 서로 마주 앉았다 The delegates of the two nations sat across the table from each other.
▶ 그 섬은 해협으로 본토와 격해 있다 The island is divided from the mainland by a strait.

격하다 激— 〈발끈하다〉 be enraged; be infuriated; 〈흥분하다〉 get [be] excited; 〈말이〉 get [become] violent
♦ 격한 감정[말] a violent emotion [language]/ 격하기 쉬운 excitable; hot-tempered / 격하여 excitedly / 격한 어조로 in a harsh tone
▶ 그는 몹시 격해 있었다 He was in a state of great excitement.
▶ 말이 격해졌다 Words ran high.

격화 激化 intensification; aggravation
—**격화하다** grow more intense; heat up; get [become] (more) violent [serious]; become intensified
▶ 두 사람 사이의 대립이 격화했다 The confrontation between the two has become more serious.
▶ 그녀의 말에 그의 감정이 격화되었다 He grew excited at her words.

격화소양 隔靴搔癢 leaving much to be desired; having an itch that one cannot scratch; unsatisfactory
♦ 격화소양의 감이 있다 feel unsatisfied; 〈사물이 주어〉 leave much to be desired
▶ 그의 설명은 격화소양의 감이 있었다 His explanation was tantalizingly off [wide of] the mark.

겪다 1 〈경험하다〉 experience; go through; undergo; meet with; taste 《the panic》
♦ 많은 고난을 겪다 experience [go through] many hardships / 여러 가지 일을 겪다 pass

through a varied experience / 겪어서 알다 learn by [from] experience
▶ 그는 전쟁 중 많은 위험을 겪었다 He went through many dangers during the war.
▶ 겪어보니 그 사람은 정직했다 On further acquaintance I found (that) he was honest [found him to be honest].
▶ 이런 추위는 겪어 본 적이 없다 This is the coldest weather (that) I have ever experienced.
▶ 실제로 겪어보지 않으면 그것이 어떤 것인지 모른다 If you don't pass through it yourself, you won't understand.
2 〈대접하다〉 feast; entertain with food and drink / 손님을 겪다 entertain [have] a guest

견 絹 1 〈깁〉 silk 2 ⇨ 견본(絹本) ■—사 silk thread —직(物) silk goods; silk(s)

견갑 肩胛 a shoulder blade ⇨ 견갑골 —관절 the shoulder joint —탈구(脫臼) dislocation of the shoulder joint

견갑골 肩胛骨 a shoulder blade; a bladebone; 〖解〗 a scapula (*pl.* ~s, -lae)

견강부회 牽強附會 a farfetched reasoning; a distorted interpretation; a sophistry
♦ 견강부회의 설 a farfetched opinion [view]
♦ 그 해석은 견강부회다 It is a strained interpretation.
—**견강부회하다** give a farfetched interpretation; strain (the interpretation)
♦ 규칙을 견강부회하여 해석하다 stretch the interpretation of a rule
▶ 그녀는 이야기를 자기에게 유리하게 견강부회 했다 She distorted [twisted] the story to her own advantage.

견고 堅固 firmness; solidity; steadiness; durableness
—**견고하다** strong; solid; durable; firm
♦ 견고한 가구 solid furniture / 견고한 기초 a solid [sound] foundation / 견고한 진지 a strong fortress; a stronghold / 견고히[하게] strongly; firmly; securely / 반석같이 견고하다 be as firm as a rock / 견고히 하다 strengthen; make *sth* firm [solid]
▶ 그는 의지가 견고하다 He has a strong will.
▶ 아군의 방비는 견고했다 The defense of our forces was strong.

견과 堅果 〖植〗 a nut ■—유(油) nut oil

견디다 1 〈참다〉 endure 《hardships》; bear; stand; put up with
♦ 견디다 못해 unable to bear any longer; running out of patience / 견딜 수 없는 unbearable; intolerable / 끝까지 견디다 hold fast to the end
▶ 더워서 못 견디겠다 It is unbearably hot.
▶ 그녀가 보고 싶어 못 견디겠다 I am dying to see her.
▶ 고문을 견디지 못해 그는 동지의 은신처를 실토했다 Unable to bear the torture, he disclosed his comrades' hideout.
▶ 더 이상은 이 고통을 견딜 수 없다 I can't bear this pain any longer.
▶ 이곳의 추위는 견딜 수 없다 I can't stand the cold here.
▶ 나는 화가 나서 견딜 수 없었다 I couldn't contain [repress] my anger.
2 〈버티다〉 hold out; stand; manage; 〈저항하다〉 resist; withstand; be proof against
♦ 고열에 견디다 stand [bear up against] intense heat / 공격에 견디다 hold out against an attack / 물[불]에 견디다 be water [fire] proof; be proof against water [fire]/ 불황에 견디다 weather the hard times / 술의 유혹에 견디다 resist [get over] the temptation to drink
▶ 그의 약한 몸으로는 여행의 피로를 견디낼 수 없었다 His feeble frame was unable to resist the fatigue of the journey.
▶ 그의 강한 체질이 오랫동안 병을 견디내게 했다 His strong constitution carried him through his long illness.
3 〈지탱하다〉 support; stand; hold on [out]; 〈오래 가다〉 last long
▶ 우리는 이만한 식량이 있으니 한 달은 견디겠다 This much food will last us one month.
▶ 그 다리는 홍수를 견디냈다 The bridge held out against the flood.
▶ 마루는 가구의 무게를 견디지 못했다 The floor could not hold [bear up under] the weight of the furniture.
▶ 그렇게 무리하게 일하면 견디지 못한다 If you keep (on) working too hard, you will lose your health.
▶ 건물은 지진에도 견딜 수 있게 지어져야 한다 Buildings should be constructed to stand even earthquakes.
4 〈살아가다〉 make a living; subsist
♦ 적은 급료로 견디어 나가다 live on a small salary
▶ 그는 적은 연금으로 그럭저럭 견디고 있다 He gets by [makes out a living] on his small pension.
▶ 우리는 적은 예산으로 견뎌낼 수밖에 없었다 We had to manage on [make shift with] a small budget.

견딜성 —性 endurance; patience; perseverance ⇨ 참을성 / 견딜성이 있는 patient; persevering / 견딜성이 없는 lacking in patience

견마지로 犬馬之勞 one's humble service 《to》
♦ 견마지로를 다하다 serve as best as one can / 견마지로를 아끼지 않다 spare no effort; do as much as one can; do the best one can
▶ 그분을 위해 견마지로를 다하겠습니다 I will render to him what little service I possibly can [such humble service as I can].

견문 見聞 〈경험〉 experience; 〈지식〉 information; knowledge; 〈관찰〉 observation
♦ 견문이 넓다[좁다] be well-informed [badly informed]/ 견문을 넓히다 enlarge one's experience; see more of the world; broaden one's horizons
▶ 우리는 여행으로 견문을 넓혔다 We widened [enriched, increased] our knowledge by traveling.
—**견문하다** observe; experience
■—록 a record of personal experiences

견문발검 見蚊拔劍 drawing the sword at a mosquito —**견문발검하다** use a sledgehammer to kill a fly [an ant]

견물생심 見物生心 (속담) Seeing is wanting. ⇌ The object gives rise to the desire. ⇌ Opportunity makes the thief.
견방 絹紡 spun silk ━사(絲) spun silk yarn
견본 見本 〈상품의〉 a sample; 〈표본〉 a specimen; 〈서적의〉 a sample copy; 〈글씨·그림의〉 an example; a model; 〈무늬 등의〉 a pattern; 〈천 조각 등〉 a swatch

解説 *sample*은 전체가 어떤 것인가를 알아볼 수 있는 부분 또는 그것의 한 개, *specimen*은 특히 표본 등 과학적인 검토의 대상이 되는 견본을 말한다. *example*은 실례(實例).

♦견본을 보내다 send [mail] a sample / 견본과 다르다 differ from sample / 견본보다 못하다 be below the sample; do not come up to the sample
▶이것들은 신제품의 견본입니다 These are samples of our new products.
▶보내온 물건은 견본과 일치하지 않았다 The article sent to us did not come up to [correspond with] the sample.
▶이 물품은 견본대로입니다 This article meet the specifications.
■상용[상품]━ a trade sample 선적━ a shipment [shipping] sample 수출━ an export sample 표준━ a standard sample 품질━ a quality sample ■━검사인(人) a sampler ━매매 sales by sample ━선적 a sample shipment ━쇄 a specimen page; an advance copy ━시(市) a sample fair : 국제 견본시 an international trade fair ━실 a sample room ━주문 a sample order; 〈견본에 따른〉 an order by sample ━책 a sample book; a pattern book ━추출 sampling ━카드 a sample card
견본 絹本 silk canvas; silk cloth for painting [drawing] on
견본조판 見本組版 specimen page composition [typesetting] ━견본조판하다 put specimen pages into type
견사 絹絲 a silk thread [yarn] ━방적(紡績) silk spinning; silk reeling ━선(腺) 〔動〕 a silk gland
견사 繭絲 〈생명주실〉 raw silk thread
견습 見習 apprenticeship; probation ♦견습 점원 a trainee salesclerk
▶그는 아직 견습 중이다 He is still on probation.
━견습하다 receive training 《in》; practice *oneself* 《in a trade》
▶그 여자는 제과점[미용실]에서 견습했다 She worked as an apprentice to a baker [apprenticed herself to a beauty parlor].
■━간호사 a student nurse; a probationary nurse ━공 an apprentice : 그는 인쇄소의 견습공이 되었다 He was apprenticed to a printer. ━기간 the probationary period; the period of probation ━기자 a junior [trainee] reporter; 《美俗》 a cub reporter ━생 an apprentice; a trainee; a probationer; 《美口》 a cub
견식 見識 〈지식〉 knowledge; information; 〈의견〉 views; an opinion; 〈안식〉 discernment; judgment

♦견식이 있는 사람 a man of insight / 견식이 있다 have a broad vision [an insight]
▶그는 자기 나름의 견식을 가지고 있다 He has opinions of his own.
견신례 堅信禮 〔가톨릭〕 the sacrament of confirmation ⇨ 견진성사
견실 堅實 steadiness; steadfastness; soundness ━견실하다 steady; sound; solid; 〈신뢰할 수 있다〉 reliable; trustworthy; 〈견실하다〉 wholesome 《girl》
♦견실한 사업 a sound line of [steady] business / 견실한 투자 a sound investment / 견실하게 steadily; soundly / 경영 방식이 견실하다 have a sound management method
▶그런 종류의 사업은 견실하다 That kind of business is stable [safe].
▶그 사업은 아주 견실하게 경영되고 있다 The business is conducted on a perfectly sound basis.
견우성 牽牛星 〔天〕 Altair (▶직녀성= Vega)
견우직녀 牽牛織女 〔天〕 the Altair and the Vega
견원 犬猿 a dog and a monkey; 〈앙숙〉 mutual enmity [hatred]
♦견원지간이다 be at enmity; be like cat and dog; hate each other like poison
▶그 두 사람은 언제나 견원지간이다 The two are leading a cat-and-dog life. ⇌ The two are on very bad terms.
견유 犬儒 〈학자〉 a Cynic; 〈냉소자〉 a cynic ■━주의 Cynicism ━학파 the Cynics
견인 牽引 traction; hauling ━견인하다 pull; draw; haul ━력 (the force of) traction; pulling power [force] ━차 a tractor; a tow car [truck]
견인불발 堅忍不拔 perseverance; fortitude; endurance
♦견인불발의 정신 an adamant will; indomitable spirit [mind]
▶그는 역경에서 견인 불발의 정신을 드러냈다 He showed invincible fortitude in adversity.
견장 肩章 a shoulder strap; 〈군복의〉 an epaulet(te)
견적 見積 an estimate; (an) estimation; calculation
♦건물의 견적 an estimate for a building / 대략적인 지출의 견적 rough estimate of the expenses / 견적 이하로 below the estimate / 견적에 의하면 according to *one's* estimation / 견적을 내다 ⇨ 견적하다 / 견적을 웃돌다 exceed the estimate
▶그에게 울타리를 칠하는 견적을 내달라고 했다 I asked him to quote a price for [to give me an estimate of the cost of] painting the board fence.
━견적하다 estimate; make [give, submit] an estimate 《of》; calculate 《at》
♦아무리 싸게[비싸게] 견적하더라도 at the lowest [highest] estimate / 줄잡아 견적하다 make a conservative estimate
▶우리는 그것을 1천만원으로 견적하고 있다 We estimate it at ten million won.
■가(假)━ a preliminary estimate 개산(槪算)━ a rough estimate 과대[과소]━ overes-

timation [underestimation] 세목— a detailed estimate 정밀— a close estimate ■—가격 an estimated value; a valuation —서 a written estimate; an estimate sheet —액 an estimated amount [sum] —원가 an estimated cost

견제 牽制 1 〈억제〉 a check; restraint; curbing ♦견제와 균형 check and balance　—견제하다 check; hold [keep] in check; restrain; curb
▶그들은 서로 견제했다 They kept each other in check.
2 〔野〕 a check; a feint
▶투수는 1루 주자를 견제 아웃시켰다 The pitcher picked the runner off first base.
—견제하다 make a feint; hold [keep] in check
♦주자를 견제하다 check a runner 《by a tossing motion》; peg a runner 《on the base》
3 〔軍〕 a diversion; containment　—견제하다 contain; make a feint; divert
■—공격〔軍〕a containing attack　—구 a feint ball [pick-off throw]: 투수는 주자를 잡으려고 1루에 견제구를 던졌다 The pitcher pegged the ball to first base trying to get the runner (out). —운동 a diversion; a diversional movement; a feint　—전술[작전] a diversionary tactic

견제품 絹製品 silk manufactures; 〈견직물〉 silk goods; silks

견주다 〈비교하다〉 compare [weigh] 《one thing》 with [against] 《another》; take *sth* for comparison; 〈겨루다〉 rival; compete 《with》
♦견주어 보면 as compared with; by comparison / 기술[힘]을 견주다 measure *one's* skill [strength] with [against] *sb*
▶고전 음악에서 그와 견줄 만한 사람은 없다 He has no equal [No one equals him] in classical music.
▶이것과 견줄 만한 것은 없다 This stands unrivaled [unchallenged, unequaled]. ⇌ Nothing can compare with it.
▶이쪽 것이 견줄 수 없을 만큼 좋다 This one is incomparably better than that.

견지 〈낚시〉 a fishing reel [spool]　♦견지질하다 fish with a roll; troll for fish

견지 見地 〈관점〉 a standpoint; a viewpoint; a point of view; an angle
♦교육적[정치적, 과학적] 견지에서 (seen) from the educational [political, scientific] point of view / 다른 견지에서 보다[생각하다] view from another angle [consider from a different standpoint]
▶이런 견지에서 보면 그것은 중요한 것이 아니다 From this point of view, that is not important.
—**견지하다 堅持**— hold fast to; maintain firmly; adhere to 《a view》; stick to
▶그는 죽을 때까지 자기 신념을 견지했다 He held fast to his belief until the day he died.

견직물 絹織物 silk fabrics [goods]; silk(s); 《英》 mercery
■—공장 a silk mill　—상 a silk merchant; 《英》 a mercer

견진성사 堅振聖事 〔가톨릭〕 the sacrament of confirmation　♦견진 성사를 받는[받은] 사람 a confirmee / 견진 성사를 베풀다 confirm

견책 譴責 a reprimand; (a) censure; (a) rebuke; (a) reproof
▶그는 직무 태만으로 견책을 받았다 He was reprimanded [reproved] for neglect of duties.
—**견책하다** reprimand; rebuke; reprove; censure

견치 犬齒 a dogtooth ⇨ 송곳니

견포 絹布 silk ⇨ 비단

견학 見學 study by observation
♦견학 가다 make a field trip to 《a museum》　—견학하다 observe; visit 《a factory》 for study [information]
▶우리는 그 공장[신문사]을 견학했다 We made a tour of [through] the factory [visited the newspaper office as part of our study].
■—공장— a tour through a factory　현장— on the spot study　—여행 a tour study; a field trip

견해 見解 an opinion 《about, on》; a view 《about, on》; an outlook 《on》; 〈개인적인〉 (口) a slant
♦시국에 관한 새로운 견해 a new slant on the situation / 견해가 일치하다[를 같이하다] agree 《with》; have the same opinion 《as》; be at one 《with》 / 견해를 달리하다 disagree 《with》; differ in opinion; have a different opinion 《from》
▶나는 그와 같은 견해다 I have [hold] the same view [opinion] as he does.
▶그것은 견해 차이다 It is a matter of opinion.
▶나는 그들과는 견해가 다르다 I do not share their opinions.
▶이 문제에 관해서는 견해가 구구하다 Opinions are divided on this question.

결다[1] **1** 〈기름이 배다〉 be oiled; be infiltrated with oil; become greasy [oily]
♦기름에 결은 종이 oilpaper; oiled paper / 때에 결은 옷 a garment greasy with grime
▶장판지가 잘 결었다 The floor paper has been well oiled.
2 〈기름에 배게 하다〉 oil (paper); infiltrate *sth* with oil　♦장판지를 걷다 oil floor-paper
3 〈손에 익다〉 get skillful (in using); become experienced (in); be quite at home (in)

결다[2] **1** 〈엮다〉 weave; braid　♦골풀로 결은 망태기 a bag woven from rushes / 삿자리를 걷다 weave a reed mat
2 〈어긋매끼다〉 stack; pile up crisscross　♦총을 걷다 stack arms

결지르다 cross; intercross; place *sth* crosswise

결질리다 1 〈엇걸리다〉 be crossed; be placed crosswise
2 〈일이 엇걸리다〉 become complicated; get entangled with each other
3 〈힘에 겹다〉 be strained; be exhausted [wrung out]

결[1] **1** 〈나무·피부 등의〉 grain; texture
♦결이 고운[거친] 돌 a stone of fine [coarse] grain / 결이 고운[거친] 천 cloth of fine [loose] texture / 결이 고운[거친] 피부 a delicate [rough] skin / 결이 거칠다 be coarse-grained; be rough-grained / 결이 곱다 be

close-grained; have a fine grain
2 ⇨ 물결, 숨결
3 ⇨ 성결(性—)
4 ⇨ 결기(—氣), 결나다

결² **1** 〈사품〉《as》an incidental result of; 《on》 the wave of
♦ 잠결에 while asleep; in *one's* sleep / 꿈결에 듣다 listen half asleep
▶ 바람결에 파도 소리가 들려온다 The wind brings with it the sound of the waves.
2 〈때〉 the time; the moment; 〈사이〉 a while
♦ 아침결에 before the morning is out; in the morning
▶ 어느 결에 1년이 지나갔다 A year has passed in a flash [before we know it].
▶ 어느 결에 날이 밝아오고 있었다 The day was dawning without our realizing it.
▶ 그들은 어느 결에 사라져 버렸다 They'd gone without our noticing it.
3 〈기회〉 an occasion; an opportunity; a chance ♦ 지나가는 결에 잠깐 들르다 drop in for a moment on *one's* way

결가부좌 結跏趺坐 〔佛敎〕 sitting with *one's* legs completely crossed (as in Buddhist statues)

결강 缺講 ▶ 김 교수는 오늘 결강입니다 Professor Kim is not giving his lecture today.
—결강하다 do not give *one's* lecture; cancel a lecture

결격 缺格 disqualification; 〔法〕 incapacity ■**—사유** a (reason for) disqualification **—자** a disqualified [an unqualified] person

결과 結果 a result; an outcome; a consequence; an effect; issue; 〈성과〉 fruits; a product; 〈결말〉 the end

> **解說** ***result***는 최종적 결과를 나타내는 일반적인 말. ***outcome***도 대략 같은 뜻으로 쓰이지만 그 결과가 주목된다는 것을 암시한다. ***consequence***는 일의 진행상 필연적으로 일어나는 결과이고, ***effect***는 어떤 원인(cause)에서 생기는 직접적 효과라는 뜻을 포함한다. ***fruit***는 특히 노력한 결과 생기는 성과임을 강조하는 말로서 흔히 복수형으로 쓰인다.

♦ 그 결과 as a result; consequently; in consequence / 문의해 본 결과 An inquiry proves that… / 원인과 결과 cause and effect / 조사 [연구] 결과 the findings of the survey [research] / 최종 결과 a final [an end] result
▶ 이 발명은 그의 다년간에 걸친 노력의 결과다 This invention is the fruit of many years of his hard work [effort].
▶ 이러한 실업자의 증가는 불경기의 당연한 결과다 This increase of the unemployed is consequent on the business depression.
▶ 결과적으로 모든 것이 잘 되었다 Everything turned out well [satisfactorily].
〈결과가〉 결과가 좋다[나쁘다] be successful [unsuccessful] / 결과가 …이 되다 result [end] in…; turn out / 뜻밖의 결과가 되다 come to [reach] an unexpected result
▶ 그 결과가 어찌 될지 나는 전연 모르겠다 I have no idea how it will turn out [what the result will be].
▶ 결과가 어떻게 되든 나는 가겠다 Whatever results follow, I will go.
▶ 일의 결과가 이렇게 되어 유감입니다 I regret that things have come to this pass.
▶ 어제 시험 결과가 발표되었다 The results of the examination were announced [published] yesterday.
〈결과는〉 실험 결과는 만족할 만한 것이었다 The result of experiment was satisfactory.
▶ 수술 결과는 실패였다 The surgical operation resulted in failure.
▶ 회담 결과는 미사일 감축이었다 The talks resulted in reducing the number of missiles [missile reduction].
▶ 선거 결과는 아무도 예측할 수 없다 No one can foresee [foretell, forecast] the outcome [results] of the election.
▶ 그런 계획에서 좋은 결과는 아무것도 나올 수 없다 Nothing good will come out of such a plan.
〈결과를〉 바라던 결과를 얻다 attain a looked-for [desired] effect; yield [produce] desirable results / 좋은[나쁜] 결과를 낳다[얻다] produce [obtain] a good [bad] result; bear [produce] good [bad] fruits / 중대한 결과를 초래하다 lead to [cause] serious [grave] consequences
▶ 그것은 의도했던 것과는 반대의 결과를 가져왔다 It produced an effect opposite to what was designed [intended].
▶ 올해는 좋은 결과를 기대할 수 없다 We can't expect a good result this year.
〈결과에[로]〉 필연적인 결과로 as a necessary consequence / 지금까지의 결과로 보아 in view of the results so far achieved
▶ 내 행동의 결과에 기꺼이 책임을 지겠다 I am ready to take [suffer, bear, answer for] the consequences of my actions.

결과론 結果論 criticism 《on past events》 based on the result; second-guessing
▶ 그것은 결과론이라고요 You can say anything after you get the result. ⇌ It's easy to be wise after the event.
▶ 결과론이지만 그 정책이 실패한 원인은 이 나라의 경제 성장력을 너무 낙관한 데 있다 Although this was not obvious until after the event, the policy failed because of the over-optimistic estimates of this country's potential for economic growth.

결구 結球 〔植〕 a head **—결구하다** bulb up; head ▶ 양배추가 잘 결구하고 있다 The cabbages are coming up well. ■**—배추** a Chinese cabbage with a head

결구 結構 〈구조〉 structure; construction; frame; 〈구성〉 a buildup 《of a story》; 〈줄거리〉 a plot 《of a novel》

결국 結局 after all; finally; in the end [long run]; ultimately; in the last [final] analysis
▶ 나는 여러 가지로 해보았지만 결국 실패했다 I tried many things, but failed after all.
▶ 그 회담은 결국 어떻게 되었습니까? How did the meeting come [turn] out?
▶ 두 사람은 5년 동안 규칙적으로 만나다가 결국

결과의 표현

1. 너무[대단히, 매우, 아주] …하므로
(1) so + 형용사[부사] + that ~
▶ 그는 몹시 바쁘기 때문에 사무실을 비울 수가 없다 He is so busy that he can't leave the office.
▶ 어제는 대단히 더웠기 때문에 아이들은 강에 수영하러 갔다 It was so hot yesterday that the children went swimming in the river.
▶ 이 문제는 매우 어려워서 나는 풀 수가 없다 This problem is so difficult that I can't solve it.
▶ 그 외국인은 말이 몹시 빨라서 무슨 말을 하는지 나는 알아들을 수가 없었다 The foreigner spoke so fast that I couldn't understand what he said.
▶ 이 호수들은 너무 작아서 지도에 나타나 있지 않다 These lakes are so small that they aren't shown in maps.

(2) such a + 형용사 + 단수 명사 + that ~ ; such + 형용사 + 복수 명사 + that ~ ; such + 형용사 + 불가산 단수 명사 + that ~
▶ 그는 몹시 바쁜 사람이기 때문에 사무실을 비울 수가 없다 He is such a busy man that he can't leave the office.
▶ 대단히 더운 날씨였으므로 아이들은 강에 수영하러 갔다 It was such a hot day that the children went swimming in the river.
▶ 그는 강연을 아주 길게 했기 때문에 많은 청중들이 잠들기 시작했다 He made such a long speech that many people began to fall asleep. ⇌ He spoke for such a long time that many people began to fall asleep. ⇌ His speech was so long that many people began to fall asleep.
▶ 테일러 박사는 아주 재미있는 강연을 하기 때문에 많은 사람들이 왔다 Dr. Taylor gives such interesting lectures that many people came. ⇌ Dr. Taylor's lectures are so interesting that many people came.
▶ 이렇게 날씨가 더우니 머지않아 장미꽃이 필 것입니다 It is such warm weather that the roses will bloom soon. ⇌ The weather is so warm that the roses will bloom soon.
▶ 그것은 대단히 아름다운 경치였으므로 모두 감탄했다 It was such beautiful scenery that everyone admired it. ⇌ The scenery was so beautiful that everyone admired it.

2. 대단히[아주] 많은 …이므로 ~
so many + 복수 명사 + that ~ (수); so much + 단수 명사 + that ~ (양)
▶ 대단히 많은 사람이 왔으므로 의자가 모자랐다 So many people came that there weren't enough chairs.
▶ 시험 문제가 아주 많았기 때문에 나는 전부 답할 수가 없었다 There were so many questions on the examination that I couldn't answer all of them.
▶ 눈이 많이 쌓여 있었으므로 그들은 스키를 (타며) 즐길 수가 있었다 There was so much snow on the ground that they could enjoy skiing.
▶ 파티가 아주 재미있어서 그녀는 언제나 참석합니다 Parties are so much fun that she always attends them.

3. 너무 …하기 때문에[지나치게 …해서] ~할 수 없다
too + 형용사[부사] to do
▶ 그녀는 너무 어려서 결혼할 수 없다 She is too young to marry. ⇌ She is so young that she can't marry.
▶ 이 커피는 너무 뜨거워서 마실 수가 없다 This coffee is too hot to drink. ⇌ This coffee is so hot that I can't drink it.
▶ 정신없이 바빠서 회신을 드릴 시간도 없었습니다 I have been too busy to find time to answer your letter. ⇌ I have been so busy that I haven't find time to answer your letter.
▶ 그는 빠른 말투로 지껄여대서 우리에게 생각할 여유를 주지 않았다 He spoke too fast to give us time to think. ⇌ He spoke so fast that he did not give us time to think.
[어법]
　so...that의 구문을 too...to ~의 구문으로 고칠 때 부정사의 목적어가 문장의 주어와 동일어[물체]를 가리킬 때에는 생략된다. 예: This coffee is so hot that I can't drink it. (it = this coffee) → This coffee is too hot to drink. (this coffee는 drink의 목적어도 된다) (▶This coffee is too hot to drink it. 이라고는 하지 않는다)

4. 너무 …하므로[사람이] ~할 수 없다; 지나치게 …해서[사람이] ~할 수 없다
too + 형용사[부사] + for sb to do
▶ 이 커피는 너무 뜨거워서 나는 마실 수가 없다 This coffee is too hot for me to drink. ⇌ This coffee is so hot that I can't drink it.
▶ 이 소설은 너무 어려워서 그녀로서는 아직 읽을 수 없다 This novel is too difficult for her to read yet. ⇌ This novel is so difficult that she can't read it yet.
▶ 그는 너무나 빨랐기 때문에 나는 그를 붙잡을 수가 없었다 He ran too quickly for me to catch him. ⇌ He ran so quickly that I couldn't catch him. (▶too가 부사와 더불어 쓰일 때는 끝에 부정사의 목적어가 나타남에 유의할 것)

5. 그러므로[그래서] ~; …하므로 ~
…, so ~
▶ 커피가 너무 뜨거워서 나는 마실 수가 없었다 The coffee was very hot, so I couldn't drink it.
▶ 그날 밤은 몹시 더워서 그들은 잠들 수가 없었다 The night was very hot, so they couldn't sleep.

결혼했다 They met regularly for five years; in the end they got married.
▶ 결국 그 사람의 말은 옳았다 What he said turned out right in the end.
▶ 나는 결국 정직한 사람이 이긴다고 믿는다 I believe that the honest will win in the long run.
▶ 어느 길로 가건 결국에는 같은 곳에 도달한다 Either road will lead to the same spot after all.

결궤하다 決潰— 〈무너지다〉 break (down); be broken; give way; collapse; burst

결근 缺勤 absence 《from office》; nonattendance 《at》
▶ 그는 건강이 나빠서 결근이 잦다 Being of delicate health, he is irregular in his attendance at the office.
—걸근하다 be absent 《from》; absent *oneself* 《from》; be [stay] away from 《work》; do not go [come] 《to the office》
▶ 열이 있어서 오늘은 결근합니다 I cannot go [come] to work today because I feel feverish. (▶ 전화 등으로 회사에 알리는 말)
▶ 나는 어제 회사를 결근했다 I was absent [stayed away] from my office yesterday.
▶ 그는 병으로 5일간 결근했다 He was absent from work [the office] for five days because he was ill.
—무단— absence without leave [notice, permission]: 무단 결근하다 absent *oneself* 《from office》 without notice [leave] **장기—** a long-term absence **—율** the rate of absenteeism **—일수** the number of absences [absent days] **—자** an absent person; an absentee; a nonattendant

결근계 缺勤届 a report [notice] of absence
♦ 결근계를 내다 report *one's* absence; tender [hand in] a report [notice] of *one's* absence

결기 —氣 a hot [quick] temper; impetuosity; impetuousness; irascibility
♦ 결기가 있다 have a hot [quick] temper / 결기를 내다 ⇨ 결내다 / 결기에 사람을 치다 beat *sb* in the heat of *one's* anger

결나다 〈성미가 나다〉 get angry; become indignant; be enraged; be offended [provoked, vexed]; have *one's* blood up ♦ 결나서 싸우다 fight in a fit of passion

결내다 give vent to *one's* anger; burst [fly] into a passion; get out of [lose *one's*] temper
♦ 툭하면 결내다 be apt to flare up; be liable to lose *one's* temper; be easily roused to temper
▶ 그가 무슨 소리를 하든지 결내지 않도록 해라 Try to keep your temper whatever he says [may say].

결단 決斷 (a) determination; (a) decision; (a) resolution ⇨ 결단력
▶ 그는 결단이 빠르다 [늦다] He is quick [slow] to make decisions.
▶ 지금이야말로 이 일에 결단을 내려야 할 때다 Now is the time to reach [come to] a definite decision about this matter.
▶ 그는 계획을 실행하기로 결단을 내렸다 He decided [determined, resolved] to carry out the plan.
▶ 틀림없다는 그의 말에 나는 드디어 결단을 내렸다 His assurance at last made me decide to venture it.
▶ 그는 아직도 가야 할지 머물러 있어야 할지 결단을 내리지 못하고 있다 He is still uncertain whether to go or stay.
—결단하다 decide; determine; resolve

결단 結團 —결단하다 form (themselves [ourselves] into) an organization
▶ 한국 핸드볼 대표팀이 결단되었다 They put together an all-Korean handball team.
■ —식 (hold) an inaugural meeting [rally] (to celebrate the formation [organization] of a delegation)

결단력 決斷力 resolution; determination; decidedness
♦ 결단력 있는 사람 a man of (firm) decision; a decisive person / 결단력이 있는 resolute; decisive / 결단력이 없는 irresolute; indecisive; lacking decision / 결단력 부족 a lack of determination
▶ 결단력 없는 사람이 책임자 자리를 맡을 수는 없다 A man who lacks decision cannot hold a position of responsibility.

결단성 決斷性 decidedness ⇨ 결단력

결단코 決斷— never; not...at all; on no account; by no means; till doomsday ⇨ 결코
▶ 결단코 그렇지 않습니다 I am positive that it is not so.
▶ 그런 일은 결단코 없다 I positively deny it.
⇒ It's a sheer [an utter] impossibility.
▶ 내 마음은 결단코 변하지 않는다 I absolutely won't [will never] change my mind.
▶ 그런 일은 결단코 하지 않겠다 I would not do it for the world.

결당 結黨 the founding [formation] of a party
—결당하다 found [form, organize] a party

결딴나다 be ruined [spoiled]; be broken [destroyed]; go to ruin [wreck]; collapse; 〈계획 등이〉 fall through
▶ 그렇게 무거운 짐을 올려놓으면 의자가 결딴난다 The chair will collapse under such a heavy burden.
▶ 그 여자는 건강이[그 집안은] 결딴났다 Her health [The family] has been ruined.
▶ 그 폭우로 벼가 결딴났다 The rice plants were ruined by the heavy rain.
▶ 태풍으로 많은 집이 결딴났다 A number of houses were destroyed by the typhoon.
▶ 나의 계획은 모두 결딴났다 All my plans fell through.
▶ 어떻게 해서 그의 집안이 결딴나 버렸나? What brought about the ruin of his family?
▶ 그 실언으로 그의 일생은 결딴나 버렸다 The slip of the tongue ruined his life.

결딴내다 spoil; ruin; destroy; break; wreck; demolish
♦ 술로 위를 결딴내다 spoil *one's* stomach with wine
▶ 상습 도박으로 그는 일생을 결딴냈다 His habitual gambling has made a wreck of his life [ruined his career].

결렬 決裂 a breakdown; a rupture
♦ 군축 협상의 결렬 a breakdown of negotiations on disarmament
―**결렬되다** break down; be broken off; come to [end in] a rupture
▶ 노사 협상[교섭]은 결렬되었다 The negotiations between management and labor broke down [were broken off].
▶ 정상회담은 핵실험 금지 문제로 결렬되었다 The summit conference blew up over the nuclear test ban.

결례 缺禮 want of respect; neglect of etiquette; lack of courtesy
―**결례하다** fail [neglect, omit] to pay *one's* compliments [offer *one's* greetings]

결론 結論 a conclusion; a concluding remark
♦ 서둘러 결론을 내리다 jump to a conclusion; form a hasty conclusion / 결론에 도달하다 come to [arrive at, reach] a conclusion / 우선 결론부터 말하다 state *one's* conclusion first
▶ 회의에서 어떤 결론이 나왔습니까? What conclusion did you come to at the meeting?
▶ 우리는 즉시 작업을 개시해야 한다는 결론을 얻었습니다 We reached the conclusion that we should start the operation at once.
▶ 우리는 정당한 근거에 입각해서 이런 결론에 도달했다 We have arrived at this conclusion on a reasonable basis.
▶ 결론적으로 말해서 그의 자만은 도저히 못 봐주겠다 To conclude [In conclusion, The conclusion is that] his conceit is unbearable.
―**결론짓다** conclude; draw [form] a conclusion
▶ 그들에게 사고의 책임이 있다고 결론짓지 않을 수 없다 It is hard to escape [We are driven to] the conclusion that they are to blame for the accident.

결리다 1 〈신체 부위가〉 feel stiff; get [grow] stiff; feel a stitch (in *one's* right side)
▶ 나는 어깨[한쪽 어깨]가 결린다 I have stiff shoulders [a stiff shoulder].
2 〈기가〉 wince 《at, under》; flinch 《from》; be daunted 《by》; be cowed [suppressed]

결막 結膜 [解] the conjunctiva (*pl.* ~s, -vae)
■ ―**염**(炎) conjunctivitis: 유행성 결막염 epidemic conjunctivitis; pinkeye ―**충혈** hyperemia conjunctiva; conjunctival congestion

결말 結末 〈결과〉 a result; an outcome; 〈끝〉 an end; a conclusion; 〈낙착〉 settlement; 〈연극 등의〉 the dénouement
♦ 행복[불행]한 결말 a happy [an unhappy] end(ing) / 결말이 나지 않다 remain unsettled; be still pending
▶ 그것이 이 이야기의 결말이다 That is the end of the story. ⇌ That is how the story ends.
▶ 국경 분쟁은 아직 결말이 나지 않았다 The border dispute has not been settled yet.
▶ 여하튼 이 사건은 결말이 났다 Anyhow, this affair came to an end [a conclusion].
▶ 이 전쟁은 결말이 어떻게 날까? How will the war end [result, come out]?
▶ 그 이야기의 결말을 아십니까? Do you know how the story ends?
▶ 빨리 그 일에 결말을 냅시다 Let's get it over with quickly.
▶ 영화는 행복한 결말로 끝을 맺고 있다 The film concludes with a happy end.
―**결말짓다** bring *sth* to a conclusion [a close, an end]; put an end to 《a strife》; settle 《a problem》
▶ 두 회사간의 분쟁은 평화적으로 결말지어졌다 The trouble between the two companies was settled in peace [came to a peaceful settlement].

결박 結縛 binding; tying; pinioning ♦ 결박을 풀다 unbind; set *sb* free
―**결박하다**[짓다] bind; tie (up) 《a thief》 with cords; pinion 《a thief》
♦ 뒷짐 결박당한 채 with *one's* hands tied behind / 단단히 결박하다 tie fast [hard] / 결박당하다 be bound [tied up]

결발 結髮 doing *one's* hair in a chignon [ʃíːnjɑn, -njɔːŋ]

결백 潔白 〈무죄〉 innocence; guiltlessness; 〈청렴〉 integrity; 〈순결〉 purity; immaculacy
♦ 자신의 결백을 입증하다 prove [establish] *one's* innocence; clear *oneself* 《from a charge》 / 끝까지[완강히] 결백을 주장하다 persist in pleading *one's* innocence
▶ 결백을 증명하기 위해 할 수 있는 일은 무엇이든 다 해야 한다 You must do all you can to prove your innocence.
―**결백하다** 〈죄가 없다〉 innocent; not guilty; 〈청렴하다〉 upright; cleanhanded; 〈깨끗하다〉 pure; immaculate
♦ 결백한 사람 a man of integrity; an upright [innocent] man
▶ 그는 자기가 결백하다고 주장했다 He insisted that he was innocent [that he was cleanhanded, that he had clean hands].
▶ 그가 결백하다는 것이 곧 판명되었다 It was soon proved that he was innocent.

결번 缺番 a missing number
▶ 6번은 결번이다 The number 6 is blank on the list.
▶ 4와 13은 불길한 숫자라고 해서 흔히 결번으로 되어 있었다 Because 4 and 13 were considered unlucky numbers, they were often omitted.

결벽 潔癖 love of cleanliness; 〈까다로움〉 fastidiousness; finicality; daintiness; 〈부정·악을 미워함〉 scrupulousness; conscientiousness
―**결벽하다** fastidious; particular; cleanly; dainty; overnice
▶ 그 정치인은 돈에 결벽했다 The politician never touched dirty money.
▶ 그는 결벽한 사람이니까 그런 돈은 받지 않을 것이다 As he is scrupulously honest, he will not accept that kind of money.

결별 訣別 parting; leave-taking ⇨ 이별, 고별

결본 缺本 a missing volume; 〈lacking, wanting〉 volume ♦ 이 전집은 제1권이 결본이다 The first volume is missing from this set.

결부 結付 linking; tying
―**결부하다** link [join] together; connect *sth* 《with》
♦ 여당과 직접 결부되어 있는 단체들 organizations with direct ties with the ruling party / 행복을 돈과 결부시켜서 생각하다 consider hap-

piness in relation to [connection with] money; associate happiness with riches
▶운명이 그들을 결부시켰다 Fate brought them together.
▶우리는 원인과 결과를 결부시키려고 한다 We look for the link between cause and effect.

결빙 結氷 ice formation; freezing
♦결빙을 방지하다 prevent ice formation; keep 《an airplane》 free of ice; 〔空〕 deice
—**결빙하다** freeze [be frozen] over; be [become] icebound [ice-locked]; 〈항구 등이〉 be closed by ice
▶호수가 결빙되었다 The lake has frozen over.
■—기 the freezing season [time]

결사 決死 preparedness for death; a "do-or-die" spirit; determination to die
♦결사의 각오로 전진하다[성을 지키다] advance [defend a castle] in the face of death / 결사의 공격을 하다 make a desperate attack / 결사의 돌격을 감행하다 make a death-defying sally [sortie]
▶그는 결사의 각오로 적지에 잠입했다 He smuggled himself into the enemy's territory, ready to die if necessary.

결사 結社 (forming) an association [a society, a fraternity]
▶결사의 자유는 헌법에 보장되어 있다 Freedom of association is guaranteed by the Constitution.
—**결사하다** form [organize] an association [a society, a fraternity]
■비밀— a secret society [organization] 정치— a political party

결사대 決死隊 a death band; a death-defying [do-or-die] corps; a suicide squad [corps, unit]; 〈대원〉 a forlorn hope 《of nine men》
♦결사대를 조직하다 organize a band determined to die / 결사대를 적진에 투하하다 airdrop a suicide squad into the enemy positions

결사적 決死的 ♦결사적인 desperate; death-defying / 결사적으로 싸우다 fight desperately; fight for *one's* life [to the death]
▶그는 물에 빠진 아이를 결사적으로 건져냈다 He risked his own life to save the child from drowning.

결삭다 soften; be softened; become mild; be mollified [soothed]

결산 決算 settlement of accounts; closing [balancing] accounts ♦2/4분기 결산 the second quarter settlement
▶결산은 1월과 7월에 합니다 We settle accounts in January and July.
—**결산하다** settle accounts; balance books [accounts]; close the books 《at the end of each year》
▶우리는 연 2회 결산합니다 We settle accounts twice a year.
■반기(半期)— a semiannual [half-yearly] settlement (of accounts) —기 a fiscal [settlement] term; a term for the settlement of accounts —액 settled accounts —위원회 a committee on accounts —일 a settling day; the day of reckoning; a closing date

결산보고 決算報告 a statement of accounts
♦결산 보고를 하다 make a report on the closing
▶나는 작년도 수지에 관한 결산 보고를 했다 I rendered an account of the last year's balance.

결석 缺席 absence; nonattendance; (口) 〈수업의〉 a cut; 〔法〕 〈궐석〉 default; nonappearance
♦결석이 잦다 be irregular in *one's* attendance
—**결석하다** be absent 《from》; absent *oneself* 《from》; 〔法〕 default; make default
▶나는 어제 복통 때문에 학교에 결석했다 I absented myself from school because of a stomachache yesterday.
▶오늘은 결석한 사람이 한 명도 없다 No one is absent today.
▶그는 지난 1년 동안 하루도 결석한 적이 없다 He has never missed a day in the past year.
■무단— absence without leave 병고— absence on account of illness 장기— a long absence ■—계 a report [notice] of absence [nonattendance]; an absence note —자 an absentee 《from class》; 〈재 판의〉 a defaulter —판결 judgment by default

결석 結石 〔醫〕 a calculus [kǽlkjələs]; a stone 《in the bladder》; a concretion ♦결석의 lithic; calculous
■신장—〈돌〉 a kidney stone; a renal calculus; a nephrolith; 〈병〉 nephrolithiasis ■—증 lithiasis

결석재판 缺席裁判 judgment by default ⇨ 궐석(—재판)

결선 決選 a final election; a runoff; 〈결승〉 a final game ♦결선에 진출하다 advance to [go into] the finals

결선투표 決選投票 《take》 a final [decisive] vote [ballot]; (美) 〈주(州) 선거의〉 a runoff primary
▶우리는 그 문제로 결선투표를 했다 We took a final [showdown] vote on the question.
▶그는 2차 결선투표에서 당선되었다 He was elected on the second ballot.

결성 結成 formation; organization
—**결성하다** form; organize 《a political party》
▶우리는 티베트 탐험대를 결성했다 We organized an expedition into Tibet.
■—식 an inaugural [inauguration] meeting [ceremony, rally]

결속 結束 union; unity; solidarity; 〈정신적인〉 spiritual bond ♦결속이 안 되다 fail to present a united front
▶그들은 결속이 잘 되어 있다 They are closely united.
▶우리 노조의 결속이 갈수록 느슨해지고 있다 The unity of our labor union is now getting less and less tight [looser and looser].
▶당내 결속을 굳게 하는[다지는] 것이 급선무다 It is of urgent necessity to strengthen [solidify] the party's unity.
—**결속하다** band [stick] together; unite; be united
♦굳게 결속되어 있다 be closely united; stand solidly together

▶ 그들은 결속하여 적에 대항했다 They united [banded] themselves together against the enemy.

결손 缺損 〈손실〉 a loss; deficiency; 〈부족〉 a (business) deficit; shortage
♦ 결손이 나다[생기다] suffer a loss 《of ten million won》
▶ 그 사업은 결국 결손이었다 The business resulted in [suffered] a loss.
▶ 이 때문에 1억원의 결손이 났다 This caused the deficit of one hundred million won.
▶ 우리 회사는 2년 연속 결손을 보았다 Our company suffered a succession of losses for two years.
▶ 문제는 결손을 어떻게 메우느냐 하는 것이다 The problem is how to make up for [cover] the deficit [loss].
■ ─액 the deficiency; the amount of loss ─처분 deficits disposal ─충당금 the reserve fund against losses [for compensation for deficits]

결승 決勝 the decision (of a contest) ⇨ 결승전
♦ 결승에 진출하다 go [move] into finals / 결승에서 이기다[지다] win [lose] in the finals
▶ 8명의 주자가 결승까지 올라갔다 Eight runners reached the finals.
■ ─선 the goal line; the finish line

결승 結繩 a knotted cord ■ ─문자 a quipu

결승전 決勝戰 the final round [game, match, contest]; the finals; a runoff (race); 〈무승부때의〉 a play-off
♦ 결승전 출전 선수 a finalist / 결승전에 나가다 run [play] in the finals; go into [reach] the finals / 결승전을 하다 decide a contest; play off [have a play-off match] 《against》
▶ 오늘 고교 야구의 결승전이 열린다 The final game [finals] of the High School Baseball Tournament will be held today.
▶ 그는 준결승에서 이겨 결승전에 진출하게 되었다 He won the semifinals and will go into the finals.
■ 준─ a semifinal game [round, match]; the semifinals 준준─ a quarterfinal game [round, match]; the quarterfinals

결승점 決勝點 〈지점〉 the goal; the home; the finish line; 〈득점〉 the (game-)winning run
♦ 결승점을 얻다 make the winning shot; 〈野〉 score the (game-)winning run / 결승점에 다다르다 get to [reach] the finish line; make [reach, hit] the goal; breast [break] the (finishing) tape

결식 缺食 going without a meal ─**결식하다** go without a meal ■ ─아동 undernourished [poorly-fed] children

결실 結實 fruitage; fructification; bearing fruit
♦ 다년간에 걸친 연구의 결실 the fruit [result] of one's years of study / 결실을 보지 못하다 bear no fruit
▶ 가을은 결실의 계절이다 Autumn is a harvest season.
▶ 결실이 있는 한 해가 되시기를 빕니다 Best wishes for a fruitful year.
▶ 우리의 노력은 결실을 보았다 Our efforts bore fruit [paid off].
─**결실하다** bear fruit; fructify; 《비유》 produce (good) results; be successful ♦ 결실하지 않는 나무 a sterile plant
▶ 다년간의 노력 끝에 그의 이상은 결실을 보았다 His ideal was realized after many years of endeavor.
■ ─기 the fruiting season

결심 決心 determination; resolution; decision
♦ 굳은 결심 a firm [a determined, an inflexible, an unshakable] resolution / 결심이 굳다 be firmly determined [resolved] 《to do》; be dead [quite] set on 《doing》 / 결심이 약해지다 be [get] weakened in one's resolution; one's resolution weakens / 결심을 굳히다 resolve firmly 《to do》; make a firm resolution; stiffen one's resolve / 설득하여 결심을 번복시키다 persuade sb out of his resolution
▶ 우리는 최후까지 싸울 결심이다 We are determined to fight to the last.
▶ 그것 때문에 그의 결심이 흔들렸다 That shook his resolution.
▶ 그 순간 내 결심이 흔들렸다 My resolution wavered at that moment.
▶ 그는 결심이 서지 않았다 He stood [remained] undecided.
▶ 아무리 설득해도 그는 결심을 번복하지 않았다 Despite all my arguments, he stuck to his decision.
─**결심하다** make up one's mind 《to do》; determine 《to do, on doing, that...》; decide 《to do》; resolve

> [解說] ***make up one's mind***는 구어적인 표현. ***determine***은 ***decide***보다 강한 결의를 나타내며, ***resolve***는 「신중히 고려한 끝에 결단을 내리다」라는 의미로 쓰이는 다소 격식차린 말이다.

♦ 굳게 결심하다 be firmly determined [resolved] 《to do》; make a firm resolve 《to do》
▶ 그는 의학 연구에 일생을 바치기로 결심했다 He made up his mind to devote his (whole) life to the study of medicine.
▶ 그는 다시는 그녀를 만나지 않기로 결심했다 He made up his mind [decided] not to see her again.
▶ 금년에는 일기를 쓰기로 결심했다 I resolved [made a resolution] to keep a diary this year.
▶ 그는 금연을 하기로 결심하고 그 결심을 지켰다 He resolved to give up smoking, and he kept his resolution.

결심 結審 the conclusion of (a) hearing [trial] ─**결심하다** close (a hearing); decide (a case) ■ ─공판 the final trial

결여 缺如 (a) lack; (a) want; (a) deficiency
♦ 상식의 결여 a want [lack] of common sense / 동정과 이해의 결여 a lack of sympathy and understanding
─**결여하다** lack 《in》; want; miss; be lacking [wanting, deficient] 《in》
▶ 그는 지성[상식]이 결여되어 있다 He is lacking [wanting] in intelligence [common sense].

▶ 당신이 실패한 것은 열의가 결여되었기 때문이다 Your failure was due to your lack of enthusiasm.
결연 結緣 forming a relationship; making a connection; 〔佛敎〕 becoming a believer in Buddhism ◆ 자매 결연 establishment of sisterhood
—**결연하다** form a relationship; establish relations 《with》
결연하다 決然 decisive; determined; firm; resolute
◆ 결연한 태도 a determined attitude / 결연히 감행하다 cross the Rubicon / 결연히 일어서다 determinedly rise to the occasion
▶ 그는 자기가 가겠다고 결연히 선언했다 He declared resolutely that he would go there.
결원 缺員 a vacancy; a vacant post [position]; an opening
◆ 결원이 생기면 if there is a vacancy / 결원을 보충하다 fill (up) a vacancy
▶ 그가 전근하는 바람에 결원이 생겼다 His transfer has caused a vacancy [left a vacant post].
▶ 그 자리는 아직 결원인 채로 있다 The position is still vacant [open].
결의 決意 determination; resolution; resolve
◆ 단호한 결의 inflexible determination; firm resolution / 결의의 표명 a declaration of resolve / 결의가 굳은 사람 a man of resolve / 결의를 굳게 하다 confirm *one's* determination; strengthen *one's* resolve; be fully determined [resolved] 《to do》 / 결의를 새로이 하다 make a fresh resolution 《to study harder》
▶ 신년을 맞을 때마다 우리는 결의를 새로이 한다 Every New Year's Day we make resolutions to turn over a new leaf.
—**결의하다** determine; resolve; make up *one's* mind; decide on 《a course of action》
결의 決議 a resolution; a decision; a vote
▶ 국회의 결의로 그 법안은 가결되었다 The bill was passed through the decision of the National Assembly.
—**결의하다** resolve; decide; pass a resolution 《for, against》; vote 《for [against] a measure》
◆ 안건을 결의하다 vote on a bill; vote for a scheme / 다음과 같이 결의함 Be it resolved [Resolved] that...
▶ 위원회는 그 법안을 폐기하기로 결의했다 The committee resolved to abolish the bill.
▶ 회의에서 결의된 사항은 다음과 같다 The following has been resolved at the meeting.
■ **부대**(附帶)— an additional resolution 불신임— a vote of nonconfidence : 불신임 결의를 하다 pass a vote of nonconfidence ■ —**권** the right of voting; the voting right —**기관** a voting [resolutionary] organ —**록** a record of resolutions; written resolutions —**문** a written resolution : 결의문을 전달하다 hand in [submit] a (written) resolution 《to》 —**사항** resolutions
결의 結義 —**결의하다** swear (to be brothers); take an oath (of brotherhood) ■—**형제** sworn [pledged] brothers
결의안 決議案 a (draft) resolution

◆ 결의안을 제출하다 move [present] a resolution / 결의안을 부결시키다 kill [vote down] a resolution / 계획에 반대[찬성] 결의안을 채택하다[통과시키다] adopt [pass] a resolution against [for, in favor of] the plan
▶ 그 결의안은 유엔 총회에서 다수의 찬성으로 가결되었다 The resolution was carried by a majority when put [submitted] to the U.N. General Assembly.
결자 缺字 an omitted word; an omission; 〔印〕 a blank (type)
▶ 이 교정쇄는 결자 투성이다 These proof sheets are full of blanks.
결장 結腸 〔解〕 the colon ■—**염** colonitis
결장하다 缺場— do not take part [participate] 《in》; do not play [compete] 《in》
▶ 나는 그 선수가 결장한 것을 알고 실망했다 I was disappointed to find that he was absent from the game [match].
결재 決裁 sanction; approval
◆ 결재가 나다 be approved; go from In-tray to Out-tray / 결재를 얻다 obtain an approval / 결재를 올리다 submit *sth* for *sb's* approval
▶ 이 계획은 판매부장의 결재가 이미 난 것이다 This plan was already approved by the sales manager.
▶ 그것은 사장의 결재를 아직 못 받았다 It remains to be sanctioned by the president.
■ —**권** the right of decision; decisive power
결전 決戰 a decisive battle [action]; a tug-of-war; a showdown; 〈경기의〉 a final game; a deciding match [race]; finals
◆ 결전의 시기 the decisive stage (of a war); the zero hour
▶ 우리는 적과 결전을 벌일 각오가 되어 있다 We are ready to fight a decisive battle with the enemy.
▶ 이번 총선에서는 양당이 결전을 벌일 것이다 The two parties will have a showdown in the coming general election(s).
—**결전하다** fight a decisive battle; fight to a finish
결절 結節 〈마디〉 a knot; 〈동식물·결핵의〉 〔醫〕 a tubercle; 〔解〕 a tuber; 〈줄기·피부의〉 〔植·醫〕 a node; a nodus 《*pl*. -di》
◆ 결절이 있는 knotted; tuberculous; nodular
■—**라**(癩) nodular [tubercular] leprosy —**종**(腫) a ganglion
결점 缺點 〈흠〉 a fault; 〈단점〉 a shortcoming; 〈문제점〉 a drawback; a defect; a blemish; a flaw; 〈약점〉 a weak point; a weakness

> [解說] 성격상의 단점이나 사물의 불완전함을 뜻하는 일반적인 말이 *fault*이고 그보다 딱딱한 말이 *shortcoming*이다. 사람이나 사물의 불쾌하거나 불편한 점을 말하는 것이 *drawback*이다.

▶ 그는 결점 투성이다 He is full of faults.
▶ 정거장에서 멀다는 것이 이 집의 (유일한) 결점이다 The (only) drawback of this house is that it is a long way from the station.
〈결점이〉 결점이 있는 faulty; defective / 결점

결점

이 없는 faultless 《works》; flawless; perfect / 결점이 없다 be free from faults; be perfect
▶ 그는 성격적으로 중대한 결점이 있다 He has a serious defect in his character.
▶ 그의 논거에는 결점이 없다 There are no flaws in his argument.
▶ 결점이 있는데도 불구하고 그는 그 여자를 사랑했다 He loved her with all her faults.
▶ 결점이 없는 사람은 없다 No one is free from faults. ⇒ There is no man but has some faults.
〈결점을〉 결점을 감추다[드러내다] conceal [expose] one's defects [faults]/ 결점을 고치다 correct [remedy, cure] one's defects [bad points]/ 결점을 보충하다 cover up sb's faults
▶ 이 논문에서는 결점을 하나도 찾을 수 없었다 I could not find a (single) flaw in this paper.
▶ 나는 결점을 고치려고 노력 중이다 I am trying to correct my bad [weak] points.
▶ 그는 항상 남의 결점을 들춰내고 다닌다 He is always finding fault with others [pointing out others' defects].

결정 決定
(a) decision; (a) determination; 〈해결〉 (a) settlement
♦결정을 내리다 make a decision 《about, over》/ 결정을 뒤엎다 reverse the decision / 결정을 서두르다 hurry in reaching a decision / 결정을 연기하다[미루다] put off [postpone] one's decision / 최종 결정에 따르다 follow the final decision
▶ 결정이 내려지는 대로 알려드리겠습니다 We will inform you as soon as the decision is made.
▶ 결정은 네가 할 일이다 It rests with you to decide.
―결정하다 decide; determine; fix; settle; set; 〈결심하다〉 resolve; 〈판정하다〉 judge

[解説] decide는 「사람이 결심하다, 사물이 사태를 결정하다」라는 뜻의 일반적인 말. determine은 decide 보다 강한 결의를 나타낸다. fix는 특히 날짜·가격·장소 등을, settle은 날짜·가격이나 사물의 조건 등을 정한다는 뜻.

♦갈 것인지 안 갈 것인지를 결정하다 decide whether to go or not / 날짜를 결정하다 fix [set] the date 《for a meeting》/ 방침을 결정하다 decide on one's policy [a course of action]/ 태도를 결정하다 determine one's attitude / 아직 어느 쪽으로도 결정되지 않다 hang [be] in the scale [balance]
▶ 가정 환경은 자녀의 성격을 결정한다 Home environment determines children's personalities.
▶ 우리는 그것을 토의한 끝에 반대하기로 결정했다 We talked it over and decided against it.
▶ 그들은 결혼 날짜를 결정했다 They fixed [set] the date of the wedding.
▶ 나는 아직 장래의 직업을 결정하지 않았다 I have not decided on my future job yet.
♦공급은 수요에 따라 결정된다 Demand determines supply.
▶ 그의 후임이 이미 결정되었다 His successor has already been chosen.
▶ 사건은 그에게 불리[유리]하게 결정되었다 The case went against [in favor of] him.
■ 의사― decision making ■―서(書) 〔法〕a written decision [verdict] ―인자 〔遺·植〕a factor of determination ―자(子) 〔遺〕a determinant ―전 a play-off; a final deciding game ―투표 the decisive [casting] vote ―판 a definitive [an authorized] edition; 〈번역본의〉 the most authentic version ever published

결정 結晶
〈결정 작용〉 crystallization; 〈결정체〉 a crystal; a grain(설탕 등의); 〈소산〉 a fruit
♦사랑의 결정 the fruit of love
▶ 이 작품은 그의 다년간에 걸친 노력의 결정이다 This work is the fruit of many years' labor on his part.
▶ 나는 돋보기로 눈의 결정을 보았다 I saw the snow crystal through a magnifying glass.
―결정하다 crystallize 《into》: become crystalline
■―계 a crystal system; a system of crystallization ―광학 crystal optics ―구조[조직] crystal structure ―면 a crystal face ―수(水) water of crystallization; combined water ―암 crystalline rock ―질 crystalline structure; crystalloid ―축 the axis of a crystal ―학 crystallography ―화 crystallization : 결정화하다 crystallize

결정권 決定權
the right of decision; decision-making authority
♦결정권을 가진 사람 a decision maker / 결정권을 쥐다 have [hold] the right [power] of decision; have decisive power
▶ 그는 그 문제에 결정권이 없다 He has no power [authority] to decide the matter. ⇒ He doesn't have the final say about [in] the matter.

결정론 決定論
〔哲〕 determinism ■―자 a determinist

결정적 決定的
decisive; definite; definitive; final; conclusive; determinate; crucial
♦결정적 순간 the crucial moment [point]; a decisive moment / 결정적 승리 a decisive victory / 결정적 증거 decisive proofs; conclusive [definitive] evidence / 결정적으로 decisively; definitely; 《speak》 with finality / 결정적인 순간에 at a decisive [crucial] moment 《in my career》/ 결정적이 되다 become decisive [definite]
▶ 우리 팀의 승리는 결정적이다 It is certain [There is no doubt] that our team will win.
▶ 그 사진기자는 미사일이 발사되는 결정적 순간을 찍었다 The cameraman took a picture of the missile at the decisive moment when it was launched.
▶ 변호사는 그녀의 무죄를 입증해 줄 결정적 증거를 제출했다 Her lawyer produced conclusive evidence of her innocence.
▶ 그것은 우리 회사에게 결정적 타격이었다 It was a decisive blow to our company.

결정타 決定打
〈권투 등의〉 a finishing [decisive] blow; 〈야구의〉 a (game-)winning hit; 〈말 등의〉 (口) a clincher

▶ 저 권투선수에게는 결정타가 없다 That boxer lacks a KO punch.

결제 決濟 settlement; 〈빚의〉 liquidation
♦ 미결제 계정 an account outstanding / 국제결제은행 the Bank of International Settlements
—결제하다 settle [square, make up] (accounts) 《with》
▶ 무역 수지는 달러로 결제한다 We settle the payments of trade in dollars.
▶ 이 청구서는 다음달에 결제하겠습니다 I will settle this bill next month.
■ **대차—** settlement of accounts; closure (of accounts): 대차 결제표 a balance sheet **부분[전액]—** partial [full] settlement **삼각—** the triple settlement **—일** a settlement [(英) settling] day **—자금** a settlement fund

결집 結集 〈집중〉 concentration; 〈조직화〉 regimentation
—결집하다 〈집중하다〉 concentrate; 〈모으다〉 collect in a mass; 〈모이다〉 gather; mass; rally (around the flag)
♦ 국민의 총의를 결집하다 regiment [orientate] people's opinions
▶ 그들은 난국을 극복하기 위해 모든 노력을 결집했다 All of them joined forces in an all-out effort to surmount the crisis.

결착 決着 end ⇨ 결말

결체 結滯 [醫] a pause [an intermission] in the pulse ▶ 그녀의 맥에 결체가 있었다 Her pulse was beating intermittently.

결체 結締 —결체하다 tie (up); bind ■ **—조직** connective tissue

결초보은하다 結草報恩— carry one's gratitude beyond the grave ▶ 결초보은하겠습니다 I shall never forget your kindness (as long as I live).

결코 決— 〈절대로〉 never; not at all; absolutely; by no means; 〈조금도〉 not…in the least; 〈어떤 이유로도〉 on no account [occasion]; 〈어떤 경우에도〉 under no circumstances; 〈어떤 의미에서도〉 not in any sense

[解說] ***never***는 가장 일반적인 부정어인데, 이 말에는 「어느 때도 …하지 않다 (not at any time)」라는 시간 관념이 포함되어 있으므로 반드시 not의 강조어는 아니다. ***not (…) at all, by no means***는 not의 부정의 뜻을 더욱 강조하는 말투로서, 정도를 나타낼 뿐 시간적 관념은 없다. ***on no account***는 「어떠한 이유가 있더라도 …하지 않다」라는 뜻.

▶ 그는 결코 바보가 아니다 He is by no means a fool.
▶ 그는 결코 당신을 속일 사람이 아니다 He is the last person to [that will] deceive you.
▶ 결과는 결코 만족할 만한 것이 아니었다 The result was far from satisfactory.
▶ 그런 행위는 결코 용서받을 수 없다 Such conduct is forbidden under no circumstances.
▶ 그는 결코 그런 짓을 하지 않는다 He would not do such a thing for (all) the world.
▶ 그 값은 결코 비싸지 않다 The price is none too high.

▶ 이것은 결코 나쁘지 않다 This is not bad in the least.
▶ 결코 그를 용서할 수 없다 I cannot forgive him on any account.
▶ 그것은 결코 그렇지 않다 I am positive that it is not so. ⇌ No, never, it isn't so.

결탁 結託 conspiracy; 〈공모〉 collusion
—결탁하다 conspire 《with》; be in collusion [league] 《with》
▶ 그 상인은 도둑과 결탁하여 장물 취득을 했다 The merchant dealt in stolen goods in conspiracy with a robber.
▶ 그는 그 악당과 결탁하여 온갖 나쁜 짓을 다 했다 He did all manner of evil things in league with that villain.

결투 決鬪 a duel; 〈총잡이들의〉 a shoot-out
♦ 결투 신청을 받다 be challenged to fight / 결투에 지다 be defeated in the duel 《with》
▶ 그는 나에게 결투를 신청했다 He challenged me to a duel.
▶ 나는 그의 결투 신청에 응했다 I accepted his challenge to a duel.
—결투하다 duel 《with》; fight a duel 《with》
■ **—입회인** a second **—자** a duelist; a dueler **—장(狀)** a (written) challenge; a cartel

결판 決判 〈판가름〉 (a) judgment; 〈결말〉 settlement; fixing (up)
♦ 결판(이) 나다 be settled [fixed, finished]; come [be brought] to an end [a conclusion] / 결판(을) 내다 settle (up) 《a quarrel》; fix (up); bring sth to a close [an end]
▶ 승패는 최후의 5분에 결판나는 것이다 The last five minutes determines the issue.
▶ 그 일은 이제 결판이 났다 It's over and done with.
▶ 두 사람 사이의 싸움은 아직 결판이 나지 않았다 The quarrel between them has not yet been settled.
▶ 이제 결판을 지어도 될 때다 It's about time we are through with it.

결핍 缺乏 〈없음〉 (a) lack [want]; (a) dearth [dɔ́ːrθ]; 〈부족〉 (a) deficiency [shortage]; scarcity
♦ 연료의 결핍 a fuel shortage / 인재의 결핍 a dearth of talent / 식량 결핍으로 고통받다 suffer from want [scanty supply] of food
▶ 당신은 비타민 C 결핍입니다 You need vitamine C.
▶ 용지 결핍으로 발행 부수에 제한이 있다 The number of copies is limited because of a shortage of paper.
—결핍하다 lack; want; be lacking [wanting] (in); be deficient (in); be scarce
▶ 현재로서는 의약품이 현저히 결핍되어 있다 Medicines are conspicuously lacking at the present time.
■ **—증** 〈비타민 등의〉 a deficiency disease

결하다 決— decide 《on, to do》; determine; settle; 〈확정하다〉 judge
♦ 승부를 결하다 decide a contest; try conclusions 《with》 / 자웅을 결하다 fight a decisive battle 《with》; fight [battle] it out 《with》; strive [contend] for mastery [supremacy]

결하다 缺— be short of; need; lack; want; be

wanting [lacking] (in); be missing
▶ 그는 상식을 결하고 있다 He lacks [is short of] common sense.
▶ 그의 대답은 성의를 결하고 있다 His reply lacks sincerity.

결함 缺陷 〈결점〉 a defect; a shortcoming; a fault(경미한); 〈미비〉 a flaw; (美口) bugs; a deformity 《of one's nature》
♦ 사회 제도의 결함 the vices of the social system / 성격상의 결함 a defect [deformity] in one's character / 육체적 결함 a physical defect / 치명적인 결함 a fatal defect / 정신적 결함이 있는 사람 a person mentally deficient / 결함이 없는 perfect; complete; faultless; flawless / 결함이 많은 badly flawed / 결함을 드러내다 betray one's weakness / 결함을 보완하다 [메우다] make good [make up for] a defect / 결함을 지적하다 point out defects 《in a machine》; indicate flaws 《in an argument》
▶ 그 사람의 논리는 결함 투성이다 There are many flaws [holes] in his reasoning.
▶ 그것은 기구상의 결함이었다 It was a defect in the mechanism.
▶ 이 기계는 결함이 너무 많다 There are too many faults [defects] in this machine.
▶ 이것이 어느 정도 결함을 보충해줄 것이다 This will make up for the defect to some extent.

결합 結合 (a) union [combination, cohesion]; (a) conjunction 《of discoveries and inventions》; 〔電·化〕 coupling; linkage; bond; bonding; 〈우주선의〉 docking; 〈원자핵의〉 fusion
♦ 분자의 결합 the bonding of molecules / 두 원소의 결합 a combination of two elements / 정신적 결합 spiritual union
—**결합하다** unite [combine] 《with》; band; conjoin
♦ A와 B를 결합하다 combine A with B; unite A and B / 두 가지를 하나로 결합하다 combine [unite] two things into one
▶ 수소와 산소가 결합하여 물이 된다 Hydrogen and oxygen unite to form water.
▶ 그 두 나라는 공통의 이해로 결합되어 있다 The two nations are linked together by common interest.
■—계수(係數) the coefficient of coupling; a coupling coefficient [factor] —공급 〔經〕 joint supply —기(器) 〔電〕 a coupler —률 〔數〕 composition rate —방식 a coupling scheme —범(죄) 〔法〕 concurrent offences —생산 〔經〕 joint and composite production —수(水) 〔生〕 combined moisture —수요 〔經〕 joint and composite demand —에너지 〔物·化〕 bond [binding] energy —음 a combination tone —재 a binding material —조직 ⇨ 결체(~조직) —체 a corporate body; a corporation —회로 〔電〕 a coupled circuit —효과 〔物·化〕 a packing effect

결항 缺航 suspension of 《ship》 service; the cancelation of a sailing; 〈항공기의〉 a flight cancelation; the cancelation of a flight
—**결항하다** do not sail [fly] (as scheduled)
▶ 태풍이 접근하고 있기 때문에 오후에는 연락선이 결항합니다 As a typhoon is approaching, the ferryboat will not sail (as scheduled) in the afternoon.
▶ 폭풍우로 그 항공편은 결항되었다 The flight was canceled because of the storm.

결핵 結核 1 〔醫〕 〈망울〉 a tubercle; 〈병〉 tuberculosis (略 T.B., t.b.)
♦ 결핵성의 tubercular; tuberculous / 결핵에 걸리다 get T.B.; contract tuberculosis; 〈앓다〉 suffer from tuberculosis
▶ 요즈음은 결핵으로 죽는 사람이 거의 없다 Few people die of tuberculosis these days.
2 〔地質〕 concretion
■—장— intestinal tuberculosis —후두— laryngeal [lǽrəndʒíəl] tuberculosis —균 a tubercle [tuberculous] bacillus —약 an anti-tuberculosis drug —요양소 a sanatorium [sanitarium] for tuberculosis; a T.B. sanatorium [hospital] —질 a (tubercular) constitution —형성 tuberculation —환자 a tubercular patient; a case of tuberculosis

결행 決行 decisive action; a resolute step
—**결행하다** carry out resolutely; carry into effect; take a resolute [decisive] step
▶ 궐기대회는 날씨에 관계없이 결행될 예정이다 The rally is to be held regardless of the weather [whether it rains or not].

결혼 結婚 (a) marriage; matrimony; a (marital) union
♦ 결혼의 marital; matrimonial / 행복한 결혼 a happy union / 결혼 전의 관계 one's premarital relations / 결혼 승낙을 받다 gain [win] (her) hand / 결혼 이야기를 꺼내다 〈본인이〉 speak [make a proposal] of marriage; 〈제삼자가〉 bring up the subject of marriage / 결혼을 거절하다 reject a (marriage) proposal / 결혼을 승낙하다 accept a (marriage) proposal; 〈여자가〉 give one's hand 《to》 / 결혼을 신청하다 propose (a marriage) 《to》 / 결혼을 약속하다 engage to marry; engage oneself 《to》 / 결혼에 성공[실패]하다 succeed [make a blunder] in marrying 《a man [woman]》
▶ 누구나 알다시피 결혼은 연애의 무덤이다 As everyone knows, marriage is death to love.
▶ 아버지는 우리의[그녀와의] 결혼을 매우 반대하십니다 My father is strongly against our marriage [my marriage to her].
▶ 그는 그녀에게 결혼을 신청했으나 거절당했다 He proposed to her [asked her to marry him], but she rejected him.
▶ 결혼을 축하합니다 Congratulations (on your wedding)! (▶ 신부에 대해서는 흔히 I wish you every happiness [the best of luck]. 라고 함)
—**결혼하다** marry; be [get] married 《to》
♦ 결혼하여 여자 a prospective bride / 갓 결혼한 just-married 《young couples》 / 부잣집 딸과 결혼하다 marry a fortune [a rich heiress] / 결혼시키다 marry 《a daughter to a man》; marry off 《a daughter》; get 《a son [daughter]》 married; unite 《a man and a woman》 in marriage
▶ 그는 늦게 결혼했다 He (got) married late in life.

▶ 언제 결혼하셨습니까? When did you get married?
▶ 그녀는 의사와 결혼했다 She got [is] married to a doctor.
▶ 그는 돈을 보고 결혼했다 He married for money.
▶ 그는 평생 결혼하지 않고 혼자 살았다 He remained unmarried [single] throughout his life.
▶ 〔會話〕「결혼한 지 얼마나 되셨습니까?」「5년 됐습니다」 "How long have you been married?" "We [I] have been married (for) five years."
▶ 그는 딸을 부하 한 사람과 결혼시켰다 He married his daughter to one of his men.
▶ 딸 넷을 결혼시키느라고 많은 비용이 들었다 It cost me dearly to marry off my four daughters.
■강제— (a) forced [coercive] marriage [match] 국제— (an) international marriage 근친— consanguineous marriage; intermarriage 매매— (a) purchase marriage 사진— (a) picture [photo] marriage 시험— a trial marriage 약탈— (a) marriage by capture 연애— a love match [marriage]: 연애결혼을 하다 get married for love 이중— bigamy 정략— (a) marriage of convenience; (an) expedient marriage; 〈정치적인〉 a political marriage 정식— a legal marriage 중매— a marriage arranged [made up] by a go-between: 중매결혼을 하다 get married through arrangement 집단— (a) group marriage 합의— (a) consensual marriage ■—기념일 a wedding anniversary —날짜 a wedding date —반지 a wedding [marriage] ring —사기 a matrimonial [marriage] fraud; a false [fake] marriage —사기꾼 a matrimonial swindler —상담 marriage [marital] counseling —상담소 a matrimonial agency [center]; a marriage bureau —상담소장 a matrimonial agent; (俗) a public lovemaker —상대 a marriage [marital] partner; one's spouse —서약 (one's) marriage [nuptial] vows —선물 a wedding gift [present] —자금 a marriage fund —적령기 the age for marriage; a marriageable [nubile] age: 결혼 적령기의 여성 a marriageable woman; a woman of marriageable age —제도 a marriage system —중매 matchmaking —중매인 a matchmaker; a go-between —지참금 a marriage portion; dowry —초야 one's first marriage night —피로연 a wedding reception —행진곡 the wedding march

결혼생활 結婚生活 a married [wedded, marital] life; wedlock
♦ 권태를 모르는 결혼생활 marriage without boredom / 행복한 결혼생활을 보내다 lead a happy married life; be happily married / 결혼생활에 들어가다 enter into the bonds of matrimony; embark in [on] matrimony

결혼식 結婚式 a wedding (ceremony); a marriage [nuptial, matrimonial] ceremony; nuptials
▶ 결혼식을 올리다 hold a wedding ceremony; perform [celebrate, solemnize] a wedding [marriage]; (俗) tie the knot / 몰래 결혼식을 올리다 have a quiet wedding / 결혼식에 초대하다 invite sb to a wedding
▶ 그들은 교회에서 결혼식을 올렸다 They (were [got]) married in a church.(▶이 경우 were married라고 하면 「목사의 주재 하에」라는 의미를 내포함)
■—장 a wedding hall

결후 結喉 the Adam's apple

겸 兼 and (also); in addition; at the same time; concurrently; as well
♦ 부엌 겸 식당 a kitchen-dining room / 부총리 겸 통일원 장관 Deputy Prime Minister and (concurrently) Minister of the National Unification Board / 서재 겸 응접실 a study-cum-drawing room; a room used both for study and for receiving visitors; a study in which one also sees one's guests / 아침 겸 점심 brunch / 주택 겸 작업장 a dwelling-cum-workshop / 침실 겸 거실 a bed-sitting-room; (俗) a bed-sitter / 편집인 겸 발행인 the editor and publisher (of a magazine) / 볼일도 볼 겸 놀기도 할 겸 partly on business and partly for pleasure; on business combined with pleasure
▶ 그는 내 운전기사 겸 비서로 일한다 He is my chauffeur besides working as my secretary.
▶ 저 가게는 제과점 겸 찻집입니다 The store is both a confectionery and coffee shop.

겸두겸두 for a double purpose ⇨ 겸사겸사

겸무 兼務 an additional [a concurrent] post [position]; plural offices
▶ 대통령은 남궁 주 프랑스 대사를 주 세네갈 대사 겸무로 임명했다 The President appointed Ambassador to France Namgung to serve concurrently as envoy to Senegal.
—하다 concurrently hold the position [post] (of); hold [take] also the post (of); serve concurrently (as)
▶ 재정 경제원 장관은 부총리 직을 겸무한다 The Minister of the Finance and Economy holds [takes] concurrently the post of a Deputy Prime Minister.
▶ 그는 경리과장과 총무과장을 겸무하고 있다 He is concurrently chief of both the accounting and the general affairs sections.

겸비하다 兼備— have both; have [possess] (A and B) at the same time
♦ 지용(智勇)을 겸비한 장수 a commander with wisdom and courage combined in him
▶ 그녀는 재색을 겸비했다 She has both beauty and intelligence. ⇌ She is beautiful as well as intelligent [is as wise as fair].
▶ 그는 문무를 겸비하고 있다 He excels at both scholarship and the martial arts.

겸사 謙辭 〈겸손한 말〉 humble words; modest speech; 〈사양〉 humble declination [refusal, denial] **—겸사하다** decline humbly; talk in a modest way

겸사겸사 for a double purpose; for two reasons; partly... and partly...
▶ 나는 일도 볼겸 관광도 할겸 겸사겸사 로마에 간다 I am going to Rome partly on business and partly for sightseeing.
▶ 자네를 만나도 보고 이야기도 해보고 하려고

겸사겸사 서울에 왔다 I have come up to Seoul for a double purpose of seeing you and of having a talk with you.

겸상 兼床 〈상〉 a table for two; 〈식사〉 a tête-à-tête [téitətéit] dinner
◆ 겸상을 받다 sit down to a tête-à-tête dinner / 겸상을 차리다 prepare [set] the table for two
─**겸상하다** take a tête-à-tête dinner; sit at the same dinner table

겸손 謙遜 modesty; humbleness; humility
▶ 겸손이 지나치면 비굴이 된다 Excessive modesty lapses into servility.
─**겸손하다** modest; humble; unassuming; 〈아랫사람에게〉 condescending
◆ 겸손한 사람 a modest person / 겸손한 태도 a humble [modest] attitude / 겸손하게 with modesty; in a modest way; humbly; modestly
▶ 그렇게 말씀하시다니 겸손하시군요 It's modest of you to say so.
▶ 그가 그렇게 말한 것은 겸손해서다 He said that out of modesty.
▶ 그는 자기가 한 일을 겸손하게 이야기했다 He spoke in a modest way of what he had done.

겸양 謙讓 modesty; humility; self-effacement
◆ 겸양의 미덕 the virtue of modesty / 겸양의 미덕을 발휘하다 behave modestly [with modesty]
▶ 지나친 겸양은 오만이다 Too much humility is pride.
─**겸양하다** humble [humiliate] *oneself*; condescend; be modest

겸업 兼業 a side business [job]; a sideline; a business on the side
─**겸업하다** pursue [follow] 《another trade》 as a side job [on the side]
▶ 그는 음식점과 식료품점을 겸업하고 있다 He runs both a restaurant and a grocery store.
▶ 그 주방용품상은 담배가게를 겸업하고 있다 The kitchenware dealer serves also as a cigarette store.
■ ─농가 a farmer with a side job; a farm family involved in another business

겸연쩍다 慊然─ abashed; embarrassed; disconcerted
◆ 겸연쩍어 bashfully; shamefacedly; shyly / 겸연쩍어 하다 be [feel] abashed; feel awkward; be [feel] embarrassed; be (put) out of countenance / 겸연쩍게 웃다 laugh to hide *one's* embarrassment / 겸연쩍게 하다[만들다] make *sb* self-conscious; put *sb* out of countenance
▶ 그렇게 칭찬을 들으면 겸연쩍다 So much praise makes me feel awkward.
▶ 사람들 앞에서 노래를 불러 겸연쩍었다 I was embarrassed to sing in front of people.
▶ 거짓말이 탄로나서 나는 아주 겸연쩍었다 I was much abashed when my lie was discovered.
▶ 그녀한테 거절을 당해 몹시 겸연쩍었다 I felt much abashed at [by] her refusal.

겸영하다 兼營─ operate 《a restaurant》 in addition 《to a hotel》; run 《a drugstore》 as well [at the same time]

겸용 兼用 a combined use
▶ 이 책상[부엌]은 식탁[식당] 겸용이다 This desk [kitchen] also serves as a table [dining room].
─**겸용하다** use *sth* both as...and...; make *sth* serve a double purpose; use in two or more ways
▶ 이 방은 서재와 거실로 겸용하고 있다 This room is used as both a study and a parlor.

겸유하다 兼有─ have both ⇨ 겸비하다

겸임 兼任 a concurrent position ⇨ 겸무, 겸직
─**겸임하다** hold the additional [concurrent] post 《of》; also hold the post 《of》; serve concurrently 《as》
▶ 그 나라에서는 국무총리가 외무부 장관을 겸임하고 있다 The Prime Minister serves concurrently as Foreign Minister in that country.
▶ 이 학교의 교장은 교감을 겸임하고 있다 The principal of this school holds the concurrent post [concurrently holds the post] of the vice-principal.

겸자 鉗子 〔醫〕 (a pair of) forceps [fɔ́ːrsəps] 《*pl.* ~, -cipes》; clamps; 〈치과용의〉 an extractor ■ ─분만 a delivery with forceps; a forceps operation

겸장(군) 兼將(軍) 〔장기〕 a double check

겸전하다 兼全─ perfect in both [all]; good at both
◆ 문무가 겸전하다 have both literary and military accomplishments; be good [excel] at both literary and military [martial] arts

겸직 兼職 a concurrent office [position]; an additional post [office]
▶ 공무원은 겸직 제한이 있다 There are restrictions on civil servants holding other jobs.
─**겸직하다** hold a position concurrently with the principal; hold two offices at a time
▶ 그는 국무총리와 외무장관을 겸직하고 있다 He concurrently holds the posts of Prime Minister and Foreign Minister.
■ ─금지 a ban for holding more than one office

겸하다 兼─ **1** 〈겸임하다〉 hold 《a post》 in addition to *one's* regular one [as an additional office]; hold 《two posts》 at once [simultaneously, concurrently]
▶ 김 선생님은 영어와 음악 교사를 겸하고 있다 Mr. Kim is both an English teacher and a music teacher.
▶ 국무총리가 국방 장관을 겸하고 있다 The Prime Minister is also (serving as) the Minister of Defense at the same time.
▶ 그는 혼자서 교장, 교사, 이사장을 모두 겸하고 있다 He is principal, teacher and chairman of board of directors all in one.
2 〈겸비하다〉 combine [unite] 《A with B》; possess both 《A and B》; 〈겸용하다〉 serve both as 《A and B》
▶ 이 강당은 체육관도 겸하고 있다 This lecture hall serves as a gymnasium.
▶ 그들은 담배 가게를 겸한 잡화점을 운영하고 있다 They have a general store which sells tobacco.
▶ 나는 쇼핑을 겸해서 시내로 산책하러 나갔다

I went downtown for a walk and did the shopping at the same time.
겸행 兼行 〈겸하여 함〉 doing more than one job at the same time ♦주야 겸행으로 일하다 work night and day [day and night]; work around the clock / 주야 겸행으로 가동시키다 set 《a machine》 on the 24-hour job
──**겸행하다** do [carry out] two or more different things at the same time; perform plural duties
겸허 謙虛 modesty; humbleness; humility
──**겸허하다** modest; humble ♦겸허하게 modestly; with modesty
▶ 겸허한 것은 좋지만 지나쳐서는 안된다 It's all right to be modest, but don't carry it to excess.
▶ 남의 충고를 겸허하게 들을 줄[자신의 행동을 겸허하게 반성할 줄] 알아야 한다 You should be humble enough to listen to others' advice [modest enough to reflect on your conduct].
겹 1 〈켜〉 a fold; a layer; a pile(쌓아올린); 〈밧줄 등의 가닥〉 a ply
♦두 겹의 twofold; double; two-ply / 여러 겹의 manifold / 담요를 두 겹으로 접다 double a blanket / 종이를 세 겹으로 접다 fold a piece of paper into three
▶ 그것을 여러 겹으로 접으시오 Fold it several times over.
2 〈이중〉 duplication; doubleness ♦겹칠 double coating / 겹으로 짠 피륙 double cloth
겹것 〈겹으로 된 것〉 a multiple-layered thing; things with linings; 〈겹옷〉 lined clothes
겹겹이 manifoldly; in many folds; one upon another; layer upon layer; ply on ply; range on range; heap(s) on heap(s); in piles
♦성을 겹겹이 둘러싸다 surround a castle thick and fast / 종이로 겹겹이 싸다 wrap 《a thing》 in several sheets of paper / 겹겹이 쌓아올리다 lay one upon another; lay in piles [layers] / 산으로 겹겹이 둘러싸이다 be surrounded by range after range of mountains
▶ 적군이 성을 겹겹이 에워싸고 있었다 There were rings and rings of enemy soldiers surrounding the castle.
▶ 그의 차는 열광적인 팬들에게 겹겹이 둘러싸였다 His car was crowded around by his ardent admirers.
▶ 전장에는 시체가 겹겹이 쌓여 있었다 Corpses [Dead bodies] lay in heaps [piles] on the battlefield.
겹꽃 a double flower
겹눈 〔動〕 compound eys=복안(複眼)
겹다 1 〈참기 어렵다〉 unrestrainable; irresistible; irrepressible; beyond *one's* control
♦눈물겨운 노력 pathetically sincere efforts / 흥에 겨워 in the excess of mirth; driven by *one's* enthusiasm / 슬픔에 겨워 in (the fullness of) *one's* sorrow [grief]; in a passion of grief / 기쁨에 겨워 눈물을 흘리다 shed tears [weep] for [with] joy
▶ 그녀는 기쁨에 겨워 덩실거렸다 She danced with joy.
2 〈힘겹다〉 beyond [above] *one's* capacity [power]; too much for *one*
▶ 나는 이 일이 힘에 겹다 I am not equal to the task. ⇌ This work is too much for me.
▶ 그에게는 힘에 겨운 일이란 없다 Nothing is beyond his power [ability].
겹두루마기 a lined Korean overcoat
겹말 tautology [tɔːtáləʤi]
겹살림 another household ──**겹살림하다** maintain more than one household
겹옷 lined clothes; clothes with a lining
겹저고리 a lined coat [jacket]
겹질리다 sprain; wrick ▶ 그 여자는 쓰러지면서 발목을 겹질렸다 She twisted [sprained, wrenched] her ankle when she fell to the ground.(▶겹질린 정도는 twist가 가장 약하고 wrench가 가장 심함)
겹집 a house with (several) wings
겹창 ──窓 a double [storm] window
겹쳐지다 1 〈포개어지다〉 be piled up; overlap each other [one another] ▶ 상자가 많이 겹쳐져 있다 There are a lot of boxes piled up. ⇌ There is a big pile of boxes.
2 〈접쳐지다〉 be folded 《in three》 ♦둘로 겹쳐지다 be doubled
겹치다 1 〈포개다〉 pile [heap] up; place [lay] one upon another
♦겹쳐서 in piles [layers]; one on top of the other; on top of one another (▶the other는 둘, one another는 셋 이상일 때 씀) / 내복을 두 벌 겹쳐 입다 wear two undershirts one over the other [one undershirts over another] / 벽돌 4개를 겹쳐 쌓다 pile [stack] up four bricks / 신문지를 2장 겹쳐서 싸다 wrap *sth* in two thicknesses [sheets] of newspaper
▶ 멀리 산이 겹쳐 있다 The mountains piled up in the distance.
▶ 나는 스웨터 위에 카디건을 겹쳐 입었다 I wore a cardigan over the sweater.
▶ 승객들이 겹쳐 넘어졌다 The passengers fell one upon another.
2 〈접다〉 fold; double (up) ♦종이를 한 번 겹치다 fold a piece of paper in two
3 〈중첩되다〉 overlap; fall on
♦고난이 겹치다 go through many hardships / 손해가 겹치다 sustain loss upon loss
▶ 경사가 겹친다 Good things come one after another [in succession].
▶ 올해는 개천절과 일요일이 겹친다 The National Foundation Day falls on Sunday this year.
▶ 두 모임이 겹쳤다 The two meetings coincided.
▶ 그는 나와 휴가가 겹쳤다 His vacation overlapped with me.
▶ 그 집안에 불행이 겹쳤다 The family had one misfortune after another [a series of misfortunes].
겹치마 a lined skirt
경 更 one of the five divisions [watches] of the night ♦삼경 midnight; 《in》 the dead [depth] of night
경 卿 Lord; Sir (▶Lord는 성에, Sir는 이름 또는 성명에 붙임); 〈대신〉 a minister ♦넬슨 경 Lord Nelson / 처칠 경 Sir Winston (Churchill) / 경들은 You all

경 經 1 〈경서〉 Chinese classics (of Confucianism)
♦시경(詩經) the Book of Odes [Poetry]
2 〈불경〉 a sutra; the Buddhist scriptures ♦화엄경 the Avatamska Sutra / 경을 읽다 recite [chant, intone] a sutra; read a service
3 〈주문〉 spells [incantations] of sorcerers ♦경을 외다 chant a spell; make an incantation
4 〈경도(經度)〉 longitude ♦동경 east longitude / 서경 25도 longitude 25 degrees west

경 京 〔數〕 ten-million billion; ten quadrillion

-경 -頃 about; (美) around; toward(s); circa ♦5시경 (at) about five o'clock / 이달 말경에 around the end of this month
▶그것은 지난 여름 7월경의 일이었다 It was in the last summer, sometime in July.
▶이 금불상은 1997년경에 발굴되었다 This gold image of Buddha was unearthed in 1997 or thereabouts.

-경 -景 ♦관동팔경 the eight tourist [scenic] attractions of the Kwandong District / 천하제일경 the most picturesque place in the world

경가극 輕歌劇 a light opera; an operetta

경각 頃刻 a moment; a minute; an instant ♦경각(지)간에 in an instant; in a split second; in the twinkling of an eye / 경각을 다투다 fight the clock
▶그의 목숨이 경각에 달렸다 His life hangs by a thread. ⇒ He is on the brink [point, eve] of death.
▶그 문제의 해결책을 찾는 일은 경각도 지체할 수 없다 Not a moment can be lost [We can't waste a moment] in finding a solution to the problem.

경각 傾角 1 ⇨ 편각(偏角) **2** (the angle of) inclination

경각 警覺 (a) warning; (a) caution; awakening —**경각하다** warn; caution; give a warning [caution] 《to》; awaken

경각심 警覺心 (self-)awakening ♦경각심을 불러일으키다 arouse [provoke] sb's attention; bring sb to 《his》 senses

경감 輕減 (a) reduction; mitigation; 〈세금의〉 abatement; 〈불안·고통의〉 (a) relief; alleviation; 〈형벌의〉 commutation
—**경감하다** lighten; reduce; relieve; alleviate; mitigate; commute 《a sentence》
♦고통을 경감하다 relieve [ease] the pain / 부담을 경감하다 lighten the burden / 세금을 경감하다 reduce [lighten] taxes
▶세금이 경감되었으면 좋겠다 We would like to have the tax reduced [lightened].
▶그러면 우리의 부담이 크게 경감될 것이다 It will greatly lighten [alleviate] our burden.

경감 警監 a police inspector; a police captain

경개 梗槪 an outline; a synopsis [sənápsəs] 《pl. -ses》; a summary; a sketch

경거망동 輕擧妄動 a rash [reckless] act; rash attempt and blind behavior
♦경거망동을 경계하다 warn sb against rashness / 경거망동을 삼가다 refrain from rash acts; be prudent in one's behavior
—**경거망동하다** do [act] rashly; commit a rash act; act on impulse
▶경거망동하지 마라 Don't act rashly [on impulse].

경건 敬虔 piety; devotion; reverence
—**경건하다** pious; devout; reverent; 〈믿음이 깊다〉 godly; God-fearing
♦경건한 기독교도 a pious Christian / 경건한 불교 신자 a pious believer in Buddhism; a pious Buddhist / 경건한 기도를 드리다 offer a devout prayer; pray devoutly 《before the altar》
▶교회당 안에는 경건한 침묵이 흘렀다 There was a reverential silence in the church.
■**—주의** Devotionalism; Pietism **—파** the Pietist

경계 境界 a boundary; a border; 〈국경〉 a frontier; 〈한계〉 the confines

〔解說〕 **boundary**는 국가·도·읍 등을 지리적으로 나누는 엄밀한 경계선(the dividing line), **border**는 경계선 및 그에 따른 지역, **frontier**는 흔히 정치적·군사적인 면에서 본 국경과 그 일대를 가리킨다.

♦낮과 밤의 경계 the confines of night and day / 시의 경계 the city limits / 경계를 정하다 fix the boundary 《between》; draw a line of demarcation 《between》 / 경계를 짓다 define boundaries; set up the borderline 《between》
▶어디가 경계인지 분명치가 않다 We can't see clearly where the boundary is.
▶이 강이 우리 마을과 이웃 마을과의 경계를 이룬다 This river forms the boundary between our town and the neighboring one.
▶여기가 미국이 멕시코와 경계를 접하고 있는 곳이다 Here the U.S. borders on [shares the borders with] Mexico.
▶한국은 북쪽으로 만주와 경계를 접하고 있다 Korea is bounded on the north by Manchuria. ⇒ Korea borders Manchuria on the north.
▶그는 3일 동안 생사의 경계를 헤맸다 He hovered between life and death for three days.
▶그는 자기 토지[소유지]의 경계에 쭉 울타리를 쳤다 He built a fence along the boundary of his estate [property].
■**—분쟁** ⇨ 국경(~분쟁) **—인(人)** 〔社〕 a marginal man **—지역** the borderland **—표** a landmark; a mete [mi:t]; a boundary stone [mark]; a demarcation post

경계 警戒 1 〈조심〉 caution; 〈예방조치〉 (a) precaution; 〈경고〉 a warning
♦경찰의 엄중한 경계 stringent police precautions / 경계를 게을리하지 않다 keep one's weather eye open / 경계를 엄중히 하다 make strict precautions
▶태풍이 우려되므로 해안 지방은 경계를 요한다 Since there is fear of a typhoon, precautions ought to be taken along the coasts.
—**경계하다** 〈조심하다〉 be cautious about 《sth, doing》; take precautions 《against》; 〈조심시키다〉 caution 《sb against error》; warn 《sb of danger》
♦경계시키다 alert 《the police》 against 《a

riot)
▶ 아버지는 내게 음주를 경계하셨다 My father cautioned me against drinking.
▶ 지진이 일어나면 화재와 해일을 특히 경계해야 한다 When an earthquake occurs, we should take special precautions against fire and tidal waves.
▶ 수상한 사람들을 경계해야 한다 You must beware of suspicious-looking men.
2 〈감시〉 watch; (a) lookout; vigilance; 〈경비〉 guard
◆ 삼엄한 경계 strict watch / 경계를 게을리하다 be off one's guard 《against》 / 경계를 늦추다 relax one's vigilance 《against》 / 경계를 엄중히 하다 keep a strict lookout 《against》; keep strict watch 《over》
▶ 전군(全軍)은 (적군에 대한) 특별 경계 태세에 돌입했다 The armed forces were on a special alert (against the enemy).
▶ 저 여자에 대해 경계를 게을리하지 마라 Keep an eye on [Guard against] that woman.
—**경계하다** 〈감시하다〉 look out 《for pickpockets》; watch 《for a thief》; be on the watch 《for》; 〈경비하다〉 guard 《against》; stand [lie] upon one's guard
◆ 늘 경계하다 keep an eye [one's eyes] out 《for surprise attacks》; keep one's eyes open / 방심하지 않고 경계하다 be ever on the lookout [alert] 《for》
▶ 등산할 때는 눈사태를 경계해라 Watch out for avalanches during the mountain climb [when you climb a mountain].
■ —**관제** warning control of lights; an air-defense precautionary order; a dimout; (美) a brownout —**색** sematic [warning, alarming] coloration; 〈특정한〉 a warning [sematic] color —**수위** the danger level 《of a river》 —**신호** 〈교통의〉 a warning [caution(ary)] signal; 〔鐵〕 a restricted speed signal —**심** wariness —**표지** a warning sign
경계 경보 警戒警報 a precautionary [preliminary] warning; 〈공습의〉 an air-raid alarm [warning]
◆ 경계경보를 발하다[울리다] issue [sound] a warning
▶ 경계경보가 내렸다 There has been a preliminary warning.
경계망 警戒網 a cordon of police; a police cordon [net]
◆ 경계망을 치다 lay a police cordon 《around an area》; block off 《an area》 / 경계망을 빠져나가다 slip through a police cordon
경계선 境界線 〈토지의〉 a boundary line; (美) a border line; a line of demarcation 《between》; 〈시대 구분의〉 a dividing line 《between》
◆ 중세와 근대의 경계선 the dividing line between the Middle and the Modern Ages / 경계선을 긋다 draw a line of demarcation / 경계선을 넘다 cross the border
▶ 미국과 캐나다의 경계선은 조약에 의해 결정되었다 The US-Canada boundary was fixed by treaties.
▶ 그때 나는 삶과 죽음의 경계선을 헤매고 있었다 I was then hovering between life and death.
경계선 警戒線 a police line [cordon] ◆ 경계선을 치다 put a police line / 경계선을 돌파하다 break through [across] the police line
경고 警告 (a) warning; (a) caution; (an) admonition; a caveat [kéiviæt]
◆ 엄중한 경고 a sharp [serious] warning / 경고도 없이 without warning / 경고를 발하다 send out a warning 《to》 / 경고를 받다 take [receive] warning 《from the police》; be warned 《against》
▶ 이게 마지막 경고인데, 그런 짓 하지 마라 I'm warning you once and for all, don't do such a thing.
▶ 그들은 내 경고를 무시했다 They disregarded my warning [caution].
▶ 그 여자는 우리의 경고에 귀를 기울이려 하지 않았다 She would not heed [listen to] our warning.
▶ 우리의 거듭된 경고에도 불구하고 그는 그 버릇을 고치려 하지 않았다 In spite of our repeated warnings, he would not mend his ways.
—**경고하다** warn; caution sb against; give sb a warning; admonish
▶ 나는 그들에게 위험한 곳에는 가지 말라고 경고했다 I gave them warning not to go to dangerous places.
▶ 그는 등산객들에게 폭풍우가 닥쳐온다고 경고했다 He warned the climbers of the approach of a storm.
■ **사전—** an advance warning ■ —**등** a warning light [flare] —**발사** 《fire》 a warning shot
경골 脛骨 〔解〕 〈정강이뼈〉 the shinbone; the tibia [tíbiə] 《pl. ~s, -iae》 ◆ 경골의 tibial
경골 硬骨 1 〈굳뼈〉 (a) hard bone
2 〈강직함〉 a firm character; firmness 《of character》; stubbornness; inflexibility
■ —**한(漢)** a man of firm character [iron will]; a man of principle; a staunch fellow
경골 頸骨 〔解〕 〈목뼈〉 the neck bone; the bones of [in] the neck; the cervical vertebrae [və́ːrtəbriː]
경골어류 硬骨魚類 〔魚〕 Teleostei ◆ 경골어류의 물고기 a teleost [téliɑ̀st]; a bony fish
경공업 輕工業 light industries ◆ 경공업 제품 light industry articles [goods]
경과 經過 1 〈시간의〉 passing; passage; lapse ◆ 오랜 시간의 경과 a long lapse of time
—**경과하다** pass; go by; elapse
◆ 20년의 세월이 경과하여 after (a lapse of) twenty years / 시간이 경과함에 따라 as time goes by; in course of time: with the lapse of time
▶ 그로부터 2년이 경과했다 Two years have passed since then.
▶ 눈깜짝할 사이에 5년이 경과했다 Five years passed very quickly.
▶ 시간이 경과함에 따라 흥분도 가라앉았다 The excitement wore off as time went by.
2 〈기한의〉 expiration —**경과하다** expire ▶ 기한이 경과했기 때문에 이 표는 무효입니다 This ticket is no good; it has expired.
3 〈일의 진전〉 progress; 〈진행〉 course 《of

events); 〈발전・전개〉 development
♦ 사건의 경과 the development of an affair / 수술 경과 the postoperation course (of a disease) / 재판의 경과 the progress of a case / 경과가 양호하다 〈환자의〉 be making satisfactory progress; be doing well [fine] / 일의 경과를 보고하다 report (to *one's* senior) how things are going / 경과를 살피다 watch the development of the affair
▶ 會話 「남편께서는 경과가 어떠십니까?」「덕분에 양호합니다. 이제 위험한 고비는 넘겼어요」 "How is your husband doing?" "He is coming along fine, thank you. He is out of danger now."
▶ 일의 경과가 어떻게 될지는 알 수 없습니다 We cannot tell how the affair will develop.
▶ 수술 후 환자의 경과는 양호합니다 The patient is doing well after the operation.
▶ 나는 교섭의 경과를 보고받았다 The progress of the negotiations was reported to me.
▶ 분쟁의 경과를 보고하겠습니다 I'll report the course of events in the dispute.
━─계정 〔商〕 deferred and accrued accounts ─배당 an accrued dividend ─시간 the time elapsed ─음 ⇨ 지남음 ─조치 interim measures

경과보고 經過報告 a progress report; 〈회의의〉 a report on the proceedings; 〈사건의〉 a report on the development of an affair; 〈수사의〉 a progress report on the investigation; a report on the developments in [of] the investigation

경관 景觀 a view [scene, sight]; (총칭) scenery
♦ 장대한 경관 a grand [thrilling] sight; a magnificent view / 경관을 해치다 destroy [spoil, injure] the scenic beauty (of a place)
▶ 신축 호텔이 경관을 해친다 The new hotel is an eyesore.
▶ 그들은 남알프스의 웅장한 경관을 즐겼다 They enjoyed the magnificent panorama of the Southern Alps.

경관 警官 a policeman ⇨ 경찰관
경교 景敎 Nestorianism ■─도 a Nestorian
경구 硬球 〔球〕 a regulation [hard] ball
경구 經口 ♦ 경구의 oral
━─백신 oral vaccine ─투약 (doses for) oral administration ─피임약 an oral contraceptive; a birth control pill; (口) the pill : 나는 경구 피임약을 먹고 있다 I am on the pill.

경구 敬具 〈친구간에〉 Yours sincerely; Sincerely (yours); 〈사무적인 편지에서〉 Cordially (yours); Yours truly; 〈관청이나 윗사람에 대해〉 Yours respectfully

경구 警句 a witty remark; an epigram; an aphorism; a witticism; a laconism ♦ 경구를 말하다 make a witty remark (about); (口) make a crack (about)
━─집 a collection of epigrams; a book of maxims

경구개 硬口蓋 〔解〕 the hard palate; the roof of the mouth

경국 傾國 endangering of a nation
━─지색(之色) a woman beautiful enough to cause the downfall of a country; a Helen of Troy

경국 經國 running a country; administration
━─지재(之才) the caliber [capacity] of a statesman; administrative talent [abilities]

경극 京劇 (a) Beijing (classical Chinese) opera; a Chinese traditional play

경금속 輕金屬 light metals

경기 景氣 1 〈형편〉 things; (the) times
♦ 경기가 어떠십니까? How's everything? ⇌ How are the times? ⇌ How are you getting along [on]?
▶ 그는 경기가 좋은 것 같다 He looks well off.
2 〈경제상황〉 business conditions; (the tone of) the market
♦ 경기가 좋아지다 (the market) pick up [look up]; become prosperous; perk up (after depression); 〈갑자기〉 boom / 경기가 나빠지다 become dull [slack]; slow down
▶ 금년도 경기 전망은 어둡다 The economic prospects for this year are dark [gloomy].
▶ 경기가 좋다 Business [The market] is brisk [active]. ⇌ Business is humming.
▶ 경기가 나쁘다 Business [The market] is dull [slow, slack].
▶ 경기가 좋아지고 있다 The market [Business] is looking [picking] up. ⇌ Business is [The economic conditions are] improving.
▶ 경기가 하락하고 있다 Business is declining.
▶ 가을에는 경기가 좋아질 것이다 Business will recover in the autumn.
▶ 그 회사는 경기가 좋다 That company is doing a good business.
▶ 전쟁 중에 철강업은 경기가 좋았다 The steel industry did a flourishing business during the war.
▶ 지금 백화점 경기는 좋다 Business at the department store is booming now.
▶ 경기는 어떻습니까? How's business? ⇌ How is your business doing?
▶ 국내 경기는 명백한 회복 기미를 보이고 있다 The domestic business shows clear signs of recovery.
▶ 이 장사는 경기를 타지 않는다 This trade is above business fluctuation.
━─가짜 a false show of activity; false [borrowed, artificial] prosperity; a fake [false] boom 벼락─ a boom (in the market) 전쟁[전후, 전시]─ a war [postwar, wartime] boom ─과열 business overheating ─대책 〈자극책〉 stimulative measures ─동향조사 a business survey ─변동[순환] a business fluctuation [cycle] ─부양책 steps to stimulate the economy; reflation measures [policy] ─상승 a business upturn [upswing] ─안정화정책 counter cyclical policy ─예측 business forecasting ─지 수[지표] a business index [barometer] ─촉진 the artificial enlivening of the market ─침체 stagnancy of business activities; economic slump ─활성화정책 an economy-invigorating policy ─회복 (a) business [(an) economic] recovery; return to prosperity; a perk-up ─후퇴 a (business) recession; a business setback: 정부는 경기 후퇴

를 수출 부진 탓으로 돌리고 있다 The government attributes the business setbacks to sluggish exports.

경기 競技 a (competitive) sport; 〈시합〉 a game; a match; a meet; a competition; 〈종목〉 an event (▶보통 야구·축구 등은 game, 권투·레슬링 등은 match, 수영은 meet라고 함)

[解說] *competition*은 능력·기술 등을 겨루는 것, *event*는 스포츠의 종목, *match*는 대항 시합을 말한다. *contest*는 심사위원이 우열을 결정하는 경기에 쓰인다.

◆경기에 이기다[지다] win [lose] a match [game]; win [lose] the day / 경기에 참가[출전]하다 take part in a contest; enter for an event; take the field
▶축구는 한국에서 인기있는 경기다 Soccer is a popular game in Korea.
▶1988년 올림픽 경기는 서울에서 개최되었다 The 1988 Olympic Games were held in Seoul.
—**경기하다** have a game [match]; play a game [match]
■근대 5종— the modern pentathlon 수상의 water [aquatic] sports [events] 10종— ten events; the decathlon 연습— a practice game; (口) a workout game 옥외[실내]— an outdoor [indoor] sport 운동— athletic sports; sporting events 육상— track and field events 주요— a main event 7종— the heptathlon ■—대회 an athletic meet; a sports meeting; 〈기술·기능의〉 a contest; a competition —시설 athletic facilities —자 a contestant; a competitor; an athlete; a player; 〈트랙의〉 a racer; 〈수영의〉 a swimmer —장 a ground; a field; a stadium; 〈투기장〉 an arena : 국립 경기장 the National Athletic Stadium —종목 a sports event; sport entries

경기 驚氣 〔韓醫〕 convulsions
경기관총 輕機關銃 a light machine gun
경기구 輕氣球 a balloon ⇨ 기구(氣球)
경기병 輕騎兵 a light cavalryman [horseman]; a hussar [hΛzɑːr]; 〈부대〉 light cavalry
경내 境內 the grounds (of a temple); the precincts; the compound; the close
◆사당의 경내(에서) (in) the precincts of a shrine / 경내 건물 precinct buildings
▶백담사의 경내는 아주 조용했다 It was very peaceful [quiet] within the precincts of the Paektamsa.
경년하다 經年— pass a year; undergo the passage of a year
경노동 輕勞動 light work [labor] ■—자 a light worker
경뇌유 鯨腦油 sperm oil; spermaceti [spəːrməséti]
경단 瓊團 〈떡〉 a rice dumpling
경대 鏡臺 a dressing table; a mirror [looking-glass] stand; (美) a dresser; a vanity
경도 硬度 hardness; solidity
▶다이아몬드의 경도는 10이다 The hardness of diamond is 10. ■—계 a durometer —시험 a hardness test
경도 傾度 〔物〕 inclination; gradient

경도 經度 1 〔地〕 longitude (略 long.)
◆경도를 측정하다 calculate the longitude 《of》
▶경도는 동경 126도 50분이다 It is situated at one hundred twenty-six degrees fifty minutes east longitude.
2 ⇨ 월경(月經)
경도하다 傾倒— 〈넘어지다〉 fall down; 〈기울여 쏟다〉 devote *oneself* to; concentrate 《*one's* mind [energy]》 on; be absorbed in
▶그는 셰익스피어에 경도되어 있다 He is an ardent admirer of Shakespeare. ⇌ He is a devoted reader of Shakespeare.
경동맥 頸動脈 〔解〕 the carotid artery; the carotid(s)
경락 競落 〔經〕 sale by auction; 〔法〕 buying by auction
—**경락하다** 〈경매인이〉 knock a thing down 《to》; 〈매수인이〉 make a successful bid, outbid 《other bidders》
▶그 건물은 100억원에 민씨에게 경락되었다 The building has been knocked down to Mr. Min for ten billion won.
▶나는 그 그림을 100만원이면 경락할 줄 알았다 I expected to be able to get the picture at the auction for one million won.
■—기일 time for objectification —물 objects knocked down —인 a successful bidder
경랍 鯨蠟 spermaceti (wax)
경량 輕量 light weight
■—급 the lightweight class: 경량급 선수 a lightweight (boxer); a light; (총칭) lightweights —콘크리트 lightweight concrete —트럭 a light truck —품 light goods —화물 light freight [cargo]
경력 經歷 a career; a record; a background; 〈이력〉 *one's* personal [life] history
〈경력이〉 경력이 다양한 사람 a man with a varied career; a man of varied experiences / 경력이 좋다[나쁘다] have a good [bad] record
▶그 분은 교사로서 경력이 뛰어나다 He has a brilliant career as a teacher [in teaching].
▶이런 사회에서는 경력이 없이는 성공할 수 없다 In this type of society, you can't hope to succeed without a good career.
▶그는 경력이 아주 다양하다 He has had a very varied [checkered] career.
〈경력을〉 경력을 조사하다 check up [trace] *sb's* career [record]
▶그의 경력을 아는 사람은 아무도 없다 Nobody knows his background.
▶그녀는 경력을 잘 쌓았기 때문에 어디든지 취직이 될 것이다 Her past record is so good that she'll be able to find a job anywhere. ⇌ She is sure to find situation anywhere, as she is a woman of commendable antecedents.
■—무대 *one's* stage career 연구— *one's* academic history —방송 〈선거의〉 a radio [television] bulletin of a candidate's career —소개 a biographical introduction
경련 痙攣 convulsions; a spasm; 〈통증을 수반한〉 (a) cramp; 〈안면의〉 a twitch; a tick
◆경련성의 spasmodic; spastic; convulsive /

경련성 마비 spastic paralysis / 경련이 일어나다 have a cramp (in one's leg); cramp up
▶ 경련이 멎었다 The spasm passed off.
▶ 오늘 아침 조깅할 때 왼발에 경련이 일어났다 My left leg cramped up while I was jogging this morning.
▶ 그녀는 눈꺼풀에 경련을 일으키고 있었다 Her eyes were twitching.
■ 강직성— tetanic convulsions; a tonic spasm 안검(眼瞼)— a nictitating spasm 안면— a (facial) tic 위— stomach cramps

경례 敬禮 a salute; a bow; salutation
◆ 거수 경례 a hand [military] salute / 경례를 받다 take [accept] the salute (of one's men); receive a salute (from) / 경례에 답하다 return [acknowledge] sb's salute
▶ 경례! (口令) Salute!
—**경례하다** salute (an officer); give [make] a salute (to); bow (to)
◆ 국기에 [장교에게] 경례하다 salute the national flag [an officer] / 차렷하고 경례하다 salute at attention
▶ 학생들은 교장 선생님께 경례했다 The students bowed to the principal.

경로 敬老 respect for the aged [the old]
■—당 a home for the aged —석 a seat for the aged; a priority [courtesy] seat —잔치 a feast [party] in deference to the aged —회 a respect-for-the aged association

경로 經路 〈길〉 a course; a route; a channel; 〈과정·순서〉 a process; a stage
◆ 비밀 경로를 거쳐 through secret channels / 같은 경로를 밟다 follow the same course / 다른 경로로 보내다 send (a thing) via another route
▶ 그는 그런 정보를 입수하는 특별 경로가 있는 것 같다 He seems to have a special channel to get that kind of information.
▶ 그는 그 정보의 입수 경로를 밝히기를 거절했다 He refused to show how [through what channel] he got that information.
■ 감염— the route of infection 외교— a diplomatic channel 입수— means of acquisition

경륜 經綸 government; administration; management; statecraft; statesmanship

경륜 競輪 〈자전거 경주〉 a bicycle [cycle] race; (美) a bike race
■—선수 a professional bicyclist; a cycle racer; a racing cyclist —장 a velodrome; a cyclodrome

경륜가 經綸家 a man of great administrative ability

경리 經理 〈일〉 accounting; accountant's business; 〈사람〉 an accounting clerk
▶ 그 여자의 경리 경력이 큰 도움이 되었다 Her accounting background came in quite useful.
▶ 그는 그 회사의 경리를 담당하고 있다 He is in charge of accounting [is an accountant] for the company.
■—과 [부] the accountants' [accounting] section [department, division] —관 〔軍〕 a fiscal officer —사무 accountant's [paymaster's] business —주임 a chief accountant —학교 a paymasters' school

경린 硬鱗 ganoid [gǽnɔid] scale ■—류(類) 〔魚〕 a ganoid (fish); a ganoidean

경마 a rein to lead a mounted horse with; a halter —**경마잡다** lead a horse with sb on it; serve as a groom ◆ 경마잡히다 have a groom lead one's horse by the halter

경마 競馬 horse racing; 〈한 경기〉 a horse race
◆ 현상 경마 a run for a stake / 경마를 보러 가다 go to the races; attend the races / 경마에 돈을 걸다 gamble [bet] on horse races; play the horses / 경마로 돈을 벌다 [잃다] make [lose] money on the turf [races] / 경마로 재산을 날리다 race one's fortune [property] away
▶ 그는 술은 안 하지만 경마는 한다 He doesn't drink but he plays the races.
■—광 a turf fan; a horse racing mania —기수 a jockey —말 a race horse; a racer; (총칭) a racing stable —장 a racecourse; a race track; the turf —팬 a track fan

경망 輕妄 rashness; flippancy; frivolousness; imprudence
—**경망하다 [스럽다]** light; flippant; frivolous; rash; thoughtless; indiscreet
◆ 경망하게 [스럽게] indiscreetly; rashly; without much thought [due reflection] / 경망한 짓을 하다 act rashly [imprudently]; commit a rash act / 경망스럽게 입을 놀리다 talk flippantly; use flippant language
▶ 그 여자는 경망한 데가 전혀 없다 There is nothing unstable [frivolous] about her.
▶ 그는 경망스럽게 입을 놀리지 않는다 He always weighs his words carefully.
▶ 남에 대해 경망스럽게 험담하지 마라 Don't say bad things about others thoughtlessly.

경매 競賣 auction; a sale at [(英) by] auction; an open [a public] sale
◆ 가구를 경매에 부치다 put the furniture up for auction / 경매에서 값을 매기다 bid a price at auction / 경매에서 중고 차를 사다 buy an old car at (an) auction
▶ 그의 재산은 대부분 경매에 부쳐졌다 Most of his fortune went under the (auctioneer's) hammer [was put up at auction].
▶ 그 사람의 집은 경매에 넘어갔다 His house was sold at auction.
—**경매하다** sell sth at [(英) by] auction; put up (an article) at auction; auction (off)
◆ 가구를 경매하다 sell the furniture at (an) auction; auction off the furniture
▶ 그 그림은 100만원에 경매되었다 The picture was sold at auction for one million won.
■ 강제— a forced [compulsory] sale by auction 부정— a mock auction ■—가격 a bid; a price offered by a bidder: 최저 경매 가격 a reserve price —공고 an auction notice —기일 the date of auction —대금 the amount of money obtained for (an article) sold by auction —수수료 an auctioneer's commission —시장 an auction market —업자 an auction dealer —인 an auctioneer —장 an auction room [house, hall] —중개인 an auction broker —처분 disposition by public sale [auction] —품 an article for sale at auction

경멸 輕蔑 contempt; scorn; disdain

解說 *contempt*는 비열·무가치하다고 생각되는 것에 대한 비난을 나타내는 뜻이 강한 말. *scorn*은 종종 강한 혐오감을 나타낸다.

♦경멸적인 웃음[표정] a scornful [contemptuous, disdainful] laugh [look] / 경멸적인 눈초리로 보다 eye *sb* with contempt; look at *sb* with scornful eyes; regard *sb* with contempt / 경멸을 나타내다 show *sb* contempt; be expressive of contempt / 경멸을 당하다 be held in [treated with] contempt; be despised / 경멸적으로 말하다 speak [talk] disrespectfully; speak in contempt
▶ 그 여학생의 행동은 급우들의 경멸의 대상이었다 Her behavior was an object of contempt of her classmates.
─경멸하다 despise; disdain; scorn; (口) look down *one's* nose at *sb* ♦경멸할 만한 despicable; contemptible; mean
▶ 그녀는 그의 태도를 경멸한다 She has contempt [scorn] for his manner. ⇒ She is contemptuous [scornful] of his manner.
▶ 가난하다고 해서 사람을 경멸해서는 안된다 You should not despise a man because he is poor.
▶ 그런 행동을 하면 경멸당한다 Such behavior will make you contemptible.
▶ 나는 겁쟁이라고 경멸당하는 것이 싫다 I hate to be looked down upon as a coward [for being cowardly].

경모 敬慕 adoration; love and respect
▶ 그 선생님은 여학생들에게 경모의 대상이다 The teacher is idolized by girl students.
─경모하다 adore; love and respect; hold *sb* in esteem and reverence
▶ 나는 지금도 내 초등학교 은사님을 경모한다 I greatly adore my grade school teacher even today.
▶ 마을 사람들은 그를 경모하고 있다 The village people have a great reverence and affection for him.

경묘하다 輕妙— light (and easy); witty; clever; smart; lambent 《wit》
♦경묘하게 lightly; wittily
▶ 문제가 경묘하다 It is written in a light and easy [witty] style.

경무 警務 police affairs ■—관 a superintendent general

경문 經文 〈불교의〉 the Buddhist scriptures; (the text of) a sutra; 〈가톨릭교의〉 prayers; 〈도교의〉 the Taoist scriptures [classics]
경문학 硬文學 metaphysical literature
경문학 輕文學 light literature
경물 景物 natural features [scenery] 《of the season》 ♦이른 봄의 경물 scenery in [features of] early spring ■—시(詩) a nature poem of the season; a seasonal poem
경미하다 輕微— slight; little; trifling; insignificant; negligible
♦경미한 문제 a trifling [trivial] matter / 경미한 부상 a slight injury
▶ 우리 측의 피해는 경미하다 The damage to us is minor.
▶ 농작물 피해는 경미했다 The crop suffered slight damage.

경박하다 輕薄— frivolous; flippant; fickle; shallow; light; flighty

解說 *frivolous*는 성질·생활 태도에 대해, *flippant*는 성질이나 일시적 언동 등에 대해, *shallow*는 인품이나 생각에 대해 쓴다.

♦경박한 노래 a frivolous song / 경박한 사람 a frivolous person / 경박한 생각 a shallow [shallow] idea / 경박한 행동 a flippant act
▶ 그녀는 경박하고 머리가 텅빈 여자다 She is a frivolous, empty-headed girl.
▶ 그 사람은 똑똑은 하지만 경박한 데가 있다 He is clever, but rather frivolous.

경백 敬白 Respectfully yours; Yours respectfully
경범죄 輕犯罪 a minor offense [crime]; a misdemeanor ■—처벌법 the Minor Offense Law
경변증 硬變症 〔醫〕 cirrhosis [səróusəs] ■—간— cirrhosis of the liver
경보 競步 a walk; a foot race; a (heel-and-toe) walking race; 〈장거리의〉 a walkathon
♦1만 미터 경보 the 10,000-meter walk (on the track [road]) ■—선수 a walker
경보 警報 a warning (signal); an alarm (signal)
♦조기 경보기(機) [레이더] an early-warning plane [radar] / 조기 경보망 an early-warning system / 경보를 발하다[내리다] give [raise] the alarm (for a fire); issue a 《flood, storm》 warning / 경보를 울리다 ring [sound] an alarm / 경보를 해제하다 cancel [call off] a 《storm》 warning; 〈공습의〉 give [sound] the all clear
▶ 그 지방 일대에는 지금 홍수 경보가 발효중이다 A general flood warning is now in operation all over the district.
▶ 기상청은 폭풍 경보를 해제했다 The Meteorological Agency called off the storm warning.
■경계— a preliminary alert; 〈공습의〉 an air defense alarm 기상— weather warning 태풍— a typhoon warning 폭풍— a storm warning [signal] 해일— a tidal wave warning 화재— a fire alarm —장치 an alarm device [system] —해제 all clear
경보기 警報器 an alarm (signal) ♦도난 경보기 a burglar alarm / 화재 경보기 a heat sensor
경복하다 敬服— admire; respect; think highly of
♦경복할 만한 admirable; estimable; worthy of admiration [esteem]
▶ 그의 냉정한 판단력에 우리는 모두 경복했다 We all bowed [took off our hats] to his cool judgment. ⇒ We had great respect [admiration] for his unprejudiced judgment.
경부 頸部 〔解〕 the neck; the cervix 《*pl*. ~es, -vices》; the cervical region
경부 京釜 Seoul and Pusan

경비

—고속도로 the Seoul-Pusan [Kyŏngbu] Expressway [Superhighway] —선 the Seoul-Pusan [Kyŏngbu] (Railroad) Line

경비 經費 〈비용〉 expense(s); cost(s); 〈지출〉 expenditure(s); (an) outlay
♦ 여행 경비 traveling expenses / 제(諸)경비 overhead expenses / 필요 경비 necessary expenses / 경비 관계로 for financial reasons / 경비를 줄이다 cut (down) [curtail] expenses; curtail [retrench] expenditures
▶ 그 사업에는 막대한 경비가 소요되었다 The project involved large expenditures.
▶ 그것은 경비가 너무 많이 들 염려가 있다 I fear it will cost too much [be too costly].
▶ 거기에 드는 경비는 내가 부담하겠다 I'll pay [cover] the expenses involved in it.
▶ 나도 경비를 분담하겠다 I'll share the expenses with you.
▶ 모든 경비를 뺀 순이익이 100만원이었다 The net profit after the deduction of all expenses was one million won.
—절감 cost reduction; curtailment of expenses; financial retrenchment

경비 警備 guard(ing); defense
♦ 경비를 강화하다 strengthen the defenses (of frontiers) / 경비를 서다 be on guard (duty) (at the gate) / 경비를 풀다 call off the guard
▶ 이 부근은 경비가 허술하다 The defense is weak around here.
▶ 국회의사당의 경비는 삼엄했다 The National Assembly building was strictly [very closely] guarded.
▶ 그들은 공항 주변의 경비를 강화했다 They tightened the security guard around the airport.
—경비하다 guard (a building against [from] robbers); keep [stand] guard (at the entrance, over a house) ♦ 해상을 경비하다 patrol [police] the sea
▶ 궁전은 경찰이 엄중히 경비하고 있었다 The palace was strictly guarded by the police [under heavy police guard].
▶ 무장 군인들이 도처에서 경비하고 있었다 Armed soldiers mounted guard [were on guard] at every place.
—실 a guardroom; a guardhouse —원[병] a guard —정 a guard ship; a patrol ship —회사 a security company

경비대 警備隊 a garrison; guards; a squad of patrolmen ■—국경— a border garrison; frontier guards 철도— railway guards 해안— coast guards

경사 傾斜 an inclination; an incline; 〈지붕 등의〉 a slant; 〈언덕 등의〉 a slope; 〈도로·철도의〉 grade; 〈배의〉 a list; 〈지층의〉 a dip
♦ 20도의 경사 an incline of twenty degrees / 가파른[완만한] 경사 a steep [gentle] slant [slope]
▶ 그 집 지붕은 경사가 가파르다 The roof of the house slopes sharply.
▶ 로켓은 적도에 대해 31도의 경사로 발사되었다 The rocket was launched with an inclination to the equator of 31 degrees.
—경사지다 incline; lean; slant; tilt; 〈도로가〉 slope; 〈배가〉 list; 〈지층이〉 dip
♦ 20도로 경사진 비탈 a slope with an inclination of 20 degrees / 경사진 inclined; slanting; sloping / 좌현(左舷)[우현]으로 경사지다 list to port [starboard] / 경사지게 하다 slope (the ground, a roof); give a slope to; slant; incline
▶ 눈이 미끄러져 내리도록 지붕이 가파르게 경사져 있다 The roof slants sharply to let the snow run off.
▶ 언덕은 기슭까지 완만히 경사져 있다 The hill slopes gently down to the foot.
▶ 그 땅은 바다 쪽으로[들판은 호반 쪽으로] 완만하게 경사져 있다 The land slopes [field descends] slowly toward the sea [shore of the lake].
■—각 an angle of inclination; a dip (angle) —계 an angle meter; 〔空〕 a clinometer —도 a gradient; (美) a grade —로(路) a slope way; a ramp —면 an inclined plane; a slope —생산방식 the priority production system —투시도 an angular perspective

경사 經絲 warp

경사 慶事 a happy [an auspicious] event [occasion]; a matter for congratulation
♦ 경사스러운 날 a happy day / 경사스럽다[롭다] happy (event); propitious (sign); auspicious (day) / 경사가 겹치다 have a series of matters for congratulation
▶ 그 집안에 경사가 났다 A matter for congratulation happened to the family.
▶ 경사가 겹쳤구나 It is like Christmas and New Year's Day have come together.
▶ 작년엔 우리 집에 경사가 많았다 There were many joyous events in my family last year.
▶ 경사스럽기 그지없습니다 Nothing is more auspicious than this.

경사 警査 a police sergeant (略 pol. sgt.)

경산부 經産婦 a multipara (pl. -rae)

경상 經常 ♦ 경상의 ordinary; regular; current; working
■—계정 a current account —비 current [ordinary] expenditures; 〈운영비〉 working expenses; operating [running] costs —세입 current [ordinary] revenue —세출 current [ordinary] expenditure [outlay] —손실 ordinary loss —수지 a current balance: 경상수지 흑자 current account surplus —예산 the regular [ordinary] budget —이익 ordinary profit

경상 輕傷 a slight injury [wound]
▶ 상처는 경상이었다 The wound was a slight one.
▶ 그는 교통사고로 경상을 입었다 He suffered a minor injury [got a slight injury, was slightly injured] in the traffic accident.
■—자 a slightly injured [wounded] person; (총칭) the slightly injured [wounded]

경색 梗塞 getting blocked [stopped up]; stoppage; blocking; tightness; 〔醫〕 infarction
♦ 경색 상태의 증권 시장 a stringent stock market / 경색 상태에 있다 be in a fix; (口) be in a (tight) box
■—금융— monetary stringency; tight-money situation [market]; tightness of money 심근

— myocardial [màiəkúːrdiəl] infarction

경서 經書 Chinese classics (of Confucianism); the Confucian classics

경석 輕石 pumice [pʌ́məs] ⇨ 속돌

경석고 硬石膏 〔鑛〕 division gypsum; anhydrite [ænháidrait] ■—플라스틱 division gypsum plastic

경선 經線 〔地〕 a meridian; a line of (terrestrial, geographical) longitude

경선 頸腺 〔解〕 the cervical gland

경성 硬性 〔物〕 hardness ♦ 경성의 hard ■—암(癌) a scirrhus [sírəs] 《pl. -rhi, ~ es》 —하감(下疳) chancre [ʃǽŋkər]

경성지색 傾城之色 a Helen of Troy ⇨ 경국(~之色)

경세 經世 governing; administration —**경세하다** administer (the affairs of state); govern 《a country》
■—가(家) a statesman; an administrator —제민(濟民) administrating the state to relieve the people's suffering —지재(之才) statesmanship; executive [administrative] ability; a talent for administration [government]

경세 警世 a warning to the world 《times, public》
♦ 경세의 서(書) an admonitory book —**경세하다** give warning to the world [public]
■—가(家) a prophet; a seer

경솔 輕率 flippancy; hastiness; rashness; 〈부주의〉 thoughtlessness; carelessness; imprudence; 〈무분별〉 indiscretion
—**경솔하다** flippant; rash; hasty; 〈부주의하다〉 thoughtless; careless; imprudent; indiscreet
♦ 경솔한 젊은이 a rash young man / 경솔한 판단 a hasty judgment / 경솔하게 lightly; rashly; hastily; 〈부주의하게〉 thoughtlessly; carelessly; imprudently; indiscreetly / 경솔한 짓을 하다 take a rash step; commit a rash act; commit an indiscretion; act thoughtlessly / 경솔하게 결론짓다[판단하다] make a hasty conclusion [judge hastily] / 경솔하게 믿다 be credulous enough to believe 《that》 / 경솔하게 언질을 주다 give a precipitate commitment / 중대한 문제를 경솔하게 처리하다 treat a serious subject with levity
▶ 그런 사람을 맹종하다니 나도 경솔했다 It was imprudent of me to follow such a man blindly.
▶ 경솔한 결정을 내리지 마라 Don't make a rash decision.
▶ 말을 경솔하게 하지 마라 Be careful about what you say. ⇌ Don't speak without thinking.
▶ 그는 남의 말을 경솔하게 믿는다 He believes too easily [readily] what others say.
▶ 그 문제는 경솔하게 취급해서는 안된다 The matter should not be taken lightly.
▶ 경솔하게 남의 험담을 하지 마라 Don't say bad things about others thoughtlessly.
▶ 그는 일을 경솔하게 처리하는 사람이 아니다 He does not treat anything lightly.

경쇠 磬 —〈아악기〉 a musical instruments made of stone or jade; 〈종〉 a handbell used by Buddhist monks

경수 硬水 〈셈물〉 hard water

경수 輕水 light water

경수로 輕水爐 a light water reactor

경승 景勝 beautiful [picturesque] scenery

경승지 景勝地 a scenic spot; a picturesque place; a place of scenic beauty ▶ 그곳은 경승지로 알려져 있다 The place is known [famous] for its beautiful scenery.

경시하다 輕視— think [make] little of; slight; neglect; belittle
♦ 문제를 경시하다 underrate the importance of a subject / 인명을 경시하다 make light of human life; attach little importance to human life / 동료들에게 경시당하다 be slighted [made light of, looked down on] by one's colleagues
▶ 그들은 그를 경시해서 회의에 부르지 않았다 They ignored [slighted] him and did not ask him to attend the conference.
▶ 소년에 지나지 않는다고 그를 경시해서는 안 된다 You mustn't look down upon him just because he is only a boy.
▶ 좋은 글을 쓰기 위해서는 한 개의 단어도 경시할 수 없다 We cannot disregard a single word if we want to write well.
▶ 그 문제는 오랫 동안 경시되었다 That matter has been treated lightly for a long time.

경식 硬式 rigid type ♦ 경식의 hard; rigid / 반경식의 semirigid 《airship》 ■—비행선 a rigid dirigible [dírɪdʒəbəl]

경식당 輕食堂 a lunchroom; a luncheonette; a cafeteria; (美) 〈카운터 식의〉 a snack bar; (英) snack counter

경식사 輕食事 a light meal; (美) a (light [quick]) lunch; a snack; a bite

경신 更新 renewal ⇨ 갱신(更新)

경신 敬神 piety; devoutness; fear of God; reverence toward God —**경신하다** revere [worship] God; be pious; be devout[diváut]

경신하다 輕信— believe hastily [credulously, lightly]; give (too) ready credence 《to》; be easily convinced ♦ 소문을 경신하다 believe rumors so easily

경심 傾心 〔物〕 metacenter

경악 驚愕 amazement; astonishment; fright; consternation; a shock
▶ 그분의 부음을 듣고 경악을 금치 못했습니다 It was with a great shock that I heard of his death.
—**경악하다** be surprised [shocked, amazed] 《at》
♦ 세상을 경악하게 한 사건 a world-shaking [most sensational] event
▶ 우리는 그 광경을 보고 경악했다 We were astonished [astounded] at the sight.
▶ 그 소식을 들었을 때의 그의 경악한 모습을 상상할 수 있겠느냐? Can you imagine how astonished [amazed] he was when he heard the news?
▶ 나는 경악하여 그를 쳐다보았다 I stared at him in surprise.

경애 敬愛 love [affection] and respect; reverent affection; veneration

♦(매우) 경애를 받다 be (much) loved and respected; be held in (great) reverence
—**경애하다** love and respect; hold *sb* in high esteem
▶우리는 모두 그분을 경애합니다 All of us love and respect [have love and respect for] him.

경어 敬語 a term of respect; an honorific (word [expression])

> 解說 영어에도 경어적인 표현은 있으나 한국어처럼 복잡하지는 않다. 겸손한 표현으로서는 ***my humble opinion [advice]*** (저의 보잘것 없는 의견[충고]), ***the likes of me*** (저 같은 것) 등의 말투가 있으나 일반적인 어법은 아니다. *Mr.*, *Mrs.*, *Ms.* 등 경칭은 존경어의 일종으로 생각해도 무방하다. 한편 공손한 표현에는 ***I am very much honored to meet you.***(뵙게 되어 영광으로 생각합니다)나 ***I am very much obliged for your help.***(도와 주셔서 대단히 감사합니다)등이 있다. 또 상대방에게 부탁이나 요청하는 경우에 쓰는 ***please***, 상대방에게 허가를 요구하는 경우에 쓰는 ***May [Can] I ...?*** 등도 공손한 표현이라고 할 수 있다.

▶윗사람과 이야기할 때는 경어를 써야 한다 You should use respectful terms [honorifics] in speaking to your seniors.

경역 境域 〈경계 지역〉a boundary; a border; 〈경계 안의 땅〉the precincts; the ground ♦신성한 경역 sacred precincts

경연 競演 a contest; a competitive performance
♦민요 경연 대회 a folk song concours [recital contest]
—**경연하다** compete 《with》; play opposite

경연극 輕演劇 a light theatrical performance

경염 競艶 —**경염하다** vie [compete] with one another in beauty
■—대회 a beauty contest

경영 經營 〈운영〉operation; working 《of a business》; running 《of a school》; 〈관리〉management; administration
♦과학적인 경영 scientific management / 경영의 재질 (have) a talent for management / 경영상의 애로 a bottleneck in management / 개인 경영의 under private management / 경영이 잘 되지 않아서 because of bad [poor, incompetent] management / 경영이 잘 되다[안 되다] be well [ill] managed
▶그는 매우 경영 능력이 있는 사람이다 He has much business [executive] ability.
▶그는 그 학교의 경영 일체를 담당하고 있다 He runs all the business end of the school.
▶아버지께서 그에게 공장 경영을 맡기셨다 My father left the operation [running] of the factory to him.
▶그의 뛰어난 경영으로 사업은 크게 번창했다 Under his excellent management the enterprise has achieved a great expansion.
—**경영하다** manage [run] 《a firm [business]》; operate 《a hotel [restaurant]》; keep 《a store [supermarket]》

> 解說 ***manage***와 ***run***은 경영 행위에 중점을 두는 말일 뿐, 그것만으로는 소주로서 회사를 경영하고 있는지 피고용인으로서 경영을 맡고 있는지를 알 수가 없다. 반면 ***own***은 소유자임을 명시하고 싶을 때 쓴다. ***run***은 상점이나 소규모의 회사 등에 대해 쓰이는 경향이 있다.

♦병원을 경영하다 run [operate] a hospital / 학교를 경영하다 keep [run] a school / 호텔을 경영하다 〈지배인이〉manage a hotel / 〈경영주가〉operate [run] a hotel / 회사를 경영하다 run a company / 클럽을 경영하다 manage a club
▶그 사람은 이 시내에서 슈퍼마켓을 경영한다 He keeps [runs] a supermarket in this town.
▶그것은 중국인이 경영하는 음식점이다 It is a Chinese-operated [Chinese-run] restaurant.
■다각— diversified [multilateral] management; multiple operation 집약— 〔經·農〕intension ■—공학 industrial engineering —권 the right of management —난 financial difficulty: 그 회사는 경영난에 빠져 있다 The firm is in financial difficulties [is finding it difficult to keep going]. —대학원 a (post)graduate school of business administration —방침 a business [management] policy; working principles —법 management —분석 financial analysis —비 operating [running] costs —수완 talent for management —전략 business strategy —진 the board of directors; the management —참가제도 participation in the management system —학 business administration —학과 the department of industrial administration —합리화 business rationalization; 〈효율화〉improving management efficiency —협의회제도 〈노사의〉labor-management council

경영 競泳 〈경기〉a swimming race [competition]; 〈종목〉a swimming [美口] swim] event
♦장거리 경영 a marathon [long-distance] swim
—**경영하다** swim a race 《with》; have a swim race 《with》
■—대회 a swim(ming) meet

경영자 經營者 a manager; an executive; 〈영업주〉a proprietor; (총칭) the management
♦경영자와 노동자(간의 분규) (disputes between) labor and management
▶그는 서투른 상점 경영자다 He is a bad store manager.
▶그 호텔은 경영자가 바뀌었다 The hotel is under new management.
■공동— a joint manager; a business partner
■—측 the management (of a company)

경옥 硬玉 〔鑛〕jadeite [dʒéidait]

경외성서 經外聖書 the Apocrypha (略 Apoc.)

경우 境遇 〈형편〉a situation; circumstances; 〈때〉a time; an occasion; a moment; 〈사례〉a case; an instance
♦그[이] 경우 in that [this] case / 대개의 경우 in most cases; in general / 만일 그렇게 되는 경우 should things come to such a pass / 지금의 경우 at this time [occasion]; as things stand [the case stands] (now) / 필요한 경우 in case

of need; when [where, if] (it is) necessary
▶ 그것은 경우 나름이다 That depends on circumstances.⇒ (口) That [It all] depends.
〈경우가〉 경우가 경우이니 만큼 느긋할 수가 없다 As it is a special case, we can't relax.
▶ 노력을 해도 보람이 없는 경우가 있다 There are cases where our efforts are not rewarded.
▶ 그것과 이것은 경우가 다르다 We must discriminate between the two cases.
〈경우에(는)〉 모든 경우에 on every occasion [all occasions] / …의 경우에(는) in case of…; in the case where…; on the occasion of…; in time of…/ 그런 경우에는 in such a case; in [under] such circumstances; on such an occasion / 내 경우에는 in my case / 어떤 경우에는 in some cases; sometimes / 위험한 경우에는 in time of danger; at a critical moment [in the moment of crisis] / 경우에 따라(서는) according to circumstances; depending on circumstances; as occasion arises [demands, requires]; as the case may be / 부득이한 경우에는 through force of circumstances
▶ 긴급한 경우에 한해 이 문을 사용해도 좋다 You can use this door [exit] only in an emergency.
▶ 경우에 따라서는 거짓말을 해도 좋을 때가 있다 Falsehood is excusable in certain circumstances.
▶ 이 규칙은 너의 경우에는 적용되지 않는다 This rule does not apply to your case.
▶ 화재의 경우에는 엘리베이터를 이용하지 마시오 In the event of fire, don't use the elevator.
▶ 비가 올 경우에는 연기하겠다 In case of rain [If it rains], we will put it off.
▶ 지금 같은 경우에는 그것을 도저히 할 수가 없다 In my present circumstances I cannot possibly afford to do it.
〈경우에나[(에)도]〉 어떤 경우에나 under all circumstances; on [at] all occasions; in any case; always / 여하한 경우에도 under [in] no circumstances; not (…) under [in] any circumstances; on no account; in no case
▶ 어떠한 경우에나 최선을 다해야 한다 We should do our best under [in] any circumstances.
▶ 정직한 사람이 손해보는 경우도 있다 There are instances where honesty does not pay.
경운기 耕耘機 a cultivator; a tiller ◆동력 경운기 a power cultivator
경운초지 耕耘草地 plowing grassland
경원하다 敬遠— keep sb [hold sb off] at a (respectful) distance; give sb a wide berth; 〈야구〉 walk [pass] (a batter) intentionally
▶ 그는 입바른 말을 잘해서 모두들 경원한다 He is so sharp-tongued that everyone keeps a respectful distance from him.
▶ 그녀는 나를 경원하는 것 같다 She seems to keep me at arm's length [keep away from me].
▶ 그는 모든 사람에게 경원당하고 있다 He is avoided by everybody.
경위 涇渭 right and [or] wrong; good and [or] bad [evil]; 〈판단·식별력〉 judgment; discernment; discrimination; good sense

◆경위야 어떻든 whether it is right or wrong; for good or bad [evil] / 경위를 따지다 discuss the rights and wrongs / 경위를 알다 know [can tell] right from wrong / 경위를 모르다 do not know what is right and what is wrong; be unreasonable / 경위에 어긋나다 be out of reason
▶ 그는 경위가 밝은 사람이다 He is a man of good sense [fair judgment]. ⇒ He knows what's what.
경위 經緯 1 〈경도와 위도〉 longitude and latitude
2 〈직물의 날과 씨〉 warp and woof [weft]
3 〈전말〉 details; particulars; circumstances
◆사건의 경위를 이야기하다 tell sb the circumstances of the case; tell the whole story [all details] of the affair
▶ 그가 파산하게 된 경위는 모르겠다 I don't know how he came to be bankrupt.
▶ 사건의 경위를 자세히 알고 싶다 I want to know all the details [the full particulars] of the case.
▶ 어떻게 된 일인지 그 경위를 내가 설명하겠다 I'll describe in detail how it came about.
▶ 경위로 보아 그 손해는 우리 쪽에서 부담하는 수밖에 없다 Under the circumstances we have no alternative but to bear the loss on our part.
━도 longitude and latitude ━선 lines of longitude and latitude ━의(儀) a theodolite [θiάdəlàit]; an altazimuth
경위 警衛 1 〈경찰 공무원의 직계〉 a Inspector; 〈국회의〉 an assembly guard
2 〈호위〉 guard; patrol; escort ━경위하다 guard; patrol; escort
경유 經由 ◆ 용산 경유 안양행 버스 a bus for Yongsan via Anyang / 익산 경유 군산행 열차 a train for Kunsan via Iksan / 시베리아 경유로 가다 go by way of [via] Siberia
▶ 그들은 배편으로 수에즈 운하 경유 나폴리로 갔다 They sailed to Naples by way of [via] the Suez Canal.
━경유하다 go via [through]; go by way of
▶ 우리는 앵커리지를 경유해서 파리로 비행했다 We flew to Paris by way of [via] Anchorage.
▶ 이 버스는 서울역을 경유해서 갑니까? Does this bus go by way of Seoul Station?
▶ 불교는 한국을 경유하여 일본에 전해졌다 Buddhism reached Japan by way of Korea.
경유 輕油 light oil; gas oil ━발동기 a light-oil motor
경유 鯨油 whale oil; train oil; whale fat
경음 硬音 【音聲】 a fortis ◆경음은 fortis; hard
경음 鯨飮 heavy [hard] drinking; swill; (口) swig ━경음하다 drink hard [deep]; drink like a fish; (口) swig; swill
경음악 輕音樂 light music
경의 更衣 changing one's dress ━경의하다 change one's dress
━일 ⇨ 탈의(~실)
경의 敬意 respect; honor; homage; regard; esteem
◆…에 대한 경의의 표시로 as a mark of respect for; out of respect for; in honor of / 경

경이

의를 표하다 pay [show] respect 《to, for》; do [pay, offer] homage 《to》
▶ 나는 그의 성실함[용기]에 경의를 표한다 I respect him for his integrity [courage].
▶ 먼저 전임자에게 경의를 표하고 싶습니다 First of all, I'd like to pay tribute to my predecessor.
▶ 연장자에게는 경의를 표해야 한다 You should show [pay] respect to your elders. ⇒ You should respect [be respectful to] your elders.

경이 驚異 (a) wonder; a marvel; a miracle; a prodigy

[解說] *wonder*는 멋지다고 마음 속으로 감탄하여 일어나는 놀라움을 의미한다. *marvel*은 인간의 힘으로는 생각할 수 없는 신비스런 것에 대한 놀라움으로, wonder보다 뜻이 강하다. *miracle*은 기적적인 것.

♦ 대자연의 경이 nature's miracles [wonders]; prodigies of nature / 경이의 눈으로 바라보다 stare in wonder 《at》; open *one's* eyes in astonishment [surprise] 《at》
▶ 인공 위성은 과학의 경이다 An artificial satellite is a scientific wonder.

경이적 驚異的 marvelous; miraculous; amazing

♦ 경이적(인) 사건 an eye-opening event; an eye-opener / 경이적인 진보를 이룩하다 make wonderful [marvelous] progress 《in》
▶ 그는 경주에서 경이적인 기록을 세웠다 He set [made, established] a sensational [wonderful, surprising] record in the race.
▶ 과학은 경이적인 발전을 이룩했다 Science has made marvelous [miraculous] progress.

경인 京仁 Seoul and Inch'ŏn
■ ―고속 도로 the Seoul-Inch'ŏn [Kyŏngin] Expressway ―선[전철] the Seoul-Inch'ŏn [Kyŏngin] (Railroad) Line [electric railway] ―지방 the Seoul-Inch'ŏn area; the Kyŏngin district(s)

경입자 輕粒子 〔物〕 a lepton

경작 耕作 cultivation; farming; tillage
♦ 경작에 알맞은 arable; tillable / 경작에 종사하다 be engaged in cultivation; cultivate the soil; follow the plow
―경작하다 cultivate; farm; till 《a field》; plow
▶ 그는 아침부터 밤늦게까지 땅을 경작했다 He cultivated the land from early in the morning until late at night.
▶ 이 밭은 경작하기 쉽다 This field plows well.
■ ―면적 the area under tillage [cultivation] ―물 farm [agricultural] products; farm crops ―자 a tiller (of the soil); a plowman; a peasant; a farmer ―지 farmland; plowland; arable [cultivated] land; land under cultivation ―지역 the area under tillage

경장 更張 reform; reformation ♦ 갑오경장 the Reformation of *Kabo*

경장 輕裝 light dress [attire, equipment] ▶ 나는 경장으로 등산을 갔다 I went mountain climbing lightly dressed [in a casual dress].
―경장하다 be lightly dressed [equipped]

경재 硬材 hardwood

경쟁 競爭 (a) competition; rivalry《▶ 전자는 목표를, 후자는 대항 의식을 강조함》; a contest; a race

♦ 선의의 경쟁 friendly rivalry / 시간과의 경쟁 a race against time / 대학 입시의 치열한 경쟁 (a) keen [severe, cutthroat] competition in college entrance examinations / 경쟁 없는 선거구 an unopposed constituency / 경쟁권 내에 있다 have a chance in the competition; be in the running / 경쟁권 밖으로 떨어지다 have no chance in the competition; be out of the running / (부당한) 경쟁을 규제[방지]하다 control [prevent] (an unfair) competition / 경쟁을 벌이다 enter into competition [rivalry] 《with》 / 경쟁을 유발하다 provoke competition [rivalry] / 경쟁에 이기다[지다] win [lose] a race; be victorious [defeated] in a competition / 경쟁에 참가하다 participate [take part] in a competition [contest]; become an entrant 《for》
▶ 지금은 경쟁의 시대라고 한다 It is said that this is an age of competition.
▶ 시장 선거는 경쟁이 치열했다 The mayoral election was sharply contested.
▶ 이 가게들 사이에 고객 유치 경쟁이 치열하다 There's keen competition between these shops to get customers.
▶ 나는 영어로는 그녀와 경쟁이 안 된다 I am no match for her in English.
▶ 그들은 호각의 경쟁을 하고 있다 They are in a close contest.
▶ 백화점들은 하계 특매 경쟁을 벌이고 있다 The department stores are rival(l)ing each other in the summer sales.
▶ 경쟁에서 최후에 승리하는 것은 노력가다 It is the hard workers that win finally.
―경쟁하다 compete 《with *sb* for *sth*》; rival 《*sb* in *sth*》; vie [cope] with 《*sb* in》
▶ 두 회사는 계약을 따내려고 서로 경쟁했다 Two companies competed [vied, were in competition] with each other for the contract.
▶ 경쟁하는 이상은 어떻게든 이기도록 해야 한다 Once you compete in anything, you must try to win.
▶ 이 가게는 가격으로는 저 가게와 경쟁할 수 없다 This store cannot rival that (one) in price.
■ ―가격― competitive pricing 가격 인하― a price cutting race; underselling competition: 회사들은 가격 인하 경쟁을 했다 The companies competed in price reduction. 과당― excessive competition 국내[대외]― domestic [foreign, overseas] competition 군비― an arms race 자유― free competition ■ ―가격 a competitive price ―국 a rival country; a competitor nation ―라운드 Competition Round 《略 CR》 ―매매 transaction by competition ―사회 a competitive society ―의식 a sense of rivalry; a competitive sense ―전략 competitive strategy ―회사 a rival company

경쟁력 競爭力 competitive power; (international) competitiveness
♦ 경쟁력이 있는 상품 competitive goods / 경

경쟁력이 부족하다 be insufficiently competitive / **경쟁력을 강화하다** strengthen [sharpen] the competitiveness 《of》 / **경쟁력을 약화시키다** weaken the competitive position 《in》
▶한국 상품은 국제 시장에서 충분히 경쟁력이 있다 Korean products are competitive enough in the international market.
▶인건비가 높아서 그 회사 제품은 세계 시장에서 경쟁력이 없다 Because of high labor costs, their products cannot compete on the world market.

경쟁률 競爭率 the competitive rate; the ratio of successful (applicants) to total applicants
▶경쟁률이 3대 1이다 There are three applicants for each opening.

경쟁상대 競爭相對 a rival; a competitor; a match 《for》
◆무역의 경쟁 상대 one's trade rival; one's competitor in trade
◆이 나라들은 값싼 노동력으로 한국에 힘든 경쟁상대가 되고 있다 These countries with their cheap labor are offering serious competition to Korea.
▶그는 교내에서는 경쟁 상대가 없었다 He couldn't find competition among his schoolmates.

경쟁시험 競爭試驗 a competitive examination
◆경쟁 시험에 합격하다 pass [succeed in passing] a competitive examination / 경쟁시험으로 선발하다 select by competitive examination

경쟁심 競爭心 a competitive spirit; a spirit of competition [emulation]
◆경쟁심을 북돋우다 arouse [stimulate] (a sense of) rivalry 《in sb》 / 경쟁심에 불타다 be incited by emulation
▶그는 경쟁심이 강하다 He is full of competitive spirit [has a strong sense of rivalry].

경쟁입찰 競爭入札 a competitive bid; a public tender ─**경쟁입찰하다** make a competitive bid 《for》

경쟁자 競爭者 a competitor; a contestant; 〈상대〉 a rival; 〈선거의〉 a rival candidate
◆사랑의 경쟁자 one's rival in love / 경쟁자를 물리치다 outdo (all) competitors
▶그 자리를 노리는 경쟁자가 많다 There are many candidates for the post.

경적 警笛 an alarm whistle; 〈기차 등의〉 a whistle; 〈자동차 등의〉 a (warning) horn; a honk; a hooter; 〈안개 경보의〉 a foghorn
◆경적을 울리다 whistle a warning; give an alarm whistle; 〈자동차의〉 sound [blow, honk] a horn; give a toot on the horn
▶경적 금지 〈게시〉 No horn [honking]!
─금지 구역 no-horn zone

경전 經典 sacred books; 〈기독교의〉 the Scriptures; the (Holy) Bible; 〈불교의〉 Buddhist scriptures; the Sutras; 〈이슬람교의〉 the Koran; the scriptures of Islam

경전기 輕電機 light electrical appliances
경전차 輕戰車 〔軍〕 a whippet tank
경정 更正 correction; revision; rectification
◆추가 경정 예산 a revised supplementary budget ─**경정하다** correct; rectify; revise
경정 警正 Superintendent
경정맥 頸靜脈 〔解〕 the jugular [dʒʌ́gjələr] (vein)

경제 經濟 **1** 〔經〕 economy
◆경제의 economic / 국내 경제의 회복 추세 the recovery trend of the domestic economy / 세계 경제의 중심지 the economic center of the world
▶나는 그 나라의 경제 사정에 훤하다 I am well acquainted with the economic conditions in that country.
▶저유가가 한국 경제의 고도 성장을 가능케 했다 Cheap oil made possible the Korean economy's high growth rate.
▶경제가 회복된 것 같다 The economy seems to have recovered.
▶가정 경제가 악화 일로에 있다 Our domestic economy is becoming worse and worse.
▶한국 경제는 고속 성장에서 안정 성장으로 전환했다 Korea's economy was switched from fast growth to stable expansion.
▶우리 나라의 경제를 안정시키기 위해서는 과감한 조치를 취하지 않으면 안 된다 We have to take drastic measures to stabilize our economy.
2 〈절약〉 thrift; frugality; economy
▶비용 경제만이 아니라 시간 경제도 생각하지 않으면 안 된다 We must consider economizing not only on money but also on time.
▶그의 아내는 경제 관념이 없다 His wife has no [lacks a] sense of economy.
■가정─ household [domestic] economy 계획 ─ planned economy 국가─ state economy 국내─ domestic economy 국민[농촌, 사회]─ national [rural, social] economy 국제─ international economy 자립─ self-supporting [viable] economy 자본주의─ capitalist economy 자유─ free economy 자유주의─ liberal economy 정치─ political economy 통제─ controlled economy ■─각료회의 an economic ministers' conference [meeting] ─개발 economic development ─개발 5개년 계획 a five-year plan [program] for economic development ─계 the economic world; economic circles; 〈재계〉 financial [business] circles ─계획 economic plan ─고문 an economic advisor ─공황 a financial panic ─과학심의회 the Economic Science Council ─관계 economic relations 《between two countries》 ─관료 economic bureaucrat ─교서[보고] 〈미국 대통령의〉 an Economic Report to Congress ─구조 an economic structure ─구조 조정 economic structural adjustment ─권(圈) an economic bloc ─기사(記事) financial news ─기자 a reporter of financial news ─단체 an economic [business] organization [group] ─대국 a great [major] economic power ─동맹 an economic league [union, alliance] ─동향 economic performance [trend] ─란(欄) the financial section [column(s)] ─력 economic strength; financial power ─마찰 economic friction ─면(面) the financial page ─문제 an economic problem [question]; 〈생

활살의〉 a matter of bread and butter —백서 an economic white paper —법칙 economic law [rule] —봉쇄 an economic blockade [sanction] —부흥 economic recovery —분석 economic analysis —사범 〈범죄〉 an economic offense; 〈범인〉 an offender of economic laws —사상 economic ideas [thought] —사절 the economic mission —사정[상태] the state of the economy; the economic [financial] conditions [situation] (of Korea); 〈개인의〉 the state of one's finances —사회 이사회 〈UN의〉 the Economic and Social Council (略 ECOSOC) —생활 economic life —성(性) economical efficiency: 경제성이 있는 commercially viable —속도 an economical speed —수역 (200-mile) economic waters 《declared by Korea》 —안정 economic stabilization —외교 economic diplomacy —원론 the principles of economics —원리 an economic principle —원조 an economic aid [assistance]: 그 나라는 우리 나라에 경제 원조를 요청했다 The country has asked for our economic aid. —위기 an economic [a financial] crisis —이론 economic theory [thesis] —인 an economic man: 전국 경제인 연합회 (略 FKI) —전(戰) an economic war; economic warfare [competition] —정의(正義) economic justice —정책 《the government's》 economic policy —제도 an economic system —조정관(실) (Office of) Economic Coordinator —조직 the economic fabric (of a country) —조치 economic measures —주의 economism —지리(학) economic geography —지표 economic indicators —통계 economic [financial] figures [statistics] —투쟁 economic strife —행위[활동] economic action [activities] —협력 economic cooperation —협력 개발 기구 the Organization for Economic Cooperation and Development (略 OECD)

경제가 經濟家 a person with a strong [keen] sense of economy; an economical [a thrifty, a frugal] person; 〈경제학자〉 an economist

경제기구 經濟機構 an economic setup [build-up] ♦경제 기구 개편 reorganization of the economic structure; shape-up of the economic setup

경제사 經濟史 an economic history; a history of (Korean) economy

경제사관 經濟史觀 historical materialism; the materialistic view of history

경제성장 經濟成長 growth of economy; economic growth
♦고도의 경제 성장 high level of (Korea's) economic growth
■—률 the rate of (Korea's) economic growth; the economic growth rate

경제적 經濟的 〈경제상의〉 economic; financial; 〈절약적〉 economical; thrifty; frugal
♦경제적 상호 의존 economic interdependence; mutual economic dependence / 경제적 이익[손실] economic gains [losses] / 경제적 자립[고립] economic independence [isolation] / 경제적인 차 an economical [economy] car / 경제적으로 economically; less expensively / 경제적인 이유로 for economic [financial] reasons / 시간을 경제적으로 쓰다 use one's time economically; be economical of one's time
▶난방에는 등유가 가장 경제적이다 Kerosine is the most economical [cheapest] for heating homes.
▶비싸도 질 좋은 물건이 결국은 경제적이다 In the long run good quality things [good articles] are economical, even if they are expensive. ⇌ An article of high price but of good quality pays in the long run.
▶그는 경제적인 이유로 학교를 그만두었다 He left school for economic reasons.

경제체제 經濟體制 an economic system
▶이것은 양국의 경제 체제의 차이에서 생긴 것이다 This is a result of the different economic systems of the two countries.

경제학 經濟學 economics; economic science
■계량— econometrics 근대— modern economics 마르크스— Marxian economics 미시[거시]— microeconomics [macroeconomics] 순수— pure economics ■—과 the department of economics —박사 〈학위〉 Doctor of Economics; 〈사람〉 a doctor of economics —원리 the principles of political economy —자 an economist; a political economist

경조 慶弔 congratulations and condolences
■—비 expenditure for gifts of congratulation and condolence —전보 a congratulatory or condolatory telegram

경조 競漕 a boat race; a regatta ♦경조용 보트 a race [racing] boat —경조하다 have a boat race; row a race

경조부박 輕佻浮薄 frivolity; levity; flippancy —경조부박하다 frivolous; flippant ▶그는 종종 경조부박한 행동을 한다 He often behaves flippantly.

경종 警鐘 an alarm bell; 〈경고〉 a warning
♦경종을 울리다 ring [sound] an alarm bell; warn
▶이것은 현대 젊은이들에 대한 경종이다 This is a warning to the young people of today.
▶이 사건은 마땅히 세인에게 경종이 되어야 한다 This incident should be a lesson for all of us.

경주 競走 a race; a run; 〈단거리의〉 a dash [sprint]
♦100 미터 경주 the 100-meter dash [race, run] / 경주에 나가다 run [compete] in a race; enter a race / 경주에 이기다[지다] win [lose] a race
▶우리는 200미터 경주에 출전한다 We are to take part in the 200-meter race [dash].
—경주하다 run [have] a race (against, with); race (against, with)
▶저 나무까지 경주하자 Let's race [have a race] to that tree.
■단거리— ⇨ 단거리(~경주) 자전거[자동차]— a cycle [an automobile] race 장[중]거리— a long-distance [middle distance] race 장애물— a hurdle [an obstacle] race ■—로(路) a track —마 a racehorse —용 자동차[자전거]

a racing car [bicycle]; a racer ―자 a runner; a racer; 〈단거리의〉a sprinter ―장 a track; a course;〈자전거 등의〉a velodrome ―종목 running events

경주하다 傾注― devote *oneself* (to); concentrate (on)
♦연구에 전력을 경주하다 devote *oneself* entirely to *one's* research; concentrate *one's* energies on [bend *one's* energies to] *one's* research
▶그는 이 사업에 전력을 경주했다 He gave all his energies to this undertaking.
▶김 신부는 그곳에서 전도 사업에 전력을 경주했다 Father Kim devoted all his energies to the missionary work there.

경중 輕重 (relative) importance [weight]
♦일[죄]의 경중 the gravity of the affairs [offense]/ 형(刑)의 경중 the relative gravity of penalties / 사물의 경중을 올바르게 인식하다 see things in their true proportions / 경중을 재다 weigh the importance [gravity] of a matter
▶일의 경중을 잘 살핀 후에 해라 Do it after weighing the importance of the matter carefully.
▶그는 일의 경중을 분별할 줄 모른다 He doesn't know what is important and what is not.

경증 輕症 a slight illness [attack]; a minor ailment; a mild case [form] (of typhoid)
♦경증의 폐렴에 걸리다 suffer a mild attack of pneumonia
▶다행히 그 사내아이의 소아마비는 경증이었다 Luckily the boy's attack of polio was not serious.
―환자 a mild [light] case (of cholera)

경지 耕地 cultivated field [area]; plowed land; plowland; 〈경작에 알맞은 땅〉arable land
■―면적 cultivated acreage [éikəridʒ]; acreage under cultivation ―정리 readjustment of arable land

경지 境地 1〈상태〉a state; a stage
♦…의 경지에 이르다 reach the state of…; attain the level of…
▶사람은 수행에 의해 무아의 경지에 이를 수 있다 One can reach [attain] the spiritual state of perfect selflessness by training.
2〈분야〉a ground; a field; a path
▶그녀는 화법에 새로운 경지를 개척했다 She cleared [broke] a new ground for the world of art.

경직 硬直 stiffness; rigidity ♦사후(死後) 경직 cadaveric rigidity; rigor mortis [rígər mɔ́:rtəs]
―경직하다 stiffen; get [become] stiff ♦경직된 사고 rigid [inflexible] ideas

경진 輕震 a weak [slight] earthquake

경진회 競進會 a competitive exhibition ⇨ 공진회(共進會)

경질 更迭 〈바꿈〉a change; a switch; a reshuffle;〈면직〉(a) dismissal ♦각료의 경질 a Ministerial change
▶머지않아 직원 경질이 있을 것이다 There will be a reshuffle of the staff in the near future.
―경질하다 change (the members); make a change (in the staff); switch (the commanders); reshuffle (the Cabinet)
♦3명의 장관을 경질하다 reshuffle three ministers / 수회 혐의로 경질되다 be dismissed from *one's* post for bribery
▶고위 공무원이 대폭 경질되었다 There was a sweeping change of top-ranking officials.
▶그 장관은 경질되었다 The Minister was dismissed.

경질 硬質 ♦경질의 hard; rigid;〈피부 등의〉 scleroid [sklíərɔid]
■―고무 hard rubber ―도기 hard earthenware; ironstone china ―비누 hard [insoluble] soap ―섬유 hard fiber ―유리 hard glass

경찰 警察〈경찰 조직〉the police;〈경찰관〉a policeman

解說 일반적으로 *police*가 경찰이라는 조직을 가리킬 때는 복수 취급한다. 보통은 the를 붙이지만 신문 영어에서는 관사 없이 쓰인다.

♦도 경찰국 a provincial police bureau / 서울 지방 경찰청 the Seoul Metropolitan Police Agency / 서울 지방 경찰청장 the Commissioner of the Seoul Metropolitan Police Agency / 경찰의 보호를 받다 place *oneself* under the protection of the police / 경찰의 수배를 받다 be wanted by the police / 전화로 경찰을 부르다 call [phone] the police / 경찰에 고발하다 complain to the police / 경찰에 넘기다[인도하다] deliver [hand over] *sb* to the police / 경찰에 신고하다[알리다] report to [inform] the police / 경찰에 연행하다[되다] take *sb* off [be taken] to a police station [to the police]/ 경찰에 출두하다 report *oneself* to the police / 경찰에 출입하다〈기자가〉work on the police beat (for a newspaper)
▶그는 경찰 신세를 진 적이 없다 He has no previous police record.
▶그에게 경찰의 손이 뻗쳤다 The police caught up with him.
▶그는 경찰의 감시를 받고 있다 The police are keeping an eye on him.
▶경찰이 그를 뒤쫓고 있다 The police are after him.
▶나는 경찰에 도난 신고를 했다 I informed the police of the theft.
▶범인은 경찰에 자수했다 The criminal gave himself up to the police.
▶홍수 이재민들은 경찰에 보호를 요청했다 The victims of the flood asked for police protection.
■―기동― the mobile police 비밀― the secret police 사법[경제]― the judicial [economic] police 수상(水上)― the water [harbor] police ―견 a police dog ―관할 구역 a police region [district] ―국가 a police state ―권 the police authority [power]: 경찰권을 발동[남용]하다 exercise [abuse] the police authority [power] ―기동순찰대 a mobile patrol police squad ―대학 the National Police College ―력 police force ―명령 a

police order —범 a police offense —법규 the police laws —병원 a police hospital —봉 a (policeman's) club; a baton; (美) a billy; (英) a (policeman's) truncheon —수첩 a policeman's pocketbook; a police officer's identification [ID] —의(醫) a police medical officer; 〈외 과의〉 a police surgeon —전문학교 National Police Academy —제도 a police system —처분 police dispositions —청 the National Police Administration —출입기자 a police reporter —학교 a police school [institute] —행위 police action —행정 police administration

경찰관 警察官 a policeman; a police officer; (英) a (police) constable; (俗) a cop; (총칭) the police

> 解說 *police officer*는 성별에 관계없이 사용된다. 특별히 성별을 구별할 경우에는 ***police-man*** (남자), ***policewoman*** (여자)이라고 한다. 경찰관에게 말을 걸 때는 "Excuse me, officer."라고 하면 된다.

♦여자 경찰관 a policewoman; a woman police officer / 경찰관 파출소 a police box; a police substation; a branch police station / 경찰관에게 미행당하다 have the police after ▶그는 경찰관 제복을 입고 있었다 I found him in police uniform. ▶사고 현장에 50명의 경찰관이 급파되었다 Fifty policemen were dispatched to the scene of the accident.

경찰대 警察隊 the constabulary [police] force ♦전투 경찰대 the combat police force unit; the combatant police unit / 전투 경찰대원 a combat policeman

경찰서 警察署 a police station; (美) a station house ♦경찰서로 연행되다 be taken [marched off, escorted] to a police station ■—장 the chief of a police station; a police chief; (美) 〈시의〉 a city marshal

경척 鯨尺 a cloth measure (=14.91 inches)

경천동지하다 驚天動地— startle the whole world; make the whole world wonder ♦경천동지할 사건 an earthshaking [a world-shaking] event; a most sensational [shocking] event

경첩 a hinge ♦경첩이 달린 문 a hinged door / 경첩을 달다 [떼다] hinge [unhinge] (a door) ▶그 문은 경첩이 빠져 있다 The door is off its hinges. ▶그 문은 경첩으로 여닫는다 The door opens [turns] on its hinges.

경청 傾聽 listening closely [attentively] —경청하다 listen (intently, attentively) to; give ear to; be all ears [attention] ▶그들은 연사의 말을 경청했다 They gave the speaker all their attention. ≒ They were attentive to the speaker. ▶그는 한 마디라도 놓칠세라 열심히 경청했다 He listened devouring every word. ▶그의 충고[연설]는 경청할 가치가 있다 His advice [speech] is worth listening to.

경추 頸椎 [解] the cervical [neck] vertebrae [vɜ́ːrtəbriː]

경축 慶祝 celebration; congratulation; felicitation ♦경축의 노래 a song of congratulation [celebration] / 경축 일색의 full of festive mood / 경축의 뜻을 나타내다 convey *one's* congratulations —경축하다 congratulate; felicitate; celebrate ♦경축할 만한 일 a happy event; an auspicious [a festive, a joyful] occasion / …을 경축하여 in celebration [honor] of...; congratulating... / 식을 거행하여 그 날을 경축하다 celebrate the day with appropriate ceremonies ▶한국에서는 정월 초하루를 성대하게 경축하는 풍습이 있다 It is customary in Korea to celebrate New Year's Day in a big way. ■—일 a flag [red-letter, festival] day; a national holiday; a gala [fete] day —행사 a celebration (event); festivities

경치 景致 〈전경〉 scenery; 〈개개의 풍경〉 a scene; a landscape (육지의); seascape (바다의); 〈전망〉 a view; a prospect

> 解說 *scenery*는 보거나 보지 않거나를 불문하고 실존하고 있는 한 지방 전체의 풍경을 의미한다. *scene*은 한 장소에서 보이는 데까지의 한 조망으로, 그 안에 사람과 그 활동이 포함되어 있는 경우가 많다: a street scene (거리의 풍경). *view*는 scenery 가운데 한 부분의 조망으로서 특히 멀리서 눈에 비치는 경치, *landscape*는 산·강·계곡·들·숲·해안 등을 포함하는 scenery 즉의 넓은 경색(景色), *prospect*는 원대한 조망을 의미한다.

♦밤 경치 a night scene / 봄 경치 spring scenery / 시골[해변]의 경치 rural [seaside] scenery / 아름다운 경치 beautiful [fine] scenery; a picturesque [charming, lovely] view / 경치 좋은 곳 a scenic place [spot]; a place of scenic beauty / 아름다운 경치에 넋을 잃다 be overpowered with the beauty of the scene ▶이 철도 연변에는 경치 좋은 곳이 많다 There are many scenic attractions [There is a lot of beautiful scenery] along this railroad line. ▶이 지방은 경치가 좋다 The scenery in this region is beautiful. ▶그곳은 경치가 좋기로 유명하다 The place is noted for its scenic beauty. ▶그 간판 때문에 경치가 보이지 않는다 The signboard blocks out the view. ▶이 호텔에서는 호수의 아름다운 경치를 즐길 수 있다 This hotel commands [has] a fine view of the lake.

경치다 〈벌받다〉 suffer torture [severe punishment]; be severely [heavily] punished; 〈혼나다〉 have a hard [rough] time of it; have [get] the worst of it; pay dearly (for) ♦경찰[선생님]한테 경치다 grilled [be sharply reproved] by a policeman [*one's* teacher (for)] ▶너 그런 짓하면[들키면] 경친다 If you do that [If you are found out], you will catch it hot.

▶ 예끼 이 경칠 놈아! God damn you!
▶ 경(을)칠 것 같으니! What's the hell! ⇒ Damn it!

경칭 敬稱 an honorific title; a courtesy title; a title of honor [courtesy]; a term of respect
♦ 경칭을 생략하다 cut out prefixes; omit honorifics / 경칭을 생략하고 부르다 call *sb's* name without (using his) title
▶ 경칭은 생략합니다 Honorifics are omitted.
▶ 그 사람들의 이름은 경칭을 붙여 불러라 Call them by their appropriate titles (of respect).

경쾌하다 輕快— light; nimble; airy; 〈리듬이〉 swinging
♦ 경쾌한 곡조 a lilting tune; a lilt / 경쾌한 동작 nimble movement / 경쾌한 리듬 a swinging rhythm / 경쾌한 멜로디 [음악] rhythmical melody [music] / 경쾌하게 lightly; nimbly; airily; cheerfully / 경쾌한 복장으로 in light clothes; lightly dressed / 발걸음도 경쾌하게 with light [springy] steps
▶ 그는 언제나 차림이 경쾌하다 He is always lightly dressed.
▶ 그는 경쾌하게 울타리를 뛰어넘었다 He nimbly jumped over the fence.

경탄 驚歎 wonder; admiration
—경탄하다 admire; wonder [marvel] 《at》; be struck with admiration [wonder]
♦ 경탄할 만한 marvelous; wonderful; admirable / 경탄하여 바라보다 look at *sb* in [with] wonder / 경탄케 하다 strike *sb* with wonder [admiration]
▶ 나는 대자연의 신비에 경탄했다 I was lost in wonder at the mysteries of great nature.
▶ 우리는 그의 심오한 지식에 경탄해 마지 않았다 His profound learning filled us with admiration [wonder].
▶ 그의 문학적 재능은 경탄할 만하다 His literary talent well deserves admiration.
▶ 이 약은 경탄할 만한 과학적인 발견이다 This medicine is a wonderful scientific discovery.
▶ 그는 그 어려운 문제를 풀어 모든 사람을 경탄케 했다 He solved the difficult problem to the wonder and admiration of all.
■ **—성(聲)** a cry of wonder; a sigh of admiration

경파 硬派 a hard-liner ⇨ 강경파

경편 輕便 convenience **—경편하다** convenient; handy; 〈가뿐하다〉 light ▶ 이 카메라는 경편해서 잘 팔린다 This camera sells well because it's easy to handle.
■ **—철도** a light [narrow-gauge] railway

경포 輕砲 a light gun

경품 景品 a premium; a bonus; a gift; 《美口》 a giveaway
♦ 경품부 대매출 a (grand) sale with gifts; a gift enterprise / 경품을 주다 offer premiums; (口) throw in
▶ 모든 상품에 경품을 붙였다 They put [set, placed] a premium on all the goods.
▶ 경품 증정 (광고) Customers offered premiums.
■ **—권** a gift coupon; a premium ticket

경풍 輕風 a light air [breeze]

경필 硬筆 a pen ⇨ 펜

경하 慶賀 congratulation; felicitation
—경하하다 congratulate 《*sb* on a matter》; offer *one's* congratulations 《to *sb* on his success》
▶ 시험에 합격하신 것을 진심으로 경하합니다 Allow me to offer you my hearty congratulations on your success in the examination.
▶ 귀교가 창립 100주년을 맞은 것은 진실로 경하할 일입니다 It is indeed a matter of congratulation that your school is celebrating the 100th anniversary of its foundation.

경하다 輕— 〈무게가〉 light; not heavy; 〈언행이〉 rash; imprudent; careless; flippant; frivolous; 〈사태 등이〉 slight; trivial; not serious; 〈중요도가〉 light; insignificant; unimportant

경합 競合 〈경쟁〉 rivalry; conflict; competition; contest; 〈연합작용〉 concurrence
♦ 치열한 경합 keen [hot, cutthroat] competition; a tight (election) race / 경합이 없는 선거구 an unopposed [uncontested] constituency
—경합하다 compete [contend] 《with *sb* for *sth*》; vie with each other 《for》; contest 《an election》; conflict; concur; 〈경매에서〉 bid against each other
▶ 국회의 의석 하나를 놓고 7명이 경합했다 Seven contested one seat in the National Assembly.
▶ 두 후보가 최후까지 경합했다 The two candidates were neck and neck until the last moment.
▶ 그 범행에는 두 가지 범죄가 경합되어 있다 The offense contravenes two laws.
■ **—과실(法)** concurrent negligence **—죄** concurrent offenses

경합금 輕合金 a light alloy

경향 京鄕 the capital and the country
♦ 경향 각지를 여행하다 travel around the country far and wide / 경향 각지에서 모여들다 come from every corner of the country

경향 傾向 〈추세〉 a tendency 《to, toward》; a trend; 〈성향·성벽〉 an inclination; a turn of mind; a disposition

| 解說 ***tendency***는 사물의 일반적·개별적 경향을, ***trend***는 오래 계속되고 있는 경향을, ***inclination***은 인간의 심적 경향을 말한다. |

♦ 물가 상승의 경향 the upward tendency [trend] of prices / 물가 하락의 경향 a drop in price trends / 현대 사상의 경향 the trend of modern thought / 급격한 인플레이션 경향 an acute inflationary trend / 최근의 입시 경향 a recent tendency [trend] in entrance examinations / 좋은 [나쁜] 경향 a good [bad] trend / …의 경향이 농후하다 show a marked trend 《toward》 / …의 경향이 있다 tend [have a tendency] to; 〈성향이〉 be disposed [inclined, apt, liable] 《to do》; have an inclination 《to do》 / 보수적 경향이 있다 tend [lean] toward conservatism; be rather conservative 《in *one's* view》 / 점차 …한 경향이 커져가다 there is a growing tendency that… / 여론의 전반적인 경향을 살피다 observe the general trend of public opinion

▶그는 우유부단한 경향이 있다 He is apt to be indecisive.
▶그녀는 과장해서 말하는[과음하는] 경향이 있다 She has a tendency to exaggerate things [drink too much].
▶그는 큰 소리로 말하는 경향이 있다 He tends to talk loud.
▶그는 게으른 경향이 있다 He is inclined to be lazy.
▶여성이 고등 교육을 추구하는 경향은 앞으로도 계속 커질 것이다 The growing tendency for women to pursue higher education will continue in the future.
▶물가는 매년 상승하는 경향을 보이고 있다 Prices show [develop] a tendency to rise every year. ⇌ Prices tend upward every year.
■—문학 tendency literature —소설[극] a tendency novel [play] —조사 a trend study

경험 經驗 (an) experience
♦교편을 잡은 경험 experience as a teacher [in teaching]/ 실무에서 얻은 경험 one's business experience / 잊을 수 없는[즐거운, 새로운, 쓰라린] 경험 an unforgettable [a pleasant, a new, a bitter] experience / 직접적인 경험 direct [firsthand, personal] experience / 첫 경험 one's first experience
▶그는 경험 삼아 그 일을 맡기로 했다 He decided to take on the job just for the experience of it.
〈경험이[은]〉 경험이 있는[없는] 사람 an experienced [inexperienced] person / 오랜 경험이 있는 의사 a doctor of long experience / 경험이 많다 have considerable [rich, wide] experience (in politics)/ 경험이 부족하다 have little experience (in); lack experience / 오랜 경험이 있다 have long experience (in)
▶나는 이런 일에는 경험이 없다 I have had no experience in [I am new to] this kind of work.
▶그 실패가 그에게 좋은 경험이 되었다 That failure was a good experience [lesson] for him.
▶이런 일에는 경험이 중요하다 Experience counts in this job.
▶경험은 가장 좋은 스승이다 Experience is the best teacher.
▶이런 경험은 처음이다 This is quite new to [quite a new experience for] me.
〈경험을〉 경험을 살리다 make good use of one's experience / 여러 가지 경험을 쌓다 accumulate various experiences / 경험을 얻다 gain [acquire] (new) experience (in); add to [increase, build up] one's experience / 호된[무서운] 경험을 하다 have a terrible experience
▶나는 해외 생활의 경험을 살릴 수 있는 직업을 갖고 싶다 I want to get a job in which I can put my experience abroad to good use.
〈경험에[으로]〉 경험에 입각한 소설 a novel based on experience / 경험으로 알다 know sth from (one's) [learn sth by] experience / 나의 경험으로는 from my own experience; My experience shows that...; in my experience
▶내 경험으로 미루어 볼 때 그 사람은 믿지 않는 게 좋다 Judging from my experience, you'd better not trust him.
—경험하다 experience; undergo; go [come] through; meet with 《adventures》
♦실제로[몸소] 경험하다 have a personal experience of / 여러 가지 일을 경험하다 pass [go] through varied experience
▶나는 외국에서 많은 곤란을 경험했다 I experienced [went through] many hardships abroad.
▶이런 더위는 여태 경험한 일이 없다 This is the hottest weather I (have) ever experienced.
▶실제로[직접] 경험해 보지 않고는 그것이 어떤 것인지 모를 것이다 If you don't pass through it yourself, you won't understand.
■사회— practical [worldly] experience 실무— business experience; experience in business —과학 empiric science —담 (tell) a story of one's (personal) experiences —론 empiricism; experientialism —론자 an empiricist; an experientialist —철학 empirical [experiential] philosophy

경험자 經驗者 an experienced person; a person with experience 《of living overseas》; (口) an old hand 《at》
▶경험자만이 그런 말을 할 수 있다 Only a person who has experienced [gone through] it can make such remarks.
▶경험자 구함 (광고) Wanted: experienced hands (in business).

경험적 經驗的 empirical; experiential ♦경험적 사실 empirical fact / 경험적 지식 empirical [experimental] knowledge

경혈 經穴 〔韓醫〕 spots on the body suitable for acupuncture

경호 警護 guard; escort; convoy
♦무장 경호 an armed guard / 군대의 경호하에 under convoy of troops / 경호 임무를 맡다 act as escort; be on guard
▶그는 경찰의 엄중한 경호를 받으며 식전에 참석했다 He attended the ceremony under heavy police guard.
—경호하다 guard; escort; convoy
▶많은 경찰들이 총리 공관을 경호하고 있다 Many policemen guard the Prime Minister's official residence.
■—대 a security guard —원 a bodyguard; a (security) guard : 대통령 경호원 a presidential guard; (美) a secret service man

경화 硬化 【굳어짐】〈물질의〉hardening; setting; induration; 〈의견·태도의〉 stiffening
—경화하다 stiffen; harden; become stiff [hard]
▶나이를 먹으면 동맥이 경화한다 The arteries harden with age.
▶그들은 갑자기 태도를 경화시켰다 They suddenly stiffened [toughened] their attitude.
■동맥— hardening of the arteries; 〔醫〕 arteriosclerosis 표면— 〔冶〕 casehardening ■—고무 ebonite; vulcanite —유(油) hardened oil —제(劑) a hardener; a hardening [setting] agent; cement —증 〔醫〕 sclerosis 《of the arteries》

경화 硬貨 a coin; hard money [currency, cash]; metallic currency; 〈총칭〉 coinage
경화기 輕火器 〔軍〕 light firearms [weapons]
경화학공업 輕化學工業 light chemical industry
경황 景況 an interesting situation
♦ 경황(이) 없다 be busy [preoccupied] for; one's mind is too much occupied (to think about other things) / 경황이 없는 틈을 타서 도망치다 make good one's escape in the confusion of the moment
▶ 그 아이는 노는 데 정신이 팔려 공부할 경황이 없다 The boy is too much absorbed in play to think of his study.
▶ 그 동안 경황이 없어서 찾아뵙지[편지도 올리지] 못했습니다 I have been too busy to call on you [so busy that I failed to write to you].
▶ 일 때문에 경황이 없어서 그 문제는 더 이상 생각해 보지 못했다 In the press of work I did not think much more about the problem.

곁 〈옆〉 the side; 〈부근〉 neighborhood; vicinity
♦ 곁의 nearby; neighboring / 곁에 in one's side; by (the side of); beside; 〈부근에〉 in the vicinity [neighborhood] 《of》; about [near] 《one's》 school; / 바로 곁에 near [close] by; close at hand / 부모 곁을 떠나다 leave one's parents [the parental roof] / 곁을 지나다 pass by 《sb, sth》 / 곁에 두다 keep (a thing) (close) at hand [at one's elbow] / 곁에 살다 live in the neighborhood / 곁에 서다 stand by the side of / 곁에 앉다 sit by sb; sit on [by] sb's side / 곁에 있다 be by sb; be at sb's side; be (near) at hand; be within one's reach / 곁에서 시중들다 wait [attend] on / 곁에 참견하다 butt in / 곁으로 다가가다 draw [come, go] near 《to sb》 / 아이를 곁으로 부르다 call a child to one's side / 곁으로 비켜서다 step aside
▶ 내 곁을 떠나지 마라 Don't leave my side.
▶ 바로 곁에 강이 흐르고 있다 Nearby flows a river.
▶ 그는 자기 아들을 곁에 두고 싶었다 He wanted to keep his son by his side.
▶ 내 곁에 꼭 붙어 있어라 Keep close to me.
▶ 나는 영원히 당신 곁에서 살고 싶습니다 I wish to live with you forever.
▶ 아이가 어머니 곁에서 자고 있었다 The child was sleeping by (the side of) [beside] his mother.
▶ 그것은 곁에서 보듯이 그렇게 쉽지는 않다 It's not so easy as it may seem to outsiders.
▶ 자네 정도는 그 사람 곁에도 못 간다 You are no match for him.
곁가지 a side branch; a lateral branch
곁노 ―櫓 sculls; sculling oars
―질 sculling
곁눈¹ 〔植〕 a lateral bud
곁눈² a side(long) glance
♦ 곁눈으로 보다 look with a sidelong glance 《at sb》; give sb a sidelong look; cast a side glance [look] 《at》; 〈흘겨보다〉 look askance 《at sb》
▶ 곁눈으로 보니까 그는 살금살금 도망치려 하고 있었다 Out of the corner of my eye I noticed that he was going away on tiptoe.
곁눈주다 〈눈짓하다〉 give a suggestion with a look; make a sign with a side glance; 〈추파를 던지다〉 give a wink (to); wink (at); make [cast] sheep's eyes 《at》
곁눈질 a side glance; a slant; 〈추파〉 an amorous glance
―곁눈질하다 cast a side(long) glance [look] 《at》; look askance 《at sb》; squint 《at》; 〈추파를 던지다〉 wink 《at》; ogle 《at》
▶ 그는 의자에 기대 앉아 지나가는 여자들을 곁눈질하고 있었다 He leaned back in his chairs, leering at the girls as they passed.
곁다리 〈딸린 것〉 a secondary thing; an appendage; 〈딸린 사람〉 a participator as an outsider
♦ 곁다리 끼다 participate as an outsider; join in a party as a special member / 곁다리 들다 say [remark] from the sidelines; put [poke, thrust] one's nose into
곁두리 〈샛밥〉 snacks for farmhands at work
곁들다 lend [give] a (helping) hand to; lend one's help to; aid; assist ♦ 일을 곁들어 주다 help sb in [with] his work / 곁들어 싸우다 take sb's part in a fight
곁들이다 1 〈다른 음식을 함께 담다〉 garnish (a dish with some vegetable); add (some vegetable) as a relish
♦ 케이크에 버찌를 곁들이다 garnish a cake with cherries / 감자 요리에 파슬리를 곁들이다 garnish boiled potatoes with parsley
2 〈겸하여 하다〉 do (things) at a time
▶ 그는 강연에 재미있는 일화를 곁들였다 He seasoned his lecture with amusing anecdotes.
▶ 그는 연설에 몸짓을 곁들였다 He accompanied his speech with gestures.
곁땀 sweat from the armpit ♦ 곁땀이 나다 sweat under the arm
곁땀내 the smell of the armpit ⇨ 암내 2
곁말 a periphrastic [an allusive] remark
곁매 blows in assistance ♦ 곁매질하다 deal blows at sb (to help the other in a fight) / 곁매를 맞다 be beaten by a third person
곁방 ―房 〈협실〉 a side chamber; a closet; 〈셋방〉 a rented room
곁방살이 ―房― living in a rented room ―곁방살이하다 live in a rented room
곁부축 a help; assistance ―곁부축하다 help sb by holding under his arm; support sb (by the armpit); 〈거들어 주다〉 lend one's help to; second (another's words)
곁상 ―床 a subsidiary dining table; a side table
곁쇠 a passkey; a master [skeleton] key
♦ 곁쇠질하다 unlock with a passkey
▶ 도둑이 곁쇠로 문을 따려고 했다 A thief tried to open the door with a skeleton key.
곁순 ―筍 lateral buds; extra sprouts [buds]
♦ 곁순 치기 nipping off extra sprouts
곁자리 a side seat; seats on either side
곁줄기 〔植〕 a side [lateral] stalk (of a vine)
곁집 a neighboring house; the next door house
곁채 an outhouse; an annex (to a main house); an attached house

계系 〔數〕 a corollary

계 戒・誡 1 〈규정〉 a command; an admonition 2 〔宗〕 〈계율〉 (Buddhist) commandments; religious precepts; discipline ♦계를 지키다[어기다] observe [break] the commandments

계係 〈부서〉 a (sub)section 《in an office》; 〈담당자〉 a clerk in charge ♦출납계〈부서〉 the cashier('s section); 〈사람〉 a cashier; a teller ■—장 the head of a section; a manager

계契 a fraternity; a (mutual) loan [benefit] club; a mutual assistance society; a mutual aid [financing] association
♦계를 조직하다 organize a fraternity; found a mutual financing association / 계를 타다 get one's share from a savings club / 계에 들다 join a loan club

계計 1 〈합계〉 the total; the sum
♦계를 내다 add up; find the total of
▶ 비용은 계 10만원이었다 The cost was one hundred thousand won in total [in all, all told].
2 〈계획〉 a plan; 〈계략〉 a stratagem ♦국가 백년지계 a permanent national policy
▶ 일년지계는 원단에 있다 The whole year's plans are made [We should make our plans for the year] on New Year's Day.

계階 a rank; a grade

-계 -系 1 〈계통〉 a system
♦신경계 the nervous system / 태양계 the solar system / 시어즈계 백화점 the Sears chain department store / 기독교계 학교 a mission(ary) [Christian] school
2 〈혈통〉 a family line; lineage; descent
♦한국계 미국인 a Korean-American; an American of Korean descent / 라틴계 국민 people of Latin origin [extraction]
▶ 나는 한국계입니다 I am of Korean descent.
3 〈당파〉 a faction; a party; a clique
♦공산계 신문 a Communist-influenced [Communist-inclined] paper / 민씨계 정치인 a politician of the Min faction / 보수계 후보자 a conservative candidate

-계 -屆 a notice; a report 《of absence》; a notification ⇨ 신고

-계 -界 a world; a community; 〈집단〉 circles 〔生〕 a kingdom; 〔地〕 a system; 〔物〕 a field
♦관계(官界) government circles; officialdom / 동물[식물, 광물]계 the animal [vegetable, mineral] kingdom / 미술계 the artistic community / 분수계(分水界) a watershed / 사교계 fashionable society; society circles / 실업계 business circles; the business world / 외교계 diplomatic circles / 정계 the political world

-계 -計 a meter; a gauge ♦속도계 a speedometer / 온도계 a thermometer / 우량계 a rain gauge

계가 計家 〈바둑〉 taking count of crosses [each territory]

계간 季刊 (a) quarterly publication ■—지 (誌) a quarterly; a quarterly magazine [journal]

계간 鷄姦 sodomy ⇨ 비역, 남색(男色)

계고 戒告 a warning; 〔法〕 notification ━━계하다 warn; give sb a warning; warn [caution] sb against sth ■—장 〔宗〕 a monition; 〈경고장〉 a written warning; a reminder

계곡 溪谷 a valley; a ravine; a gorge; 〈좁은〉 a glen; 〈깊은〉 a canyon; 〔詩〕 a dale

계관 桂冠 a crown of laurel; a laurel wreath ■—시인 a (poet) laureate

계관 鷄冠 a cock's crest ⇨ 볏¹

계관석 鷄冠石 〔鑛〕 realgar [riǽlgɑr]; sandarac [sǽndərǽk]

계관초 鷄冠草 a cockscomb =맨드라미

계교 計巧 a scheme; a trick; a plot; an artifice; a design ♦계교를 꾸미다 devise a scheme; plot; scheme / 계교를 부리다 play a trick 《on》

계궁역진하다 計窮力盡— come to the end of one's tether [wit and strength]; exhaust one's resources

계급 階級 1 〈지위의 등급〉 (a) rank; a grade; order (목사 등의)
♦군인 계급 military [naval] rank [grade] / 계급이 높은[낮은] 군인 a high-ranking [low-ranking] soldier / 계급이 높다[낮다] be high [low] in ranks / 계급이 강등되다 be degraded; be reduced to a lower grade [rank]; (美) be demoted / 계급이 오르다 be promoted; be raised in rank
▶ 대위는 소령보다 한 계급 아래다 The captain in the army is one grade lower than the major.
▶ 군대에는 여러 계급이 있다 In the army there are various ranks.
▶ 나는 그보다 계급이 위다 I rank above him. = I am higher in rank than he is.
2 〈신분〉 (a) class; estate; caste
♦계급 사회 a class society / 계급 없는 사회 a classless society / 계급 간의 대립[증오] class antagonism [hatred] / 모든 계급의 사람들 people of all classes [standings]; all classes / 계급이 다르다 belong to different classes / 계급을 철폐[타파]하다 abolish [break down] class distinctions
▶ 온갖 지위와 계급의 사람들이 그곳에 다 모였다 People of all ranks and classes gathered there.
▶ 그는 가장 교양있는 계급에 속한다 He belongs to the most cultured class.
■ 노동(자)— the working [laboring] class 무산[제4]— the proletariat [fourth estate] 부르주아— the bourgeoisie 사회— the social class; social scale [strata] 상류[중류, 하층]— the upper [middle, lower] class 양반— the yangban [genteel] caste [class] 유산[제3]— the propertied class [third estate] 유한— the leisure class 중간— the intermediate class 지배— the governing [ruling] class 지식— the intellectual [educated] class; the intellectuals; the intelligentsia; (口) the highbrows 착취— the exploiting class 특권— the privileged class ━—독재 class dictatorship ━문학 proletarian literature ━사회 a hierarchical society ━의식 class consciousness; a sense of class distinction: 계급 의식이 강하다 be strongly class-conscious ━장 a badge of

rank; an insignia; an ensign : 소령 계급장을 달아 주다 pin the insignia of a major (on the shoulder of sb) —정당 a class-based political party —제도 the class [caste] system —조직 the hierarchy; class organization —층 classes; social strata —타파 class leveling; demolishing the distinction of classes —투쟁 a class strife [struggle]

계기 計器 a meter; a gauge; an instrument
♦ 항해[공업]용 계기 a nautical [an industrial] instrument
■—반(盤) an instrument panel [board]; a gauge board; 〈자동차의〉 a dashboard —비행 an instrument flight [flying]; a blind flight [flying]; instrumental navigation : 계기 비행을 하다 fly [go] on instruments —착륙(장치) (an) instrument [(a) blind] landing (system) (略 ILS)

계기 契機 〈기회〉 a chance; an opportunity; an occasion; a turning point; [哲] a moment
♦ 이것을 계기로 with this (event) as a turning point [trigger, momentum, start] / 계기가 되다 serve as a momentum / 대화의 계기를 만들다 find an occasion to get into conversation (with)
▶ 원자탄 투하가 2차대전 종전의 계기가 되었다 The use of atomic bombs ended the Second World War.
▶ 그것은 그가 재기하는 계기가 될 것이다 It will be a good chance for him to regain his footing.
▶ 이것이 그 폭동의 계기가 되었다 This triggered (off) the riot.
▶ 그것을 계기로 나는 담배를 끊었다[재기했다] Taking [Availing myself of] that opportunity, I stopped smoking [made a comeback].
▶ 인사 이동을 계기로 그도 분발할 것이다 He will be inspired by the personnel transfer.
▶ 이것을 계기로 대화가 무르익어 갔다 This led to a familiar conversation.

계단 階段 (a flight of) stairs [steps]; a staircase; a stairway; 〈현관의〉 doorsteps; (美) a stoop

[解說] **stairs**는 집안의 위층으로 통하는 일련의 계단을 가리키며, **steps**는 집 밖에서부터 현관에 이르는 계단이나 탈것 등의 승강단을 가리킨다. 계단의 1단은 a step, a stair, 일련의 계단은 a flight of stairs [steps]다. **staircase, stairway**는 난간 등 계단에 부속되어 있는 부분까지 포함한 계단 전체를 가리킨다.

♦ 가파른 계단 a steep flight of stairs / 계단 위[아래]에서 at the top [bottom, foot] of the stairs / 계단을 오르다[내려가다] go up [down] the stairs; ascend [descend] the stairs; go upstairs [downstairs]
▶ 그는 한번에 두 계단씩 뛰어 올라갔다[내려갔다] He ran up [down] the stairs two at a time.
▶ 이 계단으로 올라가면 그의 사무실입니다 This staircase leads to his office.
▶ 나는 계단에서 굴러 떨어졌다 I tumbled [fell] down the steps [stairs].

■ 나선(식)— a spiral [corkscrew, winding] staircase; winding stairs 비상— an emergency staircase; a fire escape ■—교실 a lecture theater; an amphitheater; a classroom in tiers —식객석 seats arranged in tiers; tiers of seats; tiered seats —식농지 a terraced farm; terraced fields; a field in terraces

── 계단 ──

디딤판 코 nosing
디딤판 tread
층계참 landing
난간 handrail banister
수직널 riser
난간 동자 baluster
엄지 기둥 newel post

계도 系圖 genealogy; lineage; pedigree; a genealogical table [chart, tree]
♦ 김씨 집안의 계도를 거슬러 조사하다 trace back Mr. Kim's family line; trace back the pedigree of the Kims

계도 啓導 guidance; leading; instruction; teaching; enlightenment —계도하다 guide; lead; instruct; teach; enlighten

계란 鷄卵 an egg (⇨ 달걀) ■—덮밥 a bowl of rice topped with scrambled eggs —지(紙) 〔寫〕 albumenized paper —탕 egg soup

계략 計略 〈책략〉 a stratagem [strategy]; an artifice; a design [trick]; 〈계획〉 a plan; a scheme; 〈함정〉 a trap; a snare; 〈음모〉 a plot
♦ 그가 생각해낸 계략 a stratagem [scheme] he thought up / 계략이 뛰어난 사람 a resourceful [crafty] person / 계략을 꾸미다 make [work out] a plan; devise a stratagem [scheme] / 적의 계략을 뒤엎다 outwit [outmaneuver] the enemy; circumvent one's enemy by craft / 계략을 쓰다 adopt [use] a stratagem; resort to tricks / 계략에 걸려들다[빠지다] be entrapped; fall into sb's trap; step into snare set by sb / 계략에 빠뜨리다 entrap; ensnare
▶ 그것은 적의 계략일 것이다 That will be the enemy's trap [strategy].
▶ 우리의 계략이 들어맞았다 Our plan was a success.

▶ 그 계략이 실패했다[들통났다] The scheme failed. ⇒ The cat is out of the bag.
▶ 그가 성공한 이면에는 어떤 계략이 있음에 틀림없다 There must be some trick behind his success.
▶ 우리는 그의 계략을 간파했다 We saw through his trick [plot].
▶ 그는 무엇인가 계략을 꾸미고 있는 것 같다 I suspect he has some sort of trick up his sleeve.
▶ 나는 감쪽같이 그들의 계략에 걸려들었다 I fell into their trap completely.
▶ 네 계략에 말려들 내가 아니다 None of your games.

계량 計量 measuring; 〈무게의〉 weighing ─계량하다 measure; weigh ■─경제학 econometrics ─경제학자 an econometrician ─사(士) a certified [licensed] measurer ─스푼 a measuring spoon ─컵 a measuring cup; 〈칵테일용의〉 a jigger

계량기 計量器 a gauge [meter]; a weighing machine; a measurer ◆ 가스 계량기 a gasometer / 수도 계량기 a water gauge [meter]

계뢰 界雷 〔氣〕 a frontal thunderstorm

계루 繫累・係累 1 〈자식〉 encumbrances; 〈부양가족〉 dependents 2 〈연루〉 involvement; implication; complicity

계류 溪流 a mountain stream

계류 繫留 1 〈매어 놓음〉 mooring; (a) moorage ◆ 계류를 풀다 cast off the moorings ─계류하다 moor ⟨a boat to a buoy⟩; take up moorings ⟨at⟩
◆ 애드벌룬을 옥상에 계류하다 moor an advertising balloon to the top of a building
▶ 보트가 부두에 계류되어 있다 The boat is moored at the pier. ⇒ The boat is berthed at its [her] moorings.
2 〈미해결〉 ◆ 계류 중인 pending; outstanding; unsolved; unresolved; unsettled
▶ 그 사건은 아직도 법원에 계류 중이다 The case is still pending in court.
■─기구 a captive balloon; a kite balloon ─기뢰 a moored mine ─부표 a mooring buoy ─삭(索) a mooring cable; an anchoring rope; a bridle ─선(船) a moored [laid-up] vessel; a vessel on the berth ─장 moorings; a moorage; a berthage ─주(柱) a mooring post; an anchorage post ─탑 a mooring mast [tower]; 비행선을 계류탑에 매어두다 moor a dirigible to a mast

계륵 鷄肋 〈닭의 갈비뼈〉 chicken's ribs; (비유) something that *one* hesitates to give up even though it is of little interest

계리사 計理士 a chartered accountant ⇨ 공인 (~회계사)

계면 界面 the interface ⟨between two liquids⟩
■─장력(張力) 〔物〕 interfacial [surface, phase, boundary] tension ─화학 surface chemistry ─활성제 〔化〕 a surface-active agent; surfactant

계명 戒名 〔佛敎〕 〈생전의〉 a Buddhist name; 〈사후의〉 a posthumous Buddhist name

계명 戒命・誡命 religious precepts; commandments; discipline ■─십─ 〈모세의〉 the Ten Commandments; the Decalogue

계명 階名 〔樂〕 〈음계 이름〉 syllable names ■─창법 solmization

계명 鷄鳴 〈닭울음〉 the crowing of a cock; cockcrow(ing) (at dawn); (美) roostercrowing ◆ 계명에 일어나다 rise at cockcrow

계모 繼母 a stepmother

계몽 啓蒙 enlightenment; illumination ◆ 계몽적인 enlightening; illuminating
─계몽하다 enlighten; educate
◆ 무지한 사람들을[민중]을 계몽하다 enlighten the ignorant [public]
▶ 그들은 그 책으로 크게 계몽되었다 They were much enlightened by the book.
■─시대 the period [age] of enlightenment ─대(隊) an enlightenment squad ─문학 literature of enlightenment ─사상[사조, 철학] philosophy of enlightenment ─사상가 〈18세기의〉 an Enlightenment thinker ─주의 illuminism

계몽운동 啓蒙運動 a campaign for enlightenment; an enlightenment [edification, educational] movement [campaign]; 〈18세기 유럽의〉 the Enlightenment
◆ 국민 계몽운동 a (national) mass-education drive [campaign] / 농촌 계몽운동을 벌이다 launch a rural enlightenment drive

계발 啓發 enlightenment; edification; education; development ─계발하다 enlighten; edify; develop; illuminate; irradiate ⟨the mind⟩
◆ 지능을 계발하다 improve [cultivate] *one's* mind; develop *one's* intellectual [mental] faculties
▶ 학생들은 그의 강의를 듣고 크게 계발되었다 The students were greatly enlightened by his lecture.
▶ 나는 그와 교제하여 많이 계발되었다 I have learned a great deal by associating with him.
■─자 a developer ─적교육 developmental education

계보 系譜 (a) genealogy[dʒìːniːǽlədʒi]; (a) pedigree; lineage[líniidʒ]; a genealogical record [table]
◆ 한국 문학의 계보 genealogy of Korean literature / 계보를 조사하다 trace *sb's* genealogy [pedigree, ancestry] back to ⟨his⟩ ancestors; genealogize
▶ 그는 16세기까지 거슬러 자기의 계보를 더듬었다 He traced his genealogy [roots] back to the sixteenth century.
■─학 genealogy ─학자 a genealogist

계보 季報 a quarterly report [bulletin]

계부 繼父 a stepfather

계분 鷄糞 fowl droppings; droppings of fowls

계사 繫辭 〔論・文法〕 a copula; a copulative (verb)

계사 繼嗣 〈양자를 들임〉 adopting an heir; 〈양자〉 an adopted heir

계사 鷄舍 a coop ⇨ 닭장

계삭 繫索 〔海〕 a lasher; moorings; mooring ropes ■─이물[고물]─ a head [stern] fast

계산 計算 calculation; figures; computation; reckoning; counting; accounts; 〈고려〉 consideration

|解說| **calculation**이 계산이라는 뜻의 가장 일반적인 말. **figures**는 초보적인 가감승제에, **computation**은 전자계산기로 하는 계산 등 규모가 큰 계산을 의미한다.

♦ 내 계산으로는 in my reckoning / 계산이 빠르다[늦다, 능숙하다, 서투르다] be quick [slow, good, poor] at figures [accounts] / 계산을 맞추어 보다 check accounts / 계산을 잘못하다 miscalculate; get *one's* sums wrong; make a mistake in (*one's*) calculation(s) / 계산에 넣다 take (a thing) into account [consideration] / 계산에 넣지 않다 do not take (a thing) into account; leave (a thing) out of *one's* reckoning
▶ 계산이 맞지 않는다 These numbers don't add up. ⇒ The accounts don't tally.
▶ 계산이 얼마죠? How much (is my bill)? ⇒ Bill [(美) Check], please.
▶ 계산은 내 앞으로 달아 놓으세요 Charge it [Put it down] to my credit [account].
▶ 그녀의 역할을 계산에 넣지 않으면 안 된다 We must take her role into consideration.
▶ 우리는 그가 온다는 것을 계산에 넣지 않았다 We did not take their coming into account [consideration].
—**계산하다** calculate; compute; count; 〈합계하다〉 figure [add, sum] up; 〈견적하다〉 estimate ♦ 계산할 수 없는 incomputable; incalculable / 손익을 계산하다 make a calculation of profits and losses / 이자를 계산하다 compute interest
▶ 책상과 의자의 수를 계산해 주십시오 Please count the desks and chairs.
▶ 운임은 거리에 따라 계산된다 Freight rates are charged by distance.
■ 원가— cost accounting ■ —대 a counter; 〈슈퍼마켓의〉 a checkout counter —법 a system of measuring [calculation] —자 (數) a slide rule; (美俗) a slipstick —(조견)표 a (ready) reckoner; a calculating [numerical] table; a table book

계 산 기 計算器 a calculating [counting] machine; a calculator; a computer
♦ 계산기처럼 정확히 (analyze the facts) with computerlike precision
■ 고정프로그램— a fixed program computer 동기(同期)[비(非)동기]— a synchronous [an asynchronous] computer 디지털[계수형]— a digital computer 복합[하이브리드]— a hybrid computer 아날로그[상사형]— an analog computer 자동기록— a comptograph 전자— an electronic computer 탁상전자— an electronic desk(top) calculator ■ —산업 the computing industry —회사 a computer company

계산서 計算書 a statement of accounts; an account (of charges); an account statement; 〈청구서〉 a bill; (美) a check ▶ 계산서를 갖다 주시오 Fetch [Get] me the bill.

계산착오 計算錯誤 miscalculation; an error [a mistake] in calculation
♦ 계산 착오로 인한 전쟁 a war by miscalculation / 계산 착오를 범하다 calculate wrongly; miscalculate; make an error in calculation

계상하다 計上— 〈셈하다〉 sum [add] up; 〈할당하다〉 appropriate (a sum of money for some purpose)
♦ 내년도 예산에 계상하다 appropriate [include] (one hundred million won) in the budget for the coming fiscal year / 체육관 건설비로 10억원을 계상하다 appropriate one billion won for the building of the gymnasium / 추가 예산에 계상되다 be earmarked for the supplementary budget

계선 繫船 mooring; laying up; 〈매어 둔 배〉 a moored ship [boat]; a boat [ship] moored (to a buoy, at a pier) —**계선하다** moor (a ship to a dock); tie [lay] up; berth
■ —거(渠) a wet dock —구(具) moorings —료 quayage; moorage; mooring charges; a mooring fee —번호 a berth number —소 moorings; a moorage; a quayside —주(柱) a mooring post

계속 繫屬・係屬 〈法〉 pendency ♦ 소송 계속중 during the pendency of action; during litigation

계속 繼續 (a) continuation; continuance; succession; 〈계약 등의 갱신〉 (a) renewal

|解說| **continuation**은 보통 행동의 계속 또는 재개를 의미하며 continuance와 같은 뜻으로도 쓰인다: the continuation of broadcasting 방송의 속행. **continuance**는 상태의 지속을 의미한다: a continuance of fine weather 계속되는 맑은 날씨.

♦ 10개년 계속 사업 an undertaking extending over ten years; a ten-year program / 계속적(인) 〈끊임없는〉 continuous; uninterrupted; 〈반복적인〉 continual / 계속적으로 〈잇따라〉 in (rapid) succession; successively; one after another; 〈끊임없이〉 continuously; continually; without stopping; uninterruptedly / 빠른 걸음으로 계속 걷다 keep walking at a rapid pace / 계속 머물다 stay on / 계속 서 있다 keep standing; stay on *one's* feet / 계속 심의하다 make a continued debate (on); 〈법안을〉 carry a bill over to the next (Assembly) session / 효력을 계속 가지다 continue in effect
▶ 다음 호에 계속 To be continued.
▶ 뒷면에 계속 Over. ⇒ P.T.O.
▶ 20페이지에 계속 Continued on page 20.
▶ 앞[15]페이지에서 계속 Continued from the previous page [from page 15].
▶ 전람회는 11월 20일까지 계속 열린다 The exhibition remains open until Nov. 20.
▶ 나는 그 일에 대해 계속 생각했다 I kept thinking about it.
▶ 비가 3일간 계속 내렸다 It kept on raining for three days. ⇒ It rained for three consecutive days.
—**계속하다** continue (to do, doing); go on (with, doing); keep up

|解說| **continue**는 쉬지 않고 계속한다는 뜻과 중단했다가 다시 시작한다는 두 가지 뜻이 있다. 둘 다 다음에 doing이나 to do가 올 수 있다. **go on**은 쉬지 않고 계속한다는 뜻으로 쓰

일 때는 doing이나 with + 명사가 뒤따르고, 계속해서 새로운 일[화제]로 이어진다는 뜻으로 쓰일 때는 to do나 with + 명사가 뒤따른다. **keep (on)**은 뒤에 doing이 붙어「쉬지 않고 계속 …하다」또는「되풀이하여 계속 …하다」란 뜻을 나타낸다. 흔히 뒤에 on이 붙으면 계속의 뜻이 되어 집요함을 암시한다.

♦ 계속되는 가뭄[장마, 추위] a (long) spell of dry [rainy, cold] weather / 계속되는 불황 a continuous [lasting] recession / 네 번 계속해서 four times in succession [in a row, running]/ 닷새 동안 계속해서 for five days running; for five consecutive days / 며칠이나 계속해서 for days on end / 구독을 계속하다 renew one's subscription / 노력을 계속하다 follow up on one's effort(s) ((to do)) / 이야기를 계속하다 go on talking; keep up a conversation / 일을 계속하다 proceed [go on] with one's work / 학교를 계속하다 continue at school / 10월까지 계속되다 last until [into] October

▶ 내게 신경 쓰지 말고 일이나 계속하세요 Please don't let me interrupt your work.
▶ 그녀는 이야기를 계속했다 She proceeded [went on] with her story.
▶ 우리는 자동차 여행을 계속했다 We went on a car.
▶ 그는 쉬지 않고 일을 계속했다 He went [kept] on working without taking a rest.
▶ 그는 번역 일을 계속했다 He continued at the work of translation.
▶ 휴식 후 우리는 다시 회의를 계속했다 We resumed the meeting after a recess.
▶ 한 달 동안 쉰 다음에 일을 계속하고 싶다 After a month's rest, I want to return [go back] to work.
▶ 그는 학업을 계속하기로 결심했다 He decided to continue [stay in] school.
▶ 그 아이는 며칠 동안 계속해서 공부했다 The boy studied for days on end [running].
▶ 나는 사흘 밤을 계속해서 똑같은 이상한 꿈을 꾸었다 I had the same incredible dream for three nights running.
▶ 그 챔피언은 열 번을 계속해서 이겼다 The champion won ten successive games.
▶ 이 영화는 3개월 동안 계속해서 상영되었다 This film ran for three months [had a three-month run].
▶ 나는 현재의 일을 계속해서 하겠다 I will go on with my present work.
▶ 그는 무슨 일을 시켜도 오래 계속하지 못한다 He can stick to nothing.
▶ 이 이야기는 123페이지에 계속됩니다 This story is continued on page 123.
▶ 토의는 언제까지 계속됩니까? How long will the discussion continue [last]?
▶ 전투는 며칠을 두고 계속되었다 The battle continued for days.
▶ 그 사람의 집안에 최근 불운이 계속되었다 Recently he has had a run of bad luck in his family.
■ —기간 a period of duration —범 a continuing crime —비 a continuing expenditure —비행 duration of flight; a nonstop flight —사업 a continued program —상(相) 〔文法〕 the durative aspect —상영물 〔映〕 a holdover

계수 季嫂 one's younger brother's wife; a sister-in-law

계수 係數 〔數〕 a coefficient; 〔物〕 a modulus ((pl. -li)); a factor ♦ x의 계수 the coefficient of x ▶y의 계수를 2라고 하자 Let 2 be the coefficient of y.
■ 노동[자본]— a labor [capital] coefficient 마찰— a coefficient of friction 미분— a differential coefficient 엥겔— Engel's coefficient 연결— a coefficient of coupling 증발— a factor of evaporation 탄성— a modulus of elasticity 팽창[수축]— a coefficient of expansion [contraction] 흡수— a coefficient of absorption; the absorption coefficient ■—현상 factorial development —회로 a counter [counting] circuit

계수 計數 〈계산〉 calculation; computation; counting; 〈숫값〉 figures
▶ 그녀는 계수에 밝다 She is good at figures.
▶ 그의 이론은 계수적으로도 증명된다 His theory can also be proved mathematically.
■ —기 a calculating [counting] machine; a comptometer; an arithmometer —형전자계산기 a digital computer —회로 a scaling circuit

계수관 計數管 〔物〕 a counter
■ 가이거— a Geiger counter

계수나무 桂樹— 〔植〕 a cinnamon [cassia] tree; (비유) 〈달 속의〉 the great laurel tree in the moon

계수법 繼受法 〔法〕 an adopted law

계승 階乘 〔數〕 a factorial ♦ r의 계승 factorial r; r factorial; the factorial of r
—식 a factorial expression

계승 繼承 succession; accession; 〔法〕 inheritance
♦ 왕위 계승(권) the succession to the throne / 스페인 왕위 계승 전쟁 the Spanish Succession War
—계승하다 succeed to ((the throne)); inherit ((the estate)); take over ((the assets))
♦ 위대한 전통을 계승하다 uphold [cherish] the great traditions ((of)) / 채권 채무를 계승하다 take over [succeed to] the assets and meet the liabilities / 대대로 계승되다 be succeeded from generation to generation
▶ 그는 아버지의 작위를 계승했다 He succeeded to his father's title.
▶ 아버지가 죽자 엘리자베스 2세가 왕위를 계승했다 Upon her father's death, Elizabeth II succeeded to the throne.
▶ 우리는 많은 문화적 유산을 계승하고 있다 We have inherited various cultural legacies.
■ —사채(社債) assumed bonds —자 a successor ((to the throne)); an heir ((of liberty))

계시 an apprentice ⇨ 견습, 도제(徒弟)

계시 計時 timing; clocking —계시하다 record the time; check time; clock ((the time required accurately))
■ —기 a timer; a timing machine —원 a timer; a timekeeper

계시 啓示 〔宗〕 revelation

♦신의 계시 a revelation of God / 신의 계시로 쓴 책 writings inspired by God / 계시적인 revelatory / 계시를 받다 receive a divine revelation
—계시하다 reveal
■—문학 apocalyptic literature; apocalypses
—종교 a revealed religion

계시다 be; stay; be located
▶ 여기 계십시오 Stay here, please.
▶ 잠깐만 계시오 Please wait a minute.
▶ 아버지 계시냐 ? Is your father in?
▶ 뉴욕에는 얼마나 계셨습니까 ? How long have you been in New York?

계시록 啓示錄 〔聖〕 the Book of Revelation; the Apocalypse ▶요한— (the Book of) Revelations of St. John the Divine (略 Rev.)

계씨 季氏 your esteemed younger brother

계약 契約 a contract; an agreement; an engagement; a covenant; 〔法〕 a bond; 〈매매의〉 a bargain [deal]; 〈임대차의〉 a lease

解說 *contract*가 가장 일반적인 말로서 개인·단체·기업·국가간의 여러 가지 계약에 쓰인다. *agreement*는 폭넓게 쓸 수 있으나 법적 구속력이 없으므로 같은 계약 같은 데는 쓰이지 않는다. *bargain*은 거래[매매] 계약을 가리키고, *deal*은 구어로서 가벼운 의미의 계약·약속을 가리킨다.

♦…의 공급 계약 a contract for a supply of… / 법률상 유효한 계약 a legally binding contract / 사회 계약설 the theory of social contract / 계약대로 according to the contract; as contracted; as per contract
〈계약의〉 계약의 만료[종료] termination [expiration] of a contract / 계약(기간)의 연장 extension of a contract / 계약의 이행 performance [fulfilment] of a contract
▶ 본 계약의 유효 기간은 3년으로[12월 31일까지로] 한다 This contract shall remain in force for a period of three years [until December 31].
〈계약은〉이 계약은 3년간 유효하다 This contract is good for three years.
▶그 계약은 무효다 The contract is invalid [in null and void].
〈계약을〉 계약을 위반하다 violate a contract / 계약을 이행하다 carry out [fulfil, fill up, perform] a contract / 계약을 취소[해제]하다 cancel [annul, dissolve] a contract [an agreement] / 계약을 파기하다 break [call off] a contract
▶ 프로 야구 선수들은 팀과 1년 계약을 맺고 다 Professional baseball players are under a one-year contract to their teams.
▶ 우리는 계약을 갱신하지 않으면 안된다 We must have the contract renewed.
▶ 그는 그 일을 1000만원에 하기로 계약을 맺었다 He contracted to undertake the work for ten million won.
▶ 그 건설 회사가 이 공사 계약을 땄다 The construction company has won [received] the contract for this work.
▶ 본사는 시 당국과 신청사 건축 계약을 체결했 다 We have made a contract with the city government to build [for building] a new city hall.
〈계약에[으로]〉 계약에 조인하다 sign a contract / 3년간의 계약으로 일하다 work 《for a firm》 on [under] a three-year contract
▶ 나는 2년 계약으로 아파트를 빌렸다 I rented the apartment under a two-year lease [on a lease of two years].
—계약하다 contract 《to do, with *sb* for *sth* [doing]》; make [enter into] a contract [an agreement] 《with》; make [strike] a bargain
▶ 나는 토지 대금을 현금으로 지불하기로 계약 했다 I contracted to pay cash for the land.
▶ 우리는 그 회사와 콩 100톤을 구매하기로 계약 했다 We made a contract with the company to buy 100 tons of soybeans.
■가(假)— a temporary contract 구두(口頭)— 《make》 a verbal [an oral] contract 노동— a labor agreement 단체— a collective agreement 매매— a sales contract [agreement]; a bargain 무효[유효]— an invalid [a valid] contract 불법[적법]— an illegal [a legal] contract 서면[성문]— a written contract 수의— a private contract 쌍무[편무, 연대]— a bilateral [unilateral, joint] contract 임대— a lease; a lend-lease contract 잠정— a tentative contract; ad interim agreement 장기[단기]— a long-term [short-term] contract 정식— a formal contract; a contract under seal 판매— a sales commitment: 나는 그 회사와 판매 계약을 체결했다 I made [signed] a sales contract with the company. —가격 the contract price —갱신 renewal of a contract —고 the contract amount —기간 the term of a contract : 계약 기간이 끝났다 The contract has expired [terminated]. —노동 contract labor —(당사)자 〈일방〉 a contractor; a contracting party; 〈쌍방〉 contracting parties —보증금 ⇨ 계약금 —불이행 nonfulfilment [nonperformance] of a contract —서식 a contract form —위반 (a) breach [violation] of a contract —조건 terms (and conditions) of [under] a contract —체결 conclusion of a contract —해제 cancellation of a contract

계약금 契約金 a contract deposit; bargain money; earnest (money); 〈청약금〉 down payment
♦계약금으로 as a down payment / 새 차의 계약금을 치르다 put down money [place a deposit down, make a down payment] on a new car
▶ 나는 모터사이클 계약금 10만원을 지불했다 I made a down payment of one hundred thousand won on a motorcycle. ⇌ I put down one hundred thousand won for my motorcycle

계약서 契約書 a (written) contract; an agreement; a contract document; a bond
♦2통으로 작성한 계약서 a bipartite contract / 계약서를 교환하다 exchange written contracts 《with each other》 / 계약서를 작성하다 draw up a contract [an agreement] / 계약서에 명기하다 specify in a contract / 회사와의 계약서에 서명하다 sign a contract with a firm

계엄

▶그것에 대해서는 계약서에 아무 것도 언급되어 있지 않다 Nothing is said about it in the contract.
■매매— a contract note

계엄 戒嚴 guarding against (the threat of) danger; 〔法〕 enforcing martial law
▶전국이 계엄 하에 있다 The whole country is (put [placed]) under martial law.
■—사령관 the chief martial law administrator —사령부 the Martial Law Enforcement Headquarters

계엄령 戒嚴令 (the) martial law
◆계엄령을 펴다 place [put] (a city) under martial law; impose martial law (on the country) / 계엄령을 해제하다 lift [repeal, withdraw] martial law
▶그 도시는 현재 계엄령이 선포되어 있다 Martial law has been proclaimed in the city. ⇌ The city is now under martial law.

계열 系列 a series; a system; a chain; an order of descent; 〈대학의〉 department
◆같은 계열의 점포 stores belonging to the same chain / 현대 계열의 회사 Hyundai-affiliated firms; a business firm of [belonging to] the Hyundai group; an affiliate of the Hyundai group / 대학의 계열별 모집 admission of students to a university by department / 기업의 계열화 the systematization of enterprises
▶그 회사는 대우 그룹 계열이다 That company is a subsidiary of [is affiliated with, has an affiliation with] the Daewoo group.
▶그 화가는 인상파 계열에 속한다 The artist belongs to the Impressionist School.
■—기업〔산업〕 interrelated enterprises [industries] —회사 the affiliates; an affiliated [a subsidiary] company [firm]

계영 繼泳 relay swimming

계원 係員 an official [a clerk] in charge ◆접수계원 an information clerk; a receptionist

계원 契員 a member of a loan club [mutual financing association]

계율 戒律 (Buddhist) precepts; commandments
◆계율을 지키다〔어기다〕 observe [violate] the commandments [precepts]
▶나는 한 사찰에 묵은 적이 있었는데 거기에서는 계율이 엄격히 지켜지고 있었다 I stayed in a temple, where the precepts were strictly observed.

계인 契印 (the impression of) a seal over the joint of two sheets of paper; a tally (impression); a joint seal
◆계인을 찍다 impress a seal over the joint of two sheets of paper; affix a seal over two edges

계자 界磁 〔電〕 a field magnet ■—극 a field pole —전류 a field current —조정기 a field regulator —코일 a field coil

계장 係長 a chief clerk; the head of a section

계쟁 係爭 (a) dispute; contention; controversy; a lawsuit
◆계쟁 중인 문제 a problem [question] at issue; an issue in dispute; a pending problem / 계쟁 중이다 be in dispute; be at issue; be pending in court; be sub judice
◆그 사건은 아직도 계쟁 중이다 The suit is still disputed [in dispute].
—계쟁하다 dispute; have a dispute; engage in a controversy
—물건 property under dispute —사건 a contentious case —사실 a fact in dispute —점 the point at issue; a disputed point

계전기 繼電器 〔電〕 a relay ◆계전기식 자동 전화 교환 방식 the relay automatic telephone system

계절 季節 a season; 〈시기〉 time
◆늦은 계절 a backward season / 천고마비의 계절 the season of "high sky and plump horses" / 코스모스의 계절 the cosmos season / 해수욕의 계절 the swimming season / 계절의 꽃 flowers of the season / 계절에 어울리지 않는 폭설 the unseasonable heavy snowfall / 계절이 지난 out of season; off-season; unseasonable / 계절에 알맞은 seasonable / 계절이 바뀔 때 at the change of seasons / 이 계절에 at this time of (the) year
▶이제 바야흐로 여행의 계절이다 It is just the season for a trip now.
▶겨울은 스키와 스케이트의 계절이다 Winter is the season for skiing and skating.
▶나는 풍경 속에서 계절이 바뀌었음을 감지했다 I noted the seasonal changes [the change of the seasons] in the scenery.
▶계절이 좀 이르게 철쭉꽃이 피었다 The royal azalea blossoms came out a little too early for the season.
▶일년 중 어느 계절을 가장 좋아하십니까? Which [What] season of the year do you like best?
▶이 스포츠는 계절에 관계없이 인기가 있다 This sport is popular in all seasons [all the year round].
■—고용 seasonal employment —노동자 seasonal laborers [workers] —물 seasonable goods; things in season —변동 〔經〕 seasonal variations [fluctuations] —요리 dishes of the season —지수 〔經〕 a seasonal index —풍 a seasonal [periodic] wind; 〈인도양의〉 a monsoon

계절감 季節感 a sense of the season
▶한국인은 전래의 예민한 계절감을 잃어 가고 있다 The Koreans are losing the keen sense of the seasons which they inherited from their fathers.

계절적 季節的 seasonal ◆기후의 계절적 변화 seasonal changes of climate / 계절적으로 seasonally
■—수요 a seasonal demand —실업 seasonal unemployment

계정 計定 an account (略 a/c) ◆아무의 계정에 넣다 charge [put] (a sum) to sb's account; place [pass] to the account of sb
■당좌— a current account 대체— postal transfer account 미불— outstanding account 잡— sundry account 지급— account payable
■—과목 a title of account —잔고 the balance of accounts

계제 階梯 〈일의 단계〉 a step; 〈기회〉 an occasion; an opportunity; a chance
♦계제가 나쁜 untimely; ill-timed / 언제가 계제를 보아 at some convenient time / 어떤 계제에 by some chance / 이 계제에 with this opportunity; taking this opportunity
▶지금은 행동을 취할 계제가 아니다 This is not a good time to go into action.
▶물러나기에는 계제가 좋지 않다 This is not a proper time to withdraw.
▶그는 문제 해결을 위한 좋은 계제를 놓쳤다 He missed a perfect chance to settle the matter.
▶이 계제에 말씀드리고 싶은 것이 있습니다 Incidentally [While we're at it], there's something I'd like to talk to you about.

계좌 計座 an account ♦은행에 계좌를 트다[개설하다] open an account with a bank; open a bank account / 계좌를 종결하다 close an account with
■별도— a separate account 은행비밀— secret bank accounts

계주 契主 the organizer of a loan club [mutual financing association]

계주경기 繼走競技 a relay race ♦800미터 계주 경기 a 800-meter relay (race)

계진기 計塵器 a dust counter

계집 1 〈여자〉 a woman; a female; (총칭) the fair sex
♦계집이라면 사족을 못쓰는 사내 a man who has a weakness for woman / 계집을 좋아하는 fond of women; amorous; lustful / 계집에 미치다 be mad about a woman; be infatuated with a woman / 계집에 빠지다 give *oneself* up to a woman
2 〈아내〉 a wife
♦계집 말을 잘 듣는 사내 a fond husband / 계집을 버리다 discard [desert, leave] *one's* wife / 계집을 얻다 take 《to *oneself*》 a wife; get married to a woman
▶그는 계집 말을 잘 듣는다 He does just what his wife says.
■—자식 〈처자식〉 one's wife and children; one's family; 〈딸자식〉 one's daughter —종 a slave girl; a female slave

계집아이 a girl; a young girl; a wench; a lass; (美俗) a chick(en)
♦조속한 계집아이 a precocious girl / 계집아이 같은 사내 an effeminate fellow; (美俗) a sissy (boy)
▶그녀는 오늘 아침에 계집아이를 낳았다 She gave birth to a baby girl this morning.
▶계집아이 같이 울긴 Be a man and stop crying!

계집질 womanizing; whoring —**계집질하다** womanize; whore (around); (俗) wench; go in for amorous adventures

계책 計策 a scheme; a trick; a design; a stratagem; an artifice
♦좋은 계책 a good [clever] scheme / 계책이 다하다 be at *one's* wits' [wit's] end; be at the end of *one's* resources [tether]/ 계책이 풍부하다 be full of resources; be resourceful / 아무의 계책을 간파하다 see through *sb's* design / 계책을 생각해내다 work out [think out, invent, devise] a scheme [stratagem]/ 계책을 쓰다 adopt [use] a stratagem
▶그들은 탈세를 하려고 갖은 계책을 다 쓰고 있다 They are resorting to every stratagem to evade taxes.

계출 屆出 a report ⇨ 신고(申告)

계측 計測 measuring; measurement —**계측하다** measure ♦거리를 미터로 계측하다 measure distance by the meter
■—공학 instrumentation engineering —기(器) a measuring device [instrument, machine] —기학(器學) instrumentology

계층 階層 a class; a social stratum
♦온갖 계층의 사람들 people of [from] all classes [strata]; people on every social level; people from every walk [all walks] of life
▶그 가수는 모든 계층의 사람들에게 인기가 있다 The singer is popular with all sections and classes.
■소득— the 《low [high]》 income bracket —사회 a stratified society

계통 系統 1 〈조직〉 a system
♦계통이 선 systematic; methodical / 계통이 서지 않은 unsystematic; unmethodical / 계통을 세우다 systematize; make systematic / 계통을 세워 설명하다 give a systematic account (of)
▶그의 연구는 계통이 서 있지 않다 He lacks [has no] system in his study.
▶그는 처음으로 법의 계통을 세운 사람이다 He was the first man to systematize the law.
▶계통을 세워서 이야기를 해 주세요 Tell me your story in a systematic way.
2 〈혈통〉 a family line; lineage; genealogy; pedigree; 〈계보〉 a party; a clique
♦같은 계통의 빛깔 a color of similar shade / 뉴턴의 계통을 이어받은 학파 the Newtonian school / 계통을 이어받다 be descended 《from》; be inherited; run [flow] in the blood
▶이 부족들은 모두 같은 계통이다 All these tribes are of the same descent [stock].
▶이 언어는 인도 아리안 계통의 언어다 This language belongs to the Indo-Aryan language family.
▶그에게는 아일랜드와 잉글랜드인 계통의 피가 섞여 있다 He is of mixed Irish and English ancestry.
▶이 개는 진돗개 계통에 속한다 This dog belongs to the Chindo pedigree.
■신경[소화기]— the nervous [digestive] system 지휘— a channel [chain] of command —도 a distribution diagram; a genealogy —발생(론) phylogeny —수(樹) a family tree —오차 《物》 a systematic error —학 systematology

계통적 系統的 systematic; 〈정연한〉 methodical
♦계통적으로 systematically; on system; methodically / 독서를 계통적으로 하다 read systematically / 계통적으로 배열되다 be arranged systematically
▶나는 영문법을 계통적으로 연구하고 싶다 I'd like to make a systematic study of English

grammar.
—분류법 〔生〕 methodology —추출법 systematic sampling

계피 桂皮 cassia (bark); cinnamon
■—과자 a cinnamon-seasoned cracknel —말⇨ 계핏가루 —산 cinnamonic acid —유(油) cinnamon oil

계핏가루 桂皮— cinnamon powder

계하 階下 place below the stairs ♦계하에 엎드려 용서를 빌다 beg *sb's* pardon prostrating *oneself* below the stairs

계획 計劃 a plan; a project; a scheme [design]; 〈예정〉 a schedule [program]; 〈의도〉 an intention

> 〖解說〗 *plan*은 일반적으로 가장 넓은 의미의 말인데, 예정된 행동 계획이란 뜻일 때는 흔히 복수형이다. *project*는 대규모의 야심적인 계획·기획을 뜻한다. *scheme*은 막연한 공상적 계획이나 음모, *design*은 면밀하게 고안한 계획이나 모의, *program*은 행사 등의 실행 계획을 뜻한다.

♦국가적 계획 a nationwide plan / 막연한 계획 an indefinite plan / 빈틈 없는[조잡한] 계획 a mature [crude] plan [scheme] / 사막을 비옥하게 하는 계획 a project for making the desert fertile / 실행 가능한[불가능한] 계획 a practicable [an impracticable] plan / 원대한 계획 a far-seeing [long-range] plan / 참신한 계획 a novel [new and striking] plan / 계획 중이다 〈사업이〉 be in the planning stage; be on foot[afoot] / 〈사람이〉 be planning 《an operation》; have *sth* in contemplation
▶그 사업은 아직 계획 단계에 있다 The project is still in the planning stage.
▶그는 매사에 계획성이 없다 He has neither plan nor system in anything he does. ⇌ He never plans ahead.
▶만사가 계획대로 진행되었다 Everything worked out exactly as scheduled.
▶사업이 계획대로 실행되었다 The undertaking was carried out as planned.
〈계획이[은]〉 계획이 잘 진척되고 있다 A plan goes well.
▶계획이 진행 중이다 The plan is under way.
▶계획이 차질을 빚고 있다 The plan doesn't go well.
▶그의 갑작스런 죽음으로 우리의 계획이 들어져 버렸다 His sudden death upset our plan.
▶그의 계획은 중지되었다 His plan was dropped [canceled].
▶그의 계획은 성공했다 His plan was a success [worked well].
▶병 때문에 그의 사업 계획은 좌절되고 말았다 Illness frustrated his plans for an enterprise.
〈계획을〉 계획을 달성하다 fulfill [carry through] a plan / 계획을 뒤엎다 upset [ruin] *sb's* plan / 계획을 세우다 lay [form, work out] a plan [scheme]; make [plan] a program / 장래의 계획을 세우다 plan (up) [map out] *one's* future; 《美》 blueprint *one's* future / 계획을 실행하다 carry out [execute] *one's* plan / 계획을 진행시키다 carry forward a scheme / 계획을 포기하다 throw [fling] up *one's* cards
▶그들은 축하 파티 계획을 세웠다 They made arrangements for the celebration party.
〈계획으로〉 3년 계획으로 on a three years' program
▶우리는 5개년 계획으로 사전을 편찬하기로 했다 We decided to compile a dictionary on a five-year plan.

—계획하다 plan; make [form] a plan; scheme; map out; 〈의도하다〉 intend; contemplate; design
▶미리 계획한 대로 as planned [previously arranged] / 새 철도 부설을 계획하다 project to build a new railroad / 환영회(개최)를 계획하다 plan (to hold) a welcome party
▶우리는 금년 여름에 캐나다에 가려고 계획하고 있다 We are planning to go to Canada this summer.
▶나는 새로운 사업을 계획하고 있다 I have a new work in contemplation.
▶정부는 이 지역의 개발을 계획하고 있다 The governments is planning the development of [to develop] this region.
■단기[장기]— a short-range [long-range] plan 도시— city [《美》 town] planning 사업— a business program [project] **5개년**— a five-year plan [program]: 정부는 경제 개발 5개년 계획을 발표했다 The government published a five-year plan for economic development. 탁상— a desk plan —경제 planned economy —도 a scheme drawing —목표 the planned goal [target]: 생산은 계획 목표에 10% 미달되었다 Production was ten percent short of the planned target. —생산 planned production —설계도 a planning drawing —안 a schedule; a plan; a blueprint —입안자 a program planner —자 a projector; a promoter; 〈도시 계획 등의〉 a planner

계획적 計劃的 〈계획된〉 planned; studied 《insult》; 〈의도적〉 intentional; deliberate; calculated; 〈범죄가〉 premeditated
♦계획적(인) 거짓말 a deliberate lie / 계획적인 범죄 a premeditated crime / 계획적인 사기 a well-organized fraud / 계획적인 살인[탈세] deliberate murder [tax evasion] / 계획적으로 거짓말하는 사람 a systematic liar / 계획적으로 deliberately; intentionally; premeditatedly; by design
▶그 사건은 대규모의 계획적인 범행이었다 The case was a systematic crime carried out on a large scale.
▶그의 난폭한 행동은 계획적이었나 우발적인 것이었나? Was his violent behavior intentional [premeditated] or spontaneous?

곗돈 契— money for [from, owned by] the mutual financing association

곗술 契— wine provided by a mutual financing association

곗술에 낯내기 《속담》 playing the big shot with other people's money

고¹ 〈고리〉 a loop 《of string [ribbon]》; a bow of ribbon; a ribbon [string] tie

고² 〈그〉 that (little); 〈앞에 언급한〉 the same;

〈강조해서〉 the very
♦ 고 놈 that (little) fellow / 고 목적에 안성맞춤인 물건 the very thing for the purpose / 네가 가지고 있는 고 것과 같은 책 the same book that [as] you have / 고 모양이다 be just the same as before; be (always) like that; remain unchanged
▶ 아무리 일해도 그의 살림은 밤낮 고 모양 고 꼴이다 For all his labor, his family is as badly off as before.

고³ ♦ 머리가 아프다고 말하다 complain of a headache / 방문하겠다고 약속하다 promise to visit / 사실이 아니라고 부인하다 deny it to be true
▶ 나는 그가 정직하다고 생각한다 I think that he is honest.
▶ 가난하다고 남을 깔보아서는 안된다 You should not despise a man because he is poor.
▶ 나는 그가 성공하리라고 확신한다 I feel certain that he will succeed.
▶ 그녀는 「내일 또 오겠다」고 말했다 She said, "I'll come again tomorrow."
▶ 그렇다고 달리 좋은 방도가 있는 것도 아니다 And yet there is no other good way.
▶ 의사는 그의 증상을 신경쇠약이라고 진단했다 The doctor diagnosed his case as a nervous breakdown.
▶ 그는 나에게 돈을 꾸어 주겠다고 말했다 He offered to lend me money.

-고 1〈동작·상태·성질의 연결〉 and (also); besides; as well as; what with... and (what with)...
♦ 젊고 예쁜 여인 a lovely, young woman / 바쁘고 피곤한 busy and tired / 젊고 영리하고 게다가 부자인 young, clever and rich too / 정직하고 근면한 (both) honest and industrious
▶ 그녀는 아름답고 더구나 마음씨도 곱다 She is beautiful, and moreover [Besides being beautiful], she is good-natured.
▶ 비는 오고 배는 고프고 더 이상 한 발짝도 걸을 수가 없었다 What with rain and hunger, I was unable to walk a step further.
▶ 그 사람은 지식도 있고 경험도 있다 He has experience as well as knowledge.
2〈두 동작의 대등한 연결〉(do) and (then)
♦ 문을 열고 집 안으로 들어가다 open the door and go into the house / 택시를 타고 집으로 돌아가다 ride home in a taxi; taxi home
▶ 그는 신문을 읽고 식사했다 He read the paper and took his meal.
▶ 나는 아침밥을 먹고 외출했다 I had my breakfast and went out.
▶ 그들은 가고 우리는 남았다 They left and we remained.
3〈진행〉be ...ing; be at 《play》; be engaged in
♦ 공부를 하고 있다 be studying / 일을 하고 있다 be working at work
▶ 그 아이는 숙제를 하고 있다 The boy is doing his homework.
▶ 그는 지금 책을 읽고 있다 He is reading a book now.
▶ 그는 편지를 쓰고 있었다 He was (engaged in) writing a letter.
4〈완료〉have done; just finish ...ing

▶ 그녀는 아들을 보내고 (나서) 슬피 울었다 Having seen her son off, she cried bitterly.
5〈욕망〉want [wish] to (do); should [would] like to (do)
♦ 보고[듣고] 싶다 be curious to see [hear]/ 울고 싶다 feel like crying
▶ 그를 만나고 싶다 I want to see him.
▶ 점심을 먹고[집에 가고] 싶다 I want lunch [to go home].
▶ 당신을 만나고 싶소 I want [wish] to see you.

고 考 〈생각〉a thought; consideration; 〈연구〉studies; research(es); 〈논문〉a treatise; a monograph

고 故 the late 《Mr. Brown》; the (late) lamented...; the deceased...; 《Dr. Smith》 of blessed [happy, glorious] memory

고 高 〈높이〉height; 〈수량〉a number; a quantity 《of》; an amount; volume; 〈금액〉an amount; a sum
♦ 매상고 the sales (volume); the amount sold; the returns / 물가고 high prices of commodities / 생산고 an output; a yield 《of wheat》; an outturn / 에이커당 수확고 the yield per acre / 어획고 a haul [catch] (of fish); a fish catch

고 苦 〈고통〉(a) pain; suffering(s); an affliction; 〈근심〉anxiety; worries; (a) trouble(s); care(s); 〈고난〉hardship(s); difficulty
♦ 삼중고 a [one's] triple [threefold] handicap; (비유) a triple burden / 생활고 the difficulty of living; economic distress

고가 古家 an old house
고가 故家 a family of old standing; an old illustrious family
고가 高架 〈고가(의)〉overhead ━도로 (美) an overpass; (英) a flyover; an elevated track ━전차 an elevated [overhead] electric car ━철도 (美) an elevated (railroad [railway]); (美口) the L; (英) an overhead railway / 고가철도를 달리는 열차 (美) an elevated train / 고가철도를 타다 ride on the L ━철도역 an L station
고가 高價 a high price; costliness
♦ 고가의 기계 an expensive machine / 고가의 옷 a costly dress / 고가의 expensive; high-priced; costly; dear / 고가로 사다[팔다] buy [sell] sth at a high price
▶ 너무 고가다 The price is too high.
▶ 중고차 고가 매입 (게시) Used cars bought at good prices.
■━품 a costly [high-priced] article; a valuable : 요즘에는 고가품이 잘 팔린다 High-priced goods have been selling well recently.
고각 高角 a high angle
■━사격 a high-angle fire ━포 a high-angle gun
고갈 枯渴 〈물의〉drying up; running dry; 〈자원 등의〉exhaustion; drain
♦ 자원의 고갈 a exhaustion of resources ━고갈되다 be dried up; dry up; run dry; 〈자원 등이〉be exhausted [drained]
▶ 오랜 가뭄으로 우물이 고갈되었다 A long drought dried up the well. ⇌ The well ran

dry after a long spell of dry weather.
▶그 작가는 소재[창작력]가 고갈되었다 He has written himself out [His imagination has dried up].
▶전쟁으로 나라의 재원은 고갈되었다 The war has drained the country of its financial resources.

고감도필름 高感度— a high-speed film; a fast film; (a) supersensitive film

고개¹ 1 〈머리〉 a head; 〈목뒤〉 a neck
♦고개를 가로젓다 shake *one's* head / 고개를 한쪽으로 갸웃거리다 bend [tilt] *one's* head slightly to one side / 고개를 끄덕이다 nod; 〈찬성하여〉 nod approval [consent, agreement] / 고개를 들지 못하다 cannot hold up *one's* head (for shame) / 고개를 떨구다 hang (down) [bend, droop] *one's* head / 고개를 숙이다 turn *one's* face downward; drop *one's* head; 〈절하다〉 bow; make a bow
▶나는 그의 노력에 고개가 수그러진다 I admire [take off my hat to] him for his effort.
▶창 밖으로 고개를 내밀지 마라 Don't put your head out (of) the window.
▶그 소년은 미소를 지으며 그녀에게 고개를 끄덕였다 The boy nodded to her with a smile.
▶그녀는 슬픈 듯이 고개를 떨구다 Her head drooped sadly.
▶그는 고개를 저으며 「아니오」라고 말했다 He shook his head and said no.
▶그는 깊숙이[가볍게] 고개를 숙여 절했다 He made a deep [slight] bow.
2 〈기세〉 a trend
▶물가가 이달에 고개를 들었다[숙였다] This month prices have gone up [down].
▶그녀의 인기가 고개를 숙이고 있다 Her popularity is waning. ⇌ She is losing her popularity.
▶회원들 사이에 불만이 고개를 들기 시작했다 Discontent began to show itself among the members.

고개² 1 〈산길〉 a ridge; a (mountain) pass
♦고개를 넘다 cross a pass [ridge]; pass over the peak [crest] / 고개를 오르다[내려가다] go uphill [downhill]
2 〈고비〉 a critical moment [turn]; a crisis; a turning point
♦40고개를 갓 넘은 사람 a person just turning forty / 40고개를 넘다 be [have] turned forty; be over forty; pass *one's* forty-year milestone
▶그는 60고개를 넘었다[넘지 않았다] He is on the shady [sunny] side of sixty.
■—턱 the head [top] of a pass [slope] —티 a steep (zigzag) path [road] over a mountain (ridge)

고객 顧客 a buyer; a customer; 〈변호사 등의〉 a client; (총칭) the clientele; custom
♦국내[해외] 고객 home [foreign] customers / 단골[오랜] 고객 a regular [an old] customer / 뜨내기 고객 a casual [chance] customer / 고객이 늘다[줄다] gain [lose] customers / 고객이 많다 have a large custom; have many customers / 고객층이 좋다[나쁘다] have a good [low] class of customers / 고객을 끌다 draw [attract] custom [customers] (to a store) / 고객을 잃다[잃지 않다] lose [keep, retain] *one's* customers
▶그 호텔에는 고객이 많다 The hotel has a lot of guests.
▶그 가게는 외국인을 고객으로 하고 있다 The store is patronized by foreigners.
■—만족 customer satisfaction

고갯길 an uphill pass; an ascent
고갯짓 〈찬성의〉 a nod; 〈좌우로〉 a shake of the head —**고갯짓하다** 〈좌우로〉 shake *one's* head (in denial); 〈상하로〉 nod (in assent)

고 갱 〈프랑스의 화가〉 Gauguin, Paul (1848-1903)

고갱이 〈식물의〉 the pith; the medulla (*pl.* ~s, -lae); the heart ♦배추 고갱이 the heart of a cabbage

고검 高檢 〈고등 검찰청〉 the (Seoul) High Public Prosecutors Office

고것 〈사물〉 that; it; that one; 〈사람〉 the little thing; that guy [fellow]; (英口) that chap
▶갖고 싶으면 고것이나 가지고 가시오 Take it if you like.
▶고것 좀 보여 주시오 Show me that one.

고견 高見 1 〈탁월한 의견〉 a valuable [an excellent] opinion; a capital idea
2 〈상대방의 의견〉 your opinion [ideas, views]
▶이 문제에 대해 기탄없이 고견을 피력해 주십시오 Please feel free to express your views on [to say what you think of] this matter.
▶그 문제에 대한 선생의 고견을 듣고 싶습니다 Please let me know your views about the matter.

고결하다 高潔— noble(-minded); high-minded; lofty
♦품성이 고결한 사람 a person of noble [high] character; a high-minded man; a man of noble nature [great nobility] / 고결함을 잃지 않다 retain *one's* noble character
▶나는 그녀의 고결한 성품에 감명을 받았다 I was impressed with her loftiness.

고경 苦境 distressed circumstances ⇨ 곤경(困境)

고고 呱呱 cry of a baby at its birth
♦고고지성(之聲) the first cry of a newborn infant [baby] / 고고의 소리를 울리다 be born; come into life [being, existence, the world]
▶그는 1997년 5월 서울에서 고고의 소리를 울렸다 He was born [first saw the light of (day)] in Seoul in May, 1997.

고고 〈춤〉 the go-go [gogo] dance ♦고고를 추다 dance [do] the gogo; gogo

고고도 高高度 high altitude

고고하다 孤高— aloof from others; proud in loneliness [isolation]
♦고고한 생활 a life of proud loneliness [splendid isolation]
▶그는 홀로 고고하게 지내고 있다 He remains aloof from others.

고고학 考古學 arch(a)eology
♦고고학적 발견 an archaeological discovery / 고고학적 자료 archaeological evidence [specimens, relics] / 고고학상으로 archaeologically; from the archaeological point

of view
■—자 an archaeologist

고골리 〈러시아의 소설가〉 Gogol, Nikolai Vasilievich (1809-52)

고공 高空 a high sky; high altitude
♦고공에서 high (up) in the sky [air]; at a high altitude
▶우리는 현재 7천 피트의 고공을 비행하고 있다 We are now flying at an altitude [a height] of seven thousand feet.
■—병 〔醫〕 altitude sickness —비행 high-altitude flying [flight]

고과 考課 (do) a performance evaluation; consideration [evaluation] of services [merits]
■인사— merit [efficiency] rating ■—표 a service [business] record; a personnel record

고관 高官 a high official [officer] 《in the government》; a (high) dignitary; 〈직위〉 a high office
■—대작 〈직위〉 a high and prominent office; 〈사람〉 a high official; a man of high office; a dignitary

고관절 股關節 〔解〕 a hip joint; a coxa 《pl. ·ae》 ■—염 coxitis; coxarthritis —탈구 dislocation of hip joint

고광나무 〔植〕 a mock orange; a syringa

고굉 股肱 1〈팔과 다리〉 arms and legs 2〈사람〉 one's right-hand (man); one's trusted henchman ■—지신(之臣) a king's right-hand man; a trusted retainer

고교 高校 a (senior) high school ⇨ 고등학교

고교회파 高教會派 〔宗〕 the High Church

고구려 高句麗 〔韓國史〕 Koguryŏ

고구마 〔植〕 a sweet potato ♦ 찐[군] 고구마 a steamed [roast, baked] sweet potato / 고구마밭 a sweet-potato field [patch] / 고구마 덩굴 sweet patato runners [vines]

고국 故國 one's home(land); one's native land [country]; one's mother country
♦ 고국을 떠나다 leave one's homeland [native land]; be away from the homeland; 〈망명하다〉 go into exile / 고국을 생각하다[그리다] pine [long] for one's home / 고국에 돌아가다 [돌아오다] go [come] back to one's homeland; return [come] home
▶ 고국을 떠난지 10년이 된다 I have been away from home for ten years.
■—산천 (the mountains and rivers of) one's homeland [native country]

고군분투하다 孤軍奮鬪— fight unsupported 《against》; fight alone [a lonely battle] 《with, against》; put up a solitary struggle
▶ 대사는 총회에서 고군분투했다 The ambassador made his unaided effort in the General Assembly.

고궁 古宮 an old [ancient] palace; a time-honored palace

고귀하다 高貴— 1〈신분이 높다〉 high; noble; exalted; highborn; highly-descended; 〈혈통이〉 of noble blood
♦ 고귀한 사람 a person of high rank [(noble) birth]; the honorable person; a high [an exalted] personage / 태생이 고귀하다 be of high [noble] birth; 〈제왕·제후 등〉 be born in the purple / 고귀한 집안에 태어나다 be born into a noble family; be highborn
2〈귀중하다〉 valuable; invaluable ♦ 고귀한 생명 invaluable [the dignity of] human life

고금 古今 time past and present; ancient and modern times; all ages; any age
♦ 동서 고금의 민요 ballads of all ages and countries / 고금의 ancient and modern; 〈heroes〉 of all times [ages]; in [of] all ages / 동서 고금을 통하여 for all ages and in all places; to all times and places / 고금에 through [in] all ages; in history / 고금에 그 유례가 없다 have no parallel [equal] in history [in any age]
▶ 우리는 고금 미증유의 대전을 체험했다 We went through the greatest battle ever fought.
▶ 이것은 고금에 없던 대발견이다 This is the greatest discovery on record [in history]. ⇒ This is the greatest discovery that has ever been made.
■—독보(獨步) having no equal throughout the ages; unique for all time

고급 高級 〈계급〉 high rank; seniority; 〈정도〉 high class [grade]; select; (口) plush
♦ 고급의 〈계급이〉 of high rank; high ranking; senior 〈clerk〉; 〈정도가〉 high-class 〈articles〉; high-grade; higher; advanced; quality 〈magazine, shop〉; (口) classy 〈restaurants〉; luxury 〈food〉
▶ 그는 그 도시의 고급 주택지에 살고 있다 He lives in the select part of the city.
▶ 좀더 고급으로 보여 주세요 Show me a higher grade.
■—관 리[공 무 원] higher [high-ranking, upper-bracket] (government) officials; high functionaries —부관 〈부대의〉 a senior adjutant; 〈사령부의〉 an adjutant general —상점 a high-class [quality, fashionable] store —선원 an officer (of a ship); (총칭) the quarterdeck —양복점 a quality tailor shop —양장점 a high-class dressmaking shop —장교 a high-ranking officer; a high-ranker; senior Navy [Army] officers; (美俗) (총칭) brass; a brass hat —차(車) a high-class motorcar; a deluxe car —참모 a senior staff officer —品 goods of higher grade; a first-class [superior, choice] article; quality [high-grade] articles [goods] —호텔 a deluxe [a first-class, an exclusive] hotel

고기 1〈동물의〉 meat; flesh; 〈새의〉 poultry

> [解說] *meat*는 보통 식용으로 하는 짐승 고기를 가리킨다. 식용으로 하지 않는 살 등은 *flesh*라고 한다. flesh는 또 뼈나 가죽에 대해 살이란 뜻으로도 쓰인다. 또 식용 고기라도 생선 고기는 fish, 새의 고기는 ***poultry*** 또는 fowl로 보통 구별하며, 짐승 고기도 beef(쇠고기), veal(송아지 고기), pork(돼지고기), mutton(양고기)처럼 구분해서 쓴다.

♦ 날고기 raw meat / 냉동 고기 chilled meat / 다진 고기 minced [hashed] meat / 닭고기 chicken / 불고기 roast beef / 쇠고기 beef / 연한[질긴] 고기 tender [tough] meat / 고기 요

고기만두

리 a meat dish / 고기 한 점[파운드] a piece [pound] of meat / 고기를 썰다 cut [carve, chop] meat / 고기를 요리하다 cook meat
▶ 이 고기는 좀 오래 되었다 This meat is slightly old.
▶ 나는 잘 구워진[중간 정도로 구워진, 설구워진] 고기를 좋아한다 I like my meat well-done [medium, rare].
2 〈물고기〉 fish ◆ 고기 떼 a school [shoal] of fish
고기만두 ―饅頭 a meat bun; a rissole
고기밥 〈먹이〉 fish food; food given to fish; 〈미끼〉 a fish bait ◆ 고기밥이 되다 become food for fishes; be drowned
고기붙이 meat ◆ 고기붙이를 멀리하다 abstain from meat dishes
고기수프 gravy soup
고기압 高氣壓 high (atmospheric) pressure; anticyclone ◆ 고기압이 발달하다 a high pressure develops itself 《over》
▶ 한국 중부 지방은 고기압으로 덮여 있다 High atmospheric pressure overlies the central part of Korea. ⇌ The central part of Korea is covered by [enveloped in] a high pressure system [area].
■대륙성― the continental high pressure
■―권 a high pressure area
고기잡이 fishery; fishing; 〈낚시질〉 angling; 〈어부〉 a fisherman; a fisher ◆ 고기 잡이 가다 go fishing
▶ 오늘은 고기 잡이가 잘 되었다[되지 않았다] I (have) had a good [poor] catch (of fish) today.
―고기잡이하다 catch fish 《in a river》; fish
▶ 그들은 인천 연안에 고기잡이하러 갔다 They went out on a fishing excursion to the coast of Inch'ŏn.
■―배 a fishing boat; a fisherboat
고기칼 a carver; a cleaver; 〈정육점의〉 a butcher('s) knife
고깃간 a butcher's; a meat [butcher's] store
고깃국 meat soup; broth
고깃국물 soup; broth; gravy (soup)
고깃덩어리 1 〈짐승의〉 a lump [hunk, piece, hunch] of meat 2 〈육체〉 the flesh; the body; the fleshly envelope
고깃배 a fishing boat [vessel, craft]; a fisherboat
고깃점 a piece [slice] of meat; 〈두꺼운〉 a chop 《of meat》
고까짓 such; slight; so trifling [small, trivial]
▶ 고까짓 상처로 소동을 벌이다니 Why should you make a fuss over such a slight injury?
▶ 고까짓 일로 화내지 말게 Don't be offended at such a trifle.
고깔 a peaked hat (worn by Buddhist monks and nuns)
고깔해파리 〔動〕 a Portuguese man-of-war
고깝다 (feel) unpleasant; disgusting; reproachful; hateful
▶ 그 친구가 도와 주러 오지 않아서 고까웠다 I thought it ill of him not to have come to help me.
▶ 그녀는 고까운 듯이 나를 쳐다보았다 She looked reproachfully at me.
▶ 악의로 그런 것이 아니니 고깝게 여기지 말게 Please don't think ill [hard] of me. I meant no harm.
고꾸라뜨리다 let sb fall forward ⇨ 거꾸러뜨리다
고꾸라지다 fall [tumble] forward; topple down; fall on one's face ⇨ 거꾸러지다
◆ 술에 만취해 고꾸라지다 fall down dead-drunk / 고꾸라져 강에 빠지다 go pitching forward into the river
▶ 나는 뒤에서 밀려 고꾸라졌다 I was pushed from behind and pitched forward.
고난 苦難 distress; suffering(s); hardship(s); affliction(s)
◆ 생의 고난 the trials [ills] of life / 고난의 길을 걷다 muddle through the bitters of life / 고난을 견디다 stand [bear, endure] hardship(s) / 모든 고난을 극복하다 overcome [get over, conquer] all trials [afflictions] / 고난에 허덕이다 pant under a heavy load
▶ 이 때는 그들에게 있어 참으로 고난의 시기였다 These were indeed hard times for them.
▶ 그는 오랜 고난을 겪은 후 마침내 성공했다 After struggling through the long thorny path of life, he won success at last.
▶ 나는 어떤 고난이든 견딜 작정이다 I intend to bear any hardship.
고뇌 苦惱 gnawing; anguish; agony; distress; (an) affliction; pain
◆ 고뇌에 찬 anguished 《conscience》; 《a heart》 full of trouble
▶ 그의 얼굴에는 고뇌의 빛이 엿보였다 His face revealed an expression of distress.
▶ 그는 고뇌에 찬 일생을 보냈다 He lived a life of agony [suffering].
―고뇌하다 be in agony; suffer; be agonized [anguished]; anguish
▶ 그의 얼굴에는 고뇌하는 기색이 나타났다 A look of distress came over his face.
고니 〔鳥〕 a swan ■큰― a whooper swan 흑―a black swan
고다 1 〈푹 끓이다〉 boil down; boil sth to pulp; stew
◆ 고기[잉어]를 고다 boil meat [a carp] to pulp / 닭을 고다 stew a chicken (for a long time) / 엿을 고다 make Korean candy / 너무 고다 overdo; overboil / 고아서 과당을 만들다 boil down 《fruit juice》 into syrup
▶ 스튜를 3시간 정도 뭉근한 불에 고아라 Let the stew simmer for about three hour.
2 〈양조하다〉 brew; distill
◆ 소주를 고다 distill spirits
고단자 高段者 a high-rank holder [player]
◆ 바둑의 고단자 a high-ranking paduk player
▶ 그는 태권도에 전념하여 고단자가 되었다 He devoted himself to t'aekwŏndo and advanced to a high rank.
고단하다 tired; fatigued; exhausted; weary; worn out
◆ 고단한 일 exhausting [tiring, fatiguing] work / 몸이 고단하다 have a weary body; feel worn out [done in] / 고단하여 잠자리에 들다 go to bed fatigued

▶ 오늘은 몸이 고단하다 I feel tired today.
▶ 그는 고단한 모습으로 걷고 있었다 He was walking wearily.
▶ 몹시 고단해 보이는구나 You look done up [all in, tired out, run down, beat, fagged].

고달¹ 1 〈거만스러움〉 haughtiness; arrogance, insolence
2 〈어린애가 보챔〉 fret; peevishness; irritation; fussiness
◆ 고달을 부리다 fret; be peevish; be cross; be fussy / 고달을 부리는 아이를 달래다 soothe a fretful child

고달² 1 〈자루에 박힌 부분〉 a tang
2 〈물건의 부리〉 a ferrule

고달이 〈손잡이〉 a handle; an attached finger-loop

고달프다 〈몹시 피곤하다〉 tired [worn] out; done [used, knocked] up; very tired; utterly exhausted; 〈고되다〉 hard; 〈지겹다〉 wearisome; boring; tiresome
◆ 고달픈 나날 wearisome days / 고달픈 인생 a weary [hard] life / 고달픈 일 tiring [hard] work / 마음이 고달프다 be fatigued in mind; be mentally fatigued / 몸이 고달프다 be all worn out; have a tired body

고담 古談 a legend; an old tale [story]; folklore

고담 枯淡 ◆ 고담의 simple but refined; plain
▶ 그의 예술은 고담의 경지에 달했다 His art has attained (the realm of) subdued refinement.

고담준론 高談峻論 1 〈고상·준엄한 말〉 a noble [lofty] and stern discourse; a high and mighty talk; a lofty and puritanical discourse
―고담준론하다 discourse [talk] in a lofty and severe way [loftily and severely]
2 〈흰소리〉 tall [big] words; big talk; a tall tale [talk]; bragging
―고담준론하다 talk tall [big]; boast

고답 高踏 ◆ 고답적인 문학 highbrow literary work / 고답적인 사람들 (口) the highbrows / 고답적인 잡지 a hight-toned journal
▶ 그는 일생 동안 고답적으로 살았다 He kept aloof from the world throughout his life.
■―주의 transcendentalism ―파(派) the transcendentalists

고당 高堂 〈남의 집〉 your home [house]; 〈남의 양친〉 your parents
▶ 고당의 만복을 기원합니다 I wish you every happiness and prosperity.

고대 〈지금 막〉 just [right] now; a moment ago
▶ 그는 고대 다녀갔다 He has just been here.
▶ 고대 돌아왔습니다 I came back just now.
▶ 그 이야기는 고대 들었습니다 I have just heard it.

고대 古代 ancient [old] times; past remote ages; antiquity
◆ 고대의 ancient; 〈고풍의〉 antique / 고대의 유물 antiquities; ancient relics / 고대로부터 from [since] ancient times; from time immemorial
■―사[문학] ancient history [literature] ―소설 a story of ancient times ―인 ancient people; the ancients; (총칭) antiquity

고대광실 高臺廣室 a grand residence; a palatial mansion

고대하다 苦待― wait eagerly [impatiently] 《for》; long for; be impatient 《for》; eagerly look forward to 《an event》
◆ 고대하던 소식 the long-awaited news / 고대하는 the long-awaited-for; the long-looked-forward-to / 아무가 오기를 고대하다 long for sb to come / 학수 고대하다 be on the tiptoe with expectation
▶ 이제까지 어디 갔었니? 아버지가 너를 고대하고 계신다 Where have you been all this while? Father has been waiting impatiently for you.
▶ 학생들은 여름 방학을 고대하고 있다 The pupils are impatient [can scarcely wait] for the summer holidays to come.
▶ 고대하던 권투 프로그램이 시작된다 The long-awaited boxing program is starting.

고도 古都 an ancient city [capital]; the former capital

고도 孤島 a solitary [an isolated, a lonely] island; a remote and lonely island; 〈무인도〉 a desert island ◆ 절해의 고도 a solitary island far out on the sea

고도 高度 1 〈높이〉 (a) height; (an) altitude
◆ 4천 미터의 고도를 날다 fly at an altitude [a height] of four thousand meters / 고도를 높이다[낮추다] gain [lose] altitude / 고도를 유지하다 maintain [keep] the altitude [height] (of 1,500 meters) / 고도를 측정하다 measure the altitude
▶ 제트 여객기는 1만 미터의 고도를 비행한다 The jetliner flies at an altitude [a height] of ten thousand meters.
▶ 비행기가 착륙하기 위해 고도를 낮추기 시작했다 The plane began to descend for the landing.
2 〈정도가 높음〉 a high degree [power]
◆ 고도의 문명 a high standard of civilization / 고도로 자동화된 공장[기계화된 문명] a highly automated factory [mechanized civilization] / 고도로 진보된 사회 a highly advanced society
▶ 그것은 고도의 기술을 요한다 It requires advanced [a high degree of] technical skill.
■―비행 flight [flying] altitude ―계(計) an altimeter [altometer]; a height indicator ―기록 an altitude record ―성장 high [rapid, speedy] growth: 한국 경제의 고도 성장 high growth of Korean economy; (a) high level [rate] of Korea's economic growth ―제어(장치) 〈空〉 altitude control (system) ―측량(天) altimetry ―측량기 an altimeter

고도리 〔魚〕 a spike; a young mackerel

고독 孤獨 loneliness; solitude; isolation
◆ 고독벽(癖)이 있는 shut-in (personality); (a man) with [who has, of] a solitary temperament / 고독을 좋아하다 be fond of [like] solitude / 고독을 참다 bear solitude
▶ 그의 뒷모습에서는 깊은 고독감이 감돌았다 From the back, there was something very lonely about his form.

고동

—**고독하다** lonely; solitary; 《美》 lonesome; isolated; friendless
▶그는 고독한 생활을 했다 He led [lived] a solitary [lonely] life. ⇌ He lived in solitude.
■—**공포증** monophobia —**단신** a solitary [lonely] person; a solitary

고동 1 〈기계의 장치〉 a switch; a starter; a cock; a handle ◆**고동을 틀다[잠그다]** turn on [off] 《the water》
2 〈요점〉 the crux; the main [vital] point; the pivot
3 〈기직〉 a steam whistle; a siren
▶배가 고동을 울렸다 The ship whistled [blew a whistle].
4 〈물레의〉 the two bell-like rotating rings (on the spindle of a spinning wheel)

고동 鼓動 a beat; beating; throbbing; palpitation
◆**심장의 고동** the beat [throb] of the heart; (a) heartbeat / **심장의 고동이 들리다** hear sb's heart throbbing
▶그는 한 순간 심장의 고동이 멈췄다 His heart stopped beating for a moment.
—**고동하다[치다]** beat; palpitate; pulsate
▶나는 흥분하여 심장이 마구 고동쳤다 My heart was throbbing heavily with excitement.

고동색 古銅色 reddish brown

고되다 trying; painful; hard (to bear); tough; intense
◆**고된 노동** hard [intense] labor / **고된 생활** 〈세상〉 a hard life [world] / **고된 일** a difficult [(口) tough] job; hard [heavy] work; a toilsome [painful] task; an awful [a horrible] sweat / **고된 임무** a painful duty / **고되게 일하다** work like a dog; toil and moil
▶이 일은 몹시 고되다 This work is very tiring [fatiguing]. ⇌ This work wears me out.
▶그것은 이제까지 가장 고된 일이었다 It was the hardest [toughest] work I have ever done.

고두 叩頭 a kowtow; a deep bow
◆**고두 사죄하다** make a humble [kowtowing] apology; humbly beg pardon; apologize abjectly
—**고두하다** kowtow (to); bow deeply (to); make a bow (to)

고두밥 hard-boiled [hard-steamed] rice

고둥 〈貝〉 a snail; a spiral shellfish

고드름 an icicle ▶처마 끝에 고드름이 생겼다 [매달렸다] Icicles have formed on [hung from] the edge of the eaves.

고득점 高得點 a high mark [score] ◆**고득점을 하다** win [get] the high score [mark]
■—**자** winners of higher marks [grades, scores]; a high scorer

고등 高等 high grade; high class ◆**고등의** high; higher; advanced; supreme; 〈고급의〉 high-grade; high-class; first-class
■—**검찰청** a high public prosecutor's office —**고시** ⇨ 사법(~시험) —**군법 회의** a general court-martial —**동물** a higher animal —**비행** 《술》 aerobatics; aerial acrobatics; an acrobatic flight; stunt (flying) —**수학** higher mathematics —**판무관** a high commissioner

고등교육 高等教育 higher education ◆**고등교육을 받은 사람** a highly educated man; a college [university] graduate; 《총칭》 the intellectuals
■—**기관** an institution of higher education [learning]; higher educational institutions

고등법원 高等法院 a high court (of justice); 〈상고심〉 an appellate court ■—**장** the president of a high court

고등어 〈魚〉 a mackerel 《pl. ~(s)》; a scombroid

고등학교 高等學校 a (senior) high school; 《美口》 a senior high
▶그 아이는 고등학교 3학년이다 The boy is a third-year student in high school.
▶그는 고등학교 과정을 마쳤다 He has had a high-school education.
▶나는 2년 전에 고등학교를 졸업하였다 I graduated from (a) high school two years ago.
▶나는 1998년에 대한 고등학교에 입학했다 I entered Taehan High School in 1998.
■—**공업[상업, 여자, 농업, 인문]—** a technical [a commercial, a girls', an agricultural, an academic] high school —**내신 성적** high school records —**학생** a (senior) high-school student; 《美》 a senior high student; 《美口》 a high schooler —**야구** (senior) high school baseball —**졸업생** a high school graduate —**평준화** the academic standardization of high schools

고딕 〈建·印〉 Gothic —**식** Gothic; (in) Gothic style —**식 건축** Gothic architecture; 〈건물〉 a Gothic building —**체** 〈활자의〉 Gothic type; black letter

고라니 〈動〉 a kind of roe deer

고락 〈낙지의 배〉 the belly [abdomen] of an octopus; 〈낙지의 먹물〉 ink of an octopus; 〈먹물주머니〉 an ink bag (of an octopus) ◆**낙지가 고락을 뿜다** spurt [eject] ink

고락 苦樂 pleasure and pain; joys and sorrows
◆**인생의 고락** (experience) the sweets and bitters of life / **고락을 같이하다** share one's lot (with another); participate in sb's joys and sorrows (with him)
▶나는 세상의 고락을 다 겪었다[맛보았다] I have experienced [tasted] sweets and bitters of life.
▶우리는 고락을 같이 해 온 사이다 We have been great friends both in joy and in sorrow.

고람 高覽 〈남이 봄〉 your inspection [perusal]
▶졸작을 고람하여 주시기 바랍니다 I should like to submit [I take pleasure in submitting] my new book for your inspection.

고랑¹ 〈밭 등의〉 a trough; a furrow ◆**고랑을 짓다** make furrows in a field; furrow a field
■—**창** a narrow deep trough; a ditch

고랑² handcuffs ⇨ 쇠고랑

고래¹ 〈動〉 a whale ◆**술을 고래로 마시다** drink like a fish ▶고래가 물을 뿜었다 A whale spouted water [blew].
■**검은—** a pilot [black] whale; a blackfish **긴수염—** a finback; a fin whale **수염—** a baleen [whalebone] whale **수[암]코래** a bull [cow

whale 큰— a right whale 향유— a sperm whale; a catchalot; a black whale 혹등— a humpback (whale) 흰긴수염— a blue whale ━고기 whale meat ━기름 whale oil ━떼 a herd [school] of whales; a gam ━새끼 a whale calf ━수염 a baleen; a whalebone; 〔商〕 a whalefin ━작살 a harpoon; a gaff ━잡이 whale fishing [fishery]; whaling ━잡이배 ⇨ 포경선(捕鯨船)

고래² 〈방고래〉 flues in a hypocaust [floor heater]

고래 古來 ◆고래의 old; long-established; customary / 고래의 관습 an old [a time-honored] custom / 고래로 from ancient [early] times; from times past; traditionally; 〈태고적부터〉 from time immemorial / 고래의 누습을 타파하다 do away with the conventionalities of the past / 고래의 방식에 따르다 follow the conventional method / 고래로 유례가 없다 have no parallel [equal] in history [in any age]
▶ 인생 칠십 고래희(古來稀) Man seldom lives to be seventy years old.
▶ 이 습관은 고래로 이 지방에 전해져 온 것이다 This custom has come [been handed] down to us from ancient [early] time in this part of the country. ⇌ This is a time-honored custom in this district.

고래고래 at shouting pitch; in [with] a loud voice ◆고래고래 소리지르다 cry in a loud voice; raise a shout [one's voice] 《in a rage [huff]》; yell; roar; thunder

고래등같다 palatial; stately; magnificent ◆고래등 같은 기와집 a palatial tile-roofed house; a stately mansion

고래 싸움에 새우등 터진다 〈속담〉 An innocent bystander gets badly hurt [gets a heavy by-blow] in a Titanic struggle.

고래자리 〔天〕 the Whale; Cetus

고량 高粱 〔植〕 kaoliang; (Chinese) sorghum ■━밭 a kaoliang field ━주 kaoliang wine [spirits]

고려 考慮 consideration; (careful) thought; reflection; thinking
◆고려 중이다 〈사람이 주어〉 be considering a matter; have a matter under consideration; 〈사물이 주어〉 be under consideration; be in view / 고려를 요하다 be worth due consideration; demand deliberation / 고려에 넣다 take sb [a thing] into account [consideration]; make allowance for 《one's youth》
▶ 그 문제는 고려 중이다 The matter is under consideration.
━고려하다 consider; think [ponder] over; take account of; give consideration to; take a matter into consideration [account]; deliberate on; reflect upon
◆…을 충분히 고려하여 with due regard to…; in due consideration of…/ …을 고려하지 않고 without regard to…; regardless of…; without minding…/ 충분히 고려한 후에 after due consideration / 상대방의 사정도 충분히 고려하다 pay due regard to their convenience / 고려하지 않다 disregard; take no thought [account] of; leave a matter out of consideration [account]; pay no regard 《to》/ 고려해 볼 만하다 be worth deliberation [consideration]; deserve much consideration
▶ 그 점에 대해서는 충분히 고려했다 We have given careful consideration to that point.
▶ 교통의 지체를 고려하여 좀 일찍 출발하겠다 I will start a little early, allowing for traffic delays.
▶ 자기 나이를 고려하지 않으면 안된다 You must take your age into consideration.
▶ 그는 다른 사람을 고려하지 않는다 He shows no consideration for other people.
▶ 그것은 신중히 고려해야 할 문제다 It is a question which demands our serious consideration.
▶ 그런 제의는 고려할 가치도 없다 Such a proposal isn't worth considering.
▶ 그것은 좀 고려할 여지가 있다 It leaves some room for consideration.

고려 高麗 〔韓國史〕 Koryŏ
■━인삼 (a) Korean ginseng ━자기 Koryŏ porcelain [pottery] ━장 an ancient burial practice whereby an [a dying] old person is left to die in an open tomb

고령 高齡 an advanced [ripe, great] age
◆고령의 old; aged / 고령에도 불구하고 in spite of 《his》 great age / 80세의 고령으로 at the great age of eighty
▶ 그분은 고령이다 He is very old [advanced in age].
▶ 할머니께서는 90세의 고령으로 타계하셨다 Grandmother died at the great [advanced] age of ninety.
■━자 (총칭) the aged [old]; 〈개인〉 a very old [an aged] person ━화 aging : 고령화 사회 an aging society

고령토 高嶺土 kaolin

고로 故— accordingly; therefore; hence; consequently; and so

고로 古老 〈노인〉 an aged [old] man; an old-timer; old folks; an elder; (총칭) the aged
◆마을의 고로 an old villager; elders of the village; village seniors / 인근의 고로에 의하면 according to the aged [an old-timer] in this vicinity

고로 高爐 〔工〕 a blast [shaft] furnace ■━슬래그 blast furnace slag

고로롱거리다 be chronically ill [sick]

고료 稿料 〈원고료〉 a manuscript fee; payment for copy; copy money
◆고료가 많다[적다] 〈사람이 주어〉 be paid well [poorly] for one's writing; 〈원고가 주어〉 be paid for high [low] / 고료를 페이지[장]당 얼마로 지불하다 pay so much per page [sheet]

고루 〈균일하게〉 evenly; equally; uniformly; 〈공평하게〉 fairly; impartially; indiscriminately
◆고루 가르다 divide a thing equally; go share and share alike / 고루 나누어 주다 distribute equally [evenly]
▶ 음식을 고루 먹도록 해라 Try to eat well-balanced meals.
▶ 그 아이는 모든 과목을 고루 잘한다 The boy

does very well in every subject.
▶ 적십자사는 빈민들에게 식량을 고루 나누어 주었다 The Red Cross dispensed food equally to the poor.

고루 固陋 〈구식임〉 conservatism; fogyism; 〈완고〉 perversity; obstinacy; stubbornness; 〈옹졸〉 narrow-mindedness; bigotry
—**고루하다** bigoted; narrow-minded; stubborn; obstinate; extremely conservative ♦ 고루한 늙은이 an old fogy

고루 高樓 a lofty structure [building] ■—거각(巨閣) a lofty and stately building

고르다¹ 〈선택하다〉 choose; make choice of; select; 〈골라내다〉 pick out; single [sort] out; 〈선정하다〉 fix upon
♦ 고르고 고르다 pick and choose / 쌀에서 돌을 고르다 pick sand out of the rice [grains] / 잘못 고르다 make the wrong selection [a bad choice] / 좋은 날을 고르다 choose [fix upon] an auspicious day
▶ 내가 고른다면 녹색이다 I would take green, for choice.
▶ 이 책들 중에서 골라라 Take your pick [choice] of these books.
▶ 그는 제일 큰 사과를 골랐다 He chose the largest apple.
▶ 아버지는 그녀를 나의 아내로 고르셨다 My father fixed upon her for my wife.
▶ 어느 쪽을 고르시겠습니까? What is your choice?
▶ 나는 제2외국어로 프랑스어를 고르려고 생각한다 I'm thinking of French for my second foreign language.
▶ 골라 잡아 1,000원 All 1,000 won apiece. ⇌ Take your choice for 1,000 won.
▶ 그는 주의 깊게 말을 골라서 했다 He chose his words carefully.
▶ 친구는 주의해서 골라야 한다 You should choose your friends very carefully. ⇌ Be careful in your choice of friends.

고르다² 〈평평하게 하다〉 level (the ground); smooth; make even; 〈롤러로〉 roll; 〈불도저로〉 bulldoze
♦ 집을 짓기 전에 땅을 고르다 level ground before building / 표면을 고르다 bring a surface to a level
▶ 불도저가 둔덕을 골랐다 The bulldozer made the mound of earth level.

고르다³ 1 〈한결같다〉 uniform; even; regular
♦ 키가 고른 아이들 children of uniform height / 고르지 따뜻한 방 a room heated evenly / 고르지 않은 uneven; not uniform; unequal; irregular; 〈울룩불룩한〉 rugged / 고르게 evenly; uniformly; regularly / 이가 고르다[고르지 않다] have a regular [an irregular] set of teeth
▶ 다리의 길이가 고르지 않은 의자에 앉으면 불편하다 It is uncomfortable to sit on a chair with uneven legs.
▶ 그 사람은 모든 일을 고르게 잘한다 He is equally good at everything.
2 〈공평하다〉 equal; fair; disinterested; (口) fair and square; impartial
♦ 고르지 못한 unfair; unjust; partial; unequal / 고르게 equally; fairly; justly; impartially / 고르게 나누다 divide [distribute] 《money》 fairly [evenly]
▶ 몫이 고르지 못하다 The share is not equal.
3 〈날씨가〉 favorable [seasonable] 《weather》
♦ 고르지 못한 changeable; unfavorable; unsettled; irregular ▶ 봄 날씨는 고르지 못하다 Spring weather is changeable.

고름¹ 〈농〉 pus; purulent matter; discharge
♦ 고름이 나오다 discharge [produce] pus / 고름이 잡히다 form [generate] pus; 〈상처 등에〉 suppurate; fester / 눌러서 고름을 짜다 squeeze [press] the pus out of 《boil》
■—집 a pustule

고름² 〈옷고름〉 a breast-tie; a coat string

고리¹ 〈실·끈 등의〉 a loop; a ring; 〈사슬의〉 a link ♦ 끈으로 고리를 만들다 make a loop in (a piece of) string
■ 귀— an earring 문— a door-ring 손잡이—〈서랍의〉 a drawer handle ■—던지기 〈놀이〉 quoits; ringtoss

고리² 〈벗긴 고리버들 가지〉 split osier [willow] branches; wicker
♦ 고리에 옷을 채워 넣다 pack clothes in a wicker trunk
■—바구니 a wicker basket —장이 a wicker worker; a maker of wicker (articles)

고리³ 〈걸쇠〉 a clasp ♦ 고리를 걸다[풀다] fasten [unfasten] a clasp

고리 高利 high interest; usury; a high rate of interest
♦ 고리로 at high interest; at a high [usurious] rate of interest; 〈부당하게 높게〉 at an extortionate [exorbitant] rate of interest / 고리를 취하다 profiteer high interest / 고리로 돈을 꾸어 주다[꾸다] lend [borrow] money at a usurious rate of interest [at usury]
■—채 a usurious loan

고리눈 〈환안(環眼)〉 an eye with a white-ringed iris; 〈동그란 눈〉 big [large] round eyes
♦ 고리눈을 부릅뜨고 with (fiercely) glaring eyes

고리대금 高利貸金 〈돈〉 a loan at high interest [at a high rate of interest]; 〈업〉 usury; (口) a loan sharking; money lending
♦ 고리대금업을 하다 practice usury; lend money at usury
■—업자 a usurer; a usury man; (口) a loan shark; a Shylock

고리버들 〈植〉 an osier; a basket osier

고리삭다 too old for *one's* age; prematurely decrepit

고리짝 a bale; a wicker portmanteau [suitcase, trunk] ♦ 목화 한 고리짝 a bale of cotton

고리타분하다 1 〈냄새가〉 stinking; rancid; fetid
♦ 고리타분한 냄새가 나다 smell offensive [foul]; stink
▶ 고리타분한 냄새가 코를 찔렀다 A rancid smell greeted my nose.
2 〈진부하다〉 old-fashioned; hackneyed; trite; stale; 〈틀에 박힌〉 stereotyped; 〈말이 상투적인〉 clichéd
♦ 고리타분한 말 a hackneyed phrase; a cliché;

a trite expression / 고리타분한 생각[사상] a stereotyped [hackneyed] idea; cliché thinking; an old-fashioned [out-of-date] idea / 고리타분한 책 a musty [fusty] book / 고리타분한 학설 a worn-out [threadbare] theory

고리탑탑하다 stinking ⇨ 고리타분하다
고리 키 〈러시아의 소설가〉 Gorki, Maksim (1868-1936)
고린내 a nasty smell; a stench; a stink
♦고린내 나다 smell bad; stink / 고린내를 풍기다 give off [send out] a bad smell; emit a foul [filthy] odor
▶ 그들의 발에서 풍기는 고린내가 코를 찔렀다 The sweaty stink from their feet greeted my nose.

고릴라 〔動〕 a gorilla
고립 孤立 isolation; 〈무원〉 helplessness
♦고립 무원으로 싸우다 fight alone and unaided
—**고립하다** be isolated; stand alone [isolated]; be in isolation; 〈사회[정치]적으로〉 be quarantined
♦고립된 solitary; isolated; lone; helpless / 외부 세계로부터 완전히 고립된 be entirely cut off from the outside world [the rest of world] / 아무를 친구로부터 고립시키다 isolate sb from 《his》 friends / 고립된 생활을 하다 live in isolation
▶ 그는 동급생들로부터 고립되어 있다 He is isolated from his classmates.
▶ 그 나라는 세계로부터 고립되었다 The country was isolated from the world.
■ 국제적— 《avoid》 international isolation
■ —어 an isolated language —**정책** an isolationist policy —**주의** isolationism —**주의자** an isolationist —**화(化)** isolation; 〔外交〕 encirclement

고마움 〈감사〉 thankfulness; gratitude; 〈혜택〉 blessing 《of health》; 〈가치〉 value [virtue] 《of money》; 〈은혜〉 (a) favor
♦건강의 고마움을 알다 know [appreciate] the value [worth] of 《good》 health
▶ 병이 나빠야 비로소 건강의 고마움을 안다 It is only after we get ill that we know how blessed it is to be healthy. ⇌ No one can appreciate the bliss of health till he loses it.
▶ 나는 이제 비로소 부모님의 고마움을 알겠다 Now I understand how much I owe to my parents.

고마워하다 be thankful 《for》; be [feel] grateful 《to *one* for *sth*》; show *one's* gratitude; appreciate
▶ 그는 너의 도움을 매우 고마워한다 He is indeed thankful to you for [greatly appreciates] your help.
▶ 그는 아내의 배려에 대해 매우 고마워했다 He was very thankful [grateful] to his wife for her consideration. ⇌ He greatly appreciated his wife's consideration.

고막 鼓膜 〔解〕 the eardrum; the drumhead; the drum membrane; the tympanum 《*pl*. ~s, -na》; the tympanic membrane
♦고막의 tympanic; tympanal / 고막이 찢어질 것 같은 소리 a deafening [an earsplitting] noise / 고막이 터지다 have *one's* eardrum split [ruptured] / 고막을 파열시키다 rupture an eardrum
▶ 그는 고막이 터졌다 His eardrum burst [split]. ⇌ His tympanic membrane ruptured.
■ —염 myringitis

고만 such ⇨ 그만[1,2]
고만고만하다 much the same ⇨ 그만그만하다
고만하다 nearly same ⇨ 그만하다
-고말고 certainly; of course; indeed; sure; to be sure; surely
▶ 그렇고 말고 It's just as you say. ⇌ Of course, it is. ⇌ Oh yes, sure!
▶ 내가 가겠느냐고? 가고 말고 Will I go, you say? Sure, I will.
▶ 〔會話〕 「이 책 좀 빌려도 됩니까?」 「되고 말고요」 "May I borrow this book?" "Yes, of course [certainly]. ⇌ Sure."
▶ 〔會話〕 「나 좀 도와 주겠니?」 「도와 주고 말고」 "Will you help me?" "Sure. ⇌ With pleasure. ⇌ Certainly."
▶ 〔會話〕 「민수를 아시나요?」 「알고 말고요」 "Do you know Min-su?" "Indeed I do."
▶ 〔會話〕 「동행해도 되겠어요?」 「되고 말고요」 "Do you mind if I join you?" "Not at all. ⇌ Certainly not."

고맘때 about [around] that time ⇨ 그맘때
고맙다 1 〈대상이〉 grateful; welcome; kind; blessed
♦고마운 말씀 kind [gracious] words / 고마운 비 a welcome rain / 고마운 선물 a much appreciated present / 고마운 주인 a benevolent [kind] master / 고마운 햇빛 the blessed light of heaven / 고맙지 않은 undesirable
▶ 이것은 고마운 선물이다 This is a welcome gift.
▶ 전화란 참 고마운 것이다 What a blessed device [a happy invention] the telephone is!
2 〈내가〉 grateful; thankful; appreciative
♦고맙게도 kindly; graciously; thankfully; luckily; fortunately; I am thankful that…/ 고맙게 받다 accept 《a present》 thankfully [with thanks] / 고맙게 여기다[생각하다] be thankful [grateful] 《to *sb* for *sth*》; be obliged 《to *sb*》; appreciate 《*sb's* kindness》; gratefully acknowledge 《a favor》
▶ 대단히 고맙습니다 Thank you very much. ⇌ Thanks a lot. ⇌ I'm much obliged to you.
▶ 그렇게 말씀해 주시니 대단히 고맙습니다 It is very kind [nice] of you to say so.
▶ 편지 주셔서 고맙습니다 Thank you very much for your kind letter.
▶ 생일 파티에 초대해 주셔서 대단히 고맙습니다 It is very kind of you to invite us to your birthday party.
▶ 와 줘서 고맙다 I appreciate your [Thanks for] coming.
▶ 그렇게 해 주시면 정말 고맙겠습니다 I would be much obliged to you if you do so.
▶ 친구들이 모두 친절해서 매우 고맙게 생각하고 있습니다 All friends are very kind to me, and I am very grateful to them.
▶ 고맙게도 그 날은 개었다 Fortunately the sky cleared up that day.

▶고맙게도 저는 건강합니다 I'm happy to say I am quite well.
▶고맙게도 그는 내게 돈을 꾸어 주었다 He was kind enough to lend me some money. ⇒ He has kindly lent me money.

고매 故買 buying stolen goods; fencing ◆장물고매자 a fence; a dealer in stolen goods —고매하다 buy [deal in] stolen goods ■—품 hot goods; goods obtained by stealing

고매하다 高邁— high-minded; lofty (-minded); noble
◆고매한 기품 a noble spirit / 고매한 이상 a lofty [high] ideal / 고매한 인격자 a person of noble character / 식견이 고매하다 have exalted ideas
▶고매한 이상을 내걸어 봤자 별 수 없어 Such lofty(-minded) ideals will get you nowhere.

고명 〈양념·꾸미〉 a garnish; relish; 《美》 fixings; a seasoning for extra flavor or color
◆갖은 고명을 얹은 닭찜 cooked chicken with all the trimmings / 국수에 다진 야채 고명을 얹다 provide a bowl of noodles with a garnish of shredded [sliced] vegetables; garnish noodles with sliced vegetables

고명 高名 **1** 〈유명함〉 fame; (high) reputation; repute; renown
—**고명하다** famed; famous; renowned; noted
◆고명한 작가 a famous [famed] writer; a writer of high reputation [renown]
▶생물학자로서 그분은 세계적으로 고명하다 As a biologist he enjoys world-wide fame.
▶그분은 세계적으로 고명한 사람이다 He is world-famous (a man of worldwide fame).
2 〈존함〉 your name
▶고명은 익히 들었습니다 I have heard a great deal of you. ⇒ Your name is quite familiar to me.

고명딸 one's only daughter among (his) many sons

고모 姑母 one's father's sister; a paternal aunt; an aunt ■—부 the husband of one's father's sister; an uncle

고목 古木 an old [aged] tree ◆은행나무 고목 an old ginkgo (tree)

고목 枯木 a dead [withered] tree; 〈잎이 진〉 a bare tree

고무 鼓舞 encouragement; stimulation; incitement
◆고무적인 encouraging; inspiring; stimulative
▶한국 해운업의 미래[전망]는 고무적이다 The future [prospect] of Korean shipping business is encouraging [very bright].
—**고무하다** encourage; inspire 《sb with patriotism》; inspirit 《sb to greater efforts》; stir up 《one's mind》; stimulate; cheer 《the heart of sb》
◆사기를 고무하다 raise [arouse, stir up] the morale (of the troops)
▶지휘관은 부하들을 고무했다 The leader inspired his fellows with courage.
▶그 책은 소년들에게 모험심을 고무했다 The book inspired the boys with an adventurous spirit.

고무 rubber; 〈재료〉 gum; 〈탄성 고무〉 India rubber ◆고무를 입히다 coat sth with rubber ■생— crude rubber 아라비아— gum arabic 인조— artificial rubber 재생— reclaimed rubber 천연— natural rubber 합성— synthetic rubber —공 a (india-)rubber ball —공업 (the) rubber industry —관 a rubber tube —나무 a rubber [gum] tree; 〈관상용〉 a rubber plant —농장 a rubber plantation —도장 a rubber stamp —바퀴 a rubber tire —밴드 a rubber band —보트 a rubber boat —신 rubber shoes —액 gum water —장화 rubber boots —제품 rubber goods —줄 an elastic [a rubber] band [string] —창 a rubber sole: 고무창을 댄 구두 rubber-soled shoes —풍선 a balloon; 〈장난감〉 a toy balloon —호스 a rubber hose

고무래 〈농기구〉 a T-shaped wooden rake (for gathering (unhusked) grains)

고무지우개 an eraser; a rubber eraser; 《英》 a rubber; an india rubber
◆고무 지우개로 지우다 erase [rub out] with an eraser
▶이 연필에는 고무 지우개가 달려 있다 This pencil has an eraser.

고무풀 gum; mucilage; rubber cement; 〈사무용〉 glue
◆고무풀을 칠한 봉투 an adhesive envelope / 판지 두 장을 고무풀로 붙이다 gum the two pieces of cardboard together

고문 古文 ancient writings; 〈고전〉 classics ■—체 an archaic [a classical] style —학 study of ancient classics

고문 拷問 (physical [mental]) torture; the rack; the third degree
◆고문을 당하다 be tortured; be put to torture / 고문을 당해 죽다[자백하다] die on the rack [confess under torture]
▶어떤 고문에도 그는 입을 열지 않았다 No torture could make him speak.
—**고문하다** torture sb (on the rack); put sb to torture [the rack]; give sb the third degree
◆고문하여 입을 열게 하다 torture sb into talking
■물— water torture: 물고문을 하다 put sb to water torture ■—대 a rack —도구 instruments of torture —치사 torture resulting in death

고문 顧問 an adviser [advisor] (to); 《美》 a counselor; a consultant; a brain truster
◆고문 노릇하다 act in an advisory capacity; act as consultant 《on》 / 연극부의 고문 노릇을 하다 act as adviser for the drama club / 도시 계획의 전문가를 고문으로 두다 employ an expert on city planning as adviser
■기술— a technical adviser 대통령— an aide-de-camp to the President 법률— a juridical counselor 편집— an advisory editor ■—관 a councilor —단 an advisory group [body, council]; a brain trust; 《美》 brain trusters —변호사 a legal advisor; 〈회사의〉 a corporation lawyer [attorney]; 〈가정의〉 a family lawyer

고문서 古文書 old [ancient] manuscripts; historical [old] documents; a paleography ■—학 paleography

고물[1] 〈떡의〉 (red) bean flour (for dressing rice cake)
♦콩[팥] 고물을 묻힌 떡 rice cake dressed with soy [red] bean flour

고물[2] 〈배의〉 the stern; the poop
♦고물을 앞으로 stern foremost / 고물을 돌려서 stern on / 고물 쪽에[으로] astern; aft / 이물에서 고물까지 from stem to stern; fore and aft / 고물 쪽부터 가라앉다 sink by the stern

고물 古物 a used thing [article, item]; a secondhand article; 〈골동품〉 an antique
♦고물이 된 가구 old furniture / 고물이 된 사람 다니다 hunt for used articles
▶내 가방은 고물이 되었다 My bag has become [grown] very old.
▶그 사람은 이제 고물이 다 되어 쓸모가 없다 He is worn-out [a back number] and good for nothing.
■—상 a secondhand store [shop]; a junk shop; 〈상인〉 a dealer in secondhand articles; a junk dealer —시장 a flea market —차 a dilapidated car; (美) a flivver

고미 〔建〕 a plaster panel ceiling ■—다락 an attic; a garret —집 a house with an attic

고미 苦味 〈쓴맛〉 a bitter taste

고민 苦悶 〈심신의〉 agony; 〈마음의〉 anguish; worry; affliction
♦마음의 고민 mental affliction; anguish of heart; a weight on one's mind / 불타는 듯한 사랑의 고민 agony of ardent love / 청춘의 고민 nameless longings of youth; torments of awakened love / 고민 거리 the source of trouble / 고민스러운 표정 an agonized look / 고민 끝에 병들다 worry oneself sick
▶무슨 큰 고민이 있는 모양이구나 You seem to be immensely worried.
▶그녀는 고민이 되어 울었다 She cried out in anguish.
▶그는 고민을 잊으려고 술을 한 잔 했다 He took a drink to down his agony.
▶그녀는 심적인 고민으로 밤새 잠을 이루지 못했다 Her mental anguish kept her awake all night.
—고민하다 agonize 《over one's failure》; be in agony [anguish]; be troubled 《with》; be worried 《about》
♦사랑에 고민하다 be lovesick; languish for love; 〈실연하여〉 be lovelorn
▶나는 장래의 진로에 대해 고민했다 I was worried about the future. ⇌ I just didn't know what to do about my future.
▶그는 평생 돈 문제로 고민했다 He suffered all his life from anxiety about money.
▶너는 그렇게 고민할 필요가 없었다 You need not have worried (yourself) so much.

고발 告發 complaint; denunciation ♦…의 고발에 의해 on complaint of…
—고발하다 file a complaint 《against sb with the prosecutor's office》; inform 《the authorities against sb》
♦경찰에 정식으로 고발하다 lay a formal complaint before the police / 고발당하다 come under indictment
▶우리는 그를 고발했다 We made [filed] a complaint against him.
■—내부— an insider's disclosure; exposure from within ■—자 a prosecutor; an accuser; a complainant; a denunciator; an informant; a relator —장(狀) a bill of indictment

고배 苦杯 a bitter cup
♦고배를 마시다 drink a bitter cup; 〈쓰라린 경험을 하다〉 go through an ordeal; 〈승부에서 지다〉 be miserably defeated [beaten]; suffer a defeat
▶지난 주에 우리는 저 팀에게 고배를 마셨다 We were thoroughly [miserably] defeated by that team last week.

고백 告白 (a) confession; (a) profession; 〈자인〉 (an) acknowledgment
▶그의 사랑의 고백을 듣고 그녀는 매우 기뻤다 [놀랐다] She was overjoyed at his declaration of love [His profession of love astonished her].
—고백하다 confess (to); profess; acknowledge; make a confession [profession] 《of》
♦죄를 고백하다 confess one's crime [sin, guilt]; confess that one has committed a crime
▶그는 그 돈을 자기가 가지고 갔다고 고백했다 He confessed that he had taken the money.
▶그녀는 목사에게 죄를 고백했다 She confessed her sin to a priest.
▶그것은 무지를 고백하는 것과 다를 바 없다 That amounts to a confession of your own ignorance.
■—신앙— a confession [profession] of one's faith —서(書) a (written) confession —성사 〔가톨릭〕 the sacrament of penance; penance

고백반 枯白礬 burnt alum

고법 高法 a high court ⇨ 고등 법원

고별 告別 farewell; leave-taking; parting
—고별하다 take (one's) leave 《of》; say goodby(e) 《to》; bid farewell 《to》
▶그는 급히 우리에게 고별하고 그곳을 떠났다 He left the place, bidding us farewell in haste.
■—사 〈송별사〉 a farewell address; a valediction; 〈조사〉 a funeral oration —식 〈송별식〉 a farewell ceremony; 〈영결식〉 a funeral service —연설 a farewell address [speech] —파티[연주회] a farewell party [concert]

고본 古本 an old book (⇨ 고서) ■—시장 an old-book market

고본 稿本 〈원고를 맨〉 a manuscript; an MS.

고봉 高峰 a high mountain; a high [lofty] peak ■—준령 high mountains and steep peaks

고봉 高捧 〈말·되의〉 a heaped [heaping] bushelful; a heap (of)
♦고봉밥 a heaping bowl of cooked rice / 고봉으로 되다 give a heaping measure 《of》
▶그는 고봉밥을 순식간에 깨끗이 비웠다 He polished off a heaped bowlful of rice in no time.

고부 告訃 〈부고〉 a notice [an announcement] of sb's death; an obituary notice

고부 姑婦 a mother-in-law and a daughter-in-law
♦고부 관계 the relationship between a mother-in-law and a daughter-in-law
▶그의 집은 고부간에 사이가 별로 좋지 않다 His mother and wife don't get along so well.

고부장하다 rather [slightly] bent ⇨ 구부정하다

고분 古墳 an ancient tomb; an old burial mound; a tumulus (*pl*. ~es, -li) ♦고분을 발굴하다 excavate [unearth] an ancient tomb

고분고분 obediently; submissively; at sb's beck (and call)
▶그는 부친의 명령을 고분고분 따랐다 He readily obeyed his father's orders.
—**고분고분하다** obedient; submissive; meek
♦부모에게 고분고분하다 be obedient to one's parents

고분자 高分子 〔化·物〕 a high molecule; a macromolecule
■—물질 a (high) polymer; a macromolecular substance —전해질 a polyelectrolyte —필름 high polymer film —화학 (high) polymer chemistry —화합물 a high molecular compound —흡입체 a high polymer absorbent

고블랭직 —織 ♦수렵 장면이 그려진 고블랭직 벽걸이 주단 Gobelin tapestry depicting a hunting scene

고비[1] 〈최고조〉 the climax; the crest; the height; the peak; 〈위기〉 the crisis; the crucial moment [stage]; 〈전기〉 a turning point
♦인생의 고비 the vicissitudes of life
▶더위는 지금이 고비다 It is the hottest time in the year.
〈고비를〉 고비를 넘다 〈환자 등이〉 pass the crisis; 〈물가 등이〉 pass the crest [peak] 《of high prices》
▶여름 더위도 고비를 넘겼다 The heat of the summer has passed its peak.
▶이 일도 고비를 넘겼다 We are over the hump with this work.
▶추위도 고비를 넘긴 것 같다 It seems that the coldest season is over.
▶환자는 고비를 넘겨 쾌유 중이다 The patient has passed the crisis and is getting better.
▶우리는 이 일의 (어려운) 고비를 넘겼다 We have got over the most difficult part of this work. ⇒ (口) We are over the hump on this work.
▶그는 전쟁터에서 죽을 고비를 여러 번 맞이했다 He was often face to face with death on the battlefield.
〈고비에(서)〉 겨울 추위가 고비에 다달았다 The cold of winter has reached its climax [peak].
▶그는 마지막 고비에서 마음을 바꿨다 He changed his mind at the last moment.
■—판 a critical moment; a [an important] turning point

고비[2] 〈편지꽂이〉 a letter file [rack]

고비[3] 〔植〕 a flowering [royal] fern; an osmund

고비사막 —砂漠 the Gobi (Desert)

고뿔 (a) cold ⇨ 감기 ♦고뿔들다 catch (a) cold; take (a) cold

고삐 reins (▶보통 복수형으로 씀)
♦두 가닥의 고삐 a pair of reins / 고삐 풀린 말 a runaway horse; a riderless horse / 고삐를 늦추다 slacken [loosen] the reigns; 〈통제를 누그러뜨리다〉 relax one's supervision / 고삐를 당기다[죄다] pull on [tighten] the reins / 고삐를 잡아 말을 세우다 rein up a horse
▶그는 말 고삐를 잡고 선두에 나섰다 He held the horse by the reins and led the way.
▶그는 말 고삐를 풀어 놓아 마음대로 가게 했다 He gave the horse free rein. ⇒ He gave the horse its head.
▶그는 조금만 고삐를 늦춰 주면 게으름을 피운다 The moment you relax your supervision, he becomes lazy.

고사 考查 an examination; a test
♦고사를 보다 be tested; take [do, sit for] an examination
■인물— a character test [examination] 학력— an achievement test ■—과목[문제] examination subjects [questions] —장 an examination room [hall]; an examination site

고사 告祀 a (family) ritual for the worship of deities
♦고사를 지내다 pray to the gods [deities] for one's (family's) happiness
■—떡 rice cake offered to spirits

고사 固辭 a firm [positive] refusal
—**고사하다** refuse [decline] positively
♦고사하고 받지 않다 positively decline to accept
▶그는 대통령의 간청을 고사했다 He firmly refused the President's earnest request.
▶그녀는 장관직을 고사했다 She categorically [flatly] refused to take office as a minister.

고사 古事·故事 〈옛 사건〉 an ancient happening [event]; a historical fact [event]; 〈구전(口傳)〉 (a) tradition; folklore; 〈전설〉 a legend
♦중국의 고사 historical [ancient] events in China / 고사를 인용하다 make a reference [allude] to a historical event
▶이 말에는 고사가 있다 This word has its origin in a historical fact.
■—성어 사전 a dictionary of fables and phrases

고사 枯死 〈식물의〉 death; withering to death
—**고사하다** wither and die; 〈병으로〉 be blighted
▶오랜 가뭄으로 초목이 모두 고사했다 All the plants were withered and dead after the long drought.

고사기관총[포] 高射機關銃[砲] an antiaircraft [A.A., (口) ack-ack] machine gun

고사리 bracken; brake; fernbrake ♦고사리 같은 손 the cute [delicate] little hands (of a baby) / 고사리 캐러 가다 go bracken gathering

고사본 古寫本 an old manuscript

고사포 高射砲 an antiaircraft [A.A.] gun; (口) an ack-ack gun

■ —부대 an antiaircaft [antiair] corps —진지 an antiaircraft [A.A.] battery position —탄 an antiaircraft shell —화 antiaircraft fire; flak

고사하고 姑捨— 〈그만두고〉 apart from; setting aside; far from; let alone; on the contrary; 〈말할 것도 없이〉 not to mention; to say nothing of
▶ 그는 사과는 고사하고 오히려 내게 불평을 했다 He didn't even try to apologize. On the contrary, he complained to me.
▶ 음식은 고사하고 물도 떨어졌다 It's not a question of food. We didn't even have any water.
▶ 나는 독일어를 쓰기는 고사하고 읽을 줄도 모른다 I can't even read German, let alone [much less] write it.
▶ 그는 새 차는 고사하고 중고 차도 살 형편이 안 된다 He can't afford to buy a used car, much less [not to speak of, let alone] a new one.
▶ 우리는 야생 조류 관찰에 나섰지만 딱따구리는 고사하고 꿩도 못 보았다 We went bird watching, but we could not find even a pheasant, to say nothing of a woodpecker.

고산 高山 〈높은 산〉 a high mountain; an alp
♦ 고산의 alpine
■ —대(帶) 〔植〕 an alpine belt [zone] —병 mountain [altitude] sickness : 고산병에 걸리다 develop [suffer from] altitude sickness —생활 an alpine life —식물[동물] an alpine plant [animal]; (총칭) an alpine flora [fauna]

고살 故殺 〔法〕 (a) manslaughter; murder in the second degree (⇨ 모살) —고살하다 murder; commit manslaughter ■ —자 a murderer in the second degree

고상하다 高尙— 〈고귀하다〉 noble; lofty; 〈품위있다〉 refined; elegant; highbrow
♦ 고상한 마음 a noble mind / 고상한 목적 a lofty aim / 고상한 숙녀 a noble [an elegant, a graceful] lady / 고상한 옷 a decent suit of clothes / 고상한 잡지 a sophisticated magazine / 고상한 젊은이 a refined young man / 방을 고상하게 꾸미다 furnish a room elegantly
▶ 그녀는 옷차림이 고상하다 She is dressed elegantly [in good taste].
▶ 그는 고상한 취미를 가지고 있다 He has refined [very elegant] taste.
▶ 그녀에게는 고상한 데가 있다 There is something graceful [elegant] about her.
▶ 아무리 고상한 체 해봐도 네 바탕은 우리가 알고 있어 It doesn't make any difference what airs [graces] you put on. We know your background.

고색 古色 an antique look [appearance]
♦ 고색창연한 antique-looking; time-worn; time-honored
▶ 이 절은 고색창연하다 This temple has an antique [ancient] look about it. ⇌ This temple looks hoary [very old].

고생 苦生 **1** 〈어려운 생활〉 a hard [tough] life; privation
—고생하다 be in needy [straitened] circumstances; be badly off
♦ 고생할 때 in (the hour of) need; when one is hard up
▶ 그 당시 나는 돈 때문에 고생했다 In those days I suffered [was pinched, was hard up] for money. ⇌ I had financial difficulties in those days.
2 〈고난〉 trouble(s); hardship(s); suffering; difficulties; trials
♦ 속세의 고생 the troubles [cares] of life / 고생 10년 ten long years of hardships / 고생을 같이하다 share 《with sb》 in 《his》 hardships [distress] / 온갖 고생을 겪다 undergo [go through] all sorts of hardships [troubles]; experience [taste] the bitters of life / 고생을 견디다 endure [bear] hardships
▶ 물이 부족해서 고생이다 We are suffering from a shortage of water.
▶ 그는 고생이란 것을 모른다 He is an utter stranger to the grim realities of life.
▶ 나는 고생을 모르고 자랐다 I was brought up free from [of] care.
▶ 그는 부모에게 많은 고생을 시켰다 He has given [caused] his parents much trouble.
▶ 고생을 해봐야 사람이 된다 Adversity makes a man wise.
—고생하다 be distressed [troubled] 《by, with》; have a hard time (of it); have trouble [difficulty]; undergo [suffer, go through] hardships; be (hard) put to it

解說 *have a hard time*은 고통스러운 일을 당하다란 뜻으로, *have trouble*은 번거롭거나 힘든 일에 맞닥뜨리다란 뜻으로 쓰인다.

♦ 가족을 부양하느라고 고생하다 be hard put to it to support one's family / 이가 아파 고생하다 have trouble with one's teeth; suffer from (a) toothache / 고생시키다 put sb to 《a lot of》 trouble; give sb trouble
▶ 나는 택시를 잡느라고 고생했다 I had trouble getting a taxi.
▶ 집을 찾느라고 매우 고생했다 I had much difficulty (in) finding the house.
▶ 그들은 일 때문에 매우 고생했다 They had a hard time with their work.
▶ 이 집을 짓는 데 내가 얼마나 고생했는지 너희들은 모를 것이다 You don't know what I had to go through to build this house.
▶ 우리는 고생한 보람이 있었다 We have not suffered in vain.
▶ 젊었을 때 고생해 보는 것도 좋을 것이다 It will be good for you to go through hardships while you are young.
▶ 우리는 고생해서 강을 거슬러 올라갔다 We worked our way upstream.
▶ 고생하지 않는 사람은 없다 Everybody has his trouble.
3 〈수고〉 toil; labor; pains ♦ 헛고생 vain efforts; lost labor
—고생하다 labor; toil; take pains; work hard
♦ 고생하여 번 돈[얻은 경험] hard-earned money [experience]
▶ 이런 고생 끝에 나는 그 기술을 배웠다 Thus I learned the technique the hard way.
▶ 그의 고생은 보람이 있었다 His pains have

been rewarded.
▶ 나는 파티 준비를 하느라고 많은 고생을 했다 I took great pains with the preparations [in preparing] for the party.
━길 a thorny way; a hard row to hoe ━문 the threshold of a future filled with hardships ━살이 a hard life; a life of hardship ━주머니 a person who is never free from troubles; a person with hard luck ━티 signs [traces, the shadow] of a hard life

고생 끝에 낙이 온다 〈속담〉 No cross, no crown. ≒ No gains without pains. ≒ After a storm comes a calm. ≒ Of sufferance comes ease.

고생대 古生代 〖地質〗 the Paleozoic era ◆ 고생대의 Paleozoic

고생물 古生物 extinct animals and plants that existed in ancient times
━학 paleontology ━학자 a paleontologist

고생스럽다 苦生— hard; painful; bitter; toilsome; tough
◆ 고생스러운 삶[세상] a hard life [world] / 고생스러운 일 a hard [difficult, (口) tough] job
▶ 살아가기가 고생스럽다 It is hard to get along.
▶ 그의 삶은 고생스러울 뿐이었다 His life was full of hardships.
▶ 아무리 형편이 고생스러워도 그녀는 불평하지 않았다 No matter how trying the circumstances, she never complained.

고서 古書 an old book; the classics; 〈헌 책〉 a used [secondhand] book; 〈옛 필적〉 old handwritings
━전(시회) an exhibition of rare [old, antiquary] books ━점 a used [secondhand] bookstore

고설 高說 your opinion [view] ▶ 귀하의 고설에서 배운 바가 많습니다 I have learned greatly from your valuable suggestions.

고성 古城 an old [ancient] castle [fortress]

고성 高聲 a loud voice; a high-pitched voice
◆ 고성으로 말하다 talk in a loud [high-pitched] voice; talk loudly / 고성 방가하다 sing loudly; sing nosily without restraint

고성능 高性能 high efficiency [effectiveness]
◆ 고성능의 highly efficient; high-powered; high-performance
━라디오 a high-powered radio ━레인지 a high-efficiency range 〔(英) cooker〕 ━수신기 a high-fidelity receiver ━엔진 a high-performance engine ━폭약 high explosives ━항공기 a high-performance aircraft

고소 告訴 a charge; (an) accusation; (a) prosecution; legal proceedings; 〈민사의〉 (a) complaint; a (law) suit; an action
◆ 손해배상의 고소 a suit for damages / 고소를 수리[각하]하다 accept [reject] a complaint [charge] / 고소를 취하하다 withdraw [drop] a complaint [suit]; retract a charge
━고소하다 charge sb with a crime; accuse sb of a crime; bring an accusation [a charge] of a crime against sb (▶피해자나 법정 대리인이 주어가 됨); sue sb 《for damages》; bring [file] a suit against sb; lodge [file] a complaint against sb

〖解說〗 **charge**는 당국이 형사 사건을 고소하는 것. **accuse**는 당국이 개인이 고소하는 것으로서 형사나 민사에 모두 쓴다. **sue**는 민사상으로 고소하는 데 많이 쓴다.

▶ 그는 그 잡지사를 명예 훼손죄로 고소했다 He accused the magazine publisher of libel.
▶ 나는 손해 배상을 위해 그 회사를 고소했으나 패소했다 I brought a suit for the damages against the company, but I lost it.
▶ 그는 그 남자를 경찰에 고소했으나 2주일 후에 그것을 취하했다 He filed a complaint with the police against the man, but two weeks later he withdrew it.
▶ 그는 절도[불법 침입]죄로 고소당했다 He was accused of theft [trespassing]. ≒ He was charged with theft [trespassing].
━인 an accuser; a complainant; 〈원고〉 a plaintiff ━장 a letter [bill] of complaint; a written complaint ━절차 an accusatorial procedure

고소 苦笑 a bitter (grin, wry, forced) smile
▶ 나는 그가 아무 것도 모르는 것을 보고 고소를 금할 수 없었다 I could not suppress wry [bitter] smile at his ignorance.
━고소하다 smile a bitter smile [bitterly, grimly]; give a forced laugh

고소 高所 a high place; high ground; an elevation; heights ━공포증 (a) fear of heights; acrophobia: 나는 고소 공포증이 있다 I have acrophobia. ≒ I fear heights.

고소득 高所得 a high [large, big] income ━자 a large-income [high-income] earner; a person in the high-income bracket

고소원 固所願 ▶ 불감청이언정 고소원이다 It is just what I wanted. ≒ I couldn't ask for a better chance than this. ≒ It is a rare luck for me. ≒ It is an unexpected piece of good luck.

고소하다 1 〈맛·냄새가〉 smell [taste] like sesame; savory; pleasant in taste and smell
◆ 참깨를 볶는 고소한 냄새 the pleasant aroma of sesame seeds being roasted
▶ 그 음식은 고소한 참기름 맛이 났다 The food tasted of savory sesame oil. ≒ The food had a savor [taste] of sesame oil.
2 〈남의 일이〉 ◆ 남의 불행을 고소해하다 gloat [feel malicious pleasure] over sb's mishap
▶ 그거 고소하다 It serves [(口) Serve(s)] you [him] right!
▶ 그는 적이 꼼짝 못한 것을 생각하고 고소해 했다 He gloated quietly at the thought that his enemy had been trapped.

고속 高速 a high speed; superspeed; 〈교통〉 rapid transit ▶ 차는 고속으로 달렸다 The car traveled at high speed.
━(도)강(鋼) high-speed steel ━(도)사진 high-speed photography ━(도)시대 a speed age; an age of speed ━(도) 영화 a slow-motion picture ━중성자로(中性子爐) a fast neutron reactor ━증식로 a fast-breeder

reactor (略 FBR) ━철도 a rapid transit railway ━촬영 high-speed photographing

고속도로 高速道路 an expressway; a freeway; a superhighway; (英) a motorway
♦ 경인 고속도로 the Kyŏngin [Seoul-Inch'ŏn] Expressway / 6차선 고속도로 a 6-lane expressway / 고속도로망 the superhighway networks
■ ━입체교차로 an interchange ━중앙분리대 a median strip; (英) a central reserve [reservation] ━진입로 a ramp ━통행료 a toll ━통행료 징수소 a tollgate

고수 固守 adherence; persistence; tenacity ━고수하다 〈고집하다〉 adhere [cling] to 《the principle》; hold fast to 《one's ideal》; keep [stick] to 《old customs》; persevere [persist] in 《a course》; (口) stand pat 《on one's views》; 〈진지 등을〉 defend 《one's position》 stubbornly; hold out
♦ 자기 지위를 고수하다 stick [adhere, cling] to one's post
▶ 아버지는 지금도 옛 관습을 고수하신다 My father still holds fast to old customs.
▶ 그들은 요새를 고수했다 They tenaciously defended the fortress.

고수 高手 superiority; mastery; 〈사람〉 a good hand [master-hand]; a superior 《in》; a high-grade player; a master
♦ 바둑[장기]의 고수 a high-ranking paduk [chess] player
▶ 장기는 그가 나보다 고수다 He is better than I am at chess. ⇒ He is superior to me in chess.

고수 鼓手 a drummer; a tambour ■ 소년━ a drummer boy ━장 a drum major [〈여자〉 majorette]

고수레 〈떡 반죽할 때〉 mixing hot water in rice flour to make dough ━고수레하다 make dough sprinkling boiling water on rice flour
■ ━떡 a kind of cooked rice cake

고수레하다 〔民俗〕 scatter [spray] food and drink as an offering to a guardian deity (at a sorcerer's ritual or before a meal at an outing)

고수련 nursing ⇨ 병구완

고수머리 〈머리털〉 curly hair; a curl; frizzy [frizzled] hair; kinky hair(흑인 등의); 〈사람〉 a person with curly hair; a curly-haired [frizzy-haired] person; a curlyhead
▶ 그는 고수머리다 He has curly [frizzy] hair.
▶ 내 여동생은 날 때부터 고수머리다 My sister has had curly hair since she was born. ⇒ My sister's hair is naturally curly.

고수부지 高水敷地 the terrace land on the river; the riverside highlands

고수위 高水位 〔土・建・機〕 high-water level; flood stage

고스란히 〈있는 그대로〉 just as it was; as they [you] were; intact; untouched; 〈멀짱하게〉 safely; without damage; unhurt; 〈완전히〉 completely; entirely; all
♦ 고스란히 그대로 있다 remain intact; be just as it was / 고스란히 다 가져가다 take away everything; leave nothing behind
▶ 나는 그에게 고스란히 당했다 I was completely taken in by him.
▶ 나는 보석을 고스란히 도둑맞았다 All my jewels were stolen.
▶ 부모님은 죽은 형의 방을 고스란히 그대로 두셨다 My parents have left my dead brother's room untouched [exactly as it was].
▶ 도둑맞은 물건들이 고스란히 그대로 돌아왔다 The stolen things were all recovered in their original condition.
▶ 임자가 나서지 않아 그 돈은 고스란히 그녀의 것이 되었다 As no one claimed the money, it was all given to her.
▶ 나는 그것을 고스란히 잊고 있었다 I completely [(口) clean] forgot about it. ⇒ I forgot all about it.

고스러지다 get scraggy

고스트 〔TV〕 a ghost; a faint or secondary television image; ghosting

고슬고슬하다 properly [well] cooked; 〈서술적〉 be cooked just right; be nice to eat; be neither too hard nor too soft
▶ 밥이 고슬고슬하게 되었다 The rice is well cooked [done].

고슴도치 〔動〕 a hedgehog

고슴도치도 제 새끼가 함함하다면 좋아한다 All his geese are swans. ⇒ Every man's goose is a gander. ⇒ The owl thinks her own young fairest.

고슴도치 외 따 지듯 be deeply [up to one's ears] in debt

고승 高僧 〈학덕이 높은〉 a learned-and-virtuous priest; 〈지위가 높은〉 a high(-ranking) priest

고시 古詩 ancient [old] poems; 〈고체시〉 free verse (in ancient China)

고시 考試 an examination; a test; 〔法〕 the civil service examination
♦ 고시를 치르다[보다] take [sit for] an examination / 고시를 시행하다 examine; give [hold] an examination
■ ━검정 a certificate [qualifying, licensing] examination ━국가 a state examination ━예비 a preliminary examination ━자격 a certifying examination ■ ━과목 examination subjects ━관 an official examiner ━위원 an examiner ━위원회 an examination committee; the examination board ━장 an examination room

고시 告示 a notice; a bulletin; a notification; an announcement; a proclamation
♦ 내무부 고시 제3호 Notification No. 3 of the Ministry of Home Affairs
━고시하다 notify 《the public of sth》; give notice 《(of, that...)》; issue a notification; announce; proclaim; promulgate
▶ 그의 임관은 10월 1일자로 관보에 고시되었다 His appointment was announced in the Official Gazette dated October 1.
▶ 도서관은 내주 중에 폐관된다고 고시되었다 It has been announced that the library will be closed next week.
■ ━가격 an official price; an officially fixed price

고식 古式 an old method [custom]; ancient procedures [formalities] ♦고식을 따라서 in accordance with a time-honored procedure [rite]

고식 姑息 ♦고식적인 temporary; makeshift; stopgap; halfway
♦고식적 수단 a half [temporizing] measure; a makeshift / 고식적 정책 an expedient [a stopgap] policy / 고식책을 취하다 take stopgag [temporizing] measures; resort to makeshifts

고실 鼓室 〔解〕 the eardrum; the atrium 《pl. -ria》; the tympanic cavity ■—신경 nervus tympanicus

고심 苦心 pains; assiduities; efforts; labor
▶아들은 많은 고심 끝에 소설을 완성했다 My son, with great pains, has finished writing a story.
—**고심하다** 〈심로하다〉 be anxious 《about》; worry 《oneself》《about, over》; 〈머리를 짜다〉 rack [cudgel] one's brains 《for a good line of verse》
♦고심하여 with great pains; painstakingly; with considerable effort
▶그는 당신을 행복하게 해 주기 위해 많이 고심했다 He took great pains to make you happy.
▶우리는 그 사업을 완성시키기 위해 수년간 고심 참담했다 We took great pains for several years to finish the project.
▶정부는 새로운 재원 발굴에 고심하고 있다 The government is worrying itself about seeking a new source of revenue.
▶이 저작에는 저자가 상당히 고심한 흔적이 보인다 The author seems to have taken great pains over this work.

고십 《a piece of》 gossip 《about》
♦정계의 고십 gossip in political circles / 고십을 좋아하는 사람 a gossip; a gossipmonger / 고십 거리가 되다 give rise to 《a lot of》 gossip; cause 《some》 gossip
▶그 사건은 장안의 고십 거리가 되었다 The event has become the gossip of the town.

고아 古雅 classical grace; classicality; 〈고귀〉 antiquity —**고아하다** classical; antique and elegant ♦고아한 문체로 글을 쓰다 write in a classical style

고아 孤兒 an orphan
▶그 소년은 7살 때 고아가 되었다 The boy was left an orphan [was orphaned] at the age of seven.
▶그 여자아이는 고아나 마찬가지다 The little girl is no better than an orphan.
■전쟁— a war orphan ■—신세 orphanhood ■—원 an orphanage; an orphan home; a home for orphans

고아 高雅 elegance; refinement —**고아하다** elegant; refined

고아 〈인도 서부의 주〉 Goa ■—사람 a Goan; a Goanese

고안 考案 a design; a contrivance; a plan; a conception; 〈고안품〉 a device
▶이것은 그의 고안이오 This is his invention.
—**고안하다** devise; conceive; think out [up]; work out; design; originate
▶그는 새 기계를 고안했다 He thought up [devised] a new machine.
▶그 방법은 누가 고안했습니까? Who devised [worked out] that method?
—**자** a designer; an originator; an inventor

고압 高壓 high pressure; 〈전기의〉 high voltage [tension]
—가스 high-pressure gas —계 piezometer —보일러 a high-pressure boiler —선 a high-voltage cable; a high-tension wire [line] —송전 highvoltage transmission —전기 high-voltage [tension] electricity —전류 a high-voltage [tension] current —징책 a high-handed policy —증기기관 a high-pressure steam engine

고압적 高壓的 high-handed; strong-arm; oppressive; overbearing
♦고압적으로 high-handedly; haughtily; domineeringly / 고압적 태도를 취하다 take [adopt, assume] an overbearing attitude / 고압적으로 나오다 act [speak] high-handedly [overbearingly]
■—수단 a high-handed [oppressive, coercive] measure

고액 高額 a large amount [sum] 《of money》
—권 a large denomination bill [bank note] —납세자 a large [high] income taxpayer —소득 a high [〈자산 등의〉 large] income —소득자 a high [large] income earner; a person in a high income bracket

고야 〈스페인의 화가〉 Goya y Lucientes, Francisco José de (1746-1828)

-고야 1 〈결심〉 by all means; at all costs; without fail
▶무슨 일이 있어도 해내고야 말겠다 I will carry it out at any cost [(口) no matter what].
▶우리는 그를 구출하고야 말겠다 We will save [rescue] him at all costs [by all means].
2 〈결과〉 at last; finally; in the end
▶온갖 노력을 기울였지만 결국 실패하고야 말았다 All my efforts resulted in failure.
▶그들은 마침내 에베레스트를 등정하고야 말았다 At last they succeeded in reaching the summit of Mt. Everest.
3 〈조건〉 ▶선생이고야 그런 짓을 안 하겠지 For a teacher, of all people to do such a thing!
▶그래 가지고야 성공할 수 있겠니? The way you act, how can you expect to succeed?
▶상황이 이래 가지고야 내가 외국에 갈 수 있겠나 With the way things stand at the moment, I can't hope to go abroad.

고약 膏藥 〈붙이는〉 a (sticking) plaster; a patch; 〈바르는〉 (an) ointment; (a) salve
♦고약을 바르다 put a salve 《on》 / 벤데[상처]에 고약을 바르다 dress a cut [wound] with an ointment / 고약을 붙이다 apply a plaster 《to》; plaster / 고약을 떼다 take [peel] the plaster off; remove the plaster

고약하다 1 〈냄새・맛이〉 bad; foul; offensive; disgusting
♦고약한 냄새 a nasty [an unpleasant, a disgusting] smell / 썩은 고기의 고약한 냄새 the

stink [vile odor] of rotten meat / 고약한 냄새가 나다 smell offensive [foul]; give out a bad smell
▶이것은 맛이 고약하다 This is disgusting to the taste.
▶[會話]「썩은 계란 냄새가 어땠니?」「고약했어」 "How did the rotten eggs smell?" "They smelled bad. ⇒ They stank."
2 〈성질·행동이〉 mean; evil; wicked; crooked; vicious
◆고약한 말 a malicious [a spiteful] remark / 고약한 사람 a nasty [mean, ill-tempered] person / 고약한 성질 an ill [a bad] disposition [nature]
▶그는 혼자 오래 살아서 성격이 고약하다 Years of living alone warped his personality. ⇒ His personality became distorted because he had lived alone for many years.
▶그런 말을 하다니 그 사람들도 고약하군 It's wicked of them to say such things.
▶그 학생은 고약한 질문을 잘 한다 The student often asks nasty [embarrassing] questions.
3 〈일·날씨 등〉 ◆고약한 감기 a bad cold / 고약한 날씨 terrible [awful, nasty] weather
▶사태가 더욱 고약하게 엉켜버렸다 The situation grew more and more entangled. ⇒ The matter became quite complicated.
▶둘 사이의 관계가 고약하게 되었다 The relationship between the two went sour.

고양 高揚 exaltation; heightening ━**고양하다** exalt; enhance; uplift
◆사기를 고양하다 raise the morale (of) / 애국심을 고양하다 exalt patriotism; uplift patriotic sentiment

고양이 a cat; 〈애칭〉 a puss; a pussy ◆고양이의[같은] feline

―――――― 고양이 ――――――

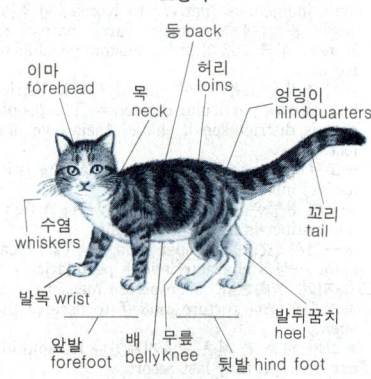

이마 forehead
목 neck
등 back
허리 loins
엉덩이 hindquarters
꼬리 tail
수염 whiskers
발목 wrist
앞발 forefoot
배 belly
무릎 knee
발뒤꿈치 heel
뒷발 hind foot

▶고양이가 목을 가르랑거린다 A cat purrs.
▶우리 집 고양이는 쥐를 잘 잡는다 Our cat is good at catching mice.
▶고양이는 야옹야옹 운다 Cats mew [meow].
▶고양이는 목숨이 아홉 있다 (속담) A cat has nine lives.
▶나는 고양이를 2마리 기른다 I have two cats.
▶도둑— a stray [an ownerless] cat 수코양이 a male cat; a tomcat; (口) a tom 암코양이 a female cat; a she-cat ■—새끼 a kitten; 〈兒〉 a kitty

고양이 목에 방울 단다 (속담) dare to undertake a formidable risk [task]

고양이 보고 반찬 가게 지키라는 격이다 (속담) It is like trusting a cat with milk [setting a fox to keep geese].

고양이 앞의 쥐걸음 (속담) be (as) timid [scared] as a rabbit

고어 古語 an old [ancient] word; an archaic word; 〈옛말〉 an old saying [adage] ■—사전 a dictionary of an ancient language

고언 古諺 an old saying [proverb]; an old saw
◆후회하지 말고 조심하라는 고언 the old saw that it's better to be safe than sorry

고언 苦言 candid [outspoken] advice; frank counsel; unwelcome [bitter, unpleasant] advice [counsel]
◆고언을 하다 give [offer] *sb* candid [unpleasant] advice / 고언을 받아들이다 swallow the bitter pill
▶나의 고언도 그에게는 허사였다 My candid counsel was wasted on him. ⇒ My frank advice had no effect on him.

고역 苦役 hard work; toil; pains; drudgery
◆고역을 치르다 go through [experience] hardships; have trouble [difficulty] 《with, in》; have a hard [difficult] time
▶사는 게 고역이다 Life hangs heavy upon me.

고열 高熱 〈신열〉 a high fever; 〈높은 열〉 (an) intense heat; a high temperature 《▶temperature는 몸의 열에도 씀》
◆고열을 내뿜다 emit high heat / 고열에 시달리다 suffer from *one's* high fever [temperature]
▶나는 심한 감기로 고열이 났다 I had a high fever [temperature] with a bad cold.
▶그녀는 고열로 헛소리를 했다 She talked wildly [She was delirious] because of a high fever.
■—반응 a pyrogenetic reaction

고엽 枯葉 a dead [dry, withered] leaf ■—제 a defoliant

고옥 古屋 an old house; an age-old [a time-honored] house

고온 高溫 a high temperature
▶이 지역은 여름은 대개 고온이다 The temperature is generally high [It is generally very hot] in summer in this region.
■—가스(냉각형 원자)로 a high-temperature gas-cooled reactor ━계 〔物〕 a pyrometer ━균 thermophile; thermophilic bacteria ━다습 high temperature and high humidity ━반응 〔化〕 a pyrogenetic [pyrogenic] reaction ━측정(법) pyrometry

고요 〈조용〉 stillness; silence; quietness; 〈평온〉 calmness; tranquility
◆죽음 같은 고요 a dead silence; silence like the grave / 폭풍 전야의 고요 the calm [hush]

▶사이렌 소리가 밤의 고요를 깨뜨렸다 The siren broke the silence [stillness] of the night.
▶호수는 여느 때의 고요를 되찾았다 The lake regained its usual calmness [tranquility].
―고요하다 〈조용하다〉 quiet; still; silent; 〈평온하다〉 calm
◆고요한 거리 a quiet street / 고요한 바다 a quiet [calm, still] sea / 고요한 밤 a quiet [silent, still] night / 고요한 아침의 나라 한국 the Land of the Morning Calm, Korea / 고요히 quietly; calmly; silently; peacefully
▶울창한 숲속은 쥐죽은 듯 고요했다 The dense wood was as silent as the grave. ⇒ A dead silence reigned in the dense wood.
▶인적이 끊긴 거리는 아주 고요했다 The deserted street was deadly silent.
▶폭풍우가 지나자 숲은 고요해졌다 After the storm a hush [dead quiet] fell over the forest.
▶그는 고향의 묘지에 고요히 잠들어 있다 He sleeps [is sleeping] peacefully in a cemetery in his hometown.

고용 雇用 employment ⇨ 고용(雇傭)

고용 雇傭 employment; an engagement
◆남녀 고용 균등법 an equal opportunity employment act for both sexes / 국내 고용의 확대 domestic employment enlargement
▶이 회사에서는 여성의 고용이 늘고 있다 The mumber of women employed by this company is on the increase.
―고용하다 employ; engage; 〈일시적으로〉 hire
▶우리는 정원사를 하루 고용했다 We hired a gardener for a day.
▶우리 회사는 경비원을 5명 고용하고 있다 Our company employs five security guards.
▶그녀는 컴퓨터 프로그래머로 고용되어 있다 She is employed [engaged] as a computer programmer.
▶이 회사에 고용되어 있는 이상 회사 규칙을 지키시오 As long as you are on the payroll of the company, you must follow the regulations.
■불완전― underemployment 완전― full employment 장기[단기]― long-term [short-term] employment 종신― lifetime [permanent] employment ―계약 an employment agreement [contract] ―관계 an employment relationship ―기간 the period of employment ―대책 employment measures ―률 hiring rate ―보험 employment insurance ―자[주] an employer; 피고용자 an employee ―정책 an employment policy ―조건 employment terms; terms of employment; 여성의 고용 조건은 좋다[나쁘다] The terms of employment for women are favorable [unfavorable]. ―촉진 acceleration [promotion] of employment

고용살이 雇傭― employment; service as an employee
―고용살이하다 be employed; work for sb; be apprenticed (to).
◆김 선생님 집에서 고용살이하다 be in service [be working as a helper] with Mr. Kim
▶그는 우리 집에서 운전기사로 고용살이했다 He served our family as chauffeur.

고용인 雇傭人 an employee
◆임시 고용인 a temporary employee / 일용 고용인 a day laborer / 고용인을 해고하다 fire [dismiss, discharge] an employee; 〈임시로〉 lay off employees

고우 故友 an old friend [(口) pal]

고운 사람 미운데 없고 미운 사람 고운데 없다 (속담) Love is blind.

고원 高原 a plateau 《pl. ~s, -eaux》; a height; a tableland (▶height와 tableland는 흔히 복수로 씀); 〈고지〉 highlands ■―지대 a plateau area; plateau country

고원 雇員 a government employee

고원하다 高遠― high-minded; noble; high; high-flown; lofty; exalted ◆고원한 이상을 간직하다 have lofty ideals

고위 高位 a high rank
◆고위 인사 a person of high rank; ranking personalities [officials]; dignitaries / 고위직에 오르다 rise to [reach, attain] a high rank ■―관리 a high government official; a government dignitary; a (high-)ranking official ―성직자 a religious dignitary ―층 people in high places; high-ranking officials ―회담 high-level talks

고위도 高緯度 a high latitude ▶런던은 고위도에 (위치해) 있다 London is (located) in the high latitude.
■―지대[지방] high latitudes; a district in a high latitude

고유 固有 ◆고유의 〈특유의〉 peculiar (to); proper (to); of one's own; 〈타고난〉 instinctive; inherent; innate; 〈특정적인〉 characteristic (of); 〈독특한〉 native (to); indigenous / 인간 고유의 권리 inherent [inalienable] rights of man / 한국 고유의 동식물 plants and animals indigenous [native] to Korea / 한국 고유의 음악[예술] music [art] native to Korea / 한국 고유의 풍속 a custom peculiar to Korea
▶이 지방은 고유의 사투리가 있다 This district has its own particular dialect. ⇒ The people of this district speak [have] their own dialect.
―고유하다 peculiar; proper; characteristic; native; inherent
▶투쟁 본능은 동물에게 고유한 것이다 A fighting instinct is innate in animals.
■―명사 〔文法〕 a proper noun ―색 〔畵〕 local color ―성 a characteristic; a peculiarity

고육지계 苦肉之計 a desperate measure ◆고육지계를 쓰다 torture oneself to deceive the enemy
▶그가 차를 판 것은 고육지계였다 He sold his car as a [in the] last resort.

고육책 苦肉策 a desperate measure ⇨ 고육지계(苦肉之計)

고율 高率 a high rate ◆고율의 이자 a high (rate of) interest ■―관세 a high tariff ―배당 a high-rate dividend ―세 high rate [percentage] taxes ―임금 high wages

고을 a district; a county; a town

고음 高音 〔樂〕 a high tone; a high-pitched sound; a note in the high key ♦고음의 high-pitched; stentorian
■—확성기 a tweeter

고의 故意 deliberation; intention; design; willfulness
♦고의의 intentional; willful / 고의적 방해 intentional interference / 고의적 탈세 willful evasion of taxes / 고의가 아닌 unintentional; accidental / 고의든 과실이든 whether by design or by accident / 고의로 intentionally; on purpose; deliberately; knowingly; by design / 고의로 의무를 태만히 하다 neglect one's duty willfully
▶고의가 아니었으니 용서하세요 Please forgive me. I didn't mean to do it.
▶고의는 아니었지만 나는 그녀의 감정을 상하게 했다 I unknowingly [unwittingly] hurt her feelings.
▶그는 고의로 답을 틀렸다 He gave the wrong answer on purpose.
▶당신을 고의로 피한 것은 아니오 I had no intention of avoiding you.
■미필적— 〔法〕 willful negligence ■—범〔범행〕 a deliberate [an intentional] offense; 〈범인〉 a deliberate offender —행위 an intentional act; an act of deliberation

고의 袴衣 〈여름 홑바지〉 men's unlined short summer trousers (of Korean clothes); men's short trousers for summer wear
♦고의춤 (thrust *one's* hands into) the waistband of summer shorts / 고의를 치켜올리다 pull [hitch] up *one's* summer short

고이 〈삼가〉 respectfully; carefully; 〈곱게〉 beautifully; nicely; gracefully; 〈소중히〉 gently; tenderly; carefully; 〈편안히〉 peacefully; in peace; 〈온전히〉 wholly; without damage; safely
♦고이 단장하다 make up [put on makeup] gracefully / 고이 돌아오다 come back safe and sound / 고이 받들다 serve *sb* carefully [respectfully, devotedly] / 고이 잠들다 〈죽다〉 pass away peacefully; die a peaceful death / 아이를 고이 키우다 bring up a child with tender care
▶아기는 엄마에게 안겨 고이 잠자고 있었다 The baby was sleeping peacefully in its mother's arms.
▶영령이여 고이 잠드소서 May your noble soul rest in peace.

고인 古人 ancient people; men of old; the ancients
♦고인이 말씀하시듯이 as they used to say in the old days; as an old saying has it

고인 故人 〈죽은 사람〉 the deceased; the departed; the dead (▶복수를 의미함)
♦고인의 유족 the family of the deceased [the dead man]; the bereaved family / 고인이 된 김 선생 the late Mr. Kim
▶민 박사는 고인이 되었다 Dr. Min is dead [no longer with us]. ⇌ Dr. Min has died [passed away].

고인돌 〔考古〕 a dolmen

고입선발고사 高入選拔考査 〈국가의〉 the state-run high school entrance examinations

-고자 〈…려고〉 for...; to 《do》; in order to 《do》; so as to 《do》; (so) that...may [can, will]
♦…하고자 하다 want [hope, wish, plan] to 《do》; would [should] like to 《do》; be anxious [eager] to 《do》
▶그는 부친을 돕고자 학교를 그만두었다 He left school (so as [in order]) to help his father.
▶그것은 내가 말하고자 했던 바다 That is what I was going to say.
▶나는 비자를 받고자 영사관에 가는 중이다 I am on my way to the consulate to get a visa.
▶그는 시험에 합격하고자 최선을 다했다 He did his best to pass the examination.

고자 鼓子 an impotent [a sterile] man; a castrated man; 〈거세된〉 a eunuch [júːnək]

고자세 高姿勢 an aggressive [overbearing] attitude; a high-handed manner
♦고자세를 취하다 assume an aggressive [overbearing] attitude; assume a high posture
▶그는 우리에게 고자세였다 He took an aggressive [an overbearing, a high-handed] attitude toward us.

고자쟁이 告者— a telltale; a talebearer; a tattletale; 〈밀고자〉 an informer; an informant

고자질 告者— talebearing; taletelling
▶그는 선생님에게 내 고자질을 했다 He told the teacher on me.
—고자질하다 tell on; tell [carry] tales 《upon, about, against》
▶누가 사장에게 내가 지각했다고 고자질했지? Who told [reported to] the boss I was late?
▶남을 고자질해서는 안 된다 You shouldn't tell on others.

고작 at (the) most; at best; at the highest; no more than; barely; only
▶그 소녀는 나이가 고작 8살이었던 것 같다 I think the girl was eight at (the) most.
▶그 모임에 나온 사람은 고작 20명이었다 There were at most [not more than] twenty people at the meeting.
▶성공한 것은 그중 고작 5명이었다 Only [No more than] five of them succeeded.
▶이 기계의 내용 연한은 고작 3년일 것입니다 This machine will last for three years at the longest.
▶고작 그 말밖에 할 수 없어요 ? Is that all you can say?
▶그의 지혜도 그것이 고작이다 That's the extent of his wisdom.
▶이게 고작입니다 This is the utmost I can do. ⇌ This is about as far as I can go. ⇌ This is the limit.
▶나는 가족을 부양하는 것이 고작이오 It is all [as much as] I can to support my family. ⇌ The best I can do is to support my family.

고장 〈장소〉 a place; 〈지역〉 a district; a locality; 〈고향〉 one's home; one's native place; 〈산지·서식지〉 the home; the habitat
♦귤[사과, 인삼]의 고장 an orange-producing [an apple-producing, a ginseng-producing]

district / 낯선 고장 a strange town [place] / 그 고장 사람 a native of the place / 그 고장의 특산품 local products / 우리 고장의 풍속 the manners and customs of our native town [place]
▶ 그는 이 고장 사정에 밝다 He is familiar with this area.
▶ 고장에 따라 풍습이 다르다 Customs differ in different localities [places, areas].
▶ 대구는 사과의 고장으로 유명하다 Taegu is famous for its production of apples.

고장 故障 〈탈〉 trouble; a breakdown; a malfunction; 〈장애〉 a hitch; (a) failure; 〈파손〉 damage
▶ 기계가 고장이다 The machine is out of order. ⇒ The machine doesn't work. ⇒ Something is wrong with the machine.
▶ 무슨 고장이죠? What's the trouble? ⇒ What's wrong?
▶ 그녀는 소화기[순환기] 계통에 고장이 있는 것 같다 She seems to have digestive [circulatory] trouble.
▶ 내 차는 고장이 났다 My car has broken down.
▶ 「會話」「그 기계가 어디 고장이 났나요?」「아니요, 아무 고장도 안 났어요」 "Is (there) anything wrong with the machine?" "No, there is nothing [Nothing is] wrong with it."
▶ 고장은 곧 고쳐졌다 The breakdown was soon fixed [repaired].
▶ 도중에 우리 차가 엔진 고장을 일으켰다 Our car developed engine trouble on the way.
▶ 고장 (게시) Out of Order.
■ 전기— (a) failure of electricity; (a) power failure 전화[엔진, 기계]— telephone [engine, mechanical] trouble —검사원 〈전선의〉 a wire tracer —차 a damaged car; a disabled [bad order] car —측정기 a fault finder

고장난명 孤掌難鳴 ▶ 고장난명이라 It takes two to wrestle. ⇒ To accomplish something one needs assistance.

고쟁이 traditional Korean loose underpants [slips, drawers, undergarment] worn by women; bloomers

고저 高低 〈높낮이〉 rise and fall; 〈기복〉 unevenness; undulations; ups and downs; 〈시세 등의〉 fluctuation
◆ 가격[기온]의 고저 fluctuations in prices [of temperature] / 목소리의 고저 〈높이〉 pitch; 〈억양〉 modulation / 고저가 없는 땅 level land
▶ 나는 요즘음 혈압의 고저가 심하다 There have been drastic ups and downs in my blood pressure. ⇒ My blood pressure has been very unstable.
■ —각 〈測〉 angle of elevation —지도 an embossment map —차 difference of altitude [elevation]

고적 古蹟 a historic site; a place of historical interest; 〈유적〉 historic remains
◆ 고적을 보존하다 preserve sites of historic value / 고적을 찾다 visit a historic spot
▶ 한강변에는 고적이 많다 There are many spots of historical interest along the Han River.

고적 孤寂 solitude; loneliness —고적하다 lonely; lonesome; solitary ■ —감 a feeling of loneliness

고적대 鼓笛隊 a fife and drum band; a drum and fife corps —장 〈남자〉 a drum major; 〈여자〉 a drum majorette

고적운 高積雲 〖氣〗 an altocumulus (*pl*. -li)

고전 古典 〈옛 서적〉 an old book; 〈최고 수준의 작품〉 a classic; 〈고전 문학〉 the classics
■ —극 classical [ancient] drama —문학 classical literature; the classics —미 classical beauty —성 classicality —어 the classical languages —연구 classical studies —음악 classical music —파 a classical school

고전 古錢 an old [ancient] coin ■ —수집 old coin collection —수집가 a collector of old coins; a numismatist

고전 苦戰 a hard battle; a desperate [an uphill] battle; 〈경기의〉 a close game [contest]; a tight [tough] game
▶ 경기는 고전이었다 It was [We had] a tight [close] game.
—고전하다 have a hard fight [tight game]
▶ 이번 선거에서 그는 고전할 거야 He will face a close contest [tough game] in the coming election.

고전장 古戰場 〈옛 싸움터〉 an old [ancient] battlefield; a historic battleground; the scene of an ancient battle

고전적 古典的 classic; classical
◆ 고전적인 아름다움 classic beauty

고전주의 古典主義 classicism ■ 신— neoclassicism —자 a classic; a classicist

고전학 古典學 the classics ■ —자 a classic; a classicist; a classical scholar —파 the classical school; the classicists

고정 固定 fixing; fixation —고정하다 fix; settle; fasten; 〈진정하다〉 calm *oneself*; calm down 《*one's* temper》

> 解説 **fix**는 단순히 움직이지 않도록 하는 것이지만 **fasten**은 단추·끈·못 등을 써서 물건을 다른 것에 부착하여 고정시키는 것을 의미한다.

◆ 고정된 책장 a built-in bookcase / 마음을 고정하다 calm *oneself*; calm *one's* mind; compose *oneself* / 선반을 벽에 고정하다 fix a shelf to a wall / 텐트를 고정하다 anchor a tent / 핀으로 고정하다 fasten *sth* with a pin
▶ 고정하시고 제 말을 들어 보세요 Please calm down [take it easy] and listen to me.
▶ 그는 그 여자에게 시선을 고정시킨 채 움직이지 않았다 He stood still with his eyes fastened on her.
▶ 책상은 마루에 고정되어 있었다 The desk was fixed [nailed] to the floor.
■ —가격 a firm [fixed] price —간첩 a resident spy —고객 a regular customer —관념 a fixed idea: 그는 그것에 대해 고정 관념을 가지고 있다 He has a fixed idea about it. —금리 a fixed interest rate —독자 a regular reader; 〈신문·잡지의〉 a regular subscriber (to): 그 작가는 고정 독자를 가지고 있다 The writer has a

fixed circle of readers. —부채 fixed liabilities —비 fixed cost(s) —석 a fixed seat —손님 a regular customer —수입 a fixed [regular] income —자본 fixed capital —점 fixed point —표 committed votes; votes which cannot be swayed —환율 제도 the fixed exchange rate system

고정 苦情 〈괴로운 상태〉 difficulties; a (sorry) plight; distress; a tough situation

고정급 固定給 a fixed salary; basic [base, regular] pay ♦고정급을 받다 be on the payroll / 고정급으로 고용하다 employ sb at fixed pay

고정자산 固定資産 fixed assets (▶복수로 씀); fixed property ■—세 the (fixed) property tax —재평가 revaluation of the fixed assets

고정화 固定化 fixation —고정화하다 fix; settle; fixate

고제 古制 the old [ancient] system ⇨ 구제도

고조 高祖 one's great-great-grandfather = 고조부(高祖父)

고조 高調 〈높은 가락〉 a high tone [pitch]; 〈기운의〉 elation; high spirits
♦감정의 고조 an uprush of emotion / 긴장의 고조 an increase of tension / 음이 더 고조로 바뀌다 change to a higher tone
—고조하다 tone up; elate; uplift ♦기운이 고조되다 get into high spirits
▶내 기분은 온통 고조되었다 All my feelings were excited to a high pitch.
▶전국에 민주화의 기운이 고조되고 있었다 There was a growing tendency toward democratization throughout the country.
▶노사간의 긴장이 고조되고 있다 Tension is building up [increasing, mounting] between labor and management.
▶그들은 고조된 사기로 경기장에 입장했다 They entered the arena in high spirits.

고조 高潮 〈조수의〉 floodtide; high tide [water]; 〈정점〉 the climax; the high point; 〈기분의〉 elevation; elation; exaltation
♦(최)고조에 달하다 reach the climax; come to [reach] the high point; arrive at its culmination
■—선 the high-water line —점 the high-water mark; the floodmark

고조모 高祖母 one's great-great-grandmother
고조부 高祖父 one's great-great-grandfather
고종사촌 姑從四寸 a cousin; a child of one's father's sister

고주망태 dead drunkenness
♦고주망태가 되다 be [get] dead drunk; be (blind) drunk as a lord / 고주망태가 되도록 마시다 get oneself blind drunk; drink oneself into oblivion; get boozy

고주파 高周波 〔電〕 high frequency (略 H.F., HF; h.f.)
■—가열 high-frequency heating; electronic heating —발전기[저항기] a high-frequency generator [rheostat] —전류 a high-frequency current —전파 high-frequency radio waves —증폭기 a radioamplifier

고증 考證 (a) historical research [inquiry, study]; historical investigation
♦탄소 동위원소에 의한 연대 고증 carbon (14) dating
▶그는 이 연극의 의상에 대한 시대 고증을 했다 He was in charge of researching authentic period costumes for the play.
—고증하다 study [ascertain] historical evidence
♦고구려 시대의 풍습을 문헌으로 고증하다 study [make investigation] on the manners and customs in the Koguryŏ era by referring to literature
■—학 the study of old documents; the methodology of historical research; 〈중국 고전의〉 a bibliographical study of Chinese classics

고지¹ 〈호박·가지 등의〉 sliced and dried pieces of squash [eggplant]

고지² 〈누룩 등의 골·틀〉 a wooden mold (for malt); a wooden frame (for soybean paste)

고지 告知 (a) notice; (a) notification; an announcement —고지하다 notify 《sb of sth》; announce 《sth to sb》
■수태— 〔基〕 the Annunciation ■—서 a notice; a bulletin : 납세 고지서 a notice for payment of tax —판 a bulletin [notice] board

고지 高地 highland(s); heights; an upland; a hill; 〈고원〉 a tableland; a plateau 《pl. ~s, -eaux》
♦105 고지 a 105-meter hill / 고지 사람 a highlander / 고지를 점령하다 capture an enemy-held [enemy-occupied] hill; (비유) gain [get] an advantage over / 고지에 살다 inhabit highland
■—훈련 high-altitude training

고지기 庫— 〈창고지기〉 a warehouse [storehouse] keeper

고지대 高地帶 a hilly section [part] (of a city); a hill; an eminence; the high elevated areas
♦도시 고지대의 식수난 water shortage in the hillside areas of a city
▶그의 집은 고지대에 있다 His house stands on high ground [a hill, a rise].

고지서 告知書 a written notice

고지식하다 simple and honest; honest to fault; tactless; very serious [earnest]
♦고지식한 사람 a (too) serious [a straitlaced] person / 고지식하게 일하다 work earnestly [conscientiously]
▶고지식한 사람은 상대하기 힘들다 A serious person is hard to get on with.
▶지금은 고지식한 사람이 손해보는 세상이다 We live in a world where simple honesty does not pay.
▶나는 농담으로 말했는데 그는 고지식하게 받아들였다 I said it as a joke, but he took me seriously.

고진감래 苦盡甘來 (속담) No pleasure without pain. ⇌ No gains without pains. ⇌ No pains, no gains. ⇌ No cross, no crown.

고질 痼疾 a chronic disease [illness]; a deep-seated disease [trouble]
♦고질적인 국제 수지 역조[재정난] chronic adverse balance of trade [financial predicament]

▶ 그 회사의 고질은 임원들간의 파벌 싸움이다 The deep-seated trouble with the company is factional strife among the directors.
▶ 그는 고질적인 천식을 앓고 있다 He is suffering from his chronic illness of (his old) asthma.
■ —병 환자 a chronic sufferer 《from》; a confirmed invalid

고집 固執 persistence; 〈주장〉 insistence; 〈집착〉 adherence; 〈아집〉 willfulness; self-will
♦ 고집이 센 obstinate; self-assertive; stubborn; uncompromising
▶ 고집 좀 그만 부려라 Enough of your stubbornness [obstinacy]. ⇌ Don't be so obstinate.
▶ 그는 고집이 세다 He is stubborn [obstinate]. ⇌ He is self-assertive.
▶ 아버지는 마침내 고집을 꺾고 우리 결혼을 승락하셨다 My father finally gave in [yielded] and consented to our marriage.
▶ 그는 자기 고집대로만 하려고 한다 He will have everything his own way.
—고집하다 persist 《in》; stick 《to》; adhere 《to》; cling 《to》; insist 《on》
▶ 그는 옛 관습을 고집했다 He clung to old custom(s) [the old way].
▶ 그는 자기 의견을 고집했다 He persisted in [held fast to, stuck to] his own opinion.
■ —쟁이[통이] a headstrong person; a person as obstinate [stubborn] as a mule; a bigot

고집불통 固執不通 extreme stubbornness [obstinacy]
♦ 고집 불통의 stubborn; obstinate; bigoted; stiff-necked / 노인의 고집불통 the stubbornness of the aged
▶ 그녀는 보기와는 달리 고집불통이다 She is much more obstinate than she appears to be.

고차 高次 ♦ 고차의 of a high order ▶ 소실된 그 문명은 고차적인 문명이었다 The lost civilization was of a higher order [was highly advanced].
■ —방정식 《數》 an equation of higher degree

고착 固着 sticking; adherence; adhesion —고착하다 adhere [stick (fast)] 《to》; be firmly fixed 《to》
■ —관념 《心》 a fixed idea; a fixation; an obsession

고찰 古刹 an old [ancient] Buddhist temple; a temple with a long history

고찰 考察 consideration; (an) inquiry; (an) examination; (a) study
♦ 윤리적[도덕적] 고찰 ethical [moral] contemplation / 청소년 범죄에 대한 하나의 고찰 a study of juvenile delinquency
—고찰하다 consider; examine; inquire into; study
♦ 신중하게 고찰하다 consider 《the matter》 carefully; give careful consideration 《to the matter》 / 모든 것을 함께 고찰하다 take all things into consideration / 주택 문제를 경제적인 측면에서 고찰하다 investigate the housing problem from an economic point of view
▶ 그것은 여러 각도에서[여러모로] 고찰해 볼 필요가 있다 It requires consideration from various angles [in all its aspects].

고참 古參 〈지위〉 seniority; 〈사람〉 a senior; a veteran; an older man in the service
♦ 고참의 senior; veteran / 고참 직원 the senior member of the staff
▶ 그는 고참 교사다 He is an experienced [a veteran] teacher.
▶ 그는 회사에서 나보다 고참이다 He is senior to me in our company.
▶ 그는 이 회사에서 고참에 속한다 He is one of the oldest [senior] members of [in] this company.
■ —병(兵) a veteran soldier; a senior comrade

고창 高唱 —고창하다 sing [chant] loudly; 〈주창하다〉 advocate; urge; emphasize ♦ 평화주의를 고창하다 advocate pacifism
■ —자 an advocate

고창 鼓脹 《醫》 tympanites; flatulence ♦ 고창성의 tympanitic; flatulent

고천문 告天文 a ritual prayer [an oath] (offered) to Heaven [God]

고철 古鐵 scrap iron; iron scraps ♦ 고철로 만들다 scrap 《an old car》; make into scrap / 차를 고철로 팔다 sell one's car for scrap [junk, its scrap value]

고체 古體 an old [archaic] style [form]; archaism

고체 固體 a solid (body); solid matter ♦ 고체의 solid / 고체화하다 solidify 《water》
▶ 드라이 아이스는 고체에서 바로 기체가 된다 Dry ice goes directly to a gas from a solid.
■ —물리학 solid state physics —연료 solid fuel

고초 苦楚 〈고난〉 hardship(s); trouble; trials (and tribulations); sufferings; distress; afflictions
♦ 고초를 겪다 suffer [go through] (hardships); have a hard time of it; have one's trials
▶ 우리는 모진 고초를 다 겪었다 We have had many scathing trials.

고초균 枯草菌 《醫》 hay bacillus

고초열 枯草熱 hay fever; rose cold [fever]; pollinosis

고추 (a) red pepper; (a) cayenne pepper; (a) hot pepper (▶조미료를 의미할 때는 a를 붙이지 않음) ▶ 이 고추는 참 맵다 This red pepper really bites.
■ —바람 a biting wind —장 hot pepper paste

고추는 작아도 맵다 《속담》 The smaller, the shrewder.

고추밭에 말 달리기 《속담》 a dog in the manger

고추보다 후추가 더 맵다 《속담》 surpass [outdo] one's teacher

고추잠자리 a red dragonfly

고춧가루 powdered red [hot] pepper

고충 苦衷 mental suffering; distress; a dilemma; 〈상황〉 a painful situation; a predicament
♦ 고충을 이해하다[알아주다] appreciate sb's painful situation; have a deep sympathy for sb's predicament
▶ 그의 고충은 이해하고도 남음이 있다 His

distress [predicament] deserves our sincere sympathy.
▶우리는 그의 고충에 동정을 금할 수 없었다 We couldn't sympathize enough with him in his distress.
고충실도 高忠實度 high fidelity (略 hi-fi) ⇨ 하이파이
고취 鼓吹 encouragement; inspiration; instillation; 〈창도〉 advocacy
—**고취하다** inspire; encourage; instill; inculcate; advocate
♦사상을 고취하다 inculcate ideas (up)on sb [in sb's mind]
▶그는 청년들에게 애국심을 고취했다 He inspired patriotism in the young [the young people with patriotism].
▶그녀는 자기 아이들에게 모두 지식애를 고취시켰다 She inculcated all her children with love of knowledge [love of knowledge in all her children].
■—**자** an advocate
고치 a cocoon ♦고치를 짓다 spin a cocoon / 고치에서 명주실을 뽑다[켜다] reel silk off cocoons ■**빈—** a pierced cocoon
고치다 1 〈수리하다〉 repair; mend; 《美口》 fix (up); patch up

> 解説 *repair*와 *mend*는 같은 뜻으로 쓰이기도 하지만, 보통 repair는 비교적 크거나 복잡한 것을 수리하는 경우에, mend는 비교적 단순한 것을 수리하는 경우에 쓰이는데, 미국에서는 보통 천으로 만든 제품을 고치는 경우를 말한다. *fix*는 구어적인 말로서 repair, mend 대신에 쓰인다.

♦기계를 고치다 repair a machine; put a machine in order / 라디오를 고치다 fix a radio set
▶그는 딸아이의 부서진 인형을 풀과 종이로 고쳤다 He mended [fixed] his daughter's broken dolls with paste and paper.
▶나는 시계[차]를 고치게 했다 I had my watch [car] repaired [《美》 fixed].
▶지금 지붕을 고치는 중이다 The roof is now under repair.
2 〈정정하다〉 correct; amend; 〈개선하다〉 improve; set right; better
♦오자[잘못된 철자]를 고치다 correct a wrong character [misspelled word] / 작문을 고치다 improve an essay / 헌법을 고치다 amend the Constitution
▶내 영어 편지의 잘못된 곳을 고쳐 주시겠어요? Could you correct the mistake in my English letter?
▶틀린 곳이 있으면 고치시오 Correct errors, if any.
3 〈바르게 하다〉 reform; rectify; correct
♦나쁜 버릇을 고치다 〈자신의〉 break oneself of a bad habit; 〈남의〉 cure sb of a bad habit / 말더듬이를 고치다 cure sb of stammering / 발음[언어 장애]을 고치다 correct bad pronunciation [a speech impediment] / 악폐를 고치다 reform abuses; redress [rectify] evils / 자기 결점을 고치다 correct one's shortcomings / 자기 행실을 고치다 reform one's conduct; mend one's ways
▶그 여자는 화장을 고치고 있었다 She was adjusting [fixing] her makeup.
▶너는 그 버릇을 고쳐야 한다 You must get over [break] that habit.
▶천성은 고쳐지지 않는다 You cannot change your nature.
4 〈바꾸다〉 change; alter; modify
♦계획의 일부를 고치다 alter a part of the plan / 시간표를 고치다 alter the schedule / 이름을 고치다 change one's name (to); assume the new name 《of》 / 생각을 고쳐 먹다 change one's mind
▶정부는 세제를 고칠 의향이 없었다 The government had no intention of reforming the taxation system.
5 〈개조하다〉 make over; remake; make anew; alter(옷 등을); 〈번역하다〉 translate
♦헌 코트를 뜯어 고치다 make over [alter] an old overcoat 《into》
▶그는 그 방을 서재로 고쳤다 He remodeled [converted, made over] the room into his study.
▶다음을 우리 말로 고치시오 Translate the following into Korean.
▶나는 리포트를 고쳐 써야 했다 I was made to rewrite my paper.
6 【치료하다】 cure; 〈상처를〉 heal
▶내 병을 고쳐 주세요 Please cure me of my illness.
▶상처를 고치는 데는 온천이 좋다 Hot spring water will heal your wound quickly.
▶가까운 장래에 암을 완전히 고칠 수 있게 될 것이다 We will be able to cure cancer completely in the near future.
고침 高枕 〈높은 베개〉 a high pillow ♦고침 안면하다 sleep in peace; rest easy; have a sound [good] sleep
고침단명 高枕短命 High pillow, short life.
고탑 古塔 an old tower; an ancient pagoda
고토 苦土 〔化〕 magnesia ⇨ 마그네슘(산화~)
고토 故土 one's homeland; one's native place; one's former territory
고토 膏土 rich [fertile] soil; fertile land
고통 苦痛 (a) pain (▶고통을 나타내는 가장 일반적인 말로, 신체의 국부적 고통은 부정관사를 붙여 표현함); 〈일시적 격통〉 a pang; 〈지속적인〉 (a) torment; (a) torture; 〈고뇌〉 suffering; distress
♦육체적[정신적] 고통 physical [mental] pain / 고통스러운 painful; hard / 고통을 누그러뜨리다[덜어 주다] ease [relieve] the pain / 고통을 느끼다 feel [suffer] pain; be in pain / 고통을 주다 give sb pain; pain sb; inflict pain on sb / 고통을 참다 bear [endure] the pain / 고통을 호소하다 complain of pain
▶그녀는 별 고통 없이 죽었다 She died without much suffering [pain].
▶몇 시간이고 앉아 있는 것은 고통이다 It's painful to keep sitting for hours.
▶이 약을 쓰면 고통이 가라앉을 것이다 This medicine will allay the pain.
▶고통이 덜해[더해]졌다 The pain has in-

creased [abated].
▶ 그는 고통으로 신음하고 있었다 He was moaning [groaning] in pain [agony].
▶ 나는 이제 아무 고통도 느끼지 않는다 I'm no longer in pain. ⇒ I don't feel pain any more. ⇒ The pain has left me.
▶ 그는 고통스럽게 숨을 쉬고 있었다 He was breathing painfully [hard, with difficulty].

고투 苦鬪 a bitter [desperate] struggle; a hard fight
▶ 오랜 고투 끝에 그는 성공했다 A long series of hard struggle brought him success.
—**고투하다** fight [struggle] hard [desperately]
▶ 그는 가난과 고투하고 있다 He is struggling hard against poverty.

고판 古版 an old edition ■—**본** an old book; old books in block print

고패 a small(-sized) pulley

고팻줄 a pulley [block] rope [cord]

고팽이 〈새끼 등의〉 a coil (of rope [wire]); 〈建〉 a scroll; scrollwork; 〈왕복〉 one round; a round-trip (route)
♦ 한 고팽이 돌다 make a round [circuit]; go one's round / 연못을 한 고팽이 돌다 walk around a pond

고평 高評 your esteemed opinion; your criticism [comments]
▶ 고평을 바라는 바입니다 I am anxious to hear your comments [criticism] (on my book). ⇒ Your comments (on the book) will be highly appreciated. ⇒ 〈증정본에〉 With the author's compliments.

고풍 古風 old fashions [manners]; old customs; an antique style; old [ancient] ways
♦ 고풍의 old-fashioned; antique; 〈낡은〉 archaic; out-of-date / 고풍스러운 가구 antique furniture / 고풍스러운 건물 an old-fashioned building / 고풍스러운 문체 archaic style / 고풍을 지키다 keep [stick] to old customs; follow the old ways; keep the traditions

고프다 hungry ♦ 배가 고프다 be [feel] hungry
▶ 배가 고파 죽겠다 I am dying of hunger. ⇒ I'm simply starving. ⇒ I'm awfully hungry.

고하 高下 〈지위의〉 rank; grade; 〈품질의〉 quality; 〈가격의〉 fluctuations ♦ 지위 고하를 막론하고 irrespective of rank
▶ 값은 고하간에 내가 사겠소 I'll buy it irrespective of its price.

고학 苦學 studying under adversity
▶ 그는 고학으로 대학을 나왔다 He worked his way through college [university].
—**고학하다** study under difficulties; support oneself while studying; pay [earn] one's own school expenses [fees]
■—**생** a working [self-supporting] student

고학년 高學年 the higher [upper] grades [classes]

고함 高喊 a shout; a yell; a roar
♦ 고함을 지르다[치다] shout; cry loudly; roar; yell
▶ 나는 목청껏 고함을 질렀다 I shouted at the top of my voice.
▶ 그는 일꾼들에게 열심히 일하라고 고함을 쳤다 He shouted to the workers to work hard.
▶ 그는 뭐라고 고함을 치고 있다 He is shouting [yelling] about something.
—**고함치다** shout; yell; roar
♦ 살려 달라고 고함치다 cry [shout, yell] out for help
▶ 「이겼다」고 그는 고함쳤다 "I won!" he cried [shouted, exclaimed].

고해 告解 〖가톨릭〗 penance

고해 苦海 〖佛敎〗 this bitter world ▶ 인생은 고해다 Life is full of hardships [rubs and worries].

고행 苦行 asceticism; religious austerities; self-mortification; mortification of the flesh; penance
▶ 그 남자는 고행 끝에 고승이 되었다 Having trained himself in asceticism, he became a high priest.
—**고행하다** practice asceticism; do penance
■—**자** an ascetic

고향 故鄕 one's hometown (▶시·군·리 어느 것에든 쓸 수 있으나 도·섬에는 쓸 수 없음); one's (old) home; 〈출생지〉 one's birthplace
♦ 마음의 고향 the spiritual home / 제2의 고향 one's second home [hometown] / 고향 사람들 folks back (at) home / 고향 자랑을 하다 boast [talk proudly] about one's hometown
▶ 그 사람들은 모이기만 하면 고향 자랑이다 Whenever they get together, they brag about their hometowns.
▶ 백두산은 한국 사람들의 마음의 고향이다 Paektusan is the spiritual home of the Korean (people).
〈고향이[은]〉 고향이 그립다 I am homesick.
▶ 〖會話〗「고향이 어디세요?」「경기도입니다」 "Where are you from? ⇒ Where do you come from? (▶Where have [did] you come from? 하면 출신지에 관계 없이「어디서 왔느냐?」가 됨) ⇒ What's your hometown? ⇒ Where is your home(town)?" "Kyŏnggi-do is my home province. ⇒ My home(town) is in Kyŏnggi-do. ⇒ I'm [I come] from Kyŏnggi-do."
▶ 고향은 언제나 아름답다 Home is always sweet.
〈고향을〉 고향을 그리워하다 be [feel] homesick; pine [long] for home / 고향을 떠나다 leave 〈one's〉 home [one's hometown]
▶ 고향을 떠난지 얼마나 됩니까? How many years is it since you left your home?
〈고향에(서)〉 고향에 돌아가다 go (back) [return] home / 고향에 편지하다 write home (to one's father)
▶ 겨울 방학에는 고향에 갈 작정이다 I'm going home during the winter vacation.
▶ 어제 고향에서 편지가 왔다 I got [received] a letter from home yesterday.
〈고향으로〉 그는 고향으로 금의환향했다 He returned to his hometown in glory [triumph]. ⇒ He returned home (as) a successful man.
▶ 나는 수원을 제2의 고향으로 생각한다 I regard Suwon as my second home.

고현학 考現學 modernology; the study on modern phenomena

고혈 膏血 sweat and blood

♦ 가난한 자의 고혈을 짜다 exploit [squeeze] the poor
▶ 왕은 폭정으로 백성의 고혈을 짰다 The king ground his subjects under his oppressive tyranny.

고혈압 高血壓 high blood pressure; hypertension; hyperpiesia
▶ 그는 고혈압이다 He suffers [is suffering] from hypertension. ⇌ He has high blood pressure.
■ ―환자 a hypertensive

고형 固形 a solid body; solidity ♦ 고형의 solid / 고형화하다 solidify; be solidified
■ ―물 a solid (body); 〔化〕 solid matter ―수프 a soup square ―식 solid food; solids ―식량 compressed food ―알코올 solid alcohol ―연료 solid fuel; solid propellant ―폐기물 solid waste

고혹 蠱惑 〈마음을 호림〉 ♦ 고혹적인 미소 a bewitching smile
▶ 그녀는 고혹적인 미소를 지으며 나와 악수를 했다 She shook hands with me with an enchanting smile on her face.

고혼 孤魂 the lonely spirit [soul] of a dead person
♦ 수중 고혼이 되다 die in water [at sea] / 고혼을 달래다 appease the lonely soul of a dead person [the dead, the deceased]

고화 古畵 an old [antique] picture [painting]

고환 睾丸 〔解〕 the testicles; the testes 《sing. -tis》 ♦ 고환의 testicular ■ ―부― the epididymis (pl. -dymides) : 부고환염 epididymitis ■ ―염 orchitis; testitis

고흐 〈네델란드의 화가〉 Gogh, Vincent van (1853-90)

고희 古稀 three score and ten; the age of seventy ▶ 우리는 아버님의 고희 잔치를 했다 We celebrated our father's seventieth birthday.
■ ―연 the celebration of one's 70th birthday

곡 曲 〈음악〉 music; 〈한 곡〉 a piece of music; 〈곡조〉 a tune; a melody; 《sing》 an air; 〈악곡〉 a composition
♦ 한 곡 연주하다 play [render] a tune 《on the piano》/ 가사에 곡을 붙이다 set a poem to music; write the music for a song / 쇼팽의 곡을 연주하다 play a Chopin's composition / 곡에 맞춰 춤추다 dance to the music
▶ 한 곡 불러 주세요 Sing us a song of some kind, please.
▶ 이것은 좋은 곡이다 This piece of music is very good.
▶ 그녀는 베토벤의 곡을 좋아했다 She was fond of Beethoven's music.

곡 哭 wailing; a moan; lamentation ―곡하다 wail; lament; moan; keen
―소리 a wail; a wailing cry

곡가 穀價 price of grain [cereals]; grain price
♦ 2중 곡가제 《enforce》 a double-tiered grain price system ■ ―변동 fluctuation in grain prices ―정책 a grain price policy

곡경 曲境 a difficult situation ⇨ 곤경

곡괭이 a pickax; a mattock ♦ 곡괭이로 땅을 파다 dig in the ground with a pickax / 곡괭이 질하다 pick; pickax

곡구 曲球 〔野〕 a curve (ball); 〔撞球〕 a fancy shot

곡두 〈환영〉 a vision; a phantom; a phantasm; an illusion ♦ 곡두를 보다 see a phantom [vision] / 곡두를 좇다 pursue phantoms / 곡두에 홀리다 be lured by an illusion

곡류 曲流 〈흐름〉 meandering; 〈물굽이〉 a winding watercourse ―곡류하다 meander; wind its way

곡류 穀類 cereals; (美) grain; (英) corn

곡률 曲率 〔數〕 curvature ♦ 곡률이 크다[작다] have a large [small] (amount of) curvature
■ ―공간― curvature of space; space curvature
■ ―원(圓) a circle of curvature ―중심[반지름] the center [radius] of curvature

곡마 曲馬 an equestrian feat ■ ―단 a (traveling) circus ―사 an equestrian

곡면 曲面 〔數〕 a curved surface ■ ―체 a solid bounded by curved surface

곡명 曲名 the title (of a musical composition)

곡목 曲目 〈개별〉 a number; a selection; 〈전체〉 a program
▶ 곡목 선택이 좋았습니다 You selected the music well.
▶ 이것은 이 악단이 연주할 수 있는 곡목들이다 This is the complete repertory [repertoire] of this band.
▶ 다음 곡목은 무엇입니까? What's the next number (on the program)?

곡물 穀物 cereals; (美) grain; (英) corn
■ ―거래소 a grain exchange ―건조기 a grain drier ―상 〈상인〉 a grain [corn] dealer; 〈상점〉 a shop dealing in grain [corn] ―시장 the grain [corn] market ―창고 a granary; a corn reserve; (美) a grain elevator

곡보 曲譜 a musical note ⇨ 악보

곡사 曲射 high-angle fire ―곡사하다 fire at a high angle ■ ―포 a howitzer; a high-angle gun

곡선 曲線 a curved line; a curve ♦ 곡선의[으로 된] curvilineal; curvilinear
▶ 곡선이 아름답다 The line is beautifully curved. ⇌ It is a beautiful curved line.
▶ 아이는 땅바닥에 긴 곡선을 그렸다 The child drew a long curved line on the ground.
▶ 공은 큰 곡선을 그리며 날아갔다 The ball flew through the air in a big arc.
■ ―운동 a curvilinear motion ―좌표 curvilinear coordinates

곡선미 曲線美 the beauty of contour [line, curves]; linear beauty; (美) curvaceousness
♦ 다리의 곡선미 the beauty of one's leg line / 곡선미가 있는 여자 a woman with a beautiful [a voluptuous, an attractive] figure; (口) a curvaceous woman

곡성 哭聲 a wail; a wailing cry

곡식 穀― cereals ⇨ 곡물

곡예 曲藝 acrobatics; an acrobatic feat; a stunt
♦ 말타기 곡예 equestrian acrobatics [feats] / 자전거 곡예 a bicycle stunt / 곡예를 하다 do [perform] stunts 《on horseback》; perform acrobatics [acrobatic feats] 《in a circus》
■ ―비행 a stunt flying; aerial acrobatics;

aerobatics; an acrobatic [aerobatic] flight / —사 an acrobat; a tumbler; a stunt performer: 줄타기 곡예사 a tightrope walker [dancer]

곡절 曲折 1 〈복잡한 사정〉 intricacies; complications; 〈부침〉 ups and downs
◆ 인생의 우여 곡절 the ups and downs of life / 많은 곡절을 거쳐 through a lot of twists and turns [ups and downs] / 곡절이 많다 be very complicated; be full of twists and turns
▶ 우리는 곡절 끝에 결론에 도달했다 We came to a conclusion after much parley [many twists and turns].
2 〈자세한 내용〉 details; particulars; the whole circumstances [story] ◆ 곡절을 설명하다 give a detailed account 《of》; give full details 《of》
3 〈까닭〉(a) reason; the whys and hows
◆ 무슨 곡절인지 for some unknown reason / 무언가 곡절이 있어서 for a certain reason; for some reason (or other) / 여러 가지 곡절이 있어서 for many reasons combined
▶ 거기에는 반드시 무슨 곡절이 있을 것이다 There must be some reason for it.

곡조 曲調 a melody; a tune; an air; strains
◆ 외기 어려운 곡조 a tune difficult to remember / 곡조가 안 맞는 노래 a song out of tune / 한 곡조 부르다 sing a tune / 가사에 곡조를 붙이다 set a song to music; write the music to a song
▶ 이 노래는 곡조가 참 좋다 This song is very melodious.
▶ 그 노래의 곡조는 이렇다 This is how the song goes.

곡직 曲直 right or wrong ◆ 불문곡직하고 without inquiring into the right or wrong / 곡직을 가리다 inquire into the rights and wrongs 《of a case》; distinguish right from wrong

곡창 穀倉 〈창고〉 a granary; 《美》 a grain elevator; 〈지대〉 a granary; a grain belt; a rice bowl; 《美》 a breadbasket
◆ 한국의 곡창 호남 평야 the Honam Plain, the granary [rice bowl] of Korea
▶ 캔자스는 미국의 대 곡창 가운데 하나다 Kansas is one of the greatest granaries in the United States.

곡척 曲尺 a carpenter's square ⇨ 곱자
곡필 曲筆 (a) falsification; (a) perversion 《of facts》; misrepresentation
▶ 그는 곡필로 권력에 아부했다 He flattered the authority by false writing.
—**곡필하다** falsify; pervert 《the truth》; misrepresent; prostitute one's pen

곡학아세 曲學阿世 prostitution of learning
—**지도**〈之徒〉an academic flatterer; an intellectual timeserver; a timeserving scholar

곡해 曲解 perversion; a strained interpretation; misinterpretation
—**곡해하다** pervert; distort; put a false [wrong] construction 《on》; interpret wrongly; misconstrue
◆ 아무의 행동을 곡해하다 put a false construction on sb's action
▶ 그는 내가 호의로 한 말을 곡해했다 He perverted my friendly remark.
▶ 그는 내 말을 곡해하고 있다 He misconstrues [twists] my words.
▶ 그것은 사실을 곡해한 것이다 It's a distortion of the fact.

곤경 困境 a difficult situation; adverse circumstances; a predicament; a dilemma; difficulties; trouble
◆ 곤경을 벗어나다 get out of a difficult situation; find a way out of trouble / 곤경에 빠지다 get into trouble [difficult situation]; (口) get into hot water / 곤경에 빠지게 하다 put sb in a difficult situation / 곤경에 처하다 be in a fix; be in trouble [difficulty, distress] / 곤경에서 구해내다 help sb out of 《his》 difficulties / 곤경과 싸우다 struggle with adversity
▶ 그 회사는 재정적으로 곤경에 처해 있다 That company is in financial difficulties.
▶ 친구의 도움으로 나는 곤경에서 벗어났다 My friend helped me out of the difficulties.

곤고 困苦 hardships; privations; sufferings
곤궁 困窮 poverty; need; want; destitution; needy [narrow] circumstances
◆ 곤궁에 처하다 get into destitution / 곤궁에 허덕이다 be in extreme distress; suffer from dire poverty / 곤궁에서 구하다 help sb out of a financial difficulty
—**곤궁하다** poor; needy; destitute
◆ 곤궁한 사람들 the poor; the needy; the destitute / 곤궁해지다 get [become] poor; be reduced to poverty; come to be badly off
▶ 그는 곤궁한 생활을 하고 있다 He is badly off [living in poverty].
▶ 그 집은 아주 곤궁한 처지에 있었다 The family was in great need [was poverty-stricken].
⇌ The family was in dire want.

곤댓짓 nodding in a haughty manner —**곤댓짓하다** nod in a haughty manner
곤돌라 a gondola ◆ 곤돌라의 사공 a gondolier
곤두박질 a headlong fall
◆ 곤두박질로 headlong; head first; headforemost
▶ 그는 벼랑에서 곤두박질로 떨어졌다 He fell head over heels from the cliff.
▶ 그는 곤두박질로 물 속에 뛰어들었다 He threw himself headlong into the water.
—**곤두박질하다[치다]** fall headlong [headforemost, head over heels]; 〈시세가〉 drop sharply
▶ 물가가 곤두박질쳤다 The prices dropped suddenly [sharply].
▶ 비행기는 곤두박질해 추락했다 The plane crashed end over end to the ground.

곤두서다 stand on end; stand upside down; bristle up
▶ 모두들 신경이 곤두서 있었다 Everyone's nerves were on edge.
▶ 너 오늘 정말 신경이 곤두서 있구나 You're really jumpy [on edge] today, aren't you?
▶ 그 이야기를 듣고 있자니 머리털이 곤두서는 것 같았다 The story almost made my hair stand on end.

▶ 그녀의 말투가 내 신경을 곤두서게 한다 Her manner of speaking gets on my nerves.

곤두세우다 set on end; set upside down; erect; bristle up
♦ 머리털을 곤두세우고 with *one's* hair erect [on end] / 성이 나서 눈썹을 곤두세우다 raise *one's* eyebrows with anger / 신경을 곤두세우다 pay all *one's* attention to
▶ 새가 깃털을 곤두세웠다 The bird ruffled up its feathers.
▶ 개가 털을 곤두세우고 으르렁거렸다 The dog growled with his hair standing on end.
▶ 그는 신경을 잔뜩 곤두세우고 있다 He is all nerves.
▶ 그가 하는 말에 그렇게 신경을 곤두세우지 마라 Don't be so nervous about his words.

곤드라지다 drop off to sleep; fall asleep dog-tired [dead-drunk]; sink into a slumber
♦ 술에 취하여 곤드라지다 drink *oneself* to sleep / 술에 곤드라지게 하다 drink *sb* under the table
▶ 그는 방안에 들어서자 마자 곤드라졌다 He sank into a slumber as soon as he got into the room.

곤드레만드레 beastly drunk; staggeringly
♦ 곤드레만드레 취하다 be (as) drunk as a fiddler [fish, lord]; be dead-drunk; be under the table / 곤드레만드레가 되도록 마시다 get *oneself* blind drunk; drink *oneself* into oblivion
▶ 그는 밤늦게 곤드레만드레가 되어 귀가했다 He came home dead-drunk late at night.

곤들매기 〔魚〕 a char(r)

곤란 困難 (a) difficulty; (a) trouble; hardships; suffering
♦ 곤란을 겪다 have difficulty (in); have trouble; be in [get into] trouble; be in difficulties; have a hard time / 곤란을 극복하다 overcome [surmount] difficulties [hardships] / 곤란을 당하다 encounter [meet with] a difficulty / 식량 부족으로 곤란을 당하다 suffer from lack of food / 곤란을 참다 bear [endure] hardships / 재정적 곤란에 빠지다 get into financial difficulties [embarrassments]
▶ 어떤 곤란이 닥쳐도 그 일을 완수해야 한다 Whatever difficulty you may find [meet], you must accomplish it somehow.
▶ 그는 곤란이 닥쳐도 주저하지 않았다 He was undaunted in the face of difficulty.
▶ 그는 돈 때문에 곤란을 받고 있다 He is hard up [pressed] for money.
▶ 우리는 재정적 곤란에 직면해 있다 We are facing financial difficulties.
▶ 그는 곤란과 싸워 정상 등정에 성공했다 He struggled with difficulties and succeeded in reaching the top of the mountain.
—**곤란하다** hard; difficult; troublesome; be in trouble [difficulties]; embarrassing; delicate; perplexing
♦ 해결하기 곤란한 문제 a difficult [hard] problem to solve; a problem difficult [hard] to solve / 곤란한 일 a difficult task; a hard [tough] job; laborious work / 곤란한 것은… The trouble is that… / 더욱 곤란한 것은 to make matters worse / 호흡이 곤란하다 breathe with difficulty; have difficulty in breathing / 곤란한 입장에 처하다 be placed in a dilemma [delicate position]; be in a fix [an awkward situation]
▶ 그 물음에 대답하기는 곤란하다 It is difficult to answer the question. ⇌ The question is hard [difficult] to answer.
▶ 그의 제안을 거절하기가 곤란했다 I found it difficult to decline his offer.
▶ 아무리 곤란해도 그녀는 희망을 잃지 않았다 No matter how hard things were, she never lost hope.
▶ 그러면 너의 입장이 곤란해질 것이다 That would place you in an awkward [a delicate, a difficult] position [situation].
▶ 신중치 못한 그의 발언이 사태를 더 곤란하게 만들었다 His careless remark made things more difficult [even worse].

곤룡포 袞龍袍 a royal robe

곤봉 棍棒 a club; a cudgel; 〈경찰의〉 a truncheon; 〈美口〉 a billy; 〈체조용의〉 an Indian club
♦ 곤봉으로 때리다 beat *sb* with a club; club; cudgel
■ —체조 Indian club exercise

곤욕 困辱 (bitter) insult; contempt; indignity; affront
♦ 곤욕을 치르다 be insulted [disgraced]; suffer a bitter insult / 곤욕을 참다 bear an extreme affront; pocket [stomach, swallow] an insult

곤이 鯤鮞 hard roe; fish eggs

곤장 棍杖 a cudgel; a stick; a club (for beating criminals)
♦ 곤장을 치다 beat *sb* with a cudgel [stick] / 곤장을 스무 대 맞다 receive twenty cudgels [strokes of the cudgel]

곤쟁이 〔動〕 a kind of tiny shrimp ■ —젓 salted tiny shrimps

곤죽 —粥 1 〈진땅〉 sludge; mire; muddiness; a quagmire
♦ 눈이 녹아 곤죽이 된 길 a slushy [slush-filled] road / 곤죽이 되다 〈길이〉 become sloppy [muddy]; 〈삶아서〉 be reduced to jelly [pulp]
▶ 이 길은 비가 오면 곤죽이 된다 This road is a mudhole [becomes muddy] when it rains.
2 〈엉망진창〉 a mess; a jumble; utter confusion
♦ 일을 곤죽을 만들다 make a mess of an affair
3 〈몸이 늘어짐〉 exhaustion
▶ 그는 곤죽이 되어 돌아왔다 He came back exhausted [dog-tired].

곤줄매기 a titmouse ⇨ 곤줄박이

곤줄박이 〔鳥〕 a titmouse (*pl*. -mice); 〈英〉 a tomtit

곤지 a rouge spot on a bride's brow
♦ 이마에 곤지를 찍다 put a rouge spot on *one's* forehead

곤충 昆蟲 an insect; a bug ■ —류 〔動〕 *Insecta*; insects —학 entomology; insectology —학자 an entomologist

곤충

- 더듬이 antenna
- 겹눈 compound eye
- 앞날개 front wing
- 뒷날개 hind wing
- 홑눈 simple eye
- 침 sting
- 뒷다리 rear leg
- 앞다리 front leg
- 가운뎃다리 middle leg
- 두부 head
- 흉부 thorax
- 복부 abdomen

곤충채집 昆蟲採集 insect collecting; (口) bugging; bughunting ─**곤충채집하다** collect insects; (口) bug ♦ 곤충채집하러 가다 go hunting for insects; (口) go bugging
■ ─가 an insect collector; (口) a bughunter

곤포 梱包 〈가마니〉 a bale; 〈포장〉 a package (略 pkg. 《pl. pkgs.》) ♦ 생사 한 곤포 one bale of raw silk ─**곤포하다** wrap sth in a straw mat and tie it up with rope

곤하다 困─ tired; weary; fatigued; exhausted
♦ 곤히 tired; exhaustedly / 곤히 자다 sleep like a log
▶ 밤을 꼬박 새웠더니 몹시 곤하다 I am worn out from staying up all night.
▶ 그 여자는 곤히 잠들었다 She fell asleep fatigued. ⇒ She fell fast asleep.

곤혹 困惑 embarrassment; puzzlement; perplexity
♦ 곤혹의 빛을 띠다 wear a worried look; look troubled [embarrassed]
▶ 그녀는 곤혹스러운 표정으로 서 있었다 She was standing with a perplexed look on her face.
▶ 그의 갑작스런 사직은 사장을 곤혹스럽게 했다 His sudden resignation upset the president.

곧 1 〈바로〉 at once; (美) right away; immediately; 〈얼마 안 있어〉 directly; soon; shortly

[解説] *at once*는 「〈우물쭈물하지 않고〉 곧」이란 뜻의 가장 일반적인 말. 이와 비슷하고 스스럼없는 말이 *right away* [*off*]로서 (美)에서는 at once보다 많이 쓰인다. *immediately*는 시간적인 간격을 두지 않고 곧이란 뜻인데, (口)에서는 흔히 강한 뜻으로 쓰인다. *directly*는 immediately와 같은 뜻이지만 (口)에서는 「얼마 안 있어」란 뜻으로 쓰인다.

▶ 지금 곧 출발하자 Let's start at once [right away].
▶ 그는 곧 돌아올 것이다 He will come back shortly.
▶ 그가 곧 올 테니 좀 더 계세요 Stay a little longer please. He will come soon.
▶ 비가 곧 올지 모르겠다 It may rain at any moment.
▶ 지금 곧 갈게 I'm coming right now.
▶ 곧 봄[크리스마스]이다 Spring [Christmas] is just around the corner.
▶ 그들은 곧 결혼합니다 They are going to get married soon [before long].
▶ 곧 1시가 된다 It will soon be one o'clock.
▶ 그 보트는 곧 가라앉을 것 같았다 The boat looked as if it was going to sink any minute.
▶ 그 약이 곧 효과를 나타냈다 The medicine took immediate effect [effect immediately].
2 〈쉽게〉 easily; readily
▶ 그것은 곧 배울 수 있다 It is easy to learn.
▶ 이런 종류의 유리컵은 곧 깨진다 Glasses of this kind break easily.
▶ 그의 집은 곧 찾을 수 있어요 You can easily [readily] find his house.
3 〈즉〉 namely; that is (to say); or; i.e.; as it were; in other words
▶ 테이프의 목소리는 곧 그 전날 전화에서 들은 그 목소리였다 The tape-recorded voice was the very same voice I heard over the phone the day before.
▶ 이곳은 구세주 곧 그리스도가 탄생한 곳이다 This is the place where the Savior, that is, Christ was born.
▶ 인간 문화의 가장 중요한 측면의 하나 곧 언어를 관찰해 보자 Let's look at one of the most important aspects of human culture, i.e., language.

곧다 1 〈사물이〉 straight; upright 《post》; erect; direct
♦ 곧은 길 a straight road / 곧은 선을 긋다 draw a straight line
▶ 자세를 곧게 하고 앉으시오 Sit up straight.
▶ 길은 몇 마일이나 곧게 뻗어 있었다 The road ran straight for several miles.
▶ 바람이 없어서 연기가 곧게 올라가고 있다 There is no wind blowing, and the smoke is rising straight up.
2 〈마음이〉 honest; straightforward; upright; righteous
♦ 곧게 honestly; straightforwardly / 세상을 곧게 살아가다 lead an honest life; pursue an honest career
▶ 그는 마음이 곧다 He has an honest mind.
▶ 그는 곧은 사람이라서 절대 거짓말을 하지 않을 것이다 He is an honest person [upright man] and would never tell lies.

곧바로 〈곧장〉 straight; direct; 〈즉시〉 at once; immediately; directly
▶ 그 남자는 곧바로 집으로 돌아갔다 He went [returned] home straight.
▶ 화살은 과녁으로 곧바로 날아갔다 The arrow went right to the mark.
▶ 그는 곧바로 우리한테 왔다 He came directly toward us.

곧바르다 〈물건이〉 straight; upright; 〈사람이〉 honest; straightforward

곧이곧대로 plainly; straightforwardly; honestly; frankly; just as it is
▶ 사실을 곧이곧대로 이야기하시오 Tell (us)

the facts as they happened [just as they are].
▶ 곧이곧대로 대답하시오 Give me a direct answer.
▶ 그 사람의 말은 곧이곧대로 들어서는 안 된다 We had better take what he says with a grain of salt.
▶ 곧이곧대로 말하면 당신은 어리석은 짓을 하고 있는 거요 To be frank (with you) [Frankly speaking], you are doing a stupid thing.

곧이듣다 take 《a thing》 for truth; accept 《a remark》 as true; swallow
♦아무의 말을 곧이듣다 take sb at (his) word(s) / 농담을 곧이듣다 take a joke seriously
▶ 그는 그녀의 말이면 무엇이든지 곧이듣는다 He swallows any story she tells.
▶ 그런 소문을 곧이들었니? Did you believe such a rumor [take such a rumor as truth]?
▶ 그의 말을 곧이듣다니 너 바보로구나 It is foolish of you to take him at his word(s).
▶ 그의 약속을 곧이들으면 안 된다 You should not take his promise seriously.

곧잘 1 〈꽤 잘〉 pretty [fairly] well; well enough; quite well
▶ 그녀는 노래를 곧잘 부른다 She sings pretty well.
▶ 그는 영어를 곧잘 한다 He speaks English fairly well.
2 〈자주〉 often; frequently; habitually; usually
▶ 그들은 토요일 밤엔 곧잘 외식을 한다 They often [usually] eat out on Saturday nights.
▶ 그는 거짓말을 곧잘 한다 He habitually tells lies.
▶ 어렸을 때 할머니는 옛날 이야기를 곧잘 해주셨다 When I was a child, my grandmother used to tell old tales to me.
▶ 그것은 그 녀석이 곧잘 쓰는 수법이다 That's his usual trick.
▶ 그것은 젊은이들이 곧잘 하는 오해다 It is a misunderstanding that young people are apt to make.

곧장 〈똑바로〉 straight; direct(ly); 〈지체없이〉 right (away); straight [right] off; without delay
♦곧장 가다 go [keep] straight on / 곧장 떠나다 leave without delay
▶ 친구한테 들르지 않고 곧장 집으로 가겠습니다 I won't drop in on my friend, but go straight home.
▶ 이 길을 100미터쯤 곧장 가면 교차점이 나온다 If you go straight along this road about a hundred meters, there is an intersection.
▶ 모퉁이를 왼편으로 돌아서 곧장 가시오 Turn sharp to the left and follow your nose.
▶ 종달새는 곧장 공중으로 치솟아 올랐다 The lark went straight high up in the sky.

곧추 upright; vertically; perpendicularly; straight; in a straight line
♦곧추 선 기둥 an upright post / 곧추 서다 stand upright [erect]; erect oneself / 곧추 세우다 set a flagpole upright / 몸을 곧추 세우다 hold oneself erect; straighten one's body / 아기를 곧추 안다 hold a baby out straight / 곧추 앉다 sit up straight
▶ 땅에 막대기를 곧추 세워라 Thrust a stick upright in the earth.

골[1] 〈성〉 anger; temper; dander
♦골이 나서 in anger; angrily / 골을 내다 get [become, grow] angry; lose one's temper; (美口) get mad (at) / 골나게 하다 make sb angry [美俗] mad]; provoke sb to anger; offend
▶ 그는 골이 나서 나한테 말도 걸지 않았다 He is so angry that he won't speak to me. ⇌ He is too angry to speak to me.
▶ 나는 그가 골을 내는 것을 본 적이 없다 I have never seen him get angry [in a bad temper].

골[2] 〈틀〉 a block; a mold; a cast
♦구둣골 a shoemaker's last / 망건골 a manggŏn mold [block] / 모자골 a hat block / 솥 골 a mold for a pot / 구두에 골을 넣다 tree a shoe

골[3] 〈접은 금〉 the crease made when a sheet of cloth, paper or cardboard is folded into two equal parts

골[4] 〈골수〉 the marrow (of a bone); the medulla 《pl. -lae》; 〈머릿골〉 brain ♦골이 비다 〈지각없다〉 have no sense / 골이 아프다 have a headache
■ 작은— the cerebellum 《pl. ~s, -la》 ⇨ 소뇌
큰— the cerebrum 《pl. ~s, -bra》 ⇨ 대뇌

골[5] **1** ⇨ 골목 **2** 〈구멍〉 a cave; a hollow ♦골로 가다 die; lose one's life **3** 〈골짜기〉 a gully; a ravine; a trough 《물결·기압의》 ♦기압골 a low pressure trough

골[6] **1** ⇨ 고을 **2** ⇨ 고랑[1]

골[7] the goal; 〈경마의〉 the winning post; 〈농구의〉 a basket ♦골을 넣다 make [score, get, win] a goal; 〈농구에서〉 score a basket; cage
■ —득실차 goal difference —라인 a goal line —키퍼 a goalkeeper —킥 a goal kick —포스트 a goalpost

골갱이 〈심〉 the core; the heart; 〈골자〉 the pith; the gist; the substance

골격 骨格 a frame; build; physique; a skeleton
♦골격이 건장한 사람 a man of stout [sturdy] build; a stalwart person / 골격이 좋은 말 a horse with plenty of bone

골고루 evenly ⇨ 고루

골골하다 suffer from a chronic disease; suffer constantly from weak health; be sick all the time
♦골골하는 사람 a chronic [an established] invalid; a sickly (and suffering) person

골다 snore
♦코를 골기 시작하다 fall to snoring / 코를 (요란하게) 골며 자다 sleep with (loud) snores / 자기 코고는 소리에 잠을 깨다 snore oneself awake
▶ 그는 코고는 버릇이 있다 He snores habitually.
▶ 제 코고는 소리가 거슬립니까? Does my snoring bother you?

골다공증 骨多孔症 〔醫〕 osteoporosis

골동품 骨董品 an antique; a curio 《pl. ~s》; a curiosity; objects [articles] of virtu; bric-a-brac; 〈시대에 뒤진 사람[물건]〉 a museum piece ♦가짜 골동품 a faked antique
■ —상 〈상점〉 a curio [curiosity] store; an

골드러시 212

antique shop; 〈상인〉 a curio [curiosity] dealer; an antique dealer ―**수집 curio hunting**: 골동품 수집 취미가 있다 take pleasure in collecting curios ―**수집[애호, 연구]가** a curioso (*pl.* ~s, -si); a virtuoso (*pl.* ~s, -si); an antiquary; an antiquarian

골드러시 gold rush

골드스미스 〈영국의 시인·극작가〉 Goldsmith, Oliver (1728-74)

골든아워 〈라디오·TV의〉(at, in) prime time ▶이 영화는 골든 아워에 방영된다 This picture will be shown in prime time.

골똘하다 absorbed [lost] (in); concentrated (on); given (to); completely taken up (with) ◆골똘히 absorbedly; intently; with an absorbed attention / 사업에 골똘하다 be engrossed in business / 골똘히 생각에 잠기다 be lost in thought ▶그는 그 문제를 골똘히 생각하고 있었다 He was brooding over the problem.

골라내다 pick [single] out; choose (from); select (out of many); sort out (the best) ▶우리는 200명의 응모자 가운데서 열 명을 골라 냈다 We selected ten people from (among) two hundred applicants. ▶그 농부는 나쁜 씨앗을 골라내고 있다 The farmer is sorting out the bad seeds.

골라잡다 choose; select; take [have] *one's* choice ▶골라 잡아 천원이오 One thousand won a piece at your choice.

골로새서 ―書 〔聖〕 The Epistle of Paul to the Colossians; Colossians (略 Col.)

골마루 〔建〕 a narrow corridor [passage, hallway]

골마지 scum ◆골마지가 끼다 form scum; scum

골막 骨膜 〔解〕 the periosteum (*pl.* -tea) ■―염 periostitis

골머리 the brain ⇨ 골치

골목 an alley; a lane; a bystreet; a side [narrow] street; an alleyway ◆막다른 골목 a blind alley / 골목 어귀 an alley entrance [mouth] ▶그 집은 막다른 골목에 있다 The house is at the end of the lane. ▶그 골목으로 들어가서 두번째 집이 그의 집이 다 The second house down that alley is his. ■―대장 the boss of the kids [youngsters] (of the neighborhood); the cock of the walk; a little lion; 〈개구쟁이〉 a bully

골몰 汨沒 absorption; immersion; engrossment ―**골몰하다** be immersed [absorbed, engrossed] in; devote *oneself* (heart and soul) to (a task) ▶그녀는 그 문제 해결에 골몰해 있었다 She was absorbed in solving the problem.

골무 a thimble; a thumbstall ◆골무를 끼다 wear a thimble

골반 骨盤 〔解〕 the pelvis (*pl.* -ves); the basin ■―부 the pelvic region

골방 ―房 a back room; a closet

골병 ―病 a disease [an injury] in the inmost part; a deep-seated disease; 〈치명타〉 a fatal blow ◆골병(이) 들다 be [get] injured internally; be seized with an incurable internal disease; have *one's* fatal [vital] parts affected

골분 骨粉 powdered bones; bone dust [meal]

골상 骨相 physiognomy; 〈인상〉 *one's* features ◆전형적인 북유럽인의 골상 a typical North European physiognomy / 골상을 보다 practice physiognomy; study [examine] *sb's* physiognomy

골상학 骨相學 phrenology; physiognomy ◆골상학(상의) phrenological; physiognomical / 골상학상[적으로] physiognomically; phrenologically; from a phrenological point of view ■―자 a phrenologist; 〈관상가〉 a physiognomist

골샌님 a man of no caliber

골생원 ―生員 〈옹졸한〉 a narrow-minded [an illiberal] man; 〈골골하는〉 a weak [sickly] man; a man in delicate health

골속 1 〈머릿골 속〉 brains; (口) gray matter **2** 〈골풀의 속〉 the heart of a rush

골수 骨髓 〔解〕 the bone marrow; the marrow (of a bone); the medulla (*pl.* ~s, -lae) ◆골수 공산주의자 a Communist to the core [backbone, marrow] / 골수에 사무치다 cut [go] deep into *one's* heart; pierce *one's* heart [the very marrow] ▶그는 병이 골수에 박혔다 The disease has taken hold of him to the marrow. ▶나는 그에게 골수에 사무치는 원한이 있다 I have a deep grudge against him. ■―염(炎) osteomyelitis ―이식(移植) bone marrow transplantation

골안개 the (morning) mist in the valley

골암 骨癌 〔醫〕 cancer of a bone

골연화증 骨軟化症 〔醫〕 osteomalacia

골염 骨炎 〔醫〕 osteitis

골오르다 get angry ⇨ 약오르다

골올리다 chafe ⇨ 약올리다

골육 骨肉 〈육친〉 (*one's* own) flesh and blood; kindred; blood relations ◆골육지간 brotherhood; sisterhood; kinship / 골육의 정 love for *one's* own flesh and blood ▶골육의 정은 어쩔 수 없다 Blood is thicker than water. ■―상쟁[상잔] domestic [family] discord [trouble]; a family quarrel; (be engaged in) an internecine feud [war] ―지친 blood relationship; blood relations [relatives]

골육종 骨肉腫 〔醫〕 osteosarcoma

골자 骨子 the gist; the main point; the substance ◆문제의 골자 the gist of the question / 계획의 골자를 말하다 outline the essential features of a plan ▶골자는 이렇다 The point is this. ▶우리는 논쟁의 골자를 알 수가 없었다 We could not make out the gist of the argument.

골재 骨材 aggregate

골절 骨折 (a) fracture (of a bone) ―**골절하다** suffer a fracture; break a bone; have a bone broken [fractured] ■―단순[복잡]― a simple [compound] fracture ―분쇄[세편]― a comminuted fracture

골절 骨節 〈뼈마디〉 a (bone) joint
골질 骨質 〔解〕 bony [osseous] tissue
골짜기 a valley; a ravine; a gorge; a dale

[解說] *valley*는 산과 산 사이에 있는 넓은 저지대를 가리키는 말. 따라서 우리나라처럼 좁고 우묵하게 들어간 지형을 말할 때는 narrow를 붙이는 것이 좋다. *ravine, gorge*는 양쪽이 절벽으로 되어 있는 지형을 가리킨다.

▶ 그는 산을 넘고 골짜기를 건너 계속 걸어갔다 He walked on, up hill and down dale.
▶ 그녀는 골짜기에 핀 한 떨기 백합이다 She is a lily in a valley.
▶ 그 골짜기에는 급류가 흐른다 A rapid stream runs in the ravine.
골초 —草 〈저질 담배〉 tobacco of low quality; cheap tobacco; 〈사람〉 a heavy [chain] smoker
골치 〈골머리〉 the brain
 ◆골치 아픈 문제 a troublesome question; a knotty problem / 골치가 아프다 have a headache; (비유) be troublesome [annoying, vexatious]
▶ 아들놈이 정말 골치다 My son is a real pain.
▶ 그것 때문에 골치를 앓았다 I racked my brains over it. ⇌ I bothered my head about it. ⇌ It gave me much trouble.
골칫거리 a headache; a (source of) trouble; a nuisance; a bother; a black sheep
▶ 형은 집안의 골칫거리다 My brother is the black sheep of the family.
▶ 두 번째 문제가 골칫거리였다 The second question baffled [was most difficult for] me.
▶ 네게 골칫거리가 되고 싶진 않다 I hate to be a trouble to you.
골탄 骨炭 animal [bone] charcoal; boneblack
골탕 —湯 1 〈골국〉 a soup made of fried ox-brain [ox-marrow] coated with flour
2 〈피해〉 a great loss [injury]; heavy [serious] damage
 ◆골탕(을) 먹다 suffer a big loss; 〈애먹다〉 have bitter experiences; have a hard [bad] time (of it); be taken in; be cheated
▶ 나는 그 녀석을 믿었다가 골탕먹었다 I was taken in, trusting that guy.
▶ 그는 악질 고리대금업자에게 걸려 골탕을 먹었다 He had a hell of time dealing with a bad [heartless] usurer.
골통 the skull; (俗) the noddle; (俗) the dome
 ◆골통이 터지다 have *one's* head hurt / 골통이 터지게 싸우다 fight hard [desperately]
골통 骨痛 〔醫〕 ostalgia; boneache
골틀리다 〈부아가 나다〉 feel [be] vexed; be in a bad humor; get angry; be displeased; be offended 《by, at》
골파 a variety of spring onion
골판지 —板紙 corrugated cardboard
골패 骨牌 domino(e)s
골퍼 a golfer; a golf player
골풀 〔植〕 a rush
골풀무 foot bellows
골풀이 venting *one's* anger ⇨ 화풀이
골프 golf ◆골프 치는 사람 a golfer; a golf player / 골프를 치다 play (at) golf; golf
■—공 a golf ball —광 a golf maniac —바지 plus fours; knickers —복 a golf coat —연습장 a golf practice range; a driving range —장 golf links; a golf course; a green —채 a golf club; 〈철제의〉 an iron; a driver; 〈목제의〉 a wood
골필 骨筆 a stencil [steel] pen; a stylus
골학 骨學 〔解〕 osteology —자 an osteologist
골함석 corrugated sheet zinc
골혹 骨— 〔醫〕 a bone tumor
골화 骨化 ossification —골화하다 ossify; be ossified
골회 骨灰 (animal) bone ash(es)
곪다 form pus; fester; come to a head
▶ 상처가 곪았다 The wound festered [formed pus].
▶ 여드름이 곪았다 The pimple has come to a head.
▶ 종기가 곪았다 The boil is ripe.
▶ 상처는 곪지 않고 아물었다 The wound has healed up without festering.
곬 1 〈한쪽으로 트인〉 a fixed direction; a set way [route]
 ◆세상사를 외곬으로 생각하다 see things from only one point of view
2 〈물 흐르는〉 a watercourse; a waterway; a channel
곯다¹ 1 〈그릇에 덜 차다〉 be [remain] unfilled; be (still) not full; be a little short of full
▶ 자루가 곯았다 The (cloth) bag is only partly filled.
2 〈굶주리다〉 go [be] hungry; be famished; starve
 ◆곯은 배를 채우다 satisfy [gratify] *one's* hunger
▶ 배를 곯아서는 아무 일도 할 수 없다 One cannot work [There is nothing done] on an empty stomach.
▶ 애들을 배곯게 할 수는 없다 My children must not be left hungry.
곯다² 1 〈상하다〉 go bad [rotten]; rot; spoil; be spoilt [spoiled]; addle(알이)
 ◆곯은 달걀 addle [bad] eggs / 곯은 바나나 rotten bananas
▶ 과일은 너무 오래 두면 곯는다 Fruit spoils if kept too long.
▶ 달걀은 곯기 쉽다 Eggs are apt to addle.
2 〈골병들다〉 suffer secret damage; suffer (an) internal injury; get injured internally
▶ 그는 폭음을 해서 몸이 곯았다 Excessive drinking did him bodily harm.
▶ 그들의 농간에 나는 되게 곯았다 I suffered heavily from their tricks.
곯리다¹ 1 〈그릇을〉 incompletely fill 《a container》; leave 《a vessel》 half-empty
2 〈배를〉 underfeed; leave *sb* to starve ▶ 식구들 배나 겨우 곯리지 않을 정도다 I barely support my family.
곯리다² 1【골병들게 하다】inflict damage upon *sb*; do harm to; cause damage to; 〈약자를〉 bully; tease; annoy; torment; be hard on *sb*
▶ 하도 건방지기에 그 녀석을 한 번 곯려 주었다

I played a trick on him to put down his pride.
▶그 아이는 엉뚱한 질문으로 선생님들을 곯려 준다 The boy perplexes [embarrasses] his teachers by asking them quite unexpected questions.
2 〈상하게 하다〉 rot; spoil; addle; make a thing stale

곯아떨어지다 〈잠에〉 fall fast asleep; fall into a deep sleep; sleep like a log; 〈술에〉 sink into a drunken slumber; drink oneself to sleep
▶그는 지쳐서 곯아떨어졌다 He fell into a deep sleep from exhaustion.
▶나는 곯아떨어져서 전화벨이 울리는 것도 몰랐다 I slept over the phone call.

곯아빠지다 **1** 〈몹시 곯다〉 be utterly rotten [spoilt]; be [get] badly addled
2 〈탐닉하다〉 be addicted to 〈drink〉; wallow in 〈pleasures〉; be given to
◆주색잡기에 곯아빠지다 give *oneself* up to wine, women, and dice; be addicted to debauchery

곰¹ thick beef soup ⇨ 곰국
곰² **1** 〈동물〉 a bear ◆흰곰 a white [polar] bear / 곰 가죽 (a) bearskin / 곰 새끼 a bear's cub **2** 〈미련한 사람〉 a slow-witted person; a slowpoke

곰곰(이) deeply; deliberately; thoroughly; seriously
◆곰곰이 생각한 끝에 after much [serious] thought; after due [mature] consideration [reflection] / 곰곰이 생각하다 think and think; think a matter over 〈and over〉; ponder 《over, on》
▶나는 그가 한 말을 곰곰이 생각해 보았다 I pondered his words carefully.

곰국 thick beef soup; thick broth of meat
곰바지런하다 unskilled yet meticulous and diligent
곰방대 a short smoking pipe
곰배팔 a disabled [deformed] arm
곰배팔이 a person with a deformed arm
곰보 a pockmarked person; a person with a pitted face
곰비임비 〈잇달아〉 in rapid succession; one after another; on [upon] the heels of another
▶참사가 곰비임비 일어났다 One disaster followed close [hard] on the heels of another.
곰삭다 **1** 〈옷이〉 wear thin; be worn out; be outworn **2** 〈젓갈이〉 get well [thoroughly] pickled
곰살갑다 kind; tender; cordial
곰살궂다 tenderhearted; warmhearted; tender; meek; cordial
곰상스럽다 meticulous; scrupulous
곰실거리다 squirm; wriggle; writhe
▶지렁이가 곰실거리며 내 손가락 사이로 빠져 나갔다 The fishworm wriggled out of my fingers.
곰치 〔魚〕 a moray
곰탕 rice in thick broth [beef soup]
곰팡 mold ⇨ 곰팡이
곰팡나다 get [become] moldy [fusty, musty]
◆곰팡난 음식 moldy food / 곰팡난 책 a mildewed book / 곰팡나지 않도록 하다 keep 〈books〉 from getting moldy
▶이 곰팡난 헌 가구를 치워 버립시다 Let's get rid of this moldy old furniture.
▶정원의 장미 봉오리가 곰팡나서 죽었다 Mildew grew and killed the rosebuds in the garden.

곰팡내 **1** 〈냄새〉 a musty [stale] smell; smell of must
◆곰팡내 나는 방 a musty room
▶이 담요에서 곰팡내가 난다 This blanket smells a bit fusty.
▶술에서 곰팡내가 난다 The wine tastes musty.
2 〈진부함〉 mustiness; staleness
◆곰팡내 나는 사상 a moss-grown idea; motheaten ideas / 곰팡내 나는 학설 an outmoded theory; a dated [an out-of-date] hypothesis
▶그것은 곰팡내 나는 이야기다 It is a hackneyed [stale, timeworn] story.

곰팡슬다 gather mold; be covered with mold; mildew
▶치즈가 곰팡슬었다 The cheese got moldy. ⇌ Mold gathered on the cheese.
▶장마철에는 곰팡슬기 쉽다 In the wet season things easily gather mold.

곰팡이 mold; mildew; must
◆검은 곰팡이 bread mold / 푸른 곰팡이 blue [green] mold / 곰팡이 투성이다 be covered with mold / 곰팡이를 없애다 remove the mold
▶온통 곰팡이가 슬었다 There is a film of mold all over it.
▶책에 온통 곰팡이가 피었다 The books got mildewed all over.

곰팡피다 gather mold ⇨ 곰팡슬다
곱¹ **1** ⇨ 곱쟁이 **2** ⇨ 곱절 **3** 〔數〕 the product
▶5와 8의 곱은 40이다 The product of 5 and 8 is 40. ―**곱하다** multiply
곱² 〈분비물〉 mucous discharge; a film of pus
▶헌데에 곱이 꼈었다 A mucous discharge formed on a sore.

곱걸다 **1** 〈노름돈을〉 bet double **2** 〈겹쳐 얽다〉 bind double
곱꺾다 〈관절을〉 bend and stretch 《a joint》; flex 《*one's* knee》
곱꺾이 bending and stretching; flexing
곱놓다 double *one's* bet
곱다¹ 〈손해보다〉 end up with a loss rather than a profit; result in a loss to *one*; suffer a loss; show a deficit
곱다² bend ⇨ 굽다²
곱다³ 〈손·발가락이〉 numb; benumbed; stiff
◆추위에 곱은 손가락 fingers numb with cold
▶추위에 손가락이 곱아 펜을 잡을 수가 없었다 My fingers were so stiff [numb] with cold that I couldn't hold my pen.

곱다⁴ **1** 〔아름답다〕 beautiful; lovely; fine; nice; 〈말·소리가〉 sweet; charming; soft; 〈살결이〉 fine; delicate
◆고운 꽃 a pretty [lovely] flower / 고운 말씨 refined language / 고운 목소리 a charming [sweet] voice / 고운 살결 a fine [delicate] skin / 고운 얼굴 a beautiful face / 곱게 차린 신부 a bride finely dressed; a bride dressed beautifully / 곱게 차려 입다 dress *one*-

self beautifully; dress up / 곱게 피다 be in beautiful bloom
▶ 언제나 참 고우십니다 How lovely you always look!
▶ 그는 언제나 글씨를 곱게 쓴다 He always writes neatly [in a clear hand].
▶ 그녀는 머리를 곱게 다듬고 나서 방을 나섰다 She arranged her hair neatly before going out of the room.
2〈마음이〉kind; tender; warmhearted; pureminded
♦ 마음씨 고운 소녀 a kindhearted [tenderhearted] girl; an affectionate girl
▶ 그 노부부는 마음씨가 고운 사람들이다 That old couple are warmhearted [pure in mind].
3〈가루 등이〉fine《flour》; fair ♦ 이 바닷가는 모래가 곱다 This beach has fine sand.

곱다랗게 1〈아주 곱게〉quite prettily [beautifully]; nicely; handsomely
♦ 곱다랗게 생긴 소년 a handsome [nicelooking] boy / 곱다랗게 생기다 be pretty [beautiful]; have nicely turned-out features
2〈깔축없이〉safely; intactly; so [such] that it is whole ▶ 집이 곱다랗게 남아 있었다 The house was safe. ⇌ The house stood intact [undamaged].
3〈깨끗이〉perfectly; beautifully; magnificently; clean ♦ 곱다랗게 잊어버리다 utterly forget

곱다랗다〈아름답다〉quite pretty; very beautiful;〈온전하다〉whole; intact; untouched; undamaged

곱돌[鑛] agalmatolite ⇨ 납석

곱드러지다 tumble [stumble]《over》♦ 돌[나무 뿌리]에 채여 곱드러지다 stumble over a stone [the root of a tree]

곱들다 cost twice as much (as); take [need] double ♦ 시간이 곱들다 take double [twice] the time / 힘이 곱들다 be twice as hard [difficult] (as)

곱들이다 pay double [twice]; spend [consume] twice (as much money as); double《one's efforts》♦ 공을 곱들이다 take twice as much trouble《as》

곱디디다 sprain [twist] *one's* ankle

곱똥 mucous feces

곱빼기 1〈음식 등의〉double measure; a double-the-ordinary dish **2**〈거듭함〉double; twice

곱사등이 a hunchback; a humpback; a crookback ♦ 곱사등이의 hunchbacked; humpbacked

곱사병 ─病 rickets ⇨ 구루병

곱살스럽다, 곱살하다〈얼굴이〉pretty; fair; charming; handsome; comely;〈마음씨가〉sweet; gentle; tender
♦ 곱살하게 생긴 소녀 a pretty [charming] girl / 곱살레 굴다 be gentle

곱새기다〈거듭 생각하다〉think over (and over) again;〈곡해하다〉misinterpret; pervert [twist]《*sb's* words》;〈오해하다〉misunderstand; misconstrue;〈고깝게 여기다〉think ill of

곱셈 (a) multiplication (↔division) ▶ 자, 곱셈 연습을 해 봅시다 Now, let's work our exercise in multiplication. ─**곱셈하다** multiply; do multiplication
■─**표** the multiplication sign

곱슬곱슬하다 curly; curled; frizzled; kinky
♦ 곱슬곱슬한 머리 a curl; curly hair ▶ 그녀는 머리가 곱슬곱슬하다 She has curly hair. ⇌ Her hair is kinky.

곱슬머리 curly hair ⇨ 고수머리

곱씹다 harp《on, upon》; rechew; repeat《a word》▶ 왜 자꾸 곱씹나? Why do you keep harping on the same subject?

곱자〈목수용〉a carpenter's square; a metal measure; a L square

곱장다리 bowlegs;〈사람〉a bowlegged person

곱쟁이 double; doubled amount ▶ 그렇게 하면 돈이 곱쟁이로 든다 It costs twice as much as that.

곱절〈…배〉times; -fold;〈갑절〉double; twofold
♦ 몇 곱절이나 many times over / 몇 곱절의 노력을 하다 redouble *one's* efforts / 곱절이 길다 [무겁다] be twice [double] as long [heavy] as《another》; be as long [heavy] again as《another》/ 원금을 곱절로 갚다 repay double the original amount
▶ 2의 네 곱절은 8이다 Four times two is (equal to) 8.
▶ 1,000은 100의 몇 곱절이냐? How many times a hundred is a thousand?

곱창 the small intestine of cattle ♦ 곱창 구이 broiled (pieces of) small intestine of cattle

곱치다〈접다〉fold;〈곱절하다〉double
♦ 신문을 곱치다 fold up a newspaper / 값을 곱치다 double the price
▶ 이 양탄자는 너무 두꺼워서 반듯하게 곱칠 수가 없다 This carpet is too thick to double up neatly.

곱하다 multiply
♦ 두 수를 곱하다 multiply two numbers together / 2에 5를 곱하다 multiply 2 by 5
▶ 7에 8을 곱하면 56이 된다 Seven (multiplied) by eight make(s) fifty-six. ⇌ Eight times seven is [make(s)] fifty-six.(▶ 2×3=6은 Twice three is six.라고 읽음)

곳 1【장소】a place;〈특정 장소〉a spot;〈현장〉a scene;〈부지〉a site;〈소재지〉a seat;〈고장〉a locality
♦ 갈 곳 *one's* destination / 그곳〈거기〉there; that place;〈상대방이 있는 곳〉your place / 사과가 많이 나는 곳 an apple-producing district / 안전한 곳 a place of safety / 옛 성채가 있던 곳 the site of an old fort / 이곳 저곳 here and there / 편리한 곳 a convenient place
▶ 여기가 내가 태어나서 자란[우리가 처음 만난] 곳입니다 This is (the place) where I was born and grew up [we first met].
▶ 여기가 사고가 난 곳이다 This is the scene of the accident.
〈곳이[은]〉여기는 젊은 사람들이 오는 곳이 아니다 This is no place for young people.
▶ 서울에는 볼 곳이 많다 There are a lot of places to see in Seoul.
▶ 그는 기거할 곳이 없다 He has nowhere to

live.
▶책상을 들여 놓을 곳이 없다 There is no room for the desk.
▶이곳은 이미 진달래가 만발했습니다 Azaleas are already in full bloom here.
▶내 집보다 나은 곳은 없다 There is no place like home.
▶그곳은 어떻습니까? How are things going on in your place?
▶그곳은 별고 없으신지요? Are you all getting along well?
〈곳을〉제 계산이 틀린 곳을 말씀해 주세요 Tell me where I went wrong in my calculations.
▶우리는 소풍하기 좋은 곳을 발견했다 We found a good spot for a picnic.
▶이곳을 지나실 때는 한 번 들르세요 Drop in when you come this way.
▶아픈 곳을 좀 보자 Show me the place where it hurts.
〈곳에〉곳에 따라 다르다 be different in different localities
▶나는 어디 공해 없는 곳에 살고 싶다 I would like to live in some pollution-free place.
▶내일 아침에는 곳에 따라 눈이 내리겠습니다 〈일기예보〉 It will snow in some places tomorrow morning.
▶이것은 건조한 곳에 두어야 합니다 You should put this in a dry place.
▶전에 연못이 있던 곳에 공원을 만들고 있다 A park is being built where there was a pond.
〈곳으로〉어디든 너 가고 싶은 곳으로 가거라 You may go wherever you like.
2 〈지점〉 a point; 〈부분〉 a part; 〈한 구절〉 a passage
▶여기가 두 도로가 교차하는 곳입니다 This is the point where the two streets cross.
▶이 책에는 어려운 곳이 많다 There are a lot of difficult passages in this book.
▶그의 논문에는 군데군데 틀린 곳이 있다 Parts of his article are mistaken.
▶필요한 곳에 동그라미를 치시오 Circle the necessary ones.
3 〈주소〉 one's address; one's home
▶사시는 곳이 어디입니까? What is your address?
▶그 사람의 이름과 사는 곳을 가르쳐 다오 Give me his name and address.
곳간 —間 a storeroom; a repository; a shed
♦곳간에 넣다 store; put in storage
곳곳 several [various] places
♦곳곳에 here and there; in (several) places; (here, there, and) everywhere / 시내 곳곳에서 in several [various] parts of the city / 곳곳을 여행하다 travel from place to place
▶나라 곳곳에 국립 공원이 있다 There are national parks scattered throughout the country.
▶그 회사는 거의 전국 곳곳에 지점이 있다 That company has its branches in almost all parts of the country.
▶사람들이 곳곳에서 모여들었다 The people flocked from far and near.
▶곳곳에서 유사한 사건이 일어났다 Similar cases occurred in various places.

곳집 **1** 〈창고〉 a storehouse; a warehouse ♦곳집에 넣다 store; warehouse **2** ⇨ 상여(상엿집)
공 a ball; 〈구(球)〉 a sphere; a globe
♦공을 던지다[받다, 굴리다] throw [catch, roll] a ball / 공을 몰다 drive a ball / 공을 차다 kick a ball; 〈축구하다〉 play soccer / 공을 치다[때리다] strike [hit, knock] a ball; bat
▶오늘 투수의 공은 아주 빠르다 The pitcher's got a lot of speed today.
▶소녀가 공을 튀기고 있었다 A girl was bouncing a ball.
▶그 아이는 공놀이를 좋아한다 The child likes to play ball.
공 公 1 〈공적인 일〉 public affairs; public [official] business
♦공과 사를 구별하다 draw the line between public and private affairs / 공과 사를 혼동하다 mix up public and private matters; 〈회사에서〉 mix company business with personal affairs
2 〈공작(公爵)〉 a prince; (英) a duke ⇨ -공(公)
3 〈2인칭〉 you (sir); sir; 〈3인칭〉 he; the gentleman
공 功 1 〈공로〉 merits; a meritorious deed; credit
♦뛰어난 공 distinguished services / 특별한 공이 있는 사람 a person of exceptional merit / 공을 치하하여 for [in recognition of] one's services / 공을 다투다 claim credit (for an invention) / 남에게 공을 돌리다 let sb take the credit (for) / 공을 세우다 render meritorious [distinguished] services; perform a meritorious deed; distinguish oneself
▶모든 것이 자네 공일세 All the credit goes [belongs] to you.
▶그는 남의 공을 가로챘다 He took credit for the work done by another.
▶그는 그 전투에서 공을 세웠다 He distinguished himself in the battle.
▶그는 나라에 큰 공을 세웠다 He rendered distinguished [meritorious] services to the state.
2 〈수고〉 exertion; efforts; labors
공 호 1 〈텅 빔〉 void; emptiness; vacancy
2 〈공간·하늘〉 the air; the sky; the space
3 〈영〉 (a) zero; (a) cipher; 〈무·허사〉 (a) naught; nothing
▶내 모든 노력은 공으로 돌아가고 말았다 All my efforts have come to naught.
▶색즉시공(色卽是空) All is vanity.
4 〈동그라미〉 a circle; an "O"
♦공을 치다 draw [describe, scribe] a circle; write an "O"; mark (a correct answer) with a circle / 공을 하나 붙이다 put a zero (to)
▶옳다고 생각되는 문장의 번호에 공표를 하시오 Draw a circle around [Enclose with a circle, Circle] the number of the sentence you think right.
5 〈공짜〉 ♦공으로 free of charge ▶그녀는 그 목걸이를 공으로 받았다 She got the necklace for nothing.
공- 公- public; open; 〈공식의〉 official ♦공문서 an official document [paper, note]; a

government paper; archives [άːrkaivz] / 공휴일 a legal holiday

공- 空- **1** 〈빈〉 void; empty ♦공병 an empty bottle **2** 〈공짜〉 free; for nothing ♦공돈 unearned money; (美俗) easy money

-공 -工 〈일꾼〉 an artisan; a worker; a mechanic ♦금속공 a metalworker / 인쇄공 a printer

-공 -公 〈공작(公爵)〉 a prince; (英) a duke; 〈존칭〉 a lord ♦웰링턴[서머싯] 공 the Duke of Wellington [Somerset]

공 〈징〉 a gong; 〈권투의〉 a bell ▶공이 울렸다 There is the bell.

공가 空家 〈빈 집〉 an empty [unoccupied, untenanted] house; a deserted house

공간 公刊 publication **—공간하다** publish

공간 空間 **1** 〈시간에 대하여〉 space; the infinite
♦공간의[적인] spatial / 무한한 공간 infinite [illimitable] space / 빈 공간 open spaces / 시간과 공간 time and space / 공간을 날다 travel through space / 시간과 공간을 초월하다 neglect [take no notice of] time and space
2 〈자리〉 〈make〉 room; 〈빈틈〉 a (vacant) space; a gap; a blank
▶여기는 차 석대가 들어갈 만한 공간이 있다 There is enough space here for three cars.
▶피아노 놓을 공간이 있습니까? Is there room for the piano?
■위상(位相)— 〔數〕 topological space; phase space ■—감각 a sense of space —개념 space idea; a concept [notion] of space —곡선 a space curve —기하학 〔數〕 space [solid] geometry —역(閾) 〔心〕 the space threshold —예술 spatial art —지각 〔心〕 space perception

공갈 恐喝 a threat; blackmail; a menace; intimidation
♦공갈 혐의로 체포되다 be arrested on a charge of blackmailing / 공갈 혐의로 피소되다 be accused of blackmail
▶그는 공갈을 당해 입을 다물고 있었다 He was intimidated into silence.
▶그는 공갈로 그녀에게서 돈을 우려냈다 He extorted money from her by (the use of) threats.
—공갈하다[치다] threaten; intimidate; menace; racketeer; blackmail; blackjack; (美口) bulldoze
♦공갈하여 돈을 빼앗다 blackmail sb of (his) money [for money]; blackjack money out of sb
▶그들은 그를 죽이겠다고 공갈쳤다 They threatened to kill him.
▶그는 공갈(을) 쳐 그 소년에게 거짓말을 시켰다 He intimidated [bulldozed] the boy into lying about it.
■—죄 (the crime of) blackmail; the crime of intimidation; extortion —취재(取財) 〔法〕 blackmail(ing); extortion by threats; (美俗) a shakedown; racketeering

공감 共感 sympathy; a response
♦공감을 느끼다 feel sympathy 《with》 / 대중의 공감을 불러 일으키다 evoke [rouse, excite] public response [sympathy] / 독자들의 공감을 얻다 win [get, gain] the sympathy of the readers
▶그 캠페인은 많은 사람들의 공감을 일으켰다 The campaign awoke sympathy in many people.
▶호소력 있는 그의 탄원은 우리의 공감을 불러 일으켰다 The eloquence of his plea aroused our sympathy.
▶호소해 보았지만 아무런 공감도 얻지 못했다 No response came to the appeal on our side.
—공감하다 sympathize with sb; respond to 《an appeal》
♦나는 그의 의견에 공감한다 I have sympathy for [with] his opinions. ⇌ I agree with him.
▶나는 그 사람의 높은 인간애의 이상에 공감했다 I sympathized with his lofty ideal of human love.

공감각 共感覺 〔心〕 syn(a)esthesia

공개 公開 opening to the public
♦공개의[적인] open (to the public); public / 공개 석상에서 in public (↔private); in a meeting open to the public / 일반에게 공개 중이다 be open [on view] to the public / 공개가 금지되다 be closed to the public
▶그녀는 공개 석상에 나가기를 좋아한다 She likes to attend public functions.
▶나는 공개 석상에서 이야기하는 데 익숙하지 않다 I am not used to speaking in public.
▶이런 일은 공개적으로 말할 수 없다 We cannot talk about this openly [freely].
—공개하다 open a thing to the public; throw a thing open to the public; 〈전시하다〉 place a thing on exhibition; exhibit; 〈신발명품 등을〉 unveil; 〈기업을〉 go public; 〈영화 등을〉 release
♦주식을 공개하다 offer shares of stock for public subscription / 회의를 공개하다 make public the proceedings 《of a committee》 / 신문기자에게 공개하다 open to the press
▶그 절의 보물들이 지금 공개되고 있다 The temple's treasures are on display [show, view] now.
▶그 공원은 일반에게 공개되어 있다 The park is open to the public.
▶그 영화는 내년에 공개될 예정이다 That movie will come out next year.
▶많은 건전 기업이 내년에 공개될 것이다 Many healthy companies will go public next year.
■기업— a business opening 주식— public offering of stock; a public sale of shares ■—강연 a public lecture —강좌 an open class; 〈대학의〉 an extension [(英) extramural] lecture —녹음 a public recording —방송 open broadcasting —법인 a corporation which is opened to public subscription —수사 an open criminal investigation : 공개 수사를 단행하다 decide to make an open criminal investigation —수업 a workshop class —시장 an open market —시장조작 open-market operations —시 합 an open tournament [game] —연설 a public address —연습 〔拳〕 a public workout —입찰 a public tender; an open bid —장(狀) an open letter —재판 a (public) trial —전시 public exhibitions —주

공것

(株) a publicly held stock ―토론 a public debate ―회의 an open session [meeting]

공것 호― a thing got for nothing; an article obtained without cost; a windfall; a godsend; a gift

♦공것으로 얻다 get [gain, receive] *sth* as a gift [without efforts]

▶공것이라고 낭비해서는 안 된다 You should not waste something just because you didn't have to pay for it.

▶공것은 없는 법이다 You never get something for nothing.

▶너무 공것을 바라지 마라 Don't expect a windfall upon the sudden.

공것이라면 양잿물도 들고 마신다 (속담) Anything given as a gift is welcome at any time.

공격 攻擊 1〈군사적인〉 an attack 《on》; an offensive; an assault 《on, against》; a strike; a raid 《on》; an aggression; an onslaught

解説 **attack**는 공격이란 뜻을 나타내는 일반적인 말. **offensive**는 공격적 태도나 자세에, **assault**는 특히 격렬한 공격에 쓰인다.

♦공격적인 offensive; aggressive / 공격을 개시하다 open [launch] an attack 《against, on》; mount an offensive / 공격을 막다 defend *oneself* against an attack / 공격을 받다 be [come] under attack [fire] 《from *one's* opponents》/ 적의 공격을 저지하다 check the advance of the enemy

▶공격이 최선의 방어다 The offensive is the best defense.

▶적의 공격이 우리의 허를 찔렀다 The enemy attack took us by surprise.

▶적의 공격에 대비하지 않으면 안 된다 We must prepare for the enemy's attack.

▶그의 태도는 공격적이 되었다 His attitude turned offensive.

―공격하다 attack; assault; make an attack [assault] 《on》; open [launch] an attack 《on, against》; mount an offensive; 〈공세를 취하다〉 take the offensive; 〈덤벼들다〉 fall on

♦적의 배후를[적을 배후로부터] 기습 공격하다 make a surprise attack on the enemy in [from] the rear

▶아군은 야간에 적을 공격했다 Our army attacked the enemy during the night.

▶그들은 적을 공격하기 시작했다 They launched an attack against the enemy.

▶우리 개가 도둑을 공격하여 쫓아버렸다 Our dog attacked the burglar and drove him off.

2 〈비난·비평〉 an attack; a charge; (a) censure; (a) criticism

♦공격의 대상 a target of [for] criticism / 공격적인 말 offensive [highly critical] language

▶그의 발언은 진보파로부터 맹렬한 공격을 받았다 His remark was criticized severely by progressives.

―공격하다 criticize; attack; censure; condemn; 〈공공연히〉 denounce; speak [talk, write] against; 〈지상에서〉 attack *sb* in print

♦신문에서 공격하다 attack [pound] *sb* in the newspaper

▶그는 정부의 정책을 공격했다 He made attack against [criticized] the government's policy.

▶그들은 의무를 다하지 않는다고 그 사람을 공격했다 They charged him with neglecting his duty.

3 〔野〕 batting (side)

―공격하다 go [come] to bat

■기습― a surprise attack 배후― a rear attack 인신― a personal attack 일제― a joint attack 정면― a frontal attack 총― a general [an all-out] attack : 적은 총공격을 시작했다 The enemy launched an all-out [a full-scale] attack. 측면― a flank attack ■―개시 시각―〔軍〕 H hour; zero hour ―군 an attacking [assailant] army [force] ―기 an attack plane; 〈공습의〉 an air raider ―력 offensive strength [ability] : 우리의 공격력이 적군[그들]보다 우세하다 Our offense is superior to the enemy's [their] striking power. ―로 a route of attack ―목표[점] an attack objective [point] ―(용)무기 offensive weapons [arms] ―정신 fighting spirit; aggressiveness ―측(側)〔野〕 the side [team] at bat ―태세 the offensive : 공격 태세를 취하다 take the offensive

공경 公卿 a court noble

공경 恭敬 respect; esteem; reverence; honor; veneration

―공경하다 respect; esteem; honor; 〈신을〉 reverence

♦공경할 만한 respectable; venerable; esteemable / 부모를 공경하다 respect *one's* parents / 스승을 공경하다 honor [pay respect to, revere] *one's* teacher [master]

▶어른[윗사람]을 공경해야 한다 You should respect [show respect for] your elders [superiors].

공고 工高 a technical high school

공고 公告 a public [an official] notice [announcement]; a (public) notification

―공고하다 notify [announce] publicly; give (out) a public notice 《of》

▶국립대 입시 요강이 공고되었다 They made a public announcement of the entrance examination requirements for the national universities.

▶입학 시험 날짜가 내일 공고될 것이다 The date of the entrance examination will be publicly announced tomorrow.

■경매[특허]― an auction [a patent] announcement

공고 鞏固 firmness; solidity; soundness; stability

―공고하다 firm; sound; solid; stable; strong

♦공고한 의지 a strong [an iron] will / 공고한 지반 firm [solid] ground / 공고한 기반을 구축하다 firmly establish *one's* sphere of influence / 기초를 공고히 하다 consolidate [solidify] the foundation 《of》/ 자기 지위를 공고히 하다 make *one's* position secure

▶양국은 우호관계를 공고히 하기로 약속했다 The two countries promised to strengthen the

bonds of friendship between them.
▶우리는 노조와의 유대를 공고히 하기를 원한다 We want to strengthen our ties with the labor union.

공공 公共 the public society; the community ♦공공의 public (↔private); common; communal / 공공의 이익을 도모하다 promote public interests [good]; work in the interests of the public / 공공을 위해 봉사하다 render services to the public; work for the public benefit
▶무엇보다 먼저 공공의 이익을 도모해라 Promote the public interests [benefit] first of all.
■—경제 public economy —기관 a public institution [organization] —기업체 a public corporation —단체 a public body [organization] : 지방 공공 단체 local [regional] public bodies —복지 (promote) public welfare —생활 community [communal] life —시설 public facilities —요금 fees for public services; 〈수도·전기료 등의〉 public utility charges [fares] : 공공 요금 인상을 억제하려고 노력하다 exert one's efforts to curb the hikes of public utility charges —위생 public health —재산 public property : 공공 재산을 소중히 해라 Take good care of public properties. —투자 a treasury [public, government] investment

공공 空空 1 〈○○〉 blanks; zero(e)s; asterisks; X's ♦007 double 0 seven
2 〈형용사적〉 a certain; unnamed; unidentified ♦○○ 기지 an undisclosed base / ○○ 부대 an unnamed unit / ○○ 사건 a certain affair / 17○○년 seventeen hundred something

공공사업 公共事業 public undertaking [enterprise]; public works; (public) utilities
■—비 public works expenditure; expenditure for public works —체 a public utility company; (美) a public-service corporation

공공심 公共心 public spirit; sense of public duty [morality]
♦공공심이 있는 public spirited / (시민의) 공공심에 호소하다 appeal to the (citizens') sense of public morality
▶그는 공공심이 투철한 사람이다 He is full of public spirit. ⇒ He is a man with plenty of public spirit.

공공연하다 公公然— open; public; open and public; avowed 〈enemy〉; overt 〈hostility〉
♦공공연한 비밀 (It is) an open secret (that...) / 공공연한 사실 a matter of common knowledge / 공공연히〈내놓고〉 openly; publicly; in public; overtly; avowedly / 〈공식적으로〉 officially; formally / 공공연히 비난하다 assail openly; denounce (in public)
▶그는 그 계획[제안]에 공공연히 반대했다 He openly opposed the plan [proposal].
▶이것은 공공연히 이야기할 수 없는 문제다 We cannot talk about this openly.
▶10대 청소년들이 공공연히 담배를 피우고 있었다 Teen-age boys and girls were smoking in public.
▶그 흉악한 범죄는 백주에 공공연히 자행되었다 The atrocious crime was committed in broad daylight.

공과 工科 the engineering department; the department of engineering
■—대학 an institute of technology; an engineering [a technical] college: 매사추세츠 공과 대학 Massachusetts Institute of Technology (略 MIT) —대학생 an engineering student

공과 功過 merits and demerits [faults]; pluses and minuses ▶그 법률[정책]은 공과가 반반이다 The merits and demerits of that law [policy] offset [are balanced against] each other.

공과금 公課金 public imposts[charges]; taxes
공관 公館 〈공적 저택〉 an official residence; 〈공용 건물〉 a public hall ♦국회 의장 공관 the official residence of the Speaker
■—재외— diplomatic offices [establishments] abroad; diplomatic and consular offices in foreign countries

공관복음서 共觀福音書 the Synoptic Gospels
공교롭게 工巧— 1 〈교묘히〉 elaborately; skillfully; deftly; dexterously; finely; cleverly
2 〈의외로·우연히〉 unexpectedly; accidentally; casually; by chance; by a lucky [an unlucky] coincidence
▶공교롭게 비가 오기 시작했다 Unfortunately it began to rain.
▶찾아뵙고 싶지만 공교롭게 독감이 걸렸습니다 I'd like to call on you, only I've caught a bad cold.
▶공교롭게 가진 돈이 없었다 It so happened that I didn't have any money with me.
▶그는 공교롭게 내가 없을 때 왔다 He had the misfortune to come when I was out.
▶그날 따라 공교롭게 그는 집에 없었다 It so happened that [Unfortunately] he was away from home on that particular day.

공교롭다 工巧— 1 〈솜씨가〉 skillful; dexterous; clever; 〈물건이〉 elaborate 《design》; delicate [ingenious] 《machine》; fine
♦공교로운 솜씨 skillfulness; dexterity; deftness; ingenuity / 공교로운 장식 elaborate decorations
2 〈의외의·우연의〉 unexpected; coincidental; well-timed [ill-timed]; casual; accidental; fortunate [unfortunate]; lucky [unlucky]
♦공교로운 때 an opportune [inopportune] time / 공교로운 실수 an unfortunate mistake
▶정말 공교로운 일치로군 It's quite a coincidence. ⇒ What a coincidence!

공구 工具 a tool; an implement ♦공구 한 벌 a set [kit] of tools
■기계[정밀, 목공]— a machine [precision, woodworking] tool 전동— a power tool —상자 a toolbox —점 a machine-parts supplier

공구 工區 〔建〕 a section of works
공국 公國 a dukedom; a duchy; a principality ♦모나코[리히텐슈타인] 공국 the Principality of Monaco [Liechtenstein]

공군 空軍 an air force; the air service; a flying corps ♦공군의 우세[절대 우세] air superiority [supremacy]
■미국— the United States Air Force (略 U.S.

A.F.) 영국— the Royal Air Force 한국— the Republic of Korea Air Force (略 ROK A.F.) ■—기 an air force plane —기지 an air base; an air force base (略 AFB) —대학 the Air Force Command & General Staff College —력 air power [might] —본부 the Air Force Headquarters —사관학교 an air-force academy —참모총장 the Air Chief of the General Staff

공권 公權 civil rights; citizenship ▶ 그는 공권을 박탈당했다 He was deprived of his civil rights. —박탈[정지] deprivation [suspension] of civil rights; disfranchisement

공권 空拳 an empty hand
♦ 적수 공권으로 with *one's* bare [naked] hands
▶ 그는 (적수)공권으로 미국으로 건너갔다 He went over to America penniless.
▶ 그는 적수 공권으로 거금을 벌었다 Though he had [Having] nothing to start with, he has made a colossal fortune.

공규 空閨 the bedchamber of a neglected [bereaved, deserted] wife
♦ 공규를 지키다 〈홀어미가〉 lead the lonely life of a deserted [bereaved] wife; 〈남편 출타 중에〉 remain true to *one's* husband in his absence / 공규를 한탄하다 complain about the lonely life of an abandoned wife

공그르다 〈떠서 꿰매다〉 blindstitch; whip 《a seam》

공극 空隙 〈빈 틈〉 an opening; a gap; a crevice 《바위의》

공글리다 1 〈다지다〉 harden; make hard; firm up; solidify; consolidate; strengthen 2 〈끝맺다〉 settle [fix (up), finish] 《a matter》 neatly

공금 公金 public funds [money]; government funds
♦ 공금을 가지고 도망치다 run away [abscond] with public money / 공금을 낭비하다 be extravagant with the public purse / 공금을 횡령하다 embezzle public funds
▶ 그는 공금을 유용했다 He misappropriated [peculated] public funds.
—횡령 embezzlement of public money

공급 供給 supply(↔demand); 〈전기·수도·가스 등의〉 service; 〈식료품의〉 provision
♦ 수요와 공급(의 법칙) (the law of) supply and demand / 전력의 공급 the supply of electricity / 공급이 끊기다 be cut off from the supply (of) / 공급을 끊다 cut off the supply (of) / 석유 공급을 받다 be supplied with oil 《by》; get a supply of oil 《from》
▶ 수요와 공급의 균형이 잘 이루어져 있다 An adequate balance between demand and supply is maintained.
▶ 요즘 석유 공급이 부족하다[과잉이다] Oil is in short [excessive] supply these days. ⇌ There is a short [an excessive] supply of oil these days.
▶ 공급이 수요를 따라가지 못한다 The supply cannot meet the demand.
—공급하다 supply [provide] 《sb with sth, sth for sb》; furnish 《with》; serve 《a town with water》
♦ 원료를 공급하다 supply 《a factory》 with material / 인력을 공급하다 supply with manpower; man up
▶ 우리는 그들에게 식량을 공급했다 We supplied [provided, furnished] them with food.
▶ 양은 양털을 공급해 준다 Sheep supply [provide] us with wool.
▶ 이것이 그 시에 가스를 공급하는 파이프라인이다 This is the pipeline which serves [supplies] the town with gas.
■—가격 a supply price —과잉[과다] an excessive supply; an oversupply; a glut : 공급 과잉으로 물가가 급락했다 Prices dropped sharply in response to the oversupply. —로(路) a channel of supply; a supply route —부족 a short supply; shortage; an undersupply —자 a supplier; a provider

공급원 供給源 a source of supply ▶ 미국은 밀의 주공급원이다 The United States is the chief source of supply for wheat.

공기 〈공깃돌〉 a jackstone; marbles; a pebble; 〈놀이〉 jackstones; marbles
♦ 공기 놀다 play [shoot] marbles [jackstones] 《with》 / 공기 놀리다 〈농락하다〉 turn [twist] *sb* round [around] *one's* (little) finger; make sport [a toy] of *sb*

공기 公器 〈공공 기관〉《abuse》 a public organ [instrument]; a public institution
▶ 매스 미디어[신문]는 사회의 공기다 Mass media are public organs [The newspaper is a public organ] of society.

공기 空氣 1 〈기체〉 air
♦ 공기의 airy; aerial; pneumatic / 바깥 공기 the air outside / 실내 공기 the air in the room / 탁한 공기 foul air / 공기의 유통이 좋은 〈나쁜〉 well-ventilated [poorly-ventilated]; airy [stuffy] / 공기가 통하지 않는 airproof; airtight / 맑은 공기를 마시다 breathe (in) fresh air / 공기에 쐬다 expose *sth* to the air; aerate
▶ 이 방은 공기가 나쁘다 The air is stale [bad] in this room.
▶ 위로 올라갈수록 공기가 차가워졌다 The air grew [became, got] cooler as we went up.
▶ 아이는 풍선[타이어]에 공기를 넣었다 The boy pumped up the balloon [tire].
▶ 그는 타이어의 공기를 뺐다 He let the air out of the tire.
▶ 그녀는 공기를 갈려고 방의 창문을 열었다 She opened the window of the room to let in (some) fresh air.
2 〈분위기〉 an atmosphere
♦ 긴장된 공기 a tense atmosphere / 불온한 공기 a disturbing atmosphere / 불쾌한 공기 an uncomfortable atmosphere
▶ 험악한 공기가 느껴졌다 I felt a threatening atmosphere.
▶ 실내는 무거운 공기에 휩싸여 있었다 There was a heavy atmosphere in the room.
■—가열[냉각]기 an air heater [cooler] —구멍 a breathing hole —돔 an air-supported dome —방석 an air cushion —베개 an air pillow —압축기 an air compressor —여과기 an air filter —요법 aerotherapy; an air cure

—욕 an air bath —저항 air resistance —전염 infection by air; aerial [airborne] infection —정화기 an air cleaner —제동기 an air [a pneumatic] brake —주머니 an air sac —총 an air gun —타이어 a pneumatic tire —펌프 an air pump

공기 空器 〈빈 그릇〉an empty vessel [dish]; 〈식사용〉a (rice) bowl
◆밥 한 공기 a bowl [bowlful] of rice
▶그는 밥 두 공기를 먹었다 He ate two bowls of rice.
▶그녀는 밥을 공기에 담아 주었다 She served boiled rice in a bowl.

공기 工期 a term [period] of construction (work)

공기업 公企業 a public [government, state] enterprise

공기오염 空氣汚染 air [atmospheric] pollution
▶이 도시는 공기 오염이 극심하다 The air pollution in this city is terrible.
▶공기 오염은 주로 자동차의 배기 가스가 원인이 되고 있다 Air pollution is caused in large part by automobile exhaust fumes.

공기조절 空氣調節 air conditioning ■—장치 an air conditioning system; 〈기계〉an air conditioner : 실내 공기 조절 장치 a room conditioning system

공납 公納 public imposts [charges]; taxes ―금 〈학교의〉regular school payment

공단 工團 an industrial complex ⇨ 공업단지

공단 公團 a public corporation

공단 貢緞 (silk) satin (without figures [patterns])

공대 工大 an institute of technology ⇨ 공과 (~대학)

공대 恭待 1〈대접〉respectful [hospitable] treatment
—공대하다 treat respectfully; treat sb with courtesy
▶그녀는 항상 남편을 공대한다 She always pays due respect to her husband.
2 〈경어〉 an honor (word); polite language; respectful address —공대하다 address respectfully; use polite language [honorific words]

공대공 空對空 ◆공대공의 air-to-air ■—미사일[로켓] an air-to-air missile [rocket]

공대말 恭待— an honorific word ⇨ 존대어

공대지 空對地 ◆공대지의 air-to-surface [air-to-ground] ■—미사일 an air-to-surface missile

공덕 公德 public morality ⇨ 공중도덕

공덕 功德 a charitable [virtuous] deed; charity; a pious act; an act of merit; virtue
◆공덕을 베풀다 practice charity [virtue]; do [perform] an act of charity / 공덕을 쌓다 accumulate [do] good [virtuous] deeds; accumulate pious acts; earn 《a great deal of》merit 《for *one's* generosity》
▶그는 생전에 가난한 사람들에게 공덕을 쌓았기 때문에 틀림없이 극락에 갈 것이다 Since he was charitable to the poor, he is sure to go to Paradise.

공덕심 公德心 public spirit [sense]; 《have》a sense of public morality [duty] ▶그 사람은 공덕심이 없다[부족하다] He has no [is lacking in] public sense [spirit].

공도 公道 1〈바른 도리〉justice; equity
◆천하의 공도 universal justice / 공도를 걷다 [따르다] take [tread, follow] the path of justice; act with justice / 공도에서 벗어나다 stray from the right path
2 〈공로〉a highway; a public way [road]

공돈 空— an unearned income; easy money; a windfall; 〈부정한〉filthy lucre; (美俗) gravy
▶공돈은 오래 못 간다 Easy [Light] come, easy [light] go. ⇌ Soon got [gotten], soon gone [spent].

공돌다 空— 〈헛돌다〉idle; run idle; 〈남아돌다〉lie wastefully [unused]; be ownerless
▶모터가 공돌았다 The motor idled.

공동 共同 cooperation; collaboration; combination; conjunction; association; partnership; union ◆공동 보조를 취하다 take joint steps 〈공동의〉common; 〈공용의〉communal; 〈합동의〉joint; concerted; united
◆공동의 관심사 matters of mutual concerns; an issue of mutual interest / 공동의 이익《을 위하여》(for) the common benefit [interests] 《of》/ 공동의 적 a common enemy 《of Korea and America》
▶그들에게는 명확한 공동의 목표가 없다 They didn't have any definite common aims.
▶아내와 나는 공동의 예금 계좌를 개설했다 My wife and I opened a joint bank account.
〈공동으로〉in conjunction [cooperation, collaboration, concert, association] 《with》; jointly
◆상점을 공동으로 경영하다 run a store in partnership with / 손해를 공동으로 부담하다 share the losses 《with another》
▶이 기숙사에서는 부엌을 공동으로 쓰고 있습니다 Everyone shares the kitchen in this dorm.
▶우리는 비용을 공동으로 부담하기로 합의했다 We agreed that we would bear the expenses jointly.
▶나는 친구와 공동으로 사업을 하기로 결심했다 I decided to do a business in association with my friend.
▶그는 친구와 공동으로 그 일을 했다 He did the work in cooperation with his friend.
▶우리는 공동으로 신제품을 개발했다 We have jointly developed the new product.
▶그들은 네 명이 공동으로 트럭을 샀다 They bought a truck between the four of them.
▶이것은 열 명의 학자가 공동으로 연구한 것입니다 This is the product of combined efforts of ten scholars.
▶우리는 공동으로 책임을 져야 한다 We must take joint responsibility for it.
■—개발 joint development —결의〈상하 양원의〉a joint resolution —관리 joint control; 《國際法》condominium —구입 (do) cooperative buying —규제수역 a jointly controlled waters [fishing zone] —기업 a joint enterprise —기자회견 a joint press [news] conference —담보 a joint mortgage —모금 the community

chest : 공동 모금을 하다 raise money for the community chest —모의〔法〕conspiracy —목적 a common cause [objective, interest] —묘지 (public) cemetery; a common burial ground —방위 joint defense —변소 a public latrine [lavatory, convenience]; 〈美〉a (public) comfort station —보험 joint insurance; coinsurance —사업 a joint enterprise [undertaking] —사회 a community —상속 joint inheritance;〈토지의〉(co)parcenary —선언 a joint declaration —소유 joint ownership; coproprietorship : 공동 소유권 joint ownership / 공동 소유사 a jolnt owner; a co-owner —수도전 a common tap; a water faucet for common use —숙박소 a public boarding house; a laborers' home —시설 public facilities; facilities for common [communal] use —시장 a common market —어업권 common fishery rights —우물 a common well —원고[피고]〔法〕a coplaintiff [codefendant] —의무 joint obligations —작업 cooperation; group work —작전 concerted [united, combined] operations —재산 joint property —전화 ⇨ 공동가입(~전화) —정범(正犯) a (joint) principal offender; an accomplice —제작 joint production; coproduction —조계(租界) an international (residence) settlement —조합 a cooperative; a co-op —주택 an apartment house ⇨ 아파트 —청부 a joint contract (for work) —출자 joint investment; pooling of funds : 공동 출자하다 jointly invest (in); pool funds —텔레비전 안테나 a communal [shared] television antenna —판매 a joint sale; joint marketing —해손(海損)〔保險〕general average (略 G.A., G/A, g.a.); gross average —행위 common action

공동 空洞 a hollow;〈동굴〉a cave; a cavern; a cavity;〈폐의〉a vomica (*pl.* -cae)
♦ 공동화하다 become hollow; lose [become devoid of] substance; get emptied of all (its) contents / 공동화한 의회 민주주의 parliamentary democracy in name only [reduced to mere form]

공동가입 共同加入〔電話〕joint subscription
■ —선(線) a party wire [line] —자 a joint subscriber —전화 a telephone on a party line; a party-line telephone

공동경영 共同經營 joint management; partnership
▶ 이 가게는 그녀와 나의 공동 경영이다 She and I run this shop in partnership. ⇌ This store is kept going jointly by her and me.
▶ 나는 그와 공동 경영을 시작했다 I entered into partnership with him.
■ —자 a business partner; a joint manager;〈소유자〉a coproprietor; a joint owner

공동생활 共同生活〈사회의〉communal [community] life;〈단체의〉collective life ▶ 그들은 2년간 공동생활을 했다 They lived together for two years.

공동성명 共同聲明 a joint statement [communiqué]
♦ 7·4 남북 공동 성명 the South-North Joint Communiqué announced on July 4, 1972 ▶ 양국은 내일 정오에 공동 성명을 발표할 예정이다 The two countries are going to issue a joint statement at noon tomorrow.

공동연구 共同硏究 joint research(es); a joint study ▶ 그들은 언어학에 관한 공동 연구를 하고 있다 They are doing joint research in linguistics.

공동전선 共同戰線 a common [united, joint] front
♦ 공동 전선을 펴다 form [make] a common front 《against》; present [put up] a united front 《against》; make common cause 《with》 ▶ 우리는 공동 전선을 펴서 그 일을 했다 We united ourselves to do it.

공동주최 共同主催 cosponsorship; joint auspices
♦ 공동 주최로 under the joint auspices 《of》; cosponsored by 《A and B》 / 신문사와 한국 대사관이 공동 주최한 전람회 an exhibition cosponsored by [held under the cosponsorship of] a newspaper and the Korean Embassy
▶ 우리는 대학과 공동 주최로 음악회를 개최했다 We gave a concert under joint auspices with the university.
■ —자 a cosponsor

공동책임 共同責任 corporate [collective] responsibility
♦ 공동 책임을 지다 share the [take a joint] responsibility 《for》; answer jointly for *sth*; be jointly responsible for 《a failure》;〈부채의〉hold joint liability 《for the debt》

공동체 共同體 a community; a communal society.
■ 도시— an urban [a town] community 운명—a community bound together by common fate 유럽— European Community (略 EC) 촌락— a rural [village] community

공동투쟁 共同鬪爭 a joint struggle ▶ 노조들은 임금 인상을 위한 공동 투쟁을 계획했다 The labor unions planned a joint struggle for higher pay.

공든 탑이 무너지랴 《속담》 Hard work is never wasted[always pays dividends]. ⇌ A man's labors will be crowned with success.

공들다 功— take[require] much labor; cost [need] strenuous efforts [exertion, labors]
♦ 공드는 일 laborious [toilsome] work; work that requires much labor
▶ 이 작품은 꽤 공든 작품 같다 This work smells of the lamp [bears traces of labor].
▶ 한 순간의 실수로 공든 탑이 무너진다 A wrong cut [One slip of the knife] will spoil the work of months. ⇌ One hour's cold will spoil seven years' warming.

공들이다 功— do elaborate work; put great care (in *one's* work); labor assiduously; spend [expend] *one's* labor
♦ 공들인 계획[장식] elaborate plans [ornaments] / 공들인 작품 an elaborate (piece of) work / 공들여 with great effort [labor, care]; elaborately; carefully / 공들여 장만한 식사 an elaborate dinner
▶ 그 일을 위해 그는 10년 동안 공들였다 He

has labored for it ten years.
▶ 공들인 보람이 하나도 없었다 All my labors were wasted [in vain]. ⇌ My labors were fruitless [unavailing].
▶ 그 여자는 언제나 공들여 화장을 한다 She always makes her toilet carefully. ⇌ Her toilet is always elaborately made.
▶ 이것은 무척 공들여 만든 옷장이다 This is a very carefully [elaborately] made wardrobe.

공떡 호— a godsend; a windfall; a thing won for nothing
▶ 공떡만 바라고 있지 마라 Don't sit there (idle) waiting for someone to drop a fortune in your lap!

공란 空欄 a blank (space); a blank column; empty space ▶ 공란을 채우시오 Fill (in) the blanks.

공람 供覽 a display; a show **—공람하다** submit 《things》 to public inspection; exhibit 《things》 before the public ♦신제품을 공람하다 display [show] new products

공랭 空冷 air cooling ♦공랭식의 air-cooled (cylinder) ■—식 엔진 an air-cooled engine —장치 air-cooling devices

공략 攻略 attack; invasion; conquest; occupation
—공략하다 attack; capture; conquer; take 《a fortress》 by storm; 〈침략하다〉 invade 《a country》
♦공략하기 어려운 impregnable (fortress) / 적진을 공략하다 carry the enemy's position; capture an enemy position

공로 公路 a public road [way]; a highway; 《美》 a highroad

공로 功勞 (meritorious) service(s); a meritorious deed; merits; credit
♦공로가 있는 meritorious; of merit / 공로를 세우다 distinguish *oneself* 《in war》; render distinguished service 《to the state》 / 공로에 보답하다 reward *sb* for 《his》 services / 공로로 훈장을 받다 be decorated for *one's* distinguished services
▶ 그는 국가[국민 복지]에 공로가 있다 He rendered distinguished service to his country [the welfare of the people].
▶ 그는 특별한 공로가 없다 He has done nothing worthy of particular notice.
■—자 a man of merits; a person who has rendered great service 《to the state》 —장(章) a distinguished service medal —주(株) 〖商〗 a bonus stock

공로 空路 an air route [lane]; an airway
♦공로로 by air; by (air)plane / 공로로 귀국하다 return home by plane [air] / 공로로 부산에서 서울로 돌아오다 fly back to Seoul from Pusan / 공로로 프랑스로 향하다 fly for France
▶ 그녀는 공로로 스페인에 갔다 She flew to Spain. ⇌ She went to Spain by air.
▶ 나는 김포에서 공로로 뉴욕으로 떠났다 I left Kimp'o by air for New York.

공론 公論 1 〈공평한 의론〉 fair criticism; an unbiassed [a disinterested] view
2 〈여론〉 public opinion; the consensus ♦국사[만사]를 공론에 따라 결정하다 refer all state affairs to [decide all affairs by] public opinion

공론 空論 an empty [a mere, an impractical] theory; a futile argument [discussion]
■탁상— an armchair [impractical] theory [argument] ■—가 a doctrinaire [doctrinarian]; an armchair philosopher

공뢰 空雷 〈공중 어뢰〉 an aerial torpedo 《*pl.* ~es》

공룡 恐龍 〖古生〗 a dinosaur ■—시대 the age of the dinosaurs

공률 工率 rate of production [work]

공리 公吏 a public official [servant]; an officeholder; a civil servant

공리 公利 public good [welfare]; the common [public] interest; the general weal ♦공리를 도모하다 promote the public interest

공리 公理 1 〈도리〉 a self-evident truth **2** 〖數〗 an axiom; a maxim
♦공리적(인) axiomatic(al)

공리 功利 utility
♦공리적(인) utilitarian; down-to-earth; practical; unsentimental; 《美俗》 hard-nosed / 사물을 공리적으로 생각하다 take a utilitarian view of things; view things in a practical [down-to-earth] way
■—주의[설] utilitarianism —주의자 a utilitarian

공리 空理 an empty [impractical] theory; doctrinairism
■—공론 doctrinarianism; academicism : 공리공론에 빠지다[흐르다] indulge in academic discussion [vain speculations]; stick to isms and ics

공립 公立 a public institution ♦공립의 public; communal; 〈지방자치제의〉 provincial; 〈시립의〉 municipal
■—학교 《美》 a public school; 《英》 a country school (▶영국에서의 public school은 명문 사립학교를 의미함)

공막 鞏膜 〖解〗 the sclera 《*pl.* ~s, -rea》; the sclerotica ♦공막의 sclerotic ■—염 sclerotitis; scleritis

공매 公賣 (a) public sale [auction]; 《美》 (a) vendue
♦공매에 부치다 put (up) 《a thing》 for public sale [for sale by public auction]; sell at [《英》 by] auction.
▶ 그녀의 재산은 공매에 부쳐졌다 Her estate was put up for public sale. ⇌ Her property was offered at public auction.
—공매하다 sell in public; sell at [《英》 by] auction
■강제— forced sale ■—장 an auction house [hall] —처분 disposition by public sale; (a) tax sale; public sale of confiscated property

공매 空賣 〖證〗 a short sale; short selling —공매하다 sell short

공맹 孔孟 Confucius and Mencius ■—지도(之道) the teachings [doctrines] of Confucius and Mencius; Confucianism

공명 公明 fairness; justice; impartiality —공명하다 fair; just; open; (open and) aboveboard ♦공명히 fairly; justifiably; honestly

■ —선거 a clean election: 이번에는 공명 선거가 이루어질 것이다 We'll have a fair election this time. —선거 운동 a campaign for clean elections

공명 功名 a great exploit; a glorious deed; a great feat; 〈무공〉 a feat of arms; 〈명성〉 credit; fame; distinction; honor
♦ 공명을 다투다 claim credit 《for》/ 공명을 세우다 perform a glorious deed; achieve a meritorious deed; distinguish *oneself* 《in》

공명 共鳴 1 〈공감〉 sympathy; unison; 〈반향〉 an echo; a response
—공명하다 sympathize 《with》; echo 《*sb's* sentiment》; respond 《to》
▶ 그는 민주주의에 공명한다 He is in sympathy with democracy.
▶ 브루노 월터는 현대 음악의 경향에 공명하지 않았다 Bruno Walter was out of sympathy with modern trends in music.
2 〔物〕 consonance; (sympathetic) resonance; 〔樂〕 resonance; a sympathetic sound
♦ 공명을 일으키다 cause [produce, set up] resonance(s)
—공명하다 be resonant 《with》; resonate
■ —관(管) a resonance tube —기 a resonator —동(胴) a resonance body —상자[실(室)] an echo chamber; a sound box —판(板) 〈악기의〉 a sound(ing) board; a resonator

공명심 功名心 ambition; aspiration(s); desire for [love of] fame
♦ 공명심에 불타다 be ambitious; be eager [thirsty] for fame / 공명심에 사로잡히다 be driven [carried away] by ambition
▶ 그는 공명심이 강하다 He is very eager for fame. ⇒ He is ambitious.

공명정대 公明正大 fairness; (fairness and) justice; (a sense of) fair play
—공명정대하다 fair; just; open [fair] and aboveboard; (fair and) square; just and fair
♦ 공명정대한 재판관[심판] a fair and square judge / 공명정대한 조치 (take) impartial measures / 공명정대한 태도 an impartial attitude / 공명정대하게 fairly; justly; aboveboard; openly; impartially / 공명정대하게 싸우다 play fair / 공명정대하게 하다 do things [deal with the matter] in a fair [an honorable, an honest] way / 공명정대하게 행동하다 behave fairly and squarely
▶ 그는 무슨 일에나 공명정대하다 He is always fair and upright in his dealings. ⇒ He is aboveboard in everything.
▶ 나는 공명정대하다 I have nothing to be ashamed of.

공모 公募 (an appeal for) public subscription; 〈모금 등의〉 a public appeal (for contributions); 〈주식 등의〉 an offer for public subscription; 〈사람의〉 public advertisement (of a post)
▶ 그 회사에서는 사원을 공모 중이다 The company is recruiting new employees publicly.
—공모하다 〈주식을〉 offer (shares) for public subscription; place (stocks) on the market; 〈기부금을〉 raise (a fund) by public subscription; 〈작품·논문을〉 invite public contribution (of)
♦ 주연 배우를 공모하다 invite applications for the leading actor / 현상 소설을 공모하다 open a prize list of novels; invite the public to join in a prize contest for best stories
▶ 우리 회사에서는 주식을 공모하고 있지 않다 We do not offer shares for public subscription.
■ —가격 〈증권〉 the offering price —채 public issues; publicly subscribed bonds

공모 共謀 (a) conspiracy; complicity; collusion
—공모하다 plot together; collude with *sb*; conspire (together, with)
♦ …와 공모하여 in conspiracy [collusion] with...
▶ 그는 자기 아내와 공모하여 사기를 쳤다 He plotted with his wife in the fraud. ⇒ He and his wife conspired together in the fraud.
▶ 그들은 공모하여 뇌물을 받아먹었다 They were acting in collusion to take bribes.
■ —자[범] a conspirator; an accomplice (in a crime): 그들은 공모자다 They are plotting together.

공목 空木 〔印〕 〈자간용〉 a spacer; 〈행간용〉 a lead; a reglet; a blind [filling] material

공무 工務 engineering works —국(局) the engineering works department; 〈신문사 등의〉 the printing bureau

공무 公務 〈공적 직무〉 official [public] duties; 〈공공 사무〉 public [state] service; government [official] affairs; official [public] business
♦ 공무에 바빠서 owing to the pressure of official duties [business] / 공무를 집행하다 exercise *one's* public duty; execute *one's* official duties / 공무를 태만히하다 neglect *one's* public duty / 공무로 출장가다 travel on public business
■ —집행 execution of *one's* official duties —집행 방해 interference with a government official in the exercise [execution, performance] of his (official) duties

공무원 公務員 〈개인〉 a public servant [official]; **(英)** a civil servant; a government employee [official]; 〈전체〉 public service personnel; the public [civil] service (▶**(美)**에서는 public을 쓰고, **(英)**에서는 civil이 보통임)

> 解說 *public official*은 일반적으로 중간적인 지위에 있는 사람을 가리키고, 그보다 지위가 낮은 사람은 *civil servant* 또는 *government employee*라고 한다. 대문자로 Government 라고 하면 지방 공무원과 구별할 때의 공무원이란 뜻이 되기도 한다. *government [Government] official*은 보통 높은 직위의 공무원을 의미한다.

♦ 중앙 공무원 교육원 the Central Officials Training Institute / 공무원이 되다 enter government [the civil] service / 공무원에 채용되다 be employed in government service
▶ 우리 형은 공무원입니다 My brother works for a government office.

■ 고급— high-ranking public officials 국가[지방]— a national [local] civil servant; 국가[지방] 공무원법 the National [Local] Public Service Law 기술[기능]직— a public official in technical [skill] post 하급— a petty official ■—시험 civil service examination

공문 公文 an official document; 〈통신〉 an official notice [dispatch, note, correspondence] ■—서식 formalities for official documents ■—전보 an official telegram

공문 孔門 the Confucian school ♦ 공문십철(十哲) the ten leading disciples of Confucius

공문 空文 a dead letter; a (mere) scrap of paper
♦ 공문으로 끝나다 end in a mere scrap of paper / 공문화하다 turn out to be a dead letter
▶ 그 조약은 공문화되어 버렸다 The treaty is now a dead letter [a mere scrap of paper].

공문서 公文書 an official document; an official paper [note]; 〈보존된〉 archives ■—위조 forgery of an official document

공물 供物 an offering (to the spirits of *one's* ancestors); a Buddhist offering [oblation]; a votive offering ♦ 공물을 바치다 make an offering to Buddha

공물 貢物 a tribute; a tributary payment
♦ 공물을 바치다 pay [offer] a tribute (to the ruler) / 공물을 바치게 하다 lay [levy] a tribute (on); impose a tribute (upon); make 《the populace》 tributary

공미 貢米 rice offered as a tribute; rice paid as taxes

공민 公民 a citizen; a burgess ♦ 공민의 자유[의무] civil liberty [duties]
■—교육 civic education [instruction]; citizenship training ■—도덕 civic virtues ■—생활 a civil life ■—학교 a civil education school

공민권 公民權 citizenship; civil [civic] rights; franchise
♦ 공민권을 빼앗다[박탈하다] disfranchise *sb*; deprive *sb* of 《his》 civil rights / 공민권을 얻다 acquire citizenship / 공민권을 주다 enfranchise *sb*

공박 攻駁 refutation; a charge; denunciation ■—공박하다 refute; attack (by argument); denounce; charge; denunciate ♦ 아무의 주장을 공박하다 refute *sb's* argument

공밥 空— a meal *one* has not paid [worked] for; a free [gratis] meal; free food ♦ 공밥을 먹다 〈놀고 먹다〉 eat idle bread; 〈식객이 되다〉 eat *sb's* salt

공방 工房 a studio (*pl.* ~s); a workshop; (프) an atelier

공방 攻防 offense and defense ■—전 an offensive and defensive battle

공방 空房 1 〈빈 방〉 a vacant [an unoccupied] room [chamber] **2** 〈공규(空閨)〉 the bedchamber of a widow [neglected wife]

공배 空排 〈바둑〉 a blank ♦ 공배를 서로 메우다 fill blanks together

공배수 公倍數 〔數〕 a common multiple ■ 최소— the least [lowest] common multiple (略 L.C.M., l.c.m.)

공백 空白 〈여백〉 a blank; blank [unfilled] space; 〈비유〉 a 《political》 vacuum 《*pl.* ~s, vacua》; a void; a gap
♦ 기억의 공백 a blank in *one's* memory / 정치[힘]의 공백 a political [power] vacuum / 공백이 생기다 leave [produce] a vacuum; make a blank 《in *one's* life》 / 공백을 메우다 fill a gap 《in》; fill up [in] a blank
▶ 그의 운전 경력에는 5년간의 공백이 있다 There is a gap of five years in his driving experience.
▶ 내각의 붕괴로 정치적 공백이 생겼다 The fall of the cabinet created a political vacuum.

공범 共犯 an accomplice 《of [with] *sb* in a crime》; a confederate; a partner; 〈행위〉 complicity 《in a crime》; conspiracy
♦ 사전[사후-] 공범 an accessory before [after] the fact / 강도의 공범 a confederate in a robbery / 공범으로 기소하다 prosecute *sb* for a party to a crime
▶ 그는 그 범죄의 공범이다 He has a hand [is a partner] in the crime.
▶ 그 범인은 공범이 있다 The criminal has an accomplice.
▶ 그녀는 그 사건의 공범으로 기소[체포]되었다 She was accused of complicity in the case [caught as a party to the crime].
■—자 an accomplice; a confederate ■—죄 complicity

공법 工法 a method of construction

공법 公法 public law ♦ 공법상의 법인 a juridical person in public law
■ 국제— international law ■—위반 breach of public law ■—학 the study of public law ■—학자 a publicist

공법인 公法人 a public judicial person; a public corporation

공병 工兵 a military engineer; (英) a sapper
■—대[대대] an engineer(ing) corps [engineering battalion]; (美) a construction battalion (略 CB) : 건설 공병대 a construction engineer corps ■—학교 the Engineering School

공보 公報 an official report [dispatch]; an official bulletin; 〈관보〉 an official gazette; 〈홍보〉 (public) information
♦ 국립 공보관 the National Information Center / 미국 공보원 the U.S. Information Service (略 USIS) / 공보에 따르면 according to an official report / 공보로 발표하다 published in a gazette
■ 선거— an election bulletin ■—국[실] the Bureau [Office] of Public Information; the Public Information Bureau [Office] ■—비서 (美) a press secretary ■—처 the Ministry of Information

공복 公僕 a public servant ⇨ 공무원

공복 空腹 〈빈 속〉 an empty stomach; 〈배고픔〉 hunger; being hungry
♦ 공복이다 be hungry / 공복을 느끼다 feel [go] hungry; (口) be starving / 공복을 채우다 satisfy *one's* appetite 《with some food》; gratify *one's* hunger 《on》 / 공복에 술을 마시다 drink on an empty stomach
▶ 그는 간식으로 공복을 달랬다 He allayed his

hunger with a snack.
▶나는 공복인 채로 잤다 I went to bed with an empty stomach.
공부 工夫 study; schoolwork; learning; work (on *one's* studies)

> 解說 ***study***가 가장 일반적으로 쓰이는 공부라는 뜻이며, ***schoolwork***는 수업・숙제 등을 전부 포함한 학업을 뜻한다.

◆계통적인[계통이 선] 공부 a systematic study / 국어 공부 the study of Korean; *one's* lesson in Korean / 공부를 열심히 하는 사람 a hard-working [an earnest] student; a hard worker / 공부를 게을리하다 neglect *one's* studies / 공부를 잘[잘못]하다 be good [poor] at *one's* studies; make good [poor] grades / 공부 중이다 be at *one's* studies [books]
▶그 아이는 공부를 제대로 하지 않는다 The boy doesn't work hard enough.
▶우리는 중학교에서 영어 공부를 시작한다 We begin the study of [begin to study] English in junior high school.
▶아버지가 내 공부를 보아 주셨다 Father helped me with my lessons.
▶공부를 게을리하지 마라 Don't neglect your studies.
▶공부만 시키고 놀리지 않으면 아이는 바보가 된다 (속담) All work and no play makes Jack a dull boy.
―**공부하다** study; learn; work at [on] (*one's* studies)

> 解說 ***study***는 학문이나 예술・외국어 등을 체계적으로 노력하여 공부한다는 뜻인 데 비해 ***learn***은 공부나 경험에 의하여 지식・기술을 습득하거나 익힌다는 뜻. ***work***는 일한다는 뜻이지만 문맥이 명확한 경우에는 study나 learn 대신으로 쓰인다.

◆법률을 공부하다 study [(英) read] law / 밤늦도록 공부하다 study till late at night; stay [sit] up late over *one's* books / 열심히 공부하다 study hard; work hard; (美口) dig 《at a subject》 / 지나치게 공부하다 overwork *oneself*; study excessively
▶그는 밤 8시부터 11시까지 공부한다 He studies from eight to eleven at night.
▶우리는 대부분 자기자신을 위해서 공부한다 We mostly study for ourselves.
▶나는 영어를 열심히 공부했다 I digged at English.
▶어머니는 나를 볼 때마다 열심히 공부하라고 말씀하신다 My mother tells me to study hard whenever she finds me.
▶그녀는 머리는 좋은데 공부하기는 싫어한다 She is bright but does not like to study.
▶그녀는 바이올린을 공부하러 빈으로 갔다 She went to Vienna to study the violin.
▶그는 지나치게 공부해서 몸을 상했다 He overworked [studied too hard] and became ill.
▶나는 대학에서 의학을 공부할 예정이다 I am going to study medicine [medical science] at college.
■시험― study for an examination : 그는 벼락치기 시험 공부를 하고 있다 He is cramming for the examination. ■―방 a study (room) ―벌레 a greasy grind; a grinder; (美俗) a dig ―시간 study hours [time]; 〈수업 시간〉 class (time)

공분 公憤 〈대중의 분노〉 indignation of the general public; 〈의분〉 public rage [resentment]; righteous [moral] indignation
◆공분을 느끼다 be morally indignant 《at, about it, with *sb*》; feel righteous indignation 《at the unfair taxation system》 / 공분을 일으키다 raise public indignation 《over》
▶저 정치가의 작태에는 공분을 느낀다 I am morally indignant at that politician's way of doing things.

공분모 公分母 〔數〕 a common denominator ■최소― the lowest [least] common denominator (略 L.C.D.)

공비 工費 the cost of construction; construction expenses
◆총 공비 2억원으로 at the total cost of two hundred million won
▶이 다리는 공비가 500억원이 들었다 This bridge was constructed at a cost of fifty billion won.

공비 公費 public expenditure [costs, expense]
◆공비로 at (the) public [government] expense [charge] / 공비를 낭비하다 waste [throw away] public money / 공비를 절감하다 reduce [curtail] public expenditure
▶그 사업은 공비로 완성되었다 The work was done at (the) public expense.

공비 共匪 〈공산 게릴라〉 Red [Communist] guerrillas ◆공비의 잔당을 소탕하다 mop up [clear out] the remnants of Communist guerrillas

공사 工事 construction; construction work; engineering work
◆공사 중이다 be under [in course of] construction / 공사를 감독하다 supervise work; direct construction / 공사를 시작하다 start 《construction》 work; set [begin] to work
▶이 길은 1킬로미터 전방에 공사를 하고 있으므로 자동차로는 갈 수 없습니다 As this road is under construction [repair] about a kilometer ahead, you can't go through by car.
▶이 공사를 완성하는 데는 약 7년이 걸렸다 It took about seven years to complete the work.
▶공사중 (게시) Under construction [repair]. ⇒ Men working [at work].
▶전방(에) 공사중 (게시) Construction Ahead.
―**공사하다** construct; do [execute] construction work 《on》; work 《at》; build
■건설― construction works 난― a difficult construction work 날림― jerry-building; flimsy [slipshod, shoddy] construction (work) 도로― road building [construction] 부정― faulty work 수리― repair work 철도― railway [railroad] construction (work) 토목― engineering [public] works ■―감독 a superintendent; an overseer ―비 the cost of construction; construction expenses [cost]

―사무소 a construction work office ―입찰 a bid for construction work ―장[현장] a field of construction work; a site of construction ―청부인 a contractor

공사 公司 〈중국의 회사〉 a firm; a company

공사 公私 public and private affairs [matters]; official and personal affairs
♦ 공사의 public [official] and private / 공사 아울러 both officially and privately / 공사 다 망하실 줄 압니다만 though I am well aware that you are very busy
▶ 그는 요즈음 공사간에 분주하다 He is very busy both in public and private [both officially and privately] these days.
▶ 자네는 공사의 구별을 분명히 하지 않으면 안 되네 You must draw a line between public and private life.
▶ 그는 이따금 공사를 혼동한다 He sometimes mixes up his public and private matters.

공사 公社 a public corporation ■ 대한 석유― the Korea Oil Corporation 대한 주택― the Korea Housing Corporation

공사 公事 official [public] affairs; official business [duty] ♦ 공사와 사적인 일을 구별하다 discriminate between public and private affairs

공사 公使 a (diplomatic) minister
♦ 각국 공사 diplomatic representatives; the heads of foreign mission / 우루과이 주재 한국 공사 the Korean Minister to [in] Uruguay
■ 대리― (프) a chargé d'affaires (ad interim) 《pl. chargés d'affaires》 전권― an envoy 특명 전권― an envoy extraordinary (and minister plenipotentiary) ―직 ministry

공사관 公使館 a legation ♦ 워싱턴[우루과이] 주재 한국 공사관 the Korean legation at Washington [Uruguay]
■ ―(부)무관 a military [naval] attaché to a legation ―(직)원 a member of a legation staff; (총칭) the staff [personnel] of a legation

공사채 公社債 〈공채와 회사채〉 bonds; public bonds and corporate debentures; 〈공사의 채권〉 public corporation bonds
■ ―시장 the bond market ―이율 a yield on corporated and public bonds ―투자신탁 a bond investment trust

공산 公算 〈가망〉 probability; likelihood; 〈가능성〉 a chance
♦ …할 공산이 크다 There is a strong probability that…; The chance are that… / 성공할 공산이 크다 stand a good chance of success / 성공할 공산이 적다 have a poor chance of success
▶ 위원회가 예산을 승인할 공산이 크다 There is a strong probability that the committee will approve the budget.
▶ 우리는 시합에 이길 공산은 별로 없다 We have not much chance of gaining the game.
▶ 그가 여기에 올 공산은 충분히 있다 There is every probability of his coming here [that he will come here]. ⇌ There is a good chance of his coming here.

공산 共産 common property; community of property
♦ 북한 공산 집단 the band of Communists in north Korea / 공산계 신문 a Communist-influenced [Communist-inclined] paper
■ ―국가 a Communist country [nation] ―군 the Communist army [force]; the Red Army ―권 the Communist bloc : 공산권 여러 나라 countries in the Communist bloc ―분자 Communist elements ―사회 a communist society ―제 a communistic system ―진영 the Communist camp ―측 the Communist side ―침략 a Communist invasion [aggression]

공산당 共産黨 the Communist Party (略 C.P.); the Communists
■ ―기관지 a Communist paper ―비밀 당원 a crypto-Communist ―선언 the Communist Manifesto ―원 a communist; a member of the Communist Party; a commie

공산명월 空山明月 1〈달〉 the bright [full] moon shining on a lone mountain 2〈대머리〉 a bald head

공산주의 共産主義 communism
♦ 공산주의의[적인] communist(ic) / 공산주의에 물든 사람 a pink
■ ―국가 a communist country [nation] ―사회 a communist community ―운동 a communist(ic) drive; a drive for the spread of communism ―자 a communist; (口) a red; a commie : 공산주의자와 싸우다 battle [struggle] against the communist

공산품 工産品 industrial products

공산화 共産化 communization
♦ 공산화를 막다 defend [safeguard] 《a country》 against Communization
―공산화하다 〈남을〉 communize; 〈자기가〉 become [turn] communist(ic)
♦ 무력으로 공산화하려 하다 try to communize 《the Korean Peninsula》 by force

공상 工商 〈공업과 상업〉 industry and commerce; 〈그 계층〉 the classes of artisans and tradesmen; the industrial and mercantile classes

공상 公傷 an injury resulting from official work; an injury incurred while at work; a wound received while on duty ■ ―연금 disability pension

공상 空想 (a) fancy; (a) fantasy; a vision; a daydream; imagination
♦ 공상적인 fanciful; visionary; imaginary / 공상에 잠기다 indulge in fancy; fall into [be lost in] thought [reverie]; be given to daydreaming
▶ 그것은 순전히 공상이었다 It was all imagination.
▶ 그때 나는 공상에 잠겨 있었다 I was lost in reverie [daydreaming] then.
▶ 그녀는 엉뚱한 공상에 사로잡혀 있었다 She was possessed by [with] wild fancies.
▶ 네 생각은 공상적이다 Yours is a fanciful [Utopian] idea.
▶ 그는 공상적인 작가였다 He was an imaginative [a fanciful] writer.
―공상하다 fancy; daydream; imagine

♦마음껏 공상하다 give full [free] play to one's imagination [fancy]
▶나는 미래의 행복을 공상해 보았다 I drew a fine picture of my future happiness.
■—가 a dreamer; a daydreamer; a visionary —과학 소설 science fiction (略 S.F.) —과학 소설가 a science fictionist —과학 영화 a science fiction film

공생 共生 〔生〕 symbiosis; commensalism; 〔鑛〕 paragenesis —**공생하다** live together [symbiotically]
■—관계 a symbiotic relationship —동물[식물] a commensal —체[생물] a symbiont; a symbion

공생애 公生涯 a public life; a public career

공서양속 公序良俗 〔法〕 good public order and customs; public order and morals

공석 公席 〈공적 모임〉 the presence of the public; the meeting; 〈공무를 보는 자리〉 a place where public affairs are attended to
♦공석에서 (speak) in public [company]

공석 空席 〈빈 좌석〉 a vacant seat; an unoccupied seat; 〈비어 있는 지위〉 a vacant post; a vacancy; an opening
♦공석을 채우다 fill (up) a vacancy / 공석으로 있다 remain vacant
▶그의 사임으로 그 자리는 공석이 되었다 His resignation left a vacancy.
▶공석은 하나도 없었다 There were no empty seats.

공선 工船 〈가공선〉 a cannery ship; a factory ship

공선 公選 〈공중 선거〉 public [popular] election; election by popular vote; official selection; 〈공명 선거〉 a fair election
—**공선하다** elect by popular vote
▶미국 대통령은 4년마다 공선한다 A U.S. president is elected every four years by popular vote.
■—의원 an elective member; (美)〈지방 의회의〉 an assemblyman —지사(知事) a publicly-elected governor

공선 孔線 〈필름의〉 (a line of) perforations; sprocket holes

공설 公設 public installation
♦공설의 public; communal; 〈시영의〉 municipal / 공설 노인정 a home for senior citizens supported by public funds
—**공설하다** install at public expense
■—기관 a public institution —시장 a public [municipal] market —운동장 a public stadium

공성 攻城 a siege —**공성하다** siege; besiege
■—군 besiegers; a besieging army —보루(堡壘) siegeworks —작전 siege operation —전 siege warfare —포 a siege gun

공세 攻勢 the offensive; the aggressive; aggression
♦공세적인 offensive; aggressive / 공세를 강화하다 step up the offensive / 질문 공세를 퍼붓다 torment sb with inquiries; assail sb with questions / 공세로 전환하다 change [switch] to the offensive
▶아군은 적에게 공세를 취했다 Our forces launched an attack on [took the offensive against] the enemy.
▶그는 사인 공세를 받았다 He was besieged by autographseekers.
▶선전— a propaganda offensive 외교— a diplomatic offensive 테러— a wave of terror [terrorism] 평화— a peace offensive

공소 公訴 〔法〕 arraignment; prosecution; accusation; public action; a criminal action
♦공소를 기각[철회]하다 dismiss [withdraw] a public action / 공소를 제기하다 institute a public action; prosecute a case
—**공소하다** prosecute; arraign; accuse
■—권 the right of arraignment —사실 a charge, a count —유지 maintenance [institution and support] of a public action —장 a written arraignment

공소하다 空疎— 〈내용이 비다〉 empty; poor in content [substance]; unsubstantial

공손 恭遜 politeness; courteousness; civility
—**공손하다** polite; civil; courteous
♦공손한 태도(로) (in) a polite attitude / 공손히 politely; courteously; in a civil way; respectfully / 공손한 말을 쓰다 use decent words [polite language] / 공손히 대하다 treat sb with courtesy [respect] / 공손히 말하다 speak politely
▶그들은 노인에게 항상 공손하다 They are always respectful [courteous] to old people.
▶남에게 공손히 해라 Be polite to others.
▶그녀는 공손히 인사를 하고 방을 나갔다 She bowed [saluted] politely [deeply] and left the room.
▶그 학생은 교장 선생님께 공손히 절을 했다 The student made a respectful [deep] bow to the principal.

공수 攻守 offense and defense; 〔野〕 batting and fielding
▶상대 팀은 공수가 다 뛰어났다 Our opponents were outstanding both offensively and defensively.
■—동맹 《conclude [enter into]》 an offensive and defensive alliance 《with》

공수 空手 empty hands ⇨ 빈손

공수 空輸 air transport; an airlift; air transportation; transportation by air
—**공수하다** transport [carry] (mail) by air [plane]; (美) fly 《goods to Africa》; airlift 《a corps》
▶구호 물자가 재해 지역에 공수되었다 Relief goods were carried to the stricken area by plane.
■—기동 여단 〔軍〕 an air cavalry brigade —부대 an airlift troop; an airborne unit [corps]; sky (army) troop —사단 〔軍〕 an airborne division —작전 airlift [airborne] operations —화물 air cargo [freight]; (美) airlift (goods)

공수래공수거 空手來空手去 "come empty, return empty"; the vanity of life

공수병 恐水病 〔醫〕 hydrophobia ⇨ 광견병(狂犬病)

공수표 空手票 a fictitious bill; (美) a bad check; 〈헛된 약속〉 an empty promise

♦공수표를 떼다 give [draw] a fictitious promissory note [bill]; (俗) fly a kite; (비유) give [make] an empty promise / 공수표로 끝나다 end in an empty pledge; prove to be an empty promise [pledge]
▶ 그의 약속은 대개가 공수표다 He often makes an empty promise.

공순 恭順 〈고분고분함〉 submission; obedience —**공순하다** submissive; obedient; docile ♦아주 공순히 (bow to the king) with all due submission

공술— a free [gratis] drink; free liquor ♦공술 먹고 취하다 get drunk at another's expense

공술 供述 testimony ⇨ 진술

공습 空襲 an air raid; an air [aerial] attack [assault]
♦공습을 받다 be air-raided; suffer an air raid / 공습으로 불타 없어지다 be burnt out in an air raid; be bombed out
—**공습하다** make an air raid (on); air-raid; attack (a town) from the air
▶ 적기가 우리 도시를 공습했다 The enemy planes made an air raid on our city.

공습경보 空襲警報 (give) an air-raid alarm; an air-raid warning [alert]
♦공습 경보를 발령[해제]하다 give an air-raid [all clear] signal
▶ 공습 경보 해제가 발령되었다 The all clear was sounded.
—**사이렌** an air-raid siren

공시 公示 public notification; an official [a public] notice
—**공시하다** make *sth* known to the public; announce publicly; publish; make public
▶ 총선거의 투표일이 공시되었다 The voting day for the general election was announced publicly.
—**송달** 〔法〕 conveyance by public announcements —**최고(催告)** 〔法〕 a public summons [peremptory notice]

공식 公式 1 〔數〕 a formula (*pl.* ~s, -lae) 2 〈정식〉 formality
♦공식의 formal; official; state / 공식으로 officially; formally; in state / 공식으로 환영을 받다 be officially feted (by)
▶ 나는 아직 공식 통고를 받은 바 없다 I have not received any official notice yet.
▶ 그 기록은 공식 인정되었다 The record was officially approved.
—**경기** a regular game [match]; 〔野〕 the pennant race —**론** formulism —**반응** (make) an official response —**발표** an official announcement —**방문** (pay) a formal visit (to); 〈국가 원수 등의〉 a state visit : 대통령은 곧 미국을 공식 방문할 예정이다 The President will shortly pay a formal visit to the United States. —**성명** (issue) an official statement (on); 〈신문에 발표하는〉 a handout —**주의** formulism; 〈형식주의〉 formalism

공식적 公式的 public; open; official; 〈정식의〉 formal
♦공식적으로 openly; publicly; in public; officially / 공식적으로나 비공식적으로나 both openly and secretly [in public and private] / 공식적인 조치를 취하다 take open measures
▶ 그것은 아직 공식적으로 발표되지 않았다 It is not officially announced yet.

공신 功臣 a worthy [meritorious] retainer; a vassal of merit

공신력 公信力 public trust ♦은행의 공신력 the credit-worthiness of banks / 공신력을 잃다 lose public confidence

공안 公安 public safety [peace (and order)]
♦철도 공안원 a security officer on the train / 공안을 유지하다 keep [maintain] public peace and order / 공안을 해치다 disturb public peace (and order)
—**경찰** the public peace police; the security police —**방해죄** breach of the peace —**사범** a public safety offender

공안 公案 〈공문의〉 a draft of a public document; 〈안건〉 a plan decided by [bill drafted in accordance with] public opinion

공약 公約 a public promise [commitment]
♦정당의 공약 the public commitment of a party / 공약을 내걸다 make [give] promise publicly / 선거 때의 공약을 실천하다 carry out [make good] an election pledge [promise] / 공약을 지키다[깨뜨리다] keep [break] the public promises [pledges]
—**공약하다** pledge [commit] *oneself* (publicly)
▶ 그 후보는 물가 안정을 공약했다 The candidate pledged himself to price stabilization [pledged to stabilize prices].
■—**선거** election [campaign] pledges : 선거 공약이란 언제나 기대할 것이 못된다 Election promises always prove to be a gross deception.

공약수 公約數 〔數〕 a common measure [divisor]; a common factor ★**최대—** the greatest common measure [divisor] (略 G.C.M., G.C.D.)

공양 供養 1 〈어른에게〉 providing with food —**공양하다** provide 《*one's*》 elders with food 2 〈부처에게〉 〔佛敎〕 offering food, flowers, etc. to Buddha; a Buddhist mass (for) —**공양하다** offer food, flowers, etc. to Buddha 3 〈스님이 음식을 먹음〉 eating food —**공양하다** eat food
—**미** a rice offering; rice offered to Buddha —**주** a person who gives alms to a Buddist temple; an offerer; a benefactor

공언 公言 (an open) declaration; profession; avowal
—**공언하다** declare openly; profess; avow
♦주저없이 공언하다 have no hesitation in stating [declaring] that...
▶ 그는 뇌물을 받아 먹은 적이 없다고 공언했다 He declared in public that he had never taken a bribe.
▶ 그는 그 불상사와 아무 관계도 없다고 공언하고 있다 He has declared in public that he has no connection with the disgraceful affair.
▶ 자넨 여전히 휴머니스트라고 공언할 수 있는가? Can you still claim to be a humanist?

공얻다 空— 〈거저 얻다〉 get for nothing; get *sth* as a gift

공업 工業 (an) industry; the manufacturing industry
♦ 공업의 industrial; technical; manufacturing / 한국 공업의 중심지 an industrial [a manufacturing] center in Korea / 공업용 로봇[다이아몬드] an industrial robot [diamond] / 공업용 알코올[원자재] industrial alcohol [raw materials] / 공업적으로 industrially / 공업을 발전시키다 promote the industries
▶ 그 나라의 자동차 공업은 위기를 맞고 있다 The country's auto(mobile) industry is facing a crisis.
■ 가내― the household industry 경[중]― light [heavy] industry 금속[기계]― the metalworking [machine] industry 전자― the electronic industry 중화학― heavy and chemical industry ■ ―가 an industrialist; a manufacturer ―경영 industrial management ―계 industrial circles; the industrial world ―고등 학교 a technical high school ―교육 technical education ―국 an industrial nation [country] ―규격 an industrial standard : 한국 공업 규격 Korean Industrial Standards (略 KS) ―단지 industrial complex : 울산 공업단지 the Ulsan Industrial Complex / 임해(臨海) 공업단지 a coastal industrial complex ―도시 an industrial city; a manufacturing town ―디자인[디자이너] an industrial design [designer] ―력 industrial might (of a nation) ―부기 industrial bookkeeping ―생산 industrial production ―선진국 an industrially advanced nation [country] ―소유권 industrial property ―시험소 an industrial laboratory [experimental station] ―약품 industrial chemicals ―용수 industrial water; water for industrial use ―정책 an industrial policy ―제품 industrial goods [products] ―지대 an industrial area; a manufacturing district [center] ―지리 industrial geography ―진흥청 the Industrial Advancement Administration (略 IAA) ―폐수 industrial effluent [waste water] ―표준화법 [法] the Industrial Standards Act ―학교 a technical [technological] school ―화 industrialization : 공업화하다 industrialize (a country) / 동남아시아는 급속히 공업화하고 있다 Southeast Asia is becoming rapidly industrialized. ―화학 industrial [technical] chemistry; technochemistry

공업 功業 an achievement; a meritorious deed; an exploit

공여 供與 giving; a grant
―공여하다 give; grant; make a grant (of)
♦ 차관(借款)을 공여하다 give [grant] (a country) a loan (of ten billion won); extend credit to (a country)
▶ 모 강대국이 그 나라에 무기를 공여한다 A certain big power gives [grants] arms to the country.

공역 公役 public service ♦ 공역을 기피하다 evade one's public service / 공역에 복무하다 enter public service

공역 共譯 joint translation ―공역하다 translate (a book) jointly [in collaboration] (with)
♦ 김 교수와 민 교수가 공역한 translated by Professors Kim and Min
■ ―자 joint translators

공역 空域 《five miles of》 airspace

공연 公演 a public performance
♦ 첫 공연 the first public performance / 한국 공연 윤리 위원회 the Korean Ethics Committee of Public Performance / 공연중인 햄릿 Hamlet on the stage
▶ 공연은 하루에 세 차례다 There are three performances a day.
―공연하다 perform publicy; play; give a public performance; 〈연극 등을〉 present; stage
♦ 인형극을 공연하다 give [put on] a puppet show
▶ 우리 교향악단이 6월에 서울에서 공연한다 Our symphony orchestra will give a public performance in Seoul in June.
▶ 그 연극은 국립극장에서 공연한다 The play will be presented at the National Theater.
▶ 그들은 하루 3회 공연했다 They performed three times a day. ⇌ They gave three shows a day.
■ 낮― a matinee; an afternoon performance 자선― a charity performance [show] 장기― a long run 추모― a memorial performance ■ ―장 an entertainment hall; an auditorium; a variety hall; (美) a vaudeville (theater); (英) a music hall

공연 共演 coacting; costarring
―공연하다 coact; costar; play together 《in a film》
♦ 제임스 딘과 엘리자베스 테일러가 공연한 영화 a film costarring [jointly featuring] James Dean and Elizabeth Taylor
■ ―자[배우] a coactor; a costar; 〈동료들〉 fellow members of the cast

공연하다 空然― useless; fruitless; futile; unavailing; vain; unnecessary; needless
♦ 공연한 걱정 an idle fear / 공연한 일 a fruitless task / 공연히 uselessly; fruitlessly; futilely; vainly; in vain; without avail / 공연한 걸음을 하다 go on a bootless errand; make a visit 《on sb》 in vain [to no purpose] / 공연한 소란을 피우다 make much ado [a great fuss] about nothing / 공연히 걱정하다 worry [trouble oneself] unnecessarily [needlessly] / 공연히 애쓰다 make vain efforts; exert oneself to no purpose / 공연히 우쭐대다 be vainly pretentious / 공연히 울다 cry for no reason at all
▶ 그 사람들과 왈가왈부해 보았자 공연한 짓이다 It is useless arguing [to argue] with them.
▶ 그들은 공연히 애만 썼다 They have labored in vain.
▶ 나는 공연히 영어 공부를 하는 것이 아니다 I don't study English without purpose.

공염불 空念佛 a fair but empty phrase ♦ 공염불을 하다 go on chant empty prayers / 공염불로 그치다 end in an empty talk; end in [prove to be] nothing but empty talk

공영 公營 public management ♦ 공영의 public; municipal ―공영하다 place [bring] 《an undertaking》 under public management
■ ―기업 〈국가의〉 a government enterprise;

〈자치제의〉 a municipal enterprise ―주택 a unit of public housing; (총칭) public housing
공영 共榮 mutual prosperity; co-prosperity
♦공존 공영 coexistence and co-prosperity
공영 共營 joint management [operation]
■―농장 ⇨ 콜호스 ―화 collectivization : 공영화하다 collectivize
공예 工藝 a technical art; technology; industrial art
■―미술 artistic handicraft; arts and crafts
■―가 a technologist; a craftsman ―기술 craft skills; craftsmanship ―미술 applied fine arts ―품 an industrial product; an art work; objects of craftwork; a craftwork ―학 technology; technics; polytechnics ―학교 a polytechnic (school); a technological school
공용 公用 〈공공용〉(for) public use; 〈공공 비용〉 public expense
■―건물 a public building ―물 objects for public use ―어 an official language ―차(車) an official vehicle: 공용차를 타고 돌아다니다 drive around in an official vehicle
공용 共用 〈공동 사용〉 common use
▶이 수도 꼭지는 공용이다 This tap [water faucet] is for common use.
―공용하다 have sth for common use; share 《the bathroom》 with sb
▶나는 이 방을 그와 공용하고 있다 I use this room in common with him.
■―물 public property ―화기 a crew-served weapon
공원 工員 a factory worker [hand]; a machine operator
공원 公園 a park; a public garden; 〈마을의 소공원〉(英) a square ♦공원을 만들다 lay out [provide] a park
■―국립― a national park 서울 대― Seoul Grand Park 어린이 대― Children's Grand Park (▶특정 공원의 명칭에는 보통 관사를 붙이지 않음) 옥상― a roof garden 자연― a wilderness [natural] park 파고다― Pagoda Park ■―묘지 a park cemetery
공위 攻圍 (a) siege ―공위하다 besiege; lay siege to ―군 a besieging army
공위 空位 1〈빈 자리〉 a vacancy; a vacant position; 〈왕위의〉 a vacant throne ♦왕위의 공위 기간 an interregnum (*pl.* ~s, -na) / 공위로 있다 be vacant
2〈명목상의 지위〉 a nominal position
공유 公有 public ownership ♦공유 건물 a public building
■―림 a public forest ―재산[물] public property [assets] ―지 land for common use; public land; a public domain : 이 공터는 시의 공유지이다 The city owns this empty lot.
공유 共有 joint [common] ownership; co-ownership; 〈재산의〉 community (of goods)
―공유하다 have [possess] a thing jointly; own *sth* jointly; hold *sth* in common
▶이 집은 나와 아내가 공유하고 있다 I own this house jointly [in common] with my wife.
▶그들은 재산을 공유하고 있다 They possess property between them [hold property in common].

■―결합 [化] a covalent bond ―물[재산] common property; property owned in common : 저것은 우리들 전체의 공유물입니다 That belongs to us all. ―자 a joint owner; [法] a co-ownership ―지 a 《village》 common; common land
공으로 空― 〈거저〉 free; without [free of] charge; gratis; gratuitously; for nothing
♦공으로 얻다 get for nothing; get free of charge / 공으로 일하다 work without pay [recompense]; work for nothing
▶그녀는 목걸이를 공으로 받았다 She got the necklace for nothing.
공의 公醫 a community doctor [physician]
공이 a pestle; a pounder; 〈총의〉 a firing pin
♦공이로 찧다 pound 《rice》 with a pestle; crush 《grains》 with a pounder
■―치기 a hammer 《of a rifle》; a cock : 총의 공이치기를 당기다 cock a gun; draw back the hammer of *one's* gun
공익 公益 the public benefit [interest, welfare]; the common [general] weal
♦공익을 도모하다 promote the public interest; work for the public good / 공익을 위해 힘쓰다 work for the public good [in the interest(s) of the public] / 공익을 해치다 be prejudicial [detrimental] to the public interest; harm the public interest
▶그분은 언제나 개인의 이익보다 공익을 앞세운다 He always gives priority to the public interest over individual interest.
■―단체 a public corporation ―대표 representatives of public interests; public welfare delegates ―법인 a public utilities corporation; (美) a public-service corporation ―사단법인 a public utility association ―사업(체) a public utility [work] ―우선 public interest first ―우선 주의 the public interest(s) first principle; the principle of "public interest first" ―재단 a public utility foundation ―회사 a public service [utility] company
공익 共益 common benefit [interest]; common good 공익을 위하여 for the common good ■―비용 [法] expenses for common profit
공인 公人 〈사회인〉 a public person [figure, character]; 〈공직자〉 a government official; a public servant; (美) an officeholder ♦공인으로서의 생활 *one's* public life
공인 公認 official recognition [approval]; authorization; legalization
♦비공인의 unofficial; unauthorized / 공인을 받다 gain official approval
―공인하다 authorize; recognize 《it》 officially 《as a world record》; approve publicly; legalize
▶이 기록은 아직 공인되지 않았다 This record has not yet been officially recognized. ⇌ We are awaiting certification of this record.
■―구 《球》 a regulation ball ―《세계》기록 an official 《world》 record ―중개사 a licensed real estate agent ―회계사 a certified public accountant 《略 C.P.A.》; (英) a chartered accountant 《略 C.A.》

공인수 公因數 〔數〕 a common factor =공통(~인수)

공일 空— 〈공짜 일〉 free service; a job in vain —**공일하다** work for nothing

공일 空日 〈노는 날〉 a holiday; 〈일요일〉 Sunday

공임 工賃 wages; pay; cost (of labor)
♦공임을 올리다 raise [increase] the wages / 공임을 내리다 cut down the wages
▶이 일의 공임을 올려 주십시오 Please increase the wages for this work [these jobs]. ▶그들은 싼 공임으로 그 공장에 다녔다 They worked at low wages in the factory.

공자 公子 a young nobleman; a young [little] prince

공자 孔子 Confucius ♦공자의 Confucian / 공자의 가르침 Confucianism; Confucian teachings / 공자 왈[가라사대] Confucius [The master] said…

공작 工作 1 〈제작〉 construction; building; engineering work —**공작하다** construct; build; make
2 〈일을 꾸밈〉 maneuvering; activities; operations
♦준비 공작을 하다 pave the way 《for》; prepare the ground 《for》
▶그의 평화 공작은 실패로 돌아갔다 His peace move ended in failure. ≒ His work for peace proved ineffective [a failure].
—**공작하다** maneuver; scheme
♦배후에서 공작하다 maneuver behind the scenes
▶그는 출세하기 위해 뒤에서 여러 가지로 공작했다 He maneuvered behind the scenes in order to rise in the world.
3 〈과목〉 handicraft ▶나는 공작 시간에 이 책꽂이를 만들었다 I made this bookshelf in my handicraft class.
■선전— propaganda maneuvers [maneuvering]; (美口) politicking; an advertising campaign 정치— political maneuvering 지하[이면]— underground activities ■금 operational funds —기계 a machine tool —대《隊》 a group of underground activities —대《臺》 a worktable —물 a building; manufactured articles —선 a repair ship —시간 a handicraft lesson —실 a workshop —원 a maneuverer; an agent —창 an arsenal —품 handicrafts

공작 孔雀 〔鳥〕 a peacock (▶좁은 의미로는 수컷을 가리킴. 암컷은 a peahen, 새끼는 a peachick라고 함); a peafowl (암수 공통)
♦꽁지를 편 공작 a peacock in his pride; a peacock with his tail spread [expanded]
■—고사리 〔植〕 a maidenhair (fern) —석 〔鑛〕 malachite [mǽləkàit]

공작 公爵 a prince; (英) a duke (▶prince는 영국 이외의 나라의 공작)
♦공작의 ducal / 웰링턴 공작 the Duke of Wellington / 비스마르크 공작 Prince Bismarck / 공작을 제수받다 be created prince
■—부인 a princess; (英) a duchess

공장 工匠 〈장인〉 an artisan; a craftsman

공장 工場 a factory; a plant; a mill; a works; a workshop

解說 *factory*는 기계로 대량 생산을 하는 공장을, *plant*는 공업적인 처리를 하는 대규모 공장을 말한다. *mill*은 제분·제지·제강·방적 등 특정 원료를 가지고 작업을 하는 공장이고, *works*는 제작소를 말하는 다소 편한 표현이다. plant, mill, works는 종종 복합어로 쓰인다.

♦공장에서 갓 나온 모터사이클 a motorcycle just off [out of] the assembly line / 공장을 폐쇄하다 close down a factory; 〈쟁의로〉 lock out / 공장에 다니다 work in [attend] a factory / 공장에서 일하다 work at a factory
■기계— a machine shop 방적— a spinning mill; a cotton mill 자동차— an automobile manufacturing plant 자동차 수리— an automobile repair shop 제지— a paper mill 제철— an ironworks; a steel plant [mill] 조립— an assembly plant 하청— an affiliated workshop; a supplier ■—감독 a factory superintendent; a foreman; a supervisor —경영[관리] factory management [control] —노동자 a factory workers [hand] —도《渡》〔商〕 ex works [factory, mill, plant]; free at factory —도 가격 the ex works price; the factory [mill] price —부지 a factory site —생산 mass production —설비 industrial equipment —용구 workshop appliances —위생 factory sanitation —장《長》 a factory [works] manager; a plant superintendent —주 the owner of a factory; a mill [factory] owner —지대 a factory district [area] —폐기물 industrial [factory] waste; 〈액체〉 industrial effluent —폐쇄 〈쟁의로 인한〉 a lockout; 〈불경기·도산에 의한〉 (factory) closure; a shutdown; a closedown

공장폐수 工場廢水 industrial sewage [waste water]; factory wastes
♦공장 폐수로 인한 하천의 오염 industrial pollution of a river / 공장 폐수로 오염되다 be polluted with industrial sewage

공저 共著 〈책〉 a joint work; 〈일〉 collaboration; joint authorship; coauthorship
♦…와 공저로 《write a book》 in collaboration with…; 《written》 under joint authorship with…
▶그는 김 교수와 공저로 경제학 책을 출판했다 He published the book of political economy under joint authorship [in collaboration] with Professor Kim.
—**공저하다** coauthor; collaborate
■—자 a coauthor; a collaborator; a joint author

공적 公敵 a public [common] enemy ♦인류의 공적 an enemy of mankind

공적 功績 services; an achievement; a meritorious deed; merits; distinguished service
♦과학상의 공적 scientific achievements / 공적이 있는 사람 a man of merit; a person of distinguished service / 공적을 기념[치하]하여 in commemoration [recognition] of sb's services / 자기 공적이라고 우기다 claim (the) credit 《for》/ 공적을 세우다 render distin-

guished services 《in war, to the state》; perform great services 《in society》
▶ 그것은 그의 공적이다[이 아니다] The credit (for that) rests with him [is not his].
▶ 이 위업을 달성한 것은 수백 명의 과학자들의 공적이다 The credit for this great accomplishment belongs [goes] to hundreds of scientists.
▶ 그는 세계 평화와 안전에 공적이 있었다 He rendered distinguished services [performed remarkable services] to world peace and security.
▶ 그는 한국의 근대화에 위대한 공적을 세웠다 He made a great contribution to the modernization of Korea.

공적 公的 〈공공의〉 public; 〈공무의〉 official; 〈공식의〉 formal
♦ 공적 지위 a public position / 공적으로 officially; publicly; in public; formally / 공적 성격을 띠다 have [be of, assume] public character / 공적으로 책임을 지다 answer publicly (for); be publicly answerable (for)
▶ 아버지는 공적 사업에 종사하고 계십니다 My father is working on a public project.
▶ 그는 공적 입장에서 그 모임에 참석했다 He attended the party in an official capacity.
■ —생애 a public career —생활 a public life

공전 工錢 〈삯〉 wages; pay
공전 公電 〈관청간 전보〉 an official telegram [dispatch]
공전 公轉 [天] revolution 《of the earth around the sun》
♦ 지구의 공전과 자전 the earth's revolution and rotation
▶ 지구는 자전과 공전을 한다 The earth revolves both on its own axis and around the sun.
—**공전하다** revolve 《around the sun》; move around the sun
▶ 지구는 365일 6시간 만에[1년에 한 번] 태양의 주위를 공전한다 The earth goes round the sun in 365 and a quarter days [in a year].
■ —속도 an orbital speed —주기 a period of revolution 《of fifty years》

공전 空前 〈전에 없음〉 ♦ 공전의 unprecedented; unheard-of; unexampled; unparalleled; record-breaking; epochal / 공전의 기록 《美》 an all-time record
▶ 금년은 공전의 대풍작이었다 We have had a record(-breaking) crop this year.
▶ 그 미술전은 공전의 대성황이었다 The art exhibition was an unprecedented [a record-breaking] success.

공전 空電 statics 《⇨ 공중(~전기)》 ■ —장애 atmospheric disturbance —제거 장치 a static eliminator

공전 空轉 1 [機] 〈자동차의〉 skidding; 〈엔진의〉 racing; lost motion —**공전하다** skid; 〈기계 등이〉 race; run idle ♦ 공전시키다 race 《an engine》
2 〈사업 등의〉 ineffective business activity; fruitless effort
—**공전하다** prove [turn out] ineffective; make a poor show 《in business》; 〈논의가〉 argue in a circle; (口) run round in circles; 〈국회가〉 be at a deadlock
▶ 국회가 한 달 동안 공전했다 The National Assembly remained idle for a month.
▶ 논의가 공전하고 있다 The argument goes round and round and gets nowhere.

공전식 共電式 [電] the common-battery system ■ —교환기[전기기] a common-battery switchboard [telephone set]

공전절후 空前絕後 〈전무후무〉 happening neither before nor after
♦ 공전절후의 명화 the greatest film of all time
▶ 이런 전쟁[이렇게 많은 참가]은 공전절후라고 할 것이다 There never was and never will be such a war [large attendance] as this.
▶ 그것은 공전절후의 업적이다 It is the first and probably the last brilliant achievement.

공정 工程 〈작업 진척도〉 the progress of work; the amount [rate] of work; 〈생산 과정〉 a process 《of manufacture》; 〈공률(工率)〉 《物》 power
♦ 공정의 반이 끝나다 be halfway through the work / 여러 공정을 거치다 go through various processes / 공정을 3분의 1 단축하다 reduce [shorten] the length of the process by one third
▶ 공정은 순조롭다 The work is progressing satisfactorily [smoothly].
▶ 공정은 약 70% 끝났다 The work is about 70 percent finished.
■ —생산 a manufacturing process ■ —관리 process [production] control —도 a flowchart; a process chart —표 progress schedule; time schedule of work; a work schedule 《for a project》

공정 公正 〈공평〉 fairness; equity; impartiality; 〈올바름〉 justice
♦ 공정을 기하기 위해 in order to do justice (to); to make (it) just and proper
▶ 어떤 일이나 공정을 기하는 것이 중요하다 It is important to be impartial [fair].
—**공정하다** just; fair; righteous 《man》; impartial; equitable
♦ 공정한 거래 fair trade [transactions] / 공정한 재판 fair courts / 공정한 조치 a fair and impartial measure / 공정한 처리 a fair [square] deal / 공정한 판단 a fair judgment / 공정한 수단으로 by fair means / 누구에게나 공정하게 대하다 treat all men justly [with justice] / 공정하게 승부하다 play fair / 공정하게 평가하다 evaluate 《sb's work》 fairly [with justice, impartially]
▶ 재판은 공정했다 The trial was fair.
▶ 나는 공정한 취급을 받지 못하고 있다 I am not getting justice.
▶ 매사에 공정한 태도로 임하지 않으면 안된다 We must be fair to everything. ⇌ We must assume an impartial attitude toward everything.
■ —가격 a fair price —거래법 the Fair Trade Act —거래위원회 the Fair Trade Commission —증서 a notarial deed

공정 公定 an official fixture; public decision;

공정가격 official regulation; government control ◆ 공정의 official; legal; (officially) fixed ―**공정하다** decide publicly; fix 《a price》
■―이율 the official [bank] rate (for interest): 공정 이율을 끌어올리다[내리다] raise [lower] the official rate ―임금 the regulation fare ―할인율 the official rate of discount ―환율 an official exchange rate

공정가격 公定價格 an official [authorized] price [rate]; an officially fixed price
♦공정 가격 이하로 팔다 sell 《an article》 under its official quotation / 공정 가격으로 팔다[사다] sell [buy] 《articles》 at official [legal] prices

공정(부)대 空挺(部)隊 an airborne unit ⇨ 공수(~부대)

공제 共濟 〈힘을 합함〉 cooperation; 〈서로 도움〉 mutual aid [benefit] ―**공제하다** aid [help] each other
■―사업 a mutual-aid project ―조합[회] a cooperative; a mutual-aid association; a benefit society; (英) a friendly society ―조합원 a member of a mutual aid association [society]

공제 控除 subtraction; deduction ◆공제 가능한 deductible 《expenses》
▶ 너는 부양 가족이 있기 때문에 세금 공제를 받게 된다 You can receive tax benefits by having legal dependents.
―**공제하다** subtract [deduct] 《from》; take away [off]
▶ 나는 교제비를 경비로 공제했다 I deducted entertainment expenses as a necessary expenditure.
▶ 집세는 내 봉급에서 공제된다 The rent is deducted from my salary [pay].
▶ 우리는 매월 봉급에서 소득세가 공제되고 있다 Our income tax is deducted from our salary every month.
■―근로 소득― an earned income credit [allowance] ―기초― the basic deduction 부양 가족― deduction [allowance] for dependents 소득세― an income tax deduction 특별― a special deduction ―액 an amount deducted 《from》; a deduction 《from one's pay》; an abatement 《of the tax》

공조 共助 mutual aid [help]; cooperation ―**공조하다** cooperate; help [aid, assist] one another

공존 共存 coexistence ―**공존하다** coexist; exist together; live and let live ▶ 그 두 종파가 공존하기는 어렵다 It is difficult for the two sects to coexist [live together].
■―평화― peaceful coexistence ―공영 coexistence and co-prosperity ―공영주의 the principle of mutual coexistence

공죄 功罪 merits and demerits ⇨ 공과(功過)
공주 公主 a (royal) princess
공준 公準 〔數·論〕 a postulate
공중 公衆 the (general) public; 〈대중〉 the masses
♦공중의 public; common; communal / 공중을 위하여 for the benefit of the public; for the public [general] good; in the public interest / 공중의 이익이 되다 be in [serve] the public interest(s) / 공중의 편익을 도모하다 consult the convenience of the public
▶ 그 여자가 공중 앞에서 그 아이를 벌줄 필요는 없었다 There was no need for her to punish the child in public.
▶ 당국은 일반 공중의 편익을 생각해야 한다 The authorities concerned should consider the convenience of the public at large.
■―목욕탕 a public bath ―보건의 a public health doctor ―위생 public health [hygiene, sanitation]

공중 空中 the air; the sky; 〈허공〉 midair
♦공중의 air; aerial / 공중에 in the air [sky], in midair / 공중을 날다 fly in [through] the air / 공중에 뜨다 float in the air / 공중에 매달리다 hang [be suspended] in midair / 공중으로 치솟아 오르다 soar up to the sky; soar skyward
▶ 공중을 마음대로 날 수 있었으면 I wish I could fly in the air [sky] freely.
▶ 풍선이 공중에 떠다니고 있다 A balloon is floating in the air.
■―감시 aerial inspection; 〈대공의〉 air surveillance ―경계 관제기 an airborne warning and control system (略 AWACS) ―곡예 an aerial stunt performance; stunt flying; aerobatics; 〈서커스의〉 an aerialist act : 공중 곡예사 an aerialist; an aerial acrobat ―관측 aerial observation ―광고 〈비행기의〉 advertising by airplane; 〈옥상의〉 a sky sign ―권 air right ―그네 a (flying) trapeze ―급유 air [air-to-air] refueling ―급유기 an air refueling tanker ―무선전화기 an aerophone ―발사 탄도탄 air-launched ballistic missile (略 ALBM) ―방전 atmospheric discharge ―부유 미생물 aeroplankton ―분해 disintegration in the air; a midair disintegration : 공중 분해하다 break up to pieces in the air; come apart while flying / 우리 계획은 공중 분해되었다 Our plan come to nothing. ―사진 an air [aerial] photo; an aerophoto ―사찰 (an) aerial inspection [investigation] ―쇼 an aerial pageant [show] ―수송 air transportation; an airlift operation ―엄호 an air cover [umbrella] ―전(戰) an air battle [combat]; aerial warfare; 〈소형 전투기의〉 an aerial dogfight ―전기 atmospheric electricity; 〔通信〕 static(s); atmospherics ―정찰 air reconnaissance; aerial scout [patrol] ―질소 atmospheric nitrogen ―질소 고정(법) nitrogen fixation ―충돌 an inflight [a midair] collision ―케이블 an aerial ropeway [cableway] ―투하 airdrop ―폭격 (aerial) bombing; an air raid : 공중 폭격을 당하다 be bombed; suffer air bombs [an air raid] ―활주 volplane; gliding

공중누각 空中樓閣 a castle in the air [in Spain]; an air [a cloud] castle; a dream
♦공중누각을 짓다 build castles in the sky; build air castles

공중도덕 公衆道德 public morality [morals]
♦공중도덕을 지키다 take care not to trouble others; act the gentleman in public

공중변소 公衆便所 a public lavatory [convenience]; (美) a (public) comfort station. ▶공중 변소 (게시) Lavatory. ⇌ Comfort Station.

공중보급 空中補給 an airlift; 〈연료의〉 air-to-air refueling ■**—물자** an airdrop

공중선 空中線 〔라디오·TV〕(美) an antenna (*pl.* ~s); (英) an aerial (wire) ■**수파(受波)—** a receiving antenna ■**—전압 [방위, 방식]** an antenna voltage [bearing, system]

공중어뢰 空中魚雷 an aerial torpedo (*pl.* ~es) ♦ 공중 어뢰를 발사하다 discharge [release] an aerial torpedo 〈at〉

공중전화 公衆電話 a public [coinbox] (tele)phone; a pay phone ▶공중 전화 (게시) Public Telephone. ⇌ (英) Call box. ■**—실** a public telephone station [booth]; (英) a call box

공중제비 空中— 1 〈재주넘기〉a somersault; a somerset; a tumble ♦ 앞공중제비 (turn) a forward somersault / 뒤공중제비 a backward somersault; 《do》 a flip-flap [flip-flop] ▶그는 멋지게 공중제비를 했다 He turned a beautiful somersault. **—공중제비하다** turn [make, do] a somersault; somersault; somerset; turn over; turn head over heels 2 〈비행기의〉a loop; looping (the loop) ♦ 공중제비 비행 a loop-the-loop flight **—공중제비하다** loop the loop; perform a looping feat ▶조종사는 네 번 공중제비했다 The pilot looped the loop four times. ▶비행기가 공중제비했다 The airplane made a loop in the air.

공증 公證 a notarial act; authentication ♦ 서류의 공증 수속을 밟다 have papers notarized **—공증하다** authenticate; attest; exemplify ■**—료** notarial fees [charges] **—(인)사무소** a notary's office **—인** a notary public (*pl.* notaries public)

공지 公知 common [universal] knowledge ♦ 공지의 known to all; widely [well, universally] known / …은 공지의 사실이다 It is (a matter of) common knowledge that… ■**—사항** the (items of) official announcement

공지 空地 vacant land; (美) a vacant [an empty] lot; (英) an empty [a vacant] plot (of land); 〈광장〉 an open space

공직 公職 (a) public office; an official position [post] ♦ 공직에 있는 사람 a holder of (public) office; a public official [servant]; an officeholder / 공직을 떠나다 leave office; leave public life / 공직에 선임되다 be elected to public office / 공직에 취임하다 take up a public office; become a government official / 공직에서 추방하다 purge *sb* from public office [service] ▶그는 공직에 있다 He is a public official [servant]. ⇌ He works for the government. ⇌ He is in the civil service. ▶그는 공직에 취임했다 He entered government service.

▶그는 정년으로 공직에서 은퇴했다 He has retired from the government [civil] service. ▶그는 공직에서 추방당했다 He was removed [purged] from public office. ■**—생활** a public career [life]; government service **—추방** purge from public service

공진 共振 〈전류의〉 resonance; 〈공명〉 (a) sympathetic vibrations; sympathy **—공진하다** resonate ■**—기(器)** 〔電〕 a resonator **—회로** 〔物〕 a resonance circuit

공진회 共進會 a competitive exhibition; a show; 〈농작물의〉 a (country) fair ■**가축—** a cattle show **농산물—** (hold) an agricultural fair

공집합 空集合 〔數〕 an [the] empty set; a [the] null set

공짜 空— 〈무료〉free [no] charge; 〈거저 얻은 물건〉 a thing got for nothing; a present; a gift ♦ 공짜의 free; gratuitous; gratis / 공짜 손님 〈관람객〉 a free spectator; 〈승객〉 a free passenger; (美口) a train jumper; a deadhead / 공짜표 a free ticket / 공짜로 free; without [free of] charge; gratis; gratuitously; for nothing / 공짜로 얻다 get [receive] *sth* for nothing [as a gift] ▶그는 공짜로 일하는 거나 마찬가지다 He almost works for nothing. ▶그는 공짜로 열차를 탔다 He got a free ride [stolen a ride] on a train. ▶공짜보다 비싼 것은 없다 Nothing costs so much as what is given us.

공차 公差 〔數〕 a common difference; 〈조폐·도량형기의〉〔機〕 legal remedy; tolerance; allowance; margin ■**—단위** 〔機〕 a tolerance unit **—한계** 〔數〕 a tolerance limit

공차 空車 1 〈빈 차〉 an empty carriage [car]; a disengaged taxi [cab]; 〔鐵〕 an idler 2 〈공짜로 타는 차〉 a free [stolen] ride ♦ 공차 타다 steal a ride on; cheat a railway; get [pinch] a free ride; (美俗) snag a pick-up

공창 工廠 〈철공장〉 an ironworks; 〈병기창〉 an arsenal ■**해군—** a naval arsenal

공창 公娼 a licensed [registered] prostitute ■**—가(街)** a red-light district **—제도** (the system of) licensed [state-regulated] prostitution **—폐지** abolition of licensed prostitution **—폐지 운동** a purification movement [campaign]; an antivice movement

공채 公債 a (public loan) bond; government securities; 〈빛〉 a public loan [debt] ♦ 6푼 이자(부) 공채 6 per cent bonds / 공채 모집에 응하다 subscribe to a loan / 공채의 상환을 청구하다 (美) call a bond / 공채를 공모하다 offer bonds for subscription / 100억원의 공채를 모집하다 float [raise] a loan of ten billion won / 공채를 발행하다[사다] issue [buy] bonds / 공채를 상환하다 redeem [sink] a loan / 공채를 청약하다 subscribe for a public loan ■**교부—** government compensation bonds **등록—** registered bonds **무기명—** blank bonds **무이자—** passive bonds **장기[단기]—** a long-term [short-term] bond [loan] ■**—금 수입** receipt from public loans **—발행 차입금** a

공책 空册 a notebook
공처 恐妻 ■—가 a henpecked [submissive] husband —증 wifephobia
공천 公薦 〈천거〉 public recommendation; 〈지명〉 party nomination 《of parliamentary candidates》
♦민주당 공천 후보자 a candidate nominated by the Democrats / 공천받은 사람 a nominee / 민주당 공천으로 입후보하다 run [stand] 《for the National Assembly》 on the Democratic ticket
—공천하다 recommend [nominate] publicly
♦후보자를 공천하다 nominate [officially adopt] a candidate
공청회 公聽會 (hold) a public hearing (on)
♦공청회는 내일 열린다 The public hearing will be held tomorrow. ■—(속)기록 hearings
공출 供出 delivery (of rice to the government); offering
♦공출을 할당하다 allot [allocate] a fixed quantity 《of rice》
—공출하다 deliver; tender; offer
♦쌀을 공출하다 deliver rice 《to the government》
▶그들은 물자 대신에 노동을 공출해야 했다 They were ordered to supply labor instead of goods.
■—가격 a delivery price ■—미 rice tendered (to the government) ■—할당 allocation of delivery quotas; 〈할당량〉 a delivery [collection] quota
공치기 a ball game; playing ball
공치다 空— 1 〈허탕치다〉 be unsuccessful; be fruitless; be (in) vain; be futile 2 〈○표를 하다〉 draw a circle; mark down an "0"
공치사 功致辭 self-praise [self-laudation] of one's good conduct; admiration of one's merit
—공치사하다 praise oneself; value one's own deed; sing one's own praises
공치사 空致辭 〈빈말〉 empty compliments
—공치사하다 pay empty compliments (to); tickle [appeal] to sb's vanity by complimenting [saying nice things to] (him)
공칭 公稱 the official name ♦공칭의 nominal; official
■—가격 the official price; a nominal price ■—능력 authorized capacity ■—마력〈物〉(略 NHP) nominal horsepower ■—부수 the official circulation ■—자본(금) nominal [authorized] capital
공탁 供託 deposition; a deposit; a trust; lodgement
♦법원에 대한 금전[재산] 공탁 payment into [deposit in] court
—공탁하다 deposit sth (in, with); give sth in trust; place (money) on deposit (in); lodge (with)
♦변호사에게 서류를 공탁하다 deposit papers with one's lawyer
■—금 a (security) deposit; deposit money; money on deposit : 공탁금을 몰수당하다 forfeit a deposit ■—물 a deposit; a deposited article ■—법〈法〉 the Deposit into Justice Offices Act ■—소 a depository; a deposit office ■—자 a depositor
공터 空— vacant land [lot]; an open space
▶놀 공터가 별로 많지 않다 There is only a little space for the playground.
공통 共通 commonness
♦공통의 common / 공통의 목적[이해] common purpose [interest] / 전체에 공통적인 성질 a characteristic common to all / 공통의 이익을 위해서 for the public good / …와 공통으로 in common with… / 만인에게 공통이다 be common to us all
▶그는 우리의 공통의 친구다 He is our mutual [common] friend.
▶그들은 공통의 이해로 결속되어 있다 They are bound together by common interests. ≒ What binds them together is their community of interest.
▶이 결점은 그들 모두가 공통으로 가지고 있다 This defect is common in all of them.
■—분모〈數〉 a common denominator : 최소공통분모 the lowest [least] common denominator (略 L.C.D., l.c.d.) ■—성 community; commonness ■—어 common language ■—의식 common consciousness ■—인자[인수] a common factor
공통점 共通點 a point of sameness
♦공통점을 발견하다 find sth in common (between the two)
▶그 두 사람 사이에는 어딘가 공통점이 있다[전혀 없다] The two have something [nothing] in common (with each other).
공판 公判 a trial; a (public) hearing
♦공판 중이다 be on (one's) trial; be under public trial / 공판을 열다[개정하다] hold (a) court
▶그 사건의 공판은 수요일에 열린다 The case will come to trial on Wednesday.
▶지방 법원은 그 사건을 공판에 붙였다 The district court brought the case to trial [put the case on trial].
▶그는 뇌물을 받은 혐의로 공판에 회부되었다 He went on trial for a graft case.
■—분리— a separate trial ■—기록 the record (of a trial) ■—기일 a fixed day for public trial; a date for hearing; a court day ■—절차 procedure in a public trial ■—정 the court (of trial); a public trial court ■—조서 a protocol for a public trial ■—청구 a demand for a trial
공판장 共販場 a joint market ■—농협[수산물]— an agricultural cooperative's [a fishery] joint market
공편 共編 coeditorship; joint compilation
▶이것은 김 교수와 한 교수의 공편으로 된 사전이다 This is a dictionary (jointly) edited by Professors Kim and Han.
■—자 a coeditor; a joint editor
공평 公平 fairness; impartiality; equity; equitability

解說 *fairness*는 개인적인 감정이나 이해에 관계 없이 공명정대함을, *impartiality*는 한쪽으로 치우치거나 편견·편파적이 아님을 의미한다.

♦공평을 기하다 try to be fair; endeavor to see justice done / 공평을 유지하다 maintain impartiality; hold the scale even / 공평을 잃다 be unfair 《to》; do *sb* an injustice; be partial [unjust] 《to》
—**공평하다** fair; impartial; unbiased; 〈정당하다〉 just; equitable
♦공평한 대우 equitable treatment 《to workers》/ 공평한 태도로 in a fair [a just, an impartial] manner / 공평한 결정을 하다 make a fair [just] decision / 공평한 의견을 말하다 give an impartial [an unprejudiced, 〈사심 없는〉 a disinterested] opinion [view] / 공평한 판결을 내리다[언도하다] give [hand down] an impartial decision / 공평하게 분배하다 distribute fairly [evenly] / 사람을 공평하게 취급하다 treat people fairly [impartially, with justice]; be impartial to / 일을 공평하게 할당하다 make a fair division of the work
▶ 우리는 그 사건을 공평한 눈으로 보지 않으면 안 된다 We must take an impartial view of the event.
▶ 세금은 모든 납세자에게 공평하지 않으면 안 된다 Taxation should be impartial to every payer.
♦공평하게 말하더라도 그가 잘못이다 Even speaking impartially, he is wrong.

공평무사 公平無私 (fairness and) impartiality; fair play —**공평무사하다** fair and disinterested

공포 公布 〔法〕 promulgation; proclamation; official announcement
—**공포하다** promulgate; proclaim; make *sth* public; announce officially
▶ 이 법률은 공포한 날로부터 발효한다 This law will be effective on and after the day of promulgation.

공포 空胞 〔動·植〕〈액포〉 a vacuole ■ —**형성** vacuolation

공포 空砲 a blank shot [cartridge]; a blank fire ♦공포를 세 발 쏘다 fire three blank shots

공포 恐怖 fear; (a) dread; (a) terror; fright; a horror; (a) panic

解說 *fear*는 불안·겁 등을 나타내는 일반적인 말, *dread*는 fear와 거의 같은 뜻이지만 싫어하는 것을 만났을 때의 싫은 기분이 들어 있다. *terror*는 매우 심한 공포, *fright*는 일시적으로 섬뜩한 느낌, *horror*는 공포를 동반한 혐오감을 나타낸다.

♦전쟁의 공포 the horror(s) [terror(s)] of war / 죽음의 공포 the fear of death / 공포의 빛을 보이다 look scared [frightened]
〈공포가[는]〉 갑자기 공포가 그를 엄습했다 A sudden fear came over him. ⇌ Suddenly he was filled with fear.
▶ 공포는 사랑보다 강하다 《속담》 Fear is stronger than love.
〈공포를〉 공포를 느끼다 be in fear [dread] of; be frightened [terrified] 《at》
▶ 나는 어두운 데 있으면 무척 공포를 느낀다 I feel great fear in the dark.
▶ 그는 그 광경을 보고 공포를 느꼈다 He was frightened at the sight.
〈공포에〉 공포에 떨다 shiver [tremble] with fear / 공포에 떨게 하다 strike terror into *sb's* heart / 공포에 질려 달아나다 run away in terror
▶ 그는 공포에 사로잡혔다 He was seized with fear. ⇌ He was terror-stricken [horror-stricken].
▶ 그는 공포에 질렸다 He became pale with fear.
〈공포로〉 공포로 기절하다 faint in terror / 공포로 떨다 shake with fear [fright, horror] / 공포로 비명을 지르다 scream with [in] terror
▶ 그녀는 공포로 미칠 것 같았다 She was frantic with terror.
—**감** (a sensation of) fear : 공포감이 엄습했다 Fear came over me. —**관념** anxiety hysteria [neurosis]; a fear complex —**시대** 〈프랑스 혁명 때의〉 the Reign of Terror —**영화** a horror movie [film] —**정치** terrorism; the reign of terror

공포심 恐怖心 fear; horror ▶ 그는 뱀에 대해 극도의 공포심을 가지고 있다 He has a great fear of [He dreads] snakes.

공포증 恐怖症 a phobia 《against》; morbid fear [dread] ♦공포증을 없애다 dissipate a phobia
■ **고소**(高所)— acrophobia **남성**— androphobia **대인**— anthrophobia **여성**— gynephobia **폐소**(閉所)— claustrophobia

공폭 空爆 (aerial) bombing ⇨ 공중(〜폭격)

공표 公表 (an) official [(a) public] announcement; proclamation; 〈발표〉 publication
▶ 그들은 그 의견의 공표를 주저했다 They hesitated to announce the opinion officially.
—**공표하다** announce officially [publicly]; make public [known]; release; give publicity 《to an affair》; 《美》 publicize; publish
♦아무의 이름을 공표하다 make the name of *sb* public / 공표되다 be published; be made known; come to light; see the light (of day) / …이라고 공표되다 be officially announced that…
▶ 의혹을 풀기 위해 사건의 진상을 곧 공표해야 한다 To clear suspicion, the facts of the case should be laid before the public at once.

공피병 鞏皮病 〔醫〕 dermatosclerosis; scleroderma

공하신년 恭賀新年 Happy New Year ⇨ 근하신년(謹賀新年)

공하다 供— offer; submit ♦열람에 공하다 submit 《a document》 to *sb's* inspection

공학 工學 engineering; technology
■ **기계**[응용, 전기, 정밀, 토목, 화학]— mechanical [practical, electrical, precision, civil, chemical] engineering **염색체**— chromosomal engineering ■ —**박사** a doctor of engineering; 〈학위〉 Doctor of Engineering (略 D. Eng.)

공학

—부 〈대학의〉 the department [faculty] of technology; (美) a school of technology —사 a bachelor of engineering; 〈학위〉 Bachelor of Engineering (略 B. Eng.) —석사 a master of engineering; 〈학위〉 Master of Engineering (略 M. Eng.) —연구소 the engineering research institute —자 an engineer

공학 共學 (美) coeducation; (英) mixed education
—공학하다 have coeducation; be coeducational [coeducated]
♦공학 대학 coeducation college [university] / 공학 대학의 여학생 a coed; a co-ed / 공학이 아닌 학교 a non-coeducational school
▶너희 학교는 공학이니? Is your school coeducational?

공한 公翰 an official letter

공한지 空閑地 unused [vacant] land; idle land; land in fallow ■—세 an idle land tax

공항 空港 an airport; an aerial port; (英) an aviation field; an aerodrome ♦공항에 착륙하다 land at an airport
■국제— an international airport : 김포 국제공항 Kimp'o International Airport ■—출입국 관리소 the airport immigration office —택시 [버스] an airport taxi [bus] —호텔 an airport hotel; an airtel

공해 公害 〈환경 오염〉 (environmental) pollution; 〈환경 파괴〉 environmental disruption
♦공해 피해자 a pollution victim / 무공해 pollution-free 《cars》; non-polluting 《technology》; chemical-free 《vegetables》 / 저공해의 low-pollution 《car》 / 공해가 없는 pollution-free 《engine, environment, pesticide》 / 공해를 방지하는 pollution-preventive 《plan》 / 공해를 제거하다 remove 《air and water》 pollutants / 공해를 방지하다 prevent [remove] environment pollution
▶공장은 공해를 일으키는 수가 많다 Factories often produce pollution.
▶우리는 공해를 추방했다 We did away with pollution.
■산업— industrial pollution 소음— noise pollution 식품— food contamination 열— thermal pollution 원자— atomic pollution 이차— secondary pollution 진동— vibration hazard
■—대책 an antipollution measure; measures against pollution —문제 a pollution problem —물질 a pollutant; a pollutional material —반대[추방] 운동 an antipollution movement [campaign, drive] —반대[추방] 운동가 an antipollution activist —방지 prevention of environmental pollution [disruption]; pollution control —방지법 〔法〕 the Environmental Pollution Prevention Act; a pollution-control [an antipollution] law —방지 시설 antipollution facilities —배출 업소 industrial firms discharging air and water pollutants —병 a pollution-caused disease; a disease caused by pollution —병 환자 victims of pollution-caused diseases —산업 a polluting industry —업소 a pollution-causing factory; a polluter —원(源) a pollutant —추방 운동 an antipollution campaign [drive]

공해 公海 〔國際法〕 the open sea; the high seas; international waters
♦공해의 자유 freedom of the seas / 공해에서 어업하다 fish in open waters / 공해상에서 핵실험을 행하다 conduct nuclear tests over international waters
■—어업 fishery in the high seas; ocean [high sea] fishery

공허 空虛 emptiness; vacancy; voidness
♦인생의 공허를 느끼다 feel the emptiness of life
—공허하다 empty; vacant; void; hollow
♦공허한 논의 argument without substance / 공허한 느낌 a hollow feeling (inside of *one*) / 공허한 말 an empty word / 공허한 생활 a life without meaning [empty of purpose]; a hollow [an empty] life / 공허한 표정 an empty [a vacant] look / 공허한 마음으로 with an empty feeling [emptiness] in *one's* heart / 공허한 느낌이 들다 feel hollow / 공허하게 웃다 give a hollow laugh
▶내 마음은 공허했다 Everything seemed meaningless to me. ⇌ My mind was blank.
▶그는 자기 인생은 공허하다고 말했다 He said that his life was empty.
▶남편이 죽은 뒤 그녀는 공허한 생활을 했다 After her husband's death, she led [lived] a hollow life.

공헌 貢獻 (a) contribution; services
—공헌하다 contribute to; make a contribution to 《the community》; render services to; conduce to 《*sb's* success》
♦국가의 복지[번영]에 나름대로 공헌하다 contribute *one's* share to national welfare [prosperity] / 스포츠 발전에 크게 공헌하다 contribute much to the development of sports
▶그는 양국간의 평화에 크게 공헌했다 He contributed much towards establishing [made a great contribution to establish] peace between the two countries.
▶그는 과학의 육성 진흥에 공헌했다 He rendered services to the cultivation and promotion of science.

공혈 供血 blood donation ⇨ 헌혈(獻血)

공화 共和 universal harmony; 〔政〕 republicanism ♦공화의 republican
■—국 a republic; a commonwealth —당 (美) the Republican Party; (口) the Grand Old Party (略 G.O.P., GOP) —당원[주의자] (美) a Republican —당 정부 a Republican Administration [Government] —정체 a republican system [form] of government —정치 republican government —제[주의] republicanism

공황 恐慌 a panic; a crisis; a scare
♦공황 상태에 있다 be in a state of panic; be panicky / 공황을 극복하다 get over a crisis / 공황을 초래하다 cause [bring to] a panic; cause great alarm / 공황에 휩쓸리다 be panic-stricken; be alarmed; be scared
▶대지진으로 사람들은 공황에 빠졌다 The great earthquake threw people into a panic [caused a scare among the people]. ⇌ People were seized with panic by the great earthquake.

▶ 공황으로 일부 은행들까지 파산했다 Even some of the banks smashed owing to the panic.
■ 금융— a financial panic 상업— a commercial panic 안정— a stabilization crisis 주식— a stock exchange [market] panic ■—가격— a panic price —시세 a panic market

공회당 公會堂 a public hall; (美) a town hall; a community center; a civic auditorium 《*pl.* ~s, -toria》

공훈 功勳 a merit; an exploit; a great [meritorious] deed; a distinguished service
♦ 빛나는[혁혁한] 공훈 brilliant exploits / 공훈이 있는 meritorious / 공훈을 세우다 do a meritorious deed; distinguish *oneself* (in); perform great deeds; render distinguished services / 공훈을 세워 훈장을 받다 be decorated for *one's* distinguished services
▶ 그는 그 전투에서 공훈을 세웠다 He distinguished himself in the battle.

공휴일 公休日 a (regular) holiday; a day off; (美) a vacation; (법정 휴일) a legal [national] holiday; (英) a bank holiday
▶ 1년에 공휴일이 며칠 있습니까? How many days off do you have a year?
▶ 다음 공휴일에 어디 갈겁니까? Where are you going away for your next vacation?

-곶 -串 a cape; a promontory; a headland; a point (of land); a spit
♦ 장산곶 Changsan Point; the headland of Changsan

곶감 a dried [cured] persimmon ♦ 곶감 빼먹듯하다 eat away [up] *one's* savings; spend up *one's* savings bit by bit

과 1 〈그리고〉 and ♦ 당신과 나 you and I / 아들과 딸 a son and a daughter
2 〈함께〉 (travel) with 《*one's* lover》; in company with; along [together] with; accompanied by
▶ 당신도 우리들과 같이 가시겠습니까? Will you come with us, too?
▶ 나는 다른 물건과 함께 책을 보냈다 I sent the book along with the other things.
3 〈합치·협력〉 with
♦ 아랍 각국과 손을 잡다 go hand in hand with the Arab countries [world]
▶ 아이들은 선생님들과 협력하여 천막을 쳤다 The children cooperated with their teachers in setting up a tent.
4 〈접촉〉 with
♦ 적과 몰래 내통하다 communicate secretly with the enemy ▶ 나는 그 회사의 중역과 개인적으로 접촉이 있다 I am in personal contact with an executive of the company.
5 〈대항〉 against; with
♦ 수학과 씨름하다 struggle with mathematics / 역경[적]과 싸우다 struggle against adversity [fight against the enemy]
6 〈관계〉 with
♦ 외국과 우호 관계를 맺다 form [establish] friendly relations with foreign nations / 은행과 거래하다 have dealings [do business] with a bank
▶ 나는 그 사건과 아무 관계도 없다 I have nothing to do with the matter.
7 〈비교〉 with
♦ 표범과 호랑이를 비교하다 compare a leopard with a tiger
♦ 원문과 네 번역문을 비교해 봐라 Compare your translation with the original.
▶ 이것과 저것은 비교가 되지 않는다 There is no comparison between this and that.
8 〈분리〉 with; from
♦ 악당들과 손을 끊다 wash *one's* hands clean of the rascals [gang]
▶ 나는 그 녀석과 손을 끊었다 I have done [am through] with him.
9 〈이동(異同)〉 (the same) as; like; (similar) to; (different) from
♦ 내 것과 같은 장갑 the same gloves as mine / 저 사람과 같이 like him / 저 사람과는 달리 in contrast with him; different from him
▶ 그 코트는 이것과 똑같다 That coat is just like this one.
10 〈혼합·연결〉 with
♦ 가스 레인지를 가스관과 연결하다 connect a gas range with a gas pipe / 설탕과 버터를 섞다 mix sugar and butter / 한 약품과 다른 약품을 혼합하다 incorporate a chemical substance with others
♦ 이것을 그것과 섞지 마라 Don't mix this up with that.
▶ 그의 방은 내 방과 복도로 연결되어 있다 His room and mine are connected by (means of) a hallway.

과 科 1 〈전공〉 a course; 〈학부·분과〉 a department; a school; 〈진료 과목〉 a department; 〈병과〉 an arm
♦ 국문과 the department of Korean literature / 문과[이과] the literature [science] course / 수학과 학생 a student majoring in mathematics; a mathematics major / 내과 the internal medicine department / 신경 정신과 the department of neuropsychiatry / 보병과 the infantry arm
▶ 그는 대학에서 무슨 과였습니까? What was his major [did he major] in college?
2 〈동식물의〉 a family
♦ 콩과 the pulse family / 고양이과 동물 animals belonging to the cat family
▶ 호랑이는 고양이과의 맹수다 The tiger is a fierce member of the cat family.

과 課 1 〈교과〉 a lesson ♦ 제5과 Lesson 5; the fifth lesson
♦ 이 과가 끝나면 시험을 치르겠다 I'm going to give you a test when we finish this lesson.
▶ 제1과부터 시작하자 Let's begin at Lesson 1.
2 〈부서〉 a section; a department
♦ 인사과 the personnel section [department] / 판매[경리]과 the sales [accounts] section
♦ [會話]「그는 어느 과입니까?」「총무과입니다」 "Which section does he work in?" "He's in the general affairs section."

과감 果敢 ♦ 과감성 〈용감〉 boldness; daring; fearless; 〈단호〉 resoluteness; decisiveness; determination
—**과감하다** bold; daring; intrepid; resolute; determined

♦과감한 공격 a daring [bold] attack / 과감하게 resolutely; daringly; in a decisive manner / 과감한 조치를 취하다 adopt drastic measures; take up a drastic measure; take a decisive [bold, resolute] step / 과감히 말하다 express oneself daringly
▶그 사람은 과감하기로 유명하다 He is well known for his intrepidity.
▶그들은 적과 과감히 맞섰다 They fought resolutely [boldly] against their enemy.

과객 過客 a foot passenger; a traveler; a wayfarer; a transient

과거 科擧 〔史〕 the civil service examination —**과거하다** 〈급제하다〉 pass the civil service examination

과거 過去 1 〈지난 날〉 the past; the bygone days; time past
♦과거의 past; bygone / 과거의 사람[것] (口) a has-been / 과거의 역사 the history of the past / 과거의 일 things of the past; past events; bygones; has-beens / 과거 5년 동안 for [during] the past [last] five years / 먼 과거에 in the distant past / 과거를 잊고 새 생활을 다시 시작하다 forget about the past and start (life) all over again / 과거를 회고하다 look back into [upon] the past / 과거에 살다 live in the past
▶그 전쟁도 이미 먼 과거의 일이 되었다 That war is far in the past.
▶과거는 돌이킬 수 없다 What is done cannot be undone.
▶과거는 과거다 Let bygones be bygones.
▶그런 일은 과거에는 아주 흔한 일이었다 Such a thing was very common in the past [in olden times].
2 〈경력(前歷)〉 one's past
♦과거가 있는 여자 a woman with [who has] a (shady) past [sth to hide]
▶그 여자는 과거가 있다고들 한다 She is rumored to have a shady past.
▶그의 과거는 모르겠다 I don't know his past.
3 〈시제〉 the past (tense); the preterit(e)
■一분사 a past participle (略 p.p.) —시제 the past tense —완료 (시제) the past perfect (tense) —진행 the past progressive —형 the past form [tense] (of a verb)

과거장 過去帳 〔佛敎〕 an obituary; a death register [roll] (in a family) ♦과거장에 기록되다 die; join the ranks of the dead; be numbered among the dead.

과격 過激 being radical [extreme, excessive] —**과격하다** 〈급진적〉 radical; 〈폭력적〉 violent; 〈과도·극단적〉 excessive; extreme
♦과격한 사상 radical [extreme] ideas / 과격한 수단 a drastic [a radical, an extreme] measure / 과격한 학생 운동 radical student activities / 과격해지다 go to extremes; go too far; be too radical [violent]
▶네 제안은 너무 과격하다 Your proposal is too drastic.
▶그는 곧잘 과격한 언사를 쓴다 He often uses violent language.
▶그는 과격한 운동으로 건강을 해쳤다 He has injured his health by taking excessive [too much] exercise.
■一분자 a radical element (※종종 복수형으로 씀) : 좌우 양파의 과격분자 extremist elements on both the right and the left —주의 〈급진주의〉 radicalism; 〈극단주의〉 extremism —주의자 a radical; an extremist —파 the radicals; a radical party; 〈러시아 혁명 때의〉 the Bolsheviks : 과격파 학생 a radical student

과공 過恭 ♦과공은 비례라 (口) It is impolite to be too modest. —**과공하다** overmodest

과꽃 〔植〕 a China aster

과남하다 過濫— 〈be〉 more than one deserves ⇨ 과람하다

과납 過納 payment in excess —**과납하다** pay excessively [in excess] ■一액 an amount paid in excess

과 냉(각) 過冷(却) 〔化〕 supercooling —**과 냉(각)하다** supercool 〈water〉; superfuse ■一액체 a supercooled liquid

과녁 a target; a mark
♦과녁의 한복판 (hit) the bull's eye / 과녁을 겨냥하다 aim at the mark [target] / 과녁을 맞히다 [빗나가다] hit [miss] the mark [target]
▶그는 권총으로 과녁을 겨누었다 He aimed his pistol at the target.
▶화살은 과녁에 명중했다 The arrow hit the mark.
■一빼기 the right opposite side : 과녁빼기 집 the house on the right opposite side; the house in the right opposite direction

과년 瓜年 1 〈나이의〉 a marriageable age; the age of marriage
♦과년찬 말 a marriageable [nubile] daughter / 과년차다 ripe for marriage
2 〈임기의〉 the last year of one's term of service

과년도 過年度 the past (fiscal [financial]) year ♦과년도의 회계 보고 the financial report for the previous year ■一지출 defrayment belonging to the preceding financial year

과년하다 過年— overage for the marriage; (be) past the marriageable age
♦과년한 말 a daughter delayed in marriage / 과년한 처녀 an old maid; a spinster

과다 過多 superabundance; plethora; (an) excess; superfluity —**과다하다** excessive; superabundant; too much [many]
♦인원이 과다한 overstaffed 〈office〉 / 여름 의류의 재고가 과다하다 be overstocked with summer clothing
■一공급— an excess of supply; oversupply 영양— excessive nutrition 위산— 〔醫〕 acid dyspepsia; hyperacidity; excess acid in the stomach 인구— ⇨ 과잉〈인구~〉 지방— excessive fat; obesity

과단 果斷 quick [prompt] decision; resolution —**과 단 하 다** decide [determine, resolve] promptly

과단성 果斷性 decisiveness; firmness of character; promptness in decision
♦과단성 있는 사람 a man of quick decision; a man of determined [decided] character; a decisive person / 과단성 있게 행동하다[있는

조치를 취하다] take prompt [quick] action; take resolute steps
▶ 그는 과단성이 없다 He is an irresolute person. ≒ He lacks decisiveness.

과당 果糖 〔化〕 fructose; levulose; fruit sugar

과당 過當 ―**과당하다** excessive;〈터무니 없는〉exorbitant;〈부당한〉undue; unreasonable;〈분에 넘치는〉undeserved
■―**경쟁** an excessive [cutthroat] competition : 과당 경쟁을 배제[억제]하다 eliminate [refrain from] excessive competitions ―**요금** an excessive charge : 나는 과당 요금을 징수당했다 I was forced to pay an excessive charge.

과대 誇大 exaggeration ⇨ 과장(誇張) ―**광고** a puff; a sensational [bombastic] advertisement; an excess [exaggerated, extravagant] advertisement [ad] : 과대 광고를 단속하다 control [check] an exaggerated advertisement

과대 過大 ―**과대하다** too big [great]; too much; excessive; extravagant; inordinate
◆ 과대하게 excessively; exorbitantly; extravagantly; unduly; too much
▶ 그는 손해액을 과대하게 추산했다 He overestimated the damages.
■―**도시** an excessively large city

과대망상 誇大妄想 delusions of grandeur ◆ 과대 망상에 빠지다 fall into expansive delusion ―**증** 〔醫〕 megalomania ―**증 환자** a megalomaniac

과대시하다 過大視― exaggerate; attach exaggerated importance (to) ▶ 그는 그 사건을 과대시하고 있다 He attaches too much importance to the affair.

과대평가 過大評價 overestimation; overvaluation; overrating
―**과대평가하다** overestimate; overvalue; overrate; think too highly of; have too high an opinion of
◆ 인격을 과대 평가하다 overestimate sb's character / 작품을 과대 평가하다 overrate [overestimate] a work
▶ 그는 자신의 능력을 과대 평가했다 He overrated [overestimated] his own ability.
▶ 그의 능력을 과대 평가하지 마라 Don't overestimate his ability.

과도 過渡 ◆ 과도적인 transitional ■―**내각** a caretaker [an interim] cabinet ―**정부** an interim government

과도 果刀 a fruit knife

과도기 過渡期 a transition [transitional] period [stage]; a period [an age] of transition
◆ 과도기적 현상 a transient phenomenon / 과도기의 문학[문화] literature [culture] in a transition period / 과도기의 한국 Korea in transition / 소년에서 성인으로 넘어가는 과도기에 during the transition from boyhood to manhood
▶ 지금은[한국 경제는 지금] 과도기다 We are [Korea's economy is] now in a period of transition.
▶ 그 나라는 사회주의에서 자본주의로 옮겨가는 과도기에 있다 The country is in the stage of transition from socialism to capitalism.

과도하다 過度― excessive; too much; immoderate; inordinate
◆ 과도한 일[노동] overwork; excessive work; too much work / 과도하게 too much; excessively; immoderately; to excess; to an undue extent / 과도한 운동을 하다 take excessive exercise / 과도하게 먹다 eat too much; overeat / 눈을 과도하게 사용하다 overtax one's eyes
▶ 그는 과도한 음주로 건강을 해쳤다 Excessive drinking ruined [undermined] his health.
▶ 내게 과도한 기대는 하지 마시오 Don't expect too much of me.
▶ 그는 과도한 요구를 했다 He made an excessive [extravagant] demand.
▶ 그런 과도한 요구는 들어줄 수 없다 I cannot satisfy such an unreasonable demand.
▶ 공부를 과도하게 하면 안된다 You must not overstudy [study too hard].

과동 過冬 wintering ⇨ 월동(越冬)

과두정치 寡頭政治 oligarchy; oligarchic government ◆ 과두 정치의 oligarchic(al)

과람하다 過濫― undeserved; unmerited; (be) more than one deserves
▶ 이렇게 과람한 보수를 받아서 황송합니다 I'm afraid I hardly deserve this sort of remuneration.
▶ 그는 사환에게 팁을 과람하게 주었다 He tipped the waiter generously [handsomely].

과량 過量 an excess (of quantity)

과로 過勞 overwork; excessive labor; overexertion; strain
▶ 신경 쇠약은 흔히 정신적 과로가 원인이다 Excessive mental labor often causes nervous breakdown.
▶ 아버지는 과로로 병이 나셨다 My father fell ill from [got sick through] overwork. ≒ My father became ill [broke down] because of overworking.
―**과로하다** overwork oneself; work too hard; exert oneself too much
▶ 당신은 요즈음 과로하고 있지 않습니까? Haven't you been working too hard lately?
▶ 부디 과로하지 않기를 바랍니다 I do hope you're not letting yourself overworked.
■―**사**(死) death from overwork

과료 科料 〔法〕 a fine; a minor fine
◆ 약간의 과료를 물고 석방되다 get off with a small [light] fine / 과료에 처하다 fine sb; impose a fine (on [upon] sb)
▶ 이 규칙을 위반하는 사람은 2만원의 과료에 처해진다 A person who violates this rule will be fined twenty thousand won.

과료 過料 a fine for default ⇨ 과태료(過怠料)

과립 顆粒 a granule ◆ 과립 모양의 granular; granulated《sugar》 ■―**형성** 〔醫〕 granulation

과망간산 過―酸 〔化〕 permanganic acid
■―**염** a permanganate ―**칼륨** potassium permanganate : 과망간산 칼륨 표백 permanganate bleaching

과명 科名 〈학과명〉 the name of a department; 〔生〕〈분류〉 a family name

과목 果木 a fruit tree ⇨ 과수(果樹)

과목 科目 1 〈학과〉 a subject; a lesson; 〈과정〉 a course (of study); 〈교과목〉 a curriculum 《*pl.* -la, ~s》
▶ 수학은 내가 좋아하는[잘하는] 과목이다 Mathematics is my favorite [strong(↔weak)] subject.
2 〈항목〉 an item ◆ 자료를 과목별로 분류하다 classify the data / 청구서를 과목으로 나누다 itemize a bill
■ 계정— items of an account 교양— the academic liberal arts subject 선택— an elective [optional] subject [course] 시험— examination subjects 입시— the subjects of the entrance examination 《for a university》 필수— a required [compulsory] subject

과묵하다 寡默— taciturn; reserved; reticent; uncommunicative ▶ 그는 과묵한 사람이다 He is a man of few words. ⇌ He is reticent [reserved]. ⇌ He is a clam [taciturn] person.

과문하다 寡聞— unread; limited in knowledge ◆ 과문해서 being poor in knowledge
▶ 과문한 탓에 그런 일은 알지 못합니다 I am too inexperienced to know anything about it.
▶ 그런 얘기는 과문해서 모르겠습니다 I am afraid I've heard nothing about it.

과물 果物 〈총칭〉 fruit; fruitage ■ —전 a fruit store [shop]

과민 過敏 sensitiveness; 〈신경의〉 nervousness —**과민하다** too sensitive [keen]; 〔醫〕 hypersensitive (to, about); oversensitive 〈신경이〉 nervous; allergic (to); 〈신경질적인〉 jumpy
▶ 그는 건강에 과민하다 He worries too much about his health.
▶ 그녀는 담배 연기에 과민하다 She is very sensitive to cigaret smoke.
▶ 그 책의 저자는 비평에 과민했다 The author of the book was sensitive to criticism.
▶ 비행기 소음으로 모두 신경이 과민해져 있었다 The noise of airplanes was grating on everyone's nerves [was getting everyone's nerves on edge].
■ 신경— morbid sensitiveness; neurosis : 그는 신경 과민이다 He is all nerves [too nervous]. ■ —성 hypersensitiveness —증 〔醫〕 erethism; hyperesthesia; allergy

과밀 過密 overcrowding; congestion; 〈인구의〉 overpopulation
—**과밀하다** overcrowded; congested; crammed; 〈인구가〉 overpopulated
▶ 그 도시의 남서부는 인구가 과밀하다 The southwestern part of the city is overpopulated [densely populated].
■ —거주 overcrowding —다이어그램 〔鐵〕 an overcrowded [a congested] train [railroad] schedule; a crammed schedule of railway operation —학급 an overcrowded class

과밀도시 過密都市 an overpopulated [overpopulous] town [city]; an overcrowded city
▶ 공업화는 과밀 도시를 탄생시킨다 Industrialization brings about overpopulated cities.

과밀지역 過密地域 an overpopulated area [region, district]
▶ 나는 서울과 같은 과밀 지역에서는 살고 싶지 않다 I don't like to live in an overcrowded [a congested] area like Seoul.

과반 過半 the greater part [number] (of) (⇨ 과반수) ▶ 목적의 과반은 성취되었다 Our purpose has practically been accomplished.

과반수 過半數 a majority; more than half 《the members》

> **解說** *majority*는 「대다수」와 「절대 다수」의 두 가지 뜻으로 쓰인다. 전자의 뜻으로는 보통 the와 함께 총칭적으로 취급한다. 후자의 뜻으로는 가산 명사 취급하여 보통 단수형으로 쓰며, 득표수나 의석수 등에 대해 쓴다.

◆ 과반수를 얻다 get [win, obtain] a [an absolute] majority / 국회에서 과반수를 차지하다 [차지하지 못하다] hold [lack] a majority in the national assembly
▶ 그 결정은 과반수의 찬성을 얻었다 The decision succeeded in finding a majority.
▶ 당선자[지원자]의 과반수는 대학[지방] 출신이었다 The greater part [majority] of the successful candidates [applicants] were university graduates [from the rural country].
▶ 위원의 과반수는 내 안건에 찬성이었다 The majority of the committee members were in favor of my plan.
▶ 회원의 과반수를 정족수로 한다 A quorum consists of a majority of the members.
▶ 의결은 과반수로 한다 The decision will be made by majority.
▶ 그는 출석 인원 3분의 2이상의 과반수로 의장에 선출되었다 He was elected chairman by a majority of two-thirds or more of those present.

과보호 過保護 overprotection; overprotectiveness
◆ 과보호 어린이 a pampered [an overprotected] child
▶ 그 아이는 과보호로 자랐다 The child grew up overprotected.
—**과보호하다** overprotect
▶ 그 부모는 아이들을 과보호한다 The parents are overly protective of their children.
▶ 그렇게 하는 것이 자녀를 과보호하는 게 아닌지 모르겠습니다 I'm afraid that to do such a thing is to give your child too much protection.

과부 寡婦 a widow; 〈상태〉 widowhood
◆ 과부가 되다 become a widow / 젊어서 과부가 되다 be widowed young / 여생을[죽을 때까지] 과부로 지내다 remain a widow for the rest of *one's* life [until death]
▶ 그녀는 전쟁으로 과부가 되었다 She became a widow [was widowed] because of the war.
▶ 남편이 죽은 후 그녀는 줄곧 과부로 지냈다 She has remained a widow [lived in widowhood] ever since her husband's death.

과부는 은이 서 말이고 홀아비는 이가 서 말이다 〈속담〉 Widows can save money, but widowers can't.

과부 사정은 과부가 안다 〈속담〉 It takes a widow to know a widow's difficulties.

과부족 過不足 overs and shorts; excess and [or] deficiency

♦과부족이 없이 neither more nor less; in proper quantities; just sufficiently / 과부족 없이 하다 avoid extremes; be moderate / 네 가지 재료를 과부족 없이 혼합하다 mix the right amounts of the four ingredients
▶그것은 과부족이 없다 It's neither too much nor too little. ⇌ It's just enough.
과분하다 過分— undeserved; unmerited; unworthy 《of》; too good 《for》
♦과분하게 undeservedly; unmeritedly; more than *one* deserves; above *one's* deserts
▶이런 사례는 제겐 과분합니다 I hardly deserve this sort of remuneration.
▶그것은 그에게는 과분한 명예다 That's a great honor he hardly deserves.
▶그런 과분한 칭찬을 받으니 송구합니다 I'm afraid I don't deserve [am not worthy of] such high praise.
▶그녀는 그에게는 과분한 아내다 She is too good a wife for him.
▶나는 그녀의 과분한 찬사에 어쩔 줄 몰랐다 I felt embarrassed by her lavish compliments.
과불 過拂 overpayment; overpaying
—**과불하다** overpay; pay too much; pay in excess
▶경리는 내게 과불해 준 사실을 깨달았다 The accountant found that he had paid me more than the due amount.
과불급 過不及 excess and [or] deficiency ⇨ 과부족
과붕산 過硼酸 〔化〕 perboric acid ■—염 a perborate
과산 過酸 〔化〕 peracidity ■—류 peracids
과산화 過酸化 ■—나트륨 sodium peroxide —납 lead peroxide —마그네슘 magnesium peroxide —망간 manganese peroxide —물(物) a peroxide; peroxyacids; dioxides —바륨 barium peroxide —수소 hydrogen peroxide —수소수(水) a hydrogen peroxide solution; oxygenated water —작용 peroxidation —질산 peroxonitric acid —철 peroxide of iron; crocus
과선교 跨線橋 an overbridge; an overpass; 《英》 a flyover
과세 過歲 celebration [observation] of the New Year —**과세하다** celebrate [observe] the New Year
과세 課稅 taxation; assessment; imposition of taxes; 〈세금〉 a tax; a duty
♦과세 대상이 되다 be subject to [liable for] taxation; be taxable; be an object of taxation; be assessable; 〈관세의〉 be dutiable / 벌칙 과세하다 place a tax penalty 《on》
▶이것은 과세 대상이다 This is taxable. ⇌ This is subject to [liable for] taxation.
▶가난한 사람들은 과세가 면제된다 The poor are exempted from taxation.
—**과세하다** tax; impose [levy] a tax [charge] 《on》; 〈관세를〉 levy duties 《on》
♦중과세하다 tax 《luxury goods》 heavily; impose [levy] a heavy tax 《on》/ 재산세를 과세하다 tax *sb's* property
▶부자나 가난한 사람이나 똑같이 과세하는 것은 불공평하다 It is unfair to tax rich and poor alike.
▶대부분의 나라에서 술과 담배는 과세된다 Alcohol and tobacco are taxed in most countries.
■**누진—** progressive tax **배당—** levying tax on stock dividends **분리—** separate taxation **소급—** back taxes **이중—** double taxation **인정—** optional taxation **자본—** a capital levy **종합—** general [consolidated] taxation **중—** heavy taxation ■**—가액** the taxable amount; 〈평가액〉 the assessed value **—거래** taxable transaction **—기간** taxable period **—대장** a tax roll **—범위** the scope of assessment **—소득** the taxable [assessable] income **—원칙** principles of taxation **—율** the tax rate **—조정** tax schedule **—최저액** a minimum taxable level; a tax floor **—특례** tax exception **—표준** tax basis **—품** a taxable article; 〈세관의〉 a dutiable [customable] article
과소 過少 ▶그는 소득을 과소 신고했다 He understated his income. **—과소하다** too few; too little ■**—생산** underproduction **—소비** underconsumption
과소 過疏 〈인구의 부족〉 underpopulation (↔ overpopulation); 〈인구의 감소〉 depopulation
♦인구 과소로 어려움을 겪다 suffer from depopulation
▶그 마을은 인구 과소가 되고 있다 The village is losing population.
—**과소하다** underpopulated
♦인구 과소한 마을 an underpopulated [a thinly populated] village
—지역 an underpopulated [a depopulated] region [area]
과소평가 過小評價 underestimation; underrating
—**과소평가하다** underestimate; underrate; belittle
▶그는 자신의 힘을 과소 평가하고 있다 He underestimates his power.
▶자신을 과소 평가하지 마라 Don't belittle yourself.
과소하다 寡少— 〈아주 적다〉 very little [few]; scanty
과속 過速 overspeed; excessive speed ♦과속으로 달리다 overspeed **—시험** an overspeed test **—차량** an overspeeding vehicle
과수 果樹 a fruit tree
▶내 동생은 과수를 재배한다 My brother grows fruit trees.
■**—원** an orchard **—재배** fruit growing [cultivation] **—재배업자** a fruit grower [farmer]; an orchardist [orchardman]
과수 寡守 a widow ⇨ 과부(寡婦)
과시 誇示 ostentation 《of *one's* power》; display 《of *one's* courage》; showing off
—**과시하다** show off (proudly) 《*one's* talent》; display 《*one's* knowledge》 ostentatiously; make a display [parade] of; parade 《*one's* wealth》
♦무력 행사로 국력을 과시하다 flaunt the nation's power by the use of arms / 권력을 과시하다 show off *one's* power
▶그는 늘 그의 해박한 지식을 과시한다 He

always makes a display of his vast knowledge.
▶ 강대국들은 서로 군사력을 과시하고 있다 The superpowers are making an ostentatious display of their military strength.

과식 過食 overeating; excessive eating; surfeit; eating too much
▶ 과식은 위장에 좋지 않다 Overeating is bad for the stomach.
─**과식하다** eat too much; overeat *oneself*; eat more than is good (for *one*)
◆ 과식하여 탈이 나다 overeat *oneself* sick / 과식히여 토하다 vomit from repletion
▶ 배가 아픈 것은 네가 과식했기 때문이다 Your stomachache comes from overeating.
■─**증(症)** bulimia; binge eating

과신 過信 overconfidence; excessive confidence
─**과신하다** be too confident (of); be overconfident (in)
◆ 자신의 능력을 과신하다 have too much confidence in *oneself*; overestimate *one's* own abilities
▶ 현대인들은 과학기술을 과신하고 있다 People today are placing too much confidence in science and technology.

과실 果實 1 〈과일〉 a fruit; 〈견과〉 a nut; 〈장과〉 a berry; (총칭) fruit
◆ 작은 과실 a fruitlet / 과실의 수확 a fruit crop / 과실을 맺다 bear [produce] fruit / 과실을 재배하다 grow fruit
2 〔法〕〈수익물〉 fruit; 〔商〕 profits
◆ 과실이 생기다 yield a profit
■**법정[천연]─** legal [natural] fruits ─**분류학** carpology ─**선별기** a fruit grader ─**송금 remittance of overseas investment returns** ─**에센스** fruit essence ─**운반선** a fruit carrier ─**주** fruit wine [liqueur] ─**채취기** fruit gather ─**학자** a carpologist

과실 過失 〈잘못·실수〉 a fault; a mistake; a blunder; an error; a misstep; 〔法〕 misfeasance; negligence
◆ 업무상의 과실 professional negligence / 작은 과실 a minor error [mistake] / 과실 책임의 원칙 〔法〕 the principle of liability arising from negligence / 과실로 by mistake [accident]; through *one's* fault; in error
▶ 그것은 내 과실이다 It's my fault.
▶ 그 화재의 원인은 과실입니까, 아니면 방화입니까? Was the cause of the fire accidental or incendiary?
▶ 그 살인이 과실인지 고의인지 알 수가 없다 There is no way of telling whether that killing was accidental or intentional.
▶ 아무의 과실도 아니다 Nobody is to blame.
〈과실이〉 사람은 누구나 과실이 있다 To err is human.
▶ 그것은 과실이 아니라 고의로 한 짓이다 It was not done by accident, but by design.
〈과실을〉 과실을 저지르다 commit an error [a blunder]; be guilty of a blunder / 과실을 아무의 죄로 돌리다 lay a fault to *sb's* charge [at *sb's* door]
▶ 그는 큰 과실을 저질렀다 He made a big mistake. ⇒ He committed a gross error [an awful blunder].
▶ 그녀는 내 과실을 눈감아 주었다 She winked at [passed over] my blunder.
▶ 그는 자기 과실을 바로잡아 보려고 하지 않는다 He doesn't try to correct his faults.
■**중─**〔法〕 gross negligence ■**─범** a careless offense; criminal negligence ─**사(死)** ⇒ 사고(~사) ─**상해(죄)** accidental [unintentional] infliction of injury

과실치사(죄) 過失致死(罪) accidental homicide, involuntary manslaughter; homicide by misadventure
▶ 그는 업무상 과실 치사 혐의로 체포되었다 He was arrested on suspicion of professional negligence resulting in death.

과언 過言 ◆…이라고 해도 과언이 아니다 It is not too much to say that…; It is no exaggeration to say that…; It can [may] safely be said that…
▶ 이 건물은 한국에서 가장 아름다운 건축물이라고 해도 과언이 아니다 It is not too much [no exaggeration] to say that this building is the most beautiful in Korea.
▶ 그는 국민적 영웅이라고 해도 과언이 아니다 It may safely be said that he is a national hero.

과업 課業 1 〈할 일〉 a task [duty]
◆ 과업을 맡기다 set [assign] *sb* to a task [job]; impose a duty upon *sb* / 과업을 맡다 take a task upon *oneself* / 과업을 완수하다 do [carry out] *one's* task
▶ 그는 그 문제를 해결해야 할 과업을 안고 있다 He has the task of solving the problem.
2 〈학과〉 a lesson; schoolwork; schoolteaching
■**─관리** task management ─**기준법** task basis method

과연 果然 〈생각한 대로〉 as *one* thought [expected]; as was [had been] expected; 〈확실히〉 sure enough; to be sure; 〈참으로〉 indeed; really
▶ 과연 그렇군 So it is, to be sure!
▶ 과연 그것은 사실이었다 It was really the case.
▶ 과연 그 아버지에 그 아들이다 He is a son worthy of his father.
▶ 그는 과연 거기 있었다 Sure enough there he was.
▶ 과연 그 팀은 첫 우승을 차지했다 The team won its first championship as we had expected.
▶ 과연 그녀는 독신이었다 She was single, just as I had thought.
▶ 과연 그가 올까요? Will he actually come?
▶ 그것이 과연 사실일까요? Is it really true? ⇒ Can it be true?
▶ 우리는 과연 다시 만나게 될까요? Shall we ever meet again?

과열 過熱 overheating; superheating
◆ 과열 입시 경쟁 excessive competition for entrance exam / 경제의 과열을 막다 prevent the economy from overheating
▶ 반체제 운동이 과열 상태에 이르렀다 The

antiestablishment movement went too far [got out of hand].
—과열하다 overheat; superheat
◆과열된 경제[엔진] an overheated economy [engine] / 과열된 과외 교육 the overheated out-of-class lessons
▶ 모터가 과열됐다 The motor is overheated.
▶ 세계 경제가 과열되고 있다 The world economy is overheating.
■—경기(景氣) an excessive economic boom —경보 a temperature alarm —기(器) a superheater —도 the degree of superheat —증기 superheated vapo(u)r

과염소산 過鹽素酸 〔化〕 perchloric acid
■—칼륨 potassium perchlorate

과오 過誤 〈잘못〉a mistake; an error; 〈과실〉a fault; 〈실패〉 a blunder; 〈죄과〉 an offense
◆과오를 깨닫다 find out one's mistake; be convinced of one's error / 과오를 뉘우치다 repent one's fault / 과오를 바로잡다 correct [remedy, amend] a fault; mend oneself / 과오를 범하다 commit offense [a fault]; err; make a mistake / 과오를 사과하다 apologize for an error [a mistake] / 과오를 인정하다 admit [acknowledge] a mistake
▶ 그것은 모두 나의 과오다 It's all my fault. ⇌ I am to blame for it all.
▶ 그는 큰 과오를 범했다 He made a terrible mistake.

과옥소산 過沃素酸 〔化〕 periodic acid ■—염 a periodate

과외 課外 extracurricular work ◆과외의 extracurricular; extracurriculum; 〈보충의〉 supplementary; outside / 과외의 독서 outside [supplementary] reading
■—강의[수업] an extracurricular lecture [lesson] (in English) —공부 out-of-school studies —활동 extracurricular [after-school, out-of-school] activities

과욕 過慾 greed; avarice; greediness; covetousness
▶ 그는 돈에 과욕이 있다 He is avaricious [greedy] for money.
—과욕하다 greedy; avaricious; covetous
◆명예[지식]에 대해 과욕하다 be greedy [hungry] for fame [knowledge]

과욕하다 寡慾— unselfish; disinterested; content with little; wantless ◆과욕한 사람 a man of few wants

과용 過用 spending too much
◆수면제 과용으로 죽다 die of an overdose of sleeping pills
—과용하다 〈돈을〉 spend too much [to excess]; be extravagant [prodigal] (with); 〈약을〉 take an overdose of a drug [medicine]
▶ 그 여자는 화장품에 돈을 과용한다 She spends too much money on cosmetics.

과원 課員 a member of the section staff; (총칭) the staff of a section
◆총무과 과원 일동 the staff of the general affairs section
▶ 이것은 경리과 과원 일동으로부터 온 것입니다 This is from the staff of the accounting section.

과유불급 過猶不及 Too much is as bad as too little. ⇌ Too much water drowns the miller.
과육 果肉 〔植〕 sarcocarp; fruit flesh; pulp
과융해 過融解 〔化〕 superfusion
과음 過淫 sexual indulgence; overindulgence in sexual pleasure —과음하다 indulge (oneself) in sex

과음 過飮 overdrinking; excessive drinking; intemperance (in drinking)
▶ 그는 과음으로 병이 났다 He drank himself sick [into illness].
—과음하다 overdrink; drink too much [to excess]; take [have] a drop too much ◆과음하여 몸을 해치다 overdrink oneself
▶ 그는 어젯밤에 과음했다 He drank too much last night.

과일 a fruit; (총칭) fruit (▶종류를 말할 때는 복수형을 쓰지만 various kinds of나 different sorts of 등과 같이 쓸 때는 단수형이 됨)
◆많은 과일 much [plenty of] fruit / 신선한 [익은] 과일 fresh [ripe] fruit / 통조림한 과일 canned fruit / 한 바구니의 과일 a basket of fruit / 과일 씨 빼는 기계 a fruit seeder / 과일 맛 fruit taste / 과일의 껍질을 벗기다 〈바나나 등〉 peel a fruit; 〈사과 등〉 pare a fruit / 과일을 따다 pick [pluck, collect, gather] fruit / 슈퍼마켓에서 과일을 좀 사다 buy some fruit at the supermarket
▶ 이 지역에서는 여러 가지 과일이 난다 This area produces a variety of fruits.
▶ 과일을 좋아하십니까? Do you like fruit?
▶ 우리는 과일을 좀더 많이 먹어야 한다 We should eat more fruit.
▶ 그 가게에서는 여러 가지 과일을 판다 They sell various fruits [various kinds of fruit] at the store.
■—가게 a fruit store [shop]; 〈노점〉 a fruit stand —나무 ⇨ 과수(果樹) —바구니 a fruit basket —벗기개 fruit peeler —샐러드 fruit salad —요구르트 fruit yogurt —장수 a fruit dealer [seller, man]; a fruiterer —재배 fruit culture —젤리 fruit jelly —주스 fruit juice —칼 ⇨ 과도(果刀)

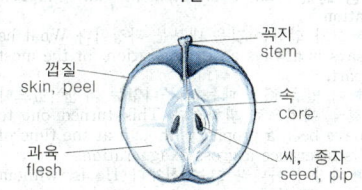
— 과일 —
꼭지 stem
껍질 skin, peel
속 core
과육 flesh
씨, 종자 seed, pip

과잉 過剩 〈잉여〉 a surplus; overabundance; superabundance; 〈과도함〉 (an) excess
▶ 우리 회사는 인원 과잉이다 Our office is overstaffed.
▶ 그들은 친절 과잉이다 They are overly [excessively] kind.
▶ 작년에 우리 나라는 쌀 과잉이었다 Our country had a surplus of rice last year.
—과잉하다 superfluous; excessive; too much;

■공급— (an) oversupply 생산— overproduction: 이 지역은 농산물이 생산 과잉이다 This district has a surplus of agricultural products. 의식— overconsciousness 인구— overpopulation: 서울은 인구 과잉이다 There are too many people in Seoul. ⇒ Seoul is overpopulated. 정력— a plethora of energy ■—노동력 surplus [redundant] labor —방위 excessive [unjustifiable] self-defense —배란(排卵) superovulation —보호 overprotection —생산 overproduction: 자동차 회사들은 금년에 과잉생산을 하고 있다 Automobile manufacturers are overproducing this year. —영양 overnutrition —인구 surplus [overflowing] population: 과잉 인구로 신음하다 groan under the burden of overpopulation —인원 superfluous personnel; supernumeraries —전자 excess electron —진료 unnecessary tests and medication —충성 excessive devotion; overloyalty —투여 〈약의〉(醫) overdosage —투자 overinvestment; overcapitalization

과자 菓子 (총칭) confectionery; sweet stuff; 〈생과자〉 a cake; 〈당과〉 (美) (a piece of) candy; 〈비스킷 등〉 a cookie; 〈파이 등〉 pastry ◆과자를 만들다[굽다] make [bake] a cake / 손님에게 차와 과자를 대접하다 serve tea and cake to a guest
▶과자 드세요 Please help yourself to the cake.
■막— a cheap cake 차— a tea cake —가게 a confectionery (shop); (美) a candy store; (英) a sweet [pastry] shop —상자 a box of cake —장수 a confectioner —접시[쟁반] a cake dish [tray]

과작 寡作 ◆과작이다 be not [far from] prolific; produce *one's* works at rare intervals
▶시인으로서는 그는 과작이다 As a poet, he is not prolific.
▶그녀는 과작하는 작가였다 She wrote very few books. ⇒ She was an unprolific writer.

과장 科長 the head [director, chief] of a department

과장 誇張 (an) overstatement; (an) exaggeration
▶그가 말하는 것은 대부분 과장이다 What he says is always an exaggeration for the most part.
▶이 말을 했을 때는 터무니없는 과장이었으나 결국 예언으로 밝혀졌다 This turned out to have been a prophecy, though at the time of its utterance a gross exaggeration.
▶과장이 아니라 그는 천재다 He is, without exaggeration, a genius.
—**과장하다** overstate; exaggerate
◆과장된 overstated; exaggerated; high-flown; inflated / 과장하여 exaggeratingly; with exaggeration; bombastically
▶그 여자는 과장해서 말하는 버릇이 있다 She has a tendency to exaggerate things.
▶그는 언제나 과장해서 말하기 때문에 친구들은 그를 믿지 않게 되었다 His constant exaggeration made his friends distrust him.
▶기자는 사실을 과장하지 않도록 조심해야 한다 Reporters should be careful not to overstate facts.
■—법 hyperbole —증(症) mythomania

과장 課長 the chief of a section; a section chief ◆김 설계과장 Chief Kim of the Design Section
■—대리 an acting chief of a section; a deputy section manager —보좌 an assistant section chief

과적 過積 overloading; overcharge
▶이 트럭은 과적이다 This truck is overloaded.
▶경찰이 과적을 감시하고 있다 The police are keeping an eye on overloading.
▶과적 차량 진입 금지 (게시) No overloaded vehicles.
—**과적하다** overload; overfreight

과전압 過電壓 overvoltage; overpotential
■—화학 chemical overpotential

과점 寡占 (經) oligopoly —수요— oligopsony [àləgápsəni] ■—가격 an oligopoly price —경제[시장] an oligopoly economy [market]

과정 過程 (a) process; a course; (醫) a period ◆성장 과정 the process of (*one's*) growth / 진화 과정 the process of the evolution (of animals) / 과정을 밟다 go through the process [stage] (of)
▶협상 과정에서 그 문제가 다루어졌다 The problem was mentioned in the process of negotiation.
▶틀림없이 포장 과정에서 착오가 약간 있었나 보다 There must have been some mistake during the packing process.
■생산[제조]— a process of production [manufacture]; a production [manufacturing] process

과정 課程 〈학과〉 a course; 〈전교과〉 a curriculum 《*pl*. -la, ~s》
◆4년 과정 a four-year course / 의무교육 과정 compulsory education course / 고교 과정을 마치다 finish a course in [of] high school (▶in 이 보통임); finish a high school (course); finish [complete] the whole course of a high school
▶그는 올봄에 대학 과정을 마쳤다 He finished [graduated from] college this spring.
▶위 사람은 본교 소정의 과정을 수료하였음을 증명함 This is to certify the above-mentioned has completed the prescribed course of this school.
■—표 a school timetable; a schedule

과제 課題 1 〈주제〉 a subject; a theme; a thesis 《*pl*. -ses》
◆논문의 과제 the subject of a thesis; a thesis subject / 과제를 주다 give (out) a subject 《for composition》 / …이라는 과제로 글을 쓰다 write a composition [an essay] on the subject of…
▶작문의 과제는 「우정에 관하여」이다 The theme assigned for the composition is "On Friendship."
2 〈해결할 문제〉 a problem; a question
◆당면 과제 an urgent problem [question]; a problem at issue / 금후의 [해결해야 할] 과제로

남겨두다 leave a problem to be solved
▶ 우리는 당면 과제의 해결을 위해 최선을 다해야 한다 We must do our best to solve the problems which confront us now.
3 〈숙제〉 homework; a home task; (美) an assignment; exercises
◆ 여름 방학 과제 summer homework [exercises] / 학습 과제 a study assignment; a school project / 과제를 주다 set sb a task; give sb an assignment 《of 10 arithmetic problems》
▶ 영문법에 관한 과제를 내주겠다 I will give you English grammar exercises.
■ —장 an exercise book; a work [homework] book

과줄 a fried honey cake

과중하다 過重— too heavy 《duty》; burdensome 《task》
◆ 과중한 노동 excessively heavy work / 과중한 부담 too great burden; a heavy burden / 과중한 부담을 지우다 overburden; burden too heavily
▶ 국민에게 과중한 세금이 부과되었다 Taxes fell heavily on the people.
▶ 그것은 내 능력으로는 과중한 부담이었다 It was a great strain on my resources.
▶ 국민은 과중한 부담에 신음했다 The people groaned under the heavy burden.

과즙 果汁 fruit juice; 〈음료수〉 a fruit drink

과찬 過讚 overpraise; excessive compliment
—**과찬하다** overpraise; speak very highly; praise [compliment] excessively

과채류 果菜類 fruits and vegetables

과칭 誇稱 (an) exaggeration ⇨ 과장(誇張)

과태료 過怠料 a fine for default; a negligence fine; a penalty fee ◆ 과태료를 부과하다 impose a 《twenty thousand won》 correctional fine

과테말라 〈나라 이름〉 Guatemala; 〈공식명〉 the Republic of Guatemala ◆ 과테말라의 Guatemalan ■ —사람 a Guatemalan

과포화 過飽和 〔化〕 supersaturation ■ —용액 〔증기〕 supersaturated solution [steam]

과표 課標 a standard of assessment; (英) a ratal ■ —액 the taxable amount; (英) the ratal

과피 果皮 the rind 《of a fruit》; the seedcase; the pericarp

과하다 科— 〈형벌을〉 impose 《a fine on sb》; inflict 《a penalty on sb》
▶ 판사는 피고에게 벌금을 과했다 The judge imposed [inflicted] a fine on the accused.
▶ 판사는 그 사람에게 어떤 벌을 과했습니까? What penalty did the judge inflict upon him?
▶ 그는 속도[주차] 위반으로 3만원의 벌금이 과해졌다 He was fined thirty thousand won for speeding [illegal parking].

과하다 課— 1 〈세금 등을〉 lay [impose, levy] 《a tax on sb》
◆ 담배에 세금을 과하다 levy [impose] a tax on tobacco / 중세를 과하다 tax 《the inhabitants》 heavily; impose heavy taxes on 《the rich》
▶ 정부는 그 수입 상품에 세금을 과했다 The government imposed taxes on the imported goods.
2 〈맡기어 하게 하다〉 assign 《a task to sb》; set; task 《sb》
◆ 학생들에게 많은 숙제를 과하다 assign [give, set] a students a lot of homeworks
▶ 네게 과해진 임무를 완수하지 않으면 안 된다 You must perform the task that has been assigned to [set for] you.

과하다 過— 〈지나치다〉 excessive; too much; beyond (all) bounds [limits]; 〈과분하다〉 too good 《for》; undue; undeserved
◆ 과한 노동 overwork; excessive [too much] work / 과한 요구 an unreasonable [excessive] demand / 과한 음주 excessive [too much] drinking / 과하게 excessively; 〈drink〉 too much; immoderately; unduly; to excess; to a fault / 과하게 긴장하여 under too much tension / 농담이 과하다 carry a joke too far
▶ 이 시계는 아이들에게는 과하다 This watch is too good for children.
▶ 저 같은 사람에겐 과한 칭찬입니다 Your praise is more than I deserve.
▶ 내가 벌인 사업은 내 힘에 과한 것 같다 I find myself unequal to what I have undertaken.

과학 科學 science
◆ 과학의 진보 development [advance] of science / 과학의 한 분야 a branch of science / 과학을 응용하다 apply science 《to industry》
▶ 과학의 발달이 반드시 인간을 행복하게 해 주는 것은 아니다 The progress of science does not always make man happy.
■ 기초— basic sciences 사회— social science 순수— pure science 응용— applied science 인문— the humanities 자연— natural [physical] science ■ —계 scientific circles; the world of science; the scientific world —관 a science museum —교육 science education —기술 science and technology; scientific technology [technique] —만능주의 scientism; almighty science —문명 scientific civilization —박물관 a science museum —사상 scientific thought —서(書) a scientific book —소설 science fiction (略 SF); 〈소설 한 편〉 a science-fiction story —수사 scientific crime detection —시대 a scientific age —연구 scientific research —영화 a science film: 공상 과학 영화 a science (fiction) film —용어 scientific terms [terminology] —위성 a science research satellite —자 a scientist —잡지 a science magazine —전(戰) scientific warfare —지식 scientific knowledge —혁명 scientific revolution

과학기술처 科學技術處 the Ministry of Science and Technology

과학적 科學的 scientific
◆ 과학적인 사고방식을 지닌 scientific-minded; science-conscious / 과학적인 방법으로 in a scientific way; scientifically / 과학적으로 생각하다 think scientifically
▶ 과학적인 조사 결과 사고의 원인이 밝혀졌다 A scientific investigation cleared up the cause of the accident.
■ —경영법 scientific management —방법 a

scientific method ―사회주의 scientific socialism ―영농(법) scientific farming

과히 過― 〈너무〉 too 〈very〉 〈much〉; extremely; excessively; to excesss; 〈英〉 overly; 〈별로〉 (not) quite; (not) very; (not) much
▶ 그의 건강 상태는 과히 좋지 않다 His condition is not very good.
▶ 나는 멜론은 과히 좋아하지 않는다 I don't like [care for] melons very [so] much.
▶ 나는 과히 바쁘지 않다 I am not so busy.
▶ 과히 걱정할 것은 없다 You don't have to worry too much.

곽 a case ⇨ 갑(匣)

곽란 癨亂 〔醫〕 cholera nostras [morbus]

관 官 〈정부〉 the government; 〈당국〉 the authorities; 〈공직〉 a government post
♦ 관을 사임하다 resign from [leave] (the) government service / 관에 있다[취임하다] be in [enter (the)] government service

관 冠 1 〈머리에 쓰는〉 a crown; a coronet ♦ 관을 쓰다 wear [put on] a crown **2** 〈족보의〉 a married man

관 貫 1 〈본관〉 a place of origin **2** 〈무게의 단위〉 a kwan (= 3.75 kg) ▶ 그 씨름선수는 체중이 40관이다 The wrestler weighs 40 kwan.

관 棺 a coffin; 〈美〉 a casket ♦ 관에 넣다 lay [rest] (a corpse) in a coffin
▶ 사람의 가치는 관 뚜껑을 덮고 나서야 안다 A man's worth is understood [settled] only when he is laid to rest.
▶ 그 사람은 이미 관 속에 한 발을 들여놓았다 He has had one foot in the grave.

관 款 〈조항〉 an article; clauses; a subsection; 〈각항·항목〉 a provision; terms

관 管 a pipe; a tube; 〈도관〉 a duct; a conduit
♦ 유리 관 a glass tube ■ 가스― a gas pipe 배수― a drainage pipe 시험― a test tube

관 館 〈푸줏간〉 a butcher's (shop) 〈美〉 a meat store [shop]; 〈요정〉 a (fancy) restaurant; 〈큰 건물〉 a large building; a hall
♦ 국립 박물관 the national museum / 도서관 the library / 미술관 an art gallery / 한국관 〈박람회의〉 the Korean Pavilion

-관 -觀 〈견해〉 a view; an outlook
♦ 사회관 one's view of social life / 선입관 (a) preconception / 세계관 an outlook on the world; a world view / 여성관 one's viewpoint on women / 인생관 one's view [philosophy] of life; one's outlook on life
▶ 그 여자의 인생관은 낙관적이면서 동시에 체념적이다 Her view of life is optimistic and at the same time she is apt to resign herself to the will of God.
▶ 그는 잘못된 결혼관을 가지고 있다 He has a mistaken idea [notion, concept] of marriage.

관가 官街 the official world; officialdom; official circles

관개 灌漑 irrigation; watering
▶ 그 강 유역은 눈 녹은 물로 끊이지 않고 관개가 된다 The river basin is continually watered [irrigated] by the melting snow.
▶ 그 지역은 관개가[관개 시설이] 잘 되어 있다 The area is well irrigated [has good irrigation facilities].
―관개하다 irrigate (paddy fields); water
■ ―공사 irrigation works ―농업 irrigation cultivation ―용수 water for irrigation; irrigation water ―용수로 an irrigation ditch [canal] ―저수지 an irrigation reservoir ―지(地) irrigated land

관객 觀客 〈행사·스포츠 등의〉 a spectator; 〈극장 등의〉 an audience (▶ audience는 집합 명사로 보통 단수 취급함); 〈총칭〉 the house
▶ 극장의 관객 a theater audience / 관객이 많다[적다] draw a large [small] audience
▶ 그 패션 쇼에는 관객이 많았다 There were a number of spectators at the fashion show.
▶ 그 영화는 관객이 많이 몰려들었다 The film drew a large audience [house].
■ ―석 a seat ―층 the strata [a type] of audience

관건 關鍵 1 〈빗장〉 a bolt; a (locking) bar **2** 〈핵심〉 a key [pivotal] point; the most important point [part]; the core [heart]
♦ 문제 해결의 관건을 쥐다 hold the key to the solution of the question
▶ 미국이 교섭 성공의 관건을 쥐고 있다 America holds the key to the success of the negotiations.

관계 官界 the official world [circles]; government circles; officialdom
♦ 관계에 있는 사람 a man in official life [in the government service] / 관계에 있다[들어가다] be in [go into, enter] government [public, 〈英〉 the civil] service
▶ 그 사람은 다년간 관계에 몸담고 있었다 He was in public life [in the government service] for many years.
■ ―쇄신 a renovation of officialdom

관계 關係 1 〈관련〉 relation; relationship; (a) connection; 〈이해 관계〉 an interest; a concern

> **解說** *relation*은 사물·사람과의 관련을 의미하는 일반적인 말로, 특히 어떤 관련인가를 문제 삼을 때 쓴다. *relationship*은 relation과 같은 뜻이지만 다소 격식을 차린 말로, 특히 관계의 상태나 정도를 문제로 삼는다. *connection*은 밀접한 관련이 있는 관계를 뜻한다.

♦ 물질과 정신의 관계 the relation between matter and mind / 수요와 공급의 관계 the relation(ship) between supply and demand / 의료 관계의 일 work connected with medicine / 관계가 없다 have no relation (to); have no connection (with) / 관계를 강화[개선]하다 cement relationship [improve relations] (with) / 관계를 끊다 cut off [sever] the connections (with) / 관계를 맺다 establish relations [connections] (with) / 관계를 유지하다 sustain a relation (to)
▶ 누구의 희망과도 관계없이 계절은 바뀐다 The season change, independent of anyone's wishes.
▶ 연령에 관계없이 콘테스트에 참가할 수 있다 You can take part in the contest regardless [irrespective] of ages.
▶ 저 분과는 어떤 관계입니까? 〈인척 관계〉

How are you related to him? ⇒ 〈교제 관계〉 What is your connection with him?
▶ 정치는 국민 생활과 매우 깊은 관계가 있다 Politics has very much to do with the life of the nation.
▶ 그 둘 사이에는 불가분의 관계가 있다 There is an indissoluble connection between the two.
▶ 한국과 중국은 옛날부터 관계가 깊다 Korea and China have long and deep ties.
▶ 그 두 가지 사건은 서로 밀접한 관계가 있었다 The two incidents were closely related to [connected with] each other.
▶ 건강과 절제는 관계가 있다 There is a relation between health and temperance.
▶ 네 말은 이 일과는 관계가 없는 말이다 Your remarks are irrelevant to this matter.
▶ 그것은 나와는 아무 관계가 없다 I have no connection with the matter. ⇒ I have nothing to do with it.
▶ 나는 그 사람과 아무 관계도 없다 I've no connection [nothing to do] with him.
─관계하다 be related (to); be connected (with); connect (*oneself*) (with); concern
2 〈관여〉 participation 《in》; involvement 《in》
▶ 그것은 너와 관계 없는 일이다 That's none of your business [concern].
▶ 나는 그 일과는 아무 관계가 없다 I'm not concerned with the matter. ⇒ I have no share in [no concern with] the matter.
─관계하다 participate 《in》; take part 《in》; be involved 《in》; have to do 《with》
◆ 범죄에 관계하다 participate in a crime / 음모에 관계하다 participate [have a hand] in a scheme; be (a) party to a plot
▶ 그는 그 사업에 관계하고 있었다 He had a share [was interested] with the enterprise.
▶ 그 건에는 관계하지 않는 것이 좋다 You should not participate [take part] in the affair.
▶ 그는 그 수회 사건에 관계되어 있었다 He is involved in that bribery case.
3 〈영향〉 influence; effect
▶ 어느 팀이 이기든 나와는 별 관계가 없다 It matters little to me which team wins.
▶ 가정 환경은 어린아이의 성격에 얼마만큼 관계가 있는가? How much influence does a child's home environment have on his personality?
▶ 기압 관계로 머리가 아프다 I have a headache caused by atmospheric pressure.
▶ 기후 관계로 이 과일은 한국에서는 나지 않는다 This fruit cannot be produced in Korea because of the climate.
─관계하다 affect; have influence 《on》
▶ 그것은 생사에 관계되는 일이다 It is a matter of life and death.
4 〈성관계〉 (sexual) relations [intercourse]; connection ◆ 깊은 관계 an intimate relationship / 불륜의 관계 an illicit relationship; illicit love / 유부녀와 관계를 가지다 have relationships with a married woman
─관계하다 have an intimate relationship; have illicit intercourse 《with》

▶ 민씨는 그 여자와 관계하고 있는 것 같다 Mr. Min seems to have relations with that woman.
■ 거래─ trade connections; business relations 국제─ international relations 대외─ foreign relations 외교─ diplomatic relations : 미국은 이란과의 외교 관계를 단절했다 America broke off diplomatic relations with Iran. 우호─ friendly relationship : 두 나라 사이에 우호 관계가 수립되었다 Friendly relationships have been established between the two countries. 인간─ human relations 인과─ the relation between cause and effect; a causal connection 적대─ hostile relations 전후─ 〈문장의〉 the context 주종─ the relationship of master and servant ■─관청 the government office concerned ─국 the nations concerned ─기관 the authorities concerned; the organs [agencies] concerned ─대명사[형용사, 부사] 〈文法〉 a relative pronoun [adjective, adverb] ─법규 the related laws and regulations ─서류 the documents related 《to the matter》; the relevant documents ─업계 related business circles ─장관 the cabinet ministers concerned ─절 〈文法〉 a relative clause ─회사 an interested concern; 〈계열의〉 a subsidiary [an affiliated] company

관계자 關係者 the persons [parties] concerned; 〈이해 의〉 an interested person [party]; 〈계약의〉 the contracting parties
◆ 관계자 각위(各位) 〈편지의 서두〉 To whom it [this] may concern / 관계자 쌍방 both parties concerned / 관계자 회합 a meeting of interested persons
▶ 관계자 외 출입 금지 (게시) No Entry [《美》 Off Limits] To Unauthorized Persons
■ 보도─ the press (interest) ■─일동 all the parties concerned; all concerned; all interested parties

관골 顴骨 〈解〉 the cheekbone ⇨ 광대뼈
관공리 官公吏 government and municipal officials; public [civil] servants [officials]
관공립 官公立 ■─학교 government and public [communal] schools
관공서 官公署 government and municipal offices; public agencies [offices]
관광 觀光 〈구경〉 sightseeing; 〈사업〉 tourism
◆ 시내 관광 city sightseeing / 관광의 계절 a tourist season
▶ 관광은 그 나라의 큰 산업이다 Tourism is a big industry in the country.
▶ 지난주에 우리는 홍콩으로 관광을 갔었다 We went sightseeing at Hong Kong last week.
─관광하다 go sightseeing; do [see] the sights (of a city); go on a (sightseeing) tour
▶ 그 여자는 하와이에 관광하러 갔다 She went to Hawaii to see the sights [for sightseeing]. ⇒ She went sightseeing in Hawaii. (▶ 이 경우에는 전치사 to를 쓰지 않음)
■─공사 a tourism corporation ─국 a country of tourist attractions ─단 a sightseeing [tourist] party [group] ─도시 a tourist city ─명소 tourist attractions ─버스 a sightseeing [《美俗》 rubberneck] bus ─사업 the

관광객

tourist industry [business, trade]; tourism —사업체 a travel bureau; a tourist agency —사증(査證) tourist visa —선(船) a sightseeing boat —시설 tourist [sightseeing] facilities —안내서 a guidebook for sightseers —안내소 a tourist information office [desk, center]; (게시) Tourist Information —안내원 a tour [sightseeing] guide —업자 a travel [tour (ist)] agent —열차 a sightseeing train —코스 a tourist route —호텔 a tourist [resort] hotel

관광객 觀光客 a tourist; a sightseer; (美俗) a rubberneck ◆관광객 유치 inducement of tourists [sight-seers]
▶제주도는 대개 봄에 관광객으로 붐빈다 Cheju-do is usually full of tourists [sightseers] in spring.
■ 외국인— a foreign tourist

관광여행 觀光旅行 a (sightseeing) tour
◆관광여행을 하다 take a sightseeing trip; sightsee; (美俗) rubberneck

관광지 觀光地 a tourist site [area]; a place for sightseeing; 〈명소〉 the sights; a tourist attraction; 〈보양지〉 a (holiday) resort
▶울릉도는 한국의 유명한 관광지의 하나다 Ullŭngdo is one of the famous sights of Korea.

관구 管區 a district under (its) jurisdiction; 〈경찰의〉 (美) a (police) precinct; 〔가톨릭〕 a province; 〔軍〕 a (military) district
—사령관 a district commander

관군 官軍 the government forces [troops]

관권 官權 government authority [power] ◆관권을 남용하다 abuse government authority; make an improper use of government power
■ —개입 government intervention

관극 觀劇 playgoing; theatergoing —관극하다 go to the theater; go to see a play; enjoy a theatrical performance ■ —회 a theater [(美) box] party

관급 官給 government supply; (美) government issue (略 GI, G. I.) ■ —품 (美) government-issue articles [equipment]; articles supplied by the government

관기 官紀 offical discipline
◆관기를 숙정하다 enforce offical discipline / 관기를 확립하다 establish rigid discipline among officials
▶관기가 해이해졌다 Official discipline became lax [relaxed].
▶오직 사건이 자주 일어나는 것을 보면 관기가 문란해진 것을 알 수 있다 The frequent corruption cases reflect the loose discipline of the office.
■ —문란 a laxity in official discipline; corruption of officialdom —숙정(肅正) (strict) enforcement of official discipline

관내 管內 ◆관내에[를] within [throughout] the jurisdiction [district] (of)
▶신임 지사가 관내를 시찰했다 The new governor made a tour of inspection through his area of jurisdiction.
▶이 경찰서 관내에서 강도 사건이[절도가] 세 건 발생했다 There were three cases of robbery [theft] in [within] the jurisdiction of this police station.

관념 觀念 1 〈개념·생각〉 an idea; a notion; a concept
◆추상적인 관념 an abstract idea / 관념적 논의 an ideal argument / 관념적인 ideological (viewpoint); ideal 《happiness》/ 관념적으로 ideally / 잘못된 관념을 가지다 have a wrong [mistaken] idea [notion, concept] 《of success》
▶그는 사생활에 대한 관념이 없다 He has no sense of privacy.
▶부유한 사람들은 가난이라는 것을 관념적으로밖에 모른다 The wealthy know poverty only in the abstract [conceptually].
2 〈…정신·의식〉 a sense; a spirit
◆국가 관념 a sense of nationality / 책임 관념 (have no) sense of responsibility
▶그 여자는 시간 관념이 없다 She takes no thought [has no sense] of time. ⇒ She has no notion of punctuality.
■ 고정— a fixed idea 《about》; a stereotype 《about》 도덕— a moral ideal : 그는 도덕 관념이 부족하다 He is devoid of moral sense. 생득[본유]— an innate idea ■ —론 〔哲〕 idealism; 〈공론(空論)〉 an empty theory; an academic argument —론자 an idealist —성 ideality —소설[시] an ideological novel [poem] —연합[心] the association of ideas —적 실재론 ideal realism —학 ideology —형태(론) ideology

관능 官能 1 〈기능〉 organic [physical, bodily] functions ◆관능의 functional / 관능적인 질병 a functional disease
2 〈감각〉 (fleshly) sense; 〈육욕〉 carnal desires [lust] ◆관능적 쾌락 sensual (↔spiritual) pleasure / 관능적인 여자 a glamor(ous) girl; (俗) a sexpot / 관능을 만족시키다 satisfy one's carnal desire / 관능을 자극하는 묘사 a sexually stimulating description
■ —미 voluptuous beauty [charm, loveliness, attraction] —소설 a sex novel —장애 a functional disorder [impediment] —주의 sensualism —파 sensualists

관다발 管— 〔植〕 a vascular bundle ⇨ 유관속 (維管束)

관대 寬大 〈너그러움〉 generosity; magnanimity; leniency; broad-mindedness; 〈용인〉 tolerance; clemency
—관대하다 generous (with, to); lenient (with); broad-minded; tolerant (of); be liberal 《to one's opponents》
◆관대한 처우[처벌] lenient treatment [a mild punishment] / 관대한 태도 a broad-minded [tolerant] attitude / 관대하게 generously; liberally; tolerantly / 관대하게 다루다 deal leniently with sb / 반대파에 대하여 관대하다 be liberal to one's opponents
▶그분은 누구에게나 관대하다 He is generous to everybody.
▶그는 내 실수에 관대했다 He was tolerant of my errors.
▶판사는 젊은 피고에게 관대한 판결을 선고했다 The judge pronounced a lenient sentence on the young offender.

▶ 그 애들은 어린아이들이니 장난을 쳐도 좀 관대해야 한다 As they are only children, you ought to be a little more lenient with them when they are naughty.
▶ 우리는 그의 관대함에 크게 감명받았다 We were deeply impressed by his generosity [broad-mindedness].
▶ 그는 포로들을 관대히 다뤘다 He dealt leniently with the prisoners.

관대 棺臺 a bier; 《英》 a feretory

-관데 ▶ 무슨 사연이 있었관데 그를 의심하느냐? On what grounds do you suspect him?
▶ 무슨 이유가 있었관데 그런 먼 곳으로 이사했느냐? How did you move to such a far-off place?
▶ 네가 무엇이관데 그런 짓을 하느냐? What on earth are you doing such a thing?

관동 關東 the Kwandong district ■**—팔경** the eight tourist [scenic] attractions of the Kwandong district

관등 官等 official rank [grade]; civil service grade
◆ 관등이 높다[낮다] be high [low] in rank; hold a high [low] position in government service / 관등이 오르다[떨어지다] be elevated [reduced] to a higher rank [lower grade]; be promoted in rank [be demoted]
■**—성명** one's official rank and name

관등 觀燈 the Lantern Festival; the celebration of Buddha's birthday ■**—놀이** merry-making at the Lantern Festival **—절** the Lantern Festival

관람 觀覽 viewing; inspection
◆ 관람이 자유롭게 되어 있다 be open to visitors [for public inspection]
▶ 그 조각품들은 일반의 관람이 허용되고 있다 The sculptures are displayed [put on display] to the public.
▶ 관람 무료 《게시》 Admission Free.
▶ 관람 시간 09:00-18:00 《게시》 Opening hours 9:00 a.m.-6:00 p.m.
■**—관람하다** see 《a tennis match》; view; watch; inspect
▶ 우리는 축구 시합을 관람했다 We watched a soccer game.
■**—자[자]** a spectator; a visitor; 《총칭》 an audience; the gallery **—권** an admission ticket **—료** an admission fee; admission

관람석 觀覽席 〈좌석〉 a seat; a chair; a box; 〈경기장 등의〉 a stand; a grandstand(정면의); a bleacher(s) (지붕이 없는)
◆ 야구장의 우익측[좌익측] 관람석 a right-field [left-field] stand

관련 關聯 relation; connection; reference; correlation; association
◆ …과는 아무런 관련도 없다 have no correlation with...
▶ 이 두 문제는 서로 밀접한 관련이 있다 These two problems are closely related to each other.
▶ 자네가 말한 것은 논의 중인 문제와는 관련이 없네 What you've said has no bearing on [no relation to, nothing to do with] the problem under discussion.

▶ 이 증거는 그 사건과 관련이 있다[없다] This evidence is relevant [irrelevant] to the case.
■**—관련하다** be connected [associated] 《with》; relate [be related] 《to》; be correlated 《to》; have a bearing 《on》
◆ 관련된 사실 related facts / 그 사건과 관련된 문제 matters connected with the incident / 이 사건과 관련하여 in connection with [in relation to, with reference to] this incident / 관련시키다 correlate 《one thing with another》; relate 《facts to events》
▶ 그 일과 관련하여 질문이 있습니다 I want to ask a question in connection with the matter.
▶ 그 여자도 그 음모에 관련된 모양이다 She seems to be involved in the plot, too.
▶ 이 사건들은 서로 미묘하게 관련되어 있다 These events are all subtly linked together.
■**—기사** a related story **—사항** related [relevant] matters; matters relevant to *sth* **—산업** allied [associated] industries **—업계** related business circle **—회사** an associated [affiliated] company

관련성 關聯性 relevancy; connection; relation
◆ 머리카락과 치아 성장의 관련성 the correlation of growth between hair and teeth / 관련성이 있다 be relevant 《to》; have relevance 《to, for》 / 관련성이 없다 be irrelevant 《to》; have no relevance 《to, for》

관례 冠禮 a coming-of-age ceremony; the capping ceremony of youths ◆ 관례를 치르다 celebrate one's coming of age [attainment of manhood]

관례 慣例 (a) custom; a usage; 〈거래·법률상의〉 (a usual) practice; 〈선례〉 a precedent; 〈인습〉 a convention
◆ 관례적인 customary; usual; conventional / 관례상 conventionally; traditionally / 관례에 따라 in accordance with the custom; according to custom [usage] / 관례를 따르다 follow [observe] 《social》 customs; follow the established procedures / 관례를 지키다[깨뜨리다] keep up [break] the custom / 관례에 어긋나다 act contrary to custom
▶ 그렇게 하는 것이 우리의 관례다 It is our custom [a custom for us] to do so. ⇌ It is customary with [for] us to do so.
▶ 크리스마스에 선물을 하는 것은 하나의 관례다 Giving presents at Christmas is an institution.
▶ 악수는 오른손으로 하는 것이 관례다 Using the right hand to shake hands is a convention.
▶ 나라마다 사회적 관례가 다 다르다 Social customs vary in different countries.
▶ 그것은 관례에 반하는 일이다 That is uncustomary [runs counter to the custom].
▶ 관례에 따라 9월에 직원들에게 상여금이 지급되었다 In accordance with custom, the employees received bonuses in September.

관록 官祿 an official salary; a stipend ◆ 관록을 먹다 receive a stipend [an official salary]

관록 貫祿 dignity; weight of character; importance
◆ 관록(이) 있는 사람 a man of dignity [gravity]; an imposing figure / 관록 있는 정치가 a

weighty [an influential] politician / 관록이 붙다 gain in dignity; gain an air of confidence [presence] ⟨as⟩; ⟨노련해지다⟩ be experienced in 《business》 / 관록이 있다 have considerable presence [an air of importance]; be [look] dignified / 장관으로서의 관록이 충분하다 be fully qualified for the portfolio
▶새로 오신 영어 선생님은 관록이 있는 분이다 The new English teacher is a man of dignity.
▶그는 사장으로서의 관록이 있다[없다] He has [lacks] dignity as president of the company.
▶그 사람은 선임자의 관록을 보여주었다 He showed what a senior could do [was made of, was supposed to]. (▶could do는 행위, 뒤의 둘은 자질에 관해 말하는 표현임)

관료 官僚 a bureaucrat; a government official; (총칭) bureaucracy; officialdom
♦고위 관료 a high-ranking official / 관료 출신의 정객 a politician from officialdom; a bureaucrat-turned politician / 관료적 형식주의[번문욕례] red tape; red-tapism; bureaucracy / 관료적인 bureaucratic / 관료 출신이다 be of bureaucratic origin / 관료화하다 bureaucratize
▶그에게는 어딘가 관료적인 데가 있다 There is something bureaucratic about him.
■직업— a career official ■—내각 a bureaucratic ministry [cabinet] —정치 bureaucratic government; bureaucracy —제도 bureaucracy —주의 bureaucratism; bureaucracy; officialism —주의자 a bureaucratist —파 the bureaucrats; the bureaucratic circles

관류하다 貫流— flow [run] through 《a city》
▶한강은 서울을 관류한다 The Han River flows through Seoul.

관리 官吏 an official; a government official [clerk]; a public [《英》 civil] servant; a public functionary; (총칭) bureaucracy; officialdom
♦고급 관리 a high (government) official; a senior civil servant / 교육부의 관리 an official of the Ministry of Education / 유능한 관리 an able official / 하급 관리 a petty official / 관리다 be in government service / 관리가 되다 become a public [civil] servant; enter the government service
▶사람들은 관리 티를 내는 사람을 싫어한다 People dislike a man who stands on his official dignity.
■—근성 bumbledom; officialism; bureaucratism —생활 an official life [career]

관리 管理 1 ⟨운영·경영⟩ management; administration; ⟨지배⟩ control; ⟨감독⟩ supervision; superintendence
♦정부 관리 기업체 a government(-controlled) [state-run] enterprise / 관리 태만 negligence of administration / 국가 관리하에 있다[두다] be [place 《a matter》] under state control
▶운동장은 관리가 구석구석 잘 안 된다 The playground cannot be fully supervised.
▶그 나라는 유엔 평화유지군의 관리하에 있다 The country is under [in] the control of the UN Peacekeeping Force.
—관리하다 manage 《an estate》; administer; control; supervise
♦회사의 사무를 관리하다 manage the business affairs of a company
▶그 사람은 그 공장[회사의 자금]을 관리하고 있다 He manages the plant [company's money].
▶이 건물은 시에서 관리하고 있다 This building is under the supervision [control] of the city.
2 ⟨돌봄⟩ charge; care
♦재산의 관리를 맡기다 entrust one's property to sb's care; place [put] one's property under sb's care [in sb's charge]
▶그 옛 건물은 관리가 잘 되고 있다 The old building is well kept [taken care of].
▶내가 돌아올 때까지 사무실 관리를 좀 맡아 주시오 I want you to take [have] charge of the office until I come back.
—관리하다 take charge of; care for
♦남의 재산을 관리하다 take charge of another's property
▶아버지는 삼촌의 재산을 관리하고 계시다 My father administers [is in charge of] my uncle's property.
■공장— control [management, supervision] of a factory 국가— state [government] control 국제— international control [trusteeship] 생산[노무]— production [labor] management 업무— business administration 외환— foreign exchange control 인사— personnel management 자금— the management of money 정부— government control 품질— quality control (略 QC) ■—가격 an administered price —권 the right of management; 《hold》 a supervisory authority 《over》 —기관 a managing agency —능력 capacity of management —무역 controlled trade —부 a management [an administrative] division —비 management expenses —사무소 a superintendent's office; a control office —사회 a control-oriented [controlled] society —자 an administrator; a manager; a superintendent; ⟨유산 등의⟩ an executor; (총칭) the management —직 an administrative [a managerial] position 《in an office》; ⟨사람⟩ an managerial officer [staff member]; a person in a managerial position; (총칭) the management (staff): 중간 관리직 a middle manager; (총칭) the middle management

관리인 管理人 an administrator; a manager; a supervisor; ⟨빌딩 등의⟩ a superintendent; 《美》 a janitor; 《英》 a caretaker; ⟨유산 등의⟩ an administrator; an executor (▶전자는 공적으로 임명된 경우이고 후자는 유언자가 지정한 경우를 말함)
■별장— a caretaker of a summer cottage 아파트— a concierge [kɑnsiéərӡ]; 《美》 a janitor; a superintendent 재산— a property custodian 토지— a real estate custodian; 《英》 a bailiff

관망 觀望 observation; watching; fence-sitting
▶이 참상을 어떻게 관망만 하고 있을 수 있겠는가? How can I be [remain] indifferent at the sight of such a tragedy?
—관망하다 observe; watch; (wait and) see; sit

[stand] by and watch
♦ 사태 진전을 관망하다 observe [watch] the developments; follow the turn of events; watch to see how a matter will turn out / 관망하는 태도를 취하다 assume a wait-and-see attitude
▶ 사태를 좀더 관망해 봅시다 Let's wait a little longer and see.
━주의 a waiting [wait-and-see] policy

관명 官名 an official title
♦ 관명을 사칭하다 assume an official title spuriously; lie about *one's* official position; assume a false title; represent *oneself* as a government official

관명 官命 official [government] orders; 〈용무〉 an official mission [business]
♦ 관명을 띠고 under official [government] orders; on official mission / 관명에 의하여 by government [official] order; by order of the government
▶ 그는 관명에 따라 해외 시찰을 갔다 He went on a foreign inspection tour under official [government] orders.
━항거 contumacy

관모 冠毛 〈새의〉a crest; 〈식물의〉a pappus (*pl*. -pi); plume; down

관목 灌木 a shrub; a bush ■ ━림 a shrubbery ━지대 a shrubbery zone

관문 關門 1 〈요새·국경 등의〉a barrier (station); a barrier-gate; a boundary gate;〈문호〉a gateway 《to the Far East》;〈검문소〉a checkpoint; a checking station
♦ 관문을 통과하다 pass [get over] a barrier; pass through a checkpoint
2 〈난관〉a difficult situation;〈장벽〉a hurdle; an obstacle; a barrier 《to success in life》
♦ 사법 시험의 관문을 돌파하다 successfully pass the state law examination / 입시의 관문을 통과하다 get through [get over the hurdle of] the entrance examination 《and enter Seoul National University》
▶ 그녀와 결혼하기 전에 그는 여러 가지 관문을 돌파해야 했다 He had to surmount various obstacles before he was able to marry her.

관물 官物 〈관청의 물품〉government property [possessions];〈관급품〉(美) governmentissue; articles supplied by the government ♦ 관물을 사사로이 쓰다 use government property for personal purposes

관민 官民 officials and people; the government and the people
♦ 관민이 협력하여 by the joint [united] efforts of government and people
▶ 관민이 일체가 되어 부정부패를 근절해야 한다 The government [officials] and the people must unite and root out corruption.

관변측 官邊側 government circles [authorities]; official quarters
♦ 관변측에 의하면 government circles say 《that》; according to official quarters
▶ 그 뉴스는 관변측에서 나온 것 같다 The news seems to have come from an official [government] source.

관보 官報 1 〈정부 인쇄물〉an official gazette; a (daily) government newsletter
♦ 관보에 실리다[나다] be published [reported] in the official gazette / 관보로 발표하다 gazette; publish [announce] by [in] the official gazette
2 〈공용 전보〉an official telegram

관복 官服 an official uniform [outfit]

관북 關北 〈지방〉 the Kwanbuk district; the northeastern part of Korea

관불(회) 灌佛(會) 〔佛敎〕 the rite of perfuming the image of Buddha on an anniversary of Buddha's birth

관비 官費 government expense(s) [expenditure] ♦ 관비의 낭비 a waste of government [public] funds
▶ 그는 관비로 프랑스에 유학갔다 He was sent to France for study at government expense.
■ ━생 a holder of a scholarship from the government ━유학생 a student studying abroad on a government grant [scholarship]; a government student abroad

관사 官舍 an official residence [house] ♦ 관사를 배정받다 be provided with an official residence

관사 冠詞 〔文法〕 an article ♦ 관사를 붙이다 give 《a noun》an article
━정[부정] a definite [an indefinite] article : 이 명사에는 부정 관사를 붙이지 않는다 This noun does not take an indefinite article.

관상 管狀 ♦ 관상의 tubular (in form); tubal; tube-shaped ■ ━기관 〔昆〕a fistula (*pl*.-lae) ━화 〔植〕 a tubular [tubulous] flower

관상 觀相 physiognomic judgment of character; phrenological interpretation
♦ 관상을 보아주다 tell *one's* fortune by physiognomy; read *one's* physiognomy
■ ━가[쟁이] a physiognomist; a phrenologist; a reader of faces ━서 a book on physiognomy ━술[학] (the art of) physiognomy; phrenology

관상 觀賞 viewing with admiration; enjoyment
━하다 admire; enjoy 《flowering plants》
♦ 열대어를 관상하다 admire [enjoy observing] tropical fish
▶ 나는 아침에 일찍 일어나서 나팔꽃을 관상한다 I get up early to enjoy the morning glories.
■ ━식물 a decorative [house] plant; an ornamental ━어 an aquarium fish

관상 冠狀 ♦ 관상의 coronal; coronary; coronate
■ ━동맥[정맥] the coronary arteries [veins] ━동맥 경화증 coronary arteriosclerosis ━동맥 혈전증 (a) coronary thrombosis;《口》a coronary ━봉합(縫合) 〔解〕a coronal suture ━톱 〈외과용〉 a trephine

관상대 觀象臺 a meteorological observatory ⇨ 기상(~대)

관생 冠省 〈편지에서〉 Dispensing with the preliminaries... / The purpose of this letter is to...

관생엽 貫生葉 〔植〕a perfoliate leaf

관서 官署 government (and municipal) offices; a government [public] office

관서 關西 〈지방〉 the Kwansŏ district; the northwestern part of Korea ■—팔경 the eight scenic attractions of the Kwansŏ district
■중앙— the offices of the central government 지방— local government offices

관선 官選 ♦관선의 chosen [appointed] by the government [authorities]; official
■—변호인 a court-appointed lawyer [attorney]; a public defender —시장 a mayor appointed by the government — 이사 〈학교 재단 등의〉 a government-appointed trustee

관설 官設 a government establishment [facility, installation] ♦관설의 established by the government ■—철도 a government(-built) railroad

관성 慣性 〔物〕 inertia ♦관성의 법칙 the law of inertia
■—모멘트 the moment of inertia —비행 〈우주선 등의〉 inertial navigation —유도 inertial guidance —질량 inertial mass —항법 장치 〔空〕 the inertial navigation system (略 INS)

관세 關稅 a tariff; customs; customs duties; a (customs) duty
♦다자간 관세 인하 교섭 the multilateral tariff negotiations (略 MTN) / 관세가 붙는 dutiable (goods); (美) customable / 관세가 붙지 않는 undutiable; duty-free; free of duty / 관세를 부과하다 levy [impose] a custom duty (on) / 관세를 징수하다 collect customs (on imported goods) / 관세를 치르고 화물을 인수하다 clear goods
▶정부는 주류에 대한 관세 인하를 발표했다 The Government announced that the custom duties on alcohol would be reduced.
▶그 나라는 내달부터 자동차의 관세를 5% 인상한다 The country will raise the duty on automobiles by five percent starting next month.
■보복— retaliatory tariffs [duties] 보호— a protective tariff 상쇄— a countervailing duty 수입[수출]— import [export] duties 신축— a flexible tariff 차별— a differential tariff 특혜[호혜]— a preferential [reciprocal] tariff ■—개정 a tariff reform [revision] —교섭 tariff negotiations —동맹 a customs union —면제품 ⇨ 면세(~품) —및 무역에 관한 일반 협정 the General Agreement on Tariffs and Trade (略 GATT) —법 〔法〕 the Customs Law [Act] —수입(收入) customs revenue —율 a customs tariff; a tariff rate: 실행 관세율 Priority rate of duty —정책 a tariff policy [measure] —조약 a tariff treaty —청 the Customs Administration —할당제 a tariff quota system —협정 a customs agreement

관세음보살 觀世音菩薩 〔佛敎〕 the (Buddhist) Goddess of Mercy; the Merciful Goddess

관세장벽 關稅障壁 a tariff barrier [wall]; a trade [custom] barrier ♦관세 장벽을 쌓다[없애다] erect [remove] a tariff wall [customs] / 관세 장벽을 높여 외국 상품을 막다 raise tariff walls against foreign goods

관솔 〈소나무의〉 a (resinous) pine knot; a resinous part of pine wood ♦관솔불 a pine torch; a fire set to pine knots

관수 官需 an official demand ■—물자 〈(medical) supplies for government use

관수 灌水 sprinkling (of water); 〈관개〉 watering; irrigation ♦나무 뿌리에 관수하다 sprinkle water at the root of a tree / 정원수에 관수하다 water the trees in the garden
■—장치 a sprinkler

관수해 冠水害 〈침수 피해〉 damage of crops by [from] a flood

관습 慣習 (a) custom; (a) usage; 〈관례〉 (a) usual [common] practice; 〈인습〉 convention; tradition
♦사회의 관습 a social custom; (social) mores / 오래 된 관습 a custom of long standing / 일반화된 관습 accepted [established] usage / 관습적인 customary; usual / 관습상 customarily; usually / 관습에 따라 according to custom; by convention / 옛 관습을 지키다 [버리다] keep up [break with] an old custom
▶이것은 그 지방의 오래 된 관습이다 This is a custom [common practice] of long standing in that district.
▶과거 100년 이래 행해지고 있는 관습에 따라 의식이 거행되었다 The ceremony was performed according to the usages of the last hundred years.
■상거래— the custom of trade; a commercial practice [usage] ■—법 (the) customary law; 〈영미의〉 (the) common law

관심 關心 〈흥미〉 (an) interest; 〈걱정〉 concern (about, over)

解說 interest는 알고 싶고 듣고 싶은 생각에서 갖는 관심을, concern은 걱정스럽게 여기며 갖는 관심을 말한다.

♦역사에 관심이 있는 historical-minded 《people》 / …의 관심의 대상이 되다 occupy the interest [attention] of… / 관심이 높아지다 take [have] a growing [an increasing] interest (in) / …에 관심을 갖다 be interested (in); be concerned about; take [have] (an) interest (in) / 관심을 기울이다 give thought (to); take [have] (an) interest (in) / 관심을 보이다 show [display] interest (in) / 관심을 끌다 arouse [awake] one's interest (in)
▶그는 음식[옷차림]에는 관심이 없는 듯했다 He seemed indifferent to food [seemed to pay no attention to his appearance].
▶그는 UFO에 관심을 가지고 있다 He is interested in UFO's.
▶젊은이들은 새 차에 큰 관심을 나타낸다 Young people show a keen [an active] interest in the new car.
▶모든 부모는 아이들의 성장에 관심을 가지고 있다 All parents are concerned about their children's growth.
▶나는 그런 일에는 아무 관심도 없다 I have no concern for [have no interest in] that sort of thing.

관심사 關心事 a matter of concern
■공동— a matter of common interest 중대— a matter of grave concern 최대— a matter of primary concern; one's greatest concern : 그

의 최대 관심사는 그녀가 자기를 어떻게 생각하느냐다 His greatest concern is what she thinks of him.
관아 官衙 a government office [agency] ⇨ 관청(官廳)
관악 管樂 the wind (music) ■ —기 《총칭》 the wind (instruments)
관여 關與 participation 《in》
—**관여하다** participate [take part] 《in》; be concerned 《in》; have *sth* to do with; have [take] a hand 《in》
♦ 계획에 관여하고 있는 사람 a participant in a plan / 경영에 관여하다 engage in management / 음모에 관여하다 join [take part] in a plot / 정사(政事)에 관여하다 participate [share] in the administration / 정치에 관여하다 participate [mix, have a part] in politics / 관여하지 않다 have no concern 《in》; have nothing to do with *sb* [*sth*]
▶ 형은 각종 사업에 관여하고 있습니다 My brother is involved [has a finger] in all sorts of businesses.
▶ 정치에 관여하지 마라 Do not get involved in politics.
▶ 그것은 네가 관여할 일이 아니다 It is no affair [concern] of yours. ⇌ It is none of your business.
관엽식물 觀葉植物 a foliage plant
관영 官營 government management [operation, control]
♦ 관영의 government-managed [government-run, government-financed, government-operated] / 관영으로 하다 nationalize; put 《an enterprise》 under government management
■ —**사 업(事業)** a government-managed [government-financed] project; a governmental enterprise [undertaking]
관외 管外 ♦ 관의 구역 the area outside the jurisdiction / 관외의 out of the jurisdiction [control] 《of》
관용 官用 〈용무〉 an official mission; government [official] business; 〈용도〉 official [public] use / 그는 관용으로 대전 출장 중이다 He is away in Taejŏn on official business.
■ —**어** ⇨ 공용(~어) —**차** ⇨ 공용(~차)
관용 慣用 usage; common use
♦ 관용적인 common; usual; ordinary; commonly used; 〈어구가〉 idiomatic; 〈습관적인〉 customary; in common [everyday] use / 관용이 되다 get into common use / 관용에 어긋나다 be contrary to usage; 〈표현이〉 be unidiomatic
▶ 그것은 관용상 허용되고 있다 It is accepted as established usage.
▶ 이 표현은 현대 영어의 관용상 올바른 것으로 간주되고 있다 This expression is sanctioned by current English usage.
■ —**구[어]** an idiom; an idiomatic phrase —**어법** idioms; an idiomatic expression —**영어** idiomatic English —**표현** an idiomatic expression
관용 寬容 《the spirit of》 tolerance; forgiveness; leniency; forbearance
▶ 관용을 바랍니다 Please be patient with us.

—**관용하다** tolerate; forgive; pardon
▶ 다른 사람들의 신앙도 관용해야 한다 We must tolerate [must be tolerant to] other people's beliefs.
관원 官員 a government [public] official [servant]; a public service personnel
관원 館員 (a member of) the staff 《of a library [an embassy]》
관위 官位 (an) official rank ♦ 관위를 박탈하다 divest [deprive] *sb* of 《his》 official rank
관유 官有 government [state] ownership ⇨ 국유(國有)
관음보살 觀音菩薩 the (Buddhist) Goddess of Mercy ⇨ 관세음보살
관인 官印 an official [a government] seal
♦ 관인을 찍다 affix [put] an official [a government] seal 《on, to》
관인 官認 government permission ⇨ 관허(官許)
관인하다 寬仁— generous; liberal; clement; broad-minded
관입 貫入 interpenetration; 〈암맥(岩脈)의〉 intrusion —**관입하다** interpenetrate
관자 貫子 〈망건의〉 headband buttons of gold or jade beads
관자놀이 貫子— 〖解〗 the temple
♦ 관자놀이의 temporal
▶ 관자놀이가 욱신거린다 The temples throb with pain.
관작 官爵 official rank
관장 管掌 charge; management; control
—**관장하다** take [be in] charge of 《a matter》; have 《a matter》 in charge; manage
♦ 공중 위생을 관장하다 manage the public health / 관장시키다 give *sb* charge of *sth*
▶ 하느님은 인간의 운명을 관장하신다 God controls [presides over] human destiny.
▶ 이 과에서는 경리 업무를 관장한다 This section takes [is in] charge of accounting.
■ —**업무** the business in *one's* charge; *one's* duty
관장 館長 a superintendent; a director; 〈도서관의〉 the chief [head] librarian; 〈박물관・미술관의〉 the curator; 〈수족관의〉 the director of an aquarium
관장 灌腸 an intestinal irrigation; (an) enema (*pl.* ~s, -mata); a clyster
—**관장하다** give [administer] an enema to 《a patient》; apply a clyster 《to》
■ —**기** an enema syringe; a clyster pump —**제** an enema; a clyster
관재 管財 administration of an estate; custodianship; 〈파산시의〉 receivership
—**관재하다** administer; put property under *one's* custody [custodianship]
■ —**국** the bureau of property custody —**인** 〈도산한 기업・법인의〉 a receiver; a trustee [custodian] 《of public property》; 〈유산・부동산의〉 an administrator 《of a will [an estate]》
관저 官邸 an official residence 《of the Prime Minister》 ■ **대통령—** the Presidential residence
관전 觀戰 —**관전하다** 〈전투를〉 witness [observe] 《a battle, a military operations》; 〈경기

를〉 watch 《a baseball game》
▶우리는 텔레비전으로 야구 경기를 관전했다 We watched the baseball game on TV.
■—기(記) a witness's account 《of a *paduk* match》
관절 關節 a joint; an articulation ◆관절의 articular 《ligaments》
▶그녀는 팔꿈치 관절이 빠졌다 Her elbow is out of joint.
▶나는 무릎 관절이 아프다 My knee hurts [pains me].
▶그는 무릎 관절을 삐었다 He sprained his knee.
■—낭 the articular capsule —동물 an articulate animal —류머티즘 articular [joint] rheumatism —부 a joint region —신경통 articular neuralgia —연골 the articular cartilage —염 inflammation of a joint; arthritis —이단[탈구(脫臼)] dislocation of a joint; disarticulation —통 arthralgia
관점 觀點 a viewpoint; an angle 《of vision》; a point of view; a standpoint
◆관점이 다르다 have a different opinion [point of view]; differ in opinion 《from》/ 다른 관점에서 보다 view 《a matter》 from a different standpoint / 문제를 새로운 관점에서 보다 look at the problem from a new angle
▶이런 관점에서 보면 그것은 중요하지 않다 From this point of view [Viewed from this angle], that is not important.
관정 管井 a tube well
관제 官制 a system [an organization] of government; government organization [setup]; 〈법규〉 official regulations
◆관제를 정하다 establish a government organization
■—개편 a reform of government organization; reorganization of the government offices
관제 官製 government manufacture ◆관제의 manufactured by the government; of government make; government-made
■—데모 a government-inspired demonstration —민의 a government-fabricated (public) opinion —엽서 an official [a government] postcard, (美) a postal card; (英) a postcard
관제 管制 〈통제〉 controlling; control ◆관제 하에 두다 bring *sth* under control 《of》
—관제하다 control
■—보도 a news blackout; news censorship: 그 당시에는 전국적으로 보도 관제가 내려져 있었다 In those days there was news censorship all over the country. 지상— ground control: 지상 관제 진입 ground-control(led) approach (略 GCA) ■—관 a [an air traffic] controller —소 〈우주선의〉 a (satellite) tracking station —장치 a controlling gear —탑 〈공항의〉 a control tower
관조 觀照 meditation; contemplation ◆ 미의 관조 contemplation of beauty —관조하다 contemplate; meditate ◆자연[인생]을 관조하다 contemplate nature [life]
관족 管足 〔動〕 a tube [an ambulacral] foot
관존민비 官尊民卑 putting government above people; the preponderance of official power; respect for the officials and disrespect for the people
◆관존민비의 폐습 the corrupt [evil] custom of making much of the government and little of the people [putting government above people]
관중 觀衆 spectators; viewers; onlookers; 〈극장의〉 the audience; 〈테니스·골프 등의〉 the gallery
◆대관중 crowds of spectators / 야구장의 관중 the audience in the ball park / 관중이 많다[적다] have a large [small] audience
▶양키즈 팀의 경기에는 언제나 많은 관중이 몰린다 A Yankees game always draws a large crowd. ⇌ There are always many spectators at a Yankees game.
▶야구장에는 많은 관중이 운집해 있었다 There was a large crowd of spectators in the ball park.
▶관중은 그의 연기에 매료되었다 The audience was [were] carried away by his acting.
관직 官職 a government [an official] post [position]; government service
▶그는 20년간 관직에 있다 He has been in government service for twenty years.
▶졸업 후 나는 관직에 들어갔으면 합니다 After graduation I hope to enter the government service.
▶그는 중요한 관직에 임명되었다 He was appointed to an important government post [office].
관찰 觀察 observation; survey; view
◆개미의 습성에 관한 관찰 observations on the habits of ants / 정확한 관찰 an accurate observation / 물체의 관찰 방법 a way of looking at [observing] things / 관찰을 잘못하다 make an incorrect observation
▶나는 그가 올바로 관찰을 했다고 생각한다 I think he made the correct observation.
▶그 생각은 관찰에 근거한 것이었다 The idea was based on observation.
—관찰하다 observe; watch; make observation 《of》; look at; view
◆내가 관찰한 바로는 according to my observation; as I see [look at] it / 관찰한 것을 기록하다 write one's observations 《on wild animals》/ 면밀히 관찰해 보면 …하다는 것을 알게 된다 Close [Careful] observation shows [reveals] that...
▶천문학자는 별을 관찰한다 An astronomer observes the stars.
▶그는 사물을 정확히 관찰한다 He observes things accurately.
■—안(眼) an observing eye 《for》; an observant eye 《for》 —자 an observer
관찰력 觀察力 (the power of) observation
◆관찰력이 부족한 사람 a man of narrow observation / 관찰력을 기르다 foster one's power of observation
▶그는 관찰력이 예리하다 He is a man of observation. ⇌ He has sharp [keen] powers of observation. ⇌ He has a sharp eye.
관찰사 觀察使 〔史〕 a (provincial) governor

관철 貫徹 accomplishment; consummation; realization; fulfilment
—**관철하다** carry through [out]; put *sth* into effect; accomplish
♦ 목적을 관철하다 achieve [carry through] *one's* purpose / 주장을 관철하다 carry [gain] *one's* point / 초지(初志)를 관철하다 realize [carry out] *one's* original object [intention]
▶ 그들은 임금 인상 요구를 관철하기로 결심했다 They determined to push through their demand for increased wages.
▶ 이것을 꼭 관철시킬 작정이다 I am determined to go through with the undertaking.

관청 官廳 a government [public] office [agency]; a government department
▶ 그의 아버지는 관청에 근무하신다 His father serves in a government office.
■ 감독— the authorities supervising the affairs (of); the supervisory office 관계[당해]— the authorities concerned: 관계 관청에 신고했습니까? Did you notify the authorities concerned? 주무— the competent authorities 행정— an administrative office ■ —가(街) a government office quarter —식 officialism; red-tapism; red tape —용어 official terminology [jargon]; officialese —집무 시간 official hours of work

관측 觀測 1 〈기상 등의〉 (an) observation; survey ♦ 남극 관측대 the antarctic expedition
—**관측하다** observe; survey; make [take] an observation; 〈처음으로〉 sight (a new star)
♦ 기상[천체]을 관측하다 make meteorological [astronomical] observations / 태양[일식]을 관측하다 make observations of the sun [a solar eclipse]
2 〈생각·의견〉 thinking; an opinion
♦ 내 관측으로는 in my opinion; as I see it; to my mind
▶ 이것은 제 희망적인 관측에 불과합니다 This is merely my wishful thinking [observation].
■ 기상— weather [meteorological] observation 천체— astronomical observation —기구 an observation balloon; (비유) a trial balloon; 〈기상 관측용의〉 a sounding balloon: 관측 기구를 띄워 올리다 send up a trial balloon —기록 a record of *one's* observations 《of, on》 —망 an observation network —소 an observatory; 〈임시의〉 an observation station [post, platform] —오차 an observational error —자 an observer —자료 observational data —지점 an observation point [site] —통 an observer: 관측통들은 …이라고 전하고 있다 Observers say that...

관통 貫通 piercing; penetration; perforation
—**관통하다** go [pass] (right) through; pierce; penetrate; perforate; 〈탄환이〉 shoot through; 〈터널이〉 tunnel through (a mountain)
♦ 총알이 팔을 관통하다 be shot through the arm
▶ 탄환이 벽을 관통했다 The bullet shot [went] through the wall.
▶ 화살은 정확히 표적을 관통했다 The arrow passed clean through the target.
▶ 그 강은 도시를 관통해서 흐른다 The river runs through the city.
▶ 터널은 아직 관통되지 않았다 The tunnel hasn't been dug through yet.

관포지교 管鮑之交 an extremely close friendship; a Damon and Pythias [David and Jonathan] friendship
▶ 그들은 관포지교의 사이였다 They were inseparable friends.

관하 管下 ♦ 관하의[에 있는] (be) under the jurisdiction [control] (of) ▶ 그것은 시 당국 관하에 있다 It is within [under] the jurisdiction of the municipal authorities.

관하다 關— 1 〈대하다〉 be connected [concerned] 《with》; be related to; bear on; concern
♦ 원예[종교, 과학]에 관한 책 a book on gardening [religion, science]; a book (which is) concerned with gardening [religion, science] / 이것에 관한 일체의 서류 all the documents referring to this matter / 환경 위생에 관한 법률 laws regarding [concerning] environmental sanitation / 나에 관한 한 (in) so far as [as far as] I am concerned
▶ 그는 경제 문제에 관한 논문을 썼다 He wrote a treatise on economic problems.
▶ 이 문제에 관한 당신의 의견을 말해 주시오 Let me hear your opinion about this issue.
2 〈관계하다〉 have [produce] an effect 《on》; affect 《*sb's* honor》; concern 《*one's* welfare》; involve 《*one's* prestige》
♦ 명예에 관한 문제 a question affecting *one's* honor / 위신에 관한 일 a point of prestige
▶ 그것은 그의 생명에 관한 일이 될지도 모른다 It may affect his life.
▶ 그것은 국가의 명예와 위신에 관한 문제다 It is a problem in which national honor and prestige are involved.

관하여 關— about; on; of; over; concerning; as to [for]; regarding; as regards; in connection with; in [with] regard to; respecting; pertaining to

> **解說** *about*이 가장 일반적인 말. *on*은 내용이 전문적이고 비중이 클 때 쓰인다. *of*는 about 대신 쓰이며, about이 상세하게 언급하는 경우에 쓰이는 데 비해 of는 간단히 언급하는 경우에 쓰인다. 예컨대 think about it이라고 하면 「그 일에 관하여 오랫동안 여러 가지로 생각하다」란 뜻이 내포되고, think of it이라고 하면 「잠시 마음 속에 떠올리다」란 뜻이 된다. *over*는 「…을 놓고」란 뜻으로 흔히 의견의 대립·불일치의 뜻이 있다. *concerning*은 about, on의 딱딱한 표현. *as to*는 〈주로 (英)에서〉 wh-절로 이어지는 경우에 많이 쓰이고, *as for*는 앞의 화제와 관련하여 다른 말을 하는 경우에 쓰이는데 대개 문장 또는 절의 첫머리에 위치한다.

♦ 그 점에 관하여 on that point / 이 일에 관하여 in regard to this subject; in this connection [respect] / 제임스 조이스에 관하여 강연하다 make a lecture on James Joyce
▶ 그는 그 문제에 관하여 내게 몇 가지를 물었다 He asked me some questions in connection

with [with regard to] the matter.
▶ 이 문제에 관하여 어떻게 생각하니? What do you think about [of] this problem?
▶ 이 문제에 관해서는 나중에 이야기하자 As for this matter, let's talk later.
▶ 그 문제에 관해서는 네게 동의할 수 없다 I cannot agree with you as regards [respecting] that matter.

관학 官學 a governmental [national] school [university]

관할 管轄 〈공권에 의한〉 jurisdiction; 〈관리·통제〉 control; competence
♦ 관할 내[외]의 within [outside] the jurisdiction (of); 〈문제가〉 within [beyond] the competence (of) / 관할에 속하는 be under the control (of); belong in the competence (of); 〈법정의〉 fall under the jurisdiction (of)
▶ 그 사항들은 우리 부서 관할이 아니다 That matters are not within the jurisdiction of our office.
▶ 국립 대학들은 교육부의 직접 관할 하에 있다 The national universities are controlled directly by the Ministry of Education.
—**관할하다** have competence (over a matter); have [exercise] jurisdiction [control] (over a district); control
▶ 그 부서는 서부 지역을 관할한다 The office has jurisdiction over the western district.
▶ 이 과는 회사의 문화 시설을 관할하고 있다 This department has jurisdiction [control] over the cultural facilities of the company.
—**관청** the competent [proper] authorities [offices] —**구역** 〈법원의〉 the district of jurisdiction; 〈경찰서의〉 a police district [(美) precinct] —**법원** a competent court —**서(署)** the police station concerned; the competent police authorities —**지(地)** jurisdiction

관할권 管轄權 (have) jurisdiction (over)
♦ 관할권을 둘러 싸고 다투다 quarrel over (their) jurisdiction
▶ 그 섬은 우리 나라가 관할권을 가지고 있다 Our country has [exercises] jurisdiction over the island.
■—**다툼** a jurisdictional dispute [controversy]

관함식 觀艦式 〖軍〗 a naval review

관행 慣行 a custom; (a) habitual [customary, traditional] practice
♦ 일반적 관행 a general practice / 관행적인 habitual; customary / 관행을 지키다 follow a custom [traditional practice]
▶ 기묘하게 들리겠지만 그것이 이 지방의 관행이다 That sounds queer, but it's the local custom.
▶ 이런 관행은 폐지되어야 한다 This practice should be done away with.
■—**범** 〖法〗 a habitual crime

관향 貫鄕 a place of origin ⇨ 본관(本貫)

관허 官許 〈정부의 허가〉 official permit; government permission [license]; 〈승인〉 approval; 〈권력자의〉 sanction
♦ 관허의 licensed; authorized / 관허를 받다 obtain an official permit
—**관허하다** authorize; approve; sanction; give official permission [recognition]; license
■—**요금** (government-)licensed charge

관헌 官憲 〈당국〉 the (government) authorities; 〈경찰〉 the police (authorities)
♦ 관헌의 간섭 official intervention / 관헌의 탄압 the pressure of the authorities
▶ 그들은 관헌의 박해를 피해 출국했다 They left the country to escape the persecution of the authorities.
■—**지방—** the local [prefectural, regional] authorities

관현 管絃 wind and string instruments

관현악 管絃樂 orchestral music ■—**단** an orchestra —**편곡(법)** orchestration

관형사 冠形詞 〖文法〗 a pre-noun

관혼상제 冠婚喪祭 the ceremonies of coming of age, marriage, funeral and ancestral worship; ceremonial occasions
▶ 관혼상제에는 많은 친척들이 모인다 Many relatives gather together on formal [ceremonial] occasions.

관후 寬厚 〈관대〉 generosity; broadmindedness; large mindedness; liberality; magnanimity
—**관후하다** 〈관대하다〉 generous; magnanimous; forgiving; 〈관용적이다〉 tolerant; large-hearted; liberal
♦ 관후한 인물 a man of magnanimity / 관후한 태도 an air of magnanimity / 관후하게 대하다 deal leniently with sb; show clemency to sb
▶ 아버지는 우리 자식들에게 관후하셨다 My father was lenient with us children.
■—**장자(長者)** a large-hearted gentleman

괄괄하다 1 〈풀기가〉 too stiff; stiffly starched
♦ 괄괄하게 풀먹인 와이셔츠 a stiffly starched white shirt
2 〈성미가〉 passionate; hot-tempered; rough; impetuous; fiery
♦ 괄괄한 남자 a man of violent temper; a rough-natured [quick-tempered] person / 괄괄한 여자 a spirited woman

괄다 〈불이〉 too high [strong]
▶ 이 스토브는 불이 괄다 This stove is very powerful.
▶ 불이 너무 괄아서 밥이 탔다 The rice was scorched because the fire was too high [intense].

괄대 恝待 a cold treatment ⇨ 냉대(冷待)

괄목하다 刮目— watch with keen interest; watch eagerly [closely]
♦ 괄목할 만한 성공 a marvelous [phenomenal] success / 괄목할 만한 일 work worthy of close attention / 괄목할 만하다 be wonderful [amazing, (美俗) eye-opening] / 괄목할 만한 산업 발전을 이룩하다 make a wonderful growth of industry
▶ 그의 새 이론은 괄목할 만하다 His new theory deserves [is worthy of] close attention.

괄시 恝視 negligence; slight; cold treatment; a cold reception
♦ 괄시를 받다 be held in [treated with] contempt
▶ 그는 어디를 가나 괄시를 받았다 Wherever he went, he was given [met with] a cold

reception.
―괄시하다 neglect; ill-treat; slight; treat *sb* coldly
▶ 너무 괄시하지 마라 Don't hold me so cheap.
괄약근 括約筋 a sphincter (muscle); a sphincteral muscle; a constrictor ◆ **방광―** the sphincter vesicae 항문― the anal sphincter; the sphincter ani
괄태충 括胎蟲 〈민달팽이〉 a slug
괄호 括弧 parenthesis [pərénθəsəs] (*pl*. -ses); a round bracket; 〈각[대]괄호〉 a square bracket; 〈중괄호〉 a brace
◆ 괄호 안의 어구 a phrase in parentheses [brackets] / 괄호를 풀다 remove the brackets [parentheses] / 괄호 안에 넣다 put 《a word》 in parentheses / 괄호로 묶다 enclose 《a word》 in parentheses
▶ 괄호 안의 부분을 우리 말로 옮기시오 Put the parenthesized passage into Korean.
▶ 번역은 괄호 안에 넣었습니다 The translation is given in parentheses.
▶ 외국어를 괄호로 묶으시오 Parenthesize foreign words.
■ 이중― double parentheses
괌 〈태평양 서부의 섬〉 Guam
광 a shed; a 《storage》 barn; a storeroom; 《英》 a lumber room; 〈곡식광〉 a granary; 〈땅광〉 a cellar
광 光 1 〈광택〉 gloss; luster; sheen; glaze; brightness
◆ 광이 나는 lustrous; bright; glossy; sheeny / 광이 나지 않는 dim; dull; dry; lusterless / 광을 내다 make *sth* glossy; glaze; give luster 《to》; burnish; polish up / 광을 없애다 take off the gloss [luster, shine]
▶ 이 테이블은 광이 난다 This table has a good polish.
2 〔物〕 〈빛〉 (a) light; 〈광선〉 a ray ◆ 월광 moonlight / 태양광 the light [rays] of the sun; sunlight
광 廣 〈넓이〉 (an) extent; (an) area; 〈나비〉 width; breadth
광 壙 〈무덤 구덩이〉 a burial hole
광 鑛 〈갱(坑)〉 a pit; a mine; 〈광석〉 an ore
-광 -狂 〈성벽(性癖)〉 a mania 《for》; 〈사람〉 a maniac; a fan; a buff; an addict
◆ 낚시[도박]광 a fishing [gambling] addict / 댄스[색정]광 a dance [sex] maniac / 야구광 a baseball fan [enthusiast] / 영화광 a film [movie] enthusiast
▶ 우리 형은 연극광이다 My brother is a theater buff.
광각 光角 〔物〕 an optic angle
광각 光覺 the light sense [sensation]
광각 廣角 a wide angle
■ ―렌즈 a wide-angle lens; a pantoscope : 초광각 렌즈 a super-wide-angle lens / 초광각 렌즈를 카메라에 장착하다 attach a super-wide-angle lens to a camera / 이 사진은 초광각 렌즈로 찍었다 This picture was taken with a super-wide-angle lens.
광갱 鑛坑 a mine; a (mine) shaft; a pit
광견 狂犬 a mad dog; a rabid dog
광견병 狂犬病 rabies; hydrophobia; lyssa
◆ 광견병 바이러스 a rabies virus / 광견병에 걸리다 be affected with rabies
■ ―공포증 lyssophobia ―예방 주사 a rabies shot; an antirabic serum injection : 광견병 예방 주사를 놓다 give 《a dog》 an antirabies injection / 광견병 예방 주사를 맞다 get an antirabies injection
광경 光景 a sight; a view; a scene; a spectacle; an prospect; (총칭) (natural) scenery

> **解說** ***sight***는 하나의 덩어리로 된 광경, 또는 인공적인 명소를 가리킨다. ***view***는 어떤 장소에서 바라보는 것을 가리키는 가장 일반적인 말. ***scene***은 눈 앞에 전개된 경치를 가리키는 말. ***prospect***는 멀리 바라볼 수 있는 곳에서의 넓은 전망.

◆ 손에 땀을 쥐게 하는 광경 a thrilling scene [spectacle] / 슬픈[무서운] 광경 a sad [horrid] sight / 장엄한 광경 an awe-inspiring sight / 하늘에서 본 광경 an aerial view / 도착 광경을 방송하다 broadcast a description of the arrival 《of》 / 광경을 보이다 present a 《fine, pitiful》 spectacle [sight]
▶ 그것은 참담한 광경이었다 It was a harrowing spectacle.
▶ 아름다운 광경이 창 밖에 펼쳐졌다 A beautiful sight unfolded outside the window.
▶ 한반도를 하늘에서 본 광경은 무척 아름답다 The air view of Korean Peninsula is very beautiful.
▶ 그 광경은 내 기억에 또렷이 남아 있다 The scenery is strongly impressed on my memory.
광고 廣告 〈상업광고〉 an advertisement; (美口) an ad; (英口) an advert; 〈선전〉 publicity; 〈알림〉 a (public) notice; an announcement
◆ 미아[분실] 광고를 내다 advertise for the recovery of a missing child [a lost article] / 일간지에 광고를 내다 put [place, run] an advertisement in a daily newspaper / 텔레비전에 광고를 넣다 insert a commercial (message) in a TV program
―광고하다 advertise 《in, for》; announce; give publicity 《to》; make *sth* widely known; 〈알림판 등에〉 put up a bill
◆ 신문[잡지]에 광고하다 advertise in a newspaper [magazine]
▶ 그 회사는 신제품을 대대적으로 광고했다 The company advertised the new product extensively.
■ ―구인― (美口) a want ad : 신문에 구인 광고를 내다 run a want ad in a paper **3행―** 〈신문의〉 a classified advertisement **신문―** a newspaper advertisement **전면―** a full-page advertisement **텔레비전―** a TV commercial ■ ―기구(氣球) an ad balloon ―기사(記事) an advertorial ―란 an advertisement [ad] column; (英) 〈사람 찾는〉 an agony column ―료 advertisement [ad] rates; advertising charges : 3회분의 광고료를 지불하다 pay for three insertions of an advertisement ―매체 an advertising medium ―문 an advertising description; a written advertisement: 광고문 작성자 a copywriter ―방송 a commercial

광공업 鑛工業 the mining and manufacturing industries

광구 光球 〔天〕 a photosphere

광구 匡救 〈바로잡음〉 correction; rectification; redress; recovery ─**광구하다** correct; rectify; redress

광구 鑛區 a mining area [field, district, concession]; diggings; a mine lot; a mining claim ─**세** a mine-lot tax

광궤 廣軌 a broad gauge; 〈구미(歐美)의〉 the standard gauge
■─**철도** 〈美〉 a broad-gauge railroad [〈英〉 railway]

광기 狂氣 madness; insanity; craziness; lunacy
▶ 그의 행동은 광기에 가깝다 His conduct borders upon madness.
▶ 그의 열의는 광기에 가깝다 His zeal verges on madness.

광꾼 鑛─ a mine worker ⇨ 광부

광나다 光─ gloss [be glossy]; shine [be shiny]; glaze; have a shine [gloss, luster, glaze]

광내다 光─ make *sth* glossy; give luster (to); polish up; burnish
♦ 광내는 가루약 polishing powder / 구두를 광내다 shine [polish] shoes / 때빼고 광내고 〈몸단장하다〉 smarten *oneself* up

광녀 狂女 a madwoman

광년 光年 〔天〕 a light-year (略 lt-yr)
▶ 지구에서 그 별까지는 4.3광년이다 That star is 4.3 light-years away from the earth.

광대 an entertainer; 〈가면극의〉 a masque performer; 〈곡예사〉 an acrobat; an acrobatic performer; a ropewalker; a ropedancer; 〈인형극의〉 a puppeteer; 〈어릿광대〉 a clown; a buffoon; a jester; 〈창극의〉 a feat singer
♦ 광대가 되다 go on [take to] the stage / 광대 노릇을 하다 play the jester [fool] / 광대 노릇을 그만두다 retire from [leave] the stage
■─**놀음** a farce; feat performance; simple entertainment ─**모자** 〈원뿔꼴의〉 a fool's cap

광대 廣大 vastness; vastitude
─**광대하다** vast; grand; magnificent; extensive; immense
♦ 광대한 토지 a wide spread of land / 광대한 평원 a vast plain

광대무변하다 廣大無邊─ immeasurable (space); infinite (wisdom of God); illimitable (ocean); boundless (universe)

광대뼈 a cheekbone; a malar
♦ 광대뼈가 나온 사람 a person with high [prominent] cheekbone ▶ 그는 광대뼈가 나왔다 He has high cheekbones.

광도 光度 intensity of light; luminous intensity; the (degree of) brightness; luminosity
♦ 별의 광도 the magnitude [brightness] of a star / 광도 1의 별 a star with a magnitude of 1.00
■─**계** a photometer ─**측정(법)** photometry

광독 鑛毒 〈독기〉 mine [mineral] pollution; 〈독물〉 pollutants produced in the 《copper》 mining process ♦ 광독의 피해 damage from mine pollution

광란 狂亂 frenzy; raving; fury
▶ 그는 아내를 잃은 후 반 광란 상태다 He has been almost mad since he lost his dear wife.
─**광란하다** be frenzied; go wild; go insane; become frantic; be beside *oneself* 《with grief》; be driven mad 《with pain》

광량 光量 the intensity of radiation ♦ 화학 광량계 an actinometer
■─**조절기** 〈필름 현상의〉 a fader ─**측정기** an actinograph ─**측정(법)** actinography; actinometry

광력 光力 illuminating power; light; 〈촉광〉 a candlepower ♦ 광력을 측정하다 measure the intensity [illuminating power] of light

광림 光臨 your esteemed visit [presence, call, company]
─**광림하다** condescend to come [be present]; honor 《*sb*, an occasion》 with a visit
▶ 금요일 만찬에 광림하여 주시면 영광이겠습니다 We request the honor of your company at dinner on Friday.

광막하다 廣漠─ vast; extensive; boundless; spacious
♦ 광막한 사막 a vast [boundless] expanse of desert / 광막한 초원 an immense expanse of grassland; 〈美〉 the vast plains [prairies] / 광막한 황야 a vast wilderness

광망 光芒 a shaft [beam] of light

광맥 鑛脈 a vein of ore; a mineral vein; a lode
♦ 매장량이 풍부한 광맥 a rich vein 《of coal》/ 큰 광맥 immense deposits
▶ 그들은 마침내 금광맥을 찾아냈다 They finally struck a vein of gold.
■─**층** a seam [vein] of ore

광명 光明 〈빛〉 light; a sunbeam; 〈희망〉 《a ray of》 hope; a bright future [prospect]
▶ 그의 앞날에는 광명이 있다 He has a bright [rosy] future before [ahead of] him. ≒ His prospects are [future is] bright.
▶ 나는 어둠 속에서 한 가닥의 광명을 본 것 같았다 I felt as if I had seen a gleam of hope before me in the dark(ness).
▶ 그는 맹인에게 광명을 되찾아주었다 He restored sight to the blind.

광명단 光明丹 red lead ⇨ 사산화삼납

광명정대 光明正大 fairness ⇨ 공명정대(公明正大)

광목 廣木 cotton (broad) cloth; 〈美〉 unbleached muslin; 〈英〉 calico

광물 鑛物 a mineral; 〈총칭〉 the mineral ♦ 희귀

한 광물 a rare mineral / 광물 표본 상자 a mineralogical cabinet / 광물성의 mineral ■ —계 the mineral kingdom [world] —면(綿) mineral wool —성(性) 섬유 a mineral fiber —성 수지[연료] mineral resin [fuel] —유 a mineral oil —자원 mineral resources: 풍부[빈약]한 광물 자원 rich [poor] mineral resources —질 mineral matter —학 mineralogy —학자 a mineralogist

광반 光斑 〔寫〕 a flare (spot); (俗) a ghost

광배 光背 a halo (around the head of a saint); 〈종교화 등의〉 a nimbus (*pl.* ~es, -bi); an aureole

광범위하다 廣範圍— extensive; wide; broad; widespread; wide-ranging (studies); comprehensive (plan); far-flung (influence); far-reaching
♦ 광범위한 개혁 a far-reaching reform / 광범위한 응용 a wide application / 광범위한 지식 extensive knowledge / 광범위한 파괴 widespread destruction / 광범위한 권한이 주어지다 be given wide power / 광범위한 영향을 주다 exercise [exert] a far-reaching influence (upon, over) / 광범위하게 논하다 discuss (a subject) at large; deal with generalities
▶ 그는 독서 폭이 광범위하다 His reading is of very wide range [covers a wide range].
▶ 그의 교제폭[지식폭]이 광범위하다 He has a wide circle of acquaintances [is widely informed].
▶ 그 연구는 매우 광범위하다 The study is very comprehensive.
▶ 피해가 광범위했다 The damage was extensive.
▶ 이 식물은 광범위하게 분포되어 있다 This plant grows [is distributed] over a wide area.

광복 光復 glorious restoration of sovereignty; 〈주권 회복〉 the restoration of independence (to a country)
—광복하다 regain (a country's) independence ■ —군 the Independence [Liberation] Army —절 Independence [Liberation] Day of Korea

광부 鑛夫 a mine worker; a miner; a digger; a pitman ■ 석탄— a coal miner

광분하다 狂奔— 1 〈미친 듯이 날뛰다〉 run wild [amuck]; run madly about; rush about 2 〈미친 듯이 뛰어다니다〉 make desperate [frantic] efforts; busy *oneself* about *sth*; be very busy (in) doing; be on the run; be absorbed in (doing)
♦ 돈벌이에 광분하다 be madly busy making money; be absorbed in moneymaking / 선거 운동에 광분하다 be heavily engaged in canvassing for an election
▶ 그들은 이면 공작에 광분했다 They rushed about madly working behind the scenes.
▶ 그는 돈벌이에 광분하고 있다 He is frantically trying to earn money.

광산 鑛山 a mine
♦ 광산 채굴을 중지하다 shut down a mine / 광산을 개발하다 develop [open up] a mine / 광산을 경영하다 run [operate] a mine
▶ 그 구리 광산은 1970년에 폐광되었다 The copper mine was closed in 1970.
▶ 아버지는 삼척에서 광산을 경영[채굴]하고 계십니다 My father runs [exploits, works] a mine in Samch'ŏk.
■ —공학 mining engineering —기사 a mining engineer [expert] —노동자 a mine worker; a miner —물 a mineral product: 광산물이 풍부한 mineral-rich (provinces); (areas) rich in meneral resources —채굴권 mining rights [concessions] —촌 a mining town; a miners' town; (美) a camp

광산 鑛産 〈광산물〉 a mineral product; minerals ■ —자원 ⇨ 광물(~자원) —지 a district full of mineral deposits

광산업 鑛山業 the mining industry; (engage in) mining ■ —자 a mine operator; a mine-owner; 〈투기적인〉 a speculator in mines

광산학 鑛山學 mining science ■ —과 the department of mining science

광상 鑛床 a (mineral) [an ore] deposit ♦ 구리 광상 a deposit of copper ■ —학 study of mineral deposit

광상곡 狂想曲 〔樂〕 a capriccio

광석 鑛石 an ore; a mineral; 〈라디오 검파용〉 a crystal
■ —검파기 a crystal [mineral] detector —분쇄기 an ore crusher —수신기 a crystal (radio) set [receiver] —운반차 a hutch —표본 a collection of ores; mineralogical specimens —화 mineralization

광선 光線 〈빛의 줄기〉 light; a ray (of light); a beam
♦ 광선의 굴절[반사] refraction [reflection] of light / 광선을 방사하다 send out light / 광선을 차단하다 cut off light; 〈갓을 씌워서〉 shade from the direct rays (of the sun)
▶ 이 필름[건판]은 광선이 들어갔다 This film [dry plate] is affected.
■ 굴절[반사]— refracted [reflected] light 살인—a death ray 엑스— ⇨ 엑스선 —분색기(分色器) a disperser —분석 spectrum analysis —여과기 a light filter —요법 〔醫〕 phototherapy —운동 photokinesis

광섬유 光纖維 optical fiber

광속 光束 a pencil of light [rays]; 〔電〕 light [luminous] flux ■ —계 an integrating photometer

광속(도) 光速(度) the velocity of light; speed of light

광수 鑛水 mineral water ⇨ 광천(~수)

광시곡 狂詩曲 〔樂〕 a rhapsody ♦ 리스트의 헝가리 광시곡 Liszt's Hungarian Rhapsodies
■ —작자 a rhapsodist

광신 狂信 (religious) fanaticism; religious frenzy
♦ 광신적인 공산주의자 a fanatical [rabid] Communist / 광신적으로 fanatically
—광신하다 believe fanatically (in); be devoted blindly (to)
▶ 그들은 지도자의 말을 광신했다 They fanatically believed what their leader said.
■ —도 a (religious) fanatic —자 a fanatic; a fanatic(al) believer (in)

광야 廣野 a wide [vast] plain

광야 曠野 a wild plain; a wilderness; 〈불모의〉 wasteland ◆광야를 헤매다 wander around in the wilds

광양자 光量子 〔物〕 a photon; light quantum (*pl.* ·ta)

광어 廣魚 〈넙치〉 a flatfish ▪말린 광어 a dried flatfish

광업 鑛業 the mining industry; mining ▪—권 a mining right —법〔法〕 the Mining Law —세 the mining tax —소 a mining station [office] —주(株) mining stocks [shares] —회사 a mining company

광역 廣域 a wide [large, broad] area ▪—경제 great-sphere economy —수사 a search (for a criminal) conducted over a wide area : 살인범에 대한 광역 수사가 진행되었다 A search for the murderer was conducted over a wide area. —행정 integrated administration of a large region

광열비 光熱費 lighting and heating expense; heat [fuel] and light expense(s); expenses for light and fuel

광염 光焰 a flame

광영 光榮 an honor ⇨ 영광(榮光)

광우병 狂牛病 mad cow disease

광원 光源 a source of light; a light source; 〈발광체〉 an illuminant; 〔電〕 a luminous source

광유 鑛油 mineral oil ⇨ 광물(~油)

광음 光陰 time (and tide); years (and months) ◆광음 여류(如流)하다 Time flies (like an arrow). ⇌ Time is fleeting.
▶일촌의 광음을 가벼이 마라 Improve [Make good use of] every minute.

광의 廣義 (in) a wide [broad, large] sense ◆광의로 해석하다 take the broad [wide] sense (of the word)
▶그 규칙을 광의로 해석하면 문제될 것이 없을 것이다 If we understand [interpret] the rule in a broad sense, it won't be any problem.

광인 狂人 a lunatic ⇨ 미치광이

광자 光子 〔物〕 a photon; a light quantum

광장 廣場 〈빈 터〉 an open space [ground]; 〈여러 길이 모여 이루는 4각의〉 a (public) square; 〈상가로 둘러싸인 넓은〉 a plaza; 〈둥근〉 a circus ◆만남의 광장 the plaza for family reunion
▶역전에 꽤 넓은 광장이 있다 There is a fairly large square [plaza] in front of the station.
▶노인과 젊은이 사이에 공통의 광장이 없다는 것은 유감스러운 일이다 It is to be regretted that there is no level of communication between the older generation and the younger generation.
▪역전— a square [plaza] in front of a station ■—공포증 agoraphobia

광재 鑛滓 slag; dross

광저기 〔植〕 a cowpea ⇨ 동부

광적 狂的 insane; lunatic; frantic; fanatic; fanatical; mad
◆광적인 신앙 fanatic belief / 광적인 신흥 종교 신자 a fanatical believer in a new religion / 광적인 열의 wild enthusiasm

광전 光電 〔電〕 photoelectricity
■—관 〈전기〉 a phototube; a photoelectric tube; 〈텔레비전의〉 a cathode-ray tube —자 a photoelectron —자 공학 photoelectronic engineering —자 방출 photoemission —효과 the photoelectric effect

광전리 光電離 〔物〕 photoionization

광전지 光電池 a photoelectric [photovoltaic] cell; a photocell

광점 光點 〔電〕 a luminous point

광정 匡正 remedy; correction; reform —광정하다 correct; set [put] *sth* right; remedy; reform
◆나쁜 버릇을 광정하다 cure [break] *sb* of a bad habit

광주 鑛主 a mineowner; a mine operator; the owner [proprietor] of a mine

광주리 a (bamboo [wicker]) basket; 〈뚜껑 있는〉 a hamper
◆한 광주리 가득한 딸기 a basketful of strawberries / 광주리를 짜다 weave [make] a basket
▶이 광주리 속에는 사과가 10개 있다 There are ten apples in this basket.

광주리장수 a peddler [hawker] with a basket of household wares

광중성자 光中性子 〔物〕 photoneutron

광증 狂症 madness; lunacy; insanity

광차 光差 〔天〕 equation of light; 〔物〕 the light equation

광차 鑛車 a tram(car); a mine car; 〈석탄차〉 a coal tub

광채 光彩 luster; brilliancy; splendor; effulgence
◆광채 나는 진주 lustrous pearls / 광채가 나다 be brilliant; be in all (its) splendor / 광채를 발하다 give off pretty colors; shed luster; shine; (비유) outshine all the others; cut a brilliant figure; stand out (among others); 광채를 잃다 lose its luster
▶그 여자의 진주 목걸이가 광채를 발했다 Her pearl necklace sparkled brightly.
▶그 여자의 눈은 광채를 잃었다 Her eyes lost their luster.

광천 鑛泉 a mineral spring ■—수(水) mineral water; (英口) minerals —요법 balneotherapy

광체 光體 〔物〕 a luminous body ⇨ 발광(~체)

광축 光軸 〔物〕 an optic(al) axis (*pl.* axes)

광층 鑛層 an ore bed

광치다 光— 〈떠벌리다〉 brag (about); talk big; make too much of (things); exaggerate; 〈광내다〉 make *sth* shine [bright]; glitter; polish; scintillate

광케이블 光— a fiber-optic cable ◆해저 광케이블 undersea fiber-optic cables

광태 狂態 scandalous [disgraceful] behavior; shameful [crazy] conduct
◆광태를 부리다 behave disgracefully; make a scandalous scene
▶그는 술마시면[취하면] 때때로 광태를 부린다 He sometimes acts wild when he drinks [he is drunk].

광택 光澤 luster; brilliance; a gloss; a shine; a polish
◆은은한 광택 quiet [subdued] gloss [sheen] /

광택이 있는 lustrous; brilliant; shining; polished; glossy; shiny / 광택이 없는 lusterless; dull; dim / 광택을 내다 burnish; glaze; polish; give luster [brilliance] 《to》 / 광택을 잃다 lose 《its》 luster; 〈금속이〉 tarnish; become tarnished

▶ 이 고양이는 털에 광택이 있다 The fur of this cat is glossy.

▶ 닦은 놋쇠는 아름다운 광택이 난다 Burnished brass has a beautiful luster.

▶ 은은 덮어 두지 않으면 광택을 잃는다 Silver will tarnish if left uncovered.

■—계(計) a glossmeter —사진 a glazed photograph —제 a brightener —지 glossy [slick, coated] paper

광통신 光通信 an optical communication
광파 光波 〔物〕 light wave
광포 狂暴 wildness; violence; frenzy; rage
—광포하다 violent; furious; wild; frenzied; berserk

◆ 상처입은 광포한 호랑이 a furious wounded tiger / 개의 광포하게 짖는 소리 the dog's frenzied barks / 광포해지다 go [run] berserk; fly into a frantic rage

▶ 환자가 광포해서 다루기 어려웠다 The patient was violent and unmanageable.

광폭 廣幅 double [extra] width 《of cloth》; a wide width
광풍 狂風 a violent gale; a raging [howling] wind [gale] ◆ 광풍으로 쓰러지다 be blown down in [by] a raging gale ▶ 광풍이 불고 있다 It is blowing a howling gale.
광학 光學 optics; optical science
■—공업 optical industry —공장 optical works; an optical shop [plant] —기기[병기] an optical instrument [weapon] —기기상(商) an optician —식 마크 판독기 〔電子〕 an optical mark reader —섬유 ⇨ 광섬유 —유리 optical glass
광합성 光合成 〔生化〕 photosynthesis ■—산물 a photosynthate
광행차 光行差 〔天〕 an aberration ■—연주(年周)[일주(日周)]— annual [diurnal] aberration
광화학 光化學 〔物・化〕 photochemistry
◆ 광화학 스모그 photochemical smog
광활하다 廣闊— spacious; vast; extensive; wide
◆ 광활한 땅[사막] a vast expanse of land [desert] / 광활한 초원 an extensive [a spacious] meadow / 광활한 평야 a vast plain [open field]
광휘 光輝 brilliancy; glory; splendor; brightness; the fire 《of a gem》 ◆ 태양의 광휘 the glory of the sun / 광휘를 발하다 shine brightly [brilliantly]; emit dazzling rays
광희 狂喜 wild joy; rapture(s); extreme delight; exultation
—광희하다 be mad [wild, frantic, beside *oneself*] with joy; go mad with joy; be enraptured 《with, over, at》 ◆ 광희하여 in *one's* wild [great] joy

▶ 그 소식을 듣고 그녀는 광희했다 She went into raptures [was overjoyed] at the news.

괘 卦 a divination sign
괘경 掛鏡 a wall [hanging] mirror
괘념하다 掛念— care; mind; take 《a matter》 to heart; be concerned 《over》

◆ 조금도 괘념하지 않다 do not care a bit [straw] 《about》

▶ 그것은 괘념치 마세요 Please pay no attention to it. ⇌ Just forget it.

▶ 비용에 대해서는 괘념하지 마라 Don't mind [concern yourself about] the expenses.

괘도 掛圖 〈도표〉 a wall chart; 〈지도〉 a wall map; 〈그림〉 a hanging picture ■—걸이 a chart hanger
괘력 掛曆 a wall calendar
괘선 罫線 a ruled line; 〔印〕 a rule mark
◆ 괘선이 있는 종이 ruled [lined] paper / 괘선이 없는 종이 plain [unruled] paper / 종이에 괘선을 긋다 rule [draw] lines on paper; rule [line] paper
괘씸하다 〈무례하다〉 insulting; rude; 〈밉살스럽다〉 hateful; detestable; damnable; 〈발칙하다〉 inexcusable; 〈건방지다〉 impertinent
◆ 괘씸한 놈 a saucy [an impertinent] fellow / 괘씸한 말 cheeky [saucy, impertinent] remarks / 괘씸하게 굴다 behave rudely [outrageously]; be rude 《to》; act disrespectfully / 괘씸하게 생각하다 hold *sb* culpable

▶ 그의 괘씸한 태도에 화가 난다 I am offended by his impertinent manner.

▶ 그 녀석은 어른한테 인사도 제대로 할 줄 모르는 괘씸한 놈이다 He is an insolent fellow who doesn't know how to greet his elders properly.

▶ 우리가 하는 일에 끼어들다니 참 괘씸한 녀석이다 It is impudent of him to cut in on what we are doing.

괘장 a sudden reversal [switch] in *one's* attitude ◆ 괘장 부치다 reverse *oneself*; suddenly switch *one's* position
괘종 掛鐘 a wall clock
괘지 罫紙 ruled paper ⇨ 인찰지
괜찮다 1 〈무방하다〉 be good enough; be all right; will do

◆ 괜찮으시다면 If you don't mind…; If it is all right for you…

▶ 연필로 써도 괜찮습니까? May I write with a pencil? ⇌ Do you mind if I use a pencil?

▶ 나는 현재의 급료로도 괜찮다 I'm 《quite》 content [satisfied] with my present salary.

▶ 5,000원[일요일]이라도 괜찮습니다 Five thousand won [Sunday] will do.

▶ 한국 말로 된 책이면 무엇이든 괜찮다 Any book will do, as long as it is in Korean.

▶ 비가 와도 괜찮다 I don't care if it rains.

▶ ▣會話▣ 「언제 돌려드릴까요?」「언제든지 괜찮습니다」 "When shall I return it to you?" "Any time will do."

▶ ▣會話▣ 「하나 더 드시지요」「괜찮아요」 "Won't you have one more?" "No, thank you. 《I've had plenty.》"

▶ 괜찮습니다 〈사과에 대한 대답으로〉 Never mind. ⇌ That's all right.

▶ 홍차가 없으면 커피도 괜찮습니다 Coffee is all right if you don't have any tea.

▶ ▣會話▣ 「여기서 담배를 피워도 괜찮겠습니까?」「그럼요」 "May [Can] I smoke here?" "Certainly." ⇌ "Do you mind my smoking [if

괜찮다

I smoke] here?" "No, I don't."
2 〈좋다〉 good; fine; fair; 〈나쁘지 않다〉 not so bad; passable
♦ 괜찮은 값 a good price / 괜찮은 솜씨 fine [good] workmanship / 괜찮은 수입 fair [handsome] income / 맛이 괜찮다 taste good
▶ 그는 영어를 괜찮게 한다 He speaks English pretty well.
3 〈안전하다〉 safe; all right; (美) O.K.
▶ 이 집은 지진이 나도 괜찮다 This house is safe from earthquake [earthquake-proof].
▶ 이 물 마셔도 괜찮은 물입니까? Is this water good enough to drink?
▶ 자, 이젠 괜찮다 〈위험을 벗어나다〉 Now we are out of the woods.

괜하다 useless ⇨ 공연(空然)하다

괭이 a hoe
♦ 괭이질하다 (dig with a) hoe / 괭이로 밭을 갈다 hoe a field; till a field with a hoe / 괭이로 파다 dig with a hoe
▶ 농부는 괭이로 땅을 일구었다 The farmer broke ground with a hoe. ⇌ The farmer hoed up the soil.

괴경 塊莖 〔植〕 a tuber; a seed=덩이줄기

괴괴망측하다 怪怪罔測— 〈괴상하다〉 very strange; strangest; most weird [mysterious, uncanny]; 〈흉측하다〉 monstrous
♦ 괴괴한 소문 the wildest [most scandalous] rumor / 괴괴 망측한 일 a (very) strange [an odd] thing; a mystery / 괴괴 망측한 운명으로 by some strange fate
▶ 그의 행동은 괴괴망측했다 His behavior was scandalous.

괴괴하다 quiet; silent; still; placid; 〈인적이 끊긴〉 deserted
♦ 괴괴한 거리 a quiet [deserted] street / 괴괴한 밤 a very silent [still] night / 괴괴해지다 be [become] as silent as the grave
▶ 주위는 괴괴했다 It was quiet all around. ⇌ All was quiet.
▶ 장내는 괴괴했다 A hush fell over the hall.

괴근 塊根 〔植〕 a tuberous [tuberose] root=덩이뿌리

괴금 塊金 a nugget

괴기 怪奇 (a) mystery; (a) wonder **—괴기하다** mysterious; grotesque; strange **■—소설** a mystery [spook] story; a ghost story; a thriller

괴까다롭다 〈문제가〉 tricky; intricate; difficult; complicated; delicate; 〈성질이〉 be fastidious [particular, choosy]; hard to please
♦ 괴까다로운 남자 a man hard to please; a fussy man / 괴까다로운 노부인 a difficult old lady / 괴까다로운 문장 a difficult passage / 괴까다로운 취미 fastidious [finicky] tastes
▶ 이것은 괴까다로운 문제다 This is a knotty [troublesome] problem.
▶ 그는 음식에 괴까다롭다 He is particular about his food.

괴나리봇짐 a traveler's knapsack; a bundle carried on *one's* back

괴다¹ 〈모이다〉 gather; collect; stay; 〈정체하다〉 stagnate; be stagnant
♦ 괸 물 (a pool of) stagnant [standing] water / 움푹한 땅에 괸 빗물 rainwater collected [gathered] in depressions
▶ 비가 온 뒤 도로의 여기 저기에 물이 고어 있었다 After the rain there were many small puddles in the road.
▶ 그녀의 눈에 눈물이 괴었다 There were tears [Tears gathered] in her eyes.

괴다² 〈발효할 때 거품이 일다〉 ferment; undergo fermentation ▶ 술이 괼 때는 거품이 부걱부걱 인다 When wine is fermented it gives off bubbles of gas.

괴다³ **1** 〈받치다〉 prop up; support; sustain
♦ 책상 다리를 돌로 괴다 support the leg of a desk with a piece of stone
▶ 그는 (두)손으로 턱을 괴고 창밖을 바라보고 있었다 He was looking out of the window with his chin resting [propped up] on the hand(s).
2 〈쌓다〉 pile up (food on a dish)
♦ 잔칫상에 음식을 괴다 pile up food on a banquet table

괴다⁴ 〈사랑하다〉 love; adore

괴담 怪談 〈무서운 이야기〉 a ghost [weird] story; (口) a spooky story; 〈이상한 이야기〉 a strange [mysterious] story

괴도 怪盜 a mysterious [phantom] thief
♦ 괴도 뤼팽 Lupin the phantom thief

괴란 壞亂 demoralization; corruption **—괴란하다** demoralize; corrupt; subvert
▶ 그들의 행동은 사회 질서를 괴란했다 Their action upset [subverted] the social order.
▶ 이런 종류의 출판물은 공중 도덕을 괴란할 우려가 있다 We fear publications of this kind have an injurious effect upon public morals.

괴력 怪力 superhuman power; marvelous [fantastic] (physical) strength; Herculean [supernatural] strength
♦ 괴력의 사나이 an uncommonly strong man; a man of Herculean strength / 괴력을 발휘하다 display uncommon strength

괴로움 〈고통〉 pain; 〈고난〉 hardship; suffering; 〈성가심〉 trouble; 〈근심〉 worry; 〈고뇌〉 agony (▶구체적인 것일 때에는 모두 가산 명사로 씀)
♦ 가난의 괴로움 hardship of poverty / 마음의 괴로움 anguish of heart; mental affliction [troubles] / 양심의 괴로움 a twinge of conscience / 인생의 괴로움 《taste》 the bitterness of life; life's trials / 청춘의 괴로움 the problems of adolescence / 해산의 괴로움 pains of childbirth / 괴로움이 있다 have worries; be in trouble / 괴로움이 없다 have no worries; be carefree / 괴로움을 겪다 go through [undergo, experience] hardships / 괴로움을 덜다 relieve *sb's* suffering / 괴로움을 참다 endure [bear] pain [suffering]
▶ 학생을 가르친다는 것은 괴로움이자 즐거움이다 To teach students is a source of pleasure as well as anxiety.
▶ 그녀와 헤어지는 것은 가슴 찢어지는 괴로움이었다 It was heartbreaking to part with her.
▶ 괴로움이 있으면 즐거움도 있게 마련이다 Every cloud has a silver lining.
▶ 그는 갖가지 괴로움을 겪어 왔다 He has gone

through various hardships.
▶ 이것은 인생의 괴로움을 맛본 사람만이 쓸 수 있는 책이다 This is the book that could be written only by a man who has tasted [experienced] the bitter side of life.
▶ 인생은 괴로움으로 가득 차 있다 Life is full of trouble(s) [worries].

괴로워하다 1 〈고통스러워 하다〉 feel [be in] pain; suffer 《from》; be afflicted 《with》; writhe in agony [pain]
♦ 가난에 괴로워하는 사람들 poverty-stricken people / 갈증으로 괴로워하다 suffer from thirst / 사랑 때문에 괴로워하다 be lovesick; languish for [with] love; 〈실연을 당해〉 be lovelorn
▶ 환자는 몹시 괴로워했다 The patient was suffering severely.
▶ 그는 두통으로 괴로워하고 있다 He is suffering from a headache.
2 〈근심하다〉 be worried [trouble] 《about》; worry *oneself* 《about, over》; 〈고민하다〉 be distressed [harassed]
♦ 돈 문제로 괴로워하다 be pressed [hard up] for money; have financial worries / 빚 때문에 괴로워하다 be harassed with debts
▶ 그들은 이 문제로 몹시 괴로워하고 있다 This question is giving them trouble.
▶ 그는 자신의 장래 문제로 괴로워하고 있다 He is worried about his future.
▶ 그는 사업 실패로 몹시 괴로워하고 있다 He is terribly distressed by the failure of his business.
▶ 그 여자는 양심의 가책으로 괴로워하고 있다 She is tormented by a guilty conscience.
▶ 그는 남모르게 괴로워하고 있다 He is eating his heart out.

괴롭다 〈고통스럽다〉 painful; tormenting; afflicting; agonizing; 〈힘들다〉 troublesome; hard; difficult; 〈난처하다〉 awkward; embarrassing; 〈고민·불안하다〉 distressed; ill at ease; troubled; uncomfortable
♦ 괴로운 마음 a troubled [an aching] heart / 괴로운 세상 a hard world / 괴로운 일 hard [strenuous] work; a hard [tough] job / 괴로운 입장 an awkward situation / 괴로운 처지 a (very) painful position [situation] / 괴로운 나머지 in *one*'s pain; driven by pain; in desperation / 경제적으로 괴롭다 suffer (from) economic distress
▶ 살아 있는 것이 괴롭다 Life hangs heavy upon me.
▶ 그들은 생활이 괴롭다 They are needy [in poverty].
▶ 병든 남편 생각에 그녀는 괴로웠다 The thought of her sick husband tormented her.
▶ 그의 중상모략이 나에게는 참 괴로웠다 His backbiting caused me a great deal of trouble.
▶ 그녀가 우는 것이 보기 괴로웠다 It was painful to see her crying. ⇌ I could not bear to see her crying.
▶ 그것은 괴로운 여행이었다 It was a painful trip.
▶ 전쟁 중에는 어머니도 괴로운 일을 겪으셨다 My mother also had a bitter experience during the war.
▶ 나는 괴로운 처지에 빠졌다 I was in an embarrassing [awkward] situation. ⇌ I found myself in an awkward [a painful] position.
▶ 무엇이 괴로운지 말해 보렴 Tell me your worries.

괴롭히다 〈고통스럽게 하다〉 afflict; torment; torture; give *sb* pain; agonize; 〈못살게 굴다〉 bully; treat *sb* harshly; harass; 〈난처하게 하다〉 vex; trouble; worry; annoy; bother; embarrass 〈병 등이〉 hurt *sb*

解説 ***trouble***은 걱정을 시키거나 폐를 끼쳐서 괴롭히는 것이고 ***worry***는 여러 가지로 불안하게 하는 것인데, 수동태로 쓰이는 경우가 많다. ***annoy, bother***는 방해하는 일을 되풀이 하거나 해서 남의 심기를 어지럽히는 것이다. annoy는 그 결과 화를 내게 하는 데 비해 bother는 반드시 그런 뜻은 없고 또 그 결과가 보다 가벼운 경우를 의미한다.

♦ 마음을 괴롭히다 〈사람이 주어〉 worry (*oneself*) [be worried] 《about, over》; be concerned about 《a matter》; 〈사물이 주어〉 oppress *one*'s heart / 약자를 괴롭히다 bully the weaker / 적을 괴롭히다 harass the enemy
▶ 아이들이란 종종 여러 모로 부모를 괴롭힌다 Children often bother their parents in many ways.
▶ 무거운 세금이 봉급 생활자들을 괴롭힌다 The weight of taxation bears hard [heavily] on the salaried workers.
▶ 그 여자는 며느리를 괴롭힌다 She is hard on her daugthr-in-law.
▶ 모기가 밤새껏 나를 괴롭혔다 Mosquitoes kept annoying me all night.
▶ 동물을 괴롭혀서는 안 된다 Don't be cruel to animals.

괴뢰 傀儡 〈꼭두각시〉 a puppet; a dummy; a marionette; 〈허수아비〉 a robot; 〈앞잡이〉 a tool; a cat's paw
♦ 괴뢰 노릇을 하다 act as *sb*'s tool / 괴뢰가 되다 become a puppet in the hand of *sb* / 괴뢰로 삼다 make a puppet of *sb*
▶ 그는 단지 괴뢰에 지나지 않고, 실제 두목은 그의 동생이다 He is just a figurehead. The real boss is his younger brother.
■ —사(師) a puppeteer; a puppet player —정권 a puppet [dummy, robot] regime —정부 a puppet [dummy, robot] government

괴리 乖離 estrangement; alienation
—**괴리하다** be [become] estranged [alienated] 《from》
▶ 과학의 진보가 인간을 종교에서 괴리시킨다 The advance of science estranges man from religion.
▶ 민심이 괴리되어 정권이 무너졌다 The government fell because it had lost touch with the people.
■ —개념 [論] a disparate concept

괴멸 壞滅 (complete) destruction; ruin; demolition; 〈전멸〉 annihilation
♦ 괴멸적인 타격을 주다 give a crushing [fatal,

deadly] blow; inflict a deathblow (on)
—**괴멸하다** be destroyed [demolished, ruined]; be wiped out; molder away; be annihilated
♦ **괴멸시키다** annihilate (an opposition force); demolish (the enemy)
▶ 됭케르크는 제2차 세계대전 중 폭격으로 괴멸되었다 Dunkirk was completely destroyed by bombs in World War II.
▶ 대지진으로 그 도시는 거의 괴멸되었다 The town was almost completely destroyed by the great earthquake.

괴문서 怪文書 a mysterious document; 〈출처불명의〉 an anonymous muckraking document; a document of obscure origin;〈불온한〉 seditious [subversive] literature
▶ 나를 중상하는 괴문서가 유포되었다 Mysterious documents were circulated to slander me.

괴물 怪物 a monster; 〈도깨비〉 a bugbear; a ghost; 〈괴상한 사람〉 a mysterious [monstrous] figure [fellow]
♦ 바다에 사는 괴물 a sea monster / 정계의 괴물 a political sphinx [wizard] / 괴물의 정체를 밝히다 unmask the apparition

괴벽하다 乖僻 eccentric; fastidious; odd; queer; strange; unusual; peculiar
♦ 괴벽한 노인 an eccentric [a queer] old man / 괴벽한 취미 fastidious taste(s)
▶ 그 시인은 괴벽하기로 유명했다 The poet was well known for his eccentricity.

괴변 怪變 〈사고〉a strange accident;〈이변〉an odd mishap

괴사 怪事 a mystery; a mysterious event; a strange case [affair]; a wonder

괴사 怪死 death from an unknown cause; a mysterious death
—**괴사하다** die a mysterious death; die from an unknown cause
▶ 그는 괴사했다 He died a mysterious death.
■—**사건** a case of mysterious death

괴사건 怪事件 a mystery; a mystery case; a mysterious event [occurrence]; strange case [affair]

괴상 塊狀 ♦ 괴상의 massive ■—**암** a massive rock —**용암** block lava —**조직** a massive structure

괴상야릇하다 怪常 quite odd [strange]; queer eccentric; most peculiar [grotesque]
♦ 괴상야릇한 경험 a quite strange experience / 괴상야릇한 조각 a quite oddly-shaped statue / 괴상야릇한 행동 strange [odd] behavior
▶ 그 괴상야릇한 풍습은 지금도 이 지방에서 보존되고 있다 That quite strange [odd] custom is still maintained in this district.

괴상하다 怪常 strange; odd; queer; peculiar; eccentric; grotesque

[解說] **strange**는 지금까지 본 적도 없이 기묘하다는 뜻을 나타내는 가장 일반적인 말. **odd, queer**는 보통의 상태에서 벗어나 색다르다는 말. **peculiar**는 다른 것과는 달라 특이하다는 느낌을 말한다.

♦ 괴상한 물건[일] a strange thing; an oddity / 괴상한 버릇 a strange [peculiar] habit / 괴상한 행동 strange [odd, queer] behavior / 괴상한 형태의 조각 an oddly-shaped statue / 괴상하게 들릴지 모르지만 It may sound strange [queer], but… / 괴상한 옷차림을 하고 있다 be fantastically dressed / 괴상한 표정을 짓다 put on a queer face / 괴상하게 보이다 look queer [strange]
▶ 그는 괴상한 녀석이다 He is an odd [a peculiar] fellow [guy]. ⇌ (口) He is a case.
▶ 그런 괴상한 질문에는 대답할 방법이 없다 I just don't know how to answer such an odd question.
▶ 그는 조금 괴상한 데가 있다 He is a bit of an eccentric.
▶ 그녀의 괴상한 행동에 그들은 진절머리를 냈다 They were all disgusted at [with] her strange [eccentric, odd, peculiar] behavior.

괴석 怪石 an oddly-shaped stone

괴수 怪獸 a monster; a monstrous animal

괴수 魁首 a ringleader; (美) a boss; a head; a head man ♦ 갱단[폭도]의 괴수 the ringleader of gangs [a mob] / 도둑의 괴수 the head [boss] of robbers

괴이쩍다 怪異 mysterious ⇨ 괴이하다

괴이찮다 怪異 natural; not strange; 〈서술적〉 be in no way peculiar; be to be expected
▶ 네가 실패한 것은 조금도 괴이찮다 It is nothing strange that you have failed.

괴이하다 怪異 strange; grotesque; weird; odd; uncanny; supernatural; mysterious
♦ 괴이한 죽음 mysterious death / 괴이한 풍문 a wild [bizarre] rumor / 괴이한 현상 a strange [mysterious] phenomenon
▶ 그의 행동은 괴이하다 His behavior is strange.
▶ 사람들은 아직도 그의 괴이한 실종에 대해 이야기하고 있다 People still talk about his mysterious disappearance.
▶ 벽에 괴이한 가면이 걸려 있었다 There was a grotesque mask on the wall.

괴인 怪人 a monster [mystery] man ♦ 복면을 한 괴인 a masked mystery man

괴인물 怪人物 a mystery [mysterious, enigmatic] person; a sphinx; a Mr. X

괴저 壞疽 〔醫〕 gangrene

괴조 怪鳥 a monstrous [a mysterious] bird

괴질 怪疾 a mysterious disease; a disease of unknown cause [origin] ♦ 유럽에 괴질이 번지고 있다 An unidentified epidemic is prevalent [raging] in Europe.

괴짜 怪 an eccentric (person); an odd [a queer] fellow [fish]; (口) a crank; (美俗) a screwball
▶ 그는 행동이 괴짜다 He is eccentric in his conduct.
▶ 그런 짓을 하다니 그 친구도 괴짜다 It is rather eccentric of him to do such a thing.
▶ 그런 행동 때문에 그는 주위에서 괴짜 취급을 당했다 People regarded him as a queer [an odd] fellow for such behavior.

괴철 塊鐵 an iron ingot

괴탄 塊炭 lump coal

괴테 〈독일의 시인·작가〉 Goethe, Johann Wolfgang von (1749-1832)

괴팍하다 乖— 〈까다롭다〉 hard to get along with; difficult [hard] to please; fastidious; crabby; fussy; 〈별나다〉 eccentric; cranky; 〈완고하다〉 obstinate; bigoted
♦성미가 괴팍한 노인 an old codger / 괴팍한 성미 a fussy temperament / 괴팍한 아이 a difficult child / 괴팍스럽게 음식을 가리다 be fastidious about food
▶그는 괴팍한 데가 있다 There is something strange [odd, peculiar] about him.

괴팍하다 乖愎— fastidious ⇨ 괴팍하다

괴한 怪漢 a suspicious(-looking) man [fellow]; a strange-looking character

괴혈병 壞血病 〔醫〕 scorbutus; scurvy
■—환자 a scorbutic

괴화 怪火 a mysterious fire; a fire of unknown [suspicious] origin

굄[1] 〈총애〉 love; affection; favor; good grace; patronage
♦굄을 받다 be loved; win sb's favor; find favor with; be patronized / 굄을 잃다 forfeit [lose] one's favor [affection]
▶그녀는 왕의 굄을 받았다 She was loved most tenderly by the king. ⇒ She was a favorite with the king.

굄[2] a prop; a support; a strut =굄대

굄대 a prop; a support; a strut

굄돌 a stone support [prop]

굄목 —木 a wooden support [prop]

굄새 〈괴어 놓은 모양〉 shape [appearance] of stacked cakes [fruits] on a plate; 〈굄질하는 기술〉 skill at cakes stacking on plates

굄질 stacking [piling up, heaping up] cakes on a plate

굉굉하다 轟轟— roaring; thundering; rumbling; booming ♦굉굉한 폭포 소리 《hear》 the roaring sound of a fall / 굉굉히 울리다 rumble; boom; roar

굉연하다 轟然— thundering; roaring; earsplitting; deafening
♦굉연히 with a roaring [terrific] sound; with a roar
▶굉연한 폭음과 함께 집이 폭파되었다[건물이 파괴되었다] The house exploded [The building was demolished] with a deafening [thunderous] roar.

굉음 轟音 a roaring sound; a boom; a deafening roar; an earsplitting sound
♦굉음을 내다 make [produce] a thundering noise / 굉음을 내며 치솟다 roar up
▶모터가 굉음을 내며 돌아갔다 The motor ran with a roaring sound.
▶기차가 굉음을 내며 지나갔다 The train thundered past [roared away].

굉장하다 宏壯— 〈크다〉 grand; magnificent; (口) 〈엄청나다〉 awful; terrible; tremendous; 〈대단하다〉 superb; excellent; (口) great
♦굉장한 더위[추위] terrible heat [cold] / 굉장한 부자 an awfully rich man / 굉장한 선물 a royal present / 굉장한 성공 a phenomenal [dazzling] success / 굉장한 인파 a tremendous turnout of people; a mammoth crowd / 굉장한 저택 a stately mansion / 굉장한 파티 a royal [grand] party / 굉장한 폭풍우 a furious storm / 굉장한 속도로 at a furious [breakneck] speed
▶노트르담 대성당은 굉장하다 Notre Dame is an imposing cathedral.
▶비행기에서 내려다본 알프스 산맥은 굉장했다 The Alps looked magnificent from the airplane.
▶그는 굉장한 힘으로 자동차를 들어 올렸다 He lifted the car with phenomenal strength.
▶그 여자는 굉장한 미인이다 She is strikingly beautiful. ⇒ She is a striking [stunning] beauty.
▶그는 굉장한 환영을 받았다 He received a lavish welcome. ⇒ He met with a wonderful reception.

굉장히 宏壯— 〈대단히〉 very (much); greatly; exceedingly; remarkably; immensely; 〈놀랄 만큼〉 strikingly; wonderfully; 〈엄청나게〉 terribly; awfully
♦굉장히 큰 사람 a great big man / 굉장히 가난하다 be deadly poor / 돈에 굉장히 궁하다 be very hard up for money; be badly in need of money / 굉장히 나쁘다 be awfully bad / 굉장히 덥다[춥다] be terribly [unbearably] hot [cold] / 굉장히 서두르다 be in a furious hurry
▶그는 굉장히 좋은 사람이다 He is an awfully nice person.
▶굉장히 피곤해 보이는 군요 You look terribly [awfully] tired.
▶그는 굉장히 화가 났다 He was wild [furious] with anger.
▶저 가수는 굉장히 인기가 있다 That singer is amazingly popular.
▶나는 굉장히 바쁘다[목이 마르다] I'm terribly busy [thirsty].
▶배가 굉장히 고프다 I'm good [rare] and hungry.
▶이것은 굉장히 맛있다 This tastes great.
▶그는 피아노를 굉장히 잘 쳤다 He played the piano very [remarkably] well.
▶나는 그것을 굉장히 좋아한다 I am very fond of it. ⇒ I like it very much.
▶그 말을 들으니 굉장히 기쁘다 I'm very [awfully] glad to hear that.

굉침 轟沈 instant sinking by explosion [a gun] —**굉침하다** sink a ship instantly by blowing it up [with explosives]

교 教 a religion ⇨ 종교

교가 校歌 a school [college] song; an alma mater ♦교가를 합창하다 sing in chorus a school [college] song

교각 交角 〔數〕〈만난 각〉 an angle of intersection; 〔電〕 a crossing angle

교각 橋脚 〔土〕 a (bridge) pier; a bent

교각살우 矯角殺牛 The remedy is worse than the evil [disease].

교감 交感 rapport; mutual response; 〔生理〕 consensus; (mutual) sympathy
■—신경 the sympathetic nerve —신경계 the sympathetic nervous system

교감 校監 an assistant principal; a head

교갑

teacher; a vice schoolmaster
교갑 膠匣 〔캡슐〕 a capsule; (프) a cachet
교과과정 教科課程 a curriculum (*pl.* ~s, -la); a course of study ♦ (3년의) 교과 과정을 마치다 complete [finish up] a (3-year) course of study ▶ 초등학교의 교과 과정에는 영어가 들어 있다 English is included in the curriculum of the elementary school.
교과(목) 教科(目) a lesson; a subject; a course of study
교과서 教科書 a textbook; (美) a schoolbook ♦ 섬인정 교과서 an authorized textbook / 국정 교과서 a national textbook / 역사 교과서 a history text(book)
■ —검인정 제도 the textbook screening system
교관 教官 an instructor; a teacher; 〈교련의〉 a drill instructor
교교하다 皎皎— bright; brilliant ♦ 교교히 brightly; bright; brilliantly ▶ 달빛이 교교하다 The moon shines bright(ly).
교구 教具 teaching tools; training aids; instruments of education
교구 教區 〔基〕 a parish; a diocese; an ecclesiastical district ♦ 교구 교회〔목사〕 a parish church〔priest〕 ■ —민 a parishioner; (총칭) the parish
교군 轎軍 a palanquin ⇨ 가마³
교권 教權 〈교육상의〉 educational authority; 〈종교상의〉 ecclesiastical authority; ecclesiasticism ♦ 교권 확립 the establishment of the educational authority
교기 校紀 school discipline
교기 校旗 a school flag [banner]
교기 驕氣 〈교만〉 a haughty attitude; a proud air ♦ 교기를 부리다 behave haughtily; assume a haughty attitude; ride the high horse
교내 校內 the school grounds; 〈대학의〉 (美) the campus ♦ 교내에서 〈교사 내〉 in the school building; 〈학교 구내〉 on the school grounds; 〈대학의〉 (美) on (the) campus
■ —운동(대)회 an interclass athletic meet —폭력 school violence; violence in schools
교단 教團 〔基〕 an order; a religious society [brotherhood]; 〈여성의〉 a religious sorority [sisterhood] ♦ 프란체스코 교단 the Franciscan order
교단 教壇 〈학교의〉 the platform; 〈교회의〉 the pulpit ♦ 교단에 서다 stand on the platform; 〈가르치다〉 (美) teach school; be a teacher
■ —생활 a teacher's life [teaching career]: 교단 생활 30년 a 30-year experience of teaching; a teaching career of thirty years
교대 交代 (a) change; an alternation; 〈근무 등의〉 a shift; 〈보초 등의〉 a relief
♦ 교대로 by turns; in turn; in relays [shifts]; alternately; in rotation (with) / 밤낮 없이 교대로 하다 work in shifts day and night; work in relays round the clock / 3교대로 8시간씩 일하다 work in three shifts of eight hours [three eight-hour shifts]
▶ 우리는 교대로 운전했다 We took turns driving.

▶ 나는 아내와 교대로 요리한다 My wife and I alternate in cooking.
—**교대하다** take *sb's* places; change places (with *one's* partner); relieve (each other)
▶ 간호사는 8시간마다 교대한다 The nurses rotate every eight hours.
▶ 누구 나와 교대해줄 사람 없습니까? Is there anyone who will take my place?
■ —시간 the changing time; a shift: 너 교대시간 언제니? When will you be relieved? ⇌ When is your shift over? —자 a shift; a relief: 야간〔주간〕 교대자 men on the night [day] shift —제 the shift system: 2교대제 a two-shift system; a double shift
교도 教徒 a believer (in); an adherent (to); a follower (of) ♦ 기독교도 a Christian / 이슬람 교도 a Mohammedan; a Moslem / 불교도 a Buddhist
교도 教導 instruction; teaching; training; guidance —**교도하다** instruct; teach; train
♦ 비행청소년을 교도하다 reform a juvenile delinquent
교도관 矯導官 (美) a (prison) guard; a jailor; a warden; (英) a prison officer; a (prison) warder; a gaoler ♦ 여교도관 (美) a female guard; (英) a (prison) wardress
교도소 矯導所 a prison; (美) a jail (▸ jail은 특히 미결수나 경범용을 가리킴); (英) a gaol; (美口) the pen
♦ 교도소에 수감하다 put (a criminal) into prison; send (a criminal) to prison / 교도소에 수감되다 be imprisoned; be put into prison; be sent to jail / 교도소에 수감되어 있다 be in prison; (口) be behind bars
▶ 그는 교도소에서 어제 출소했다 He left [was released from] prison yesterday.
▶ 그는 언젠가는 교도소에 가게 될 것이다 He will land [end up] in prison someday.
■ —장 (美) the warden [governor] of a prison
교두보 橋頭堡 〔軍〕 a bridgehead; 〈해안의〉 a beachhead
♦ 교두보를 구축하다[확보하다] establish a bridgehead [beachhead]
▶ 그들은 적의 해안에 교두보를 구축했다 They made [secured] a beachhead on the enemy shore.
교란 攪亂 disturbance; turbulence; derangement
—**교란하다** disturb; throw (the enemy) into confusion [disorder]
♦ 평화를 교란하다 disturb peace / 후방을 교란하다 harass the rear
▶ 우리는 적의 전술에 완전히 교란당했다 We were thrown into utter confusion by the enemy's tactics.
■ —전술 harassing tactics
교량 橋梁 a bridge (⇨ 다리²) ■ —공사 bridge building [construction] —공학 bridge engineering
교련 教鍊 training; (a) (military) drill —**교련하다** train; exercise; drill ♦ 교련받다 be drilled; practice drilling ■ —사격— target practice ■ —교관 a drill instructor
교료 校了 〔印〕 finishing [final] proofreading;

〈부호〉 O.K. ◆교료를 놓다 finish correcting the proof; OK ―교료하다 finish proofreading; OK ■책임― O.K. with corrections ■―쇄 an OK'd proof; a press proof

교류 交流 〈환〉 interchange; 〔電〕 an alternating current (略 AC)
◆(동서의) 문화 교류 cultural exchange (between the East and the West) / 인사의 교류 an interchange of personnel《between》/ 학자[전문가]의 교류 an exchange of scholars [specialists]
■―발전기 an AC [alternating current] generator ―전동기 an AC [alternating current] motor

교리 教理 a doctrine [tenet]; a dogma (pl. ~s, -mata); a creed ■―문답(서) (a) catechism ―신학 dogmatics; dogmatic theology

교린정책 交隣政策 a good-neighbor policy

교만 驕慢 arrogance; haughtiness; pride
―교만하다 arrogant; proudhearted; haughty
◆교만하게 굴다 bear *oneself* haughtily; act in a lordly manner / 교만하기 짝이 없다 be as proud as Lucifer
▶그는 몹시 교만하다 He is as proud as a peacock.

교모 校帽 a school cap

교모 教母 〔가톨릭〕 a Catholic sister; a nun

교목 喬木 an arbor; a tall [big, lofty] tree
■―대(帶) 〔植〕 the forest-tree zone

교묘하다 巧妙― skillful; skilled; clever; ingenious; dexterous; adept
◆교묘한 사기 a subtle deception / 교묘한 솜씨 adept performance / 교묘한 장치 an ingenious device / 교묘하게 만든 덫 a cleverly devised trap
▶우리는 그의 교묘한 속임수에 넘어갔다 We were cheated by his cunning tricks.
▶우리는 그 계획이 교묘한 데 놀랐다 We were surprised at the ingenuity of the plan.

교무 敎務 academic affairs [administration]; school affairs; 〈종교 사무〉 religious affairs
◆교무를 맡아보다 manage [take charge of] school affairs
■―과 the academic affairs section [department] ―실 a teachers' room ―주임 teacher in charge of the instruction section

교문 校門 a school gate; the gate of a school
◆교문을 나서다 〈졸업하다〉 leave school; graduate from the school

교미 交尾 copulation; pairing; coupling ―교미하다 copulate 《with》; mate 《with》; pair; 〈새 등이〉 tread 《a hen》
■―기 the mating [pairing] season [time, period]; the heat season : 교미기에 들다 〈발정하다〉 get on [in] heat

교반기 攪拌機 〔料〕 a stirrer; a churner; a whisk; a mixer; 〈칵테일용〉 a shaker

교반하다 攪拌― stir (up) 《cream》; churn 《milk》; beat [whip] 《eggs》

교배 交配 〔動·植〕 mating; 〈이종 교배〉 crossing; hybridization; crossbreeding ―교배하다 mate 《one breed with another》; hybridize; cross; crossbreed
■―종(種) a crossbred; a hybrid

교번 交番 change of shift; alternation
■―세대― 〔生〕 alternation of generations

교범 教範 〈교수법〉 teaching method; 〈교과서〉 an exemplary text; a textbook; 〔軍〕 a drill book [manual] ■―기술― a technical manual (略 TM)

교법 教法 a religious doctrine ■―사(師) 〔가톨릭〕 a Catholic missionary

교복 校服 a school uniform

교본 教本 a textbook 《on, in》 ◆운전 교본 a manual for driving / 피아노 교본 a book of études for the piano

교부 交付 delivery; grant
―교부하다 deliver; grant; hand over; issue
◆면허[허가]증을 교부하다 grant a license [permit] / 보조금을 교부하다 grant a subsidy 《to》 / 여권을 교부하다 issue a passport to [for] / 통지서를 교부하다 serve a notice on 《sb》; transfer a slip 《to》
■―금 a subsidy; a grant(-in-aid); a bounty ―자 a deliverer

교부 敎父 a Father (of the Church); a Church Father ■―철학 patristic philosophy

교분 交分 friendship; intimacy; friendly relations
◆교분이 두텁다 be good friends with; be on most intimate terms with / 옛 교분을 새로이 하다 renew *sb's* old companionship with *sb*; get in closer contact with
▶그 두 사람은 날로 교분이 두터워지고 있다 The two are growing daily in intimacy.

교사 校舍 a school building; a schoolhouse; a school ◆교사를 증축하다 extend [add to] the school building

교사 敎師 a teacher; an instructor; a preceptor; 〈초·중등 학교의〉 a schoolteacher; 〈스승〉 a master
◆가정 교사 a tutor; 〈여자〉 a governess / 댄스[승마] 교사 a dancing [riding] master [teacher] / 여교사 a woman teacher / 영어 교사 a teacher of English; an English teacher / 교사가 되다 be a teacher; 〔美〕 teach school
▶왜 교사가 되기로 결심했습니까? What has made you decide to be a teacher [to go into teaching]?
■―직 the teaching profession; instructorship; schoolteaching

교사 敎唆 incitement; instigation; 〔法〕 abetment
◆아무의 교사로 at *sb's* instigation
―교사하다 incite [instigate] *sb* 《to (commit) a crime》; 〔法〕 abet *sb* 《in a crime》
▶그들은 노동자들의 파업을 교사했다 They incited the workers to go on strike.
■―자 an instigator; an abettor ―죄 the crime of instigation : 교사죄로 on a charge of instigating 《the riot》

교사용 敎師用 《reference books》 for teaching ■―지도서 a teacher's manual

교살 絞殺 strangulation; hanging
―교살하다 strangle; strangulate; murder *sb* by strangulation; 〔口〕 choke *sb* to death
▶그녀는 그 남자에게 교살당했다 She was strangled [choked] to death by the man.

교상 咬傷 a bite; an injury by biting ♦교상을 입다 be bitten; be injured by a bite

교상 膠狀 ♦교상의 colloid(al); gelatinous ■—액 colloidal solution —체 a colloid

교생 敎生 a student teacher; a trainee [practic] teacher

교서 敎書 〈대통령의〉 a message; 〈교황의〉 a (papal) bull
♦대통령 연두 교서 〈미국의〉 the President's (annual) State of the Union Message 《to Congress》; the New Year Presidential Message [Address] / 특별 교서 a special message

교섭 交涉 1 〈흥정〉 negotiation(s); bargaining
♦단체 교섭권 the right of collective bargaining / 직접 교섭 direct negotiations / 한미 간의 교섭 negotiations between Korea and the United States; Korean-American talks / 교섭 중이다 be in [under] negotiation / 교섭을 개시하다 enter [start, open] negotiations 《with》 / 교섭을 계속하다 carry on negotiations 《with》 / 교섭을 결렬시키다[중단하다] break off [discontinue] negotiations 《with》
▶ 이 건은 교섭의 여지가 있다[없다] This matter is negotiable [nonnegotiable].
▶ 교섭이 타결되었다 The negotiations are concluded.
▶ 교섭은 교착 상태에 빠졌다 The negotiations got stalled [become deadlocked].
▶ 교섭은 실패했다 The negotiations have fallen through.
—교섭하다 negotiate 《with sb about a matter [for a purpose]》; confer [bargain] 《with》
♦인접국과 통상 확대를 교섭하다 negotiate with a neighboring country about [for] an expansion of trade
▶ 나는 집주인과 집세를 교섭했다 I bargained with my landlord about the rent.
2 〈관계〉 relation; (a) connection
♦…와 아무 교섭이 없다 have no connection [contact(s)] 《with》; have nothing to do 《with》
▶ 그와는 교섭이 오래 전에 끊겼다 I lost contact with him a long time ago.
■단체— collective bargaining : 조합은 경영자 측과의 단체 교섭권을 쟁취했다 The union won the right to bargain collective with the management. 비밀— a closed-door negotiation 예비— preliminary negotiations 외교— diplomatic negotiations ■—기관[단] a bargaining agency [party] —단체 a bargaining body; 〈국회의〉 a negotiation body —위원[대표] a delegate; a negotiating committee man —위원회 a negotiating committee

교성 嬌聲 gay voices of (young) women; seductive tones ♦교성을 지르다 utter a coquettish voice

교세 敎勢 religious influence; 〈신도의 수〉 the total number of believers

교수 敎授 1 〈가르침〉 teaching; instruction
♦피아노 개인 교수를 하다 give private piano lessons
—교수하다 teach sb 《Korean history》; instruct sb 《in cooking》; give lessons 《in French》
▶ 그는 열명의 한국인 학생에게 영어를 교수하고 있다 He gives English lessons to the ten Korean students.
2 〈사람〉 a professor; 〈총칭〉 the faculty

[解說] 미국에서는 대학의 교수·조교수·강사뿐만 아니라 중학교·고등학교 교사에게도 *professor*를 쓸 때가 있다. 영국에서는 professor는 학과나 강좌의 주임 교수란 뜻으로 쓰인다. 부를 때는 Professor ~이지만 일상적으로 Mr. [Mrs., Miss, Ms.] ~이며 그밖에 이름을 부르는 때도 많다.

♦김 교수 Professor [Prof.] Kim / 서울대학교 영문학 교수 a professor of English literature at Seoul National University
■명예— a professor emeritus 부— an associate [adjunct] professor 정— a (full) professor 조— an assistant professor 지도— an academic adviser ■—진 〈美〉 the professors; the faculty; 〈strengthen〉 teaching staff 《of a university》 —회의 a faculty meeting : 정례 교수 회의 the regular meeting of the faculty members

교수 絞首 hanging; strangulation ♦교수용 밧줄 a halter; a hempen collar —교수하다 strangle; strangulate; hang
■—대 the scaffold; the gallows; the gibbet : 교수대에 오르다 mount the gallows [scaffold]

교수법 敎授法 teaching method; a system [way] of instruction [teaching]; 《(do not) know》 how to teach 《German》
♦교수법이 좋다 be a good teacher; be experienced in teaching 《English》

교수형 絞首刑 (death [execution] by) hanging
♦교수형의 판결 a hanging verdict / 교수형에 처하다 hang sb; put to death by hanging / 교수형에 처해지다 be hanged
▶ 그는 교수형을 선고받았다 He was sentenced to death by hanging.

교습 敎習 training; teaching; instruction ♦음악 교습을 받다 take lessons in music
—교습하다 give lessons (in); train; teach; instruct
■—소 a training school [institute] 《for》: 댄스 교습소 a dancing school

교시 敎示 instruction; teaching —교시하다 instruct 《sb in sth》; teach 《sb how to do》

교신 交信 exchange of messages; communication(s); correspondence
♦…와 무전으로 교신 중이다 be in radio communication with...
—교신하다 exchange (radio) messages 《with》; communicate 《with》; conduct [open] a correspondence 《with》

교실 敎室 a classroom; a schoolroom; 〈美〉 a recitation room
■계단— a theater; an amphitheater 생물학— the department of biology 콩나물— an overcrowded classroom ■—관리 classroom control

교안 敎案 a (draft) teaching plan [program]; lesson plan ♦교안을 짜다 work out a teaching plan; form [make] a lesson schedule

교양 敎養 culture; education; refinement
♦교양이 있는 educated; cultured; ⦅a person⦆ of culture / 교양이 없는 ⦅a person⦆ without any [with no] culture / 교양을 높이다 enhance the level of *one's* culture; cultivate oneself
▶ 그는 교양이 있는[없는] 사람이다 He is a refined [an uneducated, an uncultivated, a rough] man.
▶ 그녀는 교양을 과시한다 She shows off her culture.
■—과목 cultural studies [subjects]; liberal arts —과정 a general culture course; the liberal arts course —소설 an educational novel; ⦅독⦆ a Bildungsroman —프로그램 ⦅라디오·TV 의⦆ an educational [a cultural] program —학부 the college of general education; the liberal arts school

교언 巧言 flattery; fair [fine, honeyed] words
—교언하다 flatter; use sweet words ■—영색 (令色) fine words and insinuating countenance [looks]

교역 交易 trade; commerce; ⟨물물 교환⟩ barter
▶ 최근 한중간의 교역이 활발해졌다 The Korea-China trade has become active recently.
—교역하다 trade [barter] ⦅with⦆; exchange
■—조건 terms of trade

교열 校閱 reading (and correcting); revision; revisal
▶ 원고는 지금 교열 중이다 The manuscript is under revision now.
—교열하다 revise ⦅a book⦆; look over ⦅a manuscript⦆
■—자 a reviser

교외 郊外 (in) the suburbs ⦅of⦆; ⦅on⦆ the outskirts ⦅of⦆

〖解說〗 *suburbs*는 in the suburbs of…의 형태로 쓰이는 일이 많으나, 때로 한 지역을 가리킬 때에는 a suburb of… (…의 교외다)와 같은 형태로 쓰이기도 한다. suburbs는 도시의 중심에서 가까운 곳, *outskirts*는 중심에서 멀리 떨어진 곳을 가리킨다.

♦교외 산책 a walk in the country(side) / 교외의 suburban
▶ 그는 서울 교외에 산다 He lives in the suburbs [on the (out)skirts] of Seoul.
■—거주자 a suburban resident; suburbanite —생활 a life in the suburbs; a suburban life —선 the circular line running around the metropolitan zone —주택지 a residential suburb

교외 校外 ♦교외의[에서] outside the school; out of school ■—생 an extramural student; an extension course student —활동 extramural activities

교우 交友 ⟨사귐⟩ making friends ⦅with⦆; ⟨친구⟩ a companion; an associate —교우하다 make friends ⦅with⦆; keep company ⦅with⦆
■—관계 *sb's* company : 교우 관계가 좋다 keep good company / 그는 교우 관계가 좋지 않다 He has bad friends.

교우 校友 a schoolmate; a schoolfellow; ⟨동창생⟩ a graduate ■—회 ⇨ 동창회

교우 敎友 a fellow believer; a brother ⦅*pl.* brethren⦆; a fellow Christian [Buddhist]

교원 敎員 a teacher; an instructor; ⟨초·중등 학교의⟩ a schoolteacher; a schoolmaster (남자); a schoolmistress (여자); ⟨총칭⟩ the teaching staff (⇨ 교사) ♦교원 생활 a teacher's life; a teaching career
■—시험 a teacher's license examination —양성 계획 a teacher-training program —양성소 a teacher's training school —조합 a teachers' union

교원병 膠原病 〖醫〗 collagen diseases

교원자격검정 敎員資格檢定 certification of teachers; educational certification
■—시험 an examination for a teacher's certificate [license]

교유 交遊 companionship; association; friendship; intercourse
▶ 나는 그와 교유를 끊었다 I broke with him.
—교유하다 associate ⦅with⦆; keep company ⦅with⦆

교육 敎育 education; schooling; teaching; instruction; ⟨훈련⟩ training; ⟨교양⟩ culture; ⟨버릇 들이기⟩ discipline

〖解說〗 「교육」의 뜻으로 가장 일반적인 것은 *education*이지만 「학교 교육」의 뜻으로는 *schooling*, 교육의 수단으로서 가르친다는 뜻으로는 *teaching*을 쓴다. 특수 지식을 체계적으로 가르친다는 뜻의 격식 차린 말은 *instruction*이다.

♦국민 교육 헌장 the National Charter of Education / 교육의 기회 균등 equal educational apportunity / 최고 교육을 받은 사람 a man of the highest education / 교육(상)의 educational; educative / 교육을 받지 못한 uneducated; ignorant; ⟨문맹인⟩ illiterate / 교육을 받다 be educated ⦅at a school⦆; have [get, receive] education ⦅at a college⦆
▶ 자녀 교육은 학교에만 맡겨 놓아서는 안된다 You should not entrust the education of your children only to the school.
▶ 그는 변호사가 되도록 교육을 받았다 He was educated [raised] to become a lawyer.
▶ 그는 정식 학교 교육은 거의 받지 못했다 He has had very little formal schooling.
▶ 이 회사 신입 사원은 3개월간 교육을 받은 뒤 일을 한다 The freshmen in this company are given 3-month training and then assigned to their respective jobs.
—교육하다 educate; instruct; train; teach
▶ 그녀는 자녀를 엄하게 교육했다 She disciplined her children strictly. ⇌ She gave her children a strict upbringing.
■—가정— home training [discipline] 고등— higher education 과학— scientific education [training] 기술— technical education 대학— (a) university [college] education 성인— adult education 유아— preschool education 의무— compulsory education 전문— profes-

sional [specialized] education 중등— secondary education 직업— vocational education [training] 초등— elementary [primary] education 통신— a correspondence course [school] 평생— life-long education 학교— school education; schooling ■—가[자] an educator; an educationalist —감 the superintendent of education —개혁 (a) reform of educational system; (an) educational reform —계 the educational world [circles] —공무원 an educational public service employee; (총칭) the public educational personnel and staff —과정 a course of study; a curriculum —기관 an educational institution; educational facilities —기금 an education fund —기본법 the Fundamental Law of Education —단체 an educational body —대학 a college of education; a teachers' college —법 a method of education; a teaching method;〈법률〉the Law of Education —보험 educational endowment insurance —사업 educational work —세 education tax —시설 educational facilities —심리학 pedagogical psychology —심의회 the Education Council; the Council of Education —연도 an educational [a school] year —영화 an educational film [picture]; an instructional film —프로그램〈라디오・TV의〉an educational program —학 pedagogy; pedagogics —학부 the department of education —행정 educational administration —회 an educational association

교육위원 教育委員 a member of the board of education ■〈지방〉—회 the (local) board of education; a (local) school board

교육적 教育的 educational; educative; instructive

교육정도 教育程度 a standard of education
♦ …보다 교육 정도가 낮다 have a standard of education lower than…; be beneath 《another》 in education / 교육 정도가 높다〈일반적으로〉have a high standard of education;〈개인이〉be highly educated

교의 交誼 friendship; friendly relations ▶ 당신과 영원히 교의를 맺고 싶소 I hope to be friends with you forever.

교의 校醫 a school physician [doctor]

교의 校義 a doctrine; (a) dogma; a tenet ♦ 교의상의 doctrinal; dogmatic ■—학 dogmatics

교인 敎人 a believer; an adherent; a follower (of) ♦ 기독교 교인이 되다 become a Christian

교자 交子 food set on a large table ■—상 a large table (of food)

교잡 交雜〈뒤섞임〉confusion; disorder;〈교배〉〔植〕crossing;〔動〕hybridization —교잡하다 cross; hybridize

교장 校長 a principal [director]; (英) a schoolmaster; a headmaster;〈여자〉a schoolmistress; a headmistress
▶ 그는 한국 고등학교 교장으로 임명되었다 He was appointed (the) principal of Hanguk High School.
■—대리 an acting [a deputy] principal —실 the principal's office

교장 教場 a drill [training] ground; a (military) drill field

교재 敎材 teaching materials (▶주로 복수형으로 씀)
♦ 교재를 준비하다 provide materials of instruction / 영자 신문을 읽기 교재로 쓰다 use an English paper as a reading text
■보조— teaching aids ■—비(費) expenses for teaching materials —연구 a study of teaching materials

교전 交戰〈전투〉a battle; combat; an action
♦ 교전 상태에 있다 be in a state of hostilities [war] / 교전을 중지하다 cease fire / 교전을 회피하다 avoid action
▶ 그들은 적군과 교전 중이다 They are fighting [at war] with the enemy troops.
—교전하다 fight 《with, against》; engage in a battle 《with》
■—국 warring [belligerent] nations [powers]; the belligerents —권 the right of belligerency —지 a field of battle; a battlefield; the theater of war —지대 a combat area; a war zone

교전 教典 a canon ■기독교— (Holy) Scripture; Holy Bible 이슬람교— the Scripture of Islam; the Koran

교점 交點 an [a point of] intersection; an intersecting point;〔天〕a node

교접 交接〈접촉〉contact;〈성교〉sexual intercourse; coitus [coition]
—교접하다〈접촉하다〉contact; make contact 《with》;〈성교하다〉have sexual intercourse 《with》; copulate 《with》
■—불능 impotence; impotency : 교접 불능자 an impotent (man)

교정 校正 proofreading
♦ 교정상의 실수 a proofreader's error / 교정을 세번 보다 read proofs three times; make corrections in three proofs / 교정에서 잘못된 것을 놓치다 overlook errors in proof
▶ 교정은 정확히 보았나? Did you read proofs with religious care?
▶ 교정은 몇번이나 보았습니까? How many times was the proof read?
▶ 교정필 (표시) Corrected. ⇌ O.K.
—교정하다 read [correct] proofs; proofread 《an article》; do proofreading
■—기호 proof-correction marks; proofreader's marks —원[자] a proofreader; a press reader —지 a proof sheet; proofs; a galley (proof)

교정 校訂 revision ⇨ 교열(校閱)

교정 校庭 a schoolyard;〈운동장〉a playground;〈구내〉the school [college] grounds;〈대학의〉a campus

교정 教程 1〈가르치는 과정〉a course of study; a curriculum;〈가르치는 방법〉a teaching method [technique]
▶ 운전 면허 교습은 어느 교정까지 나갔습니까? How many lessons did you take for your driver's license?
2〈교본〉a textbook; a manual

교정 矯正 correction; reform; remedy; treatment
—교정하다 corret; reform; rectify; set [put] right; set sb straight

◆난시를 안경으로 교정하다 correct *one's* astigmatism by glasses / 말더듬기를[나쁜 버릇을] 교정하다 cure [break] *sb* of stammering [a bad habit] / 발음을 교정하다 correct bad pronunciation
■—법 a remedy; a cure —시력 corrected vision [(eye)sight] —시설 a correctional institution

교정쇄 校正刷 a (galley) proof; a proof sheet
◆오식이 많은 교정쇄 a foul proof / 교정이 완료된 교정쇄 OK'd proofs; proofs marked O.K. / 교정쇄를 내다 print a proof / 교정쇄로 읽다 read 《*sb's* book》 in proof
■저자— an author's proof 최종— the final proof

교제 交際 company; friendship; association; society; acquaintance
◆교제가 넓다 know a lot of people; have a wide [large] circle of friends [acquaintances] / 교제가 서투르다 (美口) be a bad mixer / 교제를 싫어하다 unsociable; dislike company [society] / 교제를 잘하다 be tactful in society; (美口) be a good mixer / 교제를 좋아하다 be sociable; be fond of company [society]
▶그 외국 유학생은 한국 학생과의 교제를 원하고 있다 The foreign student is seeking Korean student's friendship.
—**교제하다** go (out) with; see; associate with; keep company with

解説「(이성과) 사귀다」의 뜻일 때는 *go (out) with*를 쓴다. out이 있으면 남녀의 초기[장기] 교제를 연상케 하고, out이 없으면 남녀가 결혼을 전제로 하여 교제하는 것을 연상케 한다. *see*는 미혼자·기혼자를 불문하고 이성과 빈번히 만난다는 뜻. *associate with*는 이성·동성을 불문하고 사교상 또는 직업상 교제하는 경우에 쓰인다.

◆좋은 사람과 교제하다 keep good company / 친하게 교제하다 be closely associated with *sb*; have friendly relations with *sb*
■—가(家) a sociable person; a society man [lady]; (美口) a mixer —범위 a circle of acquaintance(s) —법 social etiquette

교제비 交際費 social expenses; table money; 〈접대비〉 entertainment costs; 〈회사 지급의〉 (have) an expense account
◆식대를 교제비에 넣다 charge the meal to [put the meal on] *one's* expense account

교조 敎祖 the founder of a religion [religious sect]; 〈창시자〉 an originator
▶그는 반핵 운동의 교조적 존재다 He is an idolized figure in the anti-nuclear movement.

교조 敎條 a tenet (of faith); a dogma; a doctrine ■—주의 dogmatism; doctrinairism —주의자 a dogmatist; a doctrinarian; a doctrinaire

교졸 巧拙 skill; proficiency; degree of skill; 〈장인의〉 (quality of) workmanship
◆작품의 교졸을 논하다 comment on the skill of the work
▶같은 물건을 만드는 데도 교졸이 있다 The same thing may be made with varying degrees of skill.

교주 校主 the proprietor [founder] of a school

교주 敎主 the founder of a religion; the head [leader] of a religious sect

교지 狡智 craft; craftiness; cunning ◆교지에 밝은 사람 a crafty [cunning, tricky] person

교지 校紙 a school paper

교지 校誌 a school magazine

교지 敎旨 1〔史〕 a writ of appointment **2** ⇨ 교리(敎理) **3**〈교육의 취지〉 principles of education

교지기 校— a school janitor

교직 交織 a combined [mixed] weave; 〈혼방〉 a mixture; a mixed fabric
■면모— half wool; wool-cotton fabric; cotton and wool mixture ■—물 union cloth: 마모(麻毛) 교직물 linsey-woolsey

교직 敎職 the teaching profession; 〈대학의〉 professorship
◆교직에 있다 be a teacher; (美) teach school / 교직에 몸을 담다 enter [follow] the teaching profession; become a teacher
▶그분은 교직 생활 40년이다 He has been teaching school for forty years.
■—과정 a teacher-training course; a course of study for the teaching profession

교직원 敎職員 〈교원〉 the teaching [instructional] staff; 〈직원과 교원〉 staff and faculty; school personnel; 〈총칭〉 the faculty
◆교직원 학생 일동 the faculty and the student body / 교직원이 되다 enter [follow] the teaching profession; become a teacher
▶교직원은 그 계획에 반대였다 The faculty were against the plan.
■—회의 a teachers' [faculty] conference

교질 交迭 a change ⇨ 교체(交替)

교질 膠質 a colloid ◆교질의 〔化〕 colloid(al); gluey; glutinous; gelatinous
■—물 a jelly; gelatinoid —용액 a colloidal solution; a hydrosol —화약 colloidal powder —화학 colloid chemistry

교차 交叉 crossing; 〔通信〕 transposition; intersection; 〈염색체의〉〔遺〕 crossing-over
◆평면 교차 〈도로·철도 등의〉 (美) grade crossing; (英) level crossing / 입체 교차 grade separation; a cloverleaf (英) flyover; a two-level crossing
—**교차하다** cross [intersect] 《each other》; 〈전선을〉 transpose
■—도로 ⇨ 교차로 —법 〔通信〕 transposition —선 a cross line —승인 a cross recognition —점 a crossing; an intersection; an intersecting point; 〈사거리〉 crossroads; 〈선로의〉 a junction

교차로 交叉路 crossroads; an intersection; a crossway; a cross street
◆신호등이 있는 교차로 an intersection with traffic signals
▶교차로에 들어서려는데 신호가 바뀌었다 The light changed when I was about to enter the intersection.

교착 交錯 〈뒤섞임〉 mixture; blending; 〈엇갈려

뒤섞임〉 complication
♦ 꿈과 현실의 교착 a mixture of dream and reality / 명암[빛과 그림자]의 교착 the interplay of light and shadow
―교착하다 be complicated; be complex; be intricate; cross [mingle with] each other
▶ 불안과 희망이 교착되어 잠을 이루지 못했다 The fear and hope intermingling in my heart kept me from sleeping.
▶ 그의 최초의 반응은 기쁨과 분노가 기묘하게 교착된 것이었다 His first reaction was a strange mixture of joy and indignation.

교착 膠着 agglutination; adhesion; stalemate
♦ 교착 상태를 타개하다 break the deadlock; find a way out of the impasse / 교착 상태에 있다 be deadlocked; be at a deadlock [stalemate, standstill] / 교착 상태에 빠지다 become deadlocked; reach (a) deadlock
▶ 교섭은 교착 상태다 The negotiations are deadlocked [at a standstill].
▶ 싸움은 교착 상태에 빠졌다 The war has come to a deadlock [standstill].
―교착하다 stick 《to》; adhere 《to》; agglutinate
―어〔言〕 an agglutinative language

교체 交替 replacement; (a) change, (an) alternation
―교체하다 replace 《A with B》; change 《B for A》; shift [personnel]
▶ 감독은 그 선수를 교체했다 The manager changed the player.
▶ 우리는 부상 선수를 제때 교체해 줄만큼 인원이 많지 않다 We don't have many players enough to timely replace injured ones.
■―선수― a switch [change] of players 세대― the change of generations ■―투수 [野] a relief pitcher; a reliefer

교칙 校則 the rules of the school; school [campus] regulations [rules]
♦ 교칙에 따라[따르면] under the school regulations / 교칙을 지키다[위반하다] observe [violate] the rules of the school

교칙 敎則 rules for teaching

교탁 敎卓 a teacher's desk; a teaching desk

교탑 橋塔 a bridge tower

교태 嬌態 coquetry; flirtation
♦ 교태를 부리다 play the coquette 《with》; flirt 《with》
▶ 그녀는 만나는 남자한테마다 교태를 부렸다 She flirted with every man she saw.

교통 交通 〈왕래〉 traffic; 〈운수〉(美) transportation; (英) transport; 〈연락〉 communication
♦ 대중 교통 public transportation [(英) transport] / 중심가의 번잡한 교통 the dense [heavy] traffic of a main street / 혼잡한 도시 교통을 개선하다 improve crowded urban transport / 교통 혼잡을 덜다[완화하다] ease [relieve] traffic congestion / 교통을 차단하다 shut off [suspend] traffic; block up (the street); 〈전염병으로〉 perform quarantine / 교통을 통제[단속, 규제, 정리]하다 control [regulate] traffic / 교통에 방해가 되다 obstruct [block] traffic
▶ 교통의 흐름은 순조로웠다 There was a smooth flow to traffic. ⇌ Traffic was flowing smoothly.
▶ 우리 집은 교통이 편리하다 〈교통편이〉 My house is very convenient to public transportation. ⇌ 〈위치가〉 My house is conveniently located. ⇌ 〈오는 길이〉 My house is easy to reach [to get to].
▶ 큰 눈 때문에 1주일 동안 교통이 두절되었다 Because of the heavy snow, traffic was held up [(口) crippled] for a week.
▶ 쓰러진 나무가 한동안 교통을 방해했다 The fallen tree blocked (up) the traffic for some time.
■―경찰 traffic police ―기관 means of transportation; transport facilities; public transport ―도덕 traffic morality [morals]: 교통 도덕을 지키다 follow traffic morals ―망 a network of roads; a transportation network ―문제 a traffic problem ―방해 a traffic obstruction: 교통 방해를 하다 obstruct traffic ―법규 ⇨ 교통규칙; (美) carfare : 교통비를 지급하다 provide commutation allowances / 교통비가 많이 든다 It costs me a lot for my car-rides. ―순경 a traffic policeman [cop]; (英) a policeman on point [traffic] duty ―신고 센터 a traffic report center ―신호 a traffic signal; (英口) a stop-go sign ―신호등 a traffic light ―안전 traffic [road] safety ―안전 운동 a traffic safety campaign [drive] ―안전 주간 Traffic Safety Week ―정리 traffic control : 교통정리하는 경찰관 a policeman directing traffic [on traffic duty] ―정책 a traffic policy ―정체 a traffic tie-up; traffic congestion; a traffic jam ―질서 a traffic order ―차단 roadblocking; isolation; quarantine ―차단 구역 a quarantine district; a closed [blockaded] area ―차단선 〈전염병으로 인한〉《establish》 a sanitary cordon ―표지 a traffic sign

교통규칙 交通規則 traffic rules [regulations]; the rules of the road
♦ 교통 규칙 위반[위반자] a traffic violation [violator] / 교통 규칙을 강화[완화]하다 toughen [ease] traffic regulations / 교통 규칙을 지키다[위반하다] obey [violate] traffic rules [regulations]

교통량 交通量 the volume of 《wheeled》 traffic; traffic volume [density]
♦ 교통량이 많은 도로 a road where the traffic is heavy; a busy [crowded] street / 교통량이 가장 많은 시간 the heaviest traffic hours
▶ 교통량이 많다 Traffic is heavy [busy].

교통방송국 交通放送局 the Traffic Broadcasting Station (略 TBS)

교통사고 交通事故 a traffic [street, road] accident
♦ 교통 사고로 죽은 사람 traffic deaths; (the number of) deaths on the roads / 교통 사고를 일으키다 cause [bring about] a traffic accident / 교통사고로 죽다 be killed in a traffic accident

교통위반 交通違反 a traffic offense; violation of traffic regulations

교통과 도로를 나타내는 어휘

1. 도로
(1) 「도로」에 해당하는 주요한 영어는 road, street, avenue 등이 있는데, road는 거리와 거리를 이어주는 길이고, street는 한쪽 또는 양쪽에 가게나 집들이 늘어서 있는 한길, avenue는 일반적으로 양쪽에 가로수가 있는 큰 길을 가리킨다. 미국에서는 큰 길을 boulevard라고 하는 데도 있다.
▶ 번화가 (美) a main street; (英) a high street / 주요 도로 a thoroughfare / 골목길 [소로] a lane; an alley / 뒷골목 a back street / 상점가 a shopping street
▶ 보도 (美) a sidewalk; (英) a pavement / 산책로 a promenade; a mall (▶mall은「산책 상점가」라는 뜻으로도 쓰임)
▶ 환상 도로 a ring [loop, circular] road / 간선 도로 a trunk road; an arterial highway (▶미국의 국도는 U.S. highway)
▶ 자동차 전용도로·고속도로는 나라나 장소에 따라 여러가지로 불리지만 형식은 같다. **고속 자동차 도로** a superhighway; (英) a motorway (▶줄여서 M으로 표시); (美서부) a freeway (▶신호가 없는 도로라는 뜻); (美동부) an expressway / 유료 고속도로 a toll road; a turnpike (▶「요금 내는 길」이란 뜻도 있음) / 미대륙 횡단도로 a transcontinental highway / 주간(州間) 고속도로 an interstate highway / 진입 램프 an entrance ramp / 출구 램프 an exit ramp / 연락 도로 an access road / 본선 a main road / 휴게소 a rest area / 서비스 지역 a service area / 요금 내는 곳 a toll booth; a turnpike
(2) **기타의 길·도로**
▶ 산길 a (mountain) pass / 바이패스 a bypass / 사잇길 a bypath; a byroad / 우회로 a circuit; a detour / 진입로 an approach / 통로 a passage / 아케이드 an arcade (▶상점가의 아케이드는 a shopping arcade) / 복도 a corridor / 지름길 a shortcut / 사도(私道) a private road / 포장 도로 a paved road; a pavement / 자갈길 a gravel road / 울퉁불퉁한 길 a rough [bumpy] road
2. 교통
미국은 우측 통행 (keep to the right), 영국은 좌측 통행 (keep to the left)이다. 북미의 대부분의 십자로에서 우회전하는 경우 좌측 도로에서 직진해 오는 차가 없거나 아직 시간적 여유가 있을 때에는 빨간 신호라도 횡단 보도 (a pedestrain crossing)의 안전만 확인되면 우회전해도 무방하다. 다만 신호에「적색신호시 우회전 금지 (No Right Turn on Red)」라는 표지가 있으면 청신호를 기다려야 한다. 또 미국에서는 차의 감속을 위해 주택의 바깥 입구 부근에 요철을 해놓는 일이 있는데 이것을 bump라고 한다.
▶ 교차점 an intersection; a crossing; crossroads / 교통 신호 a traffic signal [light] / 청신호 green light; proceed signal / 황색신호 yellow light; caution signal / 적색신호 red light; stop signal / 로터리 a rotary; (英) a roundabout / 지하도 〈보행자용〉 an underground (passage); (英) a subway / 육교 an overpass / 일방통행 one-way traffic / 일방통행로 a one-way street / 차선 a lane / 8차선 도로 an 8-lane highway / 버스 전용 차선 a bus lane / 중앙 분리대 a median (strip); (英) a central reserve / 갓길 a shoulder / 자전거 (전용) 도로 a bikeway / 사이클링 도로 a cycleway
▶ 주차장 a parking lot; (英) a car park / 주차 요금 자동 징수기 a parking meter / 주차 금지 구역[견인차 이동 구역] a towaway zone; no parking zone / 주유소 (美) a gas station; a service [filling] station; (英) a petrol station (▶미국 주유소의 서비스는 3종류가 있다. 급유를 비롯, 차창 닦기, 오일 교환까지 하는 full service, 급유만 하는 mini-service, 급유를 손님이 손수 하는 self-service가 그것이다. 가솔린의 양은 리터(liter)가 아니고 갤런(gallon)으로 표시함)

표현례
▶ 뒷골목까지 차가 꽉 차서 아이들이 놀 장소가 별로 없다 Even the back streets are full of cars and children have hardly any place to play in.
▶ 이 거리는 아침 저녁 러시아워 때는 차가 꽉 들어차서 거북이걸음을 한다 During the morning and evening rush hours this street is congested, and the cars move like snails.
▶ 한국에서는 좁은 길에서도 차가 무서운 속도로 달리고 있다 In Korea, cars travel very fast even on narrow roads.
▶ 미국에서는 어디를 가더라도 거의 차를 이용한다 In most parts of the United States people use cars wherever they go.
▶ 고속도로상에서 추월할 때는 특별히 주의하지 않으면 안된다 Drivers must be very careful in passing on the expressway.

♦교통 위반 딱지 a traffic ticket / 교통 위반을 하다 break [violate] traffic rules [regulations]; commit a traffic violation; 〈보행자가〉 (美口) jaywalk / 교통 위반으로 체포되다 be arrested on a traffic charge
교통체증 交通滯症 traffic congestion; a traffic jam
▶ 우리는 교통 체증에 걸려 늦었다 We were late because we got caught in a traffic jam.
교파 教派 a (religious) sect; a denomination
♦교파적인 sectarian; denominational / 새 교파를 형성하다 form a new denominations
교편 教鞭 a birch (rod); teaching
♦교편을 잡다 be a teacher 《at》; teach at a school; (美) teach school
▶ 그는 고등학교에서 교편을 잡고 있다 He teaches at a high school. ⇌ He is a high school teacher. ⇌ He is teaching (in a) high school.
교포 僑胞 a Korean resident abroad; (총칭)

교풍

overseas Koreans ♦재미[재일]교포 a Korean resident in America [Japan]; a Korean [Koreans] (residing) in America [Japan]

교풍 校風 〈정신〉 a school spirit; school tradition [color]; 〈기풍〉 the tone of a school ♦교풍을 확립하다 establish [form] the traditions of a school / 교풍에 어긋나다 be against the traditions of a school ▶나는 그 학교의 교풍이 좋다 I like the tone [atmosphere] of the school.

교학 敎學 education and researches; 〈가르침과 배움〉 learning and teaching

교합 交合 copulation; sexual intercourse ━교합하다 have sexual intercourse

교향곡 交響曲 a symphony ♦베토벤의 제9교향곡 Beethoven's Ninth Symphony / 슈베르트의 미완성 교향곡 Schubert's Unfinished Symphony ━작곡가 a symphony composer

교향시 交響詩 (樂) a symphonic poem

교향악 交響樂 a symphony; symphony music ━단 a symphony orchestra: 국립[시립] 교향악단 The National [Municipal] Symphony Orchestra ━단원 a symphonist

교호 交互 alternation; reciprocality ♦교호의 mutual; reciprocal; 〈교체의〉 alternate / 교호로 by turns; alternately ━교호하다 be reciprocal; alternate ⟪with⟫ ━작용 (an) interaction; reciprocal action

교호계산 交互計算 (商) an account current (略 A/C, a/c) ━서 a statement of account current

교화 敎化 culture; enlightenment; edification; civilization; 〈미개인의〉 reclamation; domestication ━교화하다 cultivate; educate; enlighten; civilize; reclaim; 〈복음으로〉 evangelize ━력 educative power ━사업 educational work; an enlightenment project ━운동 educational movement; a drive for people's enlightenment

교환 交換 (an) exchange; (an) interchange; give and take; 〈물물교환〉 barter; (口) a swap; 〈대치〉 substitution; replacement; (數) commutation; 〈어음의〉 clearing ♦자동[수동] 교환 〈전화의〉 automatic [manual] switching / 포로의 교환 an exchange of prisoners / 교환 가능한 exchangeable; commutative; transferable ⟪currency⟫ ━교환하다 exchange (A for B); make an exchange; give (A for B); give and take; barter [trade] (A for B); swap ⟪stamps⟫; substitue (A for B); clear ⟪bills⟫ ♦웃돈을 얹어 주고 중고차를 새 차와 교환하다 trade a used car in for a new one ▶나는 헌 타이어를 새것과 교환했다 I replaced a worn tire by [with] a new one. ▶그 회합에서는 모두가 활발하게 의견을 교환했다 At the convention, everyone exchanged views with great enthusiasm. ▶쌀과 모피가 물물 교환되었다 Rice and fur were traded by barter. ━가격 the exchange price ━가치 the exchange value; value in exchange; exchangeability ━교수 an exchange [interchange] professor; 〈수업〉 exchange lessons ━국 〈전화의〉 (美) an central office; (英) a telephone exchange ━대 a switchboard ━렌즈 〔寫〕 an interchangeable lens ━물자 barter goods ━법칙 〔數〕 the commutative law ━소 〈어음의〉 a clearing house ━실 a telephone switchboard room ━원 a telephone operator; the "central" (operator); (美) a hello girl ━조건 a bargaining point ━학생 an interchange [exchange] student

교환 交歡 an exchange of courtesies [greetings, good wishes, goodwill] ♦한미 학생간의 교환 an exchange of greetings between Korean and American students ━교환하다 exchange courtesies [greetings, good wishes] ⟪with⟫; fraternize ⟪with⟫ ━경기 a courtesy [goodwill, friendly] game [match]

교활하다 狡猾━ cunning; sly (as a fox); tricky; crafty; wily ♦교활한 사람 a crafty [tricky] person; an old fox; a sly dog / 교활한 수단 (a) sharp practice; a shrewd trick / 교활하게 cunningly; slily; craftily / 교활하게 굴다 act craftily; act unfairly ▶그는 교활하다 He is a wily person [full of guile]. ▶그는 교활하게 혼자만 단물을 빨아 먹는다 He acts craftily and takes the lion's share.

교황 敎皇 〔가톨릭〕 the Pope; the Sovereign [Supreme] Pontiff; the Holy Father ♦교황의 papal; Apostolic ━공사 an internuncio ━권 the popedom; the papacy ━대사 a papal [an Apostolic] nuncio ━사절 an Apostolic delegate; the pope's envoy ━선거 the Pope's election ━선거회의(장) a conclave ━제도 the papal system; the Papacy ━청 the Papal court; the Holy [Papal, Apostolic] See; the Vatican

교회 敎會 〈기독교의〉 the Church; 〈건물〉 a church; a chapel (▶영국에서는 영국 국교회의 교회는 the Church of England라고 하고, 그 이외의 교회나 예배당은 모두 chapel이라고 함) ♦개신 교회 the protestant church / 감리[장로, 감독] 교회 the Methodist [Presbyterian, Episcopal] church / 로마 가톨릭 교회 the Roman Catholic Church / 교회에 다니다 go to church / 교회에서 결혼하다 be married in church / 교회에서 기도하다 pray in church ━당 a church; 〈대성당〉 a cathedral ━력 (歷) the ecclesiastical calendar ━음악 church music ━종 church bells

교회 敎誨 (an) admonition; exhortation; (an) preaching ━사(師) 〈교도소의〉 a prison chaplain [missionary]

교훈 校訓 〈학교의〉 school precepts; a motto for school discipline

교훈 敎訓 a lesson; teachings ⟪of Confucius⟫; (a) precept; 〈우화적인〉 a moral ♦산 교훈 a living lesson / 교훈적인 instructive; moral; edifying / 교훈을 얻다 learn a lesson ⟪from⟫ / 교훈을 주다 give [afford] a lesson ⟪to⟫ ▶이 사고는 나에게 좋은 교훈이 되었다 This accident was a good lesson to me. ■—극 a morality play

구 句 a phrase; 〈문구〉 an expression; 〈시〉 a line [passage, verse] ◆관용구를 사용하다 use an idiomatic phrase

구 區 〈도시의〉 a ward (➤ New York의 경우는 a borough); 〈구역〉 a district; a section [division] ◆마포구 Map'o-gu; Map'o ward / 선거구 an electoral district; a constituency; 〈美〉 an election [voting] precinct / 전국[지역]구 〈선거의〉 the national [local] constituency ■—민 the inhabitants of a ward —의회 a ward assembly —정(政) the administration of a ward

구 球 〈구체〉 a sphere; a globe; 〈공〉 a ball; 〈전구 등〉 a bulb; 〈라디오 등〉 a tube ◆구의 부피 the volume of a sphere / 5구 라디오 a five-tube radio ▶투수가 제1구를 던졌다 The pitcher threw the first pitch.

구 具 a body ◆여러 구의 시체 several bodies

구 九 nine; 〈제9〉 the ninth ◆9배(倍) nine times / 9분의 1 one [a] ninth / 십중 팔구 ten to one; in nine cases out of ten

구- 舊 old; 〈이전의〉 former; 〈전〉 ex-; one-time ◆구사상 antiquated [old-fashioned] ideas / 신구 시장(市長) the outgoing and incoming mayors ■—세대 the old generation —헌법 the abolished Constitution

-구 口 a mouth; an opening; a window; a hole; a wicket ◆개찰구 a wicket; a ticket gate / 분화구 a crater / 접수구 a reception counter; an usher's window; an inquiry [information] office / 출납구 a teller's window [cage] / 출입구 an entrance (and exit) or a gateway

-구 具 a tool; an implement ◆문방구 stationery / 방한구 an outfit for protection against cold / 운동 구 athletic goods; sporting goods; sports equipments

구가 舊家 1 〈오랜 집안〉 an old family ◆고장의 구가 one of the town's old families 2 〈옛집〉 one's former house [old home]; a house of former day

구가 謳歌 praise; glorification; eulogy; paean —구가하다 sing [chant] the praises [joys] (of); glorify; eulogize ◆인생을 구가하다 sing the joys of life / 자유를 구가하다 eulogize the blessings of liberty / 청춘을 구가하다 rejoice in the blessings of youth; sing the praises [openly enjoy the joys] of youth ▶사람들은 평화를 구가했다 People sang the praises of peace.

구각형 九角形 a nonagon; an enneagon

구간 區間 the section [district] 《between A and B》; 〈철도 등의〉 a block (of railroad track) ◆불통 구간 an impassable [a damaged] section [district] / 제4구간 공사 work on the fourth section ▶여기서는 지하철 요금이 1구간에 450원입니다 The subway fare here is 450 won (for) a section. ■—요금제 the sectional fare system

구간 舊刊 〈잡지의〉 a back number; 〈서적의〉 an old edition [publication, printing]

구강 口腔 the mouth; 〔解〕 the oral cavity ◆구강 위생 oral [dental] hygiene; the hygiene of the mouth / 구강의 oral; of the mouth ■—암 cancer of the mouth —외과 oral surgery

구강염 口腔炎 〔醫〕 stomatitis ⇨ 구내염

구개 口蓋 〔解〕 the palate; the roof [vault] of the mouth ◆구개의 palatal; palatine ■—경[연]— the hard [soft] palate ■—골 the palatine [palate, palatal] bones —수(垂) the uvula (pl. ~s, -lae) —음 a palatal (sound); 〈연구개음〉 a guttural

구걸 求乞 begging; asking for 《food, money》 —구걸하다 beg 《from door to door》; go (about) begging ▶그는 길거리에서 사람들에게 돈을 구걸했다 He begged (for) money from the people in the street.

구경 sightseeing; a visit ◆시내 구경 a tour of observation through the town / 구경이 나다 a spectacle takes place [occurs] / 서울 구경을 하다 see [do] the sights of Seoul ▶나는 이번 휴가에는 경주 구경을 할 작정이다 I'm going to see [do] the sights of Kyŏngju during the next vacation. ⇌ I'm going sightseeing in Kyŏngju on the coming vacation. ▶우리는 모두 구경만 하고 있었다 We all remained mere spectators. —구경하다 see [do] the sights 《of》; see; 〈관광하다〉 go sightseeing; 〈경기·행진 등〉 watch; visit; 〈방관하다〉 look on ◆연극[영화]을 구경하다 see a play [movie] / 싸움을 구경하다 watch a fight ▶서울에는 구경할 곳이 많다 There are lots of sights to see [places worth seeing] in Seoul.

구경 口徑 〈지름〉 a diameter; an aperture; 〈총포의〉 a caliber ◆대구경 렌즈 a wide-angle lens; a lens of large diameter [aperture] / 대[중, 소]구경 포 a large-caliber [medium-caliber, small-caliber] gun / 38구경 권총 a 38-caliber revolver / 구경 20인치 포 a gun of twenty-inch caliber; a 20-inch gun

구경 球莖 【알뿌기】〔植〕〈백합 등의〉 a bulb; 〈글라디올러스 등의〉 a corm

구경가마리 a laughingstock [byword] ▶그는 모든 사람의 구경가마리다 Everybody laughs at him. ⇌ He is ridiculed by everyone. ▶그녀는 묘한 머리를 해서 친구들의 구경가마리가 되었다 She became the laughingstock of her friends because of funny hairstyle.

구경감 a spectacle ⇨ 구경거리

구경거리 a sight; a spectacle; an attraction; a show; the object of interest ▶그 오로라[서커스]는 대단한[볼 만한] 구경거

리였다 The aurora [circus] was a great spectacle [well worth seeing].
▶그날의 구경거리는 마라톤이었다 The attraction [highlight, main event] of the day was the marathon race.

구경꾼 〈관객〉 a spectator; (총칭) the audience; 〈관광객〉 a sightseer; a visitor; 〈방관자〉 an onlooker; a viewer
▶거리는 그 행진을 보러 나온 구경꾼들로 붐볐다 The street was crowded with people watching the parade.

구고 舊稿 an old manuscript ◆구고를 고쳐 쓰다 rewrite *one's* old manuscript

구곡 舊穀 old (crop of) rice; old grain

구공탄 九孔炭 a nine-holed (coal) briquette

구과 毬果 〖植〗 a cone
■一식물 a conifer

구관 舊館 the old [older] building

구관이 명관이다 (속담) You don't know what you've got until you've lost it. ⇒ Better the devil you know than the devil you don't know.

구관조 九官鳥 〔鳥〕 a (hill) myna(h); a myna bird

구교 舊交 old friendship; old acquaintance; 〈오랜 친구〉 an old friend
▶우리 반은 3년마다 모임을 갖고 구교를 되살리고 있다 Our class holds a reunion every three years to renew our old friendship.

구교 舊敎 (Roman) Catholicism ■一도(徒) a (Roman) Catholic

구구 〈닭 부르는 소리〉 chuck-chuck

구구 九九 〈구구법〉 the rules of multiplication
■一표 the multiplication table : 구구표를 외다 say the multiplication tables; learn *one's* tables / 내 동생은 구구표를 5단까지 외웠다 My brother has learned his multiplication table up to the 5's.

구구하다 區區— various; diverse; different; conflicting; 〈사소하다〉 petty; small; trivial; 〈용렬하다〉 mean; base
◆구구한 변명 a lame [poor] excuse / 구구한 잔소리 an insignificant lecture / 의견이 구구하다 be divided [divergent] in opinion (as to)
▶한자 사용 제한에 대해서는 의견이 구구하다 Opinions are divided [Opinions differ] on restrictions in the use of Chinese characters.
▶구구한 소리 마라 Don't say silly things.

구국 救國 national salvation; salvation of *one's* country ◆구국의 병사들 the soldiers who saved the country ―**구국하다** save [rescue] *one's* country
■一운동 the save-the-nation movement [drive]

구균 球菌 〖醫〗 a coccus ((*pl.* -ci)) ◆단(單)구균 [미(微)]구균 a micrococcus / 포도상 구균 a staphylococcus

구근 球根 〖알뿌리〗〖植〗〈양파 등의〉 a bulb; 〈감자 등의〉 a tuber
■一식물 a bulbous plant

구금 拘禁 detention; confinement; custody ―**구금하다** detain; confine; keep [hold] *sb* in custody; hold *sb* under arrest
▶그 사람은 경찰서에 구금되었다 He was detained [taken into custody] at the police station.

구급 救急 first aid; rescue
■一물자 emergency supplies ―병원 an emergency hospital ―붕대 (an) emergency dressing ―상자 a first-aid kit [box] ―신호 a hurry call ―약품 first-aid medicine ―차 an ambulance (car) ―처치 first-aid treatment : 구급 처치를 하다 administer first aid (to) ―환자 ⇨ 응급(~환자)

구기 〈국자〉 a ladle [dipper]; a scoop
◆구기로 떠내다 scoop (up [out]) with a ladle [dipper]

구기 枸杞 〔植〕 a boxthorn; a matrimony vine

구기 球技 a ball game

구기다 1〈구김살이 생기(게 하)다〉 crumple; rumple; wrinkle; crease; crush
◆구겨진 옷 a crumpled dress / 구겨지다 be crumpled; become creased
▶그녀는 그 편지를 둘둘 구겼다 She crumpled (up) the letter into a ball.
▶이 천은 잘 구겨진다 This material creases easily.
▶함부로 쑤셔넣어 옷이 구겨지지 않도록 해라 Take care not to crumple your dress by packing it carelessly.
2〈살림이 꼬이다〉 be reduced to poverty; be on the decline

구기자 枸杞子 the fruit of a matrimony vine
■一나무 ⇨ 구기(枸杞)

구기적거리다 crumple [wrinkle, crease, rumple] up

구기적구기적 with a crumple [crush, rumple] ◆옷을 구기적구기적 가방에 집어넣다 crush the clothes into a baggage

구기지르다 crumple [wrinkle] up

구김살 1〈주름〉 wrinkles; rumples; creases; folds; cockles
◆구김살진 wrinkled; crumpled / 구김살지다 be crumpled; be wrinkled; become creased
▶이 천[감]은 구김살이 잘 진다[지지 않는다] This cloth [material] wrinkles easily [is wrinkle-resistant].
▶그녀는 다리미로 드레스의 구김살을 폈다 She ironed out the wrinkles on her dress.
2 (비유) ◆구김살 없는 미소 an angelic smile; 《laugh》 an innocent laugh / 구김살 없는 성격 a cheerful [fair] disposition

구깃구깃하다 crumpled; creasy; wrinkled
◆구깃구깃한 종잇 조각 a crumpled sheet of paper
▶그녀는 모자를 너무 꼭 쥐고 있어서 아주 구깃구깃해졌다 She held her hat so tightly that it became crumpled out of shape.

-구나 〈감탄〉 what; how; indeed
▶참 큰 비행기구나 What a big airplane (that is)! ⇒ How big that airplane is!
▶정말 덥구나 It's very hot, indeed.
▶향기가 참 좋구나 How lovely it smells!

구난 救難 〈구출〉 rescue; 〈선박의〉 salvage
■一선(船) a rescue ship; a salvage boat ―작업 ⇨ 구조(~작업) ―훈련 rescue training

구내 區內 ◆구내에 in the ward; within the

limit of a ward; within the section [district] / 서대문 구내에 살다 live in Sŏdaemun ward

구내 構內 〈건물을 포함한 부지〉(on) the premises; 〈교회·학교 등의〉(in) the precincts; 〈in〉 the grounds; 〈on〉 the campus
♦ 대사관 구내 the embassy compound
▶ 구내 출입 금지 (게시) Keep off the premises.
■**—역[교회]—** the station [church] precinct 학교— school grounds; 〈대학의〉 the campus ■**—방송** 〈역의〉 the station PA system (▶PA 는 public announcement의 略) **—식당** 〈학교·직장 등의〉 a refectory; a cafeteria; 〈역 등의〉 a refreshment room **—전화** an interphone; an (internal) office telephone **—전화 번호** an extension number

구내염 口內炎 〔醫〕 stomatitis

구년 舊年 the old [past] year; 〈작년〉 last year
▶ 구년에 베풀어 주신 후의에 심심한 감사를 드립니다 I have to thank you a lot for the kindness you have shown me over the past year.

구단 球團 a ball club; 〔野〕 (a corporation owning) a professional baseball team ■**—주** the club owner; the owner of a baseball team

구대륙 舊大陸 the Old World; 〈유럽〉 the European Continent

구더기 a maggot; a worm ▶ 썩은 물고기에 구더기가 들끓고 있었다 The rotten fish was full of [infested with] maggots.

구덩이 1 〈팬 땅〉 a (ground) depression; a hole; a hollow ▶ 우리는 땅에 구덩이를 팠다 We dug [made] a hole in the ground.
2 〔鑛〕⇨ 갱 (坑)

구도 求道 seeking [a search] after truth ♦ 구도심이 있는 religious minded; eager to seek after truth **—구도하다** seek [search] after truth
■**—자** a seeker after truth; an inquirer

구도 構圖 〈미술 작품의〉 composition; compositional arrangement; planning; 〈소설 등의〉 plot; 〈생활의〉 a life plan
♦ 구도를 잡다 compose; draw a rough sketch 《of》; 〈소설의〉 construct [lay out] the plot 《of a novel》
▶ 이 그림은 구도가 좋다[나쁘다] This painting is well [poorly] composed.

구도 舊都 an old capital [metropolis]; a former capital

구도 舊道 highway [an old road]

구독 購讀 subscription
♦ 구독을 신청하다 subscribe to 《a newspaper》/ 구독을 갱신하다 renew one's subscription 《to, for》
—구독하다 〈예약하여〉 subscribe to; 〈정기적으로 사다〉 take
▶ 우리는 신문을 두 가지, 잡지를 세 가지 구독하고 있습니다 We take [subscribe to] two newspapers and three magazines.
■**—료** subscription rate **—자** 〈독자〉 subscriber; reader : 이 지방 신문은 구독자가 많다 This local paper has a large circulation.

구동 驅動 drive
♦ 전륜[4륜] 구동 자동차 a front-wheel[four-wheel]-drive car [vehicle]; a car [motor vehi-cle] with front-wheel [four-wheel] drive
■**—력** driving force [power] **—륜**(輪) a driving wheel **—장치** 〔機〕 running [driving] gear **—축**(軸) the driving shaft [axle]

구두 〈단위〉 (a pair of) shoes; 〈장화〉 boots; high boots; 〈반장화〉 half boots
♦ 고무창 구두 rubber-soled shoes / 굽이 높은 [낮은] 구두 high [low] heels; high-heeled [low-heeled] shoes / 끈 매는 구두 Oxford shoes / 끈 없는 구두 slip-ons / 구두를 고치다 〈남을 시켜서〉 have one's shoes mended [repaired] / 구두를 닦다 polish [shine, black] one's shoes / 구두를 맞추다 have a pair of shoes made / 구두를 벗다 take one's shoes off / 구두를 신다 put one's shoes on
▶ 이 구두는 내게 딱 맞는다 These shoes are the just right (size) for me. ⇌ These shoes fit me perfectly.
▶ 이 구두는 좀 낀다 These shoes are a little tight for me [pinch me a little].

구두

혓바닥 가죽 tongue
장식 구멍 decorative perforations
구두끈 shoelace
장식 가죽 wing tip
창 sole
장심 shank
뒤축 heel
뒷달이 가죽 quarter

구두 口頭 ♦ 구두의 oral; verbal; spoken / 구두로 신청하다 make an application by word of mouth; apply verbally
▶ 과장에게는 구두로 보고했다 I made an oral report to the section chief.
■**—계약** a verbal contract **—시험** an oral test [examination]; 〈면접〉 an interview **—지시** verbal instruction

구두끈 a shoelace; a shoestring; a shoe tie; 〈英〉 a bootlace
♦ 구두끈을 매다 fasten [tie] one's shoes (with strings); fasten [tie] one's shoelaces; lace (up) one's boots / 구두끈을 풀다 untie one's shoestrings; unlace one's shoes [boots]
▶ 구두끈이 풀렸다 The shoestrings came loose.

구두닦기 〈닦는 일〉 shoe polishing [blacking]
■**—용구** shoeshine things **—통** a shoeshine box **—헝겊** a shoe rag

구두닦이 〈닦는 사람〉 a shoeblack; a bootblack; a shoeshine (man, woman); a boots 《호텔의》 ■**—소년** a shoeshine boy

구두법 句讀法 punctuation; pointing ◆구두법이 잘못되다 be wrongly punctuated

구두변론 口頭辯論 〔法〕 oral proceedings [argument, pleas] —**구두변론하다** plead orally

구두선 口頭禪 a fair word; a mere talk; an empty slogan ◆구두선에 그치다 be [become] mere talk [empty slogan]; end in just talk

구두쇠 a niggard; a stingy [close-fisted] fellow [person]; a miser; a skinflint; (美俗) a penny pincher; a cheapskate; a tightwad ◆구두쇠 영감 an old screw / 구두쇠다 be close [stingy] with *one's* money; be tightfisted / 지독한 구두쇠다 be as close as a vise / 구두쇠로 유명하다 be notorious for parsimony ▶참 구두쇠로구나 What a tightwad [cheapskate]!

구두심리 口頭審理 a verbal [an oral] trial; hearing —**구두심리하다** make a verbal trial; listen to a case in court

구두약 —藥 shoe [boot] polish; (shoe)blacking ◆구두약을 칠하다 black [apply polish to] *one's* shoes

구두점 句讀點 a punctuation mark [point] ▶다음 문장에 적당한 구두점을 찍으시오 Put the appropriate punctuation marks in the following sentences. ⇌ Punctuate the following (sentences) as required.

구두창 the sole of a shoe; a sole ◆구두창을 갈다 have *one's* shoes resoled (by)

구들 an underfloor heating system of a Korean house; a Korean hypocaust ◆구들을 놓다[고치다] install [repair] a Korean underfloor heating device —**방** an *ondol* room; a hot-floored room —**장** a covering stone slab of the Korean *ondol* system —**직장**(直長) a stay-at-home; a homebody

구들동티 a sudden death from no apparent cause ◆구들동티가 나다 die unexpectedly [suddenly] without any known cause

구랍 舊臘 last December; the end of last year

구래 舊來 from old times; from times past ◆구래의 old; old-time; traditional; 〈유서 있는〉 time-honored; 〈인습적인〉 conventional / 구래의 누습을 타파하다 do away with misguided practices of the past; do away with old abuses / 구래의 방법을 답습하다 follow the conventional method

구럭 a straw-net bag; 〈망태기〉 a mesh bag

구렁 a hollow; a depression; a pit; 〈구멍〉 a hole ◆자기가 판 구렁에 빠지다 fall into a pit of *one's* own digging / 타락의 구렁에 빠지다 sink into a deep pit of degradation

구렁이 1 〔動〕 a serpent; a darkish brown big snake 2 〈음흉한 사람〉 a deep one; a snake

구렁이 담 넘어가듯 (속담) realize *one's* aim [attempt, plan] in an unnoticed way; play tricks secretly [stealthily]

구렁찰 〈늦 찰벼〉 a late-ripening variety of glutinous rice

구렁텅이 a deep pit [hole]; a great hollow [hole]; 〈타락의〉 a slough ◆구렁텅이에 빠지다 sink to [reach] the bottom / 가난의 구렁텅이에서 살다 live in extreme poverty ▶그 가엾은 사람은 절망의 구렁텅이에 빠져 있었다 The sad man was in an abyss of hopelessness.

구레나룻 whiskers ◆구레나룻이 난 얼굴[사람] a whiskery face [whiskered man]

-**구려** 1 〈감탄〉 ▶솜씨도 좋구려 What excellent workmanship! ▶참 훌륭하구려 Wonderful! ⇌ Splendid! ⇌ Beautiful! 2 〈허용〉 ▶들어오시구려 Please come in. 3 〈권유〉 ▶좀 보여 주시구려 May I have a look at it? ▶드시구려 Please help yourself. ▶먼저 하시구려 Please go ahead.

구력 舊曆 the lunar calendar ⇨ 음력

구령 口令 a word of command; a verbal order ◆구령에 따라 at the word of command ▶「차려」하고 장교가 구령을 내렸다 "Attention!" the officer gave [shouted] an order. —**구령하다** command; order; give an order [a command] —**대** a drill platform

구루병 佝僂病 〔醫〕 rickets; rachitis ◆구루병에 걸린 사람 a person suffering from rickets; a rachitic (person) —**약** an antirachitic

구류 拘留 custody; detention ◆구류 중이다 be in detention; be (kept) in custody ▶그는 10일간의 구류 처분을 받았다 He was sentenced to ten day's detention. —**구류하다** take *sb* into custody; hold [keep] *sb* in custody; detain; (口) lock *sb* up ◆구류되어 심문을 받다 be detained for questioning ▶경찰은 용의자를 구류했다 The police took the suspect into custody [detained the suspect]. ▶그는 어젯밤 경찰서에 구류되었다 He was detained [kept in custody] at the police station last night.

구르다¹ 〈회전하다〉 roll; 〈굴러 넘어지다〉 tumble down; fall down ◆굴러 들어가다 roll into 《a hole》 / 재산이 굴러 들어오다 come into a big fortune ▶구르는 돌에는 이끼가 끼지 않는다 (속담) A rolling stone gathers no moss. ▶공이 상자에서 굴러나왔다 A ball rolled out of the box. ▶그 깡통은 언덕 아래로 굴러 내려갔다 The can rolled down the slope. ▶그 버스는 절벽에서 굴러 떨어졌다 The bus fell over the cliff.

구르다² 〈발을〉 tread noisily; stamp on; beat *one's* shoes (on the floor) ◆발을 구르다 stamp *one's* feet on; tread noisily; trample (the floor) / 분해서 발을 동동 구르다 stamp with vexation [chagrin]; be hopping mad ▶그는 절호의 기회를 놓치고 화가 나서 발을 굴렀다 He missed a capital opportunity and stamped his feet in anger.

구름 a cloud; (총칭) the clouds ◆검은 구름 a dark [black] cloud / 두꺼운 구름 thick clouds / 솜 같은[뭉게] 구름 fleecy

구두점의 사용법

말하고 싶은 것을 글로 표현하여 읽는 이에게 정확히 전달하기 위해서는 적절한 구두점 사용을 염두에 두지 않으면 안된다.

1. 피리어드 — Period; Full Stop (.)
 (1) 평서문이나 명령문 끝에
 I'd like to talk to him. (나는 그와 이야기하고 싶다)
 (2) 생략을 표시할 때
 ▶ 경칭·직함·인명 등에
 Mr. Hill (힐 씨) / Dr. Lee (이 박사[선생]) (▶영국에서는 Mr.나 Mrs., Dr. 등에 피리어드를 찍지 않는 일이 많음) / John F. Kennedy (존 에프 케네디)
 ▶ 기관명·국명 등에
 U.N.(= United Nations 유 엔) / U.K.(= United Kingdom 영국)
 ▶ 연월일·요일 등에
 55 B.C. (=before Christ 기원전) / Mon. (= Monday 월요일) / Aug. (=August 8월)
 ▶ 서적 등에 쓰는 약호에
 cf. (=confer 참조하라) / e.g. [íːdʒí] (=exempli gratia 예를 들면)

2. 의문부호 — Question Mark (?)
 ▶ 의문문이나 불확실한 일에
 Why didn't you come with us? (왜 우리와 함께 가지 않았습니까?)
 Muhammad was born in 570(?) and died in 632. (마호메트는 570년엔가 태어나서 632년에 죽었다)

3. 감탄부호 — Exclamation Mark (!)
 ▶ 감탄문이나 감탄사, 강한 감정 뒤에
 What a strong man he is! (그는 참으로 굳센[튼튼한] 사람이구나)
 Dear me! (아이고머니)
 This is great! (야, 굉장하군)

4. 콤마 — Comma (,)
 (1) 문장 중에서 의미의 단락을 표시하는 데
 If you go, I'll go too. (자네가 간다면 나도 가겠네)
 He speaks German, Italian and Chinese. (그는 독일어, 이탈리아어 그리고 중국어를 한다)
 (2) 삽입어구나 동격의 글에
 Mr. Kim, our homeroom teacher, teaches English. (담임인 김 선생님은 영어를 가르치신다)

5. 세미콜론 — Semicolon (;)
 ▶ 서로 관계가 있는 구나 절, 문장을 결부시키는 데
 Some people say that it is true; others say that it is false. (그것이 사실이라고 말하는 사람이 있는가 하면 거짓이라고 말하는 사람도 있다) (▶이와같이 세미콜론이 but 내지는 and의 뜻을 지니고 있는 경우가 많음)

6. 콜론 — Colon (:)
 (1) 앞의 어구를 바꾸어 말하거나 설명할 때
 Two languages are spoken in Canada: English and French. (캐나다에서는 2개 국어를 사용하고 있다. 즉 영어와 프랑스어다)
 (2) 항목이나 실례를 열거할 때
 The member nations of the EC are: France, Italy, ... (EC 가맹국은 다음과 같다: 프랑스, 이탈리아 …)

7. 하이픈 — Hyphen (-)
 (1) 그 행의 끝에서 한 단어가 분철될 때
 한 단어가 다음 행에 걸쳐질 때는 반드시 단어의 올바른 음절(syllable)에서 끊어야 함에 주의해야 한다. 짧은 단어, 예컨대 about 등은 끊지 말고 전체를 다음 행으로 넘겨야 한다.
 (2) 합성어·숫자 등에
 a brother-in-law (처남, 시동생 등) / twenty-two students (22명의 학생) / one-third of the class (그 학급의 3분의 1)

8. 아포스트로피 — Apostrophe (')
 (1) 소유격에
 Jim's dog (짐의 개) / girl's school (여학교)
 (2) 단축형에
 You'll (=you will) / '97 (=1997년)
 (3) 문자·숫자 등의 복수형에
 the 1990's (=nineteen-nineties 1990년대) (▶1990s 처럼 아포스트로피를 붙이지 않는 경우가 많음) / 3R's (=reading, writing, arithmetic 읽기·쓰기·산수)

9. 인용부 — Quotation Mark (" ", ' ')
 (1) 회화, 발음 또는 어구의 인용에
 He said, "I'm O.K." (그는 「괜찮아」하고 말했다)
 "Seeing is believing" is a well-known proverb. (「백문이 불여일견」은 유명한 속담이다)
 (2) 시·단편·책의 한 장(章)·곡명 등을 나타내는 데
 Have you read Defoe's "Robinson Crusoe"? (디포의 로빈슨 크루소를 읽어 봤니?)

---

clouds / 엷은 구름 filmy clouds; thin clouds / 구름 사이[틈] a break [rift] in the clouds; a space between the clouds / 구름에 가린 달 the clouded moon / 구름 잡는 듯한 〈애매한〉 vague; ambiguous; 〈엉뚱한〉 wild; fantastic; 〈비현실적인〉 visionary / 구름이 많은 cloudy (days) / 구름이 없는 cloudless; unclouded / 구름에 가리다 be covered with clouds; be clouded over; go [hide, disappear] behind the clouds / 구름 위로 솟다 rise above the clouds; soar into the sky
▶ 하늘에는 구름 한 점 없었다 There was not a (speck of) cloud in the sky.
▶ 구름이 낀다 Clouds build up [come up, gather, form].
▶ 구름이 걷힌다 Clouds lift [clear away].
▶ 구름이 낮게 끼어 있다 Clouds hang low.
구름다리 an overbridge; a girder bridge; an elevated bridge; (英) a flyover
구릉 丘陵 a hill; a hillock ■—지대 hilly districts; hill [hilly] country
구리 copper ◆구리를 입힌 coppered / 구리를 입히다 copper (a thing); coat (a thing) with copper ■—철사 copper wire
구리터분하다 stinking; fetid
구린내 a stinking smell; a stink; an offensive

odor
♦구린내가 나다 smell unpleasant [foul]; emit a foul odor; stink
▶구린내가 코를 찔렀다 A nasty smell greeted [assailed] my nose.
▶이것이 구린내를 없애는 최상의 방법이다 This is the best way to take out [remove, get rid of] the foul smell.

구릿빛 copper color; reddish brown (color)
♦햇빛에 구릿빛으로 타다 be (sun)tanned; be browned by the sun

구매 購買 purchase; buying
♦구매심을 일으키다 induce (a customer) to buy; arouse [excite] customers' interest
─**구매하다** buy; 〈계획적·대량의〉 purchase; 〈정부의〉 procure
─**─가격** a purchasing price ─**부** the purchasing division [department] ─**자** a buyer; a purchaser

구매력 購買力 purchasing [buying] power; 〈화폐의〉 the buying value
♦인플레이션으로 인한 구매력 감퇴 inflation's bite on buying power
▶소비자의 구매력이 떨어지고[증대하고] 있다 Consumer purchasing power is getting lower [is growing].
─**─평가지수** purchasing power parities

─**구먼 1** 〈감탄〉 참 귀엽구먼 How cute!
▶똑같구먼 Why it looks just like it!
▶큰 나무로구먼 What a tall tree!
▶자네 말이 맞구먼 Indeed, you are right.
▶여기 있구먼 Here you are!
▶아니, 자네 모르고 있었구먼 Oh dear! You didn't know that?

2 〈추측〉 I suppose; I think; I guess; I hope; I am afraid; perhaps
▶자네가 맞겠구먼 I suppose [guess, think] you are right. ≒ Probably you are right.
▶내일은 그가 오겠구먼 Perhaps he will come tomorrow.
▶그렇다는구먼 So they say.
▶그녀는 30이 넘었겠구먼 I should say she is over thirty.

3 〈의문〉 ▶케이크를 좋아하는구먼 You like cake, don't you?
▶자넨 그 일을 알고 있겠구먼 You know it, don't you?

구멍 1 〈뚫린〉 a hole; an orifice; 〈틈〉 an aperture; an opening; 〈천공〉 a perforation; 〈가늘고 긴〉 a slit; 〈동전 넣는〉 a slot
♦귓구멍 (the orifice of) an ear / 바늘 구멍 a hole made by a needle / 〈바늘귀〉 an eye (of a needle) / 빠져나갈 구멍 a loophole; a way out; a way [means] of escape / 창구멍 a chink in a paper window / 콧구멍 a nostril / 구멍을 뚫다 make a hole (in) / 구멍을 막다 stop [stuff] (up) a hole; fill [stop] a gap (with rags) / 구멍을 메우다 fill up a hole / 탈세할 구멍을 막다 plug a tax loophole / 구멍을 파다 dig a hole (in the ground)
▶네 양말에 구멍이 뚫렸다 There is a hole in your sock.
▶담뱃불이 떨어져서 바지에 구멍이 났다 A lighted cigarette burnt a hole in my trousers.
▶내 이에 구멍이 났다 I have [There is] a cavity [hole] in my tooth.
▶드릴로 판자에 구멍을 뚫었다 I drilled a hole through a board. ⇒ I made a hole through a board with a drill.
▶구멍에 동전을 넣으면 표가 나온다 Drop a coin into the slot, and you get a ticket.

2 〈결함〉 a defect; 〈맹점〉 a blind point
▶그 계획은 구멍 투성이다 There are a number of holes in the scheme.
▶그의 논리는 구멍 투성이다 There are many flaws [holes] in his reasoning.
▶국경은 구멍 투성이라 얼마든지 넘나들 수 있다 The border is porous.
▶어떤 법률이나 빠져나갈 구멍은 있다 Every law has a loophole.

3 〈결손〉 a deficit; a shortage; a loss
♦밑천에 큰 구멍이 나다 have *one's* capital badly holed / 구멍을 메우다 cover up the deficit; make up a loss
▶이것 때문에 장부상에 구멍이 났다 This caused a deficit in the account.

구멍가게 a small(-scale) shop; a small general store

구메구메 occasionally; (every) now and then; at times
▶구메구메 아이에게 젖을 먹이다 breast-feed a baby now and then

구메밥 meals provided to a prisoner through an opening of the cell door

구면 球面 〔數〕 a spherical surface
■─**경**〔거울〕 a spherical mirror ─**계** a spherometer ─**삼각법**〔기하학〕 a spherical trigonometry [geometry] ─**수차** spherical aberration ─**좌표** spherical coordinates ─**투영법**〔항법〕 spherical projection [sailing]

구면 舊面 an acquaintance; a familiar face
▶그녀와는 구면이다 I have known her from of old. ⇒ She is an acquaintance of mine.
▶그와는 구면처럼 느껴졌다 I felt as though he were an old friend.

구면체 九面體 〔數〕 an enneahedron; a solid figure having nine faces

구명 究明 investigation; study; inquiry
─**구명하다** investigate; study; inquire into
▶그 대사고의 원인을 구명하기 위하여 조사단이 구성되었다 A research group was organized to investigate [clear up] the cause of the great accident.
▶그 일은 철저하게 구명해야 한다 We must inquire [look] into the matter thoroughly.

구명 救命 lifesaving; sparing *sb's* life; 〈죄수의〉 clemency
♦구명을 요청하다[빌다] ask [beg] for *sb's* life; appeal for mercy
─**구명하다** save *sb's* life; spare *sb* from death
■─**구**(具) (美) life preserver; (총칭) lifesaving [survival] equipment ─**대**(帶) a life belt; 〈구명 동의〉 a life jacket [(美) vest] ─**벨트** a life belt ─**부이** a life buoy ─**정**(艇) a lifeboat

구명 舊名 the old name [designation]

구문 口文 a commission; brokerage ♦거래에서 5%의 구문을 받다 get [take, receive] a 5%

구문 構文 construction (of sentences); sentence structure ■분사— a participial construction ■—법[론]〔文法〕 syntax
구문 舊聞 an old story; old [stale] news ▶ 그 이야기는 구문에 속한다 It is an old story.
구문서 舊文書 an old document [record]
구물 舊物 〈옛것〉 old things; 〈전래되는 것〉 a hereditary article; heirlooms; 〈골동품〉 an antique; a curio
구미 口味 one's taste; one's palate; appetite; 〈흥미〉 one's interest
♦구미를 돋우는 tempting; inviting; appetizing / 구미를 돋우다 stimulate [tempt] one's appetite; make one's mouth water / 구미에 맞다 suit one's taste; be nice to the palate
▶ 그녀는 구미가 까다롭다 She has a delicate palate. ⇌ She is particular about her food.
▶ 그의 이야기가 내 구미를 돋우었다 His story excited [aroused] my interest.
▶ 이탈리아 요리는 내 구미에 맞지 않는다 Italian food does not suit [please] my palate. ⇌ Italian food is not to my taste [liking].
구미 歐美 Europe and America; the West; the Occident
♦구미 여러 나라 countries in Europe and America; Western countries / 구미의 European and American; Western; Occidental
■—인 Europeans and Americans; Westerners; Occidentals
구민 區民 the inhabitants [residents] of a ward ■—궐기대회 a ward rally
구박 驅迫 maltreatment; abuse ♦구박을 받다 be bullied; be abused
—구박하다 be hard on; abuse; maltreat; mistreat; annoy
♦시어머니를 구박하다 treat one's mother-in-law cruelly
▶ 신데렐라는 계모에게서 구박받았다 Cinderella was maltreated [illtreated] by her stepmother.
▶ 그녀는 며느리[의붓아들]를 구박한다 She is hard on her daughter-in-law [stepson].
구배 勾配 a slope; a slant; 〈기울기〉 an incline; 〈철도·도로 등의〉 (美) a grade; (英) a gradient; 〈지붕·계단 등의〉 a pitch
♦가파른[완만한] 구배 a steep [gentle] slope / 오르막[내리막] 구배 a rising [falling] gradient / 30°의 구배로 at [with] an incline [a gradient] of 30 degrees
▶ 도로의 구배는 1000분의 20이었다 There was a grade [gradient] of twenty in a thousand in the road.
■—표(標) a grade [gradient] post
구법 舊法 〈옛법〉 an old [ancient] law; 〈낡은 방법〉 an old [outdated] method
구변 口辯 speech; eloquence
♦구변 없는 사람 a poor speaker [talker]; an inarticulate person / 구변 좋은 사람 a glib [facile] talker; a man of many words / 구변이 좋은 eloquent; fluent; glib
▶ 그는 구변이 없어서 오해받기 쉽다 He speaks so poorly [is so awkward with words] that he is often misunderstood.

구별 區別 **1** 〈차이〉 (a) distinction; (a) difference; 〈차별〉 discrimination
♦인종, 연령, 성의 구별 없이 irrespective [regardless] of race, age, or sex; without [making no] distinction of race, age, or sex / 공사(公私)의 구별을 분명히 하다 draw a sharp line between one's public and private affairs / 선악의 구별을 못하다 have no sense of [can draw no line between] right or wrong
▶ 이 게임은 남녀노소 구별 없이 즐길 수 있다 Everyone can enjoy the game without distinction [regardless] of sex or age.
▶ 여관과 호텔은 어떤 구별이 있습니까? What is the difference between an inn and a hotel?
▶ 당시에는 계층의 구별이 매우 뚜렷했다 In those days class distinctions were very clear.
—구별하다 distinguish 《between A and B》; make a distinction 《between》; discriminate 《between two things》; tell [know] 《A from B》; 〈동일 종류를〉 differentiate; tell 《them》 apart

> 解說 **distinguish**는 「특징을 구별하다」라는 뜻의 가장 일반적인 말. **discriminate**는 미묘한 차이를 분간하여 평가한다는 뜻. **tell**은 구어적인 말이다.

♦양서와 악서를 구별하다 discriminate between good and bad books [good books from bad ones]
▶ 놀 때와 공부할 때를 구별하지 못하는 학생들도 있다 Some students don't know when to work and when to play.
▶ 이 둘을 분명히 구별해야 한다 We must draw a clear line between these two.
▶ 나는 그와 그의 동생을 구별할 수가 없다 I can't tell him from his brother. ⇌ I can't distinguish between him and his brother.
▶ 너도 이젠 옳고 그름을 구별할만한 나이가 되었다 You are old enough to know right from wrong.
▶ 그녀는 진짜 진주와 인조 진주를 구별할 줄 안다 She can tell the difference between real and imitation pearls. ⇌ She can discriminate real pearls from imitations.
▶ 그 쌍둥이 형제를 구별할 수 있습니까? Can you tell the twin brothers apart?
▶ 어느 것이 어느 것인지 구별할 수가 없다 I can't tell which is which.
2 〈분류〉 (a) classification; (a) division
—구별하다 classify [divide] 《into》
▶ 나무는 상록수와 낙엽수로 구별된다 Trees are divided [classified] into evergreens and deciduous trees.
구보 驅步 a run; 〈말의〉 a canter; a gallop (▶ gallop이 canter보다 빠른 속도임)
♦구보로 (go) at a run; 〈군대에서〉 (march) on 〔(英)〕 at] the double; 〈말이〉 at a gallop [canter]
▶ 구보 (口令) Double march!
—구보하다 run; 〈말이〉 gallop; canter; 〔軍〕 double
■—행진 the double march
구복 口腹 mouth and stomach ♦구복지계 (a)

living; a means of living / 구복을 채우다 satisfy *one's* appetite

구복이 원수라 〈속담〉 Hunger is the source of humiliation.

구부러뜨리다 bend *sth* forcefully ◆나뭇가지를 구부러뜨려 꺾다 break off a twig of a tree

구부러지다 bend; curve; be bent; be crooked ◆길의 구부러진 곳 a turn [curve, bend] in the road / 구부러진 철사 a bent [curved, crooked] wire
▶그 길은 거기서 왼편으로 구부러진다 The road turns [curves, bends] (to the) left there.
▶납은 쉽게 구부러진다 Lead bends easily.

구부리다 bend; crouch
◆손가락을 고리처럼 구부리다 crook a finger / 철사를 구부리다 bend a (piece of) wire
▶그는 철사를 둥그렇게 구부렸다 He bent the wire into a ring.
▶그는 낮은 문을 지나가려고 허리를 구부렸다 He hunched his back to get under the low gate.
▶그는 펜을 주우려고 몸을 구부렸다 He bent down to pick up the pen.

구부정하다 rather [slightly] bent ◆등이 구부정하다 be rather [somewhat] bent (in the back)
▶사람은 왜 나이를 먹으면 구부정해질까? Why do people get bent as they age?

구분 區分 〈분할〉 division; 〈구획〉 section; 〈분류〉 classification; sorting
◆시(市)의 구분 지도책 the city sectional atlas
▶종(種)은 속(屬)의 하위 구분이다 Species is a subdivision of genus.
—**구분하다** 〈부분으로 나누다〉 divide; 〈구획하다〉 section; 〈분류하다〉 classify
◆우체국에서는 우편 번호로 우편물을 구분한다 At the post office they sort mail by zip code.
▶그것은 5가지로 구분된다 It is divided into five. ⇒ It is classified into five groups.
▶한국에서는 학년이 두 학기로 구분되어 있다 The school year in Korea is divided into two terms.
▶귤은 크기로 구분되어 상자에 넣어진다 Mandarin oranges are grouped according to their size into the cartons.

구불구불 ▶그 시내는 골짜기 사이를 구불구불 흐른다 The stream winds [twists] through the valley.
—**구불구불하다** ◆구불구불한 길 a winding road / 구불구불한 강 a meandering river
▶이 길은 아주 구불구불하다 This road is full of twists and turns.

구붓하다 slightly bent [curved, twisted]

구비 口碑 (an) oral tradition; a legend; folklore
◆구비에 의하면 according to tradition; Tradition has it [says] that... / 구비로 전해지다 be handed [come] down orally [by word of mouth]

구비 具備 —**구비하다** have; possess; 〈갖추다〉 be furnished [provided, equipped] 《with》
◆모든 조건을 구비하다 fulfill all the conditions; satisfy all the requirements

▶모차르트는 태어나면서부터 음악적 재능을 구비하고 있었다 Mozart was endowed by nature with a genius for music.
▶각 테이블에는 이어폰이 구비되어 있다 Earphones have been installed at each table.
■—**서류** required documents

구빈 救貧 relief of the poor [needy]; poor relief ■—**대책[사업]** relief measures [work] —**원** a poorhouse; a workhouse —**제도** a relief system

구쁘다 〈서술적〉 feel an appetite; be hungry

구사 驅使 〈자유자재로 씀〉 free use; 〈부림〉 driving
—**구사하다** 〈능숙하게 다루다〉 use freely; 〈활용하다〉 make the most of
◆최신 기술을 구사하다 make full use of the latest technology / 영어를 자유롭게 구사하다 have a good command of English / 많은 자료를 구사하다 make free use [the most] of abundant data
▶그녀는 5개 국어를 구사한다 She has five languages at her command.
▶그는 풍부한 어휘를 구사한다 He commands a large vocabulary.
▶그는 빛의 속도를 계산하는 데 컴퓨터를 구사했다 He made the most of the computer to calculate the speed of light.

구사상 舊思想 old-fashioned [outdated] ideas

구사일생 九死一生 a narrow escape from death
▶나는 구사일생으로 살아났다 I escaped death by the skin of my teeth [by a hair's breadth].
—**구사일생하다** narrowly escape death; escape death by a hairbreadth [by the skin of *one's* teeth]
▶그는 구사일생했다 He narrowly escaped death. ⇒ He had a narrow escape from death.

구상 求償 a claim for compensation [damages] ■—**권** a right to indemnity —**무역** compensation [barter] trade —**무역 협정** barter trade agreement —**자** a claimant

구상 具象 concreteness; embodiment
◆구상의 concrete; figurative / 구상화하다 reify [ríːəfài]; exteriorize
■—**개념** a concrete concept —**시** 〔文〕 concrete poetry —**예술** the representative arts —**화(畵)** a representational painting

구상 球狀 〈공 모양〉 a spherical [globular] shape; globularity ◆구상의 spherical; globular; ball-shaped
■—**세균** 〔生〕 a micrococcus 《*pl.* -cocci》 —**체** a spheroid; a globoid

구상 鉤狀 〈갈고리 모양〉 ◆구상의 hooklike; hook-shaped ■—**골(骨)** an unciform bone —**돌기(突起)** an uncinate protuberance [projection]

구상 構想 〈계획〉 a plan; a design (면밀한); 〈생각〉 an idea; 〈줄거리〉 a plot; 〈착상〉 a conception
◆구상이 떠오르다 conceive an idea [a plan] / 구상을 다듬다 work over *one's* plan [plot, ideas]; elaborate a plan
▶이 일에 대한 앞으로의 구상은 무엇입니까?

What is your future plan [vision] in this matter?
▶ 그는 독자적인 구상을 실행에 옮겼다 He put his original idea into practice.
▶ 집필 전에 그는 그 소설의 구상을 충분히 했다 He fully worked out the theme and plot of his novel before sitting down to write.
▶ 그는 새로운 도시교통 체계에 대한 구상을 가지고 있다 He has a design for [has designed] a new urban transportation system.
―**구상하다** draw up 《a plan》; map out 《a scheme》; formulate a plan [plot] 《of》
♦ 논문을 자세히 구상하다 work out a detailed plan for one's thesis

구상나무 〔植〕 a Korean fir

구상유취하다 口尙乳臭 ―〈젖내나다〉 smelling of milk; 〈유치하다〉 babyish; childish; 〈미숙하다〉 green
▶ 그는 아직도 구상유취하다 He is still green [immature]. ⇌ He is still wet behind the ears.

구새먹다 〈나무가〉 become [get] hollow; be eaten hollow ♦ 구새먹은 나무 a hollowed tree

구새통 a hollow(ed) log; 〈굴뚝〉 a wooden chimney

구색 具色 assortment
♦ 구색을 갖추다 assort; supply [furnish] with a variety of goods / 구색을 갖춰 놓고 있다 keep [have] a well-assorted stock
▶ 그들은 문구(文具)의 구색을 풍부히 갖추어놓고 있다 They have a large assortment of writing materials.

구석 1 〈모퉁이〉 a corner; an inside corner; a nook
♦ 구석방 an inner room; a back room / 구석자리 a corner seat / 마음 한 구석에 somewhere in the back of one's mind; somewhere at the bottom of one's heart / 방 구석에 앉다 sit in the corner of the room / 소년을 방 한구석에 세워놓다 〈벌로〉 put a boy in the corner of a room
▶ 그는 다방에 가면 대개 구석 자리에 앉는다 In a coffee shop, he usually takes a seat in the corner.
▶ 방구석이 이게 뭐냐 What a messy room this is!
▶ 그는 방구석에 틀어박혀 생각했다 He shut himself (up) in [confined himself to] the room to think.
2 〈외진[외딴] 곳〉 a recess; a nook; a remote place [corner]
♦ 시골 구석 a remote rural area; a remote village; the backcountry
▶ 그는 시골 구석에 살고 있다 He lives in a remote village.
3 〈…한 점[면]〉 an aspect; a side; a point; an angle
♦ 미심쩍은 구석들 doubtful points / 모르는 구석이 없다 know sth down to the last detail
▶ 그의 이야기에는 다소 미심쩍은 구석이 있다 There are some points in his statement which do not sound quite convincing to me.

구석구석 all the corners 《of》; every corner; all over; throughout
♦ 방을 구석구석 뒤지다 search the room from top to bottom; (口) search every nook and cranny of the room / 보고서를 구석구석 살피다 give one's attention to every detail of a report
▶ 그녀는 방을 구석구석 청소했다 She gave the room a thorough cleaning.
▶ 경찰은 그 집을 구석구석 뒤졌다 The police searched every nook and cranny of the house.
▶ 나는 이 도시를 구석구석 알고 있다 I know every inch [corner] of the town.
▶ 나는 그것을 구석구석 알고 있다 I know it like a book [like the back of my hand]. ⇌ I know every detail of it.
▶ 그의 이름은 전세계 구석구석까지 알려져 있다 His name is known in every corner of the world.

구석기 舊石器 〔考古〕 a paleolith; a paleolithic stone implement ■ ―시대 〔考古〕 the Old Stone Age; the Paleolithic Age [Era] ―인 a paleolithic man

구석지다 recessed; secluded; out-of-the-way
♦ 여관의 구석진 방 a secluded room in an inn / 구석진 시골 a backcountry
▶ 산골짜기의 가장 구석진 데에 폭포가 있다 In the remotest part of the valley there's a waterfall.

구설 口舌 a gossip; 〈비방〉 slander; verbal abuse
▶ 남의 구설은 무시해버려라 Pay no attention to the gossip of scandalmongers.
▶ 그는 (남의) 구설에 올랐다 He is talked about 《by others》.

구설수 口舌數 the bad luck to be spoken ill of [to suffer words of denunciation, to be verbally abused]

구성 構成 making; (a) makeup; setup; 〈조직〉 formation; 〈조직화〉 organization; 〈구조〉 structure; line-up
♦ 이야기의 구성 the framework of a story / 인원 구성 line-up; personnel organization
▶ 그 문장은 구성이 어색하다 The sentence structure is awkward.
▶ 이 소설은 구성이 잘 되어 있다 This story is well constructed [put together].
▶ 경리과는 인원 구성이 잘못 되어 있다 The staff of the accounting section is not well organized.
―**구성하다** organize; form; make up; compose; constitute (▶ make up 이하는 구성 요소가 주어임); be made up of; consist of; be composed of (▶ 이상 셋은 구성의 대상물이 주어임)
♦ 사회[범죄]를 구성하다 form [constitute] a society [crime] / 이론을 구성하다 frame a theory
▶ 50개주가 미합중국을 구성한다 Fifty states form [constitute] the United States of America.
▶ 그 위원회는 6명으로 구성되어 있다 The committee comprises [consists of, is composed of] six members.
▶ 물질은 원자로 구성되어 있다 Matter is composed of atoms.

■—개념 〔心〕 a construct —단위 a constituent unit; a group unit —분자 a component; a constituent elements —비〔統〕the component [distribution] ratio —요소 structural elements —원 a constituent (member); a member 《of a community》—주의[파]《美》constructivism

구성지다 emotional; sentimental; enchanting
♦구성진 노랫가락 enchanting melody / 구성진 목소리 a touching voice; a full and melodious voice

구세 〔鑛〕porous ore

구세계 舊世界 the Old World, 〈유럽〉the Old Continent

구세군 救世軍 the Salvation Army ■—군인 a Salvationist —사관 a Salvation Army officer

구세대 舊世代 the old generation

구세주 救世主 the savior of the world; 〔基〕the Savior; the Redeemer; the Messiah ♦구세주의 Messianic

구속 拘束 〈속박〉(a) restriction [restraint]; binding; control; 〈감금〉confinement; 〈구류〉custody
♦구속이 없는 free; unrestrained / 구속을 받다 be placed under control; be bound; suffer restriction / 구속을 풀다 remove restrictions; set sb free
—구속하다 bind; restrict; restrain; take sb into custody; arrest; confine
▶그 규칙은 모든 공무원을 구속한다 The rule binds all public workers. ≒ All public workers are bound by the rule.
▶이 법률은 언론의 자유를 구속한다 This law restricts freedom of speech.
▶그 사람은 경찰에 구속되었다 The man was taken into by the police.
■—시간 〔勞〕actual working hours —영장 a warrant of arrest; an arrest warrant —자 a person under restraint —적부심사 review of the legality of the detention —전하(電荷) bound charge

구속 球速 〔野〕the speed of a pitched ball
♦구속을 바꾸다 〈투구가〉change one's pace

구속 救贖 〔基〕the Redemption

구속노동 拘束勞動 compulsory [forced] labor
■—시간 compulsory labor hours; "portal-to-portal" working hours

구속력 拘束力 binding power
♦구속력이 있다[없다] carry [carry no] (legal) binding force / 구속력을 갖다[잃다] have [lose] (its) binding power
▶총회의 결의는 전회원에게 구속력이 있다 Decisions taken by the general meeting are binding on all the members.

구수 口授 〈말로 전함〉oral instruction [teaching]
—구수하다 instruct [teach] orally
▶그 비법은 대대로 구수되었다 The secret (teaching) had been handed down orally from generation to generation.

구수하다 1 〈맛이〉tasty; pleasant; delightful; delicious; 〈냄새가〉nice-smelling
♦구수한 맛 pleasant taste / 커피콩을 볶는 구수한 냄새 the pleasant aroma of coffee beans being roasted
2 〈이야기 등이〉entertaining; heartwarming
♦구수한 말투로 말하다 tell (a story) in a heartwarming manner
▶그의 글은 그것 나름대로 구수한 데가 있다 His writing has a subdued charm [gentle attractiveness] all its own.
▶그는 그것을 구수하게 이야기했다 He talked about it charmingly.

구수회의 鳩首會議 a (closed-door) conference
▶그들은 그 문제에 대해 구수회의를 가졌다 They consulted [put their heads together] on the matter
—구수회의하다 counsel [hold counsel, put (their) heads] together

구순하다 friendly; 〈서술적〉be on good [friendly] terms 《with》▶그 두 사람 사이는 구순하다 The two are on good terms.

구술 口述 (an) oral statement; dictation
—구술하다 state orally; dictate
▶그는 비서에게 편지를 구술했다 He dictated a letter to his secretary
■—시험 an oral examination; 〈대학의〉a viva voce (examination) —필기〔쓰기〕writing down at sb's dictation

구슬 〈유리알〉a glass bead; 〈보석〉precious stone; a jewel; 〈진주〉a pearl
♦구슬이 구르는 듯한 소프라노 a clear beautiful soprano / 구슬을 갈다 polish a gem
■—끈 a bead string —덩 a palanquin furnished with beaded screens —땀 beads of sweat: 구슬땀을 흘리며 일하다 work with sweat running down in beads —백 a beaded bag —세공 beadwork —알 a single bead

구슬구슬하다 cooked just right; neither too hard nor too soft ▶밥이 구슬구슬하게 잘 되었다 The rice has cooked just right [properly].

구슬리다 talk sb into; sweet-talk sb into; coax; persuade; cajole; wheedle
♦구슬려서 이야기하게 하다 coax sb into talking [to talk] / 구슬려서 옷을 사게 하다 cajole sb into buying a dress
▶그는 나를 구슬려서 돈을 빌려갔다 He wheedled me into loaning him some money.
▶그녀는 남편을 구슬려서 그 조건을 받아들이게 했다 She sweet-talked her husband into accepting the condition.
▶그는 발끈해서 나가버렸으나 나중에 잘 구슬리자 집으로 돌아왔다 He left the house in a huff, but was later persuaded to calm down and come home.

구슬붕이 〔植〕a squarrose [squarrous] gentian

구슬이 서 말이라도 꿰어야 보배라 〈속담〉It takes more than pearls to make a necklace. ≒ Nothing is complete unless you put it in final shape.

구슬치기 marbles; children's games played with marbles —구슬치기하다 play at marbles

구슬프다 sorrowful; mournful; sad; unhappy
♦구슬픈 노래 plaintive song [singing] / 구슬픈 이야기 a sad story / 구슬프게 sadly; plaintively; mournfully / 구슬피 울다 weep sadly [mournfully]

구습 舊習 an old custom; an outdated practice; conventionalities
♦ 구습을 고집하다 stick to old customs / 구습을 타파하다 do away with old conventions; break through conventionalities

구시렁거리다 〈잔소리하다〉 give sb a lecture persistently; nag; 〈군소리하다〉 keep on complaining [grumbling]

구식 舊式 an old style [fashion, school]
♦ 구식의 out-of-date; outdated; old-fashioned; outmoded; (蔑) antiquated; of the [an] old type [style, school], old styled / 구식 교육법 an old-fashioned teaching method / 구식 무기 outmoded [obsolete] weapons / 구식 사고방식 an old-fashioned way of thinking / 구식 혼인 an old-fashioned [a traditional Korean] wedding
▶ 그의 생각[그 옷]은 아주 구식이다 His ideas [The clothes] are quite old-fashioned [out-of-date].
▶ 그는 구식 사람이다 He is an old-fashioned person. ⇌ He is a man of the old school.
■—쟁이 an old fog(e)y; an old-fashioned person

구신 具申 reporting 《to a superior on a matter》 in detail
—**구신하다** report in detail 《to a superior》
▶ 그는 사장에게 의견을 구신했다 He offered [gave] his opinion to his boss.
■—서 a full report

구실 1 〔史〕〈공직〉 a public office [position]; a post in the government
2 〈임무〉 a duty; an obligation; a task; a role; a function
♦ 사람 구실을 하다 discharge *one's* full duty as man; behave like a human being / 제 구실을 다하다 do [fulfil] *one's* duty
▶ 그는 자기 구실을 다하였다 He has fully performed his duties [tasks].
▶ 그는 경찰관의 구실을 게을리했다 He neglected his duties as a policeman.
▶ 나는 두 고아의 아버지 구실을 맡았다 I took on the role of father to two orphans.
▶ 이 구(句)에서는 명사가 형용사 구실을 한다 The noun functions as an adjective in this phrase.
3 〈세금〉 taxation

구실 口實 〈변명〉 an excuse; 〈핑계〉 a pretext; a plea
♦ 그럴 듯한[되지도 않는] 구실 a plausible [poor, clumsy] excuse / 빤한 구실 a transparent [an obvious] pretext
▶ 그건 구실이 안돼 That is no excuse.
▶ 그는 언제나 그럴 듯한 구실을 댄다 He always makes [finds] plausible excuses.
▶ 그녀는 교묘한 구실을 꾸며댔다 She cooked up [concocted] a clever excuse.
▶ 그는 자기 행동에 무슨 구실을 댔니? What excuse [reason] did he give for his behavior?
▶ 그는 병을 구실 삼아 학교를 조퇴했다 He left school early on [under] the pretext of being sick [that he was sick].
▶ 그는 이 일이 처음이라는 것을 실패의 구실로 삼았다 In excuse of his failure, he said (that) he was new to his work.
▶ 그것은 구실에 불과하다 That's a mere excuse.

구심 求心 1 〔物〕〈중심으로 쏠림〉 seeking the center ♦ 구심성의 centripetal / 구심적으로 centripetally 2 〈참선〉 religious meditation [contemplation] 3 〔解〕〈신경〉 afferent
■—가속도 centripetal acceleration —기 a plumbing arm —뉴런 afferent neuron —력 (exert) centripetal force —성 centripetal; a centripetal tendency —신경〔解〕an afferent [a centripetal] nerve —운동 a centripetal motion

구심 球審 〔野〕 a ball [plate] umpire; an umpire-in-chief; a referee

구십 九十 ninety
♦ 제90 the ninetieth / 90분의 1 a [one] ninetieth / 90노인 an old man of ninety; a ninety-year-old / 구십 춘광 the ninety days [three months] of spring; the happy springtime / 90대의 사람 a person of the age of 90 years; a nonagenarian

구씨관 歐氏管 〔解〕the Eustachian tube＝유스타키오관

구아 歐亞 Europe and Asia; Eurasia ⇨ 유라시아

구아슈 〈화법〉《paint in》 gouache; 〈그림〉 a gouache

구악 舊惡 a past misdeed [crime]; 〈사회악 등〉 the old [deep-rooted] evils
♦ 구악을 들춰내다 expose *sb's* past misdeeds; rake up *sb's* secret past / 구악을 일소하다 make a clean sweep of [sweep out, root out] the old evils
▶ 그들은 고관들의 구악을 폭로했다 They exposed the high officials' past crimes.

구애 求愛 courting; courtship ♦ 구애춤〈새의〉 a courtship [mating] dance
—**구애하다** try to win a woman's love; make amorous advances 《to》; court; woo
▶ 그는 그녀에게 구애하다가 퇴짜맞았다 He courted her but met with rebuff.

구애하다 拘礙— be particular about; adhere 《to》; stick 《to》
♦ 구애되는 particular; (美口) choosy; (美口) picky / 구애되지 않고 freely; irrespective of; without regard to; regardless of / 사소한 일에 구애되다 be particular about trifles; split hairs; be hairsplitting / 옛 관습에 구애되다 be unable [unwilling] to discard old customs; be wedded to the old ways / 형식에 구애되다 stick to formality
▶ 시험 성적에 너무 구애되지 마라 Don't take the results of the exam too seriously.
▶ 그는 세속적인 일에 구애되지 않는다 He is free from [indifferent to] worldly cares.

구약 口約 a verbal promise [agreement]

구약 舊約 1 〈옛 약속〉 an old promise 2 〔基〕〈구약 성경〉 the Old Testament; the Old Covenant ■—시대 the Old Testament era; Old Testament days

구어 口語 spoken [colloquial] language; a colloquial speech [word] ♦ 구어의 spoken; colloquial; conversational

구어박다

—문 a colloquial sentence; spoken language —시 a poem in a colloquial style —영어 spoken English —체 a colloquial style; colloquialism: 구어체로 쓰다 write in (a) colloquial style

구어박다 1 〈한 군데서만 지내다〉 confine oneself (in); shut oneself up (in); stay [remain] in a place
2 〈쐐기를 달구어 박다〉 heat 《a wedge》 and drive it in
3 〈이잣돈을 늘리지 않다〉 store [save] up (money); hoard

구역 區域 〈지역〉 an area; a zone; a district; a quarter; 〈한계〉 the limits; the boundary

[解説] *area*는 어떤 특징을 가진, *zone*은 어떤 목적으로 다른 것과 구별된, *district*는 행정・사법상 구분된 구역을 말한다.

♦군대 관할 구역 a military district / 배달 구역 a delivery zone / 순찰 구역 a beat / 통학 구역 a school zone / 구역 내 within [inside] the limits [boundary] 《of》/ 구역 외 outside the limits
▶이곳은 출입금지 구역이다 This area is off limits.
▶경찰이 그의 담당 구역을 순찰하고 있었다 A policeman was on his beat [making his rounds].
▶이 구역 내에서는 금연이다 Smoking is not permitted within this area.

구역 嘔逆 nausea ⇨ 욕지기

구역질 嘔逆— nauseation; vomiting
♦구역질 나는 냄새[맛] a nauseating smell [taste] / 구역질 나는 이야기 a disgusting story / 구역질나다 have [feel] nausea; be sick (at one's stomach); feel nauseated [disgusted]
▶그것은 보기만 해도 구역질이 난다 The mere sight of it is enough to turn my stomach.
—**구역질하다** vomit

구연 口演 an oral narration
—**구연하다** narrate orally; recite
▶그 이야기는 지금은 자주 구연되지 않는다 The story is not performed very often these days.
■—동화 an orally narrated fairy tale

구연 舊緣 old ties; an old connection; (an) old relationship

구열 口熱 (a) fever [temperature] in the mouth ♦구열을 재다 take [measure] one's temperature in the mouth

구옥 舊屋 an old house [building]; one's former house

구왕실 舊王室 the Royal Household of Chosŏn dynasty ♦구왕실 재산 the estate of the former Royal Household

구외 構外 ♦구외에(서) outside the compounds [premises]

구우 舊友 an old friend [acquaintance]; (口) an old pal [crony]

구우일모 九牛一毛 a drop in the bucket [ocean]; infinitesimal quantity

구운석고 —石膏 (化) plaster of Paris; calcined gypsum=소석고

구움일 〈말리기〉 drying timber (in a kiln); lumber [timber] drying in a kiln

구워지다 〈고기가〉 be roasted; 〈생선이〉 be broiled; 〈빵・과자가〉 be baked; 〈토스트가〉 be toasted; 〈오븐에서〉 be grilled
♦너무[바싹] 구워진 overdone / 덜[살짝] 구워진 underdone; 〈고기가〉 (美) rare / 잘 구워진 well-done; done brown
▶생선이 구워졌다 The fish is done.
▶고기가 구워졌다 The meat has been roasted [grilled].
▶고기기 너무 구워졌다 The meat is overdone.
▶빵이 잘 구워졌다 The bread is done just right. ⇌ The bread has baked just long enough.

구원 久遠 eternity; permanence ♦구원의 사랑 everlasting love —**구원하다** eternal; permanent; everlasting

구원 救援 〈조난・긴급시의〉 rescue; 〈어려운 처지의〉 relief; (基) salvation; redemption
♦하나님께 구원을 빌다 pray God for help / 구원을 요청하다 ask [cry] for help; seek help [relief]; call on sb for help
▶그들은 마을 사람들에게 신속히 구원의 손길을 뻗쳤다 They were quick to lend a helping hand to the townspeople.
—**구원하다** rescue; aid; help
♦구원하러 가다 go to sb's rescue; go to the rescue 《of》
▶경찰이 그들을 구원하러 나섰다 The police set out to rescue them.
■—군 relief column; 〈증원부대〉 reinforcements —투수 a relief pitcher; a reliever; (俗) a fireman

구월 九月 September (略 Sept.) ♦구월에 in September

구유 a manger; a trough

구은 舊恩 kindness shown one in the past
♦구은에 보답하다 repay sb's old favors [kindness]

구음 口音 〔音聲〕 an oral sound

구읍 舊邑 an old town; one's former town

구의 舊誼 old friendship ♦구의를 생각해서 for old acquaintance's [friendship's] sake

구이 meat [fish] roasted [broiled, grilled] with seasonings ♦생선 소금 구이 broiled [(英) grilled] fish with salt
■—갈비 roasted ribs 닭고기— broiled [roast] chicken 돼지고기— roast pork

구인 求人 a job offer; an offer of a situation
♦구인측의 요구[조건] hiring requirements [terms]
▶구인이 구직을 상회하고 있다 The number of (job) vacancies exceeds that of job hunters.
▶이 대학 학생들에게는 구인 요청이 많다 There are a lot of job offers for the undergraduates of this university.
▶구인 (게시) Help wanted. ⇌ Situations vacant.
■—광고 an advertisement for help; a help-wanted advertisement; (美口) a want ad; (英) a situations-vacant advertisement; (口) a help-wanted ad: 신문에 구인 광고를 내다 put a

want ad in the paper **—난(難)** a shortage of labor; a labor shortage: 내년에는 구인난이 심각해질 것이다 There will be a serious shortage of job applicant next year. **—란(欄)** a help-wanted column; a "Situations Vacant" column

구인 拘引 taking sb into custody; (an) arrest
—구인하다 seize and hold sb into custody; arrest
▶ 그는 신문을 위해 구인되었다 He was brought in [detained] for questioning.
■**—장(狀)** ⇨ 구속(〜영장)

구일 九日 nine days; 〈아흐레〉 the ninth day
■**—장(葬)** a burial on the ninth day after death; a funeral held for nine days

구입 購入 purchase; buying ♦새 집의 구입 the purchase of a new house
—구입하다 buy (↔sell); purchase
♦구입한 도서 books purchased / 대량 구입하다 make [effect] a heavy purchase
—가격 the purchase price **—권** a purchasing ticket [coupon] **—명세** a purchase specification **—자** a buyer; a purchaser: 대량 구입자 a heavy buyer

구작 舊作 one's old [earlier] work ♦구작을 방송 극본으로 개작하다 rewrite one's old [earlier] work for broadcasting

구잠정 驅潛艇 a (submarine) chaser

구장 球場 a ball ground [park]; a stadium; 〈야구장〉 a baseball ground; a diamond; 〈美〉 a ball park

구저분하다 filthy; squalid; sordid 《slum》; dirty; shabby

구적 求積 〔數〕 the computation of areas [volumes] 《of》 ♦구분 구적법 mensuration by parts ■**—법** mensuration; 〈넓이의〉 planimetry; 〈부피의〉 stereometry

구적 a historic site ⇨ 고적(古蹟)

구전 口傳 oral transmission; transmitting by word of mouth; 〈구비(口碑)〉 (oral) tradition ♦구전으로 by word of mouth; orally; by (oral) tradition
▶ 나는 그 소식을 구전으로 알게 되었다 I learned the news by word of mouth.
—구전하다 inform [transmit] by word of mouth; hand down orally
♦구전된 비법 a secret method handed down orally
▶ 이 이야기는 대대로 구전되어 왔다 This story has been transmitted orally from generation to generation.

구전 口錢 (a) commission ⇨ 구문(口文)

구전 舊典 an ancient code (of law); ancient customs and systems

구전심수하다 口傳心授— impart by lips and heart

구절 句節 a phrase; a passage; a paragraph

구절양장 九折羊腸 meanders; a meandering road; a winding [zigzag] path
▶ 그 길은 구절양장이다 The path is full of turns and twists.

구절초 九節草 〔植〕 Siberian chrysanthemum

구접스럽다 〈사물이〉 dirty; shabby; messy; 〈행동이〉 mean; base; nasty; filthy ♦구접스러운 방 a dirty room / 구접스러운 짓 a mean action; a shameful conduct

구정 舊正 the New Year's Day according to the lunar calendar; the lunar New Year's Day

구정 舊情 〈친구〉 an old friendship; 〈이성의〉 old love ▶ 나는 그와 10년만에 만나 구정을 새롭게 했다 I met him after ten years, and renewed our old friendship.

구정물 dirty [filthy, foul] water; used wash water; dishwater; (kitchen) slop(s) ■**—통** a slop pail

구제 救濟 relief; help; aid; 〈영혼의〉 salvation; redemption
♦실업자 구제 계획 an unemployment relief project
▶ 정부가 빈민 구제를 시작했다 The government began to give relief to the poor.
▶ 국제 연합이 난민 구제 계획에 나섰다 The United Nations launched aid programs for the refugees.
—구제하다 relieve; give relief (to); help; save
♦구제할 수 없는 unrelievable; unremediable; past salvation [redemption] / 난민[빈민]을 구제하다 give relief to the refugees [poor]
■**—기금** relief funds **—사업** relief work

구제 舊制 〈구제도〉 the old [former] system
♦구제의 학교 교육 school education under the old system

구제 驅除 extermination; destruction; stamping out
▶ 이 살충제는 흰개미 구제에 효과가 있다 This insecticide is effective in getting rid of termites.
—구제하다 get rid of; exterminate; stamp out
♦해충을 구제하다 exterminate [stamp out] harmful [noxious] insects
▶ 농부들은 화학 약품으로 진딧물을 구제한다 Farmers exterminate [get rid of] ant cows with chemicals.

구제도 舊制度 the old [former] system ⇨ 구제

구제책 救濟策 relief measures; a remedy
▶ 정부는 피난민의 구제책을 강구했다 The government took measures for the relief of the refugees.
▶ 실업자에 대한 어떤 구제책이 강구되어야 한다 Something should be done for the relief of the unemployed. ⇌ Relief measures should be taken for the jobless people.

구조 救助 rescue; succor; deliverance; 《ask [cry] for》 help
▶ 건물 맨 위층에서 몇 사람이 구조를 요청하고 있다 Several persons are crying [calling] for help from the top floor of the building.
▶ 소방대원이 그들의 구조에 나섰다 The firefighter went to their rescue.
—구조하다 rescue; save; help; salvage
▶ 그는 물에 빠진 소년을 구조했다 He saved a boy from drowning. ⇌ He rescued a boy who was drowning.
▶ 그는 그 화재에서 많은 인명을 구조했다 He saved many lives in the fire.
▶ 승객들은 침몰하는 배에서 전원 구조되었다 All the passengers were rescued from the

구조 sinking ship.
▶ 그는 화물선에 의해 구조되었다 He was picked up by a freighter.
■ 인명— 《for》 saving a life 해난(海難)— sea rescue; salvage ■ —대(隊) a rescue party [team, unit, aquad] —대(袋) an escape chute —대원 a rescue worker —망 a safety net —선 a lifeboat; a rescue ship; a salvage boat —신호 a signal [call] for help; an SOS (call); 〈항공기·선박의〉 a Mayday —원 a rescue man —자금 a relief fund —작업 relief work; rescue operations; salvage work [operations]

구조 構造 structure; construction; 〈조직〉 organization
♦ 문장의 구조 the structure of a sentence; sentence structure / 인체의 구조 the structure of the human body / 우리 사회의 구조적 모순 a structural contradiction in our society / 구조적 부패 structural corruption / 구조적 불황 a structural recession / 구조적 불황 업종 a structurally-weak industry / 구조적 실업 structural unemployment
▶ 이 건물은 구조가 복잡[단순]하다 This building is complicated [simple] in construction [structure].
▶ 로봇의 구조는 복잡하다 Robots are structurally complicated [complex in structure].
■ 사회— the structure [organization] of society; social structure 산업— industrial structure 상부— superstructure 하부— understructure; substructure; infrastructure ■ —개혁 structural reform —계산 structural calculation —론[주의] structuralism —물 a structure —선 tectonic line —식 (化) a structural formula —심리학 structural psychology —언어학 [言] structural linguistics —역학 [機] structural mechanics —지질학 tectonics —지형 tectonic landform —평야 structural (tectonic) plain —호 tectonic lake

구족 九族 the nine generations of a family; one's whole family [clan]

구존하다 具存— have one's parents still (both) alive ▶ 그의 양친은 구존해 계시다 His parents are both alive.

구좌 口座 an account ⇨ 계좌(計座)

구주 救主 〔基〕 the Messiah; the Savior; the Redeemer ■ —예수 Jesus Christ, our Savior; the Savior

구주 歐洲 Europe ⇨ 유럽

구주 舊主 one's former master [lord]

구주 舊株 〔證〕 an old stock [share]

구중 九重 1 〈아홉 겹〉 ninefold 2 〈구중 궁궐〉 the Royal Palace; the Court

구중약 口中藥 a stomatic medicine; cachou; a troche

구중주 九重奏 nonet ■ —곡 a nonet

구중중하다 filthy; dirtylooking; squalid; wet; damp ♦ 구중중한 날씨 foul [nasty] weather

구지레하다 shabby; dirty; untidy; filthy ♦ 구지레한 옷 shabby [soiled] clothes / 주제꼴이 구지레하다 be shabbily [slovenly] dressed

구직 求職 job hunting; seeking employment
▶ 내 여동생은 지금 구직 중이다 My sister is looking for a job.
▶ 구직 《게시》 Situation wanted.
—구직하다 hunt for [seek] a job; look for employment [a job]

구직광고 求職廣告 a situation-wanted advertisement; a classified ad for a job
▶ 나는 신문에 구직 광고를 닷새동안 냈다 I put a want ad [situation-wanted advertisement] in a newspaper for five consecutive days.
■ —란(欄) a work-wanted [job-wanted] column; a situation-wanted column —자 a job hunter [seeker]; a job applicant

구직신청 求職申請 an application for a situation [position, job]
▶ 몇 사람의 구직 신청이 있다 There are a few applications for the situation [position]. ⇌ A few persons came asking for employment [a position]

구질구질하다 1 〈너저분하다〉 dirty; untidy; foul; filthy; sordid
♦ 옷차림이 구질구질한 사나이 a man wearing dirty [filthy] clothes / 구질구질하게 늘어선 판잣집 a row of squalid shacks
▶ 그는 구질구질한 녀석이다 He has a mean spirit.
2 ⇨ 구중중하다

구차하다 苟且— 1 〈군색하다〉 clumsy; awkward; worthless
♦ 구차한 목숨 an ignoble existence; a humiliating life / 구차한 변명 a poor [clumsy] excuse / 남에게 구차한 소리를 하다 beg [plead] for sb's mercy; implore [entreat] sb for...
2 〈가난하다〉 poor; needy; destitute; miserable
♦ 구차한 삶을 살다 live a humble [miserable] life; lead a wretched life
▶ 그들은 살림이 구차하다 They live in poverty. ⇌ They are badly off.

구창 口瘡 a sore in the mouth

구채 舊債 an old debt; a long-standing debt
♦ 구채를 청산하다 pay off [clear] one's old debts

구척장신 九尺長身 a towering man; a very tall man; a man of towering height

구천 九天 the zenith; the heavens; 〔佛教〕 the nine celestial bodies

구천 九泉 〈저승〉 Hades; the netherworld; the other world

구청 區廳 a gu [ward] office
♦ 종로 구청 the Chongno Ward Office ■ —장 the chief [head] of a ward: 마포 구청장 the Director of Map'o Ward —직원 a ward official

구체 具體 ♦ 구체적인 사실 a concrete fact / 구체적으로 concretely; definitely; in a concrete form [way] / 구체적으로 말하면 to put it concretely; in concrete terms / 구체적인 예를 들다 give a concrete example
▶ 우리는 그것에 대한 구체적인 계획은 세우지 않았다 We have not made [formed] any concrete [definite] plan for it.
▶ 그 회의에서는 구체적인 것은 하나도 결정되지 않았다 Nothing definite was decided at the meeting.

▶ 좀 더 구체적으로 말씀해 주시겠습니까? Will you please be more specific?
■ —性 concreteness —案 a definite [concrete] plan [measure]: 내일까지 구체안을 생각해 보시오 Please think of a concrete plan by tomorrow.
구체 球體 a sphere; a spherical body; a globe ♦ 구체의 spherical
구체제 舊體制 an old order [structure, system]; the ancien régime
♦ 구체제를 폐지하다 abolish the old order
구체화 具體化 embodiment; materialization
—**구체화하다** 〈사항이〉 take (concrete) shape; materialize; 〈사항을〉 give shape (to); put (a plan) into effect
▶ 그는 자기 생각을 구체화했다 He materialized his ideas.
▶ 이 계획을 속히 구체화하지 않으면 예산은 없다 If this plan isn't actualized soon, there won't any budget for it.
▶ 그 계획은 구체화되었다 The plan materialized [was realized]. ⇒ The plan took concrete shape.
구축 構築 construction —**구축하다** build; construct ♦ 기반을 구축하다 establish [build up] the foundation
구축하다 驅逐— drive away [out]; expel ((from)); get rid of
♦ 시장에서 외래품을 구축하다 drive imported goods out of the market; throw [drive] out foreign goods from the market
▶ 악화는 양화를 구축한다 Evil money drives out good.
▶ 그들은 적군을 영토에서 구축했다 They expelled [drove] the enemy from their territory [land].
구축함 驅逐艦 a destroyer ■ 어뢰정— a torpedo-boat destroyer 호송— a destroyer escort 향도— a destroyer leader
구출 救出 rescue; saving
—**구출하다** rescue; save
♦ 위험에서[물에 빠진 사람을] 구출하다 rescue [save] sb out of danger [from drowning] / 궁지에서 구출되다 be helped out of difficulty
▶ 소방대원은 불난 집에서 소년을 구출했다 The fireman rescued [saved] the boy from the burning house.
▶ 그들은 헬리콥터를 보내 난파선의 승무원을 전원 구출했다 They sent a helicopter and rescued all the crew of a wrecked ship alive.
■ —活動 rescue operation: 구출 활동이 철야로 계속되었다 The rescue operation was continued throughout the night.
구충 驅蟲 extermination of insects; 〈체내의〉 curing of intestinal worms
—**구충하다** exterminate insects; get rid of worms; cure of intestinal worms
■ —藥[劑] an insectifuge; an insect repellent; a vermicide: 구충제를 먹다 take a vermifuge
구취 口臭 bad [foul] breath; 〔醫〕halitosis ♦ 구취가 나다 have (a) foul breath
구치 臼齒 a molar (tooth) ⇨ 어금니
구치 拘置 detention; confinement —**구치하다** detain; confine; hold [keep] sb in custody
구치소 拘置所 a prison [jail]; a detention house ■ 서울— (the) Seoul Prison
구침 鉤針 a hook
구칭 舊稱 the old name; the former title
구타 毆打 beating; a blow; 〔法〕assault and battery —**구타하다** hit; beat; give sb a blow; assault ♦ 머리를 구타하다 beat [strike] sb on the head
구태 舊態 the old [former] state of things
구태여 〈일부러〉 intentionally; purposely; 〈굳이〉 obstinately
▶ 구태여 자네가 그럴 필요는 없었다 You needn't have done such a thing.
▶ 구태여 설명할 필요는 없다 No particular explanation is necessary. ⇒ It is not particularly necessary to explain.
▶ 구태여 비교한다면 김군이 작문을 더 잘한다 If I had to compare them, I'd say that Kim is a little better at composition.
▶ 그렇게 결정했다면 구태여 바꾸라고 하지 않겠다 If it has already been decided on, I won't insist that you change it.
▶ 그 회의에는 구태여 가지 않아도 됩니다 You need not bother to attend the meeting.
▶ 나는 구태여 반대하지 않겠다 I have no particular objection to it. ⇒ I will not object to it particularly.
구태의연하다 舊態依然— remain unchanged [as it was] ▶ 그의 주장은 구태의연하다 His claims remain unchanged [the same]. ⇒ His is the same old claim.
구토 嘔吐 〔醫〕vomiting; vomiturition; emesis
▶ 배가 전후좌우로 흔들려서 승객은 모두 구토를 일으켰다 The ship rolled and pitched, and every passenger vomited [threw up].
—**구토하다** vomit; throw up (one's food)
■ —設사 vomiting and purging —劑(劑) 〈구토를 일으키는〉 an emetic; vomitive; vomitory
구투 舊套 (a) conventionalism; conventionality; stereotype ♦ 구투를 벗어던지다 shake off the bounds of convention; get free from conventionalism; get out of conventionalities
구파 舊派 the old school; 〈보수파〉 the conservatives ♦ 구파의 old style; of the old school ■ —연극 a play of the old school
구판 舊版 an old [earlier] edition ♦ 구판을 개정하다 revise an old edition
구폐 舊弊 old abuses; old evil ♦ 구폐를 바로잡다 reform old evils; 구폐를 타파하다 break down long-established abuses
구포 臼砲 〈옛 화포〉 a mortar
구푸리다 bend oneself forward; stoop
▶ 그는 구푸리고 그 종이를 주웠다 He bent (himself) down [stooped] to pick up the piece of paper.
▶ 그녀는 구푸리고 꽃내음을 맡았다 She bent [stooped] over the flower to smell it.
구풍 舊風 old customs
구하다 求— 1 〈찾다〉 look for; seek; want ♦ 셋집을 구하다 look for a house for rent [to let]
▶ 그는 지금 일자리를 구하고 있다 He is looking for a job [seeking employment] now.

▶ x의 값을 구하라 Find the value of x.
▶ 워드프로세서 조작자 구함 (게시) Wanted: a word processor operator.
2 〈요청하다〉 ask for; request; demand; claim
▶ 의견을 구하다 call for [solicit] sb's opinion / 허가를 구하다 ask (for) [request] permission 《to do》
▶ 나는 그에게 조언을 구했다 I asked him for advice [to advise me]. ⇒ I asked for [sought, requested] his advice.
3 〈얻다〉 get; have; obtain; 〈사다〉 buy; purchase
▶ 나는 저 가게에서 컴퓨터를 싸게 구했다 I bought a computer cheap(ly) at that store.
▶ 돈이면 무엇이든지 구할 수 있다 You can buy anything with money. ⇒ Money can buy anything.

구하다 救— save; help; rescue; relieve
▶ 그 의사가 소년의 목숨을 구했다 The doctor saved the boy's life.
▶ 그는 물에 빠진 아이를 구했다 He rescued [saved] the child from drowning.
▶ 내가 그녀를 곤경[위험]에서 구해 주었다 I helped her out of difficulty [danger]. ⇒ I got her out of trouble [danger].
▶ 하나님은 우리를 죄에서 구하기 위해 그리스도를 보내셨다 God sent Christ to redeem us from sin.
▶ 우리는 가난한 사람을 구하려고 모금하고 있다 We raise funds for the relief of [to aid] the poor.

구학문 舊學問 the old-type learning [education]; classical studies

구현 具現 embodiment; materialization; realization
—**구현하다** represent in concrete form; give concrete expression [form]; embody; materialize; realize
▶ 맑은 사상을 구현한다 Words embody thoughts.

구혈 甌穴 〈地質〉 a pothole

구형 求刑 the prosecutor's demands [recommendation for punishment]
▶ 검사는 피고에게 5년의 금고형[사형]을 구형했다 The prosecutor demanded five years imprisonment [the death penalty] for the accused.

구형 矩形 a rectangle ⇨ 직사각형

구형 球形 a globular form [shape] ♦ 구형의 globular; glove-shaped; spherical

구형 舊型 an old model [style, type] ♦ 구형 비행기 an outmoded plane / 구형 자동차 an old-model car; an old-fashioned car

구호 口號 a slogan; a catchword; a catch-phrase; a motto; a rallying word ♦ 한낱 구호에 그치다 end in mere gesture
▶「아시아인을 위한 아시아」가 그들의 구호다 "Asia for the Asians" is their slogan [motto].
▶ 그 정당은 「깨끗한 정치」라는 구호를 내걸고 결성되었다 The party was formed under the slogan [catchword, watchword] "Clean Politic."

구호 救護 relief; aid; rescue
—**구호하다** aid; help; rescue; relieve
♦ 부상자를 구호하다 give aid to [help] the injured [wounded] / 응급 구호하다 give first aid 《to》
▶ 그는 고아들에게 따뜻한 구호의 손길을 뻗쳤다 He extended a warm helping hand to orphans.
■—**금** a relief fund; relief money —**물자** relief goods [supplies] —**사업** relief work —**소** a first-aid [relief] station

구혼 求婚 proposal [offer] of marriage; courtship; courting; suit; wooing
▶ 그녀는 나의 구혼을 받아들였다[거절했다] She accepted [declined, refused] my proposal (of marriage).
—**구혼하다** ask sb to marry one; propose (marriage) 《to》; ask for 《a lady's》 hand; court; woo
▶ 그는 그녀에게 구혼했다 He asked her to marry him. ⇒ He proposed (marriage) to her.
■—**광고** an advertisement for a spouse: 신문에 구혼 광고를 내다 put an advertisement in a newspaper for a spouse —**자** a suitor; a wooer: 딸의 구혼자 a suitor to one's daughter / 돈이 목적인 구혼자 a fortune hunter; 《美俗》〈여자〉 a gold digger

구황 救荒 relief of the famine victims —**구황하다** give relief [aid] to the famine victims
—**작물** relief farming plants

구획 區劃 division; a section; 〈경계〉 a boundary; 〈땅의〉 a lot; 〈시가(市街)의〉 a block
♦ 행정 구획 an administrative division / 행정 구획상 in terms of administrative division
▶ 그 두 집 마당은 구획이 분명하지 않다 The division [boundary] between the two yards is unclear.
▶ 그 땅은 흰 선으로 4개의 구획으로 나누어져 있었다 The ground was divided into four parts by white lines.
—**구획하다** divide; partition; demarcate; mark off 《one lot from another》; mark out
♦ 땅을 작게 구획하여 팔다 divide up the land into small lots and sell them / 방을 둘로 구획하다 partition [divide] a room into two parts [compartments]
▶ 그 땅은 놀이터로 구획되어 있었다 The lot is marked off as a playground.

구획정리 區劃整理 〈토지의〉 land readjustment; 〈가로의〉 replanning of streets; readjustment of town lots; 〈주택지의〉 resubdivision of residential lots
▶ 이 도시는 구획 정리가 잘 되어 있다 This city has been redistricted [rezoned] effectively.
▶ 이 토지는 구획 정리 대상이다 This lot will be affected by rezoning.
—**구획정리하다** readjust the division of land [town lots]; readjust boundaries

구휼 救恤 relief ⇨ 구제(救濟)

구희 球戱 a ball game; 〈당구〉 billiards; 〈볼링〉 bowling

국 〈탕〉 soup; broth; 〈국물〉 juice ♦ 고깃국 meat soup / 된장국 beanpaste soup / 야채국 vegetable soup / 국을 먹다 eat soup / 국에 말다 put 《rice》 into soup

국 局 1 〈관청·회사의〉 《美》 a bureau; 《英》 a department (➤미국의 경우 부(ministry)에 해당함)

♦사무국 a secretariat / 편집국 an editorial board [bureau] / 1국 5과로 나누다 divide (an office) into one bureau and five sections / 국과 과로 이루어지다 be made up of bureaus and sections

2 〈전화국 등〉 ♦방송국 a broadcasting [radio, TV] station / 우체국 a post office / 전신국 a telegraph office [station] / 전화 교환국 a telephone exchange / 전화국 a telephone office / 라디오를 듣고 싶은 국에 맞추다 find [tune in] the station

3 〈바둑 등〉 a game (of *paduk* [chess])
♦대국 playing a game (of *paduk*)

-국 國 a country; a state; a nation

♦초강대국 a superpower / 개발 도상국 a developing country / 수출국 an exporter (nation) / 중립국 a neutral nation [country]

국가 國家 a state; a country; a nation; 〈정부〉 a government

> 解説 *state*는 어떤 주권 하에 통일된 국가를, *country*는 세계의 한 단위로서의 국가를, *nation*은 사회 구조나 경제 구조라는 관점에서의 국가를 뜻한다.

♦국가의 national; state; 〈정부의〉 governmental / 국가의 정책 state policy / 국가의 존망이 걸린 문제 an issue that concerns the fate of the nation / 국가에 봉사하다 serve *one's* country

▶조림은 국가 백년지 대계다 Forestation is a long-range project of the State.

■경찰[복지]— a police [welfare] state 공산[사회,자본]주의— a communist [socialist, capitalist] country 단일 민족— a racially homogeneous nation 민족— a nation-state

■경륜 statecraft —경제 the national economy —공무원 a national public official; a government official [worker; employee]; a public servant —공무원법 the National Public Service Law [Act] —권력 state power —기관 a state organ —론 the theory of the state —배상 reparation by the state —비상사태 (declare) a state of national emergency —사회주의 national [state] socialism —시험 ⇨ 국가 고시 —안보 national security —연합 a federation [union, league] of nations —주의 nationalism —주의자 a nationalist —통제주의 statism

국가 國歌 a national anthem

♦국가를 연주하다[부르다] play [sing] the national anthem / 국가를 제창하다 sing in unison the national anthem

▶군악대가 애국가를 연주하고 있었다 The Army Band was rendering the Korean national anthem.

국가고시 國家考試 a state [national] examination

♦의사 개업[교사 자격] 국가 고시 a state examination for the license of medical practice [for teacher's certificate] / 국가 고시에 합격[실패]하다 pass [fail] the state examination

국가적 國家的 national; state

♦국가적 사업 a national project / 국가적 행사 a national event; 《on》 a state occasion / 초국가적인 supernatural / 국가적 견지에서 from a national point of view

▶아름다운 자연은 국가적 유산이다 The beauties of nature are national heritage.

국거리 soup stock; materials for soup
국건더기 solid stuff [ingredients] in soup
국경 國境 the border; 《英》 the frontier (➤《美》에서는 주로 「미개척 지역」을 가리킴); (national) boundary

♦중·러 국경 the Russo-Chinese border / 국경을 넘다 cross the border / 국경을 침범하다 violate the border

▶예술에는 국경이 없다 Art has [knows] no national boundary.

▶캐나다는 남으로 미국과 국경을 접하고 있다 Canada is bordered on the south by the United States.

■—도시 a border [frontier] town —문제 a boundary [border] problem —분쟁 a boundary [border] dispute; a border conflict —선 a boundary line; a borderline —수비[경비]대 border [frontier] guards [army] —지대 the border; a border area [region]; the borderland —표시 a boundary marker

국경일 國慶日 a national holiday
국고 國庫 the national [state] treasury

▶국고가 비었다 The coffers of the state are empty.

▶의무 교육비는 전액 국고에서 부담해야 한다 The national treasury should cover all the cost of compulsory education

■—금 national funds; government money —보조 a state [government] subsidy: 이 학교는 국고 보조를 받고 있다 This school is subsidized by the government. ⇒ This school receives government subsidies. —부담 state liability: 나의 치료비는 국고 부담이다 The government pays my medical bills. ⇒ My medical bills are paid out of the national [state] treasury. —수입 national revenues: 국고 수입이 되다 go to the national treasury —지출 defrayment out of the national treasury —지출금 national treasury disbursements —차입금 a national loan

국공채 國公債 national [government] bond and public bond ♦국공채를 발행[상환]하다 issue [redeem] government and public bonds

국교 國交 diplomatic relations

♦국교를 끊다[맺다] break off [enter into, establish] diplomatic relations 《with a country》 / 국교를 정상화하다 normalize diplomatic relations 《with a country》

▶우리는 그 나라와는 국교가 없다 We have no diplomatic relations with that country.

▶1900년에 양국간에 국교가 수립되었다 Diplomatic relations were established between the two countries in 1900.

■—단절 a severance [rupture] of diplomatic relations —회복 a restoration of diplomatic relations

국교 國教 a state religion; a state church; the established church
♦ 비국교도 a nonconformist / 영국 국교도 a member of the Church of England / 영국 국교회 the Church of England; the Anglican Church

국구 國舅 the king's father-in-law

국군 國軍 the national [government] army; 〈한국군〉 the Korean Army; the Korean armed forces ♦ 국군의 날 (the Republic of Korea [ROK]) Armed Forces Day

국궁 鞠躬 ♦ 국궁 배례하다 make a deep bow ─국궁하다 bend *oneself* (forward) with respect; bow reverently

국권 國權 〈통치권〉 national sovereignty; 〈국가 권력〉 the power of the state
♦ 국권의 완전 회복 restoration of its full sovereignty / 국권을 발동하다 exercise the right of the state / 국권을 침해[주장]하다 violate [claim] national sovereignty

국그릇 a soup bowl ♦ 국그릇에 국을 떠담다 ladle soup into a bowl

국극 國劇 the national drama

국기 國技 a national sport [game] ▶ 투우는 스페인의 국기라고 한다 Bullfighting is said to be the national sport of Spain.

국기 國旗 a national flag [ensign]
♦ 러시아 국기 the Russian flag; the Hammer and Sickle / 미국 국기 the American flag; the Stars and Stripes; the Star-Spangled Banner / 영국 국기 the British flag; the Union Jack / 프랑스 국기 the French flag; the Tricolor / 한국 국기 ⇨ 태극(~기)
♦ 국기를 게양하다 hoist [put up] the national flag / 국기에 대해 경례하다 salute the national flag
▶ 그 배는 우리 나라 국기를 달고 달리고 있었다 The ship was sailing under the Korean flag.
■ ─게양식 a flag-hoisting [flag-raising] ceremony

국난 國難 a national crisis [disaster]
♦ 국난을 맞서 무기를 들다 take up arms for *one's* country / 국난을 면하다 be delivered from a national danger
▶ 그 나라는 국난에 처해 있다 The country is on the brink of a serious disaster.
▶ 그 장군이 국가를 국난에서 구했다 The general saved the nation in a (national) crisis.

국내 國內 〈국내의 domestic; internal; home / 국내에서 in [inside, within] the country
▶ 국내 (거주) 외국인 수가 급속하게 늘어나고 있다 The number of foreigners (living) in Korea is growing rapidly.
■ ─경제 domestic [home] economy ─뉴스 domestic news ─문제 a domestic problem ─방송 domestic broadcasting; the home service (of KBS) ─사정 internal affairs; the domestic situation ─산업 home [domestic] industries ─생산 domestic production ─소비 home [domestic] consumption ─소비세 an excise duty ─수요 a home [domestic] demand: 국내 수요를 충족시키다 fill [meet] the domestic need [demands] ─시장 the home [domestic] market ─여행 domestic tour ─우편물 domestic mail ─우편요금 domestic postage ─정세 the interal [domestic] (political) situation ─정책 domestic policy ─제품 homemade articles [goods] ─총생산 the gross domestic product (略 GDP) ─항공노선 a domestic air line ─항공 수송 domestic [internal] air transportation [service]

국내외 國內外 the inside and outside of a country; home and abroad ▶ 그 사건은 국내외 신문에 보도되었다 The incident was reported in domestic and foreign papers.

국도 國都 the capital (of a country) ♦ 국도를 정하다[옮기다] found [remove, transfer] a capital

국도 國道 a national road [highway] ♦ 3번 국도 Route 3

국란 國亂 a national disturbance [upheaval]; 〈반란〉 a rebellion; 〈내란〉 a civil war

국력 國力 national power [strength]
♦ 국력의 증대[쇠퇴] the growth [decline] of (Korea's) national strength / 국력을 배양하다 build up national power [strength]
▶ 한국은 국력 신장에 노력하고 있다 Korea is trying to expand its [her] national might.

국련 國聯 the United Nations ⇨ 국제연합

국록 國祿 a government stipend ♦ 국록을 먹다 be on the government payroll

국론 國論 national [public] opinion; popular discussion
♦ 국론을 양분하다 divide public opinion in two / 국론을 통일하다 create [achieve] a national consensus / 국론 통일을 도모하다 unify the public [national] opinion
▶ 국론이 들끓었다 Public opinion was greatly agitated. ⇌ There was a heated public discussion.

국리 國利 national welfare [interests, prosperity]
■ ─민복 national interests and the welfare of the people: 국리 민복을 증진하다 promote national interests and the welfare of the people

국립 國立 ♦ 국립의 〈국가의〉 national; state (▷state는 미국에서는 「주립(州立)」의 뜻으로도 쓰임); 〈정부의〉 government
─경기장 a national stadium ─공원 a national park ─극장 a national theater ─대학 a national university ─도서관 a national library ─묘지 a national cemetery ─미술관[박물관] a national museum ─병원 a national hospital ─요양소 a national sanatorium ─은행 a national bank

국말이 boiled rice [noodles] served in soup

국면 局面 〈정세〉 situation; 〈양상〉 aspect; stage; phase; 〈바둑 등의〉 the position 《on the board》
♦ 국면을 수습하다 save the situation / 국면을 일변시키다 change the whole aspect of things [situation] / 새로운 국면에 접어들다 take a new turn; enter upon a new phase
▶ 우리는 국면의 전개를 주시하고 있다 We are watching the development of the situation. ⇌ We are keeping an eye on how things

develop.
▶ 국면이 일변했다 The situation has completely changed.
▶ 국면이 우리에게 유리해졌다 Affairs took a turn favorable to us.
▶ 국면을 타개하기 위하여 수뇌 회담이 개최되었다 Summit talks were held to break the deadlock [to bring the deadlock to an end].
▶ 전쟁은 이제 새 국면으로 접어들었다 The war has now entered upon a new stage [phase].

국명 國名 the name of a country

국명 局名 〈방송국의〉 the name of a (broadcasting) station; 〈무전의〉 a call sign [signal]; call letters
♦ 국명의 표시 station identification; a station break

국모 國母 the mother of a state [one's country] 〈황후〉 the Empress; 〈왕후〉 the Queen

국무 國務 state affairs; (the) affairs of state
♦ 국무를 수행하다 conduct [administer] state affairs / 국무에 관여하다 attend to state affairs
■ —부 (美) the Department of State; the State Department —위원 a minister of state; a state minister —장관 〈차관, 차관보〉 (美) the Secretary [Undersecretary, Assistant Secretary] of State —총리 the Prime Minister; the Premier

국무회의 國務會議 〈기구〉 the State Council; 〈회의〉 a State Council meeting; a Cabinet meeting [session]
♦ 국무회의를 열다[소집하다] hold [call] a Cabinet meeting / 안건을 국무회의에 회부하다 submit a matter to the Cabinet meeting
■ 정례[임시]— a regular [extraordinary] Cabinet meeting

국문 國文 the national script; 〈한글〉 the Korean alphabet; 〈국어〉 the national language; 〈문학〉 the national literature
♦ 국문 영역 Korean-English translation / 국문 타자기 a typewriter with Korean keyboards / 국문 타자수 a typist for the Korean language
■ —법 Korean grammar; grammar of the national language

국문학 國文學 〈한국 문학〉 Korean literature
▶ 나는 대학에서 국문학을 전공했다 I majored in Korean literature at the university.
■ —과 the department of Korean literature —사 the history of Korean literature; Korean literary history —자 a scholar on Korean literature

국물 1 〈음식의〉 the liquid part of a dish; 〈국 등의〉 soup; 〈고기·물고기의〉 broth; 〈구울 때 나오는〉 gravy
♦ 김치 국물 kimch'i [pickle] juice / 맑은 국물 clear soup / 멸치 국물 anchovy stock / 국물을 우려내다 prepare stock
▶ 국물 맛이 좋다 The soup tastes good.
▶ 가다랭이포에서 국물을 우려내거라 Make broth from a dried bonito.
2 〈부수입〉 extra benefit; an additional gain; a perquisite
▶ 그는 은근히 국물을 좋아한다 He secretly helps himself to commissions.

국민 國民 a nation; the people; 〈한 나라의〉 the nation; 〈한 사람〉 a 《British》 national; a citizen 《of the United States》

> [解説] 사회적·문화적 특징 등으로 본 경우에는 ***people***이라 하고 정치적 통일체로서의 국민을 말할 때는 ***nation***이라고 한다.

♦ 한국 국민 〈전체〉 the Korean nation / 국민의 소리 the voice of the nation / 국민의 의무 an obligation of the people / 국민 적인 national / 국민에게 호소하다 appeal to the nation
▶ 나는 한국 국민이다 I'm a Korean citizen [national].
▶ 한국인은 열심히 일하는[평화를 사랑하는] 국민이다 The Koreans are a hardworking [peace-loving] people.
▶ 인플레이션은 국민의 복지를 크게 해친다 Inflation does great damages to the national welfare [well-being].
▶ 온 국민이 대통령의 죽음을 듣고 슬퍼했다 All the nation [people] grieved upon hearing the death of the President.
▶ 주권은 국민에게 있다 Sovereignty resides in [rests with] the people.
■ —가요 a national folk song —경제 the national economy —교육 national education —당 〈대만의〉 the Nationalist Party —대회 a mass meeting —도덕 national morality [morals] —성 national characteristics —소득 the national income —연금(제도) national annuity [pension] (system) —외교 diplomacy by the people; people's diplomacy —운동 a national movement —의례(儀禮) a national ceremony —장(葬) a national funeral; a public funeral service —저축 national savings —정부 〈대만의〉 the Nationalist Government —정신 the national spirit —차 a people's car —총생산(총수요, 총지출) gross national product [demand, expenditure] —총화 national solidarity; the total national unity —화합 the national harmony [reconciliation] —회의파 〈인도의〉 the All-India National Congress Party

국민감정 國民感情 (a) national [popular] sentiment [feeling]; national mood [climate of opinion]
♦ 국민 감정을 자극하다 provoke the national sentiment
▶ 그는 때로 국민 감정을 해치는 발언을 했다 He often hurt the popular [national] feeling by what he said.

국민생활 國民生活 the life of the people; people's living
♦ 국민 생활 수준 the standard of living of the people / 국민 생활을 안정시키다 stabilize national life
▶ 인플레이션은 국민 생활을 크게 해친다 Inflation does great damages to the life of the people.

국민투표 國民投票 a national [popular] vote; 〈법안 등에 대한〉 a (national) referendum; 〈기

본법 등의〉 a plebiscite
♦ 국민 투표를 요구[실시]하다 call [hold] a popular vote [referendum] 《on a matter》 / 국민투표에 부치다 put 《an issue》 to a national vote [plebiscite] / 국민 투표로 결정하다 decide 《a question》 by referendum [plebiscite]

국밥 (boiled) rice served in soup

국방 國防 national defense
♦ 자주 국방(력) independent [self-reliant] national defense (capabilities) / 국방 태세 완비 the completion of national defense preparations / 국방을 강화하다 strengthen [《美口》 beef up] the national defense
━계획 a national defense plan [program] ━과학 연구소 the National Defense and Science Institute ━비 national defense expenditure ━색 khaki (color) ━예산 the defense budget ━(분과)위원회〈국회의〉 the National Defense Committee ━장관 the Minister [《美》 Secretary] of Defense ━차관 the Vice Minister [《美》 Deputy Secretary] of Defense ━회의 the National Security Council

국방부 國防部 the Ministry of National Defense; 《美》 the Department of Defense; the Pentagon; 《英》 the Ministry of Defence
■━장관[차관] the Minister [Vice-Minister] of National Defense

국번 局番〔電話〕 a telephone exchange [office] number ♦ 시외 국번 an area code

국법 國法 the national law; the law of the country [land]
♦ 국법을 지키다[따르다] obey [abide by] the law of the country / 국법을 어기다 violate [break] a national law / 국법에 저촉되다 come into conflict with the law of the country
▶ 그것은 국법에 어긋나는 행위다 That is against national law. ⇒ That is a national offense.

국보 局報〈우체국간의〉 a service telegram;〈국의 공보〉 an official bulletin

국보 國寶 a national treasure [heirloom]
♦ 국보로 보존하다 preserve as a national treasure
▶ 이 그림은 국보급이다 This picture ranks with the national treasure.
▶ 이 절의 본당은 국보로 지정되었다 The main building of this temple was designated as a national treasure.

국부 局部 1〈일부〉 a (limited) part;〈국지적〉 a local area
♦ 국부적인 local; partial; sectional / 국부적으로 locally; partially; sectionally
▶ 그들의 영향은 국부적인 것에 불과하다 Their influence is limited to one particular locality.
2〈환부(患部)〉 the affected [diseased] part of the body [region]
3〈음부〉 the private parts; (口) the privates
■━마비 partial paralysis ━마취 local anesthesia ━마취약 local anesthetic: 그 수술은 환자의 손가락에다 바로 국부 마취약을 주사하여 행해졌다 The operation was performed under a local anesthetic, injected directly into the patient's finger. ━진찰 an examination of the affected part ━치료 local treatment

국부 國父 the father of one's [the] country

국부 國富 national wealth [resources]; the wealth of a nation ■━론〈아담 스미스의〉 The Wealth of Nations

국비 國費 national expenditure [expenses]
♦ 국비의 낭비 a waste of public funds / 국비로 at the expense [cost] of the state / 국비를 절감하다 cut [slash] governmental spending
▶ 그는 국비로 영국에 유학했다 He studied in England at government expense.

국빈 國賓 a state [national] guest; a guest of the state
♦ 국빈 대우를 하다 accord sb the treatment of a national guest
▶ 그는 국빈으로 대우[영접]를 받았다 He was treated [received] as a state guest [a guest of the state].

국사 國史 a national history; the history of a nation;〈한국사〉 the history (of Korea)
■━연표 a historical calendar of Korea ━자료 historiographical materials

국사 國事 national [state] affairs; the affairs of state
♦ 국사를 논하다 discuss the affairs of state / 국사에 참여하다 take part in the affairs of state
▶ 그는 국사에 헌신했다 He devoted himself to the interests of his country. ⇒ He took an active part in the affairs of state.
■━범〈사람〉 a political offender [prisoner]; a treason felon;〈행위〉 a political offense; a crime against the state

국산 國産 domestic [home] production;〈한국산〉 Korean production
♦ 국산의 homemade; home-produced; domestic; made in Korea
▶〔會話〕「이것은 외제 차입니까?」「아니오, 국산입니다」 "Is this a foreign car?" "No, it's Korean."
▶ 나는 오늘 국산 포도주를 한 병 샀다 I bought a bottle of domestic [Korean] wine today.
■━원료 indigenous materials ━차(車) a domestic car;〈한국산〉 a Korean car; a car made [manufactured] in Korea ━품 home products

국상 國喪 national mourning

국새 國璽 the Seal of State; the Great Seal (of the King)

국서 國書 1〈외교서신〉 a sovereign's [king's] message (to a foreign state);〈신임장〉 credentials **2**〈한 나라의 문헌〉 national literature

국선 國選 ♦ 국선의 chosen [appointed] by the government
▶ 그의 변호인은 국선이었다 His lawyer was court-appointed.
■━변호인 a court-appointed lawyer [attorney]: 국선 변호인을 배당하다 assign a defense counsel (to a defendant)

국세 局勢 1〈형세〉 the situation; aspect; phase; the state of affairs [things, play]
2〈바둑・장기 등의〉 the situation (in a game

of chess) ▶바둑은 승패를 가릴 수 없는 국세였다 The *paduk* game was anybody's guess.
국세 國稅 a national tax
♦직접[간접] 국세 a direct [indirect] national tax / 국세를 징수하다 collect national taxes
■─부가세 a surtax on a national tax ─사범 national tax offenses ─사정 assessment of a national tax ─체납 nonpayment [arrears] of national taxes ─체납 처분 disposition of national taxes in arrears
국세 國勢 〈형편〉 the state of a country [the nation]; 〈국력〉 the strength of the nation
■─조사 a national census: 국세 조사를 하다 take a (national) sensus 《of the population》 ─조사원 a census taker ─조사표 a census paper
국세청 國稅廳 the National Tax Administration ■─지방─ a regional office of national tax administration ■─장 the Commissioner of the National Tax Administration
국소 局所 a part ⇨ 국부(局部) 1
국수 thick white [wheat] noodles; soup noodles
■─장수 a noodle vender
국수 國手 1 〈명의(名醫)〉 a great doctor; an excellent [a noted] physician 2 〈바둑·장기의〉 a national champion (of *paduk*, etc.)
국수 國粹 national characteristics ♦국수적인 nationalistic ■─주의 (ultra) nationalism ─주의자 an ultranationalist
국숫물 noodle broth
국숫발 a strip of noodle
국숫사리 a coil of (boiled) noodles
국숫집 〈뽑는〉 a noodle factory; 〈파는〉 a noodle shop [restaurant]
국시 國是 a national [state] policy ♦국시를 정하다 fix [formulate, determine] a national policy
국악 國樂 Korean classical music ♦국립 국악원 the National Classical Music Institute / 국립 국악학교 the National Classical Music and Art School
■─인 a Korean classical musician
국어 國語 1 〈한국어〉 Korean, the Korean language
▶국어는 1주일에 다섯 시간 있다 We have five classes of [in] Korean a [per] week.
2 〈나라의 언어〉 a language
▶그녀는 3개 국어를 한다 She speaks three languages. ⇌ She is trilingual.
3 〈모국어〉 one's mother tongue; one's national [native] language; the vernacular
■─교사 a teacher of Korean; a Korean-language teacher ─교육 Korean language teaching ─문제 problems concerning [pertaining to] the Korean language ─사전 a Korean dictionary ─학 Korean linguistics
국에 덴 놈 물 보고도 분다 〈속담〉 Once bit(ten), twice shy.
국역 國譯 translation into Korean; (a) Korean translation
♦영문 국역 translation from English into Korean; English-Korean translation
▶다음 영문을 국역하시오 Translate [Put] the following English sentence into Korean.
─국역하다 translate [put, render] *sth* into Korean
국영 國營 state [government] operation; state management
♦국영의 〈국유의〉 state; state-owned; government owned; 〈국립의〉 national; 〈정부 운영의〉 government(al); government-operated; state-managed; state-run / 국영으로 하다 nationalize 《the mines [railroads]》; put [place] 《an enterprise》 under government [state] management
▶그 나라에서는 모든 은행이 국영이 되었다 All the banks were nationalized in that country.
■─기업 a national [state, government] enterprise ─농장 a state(-run) farm ─방송국 a government-controlled [government-operated] broadcasting [TV] station
국왕 國王 〈왕〉 a king; 〈세습 군주〉 a monarch
♦스웨덴 국왕 the King of Sweden
국외 局外 the outside; an independent position
♦국외의 outside; external / 국외에서 관찰하다 observe from the outside
■─자 an outsider; 〔法〕 a third party: 국외자의 입장에 서다 keep [stand, hold] aloof 《from》; stand outside
▶나는 국외자의 입장에서 그 문제를 생각했다 I considered [looked at] the matter from the outside [as an outsider].
국외 國外 ♦국외에[로] abroad; overseas; outside one's country / 국외로 도망치다 fly the country / 국외로 추방하다 banish; expatriate; exile; expel *sb* from the country; 〈외국인을〉 deport / 국외로 추방되다 be expelled from the country; 〈외국인이〉 be deported
▶그는 국내에서나 국외에서나 유명하다 He is famous [well-known] (both) at home and abroad.
▶나는 아직 국외로 여행해본 적이 없다 I have never traveled abroad [overseas]. ⇌ I have never been abroad [to a foreign country].
■─추방 deportation; exile; banishment: 그는 국외 추방 선고를 받았다 He was sentenced to deportation. ─추방자 an expellee
국외중립 局外中立 neutrality ♦국외 중립을 지키다 maintain [observe] neutrality / 국외 중립을 취하다 take a neutral stand
■─국 a neutral country [nation, state] ─주의 neutralism
국운 國運 the fate [destiny] of a country; the national destiny
♦국운의 융성[쇠퇴] the prosperity [decline] of a nation; the rise [fall] of a nation / 전투에 국운을 걸다 stake the fate of the nation on a battle
▶잇단 실정으로 그 나라의 국운이 기울어졌다 The country's fortunes declined because of continuing misgovernment.
국원 局員 a member of a bureau [an office]; 〈우체국·전화국등의〉 a post-office [telegraph-office, telephone-office] clerk; (총칭) the staff of a bureau

국위 國威 national prestige [dignity, honor]
♦국위에 관한 문제 a matter of national honor [prestige] / 국위를 선양[손상]하다 enhance [damage, tarnish, impair] (the) national prestige [dignity] 《abroad》

국유 國有 state [government] ownership
♦국유의 national; state; 〈미 연방 정부의〉 federal; 〈국유화된〉 nationalized; state-owned; government-owned / 국유로 하다 nationalize ■―림 a national [state] forest ―재산 national [state-owned, government] property ―철도 the national [state, government] railways

국유지 國有地 national [government-owned, state-owned, nationally-owned] land ♦국유지를 불하하다 sell (at auction) a lot in national land

국유화 國有化 nationalization
♦철강 산업의 국유화 the nationalization of steel industries
―국유화하다 nationalize
▶이란은 석유 산업을 국유화했다 Iran [The Iranian government] nationalized the oil industry.

국은 國恩 one's debt of gratitude to one's country ♦국은에 보답하다 pay one's debt of gratitude to one's country

국익 國益 national interests [benefits] ♦국익을 우선하다 give priority to national interests / 국익을 증진하다 promote [further] the national interests

국자 a scoop; a dipper; a ladle
♦국물 한 국자 a scoop of broth / 수프를 한 국자 뜨다 ladle out a spoonful of soup / 국자로 국을 뜨다 ladle [dip up] soup (into a bowl)
▶그녀는 국자로 국을 떠냈다 She dipped out the soup with a ladle.

국장 局長 the chief [director] of a bureau; 〈우체국장〉 a postmaster; a postmistress (여자); 〈방송국의〉 the head of a broadcasting station; 〈신문사의〉 the managing editor

국장 國章 national emblem

국장 國葬 a state [national] funeral ♦국장으로 하다 give [accord] sb a state funeral; hold a state funeral for sb

국적 國賊 a traitor (to one's country) ▶반전 주의자는 국적이라고 불리었다 Those who were against war were called traitors to their country.

국적 國籍 nationality; (美) citizenship; 〈선박 등의〉 registry
♦무국적자 a stateless person / 이중 국적자 a person with [of] dual [double] nationality [citizenship] / 파나마 국적의 배 a ship of Panamanian registry / 국적 불명의 〈an airplane〉 of unknown nationality / 국적을 박탈당하다 be deprived [stripped] of one's nationality / 국적을 상실하다 lose one's 《Korean》 nationality / 국적을 취득하다 acquire 《Korean》 nationality [citizenship] / 국적을 회복하다 regain [recover] one's nationality
▶ 會話 「그는 국적이 어디입니까?」「한국입니다」 "What is his nationality?" "He's a Korean."
▶그녀는 국적이 영국이다 She has British nationality. ⇌ She is a British subject [citizen].
▶그는 국적은 미국이지만 이탈리아계다 He is an American of Italian origin [Italian-American].
▶그는 일본 국적을 버렸다 He renounced [divested himself of] his Japanese nationality.
■―법 (法) the Korean Nationality Act ―변경 change of nationality ―상실자 a denationalized person ―증명서 a certificate of nationality ―회복 reinstatement of citizenship

국전 國展 the National Art Exhibition; an art exhibit(ion) sponsored by the nation [state]

국정 國定 government authorization ♦국정의 national; state; authorized by the state
■―교과서 a textbook compiled by the government; a government-designated textbook ―세율 the statutory [national] tariff

국정 國政 national administration; 〈국무〉 state affairs
♦국정을 담당하다 assume the reins of government; take the helm of state (affairs) / 국정을 수행하다 administer the affairs of state; run the government / 국정에 참여하다 participate in the national administration
■―조사권 〈국회의〉 the right to conduct investigations in relation to government

국정 國情 〈나라의 형편〉 the conditions of a country [nation, state]; 〈국내의 사태〉 the state of affairs in a country [nation]
♦미국의 국정 (be conversant with) American affairs [things American] / 국정을 시찰하다 inspect the actual condition of a country / 중국의 국정에 밝다[어둡다] be well versed in [ignorant of] Chinese affairs
▶그는 러시아의 국정에 밝다 He knows a great deal about the state of affairs in Russia. ⇌ He is well versed in Russian affairs.

국정감사 國政監査 parliamentary inspection of the administration [government offices]
♦국정 감사를 실시하다 conduct inspection of the government offices; inspect the government administration
■―권 authority to inspect the government offices ―반 a parliamentary inspection team of state administration

국제 國際 ♦국제적 견지에서 from the international point of view / 국제 감각을 몸에 익히다 acquire an international way of thinking; gain an understanding of other people's way of looking at things
■―가격 an international price ―개발국 the Agency for International Development (略 AID) ―개발 협회 the International Development Association (略 IDA) ―견본시(見本市) an International Trade Fair (略 ITF) ―결제 은행 the Bank for International Settlements (略 BIS) ―결혼 an international marriage; a mixed marriage ―경기 an international game [match] ―경쟁력 international competitive power ―경제 international economy

[economics] —경찰 the International Police (略 Interpol) —경찰군 the International Police Force —공법(公法) 〔法〕 international public law —공산당 the Communist International; the Comintern —공산주의 international communism —공항 an international airport —관계 international relations —관례 (an) international practice [usage] —관리 international control [trusteeship] —교류 international《culture》exchange —금융 international finance —기관〔기구〕 an international organization —노동기구 the Interna tional Labor Organization (略 ILO) —농업 개발 기금 the International Fund for Agricultural Development (略 IFAD) —도덕 international morals [morality] —도시 a cosmopolitan city —무역 international trade —무역 기구 the International Trade Organization (略 ITO) —문제 international affairs; an international problem; a diplomatic issue —민간 항공 기구 the International Civil Aviation Organization (略 ICAO) —박람회 a world('s) fair; an international exhibition —방송 international broadcasting —법 (public) international law; the law of nations —보호조 an internationally protected bird —부흥 개발 은행 the International Bank for Reconstruction and Development (略 IBRD) —분쟁 international disputes [controversies] —사법(私法) 〔法〕 international private law —사법 재판소 the International Court of Justice (略 ICJ) —상품 협정 an international commodity agreement —선(線) international lines —시장 an international market —신문 편집인 협회 the International Press Institute (略 IPI) —어 an international [a world, a universal] language —에너지 기구 the International Energy Agency (略 IEA) —연맹 the League of Nations —연합 ⇨ 유엔 —영화제 an international film festival —올림픽 경기 the International Olympic Games; the International Olympiad —올림픽 위원회 the International Olympic Committee (略 IOC) —음성 학회 the International Phonetic Association (略 IPA) —음표 문자 the International Phonetic Alphabet (略 IPA) —의회 연맹 the Inter-Parliamentary Union (略 IPU) —인권 연맹 the International League for Human Rights (略 ILHR) —저작권 international copyright —적십자 the International Red Cross (略 IRC) —전기 통신 위성 기구 the International Telecommunications Satellite Organization (略 INTELSAT) —전화 the international telephone service: 국제 전화를 걸다 make an international [overseas] phone call; call abroad —정세 the international situation —정치 international politics —조약 an international treaty —지구 관측년 the International Geophysical Year (略 IGY) —질서 an international order —차관〔투자〕 international loans [investment] —친선 international goodwill —통화(通貨) international currency —통화 기금 the International Monetary Fund (略 IMF) —표준화 기구 the International Standardization Organization (略 ISO) —해사(海事) 위성 기구 the International Marine Satellite Organization (略 INMARSAT) —해양법 〔法〕 the international law of the sea —협력 international cooperation —형사 경찰 기구 the International Criminal Police Organization (略 ICPO, the Interpol) —환경법 the International Environmental Law —회의 an international conference

국제무대 國際舞臺 the international stage
♦ 국제무대에 알려져 있다[있지 않다] be effective [ineffective] on the international stage

국제사회 國際社會 international society; the community of nations ♦ 국제사회의 일원이 되다 join [become a member of] the international society

국제수지 國際收支 the international balance of payments; international payments
♦ 국제 수지의 흑자[적자] a favorable [an unfavorable] balance of international payments; a《large, massive》balance of international payments surplus [deficit] / 국제 수지의 흑자[적자]국 a country with a favorable [an unfavorable] balance of international payments / 국제 수지의 불균형을 시정하다 correct the imbalance of international payments / 국제 수지를 개선하다 improve《its》balance of international payments
▶ 한국의 국제 수지는 30억 달러 흑자[적자]다 Korea's international balance of payments showed a surplus [deficit] of $3 billion.

국제적 國際的 ♦ 국제적인 운동 worldwide campaign / 국제적인 인물 a person of worldwide fame / 국제적으로 internationally; universally / 국제적 견지에서 보면 from an international point of view / 국제적 명성을 얻다 win an international reputation / 국제적으로 알려지다 be known the world over
▶ 우리는 국제적 문제를 토론했다 We discussed international [world] problems.
▶ 음악이나 회화는 국제적 예술이라고 한다 Music and painting are called international arts.
▶ 그는 국제적으로 유명한 피아니스트다 He is an internationally famous pianist.

국제화 國際化 internationalization
—국제화하다 internationalize; 〈국제화되다〉 be internationalized; become international
▶ 우리는 한국인이 (좀더) 국제화되기를 바란다 We hope that the Korean would become (more) internationally-minded.

국지 —紙 paper scraps; leftover bits of paper

국지 局地 a locality; a local area ♦ 국지적인 local; regional / 국지화하다 localize《a war》
▶ 국지적으로 큰 비가 내렸다 We had much rain regionally.
■ —전(戰) a local war; limited warfare —풍(風) local wind

국채 國債 〈부채〉 a national debt [loan]; 〈채권〉 national [government] bonds [securities]
♦ 중기 국채 기금 a medium-term government securities fund / 국채의 소화 absorption [digestion] of government bonds / 국채를 모집하다 raise [float] a national loan / 국채를 발행하다 issue government [national] bonds / 국

채를 상환하다 redeem [sink] a national loan ■ 내[외]— a domestic [foreign] loan 장기[단기]— a long-term [short-term] government bond ■ —발행고 the amount of government bond issue —정리[상환] 기금 an amortization [a consolidation] fund; a sinking fund —증권 a government [national] loan bond —현재고 the outstanding (amount of government) bond

국책 國策 a national [state] policy ♦ 국책에 따라 in line with the national policy / 국책을 수립하다 formulate a national [state] policy / 국책을 추진[수행]하다 pursue [carry out, execute] a national policy / 국책에 따르다 follow the national policy
▶ 몇몇 나라에서는 국책으로 산아 제한이 권장되고 있다 In some countries, birth control is being encouraged as a matter of [in accordance with] national policy.
■ —은행 a government-run bank —회사 a national policy concern; a state-run [state policy] corporation [company]

국철 國鐵 a national railway ⇨ 국유(~철도)

국체 國體 1〈국가 체제〉 national structure [polity] ♦ 국체를 유지하다 retain the fundamental character of the state 2〈전국 체육대회〉 the National Sports Meet

국치 國恥 a national disgrace [dishonor, humiliation] ♦ 국치를 당하다 be disgraced as a nation
▶ 그 사건은 그 나라에 국치를 초래했다 The affair has brought disgrace on the country.
■ —일 National Humiliation Day

국태민안 國泰民安 the prosperity and well-being [peace and security] of a nation
♦ 국태 민안을 기원하다 pray for the prosperity and security of the nation
—국태민안하다 enjoy national prosperity and welfare

국토 國土 a territory; a realm; a domain;〈나라〉 a country;〈토지〉 land
▶ 우리의 국토는 경지 면적의 비율이 비교적 적다 The percentage of arable land in our country is comparatively small.
▶ 한국은 좁은 국토에 과다한 인구를 안고 있다 Korea has too many people for its limited land space.
■ —계획 national land planning —보전 territorial integrity —분단 territorial division —종합개발 multipurpose land development

국토개발 國土開發 national land development
■ —계획 national land development planning; a national land development program —연구원 the Korea Research Institute for Human Settlements

국토방위 國土防衛 national defense; the defense of the country
♦ 국토 방위에 나서다 go to defend one's country / 국토 방위에 몸을 바치다 give [sacrifice] one's life to defend the country
■ —계획 a national defense program

국판 菊判 a small octavo (▶22×15cm의 크기를 가리킴);〈美〉 a medium octavo ♦ 국판 300쪽의 책 a 300-page octavo book

국풍 國風 national customs and manners

국학 國學 the study of Korean classical literature ■ —자 a Korean classical scholar

국한문 國漢文 Korean and Chinese characters ♦ 국한문을 혼용하다 use both Korean and Chinese characters (in a sentence)

국한하다 局限— localize; confine; limit; set limits to sth
▶ 빈곤은 한 지역에만 국한되어 있는 것이 아니다 Poverty is not necessarily confined to only one area.
▶ 반에서 그런 경험을 가진 학생은 일부에 국한되었다 Only a few in the class had such experiences.

국헌 國憲 the national constitution; the laws of the land ♦ 국헌을 옹호[존중]하다 defend [respect] the national constitution

국호 國號 the name of a country

국화 國花 a national flower ▶ 한국의 국화는 무궁화다 Korea's national flower is the rose of Sharon.

국화 菊花〈植〉 a chrysanthemum
■ —잠(簪) a chrysanthemum-shaped hairpin

국회 國會 a national assembly;〈입법부〉 a legislative (body);〈한국〉 the National Assembly;〈미국〉 Congress (▶보통 무관사);〈영국·캐나다 등〉 Parliament;〈일본〉 the Diet
♦ 제24차 국회 the 24th session of the National Assembly / 국회 회기 중 during the session of the National Assembly / 국회를 해산하다 dissolve the National Assembly
▶ 국회가 소집되었다 The National Assembly was convened [called in session].
▶ 국회는 지금 개회[폐회] 중이다 The National Assembly is now in session [recess].
▶ 국회는 내주에 해산한다 The National Assembly will [is scheduled to] dissolve next week.
— 모의— a mock parliamentary meeting 정기[임시]— an ordinary [extraordinary] session of the National Assembly: 제15차 임시 국회를 소집하다 call [summon] the 15th extraordinary session of the National Assembly ■ —도서관 the National Assembly Library;〈미국의〉 the Library of Congress —법 the National Assembly Law —본회의 a plenary session of the National Assembly —사무처 the Secretariat of the National Assembly —사무총장 the Secretary-General of the National Assembly —상임위원회 the National Assembly Standing Committee —소환 a summons to the National Assembly —예산결산[경제과학, 외무] 위원회 the National Assembly Budget Settlement [Economic-Science, Foreign Affairs] Committee —운영위원회 the Steering Committee of the National Assembly —의사록 the National Assembly Record —(부)의장 the (Vice-)Speaker —청원 a petition to the National Assembly

국회의사당 國會議事堂 the National Assembly building;〈미국의〉 the Capitol;〈영국의〉 the Houses of Parliament;〈일본의〉 the Diet Building; the House of the National Diet

국회의원 國會議員 a member of the National Assembly; an [a National] Assemblyman; 〈미국의〉 a member of Congress; a Congressman; a Congresswoman(여성); a Senator(상원의원); 〈영국의〉 a member of Parliament (略 an M.P.); a Lord(상원의원)
♦현직[전직] 국회의원 an incumbent [a former] Assemblyman / 인천 출신 국회의원 a member of the National Assembly for Inch'ŏn / 국회의원에 입후보하다 run for the National Assembly
■—선거 the election of members for [to] National Assembly; the Assembly [parliamentary] election; 〈총선〉 the general election

군 extra; unnecessary; needless; uncalled-for; excess ♦군걱정 needless worry; overcare

군 軍 armed forces (▶병사와 무기 등을 종합한 군대); troops; an army (▶원래 육군을 뜻하지만 흔히 군대의 총칭으로 씀)
♦미 제8군 the Eighth United States Army / 한국군 제1군 the First ROK Army / 군 당국 military authorities / 군의 military(↔ civil) / 군에 입대하다 enter [join] the army
▶중동에 UN군이 파견되었다 UN troops [forces] were sent to the Middle East.
▶삼— three branches of military service 상비— a standing army [navy, air force] 예비— reserve forces 점령— the occupation army; the army of occupation 정규— regular army 청[백]— a blue [white] team ■—사령관 an army commander

군 郡 gun; a county; a district ♦용인군 Yong-in-gun; Yong-in County / 군 행정 county administration

군 群 〈일단〉 a group; 〈군중〉 a crowd; a throng ♦군을 이루어 in a group; in groups; in crowds; in packs / 군을 이루다 flock together; congregate

군 君 1 〈호칭〉 Mr. [Mister] (▶Mr.는 성에만 붙이고 이름에는 붙이지 않음. 또 친구나 동료, 손아랫사람에게는 경칭을 쓰지 않으므로 영역할 때는 넣지 않음)
▶김 군 Kim!
▶동호 군 Hi, Tong-ho.
▶이 군, 그 문장을 크게 읽어라 Lee, read the sentence aloud.
2 〈자네(들)〉 you
♦군들 your (young) fellows
3 [史] Lord ♦연산군 Lord Yŏnsan

군가 軍歌 a military [marching] song; a war [martial] song; 〈곡〉 a martial air

군거 群居 social [gregarious] life; aggregation —군거하다 live gregariously [in flocks, together]
■—본능 a gregarious [the herd] instinct —성 gregariousness; sociability

군것 a superfluous [useless] thing; a useless object; (美) dead wood; a superfluity

군것질 eating between meals
▶살을 빼고 싶으면 군것질을 말아야 한다 If you want to lose weight, you'll have to stop eating snacks [between meals].
—군것질하다 eat between meals

군경 軍警 the military and the police ■—유가족 the bereaved families of the dead soldiers and policemen

군계일학 群鷄一鶴 a Triton among [of] the minnows; the only figure among ciphers; the sun among inferior lights

군고구마 roast [baked] sweet potatoes
■—장수 a baked sweet potato vendor

군공 軍功 military merit ⇨ 전공(戰功)

군관구 軍管區 a military district; a territory under a military jurisdiction

군국 君國 one's sovereign and country; 〈군주국〉 a monarchy

군국 軍國 a warring nation; a militant nation; a garrison state

군국주의 軍國主義 militarism ♦군국주의적 경향 a militaristic trend ■—자 a militarist

군기 軍紀 military discipline; morale among the troops
♦군기 해이 relaxation of military discipline / 군기를 지키다[어기다] maintain [violate, offend against] military discipline
▶군기가 느슨하다 The military discipline is lax.
▶군기가 문란하면 싸우기도 전에 질 것이다 If the soldiers' morals were corrupted, they would be defeated beforce the battle.
▶군기를 문란시키지 마라 Don't break military discipline.

군기 軍旗 the (regimental) colors; a standard; a battle flag; an ensign ■—수여식 the presentation of the colors

군기 軍機 a military secret; 〈서류 등〉 a classified military document
♦군기의 누설 betrayal [leakage] of military secrets / 군기상 for reasons of military secrecy / 군기를 누설하다 divulge [disclose] a military secret
▶군기가 엄중히 유지되고 있다 The military secret is maintained with great severity.
■—누설 사건 disclosure [betrayal, leakage] of military secrets; a military secret betrayal case

군납 軍納 delivery of goods to an army; the purveyance of supplies or services for an army
—군납하다 deliver goods to an army; provide (supplies or services) for an army; purvey for an army
■—불 (弗) Korean Post Exchange dollar (略 KPX dollar) —업자 a purveyor for an army; a military goods supplier; service contractors for the military —품 supplies provided by a purveyor —회사 a military purveyance firm; a military supply contract firm

군내 a stale [an unpleasant] smell; stinking smell

군단 軍團 a [an army] corps [kɔːr] 〈단수·복수 동형임〉 —제1— the First Corps ■—사령부 the corps headquarters —장 the commander of an army corps; the corps commander

군대 軍隊 armed forces (▶육·해·공군을 포함한 일국의 군대에 대해 씀); an army; troops (▶병력에 중점을 두는 경우에 씀)

◆1만 명의 군대 an army ten thousand strong; a 10,000-man army / 군대를 일으키다 raise an army / 군대에 들어가다 enlist in [join] the army / 군대식으로 하다 do *sth* in military fashion [a military way]
▶ 반란을 진압하러 군대가 파견되었다 Armed forces [Troops] were sent to pacify the rebellion.
▶ 그는 군대에 있다 He is in the military (service).
━―교육 military training ━―생활 (an) army [(a) military] life: 군대 생활을 하다 live an army life; serve in the army ━―수송선 a troopship; a (troop) transport ━―행진곡 a military march

군더더기 〈물건〉 an excrescence; something redundant; a redundancy; a superfluity; 〈사람〉 an unwanted follower; a hanger-on

군던지럽다 〈너더분하다〉 foul; nasty; disgusting; indecent; sordid

군데 〈장소〉 a place; a spot; 〈지점〉 a point; 〈부분〉 a part; 〈문장의〉 a passage; a paragraph
◆한 군데 오래 머물다 stay long in a [the same] place / 기사에서 몇 군데를 인용하다 quote several passages from an article
▶ 그는 몇 군데 상처를 입었다 He was wounded [injured] in several places. ⇌ He received several wounds.
▶ 도로에 위험한 곳이 몇 군데 있다 There are a few dangerous points on the road.
▶ 네 작문에는 두세 군데 틀린 데가 있다 There are two or three mistakes in your composition.
▶ 그녀는 노래할 때 한 군데 틀렸다 She made one mistake when she sang.
▶ 몇 군데에서 불이 났다 Fires broke out in several places.

군데군데 (in) various places; in spots; here and there; at places; sporadically
◆군데군데 나무를 심다 plant trees here and there / 군데군데 벗겨져 있다 〈페인트 등이〉 be off in places
▶ 뜰에 꽃이 군데군데 피어 있다 Flowers are blooming here and there in the garden.
▶ 벽이 군데군데 무너져 있다 The wall has crumbled in places [spots].
▶ 들에는 군데군데 집이 서 있다 Houses stand scattered [straggle] in the fields.

군도 軍刀 a military sword; (美) a saber

군도 群島 a group of islands; an archipelago (*pl.* ~(e)s)
■마셜━ the Marshall Islands 말레이━ the Malay Archipelago 필리핀━ the Philippine Islands; the Philippines 하와이━ the Hawaiian Islands

군도 群盜 a group [gang] of robbers

군돈 money spent unnecessarily; unnecessary [extra] expense ◆군돈을 쓰다 waste money; spend money to no purpose

군락 群落 〈촌락〉 a group of hamlets; a group of villages; 〔生態〕 a colony; 〔生〕 a stock; a community

군란 軍亂 an army insurrection [rebellion, revolt]

군략 軍略 strategy; a stratagem; tactics ⇨ 전략(戰略)
◆군략상의 strategic / 군략상 strategically / 군략을 쓰다 resort to a stratagem / 군략으로 이기다 outmaneuver 《the enemy》
▶ 그들은 적의 군략에 걸려들었다 They fell into the trap laid by the enemy.
■―가(家) a strategist; a tactician

군량 軍糧 (military) provisions; (food) supplies; 〈할당된〉 rations ▶ 군대는 군량이 떨어졌다 The army ran out of provisions. ⇌ The provisions for the army were exhausted.

군령 軍令 a military command [order]

군림 君臨 reigning
━―군림하다 reign 《over》; rule [lord it] 《over》; dominate
◆영화계에 군림하다 dominate [lord it over] the film world
▶ 그는 재계에 군림하고 있다 He is dominating the financial world.
▶ 영국 여왕은 군림하나 통치하지는 않는다 The English queen reigns, but does not rule.

군마 軍馬 〈군사와 말〉 soldiers and horses; 〈말〉 a military [army] horse; a (war) steed; a war horse; a charger(장교용)

군만두 饅頭 a toasted bun [dumpling]

군말 redundant [useless, superfluous] words; verbosity; redundancy
◆군말이 많은 redundant; wordy
▶ 이 책의 진가에 대해서는 군말이 필요없다 We need not emphasize the worth of this book.
━―군말하다 make an unnecessary [uncalled-for] remark

군매점 軍賣店 〔美陸軍〕 a post exchange; a PX (*pl.* PXs); a canteen

군명 君命 the orders [commands] of *one's* lord [king]

군모 軍帽 a military cap; an ammunition hat; 〈육군의〉 an army cap; 〈해군의〉 a navy cap

군목 軍牧 a chaplain

군무 軍務 military affairs; military service [duty]
◆군무에 종사하다 serve in the army [navy]; perform military duties
▶ 그는 젊었을 때 군무에 종사했다 He served in the army [navy] when he was young.
━―이탈 desertion from military service

군무원 軍務員 a civilian attached to the army [navy]; a civilian employee of the army [navy]; an army [a navy] civilian employee; a civilian in the military [naval] service

군문 軍門 〈영내〉 a camp; 〈군대〉 an army ◆군문에 들어가다 enlist in the army; enter the service

군민 軍民 the military and the people; the fighting services and the civilians

군민 郡民 inhabitants of a county; county people

군밤 a roast(ed) chestnut

군번 軍番 service number; (a soldier's) serial number (略 SN); 〈인식표〉 an identification [a dog] tag

군벌 軍閥 a military [an army] clique; a militarist party; the (powerful) militarists ■—정치 military dictatorship; militaristic government; warlordism

군법 軍法 martial [military] law

군법회의 軍法會議 a court-martial (*pl.* ~s, courts-martial); a military tribunal ◆군법회의를 소집하다 call a court-martial
▶ 그 병사는 군법 회의에 회부되었다 The soldier was tried by court-martial [court-martialed].

군복 軍服 a military [〈육군의〉 an army, 〈해군의〉 a navy, 〈공군의〉 an air-force] uniform ◆군복 차림의 장교 an officer in uniform; a uniformed officer
▶ 그는 군복을 입고 있었다 He was in military uniform.

군부 軍部 the militarists; the military authorities; army circles; (총칭) the military ◆최근 군부가 대두하고 있다 Recently the military authorities have been gaining power.

군불 a fire for heating an *ondol* ◆군불 때다 heat an *ondol* (with firewood); burn (firewood) to heat an *ondol*

군비 軍備 armaments; military preparedness ◆군비를 강화하다 reinforce armaments / 군비를 갖추다 be militarily prepared; be ready for war / 군비를 축소[확장]하다 reduce [increase] armaments
■—경쟁 an arms [armaments] race —제한 limitation of armaments —증강 military [arms] buildup —철폐 disarmaments; demilitarization —축소 a reduction of armaments; an arms reduction [cut] —통제 arms control —확장 expansion of armaments

군비 軍費 〈비용〉 war expenditure(s) [funds]; the sinews of war

군사 軍士 a soldier; a private (soldier); (총칭) (enlisted) men; the rank and file ◆브라운 장군 및 휘하 군사들 General [Admiral] Brown and his men

군사 軍使 〈전령〉 a military envoy [messenger]; the bearer of a flag of truce

군사 軍事 military affairs ◆군사상으로 (be important) in military terms / 군사상의 목적으로 for military [strategic] purposes
▶ 저 섬은 우리 나라의 방위를 위해 군사상 중요하다 That island is of strategic importance for our national defense.
■—고문 a military adviser [advisor] —고문단 the Military Advisory Group (略 MAG) —교육 military education [instruction] —기밀 military secrets —기지 a base; an army [a naval, an air] base —동맹[협정] a military alliance [pact] —분계선 the Military Demarcation Line (略 MDL) —비 war expenditure [funds] —시설 military establishments [installations] —예산 an arms budget —용어 a military term —우편 military post —원조 military aid [assistance] —위성 a military satellite —재판 a military trial; 〈군법회의〉 a court-martial —정권 a military junta [regime] —평론가 a military writer [commentator] —행동 military movements [activities]; hostile operation —행정 military administration —훈련 military drill [training]

군사 軍師 a strategist; a tactician

군사력 軍事力 military strength; armaments ◆강력한 군사력을 기르다 build a powerful military force

군사령부 軍司令部 the army [military] headquarters

군사정전위원회 軍事停戰委員會 the Military Armistice Commission (略 MAC) ◆군사 정전 위원회 유엔군측 수석 대표 the UNC [United Nations Command] senior member to the MAC meeting

군사학 軍事學 military science; 〈전술〉 tactics; 〈병법〉 strategy

군살 superfluous flesh; (口) flab ◆군살이 많이 낀 남자 a man with a lot of fat on him / 배에 군살이 끼다 put on excess weight around the waist; (口) develop a spare tire / 군살을 빼다 wear [work] off surplus fat [the fat]
▶ 나는 여름 방학 동안 이 군살을 뺄 작정이다 I'm determined to get rid of this flab during the summer vacation.

군상 群像 a large group of people; [彫] a sculptured group ◆라오콘 군상 the Laocoön group / 실업자 군상 a crowd of jobless people

군색 窘塞 〈가난〉 poverty; destitution; 〈곤경〉 straits; a fix; a sad plight
—군색하다 poor; destitute; needy; hard-up ◆군색한 변명 a poor excuse / 군색한 예산 a tight budget / 군색한 집안에 태어나다 be born in a poor family / 군색하게 살다 live on a shoestring

군생 群生 [植] gregariousness —군생하다 live in flocks [herds]; grow gregariously [in crowds] ◆군생하는 gregarious
■—동물 gregarious [social] animals —식물 gregarious [social] plants

군서 軍書 a military book; a book on strategy; 〈군기(軍記)〉 a war book

군서 群棲 [生] gregariousness
—군서하다 〈양·염소·새 등이〉 live in flocks; 〈소·돼지·말 등이〉 live in herds; live gregariously
▶ 그 당시 이 근처에는 들소가 군서하고 있었다 In those days buffaloes lived in herds around here.
■—동물 gregarious [social] animals

군세 軍勢 〈군대〉 an army; a force; troops; 〈군사력〉 military strength [power]; 〈형세〉 the military situation 〈of a country〉; 〈병사수〉 the number of soldiers
◆3만의 군세 an army 30,000 strong / 적의 군세 the enemy forces

군소 群小 ◆군소의 minor; petty; insignificant ■—국가 lesser nations —작가 minor [lesser-known] writers —정당 minor [petty] political parties

군소리 redundancy ⇨ 군말

군속 軍屬 a civilian attached to the army [navy] ⇨ 군무원

군수 軍需 military [war] supplies ■─경기 a war [munitions] boom ─공장 a munitions factory [plant] ─보급 기지 a supply complex ─산업 war [munitions] industry; armaments industry ─자재 war material ─품[물자] munitions; military supplies ─회사 a munitions company

군수 郡守 a county headman; the magistrate of a *gun* [county]

군시럽다 〈스멀대다〉 (feel) creepy [crawly]; 《feel》 ticklish; be itching

군식구 ─食口 a dependent other than a member of *one's* own family; a hanger-on (*pl.* hangers-on); 《美口》 a freeloader; a parasite; a sponger

군신 君臣 sovereign and subject; lord and vassal; ruler and ruled

군신 軍神 the god of war [arms]; a war god; 〈로마 신화〉 Mars; 〈그리스 신화〉 Ares

군신 群臣 all vassals [retainers]

군실거리다 〈스멀스멀하다〉 feel ticklish; feel itchy [creepy, crawly]

군실군실하다 feel itchy ⇨ 군실거리다

군악 軍樂 military [martial] music ♦군악을 연주하다 play military music ■─대 a military [〈해군의〉 naval] band ─대원 a bandsman ─대장 a band master

군영 軍營 a military camp; an encampment ♦군영을 설치하다 camp; encamp

군왕 君王 a king; a monarch

군용 軍用 《be used for》 military use [purposes] ■─견 an army [a military] dog ─기(機) a military plane; a warplane; 《총칭》 combat aircraft ─도로 a military road ─열차 a troop train ─지도 a military map ─철도 a military [strategic] railway

군웅 群雄 (a number of) rival leaders [barons]
▶ 그 시대에는 군웅이 할거하고 있었다 In those days there were a number of local military leaders [barons] competing with each other for power.
▶ 오늘날의 문단은 군웅이 할거하고 있다 A number of talented writers are competing with one another today.
■─할거 rivalry of warlords [local barons]: 군웅 할거 시대 the age of rival chiefs [warlords]

군원 軍援 military assistance [aid]

군율 軍律 〈군기〉 《observe》 military discipline; 〈군법〉 martial law; the articles of war
▶ 군율이 엄하다 Military discipline is very severe.

군음식 ─飮食 refreshments; a between-meals snack; a snack (between meals) ♦군음식을 먹다 eat between meals [snacks]

군의(관) 軍醫(官) 〈육군〉 an army surgeon [doctor]; 〈해군〉 a naval surgeon; 〈공군〉 a flight surgeon ▶ 그는 의과인이다 He is an army surgeon. ─장교 a medical officer

군인 軍人 a serviceman; 〈여군〉 a servicewoman; 〈육군의〉 a soldier; 〈해군의〉 a sailor; 〈공군의〉 an airman; 〈해병대의〉 a marine; 〈장교〉 a (military, naval) officer; 《총칭》 service personnel ♦군인다운 soldierly; soldierlike
▶ 그의 아들은 군인이다 His son serves in the army [navy, air force].
▶ 그는 군인 기질이 강하다 He has much of the soldier in him.
▶ 그의 말투로 나는 그가 군인 출신임을 곧 알았다 I immediately recognized him to be a veteran by his speech.
■─직업─ a professional soldier; 〈장교〉 a career officer 퇴역─ a veteran; an ex-soldier [ex-serviceman, 〈여군〉 ex-servicewoman] ─생활 a military life ─연금 a soldier's pension ─정신 the military spirit

군일 needless [unnecessary] work; extra work ─군일하다 do unnecessary [extra] work

군자 君子 a true gentleman; a man of virtue [noble character]
♦군자의 나라 a land of gentlemen / 군자연하다 assume a virtuous air; pose as a man of culture
▶ 군자는 대로행이라 A wise man never takes a short cut. ⇌ A man of virtue always sticks to a great cause.
▶ 군자는 위험한 것을 가까이 하지 않는다 A wise man never courts danger. ⇌ Discretion is the better part of valor.

군자금 軍資金 war funds; military chest; the coffers [sinews] of war; 〈운동비〉 campaign funds ♦군자금을 대다 supply the sinews of war

군자란 君子蘭 〈植〉 a Kaffir lily

군장 軍裝 (in) military uniform [equipment]; 〈전투용의〉 battle dress [kit]; combat uniform; war outfit ♦완전 군장으로 in full kit [gear]

군정 軍政 military administration [government]
♦군정을 실시하다[펴다] establish military administration; impose military rule 《on》 / 군정하에 두다 put under a military administration / 군정하에 있다 be under military administration

군제 軍制 a military system; (a) military organization

군졸 軍卒 a (common) soldier ⇨ 병졸(兵卒)

군주 君主 a king; a monarch; 〈최고 지배자〉 a sovereign ♦전제 군주 an absolute monarch ■─국 a monarchy: 입헌 군주국 a constitutional monarchy / 전제 군주국 an autocracy / 절대 군주국 an absolute monarchy ─정체(政體) monarchy; monarchism ─정치 monarchy ─제 monarchism

군중 群衆 a crowd (▶ 집합체를 가리킬 때는 단수, 군중 속의 한 사람 한 사람을 가리킬 때는 복수 취급함); the multitude; a throng; 〈폭도화할 수 있는〉 a mob
♦군중을 제지하다 keep back a crowd / 군중을 헤치고 나아가다 force [push, elbow] *one's* way through the crowd / 군중에 섞여 도망치다 slip away in the crowd
▶ 사고 현장에 군중이 모여들었다 A throng gathered at the site of the accident.

▶ 역에는 많은 군중이 그가 도착하기를 기다리고 있었다 There were a large crowd of people waiting for his arrival at the station.
▶ 군중이 흩어졌다 The crowd scattered [dispersed].
■ —대회 a (mass) rally —심리 mob [mass] psychology

군집 群集 a large group of people; a mob; 〔生態〕 a [an ecological] community —**군집하다** crowd together; swarm; throng; congregate; gather in crowds
■ —본능 the herd instinct —심리 ⇨ 군중(∼심리)

군짓 a useless [needless, unnecessary] act; a thing done uselessly [superfluously] —**군짓하다** do a useless [superfluous] act

군청 郡廳 a *gun* [county, district] office

군청(색) 群青(色) ultramarine; sea blue

군체 群體 〔生〕 a colony 《of corals》

군축 軍縮 an armament [arms] reduction; a cut in armament; disarmament ◆ 완전 군축 total [complete] disarmament
■ —협정 a disarmament agreement —회담 arms reduction [limitation] talks —회의 a disarmament conference

군침 slaver; saliva [səláivə]; slobber; drool
◆ 군침이 돌게 하다 make *sb's* mouth water; 〈부러워하게 하다〉 excite *sb's* envy / 군침을 삼키다 swallow [gulp down] *one's* saliva / 군침을 흘리다 drivel; slaver; salivate; run [dribble] at the mouth; 〈욕심내다〉 lust 《for》
▶ 음식을 보면 입에 군침이 돈다 The sight of food brings water to one's mouth.
▶ 그는 음식을 보고 군침이 돌았다 The dishes made his mouth water.
▶ 그 남자가 돈뭉치를 세는 것을 보면서 그는 군침을 삼켰다 As he watched the man count the roll of bills, he felt a strong longing for them.
▶ 이것은 음악 애호가가 보면 군침을 삼킬 만한 책이다 This is a mouth-watering book for lovers of music.

군턱 a jowl 《of a double chin》

군티 a slight flaw [speck, defect]

군표 軍票 a military scrip [currency]; an army [a war] note ■ 미— an American MPC [military payment certificate]

군함 軍艦 a warship; a war vessel; a man-of-war 《*pl.* men-》; 〈전함〉 a battleship ◆ 군함을 건조[폐함]하다 construct [scrap] a warship / 군함을 급파하다 dispatch a warship
■ —기(旗) a naval ensign; 《英》 the white ensign

군항 軍港 a naval port [base, station] ■ —사령부 the headquarters of a naval station

군호 軍號 a watchword; a (military) password; a countersign

군화 軍靴 military [army] shoes [boots]; combat boots; 《美》 G.I. shoes

굳건하다 solid; firm; strong and steady; strong-minded; stout-hearted
◆ 굳건한 기초 a solid foundation / 굳건한 의지 an iron [indomitable] will / 굳건한 정신 a stout heart; a firm spirit

굳게 hard; tightly; fast
◆ 굳게 결심하다 be firmly resolved; make up *one's* mind positively / 굳게 약속하다 promise definitely; give a solemn promise
▶ 우리는 이상이 실현될 것을 굳게 믿고 있다 We firmly believe [have a firm belief] that our ideals will be realized.
▶ 그들은 우정으로 굳게 결속되어 있다 They are closely bound up by a tie of friendship.
▶ 나는 그의 무죄를 굳게 믿고 있다 I firmly believe that he is innocent. ⇌ I am confident [convinced] of his innocence.
▶ 그는 입을 굳게 다물고 말하지 않았다 He refused to tell, shutting his mouth tight.
▶ 그들은 굳게 단결되어 있다 They are closely [firmly] united.

굳기 hardness; solidity; firmness; stiffness; toughness ▶ 그의 결심은 굳기가 보통 이상이다 His determination is unusually strong.

굳다¹ 【굳어지다】 harden; get [become] hard [firm, solid]; 〈시멘트·젤리 등이〉 set; 〈피가〉 clot; 〈우유가〉 curdle; 〈액체·용액이〉 coagulate; congeal
◆ 오래 되어 굳은 빵 stale bread / 혀가 굳다 be tongue-tied; lisp
▶ 석고는 빨리 굳는다 Plaster of Paris sets quickly.
▶ 피는 공기에 쐬이면 곧 굳는다 Blood clots easily when exposed to air.
▶ 빵[진흙]은 마르면 굳는다 Bread [Mud] hardens [cakes, stiffens] as it dries.
▶ 시멘트가 하룻밤 사이에 굳었다 The cement set overnight.
▶ 제법 돈이 굳었다 I have saved a good deal.
▶ 풀이 굳어 버렸다 The paste has hardened [become dry and hard].
▶ 나는 추위서 몸이 굳었었다 I was stiff all over from cold.

굳다² 1 〈물체가〉 hard(↔soft); solid(↔fluid); stiff; tough(↔tender); rigid
◆ 굳은 땅 hard [stiff, solid] ground / 굳은 바위 a hard rock
2 〈정신·태도가〉 firm; strong; unyielding; unshakable; fast; tight; secure
◆ 굳은 결심 a firm resolution [determination] / 굳은 신념 a firm [strong, settled] belief [conviction] / 굳은 의지 a strong [an iron] will / 정조가 굳은 여자 a chaste [virtuous] woman / 굳은 맹세를 하다 make a solemn pledge [vow, oath] / 굳은 약수를 교환하다 shake hands with a hearty grip [in firm grips] / 굳은 약속을 하다 promise definitely / 마음이 굳어 유혹에 넘어가지 않다 be adamant to temptation
▶ 내 결심은 굳다 I have a firm determination.
▶ 그는 의지가 굳다 He has a strong [firm, iron] will. ⇌ He is a man of strong will.
▶ 두 사람은 굳은 우정으로 맺어져 있다 The two are bound together by firm [strong] friendship.
3 〈표정이〉 stern; stiff; hard ◆ 굳은 표정으로 with a stern look
4 〈긴장으로〉 stiff; nervous
▶ 그렇게 굳어 있지 말고 편안히 해라 Don't be so stiff. Just relax.

굳세다
5 〈쏨쏨이가〉 frugal; thrifty; tightfisted; close-fisted; stingy ▶그는 돈에 매우 굳다 He is thrifty in spending money. ⇒ He is very tight about money.

굳세다 〈몸이〉 strong; firm; stout; 〈마음이〉 strong-minded; hardy; sturdy; stout-hearted 《man》
♦굳센 젊은이 a robust [strong, sturdy] young man / 굳센 마음으로 with indomitable [unconquerable] spirit; with the avowed intent 《to do》 / 세상을 굳세게 살아가다 face the reality of life with firm determination

굳어지다 stiffen; get [become] stiff; 〈표정이〉 freeze
♦굳어진 손 stiff hands / 세월과 함께 굳어진 우정 a friendship cemented by time / 위기에 몰려 몸이 굳어지다 〈선수가〉 choke [tighten] up in the clutch
▶나는 많은 사람 앞에서 이야기할 때면 굳어진다 I get nervous when I speak in front of many people.
▶그 말을 듣자 그의 표정이 굳어졌다 His expression hardened [stiffened] when he heard it.
▶추위로 두 다리가 굳어져서 한 발짝도 나아갈 수 없었다 My legs stiffened [got stiff] with cold and I couldn't take a step forward.

굳은살 hardened skin; 〈손·발의〉 a callus; 〈주로 발의〉 a corn; a calosity
♦발가락에 굳은살이 박이다 get a corn on a toe
▶오른 발에 굳은살이 박였다 I have a corn [callus] on my right foot.
▶〈글을 많이 써서〉 가운뎃 손가락에 굳은살이 박였다 A callus has formed on my middle finger (from writing so much).

굳이 firmly; strongly; forcibly; decisively; strictly; 〈고집스럽게〉 obstinately
♦굳이 원하신다면 if you particularly wish it; if you insist (upon it) / 굳이 묻다 inquire importunately / 아픈데도 굳이 가다 go in spite of illness
▶굳이 말하라면 내 의견을 말하겠다 I'll give you my opinion, if you insist.
▶나는 굳이 반대는 하지 않는다 I have no particular objection to it. ⇒ I will not object to it particularly.
▶생각이 없다면 굳이 권하지는 않겠다 I will not press you, if you are not inclined to do so.
▶이미 결정된 것이라면 굳이 변경하라고는 하지 않겠다 If it has already been decided on, I won't insist that you change it [on a change].

굳히다 1 〈단단하게〉 harden; make *sth* hard; 〈용액을〉 coagulate; congeal
♦진흙을 햇볕에 굳히다 harden the clay in the sun / 자갈을 시멘트로 굳히다 bind gravel with cement
▶진흙은 구워서 굳힌다 The clay is baked to harden it.
2 〈강화하다〉 strengthen; 〈공고히하다〉 solidify; consolidate; secure; 〈마음을〉 determine
♦결속을 굳히다 tighten bond of union; strengthen the unity 《of the party》 / 결심을 굳히다 make a firm decision 《to do》 / 기초를 굳히다 strengthen the basis / 국경의 방비를 굳히다 fortify the frontier / 우정을 굳히다 cement the relation 《between》 / 지반[기반]을 굳히다 strengthen [consolidate] the foundation; secure *one's* position [footing]
▶그는 작가로서의 위치를 굳혔다 He secured his position in the world of letters.
▶나는 하루 종일 그 일에 대해 생각했지만 아직 완전히 마음을 굳히지 못했다 I've thought about it all day long, but I have not yet fully determined.

굴 〔貝〕 an oyster
♦깐 굴 shelled oysters / 생굴 a raw oyster / 튀긴 굴 fried oysters / 굴을 양식하다 cultivate oysters
▶굴은 "r"자가 들어 있는 달에만 먹어야 한다 You should only eat oysters when there is an "r" in the month.
■**―껍데기** an oystershell **―양식** an oyster farming [culture] **―양식업자** an oyster farmer **―양식장** an oyster farm [bed] **―젓** 〔어리굴젓〕 salted oysters with hot pepper

굴 窟 1 〈동굴〉 a cave; 〈터널〉 a tunnel; an excavation; 〈크고 깊은〉 a cavern; a grotto (*pl.* ~ (e)s)
♦굴이 많은 산허리 a cavernous hillside / 굴을 탐험하는 사람 a spelunker; a potholer / 굴을 탐험하다 explore a cave [cavern]; spelunk / 굴을 파다 dig a tunnel 《through the mountains》; build [bore, cut, pierce] a tunnel 《through》; make a cave 《on the side of a hill》
2 〈짐승의〉 a den; a lair; a holt; an earth 〈여우의〉; a burrow 〈토끼의〉
♦굴 속에 살다[숨다] live [hide itself] in a burrow / 굴 속으로 달아나다 〈여우가〉 run to earth
3 〈소굴〉 a den; a haunt; a nest
■**아편―** an opium den [joint] ■**―탐험** 《美》 spelunking; 《英》 potholing

굴검 掘檢 an inquest of an exhumed corpse **―굴검하다** conduct [hold] an inquest of an exhumed dead body; exhume a corpse to perform an autopsy

굴곡 屈曲 bending; winding; a curve; 〈해안선 등의〉 an indentation; 〈광선의〉 refraction
♦굴곡이 진 winding; crooked; 〈길이〉 zigzag (-ging); 〈강이〉 meandering
▶이 근처 해안은 굴곡이 심하다 The coast around here frequently runs in and out. ⇒ We have a much indented shoreline about here.
▶그 길은 S자로 굴곡이 져 있다 The road curves in an S.
―굴곡하다 bend; be bent [crooked]; curve; wind; twist; zigzag
▶강은 여러번 굴곡하면서 흐르고 있다 The river bends and twists any number of times on its way downstream.
■**―부** a bend; a turn; an elbow **―작용** 〈관절의〉 flection; flexion

굴광성 屈光性 〔生〕 phototropism ♦굴광성의 phototropic

굴근 屈筋 〔解〕 a flexor (muscle)

굴기성 屈氣性 〔生〕 aerotropism ♦굴기성의

aerotropic

굴다 〈행동하다〉 behave 《toward》; act; conduct [bear] *oneself*
♦거만하게 굴다 have an imperious [arrogant] bearing 《toward *one's* underlings》 / 공명정대하게 굴다 play fair 《with *sb*》 / 남자답게 [신사답게] 굴다 behave [conduct *oneself*] like a man [gentleman] / 못살게 굴다 treat *sb* harshly; be hard on *sb* / 버릇없이 굴다 (口) carry on / 스스럼없이 굴다 conduct *oneself* without reserve / 스포츠맨답게 굴다 act [behave] in a sportsmanlike manner
▶ 그는 너에게 어떻게 굴었니? How did he behave to [toward] you?

굴다리 窟— an overhead bridge; (美) an overpass; (英) a flyover; a land bridge

굴대 a wheel axle; 〈바퀴의〉 an axle; 〈기계류의〉 a shaft ♦ 자동차의 전륜[후륜] 굴대 the front [rear] axle of a car

굴도리 a round [cylindrical] beam

굴때장군 —將軍 〈덩치 큰〉 a bulky tall fellow; a swarthy giant; 〈옷이 꺼메진〉 a dirty-clothed person

굴뚝 a chimney; 〈공장 등의〉 a smokestack; 〈배·기관차의〉 a funnel
♦ 조립 굴뚝 a chimney stack / 굴뚝의 갓 a chimney cap / 굴뚝이 둘 달린 배 a two funneled ship / (口) a two-stacker / 생각이 굴뚝 같다 covet; want *sth* body and soul; be very tempting 《to do》; be quite anxious [eager] 《to do》 / 굴뚝을 쑤시다[청소하다] sweep a chimney
▶ 굴뚝이 막혔다 The chimney is clogged up.
▶ 굴뚝에서 연기가 나고 있다 Smoke is going up [rising] from the chimney.
▶ 사고 싶은 마음은 굴뚝 같지만 돈이 없다 I really want to buy it, but I don't have enough money.

굴뚝새 〔鳥〕 a wren

굴러들어오다 roll in; 〈뜻하지 않게〉 fall in [come (in)] *one's* way
♦ 많은 유산이 굴러들어오다 be left rich [well-off] 《by the death of...》
▶ 공이 뜰에 굴러들어왔다 A ball rolled into the garden.
▶ 뜻하지 않은 재산이 굴러들어왔다 I unexpectedly came into a large fortune.

굴러떨어지다 fall down[off]; tumble down
▶ 그 노인은 계단에서 굴러떨어졌다 The old man tumbled down the stairs.
▶ 트럭이 벼랑에서 강으로 굴러떨어졌다 The truck fell over a cliff into the river.

굴렁쇠 a hoop ♦ 굴렁쇠를 굴리다 trundle [drive] 《along》 a hoop

굴레 1 〈마소의〉 a headstall; a bridle; a headgear; a halter
♦ 굴레 벗은 말 an unbridled horse / 말의 굴레를 느슨하게 해주다 give a horse the bridle / 굴레를 씌우다 put a bridle 《on a horse》; bridle; halter up / 굴레를 벗기다 take off a bridle [headgear]; unbridle; unhalter
2 〈속박·억제〉 restraint 《on》; a yoke; 〈구속물〉 fetters; 〈제한〉 (a) restriction 《on》; shackles
♦ 굴레에서 벗어나다 break from the yoke 《of》; free *oneself* from restraints; shake [cast, throw] off the yoke [fetters, shackles]; become free

굴레미 〈나무 바퀴〉 a wooden (cart) wheel

굴리다 1 〈회전〉 roll 《a ball》; trundle 《a cask》
♦ 은방울을 굴리는 듯한 목소리 a sweet, silvery voice / 눈알을 굴리다 goggle [roll] *one's* eyes / 바위를 굴리다 roll a rock 《down a hill》 / 혀를 굴리며 말하다 speak with a trill
▶ 아이들이 눈덩이를 굴리고 있었다 The children were rolling a snowball.
▶ 그는 그 통을 차있는 데까지 굴려 갔다 He rolled the barrel to the car.
2 〈방치〉 neglect; lay aside; leave 《a thing》 unattended ♦ 책을 마구 굴리다 toss a book to one side
▶ 그것을 함부로 굴리면 못쓰게 된다 If you leave it unattended, it will not last.
3 〈돈을〉 lend out; invest ♦ 돈을 굴리다 lend *one's* money out at interest; invest *one's* money profitably
4 〈운영〉 run
▶ 그는 버스 50대를 굴리고 있다 He has fifty buses running for business.
▶ 그는 땅을 굴려 큰 돈을 벌었다 He made a fortune by repeatedly buying and selling land.
5 〈깎다〉 round 《an edge》; smooth [even] a log; cut 《a piece of wood》 round; slice the edge off; round off 《the corners [angles]》

굴복 屈服 submission; surrender
—굴복하다 yield 《to》; submit 《to》; give in; 〈항복〉 surrender 《to》; bow (down) 《to》
♦ 압력에 굴복하다 yield under pressure / 굴복시키다 make *sb* give in; bring *sb* to *one's* knees
▶ 적에게 굴복하느니 차라리 죽겠다 I'd rather die than surrender to the enemy.
▶ 아무도 그의 금력에 굴복하지 않았다 No one bowed [yielded] to his money.
▶ 그는 기성의 권위에 굴복할 사람이 아니다 He is not a man to submit [bow down] to established authority.

굴비 a dried croaker [yellow corbina]

굴성 屈性 〔生〕 〈식물의〉 (a) tropism ■ —반응 a tropistic response

굴속 窟— the inside of a cave [cavern, den, tunnel] ♦ 굴속 같다 be as dark as the inside of a cave [cavern]; very dark

굴수성 屈水性 〔植〕 hydrotropism

굴신 屈伸 bending and stretching ♦ 굴신자재의 elastic; flexible; pliant **—굴신하다** bend and stretch; 〈관절이〉 flex
■ —운동 (do) bending and stretching exercises: 무릎의 굴신 운동을 하다 do knee bends

굴욕 屈辱 humiliation; disgrace; shame
♦ 굴욕을 당하다 be disgraced [humiliated]; suffer humiliation; undergo [be subjected to] humiliation / 굴욕을 안기다 humiliate; subject *sb* to humiliation; put *sb* to shame / 굴욕을 참다 eat dirt [humble pie]
▶ 나는 지난 2년 동안 굴욕을 견디어 왔다 I have been enduring humiliation [eating hum-

ble pie] for the past two years.
■—감 a sense of humiliation: 그는 심한 굴욕감을느꼈다 He felt deeply humiliated.
굴욕적 屈辱的 humiliating; insulting; disgraceful; shameful
♦굴욕적인 경험 a humiliating experience / 굴욕적인 양보 a humiliating concession / 굴욕적인 외교 humiliating [crow-eating] diplomacy / 굴욕적인 강화 조약을 맺다 conclude a humiliating [an ignoble] peace treaty 《with》
굴장 屈葬 (a) crouched [flexed] burial
굴절 屈折 bending; 〈빛·소리의〉 refraction; 〈어형의〉 inflection
—**굴절하다** bend; be refracted; undergo a refraction
♦사물을 보는 굴절된 시각 a distorted way of looking at things / 굴절시키다 refract
▶ 빛은 물[프리즘]을 통과할 때 굴절한다 Light is refracted when it passes through water [a prism].
▶ 그는 그녀에 대해 굴절된 감정을 가지고 있었다 His feelings toward her were warped.
■—각 a refracting angle; the angle of refraction —계 a refractometer —광선 a refracted ray of light [wave] —렌즈 a refractive lens; a refractor —력 〈렌즈의〉 the refractive power —률 〔物〕 refractive index; an index of refraction —망원경 a refracting telescope —어 an inflectional [inflective] language —파 a refracted wave
굴종 屈從 (servile) submission; servitude; subservience
♦굴종적인 submissive; subservient
—**굴종하다** submit (tamely, meekly) 《to》; yield 《to》; succumb 《to》; bend [bow] the knee 《to, before》
♦상사에게 굴종하다 succumb [yield, surrender] to one's superior / 굴종시키다 bring sb to one's knees
▶ 그는 순순히 굴종하는 타입이 아니다 He is not the sort of man to submit tamely.
굴지 屈指 ♦굴지의 〈제일류의〉 leading; 〈탁월한〉 outstanding; 〈저명한〉 distinguished; preeminent; one of the best (▷「굴지의」는「손가락으로 셀 수 있을 만큼 수가 적고 뛰어난」이란 뜻이므로「one of the + 형용사의 최상급」으로 표현되는 일이 많음) / 세계 굴지의 대도시 [양항] one of the largest cities [best seaports] in the world / 굴지의 실업가 a leading businessman / 당시 굴지의 화가들 the outstanding [foremost, prominent] painters of that period
▶ 그는 그 나라 굴지의 부자다 He is one of the richest man in the country.
굴지성 屈地性 〔植〕 geotropism
굴진 掘進 digging through —**굴진하다** dig through [into, under]
굴착 掘鑿 digging; boring; excavation
—**굴착하다** dig out [through]; excavate; bore
♦터널을 굴착하다 dig a tunnel 《through a mountain》
▶ 이 터널을 굴착하는 데 10년 걸렸다 It took ten years to excavate this tunnel.
■—기(機) an excavator; a [an earth] scraper —장치 drilling rigs —탑 a derrick
굴참나무 〔植〕 an Oriental species of oak
굴총하다 掘塚— open [violate] a grave; dig a grave open
굴하다 屈— 〈힘에〉 yield 《to》; submit 《to》; 〈토론에서〉 give in 《to》; 〈권위에〉 bow (down) 《to》; 〈양보〉 give way 《to》
♦굴하지 않고 undauntedly; in spite of; in defiance of / 역경에 굴하지 않다 bear up under an adversity [difficult circumstance]
▶ 그는 무엇에도 굴하지 않는 용기가 있었다 He had the courage never to submit [yield] to anything
▶ 거듭되는 실패에도 굴하지 않고 그는 마침내 그 실험에 성공했다 Never discouraged by repeated failures, he at last succeeded in the experiment.
▶ 그녀는 불행에 굴할 여자가 아니다 She is not a girl to be daunted by misfortune.
굵기 thickness; 〈크기〉 size; 〈소리의〉 depth
▶ 그 관은 굵기가 10센티미터다 The pipe is ten centimeters in diameter.
굵다 〈둥근 것이〉 big; thick; burly; 〈선 등이〉 bold; thick; 〈목소리가〉 deep; thick; 〈활자 등이〉 fat
♦굵은 가지 a thick bough / 굵은 나무줄기 a thick [wide] trunk / 굵은 다리 a thick leg; a stubby leg / 굵은 목 a thick neck / 굵은 빗방울 a large [heavy] drop of rain / 굵은 실 a thick thread / 굵고 우렁찬 목소리 a deep sturdy voice / 굵은 활자의 bold-faced; Gothic / 굵게 thickly / 굵어지다 grow bigger [thicker] / 인생을 굵고 짧게 살다 lead a short life and a merry one / 굵은 글씨로 쓰다 write thick; write in bold script [letters, strokes]
▶ 그는 팔이 굵다 He has big arms.
▶ 그는 목소리가 굵다 He has a deep voice.
굵다랗다 very thick; very big; 〈목소리가〉 very deep ♦굵다란 밧줄 a very thick rope
굵직굵직하다 all thick [big, deep] ♦굵직굵직하게 썰다 cut into big [thick] pieces
굵직하다 thickish; somewhat thick [big, 〈목소리가〉 deep] ♦굵직한 몽둥이 a thick club
굶기다 let sb go hungry [foodless]; starve
♦식구를 굶기다 let one's family go hungry [starve] / 굶겨 죽이다 starve 《an animal》 to death
▶ 애완 동물을 굶겨서는 안 된다 You should not let your pet go hungry.
▶ 처자식을 굶길 수는 없다 I can't let my family go hungry.
굶다 go hungry; be starving; miss a meal; famish
♦종일 굶다 go foodless [have not eaten] all day / 굶어 죽다 die of [from] hunger; be starved [famished] to death
▶ 나는 어제부터 굶었다 I haven't eaten since yesterday.
▶ 굶고서는 아무 것도 못 한다 You can't do anything on an empty stomach.
▶ 전쟁 중에 많은 사람들이 굶어 죽었다 Many people died of hunger [were starved to death] during the war.
굶주리다 starve; be [go] hungry; be starving;

be famished; 〈갈망하다〉 hunger [hanker, long, thirst] for [after]
♦굶주린 개 a hungry dog / 애정에 굶주린 아이 a love-starved child / 피에 굶주리다 lust after human blood
▶가뭄에 많은 사람들이 굶주렸다 Many people starved during the drought.
▶그는 지식에 굶주려 있다 He is thirsty for [after] knowledge.
▶그는 애정에 굶주려 있다 He is starved of [hungry for] affection.

굶주림 《complain of》 hunger; starvation
▶그는 한 조각의 치즈로 굶주림을 면했다 He kept off his hunger with a piece of cheese.
▶굶주림으로 많은 사람들이 죽었다 A great many people died of hunger [starved to death].

굼뜨다 slow; slow-moving; slowgoing; tardy; sluggish
♦굼뜬 동작 sluggish behavior / 굼뜬 사람 a dawdler; a laggard / 걸음이 굼뜨다 be slow of foot; be a slow walker
▶그는 일하는 게 너무 굼떠서 참을 수가 없다 He is such a slow [sluggish] worker that I am impatient with him.

굼벵이 〈애벌레〉 a (white) grub; 〈사람〉 a laggard; a sluggard; a slow(-moving) person
♦굼벵이 같은 slow(-moving); snail-slow; sluggish / 굼벵이 걸음으로 걸어가다 walk slowly; go at a snail's pace

굼벵이도 궁글[꾸부리는] 재주가 있다 《속담》 Every man for his own trade.

굼실거리다 creep about 《over one's body》; crawl over 《one》 ▶잔등이 굼실거린다 I feel something creeping up [crawling on] my back.

굼실굼실 crawling; creepling ━**굼실굼실하다** ⇨ 굼실거리다

굽 1 〈마소의〉 a hoof 《pl. ~s, hooves》 ♦갈라진 굽 cloven hoofs / 말굽 소리 hoofbeat / 말굽 자국 hoofprint / 굽이 있는 동물 a hoofed animal
2 〈신의〉 a heel; 〈그릇의〉 a foot; a stem 《of a glass》; a base ♦나막신의 굽 clog supports / 굽이 높은[낮은] 구두 high-heeled [low-heeled] shoes

굽다¹ 1 〈고기를〉 roast; 〈고기·생선을〉 broil; 〈빵을〉 bake; 〈빵 조각이나 김을〉 toast

> 解說 *roast*는 큰 고기를 시간을 들여서 굽는 경우, *grill*, *broil*은 작은 것을 불에 직접 쬐어 굽는 경우, *bake*는 특히 오븐 속에서 조리하는 경우, *barbecue*는 고기를 불에 직접 향료 맛이 나는 소스로 요리하는 경우, *toast*는 조리가 끝난 빵이나 치즈 등을 엷은 다갈색으로 눌릴 때 쓴다.

♦갓 구운 빵 bread hot from the oven / 설 구워진 rare / 알맞게 구워진 medium / 잘 구워진 well-done; well baked / 고기를 굽다 roast meat / 생선을 노르스름하게 굽다 do a fish brown / 고기를 잘 굽다 do meat thoroughly / 지나치게 굽다 overdo; overcook; overbroil
▶나는 살짝 구운 빵을 좋아한다 I like lightly toasted bread.
▶오늘 저녁 식사에는 닭을 구워 먹읍시다 Let's grill a chicken for dinner tonight.
2 〈도자기 등을〉 fire; bake; make 《china》; burn 《bricks, lime》 ♦도자기[벽돌]를 굽다 bake [fire] pottery [bricks]
3 〈숯을〉 produce; make; burn 《charcoal》
♦숯을 굽다 make charcoal; char wood / 나무로 숯을 굽다 burn wood into charcoal
▶그는 숯을 구워 생활한다 He makes a living making charcoal.

굽다² 〈휘어지다〉 bend; curve; be crooked [bent, stooped]; be curved; warp
♦굽어진 계단 a dogleg(ged) staircase / 굽은 길 a winding path / 강풍에 굽은 소나무 a pine tree tortured by storms / 나이가 들어 허리가 굽다 be bent with age; stoop from age
▶아버지는 허리가 굽으셨다 My father's back is bent (with age).
▶나는 때때로 할머니의 굽은 허리를 회상한다 Sometimes I remember my grandmother's bent back.
▶눈이 쌓여 나뭇가지가 굽어 있었다 The tree branches had been bent under the snow.
▶길은 여기서 급격히 굽어져 있다 The road bends sharply here. ⇌ There is a sharp bend in the road here.

굽달이 〈접시 등〉 a footed plate [dish]

굽도리 〈방안 벽의〉 the lower walls of a room ■ ━지(紙) a strip of paper around the walls of a room next to the floor ━**판자** 〔建〕 a mopboard; a baseboard; (英) a skirting board

굽실거리다 〈복종하다〉 truckle [yield] 《to》; bow (and scrape); 〈아첨하다〉 ko(w)tow 《to》; crouch; cringe 《at》
♦굽실거리며 in a servile manner / 상사에게 굽실거리다 humble *oneself* before *one's* superiors; cringe to *one's* superior
▶그는 언제나 상사에게 굽실거린다 He always kowtows to his superior.
▶그는 경찰관에게 굽실거렸다 He was obsequious to [cringed before] the policeman.
▶그는 굽실거려서 현재의 지위를 얻었다 He won his present post in a servile manner.

굽실하다 bow *one's* head; bow low; ko(w)tow

굽어보다 look down 《at, over》; take a bird's-eye view 《of》; overlook
♦들판을 굽어보는 산 a mountain dominating the plain / 골짜기를 굽어보다 look down into a valley
▶우리는 남산 타워에서 서울 거리를 굽어보았다 From Namsan Tower we looked down at [had a bird's-eye view of] the city of Seoul.
▶호텔에서 시내를 굽어볼 수 있다 The hotel overlooks [commands a view of] the town.

굽어살피다 be considerate of [to, toward]; be concerned about; take a kindly interest in; feel for; pay attention to
♦민생을 굽어 살피다 look into the condition of the people
▶하느님 굽어 살피소서 Heaven be my witness.
▶우리의 곤란한 입장을 굽어 살펴 주시기 바람

니다 I would like you to understand that we are in a difficult situation.
굽이 a curve; a bend; a turn; curvature; a crook; a turning
♦물 굽이 a bend [curve] in a stream [river] / 굽이마다 at every turn
▶배는 강의 굽이를 돌았다 The boat turned a bend in the river.
굽이굽이 1 〈굽이쳐〉 meandering; windingly; serpentinely
♦굽이굽이 흐르는 강 a winding [meandering] river
▶그 길은 산 사이를 굽이굽이 뻗어 있다 The path winds through the mountains.
▶시냇물이 골짜기를 굽이굽이 흐르고 있었다 The stream meandered along the valley.
2 〈굽이마다〉 at every turn [bend]
굽이돌다 make a curve (around); curve [wind] around
굽이지다 bend [curve, wind] (in); be incurved [bent]
굽이치다 〈강이〉 wind (in and out); meander; snake; 〈파도가〉 surge; swell; roll
♦굽이쳐 흐르는 시내 a winding [serpentine, meandering] stream
▶난바다에서는 파도가 크게 굽이친다 Surges run high in the open sea.
▶계곡을 따라 한 줄기의 강이 굽이쳐 흐르고 있었다 There was a river winding [meandering] through the valleys.
굽죄이다 have an uneasy conscience; feel small [intimidated] ▶저 사람에게는 굽죄인다 I still feel deeply indebted to him. ≒ I still feel I owe him a lot.
굽질리다 〈a matter〉 fail to go smoothly; 〈a research〉 make little [almost no] progress; 〈a plan〉 be foiled and twisted
굽통 1 〈발굽이〉 a hoof 2 〈화살대의〉 the bamboo butt (of an arrow)
굽히다 1 〈구부리다〉 bend (over, forward); stoop; bow (down)
♦손가락을 굽히다 hook one's finger / 책상 위에 몸을 굽히다 bend over one's desk / 허리를 굽히다 bend one's back
▶나는 몸을 굽혀 그 종이쪽지를 주웠다 I bent (myself) down [stooped] to pick up the piece of paper.
▶그는 허리를 굽혀 내게 인사했다 He greeted me by making a bow [by bowing].
▶그녀는 허리를 굽혀 꽃 향기를 맡았다 She bent [stooped] over the flower to smell it.
2 〈굴하다〉 yield (to); submit (to); give in
♦의견을 굽히다 change one's opinion / 의지를 굽히다 act against [bend] one's will / 주장을 굽히다 concede a point / 지조를 굽히다 deviate from one's principles / 주장을 굽히지 않다 hold fast to one's own views
▶필요할 때는 자신을 굽혀야 한다 We must bow to necessity.
굿 1 〈무당의〉 a service [ceremony] of exorcism; an exorcism (of demons); practices of an exorciser
―굿하다 exorcise; perform [carry out] an exorcism; drive out an evil spirit

2 〈구경거리〉 a show; a spectacle; a sight; an attraction
굿거리 (the rhythm [beat] of) tunes for an exorcism
굿 뒤에 날장구 친다 (속담) flog [mount on] a dead horse
굿 들은 무당, 재 들은 중 (속담) a person who is only too happy to be of service
굿보다 〈굿을〉 watch exorcism; 〈방관하다〉 look on; remain a spectator [an idle onlooker]; sit [stand] by and watch; be an onlooker
궁 宮 1 〈궁궐〉 a palace
2 〔天〕 a sign; 〔占星〕 a (mundane) house
♦황도(黃道) 12궁 the (twelve) signs of the zodiac
3 〔樂〕 the lowest note of the pentatonic scale
4 〔장기〕 the king; the chess position of the king
궁경 窮境 1 〈곤궁한 처지〉 adverse circumstances; a painful position; straitened [needy] circumstances
2 〈궁지〉 a difficult situation; a predicament; a fix; a dilemma; a sad [sorry] plight
궁계 窮計 the last resort ⇨ 궁여지책
궁구 窮究 thorough investigation [study, research]
―궁구하다 investigate [study] sth thoroughly; make an profound study of; make an exhaustive study of; dig into (an author); carry (it) to an extreme
궁굴다 〈보기보다 속이 너르다〉 larger than it looks; 〈서술적〉 contain more than one might expect
궁굴리다 〈너그럽게〉 think leniently; be tolerant [generous]; 〈구슬리다〉 forgive with kind words
궁궐 宮闕 the royal palace ♦궁궐같은 집 a palatial residence [mansion]; a palace of a house
궁극 窮極 ♦궁극적인 승리 a final victory / 궁극적으로 finally; ultimately; after all; in the end; in the last [final] analysis
▶궁극적인 책임은 총장에게 있다 Ultimate responsibility lies with the president.
▶그들의 궁극적인 목적은 달성되었다 Their ultimate purpose [objective] was attained.
▶궁극적으로 정의가 승리했다 Finally [Ultimately] justice triumphed.
―무기 an ultimate weapon **―성** 〔哲〕 finality **―원인** the final [ultimate] cause
궁글다 〈속이 비다〉 hollow; loose; empty ♦속이 궁근 나무 a hollow tree
궁금증 ―症 〈호기심〉 curiosity; 〈강한 관심〉a concern; 〈염려〉 anxiety; worry
♦궁금증을 풀다 gratify [satisfy] one's curiosity
▶시험 결과에 궁금증이 난다 I'm anxious about the results of the examination.
▶궁금증이 나는 일이 하나 있다 There is something that has been weighing on my mind [worrying me].
궁금하다 be [feel] curious [anxious] (to

know]; be apprehensive 《about》; 〈서술적〉 feel wonder [curious, curiosity]; wonder 《about, whether, if, when, how, who》
♦소식이 궁금하다 be anxious to hear from *sb* / 시험 결과가 궁금하다 be anxious about the result of the examination / 안부가 궁금하다 be worried [apprehensive] about *sb's* safety
▶그에게 무슨 일이 일어났는지 궁금하다 I wonder what has become of him.
▶저 여자가 누구인지 궁금하다 I wonder who that woman is.
▶누구의 생일인지 궁금하다 I wonder whose birthday it is. ⇒ Whose birthday is it, I wonder?

궁기 窮氣 a wretched [miserable, pitiable] look ♦궁기가 흐르는 wretched-looking

궁끼다 窮— suffer impoverishment; be in need [《口》 hard up]; be destitute; be in extreme poverty

궁내 宮內 《in》 the royal palace [court]
궁녀 宮女 a court lady; a maid of honor
궁도 弓道 archery; bowmanship
궁도련님 宮— the young master who knows nothing [a rich man's son who is ignorant] of the world [real life]; a green boy [youth] 《of noble birth》; a young buck

궁둥이 the buttocks; the seat 《of *one's* pants》; 《口》 the bottom; the rear; 《口》 the behind; 《美》 *one's* butt; 〈마소의〉 the rump
♦궁둥이가 가볍다 be ready [willing] to work; be quick to act / 궁둥이가 무겁다 be slow to get moving [act]; be unwilling to work; be slow in starting work / 궁둥이가 질기다 stay on and on; stay too long; overstay [outstay] *one's* welcome
▶그 여자는 궁둥이가 가볍다 She is restless [never sits still for long].
■**궁둥잇바람** lively hip-shaking **궁둥잇짓** shaking *one's* hips: 궁둥잇짓하다 shake *one's* hips

궁둥짝 both hips; the hips

궁따다 〈시치미를 떼다〉 feign ignorance; pretend not to know; (put on a poker face and) say what *one* does not mean
▶경찰관의 물음에 그녀는 아들의 소재를 모르는 척 궁땄다 In answering to the policeman's questions, she pretended to have no knowledge of her son's whereabouts.

궁륭 穹窿 〈반구형〉 a vault; cupola; a dome ♦궁륭형의 vaulted; domeshaped ■—천장 a vaulted ceiling

궁리 窮理 〈연구〉 study; research; 〈숙고〉 consideration; meditation; deliberation; thinking [pondering] over
♦궁리 끝에 after deliberation / 월 50만원으로 먹고 살 궁리를 하다 make (a) shift to live on five hundred thousand won a month
—**궁리하다** 〈연구하다〉 study; 〈생각하다〉 think 《about》; consider; deliberate on [《美》 over]; meditate 《on》; ponder over; cast about 《in *one's* mind》 《for a good plan》
♦돈벌이할 방도를 궁리하다 mull over ways and means of making money

▶나는 어떻게 해서 위기를 벗어날까 궁리했다 I pondered [thought hard] a way to get through the crisis.

궁박 窮迫 poverty; straitened circumstances; destitution; distress
—**궁박하다** be in distress; be reduced to great straits; very poor; destitute ♦재정이 궁박하다 be in financial difficulties

궁벽하다 窮僻— out-of-the-way; remote; secluded
♦궁벽한 시골 an inconvenient rural area [out-of-the-way place]; a secluded [remote] place; 《美》 the backcountry
▶나는 궁벽한 곳[마을]에 살고 있다 I live in a remote place [village]. ⇒ I live in a village far from any city.

궁상 窮狀 straitened circumstances; a sad [sorry] plight; distress; a trouble; hardships
♦옷차림이 궁상스러운 사람 a poorly [shabbily] dressed [clad] man / 궁상맞다 be miserable-looking; be shabby [poverty-stricken] / 궁상을 떨다 reveal *one's* straitened circumstances

궁상 窮相 a meager face; a poor [distressed] outlook

궁색 窮塞 poverty; straitened circumstances; distress
—**궁색하다** be poor; be destitute 《of》; be in need [distress]; distressed
♦살림이 궁색하다 be in needy [straitened] circumstances; be badly off

궁서가 고양이를 문다 《속담》 A stag at bay is a dangerous foe.

궁수 弓手 an archer; a bowman
궁술 弓術 archery; bowmanship ■—가 an archer ■—시합 an archery
궁시 弓矢 bows and arrows
궁실 宮室 a royal chamber
궁여지책 窮餘之策 the last resort; the final expedient; a desperate measure
♦궁여지책으로 as a (means of) last resort; as a desperate shift; as a last resource
▶성냥이 없어 궁여지책으로 돋보기로 불을 피웠다 I didn't have a match, so I had to resort to making a fire with a magnifying glass.

궁전 宮殿 a (royal) palace ♦버킹엄 궁전 Buckingham Palace
궁정 宮廷 the (Royal) Court; the Imperial Palace ■—문학 court literature —생활 court life —시인[화가] a court poet [painter]
궁조 窮鳥 a bird in distress
▶궁조가 쫓겨 품에 날아들면 사냥꾼도 죽이지 않는다 Even the huntsman refrains from killing a poor bird which has flown into his bosom for refuge.

궁중 宮中 the Royal Court
▶그는 여러 해 동안 궁중에서 일했다 He served at Court for many years. ■—예복 a court dress

궁지 窮地 a difficult situation; an awkward position; a dilemma; 《口》 a fix 《▶항상 부정관사 a를 붙임》; a corner
♦궁지에 몰리다 be driven [pushed] to the wall / 궁지에 빠지다 be caught in a dilemma;

(ㅁ) get into a fix [scrape, hole]; be in a (tight) corner / 궁지에 빠뜨리다 drive [push] sb into a corner
▶ 나는 궁지에 빠져 있었다 I found myself in a fix [a dilemma, an awkward position].
▶ 그는 궁지에 몰려 거짓말을 하지 않을 수 없었다 Driven into a corner, he had to tell a lie.
▶ 그들은 궁지에 몰리면 무슨 짓을 할지 모른다 They would go to any extreme if cornered.
▶ 그녀는 가까스로 궁지에서 벗어났다 She narrowly got out of difficulty [trouble].

궁체 宮體 the court style of *Hangŭl* calligraphy

궁촌 窮村 an impoverished [a deserted] village; a poor [poverty-stricken] village

궁터 宮— a palace site; the site of a [an old] palace

궁핍 窮乏 want; destitution; privation; indigence; poverty
▶ 그녀는 궁핍과 싸우고 있다 She is struggling against need.
—궁핍하다 poor; destitute; indigent; be in needy circumstances; be badly off; be in straitened circumstances
◆ 궁핍한 생활 a needy life; a life of distress [poverty, want]

궁하다 窮— 1 〈곤궁하다〉 poor; hard up; needy; destitute
◆ 돈이 궁해서 at a push for money / 생활이 궁하다 be unable to make a living / 궁해지다 grow [get, become] poor; be reduced to poverty / 궁한 처지에 있다 be in want [need]
▶ 그는 요즘 돈이 궁하다 He has been hard up [in financial difficulties] recently. ⇒ He has been short [in need] of money recently.
▶ 그들은 절대로 궁한 처지가 아니다 They are not at all badly off.
2 〈난처·당황하다〉 be in a tight squeeze; be in trouble [difficulty]; (ㅁ) be in a fix; be at a loss; be at *one's* wit's end ◆ 말이 궁하다 do not know what to say
▶ 나는 대답이 궁했다 I was at a loss for an answer. ⇒ I didn't know what to answer.

궁하면 통한다 〈속담〉 There's always a way (out). ⇒ When you are in real trouble you will find a way out. ⇒ Necessity is the mother of invention. ⇒ Want makes wit. ⇒ The darkest hour is that before the dawn.

궁합 宮合 ◆ 궁합이 좋은 well-suited 《to each other》/ 궁합이 나쁜 ill-suited; ill-matched / 궁합이 맞다 the horoscopes of a young couple agree [assure married bliss] / 궁합을 보다 compare the horoscopes of a young couple
▶ 나는 점쟁이에게 그녀와의 궁합을 보았다 I consulted a fortune-teller to find out if we would make a happy couple.

궁형 弓形 an arch; a crescent form ◆ 궁형의 arched; bow-shaped

궂기다 1 〈일이〉 not go well [smoothly]; go wrong [amiss, awry]; be unsuccessful 2 〈초상이 나다〉 be bereaved 《of *one's* grandmother》

궂다¹ 〈눈이 멀다〉 go [become] blind; lose *one's* (eye)sight

궂다² 1 〈언짢다〉 bad; disagreeable 《to》; unpleasant 《to, to do》; uncomfortable 《about》; undesirable; displeased 《at, with》
◆ 심술 궂다 be perverse; be ill-tempered / 암상 궂다 be jealous / 좋다 궂다 말이 없다 say neither good nor bad
2 〈날씨가〉 bad; foul; nasty; rough; choppy; inclement ◆ 궂은 날씨 bad weather; nasty weather

궂은고기 〈죽은 짐승 고기〉 carrion
궂은비 a vicious, untimely rain
궂은살 an excrescence; (ㅁ) flab
궂은일 1 〈언짢은 일〉 an ugly job; an untoward event; an unlucky [unfortunate] affair
2 〈흉사〉 unlucky affairs; misfortune; bad luck; unfortunate affair

권 勸 (a piece of) advice; counsel; recommendation ⇨ 권고
◆ 권을 따라 following *sb's* advice; complying with the recommendation of /…의 권으로 on [at] the recommendation of; by [at] the advice of

권 卷 1 〈책의〉 a volume; a book; a copy
◆ 제3권 the third volume; Vol. 3; Book 3 / 두 권짜리 책 a work in two volumes
▶ 이 책 열 권 주세요 I want ten copies of this book.
▶ 이 백과 사전은 열두 권으로 되어 있다 This encyclopedia is made up of [consists of, comprises] twelve volumes.
▶ 제1권은 1997년에 출간되었다 The first volume [Vol. 1] was published in 1997.
2 〈한지의 양〉 twenty sheets of traditional Korean paper
◆ 한지 세권 sixty sheets of traditional Korean paper
3 〈영화의〉 a reel ◆ 두 권짜리 영화 a two-reel picture [film]; a two reeler

-권 券 〈표〉 a ticket; a card; 〈지폐〉 《美》 a bill; 《英》 a (bank) note
◆ 식권 a meal ticket / 진찰권 a consultation card [ticket] / 천원권 a thousand-won bill [note] / 할인권 a discount ticket / 회수권 a coupon ticket

-권 圈 a sphere; a circle; a bloc
◆ 북극[남극]권 the Arctic [Antarctic] Circle / 세력권 *one's* sphere of influence / 수도권 the metropolitan area /…의 권내[권외]에 within [out of] the sphere [range] of…

-권 權 〈권리〉 rights; 〈권능〉 authority; power
◆ 선거권 the right to vote; suffrage / 소유권 ownership; title / 시민권 citizenship / 재산권 property rights / 통치권 sovereignty / 평등권 an equal right

권고 勸告 recommendation; (a piece of) advice; counsel
◆ 많은 유익한 권고의 말 many pieces [a great deal] of valuable advice / 의사의 권고로 on a doctor's advice / 권고를 따르다 follow *sb's* advice
▶ 나는 사직 권고를 받았다 I was advised [counseled] to resign.
▶ 조합은 중재위원회의 권고에 승복하지 않았다

The union did not comply with the recommendation of the arbitration committee.
—**권고하다** advise; give 《verbal》 advice 《on》; counsel; recommend
▶ 다시는 그런 일을 하지 않도록 그에게 권고해 주시오 Please advise him not to do such a thing again.
■ —**안** a recommendation —**자** an adviser; a counselor —**장** written advice; a letter of advice

권내 圏内 ◆권내에 within the range [sphere] 《of》/ 대기권내에 in the atmosphere
▶ 그 배는 지금 태풍권내에 있다 The ship is now in the typhoon area.
▶ 우리 당의 후보 50명이 당선권내에 있다 Fifty of our party's candidates have chance of being elected.
▶ 그 나라는 영국의 세력권내에 있었다 The country was within the sphere of British influence.

권농 勸農 encouragement of agriculture —**권농하다** encourage [promote] agriculture
■ —**일** Farmers' Day —**정책** an agricultural development policy

권능 權能 authority; power ◆아무에게 …할 권능을 부여하다 authorize [empower] sb to do...

권두 卷頭 the beginning [first page, opening page] of a book
◆권두에 on the first page
■ —**논문** the opening article 《of a magazine》 —**언** a foreword; a preface; an introduction

권력 權力 power; authority; influence
◆국가 권력 state authority / 절대적 권력 absolute power / 권력이 있는 powerful / 권력이 없는 powerless; without power / 권력을 잡다[잃다] gain [lose] power / 권력을 행사하다 exercise [use, wield] one's power [authority]
▶ 그는 권력 있는 자리에 오르려고 한다 He wants to get (into) power.
▶ 그는 대통령으로서 국민에게 막강한 권력을 휘둘렀다 He exercised [wielded] the great power of the President over the people.
■ —**국가** an authoritarian state —**구조** power structure —**욕** (a) desire [lust, greed] for power —**의지** 〔哲〕 the will to power —**자** a man of power [influence] —**투쟁** a struggle for power [influence]

권리 權利 a right; 〈청구권〉 a claim; 〈특권〉 a privilege; 〈영업권〉 goodwill
◆당연한 권리 a natural [due] right / 법률[종교]상의 권리 a legal [religious] right / 정당한 권리 a just [right] claim / 권리와 의무 rights and duties / 권리가 있다 have a [the] right 《to sth, to do》/ be entitled 《to sth, to do》/ 권리가 없다 have no right 《to (do) sth, of doing》; be not entitled (to) / 권리를 얻다[잃다] acquire [lose, forfeit] a right / 권리를 요구하다 claim [demand] a right / 권리를 주장하다 assert one's right / 권리를 침해하다 infringe on sb's right / 권리를 포기하다 relinquish [waive, give up] one's right / 권리를 행사[남용]하다 exercise [abuse] one's right
▶ 권리는 의무를 동반한다 Rights carry duties.
▶ 헌법에 보장된 권리는 행사해야 한다 You should exercise your rights (that are) guaranteed by the Constitution.
▶ 아무도 그 재산의 권리를 주장하지 않았다 Nobody made a claim to [on] the property.
■ —**락(落)** 〔證〕 ex right; ex warrant —**선언** 〔英史〕 the Declaration of Rights —**자** a rightful claimant —**장전** 〔英史〕 the Bill of Rights —**정지** lapse [suspension] of rights —**증서** 〈부동산의〉 a title deed; a certificate of title —**청원** 〔英史〕 the Petition of Rights

권리금 權利金 a premium; key money
◆권리금 500만원이 붙은 임대 점포 a store [shop] for rent with key money of five million won / 아주 비싼 권리금이 붙어서 at an extremely high premium

권말 卷末 the end of a book [volume] ■ —**부록** an appendix [a supplement] to a book [magazine]

권면 勸勉 encouragement —**권면하다** encourage; admonish; urge

권모 權謀 a trick; a scheme; machination
◆권모에 능하다 be full of wiles; be resourceful
■ —**가** a crafty person; a schemer; a Machiavellian —**외교** Machiavellian diplomacy

권모술수 權謀術數 trickery; Machiavellianism; craft and deceit
▶ 그는 큰 돈을 벌려고 권모술수를 부렸다 He devised tricks [trickery] to gain a large amount of money.
▶ 그는 권모술수를 써서 정권을 잡았다 He seized power by trickery [after some clever scheming].

권문(세가) 權門(勢家) a powerful [an influential] family; the great and powerful
◆권문 세가에 아부하다 curry favor with the powerful; be servile to those with influence

권법 拳法 the art of fist duel; boxing (as one of Korean martial arts)

권불십년 權不十年 Power never lasts (ten years). ⇒ Every flow has its ebb. ⇒ Pride goes [comes] before a fall.

권선 勸善 promotion of virtue; urging good [right] conduct; 〔佛教〕 soliciting contributions

권선징악 勸善懲惡 promoting virtue and reproving vice; rewarding the good and punishing the wicked; 〈이상적 정의〉 poetic justice —**권선징악하다** encourage the good and punish the evil
■ —**극** a morality play —**소설** a didactic novel; moralistic fiction

권세 權勢 power; influence ◆권세를 쥐다 seize power; hold the reins of power / 권세를 휘두르다 exercise influence; wield power
■ —**욕** ⇨ 권력(〜욕)

권속 眷属 〈딸린 식구〉 one's (whole) family; one's household; one's dependents
▶ 그는 일가 권속을 데리고 미국으로 이주했다 He emigrated to America with his whole family.

권수 卷數 the number of volumes [books]; the book [volume] number

권수 卷鬚 〈덩굴손〉 [植] a tendril; a cirrus (*pl*. -ri)

권신 權臣 a powerful vassal; an influential courtier

권외 圈外 ♦대기권외 outer space / 통신권외의 지역 a region outside of communication range / 권외에 out of the range [sphere] (of) ▶그 지방은 로마 제국의 세력권외에 있었다 The district was outside the range [out of the sphere] of the power of the Roman Empire. ▶그 어선은 태풍권외로 벗어났다 The fishing boat escaped from the typhoon area.

권운 卷雲 〈새털구름〉 a cirrus; a cirrus cloud

권위 權威 1 〈권세〉 authority; power; 〈위엄〉 dignity; prestige
♦매우 권위 있는 사전 a dictionary of great authority / 권위 있는 소식통의 정보 information received from an authoritative [authority] source / 권위 있는 책 an authoritative book / 권위가 있다 have authority (over, with) / 권위가 없다 have little authority [power, control] / 권위를 공공연히 무시하다 openly disregard the authority (of) / 권위를 인정하다 accept the authority / 권위를 잃다 lose *one's* authority (over, with)
▶요즈음은 부모의 권위가 존중되지 않고 있다 The authority of parents [parental authority] is not respected these days.
▶그 교장은 학생들에게 권위가 대단했다 The principal had great authority [power] over the boys and girls.
2 ⇨ 권위자

권위자 權威者 an (acknowledged) authority (on the subject); 〈전문가〉 an expert (on)
♦사계[전자공학]의 최고 권위자 the greatest authority in this field [on electronics]

권유 勸誘 (an) invitation; solicitation; persuasion; inducement; 〈운동〉 canvassing
♦클럽 입회 권유 an invitation to join a club / 불법적인 투표 권유 illegal canvassing for votes
▶나는 여러 번 입회 권유를 받았다 I was asked repeatedly to be a member of the society.
—**권유하다** ask; invite; solicit; canvass
♦기부를 권유하다 solicit *sb* for a contribution / 보험 가입을 권유하다 canvass *sb* for insurance
▶그는 우리 어머니께 보험 가입을 권유했다 He tried to persuade my mother to buy insurance.
■—**원** a canvassing agent; a solicitor: 나는 기부 권유원입니다 I'm soliciting [canvassing for] contributions. —**장** a letter of solicitation [invitation]; a circular

권익 權益 rights; interests ♦외국에서 자기 권익을 지키다 protect *one's* interests in a foreign country

권장 勸獎 encouragement; exhortation; recommendation
♦선생님[의사]의 권장으로 on the recommendation [on advice] of *one's* teacher [doctor]
—**권장하다** recommend; exhort; urge; encourage; advise
▶우리는 지방 산업을 육성하도록 권장했다 We encouraged the people to promote local industry.

권적운 卷積雲 〈털쌘구름〉 a cirrocumulus (*pl*. -li); a cirrocumulous cloud

권점 圈點 ♦권점을 찍다 mark 《a word》 with a small circle

권좌 權座 the seat of power; a position of power [authority] ♦권좌에 앉다 come into [be in] power; reach a position of authority / 권좌에서 물러나다 go out of power

권주 勸酒 offering (a glass of) wine (to *sb*)
■—**가** a song to offer wine; a drinking song

권척 卷尺 a tape measure; a measuring tape ⇨ 줄자

권총 拳銃 a pistol; (美) a gun; (口) a gun; 〈회전 연발식〉 a revolver
♦38구경 권총 a 38-caliber revolver; a thirty-eight / 6연발 권총 a six-chambered pistol [revolver]; a six-shooter; a six-gun / 자동 권총 an automatic revolver / 장난감 권총 a toy gun / 권총을 들이대고 at the point of a pistol; at gunpoint / 권총을 겨누다 point [aim, level] a gun (at) / 권총을 쏘다 fire [discharge] *one's* gun (at)
▶그 비행기는 권총을 든 놈들에게 납치당했다 The plane was hijacked by men armed with gun.
■—**강도** a gun-armed robber; (美口) a gunman —**자살** killing *oneself* with a gun : 그는 권총자살을 했다 He shot himself.

── 권총 ──

가늠쇠 front sight
총신 barrel
가늠자 rear sight
공이치기 hammer
총구 muzzle
실린더 cylinder
방아쇠울 trigger guard
방아쇠 trigger
손잡이, 그립 handle, grip

권층운 卷層雲 〈털층구름〉 a cirrostratus (*pl*. -ti); a cirrostratus cloud

권태 倦怠 weariness; ennui; listlessness; boredom ♦권태를 느끼다 feel tired [languid]; be bored

권태기 倦怠期 〈부부의〉 stage of ennui in married life ▶그들은 권태기에 들어섰다 They have got tired [weary] of their married life.

권토중래 捲土重來 ♦권토중래를 기하다 (regroup and) prepare to renew *one's* attack / be resolved to make a new start with redoubled efforts
▶야당측의 권토중래가 기대된다 It is hoped that the opposition parties will stage a comeback [make a recovery].
—**권토중래하다** regroup and make a fresh start with redoubled energy; resume *one's* activities with renewed efforts; make a rollback [comeback]

권유의 표현

1. …하시오
(1) 명령형
▶ 들어오시오 Come in. ⇌ Do come in.
▶ 초콜릿을 하나 더 드세요 Have another chocolate.
▶ 어서 편히 쉬십시오 Make yourself at home.
(2) Please …; …, please (명령문과 함께 쓰인다)
▶ 어서 들어오십시오 Please come in. ⇌ Come in, please.
▶ 어서 앉으십시오 Please sit down. ⇌ Sit down, please.
▶ 이쪽으로 오십시오 This way, please. (이 경우 please는 반드시 명사 뒤에 온다)
[어법]
① (1)은 허물없는 사이에 쓰는 말투다. 이것은 명령형이지만 실제는 남에게 무언가를 권유하는 뜻이므로 실례가 아니다.
② please를 끝머리에 둘 때는 반드시 그 앞에 콤마를 찍는다.

2. …하지 않겠습니까?; …하면 어떻겠습니까?
(1) Will you …?
▶ 들어오시지 않겠습니까? Will you come in?
▶ (저와) 함께 가시지 않겠습니까? Will you come with me?
▶ 오늘 저녁에 우리와 같이 식사하시지 않겠습니까? Will you have dinner with us tonight?
▶ 커피를 한 잔 더 드시겠습니까? Will you have another cup of coffee?
▶ 점심을 우리와 같이 드시지 않겠습니까? Will you join us at lunch?
▶ 【會話】 「빵을 조금더 드시지 않겠습니까?」 「아니오, 됐습니다」 "Will you have some more bread?" "No, I don't want any more."
(2) Won't you …?; …, won't you?
▶ 들어오시지 않겠습니까? Won't you come in? ⇌ Come in, won't you?
▶ 함께 가시지 않겠습니까? Won't you come with me? ⇌ Come with me, won't you?
▶ 점심을 우리와 함께 하시지 않겠습니까? Won't you join us at lunch? ⇌ Join us at lunch, won't you?
▶ 좀더 드시지 않겠습니까? Won't you have some more? ⇌ Have some more, won't you?
[어법]
① won't you를 끝머리에 두는 편이 스스럼 없는 말투다.
② 권유를 나타내는 글에서는 의문문이나 부정의문의 형식이라도 any를 쓰지 않고 some을 쓴다.
(3) Would [Wouldn't] you like + (대)명사?
▶ 한잔 드시겠습니까? Would you like a drink?
▶ 커피를 드시겠습니까? Would you like a coffee?
▶ 이 케이크를 좀더 드시겠습니까? Wouldn't you like a little more of this cake? (긍정문으로 하거나 부정문으로 하거나 의미는 변함이 없다)

3. …하지 않겠습니까?
Would you like to do?
▶ 춤을 추시지 않겠습니까? Would you like to dance?
▶ 저녁을 같이 드시지 않겠습니까? Would you like to have dinner with me?
▶ 테니스를 치지 않으시겠습니까? Wouldn't you like to play tennis? (긍정문이거나 부정문이거나 의미는 변함이 없다)
[어법]
Would [Wouldn't] you like to…?를 써서 권유를 나타내는 것은 스스럼없는 대화일 경우다.

4. …은 어떻습니까?; …은 어떻습니까?
What about …?; How about …? (…에는 명사나 do*ing*이 온다)
▶ 케이크 한 조각 어떻습니까? What [How] about a piece of cake?
▶ 휴일에 인천에 가는 것은 어떻습니까? What [How] about going to Inch'ŏn for our holidays?

5. 간접화법
(1) …하지 않겠느냐고 말했다[권했다]
invited *sb* **to do; asked** *sb* **to do**
▶ 그는 그날 저녁 자기들과 함께 저녁 식사를 하지 않겠느냐고 나에게 말했다 He invited [asked] me to have dinner with them that evening. (← He said to me, "Will you have dinner with us this evening?")
▶ 그들은 자기들과 함께 점심을 들지 않겠느냐고 우리에게 말했다 They invited [asked] us to join them at lunch. (← They said to us, "Will you join us at lunch?")
(2) …은 어떻겠느냐고 말했다
offered + 간접목적어 + 직접목적어; asked *sb* **if …would do**
▶ 그는 내게 커피 한 잔 더 어떠냐고 말했다 He offered me another cup of coffee. ⇌ He asked me if I would have another cup of coffee. (← He said to me, "Will you have another cup of coffee?")
▶ 그녀는 그에게 케이크를 좀더 들겠느냐고 말했다 She offered him some more cake. ⇌ She asked him if he would like some more cake. (← She said to him, "Would you like some more cake?")
[어법]
① 이들 구문은 Will you have…?; Would you like…?와 같이 목적어에 명사를 써서 「…은 어떻습니까?」를 의미하는 간접화법이다.
② offer를 쓰는 구문이 일반적이다.

권투 拳鬪 boxing; 〈프로 권투〉 a prizefight ━**권투하다** box 《with [against] *sb*》. ■ ━**경기** a boxing match; a fight ━**경기장** a ring ━**계** boxing circles ━**글러브[장갑]** boxing gloves

—선수 a boxer

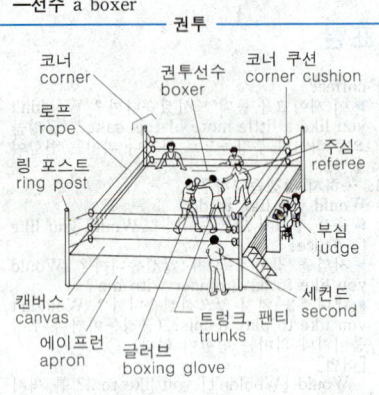

권투
- 코너 corner
- 권투선수 boxer
- 코너 쿠션 corner cushion
- 로프 rope
- 링 포스트 ring post
- 주심 referee
- 부심 judge
- 캔버스 canvas
- 세컨드 second
- 에이프런 apron
- 트렁크, 팬티 trunks
- 글러브 boxing glove

권패 卷貝 a conch 《*pl.* ~(e)s》 ⇨ 고둥, 소라

권하다 勸— 〈추천하다〉 recommend; 〈충고하다〉 advise; persuade; 〈제안하다〉 suggest; 〈내놓다〉 offer
▶나는 당신에게 이 방법을 권하오 I recommend that you take this method.
▶형은 나에게 이 사전을 권했다 My brother recommended this dictionary to me.
▶의사는 나에게 가벼운 운동을 권했다 The doctor advised me to take light exercise. ⇒ The doctor suggested that I take light exercise.
▶교수는 나에게 외국 유학을 권했다 The professor encouraged [advised] me to study abroad.
▶여승무원은 승객에게 캔디를 권했다 The stewardess offered candy to the passengers.
▶그는 내게 억지로 술을 권했다 He pressed wine on me. ⇒ He pressed me to drink the wine.

권한 權限 power; authority; 〔法〕〈관청 등의〉 competence; 〈권력의 한도〉 the limit(s) of authority [power]
◆권한이 있는 사람 a person in authority / 권한밖의 unauthorized; outside *one's* authority / 광범위한 권한을 가지다 have wide powers [broad authority] 《to do》 / 권한을 벗어나다 〔法〕 exceed *one's* competence [authority, powers]; be beyond the competence 《of》 / 권한을 위임하다 delegate authority [power] 《to》 / 권한을 주다 authorize *sb* 《to do》
▶당신은 명령할 권한이 없소 You don't have authority [power] to give orders.
▶그에게는 그럴 권한이 부여되어 있다 He is authorized [commissioned] to do that.
▶그것은 재판관의 권한을 벗어난 행위다 That exceeds the competence [authority] of a judge.
▶무슨 권한으로 내게 캐묻습니까? On what authority are you questioning me?

권한대행 權限代行 ■**대통령[총재]—** the acting President 학교장— the acting principal

권화 權化 an incarnation; (a) personification
◆악의 권화 the incarnation [personification] of evil; a devil incarnate
▶그녀는 사랑의 권화다 She is the embodiment [incarnation] of love.
▶그는 탐욕의 권화다 He is avarice itself. ⇒ He is the very personification of avarice.

궐기 蹶起 —궐기하다 rise 《against》; rouse *oneself* to action; rally
◆국민을 궐기시키다 stir up [rouse] people to action
▶학생들은 그 법안에 반대하여 궐기했다 The students rose in protest against the bill.
■**—대회** a rally: 증세(增稅) 반대 궐기대회 an anti-tax-increase rally

궐련 a cigarette; 〈엽궐련〉 a cigar ◆궐련 한 갑 a pack [packet] of cigarettes / 궐련을 피우다 smoke cigarettes; smoke a cigar / 궐련에 불을 붙이다 light (up) a cigarette
■**—갑** a cigarette case **—물부리** a cigarette holder

궐석 闕席 —궐석하다 make a default ▶피고는 재판에 궐석했다 The accused failed to appear in court.
■**—재판** judgment by default: 궐석 재판을 받다 be tried in *one's* absence / 궐석 재판에 회부하다 try *sb* in 《his》 absence

궐위 闕位 a vacancy; an unoccupied [unfilled] position [office] ◆궐위시는 in case of vacancy

궤 櫃 〈궤짝〉 a wooden chest [box]; a case; a coffer; a container; a tub ◆옷의 a clothes chest / 궤에 넣다 put [pack] *sth* in [into] a chest [box]

궤 軌 ◆궤를 같이하다 do in the same way; be the same (as)
▶그 두 사람은 궤를 같이한다 The two of them have [share] the same view. ⇒ Their opinions concur.

궤간 軌間 a (track) gauge; the gauge of a track ■**표준—** the standard gauge

궤도 軌道 1 〈철로〉 a (railroad) track; a railroad; 〈英〉 a railway track; a railway; 〈노면 전차의〉 a streetcar line; 〈英〉 a tramline
◆궤도를 부설하다 lay tracks [a line]

2 【천체 등의】 an orbit; an orbiting [orbital] path; 〈행성의〉 a circle; 〈유성의〉 a track
◆달의 궤도 the lunar [moon] orbit / 지구 주위를 도는 인공 위성 궤도 the orbit of a [an artificial] satellite around the earth / 위성의 궤도를 수정하다 adjust the orbit of a satellite / 궤도에 오르다 〈인공 위성 등이〉 go into [achieve] orbit / 궤도에 올라 있다 be in orbit / 인공 위성을 궤도에 올리다 put [place] a satellite in [into] orbit; orbit a satellite / 인공 위성을 궤도에 쏘아 올리다 launch [lift] a satellite into orbit / 궤도에서 벗어나다 go out of orbit

3 〈상궤〉 the beaten track
◆궤도를 벗어나다 stray from 《the main point》; deviate [digress] from 《the subject》 / 궤도에 오르다 〈일이〉 be started along the right lines; get going / 궤도에 올라 있다 be well under way; be on the (right) track / 궤도

에 올리다 set 《a business corporation》 on its way
▶ 계획은 궤도에 오르기 시작했다 The program is just getting under way.
■ 단선[복선]— a single [double] (railroad) track —면[축] the plane [axis] of an orbit —부설 track construction [laying] —비행 an orbital flight; orbiting —운동 an orbital motion —전자 orbital electron —차 (美) a streetcar; (英) a tram(car) —폭탄 an orbital bomb

궤란 潰爛 decomposition —**궤란하다** decompose

궤멸 潰滅 destruction; annihilation
▶ 우리는 적에게 궤멸적 타격을 주었다 We dealt our enemy a crushing [fatal] blow.
—**궤멸하다** be destroyed; be demolished; 〈전멸하다〉 be annihilated
▶ 그 도시는 대지진으로 궤멸되었다 The city was completely [totally] destroyed by the great earthquake.
▶ 또 한번 세계대전이 일어나면 전인류는 궤멸될 것이다 Another world war will annihilate the whole human race.

궤범 軌範 〈모범〉a model; an example; 〈기준〉a standard; a norm ♦ 궤범을 따르다 follow an example

궤변 詭辯 sophistry; sophism; a quibble
♦ 궤변의 sophistic; quibbling / 궤변을 농하다 use [employ] sophistry [sophisms]; quibble; chop logic
▶ 책임을 회피하려고 그는 궤변을 늘어놓았다 He used some clever talk to get out of his responsibility.
▶ 그는 궤변으로 요점을 얼버무렸다 He quibbled about the point.
■ —가 a sophist —학파 the sophists

궤양 潰瘍 〔醫〕 an ulcer ♦ 악성 궤양 a malignant ulcer / 궤양(성)의 ulcerative; ulcerous
■ 위— a gastric ulcer: 나는 위궤양이 생겼다 An ulcer has formed in my stomach.

궤적 軌跡 1 〈바퀴 자국〉a track 2 〈선인의〉the deeds of one's predecessors

궤조 軌條 〈선로〉a rail ♦ 궤조 파손에 의한 탈선 derailment caused by a broken rail

궤주 潰走 a disorderly retreat or flight following defeat; a rout
—**궤주하다** be routed; stampede
♦ 적을 궤주시키다 put the enemy to disorderly flight [retreat]
▶ 그의 연대는 궤주했다 His regiment retreated in disorder.

궤짝 櫃— a wooden box [chest] ♦ 감자를 궤짝에 넣다 pack potatoes in a box / 궤짝으로 주문하다 order sth by the case

귀 1 〈청각기관〉an ear; 〈청각〉hearing
♦ 귀의 aural; auricular / 한 쪽 귀로 듣고 한 쪽 귀로 흘리다 let 《an insult》 go in at one ear and out at the other
〈귀가〉 귀가 먹은 deaf / 귀가 따갑다 be noisy; be earsplitting / 귀가 번쩍 뜨이다 ⇨ 귀뜨이다 / 〈한 쪽〉 귀가 먹다 be deaf (of one ear) / 귀가 밝다 be quick of hearing; have quick [sharp] ears / 귀가 어둡다 be hard of hearing; have difficulty in hearing; be slightly deaf
▶ 나는 귀가 아프다 I have a pain in my ear. ⇌ I have an earache.
▶ 귀가 울린다 I have [There is] a ringing in my ears. ⇌ My ears are ringing [singing].
▶ 그녀는 귀가 작다 She has small ears.
▶ 그는 병으로 귀가 들리지 않게 되었다 He lost his hearing [He went deaf] because of an illness.
▶ 너한테 귀가 솔깃할 이야기가 있어 I have good news to tell you. ⇌ I have welcome news for you.
〈귀를〉 손으로 귀를 가리다 cover one's ears with one's hands / 귀를 쫑긋 세우다 prick up one's ears / 아무의 귀를 잡아당기다 pull sb by the ear
▶ 그들은 음악에 귀를 기울였다 (口) They were all ears listening to music. ⇌ They listened to music intently [with all their ears].
▶ 나는 귀를 기울여 들었지만 아무 것도 들리지 않았다 I listened [strained my ears], but heard [could hear] nothing.
▶ 누가 반대해도 그는 귀를 기울이지 않았다 No matter who opposed him, he wouldn't listen.
▶ 와장창 소리가 나서 나도 모르게 귀를 막았다 I covered my ears unconsciously when I heard a loud crash.
▶ 그의 말을 듣고 내 귀를 의심했다 When I heard what he said I couldn't believe my ears.
〈귀에(는)〉 귀에 연필을 꽂다 have a pencil (stuck) behind one's ear / 수화기를 귀에 대다 put [hold] the receiver to one's ear / 귀에 들어가다 reach [come to] one's ears; hear; learn
▶ 저 드릴 소리가 귀에 거슬린다 That drilling noise grates on [offends] my ear.
▶ 그에 관한 이상한 이야기가 귀에 들렸다 I heard [happened to hear] a strange story about him.
▶ 그의 말이 아직도 내 귀에 쟁쟁하다 His words still linger in my heart [ring in my ears]. ⇌ His words haunt my memory.
▶ 내 충고가 그의 귀에 거슬린 것 같다 My advice seems to have offended him.
▶ 그 이야기는 귀에 못이 박이도록 들었다 I have heard enough of the story. ⇌ I am sick and tired of hearing the story.
▶ 그것은 한국인의 귀에는 이상하게 들린다 It sounds strange to Korean ears.
▶ 목소리가 귀에 익어서 나는 전화 거는 사람이 누구인지 곧 알 수 있었다 I could guess who was speaking on the phone at once as it was a familiar voice.
▶ 나는 영어 방송이 귀에 익지 않아서 알아듣지 못한다 I can hardly understand English language broadcast because I am not used to listening to them.
2【모서리】an edge; a corner; 〈피륙의〉a selvage [selvedge] (of a fabric); a border (of cloth); 〈그릇의〉a lug
♦ 바둑판의 귀 a corner of the paduk board / 귀 달린 볼트 a lug bolt / 책장의 귀를 접다 turn down the edge of a page; dog-ear the page
3 〈바늘구멍〉 the eye of a needle ♦ 바늘 귀에

실을 꿰다 thread a needle
4 〈저고리의 아귀〉 a slit [an opening] (at the armpit of) a Korean coat [overcoat]; 〈섶끝〉 end of a neckband 《of Korean clothes》
5 〈우수리〉 an odd sum; a little extra ◆ 10만원에 귀가 달리다 be a little over one hundred thousand won

귀- 貴- 1 〈상대방〉 your (esteemed) ◆ 귀교 your school **2** 〈귀한〉 valuable; precious

귀가 歸家 coming [going] home; (a) return ◆ 귀가가 늦다 be late in coming [going] (back) home / 귀가를 서두르다 hurry back [home]
▶ 나는 귀가 중에 그를 만났다 I met him on my way home.
—귀가하다 go [come, return] home; 〈도착하다〉 get home
▶ 언제 귀가하셨지요? When did you get home?
▶ 아버님은 귀가하셨니? Has your father come [returned] home?
▶ 교실 청소가 끝나면 귀가해도 된다 You may go home after you finish cleaning the classroom.

귀감 龜鑑 a model of excellence; a paragon ◆ 교육자[군인]의 귀감 a model teacher [soldier] ▶ 그의 선행은 세상의 귀감이 되었다 His good conduct set an example for the world.

귀갑 龜甲 a tortoiseshell; the carapace of a turtle

귀객 貴客 an honored guest ⇨ 귀빈

귀거래 歸去來 homecoming after leaving *one's* government job

귀거칠다 unpleasant [offensive] to hear ◆ 귀거친 말 offensive words to hear ▶ 네 말은 귀거칠다 Your remarks are inexcusable [unpardonable].

귀걸이 〈방한용의〉 (a pair of) earmuffs; earflaps; earlaps; 〈장식품〉 an earring; a pair of earrings; an eardrop; 〈안경〉 spectacles with strings

귀결 歸結 〈결말〉 a conclusion; 〈결과〉 a result; a consequence
◆ 귀결 짓다 bring 《a matter》 to a conclusion [an end] / 귀결이 되다 come to the conclusion; end in
▶ 그가 입시에 실패한 것은 당연한 귀결이었다 It was a foregone conclusion that he would fail his entrance examination.
▶ 당연한 귀결로서 당은 두 파로 분열되었다 As a natural consequence [In the natural course of events] the party broke up into two factions.

귀경 歸京 ◆ 귀경길에 on *one's* return journey to Seoul; coming back to Seoul **—귀경하다** return to Seoul [the capital]; come [go] back to Seoul [the capital]

귀고리 an earring; a pair of earrings ◆ 귀고리를 달다 wear earrings

귀골 貴骨 〈귀인〉 a nobleman; an aristocrat; (총칭) the aristocracy; the nobility; 〈골상〉 noble features; a noble physiognomy

귀공자 貴公子 a young noble(man); a young aristocrat ◆ 귀공자다운 젊은이 a noble-looking young man; a young man with a noble [princely] appearance

귀교하다 歸校— return to school; go [come] back to school

귀국 貴國 your (esteemed) country

귀국 歸國 returning home from abroad; homecoming
◆ 귀국 보고회 a briefing [debriefing] session after *one* return from abroad / 강제 귀국을 당하다 be deported / 귀국을 명령받다 be ordered home
▶ 일행은 귀국길에 올랐다 The party left for home.
—귀국하다 return [come back, go back] to *one's* country; go [come, return] home
▶ 그는 내일 귀국한다 He comes [goes] home tomorrow.

귀금속 貴金屬 precious [noble] metals
■ **—상** 〈상인〉 a jeweler; a dealer in precious metals; 〈상점〉 a jewelry store [shop]

귀기 鬼氣 ◆ 귀기가 서린 광경 a ghostly [an unearthly, a bloodcurdling] sight

귀기울이다 listen to 《*sb*, what *sb* says》 attentively; bend *one's* ear 《to *sb*》

귀나다 1 〈일그러지다〉 be not at right angles; be distorted
2 〈의견이〉 disagree with; differ in opinion

귀납 歸納 〔論〕 induction
◆ 귀납적 추리 inductive reasoning / 귀납적으로 추리하다 reason inductively
—귀납하다 induce 《A from B》; make an induction 《from》
◆ 경험에서 일반적 원리를 귀납하다 induce general principles from *one's* experience
■ **—법** induction; the inductive method **—식** 〔數〕 a recursion formula; a recursion relation

귀넘어듣다 〈흘려듣다〉 pay no attention 《to》; take no notice 《of》; let pass; neglect; ignore

귀농 歸農 —귀농하다 return [go back] to farming ■ **—운동** a "back-to-the-land" movement

귀담아듣다 listen attentively [intently] to; be all ears; strain *one's* ears
▶ 그는 내 간청을 귀담아듣지 않았다 He turned a deaf ear to my pleas. ⇒ He would not listen to my pleas.

귀대 歸隊 ◆ 귀대 명령을 받다 be called in; 〈병사가〉 be ordered back into the ranks; 〈장교가〉 be ordered back to *one's* command
—귀대하다 return [go back] to *one's* unit [company]; 〈장교가〉 rejoin *one's* command

귀댁 貴宅 your (esteemed) home [house]

귀돌 a cornerstone; a quoin

귀동냥 learning by ear; secondhand knowledge
▶ 그는 귀동냥으로 많은 것을 배웠다 He has learned [picked up] a lot of things by listening to others.
—귀동냥하다 acquire knowledge by listening to others; listen and learn
◆ 귀동냥한 영어 English that *one* has picked up
▶ 천문학은 귀동냥한 정도입니다 I know a lit-

tle about [only a bit of] astronomy.
귀동이 貴童— a dear [loving, beloved] child
귀동자 貴童子 a beloved child ⇨ 귀동이
귀두 龜頭 〔解〕 the glans 《pl. -des》
귀때 〈그릇 주둥이〉 a spout ♦ 찻주전자의 귀때 the spout of a teapot **—그릇** a drinking vessel [container] with a spout **—동이[항아리]** a jar [pot] with a spout
귀뚜라미 〔昆〕 a cricket ♦ 귀뚜라미가 뜰에서 울고 있다 Crickets are chirping in the garden.
귀뚤귀뚤 ♦ 귀뚤귀뚤 울다 chirp; chirr; churr
귀뜨다 begin [start] to hear for the first time (in one's life); begin to receive and understand sound by using the ears
귀뜨이다 be brought to one's attention; 〈사물이 주어〉 be inviting [encouraging]
♦ 귀뜨이는 소식 welcome [encouraging, good] news / 귀뜨이는 조건 a tempting offer; inviting terms ▶ 그것은 그에게는 귀뜨이는 이야기였다 That was welcome news to him. = He was very glad [happy] to hear that.
귀띔 ♦ 귀띔을 받다 get a tip (for); receive a hint; receive confidential information ▶ 나는 그의 행방에 대해 귀띔을 받았다 I received a hint as to his whereabouts.
—귀띔하다 give sb a tip; (口) tip off; whisper; intimate ▶ 그는 사직한다고 나에게 귀띔해 주었다 He intimated to me that he intended to quit his job. ▶ 그가 그 사실을 내게 귀띔해 주었다 He tipped me off to the fact. ▶ 누군가가 도둑에게 경찰이 온다고 귀띔해 주었다 Someone tipped off the thieves that the police were coming.
귀로 歸路 the [one's] way home [back]
♦ 귀로에 on one's way home [back]; 〈여행의〉 on one's return trip / 귀로에 들르다 drop in [stop over] on one's way home / 귀로에 오르다 leave [start] for home; start on one's way home ▶ 그는 귀로를 서두르고 있었다 He was hurrying home. ▶ 그녀는 홀로 귀로에 올랐다 She made her way homeward all by herself.
귀류법 歸謬法 〔數〕 reduction to absurdity; (라) 〔論〕 reductio ad absurdum
♦ 귀류법으로 증명하다 prove sth by reductio ad absurdum
귀리 〔植〕 oats; an oat (plant) ■ **—죽** oatmeal (porridge)
귀마개 an earplug ♦ 귀마개를 하다 wear [use] an earplug
귀머거리 a deaf person ♦ 귀머거리가 되다 become deaf ▶ 그것을 못 들었다니 그 사람 귀머거리구나 He must be deaf not to have heard it.
귀먹다 become [go] deaf; be deafened; 〈상태〉 be hard of hearing; be deaf
귀면 鬼面 a devil's face; 〈탈〉 a devil mask
귀문 鬼門 the demon's gate; 〈지옥문〉 the entrance to hell
귀물 貴物 a precious [valuable] thing; a treasure; 〈희귀품〉 a rare article
귀밑 the root of the ear ▶ 그녀는 귀밑까지 빨개졌다 She blushed to the roots of her ears. ■ **—머리** hair braided behind the ears
귀밝다 (be) sharp-eared ♦ 그녀는 귀밝다 She is quick of hearing.
귀밝이(술) 〔民俗〕 wine served (on the first full-moon day of the lunar calendar year) hoping for sb to have good [sharp] ears; "ear-quickening wine"
귀부 龜趺 a turtle-shaped base (for a stone momument [pillar])
귀부인 貴夫人 your esteemed wife ⇨ 영부인 (令夫人)
귀부인 貴婦人 a lady; a noblewoman ♦ 귀부인다운 태도 ladylike manners
귀빈 貴賓 a distinguished [an honored] guest; a guest of honor ■ **—석** seats [a gallery] (reserved) for distinguished [honored] guests **—실** a (reception) room for special guests [VIPs]
귀뿌리 the root of the ear ⇨ 귀밑
귀사 貴社 your esteemed company [firm]
귀살스럽다, 귀살쩍다 all messed up; scattered; confused; distracted
귀상어 〔魚〕 a hammerhead(ed) shark
귀설다 unfamiliar; unaccustomed to hearing; strange
♦ 귀선 목소리 an unfamiliar voice / 귀선 이야기 an unusual [unheard of] story / 한국인에게는 귀선 지명 a place name unfamiliar to Koreans ▶ 귀선 소리가 들렸다 A strange sound came to [reached] my ears. = I heard [overheard] a strange sound.
귀성 歸省 homecoming; coming [going] home ▶ 그는 휴가로 귀성 중이다 He is (back) home for the holidays [vacation].
—귀성하다 go [come, return] home ■ **—객** homecoming people: 열차는 귀성객들로 혼잡했다 The train was crowded with people going home. **—버스** a bus for people going home for the holidays
귀소 歸巢 homing ■ **—본능[성]** the homing instinct
귀속 歸屬 〈복귀〉 return; reversion; 〈소관〉 jurisdiction; 〈소유〉 belonging
♦ 그 섬의 귀속 문제 the question of the title to the island
—귀속하다 〈재산 등이〉 revert ((to)); be returned; be restored; come under the jurisdiction ((of)); belong ((to)) ▶ 그 섬은 미국에 정식으로 귀속되었다 The island came formally under the jurisdiction of the U.S. ▶ 그녀의 재산은 아마 국고에 귀속될 것이다 Her property will probably revert to the state. ■ **—의식** a sense of belonging **—재산** government-vested property; property reverted to the government
귀순 歸順 submission; surrender **—귀순하다** submit; surrender ▶ 반란군은 항복하여 정부군에 귀순했다 The rebels surrendered and

swore allegiance to the government forces.
■—간첩 a surrendered espionage agent —자 a defector; a surrenderer

귀신 鬼神 〈넋〉 a (departed) soul [spirit]; 〈요괴〉 a specter; a ghost; 〈악령〉 an evil spirit; a demon; 〈비상한 전문가〉 a genius; a wizard
▶ 그는 이 회사에서 교정의 귀신이다 He is an ace proofreader [the king of the proofreaders] in this company.
▶ 이 집에는 귀신이 나온다고 한다 People say this house is haunted [a ghost appears in this house].
▶ 귀신이 나올 것 같은 밤이었다 It was a ghostly night.
▶ 나는 귀신을 믿지 않는다 I do not believe in ghosts.

귀싸대기 〈빰따귀〉 a cheek ◆ 귀싸대기를 갈기다 slap [hit, strike] *sb* on the face; box *sb's* ears

귀아프다 〈아프다〉 have a pain in *one's* ear; have an earache; 〈거슬리다〉 be unpleasant to hear; be offensive to the ear; 〈싫증나다〉 be sick [tired] of hearing
◆ 귀아프도록 잔소리하다 drum a lecture into *sb's* head; give *sb* a long lecture
▶ 나는 그 이야기를 귀아프게 들었다 I have heard enough of the story.

귀앓이 an earache =귓병

귀약 —藥 (a) medicine for earache; 〈액체의〉 eardrops
◆ 귀약을 넣다 apply eardrops

귀얄 a paintbrush

귀얄잡이 〈텁석부리〉 a bearded [whiskery] man

귀양 exile; banishment
◆ 죄인을 귀양보내다 condemn a criminal to exile / 귀양을 살다 live in exile / 귀양을 풀다 rescind *sb's* exile; release *sb* from banishment
▶ 그는 먼 섬으로 귀양갔다 He was exiled to a far-off island.
▶ 그는 귀양살다 죽었다 He died in exile.
▶ 그는 본국에서 이곳으로 귀양왔다 He was exiled [banished] from his native country to this place.
■—다리 an exile —살이 living in exile

귀에지 earwax ⇨ 귀지

귀엣고리 an earring ⇨ 귀고리

귀엣말 whispering; (in) a whisper —귀엣말하다 whisper *sth* in [into] *sb's* ear ◆ 밖으로 나가자[그리가 왔다]고 귀엣말하다 whisper to *sb* to get out [that she have come]

귀여겨듣다 listen attentively ⇨ 귀담아듣다

귀여리다 credulous; gullible
▶ 그녀는 남의 말에 무척 귀여리다 She is very credulous. = She readily takes people at their word.

귀여워하다 love; pet; make a pet of; treat *sb* with love [affection]
▶ 그 여선생님은 학생들을 귀여워한다 She is very good to [loves] her pupils.
▶ 어머니들은 흔히 자식들을 너무 귀여워한다 Mothers often pamper their children.
▶ 그녀는 그 개를 아주 귀여워한다 She loves the dog dearly. = She takes loving care of the dog.

귀염 affection; love ▶ 그 소년은 이웃 사람들의 귀염을 받고 있다 The boy is loved by his neighbors. = The boy is a favorite with his neighbors.

귀염둥이 a favorite [beloved] child; a darling child

귀염성 charm; loveliness; a lovable nature
◆ 순진한 어린애의 귀염성 the charm of an innocent child / 귀염성 없는 아이 a child without the winning ways of children; an unendearing child / 귀염성이 있는 charming; lovely; lovable
▶ 그녀가 하는 짓은 귀염성이 넘친다 She is full of loveliness in her ways.

귀엽다 cute; charming; lovely; dear; winning
◆ 귀여운 아이 a lovely little child / 귀여운 인형 a cute doll
▶ 참 귀여운 소녀로군 What a cute [pretty] girl (she is)! = How cute she is!
▶ 그녀는 귀엽게 생겼다 She has a lovely face [looks lovely].

귀영 歸營 —귀영하다 return to barracks
■—나팔 (軍) a call to quarters —시간 the time [deadline] to return to barracks

귀울다 *one's* ears ring; have a buzzing [ringing] in the ears

귀울음 ringing [buzzing] in the ears

귀의 歸依 —귀의하다 become a believer in; 〈개종하다〉 convert to ◆ 기독교에 귀의하다 embrace Christianity; be converted to Christianity / 불교에 귀의하다 become a Buddhist
■—자 a believer; a follower; 〈개종자〉 a convert

귀이개 an earcleaner; an ear pick

귀인 貴人 a noble man; an aristocrat; a man of rank; a dignitary; a VIP ■—상 a noble face [countenance]

귀일 歸一 —귀일하다 come to be united; result in [come to] one (thing); be united into one ■—법 the unitary method

귀임 歸任 return(ing) to *one's* post
▶ 대사는 내일 귀임길에 오른다 The ambassador will leave tomorrow to resume his official duties.
—귀임하다 return to *one's* post; resume *one's* official duties

귀잠 a sound [deep] sleep ◆ 귀잠 들다 be sound asleep; fall fast asleep; sleep like a log

귀재 鬼才 〈재능〉 exceptional [unusual] talent; genius; 〈사람〉 a (man of) genius; (口) a wizard ◆ 금세기 최고의 바이올린의 귀재 the greatest violinist of this century

귀저 貴著 your (esteemed) book [work]; the book you wrote

귀적 鬼籍 ◆ 귀적에 들다 die; join the ranks of the dead

귀접스럽다 〈더럽다〉 dirty; untidy; filthy; 〈인품이〉 mean; nasty; indecent

귀제비 (鳥) a striated swallow

귀족 貴族 〈개인〉 a nobleman; a noblewoman (여자); an aristocrat; (英) a peer; (총칭) the nobility; (英) the aristocracy; the peerage
◆ 귀족적인 취미 aristocratic taste / 귀족과 평

민 peers and commoners / 귀족의 noble; aristocratic
▶그녀의 남편은 귀족 출신이다 Her husband is a nobleman [of noble birth].
■—계급 the aristocratic class —기질 aristocratism —사회 the aristocracy; aristocratic circles —원 (英) the House of Lords —정치 aristocracy

귀중 貴中 Messrs. (▶Messieurs의 약어임)
♦존슨 회사 귀중 Messrs. Johnson & Co. / 서울대학교 교무과 귀중 (To) the Department of Curriculum and Instruction, Seoul National University

귀중중하다 dirty; filthy; untidy; shabby

귀중품 貴重品 an article of value; valuable things; (총칭) valuables ♦귀중품을 금고에 보관하다 keep valuables in a safe ■—(보관)실 a safe; a vault; a treasure room

귀중하다 貴重— valuable 《experiences》; precious; priceless

> 解說 *valuable*은 금액이나 그 유용성으로 보아 가치가 높다는 뜻. *precious*는 금전으로 평가할 수 없는 귀중함을 그 자체가 가지고 있다는 뜻이다.

▶그의 충고가 나의 연구에 매우 귀중했다 His advice was invaluable [most valuable] to my research.
▶귀중한 시간을 내주셔서 감사합니다 Thank you for sparing me your precious time.

귀지 earwax; (醫) cerumen ♦귀지를 후벼내다 clean the wax out of *one's* ears

귀지 貴紙 your (esteemed) paper ♦귀지 10월 3일자에 의하면 according to your paper dated October 3

귀지 貴誌 your (esteemed) magazine

귀착 歸着 1 〈귀환〉 return; coming back —귀착하다 return 《to》; come [get] back; arrive [get] home
2 〈귀결〉 a conclusion; an outcome —귀착하다 arrive at 《a conclusion》; result in; (口) boil down to
▶결국은 돈 문제에 귀착한다 Ultimately it comes [boils] down to a question of money.
▶귀착하는 바는 똑같다 It comes [amounts] to the same thing.

귀찮다 annoying; troublesome; harassing; disturbing; (美口) pesky
♦귀찮은 문제 a troublesome matter / 귀찮은 일 (bring in)a troublesome [bothersome, pesky] task / 귀찮게 persistently; annoyingly / 귀찮게 해서 미안합니다만… I am sorry to bother [trouble] you, but… / 귀찮은 질문을 하다 ask a pesky question / 귀찮아하다 feel annoyed with [at]; consider annoying / 귀찮게 굴다 behave in an annoying way; annoy [bother, trouble] *sb*
▶정말 귀찮군 What a nuisance!
▶세상이 귀찮다 I am sick (and tired) of the world.
▶그는 귀찮은 일은 아무 것도 하지 않는다 He won't do anything troublesome.
▶나는 외출하는 것이 귀찮아서 집에 있었다 I felt too tired [weary] to go out, and stayed at home.
▶공부할 때는 귀찮게 하지 말아 주세요 Please don't disturb me [Leave me alone] while I'm studying.
▶그녀는 그의 간섭을 귀찮아한다 She regards his interference as a nuisance. ⇌ She considers his interference annoying.
▶그는 목욕탕에 가는 것을 매우 귀찮아했다 He thought it too much trouble to go to the (public) bath.
▶그녀는 아이들이 졸졸 따라다녀도 조금도 귀찮아하는 것 같지 않다 She does not look at all annoyed [doesn't seem to mind at all] when children tag along after her.
▶그는 나의 질문을 귀찮아하지 않고 친절하게 대답해 주었다 He answered my questions kindly without regarding them [me] as a nuisance.

귀천 貴賤 the noble and base; the high and low ♦귀천의 구별 없이 without distinction of rank [position]; regardless [irrespective] of rank; high and low alike
▶직업에는 귀천이 없다 All (legitimate) occupations [honest trades] are equally honorable.

귀청 the eardrum ♦귀청이 떨어질 것 같은 굉음 an earsplitting [a deafening] roar

귀추 歸趨 1 〈경향〉 a tendency; a trend ♦여론의 귀추를 살피다 see the trend of public opinion / 사태의 귀추를 주시하다 watch how the situation develops
2 〈귀결〉 an outcome; a consequence ▶일의 귀추를 보고 나서 결정하자 Let's see how things turn out before we decide.

귀축 鬼畜 a brute; a savage; a fiend ♦귀축같은 인간 diabolically devil [wicked] man; a brutal [fiendish] man

귀태 貴態 a noble [princely] appearance ♦귀태가 나다 be [look] noble; be elegant [graceful]

귀퉁이 a corner; an edge ♦책상 귀퉁이 the corners of a desk

귀하 貴下 〈당신〉 you; 〈님〉 Mr.; Esquire (略 Esq.); Mrs.; Mme; Miss; Ms.(여자) ♦앤디 바우어 귀하 Mr. Andy Bauer / 샌드라 맥슨 귀하 Mrs. [Ms.] Sandra Maxon

귀하다 貴— 1 〈신분이〉 noble; aristocratic; 〈귀중하다〉 precious; valuable; 〈진귀하다〉 unique; uncommon; 〈흔치 않다〉 rare
♦귀한 경험 a unique [valuable] experience / 귀한 물건 a precious object; a rarity / 귀한 분 a person of high rank; a noble personage / 당신의 귀한 시간 your precious time
▶그의 부인은 귀한 집안 출신이다 His wife comes from an aristocratic [a noble] family. ⇌ His wife is of noble birth.
▶이것은 귀한 것이니 잃어버리지 않도록 해라 This is a very valuable thing. Don't lose it.
▶그 경험은 나에게 아주 귀한 것이었다 The experience was most valuable [most precious, of great value] to me.
2 〈귀여다〉 lovable; darling; dear ♦내 귀한 아들 my dear [darling] boy [son]

귀한 貴翰 your (esteemed) letter ⇨ 귀함
귀한 그릇 쉬 깨진다 (속담) The good die young. ≒ The fairest flowers soonest fade. ≒ Those whom God loves do not live long.
귀한 자식 매로 키워라 Spare the rod, and spoil the child.
귀함 貴函 your (esteemed) letter ◆3월 5일자 귀함 your letter of [dated] March 5
귀함하다 歸艦─ return to one's (war)ship
귀항 歸航 a return [homeward] voyage
◆귀항길에 오르다 start home; start on one's homeward voyage ─**귀항하다** make a homeward voyage; sail home
─**선** a homebound vessel
귀항 歸港 returning to port ─**귀항하다** return to port; go [come] back to port
귀향 歸鄕 going home; (美) homecoming ─**귀향하다** go [come] (back) to one's hometown; return home [to one's birthplace]
귀화 歸化 naturalization
─**귀화하다** be naturalized
▶그는 한국인으로 귀화했다 He became a naturalized Korean citizen. ≒ He was naturalized as a Korean citizen.
▶그는 귀화한 미국인이다 He is American by naturalization.
■─**식물** a naturalized plant ─**인** a naturalized person (citizen); 〔英法〕a denizen
귀환 歸還 one's return (home); 〈외국에서의〉 repatriation ◆귀환병 a returned [repatriated] soldier
─**귀환하다** return (home) ◆지구에 무사히 귀환하다 return to earth safely
▶전투기는 기지에 귀환했다 The fighter plane returned to base.
귀환자 歸還者 a returnee; 〈본국 송환자〉 a repatriate ◆미귀환자 those who haven't returned [repatriated] (from Sakhalin)
귀휴 歸休 ◆일시 귀휴 중인 근로자 a laid-off worker / 귀휴 중이다 be on leave from the service
■─**병** a soldier on leave ─**제도** 〈군대의〉 the leave [(美) furlough] system; 〈근로자의〉 the layoff system
귓가 the folded rim around the outer ear
▶그의 말이 귓가에 생생하다 His words still ring in my ears [linger in my heart, haunt my memory].
귓결 ◆귓결에 듣다 hear by chance; happen to hear ▶그가 이혼한다는 말을 귓결에 들었다 I heard [happened to hear] that he was going to get divorced.
귓구멍 the opening of the ear; an ear hole
◆귓구멍을 후비다 pick [clean] one's ears
귓등 the back of the ear
◆귓등으로도 듣지 않다 take no notice (of); pay no attention (to); ignore
▶그는 내 충고를 귓등으로 들었다 He paid no attention to [took no notice of, neglected] my advice.
귓머리 hair braided behind the ears = 귀밑 (~머리)
귓문 ─**門** the external auditory canal; the opening of the ear; a tragus (pl. -gi)

귓바퀴 the external part of the ear; a concha (pl. -chae); an auricle
귓밥 (the thickness of) an earlobe; 〈귀지〉 earwax
귓병 ─**病** an earache
귓불 an earlobe ◆귓불만 만지다 do not know what to do; be at one's wit's [wits'] end ▶그는 귓불이 두툼하다 He has thick earlobes.
귓속 the inside of the ear ◆귓속에 속삭이다 whisper in [into] sb's ear ─**다짐** a whispered promise
귓속말 whispering; a whisper
◆아무에게 귓속말을 하다 whisper to sb [in sb's ear]; whisper with [to] sb / 귓속말로 말하다 speak in a whisper [in whispers]; 〈서로〉 whisper to each other; talk in whispers
귓전 the folded rim around the outer ear
◆귓전에 대고 close to sb's ear / 귓전에서 about one's ears / 귓전에 대고 소리치다 yell into sb's ear
▶희미한 소리가 귓전에 들렸다 A faint sound reached my ears. ≒ I (over)heard a faint sound.
규격 規格 a standard
◆규격 외의 nonstandardized; substandard / 규격 미달의 substandard; below (the) standard / 규격을 통일하다 standardize
▶이 물품은 규격에 맞지 않는다 This article doesn't meet [is below, is not up to] the standards [requirements].
■─**품** a standardized article : 규격 미달품 an article below standards
규격화 規格化 standardization ─**규격화하다** standardize ◆자동차 부품을 규격화하다 standardize parts for [of] cars
규례 規例 rules (and regulations)
규명 糾明 a close [searching] examination
▶진상 규명 위원회가 구성되었다 A fact-finding committee was formed.
─**규명하다** investigate thoroughly; examine closely [minutely]; look [inquire] into (a matter); make an exhaustive study
◆사태의 진상을 규명하다 investigate the truth of the matter; inquire [look] into the true state of things
▶우리는 이 증수회 건을 철저하게 규명할 것이다 We will carry out a thorough investigation of [into] this payoff case.
규모 規模 1 〈크기〉 a scale; size; 〈범위〉 scope; 〈구조〉 structure
◆규모가 큰[작은] large-scale [small-scale]; of large [small] dimensions / 세계적인 규모로 on a world scale; on an international scale / 규모를 확대[축소]하다 enlarge [reduce] the scale
▶그 둘은 규모가 전혀 다르다 The two are quite different in scale [size].
▶그 회사의 규모는 어떻습니까? How big is that company?
▶그들은 그 운동을 전국적 규모로 계획하고 있다 They are planning the campaign on a nationwide scale.
2 〈씀씀이의 정도〉 planned spending; good (household) management ▶그녀는 규모있는

살림꾼이다 She is a good [an efficient] household manager.

규방 閨房 〈아낙네의〉 a lady's living room; women's quarters; 〈침실〉 a bedchamber
■ —문학 literature describing noble women's lives (in the feudal age); literature of the inner room

규벌 閨閥 〈처가 세력〉 a faction centered around *one's* wife's families and relatives

규범 規範 〈기준〉 a standard; a norm; 〈모범〉 a model; an example ◆ 규범적인 prescriptive / 행동의 규범이 되다 be a model of (good) behavior
■ —문법 normative [prescriptive] grammar

규사 硅砂 silica [quartz] sand; silica

규산 硅酸 〔化〕 silicic acid ■ —염 (a) silicate —점토 siliceous clay

규석 硅石 〔鑛〕 silex; silica; silicon dioxide

규소 硅素 〔化〕 silicon ■ —수지 silicone resins —화합물 a silicide

규수 閨秀 1 〈처녀〉 a maiden; a girl from a good family ◆ 이씨 댁 규수 Mr. Lee's daughter; Miss Lee
2 〈학식있는 여자〉 an accomplished lady
■ —시인[작가, 화가] a woman poet [writer, painter]

규암 硅岩 〔地質〕 quartzite

규약 規約 〈약정〉 an agreement; a contract; 〈규칙〉 rules (▶ 전체를 말할 때는 항상 복수); rules and regulations
◆ 규약을 맺다 make an agreement 《with》/ 규약을 정하다 make [lay down] rules / 규약을 지키다[위반하다] fulfill [break] the terms of an agreement
▶ 위원회는 규약의 개정을 토의했다 The committee discussed the revision of the rules and regulations.

규율 規律 1 〈질서〉 order; discipline
◆ 학교의 규율 school discipline / 규율이 엄한 strict in discipline / 규율이 있는 orderly; (well-)disciplined / 규율이 없는 disorderly; undisciplined / 규율을 유지하다 maintain discipline
▶ 그 소년들은 규율있는 생활을 하고 있다 The boys are living in an orderly life.
▶ 이 학교의 규율은 흐트러져 있다 Discipline is lax [loose, slack] at this school.
▶ 군대의 규율은 매우 엄격하다 Discipline is strictly enforced in the army. ⇌ Military discipline is very strict.
2 〈규칙〉 rules; regulations
◆ 규율에 어긋나다 be against the rules [regulations]
▶ 규율을 어기는 자는 처벌받는다 If anyone breaks a rule [fails to follow the rules], he will be punished.
▶ 규율을 지켜야 한다 You should observe the rules [regulations].

규정 規定 rules; regulations; 〈조항〉 provisions; 〈계약의〉 stipulations
◆ 개정된 규정 revised regulations / 부수 규정 supplementary rules / 직무 규정 the office regulations / 규정에 따라서 according to [in conformity with] the rules / 규정을 따르다 obey [follow] the rules / 규정을 만들다 make rules [provisions]; frame regulations / 규정을 어기다 go against [violate] the rules
▶ 제23조의 규정에 의해 그는 3만원의 벌금에 처해졌다 According to the provisions of Article 23, he was fined thirty thousand won.
▶ 기숙사의 규정으로는 10시까지 돌아와야 한다 The dormitory regulations require that you return by 10 o'clock.

—**규정하다** prescribe; 〈법률이〉 provide; 〈계약이〉 stipulate
◆ 규정된 서식 the prescribed form / 규정된 절차를 밟다 go through the necessary formalities; follow the prescribed procedure
▶ 우리 시의 건축법은 이 지역에서는 10층 이상의 건물은 짓지 못하도록 규정하고 있다 The building law in our city provides [stipulates] that no building higher than ten stories may be built in this area.
▶ 그것은 법으로 규정되어 있다 It is prescribed by law. ⇌ It is provided in the law.
■ —론 〔哲〕 determinism —액 〔化〕 a normal solution —요금 the regulation [standard] charge —종목 〈체조 등의〉 compulsory exercises —집 a directory

규정식 規定食 a (prescribed) diet ◆ 환자에게 규정식을 급식하다 put a patient on a special diet

규제 規制 control; regulation; restriction
◆ 언론 규제 법규 laws enacted to control press activities / 법적 규제를 가하다 impose legal controls 《on》
—**규제하다** control; regulate
▶ 파업은 법으로 규제되어 있다 Strikes are regulated by law.
■ 교통— traffic control: 이곳은 교통 규제가 필요하다 We need to control [regulate] traffic here. ⇌ Traffic control is needed here. 배기 가스— exhaust controls 자율— voluntary control: 수출을 자율 규제하다 control [curb] exports voluntarily

규조 硅藻 〔植〕 a diatom ■ —토 diatomite; diatomaceous earth

규준 規準 a standard; 〈판단 등의〉 a criterion (*pl.* ~s, -ria) ◆ 판단의 규준 a criterion of judgment

규중 閨中 a lady's private sitting room; a boudoir ◆ —처녀 a girl (from a good family) brought up under home discipline; an innocent girl of a good family

규칙 規則 a rule; a regulation
◆ 엄한 규칙 a rigid rule / 규칙적인 regular; orderly / 규칙대로 according to the rule / 규칙을 정하다 make [lay down, establish] rules [regulations] / 규칙을 개정하다 amend [revise] the rules / 규칙을 따르다 follow [observe, obey] the rules / 규칙을 무시하다 disregard the set rules / 규칙을 어기다 go against [break, violate] the rules / 규칙을 폐지하다 abolish a rule
▶ 이 학교는 규칙이 엄하다 This school has strict rules. ⇌ Strict discipline is enforced at this school.
▶ 예외 없는 규칙은 없다 There is no rule that

doesn't have exceptions [but has exceptions]. ⇌ There are exceptions to all rules.
▶ 우리 학교에서는 만사를 규칙대로 해야 한다 In our school we are supposed to do everything according to the rules.
▶ 만사가 규칙대로 되는 것은 아니다 Everything does not go by rule.
■ 교통— traffic rules; 〈법규〉 traffic regulations 취업— office [company] regulations ■ —동사 〔文法〕 a regular verb —위반 a breach [violation] of the rules [regulations]: 여기서 주차하는 것은 규칙 위반이다 It is against [a violation of] the rules to park a car here.

규칙적 規則的 regular; orderly ◆규칙적으로 regularly; methodically
▶ 규칙적인 생활을 해야 한다 You must lead a regular [well-regulated] life.
▶ 나는 규칙적으로 공부하고 있다 I have regular study habits.

규탄 糾彈 denouncement; censure; 〈비난〉 accusation; 〈탄핵〉 impeachment
—규탄하다 charge; accuse; denounce 《sb as a traitor》; censure
▶ 그들은 그의 수뢰를 규탄했다 They accused him of taking bribes.
▶ 그는 그 문제로 정부를 규탄했다 He censured the government on the question.

규토 硅土 〔化〕 silica; silex

규폐증 硅肺症 〔醫〕 silicosis ■ —환자 a silicosis victim; a silicotic

규합 糾合 (a) rally —규합하다 draw [call] persons together for a common action ◆동지를 규합하다 rally [call together] men of like mind

규화 硅化 〔鑛〕 silicification —규화하다 silicify; become silicified ■ —물 a silicide —석 woodstone

균 菌 a germ (▶ 일반적인 말. 의학 용어로는 다음과 같이 구별함: 세균 a microbe; 바이러스 a virus; 박테리아 bacteria; 간상균 a bacillus; 버섯 등의 균 a fungus)
◆균의 배양 bacteria cultivation / 균을 가진 사람 〈보균자〉 a germ carrier

균등 均等 equality; uniformity; evenness; 〔法〕 parity
◆교육의 기회 균등 equal opportunity in [for] education / 균등한 equal; even; uniform / 균등하게 equally; evenly; uniformly / 균등하게 나누다 divide sth equally [into equal parts] / 균등하게 비용을 부담하다 share the expenses equally
▶ 우리는 균등한 대우를 요구한다 We demand equal treatment.
■ —대표제 an equal representation —할(割) per capita rate: 이익을 균등하다 divide up the profits on a per capita basis —화(化) equalization; 균등화하다 equalize; make sth equal; (口) even sth up —화법 〔美術〕 isometric drawing

균류 菌類 the fungi ■ —학 fungology —학자 a fungologist

균분 均分 equal division —균분하다 divide [share] equally ■ —상속 inheritance by equal distribution —상속법 law of descent and distribution

균사 菌絲 〔植〕 a hypha 《pl. -phae》 ■ —체 a mycelium 《pl. -lia》

균산 菌傘 〈버섯의〉 a pileus 《pl. -lei》

균열 龜裂 a crack; a fissure; a split; a break; a rupture
◆균열이 생기다 crack; be cracked; split; break 《with》
▶ 그 건물 벽에는 균열이 있다 There are several cracks in the walls of the building.
▶ 지진으로 땅에 균열이 생겼다 The ground (was) fissured owing to the earthquakes.
▶ 노동조합의 결속에 균열이 생겼다 Cracks appeared in the labor coalition.

균일 均一 uniformity; equality
◆430원 균일 운임 a uniform fare of 430 won / 한 개 1,000원 균일로 팔다 sell at a flat rate [uniform price] of one thousand won a piece —균일하다 even; uniform; equal
◆균일한 uniform; 〈값 등이〉 flat; same / 균일하게 하다 make things uniform; equalize / 수수료를 균일하게 하다 standardize handling charges [fees]
▶ 가격은 균일하다 They are of a uniform price.
▶ 그녀는 케이크를 균일하게 나누었다 She devided the cake into equal parts [into pieces of equal size].
■ —가격 a uniform [flat] price —요금 a flat rate —요금 제도 the uniform rate system

균점하다 均霑— share in equality ◆이익을 균점하다 have [get] equal shares [allotment] of the profits

균제 均齊 symmetry; balance; harmony
◆균제된 well-balanced; symmetrical; well-proportioned
▶ 이 그림은 균제미로 유명하다 This picture is noted for its beauty of proportion [its symmetrical beauty].

균질 均質 homogeneity ◆균질적인 homogeneous ■ —우유 homogenized milk —체 a homogeneous substance

균차 均差 〔天〕 inequality; equation

균할 均割 equal division [allocation] ⇨ 균분 (均分)

균형 均衡 balance; equilibrium
◆마음의 균형 mental equilibrium / 세력의 균형 the balance of power / 수요와 공급의 균형 the equilibrium of demand and supply / 균형이 잡혀 있다 be (well-)balanced; be in balance [equilibrium] / 균형을 깨뜨리다 upset [destroy] the balance / 균형을 유지하다 keep [hold] the balance; maintain the equilibrium / 균형을 잃다 lose the balance / 균형을 회복하다 restore [regain] the balance
▶ 수출입의 균형이 잘 잡혀 있다 There is a good balance between exports and imports. ⇌ Imports and exports are well-balanced.
▶ 그는 몸의 균형을 잃고 쓰러졌다 He lost his balance and fell.
▶ 건강은 일과 놀이의 적절한 균형을 유지함으로써 가장 잘 유지된다 Health is best preserved by maintaining an adequate balance

between work and play.
■一가격 an equilibrium price 一발전 a balanced development 一예산 a balanced budget 一점 the equilibrium point

귤 橘 an orange; 〈중국 원산의〉 a mandarin (orange); a tangerine (▶mandarin의 일종) ◆귤 한 쪽 a section of a tangerine
■一껍질 (an) orange peel: 귤껍질을 벗기다 peel an orange 一나무 an orange [a citrus] tree 一농장 an orange orchard [plantation]

그¹ 1 〈그 사람〉 he ◆그의 his / 그 자신 himself / 그의 것 his / 그가[는] he / 그를[에게] him ▶ 그는 뉴욕에 있다 He is in New York.
▶ 그는 정직한 사람이다 He is an honest man.
2 〈그것〉 it; that ◆그 때문에 for that reason; on that account; consequently

그² 〈형용사적〉 that; those; the
◆그날 that [the] day / 그 때 then; (at) that time; in those days / 그 당시 (in) those days / 그 사람 that person; that [the] man [woman]
▶ 그 가방은 어디서 샀니? Where did you buy that bag?
▶ 그 남자는 누구니? Do you know who that man is?
▶ 그 때는 나도 젊었었다 I was young in those days.
▶ 내가 말하고 싶었던 것이 바로 그거다 That's exactly what I wanted to say.
▶ 그 이야기는 그만 합시다 Let's drop that subject.

그간 一間 in the meantime ⇨ 그동안

그같이 like that; (in) that way; thus; so
▶ 그같이 하는 것이 상책이다 There is nothing like doing so.
▶ 그같이 재미있는 이야기는 난생 처음이다 I've never heard a more charming story.

그건그렇고 by the way; by the by(e); well; now
▶ 그건 그렇고 다음 모임은 언제입니까? Well, then, when shall we have our next meeting?
▶ 그건 그렇고 어제 송 선생이 만났나요? By the way, did you see Mr. Song yesterday?

그것 that one; that thing; that; it
◆그것은 그렇지만 It may be so, but... / 그것은 제쳐놓고 setting it aside; apart from that; be that as it may
▶ 바로 그것이다 That's (just) it!
▶ 그것은 어느 개인 날의 일이었다 It was [happened] on a fine day.
▶ 그것은 무슨 책이니? What kind of book is that?
▶ [會話] 「그것은 뭐니?」 「지도야」 "What's that?" "It is a map."
▶ 그것을 보여주시오 Show me that one.
▶ 그것만은 못하겠다 I will do anything but that.
▶ 그것만으로는 시가 되지 않아 That alone will not make a poem.
▶ 그는 새 차를 샀다, 그것도 외제 차를 He bought a new car, and a foreign one at that.
▶ 그것보다 이것이 좋다 This is better than that.

그게 〈그것이〉 it; that ▶ 그게 어쨌다는 거냐? So what? ▶ 그게 그거다 There is little difference between the two.

그곳 that place; there; 〈상대방이 있는 곳〉 your place
◆그곳에 to that place; there; over there / 그곳에서 there; in that place
▶ 그곳은 형편이 어떤지요? How are things going on in your place?
▶ 그곳은 다들 별고 없으신지요? Are you all getting along well?
▶ 너는 월요일에 그곳을 떠나는 것이 좋다 You had better leave there on Monday.
▶ 나는 그곳까지 그녀와 함께 가지 않았다 I didn't go with her that far.

그글피 three days after tomorrow; four days from today; four days hence

그까지로 〈겨우 그만한 일로〉 by such a trifle
▶ 그까지로 걱정하지 마라 Don't worry about such a small thing.
▶ 그까지로 울면 모두가 웃을 것이다 People will laugh at you if you cry over such a little thing.
▶ 그까지로 놀랄 내가 아니다 I am not the [a] man to be startled by such a trifle.

그까짓 〈겨우 그 정도의〉 so trifling; so trivial; 〈그 같은〉 like that
◆그까짓 일 so trifling a matter; such a trivial matter; such trifles; a trifle like that
▶ 그까짓 것 Oh! It is nothing.
▶ 그까짓 일이라면 쉽게 해 줄 수 있다 That is an easy request to satisfy.
▶ 그까짓 일로 울다니 You must not weep over a trifle like that.
▶ 그까짓 일로 놀라지는 않는다 You can't surprise me with anything so trivial as that.

그끄러께 three years ago; two years before last ▶ 우리는 그끄러께 여기에 왔다 We came here two years before last.

그끄저께 three days back [ago]; two days before yesterday

그나마 at that; and that; still; even so
▶ 그 집에서는 커피 한 잔에 4천원이나 했는데 그나마 맛도 신통치 않았다 They charged four thousand won for a cup of coffee and not a very good one at that.
▶ 그는 황급히 외출했다, 그나마 행선지도 알리지 않고 He went out hurriedly, and that without saying where he was going.

그날 (on) that day; 〈강조하여〉 (on) the very [same] day; ((on)) that particular day
◆그날 그날 every day; daily; from day to day; day after [by] day / 그날 따라 on that particular day; on that day of all days (in the year) / 그날 중으로 before the day is over; by the end of the day; within the day / 그날 그날 겨우 먹고 살다 live from hand to mouth; earn a precarious living; scrape a living day by day
▶ 그날이 그날이다 Each day is just like every other day.
▶ 나는 그날로 서울로 돌아왔다 I returned to Seoul the same day.

그냥 1 〈변함없이〉 as it stands; as it is; in the same way as before; intact; still
◆그냥 그대로 있다 remain as it was; remain

그냥 intact; be left untouched / 그냥 두다 let 《it》 stand [go]; leave *sth* as it is [stands]; leave intact
▶ 부모님은 죽은 형의 방을 여러 해 동안 그냥 놔두고 계신다 My parents left my dead brother's room untouched [exactly as it was] for all these years.
▶ 그 문제를 그냥 내버려 둘 수는 없다 We cannot afford to leave [let] the matter alone. ⇒ The matter cannot be allowed to stand as it is.
2 〈줄곧〉 all the time [way]; throughout; (all) through; continuously
♦ 그냥 서 있다 keep standing; stay on *one's* feet / 그냥 울고만 있다 do nothing but cry
▶ 이제까지 그냥 여기에 있었니? Have you been here all the time?
▶ 그는 일생을 그냥 독신으로 지냈다 He remained single all through his life.

그네 a swing; (美)〈서커스의〉 a trapeze
♦ 그네를 구르다 rock back and forth a swing / 그네를 매다 put up a swing
▶ 그네를 뛰자 Let's go on a swing [have a swing].
▶ 아이 둘이 그네를 뛰고 있었다 Two children were playing on the swing.

그네(들) those people; they; them ▶ 왼쪽 방이 그네들 방이다 The room on the left is theirs.

그녀 —女 she; 〈애인〉 one's sweetheart [(口) girl] ♦ 그녀의[에게, 를] her / 그녀 자신 herself / 그녀의 것 hers

그놈 that fellow [(美) guy, (俗) bastard, (英) blighter]
▶ 그놈이 그놈이다 They're all bastards! ⇒ There is little to choose between them.
▶ 그놈은 머리가 나쁘다 That fellow [guy] is dull.

그늘 1 〈응달〉 shade; shadow
♦ 나무 그늘 the shade of a tree / 그늘에서 말리다 dry *sth* in the shade
▶ 나무 그늘에 의자가 하나 있었다 There was a chair in [under] the shade of the tree.
▶ 그늘에서 쉬자 Let's take a rest in the shade.
2 〈보호〉 protection; care ♦ 부모의 그늘에서 자라다 be brought up under the good care of *one's* parents; grow up under *one's* parents' wings
3 〈유지〉 obscurity
▶ 그녀는 평생을 그늘에서 살았다 She lived in the shadow [obscurity] all her life.

그늘지다 darken; get [be] shaded; be shady; 〈마음 등이〉 gloom; cloud; feel gloomy; look dismal
♦ 그늘진 얼굴 a gloomy face / 그늘진 오솔길 a shady path / 그늘진 쪽 the shady side 《of a street》
▶ 그는 어딘지 그늘진 데가 있다 There is something gloomy about him.

그닐거리다 1 〈피부가〉 feel itchy [creepy, crawly, ticklish]; tickle; itch
2 〈마음이〉 be on pins and needles; feel uneasy [anxious, nervous, fidgety]; be on edge; be restless [ill at ease]
▶ 내 잔등이 그닐거린다 I feel something creeping up [crawling on] my back.

그다지 〈부정·의문 구문에서 not와 함께〉 not very [as, so, particularly, (so) much]; little
♦ 그다지 잘 알지 못하는 사람 a comparative stranger
▶ 그다지 춥지 않다 It is not very cold.
▶ 나는 야구를 그다지 좋아하지 않는다 I am not particularly fond of baseball.
▶ 그것은 그다지 어려운 문제가 아니다 It is not so difficult question.
▶ 나는 이 사건에 그다지 흥미가 없다 I am not (very) much [particularly] interested in this event.
▶ 그것은 그다지 무섭지 않았다 It wasn't as scary as I expected.
▶ 그는 그다지 학식 있는 사람이 아니다 He is not much of a scholar.
▶ 그것은 내겐 그다지 중요하지 않다 It matters little to me.
▶ 그의 작품은 그다지 인기가 없다 His works are not overly popular.
▶ 그는 그다지 유명하지 않다 He is not so [very] famous.
▶ 그다지 차이는 없다 I see no great difference.
▶ 그다지 자랑할 건 못된다 It is not a thing one can well be proud of.

그달 that month; 〈강조하여〉 the very [same] month

그대 thou; you
♦ 그대의 thy; your / 그대 자신 yourself / 그대들의 것 thine; yours / 그대들은[이] ye; you; you people [folks] / 그대에게[를] thee; you
▶ 그것은 그대가 틀렸네 You are wrong there.

그대로 〈있는 대로〉 as it is [stands]; as they are; intact; untouched; 〈하던 대로〉 like that; that way
♦ 있는 그대로 두다 leave *sth* as it is [stands]; leave *sth* intact [alone, untouched] / 꼭 그대로 하다 do just like that
▶ 충돌시의 상황을 그대로 말하시오 Tell us exactly what happened at the time of the collision.
▶ 모든 것이 그대로 남아 있다 Everything remains as (it) was.
▶ 그대로 연습을 계속해라 Keep practicing just like that.
▶ 나는 들은 이야기를 그대로 말해 주었다 I told the story as I had heard it.
▶ 내 욕을 했으니 그대로 둘 수 없다 You cannot call me names and get away with it.
▶ 그 일을 그대로 둘 수 없다 We cannot afford to leave [let] the matter alone. ⇒ The matter cannot be allowed to stand as it is.
▶ 그대로 누워 계십시오 You must lie the way you are.

그도그럴것이 because; for ▶ 그는 강등되었는데 그도 그럴 것이 그는 나태했다 He was demoted because of his laziness [because he was lazy].

그동안 the while; during that time; in the meantime
▶ 그동안 줄곧 여기 있었니? Have you been here all the time?

▶ 그동안 어떻게 지내셨어요? How have you been all these days?
그뒤 〈그후〉 after that; afterward(s); at a later time; since (then); since that time; ever since; from that time on
▶ 그뒤 그가 어떻게 되었는지 아무도 모른다 Nobody knows what has become of him since then.
그득 (to the) full ⇨ 가득
그들 they ◆ 그들의 their / 그들 자신 themselves / 그들의 것 theirs / 그들에게[을] them
그들먹하다 almost [nearly] full
그따위 such; that sort [kind] 《of》; a thing [person] of that sort; such a one; 《of》 that kind
◆ 그따위 물건 that sort of goods; goods of that sort / 그따위 범죄 crimes of that nature / 그따위 협잡질 that type [form] of swindling
▶ 그가 그따위 짓을 했을 리가 없다 He can't have done such a thing.
▶ 그따위 것은 거저 줘도 싫다 I would not have such a thing as a gift.
▶ 여기서는 그따위 인간은 필요없다 We don't want his kind in here.
그때 then; (at) that time [moment]; (on) that occasion
◆ 그때의 국무총리 the then prime minister / 마침[바로] 그때 just then; just at that moment / 그때부터 since then; ever since / 그때부터 지금까지 from that date up to the present
▶ 그때 그는 나의 제자였다 He was my pupil then [in those days].
▶ 그때 나는 아무 말도 할 수 없었다 At the [that] moment I could not say anything.
▶ 나는 그때야 비로소 그 사실을 알았다 It was not till then that I knew the fact.
그때까지 till then; up to that time
▶ 그때까지 내버려 두는 것이 좋겠다 We'd better leave it until then.
▶ 그때까지는 이 일을 끝마치겠다 I'll have finished the work by that time [then].
▶ 그때까지는 별일이 없었다 So far all went well (with us).
그라비어 〔印〕 (a) photogravure; (a) gravure
◆ 그라비어 인쇄로 하다 photogravure ■ —인쇄기 a gravure press —인쇄화 a gravure picture —잉크 gravure ink
그라운드 a ground; 〈학교의〉 a playground
◆ 축구 그라운드 a football ground / 그라운드를 메운 대관중 great crowds of spectators around the stadium
■ —매너 ground manners
그라인더 〔機〕〈숫돌·연마기〉 a grinder
그라탱 (프)〔料〕 gratin [grǽtn]
◆ 마카로니[포테이토] 그라탱 macaroni [potatoes] au gratin
그랑프리 (프) the grand prix [grɑ́ːn príː]; 〈win〉 the grand prize
그래¹ 1〈대답〉 yes; all right; O.K.; indeed; so
▶ 그래, 그것이 유일한 방법이다 Yes, that's the only possible way.
▶ 그래, 정말이냐? Oh, really?
▶ 〔會話〕「너 오지 않을래?」「그래, 안 갈래」 "Won't you come?" "No, I will not."
▶ 좀 더 오른쪽으로, 그래 됐어 A little more to the right, so!
2 〈글쎄·그러니〉 well; let me see
▶ 그래 내주까지 기다릴까? Well, shall we wait until next week?
▶ 그래 이게 무슨 꼴인가? Well, what is this mess?
그래² and ⇨ 그래서
그래뉴러당 —糖 granulated sugar
그래도 but (still); however; and yet; nonetheless; nevertheless; (al)though; still; for all that
▶ 아무도 그 그림을 칭찬하지 않지만 그래도 나는 좋은 그림이라고 생각한다 Nobody praises that picture, still I think it is very good.
▶ 비록 돈 한 푼 없다해도 그래도 나는 그를 존경한다 Even if he were penniless, I would respect him nonetheless.
▶ 이상하게 들릴지 모르지만 그래도 사실이다 It may sound strange, but it is true for all that.
그래서 and; well; (and) then; (and) so; therefore; that is why...; accordingly
▶ 그래서 어쨌단 말이냐? So what?
▶ 그래서 〈어떻게 되었니〉? Well, then?
▶ 그래서 어떻게 했지? And then what did you do?
▶ 그래서 그만두고 싶다는 말이냐? And so you wish to resign?
▶ 그래서 그는 평생을 독신으로 지냈다 That is why [And so] he remained single all his life.
▶ 그는 짧게 말하라는 말을 들었다. 그래서 자기 의견을 간단히 말했다 He was told to speak briefly, accordingly he cut short his remarks.
그래야 only so; only if *one* does [says] that; ..., and
▶ 지금 떠나라. 그래야 5시까지 집에 도착할 것이다 Leave at once, and you will reach home by five.
▶ 이렇게 해라. 그래야 잘 될 거다 Do it this way [like this], and it'll work out well.
그래프 〈도표〉 a graph; a graphic chart; a (symbolic) diagram ◆ 그래프로 만들다 make a graph 《of》
■ 그림— a picture graph; a pictograph 띠— a band graph; a rectangle [component] bar graph 막대[선]— a bar [line] graph [chart] 원— a circle graph; pie chart 주상(柱狀)— a column graph
■ —대수학 graphic algebra —용지 〈모눈종이〉 graph [section] paper
그래픽 〈사진 화보〉 a graphic magazine
■ —디자이너 a graphic designer [artist] —디자인 graphic design —아트 the graphic arts
그랜드래피즈 〈미국 미시간 주의 도시〉 Grand Rapids
그랜드오페라 〔樂〕 a grand opera
그랜드피아노 〔樂〕 a grand piano ◆ 소형 그랜드 피아노 a baby grand
그랜트 〈미국 남북 전쟁 때의 북군 총사령관, 제18대 대통령〉 Grant, Ulysses Simpson (1822-85)
그램 a gram [(英) gramme] (略 g, g., gm, gr.)
■ —당량(當量) gram equivalent —분자 [원자] a gram molecule [atom] —칼로리 a gram

그러고보니 ▶ 그러고 보니 자네는 엄처시하로군 That means that you are a henpecked husband, doesn't it?
▶ 그러고 보니 그날은 눈이 왔었지 That reminds me it was snowing on that day.

그러구러 〈우연히〉 unexpectedly; accidentally; casually; by chance [accident]
▶ 그러구러 봄이 지나갔다 Spring slipped away before I realized [I was aware of it]. ⇒ Spring had slipped away without my realizing it
▶ 그러구러 그들은 같은 기차를 타게 되었다 As it happened [chanced], they took the same train.

그러그러하다 〈그저 그렇다〉 so-so; ordinary; common; moderate; tolerable; (口) (fair-to-) middling
▶ 會話 「요즘 사업은 잘 되십니까?」「그러그러합니다」 "How is your business (doing)?" "Well, it's so-so."
▶ 그 영화는 그저 그러그러했다 The movie was so-so [mildly enjoyable].

그러께 the year before last; two years ago
◆ 그러께 봄 (in) the spring before last

그러나 but; however; (al)though; 〈그럼에도 불구하고〉 in spite of; nevertheless; 〈그런데도〉 (and) yet
▶ 바람은 멈추었다. 그러나 비는 아직 오고 있다 The wind has died down, but it's still raining.
▶ 나는 더 준다고 했다. 그러나 그는 만족하지 않았다 I offered him still more, and yet he was not satisfied.
▶ 그녀는 결점이 많다. 그러나 나는 그녀를 좋아한다 I like her nonetheless for her faults.
▶ 그는 작다. 그러나 힘이 세다 Even though he is small, he's strong.

그러나저러나 〈어떻든간에〉 anyway; anyhow; in any case; at any rate; either way
▶ 그러나저러나 그것은 나에게는 너무 크다 Anyway it's too big for me.
▶ 그러나저러나 너는 죄를 면할 수 없다 You are guilty, one way or the other.

그러내다 〈그러당겨〉 rake [scrape] out ◆ 난로에서 석탄재를 그러내다 rake out the coal cinders from a stove

그러넣다 〈그러모아〉 rake in; shovel (food) into (one's mouth); bolt one's food ◆ 낙엽을 난로에 그러넣다 scrape up fallen leaves and put them into a stove

그러니까 therefore; so; for that reason; on that account; consequently; accordingly; hence
▶ 스미스 씨는 곧 본국으로 돌아갑니다. 그러니까 송별회를 한 번 해주었으면 합니다 Mr. Smith will soon return to his home country. In this connection we'd like to hold a farewell party for him.
▶ 그러니까 그는 가난한 거야 That explains [accounts for] his poverty.
▶ 그러니까 그는 친구가 많다 That is why he has so many friends.

그러니저러니 one thing and [or] another; this and that
◆ 그러니저러니 할 것 없이 without saying this and that; setting aside all objections
▶ 그러니저러니 하는 동안에 사태는 일변했다 Meanwhile [In the meantime] the situation took a new turn.
▶ 그러니저러니 하지 말고 지시받은 대로 해라 No more of your talk. Just do what you are told.

그러담다 〈그러모아〉 rake [gather, scrape] up sth into ◆ 낙엽을 가마니에 그러담다 gather up [rake together] fallen leaves into a straw bag

그러당기다 pull ◆ 머리채를 그러당기다 pull sb's hair / 밧줄을 그러당기다 pull at [on] a rope / 옷소매를 그러당기다 pull at sb's sleeve; drag sb by the sleeve

그러들이다 rake [gather] in; scrape together
◆ 닥치는 대로 그러들이다 collect haphazardly / 꾸어 준 돈을 그러들이다 collect debts

그러면 then; if (it is) so; in that case; 〈자〉 well; then; 〈그렇게 하면〉 and
▶ 會話 「이것은 당신 차요?」「아니오」「그러면 누구 것이오?」 "Is this your car?" "No, it isn't." "Whose is it, then?"
▶ 會話 「내일은 바빠요」「그러면 오늘 오세요」 "I'll be busy tomorrow." "If so, why don't you come today?"
▶ 그러면 왜 네가 하지 않니? Then [If you think so], why don't you do it yourself?
▶ 그러면 오늘은 이만 끝냅시다 Well, that's all [so much] for today.
▶ 서둘러라, 그러면 시간에 늦지 않을 거야 Hurry up, and you will be in time.
▶ 자, 그러면 시작합시다 All right [Now], let's begin.

그러면그렇지 ▶ 아, 그러면 그렇지 〈예상대로〉 Ah, that's exactly what I thought. ⇌ I thought so! ⇌ 〈만족하여〉 That's what I mean. ⇌ Well, all right. ⇌ Attaboy!
▶ 그러면 그렇지 그것이 저절로 깨질 리가 있나 I see. It cannot break of itself.

그러모으다 〈한 곳에〉 gather up [together]; scrape [rake] up [together] ◆ 부지런히 그러모으다 rake and scrape
▶ 우리는 낙엽을 그러모아 불을 피웠다 We raked up fallen leaves and made a fire.

그러므로 so; therefore; accordingly; thus; hence; for that reason; on that ground; and so; on that account [score]; that is why; such being the case

解說 so는 일상적인 접속사로서 보통 콤마 다음이나 문장의 첫머리에 쓴다. **therefore, accordingly, thus**는 접속사적인 부사로서 보통 세미콜론(;), 과 다음이나 문장의 첫머리에 쓴다. 또 일반 동사의 앞이나 조동사·be동사의 다음에도 쓰는데 그 편이 생경한 느낌을 덜 준다.

▶ 나는 그녀를 만난 적이 없다. 그러므로 그녀에 대해 그다지 알지 못한다 I've never seen her, therefore I don't know much about her.
▶ 길이 얼었다. 그러므로 천천히 운전하지 않으면 안 되었다 The road was frozen, and ac-

cordingly I had to drive slowly.
▶그는 편견이 있고, 그러므로 신뢰할 수 없었다 He was biased, and so unreliable.
그러안다 embrace [hug] *sb* tightly [close]; hold [take] 《a baby》 in *one's* arms; give a tight hug 《to》; press 《a baby》 to *one's* breast
▶나는 아기를 그러안았다 I clasped [held] the baby in my arms.
▶그는 그 소녀를 포근히 그러안았다 He held the girl to him in a warm embrace.
그러자 〈그러하자〉 thereupon; then; 〈그때〉 when; and (just) then
▶그러자 마침 경찰관이 거기를 지나갔다 Just then, a policeman happened to come along.
▶그러자 그곳에 그가 불쑥 나타났다 Just at that time, he appeared there by chance.
그러잖아도 〈그렇지 않아도〉 even if it were not so; be it otherwise; moreover; all the more; in addition 《to》; what is more; to make matters worse; on top of (it)
▶그 친구 그러잖아도 미운데 돈까지 꾸어달라네 To make himself more hateful to me, he asks me to lend him money.
▶그녀는 그러잖아도 미인인데 돈까지 많다 She is rich and beautiful as well.
▶그러잖아도 모든 것을 잃었는데 건강마저 잃었다 He lost everything, and what is more [worse], his health.
그러잡다 〈붙잡다〉 clasp; clench; clutch; grab; grasp; 〈단단히 잡다〉 grip; take [catch] hold of
▶아버지는 반갑게 그의 손을 그러잡았다 My father grasped his hand in welcome.
▶배가 좌우로 흔들렸기 때문에 그녀는 급히 난간을 그러잡았다 As the ship rolled, she hurriedly gripped the rail.
그러저러하다 so and so; such and such; and so on [forth]
♦그러저러한 이야기 such and such a story / 그러저러한 날에 on such and such a day / 그러저러한 이유로 for such and such reasons
▶사건의 경과는 그러저러했다 The course of incident was such and such.
그러쥐다 grasp; grab (up); grip; seize; take [catch] hold of; hold ♦손잡이를 그러쥐다 hold [clutch] a handle
▶그는 그것을 단단히 그러쥐었다 He seized it and held it tightly.
▶그 아이는 어머니의 손을 그러쥐고 놓지 않았다 The child grasped [gripped, clutched] his [her] mother's hand and never let it go.
▶너무 많이 그러쥐려다가는 다 잃기 쉽다 A person who grasps at too much may lose everything.
그러하다 just [quite] so; (be) so; just like that; such ⇨ 그런
▶그러한 사정이므로 같이 갈 수 없다 Such being the case [Under the circumstances], I cannot go with you.
▶그러한 미인은 드물다 One rarely sees such a beautiful woman.
▶그러한 사실은 없다 There is no such fact.
그럭저럭 somehow (or other); (美) someway; in some way (or other); (in) one way or another; by hook or (by) crook; by some means (or other)
♦그럭저럭 하는 동안에 in the meantime [meanwhile]; meanwhile / 그럭저럭 살아가다 manage to get along; live by shift(s) [*one's* wits] / 그럭저럭 합격하다 manage to pass the examination
▶우리는 위기를 그럭저럭 헤쳐나갔다 We somehow managed to weather the crisis.
▶그는 그럭저럭 대학을 졸업했다 He graduated from college somehow or other.
그런 such; like that; that kind [sort] of
♦그런 것 such a thing; a thing like that; that kind [sort] of thing / 그런 까닭으로 so; that is why; therefore
▶나는 그런 사람과 사귀고 싶지 않다 I don't want to be friends with that sort [kind] of person.
▶나는 그런 사람을 만난 적이 없다 I have never met [come across] such a man.
▶그런 때는 서로 도웁시다 Let's help each other in a case like that.
▶그런 소문은 귀담아 듣지 마라 Don't listen [pay any attention] to such a rumor.
▶세상이란 그런 거야 Such is the way of the world.
그런대로 passably; tolerably; rather; fairly; enough
♦그런대로 쓸만한 사나이 a good enough man in his way
▶그것은 그런대로 쓸모가 있다 It is useful in its own way.
▶그는 대학을 나왔으니 그런대로의 지식은 있을 것이다 I think he has a certain amount of knowledge because he is a college graduate.
▶그 영화는 그런대로 괜찮았다 The movie was so-so [mildly enjoyable].
그런데 1〈그러나〉 however; but; and yet; while
▶그 원서는 읽기 쉽다, 그런데 한국어 번역판은 이해하기 어렵다 The original is easy to read, while its Korean translation is hard to follow.
▶잘 될 줄 알았지. 그런데 실패했어 While I thought it would go well, it failed. ⇌ It failed, contrary to my expectations.
2 〈그건 그렇고〉 well; now; by the bye; by the way; incidentally
▶그런데 그 일은 어찌 되었습니까? By the bye, how does the matter stand? ⇌ Now, what has become of the matter you spoke of?
▶그런데 너의 부모님은 건강하시냐? By the way, are your parents well?
그런데도 but; however; and yet; in spite of that; (al)though; for all that
▶최선을 다했다. 그런데도 잘 되지 않았다 I did my utmost, but it didn't come off [turn out] well.
▶그는 가난하다. 그런데도 일을 하려고 하지 않는다 He is poor, and yet he will not work.
그런양으로 〈그런 모양으로〉 (in) that way; like that; in that manner
▶그런 양으로 말한다면 나는 반대할 수 없다 If you put it that way, I can't object.

그런즉 so; therefore; that's why...; for that reason ⇨ 그러므로

그럴듯하다 1 〈있음직하다〉 likely; plausible; probable; 〈겉보기만의〉 (fair-)seeming; specious
♦ 그럴 듯한 얘기 a likely story / 그럴 듯한 증거 probable evidence / 그럴 듯한 해석 a possible explanation / 그럴 듯한 표정으로 with a serious look / 그럴 듯한 거짓말을 하다 tell a plausible lie / 그럴 듯한 변명을 하다 make a plausible [specious] excuse
▶ 그의 이야기는 아주 그럴 듯했기 때문에 모두들 믿었다 His story sounded so plausible (that) everyone believed it.
2 〈상당하다〉 passable; fair; considerable; 〈남부끄럽지 않다〉 decent; respectable
♦ 그럴 듯한 연설 a speech worth hearing [listening to] / 그럴 듯한 옷차림을 하고 있다 be decently dressed

그럴싸하다 likely; plausible; probable ⇨ 그럴듯하다

그럼 1 〈그러면〉 well; in that case; then; if that is the case; if (it is) so
▶ 그럼 내일 만납시다 Well, see you tomorrow.
▶ 그럼 단념하겠다 In that case, we'll just give up.
▶ 會話 「어젯밤에는 영화 보러 가고 싶지 않았다」「그럼 왜 갔니?」 "I didn't want to go to the movies last night." "Why did you go, then?"
▶ 너 정말 아프니? 그럼 병원에 가거라 Are you really sick? If so, you had better go to the hospital.
2 〈긍정〉 indeed; yes; (美) sure; right; certainly; quite so; of course
▶ 그럼, 그렇고 말고요 Oh yes, that is true.

그렁그렁하다 1 〈눈물이〉 tearful; suffused with tears; 〈물이〉 brimful; almost full (to the brim)
♦ 눈물이 그렁그렁한 눈 eyes filled [suffused, brimming, swimming] with tears; tearful eyes / 물이 그렁그렁한 독 a jar almost full of [brimming with] water
▶ 그녀의 눈에는 눈물이 그렁그렁했다 Her eyes swam with tears.
▶ 눈물이 그렁그렁하여 잘 보이지 않았다 My eyes (were) blurred with tears. ⇌ Tears blurred my eyes.
▶ 그녀는 오렌지 주스를 컵에 그렁그렁하게 따랐다 She filled her glass full with orange juice.
2 〈국물이〉 watery; washy; thin(멀건) ♦ 그렁그렁한 수프 thin [watery] soup
3 〈뱃속이〉 feel bloated [charged, loaded] with water; be full from drinking too much water
▶ 물을 너무 마셔서 뱃속이 그렁그렁하다 I drank too much water, so I'm ready to burst.

그렁저렁 somehow ⇨ 그럭저럭

그렇게 〈수·양〉 so; so much [many]; that much [many]; that far; 〈매우〉 very; so; much; 〈방식〉 like that; in that way [manner]
▶ 會話 「그렇게 생각하오?」「아니, 그렇지 않아요」 "Do you think so?" "No, I don't think so."
▶ 꼭 그렇게 해 주세요 Please do so.
▶ 오늘은 그렇게 춥지 않다 It's not very cold today.
▶ 돈을 그렇게 많이 썼니? Did you spend that much money?
▶ 초보 영어를 가르치는 것은 그렇게 쉬운 일이 아니다 Teaching elementary English isn't all that easy.
▶ 그렇게 야단법석 떨지 마라 You needn't make such a fuss.
▶ 會話 「오늘은 그 도시에 도착 못할 걸」「그렇게 머니?」 "We won't get to that town today." "Is it that far?"
▶ 세상 일이 그렇게 뜻대로 되지는 않는 법이다 Things seldom go as one wishes [you want].
▶ 그렇게 화내지 마시오 Don't be so angry.
▶ 그렇게까지 심한 말은 안 해도 돼 You don't have to use such harsh words.
▶ 그렇게 해서 그는 가수가 되었다 In that way [And so, Thus] he became a singer.

그렇고말고 Of course!; Indeed!; Certainly!; (美) Sure!; Quite so!

그렇다 〈그러하다〉 so; (be) like that [that way]; 〈대답〉 Yes(▶긍정문이 뒤에 계속될 때); No(▶부정문이 뒤에 계속될 때)
▶ 그건 그렇다 치고 〈그런데〉 by the way [bye]; incidentally; now (then); 〈그것은 어쨌든〉 you may well say so, but...; be that as it may / 그렇다는 하나 nevertheless / 바로 그렇다 be just like that; be just [quite, exactly] so
▶ 會話 「나는 그렇게 생각하지 않는다」「나도 그렇다」 "I don't think so." "I don't either."
▶ 그렇습니까? Is that so? ⇌ Really?
▶ 그렇소 You are right. ⇌ That's right.
▶ 내가 바보면 너도 그렇다 If I am a fool, you are another.
▶ 나도 그렇다 It is also the case with me.
▶ 會話 「이것은 형용사지요?」「그렇다」 "This is an adjective, isn't it?" "Yes, that's right [you are right]."
▶ 會話 〈하숙 등에 관해서〉 「지낼 만 합니까?」「그저 그렇지요」 "Do you find it comfortable?" "Just so-so."
▶ 그는 그렇다고 대답했다 He said yes. ⇌ He answered in the affirmative.
▶ 그렇다고만 할 수는 없다 It is not always the case.
▶ 그렇지 않으면 좋겠는데 I hope not.
▶ 그렇지 않다 It is not so [the case].

그렇다고해서 yet; be that as it may; for all that; even so; nevertheless
▶ 그렇다고 해서 포기할 수는 없다 Even so [For all that], I cannot give up.
▶ 가지는 않겠다. 그렇다고 해서 섭섭지 않은 것은 아니다 I will desist from going, though I shall miss it very much.
▶ 작은 키는 아니지만 그렇다고 해서 큰 키도 아니다 He is neither short nor tall.
▶ 그렇다고 해서 네가 모임에 참석하지 않을 이유는 없다 That is no reason for (your) not attending the meeting.

그렇다면 (and) then; (and) so; 〈그런 경우는〉

그렇다면 in that case; if so; if that is the case
▶그렇다면 너는 내가 거짓말쟁이란 말이지 Then you mean to say that I am a liar.
▶그렇다면 너는 실직한 게로구나 So you've lost your job!
▶그렇다면 그는 아침 일찍 출발한 게 틀림없다 If so, he must have got started early in the morning.

그렇지 1 〈동의〉 yes; yes, it is; just so
2 〈상기〉 oh, yes; (now) I remember
▶또, 그렇지, 엽서를 10장 사다 다오 And, oh yes, get me ten postcards.
▶참 그렇지, 작년 이맘때였지 Now I remember, it was about this time last year.
3 〈동의를 구해〉 isn't it?; doesn't it?; don't you?
▶그렇지, 그것이 우리의 약속이었지? Yes, yes, that was our agreement, wasn't it?
▶매우 피곤하겠구나, 그렇지? You must be very tired, I dare say.

그렇지만 however; but; still; and yet; though; although; nevertheless; for all that; be that as it may
▶그는 젊다. 그렇지만 생각이 깊다 Young as he is, he is considerate.
▶눈이 내리고 있었다. 그렇지만 시합은 중지되지 않았다 It was snowing, but they didn't cancel [call off] the game.
▶그렇지만 그는 위인임에 틀림없다 For all that, he is certainly a great man.
▶그렇지만 그는 그 아이를 사랑한다 He loves the child, though.

그렇지않으면 else; otherwise; or (else); if not so
▶서둘러라, 그렇지 않으면 기차 놓친다 Hurry up, or (else) you will miss the train.
▶열심히 공부해라, 그렇지 않으면 낙제할거야 Work hard, or you will fail in the examination.
▶나는 즉시 갔다. 그렇지 않았더라면 그를 만나지 못했을지도 모른다 I went right away, otherwise I might have missed him.

그레고리력 —曆 the Gregorian calendar
그레고리오성가 —聖歌 the Gregorian chant
그레나다 〈나라 이름〉 Grenada; 〈공식명〉 the State of Grenada
그레셤 〈영국의 금융가〉 Sir Thomas Gresham (1519?-79) —의 법칙 [經] Gresham's law
그레이프 〈포도〉 grape —프루트 a grapefruit 《pl. ~(s)》; a pomelo —주스 grape juice
그레이하운드 〈사냥개〉 a greyhound
그레인 〈중량 단위〉 a grain
그레코로만형 —型 [레슬링] the Greco-Roman style
그려 ▶앉게 그려 Please sit down. ▶한 잔 합시다 그려 Let's have a drink, shall we?
그로기 ◆그로기 상태의 groggy / (얻어맞고) 그로기 상태가 되다 become groggy; be punch-drunk
그로스톤 〈英〉 〈중량 단위〉 a gross ton
그로테스크 grotesque(ness) —그로테스크하다 grotesque ◆그로테스크한 것 a grotesque; (총칭) grotesquerie ■—양식[무늬] 〈미술·문학〉 the grotesque

그루 1 〈나무의〉 a stump; a stock; 〈곡식의〉 stubbles 《of rice plants》
2 〈세는 단위〉 a plant; a tree ◆오렌지 나무 한 그루 an orange tree
3 〈농사의〉 a crop; a sowing
◆두 그루 농사 raising [growing] two crops; double-cropping; two crops a year; a semi-annual crop
▶이 지역은 여름에는 벼, 겨울에는 밀의 두 그루 농사가 가능하다 It's possible to grow two crops a year in this area; rice in summer and wheat in winter.

그루갈이 double-cropping; raising [growing] two crops a year; semiannual crop; 〈두번째 것〉 a second crop [sowing, planting]; an aftercrop
—**그루갈이하다** grow two crops a year; sow [plant] as a second crop

그루밭 an aftercrop field; a stubble (field); a field used again after a barely crop
그루터기 〈나무의〉 a (tree) stump; a stub; 〈벼 등의〉《a piece [clump] of》stubbles
그룹 a group; a circle ◆소그룹 a subgroup / 그룹을 이루어 in groups / 그룹을 만들다 form a group; group together / 그룹으로 나누다 divide into groups; group 《into》
■—연구— a study circle [group]

그르다 1 〈옳지 못하다〉 wrong; mistaken; unjust; untrue; blamable; 〈부당하다〉 improper; 〈잘못되다〉 incorrect; false
◆그른 답 incorrect [a wrong] answer to a question / 마음이 그른 사람 a bad [a wicked, an evil] person / 그른 생각 a false [mistaken] idea / 그른 정보 incorrect [inaccurate] information / 그른 짓 a wrong; an evil deed; a misdeed / 그른 길을 가다 take the wrong road / 옳고 그른 것을 가리다 tell [know] right from wrong; discriminate between right and wrong
▶그를 비난하다니 네가 글렀어 You are wrong to criticize him. ⇒ You are in the wrong to criticize him.
▶네 짐작은 전혀 글렀어 Your guess is quite wide of the mark.
2 〈좋지 않다〉 bad; foul; ill; unwell ◆맛이 그르다 taste bad; tasteless [flat, insipid]; be unsavory / 안색이 그르다 do not look well
3 〈가망이 없다〉 hopeless; (be) done for; (口) (be) all fouled up; unpromising
▶그가 선출되기는 글렀다 There is little chance [likelihood, probability] of his being chosen.
▶난 글렀어 I'm done for. ⇒ It's all up [over] with me.
▶시험에 합격하기는 글렀다 I am hopeless of success in the examination.
▶그 환자는 이제 글렀다 The patient has little chance to pull through [is hopeless].
▶그 애 사람되기는 글렀다 The boy is far from promising. ⇒ The child will never be a good man.

그렁거리다 ruckle; wheeze; purr
그렁그렁 ruckling; rattling (in *one's* throat)

그르치다 〈잘못하다〉 err; mistake; make [commit] a mistake [an error] (in); 〈망치다〉 spoil; ruin; mar; destroy; corrupt; 〈실패하다〉 fail (in)
♦ 건강을 그르치다 ruin [lose] one's health / 계산을 그르치다 make an error in calculation / 계획을 그르치다 spoil [ruin] a plan / 미관을 그르치다 spoil [mar] the beauty (of) / 방침을 그르치다 take a wrong course / 일생을 그르치다 make a failure [wreck, botch] of one's life; ruin one's life / 판단을 그르치다 err in one's judgment; misjudge
▶ 그는 방탕한 생활로 신세를 그르쳤다 He ruined himself by fast living.

그릇¹ **1** 〈기물〉 a container; a vessel; a receptacle
♦ 놋그릇 a brazen vessel / 밥그릇 a rice bowl / 유리 그릇 glassware / 질그릇 an earthenware / 물 한 그릇 a bowl of water
▶ 그 잼을 그릇에 담아라 Put the jam in [into] a container.
2 〈능력〉 ability; caliber; capacity
▶ 그는 사장 될 그릇이 아니다 I doubt his ability to be a president. ⇌ He is not fit to be a president.
▶ 그는 그릇이 크다 [작다] He is a man of high [low] caliber.

그릇² 〈잘못〉 by mistake; in error; wrongly; falsely; erroneously; mistakenly
♦ 사람을 그릇 보다 misjudge sb / judge sb wrongly / 그릇 전하다 give a false report [false information]; report wrongly; misinform / 그릇 판단하다 judge wrong; err in one's judgment

그릇되다 〈잘못 되다〉 become wrong; go amiss [wrong]; end in a failure; 〈망쳐지다〉 be ruined; be spoilt
♦ 그릇된 길 the wrong way; an erroneous path; an evil course / 그릇된 대답 a wrong [an incorrect] answer / 그릇된 생각 a mistaken [an erroneous] idea; a wrong opinion / 그릇된 판단 misjudgment; miscalculation / 그릇된 행실 a misdeed; an evil doing / 그릇된 문장 a sentence full of mistakes
▶ 그 계산은 아주 그릇되었다 The calculation was wildly wrong [out].
▶ 편지가 그릇된 주소로 배달되었다 The letter was delivered to the wrong address.

그리 **1** 〈그토록〉 so; so much; to that extent; to such an extent; 〈다지〉《not》 very [so]...; 〈그런 식으로〉 (in) that way [manner]
▶ 그리 서둘렀기 때문에 너는 실수를 했다 You made a miss of it because you were in too much of a hurry.
▶ 그의 건강은 그리 좋지 않다 His condition is not very good.
▶ 그리 나쁘지 않다 It is not so bad.
▶ 나는 멜론을 그리 좋아하지 않는다 I don't like [care for] melons very much.
▶ 그리 화내지 말게 Don't be so angry.
▶ 그건 그리 해야 한다 You should do it that way.
▶ 그리 생각합니까 Do you think so?
2 〈그 쪽으로〉 there; to that place; that way; in that direction
▶ 곧 그리 가겠습니다 I'm coming there soon.
▶ 그리 가면 안 된다 You must not go in that direction. ⇌ Don't go there.

그리고 and; and also; as well as; 〈그리고 나서〉 (and) then
♦ 책과 공책 그리고 연필 books, notebooks and pencils
▶ 그리고 무엇을 했니? And then what did you do?
▶ 그녀는 병이 완전히 회복되었다. 그리고 지금 건강하게 일하고 있다 She has recovered completely from her illness and is now working in good health.

그리그 〈노르웨이의 작곡가〉 Grieg, Edvard Hagerup (1843-1907)

그리니치 Greenwich [grínidʒ] ■ —천문대 Royal Greenwich Observatory —표준시 Greenwich Mean Time (略 GMT); Greenwich Time

그리다¹ 〈그리워하다〉 long [pine] for sb [sth]; be dying for sth [sb]; yearn after [for] 《one's old home》; be sick for 《one's parents》; miss 《one's dead mother》
♦ 옛날을 그리다 be nostalgic of the good old days / 죽은 아내를 그리다 miss one's departed wife / 애타게 평화를 그리다 have a great yearning [longing] for peace / 만나고 싶어서 애타게 그리다 be dying to see sb; would give anything [a lot] to see sb
▶ 그녀는 음악 선생님을 그리고 있다 She has fallen in love with the music teacher.

그리다² 【그림 등을】 draw; picture; portray; 〈채색으로〉 paint; 〈약도를〉 sketch; 〈원 등을〉 describe; 〈삼각형 등을〉 construct; 〈묘사하다〉 describe; depict
♦ 그래프를 그리다 plot (out) 《sth on squared paper》 / 눈썹을 그리다 pencil the eyebrows / 입술을 그리다 rouge [paint] one's lips / 지도를 그리다 draw a map
▶ 병풍에는 모란이 그려져 있었다 Peonies were painted on the (folding) screen. ⇌ The (folding) screen had a picture of peonies.
▶ 이 소설은 가난한 사람들의 생활을 그리고 있다 This novel depicts the life of poor people.
▶ 능선은 부드러운 호선을 그리고 있었다 The ridge of the mountain formed [described] a gentle arc.
▶ 그녀는 결혼식 장면을 마음에 그리고 있었다 She was picturing herself the scene of her wedding ceremony.

그리드 〔電〕 a grid ■ —검파 grid detection —전류 a grid current

그리마 〔動〕 a house centipede

그리스 〔機〕 〈윤활유〉 grease

그리스 Greece; 〈공식명〉 the Republic of Greece
♦ 그리스의 Greek; Grecian; Hellenic (▶ Grecian은 현재 건축·미술·사람의 얼굴 모양 및 관용구외에는 쓰이지 않음)
■ —말 Greek; the Greek language —문명 Greek civilization; Hellenism —문자 Greek letter —사람 〈한 사람〉 a Greek; (총칭) the Greeks —신화 Greek myth [mythology] —정

교회 the Greek Orthodox Church —철학 [문학, 건축] Greek philosophy [literature, architecture]

그리스도 Christ; the Messiah; the Savior ◆예수 그리스도 Jesus Christ
  ■—재림 the Second Advent (of Christ) —재림론자 a Second Adventists; an Adventist —재림설 Adventism

그리스도교 —敎 Christianity ⇨ 기독교

그리스도교화 —敎化 Christianization —그리스도교화하다 Christianize; evangelize

그리움 (a) yearning (for); (a) longing; attachment; a dear feeling; a kindly feeling; nostalgia
  ◆그리움에 사무친 곳 a longed-for place / 그리움에 사무친 longing; yearning / 그리움에 사무쳐서 longingly; yearningly / 그리움을 못 이기다 feel an irresistible yearning for [after]
  ▶할머니는 그리움에 잠겨 옛날 이야기를 하셨다 Our grandmother talked of the good old days nostalgically.
  ▶당시를 회상하니 그리움에 가슴이 메입니다 Looking back to that time, I am filled with nostalgic sweetness.

그리워하다 long for; yearn [pine] for [after]; think fondly of sb; remember fondly; miss; be sick for; thirst for
  ◆고향을 그리워하다 pine for home; be homesick / 바다를 그리워하다 have a hankering after the sea
  ▶많은 젊은이들이 도시 생활을 그리워한다 Many young people long for city life.
  ▶그들은 이 이국에서 고향을 그리워하고 있다 They long [pine] for home in this strange land.

그리저리 〈되어가는 대로〉 at haphazard [random]; without system [a plan]; in a desultory way; desultorily; in a hit-or-miss manner
  ◆그리저리 알게 된 사람 a casual acquaintance / (말을) 그리저리 둘러대다 prattle on at random; make random excuses
  —그리저리하다 do sth at random [haphazard]; do sth by trial and error

그리하여 and; then; so

그린 〈색깔〉 green; 〈골프〉 the putting green

그 린 〈영국의 소설가〉 Green, Graham (1904-91)

그린란드 Greenland

그린벨트 a greenbelt
  ■—지역 a greenbelt zone

그린피스 〈환경단체〉 Greenpeace; 〈완두콩〉 green peas

그릴 〈일품 요리점〉 a grill(room)

그림 〈독일의 동화 작가〉 Grimm, Wilhelm (1786-1859); 〈독일의 언어학자〉 Grimm, Jakob(1785-1863) ◆그림의 법칙 Grimm's law 〈게르만계 언어에서의 자음 전환의 법칙〉
  ■—동화 Grimm's fables

그림 a picture; 〈무채색화〉 a drawing; 〈채색화〉 a painting; 〈도표〉 a diagram; a chart; 〈사생화·초벌그림〉 a sketch; 〈삽화·도해〉 an illustration; a figure; a cut
  ◆그림 1 the first figure; Fig. 1 / 우리 어머니의 그림 〈어머니를 그린〉 a picture of my mother; 〈어머니가 가지고 있는〉 a picture of my mother's; one of my mother's pictures / 피카소의 그림 a picture by Picasso / 그림 같은 picturesque 《view》 / 그림이 있는 illustrated; pictorial / 그림을 그리다 draw [paint] (a picture); make a picture [drawing, painting] / 그림에 재능이 있다 have an aptitude for painting; have an eye for the picture / 그림으로 나타내다[설명하다] illustrate by a diagram [with a figure]; figure
  ▶그녀는 그림같이 아름답다 She is pretty as a picture.
  ▶아이들이 교실에서 그림을 그리고 있다 The children are drawing pictures in the classroom.
  ■—붓 a paintbrush —설명 〈캡션〉 a caption —쇠 a rule; a measure —수수께끼 a pictorial puzzle; a rebus —엽서 a picture [an illustrated] postcard; 《美》 a post card: 그림 엽서가 될 만한 풍경 picture-postcard scenery —용지 drawing paper —쟁이 a painter; an artist —족자 a picture scroll; a hanging picture —책 a picture [pictorial] book; 〈그림 이야기책〉 an illustrated story book —첩 a sketchbook —패 〈트럼프의〉 a picture card; 《美》 a face card; 《英》 a court card

그림물감 colors; pigment; paint; 〈유화용〉 oils; oil colors; oil paints; 〈수채화용〉 water colors
  ◆그림물감을 풀다 dissolve colors ■—상자 a paint box —접시 a dish for mixing paints

그림에 떡 〈속담〉 a prize beyond one's reach; 《美俗》 pie in the sky
  ▶그녀는 내겐 그림에 떡이다 She is a prize beyond my reach.

그림자 1 〈음영〉 a shadow; a silhouette

> [解說] shadow는 빛이 차단되어 생긴 검은 상을 말한다. 비유적으로도 쓰인다. silhouette는 전방으로부터의 빛으로 스크린 등에 비친 형태이다. 물이나 거울 면에 비친 그림자는 image, 사람의 모습은 figure라고 한다.

  ▶나무 그림자가 땅에 길게 드리워져 있었다 The long shadow of a tree was on the ground. ⇌ The tree cast [threw] a long shadow on the ground.
  ▶한 여인의 그림자가 장지에 비치고 있다 A woman's silhoutte is on the sliding-screen paper.
  ▶그들의 행복한 삶에 어두운 그림자가 다가오고 있었다 A dark shadow was beginning to creep over their happy life.
  ▶그 남자는 그녀를 그림자처럼 따라다닌다 The man follows her like a shadow wherever she goes.
2 〈영상〉 an image; a figure; a reflection
  ◆거울에 비친 그림자 an image in a mirror / 물에 비친 별 그림자 stars reflected in the waters / 연못에 비친 다리 그림자 the image of a bridge on the pond
  ▶백두산의 그림자가 천지에 비치고 있었다 Mt. Paekdu cast it's shadow [reflection] on Lake Ch'ŏnji.
3 〈자취〉 a trace; a sign

▶ 거리에는 사람 그림자 하나 없다 There is not a soul (to be seen) in the street.
▶ 요즈음은 폭력사건의 그림자도 비치지 않고 있다 There have not been any instances of violence recently.
▶ 적의 그림자도 보이지 않았다 There was no sign of the enemy anywhere.
■─그림 a shadow picture

― 그림자 ―
그늘 shade
그림자 shadow

그립 〈손잡이〉 a grip; 〈잡는 방식〉 grip
그립다 dear; dearest; darling; longed for; beloved; 〈서술적〉 yearn for [after] *sb*; feel yearning for *sth*; long [pine] for 《one's home》; miss *sb*
♦ 그리운 고향 one's beloved [dear old] home / 그리운 사람 one's darling [one's sweetheart]; a beloved person / 40년 전의 그리운 옛날 the nostalgic past of forty years ago / 그리운 추억 dear [sweet] memories; memories dear to one / 어머니가 그리워 울다 cry for one's absent mother
▶ 옛날이 그립다 I long [sigh] for the days past.
▶ 나는 어머니가 해주시던 요리가 가장 그립다 I miss my mother's cooking most.
▶ 집이 그립다 I miss (my sweet old) home. ⇒ I am homesick.
▶ 어머니가 그립다 My heart aches [yearns] for my dear mother.
▶ 이 사진을 볼 때마다 그리운 그녀의 모습이 떠오른다 Whenever I see this photo, I remember her beloved image.
▶ 고향이 그립지 않은 사람은 없다 There is no one who doesn't miss his old family home.
그만¹ 〈그만한〉 such a little 《thing》; so little [small] as; such 《a trifle》; as [that] much
▶ 그만 일이라면 해줄 수 있다 If that is all you want, I can do it easily.
▶ 그만 일이라면 화요일까지 할 수 있다 I can finish that much by Tuesday.
▶ 그만 일은 바보라도 안다 Even a fool knows as [that] much.
▶ 그만 일로 울면 사람들이 웃는다 People will laugh at you if you cry over such a little thing.
▶ 그만 일에 놀랄 내가 아니다 I am not the [a] man to be startled by such a trifle.
그만² 1 〈그 정도만〉 that much and no more
▶ 농담 좀 그만 해라 Do not carry your joke too far. ⇒ No more of your jokes.
▶ 비 좀 그만 내렸으면 I hope no more of raining now.
▶ 그만 지껄여라 Stop talking! ⇒ Don't talk any more!
▶ 오늘은 그만(합시다) So much [That's enough] for today.
▶ 이젠 그만 해 Enough of that!
▶ 그만 가봐야겠습니다 I must be off [going] now.
▶ 그만 (口슈) Stop!
2 〈곧장〉 immediately; at once; instantly; right away; at the moment 《of》; no sooner than; as soon as
▶ 그만 나가 Get out at once!
▶ 그는 화를 버럭 내면서 그만 가버렸다 He went off immediately in a fit of sudden temper [anger].
▶ 그녀는 남편의 사망 소식을 듣자 그만 기절해 버렸다 She fainted instantly at the news of her husband's death.
▶ 그는 나를 보자 그만 달아났다 He ran off at the moment he saw me.
3 〈도리 없이〉 unintentionally; involuntarily; 〈부주의로〉 carelessly; heedlessly; by mistake [accident]
♦ 그만 실수를 하다 make a careless mistake / 그만 그들의 대화를 엿듣다 unintentionally overhear them talking / 가난 때문에 그만 죄를 짓다 be tempted by poverty to commit a crime / 그만 …할 마음이 생기다 be tempted to...; yield to the temptation to.../ 그만 화를 내다 be betrayed into anger
▶ 나는 그만 거기를 지나쳐 버렸다 I carelessly passed it by. ⇒ I was so careless that I passed it by.
▶ 그녀는 그만 그 꽃병을 깨뜨렸다 She was careless and broke the vase.
▶ 그의 말이 그만 그녀의 감정을 해쳤다 His careless [thoughtless] remarks hurt her feelings.
▶ 그와 이야기를 하다가 그만 쓸데없는 말을 지껄인 것 같다 I'm afraid I made a bad slip when I was talking to him.
▶ 그만 정신이 없었습니다 I am sorry I was so careless.
그만그만하다 〈어슷비슷하다〉 much [nearly] the same; 〈서술적〉 be much of a muchness; (口) be six of one and half-a-dozen of others; be of a hair ♦ 나이가 그만그만하다 be about the same age
▶ 그 형제는 학교 성적이 그만그만하다 The brothers' school records nearly match.
▶ 학생들의 리포트는 다 그만그만하다 The students' papers are all more or less similar.
▶ 그 점에서는 양자는[두 사람의 솜씨는] 그만하다 There is not much to choose [little difference] between the two in that respect [in workmanship].
▶ 참석자들은 나이나 실력이 그만그만했다 All participants were of a sort of both age and competence.
그만두다 1 〈중단하다〉 stop [quit] 《doing》; cease (from) 《doing》; discontinue 《doing》; drop; 〈일시적으로〉 suspend; cut off

解說 「…하는 것을 그만두다」라고 할 때는 *stop* [*quit*] *doing*의 형태를 쓴다. *stop to* *do*라고 하면 「…하기 위해 멈춰서다」의 뜻이 되므로 주의. 들면 I stopped *smoking*.은 「나는 담배피우는 것을 그만두었다(금연했다)」의 뜻이지만, I stopped *to smoke*. 라고 하면 「나는 담배를 피우기 위해 멈춰 섰다」는 뜻이 된다.

♦ 갑자기 그만두다 cut [stop] short [suddenly]; break off / 거래를 그만두다 close an account 《with》/ 교제를 그만두다 cut [drop] acquaintance 《with》/ 이야기를 그만두다 cease [stop, leave off] talking; drop the subject / 버스의 운행을 일시 그만두다 suspend a bus service / 일을 그만두기 위해 leave [knock] off work; lay aside [cease] *one's* work;〈그날의 일을〉stop working / 전쟁을 그만두다 put an end to [terminate] the war; bring the war to an end
▶그만둬라 (口) Enough [None] of that! ⇌ Drop it! ⇌ Cut it out!
▶농담 그만둬라 None [Enough] of your jokes!
▶지난 주에 어디서 그만두었죠?〈수업에서〉Where did we leave off last week?
▶그 얘기는 이제 그만두시오 Cut (it) out, please.
▶그만뒀더라면 좋았을 텐데 I wish I had not done it.
▶그들은 연구를 그만두지 않았다 They continued [went on] with their study.
▶나는 연습을 그만두지 오래다 I have long been out of practice.
2〈하지 않다〉give [throw] up; lay aside; abandon; quit
♦그림을 그만두다 abandon the palette / 장사를 그만두다 quit *one's* business / 집을 사려다가 그만두다 give up the idea of buying a house / 학업을 그만두다 give up *one's* studies; lay aside *one's* books / 그만두게 하다 dissuade [stop] 《sb from doing》;〈악습 등을〉cure [break] 《sb of a bad habit》
▶나는 계획한 것은 어떤 일이 있어도 그만두지 않는다 I won't abandon [give up] my plan no matter what happens.
3〈사직하다〉resign 《*one's* post》; quit 《*one's* job》; retire 《from office》
▶그녀는 병 때문에 회사를 그만두었다 She left (the job [post] of) the company on account of her illness [sickness].
▶그는 가정 사정으로 학교를 그만두었다 He left [(美) quit] school for family reason.
▶그는 관계(官界)를 그만두고 실업계에 투신했다 He retired from government service and went into business.

그만이다 1〈상관 없다〉do not care [matter];〈다이다〉be the end 《of it》; no more than that
▶늦어도 그만이다 It dosen't matter if you are late.
▶나는 그것만 있으면 그만이다 That is all I want.
▶헤어지면 그만이다 That's the end of all if they take apart.
▶해 보고 안 되면 그만이다 If I try and fail, that's the end of it.
2〈충분하다〉enough; sufficient; satisfactory
▶나는 따끈한 커피 한 잔이면 그만이다 Just a cup of coffee will suffice me.
3〈더할 나위 없다〉ideal; excellent;〈최적이다〉the very; the best; the finest; superb; matchless ♦ 낚시에 그만인 장소 a capital spot for fishing
▶아주 그만이다 Excellent!
▶여기는 경기장을 만들기에 그만이다 This place is [would be] ideal for a stadium.
▶이것은 맛이 그만이다 This tastes superb.
▶그 일에는 그가 그만이다 He is just the man [He is the very man] for the job.

그만저만하다〈그저 그런 정도다〉not so bad; neither good nor bad; fair; moderate; tolerable ▶그의 성적은 그만저만하다 His grades are so-so.

그만큼 so; so much [many]; so far; that much [many]
▶그만큼 사랑한다면 결혼을 신청하지 그래? If you love her so much why don't you propose to her?
▶그만큼 공부했으니 너는 꼭 만점을 받을 거다 I'm sure you will get a perfect grade because you have studied so hard.
▶더 일하면 그만큼 더 번다 If you do more work, you are paid that much more.
▶하루 쉬면 그만큼 손해가 된다 A day's absence means so much loss.
▶일주일에 그만큼이나 필요합니까? Do you need so much [many] for one week?
▶그만큼이나 말했는데도 그는 실수를 했다 After all I had said [In spite of my advice], he made a mistake.

그만하다〈정도가〉nearly [almost] same; neither better nor worse; doing all right;〈수량이〉as much [many] as; about [much] the same
♦그만한 부자 a rich man like that; a man of such great wealth
▶내 가방도 크기가 그만하다 My bag is of the same size with it.
▶그의 병세는 그저 그만하다 He has been more or less ailing ever since. ⇌ His condition is getting neither better nor worse.
▶[회話]「경기가 어떻습니까?」「그저 그만합니다」"How is your business (doing)?" "Well, it's so-so. ⇌ Well, not too bad."
▶당신 것도 좋지만 내 것도 그만하오 Mine is as good as yours.
▶나의 성적은 그저 그만했다 My grades were neither good not bad.
▶날씨가 그만하기 다행이었다 Fortunately the weather wasn't so bad.
▶그만한 것쯤은 나도 안다 I know as much.
▶대략 그만한 정도다 That's about [the size of] it.
▶그만한 노력도 안 하고 어찌 상공하기를 바라나? How can you dream of a success without making that much of effort?
▶그만하면 충분하겠다 So [That] much will be enough.

그맘때 about [around] that time;〈당시〉in those days; 《at》that time of day [night,

그물

month, year]
▶ 사과가 제일 맛있을 때가 그맘때다 That is the time when apples taste most delicious.
▶ 그 여자는 어제도 그맘때 여기 왔다 She came here yesterday too just about that time.
▶ 그맘때의 만원은 내겐 큰 돈이었다 For me in those days ten thousand won was a big amount (of money).
▶ 그맘때는 그것은 대기록이었다 It was a great record for those days.
▶ 그맘때까지는 내 일도 끝나 있을 것이다 My work will have been finished by that time.

그물 a net; ⟨그물 제품⟩ netting; mesh
♦ 고기잡는 그물 a fishing net / 끄는 그물 ⟨저인망⟩ a dragnet / 던지는 그물 a casting net / 그물 모양의 netlike; netty / 그물을 끌어 당기다 draw (in) a net / 그물을 던지다 cast [throw] a net / 그물을 뜨다[짜다] make a net / 그물을 치다 set [stretch] a net; ⟨테니스에서⟩ put up a tennis net / 그물을 펼치다 spread a net / 그물을 피해 가다 escape a net
▶ 큰 물고기가 그물에 걸렸다 A big fish was caught in the net.
■ ─눈 a mesh of a net ─뜨기 netmaking ─바늘 a netting needle ─선반 a baggage [luggage] rack ─채[국자] a netted ladle; a skimmer ─침대 a hammock ─코 ⇨ 그물(∼눈)

그믐(날) the last day [end] of the month
♦ 그믐께 around the end of the month / 이달 그믐에 at the end [on the last day] of this month
■ 섣달─ the last day of the year; (on) New Year's Eve ■─밤 the night of the end [last day] of the (lunar) month ─칠야 a dark night of the end [last day] of the (lunar) month

그밖 ♦ 그밖의 other; additional / 그밖의 것들 the rest; the others / 그밖에 moreover; in addition; on top of that / 그밖의 조건이 같다면 other things being equal
▶ 나는 그밖의 일은 아무것도 모른다 I know nothing else.
▶ 그밖에 또 질문 있습니까? Do you have any other question?
▶ 그밖에 여섯 명의 응모자가 더 있다 In addition there are six other applicants.

그빨로 ⟨못된 버릇 그대로⟩ in one's usual nasty way

그사이 the while; (in) the interval; (in the) meantime
▶ 그사이 안녕하셨습니까? How have you been all this while?
▶ 그사이에 나는 점심을 먹었다네 I took my lunch in that while.
▶ 그사이에 그 아이는 달아났다 The boy ran away in the meantime.

그슬리다 ⟨타게 하다⟩ scorch; sear; singe; burn; ⟨연기에⟩ smoke; fumigate; ⟨검게 되다⟩ get smoked [fumigated]; get scorched
♦ 까맣게 그슬리다 char; burn to a cinder / 새를 그슬리다 singe a fowl
▶ 그는 검게 그슬린 유리로 해를 보았다 He looked at the sun through a sheet of smoked glass.

그 아비에 그 아들 (속담) Like father, like son.

그악스럽다 ⟨장난이 심하다⟩ naughty; mischievous; ⟨사납다⟩ fierce; ⟨부지런하다⟩ industrious
♦ 그악스러운 사람[짐승] a fierce person [animal] / 그악스럽게 굴다 conduct outrageously [roughly] / 그악스럽게 돈을 벌다 be all eagerness to make money; be engrossed in money-making / 그악스럽게 일하다 work too hard; overwork oneself
▶ 그 아이는 너무 그악스러워 다룰 수가 없다 The boy is too naughty to be controlled [persuaded].

그야 it; that
▶ 그야 물론이지 Of course, it is.
▶ 그야 누가 모르나 Who wouldn't know that?
▶ 그야 그렇지 That's right. ⇌ Oh, that's true.
▶ 그야 그럴 수도 있지 That's quite possible.

그야말로 ⟨참으로⟩ really; indeed; certainly; ⟨그것이야말로⟩ that is...indeed [certainly]
▶ 그의 말은 그야말로 정곡을 찌르는 것이었다 His remark really hit the nail on the head.
▶ 그야말로 힘든 일이었다 That was indeed hard work.
▶ 그야말로 구사일생이구나 You had a really narrow escape.
▶ 그야말로 내가 원하는 책이다 That is the very book that I have been looking for.

그역시 ─亦是 that [it] also [either] ▶ 그 역시 사실이다 That also is true. ▶ 그 역시 내 맘에 안 든다 I don't like it either.

그예 ⟨결국⟩ finally; ultimately; at last; after all; in the long run
▶ 그래서 그예 그는 나타나지 않았군요? So he didn't show up after all?
▶ 그는 그예 술 때문에 죽었다 Drink ended [was the end of] him.
▶ 그는 그 일로 고심하다가 그예 미치고 말았다 He took the matter too much to heart, until (at last) he went mad.

그윽하다 ⟨뜻·향기 등이⟩ deep; profound; secret; subtle ⟪perfume⟫; dim ⟪sound⟫; ⟨장소가⟩ secret; retired; hidden; (deep and) quiet
♦ 그윽한 골짜기 a secret valley / 그윽한 애정 profound affection
▶ 뜰에는 꽃 향기가 그윽하다 The garden is fragrant with the smell of flowers.

그윽히 in secret; deeply in one's heart; inwardly; quietly ♦ 그윽히 풍기는 향기 a subtle perfume / 그윽히 사모하다 love [admire] sb in one's heart

그을다 **1** ⟨햇볕에⟩ be tanned [sunbrowned]; get a tan
♦ 볕에 그을은 얼굴 a tanned face / 까맣게 그을은 deeply [well] tanned / 바닷바람에 구리빛으로 그을다 burn bronze in the salt air
▶ 그녀의 온몸은 황동색으로 그을러 있었다 Her whole body was tanned to a golden brown.
2 ⟨연기로⟩ become sooty ♦ 그을은 sooty; smoke-stained ▶ 부엌 천장은 그을러 있었다 The ceiling of the kitchen was blackened by smoke [covered with soot].

그을리다 ⟨연기로⟩ smoke; fume; fumigate;

〈볕에〉 sunburn; 〈그을음으로〉 soot; make sooty
♦ 검게 그을린 참나무 fumed oak / 쉽게 그을리는 피부 a skin that burns
▶ 램프가 천장을 그을린다 The lamp smokes the ceiling. ⇌ The ceiling is stained with soot by the lamp.

그을음 soot; black dirt
♦ 그을음이 끼다[앉다] be soot-covered; become sooty; be stained with soot / 그을음을 털어내다 sweep away [wipe off] the soot
▶ 굴뚝에 그을음이 많이 낀 것 같다 The chimney seems to have collected much soot.

그이 that person; he

그이들 those people [persons]; they; them

그저 1 〈그대로 사뭇〉 still; without ceasing [stopping]; continuously; so far
▶ 비가 그저 내리고 있다 It is still raining. ⇌ It keeps on raining.
▶ 그는 아침부터 그저 텔레비전만 보고 있다 He has been watching television all through the morning.
2 〈보통으로〉 so and so; neither so good nor so bad ♦ 그저 쓸만하다 be just passable
▶ [會話]「자네 사업은 어떤가?」「그저 그래」 "How is your business?" "It is not so good."
▶ [會話]「영화는 재미있었니?」「그저 그렇더라」 "Was the movie interesting?" "It was so and so."
3 〈단지〉 only; just; merely; simply ♦ 그저 얼간만 just a little [bit] of... ▶ 그저 농담으로 한 말이다 I said it just for fun. ⇌ I did not mean what I said.
4 〈역시·예상대로〉 just as one thought; as (was [had been]) expected
▶ 그저 그럴 줄 알았다 That is about what I thought. ⇌ I expected [thought] as much.
▶ 내 그저 그렇게 될 줄 알았지 Things have been done so just as they were expected to be.
5 〈생각없이〉 aimlessly; casually; recklessly; 〈이유없이〉 without any reason ♦ 그저 자꾸 쏘드리다 hit wildly; beat sb blind / 그저 빚을 마구 지다 go into debt recklessly
6 〈제발〉 please ▶ 그저 용서해 주십시오 Please forgive me. ▶ 그저 네가 참으렴 Won't you be patient, please?

그저께 the day before yesterday ♦ 그저께 아침[밤, 저녁] the morning [night, evening] before last

그적거리다 〈글씨·그림을〉 scrawl; scribble; dash ♦ 그적그적 scribblingly / 편지를 그적거리다 scribble a letter

그전 —前 former times [days]; the other day; the past
♦ 그전에 before; formerly; in former [old] days; in the past; before that time; prior [previous] to that time / 그전같이 as before; as usual
▶ 그 사람은 그전에 만나본 적이 있다 I have met him before.
▶ 모든 것이 그전과는 다르다 Things are not what they used to be.
▶ 우리는 그전부터 아는 사이다 We've known each other for a long time.

그제야 only then; only when [after]; not... until; for the first time
▶ 내 설명을 듣고 그제야 그는 자기가 실수한 것을 깨달았다 I had to explain it to him before he realized he had made a mistake.
▶ 그제야 나는 화재의 무서움을 깨달았다 Then I realized for the first time how horrible a fire is.
▶ 세 번이나 고함을 질렀더니 그제야 그는 창밖으로 내다보았다 He did not look out of the window until I had shouted three times. ⇌ He looked out of the window only after I had shouted three times.

그중 —中 1 〈그 가운데〉 among them (all); of them (all); of the number
▶ 그녀도 그중 한 사람이다 She is (one) of the number.
▶ 다섯 명이 부상을 당하고 그중 한 명은 중태였다 Five were wounded, and of these one was in a serious condition.
2 〈가장〉 most; best; least ▶ 나는 이것이 그중 좋다 I like this better than the others. ⇌ I prefer this to others. ▶ 나는 수학이 그중 싫다 I like mathematics least.

그즈음 about that time; around then; in those days

그지없다 〈한이 없다〉 limitless; boundless; endless; immeasurable; unfathomable; 〈표현할 수 없다〉 beyond expression [description]
♦ 그지없이 넓은 바다 the boundless expanse of the ocean / 가엾기 그지없다 be too pitiful for words / 유감스럽기 그지없다 be extremely sorry
▶ 그 경치는 아름답기 그지없다 I can't fully describe the beauty of the view.
▶ 파도타기는 통쾌하기 그지없다 Surfriding is extremely thrilling.

그쯤 1 〈그 정도〉 that [as] much; to that extent
▶ 글쎄 그쯤 되겠지 That is about right. ▶ 그쯤은 나도 안다 I know as [that] much.
2 〈장소〉 about [near] there ▶ 이것을 그쯤에 다 놓아라 Put this somewhere over there.
▶ 그쯤에서 쉬어 가자 Let's take a rest about there.

그치다 1 〈멈추다〉 stop; cease; 〈끝나다〉 end; come to a stop [an end]
♦ 그치지 않고 ceaselessly; continuously; with no break / 딱 그치다 come to a standstill; stop suddenly
▶ 바람[소리]이 그쳤다 The wind [noise] has died down [away].
▶ 비가 그쳤다 It has stopped raining. ⇌ The rain has stopped.
▶ 오늘은 비가 왔다가 그쳤다가 한다 It has been raining on and off [off and on] today.
▶ 박수가 오랫동안 그치지 않았다 The applause continued for a long time.
2 〈중단하다〉 stop; discontinue; give up; put an end (to)
▶ 그가 들어오자 그들은 말을 그쳤다 They stopped [ceased] talking when he came in.
▶ 그들은 연구를 그치지 않았다 They continued

[went on] with their study.

3 〈한정되다〉 be limited [confined] to ◆그칠 줄 모르는 욕망 unlimited desire
▶그의 나쁜 짓은 여기에 그치지 않는다 His evil doing does not stop here.
▶그의 야심은 그칠 줄 몰랐다 He had unlimited ambition. ⇌ There was no end to his ambition.

그토록 so (much); such; to that [such an] extent
▶그가 그토록 보고 싶니? Are you so anxious to see him?
▶그토록 심한 말을 할 건 없잖나 You don't have to use such harsh words.
▶그토록 일을 하는데도 그는 가난하다 He is poor in spite of all his labors.
▶그는 그토록 돈이 많은데도 불만인 것 같다 He seems discontented for all his wealth.
▶그토록 충고해도 그는 듣지 않았다 All my advice was lost upon him.

그후 —後 〈이후〉 after that; thereafter; afterward(s); subsequently; later; 〈이래〉 (ever) since; then; from that time on
◆그후 몇달 동안 during the ensuing months / 그후 3년이 지나 three years later
▶그후 그녀를 만나지 못했다 I haven't seen her ever since.
▶나는 그후 그녀가 어떻게 되었는지 모른다 I don't know what has become of her since.
▶나는 그후 죽 여기서 살고 있다 I have lived here ever since.

극 極 1 〈지구·자석의〉 a pole ◆극의 polar / 남[북]극 the south [north] pole / 양[음]극 the positive [negative] pole / 자극(磁極) a magnetic pole
2 〈절정〉 the climax; the extreme; the extremity; the height; the zenith
◆극에 달하다 reach the climax; run to an extreme; go to extremes / 절망의 극에 달해 자살하다 kill *oneself* in despair
▶그의 피로는 극에 달해 있었다 He was extremely [completely, utterly] exhausted.
▶기쁨이 극에 이르면 슬픔이 된다 Excessive joy end in sadness. ⇌ The height of joy is a sadness.
■ —궤도 a polar orbit —좌표 〔數〕 polar coordinates —지방 the polar regions

극 劇 a play; a drama ◆극으로 꾸미다 dramatize 《a story》 / 극을 공연하다 play; give [stage, perform] a play
■ —사(史)— 《stage》 a historical play 소인— private [amateur] theatricals 현대— a modern play ■ —문학 dramatic literature

극값 極— 〔數〕 the extreme value
극관 極冠 〔天〕 a polar cap
극광 極光 the aurora; the polar lights ■ 남— the aurora australis; the southern lights 북— the aurora borealis; the northern lights
극구변명하다 極口辯明— spare no pains to defend *oneself*; go to extremes in excusing *oneself*; make every sort of excuses
극구칭찬[칭송]하다 極口稱讚[稱頌]— praise [laud] *sb* sky-high [to the skies]; speak in high terms of; give the highest praise 《to》

극권 極圈 the polar circle ■ 북[남]— the Arctic [Antarctic] Circle
극기 克己 self-control; self-restraint; self-denial ◆극기의 self-controlling; self-restraining; strong-minded
■ —주의 stoicism —파 the Stoics
극기심 克己心 the spirit of self-denial; a self-denying spirit ◆극기심이 있는 사람 a man of self-restraint [strong will]
▶그는 극기심이 없다 He has no self-control.
극단 極端 an extreme; an excess; extremity
◆극단의[적인] extreme; ultra; excessive / 더위와 추위의 양극단 the extremes of heat and cold / 극단적인 수단 extremes; extreme measures; radical steps / 극단적으로 extremely; excessively; to the extreme degree
▶애증은 양극단이다 Love and hate are extremes.
▶그것은 극단적인 예다 That is an extreme case.
▶그는 극단적인 국가주의자다 He is an ultra-nationalist.
▶극단으로 치닫지 마라 Don't go to extremes [excess].
▶극단적으로 말하면 그는 세상의 쓰레기다 To put it in an extreme way, he is the scum of the earth.
극단 劇團 a dramatic [theatrical] company; a troupe ■국립— the National Drama Company 지방 순회— a provincial touring company; a troupe on the road
극단 劇壇 the stage; the theatrical world
◆극단을 떠나다 leave [go off] the stage / 극단에 나서다 come [go] on the stage; appear before the footlights
▶저 배우는 극단 출신이다 That actor comes from the legitimate stage.
극대 極大 the greatest; 〔數〕 the maximum
◆극대의 maximum; maximal / 극대와 극소 the maximum and minimum
■ —값 the maximum value
극대화 極大化 maximization —극대화하다 maximize ▶이윤을 극대화하지 않으면 안 된다 We must maximize profits.
극도 極度 the utmost limit; the extreme
◆극도의 extreme; excessive; utmost; maximum / 극도로 extremely; excessively / 극도의 신경 쇠약에 걸리다 have a nervous breakdown of the severest kind / 극도에 달하다 reach the utmost limit; be carried to an extreme / 극도로 긴장하다 be strained to the limit / 극도로 비탄하다 be in extreme grief
▶그는 극도의 피로로 쓰러졌다 He collapsed from extreme [excessive] fatigue.
▶그들은 극도로 흥분하고 있었다 They were extremely excited.
극독 劇毒 a deadly [violent] poison
극동 極東 the Far East
■ —러시아 the Russian Far East —문제 a Far Eastern question —방송 the Far East Network (略 F.E.N.) —위원회 the Far Eastern Commission (略 FEC) —자문 위원회 the Far Eastern Advisory Commission (略 FEAC)
극락 極樂 1 〈극히 안락함〉 supreme happiness;

perfect bliss
2 〈극락 세계〉〔佛敎〕 paradise (of Buddhism); the abode of the blessed; the home of the happy dead; 〔그神〕 Elysium
■ —생활 an Elysian life —왕생(往生) an easy (and peaceful) death; an easy passage into eternity —정토(淨土) the Land of Happiness [Perfect Bliss]

극락조 極樂鳥 〔鳥〕 a bird of paradise
극량 極量 〈약의〉 the maximum dose; a fatal dose
극력 極力 to the utmost; to the best of *one's* ability; as ... as possible; in every way
◆극력 반대하다 oppose stubbornly / 극력 성원하다 cheer with all *one's* might / 극력 원조하다 help as much as *one* can
▶나는 그들을 극력 설득하였으나 실패했다 I tried to persuade them in every way I could [as well as I could] but failed.

극렬 極烈 violence; severity; intensity; vehemence; fierceness
—**극렬하다** violent; severe; intense; vehement
◆극렬한 경쟁 a cutthroat [violent, keen] competition / 극렬한 언사 vehement language; high words
■ —分子 an extremist; a radical

극론 極論 an extreme argument; sophistry
—**극론하다** carry logic to extremes; make [advance] an extreme argument
▶그는 그것이 필요없다고까지 극론했다 He went so far as to deny the necessity of it.

극명하다 克明— faithful; conscientious; minute; detailed; scrupulous
◆극명한 묘사 a minute description / 문제를 극명하게 설명하다 explain a matter in detail
▶그는 관찰 결과를 극명하게 기록했다 He kept a scrupulous record of his observations.

극미 極微 —**극미하다** infinitesimal; (ultra) microscopic ◆극미한 세계 a microscopic world / 빛깔의 극미한 차이 subtle differences in color
■ —動物 an animalcule —量[數] an infinitesimal quantity [number] —速(速) a dead-slow speed

극복 克服 conquest; subjugation
—**극복하다** conquer; overcome; get over
◆온갖 난관을 극복하다 overcome many difficulties / 나쁜 습관을 극복하다 conquer [get the better of] a bad habit / 위기를 극복하다 weather a crisis
▶그는 난청을 극복하고 훌륭한 작곡을 하였다 He overcame his poor hearing and composed excellent pieces of music. ⇌ He composed excellent pieces of music in spite of his poor hearing.

극본 劇本 a play ⇨ 각본(脚本)
극북 極北 〈가장 북쪽〉 the extreme north; 〈북극〉 the North Pole ◆극북 지역 the arctic region

극비 極祕 a top [strict] secret; strict secrecy
◆극비의 top-secret; strictly secret; (美) highly classified / 극비로 with utmost secrecy / 극비로 하다 keep (a matter) a close secret; guard (a matter) with great secrecy
▶그들은 극비로 준비를 했다 They made arrangement in strict secrecy.
▶이것은 극비로 알고 계시오 You will understand this absolutely [strictly] confidential.
■ —文書 strictly confidential documents; (美) a top secret document —事項 a close secret; a top secret —情報 top secret information

극빈 極貧 extreme [dire] poverty ▶그는 극빈 생활을 하고 있다 He lives in extreme poverty. ⇌ He is as poor as a church mouse. —**극빈하다** extremely poor; destitute
■ —者 a pauper; (총칭) the destitute

극상 極上 the highest [finest] quality; the first rate [grade] ◆극상의 the best; the first-rate; extrafine; of the finest quality; choice
■ —品 an article of the best [finest, highest] quality; choice articles; the best (of its kind)

극성 極性 〔電〕 polarity ◆극성의 polar / 극성을 주다 polarize / 극성을 없애다 depolarize

극성 極盛 〈세력의〉 the height of prosperity; highly flourishing [thriving]; 〈성질 의〉 extremity ◆극성을 떨다 grow impatient; run to extreme
—**극성스럽다, 극성맞다** extreme; impatient; impetuous; mad; frantic
◆극성스러운 사람 an impatient [impetuous] person / 극성스러운 언동 intemperate conduct / 자녀 교육에 극성스러운 어머니 a mother oversolicitous for her children's education
▶그는 직공들이 쓰러질 때까지 극성스럽게 일을 시켰다 He drove the workers unmercifully until they collapsed.

극세포 極細胞 〔生〕 a polar cell
극소 極小 the smallest; 〔數〕 the minimum
◆극소의 infinitesimal; minimum
■ —값 the minimum value —量 the (irreducible) minimum —數 the minimum number; a small minority

극시 劇詩 a dramatic poem; (총칭) dramatic poetry
극심하다 極甚— intense; severe; vehement
◆극심한 경쟁 a keen competition / 극심한 더위[추위] intense heat [cold] / 극심한 통증 an acute [a severe] pain / 극심한 피해를 입다 suffer heavy losses

극악(무도) 極惡(無道) atrocity; villainy; enormity; brutality
—**극악(무도)하다** most wicked; heinous; atrocious; brutal; devilish; villainous
▶그의 극악 무도한 행위는 용서할 수 없다 His flagrant misconduct is unforgivable.

극약 劇藥 a powerful [drastic, terrible] medicine [drug]; a violent poison
극양 極洋 the polar seas ■ —漁業 the polar-sea fishery
극언하다 極言— go so far as to say...; be bold enough to say; speak in unsparing words
◆극언하자면 to put it extremely [at its most extreme]
▶극언하자면 그는 배반자다 To put it forcibly [Perhaps I am going too far in saying this, but], he is a traitor.
▶그렇게까지 극언할 필요는 없다 We need not

극영화 劇映畫 a film with a dramatic story; a drama film; a film of a play

극외권 極外圈 〔宇宙〕 the exosphere

극우 極右 the extreme right; the ultraright ◆극우의 extreme-rightist; ultraconservative; ultranationalist ■—단체 a far-right(-wing) organization; a group of the ultraright [far-right] —파 extremists of the right; ultranationalists

극작 劇作 playwriting —**극작하다** write a play [drama] ■—가 a dramatist; a playwright; a playwriter —법 dramaturgy

극장 劇場 a theater; a playhouse ■개봉— a first-run theater 국립— the National Theater 야외— an open-air theater —가 a theater district [quarter]; (美) a rialto —경영자 a theater manager; (美) a theatrical producer —식당 a theater restaurant —안내원 a theater attendant; an usher —주 a theater owner; the proprietor of a theater

극저온 極低溫 a very [an extremely] low temperature ■—물리학 very low temperature physics

극적 劇的 dramatic ◆극적인 사건 a dramatic event / 극적인 생애 an eventful life / 극적 효과를 노리다 aim at a dramatic effect
▶그것은 극적인 장면[정경]이었다 It was a dramatic scene [sight].
▶두 사람은 파리에서 극적으로 재회했다 The two met again most dramatically in Paris.

극점 極點 the extreme [highest, culminating] point; a pole; a climax

극좌 極左 the extreme left ◆극좌의 ultraleft; extreme-leftist ■—분자[파] an ultraleftist; extremists of [on] the left; extreme leftists

극중극 劇中劇 a play within a play

극지 極地 the polar regions; the pole ■—법 〔登山〕 a polar method —식물 an arctic plant —탐험 a polar expedition —횡단 비행 a transpolar flight

극진하다 極盡— cordial; warm; hearty; hospitable; devoted
▶부상자들은 극진한 간호를 받았다 The injured people were treated with tender care.
▶우리는 어디를 가나 극진한 대접을 받았다 We were received cordially [We were given a warm reception] wherever we went.
▶그녀는 아픈 친구를 극진히 간병했다 She looked after her sick friend tenderly [carefully].

극찬하다 極讚— praise *sb* sky-high ⇒ 극구칭찬하다

극채색 極彩色 rich [brilliant] coloring ◆극채색의 캘린더 a richly [gorgeously] colored calendar

극체 極體 〔生〕 a polar body

극초단파 極超短波 microwave ■—스펙트럼 a microwave spectrum

극치 極致 the acme; the perfection; the culmination; the height
◆미의 극치 the ideal of beauty; ideal beauty / 예술의 극치 the highest reach of art / 극치에 달하다 attain the highest perfection; achieve [reach] the ultimate 《in》
▶그것은 어리석음의 극치다 It's the height of folly.
▶그의 예술은 원숙의 극치에 도달했다 His art has attained the acme of maturity.

극터듬다 claw *one's* way up 《a cliff》; clamber 《up》; climb laboriously

극통 劇痛 an acute [intense] pain; a severe [sharp, keen, violent] pain; a pang; a twinge

극판 極板 〔電〕 a pole plate

극평 劇評 drama [theater] criticism

극피동물 棘皮動物 an echinoderm 《*pl*. -mata》

극하다 極— go to extremes; run to an extreme ◆사치를 극하다 be most luxurious

극한 極限 the utmost limit(s); the bounds; an extremity 《of pain》; 〔數〕 limit
◆극한을 넘다 go beyond the bounds / 극한에 이르다 reach the limit 《of patience》
▶나는 나의 능력을 극한까지 펼치고 싶다 I want to develop my faculties to the utmost limit(s).
■—상황 an extreme situation: 극한 상황에 놓이다 be placed in an extreme situation; be pushed to the limit —치 〔數〕 a limiting value —투쟁 a desperate struggle; a life-and-death struggle

극한 極寒 severe [intense, arctic] cold ◆극한의 계절 the coldest season

극형 極刑 〈최대한의 형〉 the maximum [extreme] penalty; 〈사형〉 a capital punishment; the death penalty ◆죄인을 극형에 처하다 condemn a criminal to capital punishment; sentence a criminal to death

극화 劇化 dramatization —**극화하다** dramatize ◆소설을 극화하다 dramatize a novel; make a novel into a drama; adapt a novel to the stage [into a play]

극화 劇畫 comics with a realistic narrative

극히 極— very; exceedingly; extremely; in the extreme
◆극히 어려운 책 an exceedingly [exceptionally] difficult book / 극히 중요한 문제 a very important matter; a problem of paramount importance / 극히 드물게 once in a blue moon / 극히 겸손하다 be extremely modest
▶그가 그렇게 일찍 일어나는 일은 극히 드물다 It is very rare for him to get up so early.
▶이것은 한국에서는 극히 흔한 꽃이다 This is a very common flower in Korea.

근 根 **1** 〈부스럼의〉 the core 《of a boil》 **2** 〔數〕 a root **3** 〔佛敎〕 bases of sensation ■세제곱— a cubic root 제곱— a square root

근 筋 a muscle ⇒ 근육 ■—긴장 이상증 〔病理〕 dystonia —전도 an electromyogram —조직 muscular tissue

근 斤 a *kŭn* 《= 600g》; a catty

근 近 about; almost; nearly ◆근 백리 nearly one hundred *ri*

근간 近刊 〈신간〉 a recent publication [issue]; 〈예정의〉 a forthcoming book [title] ◆근간의 recently published [issued]; latest; forthcoming; in preparation / 근간 「문학」 the latest issue [number] of *Munhak* / 근간 잡지

recently published [forthcoming] magazines ▶그 책은 근간 예정이다 The book is in preparation [will be published shortly]. ■—소개 a review of recent publications —예고 an announcement of forthcoming books; (게시) Forthcoming (▶책 제목 뒤에 씀)

근간 近間 ◆근간에 one of these days; before long ▶근간 또 뵙겠습니다 I hope we can meet again in the near future.

근간 根幹 1 〈뿌리와 줄기〉 root and trunk 2 〈근본〉 the basis 《pl. bases》; the root; 〈기조〉 the keynote 《of diplomacy》 ◆근간을 이루다 form the keynote 《of》 ▶농업은 나라의 근간이다 Agriculture is the basis of a nation.

근거 根據 a basis; foundation; ground; an authority; a reason ◆근거 있는[없는] 정보 information from a reliable [an unreliable] source / 근거 있는[없는] 주장 a well-grounded [baseless, groundless] argument ▶그녀는 그에게 근거없는 의심을 품었다 She harbored [held] a groundless suspicion against him. ▶그의 연구는 확실한 근거가 있다 His study has a firm basis. ▶의혹의 근거가 몇가지 있다 There are several reasons for suspicion. ▶그가 그 표현을 쓴 것은 근거가 있다 He has his reasons for using that expression. ▶그의 말은 사실에 근거를 두고 있다 His statement is based on fact. ▶무슨 근거로 그렇게 말할 수 있느냐? On what ground [authority] can you say that?

근거리 近距離 a short distance ◆근거리에 있는 be a short distance away 《from》 / 근거리에서 쏘다 fire at short range ▶그들은 서로 아주 근거리에 살고 있다 They live within a stone's throw [walking distance] of each other. ■—경주 a short distance race —사격 short-distance firing [shooting] —열차 a local train —전화 a short-distance (phone) call

근거지 根據地 a base (of operations); headquarters; a stronghold ◆근거지를 마련하다 establish a base

근검 勤儉 thrift and diligence [industry]; diligence and economy —근검하다 thrifty (and diligent); frugal ■—저축 thrift and saving —저축 운동 a saving movement [campaign]

근검하다 be blessed with many children

근경 近景 a near [close-range] view 《of》

근경 根莖 〈뿌리와 줄기〉 root and trunk; 〈植〉 a rootstock; a rhizome; a rhizoma 《pl. -mata》

근계 謹啓 Dear Sir; Dear Mr...; 〈회사·단체 앞〉 Dear Sirs

근고 近古 the early modern age ■—사 a history of the early modern age

근고하다 謹告— inform with respect; announce respectfully

근골 筋骨 1 〈근육과 뼈대〉 sinews and bones; 〈체격〉 build; physique; setup 2 ⇨ 체력 ◆근골이 실팍한 muscular; sinewy 《arms》; stringy 《young man》; powerfully-built

근교 近郊 the suburbs (▶보통 복수로 씀. a suburb는 특정 지구를 의미함); the outskirts; the environs; vicinity ◆근교의 suburban; neighboring / 서울과 그 근교 Seoul and (its) environs; Seoul and metropolitan area; (the) Greater Seoul (area) ▶나는 서울 근교에 살고 싶다 I'd like to live in the suburbs [a suburb] of Seoul. ■—농업 agriculture in suburban areas —도시 neighboring towns; the town around a large city

근근이 僅僅— 〈간신히〉 barely; narrowly; hardly; with difficulty; 〈고작〉 just; only ◆근근이 시험에 합격하다 scrape through the examination / 근근이 이기다 win 《a game》 by a shave ▶그 집은 근근이 살아간다 That family can just scrape along.

근기 根氣 〈인내심〉 patience; perseverance; endurance; 〈정력〉 energy ◆근기가 있는 patient; persevering; enduring / 근기가 없는 impatient; unable to carry on; lacking patience ▶그는 근기있게 노력하지 않으니까 성공하지 못한다 He doesn't succeed because he does not persevere in his efforts. ▶근기가 없으면 아무 일에도 성공할 수 없다 You can never succeed in anything without perseverance. ▶스웨터를 짜는 데는 근기가 필요하다 You need perseverance to knit a sweater.

근년 近年 (in) recent years; late years ▶근년에 없던 추운 날씨다 This is the coldest weather we have had in recent years.

근대 〔植〕 a (Swiss) chard

근대 近代 the modern age; modern times ◆근대의 modern / 근대적인 modern; modernistic / 전근대적인 premodern ■—과학 modern science —국가 a modern state [nation] —극 a modern drama [play] —문학[건축, 미술, 음악] modern literature [architecture, art, music] —사 modern history —사상 modern ideas —산업 modern industries —생활 modern life —성 modernity —여성 modern women —영어 Modern English (略 Mod. E., Mod E) —5종 경기 the modern pentathlon —인 modern people

근대화 近代化 modernization —근대화하다 modernize ▶생활 양식을 근대화하는 데는 많은 돈이 든다 It takes much money to modernize the way of life.

근동 近東 the Near East ■—제국 the Near Eastern countries

근드적거리다 shake slightly; sway gently; rock

근들거리다 swing; rock; sway; play loosely [to and fro] ◆바람에 근들거리다 be swayed by the wind; sway (about) to the wind

근래 近來 these days; recently; lately ◆근래의 late; recent / 근래의 경향 the recent [modern] tendency ▶그와 같은 정직한 소년은 근래에 드물다 An honest boy like him is rare these days.

▶그는 근래에 드물게 보는 큰 인물이다 He is the greatest man in recent years.
▶그것은 근래에 없던 큰 눈이었다 It was the heaviest snow we have had in (recent) years.

근량 斤量 weight ⇨ 무게 ◆근량을 속이다 give short weight ■—풍 ⇨ 무게

근력 筋力 muscular strength [power]; physical strength; brawn ▶우리 할아버지는 90세이신데 아직도 근력이 좋으시다 My grandfather is 90 and still going strong.

근로 動勞 work; service; 〈육체적인〉 labor ◆근로에 대한 보수 compensation for one's service —근로하다 work, labor; serve
■—계급[대중] the working class [masses] —기준법 the Labor Standard Law —봉사 labor service —소득 (an) earned income —소득세 the earned income tax —의욕 the will to work: 그 사건이 그들의 근로 의욕을 드높였다 The event heightened their will to work. —자 a worker; a working person; a laborer; (총칭) working people —조건 working [labor] conditions —포장(襃章) the Labor Medal

근류 根瘤 〔植〕 a root nodule [tubercle]
■—박테리아 root nodule bacteria

근린 近隣 the neighborhood; the vicinity
■—제국 neighboring countries

근면 動勉 hard work; diligence; industry
▶근면은 성공의 어머니다 Diligence is the mother of success.
—근면하다 hardworking; diligent; industrious ◆근면한 학생 a diligent student / 근면하게 일하다 work hard [diligently]
▶그는 근면하다 He works hard.
■—가 a hard worker; a diligent person

근모 根毛 〔植〕 a root hair; a fibril

근무 動務 work; service; duty
◆초과 근무 수당 overtime work allowance / 특별 근무 수당 specific duty allowance / 해외 근무 수당 a foreign service allowance / 근무를 충실히 하다 serve faithfully; be faithful to one's duty; attend faithfully to one's work
▶우리는 하루 8시간 근무다 We have an eight-hour day. ⇌ We work eight hours a day.
▶그는 지금 근무중이다 He is working. ⇌ He is on duty.
▶그는 근무를 게을리한다 He is neglecting his duties.
—근무하다 work; be on duty; serve
▶그는 석유 회사에 근무한다 He works for an oil company.
▶내 동생은 신문사에 근무하게 되었다 My brother got a job in a newspaper company.
▶그는 잘 근무하고 있다 He is a diligent [reliable] worker.
■—시간외— overtime (work) 야간— night duty; a night shift: 그는 야간 근무다 He works [is on] the night shift. 육상[해상]— shore [sea] service ■—능률 service efficiency —성적 one's service record: 그는 근무 성적이 좋다 He has shown good work performance. —소집 reserve training recruitment; service call —실적 service record —연한 the length of one's service —자 men in service; men on duty —조건 conditions [terms] of employment —지 수당 a service-area allowance —처 one's place of employment; one's office: 근무처가 어디십니까? Where do you work? ⇌ Where is your office? —태도 assiduity; one's conduct

근무력증 筋無力症 〔醫〕 myasthenia

근무시간 勤務時間 office [business, working] hours ▶근무 시간에 술을 마시면 안 된다 You must not drink alcohol (while) on duty.

근무평가 勤務評價 the [an] efficiency rating; work performance evaluation ▶그의 근무 평가는 별로 좋지 않았다 He was not rated very high in the performance of his duties.

근묵자흑 近墨者黑 He who touches pitch shall be defiled therewith.

근방 近方 the neighborhood ⇨ 근처

근배 謹拜 Yours truly [faithfully, respectfully, sincerely]

근본 根本 〈뿌리〉 the root; 〈근원〉 the source; 〈기초〉 the foundation; the basis; the ground; 〈본질〉 the essence
▶모든 시민의 참가가 민주정치의 근본이다 The participation of every citizen is the essence of democracy.
▶토지는 부(富)의 근본이다 Land is the basis of wealth.
▶우리는 근본까지 파들어가야 한다 We must go down to the root [source].
■—문제 a fundamental [basic] problem: 그것은 교육의 근본 문제에 관한 토론이었다 It was a discussion about the fundamental problems of education. —원리 the fundamental [basic] principle: 그들은 민주주의의 근본 원리를 모른다 They don't understand the basic principles of democracy —원인 the root cause

근본적 根本的 fundamental; basic; cardinal; 〈철저한〉 radical; drastic
◆세제의 근본적인 개혁 a drastic [radical] tax reform / 우리 외교 정책의 근본적인 변경 a fundamental change in our diplomatic policy / 실패의 근본적인 원인 the root cause of failure / 근본적으로 fundamentally; basically; root and branch / 근본적으로 개혁하다 effect a radical reform; thoroughly revolutionize; lay the axe to the root (of)
▶그 생각은 근본적으로 틀렸다 The idea is fundamentally [basically] wrong.
▶근본적인 개편이 필요하다 A thorough [radical] reorganization is needed.
▶그의 견해는 우리와 근본적으로 다르다 His view is fundamentally different from ours.

근사 近似 **1** 〈비슷한〉 approximation —근사하다 closely resemble; 〈수학〉 approximate ◆근사한 approximate; close
2 〈멋짐〉 wonderfulness; niceness —근사하다 wonderful; fine; nice; smart
▶근사한 생각이다 It's a wonderful [brilliant] idea.
■—값 an approximate value; an approximation —계산 a rough [an approximate] calculation

근생엽 根生葉 〔植〕 radical leaves

근섬유 筋纖維 〔生〕 a muscular [muscle] fiber
■—초(鞘) the sarcolemma

근성 根性 (a) nature; (a) disposition; spirit
♦근성이 비뚤어진 perverse; cross-grained / 근성이 나쁜 ill-natured
▶그는 근성이 썩어빠졌다 He is rotten at heart. ⇌ He has a mean disposition.
▶가난해지면 거지 근성이 나타나는 법이다 When a man becomes poor, he becomes mean. ⇌ Poor in money, poor in spirit.
■관료— a bureaucratic nature 노예— a servile spirit 상인— a mercenary spirit 섬나라— an insular spirit; insularism

근세 近世 modern times [ages]; recent times; latter days ♦근세의 modern; recent; latter-day ■—사 modern history

근소하다 僅少하다 〈수〉 a few;〈양〉 a little;〈사소하다〉 trifling 《cost》; insignificant; scanty
♦근소한 수입 a scanty income / 근소한 차이 a slight difference / 근소한 차로 이기다 win by a narrow margin; win by a small majority
▶예산안은 150 대 148이라는 근소한 차이로 통과되었다 The budget was passed by a narrow majority of 150 to 148.

근속 勤續 continuous [long] service
♦근속 연한에 따라 in proportion to the length of one's service
▶아버지는 장기 근속으로 표창받으셨다 My father was honored in recognition of his long service.
—**근속하다** service for long years; be in continuous serve
▶그는 기술자로 우리 회사에 30년간 근속했다 He served in our company for 30 years as an engineer.
▶김선생은 이 학교에서 30년간 근속하고 있다 Mr. Kim has been teaching at this school for thirty years.
■—년수 the length of one's service —수당 a length-of-service allowance —자 a person in long service: 10년 근속자 a person with 10 years of continuous service

근수 斤數 the weight (expressed) in kŭn;〈무게〉 the weight
♦근수가 모자라다 be short of weight; be underweight / 근수를 달다 weigh 《a commodity》 on a scale; check weight / 근수를 속이다 give short weight

근수 根數 〔數〕 a root; a radical

근시(안) 近視(眼) nearsightedness;〈英〉short-sightedness;〔醫〕myopia
♦근시의 nearsighted; shortsighted; myopic / 근시(안)적인 생각 a shortsighted [nearsighted] view
▶네 생각은 근시안적이다 You cannot see beyond your nose.
■가성(假性)— 〔醫〕false nearsightedness; pseudo-myopia ■—(안)경 《a pair of》glasses [spectacles] for a nearsighted person: 그는 10°의 근시경을 쓰고 있다 He wears concave glasses of 10°.

근신 謹愼 good behavior [conduct];〈회개〉repentance; penitence;〈자제〉self-control; self-restraint ♦근신을 명하다 order sb to put a rein on his own behavior
▶그는 근신 중이다 He is behaving himself. ⇌ He is behaving in a restrained way.
—**근신하다** behave oneself; be on one's good behavior; be penitent
♦근신하는 모습을 보이다 show one's repentance [penitence]
▶그 배우는 그 추문 후 6개월간 근신했다 After the scandal, the actor refrained from making public appearances for six months.

근실 勤實 diligence and sincerity [faithfulness]; assiduity
—**근실하다** diligent and sincere [faithful]
♦근실하게 일하다 work diligently; serve faithfully; attend to one's duties with diligence

근심 care; anxiety; worry; concern; fear
♦근심스러운 anxious; worried; uneasy / 근심이 있다 have cares [anxieties, worries]/ 근심이 없다 be free from care [worry]; be carefree / 근심이 끊이지 않다 always have sth to worry about
▶근심스러운 얼굴인데 무슨 일이오? You look worried. What's the matter with you?
▶그녀는 근심 때문에 병이 났다 She got sick from anxiety.
▶그는 술로 근심을 풀고 있다 He is drinking away his troubles.
—**근심하다** care 《about》; worry; fear; be anxious [concerned] 《about》; be troubled
♦사소한 일로 죽도록 근심하다 worry oneself to death over trifles
▶그는 따돌림당할까 근심했다 He was afraid of being left out.

근심거리 cares; a worry; an anxiety
▶딸 하나 있는 것이 항상 근심거립니다 My only daughter always weighs on my mind [is a source of anxiety].

근엄 謹嚴 sobriety; seriousness; gravity
▶우리 할아버지는 근엄 그 자체였다 Our grandfather was a [the] picture of solemnity. ⇌ Our grandfather was a man of strict morals.
—**근엄하다** stern; solemn; grave; austere
♦근엄한 사람 a grave person; a man of strict morals [dignified mien]/ 근엄한 태도 a serious [grave] manner; a dignified mien

근염 筋炎 〔醫〕inflammation of a muscle; myositis

근엽 根葉 1 ⇨ 근생엽 **2**〈뿌리와 잎〉roots and leaves

근영 近影 one's recent [latest] picture [portrait, photograph]

근왕 勤王 loyalty to the king; royalism

근원 根源 the root; the origin; the cause; the source
♦모든 악의 근원 the root of all evil / 근원을 찾다 trace sth to its origin [source]; get at [go to] the root of sth
▶금전욕이 모든 악의 근원이다 The love of money is the root of all evil.
▶해결을 위해서는 그 문제의 근원으로 되돌아가야 한다 We must go back to the origin [root] of the problem for a solution.

근위대 近衛隊 the Royal Guards; the court guards

근육 筋肉 muscle; ⟨발달한⟩ brawn
♦손[팔]의 근육 a hand [an arm] muscle / 근육의 경직 muscular rigidity / 근육이 잘 발달한 well-muscled; muscular; brawny; sinewy
▶나는 팔 근육을 발달시키기 위해 테니스를 한다 I play tennis to develop my arm muscles. ■—노동 manual [physical] labor —노동자 a manual worker [laborer] —수축 contraction of the muscles —운동 muscular motion [movement] —조직 the muscular system [tissue] —주사 an intramuscular injection —통 a muscular pain [ache] —피로 muscular fatigue

근인 近因 an immediate [a proximate] cause

근일 近日 recent [these] days
♦근일 중에 soon; shortly; in a few days; one of these days; on an early day

근일점 近日點 〔天〕 the perihelion (*pl*. -lia)
♦근일점의 anomalistic

근자 近者 these [recent] days ♦근자의 recent; late / 근자에 these days; recently; lately; of late

근작 近作 one's recent (literary) work; one's latest product

근저 近著 one's recent [latest] work

근저 根底 the root; the base; the basis; the bottom; the foundation
♦근저로부터 fundamentally; radically; (口) from the ground [bottom] up
▶이것이 그의 이론의 근저를 이룬다 This is at the root of his theory. ⇌ This forms the basis of his theory.
▶그 문제의 근저를 규명해야 한다 You should get to the bottom of the problem.
▶이 발견이 그의 학설을 근저로부터 무너뜨렸다 This discovery toppled his theory from its foundation.

근저당 根抵當 fixed collateral; a collateral security —근저당하다 give *sth* in fixed collateral [as a collateral security]

근전도 筋電圖 〔醫〕 an electromyogram (略 EMG)

근절 根絶 extermination; eradication
—근절하다 root [stamp] out; get rid of; exterminate; eradicate
♦근절할 수 있는 eradicable; exterminable / 독직을[사회악을] 근절하다 root [stamp] out bribery [social evils]
▶바퀴벌레를 근절하기는 불가능할 것이다 It will be impossible to exterminate the cockroaches.
▶그는 모든 악을 근절하려고 했다 He tried to get rid of [eradicate] all the evils.
▶그 종(種)은 전세기에 근절되었다 That species became extinct [died out] in the last century.

근점 近點 **1** ⟨가까운 점⟩ a near point **2** ⇨ 근일점 **3** ⇨ 근지점
■—거리 〔天〕 the perihelion distance —년[월] an anomalistic year [month] —이각(離角) 〔天〕 an anomaly

근접 近接 proximity; approach; 〔天〕 appulse; 〔心〕 contiguity —근접하다 approach; draw near; come [go] close (to)
♦근접한 near; close; neighboring / 근접한 도시와 마을 neighboring towns and villages / 근접해 있다 be [stand] close [adjacent] (to); be near
■—미래 〔文法〕 immediate [near] future —표시기 ⟨물체의⟩ an approach indicator

근정 謹呈 With the compliments of the author —근정하다 present *sb* with *sth*; make *sb* a present of *sth*

근제 謹製 carefully produced [prepared] (by)
♦당점(當店) 근제 과자 our carefully [meticulously] made cakes [confectionery]

근조 謹弔 I respectfully express my condolence. ♦근조 고(故) 김용만 In memorium: Kim Yong Man

근종 筋腫 〔醫〕 a myoma (*pl*. ~s, -mata)

근지럽다 itchy; scratchy

근지점 近地點 〔天〕 the perigee (point)

근직 謹直 conscientious —근직하다 conscientious; scrupulous

근질거리다 itch; feel itchy [creepy, crawly]
▶맨살에 이 스웨터를 입었더니 근질거린다 I'm wearing this sweater right next to my skin, and it itches.

근질근질하다 ⟨몸이⟩ (feel) itchy [creepy, crawly]; ⟨마음이⟩ be impatient (of); be anxious [eager] ⟨for, to do⟩; itch ⟨to do⟩
▶등이 근질근질하다 My back itches [feels itchy]. ⇌ I feel itchy on my back.
▶코가 근질근질하다 My nose tickles.
▶그에게 이 좋은 소식을 알리고 싶어 입이 근질근질하다 I am itching [have an itch] to tell him this good news.

근착 近着 recent [new] arrival
♦근착의 newly received; just [recently] arrived / 근착 도서 books which have just arrived; recently arrived books

근채류 根菜類 edible [esculent] roots; root-crops

근처 近處 the neighborhood; the vicinity
♦근처의 nearby; neighboring / 이[저] 근처에 around here [there]; in this [that] neighborhood; in these [those] parts
▶이 근처에 은행이 있습니까? Is there a bank near here [around here]?
▶우리 집은 역 근처에 있다 My house stands near [close to] the station. ⇌ My house is not far from the station.
▶근처에 오시면 들르세요 Please drop in, when you're in this neighborhood.

근청 謹聽 listening with attention —근청하다 listen to *sb* with attention; hear attentively

근촌 近村 a neighboring [nearby] village

근축 根軸 〔幾〕 a radical axis

근치 根治 radical [complete, permanent] cure —근치하다 cure radically [completely]; effect a radical [complete] cure
♦근치하기 어렵다 be hard of radical cure; hard to cure completely
▶그 병을 근치할 방법은 없다 There is no complete cure [remedy] for the disease. ⇌ It is impossible to cure the disease completely.
■—약 an eradicative medicine; a sure [radical] cure

근친 近親 a close [near] relative; 〈관계〉 close relationship; (총칭) kin
▶그는 나의 근친이다 He is a close relative of mine.
▶그의 근친중에 유명한 화가가 있다 One of his near relatives [relations] is a famous painter.
■─결혼 intermarriage (between close relatives); (a) consanguineous marriage ─상간 (相姦) incest: 근친 상간의 incestuous ─혼 금기 incest taboo

근친 覲親 a bride's (first) call at her parents' home ─근친하다 make her call on her parents after her marriage

근풀이 斤─ 〈달아서 팖〉 selling by the pound [kŭn]; 〈환산〉 figuring out the cost per kŭn ─근풀이하다 sell by the kŭn; figure out the cost per kŭn

근하신년 謹賀新年 (I wish you a) Happy New Year

근해 近海 the near seas; the neighboring [home] waters
◆근해의 coastal; coastwise / 한국 근해에서 in the sea off Korea; in Korean waters / 목포 근해에서 잡힌 고기 fish caught in the sea near Mokp'o
■─어 inshore fish ─어업 inshore fishery [fishing] ─항로 a coastal service [line] ─항로선(船) a coaster ─항행 coasting

근호 根號 〈數〉 a radical sign ■─지수 an index of a radical

근황 近況 the recent state [condition, situation]; 〈안부〉 how one is getting along
◆우리 나라 대외 무역의 근황 the recent state of our foreign trade / 시장의 근황 the recent condition of the market
▶근황을 알려 주세요 〈편지에서〉 Please let me know how you are getting along these days.

글 1 〈문장〉 writings; a composition; 〈문법상의〉 a sentence; 〈본문〉 the text; 〈문헌〉 literature; 〈문체〉 style
◆세련된 글 a polished sentence [style] / 읽기 쉬운 글 an easy [a simple] style / 글 쓰는 것을 업으로 삼다 write for a living / 생각을 글로 나타내다 express one's thoughts in writing [written words]
▶그녀는 인기 작가지만 나는 그녀의 글이 마음에 들지 않는다 She's a very popular writer but I just don't like her style.
▶돌에 새겨진 글은 아주 희미했다 The writing on the stone was very faint.
▶그녀는 글을 잘 쓴다 She writes well.
▶「21세기의 한국」이라는 제목으로 글을 쓰시오 Write a composition [an essay] on [entitled] "Korea in the Twenty-first Century."
▶그는 글을 써서 생계를 이었다 He made a living by writing.
▶나는 닥치는대로 양계에 관한 글을 읽었다 I've read all the available literature on poultry farming.
2 〈글자〉 a letter; a character; an ideograph (한자 등) ◆글을 모르다 be unlettered [illiterate]
3 〈학문〉 learning; studies; scholarship; letters
◆글이 대단한 사람 a man of great learning / 글을 배우다 study; learn; pursue learning / 글을 좋아하다 like [be fond of] learning [study] / 글 깨나 배웠다고 뽐내다 be proud of one's learning [scholarship]

글겅이 a currycomb ■─질 〈빗질〉 currying; currycombing; 〈착취〉 exploitation: 글겅이질하다 curry (a horse); clean (a horse) with a currycomb; exploit [squeeze] sb

글구멍 literary talent ◆글구멍이 크다 have a talent for learning

글귀 ─句 a phrase; a passage; a line
◆흔히 쓰는 글귀 a stock phrase / 글귀를 외다 memorize a passage
▶내가 찾고 있던 글귀가 바로 그거야 That's exactly the phrase I was looking for myself.
▶초대장에는 보통 이런 식의 글귀가 쓰여 있다 In invitations the text is usually worded in this manner.

글동무 a schoolmate; a schoolfellow; a classmate

글라디올러스 〈植〉 a gladiolus (pl. ~, ~es, ~lus, -li)

글라스 〈유리〉 glass; 〈잔〉 a glass

글라이더 〈空〉 a glider ◆글라이더를 조종하다 maneuver [control] a glider

글래드스턴 〈영국의 정치가〉 Gladstone, William Ewart (1809-98)

글래머걸 a glamor (girl)

글래스고 〈스코틀랜드의 항구도시〉 Glasgow

글러브 〈野〉 a (leather) glove; 〈拳〉 (a pair of) gloves

글러지다 1 〈잘못되다〉 be spoilt; be ruined; go wrong [amiss, awry] ◆계획이 글러지다 be baffled in one's design
▶지금까지 나는 하는 일마다 글러졌다 Everything has gone wrong [amiss] with me so far.
2 〈악화되다〉 grow [get, become] worse
▶그러면 일이 더 글러진다 That will make things worse.
▶두 사람 사이는 더욱 더 글러졌다 The relations between the two men became more and more strained.

글로방전 ─放電 〔電〕 (a) glow discharge

글로스터셔 〈잉글랜드의 주〉 Gloucestershire

글루타민 〔化〕 glutamine

글루탐산 ─酸 〔化〕 glutamic acid ■─소다 [나트륨] monosodium glutamate ─칼슘 calcium glutamate

글루텐 〔化〕 gluten

글리사드 〔登山〕 glissade

글리산도 〔樂〕 glissando

글리세린 〔化〕 glycerin(e) ■─연고 glycerine ointment

글리코겐 〔化〕 glycogen

글발 1 〈적어 놓은 글〉 jottings; notes; 〈필적〉 handwriting; penmanship ◆글발이 고르다 the letters are even 2 〈문맥〉 the context; coherence ◆글발이 서다 be coherent

글방 ─房 a private [home] school (for Chinese classics); a village school

글썽글썽 with tearful eyes
─글썽글썽하다 (one's eyes) swim with tears; be filled [brimming] with tears

♦눈물이 글썽글썽한 눈 eyes suffused [filled] with tears; moist [tearful] eyes
▶그녀는 눈물이 글썽글썽해서 나에게 그 이야기를 했다 She told me about it with tears in her eyes.
▶그 이야기를 듣고 그녀는 눈물이 글썽글썽해졌다 The story moved her to tears.

글쎄 1 〈강조·고집〉 yes; just; please
▶글쎄 맞다니까 Yes, right!
▶글쎄 해 보라구 Just try it.
▶글쎄 조용히 하세요 Please be quiet!
2 〈의심·주저〉 well; let me see; 〈생각할 때〉 ah; uh; er...
▶글쎄, 무엇이었더라 Well, what was it?
▶글쎄, 아무래도 모르겠는데 Well, I am sure I don't know.
▶글쎄, 어디다 두었더라 Let me see. — Where have I put it?
▶글쎄, 말할 수 없어요 Well, I can't tell.

글씨 1 〈필적〉 handwriting; writing; penmanship
♦알아보기 힘든 글씨 a handwriting hard to read; an illegible hand / 글씨 잘 쓰는 사람 a good penman / 여자 글씨로 쓴 편지 a letter (written) in a (delicate) female hand / 글씨를 잘[못] 쓰다 write a good [poor] hand; be a good [poor] penman / 알아보기 쉬운 글씨로 쓰다 write in an easily legible hand
▶그의 글씨는 알아볼 수가 없다 I can't read his handwriting.
2 〈쓰는 법〉 how to write; penmanship; 〈쓰는 일〉 writing ♦글씨를 가르치다 teach how to write
3 〈글자〉 a character; an ideogram (한자 등)
♦굵은[가는] 글씨 a heavy [slender] character / 작은 글씨로 쓰다 write in tiny lettering [small handwriting]
▶이 글씨는 빨간색으로 써야 했다 This character should have been written in red.
▶나는 안경을 쓰지 않으면 작은 글씨는 읽을 수가 없다 Without glasses I cannot see the small print.

글월 〈글〉 a writing; 〈문장〉 a sentence; 〈편지〉 a letter

글자 —字 a letter; a character; an ideogram (▶character는 한자와 같은 표의문자, letter는 표음문자를 가리킴)
♦글자 그대로 literally; to the letter / 글자 한 자 모르다 be unlettered [illiterate]; be an ignoramus / 아이에게 글자를 가르치다 teach a child his letters
▶그 아이는 영어 알파벳 26글자를 전부 쓸 줄 안다 The child can write all (the) 26 letters of the English alphabet.
▶국문을 영역할 때 글자 그대로 옮기려고 해서는 안 된다 You must not try to translate Korean into English word for word.
▶기차는 글자 그대로 만원이었다 The train was really packed.

글재주 literary talent [ability] ♦글재주가 있다 have a talent for writing

글제 —題 the subject [theme, title] of a composition [a poem, an article] ▶나는「세계화」라는 글제로 글을 지었다 I wrote a composition on the theme, "Globalization."

글짓기 composition ⇨ 작문

글쪽지 a slip [card] with writing on it; a memo; a note ▶그녀는 어머니 앞으로 글쪽지 하나를 남기고 가출했다 She went away from home leaving a letter behind for her mother.

글피 two days after tomorrow; three days hence

글하다 study; engage in studies

긁다 1 〈손톱 등으로〉 scratch; scrape 《off, away, out, down》
♦가려운 데를 긁다 scratch an itchy spot [place]; scratch where one itches / 머리를 긁다 scratch one's head / 긁어 구멍을 파다 scrape (out) a hole
▶그 진흙 투성이 구두를 이 헌 칼로 긁어라 Scrape your muddy shoes with this old knife.
▶그는 문의 페인트를 긁어냈다 He scraped the paint off the door.
▶나는 부엌 난로에서 등걸불을 긁어냈다 I scraped out the embers from the kitchen stove.
2 〈그러모으다〉 scrape [rake] up [together]; gather up
♦낙엽을 긁어 모으다 rake up fallen leaves; rake together dead leaves / 돈을 긁어 모으다 rake one's money together
▶남자 몇 명이 건초를 긁어 모으고 있었다 Some men were raking up hay.
▶그는 몇 년 동안 밤마다 돈을 긁어 들였다 He had raked the cash in night after night for years.
3 〈남의 마음을〉 offend; irritate; nag (at); 〈헐뜯다〉 find fault with; carp [cavil] at ♦바가지를 긁어 남편을 못살게 굴다 nag one's husband to death
4 〈착취하다〉 extort; squeeze; exploit; (美俗) sweat ♦아무한테서 돈을 긁어내다 extort [squeeze] money from sb; fleece sb of his money

긁어먹다 1 〈숟가락 등으로〉 scrape [scratch] (out) and eat; 〈이로〉 gnaw [bite] off and eat
♦수박을 숟가락으로 긁어먹다 scrape out the meat of a watermelon and eat it
2 〈재물을〉 extort; squeeze; exploit; (美俗) sweat ▶그는 가난한 사람들의 돈을 긁어먹고 산다 He lives on the money squeezed out of poor people.

긁어 부스럼 (속담) It is as if asking for trouble. ⇌ Let sleeping dogs lie. ⇌ Wake not a sleeping lion.

긁적거리다 scratch [scrape] again and again [repeatedly]

긁히다 1 〈손톱 등에〉 be scratched [scraped]
▶나는 손을 가시에 긁혔다 I got my hand scratched with the thorns.
▶나는 긁힌데 하나 없이 도망쳤다 I escaped without a scratch.
2 〈그러모아지다〉 be raked; rake ▶이 갈퀴는 잘 긁힌다 This rake rakes well.
3 〈감정 이〉 be offended [nagged, irritated]; 〈헐뜯기다〉 be found fault with; be carped [caviled]
4 〈착취당하다〉 be extorted [squeezed]; be

금¹ 1 〈선(線)〉 a line; 〈접은 자국〉 a fold; a crease ◆금을 긋다 draw a line / 손금을 보다 read sb's palm
2 〈갈라진 곳〉 a crack; a crevice; a cleft; a fissure ◆벽의 금 a crack in the wall / 우정의 금 a crack [rift] in the friendship / 금이 간 꽃병 a cracked vase
▶ 그것 때문에 두 사람의 우정에 금이 갔다 That has impaired [caused a crack in] their friendship.
▶ 이 석고는 마르면 금이 갈지도 모른다 This plaster may crack when it has dried.
금² 〈값〉 a price; a cost
◆금이 맞으면 if the price is satisfactory [moderate, reasonable] / 금이 나가다 cost much; be high in price; be dear [expensive] / 금을 놓다[매기다] name [bid] a price (for); make an offer; set a price (on); appraise
금 金 1 〈광물〉 gold; 〔化〕 aurum
◆금의 gold; made of gold; golden / 18금 gold 18 carats fine / 18금 반지 an 18-carat gold ring; a gold ring of 18 carats / 금을 함유한 auriferous / 이에 금을 씌우다 put a gold crown on a tooth; crown a tooth with gold
▶ 침묵은 금이다 (속담) Silence is golden.
▶ 그 처녀는 금이야 옥이야 자랐다 That young lady was brought up like a delicate flower [with utmost care and affection].
▶ 번쩍인다고 모두가 금은 아니다 (속담) All is not gold that glitters.
2 〈금전〉 money ▶ 일금 백만원을 영수함 Received the sum of one million won.
3 〈금요일〉 Friday
금- 今- this (time); the present (term); 〈오는〉 next ◆금세기 this century; the current century / 금월 this month; the present month
금가루 金— gold dust; powdered gold
금강력 金剛力 Herculean strength
금강사 金剛砂 emery (powder) ■ —포(布) emery cloth
금강산 金剛山 Kŭmgangsan
금강산도 식후경이라 (속담) Bread is better than the song of the birds.
금강석 金剛石 (a) diamond ◆금강석을 갈다 cut a diamond
금계 金鷄 〔鳥〕 a golden pheasant
금계 禁界 the forbidden ground; an off-limits area
금고 金庫 1 〈돈·귀중품 등을 넣는〉 a safe; a cash box; a vault (은행 등)
◆내화 금고 a fireproof safe / 대여 금고 a safe(ty)-deposit box / 휴대용 금고 a portable safe / 금고에 돈을 넣다 put money in a safe
2 〈기관〉 a cash office; a depository ◆중앙 금고 the central depository
■ —털이 〈행위〉 safecracking; safebreaking; 〈사람〉 a safecracker; a safebreaker; a safeblower
금고 禁錮 imprisonment; confinement ▶ 그는 1개월의 금고형을 받았다 He was sentenced to one month's imprisonment.
■ 중[경]— imprisonment with [without] hard labor

금공 金工 〈공예〉 metalworking; 〈사람〉 a metalworker; a metalsmith; a craftsman in metal
금과옥조 金科玉條 a golden rule ◆금과옥조로 삼다 stick fast (to); abide by (sb's advice); adhere strictly (to); recognize no other authority (than)
금관 金冠 〈왕관〉 a gold crown; 〈이의〉 a (gold) crown
◆이에 금관을 씌우다 crown a tooth with gold
금관악기 金管樂器 (a) brass (instrument)
■ —부 〈관현악의〉 the brass(es)
금광 金鑛 〈광산〉 a gold mine; 〈광석〉 (a) gold ore
◆금광을 발견하다 discover [spot, locate] gold deposits / 금광맥을 찾아내다 strike a gold vein [lode]
금괴 金塊 gold bullion; 〈천연의〉 a nugget; 〈주괴〉 a gold ingot; 〈봉상(棒狀)의〉 a gold bar
금구 禁句 a taboo word; a forbidden phrase
금권 金權 the power of money; financial influence ■ —정치[주의] plutocracy —정치가 a plutocrat
금궤 金櫃 a coffer; a strongbox
금귤 金橘 〔植〕 a kumquat; a cumquat
금기 禁忌 〈금지된 사항〉 (a) taboo; 〈금지함〉 tabooing; 〔醫〕 contraindication
◆배합 금기 약품 incompatible drugs
▶ 정치 이야기는 그의 집에서는 금기로 되어 있다 Any mention of politics is taboo in his house.
—금기하다 taboo; put sth under taboo; abstain from
금나다¹ 〈값나다〉 be priced [fixed] (at)
금나다² 〈줄이 생기다〉 crease; wrinkle; be creased [wrinkled]; 〈금이 가다〉 be cracked
금남 禁男 off-limits to men; forbidden to men; "Women Only" ◆금남의 집 a home without a man
금납 金納 cash payment; payment in money
—금납하다 pay in money
금낭화 錦囊花 〔植〕 a bleeding heart
금년 今年 this year ⇨ 올해
금년생 今年生 a baby born this year; 〈식물의〉 a plant new this year
금니 金— a gold(-capped) tooth; the gold casing of one's tooth
◆금니를 하다 have a gold tooth put in; have a tooth capped with gold
■ —박이 a person with a gold tooth
금단 禁斷 prohibition ◆금단의 열매 the forbidden fruit
■ —증상 withdrawal symptoms
금단추 金— a brass button
◆금단추를 단 제복 a uniform with brass buttons
금달맞이꽃 金— 〔植〕 an evening primrose
금닿다 〈값이 알맞다〉 be reasonable in price; 〈값이 꽤 나가다〉 have a considerable value [price]
금덩이 金— gold bullion ⇨ 금괴
금도금 金鍍金 gold plating; gilding —금도금하다 plate (a thing) with gold; gild ◆금도금한 overlaid with gold; gilt; gilded; gold-plated

금돌 金— 〔鑛〕 a gold-bearing rock; an ore rock
금동 金銅 gilt bronze ■—불상 a gilt bronze statue [image] of the Buddha
금딱지 金— a gold case [lid] of a watch; a gold watchcase
금란지계 金蘭之契 close [fast] friendship
금력 金力 the power [influence] of money [wealth]
◆무력과 금력 sword and purse / 금력으로 by employing [using] one's financial power / 금력에 좌우되다 be influenced by money
■—가(家) a plutocrat —만능[숭배] mammonism
금렵 禁獵 prohibition of hunting [shooting]
—기 a closed season; 〈英〉 a close season —조수(鳥獸) forbidden game
금렵구 禁獵區 a (game) preserve; a (bird, wildlife) sanctuary ▶여기는 금렵구다 This area is a game preserve. ≒ This is a no-hunting area.
금령 禁令 a prohibitory order ⇨ 금지령(禁止令)
금리 金利 interest; 〈이율〉 an interest rate; a rate; a rate of interest
◆은행 금리 a bank rate / 금리를 올리다[내리다] raise [lower] the interest rate [the rate of interest]
▶금리는 10퍼센트다 The rate of interest is ten percent.
▶그는 5부의 금리를 물었다 He paid 5 percent interest on a loan.
■—생활자 a rentier; a person who lives on invest income —자율화 the liberalization of interest rates —재조정 readjustment of bank (interest) rates —정책 a bank-rate policy —체계의 the structure of interest rates
금맞추다 set the price; arrange [adjust] the price 《of》
금매화 金梅花 〔植〕 an globeflower.
금맥 金脈 a vein of gold
금메달 金— a gold medal ▶그는 금메달을 땄다[획득했다] He won [was awarded, was honored with] a gold medal. ■—획득자 a gold medalist
금명간 今明間 today or tomorrow; in a day or two
금모래 〈금빛의〉 golden sand(s); 〈사금〉 gold dust
금몰 金— a gold braid; 〈美〉 gold lace ◆금몰이 달린 gold-braided; gold-laced
금문자 金文字 〈금글자〉 a gold [gilt] letter [character]; gilt lettering ◆금문자가 박힌 표지 a gold-lettered book cover; a book cover in gold letters
금물 禁物 a prohibited [forbidden] thing; a taboo
▶그 화제는 여기서는 금물이다 That topic is taboo here. ≒ You should not mention that topic here.
▶그자에게 방심하는 것은 금물이다 We must never relax our guard against him.
금박 金箔 〈엷은〉 (a) gold leaf; 〈두꺼운〉 gold foil; beaten gold ◆금박을 입히다 plate [coat] (a thing) with gold; gild
금반 今般 this time ⇨ 금번
금반지 金斑指 a gold ring
금발 金髮 golden [fair] hair; blonde [〈남자의〉 blond] hair ◆금발의 golden-haired; fair-haired; blond 《man》; blonde 《woman》
■—미인 a blonde beauty; a beautiful blonde
금방 今方 〈방금〉 just now; right now; 〈방금 전에〉 (just) a moment ago; 〈곧〉 at once; in a moment; 〈당장이라도〉 every [at any] moment
▶그 남자는 금방 나갔다 He went out just a moment ago.
▶그는 금방 돌아온다 He will be back very soon [in a few minutes].
▶나는 금방 도착했다 I arrived just now.
▶금방 비가 내릴 것 같다 It threatens to rain.
금배 金杯 a gold cup [goblet]
금번 今番 this time; lately
금보다 〈값을 알아보다〉 ask the price 《of an article》; price 《an article at a store》
금본위 金本位 the gold standard ◆금본위를 폐지하다 suspend the gold standard; go off the gold standard
■—국 a gold-using country —블록 the gold bloc —제 the gold standard system
금뵈다 1〈물건 값을〉 get sb to name his price [make an offer] 2 ⇨ 금맞추다
금부처 金— a gold [gilded] image [statue] of Buddha
금분 金粉 gold dust; powdered gold
금불 金佛 a gold image of Buddha ⇨ 금부처
금붕어 金— a goldfish ◆금붕어를 기르다 keep goldfish
■—어항 a goldfish basin [bowl] —장수 a goldfish seller [vendor]
금붙이 金— things made of gold
금비 金肥 (a) chemical [commercial] fertilizer
금비녀 金— a golden hairpin
금빛 金— (a) gold [golden] color; gold ◆금빛 찬란하다 glitter in [with] golden color
금산 金山 a gold [an auriferous] mine
금상 金像 a gold [gilded, gilt] statue
금상첨화 錦上添花 adding luster to what is already brilliant; making still more beautiful
금새 a price ⇨ 금²
금색 金色 a gold(en) color ◆금색의 golden; golden-colored
금서 禁書 a banned [forbidden] book
금석 今昔 past and present
▶나는 금석지감을 금할 수 없었다 I was struck by the way times had changed [the effects of time].
▶최근에 찾아본 고향도 아주 근대화하여 금석지감을 금할 수 없었다 My hometown that I recently visited was so modernized (that) I couldn't help being struck by the change of times.
금석 金石 1〈금속과 돌〉 metals and rocks 2〈굳음〉 being adamant(ine) [firm, unyielding] 3 ⇨ 금돌
■—문 an inscription on a stone monument; an epigraph —학 studies in ancient monumen-

금성 [天] Venus; Hesperus; the daystar
♦ 금성의 태양면 통과 the transit of Venus over the sun's disc [disk] ■—로켓[탐색기] a Venus rocket [probe].

금성철벽 金城鐵壁 an impregnable fortress
♦ 금성철벽의 팀 a solidly united team

금성탕지 金城湯池 ▶ 이 지역은 혁신 정당의 금성탕지다 This area is squarely in the progressive party's camp. ⇒ This area is a progressive party bastion.

금세 in a moment [minute]; in an instant; in no time; without delay; at once; immediately; (美口) right off [away]
♦ 금세 돌아오다 come back immediately / 금세 마음이 변하다 change one's mind in a flash

금세 今世 〈이승〉[佛敎] this world; the mundane world; this life

금세공 金細工 goldwork ■—사[장이] a goldsmith —소 a goldsmith's shop

금속 金屬 (a) metal
♦ 금속(제)의 (made of) metal; metallic / 귀[비]금속 precious [base] metals / 중[경]금속 heavy [light] metals / 금속 막대 a metal bar / 금속을 함유한 metalliferous
▶ 철은 유용한 금속이다 Iron is a useful metal.
▶ 이 상자는 금속으로 되어 있다 This box is made of metal.
■—가공 metal working —공 a metalworker —공업 metal [metalworking] industry —공학 metal engineering —광택 metallic luster —세공 metal work —수소 사이클 metal hydride cycle —원소 metallic element —인공 격자 metallic artificial superlattice —정련 metal refinery —제품 metal goods; hardware —판(版) metallograph —탐지기 a metal detector —화폐 metallic currency —피로 metal fatigue

금속성 金屬性 metallicity ♦ 금속성 소리 a metallic sound [clang]

금송화 金松花 【植】 a pot marigold

금쇠 a line-cutter

금수 禽獸 birds and beasts; animals; a beast; a brute
♦ 금수와 같은 행위 a bestial [beastly] conduct / 금수만도 못한 사람 a fellow no better than a beast; a person worse than a brute
▶ 그는 하는 짓이 금수와 다를 바 없다 He is beastly [brutish] in his conduct.

금수 禁輸 an embargo on the export [import] (of) ♦ 자동차의 금수를 해제하다 lift the embargo on (the export [import] of) cars ■—품 articles under an embargo; contraband (goods)

금수 錦繡 〈비단과 수〉 brocade and embroidery; 〈천〉 embroidered brocade ■—강산 (a land of) picturesque rivers and mountains; a land of beautiful scenery

금수출 金輸出 the export of gold ■—금지 an embargo [a ban] on gold export; a gold embargo —해금(解禁) lifting [removing] the gold embargo

금슬 琴瑟 1 〈거문고와 비파〉 a Korean harp and a lute 2 ⇨ 금실(琴瑟)

금시 今時 now; this time; the present moment
♦ 금시로 at once; immediately / 금시 발복하다 be instantly in luck's way; make one's fortune overnight / 금시 초견(初見)이다 see sth for the first time
▶ 그것은 금시 초문이다 I have never heard of that. ⇒ That's news to me.

금시계 金時計 a gold watch

금식 禁食 a fast; fasting ■—하다 fast; go without food; abstain from food ■—일 a fast day

금실 金— gold thread; spun gold

금실 琴瑟 conjugal harmony
♦ 금실이 좋다 live in conjugal harmony; be happily married; lead a happy married life

금실지락 琴瑟之樂 the pleasures of married life; conjugal happiness

금싸라기 金— a thing of great value ■—땅 an exceedingly high-priced plot of land

금액 金額 an amount [a sum] of money
♦ 막대한 금액 an infinite [enormous] sum of money / 상당한 금액 a large amount of money; a considerable [good] sum of money
▶ 피해 금액은 3억원에 달한다 The damage [loss] amounts to three hundred million won. ⇒ Three hundred million won's worth of damage was done.
▶ 이것은 금액으로 쳐서 몇 백만원에 상당하는 물품이다 This article is worth several million won.

금야 今夜 tonight ⇨ 오늘밤

금어 禁漁 prohibition of fishing [fishery] ■—구 an area closed to fishing; a no-fishing area [zone]; 〈바다의〉 a marine preserve —기(美) the closed season (for fishery); (英) the close time [season]

금언 金言 a golden [wise] saying; a maxim; an adage; a proverb

금연 禁煙 prohibition of smoking; no smoking
▶ 나는 1개월 이상 금연 중이다 I've been off cigarettes for more than a month now.
▶ 금연 (게시) No smoking. ⇒ Smoking is prohibited here. ⇒ Please refrain from smoking.
—금연하다 give up [quit] smoking
▶ 주치의는 내게 금연하라고 했다 My doctor advised me to give up [quit] smoking.
■—석 a nonsmoking seat —운동 an antismoking [antitobacco] campaign —차 a nonsmoking car; a nonsmoker

금요일 金曜日 Friday ♦ 성 금요일 [基] Good Friday / 13일의 금요일 Friday the thirteenth (▶ 서양에서는 불길한 날로 되어 있음)

금욕 禁慾 abstinence; 〈종교적인〉 asceticism; 〈성욕의〉 sexual abstinence; continence
▶ 나는 그 1년간은 완전히 금욕생활을 했다 I led a life of total abstinence (for) that year.
—금욕하다 control [repress] the passions and desires; practice asceticism
■—주의 asceticism; stoicism —주의자 an ascetic; a stoic

금월 今月 this month ▶ 금월 7일자 귀 서한을 배수하였습니다 We are in receipt of your let-

ter of [dated] the 7th of this month.
금융 金融 finance; financing; the money market
▶금융 긴축으로 기업이 경영에 큰 압박을 받고 있다 The money squeeze on [Tight money for] businesses has put strong pressure on their management.
■소액― a small loan 수출[수입]― export [import] financing ■―경색[핍박] monetary stringencing; a tight-money situation [market] ―계 the financial world; the financial circles ―공황 a financial [banking] crisis [panic] ―기관 a financial [banking] institution; a banking agency ―긴축 정책 a tight-money policy ―단 a financial syndicate ―선물거래소 a financial futures exchange ―시장 the money market ―어음 a finance bill ―완화 정책 an easy-money policy ―정세[상태] the financial [credit, money] conditions [situation] ―정책 (a) financial policy ―조직 the banking system ―채(債) a bank debenture ―통제 monetary control ―통화운영위원회 the Monetary Board ―회사 a financial company [firm]
금융거래실명제 金融去來實名制 (the) real-name financial transaction system; real-name accounting system
금융업 金融業 financial [banking] business; money lending (business) ―자 a money lender; a financier; (美) a moneyman
금융자본 金融資本 financial capital ■―가 a financial capitalist
금융자유화 金融自由化 financial liberalization.
금은 金銀 gold and silver
■―방 a goldsmith's shop ―보화 money and valuables; treasures; worldly goods: 건강은 금은 보화보다 귀하다 Health is better than wealth. ―세공 work in gold and silver; goldwork and silverwork
금의 錦衣 clothes of brocade ◆금의 환향하다 return home in glory; make *one's* triumphant journey to his homeland; go home loaded with honors
금인 金印 a gold seal
금일 今日 today (⇨ 오늘) ▶금일 휴업 (게시) Closed (for) Today.
금일봉 金―封 an enclosure [a gift] of money
▶그는 금일봉을 받았다 He got a gift of money.
▶그들은 그에게 감사의 표시로 금일봉을 주었다 They made him a gift of money in an envelope as a token of gratitude.
금자 金字 a gold letter ⇨ 금문자(金文字)
금자동이 金子童― a precious child
금자탑 金字塔 a pyramid; (비유) a monumental work [achievement] ◆출판계의 금자탑 a monumental publication
▶그는 공학상의 금자탑을 세웠다 He accomplished a monumental work in engineering.
금작화 金雀花 (植) a common broom; a Scotch broom; a genista
금잔디 金― "golden" turf; Korean lawn grass
금잔화 金盞花 a pot marigold ⇨ 금송화

금장 襟章 a collar badge [mark, ensign]; a gorget patch
금장도 金粧刀 a gold [gilded] pocketknife
금장식 金裝飾 gold(en) decoration ―금장식 하다 decorate with gold
금전 金錢 money; 〈현금〉 cash
◆금전적인 가치 cash value / 금전에 눈이 어두워지다 be blinded by money / 금전에 대범하다 be generous [liberal] with *one's* money
▶그들은 금전상의 문제로 대판 싸웠다 They had a big trouble over the money.
▶그의 금전욕은 끝이 없다 His love of money knows no bounds.
▶그와는 금전상의 거래가 없다 I have never had a financial dealings with him.
▶그는 아버지에게 금전적 원조를 바랐다 He turned to his father for financial help [support].
■―등록기 a cash register ―신탁 money trust; cash in trust ―자동 출납기 an automatic paying machine ―출납담당 a cashier; 〈은행의〉 a teller ―출납부 a cash book; an account book
금제 金製 ◆금제의 (made of) gold / 금제 식기류 gold plates ■―품 goldwork
금제 禁制 (a) prohibition ⇨ 금지(禁止)
금제품 禁制品 prohibited [banned] goods; 〈무역의〉 contraband (goods) ■전시(戰時)―contraband of war
금조 今朝 〈오늘 아침〉 this morning
금족 禁足 confinement ◆3일간의 금족을 명하다 order *sb* not to leave his house for three days; place *sb* under three days' confinement
■―령 a standstill order
금종이 金― golden paper
금주 今週 this week
◆금주나 내주 this week or next / 금주 토요일에 on Saturday this week; this Saturday / 금주 중에 some time this week; before the end of this week
▶나는 금주 중에 일을 끝내지 않으면 안 된다 I have to finish my work (within) this week.
금주 禁酒 abstinence (from) drink; 〈법률상의〉 prohibition; temperance (▶「절주」의 뜻이지만 「금주」의 뜻으로도 흔히 씀)
◆금주를 맹세하다[파기하다] talk [break] an oath [a vow] of temperance
―금주하다 give up [quit] drinking; abstain from drinking; (美俗) be on the (water) wagon
▶그는 병 때문에 금주했다 Because of illness he gave up drinking.
▶의사는 나에게 1년간 금주하라고 했다 The doctor advised me not to drink for one year.
■―가 an [a total] abstainer; a teetotaler ―동맹 a temperance union [society, league] ―운동 a temperance movement; a dry campaign ―주의 teetotalism; prohibitionism ―회 a temperance society
금주법 禁酒法 the prohibition law; Prohibition; (美) the Volstead Act; the Dry Law (▶1933년에 폐지됨)
◆금주법을 시행하다 go dry
금준비 金準備 the gold reserves

금전에 관한 표현

1. 단위
영국과 미국의 금전의 단위는 다음과 같다
미국 센트 cent (¢)
　　 달러 1 dollar ($, $)= 100 ¢
　　　　　(1997년 현재 한화 약 900원에 해당함)
　　　※ 캐나다, 오스트레일리아도 미국과 같은 단위를 쓴다.
영국 페니 penny (P) (복수 Pence)
　　 파운드 1 pound (£)= 100 P
　　　　(한화 약 1,420원에 해당함)
[어법] $, £는 숫자 앞에 붙이고 ¢, P는 뒤에 붙인다: $12; $10.15; 10¢; £7; £7.30; 20P 읽을 때는 각기 twelve dollars; ten dollars and fifteen cents; ten cents; seven pounds; seven pounds and thirty pence; twenty pence 로 읽는다.

2. 지폐와 금속 화폐
지폐는 미국에서는 보통 a bill (가산명사), 또는 총칭으로서 구어적으로는 paper money (불가산명사)이고 한장 한장은 a greenback (가산명사)이라고 한다.

영국에서는 격식을 차려서 말할 때에는 a bank note (가산명사)라고 하지만 보통은 a note (가산명사)라고 하며 구어적으로 총칭하여 paper money (불가산명사)라고 한다. 금속 화폐는 미국이나 영국 모두 a coin (가산명사)이라고 한다.

지폐의 종류는 미국의 경우 1달러, 2달러, 5달러, 10달러, 20달러, 50달러, 100달러 등이 흔히 쓰인다. 영국에서는 5파운드(fiver 라고도 함), 10파운드(tenner 라고도 함), 20파운드 등이 있다.

금속 화폐는 미국에서는 다음과 같다. ( )안은 통칭이다.
1센트화　(penny)
5센트화　(nickel)
10센트화　(dime)
25센트화　(quarter)
50센트화　(half dollar)
1달러화

영국에서는 1/2 페니(halfpenny), 1페니(penny), 2펜스(pence), 5펜스, 10펜스, 20펜스, 50펜스, 1파운드 짜리 금속 화폐가 있다.

또 영국에서는 1971년에 통화 제도가 개정되었지만 그 전에는 1파운드가 20실링(shilling), 1실링이 12펜스라는 복잡한 제도였다.

3. 거스름돈
미국이나 영국에서는 모두 상점에서 거스름돈(change (불가산명사))을 내줄 때 물건값에 거스름돈을 합쳐서 계산하여 내준다. 예컨대 5달러 지폐로 4달러 15센트어치 물건을 샀다고 하면 우선 10센트(dime)를 내주고 "Four Twenty five."라고 말하고 다음에는 50센트(half dollar)와 25센트(quarter)를 건네주고는 "Five dollars."라고 한다. 우리처럼 그 자리에서 암산으로 계산해서 내주는 일은 거의 없다.

4. 수표
한국에 비하여 미국이나 영국에서는 개인용 수표(personal [personalized] check [(英) cheque])의 제도가 발달되어 있어서 쇼핑이나 다액의 금전 수수는 물론, 슈퍼에서의 쇼핑, 레스토랑에서의 지급, 열차표 구입 등까지도 수표가 통용된다(pay by check).

이것은 사전에 거래 은행으로부터 개인용 수표장(checkbook)을 발급받아 가지고 있다가 지급 장소에서 필요한 금액을 문자와 숫자로 써넣고(write the amount in words and figures), 사인(sign)을 하거나 도장을 찍으면 현금(cash)과 마찬가지로 취급되고 더구나 수중에 지급한 증거가 남는다. 다만 당좌예금 계좌(checking [(英) current] account)에 해당 금액에 걸맞는 잔고(balance)가 있어야 한다.

5. 크레디트 카드
미국이나 영국에서는 많은 현금을 휴대하지 않고 크레디트 카드로 지급하는 것이 일반적이다. 미국에서는 charge card [plate]라고도 한다. 크레디트 카드는 신분증명서(identification card) 대용도 되므로 호텔이나 렌터카(rent-a-lcar)를 이용할 때는 반드시 제시하게 된다.

한국에서 취득할 수 있는 국제 카드는 다이너스(Diners Card), 아메리칸 익스프레스(American Express Card), 비자(VISA Card), 마스터(Master Card) 등이 있으나 현재는 모든 회사에서 한 장만 가지고도 국내, 국외 어디서든 쓸 수 있는 카드를 발행하고 있다. 미국에서는 「카드입니까 현금입니까(Cash or charge?)」라고 묻는다. How would you like to pay? (지급은 어떻게 하겠습니까?)라고도 묻는다. 카드면 "By card.", 현금이면 "In cash."라고 하면 된다. 애초에 카드로 지급할 생각이라면 「카드로 지급하려고 하는데요 (I'd like to pay by credit card.)」라고 한다. 자기 카드가 쓰일지 안쓰일지 불안할 때는 「이 카드는 쓸 수 있습니까? (Do you accept this credit card?)」라고 물으면 된다. 카드의 종류에 따라서는 거절당하는 경우도 있다. 또 카드 사용은 10달러 이상이라는 등 금액에 제한을 두는 곳도 있다.

금줄 金— 〈시계줄〉 a gold chain 《on a watch》; 〈계급장 등의〉 gold stripes 《on the sleeves》; 〈금실〉 gold thread

금지 禁止 prohibition; a ban; 〈수출입의〉 an embargo

> 解說 *prohibition*은 법률이나 규칙에 따른 금지, *ban*은 공적 권한으로 내린 금지.

◆통행 금지 구역 a restricted area / 핵실험 금지 운동 the compaign for a nuclear test ban ▶그녀는 외출 금지를 당했다 She was forbidden to go out.
▶주차 금지 (게시) No Parking.
▶통행[좌회전, U턴] 금지 (게시) No Thoroughfare [Left-turn, U-turn].
▶출입 금지 (게시) Off limits. ⇌ Private.
▶목욕 금지 (게시) No Bathing. ⇌ Bathing (strictly) prohibited. ⇌ No Bathing allowed.
—**금지하다** prohibit; ban; forbid

♦음주를 금지당하다 be (strictly) forbidden to drink
▶의사는 나에게 과격하게 운동하는 것을 금지했다 The doctor prohibited me from taking too much exercise.
▶도로 공사 때문에 통행이 금지되어 있었다 Traffic was restricted because of road contruction work.
▶이 약의 판매는 법으로 금지되어 있다 The sale of this medicine is under ban of the [prohibited by] law.
■판매— a sales ban／—조항 a forbidden clause／—품목 prohibited goods; contraband (goods)

금지령 禁止令 a prohibition order; an interdict; an embargo
♦금지령을 내리다[해제하다] issue [lift, remove] the ban [embargo] 《on *sth*》／금지령을 어기다 violate the ban [prohibition]

금지옥엽 金枝玉葉 a person of royal birth; precious sons and daughters
♦금지옥엽으로 자라다 be brought up like a prince [princess]

금촉 金— a gold pen [nib]
금추 今秋 this autumn; 《美》 this [coming] fall
금춘 今春 this spring
금치다 make [name, bid] a price 《for》; set a price 《on》

금치산 禁治産 〔法〕 incompetency ♦금치산의 incompetent／준 (準)금치산자 a quasi-incompetent person
▶그는 금치산 선고를 받았다 He was declared incompetent.
■—자 an incompetent; a legally incompetent person; an interdict: 그녀는 금치산자다 She is (an) incompetent. ⇌ She is not legally qualified.

금침 衾枕 quilt and pillow; bedclothes and a pillow; bedding
금테 金— 〈안경의〉 gold rims; 〈액자의〉 a gilded [gilt] frame
■—안경 (wear [be in]》 gold-rimmed [gilt-edged] spectacles

금파리 金— 〔昆〕 a green bottle fly; a blue-bottle (fly)
금패 金牌 a gold plaque
금품 金品 money and [or] other valuables
금하 今夏 this [next] summer
금하다 fix the price; agree on a price 《of》
금하다 禁— 1 〈못하게 하다〉 forbid; prohibit; ban; interdict; tell *sb* not to 《do》
▶관계자 외 일체의 출입을 금합니다 This place is off-limits to all except the personnel in charge.
▶이 강에서는 수영을 금합니다 Swimming in this river is prohibited. ⇌ Swimming is not allowed in this river.
▶의사는 나의 흡연을 금했다 The doctor forbade me to smoke.
▶정부는 마약 매매를 금하고 있다 The government prohibits the sale and purchase of narcotics.
▶차량 출입 금지 (게시) No vehicles. ⇌ Closed to all vehicles.

2 〈참다〉 suppress; restrain
♦기쁨을 금할 수 없다 cannot contain *oneself* for joy
▶그것을 듣고 나는 실소를 금할 수 없었다 I could not help laughing at that.
▶나는 그 극을 보고 눈물을 금할 수 없었다 I could not hold back my tears at the drama.
3 〈삼가다〉 abstain 《from》; refrain 《from》

금해금 金解禁 the lifting of the gold embargo
금혼 禁婚 prohibition of marriage
금혼식 金婚式 a golden wedding ♦금혼식을 올리다 celebrate *one's* golden wedding (anniversary)

금화 金貨 a gold coin [piece]; (총칭) gold currency [coin, coinage]
♦금화로 지급하다 pay in gold
■—본위 제도 the gold coinage system

금환 金環 a gold ring
금환(일)식 金環(日)蝕 an annular eclipse 《of the sun》

금회 今回 this time ⇨ 이번
금후 今後 from now [this time] on; in (the) future; after this
♦금후의 future; coming／금후 3년 내에 in three years from now; three years hence
▶그것은 금후의 문제다 That remains to be solved in (the) future.
▶금후는 너와 함께 일하고 싶다 I want to work with you from now on.

급 急 〈긴급〉 urgency; 〈위급〉 (an) emergency; a crisis (*pl.* crises); (a) danger; (a) peril
♦초미지급 (焦眉至急) an urgent need／급을 알리다 give [raise] the alarm
▶상황은 급을 알리고 있다 The situation is growing critical [threatening].

급 級 1 〈등급〉 a class; a grade; a rank
♦중량[경량]급 the heavyweight [lightweight] division／대사급 회담 a conference at the ambassadorial level; an ambassador-level talk／메가톤급 핵폭발 a nuclear explosion in the megaton range／10만톤급 유조선 a tanker of [in] the 100,000 ton class／장관급 인물 a man of ministerial caliber／급을 올리다 promote *sb* [move *sb* up] to a higher grade [rank]／급을 내리다 demote [reduce] *sb* to a lower grade
▶그는 나보다 한 급 위[아래]다 He is one grade above [below] me.
▶이 절은 국보급이다 This temple is ranked almost as a national treasure.
▶우리는 그녀와 같은 급이다 We are in [of] the same class as she.
▶그녀의 노래 솜씨는 프로급이다 Her singing is at a [on the] professional level.
2 〈학급〉 a class; 《美》 a grade; 《英》 a form
▶그는 나와 동급생이었다 I was in the same grade with him.

급— 急— steep 《slope》; urgent 《report》; sudden 《illness》; sharp 《attack》; swift 《current》; rapid 《stream》

급각도 急角度 an acute [a sharp] angle
♦급각도로 sharply; acutely／급각도로 방향을 전환하다 make a sharp change in direction; take a sudden turn

▶ 자동차가 모퉁이를 급각도로 돌았다 A car made a sharp turn at a (street) corner.

급강하 急降下 a sudden drop; a swoop; 〈비행기의〉 nose diving; a nose dive
―급강하하다 drop suddenly; (nose-)dive; zoom down
▶ 온도가 급강하하였다 The temperature dropped suddenly.
▶ 비행기가 급강하했다 The plane descended at a sharp angle. ⇌ The airplane flew down in a steep dive.
▶ 매가 토끼를 노리고 급강하했다 A hawk swooped down on a hare.
■**―폭격 dive bombing: 급강하 폭격하다** dive-bomb **―폭격기** a dive bomber

급거 急遽 in haste; in a hurry; hastily; hurriedly ▶ 그는 급거 상경했다 He hurried up to Seoul.

급격하다 急激― rapid; sudden; abrupt; radical
◆ 급격한 변화 a sudden change / 대도시의 급격한 인구 증가 the rapid increase in population of large cities
▶ 과학은 지난 10년간 급격한 진보를 이루었다 Science has made great strides [rapid progress] in the last ten years.
▶ 온도가 급격히 떨어졌다 The temperature has dropped suddenly.

급경사 急傾斜 a steep slope [incline]; 〈치받이〉 steep ascent [acclivity]; 〈내리받이〉 steep descent [declivity]; 〈배의〉 a heavy list ◆ 급경사의 steep; high-pitched (roof)
▶ 길은 해변 쪽으로 급경사를 이루고 있다 The road slopes [slants] steeply down to the shore.

급고 急告 an urgent notice
―급고하다 notify urgently; give an urgent notice
▶ 급고! 오늘 오후 2시에 긴급 위원회가 소집됨 (게시) Urgent.―An emergency committee meeting has been called for 2 p.m. today.
▶ 급고! 하기자들은 즉시 사무실로 출두 바람 (게시) Urgent.―The following are requested to report immediately to the office.

급급하다 汲汲― 〈서술적〉 be bent [intent] (on); be absorbed [engrossed] (in); be very anxious [eager] (to do); think only of
▶ 그들은 돈벌이에 급급해 있다 They are bent on [absorbed in] making money. ⇌ They think only of making more money.

급기야 及其也 at last; at length; after all; in the end; in the long run; finally; ultimately
▶ 그는 계속 지껄이다 급기야 목이 쉬었다 He talked till he became hoarse.
▶ 그는 급기야 마약으로 죽고 말았다 Drugs ended [was the end of] him.
▶ 질투는 급기야 비극을 초래했다 The final outcome [result] of jealousy was a tragedy.

급난 急難 〈급박한 난국〉 an imminent danger; an impending calamity

급등 急騰 a sudden rise [jump] ◆ 물가의 급등 a sudden rise in prices
―급등하다 rise suddenly [sharply]; shoot up; jump; rocket

▶ 물가가 급등했다 Prices have taken a sudden jump.
▶ 이렇게 물가가 급등해서는 월급으로 먹고 살 수가 없다 We can't possibly live on our wages because of the sharp rise in prices.

급락 及落 success or failure 〈in an examination〉; the result of an examination ◆ 급락을 결정하다 decide the result of an examination

급락 急落 a sudden drop; a sharp [steep] decline; a slump
―급락하다 drop suddenly [sharply]; slump
▶ 주식 시세가 급락했다 The stock market suffered a sharp decline.
▶ 물가가 급락했다 Prices dropped suddenly.

급랭 急冷 rapid [quick] cooling; 〔化〕 quenching **―급랭하다** cool rapidly [quickly]; quench
■**―액** a quenching liquid

급료 給料 pay; a salary; wages

> 解説 *pay*가 가장 일상적・일반적인 말로서 salary나 wage 대신에 쓰인다. *salary*는 월급・연봉으로서 정기적으로 은행 계좌에 불입되는 고정급이고, *wage*는 보통 육체 노동자에 대해 시간 단위로 계산하여 일급・주급 형태로 현금 지급하는 임금이다. 이것은 또 노동 용어로서 임금을 표시하는 가장 일반적인 말이기도 하다.

◆ 높은[낮은] 급료 high [small] pay; a high [low, small] salary / 미불 급료 unpaid wages; (美) back salary [pay] / 생활 가능한 급료 a living wage / 세금・경비를 공제한 급료 a take-home pay / 월 100만원의 급료 a salary of one million won a month / 급료 값을 하다 (口) be worth *one's* salt (▶주로 부정문에서) / 급료를 받다 receive *one's* salary; have *one's* wages paid / 급료를 깎다 cut [down] *sb's* salary / 급료를 올리다 raise [increase] *sb's* salary / 급료를 지급하다 pay salaries [wages]
▶ 저 회사는 급료가 많다 They are well paid at that company. ⇌ That company pays high salaries to the employees.
▶ 나는 급료가 5% 올랐다 My salary has gone up five percent. ⇌ I had my salary raised five percent.
▶ 너는 급료가 얼마냐? How much do you make [earn]? ⇌ What is your salary?
▶ 그는 그 회사에서 급료를 받고 있다 He draws a salary from the company. ⇌ He is in the pay [on the payroll] of the company.

급류 急流 〈급히 흐르는〉 a rapid [swift, fast] stream; a swift [strong] current; 〈격류〉 a torrent; rapids
◆ 급류를 거슬러 올라가다 go up rapids / 뗏목으로 급류를 타고 내려가다 shoot (down) the rapids on a draft / 급류에 휩쓸리다 be swept away by a strong current

급모 急募 urgent invitation **―급모하다** recruit [enlist] (personnel) hurriedly ▶ 사무 직원 급모 (게시) Office workers urgently wanted. ⇌ Urgent recruitment of office workers.

급무 急務 urgent [pressing] business; an urgent [immediate] necessity; a pressing need
◆ 초미의 급무 the pressing need of the hour

급박하다 急迫— pressing; urgent; imminent; exigent
♦급박한 국제 관계 a tense international relationship / 중동의 급박한 정세 an acute situation in the Middle East
▶식량 문제가 급박해졌다 The food question has become acute [tense, critical].

급변 急變 a sudden [unexpected] change; 〈비상시〉 an emergency; an accident
♦날씨의 급변 sudden [unexpected] changes in the weather
▶급변에 대비하여 항공모함이 파견되었다 An aircraft carrier was dispatched in readiness for an emergency [any contingency].
—**급변하다** change suddenly; take a sudden turn
♦급변하는 세계 정세 the rapidly changing world situaion
▶그의 태도가 급변했다 His attitude changed suddenly. ⇒ He changed his attitude suddenly.

급병 急病 a sudden illness ⇨ 급환
▶그 사람은 급병에 걸렸다 He was suddenly taken ill. ■—**환자** an urgent [emergency] case

급보 急報 an urgent message [report]; 〈경보〉 an alarm ♦급보에 접하다 receive the urgent news (of)
—**급보하다** send an urgent message (to); report promptly; give an alarm (for a fire); send an emergency call (of)

급부 給付 grant; a delivery; 〈보험의〉 a benefit; 〈금전의〉 payment
—**급부하다** grant; deliver; pay; provide
♦노인에게 연금을 급부하다 pay pensions to the elderly / 종업원들에게 제복을 급부하다 provide [furnish] employees with uniforms; provide uniforms for employees
■**반대**— a benefit in return (for); (비유)— a compensation (for) **의료**— a medical benefit —**기한** the duration of a benefit —**일수** a term of benefit —**제한** restriction on benefit

급부금 給付金 a benefit ♦급부금을 받다 receive [get] a benefit (from) / 급부금을 지급하다 pay sb a benefit

급비생 給費生 a scholarship student ⇨ 장학생

급사 急死 a sudden death; an untimely death
—**급사하다** die suddenly; meet with an untimely death; (口) pop off
▶그는 열병으로 급사했다 He died suddenly of a fever.

급사 急使 a courier; an express messenger; a dispatch rider

급사 給仕 〈사무실의〉 an office boy; 〈호텔의〉 a page boy; (美) a bellboy; 〈식당의〉 a waiter; a waitress(여자)
■—**장** a headwaiter; a butler

급사면 急斜面 a steep slope

급살 急煞 the most unlucky [sinister] star; the worst fate
♦급살(을) 맞다 die suddenly; meet a sudden death; drop dead; (口) pop off
▶이 급살(을) 맞을 놈아 Go to hell [the devil]! ⇒ A plague on you!

급상승 急上昇 a sudden rise; 〔空〕 a zoom; zooming; a chandelle —**급상승하다** rise suddenly [sharply]; climb steeply; skyrocket; zoom; chandelle

급서 急逝 a sudden death ⇨ 급사(急死)

급선무 急先務 the most urgent business [necessity]; the most important matter requiring immediate attention; an exigency
▶재해 지역의 재건에 착수하는 것이 급선무다 The first thing we have to do is to start the reconstruction of the stricken area.

급설하다 急設— 〈급히 설치하다〉 install《a telephone》hurriedly; lay《a cable》speedily

급성 急性 ♦급성의 acute
■—**병** an acute disease —**신장[간, 맹장]염** acute nephritis [hepatitis, appendicitis] —**인플레이션** a galloping inflation —**중독** acute poisoning —**질환** an acute disease —**폐렴[류머티즘]** acute pneumonia [rheumatism]

급소 急所 1 〈신체의〉 a vital organ; a vital part [point]; vitals ♦급소를 치다 hit sb on a vital spot
▶그는 다행히 탄알이 급소를 벗어난 것 같다 Luckily the bullet missed his vital organs.
▶공이 그의 급소에 맞은 것 같다 The ball seems to have hit him where it hurts.
2 〈약점〉 a vulnerable [weak] spot; a sore spot
▶나는 급소를 찔려서 주춤하였다 I was attacked on a vulnerable spot and flinched.
3 〈요점〉 a key point
♦문제의 급소 the main point of a question / 급소를 벗어난 질문 a question that is beside the mark / 급소를 찌른 질문 a question that touches [goes to] the heart of the matter; 〈날카로운〉 a pointed question
▶그는 급소를 잘 짚고 있다 He knows what is what.

급속 急速 rapidity; promptitude
—**급속하다** fast; rapid; speedy; quick; prompt ♦급속한 진전 rapid progress [advance] / 급속한 해결 a prompt solution / 급속히 fast; rapidly; with rapidity; quickly
▶한국의 자동차 산업은 1980년대에 급속한 발전을 했다 The automobile industry of Korea made rapid [fast] progress in the 1980's.
▶온도가 급속히 상승했다 The temperature rose suddenly [sharply].
■—**냉동** quick freezing: 급속 냉동 저장 장치 a quick-freezing storage facility / 급속 냉동한 생선[고기] quick-frozen fish [meat]

급송하다 急送— send sth in haste [by express]; dispatch; (美) ship《goods》by express; (美) express《a package》
▶이 생선은 시장으로 급송하지 않으면 안 된다 These fish must be sent to the market at once.

급수 級數 〔數〕 a series; 〈수열〉 progression
♦〈산술[기하]〉 급수적으로 증가하다 grow in arithmetic [geometrical] progression
■—**등비[기하]**— geometric progression; a geometric series **등차[산술]**— arithmetic progression; an arithmetic series **삼각**— a trigonometrical series **순환**— a recurring

series 유한[무한]— a finite [an infinite] series 조화— a harmonic series
급수 給水 water supply; 〈보일러 등의〉water feeding; 〈물〉service water; feed water
　—**급수하다** supply 《a city》 with water
　◆ 수로를 건설하여 황무지에 급수하다 build a canalage to supply water to waste land
　■ **시간**— hour-restricted supply of water: 각 가정에 시간 급수하다 supply water to each house only during limited hours 제한— regulated water supply ■ —**관** a water pipe; a service pipe; 〈보일러의〉a feed pipe —**량** the amount of water supplied —**본관** a water [service] main —**선**(船) a water boat [tender] —**소** a water station —**시설** a water system —**전**(栓) a water tap; 〈소방용의〉a hydrant; 〈보일러 등의〉a feed cock —**제한** restriction(s) on water supply —**차** a water wagon —**탑** a water tower; a standpipe —**탱크** a water tank —**펌프** a feed pump
급습 急襲 a surprise [sudden] attack; 〈경찰·군대의〉a raid; 〈軍〉〈적진으로의〉a storm
　—**급습하다** make a surprise [sudden] attack; raid; storm
　◆ 현금 수송차를 급습하다 make a surprise attack on a cash delivery car
　▶ 그들은 적을 급습했다 They made a surprise attack on the enemy. ⇌ They made a raid on the enemy position. ⇌ They stormed the enemy fort.
급식 給食 supply of food; meal service
　◆ 학교 급식 school meal [lunch]; 〈제도〉a school lunch program
　—**급식하다** provide meals
　◆ 학생[종업원]들에게 급식하다 provide (free) lunch [meals] for school children [employees]; provide [supply] school children [employees] with meals
　■ —**비** expenses for providing meals; 〈학교의〉the charge for a school lunch —**시설**[설비] facilities for providing meals
급여 給與 1 〈봉급〉pay; a salary; wages ◆ 급여가 좋다[나쁘다] be well[poorly] paid
　2 〈수당 등〉 (an) allowance; a grant; (a) supply ◆ 특별 급여 an extra allowance / 현물[현품] 급여 an allowance in kind
　—**급여하다** grant; supply; furnish; provide
　■ —**금** an allowance; a grant —**소득** (an) earned [(a) wage] income —**소득 공제** an exemption on income from salaries —**수준** a pay [wage] level —**체계** a pay [wage] system [structure]
급용 急用 〈급한 용무〉 《on》 urgent [pressing] business
급우 級友 a classmate
급유 給油 〈연료보급〉 refueling; 〈기계에〉 oiling; lubrication; 〈용기에〉 fill-up
　▶ 그 비행기는 급유 때문에 앵커리지에 기착했다 The airplane stopped over at Anchorage for refueling.
　—**급유하다** refuel; feed 《a machine》 with oil; lubricate; fill 《a tank》
　▶ 차에 급유해야 한다 We must put oil into our car.
　■ **공중**— ⇨ 공중(~급유) ■ —**기**(機) a tanker plane —**선**(船) a tanker; an oiler —**소** an oil depot; a filling [美] gas, [英] petrol) station —**장치** an oiler —**탱크** a storage tank; 〈주유의〉 an oil-feeding tank —**함** a naval tanker —**항** an oil port
급작스럽다 sudden ⇨ 갑작스럽다
급장 級長 the head of a class
급전 急電 〈급한 전보〉 an urgent telegram [telephone] ◆ 급전을 치다 wire an urgent message 《to》
급전 急錢 urgently needed money; money for immediate use
급전 急轉 a sudden change [turn] —**급전하다** change suddenly; take a sudden turn ▶ 사태가 급전했다 Things changed suddenly. ⇌ Things took a sudden turn.
　■ —**직하** sudden turn 《of affairs》; spectacular change: 그의 상태가 밤사이 급전직하로 악화되었다 His conditions took a sudden turn for the worse overnight.
급전 給電 electric [power] supply —**급전하다** supply electricity [electric power] ■ —**량** the amount [volume] of electricity supplied
급전환 急轉換 a sudden change [turn]
　—**급전환하다** change [turn] suddenly; take a sudden [abrupt] turn
　▶ 그는 계획을 급전환하지 않을 수 없게 되었다 He was forced to make a sudden change in his plans.
　▶ 정부는 경제 정책을 180도 급전환했다 The government has made a rapid and complete about-face in its economic policy.
급정거 急停車 a sudden stop
　—**급정거하다** stop suddenly [short]; come [be brought] to a sudden stop
　▶ 돌발 사태로 말미암아 버스가 급정거하는 수가 있다 Something unexpected brings a bus to a sudden stop.
　▶ 열차는 급정거하여 가까스로 사고를 면했다 The train stopped suddenly [came to a sudden stop] and narrowly avoided the traffic accident.
　▶ 그 운전자는 차를 급정거시켰다 The driver brought his car to a sudden stop.
급제 及第 success in an examination ⇨ 합격
급조 急造 hurried construction ◆ 주택의 급조 계획 a crash housing program
　—**급조하다** build in haste; build [construct] hurriedly
　◆ 급조한 막사 barracks thrown up [built] in haste / 급조된 무대 an improvised [a hurriedly built] stage / 급조한 오두막 a quickly put-up shed
급증 急增 a jump; a sudden [rapid] increase
　▶ 인구의 급증에 대한 대책이 시급하다 The populational jump calls for an immediate countermove.
　—**급증하다** increase rapidly [suddenly]; jump
　▶ 교통사고가 급증했다 The number of traffic accidents has increased rapidly [suddenly].
급진 急進 1 〈빨리 진행함〉 rapid progress [advance] —**급진하다** start suddenly; make rapid advance 2 〈과격〉 radicalism; going to

extremes ♦급진적인 radical; extreme ―당 a radical party; the radicals ―분자 a radical element ―사상 radical ideas [thought, thinking] ―주의 radicalism ―주의자 a radical ―파 radicals; a radical faction

급커브 急― a sharp curve [turn]
♦급커브지다 form [draw] a sharp curve / 급커브를 틀다 make a sharp turn (at the corner); turn (a corner) sharply
▶이 길은 급커브가 많으니 주의하시오 Be careful. This road has a lot of sharp curves.
▶길은 좌측으로 급커브졌다 The road curved suddenly to the left.
▶전방에 급커브 (게시) Warning: Sharp Curve Ahead.

급탄 給炭 supply of coal; coaling ■―소 (軍) a coaling depot ―역 a coaling station ―차 a stoker (car) ―항 a coaling port

급탕 給湯 the supply of hot water; the hot water supply (of the hotel) ―시설 a hot water supply system

급템포 急― quick tempo ♦급템포의 double-time; double-quick / 급템포로 in quick tempo; double-quick; speedily / 급템포로 진척되다 progress very rapidly

급파 急派 dispatching
―급파하다 dispatch; rush; expediate
♦현장에 구조대를 급파하다 dispatch [rush] a rescue party to the scene / 전선에 군대를 급파하다 dispatch troops to the front

급하다 急― 1 〈긴급·다급하다〉 urgent; pressing; hurried; rush
♦급한 주문 orders / 급한 볼일로 on urgent business / 급할 때는 when time is short; in case of emergency / 급한 여행을 하다 make a flying [hurried] trip
▶나는 돈이 몹시 급했다 I was in dire [urgent] need of money.
▶양국간의 형세가 매우 급해졌다 The situation between the two countries is dangerously strained.
▶그는 급한 걸음으로 올라왔다 He came up with hurried steps.
▶나는 급한 일이 생겨 모임에 참석하지 못했다 Some pressing [urgent] business turned up, so that I could not attend the gathering.
▶이건 급하지 않아 This can wait.
▶일을 급하게 하면 못 쓴다 It's no good rushing things.
2 〈성급하다〉 impatient; impetuous; quick-tempered; short-tempered
♦급한 성미 a quick [hot] temper / 성미가 급한 사람 a person of an impetuous disposition; a hothead / 급하게 결론을 내리다 jump at a conclusion
3 〈위중하다〉 serious; critical ♦급한 병 a serious illness ▶그의 병세는 급한 것 같다 His illness seems critical.
4 〈급속하다〉 swift; rapid; speedy ♦급한 흐름 a swift current; a rapid stream ▶이 강은 흐름이 급하다 The current of this river is rapid.
5 〈가파르다〉 steep; precipitous; sharp ♦급한 굽이[커브] a sharp turn [curve] / 급한 비탈 a steep slope [gradient]

급하면 부처 다리 안는다 (속담) Any port in a storm.

급할수록 돌아가라 (속담) More haste, less [worse] speed.

급행 急行 1 〈급히 감〉 fast; express; (美) hot-shot
―급행하다 go in a hurry; run (to); rush (to)
▶경찰은 사고 현장으로 급행했다 The policeman rushed to the scene of the accident.
2 〈급행 열차〉 an express (train)
♦보통[특별] 급행 열차 an ordinary [a special, limited] express (train) / 10시발 대전행 급행의 10:00 Taejŏn express / 급행으로 가다 take an express (to); travel [hurry] by express
▶ [會話] 「그 급행열차가 이 역에 섭니까?」「예, 섭니다」 "Does the express stop [call] at this station?" "Yes, it does."
―권 an express ticket ―버스 an express bus ―요금 an express charge ―정차역 an express station [stop] ―편 (send *sth* by) express

급환 急患 〈병〉 a sudden illness [disease]; 〈환자〉 an emergency [urgent] case ▶의사는 급환이 있어 왕진중이다 The doctor is out on an emergency call.

급히 急― hurriedly; in a hurry; hastily; in haste; speedily; quickly; without delay; (口) on the double
♦급히 걷다 walk hurriedly [briskly] / 급히 귀가하다 hurry [hasten] home / 급히 나가다 hurry out of (a room) / 급히 서둘러 점심을 먹다 snatch a hurried lunch / 돈이 급히 필요하다 be in urgent [immediate] need of money
▶나는 급히 가야 한다 I am in a hurry to go.
▶그는 급히 계단을 내려갔다 He hastened downstairs.
▶당신의 편지에 급히 회답을 드립니다 I hasten to reply to your letter.
▶그들은 환자를 급히 입원시켰다 They rushed the patient to the hospital.

급히 먹는 밥이 목이 멘다 (속담) Haste makes waste.

굿다¹ 〈비가 그치다〉 stop; hold up; 〈비를 피하다〉 take shelter [refuge] from (rain); shelter *oneself* from (rain)
♦처마 밑에서 비를 긋다 stand under the eaves (of a house) to get out of the rain

굿다² 1 〈선을〉 draw
♦금을 긋다 draw a line / 경계선을 긋다 draw a line of demarcation (between); demarcate / 땅에 줄을 긋다 cut [dig] a line on ground / 획을 긋다 draw a stroke (of a character)
2 〈성냥을〉 strike [scratch] (a match)
♦벽에다 성냥을 긋다 scratch a match against a wall
3 〈외상값을〉 charge (expense) to *one's* account [to the account (of)] ♦긋고 마시다 drink on credit [trust]
4 〈작정하다〉 have *one's* heart [mind] set on (doing); determine; decide

긍긍하다 兢兢― be terribly [deadfully] afraid ⇨ 전전긍긍하다

긍정 肯定 affirmation; acknowledgment

▶내 질문에 대한 그녀의 대답은 긍정도 부정도 아니었다 Her answer to my question was neither yes nor no.
—긍정하다 affirm; answer in the affirmative; answer "yes"
♦그 보고를 긍정하다 affirm the report / 긍정하지도 부정지도 않다 refuse to deny or confirm; decline either to affirm or deny
▶침묵한다는 것은 그 안을 긍정하는 것이 된다 To say nothing is to acknowledge the plan.
■**—명제** 〔論〕 an affirmative (proposition) **—문** an affirmative sentence **—판단** 〔論〕 an affirmation

긍정적 肯定的 affirmative ♦긍정적으로 대답하다 answer in the affirmative; give an affirmative answer / 인생을 긍정적으로 보다 take a cheerful view of life
■**—개념** 〔論〕 an affirmative concept

긍지 矜持 pride; dignity
♦긍지를 느끼다 feel proud / 긍지를 손상하다 hurt [wound] *sb's* pride / 한국인으로서의 긍지를 지니다 have *one's* (national) pride as a Korean / 긍지를 지키다 maintain *one's* dignity; save *one's* honor [face]

긍휼 矜恤 pity; sympathy; compassion; commiseration **—긍휼하다** take [have] pity (on); pity; sympathize 《with》 ♦긍휼히 여기다 feel compassion [pity] for

기 紀 〔地質〕 a period ♦석탄기의 the Carboniferous (period) / 쥐라기의 the Jurassic (period)

기 記 an account (of); a description; 〈기록〉 a record; 〈역사〉 a history; 〈연대기〉 annals

기 氣 1 〈기력〉 vigor; energy; spirits; 《口》 pep ♦기가 나(있)다 be full of energy [vigor, vitality]; be in high spirits / 기가 부족하다 be lacking [deficient] in energy
2 〈온힘〉 all *one's* strength [energies]; all-out efforts
▶그는 기를 쓰고 달렸다 He ran for his (dear) life.
▶그는 기를 쓰고 보트를 저었다 He rowed the boat with all his might.
▶그들은 기를 쓰고 우리 제안에 반대했다 They opposed [objected] our proposal strongly [violently].
3 〈숨〉 breath; wind
♦기가 막히다 be stifled; be dumbfounded; be astonished
▶그녀는 그의 어리석은 짓에 기가 막혔다 She was amazed at his absurdity.
▶그의 새 차는 기막히게 속도를 낸다 His new car can go at a terrific speed.
4 〈정신력〉 spirit(s); heart; will power
♦기가 꺾여 있다 be low-spirited; be in low spirits / 기가 성하다 be high-spirited / 기를 돋우다 encourage *sb*; cheer *sb* up / 기를 잃다 lose *one's* heart; be dispirited; have *one's* spirit broken / 기를 펴다 heighten *one's* spirit
▶우리는 기가 등등했다 We were elated [in high spirits].
▶우리는 실패하여서 기가 죽었다 We are depressed [in low spirits] due to our failure. ⇌ We have lost heart [courage] because of the failure.

▶그는 시합을 시작하기도 전에 상대편에게 기가 죽었다 He was overwhelmed by his opponent before the match.
5 〈정기〉 spirit; essence
6 〈객기〉 ill-advised vigor; indiscreet zeal; reckless valor; fiery temper
7 〈기미〉 a touch; a flavor; a feeling; a sign; 〈징후〉 symptom
▶나는 감기기가 있다 I have a slight cold. ⇌ I have a bit [touch] of a cold.
▶이 방은 불기가 없다 This room is unheated.
▶이것은 소금기가 모자란다 This needs a touch of salt.
▶그의 말에는 익살기가 있었다 There was a touch of humour in his speech.

기 基 〔化〕 a radical; a functional group; 〔數〕 a radix 《*pl*. ~es, radices》 ■**—산—** an acid radical [group] **수산—** a hydroxyl group [radical]

기 期 〈시대〉 a period; an age; 〈기일〉 a date; a time; 〈기간〉 a period; a term; 〈계절〉 a season; 〈회기〉 a session; a sitting; 〈단계〉 a stage
♦빙하기 the ice age / 수렵기 the hunting season / 제3기생 the third term students / 차기 국회에서 at the next session of the National Assembly

기 旗 a flag; a banner; a standard; 〈선박 등의〉 an ensign; the colors; 〈긴 삼각기〉 a pennant
♦국기 a national flag / 기를 내걸다 display [fly, hang out] a flag / 기를 내리다 lower [take down] a flag / 기를 달다 hoist [lift, put up] a flag / 기를 흔들다 wave a flag
▶기가 바람에 나부끼고 있었다 The flag was flapping [fluttering, flying] in the wind.

기 忌 〈상(喪)〉 (a period of) mourning; 〈주기〉 an anniversary of *sb's* death ♦조부의 3주기 the third anniversary of *one's* grandfather's death

기 奇 〈기이함〉 strangeness; novelty

기각 棄却 〔法〕 rejection; dismissal **—기각하다** dismiss; reject; turn down ♦신청을 기각하다 reject [turn down] an application / 항소를 기각하다 dismiss an appeal

기간 基幹 a mainstay; a nucleus 《*pl*. ·clei》 ■**—산업** basic [key] industries **—요원** key [cadre] members

기간 既刊 ♦기간의 already [previously] published [issued] ■**—도서목록** a list of books in print; a list of (previously) published books **—호(號)** back [previous] numbers

기간 期間 a period (of time); a term
♦짧은 기간 a short period / 일정한 기간내에 within a given [certain, definite] period of time / 기간을 연장하다 extend the time [period]
▶계약 기간은 몇 년이지요? How many years is the term of contract?
▶원서 접수 기간은 15일부터 25일까지다 Applications are accepted from the 15th to the 25th.
■**공시[상환]—** a period of presentation [redemption] **유효—** a term of validity: 이 표의 유효 기간은 벌써 지났다 The validity of this ticket has long since expired.

기갈 飢渴 hunger and thirst; starvation
♦기갈이 들다 suffer from [be pressed by] hunger and thirst / 기갈로 죽다 starve [be starved] to death; die of starvation
▶그는 치즈 한 조각으로 기갈을 면했다 He starved [kept] off his hunger with a piece of cheese.
기갈이 감식이다 〈속담〉 Hunger is the best sauce.

기갑 機甲 ■―**부대** armored forces; armors; panzers ―**사단** an armored division

기강 紀綱 official [government] discipline; 〈질서〉 public order; law and order
♦기강의 문란 a breach [the deterioration] of (official) discipline / 기강의 붕괴 the decline of the law of the land; decay of the moral fiber of the nation / 기강의 해이 slackness [laxity] of official discipline / 기강을 바로 잡다 improve the moral fiber; tighten discipline (among)
▶경찰의 기강을 바로잡아야 한다 We must tighten discipline within the police force.

기개 氣概 (a noble) spirit; pride; backbone; 〈口〉 guts
♦기개가 있는 high-spirited; mettlesome; proud; plucky / 기개가 없다 have no spirit [grit]; be backboneless / 기개를 보이다 show one's pluck [mettle]

기거 起居 〈일상 생활〉 one's daily life; daily living
♦기거를 함께하다 live together (under the same roof) with sb
―**기거하다** (live in a dormitory); stay (with)

기겁하다 be astonished ⇨ 기급하다

기결 旣決 ♦기결의 decided; settled; 〈法〉 convicted / 기결이다 have already decided [settled]
■―**사항[안]** a matter settled [decided on] ―**서류** documents [papers] on which a decision has already been made ―**서류함** an out-tray ―**수(囚)** a convict; a convicted prisoner

기계 棋界 paduk [changgi] circles; the paduk [changgi] world

기계 器械 an instrument; an appliance; an apparatus ―**물리**― a physical apparatus ―**의료**― medical appliances [instruments]

기계 機械 a machine; (총칭) machinery; 〈기계 장치〉 a mechanism; works 〈시계 등의〉
♦기계의 운전 시간 machine hours / 기계로 만든 machine-made
〈기계는〉 기계는 많은 노동력을 덜어 준다 Machines save (us) a lot of labor.
▶이 기계는 잘 돌아가고 있다[돌아가지 않는다] This machine runs very smoothly [does not work well].
〈기계를〉 기계를 분해하다 disassemble [dismantle] the machine / 기계를 공장에 설치하다 install a machine in a factory / 기계를 조립하다 assemble [put together] a machine
▶이 기계를 운전하기는 어렵다 It is difficult to operate [use, work, run] this machine.
▶이 기계를 조작할 줄 아니? Do you know how to work [use, operate] this machine?
〈기계에〉 이 기계에 고장이 있는 것 같다 Something seems to be wrong with this machine.
▶기계에 손대지 마시오.(게시) Hands off the machinery. ⇌ Keep away from the machine.
■**공작**― a machine tool **정밀**― a precision machine ■―**가공** machine work; machining ―**간(間)** a machine shop [room] ―**공** a mechanic; a mechanician ―**공업** the machine industry ―**공장** a machine [mechanics] shop [factory]; an engineering works ―**공학** mechanical engineering ―**공학과** a course in mechanical engineering; a mechanical course ―**기사[기술자]** a mechanical engineer; a mechanist ―**기술** machine [mechanical] technology ―**능률[효율]** mechanical efficiency ―**력** mechanical power ―**론** mechanism: 기계론적 세계관 a mechanistic world-view ―**론자** a mechanist ―**류** machines ―**문명** machine civilization ―**부품** a machine part ―**설계** the design of a machine ―**수리공** a machine mender; a repairman ―**시대** a machine age; the age of machinery ―**실** a machine [machinery] room; an engine room ―**어** 〈전자 계산기의〉 a machine language ―**유(油)** machine oil ―**제도** mechanical drawing ―**제작소** a machine shop ―**제품** a mechanical [machine] product ―**조립** assembling; fitting; erection; 〈자동차 반제품의〉 knockdown ―**조립공** an erector; a fitter ―**톱** a power saw ―**학** mechanics

기계 奇計 an ingenious [a clever] scheme; a cunning plan ♦기계를 부리다 resort to a (clever) stratagem

기계적 機械的 mechanical; machine
♦기계적인 동작 mechanical movement / 기계적으로 mechanically; automatically / 기계적으로 일하다 work mechanically
▶그는 영어 단어를 기계적으로 외웠다 He learned English words by rote.

기계체조 器械體操 apparatus gymnastics; gymnastics 〈口〉 (gym) with apparatus ♦기계체조를 하다 perform [practice] apparatus gymnastics

기계화 機械化 mechanization ♦농업의 기계화 farm mechanization ―**기계화하다** mechanize
▶이제 모든 작업은 기계화되어 있다 Now all the work is done by machine(s).

기고 起稿 drafting; 〈초안〉 draft ―**기고하다** draft; 〈쓰기 시작하다〉 begin writing [to write]; start writing [to write]; start work on a manuscript

기고 寄稿 (a) contribution
♦잡지에 기고 요청을 받다 be asked to write an article for [to contribute an article to] a magazine
―**기고하다** contribute 《to》; write 《for》
♦신문에 기고하다 write in [for] the paper [press]
■―**가[자]** a contributor: 정기 기고가 a regular contributor

기고만장 氣高萬丈 high spirits; elation
▶그들은 첫 경기에 이겨 기고만장이었다 Having won the first game, their spirits soared.
―**기고만장하다** be in high soaring spirits; be high-spirited

◆기고만장하여 in high spirits; in triumph / 성공을 거두어 기고만장하다 be elated [puffed up] with success

기골 氣骨 1 〈골격〉 the (body) frame; build ◆기골이 장대한 사람 a man of large and robust frame **2** 〈기개〉 spirit; mettle; grit ▶그는 기골이 있는 사람이다 He has backbone. ⇒ He is a solid man.

기공 技工 〈기술〉 craft; craftsmanship; skill; 〈기술자〉 an artisan; a craftsman ◆치과 기공사 a dental technician

기공 起工 the start of (construction) work; 〈토목 공사의〉 breaking ground; 〚船〛 keel laid
—기공하다 begin [start] work (construction]; begin [start] construction; 〈선박을〉 lay (down) the keel (of); 〈건축을〉 lay the cornerstone (of); 〈토목공사〉 break ground (for) ◆하수도 공사를 기공하다 begin work on a sewer system ▶주택공사가 새 고층 아파트 건축 공사를 기공했다 The Housing Corporation has broken ground on the new high-rise apartment building program.
■—식 a commencement ceremony; 〈건축의〉 the ceremony of laying the cornerstone [foundation stone]; 〈토목의〉 the ground-breaking ceremony; 〈조선의〉 the ceremony of laying down the keel

기공 氣孔 a pore; 〈식물의〉 a stoma (*pl.* ~s, -mata); 〈곤충의〉 a stigma (*pl.* ~s, -mata); 〈광물의〉 a vesicle; a gas cavity ◆기공의 stomatal

기관 汽管 〚機〛 a steam pipe

기관 汽罐 a boiler; a steam generator ■—실 a boiler room; 〈선박의〉 a stokehold; a fireroom

기관 奇觀 a wonderful [marvelous] sight; a singular [rare] spectacle
◆자연의 기관 a natural wonder / 세계 7대 기관 the seven great wonders [marvels] of the world / 기관을 이루다 present [offer] a spectacular [wonderful] sight

기관 氣管 〚解〛 the trachea (*pl.* ~s, -cheae); the windpipe ◆기관의 tracheal ■—절개(술) tracheotomy

기관 器官 〚動·植〛 an organ ◆생명 유지에 중요한 기관 a vital organ / 신체의 여러 기관 the (individual) organs of the body ◆감각— a sense organ 발성— a vocal organ 소화— the digestive organs [apparatus] 청각— a hearing organ 호흡— the respiratory organs ■—계통 an organ system —질환 an organic disease

기관 機關 1 〈엔진〉 an engine; a machine **2** 〈수단〉 a means (▶단수·복수 동형); a medium; an instrument; an agency; 〈기구(機構)〉 an organization; 〈조직〉 a system; 〈시설〉 facilities; accommodations; an institution ◆국가 최고 기관 the highest state body / 기관을 설치하다 set up an agency ▶TV는 이제 중요한 보도 기관이다 Television is now an important information medium.—
■ 가솔린— a gasoline engine 공랭[수냉]식— an air-cooled [a water-cooled] engine 교육— an educational institute 교통[운수]— transportation facilities 국제— an international agency 금융— banking facilities 내연— an internal-combustion engine 대행— an agency 보조— an auxiliary engine 심의— a deliberative body [organ] 언론— organs of public opinion 열— a heat [thermic] engine 입법— a legislative organ [body] 자치— a self body 재외— an overseas agency [organization] 전기— an electric engine 정부— a government 증기— a steam engine 행정— an executive organ 첩보— a secret service 터빈— a turbine engine 통신— means of communication 특무— the military secret service; (美) the counterintelligence corps (略 C.I.C.) 행정— administrative machinery [agencies]; the administrative system ■—고 an engine shed [house]; a locomotive depot —고장 an engine trouble [failure] —실 an engine room —원 〈선박 등의〉 a stoker; a secret service man —장 a chief engineer; 〈조직의〉 the head [chief] of an organ —효율 engine efficiency

기관단총 機關短銃 a submachine gun; (美) a burp gun

기관사 機關士 〈철도의〉 an engineman; (英) an engine driver; (美) an [a locomotive] engineer; 〈선박의〉 an engineer; 〈비행기의〉 a flight engineer
■—일등— a first engineer

기관지 氣管支 〚解〛 the bronchus (*pl.* -chi); bronchial tubes ◆기관지의 bronchial
■—경(鏡) a bronchoscope —염 bronchitis; bronchial inflammation —카타르 bronchial catarrh

기관지 機關紙[誌] a bulletin; a newspaper ◆업계의 기관지 the official bulletin of the trade association / 정당의 기관지 the official newspaper of a political party
■ 야당— an opposition paper 정부— a government organ [bulletin]

기관차 機關車 a railroad [(美) railway] engine; a locomotive (engine) ◆기관차를 운전하다 operate a locomotive
■ 전기— an electric locomotive; an electromotive 증기— a steam locomotive (engine)

기관총 機關銃 a machine gun ◆기관총으로 소사하다 machine-gun / 기관총으로 소사당하다 be machine-gunned
■—경[중]— a light [heavy] machine gun ■—사수 a machine gunner; 〈비행기의〉 an air gunner

기관포 機關砲 a (heavy) machine gun

기괴망측하다 奇怪罔測— quite strange [mysterious, weird]; fantastic; outrageous ◆기괴망측한 소리 a weird [an uncanny] sound

기괴하다 奇怪— 〈괴상하다〉 strange; mysterious; weird; queer; 〈기상천외의〉 outrageous; extraordinary; scandalous
◆기괴한 사건 an inscrutable [a strange] affair; a mystery / 기괴한 소문 a wild rumor

기교

▶그 사람의 행동은 기기하다 His behavior is strange [queer].

기교 技巧 skill; technique; art; craftsmanship; workmanship; 〈예술의〉 mechanism

◆연애의 기교 the finesse of love / 기교가 대단한 조각가 a sculptor of great skill / 기교를 부리다 exert *one's* technical skill; use art

▶이 그림은 기교 면에서는 조금도 부족한 점이 없다 This picture leaves nothing to be desired in technique.

▶그는 기교를 부린 문장을 쓴다 He writes polished sentences.

■―가[파] 〈회화·음악의〉 a technician; 〈문장의〉 a stylist; 〈나쁜 뜻의〉 a mannerist ―주의 〈예술상의〉 technicalism; mannerism

기구 氣球 balloon ◆기구를 띄우다 fly [let loose] a balloon / 기구를 타다 ride a balloon / 기구를 타고 올라가다 ascend in a balloon

■계류(繫留)― a captive [dirigible] balloon 관측― an observation balloon 광고― an advertising balloon 열― a hot-air balloon 헬륨― a helium-filled balloon ■―계류소 a balloon bed [moor]

기구 機構 a mechanism; machinery; 〈조직〉 a system; organization; 〈구조〉 structure

◆근대의 정치 기구 the mechanism [framework] of modern government / 유엔의 기구 the organization [machinery] of the United Nations / 기구를 개편하다 restructure an organization; reorganize

■국제― an international organization 당(黨)― the organization of a political party; party apparatus 유통― a distribution system 정치― a political framework; government machinery 행정[경제]― an administration [economic] structure [setup] ■―개혁 the reorganization of a system; reorganization; structural reform

기구 器具 a utensil; an implement; an appliance; an apparatus; an instrument

■난방― a heating apparatus 의료― a medical appliance; a remedial apparatus 전기― an electrical appliance 조명― lighting fixtures 주방― kitchen utensils

기구하다 崎嶇― checkered; adverse; unlucky; ill-fated

◆기구한 운명을 타고나다 be born under an unlucky star

▶그의 기구한 생애는 꼭 소설 같다 The ups and downs of his life [career] are just like something out of a novel.

기권 棄權 〈투표의〉 (an) abstention (from voting); 〈권리의〉 abandonment [renunciation] (of *one's* rights); 〈경기의〉 (a) withdrawal (from a race)

◆찬성 50, 반대 13, 기권 3(의 투표) 50 in favor, 13 opposed, 3 abstentions / 기권승을 거두다 win the game due to the opponent's withdrawal from the contest

―기권하다 abandon [give up, renounce] *one's* rights 《of》; 〈경기에서〉 withdraw 《from a contest》; be absent

▶그는 수영 경기에서 기권했다 He dropped out of the swimming race.

■―방지 prevention of abstention from voting; a voting drive ―율 an abstention rate ―자 one who abstains from voting [doesn't vote]; an abstentionist; a nonvoter; an absentee; 〈권리의〉 a releasor ―표 a blank ballot

기권 氣圈 the atmosphere ⇨ 대기권

기근 氣根 〔植〕 an aerial root

기근 飢饉 (a) famine; 〈흉작〉 failure of crops; crop failure; (a) shortage

◆기근이 든 해 〈흉년〉 a lean year / 기근으로 고생하다 suffer from a famine / 기근으로 죽다 perish with [by] famine; die of famine

■대― a great [big, severe] famine 물― shortage of water supply; a water shortage [dearth]; (a) drought 주택― shortage of housing ―재민(災民) famine-stricken people ―지역 a famine-stricken district

기금 基金 a fund; a foundation; an endowment ◆기금을 모으다 raise [collect] a fund / 기금을 설치하다 establish [set up] a fund

■공동― a common purse 구제― a relief fund 국제 아동― United Nations Children's Fund 국제 통화― the International Monetary Fund (略 IMF) ―모집 (a campaign [drive] for) raising [collection of] a fund

기급하다 氣急― be astonished [shocked]; be frightened out of one's wits; 〈소리지르다〉 cry out in astonishment [surprise]

▶그 여자는 그것을 보고 기급했다 She was frightened to see it.

▶개가 짖는 바람에 도둑은 기급하여 달아났다 The burglar was frightened away by the barking of the dog.

기기 器機 machinery and tools; (an) apparatus ■―제작소 a machinery shop [works]

기기묘묘하다 奇奇妙妙― strange; curious; queer; odd; funny; unusual; peculiar; 〈기묘하다〉 wonderful; wondrous; marvelous

◆기기묘묘한 사건 a very strange affair; a mysterious incident / 기기묘묘한 소문 a bizarre rumor

기꺼이 gladly; with pleasure [delight]; 〈자발적으로〉 willingly; voluntarily; 〈선뜻〉 readily

◆기꺼이 …하다 be willing [pleased] to do; be delighted to do; be ready to do; volunteer for…

▶그는 기꺼이 동의했다 He consented with a ready answer.

▶나는 당신을 위해서라면 무엇이든 기꺼이 하겠소 I'll be delighted to do anything for you.

▶그는 내 부탁을 기꺼이 들어 주었다 He was quite ready to comply with my request.

▶그는 기꺼이 그 일을 맡았다 He volunteered [offered (on his own account)] to do the work.

▶기꺼이 도와 드리겠습니다 I will be delighted [very happy] to help you. ⇒ I will help you with pleasure.

▶그는 나를 기꺼이 만나 주었다 He received me with a good grace.

기껍다 joyful; joyous; glad; delightful; happy; 〈유쾌하다〉 pleasant ◆기꺼운 소식 good [happy] news

▶전원 합격이라니 정말 기꺼운 일이다 I am

very happy [pleased] that everyone passed the examination.
▶ 아들의 말이 아버지를 기껍게 만들었다 The son's words pleased [delighted] his father.

기껏 1 〈힘껏〉 with all one's strength [might]; to the utmost (of one's power); as hard as one can
▶ 그는 기껏 모은 돈을 다 써버렸다 He spent the money he had saved at no small pains.
2 〈고작〉 at (the) most; at the utmost; at (the) best; merely
▶ 산 것이 기껏 이것뿐이냐? Are these all [the only ones] you bought?
▶ 기껏 한다는 소리가 그거냐? You say, at best, such a stupid thing!

기껏해야 at (the) most; at the very most; at the utmost; at (the) best; only; merely
▶ 여기서 서울까지는 기껏해야 1시간이다 It takes [will take] you one hour at most from here to Seoul.
▶ 이 정도의 책이면 기껏해야 1권에 5천원이다 The book of this kind cost not more than five thousand won a copy.
▶ 그는 기껏해야 16세다 He's about sixteen at (the) most. ⇒ He's barely [not more than] sixteen or so.
▶ 나는 기껏해야 이 정도밖에 못한다 This is the utmost I can do.

기낭 氣囊 〈어류의〉 an air bladder; 〈조류・식물의〉 an air sac; 〈비행선의〉 a gasbag

기내 機内 〈항공기의〉 the inside of a plane; the cabin
♦기내에서 in [inside] the plane / 기내의 온도를 일정하게 유지하다 maintain a constant temperature in the plane
■—반입 수하물 carryon; carry-on baggage —서비스 in-flight service —식 an in-flight meal; meal on the plane; airline food —영화 an in-flight movie

기네스북 *the Guinness Book of Records*

기념 紀念・記念 commemoration; memory; remembrance
♦기념의 commemorative; memorial / 기념으로 in memory [commemoration] (of); to the memory (of) / 기념으로 소나무를 심다 plant a pine tree in commemoration of the occasion
▶ 여행 기념으로 이 항공권을 간직하겠င다 I'll keep this air ticket as a souvenir of my trip.
—**기념하다** commemorate; honor the memory (of)
▶ 서울 올림픽을 기념하여 새 주화가 발행되었다 They issued new coins to commemorate [in commemoration of] the Olympic Games in Seoul.
■—관 a memorial hall —그림엽서 a souvenir [commemoration] picture postcard —논문집 essays (contributed) in celebration of 《the 10th anniversary of…》 —물 a souvenir; a remembrance; a memorial; a monument; a trophy; a keepsake —비 (erect) a monument (of a war); a memorial —사진 a souvenir photograph [picture] —스탬프 a commemoration stamp [postmark] —식 a commemorative ceremony —우표 a commemorative [memorial] (postage) stamp —출판(물) a commemorative publication —패(牌) a memorial tablet —품 a souvenir; a memento —행사 a memorial event; an anniversary function —호 〈잡지 등의〉 commemorative number [issue]

기념일 紀念日 a memorial day; 〈1년에 한번의〉 an anniversary; a day of remembrance
▶ 오늘은 우리의 결혼 10주년 기념일이다 This is our 10th wedding anniversary.
■—셰익스피어— Shakespeare's Day 창립— the foundation day 혁명—〈프랑스의〉 the Bastille Day

기는 놈 위에 나는 놈이 있다 (속담) Even the best man meets his match. ⇒ Everyone has somebody above him. ⇒ There is always someone better. ⇒ You cannot always outdo others.

기능 技能 (technical) skill; ability; capacity
♦특수한 기능 special [expert] skill / 기능이 우수하다 be highly skilled (in) / 기능을 닦다 improve one's skill
▶ 우리는 영어의 4기능을 완전히 익혀야 한다 We have to master the four skills of English.
■—공 a technician; a skilled worker —공양성 the training of skilled laborers —교육[훈련] technical education [training] —상(賞) a prize for technical skill; the technique award —올림픽 the International Vocational Training Competition —직 a skilled occupation

기능 機能 (a) function
♦뇌의 기능 the function(ing) of the brain / 기능적(인) functional / 모든 기능을 발휘하다 fulfill 《one's, its》 function; function / 기능적으로 쓸모가 없다 be functionally useless
▶ 당신의 신체 기관은 모두 정상적인 기능을 하고 있습니다 Every organ in your body is functioning properly.
■—생 활[생식]— vital [generative] functions 소화— digestive functions ■—검사 a functional test —심리학 functional psychology —장애 impaired functioning; a functional disorder —저하 malfunction; 〔醫〕 depression —주의 functionalism —키 function key —훈련 functional training

기니 〈나라 이름〉 Guinea; 〈공식명〉 the Republic of Guinea ♦기니의 Guinean ■—사람 a Guinean

기니비사우 〈나라 이름〉 Guinea-Bissau; 〈공식명〉 the Republic of Guinea-Bissau

기니피그 〔動〕 a guinea pig; a cavy

기다 creep; crawl
♦기어 나오다 crawl off [out of] / 기어들(어가)다 creep into / 기어 올라가다 crawl [creep, climb] up / 권력 앞에서 기다 cringe before power / 상사 앞에서 설설기다 humble [abase] oneself before one's superiors / 압제자 앞에서 설설기다 crouch to one's oppressor
▶ 아기는 풀밭에서 기어다녔다 The baby crawled around [about] on the grass.
▶ 담쟁이가 벽을 기어올라갔다 Ivy crept [was creeping] over the wall.
▶ 그는 기어서 그 구멍을 빠져 나왔다 He crawled through the hole.

▶굴에 들어가는 데는 네 발로 기어야 했다 We had to go on all fours to enter the cave.

기다랗다 〈길다〉 very long; lengthy
♦스커트를 조금 기다랗게 하다 make a skirt a bit longer; lengthen a skirt a little
▶그녀의 머리는 기다랗다 She has long hair.

기다리다 1 〈오기를〉 wait; wait for
♦신호를 기다리는 주자들 runners waiting for the sign / 기회를 기다리다 wait [watch] for an opportunity / 문이 열리기를 기다리다 wait for a gate to be opened / 오래 기다리다 have a long wait; be kept waiting long
▶우리는 역에서 오래 기다렸다 We waited a long time at the station.
▶나는 오랫동안 버스를 기다렸다 I had a long wait for a bus.
▶나는 그를 계속 기다렸다 I kept (on) waiting for him.
▶잠깐만 기다리세요 〈전화에서〉 Hold on a moment, please.
▶너무 오래 기다리셨습니다 I'm very sorry to have [that I have] kept you waiting so long.
▶ 會話 「조금만 기다려 주세요」「좋습니다」 "Wait a minute, please." "Certainly. ⇌ OK. ⇌ All right. ⇌ Sure."
▶보도진이 그를 기다리고 있었다 The reporters were waiting [lying in wait] for him.
▶다음 비행기편까지는 2시간 기다려야 할 것이다 There will be a two-hour wait before the next flight.
▶세월은 사람을 기다려 주지 않는다 (속담) Time and tide wait for no man.

2 〈기대하다〉 expect; look forward to; anticipate
▶나는 딸의 편지를 기다렸다 I anticipated getting a letter from my daughter.
▶1주일 동안 그의 편지를 기다리고 있다 I've been expecting his letter for a week.
▶학생들은 모두 방학을 몹시 기다리고 있다 All the students are looking eagerly forward to [longing for] vacations.
▶나는 그의 전화를 기다리고 있다 I am expecting a phone call from him [him to call].
▶나는 그의 성공을 기다리고 있다 I expect him to [that he will] succeed.
▶나는 기다리고 기다리던 소식을 오늘 들었다 I received the long-awaited message today.
▶나는 차례를 기다리는데 지쳤다 I got tired of waiting for my turn.

3 〈의존하다〉 count on; expect; look to
▶네가 여러 제안을 해 줄 것을 우리는 기다리고 있다 We look to you for [to make] suggestions.
▶남의 도움을 기다리지 마라 Don't count on the help of other people [others for help].

기다마하다 〈꽤 길다〉 quite long; lengthy; longish

기단 氣團 〔氣〕 an air mass ▪시베리아— the Siberian air mass ▪—발원지 an air mass source region

기담 奇談・奇譚 a strange story [tale]; a weird story; adventures

기대 期待 expectation(s); hope(s); anticipation

♦기대밖의 《be) not up to one's expectations; quite disappointing / 기대에 반하여 contrary to one's expectations / 기대를 걸다 put one's hopes in [on]; place [lay] one's hopes (on) / 기대에 부응하다 come [measure] up to (one's) expectation(s)
▶결과는 기대 이하였다 The result was below expectations.
▶우리는 그에게 큰 기대를 걸고 있다 We expect much from [of] him.
▶그는 자기 아버지의 기대를 저버렸다 He fell short of [didn't answer, ran counter to] his father's expectations.
▶그는 기대대로[이상으로] 잘했다 He has done well as we (had) expected [beyond our expectation(s)].
▶기대와는 달리 그는 낙선했다 Contrary to our expectations he failed in the election.
—**기대하다** expect; hope; anticipate

解說 ***expect***는 충분한 근거에 의거하여 상당한 확신을 가지고 「…하게 될 것이다」라고 기대하는 것인데, 나쁜 일을 예기하는 경우에도 쓰인다는 점에 유의해야 한다. ***hope***는 현실적인 근거에 입각하여 가능성이 있는 희망을 나타낸다. ***anticipate***는 닥쳐올 일을 예기하여 마음의 준비를 한다는 뜻인데, 환영 또는 불안한 감정을 나타내는 경우가 많다.

▶새 정부에 무엇을 기대하십니까? What do you want the new government to do?
▶그는 승진을 기대하고 열심히 일했다 He worked hard in expectation of promotion.
▶그녀는 그에게 도움을 기대하고 있다 She looks to him for help.
▶나는 그에게 그런 것을 기대하지 않았다 I didn't expect such thing of him.

기대감이 旗— 〈기꼭지〉 the tip [pointed end] of a flagpole [flagstaff]

기대다 1 〈몸을〉 lean against [on, over]; stand [rest] against
♦벽에 기대다 lean against a wall / 사다리를 나무에 기대어 놓다 place a ladder against the tree / 의자에 기대 앉다 lean back in a chair / 지팡이에 기대어 걷다 walk leaning on one's stick
▶그녀는 그의 어깨에 기대어 울고 있었다 She wept on his shoulder.
▶나는 난간에 기대어 강을 내려다보고 있었다 I was looking at the river below, leaning over the railing.

2 〈의지하다〉 depend on [upon]; lean [rely] on [upon] ♦친구에게 기대다 rely on a friend for help
▶그는 아직도 부모에게 기대어 생활하고 있다 He still depends on his parents for a living.
▶그녀는 기댈 사람이 하나도 없다 She has no one to depend on [turn to for help].

기도 企圖 〈시도〉 an attempt; a try; 〈계획〉 a plan; a project; a plot; a scheme; 〈사업〉 an enterprise; an undertaking
♦적의 기도를 분쇄하다 frustrate the enemy's attempt
▶대통령 암살 기도가 발각되었다 The plot to

assassinate the President was discovered.
━기도하다 plan; plot; scheme; 〈시도하다〉 attempt; try; 〈의도하다〉 intend; aim 〖at〗; contemplate; have sth in mind
♦살해를 기도하다 make an attempt on *sb's* life; plot the murder 〖of〗
▶우리 회사는 해외진출을 기도하고 있다 Our company is planning to extend our business abroad.
▶그 여자는 자살을 기도했다 She made an attempt at suicide. ⇌ She attempted to take her own life.

기도 祈禱 prayer; 〈식사 전·후의〉 (a) grace
♦아침〖저녁〗기도 the morning 〖evening〗 prayer 〖service〗; matins 〖vespers〗
▶여자는 기도 중이었다 She was praying 〖saying her prayers〗. ⇌ She was at her prayers 〖devotions〗.
━기도하다 pray; say 〖give〗 *one's* prayers; say grace ♦무릎 꿇고 기도하다 kneel 〖down〗 in prayer
■━문 a prayer; 〈주기도문〉 the Lord's Prayer ━서 a prayer 〖service〗 book; 〖가톨릭〗 a breviary; 〈성공회 등의〉 the Book of Common Prayer; the liturgy ━회 a prayer meeting

기도 氣道 the airway; the respiratory tract

기독교 基督敎 Christianity; the Christian religion 〖faith〗
♦기독교의 / 비(非)기독교도 a non-Christian / 기독교식으로 with 〖according to〗 Christian rites / 기독교를 믿다 believe in Christianity; be a Christian / 기독교를 포교하다 propagate 〖spread〗 Christianity
▶그는 기독교로 개종했다 He was converted to Christianity.
■━교회 a Christian church ━국(가) a Christian country; (총칭) Christendom ━도(徒) a Christian; (총칭) Christendom ━사회주의 Christian socialism ━선교사 a (Christian) missionary ━여자청년회 the Young Women's Christian Association (略 Y.W.C.A.) ━청년회 the Young Men's Christian Association (略 Y.M.C.A.)

기동 奇童 a wonder child; a child prodigy
▶그 아이는 기동이다 The child is a wonder.

기동 起動 **1**〈몸을 움직임〉 *one's* movements
♦기동이 자유롭지 못하다 have difficulty in moving 〖getting〗 about / 기동을 못하다 be confined to *one's* bed; be crippled
━기동하다 move; stir; get about; 〈병후에〉 be up 〖out〗 and around
▶그는 2, 3일이면 기동할 수 있을 것이다 He will be able to get up 〖leave his bed〗 in a few days. ⇌ He will be up and around 〖(英) about〗 soon.
2 〈시동〉 starting ━기동하다 start
■━기 a starter; a starting gear; a starter motor ━력 motive power

기동 機動 〖軍〗 movement
■━경찰 〈시위 진압 등의〉 the riot police; 〈경찰대〉 a riot squad ━력 mobile power; 〈기동성〉 mobility: 기동력을 발휘하다 demonstrate *one's* mobility ━배치군 Rapid Deployment Force (略 RDF) ━부대 a mechanized unit; mobile troops; a task force (略 T.F.) ━성 mobility; maneuverability ━연습 maneuvers; mobile exercises; 〈야외의〉 a field maneuver: 해군은 특별 기동 연습을 실시했다 The navy held special maneuvers. ━작전 mobile operations ━전 mobile warfare ━타격대 a special strike 〖task〗 force (ready to act) ━화 mechanization

기동차 汽動車 an internal-combustion railcar; a diesel train 〖railcar〗

기둥 〈건물의〉 a pillar; a column; a post 〖pole〗; 〈사람〉 a support; a pillar
♦나라의 기둥 the pillar of a nation / 기둥을 세우다 erect 〖set up〗 a column 〖pole, post〗
▶부친이 돌아가신 후 아들은 그 집의 기둥이 되었다 After the father's death his son became the mainstay of the family.
▶지붕은 많은 기둥으로 지탱되어 있다 The roof is supported by a large number of pillars.
■━물 a column of water ■━머리 a capital a chapiter ━목(木) logs for pillars ━뿌리 the base of a column 〖pillar〗

기둥서방 ━書房 a gigolo; a fancy man

기드림 旗━ a streamer; a pennant; a banderole; a banner

기득 旣得 ♦기득의 already acquired 〖obtained〗

기득권 旣得權 vested right; 〈권익〉 vested interests
♦기득권의 침해 in fringement of *sb's* vested right / 기득권을 잃다〖유지하다〗 lose 〖protect〗 *one's* vested right

기라성 綺羅星 glittering 〖twinkling, bright〗 stars ▶회관에는 고관들이 기라성처럼 참석해 있었다 In the hall there was a splendid array of dignitaries.

기략 機略 resource; wit; tact ♦기략이 풍부한 full of resources 〖ideas〗; resourceful; tactful / 기략으로 그 문제를 피하다 use *one's* tact to get around the problem

기량 技倆 ability; talent; skill; competence
♦기량이 있는 able; capable; competent / 기량을 발휘하다 show 〖display〗 *one's* ability 〖skill〗 / 기량을 향상시키다 improve *one's* skill
▶먼저 그의 기량을 시험할 필요가 있다 We have to test his ability first.
▶그런 일로는 그의 기량을 완전히 발휘할 수가 없다 At a job like that, he cannot bring his capacity in full play.

기량 器量 ability; talent; capacity; competence ♦기량이 있는 able; talented
▶그는 사장이 될 기량이 있다 He is competent enough to be a president.

기량계 氣量計 〖氣〗 an aerometer

기러기 〖鳥〗 a (wild) goose (*pl.* (wild) geese)
♦기러기 우는 소리 the sound of a wild goose; honk ▶기러기가 울며 머리 위로 날아갔다 The geese flew honking above.

기러기발 〈현악기의〉 a bridge

기력 汽力 steam power ♦기력으로 움직이는 기계 a machine worked by steam; a steam engine ■━발전소 a steam power plant 〖station〗

기력 氣力 **1** 〈힘〉 energy; vigor; spirit; vital force; 〈활력〉 vitality; virility
♦기력이 없다 be listless [languid]; lack in energy; be lifeless / 기력이 다하다 exhaust *one's* energy [strength] / 기력이 왕성하다 be energetic; be vigorous; be full of energy [vigor] / 기력을 회복하다 recover *one's* spirits; regain *one's* vigor
▶나는 오늘 아침은 기력이 충만하다 I'm full of energy [vigor] this morning.
▶나는 큰 병을 앓고 나서 기력을 완전히 잃었다 Since my serious illness I have completely lost my vigor.
▶나는 말할 기력도 없다 I have not energy to say even a word.
2 〔物〕 air pressure

-기로 1 〈까닭〉 on account of; because (of); as; since
▶길이 얼어 있었기로 서행해야 했다 The road was frozen and accordingly we had to drive slowly.
▶네가 떠난다기로 전송을 나왔다 Hearing that you are leaving, I have come to see you off.
2 〈조건〉 for; with; by
▶우리 제품은 품질이 좋기로 유명합니다 Our products are famous for their quality.
▶그는 글씨를 잘 쓰기로 유명했다 He was famous for his fine handwriting.
▶내가 알기로는 아무 이상도 없었다 As [So] far as I know, everything was all right.
3 〈아무리 …하더라도〉 however; whatever; no matter 〈how, who, etc.〉; even if [though]
♦아무리 재산이 많기로 however rich a man may be
▶달이 밝기로 햇빛만 하랴 No matter how bright the moonlight may be, how can it possibly rival the sun?
4 〈결정〉 ♦…하기로 하다 decide 《to do》; determine 《to do》; make up *one's* mind 《to do》; agree 《with *sb* to do》; promise 《to do》 / …하기로 되어 있다 〈당연히〉 ought to 《do》; should 《do》; 〈예정〉 be expected [supposed] 《to do》; be to 《do》; be due to 《do》
▶나는 가기로 결정했다 I have decided to go.
▶그는 담배를 끊기로 결심하고 있다 He is determined to give up smoking.
▶내일 가기로 합시다 Let's go tomorrow.
▶내 생일에 친구를 초대하기로 되어 있다 I'm planning to invite [on inviting] my friends on my birthday.
▶그는 내게 돈을 주기로 약속했다 He promised to give me some of money.
5 〈추측〉 thinking [supposing] that
▶비가 오겠기로 우산을 가져왔다 Thinking it might rain, I have brought my umbrella.

기로 岐路 〈갈림길〉 a forked [branch] road; 〈십자로〉 a crossroads (▶복수형이지만 단수 취급함)
♦기로에 서다 be [stand] at the crossroads; face two ways / 인생의 기로에 서다 stand at [come to] the crossroads [a turning point] of *one's* life

-기로서니 〈-기로의 강조〉 ▶아무리 그가 힘이 장사기로서니 그 바위를 움직일 수는 없다 However [No matter how] strong he is, he can't move the rock.
▶아무리 돈이 많기로서니 영원한 젊음을 살 수는 없다 The [Even the] richest man can not buy eternal youth.

기록 記錄 **1** 〈적은 것〉 a record; 〈문서〉 document; minutes; proceedings; archives; a note; transactions
♦인생 기록 a biography; the record of *one's* life / 기록에 남기다; chronicle leave 《an event》 on record; keep a record 《of an event》; chronicle / 기록에 오르다 be [put] on record; be recorded / 기록에서 지우다 strike 《a word》 from the record
▶그 사건의 기록은 아무 것도 없다 No record exists of the affair. ⇌ No documents are left behind concerning the event.
—기록하다 record; write down; put *sth* on record; chronicle
2 〈경기 등의〉 a record
♦우승 기록 the winning record (time) / 세계 신기록 a new world record / 신기록을 세우다 make [set, establish] a new record / 기록을 갱신하다 renew [better] *one's* record / 기록을 깨다 break [beat] the (previous) record
▶그는 마라톤의 세계 기록을 보유하고 있다 He holds the world record for the marathon.
▶그녀는 200미터 달리기에서 세계 타이 기록으로 우승했다 She won the 200 meter race with a time equaling the world record.
—기록하다 record; register
▶나는 100미터 달리기에서 12초를 기록했다 I clocked 12 seconds [for] the 100 meters.
▶어제 온도는 그늘에서 섭씨 30도를 기록했다 The temperature yesterday registered 30℃ in the shade.
▶재해가 가장 심한 곳에서는 24시간 동안에 200밀리미터의 강수량이 기록되었다 In the hardest-hit area, two hundred millimeters of rainfall were recorded in twenty-four hours.
■**—가능** 〔電算〕 write enable **—계기** a recording meter **—매체** a recording medium **—문학** documentary literature; a documentary **—밀도** recording density **—방식** recording mode **—보유자** a record holder: 100미터 달리기의 한국 [세계] 기록 보유자 the Korean [world] record holder in the 100 meter dash **—보호** write protect **—영화** a documentary film **—자** a recorder; a record keeper; 〈경기의〉 a scorer **—회로** a record circuit

기록적 記錄的 record; record-breaking
♦기록적인 호우 a record rainfall
▶작년에는 기록적인 가뭄이 들었다 We had a record-breaking drought last year.
▶물가가 기록적으로 올랐다 The prices of commodities are higher than ever before.

기뢰 機雷 a mine; an underwater mine
♦기뢰 방지 장치를 하다 provide 《a ship》 with an anti-mine device / 기뢰를 부설하다 place [lay, sow] mines 《in the sea》; mine / 기뢰에 부딪치다 strike [hit] a mine
■**계류**(繫留)**—** a moored mine **부유**(浮遊)**—** a floating [surface] mine **음향—** an acoustic [a sonic] mine **자기**(磁氣)**—** a magnetic mine

─원(原) a minefield; a field of mines **─정**〈부설선〉 a mine layer [boat]; 〈제거선〉 a minesweeper

기류 氣流 an air [atmospheric] current; an air stream; a current of air ♦기류를 타고 올라가다 soar on air current
■**난**(亂)**─** (air) turbulence; turbulent air **상승[하강]─** an ascending [a descending] air current **상층[하층]─** the upper [lower] air current **─건조기** pneumatic dryer

기류 寄留 temporary residence [domicile]
─기류하다 stay [live] temporarily 《at》 **─부**(簿) a temporary residence register **─신청서[신고]** a report of *one's* temporary residence **─자** a temporary resident **─지** a place of temporary residence [domicile]; 〖法〗 *one's* domicile of choice

기르다 **1** 〈양육하다〉 bring up; breed; support; feed; nurse; 〈양자로〉 foster

> 解說 ***bring up***은 사람을, ***raise***는 사람·동물·식물의 모든 경우에, ***breed***는 주로 가축을 기른다는 뜻으로 쓰인다. ***support***는 모든 생활 면에서 부양한다는 뜻이고 ***feed***는 먹을 것을 준다는 뜻.

♦모유로 아이를 기르다 feed a baby with [on] its mother's milk; breast-feed [nurse] a baby / 아기를 인공 영양으로 기르다 feed a baby on the bottle; bottle-feed a baby
▶그는 세 명의 고아들을 기른다 He is fostering [has adopted] three orphans.
▶그 여자는 혼자서 아이 다섯 명을 길렀다 She brought up five children by herself.
▶그는 많은 학생들을 후계자로 길러냈다 He taught [trained] many students to be his successors.
▶그런 환경에서는 훌륭한 인물을 길러낼 수 없다 You cannot develop a fine character in an environment like that.
2 〈키우다〉 have; 〈사육하다〉 breed; raise 《chickens [sheep]》; keep; feed; 〈재배하다〉 cultivate; grow

> 解說 애완동물 등에는 ***have***를 수입을 얻기 위해 기르는 경우에는 ***raise***를 쓴다. ***keep***은 〈英〉에서는 가축에만 쓴다.

▶그는 개를 두 마리 기른다 He keeps [has] two dogs.
▶그들은 농장에서 소를 20마리 기르고 있다 They raise 20 cows on the farm. ⇌ The farm raises 20 head of cattle.
▶이 물고기는 작은 지렁이로 기르면 된다 You can feed this fish on small earthworms.
3 〈함양·양성하다〉 cultivate; develop; foster

> 解說 ***cultivate***는 「재능·품성 등을 기르고 연마하다」, ***develop***는 「재능 등을 향상시키다」, ***foster***는 「곁에서 도와서 기르다」는 뜻으로 쓴다.

♦도덕심[도의심]을 기르다 cultivate *one's* moral sense / 애국심을 기르다 foster patriotism [a patriotic spirit] / 인재를 기르다 cultivate men of talent / 체력을 기르다 develop [build up] *one's* physical strength / 협동심을 기르다 cultivate [foster] a cooperative spirit
▶너는 인내심을 길러야 한다 You should train yourself to be more patient.
▶나는 여름 방학동안에 영어 실력을 기르려고 열심히 노력했다 I tried hard to make myself proficient in English during the summer vacation.
4 〈자라게 내버려두다〉 grow; wear; cultivate
♦콧수염을 기른 남자 a man having a mustache / 턱수염을 기르다 grow [cultivate] a beard / 콧수염을 기르고 있다 wear [have] a mustache / 머리털을 길게 기르고 있다 wear *one's* hair long
5 〈악화시키다〉 aggravate; worsen ♦나쁜 버릇을 기르다 take to a bad habit / 병을 기르다 worsen [aggravate] *one's* illness

기름 oil; 〈연료〉 fuel; 〈지방〉 fat; grease; 〈돼지 비계〉 lard
♦아주까리 기름 castor oil / 기름에 볶다 sauté / 기름 묻은 oily; greasy / 기름이 떨어지다 need oil; run short of (fuel) oil / 머리에 기름을 바르다 grease *one's* hair; pomade / 기름을 붓다 put [pour] oil into; feed *sth* with oil / 생선을 기름에 튀기다 fry fish (in oil) / 기름을 치다 oil *sb*; lubricate; grease
▶둘은 물과 기름 같은 사이다 The two are like oil and water. ⇌ The two don't get on [along] well together.
▶그의 작업복은 기름 투성이가 되었다 His overalls became stained all over with grease.
▶물과 기름은 섞이지 않는다 Oil and water do not mix.
▶나는 자전거에 기름을 쳤다 I oiled my bicycle.
▶그에게 그런 짓을 하면 불에 기름을 붓는 격이다 Such a thing will add fuel to his anger.
▶그가 싸움을 중재하려 했으나 불에 기름을 붓는 꼴이 되었다 His intervention added fuel to the dispute.
■**─냉각기** an oil cooler **─때** a grease stain **─병**(瓶) an oil bottle **─옷** greasy [oil-stained] clothes **─장수** an oilman **─종이** oiled paper; oilpaper **─집** an oil store [shop] **─체** an oil strainer [filter] **─탱크** an oil tank **─통** an oil cask [barrel]; an oilcan **─틀** an oil press **─흡착제** absorbent

기름기 〈고기의〉 fat (of meat); oiliness; 〈윤기〉 greasiness
♦기름기 있는 음식 rich [greasy] food / 기름기 없는 머리 unoiled hair
▶이 쇠고기는 기름기가 많다 This beef has a lot of fat in it [is very fatty].

기름먹이다 oil ♦기름먹인 천 oiled cloth; oilskins / 종이[헝겊]에 기름을 먹이다 oil a paper [cloth]

기름지다 **1** 〈기름기가 많다〉 greasy; fatty; oily
♦기름진 고기[국] fat meat [soup] / 기름진 음식 greasy [rich] food; fat diet
2 〈땅이 걸다〉 fertile; rich; productive
♦기름진 땅 rich [fat, mellow] soil; fertile land / 메마른 땅을 기름지게 하다 make bar-

기름하다 longish; somewhat long ◆기름한 얼굴４ a moderately [rather] long face; a longish face / 소매를 기름하게 만들다 make the sleeves a little longer

기리다 〈칭찬하다〉 praise; admire; extol; pay a tribute of respect to
◆ 스승을 기리다 pay a (high) tribute to one's teacher
▶ 그의 업적을 기리는 흉상이 세워졌다 A bust was erected to commemorate [〈작고한 경우〉in memory of] his accomplishment.

기린 麒麟 〔動〕 a giraffe; 〈상상의 동물〉 a kylin ■—아 a (young) prodigy; a genius —자리 〔天〕 the Camelopardus; the Giraffe

기립 起立 rising; standing up ◆ 우리는 기립을 요청받았다 We were asked to rise [stand]. —기립하다 stand up; rise; get [rise] to one's feet
■—투표 a rising [standing] vote: 기립 투표에 부치다 put 《a matter》 to a rising [standing] vote; take a rising vote 《on a matter》

기마 騎馬 horse riding ⇨ 승마(乘馬)
■—경찰 〈한사람〉 a mounted policeman; (美) a trooper; (총칭) the mounted police —대 a mounted party —민족 horse-riding people; an equestrian [a nomadic] people —병 ⇨ 기병(騎兵) —전 (play) a mock cavalry battle —행진 a cavalcade

기막히게 breathtakingly; astoundingly; stunningly; wonderfully; exceedingly; extremely; (口) awfully; terribly
◆ 기막히게 좋은 날씨 glorious weather / 기막히게 영어를 잘하다 have a wonderful command of English

기막히다 1 〈어이없다〉 amazed; stunned; astonished; dumbfounded; disgusted
◆ 기막힌 값 an unreasonable [impossible, absurd] price / 기막힌 사정 a wretched condition / 기막혀 말이 안 나오다 be so surprised (that) one cannot say a word; be dumbfounded; lose one's speech [tongue]
▶ 그 슬픈 소식에 그는 기막혔다 He was stunned by [to hear] the sad news.
▶ 모두가 그의 말에 기막혔다 Everybody was amazed [astounded] at his words. ⇌ Everybody stood agape at his words.
▶ 오늘 더위는 기막힐 지경이다 The heat today is really terrific. ⇌ (口) This heat is really something (else).
2 〈대단하다〉 breathtaking; stunning; amazing; (口) great
◆ 기막힌 경관 an excellent [a wonderful, a very fine] view / 기막힌 미인 a stunning [dazzling] beauty; a strikingly beautiful woman / 기막힌 생각 a splendid idea / 기막힌 재주 an outstanding talent
▶ 그의 새 차는 기막힌 속도를 낸다 His new car can go at a terrific speed [get up an awesome speed].
▶ 그의 연주는 정말 기막힐 정도였다 His performance was really superb. ⇌ He gave a stunning [terrific] performance.

-기만 〈오직〉 only; merely; 〈항상〉 always 〈전적으로〉 entirely; wholly; 〈그저〉 if only...; so long as...
◆ 놀기만 하다 be always idle; do nothing but play
▶ 그 아이는 울기만 하고 아무 말도 하지 않았다 The child only cried and said nothing.
▶ 그들은 만나기만 하면 싸운다 They never meet without quarrel.
▶ 그것을 보기만[생각하기만] 해도 가슴이 설렌다 The mere sight [bare thought] of it excites me.
▶ 너는 그저 열심히 공부하기만 하면 된다 All you have to do is work hard.

기만 欺瞞 〈속임〉 deception; cheat; imposture; imposition; trickery; fraud
◆ 기만적인 deceptive; deceitful; fraudulent 《act, measure》
▶ 그에게는 기만이 통하지 않는다 Deception won't work on him. ⇌ You can't put anything over on him.
—**기만하다** deceive; cheat; trick; impose sb; play sb a trick
◆ 세상을 기만하다 deceive the world
■—성 deceitfulness —술 trickery —(정)책 a deceitful [deceptive] policy —통신 deception communication

기말 期末 the end of a term ◆ 기말에 at the end of the term; at the termend
■—결산 term-end accounts —급부금 a term-end savings —시험 a term-end examination; finals

기맥 氣脈 a secret [tacit, good] understanding
◆ 기맥이 상통하다 be congenial (to, with); be like-minded; get along 《with》/ 기맥이 통하는 친구들과 어울려 in congenial friend
▶ 그 둘이는 기맥이 상통하는 것 같다 There seems to exist a secret understanding between the two.

기면 嗜眠 〔醫〕 lethargy; sleeping sickness
◆ 기면 상태에 있다 be lethargic; be in lethargy ■—성 뇌염 lethargic encephalitis; encephalitis lethargica

기명 記名 register; 〈서명〉 signature ◆ 기명 날인하다 sign and seal 《a document》 —기명하다 register 《a bond》; sign one's name; inscribe
■—이서(裏書) special endorsement —주(권) a registered [an inscribed] stock —투표 an open vote [ballot]

기명 器皿 〈그릇붙이〉 vessels and dishes

기모기 起毛機 a raising machine

기묘하다 奇妙— strange; queer; odd; peculiar; eccentric; (口) weird
◆ 기묘한 버릇 a strange [an odd, a peculiar] habit / 기묘하게(도) strangely [oddly] (enough)
▶ 모두가 그녀의 기묘한 짓에 질렸다 They were all disgusted at [with] her strange [eccentric, odd, peculiar] behavior.

기문 奇聞 strange news; a strange account [story]

기문 氣門 〔動〕 a spiracle

기문 旗門 〔스키〕 a (slalom) gate
기물 器物 〈그릇〉 a vessel; a container; 〈기구〉 a utensil; an implement
기미 freckles ♦기미가 낀 얼굴 a freckled [freckly] face ▶그녀는 얼굴에 기미가 많이 꼈다 Her face is covered with freckles. ⇌ She has a lot of freckles.
기미 氣味 〈냄새와 맛〉 smell and taste; 〈마음과 취미〉 disposition; nature; feeling; (a) sensation
기미 幾微 〈약간의 기운〉 a touch; a dash; a shade; a suspicion; 〈낌새〉 signs; indications ▶너는 약간 피곤한 기미가 있어 You look a little tired [somewhat weary].
▶물가가 오를 기미가 역력히 보인다 There is every indication that prices will go up.
▶은행 금리는 내려갈 기미가 있다 The bank rate is showing a downward tendency [a tendency to slip a little].
기미 機尾 the tail (part) of an airplane; a tail
기미독립운동 己未獨立運動 the Independence Movement in 1919
기민 機敏 ━**기민하다** smart; keen; shrewd; prompt; quick; alert; (口) cute
♦기민한 동작 quick action [movement] / 기민하게 기회를 포착하다 be prompt [quick] to seize an opportunity
▶권리를 지키는 데 기민해야 한다 You should take prompt action to defend your rights.
■━**성** smartness; quickness; promptness; readiness; alertness
기밀 氣密 airtightness; gastightness ♦기밀의 airtight; gastight
■━**복** an airtight garment [suit]; a pressure [pressurized] suit ━**실** an airtight chamber; 〈비행기의〉 a pressure [pressurized] cabin; 〈잠수함의〉 a pressure hull ━**용기** an airtight container ━**조인트** an airtight joint
기밀 機密 secrecy; a secret
♦군사[외교]상의 기밀 a military [diplomatic] secret / 기밀 정보 (a piece of) secret information / 기밀을 누설하다 let out [leak out, divulge] a secret / 기밀을 지키다 observe secrecy; keep [guard] a secret
■━**누설** leakage of (official) secrets ━**비** secret (service) funds ━**사항** confidential [exclusive] affairs ━**서류**[문서] confidential [secret] documents [papers]
기박하다 奇薄━ 〈복이 없다〉 unlucky; ill-fated; ill-starred; unfortunate
♦기박한 운명을 타고나다 be born under an unlucky star / 팔자가 기박함을 한탄하다 grieve over *one's* tough [ill] fate
▶그녀는 한평생 팔자가 기박했다 She led a very miserable existence [unhappy life].
기반 基盤 〈기초〉 a base; a basis (*pl*. -ses); a foundation; 〈발판〉 footing; foothold; 〈선거 지반〉 a constituency
♦확고한 기반 a firm basis / 기반을 굳히다 solidify *one's* footing
▶그리스도교는 그의 신앙의 기반이다 Christianity forms the basis of his beliefs. ⇌ His beliefs are rooted in Christianity.
▶민주주의의 기반은 자유를 지키려는 국민의 의지이다 The foundation of democracy is the will of the people to preserve liberty.
▶가족은 사회의 기반을 이룬다 Families form the basis of society.
▶그의 표밭은 농촌 지방을 기반으로 한다 The farming community makes up the base of his electoral support.
■━**기능** basic function ━**암** 〔地質〕 (a) bedrock ━**활동** basic activity
기반 羈絆 〈굴레·구속물〉 restraints; fetters; bonds; ties
♦애정의 기반 bonds of affection / 혈연의 기반 the ties of blood / 기반을 벗어나다 free *oneself* from restraints; shake [throw, break] off the yoke [fetters] (of)
▶1783년 아메리카 식민지는 영국의 기반에서 벗어났다 In 1783 the American Colonies threw off the yoke of England.
기발하다 奇拔━ uncommon; fanciful; novel; original
♦기발한 도안 a fantastic design; a fanciful pattern / 기발한 생각 an original [a striking, a wild; an extravagant] idea / 기발한 행동 eccentric [crazy] conduct
▶그는 가끔 기발한 생각으로 사람들을 벙벙하게 한다 He sometimes sets people agape by some original idea.
기백 氣魄 spirit; drive; soul; determination
♦기백이 있는 사람 a man of spirit / 기백에 찬 표정 a determined [spirited] look / 기백이 있다[없다] be full of [be lacking in] spirit
▶나는 그의 기백에 눌려 아무 말도 못했다 Cowed by his unmistakable determination [resolve], I couldn't say anything.
기백 幾百 〈수백〉 hundreds ♦기백만 millions (of men) / 기백명 hundreds of people ▶기백 명의 사상자가 있었다 There were several hundred casualties.
기번 〈영국의 역사가〉 Gibbon, Edward (1737-94)
기범선 機帆船 a motor-powered sailing vessel; a motor sailing vessel; a motor sailer
기법 技法 (a) technique
♦영화의 기법 cinematic technique / 유화기법을 배우다 learn the technique of oil painting
▶기법상 그는 스승을 능가했다 In technical skill he surpassed his master.
기벽 奇癖 〈괴상한 버릇〉 a queer [an eccentric] habit; an eccentricity ♦기벽이 있는 사람 a person of queer habits
기별 奇別·寄別 〈알림〉 news; information; a notice; a message; word; tidings
♦사전에 아무 기별도 없이 without previous notice / 아무런 기별도 없다 hear nothing from *sb*
▶김선생한테서 못 오신다는 기별이 방금 왔다 Mr. Kim has just sent word that he's not coming.
━**기별하다** inform 《*sb* of, that》; give *sb* notice 《of, that》; let *sb* know
▶될 수 있는대로 빨리 기별할게 I will let you know as soon as possible.
▶내가 기별할 때까지는 올 필요가 없다고 그에게 일러 주게 Tell him he need not come till I

기병 騎兵 a cavalry [mounted] soilder; a cavalryman; (총칭) cavalry ◆기병 2천명 two thousand horsemen [cavalrymen]
■—경— a light cavalryman; (총칭) light cavalry ■—대대[연대] a cavalry squadron [regiment]
기병 奇病 a strange [rare] disease ◆백만 명 중에 한 명 있다는 기병에 걸리다 contract [develop] a (rare) disease which only one person in a million has
기병 起兵 raising an army; rising in arms —기병하다 raise an army; rise in arms (against)
기보 旣報 a previous report
◆기보한 바와 같이 as previously [already] reported [announced]
▶ 기보한 대로 소방 훈련을 오늘 실시한다 As previously announced, there will be a fire drill today.
기보 棋譜 the record of a game of *paduk*
기보법 記譜法 (樂) notation
기복 起伏 ups and downs; the rise and fall; undulations
◆기복이 많은 (a life) full of ups and downs; checkered; colorful (life) / 기복이 심한 마라톤 코스 a hilly marathon course
▶ 그는 감정(상)의 기복이 심하다 He is very moody.
—기복하다 rise and fall; roll; undulate; wave
기본 基本 a basis (*pl*. -ses); the basics; foundation; the fundamentals

> [解說] ***basis***는 사물의 토대가 되는 부분의 구조를 나타내는 일반적인 말. ***foundation***은 확고한 토대를 말하며 추상적인 뜻으로도 쓴다. ***fundamentals***는 기초가 되는 원리·생각을 뜻한다.

▶ 이 공식은 물리학에서는 기본이다 This formula is basic [fundamental] to physics.
▶ 그는 수학을 기본부터 다시 배우기 시작했다 He studied mathematics starting again from the basics.
■—계획 general planning; a master plan —금 a fund; an endowment —급 a basic salary [wage, pay]; a base pay —기 basic skills —단위 a fundamental unit; a standard [base] unit —방침 a basic policy —법 a fundamental law —어휘 a basic vocabulary —요금 the base [basic] rate —원료 basic raw materials —원리 a fundamental [basic] principle —음 fundamental tone —입자 a fundamental particle —재산 permanent property; an endowment —전하량 elementary quantum of electricity
기본적 基本的 fundamental; basic
◆기본적 인간 요청 basic human needs (略 BHN) / 기본적 인권 the fundamental human rights / 기본적 오류 a fundamental error; a basic mistake / 기본적으로 fundamentally; basically
▶ 너는 기본적으로 틀렸어 You are fundamentally [basically] wrong.
기부 基部 the base; the foundation; the basal part (of); 〈하부〉 the bottom
기부 寄附 contribution; donation
▶ 다섯 대의 컴퓨터 기부가 있었다 There was a contribution of five computers.
—기부하다 contribute (to, for); donate (to); make a contribution [donation] (to, for); (口) chip in
▶ 그는 자선 사업에 200만원을 기부했다 He contributed [donated, gave] two million won to charities. ⇌ He made a contribution [donation] of two million won to charities.
■—인 a contributor; a donor —재산 an endowment —행위 donation; contribution
기부금 寄附金 a contribution; a donation; an endowment
◆기부금을 모으다 make [take up] a collection (for); collect contributions [donations]
▶ 그 고장의 몇몇 회사들이 1천달러씩의 기부금을 내겠다고 제의했다 Several local businesses have offered to chip in with one thousand dollars apiece [each].
기분 氣分 a mood; humor; temper; a feeling; thought

> [解說] ***mood***는 기분을 나타내는 일반적인 말이고, ***humor***는 변덕스러운 마음의 상태로서 일시적임을 강조한다. ***temper***는 격한 감정 특히 분노·노여움의 상태를, ***feeling***은 감정·기분을 표시한다.

◆기분 나쁜 광경 a revolting [sickening] sight / 기분 나쁜 소리 an unpleasant [a weird] sound
▶ 울고 싶은 기분이다 I feel like crying.
▶ 나는 그때 절망적인 기분이었다 I was in despair then.
▶ 그것은 네 기분에 달렸다 It depends on your mood [whether you feel like it].
▶ 기분 좋은 아침이었다 It was a pleasant morning.
▶ 그는 기분 좋은 사람이다 He is an agreeable [amiable] person.
▶ 그는 기분 좋게 나의 제안을 받아들였다 He was quite ready to accept my offer. ⇌ He willingly [readily] accepted my offer.
▶ 나는 어젯밤 기분좋게 잤다 I slept comfortable last night.
▶ 그는 나의 성공을 기분나쁘게 생각하는 것 같다 He seems displeased with my success.
▶ 그것은 주로 기분의 문제다 The problem is largely a matter of feeling.
〈기분이〉 어머니가 되니 기분이 어떠니? How does it feel to be a mother?
▶ 그는 기분이 우울해졌다 He fell into a melancholy mood. ⇌ He got depressed.
▶ 그와 함께 있으면 기분이 유쾌해진다 Being with him puts me in a cheerful mood [high spirit].
▶ 그는 기분이 좋지 않다 He is not in a good humor [out of sorts, (俗) ticked off].
▶ 뱀은 섬뜩한 기분이 든다 Snakes give me the creeps.
▶ 나는 그것을 보고 기분이 나빠졌다 I felt sick at the sight of it.

▶ 내가 약속을 지키지 않아서 그는 기분이 상했다 He was displeased when I did not keep our appointment.
▶ 그가 있으면 기분이 좋지 않다 His presence destroys the atmosphere.
▶ 지금까지 일어난 일들이 꼭 꿈같은 기분이 든다 I feel as if everything that has happened were just a dream.
〈기분을〉 기분을 돋우다 cheer [brighten, rouse] up / 남의 기분을 존중[무시]하다 respect [disregard] *sb's* feelings / 한 잔하고 기분을 내다 be gay over a cup of wine
▶ 그가 화를 내는 기분을 알겠다 I can understand why he got angry.
▶ 내가 그녀의 기분을 상하게 한 것 같다 It seems I hurt her feelings.
▶ 나는 곧 죽을 것만 같은 기분을 떨쳐버릴 수가 없다 I can't escape (the) feeling that I am going to die soon.

기분전환 氣分轉換 (a) diversion; (a) recreation; (a) relaxation
♦ 기분 전환을 위해 여행하다 go on a trip for a change [for diversion]
▶ 기분 전환 삼아 강으로 수영하러 가자 Let's go swimming in the river for a change.
▶ 산책은 훌륭한 기분 전환법이다 Walking is a good pastime [recreation].
▶ 나는 기분 전환으로 음악을 듣는다 I listen to music to relax.
―**기분전환하다** refresh *oneself* (with a song); divert *oneself* [*one's* mind]; recreate [amuse] *oneself*

기분파 氣分派 a man of moods; a moody [temperamental] person
▶ 그녀는 아주 기분파다 She is very fickle [capricious, whimsical].
▶ 그는 기분파다 He is apt to indulge in moods.

기뻐하다 be glad (at, about, of); be pleased (at, with); be happy (about, at, over); be delighted (at, with); rejoice (at, over); congratulate *oneself* (on)
♦ 어린이들이 기뻐할 만한 것 things which (would) please children / 기뻐서 날뛰다 jump [dance] with [for] joy; leap for joy
▶ 그는 그 결과를 듣고 매우 기뻐했다 He was very glad [pleased, delighted] at [to know] the results.
▶ 네가 함께 간다니 아이들이 아주 기뻐하고 있다 The children are overjoyed [very pleased] because you're coming with them.
▶ 부모님께서 당신의 합격을 매우 기뻐하실 것입니다 Your success in the examination will be a gleat pleasure [satisfaction] to your parents.

기쁘다 glad; happy; joyful; be pleased; be delighted
♦ 기쁜 날 a happy day; a joyous occasion / 기쁜 소식 happy [joyful, delightful] news / 기쁜 얼굴로 with a delightful look / 기뻐서 for [in, with] joy / 기쁘게도 to *one's* (great) joy [delight] / 기쁠 때나 슬플 때나 in joy and in sorrow / 기쁘게 하다 please; delight; make *sb* happy
▶ 당신을 다시 뵙게 되어 기쁩니다 I am glad [happy, delighted, pleased] to see you again.
▶ 당신이 와 주셔서 정말 기쁩니다 I am very glad [happy] (that) you have come.
▶ 두 시험에 다 합격하다니 얼마나 기쁘냐 How wonderful that you passed both exams!
▶ 그의 생존이 확인되어 미칠듯이 기뻤다 I was overjoyed to hear that he was alive.
▶ 나는 눈물이 나도록 기뻤다 I nearly wept for joy.
▶ 오늘은 1년 중에 가장 기쁜 날이다 This [Today] is the happiest day of (all) the year.
▶ 우리의 선물이 그녀를 기쁘게 했다 Our present delighted her [made her happy].
▶ 그녀에게서 연애 편지 답장을 받고 그는 기뻐 날뛰었다 He jumped for joy with her answer to his love letter.
▶ 그는 너무 기뻐서 말문이 막혔다 He was speechless with joy.
▶ 그를 기쁘게 하기는 참 어렵다 He is very hard to please. ⇌ It's very hard to please him.

기쁨 joy; pleasure; delight
♦ 삶의 기쁨 joy of life / 기쁨의 눈물 tears of joy; happy tears / 기쁨과 슬픔 joys and sorrows / 기쁨을 금치 못하다 be unable to contain *one's* joy; overjoy / 기쁨을 느끼다 feel happy (at); take delight (in); feel the joy of / 기쁨을 얻다 take [draw] joy (from) / 기쁨을 함께 나누다 share the joys
▶ 그의 성공은 나의 큰 기쁨이다 His success makes me very happy. ⇌ His success is a great gratification to me.
▶ 아름다운 것은 영원한 기쁨이다 A thing of beauty is a joy forever.
▶ 그녀는 혼자 기쁨을 음미하고 있었다 She was savoring her happiness all by herself.
▶ 그는 솔직히 기쁨을 나타냈다 He showed his joy quite openly.
▶ 그녀의 얼굴은 기쁨으로 빛났다 Her face [She] beamed with joy [delight].

기사 技師 an engineer; a technical expert
■ 건축— an architect 광산[토목]— a mining [civil] engineer 기계[조선, 전기, 항공]— a mechanical [a shipbuilding, an electrical, an aeronautical] engineer

기사 記事 〈기술〉 description; an account; 〈신문의〉 news; a news story [item]; an article; a report
♦ 기사를 게재하다 give [print] an account (of a fire); (美) carry a news item / 기사를 쓰다 make a report (on); write [do] an article (on) / 기사화를 금지하다 put a ban on the publication of the news (of)
▶ 모든 신문이 그 살인 사건의 기사를 싣고 있다 All newspapers carry the story of the murder case.
▶ 나는 오늘 신문에서 아동 도서에 대한 좋은 기사를 읽었다 I read a good article on juvenile books in today's paper.
■ 사회— city news; police news 서명— an article with a by-line 지방— local news 특종— a scoop; (美) a beat 특집— a feature (story [article]) 해설— a commentary (on) ■ ―게

재 금지 a press ban [embargo] ━문 a descriptive composition; a description ━체 a descriptive style ━폭주 a congestion of news [reading matter]
기사 棋士 a (professional) *paduk* [chess] player
기사 騎士 〈승마자〉a rider; a horseman;〈유럽 중세의〉a knight ■━도 knighthood; chivalry
기사보 技師補 an assistant-engineer
기사회생 起死回生 restoring from death; resuscitation; revival
♦기사회생의 영약 a wonderful medicine capable of reviving the dead; (美) a miracle [wonder] drug / 기사회생의 홈런을 치다 hit a homer to pull the game out of the fire
━기사회생하다 restore from death; revive
기산하다 起算━ reckon [count] from
♦15일부터 기산하여 30일째 되는 날에 on the 30th day counting from the fifteenth
▶ 귀하의 승급은 1개월 전으로 소급하여 기산합니다 The increase in your salary is to be reckoned from one month back.
■━일 the initial date of [for] reckoning ━점 the starting point of reckoning
기삿거리 記事━ a news item; (a piece of) news; a newsbreak; material for a news story
♦기삿거리가 되다 become a topic for the newspapers; be turned into a news story
▶ 이것은 재미있는 기삿거리다 This will make an interesting item [news article].
기상 奇想 a fantastic idea; a fanciful notion
▶ 그것은 기상천외의 생각이다 It is a most unexpected idea. ■━곡 ⇨ 광상곡
기상 起床 rising (in the morning) ━기상하다 rise; get up ▶ 나는 6시 30분에 기상한다 I get up at six-thirty in the morning.
기상 氣象 weather; atmospheric phenomena; weather conditions
♦기상의 변화 a change in the weather [in weather condition] / 기상을 관측하다 ⇨ 기상관측
■━개황 general weather conditions ━관제〈공항의〉the meteorological [met] control ━대 a meteorological observatory ━도 a weather chart [map] ━레이더 a weather radar ━사진 a weather picture (from a satellite) ━위성 a weather [meteorological] satellite ━정보 weather information ━제어 weather control ━주의보[경보] weather advisory [warning] ━청 the Meteorological Administration ━통보 weather news; a weather report ━통보관 a weather caster; a weatherman ━특보 a special weather report ━학 meteorology: 생물기상학 biometeorology ━현상 atmospheric [meteorological] phenomena
기상 氣像 nature; spirit; temperament; a disposition; (a) temper
♦자립의 기상 the self-reliant temperament / 진취적인 기상 an enterprising spirit / 기상이 낙천적인 사람들 sanguine natures
기상 機上 ♦기상에서 내려다보다 look down from an airplane
기상관측 氣象觀測 meteorological observation ♦기상 관측을 하다 make meteorological observations
■━기[선] a weather plane [ship] ━로켓 a meteorological rocket ━소 a meteorological station; a (local) weather bureau
기상나팔 起床喇叭 〔軍〕the morning bugle; the reveille
♦기상 나팔을 불다 sound [blow] the reveille / 5시 30분 기상 나팔을 불다 sound (the) 5:30 reveille
▶ 기상 나팔이 울렸다 The reveille sounded.
━시간 the [*one's*] hour of rising
기색 氣色 〈안색〉look, air, 〈기미〉an indication; a sign;〈거동〉manner; bearing;〈감정〉a feeling; sensation
♦조금도 두려워하는 기색 없이 without showing the slightest sign of fear / 기색이 변하다 change color [countenance] / 기색을 보이다 show signs of; betray (*one's* anger) in *one's* looks / 기색을 살피다 read *sb's* face [expression]; gauge [judge] *sb's* feelings [state of mind] (from his expression) / 불안한 기색을 하다 look uneasy
▶ 그것을 보는 순간 그의 기색이 변했다 The color left his face the instant he saw it.
▶ 그 사람의 표정이나 태도에서 자살을 하리라는 기색은 조금도 보이지 않았다 There was nothing in his look or manner to show that he would commit suicide.
▶ 그는 그 소식에도 성난 기색을 보이지 않았다 He showed no sign of anger at the news.
기생 妓生 a *kisaeng* ♦기생집 a *kisaeng* house / 기생을 불러 놀다 have a *kisaeng* spree
기생 寄生 parasitism ━기생하다 be parasitic (on); be a parasite (on); be a hanger-on ▶ 그 나무에 벌레가 기생하고 있다 Insects are parasitic on [live on] the tree.
■━근[뿌리] a parasitic root ━동물 a parasite; a parasitic animal ━물[체] a parasite ━식물 a parasitic plant ━화산 a parasite volcano
기생식물 氣生植物 an aerial plant; an aerophyte
기생충 寄生蟲 〈사람〉a parasite;〔動〕a parasite; a parasitic insect [worm] ♦사회의 기생충 a parasite living off the community / 식물의 기생충 a parasite living on a plant
■체내━ an entozoon (*pl*. -zoa); an endoparasite 체외━ an epizoon (*pl*. -zoa); an ectozoon (*pl*. -zoa); an ectoparasite ■━보유자 a parasite carrier
기서 奇書 a rare [strange] book
기선 汽船 a steamship (略 SS); a steamboat; a steamer;〈정기선〉a liner
♦기선 충무호 the SS Ch'ungmu / 기선을 타다 take a steamer; go on board a steamer; board a liner / 기선으로 가다 go (to Hawaii) by steamer
■━회사 a steamship company
기선 基線 the base [basal] line
기선 機先 ♦기선을 제압하다 get a head start (on the enemy); forestall (*one's* rival); take the initiative; steal a march upon (another)
▶ 우리는 적의 기선을 제압했다 We got a head

기설 既設 ♦기설의 established; existing ■—선(線) 〈철도의〉 lines in operation

기성 奇聲 a queer [peculiar] voice ♦기성을 지르다 raise [utter, give] a queer voice [sound]

기성 既成 ♦기성의 completed; accomplished; 〈현존의〉 existing; 〈만들어져 있는〉 manufactured; ready-made ⇨ 기성복
■—개념 a preconceived idea [notion] —관념 ready-made ideas —문단 existing literary circles —세대 the older generation —작가 a renowned writer; a well-known [an established] writer; a writer of standing —정당 the existing political parties; established parties —질서 an established order —품 manufactured goods; ready-made goods

기성 棋聖 a great master of *paduk* [chess]; an accomplished *paduk* [chess] player

기성복 既成服 ready-made [ready-to-wear] clothes; ready-mades; store clothes; (美) hand-me-downs; 〈싸구려〉 slops
▶ 나는 기성복 코트를 샀다 I bought a coat ready-made.
▶ 나는 기성복이 맞지 않는다 I am not what tailors call a "stock size". ⇒ Ready-made clothes don't fit me.
■—점 a ready-made(-clothing) shop; a slop-shop

기성회 期成會 an association for the realization of a plan; 〈학교의〉 a school supporting association ■—비 dues for school supporting association

기세 氣勢 spirit; 〈열의〉 ardor; 〈기운〉 energy; vigor; vivacity; dash; liveliness
♦ 맹렬한 기세로 (口) like a hundred [thousand, ton, load] of bricks; (美口) like forty; with an irresistible [overwhelming] force / 기세가 오르다 〈사람이 주어〉 be in good [high] spirits; be in good [great, fine] form; 〈사물이 주어〉 encourage; cheer / 기세가 좋다 be lively / 기세를 꺾다 〈사물이 주어〉 dispirit; discourage; dampen *one's* enthusiasm [ardor]; put a damper on / 기세를 더하다 gain [gather] strength; be fanned (by) / 기세를 돋우다 encourage; cheer; enliven; brighten; pep up / 기세를 올리다 excite [arouse] *one's* enthusiasm
▶ 그 소식을 듣고 우리는 크게 기세가 올랐다 The news cheered us greatly.
▶ 그에게 비난을 받고 우리들은 기세가 꺾였다 His reproof discouraged us [dampened our spirits].

기소 起訴 prosecution; indictment; accusation; 〈민사상의〉 litigation; legal proceedings
—**기소하다** 〈검사가〉 prosecute [indict] ((*sb* for a crime); charge ((*sb* with a crime); bring in an indictment against; 〈민사상으로〉 bring an action [a suit] ((against))
♦ 살인[수뢰]죄로 기소되다 be prosecuted [indicted] for murder [taking bribes]
▶ 그는 위조 혐의로 기소되었다 He was prosecuted [indicted] on a charge of forgery.
▶ 그는 외환 관리법 위반 혐의로 기소되었다 He was charged with violating the Foreign Exchange Control Act.
▶ 그 사건은 기소되지 않았다 The case was dropped.
■—기각 dismissal of indictment —자 an indictor [indicter]; a prosecutor —장(狀) an indictment; a bill of indictment; a written indictment

기소유예 起訴猶豫 〔法〕 suspension of indictment; stay of prosecution
♦ 기소유예가 되다 have *one's* indictment suspended
▶ 그는 기소 유예가 되었다 His indictment was shelved. ⇒ The charges against him were dropped.
—**기소유예하다** shelve an indictment; decide not to prosecute [bring charges]; (口) drop the case; dispense with a public action; stay a prosecution

기송관 氣送管 a pneumatic [dispatch] tube

기수 奇數 an odd [uneven] number ⇨ 홀수
♦ 기수의 odd(↔even); odd-numbered ■—일 days in odd numbers; odd days —회(回) an odd number of times

기수 基數 〔數〕〈서수에 대한〉 a cardinal number; 〈1부터 9까지의 정수〉 a fundamental number —사 the cardinal numerals

기수 旗手 a standard-bearer; a color-bearer; (英) an ensign; 〈올림픽 등에서의〉 a flag-bearer; a flagman
♦ 다다이즘의 기수 the standard-bearer of Dadaism [the Dadaist movement]

기수 機首 the nose of an airplane ♦ 기수를 올리다[내리다] nose up [down]; pull up [lower] the nose ▶ 비행기는 기수를 남으로 돌렸다 The plane turned its course to the south.

기수 騎手 〈승마자〉 a rider; a horseman; 〈경마의〉 a jockey

기수범 既遂犯 an accomplished [a consummated] offense [crime]

기수법 記數法 notation; the scale of notation
♦ 십진 기수법 decimal notation / 아라비아[로마] 기수법 Arabic [Roman] notation

기숙 寄宿 〈방만 빌리는〉 lodging; 〈식사까지 하는〉 board; 〈숙식〉 board and lodging ♦ 기숙제 학교 a boarding school
—**기숙하다** lodge ((at another's house, with another)); board ((with))
▶ 그는 아저씨 댁에 기숙하고 있다 He is boarding [lodging] at his uncle's [with his uncle].
■—생 a boarding [(美) dormitory] student; a boarder (▶boarder는 식사까지 제공받는 일반 하숙인에게도 씀) —인 a boarder; a lodger —학교 a boarding school

기숙사 寄宿舍 a boarding house; 〈대학의〉 a hostel; a dormitory; (口) a dorm
♦ 가족 기숙사 a dormitory for families / 독신 기숙사 apartments for bachelors / 모자 기숙사 a house for mothers and children / 학생 기숙사 students' quarters; a school dormitory / 학교 기숙사에 들다 board in the school
▶ 이 학교의 학생들은 모두 기숙사 생활을 하고 있다 All the students at this school live in the dormitory.

▶기숙사 생활을 회상하면 즐거운 기억만 난다 When I look back on my years in the (school) dormitory [at boarding school], I have only happy memories.
■―비 boarding expenses; a fee for board ―사감 a dormitory inspector [superintendent]

기술 技術 technique; skill; 〈과학·공업의〉 (a) technology; 〈美〉 (technical) know-how; 〈솜씨〉 an art; 〈학과목〉 manual training

> 解說 *technique*는 과학뿐만 아니라 기술 분야에도 미치는 전문적인 기술이다. *skill*은 훈련으로 습득한 우수한 기술을 의미한다. 특별히 과학기술에 관해서는 *technology*를 쓴다. *art*는 솜씨 또는 요령이라는 뜻을 함축한다.

♦고도의 기술 high [advanced, sophisticated] technique / 최신의 기술 the latest technique / 기술의 진보 technological [technical] advance / 기술이 늘다 improve in one's skill; show greater skill 《than before》 / 외국 기술을 도입하다 import [introduce] technological know-how from overseas / 기술을 연마하다 drill [train] one's art; improve one's skill / 기술 계통으로 나가다 follow [pursue] a technical career
▶기술이 진보하여 인간이 우주를 탐험할 수 있게 되었다 Technological advancement has enabled man to explore space.
▶그것은 기술적으로 불가능하다 It is technically impossible.
▶기술적으로는 어렵지 않지만 비용이 문제다 Though it isn't technically difficult, there is a problem of cost.
■―공업― (engineering) technology ―교육 technical education ―마찰 technological friction ―원조 technical assistance [aids] ―자 a technical expert; a technician; 〈기사〉 an engineer ―혁신 technical [technological] innovation ―협력[제휴] technical tie-up [cooperation]

기술 記述 (a) description; an account ♦기술적 과학 the descriptive science ―기술하다 describe; make [give] a description of; give an account of
■―문법 descriptive grammar ―체 a descriptive style

기술 奇術 magic; jugglery; conjuring tricks
♦기술을 부리다 juggle 《with》; play tricks; do conjuring [magic] tricks ■―사 a conjurer

기술 旣述 the foregoing ⇨ 전술(前述)
▶결과는 기술한 대로다 The results are as reported.

기스락 〈추녀끝〉 the edge of the eaves ♦기스락물 ⇨ 낙숫물

기슭 〈강의〉 the bank(s); 〈산의〉 the foot; the base; 〈호수·바다의〉 the shore; 〈대양의〉 the coast; 〈물가〉 a strand; 〈해변〉 a beach; 〈못·늪의〉 a brink; the border
♦언덕 기슭에 at the foot [bottom] of a hill / 기슭으로 ashore; to the shore / 기슭에 밀려 올라오다 be cast [washed] ashore
▶그 배는 기슭을 떠났다 The ship has left the shore.
▶강의 저편 기슭에는 개나리 꽃이 만발해 있다 Forsythias are in full bloom along the other bank [side] of the river.
▶우리는 산 기슭에서 야영했다 We camped at the foot of the mountain.

기습 奇習 a strange custom [practice]

기습 奇襲 a surprise (attack); a sudden attack 《on Pearl Harbor》
―기습하다 make a surprise attack [raid] 《on》; take 《the enemy》 by surprise; attack sb unawares
♦요새를 기습하여 함락시키다 take a fortress by surprise / 기습당하다 be taken by surprise; be attacked unawares
▶게릴라가 공군기지를 기습했다 The guerrillas made a surprise raid [attack] on the air base.
▶우리는 새벽에 적을 기습하여 대승을 거두었다 We made surprise attack on the enemy at daybreak and won a great victory.
■―부대 a surprise party; shock troops ―전 a surprise attack [raid]; guerrilla warfare

기승 氣勝 spiritedness; emulation
♦기승을 떨다[부리다] be furious [violent, rampant]; rage; increase in violence; grow more violent
▶늦더위가 유달리 기승을 부린다 The heat of late summer is more terrible than usual.
―기승하다[스럽다] unyielding; unbending; strong-minded; stouthearted
♦기승스러운 아이 a naughty [an unmanageable] boy [girl]
▶저 사내아이는 매우 기승스럽다 The boy has a strong will.

기승전결 起承轉結 〈시문의 격식〉 introduction, development, turn and conclusion
▶기승전결을 생각하고 글을 써라 Keep coherence in mind when you write your composition.

기식 氣息 ♦기식이 엄엄하다 gasp for breath; breathe feebly ▶그는 기식이 엄엄한 상태다 He is at his last gasp.

기식 寄食 parasitism; dependence; sponging
―기식하다 live with sb at 《his》 expense; sponge [hang] on sb; be sb's hanger-on; be parasitic on sb
▶나는 대학 시절의 첫 2년간은 아저씨 댁에 기식했다 I lived with my uncle at his expense for the first two years of my college.

기식음 氣息音 〖音聲〗 an aspirate; an aspirated sound

기신거리다 idle about; be sluggish; move limply [languidly] ▶술취한 그 사람은 기신거리며 일어났다 The drunken man stood up unsteadily.

기신기신 idly; sluggishly; listlessly; languidly; unsteadily; tottering and swaying

기신하다 起身― stand up; get up; rise; recover [regain] one's feet [legs]

기신호 旗信號 flag-wagging; flag signaling [semaphore]
♦기신호를 하다 signal [semaphore] with flags; flagsignal

▶ 보이 스카우트 단원들이 기신호를 하고 있었다 The Boy Scouts were signaling with flags.
▶ 너는 기신호를 할 줄 아니? Do you know how to use the semaphore (signal) system?

기실 其實 really; in reality; as a matter of fact; the truth (of the matter) is 《that…》; actually; to tell the truth

기실 汽室 a steam chamber; steam space

기실 氣室 an air chamber

기싱 〈영국의 소설가〉 Gissing, George Robert (1857-1903)

기쓰다 氣— be on *one's* mettle 《for success, to do》; make strenuous efforts; do *one's* best; exert *oneself* to the utmost; strain; struggle
♦ 기쓰고 달아나다 run (away) for *one's* life; run like the devil / 기쓰고 반대하다 oppose strongly; be (hell-)bent on opposing *sb* / 기쓰고 변명하다 try to apologize with heat
▶ 그는 꼭 이기려고 기쓰고 있다 He has got himself all psyched [pumped] up to win.

기아 棄兒 an abandoned [a deserted] child; 〈주운 아이〉 a foundling ―**기아하다** desert [abandon] *one's* child

기아 飢餓 hunger; starvation
♦ 기아선상에 있다 be starving; face [be threatened with] starvation; be on [live at] the verge [brink] of starvation; live close to the margin of starvation
▶ 그는 기아에 못이겨 도둑질을 했다 He was driven to stealing by hunger. ⇌ Hunger drove him to theft.
▶ 우리는 기아에 직면했다 Famine stared us in the face.
■―**수출** hunger export ―**임금** starvation wages ―**행진** a hunger march ―**행진자** a hunger marcher

기악 器樂 〔樂〕 instrumental music

기안 起案 drafting ―**기안하다** prepare [make out] a draft; plan 《for》; draft [draw up] a plan 《for》 ―**자** a drafter

기암(괴석) 奇岩(怪石) rocks of fantastic shape; fantastically-shaped rocks

기압 氣壓 atmospheric [air] pressure
♦ 50기압에 해당하는 압력 a pressure of 50 atmospheres / 기압 관계로 owing to the atmospheric condition
▶ 금년에 북부 지방은 기압 관계로 비가 많이 온다 This year the northern region has a lot of rain due to the prevailing pattern of atmospheric pressure.
■―**고[저]―** high [low] (atmospheric) pressure; barometric maximum [minimun] **절대**― absolute atmosphere ■―**골** a trough of low atmospheric pressure; a low pressure trough ―**배치** the distribution of atmospheric pressure; a pressure pattern

기압계 氣壓計 a barometer; a manometer; a baroscope; an air gauge ■ **아네로이드**― an aneroid (barometer)

기약 期約 promise; pledge; engagement; 〈회합의〉 appointment
―**기약하다** promise; give *one's* word [promise] 《to *sb*》; pledge *oneself* 《to *sth*, to do》
▶ 두 사람은 재회를 기약하고 헤어졌다 The two parted, promising to meet again.

기약분수 旣約分數 〔數〕 a irreducible fraction

기어 旗魚 ■―**자리** 〔天〕 the Swordfish; Dorado; Xiphias

기어 〈변속장치〉 (a) gear
♦ 4단 기어의 차 a car with four gears / 기어를 넣다 thrust the gear lever; engage the gears; put [set, throw] 《the car》 into gear; 〈고속으로〉 gear [change] up; change (up) into top (gear); 〈저속으로〉 gear [change] down / 기어를 바꾸다 change 〔美〕 shift〕 gears
■ **감속**― a reduction gear

기어가다 crawl [creep] about; 〈네 발로〉 go on all fours; crawl on (*one's*) hands and knees

기어나오다 crawl [creep] out; worm *oneself* [*one's* way] out

기어내리다 climb down; descend on hands and knees

기어다니다 creep [crawl] about [around] 《on the floor》 ▶ 아기가 잔디 위를 기어 다녔다 The baby crawled around on the grass.

기어들어가다 crawl [creep] in [into]; worm *oneself* into

기어오르다 **1** 〈벌레 등이〉 crawl [creep] up; 〈사람이〉 climb (up) 《a tree》; 〔美口〕 shinny up; clamber (over, up); scramble (up); claw *one's* way up 《a cliff》
♦ 가파른 비탈을 기어오르다 clamber up [work *one's* way up] the steep slope / 지붕에 기어오르다 climb (on) to the roof
▶ 그 남자는 밧줄을 써서 바위산을 기어올랐다 With the aid of a rope the man scrambled [climbed] up the rocky mountain.
2 〈버릇없이〉 be puffed up 《with pride》; presume on; take liberties 《with》; be overfamiliar 《with》
♦ 가만 놔두면 기어오르다 presume upon *sb's* patience

기어이 期於― by all (manner of) means; at last ⇨ 기어코

기어코 期於― **1** 〈반드시・꼭〉 by all (manner of) means; by hook or by crook; at any cost [price, risk]
▶ 무슨 일이 있어도 기어코 하고야 말겠다 I will carry it out at any cost 〔(口) no matter what〕. ⇌ I will do it, or I am a Dutchman.
▶ 그가 기어코 오고 싶다면 오게 하거라 Let him come by all means if he'd like to.
▶ 기어코 돌아가겠다면 말리지는 않겠다 If you insist on going home, I will not stop you.
▶ 기어코 그래야겠다면 하는 수 없지 If you must, (why,) you must.
2 〈마침내〉 at last; 〈결국〉 in the end; finally; at length; after all
▶ 다리의 건설은 기어코 완성되었다 The construction of the bridge was finally completed.
▶ 나는 기어코 그 문제를 풀었다 I solved the problem at last.

기억 記憶 memory; remembrance; memorization; 〈상기〉 recollection
♦ 어릴 적의 어슴푸레한 기억 dim memories [recollections] of *one's* childhood / 확실한[회

기억력

미한] 기억 an unfailing [a dim] memory / 내 기억이 틀림없다면 if I remember right(ly) [correctly]; if my memory serves me right [doesn't deceive me] / 기억을 더듬다 trace back in memory; retrace [search] one's memory (to) / 기억을 되살리다 bring back one's memory / 기억을 불러 일으키다 awaken [rub up] one's memory; recall sth to one's mind / 기억을 상실하다 lose one's memory / 기억을 새롭게 하다 refresh one's memory / 기억에 남다 remain [be retained] in one's memory; be impressed on one's memory [mind] / 기억에 새롭다 be fresh in one's memory
▶ 그녀는 우리들의 기억 속에 생생하다 She lives in our memory.
▶ 그를 전에 몇번 만난 기억이 있다 I remember seeing him several times. ⇒ I think I've seen him several times before.
▶ 그 문제에 대해서는 통 기억이 나지 않는다 My memory is perfectly blank on the subject.
▶ 그 사건은 나의 기억에 아직도 생생하다 The incident is still clear in my memory.
▶ 무슨 말을 들었는지 조금도 기억에 남아 있지 않다 What I was told went in one ear and out the other.
—기억하다 remember; be [remain, live] in one's memory; 〈잊지 않도록〉 bear [keep] in mind; 〈외다〉 learn [get] sth by heart; commit sth to memory, memorize
♦내가 기억하기로는 to the best of my memory; as far as I can remember [recollect] / 단단히 기억하다 fix [bear] sth firmly [indelibly] in one's memory [mind] / 똑똑히[어렴풋이] 기억하고 있다 have a clear [dim] recollection of; remember clearly [vaguely]
■—법 a mnemonic system —상실증 〔醫〕 amnesia —상실증 환자 an amnesiac —술 the art of memory; mnemonics [niːmániks] —용량 〔電算〕 memory [storage] capacity —장애 defects of memory —장치 〔電算〕 memory tubes: 전자기억장치 an electronic memory machine; a ticketer —중추 a memory center —착오 〔心〕 paramnesia

기억력 記憶力 (one's powers of) memory; the retentive faculty
♦놀랄 만한 기억력 a splendid [marvelous] memory / 기억력의 감퇴 failure of one's memory / 기억력이 좋다 have a good [long, strong, retentive] memory / 기억력이 나쁘다 have a poor [bad, short, weak] memory / 기억력을 상실하다 lose one's memory
▶ 그분은 노령으로 기억력이 나빠졌다 Old age has dimmed [clouded] his memory.
▶ 나는 최근 기억력이 떨어지고 있다 My memory is failing [becoming forgetful] these days.
■—이상 증진 〔醫〕 hypermnesia

기엄기엄 ♦기엄기엄 가다 go [crawl] on all fours [on (one's) hands and knees]/ 기엄기엄 산에 오르다 climb up a mountain on hands and knees
▶ 아기가 기엄기엄 기게 되었다 The baby has started crawling.

기업 企業 (a) business; an enterprise; a corporation; (an) industry

解說 *business*는 장사 또는 그것을 행하는 회사·상사·상점 등을 뜻하는 일반적인 말로. *enterprise*는 격식을 차린 말로서, 보통 수식어를 수반하여「…기업」이라는 형태로 쓰인다. *corporation*은 규모가 큰 기업에 쓰인다.

♦기업을 일으키다 plan [embark in] an enterprise / 기업을 합리화하다 rationalize an enterprise / 생산을 기업화하다 produce 《goods》 on a commercial basis [commercially]
▶ 인플레이션 때문에 기업의 경영이 곤란해졌다 Business has encountered financial difficulties because of inflation.
■국영— a government [state] enterprise 다국적— a multinational corporation 대(大)— big business [firm]; a large (-scale) [major] company; a large enterprise [corporation, company] 민간[개인]— a private enterprise 복합— a conglomerate corporation [company] 부실— an insolvent [an improperly-run] enterprise 중소— a small and medium enterprise [industry] ■—가 an entrepreneur; an enterpriser; a man of enterprise; an industrialist —가 entrepreneurship —경제학 business economics —공채 an industrial loan —농 market farming —심 a spirit of enterprise; an enterprising spirit —연합 a cartel —열(熱) a mania for enterprise; industrial fever —정비[재편성] business reorganization; industrial readjustment —조합 a syndicate —진단 management consulting —진단원 a business doctor —체질개선 improvement of industrial structure —합동 a trust; 《美口》 a combine —합리화 rationalization of enterprise —형태 a form [type] of (business) enterprise

기업 起業 〈창업〉starting a business —기업하다 organize an undertaking; start [enter on] an enterprise ■—비 initial expenses

기업공개 企業公開 a corporation's public offering [sale] of stocks [shares]; going public
♦기업 공개를 권장하다 encourage 《a corporation》to go public

-기에 1 〈…하는 데〉 for; to 《do》; with ♦ 일하기에 바빴다 be busy with [at, over] one's work ▶ 나는 여행 준비를 하기에 바빴다 I was busy getting ready for my journey.
2 〈때문에〉 on account of; owing to; as; because; because of; so...that; since
▶ 날씨가 나쁘기에 외출을 못했다 I could not go out because of [on account of] the bad weather.
▶ 지배인이 나가고 없기에 비서에게 말을 전하고 왔다 The manager was out, so I left message with his secretary.
▶ 덥기에 저고리를 벗었다 As it was warm, I took off my coat.
3 ⇒ -관데

-기에는 ♦내가 알기에는 so [as] far as I know; to the best of my knowledge
▶ 그는 겉보기에는 무뚝뚝하다 He is seemingly blunt.

그는 겉보기에는 평화로운 생활을 하고 있었다 To all outward appearances, he was living a peaceful life.

-기에망정이지 fortunately...otherwise; or (else); if not so; it is fortunate that...
▶ 즉시 출발했기에망정이지 그를 만나지 못할 뻔했다 Fortunately I started at once, otherwise I should have missed him.
▶ 열심히 공부했기에망정이지 그는 시험에 떨어질 뻔했다 He had worked hard, otherwise he would have failed in the examination.
▶ 돈이 있었기에 망정이지 창피당할 뻔했다 It was fortunate that I had some money with me, otherwise I would have to lose my face.

기여 寄與 (a) contribution; service(s)
—기여하다 contribute (to); make a contribution (to); render services (to); add (much) to; do (a lot) for《national welfare》; do much toward
▶ 산아 제한은 한국의 인구 문제 해결에 크게 기여했다 Birth control went far [a long way] toward solving Korea's population problem.
▶ 그는 세계 평화에 크게 기여했다 He made a great contribution to world peace.
▶ 그는 산업계에 기여한 바가 매우 컸다 His contributions to the cause of industry were really great.

기연 奇緣 a strange fate [chance]; a curious coincidence ▶ 여기서 너를 만나다니 참으로 기연이로구나 What a coincidence meeting you here!

기염 氣焰 〈기세〉 high spirit; 〈큰소리〉 a tall [big] talk; 〈논의〉 a heated argument
♦ 대기염 a very tall talk; a high-flown talk / 기염을 토하다 speak with great vehemence; talk big; blow hot air; deliver a fervent speech; (俗) turn on the gas
■ 만장(萬丈) high spirits

기영 機影 the sight of an airplane

기예 技藝 arts; (handi-)crafts; 〈예능〉 (artistic) accomplishments ■ —가 an artist

기예 氣銳 ♦ 신진 기예의 평론가 an up-and-coming critic / 젊고 기예있는 사람 a young and promising man

기온 氣溫 (atmospheric) temperature; (an) air temperature
♦ 기온의 급강하[급상승] a sudden drop [rise] in temperature / 기온의 변화 a change of [in the] temperature
▶ 최근에는 기온의 변화가 심하다 The temperature has been changeable recently.
▶ 기온이 섭씨 10도까지 올라갔다[내려갔다] The temperature rose [fell] to 10℃.
■ 평균— the average temperature ■ —파(波) a temperature wave

기와 a roofing tile; (총칭) tiling ♦ 기와를 이다 lay tiles on a roof; roof (a house) with tiles; tile a roof
■ 평— a plain tile ■ —공장 a tilery ■ —굽기 tile-making ■ —이기 tile-roofing; tiling ■ —장이 a tiler; a tile layer ■ —지붕 a tiled roof ■ —집 a tile-roofed house 기왓가마 a tile-kiln 기왓고랑 the channels between the rows of tiles on a roof

기왕 旣往 1 〈이전〉 the past; bygones; the bygone days; all that is gone by
▶ 기왕지사는 깨끗이 잊어버리자 Let bygones be bygones.
2 ⇨ 이왕에
■ —증 〈병〉 a disease which one had in the past; the past diseases of a patient; 〔醫〕 an anamnesis (pl. -ses)

기왕 棋王 the best player of paduk

기외 其外 〈그밖〉 the rest; the others ♦ 기외의 other ▶ 기외의 사람들은 전부 찬성했다 All the rest [others] agreed.

기용 起用 appointment; employment
—기용하다 appoint 《sb to a post》; engage; employ the service 《of》
♦ 대타로 기용하다 lift (a player) for a pinch hitter
▶ 그는 과장으로 기용되었다 He was promoted to chief of his section.
▶ 그는 우리 대학 팀의 투수로 기용되었다 He was chosen to be the pitcher of our college team.
▶ 그가 그 새 부서에 기용될 예정이다 He is to be appointed to the new position.

기우 杞憂 〈군 걱정〉 imaginary [needless, unfounded] fears; groundless apprehensions
♦ 기우를 품다 entertain groundless fears [apprehensions]; trouble oneself unnecessarily
▶ 너의 근심은 기우에 지나지 않는다 Your fears [worries] are groundless [needless].
▶ 내 걱정이 기우에 지나지 않았으면 좋겠는데 I hope my fears will prove groundless.

기우 奇遇 an unexpected [a chance] meeting; a strange encounter; 〈행운의〉 a fortuitous meeting **—기우하다** meet unexpectedly [by chance]

기우 祈雨 **—기우하다** pray for rain; offer prayers for rain
▶ 마을 사람들은 거의 매일 기우했으나 허사였다 Almost everyday the villagers prayed for rain, but in vain.

기우듬하다 slant; inclined a little; oblique; aslant; 〈서술적〉 be on the tilt
♦ 기우듬한 지붕 a slanted [sloping] roof / 기우듬히 aslant; askew; obliquely; on the [a] slant; at a tilt / 오른 쪽으로 기우듬하다 have a tilt to the right
▶ 제도판이 기우듬했다 The drawing board was slanted.
▶ 그 낡은 헛간은 한 쪽으로 기우듬했다 The old shed leaned [tilted] to one side.

기우뚱거리다 1 【흔들리다】 rock; 〈건물 등이〉 totter; 〈의자 등이〉 wobble; be shaky; be rickety; sway [move] from side to side
♦ 기우뚱거리는 의자 a shaky [wobbly, rickety] chair / 기우뚱거리며 일어서다 reel [stagger] to one's feet
▶ 배가 몹시 기우뚱거렸다 The ship was rolling heavily.
▶ 책상이 기우뚱거려서 글을 쓸 수가 없다 The table is so wobbly that I can hardly write.
2 〈흔들다〉 wobble; shake; move sth from side to side; rock; sway ♦ 몸을 기우뚱거리다

기우뚱기우뚱 swayingly; totteringly
기우제 祈雨祭 rainmaking rituals; a ritual (praying) for rain ♦기우제를 올리다 offer prayers for rain
기운 1 〈힘〉 (physical) strength; might; power; force
♦기운을 다해서 at full strength; with all one's might [strength]; with might and main / 기운이 나다 gain strength / 기운이 있다[세다] be strong; be mighty / 기운이 없다 be weak; do not have much strength / 기운을 내다 put forth one's strength / 기운을 회복하다 〈환자가〉 recover one's strength; regain strength
▶ 그는 기운이 빠졌다 His strength ebbed.
▶ 나는 접전 끝에 기운이 다 빠졌다 I was tired out [exhausted] after the tight race.
▶ 그는 너무 쇠약해서 걸을 기운도 없었다 He was so weak that he had not got the strength to walk.
2 〈원기·생기〉 vigor; energy; vitality; spirits; dash; (口) go; (美口) pep
♦기운이 왕성한 vigorous; energetic; full of energy [vitality, pep] / 기운이 나다 cheer up; become heightened in spirits; get encouraged / 기운이 없다 be in low [poor] spirits; be downhearted; be out of spirits; be in the blues / 기운이 왕성하다 be in high [good] spirits; be vigorous [energetic]; be lively [cheerful] 〈노인 등이〉 be going strong; be spry; be hale and hearty / 기운을 내다 cheer [(口) buck] up; brace oneself up / 기운을 북돋우다 cheer sb up; encourage; put sb on his mettle / 기운을 회복하다[차리다] recover [restore] one's spirits; be refreshed
▶ 그는 항상 기운이 있었는데 요새는 조금 기운이 없다 He is always full of energy [vigor, pep], but lately he has been a little depressed.
▶ 할아버지는 80세시지만 매우 기운이 좋으시다 My grandfather is going quite strong though he is eighty.
▶ 그의 말이 그녀의 기운을 크게 북돋우었다 His words greatly encouraged her.
▶ 기운을 내라 Cheer up! ⇌ (美口) Pep up! ⇌ 〈스포츠에서〉 Show your nerve! ⇌ 〈일 등에서〉 Make it snappy!
3 〈낌새〉 a sign; an indication; 〈기미〉 a touch
♦ 봄 기운 signs [indications] of (the approach of) spring / 감기 기운이 있다 have a slight [a touch of] cold
4 〈약·술 등의 효과〉 effect; efficacy
♦ 독한 기운 poisonous character; virulence / 약 기운이 빠른[느린] 약 a fast-acting [slow-acting] drug / 술 기운에 부리는 객기 Dutch courage / 술 기운에 under the influence of liquor / 기운이 빨리 퍼지다 take immediate effect; take effect rapidly; be quick in (its) action
▶ 먹는 약보다 주사가 약 기운이 빠르다 An injection would work faster than medicine.
▶ 약기운은 곧 나타났다 The medicine took effect soon.
기운 氣運 〈경향〉 a tendency; a trend
♦…의 기운이 고조되다 show a strong tendency to (do) ▶ 화해의 기운이 증대되고 있다 There is a growing tendency toward reconciliation.
기운 氣韻 〈멋〉 grace; elegance; tone; taste; refinement ♦기운이 있는 graceful; elegant; refined
기운 機運 an opportunity; a chance; the time ▶ 마침내 개혁의 기운이 무르익었다 At last the time is ripe for a reform.
기운차다 full of vitality [vigor, pep]; high spirited; vigorous; cheerful; 〈노인이〉 hale and hearty; 〈서슬걱〉 be in good [high] spirits
♦기운차게 in high spirits; cheerfully
▶ 더 기운차게 노래해라 Put more spirit into your singing! ⇌ Sing with more life!
▶ 그 아이는 기운차게 걸어서 집으로 갔다 The boy walked home in high spirits.
기울 (wheat) bran; (barley) offal
기울다 1 〈면이 쏠리다〉 incline (to); lean (to, toward); slant; tilt; have a tilt (to the left); slope (to); 〈배가 옆으로〉 list (to); heel; take a heel; keel over; careen
♦기운 지붕 a slanted [sloping] roof / 좌현[우현]으로 기울다 list [heel] to port [starboard] / 60도 기울어져 있다 be inclined at sixty degrees
▶ 우리집은 지하철 공사 때문에 조금 기울어졌다 My house has tilted a little because of the construction of the subway.
▶ 이 빌딩은 한 쪽으로 약간 기울어져 있다 This building is leaning [slanting] somewhat to one side.
▶ 꽃병이 기울어져 넘어졌다 The vase tipped over.
▶ 비행기가 기울어지면서 추락했다 The plane tilted to one side and crashed.
2 〈해·달이〉 sink; decline (toward); set; go down
♦기우는 달 the sinking [setting] moon / 지평선 아래로 해가 기우는 것을 보다 watch the sun sinking below the horizon
▶ 해가 서쪽으로 기울고 있다 The sun is going down [sinking, setting] in the west.
3 〈경향을 띠다〉 be inclined [disposed] (to, toward); lean [trend] (toward); incline (to); tend (to); have a tendency; be prone (to)
▶ 그들은 우익으로 기울고 있다 They lean [are inclined] toward [to] right.
▶ 그는 찬성 쪽으로 기울고 있다 He is leaning toward [is in favor of] it.
4 〈쇠퇴하다〉 decline; go downhill; sink; wane; ebb
▶ 잇달은 실정(失政)으로 국운이 기울었다 The country's fortunes declined because of continuing misgovernment.
▶ 사업이 기울고 있다 Our business is declining.
▶ 그 집은 가세가 기울고 있었다 The family was going downhill. ⇌ The fortune of his family was declining.
기울이다 1 〈물건 등을〉 incline; list; tilt; lean; tip; slant
♦몸을 기울이다 lean [incline] one's body (to

the right) / 술잔을 기울이다 have a drink; take [have] a cup of liquor / 앞으로[뒤로] 의자를 기울이다 tilt a chair forward [backward] / 통을 기울이다 tilt [give a tilt to] a barrel
▶ 그녀는 모자를 비스듬히 기울여 쓰기를 좋아한다 She likes to tilt a hat sideways.
2 〈마음을〉 devote *oneself* to *sth*; concentrate (*one's attention*) on *sth*
◆ 귀를 기울이다 listen / 온갖 노력을 기울이다 exert all possible efforts / 애정을 기울이다 fix [devote] *one's* affection (on) / 전력을 기울이다 concentrate *one's* energies (on); devote all *one's* energies (to) / 주의를 기울이다 pay [give] attention [heed] (to) / 전혀 귀를 기울이지 않다 turn a deaf ear (to); shut *one's* ears entirely (to)
▶ 그는 외동딸에게 깊은 애정을 기울이고 있다 He is deeply attached to his only daughter.
▶ 그는 공부에 정력을 기울이고 있다 He is devoted to study. ⇌ He is devoting himself to study.

기웃거리다 peep [peek] (into a room, through a hole); snoop; get [have, take] a peep (at) / look in on (*sb*, *sth*); 〈고개를〉 crane *one's* neck (to get a better view); incline [tilt] (*one's* head)
◆ 이웃을 기웃거리고 다니는 사람 a prowler in the neighborhood / 가게를 기웃거리다 look in at a store; show *one's* nose in a shop / 문에서 (방)안을 기웃거리다 peep [put *one's* head] in at the door / 창에서 기웃거리다 〈밖을〉 look out of the window; 〈안을〉 look in at the window
▶ 그는 여기저기 기웃거리며 돌아 다녔다 He pried about.

기웃하다 1 ⇨ 기우둠하다
2 〈조금 기울이다〉 incline [tilt, tip, slant] *sth* a little
◆ 고개를 기웃하다 incline [cock] *one's* head a little; tilt *one's* head; lean *one's* head a bit to the side; put *one's* head a bit to one side

기원 紀元 an era; an epoch

解說 서력 연호를 표시할 경우「기원 …년」은 AD이고「기원전 …년」은 BC로 나타낸다. AD는 숫자 앞에 쓰는 것이 정식이지만 뒤에 쓸 때도 있다. BC는 항상 숫자 뒤에 쓴다.

◆ 서력 기원 1392년에 in the year 1392 of the Christian era; in 1392 A.D. [Anno Domini] / 서력 기원전 37년에 in 37 B.C. [Before Christ]
기원 祈願 (a) prayer (for world peace); (a) supplication
▶ 나의 기원은 성취되었다 My prayer was answered.
—기원하다 pray (for the safety of *one's* son); supplicate
◆ 간곡히 기원하다 offer (up) a fervent prayer (for the return of *one's* health)
▶ 그를 살려 달라고 기원했다 I prayed that he might be saved.
■ **—문** 〔文法〕 an optative sentence **—법** 〔文法〕 the optative (mood) **—자** a supplicant; a

prayer
기원 起源 〈시초〉 the origin; the source; the beginning; the rise; 〈원인〉 the cause; the root; the genesis
◆ 문명의 기원 the origin of civilization / 생명의 기원 the beginnings [origin] of life / 종의 기원 *The Origin of Species* / 기원을 찾다[조사하다] trace *sth* to its origin [source] / …에 기원을 두다 originate in…; have (its) origin [rise] in…
▶ 이 관습의 기원은 중국이다 This custom is Chinese in origin.
▶ 그 기원은 분명치 않다 It is of obscure [unknown] origin. ⇌ Its origin is unknown.
▶ 이 축제의 기원은 지금부터 100여년 전으로 거슬러 올라간다 The origins of this festival go back more than a hundred years.
—기원하다 originate (from); take (its) rise in; have (its) origin [roots] (in); derive (its) origin (from); be traceable (to)
기원 棋院 a *paduk* club (house)
기율 紀律 discipline ⇨ 규율(規律)
기음 基音 〔物·樂〕 a fundamental tone
기음 氣音 〔音聲〕 an aspirate (▶[h]음)
◆ 기음의 aspirated
기음매다 weed (a field) ⇨ 김매다
기이하다 奇異— strange; queer; odd; eccentric; singular; curious; weird
◆ 기이한 경험 a strange experience / 기이한 광경 a curious sight / 기이한 행동 an unaccountable action; eccentric conduct / 매우 기이한 현상 a most singular phenomenon / 기이한 형태의 조각 an oddly-shaped statue / 기이하게도 strangely enough, strange to say / 기이하게 느끼다 feel strange
▶ 그녀는 나를 기이한 눈으로 바라 보았다 She gave me a queer [an odd] look. ⇌ She looked at me in a strange way.
기익 機翼 the wings of an airplane
기인 奇人 an eccentric (person); a queer [an odd] fellow [man]; a crank; (美口) an oddball
▶ 그는 아주 기인이다 He is really eccentric [odd].
기인 基因 〈근본적 원인〉 the root [fundamental] cause; the basic origin
기인하다 起因— come (from); originate (in); arise (from); have (its) origin [rise] in; result from; be due [owing] (to); be caused (by); spring [result] from
◆ 오해에 기인하는 반목 an antagonism caused by misunderstanding / 인종적 편견에 기인하는 증오 hatred generated [caused] by racial prejudice
▶ 이 질병은 대개 과로와 수면 부족에 기인한다 This disease is, in most cases, caused by overwork and want of sleep.
▶ 그의 성공은 끊임없는 노력에 기인한 것이었다 His success was due to [came from] his untiring efforts.
기일 忌日 〈죽은 날〉 the anniversary of *sb's* death; the deathday
◆ 아버지의 세 번째 기일 the third anniversary of my father's death
기일 期日 a date; a fixed [an appointed] day

기입

[time]; a term; 〈기한〉 a due date; a time limit

♦지불 기일 the date of payment; the term day; the due date / 기일까지 by the appointed time [day]; within the fixed date / 기일을 엄수하다 be punctual / 기일을 연기하다[앞당기다] extend [put forward] the time [term] / 기일을 정하다 fix [set] the date [term] / 기일내에 마치다 finish *sth* in [on] time

▶ 원서 마감 기일은 10월 31일이다 The application deadline is October 31st.
▶ 최종 지불 기일은 이미 지났다 The final payment is overdue.

기입 記入 entry; 〈서식의〉 filling out
──**기입하다** write (*sb's* name) in (on a voting slip); 〈빈칸에〉 fill in (an application); enter (up) (an item in an account book); make an entry of *sth* (in a register)

♦이름을 기입하다 enter *one's* name; register (*one's* name) / 대변에 기입하다 enter (an item) on the credit side / 서식[문제지]에 기입하다 fill in the blanks; (美) fill out [(英) fill in] (a form) / 원장에 금액을 기입하다 enter a sum in a ledger

▶ 기입필 (표시) Entered.
■ 차변── debtor entry; an entry on the debtor side ■──누락 an omission ──장 [簿] an entry book

기자 記者 a writer; a journalist; a news(paper)man; a newswriter; a reporter; (英) a pressman; 〈통신[특파]원〉a correspondent

♦기자를 하고 있다 be (engaged) on the staff of a newspaper; hold a reporter's job on a (local) paper

▶ 그는 워싱턴 포스트의 기자다 He is a reporter for "The Washington Post."
▶ 그는 뉴욕 주재 기자다 He is a correspondent in New York.
▶ 그는 지방 신문의 편집 기자다 He holds a desk position of a local press.
▶ 그는 사임할 의사가 없다고 기자들에게 말했다 He told the press that he had no intention of resigning.

■ 가십── a gossip writer; (俗) a keyhole reporter 수습[올챙이]── a junior reporter; (俗) a cub reporter 여── a lady reporter [journalist, writer]; (美) a news(paper)woman; (俗) a newshen 외교── a diplomatic correspondent [editor] 종군── a war correspondent 체육── a sports reporter [writer]; a sports columnist 취재── a (news) reporter; a legman (*pl.* -men); a legger 탐방── a (newspaper) reporter; an interviewer ■──단 corps of reporters; press association ──석 a press table; 〈의회 등의〉a press [reporters'] gallery; 〈경기장의〉a press stand; 〈극장·회의장의〉a press box ──증 a press card ──클럽 a press club; a journalists' club

기자력 起磁力 magnetomotive force
기자회견 記者會見 a press interview; 〈기자단 과의〉a news [press] conference

♦기자 회견을 하다 give [hold, call] a press conference; meet the press / 기자 회견을 요청하다 seek [request] a press interview (with the President)

■ 즉석── an impromptu conference with newsmen 텔레비전── a televised news [press] conference

기장¹ 〈옷의 길이〉the length of a suit; the dress length
기장² [植] (Chinese) millet
기장 記帳 〈기입〉register; (an) entry ──**기장하다** 〈장부에〉register; enter up (an item in the account book); make an entry (of *sth*); book

■ 복식── double entry ──(계)원 an entry clerk; a bookkeeper

기장 記章 a medal; 〈회원 등의〉a badge
■ 종군── a war [service] medal
기장 機長 a pilot; the captain (of the crew)
기재 奇才 〈재능〉remarkable talent; unusual ability; 〈인물〉a (a singular) genius; an outstandingly talented person ▶ 그는 문단의 기재다 He is a prodigy in the literary field.

기재 記載 〈적어 실음〉statement; mention; description; [簿] entry

♦별항 기재와 같이 as stated in a separate paragraph; as reported elsewhere
──**기재하다** record; state; mention; report; note; 〈신문·잡지에〉carry; print; 〈장부에〉enter

▶ 그 문제는 UN헌장에 기재되어 있다 The subject is stated [mentioned] in the United Nations Charter.

■──누락 an omission ──사항 items mentioned; contents : 장부의 기재 사항은 전부 정확해야 한다 All the entries in the book should be correct.

기재 機材 materials; mechanical equipment; machine parts
기재 器材 〈기계·기구의 재료〉materials for the manufacture of machinery [implements]; 〈기구와 재료〉machinery [implements] and materials

■ 통신── signal equipment
기저 基底 a base; a basis (*pl*. bases); a foundation ♦기저의 basal
기저귀 a diaper; (英) a napkin ♦기저귀를 채우다 diaper (a baby); put a diaper on (a baby) / 기저귀를 갈다 change the baby's diaper ▶ 기저귀가 축축하다 (口) The baby is wet.

■──커버 a diaper cover
기적 汽笛 a (steam) whistle; (美) a siren; (英) a hooter

♦기적을 울리다 sound [blow, give] a whistle; whistle (at the crossing)

▶ 기적이 울리고 있다 The whistle is blowing.
⇒ There goes the whistle.
▶ 배가 기적을 울렸다 The ship sounded its whistle.
▶ 기차는 기적을 울리며 떠났다 A train pulled out with a whistle.

기적 奇蹟 a miracle; a marvel; a wonder; a mystery; 〈신기(神技)〉a superhuman feat

♦설사 기적이 일어난다 하더라도 suppose a miracle happened / 기적을 이루다 achieve a miracle / 기적을 행하다 work [perform] a miracle; do [work] wonders

▶ 그가 회복된 것은 기적이었다 His recovery

was a miracle.
▶ 기적이 일어났다 A miracle occurred [came up].
▶ 이따금 기적은 일어나는 법이다 Miracles do occur from time to time.
■ —극 〈중세의〉 a miracle play
기적적 奇蹟的 miraculous
◆ 기적적인 회복 a miraculous restoration / 기적적으로 죽음을 모면하다 escape death by miracle [miraculously]
▶ 나는 기적적으로 구조되었다 I was saved miraculously [by a miracle].
기전 棋戰 〈토너먼트 방식의〉 a *paduk* tournament; 〈한 판〉 a game of *paduk*
기전기 起電機 an electrostatic generator
기전력 起電力 electromotive force (略 E.M. F., e.m.f.)
기절 氣絶 〈까무러침〉 fainting; a swoon; a fainting fit [spell]
▶ 그는 반 기절 상태에 있다 He is in a half fainting state.
—기절하다 faint (away); go faint; go off in a faint; swoon; fall [go off] into a swoon; lose consciousness [one's senses]; fall senseless [unconscious]
◆ 얼어맞아 기절하다 be stunned; be knocked unconscious / 쓰러지다 fall senseless [unconscious]; fall [drop] in a faint / 기절할 듯이 놀라다 be frightened out of one's senses [wits]
▶ 그녀는 충격으로 기절했다 She fainted from shock.
▶ 그녀는 아들의 사망 소식을 듣고 기절했다 She swooned [went faint] at the news of her son's death.
▶ 그는 그자리에서 기절했다 He fainted [fell senseless] on the spot.
기절초풍하다 氣絶—風— be absolutely astonished [amazed, astounded, staggered, (口) flabber-gasted] 《at》; one's heart leaps into one's mouth; be taken aback
▶ 나는 기절초풍하여 말문이 막혔다 I was speechless [struck dumb] with amazement.
기점 起點 〈거리 측량의〉 origin; the starting base [point]; 〈철도의〉 the railhead; the terminus (*pl.* ~es, -ni)
◆ …을 기점으로 하다 start from… / 광화문 도로 원표를 기점으로 하여 거리를 계산하다 measure the distance with the Kwanghwamun milestone as the starting point.
▶ 이 철도의 기점은 수원이다 This railway line starts from Suwon.
▶ 이 모퉁이를 기점으로 하여 거리를 측정해 주십시오 Please measure the distance using this corner as the starting point.
기점 基點 a cardinal point; a reference [a datum] point ■ **방위(方位)—** the cardinal points of the compass
기정 旣定 ◆ 기정의 established; fixed; prearranged; predetermined
■ **—사실** an established [accomplished] fact; (프) fait accompli; a settled matter **—세입** established revenue **—세출** established expenditure **—예산** the established budget

기정방침 旣定方針 the established policy
▶ 모두들 기정 방침에 따라 행동해 주기 바란다 Everybody is required to act according to the prearranged [fixed] program [plan].
기제 忌祭 a memorial service held on the anniversary of sb's death
기조 基調 〈주조〉the keynote; the underlying tone; 〈기초〉 the basis
◆ …에 기조를 두다 be based on… / 기조를 이루다 form the keynote 《of》
▶ 세계 평화가 그의 연설의 기조였다 World peace was the keynote of his speech.
▶ 인도주의가 이 소설의 기조를 이루고 있다 Humanism forms the basis [is the basic theme] of this novel.
■ **경제—** the basic economic condition ■ **—연설** a keynote address [speech] **—연설자** a keynote speaker; a keynoter
기존 旣存 ◆ 기존의 사회 조직 the existing social structure / 기존의 existing; established
■ **—시설** the existing facilities
기종 氣腫 〔醫〕 emphysema ■ **폐—** emphysema of the lung; pulmonary emphysema
기종 機種 〈비행기의〉 kinds [types] of airplanes; 〈기계의〉 a kind [type] of a machine
◆ 제조 중지된 기종 a model which is no longer being made [produced] / 신기종을 발매하다 release a new model of a machine
기주 寄主 〈기생 동식물의〉 a host (⇨ 숙주(宿主)》 ■ **—식물** a host plant
기죽다 be overawed; feel small 《in sb's presence》; be overwhelmed 《with, by》; be cowed 《by》
▶ 그녀의 능변에 나는 완전히 기죽었다 I was utterly overpowered [overwhelmed] by her eloquence.
기준 基準 〈표준〉 a standard; 〈판단 등의 척도〉 a criterion (*pl.* ~s, -ria); a yardstick; 〈기초〉 a basis (*pl.* bases)
◆ 도덕의 기준 moral [an ethical] standard / 기준을 정하다 establish standards / 기준에 맞추다 standardize
▶ 이 문제를 판단할 기준이 없다 There is no yardstick for judging this matter.
▶ 그는 합격 기준에 미달했다 He has failed to get the passing mark in the exam.
■ **—가격** a standard price **—기간** the base period **—량** a norm; standard amount **—면** a base [formation] level **—선** 〔測〕 a datum [base] line **—시세** 〈외국환〉 the central rate **—연도** the basic period [year] **—율** the basic rate **—일** the basic date **—임금** standard wages **—점** 〔測〕 a point of reference; a reference point **—지가(地價)** 《post》 standard land price
기중 忌中 (be in) mourning 《for》
▶ 기중 (게시) In Mourning.
기중기 起重機 〔機〕 a crane; 〈배의〉 a derrick; a jack ◆ 기중기로 들어 올리다 lift [hoist] *sth* with [by means of] a crane ■ **삼각—** a gin **—선(船)** a floating crane
기증 寄贈 presentation; donation; contribution
—기증하다 contribute; donate [make a dona-

기지

tion of] 《a sum of money to the school》; present 《*sb* with *sth*, *sth* to *sb*》
▶그들은 학교에 텔레비전을 기증했다 They presented the school with a TV set [a TV set to the school].
■—본[도서] a complimentary [presentation] copy; a giftbook —자 a contributor; donator; a donor; a giver —품 a gift; a donation; a present

기지 基地 a base; 〈탐험대의〉 a home ◆남극 관측 기지 an Antarctic observation base
■공군— an air(force) base 군사— a military base 미사일— a missile base 연료보급— a fueling base 영구— a permanent base 작전— a base of operations 중계— a relay base 항공— an air base 해군— a naval base ■—국 a base station —사령관 a base commanding officer —창 a base depot —촌 a military campsite town

기지 既知 ◆기지의 사실 an already-known fact
■—사항 a datum 《*pl*. data》 —수 〔數〕 a known quantity [number]

기지 機智 tact; wit; quick [ready] wits; resources
◆기지 있는 사람 a witty man; a man of wit; a wit / 기지의 번득임 a flash of wit / 기지가 있다[없다] be quick-witted [slow-witted]; have quick [slow] wits / 기지와 유머를 겸비하다 be possessed of both wit and humor
▶그의 이야기는 기지가 풍부했다 His speech was full of wit.
▶그는 순간적인 기지로 그 소녀를 구했다 He saved the little girl by his tact.

기지개 stretching 《*oneself*》
◆기지개를 켜다 stretch 《*oneself*》; stretch *one's* body with raised hands / 기지개를 켜며 하품하다 yawn with a stretch
▶수업이 끝나자 모두가 기지개를 켰다 When class was dismissed everybody stretched.
▶그 여자는 침대 위에서 기지개를 켰다 She stretched out [herself] on the bed.

기지불 既支拂 ◆기지불의 paid-up; already settled 《bill》

기직 〈돗자리〉 a straw-and-rush mat; a coarse straw mat

기진 氣盡 exhaustion; fatigue
—기진하다 be exhausted

기진맥진 氣盡脈盡 utter exhaustion
—기진맥진하다 be utterly exhausted; be worn [tired] out; 《美俗》 be pooped (out); be thoroughly spent
▶나는 기진맥진했다 I'm worn out [tired out, 《英俗》 fagged (out)].
▶나는 무거운 짐을 운반하느라고 기진맥진했다 I wore myself out carrying heavy luggage. ≒ I was exhausted [dead tired] from carrying heavy luggage.

기질 氣質 〈성격〉 a disposition; character; personality; (a) temperament; (a) nature; (a) temper; a cast [frame] of mind
◆영국인 기질 Anglo-Saxonism / 명랑하고 유쾌한 기질 a joyous and happy temperament / 온순한 기질 a mild disposition / 학생 기질 the student character; the characteristic of students / 학자[예술가] 기질인 사람 a man of a scholarly type [an artistic temperament] / 기질이 과격한 사람 a man of a fiery [violent] temperament / 기질이 착한 사람 a good-tempered [good-natured] man; a man of a good disposition / 정열적인 기질을 물려받다 inherit a warm temperament
▶그는 기질이 진취적이다 He is very independent.
▶그는 기질이 어떤 사람이냐? What sort of (a) man is he?

기질 基質 〔醫〕 a stroma 《*pl*. mata》; 〔生化〕 a substrate

기차 汽車 〈열차〉 a (railway) train; 《美》 a railroad train; 《英》 a railway carriage; 〈증기기관차〉 a steam locomotive
◆서울행 기차 a train (bound) for Seoul / 기차의 창문에서 본 경치 a scene (viewed) from a train window / 2분 차이로 기차를 놓치다 miss [lose, fail to catch] *one's* train by two minutes / 오후 3시 기차를 타다 take [board, get, get on, get into] a train at 3:00 p.m. / 마산에서 진해행 기차를 바꿔 타다 change trains at Masan for Chinhae / 기차 시간에 알맞게 be in time for a train / 기차에서 내리다 get off [out of] a train; leave [alight from] the train / 기차로 가다 go by train [rail] / 5시반 기차로 가다 take the 5:30 train; go by [on] the 5:30 train / 기차로 여행하다 travel in [by, 《美》 on] a train; make a train [railroad] journey
▶기차가 연착했다 The train is behind (time) [overdue].
▶그 기차는 탈선했다 The train was derailed.
▶이 마을에는 기차편이 있다[없다] There is [is no] railroad service available in this village.
▶기차는 제시간에 도착[출발]했다 The train arrived [departed] on schedule [time].
▶몇 시 기차로 떠납니까? What train are you going by?
▶이곳에서   기차로 20분 거리다 It is twenty minutes' train ride from here.
■—시간표 a railway timetable; 《美》 a railroad schedule —여행 railroad traveling; 《美》 a train journey [trip] —요금 a train fare; a railroad fare —표 a (railroad) ticket 기찻길 a railroad [rail] track; a railroad line

기차다 〈어이없다〉 be dum(b)founded [《口》 flabbergasted, stifled]; be stunned 《by》; be shocked 《at, by》; be astounded 《by》; 〈놀랍다〉 be wonderful
◆기차게 awfully; terribly; extremely; wonderfully; 《口》 so / 기차게 맛있다 be exceedingly palatable; be so delicious
▶그녀석 어리석은 데는 기(가) 차서 말이 안 나온다 His stupidity really staggers me.
▶원 참 기(가) 차서 Words fail me. ≒ The idea! ≒ Hoity-toity! ≒ Well, I never!

기착 寄着 stopover; 《美口》 stopoff —기착하다 stop over [break *one's* journey] 《at New York》; 〈배가〉 touch at 《a port》; make a (brief) stop 《at...for refueling》
■—지 a stopover; a place of call

기채 起債 flotation [floatation] of a loan; an

issue [issuance] of bonds
―기채하다 〈빚〉 float [raise] a loan; 〈공채〉 issue bonds
▶ 지하철을 놓기 위해 기채했다 Bonds have been issued to finance the subway construction.
■―시장 the capital market; the bond flotation market

기척 〈소리·기미〉 a sign; an indication; a trace ⇨ 인기척
▶ 사람이 오는 기척이 있다 I sensed someone approaching.
▶ 옆방에 사람 기척이 있었다 I felt [sensed] someone in the next room.
▶ 그 집에는 사람 기척이 전혀 없었다 There was no sign of life in the house.

기체 氣體 gas; vapor; a gaseous body ◆ 기체의 분자 a gas molecule / 기체의 aerial; vaporous; aeriform; pneumatic; gaseous; gasifrom / 기체가 되다 become [turn into] a gas
■―동력설 the kinetic theory of gas ―물리학 aerology ―역학 gas dynamics; aeromechanics ―연료 gaseous fuel ―온도계 a gas thermometer ―측정 (化) eudiometry ―화 vaporization; gasification; aerification : 기체화하다 vaporize; gasify; aerify

기체 機體 〈엔진 외의 전체〉 an airframe; 〈동체〉 a fuselage; the body
▶ 기체의 파손이 심했다 The airplane was badly damaged.

기초 起草 drafting
―기초하다 draft [work out the draft of] (a bill); draw up; make a draft 《of》
◆ 조약을 기초하다 make out the draft of the treaty / 헌법을 기초하다 draft a constitution
▶ 그가 평화조약을 기초했다 He made a draft of the peace treaty.
■―위원회 a (meeting of the) drafting committee ―자 a drafter; a draftsman

기초 基礎 the base; the foundation; the basis (pl. bases); the footing; the groundwork; the substructure
◆ 기초적인 basic; fundamental; elementary / …을 기초로 하여 on the basis of…; on grounds [the ground] of… / …에 기초를 두다 be based [founded] on…; rest on… / …의 기초를 쌓다 lay the foundations of; lay the groundwork for / 기초를 튼튼히 하다 consolidate [solidify] the foundation 《of, for》; make the foundation secure; put (the project) on a firm basis
▶ 기초가 흔들린다 The foundation is shaky [unstable].
▶ 너는 문법의 기초가 불충분하다 You lack a basic knowledge of grammar.
▶ 무엇이든 기초가 중요하다 Foundations are important in everything.
▶ 기초부터 영어를 시작[공부]해라 You must learn English from the beginning [ABC].
■―공제 basic deduction (from the taxable income) ―과학 (a) basic science ―대사 (代謝) basal metabolism ―산업 a basic [key] industry ―영어 the elementary course of English ―의학 the basic medical sciences ―지식 a (good) grounding (in); a basic [a fundamental, an elementary] knowledge (of) ―체온 [生理] the basal body temperature (略 BBT) ―학과 primary subjects (of study) ―훈련 a basic training

기초공사 基礎工事 foundation work; groundmaking ◆ 기초공사를 하다 lay the foundation [groundwork] 《of, for》; (비유) pave the way (for)

기초공작 基礎工作 spadework; groundwork
◆ 기초 공작을 하다 lay the groundwork 《for obtaining one's objective》

기초시계 記秒時計 a stopwatch ⇨ 스톱워치

기총 機銃 a machine gun ■―소사 machine-gun fire; machine-gunning; 〈비행기에서의〉 strafing (raids) : 기총소사를 하다 machine-gun (a house); 〈비행기로〉 strafe

기축 機軸 〈굴대〉 an axis; an axle; 〈고안〉 a plan; a device 《for》; a design 《for》; a contrivance

기축통화 基軸通貨 key currency

기치 旗幟 **1** 〈깃발〉 a flag; a banner; an ensign; an emblem; a standard (의식용); 〈군기〉 colors
▶ 그들은 자유의 기치 아래 싸웠다 They fought under the flag [banner] of freedom.
2 〈태도〉 one's attitude; one's position; one's stand; 〈정강(政綱)〉 the platform; the plank
◆ 기치를 선명히 하다 make one's attitude [position] clear; state [define, clarify] one's position 《on a matter》; assume a definite attitude; show one's hand

기침 a cough; coughing; [醫] a tussis
◆ 마른 기침 a dry cough; 〈잇달아 나오는〉 a hacking cough / 잔기침 a slight cough / 헛기침 a dry cough / 기침나다 have a cough / 기침이 낫다 get over [get rid of] one's cough / 기침으로 고생하다 suffer from [be troubled with] a cough
▶ 나는 감기가 들어서 기침이 심하게 난다 I have caught a cold and have a bad cough.
▶ 그 약으로 기침이 가라앉았다 The medicine relieved my cough.
▶ 그녀는 기침 때문에 괴로운 것 같다 She is coughing painfully.
―기침하다 cough; have a cough
◆ 심하게 기침하다 cough violently; cough one's lungs out; be taken with a fit of coughing
■―약 a cough medicine; 〈드롭·정제〉 a cough drop [lozenge]

기타 其他 and others; 〈나머지 전부〉 the others; 〈나머지 것·사람〉 the rest; 〈…등등〉 and others; and so forth [on]; and the like; and what not ◆ 기타 다수 and many others
▶ 그녀는 피아노, 바이올린, 기타 여러 가지 악기를 가지고 있다 She has a piano, a violin, and various instruments.
▶ 그는 인생, 사랑, 죽음과 기타 문제에 대해 이야기했다 He talked about life, love, death, and so on [forth].
▶ 20명은 제1교실에서, 기타는 음악실에서 대기하시오 Twenty of you are to wait in classroom No.1, and the others in the music room.

기타 a guitar ♦기타를 치다[퉁기다] play (on) the [twang a] guitar ■클래식— a classical guitar ■—연주자 a guitarist

― 기타 ―

- 헤드 head
- 감개 tuning peg
- 넥, 목 neck
- 너트 nut
- 프렛 frets
- 보디, 몸통 body
- 핑거 보드 fingerboard
- 사운드 홀 sound hole
- 현, 줄 strings
- 픽 가드 pick guard
- 브리지 bridge base

기탁 寄託 deposition; 〔法〕 bailment —**기탁하다** deposit 《sth with a bank》; entrust 《sb with sth》; commit 《sth to sb's care》
■—금 trust money; money consigned ―물 a deposit; a trust; a thing entrusted 《to another》―자 a truster; a depositor; 〔法〕 a bailor ―증서 a deposit certificate

기탄 忌憚 ♦기탄없는 의견 a candid opinion / 기탄 없는 〈솔직한〉 frank 《criticism》; 〈거리낌 없는〉 outspoken; 〈단도직입적인〉 straightforward; 〈숨김없는〉 candid 《opinion》; unreserved / 기탄없이 without reserve; unreservedly; outspokenly; frankly; candidly
▶기탄없이 의견을 말해 보시오 Speak out your thought, please. ⇒ Tell me your idea without reserve.
▶무엇이든지 기탄없이 물어보세요 Please feel free to ask me.
▶찬성인지 반대인지 기탄없이 말해 다오 Tell me frankly whether you are for or against it.
▶그는 그것에 대해 기탄없이 비평을 했다 He was outspoken in criticizing it.
—**기탄하다** hesitate; hang back; withhold; be reserved

기통 汽筒 〔機〕 a (steam) cylinder ⇨ 실린더
♦6기통 엔진[차] a six-cylindered engine [car]

기특하다 奇特— praiseworthy 《conduct》; commendable; laudable
♦기특한 마음씨 a good intention; a commendable purpose / 기특한 행동 a commendable deed / 기특하게도 what is praiseworthy of 《him》 is that...
▶그 녀석은 기특한 아이다 He is a praiseworthy boy.
▶그것은 매우 기특한 일이다 It is highly praiseworthy.
▶그는 기특하게도 열심히 공부하고 있다 He works hard like a good boy.

기틀 〈계기〉 a (most appropriate) moment; a chance; an occasion; 〈기회〉 opportunity; 〈토대·기반〉 a base; a basis 《pl. bases》; a foundation
♦이것을 기틀로 하여 with this as a turning point [trigger]; taking [availing oneself of] this opportunity / 성공의 기틀이 되다 serve as a stepping-stone [a springboard] for (future) success / 성공의 기틀을 쌓다 pave the way [lay the groundwork] for one's success / 기틀을 잡다 seize an opportunity 《to do, of doing》; take the tide (as it offers) / 문제 해결의 기틀을 잡다 get [find] a clue to a question [for solving a problem]
▶그것이 기틀이 되어 그는 인기를 되찾았다 Taking the opportunity, he made a come-back.

기펴다 氣— be [feel] relieved [animated]; feel at rest [ease]; feel [be] relaxed
♦기 못 펴다 feel constrained [oppressed]; feel uneasy 《about》; feel ill at ease
▶나치 독일에서는 사람들이 기쁘고 살 수가 없었다 In Nazi Germany they could not get along in peace [free from all anxiety].

기포 氣泡 an air bubble; 〈주물의〉 a blowhole; 〈유리의〉 a bubble
▶고여 있는 연못 물에서 기포가 일어나고 있었다 Gas bubbles were rising from the stagnant pond water.
■—고무 foam rubber —수준기(機) a spirit [bubble] level —제 a foaming agent —콘크리트 aerated concrete

기포 氣胞 〈부레〉 an air [a swimming] bladder; a (fish) sound; 〈식물의〉 an air vesicle
■—음 a vesicular murmur

기폭 起爆 —**기폭하다** explode
■—장치 a triggering device 《for a nuclear blast》; a detonator —제 the initial explosive : 그 사건이 전쟁의 기폭제가 되었다 The event triggered [led up to] the war.

기표 記票 —**기표하다** fill in [out] a ballot (paper); fill out a voting card ■—소 a polling booth

기품 氣品 〈위엄〉 dignity; 〈고아함〉 elegance; nobility; 〈세련미〉 refinement
♦기품있는 dignified; graceful; refined 《movement》; elegant; noble 《poem》
▶그 여인에게는 어딘지 모르게 기품이 있다 There is something noble about her.
▶그녀의 말씨에는 기품이 있다 She has a refined way of speaking. ⇒ She is elegant in her speech.

기풍 氣風 character; disposition; temper; 〈단체의〉 morale; 〈사회의〉 ethos; 〈정신〉 spirit; 〈분위기〉 tone; 〈특성〉 traits; characteristics
♦국민의 기풍 the traits [characteristics] of a nation / 자유로운 기풍 the liberal tone [spirit] (of the times) / 진취적인 기풍 an enterprising spirit / 기풍을 진작하다 arouse [enhance] the (national) spirit
▶나는 그 학교의 개방적인 기풍을 좋아한다 I like the liberal tone of the school.
▶그 대학에는 옛날의 기풍과 전통이 다소 남아

있다 The college retains some of its old tone and tradition.
기풍 棋風 one's way [style] of playing *paduk*
기피 忌避 〈병역 등의〉 evasion (of military service); avoidance; shirking; 〈재판관 등의〉 challenge; exception ◆배심원에 대한 기피가 a challenge to jurors
▶병역 기피는 헌법에 위배된다 Draft evasion is a violation of the Constitution.
—**기피하다** evade; shirk; shun; avoid 〈doing〉; challenge (the judge, a witness); except 《against a witness》
▶병역을 기피하다 evade [shirk] military service / 책임을 기피하다 shirk one's responsibility
■**징병[병역]**— evasion of conscription [military service]; (美) draft dodging ■**인물 [外交]** an unwelcome [unacceptable] person; (라) persona non grata —**자** an evader [a shirk] (of military service); a shirker; [法] a challenger
기필코 期必— 〈기어코〉 by all (manner of) means; at any cost; at all costs; whatever may happen; 〈꼭〉 certainly; surely; assuredly; 〈어김없이〉 without fail
◆기필코 …하다 be sure to do; never fail to do; do without fail
▶나는 기필코 그 책을 손에 넣어야겠다 I have to [must] get the book at all costs.
▶나는 기필코 그렇게 하겠다 I will do it, or I am a Dutchman.
▶기필코 너를 실망시키지는 않겠다 I'll never let you down.
기하 幾何 1 ⇨ 기하학(幾何學) 2 〈얼마〉 how much; how many ■**—공리** a geometrical axiom
기하급수 幾何級數 geometric(al) series [progression] ▶인구는 기하급수적으로 증가한다 Population increases by [in] geometric(al) progression.
기하다 期— 1 〈기한을 정하다〉 fix [decide upon] a date; set [fix] a term [time limit, deadline] (for); 〈기약하다〉 pledge; promise
▶오늘 저녁 8시를 기하여 행동을 개시하겠다 We will go into action at 8 o'clock this evening.
2 〈목표로 삼다〉 aim (at *sth*, to do); have *sth* in one's mind [in view]; 〈결심하다〉 resolve; determine; decide ◆만전을 기하다 aim at perfection
▶나는 경주에 필승을 기하고 있다 I am determined [resolved] to win the race.
기하학 幾何學 geometry
◆기하학적 도형[무늬] a geometrical figure [pattern] / 기하학적으로 geometrically
▶광장은 아름다운 기하학적 무늬로 포장되어 있었다 The plaza was paved in a pretty geometric pattern [design].
■**유클리드—** Euclidean geometry **평면[입체], 구면, 해석, 계량, 순정]—** plane [solid, spherical, analytic(al), metrical, pure] geometry **화법[도형]—** descriptive geometry ■**—자** a geometrician; a geometer —**평균** a geometric average [mean]

기한 飢寒 hunger and cold ◆기한을 모면하다 stave [keep] off (one's) hunger and cold / 기한에 떨다 suffer from hunger and cold
기한 期限 〈기간〉 a term; a period; 〈기간이 끝나는 시점〉 a time limit; a deadline; [法] 〈법률적 효력 등의〉 limitation
◆기한이 지난 overdue; expired (ticket) / 기한이 아직 안 된 [商] undue / 기한부로 with a (one-year) time limit [deadline] / 일정한 기한 내에 within a definite period of time / 기한 전에 before the time set; before the date fixed / 기한이 되다 〈지불의〉 become [fall] due; 〈만기가〉 mature / 기한이 지나다 the term expires [runs out]; pass a fixed term; 〈어음 등이〉 be overdue / 기한을 정하다 fix [set] a time limit [deadline] (for); set [fix] a term (to)
▶기한이 되면 책은 도서관에 반환해야 한다 The books should be returned to the library when they are due.
▶기한이 지나서 이 표는 무효입니다 This ticket is no good, as it has passed the time limit.
▶우리는 지불 기한을 1개월 연장했다 We have extended the term of payment by one month.
▶나는 이 아파트를 2년 기한으로 빌렸다 I rented this apartment for a period of two years.
■**—예정** the target date **유효—** ⇨ 기한(유효~) ■**—경과 어음[수표]** an overdue bill [check] —**만료** the termination [expiration] of a term
기함 旗艦 a flagship
기합 氣合 1 〈지르는 소리〉 a yell; a shout; 〈기세·투지〉 (vigor of) spirit; fight
◆기합을 넣다 〈소리치다〉 shout [yell] at *sb*; give *sb* a yell; 〈독려하다〉 urge *sb* to get a move [start] on his work / 기합과 함께 칼을 내리치다 bring down one's sword with a yell
▶그들은 기합을 지르면서 적에게 돌격했다 They charged at the enemy with a yell.
▶나는 그에게 더욱 열심히 일하라고 기합을 넣었다 I inspired [urged, encouraged] him to work much harder.
2 [軍] 〈벌〉 disciplinary punishment ◆단체 기합 disciplinary punishment upon a group / 기합을 주다 chastise; punish; discipline
기항 寄港 a call [stop, touch] at a port
—**기항하다** call [stop] 〈at〉; put in 《at》; make a call 〈at〉; make (a) port
▶그 배는 미국에 가는 길에 12일 하와이에 기항한다 The ship will call at Hawaii on her way to America on the 12th.
▶그들은 유럽의 모든 항구에 기항했다 They touched at every port in Europe.
■**—지** a port of call
기행 奇行 eccentric conduct [behavior]; an eccentricity
▶그는 여러 가지 기행이 많다 He has a lot of interesting anecdotes.
▶그 사람은 기행으로 잘 알려져 있다 He is well-known for his eccentricities [eccentric conduct].
기행 紀行 an account of a journey [trip]; a book of travels
◆유럽 기행 (a book of) travels in Europe

▶ 그는 아프리카 기행을 출간했다 He published a book on his travels in Africa.
━작가 a travel writer ━영화 a travelog
기행문 紀行文 a record of [book about] one's travels; an account of one's journey; travel sketches [notes, description]
▶ 김 교수의 기행문은 아주 재미있다 Professor Kim's travel notes are very interesting.
기형 畸形・奇型 (a) deformity; deformation; (a) malformation; 〈형태학상의〉 abnormality
♦ 기형 물고기 a deformed fish / 기형의 deformed; malformed; 〔牛〕 teratoid
━선천성━ a congenital [an inborn, an inherent] deformity ━아 a deformed [malformed] child
기호 記號 〈표・부호〉 a mark; a sign; a symbol; an emblem; 〔樂〕 〈조(調)・박자의〉 a clef; a signature
♦ 플러스 기호 a plus sign / 마이너스 기호를 표시하다 mark with a minus sign / 각 번호 앞에 ○ 또는 ×의 기호를 표시하다 put a circle or a cross before each number / 기호화하다 symbolize
▶ H는 수소를 표시하는 기호다 "H" is the symbol for hydrogen.
▶ 언어는 사상을 나타내는 기호다 Words are the signs of ideas.
▶ 이것은 무엇을 나타내는 기호입니까? What does this symbol stand for?
▶ ∞ 기호는 무한대를 표시한다 The sign ∞ represents infinity.
■발음━ a phonetic symbol [sign] 수학━ a mathematical symbol 음성━ a phonetic symbol 음악━ a musical sign 화학━ a chemical symbol ■논리학 symbolic [mathematical] logic ━론 semiotics ━법 《chemical》notation ━학 semiology
기호 嗜好 〈취미〉 (a) taste; (a) liking; fancy; gusto
♦ 색깔[의복]에 대한 기호 one's taste in color [clothes] / 기호에 따라 according to one's liking [preference] / 대중의 기호에 맞다 capture [strike, hit, catch] public fancy
▶ 사람마다 기호가 다르다 Tastes differ. ⇄ Every man has his (own) taste.
▶ 그 여자는 기호가 까다롭다 She is fastidious in her taste.
▶ 그것은 내 기호에 맞는다 It suits my taste [fancy]. ⇄ It is very much to my taste.
▶ 이 핸드백은 그녀의 기호에 맞을[맞지 않을] 것이다 This handbag will suit [will not suit] her taste [fancy].
▶ 재즈가 모든 사람의 기호에 맞지는 않는다 Jazz is not to everyone's taste.
━기호하다 have a taste [fondness, fancy] for...; have a liking for...
■━품 〈음식〉 one's favorite food; 〈차・술 등〉 table luxuries; 〈사치품〉 luxury goods; a luxury; an article of luxury
기호지세 騎虎之勢 having gone too far to retreat; having no choice but to carry on; being unable to change one's line of action
기혼 旣婚 ♦기혼의 married 《woman》 ■━자 a married person; (총칭) the married; married people: 젊은 기혼자들 young marrieds
기화 奇貨 1 〈진품(珍品)〉 a rarity; a curiosity 2 ⇨ 기화로
기화 氣化 〔物〕 vaporization; evaporation; gasification ━기화하다 evaporate; vaporize; gasify
■━기(器) a vaporizer; an evaporator; 〈내연기관의〉 a carburetor ━성 vaporability ━열 evaporation heat; the heat of vaporization ━점 the evaporation point
기화로 奇貨━ ♦ 사람이 좋은 것을 기화로 삼다 presume on sb's good nature / 아무의 무지를 〈상대가 좋은 것을〉 기화로 삼다 take (a) mean advantage of sb's ignorance [of a weaker opponent] / 아무의 약점을 기화로 삼다 practice upon sb's weakness
기회 機會 〈절호의〉 an opportunity; 〈적당한〉 an occasion; 〈돌연한〉 a chance

> 解說 (1) **opportunity**는 특정한 목적을 향해서 행동하기에 알맞은 기회: I had an opportunity to visit the museum when I was in Boston. (나는 보스턴에 있을 때 미술관을 가볼 기회가 있었다)
> (2) **occasion**은 opportunity보다 뜻은 약하지만 어떤 일을 하기에 알맞은 호기: It was a suitable occasion for introducing my daughter to him. (내 딸을 그에게 소개하기에 알맞은 기회였다)
> (3) **chance**는 원인・이유・계획 없이 우연히 기회가 도래하는 것을 말한다: If I have a chance to see him, I'll tell him so. (그를 만날 기회가 있으면 그렇게 전하겠다)

♦ 일생에 한 번 있는 기회 the chance of a lifetime / 절호의 기회 a golden [rare] opportunity / 천재일우의 기회 an opportunity in a thousand chances / 기회 있을 때마다 at every opportunity; whenever the opportunity arises [presents itself] / 기회가 있으면 if one finds an opportunity / 기회를 놓치지 않고 in due course; at the right and proper time / 기회를 보아 at a good time / 다른 기회에 some other time [day]; on another occasion / 기회만 오면 on the first opportunity / 기회가 없다 have no opportunity [chance] 《to do, of doing》/ 기회가 무르익기를 기다리다 wait for a ripe opportunity / 기회를 보는 데 재빠르다 be quick to seize an opportunity / 기회를 얻다 get a chance 《of success in life》; find [have] an opportunity 《of doing, to do》/ 기회를 놓치다 miss [lose] a [one's] opportunity; miss [lose] a [one's] chance; let a chance slip (away) [go] / 기회를 주다 afford [give, allow] an opportunity 《of》; give sb a chance / 기회를 포착하다 take advantage [avail oneself] of an [the] opportunity
▶ 지금이 기회다 Now is your [my] chance.
▶ 기회가 있으면 다시 거기에 가겠다 When I have a chance I'll go there again.
▶ 그런 좋은 기회는 두 번 다시 없을 것이다 We will never have such a golden opportunity again.
▶ 기회는 두번 다시 오지 않는다 An opportu-

nity once lost is lost for ever.
▶그와 말할 기회는 그다지 많지 않다 I don't have many occasions to talk to him.
▶이 기회를 놓치지 마라 Don't pass up this opportunity. ⇌ Don't let this opportunity slip.
▶기회를 보아 그렇게 전하도록 하겠다 I will tell him so when I have a favorable opportunity.
▶기회를 잡는 것은 어렵다 It is difficult to catch an opportunity.
▶그는 이번 기회를 이용해서 런던 구경을 했다 He took advantage of this opportunity to do the sights of London.
▶여러분께 인사드릴 기회를 얻게 된 것을 기쁘게 생각합니다 I appreciate this opportunity to voice my best wishes and greetings to you all.
▶이 기회에 감사의 뜻을 표하고자 합니다 On this occasion I would like to express my gratitude to you.
기회균등 機會均等 equality of opportunity; equal opportunity
♦교육의 기회 균등 equal educational opportunities / 여성에 대한 기회 균등 equal opportunities for women / 기회 균등을 요구하다 call for [demand] equal opportunities
━고용자 an equal opportunity employer ━법 the Equal Opportunities Act ━주의 the principle of equal opportunity
기회주의 機會主義 opportunism; fence-sitting; timeserving; wait-and-see policy
▶그들은 기회주의적인 태도로 비난을 받았다 They were criticized for their wait-and-see policy.
━자 an opportunist; a timeserver; (美) a fence sitter
기획 企劃 〈계획(함)〉 planning; a plan; a project
♦새로운 기획 a new program / 기획을 입안하다 make [form] a plan; draw up a project ━기획하다 plan; make [form, set up] a plan; work out a scheme [program]
♦여행을 기획하다 plan a trip; make plans for a trip; arrange [make arrangements for] a trip
━관리 planning and management ━력 planning ability : 기획력이 있는 사람 a person with great inventiveness ━부[과, 실] the planning department [section, office] ━성 the ability to make plans : 기획성이 있다[없다] be gifted with the ability [have little ability] to make plans ━조정실 office of planning and coordination
기후 氣候 climate; 〈날씨〉 weather

|解說| (1) *climate*는 어떤 지방・나라의 장기간에 걸친 기상적 특징・종합적인 기후를 말한다 : a tropical climate (열대성 기후)
(2) *weather*는 특정한 때와 장소에 있어서의 기상 상태・날씨다 : changeable autumn weather (변덕스러운 가을 날씨)

♦대륙성[해양성, 도서성] 기후 a continental [an oceanic, an insular] climate / 더운[건조한] 기후 a hot [dry] climate / 변덕스러운 기후 a variable climate; changeable [unsettled] weather / 불순한 기후 unseasonable weather / 좋은[온화한] 기후 a fine [mild, genial] climate
〈기후의〉 기후의 변화 a climatic change; variations in climate / 기후의 영향 a climatic influence
▶그곳은 기후의 변화가 아주 심하다 The place is subject to extreme [violent] climatic changes.
〈기후가〉 기후가 변덕스럽다 We have unpredictable weather.
▶최근에 기후가 불순하다 The weather has been unsettled [unseasonable] lately. (▶보통 weather에는 정관사 the가 붙지만 "mild weather"처럼 앞에 형용사가 붙을 때는 무관사)
▶이곳은 기후가 온난하다[좋다] We have a temperate climate here. ⇌ The climate is good here.
〈기후는〉 아프리카의 건조한 기후는 내게 맞지 않았다 The dry climate in Africa did not agree with me.
▶한국의 기후는 전반적으로 영국보다 온화하다 The climate of Korea is generally milder than that of England.
━이상— abnormal [unusual] weather ━순화 acclimation; acclimatization ━요법 climate treatment; climatotherapy ━조건 climatic conditions ━학 climatology ━학자 a climatologist
기휘 忌諱 〈꺼림〉 avoiding things; superstitious avoidance of things ━기휘하다 avoid things; taboo; shun the use of sacred names
기흉 氣胸 pneumothorax ━인공[자연]— artificial [spontaneous] pneumothorax ━요법 a pneumothorax treatment
긴급 緊急 urgency; (an) emergency; (an) exigency; 〈서류 등에〉 (美) "Rush"; (英) "Urgent"
♦긴급 발진하다 〈전투기가〉 scramble (to intercept the enemy's MIGs)
▶그 환자의 수술은 긴급을 요한다 It is urgent that the patient (should) be operated on. ⇌ The patient urgently needs to be operated on.
▶그것은 매우 긴급을 요하는 일이다 It is a matter of great urgency.
━긴급하다 urgent 《demand》; emergent 《state》; pressing [burning, exigent] 《problem》; crying 《want》
♦긴급한 필요 an urgent [a pressing] need (for) / 긴급한 경우에는 in an [in case of] emergency; in an urgent need; in time of stress
▶그는 긴급한 용무로 뉴욕으로 날아갔다 He flew to New York on urgent business.
▶나는 돈이 긴급히 필요하다 I'm in urgent need of money.
▶긴급히 구급차를 불러 주시오 Please call an ambulance immediately.
▶우리는 이 문제에 긴급히 대처하지 않으면 안 된다 We must take emergency steps to deal with this problem.
━경보 체계 an emergency warning system ━대책 《devise》 urgent countermeasures 《against a thing》 ━대통령령 an emergency

기후와 날씨

소풍가는 날
선생님: 내일 비 오면 소풍은 취소된다 The picnic will be canceled if it rains tomorrow.
학생 A: 가랑비일 때는 어떻게 됩니까? What if it's just a light rain?
선생님: 예정대로 간다 In that case, it'll be held as scheduled.
학생 B: 걱정 없어. 일기 예보에 내일 비 올 확률은 10퍼센트니까 I don't think it'll rain. The weather forecast says there's only a 10 percent chance of rain.
학생 A: 그래도 이맘때는 비가 많이 오니까 믿을 수가 없는걸 But you can't rely on that, because it rains a lot at this time of (the) year.
선생님: 지금으로서는 구름 한점 없는 맑은 날씨니까 걱정 없을게다
Well, from looks of the sky, we don't have to worry. It's beautiful; not a cloud in slight.

1. 날씨를 나타내는 주어
(1) It을 주어로 하여
▶비가 올 것 같습니다 It looks like rain. ⇌ It is likely to rain.
▶내일은 맑을 겁니다 It'll be fine tomorrow.
(2) 비·눈·바람 등을 주어로 하여
▶비는 곧 멎을 것이다 The rain will let up soon. ⇌ It will stop raining soon.
▶강풍이 불고 있다 There's strong wind (blowing). ⇌ It's blowing hard.
(3) we나 they를 주어로 하여
▶금년 여름에는 비가 많이 왔다 We have had a lot of rain this summer. ⇌ It has rained a lot this summer.
▶춘천에는 눈이 꽤 많이 온다 They have a lot of snow in Ch'unch'ŏn.
(4) the weather를 주어로 하여
▶날씨가 점점 나빠지고 있다 The weather is getting worse.

2. 날씨의 표현법
(1) 맑음, 흐림, 비
▶會話「참으로 좋은 날씨군요」「정말 그렇군요」"It's a beautiful [lovely] day, isn't it?" "Yes, it sure(ly) is."
▶날씨가 수상해지고 있다 The sky looks threatening.
▶요사이 10일간 비가 오락가락 하고 있다 It has been raining on and off for the past ten days.
▶일기예보에 의하면 저녁에 소나기가 온다고 한다 The weatherman says that we'll get showers this evening.
(2) 기온과 습도
▶금년 여름은 예년에 없이 덥다 This summer is unusually hot.
▶어젯밤은 몹시 무더워서 잠을 잘 수 없었다 It was so hot and humid last night (that) I couldn't sleep well.
▶오늘은 이번 겨울 들어 가장 추운 날입니다 Today is the coldest day we've had this winter.
(3) 바람과 눈과 폭풍우
▶바람이 일고[자고] 있다 The wind is rising [falling].
▶강릉에서는 오늘 첫눈이 내렸다 The first snow of this winter fell today in Kangnŭng.
▶눈보라[태풍] 때문에 열차 운행이 정지되었다 The trains were halted because of the blizzard [typhoon].
▶우박이 내려서 이 지방 농작물에 큰 피해가 있었다 There was hail in this region, and crops were greatly damaged.
▶플로리다에서는 허리케인 앤드루의 내습으로 많은 사망자가 나왔다 Florida was hard hit by Hurricane Andrew; many people were killed.

3. 일기 예보
▶會話「내일의 일기 예보는 어떻습니까?」「비 온 다음에 흐립니다」"What's the weather forecast for tomorrow?" "It'll be rainy, becoming cloudy later."
▶일기 예보가 맞아서 오후부터는 눈이 내렸다 Just as the weather report said, it has begun to snow this afternoon.
▶호남지방은 맑고 곳에 따라 흐릴 것입니다 The Honam area will be fair, with scattered clouds.
▶청주는 흐리고 때때로 비가 올 것입니다 Ch'ŏngju will be cloudy with intermittent [occasional] rain.
▶내일의 최고 기온은 26℃, 최저 기온은 18℃로 예상됩니다 The high (temperature) for tomorrow will be 26℃, and the low 18℃.

---

presidential decree —동의 ((make, move)) an urgent motion; ((put)) an emergency resolution —명령 an emergency order; (美) a rush order —물자 emergency goods —발진(發進) scrambling; a scramble —신호 an urgency signal —조치 ((take, issue)) emergency measures —착륙 an emergency landing —체포 (an) arrest without (a) warrant : 긴급 체포되다 be arrested on the spot —피난 emergency evacuation ((from somewhere)) —회의 ((hold, convoke)) an urgent [emergency] conference [meeting] ((of the Cabinet))
긴급사태 緊急事態 a state of emergency; an emergency
♦긴급 사태를 선언하다 declare a state of emergency / 긴급 사태에 대비하다 provide for emergencies
▷긴급 사태 발생 An emergency has arisen.
▷대통령은 긴급 사태를 선포했다 The President proclaimed a state of emergency.
긴말 a long [lengthy] boring talk; a tedious [long-winded] talk; a screed; a yarn
♦긴말을 늘어놓다 tell a long boring story; spin yarn
▶긴말은 하지 않겠습니다 I'll not bother you with a long talk. ⇌ I shall not enlarge [expa-

tiate] upon the subject.
　―긴말하다 give a tedious talk 《to》; speak long-windedly [lengthily]; dwell on *sth*
긴맛 〔貝〕 a razor clam [shell]; a solen
긴밀하다 緊密― close; intimate; tight; tightly knit 《alliance》
　♦긴밀한 접촉 close touch / 긴밀히 협력[제휴]하여 in close cooperation 《with》 / 긴밀한 연락을 취하다 keep in close contact 《with》
　▶귀국과의 긴밀한 유대가 필요합니다 We need close ties with your country.
　▶나는 내 사촌과 긴밀히 연락을 취하고 있다 I am in close contact [touch] with my cousin.
　▶그들은 긴밀히 협력하고 있다 They are in close cooperation. ⇌ They are cooperating closely.
긴박하다 緊迫― tense; acute; strained
　♦양국 간의 긴박한 관계 strained [tense] relations between the two countries / 긴박한 정세[공기] a tense situation [atmosphere] / 긴박한 국제 정세를 완화시키다 ease the tense international situation / 긴박해지다 become tense [acute]; grow strained
　▶긴박한 국제 관계가 어느 정도 완화되었다 A tense international relationship has become less acute [has been lessened] to some extent.
　▶국제 정세가 긴박해졌다 The international situation has become tense.
　▶양국 관계가 점점 더 긴박해지고 있다 The relation between the two countries are growing more and more strained.
긴병 ―病 a long [protracted] illness; a lingering [lengthy] disease; a siege of illness
　♦긴병을 앓다 suffer from a long [chronic] illness; be sick in bed for a long time
　▶아버님은 긴병에서 막 회복되셨다 My father has just recovered from a long illness.
긴병에 효자 없다 (속담) A protracted illness wears out filial devotion. ⇌ Enthusiasm is short-lived.
긴사설 ―辭說 〈수다〉a long tedious speech; a lengthy [long-winded] talk
　♦긴사설을 늘어놓다 give a long tedious talk 《to》; spin a yarn
　▶그녀는 친구와 전화로 긴사설을 늘어놓았다 She had a long talk with her friend on the telephone.
긴요하다 緊要― important; vital; 〈필요하다〉 necessary 《to》; 〈불가결하다〉 essential 《to》; indispensable 《to》
　♦긴요한 문제 a problem of vital importance
　▶그 계획의 성공을 위해서는 우리들의 협력이 긴요하다 Our cooperation is vital to the success of the scheme.
　▶그것이 긴요한 점이다 That is a point of vital importance.
　▶너는 긴요한 것을 잘 잊는다 You easily forget important matters.
　▶나는 긴요한 때에 병이 났다 I got sick at the critical moment.
　▶그것은 우리의 일상 생활에 긴요하지 않다 It is not essential to our daily life.
긴장 緊張 tension; strain; tenseness

|解說| ***tension***은 정신적인 긴장·불안감뿐만 아니라 대인관계나 정세 등의 긴장상태를 말한다. 뒤의 뜻으로는 흔히 복수형으로 쓰인다. ***strain***은 심신의 중압이나 과로 등에 의한 긴장상태를 말한다.

　♦긴장을 완화하다 relax [ease, slacken, relieve, loosen] the tension; improve the tense [strained] relations 《between》
　▶그는 한꺼번에 긴장이 풀렸다 His strained nerves relaxed all at once.
　▶그의 농담으로 긴장이 풀렸다 His joke relaxed me.
　▶양국간의 긴장은 완화될 것이다 The tension between the two countries will be loosened.
　―긴장하다 become [get] tense; be strained [tense]; (口) be on edge; get [feel] nervous; be on the strain
　♦긴장한 표정[목소리] a strained [nervous] look [voice] / 긴장된 국경지대 a tense border area [region] / 지나치게 긴장하다 overstrain *oneself*; be strained to the limit / 긴장시키다 strain; tense; make tense; key [wind] up
　▶그 선수는 시합을 앞두고 긴장하고 있다 He is strung up before the game.
　▶회의는 긴장된 분위기였다 There was a tense atmosphere in the meeting.
　▶그는 긴장된 얼굴로 상사의 말을 듣고 있었다 He was listening to his superior with a tense look.
　■―도 (lower, ease) the level of 《international》 tension ―병 〔精神病〕 catatonia ―상태 a state of tension
긴장완화 緊張緩和 〈국제간의〉the relaxation [relief] of international tensions; a détente [deitá:nt]; a thaw
　♦동서간의 긴장 완화 the East-West détente
　▶우리는 한반도의 긴장 완화를 위해 최선의 노력을 다하겠습니다 We shall make every effort to relax [ease] tensions on the Korean Peninsula.
긴지름 〔數〕 the major diameter
긴축 緊縮 (strict) economy; retrenchment; curtailment; 〈통화의〉deflation; 〈생활의〉austerity; belt tightening
　♦재정의 긴축 retrenchment in finance / 긴축 생활을 하다 lead an austere life; practice austerity
　―긴축하다 〈절약하다〉economize; 〈삭감하다〉retrench; curtail; cut down 《expenses》; 〈통화를〉deflate
　♦금융을 긴축하다 tighten the money market / 재정을 긴축하다 cut down on spending; retrench 《the nation's》 finances
　■―경영 belt-tightening management ―예산 an austerity budget ―정책 《adopt》 a retrenchment [curtailment] policy; a policy of retrenchment [austerity]; a belt-tightening [tight-financing] policy
긴축재정 緊縮財政 a reduced [curtailed] budget ♦긴축 재정 정책 a tight-money policy
　▶우리는 긴축 재정을 시행하지 않으면 안 된다 We have to tighten our belts.

긴치마 a long skirt; a maxi(skirt)
긴팔원숭이 《動》 a long-armed ape; a gibbon
긴하다 緊— 〈필요하다〉 necessary (to); indispensable (to); essential (to); 〈유용하다〉 useful; 〈긴급하다〉 urgent; pressing
♦긴한 때 (in) time [hour] of need / 긴한 문제 a very important problem / 긴한 물건 a useful object to have around; a necessary [an indispensable] article / 긴한 사람 an indispensable person
▶ 방금 긴한 볼일이 생각났다 I have just remembered something I have to do.
▶ 곧 해결해야 할 긴한 문제들이 있다 There are urgent problems which require immediate settlement.
▶ 아버지는 긴한 용무로 서울에 가셨다 My father went to Seoul on urgent business.
▶ 긴히 부탁드릴 일이 있어서 왔습니다 I have come with an urgent favor to ask of you.

긷다 〈물을〉 draw; pump
♦단수에 대비하여 식수를 좀 길어다 놓다 set aside some drinking water in case the water is shut off
▶ 그는 우물에서 두레박으로 물을 길었다 He drew water from the well with a bucket.

길¹ 1 〈통행로〉 a way; a road; 〈거리〉 a street; a thoroughfare; an avenue; 〈가도〉 a highway; a highroad; 〈통로〉 a passage; 〈코스〉 a route; 〈좁은 길〉 a path; a lane; 〈정원 등의〉 a walk; 〈산속의〉 a pass; 〈밟아 다진〉 a track
〈갈은〉 길은 거기서 두 갈래로 갈라져 있었다 There was a fork in the road there.
〈길을〉 길을 가다[걷다] walk along the road / 길을 가르쳐 주다 tell *sb* the way (to); 〈안내하여 또는 지도상에서〉 show *sb* the way (to) / 길을 고르다 level a road / 길을 내다 cut [open] a way (through a forest) / 길을 막다 stand in *sb's* way; bar the way; block the passage / 길을 묻다 ask *one's* [the] way (to a place); ask *sb* for directions (to); ask *sb* how to get (to) / 길을 비켜주다 make way [room] (for); give way (to); 〈군중이 좌우로 갈라져서〉 part; open (out) / 길을 잘못 들다 take the wrong way; go wrong way
▶ 큰 트럭이 길을 막고 있었다 A huge truck was in [blocking] our way.
▶ 그는 시내에서 길을 잃었다 He lost his way [was lost] in the town.
▶ 워싱턴 광장으로 가는 길을 가르쳐 주십시오 Will you tell me the way to Washington Square?
〈길에(서)〉 길에서 on [in] the street [road]
▶ 우리 집에서 학교로 가는 길에 우체국이 있다 There is a post office on the road I take to school.
▶ 길에서 뜻밖에 에밀리를 만났다 I ran into Emily on (英) in the street.
〈길로〉 돌아갈 때는 다른 길로 가고 싶다 I want to go another way [take a different route] on our way home.
2 〈여정〉 journey; 〈거리〉 (a) distance
♦인생길 the journey of life; life's journey / 하룻[이틀]길 a day's [two day's] distance / 10킬로미터의 길을 가다 go a distance of ten kilometers / 길을 떠나다 start [set out] on a journey
▶ 어두워졌으므로 우리는 길을 서둘렀다 As it was getting dark, we quickened our pace [step].
▶ 10킬로미터의 길이라면 3시간에 충분히 갈 수 있다 I can easily cover [walk] ten kilometers in three hours.
3 〈도중〉 ♦학교로 가는[에서 돌아오는] 길에 on *one's* way to [from] school
4 〈진로〉 a way; a course; 〈경로〉 a route; a channel; 〈수단〉 a means; a step
♦살아갈 길 a means of living / 성공의 길 the road [way] to success / 취할[택할] 길 a course to take; a course of action to follow / 후진을 위해 길을 열어 주다 make way [step aside, make room] for younger people
▶ 그것은 위험한 길이다 That's a dangerous course to take.
▶ 이것만이 당신이 살아갈 길이다 This is the only way for you to live.
▶ 그 밖에 달리 취할 길이 없다 That is the only course [way, alternative] left open to us. ⇒ We have no choice but to do so.
▶ 세계 평화의 길은 멀다 We have a long way to go [road to travel] toward world peace.
5 〈의무〉 a duty; 〈도의〉 a moral principle [doctrine]; 〈가르침〉 teachings; 〈진리〉 truth; 〈도리〉 reason
♦예수의 길을 따르다 follow the teachings of Jesus / 부처의 길을 전하다 preach the way of Buddhism / 길을 찾다 seek after truth / 올바른 길에서 벗어나다 stray from the path of virtue; (口) leave [stray from] the straight and narrow
▶ 그것이 자식으로서의 길이다 That's filial duty.
6 〈분야·직업〉 a line; a career; a profession
▶ 그는 그 길에 밝다[그 길의 전문가다] He is an authority on that subject [an expert in that field].
7 〈숙련〉 skill, dexterity

길² 〈품질의 등급〉 a class; a grade
♦윗길의 of superior grade [quality]; first-class; superior; choice / 아랫길의 of lower grade [quality]; inferior
▶ 그 물건은 윗길[아랫길]이다 The goods are of good [inferior] quality.
▶ [會話] 「좀더 나은 것을 보여 주세요」「이보다 윗길은 없습니다」 "Show me a better one." "This is the best we have."

길³ 〈옷의〉 the body (part) (of a garment)

길⁴ 1 〈사람 키의 길이〉 the height of a man; 〈깊이〉 a fathom
♦천 길 골짜기 an unfathomable ravine / 깊이 두 길 되는 물 water two fathoms deep / 한 길이나 되는 담장 man-high [man-tall] fence
2 〈길이의 단위〉 a kil

길⁵ 〈질(帙)〉 a set of volumes ♦논어 한 길 a set of the (Confucian) Analects ▶이 책은 길이 네 권이다 This book is complete in 4 volumes.

길가 the roadside; the wayside
♦길가의 roadside; wayside / 길가의 꽃[여인

길거리 a street; a road; an avenue; a thoroughfare
♦길거리의 예인[행상인] a street performer [vendor] / 길거리의 점장이 a street fortune-teller / 길거리를 쏘다니다[헤매다] roam [wander] about the streets
▶그가 죽으면 그의 가족은 길거리에 나앉을 것이다 His death will turn his family adrift.
▶길거리에서 놀지 마라 Don't play on [in] the street.

길고 짧은 것은 대 보아야 안다 〈속담〉 A real test will prove who [which] is better [greater].

길길이 1〈매우 높이〉 (pile up) high; to a great height; in a heap [pile]
♦불이 길길이 치솟다 go high up in flames
▶책이 길길이 쌓여 있다 Books are piled up high.
▶갈대가 길길이 자라고 있다 Reeds are growing tall.
2〈몹시〉 extremely; to the highest degree
♦화가 나서 길길이 뛰다 get hopping mad; (口) hit the ceiling [roof]
▶그는 그 소식을 듣고 화가 나서 길길이 뛰었다 He got as mad as a hornet at the news. ⇒ He was seething with rage at the news.

길꾼 〈노름의〉 a skilled gambler [gamester]

길나다 1〈익숙해지다〉 become accustomed to ⇨ 길들다 2 2〈윤나다〉 get [take on] a polish ⇨ 길들다 3

길년 吉年〈결혼하기 좋은 해〉an auspicious year (for marriage); 〈혼인하기 좋은 나이〉 the marriageable age

길눈 a sense of direction ♦길눈이 밝다[어둡다] have a good [a bad, no] sense of direction

길다 1〈길이가〉 long; lengthy
♦긴 연필 a long pencil / 긴 치마 a trailing skirt / 길게 눕다 lie at full length; lie down / 길게 하다 lengthen; make longer; draw long [out]; extend
▶그녀는 머리가 길다 She has a long hair.
▶그 소매는 2인치가 더 길다 The sleeve is two inches too long.
▶이 기사는 너무 길다 This article is a bit too lengthy.
2〈시간·공간적으로〉 long; prolonged (오래 끈)
♦긴 세월 계속되는 우정[습관] friendship [a custom] of long standing [many years]/ 긴 장마 a long rainy season / 길어야 3일 three days at (the) longest / 긴 눈으로 보면 in the long run
▶예술은 길고 인생은 짧다 Art is long, life is short.
▶그는 매우 긴 설교를 했다 He gave us a lengthy sermon.
▶해가 길어지고 있다 The days are getting longer.
▶길게 수다를 떨어서 미안합니다 I am sorry I've taken up so much of your time.

길동무 〈길벗〉a fellow traveler; a traveling companion
♦길동무가 되다 (happen to meet and) travel together (with); fall into company (with)
▶여행은 길동무, 세상은 인정 (속담) In traveling, companionship [good company]; in life, kindness [good will].
▶여행에는 길동무가 있어야 즐겁다 Traveling is more enjoyable with companions [company] (than alone).
▶그 사람 같은 좋은 길동무는 매우 드물다 Such a good traveling companion as he is quite rare.
—길동무하다 travel [go] with sb as a companion; travel together (with); keep sb company
▶나는 두 사람과 길동무하여 길을 떠났다 I started with two traveling companions.

길드 〈동업조합〉 a guild ♦길드의 회원 a guild member; a guildsman ♦직업— a trade [craft] guild ■—사회주의 guild socialism —상인 a guild merchant

길들다 1〈동물이〉 become [grow] tame; 〈가축으로〉 become domesticated
♦길든 고양이 a tame [housebroken] cat / 길들지 않은 undomesticated; untamed; tameless; unbroken (horse); wild
▶앵무새는 잘 길든다 Parrots get tame easily.
▶그 사람이 기르는 매는 잘 길들었다 His pet hawk is quite tame.
▶길든 곰이로군요 You have a tame bear.
▶참새는 좀처럼 길들지 않는다 Sparrows won't become tame.
2〈익숙해지다〉 get [be] used (to); grow [become] accustomed to [familiar with]; become inured to (hardships); become experienced in (teaching); 〈연장 등이〉 be broken in; be well used
♦길든 만년필 a broken-in [well-used] fountain pen / 사치에 길들다 be lapped in luxury
▶구두가 발에 길들었다 My feet got used to the shoes.
▶연장들은 모두 길들어 있었다 All the tools were well used [broken-in].
3〈윤나다〉 take [get, admit] a polish; get glossy [lustrous]; get [show] a gloss [shine, luster]
♦노상 닦아서 길들다 get a polish from constant rubbing
▶마루를 매일 닦았더니 길들었다 Daily wiping made the floor glossy.

길들이다 1〈동물을〉 tame; domesticate; reclaim (a hawk); charm (a snake); 〈훈련시키다〉 train (a dog)
♦야수를 길들이는 사람 a tamer of wild animals / 길들인 동물 a trained animal; 〈영화 등에 출연하는〉 (美) a property animal / 말을 길들이다 break in [gentle] a horse
▶그는 사자를 길들였다 He tamed a wild lion.
▶호랑이를 길들이려면 끈기가 있어야 한다 It takes patience to tame tigers.
▶그는 돌고래를 길들여 재주를 부리게 했다 He trained a dolphin to do tricks.
2〈익게 하다〉 inure; habituate; accustom;

make *sb* used [accustomed, inured] to *sth*; 〈능숙하게 하다〉 make *oneself* [*sb*] skillful [skilled, proficient] (in, at)

♦길들인 연장 a well-used tool / 몸을 새로운 환경에 길들이다 acclimate [acclimatize] *oneself* to the new environment / 몸을 추위에 길들이다 inure [accustom] *oneself* to cold
▶ 미국 영화를 보고 귀를 길들여라 Train your ear by going to American movies.
▶ 멀리 도보 여행을 하기 전에는 반드시 새 신을 길들여야 한다 Before going on a long hike, you must break in [get used to] your new shoes.
▶ 프라이팬은 오래 쓸수록 잘 길들여진다 The longer you use a frying pan, the better it becomes for cooking.
3 〈윤나게 하다〉 gloss; glaze; bring out the luster; put a gloss [polish] on; polish up; make (it) glossy
♦가구를 닦아서 길들이다 polish furniture [give a polish to furniture] by rubbing it / 마루를 닦아 길들이다 polish up [bring out the luster of] a floor

길라잡이 a guide
길래 〈오래도록〉 long; forever; for good
-길래 〈-기에〉 as ⇨ -기에; 〈-관데〉 so... that ⇨ -관데
길례 吉例 a time-honored custom ♦길례에 따라 according to time-honored custom
길로틴 a guillotine ⇨ 단두대(斷頭臺)
길리다 〈길러지다〉 be bred [fed]; be brought up; be reared [raised]; be nursed [fostered]; be cultivated (식물이)

♦모유로 길리다 be breast-fed / 우유로 길리다 be bottle-fed; be brought up on the bottle / 유모 손에 길리다 be fed by a wet nurse
▶ 그 아이는 순전히 이모 손에 길리었다 The child was brought up entirely by his aunt.

길마 〈소의 등에 얹는〉 a packsaddle ♦길마짓다[지우다] put [fix] a packsaddle on (an ox)
길모퉁이 a street corner; a turn
♦길모퉁이의 가게[우체국] a store [post office] on the street corner / 길모퉁이에(서) at [on] a street corner
▶ 그 여자는 두번째 길모퉁이를 오른쪽으로 돌았다 She turned right at the second corner.
▶ 그 두 사람은 길모퉁이에서 이야기를 나누었다 The two talked with each other at a street corner.

길목 1 〈중요한 어귀〉 an important [a key] position [place]; 〈군사상의〉 a strategic point
♦길목마다 at every strategic point; at important positions [points] / 길목을 지키다 fortify the points of strategic importance; station troops at strategic points
2 〈길모퉁이〉 a street corner; a turning of a road; (at) a turn in a road; (at) a bend of a road; a road bend
♦길목을 돌아서 두번째 집 the second house round the corner / 길목에 있는 가게 a corner store / 길목을 돌다 turn [go round] the corner; round a bend / 길목에 가게를 내다 open a shop on a street corner
▶ 모든 길목은 적군이 봉쇄하고 있다 All the street corners are blocked by the enemy troops.

길몽 吉夢 a lucky [an auspicious] dream; a dream of good [lucky] omen
길바닥 the roadbed; 〈길 가운데〉 the middle of a road ♦길바닥에 쓰러지다 fall down on the road; sink to the ground / 길바닥에서 돈을 줍다 find money on the road
길벗 a fellow traveler ⇨ 길동무
길보 吉報 good [auspicious] news; joyful [glad] tidings ♦길보를 가져오다 bring *sb* the good news (of)
▶ 그거 길보다 That's good news.
▶ 자네에게 길보가 있네 I have some (very) good news for you.
길사 吉事 〈좋은 일〉 an auspicious [a happy] event; 〈혼례〉 a wedding (ceremony)
길상 吉相 〈좋은 상〉 a lucky face; lucky physiognomy
길섶 the shoulder [edge] of a road; the roadside; the wayside
길손 a traveler; a tourist; a wayfarer; a stranger
길쌈 weaving (by hand); handweaving; handloom-weaving **—길쌈하다** weave by hand; handweave; make cloth
길안내 —案內 〈일〉 guidance; 〈사람〉 a guide **—길안내하다** show *sb* the way (to); guide (*sb* to a place); act as (a) guide
길어지다 lengthen; become [grow, be made] longer; 〈해 등이〉 draw out; extend
▶ 낮이 밤보다 길어졌다 The day has begun to gain on the night.
▶ 해가 길어지기 시작했다 The days have begun to draw out.
길운 吉運 (good) luck; good fortune; (美) a lucky break
길이¹ 〈긴 정도〉 length (of *one's* coat)

♦길이 100미터의 배 a ship 100 meters long [in length]; a 100-meter-long ship / 무릎 길이의 《an overcoat》 of knee length / 길이를 구하다 〔幾〕 rectify (an arc) / 길이를 줄이다 shorten the length (of a skirt) / 판자를 1미터 길이로 자르다 saw a board in length of a meter / 끈을 같은 길이로 세 토막으로 자르다 cut the string into three pieces of equal length
▶ 그 프로는 두 시간 길이였다 The program was two hours long.
▶ 〔會話〕 「그 밧줄은 길이가 얼마나 됩니까?」 「20미터입니다」 "How long is [What is the length of] the rope?" "It is 20 meters (long). ⇌ Twenty meters."
▶ 이 보트는 저것과 길이가 같다 This boat is as long as [has the same length as] that one.
▶ 그것들은 길이가 다 비슷비슷하다 They are about the same length.
▶ 이 막대기는 길이가 네 것의 2배다 This stick is twice as long as yours.
길이² 〈오래오래〉 (for) long; for a long time; 〈영원히〉 forever; eternally; everlastingly
♦길이 이름을 남기다 immortalize *one's* fame [name] / 길이 보존하다 preserve *sth* for good
▶ 그의 이름은 청사에 길이 빛날 것이다 His

길 안내

길 묻기의 기본 대화
A: 실례지만 이 근처에 은행이 있습니까? Excuse me, but is there a bank in this neighborhood?
B: 예, 있지요. 여기서 걸어서 5분 거리입니다 Yes, there is. It's a five-minute walk from here.
A: 어떻게 가야 하는지 가르쳐 주시겠습니까? Could you tell me how to get there?
B: 그러지요. 이 길을 곧 바로 가다가 두번째 신호에서 좌회전 하세요. 바로 앞에 있습니다 Certainly. Go straight up this street, and turn left at the second traffic light. You'll see it straight ahead.
A: 두번째라면 이 신호도 포함해서 말입니까? When you said the second, did you include this light?
B: 아니오, 이 다음에서 두번째입니다 No, the second one from here.
A: 대단히 감사합니다. 영어를 아주 잘하셔서 많은 도움이 되었습니다 Thank you very much. It was a great help that you speak English so well.

1. 길을 물을 때
▶ 실례지만 역은 어딥니까? Excuse me, but where's the station?
▶ 실례합니다. 시청으로 가는 길을 안내해 주시겠습니까? Excuse me. Could you show me the way to the City Hall?
▶ 박물관은 어떻게 가면 됩니까? How can I get to the museum?
▶ 미안합니다. 서울고등학교를 찾고 있습니다만 Pardon me. I'm looking for Seoul High School.
▶ 용산역은 이 길로 가면 됩니까? Is this the way to Yongsan Station?
▶ 귀찮게 해서 미안합니다. 길을 잃었습니다. 이곳은 무슨 거리입니까? I'm sorry to trouble you. I'm lost. What street am I on now?
▶ 구청에서 가장 가까운 지하철역은 어디입니까? What's the closest subway station to the ward office?

2. 길을 가르쳐 줄 때
▶ 버스 정류장은 파출소 정면에 있습니다 The bus stop is in front of the police box.
▶ 그것은 병원 옆[뒤]입니다 It's next to [behind] the hospital.
▶ 소방서는 극장 (길 건너) 반대쪽입니다 The fire station is across from the theater.
▶ 그 약국은 슈퍼마켓을 지나서 모퉁이에 있습니다 That pharmacy is on the corner past the supermarket.
▶ 다음 모퉁이를 우회전하여 100미터쯤 가면 그 치과 의원이 있습니다 Turn right at the next corner and go a hundred meters, and you'll find the dentist's office.
▶ 그 사무실의 정면에 커다란 영어 광고판이 있습니다 There is a large English billboard in front of the office.
▶ 공교롭게도 나는 이곳을 잘 모릅니다. 누구 다른 사람에게 물어보십시오 I'm sorry, but I don't know this area. You should ask somebody else.

3. 소요시간・거리
▶ [會話]「KBS까지 얼마나 걸립니까?」「걸어서 10분 정도입니다」 "How long will it take to get to KBS?" "It's about ten minutes' walk."
▶ 차를 타면 불과 2,3분입니다 It takes only a couple of minutes if you go by car.
▶ 김포공항까지의 거리는 얼마나 됩니까? How far is it (from here) to Kimp'o Airport?
▶ 집에서 학교까지 약 2km 된다 It is about 2 kilometers from our house to the school.

4. 탈것에 관한 안내
▶ [會話]「서울역에 되도록 빨리 도착하려면 어떻게 하면 될까요?」「지하철이 가장 좋을 겁니다」 "What's the fastest way to get to Seoul Station?" "I think the subway is (the) fastest."
▶ 그 역에 가려면 완행 열차로 다음 역에 가서 급행 열차로 갈아타면 돼 To get to that station, it's best to take a local train to the next station, and then transfer to an express train.
▶ [會話]「용산은 이미 지났습니까?」「아니오, 앞으로 두 정거장 남았습니다」 "Have we already passed Yongsan?" "No, there are two more stations to go."
▶ 신촌 가는 버스를 타시려면 길을 건너가야 합니다 If you want to get a bus for Shinch'on, you have to cross the street.

---

name will be immortalized [long noted] in history.

길일 吉日 〈좋은 날〉 a lucky day; an auspicious [a propitious] day
♦ 길일을 택하다 choose a lucky day; choose a day of good omen
▶ 두 사람은 길일을 택하여 결혼식을 올렸다 The couple held [celebrated] the wedding on a lucky day.

길잡이 1 〈길라잡이〉 a guide ♦ 길잡이 서다 act as (a) guide; guide [direct] 《sb to a place》
▶ 이번 도난 사건은 내부자가 길잡이가 되었을지도 모른다 It is possible that an insider acted as a guide in this theft.
2 〈도로 표지〉 a guidepost; a signpost; a waymark; a finger post
3 〈지침(서)〉 a guideline; a guide(book) 《to》; a handbook; a manual
♦ 문제 해결의 길잡이 an index to the solution of a problem / 초보자의 길잡이가 되다 serve as a guide to [provide guidance for] the beginners
■─별 a guiding star

길조 吉兆 〈좋은 징조〉 a good [an auspicious] omen; a lucky [favorable] sign; a happy augury ♦ 길조가 보이다 be of good omen
▶ 그것은 내게 길조다 It augurs well for me.

길짐승 〈네발 짐승〉 a quadruped; a four-footed animal; 〈모피 짐승〉 a furred animal; (총칭) furs

길쭉길쭉하다 (all) longish; (all of them) somewhat long; all rather long
♦ 길쭉길쭉한 막대기 longish sticks / 대나무를 길쭉길쭉하게 자르다 cut a piece of bamboo in long sections

길쭉이 somewhat long ♦ 길쭉이 자르다 cut (a plank) rather long [a little longer]

길쭉하다 longish; somewhat long
♦ 길쭉한 나뭇조각 a sliver / 길쭉한 지팡이 a longish stick / 길쭉한 호리병박 a long-necked gourd / 얼굴이 길쭉하다 have a longish face

길쯔막하다 somewhat long; rather long; quite longish

길쯤이 somewhat long; rather long

길찍길찍하다 =길쭉길쭉하다

길찍이 =길쭉이

길찍하다 =길쭉하다

길차다 〈쭉쭉 뻗다〉 very tall; overgrown; 〈우거지다〉 thick [dense] (forest); rank

길하다 吉 〈auspicious; propitious; good; fortunate; lucky ▶ 내 점괘가 길하게 나왔다 Good fortune was foretold for me.

길항 拮抗 〈맞버팀〉 rivalry; contention; competition; antagonism; a struggle for supremacy ―**길항하다** compete [contend, cope] (with); rival; be in conifilct (with); stand against / struggle with *sb* for supremacy
■―근(筋) 〔解〕 an antagonist ―작용(生) antagonism

길흉 吉凶 good or ill [bad] luck; fortune
♦ 길흉을 점치다 tell *sb's* fortune; read good omens or bad (from natural phenomena) / 자신의 길흉을 점치다 read *one's* own fortune
▶ 옛날 사람들은 동물의 뼈를 태워 길흉을 점쳤다 Ancient people baked bones of animals to divine whether fortune would be good or bad.

김¹ 1〈수증기〉steam; vapor
♦ 목욕탕[온천]에서 나는 김 steam (rising) from the bath [a hot spring] / 김이 무럭무럭 나는 밥 (a bowl of) steaming(-hot) rice / 김이 나다[을 내다] steam; reek; emit [give off, send up] steam / 김을 쐬다 fume; fumigate
▶ 난로 위의 주전자에서 김이 난다 The kettle is steaming [giving off steam] on the stove.
▶ 수프 접시에서 김이 났다 Steam rose from the plate of soup.
▶ 욕실 거울에 김이 서렸다 Steam formed on the bathroom mirror. ⇌ The bathroom mirror (got) steamed up.
▶ 會話 「창문을 열어 욕실에서 김이 빠지게 해라」「알았어요, 아빠」 "Open the window and let the steam out of the bathroom." "OK, Dad."
2 ⇨ 입김, 콧김
3〈냄새〉flavor; savor; smell; fume; 〈맛〉taste
♦ 김이새다 (비유) lose interest [enthusiasm] (in); *one's* enthusiasm dies down / 김새게 하다 dampen [cool down] *sb's* enthusiasm [zeal] (for) / 김이 빠지다 ⇨ 김빠지다
▶ 그녀가 반응이 없어 그는 완전히 김이 샜다 Her unresponsiveness was enough to cool down his ardor.

김² 〈해태·건태〉 laver; natural [dried] laver

〚解説〛 김의 역어로 *seaweed*를 쓰는 경우가 많지만 이는 해초 일반을 가리키는 말이다. *laver*는 바닷말에 가까운 식용 해초. 따라서 우리 나라의 말린 김을 얘기할 때는 laver를 사용하는 것이 좋다.

♦ 맛김 seasoned laver / 김 한 장 a sheet of dried laver / 김을 양식하다 grow [cultivate] laver / 김을 재다[굽다] season [toast] dried laver
■―양식 laver farming ―양식장 a laver farm ―(초)밥 (vinegared) rice rolled in dried laver

김³ 〈기회〉 an occasion; an opportunity; a chance
♦ 펜을 든 김에 while *one* is writing / 홧김에 in a fit of anger / 말이 난 김에 말씀드립니다만 I take this occasion to say...; While I am about it, I must say... / 나선 김에 들르다 look [drop] in on *one's* way
▶ 그와 통화하는 김에 나는 그녀의 소식을 물었다 When I talked with him on [over] the phone, I asked about her.
▶ 다리미질하는 김에 내 청바지도 좀 부탁해요 You can iron my jeans while you are at it. (> can은 가벼운 명령을 의미함)
▶ 외출하는 김에 뭐 해드릴 일 없습니까? Do you want anything done while I am out?
▶ 여행 이야기가 나온 김에 하는 말인데요, 유럽엔 가본 적이 있습니까? Speaking of traveling, have you ever been to Europe?
▶ 술김에 그는 상사에게 불만을 늘어놓았다 Emboldened by drink [Under the influence of alcohol], he complained to his superior.

김매다 weed (a field); remove [root out] weeds; pick weeds out (of)

김빠지다 1〈술 등이〉run vapid; become flat [insipid]; go stale; 〈차 등이〉lose its flavor; become flavorless
♦ 김빠진 맥주 vapid beer; flat beer
▶ 이 위스키는 김빠졌다 This wiskey tastes flat.
2〈일이〉flag; become dull; lose (its) relish; fall off in interest
♦ 김빠진 농담 a flat joke / 김빠진 대화 an inanimate conversation; a wishy-washy talk / 김빠진 문체 washy style / 김빠진 대답을 하다 answer vaguely [absently, in a half-hearted manner]
▶ 나는 그 선생의 김빠진 강의가 마음에 안든다 I don't like his flat lectures.

김장 〈담그는 일〉 *kimch'i*-making [preparing *kimch'i*, pickling vegetables] for the winter; 〈담근 것〉 *kimch'i* prepared for the winter ―**김장하다** prepare [make] *kimch'i* for (use during) the winter; pickle vegetables for winter use
■―감[거리] *kimch'i* stuff; vegetables and seasoning materials for *kimch'i* ―독 *kimch'i* jar [pot]; 〈김장감을 절이는〉 a pickle tub; a steeper ―밭 〈내다 파는〉 a truck farm [garden] for *kimch'i*; a kitchen garden ―철 the

kimch'i-making season; the time for pickled vegetables
김 치 *kimch'i*; pickled vegetables; Korean pickles
♦익은[덜 익은, 신] 김치 mellow [rare, sour] *kimch'i* / 김치를 담그다 prepare [make] *kimch'i*; pickle [salt] vegetables
■ 무[배추, 오이]— radish root [cabbage, cucumber] *kimch'i* [pickles] 보쌈— wrapped-up [bundle] *kimch'i*. ■—찌개 pork stew with *kimch'i*; *kimch'i* stew [soup]
김칫국 *kimch'i* juice ♦김칫국부터 마시다 count (*one's*) chickens before they are hatched; sell the skin before *one* has caught [killed] the bear [lion]
깁 silk gauze; silk
깁다 〈헝겊을 대어〉 patch (up) 《a coat》; do patchwork; 〈꿰매다〉 stitch
♦누덕 누덕 기운 양말 socks darned over and over again / 기운 옷[바지] patched clothes [trousers] / 해진 곳을 깁다 darn [stitch up] a rent / 신을 깁다 mend *one's* shoes / 터진[찢어진] 곳을 깁다 patch a tear
▶어머니는 내 낡은 바지를 헝겊을 대어 기우셨다 Mother put a patch on my old trousers.
깁스 [〈독〉Gips] 〈재료〉gyps.; gypsum; plaster of Paris; 〈석고 형〉 a plaster cast
♦깁스를 하다 wear a (plaster) cast; be put in a cast
▶그 사람은 팔에 깁스를 하고 있다 He has [wears] a cast on his arm. ⇒ He's got his arm in a cast. ⇌ His arm is in a cast.
■—붕대 a plaster bandage [cast]; a cast
깃¹ 〈외양간 등에 까는〉 litter
♦깃을 깔다 litter down 《a horse [stable]》; spread litter [straw bedding]
▶마구간에는 깨끗한 깃이 듬뿍 깔려 있었다 The stable was well littered down with fresh straw.
깃² 〈새의〉 a feather; a plume; (총칭) plumage
♦깃이 나 있는 feathered / 아직 깃이 나지 않은 unfledged / 깃이 나다 fledge / 깃이 빠지다 shed feathers; feathers come off / 깃을 갈다 molt / 깃을 다듬다 《a bird》 preen [plume] its feathers [itself]; smooth down the feathers / 깃을 뽑다 pluck feathers 《from a fowl》 / 깃으로 장식하다 decorate with a feather; wear a feather
▶닭이 깃을 곤두세웠다 The chicken ruffled up feathers.
깃³ **1** 〈옷깃〉 a collar; 〈접은〉 lapels; 〈한복의〉 a neckband
♦깃이 달린 블라우스 a blouse with a collar / 깃이 없는 코트 a collarless coat / 양복 깃에 다는 배지 a lapel badge / 깃을 달다 sew a collar on a coat / 깃에 꽃을 달다 wear a flower in *one's* lapel
▶바람이 너무 차가워서 나는 코트 깃을 세웠다 The wind was so cold that I turned [pulled] my coat collar up.
2 〈이불깃〉 the upper strip on the outside of a quilt
깃⁴ 〈화살의〉 a feather (of an arrow); a wing
♦화살에 깃을 달다 feather an arrow

깃⁵ 〈부싯깃〉 tinder; touchwood; amadou [ǽmədùː]; (美) punk
깃대 旗— a flagpole; a flagstaff
♦깃대를 세우다 set up a flagpole / 깃대에 기를 달다 run a flag up the flagpole
깃들다 build a nest ⇨ 깃들이다
깃들이다 〈새가〉 nest; build [put up] a nest; roost; (비유) lodge; dwell
▶건전한 정신은 건전한 육체에 깃들인다 A sound mind (dwells) in a sound body.
▶새들이 이 나무에 깃들였다 Some birds nest [roost, have their nests] in this tree.
깃발 旗— 〈기〉 a flag; a banner; 〈군기〉 the colors; a standard; 〈기에 단 오리〉 ribbons attached to the corners of a flag; 〈구호〉 a slogan; a motto 《*pl*. ~(e)s》
♦자유의 깃발아래 under the slogan of freedom; with "Freedom" as the slogan / 깃발을 휘날리며 with banners flying; with flying colors / 아무의 깃발 아래 모이다 flock to *sb's* standard / 깃발을 올리다 hoist [raise] a flag / 깃발을 내리다 take down a flag; strike [lower] a flag; (비유)〈항복하다〉throw up *one's* hands
▶그들은 자유의 깃발 아래 싸웠다 They fought under the flag [banner] of freedom.
▶깃발이 바람에 휘날리고 있었다 The flag was flapping [fluttering, flying] in the wind.
▶사람들은 깃발을 흔들며 일행을 환영했다 People waved flags to welcome the party.
깃저고리 〈배내옷〉 collarless [baby] clothes; clothes for a newborn baby
깃주다 litter down ⇨ 깃¹
깃촉 【動】〈날개의〉a barrel; a quill; a calamus 《*pl*. -mi[-mài]》
깃털 a feather; 〈장식용〉 a plume; 〈솜털〉 down; (총칭) plumage
♦깃털이 다 난 새 a full-fledged bird / 깃털처럼 가벼운 as light as a feather / 깃털이 나다 fledge
▶그 새는 깃털 갈이를 했다 The bird molted [shed its feathers].
▶공작은 깃털이 아름답다 Peacocks have beautiful plumage.
▶그는 깃털을 꽂은 모자를 쓰고 있었다 He wore a hat with a plume on it.
■—이불 a feather [down] quilt [bed] —침낭 a down-filled sleeping bag
깃펜 a quill pen; a quill
깊다 **1** 〈깊이가〉 deep 《cave》
♦깊은 골짜기 a deep gorge / 깊은 구멍[우물] a deep hole [well] / 깊은 산[바다]속 the depths of a mountain [the sea] / 깊은 숲 a deep forest / 이 호수의 가장 깊은 곳 the deepest part of this lake / 한없이 깊은 bottomless; fathomless
▶이 연못은 여기가 제일 깊다 This pond is (the) deepest here.
▶잔잔한 물이 깊다 (속담) Still waters run deep.
2 〈뜻·학문이〉 deep; profound
♦깊은 생각 a deep thought; a profound idea / 깊은 애정 deep affections / 깊은 연구 profound studies / 깊은 지식 (a) deep [profound]

knowledge 《of music》
▶내가 한 말은 별 깊은 뜻은 없었다 There wasn't any real [deep] meaning in what I said.
3 〈관계·정분〉 close; fast; intimate; (俗) thick
♦깊은 관계[사이] an intimate [a close] relation
▶그는 그녀와 깊은 사이다 He is deeply involved [in love] with her.
▶그와 너무 깊은 교제는 하지 않는 게 좋다 You had better not to have too much to do with him.
4 〈잠·밤이〉 ♦깊은 밤 the dead of night; midnight / 깊은 잠에 빠지다 fall into a deep [sound, heavy] sleep
▶그녀는 깊은 잠에서 깨어났다 She awoke from her deep sleep.
5 〈계절 등이〉 late ♦깊은 가을 late autumn [(美) fall]; the latter part of autumn / 가을도 깊었다 It is late autumn. ⇌ We are well into autumn.
6 〈상처가〉 serious; deep ♦깊은 상처를 입다 receive a deep wound

깊숙이 deep (down); deeply; far
♦골짜기 깊숙이 들어앉은 집 a house set deep in a valley / 장롱에 깊숙이 넣다 put deep into a chest
▶우리는 적지 깊숙이 침입했다 We went deep into the enemy's territory.
▶그 탐정은 모자를 깊숙이 눌러 쓰고 있었다 The detective wore his hat low [pulled down his hat] (well) over his eyes.
▶그는 의자에 깊숙이 몸을 파묻었다 He sagged deep in the chair.
▶탐험대는 그 나라로 깊숙이 들어갔다 The expedition advanced deep in the country.

깊숙하다 deep; in(ner)most; 〈으슥하다〉 sequestered; secluded; covert
♦깊숙한 동굴[계곡] a deep cave [valley] / 깊숙한 방 a sequestered [secluded] room; an inner room; (美) a back room / 안이 깊숙한 집 a house extending for back / 숲속 깊숙한 곳에 deep inside [in the depths of] the forest

깊어지다 **1** 〈깊이가〉 deepen; become deeper; 〈짙어지다〉 become thick [heavy]; 〈심원해지다〉 become profound; 〈강해지다〉 become intense [strong]
▶그들의 애정은 날이 갈수록 깊어졌다 Their love deepened day by day.
▶이번 여행으로 그 나라에 대한 이해가 깊어졌다 My recent trip deepened my understanding of the country.
▶그로 인해 둘 사이의 감정의 골이 깊어졌다 The gap between the two widened for it.
▶나는 그것에 대한 흥미가 더욱더 깊어졌다 I became more and more interested in it.
▶숲속의 어둠이 깊어져 갔다 The darkness deepened in the woods.
▶의심은 점점 깊어져 갔다 There has prevailed a profound suspicion.
2 〈때가〉 be advanced; be well on; ripen
♦밤이 깊어질 때까지 till the night is far advanced; into the depth of night
▶이제 가을이 깊어졌다 It is late autumn now. ⇌ Autumn is far advanced now. ⇌ We are well into autumn.
▶밤이 깊어지고 있다 The night is getting far advanced.
3 〈관계가〉 grow intimate 《with》; become deeper ♦여자와의 사이가 깊어지다 become deeply in love [thick] with a girl

깊이¹ 〈깊음〉 depth; deepness; profundity
♦바다의 깊이 the depth of the sea / 사상[지식]의 깊이 profundity of thought [knowledge] / 생각의 깊이 profundity of thought / 애정의 깊이 the depth of affection
〈깊이가〉 매우 깊이가 있는 사람 a man of great depth / 깊이가 이 정도인 곳 a place (which is) about this deep / 깊이가 없는 superficial; shallow; lacking depth / 10미터 되는 곳에 at a depth of ten meters
▶그 골짜기는 깊이가 20미터다 The valley has a depth of twenty meters.
▶ 會話 「이 수영장은 깊이가 얼마나 됩니까?」 「2미터 됩니다」 "How deep is this swimming pool?" "It's two meters deep."
▶그의 시에는 깊이가 없다 His poetry lacks [has no] depth [profundity].
▶저 사람은 어딘지 생각에 깊이가 있다 There is something profound [deep] in his thoughts.
〈깊이를〉 깊이를 알 수 없는 심연 a bottomless [fathomless, unfathomable] abyss / 강의 깊이를 재다 measure [sound] the depth of a river; take depth measurements of a river; plumb [sound] a river
▶그의 작품은 인생의 깊이를 느끼게 한다 His works make one feel the profundity of life.

깊이² 〈깊게〉 deep; deeply 《▶주로 비유적 의미로 쓰임》; dead 《asleep》; profoundly; 〈진심으로〉 heartily; sincerely; 〈강하게〉 intensely; strongly; very much
♦깊이 감명받다 be deeply impressed 《by the movie》 / 사건에 깊이 말려들다 go far into an affair / 깊이 머리를 숙이다 make a deep courtesy [bow] / 깊이 빠져들다 be taken up too much 《with gambling》 / 깊이 사랑하다 love sb deeply [dearly] / 깊이 사랑하게 되다 become deeply in love with 《a girl》 / 깊이 생각에 잠기다 be deep in thought / 깊이 숨을 쉬다 breathe (in) deep(ly); take [draw] a deep breath / 깊이 슬퍼하다 feel deep sorrow / 깊이 연구하다[배우다] study thoroughly; make a profound study 《of》 / 깊이 잠들다 fall fast asleep
▶나는 물이 나올 때까지 깊이 파내려갔다 I dug deep before I found water.
▶그 문제는 좀더 깊이 생각해 보아라 Think more deeply about the problem. ⇌ Think of the problem more deeply.
▶깊이 감사드립니다 I thank you from the depth [bottom] of my heart.
▶여러분 모두에게 깊이 사과를 드립니다 I profoundly [heartily] apologize to all of you.
▶그의 열정에 모두들 깊이 감동했다 All were deeply moved [touched] by his fervor.
▶나는 그 행위를 깊이 뉘우치고 있다 I deeply regret having done it.

까까머리 a shaven head; a shaved [tonsured] head; 〈짧게 깎은〉 a close-cropped head ◆까까머리 남자 아이 a boy with close-cut [close-cropped] hair

까까중 〈깎은 머리〉 a close-cropped head; 〈삭발한 사람〉 a close-cropped person; a shaven-headed person; 〈승려〉 a bonze
▶그 아이는 까까중이다 The boy has a close-cropped head.

까뀌 an adz(e) ◆까뀌질하다 adz(e); hew with an adz(e)

까끄라기 〈곡식 등의〉 [植] an arista 《pl. ~s, -tae》; an awn; a beard

까놓다 1 〈껍질을〉 peel [pare] off; 〈뒤집다〉 turn [place] 《a thing》 face up ◆탁자 위에 herself 카드를 까놓다 place the cards face up on the table
2 〈털어 놓다〉 unbosom *oneself* to; confide in *sb*; confide 《a secret》 to *sb*; open [unburden] *one's* heart 《to》; tell [confess] everything 《to》; speak *one's* mind
◆까놓고 말하면 frankly speaking / 까놓고 말하다 speak out; be outspoken; talk frankly; talk without reserve
▶까놓고 말하면 자네는 회사내에서 인기가 없네 To tell the truth, you are not popular in the company.
▶내 까놓고 말하지 I will be open [frank] with you. ⇌ I'll conceal nothing from you.

까다¹ 〈줄다〉 diminish; lessen; dwindle 《차차》
◆살이 까다 become [grow, get] lean [thin, thinner]; slim down; 〈병으로〉 lose flesh / 재물이 까다 *one's* fortune dwindles

까다² 1 〈껍질을〉 peel 《potatoes [a banana]》; pare; hull 《peas》; crack 《a nut》; husk
◆삶은 달걀[밤]을 까다 shell a boiled egg [chestnut]
2 〈부화하다〉 hatch 《out》; 〈품다〉 sit on 《eggs》; incubate ◆갓 깐 새새끼 a nestling; a hatching ◆암탉은 병아리를 깐다 A hen hatches 《out》 chickens.
3 〈뒤집다〉 turn out [up] ◆화투짝을 까다 turn up a card
4 〈치다〉 strike; beat; hit; knock; 〈차다〉 kick; give *sth* [*sb*] a kick; [蹴] hack ◆정강이를 까다 kick *sb* in the (right) shin ▶그는 잔등을 까였다 He was kicked in the back.
5 〈헐뜯다〉 speak ill [evil] of; depreciate 《*sb's* abilities》; write down 《글로》; 〈까아내리다〉 cry down 《a new theory》
▶그는 선거 연설에서 상대당을 호되게 깠다 In his campaign speech he really blasted the other party.
▶나는 그를 깔 수가 없다 I can speak no ill of him.
6 〈제하다〉 take away [off]; deduct; subtract
◆봉급에서 까다 deduct 《a sum》 from *sb's* pay; take 《a sum》 off *one's* salary / 원금에서 이자를 까다 deduct interest from principal
7 〈입을〉 flip *one's* lip; have a glib [clever] tongue; be full of brave talk [words]; be a glib talker
▶그는 입만 깠다 He is all talk and no action. ⇌ He never does what he says. ⇌ He makes all barks and no bite.

까다롭다 1 〈성격이〉 particular; choosy; hard to suit [please]; fastidious; overnice
◆성미가 까다로운 사람 a fastidious [particular] person; a person who is hard to please / 식성이 까다롭다 be fussy [fastidious, particular] about *one's* food; have too many likes and dislikes in what *one* eats / 의복에 까다롭다 have a fastidious taste in dress
▶그녀는 복장에 까다롭다 She is fastidious about clothing.
▶저 노인은 식성이 까다롭다 That old man is a fussy eater [is particular about his food].
2【일이】〈복잡하다〉 complicated; intricate; complex; 〈어렵다〉 hard; difficult
◆까다로운 문제 a knotty [perplexing] problem; a vexing question; a hard nut to crack / 까다로운 이론 a complex theory
▶이 문제는 좀 까다롭다 This problem is a bit difficult to solve.
▶시험은 매우 까다로웠다 The examination was very hard [extremely difficult]. ⇌ I found the examination very hard.
▶까다로운 수속에 진절머리가 난다 I'm disgusted with the complicated procedure.
▶그렇게 까다롭게 생각하지 마라 Don't take things too perplexingly.
3 〈엄격하다〉 strict [severe] 《with》; exacting; punctilious; 〈트집잡는〉 faultfinding; nagging; critical; carping
◆까다로운 규칙 a strict [stringent] rule; hard and fast rules / 까다로운 부친 a stern [strict] father / 예절에 까다로운 사람 a stickler for etiquette / 시간에 관해 까다롭다 be strict on punctuality
▶새로 오신 선생님은 학생들에게 매우 까다롭다 The new teacher is very strict [severe] with his pupils.

까닭 1 〈이유·원인〉 (a) reason; (a) cause; 〈근거〉 (a) ground(s); 〈동기〉 a motive
◆까닭 없이 reasonlessly; without reason [cause]; for no reason; 〈부당하게〉 unreasonably; without warrant / 어찌 된 까닭인지 for some unknown reason / 무언가 까닭이 있어서 for certain reasons; on certain grounds; for some reason or other / 무슨 까닭에 for what reason; why / 이런[그런] 까닭에 on this [that] account; for this [that] reason / 까닭 없이 사람을 죽이다 commit murder without provocation / 까닭 없이 시비를 걸다 make a false charge [accusation] / …할 까닭이 없다 no reason for [to do]…; can not be… / 까닭은 이렇다 The reason is that…
▶특별한 까닭 없이 학교에 결석해서는 안된다 Don't be absent from school without a good reason.
▶그의 말을 의심할 까닭이 없다 There is no reason to doubt his word.
▶불이 켜져 있으니 배터리가 나갔을 까닭이 없다 The battery can't be dead, because the lights are on.
▶그녀가 그렇게 화를 내는 데는 틀림없이 무슨 까닭이 있을 것이다 There must be some reason why she is so angry.

▶ 그가 그렇게 바쁠 까닭이 없다 He can't be so [that] busy.
▶ 그것으로 그가 불참한 까닭을 알겠다 That accounts for his absence.
▶ 올 수 없을 때는 까닭을 말하시오 Give me a reason when you can't come.
2 〈사정·연유〉 circumstances; the case
◆ 그럴 만한 까닭이 있어서 owing to unavoidable circumstances / 그런[이런] 까닭으로 such being the case
▶ 거기에는 까닭이 있다 There is a story about it.
▶ 그런 끼닭이 있으시 거질힐 수 없읐나 Under those circumstances [Such being the case] I could not refuse.

까대기 a temporary side shed [shelter]; a makeshift shack

까뒤집다 turn *sth* inside out ◆ 눈까풀을 까뒤집다 roll back *sb*'s eyelids; roll the lid back from *sb*'s eyes

까딱 1 〈고개 등을〉 ◆ 까딱도 않고 undaunted; without flinching [wincing]; calmly; coolly / 까딱도 않다 do not move a muscle; do not turn a hair; do not budge an inch; 〈태연하다〉 keep cool and calm
—**까딱하다** bob; nod (*one's head in agreement* [assent]); budge
◆ 고개를 까딱하고 인사하다 bob *one's* head (in a bow) (to)
▶ 그녀는 좋다고 고개를 까딱했다 She nodded her consent.
▶ 저 게으름쟁이는 손가락 하나 까딱하지 않는다 That lazy fellow would not stir a finger [do a stitch of work].
▶ 그는 욕을 퍼부어도 까딱하지 않았다 He remained calm [unmoved] in spite of the shower of abuse heaped on him.
▶ 그는 까딱하지 않고 전진했다 He moved forward undaunted.
2 〈자칫〉 ◆ 까딱 실수하다 make an inadvertent mistake; slip up

까딱거리다 nod (*one's* head) (to, at); agree to; nod *one's* agreement [assent] (to); bob (*one's* head) up and down
◆ 고개를 몇 번 까딱거리다 nod *one's* head several times / 알았다고 고개를 까딱거리다 nod in assent

까딱까딱하다 nod ⇨ 까딱거리다

까딱수 —手 〈바둑 등의〉 a shallow trick; an off-chance [a risky] move
◆ 까딱수를 쓰다 resort to a wild [risky] move; play a trick on *sb* / 까딱수에 넘어가다 play into the hands of 《an opponent》; fall into a trap [snare]
▶ 그것은 까딱수다 It is a short-sighted trick.

까딱없다 1 〈탈이 없다〉 safe and sound; undamaged; intact; unimpaired
▶ 불황에도 우리 회사는 까딱없다 A recession will not affect [will have no effect on] our company.
▶ 그 꽃병은 선적할 때 거칠게 다루었는데도 까딱없었다 The vase remained intact despite rough handling in shipment.
2 〈동요 않다〉 unmoved; unperturbed; undisturbed; unruffled; self-possessed; calm
▶ 그는 친구들이 무어라고 해도 까딱없다 He does not care a bit what his friends say.
▶ 그는 그 소식을 듣고도 까딱없었다 He was unmoved [unimpressed] by the news.
▶ 으르고 달래도 그는 까딱없었다 Neither threats nor coaxing could make him moved.

까딱이다 nod ⇨ 까딱거리다

까딱하면 possibly; maybe; almost; by (some) chance [possibility]
▶ 그는 까딱하면 뭘 잘 잊어버린다 He is apt to forget.
▶ 우리는 까딱하면 이기적이 되기 쉽다 We tend to selfishness.
▶ 이런 날은 까딱하면 감기 든다 You easily catch (a) cold on such a day.

까라지다 〈기운이〉 get languid; be tired out; go limp; 〈목소리가〉 become [get] hoarse [husky]; grow feeble
▶ 그녀는 지쳐서 까라졌다 She was limp with fatigue. ⇌ She was dead tired.

까르르 ◆ 까르르 웃다 laugh *one's* head off; laugh fit to kill
▶ 소녀들이 까르르 웃었다 The girls screamed with laughter.
▶ 여학생들의 까르르 웃는 소리가 밖에까지 들렸다 Shrieks of the schoolgirls' laughter was heard outside.

까르륵 〈자지러지게〉 with a bawl; squallingly
▶ 아기가 까르륵 울고 있었다 The baby was crying frantically. —**까르륵하다** burst out crying; bawl

까마귀 〈鳥〉 a crow; a raven
◆ 까마귀 떼 a flock of crows / 까마귀 울음소리 the cawing of a crow
▶ 그는 언제나 까마귀 미역감듯 목욕을 한다 He always takes a hurried bath.
▶ 까마귀가 숲에서 울고 있었다 Crows were cawing [croaking] in the grove.

까마귀 고기를 먹었나 (속담) Why are you so forgetful?

까마귀 날자 배 떨어진다 (속담) It is just a coincidence that the two events have happened at the same time.

까마득하다 remote; faraway; far distant; faraway; far distant

까마아득하다 faraway; far-off (in space [time]); far distant; remote
◆ 까마아득한 옛날에 a long, long time ago; in the remote past [far distant] in the past / 완전해지려면 아직 까마아득하다 be still far from perfect; be a long way off perfection
▶ 그곳까지 가려면 아직 까마아득하다 It is a long way yet to the place.
▶ 까마아득한 아래쪽에 폭포가 있다 There is a waterfall far below.
▶ 그것은 까마아득한 옛날의 일이었다 It happened a long time ago.
▶ 새는 벌써 까마아득하게 날아 갔다 The bird has flown far away in the sky.

까마종이 〔植〕 a (black) nightshade

까막눈이 an unlettered [uneducated] person; an illiterate (person); an ignoramus

까막잡기 〈술래잡기〉 blindman's buff [bluff]

까맣다

1 〈색이〉 pitch-black; jet-black; coal-black; inky
♦까만 눈 dark eyes / 까만 머리 jet-black hair / 까맣게 탄 charred; burnt black / 까맣게 타다 be burnt black; be charred; be burnt to a cinder; be scorched black / 까맣게 타 죽다 burnt black to death
▶그 아이는 해변에 갔다가 까맣게 타서 돌아왔다 The boy returned home from the beach tanned all over.
2 〈아득하다〉 ⇨ 까마아득하다
3 〈모르고 있다〉 utterly ignorant; 〈잊어버리다〉 forgotten
▶나는 그의 이름을 까맣게 잊었다 I forgot his name for the moment. ⇌ His name had slipped from my mind [memory].

까매지다

get [go, turn] black; blacken; get dark; darken; tan 《in the sun》
♦햇볕에 타서 까매진 소년들 sunburned [suntanned] boys / 검댕으로 까매진 천장 a ceiling blackened with soot / 햇볕에 타서 까매지다 be tanned with the sun; get [be] sun-burned
▶나는 금년 여름에는 햇볕에 타서 까매졌다 I got a good tan this summer.
▶햇볕에 까매지지 않도록 해라 Keep yourself from getting sunburned.

까먹다

1 〈껍질을〉 peel [crack, shell] and eat
♦밤[귤]을 까먹다 shell a chestnut [peel a tangerine] and eat it / 호두를 까먹다 crack a nut and eat it
2 〈밑천 등을〉 drain 《the capital》; live on *one's* capital; withdraw from 《*one's* bank account》; 〈용돈을〉 spend *one's* pocket money on
▶밑천을 300만원이나 까먹었다 I have cut into my capital up to three million won.
▶그녀는 병이 나서 저축한 돈을 다 까먹었다 Her savings were eaten up by illness.
▶그는 재산을 까먹었다 He wasted [squandered] his fortune.
♦그녀는 부모의 유산을 까먹었다 She used up [spent] all the money she had inherited from his parents.
3 〈잊어버리다〉 forget; lose
♦가사[대사]를 까먹다 go blank / 배운 영어를 까먹다 forget [lose] *one's* English
▶나는 그녀의 주소를 까먹었다 I have forgotten her address.
▶오늘 약속이 있는 것을 까먹었다 I forgot that I had an appointment today.

까무느다

level (down); ⇨ 까뭉개다

까무러치다

fall down in a faint; go faint; swoon; lose *one's* senses [consciousness]; 《俗》 pass out; 〈얻어맞아서〉 be [get] stunned
♦놀라서 까무러치다 faint with surprise / 까무러쳐 쓰러지다 fall senseless [unconscious] / 까무러칠 듯이 놀라다 be frightened out of *one's* senses [wits]
▶그는 얻어맞고 까무러쳤다 He was knocked unconscious [out].
▶그는 그 자리에서 까무러쳤다 He fainted [fell senseless] on the spot.

까무잡잡하다

darkish; rather dark; dark-complexioned; swarthy; dark-skinned
♦피부가 까무잡잡하다 be dark [dark-skinned, tanned]

까뭉개다

level (down); cut 《a road》 through 《a mountain》; dig down; demolish
♦도로를 건설하기 위해 언덕을 까뭉개다 level down a hill to construct a road
▶언덕을 까뭉개서 평평하게 했다 We leveled the hill.

까바치다

〈일러바치다〉 tell tales; tell on *sb*; 《口》 let on 《to *sb* about [that]...》
▶그는 나에 대해 선생님에게 까바쳤다 He informed on me to the teacher.
▶나는 그가 그녀를 만난 사실을 까바치지 않았다 I didn't let on that he had seen her.

까발리다

〈속을〉 pop [peel, shuck, shell] *sth* out; 〈비밀 등을〉 expose; disclose; reveal 《that》; lay bare; bring 《a matter》 to light
♦남의 비행을 까발리다 bring [put] *sb's* crime to light
▶그 회사의 내부 실정이 까발려졌다 The real condition of the company was disclosed.

까부르다

〈키질하다〉 winnow; fan
♦곡식을 까부르다 winnow grain 《from the chaff》; winnow [blow] (off) the chaff from grain

까불거리다

behave frivolously ⇨ 까불다

까불까불

frivolously; lightly; indiscreetly; flippantly; thoughtlessly
─까불까불하다 ⇨ 까불까불하는 태도 a frivolous [flippant] attitude

까불다

1 〈경망스럽게 굴다〉 behave lightly [frivolously]; 〈어린아이가〉 play [sport] with; frisk; frolic 《about》; romp about; make merry
▶아이들은 잔디 위에서 까불며 놀기를 좋아한다 Children love to romp (about) [frolic, frisk] on the lawn.
▶까불지 마라 〈어린아이에게〉 Don't be so boisterous! ⇌ Be a good boy! ⇌ 〈건방진 소리 마라〉 None of your sauce [cheek]!
2 【흔들리다】 〈불꽃이〉 flare; flicker; 〈배가〉 pitch (and toss); (dip and) heave; go up and down; 〈차가〉 jolt

까불다[1]

〈재산을〉 lose [dissipate, squander] 《*one's* fortune》; become bankrupt
▶그는 부모의 유산을 까불렸다 He used up [spent] all the money he had inherited from his parents.

까불리다[2]

〈곡식이〉 be [get] winnowed; be sifted out; 〈곡식을〉 sift out; make [let] *sb* winnow

까불이

〈아이〉 a sportive [jocose, playful] boy; 〈사람〉 a blunderer; a careless fellow; a frivolous person; 《口》 a scatter brain; a jokester; a prankster

까붊질

〈키질〉 winnowing; fanning; sifting
─까붊질하다 ⇨ 까부르다

까슬까슬하다

〈결 등이〉 hard-grained; rough; 〈촉감이〉 rough 《skin》; rugged 《surface》; sandy
♦까슬까슬한 촉감 a rough feel / 까슬까슬한 옷감 cloth of (a) rough texture

까옥

〈까마귀 소리〉 with a caw ♦까옥 까옥 울

까지

다 caw

까지 1 〈기한〉 till; until; to; 〈시점〉 by; by the time; not later than; before

解說 *till, until*은 「…까지 쭉」의 뜻. 일상어로서는 (美)에서는 until이, (英)에서는 till이 주로 쓰인다. 「(늦어도) …까지는」의 경우는 ***by, by the time, before*** 등을 쓴다.

♦ 근대까지 until [down to] modern times / 지금까지 till now; so far; up to the present; hitherto / 최후까지 to the last / 아침부터 밤까지 from morning till night / 월요일부터 토요일까지 from Monday till [(美) through] Saturday / 1시부터 3시까지 from one to three o'clock / 백살까지 살다 live to be a hundred
▶ 그는 밤늦게까지 열심히 일한다 He works hard till late at night.
▶ 8시 15분 전까지 그곳에 도착할 수 있을까요? Shall I get there by a quarter to eight?
▶ 내가 올 때까지 여기서 기다리시오 Wait here until I get back.
▶ 나는 지금까지 일 때문에 바빴다 I have been busy with my work until [till] now.
▶ 지금까지 도대체 어디에 있었니? Where have you been all this while?
▶ 저는 이달 말까지 서울에 있겠습니다 I'll stay in Seoul until [till, through] the end of this month.
▶ 찌는 듯한 더위가 9월까지 계속되었다 The heat of the summer lasted into September.
▶ 입학원서는 1월 11일까지 제출할 것 Application for admission should be presented not later than the eleventh of January.
▶ 그 토론은 밤늦게까지 계속되었다 The discussion continued to [till] far into the night.
▶ 밤까지 비가 계속 내렸다 It rained into the night.
▶ 그 표는 수요일까지 유효하다 The tickets are valid until Wednesday.
▶ 근무 시간은 8시부터 5시까지다 Working hours are from 8 a.m. to 5 p.m.
▶ 열세살까지는 소인으로 쳐도 그 이상은 다 대인이다 Up to 13 years of age you are considered a "child," but above that age everyone is an "adult."
▶ 저녁식사 때까지는 돌아오겠다 I will be back by suppertime.
▶ 일요일까지 휴업 (게시) Closed till [(美) through] Sunday. (▶till Sunday로 하면 일요일에는 개업임)

2 〈장소〉 to; 〈한정된 구간〉 as far as; 〈정도·범위〉 to the extent of; even; 〈한도〉 up to; to the limit; so much
♦ 서울까지의 차표 a ticket to Seoul / 10명 중 9명까지 nine people out of ten / 10피트의 깊이까지 가라앉다 sink to a depth of ten feet / 마지막 한 방울까지 마시다 drink (the wine) to the very last drop / 100까지 세다 count (up) to one hundred / 도둑질까지 하다 go to the length(s) of committing theft; go so [as] far as to commit theft / 천만원까지는 안 되다 do not cost so much as ten million won
▶ 그 아이는 도둑질까지 한다 The boy even steals.
▶ 어디까지 가십니까? Where are you going? ⇒ How far do you go?
▶ 물은 무릎까지 왔다 The water came up to my knees.
▶ 노인들까지 춤을 추고 있다 Even the elderly are dancing.
▶ 그렇게까지 할 필요는 없다 There is no need to go that far.
▶ 그들은 결혼하여 자식까지 둔 사이였다 Not only were they married but they had children born to them.
▶ 연령 제한은 30세까지다 There is an age limit of thirty.
▶ 회사에서 500만원까지는 빌릴 수 있다 I can get a loan of money to the extent of five million won from my company.
▶ 광주까지는 기차로 가고 그 다음은 버스를 탔다 I went as far as Kwangju by train and then took a bus.
▶ 어느 정도까지는 그를 신용할 수 있다 To some extent, we can trust him.
▶ 일부러 갈 것까지는 없다 There's no need to make a special effort to go.

3 〈더하여〉 besides; moreover; what is more; in addition (to that); 〈악화〉 what is worse; to make matters worse
▶ 설상가상으로[불행하게도] 아이까지 죽었다 What was worse [more unfortunate], her child died.
▶ 게다가 그는 병까지 났다 To make him more miserable, he fell ill.
▶ 그는 나를 저녁식사에 초대했을 뿐만 아니라 선물까지 주었다 Not only did he invite me to dinner, but he even gave me a gift.
▶ 그밖에 또 나는 상금 50만원까지 받았다 In addition I received a prize of five hundred thousand won.
▶ 그는 책뿐만 아니라 많은 그림까지 내게 주었다 He gave me books and many pictures as well.

까지다 1 〈벗겨지다〉 〈피부 등이〉 be grazed [abraded, rubbed, scraped, chafed]; 〈껍질이〉 peel (off)
▶ 나는 계단에서 굴러떨어져서 무릎이 까졌다 I fell down the steps and had my knees skinned.
2 〈여위다〉 get [become] thin; lose flesh; 〈재산 등이 줄다〉 get fewer [less, smaller]; decrease; diminish; lessen; run low

까지르다 〈싸다니다〉 hang around [about]; loiter about; gad [wander] about; (美俗) bum around

-까짓 〈…만한 정도의〉 such as; any [some] such; 〈하찮은〉 so trifling [trivial]; so little
♦ 네까짓 such as [like] you / 제까짓 such as him [her, them]
▶ 네까짓 놈이 알 수가 있겠나 Such as you wouldn't understand.

까치 〔鳥〕 a magpie ■=**걸음** a hopping walk ■=**설날** New Year's Eve ■=**설빔** children's gala dress for New Year's Eve

까치눈 a chap in the bend of a toe

까치발 〔建〕 〈선반의〉 a bracket; tripod; 〈처마

까치선 —扇 a four-color fan (used by ladies)

까칠하다 thin; haggard (face); emaciated; worn; ((look)) undernourished ▶ 그녀는 병으로 까칠해졌다 She got thin because of her illness.

까탈 〈방해〉 a hindrance; a hitch; an obstacle; an impediment; a stumbling block
♦ 까탈부리다 be a drag (on); hinder; disturb; stand in *sb's* way; throw [place] an obstacle in (another's) path
▶ 그는 이리저리 까탈을 부려 그 계약을 깨려고 했다 He tried to break off the contract on some pretext or other.

까탈스럽다 complicated; complex; intricate; difficult; hard; tiresome; troublesome
▶ 까탈스러워서 그런 일은 하지 않겠다 I won't do it. It's too much trouble [such a bother].

까투리 〈암꿩〉 a hen pheasant

까풀 the outer layer of the skin; the film; scum; skim ♦ 까풀이 지다 get a skin [film] on; be coated
▶ 그도 한까풀 벗기면 사기꾼이다 Under a thin veneer he is a swindler.

— 눈— an eyelid

깍깍 ▶ 까마귀는 깍깍 운다 Crows caw. **—깍깍하다** croak; caw

깍두기 cubed radish *kimchi*

깍둑거리다 hack [cut] (a radish) to pieces; chop (up a carrot) ♦ 깍둑거린 오이 cucumbers chopped into chunks

깍듯이 politely; courteously; civilly; with civility [respect]; respectfully; with much courtesy
♦ 깍듯이 인사하다 greet [salute] politely [deeply]; make a low [deep, polite] bow
▶ 그는 깍듯이 작별 인사를 하고 나갔다 Saying goodbye politely, he went out.

깍듯하다 polite; civil; courteous; respectful; well-mannered
▶ 그는 여자에게 깍듯한 말씨를 쓴다 He talks to women in polite language.

깍쟁이 〈인색한 사람〉 a stingy fellow; a niggard; a miser; ((美口)) a sharp customer; 〈약빠른 사람〉 a tricky person; a cunning [shrewd, calculating] fellow; a sly dog
▶ 그는 깍쟁이다 He is stingy [close-fisted].
▶ 도회지 깍쟁이들을 조심해라 Watch out for the city slickers.

깍지[1] 〈콩 등의〉 a (pea) pod; a hull; a peas(e)cod ♦ 깍지를 까다 shell (peas, beans)

깍지[2] 〈활 쏠 때의〉 an archer's thimble ♦ 깍지를 떼다 shoot [send, discharge, let fly, let off] an arrow (at)

깍지끼다 lock [hook] *one's* fingers together; interlace *one's* fingers
▶ 그는 깍지끼고 기도를 드렸다 He interlaced his fingers in prayer.

깎낫 a sickle used in cutting out a club; a whittling sickle

깎다 1 〈나무 등을〉 shave (wood); whittle (at) (a piece of wood); chip, plane (a board) (대패로); 〈껍질을〉 peel; pare
♦ 사과[배]를 깎다 pare [peel] an apple [a pear] / 연필을 깎다 sharpen a pencil
▶ 목수가 대패로 널빤지를 깎고 있다 A carpenter is planing a plank.

2 〈머리를〉 cut; clip; crop; dress; ((美俗)) shingle; bob (단발로)
♦ 머리를 깎다 〈남의 머리를〉 cut [crop] *sb's* hair (short, close); 〈남을 시켜〉 have *one's* hair cut [trimmed]; have [get] a haircut
▶ 그는 머리를 깎고 중이 되었다 He shaved his head and became a Buddhist monk.
▶ 머리 좀 깎아 주세요 I want to have my hair cut. ⇌ I want a haircut.
▶ 20분내에 머리를 깎아줄 수 있어요? Can you give me a haircut in twenty minutes?

3 〈수염·털 등을〉 shave; shear; clip off (the wool); fleece
♦ 천의 보풀을 깎다 shear cloth / 수염을 깎다 shave *oneself*; 〈남을 시켜서〉 get *oneself* shaved (by) / 양털을 깎다 shear [fleece] a sheep; shear [clip] wool from a sheep / 푸들의 털을 깎다 clip [trim] a poodle
▶ 그들은 봄에 양털을 깎는다 They shear the sheep in spring.

4 〈손톱 등을〉 cut; pare; 〈잔디를〉 mow
♦ 산울타리를 깎다 prune a hedge / 손톱[발톱]을 깎다 pare [cut, trim] *one's* fingernails [toenails]
▶ 나는 2주일마다 잔디를 깎는다 I mow the lawn [cut the grass] every two weeks.

5 〈값을〉 haggle (chaffer, bargain, ((美)) dicker) (with *sb*) over (the price); beat [knock, whittle] down (the price)
♦ 값을 많이 깎다 drive a hard bargain / 값을 25% 깎아 주다 reduce the price by [give discount of] 25 percent
▶ 현금이면 10% 깎아 드립니다 You get a 10 percent discount [We take 10 percent off] if you pay in cash.
▶ 천원만 깎아 드리지요 I'll take a thousand won off the price.
▶ 이 텔레비전은 신형이 나왔기 때문에 값을 깎아 준다 These TV are being sold at reduced prices to make way for (the) newer models.
▶ 저 백화점에서는 여름옷 값을 깎아 주고 있다 That department store is discounting all summer wear.
▶ 책값은 깎아 드리지 않습니다 There is no discount on books.
▶ 값을 좀 깎아 줄 수 있습니까? Could you give me a discount?

6 〈삭감하다〉 cut down; reduce; curtail; whittle down [away, off] ▶ 우리는 여비를 깎지 않으면 안된다 We have to cut [curtail] our traveling expenses.

7 〈손상시키다〉 disgrace; bring disgrace upon; dishonor; stain; defile; blemish
♦ 아무의 업적을 깎아 내리다 depreciate [belittle] *sb's* achievements / 위신을 깎아 내리다 injure the prestige (of); let down
▶ 그런 행위는 너의 체면을 깎는 일이다 Such conduct will disgrace you.

깎아지르다 tower up [rise] steeply

깎아지른듯하다 precipitous; very steep ♦ 깎아지른 듯한 벼랑 a steep [sheer, perpendicular] cliff; a precipice

깎이 a sharpener ■**연필―** a pencil sharpener

깎이다 1 〈깎어지다〉 be shaved [trimmed, sharpened, cut, pared, mowed]
▶이 연필은 잘 깎인다 This pencil sharpens nicely.

2 〈깎게 하다〉 make sb cut [trim]; get sb to cut [trim, pare]; have sth cut [trimmed, pared]
♦정원수를 깎이다 get sb to prune a garden tree

3 〈삭감되다〉 be cut down; be curtailed [reduced]; be bargained [beaten] down
▶사회 복지 예산이 대폭 깎였다 The social welfare budget was substantially reduced [cut].
▶우리의 급료가 대폭 깎였다 Our salaries have been slashed [chopped].
▶값이 5천원으로 깎였다 The price was beaten down to five thousand won.

4 〈삭제되다〉 be crossed out; be struck out [off]; be deleted; be erased; be blue-penciled
▶내 이름이 명단에서 깎여나갔다 My name was crossed out [crossed off, removed] from the list.

5 〈체면이〉 be disgraced; be dishonored
♦낯이 깎이다 lose *one's* honor [face]; disgrace *oneself*
▶그가 죄를 지어서 집안 체면이 깎였다 He brought disgrace on his family by committing a crime.

깐 〈가늠·속셈〉 estimation; account; a thought; an idea; something in *one's* mind
♦제[내]깐에는 in his [my] thought [estimation]; by his [my] account
▶제깐에는 대학자나 된 줄 안다 He is a savant in his own estimation.
▶그녀는 제깐에는 미인이라고 생각하고 있다 She fancies herself beautiful. ⇒ She is beautiful in her own conceit.
▶그는 제깐에는 일이 잘될 줄 알았던 모양이다 He seems to have had an idea that all would go well.

깐깐하다 〈까다롭다〉 particular; fastidious; hard to please; 〈꼼꼼하다〉 careful; meticulous; scrupulous; strict; exact; 〈깐질기다〉 tenacious; (doggedly) persistent
♦깐깐한 사람 a man of hard-grained character; a particular [persistent] person / 깐깐하게 tenaciously; persistently; fastidiously / 깐깐히 조사하다 examine carefully / 깐깐히 질문하다 pester [plague] sb with questions / 일을 깐깐히 하다 put great care into *one's* work
▶그는 너무 깐깐하다 He is too persistent.
▶우리 아버지는 매우 깐깐하시다 My father is very hard to please.

깐작거리다 1 〈깐질기다〉 persevere (in doing, with a job); be tenacious; 〈짜증나게 굴다〉 irritate; make sb impatient; get on sb's nerves
♦깐작거리는 사람 an insistent [persistent] person
▶그는 아내에게 깐작거리며 싫은 소리를 했다 He kept after [nagged] his wife with disagreeable remarks.

2 〈달라붙다〉 be sticky; be viscid; be glutinous; be adhesive

깐작깐작 〈끈적끈적〉 stickily; adhesively; glutinously; 〈깐질기게〉 tenaciously; persistently; 〈귀찮게〉 importunately
―**깐작깐작하다** ⇨ 깐작거리다
▶그녀는 깐작깐작한 사람을 좋아하지 않는다 She does not like a persistent person.
▶그는 깐작깐작하게 설명을 요구했다 He demanded an explanation persistently.

깐지다 〈깐깐하고 다라지다〉 tenacious; insistent; persistent; pertinacious; inveterate

깐질기다 tenacious ⇨ 끈질기나

깔개 〈밑에 까는〉 an underlay; 〈마루에 까는〉 a carpet; a rug; 〈방석〉 a cushion; 〈돗자리에〉 matting; 〈예식장 등의〉 a footcloth
♦마루에 깔개를 깔다 lay [put down] a carpet on the floor; cover a floor with a carpet; carpet a floor
▶나는 식탁 밑에 예쁜 깔개를 깔았다 I spread a pretty rug under the table.

깔기다 〈배설물을〉 discharge (excrements) irrespective of places; relieve [ease] nature indiscriminately; evacuate [empty] the bowels regardless of places; 〈알을〉 lay (eggs) all over
♦길바닥에 오줌을 깔기다 make [pass] water by the side of the road; go for [have] a pee on the road; (卑) piss on the road

깔깔 ♦깔깔 웃다 scream with laughter

깔깔거리다 laugh loudly [aloud]; cackle
▶그는 깔깔거렸다 〈큰소리로〉 He laughed loudly [boisterously].

깔깔하다 rough ((surface)); feel coarse ((grain)); sandy; gritty ((with sand)) ♦깔깔한 감촉 a rough [sandy] feel / 깔깔한 천 coarse cloth
▶이 종이는 깔깔하다 This paper feels rough.
▶혓바닥이 깔깔하다 My tongue is rough.

깔끄럽다 rough ⇨ 껄끄럽다

깔끔거리다 prick ⇨ 껄끔거리다

깔끔하다 〈외양이〉 clean; smart; neat and tidy [trim] (▶neat는 청결하고 정연한 것, trim은 형태가 갖추어진 것); 〈성격이〉 cleanly; dainty
♦깔끔한 가게 a tidy [spiffy] little shop / 깔끔한 사람 a stickler for cleanness / 깔끔한 성격 a sharp temper
▶그녀는 언제나 차림새가 깔끔하다 She is always neatly dressed [neat and tidy in her dress].
▶그녀는 깔끔한 것을 좋아한다 She is fond of cleanliness.
▶그는 깔끔한 사람이다 He has neat habits. ⇒ He is habitually clean and tidy.
▶그 방은 깔끔하게 정돈되어 있었다 The room was kept neat and clean.

깔다 1 〈자리 등을〉 spread; put down; lay ((a carpet on the floor))
♦돗자리를 깔다 spread a mat / 이부자리를 깔다 make a bed; put down bedding; spread [lay out] bedding / 남편을 깔고 앉다 dominate *one's* husband; keep *one's* husband under *one's* thumb / 방석을 깔고 앉다 sit [seat *oneself*] on a cushion

▶그는 방에 카펫을 깔았다 He laid [put down] carpeting in the room. ⇌ He laid the floor in the room with carpeting.
▶이 방석을 깔고 앉으세요 Please take your seat on this cushion.
2 〈자갈 등을〉 pave; pitch
♦길에 돌을 깔다 pave [cover] a road with stone / 자갈을 깔다 spread gravel; gravel (a road)
3 〈돈 등을〉 lend out 《money》 widely ♦빚을 여기저기 깔다 lend *one's* money out near and far / 외상을 깔아놓다 sell 《articles》 on credit near and far

깔딱 1 ⇨ 꿀꺽 **2** 〈숨이 끊어질 듯한 모양〉 with gasps; breathe heavily ♦숨이 깔딱 넘어가다 gasp *one's* life away

깔딱거리다 gulp repeatedly; keep gulping; gulp and gulp; 〈숨을〉 pant; breathe hard [heavily]; gasp (for breath)

깔딱하다 〈쾡하다〉 《*one's* eyes are》 drawn [sunken deep] with fatigue [hunger] ▶그는 눈이 깔딱했다 His eyes were deeply sunk [deep-set].

깔때기 a funnel ♦깔때기 모양의 funnel-shaped

깔리다 1 〈흩어지다〉 be scattered; be dispersed; 〈펴놓아지다〉 be spread; be covered
♦낙엽[자갈]이 깔린 길 a road covered with fallen leaves [paved with gravel] / 벚꽃잎이 깔린 뜰 a garden strewn with cherry blossoms petals
▶길에는 돌이 깔려 있다 The road is paved with stones.
▶땅에 낙엽이 깔려 있다 The ground is scattered with fallen leaves.
▶마루에는 융단이 깔려 있었다 The floor was laid [covered] with a carpet.
▶시내에는 경찰이 쫙 깔려 있었다 The policemen covered [swarmed] the whole city.
▶구름이 낮게 깔려 있었다 Clouds were hanging low in the sky. ⇌ The sky was covered with low-hanging clouds.
2 〈밑에〉 be buried [pressed, held] under 《a fallen tree》; be held down 《by》; be sat on 《by》 ♦바위에 깔려 죽다 be crushed to death under a rock
▶나는 인파에 깔려 죽을 뻔했다 I was almost crushed to death in the crowd.
3 〈돈 등이〉 《*one's* money》 be lent [loaned] widely; 《*one's* goods》 be sold on credit here and there

깔보다 hold *sb* cheap; underrate; underestimate; think little [nothing] of *sb* [*sth*]; belittle; slight; make light of; 〈경멸하다〉 despise; hold *sb* in contempt; look down upon [on]; look [have] down *one's* nose at *sb*
▶그들은 그를 어린애라고 깔보았다 They made light of him as a mere boy.
▶그녀는 나를 깔보는 듯한 눈으로 보았다 She gave me a contemptuous look.
▶그의 실력을 깔보아서는 안된다 You should not underestimate [undervalue, misjudge] his ability.
▶나를 그렇게 깔보지 마라 Do not hold me so cheap.

깔아뭉개다 1 〈짓눌러서〉 press down; hold [get, pin] *sb* down; pin [wrestle] *sb* to the ground [floor]; 〈밑에 깔아서〉 sit on [upon] 《a thing》 (and mash it)
2 〈일을〉 shelve; pigeonhole; put [lay, cast] on the shelf; 《美》 lay on [upon] the table
♦법안을 깔아뭉개다 pigeonhole [strangle, burke, kill] a bill
▶이 문제는 무한정 깔아뭉갤 수는 없다 This problem cannot be left on the shelf indefinitely.
▶그 계획은 당분간 깔아뭉개질 것 같다 The plan will be laid [set, put] aside for some time.

깔짝거리다 crunch; grate; scratch; 〈펜촉 등으로〉 make a scratching sound; 〈쥐가〉 gnaw 《at》
▶쥐가 상자를 깔짝거려 구멍을 냈다 The rats gnawed a hole in the box.
▶그는 비스킷을 깔짝거리며 먹었다 He munched his biscuits.

깔짝깔짝하다 grate ⇨ 깔짝거리다

깔쭉거리다 feel rough; be sandy; be rough to the touch [feel]
▶벽의 표면이 깔쭉거린다 The wall surface is rough.

깔쭉깔쭉하다 be notched; be jagged; be rugged; 〈동전 가장자리가〉 be milled ♦깔쭉깔쭉하게 하다 jag; notch; make notches (on the edge); indent; 〈동전 가장자리를〉 mill

깔쭉이 〈은화〉 a milled silver coin

깔치 《俗》 a gal; a girl friend

깜깜하다 1 〈몹시 어둡다〉 completely dark; pitch-dark 《night》; 《as》 dark as pitch [midnight]
▶터널[방] 안은 깜깜했다 It was pitch-dark [as dark as pitch] in the tunnel [within the room].
▶정전으로 방이 깜깜해졌다 The room went black when the power failed.
▶깜깜해서 아무 것도 볼 수 없었다 Nothing was to be seen in the utter [total] darkness.
▶우리는 깜깜해지기를 기다렸다 We waited for full darkness.
2 〈전혀 모르다〉 ignorant; unlearned; blank
♦아무의 소식이 깜깜하다 have no news from *sb*; hear nothing from *sb*
▶나는 스페인어는 깜깜하다 I am ignorant of Spanish.
▶그런 일에는 아주 깜깜하다 I know nothing about matters of that kind.

깜둥이 a Negro ⇨ 검둥이 2

깜부기 a smut ball; a smutted ear 《of barley》
■—불 a dying [low] fire; embers —숯 cinders; charred firewood **깜부깃병** smut; dustbrand; 〈밀의〉 bunt : 깜부깃병에 걸리다 smut; become smutted; become affected by smut

깜빡 1 〈등불이〉 with a flash; 〈별 등이〉 with a twinkle —**깜빡하다** flicker; come and go; twinkle; blink
▶등불이 깜빡하더니 꺼졌다 The lamplight flickered out.
2 〈눈을〉 with a blink [blinking]; with a

wink ♦ 깜빡 졸다 have a snatch of sleep
―**깜빡하다** 〈눈을〉 wink; blink (one's eyes); 〈졸다〉 doze; fall [go off] into a doze; drowse
▶ 그 아이는 눈도 깜빡하지 않고 나를 보고 있었다 The child was staring at me with unblinking eyes.
3 〈순간적으로〉 for a moment; momentarily; in a flash
♦ 깜빡 속다 be nicely [fairly] taken in; be taken in unawares / 깜빡 잊다 forget for the moment; 〈사물이 주어〉 escape one's momory; slip from [out of] one's memory
▶ 그는 깜빡 가스불을 끄지 않고 외출했다 He went out carelessly forgetting to turn off the gas fire.
▶ 그는 내려야 할 역을 깜빡 지나쳤다 He absentmindedly missed [failed to get off at] his station.

깜빡거리다 flicker ⇨ 깜빡이다

깜빡깜빡 with repeated blinking [flickering, wavering]
♦ 깜빡깜빡 졸다 doze off; nod [rock] in a doze
―**깜빡깜빡하다** glitter; flicker; waver; blink
♦ 깜빡깜빡하는 네온 불빛 the flickering of a neon light / 눈이 부셔서 깜빡깜빡하다 blink in the strong light
▶ 먼 도시의 불빛이 깜빡깜빡하고 있었다 The lights of a distant town are twinkling.

깜빡이다 **1** 〈별이〉 twinkle; 〈불빛이〉 shimmer; flicker; glimmer
♦ 깜빡이는 등불 a blink of light; a flickering light / 깜빡이는 별들 twinkling stars
▶ 그는 종종 장난스럽게 눈을 깜빡인다 He often winks a mischievous wink [his eyelids mischievously].
▶ 램프의 불빛이 안개 속에서 깜빡였다 The light of the lamp glimmered in the fog.
▶ 촛불이 바람에 깜빡이고 있었다 The candle was flickering in the breeze.
▶ 하늘에 별이 깜빡이고 있었다 The stars were blinking in the sky.
▶ 멀리 깜빡이는 불빛이 보였다 I saw a flickering of light in the distance.
2 〈눈을〉 blink (one's eyes); wink (significantly) (at) (▶무의식적으로 깜빡이는 것은 blink, 의식적으로 깜빡이는 것은 wink); nictitate
▶ 그녀는 갑자기 불빛이 비쳐 눈을 깜빡였다 She blinked at the sudden light.
▶ 그는 눈도 깜빡이지 않고 그 꽃 그림을 들여다 보았다 He gazed at the picture of flowers without blinking.

깜장 black

깜짝¹ 〈눈을 감았다 뜨는 모양〉 with a wink; with a blink [blinking]
―**깜짝하다** wink [blink] (one's eyes); (美) bat one's eyes [eyelids]
♦ 눈 깜짝할 사이에 in a twinkling; in the twinkling of an eye; in no time; in an instant; in a flash / 눈 하나 깜짝하지 않다 〈태연자약하다〉 be perfectly calm and collected / 눈 하나 깜짝하지 않고 보다 gaze steadily [unblinkingly] (at)
▶ 1년이 눈 깜짝할 사이에 지나갔다 A year has passed in a flash [in an instant, in the twinkling of an eye].
▶ 그녀의 모습은 눈 깜짝할 사이에 보이지 않게 되었다 She was out of sight in the twinkling of an eye [in an instant].

깜짝² 〈놀라는 모양〉 in surprise [amazement]; with a (sudden) start
♦ 깜짝 놀라서 in terror / 깜짝 놀라다 be startled out of one's wits; be shocked (at); be thunderstruck; be struck all of a heap / 깜짝 놀라 눈을 뜨다 awake with a start / 깜짝 놀라 기절하다 faint from fright / 깜짝 놀라게 하다 make sb jump; give sb a start; startle; knock the breath out of sb; strike sb dumb / 세상을 깜짝 놀라게 하다 startle the world; cause the public to gasp with surprise
▶ 그는 그 소식을 듣고 깜짝 놀랐다 He was startled at [to hear] the news.
▶ 그는 호명되자 깜짝 놀랐다 He was startled at the mention of his name.
▶ 네가 깜짝 놀랄 일이 있어 I have a surprise for you.

깜짝거리다 blink and blink (one's eyes); blink repeatedly; keep winking

깜짝깜짝 **1** 〈눈을〉 with repeated winking [blinking] ―**깜짝깜짝하다** ⇨ 깜짝거리다
2 〈놀라는 모양〉 with repeated starts ♦ 자면서 깜짝깜짝 놀라다 startle repeatedly in one's sleep

깜짝이다 wink [blink] (one's eyes); (美) bat one's eyes [eyelids]; 〈눈짓으로〉 give sb a significant wink; wink (at)
♦ 알았다는 듯이 눈을 깜짝이다 wink knowingly; give sb a knowing wink
▶ 주의해서 들으라고 그에게 눈을 깜짝였다 I winked to him to listen.

깜짝이야 Oh, dear!; Oh, shocks!; Oh my!; What a surprise!

깜찍하다 〈사람이〉 too clever [shrewd, smart, alert] (for one's age); precocious; 〈물건이〉 saucy; (small and) cute
♦ 깜찍한 모자 a saucy little hat / 깜찍한 아이 a precocious child
▶ 어린 녀석이 참 깜찍한 소리를 한다 Though a mere child, he says quite a sensible [smart] thing.
▶ 그 소녀 참 깜찍하구나 What a cute little girl!
▶ 그 아이는 나이에 비해 깜찍하다 The boy is too wise for his age.
▶ 그 여자아이는 중학생 치고는 깜찍하다 She is too forward for a junior high school girl.

깜신거리다 〈까불거리다〉 behave frivolously [flippantly]; act rashly [lightly, carelessly]

깜죽거리다 behave flippantly; act lightly [rashly, carelessly, thoughtlessly]

깡 〔鑛山〕 a percussion cap; a detonator

깡그리 〈몽땅〉 all; one and all; wholly; clean; without exception [reserve]
♦ 노름으로 재산을 깡그리 날리다 gamble away all one's property / 깡그리 뿌리뽑다 root up; exterminate sth root and all / 깡그리 잊어버리다 utterly [clean] forget

▶ 도시는 깡그리 변했다 The town has completely changed.
▶ 소지품을 깡그리 도둑맞았다 My personal effects were stolen to the last particle.
▶ 그들의 제안은 깡그리 각하되었다 All their proposals were rejected.
▶ 집들이 깡그리 파괴되었다 Every house was destroyed. ⇌ All the houses were destroyed.

깡깡이 (俗) 〈악기〉 a two-stringed fiddle ⇨ 해금

깡똥하다 undersized; dwarfish; very [unbecomingly] short
♦ 깡똥한 치마를 입고 있다 be in [wear] a very [too] short skirt
▶ 작년 옷은 내게 깡똥하다 Last year's dresses are too short for me.

깡마르다 lean; haggard; skinny; gaunt; rawboned ♦ 깡마른 사람 a skinny person; a living skeleton; a bag of bones

깡충깡충 ♦ 깡충깡충 뛰다 hop; skip; jump up and down; 〈뛰어다니다〉 romp; frisk / 깡충깡충 뛰면서 좋아하다 skip about for joy 《at》; leap [jump] for [with] joy 《at》
▶ 그녀는 그 소식을 듣고 깡충깡충 뛰면서 좋아했다 She danced [jumped] for joy at the news.

깡통 a can; (英) a tin; 〈차·담배 등을 넣는〉 a canister
♦ 빈 깡통 an empty can / 우유 깡통 a milk can / 깡통 맥주 canned beer / 깡통에 든 담배 canned tobacco / 깡통을 따다 open a tin [can] / 깡통을 차다 〈거지가 되다〉 be reduced to beggary; 〈파산하다〉 (口) go broke
■ —따개 a can [(英) a tin] opener

깡패 —牌 a gang of young roughs [toughs, hoods]; a rough; a ruffian; a blackguard; (俗) a hooligan; (美俗) a hoodlum; a scalawag; a hood; 〈폭력단원〉 a gangster; a goon
♦ 깡패 두목 a gangster boss / 깡패 집단 a group of gangsters / 깡패 패거리에서 손을 씻다 go straight; make a clean break with the gang [mob]
■ —기질 hooliganism; hoodlumism ■ —세계 the outskirts of society

깨 〔植〕 〈참깨〉 sesame; a gingili (plant); 〈들깨〉 green perilla
♦ 검은 깨 black sesame / 깨를 빻다 grind [crush] sesame seeds / 나물에 깨를 넣고 무치다 dress potherbs with sesame

깨갱깨갱 ♦ 깨갱깨갱 울다 yelp; yip; yap ▶ 꼬리를 밟혀서 강아지가 깨갱깨갱 울었다 The puppy let out a yelp when stepped on its tail.

깨깨 gauntly ⇨ 빼빼²

깨끗이 1 〈청결하게〉 clean; cleanly; neatly
♦ 방을 깨끗이 치우다 sweep a room clean; tidy up a room / 깨끗이 하다 clean; 〈정돈하다〉 put in order; tidy up
▶ 손은 언제나 깨끗이 해라 Always keep your hands clean.
▶ 그녀는 머리를 깨끗이 다듬고 방에서 나갔다 She arranged her hair neatly before going out of the room.
▶ 그는 언제나 글씨를 깨끗이 쓴다 He always writes neatly [in a clear hand].
▶ 거리를 깨끗이 합시다 (게시) Keep the town tidy.
2 〈순결하게〉 clearly; purely; cleanly ♦ 깨끗이 살다 live cleanly; live a clean life; lead a pure life
3 〈모두·완전히〉 all; quite; completely; perfectly
▶ 그는 아들의 빚을 깨끗이 갚았다 He paid [cleared] off his son's debts.
▶ 상처가 깨끗이 나으려면 1주일 걸린다 The wound will take a week to heal completely.
▶ 우리는 그 계획을 깨끗이 단념했다 We gave up the plan without any regret.
▶ 그는 접시에 있는 빵을 깨끗이 먹어 치웠다 He ate up the bread on the plate to the last crumb.
▶ 과거는 깨끗이 잊어라 Forget all about the past.
▶ 지금의 생활(방식)을 깨끗이 청산하고 싶다 I want to wash my hands completely of my present (way of) life.
4 〈정정 당당히〉 fair; clean

깨끗하다 1 〈청결하다〉 clean; tidy; neat
♦ 깨끗한 방 a clean [neat] room / 깨끗한 수건 a clean towel / 깨끗한 종이 a clean sheet of paper
▶ 이 행주는 깨끗하니? Is this dishcloth clean?
▶ 집안의 모든 것이 깨끗하고 깔끔했다 Everything in the house was neat and tidy.
▶ 깨끗한 면에서는 이 호텔이 월등하다 This hotel is superior in cleanliness.
2 〈맑다〉 clear; clean; pure; 〈오염이 없다〉 unpolluted
♦ 깨끗한 공기 clean air; unpolluted air / 깨끗한 물 clear [pure] water; unpolluted water
▶ 이 호수의 물은 아주 깨끗하다 The water in this lake is very clear [pure].
3 〈순결하다〉 pure; chaste; innocent
♦ 깨끗한 마음 a pure heart / 깨끗한 사랑 pure [Platonic] love / 깨끗한 처녀 a chaste maiden
▶ 그녀는 마음이 깨끗하다 She is a woman of pure heart [pure in heart].
▶ 그들의 사랑은 깨끗하다 Their love is pure.
▶ 그녀는 깨끗한 생애를 보냈다 She led a pure life.
4 〈정정당당하다〉 fair (and square); clean
♦ 깨끗한 선거 a clean [fair] election / 깨끗한 승부 fair [fine] play / 깨끗한 한 표 an honest vote
▶ 그의 경력은 깨끗하다 There is no stain in his personal history.
▶ 그는 깨끗한 선거를 다짐했다 He promised to conduct [hold] a clean [fair] election campaign.
▶ 깨끗한 한 표를 던집시다 Let's cast out votes conscientiously.
▶ 자, 깨끗하게 싸우자 〈경기에서〉 Come on and play fair.
▶ 그것을 할 양이면 깨끗하게 해라 If you intend to do it, do it fairly.
▶ 그는 그 경주에서 깨끗하게 이겼다 He won the race fair and square.

깨끼(옷) gossamer [silk gauze] clothes with linings; kkaekki clothes ■—(겹)저고리 a kkaekki jacket (for a young lady)

-깨나 ◆돈깨나 있다 have plenty of money / 영어깨나 하다 speak tolerable English
▶그는 프랑스어깨나 알고 있다 He has a passable knowledge of French.
▶그 집 짓느라고 돈깨나 들었다 It took a lot of money to build the house.

깨나다 1 〈잠 등에서〉 wake up; awake; 〈미몽에서〉 be awakened from an illusion [a delusion]; be disillusioned [undeceived]
◆꿈에서 깨나다 come out of a dream / 잠에서 깨나다 awake from *one's* sleep / 환상에서 깨나다 ⇨ 깨다¹ 2
2 〈의식이〉 revive; regain [recover] consciousness; return to life; come to life again; be restored [brought back to] life; be resuscitated
◆기절했다가 깨나다 regain *one's* consciousness after a fainting spell; come out of a faint / 마취에서 깨나다 come out from under the anesthesia
▶그 사람은 심장 마사지로 깨났다 He was revived by heart massage.
3 〈소생하다〉 be brightened up; be freshened; be refreshed; be invigorated
▶석달만에 비가 오니 초목이 깨났다 The trees and plants were freshened after a rainfall the first in three months.

깨나른하다 〈늘쩍지근하다〉 (feel) languid; (be) weary ▶나는 깨나른하다 I feel sluggish [listless]. ▶그는 깨나른하게 일어났다 He stood up in a languid [lazy] manner.

깨다¹ 1 〈잠 등에서〉 wake up; awake; be awakened
◆자나 깨나 asleep or awake / 잠이 덜 깨다 be half awake [asleep] / 잠[꿈]에서 깨다 wake [awake] from sleep [a dream]
▶나는 보통 아침 6시경에 깬다 I usually wake up around six o'clock in the morning.
▶무슨 큰 소리가 나서 잠이 깼다 I was awakened by a big noise.
▶다른 사람이 깨지 않도록 조용히 걸어야 한다 You must walk quietly so that the others will not wake up.
2 〈환상 등에서〉 come [be brought] to *one's* senses; be disillusioned
◆환상에서 깨다 wake from *one's* reverie [the illusion]
▶실패하여 그는 꿈에서 깼다 He was disillusioned from his dreams by his failure.
▶그의 말이 나를 꿈에서 깨게 했다 His remarks awakened me from a dream [brought me to my senses].
3 〈술이〉 sober up [off]; get [become] sober
▶이것을 마시면 술이 깬다 If you drink this, it will sober you up. ⇒ Drink this, and you will get sober.
▶밤바람을 쐬었더니 술이 깼다 The night wind sobered me up.
▶그가 술이 깰 때까지 기다리자 Let's wait till he becomes sober.
4 〈지적(知的)으로〉 be [become] civilized [enlightened, awakened]
◆무지한 사람들을 깨게 하다 enlighten the ignorant
▶신교육을 받아 사람들이 깼다 The people have been enlightened by new education.

깨다² 1 〈깨뜨리다〉 break (into [to]) pieces; crush; crack 《an egg, a nut》; smash
◆얼음을 깨다 break [crack] ice / 돌을 던져 유리창을 깨다 smash a stone through a window / 컵[접시]을 산산이 깨다 smash a glass [dish] into fine pieces [into atoms] / 유리창을 깨고 집에 들어가다 break the window into [to enter] the house / 높이 뛰기 기록을 깨다 break [beat] the record for the high jump
▶그는 컵을 마루에 떨어뜨려 깼다 He dropped a cup on the floor and broke it.
2 〈취소하다〉 cancel; dissolve; 〈어기다〉 break off [end] 《*one's* engagement》
◆계약을 깨다 break a contract / 혼담을 깨다 break up a proposed marriage
▶그와의 약속을 깨는 것은 좋지 않다 It is sinful to cancel him.
3 〈좌절시키다〉 frustrate [disappoint] *sb's* plans [hopes]; 〈파괴하다〉 break; destroy
◆침묵을 깨다 break *one's* [the] silence / 평화를 깨다 destroy the peace / 희망을 깨다 shatter *sb's* hopes
▶폭음이 밤의 정적을 깼다 An explosion broke the silence [stillness] of the night.
▶그들은 평화 회담을 깼다 They wrecked the peace negotiations.
4 〈줄이다〉 diminish; reduce; 〈망치다〉 spoil; ruin; mar
◆흥을 깨다 dampen [wet-blanket, spoil] *one's* pleasure
▶그의 말이 우리들 모두의 흥을 깼다 His remark threw a wet blanket on all of us.

깨다³ 〈부화되다〉 be hatched; hatch; 〈부화시키다〉 hatch 《an egg》
◆알에서 갓 깬 병아리 a newly-hatched [freshly hatched] chick; a chick fresh out of the shell [which has just hatched] / 알에서 깨다 hatch from [out of] the egg
▶오늘 아침 병아리 세 마리가[알이 모두] 깼다 Three chicks [All the eggs] have hatched this morning.

깨닫다 1 〈알다·인식하다〉 realize; see; understand; comprehend; become aware of [that]; 〈알아채다〉 sense [sniff] 《a danger》; scent 《a plot》; smell; get wise to 《a fact》
◆의무를 깨닫다 be conscious [aware] of *one's* duty / 진상을 깨닫게 하다 awake *sb* to the truth 《to》; convince *sb* of a truth
▶그는 자기 잘못을 깨달았다 He realized that he was mistaken. ⇒ He saw that he had made a mistake.
▶나는 세상이란 그런 거구나 하고 깨달았다 I have learned to take the world as it is.
▶나는 속은 것을 깨달았다 I found that I had been deceived.
▶그는 위험을 깨닫고 바로 그 자리를 떠났다 He sensed (the) danger and left the place at once.

▶ 깨달은 바 있어 그는 술을 끊었다 Realizing the harmfulness of the vice he has given up drinking.
2 〈종교적〉 attain spiritual enlightenment; be spiritually awakened
▶ 그가 도를 깨달은 것은 바로 그때였다 It was then that he attained spiritual enlightenment [was spiritually awakened].
▶ 그는 행자(行者)때 벌써 깨달은 바가 있었다 He was spiritually awakened [enlightened] already in his ascetic.

깨떡 a rice cake coated with sesame
깨뜨리다 crush ⇨ 깨다²
깨물다 bite; 〈앞니로〉 gnaw ▶ 그 여자는 분해서 입술을 깨물었다 She bit [gnawed] her lip in mortification. / 손톱을 깨물지 마라 Don't bite [gnaw] your (finger)nails.
깨소금 parched sesame seeds with salt
깨알 a grain of sesame; a sesame seed
♦ 깨알같은 글씨 very minute handwriting / 깨알만해서 보이지 않다 be so tiny that *one* can't see it
▶ 이 잡지는 깨알같은 활자로 인쇄되어 있다 This magazine is printed in small type.
깨우다 【깨게 하다】〈잠을〉 awaken; wake up *sb*; awake [arouse, rouse] *sb* from [out of] (his) sleep; 〈미몽에서〉 disillusion; disabuse (*sb* of an idea); undeceive; bring *sb* to (his) senses; 〈술에서〉 sober *sb* up; make *sb* sober
♦ 문을 두드려 깨우다 tap [knock] up *sb* / 흔들어 깨우다 shake *sb* out of (his) sleep
▶ [會話]「몇시에 깨워 드릴까요?」「6시 반에 깨워주세요」 "What time shall I wake you?" "Please wake me up at 6 : 30. ⇒ 〈호텔 교환원에게〉 Please give me a morning call at 6:30."
▶ 자고 있는 아기를 깨우지 마라 Don't wake (up) [arouse] the sleeping baby.
▶ 조용히 해라, 아기 깨우겠다 Be quiet or you'll wake the baby.

깨우치다 1〈깨닫게 하다〉 awake [awaken] *sb* to (the realities of life); open *sb's* eyes to *sth*; make *sb* realize [understand] *sth*
♦ 도리를 깨우치다 bring *sb* to reason / 잘못을 깨우치다 reason with *sb* on (his) mistake / 공상의 세계에서 눈앞의 가혹한 현실을 깨우치다 awake *sb* from reverie to the harsh facts before (him)
2 〈가르치다〉 teach; instruct; educate; 〈계몽하다〉 enlighten
♦ 어린이에게 글을 깨우치다 teach a child his letters / 민중[무지한 사람들]을 깨우치다 enlighten [educate] the public [ignorant]
깨죽 —粥 porridge made of ground sesame and rice
깨죽거리다 〈종알거리다〉 grumble about [at] *sth*; complain about [of] *sth*; mutter ▶ 그는 언제나 깨죽거린다 He is always complaining [grumbling].
깨지다 1〈물체가〉 break; split; smash; crack

> [解說] ***break***는 「깨지다」라는 뜻의 일반적인 말. ***smash***는 갑자기 쨍그렁거리며 갈라진다는 뜻. ***crack***은 금이 가서 갈라진다는 뜻.

♦ 깨진 꽃병[접시] a broken vase [dish] / 깨지기 쉬운 easily broken; fragile; frail
▶ 이 유리그릇은 잘 깨진다 This glass is fragile [breaks easily].
▶ 창유리가 산산이 깨졌다 The windowpane broke into [was smashed to] pieces.
▶ 그는 발 아래 얼음이 깨져 연못에 빠졌다 The ice under him cracked and he fell into the pond.
▶ 깨지기 쉬움 — 취급 주의 (표지) Fragile — Handle with care.
2 〈일 등이〉 be broken off; divide; split
▶ 균형이 깨졌다 The balance was upset [destroyed].
▶ 평화 회담[흥정]이 깨졌다 The peace talks [negotiations] were broken off.
▶ 두 나라 사이의 우호 관계가 깨졌다 Friendly relationships between the two countries were severed [ruptured].
▶ 약혼이 양가 부모의 반대로 깨졌다 The engagement was broken off because of their parents' opposition.
3 〈기록 등이〉 be broken [beaten]
▶ 이 신기록도 곧 깨질 것이다 This new record will be broken in the near future.
4 〈분위기가〉 be chilled; be spoiled
▶ 그가 있으면 흥이 깨진다 He spoils our fun. ⇒ (口) He is a killjoy [wet blanket].
▶ 그의 말로 일동의 흥이 깨졌다 His words chilled [spoiled] the pleasant atmosphere of the group.

깨지락거리다 〈음식을〉 pick at [trifle with] *one's* food; 〈일을〉 do *sth* with reluctance [half a heart]; go at *sth* reluctantly [half-heartedly, unenthusiastically]
▶ 깨지락거리지 말고 어서 먹어라 Stop picking at your food, eat it up!
깨치다 〈깨달아 알게 되다〉 perceive; realize; understand; become aware [conscious] of; 〈배우다〉 learn; master
♦ 글의 뜻을 깨치다 understand the meaning of a sentence / 진리를 깨치다 perceive a truth / 어려운 한문을 깨치다 learn [master] difficult Chinese classics
깩 Eek!; Yipe!; Yelp! —**깩하다** shriek; scream; screech
깩소리 a bit of objection [complaint, protest]
♦ 깩소리도 못하다 cannot let out the least objection / 깩소리 못하게 하다 squelch *sb*; silence
▶ 그는 깩소리 못했다 There was nothing he could say.
▶ 그의 논리에 모두 깩소리 못했다 His logic left everyone in silence.
▶ 이렇게 하면 그는 깩소리 못할 것이다 This will shut him up.
깻묵 seedcake of sesame; sesame dregs ■ 콩— bean cake
깻잎 a sesame leaf; 〈들깻잎〉 a perilla leaf
깽깽 〈깽깽거리다 yelp; (美) yip; yap ▶ 강아지가 깽깽거렸다 The puppy yelped.
꺄룩거리다 〈목을 빼다〉 make a long neck; crane (*one's* neck) (to get a better view)
▶ 그는 행렬을 보려고 꺄룩거렸다 He stretched

깍 [craned] his neck to see the procession.
깍 Eek! ⇨ 꽥
꺼끄러기 〈벼・보리 등의〉 a beard; an awn; an arista (*pl.* -tae) ◆꺼끄러기가 있는 bearded; awned; aristate
꺼내다 **1**〈물건 등을〉 draw [pull] out; take [bring] out; produce; carry out
▶ 나는 캐비닛에서 서류철을 꺼냈다 I pulled my file out of the cabinet. ⇌ I pulled [drew] out my file from the cabinet.
▶ 그는 은행에서 30만원을 꺼냈다 He drew out [withdrew] three hundred thousand won from his bank account.
▶ 비상시에는 이 상자를 꼭 밖으로 꺼내놓으시오 Be sure to take this box out in case of emergency.
▶ 그는 주머니에서 담배를 꺼내서 피웠다 He took a cigarette out of his pocket and smoked it.
▶ 그는 지갑에서 1만원권을 꺼내서 건네주었다 He took out a 10,000-won note from his wallet and handed it over.
2〈말 등을〉 bring 《a matter》 up 《for discussion》; bring out 《a question》; put *sth* before; introduce
◆이야기를 꺼내다 bring to talk 《about》; break the ice / 화제를 꺼내다 bring up a subject; introduce a subject to notice
▶ 그는 회의 중에 개인적인 이야기를 꺼내 놓았다 He dragged his own personal affairs into the discussion at the meeting.
▶ 내가 말을 꺼냈으니 내가 하겠다 As I have proposed it, I will do it.
▶ 거북해서 그 건을 꺼내기가 어려웠다 I was too embarrassed to broach the matter.
▶ 네가 말을 꺼내기를 기다렸다 I was waiting for your opening words.
▶ 언제 이 문제를 꺼내느냐가 문제다 The problem is when to broach the subject.
꺼당기다 pull; draw; haul; 〈갑자기〉 jerk; drag 《at》
◆밧줄을 꺼당기다 draw [pull] a rope; haul up [in] a rope / 소매를 꺼당기다 pull [tug] *sb* by the sleeve / 손[귀]을 꺼당기다 pull *sb's* hand [ear] / 옷을 꺼당기다 pull *sb's* collar; drag *sb* by the collar / 서로 꺼당기다 pull at each other / 힘껏 꺼당기다 pull with a sudden jerk
꺼덕꺼덕 ◆꺼덕꺼덕 마른 damp-dry; half-dry 《shirt》; damp-dried / 아직 꺼덕꺼덕 할 때 세탁물을 다림질하다 iron [press] the wash while it is still damp
▶ 옷이 꺼덕꺼덕 말랐다 The clothes are damp-dry.
꺼두르다 〈움켜쥐고 휘두르다〉 grab [grasp, clutch] and pull [drag] about; drag [shake] 《a woman by the hair》
꺼들이다 〈안으로 들이다〉 drag [pull, draw] in [into]; take in [into] ◆나무를 광에 꺼들이다 take firewood into a barn
꺼떡거리다 swagger; behave haughtily [in a cocky way]; put on airs; hold *one's* head high; assume an air of importance; give *oneself* airs
◆지위를 믿고 꺼떡거리다 magnify *one's*

office / 꺼떡거리고 걷다 walk with a swaggering gait; strut 《about, along》; walk tall
▶ 그는 언제나 꺼떡거린다 He always acts in a lordly manner. ⇌ He is always throwing his weight around.
꺼뜨리다 put out 《a fire》 by mistake; let 《the fire》 die [go] out ◆연탄불을 꺼뜨리지 않다 keep briquet fire alive
꺼리다 **1**〈싫어하다〉 loathe; dislike; have a dislike to [for]; have a distaste for; be reluctant 《to do》; 〈주저하다〉 hesitate 《to do》; scruple 《to do》; shrink from 《doing》; 〈피하다〉 avoid; shun; alienate; keep away from
◆꺼리는 풍습 a loathsome custom; an abominable custom / 남들과 사귀기를 꺼리다 shun society; dislike to see [keep] company / 남의 이목을 꺼리다 be diffident to others; avert people's eyes / 사진찍기를 꺼리다 be shy of camera; be camera-shy
▶ 그의 친구들은 그를 꺼리기 시작했다 His friends began to avoid [keep away from] him.
▶ 정직하지 못한 사람은 남을 속이기를 꺼리지 않는다 A dishonest man does not scruple to deceive others.
▶ 양심에 꺼려서 그런 일은 못하겠다 My conscience won't let me do that.
2〈금기시하다〉 taboo; put the taboo on
◆꺼리어 피하는 말 a tabooed word; a word considered to be unlucky
▶ 이 지방에는 아직도 육식을 꺼리는 풍습이 남아 있다 In this part of the country, people still maintain the taboo against eating animal flesh.
꺼림(칙)하다 be [feel] uneasy 《about》; be disgusting; weigh 《on》; have an uneasy conscience; have a sense of having done wrong; feel regret
◆말하기 꺼림칙하지만 I fear [dread] to say, but…
▶ 그는 이 일이 몹시 꺼림칙했다 This bore heavily on his mind.
▶ 무엇이 꺼림(칙)합니까? What's on your mind?
▶ 나는 그 음식을 먹기는 했으나 꺼림칙했다 I ate the food but I was not quite comfortable about it.
꺼멓다 (deep-)black ⇨ 까맣다 1
꺼메지다 become black ⇨ 까매지다
꺼벙하다 〈엉성하다〉 big and clumsy [but shaky]; hulking
꺼오다 〈끄어 오다〉 draw 《a chair》 near [up to, close to] *one*; pull [bring] nearer; drag in
꺼지다 **1**〈불이〉 go out; die out 《▶전자가 일반적, 후자는 「서서히 꺼지다」라는 뉘앙스가 있음》; be put out; be turned off 《스위치로》
◆꺼져가는 불[등불] a dying fire [failing light] / 꺼진 담배 a dead [burnt-out] cigarette / 불이 꺼지지 않게 하다 keep the fire alive [going]
▶ 불은 곧[저절로] 꺼졌다 The fire was soon put out [died down by itself].
▶ 창의 등불이 모두 꺼졌다 All the lights in the windows went out.

▶불이 꺼졌는지 확인해라 Make sure that the fire has been put out [has gone out].
2 〈거품이〉 vanish; burst; break; 〈엔진 등이〉 stop; stall ◆거품처럼 꺼지다 vanish like a bubble
▶거품은 꺼졌다 The bubbles burst.
▶기름이 다 떨어져 내 차의 엔진이 꺼졌다 The engine of my car stalled [stopped] because it was out of gas.
3 〈사라지다〉 disappear; go out of sight
▶꺼져(버려)! (口) Get lost! ⇌ Get out (of here at once)! ⇌ (口) Beat it!
▶그는 꺼져가는 소리로 대답했다 He replied in a very faint voice.

꺼지다² **1** 〈땅이〉 cave in; sink; 〈얼음판이〉 give (way); crack; 〈마루가〉 give (in)
▶어제 내린 비로 지면이 꺼졌다 The ground has sunk [caved] in because of yesterday's rain.
▶아이들의 무게로 마루가 꺼졌다 The floor gave in under the weight of the children.
2 〈눈자위가〉 become deep-set; sink in; become hollow
◆눈이 움푹 꺼진 노인 an old man with sunken eyes
▶그는 눈이 푹 꺼져 있다 His eyes are sunken (in).
3 〈배가〉 get [feel] hungry

꺼칠하다 not sleek(y) [slick]; rough; coarse; 〈수척하다〉 withered; shriveled; worn; 〈서술적〉 become haggard 《from want of sleep》; become gaunt 《from illness》; have an unhealthy complexion ◆꺼칠한 얼굴 a worn [haggard] face
▶어머니는 근심으로 얼굴이 꺼칠해지셨다 Worry has made my mother look drawn and haggard.

꺼펑이 〈덧쐬운 것〉 a cover; a covering; a hood

꺼풀 the skin ⇨ 까풀

꺽 〈트림 소리〉 with a belch [(口) burp]

꺽다리 a long-legged person; (美口) a gangling fellow; (口) a bean pole; (口) a daddy longlegs

꺽둑거리다 〈대충 썰다〉 cut [chop] 《radish》 in uneven bits [slices]

꺽둑꺽둑 ◆무를 꺽둑꺽둑 썰다 cut [chop] radish in uneven bits [slices]

꺽짓손 〈만만치 않은 수단〉 resolute and compelling means [measures, steps] ◆꺽짓손 세다 have the means to be bold and decisive; have resolute [bold] and compelling means

꺾꽂이 a cutting; 〈방법〉 (propagation by) cutting —**꺾꽂이하다** plant a cutting ▶이 나무는 꺾꽂이할 수 있습니까? Can this tree be grown from a cutting?
■—**모** a sapling grown up from a cutting; 〈꺾꽂이순〉 a cutting; a set

꺾다 **1** 〈가지 등을〉 break (off); snap
◆나뭇가지를 꺾다 break off a branch; break a branch off a tree / 붓을 꺾다 〈쓰기를〉 give up writing; 〈작가 활동을〉 give up literary activity
▶그녀는 잔가지를 꺾었다 She snapped a twig.
▶요즈음은 붓을 꺾었다 I do not write these days.
▶꽃을 꺾지 마라 Don't pick the flowers.
▶나무를 꺾지 마시오 (게시) Do not damage the trees.
2 〈억누르다〉 crush; discourage; frustrate
◆기를 꺾다 depress sb's spirit; discourage / 사기를 꺾다 depress the morale; demoralize
▶나는 그의 콧대를 꺾어 놓았다 I took him down a peg (or two).
▶그의 무관심이 나의 열성을 꺾어버렸다 His aloofness crushed my enthusiasm.
3 〈굽히다〉 yield 《to》; give in 《to》; concede
▶그는 고집을 꺾고 그녀의 요구를 받아 들였다 He finally gave in [yielded] to her request.
▶쌍방이 자기 의견을 꺾지 않았다 Both stuck fast to their own opinions.
4 〈이기다〉 beat; defeat
▶오늘 축구 경기에서 서울 대학이 도쿄 대학을 3:0으로 꺾었다 Seoul National University defeated [beat] Tokyo University three to nothing in a soccer match today.
5 〈방향을〉 turn; make a turn ◆차의 핸들을 오른쪽으로 꺾다 turn the steering wheel to the right
▶다음 모퉁이에서 왼편으로 꺾으시오 Turn (to the) left at the next corner.
6 〈접히다〉 fold; turn down; turn up ◆바지 솔기를 꺾다 turn up the hem of one's trousers / 칼라를 꺾다 turn down the collar

꺾쇠 a cramp (iron); a clamp; a clam ◆꺾쇠로 단단히 고정시키다 make 《things》 fast with cramps; fasten [hold] sth with cramps
■—**괄호** (印) a bracket

꺾어지다 **1** 〈부러지다〉 break; be broken; 〈무게로〉 give way; 〈딱하고〉 snap; [醫] 〈뼈가〉 fracture
◆한가운데서 두 동강으로 꺾어지다 break in half
▶너무 구부리지 마라, 꺾어질라 Don't bend it too far, or it will break.
2 〈접히다〉 be folded; be doubled (둘로)
▶그의 무게로 가지가 꺾어졌다 The branch broke [gave way] under his weight.

꺾이다 **1** ⇨ 꺾어지다
2 〈억눌리다〉 break (down); be discouraged; be dispirited; lose heart [courage]
◆기가 꺾이다 lose heart [courage]; be discouraged [dispirited]
▶나는 용기가 꺾였다 My heart died within me.
▶불행한 사건으로 그의 야망이 꺾였다 An unfortunate accident killed his ambition.
▶나의 모든 희망은 꺾였다 All my hopes were shattered [dashed].
▶그는 출발을 잘못해서 사기가 꺾인 것 같다 His poor start seems to have discouraged him.
▶그의 용기는 어떤 일에도 꺾이지 않았다 His courage was never shaken by anything.
▶그는 한번쯤의 실패로 꺾일 사람이 아니다 He is not a man to be daunted by a single failure.
3 〈굴복하다〉 yield [submit] 《to》; give in [bend, bow] 《to》; (口) cave in

♦금력에 꺾이다 bow to money / 역경에도 꺾이지 않다 bear up well under difficult [adverse] circumstances
4 〈방향이〉 turn; go round; round; 〈굽어지다〉 bend; curve; be bent; be crooked
▶ 강은 오른쪽으로 꺾인다 The river turns to the right.
▶ 산길은 거기서 갑자기 왼쪽으로 꺾인다 The mountain road turns abruptly to the left there.
▶ 타구는 왼쪽으로 꺾여 파울이 되었다 The batted ball flew left and crossed the foul line.

껄껄 ♦껄껄 웃으면서 (answer) with a loud laugh / 껄껄 웃다 laugh aloud [loudly]; guffaw; hawhaw

껄껄하다 〈거칠거칠하다〉 rough (surface); coarse; gritty; sandy
♦껄껄한 살결 rough skin / 껄껄한 천 coarse cloth; cloth of (a) rough texture / 껄껄한 촉감 a rough [sandy] feel
▶ 이 종이는 껄껄하다 This paper feels rough.
▶ 그의 손은 터서 껄껄했다 His hands were chapped and rough.
▶ 모래 때문에 마루가 껄껄했다 The floor felt rough with sand.

껄끄럽다 **1** 〈따끔거리다〉 prickly; pricking; irritating ▶ 이 천은 껄끄럽다 This cloth prickles (my skin). ≒ This cloth feels prickly.
2 〈껄껄하다〉 coarse; rough (surface); sandy
♦촉감이 껄끄럽다 be bristly to the touch ▶ 이 내복은 껄끄럽다 This undershirt scratches.

껄끔거리다 prick

껄떡이 〈탐욕스런 사람〉 greedy person; a covetous [an avaricious] person

껄떡하다 〈눈이〉 deep-set; sunken [hollow] (eyes) ▶ 그는 수면 부족으로 눈이 껄떡했다 His eyes were sunken deep for want of sleep.

껄렁껄렁하다 poor; worthless; trashy; rubbishy; useless; good-for-nothing
♦껄렁껄렁한 사람 a worthless [shiftless] person; a useless fellow; a wastrel
▶ 저런 껄렁껄렁한 녀석과 사귀지 마라 Don't make friends with such a good-for-nothing [useless] fellow.

껄렁이 a good-for-nothing (fellow); a useless fellow; a wastrel

껄렁패 —牌 good-for-nothing crews; a shiftless lot; scamps

껌 (a stick of) chewing gum ♦껌을 씹다 chew gum; have a chew of gum ■풍선— bubble gum

껌껌하다 **1** ⇨ 깜깜하다 **1 2** 〈마음씨가〉 black-hearted (person); crafty; scheming; evil-minded; wicked

껍데기 a shell (⇨ 껍질) ♦껍데기를 벗기다 take the shell off; (비유) take all the money [possessions] away from sb

껍죽거리다 behave haughtily [arrogantly]; assume an air of (self-)importance; put on [give oneself] airs; be too forward

껍질 〈나무의〉 (a) bark; 〈과일의〉 skin; rind (두꺼운); peel (벗겨진); 〈곡물의〉 husks (〈보통 복수형〉); 〈콩 등의〉 a hull; a shell (단단한); 〈견과의〉 nutshell

♦굴껍질 an oyster shell / 달걀 껍질 an eggshell / 달팽이 껍질 a snail shell / 땅콩 껍질 the skin of a peanut / 복숭아[사과] 껍질 the skin [peel] of a peach [an apple] / 빵 껍질 the crust of bread / 수박 껍질 the rind of a watermelon / 양파 껍질 the coats of an onion / 옥수수 껍질 husks of corn / 포도 껍질 grape-skin / 귤[사과, 바나나] 껍질을 벗기다 peel a tangerine [an apple, a banana] / 나무 껍질을 벗기다 bark a tree / 죽순 껍질을 벗기다 strip a bamboo shoot / 콩 껍질을 벗기다 shell [hull] peas
▶ 나는 토마토를 껍질채 먹었다 I ate a tomato skin and all.
▶ 그녀는 감자를 껍질채 삶았다 She boiled potatoes in their jackets [unpeeled].
▶ 감자 껍질 좀 벗겨 주세요 Will you please peel the potatoes?
▶ 나는 바나나 껍질을 밟아 미끄러졌다 I slipped on a banana peel.

-껏 **1** 〈있는 대로〉 as far [much] as possible; to the full extent (of); to the utmost (of)
♦목청껏 at the top of one's voice [lungs] / 수단껏 every possible means / 마음껏 먹다 eat to one's heart's content; make [have] a hearty meal of / 마음껏 울다 weep to one's heart's content; have one's cry out / 양껏 먹다 eat one's fill; gorge oneself 《with meat》; stuff and cramp plentifully / 재간껏 하다 do one's best [utmost] (in); do sth to the best of one's ability [as best one can] / 정성껏 대접하다 entertain sb cordially [from (the bottom of) one's heart]; keep a good house / 힘껏 일하다 work as hard as one can; do one's best [utmost]; work up to capacity
2 〈까지〉 (right) up to (now); (up) until now; till now; up to the present
▶ 나는 저렇게 예쁜 소녀를 여태껏 본 적이 없다 I have never seen such a pretty girl.
▶ 여태껏 어디 있었니? Where have you been all this while?

껑거리 〈길마의〉 a crupper
■ —끈 hip-strap strings; a crupper —막대 the crossbar of a hip strap

껑충 with a jump [leap]
▶ 그는 담을 껑충 뛰어넘었다 He jumped [sprang, leaped] over a fence.
▶ 휘발유 값이 껑충 뛰었다 The price of gasoline took a jump [has jumped (up)].
▶ 그는 개울을 껑충 뛰어넘었다 He cleared a brook in one vault.

껑충거리다 walk with bouncing [leaping] strides

껑충하다 tall and long-legged; lanky; (口) gangling ♦껑충한 소년 a lanky [gangling] boy

께 〈에게〉 to [by, for] sb
♦어머니께 온 편지 a letter for my mother / 하나님께 기도드리다 pray to God
▶ 나는 아버지께 그 책을 드렸다 I gave the book to my father.
▶ 이 편지를 선생님께 갖다 드려라 Give this letter to your teacher.
▶ 김 선생님께 올림 To [Presented to] Mr. Kim with best wishes from Min.

-께[1] 〈때〉 time; 〈무렵〉 about; around; 〈…할 즈음〉 when; while
♦그믐[보름]께 about the end [middle] of the month / 연말께 toward(s) the end of the year / 10시께 (at) about [around] ten o'clock / 일요일 저녁께 toward Sunday evening / 정오께 around noontime; toward noon / 지난달 중순께 about the middle of last month
▶6시께 또 만나자 I'll see you again (at) about six o'clock.
▶會話「그녀가 돌아온 것은 몇시였니?」「6시께였어」 "What time was it when she came?" "It was about [around] six."

-께[2] 〈장소〉 around; in and around; near; in the neighborhood of (근처에)
♦이 근처 어디께 somewhere around [about, near] here / 정거장께 near the station / 종로 네거리께 near [around] the Chongno cross; in the neighborhood of the Chongno crossroads
▶이 근처 어디께 공중전화가 있습니까? Is there a public telephone [pay phone] somewhere around [near] here?
▶저번에 그를 만난 것은 바로 여기께였다 It was right around here that I last saw him.

께끄름하다 〈꺼림하다〉 be anxious [nervous] 《about》; feel uneasy 《about》; have misgivings 《about》; 〈사물이 주어〉 weigh on *one*'s mind; lie at *one*'s heart; get on *one*'s nerves
♦뒷맛이 께끄름한 꿈 a dream remembered with discomfort
▶그에게 답장을 하지 않았더니 께끄름하다 I feel guilty about not answering his letter.
▶그 일이 께끄름해서 잠이 오지 않았다 The matter weighed so heavily on my mind that I could not get to sleep.

께느른하다 languid; weary; languourous; dull; listless; slack ♦께느른한 오후 a slack [languid] afternoon ♦오늘은 무척 께느른하다 I feel very tired [lazy] today.
▶날씨가 더워 몸이 께느른하다 The warm weather makes me feel listless [languid].

께서 from *sb* ▶아버지께서 내게 새해 선물로 이것을 주셨다 My father gave me this as [for] a New Year's gift.

께옵서 from *sb* ⇨ 께서
께적거리다 pick at *one*'s food ⇨ 깨지락거리다
께죽거리다 1 ⇨ 깨죽거리다 2 〈음식을〉 eat without appetite; pick [chew dryly] at *one*'s food
께지럭거리다 pick at [trifle with] *one*'s food ⇨ 깨지락거리다

껴안다 1 〈포옹하다〉 embrace *sb* close(ly) [tightly]; hug 《a baby》; press [clasp] *sb* to *one*'s breast; cuddle *sb*
♦꼭 껴안다 give *sb* a tight hug [close embrace]/ 목을 껴안다 throw [fold] *one*'s arms around [about] *sb*'s neck / 서로 껴안다 embrace [hug] each other; be in [go into] each other's arms
▶어머니는 아기를 꼭 껴안았다 The mother clasped her baby to her breast.
▶두 소녀는 서로 껴안고 울었다 The two girls wept in each other's arms.
▶소녀는 두 팔로 껴안을 수 없을 만큼 많은 선물을 받았다 The little girl received so many presents (that) she couldn't carry them in her arms.
2 〈일을 안아 맡다〉 take a lot of tasks upon *oneself* ♦나는 많은 일을 껴안고 있다 I've got a lot of work to do.

껴입다 wear 《more clothes》 over another; put 《more clothes》 on top of what *one* is wearing
♦내의를 석장 껴입다 wear three undershirts one over another / 옷을 지나치게 껴입다 wear too many clothes
▶추우니까 옷을 껴입고 가거라 You should pile on your clothes, it is cold outside.
▶그는 스웨터 위에 또 스웨터를 껴입고 있다 He wears one sweater over another.

꼬깃꼬깃하다 crumpled; wrinkled 《with handling》 ♦편지가 꼬깃꼬깃하게 구겨 뭉쳐져 있다 The letter is crumpled into a ball.

꼬꼬 〈兒〉 〈닭〉 a chick; 〈암탉의 울음 소리〉 clucking; cackling ♦꼬꼬하고 울다 cluck; 〈알을 낳고〉 cackle

꼬끼오 cock-a-doodle-doo ━**꼬끼오하다** cry cock-a-doodle(-doo); crow

꼬느다 1 〈치켜들다〉 lift up with a stretched arm ♦어린애를 한 손으로 꼬느다 lift a child high up in the air with one hand
2 〈벼르다〉 nurse [toy with] an idea; 〈가다듬다〉 be on standby; make ready 《to do》
▶꼬느기만 해서 무슨 소용이 있니? What's the use of just nursing your plans?

꼬다 1 〈새끼 등을〉 twist; entwist; twine; throw
♦노끈을 꼬다 twist threads into a string; braid a cord / 철사를 꼬다 twist wires together
▶우리는 짚으로 새끼를 꼬았다 We twisted pieces of straw into a rope.
▶그 철사는 잘 꼬아지지 않는다 The wire would not twist easily.
2 〈몸을〉 twist; writhe ♦사지를 꼬다 twist *one*'s limbs / 다리를 꼬고 앉다 sit with *one*'s legs crossed
3 ⇨ 비꼬다

꼬드기다 1 〈부추기다〉 tempt; allure; 〈선동하다〉 incite; abet; egg on
♦꼬드겨 …하게 하다 entice [allure, tempt] *sb* to 《do》; egg [set] *sb* on to 《an act, do *sth*》
▶다른 사내아이들이 그를 꼬드겨 싸움을 시켰다 The other boys egged him on to fight.
2 〈연줄을〉 tug at the string of a kite (to make the kite go up higher)

꼬들꼬들하다 dry and hard; (rather) hard
♦꼬들꼬들한 밥 hard-boiled rice

꼬락서니 an appearance ▶네 꼬락서니 못 보겠다 I hate to see you. ⇌ You are so disgusting. ▶네 꼬락서니를 좀 봐라 How dirty [ugly] you are!

꼬르륵 〈뱃속이〉 with a rumble; 〈액체가〉 with a gurgle
▶뱃속에서 꼬르륵 소리가 난다 (비유) I am so empty. ⇌ I can hear my stomach.
▶배가 얼마나 고픈지 속에서 꼬르륵 소리가 다

난다 I'm so hungry that my stomach's rumbling. ⇌ I am so empty that I can hear my stomach.
—**꼬르륵하다** give a growl

꼬리 1 【동물의】 a tail; 〈여우 등의〉 a brush; 〈토끼 등의 짧은〉 a scut; 〈공작 등의〉 a train
◆ 꼬리가 있는[없는] tailed [tailless]
▶ 말은 꼬리가 길다 A horse has a long tail.
▶ 강아지 한 마리가 꼬리를 흔들며 따라왔다 A puppy followed me wagging its tail.
▶ 그 말은 꼬리를 휙 휘둘렀다 The horse swished its tail.
2 〈유성·혜성의〉 a tail; a trail (of a comet); 〈끝〉 an end ◆ 무 꼬리 the end of a radish
▶ 제트기가 길게 꼬리를 남겼다 The jet left a long tail behind it.
3 (비유) 〈후미〉 the rear; 〈단서〉 a clue; 〈정체〉 one's true colors; one's real nature
◆ 꼬리에 꼬리를 물고 one after another; without a break; incessantly / 말꼬리를 잡다 pounce on sb's words / 꼬리를 잡히다 give a clue to (the police); be traced by
▶ 그는 항상 사장에게 꼬리를 친다 He is always flattering his boss.
▶ 그는 나의 말꼬리를 잡고 심하게 비난했다 He criticized me severely for a slip of the tongue.
▶ 전화가 하루 종일 꼬리를 물고 이어졌다 The phone rang continually [without a break] throughout the day.
■ —**깃털** tail feathers —**끝** a tail end; the end [tip] of a tail

꼬리가 길면 밟힌다 (속담) Evil acts are always discovered [never escape detection]. ⇌ An evil deed will be discovered.

꼬리지느러미 【動】 a caudal [tail] fin

꼬리표 —票 a label; a tag; a docket
◆ 꼬리표가 제대로 붙은 짐 properly labeled baggage / 꼬리표를 달다 fasten [(美) fix, attach] a label [tag] to (a trunk); tag [label] (one's baggage); put a label on (one's baggage)

꼬마 1 ⇨ 꼬마둥이 2 ⇨ 어린아이 3 〈소형〉 miniature (tube); midget (airplane); pocket (battleship)
■ —**스타** a baby star —**신랑** a very young bridegroom [husband] —**인형** a miniature doll —**자동차** a baby [midget] car; a minicar —**전구** a miniature (electric) bulb; a midget [fairy] lamp —**진공관** a miniature tube [bulb]

꼬마둥이 1 〈작은 사람〉 a dwarf; a midget; a small person; a shorty 2 〈어린아이〉 a little kid ◆ 「꼬마둥이」 소년 a boy nicknamed "Shorty"

꼬막 【貝】 a cockle

꼬무락거리다 move slowly ⇨ 꾸무럭거리다

꼬바기 straight through ⇨ 꼬박

꼬박 〈줄곧〉 straight through; without any break; 〈완전히〉 fully; completely
◆ 꼬박 밤을 새우다 do not sleep a wink; sit [stay] up all night [the whole night]; keep [stay, remain] awake all night / 누가 오기를 꼬박 하루를 기다리다 wait for sb to come all day long
▶ 꼬박 세 시간 동안이나 너를 기다리고 있었다 I have been waiting for you for three hours straight.
▶ 가게는 재고 정리 때문에 꼬박 1주일 동안 문을 열지 않았다 The store was closed for inventory all week.
▶ 여기서 읍내까지는 꼬박 하룻길이다 The town is a good day's trip from here.

꼬박꼬박 regularly; methodically; faithfully; obediently ◆ 일기를 꼬박꼬박 적다 make regular entries in one's diary / 집세를 꼬박꼬박 치르다 pay one's rent regularly

꼬박이 straight through ⇨ 꼬박

꼬부라뜨리다 bend (one's back); hook; curve (a wire); crook (one's arm)

꼬부라지다 1 〈구부러지다〉 bend; curve; be bent; be crooked; 〈길이〉 turn (to the right)
◆ 꼬부라진 소나무 a crooked pine (tree) / 오른쪽으로 꼬부라지다 turn [strike] to the right (hand) / 늙어 허리가 꼬부라지다 be bent (in the back) with age; stoop from age / 혀가 꼬부라지다 be tongue-tied; have an impediment in one's speech
2 〈심성이〉 get crooked; become perverse; be cross-grained ◆ 심성이 꼬부라진 사람 a perverse person; a person of vicious nature

꼬부랑글자 —字 〈서투른 글씨〉 a poor hand; "hen tracks"; 〈서양 글자〉 alphabetic letters

꼬부랑길 a winding [tortuous] path ▶ 꼬부랑길이 산을 누비고 이어져 있다 The tortuous path led on through the hills.

꼬부랑꼬부랑 meanderingly ⇨ 꼬불꼬불

꼬부랑늙은이 a bent [stooping] old person

꼬부랑하다 〈등이〉 bent; 〈길이〉 winding; 〈냇물이〉 meandering; 〈나무 등이〉 crooked ◆ 늙어 허리가 꼬부랑하다 be bowed with years; be bent with age; stoop from age

꼬부리다 〈몸을〉 stoop (over); bow; 〈물건을〉 bend; crook; curve
◆ 손가락을 꼬부리다 bend [hook] one's fingers / 안쪽으로 꼬부리다 bend [turn] in; inflect / 철사를 꼬부리다 bend a wire

꼬불꼬불 windingly; zigzag ◆ 꼬불꼬불 흐르는 시내 a meandering stream
▶ 새 고속도로는 높은 산 사이를 꼬불꼬불 지나가고 있었다 The new highway twisted through the high mountain.
■ —**꼬불꼬불하다** crooked; meandering; winding; zigzag; tortuous (curve)
▶ 나는 꼬불꼬불한 숲속의 오솔길을 더듬어 갔다 I followed a path meandering through the woods.
▶ 꼬불꼬불한 길은 산 꼭대기까지 이어져 있었다 The winding road led to the top of the hill.

꼬불탕하다 winding; meandering (lane); zigzag ◆ 꼬불탕한 길[개천] a winding road [meandering stream]

꼬붓하다 somewhat bent; slightly curved; crooked a little

꼬빡꼬빡 drowsily ⇨ 꾸벅꾸벅

꼬이다 1 〈실 등이〉 tangle; be [get] (en)tangled; be twisted; kink; (美) be snarled
◆ 넥타이가 꼬여 있다 have one's tie twisted /

꼬인 것을 풀다 untwist; disentangle; (美) unsnarl
▶실이 꼬였다 Strings were twisted.
2 〈일이〉 suffer [meet with] a setback; go wrong [amiss, awry]
▶만사가 꼬였다 Everything went against me [athwart, awry, crisscross].
▶나는 사업이 꼬여서 고생했다 I suffered from the unsatisfactory state of my business.
3 〈마음이〉 get cross; become crooked [distorted, perverse] ◆성격이 꼬이다 have a crook in *one's* character / 속[배알]이 꼬이다 get cranky; grow peevish

꼬장꼬장하다 1 〈물건이〉 straight and stiff
2 〈노인이〉 straight and strong; hale and hearty
▶70노인이지만 그분은 아직도 꼬장꼬장하시다 Though a septuagenarian, he is still vigorous and erect in figure.
3 〈성미가〉 stern; unbending; upright; incorruptible ▶그는 성미가 꼬장꼬장하다 He has a stern character [is an upright man].

꼬집다 1 〈살갗을〉 pinch; give a pinch; nip
◆세게 꼬집다 give *sb* a sharp pinch [nip] 《on the arm》 / 꼬집어 멍들게 하다 pinch *sb* black and blue
▶그녀는 내 팔을 꼬집었다 She pinched my arm.
▶나는 꿈이 아닌가 하고 내 몸을 꼬집어 보았다 I pinched myself to see if it is not a dream.
2 〈남의 잘못 등을〉 make cynical [cutting, sarcastic] remarks about *sth*; speak [talk] ironically; be cynical [sarcastic] 《about》
◆남의 잘못을 꼬집다 catch *sb* tripping; trip *sb* up / 결점을 꼬집어내다 pick [point] out *sb's* defects; pick a hole in *sb's* coat

꼬창모 〈農〉〈꼬챙이로 심는 모〉 dibbled rice seedlings; rice plants set out with a dibble

꼬챙이 a spit; a skewer; 〈농업용의〉 a dibble
◆꼬챙이에 꿰다 skewer; spit; have《a fish》on a spit [skewer]
▶우리는 생선을 꼬챙이에 꿰어 구웠다 We broiled fish on skewers [spits]. ⇒ We put a fish on a skewer and broiled it.

꼬치 1 〈요리〉 skewered stuff; food on a skewer **2** ⇨ 꼬챙이

꼬치고기 〔魚〕a barracuda (*pl.* ~s)

꼬치꼬치 1 〈깡마른 모양〉 ▶꼬치꼬치 마르다 be nothing but skin and bones; be as thin as a lath; skinny; skin and bone(s)
2 〈따지고 캐묻는 모양〉 inquisitively
◆꼬치꼬치 캐묻다 inquire of *sb* about every detail of 《a matter》; catechize *sb* to the last detail about *sth*
▶그는 내게 꼬치꼬치 캐물었다 He questioned me even to the minutest details. ⇒ He subjected me to searching inquiry.

꼬치백반 ―白飯 rice with a sidedish of skewered stuff

꼬투리 1 〈콩 등의〉 a pod; a hull; a husk; a peas(e)cod 〈완두의〉 ◆꼬투리에 든 콩 beans in the pods / 꼬투리를 까다 shell [pod] peas
2 〈담뱃잎의〉 a midrib of tobacco leaf
3 〈일의〉 cause; reason; origin《of an affair》

◆아무 꼬투리도 없이 without any reason; without cause / 오해의 꼬투리가 되다 offer a cause to incur misunderstanding / 꼬투리를 잡다 invent [make up] a pretext《for a quarrel》/ 꼬투리를 캐다 trace《an event》to its origin
▶도대체 싸우게 된 꼬투리가 뭐냐? What on earth is the bone of contention?

꼭 1 〈시각 등〉 just; right; sharp (▶시각의 뒤에 붙임); exactly; precisely
◆꼭 사흘 three days to the hour / 꼭 3마일 exactly three miles; three miles to an inch / 꼭 한가운데에 right in the center; in the very center
▶비행기는 꼭 10시에 출발했다 The plane left at ten o'clock sharp [on the dot].
▶열차는 꼭 시간대로 도착했다 The train arrived just [right] on time.
2 〈반드시〉 surely; certainly; for sure; by all means; without fail
▶그녀는 꼭 돌아옵니다 I am sure she will come back. ⇒ I know for sure [certain] she will come back.
▶〔會話〕「파티에 꼭 오세요」「꼭 갈게요」 "Be sure to come to our party." "I sure will."
▶그는 꼭 성공할 것이다 He will surely [certainly] succeed. ⇒ He is sure [certain] to succeed. ⇒ I am sure [certain] (that) he will succeed. ⇒ It is certain that he will succeed.
▶꼭 알려주세요. Be sure to let me know. ⇒ Don't fail to inform me.
3 〈단단히〉 tightly; firmly; hard; fast
◆꼭 쥐다 hold《a thing》tightly [fast]; grasp firmly
▶이 밧줄을 꼭 잡으시오 Hold this rope hard [tight].
▶그는 구두끈을 꼭 죄었다 He tied his shoelaces tightly.
▶창문은 꼭 닫혀 있었다 The window was tightly closed.
▶창문을 꼭 닫아라 Secure the window.
▶그는 입을 꼭 다물고 있다 He is clamming up.
▶그 모녀는 서로 꼭 껴안았다 The mother and daughter embraced [hugged] each other tightly.
▶내 새 구두가 너무 꼭 낀다 My new shoes are too tight for me.
4 〈딱〉 exactly; correct; 《fit, suit》to a T
◆꼭 맞는 말 a becoming word; an apt [a pertinent] remark / 꼭 맞지 않다 do not fit well
▶답이 꼭 맞는다 The answer is perfectly correct.
▶이 구두는 내게 꼭 맞는다 These shoes fit me perfectly [to a T].
▶꼭 좋을 때 왔구나 You came at just the right moment.
▶계산이 꼭 맞았다 The calculation came out exactly right.
5 〈마치〉 as if; just like
◆꼭 죽은[미친] 사람 같다 look as if dead [*sb* were mad]
▶저 구름은 꼭 사람 얼굴 같다 That cloud

looks just [exactly] like a human face.
▶그는 독일어를 꼭 독일 사람처럼 한다 He speaks German as if [as though] he were German. ≒ He speaks German just like a native.

꼭꼭 1 ⇨ 꽉 1
2 〈가득〉 to the full; with no room [not an inch] to spare ♦꼭꼭 채워넣다[눌러 담다] pack in tightly; fill chock-full; (美) jam-pack
3 〈어김없이〉 without fail; for sure; regularly ♦세금을 꼭꼭 바치다 pay one's taxes regularly; never fail to pay one's taxes / 약속을 꼭꼭 지키다 keep one's promise scrupulously; never fail to keep one's promise

꼭대기 1【맨위】 the top; the apex; 〈산의〉 the summit; 〈머리·모자의〉 the crown; 〈뾰족한 것의〉 spire
♦산 꼭대기 a mountaintop; the top [summit, peak] of a mountain / 지붕 꼭대기 a rooftop, the top of a roof
▶그 산 꼭대기는 일년 내내 눈에 덮여 있다 The mountain is crowned with snow all the year round.
▶그들은 나를 머리 꼭대기에서 발끝까지 노려보았다 They stared at me from head to toe.
▶언덕 꼭대기에서 호수가 보인다 We can see a lake from the top of the hill.
2 〈우두머리〉 a boss; the chief; the head; the leader ♦사람들의 꼭대기에 서다 be a leader of men; stand at the head of others; lead others

꼭두각시 a puppet; 〈실을 달아 놀리는〉 a marionette ♦남의 꼭두각시 노릇을 하다 act as another's tool [instrument, cat's-paw]
■—놀음 a puppet play [show]; a marionette play [show]

꼭두새벽 the peep of day [dawn]
♦꼭두새벽에 《start》 quite early in the morning; before dawn [daybreak]
▶어제는 꼭두새벽부터 손님이 찾아왔다 I had a visitor in the early hours of yesterday.
▶꼭두새벽부터 뭘 하고 있니? What do you think you are doing at this unearthly [extraordinary] hour?

꼭두서니 〈植〉 a madder; 〈빛깔〉 madder (red)

꼭뒤 1〈뒤통수 한복판〉 the back of the head
2〈활의〉 a (bow) nock

꼭뒤누르다 〈억누르다〉 suppress; have sb under one's thumb [control]

꼭뒤눌리다 〈압제받다〉 be suppressed; be dominated 《by sb》; be under sb's thumb [control]

꼭뒤지르다 〈선수치다〉 forestall; outwit; steal a march on

꼭뒤질리다 be forestalled [anticipated] 《by》; get beaten to ▶그 책을 사려다 다른 사람한테 꼭뒤질렸다 I was going to buy the book but someone bought it ahead of me.

꼭지 1 〈그릇 뚜껑의〉 a knob; 〈수도·가스 등의〉 a (stop) cock; a tap; (美) a faucet ♦꼭지를 틀다[잠그다] turn on [off] a tap
2 〈줄기〉 a stem; a stalk; 〈꽃의〉 a peduncle
3 〈거지의 두목〉 the boss 《of a band of beggars》
4 〈연의〉 a decorative strip pasted near the top of a kite
5 〈도리깨 자루〉 the pivot of a flail
6 〈묶음〉 a bunch; a bundle ♦미역 두 꼭지 two bunches [bundles] of seaweed
■젖— a nipple; a teat ■—각 〔數〕 a vertical angle —딴 the head of a group of vagrants —마리 a spinning wheel handle —점 an apex, 〔數〕 a vertex 꼭짓집 a laundry shop where laundry bundles are taken to be counted after washing

꼰질꼰질하다 overmeticulous; overscrupulous; too fussy ▶그는 무슨 일에나 너무 꼰질꼰질하다 He is too meticulous in everything.

꼴[1] 〈모양〉 a shape; a form; a figure; 〈외양〉 appearance; 〈복장〉 clothes; 〈상태〉 a state; a plight; 〈광경〉 sight; look miserable
♦꼴이 말이 아니다 be out of shape; look miserable; be put out of countenance
▶꼴 좋다 It serves [Serve] you right! ≒〈제3자를 가리켜〉 Shame on him! ≒ It served him right [damned well].
▶꼴 좀 봐라 Look at you! ≒ What a sight! ≒ What an ugly mug! ≒ What bad shape you are in!
▶그게 무슨 꼴이람 What a plight [state] he is in! ≒ What a sorry figure he cuts!
▶그 꼴이 뭐냐? How did you ever get into mess? ≒ For shame! ≒ Shame on you!
▶꼴을 보아서는 재간이 있을 것 같지 않다 Judging [To judge] from his appearance, he doesn't seem to have any talent at all.
▶꼴을 보니 일이 잘 되기는 틀렸다 As the situation stands, things look dismal. ≒ Judging from the present state of affairs the plan will come to no good.
▶이런 꼴로 실례합니다 I hope you don't mind seeing me like this.
▶그 놈은 꼴도 보기 싫다 I hate the very sight of him.
■세모[네모]— a triangle [tetragon]

꼴[2] 〈소 먹이는〉 fodder; provender; forage (grass) ♦소에게 꼴을 먹이다 fodder [give fodder to] a cow; feed a cow with fodder

-꼴 〈낱개로 따진 값〉 rate; proportion; 〈비율〉 ratio
♦하루에 천원꼴로 at the rate of one thousand won a day / 천 명에 한 사람꼴로 in the ratio of one to a thousand persons
▶하루 평균 만원꼴이 될 것이다 It will work out at ten thousand won per day.

꼴깍 at a gulp ⇨ 꿀꺽

꼴꼴 babbling; trickling; gurgling ♦꼴꼴 솟아나다 gurgle up; well up with gurgles

꼴꾼 a fodder mower [cutter]

꼴딱 ▶해가 꼴딱 넘어갔다 The night completely came on. ≒ It became quite dark.

꼴뚜기 〔動〕 a small kind of octopus ♦꼴뚜기 같은 octopal
■—장수 an octopus dealer; (비유) a bankrupt man —젓 salted [pickled] octopuses —질 a gesture of contempt made by holding up the middlefinger

꼴리다 1 〈성기가〉 stand errect; become rigid 2 〈배알이〉 be roused to anger; anger burns in *one* ♦ 배알이 꼴리다 be offended [provoked] 《at, by》; feel vexed [annoyed] 《at, with》

꼴보다 examine *sb's* face [personal appearance]

꼴불견 —不見 unsightliness; shabbiness; indecency ♦ 꼴불견이다 be unsightly [indecent]; cannot bear to see; be unable to stand [bear] the sight 《of》

꼴사납다 〈거슬리다〉 disgusting; unpleasant to the eye; 〈보기 흉하다〉 ugly; unsightly; shabby; shoddy; 〈창피하다〉 indecent; unbecoming; disgraceful; shameful
♦ 꼴사나운 광경 an ugly scene / 꼴사나운 놈 a disgusting [despicable] fellow / 옷차림이 꼴사납다 be shabbily [loudly] dressed / 꼴사납게 굴다 behave disgracefully [indecently]
▶ 그는 언제나 꼴사나운 옷차림을 하고 있다 He always wears shapeless clothes.
▶ 그는 꼴사납게 땅바닥에 쓰러졌다 He tumbled to the ground in an ungainly sprawl.

꼴짝거리다 sniffle

꼴짝꼴짝 sniffling ♦ 꼴짝꼴짝 울다 sob; sniffle

꼴찌 〈순위〉 the last; the bottom; the tail (end); 〈사람〉 the tailender
♦ 맨 꼴찌 the bottom of the bottom / 꼴찌상 a booby prize / 꼴찌 팀 the cellar-dwelling team / 꼴찌에서 둘째[셋째] the last but one [two] / 꼴찌다 be at the end [bottom] / 꼴찌를 하다 〈경주에서〉 come in [finish] last; come out bottom
▶ 나는 달리기에서는 늘 꼴찌였다 I brought up the rear [came in last] in every race.
▶ 그는 꼴찌로 졸업했다 He graduated last on the list.
▶ 그는 맨 꼴찌로 왔다 He was the last to come. ⇌ He came last.

꼼꼼쟁이 a meticulous man; an overscrupulous person

꼼꼼하다 (very) careful; scrupulous (proofreader); meticulous
♦ 꼼꼼한 성격 a meticulous nature / 꼼꼼한 솜씨 elaborate workmanship / 꼼꼼히 《do *one's* work》 carefully; elaborately; in detail

꼼지락거리다 move sluggishly; stir leisurely

꼼짝 budging; stirring
♦ 꼼짝도 하지 않다 remain motionless; do not stir [budge] an inch

—꼼짝하다 budge; stir; move (slightly); make a move
♦ 꼼짝할 수 없다 cannot move at all; cannot stir an inch
▶ 꼼짝 마라 Do not stir a step! ⇌ Do not budge an inch!
▶ 꼼짝 말고 섰거라 Stay right where you are! ⇌ Don't move from that spot!
▶ 그는 손가락 하나 꼼짝하지 않는다 He does not stir a finger.
▶ 그는 빚으로 꼼짝할 수 없다 He is up to his neck in debts.

꼼짝거리다 budge 《about》; fidget 《about》; wriggle 《about》; squirm 《in *one's* seat》
▶ 꼼짝거리지 말고 가만히 있거라 Be still and don't fidget.

꼼짝달싹 ♦ 꼼짝달싹 못하다 be in a fix [hole]; be in a tight corner [place, spot]; find *oneself* in a dilemma [predicament]; be stranded; be [get] bogged down
▶ 그는 빚으로 꼼짝달싹 못하고 있다 He is involved deeply in debt.

꼼짝못하다 1 〈몸을〉 cannot move at all; cannot move [budge, stir] an inch; be held up
♦ 감기에 걸려 꼼짝 못하다 be confined to *one's* bed [be kept in] with a cold / 무서워서 꼼짝 못하다 be unable to move with fear
▶ 열차는 눈보라로 꼼짝 못했다 The train stalled [came to a standstill] in the snowstorm.
▶ 허리가 아파 꼼짝 못하겠다 I cannot budge for the pain in my back.
2 〈기를〉 be under *sb's* thumb; be cowed
♦ 말로써 꼼짝 못하게 하다 talk *sb* down; argue *sb* into silence
▶ 그는 아내한테 꼼짝 못한다 He is tied to his wife's apron strings. ⇌ He is henpecked by his wife.
▶ 그는 주인 앞에서는 꼼짝 못한다 He is always cowed in the presence of his master.
▶ 그 말 한 마디에 그는 꼼짝 못했다 He was silenced by the one word.
3 〈곤경에 빠져〉 be in a fix; be quite helpless; be at a loss; be in a dilemma
▶ 그 회사는 자금난으로 꼼짝 못하고 있다 That company gets into a fix on account of financial difficulty.

꼼짝없이 helplessly; with no way out; without any means
♦ 꼼짝없이 굶고 있다 be starving helplessly / 꼼짝없이 붙잡히다 be held [arrested] with no way out / 꼼짝없이 죽게 되다 face the inevitable death

꼼꼼쟁이 a petty [narrow-minded] person

꼽다 count on *one's* fingers
♦ 날짜를 꼽다 count the days on *one's* fingers / 손꼽아 기다리다 wait eagerly for
▶ 그런 위인은 손에 꼽을 정도밖에 없다 Such a great man is very rare.
▶ 그는 마을에서 첫째가는 부자로 꼽힌다 He is taken to be the richest man in the village.
▶ 그는 위대한 시인으로 꼽힌다 He is reckoned [counted] among the great poets.

꼽재기 1 ⇨ 때꼽재기
2 〈미미한 것〉 a bit; a whit; a jot
♦ 꼽재기같은 놈 a small and despicable fellow / 꼽재기만큼도 …않다 no [not a, never a] whit [bit, jot]
▶ 그는 품위라곤 꼽재기만큼도 없다 There is no dignity about him.
▶ 그녀는 매력이라곤 꼽재기만큼도 없다 She is not a bit attractive.

꼿꼿이 1【사물이】 〈곧게〉 straightly; uprightly; erectly; 〈빳빳하게〉 hard; stiffly
♦ 꼿꼿이 굳은 stark and stiff / 꼿꼿이 서다 stand erect [upright] / 허리를 꼿꼿이 펴다 straighten *one's* spine
2 〈언행을〉 firmly; faithfully; honestly ♦ 꼿꼿이 버티다 stand firm; be unyielding / 꼿꼿이

살다 live honestly
꼿꼿하다 1 〖사물이〗〈곧다〉 straight; upright; erect; 〈빳빳하다〉 stiff; stark ◆꼿꼿한 나무 a straight tree / 꼿꼿한 자세로 앉다 sit in a straight posture
2 〈언행이〉 upright; unyielding; willful ◆꼿꼿한 사람 an upright man; a man of principle / 언행이 꼿꼿하다 be upright in *one's* conduct
꽁꽁¹ 1 〈언 모양〉 ◆꽁꽁 얼다 be thickly frozen (over); be frozen stiff
▶ 땅이 꽁꽁 얼어붙었다 The ground is frozen hard.
▶ 스케이트를 탈 수 있을 만큼 얼음이 꽁꽁 얼었다 The ice is strong enough to skate upon.
▶ 몸이 꽁꽁 얼어붙는 듯했다 I feel as cold as ice. ⇌ I am chilled to the bone.
2 〈묶는 모양〉 ◆꽁꽁 묶다 tie up 《a parcel》
▶ 그들은 도둑을 꽁꽁 묶었다 They bound the thief firmly hand and foot.
3 〈숨는 모양〉 getting well hidden ▶ 꽁꽁 숨어라 Hide yourself good! ⇌ Get well hidden!
꽁꽁² 〈앓는 소리〉 groaning ⇨ 꿍꿍¹
꽁무니 the tip of the coccyx 《*pl* coccyges》; the lower end of the backbone; 〈궁둥이〉 the buttocks; 〈끝〉 the tail (end)
◆꽁무니가 빠지게 달아나다 take to *one's* heels [legs]; beat a hasty retreat / 꽁무니를 빼다 flinch (from); shrink (back) (at, from); hang back (from); 〈달아나다〉 run away; run off; turn tail (and run away) / 여자 꽁무니를 쫓아다니다 dangle after [hang about] a girl; chase [run after] a woman
▶ 그는 언제나 막판에 가서 꽁무니를 뺀다 He always hangs back at the last moment.
■―바람 a tail wind; a following wind ―뼈〔解〕the coccyx
꽁보리밥 boiled barley for a meal
꽁생원―生員 an illiberal person
꽁지 the tail (of a bird); 〈공작 등의 긴〉 a train
꽁초 a cigarette [cigar] end [butt]; a stub; a half-smoked cigarette [cigar]; 《美俗》 a snipe
▶ 복도에 꽁초를 버리지 마시오 Don't throw away a cigarette butt on the floor.
꽁치 〔魚〕 a mackerel pike; a saury
꽁하다 introvert and narrow-minded; hidebound ◆꽁한 성질 introvert nature / 꽁하게 생각하다 bear in mind; feel badly [sore] 《about》
꽂다 1 〈박다〉 stick (in, into); fix (in, into); 〈절러넣다〉 drive into; stab; pierce; thrust; 〈끼워넣다〉 insert in; inset; 〈핀으로〉 pin (up)
◆땅에 기를 꽂다 fix a flag into the ground / 꽃을 꽂다 put [set, arrange] flowers (in a vase); stick a flower (in *one's* hair [hat, buttonhole]) / 자물쇠에 열쇠를 꽂다 insert [put] a key in [into] a lock / 책을 꽂다 put [set] a book (on a shelf) / 플러그를 꽂다 plug in; insert a plug (in)
▶ 머리에 꽃을 꽂아라 Put a flower in your hair.
▶ 나는 서가의 책을 이리 저리 다시 꽂았다 I rearranged the books on the shelves.

▶ 그녀는 벽에 사진을 잔뜩 꽂아 놓고 있었다 She pinned a lot of pictures up on the wall.
2 〈가로지르다〉 put 《a bar》 across ◆머리에 비녀를 꽂다 wear an ornamental hairpin in the hair
3 〈거꾸로 넘어 박히게〉 ◆짐을 메어꽂다 throw [cast] the load [burden] over *one's* shoulder
꽂을대 〈청소용〉 a gunstick; a cleaning rod; a sponge (대포의); 〈장전용〉 a rammer; a ramrod
꽂히다 be stuck [pinned, impaled]; be stabbed [pierced];〈맞히다〉hit; 〈끼이다〉 be inserted; be embedded; 〈걸리다〉 be bolted
▶ 화살이 과녁 한복판에 꽂혔다 The arrow hit the target right in the center.
▶ 칼이 나무 줄기에 꽂혔다 The knife stuck into the tree trunk.
▶ 창은 적장의 가슴에 푹 꽂혔다 The spear pierced into the enemy commander.
꽃 1 〈식물의〉 a flower; a blossom; (총칭) the bloom ◆들꽃 a wildflower / 온실의 꽃 a hothouse flower / 원예[정원]용 꽃 a garden flower / 화분에 심은 꽃 a potted flower / 일찍 [늦게] 피는 꽃 an early [a late] flower / 꽃 한 송이 a flower / 꽃의 floral / 꽃 같은 flowery; flowerlike

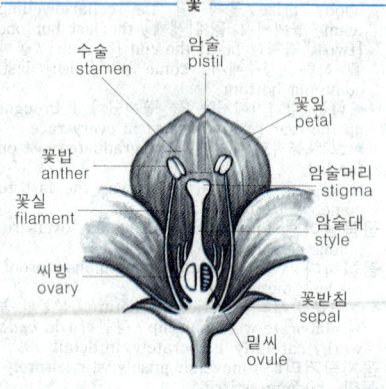

꽃 / 수술 stamen / 암술 pistil / 꽃잎 petal / 꽃밥 anther / 암술머리 stigma / 꽃실 filament / 암술대 style / 씨방 ovary / 꽃받침 sepal / 밑씨 ovule

▶ 이 백합은 흰 꽃이 핀다 This lily has a white bloom.
▶ 이 나무는 가을에 꽃이 핀다 This tree blooms [blossoms, flowers] in the fall.
▶ 살구 꽃이 피어 있었다 The apricot trees were in blossom [bloom, flower].
▶ 꽃이 졌다 The flowers have fallen [are gone].
▶ 벚꽃이 피기 시작했다 The cherry trees are beginning to blossom.
▶ 꽃들이 시들어 버렸다 The flowers withered up [away].
▶ 이 꽃은 저녁에 핀다 This flower comes out [opens] in the evening.
▶ 꽃을 꺾어 줄게 I'll pick you some flowers.
▶ 이 꽃들에게 날마다 물을 주세요 Will you

please water these flowers every morning?
▶ 꽃도 한때 사람도 한때 Roses and maidens soon lose their bloom.
2 〈비유〉〈미인〉 a fair woman; 〈정화〉 essence; spirit
♦ 기사도의 꽃 the flower of chivalry / 사교계의 꽃 a society beauty
▶ 젊음은 인생의 꽃이다 Youth is the essence [flower] of life.
▶ 이것이야 말로 근대 건축의 꽃이다 This is what modern architecture is all about.
▶ 우리는 이야기 꽃을 피웠다 We enjoyed an animated and friendly chat. ⇌ We talked on about various subjects.

꽃가게 a flower shop; a florist's; 〈노점〉 a stall of flowers ■ **—주인** a florist; a flower man
꽃가루 〔植〕 pollen; anther dust ■ **—받이** pollination **꽃가룻병** 〔醫〕 pollinosis
꽃가마 a palanquin decorated with flowers
♦ 꽃가마를 타다 get married to a man
꽃가지 a spray [sprig] of flowers
꽃게 〔動〕 a blue crab
꽃구경 flower [blossom] viewing ♦ 꽃구경 가다 go to see the flowers (at); go (out) flower viewing
꽃꼭지 〔植〕 a flower stalk ⇨ 꽃자루
꽃꽂이 flower arrangement [arranging, composition]; the art of flower arrangement
♦ 꽃꽂이를 가르치다 give lessons in flower arrangement / 꽃꽂이를 배우다 take lessons in [learn] flower arrangement
▶ 내 취미는 꽃꽂이다 My hobby is arranging flowers.
▶ 탁상 위에 꽃꽂이가 장식되어 있었다 A flower arrangement was on display on the table.
—꽃꽂이하다 arrange [set] flowers
꽃나무 a flowering tree [plant]; a flower tree
꽃놀이 a picnic for viewing flowers [blossoms]
♦ 꽃놀이 가다 go on an outing to see the flowers; go flower viewing
▶ 우리는 공원으로 벚꽃놀이를 갔다 We went to see [enjoy] the cherry blossoms at the park.
—꽃놀이하다 enjoy an outing among the flowers
꽃눈 〔植〕 a flower bud
꽃다발 a bunch of flowers; a nosegay; 〈여성복에 다는〉 a corsage; (프) a bouquet
꽃다지 **1** 〔植〕 a whitlow grass **2** 〈첫열매〉 the first fruit (of cucumber, eggplant)
꽃답다 lovely as a flower; flowery; flowerlike
♦ 꽃다운 나이 《be in》 the flower of maidenhood / 꽃다운 처녀 a girl (as) pretty as a flower; a flower of a girl; a beautiful young girl / 꽃다운 청춘 the bloom [flower, charm, glow] of youth; the springtime [prime] of life
꽃대 〔植〕 a floral axis
꽃덮이 〔植〕 the floral envelope; the perianth
꽃돗자리 a figured [fancy] mat; a flowered mat
꽃동산 a flower garden; a flowery hill

꽃말 flower [floral] language; the language of flowers ▶ 붉은 장미는 꽃말이 무엇입니까? What does the red rose mean in the language of flowers?
꽃망울 a flower bud ♦ 꽃망울이 벌어지다 a bud begins to open / 꽃망울이 지다 have [bear] buds; put forth [send out] buds
꽃무늬 a floral pattern [design]; flowering; 〔印〕 a printer's flower ♦ 꽃무늬의 floral-patterned ■ 장미— a rosette
꽃바구니 a flower basket; 〈꽃 한 바구니〉 a basket of flowers
꽃받침 〔植〕 a sepal; a calyx (pl. ~es, -lyces); a (flower) cup; a receptacle
꽃발게 〔動〕 a fiddler crab
꽃밥 〔植〕 an anther
꽃방석 **—方席** a cushion embroidered with flowers; a fancy [figured] cushion; a flowered mattress
꽃밭 a flower garden [bed]; a field of flowers
꽃병 **—瓶** a (flower) vase ▶ 그녀는 꽃병에 꽃을 꽂았다 She arranged [put] the flowers in a vase.
꽃봉오리 a flower bud; a button; 〈청춘〉 the youth
♦ 부풀어오른 장미 꽃봉오리 a swollen [fat] rose bud / 꽃봉오리 같은 소녀 a budding beauty; a young maiden / 꽃봉오리가 맺히다 have [bear] buds; put forth [out] buds / 꽃봉오리가 피다 a bud develops into flower [bursts into blossom] / 꽃봉오리를 따다 pluck a flower in the bud
▶ 꽃봉오리가 개화하고 있다 The buds are opening [bursting].
▶ 꽃봉오리가 부풀어 막 피어나려 하고 있었다 The buds were swollen to bursting.
▶ 개나리는 꽃봉오리가 부풀어 있다 The forsythia are in fat bud.
▶ 목련 꽃봉오리는 아직 단단하다 The buds of the magnolias are still tight.
꽃부리 〔植〕 the corolla of a flower
꽃불 **1** 〈파란 불꽃〉 a blazing [flaming] fire **2** 〈폭죽〉 fireworks; a fireworks display ♦ 꽃불을 쏘아 올리다 let [set] off fireworks
▶ 오늘밤 꽃불놀이가 있다 There will be a firework exhibition this evening. ⇌ Fireworks will be let off this evening.
꽃상추 〔植〕 an escarole; (美) an endive
꽃샘 〈꽃샘추위〉 chilly weather in the blooming season; a cold snap in the flowering season; a spring cold
—꽃샘하다 suddenly get cold in the flowering season
■ **—바람** a chill wind in the flowering season
꽃송이 a blossom; an open flower
꽃수레 a flower-bedecked (street)car; a decorated car; a float (in a parade); a pageant
▶ 꽃수레의 행렬이 거리를 행진했다 A procession of floats parades the streets.
꽃술 〔植〕 the pistils and stamens of a flower; 〈수술〉 a stamen; 〈암술〉 a pistil
꽃시계 **—時計** a floral [flower] clock
꽃시장 **—市場** a flower market
꽃식물 **—植物** a flowering plant

꽃실 〔植〕 a filament
꽃쌈 〈수효를 겨룸〉 a flower gathering game; 〈맞걸어 당김〉 a flower wrestle
—꽃쌈하다 play a flower game; have a flower battle
꽃잎 〔植〕 a (flower) petal; a flower leaf ◆꽃잎이 넷[열]인 tetrapetalous [decapetalous]; 4-petaled [10-petaled] 《flower》/ 꽃잎이 없는 apetalous; petalless
꽃자동차 —自動車 a floral car; a flower-bedecked automobile
꽃자루 〔植〕 a flower stalk; a peduncle
꽃자리 a figured mat ⇨ 꽃돗자리
꽃장식 —裝飾 a floral decoration; 〈탁상 등의〉 a flower piece
꽃재배 —栽培 floriculture ■—자 a floriculturist
꽃전차 —電車 a floral car; a streetcar float
꽃집 a flower shop ⇨ 꽃가게
꽃차례 〔植〕 an inflorescence; anthotaxy
꽃창포 —菖蒲 〔植〕 an iris 《pl. ~es, irides》; a flag
꽃철 the flowering [blossom] season
꽈르르 gurglingly ⇨ 꽐꽐
꽈리 1 〔植〕 a ground-cherry; 〈입에 넣고 부는 놀잇감〉 a mouth clacker ▶아이들이 뒤뜰에서 꽈리를 불고 있다 Children are blowing a ground-cherry in the backyard.
2 〈물집〉 a blister
꽉 1 〈가득〉 close(ly); tight(ly); to the full ◆젊은이들로 꽉 찬 광장 a square filled with [full of, crowded with] young people
▶그녀는 옷을 가방에 꽉 채워 넣었다 She crammed [stuffed] her bag with her clothes.
▶나는 금주에는 스케줄이 꽉 차 있다 My schedule is quite [very] tight this week. ⇌ I have a tight schedule this week.
▶주차장은 차로 꽉 차 있었다 The parking lot was jammed with cars.
▶공원은 사람들로 꽉 차 있었다 The park was overflowing with people.
▶이 근처는 집들이 꽉 들어차 있다 In this neighborhood the houses are crowded close together.
▶좌석은 이미 모두 꽉 찼다 All the seats had already been occupied [taken, filled].
▶작은 방이 사람들로 꽉 찼다 The small room was packed with people.
2 〈단단히〉 tight(ly); firm(ly); hard
◆꽉 묶다 bind [tie] sth tightly; tie fast; fasten tight / 목을 꽉 조르다 strangle sb's neck / 꽉 쥐다 grip tightly; squeeze
▶그는 입술을 꽉 다물었다 He had his lips tightly closed.
▶그 상자는 밧줄로 꽉 묶여 있다 The box is bound fast with a rope.
▶그는 내 손을 꽉 쥐었다 He squeezed my hand. ⇌ He pressed my hand hard.
▶나는 라켓을 꽉 쥐었다 I gripped the racket firmly.
▶그는 수건을 꽉 짰다 He wrung the towel hard.
▶저 집은 대개 하루 종일 창문을 꽉 닫아놓고 있다 They usually keep the windows firmly closed all day long in that house.
▶우리는 규칙에 꽉 묶여 있다 We are tied down by regulation.
3 〈굳이 참고〉 patiently ▶그는 그 고통을 꽉 참았다 He endured the pain stoically.
꽉꽉 1 〈모두 가득히〉 fully; closely
▶극장에는 관객이 꽉꽉 들어차 있었다 The theater was full [crowded] with a capacity audience.
▶광마다 곡식이 꽉꽉 차 있었다 The barns were all bursting with grain.
2 〈잔뜩 단단히〉 very firm(ly); much more tight(ly)
▶우리는 도둑을 꽉꽉 묶었다 We tied the thief (up) hand and foot.
▶그는 손목에 붕대를 꽉꽉 감고 있었다 His wrist was heavily bandaged.
꽐꽐 gurglingly; gushingly ◆꽐꽐 뿜어나오는 기름 oil gushing out 《from a well》 ▶병에서 물이 꽐꽐 쏟아져 나왔다 Water gurgled from a bottle.
꽝¹ 〈제비뽑기의〉(俗) a blank (in lottery) ◆제비 뽑기에서 꽝을 뽑다 draw a blank
꽝² 〈울리는 소리〉 with a bang [boom]; with a thump [thud]
◆문을 꽝 닫다 bang [slam] a door; close a door with a bang / 대포를 꽝 쏘다 bang off a gun; boom a gun
▶그는 벽에 꽝 부딪혔다 He bumped against the wall.
▶그는 주먹으로 테이블을 꽝 쳤다 He banged the table with his fist.
—꽝하다 bang; boom; bump; thump; crash; go bang
▶꽝하고 총성이 울렸다 Bang! went the gun.
▶폭약이 꽝하고 터졌다 Explosives blasted [went off] with a bang.
꽝꽝 bang-bang; boom-boom
◆문을 꽝꽝 두드리다 thunder at [thump on] a door / 대포를 꽝꽝 쏘다 boom a cannon repeatedly / 총을 꽝꽝 쏘다 go bang-bang with a gun [rifle]
꽝꽝거리다 1 〈자꾸 꽝꽝 소리를 내다〉 go [keep] bang-bang [boom-boom] 2 〈큰소리치다〉 talk big [tall]; talk boastfully
꽤 pretty; fairly; rather; quite; considerably

[解說] **pretty**는 일반적인 말로 긍정문에서 쓴다. **fairly**는 바람직한 것을 말할 경우에 쓰고, **rather**는 바람직하지 못한 것을 말할 경우에 쓴다. **quite**는 「예상 밖으로」의 뜻이 있으며 빈정대는 뜻을 포함하는 경우도 있다.

◆꽤 많은 금액 a considerable [substantial] sum of money / 꽤 많은 수입[재산] a handsome income [fortune] / 꽤 먼 거리 a good distance
▶그는 테스트에서 꽤 좋은 점수를 얻었다 He got a rather good mark on the test.
▶그는 꽤 좋은 그림을 그렸다 He painted a passably good picture.
▶여기서 집까지 걸어가자면 꽤 멀다 It's a good walk from here to my home.
▶할아버지는 연세가 꽤 많으십니다 My grand-

father is very [quite] old.
▶ 오늘은 꽤 덥네요 It's pretty [rather] hot today, isn't it? (➤rather의 경우 더위가 지겹다는 뜻이 포함됨)
▶ 그 길은 꽤 가파르다 The path is quite steep.
▶ 이 파이는 꽤 맛있다 This pie tastes pretty good.
▶ 우리는 꽤 오래 기다렸다 We waited for quite a long time.
▶ 그들은 꽤 잘 산다 They are fairly well off.
▶ 그 사람은 꽤 건강하다 He is reasonably healthy.
▶ 너는 그래도 꽤 잘 한 거야 You've done it pretty [fairly] well.
▶ 6월에는 비가 꽤 많이 온다 We have a great deal of rain in June.
▶ 날씨가 11월 치고는 꽤 따뜻하다 The weather is quite warm for November.
▶ 그는 꽤 나이를 먹었다 He is well on in years.
▶ 그는 꽤 알려진 인물이다 He is quite a man [somebody].

꽥 with a shout [scream, shriek, yell]
—꽥하다 yell; shout; scream
◆ 꽥하는 소리 a shout; a yell / 꽥하고 소리치다 utter [give] a shriek [shout, yell] / 꽥하며 쓰러지다 fall down with a shriek

꽥꽥 quack-quack ◆ 꽥꽥 울다 〈오리가〉 quack; 〈거위가〉 gaggle

꽥꽥거리다 〈사람이〉 shout; yell; screech; 〈오리가〉 quack; 〈거위가〉 gaggle ◆ 오리들이 꽥꽥거리는 소리 the noisy quacks of ducks

꽹과리 [樂] a (small) gong ◆ 꽹과리를 치다 strike a gong

꾀 〈지혜〉 wise counsel; wit; resource; 〈계략〉 a trick; a wile; a trap; an artifice; a stratagem 〈군략〉; 〈계책〉 a device; a design; a scheme ◆ 얕은 꾀 a shallow cunning / 꾀가 많은 사람 a man of great resource; 〈모사꾼〉 a man full of craft / 일에 꾀가 나다 get [grow] tired [weary] of a work / 꾀가 늘다 grow clever [wise, intelligent] / 꾀가 모자라다 be on the dull side / 꾀가 있다 be resourceful; be tricky; be clever; be wily / 꾀가 없다 be brainless; be harebrained; be tactless / 꾀를 빌리다 ask sb for an idea [a scheme]; pick [suck] sb's brains / 꾀를 쓰다 ⇨ 꾀쓰다 / 꾀를 짜내다 rack [cudgel, beat] one's brains / 꾀를 피우다 be idle; be [get] lazy / 꾀로 이기다 outwit sb
▶ 그는 적의 꾀에 넘어갔다 He was entrapped by the enemy. ⇌ He fell into the enemy's trap.
▶ 그는 제 꾀에 넘어갔다 He was done in his own cleverness.

꾀까다롭다 hard to please ⇨ 꾀까다롭다
꾀꼬리 〔鳥〕 an oriole ◆ 꾀꼬리 같은 목소리 a beautiful voice
꾀꼴꾀꼴 warbling and warbling ◆ 꾀꼴꾀꼴 울다 〈orioles〉 warble away; trill; sing
꾀꾀 ◆ 꾀꾀 마른 사람 a dry-bones / 꾀꾀 마르다 grow gaunt [slim]; lose one's weight
▶ 그는 오랫동안 앓아서 몸이 꾀꾀 말랐다 He has become worn out from a lengthy illness.
▶ 그는 얼굴이 꾀꾀 말랐다 His face is drawn and haggard.

꾀다¹ 〈모여들어 뒤끓다〉 gather; swarm; crowd; flock; collect; infest
▶ 그 꽃에는 진딧물이 꾄다 The flower is infested with aphides.
▶ 음식에 파리가 꾀었다 Flies collected on the food.
▶ 개미가 설탕에 새까맣게 꾀어 있다 Ants are swarming upon the sugar.

꾀다² 〈유혹하다〉 tempt; lure; entice; decoy; seduce

解說 ***tempt***는 보통 나쁜 일이나 어리석은 일에 꾀어들인다는 뜻. ***lure***는 저항하기 어려운 힘으로 끌어당긴다는 뜻으로, 나쁜 일에만 국한되지 않는다.

◆ 돈으로 사람을 꾀다 lure sb with money / 사람을 꾀어 돈을 빼앗다 coax [cajole, wheedle] sb out of money
▶ 판매원은 소녀를 꾀어 그 반지를 사게 했다 The salesman inveigled the girl into buying the ring.
▶ 불량배들은 그를 꾀어 나쁜 길로 들어서게 했다 The ruffians tempted him into vice.
▶ 그는 부잣집 딸을 꾀어 결혼했다 He tricked the daughter of a rich man into marrying him.

꾀바르다 shrewd ⇨ 약빠르다
꾀배 a fake stomachache ◆ 꾀배를 앓다 pretend to have a stomachache
꾀병 —病 pretended [simulated, feigned] illness; counterfeit [fake] sickness; malingering
▶ 그녀는 종종 꾀병을 앓는다 She sometimes shams [feigns] sickness. ⇌ She sometimes pretends to be sick [ill].
▶ 그의 병은 꾀병에 불과했다 His illness was a mere sham.

꾀보 a person full of schemes [ideas]; a wily person

꾀부리다 shirk 《one's duty》; spare oneself (the trouble of doing); grudge working; be stingy of effort
◆ 꾀부리는 사람 a shirker; a lazybones / 공부에 꾀부리다 shun real study / 힘든 일에 꾀부리다 be sly on the difficult problem / 꾀부리지 않고 일하다 work without sparing oneself
▶ 그는 그날 꾀부리고 학교에 가지 않았다 He shirked going to school that day.
▶ 그녀는 꾀부리고 일을 안했기 때문에 해고당했다 As she shirked her duty, she was fired.

꾀쓰다 use brains; use a trick; play a trick 《on》; resort to wiles [a ruse] ◆ 꾀써서 달아나다 escape by trickery

꾀어내다 decoy [(al)lure, entice] out; lure 《the child》 away 《from》
▶ 그는 그녀를 밤늦게 꾀어냈다 He lured her out late at night.
▶ 일당은 그 딸을 집에서 꾀어내려고 했다 The gang tried to entice the daughter away from home [her house].

꾀어들이다 decoy [lure] sb in [into]
▶ 나는 그들을 숲속으로 꾀어들였다 I lured them into woods.

꾀이다

▶ 그들은 호랑이를 함정으로 꾀어들이는데 성공했다 They succeeded in decoying a tiger into the trap.

꾀이다 〈꾐을 당하다〉 be lured; be enticed; be tempted ♦ 친구에게 꾀이다 be enticed by a friend

꾀잠 sham [pretended] sleep; make-believe sleep; fox sleep ♦ 꾀잠을 자다 pretend to be asleep; sham [feign, simulate] sleep

꾀죄죄하다 seedy; shabby; squalid; poor-looking; untidy ♦ 꾀죄죄한 주제(꼴)a seedy appearance; mean attire / 옷차림이 꾀죄죄히다 be shabbily [poorly] dressed

꾀피우다 shirk ⟪one's duty⟫ ⇨ 꾀부리다

꾀하다 1 【계획하다】 plan; scheme; attempt; try; devise ⟪a scheme⟫; think out; 〈나쁜 짓을〉 plot; conspire; frame up; (口) be up to ⟪do⟫
▶ 그녀는 자살을 꾀했다 She tried to kill herself. (▶결과는 불명임) ⇌ She attempted to kill herself [attempted suicide]. (▶결과적으로 실패했음을 암시함)
▶ 그들은 정부 전복을 꾀했다 They schemed to overturn the government.
▶ 그는 무엇을 꾀하고 있는 걸까 I wonder what he's up to do.
2 〈추구하다〉 seek; aim at
♦ 공익을 꾀하다 labor for the public good; promote the public interest
▶ 그는 사리를 꾀하는 사람이 아니다 He is not a self-seeking person [self-seeker]. ⇌ He never acts from selfish motives.

꾐 temptation; allurement; enticement; seduction
♦ 꾐에 빠지다 fall into [yield to] temptation; fall a victim to sb's temptation; be cajoled [wheedled]
▶ 그녀는 꾐에 빠져 부모 곁을 떠났다 She was enticed to leave her parents.
▶ 그는 꾐에 빠져 재산의 대부분을 빼앗겼다 He was coaxed out of the best part of his estate.
▶ 그는 나쁜 친구들의 꾐에 빠져 나쁜 길로 들어섰다 He was tempted [enticed] into wrong ways by the wrong company.

꾸기다 crumple ⇨ 구기다
꾸기적거리다 crumple up ⇨ 구기적거리다
꾸깃꾸깃하다 crumpled ⇨ 구깃구깃하다
꾸다¹ 〈꿈을〉 dream ⇨ 꿈꾸다
▶ 고향 꿈을 꾸다 dream about one's home / 좋은[나쁜] 꿈을 꾸다 dream a good [bad] dream
▶ 마치 꿈을 꾸는듯한 기분이었다 I felt as if I were in a dream.

꾸다² 〈돈 등을〉 borrow
▶ 나는 시계를 저당 잡히고 돈을 좀 꾸었다 I borrowed some money on my watch.
▶ 그에게 5천원 꾼 것이 있다 I owe him five thousand won. ⇌ I owe five thousand won to him.
▶ 5만원이 부족한데 그에게 꾸어야겠다 I need fifty thousand won more. I'll borrow it from him.
▶ 돈 좀 꾸어 주세요 May I trouble you for some money?

꾸드러지다 〈굳어지다〉 be dried and hardened

▶ 떡이 꾸드러졌다 The rice cake has got leathery.

꾸들꾸들하다 somewhat dry and hard ▶ 밥이 꾸들꾸들하다 Rice is half-boiled.

-꾸러기 an overindulger; a person who overdoes sth ♦ 잠꾸러기 a late riser; a sleepyhead; a heavy sleeper / 장난꾸러기 a naughty [mischievous] child; an urchin; an imp

꾸러미 1 〈꾸려 뭉쳐 싼 것〉 a bundle; a package ♦ 열쇠 꾸러미 a bunch of keys / 책 꾸러미 a package of books / 꾸러미를 만들다 make a bundle [package] / 꾸러미를 풀다 unpack; undo a package [bundle]
▶ 그녀는 결혼 선물 꾸러미를 풀었다 She unpacked the wedding presents.
2 〈긴 짚을 동인 것〉 a straw wrapper ♦ 달걀 한 꾸러미 ten eggs in a straw wrapper

꾸르륵 1 〈뱃속이 끓는 소리〉 with a rumble; 〈물이 가까스로 빠지는 소리〉 with a gurgle
♦ 꾸르륵 솟아나오다 gurgle up; well up with gurgles
▶ 뱃속에서 꾸르륵 소리가 났다 My bowels rumbled. ⇌ My belly growled.
▶ 물이 꾸르륵 소리를 내면서 물마개 구멍을 빠져나갔다 The water gurgled as it ran down the plughole.
2 〈닭이 놀라서 지르는 소리〉 with a cackle

꾸리¹ 〈실뭉치〉 a ball (⇨ 실꾸리) ♦ 실 두 꾸리 two balls [skeins] of thread

꾸리² 〈소의 무릎 위쪽 살〉 beef from upper part of fore-limbs

꾸리다 1 〈싸서 묶다〉 pack (up); do up; bundle up
▶ 짐은 다 꾸렸습니까? Have you finished packing?
▶ 우리는 모든 물건을 꾸렸다 We bundled everything up.
▶ 그들은 트렁크에 짐을 꾸려 넣었다 They packed their trunks with the things. ⇌ They packed the things into their trunks.
▶ 그는 짐을 꾸려 떠났다 He packed up his things and left.
▶ 집배원이 소포를 꾸려 주었다 The postman did the parcel up for me.
2 〈갈망하다〉 manage; deal with; have control of
♦ 살림을 꾸리다 manage household affairs / 월 70만원으로 가계를 꾸려 나가다 cover one's household expenses with seven hundred thousand won a month
▶ 그녀는 가게를 혼자서 꾸려가고 있다 She is managing the shop entirely by herself.
▶ 살림을 제대로 꾸려가기란 여간 힘든 일이 아니다 It is a hard task to manage a household properly.
▶ 그는 혼자서 그럭저럭 꾸려 나갈 것 같다 I think he can manage by himself.
▶ 그녀는 도움을 받지 않고는 꾸려 나갈 수 없을 것이다 She won't be able to manage without help.
▶ 돈을 꾸지 못하면 없는 대로 꾸려 나갈 수 밖에 없다 If I can't borrow the money, I'll have to manage without.
3 〈정돈하다〉 put ⟪things⟫ in order; put [set]

(things) to rights; tidy [do] up (a room)
♦ 매무새를 꾸미다 adjust *oneself* [*one's* dress]/ 방을 꾸미다 decorate [fix up] a room / 여장(旅裝)을 꾸미다 equip [outfit] *oneself* for a journey

꾸무럭거리다 move sluggishly ⇨ 꾸물거리다
▶ 이불 속에서 꾸무럭거리다 dally in bed / 꾸무럭거리면서 시간을 보내다 dally [putter] away *one's* time
▶ 꾸무럭거리고 있을 때가 아니다 This is no time for sitting idle. ⇌ It admits of no delay.
▶ 무엇 때문에 그렇게 꾸무럭거리는 거냐? What's taking you so long [so much time]?
▶ 나는 꾸무럭거리는 사람은 딱 질색이다 I can't bear an irresolute man.

꾸물거리다 move slowly [lazily, sluggishly]; be slow [long]; dally; dillydally; dawdle 《over》
▶ 일 가지고 어지간히도 꾸물거리는구나 You are dawdling over your work.
▶ 뭘 꾸물거리니? 어서 네 방 청소나 해 What are you waiting for? Hurry up and clean up your room!
▶ 그는 꾸물거리다가 버스를 놓쳤다 He was slow and missed the bus.
▶ 꾸물거리지 말고 해라 Don't be long about it. ⇌ Do it at once.
▶ 꾸물거릴 시간 없다 There is not a moment to be lost. ⇌ There is no time to lose.

꾸미 〈작은 쇠고기 조각〉 beef shreds (for soup, noodles, etc.)

꾸미다 **1** 〈장식하다〉 decorate; ornament; 〈화장하다〉 make (*oneself*) up; put on makeup; 〈수식하다〉 embellish; garnish
♦ 꽃으로 꾸민 방 a room decorated [blazoned] with flowers / 말을 꾸미다 use fancy [decorative] words / 문장을 꾸미다 use a flowery style; embellish *one's* style / 진열장을 꾸미다 decorate [dress] a show window
▶ 그녀는 나이보다 젊어 보이게 얼굴을 꾸민다 She makes herself up to look younger than she really is.
▶ 그녀는 보석으로 아름답게 꾸미고 있었다 She dressed herself [was decked out] with jewels.
▶ 내 방을 너무 요란하게 꾸미는 것은 싫다 I don't like to put up too many decorations in my room.
▶ 그 방은 도자기와 그림으로 아름답게 꾸며져 있었다 Ceramic pieces and pictures were beautifully arranged in the room.
▶ 방을 무엇으로 꾸밀까? What shall we decorate the room with?
2 〈꾀하다〉 scheme; plot
♦ 계략을 꾸미다 work out a scheme / 음모를 꾸미다 lay a plot [conspiracy] 《against》
▶ 아이들이 무언가 장난을 꾸미는데 그것이 무엇인지 알 수가 없다 The kids are up to some mischief but I don't know what.
▶ 그는 무언가 나쁜 짓을 꾸미고 있다 He is plotting some evil.
3 〈가장하다〉 pretend; affect; assume
♦ 꾸민 태도 an affected attitude [manner]/ 아픈 것처럼 꾸미다 pretend to be ill
▶ 그는 콧수염을 기르고 음악가처럼 꾸몄다

Wearing a mustache, he posed as a musician.
4 〈날조하다〉 invent; fabricate; make [cook] up
♦ 꾸민 일 a fabrication; a put-up job
▶ 알고 보니 그 기사는 주간지가 꾸며낸 것이었다 The report proved to be the invention [fabrication] of a weekly magazine.
5 〈조성하다〉 form; organize; set up
♦ 공원을 꾸미다 lay out a park / 새 내각을 꾸미다 form a new cabinet
▶ 그도 마침내 가정을 꾸몄다 He has set up his own home at last.
▶ 큰 길가에 가게를 하나 꾸미고 싶다 I hope to open a store on the main street.
6 〈작성하다〉 make; draw up
♦ 계약서를 두 통 꾸미다 draw up [prepare] a contract in duplicate / 서류를 꾸미다 draw up [write out] a document
▶ 그는 그 소설을 극으로 꾸몄다 He dramatized the novel.

꾸밈 〈장식〉 an ornament; a decoration; an adornment; 〈허식〉 display; show; affectation; ostentation; 〈치장〉 trimmings 《for》; trim 《on the dress》
♦ 꾸밈 없는 natural; artless / 꾸밈 없이 말하다 speak in a straightforward way; say frankly
▶ 나는 그의 꾸밈 없는 태도에 감동했다 I was deeply moved by his innocent and artless attitude.
▶ 그의 태도는 유쾌하고 꾸밈 없는 것이었다 He behaved in a pleasant, unaffected manner.
■—음[樂] ornament grace; agrements; Verzierung

꾸밈새 〈모양새〉 a shape; a form; appearance
♦ 꾸밈새가 좋은 shapely (figured); well-formed; well-shaped / 꾸밈새가 흉한 ill-shaped; ill-formed; shapeless; unseemly
▶ 소나무를 새로 심어서 정원의 꾸밈새가 좋아졌다 The garden has improved in appearance with the newly planted pine.

꾸벅 〈상체를 숙이었다 드는 모양〉 nodding
♦ 꾸벅절하다 dip a quick bow; bob *one's* head (in a bow) 《to》; bob a greeting

꾸벅거리다 〈자꾸 꾸벅이다〉 nod (in a doze); make repeated bows

꾸벅꾸벅 bowing; dozing; drowsily
♦ 꾸벅꾸벅 절하다 make repeated bows / 일하면서 꾸벅꾸벅 졸다 nod [doze] over *one's* work
▶ 그는 책을 앞에 놓고 꾸벅꾸벅 졸고 있었다 He was dozing over a book.
▶ 톰은 꾸벅꾸벅 졸다가 선생님께 들켰다 Tom was caught nodding by the teacher.

꾸어다 놓은 보릿자루 《속담》 (be like) a cat in a strange garret
▶ 교실에서 그녀는 꾸어다 놓은 보릿자루 같다 In the classroom she is tongue-tied.
▶ 그녀는 꾸어다 놓은 보릿자루 같이 앉아 있었다 She sat alone like a wallflower apart from the gay party.

꾸역꾸역 ♦ 꾸역꾸역 모여들다 crowd in; swarm about ▶ 사람들이 홀에서 꾸역꾸역 나왔다 The people came out of the hall in a stream.

꾸이다 〈꿈에〉 be dreamed [dreamt]

꾸정모기 〔昆〕 a crane fly
꾸준하다 steady; constant; persistent; ceaseless; unremitting; untiring
♦꾸준한 노력 steady [untiring, ceaseless] efforts / 꾸준한 성격 a steady [stable, solid] character / 꾸준한 우정 a constant [steadfast] friendship
▶그는 꾸준한 노력으로 목표를 달성했다 He attained the goal with unremitting efforts.
꾸준히 steadily; ceaselessly; constantly; untiringly; persistently; unremittingly
♦꾸준히 노력하다 make untiring efforts; persevere in *one's* efforts / 꾸준히 발전하다 make steady progress
▶그는 꾸준히 노력하는 타입이다 He is a hard and tireless [assiduous] worker.
꾸중 a scolding; (a) reprimand; (a) reproof; (a) rebuke; (a) reproach
♦꾸중 듣다 be scolded [reproved]; catch [have, get] a scolding; get into a row; (口) catch it (hot); (口) be told off; get it
▶그러다 들키면 너 꾸중 듣는다 You'll get told off if you're caught doing that.
▶늦어서 호되게 꾸중을 들었다 I had a good scolding for being late. ⇒ I was scolded very sharply for being late.
▶그는 학교에 지각해서 꾸중을 들었다 He got into a row for being late for school.
▶집에 늦게 돌아와서 아버지한테 꾸중을 들었다 My father gave me a good scolding for coming home late.
—꾸중하다 ⇒ 꾸짖다
꾸지람 a scolding ⇒ 꾸중
꾸짖다 scold; chide; blame; rebuke; reprove; reproach; reprimand; (口) tell *sb* off (for); talk to; yell at

解説 *scold*는 부모가 아이들을 꾸짖을 때 쓴다. *tell off*와 *talk to*는 비슷하지만 꾸짖는 투나 꾸짖을 때의 억양은 tell off 쪽이 더 엄하다. 남을 호통쳐 꾸짖을 때에는 *yell at*을 쓴다.

♦가볍게 꾸짖다 scold mildly; give *sb* a mild scolding / 호되게 꾸짖다 scold severely; give *sb* a good [sharp, severe] scolding
▶그렇게 오냐 오냐만 하지 말고 때로는 꾸짖으세요 Do not indulge so much, but scold sometimes.
▶그의 어머니는 그의 나쁜 행실을 꾸짖었다 His mother scolded him for being naughty.
▶아버지는 문을 열어 두었다고 나를 꾸짖었다 Father scolded me for having left the door open.
▶나는 너무 떠든다고 소년들을 꾸짖었다 I told the boys off for making so much noise.
꾹 1〈세게 누르는 모양〉 firmly; tightly; hard
♦꾹 누르다 press hard
2〈참는 모양〉 patiently ▶그는 모욕을 꾹 참았다 He patiently bore [put up with] the insult.
▶그녀는 말대꾸를 하고 싶었지만 꾹 참았다 She wanted to talk back, but bit her lips.
꾹꾹 to the full ♦꾹꾹 눌러 담다 fill chockfull; pack in tightly / 트렁크에 옷가지를 꾹꾹

눌러 넣다 ram [squeeze] clothes into a trunk
꿀 honey; nectar
♦꿀 먹은 벙어리 a person who could not open (his) mouth to another about something kept in (his) heart / 꿀처럼 감미로운 honey-sweet (love); mellifluous (music)
▶벌들이 이 꽃 저 꽃으로 날아다니며 꿀을 모으고 있다 Bees are getting honey, flying from flower to flower.
▶신혼인 그들에게는 하루하루가 꿀처럼 달콤하다 Being newly married, they find every day sweet like honey.
꿀꺽 1〈삼키는 소리〉 at a gulp
♦물을 단숨에 꿀꺽 들이켜다 gulp water down; drink [swallow] water down at a gulp / 꿀꺽 삼키다 gulp (down); swallow at a gulp / 침을 꿀꺽 삼키다 swallow *one's* saliva
—꿀꺽하다 make a gulping sound
2〈억지로 참는 모양〉 ♦ 분을 꿀꺽 참다 swallow [gulp down] *one's* resentment
꿀꺽꿀꺽 gulpingly ♦꿀꺽꿀꺽 마시다 gulp (down) (a glass of milk); take a long noisy drink; swill; take a swig 《at》
꿀꿀 〈돼지 우는 소리〉 gruntingly —꿀꿀하다 ⇒ 꿀꿀거리다
꿀꿀거리다 grunt; oink ▶돼지들이 꿀꿀거리고 있다 The pigs are oinking.
꿀꿀이 〈돼지〉 a pig; a swine; a hog; 〈욕심쟁이〉 a greedy, mean person
꿀떡 at a gulp ⇒ 꿀꺽 1
꿀떡거리다 gulp away; make gulping sounds
꿀떡꿀떡 gulpingly ⇒ 꿀꺽꿀꺽
꿀렁하다 1〈물이 흔들려 나는 소리〉 splash about [make a splash] inside
2〈들메서 부푼 모양〉 be baggy; be puffy ▶바지 무릎이 꿀렁하다 The trousers are baggy at the knees.
꿀리다 1〈구겨지다〉 be wrinkled; be crumpled; become creased; cockle
2〈붙인 것이 들뜨다〉 get loose [come off] at an edge
3〈옹색해지다〉 be hard up (for money); be in straitened circumstances ♦살림이 꿀리다 be ill [badly] off; (美) be poorly fixed
4〈눌리다〉 feel small [timid]; be cornered; be overwhelmed; give in; yield
♦조금도 꿀리지 않고 dauntlessly; without flinching / 말에 꿀리다 be cornered in an argument / 수량에 꿀리다 be overwhelmed by numbers
▶부자 친구를 만나면 어쩐지 꿀린다 I feel somehow small in the presence of a rich friend.
▶그녀는 테니스에서는 아무한테도 꿀리지 않는다 Nobody can beat her at tennis. ⇒ She yields to none in tennis. ⇒ She is behind none in tennis.
5〈켕기다〉 have *sth* on *one's* conscience ♦양심이 꿀리다 have scruples about 《doing》
꿀물 honeyed water
꿀벌 a (honey)bee
꿇다 〈무릎을 구부리다〉 kneel (down); go down [throw *oneself*, fall, drop] on *one's* knees
♦무릎을 꿇고 기도하다 kneel in prayer / 무릎

꿇다 〈무릎을 꿇다〉 sit [kotow] on *one's* knees / 아무의 발 아래 꿇어 엎드리다 throw [cast] *oneself* at *sb's* feet
▶ 그에게 무릎을 꿇고 가르쳐 달라야 겠다 I'll humbly ask him to teach me.

꿇리다 〈무릎을 꿇게 하다〉 make *sb* kneel (down); 〈복종하게 하다〉 bring *sb* to 《his》 knees ▶ 그를 꼭 무릎 꿇리겠다 I'll bring him to his knees.

꿇어앉다 sit on *one's* knees [legs]

꿈 a dream; 〈희망〉 a hope; 〈공상〉 a vision; an illusion; 〈백일몽〉 a daydream; a waking dream

♦ 개꿈 a silly [wild] dream; a false dream / 들어맞는 꿈 a true dream / 무서운 꿈 a frightening dream; a nightmare / 청춘의 꿈 the dreams [romantic vision] of youth / 헛된 꿈 an empty dream; a crushed hope / 꿈 많은 소녀 a girl full of romance; a starry-eyed girl / 꿈의 나라 the dreamland

▶ 이것이 꿈이냐 생시냐? Is this a dream or reality?
▶ 외교관이 되는 것이 그의 꿈이다 It is his dream [ambition] to become a diplomat.
▶ 이 모든 것이 꿈만 같다 I feel as if all this were a dream.

〈꿈이[은]〉 그 사건은 꿈이 아니고 현실이었다 The incident was not a dream, but a reality.
▶ 그녀는 장래에 대한 꿈이 없다 She has no vision for the future.
▶ 그녀의 오랜 꿈이 실현되었다 Her long-cherished dream came true [was realized].
▶ 나는 기쁜 나머지 꿈이 아닌가 싶었다 I was so overjoyed (that) I could scarcely believe my eyes.
▶ 그의 꿈은 깨졌다 His dream has been shattered. ⇌ His hopes are gone.
▶ 그 꿈은 들어맞았다[들어맞지 않았다] The dream came true [turned out false].

〈꿈을〉 꿈을 꾸다 have a dream; dream / 즐거운 꿈을 꾸다 dream a happy dream
▶ 〔會話〕「꿈을 자주 꿉니까?」「예, 때로는 무서운 꿈을 꿉니다」 "Do you often have a dream?" "Yes, I sometimes have terrible ones."
▶ 나는 이상한 꿈을 꾸었다 I had [dreamed, dreamt] a strange dream.
▶ 나는 그녀의 꿈을 꾸었다 I had a dream about her. ⇌ I saw her in a dream.
▶ 그는 요트로 태평양을 횡단하겠다는 꿈을 품고 있다 He has dreams of sailing across the Pacific in a yacht.

〈꿈에(서)[도]〉 꿈에서 깨어나다 come out of a dream; 〈미망 등에서〉 come to *one's* senses
▶ 꿈에 나는 바다에서 수영을 하고 있었다 I dreamed of swimming in the sea.
▶ 나는 꿈에 아버지를 보았다 I dreamed that I met my father. ⇌ I met my father in my dream.
▶ 인생은 한갓 꿈에 지나지 않는다 Life is nothing but a dream.
▶ 나는 시끄러운 소리에 꿈에서 깨어났다 I was awakened from my dream by a noise.
▶ 여기서 너를 만나리라고는 꿈에도 생각지 못했다 I never dreamed of meeting you here.

꿈같다 dreamy; dreamlike; visionary 《plans》; illusory
▶ 세계 일주 여행을 할 수 있다니 꿈같다 It's just like a dream to make an around-the-world trip.
▶ 꿈같은 여행이었다 It was a dream of a trip.
▶ 그것은 아주 꿈같은 이야기다 That is a story too good to be true [quite unrealistic].
▶ 나의 행복한 날들은 꿈같이 지나갔다 My happy days passed like a dream.

꿈결 〈꿈꾸는 동안〉 (the midst of) a dream; 〈꿈같은 상태〉 a dreamy [an ecstatic] state of mind
♦ 꿈결 같다 be like a dream; be dreamy / 꿈결같이 지내다 live [go about] in a dream; dream away
▶ 1주일이 꿈결 같이 지나갔다 I spent a week in a trance.
▶ 꿈결에 어떤 소리가 들렸다 I heard some noise in my dream.
▶ 나는 그의 말을 꿈결에 듣고 있었다 I was listening to him dreamily [half dreaming].

꿈꾸다 1 〈꿈을 꾸다〉 dream; have a dream
♦ 꿈꾸는 듯한 눈 dreamy eyes; a faraway look
2 〈바라다〉 dream 《of》; fancy 《*oneself*》
♦ 성공을 꿈꾸다 dream of success / 그런 날이 오기를 꿈꾸다 dream forward to such a day
▶ 그는 미래에 우주 비행사를 꿈꾸고 있다 He dreams of [fancies himself] becoming an astronaut in the future.
▶ 나는 오래 전부터 해외 유학을 꿈꾸어 왔다 I have long dreamed of studying abroad.

꿈나라 the land of dreams ♦ 꿈나라로 가다 go to *one's* dreams; fall asleep

꿈땜 a bad luck deemed to offset the bad dream ―**꿈땜하다** escape a disaster by a lesser sacrifice after having an evil dream

꿈속 ♦ 꿈속에 나타나다 appear [come] in *one's* dream; come to *one* in a dream

꿈자리 the portent [happening] in a dream; a dream
▶ 꿈자리가 좋았다[사나웠다] I had a good [bad] dream.
▶ 어쩐지 어젯밤 꿈자리가 사납더라니 I now see that the dream I had last night boded ill.

꿈틀 with a wriggle [squirm] ―**꿈틀하다** make a short writhing motion

꿈틀거리다 wiggle [wriggle] (about); squirm; wriggle *oneself*
♦ 몸을 꿈틀거리다 wriggle *one's* [its] body / 꿈틀거리며 나아가다 wriggle along; wriggle *one's* [its] way
▶ 뱀이 꿈틀거리며 오솔길을 가로질러 갔다 A snake wriggled across the path.
▶ 돌 밑에서 지렁이들이 꿈틀거리며 기어나왔다 Earthworms wriggled out from beneath a stone.

꿈꿈하다 〈축축하다〉 dampish; damp-dry (빨래가)

꿋꿋이 strongly; firm(ly); unyieldingly
♦ 꿋꿋이 버티다 take a firm stand; show a firm [an unyielding] front / 꿋꿋이 서다 stand firm

▶ 그는 꿋꿋이 역경을 견뎌 냈다 He endured adversity firmly [decisively].
▶ 그녀는 조금도 겁내지 않고 꿋꿋이 그 난국에 맞섰다 She faced the difficult situation without flinching.

꿋꿋하다 strong; firm; tough; solid; 〈마음이〉 upright; inflexible; unyielding
♦ 꿋꿋한 기상 an upright [unyielding] spirit / 꿋꿋한 의지 a strong [an iron] will / 꿋꿋한 태도 an inflexible attitude

꿍 with a thud ⇨ 쿵

꿍꽝 bang-bang ⇨ 쾅쾅

꿍꽝거리다 boom; roar ▶ 대포가 꿍꽝거리고 있었다 Guns were booming [roaring].

꿍꿍¹ 〈몹시 앓는 소리〉 with groaning; with moaning —**꿍꿍하다** ⇨ 꿍꿍거리다

꿍꿍² 〈울리는 소리〉 bang-bang ⇨ 쿵쿵

꿍꿍거리다 groan 《with pain》; moan ▶ 부상자들의 꿍꿍거리는 소리가 들렸다 I heard the injured people groan(ing). ≒ I heard the groans of the injured people.

꿍꿍이 mental arithmetic ⇨ 꿍꿍이셈

꿍꿍이셈 mental arithmetic ♦ 꿍꿍이셈이 있다 have a plot in mind; have a secret design; have an ax to grind / 꿍꿍이셈을 하다 do a mental calculation; expect

꿍꿍이속 an underhand(ed) scheme; an underlying motive; a secret scheme [design]; a plot; an intention
▶ 무슨 꿍꿍이속인지 도무지 모르겠다 I cannot quite see his motive [idea].
▶ 그에겐 뭔가 꿍꿍이속이 있는 게 틀림없다 He must have some (underhand) scheme at the back of his mind.

꿍하다 moody and taciturn; sullen ♦ 꿍해 있다 be in the sulks; be in bad humor

꿩 〔鳥〕a pheasant ♦ 수[암] 꿩 a cock [hen] pheasant / 꿩 사냥 pheasant hunting / 꿩 한 쌍 a brace of pheasants

꿩 먹고 알 먹기 《속담》 To catch two pigeons with one bean. ≒ To kill two birds with one stone.

꿰다 1 〈구멍으로 나가게 하다〉 pass [run] sth through ♦ 구슬을 꿰다 string [thread] beads / 바늘에 실을 꿰다 run [pass] a thread through a needle; thread a needle
2 〈찔러 꽂다〉 pierce; thrust
♦ 꼬챙이에 꿰다 skewer; spit / 꼬챙이에 꿰어 굽다 roast 《a piece of meat》 on a skewer [spit]
3 〈착용하다〉 slip on; put on; wear ♦ 바지를 급히 꿰다 slip on one's trousers
4 〈훤히 알다〉 know thoroughly; be versed in

꿰들다 1 〈꿰어서 쳐들다〉 skewer [spit, pierce] sth and hold it up ♦ 물고기를 작살로 꿰들다 spear a fish and hold it up
2 〈들추어 내다〉 disclose [let out]; expose 《another's fault》; dig up 《scandals》

꿰뚫다 1 〈관통하다〉 penetrate; pierce; perforate; pass [run] through
▶ 창은 기사의 방패를 꿰뚫었다 The lance penetrated the knight's shield.
▶ 화살은 그의 어깨를 꿰뚫었다 The arrow pierced his shoulder.
▶ 총알이 그의 왼쪽 허벅다리를 꿰뚫었다 A bullet went through his left thigh.
▶ 올빼미의 눈은 어둠을 꿰뚫어 볼 수 있다 Eyes of owls can penetrate the darkness.
2 〈통찰하다〉 discern; penetrate [see] into; see through
♦ 꿰뚫어 보는 듯한 눈 a penetrating eye / 아무의 마음을 꿰뚫어 보다 see into [through] sb's heart [mind]
▶ 나는 그 술책을 금방 꿰뚫어 보았다 I saw through the trick at once.
▶ 그녀는 영리한 여자라서 금방 그의 사람됨을 꿰뚫어 보았다 She was a shrewd girl and soon took his measure.
▶ 지도자는 아랫사람의 장단점을 꿰뚫어 보는 능력이 있어야 한다 A leader should have an eye for [be able to see] his subordinates.
3 ⇨ 꿰다 4

꿰뜨리다 〈해지게 하다〉 puncture; burst; wear out
♦ 공을 꿰뜨리다 burst a ball / 옷을 꿰뜨리다 wear out one's clothes
▶ 나는 그 도보 여행에서 장화 두 켤레를 꿰뜨렸다 I wore out two pairs of boots on the walking tour.

꿰매다 〈깁다〉 sew; stitch; 〈짜깁다〉 patch (up); put [add] a patch on; sew (in) a patch; darn; 〈수선하다〉 mend
♦ 옷을 꿰매다 sew garments / 터진 솔기를 꿰매다 sew up an open seam / 손으로 꿰매다 sew by hand / 재봉틀로 꿰매다 sew by machine; sew sth on a sewing machine / 꿰맨 데를 뜯다 undo a place once sewed / 천 조각을 꿰매어 잇다 sew pieces of cloth together
▶ 이 양말 좀 꿰매 주세요. Please mend [sew up] the hole in this sock. ≒ Please darn this sock.
▶ 그녀는 스웨터에 흰 장식 단추를 꿰매 붙였다 She sewed white beads on her sweater.
▶ 그녀는 비밀 문서를 드레스에 꿰매 넣었다 She sewed a secret letter into her dress.
▶ 의사는 상처를 일곱 바늘이나 꿰매야 했다 The doctor had to put seven stitches in the wound [sew up the wound with seven stitches].

꿰미 1 〈노끈〉 a string; a thin cord 2 〈꿴 것〉 things on a string ♦ 생선[엽전] 한 꿰미 a string of fish [coins]

꿰지다 〈미어지다〉 be rent [ripped] up; 〈해지다〉 be torn up; tear; 〈터지다〉 burst (open); break
♦ 쉽게 꿰지다 tear easily / 꿰진 곳을 깁다 sew up a rip / 봉지가 꿰졌다 The paper bag is broken [burst].

꿰찌르다 thrust [run] through; pierce; penetrate; plunge ♦ 단도로 가슴을 꿰찌르다 plunge a dagger into sb's breast

꿰차다 1 〈매어 달다〉 hang [suspend] a thing onto a belt; sling a thing from a belt ♦ 주머니를 꿰차다 dangle a purse from a belt
2 《俗》〈제것으로 만들다〉 make sth [sb] for one's own; latch on to

꿱 shoutingly; with a quack ♦ 꿱 소리치다 give a yell [shout] —**꿱하다** shout; yell;

quack ◆ 꽥하는 소리 a shout; a yell
꽥꽥거리다 1〈소리지르다〉 cry; yell; shout; roar; give an angry word / 사소한 일로 꽥꽥거리다 roar at [about] trifles / 화가 나서 꽥꽥거리다 roar with anger
2〈토하려고〉 keck; retch
3〈오리가〉 quack;〈거위가〉 gaggle
뀌다 release (flatulence); break; evacuate ◆ 방귀를 뀌다 break [pass] wind
끄나풀 1〈토막끈〉 a (piece of) string; a (bit of) cord
◆ 끄나풀을 풀다 untie [undo] the strings / 끄나풀로 묶다 tie with a string
2〈앞잡이〉 a tool; an instrument; an implement; a cat's-paw; an agent; a pawn
◆ 경찰의 끄나풀 a police agent / 끄나풀 노릇을 하다 work as another's instrument; act as an agent 《for》 / 끄나풀로 부리다 make a cat's-paw of *sb*
▶ 그는 보스의 끄나풀이 되었다 He made himself a minion [cat's-paw] of the boss.
▶ 그는 적의 끄나풀로 이용되었다 He was used as a tool [an agent] of the enemy.
끄느름하다 〈날이 어둠침침하다〉 cloudy; overcast; 〈불이 약하다〉 low ▶ 난로불이 끄느름하게 타고 있다 The fire in the hearth is burning low.
끄다 1〈불을 못타게 하다〉 put out; extinguish
◆ 물을 뿌려[담요를 덮어] 불을 끄다 put out [smother] a fire with water [a blanket] / 촛불[불꽃]을 불어서 끄다 blow out a candle [a flame]
▶ 그는 담배불을 발로 밟아 껐다 He stamped out the cigarette with his foot.
▶ 그는 풀밭의 불을 두들겨서 껐다 He beat out the grass fire.
▶ 야영장에서는 떠나기 전에 불을 다 꺼야 한다 You must completely put out [extinguish] the fire at the campsite before you leave.
2〈전류를 끊다〉 switch off; turn off
◆ 가스[라디오]를 끄다 turn off the gas [radio] / 전등불을 끄다 turn [switch] off a light / 엔진을 끄다 stop an engine
▶ 텔레비전을 끄고 자거라 Turn off the TV, and go to bed.
▶ 나는 라디오를 끄는 것을 잊었다 I forgot to switch [turn] off the radio.
3〈덩이를 헤뜨리다〉 crush; break; smash
◆ 얼음을 끄다 crush ice; break (up) ice / 흙덩이를 끄다 crush [break] a clod [lump] of
4〈빚을 가리다〉 pay; repay ◆ 빚을 다 끄다 pay [clear off] all *one's* debts
끄덕 〈고개를〉 with a nod ━**끄덕하다** nod; give a nod / 그렇다고 끄덕하다 nod *one's* head in the affirmative / 끄덕하고 승낙하다 show *one's* approval with a nod; nod (in) assent
끄덕이다〈머리를〉 nod (to, at); give a nod ◆ 가볍게 끄덕이다 give a slight nod / 혼자서 머리를 끄덕이다 nod *one's* head to *oneself*
▶ 그는 형의 충고를 일일이 끄덕이며 들었다 He listened to his brother's advice nodding each time.
▶ 그녀는 머리를 끄덕여 동의를 표했다 She

showed her consent by nodding to [at] me. ⇌ She nodded assent.
끄덩이 1〈머리털의〉 the ends of *one's* hair
◆ 머리 끄덩이를 잡다 seize [grab] *sb's* hair; seize *sb* by the hair / 머리 끄덩이를 끄두르다 drag [pull about] *sb* by the hair
2〈실뭉치의 끝〉 the end of a bunch of thread
◆ 실 끄덩이를 잡아당기다 pull out a thread from a bunch
끄떡¹ 〈고개를〉 with a nod ⇨ 끄덕
끄떡² 〈미동〉 ◆ 끄떡도 않다〈움직이지 않다〉 do not budge an inch; 〈기죽지 않다〉 be not at all daunted; remain unflinching; 〈태연 하 다〉 maintain [preserve] *one's* composure / 뇌물에 끄떡도 않다 be proof against bribery
끄떡없다 〈끄떡도 않다〉 unmoved; unflinching; 〈탈없다〉 safe (and sound); all right; 〈장애가 되지 않다〉 proof (against)
▶ 그들은 아무리 폭음을 해도 끄떡없다 They commit all sorts of excesses with impunity.
▶ 그는 어떤 위험이 닥쳐도 끄떡없었다 He was perfectly calm and serene in the presence of any danger.
끄르다 〈풀다〉 untie; unbind; unlace; 〈열다〉 unbutton ◆ 구두끈을 끄르다 unlace the shoes / 꾸러미를 끄르다 untie [undo] a package [bundle]; unpack / 단추를 끄르다 unbutton 《a shirt》; undo a button
끄륵 with a burp ⇨ 꺽
끄륵거리다 keep burping; belch continually
끄륵끄륵 with repeated burps
끄무레하다 〈날이 침침하다〉 cloudy; overcast; dull ◆ 끄무레한 날씨 dim and cloudy weather; a cloudy day
끄물거리다 〈날이 개었다 흐렸다하다〉 get clear and cloudy at intervals; get cloudy on and on [from time to time]
◆ 끄물거리는 날씨 unsettled weather; a partly cloudy day
▶ 날씨가 계속 끄물거릴 모양이다 It seems that the weather will remain unsettled.
끄집다 hold and pull; draw
끄집어내다 1〈물건을 밖으로 내다〉 take out; pull [draw] out; fish (out)
▶ 그는 호주머니에서 지갑을 끄집어냈다 He took out his wallet from his pocket.
▶ 그녀는 가방에 손을 넣어 돈을 한 움큼 끄집어냈다 She reached into the bag and came out with a handful of money.
2〈이야기를 시작하다〉 bring up 《a topic》; raise 《a subject》; broach
◆ 슬슬 돈 문제를 끄집어내다 lead up to the question of money / 이야기를 끄집어내다 broach a matter; introduce a topic [subject] / 대화 중에 장사 이야기를 끄집어내다 bring business matters into conversation
▶ 회의에서 그는 감원 문제를 끄집어냈다 At the conference he broached the subject of cutting personnel.
▶ 그는 잠시 망설이다가 그 문제를 끄집어냈다 He brought up the matter after some hesitation.
끄집어내리다 take [bring, carry] down ▶ 3층

에서 짐을 어떻게 끄집어내리지? How shall we bring the things down from the third floor?

끄집어당기다 draw; drag; pull ▶ 그는 의자를 식탁 앞으로 끄집어당겼다 He drew his chair up to the table.

끄집어들이다 take [bring, carry] in [into]; draw [pull] in [into] ◆ 짐을 끄집어들이다 drag a luggage in [into]

끄집어올리다 pull [take] up; draw [drag] up ◆ 가라앉은 배를 끄집어올리다 salve a sunken vessel ▶ 그는 보트를 물가로 끄집어올렸다 He drew the boat on to the beach.

끄트러기 odds and ends; odd pieces; oddments; scraps; chips ◆ 나무 끄트러기 odd pieces of wood / 천 끄트러기 remnants of cloth

끄트머리 1 〈말단〉 an end; 〈선단〉 a tip; 〈가장자리〉 an edge; the tail end; extremity
◆ 밧줄의 끄트머리 the extreme end of a rope / 끄트머리에 서다 stand at the tail end ▶ 교회는 이 길의 동쪽 끄트머리에 있다 The church is at the eastern end of this street.
▶ 그들의 대화를 끄트머리 밖에 못 들었다 I only heard the tail end of their conversation.
2 〈단서〉 a clue

끈 1 〈줄〉 a string; a cord; 〈꼬거나 짠〉 a braid; a plait; a band
◆ 가죽 끈 a strap; a thong / 끈을 매다[풀다] tie [untie] the strings / 구두 끈을 매다[풀다] lace [unlace] the boots / 끈으로 묶다 tie with a string / 트렁크를 끈으로 묶다 strap up a trunk
▶ 끈이 풀렸다 The strings came untied [loose].
▶ 내 카메라 끈이 끊어졌다 My camera strap has broken.
▶ 배낭에는 어깨에 걸치는 끈이 있다 A rucksack has straps that go over the shoulders.
2 〈연줄〉 ties; patronage; 〈俗〉 a pull ◆ 우정의 끈 the ties of friendship / 경찰에 끈이 있다 have a pull with the police / 끈이 좋다 be well-connected; have a strong [good] pull

끈기 —氣 1 〈끈끈함〉 stickiness; glutinosity; viscosity; adhesiveness ◆ 끈기가 있는 sticky; adhesive; glutinous
▶ 이 밥은 끈기가 있다 This boiled rice is sticky.
▶ 이 풀은 끈기가 없다 This paste is not sticky [lacks stickiness].
2 〈꾸준함〉 tenacity; perseverance; pertinacity; (美口) stick-to-itiveness; 〈인내력〉 stamina
◆ 끈기를 요하는 일 work which needs perseverance / 끈기 있는 tenacious; pertinacious; persevering; patient; untiring; enduring / 끈기 있게 tenaciously; pertinaciously; patiently; with perseverance
▶ 조금만 더 끈기있게 버텨 봐 Just try to stick to it a little longer.
▶ 우리는 끈기있게 교섭했다 We negotiated tenaciously.
▶ 그는 끈기가 없었다 He lacked tenacity.
▶ 그는 한 가지 일에 파고 드는 끈기가 없다 He is not steady enough to stick to one job.
▶ 영어 공부에는 끈기가 필요하다 You need tenacity [must be tenacious] when it comes to learning English.
▶ 나는 그의 끈기를 당할 수 없었다 I was not equal to his patience.

끈끈이 birdlime; lime ◆ 파리 잡는 끈끈이 종이 (a piece of) flypaper / 끈끈이로 새를 잡다 catch a bird with birdlime

끈끈이대나물 〔植〕 a catchfly

끈끈이주걱 〔植〕 a sundew

끈끈하다 1 〈끈적거리다〉 sticky; viscous; adhesive; gluey ◆ 땀으로 끈끈한 내의 a sticky undershirt / 끈끈한 송진 gluey pine resin / 끈끈한 풀 sticky [glutinous] paste
2 〈검질기다〉 tenacious; persistent ◆ 성질이 끈끈한 사람 a man of great tenacity; a stickler

끈덕거리다 be shaky [rickety]; be unsteady
◆ 끈덕거리는 의자 a shaky [rickety] chair / 끈덕거리는 이 a loose tooth ▶ 책상다리가 끈덕거린다 The legs of the table are groggy.

끈덕지다 persistent; tenacious; pertinacious; (美口) stick-to-itive
◆ 끈덕진 공격 a persistent attack / 끈덕지게 persistently; tenaciously; with persistence [tenacity] / 끈덕지게 여자를 따라다니다 dangle after a girl with grimmest tenacity
▶ 그는 내게 영화 보러 가자고 끈덕지게 졸랐다 He persistently invited me to go to the movies with him.
▶ 그는 남의 개인적인 일을 끈덕지게 캐묻는다 He is inquisitive about the personal affairs of others.

끈목 〈짠[꼰] 끈〉 a braid; a braided [plaited] cord

끈붙다 〈생계가 생기다〉 get a means of livelihood [living]; get *one's* employment

끈붙이다 provide *sb* with a means of livelihood

끈적거리다 1 〈자꾸 들러붙다〉 be sticky [gluey]; be viscous; be clammy; (口) be gooey
▶ 셔츠가 땀이 배어 끈적거린다 My shirt is sticky with sweat.
▶ 이 송진은 오랫동안 끈적거린다 This resin remains sticy for a long time.
▶ 페인트가 아직 마르지 않아서 끈적거린다 The paint is still wet and smeary.
2 〈자꾸 검질기게 굴다〉 stick (to); be tenacious; be persistent; persist (in) ◆ 끈적거리는 사람 a person of tenacity

끈적끈적 ◆ 끈적끈적 붙다 stick to [on]; adhere to; be sticky
▶ 껌이 끈적끈적 손에 들러붙었다 My hands were sticky with gum.
—**끈적끈적하다** be sticky ⇨ 끈적거리다 1, 끈끈하다 1
▶ 내 손이 기름으로 끈적끈적하다 My hands are greasy.

끈지다 persistent; pertinacious; persevering; tenacious

끈질기다 〈불굴의〉 persistent; 〈인내력이 강한〉 persevering; pertinacious; 〈집요한〉 tenacious; importunate; 〈부동의〉 steadfast; (美口) stick-to-itive

끊이다

◆끈질긴 노력 a persistent [strenuous] effort; a steadfast endeavor / 끈질긴 사나이 a man of great tenacity / 끈질긴 요구 an importunate demand
▶댐의 건설에는 끈질긴 반대가 있었다 There was stiff opposition to the construction of the dam.
▶그는 내 사무실에 취직시켜 달라고 끈질기게 졸랐다 He importuned me for a position in my office.

끊기다 be cut ⇨ 끊어지다

끊다 1 〈줄을 자르다〉 cut (off); break; sever
◆밧줄을 끊다 cut [break] a rope / 철조망을 끊다 cut [sever] barbed wire / 불에 녹여 끊다 burn off / 직각으로 끊다 cut at right angles
▶이 부분을 끊어버리자 Let's cut this section off.
2 〈관계를 그치다〉 sever 《one's connections with》; break off 《relations with sb》; break with; cut (off)
◆끊을래야 끊을 수 없는 인연 an indissoluble tie; a fatal connection / 교제[관계]를 끊다 sever [cut off] acquaintance [connection] 《with》 / 발길을 끊다 stop visiting; keep oneself away from; cease to visit / 연락을 끊다 sever [cut off] the communication 《with》 / 외교 관계를 끊다 break off [sever] all diplomatic relations
▶나는 폭력단과의 관계를 끊었다 I have broken off (my connection) with the racketeers.
▶그녀와의 관계도 끊기로 했다 I also decided to break off [sever] my relationship with her.
▶이제 그 일과는 손을 끊기로 합시다 Let's have done with it.
▶부모 자식간의 관계는 끊을래야 끊을 수 없는 것이다 Parent and child are inseparably connected.
▶두 사람은 끊을래야 끊을 수 없는 관계에 있다 They are hand in [and] glove with each other. ⇌ They are inseparably bound up with each other.
3 〈목숨을 없애 버리다〉 kill ◆남의 목숨을 끊다 take sb's life; kill sb
▶그는 스스로 목숨을 끊었다 He killed himself. ⇌ He committed suicide.
4 【중단·차단하다】 cut off; stop; shut off; intercept; interrupt; 〈스위치 등을〉 switch [turn] off; 〈전화를〉 ring off; hang up
◆가스[전기]를 끊다 cut off gas [electricity] / 갑자기 말을 끊다 break off abruptly / 보급로를 끊다 block the supply route / 전류를 끊다 switch off the electric current / 적의 퇴로를 끊다 cut off [intercept] the enemy's retreat / 회로를 끊다 kill a circuit
▶그녀는 화가 나서 전화를 끊었다 She got angry and hung up.
▶그는 잠시 말을 끊었다가 다시 시작했다 He paused a moment but soon began to speak again.
▶전화를 끊지 마세요 Please hold [hang] on. ⇌ Hold the line, please.
5 〈사다〉 buy ◆옷감을 끊다 buy a piece of cloth / 차표를 끊다 buy a ticket
6 〈그만두다〉 give up; quit; abstain from; stop

◆담배를 끊다 give up [quit] smoking / 술을 끊다 stop [give up, swear off] drinking; abstain from liquor [alcohol]
▶나는 한 달 전부터 담배[술]를 끊었다 I quit [gave up] smoking [drinking] a month ago.
7 〈말 등을 자르다〉 punctuate; mark [set] off 《a clause》 by a comma ◆이야기를 끊다 punctuate a story
▶그는 본문을 한 구절씩 끊어서 읽었다 He read the text with pauses between phrases.
8 〈수표를 발행하다〉 issue; write out ◆수표를 끊다 draw [make out] a check / 전표를 끊다 issue [write out] a sales slip

끊어주다 〈셈을 떼어 내주다〉 square [settle] accounts with sb; pay off

끊어지다 1 〈끈이 떨어져 나가다〉 be cut; break; snap
▶전구가 끊어졌다 The electric bulb has burnt out.
▶퓨즈가 끊어졌다 The fuse is gone [blown].
▶이 줄은 약하구나. 살짝 당겼는데 끊어졌어 This string is frail. It broke at a slight pull.
▶큰 고기가 걸렸는데 줄이 끊어져서 놓쳤다 I hooked a big fish, but the line snapped and it got away.
2 〈두절·차단되다〉 be cut off; be stopped [interrupted, suspended]; cease; discontinue; be disconnected
▶이 거리는 밤이 되면 인적이 완전히 끊어진다 This street is completely deserted at night.
▶산 사태로 교통이 끊어졌다 The traffic was stopped by a landslide.
▶그와의 연락이 끊어졌다 We have lost contact with him.
▶통화중에 전화가 끊어졌다 We were cut off [disconnected] in the middle of our telephone conversation.
▶그 배와의 통신이 모두 끊어졌다 All communication with the ship has been lost.
▶그의 소식이 끊어진 지 거의 6개월이 된다 I haven't heard from him for almost six months.
3 〈죽게 되다〉 die; expire
▶그는 어제 숨이 끊어졌다 He died [passed away, breathed his last] yesterday.
▶보니까 그는 숨이 끊어지려는 참이었다 I found him at his last gasp.
4 〈공급이 중단되다〉 run out; be cut off
▶급수가 끊어졌다 The supply of water ran out.
▶석유 수입이 끊어지면 한국 경제는 큰 타격을 입을 것이다 If the import of oil should be cut off, it would give a severe blow to the Korean economy.
5 〈관계가 없어지다〉 come to an end; be cut [severed]; be over [through] with; be done [finished] with ◆인연이 끊어지다 be separated; 〈부부의〉 be divorced; be finished with each other

끊이다 cease; discontinue; come to an end
◆걱정이 끊이지 않다 be never free from care
▶그녀의 집에는 손님이 끊이지 않는다 She has visitors all the time.
▶저 집안에는 말썽이 끊일 날이 없다 There is

no end of troubles in that family.
끊임없다 ceaseless; unceasing; constant; continual; continuous; endless; incessant
♦끊임없는 걱정 endless worries; unremitting care / 끊임없는 발전 continuous development / 끊임없는 주의 constant attention
▶영어에 능통하기 위해서는 끊임없는 노력이 필요하다 Constant [Unremitting] effort is necessary to have a good command of English.
▶나는 그녀의 끊임없는 잔소리에 넌더리가 났다 I was sick of her incessant [constant] nagging.
끊임없이 continuously; ceaselessly; constantly; all the time; without cessation [interruption, intermission]; without a break [letup, pause]
♦끊임없이 들려오는 소리 a continuous sound / 끊임없이 노력하다 make a constant effort / 끊임없이 담배를 피우다 be smoking all the time / 끊임없이 전화가 걸려오다 have telephone calls almost without a break / 끊임없이 지껄이다 talk without intermission [a pause]; talk on ceaselessly [continuously]
▶그는 끊임없이 불평이다 He is always [continually, constantly] making complaints. ⇒ He is grumbling all the time.
▶그들은 끊임없이 떠들고 있었다 They were incessantly making noise.
▶비가 끊임없이 내렸다 It rained without a break [continuously, incessantly].
▶적은 월요일부터 금요일까지 우리에게 끊임없이 포격을 가했다 The enemy was continuously bombarding us from Monday until Friday.
끌 a chisel ♦둥근 끌 a gouge; a scalper / 끌로 파다 chisel; cut with a chisel ▶그는 끌로 목각 불상을 조각했다 He chiseled an image of Buddha out of wood.
끌끌 〈혀를〉 tut(-tut); tsk ♦혀를 끌끌 차다 tut-tutted; go tut-tut; tsktsk
끌끌하다 〈마음이 깨끗하다〉 clean and pure; fair and clean; honest; upright
끌다 1 〈당기다〉 pull; draw; drag [tug, haul] 《at》; 〈배 등을〉 tow

解說 *pull*은 힘을 주어 순간적으로 「끌다」, *draw*는 손조롭게 얼마만큼의 시간을 두고 또는 얼마만큼의 거리에 걸쳐 「끌다」라는 뜻.

♦보트를 밧줄로 끌다 tow a boat with a rope / 배를 항구로 끌고 가다 tow a ship into the port
▶그녀가 내 소매를 잡아 끌었다 She pulled me by the sleeve. ⇒ She pulled (at) my sleeve.
▶소가 달구지를 몹시 힘들게 끌고 있다 The ox is pulling the cart as if it is very heavy.
▶두 마리의 순록이 산타클로스가 탄 썰매를 끌고 있었다 Two reindeer(s) were hauling the sled Santa Claus was in.
▶배는 밤새도록 닻을 끌고 갔다 The ship dragged its [her] anchor all night.
▶소년은 장난감 기차를 끈으로 끌고 다녔다 The boy was trailing his toy train by [on] a piece of string.
2 〈늘어뜨리고 가다〉 drag; trail
♦치맛자락을 끌다 trail *one's* skirt / 발을 질질 끌며 걷다 walk with dragging feet; scuff *one's* feet; drag *one's* feet as *one* walks
▶그는 지친 다리를 끌고 있다 He is dragging his weary legs.
▶그는 다친 다리를 질질 끌며 걸었다 He trailed along his wounded leg.
▶그녀는 진창 속을 옷자락을 끌면서 갔다 She trailed her dress through the mud.
3 〈데리고 가다〉 lead; guide; 〈연행하다〉 take *sb* to 《a place》; walk *sb* off to 《a place》
♦말을 끌다 lead a horse / 아이의 손을 끌다 lead a child by the hand
▶경찰관이 그 피의자를 경찰서로 끌고 갔다 The policeman took the suspect to a police station.
▶그를 끌고 와라 Bring him here.
4 〈미루다〉 put off; postpone; prolong; protract; delay; drag [draw] out; drag on; spin out
♦오래 끄는 병 a long disease; a lingering [protracted] disease / 오래 끌어온 협상 long-pending [long-drawn-out] negotiations / 말하는 것으로 시간을 끌다 spin out the time by talking / 지불을 끌다 put off [delay] payment / 회답을 끌다 delay *one's* reply [in answering] / 회의를 끌다 prolong [draw out] a meeting / 차일피일 끌다 put off from day to day
▶그의 병은 오래 끌었다 He was long in recovering from his illness.
▶그들은 협상을 1주일 동안이나 끌어 왔다 They have dragged the negotiation for a whole week.
▶중재는 질질 끌어 두 달이나 걸렸다 The arbitration was spun out for two months.
5 〈쏠리게 하다〉 attract; catch 《*sb's* attention》; win; draw; arrest
♦고객을 끌다 draw customers; 〈호객하다〉 try to call in customers; solicit / 눈길을 끌다 draw [attract, call] *one's* attention; catch the eye / 동정심을 끌다 arouse [evoke] *sb's* sympathy / 여자의 마음을 끌다 win the heart [love] of a woman / 인기를 끌다 catch [win, gain] popularity
▶그의 공연은 언제나 많은 관객을 끈다 His performances always draw [attract] a large crowd.
▶그에게는 어딘가 사람을 끄는 데가 있다 He has a magnetic personality. ⇒ There's something attractive [engaging] about him.
6 〈시설하다〉 lay on; install ♦논에 물을 끌다 irrigate a rice field [paddy]
▶그 별장에는 가스, 전기, 수도를 끌어 놓았다 Gas, electricity and water are laid on [installed] in the vacation house.
7 〈인용하다〉 quote 《from》; cite ♦밀턴에서 끌어온 구 a phrase quoted from Milton / 예를 끌어 오다 cite an example
끌려지다 become [get] loose; be loosened; be unfastened; come [get] untied [undone]; become unlaced
▶내 구두끈이 끌려졌다 My shoelace has come untied [undone, loose].

▶ 네 허리띠가 끌러졌다 Your belt has come loose.
끌려가다 be taken 《to》 ▶ 그는 절도 혐의로 경찰서에 끌려갔다 He was taken [(口) hauled off, walked off] to the police station on suspicion of theft.
끌려들다 be drawn [dragged] 《into》; be attracted; be allured [enticed]
♦ 이야기에 끌려들다 be drawn into the conversation / 전쟁에 끌려들다 be drawn into a war
▶ 그런 유형의 사람은 나쁜 일에 쉽게 끌려든다 A man of that type is easily led [tempted] into evil ways.
▶ 나도 모르게 그의 이야기에 끌려들었다 I was carried away by his speech. ≒ I was caught up in his speech [story].
▶ 많은 사람이 그의 이야기에 끌려들었다 A lot of people were attracted by his story.
끌리다 1 【끌어 당겨지다】 be drawn [pulled]; be tugged; 〈늘어지다〉 be dragged; trail
▶ 그녀의 긴 치맛자락이 끌리고 있다 Her long skirt is trailing (along) behind her.
▶ 그는 온 마을을 끌려 다니고 나서 처형되었다 He was executed after being dragged around (the) town.
2 〈마음이 쏠리다〉 be attracted; be charmed; be drawn
▶ 그는 그녀의 매력에 끌렸다 He was attracted [fascinated] by her charm.
▶ 나는 그의 열성에 끌려 돕기로 했다 Moved [Overcome, Touched] by his fervor, I agreed to help him.
▶ 그녀는 다른 것에 마음이 끌려 있었다 She was taken up [absorbed in] something else.
끌밋하다 〈훤칠하다〉 high in stature; handsome; good-looking ♦ 끌밋한 청년 a handsome young man / 끌밋한 풍채 a smart appearance
끌밥 chips from chiseling; chisel chips
끌방망이 a chisel mallet [hammer]
끌어내다 〈밖으로 내다〉 take out; pull [drag] out [forth]; 〈뽑아내다〉 extract; 〈연역하다〉 deduce
▶ 나는 방에서 그를 끌어냈다 I dragged him out of the room.
▶ 그는 마구간에서 말을 끌어냈다 He led a horse out of the stable.
▶ 나는 그에게서 필요한 정보를 끌어냈다 I extracted the necessary information from him.
▶ 여기서 나는 다음과 같은 결론을 끌어냈다 From this I drew [deduced] the following conclusion.
▶ 그 선생님은 학생들의 잠재능력을 끌어내는 데 소질이 있다 That teacher is good at bringing out students' latent abilities.
▶ 그는 친구한테서 약간의 사업자금을 끌어낼 수 있었다 He managed to get a little money for his business out of a friend.
끌어내리다 pull [draw, drag, haul] down
♦ 값을 천원으로 끌어내리다 reduce [lower, cut] the price to 1,000 won / 낮은 지위로 끌어내리다 reduce (an officer) to a lower grade;

lower sb in rank; demote [degrade] sb
▶ 청중은 연사를 연단에서 끌어내렸다 The audience dragged down the speaker from the platform.
▶ 우리는 적의 깃발을 끌어내렸다 We hauled [dragged] down the enemy flag.
끌어넣다 draw [drag, pull] in [into]; take [bring] sb into 《a room》; lead in
♦ 소를 외양간에 끌어넣다 lead [drag] a cow into a barn / 음모에 끌어넣다 tempt [entangle] sb into an intrigue / 자기편에 끌어넣다 win sb over to one's side
끌어당기다 draw sth near; pull [drag] up; draw 《toward》; attract; tug at
♦ 그물을 끌어당기다 draw a net / 소매를 끌어당기다 pull sb by the sleeve; tug at sb's sleeve
▶ 자석은 못을 끌어당긴다 A magnet attracts a nail.
▶ 그는 의자를 식탁으로 끌어당겼다 He drew up his chair to the table.
끌어대다 1 〈끌어다 뒤를 대다〉 raise money [funds]; finance
▶ 그는 돈을 잘 끌어댄다 He is a good fundraiser.
▶ 나는 가까스로 돈을 끌어댔다 I managed to raise the money.
▶ 그녀는 돈을 끌어대기에 바쁘다 She is busy raising funds.
2 〈끌어다 맞대다〉 bring [draw] together
♦ 살 사람과 팔 사람을 끌어대다 bring buyer and seller together
3 〈인용하다〉 cite; quote; refer to ♦ 전례를 끌어대다 cite precedents
▶ 그는 자기 견해를 입증하기 위해 많은 권위자의 설을 끌어댔다 He cited a number of authorities to prove his views.
끌어들이다 draw [pull, drag] in [into]; bring [take] sb into 《a house》
♦ 고객을 끌어들이다 solicit [draw] a customer / 자본가를 사업에 끌어들이다 interest capitalists in an enterprise / 자기 편으로 끌어들이다 win [gain] sb over to one's side; bring sb over to one's camp
▶ 그는 친구를 나쁜 일에 끌어들였다 He enticed his friend to do something wrong.
▶ 그 나라는 미국을 전쟁에 끌어들였다 The country dragged America into the war.
▶ 그를 내 편으로 끌어들이는 데 성공했다 I succeeded in winning him over to my side.
끌어안다 draw sb close to one's breast; snuggle 《a child》 to oneself [one's arms]; embrace; hug
♦ 서로 끌어안다 embrace [hug] each other; be in [go into] each other's arms
▶ 그는 소녀를 꽉 끌어안았다 He held the girl tightly in his arms.
▶ 두 사람은 서로 끌어안고 울었다 The two threw themselves into each other's arms and wept.
▶ 어머니는 아이를 끌어안고 달아났다 The mother ran away carrying her child in her arms.
끌어올리다 pull [draw] up; hoist; 〈승진시키다〉 promote 《sb to a higher position》

끌채

♦경합해서 값을 끌어 올리다 bid up the price / 펌프로 물을 끌어올리다 pump up water / 배를 해안으로 끌어올리다 beach a boat; haul a boat up (to) the beach / 침몰선을 끌어올리다 salvage a sunken vessel

▶ 우리는 크레인을 이용하여 무거운 기계를 옥상으로 끌어올렸다 We hoisted a heavy machine to the roof by crane.

▶ 그들은 그 그림 값을 1만 달러까지 끌어올렸다 They bid the price of the painting up to ten thousand dollars.

끌채 a thill; a shaft ♦끌채에 맨 말 a thiller

끓는점 —點 〖物〗 the boiling point ♦끓는점에 달하다 reach a boil; come to the boil

끓다 1 〈물 등이〉 boil; seethe

♦끓는 물 boiling water / 끓기 시작하다 come to the boil / 끓어 넘치다 boil over

▶ 난로 위의 주전자가 부글부글 끓고 있었다 The kettle was singing on the stove.

▶ 물이 끓으면 수증기로 변한다 When water boils it turns into steam.

2 〈뜨거워지다〉 become very hot; become boiling hot ▶ 방이 절절 끓는다 The room is boiling hot. ▶ 그는 몸이 펄펄 끓는다 He has a high fever.

3 〈마음이〉 fret; fume; become irritated

♦화가 나서 속이 부글부글 끓다 be convulsed with anger; boil [seethe] with rage; fret and fume

▶ 그의 젊은 피가 끓었다 His youthful blood tingled.

▶ 그 음악은 내 피를 끓게 했다 The music made my blood tingled.

4 〈뱃속이〉 rumble ▶ 배가 끓었다 The bowels rumbled.

5 〈가래가〉 rattle in the throat; make a rattling [gurgling] sound; ruckle ▶ 목에 가래가 끓는다 Phlegm obstructs [sticks in] the throat.

6 ⇨ 들끓다

끓어오르다 boil [seethe] up

▶ 나는 분노로 피가 끓어올랐다 My blood boiled with indignation.

▶ 주전자의 물이 끓어오르고 있다 The water in the kettle is boiling [on the boil].

▶ 그는 증오심이 끓어오르고 있었다 He was seething with hatred.

끓이다 1 〈물 등을〉 boil; 〈익히다〉 cook

♦국을 끓이다 make soup / 물을 끓이다 make hot water; boil water / 차를 끓이다 make [prepare] tea; draw [brew] tea / 펄펄 끓이다 boil up; bring (water) to the boil / 우유를 끓여서 살균하다 boil and sterilize milk

▶ 수프를 10분 정도 은근히 끓여라 Let the soup simmer [boil gently] for about ten minutes.

▶ 커피물 좀 끓여 주세요 Please boil some water for coffee (in a kettle).

▶ 물은 반드시 끓여 먹도록 해라 Do not fail to boil water once before you drink it.

2 〈속을〉 worry; fret; stew 《about》

▶ 무슨 일로 속을 끓이고 있는 거니? What are you worrying about? ⇒ What's on your mind? ⇒ What is bothering you?

▶ 그녀가 너무 속을 끓이다 죽을까 걱정이다 I'm afraid she'll worry herself to death.

끔벅 1 〈불빛이〉 in a twinkling —**끔벅하다** dim and flash quickly; flicker ▶ 일순간 모든 불빛이 끔벅했다 All the lights flickered for a moment.

2 〈눈을〉 blinkingly; with a wink —**끔벅하다** wink (at); blink

♦눈을 끔벅하다 wink one's eyes / 눈 하나 끔벅않고 지켜보다 gaze at sth without a wink; look steadily at sth

▶ 그는 나에게 알았다는 듯 눈을 끔벅했다 He gave me a knowing wink.

▶ 그는 놀라서 눈을 끔벅했다 He blinked his eyes in surprise.

끔벅거리다 1 〈별·불빛 등이〉 dim and flash repeatedly; flicker; twinkle

▶ 촛불이 잠깐 끔벅거리다 꺼졌다 The candle flickered a moment and went off.

2 〈눈을〉 wink; blink ♦눈을 끔벅거리다 wink [blink] (one's eyes); (口) bat one's eye(lids)

▶ 그는 눈을 끔벅거려 눈물을 떨어뜨렸다 He winked [blinked] away his tears.

끔벅끔벅 flickeringly

끔벅이다 1 〈불빛 등이〉 twinkle; flicker

▶ 멀리서 불빛이 끔벅이는 것이 보였다 I saw a blink of light in the distance.

2 ⇨ 끔벅거리다 2

끔찍스럽다 horrible ⇨ 끔찍하다

끔찍이 〈끔찍하게〉 awfully; terribly; horribly; 〈지독히〉 extremely; 〈극진히〉 kindly; cordially; heartily; devotedly ♦끔찍이 사랑하다 love very much; dote on 《one's child》

끔찍하다 1 〈참혹하다〉 horrible; cruel; dreadful; heartless; 〈소름끼치다〉 ghastly; grim; gruesome; appalling

♦끔찍한 광경 a horrible [dreadful] spectacle; a cruel [horrifying] sight; a tragic scene / 끔찍한 살인 a cruel [cold-blooded] murder / 끔찍한 죽음을 맞다 die a terrible death

▶ 그것은 생각만 해도 끔찍하다 The mere thought of it makes me shudder. ⇒ I am horrified at the mere thought of it.

▶ 끔찍한 사고가 일어났다 A terrible accident [A horrible thing] (has) happened.

▶ 끔찍한 짓을 다 하는군 It is cruel of you to do such a thing.

2 〈엄청나다〉 terrible; awful; tremendous

♦끔찍한 인파 an awful turnout of people; a mammoth crowd / 끔찍하게 크다 be awfully big [large]

▶ 오늘은 끔찍하게 춥다 It is awfully [bitterly, terribly] cold today.

끗수 —數 points; a score; 〈낱장의〉 spots; pips ♦끗수가 높은 패를 잡다 get a higher number of pips ▶ 내 끗수는 여섯이다 My point is six.

끙끙 〈몹시〉 groan; moan ▶ 끙끙 앓아 앉았자 별 도리 없다 It is no use worrying [fretting] about [over] it.

끙끙거리다 groan; moan; labor

♦끙끙거리며 물건을 나르다 drag [carry] a thing with great effort / 끙끙거리며 가파른 언덕을 오르다 toil [make one's way] up a steep hill

▶ 그는 끙끙거리며 수학 공부를 하고 있다 He is

moaning and groaning, while studying mathematics.

끙끙대다 moan (⇨ 끙끙거리다) ▶그렇게 끙끙 앨 것 없다 You don't have to worry (about it). ⇨ Take it easy. ⇨ Cheer up!

끝 1 〈마지막〉 an end; 〈모임 등의〉 a close; a finish; 〈결말〉 an ending; a conclusion; 〈기한의〉 expiration; the last

> 解說 **end**가 일반적인 말. **close**는 문어체에서 특히 행동의 끝, 때의 끝을 가리키는 경우에 쓰인다. **ending**은 이야기 등의 결말을 나타내는 경우에, **the last**는 시간의 끝, 사물의 최후의 부분을 나타내는 경우에 쓰인다.

♦이 세상의 끝 the end of this world / 20세기의 끝 the end of the 20th century / 집회의 끝 the close of a meeting / 끝에서 두번째 next to the last; last but one / 끝에 가서 finally; at last; in the end; in the long run / 끝을 잘 맺다 end well; come to a good end; make a happy ending (of)
▶이만 끝 That's that. ⇨ That's it. ⇨ 〈교실에서〉 So [This] much for today.
▶정치가로서의 그의 생애도 이제 끝이다 His political career is now at an end.
▶이런 기회를 놓치면 자네 출세는 끝일 걸세 If you miss an opportunity like this, your career will be at an end.
▶끝이 어떻게 될 지는 아무도 모른다 There is no knowing how it will end.
▶끝이 좋으면 만사가 좋은 법 〈속담〉 All's well that ends well.
▶그는 맨 끝에 왔다 He was the last to come.
▶끝으로 경청해 주신 데 대해 감사 드립니다 In conclusion, I would like to thank you for your attention.

2 〈끄트머리〉 a point; an end; a tip; an extremity; 〈펜촉 등의〉 a nib
♦연필 끝 the point of a pencil / 처마 끝 the edge of the eaves / 코 끝 the end [tip] of a nose / 혀 끝 the tip of a tongue / 끝에서 끝까지 from end to end; from one end (of...) to the other / 머리끝에서 발끝까지 from head to toe / 끝이 점점 가늘어지다 taper (to a point) / 끝이 뾰족하다 be pointed [sharp] at the end
▶손가락 끝을 바늘에 찔렀다 I hurt the tip of my finger with a needle.

3 〈한도〉 a limit; limits; bounds; an end
▶사람의 욕망에는 끝이 없다 There is no limit to a man's desire. ⇨ There are no bounds to our desires. ⇨ Human desire knows no limits.
▶어머니의 사랑에는 끝이 없다 A mother's love knows no bounds.
▶토론하기 시작하면 끝이 없다 There is no end to argument.
▶그녀는 수다를 떨기 시작하면 끝이 없었다 There was no end to her chatter.

4 〈결과〉 (in the) end; (as the [a]) result; (in) consequence
♦다년간의 노력 끝에 after many years' efforts / 노심 초사 끝에 after much thinking /

충분히 생각한 끝에 after due consideration
▶우리는 심사숙고 끝에 그 제안을 받아들였다 After careful consideration we accepted the offer.
▶그는 부친과 싸운 끝에 집을 나가버렸다 He quarreled with his father and finally ran away from home.

끝갈망 〈뒷수습〉 setting (matters) right; settlement; winding-up; windup
—**끝갈망하다** set matters right; bring matters to a settlement; wind up (one's) affairs)

끝까지 to the end; to [till] the last; throughout; to the finish
♦처음부터 끝까지 from beginning to end; from first to last / 끝까지 버티다 persist to the bitter end / 끝까지 하다 do (it) thoroughly; (口) go the whole hog / 끝까지 해보다 do one's (very) utmost
▶내 말을 끝까지 들으시오 Hear me out!
▶끝까지 싸웁시다 Let's fight it out.
▶나는 끝까지 그에게 반대하겠다 I will stand against him to the bitter end.
▶그 일을 끝까지 조사하겠다 I'll make a thorough investigation of the matter.
▶누가 무슨 소리를 하건 끝까지 그를 믿을 겁니다 I don't care what they say about him, I'll believe him to the last.

끝끝내 〈끝까지〉 to the last; to the (bitter) end; to the finish; throughout
♦끝끝내 반대하다 persist in one's opposition; (口) stick out against
▶그는 끝끝내 모른다고 버텼다 He persisted to the last, denying his knowledge (of it).
▶그는 끝끝내 독신으로 지낼 모양이다 He seems to remain single through life.

끝나다 end; come to an end; close; 〈완료되다〉 be finished [completed]; be over; 〈기한이〉 expire

> 解說 **end**는 가장 보편적으로 쓰이는 말로서 사물·행위를 완료하거나 도중에 그만두는 것을 의미한다. **close**에는 강한 완결성의 뜻은 없고 중도에 일단 끝을 맺는 경우에도 쓰인다. **be finished**는 일단 시작된 행위가 완결되어 그것이 마지막이란 뜻이 포함된다. **be completed**는 보다 격식을 차린 말로 「일체 완비하여 부족함이 없도록 끝나다」라는 느낌을 준다. **be over**는 일상 용어로서 완료 후의 상태를 강조한다.

♦비극으로 끝나다 come to a sad end; end in a sad failure / 원만하게 끝나다 be brought to a happy ending [termination]
▶수업은 5시에 끝난다 School is over at five.
▶회합은 마침내 끝났다 The meeting has come to an end at last.
▶그 일은 완전히 실패로 끝났다 It proved [ended in] a complete failure.
▶웅변 대회는 성공리에 끝났다 The speech contest ended in success.
▶오늘 일은 끝났다 The day's work is done. ⇨ (美) I am through for today.
▶만사가 끝나버렸다 All is over.
▶그는 내 말이 채 끝나기도 전에 나가버렸다

끝내

He went out without waiting for me to finish what I was saying.
▶ 일이 끝나는 즉시 가겠습니다 I will come as soon as I have finished [I am through with] my business.
▶ 시험이 끝나니 살 것 같다 The examination is over, so I feel relieved.
▶ 끝난 일을 가지고 왈가왈부해 봐야 소용없다 It is useless to flog [beat] a dead horse.
▶ 우리는 수업이 끝난 후 테니스를 했다 We played tennis after school.
▶ 일이 끝나면 가서 놀아도 좋다 You can go and play when your work is done.
▶ 도로공사는 아직 끝나지 않았다 The road construction has not been completed [finished] yet.
▶ 일은 늦어도 오늘밤 안으로 끝날 예정이다 The work is to be finished in the course of tonight at the latest.

끝내 1 〈결국〉 in the end; finally; ultimately; on top of all this; as the last consequence; after all
▶ 그들의 오랜 투쟁은 끝내 실패로 돌아갔다 Their long struggle ended in failure.
▶ 두 시간이나 기다렸으나 그는 끝내 오지 않았다 I waited for him two hours, but he did not come after all.
▶ 그는 끝내 철창 신세를 지게 되었다 He ended [wound] up behind bars.
▶ 그는 끝내 술로 인해 죽었다 Drink ended [was the end of] him.
2 ⇨ 끝끝내

끝내기 〔바둑〕 the last [concluding, clinching] moves; an ending

끝내다 finish; get [be] through 《with》; end; 〈마감하다〉 close; stop; conclude; get sth done; put an end 《to》; bring 《a thing》 to a close [an end]; 〈해결하다〉 settle
♦ 하루의 일을 끝내고 after a day's work / 논의를 끝내다 close [drop] an argument / 일[숙제, 용건]을 끝내다 finish [get through] one's work [homework, business]
▶ 그는 무사히 임무를 끝냈다 He carried out his duty without mishap.
▶ 그는 셰익스피어의 한 구절을 인용하는 것으로 연설을 끝냈다 He concluded his speech by quoting a passage from Shakespeare.
▶ 오늘 일을 끝낼 시간이 다 됐다 It's about time to call it a day [to quit working].
▶ 돈으로 끝낼 수 있는 일이라면 기꺼이 끝내겠다 If money can settle the matter, I'm willing to pay.

끝닿다 reach the end [bottom]; get to an end; touch bottom ♦ 끝닿은 데를 모르다 be boundless [endless]

끝돈 〈잔금〉 the rest [remainder] of the payment ♦ 끝돈을 치르다 pay the remaining sum

끝동 〈소매 끝의〉 a cuff ♦ 끝동을 달다 sew a cuff on a sleeve

끝마감 finish; finishing; closing; putting an end to; bringing to a close
—**끝마감하다** put an end to; bring to a close
▶ 국가를 부르는 것으로 식은 끝마감되었다 The ceremony was brought to a close by singing of the national anthem.

끝마무리 finish ⇨ 마무리
끝마치다 finish ⇨ 끝내다, 마치다²
끝막다 end; close
끝맺다 〈일을〉 finish; complete; get through with 《one's work》; 〈말을〉 conclude 《one's statement》; close 《a debate》; end off [wind up] 《one's speech》
▶ 그는 재미있는 일화를 하나 소개하고 강연을 끝맺었다 He ended off [concluded, closed] his lecture with a humorous anecdote.
▶ 끝맺기 전에 두 가지만 더 말씀 드려야겠습니다 Before I wind up, there are two more things to be said.

끝머리 (at) the end 《of a report》; a tip; the tail end; the extremity; 〈말미〉 the close; 〈서적의〉 finish
▶ 그 단어의 끝머리 글자가 빠져 있었다 The final letter of the word was missing.
▶ 내 이름은 명단의 끝머리 쯤에 있다 My name stands near the bottom of the list.

끝물 the last products of the season ♦ 끝물 딸기 late strawberries

끝수 —數 〔數〕 a fraction ♦ 끝수를 버리다 omit [ignore, round off] fractions; calculate to the nearest whole number

끝없다 endless; boundless; unlimited; limitless; infinite; everlasting; never-ending
♦ 끝없는 대양 the boundless ocean / 끝없는 야망 insatiable ambition / 끝없는 인생 여로 the endless journey of (human) life / 끝없는 토론 an interminable debate / 끝없이 boundlessly; endlessly; infinitely; to an unlimited extent
▶ 이 일을 하자면 끝없는 인내가 필요하다 You need infinite patience for this job.
▶ 그의 끝없는 불평에 진력이 났다 I'm tired of his everlasting complaints.
▶ 그들의 논의는 끝없이 이어졌다 There was no end to their argument. ⇌ There was an endless argument among them. ⇌ Their argument went on endlessly.

끝장 〈마지막〉 an end; a finish; a close; 〈낙착〉 a settlement; fixing
♦ 끝장을 보고야 마는 사람 a thoroughgoing person; a perfectionist / 끝장을 보다 see the end [conclusion] 《of》; be finished
▶ 그 가수도 이제 끝장이다 It's all over with that singer.
▶ 이것을 못 풀면 나는 끝장이다 If I can't solve this, it will be all up with me [I'm finished].
▶ 우리가 실패하면 만사 끝장이다 If we fail, that's the end of everything.

끝장나다 be ended [finished]; be closed; come [be brought] to an end; be over; come to a settlement; be settled; (口) be fixed (up)
♦ 비극으로 끝장나다 come to a sad end; end in a sad failure / 원만하게 끝장나다 be brought to a happy ending [termination]
▶ 이 전쟁은 어떻게 끝장날까? How will the war end [result]? ⇌ What will be the consequence of this war?

끝장내다 end; finish; terminate; bring sth to an end; wind up; put an end to; bring to a settlement; settle; (口) fix (up)

♦일을 끝장내다 finish *one's* work / 싸움을 끝장내다 put an end to a quarrel; settle a quarrel
▶그 문제는 속히 끝장내는 것이 좋습니다 You had better settle that question promptly.

끝판 1 〈마지막〉 the last stage 《of》; the end; the close; the finish; the finale ♦끝판에 이르다 come to an end
▶전쟁도 끝판에 가까워졌다 The war is drawing to a close.
▶토론의 끝판에 가서 싸움이 벌어졌다 A quarrel was started at the end of the discussion.
2 〈승부의 결판〉 the last round 《of a game》
♦끝판에 지다 lose a game in the last round

끼 a meal ⇨ 끼니
♦밥 두 끼분 rice for two meals / 하루 세 끼를 먹다 take three meals a day; eat three times a day
▶나는 일요일에는 두 끼만 먹는다 I take only two meals on Sunday(s).

끼끗하다 fresh and neat; smart; spruce; dapper; clear-cut; clean-cut 《features》
♦옷차림이 끼끗하다 be smartly [neatly, sprucely] dressed / 끼끗하게 생기다 have clean-cut [well-formed] features / 끼끗하게 차려 입다 dress *oneself* neat and tidy; spruce *oneself* up 《for dinner》

끼니 a meal; a repast
♦끼니마다 at every meal / 끼니 걱정은 없다 have enough to live on; be assured of livelihood / 끼니를 거르다 skip a meal / 끼니를 잇기 어렵다 find it hard to earn *one's* daily bread; be badly pressed for living / 끼니를 잇지 못하다 go without a meal
━때 a mealtime; a dinnertime

끼다¹ 〈참여하다〉 join 《in》; participate in; take part in; 〈한패가 되다〉 mix with; rub elbows [shoulders] with; 〈어깨를 견주다〉 rank with [among]
♦명단에 끼다 be on the list / 열강의 대열에 끼다 rank with [among] the great powers [world powers]; be ranked as a power / 음모에 한 몫 끼다 be a party to a conspiracy / 일행에 끼다 join the party
▶선생님도 학생들의 놀이에 끼었다 The teacher participated in the pupils' games.
▶당신이 기부금을 모금하고 있다면 나도 한 몫 끼겠소 I'll join in 《with you》 if you are raising a subscription.
▶나도 그 속에 끼어 있었다 I was among [one of] the members.
▶청중 가운데는 여자들도 상당히 끼어 있었다 There was a heavy sprinkling of ladies in the audience.

끼다² 1 〈안개 등이〉 gather; hang over; envelop; shroud; screen; veil
▶겨울에는 이 해안에 안개가 많이 낀다 We get heavy fogs on this coast in winter.
▶구름이 끼었다 Clouds have gathered.
▶산에 구름이 끼기 시작했다 The mountain is getting wrapped in clouds.
▶골짜기에 안개가 자욱이 끼어 있다 Mist is hanging over the valley. ⇌ The valley lies hidden in mist.
▶공항에는 짙은 안개가 끼어 있었다 The airport was shrouded in a heavy mist.
▶갑자기 하늘에 먹구름이 끼더니 비가 내리기 시작했다 The sky was suddenly overcast and it began to rain.
2 〈먼지 등이〉 gather; collect; be thick; be covered 《with》; be soiled [stained] 《with》
♦얼굴에 기미가 끼다 have a freckled face / 눈곱이 끼다 matter forms in the eyes; *one's* eyes are gummy [mattery] / 때가 끼다 be soiled with dirt; become dirty [filthy] / 먼지가 끼다 dust collects; become dusty / 이끼가 끼다 be mossy; become moss-grown
▶공중에 먼지가 뽀얗게 끼어 있다 The air is thick with dust.
▶그 옷에는 온통 기름때가 끼어 있었다 The clothes were smeared all over with greasy dirt.
▶헌 가구에는 먼지가 잔뜩 끼어 있었다 The old furniture was covered in dust.

끼다³ 1 ⇨ 끼우다
2 〈껴안다〉 fold *sb* into *one's* arms; hold *sb* in *one's* arms; hug; 〈팔 등을〉 fold [link] 《*one's* arms》
♦손가방을 겨드랑이에 끼고 with a portfolio under *one's* arm / 팔짱을 낀 채 with folded arms / 깍지 끼다 lock [hook] *one's* fingers together / 어린애를 끼고 자다 sleep with a child in *one's* arms [bosom]
▶그는 그녀의 팔짱을 끼었다 He linked his arm in hers.
▶두 사람은 서로 팔짱을 끼고 걷고 있었다 The two were walking arm in arm.
▶그들은 쌍쌍이 끼고 춤을 추었다 They danced holding their partners each.
▶그 사람을 너무 끼고 돌지 마시오 Don't favor him too much.
▶그는 팔짱을 낀채 생각에 잠겨 있었다 He folded his arms and was lost in thought.
3 〈착용하다〉 put on; pull on; slip on; wear
♦장갑을 끼다 pull [draw, get, put] on *one's* gloves / 반지를 끼고 있다 have [wear] a ring on 《*one's* finger》 / 장갑을 끼고 단추를 채우다 fasten a glove
4 〈따라서 가다〉 skirt along
▶나는 강을 끼고 걸었다 I walked along the river.
▶그 도로를 끼고 호텔이 줄지어 서 있다 Hotels stand in a line along the road.
▶배는 해안을 끼고 항행했다 The ship skirted along the coast.
5 〈권력 등을〉 be backed 《up》 by...; have *sb* at *one's* back; be patronized by... ♦유력자를 끼고 있다 have an influential person at *one's* back

끼뜨리다 〈흩뿌리다〉 throw 《water》 away; 〈퍼뜨리다〉 scatter about [around]

끼루룩 with a honking; honk ━**끼루룩하다** honk; have a honk

끼루룩거리다 honk and honk ▶기러기가 끼루룩거렸다 Wild geese were honking.

끼룩거리다¹ honk and honk ⇨ 끼루룩거리다

끼룩거리다² 〈목을 길게〉 make a long neck; crane [stretch out] *one's* neck; 《口》 rubberneck ♦더 잘 보려고 끼룩거리다 crane *one's* neck to get a better view

-끼리 ♦가족끼리의 모임 a family party [gathering] / 우리끼리 이야기지만 between ourselves; between you and me / 버스끼리 충돌하다 two buses run into each other
▶ 우리끼리 갑시다 Let's go by ourselves.
▶ 그 문제는 우리끼리 해결합시다 Let's settle the matter among ourselves.
▶ 승객끼리 싸우기 시작했다 The passengers began to quarrel among themselves.
▶ 이 일은 우리끼리만 알고 지냅시다 Don't say anything about it to anybody.

끼리끼리 in (separate) groups; group by group
♦ 끼리끼리 돌아다니다 walk around in separate groups
▶ 끼리끼리 해먹기 마련이다 Each group looks to its own interests [feathers its nest].
▶ 사람은 끼리끼리 모인다 (속담) Birds of a feather flock together.

끼어들다 intrude into [upon]; thrust *oneself* in; wedge (*oneself*) in [into]; 〈이야기 등에〉 break [cut] in (on)
▶ 그는 남의 일에 늘 끼어든다 He always pokes his nose into other people's business.
▶ 그녀는 우리의 대화에 자꾸 끼어들었다 She kept cutting into [in on] our conversation.
▶ 너의 사생활에 끼어들고 싶지 않다 I don't like to intrude upon your privacy.
▶ 남이 얘기하는 데 끼어드는 것은 실례야 It is rude to cut in while others are talking.
▶ 남의 싸움에 끼어들지 마라 Don't take part [be involved] in another's quarrel.
▶ 우리의 대화에 끼어들지 좀 마세요 Please don't break in on our conversation.

끼얹다 pour [splash] (on); shower [sprinkle] (on, over); dash (water on *sb*)
♦ 길에 물을 끼얹다 sprinkle a street with water; sprinkle water on a road / 몸에 물을 끼얹다 splash water on *oneself* / 머리에 모래를 끼얹다 sprinkle sand over *sb's* head
▶ 그녀는 내 머리에 물을 끼얹었다 She poured [dashed] water over me.
▶ 그는 내 등에 찬물을 끼얹었다 He dashed [threw] cold water on my back.

끼우다 get [put, let] in; put between; insert (in); 〈맞추어 넣다〉 fit [fix] (into)
♦ 신문지 사이에 광고지를 끼우다 insert a bill in a newspaper / 열쇠를 자물쇠에 끼우다 insert a key into the lock / 미닫이에 유리를 끼우다 fit a pane in a sliding door / 책 갈피에 끼우다 put (a thing) between the leaves of a book / 펜에 펜촉을 끼우다 fit a pen with a nib
▶ 자동차에 타이어를 바꿔 끼우도록 하자 Let's fit new tires to the car.
▶ 서류를 클립에 끼워 주시겠어요? Will you fasten the documents with a clip?

끼워팔기 a tie-in (sale); a combination sale

끼이다 **1**〈틈 등에〉 get between; be caught in; get jammed [hemmed] in; fit (fix)
▶ 그녀의 한복 소맷자락이 닫히는 문에 끼였다 The sleeve of her Korean clothes was caught in a door as it closed.

▶ 음식물이 잇새에 끼였다 A particle of food got caught between my teeth.
2〈양자 사이에〉 lie [get] between; be sandwiched [wedged, caught] between
▶ 나는 아름다운 두 여자 사이에 끼였다 I was sandwiched between two beautiful women.
▶ 나는 어머니와 아내 사이에 끼어 난처한 처지에 있다 Caught between my mother and my wife, I am in an awkward position.
▶ 나는 다른 두 승객 사이에 꽉 끼여 있었기 때문에 버스에서 내릴 수가 없었다 I was so tightly wedged between two other passengers, I couldn't get off the bus.
3〈구두·옷 등이〉 be tight [close]
▶ 이 웃옷은 내게 너무 끼인다 This jacket is too tight [small] for me.
▶ 새 구두가 발에 꼭 끼인다 My new shoes pinch.

끼인각 —角 〔數〕 an included [a contained] angle

끼적거리다 〈글씨 등을〉 scribble; scrawl; scratch; dash down [off]
♦ 종이에 몇 줄 끼적거리다 scribble [scrawl, scratch] a few lines on a sheet of paper
▶ 그는 공책에 뭔가 수식을 끼적거리고 있다 He is scribbling away some numerical formulas in his notebook.

끼치다¹ 〈소름이〉 feel *one's* flesh creep; shudder; get (the) gooseflesh

끼치다² **1**〈폐 등을〉 cause; occasion; give
▶ 폐 많이 끼쳤습니다 I am afraid I have put you too much trouble.
▶ 나는 어릴 때 몸이 약해서 부모님께 많은 괴로움을 끼쳤다 I was weak in my childhood and gave a lot of trouble to my parents.
▶ 그는 부모님에게 걱정만 끼치고 있다 He is a constant source of anxiety to his parents.
▶ 폐를 끼쳐 미안합니다 I am sorry to bother [trouble] you. ⇒ I am sorry to have caused you anxiety.
▶ 남에게 누를 끼치지 않도록 해라 You must not make yourself a nuisance [make a nuisance of yourself] to others.
▶ 남에게 폐 끼칠 일은 절대 하지 마라 Never do what gives others trouble [inconvenience, nuisance].
2〈남겨주다〉 hand down; leave (behind); bequeath
♦ 누명을 끼치다 leave a bad reputation [name] / 유산을 끼치다 bequeath [leave] *one's* property [fortune, estate] / 아들에게 빚을 끼치고 죽다 die leaving debts for *one's* son

끽 in a choking voice; with a scream
—끽하다 give [let out] a yell; give a scream
♦ 끽하고 쓰러지다 fall down with a scream

끽다 喫茶 tea drinking **—끽다하다** drink tea

끽소리 a yell (of protest); a squawk of complaint
♦ 끽소리 못하다 be (utterly) silenced; be completely defeated [nonplused]; be put to silence / 끽소리 못하게 하다 silence; floor; squelch; sit on; put [reduce] *sb* to silence; (口) beat *sb* all hollow
▶ 그의 논리정연한 설명에 우리는 끽소리 못했

다 His articulate explanation reduced [put] us to silence.
▶ 그는 끽소리도 못했다 He couldn't utter a word in reply.

끽연 喫煙 smoking —**끽연하다** smoke (tobacco); have a smoke

끽해야 at (the) most ⇨ 기껏해야 ▶ 그 친구 끽해야 빚 없이 사는 정도겠지 It may be all [as much as] he can do to keep out of debt.

낄낄 ◆ 낄낄 웃다 giggle; titter —**낄낄하다** ⇨ 낄낄거리다

낄낄거리다 giggle; chuckle; titter; snicker
◆ 숨어서 낄낄거리다 laugh in *one's* sleeve
▶ 저 여자들은 걸핏하면 낄낄거린다 Those women burst into giggles at the slightest provocation.

낌새 delicate signs; hint; secret devices; inner workings; a delicate turn (of the situation)
◆ 낌새를 보다 sound out [probe] the secrets of 《an affair》/ 낌새를 보이다 show signs [indications] 《of》/ 낌새를 보이지 않다 reveal no secrets; do not show the slightest sign [hint] of / 낌새를 채다 sense the secrets of 《an affair》; get scent [wind] of 《the dark connections》; find out [get at] *sb's* intimate [inmost] thoughts; smell (out) 《secrets》; sense (out) 《a danger》
▶ 정국이 달라질 낌새가 보이지 않는다 I cannot see any sign of change in the political situation.
▶ 그런 낌새는 전혀 없다 There is not the slightest suspicion of it.
▶ 우리가 무엇을 하고 있는지 이제 낌새를 챈 모양이다 He seems to have caught on to what we are up to.

낑 with a groan —**낑하다** groan; make [heave] a groan; moan

낑낑 groaningly —**낑낑하다** ⇨ 낑낑거리다

낑낑거리다 groan (and groan); moan; 〈개가〉 whine
◆ 무거운 짐을 지고 낑낑거리다 groan under a heavy load on *one's* back; groan under the load of heavy burden
▶ 개가 나를 보고 낑낑거렸다 The dog whined when he saw me.

ㄴ

- **-ㄴ가** 1 〈의문〉 ▶이것은 무엇인가? What is this?
  ▶저 사람은 누구인가? Who is that man?
  ▶아니, 김군 아닌가? Oh, you are Mr. Kim, aren't you?
  ▶그것이 늑대인가 아닌가 확인해 보자 Let's see if it is a wolf or not.
  2 〈막연한 사람·시간·장소〉 ▶내가 없는 동안에 누군가 찾아왔던 모양이다 Someone seems to have called on me in my absence.
  ▶언젠가 후회할 날이 있을 것이다 The time will come when you will repent it.
  ▶그는 이 근처 어딘가에 살고 있다 He lives somewhere about here [in this neighborhood].
- **-ㄴ가보다** 〈짐작〉 ▶그는 매우 바쁜가 보다 He seems to be very busy.
  ▶밖이 꽤 추운가 보다 It seems quite cold outside.
  ▶그런가 보다 I guess [suppose] so.
  ▶폭풍우가 다가오는가 보다 It seems a storm is approaching.
- **-ㄴ다니** 1 〈-ㄴ다느냐〉 ▶그가 왜 온다니? Do you know what he comes for?
  ▶그는 언제 돌아온다니? When do you think he will come back?
  2 〈-ㄴ다고 하니〉 ▶네가 공부를 잘한다니 기쁘다 I am delighted to hear that you are a good student.
  ▶내일 눈이 온다니 기쁘다 I am glad to hear that it will snow tomorrow.
- **-ㄴ대서** 1 〈…이므로〉 ▶증기선은 증기로 간대서 그렇게 부른다 A steamer is so called because it is run by steam.
  2 〈그렇다고 해서〉 ▶그런대서 모임에 참석하지 않을 이유는 없다 That is no reason for (your) not attending [why you should not attend] the meeting.
  ▶그런대서 가지 않을 수도 없다 Even so [For all that], I must go.
- **-ㄴ대서야** ▶그런 짓을 한대서야 그가 정신이 돈 거지 He must be out of his mind to do a thing like that.
  ▶금방 여기 있던 것을 모른대서야 말이 되는가 You can't help knowing about a thing that was here a minute ago, can you?
- **-ㄴ대야** ▶그가 먹는대야 얼마나 먹겠니, 내버려 둬라 Let him eat as much as he likes; he can't eat much anyway.
  ▶지금 떠난대야 그를 만나기는 글렀어 Even if you start now, you will not be able to see him.
- **-ㄴ데** 1 〈그리고〉 and; 〈그러나〉 but
  ▶그는 키는 큰데 힘이 세지 못하다 He is tall, but he is not strong.
  ▶그는 부잔데 만족을 모른다 He is not contented with all his riches.
  2 〈한편〉 when; while
  ▶시험이 눈 앞에 보이는데 그는 놀고만 있다 He keeps on idling when the examination is in sight.
  ▶그의 장남은 사교적인데 그 동생은 내성적이다 His eldest son is sociable, while [whereas] his younger son is more introverted.
  3 〈감탄〉 ▶날씨가 매우 더운데 It is very warm, isn't it?
  ▶훌륭한 의잔데 What a nice chair!
- **-ㄴ데도** in spite of; though; for all
  ♦젊은데도 though young; young as he is / 주의를 주었는데도 in disregard of my warning
  ▶비가 그쳤는데도 바람은 불고 있었다 Though it had stopped raining, the wind was still blowing.
  ▶불리한 조건인데도 그녀는 성공했다 In spite of her handicaps she succeeded.
  ▶나는 노력했는데도 실패했다 I failed in spite of all my efforts.
- **-ㄴ들** 〈…할지라도 어찌〉 granted [granting] that; even though [if]; though
  ▶내가 힘이 약하다 한들 너보다 약하랴 I may be weak, but I am sure I'm no weaker than you.
  ▶그가 칭찬을 많이 받았다 한들 무슨 소용이 있으랴 So he received much praise—what good is it?
  ▶간다 한들 아주 가랴 Though I leave, I'm not going away for good.
- **-ㄴ바** 〈…하였더니〉 ▶내가 들은 바 그는 선거에 다시 입후보할 것이라고 한다 I hear he's going to run for election again.
  ▶내가 알고 있는 바 이 학교는 좋은 학교다 So [As] far as I know, this is a fine school.
  ▶내가 본 바 그는 건강한 것 같다 As far as I can see, he is in good health.
  ▶그의 말을 들어본 바 사실과 틀림없다 According to what he says, it is true to the fact.
- **-ㄴ즉** since; as; now that; speaking of
  ▶알아본 즉 그녀는 부재중이었다[그의 말은 거짓말이었다] On [Upon] inquiry, I learned that she was out [what he had said proved false].
  ▶경치인즉 설악산이 한국에서 제일이다 As far as scenic beauty goes, Sŏraksan is the best in Korea.
  ▶그런즉 어떻게 하면 좋겠느냐? Well then, what would you like me to do? ⇌ Such being the conditions [circumstances], what shall we do?
  ▶남부지방에 가본즉 물 기근으로 고통받고 있었다[대풍년이었다] I went to southern part, where I realized they were suffering from a

water shortage [we had a bumper year].

-ㄴ지 1 〈불확실〉 ◆ 뭔지 꺼면 것 something black / 김 선생인지 뭔지 하는 사람 a (certain) Mr. Kim; a man named Kim or something
▶ 사람이 너무 많아서 누가 누군지 몰랐다 There were so many people that I could not tell who was who.
▶ 그가 하는 소리는 뭐가 뭔지 통 모르겠다 I cannot make head or tail of what he says.
▶ 누군지 밖에서 기다리고 있다 Someone is waiting outside.
2 〈막연한 의문〉 ◆ 충실한 개가 죽어 그는 얼마나 슬픈지 몰랐다 The death of the faithful dog left him sorrowful.
▶ 그가 어떻게 된 건지 모르겠다 I wonder what has become of him.

나¹ 〈자기〉 I; me; myself; 〈자아〉 self; ego
◆ 나의 ⇨ 내⁴ / 이전[현재]의 나 my former [present] self / 제2의 나 my second self; (라) alter ego / 나의 것 ⇨ 내것 / 나를[에게] 게 / 나라면, 나로서는 as for me; for my part / 나도 모르게 in spite of myself; involuntarily; unconsciously / 너 나 하는 사이이다 be on a first name basis 《with》
▶ 나 혼자서 책장을 방 안으로 옮겼다 I carried the bookcase into the room (all) by myself.
▶ 나쁜 것은 나다 It is I who am wrong.
▶ 會話 「거기 누구요?」 「납니다」 "Who's there?" "It's me [I]."
▶ 나는 고등학생이다 I am a high school student.
▶ 나는 커피, 너는? Coffee for me, and you?
▶ 그와 나는 같은 학교에 다니고 있다 He and I [myself] go to the same school.
▶ 나는 거울에 비친 나 자신을 보았다 I looked at myself in the mirror.
▶ 우리 아이는 나를 꼭 닮았다 My child resembles me very much.
▶ 아버지는 나에게 자전거를 사 주셨다 My father bought me a bicycle. ⇌ My father bought a bicycle for me.
▶ 會話 「지난 밤에는 잘 잤다」「나도」 "I slept well last night." "So did I [(口) Me, too]."
▶ 나도 처음에는 그렇게 생각했다 I thought so myself at first.
▶ 그는 나보다 공부를 아주 열심히 한다 He studies harder than I (do) [(口) than me].

나² 〈樂〉 B ◆ 나장조[단조] B major [minor] / 나 장조의 악장[미사곡] a movement [mass] in B major

-나 1 〈…하지만〉 but; however; though
◆ 허술하나 안락한 방 a humble but comfortable room
▶ 그녀는 얼굴은 미우나 마음씨는 곱다 She is plain, but sweet-tempered.
▶ 그는 젊으나 인정이 있다 Young as he is, he is considerate.
2 〈…든 …든〉
▶ 보나 마나 마찬가지다 There is no difference whether I see it or not.
▶ 비가 오거나 개거나 떠나겠다 We will go rain or shine [whether the weather is good or not].
3 〈의문〉 ▶ 언제 그녀를 만났나? When did you see her?
▶ 어제 어디에 갔었나? Where did you go yesterday?
▶ 가지 않겠나? Won't you go?

나가다 1 〈밖으로 가다〉 go [get] out (of); step out 《of》
◆ 방에서 나가다 go [get] out of a room / 뜰로 나가다 go out into the garden / 물건을 사러 나가다 go (out) shopping / 산책하러 나가다 go (out) for a walk / 앞으로 나가다 step forward
▶ 會話 「시시한 영화군요」「그럼 나가자」 "This is a rather boring movie." "Let's go, then."
▶ 아버지는 매일 아침 산책하러 나가신다 My father goes out for a walk every morning.
▶ 그는 아무 말 없이 방을 나갔다 He went out of [left] the room without (saying) a word.
▶ 어머니는 지금 나가고 안 계십니다 My mother is out now.
▶ 내일은 아침 7시에 나갈 예정입니다 I am leaving home at seven tomorrow.
2 〈진출하다〉 launch into; go [sally] forth into 《the world》; go upon 《the world's stage》; enter upon
▶ 그는 정계로 나가려고 하고 있다 He is planning to launch into politics.
▶ 사회에 나가면 많은 것을 배우게 된다 You'll learn a lot when going out in the world.
▶ 그는 실업계로 나간지 얼마 되지 않았다 It's not very long since he entered the business world.
3 〈근무하다〉 work 《for, at》; serve 《in an office》; be in the service 《of》; hold an office 《in》 〈관청에〉
◆ 회사에 나가다 serve a company; work for a company
▶ 그는 무역회사에 나가고 있다 He works at [for] a trading company.
▶ 어디에 나가고 있습니까? Where do you work? ⇌ Where is your office?
4 〈출석・출근하다〉 be present 《at》; attend 〈출두하다〉 appear; 〈출전・출연하다〉 play 《in》
◆ 법정에 나가다 appear in [before] court / 파티에 나가다 attend a party; be present at a party / 회사에 나가다 go to office [work] / 회의에 나가다 attend [be present at] a conference
▶ 바깥 양반은 직장에 나갔어요 My husband has gone to work.
▶ 갑자기 병이 나서 그 모임에 나가지 못했다 Sudden illness prevented [kept] me from attending the meeting.
5 〈참가하다〉 join; participate in; take part (in); enter (for) 《a concert》; 〈출마하다〉 (美) run for; (英) stand for
◆ 시합에 나가다 take part in the game / 국회 의원 선거에 나가다 run for the National Assembly
6 〈떠나다・퇴거하다〉 move away; leave; quit; 〈물러나다〉 go away; withdraw 《from》
◆ 집을 나가다 leave home [the house]; get out of the house
▶ 나가라 Go away! ⇌ Get out (of here)! ⇌ Be off with you!
▶ 우리는 이 집에서 곧 나갑니다 We will

[shall] soon move out of this house.
7 〈지급되다〉 be spent; be paid out; be out
▶지난 달에는 돈이 꽤 많이 나갔다 Our expenses last month were considerable.
▶나가는 것이 들어오는 것보다 많다 Expenses exceed receipts.
8 〈어느 정도에 이르다〉 be worth; weigh 《100 grams》
▶나는 그에게서 2천달러나 나가는 진주목걸이를 받았다 I received from him a pearl necklace worth two thousand dollars.
9 〈팔리다〉 sell
♦잘 나가는 물건 a good [quick] sell [seller] / 날개 돋친 듯이 나가다 sell like hot cakes / 잘 나가다 sell well; be in good [great] demand; 〈책이〉 have [enjoy] a large circulation
▶금년에는 가스 난로가 잘 나간다 Gas stoves are in great demand this year.
▶그것들은 보다 비싼 값에 나간다 They sell [are sold] for a higher price.
▶이런 종류의 책은 최근 잘 나가지 않는다 This kind of book has not been selling well recently.
10 〈의식·정신이 없어지다〉 become insane; lose one's senses [mind]; go mad; 〈멍해지다〉 grow absentminded
♦정신 나간 짓 a crazy act
▶그녀는 정신이 나갔다 She is mad [insane, crazy, out of her mind].
▶그는 정신이 나간 것처럼 외치고 있다 He is shouting like mad [frantically].
11 〈찢어지다·닳다〉 wear [be worn] out [off, down]; wear threadbare
♦소매끝이 나가다 be frayed in the edges of sleeves
▶이 코트는 팔꿈치가 나갔다 The elbows have worn badly on this coat.
▶그의 구두창이 나갔다 The soles of his shoes wore down. ⇌ His shoes wore down at the soles.
12 〈나아가다〉 advance; go [step] forward [ahead]; make one's way (to); 〈진척되다〉 make progress [headway]; get on [along] with 《one's studies》; improve
▶[會話]「지난 수업 시간에는 교과서 어디까지 나갔지요?」「20쪽의 5행까지 나갔습니다」"How far did we get in the textbook in our last lesson?" "We got up to [as far as] page 20, line 5, sir."
13 〈꺼지다〉 go out; be cut off; fail
▶예고도 없이 전기가 나갔다 The electricity was cut off without warning.
▶폭풍우로 시내의 전기가 모두 나갔다 The storm knocked out electricity in the town.
▶전기가 나가서 지하철 운행이 30분간이나 중지되었다 The subway stopped running for half an hour because of a power cut.
▶퓨즈가 나갔을 때는 어딘가 고장이 난 것이다 When a fuse blows (out), something is wrong.
나가동그라지다 tumble (over); fall on one's back; have oneself tripped off
♦파도에 쓸려 나가동그라지다 be carried off one's feet by the waves
▶그는 한방에 나가동그라졌다 One push sent him tumbling. ⇌ One push and he tumbled over [fell down].
▶그녀는 서둘다가 나가동그라졌다 In her hurry she tumbled over.
나가떨어지다 1 〈넘어지다〉 fall down [flat] on one's back; be knocked down; be thrown off; be hurled [flung] away [off] 《from》
♦벌렁 나가떨어지다 fall flat on one's back / 큰 댓자로 나가떨어지다 fall full length 《on the floor》 / 한방에 나가떨어지다 be knocked down at [by] a (single) blow
2 〈녹초가 되다〉 be worn [fagged, tired] out; be exhausted; 〈술에 취해〉 drink oneself down; be drunk as a lord; be dead drunk
♦술 몇잔에 나가떨어지다 be under the table [blind drunk] with a few glasses of wine
▶집에 돌아왔을 때는 나는 피곤해 나가떨어졌다 I was tired out [exhausted] by the time I came [got] home.
3 〈지다〉 fail; lose 《a game》; meet with defeat
나가자빠지다 1 〈뒤로 넘어지다〉 fall on one's back
2 〈망하다〉 go to ruin; be ruined; 〈도산하다〉 go [become] bankrupt [insolvent]; (美口) go broke
▶수많은 회사가 불경기로 나가자빠지고 있다 A large number of companies are going bankrupt owing to the depression.
3 〈손을 떼다〉 fail (to do); withdraw oneself 《from》; fall down on; back out
♦계약을 해물고 나가자빠지다 back out of a contract; withdraw from a contract; draw back [cry off] from a contract / 빚을 지고 나가자빠지다 bilk sb; (美口) jump (a bill); fail to pay [(口) run out on] one's debts [a bill]
나귀 a donkey ⇨ 당나귀
나그네 a traveler; a wayfarer; 〈타관 사람〉 a stranger; 〈방랑객〉 a wanderer; a drifter; a vagabond ■—생활 (lead) a wayfaring life 나그넷길 a journey
나근거리다 〈흔들거리다〉 sway; swing lightly
▶나뭇가지가 바람에 나근거리고 있다 The branches are swaying in the wind.
나근나근 swayingly; swingingly —**나근나근하다** 나근거리다
나굿나굿하다 1 〈태도가 부드럽다〉 mild; elegant; amiable; graceful; affable
♦나굿나굿한 동작 graceful manner [deportment] / 나굿나굿한 움직임 lithe movements 《of a ballerina》
2 〈살결이 보드랍다〉 tender; soft; smooth; velvety ♦나굿나굿한 가죽 limp leather / 나굿나굿한 살결 the soft [fair, velvety] skin / 나굿나굿한 손 supple hands
3 〈음식이 연하다〉 tender 《meat》; soft
-나기 a person from... ⇨ -내기
나깨 〈메밀의 속껍질〉 the inner husk of buckwheat ■—떡 a coarse cake made with buckwheat
나나니벌 [昆] a digger (wasp); a mud dauber; a sphecid
나날이 daily; day after [by] day; day in, day

out; from day to day ▶ 날씨가 나날이 따뜻해져 가고 있다 It's getting warmer day by day [every day].
나누기 dividing; 〔數〕〈나눗셈〉 division ▶ 다음의 나누기를 하시오 Do the following division. **—나누기하다** divide
나누다 **1** 〈가르다〉 divide 《into》; part 《into》; sever; split 《into》; 《俗》 whack 《up》
♦ 나눌 수 없는 indivisible; inseparable / 일곱으로 나누다 divide sth into seven
▶ 코치는 선수들을 두 팀으로 나누었다 The coach divided the players in two teams.
▶ 피아노 대금을 세 번[3회]에 나누어 지불했다 I paid for the piano in three installments.
▶ 그 얘기는 5회로 나누어서 게재되었다 The story was published in five installments.
2 〈구별하다〉 draw a line between; 〈분류하다〉 classify; sort out; assort
♦ 선인과 악인을 나누다 sort out the good men from the bad / 책을 항목별로 나누다 classify books according to subjects
▶ 과실과 범죄는 나누어서 생각해야 한다 We must distinguish between error and crime.
3 〈분배하다〉 distribute [divide] 《among》; share 《sth with sb》; allot 《to》; portion (out); 〈카드 등을〉 deal 《out》
♦ 돈을 둘[셋]이 나누다 divide the money between the two [among the three] / 이익을 반반으로 나누다 split (the profit) half and half [fifty-fifty] / 몫을 나누어 주다 give sb a portion 《of》
▶ 한 중소기업 경영자는 이익금을 근로자들과 똑같이 나누었다 A minor enterprisers divided the profits with the workmen.
▶ 사과를 동생에게 나누어 주었다 I shared the apple with my (younger) brother.
▶ 그는 재산을 세 아들에게 나누어 주었다 He divided his property among his three sons.
▶ 이 문장은 너무 기니 구두점으로 나누어 읽기 쉽도록 하시오 This sentence is too long, therefore you'd better break it up with punctuation so that it can be read easily.
▶ 경비를 어떻게 나눌까? How shall we divide up the expenses?
4 〈함께하다〉 share sth with sb; partake of
♦ 기쁨[슬픔]을 나누다 share one's joy [sorrow] with sb / 음식을 나누어 먹다 share food with sb
▶ 두 사람은 재회의 기쁨을 나누었다 The two shared the joy of reunion.
▶ 나는 한때 그와 인생의 고락을 나누었다 I shared the pleasures and pains of life with him for a while.
5 〈나눗셈을 하다〉 ▶ 10을 2로 나누면 5가 된다 Ten divided by two gives five. ⇌ Divide ten by two and you get five. ⇌ Two into ten goes five times.
▶ 20은 2로 나누어 떨어진다 Twenty can be divided by two without a remainder. ⇌ Twenty is (exactly) divisible by two.
6 〈주고받다〉 exchange 《words, greetings》
♦ 의견을 나누다 exchange views / 이야기를 나누다 talk 《with》; exchange a few words 《with》 / 인사를 나누다 greet each other; exchange greetings
나누이다 be divided ⇨ 나뉘다
나눗셈 〔數〕 division **—나눗셈하다** divide
나눗수 〔數〕 a divisor
나뉘다 be [get] divided; be split up; be separated; be classified ♦ 다섯 몫으로 나뉘다 be split into five portions
▶ 서울은 한강을 사이에 두고 두 부분으로 나뉘어져 있다 Seoul is divided [split] into two parts by the Han-gang.
나닐다 fly [flutter, hover] about ▶ 개똥벌레가 나닐고 있었다 Fireflies were flitting about.
나다[1] **1** 〈생기다・발생하다〉 come out [about]; come to pass; occur; take place; turn up; break out; rise; arise; spring [come] up
♦ 고장이 나다 have a breakdown; go [be] wrong 《with》 / 병이 나다 get sick; 《英》 fall [be taken] ill / 불[전쟁]이 나다 a fire [war] breaks out / 사건이 나다 an incident happens [occurs, takes place] / 사고가 나다 have an accident; an accident happens / 상처가 나다 be wounded; get hurt / 야단이 나다 have trouble [a fuss] / 탈이 나다 run into a hitch [trouble]; 〈병나다〉 get [become] ill / 홍수가 나다 have a flood
▶ 나는 열이 많이 났다 I had a high fever.
▶ 안 계신 동안에 큰일이 났습니다 Something serious happened in your absence.
▶ 그 불은 3층에서 났다 The fire started on the third floor.
▶ 굴뚝에서 연기가 나고 있다 Smoke is rising [going up] from the chimney.
▶ 기침이 심하여 나서 곤란했다 I was troubled with [by] a bad cough.
2 〈결과로서 나오다〉 leave; turn out (to be); come out; result [end] in
♦ 토지에서 나는 이익 profits issuing [accruing] from lands / 끝장이 나다 come [be brought] to an end; be finished / 능률이 나다 be efficient; improve [develop] efficiency / 동이 나다 be exhausted; run out of / 약효가 나다 tell [act, work] 《on》; have an effect 《on》 / 자국이 나다 leave a trace (behind)
▶ 이 계획에 대해 결론이 났느냐? Did you come to conclusion on this plan?
▶ 이것은 전혀 효과가 나지 않는다 This is quite fruitless. ⇌ It has no effect at all.
3 〈흘러나오다〉 flew [run] out; spring
▶ 너 코피[콧물] 난다 Your nose is bleeding [running]. ⇌ You are bleeding [running] at the nose. ⇌ You have a bleeding [runny] nose.
▶ 그녀의 이야기가 너무 슬퍼서 눈물이 났다 Her story was so pitiful that I wept.
▶ 그의 이마에 구슬같은 땀이 났다 Drops of sweat stood [There were drops of sweat] on his forehead.
4 〈뚫리다〉 be built [constructed]; be made [opened]
♦ 구멍이 나다 a hole is opened [made] / 새 길이 나다 a new road is built [opened]
▶ 그녀의 스웨터에 구멍이 났다 There's a hole in her sweater.
▶ 좀이 먹어 내 웃옷에 구멍이 났다 Moths have

eaten [made] a hole in my jacket.
5 〈잘나다〉 be outstanding [eminent] ♦난 사람 an outstanding person / 난 체하다 give [put] *oneself* airs
6 〈나돌다〉 acquire; circulate
♦명성이 나다 win fame; gain a reputation / 소문이 나다 a rumor circulates [gets abroad]
▶ 그는 시인으로 평판이 나 있다 He is famed as a poet.
▶ 그는 여색에 빠져 있다는 소문이 나 있다 He has the reputation of being a womanizer.
7 〈태어나다〉 be born; come into the world; come into being [existence]
♦내가 난 고장 my birthplace / 나서 여태까지 ever since my birth [I was born]; in (all) my born days / 한국에서 나다 be born in Korea
8 〈풍기다〉 smell; 〈우러나다〉 taste
♦맛이 나다 be tasty; taste good [nice]; be delicious / 향기[악취]가 나다 smell sweet [nasty]
▶ 간장을 치면 맛이 난다 It will taste good if you put soy sauce in it.
9 〈생겨나다〉 sound (shrill, loud); come out [forth]; make a sound [noise] ▶ 박수 소리가 난다 There is a handclap.
10 〈자라다〉 grow; 〈돋아나다〉 come out; bud (out); spring up; sprout
♦이가 나다 cut a tooth;((baby's) teeth erupt / 풀이 나다 grass grows [sprouts]
▶ 싹이 나고 있다 The buds are showing.
11 〈생산되다〉 be produced; be raised; grown
▶ 이 지역에서는 구리가 많이 난다 This area produces much copper.
▶ 이 지방은 쌀[밀]이 많이 난다 This part of the country yields much rice [wheat].
▶ 이 도에서는 정치가가 많이 났다 This province has produced [turned out] a lot of statesman. ⇌ A large number of statesman come from this province.
12 〈나타나다〉 appear; make *one's* appearance; turn [show] up
♦시장에 사과가 나다 apples appear in [on] the market
13 〈우러나오다〉 feel; occur
♦기억이 나다 〈사물이 주어〉 come into *one's* mind; remember; recollect / 심술이 나다 get cross [cranky] / 재미가 나다 become interesting; be interested (in) / 흥이 나다 get merry [excited] (over)
▶ 나는 가끔 일에 싫증이 난다 I sometimes get tired of my job.
▶ 좋은 생각이 났다 A good idea occurred to me. ⇌ I've just thought of a good idea.
▶ 나는 그 일로 몹시 화가 났었다 I was very angry about the matter.
13 〈벗어나다〉 ♦눈 밖에 나다 get out of *sb's* favor; be in *sb's* bad graces; (口) get in wrong with *sb*
14 〈게재되다〉 be recorded [registered]; be listed; be put on (a book); be given (in a program)
♦신문에 나다 appear [be printed, be reported] in a newspaper; be carried [published] in a daily
▶ 네 이야기가 잡지에 나서 읽어 보았다 I read about you in the magazine.
▶ 그 소식은 어느 신문에나 나 있다 The news is [appears, is reported] in every newspaper. ⇌ Every newspaper carries the news.
15 〈비게 되다〉 be vacated; become vacant [empty]; open up
♦방이 나다 a room is available [vacant] / 시간이 나다 have spare time / 자리가 나다 a place [job, seat] opens up [becomes available]
16 〈드러나다〉 have an air [a look]; look; show ♦시골티가 나다 wear a rustic [countrified] air; look rustic / 학자 티가 나다 have the air of a scholar; be scholarly
17 〈더해지다〉 gain (in); gather
♦기운이 나다 cheer up; take heart / 속력이 나다 gain in velocity; gather speed / 힘이 나다 gain strength
18 〈철을 지내다〉 pass (a season); tide over; go [get] through ♦겨울을 나다 pass the winter; see winter through; winter
19 〈나이가 되다〉 ♦일곱살 난 아이 a child of seven; a seven-year-old child
20 〈되다〉 ♦탄로 나다 be disclosed [revealed, exposed]

나다² **1** 〈동작의 계속〉 go on [keep] (doing)
▶ 차차 자라나면 너도 알게 될 것이다 If you grow older, you'll come to understand it.
2 〈동작의 완료〉 have (just) finished (doing); come from (doing)
▶ 한잠 자고 나니 훨씬 상쾌하다 I have had a nap and now I feel much refreshed.
▶ 숙제를 끝내고 나니 마음이 놓인다 I feel much relieved to have finished my homework.

나다니다 gad [wander] about [around]; go about [out]
♦밤에 나다니는 여자 a woman gadding about at night / 잘 나다니는 사람 a regular gadabout / 늘 나다니다 be a gadabout; be always on the go[d]; live in the street
▶ 밤에 혼자 나다니는 것은 위험하다 It is dangerous to go out alone at night.

나달 〈나흘이나 닷새쯤〉 four or five days; four days or so; several days

나돌다 〈돌아다니다〉 wander about; go [roam] about; 〈퍼지다〉 get abroad; be rumored
♦시장에 나돌다 appear on the market / 쓸데 없이 나돌다 wander about to no purpose
▶ 모조 진주가 나돌고 있다 Imitation pearls are now on sale.

나동그라지다 tumble ⇨ 나가동그라지다

나뒹굴다 tumble all about; roll over; 〈널려 있다〉 be littered [scattered] all over (the street)
▶ 빈 깡통이 그곳에 온통 나뒹굴고 있었다 Empty cans were scattered all over the place. ⇌ The place was littered [strewed] with empty cans.

나들다 go [come] in and out ⇨ 드나들다

나들이 going out; an outing; an airing; a short visit

♦나들이 준비를 하다 get ready to go out / 결혼 후 처음으로 친정집에 나들이 가다 pay the first postmarriage visit to her native home
▶ 어제는 비가 와서 나들이를 못했다 Rain kept me indoors yesterday.
━나들이하다 go out; pay a short visit 《to》; go on a (short) visit 《to》
♦이웃집에 나들이하다 go out to a neighboring house
■ 나들잇벌 one's best clothes and shoes

나들이옷 one's best clothes; a gala [holiday] dress; one's Sunday [holiday] suit [best]; a Sunday-go-to-meeting dress; a visiting wear
♦나들이옷을 입고 (dressed) in gala [one's (Sunday) best]; in one's best clothes
▶ 그는 나들이옷을 입고 파티에 참석했다 He wore his Sunday best to the party.
▶ 그의 아내는 나들이옷을 입고 외출했다 His wife went out dressed in her best clothes.
▶ 그녀는 나들이옷으로 치장하고 있었다 She was dressed up in her Sunday best.

나라 1 〈국가〉 a country; a nation; a state; 〈국토〉 a country; a land; 〈영토〉 a territory; 〈고국〉 one's native country; one's home [mother] country; one's fatherland

解說 *country*는 나라, 국토를 뜻하는 가장 일반적인 말. *nation*은 주로 사람과 관련되며, 민족 집단으로서의 국가를 말한다. *state*는 정치적 국가로서 국제법이 정의하는 독립국가를 나타낸다.

♦나라의 national / 먼 나라 a far-off land [country] / 세계의 여러 나라 the countries of the world / 신의 나라 the kingdom of Heaven [God] / 나라의 중대사 a matter of national importance / 나라를 사랑하는 마음 one's love for one's (home) country; patriotism / 나라를 다스리다 govern a nation [country] / 나라를 세우다 found [establish, build up] a country [state] / 나라를 위해 목숨을 버리다 lay down one's life for one's country / 남의 나라를 침범하다 violate the territory of another country / 나라 안을 여행하다 travel all over the country
▶ 미국은 큰 나라다 The U.S.A. is a big country.
▶ 나라 전체가 침략에 저항했다 The whole nation resisted the aggression.
▶ 두 나라는 어업 협정을 맺었다 The two nations entered into an agreement concerning fishing rights.
▶ 그는 한평생 나라를 위해 헌신했다 He devoted himself to his country throughout his life.
♦영국은 철도를 나라에서 관리하고 있다 In Britain, the railroads are controlled by the state [placed under state control].
▶ 어느 나라에서 오셨습니까? What country are you from? ⇌ What is your nationality?
▶ 먹는 습관은 나라마다 다르다 Eating habits differ from country to country.
2 〈국토〉 a country; a nation; a land; 〈영토〉 a territory
3 〈특수한 세계〉 a world; a realm
♦꿈나라 the dreamland / 달나라 the lunar world; the moon / 동화의 나라 (a) fairyland
■ ━님 the king; the monarch; the sovereign; the ruler ━일 state [national] affairs; the affairs [matters] of state

나락 奈落 Hell; Hades; an abyss; the infernal regions ♦ 나락으로 떨어지다 fall into the bottomless pit
▶ 과거 2년간 나는 절망의 나락에 빠져 있었다 I have been in the abyss of despair for the past two years.

나란하다 even; uniform; (be) in a regular line [row, file]; 〈평행하다〉 (be) parallel (to, with) ▶ 선 A와 B는 나란하다 Line A is parallel to [with] line B.

나란히 〈줄지어〉 in a (regular) line [row, file]; side by side; abreast; 〈가지런히〉 uniformly; evenly; in (good, neat, trim) order
♦철로와 나란히 뻗은 길 a road running parallel with [to] the railroad / 나란히 달리다 〈경마에서〉 run neck and neck / 나란히 서다 stand in a row [line]; line up / 두 줄로 나란히 서다 form [be drawn up in] two lines / 높이를 나란히 하다 make (them) all of the uniform [same] height / 어깨를 나란히 하다 (比肩) rank [vie] (with); bear [stand] comparison (with) / 일류 예술가와 어깨를 나란히 하다 be ranked among the artists of the highest order
▶ 많은 사람이 버스를 기다리며 나란히 서 있었다 A lot of people were waiting in line [lining] (up) for [to get on] the bus. ⇌ A lot of people were lining (up) for [to get on] the bus.
▶ 도서관 벽에는 책장들이 나란히 세워져 있다 The walls of the library are lined with bookcases.
▶ 나란히 앉으세요 Please sit side by side.
▶ 상자는 쌓지 말고 나란히 놓으세요 Don't stack up the boxes, put them side by side.
▶ 우리는 식탁[교실]에서 나란히 앉게 되었다 We happened to sit side by side [We were neighbors by chance] at table [in class].
▶ 행정력에서는 그와 어깨를 나란히 할 사람이 없다 He has no equal in administration. ⇌ For administrative skill no one can match him.
▶ 우로[좌로, 앞으로] 나란히 《口令》 Right [Left, Forward]—dress!

나래 〈농기구〉 a soil leveler [roller, grader]
■ ━질 leveling soil with a soil leveler

나루 a ferry (crossing) ♦ 나루를 건너다 cross a stream by [on a] ferry; cross a ferry
━지기 a ferryman; a ferry guard ━질 ferrying: 나루질하다 ferry ━터 a ferry crossing [point] ━턱 a ferry (moorage); ferry moorings: 나루턱에 배를 대다 draw a boat up to a ferry 나룻가 the vicinity of a ferry 나룻목 〈물목〉 the ferry narrows

나룻 〈턱수염〉 a beard; 〈구레나룻〉 whiskers
나룻배 a ferryboat; a ferry
♦나룻배로 강을 건너다 ferry across [over] a river; cross a river in a ferryboat [by ferry, on a ferry] / 나룻배로 대안까지 나르다 ferry (men) over to the other side of the river

■ ―사공 a ferryman; a ferrymaster ―삯 ferriage

나르다 【운반하다】 carry; 〈탈것으로〉 convey; 〈장거리를〉 transport; take [bring] sth to (a place)
♦ 손[수레]으로 나르다 carry sth by hand [cart] / 비행기[기차, 트럭]로 나르다 transport (goods) by air [train, truck] / 위층으로 나르다 get (things) upstairs / 피아노를 집안으로 나르다 carry a piano into the house / 테이블을 방 밖으로 나르다 carry a table out of the room
▶ 우리는 인부들을 시켜 짐을 날랐다 We engaged men to carry our baggage.
▶ 이 짐은 너무 무거워서 나 혼자서는 나를 수 없다 This baggage is too heavy for me to carry alone [by myself].

나르시시즘 〖心〗 〈자기 도취〉 narcissism

나른하다 **1** 〈피곤하다〉 languid; listless; tired; weary; heavy
▶ 몸이 나른하다 I feel lazy [languid].
▶ 더워서 몸이 나른하다 The heat makes me feel languid.
2 〈힘없이 보드랍다〉 tender; delicate; feeble

나름 ♦ 능력[사정] 나름으로 according to one's ability [to circumstances] / 자기[그] 나름대로 in one's [its] own way / … 나름이다 rest [lie] with; depend on; be dependent on
▶ 그것은 사람 나름이다 It depends on the person.
▶ 모든 것은 네가 할 나름이다 It's all up to you.
▶ 성공 여부는 너의 노력 나름이다 Whether you succeed or not depends on your effort.
▶ 값은 품질 나름이다 Prices vary with the quality.

나리¹ **1** 〈참나리〉 a tiger lily **2** ⇨ 백합(百合)

나리² 〈존칭〉 your honor; my (good) lord; sir; my honorable master; 〈왕자님〉 Your Highness
♦ 나리 같은 lordly / 나리처럼 행동하다 play the lord; act like a lord

나마 〈…라도〉 though; however; 〈…마저〉 even
▶ 늙은 마누라나마 나에게는 소중하다 Though old, she is my good wife.
▶ 그만한 비나마 와주니 크게 다행이다 Even that much of rain is of great help.
▶ 책이나마 읽으니 나는 만족한다 As [So] long as I have books to read, I am [will be] happy [satisfied].

-나마 though; however; even if
▶ 그다지 맛은 없으나마 좀 들어 보세요 These are not very tasty, but just have some anyway.
▶ 그 집은 크진 않으나마 아늑하다 Though small, the house is cozy.

나막신 《a pair of》 (wooden) clogs; wooden shoes; pattens

나맥 裸麥 〖植〗 rye=쌀보리

나머지 **1** 〈남은 부분〉 the rest; the remainder; the remnant; what is left (over); 〈잔금〉 the balance
♦ 나머지 반 the other half / 나머지 빚 balance [remainder] of one's debt / 나머지 사람들 the rest of the people / 나머지 상품 unsold stock; stock left over / 나머지 재산 the residuary estate / 나머지의 remaining; remnant / 나머지가 남지 않도록 똑같이 나누다 divide sth equally (among the members) with nothing left over
▶ 나머지 돈은 저금했다 I saved the money left over.
▶ 나머지 얘기를 마저 해다오 Go on with the rest of your story. ⇌ Go ahead.
▶ 나머지 시합 시간은 앞으로 3분밖에 없다 We have only three minutes left before the game is over. ⇌ There's only three minutes to go in the game.
▶ 나머지 고기는 모두 썩었다 The rest of the meat was all rotten.
▶ 나머지 일은 내일 합시다 Let's do the remaining work tomorrow.
▶ 나머지는 가지시오 Keep the rest for yourself.
▶ 갖고 싶은 것은 갖고 나머지는 모두 버리시오 Take what you want and throw all the rest away.
▶ 그 사고로 5명이 죽고 나머지는 중상을 입었다 In the accident, five people were killed and the rest [the others] were seriously injured.
▶ 그가 제일 큰 몫을 차지하고 나머지는 동생들에게 나누어 주었다 He took the biggest part and divided the rest among his brothers.
2 〈…한 결과〉 ♦ 기쁜 나머지 in (the excess of) one's joy / 분노한 나머지 in a fit of anger [passion] / 슬픈 나머지 in one's grief; in a passion of grief
▶ 더운 나머지 모두 물만 마시고 있었다 The heat was so intense [It was so hot], everybody was drinking a lot of water.
▶ 기쁜 나머지 그녀는 춤을 추었다 She was so happy that she danced for joy.
▶ 그녀는 너무 놀란 나머지 말을 하지 못했다 She was so surprised that she couldn't speak. ⇌ She was speechless with astonishment.
▶ 그는 일을 너무 많이 한 나머지 건강을 해쳤다 He worked so much (that) he injured his health. ⇌ Overwork ruined his health.
3 〖數〗 〈남은 수〉 remainder
▶ 20에서 5를 빼면 나머지는 15다 Five from twenty leaves fifteen.
▶ 20에서 10을 빼면 나머지는 몇인가? If you take (away) 10 from 20, what is the remainder [remains]?

나무 a tree; 〈관목〉 a shrub; 〈초목〉 a plant; 〈목재〉 wood; (美) lumber; (英) timber; 〈통나무〉 a log; 〈땔나무〉 firewood; wood for fuel
♦ 마른 나무 a dead tree / 사과[바나나] 나무 an apple [a banana] tree / 생명의 나무 the tree of life / 잎이 진 나무 a bare tree / 나무 순 a shoot; a sprout / 나무가 없는 산 mountain bare of tree; a bald mountain / 나무가 우거진 산 mountain covered with trees; a (densely) wooded [woody] mountain / 나무를 때다 burn wood / 나무를 베다 cut down [fell] a tree / 나무를 심다 plant a tree / 나무를 보되 숲은 보지 못하다 cannot [be unable to] see the wood for the trees / 나무에 물을 주다

water a plant / 나무에 오르다 climb (up) a tree / 나무하러 가다 go to gather [cut] firewood
▶ 나무는 여러 방면에 쓰인다 Wood is used in many ways.
▶ 실과로 나무를 아느니라 〔聖〕 A tree is known by its fruit.
■ —거울 a good-for-nothing (fellow) —공이 a wooden pestle —괭이 a wooden hoe —깽이 a piece of wood; a splinter —꾼 a woodcutter; a woodman; (美) a lumberman; a lumberjack; a logger —눈 tree buds [sprouts] —딸기 a raspberry —토막 a chip [piece] of wood; a stick; a board; a lath —막대기 a stick; a rod; a pole —망치 a wooden hammer; a mallet; 〈의사봉〉 a gavel —못 a wooden peg [nail] —발바리 〔鳥〕 the common tree creeper —배 a wooden ship [vessel] —상자 a wooden box [chest] —숲 a clump of trees; a grove —옹이 a knot on a tree —장수 a firewood seller; a fuel dealer —좀 〔動〕 a grain borer; a wood borer [engraver] —줄기 the trunk of a tree; a shaft —진드〔昆〕a wood louse; a jumping plant louse —토막 a piece [chip, splinter] of wood; 〈큰 것〉 a block —판자 a board —판장 a wooden wall; a board fence 나뭇가지 the branches of a tree; 〈큰 가지〉 a bough; 〈어린 가지〉 a sprig 나뭇간 a woodshed 나뭇개비 a piece of wood; a splinter 나뭇결 the wood grain: 나뭇결이 곱다[거칠다] be fine-grained [coarse-grained] 나뭇고갱이 the pith [heart] of wood 나뭇길 a woodman's path 나뭇단 a fagot; a bundle of firewood 나뭇더미 a woodpile 나뭇동 a large bundle of wood 나뭇등걸 the stump of a tree 나뭇바리 a load of wood 나뭇조각 a chip; a splinter; a piece [chip, block] of wood; a chunk (of wood) 나뭇진 sap of a tree; resin

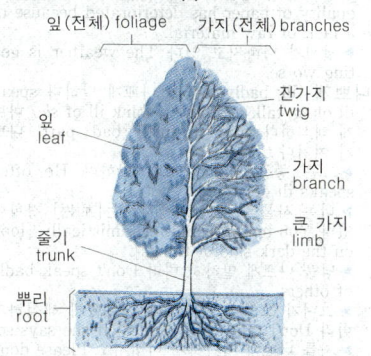

나무

잎(전체) foliage 가지(전체) branches
잔가지 twig
잎 leaf
가지 branch
큰 가지 limb
줄기 trunk
뿌리 root

나무그늘 the shade of a tree; a leafy recess [shade]; a bower
◆ 서늘한 나무 그늘 a cool shade under a tree / 나무 그늘이 많은 산책길 a shady path / 나무 그늘에서 쉬다 take a rest in the shade of [under] a tree

▶ 그는 나무 그늘에서 더위를 피했다 He took shelter from the summer heat under a tree.
나무껍질 the bark of a tree
◆ 나무껍질을 벗기다 bark a tree; strip a tree of its bark
나무늘보 〔動〕 a sloth
나무라다 reprove; rebuke (sb for sth); scold; 〈꾸짖다〉 reproach (for); 〈흠을 지적하다〉 blame (for); censure (for); accuse; 〈문책하다〉 take [call, bring] sb to task
◆ 배은망덕을 나무라다 rebuke sb's ingratitude / 버릇이 없다고 나무라다 reprove sb for his bad manners / 나무랄 데 없다 be faultless [flawless]; be impeccable; be free from blemishes
▶ 나는 그의 잘못을 나무랐다 I blamed him for his fault.
▶ 아버지는 요즈음 내가 게으르다고 나무라셨다 Father reproved me for my laziness recently.
▶ 그녀의 요리는 나무랄 데가 없다 She is a perfect cook.
나무람 a reproof; a reproach; (a) rebuke; a censure; a blame ▶ 그는 불려가서 나무람을 들었다 He was summoned to receive a reproof.
나무아미타불 南無阿彌陀佛 I sincerely believe in Amitabha; May Buddha's blessing be upon us!; 〈위험할 때〉 Save us, merciful Buddha!; 〈명복을 빌 때〉 May his soul rest in peace!
▶ 십년 공부 나무아미타불 One hour's cold will spoil seven years' warming. ≒ A hour may destroy what took an age to build.
나물 1 〈생것〉 edible greens; herbs; potherbs; salad makings ▶ 우리는 들에 나물 캐러 갔다 We went to gather herbs in the fields.
2 〈무친 것〉 cooked potherbs [greens]; vegetable with Korean dressing; herb salad
◆ 나물을 무치다 cook greens; mix greens with seasonings / 나물 먹고 물 마시고 팔을 베고 눕다 lead a simple and leisurely life
나뭇잎 a leaf (pl. leaves) (of a tree); (총칭) foliage; leafage
◆ 나뭇잎이 우거진 leafy (tree) / 나뭇잎에 가리어 hidden by the leaves
▶ 나뭇잎이 다 떨어졌다 All the leaves have fallen from the tree.
▶ 나뭇잎이 단풍 들었다 The leaves of the tree turned red and yellow.
나미비아 〈나라 이름〉 Namibia; 〈공식명〉 Republic of Namibia ◆ 나미비아의 Namibian —사람 a Namibian
나박김치 watery kimch'i made of thin-sliced radish
나발 〈나팔〉 a trumpet; a bugle ▶ 규칙이고 나 발이고 어디 있어 Regulations be hanged!
나방 〔昆〕 a moth
나변 那邊 〈어디〉 where ▶ 그 이유가 나변에 있는가? Where is the reason? ▶ 그의 진의가 나변에 있는지 알 수 없다 I cannot understand what he really means.
나병 癩病 leprosy; lepra; Hansen's disease
◆ 나병에 걸려 있다 be leprous
■ —균 a Hansen's bacillus (pl. -li) —환자 a leper; a leprous patient —환자 수용소 a leper

-**나보다** seem; look (like); appear; It seems (to me) that...; I think that...
▶ 누가 있나보다 I think someone's here.
▶ 비가 오려나보다 It looks like rain.
▶ 그는 아팠었나보다 He seems to have been ill. ≒ It seems that he was [has been] ill.

나부 裸婦 (paint) a woman in the nude; a nude woman ■—상 (像) a nude

나부끼다 〈파도처럼〉 wave; 〈펄럭거리다〉 flutter; stream; 〈팔랑거리다〉 flap; float; fly
▶ 나뭇잎이 바람결에 이리저리 나부꼈다 The leaves fluttered about in the wind.
▶ 깃발이 바람에 나부끼고 있었다 The flag fluttered [waved] in the wind.
▶ 그녀가 뛰어가자 긴 리본이 나부꼈다 Her long ribbons streamed as she ran.

나부대다 〈남신거리다〉 gabble; talk glibly [volubly]; chatter; talk glib and flippant; wag one's tongue; 〈몸을〉 keep budging nervously; fidget (about)
▶ 그녀는 몹시 나부댄다 She is such a chatterbox.
▶ 그녀는 비밀을 나부대고 말았다 She babbled out the secret.

나부대대하다 buxom; chubby-faced; have a round flat little face

나부랭이 1 〈자질구레한 조각〉 a piece; a bit; a chip; a scrap; a fag end ◆종이 나부랭이 a scrap [slip] of paper / 천 나부랭이 remnants of cloth
2 〈하찮은 존재〉 a fag end ◆관리 나부랭이 a petty official ▶ 그는 저래도 시인 나부랭이다 He is a piece [bit] of a poet.

나부시 〈천천히 내려오는 모양〉 (going down) smoothly; softly; lightly; gently
◆나부시 절하다 bow with a gentle sweep; bow from the waist; make a polite bow
▶ 새가 나무에 나부시 내려앉았다 A bird sat in a tree lightly.

나부죽하다 broad and flattish

나불거리다 1 〈나붓거리다〉 flutter [flap, stream] away; flicker ▶ 촛불이 바람에 나불거리고 있었다 The candle's flame was flickering in the wind.
2 〈경솔하게 입을 놀리다〉 talk glibly [volubly]; chatter; prattle; gabble; (口) rattle; wag one's tongue; flap about ◆입을 나불거리다 wag one's tongue
▶ 잘도 나불거리는군 How your tongue runs!

나불나불하다 flutter away ⇨ 나불거리다

나붓거리다 keep fluttering [waving, flickering, flapping]

나붙다 be posted up [stuck] (on a wall)
▶ 벽보판에 여러가지 포스터가 나붙었다 A lot of posters appeared on the wall-newspaper board.
▶ 벽에 「관계자외 출입금지」라는 게시가 나붙어 있었다 There was a notice posted up on the wall, saying "No admission except on business."

나비¹ 〈昆〉 a butterfly
◆나비 모양의 butterfly-shaped / 나비처럼 날다 fly like a butterfly
▶ 나비가 이 꽃 저 꽃으로 날아다닌다 Butterflies are fluttering from flower to flower.
■—넥타이 a bow (tie) —잠 a (baby's) way of sleeping with stretched arms —잠(簪) a butterfly-shaped hairpin —장 〔建〕 a clamp —춤 a butterfly dance

―― 나비 ――

겹눈 compound eye
촉각 antenna
날개맥 vein
미상돌기 tails

나비² 〈폭〉 width (of cloth)
나비³ 〈고양이〉 a cat; a kitty; a puss(y)
나비매듭 a bowknot; a (single, double) bow
▶ 내 여동생은 리본을 나비매듭으로 맸다 My sister tied the ribbon in a bow.

나빠지다 grow [become, get] worse; go [turn] bad; go wrong; 〈점점 더〉 grow from bad to worse; 〈품질 등이〉 spoil; become deteriorated
◆다시 나빠지다 take a turn for the worse; suffer a setback [relapse]
▶ 사태가 점점 나빠졌다 Things went worse and worse.
▶ 환자가 갑자기 나빠졌다 The patient has taken a sudden turn for the worse.
▶ 아버지의 건강은 폭음으로 서서히 나빠졌다 My father's health was undermined by excesses.
▶ 원료 부족 때문에 종이의 질이 나빠졌다 The quality of paper has deteriorated because of a lack of raw material.
▶ 날씨가 나빠지고 있다 The weather is getting worse.

나쁘게 ill; badly ◆남을 나쁘게 말하다 speak ill of sb; talk against sb; think ill of sb / 나쁘게 해석하다 take (it) in ill [bad] part / 나쁘게 여기다 take ill
▶ 그는 종종 남을 나쁘게 말한다 He often speaks ill of others.
▶ 너는 사물을 나쁘게 생각하는[보는] 경향이 있다 You tend to think pessimistically [look on the dark side of things].
▶ 남을 나쁘게 말하지 마라 Don't speak badly of others.
▶ 그녀가 그렇게 말하더라도 나쁘게 해석하지 마라 Don't take it ill [amiss] if she says so.
▶ 저를 나쁘게 생각하지 마십시오 Please don't think ill of me.
▶ 행동을 나쁘게 해서는 안된다 You must not behave badly [ill].

나쁘다 1 〈좋지 않다〉 bad; wrong; evil; ill; sinful; immoral (도덕적으로)
◆나쁜 짓 〈악행〉 a wrong; a misdeed; an evil deed; 〈악덕〉 a vice; 〈죄악〉 a sin; a crime /

쁜 친구들 bad companions / 나쁜 짓을 하다 do wrong; commit a sin [crime]
▶ 약속을 어기는 것은 나쁘다 It is not good to break your promise.
▶ 약자를 못살게 구는 것은 나쁘다 It is wrong [bad] to bully the weak.
▶ 나쁜 일은 반드시 드러나는 법 Murder will out.
▶ 나쁜 짓을 했으면 곧 사과해야 한다 You have to apologize at once when you have done wrong.
▶ 나는 나쁜 짓을 해서 꾸지람을 들었다 I was punished for my mischief.
2 〈악하다〉 bad; evil; wicked; malicious
♦ 나쁜 사람들 wicked people
▶ 그녀는 천성이 나쁘다 She is ill-natured.
▶ 그는 듣던 것보다는 나쁜 사람이 아니다 He is not so black as he is painted.
3 〈잘못이다〉 (be) in the wrong; blamable; wrong; (be) in fault
▶ 내가 나빴어 It's my fault. ⇒ I am to blame (for it). ⇒ The fault lies with me.
▶ 그는 친구에게 불리한 증언을 하는 것은 나쁘다고 생각했다 He felt it would be wrong to testify against his friend.
4 〈해롭다〉 harmful; bad; injurious; 〈악성이다〉 malignant 《influenza》; virulent 《disease》; nasty ♦ 눈에 나쁘다 be bad for [injurious to] the eyes
▶ 날씨가 농작물에 나쁘다 The weather is bad for the crops.
▶ 담배는 건강에 나쁘다 Smoking is bad for your health.
▶ 눈에 나쁘니 어두운 데서는 책을 읽지 마라 Don't read under insufficient light, for it is bad for your eyes.
5 〈건강이〉 (be, feel) unwell; (be) ill [sick]; (be) indisposed
♦ 병세가 아주 나쁘다 be dangerously [critically] ill / 심장이 나쁘다 have heart trouble; have a weak heart / 안색이 나쁘다 look pale; have a bad complexion / 위가 나쁘다 have [suffer from] stomach trouble
▶ 몸이 어디 나쁜가요? Anything wrong with you? ⇒ Is anything the matter [wrong] with you?
▶ 나는 눈이 나쁘다 I have something wrong with my eyes. ⇒ My eyes are weak.
▶ 우리 아버지는 간이 나쁘시다 My father has a bad liver.
▶ 넌 안색이 나쁘구나, 즉시 자리에 눕는게 좋겠다 You look pale, you had better lie down in bed at once.
6 〈형편·품질이〉 bad; poor; inferior; of low grade; coarse
♦ 나쁜 물건 a bad [defective] article / 품질이 나쁘다 be of bad [poor] quality
▶ 그는 재정 상태가 나쁘다 He is in a bad shape financially.
▶ 값싼 물건이 언제나 나쁜 것은 아니다 Cheap things are not always bad.
▶ 뭔가 나쁜 것을 먹은 것 같아 I am afraid I ate something bad.
7 〈머리·기억력이〉 weak; poor; feeble

▶ 그는 머리가 나쁘다 He is weak-headed [dull, stupid]. ⇒ He has a dull head.
▶ 나는 기억력이 나쁘다 I have a poor memory.
▶ 그는 공부를 하지 않았기 때문에 이번 시험 성적이 나빴다 He did not study hard and got bad marks this time.
8 〈날씨가〉 bad; foul; nasty; inclement
▶ 그날은 날씨가 나빴다 We had bad [foul, nasty] weather on that day. ⇒ The weather was bad on that day.
9 〈도로가〉 muddy; bad; rough
▶ 그 나라는 도로가 나쁘기로 유명하다 That country is notorious for its bad roads.
10 〈불길[불행]하다〉 unlucky; bad; ill; ominous; sad
♦ 나쁜 소식 bad [sad] news / 나쁜 징조 a bad [an ill] omen
▶ 오늘은 일진이 나쁜가 보다 It seems this is an evil [a bad, a black] day. ⇒ I seem to be in ill luck today.
▶ 안됐지만 당신에게 나쁜 소식이 있습니다 I'm afraid I have bad news for you.
11 〈불쾌하다〉 bad; unpleasant; disagreeable; 〈사람이 주어〉 displeased; ill-humored ♦ 기분이 나쁘다 feel out of sorts
▶ 나는 아침 차를 마시지 않으면 온종일 기분이 나쁘다 If I don't have my morning tea, I'm in a bad mood all day.
12 〈불편·불비·고장 등〉 wrong; bad; ill; out of order; 〈시기가〉 ill-timed
▶ 엔진이 어딘가 나쁘다 Something is [There is something] wrong with the engine.
▶ 이 세탁기는 상태가 나쁘다 This electric washing machine doesn't work well.
13 〈소문 등이〉 ill; bad; unsavory ♦ 나쁜 소문 an unsavory rumor
14 〈모자라다〉 deficient; insufficient; unsatisfactory; inadequate; (be) not enough
▶ 식사를 좀 나쁜 듯하게 해야 탈이 없다 Feed by measure and defy the physician.
나 삐 〈나쁘게〉 badly; ill; 〈부족하게〉 not enough; insufficiently; unsatisfactorily
▶ 가지 않는다고 해서 나쁘게 생각하지 말게 Please don't think ill [badly] of me because I'm not coming.
▶ 악의로 한 말이 아니니 그렇게 나쁘게 여기지 마시게 Don't take my words so ill [amiss] since I didn't make them out of spite.
나사 螺絲 **1** 〈나사못〉 a screw
♦ 나사를 죄다 drive a screw; tighten a screw / 나사를 뽑다 take a screw off 《a board》; unscrew 《a plate》 / 나사를 풀다 loosen a screw; slacken a screw / 나사로 죄다[고정시키다] screw sth up [down]
▶ 나사가 풀렸다 The screw has come [is] loose.
▶ 드라이버로 나사를 판자에 박았다 I drove [put] the screw into the board with a screwdriver.
2 (비유) ▶ 그는 술을 마시면 나사가 빠진다 He loses control when he drinks.
▶ 너 요새 나사가 좀 빠졌구나 You've been a bit absent-minded recently.

■수[암]— a male [female] screw; an exterior [interior] screw; a bolt [nut] 왼[오른]— a left-handed [right-handed] screw ―대가리 the head of a screw; a screw head ―돌리개 a screwdriver ―뚜껑 a screw cap ―산 a screw thread ―송곳 a screw auger

나사 羅紗 woolen cloth ―능직— twilled cloth 줄무늬— tweed ―점 a woolen draper's [dealer's] shop ―지(紙) 〈벽지 · 표지용〉 flock paper

나사 NASA [《the *N*ational *A*eronautics and *S*pace *A*dministration]

나사못 螺絲— a screw spike; a screw;〈때려박는〉 a screwnail; a drivescrew;〈대가리가 고리 모양인〉 a screw eye
―게이지 a screw gauge

나상 裸像 a nude statue [figure]

나서다 1〈앞으로 나와 서다〉step [come] forward ♦줄에서 나서다 get out of line / 한발짝 나서다 make a step forward
2〈나타나다〉appear; come out [forth]; present *oneself*; make *one's* appearance; turn up ▶그는 남 앞에 나서기를 좋아하는 것 같다 He seems fond of the limelight.
3〈떠나다〉start 《from》; leave; get out 《of》 ♦교문을 나서다 leave the school; get out of the campus / 집을 나서다 leave home; leave *one's* house
4〈가로막거나 참견하다〉intrude; interfere; obtrude; intermeddle; push [put, thrust] *oneself* forward
▶너는 이 일에 나서지 마라 You keep out of this.
▶네가 나설 일이 아니다 This is none of your business. ⇌ Mind your own business. ⇌ You have nothing to do with this matter.
▶지금이야말로 내가 나설 때다 It is time for me to take [go into] action.
5〈진출하다〉go [sally] forth into 《the world》; launch into; enter upon
♦사회개혁에 나서다 set out to reform the society / 정계에 나서다 launch into politics; enter [embark] upon a political career
6〈출마하다〉run [stand] for
♦선거에 나서다 declare *one's* candidacy 《for》; stand [come forward] as a candidate for an election; run for 《the Presidency》; 《英》stand for 《Parliament》
▶그는 나이 50세에 정계에 나서려고 결심했다 He decided to enter upon a political career at fifty.
▶그는 내년 지사 선거에 나설 것이라고 한다 They say he is going to run for governor next year.
7〈일자리 등이〉be found; turn up ♦일자리가 나서다 find a job [position]; find employment; get a place
8〈지원자 등이〉apply 《for》; make application 《for》; go in for ♦신랑감이 나서다 find a suitable bridegroom
▶아들에게 좋은 혼처가 나섰다 An offer of marriage has come up for my son.

나선 裸線 a naked electric wire; a bare wire

나선 螺旋〈소용돌이〉a spiral; a helix 《pl. ~es, helices》 ♦나선형[상]의 spiral; screw-shaped; helical
▶비행기는 나선형을 그리면서 상승하고 있었다 The plane was spiraling up into the sky.
▶연기가 나선형으로 올라갔다 The smoke spiraled up [rose in spiral].
■—강하 〔空〕 a spiral dive [descent]; a (cork)screw dive —계단 a spiral [corkscrew] staircase —(상)균 a spirillum 《pl. *-rilla*》 —성운〔天〕 a spiral nebula —운동 screw motion —체〔數〕 a helicoid; a spiral —추진기 a screw propeller

나세르〈이집트의 대통령〉Nasser, Gamal Abdel(1918-70)

나스르르하다 downy; flossy; fluey; fluffy; fuzzy ♦털이 나스르르한 담요 a woolly blanket / 털이 나스르르한 새끼 a downy young bird; a fledgling

나아가다 1〈전진하다〉advance; proceed; move [go, step] forward [ahead]; make [push, force, feel] *one's* way;〈빛 · 소리 등이〉travel

> |解説| ***advance***는 어떤 목표를 향해 나아가는 것. ***proceed***는 나아가기 시작하는 것, 또는 일단 중지했던 일을 속행하는 것을 의미한다. ***move***는 이동하는 것이고 ***move forward***는 전진하는 것을 나타낸다. ***go***는 현재의 장소에서 떠나가는 것이고, ***make one's way***는 go와 거의 같은 뜻으로 쓰이는데 자력으로 [고생해서] 나아가는 것을 암시하는 경우가 있다. 또 ***make one's way*** 대신에 ***push*** [***force***] ***one's way*** (밀어 헤치고 나아가다)나 ***feel one's way*** (손으로 더듬어 나아가다)와 같이 여러 가지 동사를 써서 나아가는 모양을 나타낼 수가 있다.

♦시대와 함께 나아가다 keep up with the times; keep abreast of the times / 시대보다 앞서 나아가다 get [go] ahead of the times; be ahead of *one's* time
▶빛은 소리보다 훨씬 빨리 나아간다 Light travels much faster than sound.
▶우리는 하루에 45킬로미터 나아갔다 We made forty-five kilometers in a day.
▶두 발짝 앞으로 나아가시오 Take [Please] two steps forward.
▶군중 사이를 헤치고 나아가기는 쉽지 않았다 It was not easy to make our way through the crowd.
▶일행은 눈 때문에 그 이상은 나아갈 수가 없다 The party could not go on any farther [further] because of the heavy snowfall.
2〈진척하다〉advance; make progress; progress; improve
▶|會話|「요전 시간에 어디까지 나아갔더라?」「14페이지 셋째 줄까지 나아갔습니다」 "How far did we get [Where did we get to] in our last lesson?" "We got (up) to page 14, line 3."
3〈진출하다〉enter upon; launch into;〈승진하다〉be promoted [raised]
♦결승전에 나아가다 go into the finals / 정계로 나아가다 enter upon a political career; go into politics

▶ 그는 재계로 나아갔다 He made his way in the business world.
▶ 요즘은 고교 졸업생의 대부분이 대학으로 나아간다 Most of the high school graduates go on to colleges these days.
4 〈형편·병세 등이〉 ⇨ 나아지다

나아지다 change [take a turn] for the better; become [get] better; take a favorable turn; pick up; improve; be improved
♦ 병세가 나아지다 take a turn for the better; take a favorable turn / 살기가 나아지다 get better off; be in easier circumstances / 학교의 성적이 나아지다 show a better school record / 솜씨가 나아지다 improve in *one's* skill 〈at, in〉; gain in skill; become more skillful
▶ 상황은 나아졌다 The situation has improved [taken a turn for the better, changed for the better].
▶ 식량 사정이 나아졌다 The food situation has improved.
▶ 경기가 나아지고 있다 Business is looking [picking] up.
▶ 그들의 경제도 곧 나아질 것이다 Their economy will pick up before long.

나약 懦弱 feebleness; feeblemindedness; effeminacy; 〈우유부단〉 irresolution
—**나약하다** weak; effeminate; emasculate; feebleminded; spiritless
♦ 나약한 남자 an effeminate man / 나약한 생활을 하다 live soft / 나약해지다 become effeminate; lapse into effeminacy
▶ 아이를 너무 나약하게 기르지 마라 Don't make your child too dependent.
▶ 소방대원은 맨먼저 나약한 어린이들을 구출했다 Firemen rescued the helpless children at first.

나열 羅列 (an) enumeration; marshaling
▶ 그것은 단지 무의미한 문자의 나열에 지나지 않는다 It is nothing but a meaningless list of letters [characters].
—**나열하다** enumerate (instances); cite 〈one example after another〉; arrange (things) in a row; set forth
♦ 통계 숫자를 나열하다 marshal statistical figures; give a wealth of statistics / 단편적인 정보를 나열하다 enumerate bits of information
▶ 그는 자기의 장점을 나열했다 He listed his own virtues [merits].

나오다 1 〈밖으로〉 come [get, turn] out; 〈잠깐〉 step out; take *one's* way out
♦ 교실에서 나오다 get out of a schoolroom / 집을 나오다 get out of the house; fly from *one's* home; leave home [the house] / 집 밖으로 나오지 않다 keep to *one's* house
▶ 그는 잠자코 방을 나왔다 He went out of [left] the room without (saying) a word.
▶ 그 소녀는 수영장에서 나왔다 The girl came out of the swimming pool.
▶ 아버지는 벌써 목욕탕에서 나오셨다 Daddy has already finished his bath.
▶ 아이들은 늘 들어갔다 나왔다 한다 Children are always popping in and out.
▶ 거리에는 사람들이 굉장히 많이 나와 있었다 The streets were extremely [very] crowded. ⇒ There were large crowds (of people) in the streets.
2 〈나타나다〉 appear; come out [forth, up, along]; make *one's* appearance; turn up; emerge 〈from, out of, on〉; come forward; present itself; 〈불쑥〉 bob up; 〈드러나다〉 be revealed; show itself; 〈화제에〉 come up 〈in *one's* discussion〉; 〈해·달이〉 rise
♦ 무대에 나오다 appear on the stage / 나쁜 버릇이 나오다 *one's* bad habit peeps [crops] out
▶ 해가 나왔다 The sun has come up.
▶ 별이 나왔다[나와 있다] The stars came out [are out].
▶ 사과가 시장에 나왔다 Apples have appeared on the market. ⇒ Apples are out on the market.
▶ 당신 호주머니에서 무엇인가 흰 것이 나와 있네요 Something white is sticking out of your pocket.
▶ 여러 가수가 차례로 나왔다가 사라졌다 Many singers appeared one after another and then disappeared.
▶ 걱정하지 마. 잃어버린 반지는 꼭 나올테니까 Don't worry. Your missing ring is bound to turn up.
▶ 화가 나자 그의 본성이 나왔다 Anger has made him betray himself.
3 〈참석·출석 하다〉 be present 〈at〉; attend; 〈참가하다〉 take part 〈in〉; participate; 〈출두하다〉 appear; 〈시합·연극 등에〉 play 〈in〉 / 〈경기 등에〉 enter; enter (*oneself*) for...
▶ 넌 그 식장에 나왔니? Did you go to the ceremony? ⇒ Were you (present) at [Did you attend] the ceremony?
▶ 전원이 나왔습니다 All members are present.
▶ 왜 나오지 않았습니까? Why did you absent yourself?
▶ 그는 100미터 경기에 나올 결심을 했다 He decided to take part in [enter] the 100meter dash.
4 〈유래하다·비롯되다〉 originate 〈in, from〉; spring [come] 〈from〉; be derived 〈from〉
▶ 증오는 흔히 오해에서 나온다 Hatred often comes from [is often caused by] misunderstanding.
▶ 이 단어는 라틴어에서 나왔다 This word is derived from Latin [of Latin origin, of Latin derivation].
▶ 그 보도는 믿을 만한 소식통에서 나온 것이다 The report comes from a reliable source.
5 〈그만두다〉 resign 〈*one's* office〉; quit; leave; withdraw; go away ♦ 회사에서 나오다 leave [resign from] a company
▶ 그는 관청에서 나왔다 He withdrew from his office.
6 〈졸업하다〉 graduate 〈from〉; leave [step out of] 〈a school〉
♦ 대학을 갓나온 여성 a woman fresh from college; a woman just [straight] out of college
▶ 그는 작년에 고등학교를 나왔다 He finished [graduated from] high school last year.
7 〈배설되다〉 be excreted; 〈분비되다〉 be dis-

charged; 〈유출하다〉 flow [run] (out); issue (forth)
♦침이 나오다 water; salivate / 코피가 나오다 bleed at the nose
▶이 만년필은 잉크가 잘 나온다 This fountain pen has a good flow of ink.
▶빛은 태양에서 나온다 Light emanates from the sun.
▶그의 팔에서 피가 흘러 나오고 있다 His arm is bleeding.
▶그녀는 때때로 나오는 대로 지껄인다 She sometimes says whatever comes into her mind.
8 〈없어졌던 것이〉 be found; turn up; be restored (to); get *sth* back
▶없어졌던 책이 나왔다 The book which was lost has been found.
▶잃어버린 줄 알았던 시계가 서랍에서 나왔다 The watch I thought I had lost turned up in the drawer.
9 〈음식 등이〉 be brought; be served; be given as a treat
▶디저트로 애플파이가 나왔다 Apple pie was served for dessert.
▶그 파티에서 술과 음식이 나왔다 We were treated to wine and food at the party. ⇌ Wine and food were served at the party.
▶점심에는 샌드위치가 나왔다 Sandwiches were served at lunch.
10 〈지급되다〉 be paid; 〈물품 등이〉 be provided (*sb* with *sth*)
♦면허가 나오다 get license; be licensed / 봉급이 나오다 get paid / 여권이 나오다 be granted a passport; have [get] *one's* passport visaed / 허가가 나오다 be granted permission; be permitted; get a permit
▶그것을 해도 좋다는 허가가 나왔다 I was given permission to do it.
▶상여금은 언제 나옵니까? When do we get our bonus?
▶금년에는 상여금이 많이 나올 것이다 We will get a good bonus this year.
11 〈길이〉 lead to; come upon [to]
▶이 길을 따라 가면 정거장이 나온다 This road leads [will take you] to the station.
▶얼마 후 한 마을이 나왔다 Soon we came to a village.
▶우리는 곧 호수로 나왔다 We soon came to a lake.
12 〈(결과로서) 생기다〉 come out (as a result); work out
▶8을 2로 나누면 4가 나온다 Eight divided by two gives four.
▶아무리 해도 답이 나오지 않는다 The problem defies solution. ⇌ It is impossible to solve the problem.
13 〈참가하다〉 join; participate in; take part in; enter for; 〈나서다〉 launch into; enter upon
♦사회에 나오다 launch into the world / 정계에 나오다 enter upon a political career; make *one's* debut on the political stage
14 〈찍히다〉 show; come out; take; be taken
▶네 얼굴은 잘 나온다 Your face takes well.
▶이 사진은 잘 안 나왔다 This photo is badly [not well] taken.
15 〈(후보로) 나서다〉 stand for; (美) run (for)
♦선거에 나오다 run for an election / 국회의원 후보로 나오다 stand for Parliament [(美) run for Congress]
16 〈게재되다〉 appear; 〈출판되다〉 come out (in); be published (in); 〈발행되다〉 be issued; 〈표·명단에〉 be listed
▶이 신문은 주 2회 나온다 This gazette comes out [is issued, is out] twice a week.
▶창간호는 20일에 나온다 The first number will come out [appear, make its appearance] on the 20th.
▶그 뉴스는 모든 신문에 나와 있다 The news is [appears, is reported] in every newspaper. ⇌ Every newspaper carries the news.
▶이 단어는 내 사전에 나와 있지 않다 This word is not given [found, listed] in my dictionary.
17 〈산출되다〉 be grown; be raised; be produced; be found
▶이 지역에서는 대리석이 나온다 This area produces marble.
▶그 지방에서는 위인이 많이 나왔다 The province has produced many a great man.
▶이제 사과가 나올 시기다 Apples will soon be in.
18 〈돌출하다〉 stick out; protrude; project
▶못이 나와 있다 A nail is sticking out.
▶그는 앞니가 나와 있다 His front teeth stick out [protrude].
▶가지가 담 밖으로 많이 나와 있다 The branches reach out far beyond the fence.
▶그는 이마가 나와 있다 He has a prominent forehead.
19 〈태도를 취하다〉 assume (an attitude); take (a move)
♦대담하게 나오다 put a bold front / 고압적인 태도로 나오다 act high-handedly; carry (a matter) with a high hand; take the high hand (with *sb*)
▶모든건 그들이 어떻게 나오느냐에 달렸다 Everything depends on what tack they take [what move they make].
▶그가 어떻게 나오는지 두고 보자 Let's wait and see what move he will take.
20 〈문제가〉 be given ▶시험에 열 문제가 나왔다 Ten questions were given in the exam.
▶시험에는 어려운 문제가 나왔다 Tough problems were given in the examination.
21 〈석방되다〉 be released
▶그는 교도소에서 나온 지 한 달 밖에 안 되었다 He was released from [let out of] prison only last month.

나왕 羅王 〔植〕 a lauan; 〈목재〉 lauan
나우루 〈나라 이름〉 Nauru; 〈공식명〉 the Republic of Nauru ♦나우루의 Nauruan ■—사람 a Nauruan
나위 〈여지〉 room; a margin; 〈필요〉 necessity ♦더할 나위 없는 perfect; good enough (for...); faultless; ideal; impeccable; unimpeachable; most satisfactory [suitable]; best fit (for) / 더할 나위 없는 바보 짓이다 be the height of folly [idiocy]; be sheer folly

▶ 그녀는 아내로서 더할 나위 없다 She is a perfect wife. ⇌ She is everything a wife should be.
▶ 그 호텔의 설비는 더할 나위 없다 The accommodation at that hotel is perfect [leaves nothing to be desired].
▶ 그들이 기뻐한 것은 말할 나위도 없다 It goes without saying that they were delighted.
▶ 좀더 부지런하기만 하면 더할 나위 없는 사람인데 If he were only a little more diligent, there would be nothing to be said against him.
▶ 그는 나에게 더할 나위 없는 남편이다 He is a perfect husband to me.
▶ 그는 그 일에 더할 나위 없는 적임자다 He is the best man for the job.
▶ 그는 더할 나위 없이 행복하였다 He was extremely happy. ⇌ He was as happy as (happy) can be.
▶ 결과는 더할 나위 없이 만족스럽다 The outcome is very satisfactory [leaves nothing to be desired].
▶ 날씨가 더할 나위 없이 좋다 This is an ideal weather. ⇌ The weather is all that could be wished for.

나이 age; years
♦ 나이 어린 소년 a boy of tender years / 나이 별로 by age group / 나이 순으로 according to age [seniority] / 나이 탓으로 from [with] age; on account of *one's* age
▶ 그들은 같은 나이다 They are (of) the same age.
▶ 너도 이제 결혼할 나이다 It's about time you were married.
▶ 그는 학교에 갈 나이다 He is old enough to go to school.
▶ 우리는 나이 차이가 많다 We are far apart in our ages. (▶나이의 위·아래가 분명하다면 I am far senior [junior] to you. ⇌ I am much older [younger] than you.로도 씀)
▶ 우리의 나이 차는 중요하지 않다 The difference in our ages is not important.
▶ 그녀는 예순 일곱이라는 나이보다는 젊어 보인다 She looks younger than her sixty-seven years old.
〈**나이가[는]**〉 나이가 지긋한 elderly; (a man) advanced in years / 나이가 젊다 be young / 나이가 지긋하다 be advanced [well up] in years / 결혼할 나이가 차다 arrive at the age of marriage; be ripe for marriage
▶ 나이가 몇입니까? How old are you?
▶ 그는 제법 나이가 들었다 He is well along [on, advanced] in years. ⇌ He is rather old.
▶ 그는 나이가 들어 허리가 굽었다 He is bent with age.
▶ 그는 나이가 나 정도 되었다 He is about my age.
▶ 나이가 나이인지라 그도 어쩔 수 없다 It can not be helped, considering his age.
▶ 나이는 먹고 싶지 않다 I don't want to get old.
▶ 여자의 나이는 알 수가 없다 I can't tell a woman's age.
▶ 나이는 속일 수 없다 Age asserts itself. ⇌ Age will tell. ⇌ One's years will not be denied.
〈**나이를**〉 나이를 먹다 grow older; grow [get, become] old; get on in years; advance in age [years] / 나이를 묻다 ask *sb's* age / 나이를 숨기다 represent *oneself* as younger than really is / 나이를 한 살 더 먹다 grow older by one year
▶ 그는 보기보다 나이를 먹었다 He is older than he looks.
▶ 그 여자는 언제 보아도 똑같은 게 나이를 먹지 않는다 She is ageless, the same every time I see her.
▶ 나이를 먹음에 따라 백발이 늘었다 As I grew older, much of my hair turned gray.
▶ 나이를 먹었지만 마음은 젊다 I am old but young at heart.
▶ 그는 나이를 먹음에 따라 원숙해졌다 He mellowed with age [as he grew older].
〈**나이에**〉 열 다섯의 나이에 at (the age of) fifteen; when *one* is fifteen (years old) / 나이에 상관없이 with no age limit / 나이에 걸맞게 행동하다 act *one's* age
▶ 그녀는 나이에 비해 젊어[늙어] 보인다 She looks young [old] for her age.
▶ 그는 나이에 걸맞지 않게 현실적이다 He is realistic beyond his years.

나이드라지드 〔藥〕 Nydrazid
나이로비 〈케냐의 수도〉 Nairobi
나이배기 a person older than he looks
나이아가라폭포 ―瀑布 the Niagara Falls
나이지리아 〈나라 이름〉 Nigeria; 〈공식명〉 the Federal Republic of Nigeria
♦ 나이지리아의 Nigerian
■ ―사람 a Nigerian
나이키 〈지대공 미사일〉 a Nike
나이터 〔野〕 a night game
나이테 〔植〕 an annual ring
나이트¹ 〈기사〉 a knight
■ ―작위 knighthood
나이트² 〈밤〉 night ■ ―가운 a nightgown; (美) a night-robe ―게임 a night game ―드레스 a nightdress ―캡 a nightcap ―클럽 a nightclub; (口) a night spot
나이팅게일 1 〔鳥〕 a nightingale 2 〈영국의 간호사〉 Nightingale, Florence (1820-1910)
나이프 a knife (*pl.* knives); 〈소형의 접는〉 a pocketknife; 〈접는 식〉 a clasp knife; 〈대형의 선원용〉 a jackknife; 〈식탁용〉 a table knife; 〈고기써는〉 a carving knife; 〈아주 작은〉 a penknife; 〈사냥용〉 a hunting knife
♦ 잘 드는 [무딘] 나이프 a sharp [dull] knife / 나이프를 갈다 sharpen [whet, grind] a knife / 나이프를 펴다 [접다] open [close] (the blade of) a knife / 나이프와 포크로 먹다 eat with (a) knife and fork / 나이프로 찌르다 stab *sb* with a knife; stick [run, plunge] a knife into *sb*; knife *sb*
▶ 이 나이프는 잘 들지 않는다 This knife won't cut (well). ⇌ This knife has a dull [a blunt] edge.
▶ 이 나이프에는 네개의 날과 병따개가 달려 있다 The pocketknife has four blades and a bottle opener.

나이프

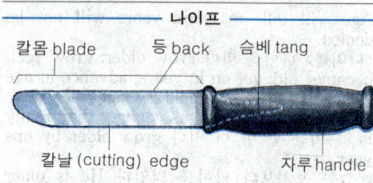

칼몸 blade, 등 back, 슴베 tang, 칼날 (cutting) edge, 자루 handle

나인 a lady-in-waiting; a lady attendant in the palace; an attendant court lady; a lady of the court; a court lady, a maid of honor

나인 〔野〕 the nine

나일강 —江 the Nile; (the) Nile River ■청[백]— Blue [White] Nile

나일론 nylon ■—수지(樹脂) nylon resin —스타킹[양말] (a pair of) nylon stockings; (口) nylons —자일 a nylon rope —제품 nylon goods; nylons

나잇값 behavior appropriate to one's age ◆나잇값도 못하다 be thoughtless for one's age; be unworthy of one's years; be unbecoming to one's age
▶나잇값을 해라 Be [Act] your age! ⇌ You ought to know better at your age.
▶나잇값도 못한 짓은 하지 마라 Stop doing things unbecoming to your age!

나잇살 a mature [an advanced] age ◆나잇살이나 먹어가지고 in spite of one's mature age; being old enough to know better

나전 螺鈿 mother-of-pearl; nacre ■—세공 mother-of-pearl work —칠기 lacquerwork [lacquer ware] inlaid with mother-of-pearl

나조 —調 〔樂〕 (the scale in) B

나졸 邏卒 a patrol(man)

나중 ◆나중의 the next; the latter; the following; later; future; coming / 나중에 afterward(s); after; later (on); some time later; after a time [while]; 〈장차〉 in the future; 〈결국〉 in the end / 나중 생각을 하다 think of the future
▶우리는 나중을 위해서 집을 장만했다 We provided the house for the future.
▶나중에 어떻게 될테지 The future will take care of itself.
▶나중에 전화하겠습니다 I will call you up later.
▶나중에 가겠다 I will come later.
▶나중에 뵙겠습니다 I will see you later.
▶그는 맨 나중에 왔다 He was the last to come.
▶너는 나중에 잘못을 깨닫게 될 것이다 You will realize someday that you were wrong.
▶그것에 대해서는 나중에 또 이야기하자 We will talk about it another time.
▶나중에 참고하기 위해 그것에 대해 듣고 싶습니다 Please tell me about that for my future reference.
▶그것에 관해서는 나중에 이야기하려고 합니다 I'm going to tell you about it later.
▶나중에는 별소리를 다 듣겠다 I never expected to hear such nonsense from you.

나중난 뿔이 우뚝하다 〔속담〕 The younger generation is better prepared.

나지리보다 look down on [upon]; hold sb cheap; think lightly [meanly] of; hold sb in contempt; make a low estimate of; look down one's nose at
▶그는 나를 나지리보았다 He looked down his nose at me.

나지막이 rather low; lowish; somewhat soft ◆나지막이 말하다 say in a low [low-toned] voice

나지막하다 rather low; lowish ◆나지막한 집 a low-built house / 나지막한 소리로 in a low voice; in an undertone; in whispers; under one's breath; 〈저음으로〉 in a low key

나직이 〈위치를〉 low; somewhat low; 〈소리를〉 softly; humbly; modestly
◆나직이 나는 새 birds of somewhat low flight / 집을 나직이 짓다 build a house low / 나직이 노래하다 sing in an undertone; croon

나직하다 〈위치가〉 somewhat low; low; lowish; 〈소리가〉 soft
◆나직한 목소리 a low voice [tone]; a subdued voice / 나직한 산 a low hill
▶이 방은 천장이 나직하다 This room has a low ceiling.
▶그 절은 나직한 언덕에 있다 The temple is (situated) on a low hill.
▶그녀는 나직한 소리로 이야기했다 She spoke in a low voice [an undertone].

나체 裸體 〈알몸〉 a naked body; a nude body ◆나체의 여자 a naked woman / 나체의 naked; nude / 완전 나체의 stark-naked / 나체로 in the nude / 나체가 되다 strip oneself of one's clothes; become (stark) naked / 화가를 위해 나체로 포즈를 취하다 pose nude [in the nude] for an artist
▶그는 그녀의 나체 사진을 찍었다 He photographed her in the nude.
■—반(半)— seminudity: 반나체의 남자 a half-naked man —미 physical beauty; the beauty of the nude —미인[모델] a nude beauty [model] —상(像) a nude statue [figure] —주의 nudism —주의자 a nudist —질주 streaking —행렬 a nude parade —화 a nude (picture) : 나체화를 그리다 paint 《a woman》 in the nude

나치 a Nazi; the Nazis ◆나치의 Nazi ■—당원 a Nazi —독일 Nazi Germany —화 Nazification : 비(非)나치화 denazification / 나치화하다 Nazify

나치즘 〈독일 국가 사회주의〉 Nazism ■네오— neo-Nazism

나침 羅針 a compass needle; the needle of a compass ■—방위(方位) a compass bearing —의(儀) ⇨ 나침반

나침반 羅針盤 a compass ◆항해용 나침반 a mariner's compass / 나침반에 표시된 방향의 points of the compass / 나침반 없이 항해하다 navigate without compass
■삼각— a triangular compass 항공— an aerocompass 회전— a gyrocompass ■—자리 〔天〕 Pyxis

나타나다 1 〈출현하다〉 appear; come in sight; show up; make one's appearance; present

[show] oneself; turn up
♦갑자기 나타나다 burst forth [out]; burst into sight / 꿈에 나타나다 appear in a dream / 불쑥 나타나다 make an abrupt appearance; pop out [up]; turn up; 〈문제 등이〉 crop out [up]
▶그는 늦게야 나타났다 He turned up late.
▶태양이 구름 사이로 나타났다 The sun came out [emerged] from behind the clouds.
▶우리 앞에 그 항구의 불빛이 나타났다 The light from the port came in sight [into view] ahead of us.
▶그 여배우가 무대에 나타났다 The actress came on stage.
▶덤불 속에서 갑자기 표범이 나타났다 A leopard burst forth out of the bush.
▶때마침 경찰관이 현장에 나타났다 A policeman made a timely appearance upon the scene.
2 〈겉으로 드러나다〉 show; appear; show [manifest, display] itself; assert [reveal, envisage, express] itself; be exposed; be revealed
♦표면에 나타나다 come to the surface; appear on the surface
▶너는 화를 내면 얼굴에 나타난다 When you get angry, it tends to show on your face.
▶그 테마는 그의 작품의 곳곳에 나타난다 The theme appears throughout his work.
▶이 사실에서 그가 믿을 만한 사람이라는 것이 나타난다 This fact shows him to be a reliable person.
▶놀라는 빛이 그의 얼굴에 나타났다 A look of surprise came over his face.
▶그의 얼굴에 피로의 기색이 나타났다 Fatigue was written on his face.
▶그의 얼굴에는 실망의 빛이 나타났다 His disappointment showed on his face.
▶그녀의 얼굴에 후회의 빛이 나타났다 Repentance revealed itself on her face.
▶그와 친해짐에 따라 그의 이기심이 점점 나타나기 시작했다 As I came to know him, his selfishness gradually began to show itself.
▶그의 견실한 성품이 나타나기 시작했다 The firmness of his nature began to assert itself.
3 〈발견되다〉 be discovered; be found (out); 〈탄로나다〉 be revealed; come [be brought] to light; be exposed [disclosed, detected]; be laid bare
▶몇가지 사실이 나타났다 A few facts have come [been brought] to light.
▶잃어버렸던 시계가 서랍에서 나타났다 My lost watch turned up in the drawer.
4 〈기록 등에 실리다〉 be mentioned; be given
▶그 역사적인 대사건은 문헌에 나타나 있다 The great historical event is mentioned in literature.
나타내다 1 〈보이다〉 show [display] (one's ability); betray (one's anger); indicate (one's approval); be indicative of (a good nature); manifest (dissatisfaction); exhibit (one's interest); bring out (invisible writing) by heat; 〈증명하다〉 prove; speak for; bespeak
♦노염을 나타내다 show one's anger / 수완을 나타내다 display one's ability
▶그는 그 모임에 갑자기 모습을 나타냈다 He suddenly appeared [showed up] at the meeting.
▶이 사실은 그의 강한 인내심을 나타내는 것이다 This fact proves [indicates] his perseverance.
▶다람쥐가 나뭇가지에 모습을 나타냈다 A squirrel appeared on a branch.
▶그는 그 회합에 모습을 나타내지 않았다 He didn't turn up at the meeting.
2 〈드러내다〉 expose (one's ignorance); show (one's true colors); disclose; betray (emotion); reveal; bare (one's heart)
♦정체[본색]를 나타내다 betray oneself; show oneself in one's true light
3 〈표현하다〉 express; give expression (to); import; convey; voice
♦생각을 말로 나타내다 put [express] one's thoughts into words / 말로 나타낼 수 없다 be inexpressible; be beyond expression
▶이 그림에서 그는 그의 애절한 슬픔을 나타내고 있다 In this painting, he expresses his deep sorrow.
▶우리의 기쁨을 말로 나타낼 수 없다 Our pleasure is beyond words.
▶그는 아직 영어로 자기의 생각을 나타낼 수가 없다 He still can't express himself in English.
4 〈의미하다〉 stand for; represent; 〈상징하다〉 symbolize ♦기호로 나타내다 represent by signs
▶비둘기는 평화를 나타낸다 The dove symbolizes peace.
▶이 기호는 무엇을 나타냅니까? What does this sign stand for?
5 〈두드러지게 하다〉 distinguish
♦이름을 나타내다 become famous; distinguish oneself; make one's name
▶음악에서 그녀는 단연 두각을 나타냈다 She distinguished herself in music.
▶그는 학계에서 두각을 나타낼 것이다 He will cut a (conspicuous) figure in the scholarly world.
나태 懶怠 laziness; idleness; indolence
—나태하다 idle; lazy (person); indolent; sluggish; slothful
▶그는 본래 나태한 인간이다 He is lazy by nature.
▶그녀는 나태한 생활을 하고 있다 She is leading a lazy [an idle] life.
■—심 a lazy mind; a disinclination to work
나토 NATO [〈North Atlantic Treaty Organization〉]
나트륨 〔化〕 sodium; natrium
나팔 喇叭 〈악단용의〉 a trumpet; a cornet; 〈군대용의〉 a bugle; a horn
♦나팔 모양의 trumpet-shaped / 나팔을 불다 blow [sound] a trumpet [bugle]; (비유) talk big; blow one's own trumpet [(美) horn] / 진군 [돌격, 후퇴] 나팔을 불다 sound the march [charge, retreat]
■—바 지 bell-bottom(ed) trousers; bell-bottoms —수 a bugler; a trumpeter : 나팔수가 진군 나팔을 불었다 The bugler signaled

나팔거리다 [sounded] the advance.
나팔거리다 flatter ⇨ 너펄거리다
나팔관 喇叭管 〖解〗 the Fallopian tube; the trumpet; the oviduct
 ■ —염(炎) salpingitis
나팔꽃 喇叭— 〖植〗 a morning glory ◆ 나팔꽃 모양의 trumpet-shaped; funnel-shaped
나팔벌레 喇叭— 〖動〗 a stentor
나팔불다 喇叭— **1** 〈나팔소리를 내다〉 blow a bugle; sound a trumpet
2 〈술 등을 병째 마시다〉 drink 《whiskey》 (straight) from a bottle; drink out of an up-ended 《beer》 bottle
3 〈소문을 퍼뜨리다〉 make known; trumpet; spread 《the news》; 〈떠벌리다〉 talk big; brag; blow hard; draw a long blow; 《美口》 blow [toot] *one's* own trumpet [horn]
4 〈어린애가 울다〉 cry; shout; yell
나팔소리 喇叭— a bugle note; a trumpet [bugle] call
 ◆ 나팔소리가 화려하게 울리는 가운데 with a flourish of bugles; with a fanfare
 ▶ 소집 나팔소리가 울려퍼졌다 A bugle [trumpet] call rang out. ⇒ A bugle [trumpet] was sounded.
나포 拿捕 seizure; capture —**나포하다** seize; capture; make a prize of ▶ 그들은 어선 세 척을 나포했다 They captured [seized] three fishing boats.
 ■ 불법— illegal seizure ■ —선(船) a captured ship; a prize
나폴레옹 〈프랑스 황제〉 Napoleon, Bonaparte (1769-1821) — 법전 the Napoleonic Code — 전쟁 the Napoleonic Wars
나폴리 〈이탈리아의 항구 도시〉 Naples ◆ 나폴리의 Neapolitan
나풋거리다 flutter lightly; flap gently ▶ 깃발이 바람에 나풋거리고 있다 The flag is flapping [fluttering] lightly in the wind.
나풀거리다 flutter [flap] roughly
나프타 〖化〗 naphtha ■ —분해 naphtha cracking
나프탈렌 〖化〗 naphthalene; naphthalin(e)
나프톨 〖化〗 naphthol
나한 羅漢 an arahant (⇨ 아라한) ◆ 5백 나한 Buddha's five hundred disciples who attained Nirvana
나한에도 모래 먹는 나한이 있다 〈속담〉 High position is no guarantee against hardship.
나화 裸花 〖植〗 an achlamydeous [a naked] flower
나훔 〖聖〗 The Book of Nahum; Nahum (略 Nah.)
나흗날 the fourth day (of a month)
나흘 **1** 〈4일간〉 four days **2** ⇨ 나흗날
낙 樂 〈즐거움〉 (a) pleasure; (an) enjoyment; (a) delight; 〈기분 전환〉 a diversion; 〈오락〉 amusement; 〈취미〉 taste; hobby
 ◆ 전원 생활의 낙 the pleasures [delights] of country life / 낙으로 하는 일 a labor of love / 독서에서 낙을 얻다 get pleasure from (reading) books / …을 낙으로 삼고 기다리다 look forward to 《the New Year》 with pleasure
 ▶ 우리 아버지는 낚시가 낙이시다 Fishing is my father's hobby [amusement].
 ▶ 그 아이는 부모의 유일한 낙이다 The boy was his parent's only hope.
 ▶ 그는 무엇보다도 여행을 하는 것이 낙이었다 Nothing gave him more pleasure than travelling.
 ▶ 음악을 듣는 것이 그에게는 큰 낙이었다 Listening to music was a great pleasure to him. ⇒ He took great pleasure in listening to music.
 ▶ 그의 주된 낙은 정원 가꾸기다 His chief pleasure [enjoyment, amusement] is gardening. ⇒ Gardening is his chief pleasure.
 ▶ 아주 가난한 생활에도 낙은 있는 법이다 The poorest life has its enjoyment.
 ▶ 나는 돈 때문이 아니라 낙으로 야채를 재배한다 I raise vegetables for love, not money.
 ▶ 나는 낙으로 그림을 그린다 I paint for pleasure [fun].
 ▶ 할아버지는 원예를 낙으로 삼고 계시다 My grandfather takes pleasure in [enjoys] gardening.
낙과 落果 〈떨어지기〉 falling of unripe fruit; 〈떨어진 과실〉 fallen fruit —**낙과하다** fruit falls
낙관 落款 a writer's [painter's] signature; a painter's sign and seal
 ◆ 낙관이 없는 그림 an unsigned painting / 작자의 낙관이 있다 bear the writer's [painter's] signature
 ▶ 이 그림에는 낙관이 없다 This picture bears neither the artist's signature nor his seal.
 —**낙관하다** sign and seal
낙관 樂觀 optimism (↔pessimism); an optimistic [a rosy] view; sanguine [optimistic] hopes
 ▶ 사태는 아직 낙관을 불허한다 The situation is still too serious for comfort.
 ▶ 그의 병은 낙관을 불허한다 His illness does not warrant any optimism. ⇒ We can't be optimistic [hopeful] about his illness.
 —**낙관하다** be optimistic 《about》; take an optimistic [a rosy] view 《of》; look on the bright side of things; have optimistic views 《on》; assume an optimistic attitude 《toward》; take things easily; paint a rosy picture 《of》
 ◆ 전도를 낙관하다 be optimistic about the future; take an optimistic view regarding the future
 ▶ 너무 낙관하면 나중에 후회할지도 모른다 If you are too optimistic, you may regret it later.
 ▶ 너무 낙관하지 마라 Don't paint too rosy a picture of things. ⇒ Don't be too sure of success.
 ■ —론 an optimistic [a rosy] view —론자[주의자] an optimist —주의 optimism
낙관적 樂觀的 optimistic; rosy; hopeful; sanguine
 ◆ 낙관적인 인생관 an optimistic [a rosy] view of life / 지나치게 낙관적이다 be too optimistic [easy-going]; paint too rosy a picture of things / 매사를 낙관적으로 보다 view [see]

things in an optimistic light; take a rose-colored view of things; take things easy
▶ 그는 매사에 낙관적이다 He takes an optimistic view [looks on the bright side] of everything. ⇌ He is optimistic about everything.
▶ 그는 이 문제의 결과에 대해 낙관적이다 He is optimistic about [has optimistic views on] the outcome of the problem.

낙길 落— an uncomplete set of books

낙낙하다 enough; sufficient ◆ 낙낙한 옷 a loose jacket

낙농 酪農 dairying; dairy farming
▶ 그는 낙농에 종사하고 있다 He runs a dairy farm. ⇌ He is engaged in dairy farming.
■ —가 a dairy farmer; a dairyman —업 dairy farming; the dairy business [industry] —장 a dairy (farm); (美) a milk ranch —품 dairy products [goods]

낙담 落膽 discouragement; dejection; despondency; dismay; 〈실망〉 disappointment
—**낙담하다** be discouraged; be disheartened [downhearted]; be dejected; lose courage [heart]; be cast down; be dispirited; be disappointed
◆ 낙담시키다 discourage; dishearten; disappoint
▶ 그는 입학시험에 떨어져 낙담했다 He was disappointed because he (had) failed the entrance examination.
▶ 부인은 남편이 죽었을 때 무척 낙담했다 When her husband died, she fell into despondency.
▶ 그는 그 소식을 듣고 아주 낙담하고 있다 He is greatly disappointed [discouraged] by the news.

낙도 落島 an outlying island; an out-island; a distant [remote] island ▶ 그 죄인은 낙도에 유배되었다 The convict was transported to a remote island.

낙락장송 落落長松 a tall and exuberant pine tree; a pine tree with trailing branches

낙뢰 落雷 the falling of a thunderbolt ◆ 낙뢰로 입은 피해 lightning damage
▶ 내 별장에 낙뢰가 있었다 My cottage was struck [hit] by lightning. ⇌ Lightning struck [hit] my cottage.
▶ 그는 낙뢰로 죽었다 He was killed by lightning
—**낙뢰하다** 〈장소 등이 주어〉 be struck by (a bolt of) lightning

낙루 落淚 the dropping of tears; shedding tears
—**낙루하다** shed [drop] tears
▶ 우리는 그 슬픈 이야기에 감동되어 낙루했다 We were moved to tears by the sad story.

낙마 落馬 a fall from a horse; (口) a spill
—**낙마하다** fall from [off] a horse; have a fall [spill] from *one's* horse
▶ 그는 경마 도중에 낙마했다 He fell [was thrown] off his horse in the race.

낙망 落望 (a) disappointment; despondency; despair; dejection; discouragement; hopelessness; (口) a letdown

—**낙망하다** be disappointed; be discouraged 《at, by》; lose (*one's*) hope(s)
▶ 그는 낙망한 나머지 자살했다 Despair led him to suicide.

낙명 落命 losing *one's* life; death —**낙명하다** die; lose *one's* life; pass away; be killed ▶ 그는 불의의 재난으로 낙명했다 He was killed [lost his life] in a sudden accident.

낙반 落磐 a cave-in; a roof-fall ▶ 낙반 사고가 나서 광부 세 사람이 죽었다 The mine roof caved in and three miners were killed. —**낙반하다** cave [fall] in

낙방 落榜 failure in an examination; (美口) flunk —**낙방하다** fail 《in》 an examination; (美口) flunk 《an exam》

낙법 落法 〖柔道〗 safe way of falling down
■ 전방(前方)— a forward fall

낙부 諾否 yes or no; consent or refusal; approval and [or] disapproval
◆ 낙부의 회답 an answer in the affirmative or negative
▶ 낙부를 즉시 우편으로 회답해 주시기 바랍니다 Please tell me whether you accept it or not by return mail.

낙상 落傷 an injury [a bruise, a hurt] from a fall —**낙상하다** fall and hurt *oneself*; get hurt from a fall

낙서 落書 scribbling; scrawling; 〈생각에 골몰하고 있을 때의〉 doodling; 〈벽・공중변소 등의〉 graffiti; 〈낙서한 것〉 a scribble; a scrabble; a scrawl
◆ 화장실 벽의 낙서를 지우다 clean the graffiti off the wall of a lavatory
▶ 벽은 낙서 투성이었다 The walls were covered with graffiti.
▶ 낙서 금지 (게시) No Graffiti. ⇌ No Scribbling.
—**낙서하다** do [write] graffiti 《on the wall》; scribble; scrabble; scrawl; (美口) doodle 《in *one's* notebook》
◆ 벽에 낙서하다 do graffiti [make scribbles] on the wall; scribble [scrawl] on the wall
▶ 아이들이 벽에 크레용으로 낙서했다 The children scribbled on the wall in crayon.
▶ 교과서에 낙서하면 안된다 Don't doodle in the textbook.

낙석 落石 〈떨어지는 돌〉 a falling rock; 〈돌이 떨어짐〉 a fall of rocks; a rock-slide
▶ 낙석으로 길이 막혔다 A fall of rocks blocked the road.
▶ 낙석 주의 (게시) Watch for falling rocks. ⇌ Beware of falling rocks.
■ —사고 a rock-slide accident; an accident caused by falling stones

낙선 落選 〈선거의〉 failure in an election; 〈전람회의〉 rejection
—**낙선하다** 〈선거에서〉 be defeated [unsuccessful] in an election; lose [fail in] an election; 〈작품이〉 be rejected
▶ 그는 총선에서 낙선했다 He was defeated [unsuccessful] in the general election.
▶ 그의 그림은 낙선했다 His picture was rejected [not accepted].
▶ 그는 불과 세 표 차이로 낙선했다 He failed

낙성

to win [missed winning] the election by only three votes.
▶ 그는 다음 선거에서 낙선할 것이다 He will lose the next election. ⇒ He won't be elected in the next election.
■—자 an unsuccessful [a defeated] candidate —작 a rejected [an unaccepted] work

낙성 落成 completion (of a building)
—**낙성하다** finish; complete; be completed; be finished
▶ 새 체육관이 낙성되었다 The new gymnasium has been completed [finished].
▶ 새 교사(校舍)는 다음 달에 낙성될 예정이다 The new school building is to be completed next month.

낙성 落城 the fall of a castle —**낙성하다** fall; surrender

낙성식 落成式 an inauguration [a completion] ceremony
♦ 낙성식을 거행하다 inaugurate [dedicate] (a new building); hold an inauguration [a completion] ceremony; celebrate the (official) opening of (a building)
▶ 이달 3일에 그 공사의 낙성식이 거행되었다 The completion of the work was celebrated on the 3rd of this month.

낙수 落水 eavesdrops (⇨ 낙숫물) ■—받이 〈평행홈통〉 an eaves trough [spout]; 〈수직홈통〉(美) a drainspout

낙수 落穗 1 〈이삭〉 fallen ears (of grain) ♦ 낙수를 줍다 glean
2 〈뒷얘기〉 an episode

낙숫물 落水— raindrops from the eaves; eavesdrops ♦ 낙숫물 소리 the pattering of raindrops [eavesdrops] ▶ 낙숫물이 떨어지고 있다 Eavesdrops are falling.

낙숫물이 댓돌을 뚫는다 (속담) Falling drops will in time drill a hole in stone. ⇒ Constant dropping wears away a stone.

낙승 樂勝 an easy win [victory]; (口) a walk-over; a walkaway
▶ 그 경기는 낙승이었다 The game was an easy victory [win]. ⇒ We won the game easily. ⇒ We had an easy win [won an easy victory] at the game.
—**낙승하다** win in a walk; win [beat] easily; win an easy victory (over); (口) win (a game) hands down; have a walkover
▶ 우리 팀은 메츠 팀에 낙승했다 Our team won an easy victory over New York Mets.

낙심 落心 discouragement; disappointment; disheartenment; frustration; dejection; despair
♦ 낙심 천만이다 be much discouraged [disappointed]
—**낙심하다** be [get] disheartened; be dejected; be discouraged; lose heart [courage]
♦ 낙심하여 disappointedly; in disappointment / 낙심시키다 dispirit; dishearten; discourage; deject; disappoint
▶ 그는 시험에 떨어져서 낙심꾼이 되고 있다 He is discouraged by his failure in the examination.
▶ 낙심하지 마라 Don't be discouraged! ⇒

Don't lose your heart!
▶ 나는 이런 사소한 실패로 낙심하지 않는다 I am not discouraged at such a minor failure.
▶ 수많은 어려움에도 낙심하지 않고 그는 옳다고 믿는 것을 해나갔다 Undaunted by many difficulties, he did what he thought was right.

낙양 洛陽 〈중국 지명〉 Loyang ▶ 그의 저서는 낙양의 지가(紙價)를 올렸다 His book appealed to the public and had tremendous sales. ⇒ His book sold immensely well.

낙엽 落葉 〈떨어진 잎〉 fallen [dead] leaves; 〈떨어지기〉 the fall of leaves
♦ 낙엽이 지다 〈나무가 주어〉 shed [lose, drop, cast] (its) leaves; 〈잎이 주어〉 leaves fall (off a tree) / 낙엽을 긁어 모으다 rake up fallen leaves
▶ 떡갈나무는 겨울에는 낙엽이 진다 Oaks shed their leaves in winter.
▶ 그 나무는 완전히 낙엽이 졌다 The tree has lost all its leaves. ⇒ The leaves are all gone off the tree.
▶ 낙엽이 지고 있다 The leaves are falling. ⇒ The trees are shedding their leaves.
■—기(期) defoliation —송 a larch (tree) —수 a deciduous tree

낙오 落伍 〈대열에서 뒤처짐〉 falling behind; straggling; 〈시대·사회에서의〉 being out of step with the times
—**낙오하다** straggle; drop [fall] out; drop [fall] behind (the others); drop to the rear
♦ 경주에서 낙오하다 drop out of a race / 대열에서 낙오하다 lag behind the line
▶ 열 사람의 주자 가운데 네 사람이 낙오했다 Four of the ten runners dropped out.
▶ 그는 트랙을 한 바퀴 돌기 전에 낙오했다 He dropped out before completing one lap (of the track).

낙오자 落伍者 〈대열 등의〉 a straggler; a dropout; 〈인생의〉 a failure ♦ 인생의 낙오자 a derelict; (social) failure; a social outcast
▶ 그는 인생의 낙오자다 He is a failure [loser] in life.
▶ 그 행군에서 많은 낙오자가 생겼다 Many soldiers dropped out during the march.

낙원 樂園 (a) paradise; Eden
♦ 어린이의 낙원 a paradise for children / 자연의 낙원 Nature's paradise; a natural paradise / 지상 낙원 an earthly paradise; a paradise on earth
▶ 그 섬은 새들의 낙원이다 The island is a paradise for birds.
▶ 그 소국은 지상 낙원이었다 The small country was an earthly paradise.

낙인 烙印 a brand; a stigma (pl. ~s, -mata)
♦ 낙인을 찍다 brand (cattle); stigmatize; (비유) brand (sb as a Communist) / 반역자라는 낙인이 찍히다 be branded (as) a rebel
▶ 소들은 모두 낙인이 찍혀 있다 These cows are all branded with a mark.
▶ 그는 사기꾼이라는 낙인이 찍혔다 He was branded [stigmatized] as a swindler.
▶ 저놈은 낙인 찍힌 악당이다 He is branded as a villain. ⇒ He is a thoroughgoing scoundrel.

낙일 落日 the setting [declining] sun; sunset;

(美) sundown
낙자 落字 an omitted word ⇨ 탈자(脫字)
낙장 落張 a missing page; a missing leaf
▶ 3페이지에서 5페이지까지 낙장이다 Pages three to five are missing.
▶ 이 책에는 4페이지의 낙장이 있다 There are four pages missing in this book.
■ **—본**(本) a book with missing pages; a defective book
낙장거리 falling outstretched on *one's* back —**낙장거리하다** fall [be thrown] flat [outstretched] on *one's* back; fall backward
낙제 落第 **1** 〈유급〉 failure (in an examination) —**낙제하다** fail in an examination; (口) flunk 〈an exam〉; stay back in the class
▶ 그는 시험에 낙제했다 He failed the examination. ⇒ (口) He flunked the exam.
▶ 그 교사는 수학에서 다섯 명을 낙제시켰다 The teacher failed [(口) flunked] five students in mathematics.
2 〈실격〉 rejection
▶ 나는 남편으로서는 낙제다 I'm a failure as (a) husband.
▶ 이런 것을 모르다니 자네는 사업가로서는 낙제야 How can you call yourself a businessman, if you don't know such things?
▶ 그 상품은 수출품으로는 낙제였다 The article was eliminated [rejected] from the list of exports.
■ **—생** a failure; a holdover; a failed student; a flunked student; (美) a repeater **—점** a failing mark [grade]: 그는 수학에서 낙제점을 받았다 He got a failing grade [mark] in mathematics.
낙조 落照 the glow of the sunset; the setting [evening, sinking] sun
▶ 이렇게 아름다운 낙조를 보는 것은 몇년만이 다 I've not seen such a beautiful sunset as this for years.
낙지 〔動〕 octopus ■ **—볶음** panbroiled octopus (seasoned with red pepper)
낙진 落塵 (atomic) fallout
낙질 落帙 an uncomplete set of books=낙질
낙차 落差 〈물의〉〔物〕 a head; a fall; a water level ♦ 낙차 100미터의 폭포 a waterfall 100 meters high
▶ 이 폭포의 낙차는 97미터다 This waterfall is 97 meters high.
▶ 물이 20미터의 낙차로 골짜기에 떨어지고 있 다 The water drops 20 meters into the gorge below.
■ **유효—** an effective [a net] head
낙착 落着 〈일의 결말〉 a conclusion; a settlement; (a) decision; an end
♦ 낙착을 보다 be settled; come to settlement [conclusion]; come to an end / 아직 낙착을 보 지 못하다 be still pending
▶ 사건은 아직 낙착을 보지 못하고 있다 The case is still pending.
—**낙착하다** be settled; come to a settlement [conclusion, close]
▶ 마침내 이 사건은 잘 낙착되었다 At last the matter was brought to a happy end.

▶ 낙착될 때까지 그와 상의하겠다 I'll have it out with him.
낙찰 落札 a successful bid
—**낙찰하다** *one's* tender 《for repairing the vessel》 is accepted [successful]; 〈사람이 주 어〉 make a successful bid 《for》; 〈사물이 주 어〉 be knocked down to *one*
▶ 그 토지는 그에게 낙찰되었다 He made a successful bid for the land.
▶ 그 건축공사의 청부는 그에게 낙찰되었다 The contract for the construction was awarded to him.
▶ 우리 회사가 그 빌딩 건설 계약을 낙찰받았다 Our company has made a successful bid for a contract for the construction of the building. ⇒ Our company has won a contract for the construction of the building.
■ **—가격** the contract price; the price of the highest bid **—물** an object knocked down **—인**[자] a successful bidder
낙천 落薦 a failure in an application 《for nomination》—**낙천하다** fail in (*one's*) application 《for nomination》■ **—자** an unsuccessful applicant [candidate]
낙천 樂天 optimism
■ **—가** an optimist; an easygoing person **—관** an optimistic [a hopeful, a rosy] view **—주의** optimism **—주의자** an optimist **—지** 〈낙토〉 a paradise
낙천적 樂天的 optimistic 《about》; easygoing; rose-colored; happy-go-lucky
♦ 낙천적인 인생관을 갖다 have an optimistic [cheerful] view of life
▶ 그는 매사에 낙천적이다 He is optimistic about everything. ⇒ He takes things easy.
▶ 그것은 매우 낙천적인 견해다 That's quite an optimistic view.
▶ 그런 낙천적인 생각은 버려라 You should discard such an easygoing view. ⇒ You shouldn't take things so easy.
낙체 落體 〔物〕 a falling body ♦ 낙체의 법칙 the law of falling bodies
낙타 駱駝 〔動〕 a camel ♦ 낙타의 혹 a (camel's) hump
▶ 아라비아산 낙타는 등에 큰 혹이 하나 있다 An Arabian camel has one large hump on its back.
■ **단봉—** a dromedary; an Arabian [a one-humped] camel **쌍봉—** a Bactrian [two-humped] camel ■ **—지**(地) camel('s) hair cloth; camlet
낙태 落胎 〔醫〕 an abortion; aborticide; a miscarriage —**낙태하다** abort; miscarry; have an abortion
♦ 낙태시키다 cause [induce] abortion; commit feticide; procure abortion
■ **—수술** a surgical operation to cause abortion: 낙태 수술을 하다[받다] perform [undergo] a criminal operation 《on》 **—아**(兒) an abortive offspring **—약** an abortive medicine [drug]; an abortifacient **—죄** aborticide; feticide; criminal abortion
낙토 樂土 (a) paradise; Heaven
낙하 落下 a fall; falling; dropping; (a)

낙하산

descent
♦ 운석의 낙하 the fall of a meteorite (on the earth) / 낙하의 법칙 the law of falling
—낙하하다 fall; drop; come down ♦ 수직으로 낙하하다 fall plumb down
▶ 비행기 파편이 그 건물에 낙하했다 Part of an airplane fell [dropped] on the building.
▶ 그 운석은 시베리아에 낙하했다 The meteorite fell in Siberia.

낙하산 落下傘 a parachute; (口) a chute
♦ 낙하산을 펴다 release a parachute / 낙하산으로 내리다 parachute (down); descend by parachute; come down in a parachute; 〈비행기에서 탈출하다〉 bail out; 〈부대가〉 make an airborne landing / 부대[식량]를 낙하산으로 섬에 투하하다 parachute troops [provisions] onto the island
▶ 낙하산으로 내리는 데는 용기가 필요하다 You need courage to make a parachute jump [come down by parachute].
■ —병 a parachutist; a paratrooper —부대 parachute troops; paratroops

낙향 落鄕 rustication —낙향하다 leave the capital [Seoul]; rusticate; retire into the country [to *one's* native place]
▶ 그는 낙향하여 살았다 He left Seoul to retire into the country.

낙화 烙畫 〈인두로 지져서 그린〉 a poker picture [work]; a pyrograph ♦ 낙화 꽃 도안을 design of flowers in poker work / 낙화를 그리다 poker

낙화 落花 〈꽃이 짐〉 falling of blossoms [flowers]; 〈진 꽃〉 fallen blossoms; 〈지는 꽃〉 falling blossoms
♦ 낙화처럼 흩날리는 눈 snow whirling down like falling blossom petals
—낙화하다 flowers [blossoms] fall [scatter]
■ —유수 fallen blossoms on a stream; (비유) mutual love [attachment]

낙화생 落花生 〈植〉 a peanut ⇨ 땅콩

낙후 落後 falling behind
—낙후하다 drop [fall, lag, be left] behind (the others); be behind [backward]; be in arrear (the times) ♦ 낙후된 lagging behind; backward 《country》
▶ 우리는 예방의학에서 세계 여러 나라에 비해 낙후되어 있다 We lag behind most countries in the world in preventive medicine.

낚다 1 〈물고기를〉 fish 《carp》; angle 《for fish》; hook
♦ 얼음을 깨고 고기를 낚다 fish through the ice / 강에서 물고기를 낚다 fish (in) a river / 지렁이를 미끼로 고기를 낚다 fish with the bait of an earthworm / 낚아 올리다 fish [hook] up; land
▶ 오늘은 많이 낚았다 I have had [made] a good catch today.
▶ 여기는 고기를 낚기에 좋은 장소가 아니다 This is not a good fishing spot.
2 〈이름을〉 ♦ 돈으로 명예를 낚다 angle for fame by money
3 〈이성을〉 decoy; entice; draw on ♦ 여자를 낚다 entice a woman; pick up a girl

낚시 〈낚싯바늘〉 a fish hook; a hook; 〈낚시질〉 fishing; angling
♦ 낚시에 미끼를 달다 put [fix] a (piece of) bait on a hook / 낚시에 걸리다 be hooked; be caught on the hook
▶ 그는 낚시 명수다 He is a good [an expert] angler. ⇌ He is good at fishing.
▶ 나는 젊었을 때는 곧잘 낚시를 즐겼다 I would often enjoy fishing while I was young.
■ 강[민물]— river [freshwater] fishing 바다— sea fishing 밤— night fishing [angling]; fishing by night ■ —꾼 an angler; a rodman; a rodster —도구 fishing tackle [gear, rig, equipment] —바구니 a creel; a fish basket —친구 a fishing companion; a fellow angler —터 a fishing place [spot] —회 a fishing [an angling, an anglers'] fraternity [club]

낚시질 fishing (with rod and line); angling
♦ 낚시질을 잘하다 be good at fishing; be a good angler / 낚시질을 좋아하다 be fond of fishing
▶ 낚시질이 그의 취미다 Fishing is his hobby.
—낚시질하다 fish (with rod and line); angle 《for carp, in a stream》
♦ 낚시질하러 가다 go fishing [angling]; go on a fishing excursion

낚시찌 a float; a quill; a cork; a bob ♦ 낚시찌가 까딱거리다[내려가다] a float bobs up and down [dips in] / 낚싯줄에 낚시찌를 달다 fix a float to a fishing line

낚싯거루 a fishing boat [skiff]

낚싯대 a fishing rod [pole]; an angling rod

낚싯바늘 a fishhook; a hook ♦ 낚싯바늘에 미끼를 달다 bait a hook; put a bait on a fishhook

낚싯밥 a bait

낚싯봉 a sink; a (fishing) sinker; a (fishing) weight; a bullet; a lead; a plummet ♦ 낚싯줄에 낚싯봉을 달다 weight a line

낚싯줄 a fishing line; a fishline ♦ 낚싯줄을 드리우다[던지다] drop [cast] a line ▶ 강둑에 여러 명의 남자가 낚싯줄을 드리우고 있다 Several men are angling on the riverbank.

낚아채다 〈낚시로〉 strike 《a fish》; 〈잡아채다〉 snatch *sth* (away) 《from, off》
▶ 그 남자는 그에게서 돈 뭉치를 낚아채 가지고 도망쳤다 The man snatched a bundle of notes from him and ran away.

난 亂 a war; a rebellion ⇨ 난리

난 欄 〈신문 등의〉 a column; a section; a page; 〈기입하는〉 a blank; a column; 〈여백〉 a space
▶ 소정의 난에 이름을 기입하시오 Please write your name in the allotted space.
▶ 이 난에는 기입하지 마시오 Do not write in this space.

난- 難- 〈곤란〉 difficult; troublesome; hard ♦ 난문제 a difficult [stiff, tough] problem [question]

-난 -難 〈곤란〉 trouble; difficulty; 〈부족〉 shortage
♦ 교통난 a traffic mess [jam, congestion] / 생활난 difficulty in making a living / 식량난 the difficulty of obtaining food / 주택난 a housing shortage / 취직난 a job shortage

-난 -欄 ♦ 스포츠난 the sports columns
난각 卵殼 an eggshell
난간 欄干 〈철책〉 a guardrail; a rail(ing); a handrail; 〈계단의〉 banisters; a parapet; a balustrade
♦ 다리의 난간 a bridge railing; the parapet of a bridge / 난간에 기대다 lean upon the handrail
▶ 난간에서 몸을 내밀면 위험하다 It is dangerous to lean over the railing.
■─동자〔建〕 a banister; a baluster ─법수(法首)〔建〕 the ornamental top of a railing

난감하다 難堪─ 〈견디기 어렵다〉 undurable; unbearable; insufferable; intolerable; 〈할 바를 모르다〉 bewildered; at a loss; at *one's* wit's [wits] end; all at sea
▶ 그에게 거절당했을 때 나는 난감했다 I was at a loss [at my wit's end] when he turned me down.
▶ 그는 그 문제를 풀 일이 난감했다 He was puzzled about how to solve the problem.

난거지 든부자 ─富者 a poor-looking rich man

난경 難境 a predicament; a difficult situation
♦ 난경을 벗어나다 weather [get through] a difficulty; get out of the predicament / 난경에 처하다 be in a fix; be in hot water
▶ 그는 어떤 난경에도 대처할 수가 있다 He is equal to any difficult situation.

난공불락 難攻不落 impregnability; inexpugnability
♦ 난공불락의 inexpugnable; unconquerable / 난공불락의 요새 an impregnable fortress / 난공불락이다 be impregnable; be hard of approach
▶ 그 요새는 난공불락으로 보였다 The fortress seemed impregnable.

난공사 難工事 a difficult construction [building] work

난관 卵管 〔解〕 an oviduct; a uterine [Fallopian] tube

난관 難關 〈곤란한 일〉 difficulty; 〈장애〉 a barrier; an obstacle; 〈넘어야 할 장벽〉 a hurdle; 〈난국〉 a difficult situation
♦ 난관을 극복하다 overcome [tide over] a difficulty; conquer all difficulties / 난관에 봉착하다 meet with a difficulty; encounter a difficult situation; 〈협상 등이〉 come to a deadlock; run into [hit, strike, come up against] a snag
▶ 마침내 그는 그 난관을 극복했다 At last he overcame the difficulty [got over the barrier].
▶ 양국의 협상은 어획 할당량에서 난관에 봉착했다 The two countries reached a deadlock over the catch quota.
▶ 그는 경쟁률이 10대 1이나 되는 입시의 난관에 도전했다 He took the fiercely competitive entrance examination which only one applicant out of ten could pass.

난구 難句 a difficult phrase; a hard passage
난국 亂局 a tumultuous situation
난국 難局 〈곤란한 상황〉 a difficult [grave] situation [position]; 〈곤란〉 a difficulty; 〈위기〉 a crisis 《*pl.* crises》; 〈교착 상태〉 a deadlock
♦ 난국을 극복[타개]하다 get over a difficulty [crisis]; weather [get through] a difficulty; break the deadlock / 난국을 바로잡아 straighten [iron] out a bad situation / 난국을 수습하다 save [settle] a difficult situation / 난국에 대처하다 deal [cope, grapple] with a difficult situation; face [meet] a difficulty / 과감히 난국에 맞서다 take the bull by the horns; rise to a crisis; stand in the breach / 난국에 처해 있다 be in a difficult situation; be in hot water; find *oneself* in a fix [tight place]
▶ 그는 침착하게 난국에 맞섰다 He faced [grappled with] the difficulty calmly.
♦ 우리는 국가의 존망에 관계되는 난국에 처해 있다 We are now facing [confronted with] a national crisis.
▶ 나는 어떤 난국에도 대처할 각오가 되어 있다 I'm fully prepared to face any difficulty [deal with any difficult situation].

난기류 亂氣流 〔氣〕 (air) turbulence; turbulent air
▶ 비행기가 지금 난기류를 만났습니다 〈기장이 승객에게〉 We are experiencing some air turbulence just now. ⇒ We have [The plane has] hit some turbulence.

난낭 卵囊 〔動〕 an ovisac; an egg case

난다긴다하다 〈보통 이상이다〉 be far above the average; 〈뛰어나다〉 be outstanding; be incomparably deft [adroit]; stand out; display versatility; 〈특히 우수하다〉 be exceptionally good
♦ 난다긴다하는 사람 a man of unusual ability
▶ 그는 운동에서는 난다긴다한다 He stands out when it comes to sports [athletics].

난당 亂黨 rioters; a mob; insurgents

난대 暖帶 the warm-temperate zone; the subtropical zone; 〈아열대〉 the subtropics
■─림 a warm-temperate forest; a subtropical forest

난데없다 〈뜻밖이다〉 unexpected; unforeseen; never dreamed of; unlooked-for; unanticipated; unthought of; 〈엉뚱하다〉 wild; eccentric; fantastic; absurd
♦ 난데없는 모임 a chance meeting / 난데없는 사건 an unforeseen [unlooked-for] event / 난데없는 손님 an unexpected visitor / 난데없이 unexpectedly; by chance [accident]; (at) unawares; suddenly; beyond expectation / 난데없이 나타나다 appear unexpectedly; make an abrupt appearance
▶ 난데없는 행운이 굴러들어 왔다 An unexpected piece of luck came our way.
▶ 여행중에 난데없는 재난을 만났다 During our travels we suffered an unforeseen misfortune.
▶ 그는 난데없이 나에게 덤볐다 He abruptly turned upon me.

난도질 亂刀─ chopping; hacking; mangling; mincing; hashing
─**난도질하다** hack [cut] to pieces; slash 《with》; mangle; hash; mince
▶ 시체가 무참히 난도질당한 채로 발견되었다 The body was found horribly mangled.

난독 亂讀 random reading ⇨ 남독(濫讀)
난동 暖冬 a mild [green] winter
▶ 난동인 해에는 벚꽃이 평소보다 일찍 핀다 A mild winter makes the cherry blossom bloom earlier than usual.
■ 이상(異常)— an unusually mild winter; an abnormally warm winter: 올해는 이상 난동이다 We are having an unusually mild winter this year. ⇌ We have an unusually [abnormally] warm weather this winter. / 이상 난동으로 야채값이 싸다 Thanks to the abnormally warm winter, vegetables are cheap.

난동 亂動 〈소동〉 a disturbance; an upheaval; a commotion; 〈폭동〉 a riot
◆ 난동을 부리다 rise in riot; raise [make] a disturbance; stir [get] up a riot; go on a rampage / 난동을 진압하다 put down a riot
▶ 경찰은 난동을 진압했다 The police got the disturbance under control.

난딱 〈손쉽게〉 easily; with ease; hands down; just like that; readily; 〈간단히〉 simply; lightly; 〈즉시〉 at once; quickly; promptly
▶ 큰 돌을 난딱 들어올리다 lift up a huge stone as if it were made of cotton / 일을 난딱 해치우다 (口) knock off a task

난로 煖爐 a stove; a heating apparatus; a heater; 〈벽난로〉 a fireplace
◆ 난로를 때다 [피우다] light a stove [heater]; start a fire in a fireplace / 난로를 쬐다 warm *oneself* by the fireplace
▶ 난로가 벌겋게 달아오르고 있었다 The stove was glowing red [burning well].
▶ 난로가 꺼졌군 The stove is out.
▶ 난롯가에만 있지 말고 밖에 나가 놀렴 Don't sit around the heater, go outside and play.
■ 가스— a gas heater [stove] 석유— an oil-stove; an oil heater 석탄[장작]— a coal [wood] stove 전기— an electric stove [heater]

난류 暖流 a warm current ◆ 노르웨이 근해의 난류 the warm currents in Norwegian waters

난리 亂離 〈전쟁〉 a war; 〈동란〉 an upheaval; 〈소동〉 disturbance; commotion; 〈반란〉 a rebellion; a revolt; 〈폭동〉 a riot; uprising; 〈혼란〉 confusion
◆ 난리통에 in the confusion of the war / 난리가 나다 have a war; a war breaks out; have a disturbance [an uproar] / 물난리가 나다 〈홍수〉 suffer from a flood; 〈물기근〉 suffer from water shortage / 난리를 가라앉히다 suppress a disturbance; quell a disturbance [a riot]; put down a revolt / 난리를 일으키다 start a war; rise in revolt; cause [make, raise] a disturbance; raise a rebellion; lead to confusion
▶ 그것 때문에 뭔가 난리가 날 것 같다 I'm afraid something serious will happen because of it.
▶ 그들은 거리에서 난리를 피웠다 They made a disturbance in the street.
▶ 난리를 진압하기 위해 기동대가 출동했다 The riot squad went into action to suppress the trouble.

난립 亂立 disorderliness; confusion; 〈입후보자의〉 running [standing] for election in a disorderly array
◆ 입후보자의 난립을 막다 check random candidacy
—**난립하다** run [stand] for 《mayor》 in great numbers
▶ 이 선거구에는 국회의원 입후보자가 난립하고 있다 The constituency is flooded with candidates running for the National Assembly. ⇌ There are too many candidates running from [standing in] this constituency.
▶ 이 부근에는 너무 많은 학원들이 난립해 있다 Too many cramming schools are competing with one another around here.
▶ 각종 빌딩이 난립해 있다 Many different sorts of buildings are jumbled up close together.

난마 亂麻 〈혼란〉 anarchy; chaos; imbroglio
◆ 난마와 같다 be in a chaotic state
▶ 그 나라의 정국은 난마와 같다 The political situation of the country is in a snarl.

난막 卵膜 (動) an egg membrane

난만 爛漫 being in full bloom; glory (of flowers)
▶ 정원은 백화난만이었다 The garden was ablaze with various colorful flowers.
—**난만하다** 〈서술적〉 be at 《their》 best; be in full bloom; be in all 《their》 glory
◆ 백화 난만한 뜰 a garden covered with all sorts of flowers
▶ 백화가 난만하다 All sorts of flowers are in full bloom [at their best].

난망 難忘 unforgettableness ◆ 난망이 never to be forgotten; unforgettable; memorable, indelible 《impressions》 ▶ 그 은혜는 백골 난망입니다 I shall never forget your kindness.

난맥 亂脈 disorder; confusion; chaos
◆ 난맥의 disorderly; chaotic; disturbed; turbulent / 난맥 상태에 빠지다 become confused; be thrown into disorder [confusion]
▶ 이 회사의 인사는 완전히 난맥 상태다 The personnel affairs of this company are in complete disorder [confusion].
▶ 시의 재정상태는 난맥 상태에 빠져 있었다 The city's finances were simply chaotic [in a chaotic state].

난무 亂舞 〈춤〉 a boisterous dance; 〈날뜀〉 rampage
—**난무하다** 〈춤추다〉 dance boisterously [wildly, madly] 《for joy》; 〈날뛰다〉 rampage; be [go] on a rampage; be rampant
◆ 폭력이 난무하는 거리 a gangster-ridden street
▶ 각종 거짓 정보가 난무했다 All sorts of false rumors were flying around.

난문 難文 a sentence [passage] hard to understand; a difficult sentence [passage]; a crabbed style

난문제 難問題 a difficult [hard] problem [question]; (口) a hard nut to crack; a knotty [thorny] problem [issue]; a puzzling question; a puzzle
◆ 난문제를 내다 put a hard question to *sb*; set a poser for *sb* / 난문제를 풀다 solve [work out] a hard problem; 〈비상수단으로〉 cut the

Gordian knot

난물 難物 〈사람〉 a man hard [difficult] to deal with; a hard character; 〈사물〉 a hard problem [case]; a hard [tough] nut to crack

난민 難民 〈이재민〉 sufferers; 〈flood〉 victims; 〈피난민〉 refugees; 〈빈민〉 the destitute
▶ 그녀는 베트남 난민이다 She is a Vietnamese refugee [refugee from Vietnam].
■해상― boat people ■―구제 the relief of the sufferers; refugee relief ―수용소 a refugee camp [reception center] ―정착사업 a refugee resettlement project; a resettlement project for needy families ―촌 a shanty quarter; a ghetto

난바다 a far-off [an open] sea; an offing
◆난바다 낚시질 offshore fishing / 난바다에 있는 섬 an off-lying island / 난바다에서 in the offing; 《ten kilometers》 offshore; out at sea / 난바다로 배를 저어 가다 pull out to sea

난반사 亂反射 〔物〕 diffused [irregular] reflection

난발 亂發 1〈난사〉 random [reckless] firing
―**난발하다** fire [shoot] at random
2〈남발〉 an excessive issue 《of currency》
◆지폐를 난발하다 overissue paper money

난방 煖房·暖房 〈덥게 함〉 heating; 〈방〉 a heated [warm] room
◆난방이 되지 않는 열차 an unheated train / 난방이 되어 있다 be heated 《by》 / 난방을 하다 [하지 않다] turn a heater on [off] / 난방 시설을 하다 install a heater 《in a room》
▶ 이 방은 난방이 잘 돼 있다[잘 돼 있지 않다] The room is well [poorly] heated.
▶ 이 방은 전기 난방을 하고 있다 This room is heated by electricity.
▶ 난방으로 방은 곧 따뜻해졌다 The room was soon warmed up by the heater.
■온수[온기]― hot-water[hot-air] heating 중앙―, ―기 central heating 증기― steam heating 지역 [복사(輻射)]― district [panel] heating ■―기구 a heater ―비 heating costs

난방장치 煖房裝置 a heating system [apparatus, arrangement]; 〈복사식 난방기〉 a radiator ▶ 그 새 건물은 중앙 난방 장치가 되어 있다 The new building has central heating.

난백 卵白 the white 《of an egg》; 〔動〕 the albumen; glair ⇨ 흰자위

난번 ―番 off duty (shift)

난봉 〈방탕〉 dissipation; a dissipated life; profligacy; 〈문란〉 a fast life
◆난봉나다 fall into vicious [evil] courses; take to fast living / 난봉 부리다[피우다] live fast; lead a fast and loose [dissipated] life; sow one's (wild) oats / 난봉으로 패가망신하다 be ruined by dissipation [debauchery]
■―꾼 a lady-killer; a fast liver; a libertine; a philanderer; a debauchee; a playboy: 저 녀석은 지독한 난봉꾼이다 That guy is a devil with girls.

난부자 든거지 ―富者― a wealthy-looking poor man

난비 亂飛 fluttering [flying] wildly around
―**난비하다** fly [flit] about

난사 亂射 random [wild] firing [shooting]

―**난사하다** fire (shots) [shoot] at random [blindly, indiscriminately]; spray bullets
▶ 그는 권총을 난사했다 He fired a pistol at random [blindly].

난사 難事 a difficulty; a difficult matter [thing]; a heavy [hard] task
◆난사중의 난사 the most difficult of all things; the hardest thing to do / 난사에 대처하다 tackle [cope with, grapple with] a difficulty [tough problem]

난사람 a prominent [a distinguished, an outstanding, an excellent, a superior, an eminent] person; a man among [of] men; a man of high [large] caliber
◆세계적으로 난사람 a world figure

난산 難産 〈출산의〉 a difficult delivery [birth]; 〈문제의〉 bringing forth with difficulty
▶ 이번 위원회의 구성은 꽤 난산이었다 The committee was organized with much difficulty.
▶ 그녀는 난산을 했다 She had a difficult delivery.
―**난산하다** 〈출산〉 have a difficult delivery; 〈일〉 bring forth with difficulty

난삽하다 難澁― difficult to understand; hard to make out [deal with]; puzzling ◆난삽한 글 a difficult passage; an article hard to understand; 〈문체〉 an esoteric style

난색 暖色 a warm color

난색 難色 disapproval; unwillingness; reluctance
◆난색을 보이다 show [express] disapproval 《of》; be oppose 《to a plan》; be reluctant
▶ 그녀의 아버지는 그녀가 외국에 가는 데 난색을 보였다 Her father was reluctant to let her go abroad.

난생 卵生 〔動〕 oviparity; oviparousness ◆난생의 oviparous ▶ 물고기는 난생이다 Fish are egg-layers. ⇌ Fish are produced from eggs.
■―동물 an oviparous [egg-laying] animal; 《총칭》 ovipara

난생처음 ―生― for the first time in one's life
◆난생 처음 당하는 일 the first experience in one's lifetime
▶ 오늘 나는 난생 처음으로 말을 탔다 Today I rode on horseback for the first time in my life.

난생후 ―生後 after one's birth; since one's birth

난선 難船 〈조난〉 a shipwreck; a wreckage; 〈조난선〉 a ship in distress; a wrecked ship ■―구조 salvage ―신호 a distress signal; an SOS

난세 亂世 turbulent [troubled, chaotic] times
◆난세의 영웅 a hero in a warlike [turbulent] age ▶ 그는 난세에 태어났다 He was born when his country was in a state of anarchy.

난세포 卵細胞 an egg cell; ovum 《pl. ova》

난센 〈노르웨이의 탐험가**〉** Nansen, Fridtjof (1861-1930)

난센스 nonsense

난소 卵巢 〔解·生〕 the ovary; the ovarium 《pl. -ria》 ◆난소의 ovarian

■ —선(腺) a nidamental gland —염 ovaritis —적출 removal of the ovary —절제술 ovariotomy —호르몬 ovarian hormones

난수 亂數 random numbers ■ —표 a table of random numbers

난숙 爛熟 1 〈과실의〉 overripeness; overmaturity —난숙하다 overripe; overmature ◆ 난숙한 full-matured / 난숙한 수박 an overripe watermelon
2 〈충분히 발달함〉 mellow ripeness; full development
—난숙하다 be fully developed; attain full maturity; be highly-developed
◆ 문화적 난숙 the mellow ripeness of culture / 난숙한 highly-developed
▶ 그의 서법은 난숙한 경지에 이르렀다 His calligraphy has reached full maturity.

난숙기 爛熟期 full maturity
◆ 문화적 난숙기에 at the apex [full glory] of civilization
▶ 로마 문명은 그때가 난숙기였다 The civilization of Rome was at [attained] its full maturity then.
▶ 그 무렵 고려는 문화의 난숙기를 맞았다 Koryŏ Dynasty's culture reached maturity then.

난시 亂視 〔醫〕 astigmatism; distorted vision
◆ 난시의 astigmatic / 난시가 있는 사람 an astigmatic
▶ 그는 난시다[난시가 있다] He is astigmatic.
■ —안 astigmatism; astigmatic eyes —안경 astigmatic glasses —측정술 astigmometry —측정기 an astigmometer

난외 欄外 the margin (of a page); 〈신문의〉 a marginal column
◆ 난외의 여백 a margin; marginal space / 난외의 주석 notes in the margin; marginal notes; marginalia / 난외에 in [on] the margin (of a page)
▶ 그는 난외에 메모를 했다 He jotted down notes in the margin.
▶ 난외에는 쓰지 마시오 Please do not write in the margin.
■ —기사 stop press news —표제 〈사전의〉a catchword; 〈일반 도서의〉 a running title

난운 亂雲 〔氣〕 a nimbus (*pl*. ~es, -bi); a rain cloud

난이 難易 hardness or ease; (relative) difficulty ▶ 두 문제의 난이는 말할 수 없다 You can't tell which problem is more difficult than the other.
■ —도 the degree of difficulty : 보수는 일의 난이도에 따라 지급한다 The remuneration is according to the difficulty of the job. ⇒ The pay depends on how hard your job is.

난입 亂入 (an) intrusion; a raid; trespass; forced entry
—난입하다 intrude [break] into; rush in; force *one's* way (into); force an entrance into
▶ 시위대가 국회의사당으로 난입했다 The demonstrators broke into the National Assembly Building.
■ —자 an intruder; a trespasser

난자 卵子 〔生〕 an ovum (*pl*. ova); an egg cell; 〈식물의〉 an ovule

난자 亂刺 ruthless [wild] stabbing —난자하다 stab *sb* ruthlessly [again and again] ◆ 단도로 난자하다 stab *sb* all over with a dagger

난잡 亂雜 〈무질서〉 confusion; disorder; pellmell; disarray; untidiness; 〈문란〉 obscenity indecency
—난잡하다 disorderly; confused; untidy; messy; pell-mell; 〈문란하다〉 indecent; loose; slatternly
◆ 난잡한 생활 a debauched life / 난잡한 행동 misconduct; immoral conduct / 난잡하게 in a disorderly manner [fashion]; confusedly; pellmell; in disorder [confusion] / 난잡하게 하다 disorder; put out of order; put into disorder / 난잡해지다 get confused; fall into disorder; get out of order; corrupt
▶ 동생의 방은 언제나 난잡하다 My brother's room is always in disorder [disorderly].
▶ 그는 술을 마시면 난잡해진다 He loses control of himself when in cups.
▶ 물건들이 난잡하기 짝이 없었다 Things were all in a jumble [in utter disorder].
▶ 마루에 책이 난잡하게 흩어져 있었다 Books were scattered in a disorderly manner on the floor. ⇒ The floor was cluttered up with books.
▶ 서류가 난잡하게 쌓여 있었다 The papers were piled up in confusion [disorder].

난장 亂帳 disarranged pages ▶ 오늘 산 책에는 몇 군데 난장이 있다 There are several pages out of place in the book I bought today.

난장 亂杖 reckless [wild] beating; merciless flogging
◆ 난장맞다 get beaten wildly; get a hard flogging / 난장치다 beat wildly [mercilessly]
▶ 마을 사람들은 그를 난장쳤다 The villagers beat the man up [black and blue].

난장판 亂場— (a scene of) confusion; a mess; a tumult; a turmoil
◆ 난장판을 이루다 go for a free-for-all; be in a turmoil
▶ 폭발사고 현장은 난장판이었다 The scene of the explosion (accident) was in turmoil [in a state of chaos].

난쟁이 a dwarf; a pygmy; a midget; 〈美口〉 a shorty

난전 亂戰 a confused fighting; a dogfight; a melee ◆ 난전을 벌이다 have [get into] a melee ▶ 양측의 싸움은 난전이었다 The fight between the two sides was chaotic.

난점 難點 〈문제점〉 a difficult [knotty] point; a rub

난제 難題 a knotty subject; a difficult problem; a hard problem to settle
◆ 난제를 안고 있다 have a difficult problem to solve / 난제에 봉착하다 meet [encounter] a thorny [difficult] problem
▶ 이것은 나에게는 난제다 This is too much [difficult] for me.
▶ 그는 난제와 씨름했다 He grappled [was at grips] with a difficult question. ⇒ He tackled a tough [hard] problem.

난조 亂調 〈음조의〉 discord; 〈혼란〉 confusion; disorder ◆ 난조를 보이다 〈투수가〉 lose con-

trol / 난조에 빠지다 be out of tune
▶ 그의 맥박이 난조를 이루고 있다 His pulse has become irregular.
▶ 주식시장이 난조다 The stock market is in confusion.
난중 亂中 ◆난중에 during a war [revolt]; in wartime ■—일기 A War Diary (by Admiral Yi Sun-shin)
난중지난 難中之難 be toughest [most difficult] problems; the hardest thing (to do)
난증 難症 a serious [malignant] case [illness]; a hard case
난처하다 難處— awkward; embarrassing; perplexed
◆난처한 입장 awkward position; a difficult situation / 난처한 표정으로 with a perplexed [troubled] look / 난처하게도 to *one's* distress [annoyance] / 난처해 하다 be embarrassed (by, with); be in trouble [difficulty]; be perplexed (at, about, with); be nonplus(s)ed
▶ 어찌 해야 할지 몰라서 매우 난처했다 I was completely at a loss what to do.
▶ 뭐라고 대답해야 좋을지 난처했다 I was at a loss for an answer. ⇌ I was perplexed because I didn't know what to answer.
▶ 호텔 예약을 하지 않아서 나는 참 난처했다 I was at my wit's [wits'] end since I had no reservation at a hotel.
▶ 난처한 질문은 하지마라 Don't ask embarrassing questions.
난청 難聽 〔醫〕bradycausia; hardness of hearing ◆난청의 hard of hearing ■—지역 〈라디오의〉 a blanket area; 〈라디오·텔레비전의〉 a fringe area (where reception is poor)
난초 蘭草 〔植〕 an orchid; 〈야생란〉 〈英〉 an orchis ■—재배가 an orchidist
난추니 〔鳥〕the male Asiatic sparrow hawk
난층운 亂層雲 〔氣〕 a nimbostratus
난치 難治 malignity ◆난치의 intractable; hard to cure; malignant; fatal / 난치성 간염 intractable hepatitis ■—병 an obstinate disease
난타 亂打 wild beating; random blows
■—난타하다 strike (a firebell) wildly [madly]; hit [beat] *sb* repeatedly; strike [knock] violently; shower *sb* with blows; rain blows on *sb*; 〈야구·권투에서〉 slug; strike blow after blow (at)
◆종을 난타하다 strike a bell violently
▶ 그 투수는 난타당해 마운드를 물러났다 The pitcher was knocked out of the box.
■—전 〈야구·권투의〉 a vicious exchange of blows; 〈美口〉 a slugfest
난투 亂鬪 a free [confused] fight; a scuffle; a scrimmage; a free-for-all (fight); a rough-and-tumble
◆노상의 난투 a scuffle in the street / 난투를 벌이다 have a free [confused] fight; come to fisticuffs [scuffles, blows]
▶ 시위대와 경찰 사이에 난투가 벌어졌다 There was a scuffle between the demonstrators and the police.
▶ 그들은 말다툼 끝에 난투를 벌였다 They progressed [went] from words to blows.
■—극 〈장면〉 a scene of violence and confusion; 〈영화·연극의〉 a fight scene
난파 暖波 a current of warm air; a warm wave
난파 難破 (a) shipwreck; wreck
■—난파하다 be shipwrecked; be wrecked
▶ 그 배는 암초에 부딪쳐 난파했다 The ship was wrecked on the hidden reef [on a sunken rock].
▶ 우리 배는 동해 연안에서 난파했다 Our ship was wrecked [We were wrecked] off the coast of the East Sea.
■—선 a wrecked ship; a ship in distress : 난파선을 구조하다 save a ship; salvage ■—신호 a signal of distress; an SOS
난폭 亂暴 violence; rudeness; roughness; wildness; an outrage
■—난폭하다 violent; rude; rough; hard; wild; outrageous; rowdy
◆난폭한 사나이 a rough [wild] fellow / 난폭한 운전 reckless driving / 난폭한 짓을 하다 do violence; assault; rough *sb* up; be rough [rude]; commit an outrage
▶ 난폭한 행동을 하지 마라 Don't use [do] violence.
▶ 그는 운전을 난폭하게 한다 He is a reckless driver. ⇌ He drives recklessly.
난필 亂筆 hasty [running, scratchy] (hand-)writing; bad (hand)writing; a scrawl; scribble
▶ 난필을 용서해 주시기 바랍니다 Excuse my writing in haste. ⇌ Excuse me for my hasty [bad] writing.
난하다 亂— 〈야하다〉 gaudy; showy; garish; loud (color); tawdry; flashy
◆난한 무늬 a showy [美 jazzy] pattern / 화장이 난한 여자 a woman wearing heavy make-up / 난한 색깔의 loud-colored
▶ 그녀는 옷차림이 난하다 She is gaily [loudly] dressed. ⇌ She is dressed in loud colors.
난할 卵割 〔生〕 cleavage
난항 難航 **1** 〈어려운 항행〉 a rough [difficult] voyage; a stormy passage [voyage]; 〈항공기의〉 a rough [hard] flight
▶ 연안에서의 항해는 난항이었다 Sailing was bad near the coast.
■—난항하다 〈배가〉 have a difficult sailing; have a rough passage
▶ 배는 격랑 속에서 난항했다 The ship sailed laboriously in a heavy sea.
2 〈일·협상 등의〉 slow progress; meeting with difficulty; hard [rough] going
▶ 새 조각(組閣)은 꽤 난항이었다 The formation of the new Cabinet was attended with considerable difficulty.
▶ 평화 협상은 난항을 거듭하고 있다 The peace negotiations are making slow progress [are going badly].
▶ 협상이 난항에 부딪혔다 The negotiations faced rough going [have a rough road ahead].
■—난항하다 〈일 등이〉 meet with a difficulty; have a rough going
▶ 그 법안 심의는 난항에 부딪혀 있다 Deliberations on the bill are facing hard going.
난해하다 難解— difficult to understand; hard

난행
to make out; knotty; abstruse; unintelligible ◆난해한 문체[시] an esoteric style [poem] / 난해한 이론 an abstruse theory
▶이 구절[책]은 매우 난해하다 This passage [book] is pretty hard [very difficult] to understand.
▶이것은 난해한 문제다 This is a difficult problem to solve.

난행 亂行 〈난폭한 행위〉 violent conduct; 〈방자한 짓〉 misconduct; immoral conduct; 〈방탕한 짓〉 profligacy; debauchery; 〈강간〉 outrage; violation
▶그의 난행은 차마 눈 뜨고 볼 수 없다 His wild life is just too much.
—**한행하다** lead a dissipated [wild, fast] life; 〈강간하다〉 violate; outrage; rape

난행 難行 〈고된 수행〉 penance; asceticism; religious austerities; 〈어려움〉 difficulty in practice
▶그는 절에서 난행고행의 수련을 했다 He practiced religious austerities at a temple.
—**한행하다** do penance; practice asceticism

난형 卵形 an egg shape; ovalness ◆난형의 egg-shaped; oviform; oval; ovate

난형난제 難兄難弟 ▶그 둘은 난형난제다 There is little to choose between the two. ≒ You find little difference between the two. ≒ The ability of the two is about the same [about equal, on a par].

난혼 亂婚 promiscuous sexual relations; 〈잡혼제도〉 a system of communal marriage

난황 卵黃 (a) yolk; the yolk [yellow] (of an egg) ⇨ 노른자(위)

날가리 a stack of grain stalks; a large pile of unhusked rice stems; an unhusked rice stack; a rick ▶날가리를 쌓다 stack up [rick] the harvested rice [grain stalks]

날알 a grain; 〈쌀알〉 a grain of rice

날¹ 1 〈하루〉 a day; 〈시일〉 time; 〈날짜〉 a date
◆그날 on the day / 다음 날 the next [following] day / 어느 날 one day / 초하룻 날 the first day of a month / 젊은날의 아버지 사진 a picture of my father in his younger days / 지난날의 추억 memories of past days / 날이 감에 따라 [갈수록] as days go by; as the days roll on / 그날그날 겨우 살아가다 live from hand to mouth; scrape a living day by day / 날을 보내다 pass one's days; pass [spend] one's time / 날을 정하다 [잡다] fix a date; fix upon the day [date]
▶중간 시험을 볼 날이 얼마 남지 않았다 We have only a few days left before the midterm exams.
▶그를 처음 만난 날은 아주 추웠다 The day that [when] I first met him was very cold.
▶갠 날에는 이 건물 옥상에서 인천시가 잘 보인다 On a fine day we can see Inch'ŏn City very clearly from the top of this building.
2 〈낮〉 (a) day
▶이 계절에는 날이 짧다[길다] In this season the days are short [long].
▶날이 밝아오고 있다 It is getting light.
▶날이 곧 저문다 It will get dark soon.
▶나는 날이 저물어서 집에 갔다 I returned home after dark.
3 〈날씨〉 the weather; atmospheric conditions ⇨ 날씨
◆궂은 날 foul [bad, rainy] weather / 좋은 날 a fine [clear] day; fine [fair, good] weather
▶날이 점점 더워진다 It is growing [getting] hotter and hotter [warmer and warmer].
▶내일 날이 좋으면 이 도시를 구경하겠다 If it is nice [fine] tomorrow, I'll see the sight of this town.
▶날이 산책하기에 안성맞춤이다 The weather is perfect [It is perfect weather] for a walk.
4 〈경우〉 a case; an occasion; a time; a moment
◆실패하는 날에는 in case one should fail; in the event of failure / 전쟁이 일어나는 날에는 in the event of a war (breaking out)
▶이것이 발각되는 날에는 나는 파면이다 If this is discovered, I will be fired.

날² 〈날붙이의〉 an edge; a blade
◆대팻날 the bit of a plane / 날카로운 날 a keen [sharp] edge / 무딘 날 a dull [blunt] edge / 날이 망가진 검 a sword with a nicked edge / 날이 잘 들다 [예리하다] have a keen [sharp] edge / 날을 세우다 put an edge 《on》; sharpen (a knife); set (a saw) / 면도날을 바꾸다 change razor blades

날³ 〈피륙의〉 the warp ◆날과 씨 warp and woof [weft]

날- 〈익히지 않은〉 raw; uncooked 《cabbage》; 〈자연 그대로의〉 crude
◆날고기 raw meat / 날달걀 a raw egg / 날로 먹다 eat (fish) raw [fresh] / 오이를 날로 먹다 eat a cucumber uncooked
▶고기를 날로 먹기를 좋아하는 사람도 있다 Some people like to eat raw meat.

날강도 —強盜 a robber; a mugger; a racketeer ▶그런 값을 부르다니 날강도와 같다 It is sheer robbery to ask such prices.
■**—질** robbery; mugging; racketeering

날강목치다 〔鑛〕 dig in vain; mine for nought; 〈비유〉 make vain efforts

날개 the wings; 〈곤충의〉 an ala 《pl. alae》; 〔쏘〕 《美》 an airfoil; 《英》 an aerofoil
◆비행기의 왼쪽 날개 the left wing of an airplane / 날개 소리 the flapping [fluttering, whirring] of wings / 날개의 길이 〈한쪽의〉 the length of a wing; 〈양쪽 날개〉 wingspan; wingspread / 날개 달린 winged / 날개 돋친 듯 팔리다 sell like fun [wildfire]; sell (off) like hot cakes / 날개 치다 flutter; flap [clap] the wings / 날개 치며 날아가다 fly with a flap of the wings / 날개를 펴다 [접다] spread [fold] the wings
▶학은 날개를 펴고 날아갔다 The crane spread its wings and flew away.

날갯죽지 a wing; the (shoulder-)joint of a wing ◆날갯죽지가 늘어지다 have a drooping wing

날것 raw stuff; uncooked food; 〈고기〉 raw meat; 〈생선〉 raw fish ◆날것으로 먹다 eat (fish) raw [fresh] ▶돼지고기를 날것으로 먹는 것은 위험하다 It is dangerous to eat raw [uncooked] pork.

날다다 〈거덜나다〉 go [come] to ruin; go broke; fail

날다¹ **1** 〈공중을〉 fly; 〈하늘 높이〉 soar; 〈새·나비 등이〉 flit; 〈날개를 파닥이며〉 flutter; 〈미끄러지듯이〉 glide; 〈표면을 스치듯이〉 skim
 ♦하늘을 나는 새 birds of the air / 파도를 스치듯 나는 갈매기 seagulls skimming the waves / 날고 있는 새 a flying bird; a bird flying in the air; a bird on the wing / 날지 못하는 새 a flightless bird / 낮게 날다 fly low / 높이 날다 soar; fly high in the air / 떼지어 날다 take wing in a flock / 그 거리를 3시간에 날다 cover the distance in three hours / 날아가 버리다 fly away [off]; wing off
 ▶그는 태평양을 비행기로 날았다 He flew the Pacific.
 ▶전투기가 음속의 2배 이상으로 날았다 The fighter plane streaked along at more than twice the speed of sound.
 ▶나비가 이 꽃 저 꽃으로 팔락팔락 날고 있다 A butterfly is fluttering [flitting] from flower to flower.
 ▶비행기는 그때 동해안을 날고 있었다 The plane was winging its way over the east coast.
 ▶많은 풍선이 하늘을 날고 있었다 There were lots of balloons [Lots of balloons were] flying through the air.
 ▶그는 당시 나는 새도 떨어뜨리는 권세를 잡고 있었다 He was then at the zenith of his power.
 ▶서류가 바람에 날아갔다 The papers blew off (in the wind). ⇌ The wind blew the papers off.
 2 〈급히 가다〉 fly; 〈서둘러 가다〉 hurry; hasten; rush; run; go very fast
 ♦나는 듯이 swiftly; like the wind / 나는 듯이 가다 fly [run, rush] to; make to dash (for)
 ▶나는 그 소식을 듣고 나는 듯이 집으로 돌아갔다 At the news I flew home like the wind.
 3 〈달아나다〉 escape; run away [off]; flee; take flight
 ▶범인은 외국으로 날았다 The criminal fled the country.
 ▶그는 빚쟁이에게 졸려서 날았다 He has given the creditors the fly.

날다² **1** 〈바래다〉 fade; discolor; lose color
 ♦잘 나는 색 a fugitive [fading] color / 날지 않는 색 a standing [fast, lasting] color / 색이 난 옷 a faded [discolored] dress
 ▶커튼이 햇빛을 받아 색이 날았다 The curtains were faded [discolored] by the sun (light).
 ▶이 색은 빨아도 날지 않는다 This color will stand wash.
 2 〈냄새가〉 lose odor; go away; die out; vanish; 〈습기가〉 evaporate
 ♦휘발유는 쉽게 난다 Gasoline is volatile.
 ▶꽃이 시들어 향기도 날아버렸다 The flower had withered, and lost its fragrance.

날다람쥐 〔動〕 a flying squirrel

날도 —度 〔地〕 degree of longitude

날도둑놈 a shameless scoundrel; a swindler; (口) a crook

날도래 〔昆〕 a caddis fly

날도마뱀 〔動〕 a flying dragon [lizard]

날들다 shine; clear up; become clear
 ▶추녀 밑에서 날들기를 기다렸다 I waited under the eaves for the rain to stop.

날떠퀴 the day's luck

날뛰다 **1** 〈뛰다〉 jump up; start up; bounce [frisk, skip] about ♦기뻐 날뛰다 jump [leap] for joy; dance with joy
 2 〈거칠게 굴다〉 act violently; run [rush] about wildly; rave [rage, ramp] about; be rampant; rampage; be riotous; 〈말 등이〉 lash out; 〈개 등이〉 be [go] wild
 ♦미친 듯이 날뛰다 rush about in a frenzy [a rage]; be [go] on a wild rampage; run amuck

날뛸판 (a) rage; (a) fury; (a) pandemonium
 ▶지금은 좋아서 날뛸판이 아니다 This is no hour for joy.

날라리 〈악기〉 a shawm; a musical woodwind instrument

날래다 〈빠르다〉 quick; speedy; swift; agile; nimble
 ♦날랜 동작 an agile [alert] movement / 날랜 말 a swift horse / 날래게 quickly; nimbly; agilely; speedily; swiftly / 걸음이 날래다 be quick [swift, fleet] of foot; have a quick step
 ▶그녀는 동작이 날래다 She is nimble.
 ▶그는 날래게 대답했다 He made a nimble reply.

날려보내다 **1** 〈놓아주다〉 fly; let fly; set free; release; 〈바람에〉 blow off [away]; have *sth* blown away ♦새장의 새를 날려보내다 set a caged bird free
 2 〈탕진하다〉 waste; throw away; dissipate [squander] (a fortune); lose

날렵하다 agile; nimble; smart; sharp; keen; cute ▶나는 그녀가 그렇게 날렵하게 행동할 줄은 몰랐다 I hadn't even imagined she could act so nimbly [agilely, quickly].

날로¹ 〈나날이〉 day by [after] day; daily; from day to day; every day
 ♦날로 나아지다 get better day by day / 날로 번창하다 enjoy increasing prosperity as time goes on
 ▶그 가게는 날로 번창하고 있다 The store is doing good business as time goes on.
 ▶사태가 날로 악화되고 있다 The situation is getting worse and worse every day.
 ▶날씨가 날로 선선해져 가고 있다 It's getting cooler day by day [every day].

날로² 〈날것으로〉 raw ♦생선을 날로 먹다 eat fish raw

날름 **1** 〈잽싸게〉 quickly; with a quick snatch
 ♦날름 먹어 치우다 eat up very quickly; gobble up every bit of food in no time
 2 〈혀를〉 ▶그 소녀는 나를 보고 혀를 날름 내밀었다 The girl stuck [put] her tongue out to me.

날름거리다 **1** 〈혀 등을〉 thrust [dart] (*one's* tongue [hand]) in and out quickly **2** 〈탐내다〉 be greedy for; have an eye for; be avaricious

날름쇠 〈총 등의〉 a tumbler; 〈무자위의〉 a valve

날리다¹ **1** 〈날게 하다〉 fly; let fly; make fly

날리다²

♦비둘기를 날리다 fly a pigeon / 풍선을 날리다 let loose a balloon / 홈런을 날리다 slam [bang out] a homer / 화살을 날리다 shoot [let fly] an arrow
▶ 아이들은 종이 비행기를 날렸다 The children flew [sailed] a paper airplane through the air.
2 〈떨치다〉 be widely [well] known; be famous [popular]
▶ 그녀는 온 세계에 명성을 날렸다 She won [enjoyed] a worldwide reputation. ⇌ Her fame spread all over the world.
▶ 그는 당시 피아니스트로서 크게 날렸다 He enjoyed great popularity as a pianist at that time.
3 〈잃다〉 lose (all); waste; throw away
♦돈을 날리다 make the money fly; lose money / 만원을 날리다 spend 10,000 won for nothing / 노름으로 전 재산을 날리다 gamble away *one's* entire fortune; lose *one's* entire fortune at the gambling table
4 〈일을〉 skimp [scamp] (*one's* work); do careless work; do slapdash
♦글씨를 날려 쓰다 write carelessly
▶ 그 벽돌공은 절대로 일을 날리지 않는다 The bricklayer is very conscientious in his work.

날리다² **1** 〈바람에〉 be blown off [away]; be wafted; 〈휘날리다〉 wave; flutter; stream; flap
▶ 내 모자가 바람에 날렸다 My hat blew off (in the wind). ⇌ I had my hat blown off (by the wind). ⇌ The wind blew my hat off.
▶ 그 여자는 바람에 머리카락을 날리며 달렸다 The woman ran with her hair streaming in the wind.
▶ 우리는 깃발을 날리며 행진했다 We marched with our flag fluttering in the wind.
2 〈일으키다〉 raise; stir up ♦먼지를 날리다 raise [stir up] dust

날림 shoddy work; slipshod [sloppy] work; scamping *one's* work; a patch-work job
♦날림으로 지은 jerry-built; of jerry-building ■—공사 a jerry-building; slapdash construction work —글씨 a scribble —집 a jerry-built [slapdash] house —치 a slipshod thing [job]

날마다 every day; day after day ▶ 그는 거의 날마다 내게 전화를 했다 He called me up almost every day [almost daily]. ▶ 나는 날마다 그 일을 했다 I worked on it day after day.

날망제 〔民俗〕 a wandering soul [ghost]
날목 —木 unseasoned [green] wood [timber]
날물 **1** 〈나가는 물〉 outflowing water **2** 〈썰물〉 an ebb tide; a low tide; the ebb
날밑 a sword guard; the guard 《of a sword》
날바람잡다 stroll [ramble] about
날반죽 cold-water dough
—**날반죽하다** knead with cold water
날밤¹ 〈새우는 밤〉 ♦ 날밤 새우다 sit [stay] up all night; pass [spend, have] a sleepless night
날밤² 〈생률〉 a raw [unroasted] chestnut
날벌레 a winged insect
날벼락 a bolt from the blue ⇨ 생벼락
날변 —邊 daily interest; interest per day
날불한당 —不汗黨 a hooligan; a rogue; a shameless rascal [scoundrel]; a barefaced villain [crook]

날붙이 an edge(d) tool; cutting instruments; (총칭) cutlery
날사이 for the past several days; these days
날삯 daily pay [wages]; a day's wage ▶ 나는 날삯 5만원을 받는다 I get [am paid] 50,000 won a day. ■—꾼 a day laborer
날새 these days ⇨ 날사이
날샐녘 dawn; daybreak; the break of day; the early hours of the morning
♦날샐녘에 at dawn [daybreak]; at the break [peep] of day; just before the sunrise / 날샐녘까지 일하다 work until daybreak [early morning]
▶ 나는 날샐녘에 일어났다 I got up at dawn [daybreak].
날서다 be edged [sharpened]; become sharp
♦날선 칼 a sharp [keen] knife
날세우다 put an edge on; give an edge to; edge; sharpen ♦날세운 칼날 a keen-edged [finely honed] blade / 칼을 면도날처럼 날세우다 whet [hone] the knife razor-sharp
날수 —數 **1** 〈날의 수효〉 (the number of) days
♦날수가 많이 걸리다 take many days [a long time]
2 〈그날의 운수〉 luck of a day; *one's* luck of the day ♦날수가 좋다[나쁘다] have a lucky [an unlucky] day
날숨 an outbreath; outbreathing; exhalation
♦날숨 쉬다 breathe out; exhale
날실 〈피륙의〉 warp (↔woof)
날쌔다 quick; prompt; agile; nimble; fleet; swift
♦날쌘 동작 an agile [alert] movement / 날쌘 짐승 a fleet animal / 날쌔게 nimbly; with dispatch; smartly; promptly / 다람쥐[족제비] 비럼 날쌔다 be (as) agile as a squirrel [weasel] / 날쌔게 행동하다 be prompt [quick] in action; move with agility
▶ 그는 날쌔게 일을 해치웠다 He finished his work in quick order.
▶ 나는 다른 소식통에게서 날쌔게 많은 정보를 얻어냈다 I quickly got a lot of information from other sources.
날씨 (the) weather; weather conditions
♦궂은 날씨 foul [bad, nasty, rainy] weather / 변덕스러운 날씨 changeable [unsettled] weather / 불순한[나쁜] 날씨 unreasonable [bad] weather / 온화한 날씨 calm [mild, genial, serene] weather / 좋은[화창한] 날씨 nice [good, fair, fine] weather / 찌푸린 날씨 a sullen sky
▶ 좋은 날씨군요 It's a nice [beautiful, lovely] day, isn't it? ⇌ It's nice [good] weather, isn't it?
▶ 금방 비라도 쏟아질 것 같은 날씨다 It is threatening weather.
▶ 산책하기에 더없이 좋은 날씨다 The weather is perfect [It is perfect weather] for a walk.
▶ 날씨 탓인지 머리가 무겁다 I feel heavy in the head, probably because of [due to] the weather.
〈날씨가[는]〉 날씨가 좋든 나쁘든 rain or shine; whatever the weather; in all weather;

in fine or foul weather / 날씨가 좋으면 if it is fine; weather permitting / 날씨가 좋아지는대로 on the first fine day
▶ 날씨가 풀렸다 The weather became warmer.
▶ 체육대회 때는 다행히 날씨가 좋았었다 We were lucky to have good weather at the athletic meet.
▶ 날씨가 나빠지고 있다 The weather is changing for the worse. ⇌ (口) The weather is going downhill.
▶ 날씨가 좋아질 것이다 The weather will improve [(口) look up, change] for the better.
▶ 이런 날씨가 당분간 계속될 것이다 This weather would hold for the time being.
▶ 내일 날씨가 좋으면 이 마을을 구경하지요 If it's nice [fine] tomorrow, I'll see the sight of this town.
▶ 비가 올 거라고 생각했는데 결국 날씨가 좋아졌다 I thought it was going to rain. But it turned out nice [it cleared up after all].
▶ 가을에는 날씨가 변덕스럽다 The weather is changeable in autumn.
▶ 내일 날씨는 어떤가요? What's the weather like tomorrow?
▶ 날씨는 여전히 꾸물거리고 있다 The weather remains [stays] as unsettled as ever.
〈날씨를〉날씨를 보다 have a look at the weather / 날씨를 예보하다 forecast [foretell, predict] the weather / 날씨를 잘 맞히다 be weather-wise / 날씨를 탓하다 put down *sth* to the weather
▶ 날씨를 봐서는 내일 비가 올 것 같다 Judging from the look of the sky, it will rain tomorrow.

날씬하다 slim; slender; lithe; delicate; thin
◆ 날씬한 몸매 a thin [slender, delicate] figure / 날씬한 미인 a slender beauty / 허리가 날씬한 여자 a slim-waisted girl / 옷차림이 날씬하다 be smartly [sprucely] dressed / 날씬해지다 become slender [slim]
▶ 그녀는 몸매가 날씬하다 She has a slim figure.
▶ 그녀는 다리가 날씬하다 She has slender [slim] legs.
▶ 그녀는 식이요법으로 날씬해졌다 She has slimmed down [become slim] by dieting.

날아가다 1 〈새 등이〉 fly away [off]; take wings
◆ 북쪽으로 날아가는 기러기들 wild geese winging northward
▶ 매가 날아가려고 자세를 취했다 The hawk posed for flight.
▶ 울새 새끼가 둥지에서 날아갔다 The young robin flew away from the nest.
2 〈없어지다〉 be gone [out]; be used up; run out; go ▶ 돈이 어느새 다 날아갔다 My money is all gone already.
3 〈파면되다〉 be dismissed [discharged, fired]
▶ 그 뇌물사건으로 몇 사람의 목이 날아갔다 As a result of the bribery scandal, several people were dismissed.
▶ 그 사건으로 교장의 목이 날아갔다 The principal lost his job [was fired] because of the incident.

날아다니다 fly about [around]
▶ 벌들이 이꽃 저꽃으로 날아다닌다 Bees flutter around from flower to flower.
▶ 나비들이 들판을 날아다니고 있다 Butterflies are flying around [about] in the field.
▶ 그는 비행기로 미국 전역을 날아다녔다 He flew all over the United States in the plane.

날아들다 fly in [into] ▶ 어제 참새 한 마리가 집안으로 날아들었다 A sparrow flew into my house yesterday.

날아오르다 fly high [up]; soar (up); take flight; rise in the air; 〈비행기가〉 take off; 〈바람에 날려〉 be blown up
▶ 참새들이 갑자기 날아올랐다 The sparrows flew up all at once.
▶ 헬리콥터가 옥상에서 날아올랐다 A helicopter rose [took off] from the roof.
▶ 센 바람에 먼지가 날아올랐다 A gust of wind stirred up the dust.

날염 捺染 (textile) printing —**날염하다** print
◆ 날염한 천 printed cotton; print; (美) calico
■ —기 a printing machine

날인 捺印 sealing; affixing 《*one's* signature》
—**날인하다** seal; put [affix] *one's* seal (to)
◆ 날인할 곳 the place for *one's* seal; (라) locus sigilli (=the place of the seal) (略 L.S.) / 서류에 날인하다 affix [put] the seal on the paper / 증서에 날인하다 seal a deed / 기명 날인하다 write *one's* name and verify it by affixing *one's* seal; sign and seal
■ —기 a stamping machine —**자** a sealer —**증서계약** a covenant; a contract under seal

날일 day labor ⇨ 날품

날조 捏造 (an) invention; (a) concoction; (a) fabrication
—**날조하다** invent; fabricate; forge; concoct; make [(口) cook, frame, turn, trump] up 《a story》; manufacture 《false news》; (口) fake 《a report》
◆ 이야기를 날조하다 invent a false story
▶ 그는 자기에게 유리하게 이야기를 날조했다 He fabricated [made up, concocted] a story to his own advantage.
▶ 그 보도는 신문이 날조한 것이다 The report is an invention of the newspaper.
▶ 그 기록은 있지도 않은 매출 신장을 나타내기 위해 날조한 것이었다 The records were faked to show an improvement in sales that didn't exist.
■ —기사 a fabrication; a fabricated report —**자** a fabricator

날줄 (a line of) longitude

날짐승 winged animals; the feathered tribe; birds; fowls

날짜¹ **1** 〈정한 날〉 a date
◆ 날짜 없는 편지 an undated letter / 날짜를 늦추다 put off the date / 날짜를 매기다 date; put a date to / 날짜를 앞당기다 advance [move up] the date / 날짜를 실제보다 앞서게 하다 antedate; predate; date forward / 날짜를 정하다 fix a date; fix upon the date [day]
▶ 이 영수증에는 날짜가 없다 This receipt has no date on it [is not dated]. ⇌ The date is not put on this receipt.

날짜·요일·연호

1. 날짜의 표현
예컨대 '1997년 9월 1일'을 표현하는 경우 다음 두 가지 방법이 있다.
미국식: 월 → 일 → 연도 순
September 1, 1997 (▶September first, nineteen ninety-seven으로 읽음)
약식 기록법: 9/1/'97
영국식: 일 → 월 → 연도 순
1st September, 1997 (▶the first of September, nineteen ninety-seven으로 읽음)
약식 기록법: (美) 1/9/'97
월명의 약기 (▶5월은 약기하지 않음)
 1월 Jan. 2월 Feb. 3월 Mar.
 4월 Apr. 5월 May 6월 Jun.
 7월 Jul. 8월 Aug. 9월 Sep(t).
 10월 Oct. 11월 Nov. 12월 Dec.

2. 연도의 표현
1945년 nineteen forty-five (네자리 수의 경우에는 두자리씩 끊어서 읽음. 단, **1900년**의 경우는 nineteen hundred로 읽음)
994년 nine (hundred) ninety-four
서기 **225년** 225 A.D.; two (hundred) twenty-five A.D. [éi díː]; (英) A.D. 225 / 기원전 **55년** 55 B.C.; fifty-five B.C. [bíːsíː] (▶B.C.는 언제나 연도 뒤에 둠)
1990년대(에) (in) the 1990s (▶nineteen nineties로 읽음) / **80년대 전[후]반** the early [late] 80s

3. ~일[월, 년]에, ~요일에
▶ 會話「당신 아버님은 언제 귀국하십니까?」「이달 5일입니다」 "When will your father come back to Korea?" "On the fifth of this month."
▶ 會話「당신은 언제 대구로 출발합니까?」「2일 아침에 출발합니다」 "When are you going to leave for Taegu?" "On the morning of the second."
▶ 제2차 세계대전은 1945년 8월 15일에 끝났다 The World War Ⅱ ended on August fifteenth, 1945.
▶ 그 사고는 13일의 금요일에 일어났다 The accident occurred on Friday the thirteenth.
▶ 체육 시간은 월요일과 목요일에 있다 We have gym class on Mondays and Thursdays.
▶ 나는 매주 토요일에 테니스 연습을 한다 I pratice tennis every Saturday.

4. 날짜를 묻고 대답하기
▶ 會話「오늘은 며칠입니까?」「6월 1일입니다」 "What's the date today?" ⇌ "What's today's date?" "It's June (the) first."
▶ 會話「오늘은 몇월 며칠입니까?」「9월 21일입니다」 "What day of the month is it today?" "It's September (the) twenty-first."
▶ 會話「당신의 생년월일을 말씀해 주십시오」「1975년 6월 2일생입니다」 "Please state your date of birth." "It's June (the) second, nineteen seventy-five."
▶ 會話「운동회는 언제 개최됩니까?」「10월 둘째 화요일입니다」 "When [On what date] will the athletic meet be held?" "It'll be held on the second Tuesday of October."
▶ 4월 10일자 편지를 받았습니다 I received your letter of April tenth.

5. 요일을 묻고 대답하기
▶ 會話「오늘은 무슨 요일입니까?」「월요일입니다」 "What day is it today?" ⇌ "What day of the week is it today?" "It's Monday." (▶of the week가 없으면「오늘은 무슨 날입니까?」라는 말도 됨)
▶ 會話「오늘은 무슨 날입니까?」「오늘은 우리 학교 창립 30주년 기념일입니다」 "What is it today?" "Today is the thirtieth anniversary of our school."
▶ 이번주 월요일에 그 영화를 보러 갔다 I went to see that movie this Monday.
▶ 會話「그 연주회는 다음주 무슨 요일에 개최됩니까?」「토요일입니다」 "What day next week will the concert be held?" "Next Saturday."
▶ 교내 야구 시합은 비 때문에 다음주 금요일로 연기되었다 On account of rain, our school's (intramural) championship baseball game has been postponed till next Friday.

▶ 정한 날짜에 꼭 오시오 Be sure to come on the fixed [stated] date. **2** 〈日수〉 (the number of) days; time ◆ 다소 날짜가 필요하다 take some time [a certain number of days] ▶ 날짜가 이렇게 빨리 가다니! How fast the days pass [go by]! ■**계약[약속]—** the date of contract [an appointment] ■**—변경선** the date line; the international date line
날짜² **1** ⇨ 날것
2 〈서투른 사람〉 a greenhorn; an inexperienced person; a new hand; a beginner; a novice
날짝지근하다 weary; listless ⇨ 늘쩍지근하다
날치¹ 〈나는 새 잡기〉 shooting a flying bird; wing shooting [shot]
■**—꾼** wing shot
날치² 〈일수빚〉 a loan payable by daily installment
날치³ 〈魚〉 a flying fish
날치기 〈행위〉 snatching; 〈사람〉 a snatcher ◆ 핸드백 날치기꾼 a handbag snatcher / 의안을 날치기로 통과시키다 rush a bill through the Assembly by surprise
—날치기하다 snatch (away) 《from, off》 ◆ 날치기당하다 have a thing snatched
▶ 물건을 날치기당하지 않도록 경계해라 Keep an eye on your belongings so that no one will swipe [snatch, walk off with] them.
■**—통과** 〈법안의〉 the unilateral passage of a bill in a lightning action; a snap passage 《of a bill》
날카롭다 **1** 〈끝이〉 pointed 《needle》; 〈날이〉

sharp [sharp-cut, sharp-edged, keen] 《knife》
♦ 날카로운 면도날 a sharp blade of a razor / 날카로운 칼 a sharp(-edged) knife; a knife with a keen edge / 날카롭고 뽀족한 끝 a sharp point / 날카롭게 sharply / 날카로워지다 get [become] sharp / 날카롭게 하다 sharpen; make sharp

2 〈민감하다〉 acute; sharp 《ear》; piercing 《eye》; keen 《sense》; 〈매섭다〉 stinging [caustic, pungent] 《sarcasm》; biting; cutting; poignant 《satire》; 〈재치가〉 trenchant; 〈머리가〉 quick; quick-witted; shrewd
♦ 날카로운 관찰 acute [keen] observation / 날카로운 눈 keen [piercing, penetrating] eyes / 날카로운 목소리 a sharp [harsh, shrill] voice / 날카로운 비판 cutting [biting] criticism / 판단력이 날카로운 사람 a man of acute judgment / 날카롭게 sharply; keenly; acutely / 날카롭게 공격하다 make hot [fierce] attacks 《on, against》; 〈말로〉 make cutting remarks 《about》
▶ 그녀는 색채 감각이 날카롭다 She has a keen sense of [sharp eye for] color.
▶ 개는 후각이 날카롭다 Dogs have a keen sense of smell.
▶ 그는 언제나 날카로운 질문을 한다 He always asks pointed [sharp] questions.
▶ 그는 날카로운 눈으로 노려보고 있다 He is glaring piercingly.
▶ 신문은 정부를 날카롭게 공격했다 The papers attacked the government bitterly. ⇌ The press leveled cutting remarks at the government.

날탕 a person with no means; a penniless person
날포 a couple of days; a few days
날품 daywork; day labor ♦ 날품을 팔다 be hired [《美》 hired out] by the day; work by the day ■ —팔이 〈일〉 work done on a daily wage basis; 〈사람〉 a day laborer [man]
날피 a poor man of loose conduct
낡다 〈오래되다〉 old; aged; antiquated; 〈써서〉 worn-out; 〈구식의〉 old-fashioned; 〈케케묵은〉 stale; hackneyed; time-worn; 〈시대에 뒤진〉 out-of-date; outdated; outmoded; outworn
♦ 낡은 가구 used [worn-out] furniture / 낡은 교사(校舍) an old ramshackle schoolhouse / 낡은 사상 an old-fashioned idea / 낡은 옷 worn-out clothes / 낡은 차 a beat-up car / 낡은 표현 a hackneyed [trite] expression / 낡은 학설 an obsolete [outdated] theory
▶ 내 가방은 너무 낡았다 My bag has become [grown] very old.
▶ 그런 사고 방식은 이젠 낡은 것이다 That kind of thinking is behind the times [is antiquated].
▶ 그는 낡은 시계를 아직도 소중하게 차고 있다 He still uses his old watch with care.

남 1 〈타인〉 other people; others; another
〈남의〉 남의 말 what people [others] say / 남의 집 other people's house / 남의 손을 빌리지 않고 without help; single-handedly / 남의 앞에서 in the presence of [before] others / 남의 손을 빌리다 ask for another's help; be helped [assisted] by another / 남의 손에 넘어가다 pass into another's possession / 남의 위에 서다 lead others / 남의 입에 오르내리다 be talked [gossiped] about; become the talk of others
▶ 그녀는 남의 이야기 하기를 좋아한다 She likes to talk about others.
〈남이[은]〉 남이 하는대로 according to custom; following the world / 남이 보고 있는데도 in spite of the presence of others; without any regard to decency / 남이야 어떻든 나는 as for myself; so far as I am concerned
▶ 남이 뭐라고 할까? What will people say?
▶ 남이 뭐라든 알게 뭐냐 I am indifferent to what other people say about me.
〈남을〉 남을 통하여 through another (person)
▶ 남을 헐뜯지 마라 Don't speak ill of others.
〈남에게〉 남에게 맡기다 leave (it) to others / 남에게서 듣다 learn from others
▶ 남에게 의지하면 안된다 You mustn't depend on others.

2 〈친척이 아닌 사람〉 an unrelated person
▶ 남보다는 제 살붙이 《속담》 Blood is thicker than water.
▶ 저 두 사람은 닮았으나 생판 남이다 Those two look alike, but they are not related (to each other).
▶ 촌수는 멀지만 그는 아주 남은 아니다 Though distant, he is still my relative.

3 〈국외자〉 an outsider; 〈관계가 없는 사람〉 an estranged person; a stranger
▶ 그는 생면부지의 남이다 He is an utter stranger to me.
▶ 그들은 이혼했으니 이젠 남이다 Since they got divorced, they have nothing to do with each other.
▶ 너는 남이니까 잠자코 있어 As you are an outsider, you had better keep silent.

4 〈나〉 me; I
▶ 왜 남의 우산을 가져갔니? Why did you take my umbrella?

남 男 〈남자〉 a man; 〈아들〉 a son
♦ 장남 the eldest [《美》 oldest] son / 차남 the second son
▶ 나는 2남 1녀를 두고 있다 I have [am blessed with] two sons and a daughter.

남 南 the south; South
♦ 남으로 south; to [toward] the south; southward / 북에서 남으로 from north to south / 남으로 면해 있다 face [look toward] the south

남 藍 〔植〕〈쪽〉 indigo; 〈쪽빛〉 indigo (blue)

남- 男- male; masculine ♦ 남동생 one's younger brother / 남탕 the men's section of a public bathhouse

남가일몽 南柯一夢 an empty dream; a day dream; an ephemeral [a fleeting] dream of prosperity; 〈덧없는 영화〉 vain glories

남경 南京 〈중국의 도시〉 Nanjing

남계 男系 the male line; the spear side
♦ 남계의 on the male line / 남계의 자손 the descendants in the male line / 남계의 조상 the ancestors on the father's [paternal] side
■ —상속 succession in the male line —친족 an agnate

남구 南歐 〈남유럽〉 Southern Europe

남국 南國 a southern country; 〈남부지방〉 the

남극 South

남극 南極 〈지구의〉 the South [Antarctic] Pole; the Antarctic; 〈대륙〉 Antarctica; 〈자석의〉 the south pole
♦남극의 antarctic
■—**관측** (an) Antarctic research [exploration] —**관측선** an icebreaker for an Antarctic research exploration [expedition] —**광** an aurora australis (*pl.* aurorae australes); the southern lights —**구**(區) 〈동물·지리학상의〉 the Antarctic Region —**권[대]** the Antarctic Circle [Zone] —**대륙** the Antarctic Continent; Antarctica —**성** the south polestar —**양[해]** the Antarctic Ocean [Sea] —**지방** the south pole region —**탐험(대)** an Antarctic expedition (team) : 한국은 남극 탐험대를 파견했다 Korea sent [dispatched] an expedition to the South Pole [Antarctica]. —**포경**(捕鯨) Antarctic whaling —**해양 생물자원 보존협약** the Convention on the Conservation of Antarctic Marine Living Resources (略 CCAMLR)

남근 男根 the penis (*pl.* ~es, penes); a phallus (*pl.* -li) ■—**숭배** phallic worship; phallicism

남기다 1 〈뒤에〉 leave (behind); 〈후세에〉 hand down; leave
♦뒤에 남겨진 가족 the bereaved family / 발자취를 남기다 leave *one's* footprints / 좋은 [나쁜] 인상을 남기다 leave a favorable [bad] impression (upon) / 기록에 남기다 place [put] *sth* on record; record / 후세[역사]에 이름을 남기다 leave *one's* name to posterity [in history]
▶그는 위대한 음악가로서 이름을 남겼다 He left behind a reputation as a great musician.
▶그는 처자를 고향에 남겨두고 서울에서 취직했다 He left his wife and children in his hometown and took a job in Seoul.
▶나 혼자만 남겨두고 다들 야유회 갔다 They went on a picnic, leaving me all alone.
2 〈예비로〉 set aside; reserve; 〈절약하여〉 save; 〈유산으로서〉 leave [bequeath] (money to *sb*)
▶아버지가 남긴 것은 빚뿐이었다 My father left nothing but debts behind him.
▶그는 돈을 한푼도 남기지 않고 다 써버렸다 He spent all the money he had.
▶그는 돌아갈 여비로 2만원을 남겨두었다 He set twenty thousand won aside for his return fare.
▶이 돈은 장래를 위해 남겨두어라 You should keep aside [reserve] this money for the future.
▶나는 일을 남겨둔 채 집으로 왔다 I came home, leaving my work unfinished [halfdone].
3 〈이익을〉 gain profit; make [get, obtain] a profit
♦5만원 남기다 make a profit of 50,000 won / 1할 남기다 clear [net] ten percent / 거래에서 [주식을 팔아서] 많이 남기다 make a large profit on a transaction [by selling stocks] / 별로 남기지 못하다 give [yield] little profit; do not pay much
▶그것을 팔면 2천 달러 남는다 It will fetch a profit [bring a gain] of 2,000 dollars.

남김없이 wholly; all; entirely; completely; all through; exhaustively; without exception [reserve]
♦한 사람도 남김없이 (one and) all; to the last man; to a man / 남김없이 먹다 eat (it) up
▶네가 알고 있는 것을 남김없이 말해라 Tell me all you know about it.
▶그는 그 돈을 한푼도 남김없이 써버렸다 He spent all the money. ⇒ He spent the money (down) to the last cent [penny].
▶그 남자는 밥을 남김없이 깨끗이 먹어치웠나 The man has licked the plate clean.
▶나는 술을 한 방울 남김없이 마셨다 I drank the wine to the last drop.

남남동 南南東 (the) south-southeast (略 S.S.E.); south by southeast

남남북녀 南男北女 The best [handsome] men are found in the south and the best [gracious] women in the north.

남남서 南南西 (the) south-southwest (略 S.S.W.); south by southwest

남녀 男女 man and woman; male and female (beings); both sexes
♦젊은 남녀 Jack and Gill [Jill]; (俗) crewcuts and ponytails / 남녀간에 between male and female
▶남녀 7세 부동석 A boy and a girl should not sit together [side by side] after the age of seven (according to Confucian rule).
▶25명의 남녀가 그 사고로 부상당했다 Twenty-five men and women [people] were injured in the accident.
■—**관계** relations between the sexes —**동권** equal rights for both sexes —**동등[평등]** the equality of the sexes —**유별** distinction between the sexes —**차별** sexual discrimination; sexism —**추니** an androgyne; a hermaphrodite

남녀공학 男女共學 coeducation ♦남녀 공학의 coeducational / 남녀공학 대학의 여학생 (美口) a co-ed
■—**학교** a coeducational [(美口) co-ed, (英) mixed] school: 우리는 남녀 공학 학교에 다닌다 We attend [go to] a coeducational school.

남녀노소 男女老少 people of all ages and both sexes; men and women of all ages ♦남녀노소를 불문하고 regardless [without distinction] of age or sex

남다 1 〈여분이 있다〉 remain; be left behind; be left (over); 〈남아돌다〉 be too many [much]; be more than enough
♦남은 것 the rest / 남은 돈 the money left over / 남은 일 the remainder of work; the remaining work / 먹다 남은 과자 leftover cake
▶7에서 3을 빼면 4가 남는다 Three from seven leaves four.
▶그의 장점은 단점을 보충하고도 남는다 His merits more than offset his demerits.
▶여비가 5천원 남았다 Five thousand won is left of the traveling expense.
▶그것을 다시 할 만한 시간은 아직 남아 있다

We still have time enough to do it over again.
▶ 냉장고에는 먹을 것이 거의 남아 있지 않다 There is [We have] almost no food left (over) in the refrigerator.
▶ 돈은 남아 있지 않다 There is [I have] no money left (over).
▶ 접시에는 아무것도 남아 있지 않았다 There was nothing left on the plate.
2 〈잔존하다〉 linger; remain; 〈잔류하다〉 remain behind; stay
♦ 귀에 남다 linger [ring] in *one's* ears / 기억에 남다 live [abide] in *one's* memory / 역사에 남다 go down in history; be written [recorded] in history / 집에 남다 remain [stay] at home / 최후까지 남다 remain [stay] to the last
▶ 그 음악은 아직 내 마음에 남아 있다 The music still lingers in my mind.
▶ 그는 언제나 방과 후에는 도서관에 남아 공부한다 He always stays after school to study at the library.
▶ 먼 산 위에는 아직 눈이 남아 있다 The snow still lies on the distant mountains.
▶ 그 풍습은 아직도 몇몇 나라에 남아 있다 The custom still remains [lingers on] in some countries.
▶ 나는 보통 밤 늦게까지 회사에 남아서 일한다 I am usually at work till late into the night at the company.
▶ 그녀의 아름다운 이미지는 오래 내 기억에 남아 있을 것이다 Her beautiful image will always remain in my memory.
3 〈살아 남다〉 be left alive; survive
♦ 뒤에 남은 처자 *one's* bereaved family
▶ 그 화재로 이 건물만 남았다 Only this building survived the fire.
▶ 그가 죽은 뒤에 아내와 두 아들이 남아 있다 He is survived by his wife and two sons.
4 〈이익이 남다〉 be profitable; be lucrative; yield profits; 〈사람이 주어〉 make a profit; make money; gain; earn
♦ 남는[남지 않는] 장사 a profitable [an unprofitable] business
▶ 그 값이라면 굉장히 남는다 At that price, it yields a nice profit.
▶ 그것은 5천원 이하로 팔아서는 남는 것이 없다 It wouldn't pay to sell it for less than 5,000 won.

남다르다 different from others; uncommon; peculiar; outstanding
♦ 남다른 기획 an unconventional [a novel] scheme / 남다른 노력 a great effort / 남다른 버릇 a strange [an odd, a peculiar] habit / 남다른 재능 (show) outstanding ability
▶ 그의 생활은 어딘가 남다르다 There is something out of common in his life.

남단 南端 the southern end [extremity, tip]; the southernmost part ▶ 공원은 시의 남단에 있다 The park is located at the southern end of the city.

남달리 unusually; uncommonly; extraordinarily; uniquely
♦ 남달리 고집이 세다 be unique in *one's* stubbornness / 남달리 열심히 일하다 work harder than others / 남달리 추위를 타다 be unusually sensitive to the cold
▶ 그는 남달리 기억력이 뛰어나다 He has an extraordinary memory. ⇌ His memory is out of the ordinary / (口) something else).

남대문 南大門 〈숭례문〉 the South Gate (in Seoul)

남독 濫讀 random reading; desultory [unsystematic] reading
▶ 대학원생에게 남독은 시간 낭비다 Reading without system [Random reading] is a waste of time for graduate students.
—**남독하다** read at random [without system, desultorily]
▶ 아무 책이나 남독하지 마라 Don't read every book that you come across [come your way].
■—**가** an omnivorous [a voracious (and indiscriminate)] reader

남동 南東 (the) southeast (略 SE) ⇨ 동남
남동생 男同生 *one's* younger brother

남루 襤褸 〈누더기〉 shabby clothes with patches; rags —**남루하다** ragged; tattered; worn-out; shabby; threadbare
▶ 그 아이는 남루한 옷을 입고 있다 The child is (clad) [goes] in rags (and tatters).
▶ 행색이 남루한 낯선 사람이 다가왔다 A stranger in ragged clothes [in rags] came along.

남매 男妹 brother and sister ▶ 그들은 남매간이다 They are brother and sister. ▶ 그는 5남매를 두었다 He has a son-and-daughter fivesome.

남모르다 be unknown to others; be unseen [hidden, secret]; 〈내심의〉 be inward [in *one's* heart]
♦ 남모르는 고뇌 inward trouble; hardships unknown to others / 남모르는 슬픔 a hidden sorrow / 남모르게 unseen; unobserved; secretly; inwardly
▶ 그녀에게는 남모르는 괴로움이 있다 She has inner troubles [hardships unknown to others].

남미 南美 South America
♦ 남미의 South American —**대륙** South American Continent —**항로** the South American line [service]

남미동 南微東 South by East (略 SbE)
남미서 南微西 South by West (略 SbW)
남바위 a hood hemmed with fur
남반구 南半球 the Southern Hemisphere
남발 濫發 an excessive [a reckless] issue; an overissue ♦ 어음[지폐]의 남발 an overissue of bills [bank notes] —**남발하다** issue excessively [recklessly]; overissue

남방 南方 the south ♦ 남방의 southern; south / 남방으로 여행하다 travel (to the) south
■—**셔츠** an aloha shirt —**인** a southerner —**지역** the southern regions —**한계선** the southern limit [barrier]; the south border: 사과 재배의 남방한계선 the southern limit of apple cultivation

남벌 濫伐 reckless deforestation —**남벌하다** cut down trees recklessly; fell trees indiscriminately; deforest

남복 男服 men's clothes; 〈여자의〉 male attire ⇨ 남장(男裝)

남부 南部 the south(ern) part; 〈미국의〉 the South ♦ 남부의 southern / 남부 사람 〈미국의〉 a Southerner / 남부 각주 〈미국의〉 the Southern States; the South

남부끄럽다 ashamed; shameful; disgraceful; scandalous; disreputable
♦ 남부끄러운 짓 a disgraceful [shameful] act / 남부끄럽지 않은 살림 a decent living / 학교 성적이 남부끄럽지 않다 do fairly well at school / 남부끄럽지 않게 차려입고 있다 be decently dressed
▶ 남부끄러워 돈을 꿔달라고 할 수 없었다 I was too embarrassed to ask for a loan.
▶ 그런 짓을 하고도 남부끄럽지 않니? Aren't you ashamed of having done such a thing?
▶ 그런 소리는 남부끄러워 못하겠다 I am ashamed to say such a thing.

남부럽잖다 well-off; well-to-do ♦ 남부럽잖게 살다 be well [comfortably] off; be well-to-do; live in plenty [abundance]; have no need to envy others

남부여대하다 男負女戴— set out for a new life carrying what remains on *one's* back and on his wife's head; set out on a wandering life

남북 南北 north and south
♦ 남북으로 흐르는 강 a river running from north to south / 남북으로 가로놓이다[에 걸쳐 있다] lie from south to north; extend north and south
▶ 칠레는 남북으로 길게 뻗쳐 있다 Chile is a country stretching out long from north to south.
■—공동성명 the joint communiqué of 4 July 1972 between the South and the North of Korea —교류 exchange between the South and the North of Korea —대화 the South-North talks [dialog] —문제 〈빈·부국간의〉 North-South problems; 〈한국의〉 Korean problems —아메리카 North and South America; both Americas —적십자회담 the South-North Red Cross conference [talks] —전쟁 〔美史〕 the Civil War —조절위원회 the South-North Coordinating Committee (略 SNCC) —통일 the 《peaceful》 reunification of Korea; the national reunification —협상 the South-North negotiations

남북정상회담 南北頂上會談 the South-North summit conference [talks]

남북한 南北韓 the South and the North of Korea; the South Korea and the North Korea

남비 a pan ⇨ 냄비

남빙양 南氷洋 〈남극해〉 the Antarctic Ocean [Sea]

남빛 藍— indigo blue ⇨ 남색(藍色)1

남사당 男寺黨 a wandering [strolling] male entertainer in traditional Korean costume
■—패 a troupe of actors

남산골샌님 南山— a poor [wretched] scholar

남상 男相 a woman's face with masculine features; an unwomanly face ♦ 남상지르다 have a mannish [unwomanly] face [look]

남새 vegetables; greens ■—밭 a kitchen [vegetable] garden

남색 男色 male homosexuality; sodomy; pederasty; buggery ♦ 남색질하다 practice sodomy ■—가 a male homosexual; a sodomite; a pederast; a bugger; (口) a homo 《*pl.* ~s》

남색 藍色 1 〈남빛〉 deep blue; indigo (blue); 〈연한〉 light blue ♦ 남색으로 물들이다 dye 《cloths》 deep blue **2** ⇨ 남색짜리

남색짜리 藍色— a newlywed woman around twenty in a deep blue skirt

남서 南西 the southwest (略 SW) ♦ 남서의 southwest; southwestern / 남서풍 a southwest [southwestern, southwesterly] wind; a southwester

남선북마 南船北馬 constant traveling; restless wandering

남성 男性 1 〈사나이〉 the male (sex); the stronger [sterner] sex; a man; manhood
♦ 남성의 male; of the male sex / 남성 중심의 사회 an androcentric society / 남성만의 파티 a stag party / 남성적인 여자 a masculine woman / 남성적인 태도 a manly attitude
▶ 그에게는 남성적인 데가 없다 He lacks manliness [masculinity].
2 〔文法〕 the masculine gender
■—미 masculine [manly] beauty —호르몬 male hormone —화(化) virilization; virilism: 남성화하다 masculinize

남성 男聲 a male voice ■—사중주[사중창] a male quartet —합창 a male chorus —합창곡 a chorus for male voices

남성용 男性用 ♦ 남성용의 men's; gentlemen's; for gentleman's use / 남성용 시계 a watch for gentleman's use; a gentleman's watch / 남성용 파자마 men's pajamas; pajamas for men / 남성용품 men's things

남실거리다 wave ⇨ 넘실거리다

남십자성 南十字星 〔天〕 the Southern Cross; Crux

남아 男兒 〈사내 아이〉 a boy; a son; 〈대장부〉 a man; a manly man ♦ 남아답게 in a manly manner ▶ 그는 한국 남아다 He is a true Korean man.

남아돌다 〈사물이 주어〉 be more than enough; be in excess; be superabundant [superfluous]; 〈사람이 주어〉 have too many [much]; have more than enough
♦ 사람이 남아도는 회사 an overstaffed firm / 남아도는 excessive; superfluous; overflowing; superabundant
▶ 그는 돈이 남아돌 정도다 He has more money than one can spend [has enough money and to spare, has money to burn].

남아메리카 南— South America

남아일언중천금 男兒一言重千金 A man's word is as good as his bond.

남아프리카 南— South Africa ■—공화국 the Republic of South Africa

남양 南洋 the South Seas ■—군도 the South Sea Islands; Oceania

남여 籃輿 an open palanquin; a sedan chair without cover

남용 濫用 (an) abuse 《of *one's* rights》; misuse; misappropriation; an extravagant [im-

proper] use 《of》
—**남용하다** abuse; misuse; misappropriate; use to excess
◆ 공금을 남용하다 misappropriate public money / 권력을 남용하다 abuse *one's* power ▶ 직권을 남용하지 마라 Don't abuse [strain, stretch] your official authority.
■ 직권(職權)— misfeasance: 직권남용죄 [法] oppression

남우 男優 〈남자 배우〉 an actor (↔an actress) ◆ 오스카상 수상 남우 an Oscar actor / 주연 남우 a leading actor

남우세 disgrace; ignominy; public derision
—**남우세하다** become a laughingstock; become the butt of ridicule
—**남우세스럽다** disgraceful; scandalous; ridiculous
▶ 남우세스런 짓을 하지 마라 Don't disgrace yourself.

남위 南緯 the south latitude (略 S.Lat.)
◆ 남위 53도 42분에 at fifty-three degrees forty-two minutes of south latitude (略 at Lat. 53° 42′S)
▶ 배는 폭발로 인하여 남위 20도 30분, 동경 170도 지점에서 침몰했다 The boat was sunk by an explosion at Lat. 20° 30′S and Long. 170°E.

남유다르다 —類— unique; peculiar; unusual; uncommon
◆ 남유다른 자질을 가진 정치가 a statesman of uncommon quality / 그녀의 남유다른 매력 her own peculiar charm / 남유달리 peculiarly; unusually; exceedingly; uncommonly; exceptionally
▶ 그는 남유달리 부지런한 사람이다 He is an uncommon hard worker.

남유럽 南— Southern Europe

-**남은** odd ◆ 여남은 ten odd / 스무남은 twenty odd

남의눈 (public) notice [attention]; observation; another's eyes
◆ 남의 눈을 피하여 secretly; in secret; by stealth / 남의 눈을 피하며 만나다 have a secret [clandestine] meeting 《with》 / 남의 눈에 띄다 attract people's attention [notice]; be conspicuous
▶ 남의 눈이 있으니 그런 짓은 하지 마라 People are watching, so don't do that.
▶ 그녀의 화려한 옷은 남의 눈을 끌었다 Her showy costume was very eye-catching [a real eye-catcher]. ⇒ Her showy dress attracted everybody's attention.
▶ 남의 눈에 띄지 않는 곳에 이것을 감추기는 곤란하다 It's difficult to hide this in a secret place.

남의달 〈해산할 다음달〉 ◆ 남의달 잡다 be a month late in childbirth

남의 밥에 든 콩이 굵어 보인다 (속담) Our neighbor's ground yields better corn than our own.

남의 손의 떡은 커 보인다 (속담) Better is the neighbor's hen than yours. ⇒ The grass is always greener on the other side of the fence.

남의일 other people's [another's] affairs [business, concern]
▶ 환경 문제는 우리에게 있어 남의 일이 아니다 Environmental pollution is a matter of great concern to us.
▶ 그는 그 사고를 남의 일처럼 생각하는 것 같다 He seems to think that the accident is no concern of his.
▶ 남의 일 같지가 않다 I feel as if it were my own affair.

남의집살이 domestic service ◆ 가정부로 남의 집살이하다 work as a live-in maid

남자 男子 a man; a gentleman; a male; (口) a guy

解說 *man*은 *woman*에 반대되는 성인 남성을 가리키는 가장 일반적인 말로, 어른이 아닌 소년이나 어린 아이에게는 *boy*를 쓴다. *gentleman*은 경의를 나타내어 정중하게 말하는 경우에 쓰이며, *male*은 주로 동·식물의 성에 중점을 두거나 통계학에서 쓰인다.

◆ 남자의 gentleman's; male; masculine / 남자 선생님 a man teacher (*pl.* men teachers) / 남자 손님 a man visitor / 남자옷 men's wear; men's clothes / 남자용품 men's things / 남자 점원 a male clerk / 남자 화장실 the men's room [toilet]; (게시) Gentlemen / 남자 같은 여자 〈활동적인〉 an aggressive woman; 〈용기있는〉 a courageous woman / 남자 중의 남자 a man among men / 남자만의 회합 a party for men only; a stag [buck] party / 남자와 여자 man and woman; men and women / 남자 빤는 여자 a spirited [firm] manly woman / 남자 같은 masculine; manly; mannish / 남자의 한창 때에 in the prime [flower] of manhood / 남자로서의 체면을 세우다[떨어뜨리다] raise [lower] *one's* reputation
▶ 나는 남자 친구가 없다 I have no men friends [boy friends].
▶ 그 여자는 남자 같은 목소리로 말한다 She speaks in a masculine voice [a manly tone of voice].
▶ 나도 자존심이 있는 남자다 I am a man of honor.
▶ 그는 45세로 한창때의 남자다 He is 45 years old and in the prime of life [manhood].
▶ 명색이 남자라면 그런 말을 듣고 분개하지 않을 사람이 있겠는가 Wouldn't he who calls himself a man burn with indignation at such words?
▶ 이 클럽은 남자 전용이다 This club is for men only. ⇌ This is a stag club.
▶ 이런 무거운 물건을 운반하는 데는 남자의 손이 필요하다 We need a man to carry this heavy stuff.
▶ 그는 어려운 경험을 통해 한 사람의 남자가 되었다 The hard experience has made a man of him.
▶ 그는 비열한 짓을 할 남자가 아니다 He is not the sort of man to do mean thing.
▶ 그는 그리 대단한 남자는 아니다 He is not much of a man.
▶ 너를 남자로 믿고 부탁하는 거다 I ask this of you because I consider you a man.

남자답다 男子— masculine; manly; manful

解說 *masculine*은 남자다운 용기・독립심・명예심을 가지고 있음을 뜻한다. *manly*는 성숙한 남성의 용기・힘 등을 의미하며 masculine 보다 기품 있는 말이다. *manful*은 manly의 뜻에 사나이다운「과단성 있는, 단호한」의 뜻이 더해진 것이다.

♦남자다운 행동 a manly(↔unmanly) act / 남자답게 행동하다 behave [act] like a man; play the man
▶그는 힘있고 남자답다 He is strong and manly [a real man].
▶나는 그의 남자다운 태도에 감탄했다 I was impressed by his manly attitude.
▶저 젊은이는 남자다워 보인다 That young man looks strong [brave].
▶그는 남자답게 행동했다 He behaved in a manly way.
▶그런 사소한 일을 걱정하는 것은 남자답지 않다 It's not manly to worry over such trifles.

남작 男爵 a baron ♦헌트 남작 (英) Lord Hunt (▶영국 이외에서는 Baron Hunt) / 남작의 작위 baronage ■━부인 a baroness: 헌트 남작부인 Baroness Hunt; (英) Lady Hunt

남작 濫作 overproduction (of literary works); excessive production
━남작하다 overproduce; produce excessively; 〈작가가〉 write many books at reckless speed; overwrite
▶그 소설가는 꽤 남작하는 편이다 The novelist writes rather excessively.

남잡이가 제잡이 (속담) A curse cuts both ways.

남장 男裝 male attire; men's clothes
▶그녀는 종종 남장을 한다 She often wears men's clothes.
━남장하다 wear [be in, put on] men's clothes; disguise *oneself* as a man; be dressed like a man
▶그녀는 남장하고 그 파티에 몰래 참석했다 She sneaked into the party disguised as a man.
■━미인 a beauty in male attire

남정 男丁 a man above the age of fifteen; a grown-up; an adult man ♦남정네 〈남자들〉 the menforks; 〈남편들〉 the husbands

남조 濫造 overproduction; 〈조제(粗製)〉 careless manufacture
━남조하다 produce in [to] excess; overproduce; manufacture carelessly
♦효력도 없는 약을 남조하다 manufacture useless medicine in profusion

남조류 藍藻類 〔植〕 the blue-green algae

남존여비 男尊女卑 male chauvinism; predominance of men over women ♦남존여비의 사회 a male-dominated society
▶그 지방에는 아직도 남존여비의 풍습이 남아 있다 The custom of treating women as inferior to men still remains in that district.

남종 男━ a manservant; a male slave

남종화 南宗畫 〔畫〕 Chinese painting of the Southern School

남중 南中 meridian transit; southing; meridian passage; culmination ━남중하다 south; cross the meridian; culminate

남중국해 南中國海 the South China Sea

남중일색 男中一色 a very handsome [good-looking] man; an Adonis

남진 南進 southward advance [movement]; southern expansion ━남진하다 advance [march, push] southward

남짓 over; above; odd; more than; upward of
♦10년 남짓 over [more than] ten years; ten years and more / 5천원 남짓 five thousand won odd; five thousand odd won / 1세기 남짓 (for) something over a century
▶나는 은행에 400달러 남짓 가지고 있다 I have 400 odd dollars [dollars odd] in the bank.
▶두 시간 남짓 기다렸으나 그녀는 오지 않았다 I waited for over two hours, but she didn't come.
▶그들은 3마일 남짓 걸었다 They walked over [more than] three miles.

남짓하다 be a bit over [above, more than]; be upward of
♦70세 남짓한 노인 an old man over seventy / 30명 남짓하다 be more than thirty people; be thirty strong
▶이 기계는 10년 남짓한 연구 끝에 겨우 완성되었다 This machine was finished as the result of over ten years' research work.
▶거기는 여기서 10킬로미터 남짓한 거리다 It is a little over 10 kilometers from here.

남쪽 南━ south (略 S)
♦남쪽의 southern; south / 남쪽에 in the southern part (of Panama) / 남쪽으로 southward; toward(s) the south / 북쪽에서 남쪽으로 from north to south / 남쪽으로 곧장 약 10마일 about 10 miles due south (of, from) / 남쪽이 바다에 면하다 face the sea on the south / 남쪽을 향하다 face [look toward] the south / 남쪽으로 가다 go [proceed] south [southward]
▶수원은 서울에서 약 40킬로미터 남쪽에 있다 Suwon is about forty kilometers south of Seoul.
▶바람이 남쪽에서 불어온다 The wind blows southerly [from the south].

남창 男唱 a song by a woman in male voice

남창 男娼 a male prostitute; a professional catamite

남천촉 南天燭 〔植〕 a sacred bamboo

남침 南侵 an invasion of the south (by); a southward invasion ━남침하다 invade the south

남태평양 南太平洋 the South Pacific

남파 南派 dispatching to the south
━남파하다 send [dispatch] 《an armed agent》 to the south
■━간첩 an espionage agent sent out (by the north) to the south

남편 男便 a husband; (口) a hubby [hub]
♦남편 있는 married / 남편 없는 single; unmarried / 남편을 욕보게 하다 bring disgrace upon *one's* husband / 남편을 잃다 lose *one's* husband / 남편을 잘 섬기다 be devoted to *one's* husband / 남편을 휘두르다 wear the

breeches [pants, trousers]
▶ 당신은 남편답지 못하다 You are not much of a husband.
▶ 그는 폭군같은 남편이다 He lords it over his wife.
▶ 그이는 내게는 이상적인 남편입니다 He is an ideal husband for me.
▶ 그녀는 남편을 깔아 뭉개고 있다 She wears the pants [breeches].
▶ 그녀는 남편을 얻지 못했다 She failed to catch a husband.

남포[1] 〈화약〉 dynamite
◆ 남포 두 개 two sticks of dynamite / 남포질하다 dynamite; blast [blow up] 《a rock》 with dynamite
▶ 남포로 다리를 폭파했다 They blew up the bridge with dynamite. ⇌ They dynamited the bridge.

남포[2] a lamp ⇨ 램프[1]

남폿불 lamplight; a lamp

남풍 南風 a south [southerly] wind; a wind from the south
▶ 남풍이 분다 The wind blows southerly [from the south].
▶ 어제는 남풍이 종일 세게 불었다 The south wind blew hard all day yesterday.
▶ 오후에는 남풍이 불 것이다 There will be a south wind in the afternoon.

남하 南下 southward advance [movement] —**남하하다** go [advance] south(ward); go down
◆ 자유를 찾아 남하하다 come to the south seeking for freedom
▶ 부대는 남하했다 The unit moved south.
▶ 일행은 반도를 남하했다 The party went south(ward) the peninsula.

남학생 男學生 a boy student; a school boy

남한 南韓 South Korea

남해 南海 the southern sea; the South Sea

남행 南行 going south; southing —**남행하다** go (down) south; south ■—**열차** a southbound train

남향 南向 a southern exposure [aspect]; a south aspect; facing the south —**남향하다** face [look toward] (the) south; be exposed to the south
■—**집** a house facing [looking (toward the)] south; a house with a southern exposure [prospect] —**판** a site facing south

남화 南畫 〔畫〕 Chinese painting of the Southern School=남종화(南宗畫)

남회귀선 南回歸線 the tropic of Capricorn

남획 濫獲 reckless [excessive, indiscriminate] fishing [hunting]; overfishing; overhunting —**남획하다** fish [hunt] recklessly [indiscriminately, excessively]; overfish; overhunt
◆ 고래[들소]를 남획하다 catch whales [hunt buffaloes] in excessive numbers
▶ 그 새는 남획으로 인해 멸종의 위기에 놓여 있다 That species of bird is endangered because of overhunting.

납 lead; 〔化〕 plumbum ◆ 납의 leaden / 납덩이 a lead [leaden] ball ■—**정련소** a lead refinery —**중독** lead poisoning —**화합물** a lead compound

납 鑞 〈땜납〉 solder ▶ 주전자의 구멍을 납으로 때웠다 I soldered the hole in the kettle.

납 蠟 wax ◆ 납을 먹인 천 waxed cloth ▶ 마루에 납을 먹였다 I waxed the floor.

납골 納骨 laying sb's ashes to rest —**납골하다** lay [place] sb's ashes to rest ■—**당** a charnel (house); an ossuary

납관 納棺 encoffining —**납관하다** place [put, lay] 《sb's body》 in a coffin; encoffin ■—**식** rites of placing a body in a coffin

납금 納金 〈지급〉 payment of money; 〈돈〉 money paid [due] —**납금하다** pay 《money》

납기 納期 〈금전〉 the time [period] for payment; 〈품의〉 the appointed date [time limit] of delivery ◆ 세금의 납기일 the date of tax payment
▶ 수업료는 납기내에 내야 한다 School fees should be paid by the due date.

납길하다 納吉— notify the bride's family of the wedding date

납덩이 a lead ingot ◆ 납덩이 같다 《비유》〈얼굴이〉 be pale; look pale; be dull as lead; 〈몸이〉 be [feel] as heavy as lead
▶ 아침에 깨어나니 손발이 납덩이처럼 무거웠다 In the morning I woke up feeling that my limbs were as heavy as lead.

납득 納得 〈이해〉 understanding; 〈수긍〉 assent; consent; 〈만족〉 satisfaction
◆ 납득이 되는 설명 a satisfactory explanation / 납득이 되지 않는 말 a story hard to understand / 납득이 가다 understand
▶ 그는 납득이 가지 않는 얼굴이었다 He looked puzzled.
▶ 충분히 납득이 갈 때까지 선생님께 여쭈어라 Ask the teacher questions again and again till you understand well.
▶ 납득이 되도록 설명해 주십시오 Please explain to my satisfaction.
▶ 그의 말은 납득이 되지 않는다 I can't understand him. ⇌ I don't agree with him.
▶ 이 문제는 납득이 될 때까지 토론하는게 좋다 We had better discuss this problem until it is mutually understood.
—**납득하다** understand; consent [assent] 《to》; be persuaded
◆ 납득하기 어려운 unconvincing 《argument》; hard to understand / 납득시키다 convince sb 《of 《his error》; reason sb in compliance / 충분히 납득시키다 give sb a clear grasp of
▶ 마침내 그도 납득한 것 같다 It seems that he, also, finally agreed.
▶ 소액의 보상으로는 그들은 납득하지 않을 것이다 They won't be satisfied with a small amount of compensation.
▶ 그런 부당한 일은 납득할 수 없다 I can't consent to [understand] such an absurdity.
▶ 외국행을 단념하도록 그를 납득시켰다 I persuaded him to give up going abroad. ⇌ I dissuaded him from going abroad.
▶ 그것이 정말이라는 것을 그에게 납득시킬 수가 없다 I cannot convince him of its truth [that it is true].

납땜 鑞— soldering —**납땜하다** solder ◆ 납땜

한 soldered ━인두 a soldering iron

납량 納涼 enjoying the cool air; cooling *oneself* ━납량하다 cool *oneself* in the (summer) breeze; enjoy the cool air
━객(客) a cool-breeze hunter; people out to enjoy a cool breeze ━유람선 summer pleasure boat ━음악회 a summer evening concert

납본 納本 〈책의 납품〉 delivery of books; 〈검열용〉 presentation of a specimen copy; a specimen copy (for censorship)
━납본하다 〈주문자에게〉 deliver books 《to》; 〈당국에〉 present a specimen copy to the authorities

납부 納付 〈세금·공과금 등의〉 payment; 〈물품의〉 delivery
━납부하다 pay; deliver
♦수업료를 납부하다 pay a tuition / 세금을 납부하다 pay *one's* taxes / 분할하여 납부하다 pay on the installment plan; pay in installments
▶클럽 회비를 즉시 납부해 주십시오 Please pay your club dues immediately.
■━분할— divided payments; payment on an installment basis ■━금(액) the amount of payment ━기한 the deadline for payment: 수업료 납부 기한은 언제냐? When is your tuition due [to be paid]? ━자 a payer

납북 拉北 ━납북하다 kidnap [abduct] *sb* to the north; hijack [skyjack] 《an airplane》 to the north
▶많은 사람들이 납북되었다 Many people were kidnaped [abducted] to the north.
━어선[어부, 인사] a fishing boat [fisherman, person] kidnaped to north Korea

납빛 lead color; lead gray ♦납빛의 lead-colored; lead-gray; leaden

납석 蠟石 〖鑛〗 agalmatolite; pagodite

납세 納稅 tax payment; the payment of tax
▶그는 납세를 지체하고 있다 He is behind [in arrears] with his taxes. = His taxes are overdue [in arrears].
━납세하다 pay *one's* taxes
━고지서 a tax notice [bill]; tax papers ━기일 the time limit for tax payment; the tax day ━대장 a tax book [list, roll] ━액 the amount of *one's* taxes ━증지 a tax payment stamp ━필 (표시) Tax Paid.

납세공 蠟細工 a waxwork ■━품 진열실 a show room of waxworks

납세신고 納稅申告 income tax returns ♦납세 신고를 하다 declare *one's* (annual) earnings for income tax; fill [make] out *one's* income tax returns ━용지 a tax form

납세의무 納稅義務 a legal obligation to pay (*one's*) taxes; liability to taxation [for tax payment]
♦납세 의무가 있다 be (legally) obliged to pay (*one's*) taxes; be liable to taxation / 납세 의무를 다하다 fulfill *one's* obligation to pay (*one's*) taxes
▶그들은 납세 의무가 면제되어 있다 They are exempt from taxation.
▶국민은 납세 의무를 진다 The people shall be liable to taxation.

납세자 納稅者 a taxpayer ♦고액 납세자 a large taxpayer ■━자진 신고— a self-assessed taxpayer

납시다 《the king》 deign to be present; appear

납신거리다 1 〈재잘거리다〉 chatter; prattle; patter; rattle; talk glibly and flippantly
▶소녀들은 남자친구에 대해 납신거리고 있었다 The girls chattered [prattled, gabbed] about their boyfriends.
2 ⇨ 굼실거리다

납유리 ━琉璃 flint glass

납인형 蠟人形 a wax doll [figure]; a waxwork ■━관 (a house of) waxworks; a wax museum

납입 納入 payment 《of a tax》; delivery 《of goods》 ━납입하다 pay 《a tax》 ■━금 〈지급된〉 money paid; 〈지급해야 할〉 money due ━품 supplies; goods for supply

납작 ━납작 받아먹다 seize upon with *one's* mouth wide open / 납작 엎드리다 lie on *one's* stomach; flatten *oneself* on the ground; lie down flat 《on *one's* belly》 / 납작 엎드려서 기어가다 creep [move] on *one's* stomach [belly]
▶그 물고기는 미끼를 납작 물었다 The fish snapped at the bait.

납작보리 〈압맥〉 pressed [rolled] barley

납작코 a pug [snub] nose; a flat [squat] nose; 〈사람〉 a flat-nosed person

납작하다 flat; low; thin
♦납작한 얼굴 (have) a flat face / 납작한 지붕 a flat roof / 납작하게 flatly; level / 납작하게 만들다 〈형태를〉 make flat [low, thin]; 〈사람을〉 snub; humble / 납작하게 하다 flatten; level / 납작해지다 〈형태가〉 be flattened; become flat; be crushed flat; 〈사람이〉 be snubbed [humbled]
▶심해에는 납작하게 생긴 물고기가 많이 살고 있다 There live a lot of flat fish in a deep sea.
▶나는 잘못하여 상자를 밟아 납작하게 짜부라뜨렸다 I carelessly stepped on the box and crushed it.
▶저 녀석의 콧대를 납작하게 해 주겠다 I'm going to bash in [flatten] that guy's nose.

납지 蠟紙 wax paper

납채 納采 betrothal presents sent by the bridegroom's family ⇨ 납폐(納幣)

납치 拉致 kidnap(p)ing; abduction; hijacking
━납치하다 take *sb* away forcibly; kidnap; hijack; skyjack
♦비행기를 납치하다 hijack [skyjack] an airplane / 인질로 납치하다 kidnap [abduct] *sb* as a hostage
▶그는 반대파에게 납치당했다 He was abducted by an opposing group.

납폐 納幣 betrothal presents [wedding gifts] sent by the bridegroom's family to the bride's family

납품 納品 delivery 《of goods》
▶그 서적은 납품을 끝냈다 We have completed the delivery of the books.
━납품하다 deliver 《goods》; supply 《an office with computers》 ♦군대에 납품하다 supply goods to the army

▶ 부품은 월요일까지 납품해 주십시오 Please deliver the parts to us [supply us with the parts] by Monday.
▶ 우리 회사는 그 병원에 기기를 납품하고 있다 We supply the hospital with equipment.
■ —서 a delivery note; a bill of goods —업자 a supplier : 관공서 납품업자 a merchant under government patronage

납회 納會 〈닊시의〉 the last [final] meeting of the year [term]; 〈증권 거래소의〉 the last [closing] session

낫 a sickle; a reaping hook; 〈큰〉 a scythe
♦ 낫으로 벼를 베다 reap rice with a sickle / 낫으로 풀을 베다 mow grass with a sickle; sickle down weeds

낫 놓고 기역자도 모르다 (속담) be completely illiterate; do not know A from B

낫다¹ 〈치유되다〉 be cured (of a disease); heal (up); 〈좋아지다〉 get well [better]
♦ 낫지 않는 incurable / 감기가 낫다 get well of a cold; get over one's cold / 저절로 낫다 heal of itself / 차츰 나아 가다 be getting better; start to get better
▶ 나는 상처를 입어도 곧 낫는다 My wound will soon heal up. ⇒ Even if I get hurt, the injury will soon heal (up).
▶ 작은 상처는 깨끗이 해두면 곧 낫는다 Small wounds heal rapidly when they are kept clean.
▶ 환자는 곧 나았다 The patient recovered quickly.
▶ 어머니의 병은 아주 나았다 Mother is quite all right [well]. ⇒ Mother has completely recovered (from her illness).
▶ 이 약으로 병이 나았다 This medicine cured me.
▶ 감기는 이제 나았습니다 I've got over my cold now.
▶ 내 위궤양은 완전히 나았다 My stomach ulcer has been completely cured [healed].
▶ 감기가 낫는 데 오래 걸렸다 It took me a long time to get over [shake off] my cold.
▶ 병이 나아 갈 때에 특히 몸조심해야 한다 You must take good care of yourself when you are convalescing [starting to get better].
▶ 이 벤 상처는 잘 낫지 않는다 This cut is slow to heal.
▶ 환자는 자기 병이 낫지 않는 병임을 알고 있었다 The patient knew his disease was incurable [past remedy].

낫다² 〈더 좋다〉 better 《than》; superior 《to》; preferable 《to》; have an advantage 《over》
♦ 아버지보다 낫다 outdo [surpass] one's father
▶ 이런 일에 관해서는 그가 너보다 낫다 He is a cut above you in this kind of affairs. ⇒ You are no match for him in such matters.
▶ 그것은 어떤 것보다도 낫다 It tops everything.
▶ 너는 무엇을 하든 그보다 낫다 You do a good job than he in everything.
▶ 이 차는 몇가지 점에서 먼저 것보다 낫다 This car has several advantages over [is superior in many points to] the old one.
▶ 기분이 좀 낫습니까? Are you feeling any better?
▶ 조금뿐이라도 없는 것보다는 낫다 Something is better than nothing.
▶ 늦더라도 전혀 안 하는 것보다 낫다 (속담) Better late than never.
▶ 그렇게 살 바에야 차라리 죽는게 낫다 I would rather [sooner] die than lead such a life.
▶ 그것보다 나은 것은 없다 Nothing can be better than that.
▶ 직접 해보는 것보다 나은 방법은 없다 There is nothing like trying it.
▶ 이 점에서는 그보다 나은 사람이 없다 He is second to none in this respect.
▶ 조심하는 것보다 나은 것은 없다 Nothing is better than caution. ⇒ Caution is the best policy.
▶ 자식을 판단하는 데 아버지보다 나은 사람은 없다 A father is the best judge of his son.
▶ 이것이 저것보다 나을 것이다 This would be better than that.
▶ 전지 요양을 하는 것이 제일 나을 것이다 You had best go somewhere for a change of air.

낫살 a mature age ⇨ 나잇살

낫잡다 〈넉넉하게 치다〉 estimate [rate] high; 〈여유를 두다〉 leave a margin; give ample measure (to)
♦ 낫잡아서 열흘 ten days at the longest / 낫잡아서 1마일 a mile at the (very) outside
▶ 낫잡아 17세쯤 되었겠지 I think she is seventeen at the most.

낫표 —標 Korean quotation marks (▶ 「」 기호의 인쇄상의 명칭)

낭군 郎君 〈남편〉《my》 dear husband

낭독 朗讀 reading aloud; a reading; a recital; 〈시 등의〉 recitation
▶ 그의 키츠 시 낭독은 훌륭했다 His recitation of Keats' poem was excellent.
—**낭독하다** read aloud; recite; declaim
♦ 시[자작시]를 낭독하다 give [do] a reading of a [one's] poem; recite a [one's] poem
▶ 그녀는 근대시를 낭독했다 She recited modern poems.
▶ 여배우는 정성을 들여 한편의 시를 낭독했다 The actress read aloud [recited] a poem with all her heart.
■ —법 elocution —자 a reader; a reciter —조 연설 a reading speech : 그는 낭독조 연설을 했다 He just read his speech. —회 a public reading : 자작시 낭독회를 하다 give a reading [recital] of one's poetry; recite [read] one's poetry

낭떠러지 a precipice; a bluff; a cliff
♦ 낭떠러지를 기어 올라가다 scale [climb up] a cliff / 낭떠러지에서 떨어지다 fall from [off] a precipice; tumble down a precipice
▶ 그 나무는 낭떠러지 끝에 서 있다 The tree stands on the edge of a cliff.

낭랑하다 朗朗— clear (and ringing); sonorous ♦ 낭랑한 목소리로 in a clear [ringing, sonorous] voice
▶ 그는 낭랑하게 그 대사를 읽기 시작했다 He began to read the lines in a clear, resonant voice.

낭만 浪漫 being romantic ♦낭만적인 생각에 잠기다 indulge in romantics

낭만주의 浪漫主義 romanticism ■신— neo-romanticism ■—문학 romantic literature —자 a romanticist

낭만파 浪漫派 the romantic school ■—시인 a romantic poet

낭보 朗報 〈회소식〉 good [happy] news; glad tidings; welcome news; a welcome report
▶그 낭보로 전시내는 온통 축제 분위기였다 The good news threw the whole city into a wild celebration.

낭비 浪費 (a) waste; a wasteful use; wastefulness; 〈사치〉 extravagance
♦정력[돈]의 낭비 waste of energy [money] / 낭비를 줄이다[그치다] reduce [stop] waste
▶이 달은 낭비 때문에 100만원의 적자다 I have gone one million won into the red from my extravagance this month.
▶거기에 가는 것은 시간과 돈의 낭비다 It is a waste of time and money to go there.
▶우리는 낭비를 좀 더 없앨 수 있을 것이다 We should be able to eliminate more of the waste.
▶그의 노력은 결국 시간의 낭비로 끝났다 His efforts resulted in his time going to waste.
▶그는 낭비로 빚을 지게 되었다 His extravagance put him in debt.
—낭비하다 waste; use [spend] 《money》 recklessly; throw away; idle [fritter] 《one's time》 away; squander *one's* money 《on》; be prodigal of
♦낭비하는 wasteful; wasting / 도박에 돈을 낭비하다 waste [squander] *one's* money on gambling; throw away *one's* money by gambling / 쓸데 없는 것에 시간과 돈을 낭비하다 waste *one's* time and money on useless things
▶그는 돈을 물쓰듯 낭비했다 He made ducks and drakes of his money.
▶그는 상속 재산을 모두 낭비했다 He trifled away his entire inheritance.
▶그들은 자연 자원을 낭비하고 있다 They are wasting natural resources. ⇌ They are wasteful of [with] natural resources.
▶그는 아르바이트로 번 돈을 낭비하고 있다 He is throwing away the money (which) he earned on the side.
▶시간을 낭비하지 마라 Save your time.
▶좋은 결과를 얻지 못한 채 3년이란 세월이 낭비되었다 Three years were wasted without any good results.
■—자 a wasteful person; a spendthrift; a waster; a prodigal

낭비벽 浪費癖 wasteful [spendthrift] habits
♦낭비벽이 있는 사람 an extravagant [a thriftless] person; a spendthrift / 낭비벽이 있다 have [be in] the habit of wasting money

낭설 浪說 《spread, circulate》 a wild [false] rumor; an unfounded [a groundless] report
♦낭설을 믿다 take rumor as it is / 낭설을 퍼뜨리다 start a rumor; spread a sensational rumor; set a false rumor afloat
▶그 소문은 순전히 낭설이다 The rumor is completely unfounded.
▶온갖 낭설이 돌고 있다 All sorts of rumors are going around [are abroad].

낭송 朗誦 recitation; reading **—낭송하다** recite; give a recitation; read aloud ♦시를 낭송하다 chant [recite] a poem loudly [in a loud voice]

낭자 娘子 〈처녀〉 a girl; a maiden; a virgin; a young woman

낭자 狼藉 〈흩어져 어지러움〉 disorder; confusion **—낭자하다** be in wild disorder; be in untidy state; be in great confusion; be scattered all over ♦유혈이 낭자하다 be all covered with blood

낭종 囊腫 〔醫〕 a cystoma (*pl.* ~s, ~ ta); a cystic tumor

낭중 囊中 (the inside of) a pocket ♦낭중 무일푼이다 be utterly penniless; have no money with *one* ■—취물 an easy task

낭창 狼瘡 〔醫〕 lupus

낭창낭창하다 〈물건이〉 pliant; pliable; flexible; 〈몸이〉 limber; supple; lithe
♦낭창낭창한 가죽 soft [pliable] leather / 낭창낭창한 나뭇가지 a flexible twig; a switch / 낭창낭창한 몸 lithe [limber] body

낭패 狼狽 〈곤경〉 trouble; difficulty; 〈실패〉 failure; a blunder; defeat
▶차가 고장나서 낭패다 We are in a fix. Our car has broken down.
▶이것 참 낭패로구나 We are in an awkward [embarrassing] position. ⇌ 〈자조적으로〉 Things have come to a pretty pass! ⇌ This is a nice business, indeed!
—낭패하다 be in trouble [difficulty]; be confused; 〈곤경에 처하다〉 be in a fix
▶그는 낭패한 기색을 보였다 He showed his confusion.
▶그녀의 사고 소식에 그는 사뭇 낭패해 했다 News of her accident upset him a lot.

낮 〈주간〉 daytime; day; 〈오정〉 noon; noonday; noontime
♦대낮[한낮] midday; high noon / 밤낮 (없이) day and night; around [round] the clock / 낮일 day work / 낮에 in [during] the day (time) / 낮에 일하고 밤에 학교에 다니다 work by day and attend school by night
▶낮에는 흐려 있었지만 밤에는 별이 보였다 It was cloudy during the day, but we could see the stars at night.
▶숲속은 낮에도 어두웠다 It was dark in the woods even in the daytime.

낮다 1 〈높이가 작다〉 low(↔high); 〈숫자가 작다〉 small
♦낮은 언덕 a low hill / 낮은 천장 a low ceiling / 낮은 코 a flat nose
▶이 주변의 산은 모두 낮다 Around here the mountains are all of low attitude.
▶가뭄으로 강의 수위가 낮다 The river is low because of the drought.
▶이곳은 해면보다 낮다 This place is below sea level.
▶들에 안개가 낮게 드리워져 있다 Fog hung low over the field.
▶버들가지가 낮게 드리워져 있다 The willow branches hang low.

▶ 그녀는 자신의 낮은 코를 싫어한다 She doesn't like her flat nose.
2 〈정도·지위가〉 low; humble; lowly; poor ◆ 낮은 생활 수준 a low standard of living / 신분이 낮다 〈태생이〉 be of low birth; 〈지위가〉 be of low social position / 낮은 수입으로 지내다 live on a low [small] income
▶ 그들은 생활수준이 낮다 Their standard of living is low.
▶ 이 나라는 교육수준이 낮다 Education is of a low level in this country.
▶ 저 분은 능력은 있는데 지위는 아직 낮다 The man still holds a minor position even though he has a lot of ability.
▶ 봉건시대에는 신분이 낮은 소작인은 경멸당하는 일이 많았다 The lowly peasants were often thought lightly of in feudal days.
▶ 그는 자기의 낮은 지위에 만족하지 않고 있다 He is not satisfied with low [humble] position he holds.
3 〈소리가 높지 않다〉 low (↔loud) ◆ 낮은 음 a low-pitched sound
▶ 그는 낮은 목소리로 말했다 He spoke in a low voice. ⇒ He talked in whispers.
▶ 그녀의 목소리는 낮아졌다 Her voice sank. ⇒ Her voice dropped to a whisper.
▶ 낮은 소리로 말하시오 Please lower your voice.

낮도깨비 〈도깨비〉 a goblin [ghost, phantom, (口) spook] haunting in broad daylight; 〈사람〉 a shameless bastard

낮도둑 a noonday [sneak] thief; (비유) a greedy person; a shark

낮말은 새가 듣고 밤말은 쥐가 듣는다 (속담) Walls [Pitchers] have ears. ⇒ Little pitcher have long ears.

낮번 一番 the day shift ◆ 낮번 들다 take the day shift

낮은말 1 ⇨ 낮춤말 **2** 〈속삭임〉 murmuring; whispers **3** 〈천한 말〉 (use) a vulgar word; vulgar language; a vulgarism

낮은음자리표 一音一標 the bass staff; f-clef

낮잠 a nap; a noon's nap; a siesta ◆ 낮잠 자다 take a nap [siesta]
▶ 점심 후 낮잠 자는 것이 내 습관이다 It is my habit to take a nap after lunch.
▶ 나는 나무 그늘에서 낮잠을 잤다 I had [took] a nap under a tree.

낮잡다 〈낮게 잡다〉 estimate [rate, appraise, evaluate] low [below cost]; underestimate; underrate
◆ 낮잡은 액수[숫자] a conservative amount [figure] / 아주 낮잡아서 at the lowest estimate

낮차 一車 〈기차〉 a day train [coach]

낮참 1 〈점심밥〉 lunch (usually for day laborers); a midday meal **2** 〈휴식 시간〉 a (one's) lunch break [hour]; a noon recess

낮추다 1 〈정도 등을〉 lower; make low; bring [let] down; 〈소리를〉 subdue; drop; lower; sink; 〈라디오 등을〉 tone down
◆ 값을 낮추다 lower [reduce, bring down] the price / 목소리를 낮추다 lower [sink] one's voice / 수준을 낮추다 lower the standard / 반음 낮추다 〔樂〕 flat (a note) by a half tone
▶ 라디오의 볼륨을 좀 낮춰주시오 Please turn the radio down.
▶ 그는 주인 앞에서는 늘 자신을 낮춘다 He is always humble in the presence of his master.
2 〈강등시키다〉 downgrade; reduce (a soldier) to a lower rank; (美) demote (to); 〈품질을 떨어뜨리다〉 degrade; debase
3 〈말을 놓다〉 speak in familiar [plain] terms
▶ 말씀 낮추십시오 Please drop honorifics.

낮추보다 look down on; have a low opinion (of); make light of; hold sb cheap [in contempt]; 〈낮잡다〉 estimate low [below cost]; undervalue; make a low estimate of
◆ 남의 능력을 낮추보다 underrate another's ability

낮춤말 〈낮은말〉 intimate [friendly] speech [terms]; 〈겸손어〉 humble [modest] words

낯 1 〈얼굴〉 a face; 〈표정〉 a look; looks; a countenance
▶ 그는 무엇인가를 묻는 낯이었다 He put on [wore] a questioning look.
〈낯이[은]〉 낯이 붉다 have a red face; be red-faced / 낯이 익다[설다] be familiar [unfamiliar] with sb
▶ 나는 부끄러워서 낯이 붉어졌다 I blushed for [with] shame.
▶ 그 소식을 듣자 그녀의 낯이 갑자기 밝아졌다 When she heard the news, her face suddenly brightened [she suddenly looked happy]. (▶ 반대로「낯이 어두워졌다」는…her face clouded over [she looked sad])
▶ 그 사람 낯은 알지만 이름은 모른다 I know him by sight, but not by name.
〈낯을〉 낯을 대하다 face each other / 낯을 들다 raise one's face; lift one's head; shoot [fling] up one's face / 낯을 익히다 become acquainted [familiar] with sb / 낯을 찌푸리다 make [(英) pull] face (at); make [give] a grimace / 낯을 찡그리다 make a wry face; frown; contort [wrinkle up, pucker up] one's face / 좋은 낯을 하다 look satisfied [pleased]; have a smile on one's face
▶ 그는 좋지 않은 낯을 하고 있다 He does not look pleased. ⇒ He wears a displeased expression.
〈낯으로〉 웃는 낯으로 with a smile on one's face; with a beaming face / 웃는 낯으로 사람을 대하다 welcome sb with a smile
▶ 그녀는 비웃는 낯으로 나를 보았다 She threw a look of contempt at me.
2 〈면목, 체면〉 face; honor; prestige
〈낯이〉 낯이 깎이다 be put out of countenance; lose one's face [reputation, honor] / 볼 낯이 없다 have no face [countenance]; be ashamed of sb / 낯이 팔려 있다 be widely known; be popular
▶ 너를 볼 낯이 없다 I'm ashamed to see you.
▶ 세상 사람들을 대할 낯이 없다 I dare not show myself [my face] in public. ⇒ How can I face people?
▶ 그런 짓을 했으니 어떻게 내가 그녀를 볼 낯이 있겠니? How can I see her after doing such a thing?

〈낯을[으로]〉 낯을 들지 못하다 be ashamed to sb; cannot face sb / 낯을 세우다 save sb's honor [face]; relieve sb from disgrace; keep sb in countenance
▶ 나는 세상에 낯을 들 수 없다 I am ashamed to show myself in public.
▶ 무슨 낯을 들고 너를 다시 보겠니? I am too ashamed on myself (ever) to see you again.
▶ 내 낯을 보아 그 애를 용서해 주시오 Please forgive the boy for my sake [just to save my face].
▶ 무슨 낯으로 그들을 만나랴 How can I ever have the face to see them?

낯가리다 〈꺼리다〉 be bashful [timid] with strangers; be afraid [shy] of strangers ◆낯가리어 울다 cry at the sight of strangers
▶ 이 아이는 아직도 낯(을) 가린다 This child is still bashful [shy] in front of strangers.
▶ 이 애는 낯가리지 않는다 This baby takes to most strangers [is sociable with everybody].

낯가죽 sense of honor [shame]
◆낯가죽이 두껍다 have lots of nerve (in one); be thick-skinned; be cheeky; be shameless
▶ 그는 낯가죽 두꺼운 거짓말쟁이다 He is an impudent [a brazen-faced, a bold-faced] liar.
▶ 나는 그런 낯가죽 두꺼운 짓은 못한다 I don't have the nerve to do such a thing.
▶ 참 낯가죽도 두꺼운 녀석이다 What an affront! ⇒ What nerve he's got!

낯간지럽다 feel embarrassed [awkward, self-conscious]; ashamed; blushed; conscience-stricken
▶ 이 작품으로 상을 받는다니 좀 낯간지럽습니다 I feel a bit embarrassed to get a prize for a work like this.
▶ 그렇게 과분한 칭찬을 하시니 낯간지럽습니다 So much praise embarrasses me [make me feel awkward].
▶ 그의 비평을 듣고 나는 낯간지러워졌다 I felt very much flattered by his comment.

낯나다 〈생색이 나다〉 gain [win] honor; get credit; reflect honor [credit] on oneself
▶ 그는 그 일로 낯났다 The work did him credit.
▶ 이것으로 그도 낯날 것이다 This will be to his credit. ⇒ This will bring him credit.

낯내다 〈생색을 내다〉 take credit to oneself (for); (口) do oneself proud [credit]; act so as to gain the respect of others
◆낯내기 위하여 기부하다 make a donation just to reflect credit on oneself
▶ 그것은 낯낼 일이 못된다 We could not get credit for that. ⇒ That is nothing to be proud of.

낯두껍다 thick-skinned; 〈철면피한〉 brazen-faced; 〈부끄러움이 없는〉 shameless; 〈뻔뻔스러운〉 saucy; audacious; cheeky; impudent
◆낯두껍게도 …하다 have the impudence to do
▶ 그에게 그런 낯두꺼운 말은 할 수 없다 I haven't the nerve [face] to say such a thing to him.
▶ 그는 낯두껍게도 또 왔다 He had the impudence [effrontery] to come again. ⇒ He was brazen-faced [shameless] enough to come again.

낯바닥 (俗) a phiz; (美俗) a pan ⇨ 낯짝

낯부끄럽다 ashamed; shameful; disgraceful
◆낯부끄러운 행위 a shameful [disgraceful] behavior [conduct]
▶ 학교를 퇴학당하다니 참으로 낯부끄럽다 It is really shameful [a disgrace] to be expelled from school.

낯붉히다 become [go] red in the face; 〈부끄러워 하다〉 blush with [for] shame; color up; 〈흥분하다〉 flush (up) with excitement; 〈성나다〉 redden [flush] with anger; get angry; turn red [crimson]
◆낯(을) 붉히는 신부 a blushing bride / 여학생처럼 낯(을) 붉히다 blush like a schoolgirl
▶ 그의 말에 그녀는 낯(을) 붉혔다 His words made her blush.
▶ 그는 성이 나서 낯(을) 붉혔다 He was red [flushed] with anger.
▶ 그는 여간해서 낯(을) 붉히지 않는다 He is slow to get angry.

낯빛 complexion ⇨ 안색(顔色)

낯설다 strange; unfamiliar; unknown
◆낯선 도시 a strange [an unfamiliar] town / 낯선 사람 a stranger / 낯선 얼굴 an unfamiliar face
▶ 나는 이곳이 낯설다 I am strange [a stranger] here. ⇒ I am quite new here [to this place].
▶ 낯선 사람이 나에게 말을 걸어왔다 A stranger spoke to me.
▶ 길에서 어떤 낯선 사람이 인사를 했다 A stranger greeted me on the street.
▶ 낯선 도시에서는 지도가 없어선 안된다 You cannot do without a map in an unfamiliar [a strange] city.

낯알다 〈얼굴을 기억하다〉 know sb by sight; know the face (of a man); remember (seeing sth [sb] before)
◆낯아는 사람이 많다 have a large [wide] acquaintance / 낯아는 사이가 되다 get to know; get [be, become] acquainted (with)

낯없다 disgrace oneself; have no face to; lose (one's) face; be in no position to; be ashamed of oneself; be in disgrace; be put out of countenance
▶ 정말 뵐 낯없습니다 I am really ashamed of myself. ⇒ I have no excuse to offer.
▶ 이런 실수를 하다니 뵐 낯없습니다 I've disgraced myself with this mistake.

낯익다 familiar ((to)); acquainted
◆낯익은 손님 a regular customer / 낯익은 얼굴[곳] a familiar face [place] / 낯익지 않은 unfamiliar; strange; new
▶ 이것은 낯익은 광경이다 This is a familiar scene to me.
▶ 그 사람은 낯익은 얼굴인데 I fancy I have seen him somewhere before. ⇒ I remember seeing him once.

낯익히다 get 《sb, a place》 familiar with oneself

낯짝 a face; (俗) a phiz; a mug; a kisser; (美俗) a pan
◆못생긴 낯짝 an ugly face

▶ 내가 무슨 낯짝을 들고 그런 것을 부탁할 수 있겠는가? I cannot with any grace ask him to do so.

낱 a piece; an item; a unit; each piece

낱개 —箇 one; a piece; each piece
♦ 낱개로 파는 loose (flowers, pencils) / 낱개로 팔다 sell (oranges) by the piece [singly]; sell loose [piecemeal]
▶ 이것들은 낱개로 1,000원입니다 These are a thousand won apiece [each].
▶ 사과는 낱개로 5센트씩 했다 The apples cost five cents apiece.

낱권 —卷 〈책의 한 권〉 a volume (in a set)

낱낱이 1 〈하나하나〉 one by one; one after another; piece by piece; from point to point; separately; individually
♦ 낱낱이 언급하다 mention one by one / 집을 낱낱이 방문하다 make a door-to-door visit
▶ 그것을 낱낱이 세기 시작한다면 끝이 없을 것이다 If you start counting them one by one, there will be no end to it.
2 〈모조리〉 without omission [exception]; each and every one; all; entirely
♦ 낱낱이 고백하다 confess all [everything] / 서랍을 낱낱이 뒤지다 rummage each and every drawers
▶ 그는 내가 하는 일에 낱낱이 트집을 잡는다 He finds faults with everything I do.
3 〈자세히〉 in detail; in full; fully; minutely
♦ 낱낱이 말하다 particularize; give full particulars / 낱낱이 보고하다 make a detailed report 《of》 / 낱낱이 설명하다 explain in detail; give full explanation
▶ 우리는 협의 사항을 낱낱이 논의했다 We discussed the items on the agenda in detail.

낱돈 small [odd] money; loose coins

낱말 〈단어〉 a word; 〈어휘〉 (a) vocabulary
♦ 기본 낱말 basic words; (총칭) a basic vocabulary / 알고 있는 영어 낱말 one's English vocabulary [word power]
▶ 나는 영어 낱말을 그다지 많이 알고 있지 않다 I don't have a very large English vocabulary.

낱장 —張 a sheet [piece] 《of paper》; a leaf 《of a book》

낳다[1] 1 〈출산하다〉 have; bear 《a child》; give birth to; 〈분만하다〉 be delivered of...; 〈새끼를 낳다〉 breed; 〈산란하다〉 spawn; 〈알을 낳다〉 lay
♦ 방금 낳은 알 a fresh [a newly-laid] egg / 아들을 낳다 give birth to a baby boy
▶ 우리집 암탉은 날마다 알을 낳는다 Our hens lay eggs every day.
▶ 그녀는 지난 달 딸을 낳았다 She had [gave birth to, bore, was delivered of] a (baby) girl last month.
▶ 댁의 개는 새끼를 몇 마리 낳았습니까? How many puppies did your dog have?
▶ 낳은 정보다 기른 정 The parent who raises you [one] is dearer than the real [blood] parent.
2 〈산출하다〉 produce; (비유) 〈불러 일으키다〉 cause; give rise to...; 〈이르다〉 lead (to)
♦ 좋은 결과를 낳다 produce [get] good results / 10%의 이자를 낳다 yield [bear] 10 percent interest
▶ 그는 한국이 낳은 가장 위대한 과학자다 He is the greatest scientist that Korea has ever produced [had].
▶ 비위생은 병을 낳는다 Unhygienic conditions cause [give rise to, lead to] disease.
▶ 이런 행동은 의혹을 낳는다 Such conduct gives rise to [arouses] suspicion.
▶ 빈곤은 흔히 범죄를 낳는다 Poverty often breeds [produces, causes, leads to] crime.
▶ 같은 원인이 때로 다른 결과를 낳는다 The same cause sometimes gives rise to different effects.

낳다[2] 〈실을 만들다〉 spin; make yarn; 〈피륙을 짜다〉 weave ♦ 명주를 낳다 weave silk / 실을 낳다 spin thread [yarn]

-낳이 〈한산낳이〉 cloth woven at Hansan; the Hansan weave

내[1] 〈연기〉 smoke; fume

내[2] 〈냄새〉 smell; (an) odor; (a) scent; 〈향기〉 (a) fragrance ♦ 기름내 the smell of oil
▶ 그의 셔츠에서는 땀내가 난다 His shirt smells [reeks] of sweat.
▶ 뭔가 타는 내가 나지 않습니까? Can't you smell something burning?

내[3] 〈시내〉 a stream; a streamlet; a brook; a brooklet; a rivulet; a current; 〈여울〉 a ford
♦ 내를 거슬러 헤엄치다 swim against the current / 내를 건너다 cross [go across] a brook; 〈걸어서〉 ford a stream; wade (across) a stream / 내를 끼고 가다 go along a stream

내[4] 1 〈나〉 I
▶ 내가 직접 저녁을 지었다 I myself made the dinner. ⇒ I made the dinner myself.
▶ 나는 나지 그가 아니에요. 내가 하고 싶은 일을 하고 싶습니다 I'm me, not him. I want to do what I want to do.
▶ 내가 맡을 테니 안심하세요 Never mind! I will take care of it.
2 〈나의〉 my ♦ 내 약속 my promise / 내 집 my home [house]
▶ 그는 내 친구다 He is a friend of mine. ⇒ He is my friend.
▶ 이것은 네 질문에 대한 내 대답이다 Here are my replies to your questions.

내[5] 內 ♦ 기한 내에 within the period (of) ▶ 3일 내에 회답을 받고 싶습니다 I'd like to have your answer within three days.

내- 來- 〈오는〉 next; coming; forthcoming
♦ 내년 next year; the coming year / 내주 목요일 next Thursday; (on) Thursday next
▶ 내년도 예산이 승인되었다 The budget for the next fiscal year has been approved.
▶ 우리는 내학기에 한국사 공부를 시작한다 We will start to study Korean history in the next semester term.

-내 throughout; all through (⇨ 내내) ♦ 그해 겨우내[여름내] throughout the winter [summer] of that year / 아침내 all morning long

내가다 take [bring] out; carry out [away]; out with *sth*; remove; 〈훔쳐 내가다〉 run away with *sth* ♦ 중요한 서류를 내가다 carry [take] out important documents

내각 內角 1 〔數〕 an interior [internal] angle 2 〔野〕 the inside (corner) ◆내각을 찌르다 pitch a ball inside

내각 內閣 a cabinet; 〈정부〉 the government
◆애틀리 내각 the Attlee Cabinet; the Cabinet headed by Attlee [Premier Attlee] / 현 내각 the present Cabinet / 내각 개편 a reshuffle of the Cabinet / 새 내각의 면모 the personnel [lineup] of a new Cabinet / 내각의 분열 a split in the Cabinet / 내각의 붕괴 the fall [dissolution, collapse] of a cabinet / 내각을 전복시키다 overthrow the Cabinet / 새 내각을 조직하다 organize [form] a new cabinet / 내각에 입각하다 accept a Cabinet post; become a Cabinet Minister
▶ 그는 이번 주말까지는 새내각의 구성을 마칠 것이다 He'll have finished forming a new Cabinet by the end of this week.
▶ 내각이 총사퇴했다 All the members of the Cabinet resigned together. ＝ The Cabinet resigned en bloc.
▶ 1년에 두 번이나 내각이 바뀌었다 The Cabinet [government] changed twice in one year.
▶ 국민은 새 내각에 큰 기대를 걸고 있다 The people have high hopes for the new government.
■ ―과도― a caretaker [an interim] cabinet 연립― a coalition cabinet 정당― a party cabinet 초당파― a nonparty cabinet ―고시 제1호 Cabinet Notification No. 1 ―령(令) a Cabinet order [decree] ―불신임 결의 a nonconfidence resolution in the Cabinet ―수반 the head of a cabinet; the Prime Minister ―총사퇴 a general resignation of the Cabinet; a resignation of the Cabinet en bloc [in a body]

내갈기다 1 〈후려치다〉 thrash; beat; hit; (美口) slug; (口) wallop; (俗) belt 2 〈글씨를〉 write hastily [carelessly]; scribble; scrawl; dash

내객 來客 〈손님〉 a visitor; a guest; a caller; (총칭) company

내걸다 1 〈밖에〉 put up; hang out 《a lantern》; hoist; display 《a flag》
▶ 그들은 깃발을 2층 창밖으로 내걸었다 They hung out a flag from an upstairs window.
2 〈목숨을〉 risk 《one's (own) life》; stake
◆목숨을 내걸고 at the risk of one's life / 회담 결과에 정치생명을 내걸다 stake one's political future on the outcome of the talks / 목숨을 내걸고 그 일을 하다 risk one's life to do the work; do the work at the risk of one's life
3 〈내세우다〉 stand for; advocate; maintain
◆슬로건을 내걸고 under the slogan 《of》 / 조건을 내걸다 give conditions
▶ 그들은 「깨끗한 정부」라는 기치를 내걸었다 They raised the banner of "clean government."
▶ 외교문제를 내걸고 그는 질문전을 개시했다 He opened the volley of interpellations with the diplomatic issue.

내것 mine
◆내것 네것을 가리다 make [draw] a distinction between meum et tuum / 내것 네것을 가리지 않다 make no distinction between meum et tuum; draw no line between what is one's own and what isn't / 내것 네것을 혼동하다 get confused as to what is one's own and what isn't / 내것으로 만들다 make sth one's own; 〈정복하다〉 master 《a foreign language》
▶ 빨간 코트는 내것이다 The red coat is mine.

내경 內徑 〈안지름〉 the inside diameter; 〈구경〉 the gauge; the caliber; the bore

내계 內界 the inner world [sphere]; the internal world

내공 內攻 〔醫〕 retrocedence; retrocession ―내공하다 strike in; retrocede
▶ 그의 병은 내공하고 있다 His disease is retroceding [striking inwards].
▶ 그는 욕구 불만이 내공하여 그런 짓을 했다 His introverted frustration made him do it.
■ ―성 질환 a retrocessive [retrocedent] disease

내공 來貢 〈조공하러 옴〉 coming to pay tribute ―내공하다 come to pay tribute

내공 耐空 endurance in flying [flight] ■ ―성 airworthiness

내과 內科 〈병원의〉 the internal medicine department; 〈내과학〉 internal medicine
―과장 the director of the internal department ―병동 a medical ward ―병원 a hospital (for internal diseases); a medical establishment ―의사 a physician; an internist; 〈개업의〉 a medical practitioner ―질환 an internal disease ―치료 internal treatment: 내과 치료를 받다 be internally treated ―환자 a medical case

내과피 內果皮 〈속껍질〉〔植〕 the endocarp

내관 內官 a eunuch [júːnək]＝내시(內侍)

내구 耐久 〈지속〉 endurance; persistence; 〈물건의〉 durability
■ ―비행[기록, 경쟁] an endurance flight [record, contest] ―소비재 consumer(s') durables; durable consumer goods

내구성 耐久性 durability; persistence; lasting quality
◆내구성이 없는 물건 an article of poor lasting quality / 내구성이 있다 be durable; be persistent; be lasting; last [hold out] long; be of lasting quality / 내구성을 시험하다 test the durability 《of sth》
▶ 손질을 잘하면 내구성이 높아진다 Good care improves durability.

내구재 耐久財 durable [hard] goods; durables
■ 비― nondurable goods; nondurables

내국 內局 an intra-ministerial bureau [office]

내국 內國 home; the home country
◆내국의 home; domestic; internal / 내국산의 homegrown; home-produced / 내국제의 of home [domestic] manufacture [make]; homemade
■ ―공채 an internal [a domestic] loan [debt]: 내국 공채를 발행[모집]하다 issue [float] a domestic loan ―무역 home [inland, domestic] trade ―세 an inland [internal] duty [tax] ―시장 ⇨ 국내(~시장) ―우편 domestic mail ―우편환 an inland money order ―인 a native ―채(債) an internal [a domestic] loan [debt] ―항로 a coastwise

service —환 domestic exchange —환어음 an inland [a domestic] bill

내굽다 bend out; be bent out

내규 內規 private rules [regulations]; bylaws
♦ 내규 제8조에 따라 according to Rule 8 of the Bylaws / 내규에 위배되다[를 위반하다] violate [infringe] the bylaw; offend against the tradition
▶ 회사에는 몇가지 내규가 있다 We have some rules governing the internal affairs of the company.
▶ 그것은 협회의 내규에 규정되어 있다 That is provided [laid down] in the bylaws of the association.

내근 內勤 office [desk] work; inside [indoor] duty
▶ 그는 내근이다 He works in the office.
▶ 그는 금년에 내근이 되었다 This year he has been transferred to a desk job.
―**내근하다** work inside [indoors]; do a desk job; be on office work
■―**경찰관** a desk policeman ―**자[사원]** a clerk; an office worker; 〈신문·잡지 등의〉 a deskman

내기 1 〈금품을 거는〉 a bet 《on》; betting; gambling
♦ 점심 내기 a bet of lunch / 천원 내기 《make》 a bet of 1,000 won / 내기에 건 돈 a bet; stakes / 내기를 크게 하다 make a big bet; play for high stakes; run [take] a great risks / 내기에 이기다[지다] win [lose] a bet / 내기로 돈을 잃다 lose money in [on] a bet
▶ 그는 내기를 좋아한다 He likes gambling.
▶ 그 일로 그와 내기를 했다 I bet him [made a bet with him] on it.
▶ 그는 내기에 빠져 전재산을 날렸다 He became a fanatic gambler and lost his entire fortune. ⇌ He gambled his entire fortune away.
▶ 내기에 손대지 마라 Don't make a bet.
―**내기하다** bet 《on》; wager 《on》; make a bet 《on》; lay down a stake
♦ 3달러 내기하다 make a bet of three dollars / 트럼프로 내기하다 gamble at cards
▶ 축구 경기에서 어느 편이 이기는지 내기하자 Let's bet on who's going to win the soccer game.
2 〈경쟁〉 a match; a bout; a race
♦ 먹기 내기 an eating contest / 술마시기 내기 a drinking bout
―**내기하다** see who will win 《in a contest》
▶ 수수께끼로 내기하자 Let's try some riddles and see which of us has the sharpest wits.

-내기 〈서울 내기〉 a person from [born in] Seoul / 풋내기 an inexperienced person

내기성 耐氣性 ♦ 내기성의 airproof

내깔기다 eject; pass [discharge] 《one's》 urine
♦ 오줌을 내깔기다 urinate; (俗) pee; piss

내남없이 without any exceptions to us all; irrespective of persons; indiscriminately; everybody; everyone ▶ 내남없이 다 같은 처지다 We are all in the same boat.

내내 all the time [way]; all along (the line); (all) through; throughout; consecutively; all during 《the winter》
▶ 그 후 내내 ever after; ever afterward / 오전 [아침] 내내 all through the morning / 1년 내내 throughout the year; all the year round / 내내 선두를 달리다 lead the race from start to finish
▶ 그녀는 3년 동안 내내 수석이었다 She has been at the top of her class for the whole three-year period.
▶ 그는 1년 내내 같은 양복으로 지낸다 He wears the same suit all the year around.
▶ 나는 지난 여름 내내 그 해변 마을에 있었다 I stayed at the seaside village all through last summer.
▶ 내내 안녕히 계십시오 Good-bye! ⇌ Farewell! ⇌ Adieu!

내내년 來來年 the year after next ⇨ 후년

내내월 來來月 the month after next

내내주 來來週 the week after next

내년 來年 next year; the coming year
♦ 내년 겨울 next winter / 내년 초 early next year / 내년의 예정표 a schedule for next year [the coming year] / 내년의 오늘 this day next year
▶ 내년 이맘때 그를 만날 수 있을 것이다 I'll be able to meet him about this time next year.
▶ 내년의 일은 아무도 모른다 There is no telling what will happen next year. ⇌ Next year is the devil's joke.

내놓다 1 〈밖으로〉 hold [stretch] out; put [take] out
♦ 창밖으로 머리를 내놓다 stick [put] one's head out of the window / 먹었던 돈을 도로 내놓다 disgorge the embezzled money
2 〈가둔 짐승 등을〉 set [make] free; free; liberate; let go [loose]; put [let] out of; release
♦ 개를 내놓고 기르다 leave a dog at large; give a dog free run of 《one's house》
3 〈드러내다〉 show; expose; bare ♦ 팔을 내놓다 bare [expose] one's arm
▶ 그 아이는 너무 더워서 배를 내놓고 잤다 It was so hot (that) the child slept with his stomach exposed.
4 〈팔려고〉 put 《a house》 on [to] sale; put up [offer] sth for sale; place sth on sale; 〈출품〉 exhibit 《one's painting》 at a show; put sth on show
♦ 내놓은 집 a house for sale
5 〈발간〉 publish; issue; bring out; 〈배출〉 produce; turn out
♦ 졸업생을 내놓다 turn out graduates / 책을 내놓다 publish a book / 훌륭한 배우를 많이 내놓다 produce [bring out] many great actors
6 〈돈을〉 pay; give; 〈기부하다〉 contribute; 〈투자하다〉 invest
♦ 병원에 거금을 내놓다 contribute a large sum to the hospital / 새 사업에 돈을 내놓다 invest money in a new enterprise
▶ 그는 체육관 건설에 거금을 내놓았다 He contributed a large sum of money for building the gymnasium.
7 〈음식 등을〉 offer 《tea》; serve 《up》; set out 《a meal》; set 《cake》 before sb
♦ 다과를 내놓다 serve light refreshments [tea

내다¹

and cake) to *sb* / 방석을 내놓다 offer *sb* a cushion / 술을 내놓다 serve wine [drinks]
▶ 그 식당은 항상 맛있는 생선요리를 내놓는다 They always serve delicious fish dishes at that restaurant.
▶ 그녀는 나에게 맛있는 커피를 내놓았다 She served me good coffee.

8 〈의견·조건을〉 present; send in; submit 〈*one's* view〉; tender; bring forward 〈up〉
◆ 동의안을 내놓다 bring forward a motion / 명함을 내놓다 present *one's* card / 의견을 내놓다 express *one's* view / 의안을 내놓다 present a bill / 조사받기 위해 내놓다 submit 〈a document〉 for *sb's* inspection
▶ 그 부인은 이혼 소송에서 아무 조건도 내놓지 않았다 In the divorce action the wife didn't make any demands.

9 〈빼놓다〉 exclude; except; leave out; 〈생략하다〉 omit
▶ 나 내놓고는 다 부자다 All are rich but [except] me.
▶ 그를 내놓고는 아무도 그 문제를 풀 수 없었다 No one except [but] him could solve the problem.

10 〈포기하다〉 give up; leave; resign
◆ 목숨을 내놓다 lay down [sacrifice] *one's* life; risk [hazard] *one's* life / 자리를 내놓다 resign from *one's* office [position] / 목숨을 내놓고 그 일을 하다 risk *one's* life to do the work; do the work at the risk of *one's* life

내다¹ 〈연기가〉 smoke; smolder; become [be] smoky ▶ 불이 벽난로에서 계속 내기만 했다 Fire was smoldering in the fireplace.

내다² **1** 〈끄집어내다〉 put out; take out; bring out; 〈제시하다〉 show ◆ 책상을 밖으로 내다 take a desk out / 차표 내세요 Please show (me) your ticket.

2 〈드러나게 하다〉 distinguish; attain distinction; raise; elevate
◆ 이름을 내다 make *one's* name known to the public; make [win] a name (for *oneself*); make *oneself* famous; distinguish *oneself*

3 〈돈을〉 give; 〈기부하다〉 contribute 〈to, toward〉; 〈투자하다〉 invest; 〈공급하다〉 supply; furnish
◆ 물건값을 내다 pay for an article / 이자를 내다 pay interest
▶ 비용은 각자 냈다 Each paid his share in the expenses.
▶ 천원만 더 내면 훨씬 더 좋은 것을 살 수 있다 You can buy a much better one if you pay 1,000 won more.
▶ 그는 반년 동안 집세를 내지 않고 있다 He has not paid the house rent for six months.

4 〈말 등을〉 put forward; set forth; start 〈a rumor〉; 〈감정 등을〉 vent
◆ 말을 내다 start talk; broach [get on] a subject / 소문을 내다 set a rumor afloat; circulate [spread] a rumor / 화를 내다 get angry (at)

5 〈발행·게재하다〉 publish; issue; bring [put] out
◆ 신문에 광고를 내다 put [place, run] an advertisement in a newspaper; advertise in [through] a newspaper / 소설을 잡지에 내다 publish a story in a magazine
▶ 나는 10년 동안 책을 한 권도 내지 않았다 I haven't had a book out in ten years.
▶ 내 이름은 내지 않겠다 I will not make your name public. = I will not mention [disclose] your name.

6 〈제출하다〉 present; send in; hand in 〈a report〉; give in 〈*one's* examination paper〉; tender 〈*one's* resignation〉; submit 〈*one's* view〉; bring forward 〈a motion〉
◆ 답안지를 내시오 Hand in [Give me] your papers.
▶ 나는 대학에 입학 원서를 냈다 I sent in [submitted] an application for admission to a university.

7 〈만들다·마련하다〉 set up; make; fix; arrange 〈for〉
◆ 벽에 구멍을 내다 make a hole in the wall; put in [make] an opening in the wall / 시간을 내다 arrange the hours; make [find] time (for *sth*, to attend the meeting) / 앉을 자리를 내다 make [arrange] a seat; make room for *sb* to sit
▶ 어떻게든 시간을 내서 찾아 뵙겠습니다 I will manage to find time to call on you.
▶ 나는 시간을 내어 양친께 편지를 썼다 I made time to write to my parents.

8 〈얻다·받다〉 get; have; take 〈out〉; receive; obtain
◆ 빚을 내다 get [take out] a loan; borrow money / 여권을 내다 have a passport issued; obtain [get] a passport / 허가를 내다 take out [get] a license
▶ 그는 식당 영업 허가를 냈다 He got a license to run a restaurant.

9 〈보내다〉 mail; post; send ◆ 초대장을 내다 send out an invitation / 편지를 내다 send a letter; post [美] mail] a letter

10 〈출품하다〉 exhibit 〈*one's* painting〉 at a gallery; put 〈an article〉 on show

11 〈음식·턱 등을〉 serve (up) 〈wine〉; offer 〈tea〉; treat
◆ 다과를 내다 serve tea and cake; serve *sb* with light refreshments
▶ 그가 한 잔 냈다 He stood us drinks.
▶ 걱정하지 마라, 이것은 내가 한턱 내는 거다 Don't worry. This is my treat.

12 〈운행하다〉 run [operate] 〈a special train〉; put out 〈a boat〉

13 〈배출하다〉 produce; yield; turn out 〈graduates〉
▶ 이 대학에서는 많은 문예 평론가를 냈다 This college has produced many fine literary critics.

14 〈힘 등을〉 exert; put [call] forth; stir [pluck] up ◆ 힘을 내다 put forth (all) *one's* strength ▶ 그는 용기를 내어 일어섰다 He plucked up his courage and stood up.

15 〈속력을〉 achieve [develop] 〈a speed of...〉; speed up
▶ 그는 고속도로에서 시속 100마일을 냈다 He made 100 miles per hour on the highway.
▶ 이 배는 40노트를 낼 수 있다 This ship can

do 40 knots.
16 〈발생시키다〉 give rise to; cause; occur
♦ 먼지를 내다 raise [stir up] dust / 많은 사상자를 내다 cause heavy casualties
▶ 불을 내지 않도록 모두 주의합시다 Let's all be careful not to start any fires.
17 〈발하다〉 issue forth [out]; send [give] out; 〈빛 등을〉 emit; 〈소리를〉 utter
♦ 김을 내다 emit [give out] steam / 부자티를 내다 give *oneself* the air of a millionaire; act the lord / 이상한 소리를 내다 make a strange noise
▶ 그 물체는 푸른 빛을 내고 있었다 The object was emitting a blue light.
▶ 그는 소리 내어 편지를 읽었다 He read the letter aloud.
▶ 시험 중에는 소리를 내지 마라 Keep your mouths closed [quiet] during the examination.
18 〈팔다〉 market; sell
♦ 쌀을 장에 내다 put rice on the market
19 〈모를〉 transplant (rice seedlings); set [bed] out (rice plants)
20 〈처음 차리다〉 open; start; set up; commence; inaugurate
▶ 이번에 이 근처에 가게를 냈다 I have just opened a store near here.
21 〈뽑다〉 put forward; select; appoint; offer
♦ 대표자를 내다 offer [put forward] a representative / 후보자를 내다 select a candidate
▶ 우리는 그를 시장 후보로 냈다 We put him up as a mayor.
22 〈비우다〉 empty; clear; 〈집 등을〉 vacate; quit; surrender ♦ 김칫독을 내다 empty a *kimchi* pot
내다³ ♦ 견더 내다 bear up; hold fast to the end / 찾아내다 find out; discover / 일을 해내다 carry the work through
▶ 나는 맹훈련을 더 이상 견더낼 수 없었다 I couldn't bear up the hard training any longer.
내다보다 **1** 〈밖을〉 look out (of, on); see from within
♦ 거리를 내다보다 look out on the street / 창 밖을 내다보다 look out of [(美) look out] the window
▶ 이 방에서는 멋진 야경을 내다볼 수 있다 You can have a fine night view from this room.
2 〈예상하다〉 foresee; look ahead; anticipate; expect; forecast
♦ 값이 오를 것을 내다보고 in expectation of a rise in price / 앞날을 내다보고 with an eye to the future / 앞날을 내다보다 foresee [forecast] the future; look ahead into the future / 정확히 내다보다 make an accurate forecast (of)
▶ 전문가들은 경기가 회복될 것으로 내다보았다 The experts have predicted that business will recover.
내다보이다 **1** 〈밖이〉 (can) be seen from within; be seen out of; show through
♦ 호수가 내다보이는 방 a room with a view of [an outlook over] the lake
▶ 그 건물에서는 항구가 잘 내다보인다 We can see the whole harbor from the building. ⇒

The building overlooks [commands a view of] the whole harbor.
2 〈예상되다〉 be anticipated [expected, foreseen]
▶ 올 여름은 무척 더울 것으로 내다보인다 It is expected (that) we will have a very hot summer this year.
내닫다 run [rush] out; break into a run
♦ 밖으로 내닫다 run [rush] outdoors / 후닥닥 내닫다 break suddenly into a clattering run
▶ 토끼가 수풀에서 내닫는 것이 보였다 I saw a rabbit jump out of a bush.
▶ 그는 교실에서 운동장으로 내달았다 He rushed out of his classroom into the playground.
내달 來— next month; the coming month; the month ahead ♦ 내달의 오늘 this day next month / 내달 5일에 on the fifth of next month
내담 來談 ▶ 본인 내담 요망 (광고) Apply in person. ⇌ Personal application (is) requested. —**내담하다** come to talk
내당 內堂 women's quarters ⇨ 내실(內室)
내던지다 **1** 〈던지다〉 throw [cast, hurl] out [away down]
▶ 그는 창 밖으로 담배꽁초를 내던졌다 He threw away a cigarette butt out (of) the window.
▶ 그는 침대에 몸을 내던졌다 He threw himself down on the bed.
▶ 그녀는 화가 나서 편지를 내던졌다 She angrily threw [flung, chucked] the letter.
▶ 그녀는 절벽에서 바다로 몸을 내던졌다 She threw herself [jumped] into the ocean from a cliff.
2 〈포기하다〉 give up; abandon; neglect
♦ 사표를 내던지다 thrust *one's* resignation at (the employer) / 지위를 내던지다 give up [resign from] *one's* position
▶ 일을 중도에 내던지지 마라 Don't give up your work halfway [before you finish the job].
▶ 그는 다른 모든 것을 내던지고 그 작품을 완성했다 Throwing everything else aside, he completed the work.
3 〈제공·희생하다〉 offer; lay down; sacrifice
♦ 자유를 위해 목숨을 내던지다 sacrifice [lay down] *one's* life for freedom / 선뜻 1억원을 내던지다 generously give a donation of a hundred million won (to) / 사업을 내던지고 쾌락을 좇다 sacrifice business for pleasure
▶ 그이를 위해서라면 내 전재산을 내던지겠습니다 I will give all I have for him.
▶ 그녀는 그를 위해서 자신의 행복을 내던졌다 She made to him a sacrifice of her happiness.
▶ 그 어머니는 자기 목숨을 내던져 아이를 구했다 The mother sacrificed her life to save the child. ⇌ The mother saved the child at the sacrifice [cost] of her own life.
내돋다 rise to the surface; come out; put forth; spring up; appear ♦ 여드름이 내돋다 pimples come out (on *one's* face)
내돌리다 pass *sth* round [from hand to hand] indiscriminately
내동댕이치다 throw out ⇨ 내던지다

내두르다 1 〈휘두르다〉 brandish 《a sword》; wave [swing] 《one's arm(s)》; wield ▶그는 지팡이를 내둘렀다 He flourished his cane.
2 〈남을 부리다〉 lead sb by the nose; have sb under one's thumb [control]

내둘리다 1 〈어지러워지다〉 feel [get] dizzy
2 〈내두름을 당하다〉 be led by the nose; be pushed around ◆남에게 내둘리다 be at sb's beck and call

내디디다 step forward; set foot 《on》; tread 《up》on; advance
◆문단에 발을 내디디다 enter upon the literary world / 새 인생에 발을 내디디다 embark on a new life / 해결을 향해 한 걸음 내디디다 take a step towards solving 《a problem》 / 인생의 첫발을 잘못 내디디다 make a wrong start in one's life
▶그녀는 가수로 무대에 첫발을 내디뎠다 She made her first appearance on the stage as a singer.
▶그는 실업계에 첫발을 내디뎠다 He took the first step into the business world.

내떨다 1 〈떨어버리다〉 shake off [down]; knock off 《the ashes of one's cigar》 2 〈뿌리치다〉 free [extricate] oneself 《from》; shake one's hand free; tear oneself away 《from》

내뚫다 pierce; go [pass, run] through; perforate ⇨ 뚫다

내락 內諾 a private agreement [consent]
◆내락을 얻다 obtain [secure] sb's informal [private] consent
▶나는 그녀와의 결혼에 아버지의 내락을 얻었다 I have my father's private consent to marry her.
—**내락하다** give a private consent
▶나는 그의 제안을 내락했다 I gave my private consent to his proposal.

내란 內亂 〈내전〉a civil war; 〈반란〉(a) rebellion; (a) revolt
◆내란을 일으키다 raise an insurrection [a rebellion] / 내란을 진압하다 put down [suppress, quell] a rebellion [an insurrection]
▶내란은 마침내 가라앉았다 The rebellion died down at last.
▶정부는 내란을 진압하는 데 온 힘을 쏟고 있다 The government is trying hard to suppress the rebellion.
■—**음모** conspiracy of a rebellion ■**—죄** high treason; treason against the state

내레이션 narration
내레이터 〈남자〉 a narrator; 〈여자〉 a narratress

내려가다 1 〈아래로〉 go [come, get] down; descend
◆바지가 내려가다 one's trousers fall down / 사다리를 내려가다 get down a ladder / 양말이 내려가다 one's socks slip down / 급히 산을 내려가다 go down [climb down, descend] a hill in a hurry; hurry down a hill / 연단을 내려가다 leave [descend from] the platform [stage] / 시골로 내려가다 go back to one's home village; move [go] down to the country / 지하실로 내려가다 descend into a cellar
▶그들은 보트를 타고 강을 내려갔다 They went down the river by boat [in a boat].
▶우체국은 이 길을 따라 500미터 정도 내려간 곳에 있습니다 The post office is about five hundred meters down this street.
2 〈가격·정도가〉 fall; drop; go down
▶야채값이 내려갔다 The price of vegetables has come down [fallen].
▶수위가 2미터 내려갔다 The water level dropped two meters.
▶내달에는 금리가 내려갈 것이다 Interest rates will be lowered next month.
3 〈온도 등이〉 drop; fall; go down
▶어젯밤에는 기온이 영하 5도까지 내려갔다 The temperature went down [fell, dropped] to five below zero last night.
▶열이 내려가고 있다 The fever is abating.
4 〈등급이〉 come down; drop; be degraded; (美) be demoted 《to》
◆아랫자리로 내려가다 sink down to a lower level / 석차가 내려가다 come down on the list
▶그는 지위가 내려갔다 He was demoted.
5 〈소화되다〉 digest ▶빨리 내려가다 be quick of digestion ▶먹은 것이 잘 내려가지 않는다 The food is slow of digestion.

내려긋다 stroke downward; draw 《a line》 down
◆몇 줄을 내려긋다 strike out a few lines / 두꺼운[가는] 2중선을 내려긋다 draw a double bold [fine] line / 평행선을 내려긋다 draw parallel lines

내려놓다 take [put] down; let down; lower; 〈선반 등에서〉 reach down
◆트럭에서 물건을 내려놓다 unload goods from a truck / 서가에서 사전을 내려놓다 take down a dictionary from the bookshelf / 난로에서 주전자를 내려놓다 take the kettle off the stove / 배에서 짐을 내려놓다 unload a ship

내려다보다 1 〈아래를〉 look down 《at, on, upon》; overlook
◆평야가 내려다보이는 산 a mountain dominating the plain / 2층 창에서 (그를) 내려다보다 look down 《at him》 from the upstairs window
▶나는 빌딩 옥상에서 차량의 물결을 내려다보았다 I looked down upon the stream of cars from the top of the building.
▶어린 누이동생이 벼랑에서 골짜기를 내려다보고 있는 것을 보고 나는 깜짝 놀랐다 I was shocked to see my little sister looking off the cliff at the valley below.
▶내 방에서는 그 호수의 전경이 내려다보인다 My room commands [overlooks] a full view of the lake.
▶우리 학교는 바다가 내려다보이는 언덕 위에 있다 Our school stands on a hill, looking down on [overlooking] the sea.
2 〈얕보다〉 look down on [upon]; despise; make light [little] of
▶그는 언제나 남을 내려다본다 He always looks down on others.

내려디디다 step upon
내려뜨리다 drop; let sth fall ▶그들은 2층에서 밧줄을 내려뜨렸다 They hung a rope down

from upstairs.
내려서다 come down on *one's* feet; go down and stand ♦ 뜰에 내려서다 go down into a garden

내려앉다 1 〈밑으로〉 take a lower seat ♦ 의자에서 내려앉다 get off a chair and sit on the floor
2 〈무너지다〉 come [fall] down; 〈벽 등이〉 crumble; give way; 〈다리 등이〉 collapse; 〈함몰하다〉 cave in; subside; 〈지층 등이〉 sink
▶ 눈의 무게로 지붕이 내려앉았다 The roof collapsed [caved in] under the weight of the snow.
▶ 사람들의 무게로 마루가 내려앉았다 The floor gave way under the weight of the people.

내려오다 1 〈아래로〉 come down; get [step] down; descend; 〈지시 등이〉 be given; be issued
♦ 계단을 내려오다 come [climb] down the stairs / 산에서 내려오다 come [climb] down a mountain / 하늘에서 내려오다 descend from heaven / 아래층으로 내려오다 come downstairs / 지하실로 내려오다 come down to the basement
▶ 아침 일찍 출발하라는 지시가 내려왔다 We were told [ordered] to leave early in the morning.
2 ⇨ 내리다¹ 2
3 〈전해오다〉 be handed down; come down 《from *one's* ancestors》
♦ 대대로 내려오다 be transmitted [handed down] for generations
▶ 이 풍습은 고려 시대부터 전해 내려온 것이다 This custom has been handed down since the Koryŏ period.
▶ 이것은 조상 때부터 전해 내려온 골동품이다 This is a curio handed down by my ancestors. ⇌ This curio has come down to me from my ancestors.

내려찍다 bring 《an ax》 down on 《a tree》
내려치다 strike from above; give a down blow; flick [swing] downward
♦ 개의 머리를 막대기로 내려치다 bring a stick down on a dog's head / 주먹으로 책상을 내려치다 hit the table with *one's* fist
▶ 그는 도둑의 어깨를 방망이로 세게 내려쳤다 He brought the bat down hard on the thief's shoulder.

내력 來歷 1 〈이력〉 *one's* career; *one's* personal history; *one's* background; 〈유래〉 a history
♦ 이 관습의 내력 the origin of this custom / 어떤 절의 내력과 고사 the history and legends connected with a temple / 행사의 내력을 캐다 trace an event to its origins
▶ 이 절에는 불가사의한 내력이 있다 This temple has a strange history.
▶ 이 관습의 내력을 아시나요? Do you know how this custom came about [what the origin of this custom is]?
▶ 역사 선생님은 그 절의 내력을 캐보려고 마음먹었다 The history teacher wanted to investigate the origin of the temple.

2 ⇨ 내림¹

내륙 內陸 inland ♦ 수도에서 100마일 내륙에 100 miles upcountry from the capital
■—국 a landlocked country; a country without a sea coast —성 기후 a continental climate; an inland climate —수운 inland water transportation —운수 inland transport —지방 inland areas

내리 1 〈아래로〉 downward ▶ 박이 지붕에서 내리 굴렀다 A gourd fell [rolled] down from the roof.
2 〈줄곧〉 all the time [way]; throughout; successively; continuously; without stopping; in a row
♦ 내리 한 달 동안 for one consecutive month; for one month running [on end, at a stretch]/ 내리 이기다 win through; win straight victories / 5시간이나 내리 일하다 work 5 hours at a stretch; make a continuous work for 5 hours / 24 시간 내리 잠자다 sleep around the clock
▶ 그녀는 일생을 내리 독신으로 지냈다 She remained unmarried until death.
▶ 그는 학급에서 내리 수석이었다 He remained at the top of the class.
▶ 나는 이틀 동안 내리 짐을 꾸렸다 I packed for two days in a row.

내리깔다 〈눈을〉 cast down [lower] *one's* eyes; look downward ▶ 그녀는 당황해서 눈을 내리깔았다 She looked down [lowered her eyes] in embarrassment.

내리누르다 1 〈위에서〉 press [push] down; press upon
2 〈압박하다〉 oppress; 《口》 clamp down; 〈윽박지르다〉 force; compel ▶ 그는 반대 의견을 내리눌렀다 He repressed opposing voices.

내리다¹ 1 〈위에서〉 come [go] down; get [step] down; descend
▶ 막이 내렸다 The curtain dropped [fell].
▶ 비행기가 공항에 내렸다 The airplane landed on the airport.
2 〈탈 것에서〉 get off; get out of; leave; alight 《from》
♦ 배에서 내리다 disembark / 비행기에서 내리다 get off [alight from] an airplane / 엘리베이터[차]에서 내리다 get out of an elevator [a car]
▶ 나는 다음 역에서 내립니다 I'm getting off at the next station.
▶ 나는 서울역에서 지하철[버스]을 내렸다 I got off the subway train [bus] at Seoul Station.
▶ 나는 말에서 내렸다 I dismounted [got down] from my horse.
▶ 승객이 모두 내릴 때까지 기다리세요 Wait for all the passengers to get off (before you get on). ⇌ Let the passengers off the train first.
▶ 우리는 역을 잘못 내렸다 We got off at the wrong stop.
3 〈눈·비 등이〉 fall 《on the ground》; come down
▶ 비[눈, 우박, 진눈깨비]가 내린다 It rains [snows, hails, sleets].

내리다²

▶ 올해는 비가 많이 내렸다 We've had a lot of rain this year.
▶ 비가 내리거나 개거나 시합은 할거다 The game will be played rain or shine [regardless of the weather].
▶ 비가 내릴 것 같다 It looks like rain. ⇒ It is threatening to rain.
▶ 지금이라도 눈이 내릴 것 같다 It is likely to snow any minute now.

4 ⟨물가 등이⟩ fall; drop; decline
▶ 이 달에는 물가가 내렸다 This month prices have gone down [have fallen].
▶ 쌀값이 내렸다 Rice has dropped in price.
▶ 야채값이 내렸다 The price of vegetables has come down.
▶ 빵값이 100원 내렸다 The bread has gone down one hundred won in price.

5 ⟨체온 등이⟩ fall; drop; go down
▶ 열이 내렸다 The fever has abated.
▶ 그의 열이 좀처럼 내리지 않는다 His fever won't go down.

6 ⟨뿌리가⟩ take [strike] root; root
♦ 뿌리가 내리다 take root (in the ground) / 뿌리가 깊게 내리다 take [spread] deep root
▶ 이 나무는 뿌리가 쉽게 내린다 This plant roots easily. ⇒ This plant takes [strikes] root easily.

7 ⟨살이⟩ lose flesh; become lean [thin] ♦ 부기가 내리다 the swelling goes down
▶ 그는 살이 많이 내렸다 He has become much thinner. ⇒ He has lost a lot of weight.
▶ 그녀는 살이 내리는 방법을 찾고 있다 She is looking for a way to reduce.

8 ⟨음식물이⟩ digest
♦ 잘 내리는 음식물 easily digestible food; light food / 밥이 내리다 food is digested; food settles
▶ 달걀 반숙은 잘 내린다 A soft-boiled egg is easy to digest.

9 ⟨명령·판결 등이⟩ be given; be issued; be ordered; be sentenced
▶ 전진 명령이 내렸다 Orders were given [issued] to advance.
▶ 그에게 무거운 판결이 내렸다 A heavy sentence was passed [sentenced] upon [on] him.

10 ⟨신령이⟩ be possessed ▶ 그 여자에게 신이 내렸다 The woman was possessed by a spirit. ⇒ The woman was in a religious frenzy.

내리다²

1 ⟨밑으로 옮기다⟩ take down; ⟨부리다⟩ unload; discharge
♦ 주전자를 불에서 내리다 take the kettle off the fire / 배[트럭]에서 짐을 내리다 discharge a ship [unload goods from a truck]
▶ 선반에서 그 상자[접시]를 내려주세요 Please take down the box [dish] from the shelf.

2 ⟨탈 것에서⟩ let... off; drop; set down
♦ 버스에서 승객을 내리다 let passengers off a bus / 부축하여 내려 주다 help sb off (a car); hand (the old woman) down from [out of] (the bus)
▶ 다음 모퉁이에서 내려주세요 Please drop me (off) [let me off, (英) put me down] at the next corner.
▶ 나는 그 아이를 부축하여 버스에서 내려주었다 I helped the child out of [off] the bus.
▶ 어디서 내려드릴까요? Where would you like to be dropped off?
▶ 승객이 내리고 있으면 버스를 앞지르지 마시오. Don't pass a bus while it is unloading (passengers).

3 ⟨커튼 등을⟩ lower; drop; pull down
♦ 닻을 내리다 cast [drop] (an) anchor / 돛을 내리다 take down [lower] a sail; ⟨급히⟩ strike sail / 셔터를 내리다 pull [roll] down the shutter / 손을 내리다 lower one's hand / 커튼을 내리다 draw [drop, bring down] the curtain
▶ 차양을 좀 내려주시오 Please lower [pull down] the shade [blinds] a little bit.
▶ 기를 내렸습니까? Did you lower the flag?
▶ 막을 내렸다 They let down the curtain.
▶ 그는 차창을 내리고 손을 내밀었다 He rolled down the car window and put his hand out.

4 ⟨값 등을⟩ bring [cut] down; reduce
♦ 값을 1,000원으로 내리다 cut [lower, reduce] the price to 1,000 won / 임금을 5만원 내리다 cut wages by fifty thousand won
▶ 값을 내리면 이건 잘 팔릴 겁니다 This will be sold well, if you lower [bring down, reduce] the price.
▶ 저 가게는 커피값을 내렸다 That store lowered the price of coffee.

5 ⟨지위·정도를⟩ lower; demote; degrade
♦ 계급을 내리다 demote sb to a lower rank / 반 음(音) 내리다 ⟨樂⟩ flatten / 수준[기준]을 내리다 lower the level [standard] / 한 음 내리다 lower the key (of a song)

6 ⟨주다·하사하다⟩ grant; give; bestow; award
♦ 관직을 내리다 confer a rank on sb / 상금을 내리다 confer a prize [an award] / 허가를 내리다 grant permission

7 ⟨명령·판결 등을⟩ issue (orders); give [lay on] (a command); pass (judgment on sb); conclude
♦ 명령을 내리다 give [issue] orders / 사격 명령을 내리다 give the word to fire / 판결을 내리다 hand down a decision (on sb, on a case); give one's verdict
▶ 그는 우리에게 곧 출발하라는 명령을 내렸다 He gave us orders to start at once. ⇒ He ordered that we should start at once.
▶ 이 문제에 어떤 결론을 내렸습니까? What conclusion did you come to on [with] this problem?
▶ 재판관은 그 범인에게 판결을 내렸다 The judge passed judgment [sentence] on the criminal.
▶ 판결은 그에게 불리하게[유리하게] 내려졌다 The case went against [in favor of] him.

내리닫이¹ ⟨아동복⟩ combinations; children's overalls with a convenience slit

내리닫이² ⟨建⟩ a sash window; push-up window

내리뜨다 cast down (one's eyes); look downward ♦ 눈을 내리뜨고 with downcast eyes

내리막 1 ⟨길의⟩ a downward path [slope]; a downhill road; a descent; ⟨철로의⟩ a declivity; a down grade ♦ 내리막 길 a downhill road

[path]
▶여기서 길은 내리막이 된다 The road descends [slopes downward] from here.
2 〈쇠퇴〉 decline; an ebb; wane
◆인생의 내리막 the downhill of life; the afternoon of life / 내리막이 되다 be on the decline; (口) have an unlucky break
▶그의 인생은 내리막 길이다 His life is on the decline. ⇌ He is over the hill.
▶8월 하순에 이르면 더위도 내리막이 된다 When it gets to be late August, the heat begins to ease.
▶경기가 내리막으로 접어들었다 Business has begun to change for the worse.
내리받이 〈지형〉 a downward slope; a descent; 〈쇠퇴〉 the wane; the decline ▶길은 내리받이였다 The road sloped down [downwards].
내리사랑 love from older toward younger members of a family; parental love [affection] toward youngsters
내리지르다 **1**〈비·바람이〉 blow [pour, fall] down violently
▶겨울에는 그 산에서 찬 바람이 내리지른다 A cold wind blows down (from) the mountain in winter.
2〈주먹·발로〉 kick [knock, beat] down
내리쬐다 beat down on; shine [blaze] down (upon) ◆따갑게 내리쬐는 햇볕 (under) a burning [scorching] sun ▶햇볕이 우리 얼굴에 내리쬐었다 The sun beat into our faces.
내리치다 strike downward; bring (a stick) down (on sb's head)
◆내리치는 듯한 비 (a) pelting [drumming] rain / 이마를 내리치다 strike straight on the forehead
▶비가 세차게 창문에 내리치고 있었다 The rain was beating [pelting] against the window.
내리퍼붓다 pour (on); rain hard; snow incessantly; fall thick (and fast)
◆내리퍼붓는 눈 a heavy snowstorm / 비가 내리퍼붓는 바닷가 a rain-swept beach / 내리퍼붓는 빗 속을 in (the) pouring rain; in a downpour
내릴톱 〈세로 켜는〉 a ripsaw
내림¹ 〈유전〉 heredity; inheritance; patrimony
▶비만증은 그 집안의 내림이다 There is hereditary obesity in the family.
▶음악을 좋아하는 것은 우리 집안의 내림이다 A love of music is in my blood.
내림² 〔樂〕 flat ◆내림 나장조[단조] (in) B flat major [minor]
내림³ a frontage; width ◆내림 여섯 칸의 집 a house with a frontage of 6 *kan*; a house 6 *kan* wide
내림 來臨 your attendance ⇨ 왕림
내림굿 〔民俗〕 a shaman's invocation rite
내림대 〔民俗〕 a wand [rod] used by a shaman to be possessed by a spirit
내림세 一勢 a fall; a decline; a downward [declining] tendency; a downtrend; a weakness; sagging
▶주가는 내림세다 The market has turned downward [weakened]. ⇌ Stock prices are falling [declining].
▶그녀의 인기는 내림세다 Her popularity is on the wane.
내림차 一次 〔數〕 a descending series [power]
내림떠보다 glare down (at)
내막 內幕 inside information [knowledge, facts]; 〈실정〉 actual conditions; (口) the lowdown
◆내막을 살피다 peep behind the scenes / 내막을 알다 see behind the screen / 내막을 폭로하다 expose a secret (of)
▶그는 정계의 내막을 알고 있었다 He knew what was going on behind the scenes [what the score was] in the political world.
▶그는 그 내막을 캐려고 했다 He tried to go behind the scenes.
▶그는 내막에 정통한 것 같다 He seems to have the inside knowledge. ⇌ He seems to be familiar with the inside story [facts].
내막 內膜 〔解〕 lining membrane
내맡기다 leave *sth* to *sb*; trust *sb* with *sth*; leave [put] *sth* in *sb's* hands
◆사업을 고용인에게 내맡기다 leave *one's* business in the charge [hands] of *one's* employees / 운을 하늘에 내맡기다 leave it to chance
▶그에게는 이 일을 내맡길 수 없다 He can't be entrusted with this job. ⇌ We can't entrust this job to him.
▶모든 것을 당신에게 내맡깁니다 I leave everything to you [in your hands].
내면 內面 the inside; the interior
◆내면의 고뇌 mental suffering / 내면적 갈등 the inner conflict / 내면적 생활 *one's* inner life / 내면적 증거 internal evidence / 내면적으로 internally / 내면화하다 internalize
▶그 두 사람은 외양은 닮아보이지만 내면은 전혀 다르다 The two look alike but they are very different inside.
▶사람은 외면으로가 아니라 내면으로 평가해야 한다 A man should be valued by what he is, not by what he looks.
▶그는 보기에는 험상궂지만 내면적으로는 착한 사람이다 He looks forbidding, but he is kind at heart.
■—관찰 an inside view; a view from inside —묘사 (an) inner description —세계 the inner world
내명 內命 private orders
◆내명을 내리다[받다] issue [receive] an unofficial [informal] orders
▶그는 사장의 내명을 받고 유럽에 갔다 He went to Europe under secret orders from the boss.
내명년 來明年 the year after next
내몰다 expel; drive [force] *sb* out; bundle off [out]; 〈직위에서〉 expel [dislodge]; oust; (口) hoof out
▶고양이를 집밖으로 내몰았다 I drove the cat out of the house.
▶그녀는 홧김에 아이들을 밖으로 내몰았다 In anger, she showed her children outdoors.
내몰리다 be driven out [away]; be expelled
내몽고 內蒙古 Inner Mongolia

내무 內務 home [domestic, internal] affairs ■ **—반** (軍) (living) quarters; barracks **—사열** an inspection of the soldiers' living quarters **—위원회** 〈국회의〉 the Home Affairs Committee

내무부 內務部 the Ministry of Home Affairs; (美) the Department of the Interior; (英) the Home Office ■ **—장관** the Minister of Home Affairs; the Home Minister **—차관** the Vice-Minister of Home Affairs

내밀다 1 〈돌출하다〉 protrude; jut out; project ◆ 바다로 내민 방파제 a pier jutting out into the sea
2 〈돌출시키다〉 push [thrust] out; stick out (of); force out ◆ 가슴을 내밀다 throw out one's chest / 혀를 내밀다 stick [thrust] out one's tongue ▶ 그는 배를 내밀고 걷는다 He walks with his stomach thrown forward. ▶ 난간 밖으로 몸을 너무 내밀지 마시오 Don't lean too far out over the railing.
3 〈남에게 미루다〉 throw (on); force; shift (on); compel ◆ 일을 남에게 내밀다 force work on sb / 책임을 남에게 내밀다 shift the blame on to another
4 〈쫓아내다〉 drive out; force out; expel; push out ◆ 사람을 방 밖으로 내밀다 push [throw] sb out of the room
5 〈서류 등을〉 submit ◆ 사표를 내밀다 tender [thrust] one's resignation / 청구서를 내밀다 render a bill for payment

내밀리다 be pushed [thrust, forced] out

내밀하다 內密— private; secret; confidential ◆ 내밀한 일 a family [private] affair [matter] / 내밀한 파티 a private party / 내밀히 secretly; in private; among one's people; confidentially; privately; in secret / 내밀히 면회를 요청하다 ask for a private interview / 내밀히 조사하다 make confidential [secret] inquiries ▶ 그들은 내밀히 계획을 추진하고 있다 They are going ahead with their plan secretly.

내밀힘 〈추진력〉 drive; pushing force; 〈배짱〉 boldness; self-confidence

내박차다 〈발길로〉 kick out hard; 〈딱 거절하다〉 reject flatly

내발뺌하다 make an excuse on; vindicate one's innocence; justify oneself; (口) put out an alibi; clear [exculpate] oneself (of, from)

내방 來訪 a visit; a call ◆ 내방중인 여행객 a tourist now on a visit (to Korea) **—내방하다** visit; call on sb; call at (a house); pay sb a visit ▶ 내방해 주시면 영광이겠습니다 I hope you will do me the honor of paying me a visit. ■ **—자** a visitor; a caller

내배다 〈젖어나오다〉 ooze out; exude; soak through; transude; saturate ▶ 그의 재킷은 땀이 내배었다 His jacket was soaked with sweat. ▶ 붕대에 피가 내배어 있었다 Blood oozed out of the bandage. ⇌ The bandage was saturated with blood.

내뱉다 〈침 등을〉 spit (out); expectorate; 〈말을〉 say sth over one's shoulder; make a parting remark ◆ 길에 침을 내뱉다 spit on the road / 내뱉듯이 말하다 say disdainfully [snappingly] ▶ 「당신이 나에 대해 어떻게 생각하든지 나는 개의치 않소」라고 그는 경찰에게 내뱉었다 "I don't give a damn what you think about me," he spat out at the policeman. ▶ 「용기가 있으면 해 봐」라고 그는 내뱉듯이 말했다 He snapped, "Do it if you dare!"

내버려두다 〈방치하다〉 leave [let] (a thing, sb) alone; let (a thing) as it is; 〈등한히 하다〉 neglect ◆ 병을 내버려두다 leave the disease untreated / 아이를 내버려두다 leave a child neglected [to himself]; let a child have his own way ▶ 그는 상처입은 동료를 내버려두었다 He deserted his injured comrades. ⇌ He left his injured comrades behind. ▶ 그는 하던 일을 내버려 두었다 He left his work unfinished. ▶ 그는 공부는 내버려두고 낚시하러 갔다 He went fishing neglecting his studies. ▶ 그건 내버려두면 시간이 해결한다 Leave it [the thing] alone, time will take care of it. ▶ 우리는 그들의 부정을 그대로 내버려 둘 수 없다 We should not let their wrongdoings go unpunished.

내버리다 〈아주 버리다〉 throw away; cast off ◆ 쓰레기를 함부로 내버리다 dump rubbish carelessly ▶ 그것은 돈을 내버리는 짓이다 It is a mere waste of money. ▶ 아직 쓸 수 있는 것을 내버리면 안된다 Don't throw away anything you can still use.

내보 內報 private information; a confidential [secret] report **—내보하다** report secretly

내보내다 1 〈나가게 하다〉 send out; let (go [get]) out; see sb out [to the door]; 〈석방하다〉 release; free ◆ 경기에 내보내다 let (the soccer team) take part in the game; let (a runner) go out (for the 400-meter race) / 사내아이들을 밖으로 내보내다 let the boys go outside ▶ 이 학교는 이미 1만명 이상의 졸업생을 내보내고 있다 This school has already sent out more than ten thousand graduates.
2 〈내쫓다〉 expel; turn out; put out; 〈셋방 등에서〉 eject (a tenant); 〈해고하다〉 dismiss; discharge; (美口) fire; (俗) sack ◆ 가정부를 내보내다 dismiss [fire] a maid / 세든 사람을 내보내다 evict [eject] a tenant from the house; put a tenant out

내복 內服 1【속옷】 underwear; underclothes; 〈여성·소아용〉 lingerie; (口) undies ◆ 내복을 입다[벗다] put on [off] underclothes / 내복을 갈아입다 change one's underwear
2 〈약을 먹음〉 internal use **—내복하다** take orally ▶ 하루 2정씩 3회 내복할 것 Take two tablets three times daily. ■ **—약** (an) internal [oral] medicine

내부 內部 the inside; the interior

♦선박의 내부 the inside of a ship / 인체의 내부 the inner [internal] parts of a human body / 내부의 internal; inside; interior / 내부에 inside; within
▶그 집의 내부를 보고 싶다 I would like to see the inside of the house.
▶간부진 내부에 대립이 있다 There is internal strife among the staff.
▶그 집은 내부도 외부와 마찬가지로 아름다웠다 The inside [interior] of the house was as beautiful as the outside [exterior].
■―기억장치 〈컴퓨터의〉 internal storage ―분열 internal discord; a split in the party ―사정 internal conditions; real conditions [circumstances]: 그는 회사의 내부사정에 밝다 He has a good inside knowledge of the company. / 도난은 내부사정에 밝은 자의 소행인 것 같다 The theft seems to be an inside job. ―인[사람] a man on the inside; an insider ―질환 an internal trouble

내부딪다 hit; knock; strike; bump
내부딪히다 get struck [hit]; get knocked [bumped]
내분 内分 〔數〕 interior division ―**내분하다** divide internally
내분 内紛 an internal trouble; domestic discord
♦정당의 내분 an intraparty strife / 내분에 시달리다 suffer from internal troubles / 내분에 휘말리다 get involved in internal trouble
▶그 정당은 내분이 끊이지 않는다 There are constant troubles within the party.
내분비 内分泌 〔生理〕 internal secretion
■―기관 an endocrine organ ―물(物) an endocrine; a hormone ―선(腺) an endocrine gland; a ductless gland ―학 endocrinology
내불다 breathe out; exhale; give out breath; breathe upon
♦거울에 입김을 내불다 breathe upon the mirror
▶그는 입김을 내불어 안경을 닦았다 He breathed on his glasses and wiped them.
내비치다 1 〈빛이〉 be transparent ♦내비치는 옷감 transparent cloth
▶얇은 옷으로 그녀의 다리가 내비쳐 보인다 Her legs are seen through her thin dress.
2 〈말을〉 hint; indicate ▶그녀는 자녀가 셋이나 있다는 것을 조금도 내비친 적이 없었다 She never gave the slighted indication that she had three children.
내빈 來賓 a guest; a visitor ▶내빈이 졸업생에게 축사를 했다 A guest offered his congratulations to the graduating students.
■―명부 a list of visitors ―석 the visitors' seats; (게시) For guests.
내빼다 (俗) scram ⇨ 달아나다
내뻗다 put forth; spread out; stretch; extend
♦손을 쭉 내뻗다 stretch out one's arms
내뻗치다 put forth; stretch; gush out; 〈물 등이〉 spout out ▶호스의 물이 내뻗쳤다 Water spouted [shot, spurted] from the hose.
내뿜다 〈물·피 등〉 gush out; spurt (out, up); 〈가스·증기·불 등〉 shoot out; blow out; 〈연기 등〉 puff out; send out [up, forth]
▶그는 담배 연기를 내뿜었다 He puffed away at a cigarette.
▶굴뚝이 연기를 내뿜었다 The chimney spouted out smoke.
▶많은 차들이 배기 가스를 마구 내뿜고 있다 Many cars freely release their exhaust gases in the air.
▶고래가 물을 내뿜고 있다 The whale is spouting.
▶화산이 불길과 연기를 내뿜고 있었다 The volcano was belching out [spewing forth] flames and smoke.
내사 内査 a secret investigation; a private inquiry
―**내사하다** make a secret investigation 《of》; make private [secret] inquiries into sth; inspect secretly
▶우리는 그의 배후를 내사하는 중이다 We are checking up on his background secretly.
▶경찰은 이 사건을 내사하기 시작했다 The police started to investigate this case secretly.
내사 來社 a visit to a company [an office]
―**내사하다** visit [come to] a company [an office] ▶10시에 내사해 주십시오 Please come to our office [company] at ten o'clock.
내산 耐酸 ♦내산성의 acid-resisting
내상 内喪 the death of one's wife
내색 ―色 〈얼굴에 드러냄〉 a revealing look; betrayal of one's emotion
―**내색하다** betray one's emotion; show [display] 《anxiety》 on one's face
▶그녀는 충격을 전혀 내색하지 않았다 Her manner showed no signs of shock. ≒ Her face did not show any sign of shock.
▶그는 불만을 내색하지 않았다 He did not betray his dissatisfaction either in his look or in his manner.
내생 内生 〔生〕 endogeny ♦내생적인 endogenous ■―식물 an endogen; an endophyte
내선 内線 〈구내 전화〉 an extension (略 ext.); 〈배선의〉 interior [indoor] wiring ▶내선 107번 부탁합니다 Give me extension 107, please. ≒ May I have extension 107, please?
■―번호 an extension number ―전화 an extension (tele)phone; an interphone
내성 内省 introspection; reflection; inward-looking ―**내성하다** introspect; reflect on oneself; turn one's thoughts inward ♦깊이 내성하다 exercise deep reflection
내성 耐性 〔醫〕 (a) tolerance 《to》 ♦내성이 있다 be tolerant; tolerate / …에 대해 내성이 생기다 develop [acquire, build up] resistance to 《insecticides》
■―균 resistant bacteria
내성적 内省的 reflective; indrawn; 〈심리학의〉 introspective
♦내성적인 사람[마음] a person [mind] of retiring desposition; a reserved person [mind]
▶그는 내성적인 성격이다 He has a retiring nature.
▶저 소녀는 너무 내성적이어서 말도 하지 못한다 That girl is too shy to speak.

내세 來世 the life after death; the other [next] world; the world to come
♦현세와 내세 this world and the other world / 내세를 믿다 believe in the world beyond the grave / 내세로 떠나다 《죽다》 go on a journey to the next world
▶대개의 젊은이는 내세를 믿지 않는다 Most young people don't believe in the life after death.

내세우다 1 〈대표를〉 support; make [have] *sb* represent; put up; stand
♦2명의 후보를 총선에 내세우다 put up two candidates in the coming general election / 회사 대표로 내세우다 have *sb* represent the firm / 후보자로 내세우다 have *sb* stand for 《the Assembly》; put up [nominate] a candidate
2 〈주장·자랑 등을〉 state; insist; claim; advocate; speak highly of; recommend; display
♦권리를 내세우다 claim [lay claim to] *one's* right(s) 《to》 / …한 조건을 내세우다 take up the position that… / 학식을 내세우다 display *one's* learning
▶그에게는 내세울 만한 재주가 없다 He has no talent to speak of.
3 〈남이 보도록〉 put [set, hang] up 《a sign》

내셔널리스트 〈국가주의자〉 a nationalist
내셔널리즘 〈국가주의〉 nationalism
내소박하다 內疏薄— mistreat *one's* husband
♦내소박당하다 be treated coldly by *one's* wife

내솟다 spring up; spout out; gush out
▶피가 상처로부터 내솟았다 Blood gushed [spurted] from the wound.
▶파열된 수도관에서 물이 내솟고 있었다 Water was spurting [gushing out] from the broken pipe.

내수 內需 domestic demand; home consumption
■—산업 an industry for domestic demand; enterprises producing commodities for domestic markets —용 원자재 raw materials for domestic demand [consumption] —확대 expansion of domestic demand: 내수확대 방안을 강구하다 take measures to boost domestic demand

내수 耐水 ♦내수의 water-resistant; 〈방수의〉 watertight; waterproof ■—성 water-proofing; water-resisting qualities
내수면 內水面 inland waters ■—어업 fresh-water fishery
내숭 wickedness; trickiness ■내숭하다, 내숭스럽다 wicked; sly; cunning; underhanded
▶그는 내숭스런 인간이다 He has a shrewd, scheming mind.
내쉬다 breathe out; exhale ♦숨을 내쉬다 breathe out *one's* breath ♦숨을 크게 들이쉰 다음 천천히 내쉬어라 Inhale [Breathe in] deeply and then exhale [breathe out] slowly.
내슈빌 〈미국 테네시주의 주도〉 Nashville
내습 來襲 an attack; an assault; an invasion; a raid
♦적의 내습에 대비하다 guard against an enemy's attack

▶우리는 스스로 적의 내습을 막아내야 한다 We must defend ourselves against the enemy invasion.
▶우리는 적의 내습을 격퇴할 수 있도록 경비를 강화했다 We tightened our defenses to fight to repulse the enemy attack.
■—내습하다 attack; assault; invade; make an attack [a raid] 《on》; 〈태풍〉 visit
내습 耐濕 ♦내습의 wetproof ▶이 타일은 내습성이 강하다 This tile is moistureproof [withstands dampness very well].
내시 內侍 a eunuch=환관(宦官)
내시 內示 an unofficial announcement ■—내시하다 show [notify] in private; announce unofficially [informally]
내시경 內視鏡 〔醫〕 an endoscope ■—검사(법) endoscopy
내신 內申 an unofficial [a confidential, a private] report ■—내신하다 report unofficially [private]
■—서 〈학교의〉 a school report on a student's record; school recommendations; a report of a student's record
내신 來信 〈온 편지〉 a letter (received); a message ▶뉴욕 지점에서 내신이 있었습니까? Did you receive a letter from the branch in New York?
내신성적 內申成績 〈고교의〉 the high school records; the academic report from high schools to colleges [universities]
내실 內室 〈거실〉 the main room; 〈안방〉 women's quarters; 〈남의 아내〉 your [his] wife
내실 內實 substance; substantiality
♦내실있는 생활 a full [fulfilling] life / 내실있는 작품 a substantial [solid piece of] work / 내실을 기하다 insure substantiality / 내실화하다 make 《a matter》 substantial [solid]
▶규모를 확대하는 것보다 내실을 기하는 것이 중요하다 It is more important to enrich the content than to enlarge the size.
내심 內心 1 〈속마음〉 *one's* (inmost) heart; *one's* real intention
♦내심으로는 at heart; in *one's* heart / 아무의 친절을 내심 고맙게 여기다 inwardly appreciate *sb's* kindness / 내심 후회하다 repent at heart
▶나는 내심 당신이 걱정됐어 I was secretly worried about you.
▶나는 내심 거절할 작정이었다 My real intention was to refuse.
▶그녀는 나에게 자기의 내심을 털어놓았다 She opened her heart to me. ⇒ She spoke her mind. ⇒ She confided in me.
▶나는 내심으로는 무서웠다 I was afraid in my heart.
2 〔幾〕 the inner center
내압 內壓 〔物〕 internal pressure
내압 耐壓 resisting pressure ♦내압성의 pressure-resistant ■—력 capacity to resist [endure] pressure ■—복 a pressure-resistant garment; 〈잠수복〉 a diving suit
내야 內野 〔野〕 the infield [diamond] ■—석 the infield stands —수 an infielder —안타[플

라이, 땅볼] an infield hit [fly, ground ball]

내약 內約 a private agreement —**내약하다** make a private agreement; 〈묵계하다〉 have a tacit understanding 《with》

내역 內譯 details ⇨ 명세(明細)

내연 內緣 an informal marriage; a marriage of consent
◆ 내연 관계 a common-law marriage / 내연의 처 a common-law wife / 내연의 남편 an unmarried husband
▶ 그들은 내연 관계다 They live together as husband and wife.
▶ 그들은 내연의 관계를 맺었다 They were married informally.

내연기관 內燃機關 an internal-combustion engine

내연터빈 內燃— an internal-combustion turbine

내연하다 來演— ▶ 베를린 교향악단이 서울에 내연했다 The Berlin Symphony Orchestra came to Seoul to give a performance.

내열 耐熱 heat-resistance; heatproof ◆ 내열(성)의 heat-resistant; heatproof; 〔治〕 refractory; 〔生化〕 thermostable ▶ 이 옷은 내열성이다 This suit is heatproof [heat-resistant].
■ —시험 a heat test; a heat-resistance test —유리 heat-resistant glass —재료 heat-resistant materials —타일 heat-resistant tile —합금 (a) heat-resistant alloy

내오다 take out; bring out ◆ 의자를 방에서 내오다 carry a chair out of the room

내왕 來往 coming and going; 〈통행〉 traffic; 〈교제〉 association
▶ 이 길은 차의 내왕이 심하다 There is very heavy [a lot of] traffic on this road. ⇌ Traffic is very heavy on this road.
▶ 그 길은 사람과 차의 내왕이 많아 건너기 힘들다 The street is so crowded with pedestrians and cars that it is hard to cross it.
—**내왕하다** come and go; go back and forth; 〈교제하다〉 have friendly relations 《with》; associate 《with》; keep company 《with》
▶ 그들은 서울과 부산을 내왕한다 They go back and forth between Seoul and Pusan.
▶ 우리는 이웃집과 내왕하며 지내는 사이가 아니다 We are not on visiting terms [We don't associate] with our next-door neighbors.

내외¹ 內外 **1** 〈안팎〉 the inside and outside; the interior and exterior; 〈국내와 국외〉 the inside and outside of the country
◆ 회사 내외의 복잡한 사정 the complicated internal and external circumstances of the company / 내외의 internal and external / 시내외의 in and around the city / 내외로부터 from within and without / 국내외로 다사다난하다 be eventful at home and abroad
▶ 그 사건은 국내의 신문에 보도되었다 The incident was reported in domestic and foreign papers.
▶ 그는 내외 사정에 정통하다 He is well versed in domestic and foreign affairs.
▶ 그는 국내외에 걸쳐 잘 알려져 있다 He is well-known both at home and abroad.
2 〈부부〉 man [husband] and wife; a (married) couple ◆ 김선생 내외 Mr. and Mrs. Kim
▶ 그들은 잘 어울리는 내외다 They are a really well-matched couple.
3 〈대략〉 about; around ◆ 100달러 내외 100 dollars or so; around 100 dollars / 1주일 내외에 in about a week [a week or so]
■ —과(科) internal medicine and surgery —동포 our countrymen both at home and abroad —자(資) 《mobilize both》 domestic and foreign capital —정책 home and foreign policy —종(從) 〈내종〉 cousins by paternal aunts; 〈외종〉 cousins by maternal uncles —채(債) domestic and foreign bonds

내외² 內外 〈남녀간의〉 avoidance of social contact between the opposite sexes —**내외하다** keep away from the opposite sex; avoid society with the opposite sex

내외간 內外間 〈부부간〉 relationship between man [husband] and wife
▶ 그들은 내외간에 사이가 참 좋다 They are an ideal husband and wife. ⇌ They get on excellently as husband and wife.

내용 內用 1 ⇨ 내복(內服) 2 **2** 〈가정용〉 domestic [household] use

내용 內容 1 〈속내·취지〉 contents; import
◆ 사건의 내용 the details of a case / 편지의 내용 the contents of a letter
▶ 그는 그 계획에 반대한다는 내용의 편지를 내게 보내왔다 He wrote me a letter saying that [to the effect that] he was against the plan.
▶ 그의 연설은 내용이 풍부[빈약]하다 His speech is full of interesting facts [contains very little matter].
▶ 그녀의 얘기는 재미있지만 내용이 없다 She is fun to listen to, but really says hardly anything.
▶ 그 책의 내용은 제2쪽에 나와 있다 The contents of the book are on the second page.
▶ 이 편지의 내용을 복사하시오 Copy the text of this letter.
▶ 회의의 내용을 가르쳐 주세요 Tell me what you discussed [talked about] at the meeting.
▶ 그 논문의 형식은 참으로 좋으나 내용에는 찬성할 수가 없다 Indeed the form of the article is good, but I don't approve of its content.
2 〈실질〉 substance ◆ 형식과 내용 form and substance [content]
■ —견본 〈책의〉 sample [specimen] pages; a prospectus; 〈출판 전의〉 advance sheets —목록 a table of contents —물 the contents: 위(胃)의 내용물 the contents of a stomach —분석 〔社·心〕 content analysis —어(語) a content word

내용연수 耐用年數 the period of durability; service life
▶ 이 기계는 내용연수가 10년이다 The life of this machine is ten years.
▶ 이 보일러는 내용연수가 지났다 This boiler is no longer serviceable.

내용증명 內容證明 certification of contents
■ —우편 contents-certified mail

내우 內憂 domestic troubles [discord]

내우외환 內憂外患 internal and external troubles; troubles from within and without

◆내우외환에 시달리다 be harassed with troubles both at home and abroad

내월 來月 next month; the coming month; 〖商〗 proximo (略 prox.) ▶내월 5일이 내 생일이다 The 5th of next month is my birthday.

내유외강 內柔外剛 ◆내유외강한 사람 a man who is tough in appearance but gentle in spirit [at heart]

내응 內應 secret communication ⇨ 내통(內通) 1

내의 內衣 an undergarment ⇨ 속옷

내의 內意 〈의도〉 one's intention [wishes]; 〈의사〉 one's personal [private] opinion

내의 來意 the object of one's visit ◆내의를 묻다 ask the object of sb's call / 내의를 알리다 tell the object of one's call

내이 內耳 〖解〗 the internal [inner] ear; labyrinth ■—염 labyrinthitis

내인 內因 an internal cause

내일 來日 tomorrow
◆내일 아침[정오, 오후, 저녁, 밤] tomorrow morning [noon, afternoon, evening, night] / 내일의 한국 the Korea of tomorrow [the future]; tomorrow's [future] Korea / 내일부터 일을 시작하다 begin one's work tomorrow
▶그는 내일 런던으로 출발한다 He is leaving for London tomorrow morning.
▶내일은 일요일이다 Tomorrow is Sunday.

내입금 內入金 part [partial] payment in advance

내자 內資 domestic fund [capital] ◆내자를 동원하다 mobilize domestic capital

내장 內粧・內裝 interior decoration [design]; 〈美〉 trim ■—공사 interior finish work

내장 內臟 the internal organs; the entrails; 〈장자〉 the intestines; the bowels; (口) insides ◆닭의 내장을 제거하다 remove the insides from a chicken
▶당신의 내장 기관에는 나쁜 데가 없습니다 You have no problems with your internal organs.
■—강(腔) a visceral cavity; a splanchnocoel —신경 the splanchnic nerve —외과 internal surgery —질환 a trouble of an internal organ; internal disease —통(痛) visceral pain —파열 a visceral cleft —포층(包層) 〖動〗 a splanchnic layer —하수증(下垂症) splanchnoptosis; abdominal ptosis —학 splanchnology —해부 splanchnotomy

내장안 內障眼 〖醫〗 〈백내장〉 cataract; 〈녹내장〉 glaucoma; 〈흑내장〉 amaurosis

내재 內在 〖哲〗 immanence ◆신의 내재 the divine immanence —**내재하다** be inherent (in); be immanent (in)

내재율 內在律 inner rhythm [cadence] ◆자유시[산문]의 내재율 inner rhythm [cadence] of free verse [prose]

내재적 內在的 immanent; intrinsic ◆내재적 가치 the intrinsic [inherent] value / 인간사회의 내재적 모순 contradictions inherent in human society

내적 內的 〈내부의〉 internal; inner; 〈본래의〉 intrinsic; 〈심리적〉 mental
◆내적 고민 mental agony / 내적 생활 one's inner life / 내적인 아름다움 the intrinsic beauty (of) / 내적 이유로 for internal reasons

내전 內殿 the innermost parts of the royal palace; 〈왕비〉 a queen; an empress

내전 內戰 a civil war ▶그 나라는 자주 내전에 휘말리고 있다 The country has often been engulfed in civil wars.

내전 來電 〈전화〉 an incoming call; 〈전보〉 an incoming telegram

내젓다 shake; wave; swing ◆팔을 내젓다 swing one's arms

내접 內接 〖幾〗 inscription —**내접하다** be inscribed; touch internally ◆내접한 inscribed / 내접시키다 inscribe (a polygon) (in (a circle))
■—다각형 an inscribed polygon; an inpolygon —원 an inscribed circle

내정 內定 unofficial [informal] decision —**내정하다** decide unofficially [informally] ▶그의 후임에 김 선생이 내정되었다 It has been informally arranged that Mr. Kim will succeed him.
▶그는 승진이 내정되어 있다 It has been unofficially decided that he will be promoted.
■—가격 〈입찰의〉 a reserve price

내정 內政 internal [home, domestic] politics [affairs]; domestic [home] administration
◆다른 나라의 내정에 간섭하다 interfere [intervene] in the domestic [internal] affairs of other countries
▶그것은 그 나라의 내정 문제다 That is an internal affair of the country.
■—(불)간섭 (non)interference in internal [domestic] affairs (of other nations)

내정 內庭 an inner court

내정 內情 domestic [internal] conditions; 〈내막〉 the inside story ▶그는 그 회사의 내정에 밝다 He is familiar with what goes on inside the company.

내조 內助 the wife's help [assistance] ◆내조 덕택으로 thanks to one's wife's help
▶나의 성공은 내조 덕택이다 I owe my success to my wife's help [assistance].
—**내조하다** help one's husband
■—자 a helpmate; a wife

내조 來朝 the visit of foreign envoy —**내조하다** 《a foreign envoy》 arrive in this country

내종 來從 a cousin by a paternal aunt

내주 來週 next week; the coming week
◆내주의 오늘 today next week; a week from today / 내주 토요일에 next Saturday; on Saturday next week / 내주중에 within [in] the next week
▶내주에는 아무런 계획도 없다 I have no particular plans for next week.

내주다 1 〈가졌던 물건을〉 give; hand over; 〈허가 등을〉 issue; grant
◆아무에게 책을 내주다 hand a book (over) to sb; hand sb a book / 여권을 내주다 issue a passport 《to》
▶구매품은 영수증과 교환하여 내주게 된다 They will give you your purchase in exchange for the receit.
▶그는 사장 자리를 아무에게도 내주지 않으려고 한다 He is trying to hang on to the post of

president.
▶나는 전재산을 아들에게 내줄 생각이다 I'm going to make over [transfer, leave] all the property to my son.
2 〈비워 주다〉 leave; vacate; move [clear] out of; make room for; 〈길을〉 make way for
♦방[집]을 내주다 evacuate [vacate] a room [house]
▶나는 한 달 후에 아파트를 내주어야 한다 I have to vacate [move out of, clear out of] my apartment in a week.
▶아무도 그 노인에게 앉을 자리를 내주려 하지 않는다 No one would make room for the old man to sit down.
▶그들은 구급차에게 길을 내주었다 They made way for the ambulance.
내주장 內主張 petticoat government; control of men by women
▶그의 집은 내주장이다 He is henpecked. ⇌ He is a henpecked husband. ⇌ His wife wears the pants in his family.
—**내주장하다** henpeck; dominate *one's* husband
내지 內地 〈안쪽 지방〉 the interior of a country; inland; 〈국내〉 home; homeland ♦내지의 interior; inland; domestic
내지 乃至 1 〈범위·정도〉 from A to B; between A and B
▶5만원 내지 10만원 정도만 기부해 주십시오 Will you please contribute between fifty and a hundred thousand won?
▶이것은 1주일 내지 2주일이면 도착할 것입니다 It will reach you in one or two weeks.
2 〈또는〉 or; and
♦경제적 내지 합리적 방법 an economic or rational method
▶파출소 내지 경찰서에 신고해 주십시오 You should report it to a police box or police station.
내진 內診 an internal examination; 〈부인과 의〉 a gynecological examination
내진 來診 a doctor's visit to a patient (⇨ 왕 진) ♦내진을 청하다 send for [call in] a doctor
▶열이 높은 것 같으니 곧 내진을 받아야 한다 You seem to have a high fever, so you should call in a doctor at once.
내진 耐震 ♦내진의 earthquake-proof 《building》 ▬**공학** seismic technology —**구조** earthquake-resistant [aseismatic] construction
내집단 內集團 〔社〕 an in-group
내쫓기다 1 〈쫓겨나다〉 be thrown [driven] out; be forced out
♦집에서 내쫓기다 be thrown out by *one's* family / 시집에서 내쫓기다 be compelled to leave *one's* husband's home / 학교[클럽]에서 내쫓기다 be expelled from school [the club]
2 〈해고·추방되다〉 be expelled [dismissed]
▶그녀는 회사에서 내쫓겼다 She was dismissed [(口) fired] by the company. ⇌ **(英口)** She got the sack from the company.
내쫓다 1 〈밖으로〉 expel; turn [drive, force] *sb* out; **(口)** throw [kick] *sb* out; 〈세든 사람

을〉 evict; eject
♦세든 사람을 내쫓다 evict; eject a tenant (from the house); force a tenant out / 집에서 고양이를 내쫓다 drive a cat out of the house
▶그는 화가 나서 손님을 내쫓았다 In anger, he showed his guest out.
▶경비원들이 모여든 기자들을 내쫓았다 The guards drove out the assembled reporters.
2 〈해고하다〉 dismiss; discharge; send *sb* packing; **(美口)** fire; **(英口)** sack; give *sb* the sack
♦회사에서 직원을 내쫓다 dismiss a clerk [kick a clerk] out of company
▶사장은 그를 즉시 내쫓았다 Boss fired him out in no time.
▶그들은 하인을 정직하지 못하다는 이유로 내쫓았다 They discharged their servant for being dishonest.
내차다 kick (away); 〈냅다 차다〉 kick hard
♦아무의 정강이를 내차다 give *sb* a hard kick on the shin
내채 內債 a domestic [an internal] loan; an internal debt ♦내채를 발행[모집]하다 issue [raise, float] a domestic loan
내처 1 〈계속〉 throughout; all the way [time]; 〈중단없이〉 without a break; continually
♦12시간의 내처 비행 12 hours' continuous flight / 내처 9시간 동안 for nine hours at a stretch / 같은 반을 내처 담임하다 continue (to be) in charge of the same class
▶3주일간을 비가 내처 온다 It has been raining continually for three weeks.
2 〈하는 김에 끝까지〉 ▶강연 후에 내처 질의 응답이 있었다 The lecture was followed by a question-and-answer session.
내추럴리즘 naturalism
내출혈 內出血 〔醫〕 internal hemorrhage [bleeding] ▶그는 가슴을 부딪혀 내출혈을 일으켰다 He was hit in the chest and suffered internal bleeding.
내치 內治 1 〈국내 정치〉 home [domestic] administration —**내치하다** administer the affairs of state **2** 〈병의〉 treatment by internal medicine —**내치하다** cure by internal medicine
내치다 1 〈물리치다〉 reject; turn down; beat off; repulse ▶그들은 그의 의견을 내쳤다 They rejected [refused to adopt] his opinion. **2** 〈내 버리다〉 throw away; throw out
내치락들이치락 1 〈변덕스럽게〉 capriciously; fickly; whimsically —**내치락들이치락하다** change *one's* mind constantly; be fickle; be capricious [whimsical]; be full of whims
▶그렇게 내치락들이치락하는 사람은 믿을 수가 없다 I can't believe such a fickle person.
2 〈병세가〉 —**내치락들이치락하다** get better one day and worse the next; have (its) ups and downs
▶그의 병세는 내치락들이치락하고 있다 His illness [condition] hangs in the balance. ⇌ He gets better one day and worse the next.
내친걸음 ♦내친걸음에 on *one's* [the] way to; in the course of; at *one's* convenience / 내친 걸음에 말하다 remark in passing

내키다¹
▶기왕에 내친 걸음이다 Over shoes, over boots, let's go through with it.
▶그와 통화하다가 내친 걸음에 그녀에 대해서 물어보았다 When I talked with him on the phone, I asked about her.

내키다¹ 〈마음이〉 feel like 〈doing〉; be in the mood 〈to do, for doing〉; be inclined 〈to do〉; be interested 〈in〉
♦내키지 않는 일 work not to *one's* liking; a job *one* is unable to put *one's* heart into
▶마음이 내키면 전화하세요 Please call me up whenever you feel like it.
▶그는 마음이 내키면 훌륭한 그림을 그린다 He paints excellent pictures when the whim is on him [when the fancy takes him].
▶지금 가는 것은 마음이 내키지 않는다 I don't feel like going now. = I'm not in the mood to go now.
▶이 일은 마음이 내키지 않는다 I don't feel inclined to do [feel interested in] this work. = I'd rather not to do this work.

내키다² 〈자리를 물리어 내다〉 remove farther; make [leave] room for

내탐 內探 a secret investigation; a private inquiry □ 내사(內査)
—**내탐하다** make [conduct] secret inquiries
▶그녀는 그들의 동정을 내탐했다 She spied on their movements.

내탕금 內帑金 money in the personal possession of the king; (英) the privy purse

내통 內通 1 〈내응〉 secret communication; 〈배반〉 betrayal; treason
—**내통하다** communicate secretly 〈with〉; betray 〈to the enemy〉
▶우리들 가운데 적과 내통하는 자가 있다 Among us there is someone who has been communicating secretly with the enemy.
2 〈남녀의 사통〉 illicit intercourse; adultery
—**내통하다** have illicit intercourse 〈with〉; commit adultery
■—자 a betrayer; 〈사통자〉 a fornicator

내팽개치다 throw out [away]; fling out ♦일을 내팽개치다 leave *one's* work unfinished; lay aside *one's* work

내포 內包 〔論〕 (a) connotation —**내포하다** 〈뜻을〉 contain; imply; involve; 〔論〕 connotate
▶그의 말은 거부의 뜻을 내포하고 있었다 His words implied rejection.

내폭 耐爆 ♦내폭성의 antiknock ■—제 antiknock; antiknock substances

내피 內皮 〔解〕〈동물의〉 the endothelium; 〈식물의〉 the endodermis

내핍 耐乏 austerity; putting up with poverty
—**내핍하다** put up with poverty
■—생활 (a life of) austerity; a hard [austere] life : 내핍생활을 하다 lead a hard life; tighten [pull in] *one's* belt —예산 an austerity budget —정책 a belt-tightening policy; an austerity measure

내한 來韓 a visit to Korea; arrival in Korea
—**내한하다** visit [come to] Korea; arrive in Korea

내한 耐寒 coldproof ♦내한성의 (winter-)hardy; cold-resistant
■—시험 a cold-resistance test —식물 a (winter-)hardy plant; a plant which can survive cold weather —장치 winterization —훈련 training to build up resistance to cold weather

내항 內港 the inner harbor
내항 內項 internal terms
내항 內航 coastal service ■—로 a coasting line [route] —선(船) a home-waters liner; a coaster —해운사업 the coastal shipping industry

내항 來航 a visit by ship 〈to〉
▶그 항구의 시민들은 퀸엘리자베스호의 내항을 환영했다 The people of the port town welcomed a visit of the ocean liner Queen Elizabeth to their port.
—**내항하다** visit this shore by ship

내항성 耐航性 〈배의〉 seaworthiness; 〈항공기의〉 airworthiness ♦내항성이 있는 seaworthy; airworthy; 〈우주선의〉 spaceworthy

내해 內海 an inland sea; an arm of the sea
내향성 內向性 〔心〕 introversion ♦내향성인 사람 an introvert

내홍 內訌 〈내분〉 internal strife
내화 內貨 local currency [money]
내화 耐火 —**내화하다** resist fire; fireproof
■—건물 a fireproof building —구조 fireproof construction —금고 a fireproof safe —도 refractoriness —벽돌 (a) firebrick; (a) refractory brick —성 fire resistance : 내화성의 fireproof; fire-resistant / 내화성이 강하다 have great resistance to fire —장치 fireproof installation; fireproofing —재 fire-resistant building materials; fireproofing —점토 fire clay

내환 內患 〈나라 안의 걱정〉 domestic troubles; 〈아내의 병〉 *one's* wife's illness ♦외우 내환 troubles at home and abroad

내후년 來後年 three years from now ♦내후년까지는 in three years

냄비 〈얕은〉 a pan; 〈손잡이가 긴〉 a saucepan
♦스튜용 냄비 a stewpot / 냄비를 불 위에 올려놓다 put a pot [saucepan] over the heat / 생선을 냄비에 끓이다 boil fish in a pan
—**국수** pot-boiled noodles —**뚜껑** a pot lid

냄새 1 【코로 맡는】 (a) smell; an odor; (a) scent; 〈향기〉 fragrance; (a) perfume; 〈음식물의〉 an aroma; 〈악취〉 a stink; a stench

〔解說〕 **smell**은 가장 일반적인 말로 갖가지 냄새를 나타내지만 수식어가 붙지 않을 때는 보통 악취를 뜻한다. **odor**는 smell을 완곡하게 나타내는 말이며 불쾌한 냄새를 가리키는 경우가 많다. **scent**는 그것 자체의 특유한 냄새이며 보통 희미한 냄새, **fragrance**는 달고 신선한 화초의 향기, **perfume**은 짙은 향수나 꽃냄새, **stink**는 지독한 악취를 나타낸다.

♦나쁜 [역한] 냄새 a bad [foul, nasty] smell; an unpleasant smell / 독한 냄새 a strong scent [smell] / 좋은 냄새 a sweet [nice] smell 〈냄새가〉 냄새가 나쁜 foul-smelling; bad-smelling; evil-smelling; stinking / 냄새가 없는

odorless; scentless / 냄새가 좋은 sweet-smelling; sweet-scented / 냄새가 나쁘다 smell offensive; have a foul smell; stink (vilely); be foul-smelling; be unpleasant [disgusting] to the smell / 냄새가 없어지다 lose the odor

▶ 이 꽃은 냄새가 좋다 This flower smells sweet. ⇌ This flower has a sweet smell [scent, fragrance, perfume].

▶ 그에게서 술 냄새가 난다 His breath smells of liquor. ⇌ I smell liquor on his breath.

▶ 그의 방은 담배 냄새가 배어 있다 His room was impregnated with the scent of tobacco.

▶ 부엌에서 가스 냄새가 난다 I (can) smell gas in the kitchen.

〈냄새를〉냄새를 맡다 smell 《a flower》; smell out; get wind [scent] of; take a smell 《at》; scent; sniff / 냄새를 없애다[빼다] take the smell 《off》; remove the odor 《from》; deodorize / 좋은 냄새를 풍기다 give out [send forth] a sweet scent [fragrance]

▶ 그녀는 언제나 향수 냄새를 짙게 풍기고 다닌다 She is always giving off a strong smell of perfume.

▶ 개가 킁킁거리고 냄새를 맡으며 먹을 것을 찾고 있었다 The dog was sniffing about, looking for food.

2 〈느낌·티·기미〉a smack; a flavor; an odor ◆ 문학적 냄새가 나는 표현 a phrase [an expression] with a literary flavor / 냄새가 몹시 나다 smell strongly [prodigally] 《of》; give off a strong smell / 관료 냄새가 짙다 smack [savor] strongly of the bureaucrat

▶ 그 프랑스인의 생각에서는 동양적인 냄새가 짙게 풍긴다 The Frenchman's opinion has a strong Oriental flavor.

▶ 그의 얘기에서 협잡꾼 냄새가 난다 His story smells of something tricky [is fishy].

▶ 물오리가 사냥꾼 냄새를 맡고 달아났다 The wild duck sensed the hunter and ran off.

▶ 신문기자가 그 회사의 비밀을 냄새 맡았다 A journalist ferreted out the secret of the company.

냅다[1] 〈연기가〉 smoky; stinging

▶ 방이 냅다 The room is smoky [full of smoke].

▶ 낙엽이 젖어있어 불이 꽤 내웠다 Because the leaves were damp, the fire was rather smoky.

▶ 불이 내워서 기침이 났다 The smoky fire made me cough.

냅다[2] 〈빠르고 세차게〉 with all one's strength [energy]; as hard as one can

◆ 냅다 도망치다 run away at full speed; run for one's (dear) life / 냅다 때리다 hit [strike] hard / 밧줄을 냅다 끌어 당기다 use all one's strength to pull a rope

냅뜨다 sally forth; venture forth; go full steam ahead

냅킨 〈식탁용〉 a (table) napkin; (英) a serviette; 〈생리용〉 a (sanitary) napkin; (英) a sanitary towel

◆ 종이 냅킨 a paper napkin / 무릎에 냅킨을 펼치다 lay [spread] one's napkin across one's lap

냇가 a streamside; the bank of a stream

냇물 〈시내〉 a stream; a brook ◆ 냇물을 건너다 wade across a stream

▶ 냇물이 말라버렸다 The stream has dried up.

냇버들 〔植〕 a purple willow; (英) a purple osier

냉 〔韓醫〕 a chill stomach; a chill; 〈대하증〉 whites; leukorrhea

냉- 冷- cold; cooled; chill(ed); 〈얼음으로 차게 한〉 iced ◆ 냉맥주 icy cold beer / 냉사이다 iced soda pop / 냉커피 iced coffee

냉가슴 冷— ◆ 냉가슴을 앓다 be (hiddenly) worried about; be afraid of; have a hidden [secret] fear [worry, anxiety]

▶ 그녀는 사고가 날까봐 냉가슴을 앓았다 She was on pins and needles (in her heart) for fear of accidents.

냉각 冷却 cooling; refrigeration

—**냉각하다** 〈차게 하다〉 cool (down); refrigerate; 〈차가워지다〉 cool (off); get cool ◆ 물을 냉각시키다 cool [refrigerate] water

▶ 에어컨이 방을 냉각시키고 있다 An air conditioner is cooling the room.

▶ 그녀에 대한 그의 정열은 차츰 냉각되었다 His passion for her gradually cooled down.

▶ 수증기가 냉각되면 물이 된다 When cooled, vapor is condensed into water.

■ —기(器) a cooler; a refrigerator; 〈자동차 엔진의〉 a radiator —기(期) a cooling-off period: 긴 냉각기가 지난 후에 그는 아내와 화해했다 After a long cooling-off period he was reconciled with his wife. —수 cooling water; (a) coolant —실 a cooling room —장치 a cooling device [apparatus] —제 a refrigerant —탑 a cooling tower —효과 a cooling effect

냉간 冷間 ■—가공 cold processing —압연 cold rolling

냉과리 half-burnt charcoal

냉기 冷氣 cold; chill; 〈찬공기〉 cool air ◆ 새벽의 냉기 the chill [coldness] of early dawn / 냉기를 느끼다 feel [have] a chill; feel cold

냉난방 冷暖房 air-conditioning ◆ 냉난방 완비 〈게시〉 Air-conditioned.

냉담 冷淡 〈무관심〉 indifference; lukewarmness; 〈냉정함〉 cold-heartedness; 〈박정함〉 cold-heartedness

—**냉담하다** 〈무관심하다〉 indifferent; apathetic; 〈냉정하다〉 cold; cold-hearted; icy; frigid ◆ 냉담한 인간 a cold-hearted man; an unfeeling person / 냉담한 태도 an indifferent attitude / 냉담하게 coolly; coldly; cold-heartedly

▶ 그는 남들의 어려움에 아주 냉담하다 He takes very little interest in the suffering of others.

▶ 그는 그녀의 노력에 대해 아주 냉담했다 He paid no attention to her efforts.

▶ 그는 내 불평에 냉담했다 He showed little interest in [paid little attention to] my complaint.

▶ 그는 그 문제가 있은 뒤부터 내게 냉담한 태도를 보이기 시작했다 He began to put the chill on me after the trouble.

▶ 그녀의 남편은 점점 냉담해졌다 Her husband's affection gradually cooled down.

냉대 冷待 a cold treatment [reception]; inhos-

♦냉대를 감수하다 submit to cold treatment / 냉대를 받다 be treated coldly; be received coldly; have a chilly reception
▶그는 회사에서 냉대를 받고 있다 He is left out in the cold in the company.
▶그는 그들에게서 냉대를 받았다 He received a cold treatment from them.
▶그녀는 그의 냉대에 발끈했다 She went mad at his cold-hearted treatment.
—냉대하다 treat [receive] *sb* coldly; give *sb* a cold reception
▶신임 과장은 그를 냉대했다 The newly-appointed section chief treated him coldly.
▶저 호텔은 행색이 초라한 손님을 냉대하기로 유명하다 That hotel is known for its cold treatment of [inhospitality to] poorly-dressed guests.

냉동 冷凍 freezing; refrigeration
—냉동하다 freeze; refrigerate; cool down
♦생선을 급속 냉동하다 freeze [refrigerate] fish quickly [fast] / 고기를 딱딱하게 냉동해 두다 keep meat frozen hard
▶이 생선들은 쉬 상하기 때문에 곧 냉동하지 않으면 안된다 You must freeze these fish at once, as they are perishable.
▶그 생선은 냉동되어 여기로 운반된다 The fish is frozen [refrigerated] and brought here.
■—건조 freeze-drying; lyophilization —건조기 a freeze dryer —고 a freezer —기 a freezer —두부 (a cake of) frozen bean curd —선 a refrigerator boat —수송 chilled transport : 생선을 냉동 수송하다 transport fish frozen —식품 frozen food —실 the freezing compartment —야 채[육] frozen vegetable [meat] —어[생선] frozen fish —제(劑) a refrigerant —컨테이너 a reefer container

냉랭하다 冷冷— 1〈차갑다〉cold; icy; chilly; freezing ▶새벽이 되니 냉랭해졌다 It became chilly toward dawn.
2〈냉담하다〉cold; cool; cold-hearted ♦냉랭한 대접 a frosty reception
▶그들은 나에게 냉랭했다 They were cold to me. ⇒ They gave me the cold shoulder.
▶그는 남에게 냉랭하게 대한다 He treats others in a cold way.

냉면 冷麵 *naengmyŏn*; buckwheat vermicelli
냉방 冷房 〈찬 방〉a cold [an unheated] room; 〈공기 조절〉air cooling; air-conditioning
♦냉방을 켜다[끄다] turn on [off] an air conditioner
▶이 방은 냉방이 너무 세다 The air-conditioning in this room is too strong.
▶냉방중. 문을 닫아 주세요 (게시) Air-conditioning is on [Space air-conditioned]. Please close the door [Keep door closed].
—냉방하다 air-condition (a room); air-cool
■—병 (be sick with) air-conditioningitis —장치 an air-conditioner; an air-conditioning unit [system]; a cooler —차 an air-conditioned car

냉소 冷笑 a cold [sarcastic] smile; a sneer
♦냉소적인 sardonic; sarcastic; mocking / 냉소조로 with a cold smile
▶그의 말은 어딘가 냉소적이었다 There was something derisive [snide] in his words.
▶그는 입가에 냉소를 띠고 그녀를 돌아보았다 He turned to her with a cold smile on his lips.
—냉소하다 sneer [jeer, mock, laugh] at *sb*
▶그들은 내 시도[실패]에 냉소했다 They sneered at my attempt [failure].

냉수 冷水 cold water
♦냉수를 끼얹다 throw [dash, pour, shower] cold water 《over, on》
▶냉수 한 컵 주세요 Give me a glass of cold water. ⇒ May I have a glass of cold water?
▶나는 냉수를 뒤집어쓴 듯한 기분이었다 I felt as if I had dashed cold water upon myself. ⇒ A cold shudder ran through me.
■—괴(塊) 〈바다의〉a cold water mass

냉수마찰 冷水摩擦 cold-water rubbing
▶나는 냉수마찰을 시작한 후 감기에 걸린적이 없다 I have never caught cold since I began rubbing myself with a cold wet towel.
—냉수마찰하다 rub *oneself* [have a rubdown] with a cold wet towel

냉수 먹고 된똥 눈다 (속담) produce something out of nothing; make something from nothing

냉수 먹고 이 쑤시기 (속담) acting as if *one* had his fill even when he is starving; enduring just for pride's sake; showing a bold front

냉수욕 冷水浴 a cold bath [shower] —냉수욕하다 take a cold bath [shower]; bathe in cold water

냉습 冷濕 1〈차고 눅눅함〉being cold and damp [moist, humid]
2 〔韓醫〕 a disease caused by cold and dampness —냉습하다 cold and moist ▶냉습한 기후는 건강에 나쁘다 A cold and damp [humid] climate is not good for our health.

냉엄하다 冷嚴— grim; stern; strict ♦냉엄한 현실 grim realities; hard facts
▶그들은 국제 경쟁의 냉엄한 현실을 모르고 있다 They don't realize the cold, hard facts of the international competition.

냉연하다 冷然— cold; icy; indifferent ♦냉연한 태도로 coldly ▶그는 냉연하게 그것을 관찰하고 있었다 He observed it with a cold attitude.

냉육 冷肉 cold meat;〈썰어 담은〉cold cuts
냉이 〔植〕a shepherd's purse [pouch]
냉장 冷藏 〈음식·약품 등의〉cold storage; refrigeration
—냉장하다 refrigerate; keep *sth* in cold storage ♦생선을 냉장하다 keep fish in cold storage
▶날고기는 냉장해야 한다 Raw meat should be kept in cold storage [refrigerated].
■—법 refrigeration —선 a cold-storage ship —실 a cold-storage room, a cool chamber —업 the cold-storage business —육 chilled meat —차 a cold-storage car; a refrigerator car; (口) a reefer —품 cold-storage goods

냉장고 冷藏庫 a refrigerator; (口) a fridge; a freezer (냉동용)
▶상하기 쉬운 것은 꼭 냉장고에 넣어 두어라

Don't forget to put the perishables in the refrigerator.

냉전 冷戰 a cold war; 〈과거 미·소간의〉 the Cold War ▶ 그들은 냉전상태에서 벗어났다 They freed themselves from a state of cold war.

냉정 冷靜 calmness; coolness; composure
♦냉정을 유지하다 keep calm [cool]; keep one's head (cool)/냉정을 잃다 lose one's presence of mind [head]/냉정을 회복하다 recover one's mental balance
▶ 그는 곧 냉정을 되찾았다 Soon he regained [recovered] his composure [self-possession].
▶ 그는 쉽게 냉정을 잃는다 He is easily upset. ⇌ He often loses his head [his presence of mind].
▶ 그는 항상 냉정을 유지하고 있다 He always keeps his head cool [presence of mind, maintains his composure].
—**냉정하다** calm; cool(-headed); composed; serene
♦냉정한 사람 a cool-headed person / 냉정한 판단력 the ability to judge coolly [calmly]/ 냉정히 calmly; coolly; composedly
▶ 그는 위험에 직면해서도 냉정했다 He was cool [kept his head cool] in the face of danger.
▶ 그는 냉정한 사람이다 He is a cool-headed person.
▶ 우리는 그 문제에 대해서 냉정한 판단을 내려야 한다 We must form a calm [cool] judgment on the problem.
▶ 그렇게 흥분하지 말고 어떻게 해야 할지 냉정하게 생각해 봐라 Don't get so excited. Be calm and consider how and what we should do!

냉차 冷茶 iced tea
냉천 冷泉 〈찬 샘〉a cold spring
냉철 冷徹 coolheadedness —**냉철하다** coolheaded ♦냉철한 두뇌 a cool head ▶ 그 저자는 현대사회를 냉철한 눈으로 보고 있다 The writer looks at modern society with a cool, realistic eye.

냉큼 〈곧〉at once; right away; immediately; 〈빨리〉quickly; swiftly
▶ 왜 꾸물대, 냉큼 시작해 What is keeping you so long? Start at once!
▶ 그는 내 청을 냉큼 들어주었다 He agreed to [granted] my request on the spot [out right, then and there].
▶ 냉큼 그 일을 끝내라 Clear up the job quickly [hurriedly]!
▶ 냉큼 나가 Get out of here right away! ⇌ You go away at once.

냉하다 冷— cold; chilly; icy
냉해 冷害 damage from [by] cold weather; cold weather damage
▶ 그 지방은 벼농사에 심각한 냉해를 입었다 The rice crop in that district has suffered serious cold weather damage [serious damage because of the cold weather].

냉혈 冷血 1〔動〕cold-bloodedness **2**〈냉혹〉 cold-heartedness; heartlessness
■—**동물** a cold-blooded animal —**한**(漢) a cold-hearted [heartless] person [guy]: 그는 냉혈이다 He is a cold-hearted guy. ⇌ His heart is a stone.

냉혹 冷酷 heartlessness; cruelty
—**냉혹하다** heartless; cold-blooded; cruel
▶ 그녀는 냉혹한 여자다 She is as cold as ice. ⇌ She is a cold-hearted woman.
▶ 그는 냉혹하게도 딸의 불운을 도와주지 않았다 He hardened [steeled] himself against his daughter's bad luck and refused to help her.

-냐 1〈의문〉▶ 넌 몇 살이냐? How old are you?
▶ 이것은 무엇이냐? What is this?
▶ 이건 네 펜이냐? Is this your pen?
▶ 넌 그 이유를 아느냐? Do you know the reason?
2〈강조·반어·감탄 등〉▶ 아니, 너냐? Why, was it you? ⇌ Oh, it was (only) you?
▶ 벌써 10시냐? My, is it already ten o'clock?
▶ 어이쿠, 난 왜 이렇게 멍청하냐, 또 틀렸잖아 Oh, stupid me! I've made a mistake again.

냠-냠 yum-yum
♦냠냠거리다 go yum-yum; eat with great relish [with gusto]
■—**이** (兒) a yummy; delicious food

냥 兩 1〈돈〉a *nyang*; a unit of old Korean coinage ♦닷 냥 five *nyang* **2**〈무게〉a *nyang*; an old Korean unit of weight

너[1] 〈2인칭〉you; thou ♦너의 your; thy / 너를 you; thee / 너에게 you; to [for] you / 너와 나 you and I ▶ 너 이리 와 Hey you, come here!
너[2] 〈넷〉four ♦너 쌀 너 말 four *mal* of rice / 너 푼 four *pun*; four pence

너구리 〔動〕a raccoon (dog)
너구리 굴 보고 피물 돈 내어 쓴다 〈속담〉 sell the skin before one has killed the bear

너그러이 generously; liberally; leniently; with a broad mind
♦너그러이 용서하다 forgive [pardon] generously; overlook; tolerate
▶ 그는 내 잘못을 너그러이 봐 주었다 He was good enough to overlook my mistakes.
▶ 그는 종파가 다른 사람에게도 너그러이 대했다 He was tolerant to those who belonged to other sects.

너그럽다 generous; broad-minded; lenient; tolerant
♦너그러운 사람 a tolerant [forgiving] person / 너그러운 판결 a lenient sentence / 너그러운 처분을 간청하다 plead for leniency [clemency]
▶ 그는 남의 의견에 너그럽다 He is tolerant of [about] other people's opinion.
▶ 그는 누구에게나 너그러웠다 He was generous to everybody.

너글너글하다 generous; moderate ▶ 그는 너글너글한 사람이다 He is a mild-mannered person.

너나없이 ▶ 우리는 너나없이 모두 같은 운명에 처해 있다 We are all in the same boat.
▶ 너나 없이 지쳐 있었다 Everyone was [All were] tired out.
▶ 너나 없이 정치인이 되고 싶어한다 Every man jack wants to be a politician.

▶우리반은[우리는] 너나없이 시험준비에 바쁘다 Everyone in the class [Everyone of us] is busy preparing for the exam.

너더댓 about four or five; several

너더분하다 1 〈지저분하다〉 untidy; messy; nasty; unpleasant
♦너더분한 방 an untidy [a messy] room / 너더분한 생활 환경 a squalid living conditions / 너더분하게 in disorder; in a mess
2 〈장황하다〉 long and boring; verbose ♦너더분하게 말하다 speak on and on; give a long-winded [lengthy, tedious] speech

너덕너덕 ♦너덕니덕 기운 헌 웃옷 a much-patched old coat; an old coat with patches all over / 옷을 너덕너덕 깁다 patch up a garment all over

너덜거리다 1 〈가닥이〉 flutter; flap ▶찢어진 옷소매가 팔을 움직일 때마다 너덜거린다 The torn sleeve of my coat is fluttering as I move my arm. 2 〈주제넘게〉 be talkative [glib]; speak well and easily; be pushy

너덜너덜 〈가닥이〉 flutteringly; flappingly; 〈주제넘게〉 freshly; forwardly

너덧 about four ♦너덧 사람 about four people; four persons or so

너도나도 both you and I
▶너도나도 같이 가자 Let's go all together.
▶너도나도 불조심하자 Let's be careful with fire.

너도밤나무 〔植〕 a beech (tree)

너럭바위 a broad and flat rock

너르다 wide (⇨ 넓다) ♦너른 캠퍼스 a large [big, vast] campus / 넓고 너른 조망 an open [a wide, an extensive] view

너머 ♦재너머 마을 a village beyond [across] the hill / 산 너머에 across [beyond] the mountain
▶그와는 10년 너머 친구다 I have been friends with him over the past ten years [for more than ten years].
▶그 일은 한달 너머 걸린다 It will take over a month.
▶공은 울타리 너머로 날아갔다 The ball went over the fence.
▶그는 안경 너머로 나를 보았다 He looked at me over (the rims of) his glasses.

너무 too; too much; excessively; to excess
▶그는 너무 열심이다 He is too [overly, excessively] enthusiastic.
▶너무 먹지 마라 Don't eat too much.
▶오늘은 너무 덥다 It is (much) too hot today.
▶너무 더워서 모두 물만 마셨다 The heat was so intense [It was so hot] that everybody was drinking a lot of water.
▶너무 서두르니까 실수를 했지 You made a mess of it because you were in too much of a hurry.
▶애기가 너무 달콤해서 믿을 수가 없다 The story is too good to be true.
▶그의 동작은 너무 꼴사납다 He is very, very awkward in his movement.
▶너무 태우지 않게 조심해야 한다, 맛이 없어지니까 Be careful not to overdo it, or it will become tasteless.
▶담배를 너무 피우면 건강에 해롭다 Too much smoking is bad for the health. ⇌ If you smoke too much [too many cigarettes], you will injure your health.

너무하다 〈도에 지나치다〉 (be) too much [hard, excessive]; (be) unreasonable [absurd]
▶그건 너무하다 That's too much [awful].
▶농담 치고는 넌 너무해 You are carrying your joke a bit [a little] too far.
▶이 더위는 너무해 It's extremely [awfully, terribly] hot. ⇌ The heat is terrible.

너벅선 —船 an open flatboat; a punt

너부죽이 flat ♦너부죽이 엎드리다 lie flat [prone]; lie with the face downward; lay *oneself* flat

너부죽하다, 너붓하다 broad and flat to some degree; somewhat broad and flat

너불거리다 flutter ⇨ 나불거리다

너붓이 calmly; politely; gracefully ♦너붓이 앉다 sit down gracefully / 너붓이 앉아 절하다 kneel down calmly and bow respectfully

너비 〈폭〉 width; breadth ♦너비 10m의 길 a street ten meters wide [broad, in width, in breadth]

너새[1] 〔建〕 a hip ■—지붕 a hip roof

너새[2] 〔鳥〕 a great bustard

너설 a rock-ribbed place; a crag; a mass of rock forming part of rugged cliff

너스래미 loose strands [strips] ♦짚신의 너스래미를 뜯어내다 pluck out the loose strips of a straw shoe

너스레 1 〈걸치는 막대기〉 a crossbar; a horizontal bar; bars [sticks] placed crosswise
2 〈허튼 소리〉 idle talk; big [tall] talk; idle remarks ♦너스레 떨다[놓다] talk nonsense; make idle talk; make a flippant remark; make a wisecrack

너스르르하다 light and airy; fluffy; flossy ⇨ 나스르르하다

너울 a veil; a piece of cloth worn by women over the head and shoulders ▶그 여자는 너울을 쓰고 있었다 The woman was wearing a veil.

너울거리다 〈물결이〉 wave; roll; swell; 〈나무나 풀이〉 flutter; swing [move] back and forth; sway
♦너울거리는 불꽃 waving flames / 바람에 너울거리는 가지 branches waving in the wind
▶바다가 너울거리고 있었다 The sea was running high. ⇌ The waves were high.
▶보리밭이 바람에 너울거리고 있었다 The barley field waved [rolled] in the wind.

너울너울 wavily; waveringly; swayingly
▶벼 이삭이 바람에 너울너울 춤추고 있었다 Ears of rice were waving [swaying] in the wind.
▶나비가 너울너울 날고 있다 Butterflies are fluttering about.

너울지다 〈물결이〉 be rough in the distance

너저분하다 〈외관이〉 squalid; shabby; disorderly; messy; 〈행동이〉 filthy; sloppy; slovenly; indecent
▶그 방은 너저분했다 The room was untidy

[messy, in a mess].
▶ 그는 너저분한 옷을 입고 있었다 He was shabbily dressed.

너절하다 1 〈허름하다〉 shabby; seedy; (口) sloppy ♦너절한 옷 shabby clothes ▶그녀는 차림새가 너절하다 She is slovenly [untidy] in appearance.
2 〈변변치 않다〉 worthless; trashy; petty ♦너절한 이야기는 그만 둬 Don't talk nonsense.
3 〈품격이〉 indecent; improper ♦너절한 농담 a dirty [an off-color] joke / 너절한 동기 mean [sordid] motives / 너절한 생각 mean thoughts / 너절한 취미 vulgar tastes

너클볼 〔野〕 a knuckle ball; a knuckler

너털거리다 1 ⇨ 너덜거리다 2 〈웃다〉 laugh loudly [heartily]

너털웃음 a hearty [coarse] burst of laughter; a burst of loud laughter
♦너털웃음을 웃다 laugh loudly and boisterously; roar with laugh(ter); burst out laughing; guffaw

너트 〔機〕 a nut ▶볼트를 너트로 제자리에 죄어라 Hold the bolt in place [Fasten the bolt] with a nut.

너펄거리다 flatter [flap, wave] (in the wind)
▶깃발이 바람에 너펄거리고 있다 The flag is flapping [fluttering, beating] in the wind.

너펄너펄 flutteringly

너풀거리다 flutter [wave, sway] lightly

너풀거리다 sway [flutter, flap] roughly ▶모자의 끄나풀이 바람에 너풀거린다 The ribbons on his hat are fluttering in the wind.

너희(들) you; you all; all of you; you people; you folks

넉 four ♦넉 달 four months / 넉 주[자] four weeks [feet]

넉가래 a wooden shovel; a snow shovel
■ ―질 shoveling with a wooden shovel : 넉가래질하다 shovel with a wooden shovel

넉걷이 raking the vines out of a garden [field] ─넉걷이하다 do the vine raking

넉잡다 ♦넉잡아 한 달 a month at most

넉넉하다 1 〈수량·규모 등이〉 enough; sufficient; ample; plenty (of); plentiful
▶시간은 넉넉하다 We have enough [plenty of] time.
▶넉넉한 식사가 공급되었다 Sufficient food was provided.
▶한 달에 80만원으로는 가족을 부양하는 데 넉넉하지 않다 Eight hundred thousand won a month is not enough [adequate] to support my family.
▶그 일은 세 사람이면 넉넉할거다 Three men will be enough for the job.
2 〈살림이〉 wealthy; well-to-do; rich; well-off; comfortably-off
♦넉넉한 가정 a well-to-do family / 살림이 넉넉하다 live well; be well [comfortably] off
▶그녀는 넉넉한 가정 출신이다 She comes from a rich [wealthy, well-to-do] family.
3 〈도량이〉 large-minded; broad-minded; lenient; generous; liberal; big-hearted ♦마음이 넉넉하다 have a lenient mind; have a broad [big] mind

넉넉히 in plenty [abundance]; enough; sufficiently; fully; generously; amply; wealthily; plentifully; richly
♦넉넉히 공급하다 supply *sth* in full measure / 넉넉히 살다 live comfortably; be well off / 옷을 넉넉히 짓다 cut clothes full; give a loose [an ample] fit
▶나는 그 임금으로 넉넉히 살아갈 수 있다 I can well afford to live on the pay.
▶아버지가 용돈을 넉넉히 주셨다 My father gave me a generous allowance.
▶그들은 넉넉히 살고 있다 They are well off [living in affluence].
▶걸어서 넉넉히 하루는 걸린다 It is a full [good] one day's journey on foot.

넉살 impudence; shamelessness; (口) nerve; (口) cheek; sauciness
♦넉살 부리다 behave shamelessly [saucily]; act brazenly [audaciously] / 넉살 좋다[스럽다] shameless; have a nerve; be brazen-faced; be impudent [cheeky] / 넉살좋게도 …하다 have the cheek [face, impudence, nerve, brass, effrontery] to (do)
▶넉살좋은 친구로군 What a nerve he has got! ⇌ What an impudent fellow he is!
▶나는 그 소년의 넉살에 놀랐다 I was surprised by the nerve of that boy.

넉자 a deerskin pad put underneath when stamping *one's* seal

넉장거리 〈벌떡 자빠짐〉 falling flat [full length, outstretched] on *one's* back

넋 a spirit; a soul
♦넋을 달래다 appease the spirit of a dead person [the dead] / 넋을 잃다 get absent-minded; forget *oneself*; be fascinated [enraptured, entranced] (by, with)
▶청중은 그녀의 노래에 넋을 잃었다 The audience was captivated by her singing.
▶나는 그녀의 아름다움에 넋을 잃고 서 있었다 I stood there captivated [enthralled] by her beauty.
▶그는 그 광경에 넋을 잃은 채 오랫동안 바라보고 있었다 He gazed enraptured at the scene for a long while.

넋두리 1 〈불평·푸념〉 a complaint; a grumble; a mutter; a murmur
▶이제 그런 넋두리는 더이상 하지 마라 Don't complain any more about it.
▶나는 그녀의 넋두리를 잠자코 듣고 있었다 I listened in silence to her tale of woe.
─**넋두리하다** 〈불평하다〉 complain (of, about); 〈주절대다〉 talk nonsense [gibberish]; gibber
2 〈무당의〉 spiritual messages narrated by a shaman
─**넋두리하다** (a shaman) convey [transmit] the words of the departed spirit to the bereaved family; call up the spirits of the dead; appear in the voice of a dead person

넌더리 an aversion; loathing; a dislike
─**넌더리나다** get disgusted (with); revolt (at); feel a repugnance (toward); be sickened (of); (口) be bored (with, by); (口) be fed up (to the back teeth) (with)
♦넌더리나는 모임 a wearisome meeting / 공

부에 넌더리나다 be sick and tired of studying / 넌더리나게 하다 make sb sick; weary
▶그에게는 넌더리난다 He wearies [bores] me to death.
▶이탈리아 요리는 이젠 넌더리난다 I don't think I'll have anything more to do with Italian food.
▶남의 빚 보증 서는 것은 넌더리난다 I know to my cost what it is to stand behind another's loan.
▶이제 비에는 넌더리난다 We are fed up with rain.

넌더리대다 weary *sb* with requests; behave disgustfully [repugnantly, revoltingly]

넌덕 witty remarks with a Homeric laughter
◆넌덕부리다 laugh a witty remark / 넌덕스럽다 chuckling and jesting; witty and amusing

넌지시 indirectly; tacitly; implicitly; secretly; quietly; softly; in a casual way [manner]
◆넌지시 말하다 hint (at); drop a hint; allude (to); suggest; insinuate; say in a roundabout way / 넌지시 속을 떠보다 beat about the bush; sound *sb* about (his) views / 넌지시 추파를 던지다 make (sheep's) eyes at *sb* secretly
▶나는 넌지시 그녀에게 손을 떼라고 말했다 I indicated vaguely that she should withdraw.
▶우리는 넌지시 그에게 주의를 주었다 We warned him in a roundabout way.

넌출 〔植〕 a bine; 〈덩굴손〉 a tendril; 〈포도 등의〉 a vine

널 1〈널빤지〉 a board; a plank (두꺼운); (총칭) boarding; planking
◆널 조각 a piece of a plank / 지붕을 널로 이은 집 a shingle-roofed house / 널을 대다 board (over); lay boards (on) / 널로 둘러치다 board up [in]; enclose with boarding
▶그 부지는 널로 둘러쳐져 있었다 The site was surrounded by boards.
2〈널뛰기의〉 a seesaw board; a teeter(ing) board; a teeter-totter
3〈관(棺)〉 a coffin; (美) a casket

널기와집 〔널지붕 집〕 a shingle-roofed house

널다¹ 〈펴놓다〉 stretch; spread out; 〈퍼서 걸다〉 hang out (a thing to air or dry it)
◆멍석에 곡식을 널다 spread grains out on a straw mat / 젖은 이불을 햇볕에 널다 spread wet bedding in the sun / 빨래를 널어 말리다 dry clothes in the sun; hang out the wash [washing] to dry

널다² 〈쥐가 쏠다〉 gnaw (a thing) into shreds

널다리 a wooden [plank-floored] bridge

널따랗다 rather wide; broad; roomy; spacious
◆널따란 공지 wide-open spaces / 널따란 초원 an extensive [a spacious] meadow / 널따란 홀[방, 길] a spacious hall [room, street]
▶소들은 널따란 초원에서 풀을 뜯고 있었다 Cattle were grazing in a broad and open meadow.

널뛰기 seesaw (play); seesawing; teeter

널뛰다 play at seesaw; seesaw; teeter

널리 widely; far and wide; broadly; 〈대규모로〉 extensively; 〈일반적으로〉 generally; universally ◆널리 선전하다 advertise extensively
▶그 책은 젊은이들 사이에서 널리 읽히고 있다 The book is widely read among young people.
▶그녀의 이름은 세계에 널리 알려졌다 Her name was widely known all over the world.
▶카뮈는 한국에서도 널리 알려져 있다 Camus is widely known in Korea, too.

널리다¹ 〈흩어져 있다〉 be spread [scattered] (over, about, around); 〈어질러져 있다〉 be littered (with); 〈널려져 있다〉 be hung out
▶줄에 빨래가 널려 있다 The wash(ing) is hung on a string.
▶빈 깡통이 여기저기에 널려 있었다 Empty cans were scattered all over the place. ≒ The place was littered [strewn] with empty cans.

널리다² extend ⇨ 넓히다

널마루 a wooden [board(ing)] floor

널방석 一方席 a large straw mat (for airing grains); an airing mat

널빈지 a board [wooden] sliding door [shutter, storm door]

널빤지 a panel (board); 〈두꺼운〉 a plank; (총칭) planking; boarding
◆널빤지를 대다 lay boards (on); board (over, up); plank (over, up) / 마루에 널빤지를 깔다 board the floor / 널빤지로 막다 board up (a room)

널찍널찍하다 all rather spacious [wide] ▶그 호텔들은 해안을 따라 널찍널찍하게 자리잡고 있다 The hotels occupy [take up] ample sites along the beach.

널찍이 rather broadly [widely, spaciously]
◆구멍을 널찍이 파다 dig a rather big hole [pit]

널찍하다 rather wide ⇨ 널따랗다

널판때기 a thick board; a plank; (총칭) planking

널판장 一板牆 a board(ing) fence; a wooden wall

넓다 1〈폭이〉 wide; broad; 〈면적이〉 large; extensive; vast; expansive; 〈방·집이〉 spacious; commodious; roomy; 〈탁 트인〉 open

> 解說 ***wide***와 ***broad***는 폭이 넓은 것을 나타내는 가장 일반적인 말. wide는 끝에서 끝까지의 거리를, broad는 wide 보다 딱딱한 말로서 표면이 널찍한 데에 중점이 있다. ***large, extensive, vast***는 면적이 넓은 것을 나타낸다. large가 면적이 큰 것을 객관적으로 표현하는 데 대하여 vast는 극단적으로 넓은 것을 말하며 보통 한정적으로 쓴다. extensive는 딱딱한 말로서 밖으로 퍼지는 식으로 넓은 것을 말한다. ***spacious***는 방 등의 둘러싸인 공간이 넓은 것을 말한다. ***roomy***는 다소 구어조의 말로서 안에 사람이나 물건이 들어간 뒤에도 여유가 있을 정도로 넓은 것을 말한다. ***open***은 가로막는 것이 없이 탁 트이게 넓은 것으로서 보통 한정적으로 쓴다.

▶우리 학교의 운동장은 매우 넓다 The playground of our school is very large [big, spacious].
2〈마음이〉 generous; broad-minded; large-minded; magnanimous
▶나는 그의 마음이 넓은데 감동했다 I was

moved by the breadth of his mind. ⇌ His broad-mindedness moved me.
3 〈범위가〉 large; wide; extensive; comprehensive ♦넓은 의미로 in a broad sense ▶그는 교제 범위가 넓다 He has a large circle of acquaintances

넓데데하다 flat [flattish] 《face》
넓어지다 widen; broaden; become wider [broader]
▶이 강은 강어귀에서 넓어진다 This river widens [broadens] at its mouth.
▶그 길은 거기서 갑자기 넓어진다 There the road widens suddenly.
넓이 1〈폭〉width; breadth ♦넓이가 3피트의 그림 a painting 3 feet in width ▶그 강[길]의 넓이는 30미터다 The river [road] is thirty meters wide [in width, in breadth].
2〈면적〉(an) area; (an) extent; dimension ▶이 땅은 넓이가 얼마나 되니까? What is the area [extent] of this land?
▶이 홀의 넓이는 50제곱미터다 The area of this hall is fifty square meters.
넓이뛰기 a broad jump ⇨ 멀리(~뛰기)
넓적넓적 〈넓적하게〉flatly; flatwise; all flat; 〈입을〉 with *one's* mouth open ♦떡을 넓적넓적 썰다 cut a rice cake into flat pieces
넓적다리 a thigh; 〈돼지고기의〉 a ham; 〈쇠고기의〉 round ■一뼈 a thighbone
넓적스름하다 rather [slightly] flat
♦넓적스름한 코 a flattish nose
넓적이 1〈사람〉a flat-faced person; a person with a flat face
2〈부사적〉flatways; flatly; flatwise
♦길바닥에 넓적이 넘어지다 fall flat upon the street
넓적하다 broad and flat
넓히다 〈넓게 하다〉broaden 《a road》; widen 《out》《a path》;〈확대하다〉extend; expand; enlarge;〈구멍 등을〉ream
♦방을 넓히다 enlarge a room / 사업을 넓히다 extend [expand] *one's* business / 시 구역을 넓히다 extend the city boundaries / 지식을 넓히다 extend [broaden] *one's* knowledge; add to *one's* stock of knowledge / 활동 범위를 넓히다 extend *one's* activities
▶그는 일을 떠맡을 때마다 경험을 넓혔다 Each job he undertook broadened his experience.
넘겨다보다 1〈욕심내다〉covet; be greedy; be avaricious; crave; lust 《for, after》; have a lust [desire] for
♦남의 재산을 넘겨다보다 covet another's property
▶남의 물건을 넘겨다보아서는 안된다 Don't covet what is not yours.
2 ⇨ 넘어다보다
넘겨씌우다 put [lay, fix] the blame on *sb*; lay the blame at *sb's* door; shift the blame 《on to》; impute the fault 《to》; charge a crime 《upon another》
▶그들은 실패의 책임을 나에게 넘겨씌웠다 They blamed the failure on me. ⇌ They laid [put] the blame for the failure on me.
넘겨잡다 guess; suppose ♦넘겨잡고 by guess; as a shot / 바로[잘못] 넘겨잡다 guess right [wrong]
▶그는 그 물음에 넘겨잡아 대답했다 He made a guess at the answer to the question.
넘겨주다 1 ⇨ 넘기다 1
2〈인도하다〉hand [turn] over 《to》; hand [pass] *sth* to *sb*
▶나는 맡아 놓은 돈을 그에게 넘겨 주었다 I delivered money in trust into his hand.
▶범인을 경찰에 넘겨주었다 The criminal was handed over to the police.
3〈양도하다〉make over; transfer; turn over; assign 《to》; convey; 〈내주다〉part with
♦아무에게 소유권을 넘겨주다 yield possession to *sb* / 채권자에게 재산을 넘겨주다 make over [transfer, leave] *one's* property to *one's* creditor
▶그는 집을 아들에게 넘겨주었다 He transferred [handed over] his house to his son.
4〈포기하다〉surrender; give [yield] up; deliver 《up》♦도시를 적의 손에 넘겨주다 yield 《up》[surrender] the city to the enemy
5〈팔다〉sell 《a thing cheap to *sb*》; dispose of *sth*
▶그는 집을 넘겨주고 양로원에 들어갔다 He sold his house and entered an old people's home.
▶나는 돈이 궁해서 집과 대지를 넘겨주지 않으면 안 되었다 I had to sell my house and land, because I was hard up for money.
넘겨짚다 make a guess; guess; conjecture; surmise; suppose; make [try] a shot in the dark
♦넘겨짚어 말하다 hazard a conjecture / 아무의 생각을 넘겨짚다 guess *sb's* intention
▶네 말은 단지 넘겨짚어서 하는 말이다 What you are saying is only guesswork [mere conjecture].
넘고처지다 be good neither for one thing nor the other; be either too long [big] or too short [small]; 〈부적합하다〉be unsuitable [unfit]; be inadequate
▶그것은 넘고처진다 It's good for neither the one thing nor the other.
넘기다 1〈너머로〉pass 《a thing》over ♦담너머로 넘기다 pass 《a newspaper》over a wall
2〈잦히다〉turn over; go over 《*one's* notes》
♦달력을 넘기다 turn over the pages of a calendar / 책장을 넘기다 turn over the leaves of a book; leaf through a book
▶5페이지까지 넘겼다 I turned to page 5.
3〈이월하다〉carry over [forward];〈연기하다〉postpone; defer; put off
♦잔액을 다음 회계 연도로 넘기다 carry the balance over to the following fiscal year
▶재판은 다음 주로 넘겨졌다 The case was adjourned until next week.
4〈시기를〉spend; pass;〈기한을〉exceed
♦상환 기일을 넘기다 overdue / 신청 기한을 넘기다 pass [miss] the deadline for application / 해를 넘기다 spend [ring out] the old year
▶이 표는 기한을 넘겼기 때문에 무효다 The validity of this ticket has expired.
5〈지탱하다〉keep [hold] over;〈극복하다〉

get through [over]; pass [go] through ♦ 난관을 넘기다 surmount a difficulty / 위기를 넘기다 pass [go through] a crisis / 하루하루를 간신히 넘기다 live from hand to mouth ▶ 그 환자는 겨울을 넘겼다 The sick person kept over [lived through] the winter.
▶ 연료는 겨울을 넘길만큼 있다 We have enough fuel to see the winter out.
6 〈쓰러뜨리다〉 throw down; fell; 〈다리를 걸어서〉 trip ♦ 나무를 잘라 넘기다 fell a tree; fell
7 〈속여〉 cheat; take in; play a trick (on) ♦ 아무를 속여 넘기다 cheat sb
8 〈목으로〉 swallow; take [get] down; drink in
넘나다 behave beyond [above] one's means [place, social standing]
넘나들다 haunt; frequent; visit often ♦ 유력자의 집을 문턱이 닳게 넘나들다 frequent the house of an influential person
▶ 저 술집에는 깡패들이 넘나든다 That bar(room) is frequented by hoodlums.
넘노닐다 wander [loiter, stroll] around [about, to and fro]; hang about [around]
넘다 **1** 〈위로〉 go over (a hill); 〈뛰어서〉 clear [take] (a hedge, a fence, a ditch); go [get] beyond; get over (a fence); hurdle [take, clear] (an obstacle); stride; 〈국경 등을〉 cross ♦ 고개[국경]를 넘다 cross a pass [the border] / 담을 넘다 go over a wall / 차로 산을 넘다 cross a mountain by car
▶ 공은 우익수의 머리 위를 넘었다 The ball sailed over the right fielder's head.
▶ 도둑은 높은 담을 넘어서 잠입했다 The thief got [climbed] over the high wall and sneaked in.
▶ 이 산을 넘으면 온천이 있다 There is a hot spring beyond this mountain.
2 〈초과하다〉 be over; exceed; rise above; go [pass] beyond (the limit); be more than ♦ 도를 넘다 go to excess; go beyond bounds; carry things too far / 한계를 넘다 pass [overstep] the limit (of)
▶ 그는 60세를 넘었다 He is over sixty.
▶ 여비가 10만원을 조금 넘었다 The traveling expenses were a little over one hundred thousand won.
▶ 회원은 백명을 넘었다 The membership exceeded [was over] one hundred.
▶ 태풍 피해는 100억원을 훨씬 넘었다 The damage from the typhoon was far in excess of ten billion won.
▶ 그녀의 수예는 취미를 넘어서 이젠 전문가에 가깝다 Her handicraft is more than a hobby. It's more like a profession.
▶ 기온이 30도를 넘으면 참기 어렵다 A temperature over 30°C is unbearable.
▶ 10만원을 넘지 않는다면 그런대로 이 구두를 살텐데 I would buy the pair of shoes if they were no more than one hundred thousand won.
3 〈때·시한이〉 be over [past]; run out; fall [become] due; expire ▶ 12시가 넘었다 It is past twelve o'clock. ▶ 계약기한이 넘었다 The contract has run out [expired].

4 〈범람하다〉 overflow; run [flow] over ♦ 강물이 둑을 넘다 the (water of a) river overflows its banks
5 〈뚫고 나아가다〉 tide [get] over; pull [muddle] through ♦ 넘을 수 없는 사랑의 장벽 an insuperable barrier to love
6 〈날이 한쪽으로 쏠리다〉 be turned [curled]; overdo ▶ 칼날이 넘었다 The edge of a knife is turned.
넘버 **1** 〈수·번호〉 a number ♦ 넘버원 (미) number 1 (略 No. 1); an ace (pilot) ▶ 각 페이지에 넘버를 매겨라 Number each page
2 〈자동차의〉 a license number; (英) (registration) number ▶ 그는 서울 넘버를 단 차를 운전하고 있었다 He was driving a car with a Seoul license plate.
넘버링머신 a numbering machine
넘보다 look down on; underrate; hold cheap; make light [little] of; think meanly [lightly] of sb; slight (⇨ 깔보다) ▶ 상대를 넘보면 안된다 Never underrate your opponent.
넘실거리다 〈파도가〉 swell; roll; undulate; surge; wave ▶ 파도가 넘실거리고 있었다 The waves were rolling [swelling].
넘어가다 **1** ⇨ 넘다 1
2 〈쓰러지다〉 go [roll] over; fall (to the ground); topple down [over]; fall (over [down])
▶ 그는 뒤로 넘어갔다 He fell on his back.
▶ 간판이 태풍으로 넘어갔다 The signboard was blown over by the typhoon.
3 〈망하다〉 collapse; be overthrown
▶ 회사가 넘어갔다 The company went bankrupt.
▶ 현 내각은 쉽게 넘어가지 않을 것이다 The present Cabinet will not fall easily.
4 〈해·달이 지다〉 sink; set; go down ♦ 넘어가는 해 the setting [declining] sun ▶ 해가 서쪽으로 서서히 넘어가고 있었다 The sun was slowly sinking [going down] in the west.
5 〈옮아가다〉 pass (into, to); drift; come [fall] (to); turn (to); 〈권리 등이〉 be transferred; pass [fall] into another's hand ♦ 화제가 딴데로 넘어가다 drift from one subject to another
▶ 그럼 다음 페이지로 넘어갑시다 Well, let's move [go] on [ahead] to the next page.
▶ 소유권은 남선생에게 넘어갔다 The ownership was transferred to Mr. Nam.
▶ 토론이 인구 문제로 넘어갔다 The discussion turned to the population problem.
6 〈속다〉 be taken in; be deceived [cheated]; be imposed upon; be tempted; be played upon ♦ 계략에 넘어가다 fall into a trap set by sb / 유혹에 넘어가지 않다 be proof against temptation
▶ 그는 마침내 유혹에 넘어갔다 He at last yielded [gave in] to temptation.
▶ 그는 내가 아무리 유혹해도 넘어가지 않는다 No matter how I entice him, that person will not be lured.
▶ 그런 수작에는 넘어가지 않는다 That trick won't do [work] with me.
▶ 그는 아첨에 넘어가지 않았다 He was above

flattery [proof against flattery].
7 〈음식물이〉 be swallowed; be drunk in; be taken [got] down; be gulped down
▶ 생선 가시가 넘어가지 않도록 주의해라 Take care not to swallow the fishbone.
8 〈잦혀지다〉 be turned over ▶ 책장이 바람에 넘어갔다 A leaf of the book is turned over by the wind.

넘어다보다 look [peep] over ♦ 담 너머 넘어다보다 look [peep] over the fence [wall] / 울타리 너머로 이웃집 뜰을 넘어다보다 see the neighbor's garden over [through] the hedge

넘어뜨리다 bring down; throw down; let fall; 〈사람을〉 throw *sb* (to the ground); knock down; floor *sb*; 〈나무를 베어〉 cut down; 〈멸망[전복]시키다〉 overthrow; ruin; 〈지우다〉 beat ⇨ 쓰러뜨리다
♦ 밀어 넘어뜨리다 push [knock] down / 바람이 나무를 넘어뜨리다 blow *sth* down / 나무를 베어 넘어뜨리다 fell a tree down; cut a tree down
▶ 그는 발을 걸어서 상대를 넘어뜨렸다 He tripped up his opponent.
▶ 내가 도둑을 넘어뜨리자 다른 사람들이 그를 묶었다 I threw the burglar down and others bound him.

넘어오다 **1** 〈넘어서〉 come over [across] 《a mountain》 ♦ 고개를 넘어오다 come across a pass / 국경을 넘어오다 come over [across] the border (line)
2 〈옮겨오다〉 transfer; come into; be made [turned] over; be passed on; change hands
♦ 내 손에 넘어온 부동산 the realty transferred to me (from) / 내 손으로 넘어오다 come into my hand [possession]
▶ 경영권이 아버지한테서 내게로 넘어왔다 The right of management was transferred from my father to me.
3 〈이월되다〉 be carried forward [over] 《to》
▶ 잔고가 금년으로 넘어왔다 The balance has been carried over to the present year.
4 〈쓰러져〉 fall [topple] (this way) ▶ 담이 뜰 쪽으로 넘어왔다 The wall toppled over toward the garden.
5 〈토하다〉 vomit; bring [fetch] up ▶ 그는 먹은 것이 다 넘어왔다 He vomited [fetched up] all he had eaten.
6 〈이쪽 편이 되다〉 come over 《on our side》
♦ 자유세계로 넘어오다 come over to [for] the free world

넘어지다 fall; come [go] down; topple; collapse; 〈사람·동물이〉 stumble [tumble] 《against, over》; trip over [on]; fall 《down, over to the ground》 ⇨ 쓰러지다
♦ 나무뿌리에 발이 걸려 넘어지다 trip [stumble, tumble] over the root of a tree / 벌렁 뒤로 넘어지다 fall on *one's* back / 큰 대자로 넘어지다 fall at full length / 바나나 껍질을 밟고 넘어지다 slip on a banana peel
▶ 그는 미끄러져서 넘어졌다 He slipped and fell down.
▶ 소년은 비틀거리며 넘어졌다 The boy stumbled and fell.
▶ 그는 넘어져 무릎을 다쳤다 He fell down and hurt his knee.
▶ 돌뿌리에 채어 넘어지지 않도록 주의해라 Take care not to trip over a stone.
▶ 어린애는 넘어질 듯이 달려갔다 A child ran away, half falling.

넘치다 **1** 〈흘러넘치다〉 overflow 《the bank》; brim over 《with》; run [flow] over 《the brim》; 〈범람하다〉 flood [inundate] 《the land》
♦ 기쁨에 넘치다 be filled with [full of] joy / 생기[원기]가 넘치다 be full of life [vigor, spirits, energy] / 행복에 넘치다 be brimming over with [brimful of] happiness / 희망에 넘치다 brim over with hope / 컵에 넘치도록 따르다 fill a glass to the brim
▶ 맥주가 잔에서 넘쳤다 The beer overflowed the glass.
▶ 호우로 강물이 넘쳤다 The heavy rain caused the river to overflow [go out of its banks].
▶ 목욕탕 물이 넘치고 있어 The bath [bathwater] is overflowing [running over, brimming over].
▶ 그녀의 눈에는 눈물이 넘쳐 흐르고 있었다 Her eyes were swimming [filled, brimming] with tears.
2 〈도를 지나치다〉 be above; exceed; be over; be more than
♦ 분에 넘치는 칭찬[영광] an undeserved praise [honor] / 분에 넘치는 생활을 하다 live beyond *one's* means
▶ 짐의 무게가 5파운드 넘쳤다 The baggage was five pounds over weight.
▶ 그에게는 분에 넘치는 영광이다 The honor is more than he deserves.

넙적 **1** 〈입을 벌리는 모양〉 with *one's* mouth agape [wide-open]
♦ 물고기가 미끼를 넙적 물었다 The fish snapped at the bait.
▶ 개구리가 파리를 넙적 잡아먹었다 A frog snapped at a fly.
▶ 개가 입을 넙적 벌려서 공을 물었다 The dog opened its mouth wide and picked up the ball.
2 〈엎드리는 모양〉 flat; low
♦ 넙적 엎드리다 lay *oneself* flat / 넙적 절하다 bow with *one's* hands laid flat on the floor; bow low
▶ 그들은 마루에 넙적 엎드렸다 They lay down (face downward) on the floor.

넙죽 flat ⇨ 넙적

넙치 〔魚〕 a flatfish; a flounder ♦ 넙치눈이 a cross-eyed person

넝마 a rag; old cloth; shred; scrap; 〈옷〉 tattered clothes; rags; worn-out clothes; tatters

넣다 **1** 〈내부로 들여보내다〉 put [take, bring] in [into]; 〈보태다〉 add 《to》; 〈채우다〉 stuff
♦ 기름을 병에 넣다 put some oil in the bottle / 공에 바람을 넣다 pump [blow] air into a ball / 바지 주머니에 양 손을 넣다 put *one's* hands in [into] *one's* trousers pockets / 안약을 넣다 drop a lotion into the eye / 차고에 자동차를 넣다 run a car into a garage / 머리속에 넣어 두다 bear [keep] *sth* in mind
▶ 그들은 서류를 금고 속에 넣었다 They sealed the documents in a strongbox.

네¹

2 〈끼우다〉 set in; insert; put 《a thing》 in [into]
♦ 신문에 광고지를 끼워 넣다 insert [stuff] bills in newspapers / 의치를 해 넣다 have a false tooth put in
▶ 100원 짜리를 동전 구멍에 넣었다 I inserted a hundred-won coin in the slot.
3 〈단체 등에〉 admit *sb* in (to); grant *sb* to membership; initiate *sb* into 《a society》; 〈학교 등에〉 send [put] to
♦ 회에 넣어 주지 않다 deny admission to 《an applicant》 ▶ 아들을 의과대학에 넣었다 I sent my son to a medical school.
4 〈포함시키다〉 include; count among [in]
♦ 이자를 넣어서[넣지 않고] inclusive [exclusive] of interest / 셈에 넣다 count in; reckon in *one's* calculation
▶ 그는 그것을 고려에 넣었다 He took it into account [consideration].
▶ 손이 모자라서 젊은 사람을 한 사람 넣었다 We hired a young man because we were short-handed.
▶ 나는 그 계획을 머릿속에 넣고 있다 I keep the project in my mind.
▶ 그 사실을 계산에 넣는 게 좋다 You had better take the fact into account.
▶ 나는 그 속에 넣지 마시오 Count me out, please.
5 〈금전을 맡기다〉 deposit 《money》; place 《money》 on deposit
♦ 은행에 돈을 넣다 put money in a bank
6 〈중간에〉 put *sb* between 《two parties》; make *sb* a mediator
♦ 중재자를 넣어 교섭하다 negotiate 《a matter》 through an intermediary / 통역을 넣어 이야기하다 talk through an interpreter

네¹ **1** 〈너〉 you ▶ 네가 잘못했다 You are to blame. ▶ 네가 틀렸어[맞았어] You are wrong [right]. ▶ 네가 한 짓이냐? Did you do it?
2 〈너의〉 your
▶ 네 이름이 뭐냐? What is your name? ▶ 네 집이 어디냐? Where do you live? ▶ 이게 네 책이냐? Is this your book?

네² 〈넷〉 four ♦ 사과 네 개 four apples / 네 번 four times / 네 사람 four people / 네 살 난 아이 a child of four (years old)

네³ 〈긍정·승낙〉 yes; certainly; of course; sure; (口) OK; O.K.; all right; 〈출석·점호의 대답〉 yes, sir; present (sir); here (sir); 〈놀람〉 O!; oh; 〈의문〉 Eh?; What?; (I beg your) pardon?
▶ 네, 알았습니다 Yes, certainly.
▶ 會話 「펜 좀 빌릴 수 있을까요?」「네, 여기 있습니다」 "May I borrow your pen?" "Sure [Yes, with pleasure]. Here it is."
▶ 會話 「너 수영 못하니?」「네, 못합니다」 "Can't you swim?" "No, I can't."
▶ 네, 물론 가겠습니다 Why yes, of course, I'm coming.
▶ 네? 뭐라고요? What did you say?

-네 〈당신네 you all / 우리네 we all / 스미스씨네 Mr. Smith and his family; the Smith family; the Smiths
▶ 나는 지금 친구네 머무르고 있다 I am staying with a friend of mine now.

네거리 crossing streets; a crossroads; an intersection
♦ 광화문 네거리 the Kwangwhamun intersection [crossing] / 네거리마다 at every crossing / 네거리에서 도로를 건너다 cross the road at the crossing [intersection] / 네거리에서 서다 stand at a crossroads / 네거리에서 오른쪽으로 돌다 turn to the right at the crossroads

네거티브 (寫) 〈음화〉 a (photographic) negative (↔positive) ♦ 네거티브 필름 (a) negative film

네구석 the four corners 《of a room》

네글리제 a negligee; (프) négligé; 〈여성용 잠옷〉 a nightgown; a nightdress

네까짓 〈네까짓 것 the likes of you; a man like you / 네까짓 놈 such a fellow [creature] as [like] you
▶ 네까짓 것한테 지겠는가? I shall never be beaten by a fellow like you.
▶ 네까짓 놈이 할 수 있겠나? It cannot be done by a character like you.

네눈박이 〈개〉 a dog with black spots above the eyes

네다리 four legs
♦ 네다리가 묶인 새끼 염소 a kid tied by the four legs / 네다리의 four-legged / 네다리를 쭉 뻗고 자다 sleep [lie] with one's limbs outstretched; 〈편안히 자다〉 sleep with ease [without cares]

네다섯 four or five

네댓 about four or five ♦ 네댓새 about four or five days

네덜란드 Netherlands; 〈공식명〉 the Kingdom of the Netherlands ♦ 네덜란드의 Dutch
■ **-령** a Dutch [Netherlandish] possession
■ **-말** Dutch ■ **-사람** a Dutchman; (총칭) the Dutch; (美) a Netherlander

네로 〈로마 황제〉 Nero (37-68)

네루 〈인도의 정치가〉 Nehru, Jawaharlal (1889-1964)

네루다 〈칠레의 시인〉 Neruda, Pablo (1834-91)

네모 a square (shape); a quadrilateral ♦ 네모난 square (face); four-cornered / 네모나다[되다] be squared (tetragonal, quadrilateral) / 네모나게 자르다 cut square
■ **-송곳** a square drill

네모꼴 a quadrilateral; a tetragon; a quadrangle ♦ 네모꼴의 quadrilateral; tetragonal

네미 〈송아지를 부를 때〉 Here-calf!; 〈욕〉 Damn it [you]!; Hang it!; Son of a bitch!

네바다 〈미국 서부의 주〉 Nevada (略 Nev., NV)

네발 four feet
♦ 네발의[달린] four-footed; quadruped / 네발로 기다 crawl [go] on hand and knees [all fours]
▶ 우리는 네발로 기면서 잃어버린 콘택트 렌즈를 찾고 있었다 We were on all fours looking for the lost contact lens.
■ **-짐승** a four-footed animal [beast]; a quadruped (animal); a beast

네브래스카 〈미국 중서부의 주〉 Nebraska (略 Nebr., Neb., NE)

네쌍둥이 —雙童— quadruplets; (口) quads

네안데르탈인 ―人 〖人類〗 a Neanderthal [niǽndərθɔ̀ːl] man; a Neanderthaler

네오- neo- ♦ 네오아이디얼리즘[로맨티시즘] neo-idealism [neo-romanticism] / 네오클래시시즘 neo-classicism / 네오파시즘 neo-fascism

네온 〖化〗 neon [níːɑn] ■―등〖燈〗 a neon lamp [light] ■―사인 a neon sign

네이블 〖植〗 a navel (orange)

네이비블루 dark blue; 〖美〗 navy blue

네이팜 〖化〗 napalm ■―탄 a napalm (bomb)

네임 a name ♦ 네임 밸류가 있는 가수 a name [well-known] singer / 네임 밸류가 있는 작가 a fiction writer of established reputation; a name writer ■―플레이트 a nameplate

네커치프 a neckerchief (pl. ~s)

네크라인 a neckline

네크리스 a necklace

네트 a net ♦ 네트를 건드리다 touch the net / 테니스 네트를 치다 put up a tennis net / 〈테니스 등에서〉 공을 네트에 닿게 하다 net the ball ■―볼 〖球〗 a net ball ―인 a net in ―플레이 net play; playing close to the net

네트워크 a network 《of railroads》 ♦ 텔레비전 네트워크 the TV networks

네팔 Nepal; 〈공식명〉 the Kingdom of Nepal ♦ 네팔의 Nepalese ■―말 Nepali ―사람 a Nepalese

네프로제 〖醫〗 〈신장증〉 nephrosis ♦ 네프로제의 nephrotic

네활개 the limbs (stretched out) ♦ 네활개치다 strut [swagger, stride] (swinging one's arms); act big; with nothing to fear; behave triumphantly / 거리를 네활개치며 돌아다니다 stride along [strut down] a street.
▶ 그들이 네활개치며 돌아다니는 꼴을 보아라 Look how they strut and swagger about!

넥타이 a tie; a necktie ♦ 넥타이를 매다 tie a necktie / 넥타이를 풀다 [고치다] untie [straighten] one's necktie
▶ 검은 넥타이를 매어라 Wear [put on] a black tie.
▶ 나는 넥타이를 느슨하게 했다 I loosened my tie.
■―나비― a bow (tie) ―핀 a tiepin; a tie tack [clip]; 〖美〗 a stickpin

넨장(맞을) 1 My goodness!; Darn it!; Damn it!; The devil!; God damn you!
▶ 넨장(맞을), 기회를 놓쳤구나 Hell! I missed the chance.
▶ 넨장(맞을), 열쇠를 잃어버렸네 Oh, dear! I've lost my key.
▶ 넨장, 또 실패했구나 Oh, no, I've made a mess of it again!
2 damned; wretched; damnable; cursed ♦ 넨장맞을 녀석 a cursed [damned, damned] fellow

넬슨 〈영국의 제독〉 Nelson, Horatio (1758-1805)

넵튠 〈바다의 신〉 〖神〗 Neptune

넷 four ♦ 넷으로 자르다 cut 《a watermelon》 into quarters [four pieces]; quarter ▶ 그녀는 그 서류를 넷으로 접었다 She folded the paper into quarters.

넷째 the fourth; No. 4 ♦ 넷째의 fourth / 넷째로 fourthly

녀석 1 〈놈〉 〖口〗 a fellow; a guy; 〖英〗 a chap; a rogue
♦ 경칠 녀석 a cursed fellow / 만만치 않은 녀석 a tough customer / 멋진 녀석 a swell guy / 묘한 녀석 a queer [an odd] fish / 불쌍한 녀석 a poor fellow [chap] / 재미있는 녀석 a jolly fellow / 저 녀석 that fellow [swine, brute]; 〖美〗 that guy / 좋은 녀석 a brick; a good sport guy
▶ 그 놈은 이상한 녀석이다 He is an odd fish.
▶ 이 바보 녀석아 You fool!
2 〈사내아이〉 a boy; an urchin; a kid ♦ 귀여운 녀석 a sweet little rascal of a boy
▶ 요 녀석 You young [little] rascal!

년 a hussy; a slut; a wench 〖英〗 crumpet; a bitch ♦ 망할 년 a damned wench / 미친 년 a crazy bitch ▶ 이 년아 You wretched slut!

년 年 a year ♦ 10년 10개월 ten years and ten months / 1998년 서울대학 졸업생 a graduate of Seoul National University in 1998 / 1년에 한번 once a year

녘 1 〈때〉 around; about ♦ 새벽녘에 around dawn; toward(s) daybreak [dawn] / 아침녘에 toward(s) morning; in the early morning / 해질녘에 about [around] sunset
2 〈방향〉 a direction; a way; in the direction of...; toward(s)...; to 《the east》 ♦ 남녘 the south; the southern way / 동녘 east; eastern ■아랫― a place in the lower part [to the south, down from here] 윗― a place in the upper part [to the north, up from here]

노¹ 〈꼰 줄〉 a string [cord] (⇨ 노끈) ■삼― a hempen cord 지― a twisted paper string

노² always ⇨ 노상

노 櫓 an oar; 〈카누용〉 a paddle; a scull ♦ 노젓는 사람 an oarsman; a rower / 노를 젓다 pull an oar; work a scull [row]; paddle 《a canoe》; scull, row 《a boat》 / 노를 저어 배를 전진시키다 propel a boat with oars
▶ 나는 노를 잘 저을 줄 안다 I can pull a good oar.
▶ 이 보트는 2개의 노를 갖추고 있다 This boat rows two oars.

노 爐 〈화덕〉 a hearth; a fireplace; 〈용광로〉 a furnace; a kiln

노 老― old; aged ♦ 노정치가 a venerable statesman / 노처녀 an old maid; spinster

노가리 〖農〗 broadcast sowing ―**노가리하다** sow seed broadcast ♦ 콩을 노가리하다 scatter beans

노간주나무 〖植〗 a juniper tree

노경 老境 old [advanced] age; one's declining years; senescence
♦ 노경에 들어서서 in one's old [advanced] age; when (one is) old; in one's declining years
▶ 그분은 노경임에도 불구하고 마음은 젊다 He is young in spirit in spite of his age.
▶ 그는 노경에 접어들었다 He has reached old age.
▶ 할아버지는 70세지만 자신이 노경에 접어들었다고는 생각하시지 않는다 My seventy-year-

old grandfather doesn't consider himself advanced in age [old].

노고 勞苦 labor; trouble; bother; pains; toil; travail(s)
♦노고를 덜어주다 save *sb* the trouble (of) / 노고를 아끼지 않다 spare no pains / 노고에 보답하다 remunerate *sb* for (his) labor / 노고를 치하하다 reward *sb* for (his) labor
▶이렇게 하면 많은 노고를 덜 수 있다 To do like this saves a lot of trouble.
▶이렇게 노고를 끼쳐 드려서 죄송합니다 I'm sorry to give you all this trouble.

노고지리 〔鳥〕 a skylark ⇨ 종다리

노곤하다 勞困 — heavy; languid; weary ♦노곤한 봄날 a lazy spring day ♦오늘은 어쩐지 노곤하다 Somehow I feel languid [listless] today.

노골적 露骨的 1 〈숨기지 않는〉 naked; plain; open; outspoken; candid; 〈단도직입적〉 blunt; direct
♦노골적인 비평 a candid remark / 노골적인 적대심 frank [open] hostility / 노골적으로 plainly; openly; unreservedly; outspokenly; bluntly; directly / 노골적으로 말하면 in plain words; to be plain with you / 사실을 노골적으로 말하다 state the facts as they are / 노골적으로 미움을 나타내다 show unconcealed hatred
▶내부의 불화는 마침내 노골적인 것이 되었다 The internal strife finally became conspicuous [came to the fore].
▶그는 노골적으로 불만을 얼굴에 나타냈다 His look plainly expressed his dissatisfaction.
▶그는 남의 결점을 노골적으로 비난했다 He criticized the defects of others openly.
▶나는 그에게 내 생각을 노골적으로 말했다 I gave him my honest opinion.
▶그는 노골적으로 우리와는 더 이상 협력하지 않겠다고 말했다 He made it clear [plain] that he was not going to cooperate with us any longer.
▶나는 그가 자네의 일을 노골적으로 비판하고 있는 것을 들었네 I heard him openly criticizing you.
2 〈음란한〉 broad; indecent; lewd; 〈선정적인〉 suggestive (picture)
♦노골적인 그림 an indecent picture / 노골적인 농담 a broad joke / 노골적인 묘사 a sexual description
▶아이들 앞에서 그런 노골적인 얘기는 하지 마라 Stop that indecent talk in front of the children.

노구 老軀 one's old age; one's old bones; an advanced age; one's old and weak limbs
♦80의 노구에도 불구하고 in spite of one's venerable [advanced] age of 80
▶그는 노구에도 불구하고 조난을 구조하러 갔다 He went to offer help in the accident in spite of his advanced age.
▶그는 노구에도 불구하고 열심히 일하고 있다 In spite of his old age he is working hard.

노구솥 a brass [copper] kettle

노그라지다 1 〈피로하다〉 be fatigued [tired]; be exhausted; be dog-tired; be worn out
♦지쳐 노그라지다 become as limp as a rag [doll] / 노그라져서 의자에 앉다 sit limply in a chair; slump down onto [into] a chair / 노그라져 잠자리에 들다 fall into bed dog-tired
2 〈정신이 팔리다〉 be addicted (to); be lost (in); (口) be dead gone (on a woman); be infatuated (with, by); lose one's heart (on); be crazy [mad] (about)

노글노글하다 1 〈유연하다〉 soft; tender; pliant; pliable; limp; flexible; supple; lithe
♦노글노글한 가죽 soft [pliable] leather / 노글노글한 몸 a lithe [limber] body / 노글노글한 어린이의 손발 the supple limbs of a child
2 〈유순하다〉 mild; meek; lamblike; docile; obedient; submissive
♦노글노글한 여성 a docile woman / 매우 노글노글한 (as) meek as a lamb

노급함 弩級艦 a Dreadnought

노긋노긋하다 〈매우 부드럽다〉 very soft [limp]; supple; elastic; very soft and flexible; 〈매우 유순하다〉 mild; gentle; docile; meek; obedient
▶그는 노긋노긋한 아이다 He is an obedient child.
▶그 소년은 노긋노긋한 성격이다 The boy has a gentle nature.

노긋하다 mild ⇨ 노긋노긋하다

노기 怒氣 indignation; anger; an angry mood
♦노기를 띠고 in anger; in a fury; in a rage / 노기 등등하다 be in a black rage; be furious with anger [rage] / 노기 충천하다 boil with rage
▶그는 노기가 치밀어 오르는 것을 느꼈다 He felt the anger rise in him.
▶그는 만면에 노기를 띠었다 He looked black [turned purple] with anger.
▶그는 노기에 찬 어조로 그렇게 말했다 He said it in an angry tone.

노기스 [〈독〉 Nonius] 〔機〕 slide [vernier] calipers

노깃 a paddle; the blade of a paddle [an oar]

노끈 〈가는〉 a string; 〈굵은〉 a cord; a hempen cord
♦삼으로 노끈을 꼬다 twist hemp into a string; braid hempen cord
▶그는 노끈으로 짐을 단단히 묶었다 He tied up the package securely with a piece of string.

노년 老年 an old age; an advanced age [life]; the winter [evening] of life; declining years ⇨ 노령(老齡) ♦노년의 old / 노년에 이르러 in one's old age [later years]; when (one is) old
■—기 senescence; old age: 노년기에 있다 be in (one's) old age

노농 勞農 〈노동자와 농민〉 laborers and farmers
■—당 the Laborers and Peasants [Labor-Farmer] party

노느다 〈가르다〉 distribute [divide (up)] (among); part (into); share (*sth* with *sb*); portion (out); split (into)
♦둘[셋]이 돈을 노느다 divide the money between the two [among the three] / 이익을

반반씩 노느다 split the profit half and half [fifty-fifty] / 음식을 노나 먹다 share food with sb / 재산을 세 아들에게 노나 주다 settle [divide] property among *one's* three sons

노느매기 apportionment ⇨ 분배(分配)

노닐다 ramble about; stroll [wander] about; saunter [lounge, loiter] along; hover [linger] about [around] 《a place》 ♦ 숲속을 노닐다 ramble [stroll] (around) in the woods

노다지¹ 〈광맥〉 a bonanza; a rich vein [mine]; 〈큰 벌이〉 a killing; a cleanup ♦ 노다지를 만나다 strike a bonanza; 〈횡재하다〉《俗》 hit the jackpot

노다지² 〈늘〉 always; ever; all along ▶ 그는 노다지 웃고만 있다 He is always smiling. ▶ 그는 노다지 담배만 피운다 He is smoking all the time.

노닥거리다 carry on [《俗》 make out] with 《*one's* girlfriend》; keep talking [chatting, chattering] playfully
▶ 그들은 남들 앞에서 노닥거리고 있었다 They are necking in public.

노닥다리 老— 〈늙다리〉 an old [aged] person; 《美》 an oldster

노닥이다 chatter playfully ⇨ 노닥거리다

노대 露臺 〔建〕 a balcony; 〈공연 때의〉 an open-air platform [stage]; a gallery

노대가 老大家 an old [a past] master 《of》; a veteran authority 《on Korean literature》
♦ 문단의 노대가들 leading figures in literary circles / 서예의 노대가 an old master of calligraphy

노도 怒濤 raging billows; angry [roaring, surging] waves; boiling waters; rough [huge] seas
♦ 노도처럼 밀려오는 군중 surging crowds / 노도를 헤치고 나아가다 advance in the face of high seas

노독 路毒 the fatigue of travel ♦ 노독을 풀다 take a good rest [refresh *oneself*] after a long journey

노동 勞動 《live by》 labor; work; toil; 〔經〕 industry
▶ 노동 후에는 밥맛이 좋다 We can enjoy our meal after work.
▶ 한국에서는 하루 8시간 노동이 보통이다 In Korea we usually work eight hours a day.
▶ 가벼운 노동은 몸에 좋다고 한다 It is said that light work is good for our health.
—**노동하다** labor; work; toil; engage in labor —**강제**— forced [compulsory] labor 경[중]— light [heavy] labor 두뇌— brain work 생산적[비생산적]— productive [unproductive] labor 시간외— overtime work 육체[정신]— physical [mental] labor 이교대제— two shift system 저임금— cheap labor ■—**가치설** the labor theory of value —**경제[경제학]** labor economy [economics] —**계약** a labor contract; a contract for labor —**관리** labor management —**권**(權) the right to labor [work] —**귀족** a labor aristocrat —**규약** 《美》 a union constitution; 《英》 constitution of a trade union —**능률** labor efficiency —**당** 《英》 the Labour Party —**당원** 《英》 a Labourite; a Labour member —**대중** the labor [laboring] mass; masses of workers —**력** manpower; labor power [force] —**문제** a labor question [problem] —**법규** labor laws; 《英》 industrial laws —**복** work clothes —**부** 〈한국 등의〉 the Ministry of Labor; the Labor Ministry; 〈미국의〉 the Labor Department —**부 장관** the Minister of Labor; 《美》 the Labor Secretary —**삼권** labor's three major [primary] rights —**수요** demand of labor —**시장** the labor market —**원가** labor cost —**위원회** a labor relations board —**의욕** will to work —**이동률[회전율]** labor turnover —**인구** working population —**재해** a labor accident —**쟁의** a labor dispute [strife]; 〈파업〉 a strike —**전선** a labor front —**절** 《美》 Labor Day; May Day —**정책** a labor policy —**조건** working [labor] conditions —**조정법** 〔法〕 the Labor Mediation Law —**지도자** a labor leader —**집약산업** labor-intensive industries —**집약성** labor intensity —**행정** labor administration —**협약** a labor agreement —**환경** labor environment —**회관** the Labor Hall

노동시간 勞動時間 working hours; the hours of labor; 〈연(延) 노동 시간 수〉 man-hours
♦ 노동시간의 단축을 요구하다 demand shorter working hours / 노동시간을 단축[연장]하다 shorten [lengthen] working hours

노동운동 勞動運動 a labor movement [campaign, drive] —**가** a labor agitator —**지도자** a labor leader

노동자 勞動者 a laborer [worker]; a workingman; a workman; 〈총칭〉 labor; the laboring [working] population
♦ 자본가와 노동자 capital and labor / 노동자의 권리 workers' [labor] rights / 노동자측과 회사측 《美》 labor and management / 노동자의 처우를 개선하다 better [ameliorate] labor conditions / 노동자를 착취하다 sweat [exploit] laborers
▶ 그들은 노동자의 권리를 지키기 위해 파업을 했다 They went on a strike in order to protect the rights of the workers.
—**계절**— a seasonal laborer 숙련[미숙련]— a skilled [an unskilled] laborer 임금— a wage earner; a wageworker 자유— a casual laborer 정신[육체]— a brain [manual] worker —**계급** the laboring [working] classes —**보호** protection of laborers —**수용소** a labor camp —**재해 보상** compensation for workmen's accident —**합숙소** a labor boarding house

노동조합 勞動組合 《美》 a labor union; 《英》 a trade(s) union
♦ 한국 노동조합 총연맹 the Federation of Korea Trade Unions (略 FKTU) / 노동조합의 운영 management [operation] of a labor [trade] union / 노동조합에 가입한 노동자 a unionized worker / 노동조합을 결성하다 form [organize] a labor [trade] union; unionize 《company employe(e)s》
▶ 우리 노동 조합도 노동절 축하 행사에 참가합니다 Our labor union will join the May Day celebration, too.
■—**간부** a union leader —**규약** a union

[trade] constitution **—법** 〔法〕 the Labor [Trade] Union Law **—원** a member of a labor [trade] union; a (trade) unionist; 《美》 a union man **—주의** trade unionism; laborism **—협의회** a council of labor [trade] unions

노두 露頭 1 〈맨머리〉 a bare head 2 〔鑛〕 an outcrop; a basset; a crop

노둔 鹵鈍 stupidity; imbecility; dullness **—노둔하다** stupid; imbecile; thickheaded

노랑 〈색깔〉 yellow; a yellow color; 〈물감〉 yellow dyes **——머리** a yellow head; yellow hair **—통이** a person with an unusually yellow complexion.

노랑가오리 〔魚〕 a stingray; a whip ray
노랑감투 〈상제의 건〉 a mourner's cap
노랑나비 〔昆〕 a yellow (butterfly)
노랑이 1 〈노란 빛의 물건〉 yellow stuff; a yellow thing
2 〈털빛이 노란 개〉 a yellow dog
3 〈구두쇠〉 a niggard; a miser; a stingy [closefisted] fellow; (口) a tightwad; a cheapskate; a skinflint ♦그는 지독한 노랑이다 He is as close as a vice.

노랗다 1 〈색이〉 yellow
♦노란 셔츠 a yellow shirt / 노란 페인트 yellow paint / 피부가 노랗다 be yellow-skinned / 노란 옷을 입고 있다 be dressed in yellow / 노랗게 되다 turn yellow
▶그는 문을 노랗게 칠했다 He painted the door yellow.
2 〈싹수가〉 ▶그는 싹수가 노랗다 He is hopeless. ⇒ He has no future. ⇒ There is a very slim chance for him. ⇒ 그 일은 싹수가 노랗다 There's not a dog's [cat's] chance.

노래 a song; 〈민요〉 a ballad; 〈성악〉 singing; 〈시〉 a poem; a verse; 〈총칭〉 poetry
♦노래를 배우다 take lessons in singing / 노래를 부르다 sing (a song); 〈콧노래로〉 hum a tune; 〈낮은 소리로〉 croon (a song) / 노래를 부르면서 일하다 sing at one's work / 노래를 불러 아기를 재우다 sing a baby to sleep / 노래로 유명하다 renowned in song
▶그것은 내가 좋아하는 노래다 That's my favorite song.
▶이 노래는 지금 유행하고 있다 This song is popular now.
▶그녀는 외국 노래를 잘 부른다 She is good at foreign songs.
—노래하다 sing (a song); chant; 〈기뻐서〉 carol; 〈콧노래로〉 hum《a tune》; 〈낮은 소리로〉 croon
♦낮은 소리로 노래하다 sing in a low voice / 목청을 돋구어 노래하다 sing at the top of one's voice / 소리를 맞추어 노래하다 sing in chorus / 피아노에 맞추어 노래하다 sing accompanied by a piano; sing to the piano / 흥얼흥얼 노래하다 hum (a tune); croon
▶그는 피아노 반주로 노래했다 He sang to the accompaniment of the piano.
—자랑 an amateur singing contest; 〈프로그램 이름〉 Amateur Singers on the Air

노래기 〔動〕 a milliped(e); a myriapod; a wireworm

노래지다 grow yellowish; turn [become, go] yellow; yellow ▶종이는 여러 해가 지나면 노래진다 Paper yellows with age.

노랫가락 〈민요〉 a popular [traditional, folk] song; a (folk) ballad; 〈무당의〉 a shaman's song

노랫소리 a singing voice; singing
♦여명을 알리는 새들의 노랫소리 the song of birds that ushers in the dawn / 노랫소리가 나무랄 데 없다 have a good [fine] singing voice
▶누군가의 노랫소리가 들린다 I hear someone singing.

노략질 擄掠— plunder; pillage; looting; despoliation; spoilage
—노략질하다 plunder; pillage; loot; strip [despoil] 《sb of sth》; ransack; ravage 《a land》
♦마을 노략질하다 sack a village / 남의 재물을 노략질하다 plunder [despoil] sb of his goods
▶폭도들은 그 구역의 상점을 전부 노략질했다 The rioters looted every shop in that district.
▶마을 전체가 적병들에게 노략질당했다 The whole village was sacked [plundered] by enemy soldiers.

노려보다 glare [scowl] at; stare fiercely 《at》; look sharply at
♦뚫어지게 노려보다 stare fixedly [hard] 《at》 / 서로 노려보다 glare at each other / 화난 눈으로 노려보다 shoot an angry look 《at》
♦선생님은 떠드는 학생을 노려보았다 The teacher scowled noisy boy.
▶그가 무서운 눈으로 노려보아 나는 몸이 오싹했다 He glared at me so fiercely (that) I was scared.
▶그렇게 노려보지 마라 Don't stare at me like that.

노력 努力 (an) effort; (an) endeavor; (an) exertion; labor; industry ♦헛된 노력 fruitless [futile] effort
▶그가 성공한 것은 노력의 결과였다 His success was the result [fruit] of effort.
▶나의 모든 노력은 수포로 돌아갔다 All my efforts went in vain.
▶그를 개심시키려는 우리의 노력은 헛수고가 되었다 Our efforts to reform [at reforming] him were unsuccessful.
▶우리는 그를 돕기 위해 온갖 노력을 다했다 We made every (possible) effort to help him.
▶그것을 하려면 많은 시간과 노력을 들여야 할 것이다 It will take a lot of time and effort to do it.
▶그는 스스로의 노력으로 그것을 했다 He did it by [through] his own efforts.
—노력하다 make an effort; endeavor; work hard 《to do》; strive for; exert [bestir] oneself
♦끊임없이 노력하다 persevere in one's efforts / …을 얻으려고 노력하다 strive [labor] for sth / 최대한으로 노력하다 exert all possible efforts; strain every nerve; do one's best [utmost]
▶그는 사업을 성공시키기 위해 노력했다 He worked hard [endeavored] to make his business a success.
▶나는 이달 말까지 그 일을 끝마치려고 힘껏

력했다 I made great efforts to finish the work by the end of this month.
▶ 나는 마감에 맞추도록 노력하겠다 I'll try to [try and] meet the deadline.
▶ 그녀는 노력한 보람이 있었다 Her efforts were rewarded. ⇒ Her efforts bore fruit.
▶ 그는 노력해서 사환에서 현재의 지위까지 올라왔다 He worked his way up from office boy to his present position.
▶ 노력하지 않으면 아무것도 달성할 수 없다 Without (making) an effort you cannot achieve anything.
■ ―가 a hard worker; a hard-working [an industrious] person ―상 a prize (awarded) for effort

노력 勞力 〈수고〉 pains; toil; trouble; 〈노동〉 labor ◆ 노력을 제공하다 offer *one's* labor [services]
▶ 이 일을 하는데는 많은 노력이 필요하다 It requires a lot of labor to do this work.
▶ 인간의 노력에는 한계가 있으므로 기계처럼 일할 수는 없다 A man cannot work like a machine, for there is a limit to his labor.

노련 老練 skil(l)fulness ―**노련하다** veteran; experienced; skilled; old
◆ 노련한 교사[선수] a veteran teacher [player] / 노련한 뱃사람 an old sailor / 노련한 솜씨 masterly skill [dexterity] / 노련한 외교관 an old hand at diplomacy / 노련한 의사 an experienced [a veteran, a skilled, an expert] doctor / 노련한 작가 a practiced [trained] writer / 낚시질에 노련하다 be an old hand at fishing
■ ―가 an expert; an experienced hand [person]; a veteran; an old hand; a master-hand

노령 老齡 old [advanced] age
◆ 노령에 이르다 grow old; attain an advanced age; reach a great age
▶ 우리 부모님은 노령이어서 그들과 함께 가실 수 없었다 My parents could not go with them because of their (old) age. ⇒ My parents were too old to go with them.
▶ 그는 노령임에도 지적 욕구가 있다 He has a desire to learn in spite of his old age.
▶ 그는 노령으로 귀가 어두워졌다 He became hard of hearing with age.
■ ―연금 an old-age pension ―학 gerontology ―화 사회 an aging society

노루 〔動〕 a roe deer ■ ―수― a roebuck ■ ―잠 a short and wakeful sleep; (美) a cat nap
노루발장도리 a claw hammer
노르께하다 tinged [stained] with yellow
노르딕종목 ―種目 〈스키의〉 a Nordic event
노르마 〔(러) norma〕〈생산 등의 기준량〉 a norm; a work [production] quota; *one's* assigned task [work] (for the day) ◆ 노르마를 정하다 set a quota (for him)
▶ 그들은 노르마를 완수했다 They fulfilled [did] their norm [quota].
▶ 나는 아직 오늘의 노르마를 완수하지 못했다 I haven't yet fulfilled my quota for today.
노르만 ■ ―인(人) a Norman; 노르만인의 영국 정복 〔史〕 the Norman Conquest
노르망디 〈프랑스 북서부의 지방〉 Normandy

노르스름하다 yellowish; creamy; cream-colored; cream
노르웨이 Norway; 〈공식명〉 the Kingdom of Norway ◆ 노르웨이의 Norwegian ■ ―말 Norwegian ―사람 a Norwegian
노른자(위) 〈난황〉 the yolk [yellow] 《of an egg》; (an) egg yolk; 〈알짜〉 the essence; the pith; the cream; the pick; the choice; the best
◆ 노른자(위)가 쌍으로 있는 계란 a double-yolked egg

노름 〈도박〉 gambling; gambling game; gaming; a game of chance
◆ 노름을 크게 하다 play for high stakes; gamble heavily; play high / 노름에 미치다 be given to gambling; indulge in gambling / 노름에서 돈을 따다 make [earn] money by gambling / 노름에서 돈을 잃다 lose [squander] *one's* money in gambling / 노름으로 패가망신하다 gamble *oneself* out of house and home; gamble away *one's* fortune
―**노름하다** gamble 《on horses》; bet 《on baseball games》; wager; play for money; play 《a game》 for stakes
■ ―꾼 a gambler; a gamester ―돈 a bet; 〈판돈〉 stakes; wager ―방 a gambling room ―빚 a gambling debt ―패 a gang of gamblers
노름판 〈open〉 a gambling house [room, place]; a gambler's den; a casino
◆ 노름판을 벌이다 start gambling; open a gambling house; gamble
▶ 경찰이 노름판을 덮쳤다 The police made a raid on the gambling place.

노릇 **1** 〈일〉 a job; a work; 〈직업〉 an occupation ◆ 선생 노릇 a teaching job; teaching
2 〈구실〉 function; 〈역할〉 a part; a role
◆ 중매쟁이 노릇을 하다 act as go-between / 주인 노릇을 잘하다 play the host well
▶ 그는 우리 야구 팀의 코치 노릇을 하고 있다 He coaches our baseball team.
노릇노릇하다 yellowish
◆ 노릇노릇하게 잘 구워지다 be beautifully browned; be done to a beautiful brown
▶ 벼가 노릇노릇하게 익어 간다 Rice is ripening yellow.
▶ 나뭇잎이 노릇노릇하게 변해 가고 있다 Leaves are turning yellow [are yellowing].

노리개 **1** 〈패물〉 a pendent trinket (worn by ladies); 〈총칭〉 trinketry
2 〈장난감〉 a toy; a plaything; 〈농락물〉 a sport; trifle
◆ 남자의 노리개가 되다 fall a prey to a man's lust; be seduced by a man; be made a plaything of a man / 여자를 남자의 노리개로 보다 regard women as the plaything of men / 여자를 노리개로 삼다 make sport [a plaything] of a woman; make a toy of a woman
▶ 우리는 운명의 노리개가 되었다 We were left at the mercy of fate.
▶ 아이가 노리개를 가지고 놀고 있다 A child is playing with a toy.
■ ―첩 a kept mistress [woman]; a young and beautiful concubine
노리다¹ 〈겨누다〉 aim for [at]; have an eye on [to]; wait for 《a chance》; be after; keep

노리다²

watch for

[解說] *aim for*가 일반적인 말이다. *have an eye on* [*to*]는「주목하다」, *wait for*는「겨누고 기다리다」, *be after*는「추구하다」라는 데서「겨누다」라는 뜻이 된다.

♦ …을 노리고 with the aim of…; with the eye on…/ 보상금을 노리다 have an eye on [be after] the reward / 재산을 노리다 have an eye upon sb's property / 방심하고 있는 틈을 노리다 watch for a moment when sb is off (his) guard / 효과를 노리다 calculate upon [be out for] an effect
▶ 갱들은 그 경찰관의 목숨을 노렸다 The gangsters had sought the policeman's life.
▶ 그는 1등상을 노리고 있다 He is aiming at [trying for] (the) first prize.
▶ 죄수는 하루 종일 탈옥할 기회를 노리고 있었다 The prisoner watched all day for a chance to escape from the prison.
▶ 그는 반격할 기회를 노리고 있었다 He was looking for a chance to counterattack.
▶ 그는 교섭을 자기에게 유리하게 진전시킬 기회를 노리고 있었다 He was waiting for an opportunity to negotiate the matter to his advantage.

노리다² 1 〈노린내가 나다〉 stinking; foul-smelling; fetid; rank; smelled like burning hair (털이 타듯); smelled like a skunk (동물의) 2 〈인색하다〉 miserly; stingy; closefisted; tightfisted; niggardly; (美俗) pinchpenny
노리착지근하다 somewhat stinking [fetid]
노린내 a stench; a stinking [fetid] smell; 〈털이 타는〉 the smell of burning hair [fat]; 〈동물의〉 the smell of a skunk
▶ 여기서 노린내가 난다 I smell a stink [stench] here.
▶ 어디서 머리털이 타는지 노린내가 났다 There was a smell of burnt [burning] hair.
노릿하다 somewhat stinking [fetid]
노망 老妄 dotage; second childhood; senility; 〈병적인〉 senile dementia [psychosis]
▶ 우리 할아버지는 노망이 드셨다 My grandfather is in his dotage [has become senile]. ─노망하다 be in [fall into] one's dotage; dote; become [be, get] senile; (俗) go gaga ♦ 노망한 노인 an old man in his dotage [second childhood]; a dotard; a senile old man
노면 路面 a road surface; the surface of a road ♦ 노면을 개수하다 resurface the road / 노면을 고르게 하다 level the surface ■ ─교통 surface traffic ─보수공사 resurfacing work ─전차 a surface car; a streetcar; (英) a tram(-car) ─포장 (re)surfacing the road; pavement ─포장기 a road surfacer
노모 老母 one's old [aged] mother
노목 老木 an old [aged] tree
노무 勞務 labor; work; service ♦ 노무에 종사하다 give one's services
■ ─과 the labor section ─관리 personnel [labor] management ─기본계약 a master labor contract ─담당 중역 a personnel manager; a director in charge of labor ─동원 mobilization of labor ─비 labor expenses [cost]
노무자 勞務者 a worker; a laborer; a workman; a working man; working people ■ ─관리 labor control ─모집 labor recruitment
노박이로 〈붙박이로〉 fixedly; steadfastly; fastened [stuck] for good; 〈끊임없이〉 always; continually; continuously; steadily
노박히다 be stuck [fastened] for good; stick to; keep (oneself) steady
노반 路盤 a roadbed
노발대발 怒發大發 violent [raving] anger; wild rage; wrath
─노발대발하다 be infuriated; boil with rage [anger]; burn with wrath; be inflamed with anger; seethe with rage; be in a towering fury
▶ 그는 아주 노발대발했다 His anger knew no bounds.
노발리스 〈독일의 시인〉 Novalis; 〈본명〉 Friedrich von Hardenberg (1772-1801)
노방초 路傍草 grass at the roadside
노벨 〈스웨덴의 화학자〉 Nobel, Alfred Bernhard (1833-96) ■ ─상 a Nobel prize [award] ─상 수상자 a Nobel prize winner [laureate]; a Nobelist ─평화상 a Nobel Peace Prize
노벨륨 〔化〕 nobelium
노변 爐邊 the fireside ♦ 노변에서 by the hearth; by the fireside [fire] ─담화 (談話) a fireside chat [talk]
노병 老兵 an old soldier; a campaigner; a war veteran; (美口) a vet ▶ 노병은 죽지 않고 사라질 뿐이다 Old soldiers never die; they just fade away.
노복 奴僕 〈사내종〉 a male slave
노부 老父 one's old [aged] father
노부모 老父母 one's aged [old] parents
노비 奴婢 〈종〉 slaves
노비 路費 〈노자〉 traveling expenses
노사 勞使 management and labor; capital and labor
▶ 노사교섭이 시작되었다 Negotiations started between management and labor.
■ ─간담회 a round-table conference between labor and management ─투쟁 a (decisive) struggle between management and labor ─협의제 the joint labor-management conference system ─협의회 a joint labor-management conference ─협조 cooperation of capital and labor [between labor and management]; labor-management cooperation: 우리는 노사협조 노선을 취해야 한다 We must take the road of labor-management cooperation.
노사관계 勞使關係 labor-management relations; the relations between labor and capital; industrial relations
▶ 노사관계는 개선되어 가고 있다 The relations between labor and management are improving. ⇌ The labor-management [The industrial] relations are improving.
노사분규 勞使紛糾 a labor-management dispute; a conflict between labor and capital
♦ 노사 분규를 조정하다 arbitrate disputes between management and labor; arbitrate labor dispute

■ —조정위원회 a labor dispute mediation committee

노상 1 〈언제나〉 all the time; always; usually; ever
♦ 부모에게 노상 걱정만 끼치다 be a constant source of anxiety to *one's* parents
▶ 그는 노상 허풍을 떤다 He always talks big.
▶ 그는 노상 지각한다 He is always late. ⇌ He comes late all the time.
2 〈반드시〉 whenever; every time; habitually
♦ 만나면 노상 싸우다 never meet without quarreling ▶ 나는 외출할 때면 노상 복장에 주의한다 I dress carefully whenever I go out.

노상 路上 ♦ 노상에서 (play) on [in] the road [street] / 노상에서 죽다 fall dead on [in] the street
■ —사고 an accident on the road; a road accident —시운전 〈자동차의〉 a road test

노상 路床 〈노반(路盤)〉 a roadbed

노상강도 路上強盜 〈행위〉 highway robbery; a holdup; 〈사람〉 a highwayman; a footpad; (美口) a holdup man
♦ 노상강도를 만나다 be robbed by a highwayman; fall in with footpads / 노상강도질을 하다 rob wayfarers; (美) hold up
▶ 이 길은 노상강도가 출몰한다 This road is infested with thieves.

노새 〔動〕 a mule

노색 怒色 an angry mood ⇨ 노기(怒氣)

노선 路線 〈버스 등의〉 a route; 〈방침〉 a line
♦ …의 노선에 따라 in line [alignment] with… / 독자 노선을 걷다 take *one's* own line / 자본주의 노선을 따르다 take [follow] the capitalist line / 정해진 노선을 가다 run on regular routes
■ 강경— a tough [hard] line 버스— a bus service route 정치— (*one's*) political line; 〈정당의〉 a party line 항공— an airline ■ —도 a route map —버스 a route bus

노섬벌랜드 〈잉글랜드 북부의 주〉 Northumberland

노성 怒聲 an angry voice; an excited voice
▶ 그는 노성을 질렀다 He shouted in anger.

노소 老少 age and youth; young and old
♦ 남녀 노소 young and old of both sexes; people of all ages and both sexes / 남녀 노소를 막론하고 without distinction [irrespective, regardless] of age or sex
▶ 많은 남녀 노소가 공원에 모여 있었다 There was a crowd of people, young and old of both sexes [men and women, young and old] in the park.
▶ 남녀 노소를 막론하고 경기에 참가해 주십시오 Please join the contest without considering age or sex.

노송 老松 an old pine tree

노쇠 老衰 decrepitude; senility; infirmity of old age; 〔醫〕 senile decay [infirmity]
♦ 노쇠를 방지하다 prevent senility; retard old age / 노쇠 현상을 보이다 show signs of decrepitude
—**노쇠하다** grow old and infirm [feeble]; become infirm with age; go [become] decrepit
▶ 노쇠하여 죽다 die of old age
▶ 우리 어머니는 이제 노쇠하십니다 My mother is infirm due to age. ⇌ My mother is stricken in years.
■ —기 senescence

노숙 老熟 maturity; mellowness; mature experience
—**노숙하다** mature; experienced; mellow
▶ 그는 화가로서 노숙한 경지에 이르렀다 He attained maturity as a painter.
▶ 그의 예술성은 노숙한 경지에 이르렀다 His artistry has come to full maturity.

노숙 露宿 camping(-out); bivouac [bívuæk]
—**노숙하다** sleep [pass the night] in the open [out of doors]; sleep rough; camp (out); bivouac
▶ 그는 산에서 길을 잃고 노숙했다 He slept in the open, having lost his way in the mountain.

노스아일랜드 〈뉴질랜드의 북섬〉 North Island

노스캐롤라이나 〈미국 남동부의 주〉 North Carolina (略 N.C.)

노스탤지어 nostalgia; homesickness ⇨ 향수(鄕愁)

노스트라다무스 〈프랑스의 예언가〉 Nostradamus (1503-66)

노승 老僧 an old [aged] priest

노심초사 勞心焦思 exertion of the mind; solicitude; worry
—**노심초사하다** exert *oneself* mentally; worry [bother] *oneself* 《about》; be worried [anxious]; rack [tax] *one's* brains
♦ 국사로 노심초사하다 devote *oneself* to the interests of *one's* country
▶ 그는 그 일에 노심초사했다 He exerted himself mentally on that job.
▶ 그런 일로 노심초사하지 마라 Don't worry yourself about such a thing.

노아 〔聖〕 Noah ♦ 노아의 방주 Noah's ark / 노아의 홍수 Noah's flood; the Flood; the Deluge

노안 老眼 aged eyes; farsightedness [long-sightedness] due to old age [advancing years]; 〔醫〕 presbyopia ♦ 노안인 사람 a presbyope; a farsighted person
▶ 나이가 들면서 노안이 점점 심해졌다 My eyesight got dimmer and dimmer with age.
■ —경(鏡) glasses [spectacles] for the aged; convex [long-distance] glasses; farsighted (eye)glasses

노약자 老弱者 the old and the weak

노어 露語 〈러시아어〉 Russian

노여움 anger; indignation; 〈은근한〉 quiet resentment
♦ 노여움을 가라앉히다 calm [appease, allay] *sb's* anger / 노여움을 사다 make *sb* angry; arouse [excite] *sb's* wrath; incur [arouse, provoke] *sb's* displeasure; offend *sb* / 노여움을 참다 restrain [hold in] *one's* anger; suppress [repress, contain] *one's* anger / …에 대한 노여움을 풀다 relent towards *sb*
▶ 상원의원의 연설이 대통령의 노여움을 샀다 A senator's speech incurred [provoked] the President's displeasure.
▶ 그는 사장의 노여움을 사서 좌천되었다 He

was demoted because he had aroused [incurred] the president's wrath.
노여워하다 resent (*sb's* actions [remarks]); take offense at; be displeased by [with, at]; feel hurt; lose *one's* temper《with *sb* for *sth*》; feel displeasure over; feel indignation over [at]
▶ 그녀는 푸대접을 받고 그에게 노여워하고 있다 She is indignant with him over the treatment she received.
▶ 그녀의 말에 너무 노여워하지 마시오 Please do not be offended by her remark.
노역 老役 the role of an aged person ▶ 그는 노역을 맡아 했다 He played [did] the part of an old man.
노역 勞役 toil; hard work [labor]
▶ 젊은이나 늙은이나 강제 노역에 끌려 나갔다 Old and young people were hunted [conscripted] for forced labor.
―**노역하다** labor; do hard work
■―**장(場)** 〈죄수의〉 a prison workshop
노엽다 displeased; unpleasant; displeasing; offensive; furious; indignant ◆ 노여운 빛을 나타내다 betray *one's* anger
▶ 나는 그의 말이 노여웠다 I was indignant (with him) about his remark. ⇌ I was indignant at [was outraged by] what he said.
▶ 나는 그를 노엽게 할 생각은 없었다 I did not mean to offend him.
노예 奴隷 1 〈자유 없는 사람〉 a slave; a bondman
◆ 노예 같은 slavish / 노예를 해방하다 set a slave free / 노예로 삼다 make a slave 《of》; enslave; enthral(l) / 노예로 팔리다 be sold into slavery; be sold for a slave / 노예처럼 부리다 use *sb* like a slave; put *sb* to a practical slave labor / 노예처럼 일하다 work like a slave; slave (away); drudge
▶ 링컨은 노예를 해방시켰다 Lincoln freed [emancipated] the slaves.
▶ 그들은 노예나 진배없다 They are no better than slaves.
2 (비유) a slave
◆ 술의 노예 a slave to drink / 금전[정욕]의 노예가 되다 become a slave to money [passion]
▶ 그는 그녀의 미모에 노예가 되었다 He became a captive to her beauty.
▶ 사람은 습관의 노예다 We are the slaves of habit.
■―**근성** a servile spirit ―**노동** slave labor ―**매매** slave trade; flesh [human] traffic ―**상인** a slaver ―**선** a slave ship; a slaver ―**소유자** a slaveholder; a slaver ―**제(도)** slavery ―**폐지론** abolitionism; antislavery ―**폐지론자** an abolitionist ―**폐지운동** an antislavery movement ―**해방** emancipation of slaves ―**해방선언** 〔美史〕 the Emancipation Proclamation
노옹 老翁 an old [aged] man
노유 老幼 the young and the old ◆ 노유를 막론하고 irrespective of age
노을 a glow ◆ 노을진 하늘 the sky aglow with the rising [setting] sun
노이로제 (a) neurosis (*pl.* -ses); (a) nervous breakdown ◆ 노이로제에 걸리다 have a neurosis
▶ 그는 입학시험 때문에 노이로제 증세가 조금 있다 He is slightly neurotic about the entrance examination.
■―**환자** a neurotic
노이즈 〈잡음〉 a noise
노익장 老益壯 a vigorous old age ◆ 노익장을 자랑하다 be hale and strong; enjoy a green old age
노인 老人 an old [aged] person; (총칭) the old [aged]; old people; old folks ◆ 노인에게 친절히 대하다 be kind to old people
▶ 그는 노인같아 보인다 He looks older than he really is [old for his age].
▶ 노인을 공경하시오 Be respectful to old people [the age].
■―**학** gerontology
노인병 老人病 the diseases of old age [aging people]; geriatric diseases; the infirmities of age
▶ 그는 노인병에 걸렸다 He suffered from a disease of old age.
■―**전문의(醫)** a geriatrician ―**학(學)** geriatrics; geriatry
노임 勞賃 wages; pay
◆ 노임을 인상[인하]하다 raise [reduce] the wages [cost of labor] / 싼 노임을 받고 일하다 work at low wages; work at poor pay / 노임 수준을 억제하다 hold [keep] down the wage level [the level of wages]
▶ 그의 회사는 노임이 높다[낮다] His company pays high [low] wages.
노자 老子 〈도교의 개조〉 Lao-tze; Lao-tsu ◆ 노자의 가르침 Taoism
노자 勞資 capital and labor ⇨ 노사(勞使)
노자 路資 〈노비(路費)〉 traveling expenses
노작 勞作 a laborious work; the product of *one's* labor; a work to which considerable labor was devoted; a work involving much elaboration; a lucubration
◆ 다년간의 노작 a work completed after many years' labor; a laborious work taking years to finish
▶ 이 소설은 아버지의 다년간의 노작이다 My father spent years in [writing] this novel.
노장 老將 an old general; a veteran general
노점 露店 a stand; an open-air stall; a (street) stall; a booth; a roadside stand
◆ 노점을 벌이다 open [keep] a street stall; engage in street stalling
▶ 축제일에는 노점이 많이 열린다 Many (street) stalls are put [set] up on festival days.
▶ 노점이 일제히 철거되었다 All the street stalls were pulled down simultaneously.
■―**가(街)** open-air stall quarters ―**상(인)** a stand keeper; a street vendor; a stallman; (美) a pitchman
노점 露點 〔物〕 the dew point=이슬점
노정 路程 〈이수(里數)〉 mileage; (a) distance; 〈여행경로〉 an itinerary; a route of travel; a course
◆ 10킬로미터의 노정 a distance of ten kilo-

meters; a ten kilometers' journey / 기차로 1시간 정도의 노정 about an hour's ride by train
■ —기(記) a traveler's guide; an itinerary
—표 a table of itinerary

노정 露呈 〈드러냄〉 exposure; disclosure; revelation —**노정하다** expose; disclose; reveal; be disclosed [exposed, revealed]; come to light; begin to show

노조 勞組 a labor union ⇨ 노동조합

노즐 〈분출구〉 a nozzle

노지 露地 the bare ground; an open field ■ —재배 raising outdoors : 노지재배한 토마토 tomatoes grown outdoor

노질 櫓— rowing; paddling; sculling —**노질하다** row 《a boat》; work 《a scull》; pull [ply] an oar; paddle 《a canoe》

노처 老妻 one's old wife

노처녀 老處女 an old maid; 〔法〕 a spinster
♦ 노처녀같은 old-maidish; spinsterish

노천 露天 ♦ 노천의 outdoor; open-air / 노천에서 in the open (air); out of doors; outdoors ▶ 그는 노천에서 야채를 팔고 있다 He sells vegetables in the open (air).
■ —교실 an open-air schoolroom [class] —극장 an open-air theater —수업 open-air classes —시장 an open-air [outdoor] market —채굴 ⇨ 노천굴 —채굴장 a strip mine

노천굴 露天掘 open-air mining; openwork; (美) opencut (英) opencast (mining); strip mining ■ —탄광 an open coal mine

노체 老體 〈노구(老軀)〉 an old body [frame]; 〈노인〉 an old [aged] person

노총각 老總角 an old bachelor

노추 老醜 aged deformity; ugliness [ill-favoredness] of old age

노출 露出 1 〈드러냄·드러냄〉 (an) exposure; disclosure; 〈광맥의〉 outcrop
—**노출하다** expose; disclose; bare; lay bare
♦ 아무의 노출된 가슴 sb's exposed chest / 피부를 노출하다 expose one's skin / 햇빛에 노출하다 expose sth to the sun / 노출되다 be exposed [disclosed, bared]; crop out
▶ 사람을 앞에서 지나치게 몸을 노출하는 것은 예의에 어긋난다 It is not decent for you to expose [bare] too much of your bodies.
▶ 석탄 광맥이 노출되었다 The vein of coal cropped out.
2 〔寫〕 exposure
■ —계 an actinometer; an exposure [a light] meter —과다[부족] overexposure [under-exposure] : 이 사진은 노출 과다[부족]다 This picture is overexposed [underexposed]. —광상(鑛床) an exposed deposit —시간 exposure time; the time of exposure : 노출 시간은 15분의 1초로 하자 Let's make the exposure time one-fifteenth of a second. —전선(電線) a bare wire —증 exhibitionism; a mania for indecent exposure; an exposure mania : 노출증 환자 an exhibitionist

노카운트 no count
▶ 그 경기는 노카운트가 되었다 The play was called no count.

노커 〈문 두드리는 쇠〉 a (door) knocker

노코멘트 no comment ▶ 그 문제에 관해서는 노코멘트다 I will make no comment on the matter.

노크 1 a knock; knocking —**노크하다** knock on [at]
▶ 그는 문을 노크했다 He knocked on [at] the door. ⇌ He gave a knock on the door.
▶ 문을 노크하는 소리가 났다 There was a knock on [at] the door.
2 〔野〕 a knock —**노크하다** knock fungoes for infield practice

노킹 〈내연 기관의〉 knocking

노타이 ▶ 그는 간편한 노타이 차림이었다 He was dressed casually without a tie. ■ —셔츠 an openneck(ed) shirt

노트¹ 1 〈필기〉 a note —**노트하다** take [make] notes of 《a lecture》; note [put, write, jot] down ▶ 나는 선생님의 말씀을 일일이 노트했다 I noted down every word the teacher said.
2 〈필기장〉 a notebook

노트² 〈배의 속도 단위〉 a knot ♦ 30노트의 배 a ship of 30 knots / 20노트를 내다 make [do, develop, log] 20 knots ▶ 이 배는 30노트를 낼 수 있다 This ship can make 30 knots.

노트북 〈필기장〉 a notebook

노티 老— signs of (old-)age
♦ 나이 치고는 노티가 나다 look old for one's age; look older than one's age [one really is]
▶ 네 그 헤어스타일은 노티가 난다 That hairdo makes you look older than your age.

노팅엄셔 〈잉글랜드의 주〉 Nottinghamshire

노파 老婆 an old woman

노파심 老婆心 grandmotherly [excessive, old-womanish] solicitude; 〈기우〉 unnecessary [useless] anxiety; solicitude for another's welfare
▶ 그녀는 다만 노파심에서 그렇게 말했다 She only said so out of concern for you.
▶ 나는 노파심에서 이런 말을 하는 거야 I say this out of kindness [for your (own) good].

노폐 老廢 superannuation —**노폐하다** super-annuated ■ —물 waste matter; wastes : 체내의 노폐물 body wastes

노포 老舖·老鋪 an old(-established) store [shop]; a store of long standing

노폭 路幅 the width of a street

노하다 怒— be [become, get] angry 《with sb, at [about] sth》; be offended 《at》; take offense; be angered; be enraged; be vexed; be stirred to anger; (美) get mad 《with sb, at sb [sth]》
♦ 불같이 노하다 burn with rage; be hot with anger [rage] / 몹시 노하여 일어서다 stand up in great [high, deep] dudgeon
▶ 그런 사소한 일 때문에 노하지 마라 Don't let such a trifling thing put you out.
▶ 어젯밤 일로 그녀는 아직도 내게 노해 있는지도 몰라 I wonder if she is still sore at me about what happened last night.

노하우 〈기술 정보〉 know-how

노형 老兄 you

노호 怒號 a roar (of anger); a bellow; an outcry ♦ 폭풍우의 노호 the raging of the storm; the howling of the wind —**노호하다** roar (in anger); howl (with rage); bellow

노화 老化 〈노쇠〉 senility; ag(e)ing; growing old —**노화하다** age
■—**방지제** 〈고무 제품의〉 an age resister; an antioxidant —**현상** 《develop》 the phenomena of ag(e)ing; a symptom of senility [age]

노환 老患 diseases [infirmities] of (old) age; geriatric diseases

노회하다 老獪 crafty; cunning; foxy ◆노회한 수단 a cunning way; a crafty method ▶그는 노회한 사람이다 He is a crafty [cunning, sly] man. ⇌ He is an old fox.

노획 鹵獲 capture; seizure —**노획하다** capture; seize; loot; pillage 《goods》 ▶우리는 적의 전차를 노획했다 We captured an enemy tank.
■—**물[품]** a spoil; a prize; a trophy; 〈총칭〉 booty; plunder

노후 老朽 —**노후하다** decrepit; superannuated; antiquated; time-worn; worn-out; overage ◆노후한 교사(校舍) an old ramshackle school house
—**선** an overage [a superannuated, a worn-out] vessel [ship] —**시설** outworn [superannuated] equipment —**차** a superannuated [decrepit] car —**화(化)** deterioration : 노후화하다 become too old for work [use]; become superannuated

노후 老後 one's old age; one's remaining years; one's declining years; the winter [evening] of life
◆노후의 낙(樂) consolation of one's old age / 노후에 in one's old age; when (one is) old ▶우리 할아버지는 노후를 편안하게 지내고 싶어 하셨다 My grandfather wanted to live comfortably in his old age. ⇌ My grandfather wanted to spend his last days [remaining years] comfortably.
▶그는 노후를 행복하게 지냈다 He spent the evening of life happily.
▶그는 노후에 대비해서 돈을 저축했다 He saved up for his old age.

녹 祿 a stipend; (a) salary; a ration of rice ◆녹을 먹다 receive a stipend

녹 綠 1 〈구리의〉 ⇨ 동록(銅綠)
2 〈쇠의〉 rust; tarnish
◆칼의 녹을 없애다 clean the rust of a knife; 〈문질러〉 rub [scour] the rust of a knife ▶쇠는 녹이 잘 슨다 Iron gathers rust [gets rusty] easily.
▶뚜껑이 녹이 슬어 열리지 않는다 The lid is rusted shut and won't open.

녹각 鹿角 an antler; a deer horn

녹나무 〔植〕 a camphor tree

녹내장 綠內障 〔醫〕 glaucoma

녹는점 —點 〔物〕 the melting [fusing] point; the point of fusion

녹다 1 〈고체가〉 melt; 〈언 것이〉 thaw; 〈양초 등이〉 run
◆녹아 없어지다 melt away / 녹아서 물이 되다 melt into water
▶눈이 햇볕에 녹았다 The snow has melted [thawed] in the sun.
▶시냇물의 얼음이 녹아버렸다 The ice in the stream has melted. ⇌ The stream has thawed.
▶아이스크림이 녹기 전에 먹어라 Eat your ice cream before it melts.
2 〈용해되다〉 dissolve; melt
▶설탕[소금]은 물에 녹는다 Sugar [Salt] dissolves in water.
▶바닷물에는 많은 염류가 녹아 있다 Sea water contains many salts in solution.
3 〈몸·마음이〉 get [become] warm(자연히); warm up(불에 쬐어)
▶그것을 생각만해도 나는 마음이 녹는다 It warms my hearts just to think of it.
▶그의 친절한 말에 내 마음이 녹았다 My heart was warmed [touched] by his kind remarks.
4 〈혼나다〉 be overcome; be overwhelmed; be broke [ruined]; get the worst of it
▶그는 어리석게 굴다가 녹았다 He paid dearly for his folly.
▶나는 주먹 한대에 녹아 떨어졌다 I was knocked out by only a blow.
5 〈주색잡기에〉 be dissipated; get ruined by dissipation
◆주색에 녹다 ruin one's health with dissipation / 술에 녹아 떨어지다 get dead drunk
▶그는 방탕한 생활로 녹았다 He ruined himself by fast living.
6 〈반하다〉 be enraptured; be gone on; be crazy; fall [go] into; be thrown into
▶그는 그 여배우의 아름다운 목소리[매력]에 녹았다 He was fascinated [stuck] by the actress's lovely voice [charm].

녹다운 a knockdown ◆녹다운시키다 knock sb down ▶그 권투선수는 녹다운당했다 The boxer was knocked down.
■—**수출** knockdown exporting: 자동차의 녹다운 수출 export of knocked-down cars

녹두 綠豆 〔植〕 a mung bean; a green gram
■—**묵** mung-bean curd

녹로 轆轤 〈선반〉 a (turning) lathe; 〈도공의〉 a potter's wheel —**공(工)** a turner —**세공** a turner's work; 〈총칭〉 turnery

녹록하다 碌碌 trifling; insignificant
▶그들의 매달 식비도 녹록하지 않았다 Their monthly food expenses ran up to a considerable sum.
▶그는 녹록하지 않은 녀석이다 He is not a person to be trifled with [made light of]. ⇌ He is a tough customer.

녹림 綠林 1 〈숲〉 a green wood **2** 〈도둑의 소굴〉 a bandits' den; a robbers' roost ■—**객** a bandit

녹말 綠末 starch; 〈英〉 farina; 〔化〕 dextrin(e)
■—**당화효소** amylase —**질** starchiness : 녹말질의 starchy; farinaceous

녹물 綠— 〈얼룩〉 rust stain; 〈색〉 rust(color); reddish brown

녹봉 祿俸 (a) salary ⇨ 녹(祿)

녹비 鹿— deerskin; buckskin ■—**장갑** buckskin gloves

녹비 綠肥 〈풋거름〉 green manure ■—**작물** 〈풋거름 작물〉 green manure crop

녹색 綠色 green; 〔詩〕 verdure ◆녹색 들판 green fields / 녹색의 green; verdant
▶그의 차는 녹색이다 His car is green.

■ —신고 〔經〕 a green return —혁명 the green revolution

녹슬다 綠— 1 〈금속이〉 rust; get [become] rusty; gather rust
▶ 칼이 녹슬었다 The knife gathered rust. ⇌ The knife rusted.
▶ 물기는 철을 녹슬게 한다 Water rusts iron.
▶ 스테인리스는 녹슬지 않는다 Stainless steel resists rust [does not rust]. ⇌ Stainless steel is rustproof.
2 〈머리·실력 등이〉 get dull [slow-witted]; weaken; (口) be rusty
▶ 내 영어는 좀 녹슬었다 My English is a little rusty. ⇌ I'm a little rusty on English.
▶ 네 재능을 녹슬게 해선 안된다 Don't let your talents become rusted.
▶ 머리가 녹슬지 않도록 수학 공부를 하고 있다 I am studying math to keep my brain alive.

녹신녹신하다 very soft and flexible; very elastic

녹신하다 soft and flexible; elastic; pliant

녹아웃 1 〔拳〕 a knockout (略 KO, K.O.) ♦상대를 녹아웃시키다 knock *one's* opponent out / 녹아웃당하다 be knocked [counted] out
2 〔野〕 knockout ▶ 우리 팀은 5회말에서 상대방의 투수를 녹아웃시켰다 Our team knocked out the opposing pitcher in the bottom of the fifth inning.

녹야 綠野 a green field; 〈초원〉 a grassland

녹엽 綠葉 a green leaf

녹용 鹿茸 the young antlers of the deer; deer antlers ♦ 녹용을 밀수하다 smuggle deer antlers

녹음 綠陰 the shade of trees; a shady nook
■ —기(期) the season of thick foliage —방초 green shades and fragrant plants

녹음 錄音 recording; (electrical) transcription —녹음하다 record (music); tape-record; 〔放〕 transcribe (a program)
♦ 녹음한 음악 recorded music / 테이프에 녹음한 audio-taped (lecture) / 테이프에 녹음하다 tape [tape-record] 《a speech》; record 《a speech》 on a tape
▶ 나는 그 시인의 시 낭송을 카세트에 녹음했다 I recorded the poet's recitation on a cassette tape.
■ 가두— 〈라디오 프로그램의〉 a "Man on the Street" interview; a street-corner transcription 동시— synchronous recording —구성 (a program of) arranged transcription —기 a recorder; a recording [transcribing] machine; 〈테이프식〉 a tape recorder —기사 a recordist; a recording engineer; a sound mixer —담당자 a (sound) recordist; a record man —대(帶) 〈필름의〉 a sound track —방송 transcription (broadcast); broadcasting by electrical transcription —실 a recording room —연설 a transcribed speech —장치 recording [sound] equipment —재생 playback —재생기 a transcription machine —테이프 a (sound) recording tape; a magnetic recording tape; 〈카세트용의〉 a cassette tape

녹이다 1 〈용해시키다〉 dissolve; melt; 〈액화시키다〉 liquefy; 〈얼음 등을〉 thaw (out)
♦ 소금을 물에 녹이다 dissolve salt in water / 초[얼음]를 녹이다 melt wax [ice]
▶ 이 약품은 쇠를 쉽게 녹인다 This chemical liquefies iron easily.
▶ 그는 설탕을 물에 녹였다 He dissolved some sugar in water.
2 〈가열하여〉 melt (down, up); fuse; smelt
♦ 쇠를 녹이다 fuse [melt] iron / 주석을 녹이다 smelt tin / 녹여서 …을 만들다 melt down 《one thing》 into 《another》
▶ 프라이팬을 불에 얹어 버터를 녹여라 Melt butter in a fryingpan over the fire.
▶ 구리와 아연을 녹이면 놋쇠가 된다 Copper and zinc are fused to make brass.
3 〈따뜻이 하다〉 warm (it) up; make (it) warm; thaw
♦ 몸을 녹이다 warm *oneself* (at the stove); get warm / 화로에 발을 녹이다 warm *one's* feet over a brazier
▶ 나는 불에 몸을 녹였다 I warmed myself at the fire.
4 〈반하게 하다〉 charm; fascinate; enchant; bewitch; captivate 《a man》; kill
♦ 살살 녹이는 눈짓 a killing wink
▶ 그녀의 미모가 그를 녹였다 Her beauty captivated him.
▶ 그녀는 눈길 한 번에 남자를 녹여버릴 만한 여자였다 She belonged to the type of those who enslave men at a glance.
5 〈낭비하다〉 squander 《away》; waste 《on, over》; throw away ♦ 도박으로 재산을 녹여 없애다 gamble away *one's* fortune; throw away a fortune in gambling

녹조류 綠藻類 〔植〕 green algae

녹주석 綠柱石 〔鑛〕 beryl

녹즙 綠汁 natural juices in green leafy vegetables ■ —기 a juicer for extracting juice from vegetables and greens

녹지 綠地 a green (tract of) land; 〈공원〉 a park; 〈나무가 무성한〉 a wooded area ♦ 녹지화하다 afforest
■ —계획 a plan for afforestation —대 (a) greenbelt; a green zone; 〈차도와 인도 사이의〉 (美) a tree lawn

녹진녹진하다 quite soft and sticky ♦ 녹진녹진한 물엿 sticky starch syrup / 녹진녹진한 성격 soft and sticky nature

녹진하다 soft and sticky; tenacious

녹차 綠茶 green tea

녹채 鹿砦 an abatis; entanglement(s)

녹청 綠靑 green rust; verdigris

녹초 1 〈맥을 못씀〉 utter exhaustion
♦ 녹초가 되다 be dead tired; be worn out; (口) be dog-tired; be exhausted / 술에 취해 녹초가 되다 (口) be dead drunk; (俗) be really plastered
▶ 나는 하루 종일 일해서 녹초가 되었다 I'm exhausted [dead tired] from working all day.
2 ⇨ 노후(老朽)

녹초 綠草 green grass

녹턴 〈야상곡〉 a nocturne

녹화 綠化 tree planting; afforestation
♦ 산림녹화운동 a tree-planting campaign [drive]; an afforestation [a forestation] cam-

녹화

paign; a campaign to make hills green
—녹화하다 plant (an area) with trees; plant trees (in an area)

녹화 錄畫 (TV) (a) video(tape) recording —녹화하다 record (a TV program) on video(tape); videotape (a TV program)
▶내가 그 드라마를 녹화해 놓겠다 I will videotape [make a videotape recording of] the drama.
■—방송(프로그램) a broadcast by transcription; a transcribed program —실 a telerecording room

녹황색 綠黃色 greenish yellow

논 a rice field [paddy]; a paddy (field) ◆논을 갈다 plow [till] a rice field / 논에 물을 대다 water [irrigate] a rice field / 논에 모를 심다 plant rice; plant out rice-seedlings

논갈이 plowing a rice field —논갈이하다 plow [till] a rice field

논객 論客 a debater; a disputant; a controversialist

논거 論據 the basis of [grounds for] an argument; data
◆…의 논거가 되다 supply arguments for… / 논거가 확실하다 be well grounded; be sound
▶그의 주장에는 논거가 없다 His claims are groundless.
▶그렇게 말하는 논거가 무엇이냐? What is the basis for saying so?
▶그의 제안을 인정하는 논거는 무엇이냐? What are the arguments for accepting his proposal?

논고 論考 a study

논고 論告 〔法〕 the prosecutor's concluding [final] argument
◆준엄한 논고 a scathing address / 논고를 개시하다 open the arguments (on a case)
▶3시에 검사의 논고가 있었다 The prosecutor addressed the court at three.
—논고하다 prosecute; (the prosecutor) address the court

논공행상 論功行賞 the official recognition of distinguished services; the grant of honors [distribution of rewards] according to the merits (of)
▶논공행상이 공평하지 못했다 The honors were not justly [fairly] distributed.
—논공행상하다 award [give, pay] rewards according to (each person's) merits; distribute [confer] honors

논구 論究 an exhaustive [a thorough] discussion

논급 論及 reference —논급하다 refer (to); enter into ▶그는 그 문제를 상세히 논급했다 He entered into a detailed discussion of the problem.

논길 a lane through rice fields; a footpath between rice fields

논농사 — 農事 rice growing [cultivation]; rice farming ▶금년에는 논농사가 잘[잘못] 되었다 This year's rice crop is good [poor].

논다 divide ⇨ 노느다

논다니 (俗) a prostitute; a whore; a harlot

논단 論壇 〈토론장소〉 a (public) platform; a rostrum; a forum; 〈언론계〉 the press; 〈평론계〉 the world of criticism; the circle of critics [publicists]
▶그는 논단의 대표적인 인물이다 He is the leader [representative] of the world of criticism.

논단 論斷 a conclusion; a verdict —논단하다 conclude; reach a conclusion

논도랑 a ditch [waterway] between rice fields

논두렁 a ridge between rice fields; a small raised area bordering a rice paddy ■—길 a footpath between rice fields

논둑 a levee

논란 論難 criticism; denunciation —논란하다 criticize (severely); denounce; refute; take to task ◆현행 세제에 대해 논란하다 denounce the present taxation system

논리 論理 logic
◆논리상 logically; from a logical point of view / 논리를 무시하고 regardless of logic / 논리에 맞지 않다 be illogical
▶그가 하는 말에는 논리의 비약이 있다 There is not much logic in what he says.
■—성 logicality —주의 logicism

논리적 論理的 logical (↔illogical); dialectic; reasonable ◆논리적으로 불가능한 일 a logical impossibility / 비 논리적인 illogical; fallacious / 논리적으로 logically; dialectically
▶네가 하는 말은 지극히 논리적이다 What you say [Your opinion] is very logical.
▶그는 아주 논리적인 주장을 했다 He produced a very logical argument.
▶남을 설득하려면 논리적으로 말해야 한다 To convince people, you should speak with logic [logically].
▶너는 문제를 논리적으로 생각해야 한다 You should consider the problem logically. ⇌ You should reason the problem out.
■—사고 logical thinking —실증주의 logical positivism [empiricism]

논리학 論理學 logic ■귀납[연역]— inductive [deductive] logic 기호[수리]— symbolic [mathematical] logic 순수[형식]— pure [formal] logic ■—자 a logician

논마지기 a small plot of rice field [paddy]
▶그는 논마지기나 부치고 있다 He cultivates some rice fields. ⇌ He is not a small-scale farmer.

논매기 weeding a rice paddy —논매기하다 weed a rice paddy; clear a rice paddy of weeds; remove weeds from a rice paddy

논문 論文 〈학회 등의〉 a paper; 〈학위 취득을 위한〉 a thesis; a dissertation; 〈학술적〉 a treatise; 〈문학적 소론〉 an essay
◆영문학에 관한 논문 a treatise [theme paper] on English literature / 논문을 발표하다 give [read, deliver] a paper / 논문을 심사하다 examine sb's paper (on) / 유전자에 관한 논문을 쓰다 write a thesis on genes / 대학에 학위 논문을 제출하다 submit a dissertation to a university
▶그는 전국 생화학학회에 3편의 논문을 제출했다 He submitted three papers to the National

Biochemistry Conference.
▶그는 박사학위를 취득하기 위해 대학에 폐암에 관한 논문을 제출했다 He presented [submitted] a dissertation on lung cancer to the university to obtain a doctorate.
■박사— a doctor's [doctorial] dissertation; a treatise for doctor's degree 석사— a master's thesis 졸업— a graduation thesis —시험 a thesis examination —제출[심사] the presentation [examination] of a thesis —집 a collection of learned papers

논문서 —文書 the title deed of rice field
논박 論駁 refutation; confutation —**논박하다** argue against; refute; confute ▶나는 그와 견해가 달랐으나 논박하지 못했다 I disagreed with his view, but I couldn't refute them.
논밭 rice paddies and dry fields; fields; a farm ▶그는 논밭을 부치고 있다 He cultivates the fields.
논배미 a plot [patch, strip] of rice field
논법 論法 argument; logic; reasoning
♦잘못된 논법 a false argument / 논법의 정확성 logicality; logical soundness / 논법에 맞다 [어긋나다] be logical [illogical]
▶네 논법은 뒤죽박죽이다 What you are saying is devoid of logic.
▶나는 네 논법에 따르지 못하겠다 I can't follow your argument.
▶나는 그가 항상 쓰는 논법에 굴복했다 I was overpowered by the argument he always uses.
▶그는 그 나름의 논법으로 상대방을 설득했다 He has managed to convince the other party through his peculiar line of reasoning.
■삼단— a syllogism 생략삼단— an enthymeme
논변 論辯 argument ⇨ 변론(辯論) 2
논보리 barley cultivated in a rice paddy (after a rice harvest); paddy-cultivated barley
논봉 論鋒 the force of an argument; a wordy attack ♦날카로운 논봉 a keen [an incisive] argument
논설 論說 〈사설〉 an editorial; 〈논평〉 (a) comment; (英) a leading article; a leader
♦극히 격렬한 논설 a highly explosive editorial / 신문의 전면에 이르는 논설 a full-page editorial / 사건을 논설로 다루다 devote a leader to the case; editorialize on the case
■—란 the editorial column —위원 an editorial writer; (英) a leader writer —주간 an editorial-in-chief
논술 論述 (a) statement; (a) discourse —**논술하다** state; set forth
■—고사 an essay-type test [examination]
논스톱 nonstop ▶이 열차는 대전까지 논스톱이다 This train goes nonstop to Taejŏn. ⇒ This is a nonstop (train) to Taejŏn.
논어 論語 the Analects of Confucius
논외 論外 ♦논의외의 〈문제가 안되는〉 out of the question; 〈주제에서 벗어난〉 beside the point [question]; irrelevant
논의 論議 〈토론〉 (a) discussion; 〈주장〉 (an) argument; (a) debate
♦활발한 논의 a lively discussion [exchange of views] / 논의가 되다 be under discussion / 열띤 논의를 벌이다 develop heated discussions
▶이것은 회의에서 논의의 대상이 될 것이다 This will become an object of discussion at the meeting.
—**논의하다** hold (a) discussion 《on》; discuss; argue 《about》; debate 《on, about》
♦문제를 논의하다 discuss a question; argue about [over] a problem
▶그 계획을 충분히 논의했다 We discussed the plan through and through. ⇒ We had a thorough discussion of the plan.
논자 論者 〈주장자〉 an advocate; 〈논쟁자〉 a debater; a disputant; 〈필자〉 the (present) writer
논쟁 論爭 a dispute; an argument; a controversy; a contention; a polemic
♦법률상의 논쟁 a dispute over a point of law / 원자력 잠수함에 관한 논쟁 a controversy over atomic submarines / 논쟁중인 문제 the question at issue / 논쟁을 조정[해결]하다 adjust [settle] a dispute / 논쟁에 끼어들다 enter into [join in] a dispute
▶이 사실에 대해서는 논쟁의 여지가 없다 This fact is indisputable [incontestable].
—**논쟁하다** dispute; argue; have a debate 《with sb on [about, over] the question [matter]》
▶나는 이 문제로 그와 심하게 논쟁했다 I had a hot argument with him on this matter.
■—자 a disputant —점 a point in dispute
논적 論敵 one's opponent [adversary] (in an argument [a debate])
논전 論戰 a dispute ⇨ 논쟁(論爭)
논점 論點 the point at issue [in question]; a point of argument
▶논점을 분명히 해라 Make your point clear.
▶그 질문은 논점에서 벗어난 것 같다 The question seems to be off [beside] the point.
▶그의 말은 언제나 논점에서 벗어나 있다 His talk is always off the point.
논제 論題 a subject [topic] of [for] discussion; a theme ▶오늘의 논제는 공해와 생활입니다 The subject under discussion today is pollution and our life.
논조 論調 a tone (of one's argument) ♦신문의 논조 press comments ▶그는 신랄한 논조로 정부 시책을 비판했다 He criticized the government policy severely [in a severe tone].
논죄 論罪 a debate in the process of finding or proving guilty
논증 論證 (a) proof; (an) argumentation; (a) demonstration
—**논증하다** prove; demonstrate
▶지구가 둥글다는 것을 그는 어떻게 논증했느냐? How did he prove that the earth is round?
논지 論旨 the point [gist] of an argument; the main point ▶논문의 논지를 원고지 2장에 쓰시오 Please write the main point of your paper on two pieces of manuscript paper.
논파하다 論破— refute; disprove; confute 《one's opponent》 ▶나는 그의 이론을 논파할 자신이 있다 I have enough confidence to

refute his theory.

논평 論評 (a) comment 《on, upon》; (a) commentary; (a) criticism ♦논평을 유보하다 reserve [withhold] comment ▶이 건에 관하여 그는 논평을 피했다 He avoided giving his views on this subject.
—**논평하다** criticize; review; comment

논픽션 nonfiction ♦베스트셀러 논픽션 a best-seller in nonfiction ■—작가 a nonfiction writer; a nonfictioneer

논하다 論— 1 〈토론하다〉 discuss; argue; dispute; debate; comment on
♦시사 문제를 논하다 comment on current topics ▶그들은 밤늦게까지 정치를 논하였다 They stayed up (until) late discussing politics. ▶그와 정치를 논하는 것은 잘못이다 It's no use discussing politics with him.
2 〈논제로 다루다〉 treat; deal with ▶그는 연금에 대해서 논했다 He talked on pensions.(▶talk about은 단순히 「이야기 하다」, on은 강연 등에서 「논하다」임) ▶그 기사는 정계의 여러 면을 논하고 있다 The article treated various aspects of the political world.

놀¹ a glow ⇨ 노을

놀² 〈파도〉 a billow; a large wave; an ocean swell ♦놀이 치는 바다 the billowing sea

놀다¹ 1 〈놀이를 하다〉 play; 〈즐기다〉 have a good time; amuse [enjoy] *oneself*

[解説] *play*는 보통 아이들이나 동물이 노는 경우, 또는 어른이 아이들과 함께 노는 경우에 쓴다. 어른이 노는 경우「즐기다」라는 뜻의 가장 일반적인 표현은 *have a good time*이다. *amuse oneself* 또는 *enjoy oneself*는 좀 딱딱한 표현으로 전자는 마음의 시름을 달래 만족하게 하다란 적극적인 뜻을 가지고 있으며, 후자는 결과적으로 즐기다란 뜻을 암시한다.

♦인형을 가지고 놀다 play with dolls / 놀며 시간을 보내다 play away *one's* time / 소꿉장난 [숨바꼭질, 야구]하며 놀다 play house [hide and seek, baseball] / 장기를 두면서 놀다 amuse *oneself* playing chess / 〈어린이가〉 놀러 나가다 go out to play / 노래부르며 놀다 divert *oneself* in singing
▶우리는 오후에는 해변에서 즐겁게 놀았다 In the afternoon we enjoyed ourselves [had a good time] at the seaside.
▶아이들이 뒷마당에서 놀고 있다 The children were playing [at play] in the backyard.
▶남들은 일하는데 그는 놀고 있었다 He was enjoying himself while the others were at work.
▶볼 일도 보고 놀기도 할 겸 왔습니다 I've come partly on business and partly for pleasure.
▶아이들은 노는 데 정신이 팔려 있다 The children are deep [absorbed] in play.
▶요즈음 일이 너무 바빠서 놀 틈이 없다 I am so busy with my work these days that I've got no time to enjoy myself.
▶거기는 놀러간 것이 아니라 일이 있어 갔습니다 I went there on business, not for pleasure.
2 〈방문·관광·체류하다〉 visit; make a trip; make [go on] an excursion (to)
▶또 놀러 오게 Come and see me again.
▶어제는 아저씨댁에 놀러 갔다 I went to see my uncle yesterday.
▶하루를 송도에 가서 놀았다 I went on a day trip to Songdo. ⇌ I spent a day at Songdo.
▶뉴욕에서 오는 길에 호놀룰루에서 이틀 동안 놀았다 On my way home from New York I spent two days in Honolulu.
3 〈유흥에 빠지다〉 make merry; have a spree; 〈방탕하다〉 lead a fast [dissolute] life
▶오늘 저녁 한 잔 하며 놀자 Let's have a spree tonight.
▶그는 독신이었을 때 꽤 놀았다 He spent a lot of time and money on pleasure when he was single.
4 〈하는 일 없이〉 be idle; idle 《time》 away; be doing nothing; take *one's* ease
♦놀고 먹다 eat the bread of idleness; live a life of ease
▶나는 자동차 사고 후 1년을 놀았다 After the car accident I spent a year doing nothing.
▶오늘은 하루종일 놀며 지냈다 I loafed about all day today.
▶나는 놀며 지낼 수 없다 I can't idle away my time. ⇌ I can't afford to be idle.
▶그는 일생을 놀면서 보냈다 He idled his life away. ⇌ He loafed through his life.
5 〈쓰이지 않다〉 be not in use; lie idle; be out of operation
♦놀고 있는 땅 land lying idle / 노는 기계 an unused machine; a machine not in use / 노는 자본 unemployed capital; idle [sleeping] funds
▶일손이 모자라서 놀고 있는 기계가 조금 있다 Due to a lack of manpower, some machines are not in use.
▶공장에는 노는 기계가 많다 There are a lot of machines lying idle in the factory.
6 〈직업을 잃다〉 be out of work [job]; be unemployed ♦놀고 있는 사람 an unemployed person; a jobless man ▶그는 요즘 놀고 있다 He is out of work these days.
7 〈박힌 것이 흔들리다〉 shake; be loose; totter; have play ▶나사못이 논다 The screw is loose.
8 〈멋대로 행동하다〉 behave as *one's* likes; act rashly as *one* pleases ♦멋대로 놀게 하다 allow *sb* to go [have] his (own) way; give *sb* a free hand
9 〈태아가〉 뱃속에서 아기가 놀기 시작한다 The child in the womb begins to move. ⇌ The child is quickening.

놀다² 〈윷 등을〉 throw; cast ♦윷[주사위]을 놀다 throw *yut* sticks [dice]; play *yut* [at dice]

놀라다 1 〈공포로〉 be frightened; be horrified; be startled; be alarmed
♦놀란 가슴 a startled state of mind / 놀라서 기절하다 be frightened out of *one's* senses / 놀라서 소리치다 cry out in surprise / 놀라서 정신을 차리지 못하다 be frightened out of *one's* wits 《by, at》

▶ 갑자기 개가 짖어대어 놀랐다 The sudden barking of a dog frightened [startled] me.
▶ 등산객들은 큰 곰을 보고 놀랐다 The climbers were frightened [horrified] to see a big bear.
▶ 나는 놀라서 말문이 막혔다 I was dumbfounded [flabbergasted].
▶ 내가 소리를 지르는 바람에 도둑은 놀라서 달아났다 My scream frightened the burglar away.
2 〈뜻밖의 일로〉 be surprised; be amazed [astonished]; be shocked; be startled
♦ …을 보고[듣고] 놀라다 be surprised at the sight [news]/ 깜짝 놀라다 be taken aback; have *one's* heart in *one's* mouth / 총소리에 놀라다 be startled at the sound of a gun
▶ 그녀가 그 제의를 거절하는 데 놀랐다 I was astonished to learn that she had refused that offer.
▶ 나는 그 소식을 듣고 놀랐다 I was surprised at [to hear] the news. ⇌ The news surprised me. ⇌ The news was a surprise to me.
▶ 내 개가 죽어 있는 것을 보고 나는 깜짝 놀랐다 To my great surprise [Much to my surprise], I found my dog dead.
▶ 양친께서 그 소식을 들으셨을 때 얼마나 놀라셨겠어요 You can imagine the shock [astonishment] of the parents when they heard the news.
▶ 그 헛소문은 놀랄 만큼 빠르게 퍼졌다 The false rumor spread very rapidly.
▶ 그는 놀랄 만큼 키가 크다 He is surprisingly tall.
3 〈감동하다〉 wonder [marvel] 〈at, that〉; be amazed at
♦ 놀랄 만한 wonderful; mavelous / 놀랄 만큼 wonderfully; marvelously / 놀라서 바라보다 stare in wonder; look with wonder at / 참으로 놀랄 만하다 be perfectly astonishing
▶ 누구나 그 건물의 장관에 놀란다 Everyone admires the splendor of that structure.
▶ 나는 그가 박식한 데 놀랐다 I was amazed at how much he knows. ⇌ I was much impressed by his learning.
▶ 그녀의 끈기에 놀랐다 I wondered [marveled] at her perseverance.

놀라움 surprise; astonishment; 〈경탄〉 wonder; 〈충격〉 shock; fright
▶ 그의 얼굴에 놀라움이 드러났다 His face showed his surprise. ⇌ He had a surprised look on his face.
▶ 남편이 체포되었다는 것을 알았을 때 그녀의 놀라움이 어떠했을까 How shocked she must have been to learn that her husband had been arrested!
▶ 그녀는 놀라움을 내색하지 않았다 She did not show her surprise.
▶ 그 소식을 들었을 때의 그의 놀라움을 상상할 수 있겠니? Can you imagine how astonished [amazed] he was when he heard the news?

놀랍다 surprising; amazing; astonishing; remarkable; wonderful; marvelous (▶ 이들은 보통 absolutely, quite 등으로 수식함)
♦ 놀라운 기억력 a remarkable [an astonishing] memory / 놀라운 뉴스 surprising [astonishing] news / 놀라운 발명 a wonderful invention / 놀라운 재간 wonderful [marvelous] talent / 놀랍게도 to *one's* surprise [astonishment, shock]; to *one's* dismay
▶ 그 약은 효력이 놀랍다 The drug works wonders.
▶ 그녀가 여배우가 되다니 놀랍다 It's amazing that she's going to be an actress. ⇌ I wonder that she should become an actress.
▶ 그것은 놀라운 사실이다 It is quite a surprising fact.
▶ 놀랍게도 방안에는 아무도 없었다 To my surprise, there was nobody in the room.
▶ 놀랍게도 그는 시험에 합격했다 To my great surprise [Much to my surprise], he passed the exam.

놀래다 〈놀라게 하다〉 surprise; take *sb* by surprise; astonish; startle
♦ 아무를 깜짝 놀래다 knock the breath out of *sb*; take *sb's* breath away / 새로운 이론으로 세상을 놀래다 startle the world with a new theory
▶ 그들을 깜짝 놀래 주겠다 I'll give them a surprise. ⇌ (口) I'll bowl them over.
▶ 너를 놀래줄 게 있는데 〈선물이나 소식을 전할 때〉 I have a surprise for you.

놀리다¹ **1** 〈놀게 하다〉 let *sb* play
♦ 아이들을 밖에서 놀리다 let [have] the children play outdoors
▶ 사장은 어제 그를 놀렸다 The boss gave him the day off yesterday.
▶ 그녀는 공원에서 아이들을 놀리며 돌보고 있었다 She was looking after the children playing in the park.
2 〈방치·쉬게 하다〉 leave [keep] *sb* [*sth*] idle
♦ 땅을 놀리다 keep a land idle / 학생들을 하루 놀리다 give schoolboys a holiday
▶ 이 기계[방]를 놀리는 것은 낭비다 It's a waste to leave the machine idle [not to use the room].
3 〈움직이다〉 move; operate ♦ 손발을 놀리다 move *one's* arms and legs
▶ 입 좀 작작 놀려라 Hold your tongue.
▶ 그는 무심결에 입을 잘못 놀렸다 He made a slip of the tongue.
4 〈조작하다〉 handle; manipulate ♦ 인형을 놀리다 manipulate [work] a puppet 《by strings》

놀리다² 〈조롱하다〉 tease; (口) kid; 〈장난치다〉 play a trick [practical joke] on; make fun of
▶ 그들은 그의 시골 사투리를 놀렸다 They made fun of his provincial dialect.
▶ 그는 너를 놀리고 있는 거야 He is teasing [kidding] you.
▶ 그는 젊은 여자를 놀리기 좋아한다 He enjoys teasing young women.
▶ 신경쓰지 마, 그는 그저 널 놀리느라고 그러는 거니까 Don't worry, he's only kidding you [teasing you, (口) having you on].

놀림 kidding; teasing; making fun of; banter
♦ 반 놀림조로 half for fun; half teasingly

놀림가마리 an object of ridicule ⇨ 놀림

놀림감 an object of ridicule; a laughingstock ♦놀림감으로 삼다 make sb an object of ridicule; hold sb up to ridicule
▶그는 친구들의 놀림감이 되었다 He was made fun [sport] of by his friends.
▶나는 놀림감이 되기는 싫다 I don't want to be (made) the laughingstock [object of ridicule].

놀부심사 —心思 perverseness; maliciousness; wickedness; ill-naturedness; stinginess ♦놀부심사로 하는 짓 vicious [wicked] practices

놀아나다 1 〈유흥·방탕하다〉 go [run] wild; become a playboy
▶그는 총각 때 꽤 놀아났었다 He spent a lot of time and money on pleasure when he was single. ≒ He played around [(口) led very dissipated life] when he was single.
2 〈남의 장단에〉 dance [do] after sb's tune
▶그녀는 그의 장단에 놀아났다 She played into his hands.

놀아먹다 1 〈놀고 먹다〉 be idle; idle away; (口) loaf
▶나는 놀아먹을 수 없으니 직장을 구해야 겠어 I'd like to find a job because I can't be idle [can't fool around].
2 〈방탕한 생활을 하다〉 live [lead] a fast [wild] life

놀음 play ⇨ 놀음놀이

놀음놀이 play; merrymaking; 〈오락〉 (a) pleasure; pastime ♦아이들 놀음놀이 children's play —놀음놀이하다 play; make merry; have fun
—판 the scene of a spree

놀이¹ 1 〈장난〉 play ▶병정놀이를 하다 play (at) soldiers / 카우보이 놀이를 하다 play cowboys and Indians
—놀이하다 play
2 〈오락·유흥〉 (a) pleasure; (a) recreation; a pastime; (an) amusement
♦들놀이 an outing; a picnic / 물놀이를 하다 play in the water; swim in a river; go bathing / 단풍놀이를 가다 go maple-viewing; go to enjoy the maple leaves
▶나는 부산에 놀이가 아니라 일 때문에 갔었다 I went to Pusan on business not for pleasure.
—놀이하다 have a pastime
3 〈경기〉 a game; a sport ♦아이들 놀이 a children's game / 야외 놀이 outdoor games / 윷놀이를 하다 play *yut*; throw *yut* sticks
▶수수께끼[주사위] 놀이를 하자 Let's play at riddles [dice].
—놀이하다 have [play] a game

놀이² 〈벌들이〉《bees》 swarming in spring

놀이꾼 〈놀음놀이 하는〉 a merrymaker; 〈행락객〉 a visitor to a pleasure resort; a person on an outing

놀이터 〈학교·공공의〉 a playground; a recreation ground; 〈행락지〉 a pleasure resort ♦어린이 놀이터 a playground for children

놀잇배 a pleasure boat

놀지다 surge ⇨ 놀치다

놀치다 surge; run high; swell; billow

♦놀치는 바다 the billowing [angry] sea

놈 1 〈사내〉《蔑》 a fellow; 《美俗》 a guy; a boy (▶어른에게 씀); 《英》 a chap
♦멋진 놈 a swell guy / 재미있는 놈 a jolly fellow / 좋은 놈 a nice fellow [guy, boy, chap]
▶불쌍한 놈 Poor fellow!
▶이 나쁜 놈 You rascal!
▶이 뻔뻔스러운 놈아 You shameless scoundrel!
▶참 어리석은 놈이군 What a stupid guy [fellow]!
▶그 놈은 아직 그것을 몰라 He still doesn't know it.
2 〈동물·물건〉 a thing; one
♦수놈[암놈] a male [female] one / 이 (망할) 놈의 개 this wretched dog
▶낚시하러 가서 큰 놈을 다섯 마리 낚았다 I went fishing and caught five big ones.
▶저 흰 놈을 주십시오 Give me that white one.

놈팡이 1 ⇨ 놈 1 2 〈실업자·건달〉 a jobless person; a bum; 〈여자의 상대〉 a girl's boyfriend; a gigolo

놉 a casual laborer paid by the day

놋 〈놋쇠〉 brass ■—그릇[기명] brass tableware; brassware —대야[대접] a brass basin [bowl] —요강 a brass chamber pot —점 a brassware shop; a braziery

놋쇠 brass 〈놋쇠의〉 brass; brassy ■—세공 brasswork —제품 brassware

놋좆 櫓— a thole(pin); an oarlock; an rowlock

농 弄 1 〈장난〉 fun; play; sport ♦농으로 (just) for [in] fun; in [for] sport; in play
▶신경쓰지마, 농으로 그런 것 뿐이야 Don't be upset. It was only in fun.
2 〈농담〉 a joke ▶농으로 말한 거야 I said it in joke.

농 膿 pus ⇨ 고름

농 籠 1 〈버들채 함〉 a wicker basket; a (wicker) trunk [suitcase]; a wardrobe trunk
2 〈장농〉 a wardrobe; a chest of drawers

농가 農家 〈집〉 a farmer's house; a farmhouse (농장주의); 〈가정〉 a farming family (전가족이 농민); a farmer's family (세대주가 농민)
▶농가는 가을에 수확으로 바쁘다 Farmers are busy harvesting in the fall.
▶그는 농가에서 자랐다 He was brought up on a farm.

농간 弄奸 a trick; wiles; an evil scheme; a wicked design ♦농간(을) 부리다 play [use] tricks
▶그녀가 너에게 농간을 부리기는 간단하다 It is easy for her to twist you around [round] her finger.
▶그는 그녀의 농간에 쉽게 걸려들었다 He fell an easy victim to her trick.
▶나는 그의 농간에 돈을 잃었다 I fell a prey to his wiles and lost my money.
—농간하다 use tricks; carry out a wicked design; lay plots; scheme

농게 籠— 《動》 a sand crab

농경 農耕 farming; 〈경작〉 cultivation ♦농경에 적합한 땅 land suitable for farming ■—민

농공 農工 agriculture and industry
농과 農科 〈학과〉 the department of agriculture; 〈과정〉 an agricultural course ━**대학** a college of agriculture
농구 農具 a farm(ing) tool; farm(ing) implements
농구 籠球 basketball ━**공** a basketball ━**선수** a basketball player ━**코트** a basketball court ━**팀** a basketball team ━**화** basketball shoes; sneakers
농군 農軍 a farmer [farmhand] ⇨ 농민
농기 農期 〈농사철〉 the farming season
농기계 農機械 agricultural machines; farm machinery
농기구 農器具 a farm(ing) tool; farm(ing) [agricultural] implements
농노 農奴 a serf; 〈신분〉 serfdom ━**━해방** emancipation of serfs
농담 弄談 a joke; a jest; fun; a wisecrack; a crack
♦ 가벼운 농담 a light jest / 농담을 좋아하는 사람 a jesting man
▶ 농담이겠지 Now you are joking.
〈농담이[은]〉 그는 농담이 통하지 않는 사람이다 He doesn't get [see] the joke. ≒ He has no sense of humor.
▶ 농담이 지나치군 You are carrying a joke too far. ≒ It is [has gone] beyond a joke.
▶ 이건 농담이 아냐 It's no joke. ≒ I mean what I say. ≒ It's no joking matter.
▶ 농담이 진담된다 What was said as a joke comes true.
▶ 농담은 접어두고 본론으로 돌아가자 Joking apart [aside], let's return to the main subject.
〈농담을〉 농담을 하다 tell *sb* a joke, joke (with *sb* about *sth*); make a crack (about) / 농담을 건네다 make a joke (at); pass a pleasantry (to)
▶ 그는 농담을 하고 있을 뿐이다 He is only joking.
▶ 어머니께서는 농담을 진담으로 받아들이셨다 My mother took the joke seriously.
▶ 그는 농담을 잘 받아 넘긴다 He knows how to take a joke.
▶ 그는 긴장을 풀려고 줄곧 농담을 했다 He kept telling jokes to ease the tension.
〈농담으로〉 농담으로 jestingly; in joke [jest]; out of fun; in fun / 반농담으로 half in jest / 농담으로 돌리다 take *sth* as a joke
▶ 나는 그저 농담으로 말했을 뿐이야 I said it only in play [fun]. ≒ I meant it for a joke.
▶ 농담으로라도 그런 말은 하지 마라 Don't say such a thing even in jest.
▶ 농담으로 한 말을 진담으로 받아들이지 말아 주십시오 Please don't take seriously what we meant as a joke.
━**농담하다** joke; crack a joke; jest; poke fun (at); pass a pleasantry
농담 濃淡 light and shade; 〈그 정도〉 a shade
♦ 그림에 농담을 나타내다 shade a picture [drawing]
▶ 이 방의 색조는 갈색의 농담을 기조로 하고 있다 The color scheme of the room makes use of several shades of brown.
━**법** 〔畫〕 shading; chiaroscuro
농도 濃度 〈액체 등의〉 〔化〕 concentration; 〔物〕 density; thickness; 〈색의〉 depth; 〈차·커피의〉 strength
♦ 높은 농도의 염분을 함유하다 contain high concentrations of salt
▶ 교차로 부근은 일산화탄소의 농도가 꽤 높았다 The air around the intersection contained a rather high density of carbon monoxide.
━**계** 〔光〕 densitometer
농들다 膿━ 〈곪다〉 maturate; form pus; suppurate; fester
농땡이 idleness; 〈사람〉 a lazy person; **(口)** a lazybones
♦ 농땡이 치다 idle away; idle about; neglect (*one's* work)
▶ 그 녀석은 항상 농땡이를 치고 있다 He is always loathing on the job.
▶ 나는 농땡이 칠 틈이 없다 I have no time to idle away.
농락 籠絡 cajolement; toying
━**농락하다** cajole *sb* into doing; entice; make *sb* (his) puppet; 〈특히 여자 등을〉 make sport (of); sport [toy] (with)
♦ 여자를 농락하다 make sport of a woman / 남자에게 농락하다 fall a prey to a man's lust
▶ 그는 결코 돈에 농락당할 사람이 아니다 He is the last man to be enticed with money.
농루 膿漏 (a) purulent discharge; pyorrhea
농림 農林 agriculture and forestry
농마 農馬 a plow horse
농목 農牧 agriculture and stock raising
농무 農務 agricultural affairs; farming; 〈행정〉 agricultural administration ━**부** [장관] 〈미국의〉 the Department [Secretary] of Agriculture
농무 濃霧 a thick [dense, heavy] fog ▶ 등산객들은 농무로 길을 잃었다 The climbers lost their way in a dense fog.
농민 農民 〈자작농〉 a farmer; 〈한 지방의〉 the farming population; 〈농장 노동자〉 a farm laborer [worker]; a farmhand; 〈소작인·소농〉 a peasant

> [解說] *farmer*는「상당한 규모의 경작지를 소유하고 있는 사람, 농장주」의 뜻이며, *farm laborer* [*worker*], *farmhand*는 farmer에 의해 고용되어 있는 사람을 가리킨다. *peasant*는 옛날의 소농 또는 개발도상국의 빈농의 이미지가 강하여 최근에는 일반적으로 쓰이지 않는다.

♦ 가난한 농민 a poor peasant; a petty farmer / 농민의 삶 a farmer's life; a peasant life
━**문학[예술]** peasant literature [art] ━**봉기** a peasants' uprising; 〈1381년 영국의〉 the Peasants' Revolt ━**사회** a farming [rural] community ━**운동** a peasant movement
농번기 農繁期 the farmer's busiest season; a busy season for farmers

■—휴가 〈학교의〉 the school holidays in the busy farming season; 〈군대의〉 a leave in the busy farming season
농법 農法 farming methods [techniques]; agricultural methods ■—유기— organic agriculture [farming]
농병아리 〔鳥〕 a grebe; a didapper
농본주의 農本主義 physiocracy; the "agriculture-first" principle; the principle of having a country's economy on agriculture
■—자 a physiocrat
농부 農夫 〈농장 노동자〉 a farm worker [laborer]; a farmhand; 〈소작농〉 a tenant farmer; a peasant; 〈자작농〉 a farmer
농사 農事 farming; farm work; agricultural affairs ♦농사를 짓다 farm; engage in agriculture [farming]
▶ 금년에는 농사가 잘 되었다 The crops are good this year.
■—꾼 a farmer; a farm laborer —시험장 an agricultural experiment station; an experimental farm —일 farm work; farming —철 the farming season
농산물 農産物 farm products [produce]; agricultural products [produce]; crops
▶ 귤은 이 지방의 주요 농산물이다 Tangerines are the main [staple] agricultural produce [products] of this district.
■—가격 farm (product) prices : 농산물 가격이 10% 급등했다 Farm product prices shot up by 10 percent. —가격유지제도 a system for shoring up farm prices —수출국 an agricultural exporter
농성 籠城 1 〈성을 지킴〉 holding a castle —농성하다 hold a castle; be besieged ▶ 적의 공격으로 우리는 오랫동안 농성했다 We stood a long siege against the attack of the enemy.
2 〈파업의 한 방법〉 a sit-in; a sit-down (strike) —농성하다 go on a sit-down (strike); stage a sit-down demonstration
▶ 근로자들은 임금 인상을 요구하며 농성했다 The workmen went on a sit-in [sit-down] strike demanding a wage increase.
■—군 a besieged army; the besieged —투쟁 a sit-down strike
농수산물 農水産物 agricultural and marine [aquatic] products; agro-fishery products; agro-marine items
농아 聾啞 deafness and dumbness; 〈사람〉 a deaf-and-dumb person; a deaf-mute; (총칭) 〈청각 장애인〉 the aurally handicapped
■—교육 education of the deaf and dumb —학교 a deaf-and-dumb school; a school for the aurally handicapped
농악 農樂 instrumental music of peasants; a farm music ■—대 a farm [peasant] band
농액 濃液 a thick liquid; a concentrated solution
농약 農藥 agricultural chemicals [medicine]; 〈살충제〉 insecticide
♦농약을 뿌리다 spread [sprinkle] agricultural chemicals
▶ 토마토에는 농약을 치지 마라 Don't dust tomatoes with insecticides.

■—생물— biological pesticide ■—살포 spreading [sprinkling] insecticides —중독 poisoning by agricultural chemicals; 〈특히 파라티온에 의한〉 parathion poisoning
농양 膿瘍 〔醫〕 an abscess; a boil
농어 〔魚〕 a sea bass; a perch
농어민 農漁民 farmers and fishermen
농어촌 農漁村 fishing and agrarian [farming] villages
농업 農業 agriculture; farming
♦농업의 기계화 mechanization of agriculture / 기계화된 농업 mechanized agriculture / 농업의 agricultural; farming / 농업에 종사하다 engage in agriculture [farming]; be a farmer
▶ 이곳은 특히 농업이 활발한 지역이다 This is a heavily agricultural district.
■—집약[조방(粗放)]— intensive [extensive] agriculture —경영 agricultural [farm] management —경제 agricultural economy —경제학 agricultural economics —고교 an agricultural high school —교육 agricultural education —국 an agricultural [a farming] country —기술 agricultural techniques —인구 the farming population —정책 (an) agricultural policy —혁명 an agricultural revolution
농업협동조합 農業協同組合 an agricultural cooperative (association) —중앙회 the National Agricultural Cooperative Federation
농예 農藝 agricultural technology; (the art of) growing plants; husbandry; 〈농업과 원예〉 agriculture and horticulture; farming and gardening —화학 agricultural chemistry
농우 農牛 a plow ox; (총칭) farming cattle
농원 農園 a farm; a plantation ♦농원을 경영하다 run [keep] a farm / 농원에서 일하다 work on a farm —주 the proprietor of a farm
농자천하지대본 農者天下之大本 Agriculture is the foundation of a nation [the basis of national existence].
농작물 農作物 the crops; farm produce [products]; agricultural produce ♦농작물을 해치다 injure the crops
▶ 금년에는 농작물이 잘 안 되었다 The crops are very bad this year. ⇌ The harvest has turned out bad this year.
농장 農場 a farm; 〈대규모 특용작물의〉 a plantation; 〈부속 건물 포함〉 a farmstead
▶ 그는 캘리포니아에서 농장을 경영하고 있다 He runs a farm in California.
▶ 그는 농장에서 일한다 He works on a farm [plantation].
■—실험— an experimental farm ■—관리인 a farm bailiff —노동자 a farm worker [laborer]; a farm hand —인도가격 〔商〕 a price ex farm —주 farmland proprietor; a farmer; a 〈cotton, coffee, sugar〉 planter
농정 農政 agricultural administration
농지 農地 farmland; agricultural [farming] land ♦농지를 개발하다 develop farmland
■—개량 improvement of farmland —개혁 a farmland [an agricultural] reform —제도 a farmland system

농지거리 弄— joking; bantering; jesting
—농지거리하다 joke; crack [make] a joke; banter; jest; poke fun 《at》; pass pleasantries 《with》
▶그는 그 여자와 농지거리하는 사이다 He is on joking terms with her.

농촌 農村 a farm [farming] village; 〈지역〉 a farm [farming, rural, agricultural] district; 〈사회〉 a rural community
♦농촌 생활 farm life / 농촌 청년 farm [rural] youth / 농촌의 완전 전기화 complete electrification of rural districts / 농촌의 rural; agricultural; agrarian
■**—경제** rural economy **—계몽** enlightenment of the farmers **—문제** the problems of farming areas **—봉사활동** enlightenment service for rural communities **—사회학** rural sociology **—인구** the rural population **—지대** an agricultural area; a rural district **—지도원** an agricultural agent; (美) a country [an extension] agent **—진흥** development of an agricultural community **—진흥청** Rural Development Administration

농축 濃縮 enrichment; concentration **—농축하다** concentrate; condense; enrich
■**—오렌지 주스** concentrated orange juice; orange juice concentrate **—우라늄** enriched [concentrated] uranium; uranium concentrate **—우유** condensed milk

농탕치다 弄蕩— carry on [flirt] with 《one's girl friend》; philander [dally, fondle] with 《sb, each other》; be jolly with 《a girl》; bill and coo; (俗) spoon
▶그들은 사람들 앞에서 [공공연히] 농탕치고 있었다 They were necking in public.

농토 農土 farmland; agricultural [farming] land; cropland ♦메마른 농토 a barren [sterile] land / 비옥한 농토 fertile land ■**—확장** expansion of farmland

농포 膿疱 〔醫〕〈고름집〉 a pustule; a pus blister ■**—진**(疹) pustular eruption

농학 農學 (the science of) agriculture
■**—과**[**부**] the agricultural department; the school 〔英〕 faculty of agriculture **—사**[**박사**]〈사람〉 a bachelor [doctor] of agriculture; 〈학위〉 Bachelor [Doctor] of Agriculture (略 B. [D.] Agr.) **—자** an agricultur(al)ist

농한기 農閑期 the agricultural off-season; the leisure season for farmers; the farmers' slack season

농협 農協 an agricultural cooperative (association) ⇨ 농업협동조합

농회색 濃灰色 charcoal gray

농후 濃厚 〈짙음〉 thickness; density
—농후하다 thick; dense; 〈영양분 등이〉 rich
♦농후한 색채 a heavy [rich] color / 농후해지다 deepen; become marked [strong, conspicuous]
▶그는 수회 혐의가 농후하다 He is strongly suspected of bribery. ⇒ There are strong suspicions that he has taken bribes.
▶우리는 패색이 농후했다 The odds were against us. ⇒ Our defeat seemed certain.
▶그의 재선 가능성이 농후해졌다 The prospects for his reelection have become very hopeful [good]. ⇒ There is a stronger possibility that he will be reelected.
■**—비료** concentrated fertilizer **—사료** concentrated fodder [feed]

높낮이 〈고저〉 high and low; 〈소리의〉 (a) pitch; modulation ♦높낮이가 있는 fluctuating; uneven / 높낮이가 없는 even; level

높다 1 〈높이가〉 high(↔low); tall; raised; lofty
♦높은 곳 a high place; a height / 높은 나무 a tall [towering] tree / 높은 산 a high [lofty] mountain / 아주 높다 be sky-high
▶파도가 높다 The waves are high. ⇒ The sea is running high.
▶세계에서 제일 높은 산은 무슨 산이냐? What is the highest mountain in the world?
2 〈지위 등이〉 high; lofty; exalted; noble; superior
♦높은 사람 a dignitary; a personage; (口) a VIP; a bigwig / 수준이 높은 학교 a school of high academic standing / 지위가 높다 be high in rank
▶그의 아저씨는 사회적 지위가 높다 His uncle has [holds] a high social position.
3 〈명성 등이〉 widely known; high
♦명성이 높은 사람 a person of high reputation / 평판이 높다 be famous; be well known
▶김선생의 그림은 프랑스에서 평판이 높은 것 같다 Mr. Kim's pictures seem to be held in high esteem in France.
4 〈소리·음성이〉 loud; high(-pitched); stentorian
♦높은 목소리 a high-pitched voice / 높은 목소리로 in a loud voice; loudly; in a treble
▶라디오 소리가 너무 높다. 조금 낮추어라 The radio is too loud. Please turn it down a little.
5 〈값·비용이〉 high (in price); expensive; high-priced
♦높은 급료 a high [large] salary / 높은 생활비 a high cost of living
▶물가가 높다 Prices are high.
▶생활비가 5년 전보다 배나 높다 Living costs are twice as high as they were five years ago.
6 〈도수·율이〉 high
♦높은 비율 a high rate / 도수 높은 안경 strong [powerful, thick] glasses / 높은 이자로 at a high interest / 체온이 높다 have a high temperature
▶환자가 열이 높다 The patient has a high fever.

높다랗다 remarkably [rather] high; lofty

높아지다 rise; be raised; get [grow, become] higher; be elevated; be promoted; increase
♦지위가 높아지다 rise in position; be raised to a higher position
▶흥분하면 혈압이 높아진다 The excitement will raise out blood pressure. ⇒ If we get excited, our blood pressure goes up.
▶고도가 높아짐에 따라 기온은 내려간다 The air grows cooler with height.

높이¹ 1 〈고도〉 height; altitude
▶그 탑은 높이가 15미터다 The tower is fifteen meters high [in height].

높이²

▶ 이 비행기는 1만 미터의 높이에서 날고 있습니다 This plane is flying at an altitude of ten thousand meters.
▶ 그는 10미터 높이에서 떨어졌다 He fell from a height of ten meters.
2 〈음성의〉 pitch; loudness (크기) ▶ 그 가수의 음성의 높이는 테너다 The voice of the singer is tenor in pitch.

높이² **1** 〈높게〉 high; highly; aloft
♦ 하늘 높이 날다 fly high up in the sky / 손을 높이 들다 hold *one's* hand up high / 높이 뛰다 [올라가다] jump [climb] high / 높이 쳐들다 raise 《a thing》 high [aloft]/ 높이 평가하다 highly appreciate [value]
▶ 그의 새 소설은 높이 평가되고 있다 His new novel is valued highly. ⇒ They think highly of his new novel.
2 〈소리를 높여〉 loud; loudly; in a high pitch; in a loud voice; in a shrill voice ♦ 소리 높이 《sing》 in a loud [high] voice

높이다 **1** 【높게 하다】 〈높이를〉 make higher; heighten; elevate; raise; 〈정도를〉 promote; lift; raise; heighten 《an effect》
♦ 가치를 높이다 enhance the value / 담장을 높이다 make a wall higher / 명성을 높이다 increase *one's* reputation / 사기를 높이다 raise [boost] morale / 수준을 높이다 raise [lift] the level / 여성의 사회적 지위를 높이다 raise women's social status / 제품의 질을 높이다 improve [better] the quality of a product
▶ 그는 화가 나서 언성을 높였다 He raised his voice in anger.
▶ 대담한 원색 사용이 효과를 높이고 있다 The bold use of primary colors has heightened the effect.
▶ 교양을 높이려면 많은 책을 읽어야 한다 You must read a lot of books to cultivate [improve] your mind.
2 〈받들다〉 respect; esteem; honor; reverence
♦ 말을 높이다 use an honorific expression [word] / 왕을 신처럼 높이다 deify a king / 높여 말하다 use polite expressions to show respect

높이뛰기 《do》 a high jump ■ 장대— a pole vault [jump]: 장대 높이뛰기 선수 a pole vaulter [jumper] 제자리— the standing high jump ■ —선수 a high jumper

높직이 rather high

높직하다 rather [somewhat] high; slightly elevated; 〈목소리가〉 rather loud

놓다¹ **1** 〈두다〉 put 《down》; set; place; lay; 〈남겨두다〉 leave behind
♦ 책을 책상 위에 놓다 put a book on the desk / 펜을 놓다 lay [put] down *one's* pen
▶ 전부 원래 있던 자리에 놓으시오 Put everything back where it belongs.
▶ 그는 명함을 놓고 갔다 He left his card.
▶ 이것을 놓을 자리가 있겠니? Is there a place for this [to put this]?
▶ 메모를 책상 위에 놓아둘테니 보아라 I'll leave the note on the desk for you to read.
2 〈잡은 것을〉 let *sth* [*sb*] go [off]; set free; turn [let] loose
▶ 그것을 놓아라 Let it go.
▶ 그는 밧줄을 놓았다 He let go 《his hold》 of the rope.
▶ 그는 핸들을 놓았다 He took his hands off the wheel.
3 〈안심하다〉 ease; set 《*one's* mind》 at ease; give 《*one's* mind》 relief
▶ 그녀의 편지에 나는 마음 놓았다 Her letter set me at ease. ⇒ I was relieved to see her letter.
▶ 이제 한시름 놓았다 Well, now I can forget about it for a while.
▶ 그 사람이라면 마음 놓고 일을 맡겨도 된다 You may trust him to do the work for you.
▶ 다가오는 시험을 생각하면 마음을 놓을 수가 없다 The thought of the coming exam worries me.
4 〈시설·가설하다〉 install; lay
▶ 마을 사람들이 내에 다리를 놓았다 The village people built a bridge across the stream. ⇒ The village people bridged the stream.
▶ 이 다리는 튼튼하게 돌로 놓았다 This bridge is solidly built of stone.
▶ 곧 전화를 놓겠습니다 We'll have a telephone installed pretty soon.
5 〈발사하다〉 fire; shoot ♦ 대포를 놓다 fire a cannon / 폭약을 놓다 fire [set off] a charge of dynamite / 한 방 놓다 fire a shot; have a shot
6 〈불을〉 set fire ▶ 적군이 성에 불을 놓았다 The enemy troops set the castle on fire [set fire to the castle].
7 〈주사·침 등을〉 ♦ 주사를 놓다 inject; give a shot [an injection to] / 침을 놓다 acupuncture; apply acupuncture
▶ 간호사는 내게 독감 예방 주사를 놓았다 The nurse gave me an injection vaccinated against the flu.
8 〈중간에 사람을 두다[보내다]〉 put in; send ♦ 첩자를 놓다 set [employ] a spy 《on》; send out a spy / 사람을 놓아 수소문하다 get information through an agent; send a person for information / 제3자를 놓아 교섭하다 negotiate through a third party
▶ 나는 그를 중간에 놓아 그 회사와 계약을 맺었다 I made the contract with the company through his mediation.
9 〈덫을〉 set; lay ▶ 우리는 여우를 잡으려고 덫을 놓았다 We set [laid] a trap [snare] for a fox.
10 〈자수를〉 ♦ 수를 놓은 블라우스 an embroidered blouse / 수를 놓다 do [lay, make] embroidery 《on》; embroider
11 〈주판·셈을〉 ♦ 주판을 놓다 use an abacus; calculate on the abacus / 비용을 놓아 보다 estimate the expense ▶ 주판을 놓아 봅시다 Let's calculate it on the abacus.
12 〈값을〉 ♦ 값을 놓다 price; name the price
▶ 당신이 값을 놓으시오 You name [set] the price.
13 〈빌려주다〉 ♦ 2푼 이자로 돈을 놓다 loan [《英》 lend] money at 2 percent interest / 사무실을 세를 놓다 lease office space
▶ 그녀는 학생들에게 방을 놓아 살고 있다 She

makes a living by renting rooms to students.
14 〈그치다〉 stop; give up; put an end to
♦붓을 놓다 quit [give up] writing; close *one's* letter / 수저를 놓다 finish *one's* meal / 일손을 놓다 stop working;〈쉬다〉take [have] a rest; rest [break] (from *one's* work)
▶일손을 놓지 마라 Go on with your work.
15 〈돈을 걸다〉 pay money for *sth*; wager
♦만원을 놓고 결혼 점을 치다 consult a fortuneteller [have *one's* fortune told] about *one's* marriage with a fee of ten thousand won
▶돈을 놓고 바둑을 두면 안 된다 It's no good to play *paduk* for money.
16 〈속력을 내다〉〈속력을 놓다 speed up ▶이 길에서는 속력을 놓을 수 있다 We can speed up [drive fast] on this road.
17 〈있는 힘을 다하다〉♦목을 놓아 울다 cry unrestrainedly [vehemently]
18 〈말을 낮추다〉♦말을 놓다 do not use polite expressions to *sb*; omit a term of respect for *sb*; relax *one's* honorifics
19 〈바둑을 접어주다〉♦석점을 놓다 accept a three-stone handicap
20 〈기르다〉raise; rear; keep ♦누에를 놓다 raise [keep] silkworms
21 〈심어 가꾸다〉sow; plant ♦참외를 놓다 sow melon seeds ▶그들은 밭에 수박을 놓았다 They seeded the field with watermelon.
22 〈기타〉♦엄포를 놓다 threaten; menace / 퇴짜를 놓다 reject; turn down / 훼방을 놓다 disturb; interfere with; obstruct
▶그는 충분한 이유도 없이 내 제안을 퇴짜 놓았다 He turned down [refused, rejected] my offer without any good reason.
▶그들은 그 문제를 놓고 열띤 논쟁을 벌였다 They had a heated [hot] dispute [argument] on the matter.
▶엄포를 놓으니까 그는 잠잠해졌다 He was intimidated into silence.
▶그의 일에 훼방을 놓지 마라 Don't disturb [hinder] him in his work.

놓다[2] 〈…해 두다〉keep; have; leave
♦등잔불을 켜놓다 leave the light burning [on] / 문을 열어 놓다 leave [keep] the door open / 방을 깨끗이 정돈해 놓다 have *one's* room clean and tidy

놓아두다 1 〈어떤 자리에〉lay; put; leave
♦몇 그루의 나무는 베고 나머지는 놓아두다 cut down a few trees and leave the others
▶책은 그대로[책상 위에] 놓아두어라 Leave the book where it is [on the table].
▶그것을 여기다 놓아 두시오 Leave it here, please.
▶그것은 그대로 놓아두면 안 된다 You must not leave as it is.
2 〈내버려두다〉keep; allow; let
▶마음대로 하게 놓아두어라 Let him have his own way.
▶홍차가 너무 묽으니 더 우러나게 놓아두시오 The tea is too weak; let it stand for a little while.

놓아먹이다 pasture [graze] 《cattle》; feed 《cattle》 by grazing; put 《sheep》 to grazing; leave 《a dog》 at large
♦놓아먹이는 닭 yard fowls / 염소를 놓아먹이다 put the goats out to pasture; turn the goats out to graze
▶여름에는 그들은 소를 산허리에 놓아먹인다 In summer they leave the cattle to graze on the hillsides.

놓아주다 let go [off]; set free; let escape
♦잡은 물고기를 놓아주다 put the fish back into the water / 새[죄수]를 놓아주다 set a bird [prisoner] free / 토끼를 들에 놓아주다 set a rabbit free [let a rabbit loose] in the field
▶치어는 놓아주되 큰 고기는 놓치지 마라 Set a fry free, but never lose a big fish.

놓이다 1 〈물건이〉be put [placed, laid, set]
♦개울에 놓인 다리 a bridge spanning a stream / 텔레비전 위에 놓인 램프 a lamp set on the TV / 식탁에 놓여 있다 be set [placed] on the table
2 〈마음이〉feel [be] relieved 《about》; feel at rest [ease]; feel easy 《about》; be relaxed
♦한시도 마음이 놓일 때가 없다 have no moment of ease
▶그가 무사히 도착해서 마음이 놓였다 His safe arrival set my mind at ease.
▶그 소식을 듣고 한결 마음이 놓였다 I was greatly relieved at the news.

놓치다 1 〈잡은[잡을] 것을〉lose; miss; fail to capture; let [turn] 《a captive》 loose; 〈들고 있던 것을〉drop 《a bottle》; let *sth* slip [go]
♦도둑을 놓치다 fail to arrest [capture] a thief / 잡은 물고기를 놓치다 lose a fish / 죄수를 놓치다 let a prisoner escape
▶1루수는 포수가 던진 공을 놓쳤다 The first baseman missed a ball thrown by the catcher.
▶놓친 고기가 더 크다 《속담》 It is the fish you lost that is biggest. ⇒ The fish that got away is always big.
▶저 놈을 놓치지 마라 Don't let him get away.
2 〈간과하다〉overlook; pass over; 〈기회 등을〉lose; miss; fail
♦놓칠 수 없는 기회 an opportunity not to be missed; a golden opportunity / 좋은 취직 자리를 놓치다 let a good position pass
▶그 팀은 우승컵을 놓쳤다 The team failed to win a trophy.
▶나는 좋은 기회를 놓쳤다 I let the chance slip by [get away]. ⇒ I missed [lost] the good chance.
▶듣다가 가장 중요한 점을 놓쳤다 I failed to hear [catch] the most important point.
▶나는 한 마디도 놓치지 않으려고 주의해서 들었다 I listened attentively so as not to miss a single word.
3 〈모습을〉lose sight of 《*one's* companions》; 〈혼적을〉lose track of
♦시야에서 놓치지 않다 keep 《a thing》 in sight; keep sight [track] of
▶우리는 번잡한 거리에서 그의 모습을 놓쳤다 We lost sight [track] of him on the busy street.
▶형사는 그 수상한 남자를 놓쳤다 The detective lost track of the suspicious man.
4 〈차를〉miss [be too late for] 《*one's* train》

▶ 나는 수원행 막차를 놓쳤다 I missed the last train for Suwon.

뇌 腦 the brain; a cerebrum; 〔解〕〈뇌수〉 the encephalon

♦ 뇌의 cerebral; encephalic / 뇌의 작용 cerebration; brain action / 뇌를 쓰는 일 brain [mental] work / 뇌를 수술하다 operate on sb's brain / 뇌를 쓰다[과중하게 쓰다] tax [overtax] one's brains

▶ 그는 뇌에 이상이 있다 He has a brain disorder. ⇌ He has something wrong in the [with his] brain.

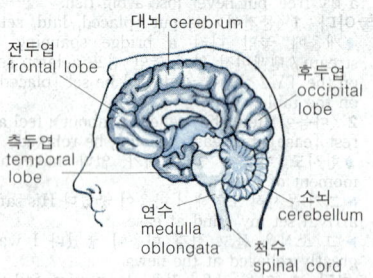

뇌

대뇌 cerebrum
전두엽 frontal lobe
후두엽 occipital lobe
측두엽 temporal lobe
연수 medulla oblongata
소뇌 cerebellum
척수 spinal cord

뇌간 腦幹 〔解〕 the brain stem
뇌격 雷擊 attacking with torpedoes; a torpedo attack ─**뇌격하다** attack with torpedoes; torpedo ♦ 적함을 뇌격하다 torpedo an enemy ship ■─기 a torpedo carrier [plane, bomber] ─전 torpedo warfare
뇌관 雷管 a percussion cap; a detonator; an exploder ■─장치 a percussion lock ─화약 percussion powder
뇌까리다 repeat; reiterate the same remark unpleasantly
뇌다 1 〈체에 치다〉 sift 《flour》 through a sieve of finer mesh

2 〈되풀이하다〉 repeat; reiterate ♦ 같은 말을 뇌다 repeat oneself; go on (and on) 《about a matter》; say over and over again; harp on the same string [topic]

뇌동 雷同 blind following ⇨ 부화뇌동(附和雷同)
뇌동맥경화증 腦動脈硬化症 〔醫〕 cerebral arteriosclerosis
뇌락하다 磊落─ openhearted; broad-minded ▶ 그는 〈호방〉뇌락한 사람이다 He is an unaffected [a frank] man.
뇌랗다 sickly yellow
뇌리 腦裡 one's mind; one's memory

♦ 뇌리에 떠오르다 cross [come across] one's mind / 뇌리에서 떠나지 않다 haunt one [one's memory]; be ever present [haunt] in one's mind

▶ 어떤 생각이 뇌리를 스쳤다 An idea occurred to me [crossed my mind].

▶ 그는 그 가르침을 항상 뇌리에 새겨 두고 있었다 He always kept [bore] that teaching in mind.

뇌막 腦膜 〔醫〕 meninges encephali ■─염 〔醫〕 cerebral meningitis
뇌명 雷名 〈뇌성대명〉 a resounding name; worldwide fame

▶ 그는 재계에 뇌명을 떨치고 있는 경영자다 He is a manager who has won wide fame [is widely known] in the business world.

뇌명 雷鳴 〈천둥소리〉 thunder; a thunderclap ▶ 요란한 뇌명이 들렸다 I heard a loud crash [clap] of thunder. ▶ 어젯밤에 뇌명이 울렸다 It thundered last night.
뇌문 雷紋 〔建〕 a fret; a meander; a key pattern ■─세공 fretwork
뇌물 賂物 a bribe; 《俗》 grease; palm oil; 《美》 graft

♦ 뇌물이 통하는 bribable; corruptible / 뇌물이 통하지 않는 unbribable; incorruptible / 뇌물을 주다[받다] offer [take] a bribe / 뇌물로 매수하다 buy off sb

▶ 그들은 그 공무원에게 뇌물을 주었다 They offered [gave] a bribe to the official.

▶ 회사는 공무원에게 뇌물을 주어 그 입찰가격을 알아냈다 The company bribed government officials into leaking the bidding price. ⇌ The company greased government officials' palms in order to leak the bidding price.

▶ 그는 뇌물을 받을 사람이 아니다 He is above bribery.

■─사건 a bribery case; a graft case ─수뢰자 a bribee; 《美俗》 a boodler ─제공자 a briber
뇌병 腦病 a brain disease; brainsickness
뇌병원 腦病院 a mental hospital ⇨ 정신병원
뇌빈혈 腦貧血 〔醫〕 (have) cerebral anemia; anemia of the brain ▶ 그녀는 일하는 도중에 뇌빈혈을 일으켰다 She had an attack of cerebral anemia in the midst of her work.
뇌사 腦死 brain death
뇌성 雷聲 thunder ─벽력 thunder and lightning
뇌성소아마비 腦性小兒痲痺 〔醫〕 cerebral infantile paralysis [polio]
뇌세포 腦細胞 〔醫〕 a brain cell
뇌쇄 惱殺 ♦ 뇌쇄적인 눈 bewitching [enchanting] eyes / 뇌쇄적인 웃음 a fascinating [seductive] smile; a smile that wins sb's heart away; a winning smile / 뇌쇄적인 눈길을 던지다 cast a killing glance [eye] 《at》 ▶ 그녀의 미모는 뇌쇄적이다 Her beauty is enchanting [irresistible].

─**뇌쇄하다** fascinate; enchant; captivate; bewitch; charm ♦ 남자를 뇌쇄시키는 힘 man-killing power

▶ 그는 그녀의 미모에 뇌쇄당했다 He was captivated with her beauty.

뇌수 腦髓 〔解〕 the brain; the encephalon 《pl. -la》
뇌수술 腦手術 a surgical operation on brain ─**뇌수술하다** do [perform, conduct] an operation on the brain
뇌신경 腦神經 〔解〕 a cerebral nerve ■─세포 a brain cell ─외과 neurosurgery ─절(節) a cerebral ganglion
뇌실 腦室 〔解〕 a cerebral ventricle

뇌연화(증) 腦軟化(症) 〔醫〕 softening of the brain

뇌염 腦炎 〔醫〕 encephalitis; cerebritis; phrenitis ◆뇌염의 발생 an outbreak of encephalitis / 뇌염을 앓다 suffer from encephalitis ■유행성— epidemic encephalitis ■—모기 a culex 《pl. -lices》

뇌외과 腦外科 brain surgery ■—의(醫) a brain surgeon

뇌우 雷雨 a thunderstorm; a thundershower ▶오늘 오후에는 뇌우가 닥칠 것이다 We'll have a thunderstorm this afternoon.
▶우리는 세찬 뇌우를 만났다 We were caught in a heavy thunderstorm.

뇌운 雷雲 a thundercloud; 〈소나기 구름〉 a thunderhead ▶뇌운이 몰려들고 있다 Thunderclouds are gathering.

뇌일혈 腦溢血 〔醫〕〈뇌출혈〉 cerebral hemorrhage; (a stroke [fit] of) apoplexy ◆뇌일혈을 일으키다 have a fit [stroke] of [be seized with] apoplexy; be stricken with a cerebral hemorrhage / 뇌일혈로 쓰러지다 have a cerebral hemorrhage

뇌장 腦漿 〈뇌속의 점액〉 the fluid in the brain

뇌장해 腦障害 a brain injury

뇌조 雷鳥 〔鳥〕 a snow grouse; a ptarmigan [táːrmigən]

뇌졸중 腦卒中 〔醫〕 cerebral apoplexy ◆뇌졸중에 걸리다 have a fit of cerebral apoplexy ■—(성) 발작 an apoplectic stroke

뇌종양 腦腫瘍 a cerebral tumor; 〔醫〕 an encephaloma 《pl. -mata》

뇌진탕 腦震蕩 〔醫〕 (a) concussion; a concussion of the brain
◆뇌진탕으로 앓다 suffer from (a brain) concussion

뇌척수 腦脊髓 〔解〕 the brain and spinal chord ■—막 〔解〕 meninges ■—막염 cerebrospinal meningitis

뇌천 腦天 〈정수리〉 the crown of the head

뇌출혈 腦出血 cerebral hemorrhage ⇨ 뇌일혈 (腦溢血)

뇌충혈 腦充血 〔醫〕 congestion of the brain; cerebral hyperemia

뇌파 腦波 〔醫〕 brain waves (▶보통 복수형으로 씀)
◆뇌파를 검사하다 check sb's brain waves; give sb an electroencephalograph test / 뇌파를 기록하다 take electroencephalogram readings
■—검사 a brain wave test ■—기록장치 an electroencephalogram ■—도 an electroencephalogram (略 EEG) ■—형 a brain wave pattern

뇌하수체 腦下垂體 〔解〕 a pituitary gland; a hypophysis ■—이식 transplanting of the pituitary gland ■—호르몬 pituitary hormone

뇌혈전 腦血栓 〔醫〕 cerebral thrombosis

뇌홍 雷汞 fulminating mercury; mercury fulminate

누 累 〈폐〉 trouble; involvement; an evil influence [effect]
◆남에게 누를 끼치다 bring [cause] troubles to others; affect sb unfavorably; implicate [get, involve] others in trouble
▶당신에게 누를 끼치지는 않겠습니다 I shall never involve you in trouble [get you into trouble, cause you trouble].
▶그렇게 하면 자기뿐만 아니라 남에게도 누를 끼치게 된다 That would bring trouble to others as well as yourself.

누 壘 〔野〕 a base ▶한 선수도 누상에 나가 있지 않다 No players have gotten to first (base).

누 〔動〕 a gnu 《pl. ~(s)》; a wildebeest 《pl. ~(s)》

누가 1 〈누구가〉 who
▶누가 왔다고 생각하니? Who do you think came?
▶너무 많은 사람이 있었기 때문에 누가 누군지 몰랐다 There were so many people that I could not tell who was who.
▶도대체 누가 꽃병을 깨뜨렸니? Who ever broke the vase?
▶누가 이 그림을 그렸는지 모르겠다 I don't know who painted this picture.
2 〈비꼼·항의〉 I; me
▶누가 안대? How should I know?
▶누가 할 말을 네가 하는 구나 You are saying what I should say. ⇌ It's me that should be saying that.
▶그러면 누가 무서워할 줄 아니? Do you think I will be afraid if you do that?

누가 累加 accumulation; a cumulative [progressive] increase; acceleration ■—누가하다 accumulate; increase progressively

누가 〈캔디의 일종〉 (프) nougat

누가 〔聖〕 〈—복음〉 the Gospel according to St. Luke (略 Luke)

누각 樓閣 a tower; a many-storied [lofty] building

누감 累減 degression ■—세[과세] degressive tax [taxation]

누계 累計 the total (amount [sum]); the cumulative total; the aggregate
◆누계 3천 8백명 three thousand eight hundred men in total [in all] / 누계 100만원에 이르다 total [amount to, run up to] one million won
▶어제로서 누계 100톤이 된다 The aggregate (amount) comes to one hundred tons as of yesterday.
■—누계하다 total; sum [add] up ◆누계하여 in the aggregate

누관 淚管 〔解〕 a tear [lachrymal] duct

누구 1 〈특정인의 경우〉 ◆누구가 who / 누구의 whose / 누구를[에게] whom
▶누구십니까? What's your name, please? ⇌ 〈전화에서〉 May I ask who is speaking, please? ⇌ Who's speaking [talking]?
▶어디 계시는 누구신지요? Who and what are you?
▶누구시더라 Excuse me, but I forget your name.
▶누구신지요? 〈손님에게〉 Who(m) shall I say?

누구누구

▶누구인가 했더니 나의 친구였다 It was no other [no less a person] than my friend.
▶그녀는 누구를 기다리고 있지? Whom [(口) Who] is she waiting for?
▶ 會話「나 선물 받았어」「누구에게서?」"I got a present." "Who from?"
2 〈일정치 않은 사람〉 ◆누군가 다른 사람 someone else / 누군가 적당한 사람 some suitable person / 누구나 everybody; everyone; 〈부정〉 no one; nobody / 누구든지 〈아무나〉 anyone; anybody; 〈모두〉 everybody; everyone
▶누구 이 책 필요한 사람 없어요? Is there anybody who wants this book?
▶누군가 찾아왔나 보다 Somebody is at the door.
▶그런 문제는 누구나 풀 수 있다 Anyone could solve such a problem.
▶누구나 결점 없는 사람은 없다 No one is free from faults. ⇒ There is no one but has some faults.
▶누구든지 이 법률을 위반한 자는 처벌 받는다 Whoever breaks this law shall be punished.
▶그것은 누구에게나 관계 있는 일이다 It is everybody's affair.
▶그는 영어에서는 누구에게도 지지 않는다 He is second to none in English.
3 〈비꼼·항의〉 I; me; someone
▶누구 놀리는 거냐? Are you kidding me?
▶누구는 밤에 자다가 오줌쌌대요 "Someone I know" wet his bed last night!

누구누구 this or that person; 〈많은 사람〉 (many) people
◆누구누구 할 것 없이 모두 each and all; everybody; every one (of them); irrespective of persons
▶누구누구가 강의에 왔느냐? Who came to the lecture?
▶누구누구가 왔는지 조사하지 않으면 안된다 You must check who has come.

누굴들 whoever; who ▶누구들 그런 생각을 했겠는가? Whoever [Who] would have thought of it?

누군지 who (it is); somebody; someone
▶누군지 비밀을 누설했다 Somebody has disclosed the secret.

누그러뜨리다 soothe, calm; pacify; soften (*one's* attitude); appease (*one's* anger)
▶그는 목소리[태도]를 누그러뜨렸다 He softened his voice [attitude].
▶의사는 나에게 치통을 누그러뜨리는 약을 주었다 The doctor gave some medicine to soothe [ease, relieve] my toothache.

누그러지다 1 〈감정 등이〉 be softened; become mild; moderate; lessen; be eased; be allayed; be calmed [cooled] down
▶아내의 설득으로 그의 완고한 태도가 누그러졌다 His obstinate attitude was softened by his wife's urging.
▶그녀의 미소로 내 마음도 누그러졌다 Her smiles disarmed me.
▶그의 자상한 말로 그녀의 마음이 누그러졌다 His tender words softened her up.
▶그녀의 깊은 설움도 시간이 가면 누그러지겠지 Her deep sorrow may be dulled in the course of time [as time goes by].
▶그는 몹시 화가 나 있었으나 차차 누그러졌다 He was very angry, but he has cooled down gradually.
2 〈날씨가〉 get milder [warmer]; become less severe; moderate; ease up; 〈바람 등이〉 abate; die down; subside; go down
▶추위[더위]가 누그러졌다 The cold [hot weather] has abated [moderated].
3 〈값이〉 get lower; decline; be on the decline
▶물가가 누그러지고 있다 Prices are on the decline. ⇒ Prices show a downtrend [downward tendency].

누글누글하다 tender ⇒ 노글노글하다
누기 漏氣 dampness; moisture; humidity
누기차다 漏氣— damp; wet; humid; moist; dampish ◆누기찬 방 a damp [humid] room / 누기찬 옷 damp clothes
누기치다 漏氣— become [get] damp [moist, wet]; dampen; moisten
▶요 근래의 오랜 비로 방이 누기쳤다 The room has become damp [wet] because of recent long rain.

누나 《a boy's》 elder [older] sister; (口) *one's* big sister; a sister ◆큰 누나 the eldest [oldest] sister

누년 累年 successive years; many years; several years; a series of years ▶—통계 annual statistics [figures]

누누이 屢屢— many times (over); unceasingly; continuously; frequently; repeatedly
▶어머니는 아이들에게 철도 근처에는 가지 말라고 누누이 타일렀다 Mother has admonished her children time and again not to go near the railroad.
▶그것을 하지 말라고 누누이 당부했었지 I have told you a thousand times not to do that.

누다 evacuate; defecate; let out [off]; relieve (nature)
◆똥을 누다 have a bowel movement; evacuate [discharge] bowels / 오줌을 누다 make [pass] water; pass [discharge] urine; urinate; (俗) pee; (卑) piss / 길가에 오줌을 누다 urinate [relieve *oneself*] in the street

누대 屢代 〈여러 대〉 successive generations
◆누대에 걸쳐 from generation to generation

누더기 rags; tatters; tattered clothes
◆누더기의 ragged; tattered; worn-out / 누더기를 걸친[입은] 사람 a person in rags / 누더기가 되다 be worn to rags / 누더기를 걸치고 있다 be (clad) in rags [tatters]
▶그는 누더기가 된 셔츠를 입고 있었다 He was wearing a shirt, worn and patched.
▶그 소년은 누더기를 입고 있었다 The boy was in rags.

누덕누덕 in patches; full of patches
◆누덕누덕 기운 바지 patchy trousers / 누덕누덕 기운 셔츠 a much-patched shirt; a shirt with patches all over / 옷을 누덕누덕 깁다 patch (up); patch and darn *one's* clothes
누되다 累— cause trouble (to)
누두 漏斗 a funnel ⇒ 깔때기
누드 (the) nude ▪—모델 a nude model ▪—사진

a nude photo [picture]: 누드 사진을 찍다 take a photograph of 《a girl》 in the nude —쇼 a nude [strip] show; a striptease
누디스트 〈나체주의자〉a nudist
누락 (an) omission
▶빈 칸을 누락 없이 기입하시오 Please fill in all the blanks (without any omission).
▶서류에 몇 군데 누락이 있었다 There were several omissions in the paper.
—**누락하다** omit; leave out ◆누락되다 be omitted; be left out; be missing
▶그의 이름이 명단에서 누락되어 있다 His name has been left off [omitted from] the list. ⇌ His name has been left out.
누란 累卵 ◆누란의 위기에 처하다 be in imminent peril [danger]; be in a most perilous situation; sit on a volcano
▶우리 나라는 지금 누란의 위기에 처해 있다 Our nation is now in a great crisis [imminent danger]. ⇌ Our country is now threatened with ruin.
누래지다 become [grow] yellow; be tinged with yellow; 〈안색 등이〉 sallow
누렁 (deep) yellow; yellow dyes ■—물 yellow water; dirty water
누렇다 quite [deep] yellow; golden yellow
▶보리가 누렇게 익었다 The barley is ripe and yellow.
누룩 malted wheat [rice]; 〈보리의〉 malt ■—곰팡이 leaven; an aspergillus (*pl.* -gilli) —밀 malt made of glutinous rice
누룽지 burnt [scorched] rice; the crust of overcooked rice; the scorched part of boiled rice
누르께하다 yellowy; yellowish; maize ◆누르께한 얼굴 a sallow face ▶그녀는 병으로 얼굴이 누르께했다 She was sallow with the disease.
누르다[1] 1 〈내리밀다〉 press (down); hold down; push; weigh on
◆여권에 검인을 누르다 stamp a passport / 국수를 누르다 make noodles; squeeze out noodles / 초인종을 누르다 push [press] the bell
▶그는 문진(文鎭)으로 종이를 눌렀다 He held paper down with a paperweight.
▶우리는 그가 움직이지 못하도록 팔다리를 단단히 누르고 있었다 We held his arms and legs down firmly so that he couldn't move.
▶무릎을 누르면 아프다 My knee hurts when I press on it.
2 〈진압·제압하다〉 put down; suppress; control; beat; defeat
◆반대를 누르다 bear down any opposition / 불평을 누르다 stifle a complaint / 폭동을 누르다 suppress [put down] a riot
▶그는 반대 의견을 눌렀다 He repressed the opposing voices [opinion].
3 〈감정을〉 restrain; control; suppress
◆격정을 누르다 restrain *one's* passions; hold *one's* passion in check; keep a rein on *one's* passions; control *oneself* / 욕심을 누르다 suppress a desire / 자존심을 누르다 put *one's* pride in *one's* pocket
▶그는 간신히 분노를 눌렀다 He managed to control his anger.
▶정부는 물가를 누르는 데 실패했다 The government failed to keep prices down [stabilize prices].
▶그는 웃음을 누르려고 애썼다 He tried to keep from laughing.
▶나는 오랫동안 불만을 눌러왔지만 더 이상 감출 수가 없다 I have long repressed my discontent, but I cannot hide it any longer.
4 〈이기다〉 beat; defeat
◆선거에서 경쟁자를 누르다 beat *one's* rival in the election / 적을 누르다 hold the enemy in check / 상대팀을 무득점으로 누르다 shut out the opposition team; hold the opposition team scoreless
▶투수는 상대팀을 산발 3안타로 눌렀다 The pitcher held the opposing team to three scattered hits.
누르다[2] 〈색깔이〉 yellow(ish); golden (yellow) ◆누른 빛 a yellow [golden] color / 누른 잎 a yellow leaf / 누른 빛이 되다 turn yellow
누르스름하다 somewhat yellow; yellowy; yellowish; maize
누르퉁퉁하다 dull yellow; subdued yellow; jaundiced; sallow ◆얼굴이 누르퉁퉁하다 look sallow; have a sallow face
누름단추 a push [press] button; 〈초인종의〉 a bell push ■—식 경보기 a push-button alarm
누름돌 a (stone) weight ◆누름돌을 얹다 place [put] a stone as a weight on *sth*; press *sth* under a stone
누리[1] 〔昆〕 a desert [migratory] locust
누리[2] 〈우박〉 hail; snow pellets
누리[3] 〈세상〉 the world; this world ◆온 누리에 in all the world; all over the world
누리다[1] 〈향유하다〉 enjoy; be blessed with
◆평화를 누리는 국민 a nation blessed with peace / 건강을 누리다 enjoy [have] good health / 장수를 누리다 live a long life / 행복을 누리다 enjoy happiness
▶이 나라는 천연 자원의 혜택을 누리고 있다 This country is blessed with natural resources.
▶이 나라 사람들은 언론의 자유를 누리고 있다 The people of this country enjoy freedom of speech.
누리다[2] 〈누린내가 나다〉 stenchful; 〈서술적〉 smell [reek] of *sth* scorched; smell burnt; have a burnt smell
누린내 〈털이 타는〉 a burnt smell; a scorched smell; a stench; 〈고기의〉 an unpleasant smell of fat [grease] ▶무언가 누린내가 난다 I can smell something burning [scorching].
누명 陋名 a false [an unjust] charge [accusation]; groundless [unfounded] suspicion
◆누명을 씌우다 accuse 《sb of theft》 unjustly [falsely]; make [bring] a false charge 《of espionage》 against *sb* / 누명을 벗다 clear *oneself* of false accusation
▶그는 탈세 누명을 썼다 He was falsely [unjustly] charged with [accused of] tax evasion.
▶그는 살인[절도]죄의 누명을 썼다 He was wrongly accused of murder [stealing].

누범 累犯 a repeated offense; the repetition of offenses; cumulative offense

누벨바그 (프) nouvelle vague; the new wave

누비 quilting; quilted work ■—옷 quilted clothes; a quilted coat —이불 a quilt —질 quilting : 누비질하다 quilt; do quilting —포대기 a baby quilt

누비다 1 〈줄지게 박다〉 quilt ◆이불을 누비다 quilt; form into a quilt
2 〈뚫고 나가다〉 thread [weave] *one's* way 《through》
▶ 아이를 따라 잡으려고 그녀는 군중 사이를 누비며 날렸다 Threading her way through the crowd, she ran to catch up with her child.
▶ 시위대가 길을 누비며 나아갔다 The demonstrators paraded (through) the street.

누상 樓上 a balcony; upstairs; the upper story

누선 涙腺 a lachrymal [lǽkrəml] gland

누설 漏泄 1 〈액체 등의〉 a leak; leakage ◆누설을 막다 stop [plug] a leak
—**누설하다** leak; let leak
2 〈비밀의〉 (a) leakage; (a) disclosure; divulgence; a leak
▶ 외교상의 비밀 누설이 국회에서 문제가 되었다 The leakage of diplomatic secret was called in question in the National Assembly.
—**누설하다** reveal; disclose; betray; divulge; let *sb* know; let out
◆비밀을 누설하다 betray [reveal, divulge, let out] a secret / 누설되다 leak (out); be divulged [disclosed]
▶ 그는 무심결에 비밀을 누설하고 말았다 He carelessly let the secret slip. ⇒ He inadvertently let the cat out of the bag.
▶ 기밀 문서가 신문에 누설되었다 A classified document has leaked out to the press.
■군기(軍機)— a leakage of military secrets
■전류 a leakage current

누손 漏損 〔商〕 leakage; ullage; 〔電〕 a leakage (loss)

누수 漏水 leaking water; leak of water ▶ 누수를 막지 않으면 안된다 We must stop a leak of water. —검출기 a hydrostat

누습 陋習 a corrupt custom ⇨ 폐습(弊習)
▶ 우리는 회사의 오랜 누습을 타파해야 한다 We must correct [break down] the long-existing abuses of our company.

누승 累乘 〔數〕 power; involution —**누승하다** raise to a given power; involve ■—근(根) a radical root

누심 壘審 〔野〕 a base umpire ■1루— the umpire at first base

누에 a silkworm
◆누에를 올리다 put silkworms on mulberry leaves to feed / 누에를 치다 rear [raise, keep] silkworms / 누에에서 생사를 뽑다 obtain raw silk from silkworms
▶ 누에가 고치를 치기 시작했다 The silkworms have begun spinning.
—고치 a cocoon —나방 a silkworm moth
—씨 silkworm eggs; a strain [breed] of silkworms —치기 sericulture; silk-farming

누옥 陋屋 1 〈누추한 집〉 a sordid [dilapidated] house; a squalid [wretched] hut; a humble cottage
2 〈자기 집〉 my (humble) dwelling [house]
▶ 이 누옥에 오신 것을 환영합니다 Welcome to my humble dwelling!

누운변 —邊 〈원금과 함께 일시에 갚는 이자〉 lump-sum payment of interest at the repayment of the principal

누울 자리 봐가며 발을 뻗어라 (속담) Stretch your arm no farther than your sleeve will reach. ⇌ Everyone stretches his legs according to his coverlet.

누워 떡 먹기 (속담) a very [quite an] easy task [job]
▶ 그런 일은 누워 떡 먹기다 That's nothing. ⇌ Nothing can be simpler [easier]. ⇌ (美俗) That's (as) easy as pie. ⇌ (英俗) I could do it before breakfast.

누워먹다 live in idleness; eat idle bread; live [lead] an idle life

누워서 침 뱉기 (속담) Curses come home to roost.

누이 1 〈손위의〉 an elder [(美) older] sister; 〈손아래의〉 a younger [little, small] sister
▶ 내 누이가 태어났다[생겼다] I have got a baby sister. —동생 *one's* younger sister

누이다¹ 1 〈눕히다〉 lay down; make *sb* lie down ◆자리에 누이다 put *sb* to bed
2 〈피륙을 찌다〉 soften; gloss; give a gloss (to) —누인[누이지 않은] 명주 glossed [unglossed] silk

누이다² 〈대소변을〉 make [let, have] 《a child》 urinate [defecate]

누적 累積 accumulation; cumulation —**누적하다** accumulate; cumulate ◆누적된 서류 accumulated papers 《on the table》 / 누적된 악폐 accumulated evils
■—적자 accumulated deficit : 100만원의 누적 적자 a cumulate deficit of one million won / 우리 회사는 누적 적자에 시달리고 있다 Our firm is suffering an increasing loss in business.

누전 漏電 an electric leakage; a leak; a short circuit; a leakage of electricity
◆누전으로 인한 화재 a fire started by a short circuit; a fire caused by a leakage of electricity / 누전을 일으키다 cause a short circuit; cause a leak(age) of electricity
▶ 화재 원인은 누전이었다 The fire was caused by a short circuit [leakage of electricity].
—**누전하다** leak; short-circuit
■—계 a leakage indicator [detector]

누증 累增 cumulation; cumulative rise [increase]; progressive increase
—**누증하다** cumulate; increase progressively [cumulatively]

누지 陋地 my place; here; this place

누지다 1 〈축축해지다〉 become damp [dampish, humid]; damp
2 〈축축하다〉 damp; dampish; humid; slightly wet ◆누진 날씨 humid weather / 누진 옷 damp clothes / 차고 누진 공기 cold and damp air

누진 累進 progressive increase; 〈지위 등의〉 successive promotion

▶ 소득세는 누진적으로 커진다 The income tax rates increase progressively. ⇌ Income taxes are imposed on a graduated scale.
—누진하다 be promoted gradually; rise step by step
▶ 그는 평사원에서 누진하여 이사가 되었다 He rose [was promoted] step by step from a mere clerk to a director.
■**—과세** progressive [graduated] taxation: 누진 과세하다 impose taxes on a graduated scale **—세** a progressive [cumulative] tax **—세율** a progressive tax rate

누차 屢次 often; successively; lots of [many] times; repeatedly; again [time] and again
♦ 누차의 successive; frequent; repeated / 누차에 걸친 재앙 a series [succession] of calamities / 누차 말한 바와 같이 as I have told you repeatedly
▶ 누차 폐를 끼쳐서 죄송합니다 I am sorry to have troubled you so often.
▶ 나는 한 번 더 해보게 해 달라고 아버지께 누차 부탁했다 I asked [begged] my father repeatedly [again and again] to let me try once more.

누추하다 陋醜 squalid; sordid; messy; grubby; untidy; shabby; filthy
♦ 누추한 오두막(집) a sordid hut / 옷차림이 누추하다 be shabbily dressed
▶ 나는 그의 누추한 외모에 놀랐다 I was surprised at his disheveled appearance.
▶ 나는 누추한 집에 살고 있다 I live in a messy [filthy] house.
▶ 누추한 곳이지만 잘 오셨습니다 I'm delighted to welcome you under the shadow of my humble rooftree.

누출 leakage; a leak ♦ 가스 누출로 인한 폭발 사고 an explosion caused by a gas leak
—누출하다 leak [ooze] out ▶ 그 파이프에서 가스가 누출된다 The pipe leaks gas.

누치 〔魚〕 a cornet fish

누타 壘打 〔野〕 a base hit ♦ 3루타를 치다 make a three-base hit

눅눅하다 damp; humid; moist; wet; clammy
♦ 눅눅한 공기 damp air / 눅눅한 담배 damp tobacco
▶ 비가 여러 날 계속 와서 방이 눅눅하다 It has been raining for days, and the room feels clammy.
▶ 창문을 열자 눅눅한 밤 공기가 흘러들어 왔다 When I opened the window, damp night air came in.

눅다 1〈반죽 등이〉 soft; tender; ductile ♦ 눅은 반죽 soft dough
2〈성질이〉 calm; quiet; peaceful; mild; gentle; placid ♦ 성질이 눅은 사람 a person of a quiet disposition; a placid-tempered person
▶ 그는 성질이 눅다 He has a mild disposition.
3〈습기로〉 damp; moist; soft with wet
▶ 이 셔츠는 눅으니 햇볕에 말려라 This shirt is damp. Dry it in the sun.
4〈날씨가 풀리다〉 become mild(er); get warm; warm up
▶ 날씨가 눅어지면 소풍 갑시다 Let's go on a picnic when it gets warmer.
5〈값이 싸다〉 inexpensive; low(-priced); cheap
▶ 시골은 일반적으로 물가가 눅다 Prices are generally lower in rural areas.
▶ 물가가 조금 눅었다 Prices have come down a little.

눅신하다 soft; tender; soft and flexible

눅이다 1〈굳은 것을〉 soften; make soft [tender]; 〈물에 적셔〉 macerate
♦ 반죽[가죽]을 눅이다 soften dough [leather]/ 빵을 우유에 담궈 눅이다 soften bread in milk
2〈마음을〉 soften; appease; ease; mollify; pacify; calm
♦ 남의 노여움을 눅이다 appease [calm] sb's anger / 아픔을 눅이다 ease the pain / 태도를 눅이다 soften one's attitude / 폭발의 충격을 눅이다 absorb the shock of the explosion
3〈적시다〉 damp; moisten; make sth damp [moist] ♦ 다리미질하기 위해 옷을 눅이다 damp clothes prior to ironing

눈[1] 1〈시각 기관〉 an eye
♦ 가는 눈 narrow eyes / 검은 눈의 소녀 a girl with dark eyes / 귀여운 눈 lovely eyes / 날카로운 눈 sharp [alert, gimlet] eyes / 눈물어린 눈 tearful [watery] eyes / 눈초리가 올라간 눈 slanting [oblique] eyes / 번쩍이는 눈 sparkling [flaming] eyes / 부리부리한 눈 big bright eyes / 왕방울 눈 saucer eyes / 움푹한 눈 deep-set eyes / 졸린듯한 눈 sleepy [heavy] eyes / 퉁방울 눈 goggle eyes / 흐리멍텅한 눈 dull [fishy] eyes / 눈 딱 감고 without hesitation
▶ 제트기는 눈 깜짝할 사이에 날아갔다 The jet plane flew away in an instant.
▶ 눈 먼 말이 제일 대담하다 Blind horse is hardiest.
〈눈의〉 눈의 ocular; optic / 눈의 근육 ocular muscle / 눈의 신경 an optic nerve / 눈의 피로 eyestrain
〈눈이〉 눈이 핑핑 돌다 be [feel] dizzy / 눈이 번쩍 뜨이는 미인 a woman of dazzling beauty / 눈이 부시다 be dazzled 《by the light》 / 눈이 아프다 have sore eyes; suffer 《from》 eye irritation / 눈이 휘둥그래지다 stare [open one's eyes wide] with [in] wonder
▶ 따님은 눈이 예쁘군요 Your daughter has pretty eyes.
▶ 모든 사람의 눈이 내게로 쏠렸다 All eyes were focused [fastened] on me.
▶ 옆 사람의 담배 연기로 눈이 따갑다 My eyes smart from my neighbor's cigarette smoke.
〈눈을〉 눈을 가늘게 뜨고 with one's eyes slightly open; (look) through half-closed eyes / 눈을 번뜩이며 with flashing eyes / 눈을 가늘게 뜨다 squint [crease, narrow] one's eyes / 눈을 감다 close [shut] one's eyes; 〈죽다〉 breathe one's last / 눈을 깜박이다 blink one's eyes / 눈을 치뜨다 glance up [upward] 《at》 / 아무의 눈을 뚫어지게 들여다보다 stare sb in the eye(s)
▶ 그는 책을 읽다가 눈을 들었다 He raised [lifted] his eyes from the book he was reading.
▶ 그녀는 그가 들어오자 수줍게 눈을 내리깔았

눈¹

다 When he came in, she lowered her eyes shyly.
▶ 그는 소파에서 잠깐 눈을 붙였다 He took [had] a nap on the sofa.
▶ 그 소년은 눈을 크게 뜨고 거대한 코끼리를 보았다 The little boy gazed at the huge elephant, (with his) eyes wide open.
▶ 노인은 눈을 부라리고 주위를 살폈다 The old man looked around with goggling eyes.
▶ 눈을 비비면 안돼! Don't rub your eye!
▶ 우리는 서로 눈을 내리깔고 지나쳤다 We passed each other with lowered eyes.
▶ 잠깐 눈을 뜨고[감고] 계십시오 Keep your eyes open [closed] for a while.
⟨눈에⟩ 눈에 쌍심지를 돋우고 with anger in one's eyes; looking daggers 《at》 / 눈에 불이 나다 ⟨아찔하다⟩ see stars; ⟨화가 나다⟩ be indignant / 눈에 티가 들어가다 have a mote in one's eye / 눈에 해롭다 be injurious to the eyes
▶ 그녀는 아무것도 눈에 들어오지 않았다 Her eyes registered nothing.
▶ 내 딸은 눈에 넣어도 아프지 않다 My daughter is the apple of my eye.
▶ 그와 이마를 부딪쳐 눈에서 불이 났다 When I lumped my head against his, I saw stars.
▶ 눈에서 사라지면 마음에서 멀어진다 ⟨속담⟩ Out of sight, out of mind.
⟨눈으로⟩ 눈으로 인사하다 (greet with a) nod; greet with one's eyes / 자기 눈으로 직접 보다 see sth with one's own eyes

2 ⟨시력·시각⟩ an eye; eyesight; sight
♦ 눈이 멀다 become [go] blind; lose one's sight [eyesight] / 한쪽 눈이 멀다 be blind in one eye / 눈을 버리다 impair one's vision [eyesight] / 눈을 멀게 하다 make sb blind / 과도한 독서로 눈을 피로하게 하다 pore one's eyes out / 눈에 보이다[보이게 되다] become in sight; come into view / 눈에 보이지 않다 be invisible; be unseen; elude the eye
▶ 그는 눈이 나쁘다 He has bad [poor] eye [sight].
▶ 그는 한쪽 눈이 보이지 않는다 He is blind in one eye.
▶ 잔 글씨를 보면 눈이 나빠진다 Small prints ruin your eye.
▶ 어두운 데서도 눈이 보이는 동물도 있다 Some animals can see in the dark.
▶ 나이를 먹어서 눈이 나빠졌다 My eyes have grown blurred with (old) age.
▶ 그의 눈은 작년부터 아주 나빠졌다 His eyesight has failed badly since last year.

3 ⟨응시·시선⟩ a look; a stare; an eye
♦ 눈이 미치는 한 as far as the eye [sight] can reach / 첫눈에 at the first sight / 눈을 떼다 look away 《from》 / 눈과 눈이 마주치다 exchange glances
▶ 그녀와 눈이 마주치자 나는 손을 흔들었다 When our eyes met [I caught her eyes], I waved to her.
▶ 거기까지는 내 눈이 닿지 않는다 That's beyond my eyeshot.
▶ 눈을 둘 데가 없다 I don't know where to rest my eyes [which way to look].

4 ⟨눈의 표정⟩ a look; an eye; a gaze
♦ 무서운 눈 threatening [menacing] eyes / 눈으로 감사하다 look at sb gratefully; thank sb with one's eyes / 눈으로 알리다 make a sign with the eye; give sb the eye / 부러운 눈으로 보다 cast an envious look 《at》 / 차가운 눈으로 보다 give sb a frigid stare / 평온한[선망의] 눈으로 돌아보다 turn to sb with a tranquil [jealous] eye [look]
▶ 골프 이야기가 나오면 그는 눈에서 빛이 난다 His eyes sparkle [flash] when it comes to golf.
▶ 경찰은 차가운 눈으로 나를 봤다 The policeman looked at me coldly.
▶ 아버지는 나를 엄한 눈으로 보셨다 Father gave me a severe look. ⇒ Father looked at me severely.
▶ 그들은 대통령이 기내로 들어가는 것을 눈으로 전송했다 Their eyes followed the President as he stepped inside the plane.

5 ⟨감식안⟩ an eye; ⟨판단력⟩ judgment; discrimination
♦ 전문가의 눈 an expert('s) eye; a professional eye / 눈이 높다 aim high / 사람을 보는 눈이 있다 be a good [fine] judge of characters
▶ 그는 그림을 보는 눈이 있다 He has an eye [a good eye] for art.
▶ 이 시를 감상하는 데는 시인의 눈이 필요하다 It needs a poet's eye [insight] to appreciate this poem.

6 ⟨관점⟩ an eye; ⟨견지·견해⟩ a point of view; a viewpoint
♦ 법의 눈으로 보면 in the eyes of the law / 다른[공평한] 눈으로 정세를 보다 look at the situation with another [an impartial] eye
▶ 우리는 그의 눈으로 보면 어린애다 We are babies in his eyes.
▶ 작가의 눈으로 보면, 이들 문학 작품은 비판할 가치가 없다 From a writer's point of view, these literary works are beneath criticism.
▶ 이것이 미국인의 눈으로 본 한국이다 This is Korea as Americans see it [as seen by Americans].
▶ 긴 눈으로 보면 그 집은 지금 사두는 게 좋을 것이다 In the long run it would be better for you to buy the house now.

7 ⟨마음⟩ eyes
♦ 서로 눈이 맞다 fall in love with each other / 눈에 들다 be in favor of sb; be in sb's favor / 눈에 삼삼하다 linger [stay] before one's eyes; be engraved on one's memory / 눈에 차다 be satisfactory / 눈밖에 나다 be out of favor 《with sb》
▶ 그것은 몹시 눈에 거슬리는 장면이었다 It was a sight too offensive to look at.
▶ 그 사건이 아직도 눈에 생생하다 The memory of the incident is still vivid [fresh] in my mind.
▶ 그 아름다운 장면이 눈에 선하다 The beautiful scene comes to [into] my mind. ⇒ I can just picture the beautiful scene.
▶ 그 장난꾸러기는 언제나 선생님의 눈 밖에 났다 The naughty boy was always out of favor

with his teacher.
8 〈주목・주시〉 (public) notice; attention; watch
▶ 우리는 그의 실수를 눈 감아 주었다 We overlooked [ignored] his mistake.
▶ 이번만은 그 말을 눈감아 주겠다 I'll pass over that remark just this once.
〈눈이〉 나는 세상 사람들의 눈이 두렵다 I am afraid of the eye of the people [the public eye].
〈눈을〉 눈을 가리다 〈속이다〉 hoodwink; blind the eyes 《of》; cheat; deceive / 눈을 감다 《못본 체하다》 shut [close] *one's* eyes 《to》; turn a blind eye 《on, to》/ 눈을 돌리다 turn [direct] *one's* eyes [attention] 《to》/ 눈을 떼다 look aside [off, away]; take *one's* eyes off 《a child》/ 눈을 뗄 수 없다 have to keep a watchful eye 《on》
▶ 그들은 선생님의 눈을 속이고 학교에서 담배를 피웠다 They smoked in the school to avoid the eye of their teachers.
▶ 잠깐 눈을 뗀 사이에 아이가 없어졌다 The child disappeared during the short time when I had taken my eyes off him.
〈눈에〉 눈에 띄다 attract [catch] *one's* attention [eye]; come [be brought] to notice
▶ 벽에 걸어놓은 작은 그림이 그의 눈에 띄었다 A small picture on the wall caught his eye.
▶ 그녀의 형편은 눈에 띄게 좋아졌다 Her condition shows 《a》 marked improvement.
▶ 그때부터 그는 눈에 띄게 변했다 There has been a visible change in him since then.
▶ 눈에 띄는 모든 것이 내게는 생소했다 Everything I saw was new to me.
9 〈자각・이성〉 reason; judgment
♦ 눈이 뒤집히다 lose *one's* sober judgment; run [go] wild [mad] / 시대에 눈을 뜨다 be awakened to the times
▶ 그는 욕심에 눈이 멀었다 Greed blinded him.
▶ 내가 단지 돈에 눈이 멀어 그런 건 아니다 I didn't do it merely for love of money.

─── 눈 ───

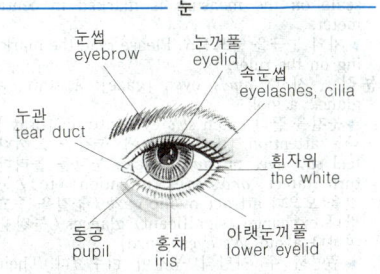

눈썹 eyebrow / 눈꺼풀 eyelid / 속눈썹 eyelashes, cilia / 누관 tear duct / 흰자위 the white / 동공 pupil / 홍채 iris / 아랫눈꺼풀 lower eyelid

눈² 〖植〗 〈싹〉 a bud; a sprout; a shoot; 〈씨눈〉 a germ ♦ 눈이 트다 《the buds》 come out
▶ 가로수가 일제히 눈이 트고 있다 The trees along the road are shooting out [putting forth] buds all at once.
눈³ **1** 〈눈금〉 a scale 《on a beam balance》; a graduation
♦ 자의 눈 the scale [graduations] on a ruler / 《저울》 눈이 모자라다 be of short weight / 《저울》 눈을 속이다 give short weight
2 〈바둑판의〉 a cross 《of [on] a *paduk* board》; 〈주사위의〉 a pip, a spot
눈⁴ 〈하늘에서 내리는〉 snow

> **解說** (1) *snow*는「눈」자체를 일반적으로 가리키는 경우에는 관사 없이, 한 번의 강설로 보는 경우에는 a가 붙는다: We had *a* heavy *snow* last winter. ⇌ We had heavy *snow* last winter. (작년 겨울에는 큰 눈이 왔다)
> (2) *snows*라고 복수형이 되면「적설(량)」, 「적설 지대」를 뜻한다: the *snows* of Mt. Everest (에베레스트 산의 적설지대)

♦ 갓 내린 눈 the freshly fallen snow / 녹은 눈 melted snow / 산봉우리의 눈 a snowcap / 싸락눈 powdery snow / 진눈 wet snow; sleet; snow mixed with rain / 함박눈 large flakes of snow; large snowflakes / 눈 경치 a snow scene; snowscape / 눈 뭉치 a snowball / 눈 축제 a snow festival / 눈 치기 snow shoveling / 눈이 많이 오는 지역 a snow district; a region of heavy snows [snowfall]
▶ 나는 1 미터나 쌓인 눈 속을 걸어서 학교에 갔다 I walked to school through the snow lying about one meter deep.
▶ 눈 때문에 오늘 아침은 모든 교통이 두절되었다 The snow stopped all traffic this morning.
▶ 그녀의 팔은 눈처럼 희었다 Her arms were as white as snow.
〈눈이〉 눈이 오는 날에 on a snowy day
▶ 눈이 온다 It snows.
▶ 눈이 오기 시작했다 It began to snow [snowing].
▶ 눈이 심하게 내리고 있다 It is snowing hard [heavily].
▶ 함박눈이 내리고 있다 Large snowflakes are falling [fluttering down]. ⇌ It is snowing in large flakes.
▶ 눈이 올 것 같다 It is going to snow. ⇌ It [The sky] looks like snow.
▶ 눈이 녹기 시작했다 The snow began to melt [thaw].
▶ 아침부터 내린 눈이 한낮에는 20 cm나 쌓였다 The snow that had been falling since morning piled up to twenty centimeters by noon.
▶ 아침에 쌓인 눈이 저녁에는 녹아버렸다 The snow which piled up in the morning melted away by the evening.
▶ 여기는 겨울에도 눈이 조금도[거의] 오지 않는다 We have no [very little, hardly any] snow here even in winter. ⇌ It never [hardly ever] snows here even in winter.
〈눈을〉 눈을 무릅쓰고 in spite of the snow / 눈을 치다 rake [shovel, sweep] away snow; clear 《a road》 of snow; remove snow / 구두의 눈을 털어내다 knock the snow from *one's* shoes / 눈을 헤치고 나아가다 plow 《*one's* way》 through the snow
〈눈에〉 눈에 갇히다 be snow-bound; be snow-stalled / 눈에 덮이다 be covered with [mantled in] snow / 눈에 묻히다 be buried under [in] the snow; be snowed under

눈

▶그 마을은 1주일 전부터 눈에 묻혀 있다 The village has been snowed in [up] for a week.
▶우리는 눈에 갇혀 이틀 밤낮을 움막에서 보냈다 We were snowed in [up] and spent two days and nights in the hut.
《눈으로》 눈으로 변하다 change to [into] snow
▶차는 눈으로 움직이지 못했다 The car got stuck in the snow.
▶큰 눈으로 우리는 산에 오를 수가 없었다 Because it snowed heavily [Because of the heavy snow], we couldn't climb the mountain. ≒ The heavy snow prevented us from climbing the mountain.

눈⁵ 〈그물 등의〉 a mesh ◆눈이 성긴[촘촘한] 그물 a wide-meshed [fine-mesh(ed)] net; a large-[small-]mesh net / 눈이 고운 체 a sieve of fine mesh ■**그물**— the meshes of a net

눈가 〈눈언저리〉 parts around the eye ◆눈가의[에] around *one's* eyes / 눈가의 주름 the lines at the corner of *one's* [the] eyes; crow's-feet

눈가리개 a bandage; 〈사람의〉 a blindfold; 〈말의〉 blinkers; (美) blinders
◆눈가리개를 하다 〈사람에게〉 blindfold [hoodwink] *sb*; bandage *sb's* eyes; 〈말에〉 put blinkers [blinders] (on a horse)
▶그들은 소녀에게 눈가리개를 했다 They put a blindfold over the girl's eyes. ≒ They blindfolded the girl.

눈가림 (a) sham; (美) (a) pretense; (a) make-believe; camouflage ◆눈가림으로 일하다 scamp [fudge] *one's* work
▶정부의 고용 정책은 눈가림에 지나지 않는다 The government employment policy amounts to nothing more than stopgap measures.
—**눈가림하다** pull the wool over *sb's* eyes; camouflage; cover up
◆골동품을 오래 된 것인양 눈가림하다 give a curio an appearance of age [an air of antiquity]

눈감다 shut [close] *one's* eyes (to); 〈죽다〉 die; pass away; breathe *one's* last / 눈감고 아웅하다 try to deceive by a transparent guile; bury *one's* head ostrich-like in the sand

눈감아주다 shut *one's* eyes (to); overlook; pass over *sth* (in silence); let (it) pass [go]; connive (at); turn a blind eye (to); wink [connive] (at)
◆무례를 눈감아주다 overlook [pretend not to see, wink at] *sb's* misbehavior / 실수를 눈감아주다 overlook [slur (over)] *sb's* fault
▶그는 내 잘못을 눈감아 주었다 He winked at my mistake. ≒ He condoned my mistake.
▶이번만은 눈감아 주겠다 I will let the matter pass for this once. ≒ We'll excuse you [give you a break] this time.
▶우리는 그의 파렴치한 행동을 눈감아주어서는 안된다 We should not overlook his unprincipled behavior.

눈거칠다 offensive [displeasing] to the eye; hateful to see; unsightly; ugly ▶그는 눈거친 녀석이다 He is an offensive guy.

눈겨룸 an outstaring game ⇨ 눈싸움¹

눈결 《at》 a glimpse [glance]; 〈잠깐 동안〉 a passing moment ◆눈결에 언뜻 보다 get [catch] a glimpse of
▶나는 그의 얼굴을 단지 눈결에 보았지만 잘 기억하고 있다 I only glimpsed at his face, but I remember it well.

눈곱 **1** 〈눈에 끼는〉 eye mucus [discharges]; eye wax; gum [matter] (in the corner of the eye)
◆눈곱이 낀 눈 a waxy [blear] eye / 눈곱이 끼다 matter forms in the eyes; *one's* eyes are gummy [mattery]
▶네 왼쪽 눈에 눈곱이 끼었다 There's some sleepy dust in your left eye.
2 〈작은 것·소량〉 a very small thing [amount]; a grain
◆눈곱만큼의 as small as a pinhead / …라곤 눈곱만큼도 없다 have not [haven't got] an ounce of 《conscience in him》; there isn't a grain of 《truth in what he says》
▶그들 사이에는 눈곱만큼의 애정도 남아 있지 않았다 Not a vestige of love remained between them.
▶나는 그것에 대해서는 눈곱만큼도 의심하지 않는다 I don't doubt it in the least [slightest degree].
▶그는 친절이라고는 눈곱만큼도 없다 He doesn't have a bit [speck] of kindness.

눈구덩이 heaped snow ⇨ 눈구멍¹

눈구멍¹ (a pit in) heaped snow ◆눈구멍 속을 헤치고 나아가다 plough (*one's* way) through the snow / 눈구멍에 빠지다 slip [tumble] in the snow

눈구멍² 〈안공〉 an eye socket; the (eye) orbit; an eyehole

눈구석 the inner corner of the eye

눈금 a scale; graduations
◆섭씨 눈금의 온도계 a thermometer with a Celsius scale / 눈금을 매기다 divide; graduate; put a graded scale (on the tube); calibrate
▶이 줄자는 눈금이 센티미터로 되어 있다 The scale on the measure is marked in centimeters.
▶자의 눈금을 읽으시오 Please read the marking on the ruler.

눈길¹ 〈시선〉 *one's* eyes [gaze]; a stare; a glance; a look
◆눈길을 끌다 catch *sb's* eyes; attract [draw] *sb's* attention [notice] / 등에 눈길을 느끼다 feel *sb's* eyes on *one's* back / 눈길을 돌리다 turn [direct] *one's* eyes [attention] 《to》 / 눈길을 모으다 attract public gaze / 눈길을 주고받다 exchange 《significant》 glances / 눈길을 피하다 avoid *sb's* eyes [gaze]
▶우연히 두 사람의 눈길이 마주쳤다 Their eyes met by chance.
▶모두의 눈길이 그녀에게 쏠렸다 All eyes were turned upon [on] her.
▶나는 그녀에게서 눈길을 돌릴 수가 없었다 I could not take my eyes off her.
▶그는 눈길을 둘 바를 몰랐다 He didn't know which way to look.

눈길² 〈눈 덮인 길〉 a snow-covered road; a snowy road

눈까풀 an eyelid ⇨ 눈꺼풀
눈깔사탕 —砂糖 toffees; taffies; (英) a sweet; a bull's-eye
♦눈깔사탕을 빨아먹다 suck on a piece of candy
눈깜짝이 a blinkard
눈꺼풀 an eyelid; the lid (of an eye)
♦윗[아랫] 눈꺼풀 the upper [lower] eyelid / 눈꺼풀의 경련 a twitching of the eyelid(s)
▶그녀는 한겹[두겹] 눈꺼풀이다 She has single-layered [double-layered] eyelids.
▶그는 애기를 하는 동안 때때로 눈꺼풀이 실룩거린다 His eyelids sometimes twitch while he is speaking.
눈꼴사납다 〈아니꼽다〉 disgusting; loathsome; hateful to see; 〈꼴사납다〉 unsightly; unseemly
♦눈꼴 사나운 행동을 하다 behave in a disgraceful [an unseemly] fashion; act dishonorably
▶그가 거드럭대는 꼴이 눈꼴사납다 I hate to see him swaggering.
▶눈꼴사나운 행동을 하지 마라 Don't disgrace yourself.
눈꼴시다 be offensive to the eye; be hateful to see; be disgusting ▶사장한테 아첨하는 꼴이라니 눈꼴시어 못 보겠다 I am sick of him licking the boss's shoes.
눈꼴틀리다 be disgusting ⇨ 눈꼴시다
눈높다 1 〈고급만 찾다〉 aiming high; desirous of things beyond *one's* means
▶그는 눈이 높아서 웬만한 사람은 거들떠 보지도 않을 거다 He aims high and will not even look at ordinary people.
2 〈안목이 높다〉 having an expert [a critical, a sharp] eye 《for》; discerning; appreciative; sharp-eyed ♦눈 높은 청중 an appreciative audience
▶그는 골동품에 눈이높다 He is quite knowledgeable about antiques. ≒ He has a good eye for antiques.
눈대중 a rough estimate; a guess; measuring with *one's* eye; eye measurement [estimation]
♦눈대중으로 at a [by] guess; by eye measure; at a rough estimate
—눈대중하다 measure with *one's* eye [by rule of thumb]
눈덩이 a snowball ▶지난 석달 사이에 그의 빚은 눈덩이처럼 불어났다 His debts have snowballed in the last three months.
눈독 eyeing; watching closely; looking over; having [keeping] an eye to
♦상금에 눈독을 들이다 be after [have an eye on] a reward / 재산에 눈독을 들이다 have an eye to the property
▶그가 정말로 눈독들이고 있는 것은 그녀의 유산이다 What he is really after is her inheritance.
▶도둑은 그 큰 차에 눈독을 들였다 The thief set his eyes on the big car.
눈동자 —瞳子 the pupil (of the eye)
눈두덩 (the protuberant part of) an upper eyelid ♦눈두덩이 붓다 have swollen eyes
눈딱부리 big round eyes; bulging eyes; 〈사람〉 a lobster-eyed [goggle-eyed] person
눈뜨다 1 〈눈을 열다〉 open *one's* eyes; 〈잠을 깨다〉 wake (up); awake
♦긴[무서운] 꿈에서 눈뜨다 wake (up) from a long sleep [dreadful dream] / 차마 눈뜨고 볼 수 없는 참상이다 be too miserable [cruel] to look at; 〈재해를 당한 사람이〉 be in a dire [miserable] plight
▶나는 동트기 전에 눈떴다 I woke up before dawn.
▶그 광경은 눈뜨고 볼 수 없는 참혹한 것이었다 The sight was to terrible [horrible] to look at. ≒ That was an unbearable sight to see.
2 〈깨달아 알다〉 awake [awaken, wake up] 《to》; be awakened to
♦성에 눈뜨다 become aware of sex; be awakened to sex [sexuality] / 진실에 눈뜨다 open *one's* eye to the truth / 현실에 눈뜨다 be awakened [have *one's* eyes opened] to the stern realities
눈뜬장님 a bat-blind person; 〈문맹자〉 an unlettered person; an ignoramus [ignəréiməs]; an illiterate (person)
눈띄다 〈두드러지다〉 stand out; be conspicuous [prominent]; be outstanding; cut a conspicuous figure
눈망울 an eyeball
눈맞다 〈눈치가 통하다〉 read each other's mind [intention]; 〈남녀가〉 fall in love with each other ▶둘은 눈이 맞아 달아났다 They fell in love with each other and ran away together.
눈 맞 추 다 〈마 주 보 다〉 exchange looks [glances] with each other; look at each other; 〈남녀가〉 make silent love to each other
눈매 the eyes; the look; the expression of the eyes
♦눈매가 고운 여자 a woman with lovely [pretty] eyes / 눈매가 시원스러운 소녀 a girl with clear [bright] eyes / 눈매가 매섭다 have hard eyes
▶그는 눈매가 고약하다 He has a sinister look (on his face).
▶그는 무서운[화난] 눈매로 그녀를 노려보았다 He glared at her with a fierce [angry] look.
눈맵시 the eyes ⇨ 눈매
눈멀다 lose *one's* sight; become [go] blind
♦눈먼 사람 a blind man / 눈먼 사랑 blind love / 돈에 눈멀다 covet money; be blinded [lured] by gain / 태어날 때부터 눈멀다 be born blind
▶그는 돈에 눈멀었다 He was blinded by the lure of gold [money].
눈물¹ 〈눈에서 흐르는〉 a tear
♦감사의 눈물 《shed》 tears of gratitude / 거짓 눈물 crocodile tears / 기쁨의 눈물 tears of joy; happy tears / 뜨거운 눈물 hot [burning, scalding] tears / 사나이의 눈물 the tears of a brave man / 피눈물 salt [bitter] tears / 회한의 눈물 tears of remorse / 눈물 어린 눈 liquid eyes / 눈물의 이별 parting in tears; tearful parting / 눈물어린 목소리로 with tears in *one's* voices
〈눈물이〉 눈물이 없는 사람 a tearless [a cold-blooded, an unfeeling] person / 눈물이 글썽해

눈물²

지다 bring tears to *one's* eyes / 눈물이 나다 tears flow; tears come into *one's* eyes / 눈물이 비오듯하다 shed a shower of tears

▶ 그는 눈물이 났다 Tears came into [formed in] his eyes.

▶ 그녀의 눈에는 기쁨의 눈물이 피어 있었다 There were tears of a joy in her eyes.

▶ 그의 얘기를 듣자니 눈물이 나오더라 As I listened to his story, I felt tears come to my eyes.

▶ 눈물이 한 방울 그의 뺨을 흘러내렸다 A tear fell [rolled, ran] down his cheek.

▶ 눈물이 흘러내려 그녀의 베개를 적셨다 The tears trickled [rolled] down and wet(ted) her pillow.

▶ 양파를 다듬고 있자니 눈물이 나기 시작했다 As I was chopping an onion, my eyes began to water.

▶ 우리는 모두 눈물이 나도록 웃었다 We all laughed until we cried [till tears came into our eyes].

⟨눈물을⟩ 눈물을 머금고 with tearful eyes / 눈물을 거두다 stop weeping / 눈물을 닦다 wipe *one's* tears away; wipe *one's* wet eyes / 눈물을 삼키다 keep [hold] back *one's* tears / 감사의 눈물을 흘리다 weep for gratitude / 거짓 눈물을 흘리다 shed [weep] crocodile tears / 회한의 눈물을 흘리다 shed bitter tears of remorse

▶ 그 소식을 듣고 모두 눈물을 흘렸다 Everybody shed tears at the news.

▶ 고아가 된 그 아이를 보니 눈물을 참을 수가 없었다 Looking at the bereaved infant, I could not hold back my tears.

▶ 그 슬픈 얘기에 나는 눈물을 흘리고 말았다 I was moved to tears by the sad story. ⇌ The sad story moved me to tears.

⟨눈물에⟩ 눈물에 젖은 얼굴 a tearful [tear-stained] face ▶ 그녀의 눈은 눈물에 젖어 있었다 Her eyes were moist with tears.

⟨눈물로⟩ 눈물로 나날[세월]을 보내다 spend *one's* days [time] in tears; live in sorrow / 눈물로 목이 메다 be choked with tears / 눈물로 헤어지다 part 《from *sb*》 in tears; take tearful leave 《of *sb*》

▶ 그녀는 눈물로 목이 메어 그 이야기를 했다 She told me about it, her voice choked with tears.

▶ 부모와 아이들은 눈물로 이별했다 The parents and the children parted in tears.

눈물² ⟨눈석이⟩ meltwater; melted snow

눈물겹다 pathetic; touching; tearful; teary

♦ 눈물겨운 광경 a moving sight; a touching [pathetic] scene / 눈물겨운 노력 pathetically sincere [painful] efforts / 눈물겨운 이야기 a pathetic [touching] story

▶ 그 사람은 눈물겨운 노력을 했다 He made strikingly strenuous efforts.

눈물지다 tears fall [flow]

눈물짓다 shed [drop] tears; weep

♦ 눈물짓게 하다 move *sb* to tears; draw tears from *sb* / 눈물지으며 신상 이야기를 하다 tell the story of *one's* life with tears in *one's* eyes [with tearful eyes]

▶ 그 슬픈 이야기에 나는 눈물지었다 I was moved to tears by the sad story. ⇌ The sad story moved me to tears.

눈바람 wind and snow; ⟨설한풍⟩ a snowy wind; ⟨눈보라⟩ a snowstorm

눈발 snow flakes ▶ 굵은 눈발이 날리고 있다 Large snowflakes are falling [fluttering down]. ⇌ It is snowing in large flakes.

눈방울 a glaring [lovely] eyeball ♦ 눈방울을 굴리다 roll ⟨goggle⟩ *one's* eyeballs ▶ 그 남자는 눈방울을 굴리며 주위를 둘러보았다 The man looked around with goggling eyeballs.

눈밭 snow-covered ground; a snowfield

눈병 —病 an eye disease; an eye trouble ♦ 눈병을 앓다 be afflicted [suffer from] an eye disease

눈보라 a spray of snow; a driving snow; a snowstorm; ⟨세찬⟩ a blizzard

♦ 심한 눈보라 a severe snowstorm; a blizzard / 눈보라가 치다 have a snowstorm; snow drifts hard / 눈보라를 만나다 be overtaken by a snowstorm

▶ 아침부터 눈보라가 치고 있다 A snowstorm has been raging since morning.

눈부라리다 look menacingly 《at》

눈부시다 1 ⟨빛이⟩ glaring; dazzling (to the eye); blinding (flash)

♦ 눈부시게 빛나다 dazzle; glare; ⟨전등 등이⟩ flare / 눈부시게 희다 be dazzlingly white

▶ 석양이 수면에 반사되어 눈부시다 The evening sun reflecting from the water is dazzling.

▶ 눈부신 전등 아래에서 많은 사람들이 즐겁게 술을 마시고 있다 A large number of people are drinking animatedly under the dazzling lights.

▶ 여름에는 햇빛이 눈부셔서 색안경을 쓴다 In summer the sunlight is bright, so we wear sunglasses.

▶ 나는 자동차 전조등이 눈부셔서 밤에는 운전하기가 두렵다 Car headlights are so blinding (that) I'm scared of driving at night.

2 ⟨황홀하다⟩ brilliant; radiant; gorgeous

▶ 그녀는 눈부신 미인이다 She is a dazzling [radiant] beauty.

▶ 그녀는 눈부시게 차려입고 있었다 She was brightly [gorgeously] dressed.

3 ⟨비유⟩ remarkable 《development》; splendid 《exploit》; brilliant 《success》

♦ 전자 기기의 눈부신 발전 a remarkable improvement in electronic equipment / 눈부신 업적을 이루다 produce splendid [wonderful, striking] achievements 《in》; achieve splendid [wonderful] things 《in》

▶ 한국의 과학 기술은 눈부신 발전을 이루었다 Korea has made remarkable [startling] progress in scientific techniques.

눈비 snow and rain

눈빛 the expression of *one's* eyes; a look (of the eyes) ♦ 호소하는 듯한 눈빛 a look of appeal

▶ 그는 눈빛을 번뜩이며 소리치고 있었다 He was shouting with a fiery look [with fiery eyes].

▶그는 상냥한 눈빛으로 나를 바라보았다 He looked at me with friendly eyes [with a warm look in his eyes].

눈사람 《make》 a snowman; a snow image

눈사태 —沙汰 a snowslide; an avalanche (of snow); a snowslip
▶눈사태가 났다 Avalanches rushed down the mountainside.
▶그들은 눈사태로 파묻혔다고 한다 They are said to have been buried under a snowslide.

눈살 the furrow [wrinkles] between the eyebrows
▶그는 그 소식을 듣고 눈살을 찌푸렸다 He knitted his brows to hear the news.
▶그의 친구들은 그의 방종한 행동에 눈살을 찌푸렸다 His friends frowned at his wild behavior.

눈석이 melted snow ⇨ 눈석임(～물)

눈석임 a thaw; the thawing of snow ■—물 melted snow; water from the thawing snow

눈설다 unfamiliar (to *one's* eyes); strange

눈속이다 blind the eyes (of); throw dust in *sb's* eyes; hoodwink; deceive

눈속임 deceiving; hoodwinking; cheating
▶나는 눈속임을 당하여 가짜 보석을 샀다 I was hoodwinked into buying fake jewels.

눈송이 a snowflake; a flake (of snow)

눈시울 the edge of an eyelid
♦눈시울이 뜨거워지는 광경 a deeply moving [touching] scene; a heart-warming [pathetic] sight; a moving spectacle
▶나도 모르게 눈시울이 뜨거워졌다 I was moved to tears in spite of myself.

눈싸움¹ 〈눈겨룸〉 a staring game [match]; an outstaring game
▶눈싸움하자 Let's play a staring game.
▶두 어린이는 눈싸움을 벌이고 있었다 The two children were having a competition to see who could stare the other out.

눈싸움² 〈설전(雪戰)〉 a snowball fight; snowballing
—**눈싸움하다** have a snowball fight [battle]; have a game of snowballing; play (at) snowballs; snowball

눈썰미 《have》 a quick eye for learning things
♦눈썰미가 있다[없다]; be quick [slow] in visual learning

눈썹 an eyebrow
▶그린 눈썹 a penciled [painted] eyebrow / 눈썹을 그리다 pencil *one's* eyebrows / 눈썹을 치켜올리다 lift an eyebrow; raise *one's* eyebrows
▶그는 눈썹 하나 까딱하지 않았다 He didn't even raise an eyebrow [bat an eyelid].
▶그는 눈썹이 짙다 He has heavy [bushy] eyebrows.
▶그녀는 눈썹을 그리고 립스틱을 발랐다 She penciled her eyebrows and put on lipstick.
▶그는 그 이야기를 듣고 눈썹을 찡그렸다 He frowned [knitted his brows] to hear the story.
■—**연필** an eyebrow pencil

눈알 an eyeball
♦눈알이 툭 불거진 개구리 a frog with goggling [protruding] eyes / 눈알을 굴리다 roll [goggle] *one's* eyes / 눈알이 튀어나올 정도로 놀라다 be frightened out of *one's* wits

눈앞 **1** 〈목전〉 ♦눈앞에 before *one's* eyes; before [in front of, under] *sb's* very eyes; in the presence of; in *one's* sight / 눈앞에 어른거리다 be haunted (by) / 눈앞에서 남을 비방하다 abuse *sb* to (his) face
▶그가 급사했다는 소식에 나는 순간적으로 눈앞이 캄캄해졌다 At the news of his sudden death, everything before me went black for a moment.
▶눈앞에 펼쳐진 경관에 우리는 매혹되었다 We were enchanted with the scene spread before us.
▶내 아이의 모습이 눈앞에 어른거린다 My child's face haunts me.
▶눈앞에서 문이 쾅 닫혔다 The door was slammed in my face.
2 〈가까운 장래〉 ♦눈앞에 닥치다 be near [close] at hand; just ahead ▶시험이 눈앞에 닥쳤다 The examination is close at hand [just around the corner].
3 〈현재〉 ♦눈앞의 immediate; present
▶눈앞의 이익만 추구하지 마라 Quit trying to gain only your (own) immediate interests.
▶그는 눈앞의 일만 생각한다 He thinks only of the present.

눈약 —藥 eyewash ⇨ 안약

눈어림 eye measurement ⇨ 눈대중

눈언저리 parts around the eye ♦눈언저리에 around the eye

눈엣가시 a very disgusting [hateful] person
♦눈엣가시로 여기다 regard *sb* as an eyesore
▶왜 그는 나를 눈엣가시 취급을 하지? Why does he always treat me like an enemy?
▶그를 눈엣가시처럼 생각하면 안된다 Don't bear him hatred.

눈여겨보다 observe [eye] carefully; watch intently; take a good [close] look (at)
♦눈여겨볼 만하다 be worth notice; be worthy of attention / 행동을 눈여겨보다 observe *sb's* behavior carefully

눈요기 —療飢 a feast for *one's* eyes; a delight [joy] to see [watch]; visual pleasure
♦눈요기가 되다 be a delight [feast, joy] to the eye; delight [please] the eye
▶그녀의 춤은 눈요기가 되었다 Her dancing was a delight to watch.
▶나는 매일 아름다운 꽃으로 눈요기를 하고 있다 Every day I feast my eyes on beautiful flowers. ⇌ Beautiful flowers delight [refresh] my eyes every day.
—**눈요기하다** feast *one's* eyes 《on》

눈웃음 a smile with [in] *one's* eyes ♦눈웃음치다 smile with *one's* eyes; 〈추파〉(口) cast [make] sheep's eyes 《at》

눈익다 familiar ♦눈익은 광경[얼굴] a familiar sight

눈자위 the rim of an eye ♦눈자위(가) 꺼지다 *one's* eyes sink; 〈죽다〉 die

눈접 —椄 〈접목〉 bud grafting; budding; inlay graft —**눈접하다** graft a bud (in, upon); bud

눈정기 —精氣 the vivacity [animation] of

the eyes; the glitter [keenness] of the eyes
♦눈정기가 있다 have lively eyes; have glittering [keen] eyes; be keen-eyed
눈주다 give sb the eye; eye sb meaningly
눈짐작 measuring with one's eye ⇨ 눈대중
눈짓 a wink; winking
♦눈짓으로 알다 make a sign with one's eyes; signal (to sb) with one's eyes
—**눈짓하다** wink (significantly) (at); make a sign with one's eye(s); eye sb meaningly; give sb the eye; cock the [one's] eye at sb ♦서로 눈짓하다 exchange significant looks
▶그녀가 눈짓하자 하인은 슬그머니 빙을 나갔다 At a sign from her eyes the servant glided out of the room.
눈초리 1 〈눈꼬리〉 the corner [tail] of the eye 2 〈시선〉 a look 《in sb's eyes》; an expression of the eyes
♦매서운 눈초리 a dreadful [menacing] look; fierce eyes / 의심스러운 눈초리로 보다 view sth with suspicious eyes; eye [regard, look on] sth with suspicion
눈총 a glare; a sharp [hostile] look; looking daggers
♦눈총 맞는 사람 an object of hatred; a hated person / 눈총(을) 맞다 be glared at; be hated [detested]/ 뭇사람의 눈총을 맞다 become a common object of hatred
눈총기 —聰氣 power of observation ♦눈총기가 있다 have a keen eyes; have a photographic memory
눈치 1 〈재치〉 tact; sense; quick wits
♦눈치가 빠르다 have quick wits; have a quick perception; be quick-witted; be tactful [sensible]/ 눈치가 없다 have no sense; have a slow perception; be slow-witted [dull-witted]; be tactless [senseless]/ 눈치있게 …하다 have the good sense to 《do》; be sensible [tactful] enough to 《do》
2 〈속마음의 태도〉 one's mind [intention, design]; one's mental attitude (toward); 〈기색〉 (facial) expression; a sign; a hint; an indication
♦눈치 코치 다 안다 be well aware of the situation; know quite well how the wind blows / 눈치 코치도 모르다 be blind to the whole situation; do not know how the wind blows / 눈치를 보이다 express (one's emotions) by outward signs; betray in one's look / 좋아하는[싫어하는] 눈치를 보이다 give [show] signs of pleasure [displeasure] / 눈치를 살피다 read [study] sb's face [countenance]
▶애들은 어른의 눈치를 살핀다 Children study the pleasure and interests of adults.
▶그는 눈치가 좀 이상했다 He was somewhat strange in his manners.
▶그녀는 슬쩍 남편의 눈치를 살폈다 She secretly studied her husband's facial expression. ⇌ She cast a furtive glance at her husband.
눈치레 〈겉치레〉 mere show; outward show; putting on a good front ♦눈치레로 for show; for the sake of appearance

—**눈치레하다** make outward show; put on a good front; dress up to appeal to the eye
눈치보다 try to read (another's) mind [face]; have a regard for sb's feelings; 〈어려워하다〉 feel constraint [small] (in sb's presence)
♦화나지 않았나 눈치보다 study sb's face to see if he is angry / 눈치보아 가며 의견을 진술하다 venture an opinion studying sb's face / 눈치보아 가며 행동하다 act according to the situation
▶아저씨 댁에 기식하고 있으니 눈치보게 된다 Living on my uncle makes me feel small.
눈치채다 sense, get [have] wind of, smell, notice
▶나는 뭔가 잘못되었다는 것을 곧 눈치챘다 I sensed at once that something was wrong.
▶그들은 우리 계획을 눈치챈 것 같다 They seem to be suspicious of our plan.
▶그의 잘못을 아무도 눈치지 못했다 His error passed unnoticed.
▶그녀에게 눈치채이지 않게 조심해라 Take care not to arouse her suspicion.
눈칫밥 a meal given [offered] unwillingly
♦눈칫밥을 먹다 eat another's salt; eat salt with sb
눈코 the eyes and the nose ♦눈코 뜰 새 없이 바쁘다 be very busy; be pressed by business [work]
눈퉁멸 〔魚〕 a round herring
눈트다 sprout ⇨ 싹트다
눈허리시다 very funny; ridiculously amusing; sidesplitting
눈흘기다 cast a reproachful [disapproving] glance 《at》 ⇨ 흘기다
눋다 scorch; be [get] scorched; burn; be burned [charred]
▶밥이 눋었다 The rice has got scorched.
▶뭐가 눋는 냄새가 난다 There's a smell of something burning.
▶눋지 않도록 계속 저어라 Stir it constantly to prevent burning [scorching].
눌러 1 〈계속하여〉 continuously; in a row; in succession; consecutively
♦눌러 앉다 continue to stay; stay on (and on); 〈유임하다〉 stay [remain] in the same position / 권좌에 눌러앉다 stay [remain] in power
▶임원들은 눌러앉기로 결정했다 The executives have decided to remain in office.
2 〈너그럽게〉 generously; magnanimously
▶저의 무례함을 눌러 용서하십시오 Please excuse me for my rudeness. ⇌ Pardon [Forgive] me for my rudeness, please.
눌러듣다 take 《sb's remark》 with kindly tolerance [with good grace]; hear leniently ♦생각없이 한 말이니 하고 눌러듣다 forgive sb for (his) thoughtless remarks
눌러보다 deal leniently with sb [sb's mistake]; treat sb with generosity [with good grace]; pass over; shut [close] one's eyes to
▶철없는 아이니 눌러봐 주십시오 Kindly forgive him since he is just a boy with little sense.
▶그는 나의 무례함을 눌러봐 주었다 He was good enough to overlook my rudeness.

눌리다¹ 1〈누름을 당하다〉be pressed [held] down
♦ 납작하게 눌리다 be pressed flat / 눌려 죽다 be crushed to death
▶ 국민은 군사정권의 압제에 눌려 지내고 있다 The people are held down by a repressive military regime.
2〈압도되다〉be overpowered [overwhelmed]; be oppressed; be suppressed; be put down
♦ 다수에 눌리다 be overwhelmed by numbers / 말에 눌리다 be overwhelmed [overpowered] by the eloquence [argument]; be talked down / 마누라한테 눌리다 be henpecked; be tied to one's wife's apron strings
♦ 작은 가게는 큰 가게에 눌려 장사가 잘 안된다 Small stores are jostled out of trade by big ones.
▶ 그의 위엄에 눌려 모두 입을 다물었다 The majesty of his appearance awed them into silence.

눌리다² 〈눌게 하다〉burn; scorch; singe
♦ 밥을 눌리다 overcook [burn, scorch] rice / 다리미질하다가 옷을 눌리다 scorch one's clothes in ironing

눌변 訥辯 slowness of speech ♦ 눌변인 사람 a poor [an awkward] speaker [talker] ▶ 그는 눌변이다 He is a poor talker.

눌어붙다 1〈타서 바닥에〉scorch ▶ 밥이 솥바닥에 눌어붙었다 The rice is burned and stuck to the bottom of the pan.
2〈한 군데 오래〉remain in the same place [position]; settle down; stay on ♦ 시골에 눌어붙어 살다 settle down in the country / 평사원으로 눌어붙어 있다 remain a mere clerk

눌은내 a burnt smell ▶ 밥에서 눌은내가 난다 The rice has a smoky [burnt] smell.

눌은밥 scorched rice (at the bottom of the pot)

눕다 lie down; lay oneself down; stretch oneself
♦ 모로[반듯이] 눕다 lie on one's side [back] / 자리에 눕다 lie in one's bed; lay oneself [repose] on the bed / 앓아 누워 있다 be ill in bed; lie on a bed of illness
▶ 나는 풀밭에 누워 하늘을 바라보기를 좋아한다 I like to lie in the grass and look up at the sky.
▶ 그녀는 지난달 말부터 병상에 누워 있다 She has been ill in bed since the end of last month.
▶ 아이들이 독감으로 누워 있다 Our children are laid up with the flu.
▶ 그는 잔디 위에 길게 누워 있었다 He was lying at full length on the lawn. ⇒ He was stretching (himself) out on the lawn.

눕히다 lay down; make [have] sb lie down
♦ 때려 눕히다 knock sb down / 상자를 눕히다 lay a box on the side / 자리에 눕히다 put sb to bed; lay sb down on the bed

눙치다 soothe [appease] 《sb's anger》 with nice words

뉘¹ 〈쌀의〉an unhulled [a half-hulled] grain of rice; rice in the husk

뉘² 〈자손 덕〉blessings from one's offspring
뉘³ a boy's sister ⇨ 누이
뉘⁴ 〈누구〉who; 〈누구의〉whose
뉘다¹ lay down ⇨ 눕히다
뉘다² make 《a child》 urinate ⇨ 누이다²
뉘렇다 sickly yellow; sallow; withered
뉘른베르크 〈독일 남부의 도시〉Nuremberg; Nürnberg
뉘반지기 〈뉘가 많은 쌀〉chaffy rice; rice containing many unhulled grains
뉘앙스 a nuance; a shade of difference 《in meaning [feeling]》
▶ 이 단어의 미묘한 뉘앙스를 아시겠습니까? Can you make out a delicate shade of meaning in this word?
▶ 이 표현의 뉘앙스를 간과하면 안된다 You must not overlook nuances in this expression.

뉘엿거리다 1〈해가〉be going [about] to set; be sinking
▶ 해가 뉘엿거린다 The sun is sinking in the west. ⇒ The sun is about to set.
▶ 지평선으로 해가 뉘엿거리고 있었다 The sun was verging [sinking] toward the horizon.
2〈속이〉feel nausea; feel sick
▶ 그것을 보기만 해도 속이 뉘엿거린다 The mere sight of it makes me sick [turns my stomach]. ⇒ My stomach turns [rises] at the mere sight of it.

뉘엿뉘엿 〈해가〉ready to set; 〈속이〉nauseatingly; sickeningly

뉘우쁘다 penitent; repentant; regretful

뉘우치다 regret; repent; be penitent 《for》; feel regret [remorse] 《for》
♦ 뉘우치는 기색도 없이 without any contrition / 깊이 뉘우치다 be smitten with remorse / 죄를 뉘우치다 be penitent for one's sin / 자기가 한 일을 뉘우치다 regret one's act; be sorry for [repent of] what one has done / 뉘우치지 않다 be impenitent
▶ 피고는 뉘우치는 빛이 없다 The accused is without remorse.
▶ 이제는 뉘우쳐도 소용없다 It's no use crying over spilt milk.

뉘 집에 죽이 끓는지 밥이 끓는지 아나 《속담》There is no knowing who is rich and who is poor.

뉴기니 〈오스트레일리아 북쪽의 섬〉New Guinea ■ —사람 a New Guinean
뉴델리 〈인도의 수도〉New Delhi
뉴딜 the New Deal
뉴멕시코 〈미국 남서부의 주〉New Mexico (略 N.Mex., N.M.)
뉴스 news
♦ 짤막한 뉴스 news in brief / 최신 뉴스 the latest news 《on》/ 뉴스의 출처 a news source
▶ 재미 있는 뉴스가 있어 Here's an interesting piece of news.
▶ 이건 뉴스거리가 되겠다 This will make news.
▶ 6시 뉴스를 들었습니까? Did you hear the six o'clock news?
▶ [會話] 「저녁 8시 텔레비전 뉴스를 보았니?」 「응, 나쁜 뉴스 뿐이더군」 "Did you watch eight o'clock news [newscast] on television

this evening?" "Yes, there was nothing but bad news this evening."
■국내[해외]— home [foreign] news 라디오[텔레비전]— a news [a newscast] on the radio [on television] 스폿— spot news 스포츠— sports news; 《美口》 sportscast 전광— an electric news tape; 《광고용의》 a sky sign ■—방송 a newscast; a news show —속보 a news flash; a news bulletin —영화 a newsreel; a news picture; a news film —원 a news source —캐스터 a newscaster

뉴스해설 —解說 news commentary ■—자 a (television, radio) (news) commentator; a news analyst

뉴욕 New York ■—사람[시민] a New Yorker —시 the City of New York; New York City —주 New York State (略 N.Y.)

뉴잉글랜드 〈미국 북동부·대서양 연안 지역〉 New England

뉴저지 〈미국 동부의 주〉 New Jersey (略 N.J., NJ)

뉴질랜드 New Zealand ■—사람 a New Zealander

뉴턴 〈영국의 물리학자〉 Newton, Sir Isaac (1642-1727) ♦뉴턴의 만유 인력의 법칙 Newton's law of universal gravitation

뉴트론 〖物〗 a neutron ⇨ 중성자(中性子)

뉴펀들랜드 〈캐나다 동부의 섬〉 Newfoundland

뉴햄프셔 〈미국 북동부의 주〉 New Hampshire (略 N.H.)

느글거리다 feel sick; nauseate ♦속이 느글거리다 feel nausea; be sick at the stomach

느긋하다 relaxed; easygoing
♦느긋하게 comfortably; at ease / 마음이 느긋해지다 feel relaxed; feel at ease
▶너도 퍽 느긋한 사람이야 You are such an easygoing man, aren't you?
▶나는 느긋하게 그 여자의 대답을 기다렸다 I looked forward patiently to her answer.
▶그는 의자에 느긋하게 앉아 쉬었다 He sat comfortably in a chair and made himself at ease.
▶그는 시골에서 느긋하게 살고 있다 He is enjoying an easy [a free and easy] life in the country.

느끼다 1 〈지각·감각〉 feel; sense; be conscious of; be sensible of [to]; experience 《inconvenience》
♦어려움을 느끼다 find difficult / 위험을 느끼다 sense danger / 필요를 절실하게 느끼다 feel keenly the necessity 《of》
▶나는 추위[피로, 시장기]를 느꼈다 I felt cold [tired, hungry].
▶그는 왼쪽발에 통증을 느꼈다 He felt a pain in his left foot.
▶나는 집이 흔들리는 것을 느꼈다 I felt the house shaking.
▶그녀는 뺨에 눈물이 흐르는 것을 느꼈다 She felt tears run down her cheeks.
▶나는 몸에 열을 느꼈다 I was aware of my feverishness.
▶나는 무엇이 내 발에 닿는 것을 느꼈다 I felt something touching my foot.
▶한 시간이 백년처럼 느껴졌다 An hour felt like a century.
▶나는 추위를 전혀 느끼지 않았다 I did not feel the cold at all.
2 〈의식·생〉 sense 《that》; feel; think
▶나는 미행당하고 있음을 느꼈다 I was aware [conscious] of being followed. ⇌ I was aware [conscious] that I was being followed.
▶그는 무슨 일이 일어났음을 느꼈다 He felt that something had happened.
▶그녀는 그가 무엇인가를 감추고 있다고 느꼈다 She felt that he was keeping something from her.
▶나는 누가 나를 감시하고 있음을 느꼈다 I felt somebody watching me. ⇌ I was aware of somebody watching me.
▶나는 스스로의 무지를 절실하게 느끼고 있다 I am fully aware of my ignorance. ⇌ I keenly realize how ignorant I am.
▶느낀 바를 솔직히 말하세요 Don't hesitate to say whatever you have in mind.
▶필요를 느끼지 않기 때문에 내 차를 갖지 않는다 I don't have my own car because I don't feel it is necessary.
▶그의 행동은 이상하게 느껴졌다 His behavior struck us as odd.
3 〈감동하다〉 be impressed 《by, with》; be moved [touched] 《by》
♦깊이 느끼게 하다 touch sb to heart; impress sb profoundly
▶나는 그때 처음으로 어머니의 사랑을 깊이 느꼈다 I had never felt my mother's love so strongly.
▶나는 그 소설을 읽고 느낀 바가 많았다 I was deeply stirred by the novel.
▶그는 깊이 느낀 바 있어 좋은 자리를 그만 두었다 He gave up his good job for some urgent reason of his own.
4 ⇨ 흐느끼다

느끼하다 1 〈맛이〉 greasy; fatty; oily ♦느끼한 음식 greasy [rich] food ▶이 요리는 너무 느끼하다 This dish is too fatty for me.
2 〈속이〉《be》 sick at the stomach; nauseous
▶기름진 음식을 먹었더니 속이 느끼하다 I feel sick [have a sick stomach] after a greasy meal.

느낌 1 〈감(感)〉 feeling; sense; 〈감촉〉 touch
♦뭐라고 말할 수 없는 느낌 an indefinable [indescribable] sensation / 느낌이 들다 feel; have a 《queer》 feeling
▶느낌이 비단 같다 It feels like silk. ⇌ It has a silklike feel.
▶이 잎사귀는 만지면 느낌이 부드럽다 This leaf feels smooth. ⇌ This leaf has a smooth feel. ⇌ This leaf is smooth to the touch.
2 〈기분〉 sentiment; feeling; a mood; 〈인상〉 an impression; 〈예술품의〉 an effect 《of a painting》
♦느낌이 어두운 그림 a gloomy-looking painting / 좋은[나쁜] 느낌을 주다 make [produce] a favorable [an unfavorable] impression on sb; impress sb favorably [unfavorably] / 한국적인 느낌을 주다 create a Korean atmosphere
▶전람회를 보신 느낌이 어떻습니까? What is

your impression of the exhibition?
▶ 그 남자를 만난 느낌이 어떻던가요? How did he impress you when you met him?
▶ 폭포 그림은 시원한 느낌을 준다 A picture of a fall creates the illusion of coolness.
▶ 사슴 때문에 경치가 우아하고 활달한 느낌이 더든다 The deer adds a touch of grace and spirit to the landscape.
▶ 이 음악은 봄의 느낌을 준다 This music produces [gives one] an impression of spring.
3 〈기미〉 a tinge; a smack
▶ 그는 성격상 좀 무난한 느낌이 있다 There is a smack of recklessness in his character.
▶ 이상한 소리가 난 듯한 느낌이 들었다 I fancied that I heard a strange noise.

느낌표 —標 〔文法〕 an exclamation mark [point]

-느냐 〈종결어미〉 ▶ 무슨 일로 왔느냐? What has brought you here?
▶ 무얼 하느냐? What are you doing?
▶ 어디로 가느냐? Where are you going?
▶ 무슨 일이 있느냐? What is the matter (with you)?

-느니 1 〈종결어미〉 ▶ 시간을 엄수해야 하느니 You should be punctual. ▶ 자식은 부모에게 순종해야 하느니 Children should obey their parents.
2 〈연결어미〉 ♦ 이러하다느니 저러하다느니 핑계를 대어 with suchlike excuses
3 〈차라리〉 rather; as soon; sooner...than
▶ 항복하느니 차라리 죽는 편이 낫다 I would sooner [rather] die than give in.
▶ 이렇게 비오는 날 외출하느니 차라리 집에 있겠다 I would stay home rather than go out on such a rainy day.

느닷없다 sudden; abrupt; unexpected; unheralded
♦ 느닷없는 말 an abrupt [unexpected] remark / 느닷없는 방문 a surprise visit / 느닷없는 짓 an unexpected behavior / 느닷없는 해고 unheralded discharge
▶ 나는 그의 느닷없는 질문에 대답이 궁해서 애먹었다 I was at a loss for a reply to his abrupt question.

느닷없이 unexpectedly; abruptly; suddenly; by surprise; 〈예고없이〉 without notice [warning]
♦ 느닷없이 나타나다 burst upon the scene [view] / 느닷없이 덤벼들다 make a sudden spring at sb / 느닷없이 뺨을 때리다 slap sb on the cheek all of a sudden / 느닷없이 해고하다 dismiss sb without notice
▶ 그녀가 느닷없이 찾아오는 바람에 난감했다 I was puzzled by her unexpected [surprise] visit.
▶ 그는 느닷없이 계획을 바꾸었다 She changed his plan abruptly.
▶ 느닷없이 폭발이 일어났다 Suddenly [All of a sudden], there was an explosion.
▶ 굵은 빗방울이 느닷없이 떨어지기 시작했다 Large drops of rain suddenly began to fall.

-느라고 〈연결어미〉 ▶ 점심 먹느라고 늦었다 Lunch made me late.
▶ 자느라고 무슨 일이 일어났는지 몰랐다 I was sound asleep, so I did not know what happened.
▶ 나는 선거운동하느라고 바빴다 I was busy (in) canvassing for the election.
▶ 그는 사과하느라고 무슨 말을 했다 He said something by way of apology.

느럭느럭 slowly; sluggishly; lazily; idly ♦ 느럭느럭 걷다 walk slowly; loiter around / 느럭느럭 움직이다 move sluggishly / 동작이 느럭느럭하다 be slow in *one's* movements
—느럭느럭하다 tardy; slow

느루먹다 make (food, provisions) last longer
▶ 가지고 있는 쌀로 3주간은 (더)느루먹을 수 있습니다 We can make the rice we have in stock last (for) three more weeks.

느른하다 languid ⇨ 나른하다
느릅나무 〔植〕 an elm (tree)
느리광이 a laggard ⇨ 느림보

느리다 1 〈더디다〉 slow; sluggish; slow-going (tortoise)
♦ 느린 공[주자] a slow ball [runner]/ 동작이 느린 slow-moving / 느리게 slow; slowly / 느린 속도로 at a slow [low] speed / 걸음이 느리다 be slow-footed / 말이 느리다 be slow in *one's* speech; be slow of speech [tongue]; speak slowly; drawl / 행동을 취하는 것이 느리다 be slow in taking action
▶ 그녀는 계산이 느리다 She is slow [poor] at figures [accounts].
▶ 그는 일하는 것이 느리다 He is slow in his work. ⇌ He is a slow worker.
▶ 투수는 느린 공을 던졌다 The pitcher threw a slow ball.
2 〈성기다〉 loose; slack

느림보 a laggard; a dawdler; 〔俗〕 a slow coach; 〔美口〕 a slowpoke

느릿느릿 1 〈느리게〉 〈walk〉 slowly; lazily; tardily
▶ 그녀는 언제나 느릿느릿 일한다 She always does her work idly.
▶ 교통 체증으로 차들이 느릿느릿 움직였다 Because of the traffic jam [congestion], vehicles were moving at a snail's pace [very slowly].
2 〈성기게〉 loose(ly); slack ♦ 느릿느릿 짜다 knit with loose stitches

느릿느릿 걸어도 황소 걸음 (속담) Slow and [but] steady [sure] wins the race.

느물거리다 talk [behave] insidiously [snakily]; act craftily [trickily]

느물느물 insidiously; craftily; snakily; trickily

느슨하다 1 〈헐겁다〉 loose; lax; slack
♦ 느슨한 매듭[붕대] a loose knot [bandage] / 구두끈을 느슨하게 매다 tie *one's* shoelaces loosely / 옷의 허리를 좀 느슨하게 만들다 make a dress with a rather loose waist; make the waist on the loose side
▶ 매듭이 느슨해졌다 The knot has come loose.
▶ 기계의 볼트가 느슨해졌다 A bolt has loosened on the machine.
2 〈마음이〉 relaxed; lax 《supervision》; loose
▶ 그의 느슨한 마음 때문에 사고가 났다 His

carelessness caused the accident.
▶ 최근에 선수들간의 규율이 느슨해지고 있다 Discipline is loose [lax] among the players these days.

느즈러지다 1 〈조인 것이〉 become [get] loose; loosen; slack(en); hang slack ▶ 걷는 동안에 구두끈이 느즈러졌다 My shoestring got loose while I was walking.
2 〈마음이〉 become remiss; relax; slack(en) ▶ 시험이 끝나면 기분이 느즈러진다 We feel relaxed after the examination.
3 〈기한이〉 be postponed; be put off; be prolonged

느지감치 rather late
♦ 아침밥을 느지감치 먹다 have a late breakfast / 아침에 느지감치 일어나다 get up rather late in the morning / 저녁에 느지감치 도착하다 arrive a bit late in the evening

느지막이 fairly [quite] late ♦ 느지막이 자다 go to bed quite late at night

느지막하다 fairly [quite] late ▶ 이런 느지막한 시간에 어딜 가는 거야? Where are you going this late?

느직이 〈좀 늦게〉 somewhat [a little] late; 〈느슨하게〉 rather loose(ly) [slack]

느직하다 1 〈좀 늦다〉 somewhat [a little] late; latish ♦ 느직한 아침 식사 a late [latish] breakfast 2 〈좀 느슨하다〉 a little loose [slack]

느타리 〔植〕 agaric
느티나무 〔植〕 a zelkova (tree)
느헤미야 〔聖〕 (The Book of) Nehemiah (略 Neh.)

늑간 肋間 ♦ 늑간의 intercostal; between the ribs ―**근(筋)**〔神經〕 the intercostal muscle [nerve] ―**신경통** intercostal neuralgia

늑골 肋骨 〔解〕 a rib; a costa (*pl.* -tae); (총칭) the ribs; 〔선체(船體)의〕 the frame

늑대 〔動〕 a wolf (*pl.* wolves) ♦ 양가죽을 쓴 늑대 a wolf in sheep's clothing; a wolf in a lamb's skin / 늑대 같은 인간 cruel and avaricious persons

늑막 肋膜 〔解〕 the pleura (*pl.* -rae) ♦ 늑막의 pleural

늑막염 肋膜炎 〔醫〕 pleurisy ■**건성[습성]**― dry [wet] pleurisy

늑목 肋木 wall bars; a stall bar; Swedish bars
늑연골 肋軟骨 〔解〕 costal cartilage
늑장부리다 dawdle (over); dally away; linger; tarry; be tardy; idle about; slow up [down]
♦ 늑장부리지 않고 without delay [lingering]; straight off / 도중에서 늑장부리다 loiter on the way / 늑장부리다가 기회를 놓치다 dally away *one's* opportunity / 늑장부리며 직무를 다하지 않다 linger in discharging *one's* duties ▶ 네가 늑장부리는 바람에 우리는 버스를 놓쳤다 You were so slow that we missed the bus. ▶ 늑장부리지 말고 곧 다녀오너라 Come back without delay. ⇌ Don't linger along the way.

늑재 肋材 〔船〕 a frame (timber); a rib; futtocks

는 ▶ 그녀는 축구선수다 She is a soccer player. ▶ 그 아이는 아직 걷지 못한다 The child can't walk yet. ▶ 그는 술은 마시지만 담배는 피우지 않는다 He drinks but doesn't smoke. ▶ 하기는 했지만 실패였다 I (really) did do it, but it was a failure. ▶ 내일까지는 끝마칠 수가 없다 I can't finish it by tomorrow.

-는 -ing ♦ 나는 새 a flying bird / 달리는 사슴 a running deer / 책상 위에 있는 책 a book on the desk / 흐르는 물 running [flowing] water

-는가 ▶ 자네 어딜 가는가? Where are you going? ▶ 그 사람 집에 있는가? Is he in [at home]? ▶ 무엇을 하고 있는가? What are you doing?

-는가보다 ▶ 비가 오려는가보다 It seems likely to rain.
▶ 그는 자기가 대단한 사람인 줄 아는가보다 He seems to think he's somebody.
▶ 그녀는 이 사실을 모르는가보다 She seems [appears] to be ignorant of this fact.

-는가하면 ▶ 비가 오는가 하면 눈이 오고, 눈이 오는가 하면 비가 온다 It can't make up its mind whether it wants to snow or wants to rain.
▶ 새들이 머리 위에서 지저귀는가 하면 다람쥐들이 발 밑을 스쳐가기도 한다 Not only are there birds chirping overhead but also squirrels darting underfoot.

-는데 1 〈연결어미〉 ▶ 그 책을 읽기 시작했는데 아주 어려웠다 I began to read the book, which I found very difficult.
▶ 그를 도와 주었는데 고맙다는 말 한 마디 없었다 I helped him, who did not thank me at all.
▶ 우리 동네에 한 사람이 있는데 재주가 비상하다 There is a man in our village, who is extraordinarily talented.
▶ 저 책을 사야겠는데 가진 돈이 없다 I have to buy that book, but I have no money with me now.
2 〈종결어미〉 ▶ 잘 하는데 You are doing well!
▶ 그 아이 잘 생겼는데 What a handsome child (he is)!
▶ 민선생이 곧 오면 좋겠는데 I hope Mr. Min will come soon.

-는데도 ▶ 그들은 비가 오는데도 외출했다 They went out in spite of the rain.
▶ 그토록 많은 결점이 보이는데도 그는 여전히 그녀를 좋아했다 With all her faults he still liked her.

는적거리다 be pulpy [flabby, squashy] from rot
는적는적 pulpily; flabbily; squashily
-는족족 every time; every [each] occasion (that it happens); whenever
▶ 그들은 만나는 족족 싸움이다 Every [Each] time those two meet, there is a quarrel.
▶ 그가 손을 대는 족족 황금으로 변했다 Everything that he touched turned gold.
▶ 나는 배우는 족족 잊어버린다 I forget as soon as I learn.

-는지 1 〈연결어미〉 ▶ 왜 거절했는지 말해 다오 Tell me why you refused.
▶ 어디가 잘못됐는지 말씀해 주세요 Will you

tell me where I am wrong?
▶ 그가 어떻게 해서 이겼는지 모르겠다 I have no idea (as to) how he won.
▶ 목욕물이 준비되었는지 알아봐 주시오 Please ask if the bath is ready.
▶ 그녀가 다음엔 언제 시작하는지 알 수 없다 I don't know when she will begin next time.
2 〈종결어미〉 ▶ 그가 집에 있을는지 I wonder if he is at home. ▶ 그는 지금 어떻게 지내고 있는지 How is he getting along, I wonder?

는지렁이 〈점액〉 mucous [viscous, sticky] liquid; mucilage; slime ♦ 달팽이의 는지렁이 the slimy trail of a snail

는질거리다 feel pulpy [mushy]; be flimsy [decomposed]

늘 always; all the time; usually
♦ 늘 바쁘다 be always busy / 늘 찾아오다 come [call] often; be a frequent visitor to
▶ 그는 늘 늦는다 He is always late. ⇌ He comes late all the time.
▶ 그에게 전화를 하면 늘 통화중이다 Whenever [Everytime] I call him, the line is busy.
▶ 외국어를 배우려면 늘 연습해야 한다 Studying a foreign language requires constant practice.
▶ 그는 늘 담배를 피우고 있다 He smokes all the time. ⇌ He is always smoking. ⇌ He smokes incessantly.

늘그막 one's old [advanced] age; one's later years; one's declining years
♦ 늘그막에 이르러 in one's old age [later years]; in the decline [evening] of one's life / 늘그막에 고生하다 have a hard time late in one's life / 늘그막에 아들을 얻다 have a son in one's old age / 늘그막에 의지할 곳이 없다 have no one to depend upon in one's later life / 늘그막에 호강하다 live in luxury in one's old age

늘다 1 〈많아지다〉 increase; multiply; gain
♦ 세력이 늘다 become more powerful; gain in influence / 수[양]이 늘다 increase in numbers [quantity] / 재산이 늘다 one's wealth increases / 체중이 늘다 gain (in) weight / 회원이 늘다 have an increased membership
▶ 수출이 작년보다 10% 늘었다 The export increased by 10 percent over last year.
▶ 외국 여행을 하는 사람의 수가 늘고 있다 The number of those who travel abroad is increasing [on the increase].
▶ 차를 사는 사람들이 늘고 있다 An increasing number of [More and more] people are buying cars.
▶ 그녀의 예금이 급속하게 늘기 시작했다 Her savings account began to grow rapidly.
▶ 그녀는 항상 체중이 늘지 않도록 조심하고 있다 She is always careful not to gain weight.
2 〈향상되다〉 improve; advance; make (good) progress
♦ 재간이 늘다 improve one's skill 《at, in》; improve in ability
▶ 내 요리솜씨가 늘었다 My skill in cooking has improved. ⇌ My cooking has gotten better.
▶ 만날 때마다 네 영어 실력이 느는구나 Your English ability is better every time I see you.
▶ 자네 술이 느는 것 같군 You seem to be able to drink more than you used to.

늘리다 increase; add (to); multiply; swell
♦ 약의 복용량을 늘리다 step up the dose / 인원을 늘리다 increase the staff [the personnel]; get more people to work / 재산을 늘리다 add to one's wealth; become richer
▶ 책을 읽어 어휘를 늘려라 Increase your vocabulary by reading.
▶ 경찰은 순찰차 수를 늘렸다 The police increased the number of their patrol cars.

늘보 a sluggard; 《美口》 a slowpoke

늘비하다 drawn up; spread out; displayed; arrayed
▶ 그 길 한쪽에는 가게가 늘비하다 On one side of the street is an unbroken succession of shops.
▶ 진열창에는 온갖 장난감이 늘비했다 A great variety of toys were displayed in the show window.

늘썽늘썽 (all) coarsely; loosely —**늘썽늘썽하다** ⇨ 늘썽하다

늘썽하다 loose (fabric); coarse (texture); large [wide] 《meshes》; coarse-woven [loose-woven] 《cloth》
♦ 늘썽한 그물 a wide-mesh(ed) net / 늘썽한 천 cloth with a loose weave [texture] / 늘썽하게 짜다 knit with large stitches

늘씬하게 severely; hard; soundly; completely
♦ 늘씬하게 패다 beat sb to a pulp [black and blue]; pommel sb to a jelly [mummy] / 늘씬하게 얻어맞다 receive a sound thrashing [severe beating]; be pommeled to a jelly

늘씬하다 slender ⇨ 날씬하다

늘어가다 1 〈수량이〉 be on the increase; be (steadily) increasing; go on increasing [growing, swelling]; 〈금액이〉 run [go] up 《to a large sum》
▶ 지출이 늘어간다 The expenditure is swelling.
2 〈실력 등이〉 be in progress; be progressing; be improving; be advancing

늘어나다 stretch; extend; lengthen; grow longer

|解說| **stretch**는 잡아당겨서 길이나 너비가 늘어나는 것, 특히 탄력성이 있는 것이 늘어나는 경우에 쓰인다. **extend**는 길이 · 기간 등에 관하여 어떤 점까지 또는 그 점을 지나서 길어지는 것을, **lengthen**은 길이 · 기간이 길어지는 것을 말한다.

♦ 잘 늘어나는 elastic [stretchy] 《nylon》 / 늘어났다 줄어들었다 하다 be elastic
▶ 고무는 잘 늘어난다 Rubber draws well.
▶ 금속은 대개 열을 받으면 늘어난다 Heat expands most metals.
▶ 생활비가 늘어난다 Living expenses increase.
▶ 의학의 발달로 수명이 늘어났다 Progress in medical science has prolonged [lengthened] our life span.

늘어놓다 1 〈벌여놓다〉 arrange; 〈진열하다〉

display; lay out
♦크기 순으로 늘어놓다 range [arrange] (books) by size / 한 줄로 늘어놓다 place sth in a row
▶우리는 의자를 한 줄에 다섯 개씩 늘어놓았다 We arranged five chairs in every row.
▶그녀는 테이블에 컵을 늘어놓고 차례로 커피를 따랐다 She lined the cups up on the table and filled them with coffee one after another.
2 〈어지르다〉 scatter (around; 《英》 about); litter; put in disorder
♦방에 옷을 늘어놓다 leave one's clothes lying about in the room / 방안에 휴지를 늘어놓다 litter a room with scraps of paper
▶아이들은 책을 늘어놓은 채 나가버렸다 The children went out leaving books scattered around [about].
3 〈열거하다〉 enumerate; itemize
♦불평을 늘어놓다 set out one's complaints / 허튼 수작을 늘어놓다 talk a lot of nonsense
▶그는 내 결점을 늘어놓았다 He listed [enumerated] my faults. ≒ He ran [went] through a list of my faults.
▶그녀는 불평을 늘어놓았다 She itemized [enumerated] her grievances. ≒ She set forth a number of grievances. ≒ 《口》 She rattled off a lot of complaints.
▶그는 자기 내력을 늘어놓았다 He spoke at length of his own personal history.

늘어뜨리다 hang down; let down (a thing)
♦축 늘어뜨리다 hang loose; dangle / 밧줄을 나무에서 늘어뜨리다 hang [suspend] a rope from a tree / 치맛자락을 늘어뜨리다 let down one's skirt; trail one's skirt
▶개는 혀를 늘어뜨리고 있었다 The dog lolled [hung] out its tongue.
▶그녀는 긴 머리를 등 뒤로 늘어뜨리고 있었다 She had her long hair flowing down her back.

늘어서다 stand in a row; line up
♦세로로 늘어서다 stand one behind another / 옆으로 늘어서다 stand side by side / 한줄로 늘어서다 form [stand] a line [《英》 queue]
▶높은 건물이 길 양편에 늘어서 있다 Tall buildings line the street on both sides.
▶많은 젊은이들이 음악회의 표를 사려고 늘어서 있었다 A lot of young people were lining [queuing] up to buy tickets for the concert.
▶대통령은 거리에 늘어선 사람들에게 손을 흔들었다 The President waved to the people lining [lined up along] the street.

늘어앉다 sit in a row; sit in line ▶정장한 신사들이 죽 늘어앉아 있었다 There was a long row of gentlemen seated in full dress.

늘어지다 **1** 〈처지다〉 hang down; dangle; droop
♦귀가 늘어진 개 a dog with low-set [flapped] ears
▶그녀의 머리는 어깨까지 늘어져 있다 Her hair falls over her shoulder.
▶눈[열매]의 무게로 가지가 축 늘어져 있다 The branches are drooping [hanging down] under the weight of the snow [fruit].
▶버드나무 가지가 거의 땅에까지 늘어져 있었다 The willow branches hung [drooped]

down close to the ground.
▶잊고 물을 주지 않아 화분의 식물들이 축 늘어져 버렸다 The potted plants were drooping, as I had forgotten to water them.
2 〈길어지다〉 lengthen; stretch
▶고무 띠가 늘어져 버렸다 The elastic band has gone slack.
▶마침내 수업이 끝나자 모두들 늘어지게 기지개를 켰다 When class was finally out, everybody stretched.
3 〈연장되다〉 be put off; be prolonged; be extended ▶기간이 늘어졌다 The term has been prolonged.
4 〈몸이〉 be exhausted; be dog-tired; be languid; languish; droop ♦축 늘어져서 (as) limp as a doll [rag]
▶나는 축 늘어져서 의자에 털썩 주저앉았다 Utterly wearied, I slumped into the chair.
▶그는 얻어맞고 축 늘어졌다 The blow left him groggy [limp].
▶그는 피곤해서 어깨가 축 늘어졌다 His shoulders drooped with tiredness.
▶그는 마루에 늘어져 누워 있었다 He was lying unconscious on the floor.
▶학생들은 모두 더위에 축 늘어져 있다 All the students are feeling weak and weary in the heat.
5 〈팔자가〉 be comfortably [well] off; live in comfort
▶그들은 팔자가 늘어졌다 They are free from care [worry]. ≒ They are now quite at their ease. ≒ They are happy-go-lucky.
6 〈잠을 푹 자다〉 ♦늘어지게 자다 sleep soundly; sleep like a log ▶늘어지게 잤더니 아주 기분이 좋다 I had a good (night's) sleep and I feel great.

늘이다 **1** 〈길이를〉 lengthen; make sth longer; stretch; extend; draw out
♦고무줄을 늘이다 stretch a rubber band / 밧줄을 2미터 늘이다 lengthen a rope by two meters; make a rope two meters longer / 수명을 늘이다 prolong [lengthen] one's (span of) life / 쇠를 늘여서 철사를 만들다 draw out an iron into wire
2 〈아래로〉 hang down; droop; suspend ♦발을 늘이다 hang a bamboo screen / 목을 늘여 칼을 받다 let one's neck droop under the sword

늘쩍지근하다 languid; weary; heavy; listless
♦온몸이 늘쩍지근하다 feel languid [lazy] all over ▶날씨가 더워 몸이 늘쩍지근하다 The heat makes me feel languid.

늘쩡거리다 be sluggish; be tardy; be slow (-moving); idle about; dawdle (over)
♦이불 속에서 늘쩡거리다 dally in bed / 일을 늘쩡거리며 하다 be lazy in doing one's work; fiddle over one's work; slack at one's work

늘컹거리다 be pulpy [flabby, limp, squashy]
늘컹늘컹 pulpily; limply —**늘컹늘컹하다** ⇨ 늘컹하다

늘컹하다 pulpy; flabby; limp; squashy

늙다 grow [get] old; age; get on [advance] in years
♦늙은 사람 an old person / 나날이 늙어가다 be getting old day by day

▶ 그는 급속히 늙어버렸다 He has grown old rapidly.
▶ 형은 앓고 나서 갑자기 늙었다 My brother has aged rapidly since his illness. ⇒ My brother's illness put years on him.
▶ 그는 늙었지만 정정하다 He is hale and hearty in his old age. ⇒ He is old in years but still hale and hearty.
▶ 어머니는 젊었을 때 고생을 해서 실제보다 늙어 보이신다 My mother had a hard time during her youth and looks older than she is [her age].

늙다리 1 〈늙은 짐승〉 an old animal ◆ 늙다리 말 an (old) nag; a hack / 늙다리 소 an old ox 2 (卑) ⇨ 늙은이

늙수그레하다 rather advanced in age; fairly old; oldish

늙어빠지다 decrepit; very [awfully] old ◆ 늙어빠진 노인 a decrepit oldster

늙은이 an old [aged] person; (口) an oldster; a crock; (총칭) the aged [old] ◆ 늙은이의 망령 an indiscretion of an old man / 늙은이나 젊은이나 (both) young and old (alike)

늙정이 (卑) an old person ⇨ 늙은이

늙히다 make sb old; let sb get old ◆ 처녀로 늙히다 let 《a girl》 pass her marriageable age; let 《a girl》 become an old maid

늠름하다 凜凜— manly; dignified; imposing; lofty; majestic; awe-inspiring
◆ 늠름한 모습 a dignified figure / 늠름한 태도 a manly attitude; an imposing air; a lofty bearing / 기상이 늠름하다 be high-spirited / 늠름한 데가 있다 have a manly [commanding] mien
▶ 그녀는 그의 늠름한 모습을 우러러보았다 She looked admiringly at his imposing figure.

늠실거리다 〈딴마음을 품고〉 squint [leer] 《at》; leer one's eye 《at》

능 陵 a royal mausoleum; a royal tomb
능 稜 〈幾〉 an angle; an edge

능가하다 凌駕— excel; surpass 〔outdo〕 《the young》; be superior to
◆ …에서 나머지 사람들을 능가하다 excel the rest in… / 훨씬 능가하다 far surpass; be far superior to 《others》
▶ 지식으로는 그가 스승을 능가하고 있다 He surpasses [exceeds] his teacher in knowledge.
▶ 그는 당대의 사람들을 훨씬 능가하는 인물이었다 He towered high above his contemporaries.
▶ 그의 업적을 능가할 만한 것은 아직 없다 His work has yet to be [not been] surpassed.

능갈치다 dissembling; deceitful ⇨ 능청맞다

능구렁이 1 〔動〕 a yellow-spotted serpent 2 〈사람〉 an insidious person; (口) a deep one; (비유) a snake

능글능글하다 sly ⇨ 능글맞다

능글맞다 sly; snaky; cunning; insidious ◆ 능글맞은 웃음 (make) an insidious smile

능금 a crab apple ■—나무 〔植〕 a crab tree —산(酸) malic acid

능놀다 〈쉬엄쉬엄 하다〉 be slow-going; linger; dawdle 《over》

능동 能動 activeness; activity ◆ 능동적이다 active; lively / 문제에 능동적으로 대처하다 grapple with a problem in an active manner [in a positive manner, actively]
■—태 〔文法〕 the active voice : 능동태 문장 a sentence in the active voice; an active sentence

능라 綾羅 twill damask and brocade

능란하다 能爛— dexterous; deft; skillful; expert; proficient; adroit
◆ 능란하게 skillfully; adroitly; dexterously / …에 능란하다 be dexterous [expert, skilled, skillful] in [at]; be good at; be master of / 글씨를 능란하게 쓰다 write a good hand; be a good hand at penmanship
▶ 그는 말솜씨가 능란하다 He is a glib speaker. ⇒ He has a glib [smooth] tongue.
▶ 그는 3개 국어를 능란하게 구사한다 He speaks three languages fluently.
▶ 그녀는 남자 종업원들을 능란하게 다룬다 She is dexterous in handling male employees.

능력 能力 (an) ability; (a) capability; (a) capacity; competence 《to do, for, in》; a talent 《for》; a faculty

> 解說 *ability*는 가장 일반적인 말로서 실제로 일을 성취하기 위한 선천적 또는 후천적인 지적・육체적 능력. *capability*는 일에 따른 잠재적 능력, *competence*는 특정한 일 등을 하는 데 필요한 적성・자격, *talent*는 특히 예술 분야에 타고난 재능을 말한다. *faculty*는 타고났거나 후천적인 특수한 종류의 재능으로 주로 《美》에서 행정과 사무 등 실제적인 능력에 대해 사용한다.

◆ 교사로서의 능력 one's competence as a teacher / 보행 능력 ability to walk / 영어 독해 〔작문, 회화〕능력 reading [writing, speaking] ability in English / 일에 대한 능력 one's competence for a task / 능력별 반편성 ability grouping; grouping students by ability / 능력이 있는 사람 an able man; a man of ability; a capable person; a person of full capacity / 능력이 있다[없다] be able [unable] to 《do》; be capable [incapable] of 《doing》; be competent [incompetent] for 《doing》 [to 《do》] / 능력을 개발하다 develop [draw out] one's ability
▶ 그에게는 그 일을 할 능력이 있다 He has the ability [capacity] to do the job. (▶ 최근에는 the ability of doing의 형으로도 씀) ⇒ He can do [is able to do, is capable of doing] the job.
▶ 그에게는 그 일을 할 능력이 없다 He has no ability to do the job. ⇒ This job is beyond his ability [capacity].
▶ 가난한 아버지에게는 배상할 능력이 없었다 The poor father was unable to pay for the damage.
▶ 이 홀은 2천명의 수용 능력이 있다 This hall seats [is seated for] two thousand. ⇒ This hall has a seating capacity of two thousand.
▶ 나는 그 문제를 풀 능력이 없다 I don't have the ability [capacity] to solve the problem.
▶ 그는 능력은 충분한데 경험이 부족하다 He is capable enough, but wanting in experience.

능률

▶교사는 학생의 능력 개발을 도와주어야 한다 Teachers should help their students (to) develop their ability [faculties].
▶만사가 네 능력에 달렸다 All [Everything] depends upon your ability.
■생산— productivity 언어[시각]— the faculty of speech [sight] 잠재— latent ability [talent]; potential [dormant] capacity 지급— solvency; the ability to pay 지적— intellectual [mental] faculties 초— supernatural power ■—급 payment based on ability —상실자 a person with a disability; a person adjudged incompetent —자 an able man

능률 能率 1 〈일의〉 efficiency
◆능률의 저하 lowering of efficiency / 능률적인 방법 an efficient method / 능률이 좋은 efficient / 능률이 좋지 않은 inefficient / 능률을 올리다[저하시키다] raise [lower] efficiency / 일의 능률을 올리다 promote [develop] the efficiency in [at] one's work / 능률을 몇 배나 올리다 multiply efficiency severalfold / 일을 능률적으로 하다 do one's work efficiently / 복잡한 절차를 능률적으로 만들다 streamline complicated procedures
▶이 방법으로 하면 능률이 훨씬 오른다 This method will make for much efficiency. ⇒ You could do it much more efficiently with this method.
▶같은 일을 오래 하면 능률이 떨어진다 Your level of efficiency will fall if you do the same thing for a long time.
▶최소의 노력으로 최대의 능률을 올리기 바란다 We want you to get maximum efficiency with minimum effort.
2 〚物〛 moment
■노동— labor efficiency 작업— work efficiency 행정— administrative efficiency ■—곡선 an efficiency curve —급 efficiency wages: 저 회사는 능률급이다 That companypays its "efficiency first" principle. —시험 an efficiency test —증진 improvement [enhancement] of efficiency

능면체 菱面體 〚幾〛 a rhombohedron ◆능면체의 rhombohedral

능변 能辯 eloquence; fluency ◆타고난 능변 unstudied eloquence / 능변이다 have a fluent [glib] tongue ▶그는 능변이다 He is honey-tongued.
■—가 an eloquent speaker; an orator

능사 能事 proper and suitable work; one's work; one's line (of business); a competent task; (sth within) one's competency
◆…을 능사로 삼다 consider sth as one's work; make it one's business to 《do》
▶돈을 모으는 것만이 능사가 아니다. 잘 쓰는 것도 중요하다 It is not everything to accumulate money; to spend it wisely is also important.
▶열심히 공부하는 것만이 능사는 아니다 Studying hard is not everything.
▶먹고 마시는 것만이 인생의 능사는 아니다 There is something in life besides eating and drinking.

능선 稜線 a ridgeline ◆능선을 따라 내려오다 come down along the ridge / 능선에 포진하다 take up [occupy] a position on the ridge of the mountain

능소능대하다 能小能大— be good at [skillful in] everything; dexterous [expert] at all things; versatile ◆능소능대한 사람 a good hand at all things

능수 能手 1 〈솜씨〉 ability; skill; dexterity; adroitness; proficiency
2 〈사람〉 a good hand 《at》; a master-hand; a person of ability; an expert (in money-making); an adept (in, at); a veteran
▶그는 그 방면의 능수다 He is a master-hand in his speciality [veteran in the line].

능숙 能熟 skill(fulness); proficiency; expertness; mastery
—능숙하다 skilled (in); skillful (at, in, with); expert 《at, in, on》; experienced (in)
◆능숙한 솜씨 great tact; 〈세공 등이〉 nice workmanship / 능숙하게 skillfully; well / …에 능숙하다 be adept in [at] / 능숙해지다 become skillful [expert]; acquire [attain] skill
▶그녀는 영어회화에 능숙하다 She is a good English speaker. ⇌ She speaks English very well.
▶그녀는 컴퓨터에 능숙하다 She is proficient at operating the computer.
▶그 아이는 암산에 능숙하다 The boy is good at mental calculation.

능욕 凌辱 1 ⇨ 모욕
2 〈강간〉 rape; violation —능욕하다 rape; violate; outrage; 〈처녀를〉 deflower ▶그 여자는 능욕당했다 She was violated [raped, sexually assaulted].

능지처참하다 陵遲處斬— hack 《a criminal》 into pieces

능직 綾織 twill; diagonal cloth

능철광 菱鐵鑛 〚鑛〛 siderite; spathic iron

능청 dissimulation; false pretenses; feigning; hypocrisy
◆능청을 떨다[부리다, 피우다] dissimulate; wear an air of innocence; play the hypocrite [fox]; feign innocence
▶정치가는 능청을 잘 떤다 Politicians are good at dissimulating.

능청맞다, 능청스럽다 dissembling; double-faced; deceitful; tricky; artful; insidious; hypocritical
◆능청맞은 사람 a deceitful person; a sly dog; an old fox / 능청스러운 웃음 a hypocritical [deceitful] smile / 능청스러운 짓 a hypocritical act

능통하다 能通— having a full knowledge 《of》; proficient; expert; skillful; skilled
◆…에 능통하다 be well versed in; be expert [proficient] in [at]; be a master of / 영어에 능통하다 have a good [fine] command of English; be well versed in English / 컴퓨터의 조작에 능통하다 be proficient at operating a computer

능필 能筆 good handwriting; skillful penmanship

능하다 能— capable; adept; adroit; dexter-

ous; competent; expert; proficient
♦용병에 능한 사람 an able commander / 처세에 능한 사람 a worldly-wise person / 만사에 능하다 be skillful in everything; be a master of all trades / 영어에 능하다 be good at English
▶그는 웅변[돈벌이]에 능하다 He is an eloquent speaker [an expert in moneymaking].
▶그는 말을 다루는 데 아주 능하다 He has a way with a horse. ⇌ He has an admirable knack of managing a horse.

능형 菱形 〔數〕 a rhomb; a rhombus 《*pl.* ~es, -bi》; a diamond (shape) ■—무늬 a diaper pattern

능히 能— capably; ably; 〈손쉽게〉 easily; with ease
♦능히 해낼 수 있다 be competent to do; be competent in [at] doing
▶그는 무슨 일이든 능히 해낼 수 있는 사람이다 He is a man capable of (doing) anything.
▶그 놈은 난폭하니까 능히 그럴 수도 있지 He can be rude enough to do so.
▶그가 능히 그 일을 할 수 있다는 것은 의심의 여지가 없다 There is no doubt of his competence for the task [to do the work].

늦- late; belated; tardy ■—가을 late autumn —겨울 late winter; the latter part of winter —곡식 late crop —봄 late spring —여름 late summer : 늦여름에 late in summer

늦게 late
♦밤늦게 late at night; at a late hour / 아침 늦게 late in the morning / 오후 늦게 late in the afternoon / 밤 늦게까지 until late at night / 밤 늦게까지 독서하다 sit up late reading [over a book] / 늦게 돌아오다 come back (home) late; be late (in) coming back
▶어제는 늦게 잤다 I went to bed late last night.
▶그는 늦게 자고 늦게 일어난다 He keeps late hours.
▶버스는 5분 늦게 도착했다 The bus arrived five minutes late [behind schedule].
▶그는 늦게 딸을 보았다 He got a daughter in his later life.
▶회의는 10분 늦게 시작되었다 The opening of the conference was delayed ten minutes.
▶어제는 늦게까지 자지 않아서 오늘 아침 나는 늦게 일어났다 I stayed up too late last night, so I got up late this morning.
▶당국은 늦게나마 그 사건을 캐기 시작했다 Though it was rather too late, the authorities began to investigate the incident.

늦다¹ 1 〈제때에 대지 못하다〉 be late; be behind time [schedule]
♦기차 시간에 늦다 be late for a train; miss a train / 약속 시간에 30분 늦다 be thirty minutes late for *one's* appointment / 학교[식사 시간]에 늦다 be late for school [dinner]
▶지금 가지 않으면 늦는다 It is high time to go.
▶기차가 사고 때문에 한 시간 늦었다 The train was one hour behind time [schedule] because of an accident.
▶서둘러라, 이러다 늦겠다 Hurry up! We shall be late.
▶늦어서 미안합니다 Excuse me for being late.
2 〈시계가〉 lose; go slow ▶이 시계는 하루에 5분이 늦다 This clock loses five minutes a day.
▶이 시계는 잘 늦는다 This watch is apt to lose.

늦다² 1 〈시간적으로〉 late(↔early)

|解説| late의 비교급·최상급은 later, latest와 latter, last의 두 종류가 있다. 전자는 시간에 관해, 후자는 순서에 관해 쓰인다.

♦늦기 전에 before 《it's》 too late / 너무 늦다 be too late (for) / 좀 늦다 be latish / 늦은 아침밥을 먹다 have a late breakfast; have breakfast late / 늦은 열차를 타다 take a later train
▶그는 걸음이 늦다 He walks slowly [slow].
▶금년엔 봄이 늦다 Spring is late in coming this year.
▶지금 가는 것은 너무 늦다 It's too late for you to go now.
▶우리 회사는 급료의 지급이 늦다 Our company is late in the payment of its wages.
▶왜 그렇게 집에 늦었니? Why do you come home so late?
▶이미 늦었으니 그만 자자 It's already late, so let's go to bed.
2 〈느슨하다〉 loose; slack
▶허리띠가 늦다 The belt is loose.

늦더위 the heat of late summer; the lingering summer heat ▶올해는 늦더위가 심하다 The heat of late summer is severe this year.

늦되다 grow [mature, ripen] late; be slow to mature ♦늦되는 과일 late fruit / 늦된 아이 a retarded child ▶금년에는 보리가 늦된다 The barley ripens late this year.

늦둥이 1 〈늦자식〉 a child born of an old couple 2 〈얼뜬 사람〉 a slow-witted [stupid] person

늦바람 〈난봉〉 old-age passion; dissipation in *one's* later [old] years ♦늦바람이 나다 take to fast living late in *one's* life; play the prodigal in *one's* later years

늦벼 late rice; a slow-maturing variety of rice

늦복 —福 good fortune in *one's* old age

늦서리 late frost

늦어도 at (the) latest; at (the) farthest ♦늦어도 5월 5일까지는 by [not later than] May 5th ▶늦어도 4시까지는 돌아오겠습니다 I will get home by four at the latest.

늦어지다 be delayed; be behind time [schedule]; 〈남보다〉 be backward in; be behind [behindhand]
♦공부가 늦어지다 get behindhand in study / 도중에서 늦어지다 be delayed on the way / 일이 늦어지다 be behind in [with] *one's* work
▶거듭 늦어진 예산위원회는 오늘 오후에 개최된다 The budget committee [committee on the budget], after repeated postponement, will meet this afternoon.
▶할 일이 많아서 여행은 늦어질 수밖에 없다 I have so much work to do (that) I have to put

off my trip.

늦잠 oversleeping; morning sleep
▶ 그녀는 일요일에는 언제나 늦잠을 잔다 She always gets up late on Sunday morning.
▶ 오늘 아침에는 한 시간이나 늦잠을 잤다 I overslept by one hour this morning. ⇒ I woke up one hour late this morning.
▶ 나는 오늘 늦잠을 자서 아침도 먹지 않고 집을 나섰다 I overslept this morning and left home without breakfast.
■ —꾸러기 a late riser; a slugabed

늦잡죄다 exercise belated control [supervision]

늦장마 a late rainy season [spell]

늦추다 1 〈느슨하게 하다〉 loosen; slacken ◆ 고삐를 늦추지 않다 slacken the reins / 고삐를 늦추지 않다 keep [hold] a tight rein 《on, over》/ 나는 허리띠를 늦추었다 I loosened my belt.
2 〈속도 등을〉 slacken; slow down ◆ 보조를 늦추다 slacken one's pace / 속도를 늦추다 slow down; reduce one's speed ▶ 기차가 속력을 늦추었다 The train slowed down.
3 〈시간적으로〉 delay; put off; postpone; adjourn; defer
◆ 대답을 늦추다 postpone one's reply / 방문을 늦추다 put off [postpone] one's visit / 시계를 10분 늦추다 set back one's watch [clock] ten minutes / 출발을 3일 늦추다 put off [defer] the departure for three days
▶ 그 공공사업은 내년으로 늦추어졌다 The public work [enterprise] was deferred [postponed] till next year.
▶ 악천후로 도로 공사의 진척이 늦춰지고 있다 Bad weather is holding up the progress of the roadworks.

늦추위 the cold of late winter ▶ 아직도 늦추위가 계속되고 있다 The cold (of late winter) still lingers.

늪 a swamp; a marsh; a bog ◆ 절망의 늪에 빠지다 be in the depths of despair

-니 1 〈열거〉 and; or
▶ 의자니 소파니 모든 것이 구비되어 있다 Everything is ready — chairs, sofas, and all others.
▶ 아이들은 동물원에서 사자니 앵무새니 펭귄이니 하는 진기한 동물과 새를 많이 보았다 The children saw in the zoo a lot of strange animals and birds such as lions, parrots and penguins.
2 〈사실〉 ▶ 자세히 보니 그것은 뱀이었다 Upon a closer look, I discovered it was a snake.
▶ 일을 끝내고 나니 벌써 열 시였다 It was already ten when I finished my work.
▶ 그녀의 안색을 보니 시험에 합격한 것 같지 않다 Judging from her look, she seems not to have passed the examination.
▶ 내가 찾아가 보니 그녀는 외출 중이었다 She was out when I visited her.
3 〈의문〉 ▶ 너 어디 가니? Where are you going (to)? ▶ 너 그 여자 좋아하니? Do you like her?

니그로 a Negro 《pl. ~es》; 〈여자〉 a Negress

-니까 1 〈강조〉 I say; I tell you ▶ 싫다니까 I tell you I don't like it. ▶ 그거 가지고는 안 된다니까 I say! It will not do.
2 〈이유〉 now that; since; because
▶ 자네가 그 말을 하니까 생각이 나네 그려 Now that you mention it, I do remember.
▶ 걸음걸이를 보니까 금방 그인 줄 알겠더라 I knew him by his walk at once.

니스 〈도료〉 varnish ◆ 니스를 칠하다 varnish (over) 《the surface》; apply varnish to 《the surface》 ■ —칠 varnishing

니스 〈프랑스의 향구도시〉 Nice

니아메 〈니제르의 수도〉 Niamey

니오브 〔化〕 niobium; 《美》 columbium

니제르 〈나라 이름〉 Niger; 〈공식명〉 the Republic of Niger ◆ 니제르의 Nigerian ■ —사람 a Nigerian

니체 〈독일의 철학자〉 Nietzsche, Friedrich Wilhelm (1844-1900)

니카라과 〈나라 이름〉 Nicaragua; 〈공식명〉 the Republic of Nicaragua ◆ 니카라과의 Nicaraguan ■ —사람 a Nicaraguan

니켈 nickel ■ —강(鋼) nickel steel —시계 a nickel-cased watch; a nickel watch

니켈도금 —鍍金 nickel plate ◆ 이 금속은 니켈 도금을 한 것이다 This metal is coated with nickel.

니코틴 nicotine ◆ 니코틴이 없는 denicotinized [nicotineless] (cigarettes) / 니코틴을 제거하다 denicotinize; remove nicotine (from)
■ —산 nicotinic acid —중독 nicotinism; nicotine poisoning: 니코틴 중독에 걸리다 become addicted to nicotine

니크롬 Nichrome ■ —선 nichrome wire

니트 ◆ 니트의 knitted (article) ■ —웨어 knitwear

니트로 〔化〕 nitro(-) ■ —글리세린 nitroglycerin(e) —기(基) a nitro group —벤젠 nitrobenzene —화 nitration —화합물 a nitro compound

니트릴 〔化〕 nitrile ■ —화합물 a nitrile compound

니힐리스트 a nihilist

니힐리즘 nihilism

닉네임 a nickname ⇨ 별명(別名)

닉슨 〈미국의 37대 대통령〉 Nixon, Richard Milhous (1913-94) ■ —독트린 the Nixon Doctrine

님 a lover ⇨ 임

-님 1 【이름·직위명 앞에】 〈남자의〉 Mr. (▶ Mister의 약어); Esq. (▶ Esquire의 약어); 〈여자의〉 Mrs. (▶ Mistress의 약어); Mme(.) (▶ Madame의 약어); Madam; Miss (미혼 여성)
◆ 김정호님 Mr. Kim Chŏng-ho, 《英》 Kim Chŏng-ho, Esq. / 사장님 Mr. President; 〈여자〉 Madam President
2 〈존경의 대상〉 esteemed; honorable
◆ 선생님 my respected teacher; Sir! / 신부님 reverend Father; Father! / 예수님 Lord Jesus / 임금님 〈3인칭〉 His [Her] Majesty; 〈2인칭〉 Your Majesty / 주인님 my honorable master

님비 NIMBY [《not in my backyard》]

닢 ◆ 가마니 두 닢 two straw bags / 동전 한 닢 a piece of copper (coin) / 엽전 열 닢 ten brass coins

ㄷ

다[1] 〔樂〕 C
■─**장조**[**단조**] C major [minor]: 다단조 교향곡 a symphony in C minor

다[2] **1** 〈모든 사람〉 all; everyone; everybody; 〈모든 것〉 everything; every…
▶ 다들 왔습니까? Is everybody [everyone] here?
▶ 여러분은 다 스포츠를 좋아합니까? Do you all [all of you] like sports?
▶ 다들 지쳤다 Everyone was tired.
▶ 그는 우리를 다 초대했다 He invited all of us.
▶ 다 내 잘못이다 I'm the only one who is to blame.
▶ 그 소식을 듣고 다 기뻐한 것은 아니다 Not all of us [them] rejoiced at the news.
▶ 나는 그 시를 다 암기하고 있다 I can recite the whole poem by heart. ⇌ I have memorized the entire poem.
▶ 사과가 다 썩어버렸다 All (of) the apples have gone bad.
▶ 우리 가족은 다 잘 있습니다 All my family are well.
▶ 나는 용돈을 다 써버렸다 I have spent the last penny of my pocket money.
▶ 그 이야기를 다 믿을 수는 없다 I don't believe every part of the story.
▶ 다 해서 얼마죠? How much are they [is it] altogether?
▶ 다 해서 3만원입니다 It comes to 30,000 won altogether.
▶ 번쩍인다고 다 금은 아니다 (속담) All is not gold that glitters.
2 〈완전히〉 perfectly; completely; entirely; fully; quite; 〈거의〉 almost; nearly
▶ 會話 「점심 아직 안됐나요?」 「곧 다 된다」 "Isn't lunch ready yet?" "It'll be ready in a minute."
▶ 이제 다 왔다 Here we are (at last).
▶ 그녀도 이젠 어른이 다 되었다 She has quite grown up.
3 〈강조·조소〉 별말씀을 다 하십니다 Not at all. ⇌ Don't mention it. ⇌ You're welcome.
▶ 별꼴 다 보겠네 What a shame!
▶ 그 주제에 양복을 다 입었네 What a sight he looks in that coat!
4 〈고작〉 at best; all [as much as] *one* can do; at (the) most
▶ 신청자는 500명 정도가 다일 것이다 There will be only about 500 applicants at the most [at best].

-다 1 〈상태·동작〉 be
▶ 그는 키가 크다 He is tall.
▶ 꽃병은 탁자 위에 있다 The vase is on the table.
▶ 잘못은 네게 있다 It is you that [who] is to blame for it.
▶ 그는 훌륭한 재능을 가지고 있다 He has [possesses] rare talents.
▶ 나는 그를 만난 적이 있다 I once saw him.
2 ⇨ -다가 1

다가 多價 〔化〕 polyvalence
◆ 다가의 polyvalent; multivalent

-다가 1 〈동작의 연속〉 ◆ 등을 굽혔다가 펴다 bend and straighten *one's* back / 울다가 잠들다 cry [weep] *oneself* to sleep
▶ 나는 그 소식을 듣고 몇번이나 웃다가 울다가 했다 I laughed and wept by turns at the news.
▶ 나는 책을 읽다가 잠들어버렸다 While (I was) reading a book, I fell asleep.
2 〈또한〉 besides; still more; and yet
▶ 그녀는 예쁜데다가 마음도 곱다 She is not only beautiful but kind. ⇌ She is kind as well as beautiful. ⇌ She is beautiful, and kind besides.

다가가다 go [get] near; walk [step] up to; come near; approach; draw near
▶ 절벽의 가장자리에 다가가지 마라 Don't go too near [close to] the edge of the cliff.

다가놓다 bring [put] *sth* close (to); bring (A) near to (B); draw *sth* near(er)
▶ 불을 네 책상 곁으로 다가놓아라 Move the light closer [nearer] to your desk.
▶ 그는 책상을 창가에 다가놓았다 He moved the desk near [close to] the window.
▶ 그는 의자를 난로쪽으로 다가놓았다 He drew his chair up to the heater.

-다가는 in case; if
◆ 이행하지 않다가는 in case of default
▶ 이 열차를 놓쳤다가는 내일까지 기다려야 해 If we miss this train, we will have to wait until tomorrow.
▶ 술을 너무 마시다가는 건강을 해친다 Drinking too much will ruin your health.

-다가도 and then
▶ 그녀는 울다가도 웃었다 She cried and (then) laughed.

다가서다 get [come, go] near(er); come [walk, step] up to; draw close (to); draw near; approach
◆ 다가서게 하다 allow *sb* to come near [approach]; let *sb* to come near / 다가서서 보다 see *sth* (from) close at hand; take a near(er) [get a closer] view of
▶ 위험! 다가서지 마시오 Danger! Keep away [out]!
▶ 내게 바싹 다가서렴 Come closer to me.
▶ 안으로 다가서 주세요 〈버스 등에서〉 Move on, please.

다가앉다 sit closer [closely]; take *one's* seat closer; sit up
▶ 좀 다가앉아 주세요 Please sit [squeeze] up

다가오다
a little closer (together).
▶ 거기는 추우니까 좀더 난로에 다가앉아라 It's cold there. Sit closer to the stove.
▶ 얘기 좀 하게 다가앉아라 Sit a little closer, so we can have a talk.

다가오다 get near 《a place》; approach; near; step [come] up to; 〈박두하다〉 draw [come] near; draw close 《to》
♦육지에 다가오다 close with the land; approach land; draw toward the shore / 다가오지 못하게 keep [hold] 《an enemy》 at bay / 점점 더 다가오다 get nearer to 《a place》 / 종말이 다가오다 draw to a close; near one's end
▶ 약속한 날짜가 다가온다 The appointed day is now close at hand [is just ahead].
▶ 시험이 3일후로 다가왔다 The examination is only three days off [away].
▶ 봄방학이 다가왔다 The spring vacation is approaching [is close at hand, is just around the corner].
▶ 폭풍우가 우리 도시에 다가오고 있었다 The storm was approaching our town.
▶ 크리스마스가 다가온다 Christmas is coming soon.
▶ 파멸이 그의 목전에 다가왔다 Ruin stared him in the face.
▶ 연말이 다가왔다 There's very little left of the year. ⇌ The end of the year is drawing near.

다각 多角 ♦다각의 many-sided; multilateral; diversified
■―경영 diversification; multiple [diversified] management [operation] ―농업 multiple agriculture; diversified farming ―무역[외교] multilateral trade [diplomacy]

다각적 多角的 multiple; various; many-sided; diversified; multilateral
♦다각적인 취미를 가진 사람 a man of diverse [many-sided] interests [tastes] / 다각적인 활동 diversified pursuit / 다각적인 문제 a many-sided problem / 다각적으로 from different angles; from various points of view / 사물을 다각적으로 생각하다 consider a matter from different points of view
■―결제(決濟) 〔貿易〕 a multilateral settlement ―핵전력 multilateral nuclear force

다각형 多角形 〔數〕 a polygon ♦다각형의 polygonal ―정― a regular polygon

다각화 多角化 〈기업 등의〉 (a) diversification
▶ 농가 소득을 증대시키기 위해서는 영농의 다각화가 필요하다 To boost farmers' income, farming should be diversified.
▶ 우리 회사는 시장 확대를 위해 제품의 다각화를 기했다 Our firm has diversified the range of products in order to extend its market.
―다각화하다 diversify
♦경영을 다각화하다 diversify business
■―전략 strategy of diversification

다갈색 茶褐色 brown (color); a dull light brown ♦다갈색의 brown; dull light brown

다감 多感 sensibility
―다감하다 passionate; sensitive; emotional; susceptible; sentimental
♦다정다감한 소녀[청년] a sentimental [susceptible, sensitive] girl [youth] / 다감한 소녀기에 in one's impressionable girlhood
▶ 그는 다감한 성질이다 He is of sentimental [emotional] nature.
▶ 그는 한 때 다정다감한 청년이었다 He was once a passionate and emotional young man.

다공 多孔 ♦다공의 porous
―성 porosity; porousness

다과 多寡 〈수〉 a number; 〈양〉 a quantity; 〈액수〉 an amount
♦금액의 다과에 관계없이 regardless of the amount involved
▶ 손해의 다과에 따라 배상금이 지급되었다 The reparations were paid in proportion to the damage suffered.
▶ 모든 주문은 다과에 관계없이 신속히 처리하겠습니다 All orders, large or small, will be promptly executed.

다과 茶菓 tea and cake; (light) refreshments
♦파티에서 다과를 대접하다 serve light refreshments at a party
■―회 a tea party; a tea: 다과회에서의 담소 a chat [talk] over tea

다구 茶具 〈여러가지의〉 tea-things; tea utensils; 〈한벌의〉 a tea set [service]
♦다구 한 벌 a set of tea-things

다국어 多國語 many languages
▶ 그녀는 다국어를 알고 있다 She knows several languages. ⇌ She is a polyglot.
―방송 a multilingual broadcast

다국적 多國籍 multinationality ♦다국적의 multinational
■―기업 a multinational enterprise

다그다 1 〈가까이 옮기다〉 bring [put] sth close 《to》; draw sth near
♦전등을 가까이 다그다 bring a light closer to oneself
2 〈날짜 등을〉 advance; move [carry] up; bring forward
♦기일을 다그다 advance [put forward] the date 《of》 / 파티 날짜를 3일 다그다 advance [move up] three days of the date of the party / 결혼식 날짜를 다그다 bring forward [advance] the wedding date

다그치다 1 ⇨ 다그다
2 〈행동 등을〉 urge; prompt; impel; spur on
♦다그쳐서 움직이게 하다 spur sb into action
▶ 그는 나에게 다그쳐 물었다 He quizzed me relentlessly. ⇌ (口) He grilled me.

다극 多極 ♦다극화한 세계 the multipolarized world / 다극의 〔物〕 multipolar

다급하다 〈몹시 급하다〉 pressing; urgent; imminent; impending
♦다급한 문제 a pressing question / 다급한 볼일로 on urgent business
▶ 사태가 다급하다 The matter is pressing [urgent].
▶ 시간이 다급하다 We are pressed for time.

다기 多岐 1 〈길〉 many branches of a road
2 〈다방면〉 many fields
♦복잡 다기한 complex and various

다기지다 多氣— gritty; plucky; daring; stouthearted; resolute

▶ 나는 그에게 대들 정도로 다기지진 못하다 I don't have the courage [nerve] to oppose him.
▶ 그녀는 그러한 시련을 겪고도 눈물 한방울 흘리지 않는 다기진 사람이다 She is really strong [tough] to be able to go through such an ordeal and not shed a single tear.

다난하다 多難 full of difficulties [troubles]; eventful
♦ 다난한 해 a hard year / 다난한 길 a thorny path / 이 다난한 시대에 in these difficult times / 국가가 다난한 때에 in a national crisis [emergency]
▶ 그의 전도는 다난하다 His future is full of troubles [difficulties]. ⇌ Many troubles lie before his future.
▶ 그는 다사다난한 일생을 살았다 He led an eventful life.
▶ 우리들의 시대는 정말로 다난하다 We live in a hard world. ⇌ It's a rough world.

다녀가다 drop in [call] on *sb*; drop in [call] at 《a place》; drop by 《a place》; stop in [by] 《a place》; come to [and] see *sb*
▶ 당신이 없을 때 어떤 여자 분이 다녀가셨습니다 A lady came to see you during your absence.
▶ 근처에 오시거든 저희 집에 좀 다녀가시죠 When you are in the neighborhood, please call on us [call at our house].

다녀오다 drop [look] in 《on *sb*, at *sb's* house》 and then come back; get [come] back 《from visiting》; go round to 《one's house》 and then return
▶ 곧 다녀와야 한다 You have to come back without 《a moment's》 delay.
▶ 곧 다녀올게 I shan't be long.
▶ 서울 좀 다녀오겠다 I'm going to run up to Seoul.
▶ [회화]「어디 다녀왔니?」「미국에 다녀왔습니다」 "Where have you been?" "I have been to America."
▶ 다녀왔습니다 Hello, here I am!
▶ 어머니, 다녀왔어요 I'm home, mother.

다년간 多年間 a long time; many a year; many years; 〈부사적〉 for [over, through] many years; for a long time
♦ 다년간의 long; of many years; of long standing / 다년간의 노력 years of efforts; one's many years' effort / 다년간의 꿈 one's long-cherished dream / 다년간의 경험 a long experience / 다년간의 연구 결과 the result [product] of one's long years of research [study] / 다년간의 소망을 이루다 realize a long-cherished desire / 다년간에 걸쳐서 for (many) years; over a period of years; through many years; over a long term of years / 다년간에 걸친 전쟁 a war of long duration
▶ 그는 다년간에 걸쳐서 언어학을 연구하고 있다 He has been studying linguistics for many years.
▶ 이 저서는 다년간에 걸친 그의 연구의 결과다 This work of his is the fruit of many years of study.

다년생 多年生 〈여러해살이〉〔植〕 perennation
♦ 다년생의 perennial (↔ annual) ■ —식물 a perennial (plant)

다뇨증 多尿症 frequent urination; 〔醫〕 polyuria
♦ 다뇨증의 polyuric

-다는 ▶ 그가 잘못했다는 것은 의심할 여지가 없었다 That he was in error was beyond doubt.
▶ 나는 그녀에게 도와 줄 수 없다는 편지를 보냈다 I sent her a letter to the effect [saying] that I could not help her.
▶ 그녀는 정신이 이상하다는 이유로 석방되었다 She was released on the grounds that she was insane.
▶ 나는 그가 정직하다는 것을 안다 I know that he is honest.

다능하다 多能 — versatile; capable of doing many things

-다니 〈뜻밖〉 how [why] should...; 〈유감〉 it is a pity that...
▶ 사태가 이 지경에 이르다니 실로 한심하다 That things should come to this pass!
▶ 런던에서 그를 만나다니 생각도 못했다 He was the last person I expected to run into in London.
▶ 그가 그렇게 젊어서 죽다니 유감천만이다 It is a great pity that he died so young.
▶ 그가 저 좋은 저택에 살고 있다니 (믿을 수 없다) Just think of him living in that fine residence!
▶ 네가 갈 수 없다니 유감이로구나 What a pity (that) you could not go!

다니다 **1**〈왕래하다〉 go to 《a place》 and back; go to and from 《a place》; 〈배가〉 ply 《between, from...to》; 〈전차·배 등이〉 run 《between》; 〈개통하다〉 be opened to traffic
♦ 도버 해협을 다니는 기선 a steamboat plying on the Straits of Dover / 목포-제주간을 다니는 배 a ship that plies between Mokp'o and Cheju / 서울·안양간을 다니는 버스 a bus which runs between Seoul and Anyang / 왼쪽으로 다니다 keep to the left / 작별인사하러 다니다 make a round calls to say good-by
▶ 이 도시에서 해변까지 기차가 다니고 있다 A railroad runs [There is a railway service] from this town to the seaside.
▶ 그는 일주일에 한 번 병원에 다닌다 He goes to hospital once a week.
▶ 그 강에는 대형 기선들이 다닐 수 없다 The river is not navigable for large steamers.
2〈통근·통학하다〉 attend 《school》; go to 《work, school》; 〈근무에서〉 《美》 commute 《to work, between Inch'ŏn and Seoul, from Inch'ŏn to Seoul》
♦ 버스로 학교에 다니다 go [commute] to school by bus / 〈교외에서〉 전철로 다니다 commute by subway / 걸어서 공장에 다니다 walk to (and from) the factory / 회사에 다니다 work for a company; be in the service of a firm
▶ 너는 어느 학교에 다니니? What school do you attend?
3〈드나들다〉 go frequently to 《a place》; frequent 《a place》; visit 《a place》 frequently; pay frequent visits to...; hang about [around,

다니엘 round]; hang out at
▶ 그는 고문서를 조사하기 위해 도서관에 다닌다 He frequently visits the library to examine old documents.
▶ 그는 스포츠를 좋아해서 체육관에 다닌다 He enjoys sports, and frequents the gym.
4 〈들르다〉 stop at 《a place》; drop in for a short visit
5 〈직무・취미로〉 ◆구경[사냥]을 다니다 go sightseeing [hunting] / 출장을 다니다 travel on (official) business 《to》; go on a business trip; make an official trip 《to》

다니엘 (聖) (the Book of) Daniel (略 Dan.)

다다르다 arrive 《at, in》; reach; gain; attain; get to 《at》; 〈수준에〉 come [be] up to 《the standard, level》
◆목적지에 다다르다 arrive at [come to] one's destination; come to one's journey's end / 완성의 경지에 다다르다 reach [attain] perfection / (산)꼭대기에 다다르다 gain [reach, attain] the summit (of a mountain) / 어떤 결론에 다다르다 arrive at [reach, come to] a conclusion
▶ 우리 선발대는 마침내 오늘 아침 일찍 에베레스트 정상에 다다랐다 Our advance party finally gained the summit of Mt. Everest early this morning.
▶ 회의에서는 어떤 결론에 다다랐습니까? What conclusion did you come to at the meeting?
▶ 즉시 작업을 개시해야 한다는 결론에 다다랐습니다 We reached the conclusion that we should start the operation at once.
▶ 적군은 야음을 틈타 아군 전초선에 다다랐다 The enemy has reached our outpost line under the cover of night.

다다이즘 (藝) dadaism; dada
다다익선 多多益善 The more, the better.
다닥다닥 in a cluster [clusters]
◆벽에 포스터를 다닥다닥 붙이다 paste up posters all over the wall; cover the wall with posters
▶ 꽃이 다닥다닥 붙어 있다 Flowers are in clusters.
▶ 많은 열매가 다닥다닥 달려 있다 Plenty of fruit hang in clusters.
▶ 그 지역은 작은 집들이 다닥다닥 붙어 있다 In that area small houses are clustered [stand] close together.

다단 多端 **1** 〈사건이 많음〉 many items; eventfulness
—**다단하다** eventful; complicated
◆복잡 다단하다 be complicated [intricate, tangled]; be a great deal of complexity 《about》
2 〈바쁨〉 pressure [press] (of business)
—**다단하다** busy
◆공무가 다단하여 owing to the pressure of official business / 용무가 다단하다 be pressed with business; be kept busy

다단식로켓 多段式— a multistage rocket
다달이 every [each] month; from month to month; monthly
◆다달이 한번씩 once a month; monthly / 다달이 (얼마씩) 붓다 pay by the month / 다달이 지급받다 be paid monthly / 이자를 다달이 내다 pay interest every month
▶ 용돈은 다달이 얼마로 정하는 편이 낫다 It is better to determine pocket money by the month.
▶ 다달이 쓰는 돈은 부모님이 보내주신다 My parents send me my monthly expenses.

다당류 多糖類 (化) polysaccharide
다대 〈헝겊 조각〉 a patch; a small piece of cloth used for patchwork
◆다대를 대다 patch [patch up] 《a cloth》; add [put] a patch on 《a coat》

다대하다 多大— much; large; great; heavy; considerable; serious
◆다대한 이익을 얻다 gain a large profit / 다대한 원조를 받다 receive a great deal of assistance / 다대한 손해를 입다 suffer a heavy [serious] loss; sustain a serious [severe] loss / 다대한 동정을 받다 obtain sb's hearty sympathy / 다대한 노력이 필요하다 require considerable labor / 다대한 영향을 받다 be seriously affected; be greatly influenced
▶ 폭풍우로 작물은 다대한 피해를 입었다 The crops suffered serious [great] damage from the storm.

다도 茶道 the tea cult [ceremony]
다도해 多島海 an archipelago (pl. ~(e)s); a sea containing a large group of islands; 〈에게해〉 the Archipelago

다독 多讀 wide [much, extensive] reading (↔〈정독〉 intensive reading)
—**다독하다** read many books; read much [a great deal, widely]
▶ 젊었을 때 다독해야 한다 You should read much [widely, extensively] while (you are) young.
■—**가** an extensive [avid] reader; a well-read man: 그는 다독가다 He is a well-read man.

다독거리다 〈물건을〉 gather 《things》 up and press in order; arrange in good order; 〈아기를〉 pat 《at, on, upon》
▶ 그녀는 아이의 등을 다독거렸다 She patted her child gently on the back.

다되다 **1** 〈떨어지다〉 be exhausted; run out; be out of stock; run [be] short 《of》; be used up; be out
◆기름이 다된 기계 a machine which has run out of oil [that needs oiling] / 다돼가다 run short [low]; there is little left 《of》
▶ 설탕이 다됐다 We ran out of sugar.
▶ 자전거 기름이 다됐다 My bicycle needs oiling.
▶ 전지가 다됐다 The battery went dead.
2 〈기한이〉 run out; expire; terminate; fall [become] due
◆기한이 다돼가다 draw to an end [a close]
▶ 시간이 다됐다 The time is up.
▶ 이틀 후면 계약 기한이 다됩니다 The contract expires [runs out] in two days.
▶ 리포트의 제출 기한이 다되었다 Your paper is overdue.

다듬다 **1** 〈매만지다〉 adorn; embellish; trim

[spruce] up
♦ 잘 다듬은 머리 well-groomed hair / 글을 다듬다 embellish *one's* writing; file *one's* composition / 손톱을 다듬다 manicure [do] *one's* nails / 얼굴을 다듬다 do [pretty up, freshen up] *one's* face
▶ 당신의 머리는 더 다듬어야 합니다 Your hair needs better care.
▶ 문장을 다듬는 데 하루 종일 걸렸다 I spent a whole day trying to improve what I have written.
▶ 그 번역을 여러 번 다듬었다 I reworked that translation a number of times.
2 〈풋성귀·나무·돌 등을〉 prune (away, off, down); trim 《off》; face; clean
♦ 다듬지 않은 옥 an uncut gem; a precious stone in the rough / 잔디를 다듬다 mow a lawn; cut the grass / 나뭇가지를 다듬다 trim the branches of a tree / 무[배추]를 다듬다 clean a radish [cabbage] / 큰 재목을 다듬다 shave a large piece of wood smoothly; 〈널빤지를〉 plane a piece of board smoothly / 돌을 다듬다 face [trim] a stone smoothly / 울퉁불퉁한 모서리를 다듬다 plane the rough edges
3 〈땅바닥을〉 level (down [up, off]); smooth 《off》; make even [smooth]; even out
♦ 길을 다듬다 level [smooth] a road / 롤러로 땅을 다듬다 smooth [level] the ground with a roller; roll a ground / 테니스 코트를 다듬다 roll a tennis court (flat)
4 〈깃털을〉 preen; plume
▶ 새가 (부리로) 깃털을 다듬고 있었다 A bird was pluming itself [its feathers].
5 〈피륙을〉 smooth 《cloth》 by pounding with clubs; full 《cloth》
♦ 다듬지 않은 가죽 an untanned [a raw] hide / 빨래를 다듬다 smooth laundered clothes / 가죽을 다듬다 tan [dress] a hide
6 〈마무리하다〉 give [add] the finishing touches (to); touch [do] up; finish off [up]
다듬이 1 〈다듬이감〉 cloth to be beaten [smoothed by pounding]
2 〈다듬이질〉 beating cloth
■ 다듬잇돌 a block [stone] for beating cloth 다듬잇방망이 clubs for beating cloth with; fulling pins [clubs] 다듬잇소리 the sound of beating cloth
다듬이질 beating cloth ─**다듬이질하다** beat cloth
다듬질 1 〈다듬기〉 the final polish; finish; the finishing touches ─**다듬질하다** give [add] the final polish 《to》; touch [do] up
2 ⇨ 다듬이질
다라지다 〈겁없다〉 bold; plucky; daring; 《口》 spunky ♦ 다라진 데가 있다 have pluck [iron nerves] ▶ 그는 체구는 작지만 다라진 사람이다 He may be small but he is a strong man.
다락 an upper story; a loft over a kitchen ─**방** a garret; an attic (room); a loft ─**집** a two-storyed house; a tower; a turret
다락같다 〈값이〉 very high (in price); expensive ♦ 다락같은 물가 soaring prices; booming prices ▶ 요즈음 물가가 다락같다 Prices are very high these days.

다람쥐 〔動〕 a squirrel
♦ 다람쥐 쳇바퀴 돌듯 하다 be repeating the same thing forever; be in a vicious circle; be no better off than before
▶ 논의는 다람쥐 쳇바퀴 돌듯 아무 진전이 없었다 The argument went round (and round) in circle without getting anywhere.
다랍다 1 ⇨ 더럽다
2 〈인색하다〉 mean; stingy; niggardly; tight; miserly; pinchpenny
▶ 그는 돈에 다랍다 He is mean over money matters. ⇌ He is greedy about money. ⇌ He is stingy (with money matters).
다랑어 〔魚〕 a tunny; a tuna
♦ 다랑어 횟감 slices of raw tuna flesh
다래 〈목화의〉 a (cotton) boll; a cotton seed pod
다래끼¹ 〈바구니〉 a fish basket; a creel; an angler's wicker basket for carrying fish
다래끼² 〔醫〕 a sty; a hordeolum 《*pl*. -la》 ▶ 왼쪽 눈에 다래끼가 났다 I have a sty on my left eye.
다래다래 danglingly in clusters
─**다래다래하다** dangle [hang] in clusters
다량 多量 a large [great] quantity; a vast amount [volume]; a great deal
♦ 다량의 가스 a large quantity of gas / 다량의 출혈 profuse [copious] bleeding / 다량의 much; a large [great] quantity of; plenty of; a great deal of / 다량으로 in abundance; abundantly; in large [great] quantities; plentifully; much / 다량의 농산물을 수입하다 import farm produce in great quantities
♦ 오렌지는 비타민 C를 다량 함유하고 있다 Oranges are rich in vitamin C.
▶ 한국은 원유를 다량 수입해야 한다 Korea has to import crude oil in large quantities [large quantities of crude oil].
■ ─**생산** ⇨ 대량생산
다루다 1 〈대우·처리·취급하다〉 treat; handle; deal with; manage 《an affair》
♦ 소년 범죄 문제를 다룬 책 a book concerned [dealing] with the problem of juvenile delinquency / 다루기 힘든 difficult [hard] to deal with; unmanageable / 다루기 쉬운 easy to deal with; easily manageable; facile / 책을 조심해서 다루다 handle books with care / 정중하게 다루다 deal with *sb* politely / 남을 함부로 다루다 handle *sb* roughly / 〈신문에서〉 뉴스를 크게 다루다 play up the news / 사회 문제를 다루다 treat of social problems / 문제를 가볍게[신중히] 다루다 deal with a matter lightly [carefully]
▶ 이 책은 문제를 실제적으로 다루고 있다 This book deals with the problem from a practical angle.
▶ 그는 사원을 다룰 줄 모른다 He doesn't know how to treat his employees.
2 〈조작하다〉 handle 《a tool》; work [operate] 《a machine》; manipulate
♦ 다루기 쉬운 easy to handle; workable; handy / 잘 다루다 handle skillfully; manipulate
▶ 이 기계는 아이들도 다룰 수 있다 Even a

다룸가죽

child can use this machine.
▶이 기계는 다루기 쉽다 This machine is easy to handle [operate, run].
3 〈무두질하다〉 work (smooth); soften; make pliant
♦다루지 않은 untanned [raw] (hide) / 가죽을 다루다 dress [tan] a hide [skin]

다룸가죽 (a) tanned [dressed] skin; leather; 〈양·사슴의〉 chamois (leather); shammy

다르다 1 〈상이하다〉 different 《from》; unlike; dissimilar 《to, from》; 〈다른〉 another; not the same
♦전혀[아주] 다르다 be quite [completely, entirely] different 《from》; differ entirely 《from》 / 조금도 다르지 않다 be quite the same; be exactly alike / 그다지 다르지 않다 make little [do not make much] difference
▶이 번역문은 원문과 다소 다른 데가 있다 The translation varies from the original in some points.
▶취미는 사람에 따라 다르다 Tastes vary from person to person.
▶그는 동생과 성격이 다르다 He differs [is different] from his brother in character.
▶품질에 따라 값이 다르다 Prices vary according to the quality.
▶내 생각은 다르다 I don't share that opinion. ⇌ I don't think so [that way].
▶그는 보통 사람과는 다른 재능을 가지고 있다 He has unusual talents.
▶그 밖에 어떤 점이 다르냐? How else [In what other respects] are they different?
▶위인은 어릴 때부터 다르다 A great man is distinguished even in his childhood.
▶나라에 따라 관습이 다르다 Each country has its own customs. ⇌ Customs differ from one country to another.
▶요금은 거리에 따라 다르다 The rates are variable according to the distance to be covered.
▶이 문제에 관해서는 의견이 다르다 Opinions vary on this issue.
▶유행은 때와 장소에 따라 다르다 Fashion varies with the time and place.
▶그때와는 상황이 다르다 Things have changed since then.
▶나와 달라서 동생은 공부를 열심히 한다 Unlike me, my brother is a hard worker.
▶또 다른 질문이 있습니까? Have you any other question to ask [put]?
▶버릇은 사람에 따라 다르다 Each has his own habit.
▶계절에 따라 값이 다르다 Prices vary with the seasons.
▶이것은 다른 사람의 모자다 This is somebody else's hat.
▶다른 이야기를 합시다 Let us change the subject.
▶이것은 견본과 다르다 This does not come up to the sample.
2 〈일치하지 않다〉 (be) not in accordance 《with》; (be) contrary 《to》
♦말과 속셈이 다르다 say one thing and mean another
▶그것은 처음 약속과 다르다 It does not agree with the original arrangement.
▶내 생활 방식은 그들과 달랐다 My way of life disagreed with theirs.
▶그의 말은 사실과 다르다 His account does not agree with the facts.
▶그는 행동과 약속이 상당히 다르다 His actions contrast strongly with his promise.

다르에스살람 〈탄자니아의 수도〉 Dar es Salaam

다름아니다 be nothing but; be no more than
♦다름아니라 …이다 It is nothing else but [than]...; It is simply that...
▶내가 지금 너에게 말한 것은 다름아니라 이 책에 쓰여 있는 것이다 What I just told you is nothing but what is written in this book.
▶다름아닌 당신 부탁이므로 최선을 다하겠소 Since it's you who are asking, I will try my best.
▶그 남자야말로 다름아닌 나의 이상형이다 He is the very person that I have been seeking as an ideal man.
▶그 사람은 다름아닌 시장이었다 It was none other [no less a person] than the mayor.

다름없다 〈서술적〉 be the same 《as》; be alike; be not different 《from》; 〈변함없다〉 never-changing; constant; unwavering; steady
♦한 집안이나 다름없다 be almost [be as good as] one of the family / 거지나 다름없다 be no [little] better than a beggar
▶그녀는 죽은 사람이나 다름없다 She is as good as dead.
▶그가 한 짓은 사기와 다름없다 What he did amounts to fraud.
▶그의 재산은 이제는 없는거나 다름없다 His fortune is practically gone.
▶그 섬에서 우리는 죄수나 다름없었다 We were virtually prisoners on the island.
▶그 두 사람은 부부나 다름없다 They are practically man and wife.
▶두 사람은 형제나 다름없다 The two are like brothers.
▶우리 집은 헛간이나 다름없다 My house is little better than a barn.
▶승부는 난 거나 다름없다 The game is practically over.
▶낡은 의자를 수리했더니 새것과 다름없었다 After he repaired the old chair, it was as good as new.
▶그 피아노는 새것이나 다름없었다 The piano was just like new.
▶그것은 공짜나 다름없다 The price is so low that the thing is as good as free.
▶그녀는 그 제안을 받아들이거나 다름없었다 She as good as accepted the offer.

다름없이 similarly; likewise; alike; equally; in the same way [manner] 《as》; without a change
♦전과 다름없이 as usual; as before; as ever; no better [worse] than before / 개를 아이와 다름없이 대하다 treat *one's* dog like (his) child
▶그는 남을 형제나 다름없이 대한다 He treats others like a brother.

▶그는 가난한 사람에게도 부자와 다름없이 친절하다 He is equally kind to the rich and the poor.
▶아버지는 자식들에게 매우 엄격했다. 어머니도 다름없이 엄격했다 My father was very strict with us children. So was my mother.

다리¹ **1**〈사람·동물의〉a leg; a (walking) limb;〈낙지 등의〉tentacles; arms
♦한 쪽 다리 one leg / 양쪽 다리 both legs / 앞다리 forelegs / 뒷다리 hindlegs / 굵은 다리 thick legs; plump legs / 다리가 긴[짧은] 동물 a long-[short-]legged animal / 다리가 길다 have long legs; be leggy [long-legged] / 다리가 짧다 have short legs; be short-legged / 다리를 뻗다[꼬다] stretch out [cross] *one's* legs / 다리를 벌리다 spread *one's* legs (apart) / 다리를 굽히다[구부리다] bend *one's* legs / 다리를 오무리다 draw in *one's* legs
▶다리가 뻣뻣해지도록 그녀의 집을 찾아다녔다 I looked for her house till my legs were stiff.
▶도시 아이들은 대개 다리가 약하다 Generally speaking, children living in cities have weak leg muscles.
▶그녀는 너무 무서워서 다리가 떨렸다 She was so frightened (that) her legs were trembling.
▶그녀는 다리가 부러졌다 She broke her leg [had her leg broken].
▶그녀는 다리를 좀 전다 She is a bit lame.
2〈책상 등의〉a leg; a leg piece
♦안경 다리 the leg of / 안경 다리 the temples [bows] of a pair of glasses / 다리가 긴 탁자 a long-legged [tall] table / 다리가 셋인 의자 a three-legged stool
■—뼈 a leg bone —살 inner thighs —통 the girth of the leg

——————— 다리 ———————

허벅다리 thigh
다리 leg
무릎 knee
장딴지 calf
아킬레스건 Achilles' tendon
정강이 shin
복사뼈 ankle
뒤꿈치 heel
발등 instep
발바닥 sole
발가락 toes
발 foot
장심 arch

다리²〈교량〉a bridge
♦〈판문점의〉돌아오지 않는 다리 the Bridge of No Return / 다리 난간 a bridge rail / 다리를 놓다 build [throw, construct] a bridge across [over] (a river); span (a river) with a bridge; bridge (a stream) / 다리를 건너다 cross a bridge; go across a bridge
▶그 강에는 다리가 셋 있다 There are three bridges across the river.
▶이 다리는 얼마나 기니? How long is (the span of) this bridge?
▶그 다리를 건너는데 차로 10분 걸린다 It takes ten minutes to cross that bridge by car.
▶무거운 차 때문에 다리가 무너졌다 The bridge gave way under a heavy wagon.
▶홍수로 다리가 떠내려갔다 The bridge was washed away by the flood.
▶누군가 양자 사이에 다리를 놓지 않으면 안된다 Someone has to bring the two parties together. ⇌ Someone has to act as an intermediary between the two parties.
■돌— a stone bridge 홍예— an arch bridge ■다릿목 (at) the foot of a bridge; (near) the approach to a bridge

다리³〈머리에 넣는〉a tress of false [artificial] hair; a hairpiece; a switch
♦다리를 넣다 put on a tress of false hair / 다리를 넣어 머리를 부풀려 보이다 use [add] a hairpiece to give *one's* hair more fullness; puff out *one's* hair with a pad of hair
■—꼭지 a bunch of false hair

다리다 iron; press
♦다린 ironed; pressed / 블라우스를 다리다 iron [press] a blouse / 바지를 다려서 주름을 펴다 press wrinkled trousers; iron out the wrinkles in a pair of trousers
▶이건 다려야겠어 This needs ironing.
▶나는 하루 종일 빨래하고 다렸소 I've been doing laundry and ironing all day.

다리미 an iron; a smoothing iron; a flatiron
♦다리미로 주름을 펴다 smooth the wrinkles with an iron / 다리미로 셔츠를 다리다 iron a shirt
■전기[증기]— an electric [a steam] iron ■—판 an ironing board

다리미질 ironing —**다리미질하다** do the ironing; iron; press
♦바지를 다리미질하다 press the trousers

다리쇠〈구멍쇠〉a trivet; a metal stand placed over a fire

다리품 walking; fee for going on an errand
♦공연히 다리품만 들이다 go in vain; get nothing for *one's* trouble / 다리품을 팔다 walk a great distance;〈심부름가다〉go on a paid errand

다림 testing the alignment;〈수직의〉plumbing;〈수평의〉level(l)ing
■—줄 a lead [plumb] line; a plumb rule —추(錘) a plumb bob; a plummet —판(板) a (carpenter's) level

다림보다〈수직을〉plumb;〈수평을〉level; test the alignment;〈이해 관계를〉keep alert to *one's* own interest

다림질 ironing ⇨ 다리미질
다릿돌 a stepping stone
-다마다 of course; sure; needless to say; certainly ⇨ -고말고
▶「파티에 가실 거예요?」「가다마다」 "Are you coming to the party?" "Yes, of course." ⇌ "Sure." ⇌ "Certainly."
다마스쿠스〈시리아의 수도〉Damascus

다만

■—검 a Damascus blade; a damask sword / —직 damask (cloth)

다만 1 〈오직〉 only; merely; simply; just; solely; but; alone; nothing but

> 解說 only는 글로 쓸 때는 보통 수식하는 어구 앞에 쓰지만 말할 때는 동사 바로 앞에 쓰는 것이 보통이다. 힘있게 강조하고 싶은 부분을 나타낸다. *merely*는 only보다 다소 딱딱한 말로서 보통 수식하는 어구 앞에 둔다. *simply*는 only, merely와 같은 뜻이지만「다른 요소를 섞지 않고 다만」이란 뜻, *just*는「그저 다만」이란 가벼운 뜻으로 회화에서 많이 쓰인다.

♦ 다만 하나의 사고 원인 the only [sole] cause of the accident / 다만 하나의 the only; the sole; single / 다만 …이라는 이유로 simply because…; for the sole reason that… / 다만 … 하기만 하면 되다 only have [need] to do; need only do; all one has to do is (to) do; have only to do / 다만 혼자서 (all) alone; (all) by oneself / 다만 만 just [only, but] once / 다만 하루라도 even for a day / 다만 울기만 하다 do nothing but cry
▶ 그는 다만 돈벌이만 생각하고 있다 All he thinks about is making money.
▶ 네가 할 수 있는 것이라곤 다만 하나뿐이다 There's only one thing you can do.
▶ 일이 이렇게 된 이상 다만 운을 하늘에 맡길 수밖에 없다 Things having come to this, there is nothing we can do but entrust our fate to heaven.
▶ 나는 다만 하루밖에 학교를 쉬지 않았다 I only missed one day of school.
▶ 나는 다만 당신을 생각해서 그렇게 했습니다 I did it only [just] for your sake [benefit].
▶ 그것은 다만 모방에 불과하다 It is a mere imitation.
▶ 다만 오고 싶어서 왔습니다 I came just [simply] because I wanted to (come).
▶ 우리는 다만 그의 명령을 따를 수밖에 없었다 There was nothing we could do but obey his order.
▶ 그것은 다만 억측에 지나지 않는다 It is merely a guess [a mere guess].

2 〈그러나〉 however; but; only; 〈조건〉 provided (that); on condition (that)
♦ 다만 …은 차한에 부재한다 Provided that the same shall not apply to…
▶ 뭐든지 주겠소 다만 이 그림만은 안 된다 I will give you anything but this picture.
▶ 다만 건강이 허락하는 경우에만 기꺼이 그것을 인수하겠다 I will be glad to undertake it, provided that I am well enough.
▶ 외출은 자유다. 다만 10시까지는 돌아와야 한다 You are free to go out; but you must be back by ten.
▶ 나는 갈 작정인데, 다만 비가 오면 그만두겠다 I am planning to go, but I'll give up if it rains.
▶ 할인은 해드리겠지만 다만 선불한다는 조건서입니다 I'll give you a discount on condition that you pay in advance.

다망 多忙 press [pressure] of work [business]
—다망하다 busy; 〈서술적〉 have a lot [a great deal] of work; have much [many things] to do; be fully occupied (with); be busily engaged (in)
♦ 다망하기 때문에 owing to pressure of business [work] / 다망한 1주일 a busy week / 다망한 생활을 하다 lead a busy life / 다망한 중에도 불구하고 despite the claims of busy life
▶ 오늘은 온종일 다망했다 I've been (kept) busy all day.
▶ 다망하신데 폐를 끼쳐 죄송합니다 I'm sorry to trouble you when you're busy.
▶ 선생님은 시험 채점을 하느라고 다망하시다 The teacher is busy marking papers.

다매 多賣 a large sale
■ 박리— small profits and quick returns

다면 多面 many sides; many faces [phases]
♦ 다면적 many-sided; versatile; multilateral
▶ 그는 활동이 다면적이다 He is active in many fields.
■ —각 a polyhedral angle

다면체 多面體 a polyhedron (*pl.* ~s, -dra)
♦ 다면체의 polyhedral; polyhedric
■ 정— a regular polyhedron

다모 多毛 hairiness; hirsuteness
♦ 다모의 hairy; hirsute ■ —증 excessive growth of hair; 〔醫〕 hirsutism

다모작 多毛作 〔農〕 multiple cropping

다목 〈나무〉 〔植〕 a sappanwood; 〈재목〉 sappanwood
■ 서양— a Judas tree

다목장어 多目長魚 〔魚〕 a brook lamprey

다목적 多目的 ♦ 다목적의 multipurpose / 다목적 가구 (a piece of) furniture with many uses
■ —댐 a multipurpose dam

다문 多聞 being widely informed
♦ 다문 박식한 사람 an erudite; a man of great learning and profound [extensive] knowledge
▶ 그는 나이에 비하면 다문 박식하다 He has a wide knowledge of many things beyond his age.

다물다 shut [close] (*one's* mouth)
♦ 꽉 다문 입 a firm [well-knit] mouth / 입을 다물다 be silent; hold *one's* tongue; stop talking; (美口) clam up; have *one's* lips closed / 입을 다물고 말하지 않다 keep *one's* mouth shut; keep silence; remain silent; (美口) clam up tight / 입을 다물고 부지런히 일하다 work steadily in silence
▶ 소년은 입을 다물고 있었다 The boy remained silent for a while.
▶ 그것에 대해서는 입을 다물고 있는 편이 좋다 You had better keep quiet about it.
▶ 왜 이제까지 입을 다물고 있었느냐? Why haven't you told me before (now)? ⇌ Why have you kept it from me?

다미씌우다 impute ⇨ 더미씌우다

다민족 多民族 ♦ 다민족의 multiracial
■ —국가 a multiracial nation [country]

다박나룻 a bushy beard; unkempt whiskers

다반사 茶飯事 an everyday occurrence

[affair]; a daily event; 〈사소한 일〉 a trifling matter
▶요즈음은 자동차 사고가 다반사로 일어난다 Car accidents are daily [everyday] happenings these days.

다발 a bundle; a bunch; 〈곡식 등의〉 a sheaf 《pl. sheaves》; 〈장작 등의〉 a fagot; 〈새끼 등의〉 a coil

解說 *bundle*은 많은 물건을 묶은 것. *bunch*는 같은 종류의 물건을 모은 것으로 특히 가지런히 묶은 것.

♦짚 한 다발 a bundle of straw / 꽃다발 a bunch of flowers; a bouquet / 한 다발에 만원 ten thousand won a bundle / 다발로 팔다[사다] sell [buy] 《things》 in a bundle / 다발로 묶다 bunch; bundle; pack into a bundle; tie up in [make up] a bundle; 〈곡식 등을〉 sheave / 지폐를 다발로 묶다 wad bank notes together
▶필요하지 않은 것은 다발로 묶으시오 Bundle up what you don't need. ⇒ Tie up in bundles [Bundle together] what(ever) you don't need.

다발 多發 occurring frequently
▶여기는 교통 사고 다발 지역이다 This is a place where accidents occur frequently.
—**다발하다** occur frequently [often]
■—**성 경화증** multiple sclerosis —**성 골수종** multiple myeloma —**성 신경염** polyneuritis; multiple neuritis

다방 茶房 a coffee shop; a teahouse ; a tearoom; a coffeehouse

解說 *coffee shop*은 미국에서는 「간이 식당」을 말하며 영국의 coffee bar, cafe에 해당하며 흔히 원두 커피를 파는 가게를 가리킨다. *tearoom*은 작은 규모의 레스토랑으로 가벼운 식사를 할 수 있는 곳이다.

다방면 多方面 〈방면〉 many quarters; 〈방향〉 many directions; 〈취미〉 versatility; many-sidedness
♦다방면에 걸친 흥미 multifarious interests / 다방면에 재능을 가진 사람 a man of many [manifold] talents / 다방면의 various; varied; many-sided; versatile; multifarious 《activities》 / 다방면으로 in many quarters [directions, fields] / 다방면으로 활동하다 work in various fields / 다방면으로 교제를 하다 have a wide [varied] circle of acquaintances
▶그는 다방면에 취미가 있다 He is a man of wide interests. ⇒ He has many-sided interests.
▶그의 연구는 다방면에 걸쳐 있다 His research covers many fields.
▶그는 다방면에서 활약하고 있다 He plays an active part in various fields.

다변 多辯 talkativeness; loquacity; garrulity; volubility
♦다변의 talkative; voluble
▶술을 마시더니 그는 더욱 다변이 되었다 Liquid made him even more talkative.
■—**가** a great talker; a prattler; a chatterbox

다변 多邊 ♦다변적(인) multilateral
■—**무역[외교]** multilateral trade [diplomacy]

다변형 多邊形 a polygon ⇨ 다각형

다변화 多邊化 diversification
♦수출시장의 다변화 diversification of export markets
—**다변화하다** diversify; extend; give variety

다병 多病 sickliness
▶재사(才士) 다병이라 Men of talent [genius] are mostly in delicate health [of weak constitution].
—**다병하다** weak; infirm; fragile; sickly; delicate ♦다병한 사람 a sickly person; a man in delicate health

다보록하다 tufty ⇨ 더부룩하다

다복 多福 great happiness [fortune]; blessedness
—**다복하다** happy; lucky; fortunate; blessed
♦다복한 생활을 하다 live [lead] a happy life; be well-to-do; live happily

다복다복 in bunches [clusters]; in groves [thickets]
—**다복다복하다** bushy; thicketed; dotted [covered] with thickets

다복솔 a bushy young pine tree (with many twigs)

다부지다 1 〈과단성 있다〉 decisive; resolute; stouthearted; staunch; firm; determined; indefatigable
♦다부진 결의 a firm resolution / 다부진 사람 a decisive [stouthearted] person / 다부지게 일하다 work hard [indefatigably]
▶다부지게 행동하라 Take prompt [quick] action on it.
▶그는 다부진 데가 없다 He is an irresolute person. ⇨ He lacks decisiveness.
▶그는 키는 작아도 사람이 다부지다 Though small in stature, he is a man of firm character.
2 〈힘들다〉 trying; hard; tough
♦다부진 일 hard work, a tough job

다분히 多分— (very) much; greatly; highly; exceedingly; to a great extent; quite a lot
▶그에게는 다분히 자기본위적인 데가 있다 He has a very selfish disposition.
▶그럴 염려가 다분히 있다 That is very much to be feared.
▶전쟁이 일어날 가능성이 다분히 있다 There is a very strong possibility that war will break out.
▶그는 시인의 소질이 다분히 있다 He has a good deal of the poet in him.

다비 茶毘 〈불교에서의 화장〉 cremation

다빈치 〈이탈리아의 화가·조각가·과학자〉 da Vinci, Leonardo (1452-1519)

다빡 rashly ⇨ 더빡

다뿍 to the full; overflowingly; brimfully

—**다뿐** 〈강조〉 ▶ 會話 「우리와 함께 가겠니?」 「가다뿐이겠어」 "Will you go with us?" "Sure!" ⇨ "Of course, I'll go!"

다사 多事 1 〈일이 많음〉 eventfulness; 〈다망〉 pressure of work [business]
—**다사하다** eventful; busy; 〈서술적〉 have

much to do
2 〈간섭이 많음〉 nosiness; meddlesomeness
—**다사하다[스럽다]** nosy; meddlesome; officious ◆다사스러운 사람 an officious person; a meddler; a busybody

다사다단 多事多端 eventfulness
—**다사다단하다** eventful; busy
◆ 다사다단한 한해[일생] an eventful year [life] / 국가가 다사다단한 이때에 in this critical hour for the country
▶ 국내외를 막론하고 다사다단하다 We are having eventful days [It is an eventful period] both at home and abroad.
▶ 그는 다사다단한 생애를 보냈다 He led an eventful life.
▶ 작년은 다사다단한 한 해였다 Many things happened [There were numerous happenings] last year. ⇌ Last year was very eventful.

다사제제 多士濟濟 a number [galaxy] of brilliant men [talents]
▶ 우리 학교 졸업생들은 다사제제입니다 Our school has produced a number of distinguished people.

다산 多産 fecundity
◆ 다산의 productive; fecund; prolific
—**다산하다** bear many young; be fecund
▶ 이 지방의 여자들은 다산한다 The women in this region have many children.
■ —계(鷄) a prolific hen; a good layer —계(系) a prolific family

다상 多相〈電〉 multiphase; polyphase
■ —전동기[발전기, 교류] a polyphase motor [dynamo, current]

다색 多色 many colors ◆다색의 multicolored; polychrome; polychromatic
■ —인쇄 multicolored printing: 다색 인쇄한 호화본 a gorgeous book printed in many colors —장식 polychromy —채색[화법] polychromy —화 a polychrome

다색 茶色 light brown; drab
◆다색의 머리 [눈] brown hair [eyes] / 다색의 brownish; light brown

다선의원 多選議員 a Congressman [an Assemblyman, a representative, a delegate] elected for many terms

다섯 five
◆〈전원〉다섯 쌍동이 quintuplets; (口) quints / 다섯째 the fifth / 다섯개 한 벌 a set of five; a quintet
▶ 내 딸은 다섯살이오 My daughter is five (years old).

다성음악 多聲音樂 polyphony
다세대주택 多世帶住宅 a multiplex house
다소 多少 1〈많은 수〉 number (수의); quantity (양의); amount (액수의)
◆다소를 불문하고 regardless of the amount; large or small / 다소에 따라서 according to the number [amount, quantity] of; in proportion to [as]/ 수입의 다소에 따라 세금을 부과하다 levy a tax on sb to the amount of (his) income
▶ 구호 물자는 다소를 불문하고 KBS에서 접수합니다 Any amount of relief goods will be accepted at KBS.
▶ 그것은 참가자의 다소에 달려 있다 It depends upon the number of participants.
▶ 다소를 불문하고 주문에는 신속하게 응하겠습니다 All orders, large and small, will be promptly executed.
2〈얼마간〉 a few; a little; some; somewhat; more or less; to some degree [extent]; in some [a] measure; (口) sort of; (口) kind of
◆프랑스어를 다소 말하다 speak French a little / 다소 병이 낫다 get somewhat better / 다소 융통성이 있다 be adaptable [flexible] to a degree
▶ 그것은 사실과는 다소 다르다 It is someway from the truth.
▶ 그는 의학 지식이 다소 있다 He has some knowledge of medicine.
▶ 나는 재즈에 대해서는 다소 알고 있다 I know something about jazz.
▶ 오늘은 다소 기분이 낫다 I feel a little [somewhat] better today.
▶ 그는 다소 이기주의적인 면이 있다 He is a bit selfish.
▶ 그 모임에는 여자도 다소 있었다 There were a few women at the meeting, too.

다소곳이〈온순히〉gently; quietly; obediently; 〈머리를 숙이고〉 with *one's* head drooped [dropped]
◆ 다소곳이 남의 충고를 받아들이다 accept another's advice obediently [without objecting] / 다소곳이 선생님의 지시를 따르다 obey the teacher quietly

다소곳하다〈고개를 숙이고〉 modest and quiet with *one's* head lowered; 〈온순한〉 modest; quiet; gentle; meek; obedient
◆다소곳한 소녀 a modest [docile] young girl / 다소곳한 태도 an obedient (and courteous) attitude
▶ 그녀는 아주 다소곳하다 She is as meek as a lamb.

-다손치더라도 (even) though [if]; although; (even) admitting [granting, supposing] that…; no matter how [what, where, who, when, which]…(may)…
◆아무리 돈이 있다손치더라도 however [no matter how] rich *one* may be / 그가 늙었다손치더라도 though he is old; old as he is / 그렇게 말했다손치더라도 even if [granted that] *one* did say so
▶ 나무가 있다손치더라도 극히 적다 There are very few trees, if any.
▶ 해고된다손치더라도 사실을 말하겠다 Even if it costs me my job [I am dismissed], I will tell the truth.
▶ 아무리 가난하다손치더라도 기가 꺾여서는 안된다 However [No matter how] poor you may be, never lose heart.
▶ 실패한다손치더라도 해볼 가치는 있다 It is worth attempting though we fail.

다수 多數 1〈많은 수〉a large [great] number; numbers; a multitude 《of relatives》; a legion [legions] 《of people》; an army 《of schoolchildren》; a host 《of friends》
◆국민의 다수 the large mass of the people /

다수의 many; many a 《man》; a great many; a lot of; a (large) number of; numerous / 다수의 힘을 믿고 by [relying on] force of numbers / 다수가 집합[참석]하다 assemble together [attend] in large numbers / 다수를 믿다 trust to numbers / 다수를 위해 소수를 희생하다 sacrifice the few to the many
▶이 숲에는 다수의 사슴이 서식하고 있다 A large number of deer inhabit this forest. ⇒ Deer are found in great numbers in this forest.
▶그는 다수의 골동품을 모으고 있다 He has a large collection of antiques.
2 〈과반수〉 the majority
◆다수의 횡포 the tyranny of the majority / 압도적[3분의 2의] 다수로 by an overwhelming [a two-thirds] majority / 다수의 학생들의 greater part [most, the majority] of the students / 다수의 의견에 따르다 agree to the views of the majority / 다수를 차지하다 command [win, get, have, hold] a majority
▶그는 4분의 3의 다수로 의장에 선출되었다 He was elected chairman by a three-fourths majority.
▶시의회는 진보론자가 다수를 차지하고 있다 The progressive hold a majority in the city council.
■**단순**— a simple majority **절대**— an absolute majority ■—**당** a majority [dominant] party [side]: 다수당 당수(黨首) the majority leader —**대표제** a majority representation system —**안** a majority proposal —**표**《poll》 a plurality [majority]
다수결 多數決 majority decision; decision by majority
◆다수결의 원칙 majority rule [principle]; rule by [of] majority / 다수결에 의한 표결 majority voting / 다수결에 따르다 accept a majority decision; abide by the decision of the majority / 다수결로 정하다 decide by (a) majority vote
▶의회제도는 다수결의 원칙을 채용한다 The parliamentary system uses the principle of decision by majority.
▶그 의안은 다수결로 통과되었다 The bill was passed by a majority decision.
■**단순**— a simple majority decision ■—**주의** majoritarianism
다수확 多收穫 a bumper crop
◆다수확의 밀 high-yield(ing) wheat
다스 a dozen 《略 doz., dz.》
◆한 다스의 연필 a dozen pencils; a dozen of pencils / 두 다스들이 상자 a box containing two dozen / 열 다스 ten dozens; a small gross / 여러 다스의 (many) dozens of... / 다스로 팔다 sell 《pencils》 by the dozen [in dozens]
▶이 연필은 한 다스 3,000원이다 These pencils are three thousand won a dozen.
▶연필이 몇 다스 있느냐? How many dozen pencils do you have?
다스리다 1 〈통치하다〉 govern; rule [reign] over 《a country》; 〈관리하다〉 manage; administer; preside over

◆집안을 다스리다 manage [regulate] a household / 나라를 다스리다 govern [rule over] a country / 국정을 다스리다 direct [conduct] the affairs of state
▶왕은 백성을 지혜롭게 잘 다스렸다 The king ruled his people wisely and well.
▶영국에서는 국왕은 군림하되 다스리지는 않는다 In Great Britain the sovereign reigns, but does not rule.
2 〈통제하다〉 control; place *sth* under *one's* control; regulate 《rivers》
◆물가와 임금을 다스리다 control prices and wages / 물을 다스리다 control floods; take flood control [river conservancy] measures
3 〈평정하다〉 quell; subdue; repress
◆폭도를 다스리다 suppress [put down] the rioters / 반란을 다스리다 subdue a rebellion
4 〈병을〉 cure; heal; remedy; set right; make whole
◆유행성 감기를 잘 다스리는 약 an effective remedy for the flu
▶이 병을 다스릴 약은 없다 There is no remedy for this disease. ⇒ This disease will yield to no remedy.
▶그들은 암을 다스리는 약을 개발중에 있다 They are developing a medicine for fighting cancer.
▶빨리 병을 다스려서 우리와 함께 다시 일할 수 있게 되기를 바랍니다 We hope you will get well as early as possible and work with us again.
5 〈죄를〉 punish
◆죄를 다스리다 punish a crime
다습 多濕 high humidity; much moisture
—**다습하다** damp; dampish; humid
◆다습한 기후 dampish weather / 고온 다습한 북태평양 기단(氣團) the hot and humid North Pacific air mass
▶올 여름은 고온다습했다 This summer has been very hot and humid.
다시 〈또 한번〉 again; once more [again]; for the second time; a second time; twice; 〈새로이〉 afresh; anew; 〈되풀이하여〉 (all) over (again)
◆몇번이고 다시 over and over (again); many times over / 언제 다시 한번 another time; some other time / 다시 방문하다 make a second visit 《to》; revisit / 다시 하다 repeat; try again; do over again [once more] / 다시 시도하다 try again; make another attempt / 다시 시작하다 begin afresh [anew]; start (all) over again / (한번 읽은 책을) 다시 읽다 read 《a book》 (all over) again / 이야기를 다시 쓰다 write a story all over again [anew] / 다시 말하다 say again; repeat
▶나는 실패했지만 다시 시도해 보았다 I failed but made another attempt.
▶어젯밤에 다시 지진이 일어났다 There was another earthquake last night.
▶언제 다시 일을 시작합니까? When will you start working again?
▶그녀는 다시 건강해졌다 She got well again. ⇒ She has recovered [regained] her health.
▶근간 다시 한번 찾아뵙겠습니다 I will call

다시금

again one of these days.
▶ 자, 다시 만나자 〈헤어질 때〉 See you again! ⇒ See you (later)! ⇒ So long!
▶ 나는 다시는 그곳에 가지 않겠다 I will never go there again.
▶ 나는 다시 주의를 받았다 I was warned for the second time. ⇒ I got a second warning.
▶ 그는 고향을 떠난 뒤 다시 돌아오지 않았다 He left his home town never to return [and never returned].
▶ 중동에서 다시 전쟁이 일어났다 Another war has broken out in the Middle East.
▶ 다시 뵐 날을 고대하고 있습니다 I'm looking forward to seeing you again.
▶ 다시 부탁하려고 왔습니다 I've come to ask you once again.
▶ 같은 실책을 두번 다시는 되풀이하지 않겠다 I swear that I shall never repeat the same error.
▶ 우리는 다시 교섭을 시작했다 We resumed negotiations.
▶ 나는 내년 여름에 미국을 다시 방문할 예정이다 I'm going to visit America for the second time next summer.
▶ 그는 인공호흡으로 다시 살아났다 He was revived by artificial respiration.

다시금 again ⇨ 다시

다시다 ♦입맛을 다시다 〈맛이 있어서〉 smack one's lips; 〈못마땅하여〉 click [clack] one's tongue / 입맛을 다시며 먹다 eat sth with much gusto [great relish]; smack appreciative lips 《over [on] a dish》
▶ 그녀의 요리에 그들은 모두 입맛을 다셨다 They all smacked their lips over her cooking.
▶ 그들은 접시에 수북이 담긴 음식에 입맛을 다셨다 They smacked their lips over the huge tray of food.

다시마 〔植〕 a (sea) tangle

다시없다 1〈견줄 것이 없다〉 unparalleled; unique; matchless; peerless; unequalled; 〈서술적〉 stand unequaled
♦그녀의 다시없는 미모 her unparalleled beauty / 다시없는 물건 a unique article; the only thing of its kind
▶ 이렇게 경치가 좋은 곳은 다시없다 The place is unequaled [has no equal] in its scenic beauty.
▶ 그런 것은 세상에 다시없다 There is nothing like [to compare with] it anywhere in the world.
▶ 그것은 범죄사상 다시없는 사건이었다 It was a case without parallel [unparalleled] in the history of crime.
2〈더 낳은 것이 없다〉 be never to happen again; be for one time only; will not be repeated
♦다시없는 기회 an opportunity one will never have again; a golden opportunity; 〈절호의 기회〉 a capital chance
▶ 지금이 다시없는 기회다 Now's the time.
▶ 이런 기회는 다시없다 We shall never have such a good opportunity again. ⇒ Such an opportunity knocks but once at the door.
▶ 그런 기회는 일생에 다시 없을 것이다 A chance like this comes but once in a lifetime. ⇒ There will never be another opportunity like this. ⇒ It is now or never.

다시증 多視症 polyopea

-다시피 〈마찬가지로〉 like; as; in the same way 《that》; 〈같은 정도로〉 almost; (pretty) nearly; all but
♦보시다시피 as you (can) see / 알다시피 as you know / 공짜로 물건을 사다시피 하다 buy sth for next to nothing / 공짜로 일하다시피 하다 work for next to no wages
▶ 함대는 거의 전멸하다시피 했다 The fleet was all but annihilated.
▶ 보시다시피 나는 돈이 없습니다 As you can see, I have no money.
▶ 그는 술집에서 살다시피 한다 He spends most of his time at the public house.

다식 多食 eating much; heavy eating; gluttony ▶ 다식은 위에 나쁘다 Heavy eating is bad for stomach.
─**다식하다** eat much; gluttonize
─■─증 〔醫〕 bulimia; polyphagia

다신교 多神教 polytheism
♦다신교적인 polytheistic
■─도 a polytheist

다실 茶室 a coffee shop ⇨ 다방(茶房)

다액 多額 a large sum [amount]
♦다액의 기부 a generous contribution / 다액의 much; a large [huge] sum [amount] of
▶ 이 사업에는 다액의 자금이 필요하다 We need a large amount of money for this project.
■─납세자 a high taxpayer; an upper-bracket taxpayer

다양 多樣 diversity; variety
─**다양하다** various; diverse; multifarious
♦다양한 직업의 사람들 men of diverse occupations / 다양한 인종 집단 various [a wide variety of] ethnic groups / 내용이 다양하다 contain a wide variety
▶ 이 단어는 다양한 뜻이 있다 This word has various meanings.
▶ 최근에는 다양한 잡지가 출판되고 있다 A great variety of magazines are published these days.
▶ 그는 취미가 다양하다 He has many-sided interests.
■─성 variety; diversity; multiformity : 문화의 다양성 cultural diversity ─화 diversification : 다양화하다 diversify

다언 多言 many words
▶ 그것에는 다언이 필요하지 않다 There is no need to dwell upon it. ⇒ We don't need to speak at length at it.

다염기산 多鹽基酸 〔化〕 polybasic acid

다용도 多用途 many purposes [uses]
♦다용도의 가구 (a piece of) furniture with many uses
■─건물[실, 댐] a multipurpose building [room, dam]

다우 多雨 much rain

다우존스 ■─산식(算式) the Dow-Jones formula ─평균주가(지수) the Dow-Jones average (price) [index] 《on the stock exchange》

다운 〔拳〕 a knockdown
♦**다운시키다** 〈권투에서〉 knock down / **다운되다** be knocked down; be downed / **다운됐다가 일어서다** climb off the canvas
▶그는 도전자를 5라운드에서 다운시켰다 He downed the challenger in the fifth round.

다운재킷 a down jacket

다원 多元 pluralism
♦**다원적** plural; pluralistic / **다원적 국가론** pluralistic conception of the State
■**─론** 〔哲〕 pluralism **─론자** a pluralist **─묘사** descriptions from different viewpoints **─방송** multiplex broadcasting; broadcasting from plural origination **─방정식** 〔數〕 a plural equation **─성** plurality

다원자 多原子 ♦**다원자의** polyatomic
■**─분자** a polyatomic molecule

다윈 〈영국의 박물학자〉 Darwin, Charles Robert (1809-82)
■**─설** the Darwinian theory; Darwinism

다윗 〔聖〕 David; the Psalmist

다육 多肉 〔植〕 fleshiness
♦**다육질[성]의** fleshy
■**─과**(果) a drupaceous [fleshy, pulpy] fruit; a drupe **─식물** a fleshy [succulent] plant

다음 the next; the second; the sequel 《of a story》; 〈형용사적〉 following; next; ensuing; coming; 〈인접한〉 adjoining; adjacent
♦**다음에** next; next time; another time / **다음 세대** the next [coming] generation / **다음부터** from now on / **다음 정거장** the next station / **다음 주**[일요일] next week [Sunday] / **다음 방** the next [adjoining] room
▶그녀의 편지에는 다음과 같이 쓰여져 있다 In her letter she writes as follows.
▶ 會話 「다음은 누구 차례냐?」「다음은 그의 차례다」"Who's next?" "It's his turn next."
▶나머지 이야기는 다음번에 하겠습니다 I will tell you the rest of this story some other day.
▶다음번까지 기다릴 수가 없다 I cannot wait for another occasion.
▶그 다음은? What (comes) next?
▶조지 워싱턴 다음의 대통령은 누구였을까? Who was the next president after George Washington?
▶이것은 다음으로 미루자 Let us save that for another time.
▶다음 분 Next, please.
▶다음 모임은 4월 20일이다 The next meeting will be held on April 20 [英] 20 April].
▶이번은 용서해 주지만 다음부터는 용서하지 않겠다 I'll forgive you this time, but not again.
▶요 다음 만날 때 돌려다오 Return it when we meet next.
▶다음번에 결과를 알려 주십시오 Please tell me the result next time.
▶식당차는 이 다음 차량이다 The dining car is the next one.
▶다음 목요일에 만나자 Let's get together next Thursday [this coming Thursday].

다음가다 be in the second place; rank [come, be] next [second] to; come [rank] after; be second to
♦**에베레스트산 다음가는 제2의 고봉** the second highest peak next to Mt. Everest / **런던 다음가는 대도시** the largest city next [second only] to London / **지위**[나이]**가 그 사람 다음가는** the man next to him in rank [age]
▶공작은 위엄에서 왕 다음갔다 The duke was next in dignity after the king.
▶나는 학급에서 키가 그녀 다음간다 I am the next tallest to her in our class.

다음날 〈이튿날〉 the next [following] day; 〈훗날〉 someday; another [some other] day; some time later
♦**사고가 있은 그 다음날에** on the day following the accident / **그 다음날 아침** the next [following] morning / **그 밤과 그 다음날 밤** that night and the next [the night after]
▶그는 그 다음날 왔다 He came on the next day.
▶눈이 온 그 다음날은 대개 쾌청하다 It is usually quite fine on the day after it snows.
▶나는 그 다음날 아침에 일찍 일어났다 I got out of bed early in the next morning.
▶그것은 다음날로 미루자 Let us leave that for another time.

다음다음 the one after the next; next but one
♦**다음다음 날** the day after next; the next day but *one*; two days after [later] / **다음다음 주** the week after next / **다음다음 달** the month after next; two months later / **다음다음 해** the year after next; two years later
▶이선생 댁은 우리집 다음다음이다 Mr. Lee lives two doors away from us [next door but one].

다음달 the next [following] month; the coming month; proximo (略 prox.)
♦**다음달의 오늘** this day next month / **다음달 10일에** on the tenth of the next month; on the tenth proximo / **다음달로 돌리다** carry 《a matter》 forward to the next month
▶그는 그 다음달에 집으로 돌아왔다 He came home the next month.

다음절 多音節 a polysyllable(↔a monosyllable) ■**─어** a polysyllabic word

다음해 the next [following, ensuing] year
♦**다음해로의 이월 잔액** the balance carried forward to the next year / **가뭄이 있던 다음해** the year after the drought / **계정을 다음해로 이월하다** carry the account forward into the next year's
▶그는 그 다음해에 태어났다 He was born the year after that [(in) the following year].

다음호 ─號 the next number [issue]
▶다음호에 계속 To be continued (in our next number).
▶다음호에 완결 To be concluded (in our next issue).

다의 多義 polysemy; ambiguity; diverse [various] meanings
■**─어** a multivocal [an ambiguous, an equivocal] word; a word with many [manifold] meanings

다이내믹하다 dynamic
♦**다이내믹하게** dynamically

다이너마이트 dynamite

다이너모

♦ 다이너마이트로 바위를 폭파하다 shatter [blow up] a rock with dynamite; dynamite a rock
▶ 다이너마이트가 2개 없어졌다 Two sticks of dynamite are missing.

다이너모 〔電〕 a dynamo

다이렉트메일 direct mail

다이빙 diving; a dive ♦ 다이빙을 잘하다 be a good diver; be good at diving
―**다이빙하다** dive
▶ 그는 안벽에서 차와 함께 바다로 다이빙했다 He drove his car off the pier into the sea and drowned himself.
■ **공중회전―** somersault diving ―**경기** a diving event; a fancy dive; a fancy diving ―**대** a diving platform

다이아몬드 〔鑛〕 (a) diamond
♦ 다이아몬드를 연마하다 cut [polish] a diamond
■ ―**가공[연마]법** diamond cutting ―**바늘** 〈전축의〉 a diamond stylus ―**반지** a diamond ring; a ring set with diamonds

다이어그램 a diagram

다이어트 a diet
▶ 나는 지금 다이어트 중이다 I'm on a diet now. ⇒ I'm dieting.
―**식품** diet food

다이얼 a dial; 〈문자반〉 a dial plate
♦ 전화의 다이얼 a telephone dial / 다이얼식 전화 a dial telephone / 라디오 다이얼을 돌리다 dial the radio; turn a dial of the radio / 라디오의 다이얼을 KBS에 맞추다 tune in to KBS; turn the radio dial to KBS

다이오드 〔電〕 a diode

다이제스트 a digest; 〈잡지〉 a magazine digest
♦「종의 기원」의 다이제스트판 an abridged version of 'The Origin of Species'; 'The Origin of Species' in digest form

다이폴안테나 〔電〕 a dipole (antenna)

다인 〔物〕 a dyne

다작 多作 abundant production; 〈많이 씀〉 prolificacy in writing
♦ 다작의 productive; prolific
―**다작하다** write many works; be prolific in writing
■ ―**가** a prolific writer [author]

다잡다 1 〈사람을〉 keep a tight rein [hand] (on); exercise close supervision (over)
♦ 부하들을 다잡아 일을 끝내다 urge one's men to push through the work / 학생들을 다잡다 put the pupils under strict discipline
▶ 그들은 다잡지 않으면 틀림없이 일을 태만히 한다 If we don't keep an eye on them, they are sure to neglect their work.
2 〈일을〉 concentrate on (a job); manage (a job); stick close to 《one's work》
3 〈마음을〉 brace oneself up (for a task); reform 《one's attitude》
♦ 마음을 다잡고 공부하다 settle [set] down to one's studies
▶ 아이들이 시끄러워서 마음을 다잡고 책을 읽을 수 없다 The children are so noisy that I cannot settle down to my reading.
▶ 그는 마음을 다잡고 새출발하기로 맹세했다

다재 多才 versatile talents; versatility
―**다재하다** versatile; many-sided; resourceful
♦ 다재(다능)한 사람 a many-sided man; a man of versatile talents
▶ 그는 다재(다능)하다 He is good [clever] at many different things.

다정 多情 1 〈인정이 많음〉 kindheartedness; warm-[tender]heartedness; tenderness
―**다정하다** affectionate; tender; kindhearted; warm-[tender]hearted
♦ 다정한 사람 a warm-hearted person; a man of heart / 다정한 편지 an affectionate letter / 다정한 말 affectionate words / 다정하게 tenderly; affectionately; warm-heartedly
▶ 그는 꽤 다정한 사람이다 He has rather a tender heart.
▶ 여자는 남자보다 다정하다 Women have warmer affection than men.
▶ 나는 아내가 어떤 낯선 사람과 다정하게 이야기하는 것을 보았다 I found my wife in an affectionate talk with a stranger.
2 〈교분이 두터움〉 close friendship; intimacy
―**다정하다** close; intimate; familiar; friendly
♦ 다정한 친구 a good [great, close] friend; a familiar; (口) a chum / …와 다정한 사이가 되다 become close friends 《with》; become familiar 《with》; come into close association 《with》/ …와 다정한 사이가 되다 be very good friends 《with》; be on good [friendly] terms 《with》; be very close 《to》/ 다정하게 closely; intimately
▶ 두 사람은 아주 다정한 사이다 They are hand and [in] glove with each other.

다정다감 多情多感 sentimentality
―**다정다감하다** emotional; passionate; sentimental ♦ 다정다감한 사람 a man of sentiment [feeling]

다정다한 多情多恨 sensibility; susceptibility; tears and regrets
―**다정다한하다** susceptive; sensitive; full of tears and regrets
♦ 다정다한한 일생을 보내다 lead a life full of tears and regrets

다정불심 多情佛心 kindheartedness; tender-[warm-]heartedness

다족 多足 〔動〕 ♦ 다족의 multiped(e)
■ ―**류** Myriapoda

다종다양 多種多樣 variety; diversity; multifariousness
―**다종다양하다** various; diverse
▶ 거기 모인 사람의 직업은 다종다양했다 The people gathered there were from all walks of life.

다중식방송 多重式放送 multiplex broadcasting

다지다 1 〈단단하게 하다〉 harden; make hard [harder]
♦ 땅을 다지다 〈달구 등으로〉 tamp (down); ram / 흙[눈]을 밟아 다지다 tread [tramp] down the soil [snow]
2 〈강조하다〉 emphasize; lay [put] stress [emphasis] 《on》; underline; underscore; make sure [certain] of [that...]/ 꼭 오라고 다지다

call sb's special attention to come / 몇 번씩이나 다지다 make doubly sure [certain] 《that...》
▶ 나는 그에게 내달에는 빚을 갚겠느냐고 다져 물었다 I pressed him for a definite answer whether he would pay the debt next month.
3 〈강화하다〉 confirm; strengthen; solidify; consolidate
◆ 터전을 다지다 strengthen the foundations [the basis]/ 사회적 지위를 다지다 consolidate one's position in society / 콘크리트를 다지다 solidify concrete
4 〈고기 등을 잘게〉 mince; hash; cut 《meat》 thin [into thin pieces]; chop (up)
◆ 잘 다진 고기 well-minced meat / 양파를 다지다 chop up a onion / 마늘을 다지다 smash (up) garlic
5 〈잠자게 하다〉 press 《seasoned food》 with a stone

다지르다 make sure that...; double-check; press for a definite answer
◆ 저녁식사 때까지 꼭 돌아오라고 그를 다질렀다 I told him again that he had to be back by suppertime.

다질리다 be assured; be double-checked; get pressed for a definite answer

다짐 an assurance; a definite promise; a pledge; vouching
—**다짐하다** assure; pledge; make sure; give [pledge] one's word
◆ 확실히 다짐하기 위해 just to make 《it》 doubly sure; to make assurance doubly sure
▶ 그는 다음 주까지는 빚을 갚겠다고 다짐했다 He gave his word that he would pay the debt by next week.
▶ 그는 다시는 도둑질하지 않겠다고 다짐했다 He pledged himself never again to steal.
▶ 내 비밀을 아무에게도 말하지 않겠다고 다짐하겠니? Will you promise [give me your word of honor] not to tell my secret to anyone?

다짐받다 get an assurance from sb; make sb pledge [promise]
◆ 그 제안에 대한 찬성을 다짐받다 obtain definite assurances of approval for the proposal
▶ 그들은 다시는 죄를 짓지 않는다는 다짐을 받고 그를 석방시켰다 They set him free on his oath that he would never commit a crime again.
▶ 나는 내일 아침에 물품을 보내줄 것을 다짐받았다 I have an assurance that the goods shall be sent tomorrow morning.
▶ 갚을 것을 다짐받고 그에게 돈을 꾸어 주었다 I lent him money on the promise that he would pay it back.

다짜고짜(로) 〈예고없이〉 without notice [warning]; 〈느닷없이〉 abruptly; suddenly; unexpectedly; without preamble; 〈까닭없이〉 whether one likes it or not
◆ 다짜고짜로 …하게 하다 force [compel] sb to do; make sb do by force / 다짜고짜로 따귀를 때리다 slap sb on the cheek all of a sudden / 다짜고짜로 집을 비워 달라고 하다 order sb out of the house without notice / 다짜고짜로 체포하다 arrest sb without giving any reason
▶ 아버지는 다짜고짜로 나를 꾸짖으셨다 Father scolded me unsparingly.
▶ 사장님은 언제나 다짜고짜로 우리를 꾸짖으신다 Our boss always takes us to task without giving us a chance to explain.

다채롭다 多彩— colorful; variegated; diversified
◆ 다채로운 경력 a colorful career
▶ 다채로운 오락행사가 있었다 There was entertainment of all sorts.

다치다 **1** 〈부상하다〉 hurt oneself; be [get] injured; get hurt; be [get] wounded
◆ 다친 다리 an injured leg / 팔을 다치다 be injured in the arm / 머리를 다치다 be wounded in the head; suffer a head injury [wound]/ 차사고로 다치다 be injured in an auto accident / 몹시[크게] 다치다 be seriously injured; be badly hurt [wounded] 《on the head》/ 다치게 하다 do harm [injury] 《to》; inflict a wound 《on》; injure; wound; hurt
▶ 그 사고로 열명이 다쳤다 Ten people were injured in the accident.
▶ 어디 다치셨습니까? Have you got hurt?
▶ 그는 교통사고로 오른쪽 어깨를 다쳤다 His right shoulder was injured [hurt] in the traffic accident.
2 〈손상되다〉 be damaged; be injured; sustain an injury

-다치더라도 even though ⇨ -다손치더라도

다카 〈방글라데시의 수도〉 Dacca

다카르 〈세네갈의 수도〉 Dakar

다큐멘터리 documentary
—**드라마** a documentary drama —**영화** a documentary (film)

다크 호스 a dark horse

다투다 **1** 〈언쟁하다〉 quarrel 《with sb about [over] sth》; exchange (angry) words; have a row 《with》; wrangle; squabble; brawl
◆ 사소한 일로 다투다 quarrel about [over] trifles
▶ 옆방에서 다투는 소리가 들렸다 I heard the voices of people quarreling in the next room.
▶ 그들은 그 물품을 어떻게 나눌 것인가에 대해 서로 다투었다 They quarreled with each other over [about] how to divide the goods.
2 〈논쟁하다〉 argue [dispute] 《with sb about [over] sth》; have a dispute [an argument]; engage in a controversy
◆ 다툴 수 없는 사실 an indisputable [undeniable] fact / 다툴 여지가 없는 indisputable; incontrovertible; incontestable / 새로운 교육제도를 두고 다투다 argue (for) a new educational system
▶ 그 결정이 시기 상조였다는데 대해서는 다툴 여지가 없다 There is no dispute that the decision was premature.
▶ 우리는 그 문제를 두고 자주 다툰다 We often dispute that point.
▶ 과학자들은 그 문제에 대해 다투고 있었다 The scientists were disputing [arguing, engaged in a controversy over] the subject.
3 〈겨루다〉 compete [vie] 《with sb for sth》;

fight; contend 《with [against] *sb* for *sth*》; struggle 《for power》

解說 *compete*가 「경쟁하다, 싸우다」라는 뜻의 일반적인 말. *fight*는 「대항심을 크게 발휘하여 격렬하게 다투다」란 뜻. *contend*는 「적의나 불만을 가지고 다투다」란 뜻으로 쓰인다.

◆시간을 다투는 문제 an urgent problem / 승리를[공명을] 다투다 contend for victory [honors] / 앞을 다투어 …하다 try to be the first to do; try to get ahead of other people 《in doing》; scramble / 앞을 다투어 사다 vie with others in buying
▶이것은 일각을 다투는 문제다 The problem does not admit of [does not brook] a moment's delay.
▶지금은 일분 일초를 다투어야 할 때다 We haven't a moment to lose.
▶그는 나와 1등상을 다투었다 He vied with me for the first prize.

다툼 1〈언쟁〉 a quarrel; a fight; a (verbal) dispute; a brawl; a wrangle; a squabble
◆말 다툼 a quarrel; an altercation; a wrangle
2〈논쟁〉 an argument; a controversy; a dispute; a debate
◆이론에 관한 다툼 a controversy over theory
3〈경쟁〉 a contest; (a) rivalry; a strife; a struggle 《for》; a competition; a contention
◆우승 다툼 a struggle for (the) victory / 공명 다툼 a contention for distinction / 예산 다툼 a struggle for a bigger share of the budget / 자리 다툼 the competition for a position / 정권 다툼 a scramble for political power

다툼질 quarreling; squabbling; arguing; controverting

다하다¹ 〈다 없어지다〉 be exhausted; run out (of); be used up [consumed, spent, gone]; give out; come to an end; be up; be out
◆힘이 다 할 때까지 while [as far as] *one's* strength lasts / 이 세상이 다하도록 to the end of time; for ever (and ever) / 수단이 다하다 have tried everything [all the means] that one can think of; come to [be at] the end of *one's* resources / 식량이 다하다 run out of food [provisions]; the food is all gone / 연료가 다하다 run out of fuel
▶그의 운[인내력]도 다 했다 His luck [patience] gave out.
▶병사들은 전투로 인해 기력이 다했다 The soldiers were used up by the fighting.

다하다² 1〈있는 대로 다 쓰다〉 use up; exhaust; do everything possible; do *one's* best [utmost]
◆온갖 수단을 다하다 try everything [every means] 《in *one's* power》; leave no stone unturned / 모든 노력을 다하다 do *one's* best endeavors / 있는 힘을 다하다 exert all *one's* powers / 갖은 도락[고생]을 다하다 drain the cup of pleasure [sorrow] to the dregs / 최선을 다하여 to the best of *one's* ability
2〈끝내다〉 end; finish; get [be] through; get through with

◆하루의 일을 다하다 finish a day's work / 과학자로서 일생을 다하다 finish a successful career as a scientist
▶네 일을 다하면 나가도 된다 You can go out when you get through with your work.
3〈이행하다〉 accomplish; complete; perform; execute; fulfill; carry out
◆임무[의무]를 다하다 fulfill [perform] *one's* duty / 책임을 다하다 fulfill *one's* responsibility / 사명을 다하다 carry out *one's* mission / 효도를 다하다 serve *one's* parents with devotion
▶그는 훌륭하게 임무를 다했다 He carried out [executed] his duty excellently.

다한증 多汗症 〔醫〕 excessive sweating; hyperhidrosis

다항 선택법 多項選擇法 a multiple choice method

다항식 多項式 〔數〕 a polynomial [multinomial] expression; a polynomial

다행 多幸 (good) luck; good fortune
◆불행중 다행 a happy feature of a misfortune
▶댁에 계셔서 아주 다행입니다 How fortunate to find you at home.
▶목숨을 건진 것이 무엇보다도 다행이다 You may bless your stars that you have escaped with your life.
―**다행하다** fortunate; lucky; happy
◆다행히 luckily; fortunately; by good luck [fortune]; as (good) luck would have it / 다행히 …하다 have the (good) fortune to do; be lucky enough to do / 다행히 일이 잘 되면 if fortune smiles upon *one*
▶다행히 좋은 일자리를 얻었다 I had the good fortune of finding [to find] a good job.
▶다행히 내 시도는 성공했다 I was fortunate enough to succeed in my attempt.
▶다행히 그는 성공했다 He had the good fortune to succeed.
▶다행히 순풍이 불기 시작했다 Fortunately, a favorable wind arose.
▶그들은 다행히 시간에 대었다 They were fortunate enough to be in time.
▶나는 다행히 시험에 합격했다 I passed the examination, I'm happy to say.
▶다행히 그를 만났다 I met him by a happy accident.
▶그는 다행히 1등상을 탔다 He was lucky [fortunate] enough to win the first prize.
▶가난해진 후로는 다행히 한번도 병에 걸리지 않았다 Luckily [By good providence], I have never been ill since poverty came in at my door.
▶그녀는 다행히 구조되었다 Luckily [Fortunately], she was saved.
▶(결석했으나) 다행히 선생님도 결근하셨다 Fortunately for me, the teacher was absent too.

다혈 多血 sanguineness; full-bloodedness
■**―증** 〔醫〕 plethora; repletion: 다혈증의 plethoric / **―질** a sanguine temperament: 다혈질의 sanguine / 다혈질인 사람 a sanguine person; a man of excitable temperament ―**한**

(漢) a hot-blooded fellow; a hothead; a hotspur

다홍 —紅 deep red; crimson
♦다홍치마 a crimson skirt

다회 茶會 a tea party

닥나무 〔植〕 a paper mulberry

닥다그르르 rollingly ⇨ 댁대구루루

닥닥 《draw lines》forcefully ⇨ 득득

닥뜨리다 face (up to); be faced with; confront; be confronted with [by]; encounter
▶우리는 생각지도 못한 난관에 닥뜨렸다 We met [ran into] unforeseen difficulties.

닥치는대로 at random; haphazardly; desultorily
♦적을 닥치는대로 쓰러뜨리다 mow [cut] down the enemy / 닥치는대로 먹다 eat anything one can put [get] one's hands on / 닥치는대로 집어 던지다 throw all the articles one can lay one's hands on
▶그는 닥치는대로 책을 읽었다 He read everything that came his way.

닥 치 다 〈다가오다〉 draw [come] near; approach; be close [near] at hand; 〈임박하다〉 hang over; be imminent; be impending; overhang; impend over
♦눈앞에 닥친 파국[위험] an imminent catastrophe [danger]/ 눈앞에 닥친 문제 a pressing [an urgent] question / 시간이 닥쳐오다 time is pressing / 임종이 닥쳐오다 one's time is drawing near
▶이 곳은 겨울이 닥쳐오고 있다 Winter is closing in on this part of the country.
▶약속한 날이 닥쳐왔다 The appointed day is close [near] at hand.
▶마감 날짜가 닥쳐오고 있다 The deadline is drawing near [approaching].
▶커다란 재난이 그에게 닥쳤다 A great misfortune [dire calamity] befell him.
▶폭풍우가 우리 도시로 닥쳐오고 있었다 The storm was approaching our town.
▶시험날이 닥쳐왔다 The examination is near at hand [is drawing near].
▶크리스마스가 닥쳐오고 있다 Christmas is coming soon.

닥터 a doctor; 《口》 a doc
♦닥터 김 Dr. Kim

닦다 1〈윤내다〉polish; give sth a polish; burnish 《metal》; rub up 《silver spoons》; brighten; scour 《a brass button》; 〈깨끗이 하다〉 brush [clean] 《one's teeth》; cleanse 《a watch》
♦은그릇을 닦다 polish silverware / 접시를 닦다 wash the dishes / 구두를 닦다 polish [《口》 shine] one's shoes; 〈닦게 하다〉 have one's shoes shined [polished]/ 구두를 반짝반짝하게 닦다 give one's shoes a good shine [polish]/ 녹을 떨어 없애다 scour rust from 《a knife》
▶나는 식후마다 이를 닦는다 I brush my teeth after every meal.
▶그녀는 집안의 놋쇠 문손잡이를 모두 닦았다 She polished all the brass doorknobs in the house.
2〈훔치다〉wipe off [out, away]; wipe clean; mop (up); 〈물기를〉 dry
♦이마의 땀을 닦다 wipe the sweat off one's brow / 눈물을 닦다 dry one's eyes; wipe one's tears away / 손수건으로 얼굴을 닦다 mop one's face with one's handkerchief / 엎질러진 물을 닦다 sop up the spilt water 《with a cloth》
▶타월로 네 손을 닦았니? Did you dry your hand with a towel?
▶창문을 깨끗이 닦는 것을 잊지 마라 Don't forget to wipe the window clean.
3 〈수학하다〉 cultivate; practice; 〈연마하다〉 improve; train
♦학문을 닦다 pursue knowledge [one's studies]/ 기량을 닦다 improve ability [one's skill]; train oneself 《in an art》/ 무술[무예]을 닦다 train oneself in military arts / 마음을 닦다 cultivate [develop] one's mind
4 〈고르게 하다〉 level; smooth; make...level; 〈롤러로〉 roll
♦길을 닦다 improve a road / 롤러로 터를 닦다 level [smooth] the ground with a roller / 운동장을 닦다 level a playground
▶이 지면은 닦을 필요가 있다 This ground needs to be leveled [rolled].
5 〈기반·토대를〉 pave the way 《for, to》; lay the groundwork 《for》; prepare the ground 《for》; solidify one's footing
♦성공의 기반을 닦다 lay the groundwork [pave the way] for one's success / 선거 기반을 닦다 nurse one's constituency; 《美》 mend [look after] one's (political) fences

닦달질 1〈닦아 세우기〉 scolding; rebuking; taking to task
—**닦달질하다** ⇨ 닦아세우다
2 〈닦음〉 polishing; shining; cleaning
—**닦달질하다** polish; shine; burnish; clean up

닦아세우다 rebuke; scold; blame; reprove; reproach; take [call, bring] sb to task 《for》
♦호되게 닦아세우다 subject sb to a severe rebuke; 《口》 give it hot / 아무의 직무태만을 닦아세우다 reproach [scold] sb for neglect of duty / 아무의 잘못을 닦아세우다 blame sb for his fault / 아무의 약속 위반을 닦아세우다 call sb to account for breaking his promise

닦음질 polishing; cleaning; burnishing
—**닦음질하다** polish; clean up; brush; scrub

닦이다 1〈윤나게〉 be polished [burnished, shined, brightened]
♦윤이 나게 닦인 구두 shoes with a high polish / 잘 닦인 마루 a highly polished [well-scrubbed] floor
▶이 마루는 잘 닦이지 않는다 This floor won't polish.
▶이 재질은 잘 닦인다 This material takes a high polish.
2 〈훔쳐지다〉 be wiped [mopped]
♦세제로 닦인 욕실 the bathroom mopped down with a cleanser
3 〈훌닦이다〉 be scolded [rebuked]; be given a good scolding
♦호되게 닦이다 have [be given] a good scolding
▶그녀는 태만했기 때문에 닦였다 She was scolded for her laziness.

▶나는 부주의했기 때문에 닦였다 I was reproached for [with] my carelessness.

단¹ 〈묶음〉 a bunch; a bundle; 〈짚 등의〉 a sheaf 《*pl.* sheaves》; 〈장작의〉 a fagot
♦볏 단 a sheaf of rice plants / 짚 한 단 a bundle of straw / 장작 한 단 a fagot of wood / 시금치 석 단 three bunches of spinach / 단으로 팔다 sell by the bundle / 단을 짓다 bundle; tie [do] up in a bundle; make into a bundle; sheave
▶나는 나뭇가지를 여러 단으로 묶었다 I've tied up [bound] the branches in several bundles.
▶우리는 짚을 난으로 묶었다 We bundled the straw.

단² a tuck ⇨ 웃단

단 段 1 〈계단〉 a step; a stair; a flight of steps [stairs]; 〈사다리의〉 a rung (of a ladder)
♦2단 침대 a double-decker (bed) / 위[아래]에서 2단째 the next to the top [bottom] stair / 3단 로켓 a three-stage rocket / 로켓의 1단을 분리하다 detach the first stage of a rocket
2 〈인쇄물의〉 a column
♦세로 2단으로 조판한 페이지 pages (printed) in double columns / 2단의 표제 a two-column heading
▶이 신문은 10단이다 This paper has ten columns to the page.
▶이 기사는 5단으로 되어 있다 This article is composed of five paragraphs.
▶그 뉴스는 3단 표제로 보도되었다 The news was reported with a three-column heading.
3 〈등급〉 a class; a rank; a grade
♦3단 기사 a *baduk*-player of the third grade
▶그는 태권도 5단이다 He holds a fifth degree black belt in Taekwondo.
4 〈넓이의 단위〉 a *tan* (=about 0.245 acres)
♦단당 수확량 production per *dan*

단 壇 a platform; a raised floor; a stage; 〈교회의〉 a pulpit; 〈제단〉 an altar
♦중앙에 단을 마련하다 lay a platform in the center / 단에 서다[오르다] stand on [climb to] the platform
▶내빈은 단 위에 앉아 있었다 The guests were seated on the platform.

단 斷 a decision; a judgment; a resolution
♦단을 내리다 give *one's* decision; make a (final) decision
▶단을 내릴 때는 바로 지금이다 Now is the time for a prompt decision.

-단 -團 〈집단〉 a body; a corps [kɔ́ːr] 《*pl.* corps [kɔ́ːrz]》; a group; a gang; 〈일행〉 a party; a team; 〈극단〉 a company; a troupe
♦사절단 a mission; a delegation / 관광단 a tourist [sightseeing] party / 조사단 a survey group / 기자단 the press corps / 평화봉사단 the Peace Corps / 발레단 the ballet (company) / 일단의 소년 a group of boys / 올림픽에 선수단을 파견하다 send a delegation of athletes to the Olympic Games
▶조사단이 조직되었다 An inquiry group [company] has been formed. ⇒ An investigation team has been appointed.

단 但 but; however; only; provided (that); on condition (that)

단 單 〈단지〉 only (one); no more than; 〈겨우〉 mere; sole
♦단 한 번 only once / 단 하나 a single one; only one / 나의 단 하나의 친구 my only [sole] friend / 나의 하나의 실례 the only [a solitary] instance (of) / 단 하룻밤이라도[하루라도] even for a night [day] / 단 하나의 신을 숭배하다 worship the one and only God / 단 한번도 …않다 never once; not even once
▶단 한번 여기에 온 적이 있다 I've been here only once.
▶나는 단 한번도 그를 만난 적이 없다 I haven't met him even once.
▶이 고대 페르시아의 유리 접시는 세계에 단 하나밖에 없다 This glass plate from ancient Persia is unique.
▶그는 믿을 수 있는 단 하나의 친구다 He is the only [sole] friend I can trust.
▶그가 나를 보러오지 않은 날은 단 하루도 없었다 Never a day passed without his coming to see me.

-단 -壇 circles; the world; a field [sphere] of human endeavor

단가 短歌 〈시조〉 a *tanga*; a kind of short poem

단가 單價 a unit price [cost]
♦단가 800원으로 at eight hundred won apiece [per piece]
▶이 품목은 단가가 500원이다 This item costs five hundred won apiece.
■**생산** — the unit cost of production

단가 團歌 the official song of an association [organization]

단가 檀家 a supporter of a Buddhist temple; a parishioner

단간 單間 a small room ⇨ 단칸

단감 a sweet persimmon

단강 鍛鋼 forged steel

단거리 短距離 a short distance; 〈사격의〉 (a) short [close] range
♦단거리에서 《shoot》 at a short distance [close range]
▶이런 종류의 트럭은 단거리 운반용으로 쓰인다 Trucks of this sort are used to carry loads a short distance.
■**-경영(競泳)** a short-distance swimming race **—경주** a short-distance race; a sprint (race); a dash **—선수** a sprinter; a sprint runner; a dashman **—수송** short-haul [short-distance, local] transportation **—이착륙기** a short takeoff and landing craft 《略 STOL》 **—탄도미사일** a short-range ballistic missile 《略 SRBM》 **—폭격기** a close-range bomber

단검 短劍 a short [small] sword; a dagger; a stiletto 《*pl.* ~(e)s》; a dirk
■**—표(印)** a dagger; an obelus 《*pl.* -li》

단것 sweet things; sweetstuff; sweetmeat; 〈과자〉 sweets
▶그녀는 단것을 좋아한다 She has a sweet tooth. ⇌ She goes in for sweets.

단견 短見 1 〈좁은 견해〉 shortsightedness; a narrow view
2 〈자기 의견〉 my (humble) opinion; my per-

sonal views [opinion]
단결 團結 unity; solidarity; union; combination
♦국민의 단결 national solidarity / 단결을 강화하다 strengthen the bond of unity [solidarity]
▶단결은 힘이다 Union is strength.
—단결하다 stand [band] together; combine; unite
♦단결한 united; leagued; combined; solid / 단결하여 in a body; in union; in *one* united body; solidly / 단결하여 일하다 work in a body
▶그들은 굳게 단결하여 그 난국에 대처했다 They united themselves firmly to cope with the difficulties.
▶국민은 단결하여 적에 대항했다 The people were banded together [united] against the enemy.
▶노동자들은 직장을 잃지 않기 위해 단결했다 The workers acted in a body in order not to lose their jobs.
■一권 [勞] the right to organize [of organization] —력 the power of unity; the capacity for united action —심 the spirit of unity; a cooperative spirit; a sense of union; (프) esprit de corps
단결에 〈즉시〉 at a breath [stretch]; at a [one] stroke; 〈기회 있을 때에〉 while there is a chance [an opportunity]; without missing the chance; before the chance slips away
♦사건을 단결에 결말내다 settle the case at a stroke
단경기 端境期 a between season; an off-crop [a pre-harvest] season
단계 段階 〈등급〉 a grade; a rank; a level; 〈순서〉 a step; a stage; 〈국면〉 a phase
♦예비적 단계 preliminary stages / 5단계 평가 grading according to five ranks / 단계적으로 step by step; by [in] stages / 지금 단계에서는 at the present stage / 4단계로 나누다 divide into four levels [ranks] / 한 단계 앞으로 진전시키다 carry 《the investigation》 a stage further
▶그 계획은 아직 실험 단계에 있다 The project is still in an experimental stage.
▶전쟁은 마지막 단계에 이르렀다 The war had reached its final stage.
▶평화 교섭은 새로운 단계에 들어갔다 The peace negotiations have now entered a new phase.
▶인권을 수호하는 것이 민주주의의 제1단계다 To defend human rights is the first step in democracy.
▶그 당시 의학은 아직 초보 단계에 있었다 In those days medical science was still in its early stage.
단골 〈손님〉 an old [a regular] customer; (口) a regular; a patron; 〈총칭〉 custom; patronage; connection; 〈집〉 a customary [regular, familiar] establishment
♦단골 가게 a permanent shop [store] / 단골 이발소 *one's* favorite barber / 단골 술집 *one's* favorite saloon [public house] / 단골 싸

전 *one's* rice dealer / 오랜 단골 a customer of long standing; an old customer / 단골이 많다 have a large custom [connection] / 큰 단골 a large patronage / 가게에 단골손님을 끌어들이다 draw custom to a store / 단골을 얻다[잃다] gain [lose] custom [a customer]
▶저 가게는 내 단골 미장원이다 That is my favorite beauty parlor.
▶단골 손님이니 값을 깎아드리죠 Since you are a regular customer, I'll cut the price.
단공류 單孔類 [動] Monotrema
♦단공류의 monotrematous
단과대학 單科大學 a college
단광 單光 [物] monochromatic rays
■一색 a monochrome; a single hue
단교 斷交 a rupture; a severance; a break of relations
—단교하다 break [cut] off relations 《with》; sever the relation 《with》
▶두 나라는 단교했다[단교 상태에 있다] The two nations severed [broke off] diplomatic relations.
■—경제— a rupture of economic relations
단교경주 斷郊競走 a cross-country race
단구 短軀 (a man of) short [small] stature
♦단구다 be short of stature
단구 段丘 [地] a terrace; a bench
■—하안(河岸)— a river terrace
단군 檀君 *Tangun*, the founding father of the Korean nation
■—신화 *Tangun* mythology
단권책 單卷冊 one volume; a single book; a one-volume edition
단궤 單軌 a monorail
■—차량 a monorail train [car] —철도 a monorail [railway]
단근 單根 **1** [化] a simple radical
2 [植] a simple root
단근질 torturing with a red-hot iron; branding **—단근질하다** torture 《a criminal》 with a red-hot iron
단급 單級 [敎] one class
■—학교 a one-class school
단기 單記 (a) single entry
■—무기명 투표 secret ballot [vote] with single entry; a single-entry ballot —투표 single voting —투표제 a single-entry ballot system
단기 單機 a single [lone] plane
♦단기비행을 하다 make a solo flight; fly solo
단기 單騎 a single [lone] horseman [rider]
단기 短期 a short time [term, period, duration]
♦단기의 brief; short; short-term; short-period; of short duration
▶이 국채는 단기의 것이다 These government loans are of short terms.
▶이번에는 단기 체류할 예정이다 I'm going to make a short stay this time.
■一강습[강좌] a short(-term) course 《in English》 —거래 short-term transaction —계약 a short-term contract —공채[사채] a short-term bond [debenture] —금리 short term rate of interest —대출 a short-term loan —보험 short period insurance —복무 a short service

─시효 short-period prescription ─어음 a short(-dated) bill [draft, exchange] ─융자 a call loan; money at call; a loan on demand ─전 a short war ─차입금 a short-term loan payable

단기 團旗 the flag of an association [organization]; an association [organization] banner

단기 檀紀 the *Tangun* Era
▶서기 1997년은 단기 4330년이다 The year 1997 in the Christian era falls on 4330 in the *Tangun* Era.

단기간 短期間 a short space of time
♦단기간에 in a short time
▶이 일은 그런 단기간에는 해낼 수 없을 것 같다 I'm afraid I cannot complete the work in such a short time.

단김에 〈단결에〉 at a breath; all at once
▶쇠뿔도 단김에 빼랬다 《속담》 Strike the iron while it is hot. ⇒ Make hay while the sun shines.

단꿈 a sweet [happy, pleasant] dream
♦단꿈을 꾸다 dream [have] a sweet dream

단내 1 〈높은 냄새〉 a burnt smell
▶단내가 난다 I smell something burning [scorching]. ⇒ There's a smell of something scorching.
▶그 비스킷은 단내가 난다 The cookie [biscuit] tastes scorched.
2 〈신열에서 나는〉 the hot foul [bad] breath (of a patient suffering from a fever)

단념 斷念 resignation; abandonment
─단념하다 give up 《an idea》; abandon; resign [reconcile] *oneself* 《to》; relinquish 《*one's* rights》
♦죽은 것으로 단념하다 give up *sb* for lost [as dead] / 운명이라 생각하고 단념하다 accept *one's* fate (philosophically); resign *oneself* to *one's* lot / 미국에 가는 것을 단념하다 give up an idea of going to America
▶나는 조종사가 되려는 생각을 단념했다 I gave up the idea of becoming a pilot.
▶비가 오기 시작했으므로 소풍 가는 것을 단념했다 Since it started to rain, we decided not to go on the picnic.
▶위통 때문에 난 술 마시는 것을 단념했다 I gave up drinking because I had a stomachache.

단단하다 1〈굳다〉 hard; firm; solid; stiff; tough

|解說| *hard*는 「매우 단단하여 쉽게 부수거나 홈을 낼 수 없다」의 뜻. *firm*은 「굳게 죄어져서 단단하다」, *solid*는 「굳어져서 단단하다」라는 뜻. *stiff*는 「뻣뻣해서 쉽게 구부러지지 않게 단단하다」는 말. *tough*는 「부수거나 자르거나 먹기 힘들 정도로 단단하고, 특히 고기 등이 물어뜯을 수 없을 만큼 딱딱하다」라는 뜻이다.

♦단단한 나무 hard wood / 단단한 땅 hard [solid] ground / 단단한 바위 a hard rock / 무쇠같이 단단한 as hard as iron / 단단해지다 harden; become solid [stiff]
▶진흙이 굳어서 단단해졌다 The clay has dried and hardened.
▶이 고기는 단단해서 먹을 수 없다 This meat is too tough to eat.
▶이 근처의 지반은 단단해 지진의 걱정이 없다 The ground around here is firm, so we need not to be concerned about earthquakes.
2 〈견실하다〉 strong; firm; steady; certain
♦몸이 단단한 사람 a man of strong physique / 그의 단단한 결심 his firm resolution
▶그의 이론은 기초가 단단하다 His theory stands on a solid [firm] basis.
▶저 회사는 단단하니 파산되지는 않을 것이다 That company is sound [solid] enough, so it couldn't go bankrupt.
▶비온 후에 땅이 단단해진다 《속담》 After a storm comes a calm.

단단히 1 〈다지는 모양〉 hard; stiff; fast
♦기반을 단단히 닦다 strengthen the foundations
▶문은 단단히 잠겨 있었다 The door shut tightly [tight].
▶그는 땅을 밟아 단단히 다졌다 He hardened the ground by stamping hard on it.
▶우리는 눈을 밟아 단단히 다졌다 We trod [tramped] down the snow hard.
▶노면의 눈은 단단히 얼어 있었다 The snow on the street was frozen hard.
2 〈죄는 모양〉 firmly; tightly
♦나사를 단단히 죄다 tighten up a screw / 짐을 단단히 꾸리다 pack a bundle tight / 밧줄로 단단히 매다 tie fast with a rope
▶그들은 내 양다리를 단단히 묶었다 They tied [bound] my legs together tightly.
▶짐의 끈을 단단히 묶어 주세요 Please tie the string of the package tightly.
▶외출할 때는 문단속을 단단히 해라 Be sure to lock up the house when you go out.
3 〈굳게〉 strongly; strictly; severely; firmly
♦단단히 결심을 make up *one's* mind; be firmly determined / 단단히 약속하다 make [give] a firm [solemn] promise / 단단히 야단 맞다 get a good scolding; be severely scolded / 단단히 재미보다 have a very good time; have great fun
▶우리는 국가 방위를 단단히 해야 한다 We must strengthen the national defense.
▶그들은 협정을 단단히 지켰다 They adhered to the contract.
▶그녀는 자기 신조를 단단히 지켰다 She held firm to her belief.

단당류 單糖類 〔化〕 a monosaccharide

단대목 單─ 〈큰 일을 앞둔 때〉 the high tide 《of》; 〈중요한 고비〉 a turning point; an important opportunity

단도 短刀 a short sword; 〈비수〉 a dagger; dirk; a poniard
♦단도를 품다[지니다] take [hold] a dagger in *one's* bosom / 단도로 찌르다 stab *sb* with a dagger
▶그는 단도를 품에 숨기고 있었다 He had a dagger concealed in his inside pocket.

단도 檀徒 〔佛教〕 《총칭》 supporters (of a temple)

단도직입 單刀直入 coming straight to the

단도(直入) point; straightforwardness
- 단도직입적인 point-blank; direct / 단도직입적으로 straightforwardly; directly; without preamble
▶ 네 얘기는 너무 단도직입적이다 You speak too bluntly.
▶ 그는 우리에게 단도직입적으로 물었다 He asked us a point-blank question.

단독 丹毒 〔醫〕 erysipelas; the rose; St. Anthony's fire ◆ 단독성의 erysipelatous
■ 창상성(創傷性)— traumatic erysipelas

단독 單獨 singleness; independence; separateness
◆ 단독의 〈독립된〉 independent; 〈개개의〉 individual; separate; 〈혼자만의〉 single; sole; 〈독력의〉 single-handed; unassisted / 단독으로 〈독립적으로〉 independently; 〈개별적으로〉 individually; separately; 〈혼자서〉 singly; alone; by *oneself*; 〈독력으로〉 single-handed(ly); unassisted / 단독으로 행동하다 act single-handed [by *oneself*] / 단독으로 적을 무찌르다 [격파하다] beat the enemy single-handed
▶ 단체 안에서는 단독 행동은 삼가야 한다 While in a group [party], you should refrain from taking arbitrary action.
▶ 외무부장관은 귀국 후 단독회견을 했다 The Minister of Foreign Affairs gave an exclusive interview when he returned home.
■ —강화 (conclude) a separate peace treaty —개념 an independent conception —경제 independent economy —기관 an exclusive organization —내각 a one-party cabinet —범 a single-handed offense —보험 simple insurance —비행 (make) a solo flight —우승자 the sole winner 《of》 —운영 unilateral operation 《of the National Assembly》 —재판 trial by a single-judge system —판사 a single judge —해손(海損) particular average (略 P.A.) —행동 (an) independent action : 단독행동을 취하다 act independently; take independent action —행위 an individual action; 〔法〕 a unilateral (juristic) act —회견 an exclusive interview

단돈 a small amount of money
▶ 난 지금 단돈 백원도 없다 I haven't even got a hundred won now.

단두대 斷頭臺 a guillotine; a scaffold; a block
◆ 단두대에 오르다 mount the scaffold; lay *one's* neck on the block
▶ 그는 마침내 단두대의 이슬로 사라졌다 He was finally sent to the guillotine.

단둘 only two persons
▶ 그들은 단둘이 남았다 The two were left alone.
▶ 그는 아내와 단둘이 살고 있다 He lives alone with his wife.

단락 段落 1 〈일단 끝남〉 an end; settlement; conclusion; a stop ◆ 단락을 짓다 bring *sth* to conclusion; fix (up)
2 〈문장의〉 the end of a paragraph; an end; a stop; punctuation
▶ 이 단락은 너무 길어서 이해하기 어렵다 This paragraph [section] is too long to follow.

단락 短絡 〔電〕 a short circuit
—단락하다 short-circuit; short

▶ 이 회로는 단락하고 있다 This circuit is affected with a short. ⇌ This is short-circuited.
■ —시험 a short-circuit test

단란 團欒 a happy (family, home) circle; a fireside circle; 〈화합〉 harmony
—단란하다 harmonious; happy; 〈서술적〉 make a happy group; sit in a happy circle
◆ 단란한 가정 a happy home / 가정의 단란한 즐거움 the pleasure of a happy home

단량체 單量體 a monomer

단려 端麗 grace; elegance; beauty
—단려하다 graceful; elegant; fine-looking; fair
◆ 단려한 용모 a graceful figure
▶ 그녀는 용모가 단려하다 She is good-looking and has a graceful figure.
▶ 그녀는 단려한 옷차림으로 나타났다 She appeared in an elegant dress.

단련 鍛鍊 1 〈쇠붙이의〉 temper(ing); forging
—단련하다 temper; forge; anneal
2 〈심신의〉 training; discipline; drilling
◆ 정신적 단련 the training of the mind
—단련하다 train; drill; discipline; school; harden
◆ 단련된 tempered; trained / 몸을 단련하다 harden *oneself* [*one's body*]; build up *one's* physique [constitution] / 마음을 단련하다 discipline [train] *one's* mind / 심신을 단련하다 train *one's* body and mind / 고난[전쟁]에 단련되다 be schooled by adversity [in war]
▶ 사회에 나가기 전에 가능한 한 심신을 단련하여라 Train yourself [your mind and body] as best (as) you can before you go into the world.
▶ 더위와 추위에 지지 않도록 피부를 단련해야 한다 You should condition your skin further against heat and cold.
▶ 피부를 단련하면 극도의 추위에도 견딜 수 있다 Our skin can be so hardened that it can stand extreme cold.

단리 單利 〔經〕 simple interest
◆ 단리로 계산하다 calculate at simple interest ■ —계산 calculation at simple interest —법 the method of simple interest —표 a simple interest table

단막 單幕 one act ■ —극[물] a one-act drama [play]; a play in one act

단말 端末 an end; a terminal

단말기 端末機 〔電算〕 a terminal

단 말 마 斷末魔 *one's* last gasp [breath, moments]; the point [hour] of death
◆ 단말마의 고통 death agonies; the agonies of death / 단말마의 고함 a death cry / 단말마에 이르다 be at death's door
▶ 그의 단말마의 고함소리가 귓가에서 떠나지 않는다 His death cry still lingers in my ear.

단맛 sweetness; a sweet taste [flavor]; a sugary taste
◆ 단맛이 나다[있다] be [taste] sweet; have a sweet taste / 단맛을 내다 sweeten; make *sth* sweet / 단맛이 들다 be sweetened

단면 斷面 a (cross) section; the cut end; 〈지층의〉 a profile

단면의 sectional / **사회의 한 단면** a social phase [slice] / **한 단면을 나타내다** reveal a cross section (of)
▶ 이 사건은 현대 사회의 어두운 단면을 드러내고 있다 This incident reveals the dark side of modern society.
■**수평[수직, 종, 횡]— a** horizontal [vertical, longitudinal, cross] section **■—도** a cross section; a sectional plan: 건물의 단면도 a sectional plan of a building **—저항 profile drag**

단명 短命 a short life; a brief span of life
♦ **단명으로 끝나다** die young; do not last long
▶ 재사(才士) 단명 Men of talent die young.
▶ 그의 단명은 과음 때문이었다 His early death was caused by heavy drinking. ⇒ He died young on account [as a consequence] of heavy drinking.
♦ 새 내각은 단명으로 끝날 것이다 The new Cabinet will be short-lived [will not last long].
—**단명하다** short-lived; ephemeral
♦ 단명한 집안 a short-lived family
▶ 그 화가는 단명했다 The painter died young.

단명수 單名數 〔數〕 a single unit number

단모음 單母音 〔音聲〕 a single vowel; a monophthong ♦ **단모음화** monophthongal / **단모음화** monophthongization

단무지 pickled radish

단문 短文 1 〈짧은 글〉 a short sentence [composition, piece]
♦ 두 단어로 된 단문 a composition of two words
▶ 다음 어구들을 써서 단문을 지어라 Make [Compose] short sentences using each of the following phrases.
2 〈글을 아는 것이 적음〉 superficial learning; shallow knowledge

단문 單文 〔文法〕 a simple sentence

단물 1 〈민물〉 fresh water
♦ 단물 고기 freshwater fish
▶ 짠물을 단물로 하는 데는 비용이 너무 든다 It is too expensive to turn salt water into fresh water.
2 〈맛이 단 물〉 sweet water [juice]; 〈실속 있는 부분〉 the cream; the lion's share
♦ 단물을 빨아먹다 skim the cream off; take the lion's share
3 〈연수(軟水)〉 soft water

단박(에) at once; immediately; instantly; quickly
♦ 일을 단박에 해치우다 finish up one's work in a jiffy / 구두가 단박 해지다 one's shoes wear out in no time at all
▶ 그만한 일은 단박에 할 수 있다 I can do that in no time.

단발 單發 1 〈한 발〉 a (single) shot; a round
♦ 단발에 at a shot
2 〈발동기의〉 a single engine
■**—기(機)** a single-engined (air)plane **—총** a single-loader; a single-shot rifle

단발 短髮 short hair; crop

단발 斷髮 bobbed hair; a bob; short hair cut
♦ 단발 머리 처녀 a girl with bobbed hair / 단발로 하다 bob one's hair; cut one's hair short (of the shoulders)
—**단발하다** bob [cut] one's hair; have one's hair bobbed
■**—령** the ordinance prohibiting topknots **—머리** a bobbed hair style

단밤 a sweet chestnut ⇨ 감밤

단방 單放 1 〈한 방〉 a single shot
♦ 사냥감을 단방에 쓰러뜨리다 down one's quarry with a single shot
2 only once ⇨ 단번
■**—치기** one's first try [attempt]; a single try [effort]; 〈최후의〉 a last [desperate] effort: 단방치기로 at a single stroke; in a single effort; at one try

단배식 團拜式 the New Year's Day celebration 《of an organization》
♦ 단배식을 갖다 observe [celebrate] the New Year's Day en masse

단백 蛋白 〈알의 흰자위〉 albumen
■**—계** an albuminometer **—뇨증** 〔醫〕 albuminuria **—석** 〔鑛〕 opal: 단백석의 opaline

단백질 蛋白質 〔生化〕 protein; albumin
♦ 단 백 질의 proteinic; proteinous; albuminous / 단백질이 풍부한 음식물 protein-rich food / 단백질이 풍부하다 be rich in albuminous substances
■ **동물성[식물성]—** animal [vegetable] protein

단번 單番 〈단 한 번〉 only [just] once; a single time
♦ 단번에 at one coup [try]; at a stroke; in a single effort; at once / 단번에 성공하다 gain success on one's first try [attempt] / 단번에 알아맞히다 guess right at once
▶ 그는 그 시험에 단번에 합격했다 He passed the exam on [at] his first attempt.
▶ 금년의 임금 인상은 단번에 결정되었다 This year's wage increase was decided in a single negotiation round [in the first round of bargaining].

단벌 單— 〈하나뿐인 것〉 a single one; the only one; 〈가지고 있는 유일한 옷〉 one's only suit; the only clothes one has
♦ 단벌 나들이 옷 one's sole Sunday best / 단벌 신사 a poor gentleman in his only suit
▶ 그는 단벌 나들이옷을 차려 입고 식에 참석했다 He attended the ceremony dressed in his sole Sunday best.

단복 團服 a uniform 《of an association》

단본위제 單本位制 〔經〕 monometallism; a single-standard system
■**—화폐** a monometallic currency

단봇짐 單褓— a handy bundle; a parcel in a wrapper ♦ 단봇짐을 싸다 wrap up one's personal belongings in a kerchief

단봉낙타 單峯駱駝 〔動〕 a dromedary; an Arabian [a one-humped] camel

단분수 單分數 〔數〕 a simple fraction

단비 a welcome [timely, long-awaited, seasonable] rain ♦ 가뭄 속의 단비 a hoped-for rain during the dry season
▶ 주말에 전국적으로 단비가 내렸다 A welcome rain fell across the nation during the

weekend.
단비 〔單比〕〔數〕 simple ratio
단비례 單比例 〔數〕 simple proportion
단사 丹砂 〔鑛〕 cinnabar ⇨ 주사(朱砂)
단사 單絲 〔紡〕 singles ⇨ 홑실
단사리별 單舍利別 simple syrup
단산 斷産 natural cessation of childbearing
—**단산하다** stop childbearing; pass the age of bearing
 ♦ 40세에 단산하다 stop her childbirth at the age of forty
단산화서 團繖花序 〔植〕 a monochasium (*pl.* -sia)
단삼 丹蔘 〔植〕 a kind of sage plant
단상 單相 〔電〕 single phase
—**교류** single-phase current
단상 壇上 (on) the platform
 ♦ 단상에서다[오르다] stand on [take] the platfrom / 의정단상에 서다 become a member of the National Assembly
 ▶ 그는 일단 단상에 오르자 말투가 전혀 달라졌다 Once he took [was on] the platform, he changed his way of speaking completely.
 ▶ 드디어 그는 의정단상에 서게 되었다 At last he become a member of the National Assembly.
단상 斷想 fragmentary thoughts; stray [random] thoughts
단색 單色 a single color; a simple hue; monochrome
 ♦ 단색의 unicolor(ed); monochromatic / 단색차(車) a monotone car; a car in a single color / 단색으로 그리다 paint in one [a single] color
 ■—광 monochromatic light —화 a monochrome —화법 monochromy
단서 但書 a proviso [prəváizou] (*pl.* ~ -(e)s); a provision; a provisory [conditional] clause; an exceptive clause
 ♦ 단서가 붙은 조건적 / …이라는 단서를 붙여서[붙이다] with [add] the proviso that…
 ▶ 그 제안은 단서를 붙여 통과시켰다 The proposal was passed with a proviso.
단서 端緖 〈실마리〉 a clue (to); a key (to); 〈발단〉 the beginning; the start; 〈기원〉 the birth; the origin; 〈범인의 자취〉 a scent; a track
 〈단서가〉 아직 단서가 잡히지 않았다 Not a clue has yet been found to it.
 ▶ 지문이 범인 체포의 단서가 되었다 The fingerprints gave a clue that led to the arrest of the culprit.
 ▶ 장물이 경찰에게 단서가 되었다 The stolen goods were a clue for the police.
 〈단서를〉 단서를 잡다 get [have] a clue (to, for) / 단서를 놓치다 lose a [the] clue (to) / 단서를 찾다 look for clues
 ▶ 경찰은 사건의 단서를 잡지 못했다 The police didn't have any clue [leads] to help them solve the case.
 ▶ 새로운 음모를 적발할 단서를 잡았다 They were on the scent of a new plot.
 ▶ 그는 문제 해결의 단서를 잡았다 He got [found] a clue that would lead to the solution

of the problem.
단선 單線 〈외줄〉 a single line; 〈단궤(單軌)〉 a single track
 ■—가공식(架空式) a single trolley system —운행 one way traffic; the single-track operation of trails —철도 a single-track railroad [(英) railway]
단선 斷線 the breaking [snapping] of a wire; disconnection
 ♦ 단선으로 on account of broken wires
 —**단선되다** be down; be snapped; snap
 ▶ 폭설로 여러 곳에서 전선이 단선되었다 The heavy snowfall caused the breaking down of power lines in several places.
 ▶ 바람 때문에 전화가 단선되었다 The telephone wires are down because of the wind.
단성 單性 unisexuality; one sex ♦ 단성의 unisexual ■—생식 unisexual reproduction; monogenesis; parthenogenesis; apomixis —잡종 〔遺〕 a monohybrid —화 a unisexual flower
단세 單稅 a single tax
 ■—주의 single-taxism
단세포 單細胞 〔動·植〕 a single cell; one cell
 ♦ 단세포의 unicellular; single celled / 단세포적인 사고방식 a single-track way of thinking / 단세포적인 인간 a person with a one-celled mind
 ▶ 그 때문에 넌 단세포적이라고 불리는 거야 That's why you are said to be simple-minded [stupid].
단소 短簫 a short bamboo flute; a pipe
 ♦ 단소를 불다 play (a tune) on the flute
단소하다 短小— small and short
단속 團束 〈규제〉 control; regulation; discipline; 〈관리〉 management; 〈감독〉 superintendence; supervision
 ♦ 단속의 대상 a subject of control / 단속의 강화 rigid enforcement of regulations / 단속 소홀로 견책되다 be reprimanded for lack of supervision / 단속을 엄중히 하다 keep strict order; tighten the control (of, over) / 단속을 할 수 없게 되다 lose control over; be unable to maintain discipline among
 ▶ 당국은 지나치게 엄중한 단속을 했다 The authorities enforced too rigid [stringent] a control.
 —**단속하다** manage; control; superintend; supervise; keep control over; keep *sth* in order
 ♦ 엄중히 단속하다 exercise strict control over; control strictly / 학생을 단속하다 keep students under control / 풍기를 단속하다 watch over [control] public morals
 ▶ 경찰은 폭력 행위를 엄중히 단속해야 한다 The police should keep [maintain] strict control over terroristic activities.
 ■—법[규칙] regulations for the control (of); disciplinary rules —자 a controller; a regulator; a superviser; an overseer
단속 斷續 intermittence
 ♦ 단속적인 intermittent; fitful; snatchy / 단속적으로 intermittently; fitfully; by snatches; at intervals
 ▶ 비가 단속적으로 오고 있다 It is raining

단속곳

intermittently [off and on].
▶ 토의는 아침부터 저녁까지 단속적으로 계속되었다 The discussion continued from morning to night with breaks now and then.
▶ 그들은 노조 지도부와 작년 가을부터 단속적으로 교섭하고 있다 They have been negotiating with the union leaders off and on since last autumn.

단속곳 單— an under-petticoat

단수 段數 1 〈바둑·유도 등의〉 the grade; the class; the rank
♦ 단수의 차이 difference in grade / 단수가 다르다 be not in a class 《with》; stand on different levels
2 〈술수〉 resource; quick wit
♦ 단수를 부리다 exercise expedient; resort to mean tricks

단수 單數 1 〔文法〕 the singular number
♦ 단수의 singular / 3인칭 단수 the third person singular / 단수와 복수 singular (number) and plural (number)
▶ 이 단어는 단수형이다 This word is in the singular.
2 〈홀수〉 a unit

단수 端數 a fraction ⇨ 끝수

단수 斷水 (a) suspension of water supply
—**단수하다** suspend [stop] the supply of water
▶ 오늘 아침 단수됐다 The water supply failed [was cut off, was suspended] this morning.
▶ 내일은 서울 시내의 일부 지역이 단수됩니다 The water will be shut off tomorrow in parts of Seoul.

단수로 短水路 〔泳〕 a short course; a 25-meter course
■—**기록** a short-course record

단순 單純 simplicity
—**단순하다** simple; uncomplicated; unsophisticated; plain
♦ 단순히 simply / 단순한 생활 a simple life / 단순한 사람 a simple-minded person
▶ 사태를 단순하게 생각지 마라 Don't take the situation simple and easy.
▶ 그녀는 어린아이와 같이 단순하다 She is as simple as a child.
▶ 그것은 단순히 구실에 지나지 않는다 It's a mere [merely an] excuse.
■—**개념** a simple concept —**림(林)** a pure forest —**승인** absolute acceptance —**재생산** simple reproduction —**점유** 〔法〕 naked possession —**(온)천** a simple spring —**평균** 〔數〕 a simple average

단순화 單純化 simplification ♦ 지나친 단순화 oversimplification —**단순화하다** simplify / 생활을 단순화하다 simplify life

단술 a sweet drink prepared with rice and malt

단숨에 單— at one stroke; in one breath; at a breath; at a heat; at a stroke
♦ 단숨에 마시다 swallow [empty the glass] at a gulf / 단숨에 일을 해치우다 finish *one's* work straight out; finish a job at a sitting / 단숨에 언덕을 뛰어오르다 run up a hill at a dash; run right up to the top of a hill / 책을 단

숨에 읽다 read a book at a stretch [sitting]
▶ 이 책은 단숨에 읽혀지지 않는다 It is impossible for me to read the book through at a stretch.
▶ 비행기를 타면 단숨에 날아간다 If you go by air, it's a short flight.

단시 短詩 a short poem [verse]; a little verse; a verselet; a sonnet
■—**작가** a writer of short verses

단시간 短時間 a short time
♦ 단시간에 in a short (space of) time / 단시간에 보고서를 쓰다 write a report in a short time
▶ 비행기 덕택에 한미간을 단시간에 여행할 수 있다 Thanks to airplanes, people can travel between Korea and the U.S. in a short time.

단시일 短時日 a short (space of) time; a short period of time
♦ 단시일에 in a short space of time; in a few days
▶ 사회개혁은 단시일에 이루어지는 것이 아니다 Social reform cannot be carried out [effected] in a day.

단식 單式 1 〈단일의 방식〉 a simple system
2 〔簿〕 single entry
3 〔數〕 a simple expression
4 〈테니스·탁구 등의〉 singles
▶ 그녀는 단식 시합에 나온다 She is going to take part in a singles match.
■—**부기** single-entry bookkeeping; bookkeeping by single entry —**인쇄** single-process offset printing —**투표** single voting —**화산** a simple volcano

단식 斷食 a fast; fasting; abstinence 《from food》
♦ 3일간의 단식에 들어가다 go on a three day fast [a fast of three days] / 24시간의 단식 a twenty four-hour fast / 단식을 중지하다 break 《one's》 fast
—**단식하다** fast; observe a fast
▶ 그녀는 3일간 단식했다 She fasted for three days.
▶ 그는 그날 하루 단식했다 He went without food the whole of that day.
■—**법** a fasting method —**요법** a starvation cure; a fasting treatment: 그는 때때로 단식요법을 한다 Sometimes he fasts for his health.
—**일** a fast day —**투쟁** a hunger strike

단신 單身 a single person
♦ 단신으로 (all) alone; by *oneself*; single-handed; unaccompanied / 단신(으로) 상경하다 come up to Seoul all alone / 단신으로 버티다 hold out single-handed
▶ 그는 단신으로 장사를 하기로 했다 He decided to start a business single-handed.
▶ 그는 워싱턴에 단신으로 부임했다 He started alone for new post in Washington.
■—**총(銃)** a single-barreled gun

단신 短身 short [small] stature

단신 短信 a brief message; brief news; a short letter

단심 丹心 sincerity; a sincere heart; single-heartedness; devotion; *one's* true heart

단심제 單審制 〔法〕 the single-trial system

단아 端雅 elegance; grace (fulness); refinement
—단아하다 elegant; graceful; refined
♦ 용모가 단아한 사람 a man of regular features / 옷차림이 단아하다 be dressed in good taste [in tasteful style]

단안 單眼 〔動〕 a stemma 《*pl.* ~s, -mata》; an ocellus 《*pl.* -celli》 ♦ 단안의 ocellar

단안 斷案 〈결정〉 a decision; 〈결론〉 a conclusion ♦ 단안을 내리다 form [make] a conclusion that.../ 최후의 단안을 내리다 give [bring in] a final verdict [judgment] / 단안을 내리지 않다 offer no conclusion

단안경 單眼鏡 a monocle

단애 斷崖 a precipice; a cliff; a bluff ♦ 단애를 기어오르다 scale [clamber up] a cliff
▶ 그 차는 단애에서 추락했다 The car fell over a precipice.

단어 單語 a word
♦ 기본 단어 basic words; a basic vocabulary / 중요 단어 most frequently used words / 단어 실력 테스트 a vocabulary test / 단어 실력을 늘리다 build up *one's* word power; increase *one's* vocabulary
▶ 그녀는 단어를 많이 알고 있다 She has a rich [large] vocabulary.
▶ 그 단어를 사전에서 찾아봐라 Look up the word in a dictionary.
■—장〔集〕 a collection of words; a wordbook

단언 斷言 assertion; affirmation; asseveration; a positive statement
—단언하다 assert (positively); affirm; declare; asseverate
♦ 단언하기를 꺼리다 hesitate to say positively; refrain from asserting; fear to affirm
▶ 단언할 수는 없지만 그녀는 분명 마중 나올 것이다 I cannot say for certain, but I believe she will come to meet us.
▶ 그는 위선자라고 나는 단언한다 I have no hesitation in saying that he is a hypocrite.
▶ 그는 그 일에 대해서는 책임이 없다고 단언했다 He asserted he was not responsible for that.

단역 端役 〈역〉 a minor roll; a small part; a bit; a walk-on; 〈배우〉 an extra; (口) a super
♦ 단역 여배우 an extra girl; a utility cinema actress / 단역을 맡아 하다 play a minor [a small, an extra] part / 단역을 배정받다 get a walk-on
▶ 그녀는 단역만 하고 있다 She always plays [acts] a small part.

단연(코) 斷然(—) 〈단호히〉 resolutely; decisively; firmly; without hesitation; 〈확실히〉 decidedly; positively
♦ 단연코 거절하다 refuse positively; give a flat refusal / 단연 뛰어나다 show decided superiority / 단연 리드하다 hold the unquestioned lead / 단연코 반대다 be dead set against 《such a plan》
▶ 나는 그의 요구를 단연 거절했다 I refused his request without hesitation.
▶ 이것은 단연 좋다 This is by far the best.
▶ 나는 단연코 담배를 끊었다 I have given up smoking once and for all.

단열 斷熱 〔物〕 insulation
▶ 이 지붕에는 단열이 필요하다 This roof requires insulation.
▶ 이것은 단열용이다 This is used for insulation.
■—감률(減率) adiabatic lapse rate —변화〔압축, 팽창〕 adiabatic change [compression, expansion] —재 an insulating material; insulation

단엽 單葉 〔植〕 a simple leaf; a single leaflet
■—(비행기) a monoplane —식물 a unifoliate plant

단오 端午 〔民俗〕 the *Tano* festival (on the fifth day of the fifth month of the lunar calendar)

단원 單元 〔敎〕 a unit
▶ 이 화학 교과서는 4단원으로 되어 있다 This chemistry book is composed of [has] four units.
■—론 〔哲〕 singularism —제도 the unit (credit) system

단원 團員 a member 《of a party, of an association》; (총칭) the company

단원제 單院制 the unicameral [single-chamber] system
■—의회 a unicameral legislature

단위 單位 1 〈길이·열량·화폐 등의〉 a unit; 〈화폐 단위로서〉 (a) denomination
♦ 화폐의 단위 a unit of money; a monetary unit / 여러 가지 단위의 경화 coins of various denominations [units]
▶ 그램은 무게의 단위다 The gram is a unit of weight.
2 〈전체의 구성 분자로서의〉 a unit
▶ 가족은 사회의 작은 단위다 The family is a small social unit [a small unit of society].
3 〈수업의 학점〉 (美) a credit; a course
♦ 필수 단위 required credits [courses]
■기본— a standard [fundamental] unit 실용— 〔物〕 a practical unit 유도〔절대〕— 〔物〕 derived [an absolute] unit 중량〔용적〕— a unit of weight [volume] —면적〔질량〕 the unit area [mass] —원(圓) 〔數〕 a unit circle —원(元) 〔數〕 the unit [identity] element —(노동)조합 a local union —행렬 〔數〕 a unit matrix

단위생식 單爲生殖 〔生〕 parthenogenesis ⇨ 단성(~생식)

단위체 單位體 〔化〕 a monomer
♦ 단위체의 monomeric

단음 單音 1 〈최소 단위의 소리〉 a single sound; a monosyllable
2 〔樂〕 a monotone; monotony; a simple tone
■—하모니카 a monotone harmonica

단음 短音 a short sound

단음 斷音 〔音聲〕 a stop; 〔樂〕 a staccato 《*pl.* ~s, -ti》 ■—기호 a staccato mark —장치 〈피아노의〉 a damper

단음계 短音階 〔樂〕 the minor (scale); the minor mode ■선율적— the melodic minor scale 자연적— the natural minor scale 화성적— the harmonic minor

단음절 單音節 ♦ 단음절의 monosyllabic
■—어 a monosyllable; a monosyllabic word —어족 monosyllabic languages

단음정 短音程 〔樂〕 a minor interval

단일 單一 singleness; unity; simplicity
♦단일의 single; sole; individual
▶이 물질은 단일 성분이다 This substance consists of only one element
―단일하다 singular; single; simple; sole
―경작 monoculture ―국가 a unitary state ―기계 a machine unit ―변동 환율제 the unitary fluctuation foreign exchange system ―세율 single tariff; single-line tariff ―신교 (神敎) henotheism; monotheism ―팀 a single team: '남북한 단일팀 single South-North team ―호봉(제) single payroll (system) ―화 simplification; unification: 단일화하다 simplify; unify ―환율 a single exchange rate ―후보 a sole candidate

단자¹ 單子 〈부조 등의〉 a list of gifts [presents]; 〈후보자 등의〉 a list of candidates

단자² 單子 〔哲〕 a monad
■―론 monadology; monadism

단자 短資 a call loan; a short-term[-dated] loan; a short loan
■―거래 call loan transaction ―시장 a call market; the short-loan market ―회사 a short-term financing company

단자 端子 〔電〕 a terminal
■―판(板) a terminal board [plate] ―함 an outlet [a terminal] box

단자 緞子 damask

단자엽 單子葉 〔植〕 monocotyledon ⇨ 외떡잎
■―식물 a monocotyledonous plant; a monocotyledon

단작 單作 〔農〕 a single crop
―지대 a one-crop area

단작스럽다 mean; dirty; stingy

단잠 a sweet [good, sound] sleep ♦단잠이 들다 fall [drop] off into sound sleep / 단잠을 자다 sleep a sound sleep / 단잠을 깨다 wake up from a sound [good] sleep

단장 丹粧 1 〈화장〉 (a) makeup; (a) toilet; 〈몸치장〉 dressing
―단장하다 put on [wear] makeup; dress oneself; outfit oneself (for)
♦단장한 시골 아낙네들 village women all decked out in their finery / 곱게 단장하고 나서다 go out beautifully dressed up; go out in gala [full] attire
2 〈장식〉 decoration; ornament; 〈칠〉 painting
▶실내의 단장 interior decoration
―단장하다 decorate; adorn; paint
♦새로 단장한 건물 a newly finished building / 새로이 단장하다 newly decorate; give a new look (to)
▶오랫만에 가보니 그 가게는 새롭게 단장되어 있더라 I found the store had been redecorated when I visited it again after a long time.

단장 短杖 〈美〉 a cane; 〈英〉 a (walking) stick

단장 團長 the leader [head] (of a party [group]); a boss; a commandant
▶X씨를 단장으로 하는 시찰단 a study group headed [led] by Mr. X

단장 斷章 〈단편적인 문장〉 a literary fragment

단장 斷腸 heartbreak; a lacerated heart
♦단장의 슬픔 heartrending [heartbreaking] grief / 단장의 비애를 느끼다 feel one's heart rent [torn to pieces]; feel as if one's heart were breaking
▶나는 단장의 슬픔을 안고 그녀와 헤어졌다 I left her with bleeding grief.

단적 端的 ♦단적인 direct; point-blank; straightforward; frank / 단적으로 directly; straightforwardly; flatly / 단적으로 말하면 frankly speaking; to be honest (with you) / 단적으로 묻다 ask sb point-blank / 단적으로 말하다 speak plainly [frankly]; go right to the point

단전 丹田 the abdomen; the hypogastrium
♦단전에 힘을 주다 concentrate one's whole strength in the abdomen

단전 斷電 〈정전〉 power failure; 〈전력 공급의 중단〉 suspension of power supply
―단전하다 shut [cut] off electricity

단절 斷絕 1 〈중단〉 (an) interruption; discontinuation; 〈종식〉 extinction
―단절하다 become extinct; cease to exist; die out
▶가문이 단절되었다 The family has died away. ≒ The family has become extinct [died out].
2 〈관계를 끊음〉 severance; (a) rupture
♦단절의 시대 the age of discontinuity / 세대간의 단절 a generation gap; the lack of communication between the young and the old generations
▶정치가와 서민의 단절감이 점점 깊어가고 있다 The credibility gap between politicians and the masses is getting wider and wider.
―단절하다 sever; cut [break] off
■국교― severance [a rupture] of diplomatic relations: 양국간의 국교가 단절되었다 Diplomatic relations between the two countries were broken off.

단점 短點 a weak point; a shortcoming; a defect; a fault; a demerit
♦장점과 단점 merits and demerits / 단점을 고치다 remedy one's defects
▶누구든지 장점과 단점이 있다 Everybody has his own virtues and faults.
▶어떤 안(案)에도 장점과 단점이 있었다 Each of the plans had its own advantages and disadvantages.
▶우리는 단점을 고치도록 힘쓰지 않으면 안된다 We must try to correct our defects.
▶그는 가끔 남의 단점을 찌른다 He often gets at other persons' weak points.
▶성질이 급한 것이 그의 단점이다 A hot temper is his weak point.

단정 端正 neatness; correctness; justness; decency; propriety
―단정하다 decent; decorous; upright; neat; just
♦옷차림이 단정한 사람 a neatly-dressed [well-groomed] person / 품행이 단정한 사람 a man of upright [good moral] character / 단정한 얼굴 a well-featured face / 단정하게 neatly; properly / 단정치 못하게 slovenly; slatternly; untidy / 단정치 못한 사람 a sloven; a slovenly person / 용모가 단정하다 have neat [classi-

cal] features
▶ 그는 단정하게 앉아 있다 He is sitting upright.
▶ 단정하게 굴어라 You must behave properly. ⇒ Behave yourself.
▶ 그녀는 단정하게 옷을 입고 있다 She is neatly dressed.
▶ 책을 다 읽고 나면 책꽂이에 단정하게 꽂아 두거라 When you've finished reading the book, please make sure you put it back in the bookcase.
▶ 그녀는 몸가짐이 단정했다 She carried herself with grace and dignity.
▶ 그는 언제나 행실이 단정하다 He is always proper in his behavior.

단정 斷定 (a) decision; (a) conclusion
◆ 단정을 내리다 form [draw] one's conclusion; make one's decision / 단정적인 언사 a conclusive remark
▶ 그것에 대해 성급하게 단정을 내려서는 안된다 You must not make [jump at] a hasty conclusion about it.
—단정하다 conclude; decide; come to [arrive at] a conclusion
▶ 그것이 그의 소행이라고 단정할 수는 없다 We cannot conclude that it was his doing.
▶ 이런 사정으로 미루어 그가 익사한 것으로 단정했다 From these circumstances, I concluded him to have been drowned.

단조 單調 〈가곡의 단일함〉 monotone; 〈무변화〉 monotony; 〈무료함〉 dullness

단조 短調 〔樂〕 a minor (key)
◆ 다 단조의 교향곡 a symphony in C minor / 단조로 in a minor key

단조 鍛造 forging —단조하다 forge

단조롭다 單調— monotonous; dull; flat; humdrum; 〈가곡이〉 monotonic; 〈억양이 없다〉 singsong
◆ 단조로운 경치 a scene lacking variety / 단조로운 빛깔 a dull [flat] color / 단조로운 생활을 하다 lead a monotonous [dull] life; live a humdrum existence / 단조로움을 깨뜨리다 break [relieve] the monotony
▶ 나는 단조롭게 살고 싶지 않다 I don't like to lead a monotonous [dull] life.

단종 sterilization; 〈거세〉 castration
■ —법 〔法〕 a sterilization law —수술 〔醫〕 a sterilization (operation): 단종 수술을 하다 sterilize sb

단좌 單坐 a single seat
■ —기(機) a single-seat(ed) plane; a single-seater

단죄 斷罪 judgment of a crime; decision on a punishment; condemnation; conviction
—단죄하다 convict; condemn; punish
◆ 단죄되다 be [stand] convicted (of a crime), be executed
▶ 그는 살인범으로 단죄되었다 He was convicted of [condemned for] murder.

단주 端舟 a (small) boat; a skiff

단주 端株 〔證〕 odd-lot [broken-lot] stocks; an odd lot

단지 a jar; a pot; a crock
■ 꿀— a honey jar

단지 但只 only; merely; alone ⇒ 다만
◆ 단지 …(일) 뿐만 아니라… not only...but also... / 단지 이름뿐이 only in name

단지 團地 a housing development; an apartment development; a housing complex
◆ 아파트 단지의 주민 dwellers [people] in modern apartments [apartment houses]
■ 공업— an industrial complex: 울산공업단지 the Ulsan Industrial Complex 주택— a collective housing area: 공무원 주택 단지 a government employees' housing area

단지 斷指 cutting a finger
—단지하다 cut one's finger

단지증 短肢症 〔醫〕 phocomelia; phokomelia
◆ 단지증의 phocomelic

단짝 a bosom [an intimate] friend; a great [close] friends; (口) a chum
◆ 단짝이 되다 become friendly 《with》; (口) chum up 《with》

단참에 單站— at a breath ⇨ 단숨에

단채 單彩 ◆ 단채의 monochromatic
■ —화 monochrome —화가 a monochromist —화법 monochromy

단처 短處 a shortcoming; a defect; a fault; a weak point

단철 鍛鐵 1 〈버리기〉 tempering iron 2 〈선철(銑鐵)에 대하여〉 malleable cast iron

단청 丹靑 〈색〉 red and blue; 〈그림·칠〉 (a) painting; a picture of many colors and designs ◆ 단청의 묘 the exquisite beauty of the painting ■ —공사 a painting work [finish]

단체 單體 〔化〕 a simple (substance)

단체 團體 1 〈일단〉 a group; a party; a body; a company; a team; a corps 《pl. ~ [kɔːrz]》

> 解説 group은 어떤 관계가 있어서 모여있는 집단이란 뜻으로 쓰는 가장 일반적인 말이다. party는 공동 목적을 위한 일시적인 집단이며 body는 계획된 방법으로 동일체인 양 행동하는 집단을 뜻한다. group, party, team은 단수가 원칙이지만 (英)에서는 하나 하나의 구성원을 가리킬 때는 복수로 취급한다: 초등학생 단체가 중국에 갈 예정입니다 A party of schoolchildren is going to China. / 그 단체는 대부분이 소년입니다 The party (美) is [(英) are] mostly a boys.

◆ 단체를 구성하다[만들다] make up a party [body] / 단체로 신청하다 apply in a body; book 《a room》 for a 《sightseeing》 party / 단체로 관람하다 go to 《a theater, a stadium》 in a party [group]
▶ 50명 이상의 단체에는 운임을 할인해 준다 For a party of not less than fifty persons reduced fares are allowed.
▶ 우리는 단체로 15명분의 방을 호텔에 예약했다 We made a hotel reservation for a group of fifteen persons.
2 〈조직체〉 an organization; a corporation; an association; a unit
◆ 단체를 조직[해산]하다 form [dissolve] an organization
■ 교섭[연구]— a negotiation [research] body

실업[자선]— a business [charity] organization **정치—** a political body [organization] ■**—경기** team sports; a team event [competition] **—경주** a team race **—관념** a sense of community life **—관람** a group viewing [inspection] **—교섭(권)** (the right of) collective bargaining: 단체교섭을 하다 bargain collectively **—보험** collective insurance **—생활** a group [corporate] life **—손님** customers coming as a group **—여행** a group tour [excursion]: 단체여행을 하다 make a group tour; travel in a party **—운동** a collective movement **—쟁의** a collective dispute **—전** ⇨ 단체(~경기) **—정신** a team spirit; esprit de corps **—할인** ⟨여행의⟩ a party-trip reduction; a group reduction **—행동** a collective action: 단체행동을 취하다 act collectively; act as a group **—협약** a collective [(英) trade] agreement **—활동** group activity **—훈련** mass training

단총 短銃 a short gun; ⟨권총⟩ a pistol; a revolver ■**기관—** a submachine gun

단추 a button
♦ 단추가 떨어지다 a button comes off [is torn out] / 단추를 채우다 fasten buttons; button (up) ⟨one's coat⟩ / 단추를 끄르다 undo [unfasten] buttons; unbutton ⟨a coat⟩ / 단추를 달다 put on buttons; sew buttons ⟨on a coat⟩ / 단추를 떼다 take off buttons ⟨on a coat⟩ / ⟨엘리베이터의⟩ 3층 단추를 누르다 push the button for the third floor
▶ 이 단추는 떨어질 것 같다 This button is loose.
▶ 바지 단추가 끌러져 있군요 ⟨완곡하게⟩ Your stable door is open.
■**금—** ⟨금으로 만든⟩ a gold button; ⟨놋쇠로 만든⟩ a brass button **누름—** ⇨ 누름단추 **배자[호박]—** a vest [an amber] stud **자개—** a shell button **장식—** a fancy button **단춧고리** a buttonhook **단춧구멍** a buttonhole: 단춧구멍을 내다 make a buttonhole

단축 短軸 〔數〕 the minor axis

단축 短縮 shortening; reduction; curtailment **—단축하다** shorten; reduce; contract; curtail; cut down
♦ 100미터 단축하다 cut the distance by hundred meters / 시간을 단축하다 reduce the time
▶ 수업시간이 10분 단축되었다 The length of a class period was cut to ten minutes.
■**생산—** output reduction **조업—** curtailment of operation **—수업** shortened school hours **—어** an abbreviation **—형** 〔文法〕 a contracted form; a contraction

단출하다 1 ⟨가족이⟩ small; simple
♦ 식구가 단출하다 have a small family
▶ 우리집은 단출한 세 식구다 Ours is a small family of three.
2 ⟨옷차림·짐 등이⟩ simple; handy; light; plain ♦ 단출한 옷차림 a plain outfit / 단출한 짐 a light baggage; a small package
▶ 단출한 짐으로 여행해라 You should travel light.

단층 單層 a single story [(英) storey]; one-story ■**—집** a one-storied house; a house of one story

단층 斷層 〔地質〕 a dislocation; a fault; a throw
■**사(斜)[사행(斜行)]—** an oblique [a diagonal] fault **소(小)—** a slip; a small fault **—면** a fault plane **—사진** ⟨뢴트겐의⟩ a tomogram **—사진법** ⟨촬영법⟩ tomography; 〔醫〕 a tomogram **—산맥** fault mountains **—작용** faulting **—지진** a dislocation earthquake

단침 短針 ⟨시계의⟩ the short [hour] hand

단칭 單稱 ♦ 단칭의 singular ■**—명사** a singular term **—명제** 〔論〕 a singular proposition

단칸 單— a small room; single room
■**—마루** a 6-foot square floor **—방** a 6-foot square room; a single room: 그의 전가족이 단간방에서 살고 있다 All the members of his family live in a single room. **—살림[살이]** (a poor family) living in a single room; a one-room household

단칼에 單— with one stroke of the sword [knife] ▶ 단칼에 목을 베다 cut off sb's head with one stroke (of one's sword)

단타 單打 〔野〕 a single (hit)
♦ 단타를 치다 single; swat a single
▶ 그는 좌익수 앞에 떨어지는 단타를 쳤다 He singled to left field.

단타 短打 〔野〕 chopping
♦ 단타 전법 the choke grip / 단타를 치다 chop (the ball)

단테 ⟨이탈리아의 시인⟩ Dante, Alighieri (1265-1321)

단파 短波 a shortwave; a short wavelength
♦ 단파로 송신하다 shortwave ⟨a message⟩ / 단파로 해외 방송을 듣다 listen to overseas broadcasts on a shortwave
■**—무전** a shortwave radio **—방송** a shortwave broadcasting: 단파방송을 듣다 listen to the shortwave broadcast (from Seoul) **—송신기[수신기]** a shortwave transmitter [receiver]

단판 單— a single round [game]
♦ 단판에 in a single round; at once; at a breath
■**—승부** a one-game[-bout] contest decided by a single round **—씨름** single-round wrestling

단판 單瓣 a single valve
■**—조개** a univalve shell **—화** a single [single-petaled, monopetalous] flower

단팥죽 —粥 sweet red-bean soup with rice cake

단편 短篇 a short piece; a sketch
■**—영화** a short film [movie]; 〈美俗〉 a shortie **—집** a collection of short stories; collected short stories ⟨of Maugham⟩

단편 斷片 a piece; a fragment; a shred; a scrap; odds (and ends)
♦ 단편적인 fragmentary; piecemeal; scrappy / 단편적인 지식 fragmentary knowledge / 단편적으로 in fragments; piece by piece
▶ 그들이 속삭이는 얘기를 단편적으로 엿들었습니다 I overheard snatches of their whispered conversation.
▶ 옛날 이야기라서 단편적으로 밖에는 생각이 나지 않아요 It is an old story, as you know, so I can only recall it fragmentarily [piece by

단편소설 短篇小說 a short story [novel]; a novelette; a sketch
■—가 a (short) story writer ／ —선집 a selection [choice collection] of short stories

단평 短評 a short criticism; a brief comment [review]
♦단평하다 criticize briefly; comment briefly (upon); make a brief comment (on)
■시사— brief comments on current events

단풍 丹楓 1〈나무〉〔植〕 a maple (tree) 2〈잎〉 red [scarlet-tinged] leaves; yellow [golden] leaves; 〈색〉 autumn(al) tints [colors]
♦단풍으로 물든 산 mountains ablaze [aflame] with autumnal tints; hills dressed up with red leaves ／ 단풍(이) 들다 turn red [yellow, crimson]; be tinged with red
▶단풍이 들어 온 산이 불타는 듯하다 The hills are aflame with autumnal tints.
■—잎 (scarlet) maple leaves

단풍나무 丹楓— 〔植〕 a maple (tree)

단풍놀이 丹楓— an excursion for viewing autumnal leaves; maple-tree viewing
▶우리는 설악산으로 단풍놀이를 갔다 We went to Mt. Sŏrak to enjoy the autumn leaves.

단합 團合 unity ⇨ 단결
■—대회 a rally to strengthen the unity

단항식 單項式 〔數〕 a monomial (expression)

단핵 單核 ♦단핵의 mononuclear
■—증 〔醫〕 mononucleosis: 전염성 단핵증 infectious mononucleosis

단행 斷行 decisive action; resolute enforcement; 〈실행〉 carrying out; execution
—단행하다 carry out (resolutely); effect; execute; enforce
♦계획을 단행하다 carry a plan into effect [execution] ／ 내각 개편을 단행하다 carry out the reshuffle of the cabinet
▶반대가 있어도 그 개혁을 단행해야만 한다 We must carry through [execute] the reform (resolutely) in spite of opposition.

단행범 單行犯 〔法〕 a single offence 〔英〕 offense》 《against the law》

단행법 單行法 〔法〕 a special law

단행본 單行本 a book; a separate [an independent] volume
♦단행본으로 발행하다 publish [bring out] 《one's work》 in book form
▶그는 최근 수필을 단행본으로 출판했다 He has recently published his essays in book form.

단호하다 斷乎— firm; decisive; determined; resolute; 〈과감한〉 drastic
♦단호한 결심 a grim [firm] resolution ／ 단호한 언사[말투] a decisive tone of voice ／ 단호한 조처를 취하다 take decisive [firm, drastic] measures 《against》 ／ 단호히 firmly; resolutely; decisively; in a determined manner ／ 단호히 거절하다 refuse point-blank [flatly]; give sb a flat refusal
▶나는 단호히 주장을 굽히지 않았다 I stuck firmly to my opinion.

단화 短靴 《a pair of》 shoes; 〔美〕 《a pair of》 low shoes

닫다¹ 〈사람이〉 run; rush; 〈말이〉 gallop; canter

닫다² 1 〈문을〉 shut; close
♦문을 닫다 shut [close] the door ／ 쾅 닫다 slam [bang] 《the door》 to [closed]; shut 《the door》 with a bang ／ 닫아 두다 keep 《the door》 shut
▶들어올 때는 반드시 문을 닫고 들어오시오 Be sure to shut [close] the door when you come in.
▶이제 가게 문을 닫을 시간이다 It is time to close the shop.
2 〈폐점하다〉 close a shop; close the door
♦(가게) 문을 닫다 (口) put up the shutters; close up [down] the store; shut up shop

닫아걸다 fasten [bolt, latch] 《a door》; lock 《자물쇠로》 ♦문을 안으로[밖으로] 닫아걸다 fasten [lock] a door from within [without]

닫치다 close (up); shut (up)
♦문을 쾅 닫치다 slam [bang] the door; shut the door with a bang

닫히다 shut; close; be shut; be closed
▶문이 저절로 닫혔다 The door shut [closed] by itself.
▶대문이 닫혀 있다 The gate is shut.
▶이 창문은 잘 닫히지 않는다 This window will not shut [close].

달 1 〈하늘의〉 the moon
♦달이 lunar ／ 그믐달 a waning moon ／ 보름달 a full moon ／ 스무날의 달 a twenty-day-old moon ／ 초승달 a new [waxing] moon ／ 달나라 the moon ／ 달무리 a halo [ring] round the moon ／ 달빛 moonlight; moonbeams ／ 달여행 a journey [flight, travel] to the moon; a lunar flight [journey] ／ 달착륙 (a) lunar landing ／ 달착륙선 a lunar module; a lunar landing craft [ship] ／ 달탐험 a lunar expedition ／ 달탐험 계획 a lunar program ／ 달의 여신 the goddess of the moon; Diana ／ 달이 뜰 무렵 at rise of the moon ／ 달이 있는[없는]밤 a moonlit [moonless] night ／ 달을 바라보다[쳐다보다] look up at the moon
▶달이 떠 있다 The moon is up [is out, has risen]. ⇌ There is a moon.
▶달이 졌다 The moon has set [gone down].
▶달이 찬다[기운다] The moon waxes [wanes].
▶달이 휘영청 밝다 The moon is shining bright.
▶며칠 달입니까? How old is the moon?
2 〈달력의〉 a month
♦큰 달 a 31-day month ／ 작은 달 a month with thirty or less days ／ 그전 달의 of the previous [preceding] month ／ 달이 바뀌면 in the month following [to come]; at the beginning of next month ／ 한 달에 한번 once a month; monthly ／ 한 달에 두번씩 twice a month; semimonthly ／ 달이면 달마다 month after month; month in and month out
▶그는 한 달에 한번은 여행한다 He makes a trip at least once a month.
3 〈임신의〉 《her》 time
♦달이 차다 be in [have gone] her full time ／ (임신) 여섯 달째다 be six months pregnant ／

달가닥 달을 덜 채우고 태어난 아기 a prematurely born infant
▶ 그녀는 달이 차서 여자아이를 낳았다 She gave birth to [delivered] a girl in the fullness of time. ⇒ At (full) term she gave birth to a girl.

달가닥 with a rattle [clatter]
♦ 달가닥달가닥 rattling; clattering / 짐수레가 달가닥 소리를 내면서 지나갔다 A cart clattered [rattled] past.

달가닥거리다 clatter; rattle; crackle
♦ 달가닥거리는 소리 a clatter; clattering; a clack; a rattle / 달가닥거리는 타자기 소리 the clatter [rattle] of a typewriter / 달가닥거리며 with a clatter [rattle]
▶ 바람 때문에 덧문이 달가닥거리고 있다 The wind is rattling the shutter.

달가당 with a clang [clink, rattle]
♦ 달가당하고 떨어지다 fall with a clang
▶ 무엇인가 달가당 떨어졌다 Something fell with a thud [thump].

달가당거리다 clink; clang; clatter; rattle
♦ 달가당거리는 clinking; clangorous / 달가당거리는 차 a rickety car

달갑다 satisfactory
♦ 달갑지 않은 undesirable; objectionable / 달갑지 않은 손님 an unwelcome visitor [guest]/ 달갑지 않은 호의 an unwanted [unwelcome] favor
▶ 우리는 달갑지 않은 소식을 받았다 We received an unfavorable message.
▶ 그녀는 달갑지 않았으나 그 개를 돌보기로 했다 She agreed reluctantly to take care of the dog.

달개 a penthouse

달걀 an egg
♦ 달걀 껍데기 an eggshell / 달걀 부침 a fried egg; an eggroll / 날[생]달걀 a raw egg / 삶은 달걀 a boiled egg / 반숙한[완숙한] 달걀 a soft-[hard-]boiled egg / 갓 낳은 달걀 a newly-laid egg / 달걀 모양의 egg-shaped; oval / 달걀을 낳다 lay an egg / 달걀을 품다 sit on an egg; brood / 달걀을 (닭에게) 품게하다 set a hen on eggs / 달걀을 깨다 break an egg
▶ 암탉이 달걀을 낳기 시작했다 The hen started laying.
▶ 달걀을 2개 깨어 잘 휘저어라 Break two eggs and beat them.
▶ 달걀을 어떻게 요리할까요? How do you like your eggs done?

달걀로 백운대 치기 〈속담〉 It's running one's head against a wall.

달걀로 치면 노른자다 〈속담〉 the basic point; the key post

달걀 섬 다루듯 하다 〈속담〉 being very careful; handling with utmost care

달게받다 tolerate; endure; submit to; put up with
♦ 책망을 달게 받다 take *one's* reproof in good part; receive [bear] a reprimand calmly / 벌을 달게 받다 submit *oneself* passively to punishment
▶ 누구도 이런 모욕을 달게 받지는 않을 것이다 No one would submit silently to such an insult.

달견 達見 〈견식〉 farsightedness; clear-sightedness; foresight; 〈의견〉 an excellent view; a fine idea

달곰새금하다 sweet-sour (flavor)

달곰쌉쌀하다 bitter-sweet (flavor)

달관 〈멀리 내다봄〉 a farsighted [long] view; a broad outlook; 〈높은 견식〉 philosophic ripeness; a philosophic view

—**달관하다** take a farsighted [long] view of; have a broad outlook; take things philosophically
♦ 장래를 달관하다 take a farsighted view; see far into the future
▶ 그는 인생을 달관하고 있다 He takes a philosophical view of life.

달구 a (ground) rammer

달구다 heat; make hot
♦ 부젓가락을 빨갛게 달구다 heat a tong red-hot / 오븐을 350도까지 달구다 heat the oven to 350 degrees / 철판을 전기로 달구어 끓다 burn off an iron plate with electricity

달구지 a cart
♦ 소달구지 an oxcart / 달구지를 끌다 draw a cart / 달구지에 싣다 load a cart (with) / 건초를 달구지로 농장까지 나르다 cart hay [carry hay in a cart] to the farm

달구질 pounding [ramming, beating down] earth —**달구질하다** pound [ram, beat down] earth with a rammer; harden

달그락 with a rattle [clatter]

달그락거리다 rattle; clatter; crackle
▶ 짐수레가 달그락거리면서 지나갔다 A cart clattered [rattled] past.

달그랑 with a clink [clang, rattle]
▶ 그들은 컵을 서로 마주치고 건배했다 They clinked (their) glasses and drank a toast.

—**달그랑거리다** clink; clang; rattle

달다¹ 1 〈졸아들다〉 be boiled down [dry]; boil down
▶ 탕약이 다 달았다 The decoction is parched up.
2 〈뜨거워지다〉 become (red-)hot; 〈벌겋게〉 glow
♦ 벌겋게 단 red-hot (iron) / 벌겋게 단 숯 glowing charcoal / 벌겋게 단 부젓가락 red-hot [burnt] tongs
▶ 쇠꼬챙이가 열로 빨갛게 달아 있다 An iron skewer glows with heat.
3 〈화끈해지다〉 feel hot [warm]; flush; burn
♦ 흥분해서 얼굴이 달다 flush with excitement / 부끄러워서 얼굴이 달다 blush with [for] shame
▶ 열이 있어 몸이 단다 I feel hot with fever.
▶ 그녀의 얼굴은 불에 빨갛게 달았다 Her face was fire-flushed.
▶ 술을 마셨더니 얼굴이 단다 My cheeks are flushed with wine.
4 〈마음이〉 be [feel] irritated (at, by, with); be fretful; fret [be in a fret] (about, at, over); 〈안달〉 be [feel] impatient (at, by, for, with)
♦ 애인이 보고 싶어 애가 달다 be dying to see *one's* sweetheart / 직장을 구하려고 몸이 달아

돌아다니다 run about eagerly to seek employment
▶그의 말투는 나를 애가 달게 한다 His way of talking irritates me [is irritating].
▶그녀가 무슨 일로 애가 다는지 이상하다 I wonder what she is so impatient [fretful] about.

달다² 1 〈걸다〉 hang; suspend; put [hang] up
♦간판을 달다 hang [put] up a signboard / 국기를 달다 hoist [raise] the national flag / 돛을 달다 hoist [spread, put up] a sail / 문패를 달다 put up a name plate 《at the gate》 / 천장에 모빌을 달다 hang [suspend] a mobile from the ceiling / 두 나무 사이에 해먹을 달다 sling [hang] a hammock between two trees
▶그녀는 창에 커튼을 달고 있다 She is hanging a curtain on the window.
▶바람 부는 곳에 달아 두면 금방 마릅니다 Hang it in the wind, and it will soon dry up.
2 〈부착시키다〉 fix [affix, attach, tag] 《one thing to another》; set [put] 《one thing on another》; fit 《up》; 〈연결하다〉 stick; fasten; join 《one thing to another》
♦명찰을 달다 attach [affix] a name tag 《to》 / 훈장을 달다 wear a decoration / 문에 벨을 달다 fix a bell on the door / 벽에 선반을 달다 put up a shelf on the wall / 셔츠에 단추를 달다 sew a button on [to] a shirt / 열차에 기관차를 달다 couple an engine to a train / 트렁크에 꼬리표를 달다 fasten [attach, fix] a label [tag] to a trunk
▶나는 차에 스노 타이어를 달았다 I equipped my car with snow tires.
▶그녀는 옷깃에 브로치를 달고 있었다 She wore a pin on her collar.
▶장군은 병사의 가슴에 훈장을 달아 주었다 The general pinned a decoration on the breast of the soldier.
▶단추가 떨어졌으니 다시 달아 줘요 This button has come off, so put it back on.
3 〈덧붙이다〉 add [annex, append] 《one thing to another》; 〈기입하다〉 enter 《in a book》
♦단서를 달다 annex a proviso 《to a deed》 / 주(註)를 달다 add [annex, append] notes 《to a book》; annotate / 외상을 달다 put down [charge] to one's credit account / 장부에 달다 enter 《an item》 in a book; keep accounts / 한자에 한글로 토를 달다 show the reading of a Chinese character in Hangul / 달아놓고 물건을 사다 buy a thing on credit
▶계산은 내 앞으로 달아 두시오 Charge it [Put it down] to my account.
4 〈정하여 붙이다〉 give; attach
♦제목을 달다 give a title 《to》; entitle 《a book》; attach a headline 《to》

달다³ 〈무게를〉 weigh; measure
♦무게를 달다 weigh; measure the weight 《of》 / 저울로 달다 weigh sth in the balance [on the scales] / 달아서 팔다 sell sth by weight
▶나는 목욕 하고나서 체중을 달아 보았다 I weighed myself after a bath.
▶온스는 무게를 다는 단위다 Ounce is a unit of measuring weight.

달다⁴ 1 〈맛이〉 sweet; sugary; sweet-flavored
♦단 것 sweet things; sweet-stuff; 〈과자〉 sweets; (美) candy / 너무 단 홍차 sugary tea / 설탕으로 달게 하다 sweeten 《coffee》 with sugar
▶나는 커피를 달게 마신다 I like my coffee sweet.
2 〈입이〉 have a good appetite
♦(음식을) 아주 달게 먹다 eat with gusto [keen relish]
3 〈흡족하다〉 satisfactory; gratifying
♦달게 자다 sleep soundly / 달게 받다 submit to ⇨ 달게 받다

달단 韃靼 〔史〕 Ta(r)tary
■一사람 a Ta(r)tar

달달 1 〈휘젓는 모양〉 stirringly
♦깨를 달달 볶다 toast [parch] sesame seeds thoroughly
2 〈들볶는 모양〉 persistently; pressingly
▶그는 돈을 더 달라고 나를 달달 볶았다 He pestered [importuned, pressed] me for more money.
3 〈뒤지는 모양〉 thoroughly; throughout
♦서랍을 달달 뒤지다 ransack [rummage in] drawers 《for》

달도 차면 기운다 (속담) Every flow hath its ebb.

달라다 ask; request; beg; call upon sb to 《do》; pray for; entreat; plead for
♦도와 달라다 ask sb for help; call for help / 돈을 달라다 ask for money / 책을 빌려 달라다 ask sb to lend a book / 해 달라는 대로 at sb's request; as requested
▶그는 내 누이를 달라고 말했다 He asked (for the hand of) my sister in marriage.

달라붙다 stick [cling] 《to》; hold on to; fasten oneself on; be [stick] close together
▶내 구두창에 껌이 달라붙었다 Chewing gum got stuck to the sole of my shoe.
▶젖은 블라우스가 그녀의 살갗에 달라붙었다 The wet blouse clung to her skin.
▶2개의 판자는 접착제로 달라붙어 있었다 The two boards were glued tightly together.
▶온 식구가 모내기에 달라붙었다 The whole family stuck to [at] bedding out young rice plants.

달라이라마 the Dalai [Grand] Lama

달라지다 become different; change; undergo a change; be changed; 〈일부가〉 be altered; 〈여러 가지로〉 vary; turn into
♦달라지지 않다 be [remain] unchanged; be the same 《as before》; be constant
▶날씨가 갑자기 달라졌다 The weather changed suddenly.
▶그의 의견은 쉽게 달라진다 His opinions are variable. ⇌ He changes his mind easily.
▶그는 결혼 전과는 사람이 달라졌다 He has changed since he got married.
▶이 도시는 지난 5년간에 크게 달라졌다 This town has changed [altered] a great deal in the last five years.
▶세상 참 많이 달라졌구나 How the world has changed!
▶그의 태도는 지난 1년 동안에 많이 달라졌다

His attitude has changed [altered] a lot in the past year.
▶너는 몰라보게 달라졌다 You have changed almost beyond recognition. ⇌ You have changed so much that I hardly recognized [knew] you.

달랑 1 〈매달려〉 hanging (down); dangling
▶저 나뭇가지에 무엇인가 달랑 매달려 있다 Something is hanging down [dangling] from a branch of that tree.
2 〈홀로〉 lonely; alone
▶그는 달랑 혼자 남았다 He was left alone [all by himself].
3 〈뜨끔하게〉 shivering

달랑거리다 〈행동이〉 be frivolous [flippant]; be restless; 〈부주의한〉 be careless; 〈사려가 없는〉 be thoughtless; 〈경솔한〉 be hasty; be rash
▶그녀는 달랑거린다 She is careless [is a careless girl, behaves carelessly].

달랑달랑 〈행동이〉 frivolously; flippantly

달랑달랑하다 1 〈부족하게 되다〉 run [fall, go] short of
▶물[식량]이 달랑달랑한다 We are running out [short] of water [food].
2 ⇨ 달랑거리다

달랑하다 〈뜨끔하다〉 feel a shock; be shocked (at, by); get a start
▶그 소식을 듣고 가슴이 달랑했다 The news gave me a start.

달래 〔植〕 a wild rocambole

달래다 1 〈위로하다〉 soothe; pacify; appease; placate; comfort; dandle (a baby)
♦달래기 쉬운 appeasable; placable / 달래기 어려운 inappeasable; implacable / 기분을 달래다 divert *oneself* (by singing); get [take] *one's* mind off (*one's* sorrow) / 성난 사람을 달래다 soothe [calm down] an angry person / 우는 아이를 달래다 soothe a crying child
▶아버지는 술로 슬픔을 달랬다 My father drowned his sorrows in drinking.
▶그녀는 외로울 때는 언제나 음악으로 마음을 달랜다 She always comforted herself with music when she was lonely. ⇌ She always consoled herself by listening to music.
2 〈살살 꾀다〉 coax; humor; cajole; wheedle; 〈비위를 맞추어〉 fondle
♦아이를 달래어 약을 먹이다 [학교에 보내다] coax a child to take a medicine [to school]
▶그녀는 우는 아이를 달래어 재웠다 She coaxed the crying child into going to sleep.
▶그를 가까스로 달래어 돌려보냈다 I had great difficulty in persuading him to return home.

달러 a dollar; (美) a buck
♦미국 달러 U.S. dollar / 싱가포르 달러 Singapore dollar / 캐나다 달러 Canadian dollar / 호주 달러 Australian dollar / 1달러 은화 (美俗) a cartwheel / 5달러 지폐 a five-dollar bill [note]; a fiver / 5달러 금화 a half eagle / 10달러 지폐 a ten-dollar bill [note]; (美俗) a sawbuck / 20달러 금화 a double eagle / 1천 달러 (美俗) a grand
♦달러를 벌다 earn dollars / 달러로 지불하다 pay in dollars
▶달러가 900원으로 올랐다[내렸다] The dollar has risen [fallen] to nine hundred won.
▶지금 서울에서는 1달러가 900원으로 거래되고 있다 Right now in Seoul the dollar is being traded at nine hundred won.
■─권(圈) a dollar bloc ─대부[차관] a dollar loan ─방위 the defense of the dollar ─부족 a dollar shortage ─시세 the exchange rate of the dollar ─외교 dollar diplomacy ─위기 a dollar crisis ─자금 dollar funds ─지역 a dollar area

달러박스 〈돈상자〉 a money box; a cashbox; a strongbox; 〈후원자〉 a financial supporter [backer]; 〈돈벌게 해주는 것〉 a gold mine
▶그녀에게는 김선생이라는 달러박스가 있다 She has a patron in Mr. Kim.
▶그 여자는 저 영화회사의 달러박스다 She is like a gold tree to that film studio.
■─스타 a box-office star.

달려가다 run [rush, hasten, hurry] to (the place, the scene); run [rush] up to *sb*
♦의사에게 달려가다 run for the doctor / 차를 몰아 현장으로 달려가다 rush [hasten] to the scene in a car / 시내까지 달려가다 take a run to downtown
▶우리는 병원으로 달려갔다 We hurried to the hospital.
▶경찰이 곧 사고 현장으로 달려갔다 The police rushed to the scene of the accident.
▶우리는 그를 도우러 달려갔다 We ran to his aid.

달려나가다 run [rush] out; run [scamper] off; fly out [away] ♦거리로 달려나가다 rush into the street

달려들다 〈불시에〉 pounce on *sb*; throw *oneself* into another's arms

달려오다 come running; hasten [hurry, rush] to (a place)
▶그는 역에서 달려왔다 He came running from the station.
▶아이들이 달려왔다 The children came running.
▶나는 만사를 제쳐놓고 이리로 달려왔다 I dropped everything and beat it over here.

달력 ─曆 a calendar; an almanac
▶달력상으로는 2주전부터 봄이다 According to the calendar, it has been spring for two weeks.

달로켓 a lunar [moon] rocket; a mooncraft; 〈탐사기〉 a moon probe

달리 differently; in a different way; 〈갖가지로〉 variously; 〈따로〉 separately; apart; 〈특별히〉 specially; particularly; 〈더욱〉 additionally
♦달리 특정하지 않으면 unless otherwise specified / 기대와는 달리 contrary to *one's* expectations / 달리 할 일이 없다[있다] have nothing [something] else to do / 달리 갈 곳이 없다 have nowhere to go
▶생각과는 달리 자금이 충분히 모이지 않았다 Contrary to our expectations, we could not raise the necessary funds.
▶내 누이는 나와는 달리 부지런하다 My sister is a hard worker, unlike myself.
▶그는 달리 결론을 내릴 수 없었다 He

couldn't conclude otherwise.
▶ 달리 통지가 없으면 모든 회합은 서울 사무소에서 합니다 Unless otherwise notified, all meetings will be held in the Seoul office.
▶ 이 소나타는 예상과는 달리 쉬웠다 I found this sonata easier than I had expected.
▶ 나는 달리 말할 것이 없소 That's all I want to say. ⇌ I have nothing more [further] to say.
▶ 달리 방법이 없다 There is nothing for it but to do that. ⇌ We have no choice [There is no other way] but to do that.

달리기 a run; 〈경주〉 a race; a footrace
◆ 달리기 선수 a runner; a racer; 〈단거리의〉 a sprinter ▶ 나는 그와 달리기를 했다 I ran a race with him.

달리다[1] 〈매달리다〉 hang down; dangle; be suspended
▶ 램프가 천장에 달려 있었다 A lamp was hanging [suspended] from the ceiling.
▶ 저 나뭇가지에 무엇인가 달려 있다 Something is hanging down [dangling] from a branch of that tree.
▶ 귤이 가지마다 주렁주렁 달려 있다 The branches are heavily laden with tangerines.
▶ 처마에 달린 풍경이 울리고 있다 The wind-bell hanging from the eaves is tinkling.
2 〈좌우되다〉 depend 《on, upon》; hang on; rest 《with》
◆ 우승이 달린 경기 the game to decide the championship
▶ 성공 여부는 너의 노력에 달려 있다 Whether you succeed or not depends on your efforts.
▶ 국가의 운명이 그들의 어깨에 달려 있다 The destiny of the nation rests [falls] on their shoulders.
▶ 그의 운명은 배심원의 평결에 달려 있었다 His fate hung on the jury's decision.
▶ 가게의 흥망이 그의 장사 수완에 달려 있다 The prosperity of the store depends on his commercial ability.
3 〈우수리가〉 be tacked on 《to a round sum》
◆ 예산은 백만불 귀가 달리다 be tacked another million dollars onto the budget

달리다[2] **1** 〈붙어 있다〉 be attached; be fixed
◆ 꼬리표가 달린 트렁크 a trunk with a tag attached / 벽에 붙박이로 달려 있는 책장 built-in bookshelves
▶ 이 책장에는 서랍이 두개 달려 있다 This bookcase has two drawers.
▶ 그 가방에는 꼬리표가 달려 있었다 The bag had [carried] a label. ⇌ There was a label attached to the bag.
▶ 이 열차는 여덟량이 달려 있다 This train is eight cars [《英》 carriages] long. ⇌ This train is made up of eight cars [carriages].
▶ 이 열차에는 식당차가 달려 있지 않다 This train doesn't have a dining car (attached).
2 〈가설되다〉 be furnished; be installed; be set [put] up
▶ 이 문에는 자동자물쇠가 달려 있다 This door has an automatic lock.
▶ 각 탁자에는 이어폰이 달려 있다 Earphones have been installed at each table.
▶ 방마다 냉방기가 달려 있다 Each room has an air-conditioner.
3 〈첨가되다〉 be added [affixed, appended]
▶ 그 책에는 자세한 주가 달려 있다 The book is fully annotated.
▶ 그 책에는 용어집이 달려 있다 A glossary is appended to the book.

달리다[3] 〈나른해지다〉 feel languid; be dull; be heavy
▶ 잠을 자지 못했더니 눈이 달린다 My eyes feel heavy [are drawn] from lack of sleep.

달리다[4] **1** 〈부치다〉 be [fall] behind; be not enough; be no match [equal] for
◆ 실력이 달리다 be poor [wanting] of ability / 힘이 달리다 be not strong enough; be beyond *one's* power [capacity]
▶ 나는 영어 실력이 달린다 I am weak in [poor at] English.
▶ 그 일에는 내 능력이 달린다 The task is beyond my power(s). ⇌ I'm not equal to the task.
2 〈부족하다〉 〈사물이 주어〉 be in short supply; be insufficient; 〈사람이 주어〉 lack; be lacking in; be [come, fall] short of
◆ 돈[식량]이 달리다 be short [scant] of money [food]/ 일손이 달리다 be shorthanded; be short of hands
▶ 우리는 연료가 달렸다 We didn't have enough fuel.
▶ 가족을 부양하기에는 그의 수입이 달린다 His income is not enough [sufficient] to support his family.
▶ 우리는 자금이 달린다 We are pressed for funds.
▶ 자격있는 교사가 달린다 There is a shortage of qualified teachers.

달리다[5] **1** 〈사람·동물이〉 run; dash; rush
◆ 달려가다 go running; run 《to》; rush 《for》 / 전속력으로 달리다 run [dash] at full [top] speed
▶ 그들은 계단을 달려 올라[내려] 갔다 They ran up [down] the stairs.
▶ 그는 반에서 가장 빨리 달린다 He is the fastest runner in his class.
▶ 버스정류장까지 달리자, 시간이 없어 Let's dash to the bus stop. We have no time.
2 〈교통수단이〉 run
▶ 이 차는 아직 달릴 수 있다 This car can still run all right.
▶ 원자력선은 원자 에너지로 달린다 A nuclear powered ship runs on atomic energy.
▶ 이 열차는 서울·부산간을 4시간만에 달린다 This train covers the distance between Seoul and Pusan in four hours.
▶ 이 차는 1리터로 10킬로미터를 달린다 This car does ten kilometers to a liter.
▶ 이 배는 시속 30노트로 달린다 This boat does 30 knots an hour.
3 〈달리게 하다〉 drive; drive fast
▶ 말을 달리다 drive [gallop] a horse
▶ 그는 역까지 차를 전속력으로 달렸다 He drove (his car) to the station at top speed.
▶ 사고가 났을 때 그는 시속 100 킬로미터로 차를 달리고 있었다 He was driving as fast as a

hundred kilometers an hour when the accident occurred.

달리아 〔植〕 a dahlia

달리하다 differ 《from》; be different 《from》; vary; be dissimilar 《in》; 〈차별두다〉 discriminate
♦ 지위를 달리하다 be in different social stations / 인생관을 달리하다 view things from a different angle [side]; have a different view of life / 대우를 달리하다 treat *sb* differently 《from others》; discriminate 《in favor of, against》 / 문화 수준을 달리하는 사람들 people on various levels of culture
▶ 나는 그와 의견을 달리한다 He and I differ in opinion. ⇌ I differ from him in opinion.

달마 達磨 〔佛敎〕 〈달마대사〉 Dharma

달마다 every month; monthly; each month

달막거리다 shake

달맞이 〔民俗〕 welcoming [viewing] the first full moon —**달맞이하다** welcome [view] the first full moon

달맞이꽃 〔植〕 an evening primrose

달무리 a ring; the halo of the moon
▶ 오늘밤에는 달무리가 졌다 The moon has a ring around it tonight. ⇌ There is a halo around the moon tonight.

달밤 a moonlight [moonlit] night
♦ 달밤의 moonlight / 달밤에 on a moonlit night / 달밤에 산책하다 walk under [in] the moonlight
▶ 그 날은 밝은 달밤이었다 It was a bright moonlight night. ⇌ There was a bright moon that night.
▶ 우리는 달밤에 해변을 걸었다 We walked along the beach in the moonlight.

달변 —邊 a monthly interest

달변 達辯 eloquence; fluency

달빛 moonlight; moonshine; 〈한줄기의〉 a moonbeam
♦ 달빛에 비친 정원 a moonlit [moony] garden / 달빛에 책을 읽다 read by (the) moonlight / 달빛을 받다 be bathed in [be flooded by] the moonlight
▶ 호수가 달빛을 받아 은색으로 보였다 The lake looked silver in the moonlight.
▶ 커튼을 열자 달빛이 흘러 들어왔다 When the curtain was opened, the moonlight streamed [flowed] into the room.

달삯 monthly wage(s)

달성 達成 attainment; achievement —**달성하다** achieve; attain; accomplish; carry out
▶ 그 목적은 달성하기 힘들다 The object is beyond attainment.
▶ 우리는 마침내 목적을 달성했다 We attained [accomplished, realized] our purpose at last.

달싹하다 move slightly; budge ⇨ 꼼짝(~하다) ♦ 달싹하지도 않다 do not budge an inch; won't give an inch; stand like a rock

달아나다 1 〈도주하다〉 run away; get way 《from》; escape 《from》; break [get] loose
♦ 몰래 달아나다 slip off [away]; sneak away / 허둥지둥 달아나다 rush away; make a quick escape
▶ 그는 내 돈을 모두 가지고 달아났다 He got away with all my money.
▶ 교도소에서 죄수 한 사람이 달아났다 One of the inmates has escaped from the prison.
▶ 범인은 이미 국외로 달아났다 The culprit has already fled the country [run away abroad].
▶ 사자가 달아났다고 들었다 I heard a lion has broken [got] loose.
▶ 개가 짖자 아이들은 집으로 달아났다 When the dog barked at them, the children scurried [ran] back to their home.
▶ 그녀는 남자 친구와 달아났다 She eloped [ran away] with her boyfriend.
2 〈떨어져 나가다〉 come off
♦ 웃옷의 단추가 달아났다 A button has come off my coat. ⇌ A button on my coat has come off.
3 〈사라지다〉 vanish
▶ 커피 때문에 잠이 달아났다 Coffee kept me awake.
▶ 위기에 처하자[위기가 닥치자] 용기가 달아났다 My courage failed me at the crucial moment.
▶ 이제 기다릴 생각이 달아났다 I don't feel like waiting any longer.

달아매다 hang (down); suspend
♦ 천장에 램프를 달아매다 swing a lamp from the ceiling

달아보다 〈무게를〉 weigh *sth*; check the weight of; 〈능력을〉 test (out)
♦ 자기의 체중을 달아보다 weigh *oneself* / 짐을 달아보다 weigh a baggage / 남의 능력을 달아보다 put *sb* through (his) paces

달아오르다 1 〈물건이〉 become red-hot; glow; become [get] heated
♦ 달아오른 쇠 red-hot iron
2 〈몸이〉 feel hot [warm]; burn; be all aglow; flush
▶ 열로 몸이 달아오르는 기분이다 I feel hot with fever.
▶ 목욕하고 나니 몸 전체가 달아올랐다 My body was all in glow [I felt warm all over] after taking bath.

달음박질 running (fast) —**달음박질하다** run; rush; dash; race; dart

달이다 boil down; decoct; extract [take out] the essence by boiling; infuse
♦ 약을 달이다 make [prepare] a medical decoction / 뿌리를 달이다 decoct the root / 차를 달이다 infuse tea (leaves); draw [brew] tea

달인 達人 〈기예에 숙달한〉 an expert; a master; a master-hand; 〈인생을 달관한〉 a master mind; a philosopher
♦ 무예의 달인 a master of [an expert in] the martial arts / 검술의 달인 a master fencer / 활의 달인 an expert at archery; an expert archer

달착지근하다 somewhat [rather] sweet; sweetish

달창나다 1 〈닳다〉 wear out; be worn out; 〈해지다〉 become threadbare; tatter
♦ 달창난 구두 a pair of worn-out shoes
2 〈바닥나다〉 run out; be all gone

▶ 뒤주가 달창났다 We have no rice in store at our house. ⇌ We are almost out of rice. ⇌ Our supply of rice is running low.

달치다 1〈너무 달다〉get too hot; get overheated 2〈바싹 졸이다〉boil sth hard [dry]; boil down [away]

달카닥 clatteringly ⇨ 덜커덕

달카당 with a clang ⇨ 덜커덩

달콤하다 sugary; sweet-flavored; honey(ed)
♦ 달콤한 꿈 a sweet dream / 달콤한 말 sugared words; honeyed words; endearing words / 달콤한 말에 넘어가다 be imposed upon by honeyed words [tongue] / 달콤한 소리로 속삭이다 whisper sweet things in *one's* ear
▶ 많은 여자가 그의 달콤한 말에 넘어갔다 Many women were deceived by his honeyed words [smooth talk].

달팽이 〔動〕 a snail
▶ 달팽이가 지나간 자국 a snail track / 달팽이처럼 느릿느릿 (proceed, walk) at a snail's pace
♦ 식용— an edible snail; an escargot ■ —껍데기 a snail shell

달포 a month odd
▶ 그가 하와이에 간지 달포가 된다 It is about a month since he went to Hawaii.

달필 達筆 good handwriting; a good hand
▶ 그는 달필이다 He writes a good hand. ⇌ He is good [skillful] at handwriting. ⇌ He has good handwriting.
▶ 그녀는 달필로 정평이 나있다 She is established as a good calligrapher.
▶ 메모는 가늘게 달필로 적혀 있었다 The note was written in a small, skillful hand.
■ —가 a good [skillful, nimble] penman [calligrapher]

달하다 達— 1〈도달하다〉reach; arrive at [in]; get to
♦ 성숙[노령]에 달하다 reach maturity [oldage] / 결론에 달하다 arrive at [reach] a conclusion / 목적지에 달하다 reach [arrive at] *one's* destination
▶ 나의 공포는 극도에 달했다 My fear was at its height.
▶ 그의 기법은 아직 완전한 경지에는 달하지 못했다 His technique has not yet reached [arrived to] perfection.
▶ 머지않아 그의 일은 최고 수준에 달할 것이다 It will not be long before his work comes up to the highest possible standard.
2〈수량이〉reach; amount to; come (up) to
♦ 천문학적인 숫자에 달하다 run into astronomical figures
▶ 손해는 1억원[억대]에 달했다 The damage amounted to a hundred million won [ran into hundreds of millions of won].
▶ 그 도시의 인구는 500만에 달했다 The population of the city reached five million.
▶ 모금액은 아직 목표에 달하지 못하고 있다 The amount donated still fails short [is still short] of the goal.
3〈이루다〉attain; accomplish; achieve; realize
▶ 그들은 성공적으로 목적을 달했다 They have attained [achieved, realized] their purpose with success.

닭 〔鳥〕 a domestic [garden] fowl; (美) a chicken; 〈암탉〉a hen; 〈수탉〉a cock [rooster]
♦ 산란용 닭 a laying hen / 알을 잘 낳는[낳지 않는] 닭 a good [bad] layer / 놓아 먹이는 닭 yard fowls / 닭을 치다 keep hens; (美) raise [breed] chickens / 암탉이 울다 henpeck; dominate *one's* husband
■ —고기 chicken; fowl

닭벼슬이 될망정 쇠꼬리는 되지 마라 (속담) Better be the head of an ass than tail of a horse.

닭 소 보듯, 소 닭 보듯 (속담) look at each other in silence

닭싸움 a cockfight; cockfighting ♦ 닭싸움시키다 hold a cockfight

닭의장풀 〔植〕 a dayflower; a spiderwort

닭 잡아먹고 오리발 내놓기 (속담) fooling people with dubious evidence which cannot positively be denied

닭장 —欌 a coop; a hencoop; a henhouse; a chicken house; a hencote; a roost
♦ 닭장에 넣다 house chickens [fowls]

닭 쫓던 개 지붕 쳐다보듯 (속담) be frustrated in *one's* attempt

닮다 resemble; be [look] like (another); be alike; take after 《*one's* father》; have a likeness 《to》; be similar 《to》
♦ 꼭 닮다 be as like as two peas; be the very image (of); be the exact counterpart (of) / 용모가 닮다 present *sb* 《facial》 resemblance 《to》 / 닮은 점이 많다 gave many points of likeness 《to》 / 닮은 데가 있다 bear some resemblance 《to》; have some similarities 《between》 / 전혀 닮은 데가 없다 do not bear the slightest resemblance 《to》; be quite unlike [different from] 《another》
▶ 이 아이는 누구를 닮았지? Who(m) does this baby take after?
▶ 저 부부는 서로 닮았다 That husband and wife resemble each other closely [are two of a kind].
▶ 나는 아버지보다 어머니를 많이 닮았다 I take after mother more than father.
▶ 너는 30년 전의 네 아버지를 그대로 닮았다 You look exactly as your father did thirty years ago.
▶ 이것은 그것과 모양이 닮았다 This resembles that in shape.
▶ 그들은 서로 성격이 닮은 데가 많다 They are much alike in character.
▶ 그는 부친을 닮아 근면하다 He is hardworking like his father.
▶ 그는 양친을 닮지 않아 겁이 많다 He is timid unlike his parents.

닮은꼴 〔幾〕 a similar [like] figure

닳다 1〈해지다〉wear [be worn] out [down, off]; be rubbed down
♦ 닳아 해진 worn-out; threadbare; frayed / 입이 닳도록 말하다 tell over and over again
▶ 이 양말은 뒤축이 닳아 얇아졌다 These socks are worn thin at the heels.

▶ 그의 웃옷 소매는 너무 닳아 꿰맬 수 없다 The sleeves of his coat are frayed beyond repair.
▶ 건강에 조심하라고 어머니는 입이 닳도록 말씀하신다 My mother tells me over and over again to take care of my health.
2 〈세상사에〉 be over-sophisticated
▶ 그녀는 어려서부터 워낙 고생을 많이했기 때문에 아주 닳고 닳았다 She has suffered such hardships [has had such a hard time of it] since she was a child that she has become shrewd and sly.
▶ 그녀는 도회지에 살면서 많이 닳았다 She became quite sophisticated through living in town.
3 〈졸아들다〉 be boiled down; get dry
▶ 수프가 닳았다 The soup has boiled down.

닳리다 1 〈해뜨리다〉 wear away [down]; rub off [down]
♦ 구두 뒤축을 닳리다 wear [run] one's shoes down at the heels / 지우개를 닳리다 rub the eraser off / 붓을 뭉툭하게 닳리다 wear a brush to a stump
2 〈졸이다〉 boil down; boil dry
♦ 국물을 닳리다 boil the soup away
3 〈피부를〉 make 《one's cheeks》 flush

담 〈벽돌 등의〉 a wall; a fence
♦ 돌[벽돌] 담 a stone [brick] wall / 흙 담 a mud [an earthen] wall / 담을 쌓다 build [set up] a wall / 담을 두르다 wall in 《a place》; surround 《a house》 with a wall
▶ 그는 집 둘레에 담을 둘렀다 He put [built] a fence around his house.
▶ 그는 담을 두른 집에 살고 있다 He lives in a walled-in house.
▶ 무너져가는 담을 넘어 도둑이 들었다 A thief jumped over the crumbling fence and went into the house.

담 痰 1 〈가래〉 phlegm; sputum 《pl. ~s, -ta》
♦ 피가 섞인 담 bloody phlegm / 담이 생기다 raise [have] phlegm / 담을 뱉다 spit out phlegm; cough out [bring up] phlegm; clear the throat of phlegm
▶ 그는 목에 담이 걸려 기침을 했다 Phlegm caught in his throat and he coughed.
2 〈담병〉 congestion
♦ 담의 congestive / 가슴에 담이 들다 suffer from the breast congestion
■ —약 expectorant (medicine)

담 膽 the gallbladder; 〈담력〉 courage; pluck; grit; nerve ⇨ 담력

-담 -談 a talk; a story; a tale
♦ 모험담 a tale of an adventure; an adventure story / 성공담 a success story / 괴기담 a mystery story / 여행담 an account of one's travels

담갈색 淡褐色 light brown (color)

담그다 1 〈액체 속에〉 soak; steep; dip
▶ 그는 발을 물에 잠깐 담갔다 He dipped his foot into water.
▶ 그녀는 콩을 하룻밤 물에 담가놓았다 She soaked the beans in water overnight.
2 〈음식을〉 ♦ 통째로 담근 무 a radish pickled whole / 김치를 담그다 prepare [make] kimch'i; pickle [salt] vegetables / 술을 담그다 brew [make] rice wine / 젓갈을 담그다 preserve fish with salt
▶ 콩으로 간장을 담근다 Soybean is made into soy.

담금질 〔冶〕 quenching; tempering
—담금질하다 quench; temper
▶ 달군 강철은 담금질한 다음 경화시킨다 We quench hot steel before hardening it.

담기다 1 〈그릇에〉 be filled; be put in; be heaped
♦ 주발에 가득 담긴 밥 a single helping of rice in a bowl / 사과가 가득 담긴 쟁반 a tray with a heap of apples on it; a tray heaped with apples
▶ 이 병에는 얼마나 담길까? How much will this bottle hold?
▶ 이 병에는 2리터가 담긴다 This bottle holds two litters.
▶ 이 병에는 무엇이 담겼지? What is in this bottle?
2 〈포함되다〉 be included
▶ 그의 책에는 그의 초기 논문도 담겨 있다 His book incorporates his earlier essays.
▶ 이 책에는 광범위한 문제가 담겨 있다 This book covers a wide range of topics.
▶ 이 속담에는 적어도 두 가지 뜻이 담겨 있다 This proverb implies at least two things.

담낭 膽囊 〔解〕 the gallbladder; the gall
■ —관 the cystic duct —염 〔醫〕 cholecystitis

담녹색 淡綠色 light [pale] green

담다 1 〈그릇에〉 put in; fill; keep in; 〈음식을〉 serve; dish up [out]; 〈병에〉 bottle
♦ 병에 담은 bottled / 통에 담은 barreled / 반만 담은 half-full / 대야에 더운 물을 담다 pour hot water in [into] the tub / 모자를 통에 담다 put a hat in [into] a box / 귀중품을 곽에 담다 keep one's valuables in a box / 밥을 그릇에 담다 fill rice in a bowl; dish up rice / 밥을 조금만 담아내다 serve small helpings of rice
▶ 그녀는 공기에 밥을 가득 담았다 She filled a bowl with rice. ⇌ She served a bowl full of rice.
▶ 어머니는 쟁반에 밤을 가득 담으셨다 My mother heaped the tray with chestnuts.
2 〈포함시키다〉 put into; include
♦ 그 기획에는 우리의 여러 아이디어가 담겨졌다 All our ideas were incorporated into the project.
3 〈입에〉 speak; say; mouth 《a bad word》
♦ 입에 담지 못할 말 abusive [foulmouthed] language
▶ 그는 입에 담지 못할 말로 나를 욕했다 He jeered at me in filthy words.
▶ 그것은 입에도 담지 못할 이야기다 The story is too odious to tell.

담담하다 淡淡— 1 〈마음이〉 cool; quiet; serene; indifferent
▶ 지금 내 심경은 담담합니다 Now I am in a serene state of mind.
▶ 그는 명성이나 부에는 아주 담담하다 He is quite indifferent to fame and riches.
▶ 그는 담담한 어조로 말했다 He talked in quiet tones.
2 〈물이〉 clear; 〈달빛이〉 bright; 〈맛·색채가〉

light; simple
♦ 담담한 맛[음식] light [plain] taste [food]

담당 擔當 charge; undertaking
▶ 그 학급 담당은 누구입니까? Who is in charge of the class?
▶ 영어 담당은 김선생님입니다 Mr. Kim teaches us English.
—**담당하다** take [assume, have] charge (of); take *sth* in *one's* charge; be in charge of; 〈의사가〉 serve 《a large district》
♦ 국제법을 담당하다 teach international law / 담당시키다 give *sb* charge of; put *sb* in charge of; assign 《*sb* for a new task》/ 한 주에 5시간을 담당케 하다 allot 《a teacher》five hours a week
▶ 이 판매원은 호남 지구를 담당하고 있다 This salesman works [covers] the Honam district.
■ —**검사** the prosecutor in charge —**구역**〈경찰관 등의〉 *one's* round; *one's* beat;〈판매원의〉 *one's* territory;〈배달원의〉 *one's* walk —**시간**〈수업의〉 *one's* class hours —**아나운서** the announcer in charge —**업무[사무]** the business in *one's* charge; *one's* duty —**자** a person in charge (of)

담대하다 膽大— daring; bold; plucky; audacious;〈서술적〉 be a man of pluck

담력 膽力 courage; boldness; nerve; pluck; (口) guts
♦ 담력이 있는 brave; courageous; bold; daring / 담력이 없는 timid; cowardly / 담력을 시험하다 put *one's* courage to the test
▶ 나는 그녀의 담력에 놀랐다 I was surprised at her (daring) pluck.
▶ 그것을 할만한 담력은 내게 없다 I don't have the nerve [have nerve enough] to do that.

담론 談論 discussion; argument; discourse
—**담론하다** discuss; argue; discourse

담박하다 淡泊 1〈음식·색 등이〉light; plain; simple
♦ 담박한 맛 light [plain] taste
▶ 나는 여름에는 담박한 음식이 좋다[을 좋아한다] I prefer light food in summer.
2〈성품이〉frank; openhearted; indifferent
♦ 담박한 사람 an openhearted [a frank] person
▶ 그는 명예나 부에는 담박한 사람이다 He is indifferent to fame or wealth.

담배 tobacco;【植】a tobacco 《*pl.* ~(e)s》;〈엽궐련〉 a cigar;〈권련〉 a cigaret(te)
♦ 독한[순한] 담배 strong [mild] tobacco / 살 썬 담배 cut tobacco / 파이프[쌈지] 담배 pipe tobacco / 잎담배 leaf tobacco / 씹는 담배 chewing tobacco / 필터 달린 담배 a filter (-tipped) cigarette / 담배 한 개비 a cigarette / 담배 한 갑 a pack 《(英) packet》of cigarette / 담배 한 대 a fill [smoke] of tobacco / 담배를 피우지 않는 사람 a non-smoker / 줄담배를 피우는 사람 a chain smoker / 담배를 입에 물고 with a cigarette in *one's* mouth / 담배에 불을 붙이다 light a cigarette / 담배를 권하다 offer *sb* a smoke / 담배를 말다 roll (tobacco into) a cigarette / 담배를 재배하다 cultivate [raise] tobacco / 담배(연기)를 깊이 들이마시다 draw deeply on *one's* cigarette / 담배를 뻐끔뻐끔 피우다 puff at *one's* pipe [cigar, cigarette] / 담배를 몇 모금 빨다 take several pulls on [from] *one's* cigarette
▶ 담배 (한 대) 피우고 싶다 I want to smoke. ⇌ I want to have a smoke [puff].
▶ 그는 성냥을 그어 담배에 불을 붙였다 He struck a match to light (up) a cigarette.
▶ 會話「담배 한 대 어떻습니까?」「괜찮습니다. 나는 담배를 피우지 않습니다」"How about a cigarette?" "No, thank you."
▶ 會話「담배 피워도 됩니까?」「물론이지요」 "May I smoke?" ⇌ "Do you mind if I smoke?" "Yes, of course." ⇌ "No, not at all."
▶ 그는 담배를 너무 피운다 He is a heavy smoker.
▶ 나는 담배를 끊었다 I gave up smoking.
▶ 담배로 목숨을 잃을 수 있습니다 Smoking can kill you.
▶ 담배 연기는 담배를 피우지 않는 사람에게 치명적 폐질환을 유발한다 Tobacco smoke causes fatal lung disease in non-smokers.
■ —**꽁초** a cigarette butt [stub, end];《美俗》a snipe : 담배꽁초를 발로 밟다 crush a cigarette butt under *one's* foot —**물부리** a mouthpiece of a pipe; a cigarette holder —**설대** a pipestem —**쌈지** a tabacco pouch —**연기** tobacco [cigarette] smoke: 담배연기를 내뿜다 blow smoke from *one's* cigarette / 담배연기를 둥글게 뿜어내다 blow a smoke ring into the air **담배 가게** a tobacco shop; a cigar store; 《英》a tobacconist's (shop) **담뱃갑** a cigarette case; a cigar case; a tobacco box

담뱃대 a (tobacco) pipe
♦ 담뱃대를 털다 knock the ashes off *one's* pipe / 담뱃대를 물다 have a pipe in *one's* mouth / 담뱃대에 불을 붙이다[담배를 담다] light [fill] *one's* pipe

담뱃불 a light for *one's* cigarette [pipe]; the light of a cigarette [pipe]
♦ 담뱃불을 빌리다 borrow a light for *one's* cigarette / 담뱃불을 붙이다 light (up) a cigarette / 담뱃불을 붙이려고 성냥을 켜다 strike a match for a cigarette / 담뱃불을 끄다 put [snuff] out *one's* cigarette
▶ 담뱃불 좀 빌립시다 Please give me [Let me have] a light.

담뱃재 cigarette ash
♦ 담뱃재를 털다 flick the ashes from a cigarette; knock the ashes off *one's* pipe

담뱃진 —**津** (tobacco) tar; nicotine
▶ 담뱃대에 담뱃진이 끼어 있다 The pipe is choked with nicotine.

담벼락〈담·벽의 겉표면〉the surface of a wall;〈사람〉a man of dull apprehension; a block; a blockhead
▶ 담벼락하고 말하는 셈이다 (속담) You might as well speak to a stone wall as talk to him.

담보 擔保 (a) security; (a) mortgage; a guarantee; a warrant; a surety; a cover
♦ 담보없이, 무담보로 without security /〈담보를〉담보를 잡다 take security; secure *oneself* from loss / 충분한 담보를 잡고 돈을 빌려주다 lend money on ample [good] security /〈담보로〉담보로 잡히다[넣다] lay [put] to

담불 pledge; give [offer] as a security [in security] (for); put up as security; mortgage / 토지를 담보로 잡히다 mortgage land; offer land as a security / 담보로 잡다 receive [take] *sth* as security / 집을 담보로 돈을 빌리다 borrow money on (the security of) *one's* house ▶ 나는 담보[무담보]로 돈을 빌렸다 I borrowed money on [without] security.
■ 대물— impersonal security 대인— personal security 이중— a double mortgage: 우리 집은 이중담보로 잡혀 있다 Our house is under double mortgage. 제일— the underlying mortgage ■—계약 a warranty —권 a security right; a hypothec —대출 loan on [against] security —물 a security; 〈근저당〉 (a) collateral (security) —물권 real rights granted by way of security —부 사채(社債)[채권] a mortgage debenture [bond] —인 a guarantor; a voucher —증서 a warranty deed

담불 〈곡식 무더기〉 a pile [heap] of corn [cereals]

담비 〈動〉 a marten; a Korean sable
■ 검은— a sable 흰— an ermine ■—가죽 marten; sable

담뿍(이) plenty ⇨ 듬뿍(이)

담석 膽石 〈醫〉 a gallstone; a biliary calculus; a cholelith ■—증 cholelithiasis

담세 擔稅 bearing tax
■—능력 tax-bearing capacity; taxpaying ability —자 〈英〉 a ratepayer; a taxpayer

담소 談笑 a chat; chatting; a familiar [friendly] talk; a confabulation
—담소하다 talk pleasantly 《with》; chat 《with》; have a pleasant chat 《with》; confabulate 《with》
▶ 옛 친구와 담소하는 것만큼 유쾌한 일은 없다 Nothing is pleasanter than having a lively talk with an old friend.
▶ 문제는 담소하는 동안 해결되었다 The question was settled during a friendly talk.
▶ 그들은 잠시 담소했다 They enjoyed [had] a pleasant [friendly] chat with each other for a while.

담수 淡水 〈민물〉 fresh water
◆ 염수를 담수로 만들다 turn salt water into fresh water ■—어[호] a fresh-water fish [lake]

담요 毯— a blanket; a rug
▶ 나는 담요를 뒤집어 쓰고 잤다 I slept wrapped in a blanket.
▶ 그녀는 아기에게 담요를 덮어 주었다 She laid a blanket over her baby.

담임 擔任 charge; responsibility
▶ 이 학급의 담임은 누구입니까? Who is taking [in] charge of this class? ⇒ Who teaches this class?
—담임하다 take [be in] charge of
■ 학급— a class [homeroom] under *one's* charge ■—교사 a teacher in charge (of a class); a homeroom teacher

담자색 淡紫色 light purple

담쟁이(덩굴) 〈植〉 (an) ivy
◆ 담쟁이덩굴에 휘감긴 건물[벽] an ivied [ivy-mantled, ivy-covered] building [wall]

담즙 膽汁 〈쓸개즙〉〈生理〉 bile; gall; choler
◆ 담즙의 bilious; biliary
■—병 biliousness; a bilious complaint —산 bile acid —질 (a man of) choleric [bilious] temperament

담차다 膽— bold; daring; plucky; full of courage [pluck]
◆ 담찬 계획 a bold [daring] attempt [plan] / 담찬 등산가 an adventurous climber / 담차게 사태에 직면하다 face a situation fearlessly

담채 淡彩 〈엷은 채색〉 light [thin] coloring; weak coloring
◆ 담채를 하다 apply thin coloring 《to》
▶ 그는 묵화에 담채를 했다 He applied thin coloring to the Indian-ink drawing.
■—화 a wash drawing; a drawing in ink and wash; a light-colored picture

담청색 淡靑色 light [pale] blue
◆ 담청색의 light-[pale-]blue

담판 談判 negotiations; a parley
▶ 담판은 결렬되었다 The negotiations have broken down.
—담판하다 negotiate [discuss] 《with》; have talks 《with》
▶ 우리는 그 문제에 대해 그들과 담판했다 We talked over the matter with them. ⇒ We had a meeting with them to discuss the matter.

담합 談合 consultation; (a) conference; 〈입찰에서〉 artful prebidding arrangement
◆ 담합에 의해 by mutual consent
—담합하다 consult [confer] with; hold a conference [consultations] 《on》
◆ 입찰에 관해 담합하다 confer on the bidding
▶ 그들은 무언가 담합하려고 하는 것 같다 They seem to be trying to reach some kind of arrangement.

담홍색 淡紅色 pink; rose pink; pale rose-color; salmon pink [red]
◆ 담홍색의 pink; rose-colored; salmon-pink
▶ 그녀의 뺨은 맥주를 마신 탓으로 담홍색이 되었다 Her cheeks are slightly flush with beer.

담화 談話 (a) talk; (a) conversation
◆ 노변 담화 a fireside talk [chat]
▶ 교섭 경과는 수상에 의해 담화 형식으로 발표되었다 The outcome of the negotiations was aired [given out] by the Prime Minister in the form of an informal talk.
▶ 아버지께서는 지금 손님과 담화 중이시다 My father is now talking with a visitor.
■—체 a conversational [colloquial] style

담황색 淡黃色 straw color; light [pale, lemon] yellow; citrine
◆ 담황색의 citrine; light-[lemon-]yellow

답 答 〈대답〉 (give) an answer; (give, make) a reply; 〈반응〉 (make) a response; a rejoinder; 〈해답〉 an answer (to); a solution (to)
◆ 분명한[종잡을 수 없는] 답을 하다 give a definite [ambiguous] answer (to a question) / 답을 내다 get [work out] an answer [a solution]; find an answer (to a question) / …이라는 답이 나오다 we have…for the answer
▶ 몇 번이나 문을 두드렸지만 답이 없었다 I knocked at the door again and again but there was no response. ⇒ I knocked and

knocked but no one came to answer the door.
▶그것은 답이 되지 못한다 That is not quite the answer.
▶너의 답이 옳다[틀리다] Your answer is right [wrong]. ⇌ Your answer is correct [incorrect].
▶이 문제의 답은 다음 페이지에 있습니다 The answer to this question [solution to this problem] is on the next page.
—답하다 answer; reply; solve
◆질문[편지]에 답하다 answer [reply to] a question [a letter]

-답다 like; becoming to; worthy of; -ly; -like
◆꽃다운 소녀 a flower-like girl; a girl as lovely as a flower / 신사다운 행동 gentlemanly conduct / 학생답지 않은 행실 a conduct unbecoming to [unworthy of] a student / 숙녀다운 ladylike / 신사다운 gentlemanly / 숙녀다운 태도로 in a ladylike manner / 신사[남자]답게 행동하다 behave like a gentleman [man]
▶그는 남자다운 사람이다 He is a masculine type.
▶과연 그 사람답다 It is really worthy of him.
▶거짓말을 하다니 너답지 않다 It isn't like you to tell a lie.
▶그는 정말로 학자다운 학자다 He is truly worthy of the term "scholar."
▶날씨가 제법 봄다워졌다 The weather has become very springlike.
▶이 도시에는 극장다운 극장이 없다 There is no theater worthy of the name [to speak of, worth mentioning] in this town.
▶그는 군인답게 죽었다 He died like the soldier that he was.
▶학생이면 학생답게 행동해라 If you are a student, behave like one.
▶그런 짓은 숙녀답지 않다 That's quite an unladylike thing to do.

답답하다 沓沓— 1 〈숨이〉 stuffy; suffocating; choking; stifling; close; 〈옷 등이〉 tight 《coat》; 〈가슴이〉 《feel》 oppressed; heavy
◆답답한 분위기 an oppressive atmosphere / 답답한 느낌 a choking sensation / 답답한 느낌이 들다 feel chokey [suffocating] / 비좁아 답답하다 〈장소가 주어〉 be too cramped for comfort; 〈사람이 주어〉 feel cramped in a confined space / 가슴이 답답하다 have a heavy feeling [feel heavy] in one's [the] chest; feel a pressure on one's chest / 답답한 가슴 속을 풀다 divert one's mind from one's cares; drive away [dispel] one's gloom
▶걱정 때문에 그들은 가슴이 답답했다 Cares weighed heavily upon them.
▶이런 집에 4인 가족이 살기에는 좀 답답하다 This house is a little too small for a family of four (to live in).
▶회의 분위기는 답답했다 The meeting was enveloped in an oppressive atmosphere.
▶방안이 너무 답답하다. 창문 좀 열자 The room is too stuffy. Let's open the windows.
2 〈사람됨이〉 hidebound; unadaptable; straitlaced; drawling; slow (going); sluggish
◆답답한 사고 방식 a narrow [rigid] view of things / 답답한 사람 an unadaptable [intolerant, illiberal] man; a man of no resources / 말을 답답하게 하다 drawl; speak with a drawl
▶답답한 생각을 버리지 않으면 시대에 뒤떨어질 것이다 You will find yourself behind the times if you stick to such a narrow view of things.
3 〈속답다〉 《feel》 impatient; irritating; irritable; restless; anxious; uneasy
▶시간이 참 답답하게도 가지 않는 구나 How slow the time passes!
▶그의 느린 말투 때문에 답답하기 짝이 없었다 I got irritated by his slow speech.
▶그는 답답해서 우리 말에 끼어들었다 He grew impatient and interrupted us.
▶그에게서 소식이 없어 답답하신가보군요 Something is fretting you. Can it be his long silence?
▶그녀는 답답해서 사전을 쭉 훑어 보았다 She impatiently leafed through the dictionary.
▶우리는 하고 싶은 말을 할 수 없기 때문에 답답하다 We are [feel] irritated and impatient because we cannot say what we want to say.

답례 答禮 a return call; 〈선물〉 a return present
▶선물의 답례로 그에게 무엇을 주면 좋을까? I wonder what I should give the man in return for his present.
▶너는 그녀에게 어떤 식으로든 답례를 해야 한다 You should make her some present or other in return.

답배 答— a reply [an answer] to (a letter from) one's inferior
—답배하다 answer [reply to] a letter from one's inferior

답변 答辯 〈대답〉 a reply; an answer; 〈변명〉 an explanation; 〈피고의〉 a defense; a plea
◆답변의 책임 answerability / …에 대한 답변으로 in answer to… / 답변에 궁하다 be at a loss for an answer [explanation] / 답변을 요구하다 call sb to account; demand an explanation of sb / 답변을 잘하다 be clever in reply
▶난 답변을 할 수가 없었다 I didn't know what explanation to make.
—답변하다 reply; answer; make a reply; make (an) answer; give an answer; 〈변호하다〉 defend [explain] oneself
◆총리를 대신하여 답변하다 reply for the Prime Minister
▶저는 당신 질문에 답변할 처지가 못됩니다 I am not in a position to answer your question.
▶뭐라고 답변하겠느냐? What have you to say to that?
■—서 a written answer [reply, refutation]; 〈피고의〉 《present》 a defense —자 an answerer; a pleader

답보 踏步 stepping; stamping; 〈정체〉 a stalemate; a standstill
◆답보 상태에 있다 be at a standstill; be in a stalemate
▶경기는 앞으로 답보 상태가 될 것 같다 I'm afraid the market will be a standstill in the future.
—답보하다 step; stamp; 〈정체하다〉 come to a standstill

답사 答辭 an address in reply; a (formal) reply; 〈졸업식의〉 《美》 a valedictory
♦답사를 하다 read the reply; read a prepared address in reply
▶그는 졸업생을 대표해서 답사를 했다 He delivered the valedictory [made the farewell speech] representing all the graduating students.
—**답사하다** make a formal reply (to the congratulatory address); 〈졸업식에서〉 《美》 deliver a valedictory

답사 踏査 a survey; 〈탐험〉 (an) exploration; 〈실지조사〉 a field investigation; 〈측량〉 〔土〕 reconnaissance
—**답사하다** survey; make a survey of; investigate; 〈광산의 가망성을〉 prospect; explore
♦현지 답사하다 make an on-the-spot survey [a field investigation] / 고적을 답사하다 explore a historic site
▶학생들은 사적을 현지 답사했다 The students made a field investigation of the historic scene.

답습 踏襲 following (a former policy)
—**답습하다** follow in the steps of *sb*; follow; follow suit; 〈모방하다〉 imitate

답신 答申 a report; 〈배심원의〉 the reply [return] (of the jury)
—**답신하다** report; submit a report (to a minister); report (back) the findings (of the committee) to (the Prime Minister); 〈배심원이〉 return (*sb* guilty)
▶심의회는 그 문제에 대해 총리에게 답신했다 The council reported [submitted a report] on the issue to the Prime Minister.
■—**서** a report (of an inquiry); a finding
—**안** a draft report; the draft of a report

답신 答信 a reply; an answer; 〈전신의〉 a reply telegram
♦답신료로 600원 짜리 우표를 동봉하다 enclose a six-hundred-won stamp for return postage
—**답신하다** reply to [answer] a letter; send a reply (telegram) (to)

답안 答案 〈해답〉 an answer; a paper; 〈답안지〉 an examination [exam] paper
♦백지 답안 a blank paper / 수학 답안 a paper in mathematics / 훌륭한 답안 a good paper / 답안을 채점하다 grade [mark] examination papers
▶나는 벌써 답안지를 냈다 I have already handed in my paper.

답장 答狀 an answer; a (written) reply; a reply letter
▶한달 전에 그에게 편지를 냈는데 아직 답장이 없다 I wrote to him a month ago, but I haven't heard from him yet.
▶나는 곧 답장을 쓰겠다 I'll write an answer right away.
▶이 편지에는 답장을 하지 않겠다 I'll leave this letter unanswered.
♦답장을 기다리겠습니다 I am looking forward to hearing from you [your reply].
—**답장하다** answer [reply to] a letter
▶즉시 답장해 주십시오 Please answer my letter by return of mail.

답전 答電 a reply telegram [cable, telex, wire]; an answer to a telegram
▶나는 승낙하는 답전을 쳤다 I cabled (back) my consent [agreement, acceptance].
—**답전하다** answer [reply to] a telegram; wire [telegraph] back; reply by cable [telex, telegram]

답지하다 遝至— 〈몰려들다〉 rush in; flood in; come with a rush; rush to (a place); be flooded with; come pouring in
♦신청이 답지하다 be flooded with applications
▶전국에서 항의 편지가 답지했다 Letters of complaint poured [flooded] in from all over the country.
▶모피 코트 주문이 답지하고 있다 There is a rush [a flood of orders] for fur coats.

답치기 ♦답치기 놓다 act thoughtlessly [rashly, recklessly, blindly, on impulse]; go it blind

답파 踏破 traveling on foot
—**답파하다** traverse; travel on foot; tramp
♦산꼭대기를 답파하다 surmount [scale] the summit (of a mountain) / 사막을 답파하다 traverse a desert
▶일행은 전국을 답파했다 The party traveled through the country on foot.

닷 five (⇨ 다섯) ♦닷 되[말] five *doe* [*mal*]

닷곱 five *hob*; half a *doe*

닷새 〈5일간〉 five days; 〈초닷샛날〉 the fifth day (of a month)

당 唐 〔史〕 Tang (618-907)
♦당대 the Tang age

당 黨 〈정당〉 a (political) party; 〈파벌〉 a faction; 〈집단〉 a group; 〈도당〉 a clique; 〈동맹〉 a league
♦공화당 《美》 the Republican party / 민주당 《美》 the Democratic party / 전당대회 《美》 (hold) a party convention; 《英》 a party conference / 당 중진 leaders of a party / 당출신의 시장 a mayor of party extraction / 당규 party regulations [rules] / 당내 파벌 an intraparty faction / 당의 방침에 따르다 toe the party line / 당을 해산하다 dissolve the party / 당을 조직하다 form a party [faction] / 당을 탈퇴하다 leave [secede from, quit] the party / 당을 대표[재 정비]하다 represent [realign] a party / 당에 가입하다 join [enter] a party
▶그 당의 정책은 자유주의다 The party line is liberal.
▶그는 공화당의 공천 후보자다 He is on the Republican ticket.

당- 當 〈이〉 this; 〈그〉 that; the said; 〈현재의〉 the present; 〈문제의〉 in question; at issue
♦당(년) 20세 twenty years old (at the time) / 당자 the said person; the person concerned / 당대학에서는 at our [this] university / 당연구소의 연구원들 research fellows affiliated with this institute
▶당자는 아무것도 몰랐다 He himself [The person directly concerned] knew nothing about it.

-당 -當 per...; a; the; (for) each; apiece (▶ per는 상용어로, 일반적으로 《美》에서는 a, 《英》

에서는 the를 쓰는 경향이 있음)
♦ 일[연]당 per diem [annum] / 인구 1인당 per head of population / 일당 50,000원 fifty thousand won a [per] day / 개당 1,000원 one thousand won apiece
▶ 회비는 1인당 5,000원이다 The fee is five thousand won per person.
▶ 보수는 한 시간당 2달러로 한다 The pay will be two dollars an hour.
▶ 이 차는 1갤런당 35마일을 달린다 This car runs 35 miles per gallon.
▶ 그 멜론은 한 개당 5,000원 했다 The melons cost five thousand won apiece.

당고하다 當故— lose *one's* parent; go into [take to, put on] mourning *one's* parent

당과 糖菓 sweetmeats; bonbon; confection; (美) candy; (英) sweets ■—류 confectionery

당구 撞球 《play》 billiards; (英俗) pills; 〈돈내기〉 pool
♦ 당구치는 사람 a billiardist; a billiard player / 당구치다 play (at) billiards; have a game of billiards / 당구에서 이기다[지다] win [lose] a game of billiards
▶ 당구를 칩시다 Let's play billiards.
■—공 a billiard ball —대 a billiard table —장 a billiard room [saloon, hall]; (美) a poolroom —채[큐] a (billiard) cue

당국(자) 當局(者) the authorities (concerned); the competent authorities; a person in authority [power]
♦ 미국 정부 당국자 a U.S. authority / 당국의 지시에 따라 by order of the authorities (concerned) / 당국의 허가를 얻다 obtain the sanction of the authorities / 당국에 진정하다 petition [make an appeal to] the authorities
▶ 관계 당국과 접촉하겠다 I will contact the authorities concerned.
▶ 당국에 신고했습니까? Did you notify the authorities concerned?
■경찰— the police authorities 군[시]— the military [municipal] authorities 군수사— the Army investigation authorities 정부— the Government authorities 학교— the school authorities [administration]

당권 黨權 party hegemony
■—싸움 a strife for party hegemony

당규 黨規 the party regulations [rules]; the regulations of a party

당근 〔植〕 a carrot

당기 黨紀 〈당의 규율〉 party discipline
♦ 당기를 문란하게 하다[숙정하다] break [enforce] party discipline
■—위반[문란] a breach [the degradation] of party discipline

당기 當期 this [the current, the present] term [period]
■—결산 the settlement of accounts for this term —배당 the dividend for [of] this term —손익 the profits and losses for this term —순(이)익 the net income

당기다¹ 1〈끌다〉 draw; 〈자기 쪽으로〉 pull; haul; 〈세게〉 tug; 〈무거운 것을〉 drag; 〈갑자기〉 jerk
♦ 그물을 당기다 draw a net / 밧줄을 당기다 pull [tug] at a rope / 방아쇠를 당기다 pull a trigger; trigger 《a rifle》 / 커튼을 당기다[치다, 닫다] draw a curtain / 고삐를 꽉 당기다 jerk reins / 난롯가로 의자를 당기다 draw a chair up to the fire
▶ 그의 소매를 당겨라 Pull him by the sleeve. ⇌ Pull [Tug] at his sleeve.
▶ 화재시에는 이 레버를 당기시오 Pull this lever in case of fire.
▶ 너무 팽팽하게 당기면 끊어진다 If you strain it too hard, it will break.
▶ 자석은 쇠를 당긴다 A magnet attracts iron.
2〈시간·날짜를〉 advance; move [carry] 《a day》 up [forward]
▶ 그는 일정을 당겨서 돌아왔다 He came back earlier than scheduled.
▶ 그들은 결혼식(날짜)를 6월 5일에서 5월 5일로 당겼다 They advanced [moved up] (the date of) the wedding from June 5 to May 5.

당기다² 〈입맛이〉 stimulate [whet, tempt] 《*one's* appetite》; be stimulated
♦ 식욕이 당기는 음식 an appetizing food / 구미가 당기는 지위 a tempting post
▶ 운동을 했더니 식욕이 당겼다 Exercise gave me a good appetite.

당나귀 唐— an ass; a donkey (➤ 일상어로는 보통 donkey를 씀) ♦ 수탕나귀 a male ass; a jackass / 암탕나귀 a jenny donkey; a jennet

당내 黨內 ♦ 당내의 알력 an intraparty conflict [trouble, strife] / 당내의 intraparty / 당내의 사정으로 for intraparty reasons [considerations] / 당내의 의견을 통일하다 reach a consensus inside [within] the party

당년 當年 〈금년〉 this [the current] year; 〈그 연대〉 that year; those years
▶ 그녀는 당년 30세다 She is thirty years old now.
▶ 그는 당년 20세의 대학생이다 He is a college student, twenty years old this year.
■—치 products of the year; the year's growth —치기 goods which last only one year; the year's wear

당뇨 糖尿 glycosuria; glucosuria

당뇨병 糖尿病 〔醫〕 diabetes [dàiəbíːtiːz, -təs]; sugar diabetes
♦ 당뇨병 증세 diabetic symptoms / 당뇨병의 diabetic / 당뇨병에 걸리다 suffer from diabetes; be diabetic
■—환자 a diabetic

당닭 唐— 〔鳥〕 a bantam; 〈사람〉 a humpty-dumpty

당당하다 堂堂 1〈웅대한〉 grand; 〈위압하는 듯한〉 imposing; 〈위엄이 있는〉 stately; dignified
♦ 당당한 대저택 a grand [an imposing, a stately] mansion / 당당한 체격 a splendid physique / 풍채가 당당한 사람 a man of commanding presence / 보무가 당당하다 march [advance] in fine array
2〈정정당당하다〉 fair; square; open
♦ 당당한 권리 a lawful right / 당당한 승부 fair play

당당히 堂堂 1〈멋지게〉 grandly; 〈위엄있게〉 majestically; in a dignified style

▶ 한국 선수단은 당당히 행진하며 입장했다 The Korean players marched grandly into the field.
2 〈용감히〉 bravely; boldly; 〈정정당당하게〉 fair (and square); 〈자신있게〉 confidently; 〈공공연히〉 openly
♦ 당당히 싸우다 play fair / 당당히 싸워 이기다 play fair and win a game
▶ 당당히 자기 의견을 내세워라 Express your opinion confidently.
▶ 그는 당당히 적과 싸웠다 He fought the enemy bravely.
▶ 그들은 당당히 싸웠다 They fought fair in the battle. ⇌ They played fair.

당대 當代 1 〈한평생〉 one's whole life; one's lifetime
♦ 당대에 이룩한 그의 업적 his lifetime achievements / 당대에 부자가 되다 get rich in one's own lifetime
2 〈이 시대〉 the present age
♦ 당대의 작가들 contemporary writers; writers of the day / 당대의 present; contemporary; of the present age; of the day

당도 當到 coming; arrival
—**당도하다** come (upon); arrive 《at, in》; get to; 〈목적지에〉 reach; 〈기회가〉 offer [present] itself; occur
♦ 목전에 당도한 재난 a pressing [an impending] disaster
▶ 때가 당도했다 The time has [is] come.

당돌하다 唐突— 1 〈다부지다〉 bold; daring
▶ 나이는 젊지만 그는 아주 당돌하다 Though young, he is quite a daring guy.
2 〈무례하다〉 rude; abrupt; blunt
♦ 당돌한 태도 rude manners
▶ 그는 당돌하게도 내게 그런 질문을 했다 He was rude enough to ask me such a question as this.

당두하다 當頭— draw near; be near [close] at hand ⇨ 박두하다
▶ 여름이 당두하고 있었다 Summer was drawing near. ⇌ It was almost summer.
▶ 시험이 당두하고 있다 Examinations are close at hand.

당락 當落 one's electoral fortunes; the result of an election; success or failure in an election
♦ 당락의 가능성은 반반이다 have only a fifty-fifty chance of success in the election
▶ 그는 당락 선상에 있다 He has a fifty-fifty chance of being elected.
▶ 아직 당락이 판명되지 않은 후보가 많다 There are many candidates whose success or failure in the election is not yet known.
▶ 당락은 언제 알 수 있느냐? When will the results of the election be known?

당략 黨略 the policy of a party; a party policy; party politics
♦ 당략상 as a matter of party policy

당량 當量 〔化〕 an equivalent; an equivalence
■ 화학— a chemical equivalent

당론 黨論 the view [platform] of a party; a party opinion
▶ 이 점에 관해서는 당론이 구구하다 Party opinions vary [differ] on this point. ⇌ Party opinions are divided on this point.
▶ 당론은 정부에 찬성하는 방향으로 기울어져 있다 The platform of the party is favorable for the Government.

당류 糖類 sugars; 〔化〕 saccharide

당리 黨利 the party interests; partisan politics
♦ 당리 당략에 치우치다 put party interests first; be too much swayed by the party interests / 당리 당략에 전념하다 play partisan [party] politics / 당리를 도모하다 promote [advance] the party interests

당면 當面 facing
♦ 우리나라의 당면 문제 the problems with which our country is confronted [faced]
—**당면하다** face; confront
♦ 당면한 문제 the present problem; an urgent [a pressing, a present, an immediate] problem; the matter [question] at hand / 당면한 급선무 the most urgent task; immediate [pressing] necessity / 당면한 present; pressing; immediate; urgent / 당면한 목적을 달성하기 위하여 to serve a present object
▶ 당면한 필요를 충족시키는데는 그것으로 충분하다 That's enough to meet the immediate [pressing] need.

당면 唐麵 Chinese noodles

당명 黨命 an order of a party; a party order [policy]
♦ 당명을 어기다 act against a party policy

당목 唐木 Chinese cotton goods; cotton (cloth)

당무 黨務 party affairs
■—위원 an executive member of a party
—회의 the executive committee of a party; 〈모임〉 an executive committee meeting of a party

당밀 糖蜜 theriac; 〈순수한〉 syrup; 〈순도가 다소 낮은〉 golden syrup; 《美》 molasses (▶단수 취급); 《英》 treacle

당방 當方 〈우리들〉 I; we; 〈우리쪽〉 our party
♦ 당방의 실수 my error; an oversight on our part / 당방의 my; our; on my [our] part
▶ 당방의 실수로 연락을 취할 수가 없었다 Through a slipup on our part, we were unable to contact them.

당번 〈근무〉 being on duty; 〈보초〉 being on guard [watch]; 〈근무자〉 sb on duty ▶ 누가 오늘밤 당번이냐? Who is on duty tonight?

당부 付 〈부탁〉 a request; an entreaty
▶ 나는 당신의 당부를 받고 그렇게 했습니다 I did so at your request.
—**당부하다** ask [request, tell, solicit, beg] sb to do sth; make a request 《for》
♦ 재산 관리를 친구에게 당부하다 entrust a friend with the care of one's property / 뒤처리를 해달라고 당부하다 ask sb to take care of [settle] the matter [problem]/ 신신 당부하다 request earnestly; make an earnest request (to sb for sth)
▶ 자네에게 당부할 일이 있네 I ask you a (big) favor. ⇌ May I ask you a (big) favor?
▶ 여러분에게 당부하고 싶은 말은 그것을 비밀로 해달라는 것이오 What I request of you is

that you should keep it secret.
▶ 그에게 그렇게 하도록 당부했다 I asked him to do that.
▶ 만사 실수가 없기를 당부한다 Make sure [See (to it)] that nothing is amiss.
▶ 나는 그에게 편지를 전해달라고 당부했다 I asked him to deliver a letter.

당분 糖分 (the amount of) sugar; sugar content
♦ 당분이 많은 음식 sugar-rich foods / 당분이 적은 포도 grapes low in sugar / 당분의 saccharic; saccharine / 당분을 함유한 sugary; saccharated / 당분을 함유하다 contain sugar / 소변의 당분 검사를 받다 have one's urine examined for sugar
▶ 너는 너무 많은 당분을 섭취한다 You take too much sugar.
▶ 의사는 내게 당분 섭취량을 줄이라고 말했다 The doctor told me to cut down on my sugar intake.
▶ 너는 당분을 함유한 음식을 삼가는 것이 좋다 You may as well be moderate in eating sugary food.

당분간 當分間 for the time being
▶ 나는 당분간 여기에 있을 작정이다 I'll stay here for some time.
▶ 당분간 뵙지 못하겠습니다 Good-by for the present.
▶ 나는 당분간 호텔에서 지내지 않으면 안된다 I have to live at a hotel for the time being.

당비 黨費 party expenditure [expenses]; 〈당원이 부담하는〉 a party membership fee

당사 當社 〈이 회사〉 the firm [company]; 〈우리 회사〉 our company [firm]
♦ 당사 제품 our company's products; the products of our company

당사 黨舍 the headquarters of a party
당사국 當事國 the country concerned
당사자 當事者 the person [party] concerned [interested]; the said person; an interested party; 〈소송의〉 a party (to a suit)
▶ 그들은 그 소송 사건의 당사자였다 They were the parties to the lawsuit.
■ 결혼— the contracting parties in a marriage 소송— a party to a suit ■ 일동 all concerned

당선 當選 〈선거에서의〉 one's election (to); success in (an) election; 〈현상(懸賞) 등에서의〉 winning a prize
♦ 당선의 가망이 있다 have a (good) chance of winning [be likely to win] the election
▶ 그의 대통령 당선은 확실하다 He will surely be elected as [to be] president.
—**당선하다** 〈선거에서〉 be elected; win an election; 〈현상 등에서〉 win a prize
▶ 그는 국회의원으로 당선되었다 He was elected to the National Assembly.
▶ 그는 최고 득표로 당선되었다 He was returned at the head of the poll.
▶ 그녀는 현상 논문에서 1등으로 당선됐다 She won (the) first prize in an essay contest.
■ —자 〈선거의〉 a successful candidate; 〈현상 등의〉 a prize winner

당세 當世 the present time [day, age]; the day; the time
♦ 당세의 젊은이들 the young people of today; present-day youths / 당세의 up-to-date; present
▶ 이것이 당세 유행하는 옷이다 This is the latest style.

당세 黨勢 party power; the strength [size] of a party; party influence
♦ 당세를 확장하다 expand the strength [extend the prestige] of a party; enhance the party prestige

당수 黨首 the leader [chief, head] of a political party; a party's chief; a party leader
■ —회담 a party leaders' talk; a meeting of the heads of the various parties

당숙 堂叔 a male cousin of one's father=종숙(從叔)

당시 唐詩 poems of Tang period; Tang poetry
당시 當時 in those days [times]; at the [that] time; time
♦ 당시의 여론 the then current opinion / 당시 교장선생님 the then principal of the school / 당시의 then; of those days [times]; at that time
▶ 당시 나는 아이였다 I was a child then [at the time, in those days].
▶ 당시의 과학자들은 그것이 무엇인지 알 수 없었다 The scientists of those days couldn't understand what it was.
▶ 그가 당시의 대통령이었다 He was the then President.
▶ 내가 태어났을 당시는 텔레비전이 없었다 TV didn't exist at that time I was born.
▶ 그 당시 그는 아직 학생이었다 He was still at school then [at that time].

당신 當身 **1** 〈2인칭〉 you; 〈부부·연인 사이의〉 (my) dear; (my) darling
♦ 당신의 your (friend); (a friend) of you / 당신들 둘 다 both of you
▶ 실례합니다만, 당신이 이것을 잃지 않으셨나요? Excuse me, sir, don't you lose this?
▶ 당신, 저 흰 모자를 쓴 여자는 누구예요? My darling, who is the lady wearing that white hat?
▶ 당신, 좀 와서 도와주지 않겠어요? Won't you come and help me, dear [darling, honey]?
▶ 그녀가 그 신임을 받을 만하다는 것은 당신 자신이 알고 있소 You yourself know that she deserves the credit.
2 〈그 어른〉 he; she; himself; herself

당야 當夜 〈그날밤〉 the [that] night; the same [very] night

당연하다 當然— 〈공정하다〉 proper; right; just; fair; 〈합당하다〉 justifiable; reasonable; 〈자연스럽다〉 natural
♦ 태만의 당연한 결과 the natural result [consequence] of negligence
▶ 그것은 당연하다 It is a matter of course.
▶ 우리는 언론의 자유를 당연한 것으로 알고 있다 We take freedom of speech for granted [as a matter of course].
▶ 그는 당연한 보응을 받았다 He got what he deserved. ⇌ It served him right.
▶ 부모가 자녀를 기르는 것은 당연하다 It is

natural for parents to bring up [raise] their child.
▶ 그가 화내는 것은 당연하다 It is natural that he should be [get] angry.
▶ 자네가 그런 말을 하는 것도 당연해 You may well say that.
▶ 그가 실패한 것은 당연해 It is no wonder that he failed.

당연히 當然— of course; no wonder; no doubt; justly; properly; naturally; rightly
♦ 당연히 가야 할 길 the proper [natural] way to go
▶ 그가 당연히 받아야 할 벌이다 He deserves the punishment. ⇒ It serves him right.

당원 黨員 a member of a party; a party man [member]; a partisan
♦ 당원이 되다 join a party; affiliate *oneself* with [to] a party
■ —명부 a list of the party members

당월 當月 〈이달〉 this [the current] month; 〈그달〉 that month
♦ 당월 10일 the tenth instant [inst.] / 당월호 잡지 the current issue of the magazine
▶ 나는 그것을 당월 중에 끝마치겠다 I will finish it this month [within the month].

당위 當爲 〔哲〕 what should be; what *one* should do

당의 糖衣 sugar coating
♦ 환약에 당의를 입히다 sugarcoat a pill —정(錠) a sugarcoated pill [tablet]

당의 黨議 〈강령〉 a party policy; 〈결의〉 a party decision; 〈회의〉 a party council [conference]
♦ 당의로 결정되다 be decided at a party council / 당의에 자문하다 bring 《a matter》 before a party council

당일 當日 〈그날〉 that day; 〈바로 그날〉 the very day 《of》; 〈정해진 날〉 the appointed day
♦ 당일표 a ticket sold on the day 《of performance》; (英) a day ticket
▶ 이 표는 발행 당일만 유효합니다 This ticket is valid [good] only for day of issue. ⇒ Valid [Good] for the day of issue only.

당일치기 當日— ♦ 당일치기 여행 a day's trip / 당일치기 일 a day's work / 당일치기로 same in a day
▶ 그는 당일치기로 영어 시험 공부를 했다 He crammed for an English examination.

당자 當者 the person [man] himself; the person concerned [in question] ⇨ 당사자
▶ 당자는 (그것을) 전혀 모르고 있네 He himself has no idea (of it), you see.

당장 當場 ♦ 당장의 필수품 immediate needs [requirements] / 당장의 present; immediate; temporary; current / 당장은 for the time being; for the present; temporarily
▶ 당장은 그것으로 족할 것이다 That will do for the present.
▶ 당장의 비용은 이것으로 족하다 This will take care of [cover] our immediate expenses [our expenses for the moment].
▶ 우리는 당장 먹고 사는데는 곤란을 받지 않았다 We had enough to live on for the time being.
▶ 당장 잔금을 치르시오 Pay (me) the balance this very moment.

당쟁 黨爭 party strife [rivalry]; faction
♦ 당쟁을 일삼다 be given to party squabbles / 당쟁에 초연하다 keep clear of [stand aloof from] party strife

당적 黨籍 the party register
♦ 당적을 박탈하다 expel *sb* from the party; strike 《*sb's* name》 off the party register / 당적을 옮기다 come [go] over to another party / 당적을 떠나다 disaffiliate *oneself* from *one's* party
■ —증명서 a certificate of party membership

당점 當店 〈이 상점〉 this [our] store [shop]
♦ 당점이 자랑하는 요리 our speciality; the chef's specials

당조짐하다 exercise rigid [strict] control 《over》; control *sth* [*sb*] strictly; crack down on 《gamblers》; keep *sb* under strict control; exercise close supervision 《over》

당좌 當座 a checking account [deposit] ⇨ 당좌예금
♦ 은행에 당좌를 트다 (美) open a banking [bank] account; open a current account with a bank
■ —계정 a current account (略 C/A) —대부 a loan on short notice; an on-the-spot loan; a cash credit —대부금 a call loan —대월 (an) overdraft; an overdrawn account —수표 (美) a check; (英) a cheque

당좌 예금 當座預金 a checking account [deposit]

당지 當地 this place [city, town, country]; these parts; here
♦ 당지에서는 here; in this place
▶ 당지에 오시면 꼭 들러주십시오 Please drop in when you happen to come to our town.

당지기 堂— the janitor of a private school [a temple]; a shrine keeper

당직 當直 duty; watch
♦ 당직을 교대하다 relieve the watch / 당직을 인계하다[인수하다] hand [take] over a duty
▶ 나는 오늘 저녁 당직이다 I am on duty tonight.
—당직하다 be [go] on (night) duty; carry on duty; 〈선원이〉 keep watch
▶ 어제 나는 당직했다 I was on (duty) yesterday.
■ —사관 〈상선의〉 an officer on watch [duty]; a duty [watch] officer —수당 night duty pay —의사 a duty doctor —자 a person [an official] on duty; a duty man —장교 an orderly [a duty] officer; an officer of the day [guard]; 〈해군의〉 a watch officer

당직 黨職 a party post
■ —개편 reorganization of a party's hierarchy —자 a party executive; an executive staff member of a party

당질 堂姪 a son of a male cousin ⇨ 종질(從姪)

당집 堂— 〈신전〉 a temple; a shrine; 〈모이는 곳〉 a hall

당차다 short but stout; be small but sturdy built

당착 撞着 〈앞뒤가 맞지 않음〉 contradiction; inconsistency; a clash; a conflict
—**당착하다** contradict; be inconsistent ((with)); conflict [clash] with; be anomalous; be at variance ((with))
♦ 자가 당착하다 contradict *oneself*

당첨 當籤 prize winning
—**당첨하다** win a prize; draw a winning [lucky] number
♦ 1등에 당첨되다 win first prize
▶ 내가 추첨에 당첨됐다 The lot fell on me.
▶ 그는 복권이 2등에 당첨됐다 He won (the) second prize in a (public) lottery.
■—권 a winning [prize] ticket —률 the ratio of winning numbers —번호 winning [lucky] numbers —자 the winner of the prize; the drawer of the lucky number

당초 當初 the beginning ⇨ 애초
♦ 당초의 계획 the original plan

당초(문) 唐草(紋) an arabesque (pattern, design)

당치않다 當— 〈불합리하다〉 absurd; unreasonable; 〈부당하다〉 undeserved; unfair; unjust; improper; unjustifiable; undue; unmerited; 〈용납되지 않다〉 outrageous; preposterous
♦ 당치않은 권력 행사 undue use of power / 당치않은 벌 an undeserved punishment / 당치않은 생각 an absurd [a preposterous] idea / 당치않은 처사 unfair measures; an improper step / 당치않게 unreasonably; ridiculously; absurdly / 당치않은 말을 하다 talk nonsense
▶ 우리는 너의 당치않은 요구를 받아들일 수 없다 We will not accept your excessive [unjustifiable] demands.
▶ 그게 무슨 당치않은 소리냐? Where is the sense of it?
▶ 그가 그런 것을 요구하다니 당치않다 It is unreasonable of him to demand such a thing.
▶ 나보고 사과하라니 당치않은 소리다 Apology on my part is out of the question.
▶ 그를 책하는 것은 당치않다 You cannot justly blame him.

당파 黨派 〈붕당〉 a party; 〈도당〉 a faction; a junto; a clique; a league
♦ 비당파적 nonparty; nonpartisan / 당파적인 party-[factious-]spirited; factious; factional / 당파색이 없는 nonpartisan (diplomacy); independent / 당파로 갈리다 split into factions / 당파를 짜다 form a party [faction, clique]
▶ 그 당에는 몇개의 유력한 당파가 있다 There are several powerful factions in the party.
■—심[근성] party feeling [spirit]; partisan spirit [prejudice]; partisanship —싸움 party dispute [strife]; faction: 당파싸움을 일삼다 be given to party squabbles

당폐 黨弊 party evils
♦ 당폐를 없애다 eliminate party evils

당하다¹ 當— 1〈겪다, 만나다〉 encounter; experience; meet (with) (▶meet with는 불행한 사고에 한함); suffer
♦ 곤란을 당하다 encounter difficulties / 모친상을 당하다 have *one's* mother die; suffer the loss of *one's* mother / 재난을 당하다 encounter [experience] a disaster / 수모를 당하다 suffer an insult
▶ 홍수 때문에 그 마을은 큰 피해를 당했다 The village suffered heavy damage from the flood.
▶ 그 사고로 통행인이 피해를 당했다 Some passersby were injured in the accident.
▶ 그들은 부산으로 가는 도중에 차사고를 당했다 They met with a car accident on their way to Pusan.
▶ 그는 불행한 일을 당했다 Something terrible happened to him.
2 〈지다〉 be beaten; be defeated; 〈속다〉 be cheated; be deceived; 〈매맞다〉 be struck; suffer a blow
▶ 나는 감쪽같이 당했다 I was fairly caught. ⇌ I was fooled. ⇌ I was taken in.
3 〈감당하다〉 match; rival; cope with; be equal to
▶ 이 아이들은 내가 당해내지 못한다 These children are beyond my control.
▶ 이 일은 내가 당해내지 못할 것 같다 I'm afraid this job is too much for me.
▶ 지금은 내 몸이 둘이라도 못당할 지경으로 바쁘다 This is the busiest time when I wish I had two bodies.

당하다² 當— 〈사리에 맞다〉 reasonable; fair; right; rational; sensible
♦ 당한 말을 하다 talk [speak] sense

—**당하다 當**— suffer; receive; sustain; incur; undergo; be afflicted with
♦ 피해당한 곳 the stricken area [district]/ 부상당하다 be injured [wounded]; get hurt / 저격당하다 be shot ((in the head)) / 체포당하다 be arrested [caught, apprehended]/ 구타당하다 receive [get] a blow; be struck / 침략당하다 be invaded / 무시당하다 be despised / 도난당하다 be stolen; have ((a thing)) stolen; be robbed ((of a thing)) / 처벌당하다 be punished / 거절당하다 be rejected; be turned down; meet with a refusal / 습격당하다 be attacked
▶ 그는 낙석에 부상당했다 He was injured by falling rocks.

당해 當該 ♦ 당해의 proper; 〈관계의〉 concerned; 〈소관의〉 competent
■—관청 the proper [competent] authorities; the authorities concerned —인물 the said person

당헌 黨憲 the party constitution
♦ 당헌에 규정된 대로 as implied [stipulated] in the party constitution

당혹 當惑 〈곤혹〉 perplexity; embarrassment; 〈진퇴양난〉 dilemma; 〈혼란〉 confusion
—**당혹하다** be perplexed; be embarrassed; be puzzled; be confused ((by)); be [put] in a difficult position; be nonplussed; be at *one's* wit's [wits'] end
▶ 그녀는 그의 요구에 당혹하고 있다 She is in perplexity over his request.
▶ 나는 무엇이라고 말해야 할지 당혹했다 I was at a loss as to what to say [for words].
▶ 그녀는 당혹한 얼굴빛으로 서 있었다 She was standing with a perplexed look on her face.

당화 糖化 〔化〕 saccharification

―당화하다 make into sugar; saccharify; saccharize; convert *sth* into sugar
♦전분을 당화하다 saccharize starch
■―효소 diastatic enzyme

당황하다 唐慌― be nervous; be flustered; (口) be in a dither; get all shook-up
♦당황하여 in a flurry; in confusion; in panic; in perplexity
▶나는 어떻게 대답해야 할지 몰라 잠시 당황했다 I didn't know how to answer for a moment.
▶그의 태도가 급변했기 때문에 나는 당황했다 The sudden change in his attitude confused [upset] me.
▶그 소식에 그는 당황했다 He was upset [disconcerted] at the news.
▶나는 그 소식을 듣고 [그 광경을 보고] 몹시 당황했다 I was utterly confounded at the news [sight].
▶나는 당황해서 질문의 뜻을 잘못 이해했다 I was in a confused state of mind and misunderstood the question.
▶그의 질문이 그녀를 당황하게 했다 He threw her into confusion by his question.

닻 an anchor
♦닻을 올리다 unmoor a ship; weigh anchor

닿다 reach
♦손이 닿는[닿지 않는] 곳에 within [beyond, out of] one's reach
▶그의 진심이 그녀의 가슴에 와 닿았다 His sincerity went home to [touched] her heart.
▶그물 선반에 손이 닿느냐? Can you reach the rack?
▶그 장대는 처마까지 닿는다 The pole reaches to the eaves.

닿소리 a consonant (sound) ⇨ 자음(子音)

대¹ 1 〈줄기〉 a stem; 〈벼·대나무 등의〉 a culm; a stalk; a pipe; 〈완두 등의〉 (英) a ha(u)lm; 〈사탕수수 등의〉 a cane ;〈막대〉 a staff; a rod; a pole; 〈담뱃대〉 a pipe
♦펜대 a penholder / 저울대 a balance beam
2 〈줏대〉 spirit; mettle; backbone; 〈담력〉 pluck; courage; (口) guts; grit
♦대가 센 사람 a man of spirit [backbone]; a man with guts [grit] / 대가 센 daring; bold; plucky; audacious / 대가 약한 fainthearted; weak-kneed; cowardly; backboneless
3 〈담배의〉 a smoke; a puff; a whiff
♦한 대 피우다 smoke a pipe; have [take] a smoke [puff] / 한 대 권하다 offer *sb* a smoke
4 〈주먹 등〉 a blow; a punch; a hit
♦한 대에 at a [one] blow [stroke]; by a (single) blow / 한 대 먹이다 strike [deal, give] *sb* a blow
▶그의 코에다 한대 먹였다 I gave him a punch on [in] the nose.
5 〈주사의〉 a shot; an injection
♦캠퍼를 두 대 주사하다 give *sb* two camphor injections [two shots of camphor]
▶해외에 나가기 전에 의사에게 주사를 몇 대 맞았다 I had several injections [(口) got several shots] by [from] the doctor before going overseas.

대² 〔植〕 (a) bamboo
♦대를 쪼개다 split a bamboo
▶그 가구는 대로 만든 것이다 The furniture is made of bamboo.
■―껍질 a bamboo sheath ―꼬챙이 a pointed bamboo stick ―나무 세공 bamboo work ―마디 a bamboo joint [node] ―바구니 a bamboo basket ―바늘 a bamboo needle ―비 a bamboo broom ―숲 a bamboo thicket [grove] ―울타리 a bamboo fence ―창 a bamboo spear 댓잎 a bamboo blade 댓줄기 a bamboo stalk

대 大 〈큼〉 largeness; bigness; greatness; 〈크기〉 large size; 〈큰 것〉 a big thing
♦대짜의 large; big; 〈거대한〉 huge; giant; gigantic / 대를 위해 소를 희생하다 sacrifice small things to save great ones
▶대는 소를 겸한다 The greater [larger] also serves for the lesser [smaller].
▶[會話]「크기는 어떤 것이 있습니까?」「대중소의 세가지가 있습니다」 "What sizes do you have?" "We have three sizes, large, medium and small."

대 代 〈세대〉 a generation; 〈시대〉 an age; an era; 〈왕위의〉 a reign ⇨ ―대(代)
♦어버이[자식]대 the parental [filial] generation / 대를 이을 사람 a successor 《to》; heir (남자); an heiress(여자) / 대를 잇다 succeed to the house / 대가 바뀌다 〈가장이〉 be succeeded (by the son); 〈군대의〉 change hands [the head]/ 대가 끊어지다 a family line breaks; a line dies out
▶그의 집안은 아버지대에는 번창했었다 His family prospered in his father's days.
▶그의 집안은 여러 대째 이 마을에 살고 있다 His family has lived in this town for (many) generations.

대 隊 〈일단〉 a party; a company; a corps 《*pl.* ~[kɔ́ːrz]》; a body 《of troops》; a unit; a squad; 〈악대 등의〉 a band; 〈경찰관 등의〉 a force
♦소[중·대]대 a platoon [company, battalion]/ 구조대 a rescue party / 선발대 an advance party;〈군대의〉 an advance contingent / 탐험대 an expedition (team)/ 항공대 a flying corps / 대를 짓다 form a party [company]
▶학생들의 일대가 산을 오르고 있었다 A party of students was [were] climbing up the mountain.

대 對 1 〈반대되는 것〉 the opposite
2 〈짝〉 a pair; a counterpart; a parallel; 〈쌍〉 a couple
3 〈상대〉 versus (略 v., vs); against; between; toward; to
♦지대지 미사일 a ground-to-ground [surface-to-surface] missile / 지대공 미사일 a ground-[surface-]to-air missile / 공대지 미사일 an air-to-ground[-surface] missile / 공대공 미사일 an air-to-air missile / 빈자 대 부자의 대립 a confrontation of the poor against the rich / A대학 대 B대학의 농구 시합 a basketball game between A University versus B University
4 〈비(比)〉 to; (as) against
♦100표 대 250표 250 votes against 100 / 3대 1

로 이기다 win (a game) by [with] a score of 3 to 1 / 3대 1로 지다 lose a game by [with] a score of 3 to 1
▶나는 그와 1대 1로 이야기했다 I talked with him in person.

대 臺 1〈받침대〉a stand; a rest; a pedestal; a base; a support;〈시렁〉a rack;〈탁자 등의〉a table
◆당구[탁구]대 a billiard [ping-pong] table / 악보대 a music stand / 진열대 a display stand [counter]
▶그들은 작업대에서 기계를 수리중이다 They are repairing a machine at the worktable.
2〈액수〉a level; a mark
◆백만원대에 달하다 touch [rise to] the level of a million won; reach [hit] the one million won mark [level]
▶광산주는 만원대로 떨어졌다 The mine stocks sagged to the ten thousand won level.
▶하루 매상이 백만원대를 돌파했다 The daily sales have reached the million won mark [level].
3〈대수〉발동기 5대 five motors / 트럭 10대 분의 화물 ten truckloads of goods / 자동차가 세 대 있다 have three cars

대- 大- 1〈큰〉big, large; great;〈거대한〉grand; large-scale 《scheme》; wholesale
◆대가족 a large family / 대서울 Great Seoul / 대승리 a sweeping [great] victory;〈선거의〉a landslide / 대시합 a big event / 대평원 a vast plain
2〈중대한〉grave; serious
◆대죄 a deadly [mortal] sin; a serious crime
3〈심한〉heavy; severe; serious; gross
◆대손실 a heavy [stupendous] loss / 대실책 a terrible mistake / 지진으로 생긴 대파괴 the great destruction caused by an earthquake
4〈뛰어난〉great; prominent
◆대작곡가 a great composer / 대가수 a prominent singer

-대 -代 1〈세대〉◆제5대 the fifth generation / 그의 5대 후손 his descendant in the fifth generation / 10대의 사람 a teenager; a teenage(d) boy [girl] / 나이 40[50]대에 at one's forties [fifties] / 제40대 미국 대통령 로날드 레이건 Ronald Reagan, the 40th President of the United States
▶링컨은 미국의 몇대 대통령입니까? Where does Lincoln stand in the order of the American presidents?
▶그는 아직 20대를 넘지 않았다 He is not yet out of his twenties.
2〔地質〕an era; a period
◆신생대 the Cenozoic [Cainozoic] era [period]
3〈연대〉◆1920년대에 in the 1920s [1920's] / 1980년대 말에서 1990년대 초에 in the late 1980s and early 1990s / 1960년대 중반에 in the mid-1960s
4〈대금〉a price;〈요금〉a charge; (a) rate; a fee; a fare; (a) rent
◆버스대 a bus fare / 식사대 food expenses;〈하숙의〉(the charge for) board

-대 -帶 a zone; a region;〔解〕a girdle
◆한[온]대 the frigid [temperate] zone

대가 大家 1〈큰 집〉a mansion; a great house;〈명문〉a distinguished [great] family;〈부호〉a rich [wealthy] family
2〈거장〉a (great) master 《in, at》;〈권위자〉an authority; an expert; a leading figure;〈대학자〉a great [an eminent, a distinguished] scholar
◆교육계의 대가 a leading figure in the educational world / 그림의 대가 a great [master] artist [painter] / 문단의 대가 an eminent [a distinguished] writer [author]; a great man of letters / 음악의 대가 a great musician; a maestro / 대가인 체하다 pose as [pretend to be] an authority; put on the airs of a great master / 대가가 되다 attain eminence [greatness] / 그 분야의 대가로 인정받고 있다 be an acknowledged [a recognized] authority on the subject

대가 代價〈대금〉price; cost;〈희생〉cost
◆대가를 치르다 pay the price 《for》; pay for sth / 어떠한 대가를 치르더라도 at any cost
▶내 노력에 대한 대가는 아무것도 없었다 I got nothing for my efforts.

대가극 大歌劇〔樂〕a grand opera=그랜드 오페라

대가다〈정각에〉arrive on time;〈늦지 않게〉be [arrive] in time 《for》
◆막차 시간에 대가다 catch [make] the last train / 수업 시간에 대가다 arrive at school on time / 약속한 시간에 대가다 present oneself at the appointed time

대가리〈머리〉the head;〈물건의〉the top [head, point, tip] 《of》
◆돼지 대가리 the head of a pig / 망치 대가리 a hammerhead / 생선 대가리 the jowl / 콩나물 대가리 the tips of bean sprouts / 대가리에 피도 안 마른 녀석 a young and inexperienced fellow; a greenhorn / 대가리를 싸매고 덤비다 make a desperate effort

대가족 大家族 a large [big] family; an extended family
◆대가족을 거느리고 있다 have a large family to support
▶그녀의 가족이 우리보다 대가족이다 Her family is larger than ours.
■—제도 an extended family system

대각 對角〔幾〕the opposite angle

대각거리다 clatter; crack; crackle; clack; clink; rattle
◆그릇이 대각거린다 Dishes are clattering.

대각선 對角線 a diagonal line
◆대각선 무늬의 천 a cloth with a diagonal pattern / 대각선으로 diagonally / 대각선을 긋다 draw a diagonal

대간첩작전 對間諜作戰 a counter-espionage operation

대갈¹ a horseshoe nail
대갈² the head ⇨ 대가리

대갈 大喝 a loud [thundering] cry
◆대갈 일성으로 in a thunderous shout
—**대갈하다** shout (in a thunderous voice); yell; roar; bellow

대감 大監 His [Your] Excellency

대감독 大監督 〔基〕 an archbishop

대강 大綱 1 〈강령〉 general [fundamental] principles; 〈대요〉 the main points; an outline; a summary; a gist; the substance; general [principal] features; 〈논문의〉 a synopsis
♦강의의 대강 the syllabus of a lecture / 대강을 정하다 lay down fundamental principles / 대강을 말하다 outline; give [sketch] an outline of
2 〈거의・대부분〉 nearly; almost; 〈대충〉 roughly; about; approximately; 〈대체로〉 generally; in general / 대강 이야기하다 give a short sketch (of) / 대강 어림잡다 make a rough estimate (of) / 대강 훑어보다 glance [run one's eyes] over (a letter); run over (a morning paper); skim through (a book)
▶나는 일을 대강 끝냈다 I have finished most of my work.
▶그것이 어떤 것인지 대강 알고 싶소 I would like to get some idea (of) what it is like.
▶회의 결과는 대강 다음과 같다 The result of the conference may be summarized as follows.

대강 代講 teaching as a substitute
▶오늘만 존슨 선생의 대강을 부탁합니다 Please substitute for Mr. Johnson [take Mr. Johnson's class(es)] just for today.
—**대강하다** teach for [in place of] (another); lecture as a substitute

대강령 大綱領 fundamental [first] principles; general rules [principles]

대갚음 對— revenge; retaliation; repayment [requital] in kind; tit for tat; measure for measure
—**대갚음하다** retaliate; revenge; give [pay] sb tit for tat
♦폭력을 대갚음하다 answer violence with violence
▶그에게 대갚음해주었다 I got my revenge on him. ⇒ (口) I got even with him.

대개 大概 1〈대부분〉 most (of); the [a] greater [major] part (of); a great [large] portion (of); the majority (of)
♦대개의 사람들 most people
▶그것들은 대개가 장식품이다 Most of them are ornaments.
▶그곳의 거주민은 대개가 중국인이다 The residents there are for the most part Chinese.
2〈대체로〉 generally (speaking); in general; 〈대부분〉 mostly; for the most part; 〈주로〉 mainly; prinicipally; chiefly; 〈거의〉 nearly; about; almost
▶학생들은 대개 이 사전을 가지고 있다 Most students have this dictionary.
▶이 방의 책들은 대개 다 읽었다 I read almost all (of) the books in this room.
▶나는 대개 여기 있지만 때로는 외출할 때도 있다 I'm here most of time, but I go out now and then.
▶그는 저녁에는 대개 산책을 한다 He usually takes a walk in the evening.

대개념 大概念 〔論〕 a major concept

대거 大擧 〈큰 기획〉 a great enterprise; 〈공동 노력〉 a united effort; 〈부사적〉 in a body; in (great) force; in a great mass; in large [great] numbers
♦대거 공격하다 attack (the enemy) in full force; take the offensive on a large scale; mass-raid

대검 帶劍 〈칼을 참〉 a sword at one's side; wearing a sword
♦대검을 허락[금지]하다 allow [forbid] sb to wear a sword
—**대검하다** wear a sword [saber]; be armed with a sword

대검찰청 大檢察廳 the Supreme Public Prosecutor's Office

대견하다 〈흡족하다〉 (be) satisfied; contented; content; 〈훌륭하다〉 wonderful; excellent; admirable; praiseworthy; great; 〈소중하다〉 valuable; dear; precious
♦대견하게 여기다 be proud of; take sb [sth] admirable [laudable]; make much [highly] of / 결과를 대견하게 여기다 express one's satisfaction at [with] the result
▶초등학생으로서는 대견한 일이다 For a schoolchild, this is quite an achievement.

대결 對決 confrontation; a face-to-face meeting; (美) a showdown; a contest; a match
♦여야의 대결 confrontation between the ruling party and the opposition parties
▶아랍과 이스라엘의 대결이 심각하게 되어가고 있다 The confrontation between the Arab and Israel has become serious.
—**대결하다** confront (with); have a showdown (with); stand face to face (with); have a contest [match] (with)
▶피고와 원고를 대결시켰다 The accused was confronted with his accuser.

대경 大驚 great astonishment
—**대경하다** be greatly astonished [surprised]; be startled [astonished]; be amazed; be speechless [struck dumb] with amazement

대경실색 大驚失色 turning pale with astonishment
—**대경실색하다** turn pale with astonishment [fear]; be startled [frightened] out of one's wits; be dumbfounded
▶우리는 그 소식을 듣고 대경실색했다 We were astounded at the news.

대계 大計 a far-reaching [far-sighted] policy; a long-range plan; a great plan
♦국가의 백년 대계를 세우다 make [lay out] a great plan for the grand future of the nation; establish a great national policy on a long-range basis

대계 大系 an outline
♦세계사 대계 an outline of world history / 지리학 대계 compendium of geography

대고 〈자꾸〉 persistently; tenaciously; importunately; without intermission; (美口) without a letup
♦대고 조르다 ask for urgently [repeatedly]; pester; nag / 대고 지껄이다 chatter ceaselessly; talk without a pause
▶그는 돈 달라고 어머니한테 대고 졸랐다 He pressed [pestered] his mother for money.

대고모 大姑母 a great-aunt [grandaunt] (on

대공 大公 a grand duke; an archduke
■ 룩셈부르크 대공 the grand duke of Luxembourg
■―국 an archduchy; a grand duchy ―비 a grand duchess

대공 大功 a great merit; meritorious [distinguished] services
▶ 그는 나라를 위해 대공을 세웠다 He rendered distinguished [meritorious] services to the state.

대공 對空 ◆ 대공의 anti-aircraft; 《美》 anti-air
―레이더 an air search radar ―방어 anti-aircraft defense ―사격 antiaircraft fire ―십자포화 《軍》 a box barrage ―진지 an anti-aircraft position [emplacement] ―포[미사일] an anti-aircraft gun [missile] ―포화 anti-aircraft [AA] fire

대과 大過 a serious [grave, gross] error [mistake]; a blunder
◆ 대과 없이 근무하다 serve without (making [committing]) any serious mistakes [errors]
▶ 그는 30여년을 대과 없이 근무했다 He served creditably for more than thirty years.

대과거 大過去 〔文法〕 the past perfect tense; the pluperfect (tense)

대관식 戴冠式 a coronation (ceremony)
◆ 대관식을 거행하다 hold [perform] a coronation (ceremony)

대관절 大關節 〈도대체〉 (how, what, why) on earth [in the world, in the name of God, the devil]
▶ 대관절 그것은 누구일까? Whoever can it be?
▶ 너는 대관절 왜 그런 짓을 저질렀니? Why in the world [on earth] did you do that? ⇌ Whatever made you do that?
▶ 그는 대관절 무엇을 원하는 것인지 모르겠다 I don't know what the hell he wants.
▶ 대관절 어디서 그 옷을 샀니? Where on earth did you buy that dress?
▶ 대관절 어떻게 된 일이냐? What on earth [the deuce] is the matter? ⇌ What in the world has happened?

대괄호 大括弧 a (square) bracket ([,]); 〔數·樂〕 a brace (《, 》)

대교 大橋 a large [big] bridge (over the Hangang)

대구 大口 〔魚〕 a cod (pl. ~(s)); a codfish; a gadoid
■ 통― (a) dried cod 훈제― smoked cod [haddock]
■―알 cod roe ―잡이 cods fishery

대구 對句 〈시의〉 a couplet; 〈대조의〉 an antithesis (pl. -ses) ◆ 대구를 이루다 form [make] an antithesis (to)

대구루루 rolling ⇨ 때구루루 ◆ 대구루루 구르다 roll over (and over) / 언덕을 대구루루 굴러 가다 go rolling down the hillside
▶ 탁구공이 탁구대에서 대구루루 굴러 떨어졌다 The pingpong ball rolled off the table.

대국 大局 the general [whole] situation; the main issue
◆ 대국적으로는 on the whole; generally [roughly] speaking / 대국적으로 보다 take a wide view of; see sth in perspective / 대국을 잘못 판단하다 take a wrong view of things; miss the main point of things

대국 大國 a large country; a great country [nation]; 〈강대국〉 a big [great] power
◆ 경제 대국 an economic superpower

대국 對局 1 〈국면에 대한〉 confronting the situation
―대국하다 confront [face] the situation; tackle [deal with, cope with] the matter
2 〈바둑·장기의〉 a game of paduk [changgi, chess] (with)
―대국하다 play (a game of) paduk [changgi, chess]
▶ 그는 내일 국수와 대국한다 He has a match with the champion tomorrow.

대군 大君 a (Royal) prince

대군 大軍 a large [big] army; a large [vast] force ◆ 적의 대군 a large enemy force / 대군을 거느리다 lead [command] a large [powerful] army

대군 大群 a large crowd [herd, flock, shoal, school] ◆ 메뚜기의 대군 a vast swarm of locusts / 물고기의 대군 large schools of fish / 철새의 대군 a large flock of migratory birds

대굴대굴 rolling ⇨ 데굴데굴

대궁 leftover rice [leftovers] in a bowl

대권 大圈 a great circle
―항로 the great-circle course [route]: 대권 항로를 날다 fly the great-circle route ―항법 great-circle sailing

대권 大權 the supreme power; the sovereign authority; sovereignty; the royal prerogative [authority, power]; 〈통치권〉 the governing power
◆ 병마의 대권 the supreme authority over the armed forces / 국가의 대권을 장악하다 hold the supreme power of the state; reign supreme in the land

대궐 大闕 〈궁궐〉 the royal palace
◆ 대궐같은 집 a palace of a house; a palatial building; a house of palatial splendor

대규모 大規模 a large scale
◆ 대규모의 large-scale; grand-scale; massive / 대규모로 on a large [a grand, a huge, an extensive] scale; in a big [large] way
▶ 우리는 7년이 걸리는 대규모 공사를 맡았다 We accepted a major construction project that would take seven years to complete.
■―작전 large-scale operations

대글대글하다 rather thick [big, large] among thin [small] things

대금 大金 a large [an enormous] sum of money; a lot of money; a mint of money
▶ 백만원이면 저한테는 대금입니다 A million is won a mint of money for me.

대금 大笒 〈악기〉 a large (cross) flute; a large fife

대금 代金 a price; (a) charge; a bill; a fee
◆ 대금을 받다 receive payment (of); be paid (for) / 대금을 재촉하다 press sb for payment / 대금을 청구하다 ask sb to pay for sth; bill sb for sth / 대금을 치르다 pay for 《an

대금 article); pay the price ((for))
▶대금은 필요 없습니다 It is free of charge.
▶이 옷의 대금은 얼마입니까? What is the cost [price] of the dress? ⇒ How much should I pay for the dress?

대금 貸金 〈돈〉 a loan; an advance; 〈돈놀이〉 money-lending; 〈고리의〉 usury
♦대금을 회수하다 collect debts; collect [call in] loans
—**대금하다** make a loan [an advance] ((to)) ■**당좌**— a call loan; call money; money at [on] call 장기[단기]— a long-term [short-term] loan 정기— a time loan —업 money-lending business —업자 a money lender; a usurer

대금교환 代金交換 (美) collect on delivery (略 C.O.D.); (英) cash on delivery (略 C.O.D.)
■—우편 C.O.D. mail [(英) post]: 대금교환 우편으로 소포를 보내다 send a parcel C.O.D.

대기 大氣 〈지구 둘레의〉 the atmosphere; 〈공기〉 the air ♦대기의 압력 atmospheric pressure / 대기의 atmospheric(al)
■—관측 aeroscopy —론 aerology —차 〔天〕 refraction

대기 大器 〈큰 그릇〉 a large vessel; 〈인재〉 a great talent; a man of (great) caliber; a person of great ability; 〈앞날의〉 a man of great promise

대기 待機 waiting for a chance
♦대기 명령을 내리다 alert; order to stand by / 대기 상태에 있다 be standing; be ready ((to do)); 〈함대·공군 등이〉 be on alert status / 대기 자세를 취하다 assume a posture of standing by
—**대기하다** stand ready ((for, to do)); hold *oneself* in readiness; stand by; keep attending on; be in constant attendance on; wait for an opportunity; be on the waiting list
▶500명의 경찰관이 출동을 위해 대기하고 있었다 Five hundred police were on the alert for their movement.
■—기간 a waiting period —료 the fee for the waiting time —발령 an order of placement on a waiting list —시간 waiting time —실 a waiting room; the adjoining room; an antechamber —차관(借款) a standby credit

대기권 大氣圈 the atmosphere
♦대기권 내의 핵실험 nuclear tests in the atmosphere; the atmospheric testing of nuclear weapons / 대기권 밖의 우주에서[로] from [into] outer space / 대기권 밖으로 나가다[로켓을 발사하다] venture [launch a rocket] into outer space
▶로켓은 대기권으로 재돌입했다 The rocket reentered the atmosphere.

대기만성 大器晚成 ♦대기 만성형의 사람 late bloomer; late developer
▶그는 대기만성형이다 He is slow to mature [come into his own]. ⇒ He is a late developer [bloomer]

대기명령 待機命令 awaiting orders; pending appointment; 〈공무원 등의〉 being placed on the waiting list
♦대기명령중에 있다 be placed on the wait-ing list
▶그는 목하 대기명령중에 있다 He is awaiting further instructions [orders].

대기업 大企業 a large company [enterprise, corporation]; 〈자회사를 거느린〉 a conglomerate; (총칭) big business; major companies [firms]

대기오염 大氣汚染 air [atmospheric] pollution
♦방사능 낙진에 의한 대기오염 air pollution by radioactive fallout / 자동차의 배기 가스에 의한 대기오염 atmospheric contamination by exhaust gases from cars
■—도 a degree of air pollution —방지법 〔法〕 the Air Pollution Control Act; 〔英美法〕 Clean Air Act —방지책 measures against air pollution —지구 an air-polluted area

대길 大吉 very good luck; excellent luck; a great stroke of luck
—**대길하다** very lucky; very auspicious

대꼬챙이 a pointed bamboo stick; a bamboo skewer [spit]

대꾸 a retort ⇨ 말대꾸

대나무 〔植〕 a bamboo (tree) ⇨ 대²

대낚(시) pole-and-line fishing [angling]

대 남 對南 —간첩 an espionage agent against the South —공작 clandestine [espionage] operations against the South —방송 (propaganda) broadcasting toward the South

대납 代納 〈대리 납부〉 payment by proxy; 〈물납(物納)〉 payment in kind
—**대납하다** pay for another; pay in kind
♦상속세를 토지로 대납하다 pay an inheritance tax in land

대낮 〈백주〉 broad daylight; 〈정오〉 high noon; midday
♦대낮에 in broad [full, open] daylight; in the daytime / 대낮처럼 밝다 be as bright as day [noontime]
▶그 살인은 대낮에 자행되었다 The murder was committed in broad daylight.

대내 對內 ♦대내의 domestic; home; interior
■—문제 domestic problems [issues]; home affairs —정책 a domestic [home] policy

대농 大農 〈부농〉 a wealthy farmer; 〈큰 농사〉 large-scale [extensive] farming

대뇌 大腦 〔解〕 the cerebrum (*pl.* ~s, -bra)
■—각 the pedunculus cerebri —반구 a cerebral hemisphere —생리학 cerebral physiology —피질 the cerebral cortex

대님 a pair of ankle bands (for traditional Korean clothes)
♦대님을 매다 tie ankle bands; bind *one's* trousers with ankle bands [around the ankles]

대다¹ 1 〈접촉시키다〉 put; apply; hold; place; press
♦컵을 입에 대다 set [put] a glass to *one's* lips; put *one's* lips to a glass / 문에 귀를 대다 press *one's* ear against the door / 수화기를 귀에 대다 hold [apply, put] a receiver to *one's* ear / 가슴에 청진기를 대다 put a stethoscope to *sb's* chest
▶그녀는 손수건을 눈에 대었다 She held [put]

her handkerchief to her eyes.
2 〈만지다〉 touch; lay [put] one's hand 《on, against》
▶ 손 대지 마시오 《게시》 Hands off! ⇌ Don't touch!
◆ 맹인(盲人)은 촉감으로 물건을 분간한다 Blind people recognize things by feeling [touching] them.
3 〈비교하다〉 compare with; make a comparison with
▶ 머리가 좋기로는 나는 그와는 댈 것이 못된다 I'm no match for him in intelligence.
4 〈착수하다〉 start 《doing》; set about 《doing, to do》; begin 《to do》; set one's hand to sth; 〈시도하다〉 try one's hand 《at》
◆ 사업에 손을 대다 start [embark in] a business [an enterprise] / 정치에 손을 대다 dabble [meddle] in politics
▶ 이 문제는 하도 어려워 어디서부터 손을 대야 할지 모르겠다 This problem is so difficult that I don't know where to begin.
5 〈먹다〉 eat; taste
◆ 술을 입에 대지 않다 do not drink wine
◆ 이런 맛있는 요리를 입에 댄적이 없다 I've never tried [tasted, eaten] such nice food.
▶ 지금은 아무것도 입에 대고 싶지 않다 I don't want to take anything now. ⇌ I don't care to eat now.
6 〈대면·연결시키다〉 link 《together》 《with》; connect 《with, to》; bring into contact 《with》
◆ 톰을 좀 대주십시오 〈전화에서〉 May I talk to Tom, please? ⇌ Please get [《英》put] me through to Tom.
7 【도착시키다】〈차를〉 drive [draw, pull] up; 〈배를〉 put ashore; 〈시간에〉 arrive [be] in time 《for》; make it
◆ 차를 은행 앞에 대다 park a car in front of a bank / 배를 부두에 대다 lay [bring] a ship alongside the pier
▶ 그는 저녁 식사에 대어 귀가했다 He came home in time for dinner.
8 〈향하게 하다〉 direct; aim
◆ 아무의 얼굴에 침을 뱉다 spit in sb's face / 새에 대고 총을 쏘다 shoot at a bird
▶ 그래 그건 누구에게 대고 하는 말이냐? And who is that remark aimed at?
9 〈의지하다〉 lean against
◆ 벽에 등을 대고 with one's back against the wall
10 〈구실 등을〉 do; make
◆ 핑계를 대다 find [make] an excuse for oneself
11 〈고용하다〉 hire; employ
◆ 변호사를 대다 provide sb with a lawyer; retain a lawyer for sb
▶ 그는 딸에게 좋은 가정교사를 대주었다 He provided his daughter study with [under] a good tutor.
12 〈덧대다〉 put; line; apply
◆ 구두에 밑창을 대다 fix a sole on one's shoes / 상처에 거즈를 대다 apply gauze on the wound / 오버코트 안에 털가죽을 대다 line an overcoat with fur
대다² 1 〈물을〉 draw 《water》 into; water; irrigate
◆ 논에 물을 대다 irrigate a rice field / 사막에 물을 대다 irrigate the desert; draw water into the desert
2 〈공급·후원하다〉 supply [provide, furnish] sb [sth] with
◆ 공장에 부품을 대다 supply parts to a factory / 쌀을 대다 supply 《the house》 with rice
◆ 아버지가 개점 자금을 대주셨다 My father supplied me with the funds to open the store.
▶ 여행 경비는 누가 대는 거냐? Who is to pay the travel expenses?
대다³ 1 〈말하다〉 speak; tell; 〈사실대로〉 tell the truth; confess
◆ 자기 이름을 대다 tell sb one's name; introduce oneself / 증거를 대다 give evidence / 이유를 대다 give a reason
▶ 바른대로 대라 Tell me the truth.
▶ 이젠 본심을 대야 할 것 아니냐? Isn't it about time you told me your real intentions?
2 〈일러주다〉 tell; show; indicate
▶ 가장 가까운 길을 대드리죠 I will tell you the shortest way.
대다⁴ ◆ 먹어대다 eat greedily; eat up hungrily / 웃어대다 laugh a heavy laugh; laugh one's head off; go into fits of laughter / 하염없이 울어대다 cry one's heart out
▶ 그의 실수를 너무 놀려대지 마라 Don't make too much fun of his failure.
대다수 大多數 the majority; a large [great, heavy, crushing] majority; the greater part 《of》; the mass [bulk] 《of》
◆ 압도적 대다수 an overwhelming majority / 대다수를 차지하다 hold [form] a large majority
▶ 대다수의 사람은 그렇게 생각한다 Most people think so.
▶ 여기서는 대다수의 학생이 영어를 한다 Most of the students here speak English.
▶ 위원의 대다수는 그 안에 반대했다 The majority of the committee was [were] against the proposal.
▶ 회의는 온건파가 대다수를 차지하고 있었다 The moderates commanded a large majority at the meeting.
대단원 大團圓 the (grand) finale; the end; 〈비극의〉 a catastrophe
◆ 대단원의 막이 내리다 come to an end
▶ 그 연극은 행복하게 대단원의 막을 내렸다 The drama ended happily [came to a happy ending].
대단찮다 1 〈많지 않다〉 not (so) many [much]; 〈크지 않다〉 not (so) large [huge, big, great]
◆ 대단찮은 돈 a small sum of money / 재간이 대단찮다 have little ability [talent]
▶ 내 수입은 대단찮다 My income is nothing much.
▶ 손해는 대단찮다 There is not much damage. ⇌ The damage is not serious.
▶ 돈을 잃었지만 대단찮은 액수요 I lost some money, but it wasn't much.
2 〈대수롭지 않다〉 of little importance [value, use]; insignificant; trivial; 〈평범하다〉 ordinary; mediocre

대단하다

♦대단찮은 사람 a person of no importance; an ordinary man / 대단찮은 일 a matter of little importance; a trivial matter [affair]; a trifle thing / 대단찮게 여기다 think [make] little 《of》

▶그는 대단찮은 학자[작가]다 He is not much of a scholar [writer]. ⇒ He is a third rate scholar [writer].

3 〈병 등이〉 not serious [grave, acute]; slight
♦대단찮은 감기[부상] a slight cold [wound]
▶그의 병은 대단찮다 He is not seriously sick.

4 〈추위 등이〉 not severe [hard, tense]; mild; moderate
▶대단찮은 추위[더위]다 It is not so cold [hot].

대단하다 1 〈많다〉 many; much; huge; enormous; a great [large, good] number of

♦대단한 금액 a colossal [huge, vast] sum / 대단한 비용 enormous [immense] expense; huge [stupendous] cost / 대단한 손실 a tremendous loss / 대단한 인파 an immense crowd of people

▶이 초판본에는 대단한 값이 매겨져 있다 This first edition bears an extraordinary [incredible] price.

2 〈중대하다〉 important; serious; grave
♦대단한 일 a serious [an important] matter
▶그것은 대단한 경험이었다 It was quite an experience.
▶내가 어떤 대학을 나왔는지는 대단한 일이 아니다 It matters very little what college you graduated from.

3 〈병 등이〉 serious; grave; 〈날씨 등이〉 severe; intense; violent
♦대단한 병 a serious [severe] illness [disease] / 대단한 추위 [더위] a severe cold [heat] / 대단한 고통 [기근] a severe pain [famine] / 대단한 감기에 걸려 있다 have a bad cold
▶감기가 들었지만 대단하지는 않다 I have a cold, but it's nothing [it's not] serious.

4 〈뛰어나다〉 great; grand; 〈놀랍다〉 wonderful; amazing; awful
♦대단한 학자 a great [an eminent] scholar
▶그녀는 대단한 미인이다 She's very [really] beautiful. ⇒ She is a real [stunning] beauty.
▶대단한 녀석이구나 What a man! ⇒ Such a man!
▶그는 재주가 대단하다 He is terribly talented.

대단히 very; (very) much; a great deal; greatly; extremely; highly; terribly; awfully
▶대단히 미안합니다 I'm terribly sorry.
▶도와주셔서 대단히 감사합니다 Thank you very much for your help.
▶오늘은 대단히 춥다 It is very [terribly, awfully] cold today.
▶그는 대단히 지쳐 있다 He is very tired. ⇒ He's tired out.
▶그녀는 지금 대단히 행복하다 She is very [so, most] happy now.
▶그는 대단히 흥분하고 있었다 I found him very excited.
▶그의 실패 소식을 듣고 대단히 놀랐다 I was greatly surprised to hear his failure.
▶그는 대단히 큰 잘못을 저질렀다 He has made a terrible mistake.
▶그곳은 대단히 아름다운 곳이다 It's a extremely beautiful place.
▶그녀는 음악을 대단히 좋아한다 She is a passionate lover of music.

대담 大膽 boldness; daring; audacity
—**대담하다** bold; daring; dauntless; fearless; stout-hearted; hardy; courageous; 〈모험적〉 adventurous

♦대담한 생각 a daring idea; a bold idea / 대담한 시도 a bold attempt; an adventurous undertaking / 대담 무쌍한 dauntless, fearless, daredevil; death-defying / 대담하게 boldly; fearlessly; daringly; courageously; adventurously / 대담하게 …하다 be bold enough 《to》 / 대담하게 나오다 show [present] a bold front / 대담하게 말하다 speak out; venture to say

▶강도수법이 해마다 대담해지고 있다 Robbery is getting bolder every year.
▶그는 때때로 대담한 행동을 한다 He sometimes takes a bold action.
▶그는 대담하게도 그 강을 헤엄쳐 건넜다 He was bold enough to swim across the river.

대담 對談 a talk; a face-to-face talk; a conversation; a dialogue; a colloquy; 〈회견〉 an interview
—**대담하다** talk with; converse with; have a talk [conversation] with; interview; have an interiew with
▶그는 존슨씨와 그 계획에 대해 장시간 대담했다 He had a long talk with Mr. Johnson about the plan.

대답 對答 an answer; a reply; a response
♦대답으로서 for an answer / 이도 저도 아닌 대답을 하다 give a noncommittal [vague] answer / 분명한 대답을 하다 have a definite reply / 아무 대답도 하지 않다 make no reply [answer]; answer sb nothing
▶문을 두드렸으나 아무 대답도 없었다 I knocked at [on] the door, but there was no answer.
▶가슴이 벅차서 정작 대답도 못했다 I was too excited to answer properly.
▶한 달 전에 그에게 편지했는데 아직까지 대답이 없다 I wrote to him a month ago, but I haven't heard from him yet.
—**대답하다** reply; answer; make [give] an answer [a reply]; respond 《to》
♦대답할 수 없는 unanswerable / 그렇다[아니다]라고 대답하다 give an affirmative [a negative] answer; answer in the affirmative [negative] / 어려운 질문에 대답하다 answer [reply to] a difficult question
▶호명하면 대답하시오 Answer when your name is called, please.
▶그는 뭐라고 대답했죠? What was his answer?
▶나는 뭐라고 대답해야 좋을지 몰랐다 I did not know what to say in reply. ⇒ I was at a loss for an answer.
▶나는 감히 「아니오」라고 대답했다 I ventured to answer "No."

대대 大隊 a battalion
■공병— an engineering battalion 비행— a squadron: 비행 대대장 a squadron commander ─기 a battalion flag ─부관 a battalion adjutant ─장 a battalion commander

대대 代代 ♦대대의 a hereditary article; a heirloom / 대대로 for generations; generation after generation; from generation to generation
▶그 집안은 대대로 의학에 몸담고 있다 That family has been in medicine for generations.
▶그들은 대대로 불교를 믿었다 Their hereditary religion was Buddhism.

대대손손 代代孫孫 all ages (to come); all generations; eternity

대대적 大大的 great; grand; gigantic; wholesale; sweeping 《victory》; 〈대규모의〉 large-scale
♦대대적으로 on a large [gigantic] scale; on an extensive scale / 대대적으로 선전하다 carry on an extensive [a large scale] advertising campaign 《about》
▶그 소식은 신문에 대대적으로 보도되었다 The news made the headlines. = The newspapers treated it as top headline news.

대덕과학단지 大德科學團地 the Taedŏk Science Town

대도 大道 〈큰 길〉 a highway; an avenue; a main road [street]; 〈정도(正道)〉 a great (moral) principle; a great cause

대도시 大都市 a big [large, great] city; a metropolis
♦인구 천만의 대도시 a big city with a population of 10 million

대독 代讀 reading by proxy
─대독하다 read for [on behalf of] 《another》
♦시장의 메시지를 대독하다 read the message for [on behalf of] the mayor

대동 帶同 accompaniment
─대동하다 be accompanied by; take 《another with *one*》; take [have] sb along
▶국무총리는 외무부장관을 대동하여 미국으로 떠났다 The Prime Minister left for the United States accompanied by the Foreign Minister.

대동단결 大同團結 unity; union; coalition; solidarity; grand alliance
─대동단결하다 unite for a common purpose; be (firmly) united; solidify; stand together
▶그들은 공통의 적에 맞서 대동단결했다 They united together against a common enemy.

대동맥 大動脈 〔解〕 the aorta 《*pl.* ~s, -tae》; 〈큰 간선〉 the main artery
♦교통의 대동맥 the main artery for traffic

대동사 代動詞 〔文法〕 pro-verb

대동소이 大同小異 substantial identity with minor differences; general similarity
─대동소이하다 much the same; almost identical; quite similar
▶이 점에서 둘은 대동소이하다 There is not much to choose [There is little [not much] difference] between the two in this respect.

대두 大斗 〈열 되들이 말〉 a ten-*doe* measure; a large (dry) measure

대두 大豆 a soy(bean); a soya [soja] (bean)
■─유 soy bean oil; soya-bean oil

대두 擡頭 rise
♦민족주의의 대두 the rise of nationalism
─대두하다 raise [show] *one's* [its] head; come to the fore [front]; be on the rise
▶당시 자본주의가 대두하고 있었다 Capitalism was on the rise then.

대들다 turn on [upon]; challenge; defy; rise against; raise [lift up] *one's* hand against
▶그 말을 듣고 그는 주인에게 대들었다 Hearing that, he turned [fell] upon his master.
▶그는 약속을 어겼다고 내게 대들었다 He flew at me for breaking my promise.
▶그 주정뱅이에게 무례하다고 나무랐더니 내게 대들었다 The drunk turned on me when I told him he was being rude.

대들보 大─ 1 〔建〕 a girder; a crossbeam; a summer
2 〈사람〉 a mainstay; a pillar
♦나라의 대들보 the pillar [main prop] of the state / 집안의 대들보 the (chief) bread-winner of a family
▶그들은 집안의 대들보를 잃었다 They lost the chief supporter of the family.

대등 對等 equality; an equal [the same] footing; equal [even] terms; parity; 〔數〕 equivalent
─대등하다 equal; 《be》 on an equal status [footing]; even
♦대등한 권리[조건] equal rights [terms]/ …와 대등하다 be on a level [a par, equal terms] with / 대등하게 on equal terms; on an equal footing
▶인간은 태어나면서부터 대등하다 All men are born equal.
▶모든 국민은 법 아래 대등하다 All of the people are equal under the law.
▶그녀는 능력에 있어서는 그와 대등하다 She is equal to [equals] him in ability. = She is his equal in ability.
■─조약 a treaty on equal terms

대뜸 〈즉석에서〉 offhand; on the spot; 〈즉시〉 at once; immediately; promptly; instantly; outright; in an instant; in no time; 〈하자마자 곧〉 as soon as
♦대뜸 대답하다 answer at once [right away]; give a ready answer / 대뜸 승낙하다 give a ready consent; consent immediately
▶그녀는 대뜸 거절했다 She declined then and there. = She lost no time (in) saying no.

대략 大略 1 〈개략〉 an outline; 〈요약〉 a summary; a gist; an epitome
♦대략을 말하다 outline; sum up; describe roughly [in outline]; summarize; give an outline [a summary] of
▶내가 우리 계획의 대략을 말하겠소 I will give you an outline of our plan.
▶첫째 날에 강사는 그 과정을 대략 알려주었다 On the first day, the instructor gave us a syllabus for his course.
2 approximately; cursorily; 〈대충〉 about; mostly; nearly; roughly; in the main; in substance; on the whole
▶그 건은 대략 다음과 같다 The case may be

summarized [briefly summed up] as follows.
▶일은 대략 끝났다 My work is almost [practically] finished.
▶그 차를 고치는데 대략 얼마 들겠습니까? What is a rough estimate to fix the car?

대량 大量 a large quantity 《of》; a huge [an enormous] quantity; a large amount; a lot 《of》; (口) a pile 《of》
♦대량으로 in large [great] quantities; in bulk / 대량(으로) 득점하다 〈야구에서〉 score a lot of runs / 대량 득점으로 상대팀을 격파하다 beat the opposing team by a large score
▶항공기는 날마다 대량의 연료를 소비한다 Planes consume a large [a huge, an enormous] quantity of fuel every day.
■—거래 a large transaction; voluminous business —구매 bulk purchase; heavy buying —소비 mass consumption —수요 a large demand —수요자 a large user —주문 a bulk [large, big] order —판매 mass sale —해고[검거] mass discharge [arrest]

대량 생산 大量生産 mass [large scale] production; production on a large scale
▶요즘은 컴퓨터도 대량 생산된다 Today even computers are mass-produced [produced on a large scale].
—대량생산하다 mass-produce
■—자 a mass-producer

대량 학살 大量虐殺 mass murder [killing]; 〈어떤 민족에 대한〉 massacre; genocide

대렵 大獵 a big bag; a large take

대령 大領 〈육군·해병대〉 a colonel (略 Col.); 〈해군〉 a captain (略 Capt.); 〈공군〉 (美) a colonel; (英) a group captain

대령하다 待令— wait for an order [a command]; be on standby for an order; stand ready to carry out an order
♦가마를 대령하다 get a palanquin [sedan chair] ready 《for》

대례 大禮 〈국가의〉 a state ceremony; a grand ceremony; 〈결혼식〉 a marriage ceremony [service]
■—모(帽) court hat —복 court dress

대로 1 〈…처럼〉 as; like; 〈그대로〉 as it is; as it stands; intact; 〈본떠서〉 after
♦종전 대로 as hitherto / 있던 대로다 remain as it was / 들은 대로 이야기하다 tell a story just as one heard it / 생각 대로 이야기하다 speak just as one feels / 본 대로 이야기하다 tell as one saw it
▶내 방은 그대로 놔 두시오 Leave my room as it is.
▶그 창문은 열어둔 대로였다 The window had been left open.
▶결과는 예상한 대로였다 The results were what we had expected.
▶봐? 내가 말한 대로지 See? What did I tell you?
2 〈…에 따라〉 as; according to [as]; in accordance with; pursuant to; true to
♦규칙 대로 according to the rule / 약속 대로 as promised / 예정대로 as scheduled; as previously arranged; in accordance with prearranged plan
▶내가 말한 대로 해라 Do just as [like] I have told you.
▶그의 충고[제안] 대로 하지 그래 Why don't you follow his advice [suggestion]?
▶계획 대로라면 벌써 끝났어야 하는데 If things had gone according to plan, it should have been finished long ago.
3 〈즉시〉 as soon as; directly
♦기회가 있는대로 at [on] the first opportunity / 날이 개는 대로 as soon as it becomes fine; on the first [next] fine day
▶집에 가는 대로 그에게 답장을 써야지 I'll write him an answer as soon as I get home.
4 〈원하는 대로〉 as one pleases; at will
♦먹고 싶은 대로 먹다 eat one's fill [to one's heart's content]; eat as much as one likes
▶너 하고 싶은 대로 해라 You can do as you like [please, wish].
▶만사가 내가 바라 던대로 되었다 Everything has turned out just as I wished.
5 〈족족〉 every [each] time; whenever; as often as
♦하는 대로 실패하다 fail in every attempt [at every step]; fail in everything one does
6 〈따로〉 apart; separately
♦자기식대로 하다 do a thing in one's own fashion [way, manner, style]
▶나는 나대로 하겠다 I'll do it my way [in my own way].

대로 大怒 great anger; wild rage; wrath; fury
—대로하다 be very angry; (口) got mad
▶그는 그 말에 대로했다 He got as mad as a hornet at the words.

대로 大路 〈큰길〉 a main [broad] street; a highway; a main thoroughfare
▶군자는 대로행이라 A wise man never takes a shortcut.

대롱 a bamboo tube; 〈관〉 a pipe; 〈물레의〉 a spool

대롱거리다 dangle; swing; sway to and fro; hang loosely
▶저 나뭇가지에 무엇인가가 대롱거리고 있다 Something is dangling [hanging down] from a branch of that tree.

대롱대롱 danglingly; dingle-dangle; swayingly to and fro
▶호리병박 하나가 시렁에 대롱대롱 매달려 있다 A gourd is dangling from the trellis.

대류 對流 〔物〕 a convection (current)
♦대류의 convective / 대류시키다 circulate (warm air) by convection; convect
■—난방기 a convection type heater; a convector —전류 a convection current

대류권 對流圈 〔氣〕 the troposphere
♦대류권의 tropospheric

대륙 大陸 a continent
♦대륙의 continental / 대륙간의 intercontinental
■신— the New Continent 아시아[유럽]— the Continent of Asia[Europe]; the Asian [European] Continent 암흑— the Dark Continent —간 탄도탄 an intercontinental ballistic missile (略 ICBM) —법 the Continental law —분수계 the continental divide —사면 conti-

nental slope —식 [주의, 사상] continentalism —이동설 [地] continental drift theory —정책 continental politics —화(化) continentalization: 대륙화하다 continentalize; be continentalized —횡단 철도 a transcontinental railway; (美) a coast-to-coast railroad

대륙붕 大陸棚 a continental shelf

대륙성 大陸性 continentality ◆대륙성의 continental —기후 a continental climate

대륙적 大陸的 continental; (비유) large-minded
◆대륙적 사상 continentalism / 대륙적 풍경 a continental landscape
▶시베리아 기후는 전형적으로 대륙적이다 The weather in Siberia is typically continental.

대리 代理 〈행위〉representation; agency; proxy; [法] procuration; 〈사람〉 an agent; 〈회의 등의〉 a representative; 〈직권을 가진〉 (pl. -ties); 〈투표 등의〉 a proxy (pl. -xies); 〈대역〉 a substitute
◆의장 대리〈부의장〉 a deputy chairman; 〈임시의〉 the acting chairman / 광고 총대리점 the sole advertising agency / 대리로 by deputy; by proxy; [法] by [per] procuration (略 per pro(c).); in deputation / …의 대리로(서) as proxy for…; in [on] behalf of…
▶나는 병이 난 김선생의 대리로 여기에 왔습니다 I am here for [in place of] Mr.Kim, who is sick.
▶나는 그녀의 대리로 서류에 서명했다 I signed the paper for her by proxy.
▶김선생이 우리 선생의 대리를 보았다 Mr.Kim acted for our teacher.
—**대리하다** act [substitute] for; act in another's place [behalf] of; take another's place; stand [be] proxy for; stand in the place of; replace
◆대리시키다 substitute *sb* for 〈another〉; make 〈another〉 *one's* proxy; deputize 〈*sb* to do *sth*〉; [法] subrogate
▶나는 주인을 대리하여 일하고 있습니다 I am acting for my master.
■—**권** the right [power] of representation [attorney]; agency —**대사** a chargé d'affaires; an acting ambassador —**소송** a lawsuit by proxy [attorney] —**업** (commission) agency; an agent's business —**업자** an agent —**위임권** (the) power of attorney —**위임장** a letter of attorney —**전쟁** a proxy war —**투표** voting by proxy —**판매** sale by agent

대리공사 代理公使 a chargé d'affaires (pl. chargés d'affaires) (of a legation); an Acting Minister

대리석 大理石 [鑛] marble
■**인조[모조]—** scagliola; artificial marble —**기둥** a marble pillar —**상** a marble statue; a statue of [in] marble —**조각품** 〈여러 가지〉 marbles

대리인 代理人 a representative; 〈직무의〉 a deputy; 〈투표·주주총회 등의〉 a proxy; 〈거래의〉 an agent; 〈법정의〉 an attorney; a substitute; an alternate; [法] a procurator; a proctor
■**법정—** a legal representative 총—a universal agent; a general [sole] agent 특별—a special attorney [representative]

대리점 代理店 an agency; an agent
◆대리점을 설치하다 establish an agency
▶그 가게가 우리 회사의 대리점입니다 The firm holds the agency for our company.
■**독점—** an exclusive [a sole] agency 《for a company, for a product》 **총—** the general agent 판매— a selling agent

대립 對立 (an) opposition 《to》; (a) confrontation 《between》; 〈반목〉 antagonism
◆민족간의 대립 the antagonism of *one* race against another
▶고용자와 종업원 사이에 끊임없는 대립이 있었다 There was constant antagonism between the employer and employees.
—**대립하다** be opposed to 《each other》; be set up in opposition 《to》; be confronted with 《each other》; be pitted against 《each other》; be antagonistic to 《each other》
◆…와 대립하여 in opposition to…; in rivalry with… / 대립시키다 set 《one》 against 《another》
▶중요한 점에서 우리 의견은 날카롭게 대립해 있다 We have sharply divided opinion on an important point.
■—**감정** a feeling of confrontation [rivalry] —**개념** a coordinate concept —**관계** antagonistic relationship —**유전자** allele —**자** an opponent

대마 大馬 〈바둑에서〉 a large group of stones
▶대마 불사(不死) Large groups of stones are seldom captured.

대마 大麻 [植] hemp ⇨ 삼
■—**씨** hempseed —**유**(油) hempseed oil —**인**(仁) hempseed

대마루 1 〈지붕의 가장 높은 마루〉 the ridge of the roof **2** ⇨ 대마루판

대마루판 〈끝판〉 a decisive moment; a critical [crucial] moment; the eleventh hour

대마초 大麻草 〈식물〉 hemp; 〈흡연물〉 a hemp cigarette; 〈마리화나〉 marijuana; marihuana; hashish
▶인기 영화배우가 어제 상습적 대마초 흡연 혐의로 구속되었다 A top movie star was arrested yesterday on suspicion of habitually smoking hemp.
■—**사범** an offender of the law of hemp control —**흡연자** a hemp [marijuana] smoker

대막대기 a bamboo stick [pole]

대만 臺灣 Taiwan; Formosa
◆대만의 Taiwanese; Formosan
■—**인[사람]** a Taiwanese; a Formosan; a native of Taiwan [Formosa] —**해협** the Taiwan [Formosa] Strait

대만원 大滿員 a full house; an overflowing house; a crowded [packed] audience; a large attendance
◆대만원을 이루다 have a crowded audience
▶극장은 대만원이다 The theater is bursting with people.
▶열람실은 언제나 대만원이다 The reading room is always well patronized.

대망 大望 (an) ambition; (an) aspiration; a great desire
◆대망을 품은 사람 an ambitious man; an aspirant / 대망을 품다 be full of ambitions /

대망을 이루다 realize one's supreme ambition
▶ 사람은 누구나 대망을 품고 있어야 한다 Everybody should have an ambition.
▶ 그 여자는 일급 동시통역자가 되겠다고 하는 대망을 실현했다 She realized her ambition [aspiration] to be a first-rate simultaneous interpreter.
▶ 그 소년은 제2의 에디슨이 되겠다는 대망을 품고 있었다 The boy had an ambition [was ambitious] to become another Edison.

대망 待望 expectation; eager waiting; anticipation
♦ 대망의 hoped-for; long-awaited; long-cherished [-expected, -sought] / 대망의 경기 회복 the hoped-for business recovery
▶ 대망의 딸아이가 태어났다 The long-awaited [hoped-for, long-expected] baby girl was born.
━**대망하다** expect; (eagerly) wait for; look forward to
▶ 집에 돌아가기를 대망하고 있다 I'm looking forward to going home.

대매출 大賣出 a sale; a bargain sale; 〈특별 매출〉 a special sale
♦ 대매출[대염가매출]하다 sell *sth* at a greatly reduced price; sell *sth* dirt cheap

대맥 大麥 ⇨ 보리

대머리 〈머리〉 a bald head; 〈사람〉 a bald-headed person; a baldpate
♦ 대머리의 bald-headed; baldpated / 젊어서 벗어진 대머리 a premature baldhead / 대머리가 되다 become baldheaded
▶ 그는 대머리다 He is bald-headed.
━**총각** a bachelor prematurely bald

대면 對面 1 〈면회〉 an interview; (a) meeting
▶ 첫 대면 the first meeting [interview] / 첫 대면하는 손님 a new [unfamiliar] customer
━**대면하다** interview; meet; see; have an interview with
2 〈마주 봄〉 facing; 〔法〕 confrontation
▶ 나는 유명한 학자와 대면했다 I had an interview with a famous scholar.
▶ 고교시절의 친구들과 20년만에 대면했다 I met some high school friends after a twenty-year interval.

대명 大命 a royal command [mandate]
♦ 대명을 받들어 in obedience to the king's command / 대명을 내리다 issue a royal mandate

대명 待命 awaiting orders ⇨ 대기 명령

대명사 大名辭 〔論〕 the major term

대명사 代名詞 〔文法〕 a pronoun
♦ 대명사의 pronominal / 대명사로서 pronominally
▶ 그의 이름은 부(富)의 대명사가 되었다 His name has become a synonymous with wealth.
■ **부정[의문, 관계]―** an indefinite [an interrogative, a relative] pronoun 인칭[재귀, 지시]― a personal [reflexive, demonstrative] pronoun

대모 代母 〈가톨릭〉 a godmother

대모 玳瑁 1 〔動〕 a hawksbill (turtle)
2 〈대모갑(甲)〉 a tortoiseshell
■ ―**갑 세공** tortoiseshell work

대모집 大募集 a wholesale employment; an extensive employment
━**대모집하다** invite a large number of; advertise widely for

대목 1 〈시기〉 the best [busiest, highest] season; 〈상인의〉 a rush period
♦ 섣달 대목 the very end of the year / 대목 날 the busiest day; a big day / 대목을 노리고 물건을 쌓아두다 stock goods to provide for the rush period
2 〈고비〉 the most important occasion; the vital point; a critical stage
▶ 이제부터가 가장 어려운 대목이다 Now we have come to the most difficult part of the work.
3 〈문장의〉 a passage; a paragraph
♦ 재미있는 대목 an interesting passage
■ ―**장** a fair preceding a fete day; 〈연말의〉 a year-end fair

대목 大木 〈큰 공사의〉 a master carpenter

대목 臺木 〈접본(椄本)의〉 a (parent) stock
♦ 대목에 접목하다 insert a graft into a stock / 대목에 접목되다 be grafted on a parent stem

대못 大― a big [large] nail; a spike
♦ 대못을 박다 spike 《a beam》

대문 大門 a gate; the front gate; the main entrance
♦ 으리으리한 대문이 있는 집 a house with a stately gate / 대문을 닫다[걸다] close [lock] the front gate

대문 밖이 저승이라 〈속담〉〈사람은 언제 죽을지 모른다〉 Death keeps no calendar.

대문자 大文字 〈로마자의〉 a capital letter; 〔印〕 an uppercase letter
♦ 대문자로 쓰다 write 《a word》 in [with] capital letters; capitalize
▶ 독일어에서는 명사의 첫글자를 대문자로 쓴다 In German, nouns are spelled with a capital initial.

대문장 大文章 〈글〉 masterful [magnificent] writing; 〈사람〉 a good [master] writer; a master of (literary) style

대문짝 大門― 〈문학〉 a flap; a (door) leaf; 〈문〉 a gate
♦ 대문짝만하게 in huge letters; conspicuously / (표제 등을) 대문짝만하게 내다 play up 《the news》 with a banner; banner / 신문에 대문짝만하게 나다 go into headlines

대물 代物 a substitute
■ ―**변제** payment in substitutes

대물 對物 objects; reality
♦ 대물의 real; objective
■ ―**경[렌즈]** an object lens [glass]; an objective (lens[glass]); a field lens ―**담보** security against a thing ―**변제** payment in substitute ―**세** a real tax ―**소송** 〔法〕 real action ―**신용** real credit

대물리다 代― hand down; transmit; leave; bequeath
♦ 대물린 재산 inherited property; patrimony / 자손에게 대물리다 hand down to posterity / 아들에게 대물리다 transmit from father to son / 재산을 대물리다 leave [bequeath] property

대미 對美 ♦대미의 toward America; with America; American / 우리나라의 대미정책 our policy toward America; our American policy ■—관계 relations with America: 우호적인 대미관계를 유지하다 maintain amicable relations with America —무역 trade with America —수출 exportation to America —환율 the exchange rate on America; the won-dollar rate

대민 對民 ♦대민 봉사 활동 service for public welfare

대바구니 a bamboo basket; ⟨큰 것⟩ a bamboo crate

대바늘 a bamboo (knitting) needle

대받다 代— 1 ⟨상속받다⟩ inherit ⟨property⟩; succeed [accede] to
♦재산을 대받다 inherit some property
2 ⟨계승하다⟩ succeed to; continue
♦아버지의 사업을 대받다 succeed to one's father's business

대발회 大發會 〖證〗 the first session of the new year

대밭 a bamboo thicket [grove]

대백로 大白鷺 〖鳥〗 the great egret; common egret; great white heron

대번에 ⟨단숨에⟩ at a breath; all in a breath; ⟨한번에⟩ at one time; ⟨일거에⟩ at a stroke; at one blow; by [at] one effort; at one try; ⟨곧⟩ at once; in a moment; in no time; ⟨서슴지 않고⟩ without hesitation; ⟨쉽사리⟩ easily; without difficulty [effort]
♦쟁점을 대번에 결정하다 decide the issue at a stroke / 대번에 쓰러뜨리다 knock sb down at a single blow / 대번에 알아맞히다 guess (right) at once
▶우리는 일을 대번에 해치웠다 We finished the job at one standing.
▶나는 그곳의 형편을 대번에 알아차렸다 I took in the scene with a single glance.

대범스럽다 大汎— broad-minded ⇨ 대범하다

대범하다 大汎— bighearted; large-hearted; large-minded; broad-minded; liberal; generous; magnanimous; open-hand(ed)
♦대범한 태도 an air of magnanimity; free and open manners / 대범하게 행동하다 take a tolerant [benevolent] attitude ⟨toward⟩; act magnanimously / 대범하게 돈을 쓰다 be generous [liberal] with one's money

대법관 大法官 a justice of the Supreme Court; ⟨영국의⟩ Chancellor of English; Lord (High) Chancellor (略 L.(H.) C.)

대법원 大法院 the Supreme Court; ⟨영국의⟩ the Supreme Court of Judicature; ⟨프랑스·벨기에 등의⟩ the Court of Cassation
♦대법원에 상고하다 appeal to the Supreme Court
■—장 the Chief Justice [President] of the Supreme Court —판사 a justice of the Supreme Court

대법회 大法會 1 ⟨설법회⟩ a large Buddhist lecture meeting
2 ⟨재 올림⟩ Buddhist high mass; a great memorial service
♦대법회를 열다 celebrate [hold] high mass

대변 大便 ⟨美⟩ feces [fíːsìːz]; ⟨英⟩ faeces; fecal matter; ⟨동물의⟩ dung; excrement(s); ⟨새의⟩ droppings
♦대변을 보다 defecate; have (a) bowel movement; relieve oneself; evacuate the bowels; ⟨동물이⟩ dung / 대변을 보러 가다 go to the lavatory; ⟨美⟩ go to the toilet / 대변이 마렵다 want to go to the toilet; have a call of nature
■—검사 an examination of the feces: 대변 검사를 하다 examine sb's feces [stool] —기 a toilet stool [bowl]

대변 代辯 ⟨대신하여 말함⟩ speaking for sb; speaking by proxy
—**대변하다** speak for ⟨another⟩; be a spokesman [mouthpiece] of ⟨another⟩; act as (a) spokesman of ⟨another⟩
▶아들이 어머니의 의견을 대변했다 The son spoke for [on behalf of] his mother.
■—자 a spokesman; a mouthpiece: 신문은 여론의 대변자다 The newspaper is the voice of public opinion.

대변 貸邊 〖簿〗 the credit [creditor] (略 cr.); ⟨대변란⟩ the credit [creditor] side
♦10만원을 대변에 기입하다 enter one hundred thousand won on the credit side; credit one hundred thousand won to sb
▶80만원을 센트럴 회사의 대변에 기입해 주시오 Credit Central Trading with eight hundred thousand won. ⇌ Enter 800,000 won to the credit of Central Trading.
■—계정 a credit side —기입 credit entry —잔액 a credit(or) balance —전표 a credit note

대변 對邊 〖數〗 the opposite side[edge]; the subtense

대변인 代辯人 ⟨대변자⟩ a spokesman; ⟨여성⟩ a spokeswoman; a mouthpiece
♦민중의 대변인 a spokesman for the masses / 외무부 대변인 a Foreign Ministry spokesman; a spokesman for [of] the Ministry of Foreign Affairs
▶신문은 여론의 대변인이 되어야 한다 The newspaper must speak for the public.

대변하다 代辯— ⟨대신하여 변상함⟩ compensate on behalf of sb
▶그가 입힌 손해는 내가 대변하겠습니다 On his behalf I will compensate you for your loss.

대별 大別 a general [broad] classification
—**대별하다** classify [divide] roughly [broadly]; make a general classification; divide into main classes [principal groups]
▶그의 수집은 두 종류로 대별된다 His collection can be divided broadly [roughly] into two categories.

대보다 ⟨비교하다⟩ compare ⟨A with B⟩; make a comparison ⟨between A and B⟩; ⟨대조하다⟩ contrast ⟨A with B⟩
♦…와 대보면 in comparison with...; as compared with... / 키를 대보다 compare heights; measure oneself with ⟨another⟩

대보름(날) 大— the fifteenth January by the lunar calendar
■—달 the year's first full moon

대본 大本 the great foundation; the primal

대본 basis; the basic [cardinal] principles
♦국가[인류]의 대본 the foundation of the state [human morality]
▶농자는 천하의 대본이다 Agriculture is the foundation of a nation.

대본 貸本 a book for lending; (美) a rental book; (英) a book for hire
■—서점 (美) a rental [lending] library; circulating library: 대본 서점을 하다 keep a circulating library —업 the book-lending business

대본 臺本 〈연극의〉 a playbook; 〈영화·방송 등의〉 a script; a scenario (*pl.* ~s); 〈오페라의〉 a libretto (*pl.* ~s, -ti)
■방송— 〈라디오·TV〉 a script
■—작가 〈영화의〉 a scriptwriter; a scripter; a scenarist; a screenwriter; 〈오페라의〉 a librettist

대본산 大本山 〔佛敎〕 〈절의〉 the home temple; the headquarters (of a sect)

대부 代父 〔가톨릭〕 a godfather
♦대부가 되다 stand godfather (to)

대부 貸付 lending; loan
—대부하다 lend; loan; advance; make a loan

대부분 大部分 1 〈명사적〉 most (of); the greater [best, major] part (of); large [major] portion (of); the bulk (of); the majority (of)
▶학생의 대부분이 그 운동에 참가했다 The majority [Most] of the students took part in the movement.
▶비용의 대부분은 회원의 기부였다 The bulk of the expenses was collected from the members.
▶제방의 대부분은 파괴되었다 The greater part of the embankment collapsed [gave away]
▶그는 일생의 대부분을 외국에서 지냈다 He spent the better part of his lifetime abroad.
2 〈부사적〉 mostly; largely; for the most part; in large part
▶참석자는 대부분 대학생이었다 Those present were, for the most part, university students.
▶청중은 대부분 아이들이었다 The audience consisted mainly of children.
▶유럽의 대부분의 집은 석조다 Most houses in Europe are made of stone.

대부인 大夫人 your [his, her] (esteemed) mother

대북 臺北 Taipeh; Taipei

대북 對北 ■—방송 propaganda broadcast beamed at north Korea; broadcast to the north

대분수 帶分數 〔數〕 a mixed fraction

대불 大佛 a great image of Buddha; a huge [colossal] statue of Buddha

대비 a bamboo broom

대비 大妃 a queen dowager; a queen mother

대비 對比 1 〈대조〉 contrast; contradistinction
♦색의 대비 color contrast; contrast of colors
—대비하다 contrast; set (A) against (B)
▶번역을 원문과 대비해볼 필요가 있다 You should compare the translation with the original
2 〈비교〉 comparison; a side-by-side comparison (of A and B)
—대비하다 compare; draw (A) into comparison with (B)
3 〔地質〕 correlation

대비 對備 〈준비〉 provision (for, against); preparation(s) (for); preparedness (for); 〈방비〉 defenses
♦비상시를 위한 대비 provision against emergencies / 갑작스런 지출에 대한 대비 provision against unforeseen expenses / 대비가 되어 있다 be prepared [ready] (for)
—대비하다 provide (for, against); prepare (for); make preparations (for)
♦흉년에 대비하여 by way of precaution against a bad year / 만일에 대비하여 저축하다 lay up money against a rainy day / 노후에 대비하여 저축하다 save money for *one's* old age
▶그는 최악의 경우에 대비하고 있다 He is prepared for the worst.
▶만일에 대비하여 그들은 각서를 교환했다 By way of precaution they exchanged notes.

대사 大事 1 〈큰일〉 a great thing; a grand enterprise; a great undertaking [task]; 〈중요한 일〉 an important matter; a serious affair
♦대사를 이루다 achieve a great thing
2 〈혼례〉 a marriage ceremony
♦대사를 치르다 hold a marriage

대사 大使 an ambassador; 〈여성〉 an ambassadress
♦브라운 대사 부처 Ambassador and Mrs. Brown
▶한국은 중국에 대사를 파견하였다 Korea dispatched an ambassador to China.
■대리— (프) a chargé d'affaires 무임소— an ambassador-at-large 순회 [이동]— a roving ambassador 전권— an ambassador plenipotentiary 주미— an ambassador to the United States 특명전권— an ambassador extraordinary and plenipotentiary 특파— an ambassador extraordinary —급 회담 an ambassadorial [ambassador-level] conference; talks on the ambassadorial level —부인 an ambassadress

대사 大師 a saint; a great Buddhist priest; a great teacher of Buddhism
♦원효 대사 the Buddhist Saint Wonhyo

대사 大赦 an amnesty; a general amnesty; oblivion; 〔가톨릭〕 indulgence
♦대사를 받아 출옥하다 be released from prison on a general pardon
—대사하다 proclaim an amnesty; grant a general amnesty (to)
■—령 a decree of amnesty [oblivion]: 대사령을 내리다 grant an amnesty (to)

대사 代謝 metabolism ⇨ 신진대사
■—작용[기능] metabolism

대사 臺詞 〈연극 등의〉 speech; words; *one's* lines; *one's* part
♦대사를 말하다 read *one's* lines; speak *one's* part / 대사를 잊다 forget *one's* lines / 대사를 외다 study *one's* part / 대사를 잘못 말하다 bungle in *one's* lines
■독백— a monolog(ue); a soliloquy

대사관 大使館 an embassy

♦ 대사관을 두다 [설치하다] post an embassy (in)
  ■ 미국— the American Embassy 주미 한국— the Korean Embassy at Washington ■ —원 (a member of) the embassy staff —참사관 a council(l)or [counsel(l)or] of an embassy
대상 大祥 the second anniversary of *sb*'s death
대상 大賞 the grand prize; (프) the grand prix
대상 代償 **1** 〈변상〉 compensation; reparation; indemnification; a consideration; (라) a quid pro quo
  ♦ …의 대상으로서 in compensation for; in return for; as a quid pro quo for / 대상을 요구하다[주다] demand [pay] compensation (for)
  ▶ 어떠한 대상을 치르더라도 그 목적을 달성하지 않으면 안된다 We must achieve our aim at any price [at any cost, at all costs].
  —대상하다 compensate (*sb* for a loss); make compensation for; pay an indemnity
  2 〈대리 변상〉 compensation for *sb*; vicarious compensation; 〖宗·心〗 substitution
  —대상하다 compensate on behalf of *sb*
대상 帶狀 ♦ 대상의 zonal; belt-shaped
  ■ —지수(指數) a zonal index
대상 隊商 a caravan
대상 對象 the object; the subject; 〈목표〉 a target
  ♦ 공격[비판]의 대상 a target [subject] of attack [criticism] / 과세의 대상 property liable for taxation; an object of taxation / 선망의 대상 an object of envy / 신앙의 대상 the object of worship / 조사(의) 대상 the subject of investigation / 과학적 연구의 대상 an object of scientific study / 연소자를 대상으로 하는 잡지 a magazine intended for juvenile readers
  ▶ 그는 조소의 대상이 되었다 He became a laughingstock [the butt of derision].
  ▶ 이 책은 어린이를 대상으로 쓴 것이다 This book is intended for children.
  ▶ 우리는 이것들을 과학적인 연구 대상으로 삼았다 We made these things an object of scientific study.
대생 對生 〖植〗 opposition ♦ 대생의 opposite; adverse —대생하다 grow in opposition ■ —엽 opposite leaves
대서 大暑 the 12th of the 24 seasonal divisions of the year
대서 代書 writing for [on behalf of] *sb*
  —대서하다 write [draw up] for *sb* 《a contract》
  ■ —인 a scribe; a scrivener; a public letter-writer : 대서인을 시켜서 신청서를 쓰다 have an application written by a scrivener
대서양 大西洋 the Atlantic Ocean
  ♦ 대서양의 Atlantic
  ■ —조약 the Atlantic Pact; 북대서양 조약기구 the North Atlantic Treaty Organization (略 NATO) —함대 the Atlantic Fleet —항로 an Atlantic line; a transatlantic route —헌장 the Atlantic Charter —회담 the Atlantic Conference —횡단비행 a transatlantic flight
대서특필 大書特筆 special mention [writing]; 〈신문 등의〉 featuring
  —대서특필하다 write specially; 〈신문 등에서〉 publish 《the news》 with heavy headlines; play up 《the event》 with a banner; feature; banner
  ▶ 대서특필할 만한 것이 아무것도 없다 There is nothing worthy of special mention.
  ▶ 신문들은 대구 가스 폭발 사고를 대서특필하고 있다 The newspapers are headlining the deadly gas explosion in Taegu.
대석 臺石 a pedestal (stone); a footstone
대선 大船 a vessel
대선 貸船 hiring out boats; 〈배〉 a boat on [for] hire —대선하다 hire out boats ■ —료 boat hire —장 a boat-hiring place
대선거구 大選擧區 a major constituency
  ■ —제 a major constituency system
대설 大雪 **1** 〈큰눈〉 a heavy (fall of) snow; a heavy snowfall
  2 〈절기〉 "the heavy snowfall"; the 21st of the 24 seasonal divisions of the year
대성 大成 **1** 〈완성〉 completion; accomplishment
  ▶ 그의 그 연구는 마침내 대성을 거두었다 He accomplished his researches on it at last.
  —대성하다 complete; accomplish; bring to completion; 〈이루어지다〉 be completed; be accomplished; be brought to completion
  ♦ 사업을 대성하다 accomplish [achieve] *one's* work
  2 〈사람이〉 attainment of greatness
  ▶ 그는 대성의 싹이 보인다 He promises to achieve great things. ⇒ He has in him the makings of a great man.
  —대성하다 attain [come] to greatness; become a great person
  ▶ 그는 학자로서 대성했다 He became a great scholar.
  ▶ 그녀는 가수로 대성할 것이다 She will be crowned with success as a singer.
  ▶ 그는 실업계에서 반드시 대성할 것이다 I am sure he will attain to greatness in the business world.
  ▶ 아무래도 나는 그가 대성할 것 같지 않다 I am afraid he will never do well.
대성 大姓 a noted [an illustrious] family name; the family name of a prosperous [noted] clan
대성 大聖 a great sage; 〈인도의〉 a mahatma; 〈공자〉 Confucius, the Great Sage
대성 大聲 a loud [stentorian] voice
  ♦ 대성 통곡하다 weep aloud; wail; lament at the top of *one's* voice
대성공 大成功 a great [big, brilliant] success; a big [smash] hit
  ♦ 대성공을 거두다 win [gain] a great success; (口) hit the jackpot
  ▶ 그의 사업은 대성공이었다 His business was [became] a great success.
  ▶ 이번 연극은 대성공이다 The new play is a great success [hit]. ⇒ The new play is a big box-office hit [success, riot].
대성황 大盛況 prosperity; a great success
  ▶ 그 모임은 홀이 꽉 찰 정도로 대성황을 이루었다 The meeting was a great success, with the

hall crowded to capacity.

대세 大勢 the general situation; the general tendency; the trend; the current
♦ 세계의 대세 the general situation of the world; the trend of international affairs / 대세를 따르다 follow the general trend; swim with the tide [stream, current] / 대세를 살피다 take a general view of things / 대세를 파악하다 grasp [understand] the situation / 대세에 순응하다 adapt *oneself* to (the trend of) the times / 대세에 역행하다 go against the current; swim against the stream
▶ 대세는 이미 결정되었다 The end is now in sight. ⇌ The matter [issue] is as good as settled.
▶ 시합은 대세가 거의 결정되었다 The game is almost decided.
▶ 대세는 우리에게 유리[불리]하다 The general situation is [not] favorable to us. ⇌ The tide (of public opinion) has turned in our favor [against us].
▶ 정오까지는 선거의 대세가 판명될 것이다 We will know the general outcome of the election by noon.

대소 大小 large and small sizes; 〈크기〉 (relative) size; dimensions; magnitude
♦ 대소의 섬들 islands of various [all] sizes / 대소에 관계 없이 regardless of size; whether large or small
▶ 여러 가지의 대소 셔츠가 있다 There are shirts of various sizes. ⇌ Shirts are in all sizes.
▶ 그것은 대소에 따라 값이 다르다 The price varies according to size.
▶ 값은 대소에 관계 없이 모두 같다 They are (of) the same price, regardless of size.
▶ 그 내해에는 대소 합쳐 백 개 이상의 섬이 있다 There are more than one hundred islands, large and small, in the inland sea.
▶ 일의 대소를 불문하고 보고하시오 Report everything whether it is important or not.

대소 大笑 a roar [burst] of laughter; a loud [great] laughter; a hearty [good] laugh; a convulsive laughter
―**대소하다** roar with laughter; burst out laughing; laugh a hearty laugh (over, at)

대소 對訴 〖法〗 a cross action ⇨ 맞고소
■ 이혼― a counter divorce action

대소동 大騷動 an uproar; a turmoil; a tumult; a great disturbance [commotion, stir, (口) fuss]; great excitement [trouble]; much ado; a clamo(u)r; a considerable agitation
♦ 대소동을 벌이다 make a tumult; make [put up] a (great) fuss 《about, over》; make much ado 《about》
▶ 모임에서 대소동이 벌어졌다 There was a great stir at the meeting.
▶ 그것 때문에 대소동이 일어났다 It caused serious trouble. ⇌ It created [excited] a considerable agitation.

대소변 大小便 feces [fíːsiːz] and urine
♦ 대소변을 보다 relieve *oneself* [nature]; go to the bathroom; visit the lavatory

대소사 大小事 matters great and small; all sorts of matters; any and every thing
♦ 대소사를 맡기다 leave everything to *sb's* care [discretion]

대소수 帶小數 〖數〗 a mixed decimal

대소쿠리 a bamboo basket

대속 代贖 redemption [expiation, atonement] on behalf of another; atonement for [expiation of] another's sin(s); 〈예수의〉 the (Vicarious) Atonement; the Redemption
―**대속하다** redeem; atone for [expiate] another's sin(s) [offense]

대손 貸損 a bad debt; an irrecoverable debt; a dead loan
♦ 대손이 되다 become irrecoverable
■ ―상각 계정 bad debt account ―준비금 a bad debt reserve

대수 大數 **1** 〈큰수〉 a great [large] number **2** 〈대운〉 great fortune; good luck

대수 代數 〖數〗 algebra; literal arithmetic
♦ 대수적 해법(解法) an algebraic(al) solution / 대수로 풀다 solve 《a problem》 algebraically
■ 논리― algebra of logic ■ ―방정식 [기호] an algebraic(al) equation [symbol, sign] ―식 [곡선, 함수] an algebraical expression [curve, function] ―책 an algebra (book) ―학자 an algebraist

대수 臺數 the number 《of cars》
▶ 자동차 대수가 급속히 증가하고 있다 The number of cars is increasing rapidly. ⇌ Cars are rapidly increasing in numbers.

대수롭다 important; significant; valuable; useful
♦ 대수롭지 않은 일 a matter of no importance [weight, consequence, account]; a trivial [trifling] affair [matter]; a trifle / 대수롭지 않은 물건 a trifling thing; a little thing; a trifle; trivial [poor] stuff / 대수롭지 않은 사람 a worthless [an insignificant, a good-for-nothing] fellow; a person of no importance / 대수롭지 않은 trifling; trivial; insignificant; inconsiderable; valueless; unworthy; worthless / 대수롭게 여기다 think [make] much of; attach importance to; hold *sb* in high regard / 대수롭지 않게 여기다 have no regard for; think [make] little [light] of; slight
▶ 그는 대수롭지 않은 일에도 곧잘 화를 낸다 He gets angry at the merest trifle.
▶ 그녀는 내 말을 대수롭게 듣지 않는다. 언제나 한 귀로 듣고 한 귀로 흘릴 뿐이다 She never takes what I say seriously. It just goes in one ear and out the other.
▶ 그녀는 대수롭지 않은 일에도 참견한다 She interferes even in little things.
▶ 객지에서는 대수롭지 않은 친절에도 고마움을 느끼게 된다 When you are a stranger, a little kindness makes you happy.
▶ 대수롭지 않은 일로 법석대지 마라 Don't make a fuss about trifles!

대수술 大手術 〖醫〗 a major operation

대숲 a bamboo thicket [grove]; a clump of bamboos

대승 大乘 〖佛敎〗 Mahayana; the Great Vehicle

▶ 대승적 견지에서 문제를 해결하지 않으면 안 된다 We have to settle the matter from a broader viewpoint.
■ —경 the Mahayana Sutras / —불교 Mahayanist Buddhism

대승 大勝 1 〈썩 나음〉 great superiority
—**대승하다** be much better 《than》; be far superior 《to》
2 〈이김〉 a great [signal, decisive] victory; 〈선거의〉 a landslide [sweeping] victory; a sweep
♦ 7대 0의 대승 a great victory with [by a score of] seven to nothing / 대승을 거두다 achieve a great victory
—**대승하다** gain [win] a great [signal] victory; win big; 〈선거에서〉 win a landslide 《over》
▶ 우리 팀이 10대 0으로 대승했다 Our team won a great victory by a score of 10 to 0.

대시 1 〈역주(力走)〉 a dash
▶ 그는 출발시 대시가 좋았다 He started with a good dash.
—**대시하다** dash
2 ⇨ 줄표
♦ 대시를 붙이다 put a dash
3 〔數〕 a prime 《>A′는 A prime, A″는 A double prime으로 읽음》

대식 大食 gluttony; voracity
▶ 대식은 건강에 좋지 않다 Eating much is not good for the health.
—**대식하다** eat much; eat heavily [gluttonously, voraciously]; eat like a horse; cram [stuff] *oneself*; gormandize; gluttonize
♦ 대식하는 gluttonous; ravenous; voracious
■ —가[한] a big [heavy, hearty] eater; a glutton; a gormandizer

대신 大臣 a minister; a Cabinet minister; a Cabinet member; 《英》 a Secretary
♦ 대신의 직 ministership; a Cabinet position; a portfolio / 대신의 ministerial / 대신이 되다 become [be appointed] a (Cabinet) minister; enter the Cabinet; receive a portfolio

대신 代身 1 〈대리·대용〉 substitution; vicariousness; 〈대용품·대리인〉 a substitute; (口) a sub; 〈대리인〉 a deputy; a proxy; 〈교대자〉 a relief
♦ 가는 대신에 instead of going / 버터 대신에 마가린을 쓰다 substitute butter by margarine / 고기 대신에 생선을 먹다 eat fish in the room of meat / 남 대신에 투표하다 vote in the name of another
▶ 네가 못 가면 내가 대신 가마 If you can't go, I'll go instead (of you).
▶ 당신 어머님께 내가 대신 말씀 드리죠 I'll speak to your mother on your behalf [on behalf of you].
▶ 램프 대신 전등이 쓰이게 되었다 Electric lights came to be used in place of lamps.
▶ 그는 직접 오지 않고 대신 동생을 보냈다 He sent his brother instead of coming himself.
▶ 그 사람이 내 대신 그것을 했다 He did it on my behalf.
▶ 우리는 프랑스어 대신 독일어를 배웠다 We learned German instead of French.
▶ 네 대신에 누군가를 채용해야 된다 I shall be obliged to get someone in your place.
▶ 통나무를 의자 대신 썼다 A log did for my seat.
▶ 이 방은 사무실 대신이다 This room will serve for the office.
▶ 장군은 참석할 수 없었지만 대신 부관을 보냈다 The general was unable to attend, but he sent his deputy as a substitute.
—**대신하다** take *sb's* place; take the place of; replace; substitute [be substituted] for; 〈교대하다〉 relieve *sb*
♦ 일동을 대신하여 on behalf of the company / 아무를 대신하다 take *sb's* place; stand in *sb's* shoes; act [sub] for *sb*
▶ 나뭇잎으로 접시를 대신했다 A leaf served as a plate.
▶ 기계가 육체 노동을 대신하게 되었다 Machinery took the place of manual labor.
▶ 어머니의 사랑을 대신할 수 있는 것은 없다 Nothing can replace a mother's love.
▶ 뭔가 이에 대신할 것을 찾아야겠다 I must find some substitute for this.
▶ 아버님을 대신하여 심심한 감사를 드립니다 I thank you heartily in the name of my father.
▶ 그를 대신할 만한 사람을 구할 수가 없다 We cannot find a substitute for him.
▶ 서면으로 인사를 대신하겠습니다 Please allow me to send you a letter instead of [in place of] paying you a visit.
2 〈대상(代償)〉 compensation; return; 〈교환〉 exchange
♦ 대신에[으로] in compensation 《for》; in return 《for》; in exchange 《for》
▶ 어제 깬 컵 대신에 하나 사드리겠습니다 I'll replace the cup I broke yesterday.
▶ 미국 우표를 보내주십시오. 대신 한국 우표를 보내드리겠습니다 Would you send me some American stamps? I'll let you have some Korean ones in exchange.
▶ 그녀가 가사를 돌봐주는 대신 나는 그녀에게 영어를 가르쳐 주고 있다 I teach her English in exchange for [in return for] her help with housekeeping.
3 〈한편〉 but; though; while
▶ 이것은 비싼 대신에 질깁니다 This wears longer, though a bit expensive.
▶ 나는 적도 많지만 대신에 친구도 많다 I have as many friends as enemies.
▶ 그는 두뇌가 명석한 대신 몸이 튼튼하지 못하다 He has a sharp mind, but he's not strong physically.
▶ 가르치는 것은 힘이 드는 대신에 낙이 있다 The pleasure of teaching makes up for the toil.

대실 貸室 a room [hall] on [for] hire
■ —료 room charge; 〈호텔의〉 hotel charge

대심 對審 〔法〕 confrontation in court
▶ 내일은 원고와 피고의 대심이 있겠습니다 Tomorrow the accused and his accuser [the plaintiff and the defendant] will confront each other in court.

대심원 大審院 〈미국의 대법원〉 the Supreme Court of the United States

대싸리 〔植〕 a broom cypress =댑싸리

대아 大我 〔哲〕 absolute ego; the higher self; *one's* larger self; 〔佛敎〕 *one's* true self; (산) Atman

대안 代案 an alternative plan
♦ 대안을 내다 make [work out] an alternative plan [measure]

대안 對岸 the other [opposite] side 《of a river》; the opposite bank [shore]
▶ 어떻게 하면 강의 대안에 닿을 수 있을까? How can I get to the other side of the river? / 대안의 송림이 보입니까? Do you see the pine wood on the opposite bank?
▶ 이 사건을 대안의 불 보듯 할 수는 없다 We must not look on the incident with (utter) indifference.

대안 對案 a counterproposal
♦ 대안을 제시하다 make a counterproposal / 대안을 짜다 work out a countermeasure
▶ 이것을 그들에게 대안으로 내놓읍시다 Let's counter their plan with this proposal.

대안렌즈 對眼— an eyepiece ⇨ 접안렌즈

대야 a basin; a (wash)tub; (美) a washbowl; (英) a washbasin

-대야 〈-다고 하여야〉 ▶ 열심히 한대야 도와주지 I will help you only if you exert yourself.
▶ 공부를 한대야 책을 사주지 I won't buy you books unless you are ready to study.
▶ 쇳덩이가 솜뭉치보다 무겁대야 말이 되지 To make sense you have to say that the metal is heavier than the cotton.

대양 an ocean; (詩) the main
♦ 대양 저쪽에 있는 대륙 a transoceanic continent / 대양의 oceanic / 대양의 한가운데서 in the middle of the ocean / 대양을 가로질러 across the ocean / 대양을 항해하다 sail [plow] the ocean
■ —도(島) an oceanic island —항로 an ocean line —항로선 an ocean liner —횡단비행 a transoceanic flight

대양주 大洋洲 Oceania ♦ 대양주의 Oceanian
■ —사람 an Oceanian

대어 大魚 a large [big] fish; a big-game fish
♦ 대어를 놓치다 miss a good chance of success
▶ 그는 대어를 낚았다 He landed a big fish.
■ —낚시 big-game fishing —상 the prize awarded to the most successful angler of the day; the award for catching the biggest game fish

대어 大漁 a large [big, good] catch (of fish); a good [rich] haul
♦ 대어를 하다 have a large [big] catch (of fish); make a rich haul

대어 對語 an antonym
▶ 삶의 대어는 죽음이다 The antonym of "life" is "death."

대언장담 大言壯談 big [tall] talk ⇨ 호언장담 (豪言壯談)

대업 大業 a great work [enterprise]; a great deed [achievement]; a great [mighty, gigantic] task
♦ 건국의 대업 the great work of founding the state / 대업을 맡다 take charge of a great task / 대업을 이루다 achieve a great work

대여 貸與 lending; a loan
—대여하다 lend; lease; loan; give the loan of *sth*; grant the use of *sth*
♦ 무료로 대여하다 lend free; loan *sth* without charge
■ 무기—법 (美) the Lend·Lease [Lease·Lend] Act ■ —금 a loan —자 a lender —장학금 a loan scholarship

대여섯 about five or six

대역 大役 〈임무〉 an important duty [task]; 〈역할〉 an heavy role [part]; 〈사명〉 an important [a great] mission
♦ 대역을 맡다 undertake [take up, accept] an heavy part / 대역을 완수하다 perform [discharge, accomplish] an important duty
▶ 그에게 대역이 맡겨졌다 He was charged with an important task.
▶ 나는 새 지점 창설의 대역을 맡았다 I was charged with the important mission of establishing a new branch.
▶ 그는 햄릿이라는 대역을 훌륭히 해냈다 He played the important part of Hamlet splendidly.

대역 大逆 〈죄〉 high treason; 〈악행〉 bestial wickedness
■ —무도[부도] heinous [bestial] wickedness —죄 high treason; lese majesty; (프) lèse majesté / 대역죄로 사형 선고를 받다 be sentenced to death on a charge of high treason

대역 代役 〈행위〉 substitution; 〈사람〉 a substitute actor [actress]; a substitute; an understudy; 〔映〕 a stand-in; a double
▶ 내가 그의 대역을 했다 I filled in for him.
▶ 나는 그의 대역으로 주인 노릇을 했다 I acted as host in place for him.
▶ 신인이 그녀의 대역으로 오필리아 역을 했다 A new face played the part of Ophelia as a substitute for her.

대역 對譯 a translation printed side by side with the original (text); a text 《of Lost Paradise》 with its 《Korean》 translation (printed) on the opposite page
▶ 이 책은 대역본이다 This book is in bilingual.
▶ 이 책은 영한 대역으로 되어 있다 In this book the English original has its Korean translation on the opposite side.
■ —판 a bilingual edition [version]; an interlinear edition

대연습 大演習 (hold) grand maneuvers

대열 隊列 a file ⇨ 대오(隊伍)

대엿 about five or six =대여섯

대엿새 about five or six days

대영제국 大英帝國 the British Empire

대오 great [divine] enlightenment; spiritual awakening [enlightenment]
—대오하다 be spiritually awakened; attain divine enlightenment [spiritual awakening]

대오 隊伍 〈대열〉 a file; the ranks; a line; 〈행렬〉 a procession; 〈대형〉 (a) formation
♦ 대오 정연하게 in regular ranks; in perfect order / 대오를 짓다 form ranks [a column]; line up / 대오를 흐트러뜨리다 break the line

[column, ranks]
▶우리는 대오를 지어 거리를 행진했다 We marched in rank and file on the street. ⇌ We paraded in line on the street.

대오다 come [arrive] on time; get [be] (here) on time ♦약속 시간에 대오다 come at the appointed time
▶3시까지 대오시오 Please be here by three.

대오리 a strip of bamboo; a bamboo strip

대왐풀 [植] a bletilla ⇨ 자란(紫蘭)

대왕 大王 〈위대한 왕〉 a great king; 〈선왕〉 the late king ♦염라 대왕 Yama; the King of Hell / 세종[알렉산더] 대왕 Sejong [Alexander] the Great

대외 對外 ♦대외적인 outside; foreign; external; international; oversea(s); abroad
■—거래 foreign transactions [business] —경제협력 economic assistance —관계 foreign [international] relations —권익 foreign [overseas] rights and interests —무역 foreign [overseas] trade —문제 international issues —방송 broadcasting abroad; a broadcast beamed overseas —정책 a foreign [an external, an exterior] policy —투자 overseas investment

대외원조 對外援助 a foreign aid; an aid to a foreign country
—법 (美) the Foreign Assistance Act

대요 大要 〈요지〉 an outline; a summary; a gist; an epitome; an abstract; (프) a résumé; a précis; 〈개요〉 a general idea
♦문제의 대요 the sum and substance of the matter / 한국사 대요 an outline of Korean history / 질문에 대한 회답의 대요 the general tenor of the answers to a question / 대요를 설명하다 describe [give] the outline (of) / 대요를 말하다 give a summary [an outline] of; sum up; epitomize; summarize; outline
▶당신의 논문의 대요를 말해 보시오 Give the summary [outline] of your paper.
▶나의 해외 여행의 대요를 기술하겠다 I will outline my trip abroad.

대욕 大慾 avarice; greed; covetousness; avidity; rapacity

대용 代用 substitution
♦의자 대용으로 in place of a chair; (in substitution) for a chair
▶그것은 침대 대용이다 It serves as a bed. ⇌ You can use it for a bed.
▶나는 마가린을 버터 대용으로 쓴다 I substitute margarine for butter.
▶밀가루가 쌀 대용으로 많이 이용된다 Flour is in great demand as a substitute for rice.
—대용하다 substitute 《A for B》; use 《one thing》 for 《another》
♦종이를 천으로 대용하다 substitute paper for cloth
■—가능성 substitutability —식 substitute food; 〈쌀의〉 a rice substitute —어(語) [文法] a substitute —품 a substitute (for); a substitute article [product]; an ersatz

대우 [農] catch cropping; planting 《beans》 in [between] the rows of wheat [barley] field
■—콩[팥, 깨] beans [red beans, sesame] planted as a catch crop with wheat [barley]

대우 待遇 1 〈취급〉 treatment; dealing; 〈접대〉 reception; entertainment
♦따뜻한 대우를 받다 be warmly received; meet with a cordial reception / 파격적인 대우를 받다 enjoy exceptionally good treatment / 신사 대우를 하다 treat sb as a gentleman / 지위에 합당한 대우를 하다 do sb the honor due to 《his》 position; do sb due honor
▶그 집은 손님에 대한 대우가 좋다[나쁘다] They are hospitable [inhospitable] to visitors at that house.
▶나는 그에게 공정한[부당한] 대우를 받았다 I received impartial [unfair] treatment from him.
—대우하다 treat; receive; entertain
♦동등하게 대우하다 treat sb on the same footing with [as] 《another》
2 〈급료〉 pay; salary; remuneration
♦대우를 개선하다 raise [increase] sb's pay; give better treatment to 《workers》
▶그 회사는 대우가 좋다[나쁘다] That company pays their employees liberally [poorly]. ⇌ The employees are well [poorly] paid at that company.
■—과장— an associate section chief 차별— discriminative treatment ■—개선 the improvement [betterment] of labor conditions; a raise of salary —문제 the question of pay [treatment]

대우 對偶 1 〈짝〉 a pair **2** [數] contraposition **3** [論] opposition; antithesis
■—법 (修) antithesis —법칙 the law of contraposition

대우주 大宇宙 [哲] the great universe; the macrocosm

대우파다 [農] plant a catch crop with wheat [barley]

대운 大運 great fortune; wonderfully good luck

대웅성 大熊星 [天] (stars of) the Great Bear; Ursa Major

대웅전 大雄殿 [佛敎] the main building of a temple (where the image of Buddha is enshrined)

대원 大圓 [數] a great circle

대원 大願 an earnest prayer; a great desire; one's cherished desire

대원 隊員 a member (of a party)
♦구조대 대원 a member of the rescue party

대원수 大元帥 the generalissimo (pl. ~s); the commander in chief (略 C. in C.) of the Army and Navy

대원칙 大原則 the broad [dominant] principle

대월 貸越 overdraft ⇨ 당좌(~대월)

대위 大尉 [軍] 〈육군〉 a captain; 〈해군〉 a lieutenant; 〈공군〉 (美) a captain; (英) a flight lieutenant
♦대위 직[계급] a captaincy; a lieutenancy

대위법 對位法 [樂] counterpoint
♦대위법의[(적)인] contrapuntal
■—이중— double counterpoint —작곡가 a contrapuntist

대유성 大遊星 〔天〕 the major planet=대행성

대응 對應 1 〈상대〉 facing each other; confrontation; opposition
—**대응하다** face [confront] each other; be opposed ((to)); tackle; deal with; cope with
◆폭력에는 폭력으로 대응하다 oppose violence to violence / 시류에 대응하다 keep up with the trend of the times
▶우리는 항상 새로운 정세에 대응해 나가야 한다 We should always cope with the new situation.
2 〈상당〉 equivalence
—**대응하다** be equivalent to
▶그 한국어에 대응하는 영어는 없다 The Korean phrase has no close equivalent [counterpart] in English.
▶영국의 퍼블릭 스쿨은 한국의 고등학교에 대응한다 The public schools in Britain correspond to the senior high schools in Korea.
3 〔數〕 correspondence
—**대응하다** correspond to; answer to
◆대응하는 두 개 corresponding sides

대의 大義 a great [noble] cause; a great duty; justice; a just and righteous cause
◆대의를 밝히다 recognize *one's* highest duty (to *one's* sovereign) / 대의를 위해 죽다 sacrifice *oneself* for the sake of justice; sacrifice *one's* life in a great cause

대의 大意 〈요지〉 the gist; the (main) purport; the substance; 〈개요〉 the general idea [purport]; an outline; a summary; a synopsis; a résumé
◆대의를 적다 make a résumé / 대의를 말하다 give an outline (of)
▶이 문단의 대의를 적으시오 Write [Give] the general idea of this paragraph.
▶이 논문의 대의를 400자 이내로 적으시오 Write a summary [synopsis, résumé] of this paper in four hundred words or less.
▶이 이론의 대의는 이렇다 In substance [outline], the theory is as follows [like this].

대의 代議 representation
■—원 a representative; a delegate —정치 a representative [parliamentary] government —제도 a representative [parliamentary] system

대의명분 大義名分 a just and great cause; the highest duty
▶그의 행동은 대의명분이 서지 않는다 His conduct cannot be justified. ⇒ He has no cause for such conduct.

대인 大人 1 ⇨ 거인(巨人)
2 〈어른〉 an adult; a grown-up (person)
▶입장료 대인 5천원 《게시》 Admission : 5,000 won per adult.
3 〈인물〉 a great [magnanimous] man; a big [generous, broad-minded] person; 〈군자〉 a man of virtue; 〈남의 아버지〉 your [his] father
▶그에게는 대인의 풍격이 있다 There is an air [a look] of magnanimity about him. ⇒ He impresses us as a man of great character. ⇒ He carries himself like a man of substance. ⇒ He has all the qualities we find in a fine gentleman.

대인 代印 〈찍기〉 signing per [by] procuration; 〈찍는 도장〉 a seal set by proxy
◆대인을 찍다 sign (for another); set a seal by proxy

대인 對人 ◆대인(용)의 antipersonnel
■—공포증 anthrophobia —권(權) [신용, 담보] personal rights [credit, security] —무기 an antipersonnel weapon

대인관계 對人關係 personal relations [relationships]
▶그는 대인관계에 신경을 많이 썼다 He was very careful about personal relations.
▶그는 대인관계가 원만하지 않다 His personal relationships are not going well.

대인기 大人氣 great popularity; a great success; a (big) hit
◆대인기를 끌다 be very popular; enjoy great popularity; make a great hit; be very successful
▶이번 공연은 대인기다 The performance has created a sensation [has a great run].
▶그는 학생들한테 대인기다 He is very popular [a great favorite] with the students.

대인물 大人物 a great man [character, figure]; a man of great caliber ◆역사상의 대인물들 great personalities of history

대일 對日 〈부사적〉 toward [with] Japan ◆한국의 대일 외교 정책 Korea's diplomatic policy toward Japan
■—관계 relations with Japan —무역 trade with Japan —청구권 the claim to Japan

대일감정 對日感情 the feeling [sentiment] toward Japan
▶그들의 대일감정이 악화되었다 Their feelings toward Japan have changed for the worse.
▶대일감정이 아주 나쁘다 The feeling is very bad toward the Japanese. ⇒ The anti-Japanese sentiment is mounting [growing].

대임 大任 〈임무〉 a great task; an important duty [task]; 〈요직〉 an important office; 〈사명〉 an important mission
◆대임을 맡다 undertake a great task / 대임을 맡기다 entrust *sb* with an important task / 대임을 완수하다 carry through [perform, acquit *oneself* of] a great task; fulfill a great mission
▶그는 대임을 띠고 미국으로 떠났다 He left for America on an important mission.

대입 代入 〔數〕 substitution —**대입하다** substitute
▶y에 3을 대입하다 substitute 3 for y

대자 大字 a large character [letter]; 〈대문자〉 a capital letter

대자 帶磁 〔物〕 magnetization = 자기(磁氣)(~화)

대자대비 大慈大悲 〔佛敎〕 great mercy and compassion
◆대자대비하신 관세음보살 Avalokitêsvara of Great Love and Great Mercy

대자보 大字報 a big-character paper [poster]; a wallposter; a wall newspaper

대자연 大自然 creation; Mother Nature; (Mighty)

Nature
▶ 나는 시베리아에서 대자연의 웅대함에 깊은 감명을 받았다 I was much impressed with the grandeur of Mother Nature in Siberia.

대작 大作 〈걸작〉 a masterpiece; a monumental [great] work; 〈대형의〉 a work [picture, sculpture] of large size; a voluminous work
▶ 그녀는 나이 50에 마침내 대작을 그렸다 She painted a great picture at last at (the age of) fifty.
▶ 그는 막 1,000 페이지가 넘는 대작을 탈고했다 He has just completed a voluminous work of over a thousand pages.
▶ 그는 200호 짜리 유화 대작을 완성했다 He finished a large oil painting, size two hundred.

대작 代作 1 〈행위〉 ghostwriting; vicarious writing; writing [composing] for 《another》; 〈작품〉 a vicarious work
—**대작하다** write [compose] for 《another》; ghostwrite; ghost
▶ 그의 조수가 그의 논문을 대작하고 있다 His assistant has been ghostwriting his article.
2 〔農〕 ⇨ 대파(代播)
■ —**자** a ghostwriter —**물** a ghostwritten work

대작 對酌 drinking together (facing each other) —**대작하다** drink together; exchange drinking cups

대잠 對潛 ■ —**미사일** an antisubmarine missile —**초계기**(哨戒機) an antisubmarine patrol plane

대장 大將 1 〔軍〕〈육군〉 a general; 〈해군〉 an admiral; 〈공군〉〈美〉 a general; 〈英〉 an air chief marshal
2 〈우두머리〉 a head; a chief; a boss; a captain
▶ 여기서는 내가 대장이다 I'm cock of the roost around here.

대장 大腸 〔解〕 the colon 《pl. ~s, -la》; the large intestine
■ —**균** a colon bacillus; Escherichia coli —**염** colitis —**카타르** catarrh of the colon

대장 隊長 a captain; a leader; a (troop) commander; a commanding officer 《略 C. O.》
■ —**소[중, 대]**— a section [company, battalion] commander **탐험**— the leader of an expedition

대장 臺帳 〈회계원장〉 a ledger; 〈등록대장〉 a register; 〈토지대장〉 a cadastre; a terrier; a land register

대장간 —間 a blacksmith's shop; a smithy
대장간에 식칼이 논다 〈속담〉 The shoemaker's wife goes barefoot. ⇒ A shoemaker is always ill shod. ⇒ The tailor's wife is worst clad.

대장경 大藏經 〔佛敎〕 the complete collection of Buddhist Sutras, Laws and Treatises; Tripitaka ■ **팔만**— the Tripitaka Koreana

대장부 大丈夫 a manly man; 〈용사〉 a heroic [brave] man; 〈큰 인물〉 a great man
♦ **대장부다운** manly; manful; heroic
▶ 대장부답게 굴어라 Be a man. ⇒ Play the man. ⇒ Behave [Act] like a man.

▶ 대장부라면 그런 짓은 못한다 You should be man enough not to do a thing like that.
▶ 그는 대장부다움을 보였다 He showed himself a hero.

대장장이 —匠— a blacksmith; a smith

대저 大著 〈명저〉 a great work; a masterpiece; 〈방대한〉 a voluminous work

대저울 a beam balance; a steel yard

대적 大敵 〈강적〉 a great [powerful, formidable] enemy; an invincible foe; an archenemy; 〈경쟁상대〉 a formidable rival [opponent]; 〈다수의 적〉 a large group of enemies; a mass of enemies
♦ **민주주의의 대적** the most deadly foe of democracy
▶ 부주의는 교통 안전의 대적이다 Carelessness is a great menace to traffic safety.
▶ 대적이라고 겁내지 말고 소적이라고 경시하지 마라 Don't fear a powerful enemy and don't underrate a powerless enemy.

대적 對敵 1 〈적대〉 hostility; antagonism; contention
—**대적하다** be hostile (to); contend against; be antagonistic (to)
2 〈겨룸〉 rivalry; (a) competition; emulation; a contest; 〈적수〉 a match; an equal
—**대적하다** 〈겨루다〉 rival; contend [compete] 《with》; 〈필적하다〉 be a match for; be equal to
♦ **대적할 사람이 없다** have no equal [match, parallel]; be without a match; be peerless
▶ 너는 그와 대적할 상대가 못된다 You are no match for him.

대전 大典 1 〈의식〉 a state [great] ceremony [function]; 〈즉위 의〉 (the ceremony of) enthronement; a coronation
2 〈중대한 법전〉 a canon

대전 大殿 〈궁전〉 a royal palace; 〈대전마마〉 His [Your] Majesty the King

대전 大戰 a great war; 〈전투〉 a great battle; 〈세계대전〉 a World War
♦ **제1차 세계대전** the First World War; World War I; the Great War / **제2차 세계대전** the Second World War; World War II; the Second War

대전 帶電 〔物〕 electrification
▶ 금속은 대전이 잘 된다 Metal is easily charged with electricity.
—**대전하다** charge with electricity; electrify; take a charge
■ —**체** an electrified body

대전 對戰 fight; match; competition
—**대전하다** encounter (the enemy); fight 《with》; compete 《with》; play a match 《against》; play 《another》; face
▶ 우리는 준결승에서 A팀과 대전했다 We had a game with A team in the semifinal.
▶ 우리는 강적과 대전하게 되었다 We were confronted with [by] a formidable enemy.
■ —**료** fight money —**성적** the result of a game [match]

대전제 大前提 〔論〕 the major premise 《of syllogism》; the sumption

대전차 對戰車 ♦ **대전차용의** antitank

■—미사일[지뢰] an antitank missile [mine] —포 an antitank gun; a bazooka —호 an antitank trench

대절 貸切 (美) reserving; (英) booking ⇨ 전세(專貰)

대접 a (soup) bowl
♦ 국 한 대접 a bowl of soup

대접 待接 〈대우〉 reception; treatment; 〈환대〉 hospitality; entertainment
♦ 극진한 대접 cordial [hearty] hospitality / 푸짐한 대접 generous treatment / 융숭한 대접을 받다 be given [accorded] hospitable treatment [a cordial reception]
▶ 그의 집에서 저녁 대접을 잘 받았다 I was treated to a good dinner by him and his family.
▶ 대접 잘 받고 갑니다 Thank you for your kind hospitality.
▶ 그렇게 친절한 대접을 받으리라고는 생각지 못했어요 I didn't think that I'd receive such a kind reception.
▶ 대접이 번번치 못해서 죄송합니다 I am sorry I have not been much of a host to you. = I wish I could have entertained you better.
—**대접하다** 〈대우하다〉 treat; receive; 〈환대하다〉 entertain; show [give] sb hospitality
▶ 교수님댁에서 차와 케이크를 대접받았다 We were served tea and cake at the professor's house.
▶ 그들은 나에게 저녁을 대접했다 They treated [entertained] me to dinner.
▶ 그들은 외국에서 온 그 손님을 따뜻이 대접했다 They gave the foreign guest a warm reception.
▶ 술 한 잔 대접하겠습니다 I'll buy you a drink.

대정맥 大靜脈 〖生〗 the main vein; the vena cava (*pl.* venae cavae)

대제 大帝 a great emperor
♦ 이반 대제 Ivan the Great

대제 大祭 a great religious ceremony [service]

대제사장 大祭司長 a high [chief] priest

대조 大潮 the flood tide; the spring tide; the major tide

대조 對照 (a) contrast; (an) antithesis; 〈비교〉 (a) comparison; 〈맞추어보기〉 (a) collation
♦ 명암 대조 the contrast between [of] light and shade / 이론과 실제의 대조 the antithesis between theory and fact / 좋은 대조 an excellent [a great] contrast / 대조적인 contrastive / …와 대조적으로 in contrast to… / 대조를 이루다 form [present] a contrast 《with》; be in contrast 《to, with》
▶ 자목련화가 푸른 하늘과 아름다운 대조를 이루었다 The red magnolia blossoms were in beautiful contrast to the blue sky.
▶ 흑과 백은 대조적이다 Black is a contrast to white.
—**대조하다** contrast [compare] 《A with B》; set 《A against B》
♦ 원장[원문, 원고]과 대조하다 compare with [refer to] the ledger [text, manuscript] / 두 사본을 대조하다 collate the two manuscripts
▶ 그 번역을 원문과 비교 대조해 주십시오 Compare the translation with the original.
▶ 우리는 물건과 견본을 대조해 봤다 We compared the article with the sample.

대종 大宗 1 〈계통〉 the lineage of the head [main] family
2 〈사물의 주류〉 the main items
♦ 수출의 대종 the staple article for export / 대종을 이루다 form 《(its) majority》

대종상 大鍾賞 Grand Bell (best film) Awards

대좌 對坐 sitting opposite [face to face]
—**대좌하다** sit opposite 《to sb》; sit face to face [(프) vis-à-vis 《with sb》

대좌 臺座 a pedestal; a plinth

대죄 大罪 a great [grave, heinous] crime; a grave offense; a felony; 〈종교·도덕상의〉 a great [mortal] sin
♦ 대죄를 범하다 commit a great crime
—인 a felon; a great offender; an atrocious criminal

대죄하다 待罪— wait for the judgment

대주 大酒 heavy [deep, hard] drinking
—가 a heavy [hard] drinker; a soaker; a boozer; a guzzler; a toper

대주 貸主 a lender; 〈채권자〉 a creditor; 〈부동산의〉 a lessor

대주교 大主敎 〖가톨릭〗 an archbishop; 〈수석대주교〉 a primate ♦ 캔터베리 대주교 the Archbishop of Canterbury

대주다 supply [provide, furnish] 《sb with sth》
♦ 돈을 대주다 give sb financial aid; finance sb / 학비를 대주다 provide 《a student》 with (his) school expenses / 한 달에 20만원씩 대주다 allow sb two hundred thousand won a month / 밑천을 대주다 furnish sb with funds

대주자 代走者 〖野〗 a pinch runner

대중 〈어림함〉 a rough estimate [calculation]; 〈추측〉 conjecture; guess; 〈표준〉 a standard; a yardstick; consistency
♦ 대중을 잡다 make a rough estimate / 대중이 틀리다 make a miscalculation
▶ 그의 말은 대중을 잡을 수가 없다 I can't make head or tail of what he says.
—**대중하다** make [form] a rough estimate [calculation] 《of》

대중 大衆 the (ordinary) people; the (general) public; the masses; the mass of people

> 解說 *the people*은 국가나 자치단체를 구성하는 일반 사람들. *the public*은 합리적인 판단을 할 줄 알며 건전한 민주주의를 유지해 나가는 사람들. *the masses*는 사회기구를 이해하지 못하며 매스컴에 놀아나는 사람들로서 때때로 경멸적으로 사용된다.

♦ 대중의 소리 public opinion / 대중 취향의 영화 a movie for the masses / 대중을 위한 정당 a party for the masses / 대중적인[취향의] for the masses; for popular use / 대중에게 맞는 suited for the use of the general public; appealing to the masses / 대중의 마음을 사로잡다 have a strong hold on the public / 대중의 지지를 얻다 have a mass support; have the support of the public / 대중을 우롱하다 fool

the public / 국민 대중에게 호소하다 address the mass of people
▶ 그의 연설은 대중의 지지를 얻었다 His speech won popular support. ⇌ His speech appealed to the (general) public.
▶ 그의 작품은 대중의 취향에 맞지 않는다 His works do not appeal to the common taste.
▶ 한국의 일반 대중은 그의 정책을 지지하는 것 같다 The general public of Korea seems to favor his policies.
■ 근로— the working classes [masses] 일반— the general public ■—가요 a popular song —과세 mass tax; taxation on the general public —문학 popular literature —사회 a mass society —성 popularity —소설 a popular novel [story] —식당 an eating place [house]; a chophouse; a cheap restaurant —심리 ⇨ 군중(~심리) —오락 mass entertainment —운동 a mass movement : 대중 운동을 일으키다 start a mass movement [people's drive] —음악 popular music —작가 a popular writer; a dime novelist —잡지 a popular magazine —전달 mass communication —정당 a mass party —집회 a mass rally —판 ⇨ 보급 (~판)

대중 對中 〈부사적〉 toward [with] China
◆ 한국의 대중 관계 Korea's relations with China / 대중무역의 발전 expansion of China trade [trade with China]

대중없다 〈일정치 않다〉 irregular; unsettled; indefinite; unfixed; 〈변하기 쉽다〉 inconstant; changeable; 〈종잡을 수 없다〉 inconsistent
◆ 대중없는 말 inconsistent remarks; a pointless statement / 대중없는 수입 an irregular income
▶ 점심 시간은 대중없습니다 There is no fixed rule about the hour of lunch.
▶ 그는 하는 짓이 대중없어 믿을 수가 없다 He is so inconsistent in his behavior that you can never depend upon him.

대중화 大衆化 popularization
◆ 과학의 대중화 popularization of science
—대중화하다 popularize; make 《a thing》 popular; be popularized
▶ 전화는 대중화되어 있다 The telephones have come into widespread use [are widely used].

대증요법 對症療法 〔醫〕 allopathy; a symptomatic [expectant] treatment
◆ 대증요법을 하다 treat symptoms as they appear; meet symptoms as they call for attention
▶ 정부의 시책은 일시적인 대증요법에 지나지 않았다 The government's policy served to do little more than to patch over each problem temporarily when it arose.

대지 大旨 an outline ⇨ 대의(大意)
대지 大地 the earth; the ground; (詩) mother earth
◆ 대지를 밟다 tread on the ground
대지 大志 an ambition; an aspiration 《to do》
▶ 대지를 품어라 Be ambitious.
▶ 그는 사회 개혁자가 되겠다는 대지를 품고 있었다 His ambition was [He aspired] to be a great social reformer.

대지 垈地 a (building) site; ground; a plot; a lot
◆ 대지 선정 the selection of a site / 대지를 확보하다 secure the location (for)
■ —계획 site planning —면적 plottage

대지 貸地 land for rent [(英) to let]

대지 對地 ◆ 공대지 공격 an air-to-ground attack / 지대지 미사일 a ground-to-ground missile
■ —공격 an attack from the air; an air raid —속도 〔空〕 ground speed

대지 臺地 〈고원〉 a plateau 《pl. ~s, ~x》; a tableland; 〈고대(高臺)〉 a height; a rise
◆ 용암— a lava plateau

대지 臺紙 ground paper; 〈두꺼운 종이〉 pasteboard; board; 〈사진의〉 a mount; 〈그림의〉 a mat
◆ 사진을 대지에 붙이다 mount a photograph

대지주 大地主 a great [big, large] landowner; (英) a squire

대진 代診 a doctor's assistant; an assistant doctor
▶ 오늘 그는 주치의의 대진을 했다 He examined patients today in place of the physician in charge.
—대진하다 examine 《a patient》 in sb's place
▶ 나는 선생님이 계시지 않을 때 환자 두 명을 대진했다 I examined two patients on behalf of the doctor while he was absent.

대진 對陣 the confrontation of armies; 〈경기〉 a match; a competition
▶ 좋은 대진이었다 It was a good match.
—대진하다 confront [face] each other; encamp facing each other

대질 對質 〔法〕 confrontation; a face-to-face questioning
—대질하다 confront 《one's accuser》; stand face-to-face (with)
◆ 피고와 원고를 대질시키다 confront the accused with the accuser; bring the accused face-to-face with the accuser
■ —심문 (a) cross-examination

대집행 代執行 〔法〕 execution by proxy

대짜 大— a big one; a big thing
◆ 대짜 못 a big nail

대쪽 split bamboo
◆ 성미가 대쪽같은 사람 a straightforward person; a man of frank disposition; a single-minded person

대차 大差 a great [wide] difference; a great discrepancy [disparity]
◆ 대차가 있다 be much [very] different 《from》; differ much [a great deal] 《from》 / 대차가 없다 make little [no great] difference; be much the same / 대차가 나다[생기다] make a great difference / 대차를 내다 gain a great [long] lead (on others)
▶ 그의 의견과 내 의견에는 대차가 없다 There is no wide difference between his opinion and mine.
▶ 우리 팀은 7점이라는 대차로 이겼다 Our team won the game by the wide margin of seven points.

대차 貸借 (a) loan; 〈장부상의〉 debit and credit; 〈건물 등의〉 letting and hiring
♦장부상의 대차 a book account/ 대차가 없다 be square with 《another》/ 대차를 대조하다 balance / 대차를 차감하다 balance account / 대차를 결산하다 strike a balance; sum up the debtor and creditor account
▶이것으로 대차가 없어진다 This will settle the account. ⇌ This will put [make] us even [quits].
▶두 사람 사이에는 대차 관계가 있다 The two have accounts to settle with each other.
■사용— loan of use ■계약서 〈버스 능의〉 a charter ─계정 a debtor and creditor account ─기한 the term [period] of a loan ─소송 an action for debt ─인 lessor and lessee; lender and borrower; debtor and creditor

대차대조표 貸借對照表 a balance sheet (略 B/S, b.s.); a position statement
♦대차대조표를 작성하다 draw [make] up a balance sheet
■감사 balance sheet audit

대차륜 大車輪 〈철봉의〉 a giant swing

대찰 大刹 a large [great] Buddhist temple; a Buddhist cathedral

대창 a bamboo spear

대책 對策 a countermeasure; a counterplan; a countermove
♦대책을 강구하다 consider a counterplan; devise a countermove; take a countermeasure; take a measure to meet the situation
▶정부는 불황대책을 강구할 것을 약속했다 The government has promised to take measures to counter depression.
■수해— flood-control measures 실업— an unemployment countermeasure 인플레이션— an anti-inflation measure; a measure to counter inflation

대처 大處 a city; a town =도회 (～지)
■─사람 a townsman; (총칭) townsfolk

대처승 帶妻僧 a married Buddhist priest

대처하다 對處─ cope [deal] 《with》; tackle; meet; move 《against》; manage; treat
♦긴급사태에 대처하다 meet the emergency / 긴박한 상황에 잘 대처하다 cope [deal] effectively with a tense situation
▶그것에 대해서는 대처할 방법이 없다 There is nothing that can be done about it.

대척 對蹠 ♦대척의[적인] antipodal; directly [diametrically] opposite
▶그는 이 점에서 김선생님과 대척이다 He is diametrically opposed to [just the opposite of] Mr. Kim in this respect.
■─점[지] the antipodes; antipodal points; [無線] the antipode

대첩 大捷 a sweeping [great, complete, decisive, signal, sensational] victory
♦행주 대첩 the Great Victory at the *Haengju* Castle
─대첩하다 win a sweeping [great] victory

대청 大靑 [植] a woad; a pastel

대청 大廳 a hall

대청소 大淸掃 general (house) cleaning; cleaning up; housecleaning ♦대청소를 하다 carry out a general (house) cleaning; clean the whole house

대체 大體 1 〈기본 줄거리〉 the principal parts; the main point(s); 〈취지〉 the purport; 〈개략〉 an outline; a summary; an epitome; the substance
♦대체의 뜻 general meaning / 대체적인 원칙 general principles / 대체적인 general (idea); main (points); rough (estimate) / 대체적으로 ⇨ 대체로
2 〈대관절〉 on earth; in the world

대체 代替 substitution; 〈교체〉 alternation; replacement
─대체하다 substitute 《one thing for another》; replace 《with》; alternate 《with》
♦헌 타이어를 새것으로 대체하다 replace a worn tire by [with] a new one
■─물 [法] a substitute; fungible ─식량 substitute food (for rice) ─에너지 an alternative energy ─집행 an alternation execution ─효과 [經] substitution effect

대체 對替 [商] change; changeover; transfer
♦대체로 송금하다 send money by postal transfer
─대체하다 change (a bill); transfer; switch [change] over (to)
♦가불금을 손익 계정에 대체하다 transfer temporary payments to a profit and loss account
■─계정 (計定) a transfer account ─계정 거래 transfer account transaction ─전표 a transfer slip

대체로 大體─ generally; in general; on the whole; for the most part; approximately; almost
♦대체로 말해서 generally [broadly] speaking / 대체로 보아 on the whole; taken as a whole
▶대체로 나는 그 결과에 만족하고 있다 On the whole I am satisfied with the result.
▶대체로 말해서 그런 사람이 많다 Generally speaking, there are many people like that.
▶대체로 그의 사업은 잘 되고 있다 By and large his business is going well.
▶성적은 대체로 우수한 편이다 The results are on the whole excellent.
▶금년의 작물 수확은 대체로 좋은 것 같다 The harvest this year seems generally good.
▶이 지역 사람들은 대체로 살색이 희다 People in this area are on the whole pale in color.

대체저금 對替貯金 transfer savings; post-office saving transfer

대추 〈열매〉 a jujube
▶그는 대추씨 같다 He is short but is (as) hard as nails.
■─나무 [植] a jujube tree

대추야자나무 [植] a date palm

대출 貸出 〈금전의〉 a loan; 〈가불〉 an advance; 〈도서의〉 lending service
♦대출 중에 있다 〈도서관의 책 등이〉 be out on loan / 도서관의 대출을 이용하다 use the lending service of a library
▶은행은 다액의 대출을 해주고 있다 Banks are accommodating a volume of loans.
▶그 책은 대출 중입니다 That book is checked

—**대출하다** loan (out); advance; lend
▶ 이 책을 대출 받을 수 있을까요? May I have the loan of this book?
▶ 학교 도서관에서는 책을 1주일 동안 대출할 수 있다 We can borrow [check out] a book for a week from our school library.
■ **부당**— an illegal advance **비상**— an emergency advance **—계** a lending clerk; 〈부서〉 the lending section **—규칙** 〈도서의〉 the rules for borrowers **—금** loaned [advanced] money : 장기[단기] 대출금 long-[short-]term loan / 대출금을 회수하다 collect [call in] loans **—금리** the interest on a loan **—능력** banking power **—책** a book on loan **—료** a rental fee **—액** an amount of loans **—초** an over loan

대충 roughly ⇨ 대강(大綱) 2

대충 代充 (a) supplement by substitution
—**대충하다** substitute 《A for B》; fill up [supplement] with substitutes

대충자금 對充資金 collateral funds [money]; a collateral loan; a counterpart fund

대취 大醉 dead drunkenness
—**대취하다** get dead drunk
▶ 아버지는 대취하셨다 My father was blind [dead] drunk.

대치 代置 replacement
—**대치하다** replace 《A with B》

대치 對峙 confrontation
—**대치하다** stand face to face with; be pitted against each other; hold *one's* own against 《*one's* antagonist》; hold *one's* ground against 《the enemy》; take a stand against; hold out against 《the Government forces》; square off 《against》
♦ 대치하고 있는 두 거봉 two lofty peaks facing each other
▶ 양군이 대치했다 The two armies confronted [faced] each other.
▶ 양쪽이 서로 대치하여 굽히지 않는다 Neither would yield to the other in their rivalry.

대치 對置 contraposition
—**대치하다** oppose [set] *sth* against 《another》
♦ 사회주의를 자본주의와 대치하여 고찰하다 contrast socialism with capitalism

대칭 對稱 1 〔數〕 symmetry
♦ 좌우 대칭의 무늬 a symmetrical pattern / 대칭적(으로) symmetrical(ly)
▶ 이 두 점은 x축에 대해서 대칭이다 These two points are symmetric with respect to the x-axis.
2 〔文法〕 the second person
■ **평면**— plane symmetry **—도형** a symmetrical figure **—률** symmetric law **—면** planes of symmetry **—배광(配光)** 〔電〕 symmetrical light **—배열** 〔電〕 symmetrical arrangement **—변환** symmetric transformation **—식** 〔數〕 a symmetric(al) expression **—점** a point of symmetry; a symmetric point **—축** an axis of symmetry **—함수**[삼각형] a symmetrical function [triangle]

대타 代打 〔野〕 pinch-hitting
♦ 대타로 나가다 pinch-hit 《for》
■ **—자** a pinch hitter

대토 代土 〈땅의〉 a substitute land; 〈교환〉 exchange of land

대통 —桶 〈담배통〉 the bowl of a 《tobacco》 pipe

대통 大通 being wide open; success; prosperity **—대통하다** be wide open; be successful; prosper
♦ 운수가 대통하다 have a spell of extremely good luck; fortune turns in *one's* favor
■ **—운** great good luck; a great stroke of luck

대통 大統 the Royal line **—대통을 잇다** succeed to the Royal line [the Throne]

대통령 大統領 the President; the Chief [Federal] Executive
♦ 대통령의 임기 a presidential term / 대통령의 지위[직] presidency; presidential chair [office]/ 대통령의 presidential / 대통령에 선출되다 be elected president / 대통령후보에 지명되다 be nominated for the president
▶ 그는 대통령 선거에 출마한다 He will run for the Presidency.
▶ 그는 대통령에 취임했다 He was sworn in as President.
▶ 그는 대통령에 당선됐다 He was elected President.
▶ 미국에서는 대통령의 임기는 4년이다 In the United States of America the President holds office for four years.
■ **—거부권** a presidential veto **—경호실(장)** (the Chief of) the Office of the Presidential Security **—관저** the Executive [Presidential] Mansion; the Presidential residence; 〈한국의〉 the Blue House; 〈미 국의〉 the White House **—교서** a Presidential message; the President's message **—권대행** the acting President **—당선자** 〈취임 전의〉 the president-elect **—령(令)** a Presidential decree; an executive order **—비서실** the Presidential Secretariat **—비서실장** the Chief Presidential Secretary; the Presidential Secretary-General **—선거** a presidential election: 대통령 선거의 해 a presidential (election) year **—선거전** a presidential election campaign **—영부인 (美)** the first lady **—입후보자** a candidate for the presidency; a presidential nominee [candidate, contender] **—특별 보좌관** the Special Assistant 《for the Foreign Affairs》 to the President

대퇴 大腿 〔解〕 the thigh; the femur 《*pl.* ~s, femora》
■ **—골** a thighbone; a femur **—근** the femoral muscle **—부** the femoral region

대파 大破 1 〈파손〉 dilapidation; ruin; serious damage; havoc
—**대파하다** be greatly [heavily] damaged; be crippled; be wrecked; be smashed
▶ 그 사고로 그의 차는 대파했다 His car was badly damaged [smashed up] in the accident.
2 〈격파〉 a crushing defeat
—**대파하다** defeat utterly; (put to) rout; crush down; smash

대파 代播 〔農〕 sowing a substitute plant
—**대파하다** plant 《a paddy with corn》 in substitution 《for rice》

◆논에 메밀을 대파하다 sow the paddy with buckwheat in substitution ((for rice))
대판 大— a large [big, grand, huge] scale
◆대판 싸움 ((have)) a big quarrel [fight] / 대판으로 on a large [an extensive] scale; in a big [large] way
대패 ⟨공구⟩ a plane
◆대패로 밀다 plane ((a board)); plane away [off, down] ((a board))
■—질 planing 대팻날 a plane iron 대팻밥 (wood) shavings; ⟨포장용⟩ woodwool; (美) excelsior 대팻손 the handle of a plane 대팻집 a plane stock
대패 大敗 a crushing [heavy, serious, severe, complete] defeat; an utter defeat [rout]
—대패하다 sustain [suffer, meet with] a crushing defeat; be routed; be put to rout; be beaten hollow
▶그 당은 선거에서 대패했다 The party was defeated soundly [sustained a crushing defeat] in the election.
▶우리는 야구 시합에서 대패했다 We were completely defeated in the baseball game.
대포 1 drinking from a large cup
2 ⇨ 대폿술
■대폿값 drink money [penny]; ⟨팁⟩ a tip 대폿잔 a large cup; a goblet; a bowl 대폿집 a grogshop; a groggery
대포 大砲 1 ⟨무기⟩ a gun; a cannon ((pl. ~s, ~)); ((총칭)) artillery
◆대포 소리 the roaring [boom] of guns / 대포를 쏘다 fire a gun
▶포병대가 대포를 발사했다 The artillery fired their guns.
▶대포 소리가 온 마을에 울려퍼졌다 The booming of guns resounded all over (the) town.
2 ⟨거짓말⟩ a (big) lie; ⟨허풍⟩ a brag; tall [big] talk; (美俗) hot air
◆대포를 놓다 ⟨거짓말하다⟩ lie; tell a lie; ⟨허풍떨다⟩ brag; talk big [tall]
대폭 大幅 1 ⟨큰 폭⟩ full breadth; double width
2 ⟨썩 많이⟩ sharply; steeply; by a large margin
◆대폭 삭감 a sharp cut; a drastic retrenchment / 대폭 인상 a steep raise; a sharp increase; a heavy boost / 대폭적인 임금 인상 a big [substantial] raise in pay [salary]/ 가격의 대폭인 인하 sharp reductions in prices / 대폭적인 하락 a big fall ((in prices)) / 대폭적인 large; big; sharp; steep; wholesale; substantial
▶정부는 대폭적인 양보를 강요당했다 The government was pressed for a considerable concession.
▶눈 때문에 야채값이 대폭 올랐다 The price of vegetables has risen sharply because of the snow.
▶노조는 대폭적인 임금 인상을 요구하고 있다 The labor union is demanding a substantial wage hike.
대폿술 liquor in a large cup
대표 代表 representation; ⟨대표자⟩ a representative; a delegate; ⟨대표단⟩ a delegation
◆국가 대표 선수 a member of the national team; a national athlete / 국가 대표팀 the national ((soccer)) team / 다수[비례] 대표제 a majority [proportional] representation system / 대표적인 인물 a representative person / 대표적인 representative; typical; model; exemplary / 대표를 보내다 send delegates [a delegation] ((to a conference))
▶당신네 당의 대표는 누구입니까 ? Who represents your party? ⇌ Who is the representative of your party?
▶한국은 그 회의에 다섯 명의 대표를 보냈다 Korea sent five delegates to the conference.
▶각 당의 대표는 아직 나타나지 않았다 The delegates of every party have not appeared yet.
—대표하다 represent; be representative of; stand for; act as a representative; typify
▶그는 우리 학급을 대표한다 He is a representative of our class. ⇌ He represents our class.
▶그는 학급을 대표하여 학생회에 참석했다 He represented his class at the student council meeting. ⇌ He attended the student council meeting as the representative of his class.
▶그는 가족을 대표하여 환영 인사를 했다 He made a speech of welcome on behalf of his family.
▶이것은 16세기의 영국 교회를 대표하는 건물이다 This is typical to [typifies] the sixteenth century English churches.
▶이것은 시대 정신을 대표하는 책가운데 하나다 This is one of the books which typify [are typical of] the spirit of the age.
■졸업생— the representative of the graduating class; ⟨고별사를 하는⟩ (美) a valedictorian 종업원— a representative of the employees 학생— a student representative ■—단 a delegation —번호 ⟨전화의⟩ a key number —사원 a representative partner —이사 the chief director; the chairman of a board of directors —작 the masterpiece ((of)); the most important work ((of))
대표부 代表部 a mission
■무역— a trade mission
대푼 a penny; a tiny sum; a red cent
■—변 one persent interest —짜리 a thing of little value —쭝 a pennyweight
대풍 大風 a strong [violent, big, heavy, high] wind; ⟨질풍⟩ a gale; ⟨폭풍⟩ a hurricane; ⟨태풍⟩ a typhoon
▶대풍이 발생했다 A strong wind formed [was born].
▶대풍이 불고 있었다 A gale was blowing.
대풍 大豊 a bumper [heavy, record] crop; a rich [an abundant] harvest; a large yield ((of fruit))
▶올해 사과는 대풍이었다 This has been a bumper [fruitful] year for apples.
대피 待避 taking shelter
▶우리는 대피 훈련을 받았다 We were trained in taking refuge.
—대피하다 shelter; take [find] shelter [cover]; ⟨鐵⟩ shunt
◆폭풍으로부터 대피하다 find [take] shelter

from a storm
▶ 배는 태풍을 피해 안전한 항구로 대피했다 The ship found shelter in a safe harbor from a storm.
▶ 그들은 그 열차를 옆 선로로 대피시켰다 They shunted the train to the siding.
■—소 a shelter; 〈도로의〉 a turnout: 방사성 강하물 대피소 a fallout shelter / 핵폭탄 대피소 a nuclear-bomb shelter —역 a shunting station —호(壕) a dugout; a (bomb) shelter; a shelter trench

대피선 待避線 〖鐵〗 a (railroad) siding; a siding (track); a sidetrack; a turnout
♦ 열차를 대피선에 넣다 sidetrack a train

대필 代筆 ghostwriting; writing for (another)
▶ 나는 아버지의 대필을 했다 I wrote a letter for my father.
▶ 그 여자의 최근의 편지는 분명 대필이었다 Her last letter was obviously written by someone else.
—**대필하다** ghostwrite; write (a letter) for (another); write (a letter) to (another's) dictation
♦ 아무의 편지를 대필하다 write a letter for sb
■—인 someone who writes (a letter) for another

대하 大河 a big [large] river
■—소설 a long novel; a roman-fleuve; a saga (novel)

대하 大蝦 〖動〗 a (spiny) lobster

대하 帶下 〖醫〗 a discharge from the womb
■—증 leucorrhea

대하다 對— 1 〈마주하다〉 face; confront; be opposite to
♦ 서로 얼굴을 대하다 face [confront] each other / 마주 대하고 앉다 sit opposite (each other, to sb); sit face to face 〖프〗 vis-à-vis〗 (with)
2 〈응대·접대하다〉 treat; receive; act (well, ill) toward sb
♦ 양친을 대하는 태도 one's attitude toward(s) one's parents / 친절히 대하다 act kindly toward sb / 예로써 대하다 treat sb with due courtesy / 따뜻이 대하다 receive sb with warmth / 심하게 대하다 treat sb unkindly [harshly]; be hard on [cruel to] sb / 후히 대하다 treat sb generously
▶ 모든 사람을 정직하게 대하라 Deal honestly with all men.
3 〈대항하다〉 oppose
▶ 적은 전력을 다하여 우리를 대했다 The enemy directed its whole strength against us.
4 〈대상으로 하다〉 ♦ 사회에 대한 책임 one's duty to society / 시험에 대한 준비 preparations for an examination / 종교에 대한 서적 books on religion / 질문에 대한 답 an answer to a question / 시사문제에 대한 강연 a lecture on current affairs / 선생님에 대한 태도 one's attitude toward one's teacher / 세 사람에 대한 한 대의 차 a car to every three persons / 1,000원에 대해 50원의 수수료 a commission of fifty won for a thousand won / …에 대한 toward; to; against / 이 일에 대하여 about this; regarding [concerning, respecting] this; with [in] regard to this matter
▶ 그는 그것에 대하여 전혀 무관심하였다 He was utterly indifferent to it.
▶ 그 분의 학식에 대하여 십분 경의를 품고 있습니다 I have great respect for his scholarship.
▶ 아동심리학에 대하여 많은 흥미를 가지고 있다 I am much interested in child psychology.
▶ 민중은 압제에 대해 들고 일어났다 The people rose against tyranny.
▶ 협조에 대하여 진심으로 감사드립니다 Thank you very much for your cooperation.
▶ 그의 100표에 대해서 나는 200표를 얻었다 I got two hundred votes to [against] his one hundred.
▶ 사망률은 천명에 대해 다섯 명 비율이다 The death rate is five per a thousand.
5 〖數〗 〈현(弦)·삼각형의 변이 호(弧)·각에〉 subtend

대학 大學 a university (*pl.* -ties) (略 univ.); a college (略 col.); 〈英俗〉 a varsity

┌─────────────────────────────────┐
│ **解説** ***university***는 석사(碩士) 이상의 학위를 │
│ 줄 수 있는 권한을 가지고 있는 종합대학, │
│ ***college***는 단과대학을 가리킨다. 그러나 종합 │
│ 대학을 특히 강조하지 않고 넓은 의미로 「대 │
│ 학」을 가리킬 때는 대학 이름에 university가 │
│ 붙는다 하더라도 college를 쓰는 것이 보통이 │
│ 다. 건물이나 장소가 아니라 기능으로서의 대 │
│ 학 교육을 가리킬 경우, college는 보통 관사 │
│ 없이, university는 보통 〈美〉에서는 the를 붙 │
│ 이고 〈英〉에서는 관사 없이 쓴다. 따라서 학생 │
│ 또는 교사가 「대학에 다니다」는 go to col- │
│ lege, 〈美〉 go to the university, 〈英〉 go to │
│ university와 같이 말한다. 다만, 수식어를 붙 │
│ 여 특정 또는 불특정 대학을 가리킬 때는 │
│ 〈美〉·〈英〉 모두 보통 관사를 붙인다: go to a │
│ good [the, a] college [university] (좋은[그, │
│ 어떤] 대학에 다니다). 또한 일반적으로 전문 │
│ 대학, 대학원을 가리킬 때 〈美〉에서는 대학을 │
│ school이라 하기도 한다: the School of Law; │
│ the Law School (법학부) │
└─────────────────────────────────┘

♦ 대학 생활 college [campus] life / 대학 입시 (take) a college entrance exam [examination] / 대학의 자유 academic freedom / 대학의 자치 university autonomy / 대학 시절에 〈美〉 while in college; 〈英〉 while at university
▶ 그는 K대학 영문과 학생[교수]이다 He is a student [professor] of English literature at K University.
▶ 대학은 여기서 멀다 The university [college] is a long way from here.
〈대학을〉 대학을 졸업하다 graduate from [finish, 〈英〉 leave] college / 대학을 중퇴하다 drop out of [leave, 〈口〉 quit] college (▶leave the college는 「하교하다」의 뜻)
▶ 그는 대학을 갓 나왔다 He is fresh from college.
〈대학에(서)〉 대학에 진학하다 go on to college / 대학에 들어가다[입학하다] get into [enter] college; enter (the) university / 대학에 다니다 go to [be in] college [(the) university] / 대학에서 공부를 시작하다 begin [start]

college / 대학에서 미술을 공부하다 study fine arts at college
▶ 그녀는 대학에 재학중이다 She is in [at] college [a university].
▶ [會話]「그는 어느 대학에 다니니?」「고려 대학이야」 "Where does he go to university? ⇌ What university does he go to?" "He goes to Korea University."
■ 가정— a college of domestic science [home economics] 공과[농과, 문리과, 미술, 법과, 상과, 수산, 수의과, 약학, 음악, 의과, 치과, 항공]— a college of engineering [agriculture, liberal arts and science, fine arts, law, commerce, fishery, veterinary medicine, pharmacy, music, medicine, dentistry, aviation] 국립— a national university [college] 사범— a teacher's college 여자— a women's university 초급— a junior college ■ —가 a university [college] town —교수 a university [college] professor —교수회[단] the faculty of a university; the college staff —구내 a university campus —모자 a college cap; a square [trencher] cap —병원 a university hospital; a teaching hospital —졸업생 a college [university] graduate; a university man [woman]: 하버드 대학 졸업생 a Havard graduate —진학률 a college-going rate —총장 a university president; the president [chancellor] (of a university) —출신자 a university man; a university [college] graduate; a collegian —학장 a dean; a president

대학교육 大學教育 a university [college] education; college training
◆대학교육을 받다 get a college education; acquire college training

대학생 大學生 a university [college] student; a college man [woman]; an undergraduate; a collegian

대학 수학능력 시험 大學修學能力試驗 the college (academic) aptitude test

대학원 大學院 a graduate [postgraduate] school; the postgraduate course
◆대학원에 들어가다 become a graduate student; pursue the postgraduate course / 대학원에서 연구하다 do graduate work
■ —과정 the graduate [postgraduate] course (of a university) —생 a graduate [postgraduate] student; (美俗) a grad student

대학자 大學者 a great [prominent, profound] scholar; an erudite man; a savant

대한 大寒 1 〈추위〉 an intense [freezing] cold 2 〈절후〉 the last of the 24 seasonal divisions according to the lunar calendar (about 21st of January)

대한 大韓 Korea
■ —민국 the Republic of Korea (略 R.O.K.) —해협 the Straits of Korea

대한 對韓 〈부사적〉 toward [to, with] Korea
◆대한원조 (economic, military) aid to Korea / 중국의 대한 외교 정책 China's diplomatic policy toward Korea

대합 大蛤 〔貝〕 a (large) clam
■ —구이 baked clams

대합실 待合室 〔역 등의〕 a waiting room; 〈은행 등의〉 a lobby
◆1등 대합실 the first-class waiting room

대항 對抗 opposition; antagonism; (a) rivalry; counteraction; difiance; resistance; confrontation
◆학급 대항 시합 an interclass [an intercollegiate] match / 한미 대항 야구시합 a Korea versus [v., vs.] America baseball game; a baseball game between Korea and America; the Korea-U.S. baseball game
—대항하다 oppose; antagonize; confront; face; meet; set up against; pit *oneself* against; emulate; rival; cope [vie] with
◆…에 대항하여 in opposition to…; in rivalry with…; against…/ 대항시키다 match; pit [set up] (against)
▶ 힘에는 힘으로 대항한다는 것이 그의 신조다 His principle is to counter [meet] force with force.
▶ 작은 가게들은 싼값으로 슈퍼마켓에 대항했다 Small stores competed with the supermarket by selling goods cheap.
■ —동맹[단체] a counter alliance [organization] —력 opposing power —마 〔競馬〕 a rival horse (in a race) —자 an antagonist; a rival; an opponent; an emulator —품 competitive goods —행위 a counteraction

대항책 對抗策 a counterplot; a countermeasure (against); a countermove
◆대항책을 강구하다 take a countermeasure; form a counterplot

대해 大害 great damage [loss]; great harm; great injury
▶ 그 태풍으로 말미암아 이 지방의 벼농사는 대해를 입었다 The typhoon has done much damage to the rice plants in these regions.

대해 大海 an ocean; the sea; (詩) the main; the deep
◆망망한 대해 a boundless expanse [stretch] of water

대행 代行 vicarious execution
◆교장 대행 the acting principal
—대행하다 execute (business) for (another); act for *sb*
◆아버지를 대행하다 act for *one's* father
▶ 그는 1년간 대학총장을 대행했다 He was the acting president of the university for one year.
▶ 우리는 보험회사의 업무를 대행하고 있다 We handle [execute] business for an insurance company.
■ —기관 an agency; a substitute machinery —업무 agency business —자 a proxy; an agent

대행성 大行星 〔天〕 the major planet

대헌장 大憲章 〔史〕 the Magna Charta [Carta]; the Great Charter

대현 大賢 a man of great wisdom; a sage
▶ 대현은 때로 대우(大愚)와 같다 A great sage is often taken for a great fool.

대형 大兄 Mr. …; you

대형 大型 a large [full] size; oversize
◆대형 선수의 발굴 discovery of a mammoth [tall-statured] athlete / 대형의 large; big; of

large size; large-sized; king-size(d) / 초대형의 extra-large; supersize(d)
▶ 최근 냉장고는 대형화되고 있다 Refrigerators are made bigger these days.
▶ 오랫만에 대형 선수가 나타났다 For the first time in many years a great player emerged.
■一버스 a coach 一선박 a large vessel 一주(株) a large-capital stock 一차 a large-size [big] car 一트럭 a heavy-duty truck

대형 隊形 (a) formation; order
♦ 대형을 흐트러뜨리지 않고[정연히 하고] in good formation [order] / 대형을 유지하다 keep [put] the formation
▶ 대형이 흐트러져 있다 The formation is in disorder.
■밀집— (a) close formation 전투— (a) battle formation

대혹성 大惑星 〔天〕the major planet＝대행성(大行星)

대화 大火 〈큰불〉a big fire

대화 大禍 a great disaster; calamity ♦ 대화를 입다 meet with a calamity [misfortune]

대화 對話 〈회화〉conversation; a talk; (a) colloquy; 〈두 사람의〉a dialog(ue); a duolog
♦ 세 사람의 대화 a trialog / 야당과[노사간에] 대화를 갖다 have a dialog with the opposition [between labor and management]
▶ 그들은 그 문제에 관해 대화를 가졌다 They carried on a dialog concerning the problem.
—**대화하다** dialog; engage in a dialog 《with》; talk [converse] 《with》; have [hold] a talk [conversation] 《with》
▶ 나는 그와 대화했다 I talked [had a talk] with him.
▶ 그들은 영어로 대화했다 They were talking in English.
■남북— a South-North dialog ■—극 a dialogic play

대화체 對話體 dialogic [conversational] style
♦ 대화체의 dialogic(al); dialogistic(al); written in dialog (form)

대황 大黃 〔植〕a rhubarb

대회 大會 〈큰 모임〉a mass meeting; a great [large] meeting; 〈특정한 목적을 위한〉a rally; a congress; 〈총회〉a general meeting [assembly]; 〈정기〉a meet
♦ 대회를 개최하다 hold a mass meeting / 대회에서 연설하다 address a large assembly
■국민— a popular mass meeting; 〈정당 주최의〉a political rally 국제— a world jamboree 기념— a commemoration meeting 당— a party convention 시민— a mass meeting of citizens 연차— an annual meeting 전당— a National Convention ■—신기록 《set》a new meet record

대회전경기 大回轉競技 〔스키〕(the) giant slalom

대흉 大凶 **1** 〈매우 불길함〉singular ill fortune; a dark omen; great bad [ill] luck
—**대흉하다** ill-omened; extremely unlucky; unusually ominous [portentous, sinister]
▶ 점쟁이는 내 운세를 대흉하다고 점쳤다 The fortune-teller said my future was black.
2 〈극악함〉an atrocity; brutality
—**대흉하다** atrocious; brutal
3 〈심한 흉작〉an unusually bad harvest [crop] ■—년 an extremely lean year 《for the rice crop》

댁 宅 1 〈남의 집〉your [his] house; 〈가족〉your [his] family
♦ 김선생댁 따님 Mr. Kim's daughter
▶ 여기가 Y씨댁입니까? Is this where Mr. Y lives?
▶ 댁은 어디십니까? Where do you live?
▶ 댁이 어디라고 하셨죠? Where did you say your house is?
2 〈당신〉you
▶ 이것은 댁의 것입니까? Is this yours?
▶ 댁의 존함은 무엇입니까? What is your name? ⇒ May I ask your name?
▶ 댁의 말씀이 옳습니다 You are right.
3 〈남의 부인〉Mrs. ...; the wife of sb
♦ 김선생댁 Mrs. Kim; the wife of Mr. Kim

댁내 宅內 your [his] esteemed family
▶ 댁내가 두루 평안하십니까? Is everyone in your family well? ⇒ Are you all getting along well?

댁네 宅— your [his] wife

댁대구루루 rollingly; tumblingly
♦ 댁대구루루 굴러가다 roll over and over / 선반에서 댁대구루루 굴러 떨어지다 roll [tumble] down from the shelf

댄서 a dancer; a dancing girl; 〈직업적인〉a taxi dancer

댄스 a dance; dancing
♦ 댄스 상대 one's dancing partner
▶ 그녀와 댄스를 I danced with her. ⇒ I had a dance with her.
▶ 저의 댄스 상대가 되어 주시겠습니까? May I have the next dance with you?
■—교사 a dancing instructor; a dancingmaster; 〈여자〉a dancing mistress —교습소 a dance studio —파티 a dance; a dancing party; a ball; 〈고교·대학의〉a prom: 이 호텔에서는 매일밤 댄스파티가 열린다 Dances are held at the hotel every evening. —홀 (美) a dance hall; (英) a dancing saloon: 비밀댄스홀 an underground dance hall

댈러스 〈미국의 도시〉Dallas

댐 a dam
♦ 강에 댐을 건설하다 build [construct] a dam across a river; dam a river / 강을 댐으로 막다 dam (up) a river
▶ 이 강에 댐을 건설할 계획이 있다 They are planning to dam this river [build a dam across this river].
■ 다목적[수력 발전용]— a multipurpose [hydroelectric] dam 저수— a water-storage dam ■—건설용 부지 a damsite

댑싸리 〔植〕a broom cypress

댓 〈댓 권〉about five volumes

댓개비 a bamboo split [skewer, broach]; a piece of split bamboo

댓돌 臺— terrace stones

댓바람에 〈단번에〉at a stroke [heat]; all in a breath; at once; immediately; quickly
♦ 댓바람에 일을 해치우다 finish one's work at a stroke [straight out]/ 댓바람에 언덕을 뛰어

오르다 go up a hill with one rush [at a cash]
▶ 사고 소식을 듣자 그는 댓바람에 현장으로 달려갔다 On hearing of the accident, he hurried to the scene at once.

댓새 about five days

댓진 —津 tobacco tar accumulated in a pipe

댕기 a pigtail ribbon ◆ 댕기를 드리다 wear [put on] a pigtail ribbon

댕기다 1 〈불을 옮겨 붙이다〉 light; kindle; ignite
◆ 담뱃불을 댕기다 light a cigar [cigarette]
2 〈불이 옮겨 붙다〉 catch [take] fire; be ignited; be kindled; spread to
▶ 마른 나무에는 불이 잘 댕긴다 Dry wood catches fire easily.

더 〈수량·정도〉 more; some more; 〈시간〉 longer; 〈거리〉 farther; 〈더욱〉 further (▶구어에서는 정도·거리에 모두 further를 쓰기도 함); still [much] more; 〈부정어와 함께〉 less; still [much] less
◆ 더 많이 〈양〉 much more; 〈수〉 many more / 더 생각한 뒤에 after further consideration / 하나 더 많다 be too many by one; be one too many
▶ 과자 좀 더 주십시오 Please give me some more cookies.
▶ 난 더 할말이 없다 I have nothing more to say.
▶ 나도 키가 꽤 크지만 형은 더 크다 I'm tall enough, but my brother is still taller.
▶ 여러분, 앞으로 더 가까이 오십시오 Everybody, please come a little closer to the front.
▶ 넌 잠을 더 자두는 게 좋겠어 You'd better get [have] some more sleep.
▶ 그 얘기를 더 들려주십시오 Get on with the rest of your story.
▶ 그것은 더 연구할 필요가 있다 It requires further research.
▶ 보지 말라고 하면 더 보고 싶어지는 게 사람의 마음이다 When we are told not to look at anything, we are all the more tempted to see it.
▶ 나는 더 이상은 걸을 수가 없다 I can walk no further.
▶ 그들은 도로를 3마일 더 연장했다 They extended the road for three more miles.

더가다 〈지나쳐 가다〉 go too far; go [walk] past [beyond] (one's destination); 〈시계가〉 gain; go [run] too fast; 〈정도〉 exceed; go farther; last longer; be more than
▶ 우리는 두 정거장을 더갔다 We were carried two stations [stops] beyond our destination.
▶ 조금 더 가서 쉬자 Let us walk a little farther before we take a rest.
▶ 나는 저것보다 이것에 마음이 더간다 I like this better than that. ⇒ I prefer this to that.
▶ 나는 이 모자에 마음이 더간다 I like this hat better.
▶ 내 시계는 하루에 5분씩 더간다 My watch gains five minutes a day.

더구나 moreover ⇨ 더군다나

더군다나 moreover; even [all the] more; in addition; besides; furthermore
▶ 그녀는 아름답고 현명하며 더군다나 매우 친절하다 She is beautiful, clever, and very kind besides.
▶ 그는 학벌이 없으며 더군다나 경험도 없다 He has no scholarship, to say nothing of [not to speak of, much less] experience.
▶ 비가 오는데, 더군다나 바람까지 분다 It is raining and, what's more, the wind is blowing too.
▶ 한치 앞도 안 보이는 어둠에, 더군다나 비바람까지 심해졌다 It was pitch-dark and, what was worse, the rainstorm grew in violence.

더그매 an empty space between the roof and the ceiling; the attic
◆ (쥐가) 더그매에서 날뛰다 (rats) scramble among the beams
▶ 제비가 더그매에 둥지를 쳤다 Swallows built a nest in the ceiling.

더그아웃 〔野〕 a dugout

더껑이 〈굳어진 꺼풀〉 scum; cream; skim; film; an incrustation
▶ 죽이 식으면 더껑이가 앉는다 A skim forms on the porridge when it gets cool.
▶ 우유의 더껑이를 걷어내라 Skim the cream from [off] milk.
2 ⇨ 더께

더께 encrusted dirt

더넘스럽다 a little too large (for); overlarge

더느다 brail (string, thread) in two piles

-더니 1 〈원인·이유〉 as; so; since; because (of); owing to; but now [then]; and now [then]
▶ 그는 열심히 공부하더니 시험에 수석 합격했다 He studied so hard that he topped the list of successful examinees.
▶ 한참을 쉬었더니 몸이 거뜬하다 I've had a bit of rest and now I feel wonderfully refreshed.
▶ 바람이 불더니 비가 온다 First the wind and now the rain.
▶ 그는 한 번 가더니 소식이 없다 We've had no word from him at all since he left.
▶ 내가 할말을 다 하고 났더니 이제 가슴이 후련하다 Now that I have had my say I feel much relieved.
2 〈회고〉 used to be... (but now...)
▶ 그때는 낚시꾼도 드물더니 Then there used to be very few anglers (but now any more).
▶ 그 전에는 이곳이 연못이더니 This used to be a pond.

더더군다나 moreover ⇨ 더군다나

더더귀더더귀 (grow) in clusters ⇨ 더덕더덕 1

더덕 〔植〕〈학명〉 Codonopsis lanceolata
■—바심 crushing tŏdŏk root

더덕더덕 1 ⇨ 다닥다닥
2 〈짙게〉 thickly; thick
▶ 그녀는 언제나 분을 더덕더덕 바른다 She always powders her face thickly.
▶ 그 아이의 손가락엔 풀이 더덕더덕 묻어 있다 The child's fingers are sticky with paste.
▶ 그는 흠집이 있는 곳에 페인트를 더덕더덕 칠했다 He daubed on the paint where there was a flaw.

더덜거리다 stammer ⇨ 더듬거리다 2

더뎅이 a scab; a slough ▶ 부스럼에 더뎅이가

앉았다 A scab formed over a boil.
더듬거리다 1 〈손으로〉 grope; fumble for; feel about for
♦어둠 속에서 문고리를 찾느라 더듬거리다 grope about in the dark for a doorknob
▶나는 책을 찾느라 어두운 방에서 더듬거렸다 I was groping for a book in a dark room.
2 〈말을〉 stammer; stutter; falter
♦더듬거리며 말하다 stammer out (a few words); falter out [forth] ((that...))
▶그 학생은 교과서를 더듬거리며 읽었다 The student read the textbook falteringly.
더듬다 1 〈손으로〉 grope ((for)); feel ((after, for)); fumble ((in the darkness)) for *sth*
♦(맹인 등이) 지팡이로 길을 더듬다 feel the way with a cane / 어둠 속에서 더듬어 가다 feel [grope] *one's* way in the dark / 성냥을 더듬어 찾다 grope [fumble, feel] for the matches
2 〈말을〉 stammer; stutter; falter
♦말을 더듬으며 stammering(ly); stuttering-(ly) / 말더듬이를 교정하다 correct stammering
▶그는 몹시 말을 더듬는다 He stammers badly.
▶그는 말을 더듬으며 싫다고 말했다 He stammered out a negative answer.
3 〈자취·기억 등을〉 follow (up); trace; retrace; tread; fumble
♦우리가 더듬어 온 길 the path we have followed / 기억을 더듬다 try to recall; retrace *one's* memory / 근원을 더듬다 trace *sth* to its origin [source]; get at [go to] the root of *sth* / 인류의 역사를 더듬다 trace the history of mankind
더듬더듬 1 〈손으로〉 gropingly; fumblingly; by feel
♦더듬더듬 걸어가다 go feeling around; grope *one's* way along
▶나는 어두운 복도를 더듬더듬 걸어갔다 I groped [felt] along the dark hallway.
2 〈말을〉 stammeringly; stutteringly; falteringly
▶그 노인은 더듬더듬 자기 신세타령을 했다 The old man told all about himself falteringly.
더듬이¹ a stammerer ⇨ 말더듬이
더듬이² [蟲] a feeler ⇨ 촉각
▶달팽이가 더듬이를 내밀었다[움추렸다] The snail has stuck out [drawn in] its horn.
더디 〈늦게〉 late; behind time [schedule]; 〈느리게〉 slow(ly); tardily; sluggishly
♦목적지에 더디 도착하다 reach *one's* destination late / 더디 일하다 work slowly [sluggish-ly]; be slow in *one's* work
▶그는 더디 돌아온다 He is long in returning.
▶봄이 더디 온다 Spring is long in coming. ⇌
더디다 1 〈늦다〉 late; tardy; dilatory; behind time [schedule]; 〈서술적〉 take a long time
2 〈느리다〉 slow; tardy; retarded
♦걸음이 더디다 go at a slow pace; be slow-[heavy-]footed; be slow of foot; be a slow walker; make poor time / 일이 더디다 be slow in *one's* work / 진보가 더디다 make (but) slow progress
▶아버지께 편지를 했지만 그 답장은 아주 더뎠다 I wrote a letter to my father but the reply took a long time coming.
-더라 ▶서울대공원에는 동물이 많더라 I found a great many animals at the Seoul Grand Park.
▶그들은 금년 봄에 결혼한다고 하더라 I hear [People say] (that) they will get married this spring.
▶그 일은 참 고되더라 It was hard work, I tell you.
▶그는 한 밑천 벌었다고 하더라 It is said that [I hear] he has made a fortune.
▶이 개는 네가 하는 말을 알아듣는다고들 하더라 They say this dog understands what you say.
▶그는 곧 미국에 간다더라 They say [It is said, I have been told] that he is going to America pretty soon.
-더라도 though; although; (even) if; however; no matter how [what, which, where, when, who]... (may)...
♦무슨 일이 있더라도 whatever may happen; come what may / 그것이 사실이라 하더라도 granting [supposing] it to be true [that it is true] / 비가 오더라도 if it rains; in spite of the rain
▶네가 아무리 열심히 노력하더라도 그를 이길 수는 없다 No matter how hard you try, you cannot beat him.
▶그가 무슨 말을 하더라도 들어서는 안된다 Whatever he may say [No matter what he says], you must not listen to him.
▶비록 그것이 사실이라 하더라도 증거가 없다 Even granting [granted] that it is true, there is no evidence.
-더라면 〈가정〉 if (only); 〈희망〉 I wish
▶네가 내내 달려갔더라면 시간에 대었을텐데 If you ran all the way, you'd get there in time.
▶그 돈이 없었더라면 나는 굶어죽었을 거야 If it had not been for [But for, Without] the money, I would have been starved to death.
▶좀더 그녀를 자주 문병했더라면 좋았을 것을 I wish I'd gone to see her in the hospital more often.
▶내가 새였더라면 좋았을 걸 I wish I were a bird.
▶이 방이 좀더 컸더라면 좋았을 걸 I wish this room were a little larger.
더러¹ 1 〈얼마쯤〉 a little; 〈의문문·조건절에서〉 any; a bit; some; to some degree; 〈일부분〉 partially; partly; 〈제법〉 fairly; rather
♦이름이 더러 알려진 사람 a man of some note
▶나는 스페인어를 더러 알고 있다 I have some knowledge of Spanish.
▶물가는 더러 내렸지만 인플레이션은 계속되고 있다 Prices have dropped to a certain extent [degree], but the inflation continues.
▶그 사고는 나에게도 더러 책임이 있었다 The accident was partly my fault.
▶그 일에 관해서 더러 알고 있다 I know something about it.

더러² 2 〈이따금〉 sometimes; once in a while; occasionally; now and then; at times; at moments; from time to time
▶ 그에게서 더러 소식이 온다 I occasionally hear from him.
▶ 그를 더러 만납니까? Do you see anything of him? ⇌ Do you see him once in a while?
▶ 저는 더러 부모님께 편지를 씁니다 I write to my parents occasionally.

더러² 〈…에게〉 to *sb*; toward
▶ 어머니는 나더러 6시까지 집에 돌아오라고 하셨다 Mother told me to be home by six.
▶ 그는 나더러 빨리 출발하는 것이 좋다고 권했다 He advised me to start early.

더러움 〈부정〉 uncleanness; impurity; defilement; 〈오염〉 pollution; a stain; a spot; a blot; 〈오점·오욕〉 a stain; a blot; disgrace
♦ 더러움이 없는 pure; stainless; undefiled; spotless; clean; pure; unsullied / 더러움을 모르는 innocent; naive
▶ 흰 셔츠는 더러움이 빨리 눈에 띈다 A white shirt quickly shows any stains.
▶ 그 더러움은 쉬이 지지 않는다 The stain won't come out easily.
▶ 이 더러움을 물로 씻어라 Wash this dirt off.
▶ 그의 인격에는 한 점의 더러움도 없다 There is not a blot on his character.

더러워지다 1 〈물건이〉 become [get] dirty [filthy]; be soiled [spotted]; be stained; be polluted; become unclean; be blemished [smudged]
♦ 더러워진 공기 foul air / 잉크로 더러워진 식탁보 a tablecloth stained with ink / 더러워진 unclean; filthy; dirty / 쉬이 더러워지다 be easily soiled; soil easily
▶ 비 때문에 창문이 더러워졌다 The rain blurred the windows.
▶ 내의가 땀으로 더러워졌다 My underwear is soaked with sweat.
▶ 합성섬유는 쉬이 더러워진다 Synthetic material stains easily.
▶ 더러워진 손으로 이 드레스를 만지지 마시오 Don't touch this dress with your dirty hands, please.
2 〈마음·사람이〉 become mean [base, low, sordid, despicable, dirty]
♦ 마음이 더러워지다 become meanspirited [base-minded] / 사람이 더러워지다 become a mean [base, low, dirty] character
3 〈이름·명성 등이〉 be soiled [sullied, befouled, dishonored, disgraced]
▶ 그런 짓을 하면 자네 이름이 더러워지네 That would bring disgrace upon your good name.
▶ 그런 행위를 하면 우리 학교의 전통이 더러워질 것이다 Such a deed would disgrace [defile] the tradition of our school.
4 〈순결이〉 become unchaste; lose *one's* chastity [(virginal) purity]; lose *one's* maidenhood; be deflowered

더럭 all at once; suddenly; all of a sudden
♦ 더럭 겁이 나다 be seized with fear all of a sudden / 더럭 화를 내다 have a fit of anger; fly into a rage
▶ 그는 더럭 의심이 났다 A doubt rushed into [upon] his mind. ⇌ A question burst upon him.
▶ 그는 그 일을 끝내자 더럭 병이 났다 He suddenly fell sick after he had completed the work.

더럭더럭 importunately; tenaciously; pertinaciously
♦ 더럭더럭 조르다 importune [pester, press] *sb* 《for *sth*, to do》; ask *sb* importunately 《for *sth*, to do》

더럼 a stain ⇨ 더러움

더럼타다 be easily soiled; soil easily
♦ 쉬이 더럼타는 옷 clothes easy to get soiled
▶ 흰 옷은 쉬이 더럼탄다 A white dress is easily soiled [shows the dirt easily].

더럽다 1 〈불결·부정하다〉 dirty; filthy; grubby; foul; unclean; soiled; nasty; stained; grimy; squalid
♦ 더러운 방 a dirty [foul] room / 더러운 옷 soiled clothes / 더러운 변소 a filthy toilet / 더러운 돈 filthy lucre; ill-gotten [tainted] money
▶ 그의 방은 언제나 더럽다 His room is usually untidy.
▶ 공해 때문에 이 강물은 더럽다 The water in this river is polluted.
▶ 더러운 손으로 만지지 마라 Keep your dirty hands off it.
2 〈상스럽다〉 nasty; disgusting; indecent; vulgar; obscene; 〈지저분하다〉 gross; filthy; 〈비열하다〉 mean; ignoble; base; low; 《美》 dirty
♦ 더러운 소리 a filthy [an indecent] talk; nasty words / 마음이 더러운 사람 a person of base mind; a meanspirited person / 더러운 생각 a mean idea
▶ 그들은 나에게 더러운 속임수를 썼다 They played a dirty trick on me.
▶ 나는 그런 더러운 소리가 듣기 싫다 I hate hearing such a filthy [dirty] talk.
3 〈인색하다〉 stingy; niggardly; sordid; tightfisted; closefisted; greedy of money
♦ 돈에 더러운 사람 a stingy person; a niggard; a miser
▶ 그는 돈에 더럽다 He is mean about money [over money matters].
4 〈비겁하다〉 foul; unfair; 〈창피하다〉 ignominious
♦ 더러운 방법을 쓰다 use underhand methods; 《口》 play dirty; 《口》 do the dirty on *sb* / 더럽게 이기다 win by foul play; win unfairly / 더럽게 지다 be ignominiously defeated; be a bad loser

더럽히다 1 〈불결하게〉 make *sth* dirty [unclean]; stain; soil; foul; defile; taint; contaminate; pollute 《air, water》
♦ 책[옷]을 더럽히다 soil a book [*one's* dress] / 하수로 강물을 더럽히다 contaminate a river with sewage
▶ 담배 연기는 방의 공기를 더럽힌다 Cigarette smoke pollutes the air in the room.
▶ 나는 넘어져서 옷을 더럽혔다 I fell down and got my clothes dirty.
▶ 새 옷을 더럽혀선 안된다 Don't make [get] your new dress dirty.
▶ 공장 폐수가 흔히 강물을 더럽힌다 Rivers are

often polluted by waste from factories.
2 〈명예 등을〉 disgrace; bring disgrace on; dishonor; sully; defile; tarnish; 〈신성을 모독하다〉 profane 《a church》

♦이름을 더럽히다 soil *one's* reputation; stain [disgrace] *one's* name / 가문을 더럽히다 bring disgrace on [be a disgrace to] *one's* family / 조상의 이름을 더럽히다 disgrace the good name of *one's* ancestors
▶ 그의 행위는 가문을 더럽혔다 His behavior brought shame [disgrace] on his family.

더미 a heap; a pile; 〈축적〉 an accumulation 《of knowledge》; 〈건초·볏짚 등의 가리〉 a stack; a rick

♦돌[책]더미 a pile of rocks [books] / 쓰레기더미 a rubbish [trash, dump] heap / 짚더미 stack of straws

더미씌우다 〈넘겨 지우다〉 impute; shift; shuffle off; pass the buck 《to *sb*》 ⇨ 전가(轉嫁)(~하다)

더벅머리 〈머리〉 disheveled [unkempt, bushy] hair; 〈아이〉 a boy with disheveled hair [who still has his hair loose]
▶ 그녀는 더벅머리 남자를 싫어한다 She hates thickly-haired men.

더부룩이 〈수염·머리 등이〉 in tufts; tufty; fringy; bushy; thick(ly); 〈풀 등이〉 thick(ly); rankly

♦머리를 더부룩이 기른 남자 a man with long unkempt hair / 수염을 더부룩이 기르고 있다 have a shaggy beard

더부룩하다 1 〈머리·수염 등이〉 tufty; fringy; bushy; thick

♦수염이 더부룩한 남자 a man with a shaggy beard / 더부룩한 머리 tufty [thick] hair; a profusion [wealth] of hair

2 〈풀 등이〉 thick, rank 《weeds》; rampant 《grass》
▶ 뜰에 풀이 더부룩하다 The garden is overgrown with grass.
▶ 빈 집의 뜰에는 풀이 더부룩했다 Wild grass was rank in the garden of the empty house.

3 〈서술적〉 be [lie, sit] heavy on *one's* stomach; be hard to digest; be not easily digested

♦위에 더부룩한 음식 heavy food / 배가 더부룩하다 sit [lie] heavy on the stomach

더부살이 a resident [living-in] servant; a domestic (servant) ♦더부살이 점원[하녀] a live-in [resident] clerk [maid] / 더부살이를 하다[살다] become [work as] a domestic help

더불다 1 〈함께 하다〉 partake of; share with
2 〈동행하다〉 accompany *sb*; go with *sb*; take [bring] *sb* with; keep *sb* company; be accompanied [attended] 《by》

더불어 1 〈함께〉 together ♦더불어 일하다 work together / 더불어 살다 live together; live under the same roof / 더불어 기뻐하다 rejoice together / 더불어 가다 go side by side / 더불어 노래하다 sing in chorus / 더불어 하다 join *sb* in doing

2 〈…와 함께〉 with; together [along] with; 〈…에 따라서〉 as; with

♦나이와 더불어 with (the) years; with age; as *one* grows older / 그와 더불어 고락을 같이 하다 share joy and sorrow with him
3 〈한가지로〉 alike; equally
▶ 노소가 더불어 뛰었다 They ran, irrespective of age [young and old alike].
4 〈상대하여〉 with; against
♦적과 더불어 싸우다 fight with [against] the enemy

더블 〈이중의〉 double
♦더블(-폭)의 천 cloth of double width
■—베드 a double bed —보기〔골프〕 a double bogey —상의 a double-breasted coat —스템〔스키〕 the double stem; the snowplow —스틸〔野〕 a double steal —펀치〔拳〕 a one-two (punch) —폴트〔테니스〕 a double fault —플레이〔野〕 a double play; a twin killing : 더블플레이하다 double up —헤더〔野〕 a double-header; a twin bill

더블린 〈아일랜드의 수도〉 Dublin
■—시민 a Dubliner

더블유비시 〈세계복싱평의회〉 WBC [〔the *W*orld *B*oxing *C*ouncil]

더블유비에이 〈세계복싱협회〉 WBA [〔the *W*orld *B*oxing *A*ssociation]

더블유에이치오 〈세계보건기구〉 WHO [〔the *W*orld *H*ealth *O*rganization]

더블유티오 〈세계무역기구〉 WTO [〔*W*orld *T*rade *O*rganization]

더블즈 〔테니스〕 doubles ■—시합 (a) doubles (match)

더비 〔競馬〕 the Derby ■—말 a Derby racer

더빙 〈재녹음〉 〔映·TV〕 dubbing(-in)
—더빙하다 copy; dub 《a tape》
▶ 그 영화는 우리말로 더빙되어 있다 The movie is dubbed in Korean.

더뻑 〈경솔하게〉 rashly; indiscreetly; 〈사려없이〉 thoughtlessly; blindly; recklessly; unreasonably; indiscriminately

♦더뻑 믿다 believe too readily / 제안을 더뻑 받아들이다 jump [snatch] at a proposal blindly; snap up an offer
▶ 남과 더뻑 약속하지 마라 Don't make rash promises.

더뻑거리다 act rashly [recklessly]; act on impulse ▶ 그는 더뻑거리는 사람이 아니다 He is not the sort of person to act rashly.

더뻑더뻑 rashly; recklessly; thoughtlessly; blindly

♦아무 일에나 더뻑더뻑 손을 대다 try recklessly to do everything / 더뻑더뻑 돈을 쓰다 spend *one's* money freely [recklessly, like water]; be lavish with *one's* money

더뿌룩하다 tufty ⇨ 더부룩하다

더새다 stay overnight; stay for the night; stay the night; take a lodging for the night; spend [pass] the night (on *one's* journey)
▶ 우리는 항구 근처의 여관에서 더샜다 We stayed [put up] at an inn [a hotel] near the harbor.

더스트슈트 〈英〉 a dust chute; 〈美〉 a trash [refuse, rubbish] chute

더스트코트 a duster; 〈英〉 a dustcoat

더없이 most of all; extremely; best (of all); supremely; superlatively; in the last degree
♦더없이 기뻐하다 be delighted beyond mea-

더욱 sure; be only [but] too pleased / 더없이 행복하다 be as happy as happy can be
▶ 그녀는 더없이 행복하다 She is as happy as happy can be. ⇒ She is extremely happy.
▶ 다시 그를 만나면 더없이 기쁠거야 Nothing will give me more pleasure than to see him again.
▶ 그는 더없이 진지한 사람이다 He is the most serious man I've ever met.

더욱 more; still [much] more; more and more; farther; further; all the more 《because, for》; 〈부정〉 still [much] less
◆ 더욱 힘드는 일 (much) harder work / 더욱 중요한 것은 what is more important / 더욱 좋다[나쁘다] be so much the better [worse]/ 더욱 좋게 만들다 make 《it》 even better / 더욱 노력하다 make greater [further] efforts; work harder than ever
▶ 그것은 더욱 어렵다 It is still more difficult.
▶ 내일 날씨는 더욱 나쁠 것이다 The weather for tomorrow will be even worse.
▶ 그는 학문도 없지만 경험은 더욱 없다 He has no scholarship, to say nothing of [not to speak of, much less] experience.
▶ 네가 결점이 있어서 나는 더욱 너를 좋아한다 I like you all the better for your faults.
▶ 막내둥이라서 더욱 귀엽다 I love him the more because he is my youngest child.
◀ 더욱 곤란한 것은 그가 항상 실수를 되풀이하는 것이다 What is worse, he always persists in his error.

더욱더 more and more; still [even] more; all the more; increasingly; growingly; more than ever [before]; 〈부정〉 still less
◆ 더욱더 번영하다 become more and more prosperous / 더욱더 나빠지다 go from bad to worse; be worse than ever
▶ 바람은 더욱더 심해졌다 The wind blew harder and harder. ⇒ The wind raged with growing intensity.
▶ 겨울이 되면 더욱더 추워진다 When winter sets in, it becomes increasingly colder.
▶ 소매값이 더욱더 오르고 있다 The retail prices are rising higher and higher.
▶ 높이 올라가면 올라갈수록 공기는 더욱더 희박해진다 The higher we go up, the thinner the air becomes.
▶ 생각하면 생각할수록 난 더욱더 모르겠다 The more I think about it, the less I understand it.
▶ 빠르면 빠를수록 더욱더 좋다 The sooner, the better.

더욱이 and; besides; more; still more; all the more; moreover; further(more); as well; in addition (to that); particularly; especially; what's more
◆ 더욱이 곤란한 일은 what is worse; to make (the) matters worse
▶ 그녀는 미인이고 더욱이 재원이다 She is pretty, moreover, she is intelligent.
▶ 그건 영어로 쓰여 있다. 더욱이 서투른 영어로 It is written in English, and poor English at that.

더워하다 complain of the (summer) heat; be sensitive to the heat; feel the heat (very much); feel hot; swelter
▶ 그는 언제나 더워한다 He is always complaining about the heat.
▶ 그는 뚱뚱해서 여름에는 유달리 더워한다 Being so fat, he is particularly susceptible to the summer heat.

더위 1 〈날씨〉 heat; warmth; hot weather
◆ 대단한 더위 great heat / 찌는 듯한 더위 steamy heat / 무더운 더위 sultry [sweltering] heat / 더위 타는 사람 a person who is sensitive to [can't stand] the heat / 타는 듯한 더위 scorching [parching, fiery] heat / 숨막힐 듯한 더위 suffocating [stifling] heat / 더위에 시달리다 be affected by the heat; suffer from hot weather / 더위를 타다 be sensitive to the heat; feel hot; feel the heat; complain of the (summer) heat / 더위에 지다 succumb to the heat / 나무 아래서 더위를 피하다 shelter from the heat under a tree / 더위를 참다[견디다] do not mind the heat; bear [stand, withstand] the heat
▶ 오늘은 더위가 대단하군요 How hot it is today! ⇒ Today's heat is terrible, isn't it?
▶ 이 더위에 잘 지내시기를 바랍니다 I hope you are getting along well [on all right] in this heat.
▶ 더위로 기운이 하나도 없다 I feel quite enervated by this sweltering heat.
▶ 이 더위에서는 공부할 수가 없다 I can't study in this heat.
2 〈병〉 heatstroke; heat prostration; 〈일사병〉 sunstroke
◆ 더위 먹다 suffer from [be affected by] heatstroke; 〈일사병에 걸리다〉 be sunstruck; have [be affected by, suffer from] sunstroke

더치다 become [grow, get] worse; be seized with a relapse; recur
◆ 병이 더치다 one's illness worsens; take a bad turn; take a turn for the worse; have a relapse; relapse into illness
▶ 그는 병이 더쳤다 He has had a relapse. ⇒ His illness has recurred.
▶ 그는 암이 더쳤다 He got cancer again. ⇒ He had a recurrence of cancer.

더킹 〔拳〕 ducking
더펄개 a shaggy dog; a poodle
더펄거리다 1 〈머리가〉 bounce up and down 2 〈사람이〉 act briskly [rashly, thoughtlessly, carelessly, on impulse]
더펄이 a scatterbrain; a madcap; a reckless fellow; a daredevil
더하기 〔數〕 add; adding up
◆ 더하기를 하다 add up 《figures》 ▶ 그는 더하기를 잘한다 He is good at addition [doing sums].

더하다¹ 1 〈심해지다〉 grow violent [severe, intense]; increase in violence [severity, intensity]; become worse [aggravated]; 〈비바람 등이〉 gather (force)
◆ 병세가 더하다 take a bad turn; take a turn for the worse / 추위[더위]가 더하다 get colder [hotter]
▶ 그녀에 대한 나의 사랑은 더해갔다 My love

for her grew.
▶ 비바람이 더해진다 The storm is gathering.
▶ 더위가 날로 더해간다 It is getting hotter and hotter every day.
2 〈덧셈하다〉 add 《one number to another》; 〈합계하다〉 add [sum] up
▶ 10에 5를 더하면 몇이냐? If you add five to ten, what number do you get?
▶ 3에 5를 더하면 8이 된다 Three and five make [are] eight. ⇌ Three plus five is eight.
▶ 15에 25를 더하면 40이 된다 Twenty-five added to fifteen makes [is, equals] forty.
▶ 처음에는 10명이었으나 늦게 온 사람을 더해서 결국 16명이 되었다 At first there were ten people but altogether, adding those who came late, there were sixteen.
3 〈증가하다〉 increase; add to; augment; gain; grow
◆세력을 더하다 gain in influence; gather strength / 속력을 더하다 speed up; gather [pick up] speed
▶ 그 젊은 가수는 인기를 점점 더해 갔다 The young singer has gradually increased in popularity.
▶ 나날이 추위가 더해가고 있다 It's getting colder (and colder) every day.

더하다² 〈비교〉 more; much; all the more [better, worse]
▶ 그녀는 내가 예상한 것보다 더한 미인이었다 She was a far more beautiful woman than I had expected.
▶ 그도 술꾼이지만 그의 아버지는 더한 술고래다 He is (quite) a drinker, but his father is an even heavier drinker.
▶ 이것은 내구성이 저것보다 더하면 더했지 떨어지지 않는다 This is no less durable than that.

더한층 一層 still [much, even] more; all the more; 〈부정〉 still [much] less
◆더한층 노력하다 make even greater efforts; work harder (than ever) / 더한층 좋다[나쁘다] be so much the better [worse]
▶ 대학에 들어간 후 그는 더한층 공부하기 시작했다 After entering the university, he began to study (even) harder.
▶ 그가 참가해 준다면 더한층 좋다 If he joins us, so much the better.

더할나위없다 〈완전하다〉 perfect; 〈만족스럽다〉 most satisfactory; 〈알맞다〉 best fit (for); most suitable (for); 〈탁월하다〉 excellent; superior; 〈이상적이다〉 ideal; capital; 〈최고다〉 the best; the finest; the greatest; unsurpassed; peerless; supreme; superb
◆더할 나위 없는 미인 a woman of unsurpassed beauty / 낚시하기에는 더할 나위 없는 날씨 a capital weather for angling
▶ 제가 이 국제회의를 주재하게 되어 더할 나위 없는 영광입니다 It is the greatest honor for me to chair this international conference.
▶ 다시 그를 만난다니 더할 나위 없는 즐거움이다 Nothing will give me more pleasure than to see him again.
▶ 그 사람은 더할 나위 없는 진지한 사람이다 He is the most serious man I've ever met.
▶ 날씨는 더할 나위 없었다 The weather was at its best. ≒ The weather was all that could be wished for.

더할나위없이 perfectly; satisfactorily; impeccably; most (of all); best (of all); extremely; supremely; superlatively; in the last degree
◆더할 나위 없이 아름다운 꽃 the finest possible [imaginable] flower / 더할 나위 없이 중요한 the most important; of sovereign importance

덕 〈시렁〉 rack [shelf] (for drying grain)

덕 德 **1** 〈미덕〉 (a) virtue; goodness; moral excellence; a merit
◆매우 덕이 높은 사람 a man of exceptional virtue; an extremely virtuous man / 덕이 있는 virtuous; respectable / 덕을 갖추다[지니다] possess [be invested with] virtue / 덕을 기르다[닦다] cultivate virtue [moral character]
▶ 온 마을이 그의 덕에 감화되었다 The whole village was influenced by his virtue.
▶ 그는 경솔한 행동을 해서 할아버지의 덕을 손상시켰다 His reckless conduct impaired the reputation of his grandfather.
2 〈은혜·덕택〉 benevolence; good; kindness; mercy
◆남의 덕으로 살다 live on charity [the bounty of others]
3 ⇨ 공덕(功德)
▶ 그는 고아들에게 덕을 베풀었다 He was benevolent [good] to the orphans.

덕기 德氣 virtuous mien
덕담 德談 well-meant [well-wishing] remarks
덕대 【鑛】 a subcontractor of mining
■—갱(坑) a rented part of a mine
덕량 德量 virtuous mind; generosity; broad-mindedness
덕망 德望 (a) moral influence
◆덕망이 있는 사람 a person renowned for his virtues; a paragon (of virtue) / 덕망이 없는 사람 a man of loose morals / 덕망이 있다 have a moral influence; be renowned for one's virtues; have [enjoy] high reputation as a man of virtue
■—가 a man of high (moral) repute
덕목 德目 (a) virtue; moral principles
◆남의 덕목을 나열하다 enumerate a person's virtues
덕분 德分 indebtedness ⇨ 덕택(德澤)
▶ 날씨가 좋은 덕분에 운동회는 대성공이었다 Thanks to fine weather, the athletic meet was a big success.
▶ 그가 노력한 덕분에 그 계획은 성공했다 Thanks to his efforts, the project has been a success.
▶ 당신이 도와준 덕분에 시험에 합격할 수 있었습니다 Thank you very much for helping me (to) pass the examination.
▶ 나는 그것을 오직 하나님의 덕분이라고 믿습니다 I believe that it was only by the grace of God.
▶ 덕분에 건강합니다 I'm quite well, thank you.

덕석 a straw rug for cattle; 《총칭》 straw matting for cattle; 〈한 장〉 a straw mat for cattle

덕성 德性 moral character [nature]; (a) virtue
♦덕성이 높은 사람들 virtuous people; people of high moral character / 덕성을 기르다 [함양하다] cultivate [foster] moral character / 덕성스럽다 be virtuous; be good-natured; be kind-hearted

덕스럽다 德— virtuous; respectable; gracious; dignified; refined; benignant
♦덕스러운 사람 a man of virtue; a virtuous man / 덕스럽게 생기다 have respectable features; have a refined [noble] look

덕용 德用 ♦덕용의 economical; saving
■—品 an economical article

덕육 德育 moral education [culture, training]
♦덕육을 중히 여기다 attach importance to moral culture

덕의 德義 〈덕성과 신의〉 morals; morality; integrity
♦덕의가 있는 사람 a man of unimpeachable morality [morals]
■—心 moral sense; a sense of honor

덕적덕적, 덕지덕지 thickly; heavily; lavishly
♦벽에 페인트를 덕적덕적 칠하다 daub paint on a wall / 때가 덕적덕적 끼어 있다 be thickly covered with dirt [filth, grime]
▶그녀는 덕적덕적 화장했다 Her face is thickly [heavily] made-up.
▶벽에는 포스터가 덕지덕지 붙어 있었다 The wall was covered with posters.

덕택 德澤 〈신세〉 indebtedness; 〈은혜〉 grace; favor; patronage; 〈도움〉 help; aid; assistance; 〈후원〉 support; backing
♦덕택으로 thanks to sb; thanks to sb's patronage; by sb's favor [help, aid]; through [by] sb's assistance; by sb's kind influence; through sb's efforts; 〈이유·원인〉 due to; because of; owing to; by [in] virtue of
▶내가 살아난 것은 하나님의 덕택이라고 생각한다 I think what saved me was the grace of God.
▶덕택으로 모두 잘 있습니다 We are all well and fine, thank you.
▶덕택으로 사업은 잘 돼가고 있습니다 We owe the prosperity of this business to you. ⇒ Thanks to you, the enterprise is going on swimmingly.
▶그들은 그의 덕택으로 산다 They depend upon him for their living.
▶당신 덕택으로 젖지 않았습니다 Thanks to you, I didn't get wet.
▶당신 덕택으로 빚도 완벽히 갚았습니다 Luckily, I was able to repay my loan completely.
▶그의 덕택으로 내가 이만큼 되었다 He has made me what I am. ⇒ He has been the making of me. ⇒ What I am I owe to him.
▶내가 성공한 것은 당신 덕택입니다 I owe my success to you. ⇒ I am greatly indebted to you for my success.
▶위기를 극복한 것은 당신 덕택입니다 I owe it to you that I was able to overcome my difficulties.

덕행 德行 virtuous [moral] conduct [deed, act]; virtue; goodness
▶그의 덕행은[에 관해서는] 널리 알려져 있다 He is renowned for his virtue.

덕화 德化 moral influence [reform]
—덕화하다 influence [reform] by a virtuous example

덖다[1] 〈때로 찌들다〉 become dirty [filthy, grimy, grubby]; become soiled; be begrimed

덖다[2] 〈볶다〉 parch 《beans》; roast 《tea, nuts, coffee beans, etc.》

-던고 〈과거의 의문〉 ▶그것이 길던가 짧던가? Was it long or short?
▶그는 어느 쪽으로 가던가? In what direction did he go?
▶내가 그것을 어디에 두었던가? Where did I leave it, I wonder?
▶저 여자는 누구였던가? I wonder who that woman was.
▶이것은 너의 책이 아니었던가? Wasn't this your book?

-던걸 〈회상·감탄〉 ▶그녀는 굉장한 미인이던걸 She was a stunning beauty, indeed.
▶일이 고되던걸 It was work, I tell you.
▶매우 어렵던걸 It was difficult [hard]

-던데 1 〈연결어미〉 but; though
▶그가 아까 오던데 아무데도 안 보이네 I saw him coming, but I can find him nowhere.
▶그는 그것을 모를 만큼 바보가 아니던데 He was not such a fool but knew it.
▶사람은 젊던데 아주 똑똑하더라 Young though he was, he was very wise.

2 〈종결어미〉
▶손해는 대단치 않던데 The loss was far less than we feared.
▶책은 재미있던데 I found the book interesting.

-던들 if only; if it had happened that...
▶비가 오기만 했던들 If only it would rain!
▶알고만 있었던들 If only I [I only] had known!
▶그의 주소를 알고 있었던들 너에게 알려줄텐데 If I knew his address, I'd give it to you.
▶빨리 의사에게 보였던들 그는 죽지 않았을 텐데 If he had been sent to the doctor right away, he wouldn't have died.
▶내내 달렸던들 시간에 대어 거기에 도착했을 텐데 If you had run all the way, you'd gotten there in time.
▶당신의 도움이 없었던들 나는 실패했을 거요 If it had not been for [But for, Without] your help, I should have failed.

던적스럽다 〈비천하다〉 mean; base; sordid; 〈다랍다〉 stingy; miserly; 〈추잡하다〉 filthy; dirty (-looking); foul; indecent; obscene
♦던적스러운 사람 a man of low [mean] character / a low-minded [meanspirited] person / 던적스러운 속임수를 쓰다 use a dirty trick; use underhanded methods / 돈에 던적스럽다 be grasping; be greedy about money / 던적스러운 말을 하다 use a filthy [dirty] language / 던적스러운 생각을 하다 have a mean idea
▶그는 그런 던적스러운 짓을 할 사람이 아니다 He is above such meanness.

던져두다 〈방치하다〉 leave sb [sth] as he [it] is; put [throw] aside; 〈하던 일을〉 lay aside;

leave sb; leave sth 《undone》; neglect
♦하던 일을 던져두다 leave [let] one's work undone [unfinished]
▶가방은 책상 위에 던져진 채였다 His bag was lying on the desk as he had left it.
-던지 《과거의 의문》 ▶그가 누구였던지 생각이 나지 않는다 I cannot remember who he was.
▶그녀가 안경을 썼던지 안썼던지 기억이 나지 않는다 I don't remember whether or not she was wearing spectacles.
▶우연이었던지 고의였던지 하여튼 그는 왔다 He came anyway, whether by accident or design.
던지기 a throw; throwing
■원반— a discus throw
던지다 1 〈물건을〉 throw 《away》; 〈가볍게〉 toss; 〈세게〉 fling; hurl; cast; 〈투수가〉 pitch; 〈창 등을〉 dart; hurl; 〈메어다꽂다〉 throw [fling] down

> 解說 **throw**는 「던지다」라는 뜻의 가장 일반적인 말이다. **fling**과 **hurl**은 throw 보다 세차게 던진다는 뜻으로 fling은 때로 감정적으로 난폭하게 내던진다는 뜻을 내포하며 hurl은 크고 무거운 물건을 멀리 던지는 맹렬한 힘을 강조한다. **pitch**는 주로 야구 등에서 목표를 향해 공을 던진다는 뜻이다.

♦돌을 던지다 throw [fling] a stone 《at》; stone sb / 주사위를 던지다 shoot [throw, cast] a die / 창을 던지다 hurl [dart] a javelin / 그물을 던지다 cast a net; throw a casting net
▶제2구, 던졌습니다 Now the second pitch. Pitch!
▶그녀는 남동생한테 계란을 던졌다 She threw [flung] some eggs at her brother.
▶소년은 개한테 뼈다귀를 던졌다 The boy tossed the dog a bone.
▶투수는 커브를 던졌다 The pitcher delivered a curveball.
▶창문에서 휴지를 던지지 마라 Don't throw wastepaper from the window.
▶신문 배달원이 창문으로 신문을 던져 넣었다 The newsboy threw the paper in at the window.
2 〈투표하다〉 cast a ballot; ballot 《for》; 《美》 vote; 《美》 cast a [one's] vote 《for》; poll
♦깨끗한 한 표를 던지다 cast an honest [a fair, a clean, a conscientious] vote / 찬성표 [반대표]를 던지다 vote for [against]; ballot for [against]
3 〈시선·웃음 등을〉 cast 《at》; sent 《at》
♦시선을 던지다 cast a glance 《at》; turn [direct] one's eyes 《to》; look toward / 미소를 던지다 smile at sb / 추파를 던지다 cast an amorous glance 《at》; wink 《at》
4 〈몸을〉 throw [cast] oneself 《into a river》; 《비유》 enter [launch] 《into politics》
▶그녀는 그의 품안에 몸을 던졌다 She sank into his arms.
5 〈버리다〉 abandon; throw [give] up
♦지위를 던지다 throw up [resign from] one's position / 목숨을 던지다 lay down one's life
던지럽다 mean; base; foul; filthy; dirty
덜 less; incompletely; little; insufficiently
♦덜 익은 과일 green [unripe] fruits / 덜 구워진 half-roasted; 〈고기가〉 half-done; underdone; rare; 〈빵이〉 half-baked / 덜 마른 half-dried; unseasoned 《wood, timber》
▶돈이 덜 드는 방법은 없을까? Isn't there a cheaper [less expensive] way?
▶그의 새 사무실은 전의 것보다 덜 편리하다 His new office is less convenient than his old one.
▶그는 덜 구워진 고기를 좋아하지 않는다 He doesn't like meat underdone.
▶오늘은 어제보다 덜 덥다 It is less warm today than yesterday.
덜거덕 with a rattling [clattering, crunching] sound [noise] ⇨ 달가닥
덜거덕거리다 rattle; clatter ⇨ 달가닥거리다
▶바람에 창문이 덜거덕거렸다 The wind rattled the window.
▶마차가 덜거덕거리며 지나갔다 A wagon rattled on.
▶부엌에서 식기류가 덜거덕거리는 소리가 들렸다 I heard cutlery clattering in the kitchen.
덜거덩 with a clang ⇨ 달가당
덜거덩거리다 rattle ⇨ 달가당거리다
▶짐수레는 덜거덩거리며 멈춰 섰다 The cart stopped with a jolt [jolted to a stop].
▶그 남자는 문을 덜거덩거렸다 The man rattled the door.
덜그럭 with a rattling [clattering] noise [sound] ⇨ 달그락
덜그럭거리다 rattle; clatter ⇨ 달그락거리다
♦닻을 덜그럭거리며 올리다 rattle up the anchor
▶바람에 덧문이 덜그럭거린다 The wind is rattling the shutters.
덜그럭덜그럭하다 ▶누군가가 문을 덜그럭덜그럭 두드리고 있다 Someone's rapping [tapping] on [at] the door.
덜다 1 〈빼다〉 subtract; deduct 《from》; take off; 〈수량을 줄이다〉 decrease; lessen; abate; 〈수·크기·정도를〉 reduce
♦50에서 20을 덜다 subtract 20 from 50 / 분량을 덜다 decrease the quantity 《of》 / 수를 덜다 reduce [decrease] the number / 무게를 덜다 reduce [lessen] the weight
▶천만원 덜어 주시오 Cut it down 1,000 won.
▶나는 다이어트로 체중을 덜고 있다 I am reducing [losing weight] by dieting.
2 〈경감하다〉 lessen; ease; relieve; lighten; 〈절약하다〉 save; spare; curtail; 〈지출을〉 cut 《down》
♦무거운 짐을 덜다 lessen the burden / 고통 [근심, 슬픔]을 덜다 ease [allay] the pain [anxiety, grief] / 수고를 덜다 save sb trouble; save labor / 교통난을 덜다 relieve traffic congestion; ease a traffic jam / 경비를 덜다 cut down on [curtail] expenses
▶기계는 많은 시간과 노력을 덜어준다 Machinery saves us much time and labor.
덜덜[1] 〈떠는 모양〉 tremblingly; shiveringly; shakingly; quiveringly

♦손을 덜덜 떨면서 with trembling hands / 추워서 덜덜 떨다 shiver with cold; quiver from cold / 무서워서 덜덜 떨다 shudder in horror; tremble with [for] fear
▶그는 공포[노여움] 때문에 덜덜 떨고 있었다 He was trembling with fear [anger].
▶손이 덜덜 떨려서 글씨를 잘 쓸 수가 없었다 My hands were shaking so badly that I could not write well.
▶나는 무릎이 덜덜 떨렸다 My knees knocked together.

덜덜² 〈구르는 소리〉 rumbling; rolling; rattling
♦(수레가) 덜덜 굴러가다 rumble along [up, down]
▶짐마차가 덜덜거리며 지나갔다 A cart rattled as it went away. ⇌ A cart rattled away.

덜되다 1〈서술적〉 be no good; be wretched [poor, sorry, sad] stuff; be not up to the mark; be a failure
♦덜된 놈 a greenhorn; a fool; a stupid fellow; a blockhead; a bonehead; a good-for-nothing (fellow); a wretched fellow; a silly ass / 덜된 소리를 하다 talk nonsense [rot]; say silly things
▶저 소녀는 좀 덜되었다 She isn't very bright. ⇌ (口) She's a bit short on brains.
2〈설익다〉 unripe; unmellow; immature; green
♦덜된 과일 green [unripe] fruits
3〈미완성되다〉 unfinished; incomplete; not completely done; imperfect
♦덜된 밥 half-boiled rice / 덜된 작품 an unfinished work ((of art)) / 덜된 채로 있다 be left unfinished / 일이 덜되다 one's work is not finished
▶저 건물은 아직 덜되었다 The building is not yet finished.
▶그 시는 아직 덜되었다 The poem is unfinished [undone]. ⇌ The poem is not completed yet.

덜렁거리다 1〈소리가〉 jingle; clink
2〈행동이〉 act hastily [rashly, thoughtlessly, carelessly]; behave lightly [frivolously]
♦덜렁거리는 사람 a flighty [hasty] person; a hasty [careless] person; a bustling fellow / 덜렁거리고 쏘다니다 hustle [bustle] about; go around restlessly
▶그는 정말로 덜렁거린다 He is so careless. ⇌ He is such a scatterbrain.
♦덜렁거리는 사람은 사절한다 I have no use for people who act rashly.

덜렁쇠,덜렁이 a restless person; a heedless person; a flighty [hasty, bustling] person; a blunderer; (口) a scatterbrain; (口) a birdbrain

덜렁하다 1〈소리가〉 ring; jingle; tinkle
2〈가슴이〉 be startled; get a start; be taken aback; feel a shock; be shocked ((at, by)); get a start [turn]
♦가슴이 덜렁하다 one's heart leaps into one's mouth; be frightened [startled] out of one's wits
▶그가 바로 맞혔을 때 내 가슴이 덜렁했다 I was startled when he guessed right.
▶어둠 속에서 누군가 다가오는 것을 보고 가슴이 덜렁했다 I was frightened [scared, shocked] to find someone approaching in the dark.
▶그 소식을 듣고 가슴이 덜렁했다 My heart turned over at the news.
▶그의 말에 가슴이 덜렁했다 I was shocked at his words. ⇌ His words gave me a shock [start].

덜리다 1〈줄다〉 be subtracted [deducted]; be taken off [away, from]
2〈경감·완화되다〉 be reduced; become less; lessen; loosen; decrease; be mitigated [alleviated]; become mild [less severe]; be allayed [eased]; become lower
▶내 아픔이 덜렸다 My pain is eased.
▶그의 걱정이 덜렸다 His anxiety is eased.

덜먹다 1〈다 먹지 않다〉 do not eat up; 〈실컷 먹지 않다〉 do not eat heartily [one's fill]
2〈행동이〉 act improperly and impudently
3〈나이를〉 be younger than sb

덜미 the back [scruff] ((of the neck)); the nape ⇨ 뒷덜미
▶그는 소년의 덜미를 잡았다 He seized the boy by the scruff of his neck.

덜미잡이하다 grab [take, seize] sb by the scruff of ((his)) neck [by the collar]

덜어내다 take out [away] ♦가마니에서 쌀을 덜어내다 take some rice out of a rice bag / 숟가락으로 죽을 덜어내다 spoon some gruel out of a bowl

덜커덕 clatteringly; rattlingly —**덜커덕하다** clatter; rattle; make a clattering [rattling] sound

덜커덕거리다 keep clattering; clatter; rattle
♦(차가) 덜커덕거리다 bump; be bumpy; jolt / 미닫이를 덜커덕거리며 닫다 shut the sliding door noisily
▶짐마차는 울퉁불퉁한 길을 덜커덕거리며 지나갔다 The cart bumped along the rough road.
▶우리 차는 산길을 덜커덕거리며 달렸다 Our car rattled along the mountain road.

덜커덕덜커덕 clatteringly; rattlingly

덜커덩 clatteringly; rattlingly; lumberingly; clangingly; with a clang [bump, bang]
♦문을 덜커덩 닫다 close a door with a bang [bump]/(차가) 덜커덩 움직이다 jerk [get jerkily] into motion / 덜커덩 서다 jerk to a stop
—**덜커덩하다** clatter; rattle; rumble; clang; bang; bump
▶나는 차 뒤에서 무언가 덜커덩하는 소리를 들었다 I heard something bang [thud] at the back of my car.

덜커덩덜커덩 clatteringly; rattlingly; lumberingly; with a clattering [rattling] noise
—**덜커덩덜커덩하다** clatter; rattle; clang; rumblingly
▶창문이 바람에 덜커덩덜커덩했다 The window rattled in the wind.
▶낡은 차가 울퉁불퉁한 길을 덜커덩덜커덩하며 달렸다 The old car bumped along the rough road.

덜컥 1 ⇨ 덜커덕 2〈급작스럽게〉 suddenly; all of a sudden; unexpectedly
♦덜컥 죽어버리다 die suddenly [a sudden

death]; (口) drop dead / 덜컥 겁이 나다 be seized with fear all of a sudden / 가슴이 덜컥하다 be shocked 《at》; be startled 《at》; feel a shock; get a start
▶ 아버지가 뇌출혈로 덜컥 돌아가셨다 My father died suddenly of a stroke [a sudden death from apoplexy].
▶ 그는 호명되자 가슴이 덜컥했다 He was startled at the mention of his name. ⇌ He showed a startled look when he was called.
▶ 그 청년은 외국에서 덜컥 죽었다 The young man died suddenly abroad.

덜퍽지다, 덜퍽스럽다 plentiful; ample; rich; abundant; affluent; 〈몸집이〉 big and heavy; plump; portly; buxom; corpulent; 〈건장하다〉 massive; stout; sturdy

덜하다 1 〈줄다〉 decrease; diminish; lessen; abate
▶ 어두워지니까 더위가 덜하다 The heat diminishes as it gets dark.
▶ 추위가 갑자기 덜해졌다 The cold weather suddenly gone.
▶ 내 복통이 덜해졌다 My stomachache is much better.
▶ 나는 볼링에 대한 흥미가 덜해졌다 My interest in bowling has declined.
▶ 그에 대한 그녀의 애정이 덜해졌다 Her love for him has cooled down.
▶ 그에 대한 우리의 존경심은 차츰 덜해졌다 Our respect for him became less and less.
2 〈줄이다〉 decrease; reduce; diminish; lessen; abate; 〈수를〉 subtract 《from》
♦ 노력을 덜하다 relax (in) [ease up] *one's* efforts; slack off / 지출을 덜하다 curtail [cut down] the expenses

덤 an addition; a premium; a supplement; an accessory; an extra; 〈경품〉 something thrown in; a throw-in; a bonus
♦ 덤의 supplementary; additional / 덤으로 in addition 《to》; on top of *sth*; into the bargain / 덤으로 넣다 throw *sth* in 《for good measure》
▶ 이것은 덤입니다 This is a free [an uncharged] addition. ⇌ This is free [for nothing].
▶ 열 권을 사면 한 권을 덤으로 더 드리지요 If you'll take ten copies, I'll throw in another.
▶ 가구를 샀더니 왁스를 덤으로 주더라 When I bought the furniture, they throw in the wax (for free).

덤덤탄—彈 a dumdum (bullet); a softnosed bullet

덤덤하다 1 〈말이 없다〉 quiet; silent; taciturn; reticent; speechless; closemouthed; mum; 〈서술적〉 keep [remain] silent; hold *one's* tongue; (口) keep *one's* mouth shut; keep dumb
♦ 덤덤한 사람 a reticent person; a person of few words / 모욕을 당하고도 덤덤하다 take an insult lying down
2 〈차분하다〉 calm; serene; placid; peaceful; 〈탐탁하지 않다〉 ordinary; common
♦ 덤덤한 생활 ordinary life; a serene life
3 〈맛이〉 have not much flavor; plain; flat (to the taste)

▶ 이 배는 덤덤하다 This pear is tasteless [is insipid, has little flavor].

덤벙 splashing; with a plop [splash]
♦ 덤벙 물에 떨어지다 drop into 《the water》 with a plop [a dull splash]
▶ 그는 덤벙 강에 빠졌다[뛰어 들었다] He fell [plunged] into the river with a plop.
—**덤벙하다** plop [flop, plump, plunge, splash] into 《the water》

덤벙거리다 1 〈까불다〉 behave carelessly; act frivolously [rashly, flippantly, lightly]; frivol; bustle; make a fuss
♦ 덤벙거리는 사람 a careless [heedless] person; a scatterbrain / 덤벙거리는 frivolous; slapdash; hasty; scatterbrained; rash; light; flippant; careless; incautious / 덤벙거리며 일을 함부로 하다 do *one's* work carelessly
2 〈물에서〉 splash; make a splash; splatter; spatter
♦ 진창길을 덤벙거리며 걷다 splash along in slush [mud] / 발을 물에 담그고 덤벙거리다 dabble *one's* feet in the water

덤벙덤벙 1 〈경솔히〉 frivolously; flippantly; rashly; hastily; lightly; too readily; imprudently; carelessly; thoughtlessly 2 〈물에서〉 splashing; splattering

덤벼들다 1 ⇨ 덤비다 1
▶ 독수리가 토끼에게 덤벼들었다 The eagle swooped (down) upon a hare.
▶ 그는 화가 잔뜩 나서 나에게 덤벼들었다 He turned upon me in a fury.
▶ 그들은 뒤에서 그에게 덤벼들었다 They grabbed him from behind.
▶ 술 취한 사람이 갑자기 덤벼들었다 The drunken man suddenly turned upon me.
2 〈일에〉 begin; start (in); set [go] about; set [turn, put] *one's* hand to; set *oneself* to work [on job]; tackle 《the work》
▶ 우리는 지금 막 일에 덤벼들었다 We've just begun our work [set to work, started our work].

덤불 a thicket; a bush; a shrub; 〈관목의〉 a shrubbery
♦ 가시 덤불 a thorny thicket / 덤불이 있는 뜰 a garden planted with trees

덤불자작이 (植) a birch

덤비다 1 〈대들다〉 go at; turn [fall] upon [on]; defy; challenge; fling [throw] *oneself* upon; be [come] down on [upon]; 〈공격하다〉 attack; assault; assail; charge; 〈싸움을 걸다〉 pick a quarrel [fight] 《with》; 〈짐승 등이〉 spring [jump, leap, pounce, fly] upon [at]; rush [bounce] upon
▶ 그 개는 그의 목을 향해 덤볐다 The dog jumped [sprang, leapt] at his throat.
▶ 소년들은 도둑에게 덤볐다 The boys jumped [sprang] on the thief. ⇌ The boys threw [hurled, flung] themselves on the thief.
▶ 자 덤벼라 Come on!
▶ 그는 아무것도 아닌 일을 가지고 내게 덤볐다 He turned on me for nothing.
▶ 그는 상사에게 정면으로 덤볐다 He defied his boss openly.
▶ 그는 내게 덤볐다 He turned [defied] on me.

2 〈서두르다〉 hurry; hasten; be in a hurry; make haste; be hurried; be in hot haste; be hasty
♦덤비지 말고 calmly; with calmness [composure]
▶덤비지 마라 Don't hurry [rush]. ⇌ Take your time. ⇌ Get yourself together. ⇌ Take it easy. ⇌ Steady on. ⇌ Keep your shirt on.

덤터기 ♦덤터기 쓰다 have the blame shifted on to *oneself*; take a weight upon *oneself* / 덤터기 씌우다 shift the blame [the weight] on to 《another》; put [lay, fix] the blame on *sb*; lay the blame at *sb's* door; **(俗)** pass the buck 《to》
▶그는 부하의 죄를 덤터기 썼다 He took a subordinate's guilt on himself.
▶그는 어떻게 해서 동생의 부채를 덤터기 쓰게 되었는가? How did he come to shoulder his brother's debts?

덤프차 —車 a dump truck [(美) lorry]; a dump car (▶dump car는 철도의 화차)

덤핑 (商) dumping; underselling
▶그 회사는 지금 해외시장에서 덤핑 공세를 하고 있다 The firm is now conducting offensive dumping on overseas markets.
—**덤핑하다** dump; sell (goods) at sacrifice price; undersell
▶그들은 해외시장에서 잉여상품을 덤핑하려 하고 있다 They are trying to dump surplus goods on overseas markets.
■—방지 관세 anti-dumping duties —시장 a dumping field [market] —전 a dumping war

덥다 hot (↔ cold); warm; 〈무덥다〉 sultry
♦더운 날 a hot day / 더운 물 hot water / 무척 덥다 feel the heat very much / 더워서 헐떡거리다 gasp in the sweltering heat
▶찌는듯이 덥다 It is steaming hot.
▶나는 더운 것은 아무렇지도 않다 I don't mind the heat.
▶오늘은 무덥다 It's sultry today.
▶더워서 숨이 막힐 지경이다 It is stifling hot.
▶더워서 잠을 잘 수가 없다 It's so hot (that) I can't sleep.
▶나날이 더워지고 있다 It's getting hotter day by day.
▶지금이 한창 더울 때다 The summer is now at its hottest.
▶더워서 못견디겠다 The heat is unbearable. ⇌ It is unbearably hot. ⇌ I can't stand the heat. ⇌ I am dying of the heat.
▶더워지기 전에 떠납시다 Let's go out before it gets hot.

덥석 〈급히〉 quickly; suddenly; all of a sudden; all at once; hastily; 〈단단히〉 tightly; firmly
♦덥석 물다 snap (at *sth*); sink its [*one's*] teeth into 《*sb's* arm》 / 덥석 잡다 grab; grasp; seize violent hold (of)
▶그는 내 두 손을 덥석 잡았다 He grabbed both my hands with his own.
▶사자가 먹이를 덥석 물고 있다 The lion is biting at the bait.
▶개가 내 손을 덥석 물었다 The dog bit me on the hand.

덥적거리다 1 〈남의 일에〉 meddle 《with [in] *sb's* affairs》; interfere in [with]; poke *one's* nose 《into *sb's* business》
♦덥적거리는 사람 a busybody; a meddlesome [an officious] person; a meddler / 덥적거리는 interfering; meddlesome; officious; **(口)** nos(e)y
▶남의 일에 덥적거리지 마라 Mind your own business.
▶그는 언제나 남의 일에 덥적거린다 He is always meddling (in other people's affairs).
2 〈붙임성 있게〉 make *oneself* agreeable [delightful] to 《another》; **(俗)** talk turkey
▶그녀는 남에게 덥적거린다 She has a gentle manner toward others. ⇌ She has an affable way with people.

덥적덥적 1 〈남의 일에〉 meddlesomely; nosily; interferingly; officiously **2** 〈붙임성있게〉 amiably; affably; friendly; sociably; winningly

덧 a short time ⇨ 어느덧

덧가지 a double branch

덧거름 topdressing

덧나다 1 〈치아 등이〉 (a tooth) grow beyond the rest [others]; grow to one side
2 〈병이〉 worsen; get complicated; get [grow] worse; go from bad to worse; take a bad turn; change [take a turn] for the worse; be aggravated; 〈종기가〉 become [get] inflamed; 〈곪다〉 form [generate] pus; fester
♦덧난 상처 a festering [purulent] wound
▶감기가 덧나서 낫는데 어려움을 겪었다 My cold grew worse and I had a hard time getting rid of it.
▶상처가 덧났다 The wound has festered [formed pus].
▶할퀸 자국이 덧났다 The scratch festered.
▶감기가 덧나서 폐렴이 되었다 His cold developed into pneumonia.
3 〈노영이〉 get angry; be offended [provoked]

덧날 a wedge (of a plane); back iron ■—막이 a metal bar [band] over the back iron

덧내다 1 〈병을〉 worsen; make 《a disease》 worse; cause to take a bad turn; aggravate; 〈종기 등을〉 inflame
♦병을 덧내다 aggravate an illness / 종기를 건드려 덧내다 make a boil [tumor] worse by fiddling with it / 감기를 덧내서 죽다 die from a neglected cold
2 〈덧들이다〉 offend; stir [provoke] *sb* to anger

덧니 (美) a snaggletooth (*pl*. -teeth); 〈큰〉 a bucktooth; a snag tooth; a protruding [prominent] tooth; a projecting tooth; 〈겹친〉 a double tooth ♦덧니 나다 cut a snaggletooth; get a snag [double] tooth through
■—박이 a person with a snaggletooth

덧달다 hang over [upon] another; attach 《one thing》 on top of 《another [the other]》
♦덧달리다 be hung over [upon] another

덧대다 put [attach, place] 《one thing》 over [upon, on top of] 《another》; add [join] 《on a board, a prop, a layer》

덧문 —門 an outer [a double] door [window]; a storm [rain] door [window]; a shutter ♦ 덧문을 열다[닫다] open [shut, close] the shutters

덧버선 outer socks; outer Korean socks

덧보태다 add 《one thing to another》; supplement ⇨ 덧붙이다
▶ 선생님이 나의 작품에 몇 마디 덧보태서 정정하셨다 The teacher added some words to my composition to improve it.

덧붙다 adhere [stick, cling] to *sth* in addition

덧붙이다 1 〈더 붙이다〉 add [attach, stick] 《a thing to another》; supplement; join [fix] 《a thing on top of another》; affix; append; annex
♦ 벽에 널빤지를 덧붙이다 fix planks on a wall
▶ 꽃다발을 덧붙여 선물이 배달되었다 A bouquet was delivered together with the present.
2 〈보태어 말하다〉 add 《that...》; say *sth* in addition; make an additional remark
♦ 덧붙여 말하자면 to make an additional remark; it may be said in this connection [in passing] that...; by the way
▶ 한 마디 덧붙이고 싶다 I would like to say one more word.
▶ 이밖에 덧붙여 말할 것이 있느냐? Do you have anything else to add?
▶ 이 사진에는 설명을 덧붙이는 편이 좋다 It would be better to put an explanation with this picture.

덧셈 〔數〕 addition (↔ subtraction); adding up ━**덧셈하다** add up (figures)

덧신 《a pair of》 (indoor) slippers; overshoes; galoshes; 〈고무로 된〉 rubbers; gumshoes; gums

덧신다 put on [wear] overshoes [outer socks]

덧양말 ━洋襪 outer socks

덧없다 1 〈속절없다〉 short-lived; uncertain; passing; fleeting; fugitive; momentary; transient; transitory
♦ 덧없는 사랑[기쁨] a short-lived love [joy] / 덧없는 인생 transient life / 덧없는 세상 this changeable world; the transient world; transient life
2 〈허무하다〉 vain; empty; hopeless
♦ 덧없는 꿈 an empty dream / 덧없는 노력 vain efforts
▶ 그것을 얻으려고 덧없는 희망을 가졌었다 I had a vain hope to get it.
▶ 아직 젊은데도 그는 인생의 덧없음을 깨달았다 Though young, he realized the vanity of life.
▶ 인생은 덧없는 것이다 All is vanity in life. ⇌ Life is nothing but an empty dream.
3 〈자취·근거없다〉 unfounded; groundless; baseless

덧없이 transiently; fleetingly; transitorily
▶ 세월은 덧없이 흐른다 Time passes fleetingly [before we know it].

덧옷 a smock; 《英》 an overall

덧입다 put on [wear] 《a coat》 over a garment

덧저고리 an outer jacket [coat]

덧줄 〔樂〕 a leger line; an added line

덩굴 〔植〕 a bine; 〈포도 등의〉 a vine; 〈고구마 등의〉 a runner; 〈땅에 붙어서 뻗는〉 a creeper; 〈덩굴손〉 a tendril
♦ 등나무 덩굴 a wisteria vine / 덩굴이 뻗다 a vine creeps [climbs, trails, runs]
━一植物 a winder; a liana; a liane

덩굴손 〔植〕 a tendril; a cirrus

덩굴장미 ━薔薇 a climbing rose; a rambler

덩굴지다 grow creepers; creep; put on vines; run
▶ 호박이 지면에 덩굴지고 있었다 Pumpkin vines spread over the ground.
▶ 담쟁이 덩굴이 벽에 덩굴지고 있었다 Ivy crept [was creeping] over the wall.
▶ 포도는 덩굴진다 A grapevine grows [puts out] creepers.

덩그렇다 1 〈높고 헌거롭다〉 high and big; imposing; solitary; lonely; lonesome
▶ 고층 빌딩이 시내에 덩그렇게 서 있다 A skyscraper towers [rises] high over the town solitarily.
▶ 언덕 위에 집 한 채가 덩그렇게 서 있다 A lonely [solitary] house towers high over the hill.
2 〈텅비어 있다〉 big and hollow [empty]; bare; deserted
♦ 덩그런 집 a big and empty house / 덩그런 방 a bare and deserted room
▶ 나 혼자 덩그런 교실에 남아 있었다 I remained in an empty classroom alone.

덩달다 imitate [follow] *sb* blindly; go along with the others; do the same as *sb* does; follow suit; echo; follow the crowd; chime in
♦ 덩달아 울다 weep in sympathy
▶ 그녀가 노래를 부르자 다른 사람들도 덩달아 불렀다 She began to sing and all the rest chimed in.
▶ 그녀는 노파의 이야기를 듣고 덩달아 울었다 When she heard the old woman's story, she wept [cried] for company [in sympathy with her].

덩덩 〈북소리〉 rub-a-dub; rataplan; 〈문 등을 두드리는 소리〉 rat-tat(-tat); tum-tum; tum-tumming
♦ 덩덩하는 북소리 the rub-a-dub of a drum / 덩덩 북을 치다 beat away on the big drum; beat a drum loudly; rataplan; tom-tom

덩실거리다 dance lively [merrily, lightly] (for joy) ▶ 아이는 기뻐서 덩실거렸다 The child danced [jumped, leapt] for [with] joy [skipped about for joy].

덩실덩실 (dance) lively; joyfully; lightly; light-heartedly

덩어리 1 〈뭉쳐진 덩이〉 a lump; a mass; 〈흙의〉 a clod; a gobbet 《of meat》
♦ 금 덩어리 a lump [nugget] of gold; 〈주괴〉 a gold ingot / 흙 덩어리 a lump of clay / 핏 덩어리 a clot of blood
2 〈떼〉 a clump; a cluster; 〈집단〉 a group; a crowd; a flock
♦ 《사람들이》 한 덩어리가 되어 united; in a body [group]
▶ 전원이 한 덩어리가 되어 일했다 All of them worked as a group.
━ 골칫━ 〈사람〉 a troublesome fellow 욕심━ 〈사람〉 a very greedy person; a lump of ava-

rice [selfishness]; (be) avarice itself

덩어리지다 lump; mass; cake (on); become solid [still]; get [go] firm [hard]; form a mass; turn into [become] a solid [hard] mass; form [harden] into a mass; 〈엉기다〉 congeal; coagulate
- ♦ 딱딱하게 덩어리지다 form a hard mass
- ▶ 풀이 덩어리졌다 The paste thickened.
- ▶ 피가 상처에 덩어리져 있었다 Blood had congealed [caked] around the wound.

덩이 a lump; a mass; 〈흙의〉 a clod ⇨ 덩어리
덩이줄기 [植] a tuber; a seed
덩이뿌리 [植] a tuberous [tuberose] root
덩지 bulk ⇨ 덩치
덩치 bulk; physique; build; frame; (physical) make; size; volume
- ♦ 덩치가 큰 사람 a big [bulky] fellow; a hulk of a man / 덩치가 큰 하마 a hippopotamus of great bulk / 덩치가 큰 big(-bodied); of large build
- ▶ 덩치 크고 지혜로운 자 없다 (속담) Big body, little wit.

덫 a snare; a hook; 〈창애〉 a trap (for rats); a gin
- ♦ 덫을 놓다 set [lay] a snare [trap] (for) / 덫에 걸리다 be caught in a trap; fall into a snare [trap]; be trapped [entrapped] (by sb, into doing) / 제가 놓은 덫에 제가 걸리다 be hoisted with [by] one's own petard / 덫으로 잡다 entrap; snare; gin; ensnare; catch in a trap [snare]
- ▶ 족제비를 잡으려고 덫을 놓았다 We set [laid] a trap for weasels.
- ▶ 큰 쥐가 덫에 걸렸다 A big rat was caught in the trap.
- ▶ 이 사자는 덫으로 잡았다 This lion was caught in a trap.
- ■ 쥐— a rattrap; a mousetrap

덮개 a cover; a covering (for a seat); 〈침구〉 bedding; bedclothes; a quilt; bedcovers; a coverlet; a comfort(er); 〈차양〉 a shade
- ♦ 덮개가 있는 covered / 덮개가 없는 uncovered; bare / 덮개를 덮다 cover / 덮개를 벗기다 uncover; take the cover off sth

덮다 1 〈씌우다〉 cover (with); put (a thing) on; overspread; veil; overlay
- ▶ 뚜껑을 덮다 put a lid on (a pot) / 이불을 덮다 put on bedclothes; cover oneself with bedclothes; draw bedclothes over / 아기에게 이불을 덮어주다 spread a quilt over the baby
- ▶ 농부는 씨를 뿌리고 흙을 덮었다 After sowing the seeds, the farmer covered them with soil.

2 〈감추다〉 hide; conceal; cover up; keep (a matter) secret
- ♦ 죄를 덮어주다 cover up sb's crime; keep sb's crime secret
- ▶ 그는 그 사실을 덮어두고 최후까지 말하지 않았다 He hid that fact and kept it secret to the very end.

덮밥 〈계란 덮밥〉 a bowl of rice capped [topped] with eggs / 장어 덮밥 a bowl of boiled eel and rice

덮어가리다 cover; cloak; conceal; hide sth from sight with a cover; hide [conceal] sth under a cover

덮어놓고 〈무턱대고〉 reckless of the consequences; recklessly; rashly; thoughtlessly; without asking any reason; without giving any explanation; immoderately
- ♦ 덮어놓고 책을 읽다 read books at random / 덮어놓고 가라고 하다 ask sb to go without telling why
- ▶ 그녀는 덮어놓고 돈을 쓴다 She spends money like water.
- ▶ 범인은 덮어놓고 발포했다 The criminal fired his gun blindly [at random].
- ▶ 그는 덮어놓고 약속을 한다 He is too ready to make promises.
- ▶ 그 일을 그렇게 덮어놓고 하면 안된다 It will not do to go about it in that random way.
- ▶ 그는 대중가요를 덮어놓고 싫어한다 He has a silly prejudice against popular songs.

덮어두다 ignore; disregard; let go; lay aside (a question); overlook (sb's faults); pass (sb's sin) over; leave (a matter) unnoticed [out of consideration]; take no notice of; shut one's eyes to
- ♦ 남의 잘못을 덮어두다 shut one's eyes to sb's fault; overlook sb's mistakes
- ▶ 이 문제를 그냥 덮어둘 수는 없다 I cannot pass over [by] this question in silence.
- ▶ 미성년자이므로 그의 범행은 덮어두었다 As he was a minor [under age], his offence was overlooked.

덮어쓰다 1 〈글씨본을〉 trace an undercopy letter by letter ♦ 글씨본을 덮어쓰다 trace penmanship models 2 ⇨ 뒤집어쓰다

덮어씌우다 1 〈가리다〉 cover (with); put (a thing) on; plate sth (with gold); put (a quilt) on [over] sb
- ♦ 흙을 덮어씌우다 cover sth (with earth) / 이에 금을 덮어씌우다 put a gold crown on a tooth; crown a tooth with gold

2 〈죄 등을 남에게〉 put [pin] the guilt on sb; lay the blame on sb's door; shift (the blame) on to sb; charge (the guilt) on sb

덮이다 〈가려지다·얹히다〉 be [get] covered with; be put on; be veiled; hang over sth; 〈겹치다〉 get overlapped; be hidden [concealed]; be wrapped [enfolded]; 〈꼭대기가〉 be crowned [capped] with (snow)
- ▶ 하늘은 검은 구름으로 덮여 있었다 The sky was overcast with black clouds.
- ▶ 나뭇가지가 개울에 덮여 있었다 The trees spread their branches over the brook.
- ▶ 들은 온통 눈으로 덮여 있었다 The fields were covered with snow all over.

덮치다 1 〈겹쳐누르다〉 throw [cast] sth over; hold [press] sth down; lean on sb; pin sb to the floor; overlap one another; 〈습격하다〉 attack; assail; assault; raid; strike [go] at; 〈독수리 등이 먹이를〉 fall [set] on; fall [swoop, pounce] upon; descend on; 〈재해·병 등이〉 infest; visit; hit; strike; sweep
- ♦ (경찰이) 노름판을 덮치다 (the police) raid [make a raid upon] a gambling den
- ▶ 적이 그 도시를 덮쳤다 The enemy assailed

[assaulted] the city.
▶ 사냥개가 먹이를 덮쳤다 The hounds descended on their prey.
▶ 기근이 그 지방을 덮쳤다 Famine swept over the area.
▶ 태풍이 그 도시를 덮쳤다 The typhoon hit the town.
▶ 그 나라에는 오랜 가뭄이 덮쳤다 A long drought visited the country.
2 〈동시에 닥치다〉 come [happen] all at the same time
▶ 그들에게 여러가지 불행이 덮쳤다 They had a series [chapter, spell] of misfortunes.
▶ 엎친데 덮친다 (속담) Misfortune never comes singly. ⇌ One misfortune rides upon another's back.

데 〈곳〉 a place; 〈좁은〉 a spot; 〈점〉 a point; 〈현장〉 scene; 〈소재지〉 a seat; 〈지방〉 locality; a district; an area; 〈특징〉 a feature; an aspect; 〈대목〉 a passage; 〈부분〉 a part; 〈경우〉 a case; an occasion; a time; a moment; a circumstance
♦ 아픈 데 a sore spot / 위험한 데 a dangerous spot / 길의 울퉁불퉁한 데 a rough place in the road / 사람이 있는데서 in the presence of others; in public / 성이 있었던 데에 on the site of the castle
▶ 그는 위선적인[심술궂은] 데가 있다 He has a tinge of hypocrisy [malice].
▶ 그는 일 때문에 전국 안 간 데가 없다 His work took him all over the country.
▶ 우리가 틀린 데를 말씀해 주시오 Tell us where we are mistaken.
▶ 사치스러운 데라고는 없다 There is nothing which savors of luxury.
▶ 나는 부서진 데를 수리했다 I repaired the broken part.
▶ 이것이 그 사람다운 데다 This is a distinctive feature of his.
▶ 그에게는 어딘지 우스꽝스러운 데가 있다 There is something comical about him.
▶ 그녀의 태도에는 좀 냉담한 데가 있었다 There was a certain [a streak of] coldness in her manner.
▶ 이 페이지에는 더 이상 쓸 데가 없다 There is no more space to write in on this page.
▶ 모두가 앉을 데가 없다 There is not enough room for everyone to sit down.

데구루루 rolling; rumbling ⇨ 때구루루
데굴데굴 rolling; rumbling
♦ 데굴데굴 구르다 roll over (and over); 〈아파서〉 writhe in pain / 데굴데굴 굴러 떨어지다 roll down 《the hill》 (one after another)
▶ 그는 그 광경을 보고 데굴데굴 구르며 웃었다 He was convulsed with laughter at the sight.
▶ 공이 길 건너로 데굴데굴 굴러갔다 The ball rolled across the road.
♦ 아이들은 운동장에서 폐타이어를 데굴데굴 굴리고 있었다 The children were rolling used tires around the athletic field.
데그럭거리다 keep clattering ⇨ 때그락거리다
데꺽(데꺽) **1** 〈소리〉 cracklingly; rattlingly; with a snap [snaps];

데려가다

2 〈손쉽게·재빨리〉 without any trouble [difficulty]; very easily; with ease; readily; quickly (and easily); without effort; as if it was nothing (to *one*)
♦ 일을 데꺽 해치우다 make short [quick] work of *one's* business / 데꺽 팔리다 sell quickly; find quick sales
▶ 그들은 여러 의안을 데꺽 통과시켰다 They rattled the bills through the House.
▶ 그는 문제를 데꺽 풀었다 He solved a problem just like that.
▶ 그는 큰 돌을 데꺽 들어 올렸다 He lifted the big stone without any difficulty.
▶ 내가 그런 것을 어떻게 데꺽 승낙할 수 있겠는가? How can I accept such a thing so readily?

데님 〈織〉 〈면포〉 denim ♦ 데님 바지 denim jeans [pants]
▶ 그녀는 데님제 작업복을 입고 있다 She is dressed in denims.

데다 **1** 〈불·열에〉 be [get] burnt; have [suffer] a burn; burn *oneself*; 〈부젓가락 등으로〉 be [get] scorched; 〈뜨거운 물에〉 be [get] scalded
♦ 덴 자국 the scar of a burn [scald] / 손을 데다 get burnt in the hand; burn *one's* hand / 몹시 데다 be badly burned
▶ 불에 덴 아이는 불을 무서워한다 (속담) The burnt child dreads the fire.
▶ 나는 뜨거운 물에 손가락을 댔다 I scalded my fingers with hot water.
▶ 욕조의 물은 델 정도로 뜨거웠다 The water in the bathtub was scalding hot.
2 〈혼나다〉 have a bitter experience; have had enough 《of》; find [know] 《it》 to *one's* cost
▶ 그 아들 녀석에게는 부모도 데었다 His parents didn't know what to do with [couldn't handle] the boy.
▶ 그 장난꾸러기에게 데었다 The naughty boy is quite a handful.

데데하다 〈시시하다〉 (be) of little importance; worthless; valueless; good-for-nothing; insignificant; trivial; unimportant; poor; trashy; unsatisfactory
♦ 데데한 것[일] a matter of no importance; a trifling thing; trifles; poor stuff / 데데한 녀석 a person who is not worth bothering about; a person of no importance [account]; a good-for-nothing fellow; a nobody; (口) no good / 데데한 소리를 하다 talk nonsense; say silly things
▶ 그는 데데한 일을 걱정한다 He worries about trifles [little things].
▶ 그 학설은 데데하다 That theory is not worth serious consideration [attention].

데드라인 〈한계·마감〉 a deadline
데려가다 take [bring] *sb* with 《*one*》; be accompanied by *sb* along; 〈연행하다〉 walk 《a man》 off; take [walk] 《a suspect to a police station》; 〈도로〉 take back; bring back; make *sb* come back; 〈집으로〉 take *sb* home
▶ 그녀는 어린애를 유치원에 데려가고 데려온다 She takes her child to and from the kinder-

데려오다

garten.
▶ 경찰관은 좀도둑을 데려갔다 The policeman took away the sneak thief.
▶ 산책하는 데 개를 데려가거라 Take the dog out for a walk.
▶ 자동차로 아이들을 학교에 데려간 후 나는 회사에 간다 I drive to work after I take my children to school.
▶ 나를 데려가 주세요 Let me go with you. ⇒ May [Can] I come with you?

데려오다 bring *sb* with *one*; come in company with; fetch; 〈도로〉 take *sb* back; bring back; 〈집으로〉 fetch [get] *sb* home; 〈불러오다〉 send for
♦ 어린애를 학교에서 데려오다 bring *one's* child from school / 의사를 데려오다 bring [go and fetch] a doctor / 의사를 데려오도록 사람을 보내다 send for a doctor

데리다 take with; bring with; be accompanied [attended] by
♦ 데리러 가다 go for *sb*; go to fetch *sb*; call for *sb* / 데리고 돌아가다 take [bring] back; take *sb* home / 〈집에〉 데려다 주다 see *sb* to (a house); escort *sb* home / 산책에 데리고 나가다 take *sb* out for a walk / 이리저리 데리고 다니다 take [lead] *sb* about
▶ 그는 딸을 데리고 나갔다 He went out with his daughter.
▶ 저를 데려다 주세요 Take me with you.
▶ 품행이 좋지 않은 여자를 데리고 들어오지 마라 Don't bring in a woman of doubtful character.
▶ 나는 아이를 데리고 장보러 가겠다 I'll take my child out shopping.

데릭(기중기) —(起重機) a derrick; a derrick crane

데릴사위 a man who marries into his wife's family; a son-in-law taken into the family
♦ 데릴사위로 들어가다 become a member of *one's* wife's family
▶ 그는 김씨집의 데릴사위가 되었다 He married Mr. Kim's daughter and was adopted into his family.

데릴사윗감 **1** 〈얌전한 젊은이〉 a young man of good [irreproachable] conduct; a young man of good behavior; a well-behaved young man
2 〈미운 놈〉 a detestable fellow; a repulsive wretch

데마(고기) 〈선동행위〉 demagogy; 〈허위선전〉 a false [groundless] rumor [story]; 《美》 a grapevine
♦ 데마를 퍼뜨리다 circulate a false rumor / 데마에 현혹되다 be misled by a false rumor

데면데면하다 unmindful 《of》; unscrupulous; careless 《about, of》; inattentive 《to》; half-hearted; indifferent 《to》; nonchalant
▶ 그는 옷차림에 데면데면하다 He is careless about his personal appearance. ⇒ He does not care how he looks.

데모 a demonstration; (口) a demo (*pl.* ~s)
♦ 전쟁 반대[공해 방지] 데모 an antiwar [antipollution] demonstration / 데모(군중)을 해산시키다 disperse a demonstration (crowd);

break up a parade / 데모를 진압하다 put down a demonstration / 데모에 참가하다 join a demonstration
—**데모하다** demonstrate 《against》; hold [stage] a demonstration
▶ 그들은 전쟁에 반대하여 데모했다 They demonstrated [held demonstration] against war.
♦ 관제[위장]—a government-organized [disguised] demonstration 동정[가두]—a sympathy [street] demonstration ■ —**대** demonstrators

데모크라시 democracy ⇨ 민주주의 ◆**데모크라시의** democratic

데모크리토스 〈고대 그리스의 철학자〉 Democritus (460?-370? BC)

데모 행진 —行進 a demonstration parade [march] ♦ 학생 데모 행진 a student parade / 데모행진을 하다 demonstrate in a march

데뷔 〈첫 등장〉 *one's* debut; *one's* first appearance on the stage
▶ 이 소설은 그의 데뷔 작품이다 This is the novel with which he made his literary debut.
—**데뷔하다** make *one's* debut 《on the stage》; debut; come out
♦ 문단에 데뷔하다 make *one's* debut in letters
▶ 그녀는 16세 때 사교계에 데뷔했다 She came out [made her debut in society] at sixteen.

데삶다 boil 《an egg》 soft [lightly]; parboil
♦ 데삶은 계란 a half-[soft-]boiled egg; a half-done [half-poached] egg / 데삶은 고기 underdone meat / 데삶은 half-boiled; half-cooked; half-done

데생 〔美術〕 (프) 〈소묘〉 dessin; a drawing; a (rough) sketch —**데생하다** sketch; make a sketch
▶ 그녀는 그 정물을 데생했다 She made a rough sketch of the object at rest.

데설궂다 〈자상하지 않다〉 rude; careless; thoughtless; unrefined; unmannered; rough; broad; sketchy; loose

데스마스크 a deathmask ♦ 데스마스크를 뜨다 make a deathmask 《of》

데스크 〈책상〉 a desk; 〈호텔의 프런트〉 the desk; 〈신문사의 편집부〉 (美) the (copy) desk
▶ 그는 외신부 데스크에서 일한다 He is a deskman in the foreign news department.

데시- deci- (▶ 10분의 1의 뜻)

데시그램 a decigram (略 dg)

데시리터 a deciliter (略 dl)

데시미터 a decimeter (略 dm)

데시바 〔氣〕 a decibar

데시벨 〈음의 강도의 단위〉 a decibel (略 db)

데알다 〈대충 알다〉 have a superficial knowledge 《of》; have a smattering of *sth*; know *sth* by halves
♦ 외국어를 데알다 dabble in foreign language / 데아는 지식을 과시하다 parade *one's* superficial [imperfect] knowledge
▶ 그는 많은 것을 알고 있으나 모두 데아는 것 뿐이다 He knows about a lot of things but his knowledge is all superficial.
▶ 그녀는 경제학을 다만 데알고 있을 뿐이다 She has only got a smattering [superficial

데우다 heat [warm] (up); make *sth* warm [hot]
♦ 물을 데우다 heat (up) water / 다시 데우다 rewarm; warm over; reheat / 술을 데워[데우지 않고] 마시다 drink wine hot [cold] / 미리 데우다 preheat
▶ 나는 그 물을 90도까지 데웠다 I heated (up) the water to 90 degrees.

데이비스컵 the Davis Cup ■—쟁탈전 a Davis Cup tournament (series) —참가선수 a Davis Cup player

데이지 〔植〕(美) an English daisy; (英) a daisy

데이터 data (▶*datum*의 복수로 (美)에서는 this data처럼 단수로 취급) ■ 초기— 〈컴퓨터의〉 the initial data ■—뱅크 a data bank —처리장치〔電子〕 a data processing machine; a data logger —통신 data communications

데이트 a date
♦ 데이트 상대 one's date / 데이트 나가다 go out on a date / 데이트 중이다 be on a date —데이트하다 date 《with》 《a girl》; have [make] a date 《with》
▶ 나와 데이트합시다 Can I ask you for a date?

데치다 parboil; scald ♦ 데친 시금치 boiled spinach / (뜨거운 물에) 야채를 데치다 parboil vegetables (in hot water)

데카당 decadence;〈사람〉a decadent ♦ 데카당식의 인생 a decadent life ■—문학 decadent literature —파 the decadents

데카르트 〈프랑스의 수학자, 철학자〉 Descartes, René (1596-1650)

데카리터 a decaliter
데카메론 〈보카치오의 소설〉 *The Decameron*
데카미터 a decameter
데칸고원 —**高原** Deccan Plateau
데커레이션 〈장식〉 (a) decoration
♦ 크리스마스— Christmas decorations ■—케이크 (a) fancy cake; (a) decorated cake

데탕트 〈긴장완화〉(프) détente
데퉁바리 a clumsy person; a dunce
데퉁스럽다, 데퉁하다 clumsy; stupid; awkward; unrefined; tactless

덱 〈갑판〉 a deck;〈열차의〉platform;〈트럼프 한벌〉a pack;〔電算〕〈천공한 카드 묶음〉a deck;〈테이프의〉a tape deck
■—체어 a deck chair

덱데구루루 rolling
덴가슴 a horror-stricken [frightened] state of mind; a nightmarish memory; a bitter experience

덴마크 Denmark;〈공식명〉the Kingdom of Denmark ♦ 덴마크(사람·말)의 Danish ■—말 Danish; the Danish language —사람 a Dane

덴버 〈미국 콜로라도 주의 주도〉 Denver
■—시민 a Denverite

델라웨어 1〔植〕〈미국산 포도〉 a Delaware
2 〈미국 동부의 주〉 Delaware (略 Del.)
♦ 델라웨어주의 Delawarean; Delawarian
■—사람 a Delawarean; a Delawarian

델리 〈인도 북부의 도시〉 Delhi
델리킷하다 delicate; sensitive

解說 「델리킷한 문제」는 *delicate* matter로 표현하면 되지만 「델리킷한 신경」이라고 말하는 경우의 「델리킷」은 「예민한」의 뜻이므로 *sensitive*라고도 해야한다. 사람에 대해 delicate를 쓰면 「연약한」「허약한」의 뜻으로 취급되기 쉬우므로 주의가 필요.

♦ 델리킷한 일[입장] a delicate matter [situation]
▶ 그녀는 신경이 델리킷한 여자다 She is a very sensitive woman. ⇌ She is easily upset.

델린저현상 —**現象**〔物〕the Dellinger phenomenon

델타 〈삼각주〉 a delta ♦ 나일강의 델타 지역 the Nile Delta ■—지대[평야] a delta land [plain]

뎅겅, 뎅그렁 clang ⇨ 땡그랑거리다
뎅그 열 —**熱**〔醫〕〈열병〉dengue [dandy] (fever)

도 1〈또한, 역시〉too; also;〈및, …도…도〉and; as well as; both…and

解說 *too*는 보통 문장 끝에 오지만 뜻이 혼동되기 쉬울 때는 수식어 뒤에 둔다. *also*는 too보다 형식을 차리는 말. 부정문에서는 too를 쓸 수 없고 보통 *either*를 쓴다.
*both A and B*는 「A와 B 둘 다」라는 표현으로 A and B를 강조하는 말. A와 B 부분에는 보통 같은 역할을 하는 어구가 온다.
both A and B를 부정문으로 만들 경우 A, B의 양쪽을 부정하면 *neither A nor B* 또는 *not…either A or B*라 쓰고, 「A와 B 모두가…한 것은 아니다」처럼 한쪽만을 부정하면 *not…both A and B*라 쓴다.

▶ 그의 부친도 우리 아버지도 우리 계획에 찬성하셨다 Both his father and my father agreed to our plan.
▶ 너도 거기 있었니? Were you there also?
▶ 그의 누이도 미국에 갔다 His sister also went to America.
▶ 오늘은 좋은 날씨다 It's fine again today.
▶ 그녀는 주부이자 피아니스트이기도 하다 She is not only a housewife but (also) a pianist. ⇌ She is a pianist as well as a housewife.
▶ 나도 야구를 좋아해 I too like baseball.
▶ 그녀는 피아노도 바이올린도 연주한다 She plays the piano and the violin.
▶ 너에게도 주겠다 I'll give it to you too.
▶ 그는 영어도 알고 프랑스어도 안다 He understands both French and English.
▶ 그는 내게 돈도 주고 옷도 주었다 He gave me clothes as well as money.
▶ 내가 바보라면 너도 바보다 If I am a fool, you are another.
▶ 會話 「오늘은 피곤해」「나도 그래」 "I'm tired today." "So am I. ⇌ I am too. ⇌ Me too."
▶ 會話 「휴가 잘 지내요!」「너도!」 "Have a good holiday!" "And you (too)! ⇌ Yes, same to you!"
▶ 會話 「그를 파티에서 만났어」「나도 그래」 "I met him at a party." "So did I."

2 〈부정형〉 not …either; neither; …nor

▶네가 가지 않으면 나도 가지 않겠다 If you don't go I'll not go, either.
▶나는 아무도 보지 않았고 아무것도 듣지 않았다 I didn't see anyone or hear anything. ⇌ I saw no one and heard nothing.
▶아무도 그의 이야기를 믿지 않는다 Nobody believes his story.
▶그녀는 카레라이스도 만들 줄 모른다 She cannot make even curry and rice.
▶그는 영어도 일본어도 할 줄 모른다 He can speak neither English nor Japanese.
▶[회화]「그는 이 책을 잘 읽지 못해」「나도 그래」 "He cannot read this book well." "I can't read it either. ⇌ Neither [Nor] can I. ⇌ Not me. ⇌ Me neither."
3 〈조차〉 even; 《without》 so much as
▶그는 일요일에도 일해야 했다 He had to work even on Sunday.
▶그녀는 자기 이름도 쓸 줄 모른다 She can't even [so much as] write her own name.
▶나는 학생 때 한번도 지각한 적이 없다 When I was a student, I was never late even once.
4 〈어느 쪽이나〉 either…or
▶이 책은 네가 읽어도 좋고 안 읽어도 좋다 You may either read this book or not.
▶어느 길로 가도 역으로 가게 될 것이요 Either road [Both roads] will take you to the station.
5 〈비록 …이라도〉 even if [though]; though; notwithstanding; no matter 《who [what]》
▶눈이 그치지 않더라도 가야 할 것 같다 I will have to start, even if [though] it doesn't stop snowing.
▶어디에 가더라도 행선지를 알려라 Keep us informed of your whereabouts, wherever you go.
▶오지 않아도 된다 You need not come. ⇌ You may stay (at) home.
▶아무리 피곤해도 수업 중에 졸면 안된다 No matter how tired you are, you must not doze off in class.
▶지금 그에게 그렇게 말해도 소용없다 There is no use saying it to him now.
▶슬기로운 사람도 실수를 할 때가 있다 Even a wise man makes mistakes sometimes.
▶원숭이도 나무에서 떨어질 때가 있다 《속담》 Even Homer sometimes nods.
6 〈기타〉 그는 친절하게도 나를 도와주었다 He was kind [good] enough to help me.
▶덥기도 해라 How hot it is!
▶아! 달도 밝다 How brightly the moon is shining!

도 度 1 〈각도·온도·경위도〉 a degree
◆30도의 각 an angle of thirty degrees / 영하 [상] 8도 eight degrees below [above] zero / 섭씨 5도 five degrees C; 5°C / 북위 38도 thirty eight degrees [38°] north latitude; latitude 38°N / 동경 120도 longitude 120°E
▶90도의 각은 직각이다 A ninety-degree angle is called a right angle.
▶서울은 동경 127도 북위 37도 50분이다 Seoul's longitude is a hundred twenty·seven degrees east and its latitude is thirty-seven degrees fifty minutes north.
▶물은 섭씨 100도에서 끓는다 Water boils at 100°C [one hundred degrees Centigrade].
▶지금 온도는 응달에서 28도다 The mercury registers [stands at] 28° in the shade.
2 〈(렌즈의) 만곡도〉 a degree; a diopter
◆5도 이상의 근시인 사람 myopes of five diopters or more / 18도의 안경 spectacles of eighteen degrees
▶네 안경은 몇 도니? What is the degree of your concave lenses?
3 〈음정〉 a degree
◆3도의 화음 triad; common chord
4 〈알코올분〉 proof (▶100% alcohol을 미국에서는 200°, 영국에서는 175°로 나타냄)
▶이 위스키는 40도다 This whisky is forty proof.
5 〈횟수〉 the number of times
◆3색도 인쇄법 the three-color process / 다색도 인쇄의 호화판 서적 a gorgeous book printed in many colors
6 〈정도〉 a degree; an extent; 〈한도〉 a limit; 〈절제〉 moderation
◆도를 지키다 be moderate; keep within bounds; be temperate / 도를 넘다 [지나치다] go to excess; go too far; go beyond bounds; be immoderate [intemperate] in 《drinking》; exceed the limits
▶커피는 도가 지나치지 않으면 해가 되지는 않는다 Coffee isn't harmful if it's taken in moderation.
▶공부도 도를 지나치면 건강에 해롭다 Too much study is bad for your health.
▶그녀의 장난은 도가 지나치다 She carries her jokes too much [too far].

도 道 1 〈행정구역〉 a province; a do
◆강원도 Kang-won-do / 출신도 one's native province; the province one's comes from / 도(립)의 provincial 《park》 / 도당국 the provincial authorities / 도지사(知事) a (provincial) governor / 도행정 provincial administration
2 〈걸어야 할 길〉 a duty; 〈진리〉 truth; 〈도리〉 reason; 〈정의〉 justice
◆도를 구하다 seek after truth / 도를 깨닫다 perceive a truth / 도를 닦다 cultivate one's moral sense / 공자의 도를 펴다 expound the teachings [doctrines] of Confucius; preach [propagate] Confucianism / 도에 어긋난 짓을 하다 misconduct oneself
3 〈기예〉 an art; a craft; an (artistic) accomplishment
◆궁도 archery; bowmanship

도 〔樂〕 do; doh
■이동[고정]— movable [fixed] do

-도 度 〈연도〉 a year (period); a term
◆금년도 the current year / 내년도 next year / 내년도 예산안 the budget bill for the next fiscal year

-도 圖 〈그림〉 a picture; 〈설계도〉 a plan; 〈도표〉 a diagram; a chart; a graph; a design; 〔幾〕 a figure
◆제1도 the first figure; fig. 1

도가 都家 〈도매집〉 a wholesale store [house, firm]; 〈집합소〉 a guild's house
도가 道家 a Taoist

도가니¹ 〈녹이는〉 a crucible; a melting pot
♦쇠를 도가니에 넣고 녹이다 melt metal in a crucible
▶ 미국은 인종의 도가니라고 한다 The United States is said to be a melting pot of races.
▶ 장내는 흥분의 도가니가 되었다 The audience went wild with excitement. ⇒ The audience was thrown into a state of feverish [wild] excitement.
도가니² 〈무릎도가니〉 (the meat on) the kneebone of cattle
도가머리 〈새의〉 a crest (of a bird); 〈사람의〉 disheveled hair; unkempt [uncombed] hair
도각 倒閣 overthrowing [unseating] the Cabinet ♦도각 운동 a movement to overthrow the Cabinet
—도각하다 overthrow [unseat] the Cabinet
도감 圖鑑 a picture [a pictorial, an illustrated] book
■ 동물[식물]— an illustrated animal [plant] book 사회과— a picture book of social studies
도강 渡江 crossing (of) a river
—도강하다 cross [go across] a river ♦헤엄쳐 [걸어서] 도강하다 swim [wade] across a river —훈련 a river-crossing exercise
도개교 跳開橋 a drawbridge; a bascule bridge
도거리 the gross; bulk; mass
♦도거리로 in [by] the lump; in one [a] lot; in a [the] mass; in bulk; in the gross / 도거리로 사다 buy by [in] bulk; buy wholesale / 일을 도거리로 맡아하다 do work by the job
■ —일 job work; piecework; work done by contract [by the job]
도검 刀劍 swords; cold steels
■ —감정가 a judge [connoisseur] of swords
도경 道警 the provincial police (headquarters)
도계 道界 a provincial border; the province limits
도공 刀工 a swordmaker; a swordsmith
도공 陶工 a potter; a ceramist; an earthenware [a porcelain] maker
■ —술 ceramics; pottery
도관 導管 a pipe; a conduit (pipe); a duct; 〈식물의〉 a vessel
도괴 倒壞 collapse; destruction
—도괴하다 fall down; collapse; crumble; be destroyed; be level(l)ed [razed] (to the ground)
▶ 지진으로 수백 호의 집이 도괴했다 Hundreds of houses were destroyed by the earthquake.
■ —가옥 a collapsed house
도교 道教 Taoism ■ —신자 a Taoist
도구 道具 1 〈연장〉 a tool; an implement; an instrument; a utensil; an appliance; outfit; kit

解說 대개 *tool*은 동력 없이 손으로 사용하는 것을 말하는데 해머나 드릴 등, 특히 장인(匠人) 등이 사용하는 도구를 가리킨다. *implement*는 tool 보다 큰 것을 말하는데 특히 괭이·쟁기 등 구조가 단순한 도구를 말한다. *instrument*는 의료용 메스나 온도계 등 정밀하고 학술적인 일에 쓰이는 도구로서 보통 동력을 쓰지 않는 것을 말한다. *utensil*은 요리·청소 등에 쓰이는 가정용 도구를 일컫는 다소 딱딱한 말. *outfit*, *kit*는 어떤 목적을 위해 필요한 도구 한벌을 말한다.

♦ 가재 도구 household goods; furniture / 장사 도구 the tools of *one's* trade; *one's* trade outfit / 필기 도구 writing utensils / 도구 상자 a toolbox; a (workman's) kit; a workbox
▶ 목수의 도구는 장도리·톱·대패 등이다 Carpenter's tools include hammers, saws, planes, etc.
2 〈수단·방편〉 a means; a tool
♦ 아무를 도구로 이용하다 use *sb* as tool; make a tool [cat's paw] of *sb*
▶ 예술이 선전 도구로 될 때가 있다 At times art is used as a vehicle [tool] of propaganda.
도굴 盜掘 〈무덤의〉 grave robbery; 〈광물의〉 illegal [bootleg] mining
—도굴하다 rob a grave; mine illegally
♦남의 석탄을 도굴하다 dig coal illegally from another's land
도규 刀圭 〈약순갈〉 a medicine spoon; 〈의술〉 medicine
■ —가 a medical man; a physician —계 the medical profession [world]; medical circles : 도규계의 대가 a great physician —술 the medical art
도그마 a dogma (*pl.* ～s, -mata); dogmatism
도금 鍍金 plating; gilt; gilding; coating
▶ 도금이 벗겨졌다 The gilt is off [has come off].
—도금하다 plate; gild; engild
♦도금한 숟가락 a plated spoon / 도금한 목걸이 a gilt chain / 구리에 은을 도금하다 plate copper with silver
■ 금[은]— gold [silver] plating 전기— electroplating; galvanizing ■ —공 a plater; a gilder; a galvanizer —술 the art of plating [gilding] —액 a plating solution —제품 plated ware
도급 都給 a contract (for work); undertaking
♦ 도급(을) 주다 put out (the work) to contract; give out a contract (for the work) / 도급(을) 맡다 contract 《for the work》; undertake / 주택 건축을 도급맡다 have a contract to build a house / 도급으로 건축하다 build by contract
▶ K건설이 이 공사를 도급맡았다 The K Construction Company has received [has won] the contract for this (construction) work.
■ —가격 a contract price —공사 contract work; construction work done on contract —업 contracting business —인 a contractor —일 contract work; a contract job
도기 陶器 (a piece of) china; chinaware; earthenware; ceramics; ceramic ware
♦ 도기 꽃병 a china vase / 도기의 china; ceramic
■ —공장 a pottery —류 crockery; pottery —상 〈상인〉 a crockery [china] dealer; 〈상점〉 a chinashop
도깨비 a goblin; a hobgoblin; a bog(e)y; (美) a bugaboo; an apparition; (口) a spook; an

도깨비바늘 〔植〕 Spanish needles [grass]

도깨비방망이 a magic mallet; a mallet of luck

도깨비불 **1** 〈인화(燐火)〉 phosphorous light; phosphorescence; 〈귀화(鬼火)〉 a jack-o'-lantern; a will-o'-the-wisp; an elf fire; a fatuous fire; a friar's lantern; 〈묘지 등의〉a death fire [flame, light]
2 〈화재〉a fire of unknown origin; a mysterious fire

도깨비엉겅퀴 〔植〕a blessed (horse) thistle

도꼬마리 〔植〕a cocklebur(r); a burweed

도끼 an axe; 〈美〉an ax; 〈손도끼〉a hatchet; a hack; a chopper
♦도끼질하다 wield [strike with] an ax
▶ 믿는 도끼에 발등 찍힌다 (속담) In trust is treason. ⇒ Be betrayed by a trusted follower.

도끼눈 glaring eyes; 〈눈짓〉a sharp look; a glare; staring with anger [hatred]
♦도끼눈으로 보다 glare fiercely at; glower at; look fiercely

도나우 〈강이름〉the Donau [Danube] River

도난 盜難 being the victim of robbery [theft, burglary]
♦도난 방지용 자물쇠 a burglarproof [an antitheft] lock / 도난 방지의 burglarproof / 도난(을) 당하다 be robbed; fall a victim to a theft / 도난 신고를 하다 report a burglary [theft] to the police
▶ 그는 수금한 돈을 도난 당했다 He was robbed of the money he had collected.
▶ 도난 사건이 열 건 발생했다 There were ten cases of robbery.
■ —경보기 a burglar alarm —품 a stolen article [object] —피해자 a victim of robbery [theft, burglary]

도내 道內 ♦도내의[에서] in [within] the province

도넛 a doughnut ♦〈도시 주변의〉도넛화 현상 urban sprawl

도달 到達 〈도착〉arrival; reaching; 〈달성〉attainment
—**도달하다** arrive at [in]; reach; come to; get to [at]; attain
♦목적지에 도달하다 reach a destination / 같은 결론에 도달하다 arrive at [come to, reach] the same conclusion
▶ 마침내 우리는 합의에 도달할 수 있었다 We were finally able to come to an agreement.

도당 徒黨 a gang; a clique; a league; a faction; a set
♦도당을 지어 (do sth) in a gang / 도당을 짓다 band together; form a gang [faction]; be banded in party; conspire (with, against); (口) gang up

도대체 都大體 (what [why, how]) on earth [in the world, in the name of God [goodness], the hell]
▶ 도대체 너는 누구냐? What on earth are you?
▶ 도대체 어디에 갔었느냐? Where the devil have you been?
▶ 도대체 어찌된 영문이냐? What on earth [in the world] is the matter? ⇒ Whatever is the matter?
▶ 도대체 그가 무얼 원하는지 모르겠다 I don't know what the hell he wants.
▶ 도대체 어쩔 셈으로 그러느냐? What the devil [Just what] do you mean by doing that?
▶ 도대체 그는 영어를 알고 있는거냐? Does he know any English at all?

도덕 道德 morals; morality; ethics
♦도덕의 타락 moral decline; demoralization / 성도덕의 퇴폐 the corruption of sex(ual) morals
♦도덕이 땅에 떨어졌다 Morality has lost its hold on the people.
■ 공중— public morals : 공중도덕을 지키다 conform to public morals [morality] 사회[국민, 상]— social [national, commercial] morality ■ —가 a virtuous man; a man of virtue; a moralist —관념 a moral sense; a sense of morality: 그는 도덕관념이 없다 He lacks a moral sense [sense of morality]. —교육 moral education —군자 a gentleman renowned for his virtue; a virtuous man; a moralist —률 (a) moral law; (an) ethical code —시간 〈학교의〉a good citizenship class —심 a sense of morality; a moral sense : 그는 도덕심이 강[약]하다 He has a keen [weak] sense of morals. —원리 moral principles [law] —의식 moral consciousness —재무장운동 the Moral Rearmament movement(略 MRA movement) —주의 moralism —철학 moral philosophy; ethics

도덕상 道德上 morally; from a moral point of view
♦도덕상의 문제 a moral question / 도덕상의 moral; moralistic; ethical
▶ 네 행동은 도덕상 옳지 않다 Your action is immoral [morally wrong]. ⇒ Your action is wrong from a moral point of view.

도덕적 道德的 moral; moralistic; ethical
♦도덕적 감화[기준] moral influence [standards]/ 도덕적 관점 a moral point of view / 도덕적 제재 moral restraint [sanctions]

도데 〈프랑스의 소설가〉Daudet, Alphonse (1840-97)

도도하다 proud; arrogant; haughty; overbearing; lordly
♦도도한 여자 (口) a snooty [stuck-up] woman / 도도한 태도 a haughty [proud] attitude / 도도하게 proudly; arrogantly; haughtily; with a lordly air / 도도하게 굴다 assume a haughty attitude; hold one's head high; ride [mount] the high horse

도도하다 陶陶— pleased; happy; jolly
♦취흥이 도도하다 be gay with wine; be gloriously drunk

도도하다 滔滔— **1** 〈물이〉rushing; rapid; swift
♦큰 비가 온 뒤의 도도한 탁류 a gush of

muddy water after a heavy rain / 도도히 with a rush; rapidly; swiftly
▶ 강물은 도도하게 흐르고 있었다 The river flowed swiftly [in torrents].
2 〈언변이〉 eloquent; fluent; effusive
◆ 도도한 언변 a flood of eloquence [words]; flowing eloquence / 도도히 eloquently; fluently; flowingly
▶ 그의 변설은 도도하여 그칠 줄 몰랐다 His tongue went nineteen to the dozen.

도두 〈높게〉 high
◆ 둑을 도두 쌓다 build a dike high / 책을 도두 쌓아 올리다 pile books in heaps

도둑 1 〈도둑놈〉 a thief 《pl. thieves》; 〈좀도둑〉 a pilferer; a filcher; a shoplifter; 〈밤도둑〉 a burglar; 〈강도〉 a robber
◆ 자동차 도둑 a car thief / 도둑 맞다 〈사람이 주어〉 have *sth* stolen; be robbed of 《*one's* purse》; 〈물건이 주어〉 be stolen / 도둑을 잡다 catch [arrest] a thief
▶ 그는 지갑을 도둑맞았다 He had his purse stolen.
▶ 요전날에 그녀의 집에 도둑이 들었다 Her house was robbed [broken into] the other day.
▶ 어젯밤엔 여러 곳에 도둑이 들었다 There were many burglaries last night.
▶ 도둑이야 Stop thief!
2 ⇨ 도둑질

도둑고양이 a stray [an ownerless] cat; an alley cat
▶ 그녀는 그 도둑고양이에게 정이 들게 되었다 She came to feel some attachment to the stray cat.

도둑놈 a thief ⇨ 도둑 1

도둑이 제 발이 저리다 〈속담〉 A guilty conscience needs no accuser.

도둑장가 a secret marriage [consummation]
◆ 도둑장가를 들다 get married secretly; consummate a marriage secretly

도둑질 〈절도〉 theft; thievery; stealing; 〈강도질〉 robbery; burglary; 〈좀도둑질〉 pilfering; filching
▶ 그는 소년들에게 도둑질을 시키다가 체포되었다 The man was arrested for forcing the boys into theft.
▶ 그는 도둑질로 감옥에 갔다 He was sent to prison for theft.
▶ 요즈음은 도둑질이 별로 없다는 소식이다 Recently not many cases of theft have been reported.
━도둑질하다 commit theft; steal 《*sth* from *sb*》; pilfer 《*sth* from a shop》; **(**口**)** filch; 〈강탈하다〉 rob 《*sb* of *sth*》
◆ 도둑질하러 들어가다 break into 《a house》; burglarize 《a house》 / 도둑질하게 되다 take to thieving

도드라지다 1 swell; protrude; stand out (from the surface); heave (up); become elevated; be embossed
◆ 무늬가 도드라지다 stand out in (bold) relief / 종이에 무늬를 도드라지게 넣다 emboss the paper with a design.
▶ 종기가 목에 도드라졌다 A swelling has appeared on my neck.
2 ⇨ 두드러지다 1

도떼기시장 —市場 an open-air market; a flea market
▶ 이곳은 언제나 도떼기시장처럼 붐빈다 This area is bustling with activities [is alive with people] all the time.

도라지 〈植〉 a Chinese [broad] bellflower; a balloonflower; 〈뿌리〉 the root of a broad bellflower ◆ 도라지를 캐다 dig up the roots of balloonflowers
━—나물 cooked roots of balloonflowers

도락 道樂 1 〈취미〉 a hobby; a pastime; *one's* favorite amusement [diversion]; relaxation
◆ 도락삼아 우표를 수집하다 collect stamps as a pastime [for fun]
▶ 나는 다만 도락으로 유화를 그립니다 I paint oil pictures only as a hobby [pastime, diversion].
2 〈주색에 빠짐〉 dissipation; prodigality; amorous pursuits
◆ 도락에 빠지다 be dissipated; lead a loose and dissolute life; play the prodigal; live a fast [riotous] life

도란거리다 have a pleasant chat [talk] 《with》; murmur [mutter] together; talk [chat] in an undertone [in a whispering tone]

도란도란 in (affectionate) whispers
▶ 두 친구는 구석에 앉아 도란도란 이야기하고 있었다 The two friends sat in a corner and chatted away to each other.
▶ 방에서 도란도란 이야기하는 소리가 들린다 The room is all abuzz with murmur.
━도란도란하다 murmur [mutter] together ⇨ 도란거리다

도란형 倒卵形 an obovoid [obovate] form

도랑 a ditch; a gutter; 〈하수의〉 a drain; a gully
◆ 도랑을 메우다 fill in a ditch / 도랑을 치다 ditch; clear out a ditch / 도랑을 파다 dig a ditch; trench; gully
▶ 큰 비로 도랑이 넘쳤다 The gutter [drain] overflowed in the heavy rain.
■━물 ditch water ━창 a dirty [filthy] ditch

도래 到來 arrival; advent
◆ 호기의 도래를 기다리다 wait for a good opportunity
━도래하다 come; arrive; 〈기회가〉 offer [present] itself; occur

도래 渡來 1 〈사람의〉 a visit
━도래하다 come over [across] the sea; cross over (to Korea); visit
2 〈사물의〉 introduction; importation
◆ 기독교의 한국에의 도래 the introduction of Christianity in Korea
━도래하다 be introduced (into); be brought over 《from》
▶ 불교는 384년에 백제에 도래했다 Buddhism was introduced into Paekche in three hundred and eighty-four.

도래송곳 a spiral-drill; a gimlet

도량 度量 magnanimity; generosity; liberality
◆ 도량이 넓은 magnanimous; generous; liberal; tolerant; broad-[large-]minded / 도량이

좁은 narrow-minded; small-minded; mean-spirited
▶ 그녀에게는 남편을 용서할 도량이 없었다 She was not tolerant enough to forgive her husband.

도량 跳梁 rampancy; domination
▶ 마을 사람들은 폭력단의 도량을 가만두지 않았다 The townspeople did not let gangsters have their own way.
―도량하다 prevail; domineer

도량 道場 〔佛敎〕 a Buddhist seminary

도량형 度量衡 weights and measures
■ ―검사관 a sealer (of weights and measures) ―검사소 the Weights and Measures Examination Institute; the Bureau of Standards ―기 measuring instruments ―법 measurement : 미터 도량형법 the metric system of weights and measures ―표 tables of weights and measures ―학 metrology

도레미파 the (musical) scale; 〈계이름〉 do, re, mi, fa, sol, la and si; 〈초보〉 the rudiments of music ―연습 a solfège; a solfeggio (pl. ~s, -gi) ―창법 Solmization; sol-fa

도려내다 scoop [scrape] out; gouge out; hollow out; excavate
♦ 코르크를 둥글게 도려내다 gouge a cork / 사과의 썩은 곳을 도려내다 scoop out a bruised part of an apple
▶ 그들은 통나무를 도려내어 카누를 만들었다 They hollowed out a log to make a canoe.
▶ 마음을 도려내는 듯한 외로움이 그녀를 엄습했다 Heartrendering [Acute] loneliness overcame her.

도련 刀鍊 trimming; cutting the edge (of paper) even ―도련하다 trim [cut] the edge (of paper) even
■ ―칼 a paper-trimming knife

도련님 1 ⇨ 도령 2 〈주인의 아들〉 a young master 3 〈시동생〉 an unmarried younger brother of one's husband

도령 an unmarried young man; a young gentleman; a bachelor

도령 道令 a provincial ordinance

도로 1 〈되돌아서〉 back; (over) again
♦ 오던 길을 도로 가다 go back over one's way; go back where one came / 도로 주다 give back; return back / 도로 빼앗다 take [win] back; recapture / 좌석에 도로 앉다 go back to [resume] one's seat / 잃었던 돈을 도로 찾다 get one's lost money back
▶ 언제 일을 도로 시작할 겁니까 ? When will you start working again [be back at work]?
2 〈먼저대로〉 as (it was) before; as usual [ever]
♦ 제자리에 도로 갖다 놓다 put sth back in its place [where it belongs] / 도로 건강해지다 become as healthy as before; be restored to health
▶ 마을은 평온을 도로 찾았다 The town recovered its normal calm. ⇌ The town was restored to peace and quiet.

도로 徒勞 vain [fruitless] effort; lost labor; vain [empty] attempt; waste of labor
♦ 도로에 그치다 prove futile [fruitless]; come to nothing [naught]
▶ 우리의 노력은 도로였다 Our efforts have been useless [futile, a waste].

도로 道路 a road; a way; 〈가로〉 a street; 〈대로·공로〉 a thoroughfare; a highway
♦ 도로의 개통 the (formal) opening of a new road / 도로상에서 on the road; on [in] the street / 도로를 개통하다 (막다) open [block] a road / 도로를 건설하다 construct [build, make] a road / 도로를 파헤치다 tear up a road / 도로를 보수하다 repair [mend, improve] a road / 도로를 횡단하다 walk across a road [street] / 좌측 도로로 걷다 walk on the left side of the road
▶ 도로 공사중 (게시) Under construction.
▶ 오전 중에는 도로 혼잡이 덜했다 There was not much traffic on the street(s) in the morning.
■ ―고속 an expressway; (英) a motorway 비포장― a dirt road 유료― a toll road 포장― a paved road ―경주 a road race; road racing ―계획 a road plan ―교통 road traffic ―교통법 〔法〕 the Road Traffic Law ―망 a network of streets [roads] ―보수(공사) road [street] repair [improvement] ―이정표 a milepost; a milestone ―지도 a road map ―청소기 a road sweeping machine ―포장 pavement of a road [street] ―표지 a road sign

도로건설 道路建設 street [road] construction [works] ―기사 a road engineer ―계획 a road-building program ―장비 road construction equipment

도로아미타불 ―阿彌陀佛 ♦ 도로아미타불이 되다 lose all (that) one has gained ▶ 결국 나로서는 도로아미타불이었다 After all I was not better off than before.

도록 圖錄 a picture [pictorial] record; a record in pictures

-도록 1 〈목적〉 (so as) to (do); in order to (do); so that one may (do); that one might (do)
♦ 하지 않도록 (so as) not to (do); that...may not (do)
▶ 나는 급행을 탈 수 있도록 집에서 일찍 떠났다 I left home early so that I could catch the express train.
▶ 내일 꼭 오도록 하게 Be sure to come tomorrow.
▶ 나는 그가 무사히 거기 도착하도록 기도했다 I prayed to God that he might arrive there safe(ly).
2 〈…때까지〉 till; until; to; up [down] to
▶ 목숨이 다하도록 싸우다 fight to the last drop of one's blood
▶ 오래도록 사십시오 ! May you live a long life!
▶ 그는 밤늦도록 공부한다 He sits up studying till late at night.
3 〈가능성〉 as much [far] as one can; as much [far] as possible
▶ 되도록 빨리 여기 오도록 해라 Come here as soon as possible [you can].
▶ 이 기회를 되도록 많이 이용하시오 You'd better make the most of the opportunity.

도롱뇽 〔動〕 a salamander
도롱이 a straw raincoat
도롱이벌레 〔昆〕 a bagworm
도롱태 〈수레〉 a handcart; a pushcart; 〈바퀴〉 a wheel
도료 塗料 paints; paint and varnish
♦벽에 도료를 칠하다 paint the walls / 문의 도료를 벗기다 scrape the paint off the door
■ **발광[야광]—** luminous [fluorescent] paint
■ **—분무기** a paint sprayer **—희석제** a thinner; a paint diluent
도루 盜壘 〔野〕 base stealing; a stolen base
♦도루를 잘하다 be clever at stealing bases
—도루하다 steal a base
▶ 그는 도루하여 2[3]루에 진출했다 He stole second [third].
도루묵 〔魚〕 a sandfish
도륙 屠戮 massacre; slaughter; butchery
♦집단 도륙 mass slaughter
—도륙하다 slay; massacre; slaughter; butcher
▶ 온 마을이 도륙당했다 The whole village was massacred.
도르다¹ 〈토하다〉 vomit; throw up; cast up
♦먹은 것을 도르다 throw up what *one* has eaten
도르다² 〈분배하다〉 distribute; hand round [out]; serve out [round]; deal out
♦기념품을 도르다 hand out [round] souvenirs / 화투짝을 도르다 deal cards 《to the players》
도르다³ 〈변통하다〉 contrive; manage; (make) shift; shift and contrive
♦돈을 도르다 raise enough money / 소요 금액을 도르다 raise money to make up the required sum
도르래 〈활차〉 a (movable) pulley; a block; 〈장난감〉 a pinwheel
도르르 round and round; with a twirl
♦종이를 도르르 말다 roll paper up round and round / 담요를 도르르 말다 roll up a carpet / 도르르 말리다 roll itself
도리 建 a beam; a girder
도리 道理 **1** 〈이치〉 reason; 〈정당〉 right; 〈정의〉 justice; 〈진리〉 truth; 〈본분〉 (a) duty; obligation
♦자식으로서의 도리 filial duty; obligation as a son / 도리상 in reason; in [by, from] the nature of things; as a matter of course / 도리에 맞다 stand to reason; be reasonable / 도리에 어긋나다 be contrary to [inconsistent with] reason; be unreasonable / 도리에 어긋난 짓을 하다 misconduct *oneself*; do wrong
▶ 그는 도리를 안다 He knows what is right and what is wrong. ⇌ He knows what's what.
▶ 공부하는 것이 학생의 도리다 It is a student's duty to study. ⇌ A student's duty is to study.
▶ 나는 아버지로서의 도리를 다했다고 생각한다 I think I have done what is expected of me [my duty] as a parent.
2 〈방도〉 a way; a method; the ways and means; 〈대안〉 an alternative
♦(할) 도리가 없다 have no way (of doing [to do]); have no alternative

▶ 話 「왜 그에게 돈을 줬어요?」「딴 도리가 없었어」 "Whatever made you pay him?" "It couldn't be avoided."
▶ 그녀에게 진상을 말할 수밖에 도리가 없다 There is nothing for it but to tell her the truth.
도리깨 a flail ♦도리깨질하다 flail; thresh [thrash] with a flail; thresh grain
도리다 1 ⇨ 도려내다
2 〈지우다〉 strike [cross] out; erase; rub out
♦명부에서 이름을 도리다 cross [strike] a name from a list
도리도리 〈아기에게 도리질을 시킬 때〉 Shake (your) head!
도리스식 —式 〔建〕 Doris (type [style])
♦도리스식의 Doric (order)
도리어 〈반대로〉 on the contrary; instead; 〈오히려〉 rather; all the more [better, worse]
▶ 도리어 제가 사과해야겠습니다 It is for me rather than for you to apologize.
▶ 약을 먹었더니 도리어 병이 도졌다 Although I took the medicine, I became even more ill.
▶ 도로가 혼잡할 땐 자동차보다는 걷는 편이 도리어 낫다 When (the) roads are congested, it is better to walk rather than go by car.
▶ 충고가 도리어 해가 됐다 My advice turned out harmful after all.
▶ 그는 잠자코 있었기 때문에 도리어 우리의 관심을 끌었다 He attracted our attention (all) the more because he kept silent.
▶ 너무 야단을 치면 아이에게는 도리어 해가 된다 If one scolds too severely it does a child more harm than good.
도리질 shaking head for fun; headshake
—도리질하다 〈a baby〉 keep shaking *one's* head for fun / 아이가 도리질하게 되었다 The baby has begun to headshake.
도립 倒立 〔體操〕 a handstand; handstanding
—도립하다 stand on *one's* hands; do a handstand
도립 道立 ♦도립의 provincial
■ **—공원** a provincial park **—도서관** a provincial library **—병원** a provincial hospital
도마 a chopping [cutting] board [block]
도마뱀 〔動〕 a lizard
♦**—붙이** 〔動〕 a gecko; a wall [house] lizard
도마에 오른 고기 〈속담〉 a doomed fish on the dresser; being left to *one's* fate; being at the mercy of fate
도막 a piece ⇨ 토막 1
도말 塗抹 **1** 〈발라 가림〉 painting out [over]
—도말하다 coat [cover] with; paint over 《with》; paint out
2 〈임시변통〉 a makeshift; a patchwork
—도말하다 make shift 《with》; patch up; temporize
■ **—제(劑)** a liniment; an embrocation
도망 逃亡 escape; flight; (口) runaway; (口) getaway; desertion; decampment; elopement
♦도망중인 살인범 a murderer on the run
—도망하다[치다] escape; flee; run away [off]; get away; desert 《a ship》; decamp 《for, to》; elope 《from》
♦간신히 도망치다 escape with bare life / 슬그

머니 도망치다 sneak away; slink [shirk] off / 허둥지둥 도망치다 run away in a flurry / 목숨을 걸고 도망치다 run [flee] for one's life / 여기저기로 도망치다 run [flee] from place to place [this way or that] / 정부(情夫)와 도망치다 elope with a lover / 도망치게 하다 let sb escape; help sb get away / 미처 도망치지 못하다 fail to escape [get off]; be left behind
▶ 그는 내 카메라를 가지고 도망쳤다 He has got away with my camera.
▶ 범인은 이미 외국으로 도망쳤다 The culprit has already fled the country [run away overseas].
▶ 운전사는 사고현장에서 도망쳤다 The driver drove away from the accident.
■—병 a runaway [fugitive] soldier; a deserter —자 a runaway; a fugitive; an absconder; a deserter; an escapee

도망범죄인 逃亡犯罪人 〔法〕 a fugitive from justice; a fugitive criminal [prisoner]; a runaway ■—인도〈국제간의〉extradition

도맡다 1〈혼자서 맡다〉undertake alone; take all upon oneself; shoulder sth alone; take [bear] responsibilities by oneself ((for sth)); run the whole thing
◆ 책임을 도맡다 take the whole responsibilities alone / 남의 빚을 도맡다 shoulder sb's debts
▶ 그는 그 일을 혼자 도맡았다 He took the task upon himself single-handed [alone, by himself].
▶ 모든 문제는 내가 도맡는다 I'll handle all the problems by myself.
2〈도거리로 맡다〉take over (the whole)
◆ 주택 건축을 도맡다 have a contract to build a house

도매 都賣 wholesale
◆ 도매값으로 at the wholesale (price) / 도매로 사서 소매로 팔다 buy wholesale and sell retail
▶ 이것은 도매로 10,000원이오 This sells for ten thousand won wholesale.
—도매하다 sell (by [(美) at]) wholesale; wholesale
■—가격 a wholesale price; a trade price —물가(지수) wholesale price (index) —시장 a wholesale market —업 whole sale business [trade]

도매상 都賣商 〈영업〉a wholesale business [trade]; 〈상인〉a wholesale dealer [merchant]; a wholesaler; 〈가게〉a wholesale house [store, firm]
◆ 전기기구 도매상 a wholesale electric appliance firm / 도매상을 경영하다 carry on a wholesale trade [business]

도면 圖面 a drawing; a sketch; 〈설계도〉a plan; 〈청사진〉a blueprint
◆ 도면을 그리다 draw a plan

도모 圖謀 planning; devising; contriving; designing; scheming
—도모하다 plan; attempt; contrive; scheme; plot; 〈애쓰다〉labor [work, strive] ((for))
◆ 공익을 도모하다 labor for the good of the public / 사리(私利)를 도모하다 seek [try to advance] one's own interests / 자살을 도모하다 attempt suicide
▶ 그들은 시장의 확대를 도모하고 있다 They are planning ways to expand their market.
▶ 일을 도모함은 사람이나, 일의 성사는 하늘에 달려 있다 Man proposes, God disposes.

도목수 都木手 a master carpenter

도무지 utterly; entirely; quite; altogether; 《not》at all; 《not》in the least
◆ 도무지 모르겠다 be wholly at a loss; cannot make head or tail of sth / 도무지 소식이 없다 have been silent so long / 도무지 불가능하다 be utterly impossible
▶ 그의 말은 도무지 알아들을 수가 없다 I can't catch [understand] him at all.
▶ 그것이 뭣인지 도무지 모르겠다 I don't have the faintest [slightest, least, remotest] idea what it is.
▶ 그의 행방은 도무지 모르겠다 His whereabouts are [is] entirely unknown.
▶ 그 아이는 도무지 낯을 가리지 않는다 The child is not at all [in the least] shy with strangers.
▶ 저 녀석은 도무지 쓸모가 없다 He is of no use whatever. ⇌ He is good for nothing. ⇌ He is completely useless.

도미 〔魚〕 a sea bream

도미 渡美 going to America; a visit to America
—도미하다 go (over) to America; visit America; leave for America; 〈이주하다〉emigrate to America
■—유학생 a Korean student studying in the U.S.A. —의원단 a parliamentary mission to America

도미노 dominoes ◆ 도미노 놀이를 하다 play dominoes —이론 the domino theory

도미니카 Dominica;〈공식명〉the Dominican Republic ◆ 도미니카의 Dominican
■—사람 a Dominican

도미니크수도회 —修道會 〈가톨릭〉the Dominican order

도민 島民 the islanders; the inhabitants of an island

도민 道民 the residents [inhabitants] of a province

도박 賭博 1〈노름〉gambling; gaming; a gambling game
◆ 도박으로 돈을 잃다 lose one's money gambling / 도박으로 돈을 따다 make [earn] money by gambling / 상습 도박 혐의로 체포되다 be arrested on suspicion of habitual gambling
2〈모험〉a speculation; a venture; a hazardous attempt
◆ 도박을 하다 take the risks [a chance, chances]; run a risk; stake one's all ((on))
▶ 인생은 도박이다 Life is a game of chance.
■ 사기— fraudulent gambling : 사기 도박꾼〈카드놀이의〉a cardsharp(er); a rook ■—꾼 a gambler; a gamester —단 (round up) a gambling group —상습자 a confirmed [habitual] gambler —장 a gambling house [hall, den]; a gaming house; a casino —죄 the crime of gambling

도박성 賭博性 an inclination to gambling; a habit of gambling ♦도박성을 띤 오락 a recreational game bordering on gambling

도발 挑發 provocation; incitement; encouragement; stirring up
—**도발하다** arouse; provoke; stir up; incite; stimulate; be provocative of
♦전쟁을 도발하다 provoke [set off, touch off] a war

도발적 挑發的 provocative; suggestive 《novel》; inflammatory 《speech》; seditious 《writings》 ♦도발적 언사 provocative [incendiary] remarks / 도발적인 태도를 취하다 take a provocative attitude

도배 徒輩 (口) fellows; (口) guys; a gang; a company; a party; a group
♦불량한 도배와 사귀다 keep bad company

도배 塗褙 papering 《of the walls and ceiling of a room》; paperhanging; wallpapering
—**도배하다** cover with paper; paper [hang paper on] 《the walls [ceiling] of a room》; decorate with paper
♦방을 새로 도배하다 repaper [redecorate] a room
■—장이 a paperhanger; a paperer —지 wallpaper

도배장판하다 塗褙張板— paper [cover with paper] the walls, ceiling and floor of a room

도백 道伯 a provincial governor ⇨ 도지사《道知事》

도버해협 —海峽 the Strait of Dover

도벌 盜伐 the secret felling of trees
▶ 삼림 도벌이 잦았다 Trees were frequently stolen from the forest.
—**도벌하다** fell trees in secret; cut down trees without a license [permission]

도범 盜犯 〈범죄〉theft; robbery; burglary;〈범인〉a thief; a burglar; a robber

도법 圖法 drawing; draftsmanship —투시— perspective drawing 투영— projection

도벽 盜癖 thievish habits; a proclivity to steal; kleptomania; (口) sticky fingers
♦도벽이 있는 사람 a kleptomaniac / 도벽이 있다 have thievish habits; be kleptomaniac; (口) have sticky fingers

도별 道別 classification by province
♦도별로 by province —인구표 a population chart 《broken down》 by province

도보 徒步 walking; going on foot; pedestrianism
♦도보로 on [by] foot; afoot / 도보로 가다 go [travel] on foot; walk 《to》; (美) hike / 도보로 통학[출근]하다 walk to school [office]; go to school [office] on foot
▶ 우리 집은 역에서 도보로 15분이다 My house is a fifteen-minute walk from the station.
—경주 a foot race —운동 walking [pedestrian] exercise

도보여행 徒步旅行 a walking tour; a walking trip; hiking
♦도보여행을 하다 go on a walking tour; travel on foot; make a journey on foot

도부 到付 〈행상〉peddling; hawking; an itinerant trade
—**도부하다**[치다] peddle; hawk; go around hawking [peddling]
♦건어물을 도부치다 peddle dried fish from town to town
■ 도붓장수 a street vendor; a peddler; a hawker; an itinerant vendor [trader]

도사 道士 〈도교의〉a Taoist priest;〈불교의〉an enlightened Buddhist monk [priest];〈도를 닦는 사람〉an ascetic

도사 導師 a spiritual guide in Buddhism; a guru; a priest

도사공 都沙工 a chief boatman

도사리다 1 〈다리를〉sit [squat (down)] cross-legged [tailor fashion]; sit with one's legs crossed; cross one's legs
2 〈마음을〉quiet; calm (down)
♦마음을 도사리다 gather [collect] one's wits [senses]; calm oneself [one's mind]; compose oneself
3 〈뱀 등이〉coil itself (up)
▶ 큰 뱀이 바위 옆에 도사리고 있다 A big snake has coiled itself up [is coiled up] by a rock.
4 〈생각 등이〉lurk 《in》; be harbored; be rooted
♦두 사람 사이에 나쁜 감정이 도사리고 있다 There are ill feelings estranging the two.

도산 倒産 1 ⇨ 파산《破産》
2 [醫] cross birth

도산매 都散賣 wholesale and retail —도산매하다 sell 《by [(美) at]》 wholesale and retail

도살 屠殺 slaughter; butchery;〈학살〉massacre
—**도살하다** slay; slaughter; butcher; massacre
■ 밀— illegal butchery: 밀도살 행위를 적발하다 pick up illegal butchery practices ■—업 butchery —자 a slaughterer; a butcher —장 a slaughterhouse; a butchery

도상 途上 —발전도상국가는 developing countries; countries on their way to development
▶ 레저 산업은 발전 도상에 있다 The leisure industry is becoming more and more prosperous.

도상 圖上 —실습 a map exercise —작전 a war game; tactics on the map(s)

도색 桃色 rose 《color》; pink;〈외설〉obscenity
♦도색의 peach-[rose-]colored; rosy; pink;〈외설적인〉pornographic; obscene
■—문학 erotic literature; pornography —본(本) an obscene book; (총칭) erotica —사진 an obscene picture; pornography —영화 a sex film; (俗) blue movies —영화관 a sex kino —유희 sex play; an amorous affair —잡지 a yellow journal; a pornographic [dirty] magazine

도서 島嶼 islands; isles; islets ■—민 an islander; an islesman —여행 a tour of the islands

도서 圖書 books;〈간행물〉publications;〈문헌〉literature
■ 교양— cultural books; books of cultural studies 신간— new books 아동— children's books 참고— reference books 추천— recommended [suggested] books ■—목록 a catalog

도서관

of books [publications]; a publication list [catalog] —복사필름 a bibliofilm —비 a book budget —상품권 a book coupon [(英) token]《for 5,000 won》—실 a library; a book room —열람권 a library permit —열람료 a library admission fee —열람실 a reading room —열람자 a reader; a visitor —전시회 a book exhibition; a book show —출판업 publishing [book] business; publishing [book] industry —출판업자 a publisher —출판회사 a publishing house [company, concern]; a book concern —카드 a book card —학 bibliography; bibliology

도서관 圖書館 a library
♦도서관에서 책을 찾다 search a library / 도서관에서 《책을》 빌려오다 get 《books》 out of library
▶책을 대출하려고[반환하려고] 도서관에 갔다 I went to the library to borrow [return] books.
■공공[무료]— a public [free] library 국회— the National Assembly Library; 《미국의》 the Library of Congress 대학[학교]— a university [school] library 순회— a traveling 《美》 a mobile] library; 《英》 a bookmobile
—원 a library clerk; a librarian —장 the director [curator] of a library; the 《chief [head]》 librarian —학 library science

도서다¹ 〈건물이〉 heal up
도서다² **1**〈사람이〉 return; come back
2〈바람이〉 change; shift; veer
3〈태아가〉 quicken; (the fetus) begin to move; show life by movements
4〈젖이〉 《a mother's milk》 start flowing after childbirth

도선 渡船 a ferry《boat》; 〈건네주기〉 ferrying
—료 ferriage; a ferry charge —장 a ferry

도선 導船 pilotage; piloting
—도선하다 pilot 《a boat》 ■—사 a pilot

도선 導線 〔電〕 a leading [conducting] wire; a lead 《wire》; a conductor

도설 圖說 an explanatory diagram 《of insects》; a diagrammatic chart; a diagram; an illustration ⇨ 도해(圖解)

도섭 caprice; whim; fancy; fickleness
♦도섭을 부리다 show fickleness; be willful —도섭스럽다 capricious; whimsical; full of whims; fitful; wanton; fanciful

도섭 徒涉 wading
—도섭하다 walk in [through] water; wade 《across a stream》; ford 《a river》

도성 都城 a castle town; 〈서울〉 a capital city

도소주 屠蘇酒 the New Year's ceremonial wine

도수 度數 **1**〈횟수〉 (the number of) times; the frequency
♦사용 도수가 많은 단어 the words frequently used; words of high frequency
2〈온도 등의〉 the degree; 〈렌즈의〉 a degree; a diopter
♦도수 없는 안경 plain glasses; plain-glass spectacles / 도수 높은 안경 powerful spectacles / 안경의 도수를 높이다 use stronger lenses / 안경의 도수를 맞추다 adjust the lenses to one's eyes

3〈알코올의〉 proof
♦도수 높은 위스키 high-proof whisky
4〈눈금〉 graduation ⇨ 눈금
■—계 a (counting) register; 〈전화 통화의〉 a message [call] register; a service meter —분포 frequency distribution —요금 message [call] rates —제 〈전화〉 the message-[call-]rate system; time-charge system

도수 徒手 an empty hand; bare hands
♦도수로 bare-handed; with bare hands
■—공권(空拳) one's bare hands ⇨ 적수(赤手) —체조 gymnastic exercises without apparatus, 〈경기종목〉 free standing exercises

도수 導水 〔土〕 water conveyance —도수하다 conduct water 《into》 ■—관 an aqueduct

도수장 屠獸場 a butchery; a slaughterhouse

도술 道術 Taoist magic; magical arts

도스토예프스키 〈러시아의 소설가〉 Dostoevski, Feodor Mikhailovich (1821–81)

도스패소스 〈미국의 소설가·극작가〉 Dos Passos, John (1896–1970)

도승 道僧 a Buddhist monk who has attained spiritual enlightenment [awakening]

도시 都市 a city; a town; an urban community; towns and cities
♦도시의 발달 the growth of cities [urban communities] / 도시의 municipal; urban; city; town / 도시간의 intercity 《railway, bus》
■거대— a megalopolis 공업— an industrial [a manufacturing] town [city] 관광— a tourist city 국제— a cosmopolitan city 근대— a modern city 대[중, 소]— a large [medium-sized, small] city [town] 대학— a university [college] town 상업— a business town 위성— a satellite city 자매— 《美》 a sister city; 《英》 a twin town 전원— a garden city —가스 city gas —개발 urban development —게릴라 an urban guerrilla —경제 urban economy —공학(과) urban engineering [construction] (department) —국가 a city state —문제 urban problems —사회학 urban sociology —생활 city [town, urban] life —위생 urban sanitation —인 a townsman; a city man [dweller]; an urbanite —인구 urban population —재개발 urban renewal [redevelopment] —전입 inflow into urban areas —행정 municipal administration

도시 圖示 (an) illustration; graphic(al) representation
—도시하다 illustrate; show by [in] a diagram; show in a graphic form
♦시청의 위치를 도시하다 draw a diagram [map] to show the location of the town hall
■—마력[효율] indicated horsepower [efficiency]

도시 都是 at all; on earth; ever ⇨ 도무지

도시계획 都市計劃 urban planning; 《美》 city [《英》 town] planning
■—과 the City-Planning Section —구역 a town planning area —법 the Town Planning and Zoning Act —위원회 the City Planning Committee

도시락 〈상자〉 a lunch box; 〈옛날의〉 a small willow basket 《for carrying food》; a lunch

basket
◆도시락을 먹다 eat [have, take] lunch; eat box lunch / 도시락을 가지고 가다 take [carry] lunch with one
■─밥 food packed in a lunch box; a box lunch

도식 徒食 living in idleness; leading an idle life ⇨ 무위(~도식)

도식 圖式 a diagram; a graph; a schema (pl. -mata); a chart; a figure
◆도식으로 나타내다 put into the form of a diagram [graph]; show in a diagram; diagrammatize; schematize
▶ 그의 사고는 너무 도식적이다 His way of thinking is too simplistic.
■─화 diagraming; graphing; schematization: 도식화하다 diagrammatize

도신 刀身 a sword blade; the blade [flat] of a sword

도심 都心 the heart [center] of the city; the downtown ◆서울의 도심 downtown Seoul
■─지대 the downtown [midtown] area

도싯(셔) 〈영국 잉글랜드의 주〉 Dorset(shire)

도안 圖案 a design; an ornamental design; a sketch; a plan; a pattern
◆도안을 만들다 design; draw [make] a design (for, of) / 도안을 현상 모집하다 collect [invite] designs by prize competition
■─가 a designer ─용지 design paper ─화 making a pattern: 꽃을 도안화하다 make a pattern of flowers

도야 陶冶 training; cultivation; education
◆인격의 도야 character building
─도야하다 train; cultivate; educate; mold; build up
◆자기 인격을 도야하다 form [mold, train, build (up)] one's character

도약 跳躍 a jump; a spring; a leap; a skip; 〈경기〉 jumping
─도약하다 jump; leap; skip; 〈말이〉 prance
■─단계 〔經〕 the take-off stage ─선수 a jumper ─운동 a jumping exercise ─자 a jumper; a leaper ─종목 a jumping event ─판 a springboard; a leaping board

도양 渡洋 crossing the sea
■─작전 transoceanic [oversea(s)] operations [maneuvers] ─폭격 transocean(ic) bombing; a transoceanic raid; oversea(s) [ocean-hopping] bombing

도열 堵列 a line (of men)
─도열하다 form a line; line up; stand in a line
◆길 양쪽에 도열하다 line [be drawn up on] either side of the road / 사람들을 길에 도열시키다 line people along a street

도열병 稻熱病 〔植〕 rice blast disease; rice blight

도예 陶藝 ceramic art; ceramics
■─가 a potter; a ceramist ─품 works of ceramic art; ceramic works

도와 陶瓦 a (roofing) tile

도와주다 1 〈조력하다〉 help sb 《(to) do》; help 《with》; give help [aid] 《to》; aid; assist; give [lend] a helping hand 《to》
◆일을 도와주다 help in [with] sb's work
▶ 나는 그가 일어서는 것을 도와주었다 I helped him (to) get up. ⇌ I helped him to his feet.
▶ 그녀는 내가 아이 기르는 것을 많이 도와주었다 She's helped me a lot [She's been a lot of help (to me)] in bringing up my children.
2 〈구제하다〉 relieve; give relief to; 〈구조하다〉 rescue; help out
◆가난한 사람을 도와주다 relieve [give relief to] the poor / 곤경에 빠진 사람을 도와주다 help sb out of difficulties

도외시 度外視 disregarding
─도외시하다 disregard; leave sth out of account [consideration]; ignore
◆여론을 도외시하고 in disregard of public opinion
▶ 그들은 채산을 도외시하고 사진집을 출판했다 They published a collection of pictures irrespective of expense.
▶ 그 건은 도외시해도 된다 That matter may be left out of consideration. ⇌ That matter doesn't have to be brought up.

도요새 〔鳥〕 a snipe

도용 盜用 surreptitious use; plagiarism
─도용하다 use by stealth; make a fraudulent use of
◆남의 아이디어를 도용하다 steal [plagiarize] another's idea
▶ 그는 계약서에 사장의 인감을 도용했다 He made improper use of the president's seal on a contract.

도움 1 〈조력〉 help; aid; assistance; 〈후원〉 support
◆아무에게 도움이 되다 be of help to sb; be helpful to sb / 아무에게 도움을 청하다 ask sb for help; turn [look] to sb for help / 도움을 받다 have [receive] help 《from》
▶ 그의 충고가 큰 도움이 되었다 His advice was very helpful to me.
▶ 좋은 사전은 말 공부에 크게 도움이 된다 Good dictionaries are a great help in a study of languages.
▶ 누군가의 도움을 받아야겠다 I will get someone to help me.
▶ 나는 아무 도움도 받지 않고 그것을 해냈다 I did it without (any) help.
2 〈구원〉 relief; rescue
▶ 피해 지역에서 도움을 청해 왔다 Aid was requested from the stricken area.
▶ 도움을 청하는 난민이 해상을 표류하고 있었다 Refugees seeking relief was adrift on the sea.
3 〈효용〉 use; service; utility
◆도움이 되다 be useful [effective]; be of use [service] / 도움이 되지 않다 be useless; have no effect

도움닫기 〈스포츠〉 an approach run
■─높이뛰기 a (running) high jump ─멀리 뛰기 a (running) long jump

도원경 桃源境 Shangri-la; the hidden Paradise

도유 塗油 (applying) anointment; inunction; anointing

도읍 都邑 〈수도〉 a capital; a metropolis; 〈도회지〉 a city; a town
─도읍하다 found a capital; 〈왕이〉 choose

《Hanyang》as the capital of the country

도의 道義 morality; morals; moral principles
♦도의적 책임 moral responsibility / 도의적(인) moral / 도의적으로 봐서 morally speaking; from the moral point of view / 도의를 존중하다 have high [strong, keen] moral sense / 도의에 어긋나다 be against public morals; be contrary to accepted standards of morality
▶도의가 땅에 떨어졌다 People have lost their sense of morality. ⇒ Morality has lost its hold on the people.

도의심 道義心 moral sense; a sense of morality
▶우리는 그의 도의심에 호소했다 We appealed to his moral sense.
▶그는 도의심이 강한 사람이다 He is a man of strict morality.

도의원 道議員 a member of a provincial assembly ⇨ 도의회(~의원)

도의회 道議會 a provincial assembly ■—의원 a member of a provincial assembly; a provincial assemblyman

도일 渡日 a visit [trip] to Japan
—**도일하다** visit [go (over) to] Japan

도일 〈영국의 추리작가〉 Doyle, Sir Arthur Conan (1859-1930)

도입 導入 introduction
♦서양문화의 도입 the introduction of Western culture
—**도입하다** introduce
▶그들은 독일에서 새 기술을 도입했다 They introduced the new technology from Germany.
■외자— introduction of foreign capital ■—부 the introduction; the introductory part

도자기 陶瓷器·陶磁器 ceramic ware; ceramics; china and porcelain; pottery; a piece of pottery
■—공 a potter; a ceramist —제조소 a pottery

도작 盜作 plagiarism ♦남의 논문의 도작 plagiarism of another person's treatise ■—자 a plagiarist

도장 道場 a training hall; an exercise hall; a gymnasium (*pl.*~s, -sia)
■펜싱[레슬링]— a fencing [wrestling] hall

도장 塗裝 painting; coating
▶문의 도장이 벗겨지고 있다 The paint is peeling off the door.
—**도장하다** paint; coat [cover] with paint
♦개집을 빨갛게 도장하다 paint the dog house red
■—공 a painter (and decorator) —공사 painting; painter's work

도장 圖章 a seal; a stamp; a name seal
♦도장을 찍다 seal; affix [stamp, put] *one's* seal (to) / 도장을 새기다 〈남을 시켜서〉 have *one's* seal cut [engraved]
▶그 책에는 김선생의 도장이 찍혀 있다 The book bears [is affixed with] the seal of Mr. Kim.
▶이름 뒤에 도장을 찍으시오 Put your signature stamp after your name.
■인감— a registered seal ■—주머니 a seal case —칼 a seal graver

도저하다 到底— **1** 〈썩 좋다〉 good; fine; excellent
2 〈극진하다〉 perfect; thorough

도저히 到底— 〈아무리 해도〉 (not) possibly; (not) at all; not nearly (so);〈전혀〉 utterly; absolutely
♦도저히 비교가 되지 않다 cannot for a moment compare with; be beyond all comparison / ···은 도저히 있을 수 없는 일이다 It is most unlikely [out of the bounds of possibility] that...
▶나로서는 도저히 그것을 생각할 수 없다 I cannot possibly [hardly] think of it.
▶그것은 상식으로는 도저히 헤아릴 수 없다 That goes beyond the bounds of common knowledge.
▶이 더운 날씨는 도저히 참을 수 없다 I really can't stand this hot weather.

도적 盜賊 a thief; 〈절도〉 a robber; 〈강도〉 a burglar; a house breaker

도전 挑戰 challenge; defiance; provocation
♦도전적(으로) challenging(ly); defiant(ly); provocative(ly); aggressive(ly) / 도전적 태도를 취하다 assume [take] a defiant [provocative] attitude 〈toward〉
▶챔피언은 그의 도전에 응했다 The champion accepted his challenge.
—**도전하다** challenge; make a challenge; bid defiance 〈to〉
♦세계기록에 도전하다 try [attempt] to get the world record
▶그는 이번 겨울 등반에 도전할 작정이다 He's going to challenge a mountain this winter.
▶나는 서울 대학 입시에 다시 도전하겠다 I will try to pass the entrance exam of Seoul University again.
■—자 a challenger —장 a (written) challenge

도전 導電 electric conduction; conduction of electricity ■—도 conductivity —성[율] conductivity —체 an electric conductor

도정 道政 provincial government [administration]

도정 道程 〈거리〉 the distance; mileage; 〈여정〉 a journey; an itinerary; a route; 〈과정〉 a process ♦450킬로미터의 도정 a distance of 450 kilometers
▶성공에의 도정은 쉬운 것이 아니다 The path to success is not an easy one.

도정 搗精 (rice) polishing by pounding; pounding; hulling
♦도정이 덜 되다 be insufficiently pounded
—**도정하다** polish (rice) by pounding
■—공장 a rice(-polishing) mill

도제 徒弟 an apprentice
♦도제가 되다 become an apprentice 〈to〉; be apprenticed 〈to〉; apprentice *oneself* 〈to〉; go apprentice / 도제를 두다 take apprentices
■—기간 *one's* apprenticeship —제도 apprenticeship; an apprentice system

도제 陶製 ♦도제의 china; porcelain; ceramic; earthen ■—타일 a ceramic tile —파이프 〈흡연용의〉 a clay pipe

도주 逃走 (a) flight; (a) desertion; (an) escape ⇨ 도망

도중 途中 ◆도중에(서) on the way 《to, from》; on *one's* way 《to》; on [en] route 《to, from》; in the middle of; in the course of; halfway; midway / 학교에 가는 도중에 on *one's* way to school / 등산[하산]하는 도중에 on *one's* way up [down] the mountain / 도중에 그만두다 give up halfway; do not go all the way / 도중에서 되돌아가다 turn back halfway [midway]
▶ 이야기 도중 죄송합니다만 지금 몇시입니까? I'm sorry to interrupt you, but what time is it now? ⇌ Excuse me for interruption, but what time is it now?
▶ 그는 회의 도중 무단으로 자리를 떴다 He left during the conference without leave.
▶ 그녀는 이야기 도중 말을 멈췄다 She paused in the middle of her talk. ⇌ She paused midway through her talk.
▶ 그는 내가 이야기하는 도중 내내 껌을 씹고 있었다 He was chewing gum all the time I was talking.

도중하차 途中下車 a stopover; (美) a layover ─도중하차하다 stop over; make a stopover; stop off; break *one's* journey; (美) lay over
◆대전에서 도중하차하다 stop over [make a stopover] at Taejŏn

도지다 〈재발하다〉 regress after partial recovery from illness; 〈사람이 주어〉 have [suffer] a relapse [return] 《of a disease》; suffer a setback; take a critical [serious] turn
▶ 그의 병이 도졌다 He has had a relapse. ⇌ His illness has recurred.
▶ 병이 도지지 않도록 조심하세요 Take good care not to have [suffer] a relapse.

도지볼 〔競〕 dodge ball

도지사 道知事 the governor of a province; a provincial governor
◆경기도지사 이선생 Mr. Lee, Governor of Kyŏnggi-do

도착 到着 arrival
─도착하다 arrive at [in, on]; 〈도달하다〉 get to; reach; 〈편지·화물이〉 come to hand

> [解說] *arrive*는 「도착하다」란 뜻의 가장 일반적인 말. arrive 다음에 전치사로는 보통 좁은 장소일 때는 at, 넓은 장소일 때는 in을 쓰는데 장소의 좁고 넓음은 물리적인 것이 아니라 심리적으로 파악한 것이어서 예컨대 대도시라도 통과도중의 한 지점으로 생각할 때는 at을 쓰고, 도착지점이 아니라 체재한다는 생각이 가미될 때는 in을 쓴다. 따라서 「런던에 도착하다」는 arrive at [in] London의 두 가지가 다 가능하다. on은 continent, island, moon, shore, scene, platform 등과 같이 장소의 표면이 의식될 때에 쓰인다. *get to*는 arrive at 보다 구어적이고 흔히 노력하여 도착한다는 뜻이 내포된다. *reach*는 약간 딱딱한 말로 어떤 노력을 해서 도달한다는 뜻이다. 따라서 「인류가 달에 도착했다」는 Man reached [got to] the moon.이라 하고 arrive를 쓰지 않는다.

◆도착하는 즉시 upon arrival; as soon as *one* arrives; immediately on *one's* arrival / 도착순으로 in order of arrival / 무사히 도착하다 〈물품이〉 arrive in safety; arrive in good condition [order] / 10시 기차로 도착하다 arrive by [美] on] the 10 o'clock train
▶ 기차는 정시에 도착하였다 The train got in [pulled in] on time [(美) schedule].
▶ 악천후로 비행기가 도착하는 것이 늦어졌다 The bad weather delayed the plane's arrival.
■─시간 the arrival time ─역 a destination (station); 〈물품의〉 the receiving station ─예정시간 estimated time of arrival (略 ETA) ─지점 *one's* destination; a place of arrival ─항 a port of arrival

도착 倒錯 〔醫〕 perversion
■─성적─ sexual perversion: 성적도착자 a (sexual) pervert [invert]

도처(에) 到處(─) everywhere; wherever *one* goes; all over 《the world》; throughout 《the country》; far and wide [near, nigh]; in every quarter; here, there, and everywhere
◆세계 도처에 all parts [every corner] of the world
▶ 우리 회사는 전국 도처에 지점이 있다 We have branches throughout the country.
▶ 친선 사절은 도처에서 환영을 받았다 The goodwill mission was welcomed wherever they went.
▶ 로마에는 도처에 유적이 있다 Rome abounds with relics.

도청 盜聽 〈전화의〉 (wire) tapping; bugging; 〈엿들음〉 eavesdropping
─도청하다 tap 《the telegraph [telephone] wire》; wiretap; eavesdrop (on) 《a conversation》; (美俗) bug 《a conversation》
▶ 그녀는 그들의 대화를 도청했다 She listened in on their conversation.
■─사건 a wiretap scandal ─자 a wiretapper

도청 道廳 a provincial office [government]
■─소재지 the seat of a provincial office; a provincial capital

도청기 盜聽器 〈대화의〉 a concealed microphone; 〈전화의〉 a wiretapping device; 〈벽에 장치한〉 a wall-snooper; (美俗) a bug
▶ 회의실에는 도청기가 설치되어 있었다 The conference room was bugged.

도체 導體 a conductor
■─반─ a semiconductor ─부─ a nonconductor 양(良)[불량]─ a good [bad] conductor

도축 屠畜 slaughter; butchery ⇨ 도살(屠殺)

도취 陶醉 **1** 〈술에 취함〉 intoxication
─도취하다 be intoxicated
2 〈감정에 젖음〉 (an) ecstasy; fascination; rapture
─도취하다 be fascinated [charmed, carried away] 《by》; be enraptured 《with》; be in rapture [ecstasies] 《over》
◆자연의 아름다움에 도취되다 be intoxicated with [fascinated by] the beauty of nature / 아름다운 음악에 도취되다 be fascinated by the beautiful music
▶ 그녀의 아름다운 목소리에 나는 도취되었다 I was carried away by her beautiful voice.

■ 자기— self-intoxication: narcissism: 자기도취자 a narcissist
도치 倒置 turning upside-down; 〔文法〕 inversion —도치하다 invert; reverse; put upside-down
♦ 두 단어의 순서를 도치하다 invert [reverse] the order of the two words
도킹 〈우주선의〉 docking; space linkup
♦ 도킹을 풀다 undock 《from》
—도킹하다 dock 《with the command module》
도탄 塗炭 misery; distress
♦ 도탄에 빠지다 fall into [be in] great misery; suffer [be in] the distress; be reduced to the greatest misery / 도탄에 빠진 백성을 구하다 save the people from distress
도태 淘汰 〈가려냄〉 selection; washing out useless elements; weeding out
—도태하다 select; weed out; screen; sift 《the good from the bad》
♦ 과잉 인원을 도태하다 dismiss superfluous [redundant] employees; weed out superfluous personnel [officials] / 무능한 공무원을 도태하다 weed out [dismiss] incompetent officials
▶ 환경의 변화에 적응하지 못하는 동물은 도태된다 Animals that cannot adapt to changes in the environment will die out.
■ —작용 sifting-[weeding-]out process
도토 陶土 potter's clay; porcelain [china] clay; kaolin(e)
도토리 an acorn
▶ 그들 모두는 도토리 키재기다 There is nothing to choose between [(from) among] them. ⇌ They are all nearly alike.
▶ 그는 개밥에 도토리다 He is an outcast [a left-out person].
도톨도톨 rough; ruggedly; unevenly
—도톨도톨하다 rough; rugged; uneven; pimply; granular; granulated
♦ 도톨도톨한 나무껍질 a rugged bark / 도톨도톨하게 만든 가죽 granulated leather / 도톨도톨하게 만들다 granulate
▶ 그의 얼굴에는 여드름이 도톨도톨 나 있다 His face is covered with pimples.
도통 都統 1 ⇨ 도합
♦ 도통 15개 fifteen in all / 도통 10만원이 되다 total (up to) 100,000 won
2 〈전혀〉 (not) at all; absolutely
▶ 그 사람에 관해선 도통 모른다 I know absolutely nothing about him.
▶ 요즈음 그를 도통 못 만난다 I have seen nothing of him of late.
▶ 그는 선거 쯤은 도통 마음에도 없다 He doesn't give a damn about the election.
도통 道通 spiritual awakening [enlightenment] —도통하다 be spiritually awakened; attain higher perception [spiritual enlightenment]
♦ 그 일에 도통하다 be well [deeply] versed in the matter; be conversant with the matter
도판 圖版 a plate; a figure; an illustration; 〈삽입도〉 an inset
♦ 도판 다수 삽입 profusely illustrated
도포 塗布 application —도포하다 apply 《an ointment to the skin》; spread
■ —약[제] (an) ointment; (an) endermic liniment
도포 道袍 Korean full-dress attire (in olden days); a gentlemen's robe [gown]
도표 道標 a guidepost; a signpost; a fingerpost; a milestone
♦ 도표를 세우다 set up a guidepost [signpost] / 도표를 따라가다 follow the signposts
도표 圖表 a chart; a diagram; a graph
♦ 도표의 diagrammatic(al); graphic / 도표를 만들다 draw a chart [diagram] / 도표로 나타내다 chart; show [represent] on a chart; put (figures) into the form of a diagram; diagrammatize; represent by a chart
■ 막대— a bar chart [graph] 선— a line graph 역사— a historical chart 점— a scatter [dot] diagram 통계— a statistical chart
도품 盜品 〈장물〉 stolen goods [things]; spoils; hot goods; the goods
■ —시장 a thieves' market
도플러효과 —效果 〔物〕 the Doppler effect
도피 逃避 (an) escape; 〈회피〉 evasion; (a) flight
♦ 도피(적) 생활 an escape life / 현실로부터의 도피 an escape from reality
—도피하다 flee; escape; fly; evade
♦ 사회로부터 도피하다 seclude *oneself* from society / 애인과 함께 도피하다 elope with *one's* lover
▶ 경찰은 범인이 도피하기 직전에 붙잡았다 The police arrested the criminal just before his bolt.
■ —결혼 a runaway marriage [match] —구 a way of escape; a wayout; a loophole —문학 escapist literature —생활 a life of escape from the world —여행 a runaway trip; an escape journey —자 a runaway; a fugitive; a refugee —장소 a place of refuge; a bolt-hole —주의 escapism —주의자 an escapist
도핑 〈운동선수의 흥분제 복용〉 doping
■ —검사 a dope check
도하 都下 the capital; the metropolis
♦ 도하의 각 중학교 the middle schools in the capital [in Seoul] / 도하의 in Seoul; in the metropolitan area
도하 渡河 the crossing [fording] of a river
—도하하다 cross [ford] a river
■ —기재(器材) river-crossing materials —작전 a river-crossing[-fording] operation: 우리는 도하작전을 강행했다 We forced river-crossing operations.
도학 道學 1 〈도덕에 관한 학문〉 moral philosophy [science]
2 〈도교〉 Taoism; 〈유학(儒學)〉 Confucianism
■ —군자 a virtuous gentleman; a man of virtue —자 a moralist; a Taoist
도함수 導函數 〔數〕 a derivative; a derived function
도합 都合 〈모두 합한 셈〉 the total; the sum total; 〈부사적〉 in all; all together; all told; totally
▶ 출석자는 도합 50명이었다 In all, fifty people attended.
▶ 비용은 도합 10만원이었다 The costs totaled one hundred thousand won.

▶도합 48명이 행방불명이다 A total of 48 are still missing.
도항 渡航 a passage; a voyage; a sailing; a crossing
♦도항절차를 밟다 arrange passage; go through due formalities for a passage
―도항하다 make [take] (a) passage 《to》; make a voyage 《to》; go across 《to》; cross the water
■―자 a passenger; a visitor
도해 圖解 an illustration; an explanatory diagram; a diagrammatic chart
♦도해의 diagrammatic; 〈그림이 든〉 pictorial
―도해하다 illustrate; diagram; show by a diagram [in a graphic form]
▶그것을 도해하면 다음과 같다 It is graphically shown as follows.
▶선생님은 인공위성의 궤도를 도해해 주셨다 The teacher showed the orbit of a satellite using a picture.
도형 圖形 a figure; a device; a diagram
♦도형으로 나타내다 show in [by] a diagram; figure
■기하학적― a geometrical figure; a geometric design 평면[입체]― a plane [solid] figure ■―기하학 descriptive geometry
도화 桃花 a peach blossom
도화 圖畵 〈그리기〉 drawing; 〈그림〉 a drawing; a picture
■―지 drawing paper
도화선 導火線 1 〈폭약의 심지〉 a fuse; a blasting [detonating] fuse; a (powder) train
♦도화선을 달다[붙이다] put a fuse to; lay a train (of powder) / 도화선에 불을 붙이다 light [fire] a fuse
2 〈직접 원인〉 a cause; an incentive; the origin 《of a quarrel》
♦도화선이 되다 prove an incentive to; cause; occasion; touch off
▶영토문제가 전쟁의 도화선이 되었다 The territorial problem gave rise to [led to] war.
▶그의 방해가 도화선이 되어 회장 안은 혼란에 빠졌다 His interruption was a cause for confusion in the assembly hall.
도회 都會 a town; a city

> **解說** town은 village보다는 크고 city보다는 작은 자치단체다. 행정상의 단위로는 city는 「시」, town은 그 아래의 「읍」에 해당하지만 일상에서는 엄격하게 구별하지 않는다. 또 the country(시골)의 대립개념으로 city나 town을 다 쓰는데, town은 상업지구(downtown)의 뜻으로도 쓰인다.

♦도회에서 자란 아이 a city-bred child / 도회의 urban / 도회풍의 urbane
▶도회에는 공기가 오염돼 있다 Air is polluted in cities.
■―문학 urban literature ―병 a city disease ―생활 urban [town, city] life: 도회생활은 시골생활보다 편리해서 좋다 City life is much more convenient than country life. ―인 a townsman; townspeople; townsfolk ―정서 an urban atmosphere ―지 a city; a town ―풍 urban [city] manner; urbanity ―화 urbanization

독¹ an earthenware pot; a crock; 〈족자리가 없는〉 a jar; 〈족자리가 있는〉 a jug; 〈작은 것〉 an urn; 〈술독 등 큰 것〉 a vat
독² 〈선거(船渠)〉 a dock
♦부(浮)독 a floating dock / 건식(乾式)독 a dry [graving] dock / 독에 들어가다 go into dock / 배를 독에 들이다 dock a ship; put a ship into dock
▶그 배는 독에서 나왔다 The ship came out of dock.
■―사용료 dockage; dock dues
독 毒 1 〈일반적인 독물〉 (a) poison; 〈뱀·전갈·거미 등의〉 venom
▶갑의 약은 을의 독 《속담》 One man's meat is another man's poison.
〈독이〉 독이 있는 버섯 a poisonous mushroom / 독이 있는 뱀 a venomous snake / 독이 없는 뱀 an innocuous snake / 독이 있어 보이는 poisonous-looking / 독이 있는 poisonous; venomous; 〈유해한〉 harmful; injurious / 독이 없는 innoxious; innocent; harmless
▶독이 곧 퍼졌다 Poison took instant effect.
▶독이 그의 전신에 퍼졌다 The poison went around his system.
〈독을〉 독을 탄 음료 a poisoned drink / 독을 먹이다 administer poison to; poison sb / 독을 마시다 take poison / 독을 중화하다 counteract (the effect of) poison / 독을 마시고 자살하다 kill *oneself* by taking poison
▶이 약은 독을 해소한다 This medicine is an antidote for poison.
▶독으로 독을 없이한다 Counteract poison with poison. ⇌ Fight fire with fire.
2 〈해치는 성분〉 harm; injury
▶과식은 몸에 독이다 Eating too much is harmful to [bad for] your health.
▶이 책은 소년에게는 독이다 This book poisons [harms] young minds.
▶이 책은 독도 약도 되지 못한다 This book is neither good nor bad.
▶그의 말에는 독이 있다 He has a malicious tongue.
독가스 毒― poison gas; poisonous gas; toxic smoke; noxious gas
♦독가스를 맡다 be gassed / 독가스를 사용하다 use poison gas / 독가스로 적을 공격하다 gas the enemy
■―공격 a gas attack ―전 (poison-)gas warfare ―탄 〈포탄〉 a poison-gas shell; 〈폭탄〉 a gas bomb; a gas shell
독감 毒感 〈유행성〉 influenza; 《口》 flu; 〈지독한〉 a bad [nasty] cold ♦독감에 걸리다 contract [catch, get] flu [a bad cold] ▶독감이 유행하고 있다 There's a lot of flu about.
독거 獨居 solitude; a solitary life
―독거하다 live alone [by *oneself*]; live in solitude; lead a solitary life
■―성동물 a solitary animal; a hermit
독경 讀經 [佛教] sutra chanting
―독경하다 chant [recite] Buddhist sutras [scriptures]
독과점 獨寡占 monopoly and oligopoly

독극물

■―품목 monopoly-oligopoly items: 독과점 품목으로 지정하다 designate as monopolistic and oligopolistic items ―회사 oligopolists

독극물 毒劇物 toxic chemicals

독기 毒氣 1 〈독기운〉 noxious air; poisonous gas [vapor]
♦ 독기 있는 poisonous / 독기에 노출되다 be exposed to poisonous air
2 〈악의〉 malice; spite
♦ 독기 있는 말 malicious words; poisonous tongue
▶ 그녀의 목소리에는 독기가 있었다 She has a malicious tongue.

독나방 毒― 〔昆〕 a poisonous moth; an oriental tussock moth; a brown-tail moth

독녀 獨女 an only daughter ⇨ 외딸

독농가 篤農家 an exemplary good farmer; a most efficient farming producer; an industrious farmer; a diligent [hardworking] farmer

독단 獨斷 1 〈전단(專斷)〉 an arbitrary decision
♦ 독단적인 arbitrary; peremptory / 독단적인 말을 하다 lay down the law / 독단으로 정하다 decide (it) arbitrarily [for *oneself*, on *one's* own judgement]
▶ 나는 그것을 독단으로 정했다 I decided the matter arbitrarily.
▶ 그는 독단으로 집회를 연기했다 He postponed the meeting at (his own) discretion.
―독단하다 decide arbitrarily [for *oneself*]; decide on *one's* own judgment [responsibility]
2 〈주관적 판단〉 dogmatism
♦ 독단적 발언 a dogmatic assertion / 독단적 (인) dogmatic / 독단적으로 dogmatically; on *one's* own judgment
▶ 그는 독단적이어서 남의 의견을 듣지 않는다 He is too opinionated to listen to what others say.
―독단하다 dogmatize
▶ 그는 내가 도와줄 거라고 독단하고 있다 He takes my help for granted.
▶ 그는 스스로가 지도자로 독단하고 있다 He is posing as a leader.
■―론 a dogma; dogmatism ―론자 a dogmatist

독도 獨島 Tokto

독두 禿頭 a bald head ⇨ 대머리

독려 督勵 encouragement
―독려하다 encourage; stimulate; urge
♦ 부하를 독려하여 작업을 서두르다 urge *one's* men to push the work
▶ 그를 독려하여 다시 한번 그것을 하도록 하는 것이 너의 임무다 It is your duty to encourage him to try it again.
▶ 코치는 선수들이 더 연습하도록 독려했다 The coach encouraged [urged] the players to practice more.

독력 獨力 *one's* own efforts; single-handed efforts
♦ 독력의 independent / 독력으로 by *oneself*; on *one's* own; for *oneself*; unaided; alone; single-handed / 독력으로 하다 do *sth* single-handed [on *one's* own]; 〈독립하다〉 stand on *one's* own legs

독립 獨立 1 〈자립〉 independence; self-help; 〈독립독행〉 self-reliance
♦ 경제적 독립 economic independence / 독립의 independent / 독립하여 independently ((of)); 〈스스로〉 for *oneself*; alone; 〈남의 도움을 받지 않고〉 on *one's* own
―독립하다 become [be] independent of; stand on *one's* own legs [feet]; stand alone; set up for *oneself*
♦ 독립하여 영업하다 set up [engage in] business on *one's* own (account) / 독립하여 가정을 꾸려가다 keep house for *oneself*
▶ 그는 이제 독립해도 될 나이다 He is old enough to be doing for himself [to be on his own].
▶ 당시 한국은 경제적으로 독립하지 못했었다 Korea could not economically stand on her own legs at that time.
▶ 그는 18살 때 독립했다 He set out on his own [became independent of his parents] when he was eighteen.
▶ 우리 아들은 학교 졸업 후 6년 만에 드디어 독립했다 It has been six years since my son graduated from school, and now finally, he is independent.
2 〈정치적〉 independence; freedom
♦ 독립을 선언하다 declare independence; declare (itself) independent / 독립을 인정하다 recognize the independence (of) / 독립을 시켜 주다 give [grant] independence ((to))
―독립하다 become (free and) independent
▶ 미국은 1776년에 독립했다 The United States of America became independent in 1776.
▶ 인도는 1947년 영국으로부터 독립했다 India became independent of Britain in 1947. ⇌ India won [gained] independence from Britain in 1947.
3 〈자활〉 self-support
4 〈분리〉 separation; 〈고립〉 isolation
―독립하다 be separated from; separate from; be isolated from
▶ 그 건물은 딴 건물과는 독립되어 있다 The building is separated from the rest.
■―가옥 a detached house ―국(가) an independent nation [country]; a sovereign nation ―군 an army for national independence ―권(權) right of independence ―기념일 〈미국의〉 Independence Day; the Fourth of July ―독보 ⇨ 독립독행 ―변수 〔數〕 an independent variable ―분사구문 〔文法〕 an absolute participial construction ―생계 self-support: 독립 생계를 영위하다 support *oneself*; earn *one's* own living ―생계자 a self-supporter ―생활 an independent life ―선언 〈미국의〉 the Declaration of Independence ―심 an independent spirit: 독립심이 없다 lack the spirit of independence ―어 〔言〕 a free-standing [an independent] word ―운동 an independence movement ―전쟁 〈미국의〉 the War of Independence (▶(英)에서는 the War of American Independence라고 함) ―투사 〈한국 등의〉 a fighter for national independence

독립국가연합 獨立國家聯合 the Commonwealth of Independent States (略 CIS)

독립독행 獨立獨行 independence; self-reliance
♦ 독립독행의 self-reliant
―**독립독행하다** rely on *oneself*; be self-reliant; stand on *one's* own legs; paddle *one's* own canoe
♦ 독립독행하는 사람 a self-reliant person

독립채산제 獨立採算制 a self-supporting accounting system
♦ 독립채산제로 on a self-paying basis

독목교 獨木橋 a single-log bridge ⇨ 외나무다리

독목주 獨木舟 a canoe ⇨ 마상이

독무 獨舞 a solo (dance)

독무대 獨舞臺 1 〈단독 연기〉 playing alone [by *oneself*]
▶ 그 연극의 저 유명한 장면에서는 그의 독무대가 된다 He has the stage all to himself during the famous scene of the play.
2 〈독장치는 판〉 the sole master of the stage [field]
3 〈경쟁자가 없음〉 *one's* unrivaled sphere of activity; *one's* monopoly
♦ 독무대다 stand unchallenged; be unrivaled [without a rival]
▶ 그 경주는 그의 독무대였다 He had no rival [was without a rival] in the race.
▶ 아이스하키에서는 10년간 그 팀이 독무대였다 That team was without a rival [unrivaled] in ice hockey for ten years.
▶ 아프리카 얘기만 나오면 그의 독무대다 When it comes to Africa, he monopolizes the conversation.

독물 毒物 1 〈독성 물질〉 a poison; a poisonous substance [agent]
♦ 독물을 제거하다 remove the poison 《from》; detoxify
2 〈사람〉 a vicious [ferocious] person
■―검출 detection of poisonous substances
―공포증 toxiphobia ―학 toxicology

독미나리 毒― 〔植〕 a hemlock

독방 獨房 〈혼자 거처하는 방〉 a single room; a room to *oneself*; 〈교도소의〉 a (condemned) cell; a solitary [an isolation] cell
♦ 독방에 감금되다 be placed in solitary confinement
▶ 당신이 거처할 독방을 예약해 두었습니다 I've reserved [(英) booked] a single for you.
■―감 solitary confinement [imprisonment]; (口) solitary ―제 the solitary imprisonment system

독백 獨白 a monolog(ue); a soliloquy ―**독백하다** soliloquize; utter a soliloquy; say to *oneself*

독버섯 毒― a poisonous mushroom; a toadstool

독벌레 毒― a poisonous insect ⇨ 독충

독법 讀法 〈읽는 법〉 (the way of) reading; 〈발음〉 pronunciation

독보 獨步 ♦ 독보적인 unique; matchless; peerless; unparalleled; unequaled; unrivaled; unchallenged
▶ 그의 업적은 고금 독보다 His achievements stand unique [have no rival].
▶ 그는 현대 교향악의 지휘자로서 독보적인 존재다 He stands alone as a conductor of modern symphonic music.

독본 讀本 a reader; a reading book; a textbook ♦ 영어― an English reader

독부 毒婦 a wicked woman; a she-devil

독불 獨佛 France and Germany
♦ 독불의 Franco-German; German-French 《dictionary》

독불장군 獨不將軍 1 〈제 주장만 하는 사람〉 a man of self-assertion; a self-righteous man
▶ 그는 종종 독불장군처럼 군다 He often behaves self-righteously [in a self-centered way].
2 〈따돌림받는 사람〉 a person left out in the cold; an outcast; an isolated man
▶ 그는 정계의 독불장군이다 He is a political loner.

독사 毒蛇 a poisonous snake; a venomous serpent; a viper; an adder

독살 毒殺 poisoning; killing by poison ―**독살하다** poison; kill [murder] *sb* by [with] poison
▶ 장군은 독살당했다 The general was poisoned to death.
■―사건 a poisoning case ―자 a poisoner

독살림 獨― an independent life
―**독살림하다** live independently; keep house for *oneself*
▶ 막내아들은 부모를 떠나 독살림했다 The youngest son lived independently of his parents. ⇌ The youngest son supported himself without relying on his parents.

독살부리다 毒殺― act spitefully [malignantly, venomously]; give vent to *one's* spite

독살스럽다 毒殺― venomous; spiteful; malicious; vicious; malignant
♦ 독살스러운 여자 a wicked [spiteful, vicious] woman / 독살스럽게 spitefully; malignantly; acrimoniously / 독살스럽게 말하다 use spiteful [virulent] language

독생자 獨生子 〔基〕 (Jesus Christ,) the only-begotten son (of God)

독서 讀書 reading
♦ 체계적인[계통을 세운] 독서 systematic reading / 즐기기[오락을] 위한 독서 reading for pleasure / 독서를 좋아하는 사람 a booklover / 독서에 몰두하다 be buried in a book; be absorbed in reading / 독서를 좋아하다 be fond of reading
▶ 가을은 독서에 가장 좋은 계절이다 Autumn is the best season for reading.
▶ 그는 언제나 독서에 몰두한다 He is always buried in his books. ⇌ He always has his nose in a book.
▶ 그의 독서 범위는 매우 넓다 His reading is of very wide range. ⇌ He is an extensive reader.
―**독서하다** read 《a book》
♦ 독서하지 않는 사람 an unread person; a nonreader
▶ 요즘 젊은이들은 별로 독서하지 않는다 Young people nowadays do not do much reading.
■―가 a (great) reader; a well-read person; a

독선

person of wide reading ―경향 readers' interests ―계 the reading public ―광 a bookworm; a literary glutton ―력 《cultivate one's》 reading ability: 독서력을 키워라 Cultivate your reading ability. ―법 a method of reading (a book) ―실 〈도서열람실〉 a reading room ―욕 a desire for reading ―인 a reader of books ―주간 Book Week ―회 a reading club [circle]

독선 獨善 self-righteousness; self-complacency; self-complacency
♦독선적(인) self-righteous; self-complacent; self-opinionated; self-justified / 독선적인 태도 a self-righteous attitude / 독선적으로 이야기하다 speak self-righteously
―관료 a self-righteous bureaucrat ―주의 self-righteousness; (self-)complacency

독설 毒舌 a stinging [blistering] tongue; a malicious [poisonous] tongue; malicious [abusive] language
♦독설을 퍼붓다 use one's malicious tongue; speak with acrimony; speak venomously [daggers] (to sb)
■―가 a malicious person: 그는 대단한 독설가다 He has a terribly poisonous [sharp] tongue.

독성 毒性 virulence; toxicity; poisonous [toxic] character ♦독성이 있는 virulent; poisonous; toxic; toxicant / 독성이 강한 화학약품 a highly toxic chemical
▶ 그 약은 독성이 극히 약하다 The toxicity of the drug is very low.
▶ 이 식물은 독성이 있다 This plant is poisonous.
■―궤양 (a) virulent ulcer ―완화 mollification of virulence ―완화제 a safener

독소 毒素 poisonous matter; a toxin
■ 항(抗)― an antitoxin(e)

독송 讀誦 recitation; intonation
―독송하다 read aloud; recite; intone

독수 毒手 a vicious means [clutch]
♦악인의 독수에 걸리다[를 벗어나다] fall into [escape from] the clutches of a villain

독수공방 獨守空房 〈남편 출타중의〉 a lonely life in one's husband's absence; 〈독거〉 a solitary life; a lonely life in separation; a widowed life
―독수공방하다 live in solitude with one's husband away from home; lead a solitary life; live as a widow

독수리 禿― 〖鳥〗 an eagle; a vulture
♦독수리 둥지 an aerie [éori]; an aery / 독수리 새끼 an eaglet / 독수리같은 vulturous
―자리 〖天〗 the Eagle; Aquila

독순술 讀脣術 lip reading ♦독순술을 하는 사람 a lip-reader / 독순술로 이해하다[알다] lip-read

독습 獨習 self-study; self-education; self-teaching
♦독습으로 익힌 컴퓨터 지식 knowledge about computers acquired through self-study [self-teaching]; self-taught knowledge about computers
―독습하다 teach oneself (typing); study

without a teacher; learn [practice] by oneself
♦기타를 독습하다 learn to play the guitar by oneself
▶ 그는 영어를 독습하고 있다 He teaches himself English. ⇒ He is studying English by himself [without a teacher].
▶ 그는 라틴어를 책으로 독습했다 He teached himself Latin from a book.
―자 a self-taught person; an autodidact

독시 毒矢 a poisoned [venomed] arrow

독식 獨食 monopoly ―독식하다 monopolize; engross; have [keep] sth to oneself

독신 獨身 single life; celibacy
♦독신의 single; unmarried; celibate / 독신으로 살다 live [remain] single; live as an unmarried man [woman]; lead a bachelor's [spinster's, single] life / 독신으로 마음 편히 살다 live in single blessedness
▶ 그녀는 일생 독신으로 지냈다 She remained unmarried [single] all her life.
■―생활 celibacy; 〈남자〉 bachelorhood; 〈여자〉 spinsterhood ―자 an unmarried person; 〈남자〉 a single man; a bachelor; 〈여자〉 a single woman ―자 아파트 a bachelor apartment house ―주의자 a person who favors [believes in] celibacy; a celibate

독신 篤信 devotion; earnest belief ―독신하다 believe earnestly; be devoted to 《a religion》
―자 a devout believer (in); a devotee (of)

독신 瀆神 blasphemy; desecration; sacrilege
♦독신적인 blasphemous; sacrilegious ―독신하다 blaspheme God

독실 獨室 a single room ⇨ 독방 (獨房)

독실 篤實 sincerity; faithfulness ―독실하다 sincere; faithful; true ♦독실한 사람 a sincere person; a true gentleman / 독실한 신자 a devout [an earnest] believer; a devotee (of)

독심술 讀心術 mind [thought] reading; telepathy ▶ 그는 독심술에 능하다 He is very good at reading other people's minds. ■―사 a mind [thought] reader; a telepathist

독아 毒牙 a (poison) fang ♦악당의 독아에 걸리다 fall victim [a prey] to a scoundrel / 독아를 벗어나다 get out of sb's clutches

독 안에 든 쥐 《속담》 ▶ 그는 독안에 든 쥐와 같다 He is trapped like rat. ⇌ He is in a hopeless fix.

독액 毒液 poisonous liquid [juice, sap]; 〈독사 등의〉 venom

독약 毒藥 a poisonous drug [medicine]; a poison
♦독약을 타다 mix a poison 《with sth》; put poison into 《food》; poison 《food》 / 독약을 먹다 take poison / 독약을 먹이다 poison sb
▶ 포도주에 독약이 들었다 The wine was laced with poison. ⇌ The wine was poisoned [had poison in it].

독어 獨語 1 〈혼잣말〉 monologue; soliloquy 2 ⇨ 독일(~어)

독연 獨演 a solo performance; a recital; a solo 《pl ~s, -li》 ―독연하다 give a solo performance; perform alone
■―자 a soloist; a solo performer ―회 ⇨ 독주(~회)

독오르다 毒— become poisonous [venomous]; become spiteful

독일 獨逸 Germany; 〈공식명〉 the Federal Republic of Germany (略 F.R.G.) (▶1990년 10월 동독과 서독이 독일연방공화국으로 통일함)
♦독일의 German; Germanic
■—어 German; the German language —인[사람] a German; the Germans; the German people —제품 a German production —통일 German unification

독자 獨子 the only son 《of Mr. A》; one's only son

독자 讀者 a reader; 〈구독자〉 a subscriber; 〈독자 대중〉 the reading public; 《총칭》 the audience; the readership
♦독자의 소리 the readers' voice / 독자가 많다 〈신문·잡지가〉 have a large circle of subscribers; have [enjoy] a large circulation; 〈책이〉 be widely read
▶그 잡지는 많은 독자를 확보하고 있다 The magazine has a large circulation.
■ 일 반— general readership —란 the readers' column; letters to the editor —층 a class of readers [subscribers]

독자 獨自 **1** 〈저 혼자〉 one's self
♦독자의 personal; individual / 독자적 견해 one's personal views / 독자(적) 행동을 취하다 act independently of others; go [take] one's own way
2 〈독특성〉 originality; uniqueness
♦독자적인 수영법 an original [one's own] way of swimming / 독자적인 문체 an original [a peculiar, a unique] style / 독자적인 입장에서 from an independent standpoint
▶그는 독자적인 연구를 계속해 나갔다 He continued his research independently [in his own way].
▶이 수필은 저자의 독자적인 유머가 곳곳에 보인다 This essay is jeweled everywhere with the writer's unique humor.

독자성 獨自性 originality; individuality
▶이 계획에는 독자성이 없다 This plan lacks originality.
▶그 민족은 독자성이 있다[없다] The race has maintained [has lost] its identity.

독작하다 獨酌— drink alone [by oneself]; help oneself to wine

독장수셈 an unreliable account; a fruitless [vain] effort ♦독장수셈을 하다 count chickens before they are hatched; sell the skin before one has killed the bear

독장치다 獨場— be the sole master of the situation; play a one-man show; stand unchallenged [without a rival]; reign supreme 《in》

독재 獨裁 dictatorship; despotism; autocracy; absolute rule; absolutism
♦나치 독재 the Nazi dictatorship / 독재의[적인] dictatorial; autocratic; despotic / 독재적으로 dictatorially; despotically; autocratically / 독재 정치를 펴다 impose one-man rule 《on》
▶독일은 한때 히틀러의 독재하에 있었다 Germany was once under Hitler's despotic rule [control].
—독재하다 have 《a country》 under one's despotic rule; hold an absolute authority 《over a project》
■—국가 a despotic state; an autocratic nation —군주 a despotic monarch; a despot; an absolute ruler —군주국 an absolute monarchy; a royal dictatorship —자 a dictator; an autocrat; a despot —정치 dictatorship; dictatorial government —주의 dictatorship; despotism

독전 督戰 urging the soldiers to fight vigorously; leading in battle —독전하다 urge the soldiers to fight (still more) vigorously
■—대 a supervising unit; a command group behind the front lines

독점 獨占 exclusive possession; (a) monopoly; monopolization; engrossment
♦독점적인 monopolistic; exclusive / …의 독점물이 되다 become the exclusive property of…
—독점하다 have [keep, appropriate] sth to oneself; obtain the exclusive possession of; monopolize; make a monopoly of
♦이익을 독점하다 get all the benefits without division; monopolize the profit / 생사 시장을 독점하다 monopolize the (raw) silk market / 서울의 식육 시장을 독점하고 있다 corner [have a monopoly on] the Seoul meat market
▶나는 이 큰 방을 독점하고 있다 I have this big room all to myself.
▶800미터 경주에서는 1위에서 4위까지 미국 선수가 독점했다 The American athletes swept the first four places in the 800-meter race.
■—가격 a monopoly [monopolistic] price —권 (the right to) a monopoly; an exclusive [a sole] right: 이 회사는 석유 판매의 독점권을 가지고 있다 The firm has a monopoly on [《英》of] oil sales. —금지법 《法》 the Antitrust Law; the Antimonopoly Act —도 (度) the degree of monopolization —사업[기업] a monopolistic enterprise [undertaking] —시장 a monopolistic market —욕 a desire for exclusive possession: 독점욕이 강하다 have strong monopolistic desires —자 a monopolizer; a monopolist; a sole owner —자본 monopolistic capital —적 경제 monopoly economy —주의 monopolism —화 monopolization —회사 a monopoly

독점판매 獨占販賣 an exclusive sale
♦독점판매를 하다 make an exclusive sale 《of》 / 독점판매권을 주다 give the sole selling rights [the franchise] / 독점판매의 특약을 맺다 enter into a special contract for the sole agency
■—인 a sole agent [distributor] —점 a sole agent [agency]

독종 毒種 〈사람〉 a cold-blooded [malicious] person; 〈동물〉 a fierce animal; 〈식물〉 a nasty [poisonous] plant; 〈품종〉 malicious offspring; a bad seed

독주 毒酒 〈독한 술〉 strong [hard] liquor; 〈독을 탄 술〉 poisoned liquor

독주 獨走 〈혼자 뜀〉 running alone; 〈낙승〉 a walkaway; a walkover; 《get》 a runaway (victory)

▶ 레이스는 그의 독주였다 He won the race in a walkover.
—독주하다 run alone [without a rival]; leave others far behind; have a walkover
▶ 35킬로미터 지점에서부터 그는 독주하기 시작했다 He began to leave all the other runners far behind after 35km from the starting point.
▶ 금년도 페넌트 레이스에서는 타이거즈팀이 독주할 것이다 The Tigers will get a runaway victory in the pennant race this year.

독주 獨奏 a recital; a solo; a solo performance
—독주하다 play [give] a solo; play alone
◆ 플루트를 독주하다 play a solo on the flute
■—곡 a solo —자 a soloist —회 a solo; a recital: 바이올린[피아노] 독주회를 열다 give [hold] a violin [piano] recital

독지가 篤志家 〈자선가〉 a benevolent person; a philanthropist; a charitable man; 〈솔선자〉 a volunteer; 〈후원자〉 a supporter
◆ 익명의 독지가 an anonymous benefactor
▶ 이 사업에 독지가의 찬조를 바랍니다 We solicit the support of those who are specially interested in the project.

독직 瀆職 (official) corruption; corrupt practices; bribery; (美) graft
▶ 정부 고관의 독직이 발각되었다 Corruption was discovered among high government officials.
—독직하다 practice corruption; take a bribe; graft
■—공무원 a corrupt official; a grafter —사건 a corruption scandal; a bribery [graft, corruption] case —죄 the crime of bribery; a charge of misconduct in office —행위 corrupt practices

독차지 獨— exclusive possession; having [keeping] all to *oneself*; monopoly
—독차지하다 have [keep] all to *oneself*; possess exclusively; monopolize; engross
◆ 유산을 독차지하다 have all the inheritance to *oneself* / 이야기를 독차지하다 monopolize [engross] the conversation / 이익을 독차지하다 take all the profit
▶ 그는 상품을 독차지했다 He carried away all the prizes.

독창 獨唱 a (vocal) solo; a recital —독창하다 sing (a) solo; sing [give] a vocal solo
■—곡 a solo piece —자 a soloist; a solo singer —회 (hold) a (song) recital

독창 獨創 originality; (original) creation
◆ 독창적(인) original; creative / 독창적인 견해 an original idea / 독창적인 연구 a trailblazing study / 놀라울 만큼 독창적인 작품 a strikingly original work; a work of striking originality
—독창하다 create uniquely; originate
■—력 creative [inventive] power: 저 작가는 독창력이 풍부하다 That writer is very original. —성 originality

독채 獨— (live in) an unshared [a separate] house

독초 毒草 〈독풀〉 a poisonous herb; a baneful plant; a noxious plant; 〈독한 담배〉 strong tobacco

독촉 督促 urge; demand; pressing; importunity; 〈빚의〉 dunning
—독촉하다 press [prod] *sb* for *sth*; urge 《*sb* to do》; dun
◆ 빚을 갚으라고 독촉하다 dun *sb* for the payment of a debt
▶ 그에게 빚을 갚으라고 독촉했다 I pressed [pushed] him for payment of his debt.
▶ 나는 그에게 서둘러 답장을 달라고 독촉했다 I demanded a prompt answer of him.
▶ 세탁소에서 아직도 셔츠를 가져 오지 않으니 전화해서 독촉해야겠다 As the laundry has not yet brought my shirt, I will telephone and hurry them up.
▶ 빌린 돈을 빨리 갚으라고 독촉해 와서 나는 궁지에 몰려 있다 I am in a jam, being urged to pay the debt.
▶ 그는 그녀에게 집세를 독촉했다 He pressed [(口) hounded] her for [to pay] the rent.
■—수수료 a 가산(~금) —장 a reminder; a demand note; a dun; 〈빚의〉 a dunning letter [note]

독충 毒蟲 a poisonous [noxious] insect

독침 毒針 〈곤충의 독바늘〉 a poison sting(er); 〈독을 묻힌 바늘〉 a poisoned needle
◆ 독침에 쏘이다 get stung 《by a bee》 / 독침으로 찌르다 prick with a poisonous needle

독탕 獨湯 a private bathroom ◆ 독탕에서 목욕하다 take a bath in a private bathroom

독특하다 獨特 peculiar (to); special; original; unique; characteristic (of)
◆ 독특한 재능 a special talent / 독특한 묘기 one's unique skill / 그 지방의 독특한 억양 the accent peculiar to [characteristic of] that district / 그의 독특한 방법으로 in the way of his own; in his own way
▶ 그의 말하는 투는 독특하다 His manner of speaking is distinctive.
▶ 이 과일은 독특한 향기가 있다 This fruit has a characteristic smell.
▶ 사계절이 각각 그 나름의 독특한 정취가 있다 Each season has its own features.

독파하다 讀破— read 《a book》 through; read 《a book》 to the last page; finish reading 《a book》; go through 《a volume》

독판 獨— 〈독무대〉 one's unrivaled sphere of activity; one's monopoly ◆ 독판치다 stand unchallenged [unrivaled]; monopolize ⇨ 독장치다

독필 毒筆 a spiteful pen; a pen dipped in gall
◆ 독필을 휘두르다 wield a spiteful pen; dip one's pen in gall

독하다 毒— 1 〈유독하다〉 poisonous; venomous; toxic; noxious
◆ 독한 가스 poisonous gas
2 〈강력하다〉 strong; severe; intense; sharp
◆ 독한 술 a strong [potent] wine / 독한 담배 strong tobacco / 독한 냄새 a sharp [strong] odor (of gas)
3 〈악독하다〉 malicious; spiteful; bitter; vicious; venomous; atrocious
4 〈굳세다〉 firm; dogged; tough; unflinching;

unyielding
♦독한 마음 firm resolution / 마음을 독하게 먹고 공부하다 study with firm resolve
독학 篤學 a love of learning; devotion to *one's* studies —**독학하다** devote *oneself* to *one's* studies; study hard [assiduously]
■—자 a diligent student; a devoted scholar
독학 獨學 self-education; self-instruction
▶그는 독학으로 그리스어를 배웠다 He learned Greek on his own.
—**독학하다** study by *oneself*; teach [educate] *oneself* (how to read and write); study without a teacher
♦독학한 영어 English self-taught
▶그는 프랑스어를 독학했다 He studied French without a teacher [(all) by himself]. ⇒ He taught himself French.
■—자 a self-educated[-taught] man; a learner without a teacher; an autodidact
독항선 獨航船 a catcher (boat)
독해력 讀解力 ability to read and understanding; reading comprehension
♦독해력 테스트 a reading comprehension test
독행 篤行 good deeds; charitable work; upright conduct
독행 獨行 1〈혼자 힘으로 일을 함〉self-reliance; pursuing [taking] a course of *one's* own choice; going *one's* (own) way
—**독행하다** act independently; pursue [take] a course of *one's* own choice
2〈혼자 길을 감〉going alone [by *oneself*]; a solitary [companionless] journey
—**독행하다** go alone [by *oneself*]; travel companionless [without a companion]
독혈 毒血 bad [toxic] blood
■—증〔醫〕tox(a)emia; blood poisoning
독화살 毒— a poisoned [venomed] arrow = 독시
독회 讀會 reading
♦제1〔제2, 제3〕독회 the 1st〔2nd, 3rd〕reading; the committee [discussion, voting] stage
▶의안은 제1 독회에 회부되었다 The bill was read for the first time.
▶의안은 제2 독회를 생략하고 가결되었다 The bill was passed, the discussion stage having been dispensed with.
독후감 讀後感 *one's* impressions of a book [an article] ♦독후감 리포트 a book report
돈 〈금전〉money; gold;〈현금〉cash;〈경화〉coin;〈지폐〉(美) a bill; (英) a bank note;〈자금〉funds;〈재산〉wealth; riches;〈통화〉currency

|解說| (1) **money**는 보통 단수형으로 a를 붙이지 않으나 통화의 종류를 나타낼 때는 가산명사로서 different moneys of different countries (여러 나라의 다른 돈)로 사용한다.
(2) moneys 또는 monies와 같이 복수형으로 쓸 때는 보통「(정부 등의) 재원, 기금」의 뜻. tax moneys (세 수입), foreign aid monies (외국 원조 자금) 등을 나타낸다.

♦많은〔적은〕돈 a large [small] sum of money / 부정한 돈 ill-gotten gains;《俗》filthy lucre / 돈 걱정 pecuniary [financial] anxiety / 돈 문제 money [pecuniary] matters / 돈 타령 a song of money; talking about money all the time
▶시간은 돈이다 Time is money.
▶그는 돈 많은 집에서 태어났다 He was born rich.
〈돈의〉돈의 위력 the power of the purse / 돈의 유통 the circulation of money / 돈의 힘으로 by force of money
▶그는 무슨 일이든 돈의 힘으로 해결하려고 한다 He tries to settle everything with money [through the power of money].
〈돈이〉돈이 있다 have money; be in funds; have plenty of money; be rich; be well off / 돈이 없다 have no money; be out of funds; be poor; be badly off / 돈이 모이다 come to have some money saved / 돈이 벌리는 일 a fat job; lucrative [profitable] work / 돈이 생기다 grow [get] rich; make money / 돈이 들다 be expensive; be costly; cost *one* much [a great deal of] money / 돈이 달리다 be short of money; be hard up (for money)
▶돈이 말하다, 돈이면 다된다 Money talks.
▶돈이 많으면 근심도 많다 (속담) Much coin, much care.
▶돈이 거짓말한다 (속담) Debtors are liars.
▶돈이 장사라 (속담) Money is power.
▶돈은 돌고 돈다 (속담) Money comes and goes. ⇒ Money is always changing hands.
▶돈이 떨어지면 정분도 떨어진다 (속담) When poverty comes in, love flies out. ⇒ Money gone, friends gone.
▶그 사전을 살만한 돈이 없다 I don't have enough money to buy the dictionary (with).
▶오늘은 돈이 없으니 내일 지불하겠소 I have no money (with me) today, so I'll pay you tomorrow.
▶지금 그것을 팔면 돈이 된다 If you sold that now you'd get a lot of money for it.
▶돈이 생기지 않는 일을 하는 것은 어리석다 It is absurd to do a job that does not pay.
▶돈이 아쉽다 I need money badly! ⇒ If only I had money enough!
▶마침 가진 돈이 없다 I have no money about [with] me.
〈돈을〉돈을 벌다 make [earn] money / 돈을 쉽게 벌다 make money with wet fingers; make easy money / 돈을 많이 벌다 make [amass] a fortune / 돈을 모으다 save [hoard] money; amass money; fatten *one's* purse / 일해서 돈을 벌다 earn an honest money / 돈을 낭비하다 waste money; make the money fly / 돈을 빌려주다 lend *sb* money / 돈을 변통하다 manage to raise money / 돈을 물쓰듯하다 spend *one's* money recklessly [freely] 《on》; squander *one's* money 《on》/ 돈을 부치다 remit money 《through a bank》; send money 《by postal order》/ 담보물을 잡히고 돈을 빌리다 borrow money on *one's* property / 돈을 갚다 repay [pay back] money; return money / 돈을 보고 결혼하다 marry *sb* for money; marry money / 돈을 은행에 맡기다 put [deposit] money in a bank / 돈을 걸다 bet

with money; bet money 《on》/ 돈을 뿌리다 fling money about
▶ 돈을 좀 빌려주지 않으시겠습니까? Will you lend me some money?
▶ 그는 돈을 물쓰듯한다 He spends money like water. ⇌ He is too free with his money. ⇌ He is a spendthrift.
▶ 차를 사려고 돈을 모으고 있다 I am saving money to buy a car. ⇌ I am saving (up) money for a car.
▶ 시계를 팔아 돈을 만들었다 I sold my watch to get some money.
▶ 그 불쌍한 아이들을 위해 돈을 마련했다 We raised money for the poor children.
▶ 나는 고리로 돈을 빌렸다 I borrowed money at high interest.
▶ 빌렸던 돈을 갚았다 I paid back the money I had borrowed.
▶ 없는 돈을 털어 그에게 줄 선물을 샀다 I spent what little money I had to buy a present for him.
▶ 그녀는 추리소설을 써서 돈을 벌고 있다 She makes [earns] money by writing detective stories.
▶ 피아노 살 돈을 입학금으로 썼다 I used the money I was going to buy a piano with to pay the school entrance fee.
▶ 나는 많은 돈을 들여 책을 샀다 I spent a large sum of money on books.
▶ 그는 투기로 돈을 탕진해버렸다 He has run out of money in (a) speculation.
▶ 저쪽에서 돈을 지불해 주십시오 Please pay over there.
▶ 나는 아르바이트를 해서 돈을 벌어야 한다 I have to earn money by (doing) a part-time job.
▶ 너를 위해서라면 기꺼이 돈을 내놓겠다 You are welcome to my money.
〈돈에〉 돈에 구애받지 않고 sparing no money; without regard to cost / 돈에 팔리다 sell *oneself* / 돈에 정신이 없다 be eager for money; be venal / 사랑에 속고 돈에 울다 be lucky neither at cards nor at love
▶ 그는 돈에 쪼들리고 있다 He is pinched [hard up, pressed] for money.
▶ 나는 돈에 쪼들려 집을 팔았다 I sold the house because I was short of money.
▶ 그는 돈에 눈이 멀어 도둑질을 했다 He stole because he was blinded by money.
▶ 그는 돈에 궁색하지 않다 He is well-to-do [well off].
〈돈으로〉 돈으로 따져 in money value / 돈으로 살 수 없는 priceless; beyond price / 돈으로 매수되지 않는 사람 a soul above money / 돈으로 학교에 들어가다 buy *one's* way into a school / 돈으로 바꾸다 turn [convert] *sth* into money / 수표를 돈으로 바꾸다 cash a check / 증권을 돈으로 바꾸다 sell [realize] securities / 돈으로 지불하다 pay in money
▶ 그는 자기 돈으로 시집을 출판했다 He had his poems printed at his own expense.
▶ 나는 그 책을 내 돈으로 샀다 I bought the book with my own money.
▶ 그것은 미국 돈으로 100달러다 It costs 100 dollars in U.S. currency.
▶ 그는 돈으로 유혹당할 사람이 아니다 He is not a man who can be seduced by [with] money.
▶ 사람의 목숨은 돈으로 바꿀 수 없다 Money cannot pay for *one's* life.
▶ 자기 돈으로 해외여행을 가야 한다 You should go abroad at your own expense.
〈기타〉 돈 때문에 for (love of) money / 돈 때문에 일하다 work merely for money / 돈과 인연이 없다 be doomed to poverty / 돈과 명예를 바라다 desire for wealth and fame
■—궤 a cash [money] box —꿰미 a string of coppers —지갑 a wallet; a pocketbook —치기 (play) chuck-farthing; coin-tossing —표 〈수표·어음 등〉 a voucher; a check

돈 〈무게의 단위〉 a *don* (=3.7565 grams, 0.1325 ounces)

돈 〈강 이름〉 the Don River

돈구멍 1 〈돈줄〉 a source of money; a source of income ◆돈구멍을 뚫다 find a way of getting [raising, borrowing] money **2** 〈금속 화폐에 뚫린 구멍〉 a hole in the middle of a coin

돈내기 a bet; gambling ▶ 돈내기 바둑은 좋지 않다 It's no good to play *paduk* for money [gamble at *paduk*].

돈냥 —兩 a small sum of money ⇨ 돈푼

돈놀이 money-lending (business); 〈고리 대금업〉 usury —**돈놀이하다** loan; run money-lending business; practice usury —**꾼** a moneylender; a moneymonger; 〈고리 대금업자〉 a usurer

돈대 墩臺 a high place; a high ground; a mound of earth ▶ 그의 집은 돈대 위에 있다 His house stands on a high ground.

돈더미 a heap of money ◆돈더미에 올라 앉다 get [become] rich suddenly; gain quick riches

돈독 —毒 an unhealthy taste for money; mercenariness
◆돈독이 오르다 acquire an unhealthy taste for money; become mercenary / 돈독이 오른 사람 a person of mercenary spirit; a money-grubber

돈독하다 敦篤— gentle and sincere; courteous; affable; friendly ◆한미 관계를 돈독히 하다 promote friendly relations between Korea and America
▶ 그는 우정이 돈독한 사람이다 He is true to his friends.

돈만 있으면 개도 멍첨지라 (속담) Money makes (the) man.

돈만 있으면 귀신도 부릴 수 있다 (속담) A golden key can open any door. ⇌ Everything can be settled by money even in Hell. ⇌ Money makes the mare (to) go.

돈맛 the charm of money; a love of money
◆돈맛을 알다 be charmed by money; learn the value [charm] of money / 돈맛을 들이다 get [acquire] a taste for money
▶ 돈맛을 알면 사람이 인색해진다 One grows stingy when one learns the charm of money.

돈머리 〈돈의 액수〉 a (given) sum [amount] of money ◆돈머리를 맞추다 round the sum off / 돈머리가 모자라다 be short to make up

돈모 豚毛 swine [hog] bristles ▶ 이 솔은 돈모로 만든다 This brush is made of swine bristles.

돈바르다 (be) narrow-minded; fussy

돈방석 ◆돈방석에 앉아 있다 have plenty of money; be well-off

돈벌이 moneymaking
◆돈벌이에만 급급하다 be too much bent on moneymaking / 돈벌이를 잘하는 사람 a moneymaker; (俗) a golden thumb
▶ 그 일은 돈벌이가 된다 That's a fat job.
▶ 그는 돈벌이를 잘한다 He is clever at making money. ⇒ He is a moneymaker.
▶ 저 사람은 돈벌이에 열심이다 He is bent on making money. ⇒ He is anxious to get rich.
▶ 저 회사는 돈벌이밖에 모른다 That company is bent solely upon profit.
—**돈벌이하다** make money; make a fortune
◆돈벌이하러 해외로 나가다 go abroad to make money

돈벼락맞다 get [become] rich suddenly; gain quick riches; strike a bonanza

돈복 —福 bliss with money; good luck in moneymaking ◆돈복이 있다 be blessed with a chance to make money / 돈복이 터지다 hit a source of wealth

돈사 豚舍 a pigsty; a pigpen

돈사 頓死 a sudden [an untimely] death
—**돈사하다** die suddenly; die a sudden [an unexpected] death

돈세탁 money laundering; money-washing

돈수 頓首 〈편지의 맺음말〉 Your's (very) respectfully [truly]; Sincerely Yours; Respectfully yours

돈아 豚兒 〈자기 아들〉 my son; my boy

돈육 豚肉 pork

돈이 돈을 번다 (속담) Money begets Money. ⇒ Money draws money.

돈이 없으면 적막 강산이요, 돈이 있으면 금수 강산이라 (속담) Money makes a man free everywhere.

돈좌 頓挫 a setback; a check —**돈좌하다** be checked; receive a setback; be brought to a standstill

돈주머니 a (coin) purse; a moneybag; a pocketbook
◆묵직한 돈주머니 a plump [fat] purse / 돈주머니가 가볍다 have a light purse / 돈주머니를 털다 empty *one's* purse to the last penny; clear *one's* purse out
▶ 우리 집에서는 아내가 돈주머니를 움켜쥐고 있다 My wife holds the purse strings in my family.

돈줄 a source of revenue; financial resources; 〈전주〉 a rich patron; a financial supporter
◆돈줄을 잡다 find a supplier of funds [a financial supporter]
▶ 돈줄을 잡았기 때문에 사업이 회복되어 가고 있었다 As he struck oil, business was picking up.

돈지랄하다 spend money in a crazy way

돈키호테 Don Quixote

◆**돈키호테식의** quixotic(al)

돈푼 a small sum of money; a small fortune
◆돈푼깨나 모으다 save a pretty penny; make a small fortune
▶ 돈푼깨나 있다고 으스대지 마라 Don't boast yourself of your small fortune.

돈후안 〈방탕아〉 a Don Juan; a libertine
◆돈 후안 형의 a Don Juan type
▶ 그는 돈후안이니까 조심해라 Do be careful as he is a Don Juan.

돋구다 1 〈더 높이다〉 raise; make higher
◆안경의 도수를 돋구다 make *one's* glasses stronger / 목청을 돋구다 raise [lift (up)], put forth] *one's* voice; raise *one's* pitch
2 ⇨ 돋우다

돋다 1 〈솟아 오르다〉 rise; come up
▶ 해는 동쪽에서 돋는다 The sun rises [comes up] in the east.
2 〈생겨 나오다〉 grow; bud; sprout; spring up; come up; shoot (forth)
◆날개가 돋다 grow wings / 이가 돋아나다 cut a tooth
▶ 싹이 돋았다 The buds are out.
▶ 새 잎이 돋았다 The new leaves have shot forth.
▶ 뜰에 잡초가 돋기 시작했다 Weeds have started growing in the garden.
▶ 사슴의 뿔이 돋아나고 있다 The deer is sprouting a horn.
▶ 갓난아기의 이가 하나 돋았다 The baby has cut a tooth.
3 〈우툴두툴하게 내밀다〉 break out; come out; erupt; form
◆여드름이 돋다 pimples break [come] out 《on [in] *one's* face》 / 좁쌀 같은 것이 돋다 have rashes 《on the arm》

돋보기 1 〈노안용〉 glasses [spectacles] for the aged; convex [long-distance] glasses; 〈독서용의〉 reading glasses (for the aged)
▶ 그는 돋보기를 끼고 책을 보고 있다 He is reading with his reading glasses on.
2 〈확대경〉 a magnifying glass; a magnifier
◆돋보기로 보다 see through a magnifying glass; take a close look 《at》 through a magnifier

돋보이다 look better (than actually is); improve [be improved] in appearance; look [show] to advantage
◆돋보이게 하다 show to advantage; set off; make *sth* look better
▶ 가구를 이렇게 놓으니 한결 돋보인다 The furniture looks much better in this position.
▶ 이 바탕에서는 붉은 색이 가장 돋보인다 In this pattern red is the predominant color.
▶ 이 그림을 벽에 걸면 이 방이 한결 돋보일 겁니다 If you hang this picture on the wall, this room will look better [improve in appearance].
▶ 검은 머리가 흰 피부를 돋보이게 한다 Dark hair sets off a fair complexion.
▶ 그 자줏빛 옷이 그녀를 돋보이게 한다 That purple dress sets her off to advantage. ⇒ She looks better in that purple dress.
▶ 나무들이 건물의 아름다움을 돋보이게 해준다

돋우다 1 〈심지를〉 raise; lift (up)
♦ 등잔의 심지를 돋우다 turn up the wick; screw up a lamp
2 〈자극하다〉 irritate; stimulate; incite; excite; provoke; aggravate
♦ 감정을 돋우다 stimulate [stir up] *sb's* sentiment [feelings] / 화[부아]를 돋우다 aggravate *sb* to anger / 식욕을 돋우다 tempt [stimulate] *one's* appetite / 호기심을 돋우다 excite *one's* curiosity
3 〈높이다〉 raise; heighten
♦ 땅을 돋우다 raise the ground level / 베개를 돋우다 make *one's* pillow higher; raise *one's* pillow
4 〈고무하다〉 raise; lift; elevate; heighten; encourage; cheer up; inspire; inspirit
♦ 기운을 돋우다 raise [lift] *one's* spirits; cheer up; invigorate / 사기를 돋우다 heighten [stir up] the morale 《of troops》 / 용기를 돋우다 encourage; embolden; give *sb* courage; put *sb* on his mettle
5 〈부추기다〉 abet; incite; instigate; stir up; egg on
♦ 싸움을 돋우다 egg *sb* on to fight 《with another》; make 《persons》 quarrel

돋을무늬 a raised figure; an embossed figure
♦ 돋을무늬를 내다 emboss; raise

돋을새김 relief ⇨ 부조《浮彫》

돋치다 1 〈돋아서 내밀다〉 grow; come out; rise [sprout] up
♦ 가시 돋친 말 stinging [barbed] words; harsh language / 날개가 돋치다 grow wings / 날개 돋친 듯 팔리다 sell like wildfire [hotcakes]
2 〈값이 오르다〉 rise [jump] in price

돌¹ 〈주년《周年》〉 an anniversary
♦ 창립 열 돌 맞이 기념행사를 하다 observe the tenth anniversary of the opening
▶ 집을 지은 지 두 돌이 된다 It is two years since I built the house.
▶ 이 회사는 20돌을 맞는다 This company is going to celebrate the 20th anniversary.
2 〈첫돌〉 the first birthday
♦ 돌을 맞다 mark [celebrate] *one's* first birthday
▶ 우리 아기의 돌이 다가온다 The first birthday of our baby is coming around.

돌² **1** 〈천연의〉 a stone; a pebble; 《美口》 a rock; 〈쌀 등에 섞여 있는〉 a grit; 〈라이터의〉 a flint
♦ 돌의《같은》 stony; lithic / 돌이 많은 stony; full of stones / 돌처럼 차가운[단단한] (as) cold [hard] as (a) stone / 돌이 되다 turn to stone; petrify / 돌을 깔다 pave 《the road》 with stone / 돌을 던지다 throw a stone at 《a dog》; pelt *sb* with a stone / 돌을 떠[잘라]내다 quarry (out) stones / 돌에 새기다 carve [cut] in stone / 돌로 쳐죽이다 stone *sb* to death
▶ 쌀에 돌이 있다 There are grits in the rice.
▶ 돌처럼 딱딱해서 먹을 수가 없다 It's as hard as a rock, so I can't eat it.

돌감 〈야생감〉 a wild persimmon
돌개바람 a whirlwind ⇨ 회오리바람
돌격 突擊 a dash; a rush; a charge; an onrush
♦ 우리는 돌격해서 요새를 점령했다 We rushed a fort. = We carried a fort with a rush.
—**돌격하다** charge 《at, on》; rush [dash] 《at》; make a dash at; make an assault (up)on
▶ 아군은 적을 향해서 돌격했다 Our troops made a dash at [for] the enemy.
▶ 기병대는 적진으로 돌격했다 The cavalry rushed to the enemy's position. = The cavalry charged the enemy.
■ —나팔 charge: 돌격 나팔을 불다 sound the charge —대 a storming party [corps]; a shock troop

돌계단 —階段 (a flight of) stone steps; a stone stairway; 〈한 단〉 a stone step
▶ 돌계단을 올라가면 붉은 색의 새집이 나온다 A flight of stone steps leads you to a red birdhouse.

돌고래 〔動〕 a dolphin; a porpoise
—**자리** 〔天〕 the Dolphin; Delphinus

돌관 突貫 〔軍〕 a charge; a rush
—**돌관하다** charge forward with a shout; charge 《on》; rush 《at》

돌관공사 突貫工事 rush [lightning] work
♦ 돌관공사를 하다 rush the construction work
▶ 그 다리는 돌관공사로 건설되었다 The bridge construction was a rush job.

돌기 突起 a projection; a prominence; a protuberance; a boss; 〔生〕 a process; 〔解〕 a promontory
—**돌기하다** project; protrude; rise
♦ 돌기한 projecting 《teeth》; protuberant; prominent; salient
■ —충양 vermiform appendix

돌기둥 a stone pillar [column]

돌다 1 〈회전하다〉 turn (round); go round; circle; revolve; rotate; spin
▶ 지구는 돈다 The earth turns.
▶ 달은 지구의 주위를 돈다 The moon turns around the earth.
▶ 지구는 자전하면서 태양의 주위를 돈다 The earth, rotating on its own axis, goes around the sun.
▶ 그는 발뒤축으로 빙글 돌았다 He turned on his heel(s).
▶ 팽이가 조용히 돌고 있다 The top is spinning silently.
▶ 선풍기가 세게 돌고 있었다 The (electric) fan was working hard.
▶ 비행기는 공항의 상공을 세 번 돌았다 The airplane circled above the airport three times.
▶ 발레리나는 스커트를 휘날리며 멋지게 돌았다 The ballerina turned round beautifully with her skirt waving about her.
2 〈순찰하다〉 make a round; go (on) *one's* rounds; walk *one's* beat; patrol; 〈유람하다〉 make a tour; tour; travel about
♦ 공원을 한 바퀴 돌다 take a walk through the park / 야경을 돌다 go [make] *one's* rounds at night / 호남 지방을 돌다 make [take] a tour of the Honam district
▶ 나는 매일 농장을 한 바퀴 돈다 Every day I make a round of the farm.
▶ 이 호텔에서는 경비원이 끊임없이 구내를 돌고 있다 Security guards constantly patrol this

hotel.
▶ 경찰관이 순찰을 돌고 있다 The policeman is on the beat.
▶ 이번 가을에는 한 달 정도 유럽을 돌 예정이다 This autumn I am going to tour Europe for a month or so.
3 〈방향을 바꾸다〉 turn (about); make a turn; 〈전향하다〉 swing; switch (over)
♦ 뒤로 돌다 turn round [around] / 오른쪽[왼쪽]으로 돌다 turn to the right [left] (hand); turn right [left] / 모퉁이를 돌다 turn [go round] the corner / 정부 지지로 돌다 swing over to the Administration
▶ 차는 급커브를 돌았다 The car turned the curve all of a sudden.
▶ 그 집은 모퉁이를 돈 곳에 있다 The house stands round [around] the corner.
▶ 담배 가게를 따라 왼쪽으로 돌면 병원이 나옵니다 Turn to the left along the cigar store, and you will find the hospital.
4 〈우회하다〉 go round; detour; go by a detour; take a roundabout way; go a long way about
♦ 많이 돌다 make a long circuit [detour] / 산을 돌아서 가다 go round [bypass] a mountain
▶ 배는 케이프 혼을 돌아 인도양으로 향했다 The ship went round Cape Horn and headed toward the Indian Ocean.
▶ 모스크바로 돌아서 런던으로 갈 예정이다 I intend to go to London via [by way of] Moscow.
5 〈약・술 기운 등이〉 take effect
♦ 기운이 돌기 시작하다 begin to feel the effect 《of》 / 술 기운이 돌다 grow [become, get] tipsy; feel intoxication coming on; feel the effect of drink
▶ 독이 그의 온몸에 돌았다 The poison has passed into his system.
▶ 술 기운이 도니 기분이 좋았다 I felt good as the wine took hold.
6 〈유통・순환하다〉 circulate; pass current; 〈차례로〉 pass
♦ (물건이) 돌고 돌아 passing through many hands / 술이 몇 순배 돈 다음에 after the cup has circulated a few times; after wine has gone round several times / 피가 돌다 the blood circulates / 회람장이 돌다 a circular passes
▶ 돈이란 돌고 도는 것이다 Money will come and go.
▶ 불경기라서 돈이 잘 안 돈다 Money is tight owing to the trade depression.
7 〈소문이〉 spread (abroad); be in circulation; be abroad; circulate
♦ …이라는 소문이 돌고 있다 a rumor is abroad [current, in circulation] about...
8 〈돌림병이〉 prevail; be prevalent [widespread]
▶ 감기가 돈다 A cold is making the rounds.
▶ 전국적으로 독감이 돌고 있다 Influenza is prevailing throughout the country.
9 〈생기다〉 bear; yield; produce
♦ 얼굴에 화색이 돌다 have a good [healthy] complexion; 《美》 look rosy / 윤기가 돌다 be glossy [lustrous]
▶ 내 눈에 눈물이 핑 돌았다 Tears stood [gathered] in my eyes.
10 〈몸의 기능이〉 work; function; operate
♦ 혀가 잘 돌다 be oily-tongued; have a glib tongue / 머리가 잘 돌지 않다 be slow-[half-]witted; be dull-brained; be slow of understanding / 혀가 잘 돌지 않다 be tongue-tied; be inarticulate; lisp
▶ 그는 머리가 잘 돈다 He is quick-[sharp-]witted. ⇌ He has a clever head [nimble brain].
▶ 그 애는 혀가 잘 돌지 않는 말로 기도를 올렸다 The child lisped out his prayers.
11 〈현기증이 나다〉 be [feel] dizzy; get [feel] giddy ♦ 눈이 뱅뱅 돌다 feel dizzy [giddy]; *one's* head reels [swims]
▶ 나는 바빠서 눈이 돌 지경이다 I am in a whirl of businesss.
12 〈미치다〉 go off *one's* head; 《俗》 be off *one's* nut [rocker]; 《口》 go barmy; 《英俗》 go balmy; go [become] mad [insane]
▶ 머리가 돌 것만 같다 I feel like I'm going to lose my mind [go crazy].
▶ 그는 머리가 좀 돌았다 He is touched in the head.
▶ 그런 짓을 하다니 그 노인 정신이 좀 돈 모양이군 The old man must have a screw loose to do such a thing.

돌다리¹ 〈조그만 다리〉 a low bridge over a brook
돌다리² 〈석교〉 a stone bridge
돌다리도 두드려 보고 건너라 《속담》 Look before you leap. ▶ 그는 돌다리를 두드려 보고도 건너지 않을 사람이다 He is the sort of man who won't risk anything.
돌담 a stone wall
♦ 돌담을 두르다 surround with a stone wall; wall round with stone
돌담불 a heap [pile] of stones; a rock pile
돌대가리 **1** 〈우둔한 사람〉 a stupid fellow; a blockhead; 《口》 a pumpkin head **2** 〈완고한 사람〉 an obstinate [incorrigible] person
돌덩이 a (piece of) stone; 《美口》 a rock
♦ 돌덩이 같다 be hard as a rock [granite, brick]
돌도끼 〖考古〗 a stone ax(e)
돌돌 1 〈마는 모양〉 into a roll [scroll, ball]
♦ 종이를 돌돌 말다 roll up [twirl] a sheet of paper / 머리를 돌돌 말다 curl *one's* hair
2 〈구르는 모양〉 with a twirl [whirl]
♦ 돌돌 구르다 roll over and over / 물레바퀴가 돌돌 돌아가는 소리 the whirl of a spinning wheel
3 〈뭉치는 모양〉 ♦ 돌돌 뭉치다 solidify unity
돌떡 rice cake made for a baby's first birthday
돌라대다 give an evasive answer ⇨ 둘러대다
돌라막다 enclose ⇨ 둘러막다
돌라방치다 substitute; replace; change
돌라서다 stand in a circle ⇨ 둘러서다
돌라싸다 surround ⇨ 둘러싸다
돌라앉다 sit round ⇨ 둘러앉다
돌라주다 distribute; share (out); serve out

돌라치다

[round] 《food》; deal out
♦전단을 돌라주다 distribute handbills / 선물을 돌라주다 share gifts 《among》 / 트럼프 카드를 돌라주다 deal cards 《to the players》

돌라치다 substitute ⇨ 돌라방치다

돌려나기 〔植〕 verticillation

돌려내다 1 〈빼돌리다〉 win [gain, bring] over; 〈꾀어내다〉 lure away; tempt in; entice into
♦다른회사의 직공을 돌려내다 hire a worker away from another company
2 〈따돌리다〉 leave *sb* out in the cold

돌려놓다 change the position 《of》; change direction; turn 《about》; shift; veer 《round》
♦책상을 돌려놓다 put a desk the other way round / 의자들을 돌려놓다 rearrange a set of chairs

돌려보내다 send back; return ♦심부름꾼을 돌려보내다 send back a messenger
▶그는 아내를 친정으로 돌려보냈다 He sent back his wife to her parents.
▶여자를 밤에 혼자 돌려보내면 안된다 You should not send a girl back home alone at night.
▶그 상품은 견본과 달라서 돌려보냈다 The article was sent back as not being up to sample.

돌려보다 have a look at *sth* by turns passing it around; read and pass on; send round 《a notice》 ♦책을 돌려보다 pass a book around reading it in turns

돌려쓰다 〈빌리다〉 borrow 《*sth* from *sb*》

돌려주다 1 〈반환하다〉 return; give [pay] back ♦돈을 돌려주다 pay *one's* debt; pay the money back / 빌린 책을 돌려주다 return *sb* a borrowed book
▶주운 물건은 떨어뜨린 사람에게 돌려주어야 한다 One should return [give back] a thing that one picks up to the person who dropped it.
▶이 테이프는 다음 일요일에 돌려주겠다 I will return this tape to you next Sunday.
2 〈빌려주다〉 lend; accommodate 《*sb* with a loan》

돌려짓기 〔農〕 crop rotation; rotation [shift] of crops —**돌려짓기하다** rotate crops
▶농부는 감자와 토마토를 돌려짓기하고 있다 The farmer rotates potatoes with tomatoes.

돌리다[1] 1 〈회전시키다〉 turn; spin; revolve 《a wheel》; wheel; whirl; rotate
♦팽이를 돌리다 spin a top / 프로펠러를 돌리다 rotate [spin] a propeller / 지팡이를 빙빙 돌리다 whirl a stick / 손잡이를 오른쪽으로 돌리다 turn the knob to the right / 시계바늘을 앞으로[뒤로] 돌리다 set [put] the hands forward [back]
▶나사를 한번 더 돌리시오 Give another turn to the screw.
▶나는 병마개를 돌려 뺐다 I turned the cap of the bottle off.
▶그는 의자에 앉은 채 몸을 빙 돌렸다 He wheeled around in his chair.
2 〈방향을 바꾸다〉 turn 《about, around, over, toward》; shift; veer 《round》; direct 《to, toward》; wheel; screw

♦고개를 돌리다 turn *one's* head around / 시선을 돌리다 avert [turn away] *one's* eyes 《from》 / 등을 돌리다 turn *one's* back 《to, on》; 〈변절하다〉 change about [*one's* coat]; turn round; 〈도중에서〉 turn back on the way out / 뱃머리를 돌리다 veer [wind] a ship / 기수(機首)를 남쪽으로 돌리다 head for the south; take a southern course
▶배를 기슭 쪽으로 돌립시다 Let's steer the boat toward shore.
▶얼굴을 이쪽으로 돌리세요 Please turn your face toward me.
▶그는 고개를 돌려 나를 보았다 He screwed his head round to see me.
▶나는 달리는 여우를 향해 총부리를 돌렸다 I pointed my gun at a running fox.
▶그는 차의 방향을 급히 돌려서 사고를 피했다 He averted the accident by a quick turn of the car.
3 〈차례로 전하다〉 send [pass, hand] round
♦다음으로 돌리다 pass on to the next / 술잔을 돌리다 pass the wine cup round / 회람장을 돌리다 pass on a circular notice / 책을 돌려가며 읽다 circulate a book
▶그들은 위스키 한 병을 돌려가며 마셨다 They passed around a bottle of whiskey.
▶의장은 돌려가며 하기로 하자 We'll be chairman by turns.
▶그 사진을 모두가 돌려가며 보았다 The photograph was passed (a)round for everyone to see.
4 〈생각을〉 think better of; change; alter
♦마음을 돌리다 change *one's* mind 《from》; reconsider *one's* resolution / 마음을 돌려 새사람이 되다 turn over a new leaf; mend *one's* ways / 설득해서 마음을 돌리게 하다 talk [persuade] *sb* out of 《his》 resolution
▶나는 생각을 돌려 도중에서 되돌아왔다 I changed my mind and turned back halfway.
5 〈원인·책임을〉 attribute [ascribe] to; set [put] down *sth* to *sb*; impute 《a crime》 to *sb*
♦성공을 행운으로 돌리다 attribute [credit] *one's* success to luck / 실패를 운이 나쁜 탓으로 돌리다 ascribe [impute] *one's* failure to bad luck
▶의사는 그의 병을 과음한 탓으로 돌렸다 The doctor attributed the cause of his illness to his overdrinking.
▶그는 자기의 실패를 병 탓으로 돌렸다 He imputed his failure to ill health.
6 〈영광을〉 bring; yield; concede
♦영광을 하나님께[모교에] 돌리다 bring glory to God [*one's* alma mater] / 승리의 영광을 조국에 돌리다 yield [give] the palm (of victory) to *one's* fatherland
7 〈미루다〉 defer; postpone; put off
♦뒤로 돌리다 let *sth* wait [stand over]; hold over / 뒤로 돌려지다 be put off; take a backseat to 《another problem》 / 의안의 토의를 뒤로 돌리다 sidetrack the discussion of a bill
▶그건 나중으로 돌려도 된다 That can be left over. ⇌ That can wait. ⇌ You can let it wait.
▶그건 뒤로 돌리고 이 문제부터 검토합시다

Let's discuss this matter first, leaving that till later on.
8 〈도르다〉 deliver; distribute; send out
♦신문을 돌리다 deliver newspapers/ 초청장을 돌리다 send out invitations
▶선생님은 학생들에게 시험지를 돌렸다 The teacher distributed [passed out, handed out] examination papers to the students.
▶괴상한 옷차림을 한 사람이 전단을 돌리고 있었다 A man in a strange costume was distributing [giving out] handouts [handbills].
9 〈회부하다〉 transmit; send round 《a bill to》; refer 《a matter to》
♦서류를 담당자에게 돌리다 send the papers over to the man in charge / 사건을 다른 부서로 돌리다 refer a matter to another office / 의안을 위원회로 돌리다 refer a bill to a committee
10 〈전임시키다〉 transfer
▶그는 인사과로 돌려졌다 He was transferred to the personnel (affairs) section.
11 〈충당하다〉 divert 《*sth* to some other purpose》; appropriate [apply, assign] 《to》
▶그의 기부금은 도서비로 돌려졌다 His donation was earmarked for (the purchase of) books.
12 〈가동·운영하다〉 run; work; operate; drive; set [put] in motion ♦공장을 돌리다 operate a plant / 기계를 돌리다 set a machine in motion; run [work] a machine
13 〈기타〉 ♦농담으로 돌리다 treat [take] *sth* as a joke / 백지로 돌리다 bring to [set at] naught

돌리다² **1** 〈병의 고비를 넘기다〉 turn the corner; pass the crisis [critical point]; take a turn for the better; be over the hump
▶열이 내리면서 그는 병세를 돌렸다 He turned the corner with the fever passed.
2 〈쉬다〉 ♦한숨 돌리다 after a pause / 잠시 숨을 돌리다 take [have] a rest [breather]
▶한숨 돌리고 나서 다시 일을 시작하자 Let's have a little rest, and start again.
▶빚을 다 갚았으니 이제 숨 좀 돌리겠다 I can breathe easy now that I have paid all my debts.
3 〈노여움이 풀리(게 하)다〉 cool down
▶그녀의 말이 그의 노여움을 돌렸다 Her words appeased [softened, pacified] his anger.
4 〈변통하다〉 borrow ♦땅을 담보로 돈을 돌리다 borrow [raise] money on *one's* estate
▶백만원쯤 돌릴 수 없을까요? Can you afford to lend me one million won?

돌림 1 〈교대〉 turn; rotation ♦돌림으로 alternately; in turn; by turns; by [in] rotation
2 〈따돌림〉 exclusion; ostracism
♦돌림을 받다 be left out in the cold; be excluded; incur ostracism
3 〈전염병〉 something passed round
■ —**병** an epidemic; 〈가축의〉 an epizootic —**자(字)** 〈항렬자〉 a letter of *sb's* given name which is common to the same generation of 《his》kinsfolk(s) —**쟁이** a person left out in the cold; 〈사회적으로〉 an [a social] outcast —**턱** a treat given by turns; 《provide》 a round of entertainment —**판** a circular notice —**편지** a circular letter

돌림노래 〔樂〕 a troll; a round
돌매 a hand mill ⇨ 맷돌
돌멘 〈고인돌〉 a dolmen; a cromlech
돌멩이 a (small) stone; a cobble(stone); 《美口》 a rock
돌멩이질 stone-throwing; stone-slinging
—**돌멩이질하다** sling [throw] a stone 《at》; pelt *sb* with stones; pelt stones at
돌무더기 a pile [heap] of stones
돌무덤 a stone grave; a cairn
돌미나리 〔植〕 wild parsley
돌미륵 —**彌勒** a stone Buddhist image
돌반지기 〈잔돌이 많은 쌀〉 gritty rice
돌발 突發 a burst; an outbreak
♦돌발적인 sudden; unexpected; unforeseen / 돌발적으로 suddenly; unexpectedly / 돌발(적인) 사태에 대비하다 be prepared for the unexpected (to happen)
▶그런 돌발 사고는 막을 방도가 없다 There is no way of preventing such a totally unforeseen accident.
—**돌발하다** break out; burst forth [out]; occur suddenly
▶중동에서 전쟁이 돌발했다 A war broke out in the Middle East.
돌배 〈야생배〉 a wild pear
돌변 突變 a sudden change [turn]
—**돌변하다** change suddenly; undergo a sudden change; take a sudden turn
▶날씨가 돌변했다 The weather suddenly changed.
▶그녀의 병세가 돌변했다 〈악화했다〉 Her condition has taken a sudden turn for the worse.
▶그것을 듣고 그의 태도가 돌변했다 He changed his attitude suddenly, when he heard it. ⇌ His attitude changed suddenly on hearing it.
돌보다 take care of; look after; care for; attend (to); tend
♦양을 돌보는 목동들 shepherds tending their sheep / 아기를 돌보다 nurse [look after] a child; baby-sit
▶딸이 아프기 때문에 당분간 우리가 손자들을 돌보기로 했어요 As our daughter is ill, we decided to keep our grandchildren under our care for some time.
돌부리 a jagged edge [point] of a stone
♦돌부리를 차고 넘어지다 trip over the edge of a stone
돌부리를 차면 발부리만 아프다 《속담》Don't kick against the pricks [goad]. ⇌ Don't cut off your nose to spite your face.
돌부처 1 a stone (image of) Buddha
▶그는 돌부처 처럼 말이 없다 He is as silent [taciturn] as a stone Buddha.
2 〈고집센 사람〉 a stubborn person
돌비 —碑 〈기념비〉 a stone monument; 〈묘비〉 a tombstone; a gravestone
돌비늘 〔鑛〕 mica ⇨ 운모
돌비알 a rocky precipice; a rock wall
돌사닥다리 a stony [rugged] mountain path

돌산 —山 a rocky mountain; 〈채석장〉 a quarry
돌상 —床 a feast table for a baby's first birthday
돌샘 a rock spring; a spring gushing out of stony ground
돌소금 rock salt ⇨ 암염(岩鹽)
돌솜 〔鑛〕 asbestos ⇨ 석면(石綿)
돌싸움 a fight with stone missiles; a stone-slinging fight
—**돌싸움하다** fight with stone missiles
돌쌓기 〔建〕 (stone) masonry; masonwork; stone bond
돌아가다 1 〈되돌아가다〉 go [turn] back; return; 〈물러나다〉 leave
♦집으로 돌아가다 go (back) home / 돌아갈 채비를 하다 prepare *oneself* for going home [back] / 본론으로 돌아가다 return to the subject / 정상적인 상태로 돌아가다 return [be restored] to the normalcy [normal conditions] / 제 자리로 돌아가다 resume [go back to] *one's* seat /(죽어서) 흙으로 돌아가다 fall back to dust
▶이제 돌아가도 좋다 You may leave now.
▶곧장 집으로 돌아가야 한다 You had better go straight home.
▶이제 돌아가 봐야겠습니다 I must be going home now. ⇌ I must say good-bye now.
▶어린 시절로 돌아가고 싶다 I wish I were a child again.
2 〈죽다〉 die; pass away; be dead; breathe *one's* last; depart (from) this life
▶그분은 돌아가셨다 He is dead and gone.
▶아버님이 돌아가신 지도 어언 20년이다 It is twenty years since my father died.
▶돌아가신 아버님을 대신하여 감사 드립니다 I thank you on behalf of my deceased [dead] father.
3 〈우회하다〉 go round (a place); go by a roundabout way
▶도로 공사 때문에 귀가할 때 멀리 돌아갔다 Because of road repairs, I went home by a roundabout way.
▶그 길로 가면 멀리 돌아가게 된다 That road goes the long way (around).
4 〈귀착하다〉 come to; arrive at; result [terminate, end] in; lead to
♦실패로 돌아가다 result [end] in (a) failure; prove a failure
▶승리의 영광은 그에게 돌아갔다 The laurel of victory crowned him.
▶내무장관 자리는 김박사에게 돌아갔다 For the Portfolio of Home Affairs the choice has fallen upon Dr. Kim.
▶나의 모든 노력은 수포로 돌아갔다 All my efforts have come to nothing [naught]. ⇌ All my efforts ended in vain.
5 〈책임·욕 등이〉 fall (upon); attribute (to); ascribe (to); set [put] down (to)
▶그렇게 하면 책임이 너한테 돌아간다 If you do that, you will be held responsible for it.
▶아들의 잘못으로 욕이 아버지한테 돌아갔다 The misdemeanor of the son brought disgrace to his father.
6 〈작용하다〉 work; operate; come into play
♦잘 돌아가지 않다 fail to operate [work] properly
▶기계는 잘 돌아가고 있다 The machine is working [running] smoothly.
7 〈되어가다〉 turn out; develop
▶일이 어떻게 돌아가는지 두고 보자 Let's wait and see how the matter develops [things turn out].
▶사태가 엉뚱하게 돌아가고 있다 The situation takes a turn for an unexpected result.
8 〈차례로 하다〉 do *sth* by turns; take turns
♦돌아가며 in turn; by turns; by [in] rotation / 돌아가며 일하다[망보다] work [watch] by turns
▶우리는 돌아가며 이야기했다 We took turns in telling a story.
9 〈분배되다〉 go (a)round
▶음식은 모두에게 돌아갈만큼 있습니까? Is there enough food to go (a)round?
돌아눕다 turn (over) on *one's* side (in bed)
▶아이는 잠결에 그 소리를 듣고 돌아누웠다 The child turned in his sleep at the noise.
▶나는 잠결에 돌아눕다가 방바닥으로 떨어졌다 While turning in my bed, I fell on the floor.
돌아다니다 1 〈쏘다니다〉 wander [roam] about; walk [go] about; get [hang, pace] around; gad about
♦여기저기 돌아다니다 knock about here and there; wander [tramp] from place to place / 하는 일 없이 돌아다니다 gad about idly / 산속으로 돌아다니다 wander about in the mountains
▶그들은 시골을 두루 돌아다녔다 They roamed [wandered] about the countryside.
▶사냥꾼은 사냥감을 찾아 숲속을 돌아다녔다 The hunter ranged a forest in search of game.
▶어디를 그렇게 돌아다녔니? Where have you been wandering about?
▶그는 방안을 이리저리 돌아다니며 생각을 정리하려고 했다 He tried to get his ideas into shape, pacing up and down the room.
2 〈퍼지다〉 get about [abroad, around]; go the rounds; 〈병이〉 prevail; be prevalent
돌아다보다 look back 《at》 ⇨ 돌아보다 1
돌아들다 1 〈돌아오다〉 come back; return; find *one's* way back 《to》
▶저녁이면 새들이 제 둥지로 돌아든다 In the evening the birds fly back to their nests.
2 〈흐르는 물이〉 curve in; make a bend
▶강물이 산 기슭으로 돌아든다 The river curves in toward the foot of the mountain.
돌아보다 1 〈돌아다보다〉 look back 《at》; turn round; 〈어깨너머로〉 look over *one's* shoulder
♦흘끗 돌아보다 cast a hasty glance behind [backward]; look back for a second
▶그는 뒤도 돌아보지 않고 방을 나가버렸다 He went out of the room without looking back.
▶그녀는 지나가는 사람들이 모두 돌아볼 만큼 미인이다 She is such a beauty that everybody turns to look at her when she passes.
2 〈돌이켜 보다〉 look back upon (the past); recollect; retrospect; review; reflect upon
♦1980년대를 돌아보다 review the 1980's / 학창 시절을 돌아보다 look back upon *one's*

돌이키다

school days
▶노인은 자기의 과거를 돌아보았다 The old man reflected on his past.
▶과거를 돌아보면 가끔 부끄러울 때가 있다 I am sometimes ashamed on looking back upon the past.
3 〈돌보다〉 take care of; look after
◆가정을 돌아보지 않다 neglect [think little of] *one's* home / 자기의 목숨을 돌아보지 않다 sacrifice *one's* life; act with total disregard for *one's* own interests
▶그는 일에 쫓겨 가족을 돌아볼 겨를이 없다 He is too busy rushing about his job to pay any attention to his family.
4 〈살피며 돌다〉 make a round; go *one's* round; walk *one's* beat; patrol
◆공장을 돌아보다 visit [go] round a factory / 학교를 돌아보다 make a round of a school for inspection
◆공장장은 하루 한번은 반드시 공장을 돌아본다 The factory superintendent makes a point of touring the factory once a day.

돌아서다 1 〈등을 돌리다〉 turn *one's* back ((on)); turn away [the other way]; turn on *one's* heels; 〈방향을 바꾸다〉 turn round ((toward)); turn about
◆적을 보고 돌아서다 turn *one's* back upon the enemy
▶그는 두세 발짝 걷고는 돌아섰다 He walked two or three steps, and turned about [round].
▶그녀는 돌아서서 울기 시작했다 She turned round and began to cry.
▶그는 갑자기 돌아서더니 강물로 뛰어들었다 He turned around suddenly and jumped into the river.
2 〈등지다〉 turn against *sb*; give *sb* the back; turn *one's* back
3 〈병세가 좋아지다〉 be progressing favorably; take a turn for the better; take a favorable turn

돌아앉다 sit the other way round; sit with *one's* back to *sb*

돌아오다 1 〈귀환하다〉 come back; get [be] back; return
◆되돌아오지 않는 청춘 *one's* irrevocable youth / 돌아오는 길에 on *one's* way back [home]; on route back to ((Seoul)) / 해외에서 돌아오다 return from abroad / 늦게 돌아오다 be late in coming home / 다시는 돌아올 수 없는 길을 떠나다 〈죽다〉 go on *one's* last journey; depart from this life; die
▶곧 돌아오겠습니다 I'll be back in a moment. ⇌ I won't be long.
▶빨리 돌아오너라 Don't tarry [be long] on the way.
▶네가 돌아올 때까지 기다리겠다 I'll wait till your return [you come back].
▶그는 떠난 후 다시는 돌아오지 않았다 He has gone [left] never to return.
▶나는 5년 만에 고향 마을로 돌아왔다 I returned to my native village after five years' absence.
▶내 아들은 3년 후에 딴 사람이 되어 돌아왔다 My son came back a changed man after three years.
2 〈우회하다〉 come the roundabout way ((to))
◆산을 돌아오다 come around a mountain
▶뒷문으로 돌아오세요 Step around to the back door.
3 〈때·차례 등이〉 come again; come round; return ▶마침내 그의 차례가 돌아왔다 At last his turn came ((round)).
4 〈결과 등이〉 fall ((up))on; be imposed on
◆욕이 돌아오다 be smirched with dishonor
▶집안의 생계를 꾸려나갈 책임이 그녀에게 돌아왔다 It devolved upon her to keep the home fires burning.
5 〈배당되다〉 fall ((to)); be allotted
▶내게는 이것밖에 돌아오지 않았다 This much has fallen to my lot.
6 〈회복되다〉 return ((to)); revert ((to)); recover
◆정상으로 돌아오다 return to normal / 제 정신으로 돌아오다 come [return] to *oneself*; recover *one's* senses

돌알 1 〈수정알〉 a crystal lens (of eyeglasses)
2 〈삶은 달걀〉 a hard-boiled egg

돌연 突然 〈갑자기〉 suddenly; all at once; all of a sudden; 〈뜻하지 않게〉 unexpectedly; 〈예고 없이〉 abruptly; without notice [warning]

解說 ***suddenly***는 갑자기 예기치 못했던 일이 생기는 것. ***all at once***와 ***all of a sudden***은 suddenly와 거의 같은 뜻으로 쓰이는데 all of a sudden 쪽이 구어적이고 보다 강한 뜻이 된다. ***unexpectedly***는 생각지 않았던 일이 생기는 것을 말하는데, 대비가 충분치 못함을 암시한다. ***abruptly***는 아무런 예고도 없이 갑자기 변화가 생기는 것을 이르며 흔히 불쾌[불리]한 결과를 암시한다.

▶그녀가 돌연 집으로 돌아왔다 She came back home unexpectedly.
▶한밤중에 돌연 사이렌이 울렸다 The siren rang out without notice in the middle of the night.
▶돌연 슬픈 소식이 날아왔다 The sad news came as a surprise.
—돌연하다 sudden; abrupt; unexpected
◆돌연한 공격[변화] a sudden attack [change] / 돌연한 죽음 an abrupt [a sudden] death / 돌연히 나타나다 burst upon the scene [view]
▶나는 돌연한 질문에 당황했다 I was puzzled by the unexpected question.
▶그의 돌연한 방문에 당황했다 I was embarrassed at his sudden visit.

돌연변이 突然變異 〔生〕 (a) mutation ◆돌연변이를 일으키다 mutate; sport ■**—설** the theory of mutation **—체** a mutant; a sport

돌옷 〈이끼〉 rock moss

돌이키다 1 〈고개나 몸을〉 turn *one's* face [head]; turn around; look over *one's* shoulder
◆고개를 돌이키다 turn *one's* head; turn round
2 〈바꾸다〉 change ((*one's* mind)); reverse ((a decision)); 〈재고하다〉 reconsider; think over ((again)); think twice; think better of
3 〈회상하다〉 look back upon; review; retrospect; 〈반성하다〉 reflect on *oneself*

돌입

♦ 돌이켜 생각하면 on [upon] second thought; on reflection/ 과거를 돌이켜 보다 look back into [upon] the past/ 자기의 행위를 돌이켜 보다 reflect on *one's* own conduct
▶ 나는 돌이켜 보아 양심에 찔리는 데가 없다 I have an easy conscience.
▶ 지난날을 돌이켜 보면 별별 일이 다 생각난다 When I look back on my past, I am reminded of a variety of things.
4 〈원래 상태로〉 get back; recover; regain; retrieve; restore
♦ 돌이킬 수 없는 과거 the irrevocable past / 돌이킬 수 없는 과오를 저지르다 commit [make] an irreparable [a fatal] mistake [error]
▶ 이미 저지른 일은 돌이킬 수 없다 What is done cannot be undone.
▶ 후회해 봤자 돌이킬 수 없는 일이다 No repentance will mend matters. ⇒ Regrets will not mend matters. ⇒ 〈속담〉 It is no use crying over spilt milk.

돌입 突入 inrush; a thrust 《into》 —**돌입하다** rush [dash, run] in [into]; break [plunge] into
▶ 양국은 전쟁에 돌입했다 Two nations broke into war.
▶ 우리는 적진으로 돌입했다 We broke into the enemy line. ⇒ We dashed into the enemy's position.
▶ 노조는 파업에 돌입했다 The labor union plunged [rushed headlong] into a strike.

돌잔치 a baby's first-birthday party [feast]; the birthday party for a one-year-old baby
♦ 돌잔치를 벌이다 give a party in celebration of a baby's first birthday

돌잡히다 let the baby celebrate its first birthday by choosing one thing out of various articles spread on the table before it

돌장이 a mason; a stonemason; a stonecutter
돌쟁이 〈첫돌이 된 아이〉 a one-year-old baby
돌절구 a stone mill [mortar]
돌절구도 밑빠질 때가 있다 〈속담〉 Nothing lasts forever.
돌제 突堤 a jetty; a breakwater; a quay
돌진 突進 a rush; a dash; a charge; an onrush —**돌진하다** rush [dash] (forward); make a dash; charge 《at》; storm
♦ 돌진하는 차 an onrushing car / 무모하게 돌진하다 rush headstrong / 적을 향해 돌진하다 charge [rush at] the enemy; make a dash at the enemy
▶ 그는 결승점을 향해 돌진했다 He made a wild rush [dash] to the goal.
▶ 그는 돌진해 오는 열차에 몸을 던졌다 He threw himself in front of the oncoming train.
돌짬 a crevice [crack, chink] on a stone
돌쩌귀 a hinge; a butt
돌쩌귀에 녹이 슬지 않는다 〈속담〉 A rolling stone gathers no moss.
돌출 突出 protrusion; projection; prominence; salience
—**돌출하다** protrude; project; jut out [forth]
♦ 바다로 돌출한 반도 a peninsular jutting out into the sea / 길 위로 돌출한 발코니 a balcony that projects over the street
■ —**물** a projection —**부** a protrusion; a projecting [salient] part; 〈산·바위 등의〉 a spur

돌층계 —層階 stone steps ⇨ 돌계단
돌칼 〔考古〕 a stone blade; a blade tool
돌파 突破 1 〈뚫고 나감〉 breakthrough
—**돌파하다** break [smash] through; breach
♦ 적의 포위망을 돌파하다 break through the enemy's siege / 경찰의 비상[경계]선을 돌파하다 break through the police cordon
2 〈극복〉 surmounting —**돌파하다** surmount; overcome
♦ 난관을 돌파하다 surmount obstacles; tide over [overcome] a difficulty
3 〈수량의 초과〉 passing —**돌파하다** pass; exceed; rise above; top ♦ 백만원대를 돌파하다 break a million won line
▶ 지원자는 천명을 돌파했다 The number of the applicants exceeded one thousand.
▶ 서울의 인구는 천만을 돌파했다 The population of Seoul passed the ten-million mark.
■ **중앙—** a frontal breakthrough **—작전** 〔軍〕 breakthrough operations; a breakthrough

돌파구 突破口 a breach; a breakthrough
♦ 돌파구를 만들다 break through; find a way out 《to resume the deadlocked talks》
▶ 그가 그 돌파구를 열었다 He took the initial step in breaking the barrier.

돌팔매 a throwing stone
돌팔매질 stone throwing [slinging]
—**돌팔매질하다** throw [fling, hurl, sling] a stone 《at》

돌팔이 an itinerant trader ■ —**선생** an incompetent teacher **—의사** a quack (doctor)
돌풍 突風 a (sudden) gust (of wind); a rush of wind; a squall ♦ 돌풍에 날리다 be blown by a gust
돌확 〈돌절구〉 a stone mortar
돔 〈반구형 지붕〉 a dome
돕다 1 〈조력하다〉 help; aid; assist; give [lend] a helping hand 《to》

> **解說** **help**는 「돕다」란 뜻의 가장 일반적이고 강한 말. **aid**는 보통 단체 등에 대해 「공적인 금전적 원조를 하다」의 뜻. **assist**는 「보조적인 일을 하다」의 뜻.

♦ 서로 돕다 help each other [one another] / 가게 일을 돕다 help in the shop
▶ 그는 한번도 나를 도운 적이 없다 He has never once helped me.
▶ 저를 좀 도와주시겠습니까? Will you please help me?
▶ 하늘은 스스로 돕는 자를 돕는다 〈속담〉 Heaven helps those who help themselves.
2 〈구제하다〉 relieve; give relief to; give [lend] a helping hand 《to》
♦ 가난한 사람을 돕다 relieve the poor; help the needy / 곤경에 처한 사람을 돕다 help a person out of difficulties
3 〈기여·증진·촉진하다〉 promote; contribute to; conduce to
♦ 생활비를 돕다 give [contribute, chip in] some money for living expenses / 소화를 돕다 aid [help] digestion / 사회의 발전을 돕다

돗바늘 a darning [matting] needle; a bodkin
돗자리 a (rush) mat; matting
♦돗자리를 깔다 spread a mat (on a floor) / 돗자리를 짜다 weave [make] a mat
■꽃— a figured mat; fancy matting

동¹ 1 〈사물의 조리〉 logic; reason; consistency ♦동이 닿지 않는 말 illogical [unreasonable] remarks / 동이 닿다 stand to reason; square with logic; be reasonable; be logical
▶그가 말하는 바는 동이 닿지 않는다 He is not governed by logic.
2 〈옷의〉 cuffs ♦끝[소맷]동 the cuffs of a sleeve
3 〈끝장〉 an end; a close; a finish
♦동이 나다 be exhausted; be used up; be out
4 〈동안〉 (a space of) time; a period; a span
♦동이 뜨다 have an interval (between); the interval is longer than usual
▶그 여자 수금하러 오는 것이 이번엔 좀 동이 뜨구나 She is later than usual this time in collecting money.

동² 1 〈묶음〉 a bundle; a bunch; a load
♦붓 한 동 a bundle of 10 writing brushes / 무명 두 동 two bundles [100 *pil*] of cotton cloth / 곶감 한 동 a load of 10,000 dried persimmons
2 〈윷놀이의〉 one of the four rounds necessary to complete a game of *yut*

동 東 the east ⇨ 동쪽
♦동으로 가다 go to the east; 〈동쪽에〉 on the east / 동이 틀 무렵에 at the break of dawn; at the first sign of daylight/ 동에 번쩍 서에 번쩍 하다 make frequent appearance here and there
▶동이 튼다 Day breaks. ⇌ It dawns.

동 洞 〈마을〉 a village; 〈행정구역〉 a *tong*
동 胴 〈몸통〉 the trunk (of a body); 〈옷의〉 the body; 〈갑옷의〉 a plastron
▶저고리의 동이 길다 The coat has a long waist.

동 棟 〈집채〉 ♦2동 two buildings [houses] / 3동의 2층 the second floor of building No. 3
▶그 화재로 가옥 세 동이 전소했다 Three houses were burned to ashes in the fire.

동 銅 copper (⇨ 구리) ■—관 a copper tube [pipe] —세공 copperwork —세공인 a coppersmith

동 同 〈똑같은〉 equal; 〈위와 같은〉 the same; the said; 〈문제의〉 in question; at issue
♦동인(同人) the same [said] person / 보석, 귀금속류 및 동제품 jewelry, precious metal and articles thereof / 동회사 the same company; (the) said corporation / 동일 동시에 at the same time on the same day

동가 同價 〈같은 값〉 the same price [cost]
동가리톱 a crosscut saw
동가식서가숙하다 東家食西家宿— lead a vagabond [wandering] life; live as a tramp
♦동가식서가숙하는 사람 a man who has no fixed abode; a wanderer; a vagabond; a tramp

동감 同感 〈같은 느낌〉 the same sentiment [feeling]; sympathy; 〈찬동〉 agreement; concurrence
♦동감이다 feel the same way (as); sympathize with; agree [concur] with; be of the same opinion
▶그 점은 나도 동감이다 I'm with you on that.
▶나도 전적으로 동감입니다 I quite agree with you. ⇌ I am entirely at one with you.

동갑 同甲 the same age; 〈사람〉 a person of the same age
▶우리는 동갑이다 We are of the same age.
▶나는 자네 춘부장과 동갑이라네 Your father and I are the same age. ⇌ Your father is the same age as I.

동강 a (broken) piece
♦양촛동강 a candle end / 동강 나다 go [be broken] to pieces / 동강 치다 cut in pieces / 세 동강으로 자르다 cut *sth* into three pieces
▶그의 연필이 두 동강 났다 His pencil was broken into two pieces.
■—치마 a short [knee-length] skirt

동강동강 into pieces; piece by piece ♦동강동강 자르다 cut *sth* into pieces
▶태피가 동강동강 부러졌다 The taffy was broken into pieces.

동개 〈화살통〉 a quiver ■—살 a large-feathered arrow for the cavalry bow —활 a cavalry bow

동갱 銅坑 a copper mine
동거 同居 living together; 〈남녀의〉 cohabitation
—동거하다 live together; share [live in] the same house; take *one's* abode (with); 〈남녀가〉 cohabit with
▶그는 숙모 집에 동거하고 있었다 He lived with his aunt. ⇌ He was staying at his aunt's.
▶그들은 결혼 전에 3년 동안 동거하고 있었다 They were cohabiting for three years before their marriage.
■—인 a person living together with *one*; a person living under the same roof; 〈동서자〉 a cohabitant; an inmate

동격 同格 〈같은 자격〉 the same rank [standing, status]; an equal footing; equality; 【文法】 apposition
♦동격의 equal (in position); equivalent (to); 【文法】 appositive / 동격인 사람 *one's* equal [peer] / …과 동격이다 be on a par (with); be [stand] on an equality [equal footing] (with)
▶그는 자격상으로는 나와 동격이었다 He was equal in rank with me.
▶이 단어는 저 단어와 동격이다 This word is [stands] in apposition with that word.
■—명사 an appositive; a noun in apposition
—어 an appositive

동결 凍結 freezing; a freeze (of, on)
♦동결을 풀다 unfreeze; defreeze
—동결하다 freeze (up)
♦임금과 물가를 100일간 동결하다 impose a 100-day freeze on wages and prices
▶그의 해외 자산은 동결되었다 His assets abroad were frozen.
■물가— freezing [pegging] of prices 임금—wage freeze; freezing of wages : 임금 동결 정

책 a wage-freeze policy / 자산— freezing of assets [credits]

동경 東經 east longitude
◆동경 180도 the 180th degree of east longitude; the international date line / 동경 30도 12분에 at thirty degrees twelve minutes of east longitude; at long. 30°12′ E

동경 憧憬 yearning; longing; aspiration; adoration; admiration
▶그는 소년들의 동경의 대상이다 He is the object of the boys' adoration.
▶대부분의 사람들은 미에 대한 동경심을 가지고 있다 Most people have a yearning for beauty.
—**동경하다** yearn for [after]; long for; aspire after
◆동경하는 남성 the man of one's dreams / 동경하는 직업 a longed-for [coveted] job / 도시 생활을 동경하다 yearn [hanker] after city life / 영화배우를 동경하다 admire a movie star
▶그는 자유를 몹시 동경하고 있다 He has a great yearning [longing] for liberty.

동경이 東京— 〈개〉 a short-tailed dog

동계 冬季 the winter season [months] ■—올림픽 the Winter Olympic Games —휴가 the winter vacation; winter holidays

동계 同系 ◆동계의 akin 《to》; of the same stock; cognate
■—회사 an affiliated concern [company]

동계 動悸 palpitation; pulsation; throbbing; thumping
▶심장의 동계가 심하시군요 Your heart beats [throbs] violently.
—**동계하다** beat; palpitate; throb; thump

동고동락하다 同苦同樂— share one's lot 《with another》; share the sweets [pleasures] and bitters [pains] of life 《with》
▶우리는 오랫동안 동고동락해 온 사이다 We have been great friends both in joy and in sorrow for a long time.

동고비 〈鳥〉 a nuthatch; a tree runner

동곳 〈상투의〉 a topknot pin; a hairpin 《worn by men》 ◆동곳을 꽂다 wear a hairpin in one's topknot

동공 瞳孔 [解] the pupil; the apple of the eye
▶그녀의 동공은 이미 열려 있었다 The pupils of her eyes were already dilated.
■—막 the pupillary membrane —반사 a pupillary reflex —축소[확대] contraction [dilation] of the pupil

동광 銅鑛 〈광산〉 a copper mine; 〈광석〉 copper ore; crude copper

동구 洞口 the approach to a village; a village entrance
◆동구 밖 〈on〉 the outskirts of a village

동국 同國 〈같은 나라〉 the same country; 〈그 나라〉 that [the said] country
■—인 a fellow countryman; a compatriot; a man of one's own nation

동국 東國 〈한국〉 the Nation of the East; Korea

동굴 洞窟 a cave; a cavern; a grotto 《pl. ~ (e)s》

◆동굴의 입구 a cave mouth / 동굴에 사는 사람 a cave dweller; a caveman / 동굴을 탐험하다 explore a cave [cavern]; spelunk
▶우리는 그 동굴 벽에서 동물 그림 몇 개를 발견했다 We found some pictures of animals on the wall of the cave.
■—벽화 a wall painting in a cave; 〔考古〕 a graffito —탐험 spelunking —탐험가 a spelunker

동궁 東宮 〈세자궁〉 the Crown Prince's Palace; 〈왕세자〉 the Crown Prince

동권 同權 equal rights; equality of rights; 〈법률상의〉 isonomy
■—남녀 equal rights for men and women; the equality of the sexes 《in law》: 남녀 동권주의 feminism / 남녀 동권주의자 a feminist

동그라미 **1** 〈원〉 a circle; a ring
◆동그라미를 그리다 draw [describe] a circle / 동그라미를 치다 enclose 《a word》 with a circle; encircle
▶바른 답의 번호에 동그라미를 치시오 Put a circle around the number of the correct answer.
2 〈俗〉 〈돈〉 lucre; chink; clink; tin; the needful
■—표 the circle symbol

동그라지다 fall [tumble] over; fall [roll] head over heels
◆미끄러져 나가동그라지다 slip and fall 《head over heels》
▶겨우 걷기 시작한 아기는 늘 동그라지기만 한다 The baby just learning to walk is always tumbling over.

동그랗다 round; rotund; 〈고리 모양의〉 circular; 〈공 모양의〉 globular; spherical
◆동그란 눈 round [beady] eyes / 동그란 얼굴 a round [moon] face / 눈을 동그랗게 뜨고 with one's eyes wide-open
▶동그랗게 앉읍시다 Let's sit in a circle.
▶이 말을 발음하자면 입술을 더욱 동그랗게 해야 합니다 You must round your lips more (closely) to pronounce this word.

동그마니 〈외따로〉 lonely; alone; 〈홀가분히〉 light and alone; lightly; easily

동그스름하다 somewhat round; roundish; rounded
◆동그스름한 얼굴 a roundish face

동근 同根 〈같은 뿌리〉 the same root(s)
◆동근으로부터의 파생어 words derived from the same root

동글납작하다 round and flat 《face》

동글동글하다 round; circular; globular
◆동글동글한 눈깔사탕[조약돌] round toffies [pebbles]

동급 同級 the same rank [level]; equality; 〈학급의〉 the same class [grade]
■—생 a classmate; a classfellow

동기 冬期 the winter season ⇨ 동계 (冬季)

동기 同氣 〈형제 자매〉 siblings ◆동기간 sibling relationship / 동기간의 우애 brotherly [sisterly] affection; fraternal love
▶그들은 동기간이다 They are siblings.

동기 同期 the same period [term]; 〈학교의〉 the same class; 〔電〕 synchronism
▶우리는 대학 동기다 We were in the same

class at the university.
▶ 우리는 입사 동기다 We entered the company in the same year.
▶ 작년 동기와 비교해서 매출이 줄었다 Sales have fallen off (as) compared with the corresponding [same] period of last year.
■ 一생 a classmate; a graduate in the same class

동기 動機 a motive; an inducement; an incentive
♦ 범죄의 동기 the motive of [for] *sb's* crime / …이 동기가 되어서 prompted [motivated, actuated] by... / 개인적인[불순한] 동기에서 from a personal [an interested, an ulterior] motive
▶ 이런 일을 한 동기가 무엇입니까? What caused [motivated] you to do this?
▶ 그의 동기는 좋다 He means well. ⇌ His intentions are good.
▶ 무슨 동기로 아프리카에 가셨습니까? What motivated you to go to Africa?
▶ 나는 순수한 동기에서 말하고 있는 것이다 I am speaking from a disinterested motive.
■ 一분석[조사] 〔經〕 motivation(al) research

동기 童妓 〈어린 기생〉 a child *kisaeng*; a young apprentice entertainer

동기 銅器 a copper [bronze] utensil; copperware

동나다 〈떨어지다〉 run out of; be used up; be exhausted; be consumed; 〈매진되다〉 sell out; be sold out of stock
▶ 자금[식량]이 동났다 We have run out of funds [provisions].
▶ 재고품이 동났다 We are cleared of all stock.

동남 東南 the southeast
♦ 동남의 southeast (side); southeastern ((districts)); southeasterly ((course)) / 동남으로 southeastward(s)
■ 一동 east-southerly (略 ESE) 一풍 a southeast [southeasterly] wind; a southeaster 一향 a southeast exposure [aspect]

동남아시아 東南— Southeast Asia
■ 一조약기구 the Southeast Asia Treaty Organization (略 SEATO)

동내 洞內 inside a village; the whole village

동냥 begging; 〈탁발승의〉 mendicancy; 〈시혜물〉 an alms; 〈美口〉 a handout
♦ 동냥다니다 go (about) begging; go round as a beggar / 동냥을 주다 give food [money] to a beggar / 동냥을 받다 receive food [money] as a beggar
一동냥하다 beg ((food, money)); beg *one's* bread
■ 一아치 a beggar; a mendicant 一자루 a beggar's [mendicant's] bag 一중 a mendicant (priest) 一질 begging; mendicancy

동냥은 안 주고 쪽박만 깬다 〈속담〉 only find faults with *sb* without complying with his request

동네 洞— a [*one's*] village; 〈사는 근처〉 the neighborhood
♦ 작은 동네 a hamlet / 큰 동네 a large village / 동네 사람 a villager; 〈복수〉 village folk [people]; people living in the same street; 《총칭》 the whole village / 동네 어른들 elders of *one's* village / 동네의 모임 a neighbors' meeting; a neighborhood get-together / 동네의 소문 (a) neighborhood gossip / 동네 어귀에서 on the outskirts of a village / 같은 동네에 살다 live in the neighborhood [the same block]
▶ 온 동네가 벌컥 뒤집혔다 The whole village is in an uproar.

동네 색시 믿고 장가 못 든다 〈속담〉 Wanting the improbable often leads to frustration.

동년 同年 〈같은 해〉 the same year; 〈그 해〉 that [the said] year
♦ 동년에 in the same year; in that year

동년배 同年輩 〈같은 또래〉 (about) the same age ♦ 동년배의 사람들 people of about the same age; people in the same age bracket

동녘 東— the east; the eastward
♦ 동녘 하늘 the eastern sky

동단 東端 the east(ern) end; the eastern extremity [tip] ♦ 시의 동단에 있는 공원 the park at the east(ern) end of the city

동당거리다 keep drumming and twanging ⇨ 똥땅거리다

동닿다 1 〈끊이지 않고 이어지다〉 come [follow] in succession
2 〈조리가 서다〉 stand to reason; be logical; be reasonable
♦ 동닿지 않는 말 illogical [incoherent, unreasonable] remarks / 동닿지 않는 변명 a lame excuse / 동닿지 않는 대답을 하다 answer irrelevantly / 동닿지 않는 말을 하다 talk nonsense; talk incoherently; contradict *oneself*
▶ 그것은 전혀 동닿지도 않는다 That's against all reason.

동대다 1 〈떨어지지 않게 대다〉 supply in regular succession; furnish regularly
♦ 학비를 동대다 supply *sb* with ((his)) school expenses / 이자를 동대어 갚다 pay the interest regularly [punctually]
▶ 이 쌀을 가지고는 다음 추수 때까지 동댈 수 없을 것 같다 I am afraid the rice won't last until next harvest time.
2 〈조리가 닿게 하다〉 make fit in; make ((*one's* story)) consistent [coherent]; make ((it)) reasonable [logical, plausible]

동댕이치다 1 〈내던지다〉 fling; hurl; throw [cast] away
♦ 홧김에 재떨이를 동댕이치다 throw away [fling, hurl] an ashtray in anger
2 〈그만두다〉 give [throw] up; (口) chuck up
♦ 일자리를 동댕이치다 throw over *one's* job / 하던 일을 중도에 동댕이치다 give [chuck] up *one's* work halfway through

동동 ♦ 발을 동동 구르다 stamp the ground / 분해서 발을 동동 구르다 stamp with vexation [chagrin] / 추워서 발을 동동 구르다 jump up and down for [stamp (*one's* feet) from] cold / 화가 나서 발을 동동 구르다 stamp (*one's*) foot in anger

동동거리다 stamp (*one's* feet) ((on the ground)); beat [thump] *one's* shoes ((on the floor))
▶ 우리는 추워서 동동거리며 기다려야 했다 We

had to wait, stamping to keep warm.
동등 同等 equality; parity
♦대졸 또는 동등 이상의 학력 소유자 a person with attainments equal to or higher than the college graduate
—동등하다 equal; equivalent; coordinate
♦동등한 권리 equal rights / 동등한 대우 equal treatment / 고졸 또는 그와 동등한 학력 소유자 high school graduates or the equivalent / 동등한 입장에서 on an equal footing; equally; on the square
▶그 회사는 남녀를 동등하게 대우한다 The company treats men and women equally.
▶양국은 군사력 면에서 동등해졌다 The two countries reached parity in military strength.
동떨어지다 〈거리가 멀다〉 be far [wide] apart (from); be remote (from); be far [distant] (from); 〈성질이 다르다〉 be (widely) different (from)
♦동떨어진 곳 a remote [an out-of-the-way] place / 동떨어진 소리 a remark wide of the mark; an absurd remark
▶그는 인가에서 동떨어진 외딴 오두막에서 살고 있다 He lives in a solitary cottage far from the village [human habitation].
▶나는 내 취미와는 아주 동떨어진 일을 하고 있다 I am engaged in a work quite alien to my taste.
▶그의 증언은 진실과는 동떨어진 것이었다 His testimony was far removed [quite different] from the truth.
▶그들의 주장은 서로 완전히 동떨어져 있다 Their contentions are poles apart.
동뜨다 1 〈뛰어나다〉 superior; surpassing; outstanding; extraordinary; exceptional
♦성적이 동뜨다 be out and away [by far] the best student (in the class)
▶그는 동뜨게 재간이 있는 사람이다 He has an exceptional [extraordinary] talent.
▶그녀는 동뜨게 영어를 잘한다 〈키가 크다〉 She is exceptionally good at English [tall].
2 〈사이가 뜨다〉 ⇨ 동안뜨다
▶두 동네는 사이가 동떠 있다 The two villages are far apart from each other.
동란 動亂 agitation; an upheaval; (a) disturbance; commotion; a riot
♦동란을 일으키다 cause a disturbance [riot]; rise in riot / 동란을 진압하다 quell a disturbance [riot]
■ 6.25— ⇨ 한국전쟁
동량 棟梁 1 〈기둥과 들보〉 a pillar and a beam
2 ⇨ 동량지재
동량지재 棟梁之材 a pillar 《of the state》; the chief support
동력 動力 〔電〕 electric power; 〔機〕 (motive) power; 〔力學〕 dynamic (force)
♦동력으로 움직이는 power-driven / 동력을 공급하다 supply (electric) power 《to a factory》 / 동력으로 공장을 움직이다 power a plant / 태양 전지를 동력으로 쓰다 use solar batteries for power
■ —계 a dynamometer —로 a power reactor; 〈발전용 원자로〉 an atomic (power) pile —료(料) power rate —사정 power condition —선 a power vessel; a powerboat —선반 a power lathe —원 a power source —장치 a power plant —회선 a power circuit
동렬 同列 the same rank [file] ♦…와 동렬에 두다 place on the same level with; put in the same category with
동록 銅綠 green [copper] rust; verdigris; 〈청동기의〉 patina
동료 同僚 a colleague; an associate; a fellow worker; a co-worker

> 解說 *colleague*는 전문직의 사람이나 회사의 임직원이 쓰는 경우가 많다. *associate* (business associate라고도 함)는 사업상 어떤 관계를 가진 사람을 가리키며 같은 뜻으로 business friend를 쓰는 사람도 있다. *fellow worker, co-worker*는 모두 같은 직장에서 일하는 사람을 가리키는데, 이 말들에서는 친밀감을 느낄 수 있다.

▶그는 직장 동료들과 자주 술 마시러 간다 He often goes drinking with his fellow workers at the office.
■ —의식 a fellow feeling
동류 同類 〈동종〉 the same class [kind, category]; 〈비슷한 것〉 a like (of); 〈한패〉 an accomplice; a gang
♦동류의 of the same class; similar / …과 동류다 belong to the same class with; be in the same category as
▶바이올린과 첼로는 동류의 악기다 The violin and the cello are related instruments.
▶그도 동류임에 틀림없다 He must be one of the party.
■ —의식 〔社〕 consciousness of kind —항 〔數〕 a similar [like] term
동륜 動輪 〔機〕 a driving [traction] wheel
동률 同率 the same ratio; a tie
동리 洞里 a village ⇨ 동네
동마루 棟— the ridge of a tiled roof
동맥 動脈 〔解〕 the artery ♦동맥의 arterial
▶네덜란드에선 수로가 상업의 동맥이다 In the Netherlands waterways are the arteries of commerce.
▶동맥이 경화되었다 The artery hardened.
■ —경화증 〔醫〕 hardening of the arteries; arteriosclerosis 《*pl.* -roses》 —관 an arterial tube —류(瘤) 〔解〕 an aneurysm [aneurism] —염 arteritis —절개술 arteriotomy —혈 arterial blood —혈화 arterialization
동맹 同盟 an alliance; a league; a union; a confederation; a confederacy
▶프랑스는 영국과 동맹을 맺었다 France made [formed, concluded] an alliance with England.
▶양국은 서로 동맹을 맺고 있었다 The two countries were leagued together [with each other].
—동맹하다 make [enter into, form] an alliance with; ally (*oneself*) with; be allied with
♦…과 동맹하여 in league [alliance] with…; leagued with…
■ 공수(攻守)— an offensive and defensive alliance 관세— a customs league 군사— a

동등 비교의 표현

1. ~와 같은 (높이, 길이 등); ~와 같이 (재미있는, 능숙한 등)
   ▶ 아들의 키는 내 키와 같다 My son is as tall as I am.
   ▶ 민선생님은 나의 부친과 거의 같은 연배시다 Mr. Min is almost as old as my father.
   ▶ 그녀는 그에 못지 않게 테니스를 잘한다 She plays tennis as well as him.
   ▶ 나와 그는 체중이 같다 I weigh as much as he does.
   [어법]
   ① 스스럼없는 글에서는 as 다음에 인칭대명사가 오는 경우 주격 대신에 목적격을 많이 쓴다.
   My son is as tall as me. / She plays tennis as well as him.
   ② as 다음에는 동사를 생략할 수가 있다.
   My son is as tall as I (am).

2. ~와 같은 정도로 …하기 쉽다[…하기 힘들다]
   as + 형용사 + to do + as ~ (동사는 타동사 또는 자동사 + 전치사)
   ▶ 이 책은 그 책만큼 읽기 쉽다 This book is as easy to read as that one.
   ▶ 이 책은 그 책만큼 구하기가 힘들다 This book is as hard to get as that one.
   ▶ 이 단어는 그 단어만큼 발음하기 어렵다 This word is as hard [difficult] to pronounce as that one.

3. ~와 같은 정도로 많이
   (같은 수, 같은 양을 나타낸다)
   as many + 복수명사 + as ~ (수)
   as much + 단수명사 + as ~ (양)
   ▶ 나는 그만큼 레코드를 가지고 있다 I have as many records as he does.
   ▶ 이 책의 쪽수는 그 책과 같다 This book has as many pages as that one. ⇌ There are as many pages in this book as in that book.
   ▶ 그녀는 언니만큼 옷치장에 돈을 쓴다 She spends as much money on clothes as her sister does.
   ▶ 겨울에 그들은 우리만큼 석유를 쓴다 They use as much oil as we do in winter.

4. ~만큼 …하지는 않다
   not + as [so] + 형용사[부사] + as ~
   ▶ 이 양복은 저 양복만큼 비싸지는 않다 This suit is not as [so] expensive as that one.
   ▶ 나는 당신이 생각하고 있는 만큼 젊지는 않아요 I am not as [so] young as you think.
   ▶ 그녀는 내 여동생만큼 노래를 잘 부르지 못한다 She doesn't sing as [so] well as my sister does.
   ▶ 이 문제는 네가 생각하는 것만큼 쉽지 않다 This question is not as [so] easy to answer as you think.
   ▶ 그녀는 언니만큼 옷치장에 돈을 쓰지 않는다 She doesn't spend as [so] much money on clothes as her sister does.

5. ~만큼 …한 것은 없다
   (1) Nothing is so [as] + 형용사 + as ~
   ▶ 인생에 있어서 건강 만큼 중요한 것은 없다 Nothing is so important in life as health. ⇌ Nothing is more important in life than health.
   ▶ 등산 만큼 상쾌한 것은 없다 Nothing is so pleasant as climbing mountains. ⇌ Nothing is more pleasant than climbing mountains.
   ▶ 사랑을 받는 것만큼 좋은 일은 없다 Nothing is so nice as to be loved. ⇌ Nothing is nicer than to be loved.
   (2) Nothing+동사+so[as]+명사+as ~
   ▶ 그들에게는 스키만큼 즐거운 것은 없다 Nothing gives them so much fun as skiing. ⇌ Nothing gives them more fun than skiing.
   [어법]
   같은 뜻일 때는 「비교급… + than ~」으로도 나타낼 수 있다.

6. 될 수 있는 대로…; 마음 내키는 대로
   as…as + 주어 + can; as…as possible; as…as + 주어 + like (as 다음의 주어는 글의 주어와 같은 것을 쓴다)
   ▶ 될 수 있는 대로 빨리 오시오 Come as soon as you can. ⇌ Come as soon as possible.
   ▶ 문에서 될 수 있는 대로 멀어져서 앉읍시다 Let's sit as far as possible [as far as we can] from the door.
   ▶ 캔디를 마음 내키는 대로 먹어도 괜찮아요 You can take as much candy as you like.
   ▶ 그는 커피를 실컷 마셨다 He drank as much coffee as he liked.

7. 이전[옛날] 만큼 …하지 않다
   not as [so]…as + 주어 + used to
   ▶ 그녀는 옛날 만큼 예쁘지 않다 She isn't as beautiful as she used to be. (▶술어동사가 be동사일 때는 used to be로 함)
   ▶ 이 근처는 옛날 만큼 한적하지는 않습니다 This neighborhood isn't as quiet as it used to be.
   ▶ 아버지는 예전만큼 담배를 피우지 않으신다 My father doesn't smoke as [so] much as he used to.
   ▶ 그 분은 예전만큼 자주 찾아오지 않습니다 He doesn't visit us as often as he used to.

8. ~년전[젊었을 때] 처럼 …하지는 않다
   not as [so]…as + 주어 + 동사 + 부사구[절]
   ▶ 그는 몇년 전처럼 건강하지 않다 He isn't as healthy as he was several years ago.
   ▶ 그는 젊었을 때처럼 술을 많이 마시지 않는다 He doesn't drink as [so] much as he did when he was young.
   ▶ 그는 내가 처음 만났을 때처럼 젊게 보이지는 않는다 He doesn't look as [so] young as he did when I first met him.
   [어법]
   clause에서는 술어동사가 be동사인 경우에는 I was, he was, they were 등의 꼴로, 그 밖의 경우(완료형은 제외)에는 I did, he did, they did 등의 꼴로 쓴다.

military alliance 방위― a defense alliance 삼국― a triple alliance ■―국 an ally; an allied power [country]; a confederate ―군 an allied army; allied forces ―조약 a treaty of alliance ―휴학 a strike of students; a school [college] strike

동맹파업 同盟罷業 a (labor) strike; (美) a walkout; (英) a turnout
♦동맹파업 중인 노동자 the workmen on strike / 동맹파업 중이다 be on strike / 임금 인상을 요구하며 동맹파업을 일으키다 go on a strike for higher wages [pay] / 동맹파업을 중지하다 call off a strike
―동맹파업하다 strike; go on (a) strike; (美) walk out
■―자 a striker; (英) a turnout ―파괴자 a strikebreaker; a scab; a rat

동메달 銅― a copper medal; a copper medallion; 〈경기에서의〉 a bronze medal

동면 冬眠 hibernation; winter sleep
▶곰은 동면 중이다 Bears are now in hibernation.
▶개구리는 동면에 들어갔다 Frogs have gone into hibernation.
▶만물이 동면에서 깨어나고 있다 Everything is awake from a long winter sleep.
―동면하다 hibernate
―동물 hibernating [hibernant] animals; hibernants ―장소 a hibernaculum 《pl. -la》; a hibernacle

동명 同名 〈같은 이름〉 (a person with) the same name; 〈같은 제목〉 the same title
▶이것과 동명의 소설이 여러 개 있다 There are several novels by the same name [with the same title] as this.

동명 洞名 the name of the village [*dong*]

동명사 動名詞 《文法》 a gerund
―동명사의 gerundial

동명이인 同名異人 a person of [with] the same name; a [*one's*] namesake; a homonym
▶그들은 동명이인이다 They are different persons of the same name.
▶그녀는 동명이인이었다 She was a different person with the same name.

동명태 凍明太 a frozen pollack

동무 a friend, a comrade; (口) a pal; a chum; a buddy; a mate; a companion; 〈교우〉 a circle; a company
♦동무가 되다 become [make] friends with *sb* / 동무가 없다 have no companion [friend]; be companionless; be friendless / 동무를 삼다 make a friend of *sb*
▶동무 삼아 나도 가겠소 I'll come to keep you company.
―동무하다 make a friend [companion] of; make friends with; keep company with; keep *sb* company
▶우리 동무하자 Let's make friends with each other.
■―길― a fellow traveler 말― a companion to talk with ―장사 〈동업〉 business in partnership ―장수 〈상인〉 traders in partnership

동문 同文 an identical text [passage]
▶이하 동문 The following [rest] is the same as above. ⇌ Same as above.
▶그와 동문의 편지가 나한테도 왔다 I too received a letter of the same content (as that).
■―전보 a multiple [an identical] telegram ―통첩 an identic note; a circular note

동문 同門 an alumnus 《pl. -ni》; 〈여자〉 an alumna 《pl. -nae》 ■―회 an alumni association

동문서답 東問西答 an irrelevant answer; an incoherent reply
▶우리는 서로 동문서답을 하고 있구나 I talk of chalk, and you talk of cheese
―동문서답하다 give an irrelevant [incoherent] answer to a question

동문수학하다 同門受學[修學]― study under the same teacher [master] 《with》

동물 動物 an animal; 〈짐승〉 a beast; a brute; 〈총칭〉 animal life

> [解說] *animal*은 넓은 의미로 식물에 대한 동물을 가리키는데, 일상 용어에서는 좁은 의미로 인간에 대한 동물이나 포유류로서의 동물을 가리키는 일이 많다. *beast*와 *brute*는 인간 이외의 고등 포유류를 나타내는데, beast는 문어적인 말로서 크고 위험한 동물, 특히 네발 짐승을 가리키는데 비해 brute는 그냥 큰 동물을 말하며 동정심을 내포하는 일이 많다.

♦동물적인 animal; brutal; beastly / 동물 취급하다 treat *sb* like a beast / 동물의 생태를 관찰하다 observe animal life / 동물을 기르다[길들이다] keep [domesticate] animals / 동물을 애호하다 be kind to animals
▶인간도, 새도, 벌레도 모두 동물이다 Men, birds and insects are all animals.
▶그는 동물적 본능으로 위험을 감지했다 He sensed the danger by an animal instinct.
▶그에게는 동물적인 직감력같은 것이 있다 He has a kind of animal intuition.
■고등[하등]― the higher [lower] animals; 〈개개의〉 a high [low] animal 육식[초식]― a carnivorous [herbivorous] animal 태생― a viviparous animal ■―계 the animal kingdom [world] ―분류학 zootaxy; zoological taxonomy ―상(相) (the) fauna ―생태학 zoo-ecology ―숭배 animal worship; zoolatry ―시험 《subject a medicine to》 a biological test ―실험 《conduct》 tests [experimenting] on animals; animal experimentation ―애호가 an animal lover ―애호회[학대 방지회] the Society for the Prevention of Cruelty to Animals (略 S.P.C.A.) ―요법 therapy with animals ―조직 animal tissue ―지(誌) a fauna 《pl. ~s, -nae》; zoology ―질 animal matter ―학 zoology ―학대 cruelty to animals ―학자 a zoologist ―해부학 zootomy; animal anatomy ―화(化) animalization ―화(畫) an animal painting

동물성 動物性 animal nature; animality
■―단백질 animal protein ―섬유 an animal fiber ―식품 animal food ―지방 animal fat

동물원 動物園 zoological gardens; (口) a zoo
▶그는 아이들을 동물원에 데리고 갔다 He took

동민 洞民 the inhabitants of a *tong*, the villagers; the village folk

동바리 〈짧은 기둥〉 a supporting post; a short pillar; 〈갱도의〉 a mine pillar; a pitprop; a puncheon

동박새 〔鳥〕 a white-eye; a silvereye

동반 同伴 company
—**동반하다** accompany; go (in company) with; go in *sb's* company
▶ 그는 가족을 동반하고 있다 He is accompanied by his family.
▶ 그는 부인을 동반하고 도미했다 He went to America, accompanied by his wife.
—**자** a companion

동반구 東半球 the eastern hemisphere

동방 東方 the east; the eastward; 〈동양〉 the Orient
♦ 동방의 east; eastern / 동방 견문록 *The Eastern Travels* (by Marco Polo) / 동방으로 toward the east; eastward(s); to the eastward / 빛은 동방으로부터 〈타고르의 시구〉 Light from the East
■ —**교회** 〈그리스 정교회〉 the Eastern [Orthodox] Church —**예의지국** the country of courteous people in the East; Korea

동방 東邦 〈동쪽 나라〉 an eastern country; an Oriental nation; 〈한국〉 Korea

동방 洞房 〈침실〉 a bedroom; 〈동방화촉〉 sharing bed on the bridal [first] night

동방구리 a potbellied jar

동배 同輩 *one's* equal; a peer; a fellow; a comrade ▶ 동배 중에서 뛰어나다 rise above *one's* fellows

동백 多柏 〔植〕 camellia seeds
■ —**기름** 〔油〕 camellia oil (used to dress hair)
—**꽃** a camellia (flower): 동백꽃이 한 송이 두 송이 피기 시작했다 Camellias are coming out one after another. —**나무** a camellia (tree)

동병상련 同病相憐 Fellow sufferers pity [sympathize with] each other. ⇒ Misery loves company.

동복 多服 winter clothes [clothing]; winter wear; a winter suit [〈여성용〉 dress, 〈학생용〉 jacket]

동복 同腹 children born of the same mother
■ —**형제**[**자매**] brothers [sisters] of the same mother; uterine brothers [sisters]

동복 童僕 a boy servant; a page

동봉하다 同封— enclose [inclose] (a letter)
♦ 동봉한 편지 the enclosed letter / 편지에 사진을 동봉하다 enclose a photo with [in] a letter / 동봉하여 보내다 send under the same cover
▶ 원서를 동봉합니다 I enclose my application herewith.
▶ 500달러 수표를 동봉합니다 I send you herewith a check for $500. ⇒ Enclosed please find a check for five hundred dollars.

동부 〔植〕 a cowpea; a southern pea

동부 東部 the eastern part; 〈미국의〉 the East
♦ 동부의 eastern / 동부 사람 an Easterner / 동부 해안 the east coast
▶ 그녀는 동부 출신이다 She is from the East.

동부 胴部 〈몸통〉 the body; the trunk; 〈조각상의〉 the torso 《*pl.* ~ (e)s, -si》; 〈기계의〉 the drum; the barrel

동부인하다 同夫人— go out with *one's* wife; take *one's* wife along [with]; be accompanied by *one's* wife
▶ 그는 동부인하여 파티에 참석했다 He attended the party with [accompanied by] his wife.
▶ 그는 일요일이면 반드시 동부인하여 외출한다 On Sundays he never fails to go out in company with his wife.
▶ 동부인하여 왕림해 주시기 바랍니다 Please come to see us with your wife. ⇒ 〈정식 초대장〉 We request the pleasure of your company and that of Mrs. 《Min》.

동북 東北 the northeast ♦ 동북의 northeast; northeastern; northeasterly —**동** east-northeast (略 ENE) —**지방** the northeastern provinces [districts] —**풍** a northeasterly wind; a northeaster —**향** a northeast exposure

동분모 同分母 〔數〕 a common denominator ⇨ 공분모 (共分母)

동분서주하다 東奔西走— run [bustle] about; busy *oneself* about *sth*; bestir *oneself* 《in a matter》
▶ 그들은 모금하느라고 동분서주했다 They busied themselves to raise funds.
▶ 그는 사회복지를 위해 동분서주하고 있다 He is always on the move, working for social services.

동사 同社 〈같은〉 the same company; 〈앞서 말한〉 the said [above-mentioned] firm

동사 凍死 death from (the) cold
—**동사하다** die of cold; freeze [be frozen] to death
▶ 두 명의 등산가가 산에서 동사했다 Two climbers froze to death in the mountains.
■ —**자** a person frozen to death —**체** a frozen body

동사 動詞 〔文法〕 a verb
♦ 동사(형)의 verbal
■ —**규칙**[**불규칙**]— a regular [an irregular] verb 완전[불완전]— a complete [an incomplete] verb 자[타]— an intransitive [a transitive] verb —**변화**[**활용**] conjugation

동사무소 洞事務所 the office of a *tong*; a *tong* [village] office

동산 a hill [hillock] (behind a house)
—**바치** a gardener

동산 動産 movable property; movables; personal estate [property, effects]
■ —**보험** property insurance —**압류** a distrainment; distraint; personal distress

동산 銅山 〈동광〉 a copper mine

동삼삭 冬三朔 the three winter months

동상 同上 〈위와 같음〉 the same as (the) above; ditto (略 do.)

동상 凍傷 frostbite; 〈가벼운〉 chilblains
♦ 동상에 걸리다 be [get] frostbitten; get [have] chilblains (on *one's* feet)
▶ 발가락이 동상에 걸렸다 My toes are frostbitten. ⇒ I have frostbite on my toes. ⇒ I'm suffering from frostbite in my toes.

동상 銅像 《erect [set up]》 a bronze statue; a statue in bronze

동상례 東床禮 〈신랑이 신부 집에서 베푸는〉 a wedding reception at the bride's house

동상이몽 同床異夢 ▶그 부부는 동상이몽의 생활을 하고 있다 The couple have the same bed but different dreams. ⇌ The couple live together but think differently.

동색 同色 〈색깔〉 the same color; 〈파벌〉 the same faction

동색 銅色 copper color ■—인(人) a redskin —인종 a copper-colored race

동생 同生 a (younger) brother [sister]; one's little [(口) kid] brother (▶이 표현은 성인의 경우에는 쓰지 않는 것이 보통임)

> [解說] 우리 말에서는 「형」과 「남동생」을 구별하지만, 영어에서는 보통 구별하지 않고 그저 **brother**라고만 한다.

♦가운데 동생 one's middle brother [sister]/ 막내 동생 one's youngest brother [sister] / 큰 동생 one's next younger brother [sister]

동서 同書 〈그 책〉 the said book ♦동서에서 〈출전을 나타내어〉 ibidem (略 ib., ibid.)

동서 同棲 〈같이 삶〉 living together; cohabitation ▶그들은 동서중이다 They are living together like husband and wife.
—동서하다 live together; cohabit with; live with; share bed and board with

동서 同壻 〈남자〉 the husband of one's wife's sister; a brother-in-law; 〈여자〉 the wife of one's husband's brother; a sister-in-law

동서 東西 (the) east and (the) west; 〈동양과 서양〉 the East and the West; the Orient and the Occident; 〈과거 공산권과 서방측〉 the East and the West

> [解說] 우리 말에서는 「동·서·남·북」의 순으로 말하지만 영어에서는 보통 **north, south, east and west**의 순서가 되고, 각각 **N,S,E,W**로 약해서 표시한다. 또 「동북」이나 「북동」이나 모두 **northeast**로, 「남동」이나 「동남」이나 모두 **southeast**라고 하고, 「동서」는 **east and west**, 「남북」은 **north and south**라고 한다.

♦동서의 관계[대립] the East-West relations [confrontation] / 동서를 막론하고 throughout [all over] the world; for all countries of the world / 동서간의 긴장을 완화하다 ease East-West tensions [the tensions between the East and the West]
▶이 공원은 넓이가 동서로 2킬로미터다 This park is two kilometers broad from east to west.
▶이러한 사실은 동서를 불문한다 This is true of all parts of the world.
▶그 섬은 동서로 가로 누워[길게 뻗어] 있다 The island lies east and west [stretches from east to west].
▶그 강은 동서로 흐른다 The river runs [flows] from east to west.

■—남북 the (four) cardinal points; north, south, east and west; 〈사방〉 the four quarters: 동서남북도 모르다 do not know chalk from cheese [one's right hand from the left]

동서고금 東西古今 all ages and countries; all times and places
♦동서고금의 노래[문화] the songs [cultures] of all ages and countries / 동서고금을 막론하고 across the ages and in all countries of the world; for all ages and countries [time and places]
▶그런 흉악한 범죄는 동서고금에 유례가 없다 We have never heard of such a brutal crime for all ages and in all places.
▶그와 같은 진리는 동서고금에 통한다 The truth is applicable to all times and places. ⇌ The truth holds true in all ages and countries.

동석 同席 —동석하다 sit with sb; sit in company with sb
▶나는 그 모임[파티]에서 그녀와 동석했다 I sat at the same table with her at the meeting [party].
▶나도 동석했다 I was among [one of] the company.
▶그 사람과 동석하는 것은 사양하겠습니다 I must be excused from being in his company.
▶그녀와 동석하면 지루하지가 않다 In her company we are never bored.
▶우리는 동석할 기회가 많습니다 We are often in each other's company.
■—자 those present; the (present) company

동선 同船 〈같은 배〉 the same ship; 〈그 배〉 the said ship; 〈한 배를 탐〉 sailing on the same ship
—동선하다 take [be on board] the same ship; sail on [in] the same vessel
▶나는 그와 동선했다 I took [was on board] the same ship with him.
■—자 a fellow passenger; a shipmate

동선 銅線 copper wire

동설 同說 the same [said] opinion [view, theory]

동성 同性 the same sex; one's own sex
▶그 여자는 동성간에는 평판이 좋다 She is well spoken of among her own sex.

동성 同姓 the same surname [family name]
▶그녀는 나와 동성이다 She has the same surname as myself.
▶그 마을에는 동성인 사람들이 많다 There are a lot of persons of the same surname in the village.
▶그와 나는 동성이지만 친척은 아니다 He is my namesake, but he is no relation to me [we are not related].
■—동명인(同名人) a person of the same family and personal name ―동본 the same surname and the same family origin ―인(人) a namesake; a person of the same surname as oneself

동성애 同性愛 〈남성끼리의〉 homosexuality(↔ heterosexuality); 〈여성끼리의〉 lesbianism
♦동성애의 homosexual (↔ heterosexual); lesbian

■—자 a homosexual; (俗) a homo ((pl. ~s)); a gay; 〈여자〉 a lesbian
동소체 同素體 〔化〕 an allotrope
동수 同數 the same number
♦찬반 동수의 투표 a (20-20) tie vote / 찬반 동수인 경우에는 in case of a tie
▶찬반이 동수였다 There was an equal number of yeas and nays. ⇒ The vote was equally divided between the yeas and nays.
동숙 同宿 lodging [staying] together
—동숙하다 stay in the same room with *sb*; share a room ((with *sb* at an inn)); stay at the same hotel; live in the same lodging house; lodge in the same house ((with))
▶그 호텔에서 나는 그와 동숙했다 I shared a room with him at the hotel.
▶우리는 우연히 같은 호텔에 동숙하게 되었다 We happened to put up at the same hotel.
■—인[자] 〈호텔 등의〉 a fellow guest; 〈하숙 등의〉 a fellow lodger [boarder]; a roommate
동승 同乘 riding together
—동승하다 ride together; ride with another (in the same car); share ((a carriage))
▶우리는 그 버스에 동승했다 We rode on the bus together.
▶나는 그녀와 동승하여 해운대에 갔다 I went to Haeundae in the same car with her.
■—자 a fellow passenger
동시 同時 the same time
■—방송 simultaneous broadcasting; a simulcast —선거 the simultaneous elections —선택 coincident selection —성 〔發生〕 simultaneity; synchronism —통역 (make) simultaneous interpretation —통역자 a simultaneous interpreter
동시 凍屍 a frozen corpse [body]; the corpse of *sb* frozen to death
동시 童詩 children's verse; (a) nursery rime [rhyme]
동시녹음 同時錄音 synchronous recording
—동시녹음하다 record simultaneously
동시대 同時代 the same age [period]
♦동시대의 contemporary; of the same age; contemporaneous / 동시대의 사람 a contemporary; a coeval / 동시대의 작가들 contemporary [coeval] writers / 프랑스 혁명과 동시대의 사건 an event contemporaneous with the French Revolution
▶그들은 우리와 동시대의 사람이다 They are our contemporaries.
▶헤밍웨이는 포크너와 동시대의 사람이다 Hemingway is a contemporary of Faulkner. ⇒ Hemingway lived in the same age [period] as Faulkner.
동시상영 同時上映 a double feature; a two-picture program; 〈흥행〉 a double-featured show ♦동시상영 영화를 보러 가다 go to a double-featured movie
동시에 同時— 1〈같은 때에〉 at the same time; simultaneously ((with)); concurrently ((with)); synchronously
♦…과 동시에 일어나다 coincide with; synchronize with
▶그들은 동시에 출발했다 They started at the same time.
▶그들은 서로 동시에 쳤다 They hit each other at the same time.
2〈즉시〉 as soon as; the moment [instant]
▶그가 역에 도착함과 동시에 기차가 떠나 버렸다 The train had left just as he arrived at the station.
▶목적지에 도착함과 동시에 그는 그 자리에 쓰러졌다 On arriving at his destination, he fell down on the spot.
▶어머니가 돌아오심과 동시에 나는 외출했다 I went out the moment Mother came home.
3〈한꺼번에〉 at a [one] time; at once
▶아무도 두 가지 일을 동시에 할 수는 없다 No one can do two things at a time.
4〈…하기도 …하기도〉 both... and; not only... but (also); 〈한편〉 while; on the other hand
▶그 여자는 주부인 동시에 작가다 She is a housewife and a writer.
▶약은 몸에 이로운 동시에 해로울 수도 있다 Medicine may be good for our health, but at the same time it can be dangerous.
▶이 책은 재미있는 동시에 유익하다 This book is both interesting and instructive.
▶수영은 즐거운 운동이긴 하지만 동시에 위험도 따른다 Swimming is a pleasant sport, but, on the other hand, it is attended with danger.
동식물 動植物 animals and plants; 〈어느 지역·시대의〉 fauna and flora
■—계 the animal and vegetable kingdoms
동실 同室 the same room [chamber]
동실동실 buoyantly ⇨ 둥실둥실
동심 同心 〈같은 마음〉 the same mind; 〈마음을 같이 함〉 like-mindedness; accord; 〈중심이 같음〉 concentricity
■—원 〔數〕 concentric circles
동심 童心 the child's mind [heart]; the juvenile mind; *one's* child heart
♦동심을 좀먹다 destroy the innocence of a child's mind / 동심으로 돌아가다 be [become] a child again; recover the innocence of a child / 동심에 상처를 주다 offend the child heart; hurt the feelings of children
▶그 여자는 나이를 먹어도 동심을 잃지 않았다 She never lost her childlike innocence.
▶나는 동심으로 돌아가 회전목마를 즐겼다 I became a child again and enjoyed the merry-go-round.
동씨 同氏 the said person; he
♦동씨(의 말)에 의하면 according to him; in his opinion
동아 〔植〕 a wax gourd; a white gourd
동아 冬芽 〔植〕 a winter bud
동아리 1〈부분〉 a part; a portion
♦윗[아랫]동아리 the upper [lower] part
2〈무리〉 a group; a set; (a) league; faction; colleagues; companions composed of the people with the same purpose
동아 속 썩는 것은 밭 임자도 모른다 〔속담〕 The anxiety deep in one's mind escapes the notice of even the most intimate friend.
동아시아 東— East Asia; 〈극동〉 the Far East
♦동아시아의 East-Asian; Far Eastern / 동아시아 각국 the East-Asiatic countries

동아줄 a thick and durable rope; a hawser; a stay

동안 〈기간〉 (a space of) time; a period; a span; (a) while; 〈간격〉 an interval; 〈부사적〉 for; during; while; on the [*one's*] way
♦그(럭저럭 하는) 동안 in the meantime / 대학에 다니는 동안 while in college / 사는 동안 while *one* lives /(과거) 3년 동안 for (the past) three years (▶「그 3년 동안」이라고 할 때는 during the three years임) / 여러 해 동안 for (many) years / 오랫동안 for a long time / 삼간 동인 for a short time; for a (little) while; for a moment [minute]/ 60년이란 긴 세월 동안 for sixty long years / 내가 살아 있는 동안은 as [so] long as I live / 말을 하는 동안에 in the course of conversation / 일정 기간 동안에 within a certain [given] period of time / 책을 읽는 동안에 while (I was) reading / 휴가 동안에 during the vacation
▶ 나는 거기서 3일 동안 묵었다 I stayed there (for) three days. (▶계속을 나타내는 동사 뒤에서는 종종 생략됨)
▶ 나는 2년 동안 그를 만나지 못했다 I haven't seen him for [(美) in] two years. (▶in은 no, not, first, only와 함께 쓰임)
▶ 지난 10년 동안 로켓은 급속한 발전을 이룩했다 Rockets have made rapid progress during [for] the past ten years.
▶ 그 일을 3일 동안에 끝내시오. Finish the work within three days.
▶ 살아 있는 동안 은혜는 잊지 않겠습니다 As long as I live, I shall never forget your kindness.
▶ 그 동안 안녕하셨습니까? How have you been since I saw you last?
▶ 나는 대구까지 가는 동안 줄곧 서서 갔다 I stood [had to stand] all the way to Taegu.
▶ 당신이 없는 동안 스미스 씨라는 분이 찾아 왔었습니다 A Mr. Smith called while you were out [during your absence, in your absence].
▶ 그는 여름 동안 쭉 그 가게에서 일했다 He worked at the store throughout [(all) through] the summer.
▶ 나는 여름 동안에 세번 홍도에 갔었다 I went to Hongdo three times during the summer.
▶ 내가 이야기하는 동안 그는 줄곧 껌을 씹고 있었다 He was chewing gum all the time I was talking.

동안 東岸 the east coast; the east bank ((of a river))

동안 童顔 a boyish [childish] face; a baby [childlike] face
♦동안의 청년 a boyish-looking youth
▶ 그 분은 아직도 동안이다 He still has a childlike face. ⇌ He is still juvenile-looking.

동안뜨다 〈오래다〉 have an interval between; 〈멀다〉 be far apart

동압력 動壓力 dynamic pressure

동액 同額 the same amount ((of money)); a like sum
♦동액의 equivalent in amount
▶ 그 회사에서는 봉급이 남녀 동액이다 Men and women are paid the same salary [paid equally] at the company.

동양 東洋 the Orient; the East

解說「동양」과「서양」은 대체로 우랄 산맥을 경계로 삼고, 특히 한국·중국·일본 등을 포함하는「극동」을 말할 때는 **the Far East** 또는 **Eastern Asia** 라고 한다.

♦동양의 Eastern; Oriental; of the East [Orient]/ 동양의 신비 the mystery of the Orient / 동양의 풍속 the Eastern manners / 동양적인 사고 방식 an Oriental way of thinking
━무역 Eastern trade ━문명[미술] Oriental civilization [art] ━문제 an Oriental [Eastern] question ━사(史) Oriental history ━사상 Eastern ideas; Orientalism ━인(人) an Oriental; (총칭) the Orientals ━제국 the Eastern [Oriental] countries [nations] ━통 an Orientalist; an authority on Oriental affairs ━풍 Orientalism ━학 Oriental studies ━학자 an Orientalist ━화(化) orientalization : 동양화하다 orientalize ━화(畫) an Oriental painting [drawing]

동업 同業 the same trade [profession, calling]/ profession은 의사·변호사·교수 등의 경우에 씀)
▶ 그 사람은 김 선생과 동업으로 사업을 했다 He did business in partnership with Mr. Kim.
━동업하다 do [engage in] business in partnership; run business together
▶ 동업하는 정의로 이 일은 비밀로 해 주십시오 Please keep this to yourself out of professional courtesy.
━조합 a trade association; a (craft) guild

동업자 同業者 a person of [in] the same trade [profession, business]; a fellow trader [businessman]; 〈공동 영업의〉 a partner; an associate
♦동업자간 가격 the trade price / 동업자 단체 trade association / 동업자 할인 trade discount / 동업자가 많은 사업 a crowded profession [trade]/ 동업자 브라운 씨 Mr. Brown who is in the same trade [line of business]
▶ 우리는 동업자다 We are in the same line of business [trade].
▶ 그 사람은 동업자 사이에 평판이 좋다 He is popular in the trade [among those in the same trade].

동여매다 bind ((to a stake)); bind *sth* together; fasten ((to a post))

동역학 動力學 〈物〉 kinetics; dynamics

동옷 a coat ⇨ 동저고리

동요 動搖 1 〈흔들림〉 shaking; trembling; 〈배의〉 rolling (좌우로); pitching (상하로)
━동요하다 tremble; shake; stir; quake; rock; 〈차가〉 jolt; 〈배가〉 pitch and roll
2 〈불안〉 restlessness; unrest; agitation; 〈소요〉 disturbance; commotion; (a) tumult; 〈움직임〉 fluctuation
♦마음의 동요 restlessness of mind / 물가의 동요 fluctuation in price / 사상의 동요 an agitation of thought / 동요를 일으키다 cause [create] unrest; create a commotion / 마음의 동요를 진정시키다 calm *oneself* / 정치적 동요를 야기하다 produce political unrest [a political

disturbance]
▶ 아무도 그녀의 심리적 동요를 눈치채지 못했다 Nobody noticed her mental disturbance.
▶ 유언비어는 사회의 동요를 야기한다 Wild rumors cause social unrest.
▶ 그의 발언은 실업계에 동요를 일으켰다 His remark has brought about disturbances in the business world.
—**동요하다** be restless; be unsettled; be agitated; be shaken (up); be disturbed; be upset; 〈세상이〉 be in commotion
▶ 그는 그 소식을 듣고 몹시 동요했다 He was badly shaken (up) by [at, with] the news. = He was very upset about [over, to hear] the news.
▶ 온 나라의 인심이 동요하고 있다 Public unrest prevails throughout the country.
▶ 그녀의 마음은 동요하고 있었다 Her mind was wavering.
▶ 그들은 동요하지 않고 목적을 향해 나아갔다 They never wavered from their purpose.

동요 童謠 a children's song; a nursery song [rhyme]
■ —**작가** a writer of juvenile songs; a poet of the nursery —**집** nursery rhymes

동원 動員 mobilization
♦ 노동력[학생]의 동원 labor [student] mobilization / 동원을 해제하다 demobilize / 동원이 가능한 사람이 많다 have many persons in reserve
▶ 육군은 동원 상태에 들어갔다 The army went into a state of mobilization.
▶ 이 공군기지의 전투기들은 언제든지 동원이 가능하다 The fighters from this air base can mobilize at any time.
—**동원하다** mobilize 《troops》; set 《an army》 on a war footing; call out; 〈관객을〉 draw
▶ 그 연극은 많은 관객을 동원했다 The play attracted [drew] a large audience.
▶ 전 경찰을 동원하여 폭동을 경계하게 하였다 All the police were sent out on the alert for the riot.
▶ 아이들까지 동원하여 대청소를 했다 Even the children were pressed into service for the great cleanup.
▶ 예비군이 동원되었다 An reserve army was mobilized.
▶ 우리는 그들의 일을 돕기 위하여 동원되었다 We were urged to help them with their job.
■ **산업—** industrial mobilization **인력—** labor [manpower] mobilization ■ —**계획** a mobilization plan —**해제** demobilization

동원령 動員令 mobilization order(s)
▶ 그날 육군 수송대에 동원령이 내렸다 Orders for the mobilization of the Army Service Corps were issued.
■ **국가—** 《promulgate》 National Mobilization Order

동원체 動原體 centromere; kinetochore
동월 同月 〈같은 달〉 the same month; 〈그 달〉 the said month
동위 同位 the same rank [position]; 〔數〕 the same digit
♦ 동위의 coordinate; corresponding

■ —**각** 〔數〕 corresponding angles —**원소** 〔物〕 an isotope : 방사성 동위원소 a radioactive isotope; a radioisotope

동유 桐油 tung oil ■ —**지** oilpaper
동음 同音 the same sound; homophony ♦ 동음의 homophonic ■ —**어** a homophone —**이의어** 〈異義語〉 a homonym

동의 同意 〈같은 의견〉 the same opinion; 〈의견의 일치〉 agreement; 〈승인〉 consent; assent; 〈찬성〉 approval
♦ 동의를 얻어서 with 《another's》 consent [approval] / 동의를 구하다 ask [seek] sb's agreement [consent] / 동의를 얻다 get [obtain, win] sb's consent [approval] / 머리를 끄덕여 동의를 나타내다 nod in agreement [consent, approval]; nod 《one's head》 in assent
▶ 그는 부모의 동의를 얻어 그 여자와 결혼했다 He married her with his parents' consent [approval].
▶ 그의 동의를 얻기는 어려웠다 It was difficult for me to obtain his consent.
—**동의하다** agree 《with, to, on》 (▶ agree 다음에 사물이 올 때는 to, 사람이나 의견이 올 때는 with, 결정 조건이 올 때는 on을 씀); consent 《to a proposal》; assent 《to》; approve of 《a plan》
♦ 제시된 조건에 동의하다 agree on the asked terms / 아무의 의견에 동의하다 agree with sb [sb's opinion] / 제안에 동의하다 agree [accede] to a proposal
▶ 부모가 결혼에 동의하지 않았다 Parents did not agree to [approve of] the marriage.
▶ 그 점에는 나도 동의합니다 I agree with you on that point.
▶ 그들은 그를 돕는데 동의했다 They agreed [consented] to help him.
▶ 참석자 모두가 동의했다 All those present were of the same opinion.
▶ 그는 그 제안에 동의했다 He okayed the proposal.
▶ 그에게 전적으로 동의할 수는 없다 I cannot agree with him in every respect [go all the way with him].
■ —**서** a written consent —**자** an assentient; an assentor; an approver

동의 同義 synonymy [sənǽnəmi]; synonymity; the same meaning
♦ 동의의 synonymous 《with》; synonymic(al); having 《of》 the same meaning
■ —**유전자** multiple gene; polymeric gene

동의 胴衣 a vest; a jacket; a waistcoat
■ **구명—** a life jacket [vest]

동의 動議 a motion
♦ 김 선생의 동의로 on Mr. Kim's motion / 동의에 찬성하다 second a motion / 동의를 가결하다[성립시키다] adopt [carry] a motion / 동의를 기립 표결하다 put a motion to a standing vote / 동의를 철회하다 withdraw a motion / 휴회 동의를 내다 make a motion to adjourn the meeting [that the meeting adjourn]; move (for) an adjournment
▶ 동의가 가결[부결, 성립]되었다 The motion was adopted [rejected, carried].
▶ 그 동의에 찬성합니다 I second the motion.

동의어

—동의하다 make a motion; move
▶ 이 회의의 휴회를 동의합니다 I move that this meeting be adjourned.
▶ 의장, 즉시 표결할 것을 동의합니다 Mr. [Madam] Chairman, I move that we take an immediate vote.
■**—긴급—** an urgent motion ■**—제출자** the mover

동의어 同義語 a synonym (↔ antonym)
▶ 'big'은 'large'의 동의어이다 'Big' is a synonym for [of] 'large'.
▶ 이 말의 동의어를 말해 보아라 Give a word synonymous with this word.

동이 a (round) jar ■**물—** a water jar

동이다 bind; tie [do] up; fasten; 〈끈으로〉 cord
♦ 상자[짐]를 끈으로 동이다 cord (up) a box [bundle] / 볏단을 동이다 bind rice into a sheaf

동인 同人 1 〈같은 사람〉 the same person; 〈그 사람〉 the said person; the person in question 2 〈뜻을 같이 하는 사람〉 a coterie; a clique; a member (of a literary coterie); a comrade; an associate; a colleague
♦ 잡지「시대」의 동인 a member of the staff of the magazine *Sidae*
■**—잡지** a literary coterie magazine; a little magazine

동인 動因 a motive; motivation; a cause; an incentive (to an action)
♦ 이 범죄의 동인 the motive for this crime / 개인적인[금전적인] 동인에서 from personal [mercenary] motives
▶ 그 사건과 동인이 되어 그는 회사를 사직했다 That incident motivated [caused] him to resign the company.

동인도 東印度 the East Indies ♦ 동인도의 East-Indian
■**—회사** the East India Company

동일 同— 〈꼭같음〉 sameness; identity; oneness; equality; indiscrimination
♦ 동일의 same (as, that); identical (with) / 동일 인물 one and the same person; the identical person / 동일 노동에 대한 동일 임금 equal pay for equal work / 동일 수준이다 be on a level (with *sb*) / 동일인임을 증명 [확인]하다 identify *sb* as
▶ 이 두 범죄는 동일범의 소행이다 The same person committed these two crimes.
▶ 지킬 박사와 하이드 씨는 동일 인물이다 Dr. Jekyll and Mr. Hyde are one and the same person.
▶ 사진만 가지고 동일 인물임을 확인하기는 곤란하다 It's difficult to identify people only from pictures.
—동일하다 identical; equal; the same (▶강조하여 the very same, one and the same의 형태로도 씀)
♦ 동일하게 equally; without discrimination / 양자를 동일하다고 보다 consider the two as one and the same thing / 동일하게 취급하다 treat *sb* without discrimination
▶ 영과 혼은 동일하다 The spirit is one with the soul.
▶ 개와 늑대는 동일한 과에 속한다 The dog belongs to same family as the wolf.
▶ 그 둘의 능력은 동일하다 The two are equal in ability.
▶ 나를 그런 사람들과 동일하게 보면 곤란하다 I don't like to be classed with them.
■**—개념** an identical conception **—과정설** uniformitarianism **—성** identity **—원리** [論] the principle of identity **—화** identification

동일 同日 〈같은 날〉 the same day [date]; 〈그 날〉 the said day ♦ 동월 동일 the same day of the same month

동일시하다 同一視— put *sth* in the same category [class]; identify *sth* with (another); regard (A) in the same light with (B); class (A) with (B)
♦ 자신을 영화 주인공과 동일시하다 identify *oneself* with the hero of the film / A와 B를 동일시하다 place A and B in the same category
▶ 이 문제들은 동일시하여도 좋은 문제들이다 These problems could be put in the same category.
▶ 이 두 사람을 동일시해서는 안된다 These two persons should not be viewed [looked at] in the same light.

동자 童子 a child; a (young) boy
■**—중** a young Buddhist monk; a priestling

동작 動作 motion; action; movement(s); 〈거동〉 carriage; bearing; behavior; deportment; manners; 〈몸짓〉 gesture; [倫] an act
♦ 느린 동작 slow motion [movement] / 우아한 동작 graceful deportment
▶ 그는 동작이 민첩하다[느리다] He is quick [slow] in movement [action].
▶ 그녀는 동작이 매우 우아하다 She is very graceful in her movements.
▶ 그 여인은 나에게 우아한 동작으로 인사했다 The lady greeted me gracefully [in a graceful manner].
—동작하다 move; act; bear [carry] *oneself*

동장 洞長 a *tong* [village, town] manager [headman]; the chief of a *tong* office

동장군 冬將軍 the rigors of winter; rigorous winter; General Winter; Jack Frost
♦ 동장군의 방문 the advent of General Winter [Jack Frost]

동저고리 a (man's) coat; a jacket
♦ 동저고릿바람으로 나다니다 go around in informal wear; go about in *one's* shirt sleeves

동적 動的 dynamic (↔ static); kinetic
♦ 동적인 표현 dynamic expressions
▶ 그는 인간의 심리를 동적으로 파악한다 He understands human psychology in motion.
■**—밀도** 〈인구의〉 dynamic density **—평형** dynamic equilibrium [balance]

동전 銅錢 a copper coin; a copper; (美俗) a red
♦ 10원짜리 동전 a ten-won coin [copper] / 구멍뚫은 동전 a perforated coin / (공중 전화기 등의) 동전 넣는 구멍 (drop a coin in) a slot / 동전 투입식 세탁소 a coin laundry / 동전 한 푼 없다 be penniless; have not a penny; have no money at all
▶ 동전 한 푼 안 남기고 다 써버렸다 I spent my last penny.
▶ 이 기계는 동전 투입식이다 This is a coin-operated machine.

▶동전 바꾸어 드립니다 《게시》 Change made here.
▶동전은 현관 판매대에 준비되어 있음 《게시》 Coin exchange at cashier's counter in entrance.
■―교환기 a coin changer: 동전 교환기 가동중 《게시》 Coin changer: in operation. ―지갑 a coin purse ―통 a coin box

동전기 動電氣 dynamic [voltaic, galvanic, current] electricity

동절 多節 the winter season; winter; wintertime

동점 同點 〈같은 점수〉 the same mark [grade, score]; 〈무승부〉 a tie; a draw
▶그 선수는 동점 홈런을 쳤다 He swatted the (game-)tying homer.
▶양팀은 9회말에 동점이 되었다 The teams tied [drew] at the second half of the ninth inning in the game.
▶축구에서 한국은 브라질과 동점이 되었다 Korea tied (with) Brazil in soccer.
▶나는 영어 시험에서 그녀와 동점을 받았다 I got the same score as she did on the English test.
▶경기는 2대 2 동점으로 끝났다 The game ended [finished] in a tie with a score of 2 to 2.
■―결승시합 a play-off ―타 〔野〕 the game-tying hit; a score-tying blast

동점 東漸 eastward advance [movement]; eastern penetration [drive]
―동점하다 advance [spread, proceed] eastward
▶페르시아 문명이 차츰 동점했다 Persian civilization gradually spread [advanced] eastward.

동정 a collar strip (for a Korean jacket)

동정 同情 sympathy; pity; compassion; fellow feeling

|解説| **sympathy**는 남의 슬픔이나 괴로움 등에 공감하고 함께 나누는 기분을 나타낸다. **pity**는 어려운 처지에 있는 사람을 불쌍히 여기는 마음과, 때로는 얕보는 기분을 나타낸다. **compassion**은 앞의 두 단어보다 딱딱한 말로서 적극적으로 돕고 싶다는 기분. sympathy 보다는 더 깊은 동정심을 나타낸다.

♦깊은 동정 deep [profound] sympathy / 따뜻한 동정 warm sympathy / 마음으로부터의 동정 hearty [heartfelt, sincere] sympathy / 동정 어린 눈길[말] sympathetic looks [words] / 동정적인 sympathetic; compassionate / 동정적으로 sympathetically; in sympathy / 동정을 끌다 arouse sb's sympathy / 동정을 나타내다[보이다] express [show] one's sympathy [pity] (for, toward) / 동정을 베풀다 extend one's sympathy 《to one's neighbors》 / 동정을 사다 [받다] win [gain, excite] sb's sympathy
▶사람들의 동정이 그녀에게 쏠렸다 Public sympathies were centered on her.
▶그 여자는 그 고아에게 동정이 갔다 She sympathized with the orphan.
▶그는 수재민들에게 동정을 금치 못했다 He could not help pitying the flood victims.
▶나는 너에게 동정을 구하고 있는 것이 아니야 I am not begging for your mercy.
▶네 동정 같은 건 필요 없다 I don't want any of your pity. ⇌ Don't have compassion [take pity] on me. ⇌ Don't pity me.
▶그는 동정보다 도움이 필요했다 He needed help more than sympathy.
▶그는 그녀의 불행에 동정적이다 He is sympathetic [compassionate] to her misfortune.
―동정하다 sympathize with; feel sympathy for; be sympathetic with [of]; take pity upon; have sympathy with [for]; have compassion on
♦마음으로부터 동정하다 sympathize from the bottom of one's heart / 동정할 만하다 deserve one's sympathy [pity]
▶자네를 진심으로 동정하네 You have all my sympathy.
▶우리들은 모두 그 부모를 여읜 아이를 동정했다 We all sympathized with the child who had lost his parents.
▶나는 그들을 전혀 동정하지 않는다. 자업자득이니까 I feel no pity for them at all. They got what they deserved.
▶우리는 그를 동정하고 있다 Our sympathy goes out to him.
■―자 a sympathizer; a well-wisher ―파업 a sympathy strike : 동정 파업을 하다 go on strike in sympathy 《with》 ―표 《win》 a sympathy vote; a vote of sympathy

동정 動靜 movements; a state of affairs [things]; the goings-on; development(s)
♦교육계의 최근의 동정 recent developments [trends] in educational circles / 적의 동정을 살피다 watch [feel out, spy on] the movements of the enemy
▶그 여자의 그 이후 동정은 모르겠습니다 I have no idea about what has become of her since then.
▶그는 정계의 동정에 밝다 He knows well about the situation of political circles [development of political affairs].

동정 童貞 chastity; virginity
♦동정을 지키다[잃다] keep [lose, surrender] one's chastity [virginity]
▶그 화가는 죽을 때까지 동정이었다 The painter had no carnal knowledge of woman all his life.
■―남 a (male) virgin ―녀 a virgin; 〈성모〉 the Virgin (Mary) ―설 the Virgin Birth

동정세포 ―細胞 collar cell; choanocyte

동정심 同情心 a sympathetic feeling; sympathy; compassion
♦동정심이 많은 sympathetic; feeling; compassionate; kindhearted; warmhearted / 동정심이 없는 unsympathetic; pitiless; coldhearted; unfeeling / 동정심이 많은 사람 a man of ready sympathies / 동정심이 생기다 feel compassionate; be moved to sympathy [pity] / 동정심에 호소하다 appeal to sb's sympathy
▶그는 동정심이 없다 He has no pity. ⇌ He lacks compassion.
▶그는 아주 동정심이 많은 사람이다 He is an

extremely compassionate man.
동제 銅製 ◆동제의 copper; made of copper ■—品 copper goods [manufactures]
동조 同調 1 〈보조를 같이함〉 alignment —동조하다 align *oneself* (with); follow suit; act in concert (with); be in sympathy (with); side (with)
◆당의 방침에 동조하다 act in concert with the party's policy
▶그가 회사를 그만둘 때 나도 동조했다 When he left the company, I followed suit.
▶나는 그의 의견에 동조하지 않는다 I do not sympathize with his opinion.
▶그의 설득에 동조하는 자는 없었다 No one yielded to his persuasion.
2 〔電〕 syntony; tuning; 〈영화·텔레비전 등의〉 synchronism
◆(음성과 화면이) 동조하지 않다 be not in synchronize; be not in synchronism 《with》
■—기 a tuner —자 a sympathizer; a fellow traveler —회로 a turning circuit
동족 同族 〈종족〉 the same race [tribe]; *one's* kind; 〈일족〉 the same family; 〈혈족〉 the same blood; consanguinity
■—결혼 endogamy; consanguineous marriage —계열 homologous series —목적어 〔文法〕 a cognate object —언어 cognate languages —체 〔化〕 a homologue —회사 a family partnership 〔concern〕; an affiliated [a family] company; a family corporation
동족상잔 同族相殘 a fratricidal war; an internecine struggle
◆동족상잔의 비극을 겪다 experience the tragedy of fratricidal war
▶육이오 전쟁은 동족상잔의 싸움이었다 The Korean War was a fratricidal struggle.
—동족상잔하다 engage in a fratricidal war; prey on each other
▶쥐는 동족상잔한다 Rats feed [prey] on each other [one another].
동종 同種 the same kind [sort, description]; 〈동종임〉 homogeny
◆동종의 of the same kind [sort]; of the same family [species]; similar (in kind) / 동종의 사과 apples of the same kind [sort]; the same kind [sort] of apples / 동종 동문의 《a nation》 of the same race and language; homogeneous in race and characters
▶동종의 범죄가 증가했다 Crimes of the same kind have increased.
■—교배 〔生〕 close [in-and-in] breeding —기생 autoecism
동주 同舟 taking the same boat
동중국해 東中國海 East China Sea
동중원소 同重元素 〔化〕 an isobar
동지 冬至 the winter solstice
▶오늘이 동지다 Today is the winter solstice.
■—선(線) 〔天〕 the tropic of Capricorn —설달 November and December by the lunar calendar; the last two lunar months —점 〔天〕 the winter solstice —팥죽 red bean gruel taken on the winter solstice
동지 同地 〈같은 곳〉 the same place [district]; 〈그곳〉 the (said) place

동지 同志 〈뜻이 같음〉 the same mind; 〈뜻이 같은 사람〉 the congenial spirit; a friend; a comrade; a like-minded person; a fellow thinker
◆동지를 규합하다 rally kindred spirits; muster men under *one's* banner
동진 東進 marching [proceeding] east; 〈천체의〉 easting —동진하다 move [march, advance] eastward; proceed east
동질 同質 the same quality [nature]; homogeneity
◆동질의 문화 a homogeneous culture / 동질의 of the same quality; homogeneous (↔ heterogeneous)
▶동질의 사건이 연속적으로 일어났다 Accidents of the same sort happened one after another.
■—이상 〔鑛〕 polymorphism; dimorphism
동짓달 冬至— November by the lunar calendar; the 11th lunar month
동쪽 東— the east (略 E)

> 解說 동·서·남·북을 말할 때 지리상, 특히 정치상의 명확한 경계에는 ***north, south, east, west***를, 보다 막연한 경계에는 ***northern, southern, eastern, western***을 쓰는 경우가 많다: East Asia (동 아시아) / Southern France (남 프랑스) / an east window (동쪽 창) / on the east coast (동쪽 해안에서) / in the eastern sky (동쪽 하늘에) / the eastern half of the country (그 나라의 동반부)

◆동쪽으로 가는 기차 a train bound east; an eastbound train / 동쪽의 east; eastern; easterly / 동쪽에 in the east; on the east (side) / 동쪽으로 to the east / 동쪽으로 가다 go east [eastward] / 동쪽으로 향해하다 sail east [to the east, eastward] / 동쪽 출구로 역을 빠져나오다 leave the station through the east exit
▶그 마을은 수원 동쪽 약 30킬로미터 지점에 있다 The village is (located) about 30 kilometers (to the) east of Suwon.
▶동쪽 하늘이 밝아온다 The eastern sky becomes light.
▶그의 집은 우리 집 동쪽에 있다 His house is on the east side of mine.
▶내 방은 창이 동쪽에 있어 아침 햇빛이 들어온다 My room has a window on the east side and gets the morning sun.
▶그 새들은 동쪽에서 날아왔다 The birds flew from the east.
▶해는 동쪽에서 떠서 서쪽으로 진다 The sun rises in the east and sets in the west.
▶여기서 동쪽으로 1킬로미터 가면 주유소가 있습니다 If you go one kilometer east from here, there is a filling station.
동차 同次 ◆동차의 homogeneous ■—방정식 a homogeneous equation —식 a homogeneous expression
동차 童車 a baby carriage ⇨ 유모차
동착 同着 ◆동착이 되다 arrive at the same time 《with another》; hit [reach] the goal on the same instant
▶그들은 동착이 되었다 They reached the

동창 同窓 a schoolmate; a schoolfellow
▶ 나는 그와 대학 동창이다 He is an alumnus of my college. ≒ He and I studied at the same college. ≒ I attended the same college as he did.

동창 東窓 a window facing east; the east window

동창생 同窓生 a schoolfellow [schoolmate]; a graduate; 〈남자〉 an alumnus [əlʌ́mnəs] 《pl. -ni [-nai]》; 〈여자〉 an alumna [əlʌ́mnə] 《pl. -nae [-niː, -nai]》

동창회 同窓會 〈조직〉(美) an alumni association; (英) an old boys' [girls'] association [society]; 〈모임〉(美) an alumni reunion [meeting]; (英) an old boys' [girls'] reunion ■ —지(誌) an alumni bulletin

동천 東天 the sky in the east; the eastern sky
▶ 동천이 붉게 물들었다 The eastern sky is tinged with crimson.

동철 冬鐵 〈나막신 굽에 박는 징〉 crampons; spikes; 〈말편자에 박는 징〉 horseshoe spikes

동체 同體 〈한 몸〉 one body; 〈같은 물체〉 the same substance ⇨ 일심동체

동체 胴體 〈몸통〉 a trunk; 〈조각의〉 a torso (*pl.* ~s, -si); 〈뼈대〉 a shell; 〈기체〉 a body; a fuselage; 〈선체〉 a hull
▶ 비행기의 동체가 두 동강이 났다 The body of the airplane was severed in two.

동체 動體 a moving body; a body in motion ■ —사진 a photochronograph

동체착륙 胴體着陸 a belly landing
♦ 동체 착륙을 하다 make a belly landing; belly-land / 비행기를 동체 착륙시키다 belly-land a plane
▶ 우리 비행기는 부득이 동체 착륙을 감행했는데 다행히 일행은 모두 무사했다 Our plane was forced to make a belly landing, but luckily all of us were safe.

동축 同軸 the same axle
■ —원 coaxal [coaxial] circles —케이블 a coaxial cable

동치 同値 〈數〉 the eqivalent ⇨ 등치(等値)

동치미 watery radish *kimch'i*; chopped radishes pickled in salt water

동침하다 同寢— sleep [lie] together; bed (with); share the same bed (with)

동태 凍太 a frozen pollack ⇨ 동명태

동태 動態 movement; dynamic state
♦ 여론의 동태 the drift [trend] of public opinion
▶ 정부는 5년마다 인구 동태를 조사한다 Government investigates the movement of population every five years.
■ —경제 dynamic economy; mobile economy; 동태 경제학 dynamic economics —인구 a dynamic population —통계 dynamic statistics; 인구 동태 통계 vital statistics

동토 凍土 〈언 땅〉 frozen land [soil] ■ —층 a freezing land layer

동통 疼痛 a (sharp) pain; an ache
▶ 그는 옆구리에 심한 동통을 느꼈다 He felt [had] a terrible [an accutte] pain in the [his] side.

동트기 東— daybreak; dawn

동트다 東— break; dawn; begin to grow light
♦ 동트는 하늘 the dawning sky / 동틀 녘에 at the first gray of dawn; in the gray of the morning; at daybreak [dawn]
▶ 동튼다 It [Day, Morning] dawns.
▶ 동틀 녘에 새들이 지저귀기 시작했다 The birds began to sing at dawn.
▶ 그는 동틀 녘 조금 전에 나섰다 He set out a little before daybreak.

동티 1 〈지신(地神)의 재앙〉 retribution from the earth gods
2 〈자초한 걱정〉 trouble brought on *oneself* gratuitously
—**동티나다** 〈재앙이 생기다〉 incur the divine wrath; bring evil [a curse] upon; 〈일이 잘못되다〉 get into trouble; incur trouble; 〈비밀이 탄로나다〉 be out [revealed, disclosed]

동파 同派 1 〈같은 파〉 the same clan [faction, clique]; the same school
2 〈그 파〉 the said clan; that sect

동파이프 銅— a copper pipe

동판 銅板 sheet copper; a copper sheet

동판 銅版 a copperplate
■ —인쇄 a copperplate [an etching] printing: 동판 인쇄하다 print from copperplates —조각 (술) chalcography; copperplate engraving —화 a copperplate print

동편 東便 the east [eastern] side

동포 同胞 〈형제 자매〉 brothers; brethren; 〈한 겨레〉 fellow countrymen; *one's* countrymen; compatriots; 〈같은 인간〉 fellowmen; fellow creature
▶ 7천만 동포에게 고함 A word for our seventy million compatriots!
■ —사해(四海)— universal [world] brotherhood 재일[재미]— Korean residents in Japan [the U.S.A.] 해외— Koreans abroad ■ —애 brotherly [fraternal] love; fellow feeling; fraternity

동풍 東風 the east wind; an easterly wind; (詩) the east
▶ 동풍이 분다 The east wind is blowing. ≒ The wind is in the east.
■ 마이(馬耳)— complete indifference; praying to deaf ears

동하다 動— 1 〈움직이다〉 move; budge; stir
2 〈흔들리다〉 be shaken; be perturbed; be upset; be moved [touched, influenced, affected]
♦ 〈마음이〉 동하기 쉽다 be easily affected [moved, influenced] 《by》; be sensitive 《to》 / 동하지 않다 keep calm; remain unruffled [unperturbed] / 유혹에 동하지 않다 be proof against temptation / 아첨에 동하지 않다 be above flattery
3 〈마음·구미가 당기다〉 have a desire 《for, to do》; be eager 《about, to do》; want 《to do》; have a mind 《to do》
♦ 구미가 동하다 feel an appetite 《for》; tempt 《offer》 / 여자에게 마음이 동하다 feel desire for a woman; take a fancy to a woman

동하중 動荷重 〈物〉 a dynamic load

동학 同學 〈동창생〉 *one's* schoolmate; *one's* schoolfellow; a companion in *one's* studies

▶ 나와 존은 동학의 친구다 John and I are companion in our studies.
▶ 그들은 동학이다 They are schoolmates [schoolfellows].

동항 凍港 an icebound port
■ —부 an ice-free port

동해 東海 the East Sea

동해 凍害 frost damage 《of vegetables》

동해안 東海岸 the east coast

동행 同行 going together; traveling together
♦ 동행인의 한 사람 one of the party / 다섯명의 동행인 a party of five (travelers) / 동행이 되다 fall into company; join company
— 동행하다 go [come] with; accompany *sb*; go in company with; go in *sb's* company; travel together; 〈호위·호송〉 escort
♦ …와 동행하여 (in company) with…; accompanied by…
▶ 그는 경찰서까지 동행할 것을 요구당했다 He was asked to come to the police station.
▶ 그녀는 곧잘 남편과 동행하여 야구를 보러갔다 She often went to the ball game with her husband.
▶ 제가 공항까지 동행해 드리겠습니다 I will accompany [go with] you to the airport.
▶ 그와 동행하여 시내까지 갔다 I accompanied [went with] him to town.
■ —자 a fellow traveler; a (traveling) companion —친구 ⇨ 길동무

동향 同鄕 the same village [town, district, province]
▶ 우리는 동향이다 We are [come] from the same town.
▶ 그녀와 나는 동향이다 She is [comes] from the same district as I.
▶ 그와는 동향이기 때문에 친해졌다 I became friendly with him because we came from the same part of the country [hometown].
■ —인 a man from the same place with *one*: 그와 나는 동향인이다 He hails from my province. ⇌ He is [comes] from the same province as myself.

동향 東向 an eastern exposure [aspect]; facing east
▶ 내 방은 동향이다 My room faces [looks] (to the) east.
▶ 그의 집은 동향이다 His house faces east [to the east].
— 동향하다 face east; look toward the east; orient
■ —집 a house facing east —판 a ground [lot] facing east

동향 動向 〈경향〉 a trend; a tendency; 〈움직임〉 movement; attitude
♦ 경제계의 동향 economic trends / 적의 동향 the movements of the enemy / 여론의 동향에 주의하다 keep an eye on [pay attention to] public opinion trends
▶ 그는 경제계의 동향에 매우 민감하다 He is very responsive to economic trends.
▶ 정치가는 시대의 동향에 민감하지 않으면 안 된다 Politicians must be sensitive to the movements of the times.

동혈 洞穴 〈동굴〉 a cave; a cavern; a grotto 《*pl.*~(e)s》; 〈인공의〉 an excavation

동형 同形 〔化〕 isomorphism; the same shape [form]
♦ 동형의 〔化〕 isomorphous; isomorphic
▶ 이 두 물체는 완전히 동형이다 These two things are exactly (of) the same shape.
■ —화합물 isomorphous compound

동형 同型 the same type [pattern]; a similar type
▶ 저 두 사람은 동형의 인간이다 They are of the same kind [type].
▶ 두 사람은 동형의 구두를 샀다 The two bought shoes of the same style.
▶ 동형의 사기 사건이 빈번히 일어났다 Fraud cases of similar pattern [type] occurred frequently.
■ —배우자 a homogamete

동호 同好 the same taste
— 동호하다 be interested in the same subject; share the same taste [interest]
■ —인 persons of [having] the same taste; persons interested in the same subject; a friend of similar tastes —회 an association of like-minded persons: 음악 동호회 a music-lovers' society [club] / 테니스 동호회 a tennis club

동화 同化 **1** 〔生〕 assimilation; anabolism
♦ 음의 동화 assimilation of a sound (to another)
— 동화하다 assimilate 《with, to》 (↔ dissimilate)
♦ 동화할 수 있는 assimilable / 동화하지 않는 unassimilated / 여러 나라의 사상을 동화하다 assimilate various foreign ideas
▶ 음식물은 동화되어 영양이 된다 Food is assimilated into nourishment.
▶ 그들은 그 지방 사람들과 동화되지 않았다 They didn't assimilate [adapt themselves] with the local people.
2 〈순응〉 adaptation
— 동화하다 adapt *oneself* 《to》
♦ 동화하기 쉬운[어려운] adaptable [inadaptable]
■ —녹말 assimilated starch —력 the ability to assimilate; assimilative power —색소 assimilatory pigment —성 assimilability —작용 〔生〕 assimilation: 탄소 동화작용 〔生〕 carbon dioxide assimilation —조직 〔植〕 an assimilation tissue

동화 動畫 an animation; an animated film [cartoon] ■ —제작자 an animator

동화 童話 a nursery tale [story]; a juvenile story; a fairy tale
♦ 동화의 나라 fairyland
■ —극 a juvenile [fairy] play; a play for children —작가 a writer of juvenile stories; a fairy-tale writer —집 a collection of fairy tales

동화 童畫 〈아동화〉 a nursery [juvenile] picture

동화 銅貨 a copper coin ⇨ 동전

동활차 動滑車 a movable pulley ⇨ 움직도르래

동회 洞會 a *tong* office ⇨ 동사무소

돛 a sail; a canvas

♦돛을 올리다 hoist [put up, spread] a sail / 돛을 달다 set a sail / 돛을 내리다 lower [take down] a sail / 돛을 펴다[감다] unfurl [furl] a sail / 바람을 가득 안은 돛 a full sail; a sail well taut / 순풍에 돛을 달고 달리다 sail before the [a fair] wind; be under easy sail
▶ 우리 요트는 순풍에 돛을 달고 달렸다 Our yacht sailed before a fairy wind.
▶ 순풍에 돛단듯이 일이 잘 돼간다 It's all plain sailing.
삼각— a jib 흰**—** a white sail
돛단배 a sailboat; a sailer; a sailing ship [vessel]
돛대 a mast; a stick
▶ 그 배는 폭풍우로 돛대를 잃었다 The ship was dismasted in the storm.
▶ 돛대가 부러진 그 배를 본 원주민들은 불길한 징조라고 믿었다 When the natives saw the dismasted vessel, they believed it an unlucky omen.
돛배 a sailboat ⇨ 돛단배
돛새치 〔魚〕 a sailfish
돼지 1 a pig; 〈거세한 수돼지〉 a hog; a swine (▶단수·복수 동형); 〈거세하지 않은 수돼지〉 a boar; 〈암돼지〉 a sow [sáu]

解説 *pig*는 (英)에서는 돼지를 뜻하는 가장 일반적인 말이지만 (美)에서는 120파운드 이하의 「새끼돼지」를 뜻한다. *hog*는 (美)에서는 「어미돼지」를 가리키지만 (英)에서는 식용으로 거세한 수돼지를 가리키는 경우가 많다.

♦돼지같은 piggish; hoggish; swinish / 돼지처럼 piggishly; hoggishly; swinishly / 돼지 처럼 (게걸스럽게) 먹다 eat greedily; eat like a hog; devour; feed *one's* food 《down》 / 돼지처럼 뚱뚱하다 be fat as a pig
▶ 그는 돼지를 치고[기르고] 있다 He raises [breeds] hogs [pigs].
▶ 돼지가 꿀꿀거린다 The hog is grunting. ⇌ The pigs are oinking.
▶ 저 자는 돼지처럼 게걸스럽게 먹는다 He eats like a hog [pig]. ⇌ He makes a pig of himself.
▶ 돼지에게 진주 (속담) To cast [throw] pearls before swine. ⇌ It's like casting pearls before swine.
2 (비유) 〈뚱보〉 a fat person; a fatty; 〈대식가〉 a greedy [grasping] person
■ **새끼—** a piggy; a pigling; a hogling; a piglet; a young pig [hog] : 한 배의 새끼돼지 a farrow; a litter of pigs 식용**—** a porker; a swine **—가죽** pigskin **—고기** pork; hog meat **—불고기** roast pork **—비계[기름]** lard; hog fat **—새끼** ⇨ 새끼 돼지
돼지감자 〔植〕 an [a Jerusalem] artichoke
돼지우리 a pigsty; a pigpen; (美) a hogpen; a pigsty
♦돼지우리같은 집 a shack; a pigpen; a hovel
되 1 〈계량기〉 a (one-*toe*) measure; a measuring cup [basket] 〈곡물용〉 a dry measure; 〈액체용〉 liquid measure
2 〈용량 단위〉 a unit of measure; a *toe* (= 1/10 *mal* =0.477 U.S. gallon)

♦쌀 석되 three *toe* of rice / 되로 팔다 sell by the measure / 되로 주다 give *sb* good measure / 되를 속이다 give short measure
되- 〈다시·도로〉 re-; again; back; 〈도리어〉 reversely; conversely; on the contrary; in return
♦되돌려 보내다 send *sb* back / 되묻다 ask back [in return]; throw back a question / 되사다 buy back; repurchase / 되쏘다 shoot back; 〈빛을〉 reflect / 되씹다 〈음식을〉 chew again and again; chew well; 〈말을〉 say over again / 되감다 rewind / 되던지다 throw [hurl, cast] back / 되돌려주다 return 《*sb* a borrowed book》; give [hand] back / 되튀다 rebound 《upon》; recoil 《on》; spring back / 되찾다 regain / 되심다 reship
-되 1 〈도리어, 반대로〉 though; but; although
▶ 그는 가난하되 거짓을 모르는 사람이다 Though (he is) poor, he is above telling a lie.
▶ 그녀는 아름답기는 하되 지성미가 없다 Although (she is) beautiful, she lacks intellectual beauty.
▶ 그 꽃은 아름답기는 하되 향기가 없다 The flower is lovely; only, they have no scent.
▶ 그는 돈은 많되 쓸 줄을 모른다 He has a lot of money, but he doesn't know how to spend it.
2 〈조건〉 if; when
▶ 오기는 오되 동생을 데리고 와라 If you want to come, bring your brother with you.
▶ 보기는 보되 만지지는 마라 You may look at it, but don't touch it.
3 〈부연〉 and that
▶ 그는 그것을 하되 훌륭하게 해냈다 He did it, and that very well.
▶ 비가 오되 억수같이 온다 It is raining and that in torrents.
되강오리 〔鳥〕 a grebe ⇨ 농병아리
되개고마리 〔鳥〕 a red-tailed shrike
되걸리다 〈다시 병들다〉 relapse 《into illness》; be seized with a relapse; be attacked 《by a disease》 again
♦감기에 되걸리다 catch [contract] a cold again; be attacked by a cold again; catch more cold; recatch a cold
▶ 그는 병이 회복되는 듯하더니 되걸렸다 He seemed to be getting round but had a relapse [return, second attack] of the disease.
되글을 가지고 말글로 써먹는다 (속담) use *one's* learning to the best advantage; take full advantage of *one's* little knowledge.
되넘기다 〈되팔다〉 resell; buy *sth* and sell it again 《to》 ♦기름을 사서 되넘기다 resell oils
되놈 〈중국 사람〉 a Chinese; (蔑) a Chinaman; (俗) a Chink
되뇌다 say over again; repeat
♦같은 소리를 되뇌다 harp on the same string; repeat the same thing
▶ 그의 말은 남이 한 말을 되뇌는데 지나지 않는다 He merely parrots what others have said.
▶ 그는 서양 학자의 견해를 되뇌고 있다 He repeats the views of Western scholars.
되는대로 1 〈함부로〉 at random; without thinking; haphazardly; 〈성의없이〉 lukewarmly

되다¹

♦되는대로 지껄이다 talk irresponsibly [at random]; say whatever comes into one's head /(일을) 되는대로 하다 do sth at random haphazardly
▶ 그는 되는대로 대답했다 He gave a random [haphazard] answer.
▶ 그는 그 문제에 관해 되는대로 비평했다 He made random remarks on the matter.
▶ 그녀는 되는대로 책을 펼치고 읽기 시작했다 She opened the book at random and began to read it.
▶ 그 얘기는 모두 그가 되는대로 지어낸 것이다 The whole story is his invention.
2 〈되어가는 대로〉♦ 일을 되는대로 내버려두다 leave a matter to take [run, follow] its own [natural] course; allow (the situation) to develop in its own way / 되는대로 살아가다 ride with the tide; live in a happy-go-lucky way; resign [abandon] *oneself* to fate

되다¹ **1** 〈지위·신분을 얻다〉 be; become; make; get; turn; grow; go

解說 (1) 「되다」의 뜻으로는 **become**과 **get**이 널리 쓰이는데 get이 구어적이다. **turn**은 「변화하다」의 뜻으로서 변화하여 달라진다는 점을 강조한다. **grow**는 「점차」「점점」이란 과정을 나타내고, **go**는 turn보다 구어적인 표현으로서 주로 바람직하지 못한 상태로의 변화나 또는 급격하거나 뚜렷한 변화를 나타내는 경우가 많다: go bald (대머리가 되다) / go mad (정신이 이상하게 되다)
(2) 「…이 되다」는 흔히 다음과 같이 표현한다. ① 수동태: be [get] fired (면직되다) ② 관용구: carry a chip on *one's* shoulder (시비조가 되다) ③ 기타 동사: miss (him, it) (그리워하게 되다) / feel lonely (쓸쓸하게 되다)

♦부자가 되다 become [grow] rich
▶ 그는 훌륭한 젊은이가 되었다 He has grown up to be a fine young man.
▶ 그는 어떻게 되었니? What has become of him?
▶ 당신은 좋은 아내가 될 것입니다 You will make a good wife.
▶ 우리 아들은 의사가 되기를 원하고 있어요 My son wants to be [become] a doctor.
▶ 우리 딸은 벌써 두 아이의 엄마가 되었지요 My daughter has already become [is] the mother of two children.
2 〈상태가 되다〉 get; become; turn; reduce
♦잘 되다 get better / 잘못 되다 get worse; worsen / 눈이 보이지[귀가 들리지] 않게 되다 go blind [deaf]; lose *one's* sight [hearing]
▶ 이 장소는 좋은 피서지가 될 것이다 This place will make a nice summer resort.
▶ 그의 재산은 모두 재가 되어버렸다 Everything he had was reduced to ashes.
▶ 쐐기벌레는 나비가 된다 A caterpillar turns [metamorphoses] into a butterfly.
3 〈때가 오다〉 ▶ 나는 곧 열일곱 살이 된다 I'll very soon be seventeen.
▶ 그녀는 다음 생일로 스무 살이 된다 She'll be twenty (years old) next birthday.
▶ 곧 정오가 된다 It will soon be twelve noon.

4 〈변하다〉 turn (into, out); change; develop
▶ 가을에는 나뭇잎이 누렇게 된다 The leaves turn yellow in autumn.
▶ 얼음이 녹아 물이 되었다 The ice has melted.
▶ 눈은 곧 비가 되었다 The snow soon turned [changed] to rain.
▶ 그의 감기는 폐렴이 되었다 His cold developed into pneumonia.
5 〈성립·구성하다〉 consist of; be composed [made up, formed] of; form
▶ 물은 산소와 수소로 되어 있다 Water consists of oxygen and hydrogen.
▶ 운영위원회는 일곱 명의 멤버로 되어 있다 The steering committee is composed of seven members.
▶ 이 책은 열다섯 장의 지도와 그 해설로 되어 있다 This book comprises fifteen maps and their explanations.
6 〈성취하다〉 succeed; be accomplished; be attained
♦일이 잘 되다 be successful; go well; work [come off] well / 잘 되지 않다 go badly [amiss, wrong]; be unsuccessful
▶ 모든 일이 잘 되었다 All went well with us.
▶ 이 설계도까지 손에 넣었으니 일은 다 된 셈이다 Success is almost ours since we've got this plan.
7 〈결과를 가져오다〉 turn out; result [end] in
♦현실이 되다 come out true / 무용하게[폐지] 되다 fall into disuse
▶ 꿈이 현실로 되었다 The dream has come true.
▶ 시합은 무승부가 되었다 The match resulted in a draw.
▶ 근심 때문에 그 여자는 담배를 피우게 되었다 Her troubles led her to smoke.
▶ 그것은 결국 같은 일이 됩니다 It comes to the same thing.
▶ 그가 마지막 입은 부상이 치명상이 되었다 The last wound he received proved fatal.
▶ 일이 그렇게 되지는 않았다 Things didn't work out that way.
▶ 나는 일이 그렇게 되리라고는 생각하지 못했다 I never expected things would come to this pass [take such a turn].
8 〈수량에 미치다〉 come to; amount; make
▶ 6에 3을 더하면 9가 된다 Six and three makes [markes] nine.
▶ 이것으로 지원자는 서른 명이 된다 This makes thirty applicants.
▶ 이 일은 일당 3만원이 된다 This job pays thirty thousand won a day.
▶ 7에서 3을 빼면 4가 된다 Three from seven leaves four. ⇌ Seven minus three is four.
▶ 그 그림이 30만원이 되었다 The picture brought in three hundred thousand won.
▶ 3에 3을 곱하면 얼마가 됩니까? How much is three times three?
▶ 모두 얼마가 됩니까? How much does all that come to [add up to]? ⇌ What do you make the total?
9 〈구실을 하다〉 act as; impersonate; play the role [part] of; serve as [for]
♦햄릿역을 하게 되다 play the part of Ham-

let; impersonate Hamlet
▶알코올은 소독약이 된다 Alcohol acts as a disinfectant.
▶이 지팡이는 무기도 된다 This stick will serve as [for] a weapon.
▶긴 의자가 침대 대용품이 되었다 The couch served as a bed.
10 〈경과하다〉 elapse; pass; it is 《a month》 since ♦몇 백년 된 나무 a tree centuries old
▶그가 죽은지 벌써 5년이 되었다 It has been five years since he died. ⇒ Five years have elapsed since he died.
▶서울에 온지 얼마나 되었니? How long have you been in Seoul?
▶1주일 있으면 여기서 산지 만 1년이 된다 In another week I shall have lived here for a full year.
▶벌써 그렇게 되었나요? Was it so long ago, I wonder?
11 〈나이를 먹다〉 attain; reach; turn
♦서른이 되다 enter upon [attain] one's thirtieth / 서른 살이 다 되어가다 be on the short side of thirty; be nearing thirty
▶그는 마흔살이 못된다 He is under forty.
▶그녀는 아직 쉰살이 안되었다 She is on this side of fifty.
12 〈시작하다〉 begin to 《do》; come [get] to 《do》; learn to 《do》; set in
▶처음 만났을 때부터 그녀를 좋아하게 되었다 I began to like her from the first time we met.
▶어떻게 해서 술을 마시게 되었습니까? How did you come to start drinking?
▶언제부터 담배를 끊게 되었나요? When did you give up smoking?
▶나는 중학생 시절에 시를 쓰게 되었다 I began to write poetry when I was in middle school.
▶그는 요즘 부쩍 미남이 되었다 He has grown much more handsome recently.
13 〈자라다〉 grow; thrive; prosper
▶올해는 벼가 풍작이 되었다 We have had a good crop of rice this year.
▶이 지방에서는 복숭아가 잘 된다 Peaches grow well in this area.
▶아주까리는 어떤 땅에서나 잘 된다 The castor-oil plant thrives in almost any soil.
14 〈인적 관계가 되다〉 be related to; be a relative
♦먼 일가가 되다 be a distant relative
▶저 분이 부인 되시나요? Is that [she] your wife?
▶그분과는 어떻게 되시나요? What relation is he to you? ⇒ How are you related to him?
▶그분은 외가쪽으로 친척이 되십니다 He is related to [connected with] me on my mother's side.
15 〈다하다〉 come to an end; run out; be out [up]; be used up
▶연료가 다 되었다 The gasoline [fuel] is [has run] out.
▶계약 기한이 다 되었다 The contract has run out [expired]. ⇒ The lease is out.
▶나는 돈이 다 되었다 I have run through all my money. ⇒ My money come to an end.
▶이 자전거도 이제 다 되었다 This bike has seen its day. ⇒ This bike has served its time.
16 〈해도 좋다〉 may 《do》; 〈…하지 않아도 좋다〉 need not 《do》; have no need of 《doing》
♦가도 되다 may go / 가지 않아도 되다 need not go
▶이 돈은 없어도 된다 I can do [manage] without the money.
▶그렇게 하면 다시 나가지 않아도 된다 That will save you going out again.
▶나는 가지 않아도 된다 I need not go. ⇒ There is no need of my going.
17 〈충분하다〉 be enough; be sufficient; will do; answer [serve] the purpose
▶이것이면 된다 This will do. ⇒ This will serve [answer for] my purpose.
▶만원만 있으면 됩니다 Ten thousand won will do [answer the purpose, be enough for the purpose].
18 【가능하다】 〈사람이〉 can 《do》; be able to 《do》; be capable of 《doing》; 〈사물이〉 be possible
♦될 수 있는대로 as...as possible / 될 수 있는 대로 정확한 계산 the most accurate calculations available
▶제 힘으로 될 수 있는 것은 무엇이든지 하겠습니다 I will do anything in my power everything I can.
▶될 수만 있으면 외국에서 공부하고 싶다 I'd like to study abroad, if possible.
▶이 기회를 될 수 있는대로 이용하십시오 You'd better make the most of this opportunity.
19 〈타당하다〉 proper; adequate
▶이 문장은 돼먹지 않았다 This sentence makes no sense at all [is complete nonsense].
▶그녀가 하는 짓은 돼먹지 않았다 What she does is ridiculous.

되다² 〈되질하다〉 measure
♦말[되]로 되다 measure 《rice》 with a *mal* [*toe*] measure / 수북이 되어 주다 give *sb* full measure / 빠지게 [속여서] 되어주다 give *sb* short measure / 되어서 팔다 sell by the measure

되다³ 1 〈빡빡하다〉 hard; thick; stiff; tough
♦된 죽[풀] thick gruel [paste] / 되게 반죽하다 give stiff consistency by kneading or churning
▶밥이 좀 되다 The rice is boiled rather hard [rather hard-boiled].
▶풀을 되게 쑤어라 Make the paste thick [stiff].
2 〈팽팽하다〉 tight; taut; tense
♦줄을 되게 당기다 tighten a rope; stretch a rope tight
▶밧줄이 되다 A rope is taut.
3 〈고되다〉 hard; tough; laborious; toilsome
♦된 일 hard [heavy] work; a tough job [task] / 된 등반길 a toilsome climb up the mountain / 된 생활 a hard life / 병의 된 고비를 넘기다 pass the crisis of an illness
4 〈심하다〉 severe; intense; violent; strong; bitter
♦된 감기 a bad cold / 된 바람 a strong [violent] wind / 된 벌 a severe punishment / 된 추위 severe [intense] cold / 되게 〈매우〉 very;

-되다

〈심하게〉 severely; hard; soundly; 〈많이〉 much; heavily / 되게 야단맞다 be scolded severely; be given a good scolding / 되게 술을 마시다 drink heavily [hard]/ 되게 가난하다 be awfully poor; be as poor as a church mouse / 되게 다치다 be severely wounded / 되게 덥다[춥다] be terribly [awfully, extremely] hot [cold] / 되게 비싸다 be very high in price; be very dear / 되게 머리가 아프다 have a severe headache
▶ 나는 되게 운이 좋았다 I had capital luck.
▶ 그는 넘어질 때 머리를 되게 부딪쳤다 He got a nasty knock on the head when he fell.
▶ 그런 녀석은 되게 혼내줘야 한다 Such a fellow deserves the severest possible punishment under the sun.

-되다 1 〈동사적 명사에 붙어〉 be (expected); get (ready)
◆ 번역되다 be translated [put] into (English) /(병세가) 악화되다 take a serious turn; change [take a turn] for the worse / 완쾌되다 be completely cured (of a disease); recover (completely) / 해고되다 be [get] dismissed [discharged]/ 해결되다 be solved [settled]; come to a settlement / 공인되다 gain official approval
▶ 그 영화는 지금 상영되고 있다 The film [movie] is now on (show).
▶ 데모가 전국으로 확대되었다 The demonstration spread throughout the country.
2 〈형용사적 명사·부사적 어근에 붙어〉 be
◆ 망령되다 be foolish [unreasonable, silly]; 〈노인이〉 be senile [doting]; be in one's dotage [second childhood] / 막되다 be ill-mannered[-bred]; be wild / 속되다 be vulgar [low]; be worldly / 참되다 be true [honest, faithful]/ 헛되다 be vain [futile, fruitless, empty]

되다랗다 quite thick [hard, heavy]
되대패 a round plane; a circular plane
되도록 1 〈가급적〉 as...as possible [practicable]; as...as one can; 〈될 수 있으면〉 if possible [practicable]; if it can be so arranged; if circumstances allow; 〈부정(否定)〉 no more than one can help
◆ 되도록 빨리 as soon [quickly, promptly] as possible; at one's earliest (possible) convenience / 되도록 많이 as much [many] as possible / 되도록 싸게 팔다 sell as cheaply as possible
▶ 되도록 빨리 답장을 주시오 Please reply at your earliest convenience. ⇌ Please let me have your answer as soon as possible.
▶ 되도록 늦지 않도록 하시오 Don't be longer than you can help.
2 〈될 수 있도록〉 (so as) to (become); (so [in order]) that one may (become)
◆ 교사가 되도록 돕다 help sb (to) become a teacher / 챔피언이 되도록 노력하다 try to be a champion; try to win [gain] a championship
▶ 위대한 인물이 되도록 노력해라 Try hard to be a great man.

되돌아가다 1 〈되짚어가다〉 turn [go] back (to); return (to); backtrack; retrace one's steps [way]
◆ 온 길을 되돌아가다 retrace one's steps [way]; turn back the way one has come / 도중에서 되돌아가다 turn back halfway [on the way out]
▶ 폭풍 때문에 배는 항구로 되돌아갔다 Owing to the storm the ship put back to port.
▶ 사람은 나이가 들면 어린애로 되돌아간다 When one grows old, one enters a second childhood.
▶ 우리는 학창시절로 되돌아간 듯이 법석을 떨었다 We had an uproarious [a hilarious] time acting just like schoolboys again.
2 〈본디 상태로 되다〉 go back(ward); turn back; return (to); revert (to)
◆ 야만 상태로 되돌아가다 relapse [back] into savagery / 나쁜 길로 되돌아가다 relapse into vice / 본론으로 되돌아가다 return [revert] to the main subject / 제자리로 되돌아가다 resume [return to, go back to] one's seat
▶ 내가 지난주에 말한 화제로 되돌아가자 Let's return to the subject I spoke of last week.
▶ 여기까지 온 이상 우리는 되돌아가지는 못합니다 We have come so far (that) there can be no turning back.
▶ 그녀는 집안으로 되돌아갔다 She retreated into the house.
▶ 나는 돈지갑을 놓고 온 것이 생각나서 집으로 되돌아갔다 I remembered I (had) left my wallet in my house, and went back for it.

되돌아보다 look back (at); look over one's shoulder; turn one's head; turn round; look again
◆ 옛날을 되돌아보면 in retrospect / 과거를 되돌아보다 think back to the past days; think backward; look back upon the past / 자신의 행동을 되돌아보다 review one's conduct
▶ 나는 시간이 다 될 때까지 몇 번씩 답안을 되돌아보았다 I read my (exam) paper over and over again before time ran out.

되돌아오다 come back (to); return (to); 〈상품이〉 be sent back; 〈분실물이〉 be restored [recovered]; 〈비난이〉 boomerang; 〈수영경기에서〉 make a turn
◆ 본론으로 되돌아오다 return to one's main point / 본심으로 되돌아오다 come to oneself; recover one's senses
▶ 분실물은 주인에게로 되돌아왔다 The lost article was restored to its owner.
▶ 그는 정계로 되돌아왔다 He returned to the political world.
▶ 그는 대사의 지위로 되돌아왔다 He was reinstated in his post as (an) ambassador.

되똑거리다 totter; wobble; be shaky [rickety, unsteady, unstable]
◆ 되똑거리는 의자 a rickety [shaky] chair
▶ 어린애가 되똑거리며 걸어간다 The child is walking with tottering steps.

되똑되똑 totteringly; unsteadily; unstably
▶ 아기가 되똑되똑 걷기 시작했다 The baby took a few tottering steps.

되레 on the contrary ⇨ 도리어
되로 주고 말로 받는다 〈속담〉 Sow the wind and reap the whirlwind.

되롱거리다 dangle ⇨ 대롱거리다
되묻다 1 〈다시 묻다〉 ask again; inquire again
▶ 그는 내 이름을 되물었다 He asked for my name in return.
2 〈반문하다〉 ask back; throw a question back (at *sb*)
▶ 나는 그것을 세 번 되물었다 I inquired about it three times.
되바라지다 precocious; pert; saucy; forward; cheeky
♦ 되바라진 아이 a precocious boy / 되바라진 녀석 (口) a sassy kid; (口) a squirt / 되바라진 소리를 하다 say pert things
▶ 웬일인지 저 집 아이들은 되바라져 있다 Somehow or other their children are sophisticated [worldly-wise].
▶ 그 마을 사람들은 되바라져 있지 않다 The people in the village are naive and unsophisticated.
되부르다 call back; recall
되살다 1 〈더부룩하다〉 be not digesting; be heavy on *one's* stomach; feel uncomfortable (because of indigestion)
2 〈소생하다〉 come to *oneself* [*one's* senses]; be brought (back) to life; be restored (from death) to life; return to life; revive; resuscitate; 〈싱싱해지다〉 be freshened
♦ 실신 상태에서 되살아나다 revive from a swoon / 인공호흡으로 되살아나다 be resuscitated by artificial respiration / 꺼져가던 불이 되살다 a dying fire flames up again
▶ 비가 와서 초목이 되살아났다 The grass and plants have been freshened after a rainfall. ≒ The rain has reinvigorated the withered plants.
▶ 그 책을 보고 어릴적 기억이 되살아났다 The book reminded me [put me in mind] of my childhood.
3 〈재결합하다〉 be reunited; return to former relations (with a wife)
되살리다 〈소생시키다〉 raise *sb* from the death; restore *sb* to life; bring *sb* to life [(*his*) senses]; revive; resuscitate; 〈기억나게 하다〉 wake [recall, bring back] (*one's* memories); call back the memory of; call *sth* to mind [memory, remembrance]; 〈싱싱하게 하다〉 freshen
되새 〔鳥〕 a mountain [bramble] finch; a brambling
되새기다 〈내씹다〉 chew over and over again (because of poor appetite); 〈반추하다〉 ruminate; chew the cud; 〈곰곰이 생각하다〉 meditate (on, upon); ruminate (about, of, upon, over)
♦ 과거를 되새기다 meditate on *one's* past
▶ 남녀노소 할것 없이 고통스러웠던 6·25의 역사를 잠시 되새겼다 Men and women, old and young alike, relived for a while the painful history of the Korean War.
되솔새 〔鳥〕 a pale-legged willow warbler [wren]
되쏘다 〈다시 쏘다〉 shoot back; 〈반사하다〉 reflect; 〈되받아 치다〉 retort [retaliate] (upon); give [pay] *sb* tit for tat

되씌우다 〈허물을 남에게 넘기다〉 put [lay, thrust] (the blame) on *sb*; shift (the blame) on to *sb*; (俗) pass the buck (to)
♦ 절도죄를 되씌우다 impute the theft to *sb*
▶ 네 잘못을 내게 되씌우려 하고 있다 You are trying to put the blame on me when you are to blame yourself.
되씹다 1 〈말을 되풀이하다〉 repeat; reiterate; tell the same story over again
▶ 그는 여전히 똑같은 얘기만 되씹고 있다 He is still harping on the same topic.
2 ⇨ 되새기다
되알지다 1 〈억짓손이 세다〉 forcing; coercive; aggressive; pushing
2 〈벅차다〉 beyond *one's* power; above *one's* ability; more than *one* can do
되어가다 1 〈거의 이루어져가다〉 go (on); work; progress; advance
♦ 잘 되어가다 go well [all right]; work well; go on smoothly [without a hitch] / (매사를) 되어가는 대로 하다 have the haphazard way of doing everything; follow a hit-or-miss method / 되어가는대로 내버려두다 leave (a matter) to take its own course
▶ 그 계획은 잘 되어가고 있다 The project is in full swing.
▶ 계획대로 잘 되어갑니까? Does the plan work well?
▶ 만사 잘 되어갈 것이다 Everything will go off smoothly.
2 〈거의 완성되어가다〉 be getting finished [completed]
▶ 연이 다 되어간다 The kite is being finished.
▶ 동상이 거의 되어가고 있다 The bronze statue is nearly completed.
3 〈거의 다 되다〉 be getting; be on the verge [brink] of
▶ 점심때가 다 되어간다 It is almost [well-nigh] noon.
▶ 저녁때가 되어가고 있다 Evening is just falling.
▶ 그가 미국으로 떠난지 3년이 되어간다 It is almost three years since he went to America.
되우 〈몹시〉 very; exceedingly; heavily; severely; hard; extremely
♦ 되우 덥다 be exceedingly hot / 되우 바쁘다 be very busy / 되우 피로하다 be very tired / 되우 꾸짖다 scold severely
되잖다 poor; wretched; (be) no good; absurd; nonsensical
♦ 되잖은 수작 an absurd remark; silly talk; nonsense / 되잖은 녀석 wretched fellow; a good-for-nothing / 되잖은 핑계 a poor [lame] excuse / 되잖은 소리를 지껄이다 talk rot [nonsense]
되지기[1] 〈데운 밥〉 reheated rice
되지기[2] 〈논밭의 넓이〉 paddy land enough to grow one *toe* of seed rice
되지못하다 1 〈다 이루어지지 못하다〉 be short of; be less than; be under; be not made; be not finished [completed, accomplished]
♦ 열살이 되지 못하다 be under ten (years old)
▶ 미국 간지 1년이 되지 못하여 다시 돌아왔다 He came back home less than a year after he

went to America.
▶ 지식만으로는 교사가 되지 못한다 Knowledge alone does not qualify one for [to be] a teacher.
2 〈건방지다〉 (be) impudent; conceited; forward; pert; saucy
◆ 되지 못한 놈 a cocky guy; a conceited pup; 〈욕으로〉 a wretched fellow; a bastard / 되지 못하게 굴다 act fresh [smart]; behave indecently [impudently, overbearingly]
▶ 되지 못한 수작 마라 Don't talk fresh! ⇒ None of your foul [impudence] now!

되지빠귀 〔鳥〕 a gray-backed thrush

되직하다 〈조금 되다〉 somewhat thick; stodgy
◆ 밥을 되직하게 짓다 boil [cook] rice a bit too hard
▶ 죽이 되직하다 The gruel is rather thick.

되질하다 measure (rice) with a *toe*

되짚어 back; returning right away
◆ 되짚어 가다 ⇨ 되돌아가다 / 되짚어 보내다 send right back; send back at once / 되짚어 오다 come [return] (right) back
▶ 이 열차는 부산에서 되짚어 돌아온다 This train goes as far as Pusan and then returns.

되찾다 get [take] back; regain; restore; recover; retrieve
◆ 〈분실물을〉 남에게서 되찾다 take back *sth* from *sb* / 예전 지위를 되찾다 retrieve *one's* former position / 저당잡힌 물건을 되찾다 redeem a mortgage [pawned goods]; take [get] a thing out of pawn / 진지를 되찾다 reoccupy a fort / 질서를 되찾다 reestablish [restore] order
▶ 지나가버린 유년시절은 되찾을 수 없다 We can't go back to our childhood days.

되통스럽다 awkward; clumsy; tactless; bungling; (口) harum-scarum
◆ 되통스러운 사람 a bungler; a botcher; a harum-scarum / 하는 짓이 되통스럽다 be awkward in *one's* movements
▶ 그는 사람이 되통스러워 하는 일마다 실수를 저지른다 He is so clumsy that he makes a bungle of everything he does.

되풀이¹ 〈반복〉 (a) repetition; a repeat; reiteration
—**되풀이하다** repeat; reiterate; do [go] *sth* over again
◆ 되풀이하여 repeatedly; over and over (again); again and again / 잘못을 되풀이하다 repeat *one's* mistake; make the same mistake again (and again) / 되풀이하여 말하다 repeat; say over again; reiterate; 〈같은 말을〉 harp on the same string / 같은 것을 되풀이하다 repeat the same thing / 세 번 되풀이하여 읽다 read three times over
▶ 역사는 되풀이한다 History repeats itself. ⇒ History is the record of repetition.
▶ 그 여자는 그 얘기를 두 번 되풀이했다 She went over the story two times [twice].
▶ 내가 말하는 것을 되풀이해 주세요 Please repeat after me.
▶ 같은 잘못을 되풀이하지 마라 Don't make the same error twice.
▶ 그녀는 남편의 편지를 되풀이해서 읽었다 She read her husband's letter again and again.
▶ 되풀이해서 연습하면 는다 We make progress by repetition.
▶ 다시 한 번 되풀이해서 말해 보게 Say it over.
▶ 나는 책을 처음부터 되풀이하여 읽기로 하고 있다 I make it a rule to reread books from the start.
▶ 내가 떠날 때 그녀는 「여름 휴가에는 꼭 그와 함께 와」라고 되풀이하여 다짐했다 When I was leaving, she kept repeating, "Please be sure to come along with him for summer vacation."

되풀이² 〈되로 풀기〉 figuring out the cost of *sth* by the *toe*; 〈되로 팔기〉 selling by the *toe*
—**되풀이하다** calculate the cost (of grain) by the *toe*; sell by the *toe*

된똥 hard excrements [feces]

된바람 〈강풍〉 a strong [severe, high] wind; a gale; 〈뱃사람의 말〉 a north [northerly] wind

된밥 hard-boiled rice

된비알 a steep slope [hill]; a very steep road [cliff]

된서리 a heavy [hard, severe] frost
◆ 된서리 맞다 suffer from a heavy frost; 〈타격받다〉 receive a bitter blow; be hard [severely] hit (by); be severely affected (by); sustain great damage
▶ 그는 지난 번 장사에서 된서리를 맞았다 He suffered quite a setback on the last deal.
▶ 소매치기들은 경찰의 일제 검거로 된서리를 맞았다 Pickpockets were hard hit by a police roundup.

된서방 ―書房 an overbearing [a harsh] husband ◆ 된서방 맞다 get married to a brute; (비유) be treated harshly [cruelly]; suffer an ordeal

된소리 〔音聲〕 a fortis (*pl*. -tes)

된장 ―醬 *toenjang*; soybean paste
▶ ―국 beanpaste potage [soup]

될뻔댁 ―宅 a person who just missed a chance of success

될성부르다 promising; hopeful

될성부른 나무는 떡잎부터 알아본다 (속담) Genius displays itself even in childhood. ⇒ Sandalwood is fragrant even in seed leaf.

됨됨이 1 〈사람의 생긴 품〉 *one's* nature; (a) personal character; (a) personality; 〈외모〉 personal appearance
◆ 됨됨이가 좋은[나쁜] 학생 bright [dull] student / 됨됨이가 귀골스럽다 look noble; have the appearance of a high personage
▶ 저분의 자녀들은 모두 됨됨이가 좋군요 His children are all bright.
▶ 이것으로 그의 됨됨이를 알 수 있다 This shows what he is made of [what he is (like)]. ⇒ This is characteristic of him.
2 〈물건의 생긴 품〉 makeup; workmanship
▶ 됨됨이가 시원찮다 The make is poor. ⇒ It is of bad make.
▶ 이 옷장은 됨됨이가 조잡하다 This wardrobe is cheap in make.
▶ 이 캐비닛은 됨됨이가 좋다[나쁘다] This cabinet is well [badly] made.

뒷박 1 a *toe* ⇨ 되 2 a gourd bowl used as a measure ♦ 쌀을 뒷박으로 사다 buy rice by the *toe* [in small quantities]

뒷술 about one *toe* of liquor; (rice) wine sold by the *toe*

두 two; a couple (of)
♦ 두 가지 〈종류〉 two kinds (of); 〈방법〉 two ways / 두 사람 two persons / 두 내외 a (married) couple; husband [man] and wife / 두 번 twice; two times / 두 번째 a second time / 우유 두 잔 two glasses of milk
▶ 두 주인을 섬기기는 어렵다 No man can serve two masters.
▶ 이 단어에는 두 가지 뜻이 있다 This word has a double meaning.

두 頭 1 〈골치〉 ▶ 아이고 두야! What a headache [trouble, nuisance]!
2 〈마리〉 a head (▶단수·복수 동형)
♦ 소 열 두 ten head of cattle
▶ 우리 집에서는 소 삼십 두를 기르고 있다 I have [keep] thirty cows at my place. ⇌ I have thirty head of cows at my place.

두각 頭角 1 〈머리 끝〉 the top of the head
2 〈뛰어남〉 prominence; conspicuousness
♦ 두각을 나타내다 make [cut] a conspicuous [brilliant] figure; distinguish *oneself* (in); stand head and shoulders (above others); rise into prominence; stand out; lead all the rest
▶ 그는 동료들 사이에서 단연 두각을 나타내고 있다 He stands a giant among his colleagues. ⇌ He towers above his fellows.
▶ 그는 실업계에서 두각을 나타냈다 He became distinguished in business circles.
▶ 그는 그의 분야에서 두각을 나타내기 시작했다 He began to rise in his field.
▶ 그녀는 파티에서 두각을 나타냈다 She made herself conspicuous at the party.
▶ 그는 학자로서 두각을 나타냈다 He assumed greater prominence as a scholar.

두개 頭蓋 [解] the cranium (*pl.* ~s, -nia); the skull; the brainpan ♦ 두개의 cranial; cephalic ─근 cranial muscles ─수술 craniotomy ─절개술 craniotomy

두개골 頭蓋骨 the skull; the cranium (*pl.* ~s, -nia); the cranial bone
─골절 a skull fracture: 두개골 골절을 당하다 suffer a skull fracture; have *one's* skull fractured ─연구 craniology ─측정기 a craniometer

두건 頭巾 a mourner's hempen hood
♦ 두건을 쓰다 put on [wear] a hood

두겁 an ornamental cap at the tip of a long and slender object; 〈붓두껍〉 a writing brush cap

두겁조상 ─祖上 *one's* most distinguished ancestor

두견 杜鵑 1 〈鳥〉 ⇨ 두견이
2 〈植〉 〈진달래〉 an azalea

두견이, 두견새 杜鵑─ 〈鳥〉 a (common, little) cuckoo (*pl.* ~s)

두고가다 leave *sth* (behind); forget
♦ 탁자 위에 명함을 두고가다 leave a card on the table

두고두고 〈여러 차례〉 many times; from time to time; over and over (again); 〈오래도록〉 (for) long; for a long time; 〈영원히〉 forever; eternally; for good (and all)
♦ 두고두고 생각하다 think continually of [about] *sth*; turn *sth* over and over in *one's* mind / 두고두고 먹다 keep *sth* and eat (it) sparingly
▶ 은혜는 두고두고 잊지 않겠습니다 I shall be grateful to you as long as I live. ⇌ I shall always remember your kindness to me.
▶ 그것은 두고두고 쓸 수 있다 It can be used many and many times.
▶ 그것은 두고두고 잊혀지지 않는다 The memory always haunts me.

두고보다 〈지켜보다〉 watch (intently); keep (a good) watch (over)
▶ 두고보자 See how things will shape up. ⇌ Watch and wait.
▶ 그는 「두고보자」는 말을 남기고 돌아갔다 He went away with the parting threat, "You shall pay [smart] for this."

두고오다 leave *sth* behind; forget; mislay; misplace ♦ 책을 두고오다 mislay *one's* book
▶ 나는 지하철 안에 가방을 두고왔다 I left my bag (behind) on [(英)] in] the subway.

두골 頭骨 the skull ⇨ 두개골

두근거리다 throb; beat (fast); palpitate; pulsate; pulse
♦ 가슴이 두근거리다 *one's* heart palpitates [throbs, beats] violently; 〈불안하여〉 feel nervous (without any known cause); 〈겁이 나서〉 have *one's* heart in *one's* mouth / 두근거리는 가슴을 가라앉히다 calm *one's* agitated breast; compose [collect] *oneself*
▶ 입상의 기쁨으로 내 가슴이 두근거렸다 My heart throbbed with joy at winning the prize.
▶ 그 남자의 모습을 보고 그녀는 가슴이 두근거리는 것을 느꼈다 She felt her heart throbbing at the sight of the man.
▶ 그녀의 가슴은 기대로 두근거렸다 Her heart fluttered [beat fast] in anticipation.
▶ 웬일인지 가슴이 두근거린다 Somehow I feel uneasy.
▶ 내 이름을 부르는 소리를 듣자 가슴이 두근거렸다 My heart beat when I heard my name called.
▶ 가슴을 두근거리며 막이 오르기를 기다렸다 I waited for the curtain to rise with my heart beating in excitement.

두근두근 pit-a-pat; palpitating; throbbing
─두근두근하다 ⇨ 두근거리다

두꺼비 〈動〉 a toad ─기름 toad's grease ─씨름 the seesaw match; a tie game

두꺼비 꽁지만하다 〈속담〉 be shallow [superficial] in *one's* learning [talent]

두꺼비집 〈電〉 a fuse box; a (safety) cutout

두꺼비 파리 잡아먹듯 〈속담〉 eat up anything in a twinkling

두껍다 thick; bulky; stout
♦ 두꺼운 책 a thick book / 두꺼운 입술 full [thick] lips / 두꺼운 벽 a heavy [solid] wall / 두껍게 thickly / 낯이 두껍다 be brazen(-faced); be shameless [cheeky] / 두껍게 하다 thicken; make thicker

두껍닫이

▶ 그는 고기를 두껍게 썰었다 He cut the meat into thick pieces.
▶ 겨울에는 두꺼운 오버코트를 입는다 In winter we put on thick overcoats.

두껍닫이 a sliding door pocket; a boxing; a box

두께 thickness
◆ 두께가 두껍다[얇다] be thick [thin]
▶ 그것은 두께가 얼마나 됩니까? How thick is it? ⇒ What is the thickness?
▶ 이 벽은 5cm의 두께다 This wall is five centimeters thick. ⇒ This wall has a thickness of five centimeters.
▶ 두께는 모두 같습니다 They are all of the same thickness.
▶ 그린란드의 빙하는 어떤 곳은 두께가 1.5킬로미터 이상이 되기도 한다 The Greenland glacier reaches a thickness of more than 1.5 kilometers in some places.

두뇌 頭腦 a head; brains
◆ 치밀한 두뇌 a close head / 예민한 두뇌 an acute intellect / 두뇌 플레이 a play with brains / 두뇌가 모자라다 have a poor [bad, dull] head; be dull-brained / 두뇌를 쓰다 use one's brains [head]; use mental power / 두뇌를 요하다 require brains
▶ 이 일을 해내려면 명석한 두뇌가 필요하다 It takes an excellent brain to accomplish this task.
▶ 그의 두뇌는 실무에 적합하다 He has a good head for business.
▶ 그는 수학적인 두뇌를 가지고 있다 He has a head for mathematics.
▶ 그는 두뇌가 명석하다 He is bright. ⇒ He has a clear head. ⇒ He is clear-headed.
■ ─노동자 a brain worker ─유출 brain drain ─회귀 brain reverse

두다¹ 1 〈놓다〉 put; place; set; position
▶ 이것을 어디다 둘까요? Where shall I put this?
▶ 분명히 여기에 뒀는데 찾을 수가 없다 I am sure I put it here, but I cannot find it.
▶ 그 짐을 둘 데가 없다 I can find no room for the baggage.
2 〈남겨놓다〉 leave (behind)
▶ 우산을 어딘가에 두고 왔나보다 I'm afraid I've left my umbrella (behind) [lost my umbrella] somewhere.
▶ 기차 안에 두고 내린 물건들이 많다 There are lots of things left in trains.
▶ 오늘 밤에는 아이들을 집에 두고 나갈 작정입니다 We're going out this evening with the children left at home.
▶ 그는 아내를 한국에 둔채 미국으로 갔다 He went to America leaving his wife (behind) in Korea.
▶ 그는 가족을 부산에 두고 서울에서 살고 있다 He has left his family behind in Pusan, and is living in Seoul.
3 〈원상태대로 있게 하다〉 leave; allow; let; keep; have
◆ 일을 손대지 않고 두다 leave one's work undone / 문을 열린채 두다 leave the door open

▶ 그대로 두어라 Leave it as it is. ⇌ Leave it alone.
▶ 말하지 않고 그대로 두는게 좋다 It had better be left unsaid.
▶ 하고 싶은대로 하게 돼라 Let him do as he pleases [likes].
▶ 그는 하던 일을 그대로 두고 외출했다 He went out, leaving work half done.
▶ 그들의 무례를 그대로 두어서는 안된다 You shouldn't leave their bad manners uncorrected.
4 〈마음 속에 지니다〉 cherish; bear; entertain; hold; have
◆ 의심을 두다 harbor suspicion / 마음을 두다 have a mind to; be determined to / 학문에 뜻을 두다 set one's heart on learning
▶ 당신의 일을 언제나 마음에 두고 있습니다 I always keep you in mind.
▶ 그가 하는 말을 너무 마음에 두지 마십시오 Don't worry too much about what he says.
5 〈바둑 등을〉 play 《chess, paduk》; move 《a chessman》
◆ 바둑을 잘 두다 play paduk skillfully / 네 점 놓고 두다 accept a four-stone handicap
▶ 한 판 두지 않으시겠습니까? How about (playing) a game?
▶ 먼저 두시지요 Take the first move.
▶ 이번에는 네가 둘 차례다 The next move is with you.
6 〈고용하다〉 employ; hire; 〈데리고 있다〉 engage; keep; 〈묵게 하다〉 lodge; take in
▶ 하인을 셋 두다 keep three servants / 좋은 아들을 두다 be blessed with a good son
▶ 타이피스트를 한 사람 두고 싶은데요 We want to hire a typist.
▶ 새 비서를 두었다 We employed a new secretary.
▶ 하숙인을 몇 사람이나 두고 있습니까? How many boarders have you taken in?
▶ 하숙인을 두 사람 두고 있습니다 I have [I've taken in] two boarders.
7 〈넣다〉 put in; add; stuff
◆ 밥에 팥을 두다 put red beans in the rice / 이불에 솜을 두다 stuff a quilt with cotton
8 〈수결을〉 sign (a document); put one's written seal [signature] to
9 〈간격을〉 ◆ 간격을 두다 leave a 《wider》 space between 《the lines》
▶ 불과 1미터 간격을 두고 이웃에 집이 들어섰다 A house was built just one meter from mine.
▶ 10미터씩 간격을 두고 집을 짓고 있다 They are building the houses ten meters apart.
▶ 두 나라 대표는 테이블을 사이에 두고 마주 앉았다 The delegates of the two nations sat across the table from each other.
10 〈차이·중점을〉 lay; put; place
◆ 차이를 두다 make a difference / 중점을 두다 lay [put, place] emphasis [stress] 《on》 / 단테를 괴테 위에 두다 rank [put] Dante above Goethe
11 〈설치하다〉 set up; have; provide
▶ 방마다 텔레비전을 두었다 We have provided each room with a TV (set).
▶ 내월부터 사내에 광고부를 두기로 했다 We

have decided to set up [have] an in-house advertising department starting next month.
▶세계 각지에 지점을 두고 있다 We have branch offices all over the world.
12 〈보존하다〉 keep
▶이 고기는 너무 오래 두면 안된다 This meat can't be kept long.
▶이것은 어둡고 서늘한 곳에 두어라 Keep this in a dark, cool place.
▶이 생선을 내일까지 두어도 괜찮을까? Will this fish keep overnight?
▶이 종류의 소세지는 장시간 둘 수 있습니다 This kind of sausage keeps [can be kept] for a long time.
13 〈지칭하다〉 name; mean
▶너를 두고 하는 말이다 It means you.
▶「노랑이」란 나를 두고 하는 말이었다 When he said the miser, he meant me.
14 〈다짐하다〉 pledge; give a pledge
▶하나님을 두고 내 결백을 맹세합니다 I swear by God that I am innocent.

두다² 〈동작의 결과가 이어져〉 ◆미리 조사해 두다 examine beforehand; have (it) examined before...
▶그것도 알아두면 써먹을 날이 있을 거다 If you learn how to do it, you would have a chance to make use of it.
▶맛은 없지만 그냥 먹어두자 It is not very tasty but let's eat it up anyway.
▶그가 자리를 확보해[예약해] 두었다 He has saved [reserved] a seat for me.
▶방의 온도를 1년 내내 일정하게 해둘 필요가 있다 The room temperature has to be constant all the year round.
▶듣지 않은 것으로 해두겠다 I'll just pretend I didn't hear it. ⇌ I will say I have not heard about it.

두더지 〈動〉 a mole ■—가죽 a moleskin ─굴 a mole('s) tunnel ─전술 tunneling tactics
두더지 혼인 같다 〈속담〉 cherish an empty hope; build a castle in the air
둘덜거리다 grumble ⇨ 투덜거리다
두렁 〈논·밭의〉 a bank; a levee; 〈신체의〉 a raised part of the body; a mound
◆논두렁 a levee; a ridge between rice fields / 밭두렁 a bank around a field
두렁에 누운 소 〈속담〉 a person in easy circumstances
두두룩이 **1** 〈볼록하게 올라온 모양〉 protuberantly; protrusively
◆흙을 두두룩이 쌓아올리다 pile [heap] earth up into a small mound / 젖가슴을 두두룩이 내밀다 her breasts stand out from the chest
2 〈많이〉 much; plenty; satisfactorily
◆돈을 두두룩이 집어주다 give plenty of money / 팁을 두두룩이 주다 tip 《a porter》 handsomely
두두룩하다 swollen; protuberant; raised; elevated; heaved; high
◆젖가슴이 두두룩한 busty; round-bosomed / 두두룩한 젖가슴 full breasts / 두두룩한 지갑 a well-filled purse / 두두룩해지다 swell (out); bulge; become protuberant
두둑 〈밭 사이의 둑〉 a bank; a levee; a ridge between fields; 〈이랑〉 ridges (in plowed ground)
■—길 a footpath (between fields)
두둑이 plenty ⇨ 두두룩이
두둑하다 **1** 〈두껍다〉 thick; heavy
▶밖이 꽤 추우니 두둑하게 입고 나가거라 It's pretty cold outside, so you had better bundle up.
2 〈풍부하다〉 plenty; quite a lot; ample; satisfactory
◆두둑한 보수 an ample reward; a fat salary / 두둑한 사례를 받다 be given a liberal [handsome] reward / 돈이 두둑하다 have plenty of money; have a plump purse
두둔하다 back (the weak); cover [screen] (a guilty person); support; give support to; stand by; side with; 〈변호하다〉 speak up for
◆자기 자식을 두둔하다 back one's own child (in a quarrel) / 약자를 두둔하다 stand by the weak [underdog] / 부하를 두둔하여 말하다 talk in favor of [in defense of] one's subordinate
▶그를 두둔하는 사람은 아무도 없었다 No one stood [spoke] up for him.
두둥실 floating gently [lightly]; buoyantly; in an airy manner ◆두둥실 높이 떠 있는 기구 a balloon floating on high
▶달이 두둥실 떠오르고 있었다 The moon was rising buoyantly.
▶망망 대해에 일엽편주가 두둥실 떠있다 A small boat is floating lightly on the boundless expanse of water.
두드러기 〈醫〉 hives; nettle rash; urticaria
◆두드러기가 돋다 break out in a rash; get nettle rash; have urticaria; form wheals
▶상한 생선에 중독되어 두드러기가 돋았다 Being poisoned by bad fish, I had a breaking-out.
두드러지다 **1** 〈뚜렷·현저하다〉 conspicuous; prominent (figure); marked; outstanding; remarkable (fellow); notable (person); striking; exceptional; 〈서술적〉 stand out; cut a brilliant figure
◆두드러지게 conspicuously; prominently; strikingly; in a striking contrast; remarkably / 두드러지게 눈에 띄다 be conspicuous; stand out conspicuously; cut a conspicuous [brilliant] figure
▶그는 그의 학급에서 두드러지게 영어를 잘한다 He is far ahead of his class in English.
▶그는 영어 회화에서 두드러진 향상을 보였다 He has made a marked [remarkable] improvement in English conversation.
▶이 둘 사이에는 두드러진 차이가 없다 There is no remarkable difference between the two. ⇌ The two are not noticeably different.
▶그의 큰 키가 두드러지게 눈에 띄었다 His tall figure attracted attention among all others.
▶근년에 지원자 수가 두드러지게 증가했다 The number of applicants has markedly increased in recent years.
▶이 저수지의 수위가 두드러지게 내려갔다 The water level of this reservoir has dropped considerably.

2 〈내밀다〉 swell; protuberate; protrude; stand out (from the surface)
♦ 종이에 무늬를 두드러지게 넣다 emboss the paper with a design
▶ 뾰루지가 두드러졌다 A boil was swollen up.

두드리다 strike; beat; hit; 〈똑똑〉 knock; rap; 〈가볍게〉 tap (at, on); 〈세게〉 pound
♦ 가슴을 두드리다 〈분해서〉 beat the breast; 〈의사가〉 tap [sound] *sb's* breast / 문을 가볍게 [세게, 쾅쾅] 두드리다 tap [rap, pound] at the door
▶ 누가 문을 두드리고 있다 Someone is knocking at [on] the door. ⇌ There is a knock at the door.
▶ 그 남자는 화가 나서 탁자를 두드렸다 The man pounded the table in anger.
▶ 그는 그녀의 어깨를 톡톡 두드렸다 He tapped her on the shoulder.
▶ 비가 창문을 두드리고 있다 The rain is beating against [whipping] the windows.
▶ 그들은 북을 두드리고 있다 They are beating the drums.
▶ 양탄자를 두드려 먼지를 털었다 I beat the dust out of the carpet.
▶ 문을 세 번 두드리는 소리가 들렸다 We heard three knocks on the door.

두들기다 strike repeatedly; beat; pound; batter; deal [give] repeated blows
♦ 두들겨 내쫓다 beat and drive out / 불을 두들겨 끄다 beat out a fire; put out [extinguish] a fire by beating / 문을 두들겨 부수다 batter the door down / 몹시 세게 두들기다 beat [pommel] *sb* to a jelly
▶ 그 정치가는 신문에서 두들겨 맞았다 The politician was attacked [criticized] in the newspapers.
▶ 대장장이가 쇠를 두들겨 펴고 있다 A blacksmith is hammering iron out.

두랄루민 〔化〕 duralumin
■ —판 a duralumin plate

두런거리다 whisper to each other ⇨ 도란거리다

두런두런 in whispers ⇨ 도란도란

두렁 a ridge between (rice) fields; a levee
♦ 두렁에 든 소다 (비유) have plenty to eat wherever *one* goes
■ —길 a footpath between rice fields

두렁이 swaddling clothes; a baby's skirt

두렁허리 〔魚〕 a kind of freshwater eel

두레 1 〈물 푸는 기구〉 a scoop (used in irrigation) **2** 〈농사꾼들의 모임〉 a group of farmers organized for mutual help in the busiest season; a cooperative farming team

두레박 a well bucket ♦ 두레박으로 물을 긷다 draw water 《from a well》 with a bucket
■ —줄 a well rope —틀 a (well) sweep; 〈이집트 등지의〉 a shadoof

두레박질 drawing water with a well bucket
—두레박질하다 draw water 《from a well》 with a bucket

두레질 irrigation by scooping —두레질하다 irrigate 《paddy fields》 by scooping

두려움 〈공포〉 (a) fear; (a) fright; (a) dread; horror; (a) terror; 〈염려〉 apprehension(s); anxiety; 〈외경(畏敬)〉 reverence; veneration; awe

|解說| *fear*는「자기 몸에 위험을 느껴 두렵다고 생각하는 감정」, *fright*는「돌연한 심한 공포」를 말한다. *dread*는 특히「위험이 닥쳐오고 있다는 공포」, *horror*는「깜짝 놀랄 정도 또는 매우 싫은 기분이 드는 강한 두려움」, *terror*는「자기 몸에 다가오는 소리가 끼칠 정도의 강한 공포·두려움」의 강도를 나타낸다. fear, dread, terror의 순으로 강해진다.

♦ 죽음에 대한 두려움 the fear of death / 시험에 떨어지지 않을까 하는 두려움 a dread of failing in the examination / 두려움 때문에 out of fear; from fear; in horror [fright] / 두려움을 모르다 be fearless [dauntless]; be stranger to fear / 두려움을 품다 entertain fears [apprehension, misgivings] / 두려움에 휩싸이다 be seized with fear; be struck with horror / 두려움으로 부들부들 떨다 tremble like a leaf in terror; shake with fear [fright, horror]
▶ 갑자기 두려움이 그를 엄습했다 A sudden fear came over him. ⇌ Suddenly he was filled with fear.
▶ 나는 어두운데 있으면 대단히 두려움을 느낀다 I feel great fear in the dark.
▶ 그는 두려움으로 새파랗게 질렸다 He became pale with fear.

두려워하다 1 〈무서워하다〉 fear; dread; be afraid [fearful] of; be frightened [scared, terrified] at; have a horror [dread] of
♦ 몹시 두려워하다 have a holy horror of; be in mortal fear of / 두려워하지 않다 do not fear; be unafraid of; be unterrified / …을 두려워하다 be [live] in constant fear of… / 야단맞을 [매맞을] 것을 두려워하다 (口) funk a scolding [whipping] / 죽음도 두려워하지 않다 defy death
▶ 그녀는 뱀을 무척 두려워한다 She is very (much) afraid [frightened, scared] of snakes. ⇌ She has a great fear [terror] of snakes.
▶ 불에 덴 아이는 불을 두려워한다 A burnt child dreads the fire.
▶ 아무것도 두려워할 필요가 없다 You have nothing to be afraid of.
▶ 그는 법도 두려워하지 않는다 He defies the laws. ⇌ He sets the laws at defiance.
▶ 그런 녀석을 두려워하면 안된다 You should not be afraid of a man like him.
▶ 그 정도의 위험은 두려워할 것이 못된다 The sort of risk is not to be feared.
▶ 나쁜 짓 한 것이 없다면 아무것도 두려워할 것이 없을 게 아닌가 If you haven't done anything wrong, you should have nothing to fear.
2 〈근심·걱정하다〉 fear; be afraid of; apprehend; be apprehensive of
♦ …하지 않을까 두려워하여 for fear 《of doing, that [lest]…should do》; fearful of 《getting infected》
▶ 병이 나지 않을까 두려워하는 것은 어리석은 일이다 It's foolish to worry too much about falling ill.
▶ 실패를 두려워하다가는 큰 일은 아무 것도 못

한다 You'll never be able to do anything great if you are afraid of failure.
3 〈경외(敬畏)하다〉 stand in awe of; be struck with awe
♦ 어른을 두려워하다 stand in awe of one's elders; venerate one's elders / 어른을 두려워할 줄 모르다 be defiant of one's elders; do not pay due respect to one's elders
▶ 그는 아버지를 두려워하고 있다 He is in awe of his father.

두렵다 1 〈무섭다〉 fearful; scared; frightened; terrified; 〈서술적〉 be afraid of
♦ 탄로날까봐 두려워서 in fear of discovery / 두려워지다 be [get] frightened [scared]; have [get] frightful / 두려워서 몸을 움츠리다[떨다] shrink [shudder] for fear
▶ 나는 캄캄한 데가 두렵다 I'm afraid of the dark.
▶ 나는 비행기 타는 것이 두렵다 I'm afraid [scared] of flying (in a plane).
▶ 나는 그녀가 화를 내지 않을까 두려웠다 I was afraid [scared] that she might [would] be angry. ⇌ I was afraid [scared] of her anger.
▶ 그는 야단맞을까봐 두려웠다 He was afraid of being scolded.
▶ 나는 죽는 것이 두렵다 I am afraid [scared] of death in the last.
2 〈염려스럽다〉 feared; fearful; apprehended; 〈서술적〉 be afraid of
▶ 그는 실수를 할까바 두려웠다 He was fearful of making a mistake.
▶ 그렇게 두려운 사업에는 참가할 수 없다 I can't take part in such audacious business.
3 〈경외스럽다〉 awed; awe-some

두령 頭領 a boss; a chief; a head; a leader; a master; a captain

두루 〈골고루〉 all over; all around; thoroughly; throughout; 〈일반적으로〉 generally; universally; 〈널리〉 widely; extensively; far and wide
♦ 두루 찾다 make a wide search; search every corner (of a place for sth) / 온 세계에 두루 알려지다 be known all over the world
▶ 그에게 서울을 두루 구경시켜 주었다 I showed him round [all over] Seoul.
▶ 나는 세계를 두루 여행했다 I have traveled extensively [far and wide] in the world.
▶ 노인은 자기의 미래에 관해 두루 생각해 보았다 The old man thought about his future.
▶ 이것은 두루 알려진 사실이다 This is a fact generally known [known extensively].

두루마기 a Korean overcoat

두루마리 〈둘둘 만 종이〉 a roll of paper; a scroll; 〈족자〉 a hanging scroll ♦ 두루마리를 펴다[말다] unroll [roll up] a scroll
■—구름 ⇨ 권운(卷雲) —화장지 a toilet roll; a roll of toilet paper

두루뭉수리 1 〈어떤 형체를 이루지 못한 사물〉 an object of nondescript shape; an unshapely thing; a mess ♦ 두루뭉수리를 만들어 놓다 make a mess out of it
2 〈변변치 못한 사람〉 a nondescript; a good-for-nothing (fellow); a nobody

두루미 〈鳥〉 a crane; a white crane with a red crest ■재— a white-naped crane 흑— a hooded crane —자리〈天〉 the Crane

두루미 꽁지 같다 (속담) have a short thick beard

두루미냉이 〈植〉 a chorogi; a Chinese artichoke

두루춘풍 —春風 ♦ 두루춘풍이다 be affable to everybody; be always genial to everybody

두루치기 1 using a thing for a variety of purposes; alternate use of a thing
2 〈조갯살 등을 데친 음식〉 a kind of bouillabaisse

두류 逗留 a stay; a stop; a sojourn
—두류하다 stay (at, in)

두르다 1 〈둘러싸다〉 enclose (with, in); surround (with, by); encircle; gird
♦ 해자를 두른 성 a castle enclosed [girded] by [with] a moat / 담[울타리]을 두르다 surround (a house) with a wall [fence]
▶ 그의 집은 높은 담이 두르고 있다 His house is surrounded with [by] high walls.
2 〈입다·차다〉 gird; engirdle; wear
♦ 치마를 두르다 wear a skirt; put on one's skirt / 완장을 두르다 wear an armband / 허리에 띠를 두르다 bind a belt about [round] one's waist / 머리에 수건을 두르다 tie a rolled towel around one's head
▶ 그녀는 목에 스카프를 두르고 있었다 She had a scarf around her neck.
3 〈돌리다〉 twirl [turn] (round); whirl; wheel; revolve
♦ 물레를 두르다 turn a spinning wheel
4 〈마음대로 다루다〉 wield; have sb under perfect control; turn sb round (his) little finger
5 〈변통하다〉 make (a) shift (with); shift; contrive; borrow [raise] 《money》
♦ 돈을 두르다 raise [borrow] money; find funds / 돈을 둘러주다 lend money; accommodate sb with money
6 〈속이다〉 deceive; cheat; swindle; trick; take in sb; play a trick on

두르르 1 〈말리는 모양〉 (form) into a roll; (wrap) round (on itself) ♦ 지도[천]를 두르르 말다 roll up a map [the cloth]
2 〈바퀴가 구르는 소리〉 with a rumble
▶ 마차가 두르르 굴러갔다 A carriage rumbled [rolled] along.

두르풍 —風 a cape; a shawl; a mantle

두름 a string (of fish, of dried vegetables)
♦ 굴비 한 두름 a string of 20 dried corbinas

두름성 —性 resourcefulness; adaptability; versatility
♦ 두름성이 있는 able; resourceful / 두름성이 있는 사람 a man of ability; a resourceful man; a good provider / 두름성이 없다 shiftless; resourceless
▶ 그는 두름성이 있어 돈을 잘 마련한다 He is resourceful and very good at raising money.

두릅 edible shoots of a fatsia

두릅나무 a Japanese angelica tree; a fatsia

두리기 dining together seated around a table
■—상 a round table set for a group of people

두리기둥 〈建〉 a round [cylindrical] pillar; a

column
두리목 —木 round timber [lumber]
두리반 —盤 a (large) round dining table
두리번거리다 look (a)round; stare about
♦두리번거리며 찾다 look around for *sth* / 두리번거리며 걷다 walk along gazing around *one*
▶바보처럼 두리번거리지 마라 Don't look about in that idiotic fashion.
두리번두리번 looking around restlessly [nervously]; with unsteady eyes; goggle-eyed
▶그는 불안스럽게 두리번두리번 주변을 살폈다 He looked around uneasily.
—**두리번두리번하다** ⇨ 두리번거리다
두마음 duplicity ⇨ 이심(二心)
두말 a double tongue; equivocation
♦두말 말고 without saying anything further; here and now
▶두말 말고 열심히 해 Work hard without making complaints.
▶두말 말고 어서 돈을 내라 Pay me the money here and now.
—**두말하다** be double-tongued; break [go back on] *one's* word [promise]; say this or that
♦두말하지 않고 without saying this or that; without complaint [grumbling]; without objection [question] / 두말 할것 없이 of course; without saying this or that / 두말 하지 않다 keep *one's* word; be as good as *one's* word / 한 입으로 두말하다 keep two tongues in one mouth; speak out of both corners of mouth; tell a lie
▶나는 두말하지 않는다 When I say "yes" I mean it.
▶남자가 두말 하랴 A gentleman never goes back on his word. ⇌ The gentleman can never be double-tongued.
두말없이 〈즉각〉 readily; without hesitation; 〈군말 없고〉 without asking questions; 〈딱 잘라〉 point-blank; flatly
♦두말없이 승낙하다 consent readily; give a ready consent / 두말없이 거절하다 refuse point-blank; give *sb* a flat refusal / 두말없이 거절당하다 meet with a square rebuff
▶그는 두말없이 동의했다 He was only too glad to consent.
두멍 a water tub; a large water jar
두메 an out-of-the-way mountain village; remote countryside; 〈美〉 the backcountry [backwoods] ♦두메에 살다 live in the backcountry [remote countryside]
두멧구석 an out-of-the-way corner of a mountain district; remote backwoods
두멧사람 a deep countryman; a person who lives in an out-of-the-way place; 〈美〉 a backwoodsman
두목 頭目 a boss; a captain; the chief; the head; a leader; a big shot
♦깡패 두목 a gangleader; 〈俗〉 a big gun / 산적 두목 a bandit captain / 소매치기 두목 a master pickpocket / 두목과 부하 a boss and his henchman / 두목이 되다 boss it over other people

두묘 痘苗 〔醫〕 vaccine; the vaccine lymph [virus]
두문불출 杜門不出 confining *oneself* at home; a stay-at-home life
—**두문불출하다** confine *oneself* at home; lead a stay-at-home life; be in the seclusion of *one's* own home
두문자 頭文字 the first letter 《of a word》; an initial letter; the initials 《of *one's* name》
♦두문자를 적은 손수건 an initialed handkerchief / 두문자를 맞춰 만든 약어 an acronym 《▶예를 들면 the United Nations Educational, Scientific, and Cultural Organization의 약어 UNESCO와 같은 것》
두미 頭尾 the head and tail; beginning and end ♦두미 있게 be incoherent / 두미없이 이야기하다 tell an incoherent story
두발 頭髮 hair (of the head) ⇨ 머리털
두방망이질 beating with both hands; 〈두근거림〉 pounding of *one's* heart; throbbing; the (heavy) thumping of the heart
♦두방망이질 치다 pound; throb
▶그 소식을 듣고 내 가슴은 두방망이질쳤다 My heart beat quick [went pitapat] at the news.
▶나는 기뻐서 가슴이 두방망이질 쳤다 I felt my heart beating with joy.
두번 〈2회〉 twice; two times; 〈다시〉 again
▶나는 그 영화를 이미 두 번이나 보았다 I have already seen that movie twice.
▶네 얼굴은 두번 다시 보고 싶지 않다 I don't want to see you again.
▶이곳에는 두번 다시 오지 않겠다 I will never come here again.
두번째 the second time
♦두 번째로 for the second time
▶뉴욕 방문은 이번이 두번째입니다 This is my second visit to New York.
▶그 이야기를 듣는 것은 이번이 두 번째다 This is the second time (that) I've heard of the story.
▶이것은 그의 두 번째 소설이다 This is the second novel that he wrote.
▶그에게 돈을 빌려준 것은 그것이 두 번째였다 That was the second time I had lent him money.
▶그는 끝에서 두번째로 도착했다 He was the last but one to arrive.
두벌갈이 〔農〕 a second plowing [sowing]
—**두벌갈이하다** make a second plowing; till a second time; plow again
두벌주검 an examined [a dissected] corpse
두부 豆腐 bean curd ♦두부 한 모 a cake of bean curd / 두부 찌꺼기 bean curd refuse ■—장수 a bean curd dealer [seller] —저냐 fried bean curd
두부 頭部 the head ♦두부의 cephalic
▶그는 어제 교통사고로 두부에 부상을 입었다 He was injured [wounded] in the head in the traffic accident yesterday.
두부 살에 바늘 뼈 (속담) be very delicate [fragile]
두 사이 1 〈간격〉 a space between two 《objects》 ♦두사이에 끼이다 get in between;

be caught in the middle
2 〈관계〉 the relation [relationship, terms] between two persons
◆두사이가 좋다[나쁘다] be on good [bad] terms / 두사이가 버그러지다 be estranged from each other; split up

두상 頭上 〈머리〉 one's head; 〈머리 위〉 the top of one's head; the crown
▶ 두상에 on [over] the head

두상화 頭狀花 〔植〕 a capitate(d) flower; capitulum (pl. -la); a flower head

두서 頭書 〈머리말〉 a preface; 〈본문 앞에 쓴 글〉 a superscription
◆두서의 superscript; 〈상기의〉 foregoing; above-mentioned / 두서에 적은 바와 같이 as mentioned above
▶ 두서의 건에 대한 귀사의 의견을 바랍니다 Please let me know your opinion about the matter I mentioned above.

두서너 two or three; a few; some
◆두서너 마디 a few words / 두서너 번 two or three times / 두서너 사람 some [a few] people / 두서너 집 건너 a few doors away
▶ 그는 친구가 두서너 명 있다 He has a few friends.
▶ 두서너 마디만 말씀드리겠습니다 Allow me to speak just a few words.

두서넛 two or three; a few
▶ 두서넛씩 in two or three

두서 없다 頭緖— incoherent; rambling; absurd; wandering; wild
◆두서없는 설명 an incoherent explanation / 두서없는 이야기 a rambling [wild, skimble-skamble] talk / 두서없이 incoherently; in a rambling manner / 두서없는 말을 하다 make a rambling [pointless] speech; talk in a rambling way; wander in one's talk; make incoherent remarks
▶ 그의 말은 두서(가) 없다 What he says is without rhyme or reason [does not make sense].
▶ 그 사람의 두서없는 말에는 많은 교훈이 담겨져 있다 His rambling talk has many lessons in it.

두성 頭聲 〔樂〕 head voice
■—음역 the head register

두세 two or three 《men》; a few ◆두세 번 two or three times; more than once
▶ 놀이터에서 아이들이 두세 명 놀고 있었다 Some children were playing in the playground.

두셋 two or three ▶ 두셋 쯤은 당해낼 수 있다 I can cope with [am strong enough to be a match for] two or three.

두손 two hands; both hands
◆두손을 들다 (비유) give up [in]; throw up one's hands; take off one's hat 《to》; admit one's inferiority 《to》/ 두 손 모아 빌다 pray with one's hands pressed together / 두 손을 내밀다 [벌리다] extend [open] one's hands / 두 손에 쥐다 hold sth in both hands / 두 손으로 상자를 들어올리다 use both hands to lift a box / 두 손으로 잡다 hold sth with both hands
▶ 그 남자는 두 손을 호주머니에 찌르고 거기서 있었다 The man stood there, hands in pockets.

두손매무리 doing 《one's work》 slapdash; scamping
—두손매무리하다 do 《one's work》 slapdash [in a slipshod manner, in a haphazard manner]; scamp 《one's》 work

두수 頭數 the number of heads

두약 杜若 〔植〕 an alpine tree

두어 about two; a couple of ◆두어 달 about two months / 두어 마디 a few words / 두어 사람 a couple of people or so

두어두다 〈돌보지 않다〉 neglect 《one's work》; lay aside; 〈내버려두다〉 leave [let] sb [sth] alone (unattended); let sth as it is [stands]
▶ 가만 두어두어라, 그 녀석 울겠다 Leave him alone or he will cry.
▶ 제멋대로 하게 두어두렴 Let him have his own way.

두억시니 a demon; a devil

두엄 compost; barnyard [farmyard] manure; muck ◆밭에 두엄을 주다 compost [manure] a field
■—걸채 a compost rack —더미 a compost heap [pile] —발치 a compost pit; a muck bog —자리 a compost yard [dump] —풀 grass for compost

두엇 about two ⇨ 두어

두운 頭韻 〔詩〕 alliteration
◆두운을 맞추다 alliterate
▶ 'pipe'와 'pet'은 두운을 맞추고 있다 'Pipe' alliterates with 'pet'. ⇌ 'Pipe' and 'pet' alliterate.
■—법 alliteration —시 an alliterative verse

두유 豆乳 soybean milk

두이레 the fourteenth day after a baby's birth [of a baby's life]

두절 杜絶 stoppage; cessation; suspension; interruption
—두절하다 be stopped; be blocked; be interrupted; be paralyzed; be cut off
▶ 서신 왕래가 두절되었다 The correspondence dropped.
▶ 큰 눈으로 교통이 두절되었다 All the transportation service were blocked [suspended] because of the heavy snow. ⇌ Traffic was held up [paralyzed] by the heavy snow.
▶ 그 이후 그에게서 소식이 두절되었다 I [We] have heard nothing from him since then.
▶ 갑자기 통신이 두절되었다 Radio communication was abruptly cut off.

두족류 頭足類 〔動〕 the Cephalopoda
◆두족류의 동물 a cephalopod

두주 斗酒 kegs of wine ▶ 그는 두주를 불사한다 He drinks like a fish.

두주 頭注 a headnote ◆두주를 달다 give headnotes 《to》; put a headnote (in a book)

두텁다 〈정리·인정 등이〉 warm; kind; affectionate; cordial; hearty; deep
◆인정이 두터운 사람 a warm-hearted person / 정이 두텁다 be very friendly; be (kind and) warmhearted; be cordial 《to sb》/ 우의를 두텁게 하다 deepen the friendship
▶ 그는 우정이 두텁다 He is loyal [faithful] to

his friends.
▶그 집 식구들은 인정이 두텁다 His family have warm hearts [are warm-hearted].
두통 頭痛 (a) headache; [醫] cephalalgia
◆머리가 빠개지는 듯한 두통 a splitting [racking] headache / 두통이 잘 나다 be subject to headaches / 두통을 호소하다 complain of a headache / 잠을 자서[산책하여] 두통이 나았다 sleep [walk] off the headache
▶약간[몹시] 두통이 난다 I have a slight [bad] headache. ⇌ I'm suffering from a slight [bad] headache.
▶그 여자는 두통이 떠나지 않는다 She has a chronic headache.
■─편 (a) migraine (headache) ■─약 a headache specific
두통거리 頭痛─ a headache; the source of trouble; a nuisance; a thorn in one's side [flesh]
▶교통 문제야말로 우리의 두통거리다 The traffic problem is a real headache [source of anxiety] to us.
▶자금 부족이 그의 큰 두통거리다 Lack of money is a big headache to him.
▶그는 가족에게 두통거리다 He is a great distress to the family.
두툴두툴하다 rough ⇨ 도툴도툴
두툼하다 thick; heavy
◆두툼한 돈 뭉치 a thick [massive] stack of bills / 두툼한 외투 a thick [heavy] overcoat / 두툼한 입술 full lips / 두툼한 책 a thick [bulky, voluminous] book [volume]
두호 斗護 patronage; protection; favor
◆어느 재력가의 두호 아래 under the patronage of a rich man
─두호하다 protect (the weak); patronize; favor; take sb under one's wing
▶그가 그녀를 두호해 주었다 He stood up for her.
둑 a bank; an embankment; a dike; 〈논밭의〉 a ridge (between the fields); a levee
◆강둑 a riverbank / 논둑 a ridge around a rice field; a levee / 철롯둑 a mound for railroad / 둑길 a causeway; a bank path; a dike / 둑을 무너뜨리다 break (down) a dam [riverbank] / 둑을 쌓다 construct [build (up)] a dam [bank]; embank (a river)
▶강물이 넘쳐 둑이 무너졌다 The river overflowed and its bank was washed away.
둑중개 〔魚〕 a miller's-thumb; a sculpin
둔각 鈍角 〔幾〕 an obtuse angle
■─삼각형 an obtuse triangle
둔감 鈍感 insensibility; stolidity; obtuseness of feeling
─둔감하다 insensitive; insensible (to, of); thick-skinned; dull; stolid; obtuse; thickheaded
◆미에 둔감하다 be insensitive to beauty / 둔감해지다 〈사람이〉 become insensitive; 〈감각이〉 become dull
▶그 여자는 둔감해서 유머가 통하지 않는다 He is so dull that he fails to see a joke.
▶그 여자는 자신에 대한 소문에 둔감했다 She was deaf to the gossip around her.

▶나는 소음에 길들여져 귀가 둔감해졌다 I am dull of hearing, as I have got accustomed to noise.
둔갑술 遁甲術 the art of changing oneself
둔갑하다 遁甲─ take the form [shape] (of); turn [change, transform] oneself (into sth)
◆사람으로 둔갑한 여우 a fox in the shape of man; a fox in [assuming] human shape [form]
▶여우가 처녀로 둔갑했다 A fox took [assumed] the form of a girl. ⇌ A fox changed itself into a girl.
둔기 鈍器 a blunt [dull] weapon ◆둔기로 치다 hit [strike] sb with a blunt instrument
▶그는 둔기로 살해되었다 He was killed with a blunt instrument.
둔덕 a (small) mound; a low hill; a hillock
◆둔덕진 mounded; hillocky / 둔덕지다 form [become] a mound; become hilly
둔부 臀部 〈불기〉 the buttocks; the hip; the rump; [解] the nates [néitiːz]; [解] the coxae [káksiː, -sai] ◆둔부의 gluteal
둔사 遁辭 〈변명〉 an excuse; a subterfuge; 〈책임 회피〉 an evasion; an evasive answer
◆둔사를 늘어놓다 give an evasive answer; excuse oneself
▶그의 설명은 단지 둔사에 지나지 않았다 His explanation was only a mere evasion [excuse].
둔세 遁世 seclusion [retirement] from the world; escape from society
◆둔세 생활을 하다 live secluded [in seclusion, apart] from the world
─둔세하다 retire [seclude oneself] from the world; renounce the world; escape from society; go into seclusion
■─출가 monastic seclusion ■─자 a recluse; a hermit
둔재 鈍才 〈재주가 둔함〉 dullness; stupidity; 〈재주가 둔한 사람〉 a dull [stupid] person; a dullard; (美口) a dumbbell ◆둔재의 slow-[dull-]witted; dull; stupid
둔전 屯田 a garrison farm; a farm cultivated by troops regularly stationed in the area
■─병 a farm soldier
둔주 遁走 〈도주〉 flight; abscondence; running away ─둔주하다 flee; run away; escape; take (to) flight
둔주곡 遁走曲 〔樂〕 a fugue
■─작곡가 a fuguist
둔중하다 鈍重─ heavy and clumsy; ponderous; logy; 〈우둔하다〉 bovine; dull
◆둔중한 모습 a ponderous figure / 둔중한 걸음걸이 (with) a heavy [leaden] step
둔치 〈물가〉 the waterside; the water front; the water's edge
둔탁하다 鈍濁─ dull; thick; dead
▶뭔가 둔탁한 소리가 들렸다 A dull [dead] sound was heard.
둔통 鈍痛 a dull pain ▶나는 위장에 둔통이 있다 I feel a dull pain in the stomach.
둔팍하다 鈍─ thickheaded; slow-witted; stolid; dull; stupid
둔패기 〈아둔패기, 바보〉 a dull [slow-witted]

person; a thickhead

둔하다 鈍― 1〈머리·성질 등이〉 dull; slow; stupid; thickheaded; slow-witted
♦ 둔한 통증 a dull pain / 머리가 둔한 사람 a dull [stupid] fellow; a slow-witted [thick-headed] person; a dolt; a dullard / 감각이 둔하다 be insensitive
▶ 그는 머리 회전이 둔하다 His head works slowly.
▶ 그는 감성이 둔하다 He is slow to notice things. ⇒ He isn't very perceptive.
▶ 그 아이는 둔한 아이다 He is a dull boy.
2 〈동작·상태 등이〉 slow; sluggish; inactive; inert
▶ 나는 운동 신경이 둔하다 I have slow reflexes.
▶ 그는 동작이[일하는것이] 둔하다 He is slow in movement [doing things].
▶ 그 아이는 둔하게 두꺼운 외투를 껴입고 있었다 The child was all wrapped up in a heavy coat.
3 〈소리가〉 thick
♦ 둔한 소리 a thick sound

둔해지다 鈍― become [grow] dull; become blunt
♦ 솜씨가 둔해지다 become less capable
▶ 한동안 연습을 쉬었더니 솜씨가 둔해졌다 Since I haven't practiced for some time, my skill has dulled. ⇒ I am out of practice, and so I've become rather rusty.
▶ 술을 마시면 머리가 둔해진다 Drinking dulls the senses [muddles one's brains].

둔화 鈍化 blunting; slowing down
▶ 이 도표는 한국 경제의 둔화를 보여주고 있다 This diagram shows a slowdown in the Korea economy.
―둔화하다 become [get, grow] dull
♦ (감각을) 둔화시키다 dull [blunt] the ⟪sb's⟫ senses
▶ 경제 성장률이 둔화되었다 The rate of economic growth has slowed.

둘 two ♦ 둘 건너 [걸러] in [at] every third place / 둘 다 both (...and...); 〈부정〉 neither (...nor...) / 둘씩 by [in] twos; two by [and] two; two at a time / 둘로 접은 twofold; twice-folded / 둘 중에서 하나를 고르다 choose between the two / 둘로 자르다 [쪼개다] cut [divide] sth in two [into two parts, in half, into halves]
▶ 학생 둘이 수업을 빼먹었다 Two students cut class.
▶ 그 둘은 잘 어울리는 부부다 They are a well-matched couple.
▶ 나는 그 여자와 둘이 영화 구경을 갔다 I went to a movie with her.
▶ 그는 부인과 둘이서만 살고 있었다 He lived alone with his wife.
▶ 의견이 완전히 둘로 갈라졌다 Opinions were completely divided. ⇒ There was a division of opinion.
▶ 그녀는 종이를 둘로 접었다 She folded the paper in two.
▶ 이 수박[사과]을 둘로 쪼개 [잘라] 주세요 Please divide [cut] this watermelon [apple] in two.
▶ 그들은 둘 다 수영을 못한다 Neither of them can swim.
▶ 우리는 둘 다 몹시 배가 고팠다 Both of us were [We were both] very hungry.
▶ 둘씩 산책하고 있는 사람들이 대부분이었다 Most of the people were walking in pairs.

둘― 〈새끼·알을 못배는〉 sterile; barren
♦ 둘암소 [암탉] a sterile cow [hen]

둘도없다 〈유일하다〉 only; unique; 〈비길 데 없다〉 peerless; matchless; unparalleled; 〈바꿀 수 없다〉 something that cannot be replaced; irreplaceable
♦ 둘도 없는 고문서 an irreplaceable [a most precious] ancient document / 둘도 없는 미인 a peerless [matchless] beauty / 둘도 없는 용사 a peerless hero / 둘도 없는 친구 one's best [bosom] friend / 당대에 둘도 없는 시인 the greatest [unrivaled] poet of the day
▶ 이런 보석은 둘도 없다 This jewel is matchless. ⇒ This is the most unique jewel.

둘되다 〈미련하다〉 stupid; dull; stolid; thick-headed; dull-witted

둘둘, 뚤뚤 ♦ 둘둘 감다 wind ⟪a rope⟫ round sth / 둘둘 말다 roll up ⟪a carpet [sheet of paper]⟫; coil; uproll / 둘둘 구르다 ⟪a wagon⟫ rumble / 잡지를 둘둘 말아서 치다 hit sb with rolled magazine
▶ 판지는 둘둘 말면 으레 구겨진다 Cardboard won't roll without creasing.

둘러대다 1〈꾸며대다〉 make [give] an evasive answer; cook up [concoct] an excuse; talk oneself out of ⟪the difficulty⟫; explain away ⟪one's strange behavior⟫; sophisticate
♦ 그럴 듯한 이유를 둘러대다 cook up a good reason / 잘못을 둘러대다 gloss over [explain away] one's mistake
▶ 그는 돈을 못갚는 이유를 둘러댔다 He put up good reasons why he hasn't been able to return the money.
▶ 그는 지각한 이유를 그럴 듯하게 둘러댔다 He made up a clever excuse for being late.
▶ 나는 말을 둘러대서 곤경을 모면할 수 있었다 I was able to talk myself out of the difficulty.
▶ 그런 실수를 둘러댈 수 있다고 생각하니? Can you make any excuse for [explain away] such an error?
2 〈변통하다〉 manage to get ⟪a loan⟫; make (a) shift ⟪with⟫
♦ 돈을 둘러대다 get money somehow
▶ 나는 컴퓨터를 사려고 돈을 둘러댔다 I swung a loan in order to buy a computer.
▶ 여기 저기서 둘러대어 겨우 300만원을 마련했다 I barely managed to raise three million won from various sources.

둘러막다 enclose; surround; shut in; fence [rope off] ⟪a garden⟫; wall in; environ
♦ 돌담으로 집을 둘러막다 enclose a house with stone walls / 철조망으로 둘러막다 fence ⟪the pastureland⟫ with barbed wire

둘러메다 (lift and) carry ⟪a bag⟫ over ⟪the shoulder⟫; bear [carry] sth on one's shoulder (▶ 양어깨인 경우에는 shoulder가 복수가 됨)
♦ 카메라를 둘러메고 with a camera hanging

from one's shoulder / 짐을 둘러메다 shoulder a pack / 총을 둘러메고 행진하다 march with guns on one's shoulder
▶ 나는 그것을 어깨에 둘러메고 날랐다 I carried it on my shoulder.

둘러보다 look around [(英) round]; look about; give [take] a look [glance] around; make a survey (of); survey
♦ 좌중을 둘러보다 survey those present; look from one to another of the company / 집을 한 바퀴 둘러보다 take a look around a house / 차 안의 사람들을 둘러보다 look around at the people in the car
▶ 그는 주위를 주의 깊게 둘러보았다 He looked around him cautiously.
▶ 나는 빈 자리가 있는지 교실을 둘러보았다 I looked around the classroom for an empty seat.

둘러서다 stand in a circle
▶ 병사들은 지휘관을 중심으로 둘러섰다 The soldiers stood in a circle [formed a ring] around the commander.

둘러싸다 1 〈에워싸다〉 surround; enclose; encircle; crowd round; beset; embosom; shut in; fence 《a garden》; wall in
♦ 숲으로 둘러싸인 호수 a lake encircled with [by] woods / 그를 둘러싼 5인의 여성 the five women around him / 친구들에게 둘러싸여 with one's friends around one
▶ 군중들이 버스 사고 현장을 둘러쌌다 The crowd surrounded [clustered around] the scene of a bus accident.
▶ 기자들이 그 여배우를 둘러쌌다 The reporters gathered around [surrounded] the actress.
▶ 그들은 탁자를 둘러싸고 앉아 있었다 They sat [were seated] around the table.
▶ 그를 둘러싸고 있는 상황이 불리했다 The circumstances surrounding him were unfavorable (to him).
▶ 한국은 3면이 바다로 둘러싸여 있다 Korea is surrounded [bounded] by the sea on three sides [on all sides but one].
▶ 그 학교는 높은 생울타리로 둘러싸여 있다 The school is surrounded [is enclosed] by a high hedge.
▶ 그 노인은 손자들에게 둘러싸여 웃고 있었다 The old man was smiling, encircled [ringed around] by his grandchildren.
2 〈포위하다〉 besiege; lay siege 《to》; surround; envelop; invest
♦ 요새를 둘러싸다 lay siege to a fortress / 적을 둘러싸다 surround the enemy
▶ 적군이 마을을 둘러쌌다 The enemy troops besieged the town.
▶ 우리는 사방이 적에게 둘러싸여 빠져나갈 길이 없었다 As we were besieged by the enemy on all four sides, there was no way to escape.
3 〈관계·문제를〉 surround
♦ 김 교수의 실종을 둘러싼 비밀 a secret surrounding Prof. Kim's disappearance / 자금의 출처를 둘러싼 소문 rumors concerning the source of the money / 유산을 둘러싸고 싸우다 fight over a legacy
▶ 그의 제안을 둘러싸고 활발한 토론이 벌어졌다 A lively discussion took place on [regarding, concerning] his proposal.

둘러쌓다 pile sth up in a circle
♦ 성벽을 둘러쌓다 wall a castle

둘러쓰다 1 〈머리에〉 wear (it) round the head; 〈몸에〉 get (it) all over oneself; wrap oneself up; on [upon] 《oneself》
♦ 담요를 둘러쓰다 wrap oneself up in a blanket / 먼지를 둘러쓰다 be covered with dust / 머리에서부터 이불을 둘러쓰다 pull the bedclothes over one's head
2 〈빈통하다〉 borrow 《sth, money》
♦ 어찌어찌 돈을 둘러쓰다 find the money somehow

둘러앉다 sit round [around]; sit in a circle [ring]; gather around in a circle
♦ 식탁[불가]에 둘러앉다 sit [be seated] around the table [fire]
▶ 우리는 식탁에 둘러앉아 차를 마셨다 We sat around the table drinking tea.
▶ 우리는 오래간만에 만난 친구들과 둘러앉아 이야기를 나누었다 We sat around and talked with friends whom we hadn't seen for a long time.

둘러엎다 1 〈엎어버리다〉 overturn; overthrow; upset; turn upside down; turn over
♦ 밥상을 둘러엎다 overturn a (dining) table; throw a table over
▶ 반군은 정부를 둘러엎었다 The rebels overturned the government.
2 〈중단하다〉 break up; give up
♦ 살림을 둘러엎다 do away with a home; break up a household / 장사를 둘러엎다 quit one's business
▶ 그 남자는 가게를 둘러엎고 서울로 갔다 The man closed down his shop and went to Seoul.

둘러차다 〈허리에〉 tie [wear] sth round one's waist; attach sth around one's waist

둘러치나 메어치나 일반 (속담) It makes no difference which we choose.

둘러치다 1 〈둘러막다〉 surround [enclose] 《a garden with a fence》; encircle; put around
♦ 벽에 병풍을 둘러치다 put a screen around the wall / 공터에 목책을 둘러치다 enclose a vacant lot with a picket fence; palisade a vacant lot / 잠자리에 커튼을 둘러치다 draw a curtain around the bed
▶ 나는 집에 담을 둘러쳤다 I surrounded my house with walls.
▶ 홍백의 줄무늬 장막이 둘러쳐져 있었다 The curtain in red and white stripes was stretched around.
2 〈내던지다〉 throw hard; fling; hurl
♦ 땅바닥에 둘러치다 hurl [throw] sb to the ground
3 〈휘둘러 치다〉 bring 《a stick》 down 《on sb's head》

둘레 (a) circumference; girth; surroundings
♦ 둘레가 1000 미터다 be 1000 meters in circumference / 연못 둘레를 한 바퀴 돌다 go [walk] round a pond / 모닥불 둘레에 앉다 sit around a bonfire
▶ 그 나무 [이 호수]는 둘레가 4미터[킬로미터]

다 The tree measures [This lake is] four meters [kilometers] around.
▶ 나는 우리 집 둘레에 울타리를 치게 했다 I had a fence built around my house.
▶ 성 둘레에는 해자가 파여져 있다 A moat runs around the castle.

둘레둘레 ♦둘레둘레 살펴보다 stare around; look about wanderingly / 둘레둘레 앉다 sit around [in a circle]

둘리다 1 〈속다〉 be cheated; be taken in; get deceived
▶ 우리는 그 여자의 순진한 모습에 쉽게 둘렸다 We were easily deceived [taken in] by her innocent looks.
2 〈둘러막히다〉 be surrounded [enclosed, encircled, encompassed]
♦높은 산들에 둘린 골짜기 a valley enclosed by high mountains
▶ 그 고대 도시는 성벽으로 둘려 있었다 The ancient city was encircled with walls.
▶ 그 연못은 숲에 둘러 있다 The pond is encircled by woods.
3 〈휘둘리다〉 be swayed; be wielded; be controlled
♦남에게 둘리다 be swayed by *sb* [under *sb's* thumb]

둘신 (商標) 〖化〗 Dulcin
둘째 the second; number two; No. 2; 〈경기 등의 2위자〉 a runner-up
♦둘째 형 [누나] *one's* second eldest brother [sister] / 한국에서 둘째로 큰 도시 the second largest city in Korea / 둘쨋번 집 the second house / 둘째로 secondly; in the second place
▶ 그 문제는 둘째다 That's a secondary matter.
▶ 채산은 둘째 문제다 Profit is of secondary importance.
▶ 둘째로 온 사람은 모스씨였다 Mr. Morse was the second to come. ⇌ Mr. Morse came second.

둘치 〈새끼 못 배는 암컷〉 a sterile female animal
둘하다 dull; clumsy; stupid; gawky; awkward
♦둘한 사람 a clumsy [gawky] person / 둔한 솜씨 poor skill

둥¹ 〈하는 둣 마는 둣〉 ♦남의 말을 듣는 둥 마는 둥하다 listen to *sb* in an absent sort of way; pay little attention to *sb's* talk
▶ 나는 갈 둥 말 둥한다 I have half a mind to go.
▶ 비가 오는 둥 마는 둥했다 The rain was only a drizzle.
▶ 그 소년은 아침을 먹는 둥 마는 둥하고 학교에 갔다 The boy went to school, taking a hasty breakfast.
▶ 그들은 찾는 둥 마는 둥하다가 집으로 돌아갔다 After a halfhearted search, they went home.
2 〈말이 많음〉 ▶ 그녀는 바쁘다는 둥 아프다는 둥 약속을 통 지키지 않는다 She never keeps her promises, saying she is too busy, or she is not well, or something. ⇌ She keeps breaking her promises on the pretext of pressure of business, ill health or whatnot.

둥² 〈북소리〉 turn; with a boom
♦북을 둥하고 울리다 give a beat [boom] on a drum; thump a drum; turn

둥개다 〈쩔쩔매다〉 find difficulty to deal with; do not know what to do 《with》; labor [slave] over; have a hard time; be embarrassed with
♦일을 둥개다 have a hard time doing *one's* work; slave over *one's* work / 문제를 푸느라고 둥개다 find difficulty in solving a problem

둥구나무 a big [giant] shade tree
둥굴대 a rounded strickle
둥굴레 〖植〗 a Solomon's seal
둥굴이 〈껍질 벗긴 통나무〉 a barked log
둥그러지다 tumble 《over, down》; have a tumble; fall 《against a bucket》
♦계단에서 둥그러지다 tumble down the stairs
▶ 그는 나무 뿌리에 걸려 둥그러졌다 He tumbled over the root of a tree.
▶ 그 소년은 길에 둥그러졌다 The boy toppled over onto the street.

둥그렇다 round ⇨ 둥그랗다
둥그레모숨 〖農〗 four handfuls of rice seedlings bound in a bundle
둥그스름하다 roundish; somewhat round [circular]
▶ 위험하니까 날카로운 모서리를 둥그스름하게 하는 것이 좋다 You had better round off the sharp corners because they are dangerous.

둥근톱 a circular [disc] saw; 〈외과용〉 a trepan; 〈자루가 있는〉 a trephine
둥글다 〈원형의〉 round; rotund; 〈고리 모양의〉 circular; 〈구형의〉 globular; spherical
♦둥근 얼굴 a round [moon] face / 둥근 지붕 [천장] a dome; a cupola; a vault / 둥근 창 a circular [round] window / 둥글게 자르다 cut *sth* round / 둥글게 in a circle [ring]
▶ 지구는 둥글다 The earth is spherical.
▶ 저쪽에 보이는 건물은 모양이 둥글다 The building you can see over there has a circular shape.
▶ 나는 얼굴이 둥근 여자를 좋아하는 편이다 I rather like a woman with a round face [moon-faced woman].

둥글둥글 1 〈모양이〉 round
2 〈원만하게〉 peacefully; amicably; harmoniously; smoothly
—**둥글둥글하다** harmonious; amicable; peaceful; 〈인격이〉 well-rounded; affable; sociable
♦둥글둥글한 태도 smooth [bland, suave, affable] manner
▶ 그는 사람이 둥글둥글하다 He has well-rounded corners.
▶ 그 사람은 요즈음 둥글둥글해졌다 Recently he has become sociable.

둥글리다 make *sth* round; make round 《into a ball》; 〈깎아서〉 round off
♦눈을 둥글리다 make a ball of snow; make a snowball / 날카로운 책상 모서리를 둥글리다 round off the sharp-pointed edge of a table
▶ 나는 돌의 모서리를 깎아 둥글렸다 I rounded off the edges of the stone.
▶ 그 모음을 발음할 때는 이렇게 입술을 둥글려라 When you pronounce that vowel, round your lips like this.

둥글뭉수레하다 round and blunt-tipped; round at the end
둥글번번하다 round and well-featured
둥덩실 (float) lightly ⇨ 둥실
둥둥¹ 〈북소리〉 rub-a-dub; rataplan; tom-tom; 〈큰 북 둥〉 boom, boom, boom
  ♦북을 둥둥 울리다 beat a drum boom-boom; beat a big drum
둥둥² buoyantly ⇨ 둥실
둥실 (float) lightly; buoyantly
  ▶밤 하늘에 달이 둥실 떠 있다 The moon floats in the night sky.
  ▶흰 구름이 하늘에 둥실 떠돌고 있다 White clouds are floating lightly in the sky.
둥실둥실 buoyantly ⇨ 둥실
둥실둥실하다 corpulent; plump; rotund
  ♦둥실둥실한 얼굴 a plumpy face / 둥실둥실하게 살찐 돼지 a pig of marvelous rotundity
  ▶얼굴이 아주 둥실둥실해졌구나 How your cheeks have plumped up!
둥싯거리다 move slowly; waddle
  ♦몸이 비대해서 둥싯거리다 be fat and move slow
  ▶배가 둥싯거리며 항구로 들어왔다 The ship waddled into port.
둥싯둥싯 waddlingly; with waddling gaits [step]; sluggishly; slowly
  ♦둥싯둥싯 걷다 waddle; walk [move] with an awkward, swaying motion
둥어리막대 〈길마의〉 a packsaddle rack; a stick attached to a packsaddle
둥우리 1 〈바구니〉 a basket [crate] made of straw, bamboo or the like
  2 〈둥지〉 a nest; 〈새장〉 a cage; a coop; 〈상자형〉 a nest(ing) box
  ■대— a bamboo basket
-둥이 ♦귀염둥이 one's dear [precious] child / 막내둥이 the youngest child [son, daughter] / 쫄랭둥이 a frivolous [cheeky] urchin / 해방둥이 a child born in the year of Liberation of Korea in 1945
둥주리감 〈둥근 감〉 a round persimmon
둥지 a nest ♦새 둥지 a bird's nest / 둥지에 들다 nest; settle in the nest / 둥지를 틀다 [치다] build [make] a nest; nest (in a tree)
  ▶까치 두 마리가 이 나무 꼭대기에 둥지를 틀고 있다 Two magpies have their nests at the top of this tree.
둥치 〈밑동〉 the butt; the base of a tree trunk
  ♦나무를 둥치부터 잘라 넘기다 cut down [saw off] a tree at the base [root]
둥치다 〈함께 동이다〉 tie [wrap] up together; 〈깎아버리다〉 cut off the unnecessary [worthless] part; trim
뒈지다 die ⇨ 죽다
  ▶뒈져라 Go to hell [the devil]! / ▶너 같은 놈은 뒈져 버려라 Drop dead, you bastard!
뒝박 a gourd = 뒤웅박
뒝벌 〖昆〗 a bumblebee (英) a humblebee
뒤 1 〈뒤쪽〉 the back; the rear
  ♦뒤의 back; hind; rear; posterior; backward / 맨 뒤의 hindmost / 가게 뒤(쪽)에 있는 방 a room in the rear of a shop
  〈뒤를〉 뒤를 돌아(다)보다 look back [around] (at); look behind / 뒤를 쫓다 follow (up); pursue; run after *sb*; 〈口〉 tail (after) *sb*
  ▶그녀는 말없이 내 뒤를 따랐다 She followed me without a word.
  ▶적에게 뒤를 보이지 마라 Don't turn your back upon your enemy.
  〈뒤에〉 바로 뒤에 close behind / 행렬의 맨 뒤에 at the tail of a queue / 마을 뒤에 있는 산 a hill to the rear [at the back] of the village / 뒤에 처지다 drop [lag] behind 《the others》 / 뒤에 숨다 hide behind 《a person, a door》
  ▶네 뒤에 서 있는 사람이 누구냐? Who is it standing behind you?
  ▶학교 뒤에 큰 은행나무 한 그루가 있었다 There was a huge gingko tree at the back of the school.
  〈뒤에서〉 뒤에서 따라가다 go behind; follow *sb* / 뒤에서 밀다 push 《a cart》 from behind
  ▶뒤에서 그렇게 세게 밀지 말아요 Don't push me so hard from behind.
  ▶그녀는 뒤에서 그들을 따라갔다 She followed them in the rear.
  ▶뒤에서 누가 부르고 있다 Someone is calling from behind.
  〈뒤로〉 뒤로 물러나다 get [step, draw] back; back away 《from》 / 한 발 뒤로 물러서다 take a step backward / 뒤로 넘어지다 fall (down) backward; fall on one's back / 고향을 뒤로 하다 leave one's home (behind him)
  ▶좀더 뒤로 물러서시오 Step back a little more, please.
  ▶지금은 한 발짝도 뒤로 물러설 수 없다 I can't yield an inch now.
  ▶2보 뒤로 (口令) Two steps backwards!
  ▶뒤로 돌아 (口令) Turn to the right about! = About turn!
  2 〈시간적으로〉 ♦그 뒤 since then; thereafter / 사흘 뒤 three days later [after] / 10년 뒤의 한국 Korea ten years hence / 폭풍 뒤의 고요 a calm after the storm
  ▶비 온 뒤라 길이 젖어 있었다 The roads were wet after the rain.
  ▶그 뒤는 어떻게 됐는지 기억이 나지 않는다 I can't remember how the matter ended.
  〈뒤에〉 2, 3일 뒤에 a few days after [later]; after a few days / 아침 식사 뒤에 after breakfast / 훨씬 뒤에 long after
  ▶당신은 뒤에 후회할 겁니다 You will be sorry for it later.
  ▶그것은 뒤에 안 일이다 It was discovered afterwards.
  ▶그는 뒤에 큰 인물이 되었다 He became a great man later on.
  ▶그날부터 이틀인가 사흘인가 뒤에 그를 만났다 I met him two or three days after that day.
  3 〈순서적으로〉 ♦뒤의 the next; the following; the succeeding; 〈후자의〉 the latter / 뒤로 next; after / 뒤로 미루다 defer; postpone; put off; adjourn
  ▶그녀는 맨 뒤에 모임에 참석했다 She was the last to attend [who attended] the meeting.
  ▶재난이 뒤를 이어 일어났다 One calamity followed close on the heels of another.
  ▶사람들에게는 하기 싫은 일은 뒤로 미루는 경

향이 있다 People are apt to postpone the work they dislike.
▶ 그것은 뒤로 돌립시다 It can wait. ⇌ Let it wait. ⇌ We will leave the matter till later on.
4 〈뒷일〉 future
▶ 뒤를 잘 부탁하오 〈여행을 떠나는 사람이〉 Please look after my affairs while I am away.
5 〈결과〉 consequences; results
▶ 뒤는 내가 맡겠다 I will answer for the consequences.
▶ 뒤야 어찌 되건 내 알 바 아니다 I don't care what may come [will become] of it. ⇌ What happens afterward(s) is of no concern to me. ⇌ After me [us] the deluge.
6 〈나머지·여타〉 the rest; the remainder
▶ 뒤는 말하지 않아도 잘 아시겠죠? You can well understand the rest, can't you? ⇌ You know what I mean even if I don't explain it further.
▶ 그는 그렇게 말하고는 뒤를 얼버무렸다 Saying that, he evaded the point.
▶ 그 뒤는 상상에 맡기겠다 The rest may be left for you to imagine.
▶ 그 마을까지는 차로 가고 그 뒤는 걸어갔다 I went by car as far as the village and walked the rest of the way.
7 〈자손〉 a descendant; a descent; posterity; offspring
▶ 그 집은 뒤가 끊어졌다 The family became extinct. ⇌ The family line broke.
8 〈후계·후임〉 succession; a successor
▶ 그에게는 뒤를 이을 사람이 없다 He has no heir to succeed him.
▶ 그는 아버지의 뒤를 이어 회사 사장이 되었다 He became president of the company in succession to his father.
9 〈배후〉 background; the back
▶ 뒤에서 조종하는 자가 누구냐? Who pulls the wires [strings] (from behind)?
▶ 뒤에서 남의 욕을 하지 마라 Don't speak ill of others behind their backs [in their absence].
▶ 뒤에서는 모두 너를 비웃고 있다 Everyone is laughing at you behind your back.
10 〈뒷바라지〉 support; backing
♦ 뒤를 밀어주다 give support to; back (up) / 공부하는 아들의 뒤를 대다 pay school expenses for *one's* son / 아들이 뒤를 대주어 생활하고 있다 be supported by *one's* son
▶ 그에게는 뒤를 대주는 큰 부자가 있다 He is backed by a millionaire.
11 〈행방〉 a trace; a track; a trail
♦ 뒤를 밟다 track [trail, shadow] *sb*; dog *sb's* steps; follow in *sb's* track / 형사에게 뒤를 밟게 하다 put the detective on *sb's* track
12 〈사후〉 ♦ 뒤에 남은 가족 the bereaved family / 뒤에 남다 survive (*one's* parents)
13 〈대변〉 feces; fecal matter; stool
♦ 뒤가 마렵다 have a call of nature; want to go to the toilet / 뒤를 보다 relieve [ease] nature [*oneself*]; move the bowels; respond to the call of nature / 뒤 보러 가다 go to stool; 〈美〉 go to the toilet
▶ 오늘은 뒤를 두 번 봤다 My bowels were open twice today.
▶ 뒤 보러 갈 적 마음 다르고 올 적 다르다 〈속담〉 Danger past, God forgotten.

뒤구르다 1 〈뒷끝을 다지다〉 settle; set (matters) right; wind up (*one's job*) and make sure that everything is all right
2 〈총포가〉 kick; recoil; rebound
▶ 총이 몹시 뒤구른다 The gun kicks badly.

뒤꼍 a back [rear] garden; 〈美〉 a backyard
♦ 〈집〉 뒤꼍에서 놀다 play in the backyard

뒤꼭지치다 strike *sb* on the back of (his) head

뒤꽁무니 the rear end ⇨ 꽁무니

뒤꽂이 〈쪽의〉 a chignon accessory

뒤꿈치 the heel ⇨ 발뒤꿈치

뒤끓다 1 seethe; boil up [over]
▶ 주전자의 물이 뒤끓고 있다 The water of kettle is boiling up [over].
2 〈우글거리다〉 swarm; flock; be infested with; be crowded [jammed] (with people)
▶ 식료품 매장은 고객들로 뒤끓었다 The food area was crowded with customers.
▶ 역은 행락객으로 뒤끓고 있다 The station is overcrowded with holidaymakers [vacationists].
2 〈비유〉 seethe; be in an uproar [a ferment]; stir
▶ 그의 우승 소식에 온 시내가 뒤끓었다 The whole town was in an uproar at his victory.
▶ 그 문제로 전국이 뒤끓었다 The whole country seethed [was in a ferment] over the question.

뒤끝 〈결말〉 an end; a conclusion; 〈해결〉 (a) settlement; (a) decision; 〈후유증〉 aftereffect
♦ 〈일의〉 뒤끝을 맺다 bring (a matter) to an end [a conclusion]; complete [finish] (*one's* work); bring (*one's* work) to conclusion
▶ 그는 항상 맡은 일의 뒤끝을 맺지 못한다 He always fails to finish the job he has undertaken.
▶ 이 술은 뒤끝이 나쁘다 This liquor has [leaves] nasty aftereffects.

뒤넘기치다 〈넘어뜨리다〉 throw [cast, fling] *sb* backward; 〈뒤엎다〉 upset; overturn (a table); turn over

뒤넘다 〈넘어지다〉 fall backward; fall on *one's* back; 〈뒤집히다〉 tumble [turn] over; overturn; upset

뒤넘스럽다 〈건방지다〉 presumptuous; impertinent; impudent; overbearing; cheeky; saucy; pert; perky; forward; haughty; (口) uppish

뒤놀다 1 〈혼들리다〉 shake; sway; totter; quake; reel; be shaky [rickety]
▶ 책상다리가 뒤논다 The legs of a table are rickety.
▶ 배가 물결에 뒤논다 The boat rolls heavily in the waves.
2 〈돌아다니다〉 wander; roam; rove

뒤늦다 late; tardy; belated; delayed
♦ 뒤늦은 경고 a belated warning / 뒤늦은 꾀 a fool's afterthought / 뒤늦게 나타나다 make a tardy appearance / 뒤늦은 사과를 하다 offer a

뒤대 belated apology
▶ 그의 출마 선언은 뒤늦은 감이 있었다 He was rather tardy in announcing his candidacy.
▶ 나는 뒤늦게나마 화재 현장으로 달려갔다 I ran to the scene of the fire none too soon.
▶ 뒤늦게나마 감사의 말씀을 드립니다 〈편지에서〉 I would like to offer you my belated thanks. ⇒ I'm sorry that I am so late in thanking you. ⇒ I should have thanked you sooner.

뒤대 the northern part (of); the northern district [area]; the northland ◆뒤대에서 피난 온 사람 a refugee from the north

뒤대다[1] 〈비꾸로 말하다〉 make ironical remarks 2 〈거꾸로 가르치다〉 misinform; tell a lie; make a false statement

뒤대다[2] 〈대주다〉 supply (with); provide (with); assist; help
◆돈을 뒤대다 supply sb with money; give sb financial aid / 학비를 뒤대다 supply sb with (his) school expenses

뒤덮다 cover (over, up); overspread; overlay; hang over
◆산꼭대기를 뒤덮은 구름 clouds hanging over the top of the mountain
▶ 홍수가 온 마을을 뒤덮었다 The flood has spread over the whole village.
▶ 먹구름이 하늘을 뒤덮고 있었다 The sky was overcast with black clouds. ⇒ Black clouds obscured the sky.
▶ 흐린 하늘이 바다를 낮게 뒤덮고 있었다 The overcast sky hung low over the sea.

뒤덮이다 be covered (all over) (with); be overspread [overlaid]; be hung over; be veiled
◆정상이 눈으로 뒤덮인 산 a mountain whose top is covered with snow / 얼음으로 뒤덮이다 be coated [covered] with ice / 눈으로 뒤덮이다 be blanketed [covered all over] with snow
▶ 골짜기는 안개로 뒤덮여 있다 The valley is enveloped in mist.
▶ 그 건물은 담쟁이덩굴로 뒤덮여 있다 The building is overgrown with ivy.

뒤돌아보다 1 〈뒤를〉 look back (at, toward); turn about to see; take a backward glance (at)
▶ 그녀는 지나치는 사람마다 뒤돌아볼 정도로 미인이다 She is such a beauty that everybody turns to look at her when she passes.
▶ 그는 우리를 몇 번이고 뒤돌아보면서 작별 인사로 손을 흔들었다 He looked back toward us again and again, waving his hand in farewell.
2 〈과거를〉 look back on [upon]; reflect on [upon]
◆과거를 뒤돌아보다 look back upon the past; think backward; think back to the past days / 30년 전을 뒤돌아보다 look back over a distance of thirty years
▶ 지난 날을 뒤돌아보면 별별 생각이 다 난다 When I look back on my past, I am reminded of a variety of things.

뒤따르다 follow (along behind); run after
◆바싹 뒤따르다 follow on; run after sb closely
▶ 그녀는 남편을 뒤따라 프랑스로 갔다 She followed her husband to France.
▶ 뒤따라 갈테니 걱정하지 마라 Don't worry. I'll join you later.
▶ 한 떼의 기마 경찰이 뒤따랐다 A group of mounted policemen brought up the rear.
▶ 많은 소년 소녀가 서커스 행렬을 뒤따랐다 Many boys and girls tailed after the circus procession.

뒤딱지 〈시계의〉 the back lid (of a watch)

뒤떠들다 make a (loud) noise; clamor; fuss (over a matter)

뒤떨다 shake; shudder; quiver; tremble; shiver (with cold); be all of a tremble

뒤떨어지다 1 〈뒤에 처지다〉 be (a long way) behind; 〈뒤에 남다〉 leave (behind)
◆혼자 뒤떨어지다 be left (all) alone / 행군에서 뒤떨어지다 fall out while on the march
▶ 모두들 떠났으나 그만이 뒤떨어졌다 All left but he was staying behind.
▶ 그녀는 멀찌감치 뒤떨어져서 그를 따라갔다 She followed a long way behind him.
2 〈시대·유행에〉 get [fall, lag, drop] behind; be in arrear of (the times)
◆시대[유행]에 뒤떨어지다 be behind the times [fashion] / 시대에 뒤떨어지지 않도록 하다 keep abreast of the times; keep up with the times
▶ 이 나라의 교육은 아직 뒤떨어져 있다 This country is still backward in education.
▶ 북한의 생활 수준은 남한보다 훨씬 뒤떨어져 있다 North Korea's living standard lags far behind South Korea's.
▶ 요즘 그런 시대에 뒤떨어진 생각은 통하지 않는다 Such old-fashioned [antiquated] ideas are no good nowadays.
3 〈학력·지능이〉 be inferior; be worse than; be below; fall behind; be behindhand
◆수학이 특히 남보다 뒤떨어지다 be behind the others in mathematics above all / 다른 아이들보다 지능이 훨씬 뒤떨어지다 be far beneath the other children in intelligence
▶ 나는 영어에서는 남에게 뒤떨어지지 않는다 I am second to none in English.
▶ 그는 병 때문에 공부가 뒤떨어졌다 He is backward in his studies as he was ill. ⇒ He dropped back in school because of illness.

뒤뚝거리다 stagger; walk unsteadily; totter
▶ 그는 다시 뒤뚝거리며 걷기 시작했다 He began to walk again with unsteady steps.

뒤뚱거리다 stagger; totter; falter; waver

뒤뚱뒤뚱 totteringly; staggeringly
◆뒤뚱뒤뚱 걷다 stagger along; walk with faltering steps

뒤뚱발이 a person who totters [staggers] along; a person who walks with tottering steps

뒤뜰 a back [rear] garden; (美) a backyard

뒤란 the rear [back] of a house; a backyard

뒤룩거리다 1 〈눈을〉 goggle
◆뒤룩거리는 눈 goggle [glaring] eyes / 눈을 뒤룩거리다 goggle [roll] one's eyes (on)
▶ 그는 눈을 뒤룩거리며 주위를 둘러봤다 He looked around staringly [with glaring eyes].
2 〈몸을〉 sway [waddle] (one's body)

3 〈성나서〉 make angry gestures; jerk with anger

뒤룩뒤룩 〈눈알을〉 glaring; 〈몸을〉 swaying; waddling
♦뒤룩뒤룩 걷다 walk swaying one's body; lump along / 살이 뒤룩뒤룩 찌다 be fat as a football [pig]

뒤룽거리다 dangle; hang loose; sway (to and fro)

뒤미처 〈바로 뒤이어〉 right [immediately] after; soon [shortly] after; close [hard, hot] on the heels 《of sb》
♦뒤미처 달려오다 hurry to 《the place》 at the eleventh hour
▶ 그녀는 뒤미처 그를 쫓아갔다 She followed him shortly after he has left.
▶ 그가 집에 돌아오자 뒤미처 그의 동생도 도착했다 Shortly after he had come back home his brother arrived.
▶ 뒤미처 그도 사직했다 He too, soon after the other, resigned his post.

뒤바꾸다 reverse; invert; turn around; switch / 순서[자리]를 뒤바꾸다 reverse the order [their positions]/ 신을 뒤바꿔 신다 〈좌우를〉 have the right shoe on the wrong foot

뒤바뀌다 be reversed; be changed to the opposite; be inverted
♦순서가 뒤바뀌다 be topsy-turvy; be out of order
▶ 상황이 뒤바뀌었다 The situation reversed itself.
▶ 우리의 입장이 뒤바뀌었다 Our positions have been reversed.
▶ 모든 것이 뒤바뀌었다 Everything has turned topsy-turvy.
▶ 형세는 그들에게 유리하게 뒤바뀌었다 The tables were turned in their favor.

뒤바르다 〈종이 등을〉 paste (up) all over; 〈등을〉 paint [powder] 《one's face》 thick(ly); 〈칠 등을〉 daub all over; besmear; smear

뒤받다 〈되받다〉 stand up to a scolding; scold back; talk [answer] back; retort

뒤밟다 〈미행하다〉 follow; dog; shadow; trail; tail (after); track
▶ 경찰은 문제의 사나이를 뒤밟았다 The police followed the man in question.
▶ 나를 뒤밟는 자가 있는 것 같다 I seem to be shadowed [followed, trailed] by somebody.
▶ 그는 앞서거니 뒤서거니 하며 나를 뒤밟았다 He shadowed me, now ahead and now behind.

뒤버무리다 mix (up); jumble (up) together
♦나물을 뒤버무리다 mix up vegetables

뒤범벅 a medley; a jumble; a hotchpotch; a mess; a muddle; a pell-mell
♦뒤범벅을 만들다 jumble (up) together; mix up; make a mess / 뒤범벅(이) 되다 be mixed up; be jumbled together; go to pie
▶ 그 기사는 사실과 허구의 뒤범벅이었다 That article mixed fact and fiction.
▶ 그들은 뒤범벅이 되어 싸웠다 They fought in a confused mass.
▶ 방안은 뒤범벅이 되어 있었다 The room was in a terrible mess.
▶ 모든 것이 뒤범벅이 되어 있다 All sorts of things are jumbled [mixed] up together.
▶ 그는 기대와 불안이 뒤범벅이된 기분이었다 He had mixed feelings of hope and anxiety.

뒤보다[1] 〈용변을 보다〉 evacuate the bowels; have a bowel motion [movement]; ease nature [oneself]; go to stool; do one's needs
♦뒤보러 가다 go to the lavatory [toilet]

뒤보다[2] 〈잘못 보다〉 mistake 《A for B》; misread; misjudge; misview

뒤보다[3] take care of ⇨ 뒤보아주다

뒤보아주다 take care of; look [see] after; help
♦불쌍한 고아를 뒤보아주다 take care of a poor orphan / 동생의 산수 공부를 뒤보아주다 help one's brother with his arithmetic

뒤뿔치다 work under sb; do hackwork 《for》; serve for hire

뒤서다 **1** 〈뒤를 따르다〉 follow sb; follow at 《another's》 heels
♦앞서거니 뒤서거니 하며 now ahead and now behind / 뒤서서 가다 go in the rear / 뒤서게 하다 bring to heel
2 ⇨ 뒤지다[1]

뒤섞다 mix; jumble (together, up); mingle; blend; compound (this and that)
♦희극과 비극을 뒤섞은 연극 a drama blended of comedy and tragedy / 흙과 모래를 뒤섞다 mix earth with sand / 카드를 뒤섞다 shuffle [ruffle] the cards
▶ 번호순으로 되어 있으니 뒤섞지 않도록 하시오 They are in numerical order, so please don't jumble them.

뒤섞이다 be mixed [intermixed]; be jumbled; mix in a confused way; commingle
▶ 서류가 뒤섞이지 않도록 주의하시오 See (to it) that the papers do not get mixed.
▶ 프랑스어와 영어 문법이 마구 뒤섞여 있었다 French and English grammar was all jumbled [mixed] up.
▶ 가장무도회에서는 남녀가 어지럽게 뒤섞여 열광적으로 춤을 추었다 At the masquerade the men and women were mixed in confusion and danced frenziedly.
▶ 그는 그 무리에 뒤섞여 달아났다 He mingled with the crowd and ran away.

뒤숭숭하다 **1** 〈정신이 어수선하다〉 restless; disturbed; distracted; nervous; uneasy; troubled
▶ 마음이 뒤숭숭해서 아무것도 못하겠다 I am restless and don't feel like doing anything.
▶ 마음이 뒤숭숭할 때는 무엇을 하든 실패하게 마련이다 One is sure to fail in anything when disturbed in mind.
▶ 그런 일로 마음이 뒤숭숭해지다니 넌 수양이 덜 됐구나 You are not sufficiently trained yet to have your mind distracted by such a thing.
▶ 참으로 뒤숭숭한 세상이다 What troubled times we live in!
▶ 세상이 갈수록 뒤숭숭해진다 Social unrest is gradually spreading among the masses.
2 〈물건이 흩어져 있다〉 confused; messy; untidy ♦뒤숭숭한 방 a messy room; a room in disorder

뒤안길

▶그의 방은 언제 보아도 뒤숭숭하다 His room is always in disorder [confusion].

뒤안길 〈뒷길〉 a back street [lane]; a byway; a byroad; (비유) the dark side 《of life》
♦인생의 뒤안길을 걸어온 사람 a person who has lived on [who has seen] the dark [seamy] side of life / 인생의 뒤안길을 가다 live a shady life; live outside the mainstream of society

뒤어금니 [解] a (true) molar (tooth)

뒤엉키다 1 〈실 등이〉 get [become] entangled; get [become] raveled
♦뒤엉킨 실을 풀다 untie entangled knots; unravel a thread
▶나무와 덤불이 온통 뒤엉켜 있었다 The trees and bushes were all tangled together.
2 〈이야기 등이〉 get confused [mixed]; 〈사건 등이〉 get complicated; become involved
♦복잡하게 뒤엉킨 사태 a labyrinthine state of things / 복잡하게 뒤엉킨 인생 the raveled skein of life / 뒤엉킨 문제를 해결하다 settle a complicated problem

뒤엎다 upset; overthrow; overturn; turn over
♦밥상을 뒤엎다 overturn a dining table / 찻잔을 뒤엎다 upset the teacup / 정설(定說)을 뒤엎다 explode [overthrow] the established theory / 판결을 뒤엎다 overrule a decision; reverse a sentence
▶등잔을 뒤엎지 않도록 주의하시오 Take care not to turn over the lamp.

뒤웅박 a gourd

뒤잇다 follow; succeed; occur in succession
♦뒤이어 then; subsequently; continuously; continually; successively; in succession
▶예정대로 뒤이어 민 교수의 연설이 있었다 As the next item on the program, Professor Min made a speech.
▶강연이 끝나고 뒤이어 여흥이 베풀어졌다 The lecture came to an end, and then an entertainment followed [was given].

뒤적거리다 ransack; rummage; 〈책 등을〉 browse; 〈더듬다〉 fumble [feel, fish] 《in》
♦서류를 뒤적거리다 rummage among papers / 책을 뒤적거리다 turn over the leaves of a book; browse through a book
▶그는 라이터를 찾느라 호주머니를 뒤적거리고 있었다 He was fumbling in his pocket for the lighter.

뒤적뒤적하다 fumble ⇨ 뒤적거리다

뒤적이다 rummage ⇨ 뒤적거리다

뒤져내다 rummage out; hunt [seek, search] out ♦벽장에 감춰둔 돈을 뒤져내다 seek out money put away in a closet

뒤져보다 search [look, hunt] 《for》; make [prosecute] a search 《for》; rummage 《a house for a thing》
♦돈이 있나 호주머니를 뒤져보다 fumble [fish] in one's pocket to see if there is any money
▶나는 집안을 샅샅이 뒤져보았지만 그것을 보지는 못했다 I searched all over the house, but I could not find it.
▶그는 옛 기록을 뒤져보기를 좋아한다 He is fond of raking through old records.

뒤조지다 settle 《a matter》 securely; bring 《a matter》 to a secure finish

뒤주 a rice chest [bin]

뒤죽박죽 (in) disorder [confusion]; topsy-turvy; higgledy-piggledy; pell-mell; all mixed [jumbled] up
♦뒤죽박죽을 만들다 mix [jumble] up [together]; turn 《things》 topsy-turvy / 뒤죽박죽이 되다 get confused; be jumbled [mixed] up
▶세상이 뒤죽박죽이 되었다 Things have become topsy-turvy.
▶항목의 순서가 뒤죽박죽이다 The order of entries is utterly without rhyme or reason.
▶모든 것이 뒤죽박죽이다 All is in confusion.

뒤쥐 [動] a shrew; a shrewmouse 《pl. -mice》

뒤지 一紙 〈화장지〉 toilet [privy, lavatory] paper; toilet tissue

뒤지다¹ 〈뒤떨어지다〉 fall [drop, lag] behind 《another》; fall back; be backward; be behind 《others》; be inferior [second] 《to》
♦지능이 뒤지는 아이 a backward [(mentally) retarded] child / 시대에 뒤지다 get behind the times [the age]; go out of date; become old-fashioned / 아무에게도 뒤지지 않다 yield [be second] to none / 외국에 뒤지지 않다 keep up with [abreast of] all other nations
▶이 나라는 중공업 개발에서 뒤져 있다 This country is slow in developing its heavy industries.
▶우리는 예방의학에서 뒤져 있다 We lag behind in preventive medicine.
▶이 수족관은 세계의 그 어느 것에도 뒤지지 않는다 This aquarium ranks with any in the world.

뒤지다² 〈찾다〉 search 《for》; ransack; rummage 《in》; fumble 《in》
♦남의 몸을 뒤지다 search sb 《for a hidden weapon》 / 서랍을 뒤지다 ransack [rummage] a drawer 《for jewelry》 / 헌책방을 뒤지고 다니다 poke around secondhand bookstores; hunt for secondhand books / 호주머니를 뒤지다 fumble [feel, fish] in one's pocket 《for a key》 / 샅샅이 뒤지다 search thoroughly 《for》; comb (out) 《for》
▶그들은 편지를 찾아내려고 내 방을 구석구석 뒤졌다 They ransacked my room to find the letter.
▶만년필이 보이지 않아 서랍을 샅샅이 뒤졌다 I couldn't find my fountain pen, and rummaged through the drawer.
▶경찰은 살인범을 색출하기 위해 그 마을을 샅샅이 뒤졌다 The police have combed (out) the village for the murderer.

뒤집개질 turning 《a thing》 over; overturning; overthrowing; upsetting —**뒤집개질하다** upset; overturn; tip [turn] over; overthrow

뒤집고 핥다 know inside out [in detail]

뒤집다 1 〈안팎을〉 turn 《a sock》 inside out; turn the other side; turn wrong side out; 〈위아래를〉 turn upside down; reverse
♦뒤집어 말하면 to put it the other way / 뒤집어 생각해 보면 if you consider it from the opposite point of view / 부침개를 뒤집다 turn

a pancake upside down / 주머니를 뒤집다 turn *one's* pocket (inside) out / 카드를 뒤집다 turn up a card / 양말을 뒤집어 신다 put on *one's* socks inside [wrong side] out
▶ 소년은 코트를 뒤집어 입고 있었다 The boy wore his coat inside out.
▶ 여러분, 답안지를 뒤집어 놓으세요 Everyone, put your examination paper face down.
2 〈바꾸다〉 reverse 《the order》; invert; switch
3 〈뒤엎다〉 upset; overturn; overthrow
♦ 판결을 뒤집다 overrule a decision / 학설을 뒤집다 upset [overthrow] a theory
▶ 상자를 뒤집어 놓고 식탁으로 쓰자 Let's set [turn] the box upside down and use it as a table.
4 〈혼란시키다〉 raise [make] a disturbance; throw into confusion
▶ 그 소식은 온 집안을 발칵 뒤집어 놓았다 The news threw the whole house into utter confusion.

뒤집어쓰다 1 〈얹어 쓰다〉 put [have] on; wear; draw [pull] *sth* over *one's* head
♦ 모자를 뒤집어쓰다 wear a hat
♦ 〈푹 덮다〉 put on; cover with; draw over
♦ 담요를 뒤집어쓰다 wrap *oneself* up [be wrapped up] in a blanket / 이불을 뒤집어쓰다 pull the bedclothes over *one's* head
3 〈내리 덮다〉 pour 《water》 on 《*oneself*》; be covered 《with》
♦ 먼지를 뒤집어쓰다 be covered with dust / 물을 뒤집어쓰다 pour water upon *oneself* / 온몸에 흙탕물을 뒤집어쓰다 be covered [splashed] all over with muddy water
▶ 책들이 흠뻑 먼지를 뒤집어쓰고 있었다 The books were covered with dust.
4 〈넘겨 받다〉 take 《another's fault》 upon *oneself*
♦ 억울한 죄를 뒤집어쓰다 be falsely accused
▶ 네가 그녀석의 허물을 뒤집어쓸 필요는 없다 You don't have to take his guilt on yourself.

뒤집어씌우다 〈물건을〉 cover 《a thing》 with 《another thing》; 〈죄 등을〉 lay the blame on 《*sb* for *sth*》; blame 《the accident》 on *sb*
▶ 그는 책임을 친구한테 뒤집어씌웠다 He passed the buck onto his friend.

뒤집히다 1 〈뒤집어지다〉 be turned [turn] inside out; be turned over
▶ 내 우산이 바람에 뒤집혔다 The wind has blown my umbrella inside out.
▶ 네 옷이 뒤집혔다 Your dress is wrong side out.
2 〈바뀌다〉 be reversed; be changed
▶ 순서가 뒤집혔다 The order is reversed [changed].
▶ 형세가 뒤집혔다 The tables were turned in our [their] favor.
3 〈전복되다〉 be upset; be overturned; topple [turn] over; capsize 《배가》; be reversed; be overruled; be exploded 《결정 등이》
▶ 차가 인도에 뛰어들어 뒤집혔다 The car ran over the sidewalk and turned upside down.
▶ 그 이론은 새로운 발견으로 뒤집혔다 The theory was overthrown by the new discovery.
▶ 배가 뒤집혀 세 사람이 익사했다 The boat capsized and three men were drowned.
▶ 현정권이 곧 뒤집힐지도 모른다 The present government might be tumbled from power [overthrown] before long.
4 〈야단이 나다〉 be in 《an》 uproar; be turned topsy-turvy
♦ 세상이 발칵 뒤집힌 사건 a sensational [much talked about] affair
▶ 그 부정 사건으로 나라가 발칵 뒤집혔다 The scandal created a sensation among the whole nation.
5 (비유) 〈눈이 뒤집힌 군중 a frenzied crowd / 눈이 뒤집히다 lose *one's* sober judgment; lose *one's* mind 《wits》 / 속이 뒤집히다 feel nausea; have a sick stomach
▶ 그 일 때문에 속이 뒤집힌다 I am very (much) upset about the incident. ⇌ The incident quite upsets me.

뒤쪽 the backside; the rear

뒤쫓다 run after; pursue; chase; follow; track; trail; hunt up
♦ 범인을 뒤쫓고 있다 be on the track [trail] of a criminal / 뒤쫓아 가다 start in pursuit / 뒤쫓아 붙잡다 track down 《a criminal》

뒤차 ―車 〈다음 차〉 the next train; 〈뒤따라가는 차〉 a car [vehicle] running behind 《another》

뒤채¹ 〈뒤편 집채〉 a backhouse; a backyard annex; the back wing

뒤채² 〈뒤에서 메는 채〉 the rear poles of a palanquin [sedan chair]

뒤채다 〈남아돌다〉 be superabundant; be in excess; be met with everywhere; 〈발길에 걸리다〉 get in *one's* way; be so much [many] that it obstructs the way

뒤처리 ―處理 settlement 《of an affair》; dealing with the outcome; winding-up
♦ 사건의 뒤처리를 하다 settle an affair / 화재 (현장)의 뒤처리를 하다 clear 《the scene of》 the debris of a fire / 파산한 회사의 뒤처리를 하다 clear [wind] up the affairs of a bankrupt company
―**뒤처리하다** settle; set 《matters》 right; put 《things》 in order; wind up 《*one's* affairs》; deal with the aftermath [outcome]

뒤척이다 ransack; rummage 《in》 ⇨ 뒤적거리다

뒤축 〈구두 등의 발뒤축 부분〉 a heel; 〈발뒤축〉 the heel
♦ 뒤축이 높은[낮은] 구두 high-[low-]heeled shoes / 뒤축을 대다 put a heel on; heel
▶ 내 구두 뒤축이 닳았다 The heels of my boots are worn out. ⇌ My shoes are down at heels.

뒤치다 turn 《over》; upset; overturn
♦ 자다가 몸을 뒤치다 turn [heave] (over, round) in sleep; toss about in bed; 〈잠 못 이루고〉 toss and turn sleepless in bed / 엎어진 책상을 뒤쳐 놓다 turn over an upturned table

뒤치다꺼리 1 〈보살핌〉 looking after; taking care of; patronage; helping 《from behind》; providing for
♦ 대가족의 뒤치다꺼리를 하다 provide for a large family / 아이들 뒤치다꺼리를 하다 take

뒤치락거리다

care of one's children
—**뒤치다꺼리하다** look after; take care of; patronize; help (from behind); provide for
2 ⇨ 뒤치리

뒤치락거리다 turn over from one side to the other (⇨ 뒤치다) ♦ 몸을 뒤치락거리며 잠을 못 이루다 thrash about in bed unable to sleep

뒤탈 —頉 after trouble; later [future] trouble ♦ 뒤탈이 두려워 for fear of later troubles / 뒤탈이 없도록 하다 leave no seeds of future trouble
▶ 뒤탈이 없도록 문제를 해결해 주시오 Please settle the matter so that there may be no trouble left behind.
▶ 이 일로 뒤탈이 생기지 않았으면 합니다 I hope I won't get into trouble for this.

뒤통수 the back (part) of the head; [解] the occiput 《pl. ~s, occipita》 ♦ 뒤통수를 치다 strike sb on the back of one's head; 〈낙담하다〉 be disappointed; be dejected

뒤통스럽다 bungling; clumsy; awkward; thickheaded
♦ 뒤통스러운 짓 a blunder
▶ 사람이 뒤통스러워 하는 일마다 그르친다 He is such a thickheaded fellow that he makes a bungle of everything he does.

뒤틀다 1 〈비틀다〉 twist; warp; screw; wrench; distort
♦ 고통으로 몸을 뒤틀다 be convulsed with pain; writhe in great agony / 허리를 왼쪽으로 뒤틀다 twist [turn] one's hip to the left
2 〈망쳐 놓다〉 thwart; baffle; foil; frustrate
♦ 아무의 계획을 뒤틀어놓다 thwart [baffle] sb's plan

뒤틀리다 1 〈사납고 험해지다〉 become perverse; get distorted; become crooked; get warped
▶ 겹친 불행 때문에 그녀의 성격이 뒤틀렸다 Her character was warped by repeated misfortunes.
2 〈비틀리다〉 be twisted; be distorted [wrenched]; grow [become] warped
♦ 충돌로 프레임이 뒤틀린 자동차 a car whose frame is distorted by a collision / 무릎이 뒤틀리다 get one's knee wrenched
▶ 열로 인해 판자가 뒤틀렸다 The heat has warped the boards.
3 〈틀어지다〉 miscarry; be baffled [thwarted]; be frustrated
▶ 그의 계획은 뒤틀렸다 His plan miscarried [was thwarted].

뒤틀어지다 1 〈물건이〉 《one's》 limbs》 twist; warp; go awry
2 〈일이〉 fail; miss; go wrong [amiss]
▶ 계획이 뒤틀어졌다 The plan has gone wrong [amiss].

뒤편 —便 the back side ⇨ 후방(後方)

뒤폭 —幅 〈옷의 뒤편 조각〉 the back (piece) of a garment 2 〈세간의 뒷막이〉 the back (piece) of a box [chest]

뒤표지 —表紙 the back cover (of a book)

뒤흔들다 1 〈몹시 흔들다〉 shake [swing, sway] violently [hard]; jolt; convulse
♦ 지축을 뒤흔드는 굉음 a deep earthshaking rumble / 멱살[어깨]을 잡고 뒤흔들다 shake sb by the coat collar [the shoulder]
▶ 지진이 그 섬을 뒤흔들었다 An earthquake convulsed the island.
▶ 폭격은 천지를 뒤흔들 정도로 맹렬했다 The bombing was fierce enough to shake heaven and earth.
2 〈어지럽히다〉 disturb; agitate
♦ 마음을 뒤흔들다 disturb sb's mind / 세계를 뒤흔들 만한 대사건 a big incident that may shake the world

뒤흔들리다 1 〈물건이〉 be shaken [swayed] violently; jolt
▶ 길이 나빠 차가 뒤흔들렸다 The car swayed because of the rough road.
▶ 지진으로 집이 뒤흔들렸다 Houses were shaken by the earthquake.
2 〈교란되다〉 be disturbed [agitated, shaken]
♦ 결심[마음]이 뒤흔들리다 one's resolution shakes [mind is disturbed]

뒷간 a water closet; a privy; a lavatory; (美) a toilet (room)

뒷간에 갈 적 맘 다르고 올 적 맘 다르다 《속담》 The danger past and God forgotten.

뒷갈망 settlement 《of an affair》 ⇨ 뒤처리

뒷갈이 plowing the field after harvesting

뒷거래 —去來 backdoor dealings ⇨ 암거래(暗去來)

뒷거름 (an) additional manuring

뒷거리 a back street; a side street

뒷걱정 after worries —**뒷걱정하다** worry about an aftermath

뒷걸음질 stepping backward; taking backward steps
—**뒷걸음질하다** step backward; step back
▶ 갑자기 크게 떠드는 소리가 들려 그는 뒷걸음질했다 Suddenly he heard a loud noise, and stepped back.

뒷걸음질치다 1 〈물러서다〉 step [move, walk] backward; step [draw] back
▶ 그는 몇 발짝 뒷걸음질쳤다 He drew back a few paces [steps].
2 〈꽁무니를 빼다〉 shrink back; back away 《from》; flinch [recoil] 《from》
▶ 소년은 개를 피해 뒷걸음질쳤다 The boy shrank (back) from the dog.
▶ 말은 자동차에 겁을 먹고 뒷걸음질쳤다 The horse shied at the car.

뒷결박 —結縛 tying sb's hands behind 《his》 back

뒷경과 —經過 later developments ⇨ 경과

뒷고대 the back of a collar

뒷골목 a back street; a side street; an alley
♦ 뒷골목 인생 a sordid life

뒷공론 —公論 1 〈사후(事後)의〉 a futile rehash of an event; a postmortem (debate, discussion)
▶ 뒷공론은 제발 그만 두시오 Please spare me the after-the-fact commentary!
▶ 지금은 무슨 말을 해도 뒷공론에 지나지 않는다 At this point, anything you say is no more than hindsight.
—**뒷공론하다** hold a fruitless debate after the event; flog a dead horse
▶ 이제 와서 뒷공론해봐야 소용 없다 It is too late now. What is done is done.

2 〈험담〉 criticizing [speaking ill of] *sb* behind *one's* back; backbiting
—**뒷공론하다** criticize [speak ill of] *sb* behind *one's* back [in *one's* absence]; stab *sb* in the back; backbite

뒷구멍 〈뒷문〉 a back door [way]; a rear entry; 〈부정 수단〉 backstairs channels; an illegitimate [irregular, unfair] way; unjust [unlawful] means
♦ 뒷구멍으로 하는 계약 a backdoor contract / 뒷구멍으로 들어가다 enter by the back door / 뒷구멍으로 돈을 먹이다 bribe *sb* secretly
▶ 뒷구멍 영업을 하는 곳이 몇군데 있다 There are some places that have under-the-counter business.
▶ 그는 뒷구멍으로 슬그머니 빠져나갔다 He sneaked out by the back door.
▶ 그는 뒷구멍으로 입학했다 He entered the school through backstairs channel.

뒷길¹ **1** 〈뒤에 있는 길〉 a back street; a byroad
2 〈장래〉 *one's* future; prospects
♦ 뒷길을 생각하다 think of *one's* future
3 〈부정한 수단〉 unjust [unfair, unlawful] means

뒷길² 〈웃옷의 뒤판〉 the back piece of an upper garment

뒷날 the future ⇨ 후일(後日)

뒷눈질 a backward glance —**뒷눈질하다** glance [look] back 《at》; take a backward glance 《at》

뒷다리 a hind [rear] leg ▶ 그 개는 뒷다리로 서 있다 The dog is standing on its hind legs.

뒷담 the wall in back; a back fence

뒷담당 —擔當 answering [taking responsibility] for the aftermath; taking care [charge] (of it)
▶ 뒷담당은 내가 하겠다 I will answer for the consequences [result].
▶ 자네가 손해를 보면 내가 뒷담당을 하겠다 I am willing to answer for your possible losses.
—**뒷담당하다** answer for the aftermath 《of an affair》

뒷대문 —大門 a back [rear] gate

뒷덜미 the nape [scruff]; the back of *one's* neck ♦ 뒷덜미를 잡다 seize [take, grasp] *sb* by the nape

뒷돈 supply of money; ready money; funds; capital; stakes
♦ 노름의 뒷돈을 대다 supply *sb* with gambling stakes / 장사의 뒷돈을 대다 finance a business; provide money for a business
▶ 뒷돈을 대지 못해 사업이 중단되었다 The enterprise was abandoned owing to lack of funds.

뒷동산 a hill at the back 《of *one's* home [the village]》

뒷마감하다 wind up; bring to a finish; complete ♦ 회계를 뒷마감하다 close an account

뒷마구리 the rear crossbar of a saddle rack
뒷마당 a backyard; a rear garden [ground]
뒷마루 a rear floor; the floor in the back
뒷말 backbiting ⇨ 뒷공론
뒷맛 (an) aftertaste
♦ 뒷맛이 좋다 leave a pleasing taste in *one's* mouth; leave a pleasant aftertaste / 뒷맛이 나쁘다 leave a bad [an unpleasant] aftertaste; leave an uncomfortable [a nasty] taste in *one's* mouth
▶ 그것은 뒷맛이 고약했다 It left a bad taste [aftertaste] in my mouth.
▶ 그 사건은 전국민에게 개운치 않은 뒷맛을 남겼다 The event left a gloomy impression on all the nation.

뒷맵시 *one's* appearance [figure] from the back ♦ 뒷맵시가 곱다 look fine [graceful] from behind / 뒷맵시가 없다 look poor [ungainly] from behind

뒷머리 **1** 〈물건의〉 the back part [end] 《of》
♦ 책상의 뒷머리 the back end of a table
2 〈행렬의〉 the rear; the end
♦ 줄의 뒷머리 the rear [end] of a row
3 〈뒤쪽의 머리털〉 hair on the back of the head; back hair
4 ⇨ 뒤통수

뒷면 —面 the reverse [other] side; the back (side); 〈동전의〉 the tail
♦ 엽서의 뒷면 (on) the back of a postal card / 레코드판의 뒷면 the flip side of a phonograph record
▶ 뒷면을 보시오 《게시》 See back page. ⇌ See the reverse side. ⇌ Please turn over. (略 P.T.O.)
▶ 표지의 뒷면에 약어표가 있다 A list of abbreviations is given on the back [inside] of the cover.
▶ 국명은 동전의 뒷면에 있다 The name of the country is on the reverse side of the coin.

뒷모습 the sight of *one's* back; *one's* appearance from the back; *one's* back [rear] view
▶ 네 뒷모습은 네 아버지를 꼭 닮았다 You look just like your father from behind
▶ 달리는 그녀의 뒷모습을 보았다 I caught sight of her back as she ran along.

뒷모양 —貌樣 the sight of *one's* back ⇨ 뒷모습

뒷목 〈타작 후의 찌꺼기〉 leavings after threshing; grain tailings (on a thrashing floor)

뒷문 —門 a back [rear] gate [door]; the rear entrance; a postern (gate)
♦ 뒷문으로 도망치다 escape [run away] by the back door [gate] / 뒷문으로 입학하다 obtain a backdoor admission 《to a school》

뒷물 a hip bath —**뒷물하다** bathe *one's* private parts

뒷밀이 〈일〉 pushing (from behind); 〈사람〉 a person who pushes 《a cart》; a pusher —**뒷밀이하다** push 《a cart》

뒷바라지 supporting; looking after; taking care of
—**뒷바라지하다** look after; take care of; provide for; support
♦ 아들의 살림을 뒷바라지하다 provide *one's* son with daily necessaries / 환자를 뒷바라지하다 attend [wait on] a patient
▶ 그녀는 아이들 뒷바라지하기에 바쁘다 She is busy with the care of her children.

뒷바퀴 a rear [back] wheel

뒷받침 〈후원〉 backing; support; 〈증명〉 proof;

evidence; substantiation; 〈보증〉 guarantee; endorsement; 〈기반〉 foundation

♦유력한 뒷받침 strong backing / 기소의 뒷받침이 되는 증거 evidence that justifies indictment / 사실의 뒷받침이 없는 주장 an argument not founded [founded] on facts; an argument unsupported by facts

▶ 당신의 주장에는 사실의 뒷받침이 없다 Your argument is not supported by [based on] facts.

▶ 이 모험적인 사업에는 그의 아버지의 뒷받침이 있었다 His father was behind him in this venture.

▶ 재정적인 뒷받침이 없어지자 그들의 계획은 무너졌다 Their plans collapsed when they lost financial backing.

—**뒷받침하다** back (up); support; endorse; substantiate; give substance to 《words》; add support to 《the rumor》

♦견해를 뒷받침하다 endorse sb's view / 말을 행동으로 뒷받침하다 back up one's words with deeds / 통계를 가지고 자기의 주장을 뒷받침하다 fortify one's case with statistics / 사실을 뒷받침해 주는 증거를 확보하다 secure evidence supporting the fact

▶ 그것을 뒷받침할 이론이 없다 There is no theory to prove it.

▶ 그 과학자는 자기의 이론을 뒷받침할 많은 실험 데이터를 제출했다 The scientist produced much experimental data as evidence for his theory.

뒷발 a hind foot; heels; a hind leg
뒷발굽 a hind hoof; a heel 《of a horse》
뒷발질 kicking with one's heel —**뒷발질하다** kick with one's heel; make a heel
뒷방 —房 an inner [a rear] room; 《美》 a back room
뒷보증 —保證 endorsement ⇨ 배서(背書)
뒷북치다 fuss about belatedly; pother after the event ▶ 미련한 놈 뒷북친다 Fools are wise after the event.
뒷사람 a person behind one; 〈뒷세대의〉 a person of a later [following] generation
뒷생각 afterthoughts
뒷소문 —所聞 gossip [a rumor] following the event; later tidbits 《of news [information]》; an after-talk
뒷손 illegal [false] reach; a dirty hand 《for money》; acceptance 《of sth》 on the sly

♦뒷손을 벌리다 demand 《money》 under a counter; be ready to accept on the sly; be open to bribery

뒷손가락질하다 point after sb; point a finger of scorn at sb; talk about sb with scorn

♦뒷손가락질 받다 have the finger of derision pointed at; be talked 《in contempt》; be an object of 《public》 contempt

▶ 사람들한테 뒷손가락질 당할 일은 하지 마시오 Don't do anything that might make people talk 《about you》.

뒷수쇄 —刷 winding-up ⇨ 뒤처리
뒷수습 —收拾 settlement 《of an affair》 ⇨ 뒤처리
뒷심 1〈조력〉 supporting behind one's back; help [aid, assistance] from behind; backing-up

♦뒷심이 든든하다 have a strong [good] backing / 뒷심이 있다 have sb at one's back

2〈저력〉 power to resist [sustain]; stamina
뒷이야기 a sequel 《to a story》 ♦사건의 뒷이야기 a sequel to an event
뒷일 〈장래의〉 future affairs; 〈사후의〉 one's affairs after his death

♦뒷일을 생각하다 have the (distant) future in view; 〈자손을〉 have the welfare [interest] of posterity at heart

▶ 뒷일은 책임질 수 없다 I won't take responsibility for what may happen later on.

▶ 뒷일은 네게 맡기겠다 I'll leave the rest to you.

▶ 그는 나에게 뒷일을 부탁했다 He has asked me to look after his affairs when he's gone.

▶ 뒷일을 부탁합니다 See (to it) that all is well after my departure.

▶ 뒷일이야 누가 알 수 있겠는가 There is no knowing what will happen in the distant future.

뒷자락 the back hem [rear train] of one's clothes; 〈치마의〉 the rear skirt
뒷자리 a back seat; a seat at [in] the back
뒷전 1〈굿의 마지막 거리〉 the last stage of an exorcism

2〈뒤쪽〉 the back; the rear
♦뒷전에 멀찍이 앉다 sit far back

3〈배후・이면〉 the back
♦뒷전에서 조종하다 pull the wires [strings] from behind / 뒷전에서 혈뜯다 speak ill of sb behind one's back; backbite sb

4〈미룸〉 negligence ♦뒷전으로 돌리다 lay aside 《one's work》; leave sth out of account [consideration]

▶ 그 아이는 공부는 뒷전이다 The boy neglects [ignores] his studies.

뒷전놀이 1〈무당이 뒷전 놀다〉 perform the last stage of an exorcism

2〈뒤치다꺼리하다〉 wind up; take care of the aftermath; deal with the outcome

뒷정리 —整理 arrangements for the end; after adjustment; clearance work; winding-up —**뒷정리하다** arrange to end; wind up 《one's affairs》;〈청소〉 clear away;〈처리〉 dispose of

뒷조사 —調査 〈내사〉 a secret investigation [inquiry] —**뒷조사하다** investigate secretly [in secret]; throughly investigate; make secret inquiries into 《a matter》

뒷줄 1〈뒤쪽 줄〉 the row behind; a back [rear] row ▶ 나는 맨 뒷줄에 앉았다 I was seated in the last row.

2〈배후 세력〉 a patron; a backer; a pull
뒷지느러미 an anal fin
뒷질 〈앞뒤로 흔들림〉 a pitch; pitching —**뒷질하다** pitch
뒷짐 folding one's hands behind one's back

♦뒷짐 지다 fold one's hands behind one's back / 뒷짐 지우다 make sb fold 《his》 hands behind 《his》 back; 〈결박 짓다〉 tie sb's arms behind 《his》 back

뒷짐결박 —結縛 〈뒷짐박〉 tying sb's hands

behind (his) back —뒷짐결박하다 tie *sb's* hands behind (his) back

뒷집 the house behind; a house in [at] the back of *one's* own

뒹굴다 1 〈누워서 구르다〉 roll [tumble, toss] about; wallow; welter; 〈뒤틀다〉 writhe
♦ 마루 위에서 뒹굴고 있는 새끼 고양이 pussies tumbling about on the floor / 침대 속에서 뒹굴다 toss and tumble in bed
▶ 모터사이클이 미끄러져 뒹굴었다 The motorcycle slipped and rolled over.
▶ 돼지 새끼들이 진창 속에서 뒹굴고 있었다 Little pigs were wallowing [weltering] in the mire.
2 〈빈둥거리다〉 idle [loaf] *one's* time away; be on the loaf; (美) loaf around; live at ease
♦ 평생을 뒹굴며 보내다 drift aimlessly through life
▶ 그는 아무것도 하지 않고 뒹굴고 있다 He leads an idle life.

듀공 〔動〕 a sea pig [cow]; a dugong

듀스 〔競〕 deuce ▶ 듀스가 되었다 The game went to deuce.

듀엣 〔樂〕 〈이중주〉〔唱〕 a duet

드나나나 whether (*one* is) in or out; whether *one* is at home or stays out; out and home
▶ 드나나나 걱정 뿐이다 I have nothing but troubles, whether at home or abroad.

드나들다 1 〈출입하다〉 go [come] in and out; 〈자주 가다〉 go often; frequent (a house)
♦ 드나드는 배 ships going in and out / 드나드는 사람이 많은 곳 a place with a lot of people coming and going / 우리 집에 드나드는 세탁업자 a laundryman serving my family / 술집에 드나들다 hang out [around] a bar; frequent a pub / 유력인사의 집에 드나들다 frequent the house of an influence from interested motives
▶ 그는 민 박사의 집에 자주 드나든다 He frequents Dr. Min's house.
▶ 그의 집에는 드나드는 사람이 많다 There are a large number of visitors to his house.
▶ 경찰은 그 집에 드나드는 모든 사람을 지켜보았다 The police watched everyone going in and out of the house.
2 〈갈아들다〉 be frequently changed
▶ 그 집에는 가정부가 자주 드나든다 Housemaids are frequently changed in that family.
3 〈들쭉날쭉하다〉 be indented; be not straight; have a zigzag direction [course]
▶ 모를 심은 줄이 드나든다 The row of planted rice is irregular.

드날리다 1 〈이름이〉 (*one's* name) resound [echo] far and wide; come to fame; become famous [popular]; 〈이름을〉 have *one's* name up; win [earn] fame; win a reputation
♦ 명성이 전국에 드날리다 be popular throughout the country / 이름이 온 세상에 드날리다 be known all over the world / 온 세상에 이름을 드날리다 gain a worldwide reputation; win [enjoy] worldwide fame
▶ 그는 그 작품으로 일약 명성을 드날리게 되었다 He came to fame suddenly through that work.
▶ 그의 명성은 전국에 드날렸다 His name echoed throughout the country.
2 〈집어들어 날리다〉 hold [pick] up *sth* and make (it) fly

드넓다 spacious (garden); wide; broad; open; extensive; vast
♦ 드넓은 길 a broad street / 드넓은 방 a large [spacious] room / 드넓은 집 a large [roomy] house
▶ 드넓은 들판이 서쪽으로 몇 마일이고 뻗어 있었다 An open field stretched for miles westward.

드높다 high; lofty; eminent
♦ 드높은 이상 lofty ideals / 하늘에 드높이 high in the air; (美) way up in the sky
▶ 교육 개혁을 요구하는 소리가 드높다 There are loud cries demanding a reform of education.

드디어 at last; at length; finally; in the end
▶ 대표단은 드디어 내일 서울을 떠난다 Tomorrow the delegation is finally leaving Seoul.
▶ 드디어 졸업식이 다가왔다 The graduation is at length near at hand.
▶ 드디어 결단을 내려야 할 때가 왔다 There comes a time when I must make a decision.

드라마 a drama; a play
■ 라디오— a radio play 인간— a human drama 텔레비전 연속— a television serial drama 홈— a drama of home life; (美) a soap opera

드라이버 〈운전기사〉 a driver; 〈나사돌리개〉 a screwdriver

드라이브 a drive; a motor ride —드라이브하다 drive; take [have] a drive (to) ■—웨이 a driveway

드라이브인 (a) drive-in

┌───┐
│ 解說 ***drive-in***은 차에 탄 채로 식사할 수 있는 │
│ drive-in restaurant이나 차에 탄 채로 영화를 │
│ 볼 수 있는 drive-in theater를 가리킨다. 따라 │
│ 서 차에서 내려서 들어가는 레스토랑은 road- │
│ side restaurant이라고 말하는 것이 정확하다 │
└───┘

♦ 드라이브인 극장 a drive-in theater / 드라이브인 식당 a drive-in restaurant [lunch counter] / 드라이브인 은행 a drive-in bank

드라이아이스 dry ice

드라이어 a (hair) drier; a dryer

드라이클리닝 dry cleaning
♦ 코트를 드라이클리닝 보내다 send *one's* overcoat to the (dry) cleaner's
—드라이클리닝하다 dry-clean; dry-cleanse
■—업자 a dry cleaner

드래그번트 〔野〕 a drag bunt

드래프트 a draft
♦ 드래프트에서 1위로 뽑힌 선수 the 《baseball》 player who was picked first in the draft [who was drafted first]
■—제(制) the draft system —회의 a draft conference

드러나다 1 〈겉으로 나타나다〉 come out; come into view; appear; emerge (from); be exposed; be revealed; crop out 〈광맥이〉
▶ 그녀의 어깨가 드러났다 Her shoulders were exposed [bared].

►두 사람 사이의 대립은 완전히 드러났다 The conflict between the two has become quite open [public].
►그의 얼굴에 개전의 빛이 드러났다 Repentance was written upon his face.
2 〈밝혀지다〉 be [become] known; be found (out); be discovered [disclosed, revealed, exposed]; come to light; emerge; be laid bare
♦업적이 드러나다 one's achievements become known / 이름이 세상에 드러나다 become famous in the world
►마침내 그의 악행이 드러났다 At last his wrongdoing came to light.
►조사 결과 몇 가지 중요한 사실이 드러났다 Some important facts emerged as a result of the investigation.
►비밀이 드러났다 The secret got out.
►시험 결과 그의 실력이 바닥이 드러났다 As a result of the examination his pretense to knowledge was found false.
►비밀이 드러나게 하면 안된다 We must not let the secret get out.

드러내다 **1** 〈노출하다〉 〈신체·모습 등을〉 expose; bare; lay bare [open]
♦가슴을 드러내다 bare [expose] one's breast / 넓적다리를 드러내다 expose one's thigh / 모습을 드러내다 appear; show oneself; come in sight; come into view / 이를 드러내다 show [bare] one's teeth; grin
►한라산이 구름 사이로 모습을 드러냈다 Mt. Hanra appeared from between the clouds.
►그녀는 숄을 벗어 어깨를 드러냈다 She took off her shawl and exposed her shoulders.
►개가 이를 드러내고 으르렁거렸다 The dog growled, baring [showing] its teeth.
►그녀는 맨발인데다 가슴까지 드러내고 있었다 She was barefooted, and, what is more, her chest was completely bared.
►아이는 배를 드러낸 채 자고 있다 The child is sleeping with its belly uncovered.
2 〈성질·본색을〉 express; reveal; show; betray
♦드러내놓고 반대하다 oppose publicly; offer an open opposition / 본성을 드러내다 reveal one's true character / 본심을 드러내다 disclose one's real intention; reveal one's real motive / 불만을 드러내다 wear a discontented look; betray one's dissatisfaction / 자기의 무지를 드러내다 betray one's ignorance
►술에 취하면 사람은 본성을 드러낸다 One's true self is revealed when he drinks.
►그는 마침내 정체를 드러냈다 He at last showed himself in his true colors.
3 〈보이다〉 show; display; exhibit; indicate; manifest; 〈증명하다〉 prove; speak for
►이 점이 그의 정직함을 드러내 준다 This proves [speaks for] his honesty.
►그는 있는 재간을 다 드러내 보였다 He displayed all his talents [skills].
►이것은 분명히 그가 법률에 대해 무식함을 드러내고 있다 This is a positive proof of his legal ignorance.
4 〈폭로하다〉 reveal; disclose; divulge
♦회사의 내막을 드러내다 disclose the inside secret [story] of a company / 비밀을 드러내다 reveal [divulge] a secret / 흉계를 드러내다 lay bare one's evil design

드러눕다 lie (down); lay oneself down
♦감기로 드러눕다 be laid up with a cold / 병으로 드러눕다 be laid up with illness; be ill [sick] in bed / 마루에 드러눕다 lie (on) the floor; stretch [lay] oneself on the floor / 길게 드러눕다 lie at full length; stretch oneself
►나는 피곤하여 풀밭에 드러누웠다 I lay [threw myself] down on the grass since I was tired.
►고양이는 침대 위에 길게 드러누웠다 The cat lay full length on the bed
►드러누워서 책을 읽으면 눈에 해롭다 It's bad for your eyes to read lying down.

드러머 〈북 치는 사람〉 a drummer

드러쌓이다 be heaped up; be piled up; accumulate; 〈눈·먼지 등이〉 lie (on)
►할 일이 드러쌓였다 I have a pile of work to do.
►눈이 석자나 드러쌓였다 The snow lay three feet deep (on the ground).
►창고에 쌀이 드러쌓여 있다 Rice is piled up in the warehouse.

드럼[1] 〔樂〕 〈북〉 a drum
드럼[2] 〔통〕 a drum
  ―통 a drum (can)

드렁거리다 snore ⇨ 드르렁거리다
드렁드렁 snoring (loudly) ⇨ 드르렁드르렁
드레스 a dress ♦흰 드레스를 입은 부인 a lady in a white dress
►그녀는 자기 드레스는 자기가 전부 해 입는다 She makes all her own dresses.
  ―리허설 a dress rehearsal ―메이커 a dressmaker; a couturier (남성); a couturière (여성)

드레싱 〔料〕 (a) dressing
드로어즈 (a pair of) drawers; bloomers; underpants
드롭 〔野〕 (hurl, hit) a drop; a drop curve
드롭스 〈사탕〉 drops
드르렁거리다 keep snoring (through one's nose) ♦드르렁거리기 시작하다 fall to snoring
►그는 그날 밤 코를 드르렁거리며 잤다 He snored the night away.

드르렁드르렁 snoring (loudly, terribly) ♦코를 드르렁드르렁 골다 snore loudly [terribly]; (口) blow [snore] like a grampus

드르르[1] 〈막힘없이〉 smoothly; without a hitch; fluently; 〈순조롭게〉 swimmingly
♦드르르 외다 say by heart without a single break / 글을 드르르 읽다 read a passage smoothly
►소년은 암기한 연설을 드르르 외었다 The boy rattled off the speech which he had learnt by heart.

드르르[2] **1** 〈미끄럽게 구르는 소리〉 smoothly; slipperily; rolling along
♦문을 드르르 열다 open the door smoothly / 드르르 열리다 open smoothly
2 〈떠는 모양〉 tremblingly; shiveringly
♦드르르 진동하다 tremble all over; shiver like a jelly
►그 폭발 때문에 창유리가 드르르 떨렸다 The explosion made the windowpanes tremble.

드리다[1] 〈쭉정이 등을 날려 보내다〉 winnow (grain from the chaff by blowing air on it)

드리다[2] 〈꼬다〉 braid; plait; twist together; twine ♦밧줄을 드리다 make [twist] a rope

드리다[3] **1** 〈주다〉 give; offer (up); present; serve
♦선생님께 선물을 드리다 give [send] a present to one's teacher / 아버지께 진지를 드리다 serve one's father with dinner / 축하를 드리다 offer one's congratulations
▶ 싸게 드리겠습니다 I will let you have it very cheap.
▶ 얼마 드리면 됩니까? How much do I have to pay?
▶ 맥주 좀 드릴까요? Will you have some beer?
▶ 무엇을 (보여) 드릴까요? 〈가게에서〉 What can I show you, sir?
2 〈정성을 바치다〉 devote; dedicate
♦기도드리다 offer (up) a prayer 《to God》 / 불공드리다 offer [hold] a Buddhist mass

드리다[4] 〈방 등을 만들다〉 make; build; construct; add; put in [over] ♦마루를 드리다 make a floor; floor ▶ 광이 있던 자리에 새로 방을 하나 드렸다 I have turned the storeroom into a living room.

드리다[5] 〈가게 문을 닫다〉 close the shop; put up the shutters ♦가게를 하루 드리다 close the store for the day

드리다[6] let down ⇨ 드리우다 1

드리다[7] 〈조동사로〉 ♦보여 드리다 submit a thing for sb's inspection / 알려 드리다 inform sb of a matter; let sb know
▶ 어머니 일을 도와 드려라 Help your mother with her work.
▶ 그분께 길을 가리켜 드렸다 I have shown the gentleman the way.
▶ 댁에까지 모셔다 드릴까요? Shall I see you home?

드리블 〖球〗 a dribble; dribbling ─**드리블하다** dribble

드리없다 〈일정하지 않다〉 irregular; variable; unfixed; changeable
♦드리없이 irregularly; variably / 값이 드리없다 have no fixed prices; prices are irregular / 수업을 드리없이 시작하다 start class at no fixed time / 드리없이 팔다 sell at irregular prices

드리우다 **1** 〈늘어뜨리다〉 hang (down); let down; suspend
♦낚싯줄을 드리우다 drop a line; cast a line for (fish) / 발을 드리우다 let down a bamboo blind / 커튼을 드리우다 draw [let] down a curtain
▶ 기가 드리워져 있다 A flag is hanging down.
▶ 그 방에는 검정빛 커튼이 드리워져 있었다 The room was hung with a black curtain.
2 〈교훈을 베풀다〉 give (to an inferior); grant; bestow (on, upon)
♦교훈을 드리우다 give a moral lesson; grant a favor of giving lesson / 은혜를 드리우다 bestow a favor on sb
3 〈남기다〉 leave (one's name)
♦이름을 후세에 드리우다 leave one's name to posterity; immortalize one's name; win immortal fame
4 〈댕기를 물리다〉 ribbon ♦댕기를 드리우다 wear [put on] a pigtail ribbon

드릴 〖송곳〗 a drill

드맑다 very clear ♦드맑은 하늘 a clear [serene] sky

드문드문 **1** 〈시간적으로〉 once in a (long) while; at long [rare] intervals; occasionally; now and then; on rare occasions
♦드문드문 찾아오다 show up once in a long while
▶ 손님이 드문드문 있습니다 We have visitors once in a while.
▶ 그런 일이 드문드문 일어난다 Such a thing happens from time to time.
▶ 기회가 있으면 드문드문 음악회에 간다 I go to the concert from time to time when an occasion presents itself.
▶ 그녀의 소식은 드문드문 듣고 있다 I hear things now and again about her.
2 〈공간적으로〉 at intervals; sparsely; thinly; here and there
♦드문드문 분산된 인구 a thinly scattered population / 나무를 드문드문 심다 plant trees at intervals [here and there] / 털이 드문드문 나다 be thinly haired [covered with hair]
▶ 그곳에는 농가가 드문드문 있다 There are scattered farmhouses there. ⇌ The place is sparsely dotted with farmhouses.
▶ 그 산에는 나무가 드문드문 나 있다 The hill is sparsely wooded.

드물다 〈수효가 적다〉 scarce; few (and far between); 〈진귀하다〉 rare; uncommon; unusual; 〈특이하다〉 unique
♦보기 드문 사건 [미인] a rare event [beauty] / 보기 드문 웅변가 a person gifted with rare eloquence / 드물게 in rare cases; on rare occasions; uncommonly / 드물게 일어나는 일 a rare [an uncommon] occurence
▶ 그가 약속 시간에 늦는 일은 드물다 He is seldom [rarely] late for the appointed time.
▶ 읽을 가치가 있는 책은 있다고 해도 드물다 Few books, if any, are worth reading.
▶ 그가 화를 내는 것은 드문 일이다 It is unusual for him to get angry.
▶ 그는 드물게 보는 수완가다 He is a man of rare [exceptional] ability.

드새다 pass the night 《at an inn》; stay for the night; lodge (in)
♦하룻밤 드새다 stay overnight; get accommodation [take a lodge] for the night / 하룻밤 드새기를 청하다 ask sb for a night's lodging

드세다 〈세력이 강하다〉 powerful; influential; 〈집터가 나쁘다〉 evil; ill-omened; 〈성정이 사납다〉 wild; savage; violent
♦드센 여자 a woman of violent temper
▶ 그곳은 터가 드세다 The place has an unlucky aspect.
▶ 그는 당내에서 상당히 세력이 드세다 He has [wields] much power [influence] in the party.

드잡이 **1** 〈싸움〉 a scuffle; a grapple; handgrips; a wrestle; a grappling; a rough and

tumble fight
▶경찰과 구경꾼들 사이에 드잡이가 벌어졌다 There was a scuffle between the police and spectators.
▶그들의 말다툼은 끝내 드잡이가 되었다 Their quarrel ended in scuffling. ⇒ They proceeded from words to grips [grapples].
━드잡이하다 scuffle; grapple 《with》; come to grapples [handgrips, grips] 《with》
2 〈빚대신 가져 감〉 seizure; attachment; distraint ━드잡이하다 seize *sb's* kitchen utensils for debts; attach; distrain

득 1 〈긋는 모양〉《draw a line》forcefully; with pressure
2 〈어는 모양〉《freeze》hard [solid, fast]
3 〈긁는 모양〉 harshly; with a harsh noise
▶그는 벽에 성냥을 득 그었다 He scratched a match on the wall.

득 得 (a) profit ⇨ 이득
♦득이 되다 turn [prove] to *one's* profit; bring profit 《to》; do *sb* good / 득을 보다 profit; gain; benefit; do well [nicely] out of 《a war》
▶그런 짓을 해서 대체 어떤 득이 있나? What is the use of doing such a thing?
▶그렇더라도 득이 되지 않을걸 It will not be profitable. ⇒ It will not benefit you.
▶이 일은 득이 되지 않는다 This work does not pay.
▶사두면 그만큼 너에게 득이 된다 It would be advantageous to you to buy it.
▶나는 십만원의 득을 보았다 I made a profit of one hundred thousand won.
▶지름길로 가면 1마일 득을 본다 You save a mile by taking a short cut.

득남 得男 begetting of a son ⇨ 생남(生男)
▶자네의 득남 소식을 들었네 I have heard of your begetting a son.

득녀 得女 begetting of a daughter ⇨ 생녀(生女)

득달같다 〈지체없다〉 prompt, ready; 〈서슴지〉 be right on time
♦득달같이 without loss of time / 득달같이 대령하다 present *oneself* promptly; make *oneself* ready for order of [to]

득도 得度 〖佛教〗 attaining Nirvana ━득도하다 attain Nirvana

득도 得道 attainment of salvation; finding the truth; spiritual awakening [enlightenment]
━득도하다 attain salvation; find the truth; achieve spiritual awakening [enlightenment]

득돌같다 〈뜻대로 꼭 맞다〉 quite satisfactory; perfect

득득 1 〈긋는 모양〉《draw a line》again and again forcefully [firmly, fast]
♦줄을 득득 긋다 draw line after line forcefully
2 〈긁는 모양〉《scratch, scrape》again and again; with harsh noises
♦득득 긁다 scrape and scrape; scratch violently / 솥바닥을 득득 긁다 scratch (repeatedly to clean up) the bottom of a cauldron
3 〈얼어붙는 모양〉《freeze》solid all over
♦얼음이 득득 얼어붙다 freeze up solid all over; be frozen hard [fast]

득롱망촉 得隴望蜀 insatiable ambition; limitless greed ▶득롱망촉이다 Give him an inch and he'll take an ell.

득명하다 得名— gain fame; make *one's* reputation; become famous ▶이 작품으로 그는 크게 득명했다 The work won him great fame.

득문하다 得聞— 〈얻어듣다〉 hear of; catch wind of; be informed of ♦득문한즉 I'm told that...; I hear that...; from what I hear

득보기 〈못난 사람〉 a fool; an idiot; a moron

득세 得勢 1 〈세력을 얻음〉 gaining power [influence]; getting strength [force]
━득세하다 gain [acquire, obtain] power [influence]; become influential [powerful]
▶그의 발언으로 개혁의 요구가 득세하게 되다 His speech gave great impetus to the demand for reform.
2 〈국면이 좋아짐〉 turning to *one's* advantage
━득세하다 turn to *one's* advantage; take a favorable turn
▶그는 하는 일마다 득세했다 Everything turned to his advantages [profits].

득승 得勝 a victory; a triumph; a success
━득승하다 〈전쟁 등에서〉 win a battle; win a victory; 〈경기·게임에서〉 end in *one's* victory; win a game [race]
♦투표에서 득승하다 beat *sb* at the poll

득시글 in swarms; swarming
━득시글득시글하다 be swarming 《with》; be crowded [teeming] 《with》; be alive 《with fish》; 〈벌레 등이〉 squirm [wriggle about] in a swarm
♦구더기가 득시글득시글하다 swarm with maggots; maggots swarm
▶그는 옷에 이가 득시글득시글했다 His clothes were covered with lice all over.

득실 得失 〈얻음과 잃음〉 gains and losses; 〈이익과 손해〉 profits and losses; 〈성패〉 success and failure; 〈장단점〉 merits and demerits; advantages and disadvantages [shortcomings]
♦득실을 떠나서 leaving [without considering] the personal interest / 득실을 재다 weigh the advantages and disadvantages / 제출된 안(案)의 득실을 논하다 discuss the advisability of the proposal
▶득실이 거의 반반이다 The gains and losses are about even [on a par].

득실득실 swarming ⇨ 득시글득시글

득의 得意 1 〈뜻을 이뤄 만족함〉 satisfaction
2 〈뜻을 이뤄 뽐냄〉 pride; triumph; elation
♦득의만면 an exultant air / 득의만면하여 proudly; in triumph; triumphantly / 득의의 미소를 짓다 smile in triumph
━득의하다 take pride 《in》; be proud 《of》; feel elated; congratulate *oneself* 《on, upon》; swell up

득의양양하다 得意揚揚— as happy as a king; as proud [pleased] as a peacock
♦득의양양한 태도 a triumphant air; a complacent look / 득의양양하여 proudly; in triumph; triumphantly
▶그는 득의양양한 태도로 말했다 He spoke in

a triumphant manner.

득점 得點 〔競〕 a point; a goal; 〔野〕 runs; 〈시험 등의〉 a mark; 〈총칭〉 a score
♦득점이 없다 score nothing; be [go] scoreless / 득점 없이 끝나다 end scoreless / 득점을 기입하다 keep (the) score; score the runs / 득점을 거듭하다 build [pile] up points / (상대팀에게) 득점을 주지 않다 〔野〕 shut out
▶ 득점은 7대 2로 우리 학교의 승리였다 The score was 7 to 2 in favor of our school.
▶ 우리는 5대 4의 득점 차로 이겼다 We won the game by [with] a score of 5 to 4.
▶ 그 팀의 득점은 5점이었다 The team scored five points.
▶ 우리는 상대팀을 무득점으로 눌렀다 We held the opposing team scoreless. ⇌ We shut out the opposing team.
▶ 그는 수학은 학급에서 최고 득점을 했다 He got the highest score [〈英〉 marks] in mathematics in our class.

─득점하다 score (a point); make [earn] a score
♦대량 득점하다 score many points; make a good score [record]; 〔野〕 score a lot of runs / 한 점 득점하다 gain a point (over); score a point (against)

득책 得策 a good policy; the best plan [way, policy]; advisability ♦득책이다 be wise; be advisable [politic]; be a good policy
▶ 일행에 합류하는 것이 득책이라고 생각한다 I think it advisable [better] to join the group.
▶ 모르는 체하는 것이 득책일 것 같다 I would be wise to play innocent.

득표 得票 the number of votes polled [got, obtained]
♦득표 운동을 하다 canvass for votes
─득표하다 poll [get, win, obtain] votes
♦대량 득표하다 poll a large vote / 남보다 많이[적게] 득표하다 get more [less] votes than another; 〈美〉 run ahead of [behind] another's ticket
■최고— the highest poll: 최고 득표로 당선되다 be elected (to) with the highest poll; lead the ticket; be returned at the head of the poll
■─차 plurality [majority] over one's rival candidate

득표수 得票數 the number of votes (obtained [polled]); the polling score
▶ 그의 득표수는 다른 후보자보다 현저하게 많았다 His polling score was far larger than that of any other candidate.
▶ 그의 득표수는 100만에 달했다 He polled over one million votes.
■법정— the legal number of votes; the legally required minimum number of votes [points]

든 even ⇨ 든지 ▶ 무엇이든 명령만 내리십시오, 분부대로 하겠습니다 I shall obey whatever orders you give me.

-든 either...or ⇨ -든지 ▶ 네가 가든 안 가든 나는 가겠다 Whether you go or not, I will go myself.

든거지 난부자 —富者 a rich-looking poor man; a person who looks rich but is really poor

든든하다 1 〈단단하다〉 firm; solid; secure; steady
♦재정이 든든한 회사 a solid company / 든든한 담보 a gilt-edged [good] security / 방비를 든든하게 하다 strengthen the defenses
▶ 기초가 든든하다 The foundation is secure [solid, firm].
▶ 든든한 회사니까 돈을 빌려줘도 안전하다 That is a solid company, so it is safe to loan them money.
2 〈굳세다〉 strong; robust; stout; hardy
3 〈미덥다〉 secure; confident; reassuring; reliable; safe
♦든든한 자리 a safe position / 마음이 든든하다 feel reassured [confident, secure]; be inspired with confidence
▶ 그 말을 들으니 마음이 든든하다 It is heartening [encouraging] to hear that.
▶ 당신과 같이 있으면 마음이 든든합니다 I feel secure [reassured] when I am with you.
▶ 당신이 도와 주신다니 마음이 아주 든든합니다 Your help will greatly embolden [encourage] me.
4 〈배가 부르다〉 full
♦속이 든든하다 have a full stomach [belly]; feel replete; have the stomach full
▶ 속이 든든하지 않으면 일을 할 수가 없다 One cannot work on an empty stomach. ⇌ A full belly counsels well.

든든히 1 〈굳세게〉 strongly; robustly; firmly
♦집을 든든히 짓다 build a house durable
2 〈미덥게〉 securely; safely; reassuringly; confidently; reliably ♦마음 든든히 생각하다 feel reassured [secure]; feel emboldened
3 〈배부르게〉 fully; to repletion
▶ 밥을 든든히 먹다 take a full meal

든번 —番 being on duty; one's time
♦든번이다 be on duty; be one's turn to be on duty; be on a shift

든부자 난거지 —富者— a poor-looking rich man; a person who looks poor but is really rich; a rich man in disguise

든지 1 〈열거〉 either...or; whether...or
♦사과든지 배든지 either apples or pears / 정말이든지 거짓말이든지 whether (it be) true or not
▶ 이거든지 저거든지 둘 중 하나를 가져라 Take one of the two, either this one or that one.
2 〈…까지도〉 even; even if [though]
▶ 내가 할 수 있는 일이라면 무엇이든지 해서 너를 돕겠다 I am willing to do everything in my power to help you.
▶ 우리는 언제든지 출발할 준비가 되어 있다 We are ready to start at a moment's notice.
▶ 언제든지 좋을 때 오십시오 Come whenever [(at) any time] you like.

-든지 1 〈…더라도〉 even if; although; though; no matter 〈who, what, when, where, how〉
♦어디로 가든지 wherever [no matter where] you may go / 누가 뭐라고 하든지 whatever others may say (about, of) / 어떻게 해서든지 at all costs; at any cost; by any means
▶ 무슨 일이 있든지 오늘은 나가지 마라 Don't

든직하다 712

go out today no matter what happens.
2 〈선택〉 or; either...or; whether...or
♦비가 오든지 안 오든지 간에 whether it may rain or not; rain [wet] or shine
▶그에게 정보를 치든지 편지를 내든지 해야 한다 You must either wire or write to him.
▶가든지 오든지 마음대로 하게 Come or go, whichever you please.

든직하다 grave; serious; sedate; imposing; dignified
♦든직한 인물 a man of substance; a sedate [grave] man / 든직한 태도 a grave and serious attitude
▶그는 든직한 인상을 주는 사람이다 He impresses one as being a man of depth.

들그럽다 noisy; clamorous; boisterous; uproarious; vociferous; tumultuous
♦들그러운 소리 (a) noise; (a) discord

듣기 좋은 노래도 한두 번이지 (속담) The best fish smells after three days.

듣다¹ 〈방울져 떨어지다〉 drip; drop; dribble; fall in drops ♦빗방울이 듣다 raindrops fall; rain is dripping
▶땀이 이마에 듣는 것을 느꼈다 I felt the sweat trickle down my brow.

듣다² **1** 〈효험이 있다〉 be effective; take [have] effect on; be good 《for a cold》; 〈약이〉 be efficacious; act [work, tell] 《on》
♦만병에 듣는 약 a panacea; a cure-all / 놀랄 정도로 잘 듣다 work wonders / 뇌물이 듣다[안 듣다] be susceptible to bribery [be proof against bribes] / 듣지 않다 fail to work; be no good 《for》; have no effect 《on》
▶그 약은 아주 잘 듣는다 The medicine acts marvelously well.
▶이 약은 간장에 잘 듣는다 These pills are very good for the liver.
▶이 약은 내게는 듣지 않는다 This medicine has no effect on me.
▶그 항생물질은 단번에 들었다 The antibiotic worked at once.
2 〈정상적으로 움직이다〉 work; act
♦오른손이 말을 안 듣다 lose the use of *one's* right arm; *one's* right hand is out / 몸이 말을 안 듣다 be disabled; cannot help *oneself*; be helpless
▶브레이크가 안 듣는다 The brake refuses to act [work].

듣다³ **1** 〈소리를〉 hear 《music》; listen to; give (an) ear to; heed
♦아무가 듣는 데서 in the audience of *sb*; in *sb's* audience / 연설을 듣다 hear a speech [an address]; listen to a speech / 듣기 거북하다 be unpleasant to the ear / (연속) 강의를 듣다 hear a course of lectures / 비오는 소리를 듣다 listen to it rain / 얘기를 열심히 듣다 hang on *sb's* words / 건성으로 듣다 hear *sb* inattentively [with half an ear] / 라디오를 듣다 listen to [on] the radio / 잘못 듣다 hear amiss; mishear; be misinformed 《about》 / 듣기 좋은 소리를 하다 say pleasant [agreeable] things; tickle *sb's* ear / 듣지 못하다 fail to hear; leave *sth* unheard / 들으려 하지 않다 turn a deaf ear 《to》

▶들으려고 하면 들린다 If you listen, you can hear it.
▶그가 듣는 데선 그런 말 하지 말게 Don't say things like that in his hearing.
▶나는 그가 우는 소리를 들었다 I heard him cry [crying].
▶내 말을 귀담아 들으세요 Mark my words. ⇒ Listen [Give heed] to what I say [I am going to say].
▶그가 하는 영어를 들으면 영국인으로 착각할 정도다 To hear him speak English, one would take him for an Englishman.
▶그가 하는 말을 주의해 들었다 I paid attention to him [what he said]. ⇒ I listened carefully to him [what he said].
2 〈소식 등을〉 hear of [about]; be informed [told] of [about]; learn *sth* from [of] *sb*; understand; 〈사물이 주어〉 come to *one's* ears
♦들은 바로는[듣자하니, 듣기로는] from what I hear; I hear [we learn] 《that...》; I'm told 《that...》 / 소문으로 듣다 hear of 《a matter》; hear say; learn 《news》
▶그런 얘기는 들어본 적이 없다 I've never heard of such a thing.
▶듣는 것과 보는 것은 크게 다르다 There is a great difference between what I hear and what I see.
▶그 점에 관해서는 아무것도 듣지 못했다 I had no information on the point.
▶나는 그 소식을 듣고 놀랐다 I was surprised when I heard the news.
▶그 사람은 결혼했다고 들었다 I hear he was married.
3 〈칭찬·꾸지람 등을〉 ♦칭찬을 듣다 be praised [admired, extolled, applauded] 《by》; be spoken well [highly] of / 꾸지람을 듣다 be scolded [reproved, rebuked]; catch [get] a scolding
▶칭찬을 듣고 화낼 사람은 없다 Nobody feels offended at compliments.
▶그 따위 짓을 하면 꾸지람을 듣는 정도가 아닐 걸 If you do a thing like that, you can't get away with a mere scolding.
4 〈이르는 말대로〉 obey; follow; take 《*sb's* advice》; grant 《*sb's* request》; comply with [accede to] 《a demand》
♦명령을 듣다 obey orders / 남의 말을 안 듣다 will not listen to what others say; will not take advice from others
▶딸은 어머니의 충고를 듣지 않았다 Her daughter rejected [turned a deaf ear to] Mother's advice.
▶이 아이는 부모의 말을 잘 듣는다 This child obeys his parents. ⇒ This child minds [does] what his parents tell him.
▶그의 충고를 듣고 담배를 끊었다 Following [Taking] his advice, I gave up smoking.
▶그는 비가 오는데도 가겠다고 우기고 듣지 않았다 He insisted on going out despite the rain.
▶이르는 말을 듣지 않으면 벌 주겠다 If you won't obey, you'll be punished.

듣다못해 ▶그는 아내의 바가지를 듣다못해 밖으로 나가 버렸다 Fed up with his wife's nag-

ging, he went out.
▶ 모욕을 듣다못해 그녀는 대들었다 Unable to let the insult go by, she turned upon him.

들¹ a field; 〈전야〉 the fields; 〈평야〉 a plain
♦ 넓게 펼쳐진 들 a stretch [an expanse] of plains / 산에도 들에도 in the mountains as well as on the plains / 들에 일하러 나가다 go to work in the fields
▶ 들에 나가 꽃을 따자 Let's go out to the fields and pick some flowers.
▶ 양친은 동트기 전부터 들에 나가 일하십니다 My parents go out to work in the field before dawn.

들² 〈등등〉 and so on [forth]; and others [other things] (of the same kind); and [or] the like; and what not; **(라)** et cetera (略 & c., etc.)
♦ 가령 …들 such as…; …for example / 사과며 배 들 apples, pears, and what not
▶ 우리는 동물원에 가서 코끼리, 호랑이, 곰 들을 보았다 We went to the zoo and saw elephants, tigers, bears, and the like.
▶ 나는 나이프니 사과니 확대경 들을 가져 왔다 I brought with me a knife, apples, a magnifying glass, and [or] what not.

-들 ♦ 우리들 we / 너희들 you / 사람들 people; other people; others / 어린이들 children / 의사들 doctors
▶ 잘들 했습니다 You all did well.
▶ 이리들 오너라 You boys [girls, people, folks] come here.
▶ 놀러들 가자 Let's all go out to play.
▶ 아이들은 제각기 기를 들고 있다 Each child has a flag.
▶ 이 애들은 우리 애들입니다 These are my young ones.

들개 〈야생의〉 a wild dog; 〈집 잃은〉 a stray dog ♦ 우리는 지금 들개를 사냥하고 있다 We are rounding [hunting] up stray [homeless] dogs now.

들것 a stretcher; a litter
♦ 들것으로 나르다 carry sb on a stretcher / 부상자를 들것에 싣다 put a wounded man on a stretcher
 ■ **-경주** a stretcher race **-부대** a stretcher party; a litter team

들고뛰다 run away ⇨ 달아나다
들고빼다 run away ⇨ 달아나다
들고튀다 run away ⇨ 달아나다
들고파다 study hard; work hard [steadily] 〈at〉; 〈口〉 dig 〈into, at〉
들국화 —菊花 a wild chrysanthemum [aster]
들기름 perilla oil
들길 a field path; a path [track] across a field
들까부르다 1 〈키질하다〉 winnow [fan] briskly 2 〈몹시 흔들다〉 move sth up and down briskly; 〈아기를〉 dance; dandle ♦ 우는 아기를 들까부르다 dandle a crying baby
들까불다 winnow briskly ⇨ 들까부르다
들까불리다 be winnowed briskly; be moved up and down briskly
▶ 배가 거친 파도에 들까불렸다 The ship (was) tossed about on a stormy sea.

들깨 〔植〕 a perilla; 〈씨〉 perilla seeds
들꽃 〈야생화〉 a wild flower
들꿩 〔鳥〕 a hazel grouse [hen]
들끓다 1 〈많이 모이다〉 swarm 《around, about, over, through》; gather 《around》; crowd; 〈해충·도둑 등이 설치다〉 infest
♦ 바퀴가 들끓다 〈장소가 주어〉 《a room》 swarm [be overflowing, be crowded] with cockroaches / 쥐가 들끓다 《a house》 infest with rats / 파리가 들끓다 be infested with flies
▶ 설탕에 개미가 들끓고 있다 Ants are swarming upon the sugar.
▶ 늪에는 모기가 들끓고 있었다 The marshes were swarming with mosquitoes.
▶ 바닷가는 여름 휴가 동안에는 아이들로 들끓는다 The beach swarms with children during the summer holidays.
▶ 가게 앞에는 사람들이 들끓고 있었다 There was a big crowd of people about the store.
2 〈술렁거리다〉 be excited; seethe; ferment; be in an uproar
♦ 들끓는 소동 an uproar; a ferment
▶ 그 문제로 온 나라가 들끓었다 The whole country seethed [was in a ferment] over the question.

들날리다 〈널리 펼치다〉 make famous; be well-known; win reputation [renown]
♦ 명성을 들날리다 come to fame; win fame / 온 세상에 이름을 들날리다 be known all over the world; win [enjoy] a world-wide fame [reputation]
▶ 김선생은 요즘 유행가로 이름을 들날리고 있다 Mr. Kim has gained his musical reputation by popular songs.
▶ 그의 이름은 국내외에 들날리고 있다 His name is known both at home and abroad.

들녘 a plain; an open field; a flat country
들놀이 a picnic; an outing ♦ 들놀이 가다 go (out) on a picnic; go picnicking
—들놀이하다 picnic; have [be on] a picnic

들다¹ 1 〈들어가다〉 go in [into]; get in [into]; come in [into]; enter
♦ 잠자리에 들다 go to bed / 범주 안에 들다 fall under [come within] the category 《of》 / 사정 거리 안에 들다 come within range 《of fire》
▶ 어서 안으로 드시지요 Please come in.
2 〈안에 담기다〉 hold; contain; 〈포함하다〉 be included; be among; 〈수용하다〉 accommodate
♦ 병에 든 물 water in a bottle / 30,000원이 든 지갑 a purse with 30,000 won in it / 계산에 들다 count; be taken into account
▶ 지갑에는 돈이 많이 들어 있었다 The wallet had a lot of money in it.
▶ 편지 속에는 몇 장의 사진이 들어 있었다 The letter contained some pictures. ⇒ Some pictures were enclosed in the letter.
3 〈입주하다〉 settle 《at, in》; move in; 〈투숙하다〉 put up 《at》
♦ 새 집에 들다 settle in a new house / 호텔에 들다 put up at a hotel; register [check in] at a hotel / 셋방에 들다 rent [take] a room
▶ 그 집에는 아직 사람이 들지 않았다 That

들다²

house remains unoccupied [vacant].
4 〈풍습·절기가 돌아오다〉 set in; begin; come (around)
▶ 금년에는 윤달이 들어 있다 A leap month sets in this year.
▶ 금년에는 풍년이 들었다 We have had a good harvest this year.
▶ 이 달에 춘분이 들어 있다 This month contains the vernal equinox.
▶ 장마가 들었다 The rainy season has set in.
5 〈물감·빛이 스며들다〉 dye; be dyed; take (up) color; 〈감염되다〉 be stained
♦ 물이 잘 들다[들지않다] dye well [badly] / 피로 물들다 be stained with blood / 악에 물들다 be stained with vices; sink in vices
6 〈마음에 꼭 맞다〉 be pleased [satisfied] 《with》; 〈사물이 주어〉 be satisfactory; be acceptable to *sb*; be to *one's* taste; suit [catch, take, strike] *one's* fancy
♦ 마음에 드는 집 a house to *one's* taste / 마음에 드는 여자 a woman after *one's* heart / 마음에 들도록 to *one's* satisfaction; (so as) to please *sb* / 마음에 들지 않다 〈사람이〉 do not like; be dissatisfied [displeased] with; 〈사물이〉 be against [not to] *sb's* taste [liking]; be unsatisfactory
▶ 모든 사람의 마음에 다 들기는 어렵다 It is hard to suit everybody.
▶ 이것이 제일 마음에 든다 This suits my taste best. ⇌ I like this best.
▶ 이 물건들은 내 마음에 들지 않는다 These goods don't commend themselves to me.
7 〈소용되다〉 take; want; need; require; cost; be needed [required]
♦ 비용이 얼마가 들더라도 at any cost; regardless of expense / 힘이 들다 be hard [toilsome, tough, trying]; require much effort / 비용이 많이 들다 cost a great deal
▶ 5만원도 들지 않을 것이다 It will cost less than fifty thousand won.
▶ 그 일을 하는 데는 힘이 많이 든다 It takes a lot of trouble to do the work. ⇌ The work takes [requires] a lot of trouble to do.
▶ 이 집을 짓는 데 많은 시간과 돈이 들었다 This house cost [took] (us) a lot of time and money to build.
▶ 그 다리를 완성하기까지는 30억원이 들었다 The bridge was completed at the cost of three billion won. ⇌ It cost three billion won to construct the bridge.
8 〈병이 나다〉 ♦ 병이 들다 fall ill [sick]; be affected by a disease
▶ 그는 감기가 들었다 He had an attack of influenza.
▶ 감기가 들면 입맛이 없다 A cold dulls *one's* taste.
9 〈맛이 알맞게 되다〉 (a taste) set in; get a taste (to it); be seasoned with; ripen
♦ 맛이 들다 become good [pleasant] to the taste; 〈익다〉 get [become] ripe [mellow] / 술 맛이 들다 wine mellows
▶ 사과가 맛이 들었다 The apples got some flavor in them.
▶ 김치가 맛이 들었다 *Kimchi* has ripened.

10 〈버릇이 생기다〉 take to a habit; get [fall] into a habit 《of》
♦ 담배를 피는 나쁜 버릇이 들다 take to the bad habit of smoking
▶ 한번 든 버릇은 고치기 힘들다 Once formed, habits are difficult to change.
11 〈가입하다〉 join; enter; go into; 〈단체의 성원이 되다〉 associate *oneself* 《with》; 〈합격하다〉 enter; pass into
♦ 보험에 들다 insure *oneself*; take out (a policy of) insurance 《on》 / 클럽에 들다 enter [join] a club; become a club member / 대학에 들다 enter a college / 조합에 들다 join an association
▶ 나는 생명보험에 들었다 I have taken out life insurance (on myself).
▶ 그는 서울대에 들었다 He passed [succeeded in] the entrance examination for [of, to] Seoul National University.
12 〈침입하다〉 visit; attack; break into
▶ 어젯밤 우리 집에 도둑이 들었다 A burglar broke into my house last night. ⇌ My house was broken into last night.
13 〈햇볕 등이〉 come in; shine into; pour in [into]
▶ 이 방은 볕이 잘 든다 This room gets a lot of sun.
▶ 이 방은 햇볕이 잘 들지 않는다 This room gets very little sun [sunshine].
14 〈어떤 상태에 처하다〉 become; get; grow; come round; set in
♦ 멍이 들다 get bruised / 잠이 들다 go to sleep; fall asleep / 정신이 들다 come to *oneself*; recover [regain] *one's* senses / 철이 들다 become [get] intimate with; become attracted to (a woman); become to love *sb*
15 〈어떤 행동을 하다〉 act
♦ 중매를 들다 act as (a) go-between [middleman]; arrange a match [marriage] 《between A and B》 / 역성 들다 side with *sb*; take side with; stand up for / 시중 들다 wait upon; attend on
▶ 그는 언제나 가장 강한 자의 편을 든다 He always sides with the strongest party.
16 〈생각이 나다〉 ♦ 생각이 들다 come across [into] *one's* mind; come into *one's* head / 잡념이 들다 be lost in idle thoughts / …이라는 느낌이 들다 have a feeling that...

들다² 〈날붙이가〉 cut (well); be keen; be sharp
♦ 잘 드는[안 드는] 칼 a sharp [dull] knife / 들지 않게 되다 become dull; lose (its) edge / 칼이 잘 드는지 시험해 보다 test the sharpness of a sword
▶ 가위는 제대로 사용하면 잘 든다 Scissors are sharp if they are used right.

들다³ 1 〈날씨가〉 clear (up); become clear
▶ 날이 들 것 같다 It is going to be fine. ⇌ The weather looks promising.
▶ 날이 든다 It [The weather] clears up.
2 〈땀이〉 cease; stop ♦ 땀이 들다 stop sweating

들다⁴ 1 〈위로 올리다〉 raise; lift (up); put [set] up; hold up; hoist

◆돌을 들다 lift (up) a stone / 얼굴을 들다 raise one's face; look up / 머리를 들다 raise [lift up] one's head / 손을 들다 raise [lift] a [one's] hand; 〈찬성하다〉 show one's hand
▶ 이 상자는 너무 무거워서 들 수 없다 This box is too heavy for me to lift.
▶ 손들어 Hands up!
2 〈손에 쥐다〉 hold 《a book in one's hand》; have sth in one's hand; 〈휴대하다〉 take [have, carry] sth with [about] one
◆지팡이를 들고 with a stick in one's hand / 펜을 들다 take a pen in one's hand; write / 들고 다니다 carry about one / 들고 나오다 take [bring] out; carry out [away] / 차안에 들고 들어가다 take [bring, carry] 《one's baggage》 into a car
3 〈먹다〉 take; help oneself to; have; eat; 〈마시다〉 drink
◆점심을 들다 take 《one's》 lunch
▶ 뭣 좀 드시지요 Won't you have something to eat?
▶ 아침에는 뭘 드셨습니까? What did you have for breakfast?
▶ 아침에는 빵과 우유와 달걀을 들었습니다 I had bread, milk and egg for my breakfast.
▶ 파이를 좀 더 드시지요 Help yourself to some more pies.
4 〈예증하다〉 give 《an example》; mention 《a fact》; produce 《evidence》; 〈인용하다〉 quote 《a passage from a book》; cite 《an instance》
◆예를 들다 cite [give] an instance [example] / 이유를 들다 adduce reasons; state a reason / 이름을 들다 mention sb's name
▶ 여기에 전원의 이름이 들어 있다 All persons are named here.

들들 1 〈볶는 모양〉 stirringly ◆깨를 들들 볶다 parch sesame-seed turning upside down
2 〈사람을 볶는 모양〉 annoyingly; tiresomely; 《ask》 importunately
◆사람을 들들 볶다 importune sb 《for money》; trouble [pester, plague] sb 《with questions》
3 〈뒤지는 모양〉 ransackingly ◆집안을 들들 뒤지다 ransack the house; search the whole house

들떠들다 make a noise; make (a) din; raise a clamor; be noisy ▶ 그렇게 들떠들지 마라 Don't make such a noise [fuss].

들뜨다 1 〈붙은 것이〉 come off [undone]; get loose [free]; become unfastened
◆장판이 들뜨다 a layer of oil paper comes off the floor
2 〈마음이 들썩거리다〉 grow restless [unstable, unsteady]; tread [walk] on air; 《one's mind》 wander
◆들뜬 마음 a restless [fickle] heart / 들뜬 목소리로 말하다 speak in an excited [high-pitched] voice / 희소식으로 마음이 들뜨다 be buoyed up by good news
▶ 우리는 들떠서 잠 한숨 못 잤다 We were wakeful and restless. ⇌ We had [passed] a restless night.
▶ 봄이 되면 마음이 들뜬다 My mind wanders when spring comes.
▶ 그는 수학여행으로 들떠 있다 He is being carried away [captivated] by the school excursion.
▶ 기쁜 소식으로 나는 마음이 들떴다 The good news cheered me.
3 〈살이〉 sallow and swell ◆누렇게 들뜬 얼굴 a sallow and swollen [bloated] face

들뜬상태 — 狀態 〔化·物〕 excited state

들라크루아 〈프랑스의 화가〉 Delacroix, Ferdinand Victor Eugène (1798-1863)

들락날락하다 come and go incessantly; go in and out frequently
▶ 아이들은 늘 들락날락한다 Children are always popping in and out.
▶ 쥐가 들락날락하며 밤을 다 물어갔다 Going in and out, back and forth, the rats carried away all the chestnuts.

들랑거리다 keep going in and out

들러리 1 〈신랑의〉 a best man; a groomsman; 〈신부의〉 a bridesmaid ◆들러리 서다 serve as a best man [bridesmaid]
2 (비유) a setoff; a foil
◆들러리가 되다 serve as a setoff 《for》; act as a foil 《for》

들러붙다 stick to; adhere to; cling to
▶ 껌이 옷에 들러붙었다 A chewing gum stuck to the clothes.
▶ 덩굴식물이 벽에 들러붙어 있다 The creepers cling to the wall.

들레다 make a noise; shout; clamor

들려주다 tell; inform 《sb of [about] a matter》; let sb hear [know] 《of》
◆피아노를 쳐 들려주다 play the piano for sb / 책을 읽어 들려주다 read sb a book; read a book to sb / 노래를 들려주다 sing for sb / 연주하여 들려주다 play for sb; give sb a tune
▶ 재미있는 이야기를 좀 들려주십시오 Tell us some interesting story.
▶ 이것은 아이들에게 들려줄 이야기가 아니다 This is not a story for children.
▶ 그 일에 관해 들려주렴 Tell me all about it.

들르다 〈방문하다〉 call at 《a house》; step at 《a place》; 〈지나다가〉 drop in 《on sb, at a place》; drop into 《an office》; stop [come] by; 《美》 go by 《a house》
◆목포에 들르다 stop off at Mokp'o; drop off 《the train》 at Mokp'o / 잠깐 들르다 run in for a minute
▶ 또 들르겠습니다 Let me call on you again.
▶ 또 들러주십시오 Drop in again, please.
▶ 부디 들러주십시오 Please come and see us.
▶ 나는 아주머니 가게에 들렀다 I dropped by my aunt's store.
▶ 이쪽에 오실 때는 들러주십시오 Look us up when you get down [come] our way. ⇌ Please drop in 《on us》 when you happen to be in this neighborhood.

들리다[1] **1** 〈사람이 주어〉 (can) hear 《sb speaking》; catch; 〈소리가 주어〉 be heard; be audible; reach [fall on] one's ear; meet [greet] the ear
◆들려오다 reach one's ear; come into hearing / 들리지 않다 cannot hear 《sb, what sb says》; 〈소리가 주어〉 cannot be heard; be inaudible / 들리지 않게 되다 〈귀가〉 lose one's

들리다²

hearing; 〈소리가〉 die away
▶ 새가 지저귀는 소리가 들린다 I hear a bird singing. ≒ A bird is heard to sing.
▶ 구급차의 사이렌 소리가 들린다 There goes a siren of an ambulance!
▶ 옆집 사람의 코고는 소리가 얇은 벽을 통해서 들려왔다 My neighbor's snoring was audible through the thin wall.
▶ 부르면 들리는 곳에 있어 주시오 Please keep within earshot.
▶ 그는 오른쪽 귀가 잘 들리지 않는다 He has a hearing trouble in his right ear.
▶ 이상한 소리가 들렸다 I heard a strange sound.
▶ 내가 말하는 소리가 들립니까? Can you hear me [what I'm saying]?
▶ 시끄러워서 텔레비전 소리가 들리지 않는다 It's so noisy I can't hear the television.
▶ 소음 때문에 강사의 말소리가 들리지 않았다 The noise drowned out the lecturer's voice.
▶ 요즘은 귀가 잘 들리지 않는다 I've been going deaf recently. ≒ My hearing has become worse recently.
▶ 나는 선천적으로 왼쪽 귀가 들리지 않는다 I am naturally deaf in my left ear.
▶ 그의 발소리는 멀어지더니 드디어 들리지 않게 되었다 The sound of his footsteps faded away into the distance.
▶ 북소리 때문에 현악기 소리가 들리지 않았다 The drums killed the strings.
▶ 라디오 소리가 2층까지 들려왔다 The sound of the radio came floating upstairs.
▶ 잘 들리지 않으니 큰 소리로 말해라 Speak louder — I can't hear you.
▶ 그 전화는 잘 들리지 않는다 The telephone isn't clear.
2 〈울리다〉 sound (strange, reasonable); ring (true, false)
▶ 네 말은 빈정거리는 말로 들린다 What you say sounds ironical.
▶ 그의 말은 정말[거짓말] 처럼 들린다 His words ring true [false].
3 〈소문 등이〉 be said [told]; be rumored; come to *one's* ears [knowledge]
♦ 들리는 바로는 according to the report [rumor]; It is said that...; from what I have heard...
▶ 네 소식이 종종 들렸다 I've often heard of you.
▶ 들리는 바로는 그는 인격자라고 한다 He is said to be a man of character.
▶ 그가 돈을 많이 모았다는 소문이 들린다 They say [It is said] that he has made a lot of money.

들리다² **1** 〈귀신 등이 들러붙다〉 be possessed (by [with] an evil spirit); be obsessed 《by》; be haunted 《by》; be bewitched
▶ 그는 신들린 사람처럼 싸웠다[공부했다] He fought [studied] like one possessed.
▶ 사람들은 그에게 악마가 들렸다고 생각했다 People thought the man was possessed by a devil.
2 〈병이 덮치다〉 be taken ill; be attacked [affected] by 《a disease》; be besieged with 《a disease》; suffer from; catch
♦ 감기(가) 들리다 catch [take, get] (a) cold; have an attack of flu
▶ 그녀는 중병이 들렸다 She is suffering from a serious illness.

들리다³ 〈바닥나다〉 be exhausted [used up]; run out
♦ 밑천이 들리다 come to the end of *one's* money [capital] / 석유가 들리다 run out of kerosine; the kerosine is all gone

들리다⁴ **1** 〈올려지다〉 be lifted (up); be raised
▶ 책상 다리가 들렸다 The legs of the desk were lifted.
▶ 차가 잭으로 들렸다 The car was jacked up.
2 〈올리게 하다〉 let *sb* raise [lift (up)] *sth*

들리다⁵ **1** 〈갖게 하다〉 let *sb* have [take, hold]
▶ 그 사람 손에 들리면 무딘 칼도 날카로워진다 A dull blade becomes a sharp weapon in his hands.
2 〈운반시키다〉 get *sb* to take [carry] *sth*
♦ 가방을 들리다 have *sb* carry a bag / 누이에게 선물을 들려보내다 send [offer] a present by *one's* sister

들먹거리다 **1** 〈물체가〉 move up and down; shake; sway; quake
▶ 바위가 들먹거린다 A rock shakes.
2 〈물체를〉 move *sth* up and down; shake *sth*
♦ 바위를 들먹거리다 shake a rock
3 〈몸이〉 〈*one's* shoulders [buttocks]〉 move up and down; 〈마음이〉 become restless; be fidgety; be excited [tempted] (to do); be inclined (to do); be eager 《to》
♦ 어깨가 들먹거리다 *one's* shoulders twitch / 궁둥이가 들먹거리다 *one's* buttocks move up and down
▶ 그는 잠실 종합운동장에 가고 싶어서 들먹거리고 있다 He is impatient [all eagerness] to go to the Chamshil Sports Complex.
4 〈몸을〉 move 〈*one's* shoulders〉 up and down; 〈마음을〉 make *sb* restless [fidgety]; stir up; incite; instigate; put *sb* up to; egg *sb* on (to do)
♦ 어깨를 들먹거리다 move *one's* shoulders restlessly / 아무의 마음을 들먹거리다 excite *sb*; make *sb* eager to
▶ 누가 그녀를 들먹거리며 장난치게 했니? Who put her up to the prank?
▶ 그녀는 어깨를 들먹거리며 울었다 Sobs shook her.
5 〈상처가〉 ache; smart; tingle; throb with pain
6 〈언급하다〉 mention; make mention of; speak of; refer to; specify by name
▶ 그 사람까지 들먹거릴 필요 없지 않니? You don't have to mention his name.
▶ 나는 그 문제를 들먹거리기 싫어 I hate to mention it.

들먹들먹 in a moving up and down; shakingly; 〈마음이〉 buoyantly; excitedly; restlessly
—들먹들먹하다 ⇨ 들먹거리다
▶ 너희들은 왜 들먹들먹하고 있니? Why are you in a fidget?

들먹이다 move up and down ⇨ 들먹거리다

들보 〔建〕 a girder; a beam

들볶다 annoy; tease; harass; torment; pester; fret *sb* badly [harshly]; be hard [severe] on *sb*; be cruel to *sb*; treat *sb* roughly; 〈재촉하여〉 urge 《*sb* to do》; press 《*sb* for *sth*》
♦못살게 들볶다 make it too hot for *sb* / 강아지를 들볶다 torment a small dog; be cruel to a puppy / 제의를 받아들이라고 들볶다 urge *sb* to accept an offer /돈을 내라고 들볶다 press *sb* for payment (of money); pester *sb* for money / 빚쟁이에게 들볶이다 be tormented [hounded] by a pressing creditor
▶그는 아이에게 들볶여 장난감을 사주었다 He was pestered by his child to buy a toy for him.
▶저 아이를 들볶지 말게 Stop teasing that child.
▶아이들은 약자를 들볶는 경향이 있다 Children tend to bully [pick on] the weak.
▶한 무리의 소년들이 시골에서 온 소년을 들볶아 그를 울게 했다 A group of boys teased the boy from the country and made him cry.

들부수다 knock [strike] to pieces; break [batter] down [to pieces]; smash (up); crush; destroy
♦그릇을 들부수다 smash dishes / 닥치는 대로 들부수다 destroy everything *one* can lay *one's* hands on
▶그들은 낡은 건물을 들부수었다 They pulled down the old building.

들뽕나무 a wild mulberry tree

들새 a wild bird; (총칭) wild fowl
♦들새 도감 a pictorial book of wild fowl

들소 〔動〕 a bison (▶단수·복수동형); a wild ox; 〈북미산의〉 a buffalo

들썩하다 1〈약간 들리다〉 turned up [lifted (up), raised] a little [slightly]
▶이불 귀가 들썩하다 The corner of the quilt is a bit turned up.
2〈시끄럽다〉 noisy; boisterous
▶이웃 아이들은 언제나 들썩한다 My neighbor's kids are always making noise.
3〈그럴듯하다〉 plausible; specious

들쑤시다 1〈몹시 아프다〉 sting; ache; throb with pain; tingle [smart] (with pain)
♦들쑤시는 상처 a sore cut; a painful wound
▶머리[배]가 때때로 들쑤신다 My head [stomach] aches on and off.
▶어제 덴 데가 들쑤신다 It smarts [stings] where I burned myself yesterday.
▶이가 들쑤신다 My tooth stings. ⇌ I have an awful toothache.
2〈막대기로 찌르다〉 poke hard (at); pick (at); prod
▶나는 난로의 석탄을 들쑤셔 타게 하였다 I poked the coals in the stove up into a blaze.
3〈샅샅이 뒤지다〉 ransack; rummage (in); search thoroughly
♦서랍 속을 들쑤시다 ransack [rummage in] desk drawers / 서류를 찾으려고 들쑤시다 rummage around for papers
4〈부추기다〉 instigate; incite; stir up; needle; urge on; egg [set] *sb* on (to do, to *sth*)
♦아무를 들쑤셔 …하게 하다 set [needle] *sb* to (do) / 들쑤셔서 싸움을 붙이다 stir up a fight / 허영심을 들쑤시다 inflate the vanity

들쓰다 1〈덮어쓰다〉 put on [pull up] *sth* all over *oneself*
♦담요를 들쓰다 pull a blanket over *one's* head / 이불을 들쓰고 자다 sleep with the bedclothes (pulled) over *one's* head
2〈물 등을〉 pour 《water》 on [upon, over] *oneself*; be covered with
▶나는 차가 지날 때 흙탕물을 들썼다 The passing car splashed muddy water on me.
▶선반이 먼지를 들쓰고 있었다 The shelf was covered with (a layer of) dust.
3〈모자 등을〉 wear [put on] 《a cap》 casually
♦모자를 들쓰고 나서다 go out wearing a hat casually
4〈허물·책임 등을〉 take 《blame, responsibility》 upon *oneself* ♦남의 허물을 들쓰다 take another's fault upon *oneself*
▶그는 부하의[두목의] 죄를 들썼다 He took a subordinate's [his boss's] guilt upon himself.

들씌우다 1〈씌우다〉 pull up *sth* all over *sb*; put 《a guilt》 on [over] *sb*; cover 《with》
♦이빨에 금을 들씌우다 cap [crown] a tooth with gold / 머리에 이불을 들씌우다 pull the bedclothes over *sb's* head
2〈물 등을〉 pour [throw] 《water》 all over *sb*; cover *sb* all over with 《dust》
▶그는 술주정꾼의 얼굴에 물을 들씌웠다 He poured water over the drunk's face.
3〈모자 등을〉 put 《a hat》 on 《*sb's* head》 casually
4〈죄 등을〉 impute (the crime to another); charge 《a guilt [crime] to another》; shift 《a responsibility on another's shoulders》

들어가다¹ 1〈안으로〉 go [get] in; go [get] into; come in [into]; enter 《a room》; walk [step] in [into]; turn in; let *oneself* in; make *one's* entry into 《a place》; 〈억지로〉 break into; intrude [crush] into; enter forcibly [by force]; find *one's* way into
♦혼잡한 홀 안으로 억지로 들어가다 force *one's* entry [way] into a crowded hall / 몰래 들어가다 sneak [slip] into 《a room》 / 물[풀]에 들어가다 enter [go into] the water [swimming pool] / 항구에 들어가다 〈배가〉 enter [make] port; come into port / 기어 들어가다 creep [crawl] into [under] / 들어가게 하다 let *sb* enter; allow *sb* to get into
▶들어가도 됩니까? May I come in?
▶열차가 터널에 들어갔다 The train went into [in] the tunnel.
▶용무자외 들어가지 말 것 《게시》 No admittance except on business. ⇌ Keep out.
2〈틈·속·사이로〉 go through; be inserted; be lodged; enter; 〈뚫고〉 penetrate 《into》
▶바늘귀에 실이 들어간다 A thread goes through the eye of a needle. ⇌ A needle is threaded.
▶총알이 벽을 뚫고 들어갔다 A bullet penetrated [was lodged in] a wall.
3〈패다〉 sink; be sunk(en); become dented; cave in; sag; be [become] hollow
▶그 사고로 차의 문이 쑥 들어갔다 The door

들어가다²

of my car was dented in the accident.
4 〈가입하다〉 join; enter; go into; associate *oneself* with 《a society》; 〈입사하다〉 join; find [take] service in [with]; be employed 《by》; 〈입학하다〉 enter 《a school》
♦ 군대에 들어가다 enter [join, go into] the army / 대학에 들어가다 enter [pass into, get into] a college
▶ 내 여동생은 내년에 학교에 들어간다 My (little) sister will start school next year.
5 〈포함되다〉 be included; be counted among; be contained; enter; go into
▶ 이 알약에는 비타민 C가 들어가 있다 This tablet contains vitamin C.
▶ 지갑에 돈이 많이 들어가 있었다 The wallet had a lot of money in it.
▶ 편지 속에 사진이 들어가 있었다 The letter contained some pictures.
6 〈수용하다〉 accommodate; house; hold
▶ 책들이 그 상자에 들어갈까? Will the books go into that box?
▶ 이 방에는 백명의 손님이 들어간다 This room can accommodate a hundred guests.
▶ 이 오두막에는 도저히 우리가 모두 들어갈 수 없다 This shack will never house us all.
7 ⇨ 들다¹ 7
8 〈접어들다〉 begin; set in; enter 《into, upon》
♦ 새 단계로 들어가다 enter upon a new stage / 새 생활로 들어가다 enter upon a new life / 새 학기에 들어가다 the new term begins [has begun]
▶ 장마철에 들어갔다 The rainy season has set in.
9 〈기타〉 ▶ 내가 나타나자 그의 기세는 쑥 들어가고 말았다 As soon as I showed up, he was suddenly daunted [dispirited].

들어가다² 〈몰래 가져 가다〉 make [walk] off with *sth*; run [go, walk] away with; steal *sth* off ♦ 남의 책을 들어가다 make off with another's book

들어내다 1 〈내놓다〉 lift out; take [bring, get, carry] out; remove
♦ 중요 서류를 들어내다 carry [take] out important documents / 남몰래 들어내다 smuggle *sth* out of 《the house》
2 〈쫓아내다〉 expel; turn [put, drive] out; 〈셋방 등에서〉 evict [eject] 《a tenant from the house》

들어맞다 1 〈적합하다〉 fit; fit into ; fit in 《with》; be fit [fitted] 《for》; suit; be suited 《to》; 〈신발 등이〉 be suitable 《to》; go on
♦ 목적에 들어맞다 serve [suit] *one's* purpose
▶ 이 신발은 발에 안 들어맞을 것이다 These shoes won't go on.
2 〈일치하다〉 fit together; agree [accord] 《with》; be in accord 《with》; coincide [tally] 《with》; answer to; correspond 《with》; harmonize 《with》
▶ 너의 이야기는 그의 이야기와 들어맞지 않는다 Your story disagrees [does not agree] with what he says.
▶ 그는 말과 행동이 들어맞지 않는다 His words do not accord [correspond, coincide] with his actions.
▶ 그 남자는 인상서와 들어맞았다 The man met [answered (to)] the description.
3 〈정확하다〉 be right; be correct
▶ 계산이 꼭 들어맞는다 The accounts are quite correct.
▶ 너의 계산은 나의 것과 들어맞는다 Your figures agree with mine.
4 〈적중하다〉 hit the target; make a good hit; 〈평이〉 hit it 《right》; 〈추측이〉 guess right; hit the truth; 〈예상이〉 prove (to be) right; come [turn out] true; 〈계략이〉 take; work
▶ 그의 경제 예측은 들어맞았다 His forecast about economy proved right.
▶ 그의 추측은 들어맞았다 He guessed right.
5 〈적용되다〉 apply 《to》; go 《for》; be applicable 《to》; hold true 《of》; hold good 《of, for》; 〈해당하다〉 conform 《to》; be in accordance 《with》
▶ 이 규칙은 외국인에게는 들어맞지 않는다 We cannot apply this rule to foreigners. ⇒ This rule cannot be applied [be applicable] to foreigners.
▶ 거기에 들어맞는 영어 표현은 없다 There is no corresponding expression 《for it》 in English.

들어먹다 1 〈탕진하다〉 eat *sb* [*oneself*] out 《of》; eat 《*sb, oneself*》 up; consume; use up; squander; go [run] through 《*one's* fortune》
♦ 도박[술]으로 가산을 들어먹다 gamble [drink] away *one's* fortune
▶ 그들이 우리 가산을 들어먹었다 They ate us out of house and home.
▶ 비축한 식량을 다 들어먹었다 We had consumed all the provisions [food] that we had stored up.
2 〈횡령하다〉 pocket; embezzle; divert 《another's money》 into *one's* own pocket
♦ 공금을 들어먹다 embezzle public money [funds] / 아무의 재산을 들어먹다 misappropriate *sb's* property

들어박히다 1 〈빠지다〉 fall [plunge, stick] into; be stuck; 〈총알 등이〉 be lodged
♦ 도랑에 들어박히다 〈자동차 등이〉 be mired in a ditch
2 〈집에〉 stay in [at home]; keep [confine *oneself*] indoors; shut *oneself* up 《in》; remain in seclusion
♦ 방에 들어박히다 keep to *one's* room
▶ 그는 집에만 들어박혀 있다 He stays indoors. ⇒ He seldom goes out.

들어붓다 1 〈비가〉 rain in torrents [cats and dogs]; pour down; fall [rain] heavily
♦ 들어붓는 비 a pouring (driving, heavy) rain; a downpour (of rain);(a) torrential rain
2 〈물 등을〉 pour 《water》 into [on, out of] *sth*
♦ 욕조에 물을 들어붓다 pour water into a bathtub / 아무에게 물을 들어붓다 pour water upon [over] *sb*
▶ 그는 맥주를 단숨에 들어붓듯이 마셨다 He drank beer (straight) from a bottle. ⇒ He swigged beer from a bottle. ⇒ He swallowed beer in one swig.

들어서다 1 〈안쪽으로〉 enter; come [go, get)

into; step in
♦마당에 들어서다 step [walk] into a garden / 캠퍼스에 들어서다 enter the campus
2 〈자리잡다〉 occupy; hold; take (up)
▶호텔들은 해안을 따라 아름다운 장소에 전부 들어서 있다 The hotels occupy [take up] all the beautiful sites along the beach.
▶그 지역에는 거의 다 공장이 들어서 있었다 Most of the areas were occupied [were taken up] by factories.
▶이제는 그곳에도 집이 많이 들어서 있다 The place is much built up now.
3 〈접어들다〉 begin; set in
▶굴은 지금 제철에 들어섰다 Oysters are now in season.
▶이달에 들어서서 아주 더워졌다 The weather has been extremely hot since the beginning of this month.
▶내일부터 신학기에 들어선다 The new semester begins tomorrow.
4 〈대들다〉 stand [rise] against; stand up to; defy

들어앉다 1 〈안으로〉 get [come] in and sit; 〈다가앉다〉 sit closer [nearer] (to)
▶좀 더 들어앉아 주십시오 Please sit [squeeze up] a little closer (together).
2 〈위치하다〉 be situated [located]; lie
▶그 나라의 수도는 북쪽으로 조금 들어앉아 있다 The nation's capital is located [is situated, lies] somewhat to the north.
3 〈집에〉 keep to the house; keep [stay] indoors; 〈은퇴하다〉 retire (from); go into retirement
▶그는 사업을 그만두고 들어앉았다 He retired from business.
4 〈직책에〉 take office; take up (*one's*) post; settle down; 〈후임으로〉 succeed; sit in *sb's* place
♦사장직에 들어앉다 settle down to [into] the post of president / 후임으로 들어앉히다 put [install] *sb* in (another's) place
▶그는 본래의 자리에 들어앉았다 He was reinstated in his former position.

들어오다 1 〈안으로〉 enter; step in; come [get] in; come [get] into; turn in; let *oneself* in; 〈도둑 등이〉 break in [into]; find *one's* way into; 〈억지로〉 force *one's* entry [way] into
♦들어오게 하다 let *sb* enter; allow *sb* to come into / 혼잡한 홀 안으로 억지로 들어오다 force *one's* way into a crowded hall
▶어서 들어오세요 Please come in [(美) come on in].
▶바람이 들어오게 문을 좀 열어 두어라 Leave the door slightly open [ajar] for the some air to let in.
▶여기는 틈새기 바람이 들어온다 It's drafty here.
▶이 창문으로는 내 방에 충분한 햇빛이 들어오지 않는다 This window doesn't let in [admit] enough sunlight to my room.
▶구두에 물이 들어왔다 Some water got into [in] my shoes.
▶들어오지 마시오 (게시) No Admittance.

2 〈끼어들다〉 join (in); enter; participate in; take part in; 〈입사·입회하다〉 join; come into; be employed (by)
▶그는 우리 클럽에 들어왔다 He joined our club.
▶사원 한 사람이 새로 들어왔다 A new member has joined our company.
3 〈설치되다〉 be laid on; be installed
▶이 집에는 언제 전화가 들어옵니까? When will the telephone be installed in this house?
4 〈수입이〉 have; get; receive; make
♦한 달에 천달러가 들어오다 get [receive, have an income of] 1,000 dollars a month
5 〈눈에〉 come into sight [view]; be seen
▶그것이 내 눈에 들어왔다 My eye(s) fell on [caught] it.

들어올리다 raise; lift (up); give (a stone) a lift; hold [put, boost] up
♦잭으로 들어올리다 jack up (a car) / 우승컵을 높이 들어올리다 lift [hold] up the championship cup high above *one's* head
▶그는 모자를 조금 들어올리고 부인에게 인사했다 He raised his hat a little to the lady.
▶그는 손을 높이 들어올렸다 He raised his hands high.

들어주다 〈요청을〉 comply with (*sb's* request); grant [concede] (a request); hear [answer] (*sb's* prayer)
♦들어주지 않다 refuse (to be persuaded); turn a deaf ear to (*sb's* request)
▶네 부탁을 들어주마 I'll grant your wish.
▶하나님은 꼭 나의 기도를 들어주시리라고 믿는다 I am sure God will hear [answer] my prayer.
▶너의 부탁을 들어줄 수는 없다 I'm afraid I can't give you what you want.

들어차다 fill (with); become full (of); be filled [replete] (with); be busy [pressed] with; be packed; be stuffed; be crowded (with); be jammed
♦가득 들어차다 be packed to the full; be chock-full (of)
▶이 근처에는 집이 들어차 있다 This is a built-up area.
▶가게에는 손님들이 들어차 있었다 The shop was crowded [busy, filled] with customers.

들엉기다 stick together to form a thickened mass; solidify; congeal; clot; 〈우유 등이〉 curdle; 〈시멘트 등이〉 set; coagulate

들여가다 〈안으로〉 bring [take] in (a thing); carry (a thing) into (a room); 〈사다〉 buy
▶사과를 좀 들여가시지요 Won't you buy some of the apples?
▶누가 그 가방을 들여갔니? Who carried the bag on [brought the bag in]?

들여놓다 1 〈물건을〉 take [bring, get, carry] in; 〈사들이다〉 buy (in); purchase; lay in
♦가구를 방에 들여놓다 bring furniture in a room
▶차를 차고에 들여놓아라 Put the car in [into] the garage, will you?
▶계란과 밀가루 중 어느 것을 먼저 들여놓겠니? Which will you buy in first, the eggs or the flour?

들여다보다

2 〈발을〉 set foot 《in, on》; put *one's* foot 《in, on》; step into
♦ 진흙탕 속에 발을 들여놓다 step into the mire / 새로운 인생에 발을 들여놓다 embark [set forth] on a new life
▶ 탐험대는 인적미답의 땅에 발을 들여놓았다 The expedition set foot in unexplored regions.
3 〈사람을 들이다〉 let [allow] in; admit; receive; show [usher] in

들여다보다 1 〈안을〉 look in [into]; peep [peek] into 《a room》; peep through 《a hole》
♦ 방을 들여다보다 look [peep] into a room / 현미경으로 들여다보다 look through a microscope / 냉장고를 들여다보다 look in a refrigerator / 환히 들여다보이다 be seen through clearly; be fully exposed to view
▶ 그녀는 하루에 거울을 여러번 들여다본다 She looks into [at herself in] the mirror many times a day.
2 〈빤히〉 gaze 《at, on》; stare 《hard》 《at》; look hard [fixedly] 《at》; 〈자세히〉 look over; look into; examine closely [carefully]
♦ 얼굴을 들여다보다 stare *sb* in the face; keep *one's* eyes fixed upon *sb's* face
▶ 그는 경기를 열심히 들여다보고 있었다 He was watching the game intently.
▶ 그녀는 그 사진을 들여다보고 있었다 She kept her eyes fixed on the picture.
3 〈들르다〉 look [drop, call] in 《on, at》; look *sb* up
♦ 상점을 들여다보다 have a peep [look in] at the shop; show *one's* nose in a shop
▶ 도중에 몇군데 책방을 들여다보았다 On the way I looked in at [dropped by, dropped in at] some bookstores.

들여보내다 send 《*sb*, a thing》 into; show... into; let [allow] *sb* in [into]; admit
♦ 입장권을 가진 사람만 들여보내다 admit those only who have a ticket / 들여보내지 않다 close [shut] the door against [to] *sb*
▶ 그녀는 그를 방으로 들여보냈다 She showed him into the room.
▶ 그의 비서는 나를 그의 방으로 들여보내려고 하지 않는다 His secretary wouldn't let me into [admit me to] his room.
▶ 손님을 들여보내라 Show the guests in.

들여앉히다 1 〈외출을 막다〉 keep *sb* from going out; confine *sb* to [in] 《a room》
2 〈여자를〉 keep 《a mistress》; have [make] 《a woman》 settle down in *one's* home

들여오다 1 〈안으로〉 bring in; carry in; take in / 책을 서재로 들여오다 carry [bring] books into *one's* study / 상을 들여오다 carry in a dinner table
2 〈사들이다〉 buy; get (in); lay in; stock (goods); 〈수입하다〉 import
♦ 중국에서 밀을 들여오다 import wheat from China
▶ 우리나라는 브라질에서 커피를 들여오고 있다 Our country imports coffee from Brazil.

들은귀 picked-up experience [information]
♦ 들은귀가 있는[없는] 곡 a familiar [an unfamiliar] tune / 들은귀가 밝다 have alert ears / 들은귀가 있다 ring a bell
▶ 그의 이름은 들은귀가 있는데 얼굴이 생각나지 않는다 I've heard his name [His name rings a bell], but I can't remember his face.

들은풍월—風月 learning by (the) ear; secondhand knowledge; knowledge picked up by listening to others (without real study)
♦ 들은풍월로 배우다 pick *sth* up from others [others' conversation]; learn about *sth* by listening to what people say / 들은풍월로 알다 know *sth* secondhand

-들이 〈용량이 정해진 경우〉 ♦ 계란 두 다스들이 상자 a box of [containing] two dozen eggs / 한 말들이 자루 a sack holding a *mal*; a one-*mal* bag / 2리터들이 병 a 2-liter bottle

들이굽다 bend toward inside; bend inward; bent in
▶ 팔은 들이굽게 되어 있다 One's arms are to bend toward oneself.

들이다 1 〈안으로〉 let [allow] in; admit; show [usher] in
♦ 집에 들이다 let *sb* into *one's* house / 바람을 들이다 let fresh air in / 손님을 응접실로 모셔 들이다 usher [show] a visitor into the drawing room
▶ 그는 아무도 방에 들이지 않는다 He admits no one to his room.
▶ 그녀는 그를 방으로 들였다 She showed him into the room.
2 〈입회·입당시키다〉 let join; let participate; admit; let in
♦ 새 회원을 들이다 admit a new member
3 〈돈 등을〉 invest (capital in); lay out (capital); spend [expend] (money on *sth*); put in; 〈시간을〉 take time; 〈노력을〉 take pains; make efforts
♦ 비용을 덜 들이다 make (it) less expensive / 힘을 들이다 put in effort; throw *oneself* into / 많은 비용을 들이다 spend [lay out] a large amount of money (on) / 큰 돈을 들여서 사다 give [pay] large sum for (a thing)
▶ 여자들은 화장하는데 많은 시간을 들인다 It takes a lot of time for women to put on their make-up.
▶ 이 일에 더 이상의 시간[돈]을 들일 수는 없다 We can't afford to spend any more time [money] on this affair.
▶ 그는 그 소설을 쓰는데 3년의 공을 들였다 He spent three years (in) writing the novel. ⇒ It took him three years to write the novel.
▶ 그런 장난감에 돈을 들이지 마라 Don't waste money on a toy like that.
4 〈고용인을〉 employ; engage; take *sb* into *one's* service; 〈양자를〉 adopt; take *sb* into the family
▶ 그는 조카를 양자로 들였다 He adopted his nephew as a son.
5 〈들여놓다〉 take in; bring in; carry in
6 〈맛을〉 get [acquire] a taste (for); take a liking (for, to)
♦ 돈에 맛을 들이다 get a taste for money / 좋은 습관을 들이다 get *oneself* into good habits / 노름에 맛을 들이다 take to gambling
▶ 젊었을 때 좋은 습관을 들여라 Try to form

[develop] good habits while (you are) young.
▶ 한번 투기에 맛을 들이면 여간해서 그만둘 수 없다 Once you are successful in speculation, it is hard to leave off.
▶ 나쁜 습관을 들이지 않도록 조심해라 Be careful not to pick up bad habits.
7 〈잠을〉 invite [induce] (sleep); put [send] *sb* to (sleep)
♦ 자장가를 불러 애기를 잠들이다 lull [lullaby] a baby to sleep; sing a baby to sleep
8 〈물감을〉 dye
♦ 천에 빨간 물을 들이다 dye cloth red / 검정 물을 들이다 dye (a thing) (in) black
▶ 그녀는 머리를 금발로 물들였다 She has her hair dyed blond(e).
9 ⇨ 길들이다 1
10 〈땀을〉 let (sweat) cool off; cool *oneself*; cool off
▶ 우리는 골짜기의 개울물에 들어가서 땀을 들였다 We cooled off in the mountain stream.

들이닥치다 rush in; come on; descend upon; raid; make a rapid approach to; 〈여럿이〉 throng; storm (a place)
♦ 뜻밖의 손님이 들이닥치다 be visited by unexpected guests; be visited by uninvited guests / 적이 들이닥치다 be suddenly attacked by the enemy
▶ 관광객이 그 레스토랑에 들이닥쳤다 Tourists crowded into [thronged to] the restaurant.

들이대다 1 〈물건·증거 등을〉 thrust (a thing) before *sb*
♦ 증거를 들이대다 thrust proofs before *sb*; confront [face] *sb* with the proof / 권총을 들이대다 point [aim, level] a revolver at *sb*; cover *sb* with a pistol / 등에 총을 들이대다 stick [(口) poke] a gun into *sb's* back / 무리한 요구를 들이대다 level an unacceptable demand at *sb*
▶ 그들은 칼[총]을 들이대고 나를 협박했다 They threatened me at knifepoint [gunpoint].
▶ 그에게 증거를 들이대고 자백시켰다 We confronted him with the evidence [thrust the evidence at him] and made him own up.
2 〈대들다〉 defy [set *oneself*] against] *sb*; resist openly; protest; go at; challenge
▶ 우리는 그에게 진상을 밝히라고 들이댔다 We pressed him to disclose the truth.
▶ 그는 상사에게 맞대놓고 들이댔다 He defied his boss openly.
3 〈공급하다〉 supply *sb* continuously 《with》

들이마시다 1 〈기체를〉 breathe in; inhale; draw [take] in
♦ 연기를 들이마시다 inhale smoke / 담배연기를 깊이 들이마시다 take a deep pull [drag] at a cigarette / 산소를 들이마시고 탄산가스를 내쉬다 inhale oxygen and exhale carbon dioxide
▶ 그는 신선한 공기를 가슴 깊이 들이마셨다 He breathed fresh air deep into his lungs.
2 〈액체를〉 suck in [up]; drink (in); swallow up; swig; take a deep swig; gulp down; down
♦ 물[술]을 들이마시다 drink water [wine] / 단숨에 들이마시다 swallow (empty the glass) at a gulp / 맥주 한 병을 들이마시다 drink a bottle of beer to the dregs

들이맞추다 get [put, let] in; fit *sth* in [into]
♦ 파이프 B를 파이프 A에 들이맞추다 fit pipe B in pipe A

들이몰다 1 〈몰아넣다〉 drive in [into]; chase into; shoo in
♦ 돼지를 울 안으로 들이몰다 drive a pig in the sty
▶ 그는 소를 울 안으로 들이몰았다 He drove the cattle into an enclosure [a corral].
2 〈심하게 몰다〉 drive fast [violently]; make [let] run
♦ 말을 들이몰다 gallop a horse; drive [spur] a horse on / 차를 들이몰다 hasten [drive fast] (to a place) in a car

들이밀다 〈안으로〉 push [thrust, force, shove, put] in; 〈마구〉 push [thrust] hard
♦ 비디오에 카세트를 들이밀다 push [press] a videocassette in [into] a videoplayer
▶ 들이밀면 두명쯤은 더 들어간다 If we squeeze them in, there is still room for about two more.

들이밀리다 1 〈안으로〉 be pushed [thrust, shove] in [into]
▶ 그는 방 구석으로 들이밀렸다 He was pushed (into) the corner of a room.
2 〈한 곳으로〉 gather [flock] (together); crowd; make [rush] for
♦ 사방에서 들이밀리다 flock from all [various] quarters
▶ 관광객들이 가게에 들이밀렸다 The tourists besieged the store.
▶ 서울역에 관광객들이 들이밀렸다 Seoul Station was deluged with tourists.

들이박다 drive [strike] in [into]; ram *sth* into; ram down (a stake); 〈쐐기 등을〉 wedge in
♦ 못을 들이박다 drive [hammer] a nail into (a wall)

들이받다 dash against; 〈동물이 뿔로〉 gore; ram against [into]; knock [run, strike] against; run into; butt (into); bunt
♦ 승용차로 버스를 들이받다 ram a car into a bus / 자동차로 담벼락[전주]를 들이받다 run [crash] a car into a wall [an electric pole] / 머리로 들이받다 give *sb* a butt of head / 뿔로 들이받다 horn; bunt (it) with horns
▶ 트럭은 담을 들이받아 무너뜨리고 나서야 멈췄다 The truck crashed through the fence and finally stopped.
▶ 염소 한 마리가 뿔로 나무를 들이받고 있었다 A goat was butting a tree with his horns.

들이부수다 knock to pieces ⇨ 들부수다

들이불다 1 〈이쪽으로·안으로〉 blow this way; blow (in)
2 〈세차게〉 sweep along [over]; blow [howl] about; rage
▶ 틈새기 바람이 침실로 들이불었다 A draft blew into the bedroom.
▶ 강풍이 들이불면 비도 들이친다 When strong winds blow in, the rains also drive in hard.

들이붓다 〈부어넣다〉 pour down [into]; 〈마구〉 pour profusely

♦식물에 물을 들이붓다 water the plants / 유리컵에 우유를 들이붓다 pour milk into a glass

들이빨다 suck in [up]; inhale; suck hard; imbibe
♦젖을 들이빨다 suck the breast hard

들이쉬다 〈숨을〉 inhale; breathe [draw, take] in; absorb
♦숨을 깊이 들이쉬다 take [draw] a deep breath
▶그는 신선한 공기를 깊이 들이쉬었다 He took [drew] a deep breath of fresh air.

들이쌓이다 pile (up); lie in a heap; heap [be heaped] up; accumulate
▶책이 높게 들이쌓여 있었다 The books piled up high.

들이쑤시다 1〈아프다〉 sting; tingle [smart, throb] with pain; rankle; ache
♦들이쑤시는 아픔 a smarting pain
▶골치가 들이쑤신다 My head aches awfully.
▶옛 상처가 들이쑤신다 My old wound aches.
▶벤 자리가 들이쑤신다 My cut stings.
2〈구멍 등을〉 poke hard at; prod; pick
3〈부추기다〉 instigate; incite; stimulate; stir [work] up; agitate; 〈감정 등을〉 kindle; inflame
♦들이쑤셔 싸움을 붙이다 stir up 《them》 to fight
▶누가 노동자를 들이쑤셔서 파업을 하게 했는가? Who prompted [incited] the workers to go on strike?
4〈뒤지다〉 dig up; rummage 《in》
♦책상 서랍을 들이쑤시다 ransack [rummage in] the desk drawers / 서류를 들이쑤시다 rummage among the papers / 꼬치꼬치 들이쑤시다 poke and pry into

들이지르다 1〈세게 지르다〉 push [thrust] hard; strike [beat] hard; 〈차다〉 kick hard; give a hard kick 《on the shin》
♦머리를 들이지르다 strike [beat] sb on the head / 옆구리를 들이지르다 give a hard kick on the side / 몽둥이로 가슴을 들이지르다 push hard in the chest with a stick
2〈탐식하다〉 devour (gluttonously); eat voraciously [like a pig]; eat greedily [ravenously]; eat away with wolfish greediness
3〈고함치다〉 yell (out); shout; bawl; roar; cry in a loud voice

들이치다 drive in(to); be driven [blown] in
♦비가 방으로 들이치다 rain into the room
▶그는 들이치는 빗속을 무릅쓰고 나갔다 He went out into the driving rain.
▶강풍으로 비가 들이치기 시작했다 Because of the strong wind, the rain began to come down diagonally.

들이켜다 drink (down); drink deep; gulp down; take [have] a pull at 《liquor》; toss off
♦꿀꺽꿀꺽 들이켜다 drink drafts 《of》; gulp; swill; guzzle 《beer》 / 단숨에 들이켜다 drink 《a glass of wine》 at one [a] gulp; gulp down; empty 《one's glass》 in one draft / 맥주 한 병을 단숨에 들이켜다 drink a bottle of beer in one breath / 쭉 들이켜다 take a long pull at drink 《a glass》 dry
▶그는 술로 시름을 달래기 위해 위스키를 들이켰다 He tossed off glasses of whisky to drown his sorrow.

들이키다 〈안으로 다그다〉 bring (a thing) near (to); tug [draw, take, pull] in
♦발을 들이키다 draw in one's legs / 손을 들이키다 withdraw one's hand / 머리를 들이키다 pull in one's head

들이퍼붓다 〈눈·비가〉 snow [rain] hard [heavily]; pour down; fall thick
▶비가 들이퍼붓었다 It rained cats and dogs.
▶비가 나뭇잎에 들이퍼붓고 있다 It is raining very fast on the leaves.
▶이거 비가 지독하게 들이퍼붓는군 It's raining in torrents [in cataracts, in buckets].

들일 farm work [labor]; work in the fields; field labor
♦들일을 하다 do farm work; work on the farm
▶아버지는 들일을 하러 나가셨습니다 My father is working out in the fields.

들입다 recklessly; rashly; frantically; madly; like mad
♦들입다 공부하다 work like fury; 《口》 dig into one's subject / 들입다 밀다 give a hard [violent] push / 들입다 돈을 쓰다 spend money recklessly / 들입다 책을 읽다 read books at random / 들입다 일하다 work like crazy [hell]

들장미 ―薔薇 〔植〕 a wild rose; a brier [briar]

들쥐 〔動〕 a field [meadow] mouse

들짐승 a wild [feral] animal [beast]

들쩍지근하다 somewhat sweet; sweetish

들쭉날쭉 jaggedly; ruggedly
―**들쭉날쭉하다** uneven; notched; corrugated; milled; jagged; indented
♦가장자리가 들쭉날쭉한 잎 a leaf with a serrated margin / 들쭉날쭉한 상어의 이빨 the jagged teeth of a shark / 들쭉날쭉한 해안선 an indented coastline

들창 ―窓 an awning window; a push-up window
■―눈이 a person who is always lifting his eyes ―코 a turned-up nose; an upturned nose; 〈사람〉 a person with an upturned nose

들추다 1〈폭로하다〉 disclose [divulge, let out] 《a secret》; expose; uncover; reveal; rake up; dig up; ferret out 《sb's secret》; pry into; peck at sb's faults; lay bare; bring to light
♦아무의 잘못을 들추다 expose sb's fault / 서류철을 일일이 들추다 dig through the files / 아무의 정체를 들추다 ummask sb; disclose sb's identity / 추문을 들추다 bring a scandal to light
2〈뒤지다〉 ransack; rummage 《in》; search
♦서랍을 들추다 ransack [rummage in, root about in] a drawer 《for》
▶개가 쓰레기통을 들추고 있었다 A dog was rummaging through the garbage can.

들추어내다 1 ⇨ 들추다 1
♦아무의 불미한 과거를 들추어내다 dig up sb's disreputable past / 사생활을 들추어내다 lay bare (another's) private life

2 〈찾아내다〉 find out; discover; hunt [seek] out; rummage out
♦ 남의 비밀을 들추어내다 pry a secret out of *sb*; ferret [worm] out; dig up; grub (out) / 남의 결점을 들추어내다 find fault with *sb*; peck [pick] at *sb's* fault; pick holes in a person's coat [character]

들치기 〈행위〉 lifting; shoplifting; 〈사람〉 a shoplifter; a lifter
—**들치기하다** shoplift; lift [steal] goods
♦ 들치기하다가 잡히다 be caught lifting *sth*

들치다 raise; lift; hold up (the end of)

들큼하다 〈달콤하다〉 sweetish; somewhat sweet

들키다 be found (out); be discovered; be detected; be sought out; be caught 《doing, in the act of doing》
♦ 현장에서 들키다 be caught red-handed [in the act]
▶ 그는 선생님께 들키지 않고 교실에서 빠져나갔다 He got out of the classroom unobserved by the teacher.

들타작 —**打作** threshing in the field

들통 —**桶** a pail; a bucket

들통나다 be detected [revealed; disclosed]; come [be] out; come [be brought] to light; give *sth* [*sb*] away
▶ 그의 필적으로 그는 들통났다 His handwriting gave him away.
▶ 그의 사투리로 그의 고향이 들통났다 His accent gave him away.

들판 〈평원〉 a plain; a field

들풀 wild grass ♦ 들풀도감 a pictorial book of wild grass

듬북(이) plenty; much; quite a lot; brimfully; full (to the brim)
♦ 사례를 듬뿍 받다 be given a liberal [handsome] reward; be rewarded generously / 돈을 듬뿍 벌다 make a lot of money / 팁을 듬뿍 주다 tip 《a porter》 handsomely / 술을 듬뿍 붓다 pour wine full to the brim / 밥을 듬뿍 담다 heap 《a bowl》 with rice; fill 《a bowl》 full of rice
▶ 그는 급료를 듬뿍 받고 있다 He gets good wages.
▶ 그는 보상을 듬뿍 받았다 He was well rewarded.
▶ 그는 그 거래에서 듬뿍 벌었다 He made a large profit on the transaction.
—**듬뿍하다** full; brimful; plenty
▶ 사례는 듬뿍 하겠습니다 I assure you a handsome [large] gratuity.

듬성듬성 sparsely; thinly; sporadically; scatteredly; 〈순서없이〉 without order; at random; here and there; 〈간격을 두고〉 at intervals
♦ 털이 듬성듬성 나 있다 be thinly haired [covered with hair] / 나무를 듬성듬성 심다 plant trees sparsely
—**듬성듬성하다** sparse; thin; scattered; sporadic
▶ 나무가 듬성듬성하게 심어져 있다 The trees are planted at intervals.

듬쑥 full; greedily
♦ 그릇에 밥을 듬쑥 담다 fill a bowl full of rice
▶ 소녀는 과자를 듬쑥 그러쥐고 입에 넣었다 The girl grasped a greedy handful of cake and put it into her mouth.
▶ 그는 동전을 한주먹 듬쑥 움켜쥐었다 He seized all the coppers that his fist can hold.
▶ 그녀는 야채를 듬쑥 먹었다 She ate vegetable a lot.

듬쑥하다 grave ⇨ 듬직하다

듯 ♦ 자는 듯 마는 듯하다 have an interrupted sleep
▶ 너무 적어서 먹은 듯 만 듯하다 I ate so little that I am hardly satisfied.
▶ 비가 올 듯 말 듯했다 There was no telling whether it would rain or not.
▶ 짙은 안개로 앞이 보일 듯 말 듯했다 We could scarcely see through the thick fog.

듯싶다 〈…인 듯 생각되다〉 seem; appear 《to be》; 《It》 looks 《like》; it seems (to me) that; 〈…일[할] 것 같다〉 be likely 《to》; probably
▶ 아무리 보아도 상인인 듯싶다 He is a merchant to all appearances.
▶ 이 책은 유익한 듯싶다 This book seems to be useful.
▶ 눈이 올 듯싶다 It looks like snow.

듯이 as if; as though; like; as...as; as
♦ 기쁜 듯이 with a glad look / 슬픈 듯이 with a sad air / 만족스러운 듯이 with evident satisfaction / 갖고 싶은 듯이 with wistful eyes (at) / 아무 일도 없었던 듯이 as if nothing had happened / 미친 듯이 달리다 run like [as if *one* were] mad / 죽은 듯이 보이다 look as if dead; be more dead than alive / 빚을 줄 듯이 말하다 talk as if *one* would give a loan
▶ 그 소녀는 쇼윈도 안에 있는 인형을 갖고 싶은 듯이 보았다 The girl looked with wistful eyes at the dolls in the window.
▶ 그는 마치 보고 온 듯이 말한다 He talks as if he had been there to see it himself.
▶ 그는 나를 때릴 듯이 노려보았다 He glared at me as if he was going to strike me.
▶ 눈물이 비오 듯이 쏟아진다 Tears pour down like rain.
▶ 삶이 있듯이 죽음이 있다 As a man lives, so he dies.

듯하다 **1** 〈…같이 보이다〉 look (like); appear; seem; 〈…할[일] 것 같다〉 be likely 《to》; probably

解說 추정이나 추측을 나타내는 「…인 듯 하다」에는 *I think* (…라고 생각하다), *look like* (…할 것 같다), *seem* (…로 생각되다), *appear* (외견상 …같이 보이다) 등이 해당된다. I hear, I've heard, I've been told나 They say도 그런 뜻을 나타내지만, 이들은 모두 정보 출처를 명백히 밝히고 싶지 않을 경우에 쓸 때가 많다. 일반적으로 My father told me (아버지의 말씀으로는), According to the weather reporter (일기예보에 따르면), According to today's newspaper (오늘 신문에 의하면) 처럼 구체적으로 말하는 것이 보통이다.

♦ 상인인 듯하다 look like a merchant / 머리가 깨질 듯하다 feel as if *one's* head were bursting

▶ 비가 올 듯하다 It looks like rain.
▶ 날씨가 갤 듯하다 The weather is likely to clear up.
▶ 그는 가기로 작정한 듯하다 It looks like he means to go.
▶ 저것은 짐의 목소리인 듯하다 That sounds like Jim's voice.
▶ 그는 병이 있는 듯하다 He seems to be ill.
2 〈당장 …할 듯하다〉 be ready 《to do》; be going 《to do》; be on the point of 《doing》
♦ 금방 피어날 듯한 꽃봉오리 a bud just ready to burst / 당장 붕괴할 듯한 집 a house ready to collapse
▶ 금방 비가 올 듯하다 It threatens to rain.
▶ 배는 침몰할 듯했다 The boat was ready to sink.
▶ 슬퍼서 가슴이 메어질 듯했다 My heart was almost burst with grief.

등 〈몸·물건의〉 the back
♦ 등 뒤에서 욕하는 사람 a backbiter / 등을 맞대고 앉다 sit back to back with each other / 국민의 신망을 등에 업다 be backed by the confidence of the people / 등의 단추를 끄르다 undo the buttons in the back / 등을 돌리다 turn *one's* back 《on, to》 / 등을 펴다 straighten *one's* back / 적에 등을 보이다 turn *one's* back on the foe; beat a retreat / 등을 밀다 wash *one's* back
▶ 그는 내 등을 가볍게 두드렸다 He patted me on the back.
▶ 등을 꼿꼿이 펴라 Straighten your back.
▶ 곤란할 때 도와준 사람에게 등을 돌리지 마라 Don't turn your back on those who helped you in need.
▶ 그는 나에게 등을 돌리고 앉았다 He sat with his back toward me.
▶ 나는 등에 배낭을 짊어지고 산에 올랐다 I climbed the mountain with [carrying] a knapsack on my back.

등 藤 〖植〗〈나무〉 a rattan; 〈줄기〉 a cane ♦ 등 의자 a cane chair

등 等 1 〈등급〉 a class; a grade; a degree
♦ 1[2, 3]등 the first [second, third] class [grade] / 1[2] 등상 the first [second] prize / 경주에서 2등이 되다 win second place [come out second] in a race / 3등으로 떨어지다 drop to third place / 벌점 1등을 감하다 reduce the penalty by one degree; commute the sentence by one degree
▶ 이 그림은 전람회에서 1등 상을 받았다 This painting was awarded first prize at the exhibition.
▶ 〘會話〙「몇 등석으로 여행하시겠습니까?」「1등석으로 가겠습니다」 "What class are you traveling?" "I am traveling first class."
2 〈따위〉 and so on [forth]; and the like; etc. (▶ and so forth로 읽는다. 라틴어 발음은 [etsétərə]); such as; and [or] such; and suchlike
♦ 책과 사전 등 books, dictionaries, and so on [and the like]; books, dictionaries, etc. / 시계, 카메라 등의 정밀 기계 precision instruments, such as watches, (and) cameras / 달, 별 등의 천체 heavenly bodies—the moon, the stars, for example

▶ 그는 내 이름, 나이, 주소 등을 물었다 He asked me my name, my age, my address, and so on [forth].

등 燈 a light; a lamp; an electric light; 〈초롱〉 a lantern
♦ 등을 켜다 light the lamp; 〈전등을〉 turn [put, switch] on the light / 등을 끄다 put out the lamp; 〈전등을〉 turn [switch] off [put out] the light / 60와트짜리 등 두 개를 달다 use two 60-watt lamps
▶ 등이 꺼졌다 The light has gone out [is out].

등가 等價 〖物〗 an equivalent; 〖經〗 parity

등각 等角 〖幾〗 equal angles ♦ 등각의 equiangular ■ —형〖삼각형〗 an equiangular figure [triangle]

등갓 燈— a lampshade

등거리 等距離 equal distances; equidistance
♦ 등거리의 equally distant 《from A and B》; equidistant / 등거리에 at equal distances ■ —외교 equidistant diplomacy

등걸 〈나무의〉 a stump; 〈수확한 뒤의 보리 등의〉 stubble; a stub ◆ —불 a stump fire; 〈깜부기불〉 embers; a dying [low] fire ◆ —숯 charcoal made from stumps

등걸잠 sleeping with *one's* clothes on [without changing dress]

등겨 chaff

등고선 等高線 〖地〗 a contour (line) ♦ 등고선을 그려 넣다 draw contour lines on a map; contour / —지도 a contour map

등골 1 〈등줄기〉 the hollow along the spine; the line of the back
♦ 등골이 오싹해지는 광경 a spine-chilling sight / 등골이 오싹해지다 be chilled to the marrow [bone]
▶ 등골이 아프다 I have a pain in my back.
▶ 그 무시무시한 이야기에 나는 등골이 오싹해졌다 A cold shiver [chill] ran down my spine when I heard the weird story. ⇒ The weird story sent a chill up my spine.
2 〈등골뼈〉 the backbone; 〈척수〉 the spinal cord [marrow]
♦ 등골이 빠지는 일 a painstaking task; a tough job; a laborious [toilsome] task / 등골이 빠지다 suffer extremely; have a very hard time of it

등골나물 〖植〗 a boneset

등과 登科 passing the higher civil service examination —등과하다 pass the higher civil service examination

등교 登校 attending school; school attendance —등교하다 go to school; attend school
▶ 나는 매일 버스로 등교한다 I go to [attend] school by bus every day.
▶ 수험자는 9시까지 등교하기 바랍니다 The examinees are expected to present themselves by nine.
▶ 등교할 때 차 조심해라 Watch for the passing traffic when you are on your way to school.

등귀 騰貴 a rise; appreciation
♦ 땅값의 등귀 the appreciation of land value —등귀하다 rise; go up; soar

등극 登極 accession 《to the throne》; enthronement —등극하다 accede to the throne; ascend [mount] the throne

등긁이 a back scratcher; a scratchback

등급 等級 a class; an order; a grade; a rank; a degree; 〈별의〉 magnitude
♦등급을 매기다 grade; classify; graduate / 1, 2, 3으로 등급이 매겨지다[매겨져 있다] be graded 1, 2, 3
▶등급에 따라 값도 다르다 The prices differ according to the class.
▶생사는 생사검사소의 규칙에 따라 등급이 매겨진다 Silk is graded according to the rules of the Raw Silk Conditioning House.
▶이런 상품에는 등급을 매기기가 어렵다 It is not easy to grade these sort of articles.

등기 登記 registration; registry
♦미등기의 unregistered / 등기가 되어 있다 be registered; be on the record / 가옥 등기를 말소하다 cancel the registration of a house
▶이 소포를 등기로 부쳐 주십시오 Will you please register this parcel? ⇌ I'd like to have this parcel registered.
—등기하다 register; have [get] sth registered; effect [make] registration; enter 《in a book》
■국내[국제]— domestic [international] registration 선적(船籍)— registration of nationality (of a ship) ■—료 a registration fee —말소 cancellation of registration —번호 the registered number; a registration number —부 a register (book) —사항 matters required to be registered —소 a registry (office) —용지 a registration form; a registry folio (pl. ~s) —절차 the formalities of registration —편지 [소포] a registered letter [parcel, package] —필 (표시) Registered —필증 a registration certificate

등기우편 登記郵便 registered post [《美》 mail]
♦등기우편으로 부치다 send 《a letter》 registered [by registered mail]/ 등기우편으로 하다 have [get] 《a letter》 registered
■—료 a registration [registry] fee —영수증 a registration receipt

등꽃 藤— 〔植〕 a wisteria

등나무 藤— a wisteria; a wistaria ■—덩굴 wisteria vine —시렁 a wisteria trellis

등넘기 leapfrog ♦등넘기를 하다 leapfrog

등단하다 登壇— mount [go on, step up on] the platform; take [mount] the rostrum

등달다 get all hot and bothered; fret [stew]; be in [get into] a stew; be irritated [impatient]; be upset
▶그 일로 등달아 할 필요는 없다 You need not fret yourself about that.
▶그는 꾸어 준 돈을 받지 못해 등달아 있다 He is all hot and bothered because he can't collect the money he lent out.
▶그는 손실을 회복하려고 등달았다 He was impatient [eager] to make up (for) the loss.

등닿다 1 〈의지하다〉 rely upon; have backing; be supported; lean on; depend on; shelter oneself under 《the man of influence》
▶그는 등닿는 친구 한 사람만을 믿고 상경했다 He came up to Seoul with a single acquaintance to look to for assistance.

2 〈마소의 등이 벗어지다〉 be grazed; be abraded; be chafed; be rubbed raw

등대 等待 waiting —등대하다 wait for; await; be [get, stand] ready for 《an order》

등대 燈臺 a lighthouse; a beacon; a light tower; 〈詩〉 a pharos ■—선 a lightship; a lightboat —지기 a lighthouse keeper; a lighthouse man

등대다 lean [depend, rely] on sb's authority [power, influence]; turn [look] to sb's power
▶그는 아버지의 위세에 등대고 뽐내고 있다 He is giving himself airs under the shelter of his father's influence.

등댓불 燈臺— a beacon lamp

등덜미 the upper part of the back
♦등덜미를 치다 pat sb on the back

등등 等等 and so on [forth] ⇨ 등(等) 2
▶그 방에는 책상, 의자 등등이 있었다 We found desk, chairs and what not in the room.
▶그는 인생, 사랑, 죽음 등등에 대해서 이야기했다 He talked about life, love, death, and so on [forth].

등등거리 藤— a rattan undershirt (worn in summer)

등등하다 騰騰— 〈서슬이 푸르다〉 mighty; powerful; influential; 〈의기양양하다〉 triumphant; exultant; (be) on one's high horse; mount [ride] the high horse; riding high
♦기세가 등등하다 show one's spirit [nerve]; be in high spirits [feather]/ 살기등등하다 be bloodthirsty; be all in a truculent mood; reek of murder
▶그는 노기가 등등했다 Fury and anger filled his heart [head].

등딱지 a carapace

등락 騰落 rise and fall; fluctuations
♦주가의 등락 the fluctuations of stock prices

등량 等量 an equal quantity [amount]
♦등량의 소금과 설탕 an equal amount of salt and sugar / 등량으로 〈처방전에서 약을〉 ana (略 aa)

등록 登錄 registration; entry; record
♦유권자의 등록 registration of voters / 미등록의 unregistered 《trademark》
▶나는 차의 등록을 마쳤다 I have already registered my car.
—등록하다 register; enter; make an entry; enroll; put on record
♦토지대장에 등록하다 enter in the cadaster / 상표를 특허청에 등록하다 register a trademark with the Patent Office / 회원으로서 등록하다 enroll [register] as a member
▶그는 치과의사로 등록했다 He registered himself as a dentist.
▶그녀는 졸업생 명부에 등록되어 있지 않았다 She was not listed among the graduates.
■상표[실용신안, 의장, 판권]— registration of trademark [utility model, design, copyright] 주민— the resident registration : 주민등록증 a resident card [certificate] ■—금 a registration fee; 〈학교의〉 tuition (fees) —말소 cancellation of a registration —번호 a registration number —부 a register; a roster —상표 a registered trademark —세 a regis-

등록세 tration tax ―의장 a registered design ―자 a registrant ―제 a registration system ―증(서) a certificate of inscription ―필 (표시) Registered

등롱 燈籠 〈달아놓는〉 a hanging lantern; a garden lantern; 〈들고 다니는〉 a hand lantern; 〈신전의〉 a sacred [dedicatory] lantern
♦등롱에 불을 켜다 light a hanging lantern

등마루 the ridge of the spine

등명 燈明 a sacred light
♦등명을 올리다 offer a light (to a god)

등반 登攀 climbing; ascent
▶소수의 인원으로 구성된 일대가 에베레스트 등반을 계획중이었다 A small party was planning to ascend Mt. Everest.
―등반하다 climb (up); scale; make the ascent of; clamber up
▶그들은 히말라야를 등반했다 They climbed the Himalayas.
■―대 a climbing party ―자 a climber

등받이 the back of a chair

등변 等邊 〔數〕 equal sides ♦등변의 equilateral ■―다각형 an equilateral polygon ―삼각형 an equilateral triangle ―형 an equilateral (figure)

등본 謄本 an attested [a certified] copy; a transcript; a duplicate; 〔法〕 a tenor
♦등본을 신청하다 apply for a copy / 등본을 떼다 get [obtain] an attested copy
■호적― a (certified) copy of one's [the] domiciliary [family] register

등분 等分 division into equal parts
―등분하다 divide [share] equally; divide into (two, three) equal parts
▶그녀는 사과 하나를 2등분했다 She cut an apple into exact halves.
▶그의 재산은 3등분되었다 His property was divided into three equal parts.
▶비용은 등분하여 부담합시다 Let's bear an equal share of the expenses. = Let's share the expenses equally.

등불 燈― a lamp; a lamplight ⇨ 등(燈)
♦등불 밑에서 독서하다 read by lamplight

등비 等比 〔數〕 an equal [a geometric(al)] ratio ■―수열 a geometric sequence ―중항 a geometric mean

등비급수 等比級數 〔數〕 a geometric series
♦등비급수적으로 《grow》 in geometric series

등뼈 the backbone; the spine; the chine; the spinal 〔vertebral〕 column
■―동물 a vertebrate (animal)

등사 謄寫 〈베껴씀〉 copy; transcription; reproduction; 〈등사판 인쇄〉 mimeographing
―등사하다 copy; transcribe; reproduce; mimeograph
■―물 mimeographed material ―(원)지 stencil paper; a stencil ―판 a mimeograph : 등사판 인쇄의 mimeographed

등사기 謄寫機 a mimeograph; a ditto [copying] machine ♦등사기로 밀다 mimeograph 《an article》; make [run off] copies 《of a leaflet》 on a mimeograph

등산 登山 mountainclimbing; mountaineering
▶나는 종종 혼자 등산을 간다 I sometimes go mountainclimbing [mountaineering] alone.
―등산하다 go up [climb, ascend, scale] a mountain; make an ascent of a mountain
♦지리산을 등산하다 climb [ascend] Chirisan
■―가 a mountaineer; an alpinist ―가 a mountaineering [climbing] party ―로 a path up a mountain ―열 a craze [passion] for mountaineering ―장비 mountain-climbing equipment ―지팡이 an alpenstock ―철 the mountain-climbing [mountaineering] season ―철도[전차] a mountain railway [trolley] ―화 mountaineering boots

등살 the flesh [muscle] of one's back
♦등살이 꼿꼿하다 be in a fix [quandary]

등살바르다 feel heavy in one's back; have a stiff back; have stiff back muscles

등성마루 the ridge (of the spine); the top of the back; the line of the backbone; a ridge

등성이 a ridge ⇨ 산등성이

등세공 籐細工 rattanwork; canework
■―품 rattanwork; a canework

등소평 鄧小平 〈중국의 정치가〉 Deng Xiaoping (1904-97)

등속 等速 〔物〕 uniform velocity
■―(도)운동 uniform motion

등속 等屬 and so on [forth]; and [or] the like; and such like
▶그 가게에서는 과일 등속을 팔고 있다 Fruits and other things are sold at that store.

등수 等數 a grade; a rank; a rate
♦등수를 매기다 grade; graduate; rate; rank
▶그는 자기 반에서 등수가 5등 이내였다 He ranked among the top five in his class.

등식 等式 〔數〕 an equality

등신 等身 life size ■―상(像) a life-size statue

등신 等神 a fool; a dunce; a noodle; a blockhead; (口) a stick ♦등신 같은 foolish; stupid; silly / 등신 같은 짓을 하다 do a stupid thing; make a fool of oneself
▶이 등신아 You fool [noodle, stupid thing]!

등신대 等身大 ♦등신대의 동상 a life-size bronze statue / 등신대의 초상화를 그리다 paint a life-size portrait

등심 ―心 meat around the backbone of cattle; (the upper part of) sirloin

등심 燈心 〈심지〉 a (lamp)wick

등쌀 annoying; bothering; pestering; harassing ▶모기 등쌀에 잠을 잘 수가 없다 The mosquitoes are so annoying that I can't sleep.

등쌀대다 bother; annoy; harass; pester; molest
♦신체장애자에게 등쌀대다 be hard on disabled persons

등압선 等壓線 〔氣〕 an isobar; an isobaric line

등어선 等語線 〔言〕 an isogloss

등에 〔昆〕 a horsefly; a gadfly

등온선 等溫線 〔氣〕 an isothermal line; 〔氣·物〕 an isotherm

등외 等外 a failure; 〈경기의〉 an also-ran
♦등외의 〈경기에서〉 unplaced; 〈품질이〉 off-grade; substandard / 등외로 떨어지다 be [run] unplaced; fail to win a prize; 〈예선에서〉 be eliminated; 〈품평회 등에서〉 be judged to be below standard

▶ 그것은 등외로 떨어질 게 틀림없다 It is sure to fall under the regular grades.
등용 登用 〈임용〉 appointment; 〈승진〉 elevation; promotion; advancement
♦ 인재 등용의 길을 열다 make all careers open to talent; open up opportunities for the talented / 신인의 등용을 방해하다 obstruct the rise of new talent
—**등용하다** appoint 《*sb* to a position》; promote [advance] 《*sb* to a higher position》; elevate
♦ 인재를 등용하다 take men of talent 《into government service》; engage men of ability; raise men of ability to higher positions / 법관으로 등용되다 be appointed (as a) judge; be elevated [raised] to the bench
등용문 登龍門 a gateway to success; an opening to (all) honors
▶ 이 콩쿠르는 많은 음악가의 등용문이 되어 왔다 Success in this contest has been the first step to a successful career for a number of musicians.
등원 登院 attendance at the House
—**등원하다** attend the House
등위 等位 1 ⇨ 등급(等級)
2 ⇨ 동위(同位)
■ —절[접속사] 〖文法〗 a coordinate clause [conjunction]
등유 燈油 《美》 kerosene; 《英》 paraffin oil; lamp oil
등의자 籐椅子 a cane chair
등자 鐙子 stirrups ♦ 등자를 밟다 rest [have] *one's* feet on the stirrups / 등자를 헛밟다 miss *one's* stirrups
등잔 燈盞 an oil cup for a lamp; a lamp-oil container ■ —기름 a lamp oil —불 a lamplight
등잔 밑이 어둡다 《속담》 The beacon does not shine on its own base. ⇌ At the foot of the candle it is dark. ⇌ One must go abroad to hear of home.
등장 登場 1 〖劇〗 entrance on the stage; entry
♦ 맥베스 등장 〈각본에서〉 Enter Macbeth.
—**등장하다** enter the stage; come [appear] on (the) stage; make an entrance
2 〈출현〉 advent; appearance
♦ 신무기의 등장 the advent of new weapons
—**등장하다** appear; show up; make an [*one's*] appearance; put in an [*one's*] appearance
▶ 그녀는 연예계에 혜성처럼 등장했다 She made a comet-like appearance in the world of entertainment.
▶ 이 사건에는 정계의 거물들이 속속 등장한다 Political bosses figure in this case one after another. ⇌ A lot of political bigwigs are involved in this case.
■ —인물 characters; the cast; (라) dramatis personae
등재 登載 registration; record
—**등재하다** register; record
등정 登頂 climbing to the summit
▶ 그는 한국인으로서는 최초로 에베레스트 등정에 성공한 사람이다 He was the first Korean to reach the summit of Mt. Everest.
—**등정하다** climb to the summit; reach [gain] the top of a mountain
등정 登程 starting [setting out] on a journey; departure —**등정하다** start [set out, set off] on a journey [trip]; depart
등줄기 the line of the backbone
▶ 가끔 등줄기가 쿡쿡 쑤시고 아프다 I often have a sharp pain in my back.
▶ 어두운 곳에서 하얀 물체가 움직이는 것을 보았을 때 등줄기에서 식은땀이 흘렀다 A cold shiver ran down my spine when I saw something white moving in the darkness.
등지 等地 (and) like [other] places
♦ 인천, 목포, 부산 등지에서 from Inch'ŏn, Mokp'o, Pusan and like [other] ports
등지느러미 a dorsal fin
등지다 1 〈틀어지다〉 become estranged [alienated] 《from》; break [split] 《with》; fall out 《with *sb* about trifles》
♦ …와 등지고 있다 be on bad terms with *sb*; be at odds with *sb*
♦ 형제가 서로 등진지 오래다 It has been a long time that the two brothers are at odds.
▶ 통상회담의 결렬로 인해 양국은 서로 등지게 되었다 The breakdown of the trade talks impaired the relations between the two nations.
▶ 사소한 오해로 평생의 친구와 등지게 되는 일이 있다 Slight misunderstanding may sever lifelong friends.
2 〈배반하다〉 rise against; turn against [on]; betray; 〈돌아서다〉 turn *one's* back on; 〈떠나다〉 leave
♦ 고향을 등지다 leave *one's* home behind (one) / 나라를 등지다 turn against *one's* country; leave *one's* native country / 세상을 등지다 turn *one's* back on [upon] the world; renounce [forsake] the world / 세상을 등지고 살다 live apart from the world; live in isolation
▶ 친절히 대해준 사람들을 등지지 않도록 해라 Don't turn your back on those who were kind to you.
▶ 그는 세속을 등지고 공부에 전념했다 He devoted himself to his study without hearing about worldly affairs.
3 〈등뒤에 두다〉 《*one's* back》 lean against
♦ 관중을 등지고 with *one's* back to the audience / 벽을 등지고 앉다 sit with *one's* back against the wall
▶ 그 도시는 산을 등지고 있다 The town has [lies with] hills at the back.
▶ 우리는 산을 등지고 사진을 찍었다 We had a photograph taken with mountains in the background.
등질 等質 homogeneity ♦ 등질의 homogeneous
등짐 a pack [burden] carried on *one's* back; a backpack ♦ 등짐을 지다 carry a burden on *one's* back; backpack ■ —장수 a peddler; a packman
등차 等差 〈같은 차〉 equal difference; 〈차등〉 gradation ■ —급수[수열] 〖數〗 an arithmetic series [sequence] —중항 an arithmetic mean

등창 —瘡 an abscess [a tumor] on *one's* back
등청 登廳 attendance at office
—**등청하다** attend the [*one's*] office; go [come] to *one's* [the] office
▶ 시장은 아침 8시에 등청한다 The mayor goes to the office at eight in the morning.
■—**일** the day for *one's* attendance at office
등촉 燈燭 a lamplight and a candlelight; a (lighted) lamp
등축 等軸 an equal axis 《*pl*. axes》
■—**정계**(晶系)〔結晶〕 the isometric system
등치 等値 equal value; equivalence; equivalent; equipollence ◆ 등치의 equivalent; equipollent
등치다 1〈등을 두드리다〉 pat [slap] *sb* on the back
2〈위협하여 빼앗다〉 extort 《money from *sb*》; pinch; blackmail; squeeze; wring 《screw, bully》《money out of *sb*》;《美俗》racketeer
◆ 등쳐먹고 살다 live by racketeering
▶ 그 협박범은 그에게서 막대한 돈을 등쳐먹으려고 했다 The blackmailer tried to extort a large sum of money from him.
등태 a (straw) back pad (for carrying a burden on the back)
등판하다 登板— 〔野〕 take the plate [mound]; go to the mound;〈구원투수로〉come in [up] to pitch
▶ 그는 어제 시합에 등판했다 He was a pitcher in yesterday's game. = He took the plate [mound] in yesterday's game.
등피 燈皮 a (lamp) chimney;〈둥근 것〉a globe
▶ 그는 낡은 램프를 끌어내 등피를 닦기 시작했다 He took out an old lamp and began to clean its chimney.
등하불명 燈下不明 《속담》 The beacon does not shine on its own base. = At the foot of the candle it is dark. = One must go abroad to hear of home.=등잔 밑이 어둡다
등한시하다 等閑視— ignore; neglect; make light of; slight; disregard
▶ 그는 가정을 등한시했다 He took no heed of his family. = He paid little attention to his family.
▶ 그것은 등한시할 일이 아니다 It is not to be lightly disregarded. = It shouldn't be lightly neglected [ignored].
등한하다 等閑— negligent; neglectful; careless ◆ 등한히 하다 neglect; slight; disregard / 공부를 등한히 하다 neglect *one's* studies / 일을 등한히 하다 slight *one's* work
▶ 환자 방문하는 것을 등한히 하지 마라 Don't neglect to call on a patient.
▶ 경고를 등한히 한 사람들이 참화를 입었다 Those who ignored [disregarded] the warning met with disaster.
등허리 〈등과 허리〉 the back and the waist;〈허리의 등쪽〉 the back of the waist
등현례 登舷禮 〈해군 예식의 하나〉 manning the side [yards]; a salute from deck
등호 等號 〔數〕 an equal(ity) sign
등화 燈火 a light; a lamplight
▶ 등화가친지절(可親之節)이 되었다 The good season for reading is on [here]. = We are now in the best season for reading.
■—**신호** a light signal; signaling by a flashlight
등화관제 燈火管制 light control; control of lights; control over lighting; a blackout; a brownout; a dimout ◆ 등화관제용의 검은 휘장 a blackout curtain / 등화관제하의 도시 a blacked-out city
▶ 등화관제가 해제되었다 The blackout was up.
—**등화관제하다** black [brown, dim] out
-디 1〈형용사의 강조〉 very; awfully; terribly
◆ 김디 김은 deep-black; (as) black as coal [pitch]/ 짜디 짠 terribly salty / 춥디 추운 awfully [severe] cold
2〈의문〉▶ 여기서 얼마나 멀디? How far is it from here?
▶ 얼마나 크디? How big was it?
▶ 그는 온다디? Is he coming?
디기탈리스 〔植〕 digitalis; a (common) foxglove
디너파티 a dinner (party)
디노미네이션 〈화폐 단위명의 변경〉 redenomination; changing of denominations (▶ denomination은 단순히 「화폐 단위명」의 뜻. 평가 절하는 devaluation)
디데이 (the) D-day 《for a military coup》
디도서 —書 〔聖〕 The Epistle of St. Paul to Titus 《略 Tit.》
디디다 1〈밟다〉 step on; tread on [upon]
◆ 땅을 디디다 step on the ground / 한 발짝 내어 디디다 take a step forward / 발을 헛 디디다 miss *one's* foot [step]; make [take] a false step / 정계에 발을 디디다 enter into politics; enter upon a political career
▶ 나는 지금까지 프랑스 땅을 디뎌보지 못했다 I have never set foot in France [on French soil] before.
▶ 버스간에서 발을 잘못 디뎌 여자의 발을 밟았다 I stepped on a woman's foot in the bus by mistake.
▶ 그는 달에 발을 디딘 최초의 인간이었다 He was the first human being to set foot on the moon.
2〈덩이로 만들다〉
◆ 누룩을 디디다 tread malted flour paste into cakes
디디티 DDT 〔*d*ichloro-*d*iphenyl-*t*richloroethane〕
디딜방아 a treadmill
디딤돌 a stepping-stone
◆ 출세를 향한 첫번째 디딤돌 a first stepping-stone on the path to success / 남을 디딤돌 삼아 출세하다 improve *one's* position at the expense of another / 장차 성공하는 디딤돌이 되다 serve as a stepping-stone for future success
디럭스 deluxe 《cars》
■—**판(版)** an edition deluxe; a deluxe edition
디렉터 a director
디멘션 〔物〕 a dimension
디모데 〔聖〕 Timothy 《略 Tim.》
■—**전서〔후서〕** The First [Second] Epistle of St. Paul (the Apostle) to Timothy

디밀다 put in ⇨ 들이밀다 ♦얼굴을 디밀다 put in an appearance; make one's appearance
▶그들은 그에게 청구서를 디밀었다 They stuck him with the bill.

디스카운트 (a) discount —**디스카운트하다** give sb a 《10 percent》 discount 《on sth》 ■**―세일** discount sale

디스코 〔美〕〔樂〕 disco 《pl. ~s》; a discotheque

디스크 a disk; a disc ■**―자키** a disk [disc] jockey; 〔口〕 a deejay

디스템퍼 〈강아지의 전염병〉〔獸醫〕 distemper ♦디스템퍼에 걸리다 get distemper

디스토마 〔動〕 a distoma; a distome; flukes ♦간(肝)― a liver fluke ■**―증** distomiasis

디아스타아제 〔生化〕 diastase

디엔에이 〈디옥시리보핵산〉〔生化〕 DNA [*d*eoxyribo*n*ucleic *a*cid]

디오니소스 〔그神〕 Dionysus; Dionyos

디옥시리보핵산 **―核酸** 〔生化〕 deoxyribonucleic acid 《略 DNA》

디자이너 a designer; a stylist ■**상업[공업]―** a commercial [an industrial] designer

디자인 a design; designing —**디자인하다** design 《a dress》 ■**그래픽―** (a) graphic design **상업[공업]―** a commercial [an industrial] design

디저트 (a) dessert ♦디저트용 나이프[스푼, 포크] a dessert knife [spoon, fork] ♦아이스 크림이 디저트로 나왔다 Ice cream was served as dessert. ■**―코스** the dessert

디젤기관 **―機關** a diesel 《engine [motor]》 ■**―차** a diesel-electric locomotive; a diesel

디지털 digital ■**―시계** a digital clock [watch] **―컴퓨터** a digital computer **―통신** digital communications

디프테리아 〔醫〕 diphtheria ♦디프테리아 예방의 antidiphtheritic / 디프테리아에 걸린 suffering from diphtheria ■**―증상** diphtherial symptoms

디플레이션 〈통화수축〉 deflation ♦디플레이션을 막다 prevent deflation ♦―정책 a deflationary policy [measure]

디피이 D.P.E. [*d*eveloping, *p*rinting, and *e*nlargement]; 〔寫〕 film [photo] processing

> 〔解說〕 우리나라에서는 필름의 현상(development), 인화(printing), 확대(enlargement)를 그 머리글자를 따서 **D.P.E.**라고 하지만, 영어에는 이런 의미의 약어는 없다. 다만 광고·간판 등에 동사인 develop, print, enlarge 등을 쓰는 경우가 있다.
> 위의 세 가지 공정을 가리켜 photo [film] *processing*이라고 하고 D.P.E.를 업으로 하는 상점을 photo [film] processing shop이라고 한다.

딕실랜드재즈 Dixieland jazz
딕터폰 (商標) a Dictaphone
딜레마 a dilemma ♦딜레마에 빠지다 fall into a dilemma; be in a dilemma; be on the horns of a dilemma
딜레탕트 〈예술 애호가〉 a dilettante 《*pl.* ~s, -ti》
딩딩하다 1 〈힘이 세다〉 mighty; strong; robust; sturdy; stout
▶노인은 아직 딩딩하다 The old man is still hale and hearty.
2 〈단단하다〉 hard; solid; firm; 〈팽팽하다〉 tense; taut; 〈서술적〉 be stretched to the full
▶배가 불러 딩딩하다 I have a full stomach.
▶그녀는 젖이 불어 딩딩했다 Her breast was swollen with milk.
▶종기가 밑이 들어 딩딩했다 The abscess was deep-rooted and hard.
3 〈기반이 튼튼하다〉 stable; secure; solid; firm ♦딩딩한 부자 a solid man / 살림이 딩딩하다 be well off / 재정적 배경이 딩딩하다 have a stable backing of finance

따갑다 1 ⇨ 뜨겁다
2 〈쑤시다〉 tingly; stinging; smart; prickly; pricking
♦연기때문에 눈이 따갑다 My eyes smart with smoke.
▶벌에 쏘인 데가 따갑다 The spot stung by the bee is tingling.
▶그 이야기는 귀가 따갑도록 들었다 I am sick (and tired) of hearing the story. ≑ I have heard enough of the story.

따개비 〔動〕 a barnacle; an acorn shell
따귀 a cheek ♦따귀를 때리다 slap sb on the cheek [in the face]
▶나는 그의 따귀를 후려갈겼다 I gave him a box on the ear. ≑ I slapped his face.
▶나는 따귀를 맞았다 I got slapped on the cheek.

따깜질 picking away at 《a mass》 —**따깜질하다** 〈조금씩 뜯어내다〉 take away little by little [bit by bit]; pick 《away》

따끈따끈하다 warm; (piping) hot
♦따끈따끈한 감자 potatoes hot from the oven
따끈하다 hot; heated
♦따끈한 커피 hot coffee / 따끈한 엽차 steaming hot tea / 따끈히 warmly; hot; good and hot / 청주 한 병을 따끈히 데우다 heat a bottle of *ch'ŏngju*
▶나는 음식은 따끈한 것이 좋다 I like my food hot.
▶우유를 따끈히 데워 주시겠습니까? May I please have my milk hot?

따끔거리다 sting; tingle; prick; prickle
♦따끔거리는 상처 a sore cut / 귀가 따끔거리다 have a sharp pain in one's ear
▶내 눈이 따끔거린다 I have a throbbing pain in my eye.
▶햇볕에 탄 등이 따끔거린다 My sunburn back smarts [tingles].
▶그는 상처가 따끔거려 잠을 이루지 못했다 The smart of the hurt kept him awake.

따끔따끔 ♦따끔따끔 아프다 have a sharp [throbbing, tingling] pain; be stinging
▶옆구리가 따끔따끔 아프다 I have stitches [a stick] in my side.
—**따끔따끔하다** ⇨ 따끔거리다
▶이 약을 바르면 좀 따끔따끔합니다 This medicine stings when you apply it.

따끔하다 1 〈아프다〉 stinging; tingly; prickly; pricking
♦바늘로 따끔하게 찌르다 prick with a needle

2 〈호되다〉 severe; harsh; sharp; caustic
♦ 따끔한 비평 (a) harsh [caustic] criticism / 따끔한 맛을 보다 have a bitter experience [a hard time of it] / 따끔한 맛을 보여주다 make *sb* smart 《for it》; give *sb* a lesson [a good licking] / 따끔하게 꾸중을 듣다 be severely [warmly, roundly] scolded
▶ 아버지는 아들을 따끔하게 야단쳤다 Father gave his son a sharp [good] scolding.
▶ 그 말이 따끔하게 아픈 데를 찔렀다 The words really fingered the sore spot.
▶ 이번에야말로 그를 따끔하게 혼내줄 테다 This time I'll drive him to a corner [wall].

따님 your daughter ♦ 댁의 따님 your daughter

따다¹ 1〈잡아 떼다〉pick; pluck; nip 《off》; gather
♦ 꽃을 따다 pick a flower / 딸기를 따다 pick strawberries / 밤 따러 가다 go gathering nuts; go chestnuts gathering
▶ 이 꽃을 조금 따도 괜찮겠습니까? May I pluck some of these flowers?
▶ 그녀는 뜰에서 꽃을 조금 땄다 She gathered some flowers from the garden.
▶ 곧 새싹을 따내야겠다 I shall have to nip off the shoots soon.
2〈터뜨리다〉open; lance
♦ 종기를 따다 open an abscess [a boil]
3〈개봉하다〉open; unseal
♦ 깡통을 따다 open a tin [can]
▶ 병마개를 따 주시오 Please open the bottle for me. ⇌ Please open me the bottle.
4〈말·글에서〉quote; steal; extract; pick out
♦ 남의 글귀를 따다 steal another's words; plagiarize / 요점을 따다 pick out the main points; sum up / 밀턴의 글에서 따다 extract [excerpt, quote] from Milton's writings; make an extract from Milton's writings
▶ 그 별은 로마의 미의 여신 이름을 따서 명명되었다 The star was named for the Roman goddess of beauty.
5〈노름 등에서〉gain; get; win 《by gambling》
♦ 속임수로 돈을 따다 rook *sb*
6〈얻다·받다〉get; obtain; gain; take; secure
♦ 만점[백점]을 따다 get [score] full marks / 금메달을 따다 be awarded a gold medal 《at an exhibition》/ 박사 학위를 따다 take a doctor's degree / 면허를 따다 take out a license
▶ 우리 아들은 수학에서 좋은 점수를 땄다 My son got good marks in math(ematics).

따다² 1〈만나주지 않다〉pretend to be out; feign absence; be "not at home" to *sb*; refuse to see 《a caller pretending to be away from home》
▶ 그는 귀찮은 손님은 언제나 따버린다 He is always out to unwelcome guests.
2〈따돌리다〉leave *sb* out; exclude; 〈미행자 등을〉give *sb* the slip; shake off 《*sb* following *one*》; throw [put] 《a detective》off the scent
▶ 그들은 나를 따버리고 자기들끼리만 소풍을 갔다 They all went off on a picnic, alone leaving me out.

따다³ 〈다르다〉different; alien; another
♦ 언제고 딴 날 some other day / 딴 가게에서는 at other stores / 딴 상자에 넣다 put *sth* in another box
▶ 딴 것 좀 봅시다 Show me another, please.
▶ 그것과 이것은 전연 딴 문제다 That is one thing and this is another. ⇌ They are entirely different things.
▶ 우리는 같은 하숙집에 들어 있지만 서로 딴 방을 쓰고 있다 We are living in the same lodging house, but we have different rooms.
▶ 의도와는 전연 딴 결과가 되었다 It had an effect entirely alien from the one intended.

따돌리다 leave *sb* out 《in the cold》; cut *sb* out; leave *sb* severely alone; put *sb* on one side; exclude; shun; 〈사회적으로〉ostracize; blackball
♦ 따돌림을 받는 사람 a black sheep; a person left out in the cold / 따돌림을 받다[당하다] be shunned by all; be ostracized; be boycotted 《by the villagers》
▶ 그들은 나를 따돌리고 말상대조차 하지 않았다 They left me entirely out of their conversation.
▶ 그는 마을 사람들에게 따돌림을 받고 있다 He is the pest to the villagers. ⇌ He is alienated from the villagers.

따뜻이 1〈덥게〉warmly; hot
♦ 몸을 따뜻이 하다 keep *oneself* warm; dress warm
2〈온정으로〉warmly; kindly; heartily
♦ 따뜻이 맞이하다 give *sb* a warm [cordial] reception; receive *sb* with warm hands
▶ 집주인은 그를 따뜻이 맞았다 The master of the house was very hospitable to him. ⇌ He was well received by the host.

따뜻하다 1〈덥다〉warm; mild
♦ 따뜻한 겨울 a soft [mild] winter / 따뜻한 날씨 warm weather / 따뜻한 남쪽 나라 a warm southern country / 불[볕]에 쬐어 몸을 따뜻하게 하다 warm *oneself* at the fire [in the sun]
▶ 금년 겨울은 따뜻하다 This is a mild winter. ⇌ We're having a mild winter this year.
▶ 그녀는 옷을 따뜻하게 입고 있다 She is wearing warm clothes. ⇌ She is warmly dressed.
▶ 방이 기분 좋을 만큼 따뜻해졌다 The room was comfortably heated up.
2〈온정이 있다〉kindly; genial; cordial; heart-warming 《kindness》
♦ 따뜻한 가정 a cheerful [sweet] home / 따뜻한 마음 a warm [kindly] heart / 따뜻한 환영 a cordial [hearty] welcome; a warm reception / 따뜻한 손길을 뻗치다 extend friendly help to 《the poor》/ 부모[형제]의 따뜻한 정을 모르다 be a stranger to parental [fraternal] affection
▶ 그는 엄해 보이지만 실제로는 마음이 따뜻하다 He appears to be strict, but actually he is a warm-hearted person [a person with a warm heart].
▶ 먼저 따뜻한 환대에 감사드립니다 First, I'd like to thank you for your hearty hospitality.
▶ 그는 따뜻한 가정에서 자란 게 틀림없다 He must have been brought up in a genial [happy] family.
▶ 우리는 가는 곳마다 따뜻한 대접을 받았다 We were received warmly [received a hearty

따라가다 1 〈바로 뒤에서〉 follow; follow at 《another's》 heels; 〈함께〉 go (along) with; accompany; 〈뒤를 밟다〉 shadow; track; tag [trail] along
♦아버지를 따라가다 go (along) with *one's* father / 사절단을 따라가다 accompany a delegation; join the retinue of a mission
▶우리는 그를 따라갔다 We followed [went after] him.
▶나는 너를 따라가고 싶다 I'd like to go [come] with you.
▶그녀의 뒤를 졸졸 따라가는 개를 봐라 Look at the dog tagging at her heels.
2 〈쫓아가다〉 keep up with; catch up with [to]
▶네가 너무 빨리 걸어서 따라가지 못하겠다 You walk so fast I can't keep up with you.
▶강의가 너무 어려워 따라갈 수 없었다 The lecture was too difficult for me to follow.
▶반 친구들을 따라가기 위해서 메리는 열심히 공부하지 않으면 안되었다 Mary had to study hard in order to catch up with her classmates.
3 〈겨루다〉 compete with; be a match for; equal; rival
♦따라갈 사람이 없다 be peerless; be without a peer
▶수학에서는 그를 따라갈 사람이 없다 No one can compete with him in mathematics.
따라다니다 follow *sb* about [around]; shadow; dangle about [after] 《a woman》
▶그는 늘 여자 꽁무니만 따라다닌다 He is always dangling after [about] a girl.
따라붙다 overtake; catch up with [to]; come level with; 〈점점〉 gain (up)on
♦경주에서 선두 주자를 따라붙다 gain on the leader in a race
따라서 1 〈그러므로〉 accordingly; consequently; therefore; hence; for that reason
▶당신은 미국 시민이오. 따라서 한국에서는 선거권이 없소 You are a U.S. citizen. Therefore you don't have the vote in Korea.
2 〈…대로〉 according to; in obedience to; in accordance [conformity] with
♦지시에 따라서 in accordance with *sb's* instructions / 필요에 따라서 as occasion calls [demands]; as the need arises / 자기 능력에 따라서 according to *one's* ability / 법에 따라서 처단하다 punish according to [in accordance with] the law
▶그는 그녀의 요청에 따라서 계획의 일부를 바꿨다 He altered [changed] the plan according to her request.
▶그는 자기의 원칙에 따라서 행동했다 He acted up to his principle.
▶그는 학칙에 따라서 퇴학당했다 He was expelled from school according to the school regulations.
3 〈…에 비례하여〉 in proportion to [as]; according as; as
▶가격은 수요에 따라서 결정된다 The price is decided depending on (the) demand.
▶돈이 많아질수록 그에 따라서 걱정도 느는 The richer you are, the more anxieties you will have.
▶방의 크기에 따라서 목소리도 조절해야 한다 We must modulate our voice according to the size of the room.
▶나이를 먹는데 따라서 지혜가 생긴다 Sense [Wisdom] comes with age.
4 〈…을 끼고〉 along
♦선로를 따라서 along the tracks / 산울타리를 따라서 along by the hedge / 강둑을 따라서 가다 go along the river bank
▶강을 따라서 길이 하나 나 있다 A path runs along the river.
따라오다 1 〈뒤쫓아오다〉 follow; come (along) with; tag along after; accompany
▶개는 역까지 나를 따라왔다 The dog followed [tagged along after] me to the station.
▶따라오게 Come (along) with me ! ⇒ Follow me!
▶점원은 입구까지 따라와서 깍듯이 인사했다 The clerk accompanied us to the entrance and made a very deep bow.
▶그는 우리를 따라오느라고 애를 썼다 He had a hard time catching up with us.
2 〈남이 하는 대로〉 follow (suit); do likewise [the same]; catch up
3 〈겨루다〉 compete; rival; equal; be match for
♦따라올 사람이 없다 have no equal [match]; be without a match
따라지 1 〈땅보〉 a dwarf; a shorty; a midget
2 〈끗수〉 one point; the lowest point [hand] (in a card game)
3 〈따분한 존재〉 a miserable existence
■—목숨 a life lived under another's thumbs; slavish life; a life in bond —신세 a wretched life; a life of bare subsistence
따로 1 〈분리하여〉 separately; apart
♦…와는 따로 apart [aside] from…/ 따로 살다 live separately / 따로 만나다 see 《them》 separately / 따로 걷다 walk apart
▶이 넥타이 두 개는 따로 싸주세요 Please wrap up these two neckties separately.
▶그녀는 파티용 드레스 살 돈을 따로 떼어놓았다 She set aside some money to buy herself a party dress.
▶이것은 그것과는 따로 논해야 한다 This must be discussed separately from that.
2 〈별도로〉 extra; additionally; in addition; besides
▶그에게는 따로 백만원의 수입이 있다 He has an additional income of a million won.
▶방세는 십만원이고 식비는 따로 낸다 Lodging costs a hundred thousand won and board extra [board is an extra].
▶급행열차는 따로 돈을 더 내야 한다 You have to pay extra for an express train.
3 〈특별히〉 particularly; specially
▶따로 볼 일은 없다 I have nothing particular to do. ⇒ I've nothing very special to attend to.
▶따로 이렇다 할 일은 일어나지 않았다 Nothing mentionable has happened.
따로따로 apart; separately; severally; singly;

따르다¹

one by one; individually
▶ 자매는 따로따로 앉았다 The sisters sat apart [took separate seats].
▶ 그 부부는 현재 따로따로 살고 있다 That couple is living separately now.
▶ 이것을 하나씩 따로따로 싸주세요 Please wrap these one by one [each of these separately].
▶ 그들은 모두 따로따로 행동을 취했다 They acted each in his own way.
▶ 함께 오지 말고 따로따로 오너라 Come one by one, not all at once.
▶ 상품은 우리에게 따로따로 수여되었다 The prizes were awarded to us respectively.
▶ 목격자들은 따로따로 소환되었다 The witnesses were summoned one at a time.
▶ 죄수들은 따로따로 수용되어 있다 The prisoners are kept separate one from another.

따르다¹ 1 〈뒤를 좇다〉 follow; go [run] after; follow at 〈another's〉 heels; track; shadow
◆ 뒤를 따르다 go after sb; follow about [around] sb / 대세를 따르다 follow the general trend; swim with the tide / 유행을 따르다 follow [run after] the fashion / 형사를 따르게 하다 set a detective on sb
▶ 나는 그를 따라 다방으로 들어갔다 I followed him into a coffee shop.
▶ 장관의 뒤를 따라 차관도 사임했다 The Vice-Minister resigned, following the Minister's suit.

2 〈본뜨다〉 follow; follow suit; model oneself 〈on, after〉; tread in sb's steps
◆ 선례를 따르다 follow a precedent / 선인(先人)을 따르다 follow in the footsteps [wake] of one's forefathers / 남의 예를 따르다 follow another's example / 그 마을의 관습에 따르다 conform to the customs of the town

3 〈입각·의거하다〉 depend [turn, hang] on; be based [founded, grounded] on sth
◆ 따라야 할 기준 a rule to go by; an authoritative rule / 사실에 따른 이야기 a story based upon fact / 법에 따라 처리하다 deal with sb according to the law; bring sb to justice
▶ 한영 양문(兩文)에 차이가 있을 경우에는 영문에 따른다 The English version will prevail if discrepancies exist between it and the Korean version.

4 〈좋아하여 붙좇다〉 take 〈kindly〉 to sb; be fond of
◆ 여자들이 따르다 be much sought after by girls [women] / 따르게 하다 make [get] 〈another〉 attached to one; make oneself dear to sb
▶ 아이들이 그를 무척 따른다 The children love [are very attached to] him.
▶ 그는 아이들이 잘 따르는 타입의 사람이다 He is the sort of person that children take to instinctively.
▶ 이 원숭이는 누구한테나 잘 따른다 This monkey is easily tamed to anybody.

5 〈수반하다〉 accompany; follow; be followed by; attend on; be attendant on [upon]; be attended [accompanied] by; be consequent upon

◆ …에 따르는 폐단 the evil effects attendant upon…/ 위험이 따르는 직업 a hazardous job
▶ 권력에는 책임이 따른다 Power carries (with it) responsibility.
▶ 악덕에는 재앙이 따른다 Miseries are attendant on vice.
▶ 여자들에게는 허영이 따르게 마련이다 Vanity is a vice peculiar [common] to women.
▶ 그 사업에는 많은 어려움이 따랐다 The enterprise was attended with much difficulty.

6 〈복종·준수하다〉 obey; conform (oneself) to; abide by 〈the rules〉; act (up)on
◆ 규칙을 따르다 comply with the rule / 원칙에 따르다 act on a principle / 법을 따르지 않다 defy the law / 다수결에 따르다 abide by the decision of the majority

7 〈견주다〉 compete with; be a match for; equal; rival
▶ 재능에 있어서는 그를 따를 사람이 없다 No one can compare with him in talent.

따르다² 〈붓다〉 pour 〈out, in〉; fill 〈a cup with tea〉; put 〈water in a bowl〉
◆ 차를 따르다 pour out (a cup of) tea / 술을 따르다 fill a cup with wine
▶ 그녀는 보온병에서 더운 물을 따랐다 She poured hot water from [out of] the thermos.
▶ 그에게 술 한 잔을 따라주었다 I poured him a drink.
▶ 한 잔 더 따를까요? You want a refill?
▶ 차를 따를 때는 엎지르지 않도록 조심해라 Be careful not to spill when pouring tea.

따름 ◆ …ㄹ 따름이다 It is just [only] that…
▶ 그는 일개 서기일 따름이다 He is nothing but a clerk.
▶ 나는 사실을 말했을 따름이다 I said only what was true.
▶ 나는 해야 할 일을 했을 따름이다 I simply have done what I ought to do.
▶ 그저 훌륭할 따름이다 It is just splendid.

따리 〈아첨〉 flattery; adulation; toadyism; lipsalve; sycophancy ◆ 따리 붙이다 flatter; toady; curry favor with
■ —꾼 a flatterer; a toady; a sycophant

따먹다 1 〈과일을〉 pick [pluck] 〈a peach〉 and eat
2 〈장기·바둑 등에서〉 take; catch; get; seize
3 〈여자를〉 (俗) defile [trifle with] 〈a girl's〉 chastity; seduce [dishonor, ruin] 〈a girl〉

따발총 —銃 a Russian submachine gun

따분하다 1 〈느른하다〉 languid; weary; listless; dull; heavy; enervated
▶ 날씨가 더워 따분하다 The heat makes me feel languid.

2 〈생기없다〉 boring; tiresome; tedious; irksome; wearisome; weary; dull; insipid; dreary
◆ 따분한 사람 a dull [tedious] fellow; a bore / 따분한 세상 a dreary world; wearisome life / 따분한 이야기 a boring tale; dull talk / 사는 것이 따분해지다 get tired of living
▶ 편지 쓰는 건 따분하다 It irks me to write letters.
▶ 그녀는 나이가 들면서 인생이 따분해졌다 She has grown weary of life with age.
▶ 그는 그 따분한 도시 생활에 진력이 났다 He

is sick and tired of life of that dull town.
▶ 그녀는 정말 따분한 여자였다 She was a dead [most crashing] bore.
3 〈난처하다〉 embarrassing; awkward; helpless
▶ 나는 돈이 없어서 따분하다 I am hard up for money.
▶ 이거 참 따분하게 됐군 What a most awkward case this is! ⇒ Things have come to a peculiar pass.

따스하다 somewhat warm; mild; genial
◆ 따스한 겨울 a soft [mild, green] winter / 따스한 날씨 mild [warm] weather / 따스한 빛깔 a warm color

따습다 comfortably warm; nice and warm
◆ 몸을 따습게 하다 keep *oneself* warm

따오기 〔鳥〕 a ibis

따옴표 —標 〔言〕 quotation marks

따위 1 〈등등〉 and [or] the like; and so forth [on]; and others [other things]; (口) and what not; et cetera (略 etc.)
◆ 가령 …따위 such as…; for example / 사과, 배 따위 apples, pears, and what not
▶ 밀, 귀리 따위는 곡류다 Wheat, oats and the like are cereals.
▶ 그는 그림이며 음악이며 산수 따위를 배웠다 He studied painting, music, arithmetic, and the like.
2 〈…같은〉 such (a thing) like [as]…; the like (of…); 《of》 the sort
◆ 이 따위 물건 an article of this kind [sort] / 너 따위 바보 such a fool like you
▶ 난 네 도움[동정] 따위는 필요 없다 I don't need your help [sympathy].
▶ 그녀는 그 따위 짓은 하지 않았다 She did no such thing.
▶ 이 따위 인간은 실패하기 마련이다 A man of this type tends to fail.
▶ 너 따위가 나설 일이 아니다 That is none of your business.

따지다 1 〈시비를 가리다〉 call (it) in question; distinguish [discriminate] 《between right and wrong》
◆ 잘잘못을 따지다 argue about whether it is right or wrong; distinguish between right and wrong / 면전에서 따지다 run *sb* down to 《his》 face / 뉴스에서 진위를 따지다 verify the news / 미심쩍은 점을 따지다 inquire into a doubtful point; have a doubtful point explained 《by *sb*》
2 〈숫자를 헤아리다〉 count; calculate; compute; reckon
◆ 비용을 따지다 calculate expenses / 손익을 따지다 reckon [calculate] the profits and losses / 이자를 따지다 compute [reckon] interest; take the interest into account

딱¹ 〈소리나게〉 with a bang [crack, snap]
◆ 머리를 딱 부딪치다 bump *one's* head against 《a wall》; crack *one's* head on 《a post》
▶ 가지가 딱 부러졌다 The branch broke with a snap.
▶ 정원사는 잔가지 하나를 딱 분질렀다 The gardener snapped off a twig.
▶ 아빠가 내 머리를 딱 때렸다 Dad gave me a whack on the head.

딱² **1** 〈갑자기〉 suddenly; unexpectedly
◆ 딱 마주치다 come [stand] face to face with *sb*; (美) run up against *sb* / 딱 멈춰서다 stop suddenly [short]; come to a standstill
▶ 나는 그 노인과 길에서 딱 마주쳤다 I ran against [across] that old man on the street.
2 〈단호히〉 positively; decisively; resolutely; flatly; definitely
◆ 딱 잘라 거절하다 refuse positively [flatly]; give a flat [point-blank] refusal / 딱 잘라 말하다 speak flatly / 딱 잡아떼다 give a flat denial / 딱 결심하다 make a grim [firm] resolution; make up *one's* mind definitely
▶ 그의 부탁을 딱 잘라 거절할 수가 없었다 I couldn't give a flat refusal to his request.
▶ 회사측은 노조측의 요구를 딱 잘라 거절했다 The management definitely refused the demands of the union.
3 〈완전히〉 perfectly; completely; entirely
◆ 담배를 딱 끊다 give up [quit] smoking once for all
▶ 그후 그는 발길을 딱 끊었다 It was his last visit.
▶ 아첨은 딱 질색이다 Flattery is my greatest abhorrence.

딱³ **1** 〈활짝 벌어진 모양〉 with an outward thrust ◆ 입을 딱 벌리고 with *one's* mouth wide-open; agape / 놀라서 입을 딱 벌리다 be agape with wonder [surprise] / 두 눈을 딱 부릅뜨다 open *one's* eyes wide
▶ 미개인들은 입을 딱 벌리고 비행기를 바라보았다 The savages gaped at the airplane.
2 〈정확히 들어맞는 모양〉 perfectly; exactly; just; accurately; precisely; to a T
◆ 딱 맞는 옷 a well-fitting suit / 딱 백만원 neither more nor less than a million won; just a million won / 딱 2시간 two hours to a minute; exactly two hours
▶ 내 구두는 발에 딱 맞는다 My shoes are an excellent fit.
▶ 이 책은 어린아이들에게 딱 맞는다 This book is just right for little children.
▶ 그녀는 딱 7시에 나타났다 She appeared [turned up] exactly at seven.
▶ 어머니는 수박을 딱 두쪽으로 잘랐다 Mother cut the watermelon right in half.
▶ 그가 한 말이 딱 들어맞았다 His remark really hit the nail right on the head.
3 〈굳세게 버티는 모양〉 firmly; stubbornly
◆ 딱 버티고 서다 stand firm 《against》; won't yield [budge] a step [an inch]

딱따구리 〔鳥〕 a woodpecker

딱딱 1 〈마주치는 소리〉 with bangs [claps, cracks, crashes]
◆ 손뼉을 딱딱 치다 clap *one's* hands continuously
▶ 돌을 딱딱 부딪쳐 신호를 했다 I gave a signal by knocking [hitting] stones together.
2 〈부러지는 소리〉 with snaps [cracks]
◆ 딱딱 부러지다 snap in [to] pieces
▶ 형은 손가락 마디를 딱딱 꺾는 버릇이 있었다 My brother had a habit of cracking his finger

joints.
딱딱거리다 〈을러대다〉 snarl; speak harshly [roughly]; be strict [severe] with *sb*
▶ 그 순경은 누구에게나 딱딱거린다 That policeman is severe with everybody.
▶ 나한테 그렇게 딱딱거리지 마라 Don't snarl at me like that. ⇌ Don't speak so harshly to me.
딱딱이 wooden clappers ♦ 딱딱이를 치다 beat [strike] clappers; clap wooden clappers
딱딱하다 1 〈단단하다〉 hard; solid; dry and hard
♦ 딱딱한 나무 hard wood / 딱딱한 씨 a hard seed / 돌처럼 딱딱하다 be hard as a rock [brick] / 딱딱해지다 become hard [hardened, solid]; harden; be dried and hardened
▶ 떡이 딱딱해졌다 The rice cake has got leathery.
2 【부자연스럽다】 〈엄하다〉 severe; strict; stern (look); rigid; 〈융통성 없다〉 hard-boiled; hidebound; leathery; 〈어색하다〉 awkward; uncomfortable; 〈격식을 차리다〉 stiff; formal; ceremonious; (美口) stuffy; 〈문장 등이〉 hard; stiff; bookish
♦ 딱딱한 규율 rigid [stiff] discipline / 딱딱한 교사 a severe teacher / 딱딱한 보수주의자 a hard-boiled conservative / 딱딱한 분위기 an uncomfortable atmosphere / 딱딱한 말씨 formal language / 딱딱한 문장 a stiff [hard] style (of writing) / 딱딱해지다 become formal; (口) freeze up / 아이들에게 딱딱하게 굴다 be stern to one's children / 딱딱한 인사를 나누다 exchange formal greetings / 딱딱한 얼굴을 하다 look grave [solemn]
▶ 그는 어지간히 딱딱한 사람이다 He is very punctilious.
▶ 그는 딱딱한 이야기만 한다 He only talks about serious subjects.
▶ 이런 딱딱한 이야기는 그만 합시다 Let's stop this formal talk.
▶ 그는 딱딱한 태도로 말했다 He spoke in a stiff manner.
▶ 이 학교 학생들은 딱딱한 규율에 꽉 묶여 있다 The students of this school are strictly bound by hard-and-fast rules.
딱바라지다 〈몸이〉 be short and thick [plump]; be stocky; be chunky; 〈그릇이〉 be wide and shallow
♦ 딱바라진 사나이 a stocky [stockily-built] man; a short and stout man; a chunky fellow / 가슴이 딱바라지다 have a broad chest; be broad of chest
딱부리 a goggle-eyed person ⇨ 눈딱부리
딱새 〈鳥〉 a redstart
딱성냥 a lucifer [friction] match ♦ 딱성냥을 긋다 strike [scratch] a friction match; light a friction match
딱정벌레 〈昆〉 a ground beetle
딱지[1] 1 〈상처의〉 a scab; a crust
▶ 상처에 딱지가 앉았다 The wound scabbed over.
▶ 부스럼에 딱지가 앉았다 A scab has formed over the boil.
▶ 마침내 딱지가 떨어졌다 At last the scab fell off [peeled away].
2 〈종이의 티〉 a fleck in paper
▶ 종이에 딱지가 많이 붙어 있다 There are many flecks in the paper.
3 〈껍데기〉 a shell; a crust; a carapace
♦ 게딱지 the shell of a crab / 거북의 등딱지 (a) tortoise [turtle] shell
4 〈시계의 겉뚜껑〉 a (watch) case
♦ 금딱지 시계 a gold watch; a watch in a gold case / 시계의 뒤딱지 the back of a watch case
딱지[2] 〈거절〉 rejection; refusal; 〈퇴짜〉 a rebuff
♦ 딱지 놓다 refuse; reject; snub; give *sb* a rebuff; 〈구혼자에게〉 give (a suitor) the mitten; kick (*sb's* proposal) / 딱지 맞다 be refused [spurned, rejected]; suffer [meet with] a rebuff; get snubbed; 〈구혼자가〉 get the mitten; be kicked
딱지 —紙— 〈우표·증지 등〉 a stamp; a label; a sticker; 〈꼬리표〉 a tag; 〈교통 위반〉 a ticket
♦ 딱지 붙은 〈소문난〉 notorious; marked; regular / 딱지를 떼다 give *sb* a ticket; issue a check ticket / 교통 위반자에게 딱지를 떼다 ticket a traffic offender
▶ 그는 딱지 붙은 사기꾼이다 He is a notorious swindler.
▶ 그는 이 장사에서는 딱지가 붙어 있다 He is a marked man in this line.
♦ 우표— a postage stamp
딱총 —銃— a popgun; a firecracker
딱총나무 —銃— 〈植〉 an elder (tree); an elderberry
딱하다 1 〈가엾다〉 pitiable; pitiful; poor; too bad
♦ 딱하게도 sorry [sad] to say / 딱하게 여겨 out of pity [sympathy]; in pity (of) / 보기에 딱하다 be pitiful to see / 딱하게 여기다 be [feel] sorry (for that…); feel sympathy (for); sympathize (with) / 딱한 사정을 호소하다 appeal for another's sympathy; plead for mercy
▶ 딱하게도 그 노인은 말을 하지 못했다 The poor old man was not able to speak.
▶ 그것은 보기 딱한 광경이었다 It was a pitiful scene to see.
▶ 그것 참 딱하게 됐구먼 That's too bad! ⇌ I am sorry to hear that.
2 〈난처하다〉 awkward; annoying; embarrassing; troubled
♦ 딱한 처지 an awkward situation; a fix / 딱한 처지에 있다 be awkwardly situated; be in a plight [predicament]; be in a fix
▶ 그는 처지가 딱하다 He is in a painful [an awkward] position.
▶ 딱하게도 내게 돈이 없다 The trouble is that I have no money.
▶ 내 딱한 입장도 좀 생각해 주게나 You might have a little consideration for my painful position.
딴[1] 〈…로서는〉 ♦ 내 딴에는 as for myself; on my part; in my thought
▶ 그는 제 딴엔 잘 한다고 생각하고 있다 He fancies himself to be doing it well.
▶ 그 여자는 제 딴엔 미인이라 생각하고 있다

She fancies herself a beauty. ⇌ She is beautiful in her own conceit.
▶ 내 딴엔 최선을 다한다고 한 것이 이렇게 되었다 Poor as the job is, I have done my best.

딴² 〈다른〉 another; other; different; else; separate
♦ 딴 날 some other day / 딴 방법 another method; a different way / 딴 수작 irrelevant remarks / 딴 종이에 쓰다 write on another [a separate] sheet (of paper)
▶ 딴 이야기를 합시다 Let us change the subject.
▶ 그것은 딴 문제다 That is another matter.
▶ 딴 질문 있습니까? Do you have any other questions (to ask [put])?
▶ 딴 일이라면 몰라도 이것만은 못 하겠다 I will do anything but this.

딴것 something else; another one; a different thing; the other; the others; the rest
♦ 딴것은 젖혀놓고 first of all; before everything [anything] else
▶ 딴것을 좀 보여 주세요 Please show me some others.
▶ 딴것은 아무것도 모른다 I know nothing else.

딴꽃가루받이 〖植〗 cross-pollination=타가수분(他家受粉)

딴데 somewhere else; some other place; another place
♦ 딴데를 보다 look [turn] away [aside] / 이야기를 딴데로 돌리다 turn the subject
▶ 그것은 딴데서 샀다 I bought it elsewhere.
▶ 저 가게는 딴데보다 훨씬 싸다 They sell much cheaper than other stores.
▶ 그녀는 정신이 딴데 있었다 Her mind was faraway [somewhere else].
▶ 나는 지금 딴데 약속이 있어서 못 가겠다 I have an engagement now somewhere else so I won't be able to go.

딴마음 〈다른 생각〉 any other intention; 〈배반하는 마음〉 a double heart; duplicity; treachery
♦ 딴마음이 있는 double-faced; double-dealing; treacherous / 딴마음이 없는 single-hearted; sincere; devoted / 딴마음이 있다 have an axe to grind; have an ulterior motive / 딴마음이 없음을 분명히 하다 make clear that *one* bears no malice / 딴마음을 품다 have two faces; play (a) double game
▶ 딴마음이 있어 그렇게 말한 것은 아니었다 I meant no harm in saying that. ⇌ I had no hidden motive in saying so.

딴말 1 〈관계없는 말〉 an irrelevant [improper] remark; an absurd remark
♦ 딴말을 하다 digress [wander] from the main subject
▶ 넌 딴말을 하고 있어 You are talking nonsense. ⇌ You are getting off on a tangent.
2 〈뒤집는 말〉 duplicity
♦ 딴말을 하다 break [go back on] *one's* word [promise]; be double-tongued
▶ 나중에 딴말 해도 소용 없다 You know, it's no use regretting afterwards [crying over spilt milk].
▶ 그렇게 굳게 약속했으니 지금 와서 딴말은 못

하겠지 After his solemn promises he cannot back down now.

딴맛 〈다른 맛〉 a different taste; 〈색다른 맛〉 a particular [peculiar] taste

딴사람 1 〈다른 사람〉 another person; someone else; a different person
♦ 딴사람들 the others; the rest 《of the company》 / 딴사람은 모르거니와 나로서는 for my own part; I don't know about others, but...
▶ 딴사람이 아니라 바로 사장이었다 It was nothing less [no less a personage] than the president.
▶ 그것은 누군가 딴사람이 해야 한다 Somebody else ought to do that.
▶ 제복 차림의 형은 아주 딴사람처럼 보였다 My brother looked quite another person in his uniform.
2 〈달라진 사람〉 a different [new] being; a changed being [man]
▶ 그는 아주 딴사람이 되었다 He is now a new being.
▶ 그는 10년 전과는 아주 딴사람처럼 보인다 He looks quite different from (what he was) ten years ago.
▶ 그녀는 완전히 딴사람이 된 것같다 She seems to be quite another person now.

딴살림 living apart; a separate living [livelihood]
—**딴살림하다** live in a separate house; live apart (from); establish a separate home
▶ 형제가 각기 딴살림한다 Each brother has his own home.

딴생각 〈다른 생각〉 another idea; a different intention; some other intention; 〈엉뚱한 생각〉 an ulterior motive; a secret purpose; an axe to grind ♦ 딴생각이 있다 have an ulterior motive [an axe to grind]

딴소리 an absurd remark ⇨ 딴말

딴은 〈과연〉 well; indeed; really; I see; to be sure
▶ 딴은 그렇다 Well, so it is. ⇌ Indeed you are right. ⇌ To be sure!
▶ 딴은 네 말도 그럴 듯하다 Hearing what you say, it sounds quite reasonable.
▶ 딴은 좋은 방법이지만 실행이 어렵다 A good plan, to be sure, but it is hardly practicable.

딴전 〈관계없는 언동〉 irrelevant remarks; an irrelevant act; 〈화제의 일탈〉 digression; deviation
♦ 딴전 보다 neglect *one's* duty; be negligent of *one's* duties / 딴전 부리다 make irrelevant [unrelated] remarks; miss [get off, get away from] the point; 〈시치미떼다〉 pretend ignorance 《of》; pretend indifference 《to, toward, about, as to》

딴쪽 〈다른 쪽〉 another [a different] direction; the other side

딴청 irrelevant remarks ⇨ 딴전

딴판 a completely different state of affairs; a quite unrelated situation
▶ 실제로 본 것은 들었던 것과 전연 딴판이었다 What I actually saw was something quite different from what I had heard.
▶ 한때 평화로웠던 시골이 완전 딴판으로 변했

딸

다 The once peaceful countryside has been entirely transformed.
▶그는 사람이 옛날과는 딴판이다 He is quite another man now.
▶그러면 완전 딴판이 된다 That makes all the difference in the world.

딸 a daughter
♦맏[막내]딸 one's first [last] daughter / 딸을 낳다 give birth to a daughter / 딸을 시집 보내다 marry off one's daughter

딸가닥 with a rattle ⇨ 달가닥
딸가닥거리다 clatter ⇨ 달가닥거리다
딸가당 with a clang ⇨ 달가당
딸가당거리다 clink ⇨ 달가당거리다
딸기 〔植〕 a strawberry ♦딸기를 따다 pick strawberries
■—밭 a strawberry bed [patch] —코 a red-spotted [red-speckled] swollen nose; a strawberry nose

딸꾹질 a hiccough; a hiccup ♦딸꾹질을 시작하다 get the hiccups; have an attack of hiccups / 딸꾹질을 멈추다 stop one's hiccups / 딸꾹질을 참다 catch a hiccup ─**딸꾹질하다** hiccough; hiccup; have the hiccups

딸랑딸랑 jingle-jingle; tinkle-tinkle; ting-a-ling
▶종이 딸랑딸랑 울렸다 The bell jingled.
▶양의 목에 단 방울이 산 속으로 딸랑딸랑 울려 퍼졌다 The sheep's bells tinkled through the hills.
─**딸랑딸랑하다** jingle; tinkle
♦딸랑딸랑하는 방울소리 the jingling of a bell

딸리다 〈부속되다〉 be attached [annexed] to; belong to; go with
♦시계가 딸린 라디오 a radio with a clock built in / 가구가 딸린 셋집 a furnished house to let / 나에게 딸린 식구 my (own) family; a family depending upon me / 아이한테 유모를 딸려 보내다 send a child accompanied by his nurse
▶이 책장에는 서랍이 둘 딸려 있다 This bookcase has two drawers.
▶그에게는 딸린 가족이 많다 He has a large family to support.
▶국회의원 한 사람에게 두 명의 비서가 딸린다 A member of the National Assembly is provided with two secretaries.

딸자식 ─**子息** 〈자기의〉 my daughter

땀¹ 〈흘리는〉 sweat; perspiration
♦구슬땀 beads of sweat / 식은땀 a cold sweat; night sweat / 진땀 a sticky [clammy] sweat / 땀 흘려 번 돈 money earned by the sweat of one's brow / 땀투성이가 되다 be soaked with perspiration; be bathed in perspiration; be all in the sweat
▶우리는 매일 땀 흘려 일하지 않으면 안된다 We must toil and sweat every day.
▶그는 20년 동안 땀 흘려 일해서 돈을 모았다 For twenty years, he has been saving money by [in] the sweat of his brow.
〈땀을〉 땀이 나다 〈사람이 주어〉 perspire / 땀이 많이 나다 sweat profusely [freely, copiously] / 옷에 땀이 흠뻑 배다 one's clothes are soaked [wet] with sweat; one's clothes are all sweaty / 땀이 배어 끈적거리다 be clammy with sweat; become moist with perspiration
▶등에서 땀이 줄줄 흘렀다 Perspiration was running [streaming] down my back.
▶그의 이마에는 구슬 같은 땀이 맺혔다 Great beads [drops] of perspiration stood on his forehead.
▶그녀의 얼굴에서 땀이 뚝뚝 떨어지고 있었다 Sweat was dripping from her face.
▶어제는 약간 땀이 날 정도로 따뜻했다 It was warm enough yesterday to make us slightly sweaty.
〈땀을〉 땀을 많이 흘리는 사람 a great sweater; one who perspires freely / 땀을 흘리다 sweat; be in a sweat; break into a sweat; perspire / 땀을 뻘뻘 흘리다 sweat [perspire] profusely; be dripping with sweat / 땀을 씻다 wipe sweat away / 이마의 땀을 닦다 mop one's brow; wipe (the) perspiration from one's forehead / 땀을 내어 감기를 떼다 sweat out a cold
▶나는 땀을 잘 흘린다 I sweat easily.
▶매일 한 번 땀을 흘리면 몸에 좋습니다 A sweat every day is good for you.
▶우리는 손에 땀을 쥐고 게임을 구경했다 We watched the game breathlessly [in breathless suspense].
〈땀에〉 땀에 젖어 끈적끈적한 손 a sweaty hand / 땀에 흠뻑 젖어 sweated all over; bathed in perspiration; drenched in sweat / 땀에 젖다 be wet with perspiration; be drenched [soaked] in [with] sweat
▶셔츠가 온통 땀에 젖었다 My shirt was thoroughly soaked with sweat.
▶그는 땀에 흥건히 젖을 정도로 열심히 일했다 He worked so hard (that) he was bathed in perspiration.

땀² 〈바느질의〉 a stitch

땀기 ─氣 a bit [trace] of sweat ♦손에 땀기가 있다 have a bit of sweat in one's palm; one's palm is a bit moist [sweaty]

땀나다 1 〈땀이 나다〉 the sweat comes out; the perspiration oozes out 《of one》; 〈사람이 주어〉 sweat; perspire
♦몹시 땀나다 perspire profusely [freely, copiously]
▶구두를 신고 있으면 발에 땀난다 My feet get sweaty in my shoes.
2 〈힘들다〉 be hard; be toilsome; take pains
▶그 숙제는 정말 땀나더라 The homework was really a horrid sweat.

땀내 the smell of sweat
♦땀내 나는 옷 clothes stinking with [of] sweat / 땀내 나는 손수건 a sweaty handkerchief / 땀내 나다 smell [stink] of sweat
▶그는 항상 땀내 나는 옷을 입고 있다 He always wears sweaty clothes.
▶그의 셔츠에서 땀내가 물씬 난다 His shirt smells really sweaty.

땀내다 induce perspiration; work up a sweat; sweat 《a patient》; throw sb into a sweat
♦이불을 쓰고 땀내다 work up a sweat covering oneself with bedclothes / 땀내어 체중을

줄이다 sweat off *one's* surplus weight [fat]
▶ 땀내면 나올 것이다 A sweat will do you good.
▶ 푹 땀내면 흔히 감기는 떨어진다 A good sweat often cures a cold.

땀들이다 cool (and refresh) *oneself*; cool off; dry *one's* sweat

땀등거리 a sweat shirt; underwear (for sweat) ⇨ 땀받이

땀띠 prickly heat; (美) (a) heat rash
▶ 누이는 매년 여름이면 땀띠가 난다 My sister gets heat rash every summer.
■—약 prickly heat powder; talcum powder

땀받이 a sweat shirt; 〈모자 안에 댄〉a sweat-band

땀방울 beads [drops] of sweat
▶ 그의 얼굴에 땀방울이 맺혔다 Drops of sweat gathered on his face.

땀빠지다 have a hard time of it ⇨ 땀빼다
♦ 땀빠지게 일하다 sweat away at a job; toil and moil

땀빼다 〈애를 먹다〉suffer severely; sweat (it out); have a hard time of it
▶ 거짓말을 했다가 땀뺐다 I sweated for the lie I had told.
▶ 그 문제를 푸느라고 땀뺐다 I took great pains to solve the problem. ⇌ I had a hard time in solving the problem.

땀질하다 chisel [knife, cut] out [off, away] unnecessary parts of 《wood》

땅[1] **1**〈대지〉the earth; 〈육지〉land; 〈땅바닥〉the ground
♦ 하늘과 땅 heaven and earth / 땅에서 50여 미터 위에 fifty and some odd meters above the ground / 땅에 구덩이를 파다 dig a hole in the ground / 땅이 꺼지다 the ground gives way [collapses, sinks] / 땅에 묻다 bury 《a thing》 in the ground
▶ 땅이 말라 먼지가 잘 일어난다 Dust rises easily because the ground is dry.
▶ 그는 불도저로 땅을 평평하게 했다 He leveled the ground with a bulldozer.
▶ 언 땅을 파기는 어렵다 It is difficult to dig the ground when it is frozen.
2〈토지〉land; a piece [lot, plot] of land; a landed property
♦ 땅부자 a great land owner / 넓은 땅 a large tract of land; broad acres / 3만평의 땅 a lot of thirty thousand *p'yŏng* / 금싸라기같은 땅 ground which is worth its weight in gold / 젖과 꿀이 흐르는 땅 land of milk and honey / 땅을 개간하다 clear [exploit] the land [ground] / 땅을 놀려 두다 keep land idle
▶ 이 땅은 넓이가 얼마나 될까? I wonder how large this land is.
▶ 그는 교외의 땅을 얼마쯤 샀다 He has bought some [a piece of] land in the suburbs.
3〈토양〉soil; earth; land
♦ 기름진 땅 fertile [rich] soil / 메마른 땅 poor [barren] soil / 땅을 갈다 till the soil; cultivate land / 땅을 걸우다 enrich [fertilize] the soil
▶ 이 땅은 토마토 재배에 적합하다 This soil is fit for the cultivation of tomatoes.
4〈영토〉(a) territory; a land

♦ 외국 땅을 밟다 set foot on foreign soil; enter a foreign country / 이국 땅에서 죽다 die in a strange land [a foreign country]
▶ 그는 3년만에 고국 땅을 밟았다 He stood on the ground of his homeland after three years' absence.
▶ 그 사절단은 우리 땅을 떠났다 The mission left our shores.
5 (비유) ▶ 도덕이 땅에 떨어졌다 Morality is at a low ebb.
▶ 그의 명성은 완전히 땅에 떨어졌다 He has entirely lost his reputation.
▶ 그는 땅이 꺼져라고 한숨을 내쉬었다 He gave [let out] a deep sigh.
■—사기꾼 a land swindler; a fake land broker

땅[2]〈총소리〉bang; with a bang; 〈쇳소리〉clang; with a clang
♦ 총을 땅 쏘다 bang a gun / (권총 등이) 땅 하고 울리다 go bang

땅값 land price ⇨ 지가(地價) ▶ 땅값이 치솟고 있다 Land prices are skyrocketing.

땅강아지 〔昆〕 a mole cricket

땅개〈개〉a dog built short; a dog with short legs; 〈사람〉a man of short stature

땅거미[1]〈저녁 어스름〉dusk; (evening) twilight
♦ 땅거미질 때 [무렵]에 in the gathering dusk; at dusk; toward evening; as dusk falls
▶ 땅거미가 지고 있었다 The dusk was gathering [falling, closing in].

땅거미[2]〔動〕a ground spider

땅광〈지하실〉a cellar

땅굴 —窟 a tunnel; an underground way [passage]
♦ 땅굴을 파다 build [bore, excavate] a tunnel 《through a mountain》
▶ 이것이 북한이 비무장지대에 몰래 파놓은 땅굴입니다 This is the tunnel the North Korean infiltrators have secretly dug under the Demilitarized Zone [DMZ].

땅기다 be cramped; have a cramp [stitch]
♦ 근육이 땅기다 have a cramp in the *one's* muscle / 옆구리가 땅기다 have a stitch in the *one's* side

땅꾼 a snake catcher [dealer]

땅내 the smell of soil; smelling of the ground
♦ 땅내 맡다 〈식물이〉take [strike] root; 〈동물이〉settle down in a place

땅덩이 land; 〈지구〉the earth; 〈국토〉a territory; 〈대륙〉a continent
▶ 러시아는 땅덩이가 크다 Russia has a large territory.

땅딸막하다 short and thick; fat and short; stumpy; chunky; pudgy; thickset; stocky; stodgy

땅딸보 a pudge; a stocky [dumpy] person; a chunky fellow

땅땅〈총성〉bang-bang; 〈쇳소리〉clang-clang
♦ 총을 땅땅 쏘다 keep banging a gun / 쇠를 땅 땅 두드리다 beat iron clang-clang

땅땅거리다 1〈큰소리치다〉talk big [tall, high and mighty, high-handedly]; brag; swagger

▶그는 대학에 들어갈 자신이 있다고 땅땅거리고 있다 He is bragging that he is confident to pass the college entrance exam.
▶땅땅거린다고 무서워할 내가 아니다 I am not the man to flinch at your high-handed talk.
2 ⇨ 땡땡거리다

땅뙈기 a patch of land; a small plot [piece] of land [field]

땅마지기 a few acres of field
▶그 사람 처자식 먹여 살릴 만한 땅마지기는 가졌다 He has a few acres of field, just enough to support his family.

땅바닥 the surface of the earth; the ground
♦땅바닥에 앉다 sit [squat] on the (bare) ground

땅벌 〔昆〕 a digger wasp; a sphex

땅벌레 〔昆〕 a grub; the larva of a ground beetle

땅볼 〔野〕 a grounder; a bounder
♦땅볼을 치다[잡다] knock [take] a grounder / 땅볼 안타를 치다 hit into the dirt
▶그는 유격수 앞으로 강한 땅볼을 쳤다 He hit a hard grounder to the short.

땅세 ―貰 land [ground] rent
♦땅세가 비싼 high-rented

땅속 ♦땅속의 보물 buried [underground, hidden] treasure / 땅속의 underground; subterranean / 땅속 깊이 뿌리를 내리는 나무 a tree striking root deep into the ground / 땅속에 묻히다 be buried in the earth [ground] / 땅속에서 파내다 dig out of the ground; unearth (treasures) / 땅속에서 일하다 work underground
▶매미는 애벌레기를 땅속에서 보낸다 Cicadas in the larval stage live underground [in the ground].

땅울림 a rumbling of the earth; 〈hear〉 subterranean rumbling

땅임자 a landowner; a landholder

땅재주 tumbling; a somersault; a somerset
♦땅재주를 넘다 perform [make] a somersault; somersault; tumble

땅콩 a groundnut; 〈美〉 a peanut ■―버터 peanut butter ―장수 a peanut vendor

땅파기 1 〈땅파는 일〉 digging the soil [earth]
2 〈어리석은 사람〉 a block-head; an ignorant person

땅파먹다 engage in farming [mining]; do farm [mine] work for a living; dig dirt for a living

땅풍뎅이 〔昆〕 a kind of ground beetle

땋다 〈머리를〉 braid 〈one's hair〉; plait
♦머리를 땋아 늘인 소녀 a girl with a plait [two plaits] (of hair) hanging down her back
▶그녀는 머리를 땋아 늘어뜨리고 있다 She wears her hair in plaits. ⇒ She has her hair hanging down the shoulder.

때¹ 1 〈시간·시각〉 time; an hour
♦식사[점심]때 meal [lunch] time
〈때가〉 때가 되면 [오면] in due course of time; in (due) time; with time / 때가 지남에 따라 as time goes by; in the course of time / 때가 가다 time passes [goes by, flies]
▶때가 지남에 따라 그 기억도 희미해졌다 As time passed, the memory of it became dim.
▶우리는 카드놀이에 정신이 팔려 때가 가는 줄도 몰랐다 We were so absorbed in playing cards that we had forgotten all about the time.
〈때를〉 때를 가리지 않고 at all times / 때를 정하여 at a fixed time; at regular intervals / 때를 어기지 않고 punctually; on time / 때를 보내다 pass one's time; spend time (in) / 때를 같이하다 agree in time
▶이 수탉은 때를 잘 맞춰서 운다 This rooster crows well.
▶이 괘종시계는 정확히 때를 알린다 This clock keeps [marks] accurate time.

2 〈…한 때·경우〉 a case; an occasion; a season; time; a conjuncture
♦위기 존망의 때 the critical moment / 때에 따라서는 as occasion requires [demands]; as the case may be / 때와 장소에 따라서는 should time and circumstances permit / 때와 장소를 가리지 않고 without the least respect [regardless] of time and place / 필요한 때에 in case of need; as occasion calls [demands] / 마침 좋은 때에 just at the right moment; just in time (for) / 위험[위급]한 때에 in (the) time [in times] of danger; at a critical moment / 무슨 일이 있을 때는 should emergency arise; in case [time, the hour] of need / 내가 실패했을 때는 in case I should fail / 좋지 않은 때에 오다 come at an unfavorable moment [time]
▶저녁을 먹고 있을 때 전화가 걸려 왔다 The telephone rang while I was having supper.
▶집을 나설 때는 날씨가 쾌청했다 The weather was lovely when I left home.
▶지금은 탁상공론이나 하고 있을 때가 아니다 This is no time for vain discussion.

3 〈기회〉 an opportunity; a chance; 〈시기〉 a season; (a) time; a moment
♦때를 얻지 못한 사람 a person who is out of tune with the times / 때를 못 만난 영웅 an unappreciated hero / 때가 나쁜 inopportune; unseasonable / 때를 얻은 timely; well-timed; opportune; seasonable / 때를 잘못 만난 ill-timed; untimely; inopportune; unseasonable / 때를 보아 at some convenient time; at a favorable opportunity / 때를 기다리다 wait [bide] one's time; wait for time (to do); wait for a favorable chance / 때를 노리다 watch for opportunity / 때를 놓치다 miss [lose, fail to catch] an opportunity / 때를 만나다 have luck; have one's day [time of prosperity]; be fortunate / 때를 놓치지 않다 save the tide / 때가 무르익기를 기다리다 wait for a ripe opportunity; wait till the ripe moment comes
▶무엇이나 다 때가 있는 법이다 There is a time for everything.
▶때가 오면 알게 된다 Time will show [tell].
▶자 때가 왔다 Now the time [chance] has come. ⇒ Now is the time [chance].
▶지금이야말로 우리가 궐기할 때다 It is high time for us to stand up.

4 〈철〉 season; time of the year
♦파종 때 seedtime; the seeding season / 추수 때 the harvest time / 내년[작년] 이맘 때 this

time next [last] year / 꽃 피는 때 the time of flowering; the flowering time / 때 아닌 더위 unseasonable heat
▶ 벚꽃이 조금 때 이르게 피었다 The cherry blossoms came out a little too early for the season.
5 〈시대·당시〉 the times; the time; the day
♦ 어느 때인지 at some unknown time / 그 때에는 in those days; at that time; then / 젊었을 때에 when (one was) young; in one's youth / 학교에 다니던 때에 in one's school days / 2차 대전 때에 at the time of the 2nd World War / 어릴 때부터 since one's childhood
▶ 때는 세종 15년이었다 It was in the 15th year of Sejong.
▶ 어릴 때부터 병을 앓은 적이 없다 I have never been sick [ill] since I was a child.
6 〈끼니〉 a meal; mealtime
♦ 두 때를 굶다 miss [skip, do not have] two meals / 때를 거르다 go without a meal / 간신히 때를 잇다 eke out a scanty livelihood [poor existence]
7 〈시제〉【文法】 the tense
♦ 때를 나타내는 temporal 《adverbs》
때² **1** 〈더러움〉 dirt; filth; grime
♦ 때가 끼다 [묻다] be soiled with dirt; become dirty [filthy]; become soiled / 때를 씻다 wash off the dirt / 때를 벗은 〈세련된〉 polished (in manners); refined; urbane; smart; 〈시골티를 벗은〉 free from boorishness / 때를 벗지 못한 unpolished; unrefined; uncouth; rustic; raw
▶ 흰 옷은 때를 잘 탄다 White clothes pick up dirt easily.
▶ 참, 때도 많이 나온다 Oh! What a lot of dirt rolls [comes] off!
2 〈인색함〉 meanness; stinginess
▶ 그는 하는 짓에 때가 끼었다 There is something mean in what he does.
3 〈누명〉 a false [an unjust] charge; 〈오명〉 a slur; a stain; a blot; disgrace; dishonor
♦ 도둑의 때를 벗다 clear oneself of a false charge of theft
때가다 〈잡혀가다〉 be taken 《to the police station》; be arrested
때구루루 rolling; rumbling; with a rolling [rumbling] sound
♦ 때구루루 구르다 roll over and over; keep rolling / 때구루루 굴리다 roll 《a ball》 over 《the floor》
때굴때굴 rolling ⇨ 데굴데굴
때그락거리다 keep clattering [rattling]; clatter; rattle
▶ 그릇이 때그락거린다 Dishes are clattering away.
▶ 상자 속의 연필이 때그락거린다 Pencils rattle in a box.
때그락때그락 clattering(ly); rattling(ly)
때까치 〔鳥〕 a shrike; a butcherbird
때깔 the shape and color of cloth; the color and charm of cloth; the colorful pattern
때꼽재기 (bits of) dirt; filth; grime
때꾼하다 sunken [hollow] from exhaustion
♦ 때꾼한 눈 sunken [hollow] eyes

때다¹ 〈불을〉 burn; kindle; make [build] a fire
♦ 난로를 때다 make a fire in the stove / 방에 불을 때다 heat the room
때다² solder ⇨ 때우다
때때로 sometimes; occasionally; once in a while; from time to time; now and then; off and on; on and off

> 解說 ***sometimes***는 「때때로 …하다」라는 긍정적인 함축성이 있는데 대해 ***occasionally***는 그보다 빈도가 낮고 「간혹 …할 뿐」이라는 부정적인 함축성이 있다. 이 두 단어의 위치는 always와 같은 위치에 쓰이는데, 부정어 앞에 쓸 수도 있으며, 문장의 어디든 임의로 쓰인다.

♦ 때때로 들르다 drop in once in a while
▶ 나는 때때로 그를 방문한다 I call on him from time to time.
▶ 때때로 소나기가 오겠습니다 There will be showers from time to time.
▶ 때때로 기회가 있으면 연주회에 간다 I go to the concert from time to time when an occasion presents itself.
때때옷 a colorful festive dress for children
때때중 a young Buddhist monk
때려눕히다 knock [strike, batter] sb down; stretch sb on the ground; send sb sprawling
♦ 여지없이 때려눕히다 pommel sb to a jelly
때려부수다 break [batter] down 《a house》; smash (up, down); knock [strike] sth to pieces
♦ 문을 때려부수다 batter the door down / 인습을 때려부수다 break old customs
▶ 그는 울타리를 때려부쉈다 He smashed down the fence.
▶ 아이들이 망치로 장난감을 때려부쉈다 The children smashed a toy with a hammer.
▶ 경찰은 자물쇠가 채워진 문을 때려부쉈다 The police broke down the locked door.
때려죽이다 knock [strike, beat, club] sb to death; strike sb dead; beat [thrash] the life out of sb
때려치우다 〈그만두다〉 give [throw] up; quit; abandon; relinquish
♦ 장사를 때려치우다 quit one's business / 직장을 때려치우다 throw up one's job / 학교를 때려치우다 give up [withdraw from] school
때로(는) sometimes; occasionally; at times; in some cases; on (some) occasion; once in a while
▶ 때로 큰 고기가 걸리는 일도 있다 You catch a big fish at times.
▶ 때로는 인생이 무의미한 것 같고 또 때로는 인생에 의미가 있는 것도 같다 Sometimes life appears senseless, and sometimes it seems to have meaning.
때리다 **1** 〈치다〉 strike; beat; knock; hit; thrash; give [deal, deliver] sb a blow; punch
♦ 호되게 때리다 give sb a good thrashing; strike sb hard / 녹초가 되도록 때리다 beat sb to jelly / 멍이 들도록 때리다 beat sb black and blue / 머리[얼굴]를 때리다 hit sb on the head [in the face] / 귀싸대기를 때리다 give sb

a box [lick] on the ear / 얼굴을 찰싹 때리다 give *sb* a nice slap in the face
▶ 때릴테면 때려봐! Strike me if you dare!
▶ 그는 아이의 볼기를 찰싹 때렸다 He spanked her child on the buttocks.
▶ 그는 몹시 화가 나서 아들의 따귀를 때렸다 He got very angry and struck his son on the ear.
▶ 빗발이 창문을 세차게 때렸다 The rain lashed [beat] against the window.
▶ 그는 오늘 공을 잘 때리고 있다 He is hitting the ball well today.
2 〈비난하다〉 attack; charge; criticize; denounce
♦ 신문에서 때리다 write against *sb*; attack [pound] *sb* in the newspaper

때마침 just in time; at the right moment; in the nick of time; in good time; 〈다행히〉 fortunately; luckily; as good luck would have it
▶ 때마침 강풍이 불기 시작했다 Just then a strong wind began to blow.
▶ 나는 때마침 지나가던 택시를 잡아탔다 I took a taxi which fortunately happened to be passing by.
▶ 때마침 비가 내려 야구 경기는 중단되었다 As it started raining, the baseball game was called off.

때맞다 timely; well-timed; seasonable; opportune
♦ 때맞은 말 a seasonable [an opportune] remark / 때맞은 비 a timely [seasonable] rain / 때맞은 원조 timely aid [help] / 때맞게 just in time; in good time; at the right moment; at a proper time

때문 ♦ …때문에 because (of); on account of; by reason of; owing to; due to; thanks to; as; for; since / 신병 때문에 on account of illness / 부주의[태만] 때문에 through carelessness [negligence] / 그[이] 때문에 for that [this] reason / 달리 좋은 것이 없기 때문에 for want of a better *one*
▶ 너 때문에 몹시 걱정했다 You have caused me great anxiety.
▶ 짙은 안개 때문에 그들은 착륙하지 못했다 Owing to the dense fog, they were not able to land.
▶ 우리는 비 때문에 출발을 연기했다 We put off our departure because of the rain.
▶ 할 일이 많기 때문에 일요일에 낚시질하러 갈 수가 없다 Since I have a lot of work to do, I can not go fishing on Sunday.
▶ 시험이 다가오기 때문에 열심히 공부해야 한다 The test is approaching, so I have to study hard.
▶ 그것은 지면이 없기 때문에 여기서 논할 수 없다 It cannot be discussed here for lack of space.
▶ 산이 귀중한 것은 높기 때문이 아니라 나무가 있기 때문이다 A mountain is valuable, not because it is high, but because it is wooded.

때묻다 be defiled; be soiled; be stained; become dirty [filthy, grimy]
♦ 때묻은 정치가 a tainted politician / 때묻지 않은 undefiled; stainless; clean; pure / 조금도 때묻지 않은 생활을 하다 lead a life pure from any blemish

때물 boorishness; rudeness; rusticity
♦ 때물을 벗은 사람 a polished [refined] person / 때물을 벗다 be polished [refined]

때아닌 unseasonable; untimely; unexpected; inopportune; out of season
♦ 때아닌 꽃 a blossom out of season; off-season flowering / 때아닌 손님 an unexpected visitor / 그녀의 때아닌 죽음 her untimely death / 때아닌 시각에 at an unseasonable hour; at an ungodly hour / 때아닌 꽃이 피다 bloom out of season
▶ 그들은 때아닌 천둥소리에 놀랐다 They were surprised at the unseasonable thunder.

때없이 regardless of the time; at irregular intervals
♦ 때없이 들락날락하다 go in and out regardless of the time / 때없이 돈을 달라고 하다 ask for money at an improper hour

때우다 1 〈땜질하다〉 solder; tinker; braze; 〈깁다〉 patch up; darn
♦ 냄비를 때우다 tinker [solder] a pan
2 〈대강 처리 넘기다〉 make shift 《with》; manage 《with》; substitute
♦ 도넛으로 점심을 때우다 substitute doughnuts for regular lunch; make a lunch of doughnuts / 저녁을 국수로 때우다 dine off a bowl of noodle
3 ⇨ 액땜(∼하다)

땔감 fuel

땔나무 firewood; kindling (wood)
■ ─꾼 a firewood gatherer; 〈소박한 사람〉 a simple [naive] person

땜¹ 〈액땜〉 an escape 《from》
─땜하다 forestall 《a disaster》 with a lesser sacrifice
■ 액─ an escape from evil [a calamity]

땜² tinkering ⇨ 땜질
─납 solder; pewter : 땜납으로 때우다 solder ─인두 a soldering iron [copper] ─장이 a tinker; a tinsmith

땜질 1 〈냄비 등의〉 tinkering; soldering
─땜질하다 tinker; solder; mend (kettles)
2 〈옷 등의〉 a patchwork
─땜질하다 patch up 《a paper screen》
3 〈미봉책〉 a makeshift; a patchwork; a stopgap ─땜질하다 temporize

땟국 dirt; filth; soil; grime
♦ 땟국이 흐르는 옷 soiled [dirty] clothes / 얼굴에 땟국이 끼다 have dirt on *one's* face

땟물 1 〈몸〉 figure; form; shape; appearance
♦ 땟물이 훤하다 have a good [graceful] figure; be fair of form; be smart
2 〈더러운 물〉 dirty [filthy] water; washings

땡¹ 1 〈노름판에서〉 two cards of the same denomination; a pair
♦ 땡잡다 hold a pair
2 〈행운〉 (a stroke of) good fortune; (美) a lucky [good] break ■ 장─ a pair of tens

땡² 〈소리〉 a clang
♦ 땡 소리 나다 clang; clangor

땡감 an unripe [astringent] persimmon

땡그랑거리다 clang; jingle; ring; tinkle

▶ 풍경이 땡그랑거리기 시작했다 A wind bell began to tinkle.
▶ 빈 깡통이 땡그랑거리며 굴러갔다 An empty can went clattering along the road.

땡땡 〈종소리〉 ding-dong; clang-clang
◆ 땡땡 울리는 종소리 the clanging of a 《school》 bell / 땡땡 울리다 ding-dong; ring; clang
▶ 종이 땡땡 울린다 The bell is ringing. ⇌ The bell clangs.
▶ 시계가 땡땡 친다 The clock is chiming.

땡땡이 〈장난감〉 a toy drum; a rattle

땡땡하다 hard; tight; taut; compact
◆ 땡땡한 감[근육] a hard persimmon [muscle] / 배가 땡땡하도록 먹다 stuff [load] one's stomach with food; stuff [gorge] oneself with food; eat one's fill
▶ 암소의 젖이 불어나서 땡땡하다 The udders of the cow are bursting with milk.

땡잡다 〈수나다〉 make a lucky [big] hit; run into good luck; strike a bonanza; (美) hit the jackpot; (口) make a killing
◆ 주식으로 땡잡다 make a killing in stocks
▶ 듣자 하니 자네 증권에서 땡잡았다면서 I hear you've pulled off a nice pile on the stock market.

떠가다 float [fly] away

떠꺼머리 a pigtail
■─총각[처녀] an old bachelor [maid]

떠나다 1【장소를 옮겨가다】〈출발하다〉 leave; start (off); depart 《from》; set off [out]; take leave of; go away [off]; 〈열차 등이〉 pull out; 〈비행기가〉 take off; 〈배가〉 set sail; sail out; clear 《port》; 〈떨어지다〉 separate; part from [with]; 〈분해되다〉 fall apart
◆ 고향을 떠나다 leave one's native place; leave home / 한국을 떠나다 leave [depart from] Korea / 여행을 떠나다 start on a journey; leave on a trip / 미국으로 떠나다 leave [depart, sail] for America / 아침 일찍 떠나다 start early in the morning / 멀리 떠나 살다 live far apart
▶ 언제 떠나십니까? When are you leaving?
▶ 이제 우리가 떠나야 할 때다 It is time we left [for us to leave].
▶ 그는 말없이 떠났다 He went away without a word.
▶ 그 아이는 어머니 곁을 떠나지 않는다 The child is always at his mother's side.
▶ 그는 고향을 떠나 부산으로 갔다 He left his hometown for Pusan.
▶ 그녀는 고향을 떠나 하숙 생활을 하고 있다 She lives in a lodging away from her hometown.
▶ 고향집을 떠난지 10년이 된다 It is ten years since I left home.
▶ 사람들이 하나 둘 떠나고 어느새 그녀와 나만 남았다 One by one the people left and soon I was alone with her.
2【관계를 끊다】〈물러나다〉 resign (from) 《one's post》; leave [quit, relinquish] 《one's post》; 〈벗어나다〉 be estranged from; cut oneself off
◆ 이해 득실을 떠나 from a disinterested motive / 속세를 떠나서 away from the tainting influence of the world / 부모 슬하를 떠나다 leave one's parental roof [home] / 공직을 떠나다 retire [resign] from public life / 회사를 떠나다 leave (the service of) the company
▶ 직장을 떠나야 할 날이 왔다 The day has come for me to quit my job [to resign from my office].
▶ 정치를 떠나서 이 문제를 생각할 수는 없다 It is impossible to consider this matter apart from politics.
▶ 민심은 이미 현정부로부터 떠났다 Public opinion is estranged from the government.
3〈죽다〉◆ 세상을 떠나다 die; pass away [on]; be gone; depart (from) this life
4〈잊혀지다〉 be forgotten; pass out of mind
▶ 그 생각이 뇌리에서 떠나지 않는다 The idea haunts me. ⇌ I cannot get rid of the idea.
▶ 그 날의 참혹한 광경이 머리에서 떠나지 않는다 I cannot forget the cruel sight of that day.

떠내다 1〈액체를〉 scoop (up); dip up [out]; ladle out
◆ 국물을 떠내다 ladle [spoon up] soup / 국자로 수프를 떠내다 dip out soup with a ladle
2〈나무 등을〉 scoop up; 〈돌을〉 quarry (out)
◆ 뗏장을 떠내다 scoop up a piece of sod [turf]

떠내려가다 be washed [swept, carried, borne] away; drift (away) [down]
◆ 바다로 떠내려가다 be washed out to sea / 하류로 떠내려가다 be carried down the river
▶ 어젯밤의 호우로 다리가 떠내려갔다 The torrential rain last night carried the bridge away.

떠다니다 1〈하늘·물 위를〉 float (about); fly (about); drift (about)
▶ 하늘에는 구름이 떠다녔다 The clouds floated across the sky.
▶ 배는 물결치는 대로 밤새 떠다녔다 The ship drifted about all night at the mercy of the waves.
2 ⇨ 떠돌다

떠다밀다 push; thrust; shove; force aside
◆ 사람을 떠다밀다 push people aside / 떠다밀고 들어가다 break into / 아무를 물로 떠다밀다 push sb into the water

떠돌다 1〈방랑·배회하다〉 wander; roam; rove; tramp 《abroad》; be a bagabond
◆ 떠도는 wandering 《musician》; roaming
▶ 그는 20년 동안이나 이곳 저곳을 떠돌았다 He drifted from place to place for twenty years.
▶ 그는 여러 회사를 떠돌았다 He moved from company to company.
2〈소문이 나다〉 get about [abroad, around]; go the rounds; get [take] air
▶ 그녀에 대한 이상한 소문이 떠도는 거 너 아니? Do you know that strange rumors about her are in the air?
▶ 하는 짓이 그렇고 그래서 그에게 나쁜 소문이 떠돌았다 His conduct gave rise to scandals.
3〈물 위를 배회하다〉 drift (about, away); be adrift; float; 〈공중을〉 float (in the sky); hover

▶ 구름이 하늘에 떠돌았다 The clouds floated across the sky.
▶ 그 배는 바다를 떠돌고 있었다 The boat was drifting about in the sea.
▶ 대기에는 희미한 봄기운이 떠돌고 있다 There is a faint suggestion of spring in the air.

떠돌이 〈방랑자〉 a wanderer; a vagabond; a tramp; a vagrant; a waif; a drifter; 〈부랑자〉 《美》 a hobo
▶ 그에게는 다소 떠돌이 기질이 있다 He has a dash [touch] of the Bohemian in him.
━**노동자** a traveling [wandering] laborer; a drifter; a job-hopper ━**별** ⇨ 행성(行星) ━**생활** a wandering life

떠들다¹ 1 〈시끄럽게 지껄이다〉 gabble boisterously [clamorously]; gaggle; wag *one's* tongue [jaw] 《noisily, wildly》; 〈시끄럽게 하다〉 make a noise [hubbub]; raise a clamor; be boisterous [uproarious, clamorous], clamor; 〈외치다〉 cry; shout; utter a cry
♦ 〈여럿이〉 와글와글 떠들다 make much noise; be noisy / 술마시고 떠들다 have [go on] a spree; (drink and) make merry
▶ 아이들이 떠들며 뛰놀고 있다 The children are romping about.
▶ 그는 한시간 동안이나 계속 떠들었다 He rattled on for an hour on end.
▶ 그렇게 떠들지 마라 Don't make such a noise.
▶ 너무 떠드는구나, 조용히 해 You're making too much noise. Shut up!
2 〈요구·반대하여〉 clamor
♦ 임금 인하에 반대하여 떠들다 clamor against a wage cut.
▶ 그 젊은이는 입장시켜달라고 떠들었다 The young man clamored for admission.
3 〈소란피우다〉 《美》 kick up a row; raise a dust [racket]; make a disturbance; 〈법석 대다〉 make much ado; bustle 《about》; (make a) fuss 《about》
▶ 하찮은 일로 떠들지 마라 Don't make a fuss about trifles.
▶ 이것은 신문에서 떠들었던 문제다 This matter was noised about in the newspaper.
▶ 그렇게 떠들 것까진 없잖아? What's the use of making such a stir?
▶ 이제 와서 떠들어야 소용없다 It's too late to make a fuss now.
4 〈소문나다〉 be rumored; gossip [talk] about; be in everybody's mouth
▶ 그 장관은 그만둘거라고들 떠들고 있다 A rumor is current [afloat, in the air] that the minister will resign.

떠들다² 〈조금 쳐들다〉 turn up [lift, raise] an edge of 《an object》
▶ 나는 모기장을 떠들고 잠자는 아기를 들여다 봤다 I lifted up a corner of the mosquito net and looked at the sleeping baby.

떠들썩거리다 〈소란하다〉 all make noise; make a hubbub; 〈술렁대다〉 all make an uproar; make a row; agitate ⇨ 떠들다¹, 떠들썩하다¹
♦ 몹시 떠들썩거리다 make a hell of a noise / 하찮은 일로 크게 떠들썩거리다 make a great fuss about trifles; raise a storm in a teacup
▶ 종업원들이 월급을 인상하라고 떠들썩거리고 있다 The employees are making an uproar clamoring for a raise of their salaries.

떠들썩하다¹ 1 〈시끄럽다〉 noisy; boisterous; uproarious; clamorous
♦ 떠들썩한 교실 a noisy classroom / 떠들썩한 선거운동 an election campaign with fife and drum / 떠들썩하게 noisily; boisterously; clamorously; uproariously
▶ 이웃집 아이들은 언제나 떠들썩하다 My neighbor's kids are always making noise.
▶ 어젯밤에는 떠들썩해서 잠을 자지 못했다 The noise kept me awake last night.
▶ 바깥이 떠들썩하다. 무슨 일일까? There's a hubbub outside. What's happened [the matter]?
2 〈어수선하다〉 turbulent; troubled; disturbed; unquiet; agitated
▶ 나라 안이 떠들썩하다 The whole country is in (a) turmoil [a state of unrest].
▶ 세상이 떠들썩하다 We are living in troubled times.
3 〈야단스럽다〉 excited; agog; agitated; 〈여론·소문이〉 sensational; much discussed; making the rounds 《of》; noised about; 《be》 abroad
▶ 이것이 세상을 떠들썩하게 한 사건이다 This is a sensational [much-talked-about] affair.
▶ 이 사건은 세상을 떠들썩하게 했다 The event has kept the world astir.

떠들썩하다² 〈떠들려 있다〉 slightly lifted [raised]
▶ 이불 끝이 좀 떠들썩하다 The end of quilt is slightly raised.

떠들어대다 be terribly noisy; raise a clamor; raise [make] an uproar; fuss about
▶ 그는 늘 하찮은 일로 떠들어댄다 He always makes a fuss about trifles.

떠들치다 1 lift an edge of
2 〈비밀을 들춰내다〉 disclose; divulge; reveal; expose; lay bare
♦ 비밀을 떠들치다 reveal a secret

떠름하다 1 〈조금 떫다〉 somewhat astringent [puckery, rough]
♦ 떠름한 감 a puckery persimmon / 떠름한 포도주 rough wine
2 〈심드렁하다〉 glum; sullen; sulky; sour; 〈마음 내키지 않다〉 indisposed; reluctant; 〈미심쩍다〉 doubtful; suspicious; questionable; unreliable
♦ 떠름하게 대답하다 give a halfhearted answer / 떠름한 얼굴을 하다 make a glum [wry] face; look grim [sullen]
3 【마음에 걸리다】 〈사람이 주어〉 feel uneasy 《about》; be anxious [nervous] 《about》; 〈사물이 주어〉 weigh on *one's* mind
▶ 그의 말이 나에게 무척 떠름하다 His remarks weigh heavily with me.

떠맡기다 1 leave [commit] 《a matter》 to *sb's* care; entrust *sb* with 《a task》; saddle *sb* with; 〈가짜 등을〉 impose *sth* on [upon] *sb*
♦ 아무에게 일을 억지로 떠맡기다 force [thrust, shove (off)] work on *sb* / 어린애를

시어머니에게 떠맡기다 commit one's child to the care of one's mother-in-law / 나쁜 물건을 떠맡기다 palm [impose] a bad article upon sb / 말썽거리를 떠맡기다 saddle sb with an encumbrance
▶ 그는 끔찍한 일을 내게 떠맡겼다 He forced [thrust] his odious work on me.

떠맡다 1 〈남의 일을 맡다〉 undertake; assume; take on 《a job》; take 《a job》 on oneself; 〈담당하다〉 be charged with; take charge of; 〈인수하다〉 take over 《another's business》; 〈계승하다〉 succeed to 《a business》
♦ 일을 떠맡다 undertake a job; take a job on oneself / 의장의 역할을 떠맡다 accept [take on] post of chairman / 사건의 처리를 떠맡다 agree to take care of an affair / 〈변호사가〉 사건을 떠맡다 undertake [be entrusted with] a case / 업무를 떠맡다 take over sb's business
▶ 광고하는 것은 내가 떠맡겠다 I will take it on myself to give publicity to it.
▶ 그 아기는 내가 떠맡겠다 I will take charge of the baby.
2 〈책임지다〉 answer for; take responsibility for; hold oneself responsible for; 〈보증하다〉 guarantee
♦ 부채를 떠맡다 hold oneself liable for a debt; 〈남의 부채를〉 shoulder another's debt
▶ 자네가 손해를 본다면 내가 떠맡겠네 I'll answer [make up] for your possible losses.
▶ 자금 조달은 내가 떠맡겠다 I'll see (to it) that the funds are raised. ⇌ I'll undertake to raise the funds.

떠메다 〈어깨로〉 lift sth up on one's shoulder; carry [take, bear] sth on the shoulder

떠밀다 push ⇨ 떼밀다

떠받다 1 〈머리·뿔로〉 butt; 〈뿔·엄니 등으로〉 gore; 〈뿔로〉 horn
♦ 머리로 떠받다 butt sb with one's head
▶ 소가 그를 떠받았다 A bull butted him.
2 ⇨ 떠받치다

떠받들다 1 〈쳐들어 올리다〉 raise up; hold up; lift (up); hoist; (口) boost
♦ 떠받들어 담을 넘게 하다 boost sb over a wall [fence]
2 〈공경하다〉 revere; respect; look up to; 〈추대하다〉 set up; set sb on a pedestal; 〈소중히 여기다〉 hold sb dear; make [think] much of; have a great regard for [for]; 〈섬기다〉 serve faithfully; take good care of
♦ 어른으로 떠받들다 revere [set up, look up to] sb as one's elder / 부모를 떠받들다 be filial [devoted] to one's parents; be a good son [daughter] to one's parents / 스승으로 떠받들다 look up to sb as one's teacher

떠받치다 support; bolster [shore, prop] up
♦ 기둥으로 벽을 떠받치다 support a wall with a post / 지팡이로 몸을 떠받치다 support oneself with a stick
▶ 그녀는 손으로 턱을 떠받치고 창 밖을 내다보고 있었다 She was looking out of the window, resting her chin on her hands.

떠버리 〈수다쟁이〉 a rattler; a chatterbox; 〈허풍선이〉 a boaster; a braggart; (口) a gasbag

떠벌리다 1 〈과장하다〉 brag; exaggerate; blow; talk big [tall]; 〈떠들어대다〉 wag one's tongue [jaw(s)]; rattle on [away, off]
▶ 그는 술에 취하면 벌써 아내 얘기를 거침없이 떠벌린다 When he gets drunk, he is ready to speak amorously [fondly] of his wife.
2 〈크게 차리다〉 set up sth on a large scale

떠보다 1 〈저울로 달아보다〉 weigh sth; check the weight
2 〈사람됨을 알아보다〉 try [test] sb's character [caliber]; size up sb
♦ 아무의 역량을 떠보다 put sb through 《his》 paces
3 〈남의 속을 가늠하다〉 sound; fathom; feel
♦ 아무의 속을 떠보다 sound (out) [feel] sb [sb's views] (on a matter); fathom sb's thoughts; throw [put] out a feeler / 아무의 속을 넌지시[슬쩍] 떠보다 sound sb's opinion in a roundabout way; beat about the bush
▶ 적의 사정을 떠볼 필요가 있다 We need to spy on the enemy's movements.
▶ 그의 속마음을 떠보았나? Have you sounded him out?

떠오르다 1 〈위로 솟아오르다〉 rise [come up] to the surface 《of water》; surface; float; 〈다시〉 refloat; be refloated; 〈공중에〉 rise; rise to [in] the sky
▶ 잠수함이 수면으로 떠올랐다 The submarine rose [came] to the surface.
▶ 익사체는 아직 떠오르지 않았다 The drowned body hasn't been recovered yet.
▶ 지평선 위로 태양이 떠오르고 있다 The sun is rising [going up] above the horizon.
▶ 그는 물 속으로 뛰어들더니 숨을 쉬려고 수면으로 떠올랐다 He dived into the water and came up to the surface for air.
2 〈생각이 나다〉 come [flit, flash, shoot] across [into] one's mind; come into one's head; occur to one; hit [strike] one; burst [dawn] upon one
▶ 그 생각이 문득 머리에 떠오른다 The idea pops into my head.
▶ 이 말을 들으면 언제나 대학 시절의 사건이 머리에 떠오른다 This word always reminds me of an incident in my college school days.
▶ 좋은 생각이 떠올랐다 A capital idea occurred to [burst upon, struck] me. ⇌ I hit upon an excellent plan.
▶ 수사관들 심중에 그의 이름이 떠올랐다 His name came [flashed] across the minds of the Criminal Investigators.
3 〈나타나다〉 ▶ 그녀의 입가에는 상냥한 미소가 떠올랐다 There was a sweet smile playing about her lips.
▶ 그 산은 안개 속에서 커다랗게 떠올랐다 The mountain loomed large in the mist.
▶ 그 산은 푸른 하늘을 배경으로 하여 뚜렷하게 떠오르고 있다 The mountain is standing out in sharp relief against the blue sky.

떠죽거리다 〈젠 체하고 지껄이다〉 boast; talk boastfully [big]; swagger; 〈싫은 체하고 사양하다〉 make an outward show of declining

떠지다 1 〈눈이〉 《one's eyes》 open; wake (up); (become) awake; (비유) come [be

떡¹

brought] to *one's* sense; awake from an illusion ♦현실에 눈이 떠지다 be awakened to the stern realities 《of life》
떡¹ 1〈먹는〉 rice cake
♦갓 빚은 떡 rice cake fresh from the dresser / 떡을 빚다 shape dough for cakes / 떡을 치다 pound steamed rice into cake
2 (비유) ♦남을 떡 주무르듯 하다 lead *sb* by the nose; turn [twist] *sb* round [around] *one's* (little) finger; have *sb* well in hand / 그림의 떡 (a) pie in the sky
▶나는 웬 떡이냐 하고 그 제의를 승락했다 I jumped at the proposal.
▶이게 웬 떡이냐? What a welcome windfall! ⇒ It's a gift from the gods.
■가래─ a bar rice cake ■─가래 a piece of rice cake ─가루 rice flour: 떡가루를 빻가 pound rice into flour / 떡가루를 반죽하다 knead dough / 떡가루를 찌다 steam rice flour ─고물 covering [coating] for rice cakes ─국 rice-cake soup (prepared with slices of rice cake, beef, eggs, etc.) ─만두국 rice cake and dumpling soup ─메 a mallet used to pound rice for cakes ─방아 a rice-flour mill: 떡방아를 찧다 make rice flour; pound rice into flour ─보 a person who is crazy about rice cakes ─볶이 a broiled dish of sliced rice cake, meat, eggs, seasoning, etc. ─산적 shish kebab made of sliced rice cake and meat ─살 various forms used to press patterns [designs, markings] into rice cake ─소 stuffing (for rice cakes) ─쌀 rice for making rice cake ─집 a rice-cake shop ─충이 ⇨ 떡(～보)
떡² 1〈벌어진 모양〉 wide (open); 〈split〉 widely
♦입을 떡 벌리고 with *one's* mouth wide open
2 〈들어맞는 모양〉《fit》 exactly; to a T
3 〈버티는 모양〉 firmly; resolutely
♦떡 버티고 서다 stand firmly [fast]; take a firm stand
떡갈나무 〈植〉 an (evergreen) oak (tree)
떡국이 농간한다 (속담) Years know more than books.
떡밥 (a) paste bait; paste
떡벌어지다 1〈퍼지다〉 spread (out); extend; widen; stretch; outstretch
♦가슴이 떡벌어지다 have a broad chest; be broad of chest / 어깨가 떡벌어지다 be broad-[square-]shouldered
2 〈널리 소문나다〉 get about [abroad, around]; go the rounds; get [take] air; be abroad [current, in circulation] 《about》
3 〈활짝 열리다〉 open wide; be wide-open; gape; 〈터져서〉 burst [split] open
♦놀라서 입이 떡벌어지다 be agape with wonder [surprise]; be in open-mouthed amazement
떡심 1〈힘줄〉 a tendon; a sinew; tough part of beef **2** 〈끈질긴 사람〉 a man of stubborn nature; a stiff-necked fellow; a tough guy
떡쑥 〈植〉 a cottonweed; a cudweed
떡잎 〈植〉 a seed leaf [lobe]; a cotyledon; a young leaf; 〈싹〉 a bud; a sprout
▶될성부른 나무는 떡잎부터 알아본다 (속담)

Genius displays itself even in childhood. ⇒ A fine child becomes a fine gentleman.
떡 줄 놈은 생각도 않는데 김칫국부터 마신다 (속담) Don't count your chickens before they are hatched.
떡판 ─板 1〈떡치는 판〉 a pounding board for making rice cakes; 〈절편판〉 a wooden rice-cake mold **2** 〈여자의 엉덩이〉 a woman's buttocks [bottom]
떡 해 먹을 집안 (속담) a troubled [trouble-ridden] family
떨거지 *one's* relatives [kindred, kinsmen]
떨기 a bunch; a cluster; a root; a plant
♦한 떨기 장미 a cluster of roses
떨다¹ 〈몸을〉 tremble; quiver; quake; shake; shiver; 〈전율하다〉 shudder; thrill; 〈목소리를〉 wobble; 〈진동하다〉 vibrate
♦와들와들[사시나무 떨듯] 떨다 tremble all over [like an aspen leaf]; be all of [in] a tremble; shiver like a jelly / 흥분하여 몸을 떨다 tremble with excitement
▶그 아이는 공포로 몸을 떨고 있었다 The child was trembling with [for] fear.
▶그 여자는 뱀을 보고 벌벌 떨었다 She shuddered at the sight of the snake.
▶그는 입술을 떨며 화를 냈다 His lips trembled in anger.
▶그는 추위로 몸을 덜덜 떨고 있다 He is shivering all over with cold.
떨다² 1〈붙은 것을〉 shake down; brush 《dust》 off 《one's coat》; 〈담뱃재 등을〉 knock off
♦먼지를 떨다 dust 《furniture》; shake [beat] off the dust / 자리〈담요〉를 떨다 shake [beat] a mat [blanket] / 저고리의 먼지를 솔로 떨다 brush *one's* jacket
▶그는 책장의 먼지를 떨었다 He dusted the bookcase.
▶그는 바지에 붙은 진흙을 떨었다 He beat the dirt [mud] from his trousers.
2 〈공제하다〉 deduct; take off; cut off
♦월급에서 세금을 떨다 take tax off *one's* pay
3 〈팔다 남은 것을〉 sell [clear] off [out]; dispose of; close out 《a stock of shoes》
♦재고품을 떨다 clear out a stock; have a clearance sale
4 〈우수리를〉 cut off [cast away, omit, discard] 《fractions》
♦우수리를 떨고 800원만 주다 give only 800 won knocking off the odd sum
5 〈주판·셈을〉 calculate anew; 〈전자계산기의〉 clear
6 〈주머니·돈을〉 empty
♦주머니를 떨다 empty *one's* purse
떨다³ 〈애교 등을〉 display; pretend; show
♦애교를 떨다 display *one's* charm; turn on the charm; be profuse of *one's* smiles / 수다를 떨다 wag *one's* tongue; rattle on / 엄살을 떨다 pretend to be in pain / 극성을 떨다 grow impatient; get upset
떨떠름하다 1〈맛이〉 astringent; puckery
▶이 감은 떨떠름하다 This persimmon has a very puckery taste.
2 〈내키지 않다〉 indisposed 《to do, for》; reluctant; unwilling

▶어두운 길을 혼자 가기가 떨떠름하다 I am scared of going my way alone in the dark.
▶그는 우리와 함께 가는 것이 떨떠름한 모양이다 He seems to feel indisposed to come with us.
3 〈꺼림칙하다〉 uneasy; concerned; anxious; nervous; 〈서술적〉 weigh on *one's* mind; lie at *one's* heart
▶일은 해결되었으나 뒷맛이 떨떠름하다 The matter was brought to a settlement but it makes me uncomfortable.

떨떨하다 1 〈천하다〉 mean; shabby; humble; wretched; unbecoming; indecent ♦ 떨떨한 사내 a good-for-nothing (fellow) / 옷맵시가 떨떨하다 be shabbily [poorly] dressed
2 〈내키지 않다〉 disinclined 《to do》; reluctant 《to do》; 〈서술적〉 be in no mood [humor] 《to do》; have no inclination 《to do》
▶거기에 가기가 떨떨하다 I'm not very keen on going there.

떨리다[1] 〈몸이〉 shake; tremble; shiver; shudder; quiver; 〈목소리 등이〉 wobble; waver; 〈현(絃) 등이〉 vibrate; 〈이가〉 chatter
♦ 떨리는 손 trembling [shaky] hands / 떨리는 목소리 a trembling [quavering] voice / 추위서 떨리다 shiver with [from] cold; quiver from cold / 무서워서 떨리다 tremble from fear; shiver with fright / 사지가 떨리다 tremble in every limb / 덜덜 떨리다 be all of [in] a tremble; be (up) on the tremble / 떨리는 목소리로 노래하다 sing with a quaver [trill]; quaver; trill / 떨리는 소리로 몇 마디 하다 quaver out a few words / 떨리는 손으로 붙잡다 take *sth* with trembling [quivering] fingers
▶나뭇잎이 바람에 떨리고 있다 The leaves are trembling in the wind.
▶그의 목소리는 분노로 떨리고 있었다 His voice was shaking [trembling, quivering] with anger.
▶그것을 생각하는 것만으로도 몸이 떨린다 The very thought of it makes me tremble.
▶현(絃)이 떨렸다 The string vibrated.
▶나는 추위[공포]로 이가 덜덜 떨렸다 My teeth chattered with cold [fright].

떨리다[2] **1** 〈떨어지다〉 be shaken [beaten, brushed] off; come out [off]; be removed
▶담요의 먼지가 잘 떨리지 않는다 The dust in the blanket won't come out.
2 〈제거되다〉 be excluded [eliminated, removed, left out]; 〈쫓겨나다〉 be dismissed [discharged, expelled]; get fired; (口) get sacked
♦ 채용시험에서 떨리다 be plucked in the examination for service / 공직에서 떨리다 be removed [ousted] from public office; be purged from public life
▶지원자의 20명 이상이 시험에서 떨리었다 More than twenty candidates were plucked in the examination.

떨어내다 beat off; shake [strike] off
♦ 먼지를 떨어내다 brush off dust; dust 《*one's* coat》 / 나무에서 열매를 떨어내다 shake down fruits from a tree; shake fruits off the tree

떨어뜨리다 1 〈아래로〉 drop; let fall [drop]; throw down; dump; 〈고개를〉 hang; drop; droop
♦ 폭탄을 떨어뜨리다 drop bombs (on) / 컵을 떨어뜨리다 let a cup fall; drop a cup / 나무를 흔들어서 밤을 떨어뜨리다 shake chestnuts off a tree / 고개를 떨어뜨리고 with a hanging head; with *one's* head dropped
▶그 접시를 마루에 떨어뜨리면 산산조각이 날 것이다 If you drop the dish on the floor, it will break into pieces.
2 〈놓치다〉 miss 《*one's* hold》; let slip; drop
♦ 공을 떨어뜨리다 miss [fail to catch] the ball; fumble 《a grounder》; 〈받았다가〉 muff
3 〈흘리다〉 drop; lose
♦ 손수건 떨어뜨렸어요 You dropped your handkerchief.
▶지갑을 어딘가 이 근처에 떨어뜨렸다 I lost my wallet somewhere around here.
4 〈하락시키다〉 debase; abase; degrade; depreciate; reduce; lower; detract 《from *one's* merit》; take from 《the value》; 〈저하시키다〉 make worse; deteriorate
♦ 지위를 떨어뜨리다 degrade; demote; reduce 《an officer》 to lower grade / 품위를 떨어뜨리다 lose dignity; demean *oneself* / 인기를 떨어뜨리다 detract from *one's* popularity / 가치를 떨어뜨리다 detract *sth* from the value; impair [detract] the value / 물가를 떨어뜨리다 lower [bring down, reduce] price / 화폐의 가치를 떨어뜨리다 devaluate [devalue] currency / 품질을 떨어뜨리다 lower in quality; deteriorate
5 〈낮추다〉 lessen; decrease
▶그는 자동차의 속도를 떨어뜨렸다 He slowed down his car.
6 〈소비하다〉 scatter; spend
♦ 유럽인 관광객이 떨어뜨리고 가는 돈 the dollars [money] scattered [spent] by European tourists
7 〈빠뜨리다〉 let fall [get] into; 〈속여서〉 entrap; entice; take in
8 〈탈락시키다〉 reject 《a candidate》; fail; sift out; eliminate; weed out
♦ 지원자의 반수를 떨어뜨리다 fail half the candidates
9 〈앞지르다〉 leave 《another》 behind; outstrip; outrun; outpace; get [pull] ahead of 《another》; outsail 《another ship》
♦ 경주에서 다른 선수를 모두 떨어뜨리다 outstrip all the other runners in the race
10 〈함락시키다〉 take; capture; reduce; carry
♦ 요새를 떨어뜨리다 reduce a fort / 적의 진지를 떨어뜨리다 carry an enemy position
11 〈해어뜨리다〉 wear out [down] 《*one's* clothes》
12 〈달리게 하다〉 exhaust; use up; run out; run through [short]
♦ 쌀을 떨어뜨리다 use the rice up; run out [short] of rice / 돈을 떨어뜨리다 run out of money

떨어먹다 eat 《*oneself*》 up; use up [spend all] 《*one's* money》; go [run, squander] through 《*one's* fortune》 ♦ 가졌던 돈[재산]을 떨어먹다 run through all *one's* money [fortune]

▶형은 부모가 남겨놓은 재산을 다 떨어먹었다 My elder brother made away with the estate left by our parents.
▶이러다가는 얼마 안 가서 집이고 땅이고 다 떨어먹겠다 At this rate he will soon eat himself out of house and land.

떨어지다 1 〈낙하하다〉 fall; drop; get [have] a fall; come [go] down; be down; 〈추락하다〉 crash; 〈액체가〉 drip
♦의자에서 떨어지다 fall off a chair / 비가 뚝뚝 떨어지다 fall in drops / 거꾸로 떨어지다 fall headlong [head foremost] / 벼랑에서 떨어지다 fall over a precipice / 말에서 떨어지다 fall from [come off] a horse / 계단에서 굴러 떨어지다 fall down [off] the stairs; fall downstairs
▶포크가 식탁에서 마루에 떨어졌다 A fork dropped [fell] from the table to the floor.
▶거실에 먼지가 떨어져 있다 There's some dirt in the hall.
▶그녀의 눈에서 눈물이 떨어졌다 Tears dropped [dripped] from her eyes.
▶그 비행기가 산허리에 떨어졌다 The plane crashed [went down, fell] on the hillside.
▶힘든 일을 하고 났더니 이마에서 땀방울이 떨어진다 After the hard work, sweat is dropping from my brow.
▶관광버스가 벼랑에서 강으로 거꾸로 떨어졌다 The sightseeing bus fell headlong over the precipice into the river.
▶한 아이가 2층에서 떨어져 다쳤다 A child fell from the second story and hurt himself.
2 〈해·달이〉 지다〉 set; sink; go down
▶해는 서산에 떨어졌다 The sun has sunk behind the western mountains.
3 〈실패하다〉 fail; lose; be unsuccessful; be defeated; lose
♦시험에 떨어지다 fail [《美口》 flunk] (in) an examination / 선거에 떨어지다 be defeated in an election; be beaten at the polls
▶그는 이번 선거에서 떨어질 것이다 He'll be defeated in the election next time.
▶1차 시험에는 합격했지만 2차 시험에서 떨어졌다 I was success in the first screening, but failed (in) the second [to pass the second] examination.
▶면접시험에서 약 30명의 지원자가 떨어졌다 About thirty (out) of the candidates were rejected after an oral test.
4 〈낮아이〉 go down
▶학교 성적이 떨어졌다 My school record got worse.
5 〈분리되다〉 separate; part from [with]; fall apart
♦줄에서 떨어져 나오다 fall out of (the) line / 가족과 떨어져 살다 live separated from one's family
▶그들 둘은 서로 떨어질 수 없는 사이다 They are inseparable (from each other).
6 〈붙었던 것이〉 come off; come apart; be off; become disjoined
♦표지가 떨어진 책 a book with the covers off
▶인형의 코가 떨어졌다 The nose of the doll has come off.
▶겨울이 되면 대개의 나무는 잎이 떨어진다 Most trees shed their leaves in winter.
7 〈사이가〉 be estranged [distant] from; cut oneself off [from]
▶민심은 이미 현정부에서 떨어져 나갔다 Public opinion is estranged from the Government.
8 〈거리가〉 be (a long way) off; 〈시대가〉 be (a long time) ago [back]
▶1마일 떨어져 있다 be a mile away 《from》 / 하늘과 땅만큼 떨어져 있다 be poles apart
▶한길에서 좀 떨어진 곳에 큰 소나무가 있다 There stands a big pine tree a little way off the road.
▶그것은 조금 떨어져서 보면 더 잘 보인다 It looks better at a distance.
9 〈손에 들어오다〉 fall into; 〈사람을 주어〉 win; secure; carry away
♦남의 수중에 떨어지다 fall into another's hands
▶입찰이 우리에게 떨어졌다 Our tender was accepted.
▶경매에서 그 가구가 그의 손에 떨어졌다 At the auction, the furniture was knocked down to him.
10 〈하락하다〉 go down; fall; drop; be debased; 〈기력 등이〉 decline; break down; 《美口》 go downhill; 〈열등하다〉 be inferior (to); 〈미달하다〉 do not come up to; fall short of; 〈뒤떨어지다〉 fall [drop, hang] behind
♦인기가 떨어지다 lose one's popularity; fall in popularity; fall into disfavor / 사회적 신용이 떨어지다 lose public confidence / 아무에게도 떨어지지 않다 be [rank] second [inferior] to none
▶매상이 떨어졌다 The sales have dropped [fallen] off.
▶그녀는 인기가 떨어지고 있다 She is falling in popularity. ⇒ Her popularity is falling [on the skids].
▶소매점의 손님이 뚝 떨어졌다 Business dropped off drastically in the retail stores.
▶요즘 그의 연기는 평판이 떨어졌다 Recently his performance has become less popular.
▶여자는 남자보다 체력이 떨어지게 마련이다 Women are naturally inferior to men in physical strength.
▶그 은행의 신용이 꽉 떨어졌다 The bank's credit was badly shaken.
▶값은 전과 같지만 품질이 떨어졌다 The price is the same, but they've lowered the quality.
▶인플레가 되면 돈의 가치가 떨어진다 The value of money lessens during inflation.
▶이것은 견본보다 떨어진다 This does not come up to the sample.
▶그는 수학이 제일 떨어진다 He is behind the others in mathematics above all.
11 〈함락하다〉 fall; be reduced
▶요새가 적의 수중에 떨어졌다 The fortress fell to the enemy.
12 〈남다〉 be left (over, behind) 《from》; remain; 〈꼭 나뉘다〉 be divisible; can be divided 《by》
▶그 빚을 갚고서도 상당한 돈이 떨어졌다 There was a considerable [sizable] sum left

over after paying the debts.
▶ 91은 13으로 나뉘어 떨어진다 Ninety one is (exactly) divisible by thirteen.
13 〈가격이〉 fall; drop; go down; decline; sag; depreciate
♦ 값이 떨어지다 fall in price / 백원이 떨어지다 fall off by 100 won
▶ 기름값이 지난달보다 조금 떨어졌다 Prices of oil have shown a slight decrease against the previous month.
14 〈열・온도가〉 drop; fall; go down
▶ 그는 열이 떨어지지 않는다 There is no abatement in his fever.
15 〈해지다〉 wear out; be worn out
♦ 다 떨어진 구두 worn-out [dilapidated] shoes
▶ 이 옷은 여러 해가 되어도 떨어지지 않을게다 This suit will hold its shape for (many) years.
16 〈바닥나다〉〈사람이 주어〉 run [get] out of; be [run] short of; be out of
♦ 용돈이 떨어지다 run out of pocket money / 쌀이 떨어지다 run out of rice; rice is exhausted [used up, all gone]
▶ 그 물건은 떨어졌습니다 The article is out of stock [is all sold out].
▶ 설탕이 떨어졌다 We're out of sugar.
▶ 물건을 이것저것 사다보니 결국 돈이 떨어지고 말았다 I bought one thing after another and finally ran out of money.
17 〈술수에〉 fall into; be deceived; be taken in
♦ 계략에 떨어지다 fall into a snare
▶ 그는 적의 책략에 떨어졌다 He was caught in the enemy's trap.
18 〈병・버릇 등이〉 be gone; be got rid of; be got over; be shaken off
▶ 나쁜 버릇은 좀처럼 떨어지지 않는 법이다 A bad habit is hard to get rid of.
▶ 감기가 여간해서 떨어지지 않는다 I can't shake off [get over] my cold.
19 〈유산하다〉 abort; miscarry; 〈사람이 주어〉 have a miscarriage
♦ 애가 떨어지다 have an abortion [a miscarriage]
20 〈끝나다〉 be finished; be completed
▶ 내일이면 일이 다 떨어진다 The work will be finished tomorrow.
21 〈터지다〉 rend; ; break; pierce; split; burst
♦ 귀청이 떨어질 것 같은 ear-splitting; ear-piercing; deafening
22 〈부합하다〉 tally with; check up with; coincide with; accord with; correspond with
▶ 상품은 송장(送狀)과 맞아 떨어지지 않는다 The goods do not tally with the invoice.
23 〈교부받다〉 be granted
▶ 드디어 여권이 떨어졌다 I was granted [given] my passport at last.
24 〈끊어지다〉 ♦ 밥줄이 떨어지다 lose *one's* means of livelihood / 숨이 떨어지다 breathe *one's* last; expire; die
▶ 그는 막 숨이 떨어지려는 참이었다 He lay at the point of death.

떨이 sacrifice [cut-price] goods; a bargain; (remaining) articles offered at marked-down [reduced] prices
♦ 떨이 야채 remaindered [dumped] greens; vegetables sold in remainder
▶ 떨이로 팝니다 Surplus stock for sale at a (great) sacrifice.
■ ─판 a clearance [rummage] sale

떨치다¹ **1** 〈널리 알려지다〉 be widely felt [known]; become well known; be wielded
▶ 그의 명성은 나라 안팎에 떨치고 있다 His name is known both at home and abroad.
2 〈널리 들날리다〉 make well known in the world; wield 《power, influence, etc.》
♦ 명성을 천하에 떨치다 win [enjoy] a world-wide reputation / 맹위를 떨치다 rage with all *one's* force / 위세를 떨치다 exercise [wield] *one's* authority over 《others》
▶ 태풍이 맹위를 떨쳤다 The typhoon raged in all its fury.
▶ 그는 천하에 악명을 떨치고 있다 He is notorious throughout the country.

떨치다² 〈흔들어 떨어뜨리다〉 shake off; beat
▶ 그는 몸을 떨쳐 자리에서 일어났다 He tore himself away from the seat.

떫다 astringent; puckery; rough
♦ 떫은 감 an astringent persimmon / 감의 떫은 맛을 우려내다 remove the astringency of persimmons
▶ 이 포도주는 떫은 맛이 난다 This wine tastes rough.
▶ 그는 떫은 얼굴을 했다 He looked sullen. ⇌ He made a glum face.
▶ 익지 않은 감은 아주 떫게 마련이다 The persimmon is usually extremely astringent when unripe.

떳떳이 〈당당하게〉 honorably; in an honorable way; fairly (and squarely); openly; aboveboard; with a clear [clean] conscience; 〈정당하게〉 right(ly); justly
♦ 떳떳이 행동하다 play fair; act fair and square / 떳떳이 싸우다 fight openly and squarely / 떳떳이 이기다 play fair and win a game; win a game fairly / 떳떳이 지다 be a good loser

떳떳하다 〈당당하다〉 honorable; fair; square; open; aboveboard; 〈깨끗하다〉 upright; clean-handed; 〈정당하다〉 right; rightful; just
♦ 떳떳한 시합 fair play; a fairly contested match / 떳떳한 행위 an aboveboard action; an honorable deed; right conduct / 떳떳하지 못한 거래 a shady deal / 양심에 비추어 떳떳하다 have a clear [clean] conscience; feel no prick of conscience / …하기를 떳떳하게 여기지 않다 be too proud to 《do》; disdain to 《do》
▶ 떳떳하게 겨루자 Let's play fair.
▶ 그의 행동은 떳떳하다 His action is open and aboveboard.
▶ 나는 그 일에 관해 떳떳하지 못하게 생각하고 있다 I feel guilty about that.
▶ 떳떳하지 못한 일은 하지 않았다 I have done nothing to be ashamed of.
▶ 그는 무엇인가 떳떳하지 못한 일을 하고 있다 He is engaged in something shady.

떵떵거리다 〈호화롭게 지내다〉 live in grand [extravagant] style; live like a prince

▶ 그는 이제 큰 집을 사서 떵떵거리며 산다 Now he has bought a mansion and is living on the fat of the land.

떼¹ 〈무리〉 a group; a troop; a crowd; a throng; 〈다수의〉 a multitude; 〈폭도 등의〉 a mob; a gang; 〈말·소 등의〉 a herd; 〈양의〉 a flock; 〈이리·사냥개의〉 a pack; 〈물개·고래 등의 작은 때〉 a pod; 〈몰려가는 가축의〉 a drove; 〈새의〉 a flock; 〈날고 있는〉 a flight; 〈메추라기 등의〉 a bevy; 〈물고기의〉 a school; a shoal
♦ 소[코끼리] 떼 a herd of cattle [elephants] / 고기 떼 a school [shoal] of fish / 비둘기 떼 a flock [flight] of pigeons / 파리[벌] 떼 a swarm of flies [bees] / 떼를 짓다 form groups; flock; band together; crowd; swarm; 〈물고기가〉 school / 떼를 지어, 떼로 in a bundle [bunch] / 떼 지어 살다 live in herds [flocks] / 떼지어 모이다 flock [throng] together
▶ 비둘기가 떼를 지어 날아올랐다 Pigeons flew up in crowds.
▶ 광장에는 200명의 학생이 떼지어 모였다 A huge throng of 200 students came together in the square.
▶ 양떼가 오고 있다. 길을 비켜 주자 A flock of sheep is coming. Let's make way for them.

떼² 〈잔디〉 sod; turf ♦ 떼 한 장 a sod; a turf / 떼를 뜨다 cut out sod; cut [tear] turfs (from) / 떼를 입히다 sod; turf

떼³ a raft ♦ 떼를 만들다 make a raft (of) / 떼를 띄워 보내다 send a raft along the stream / 떼를 타고 가다 travel by raft; cross [go down] (a river) by craft

떼⁴ 〈억지〉 an impossible [unreasonable, unjustifiable, importunate] demand [claim]; a persistent demand [assertion]
♦ 떼를 쓰다 ask for the impossible; fret; pester (sb to do); tease [importune] (sb for sth)
▶ 넌 언제나 떼만 쓰는구나 You are always asking me for something.
▶ 그는 돈을 더 달라고 어머니에게 떼를 썼다 He importunately asked his mother for more money.

떼거지 〈거지〉 a bunch of beggars; 〈이재민〉 a great number of victims of a disaster

떼과부 —寡婦 a lot of widows
▶ 전쟁으로 떼과부가 생겼다 The war widowed many women. ⇌ A great many women were widowed by the war.

떼다 1 〈붙은 것을〉 take off; strip [tear] off; remove
♦ 간판을 떼다 remove a signboard / 우표를 떼다 take the stamp off / 포스터를 떼다 clear (a pole) of bills / 붙인 종이를 찢어 떼다 tear off the paper / 달력을 한 장 떼다 tear off a leaf from a calender
2 〈간격을 두다〉 detach; keep apart; keep (one thing) from (another); leave a space [an opening] (between); space (the lines); 〈분리〉 part; separate; disconnect; 〈격리〉 isolate
♦ 행간을 떼다 leave spaces between lines; 〈조판할 때〉 space the lines / 손을 떼다 〈관계를 끊다〉 get sth off one's hands; wash one's hands of; sever connection with; cease to do with (it); withdraw oneself (from...) / 나무를 1미터씩 떼어서 심다 plant trees a meter apart [at intervals of a meter]
▶ 이 문제는 다른 것과 떼어 토의하자 Let's discuss this problem separately (from the others).
▶ 병든 돼지는 따로 떼어 놓아야 한다 We should keep sick pigs apart [away] from the others. ⇌ The sick pigs should be isolated from the others.
▶ 그 군인은 어린아이를 부모에게서 떼어 놓았다 The soldier took a little child away from its parents.
▶ 저 두 사람은 당분간 떼어놓는 것이 좋겠다 It's preferable to separate those two for a while.
▶ 나는 이 사전을 손에서 뗄 수가 없다 I cannot do without this dictionary.
3 〈봉한 것을〉 open; unseal; cut (a letter) open
♦ 봉함을 떼다 open [break, take off] the seal / 입을 떼다 open one's mouth to talk; be the first to speak; open the conversation; break the ice / 함부로 봉을 떼다 tamper with the seal
▶ 편지를 받자 그는 곧 봉함을 떼었다 As soon as he received the letter, he took off the seal.
4 〈빼다〉 subtract (from); deduct [subduct, detract] (from); take away [off]
♦ 봉급에서 일정액을 떼다 take a sum off one's pay; deduct a sum from one's salary
▶ 그는 이자를 미리 떼고 꾸주었다 He loaned money with the interest deducted in advance.
5 〈거절하다〉 refuse (a request); reject; turn down; decline
▶ 그녀의 청을 잡아 뗄 수가 없었다 I could not decline her request.
6 〈수표·어음 등을〉 issue [write out, make out, draw] (a check)
♦ 어음을 떼다 draw a bill [draft] (upon sb for a sum) / 수표를 떼다 issue a check / 영수증을 떼다 give sb a receipt (for); make out a receipt (for)
▶ 나는 친구에게 백만원짜리 수표를 떼어 주었다 I have issued a check for a million won in favor of my friend.
7 〈관직 등에서 물러나게 하다〉 deprive [strip] sb of (his office); divest sb of (his rank)
8 〈낙태하다〉 ♦ 아이를 떼다 abort a baby; commit feticide; have an (artificial) abortion (performed)
9 〈병을〉 cure (a disease); 〈성가신 것을〉 get rid of (a nuisance)
♦ 학질을 떼다 cure malaria; get rid of malaria
10 〈끊다〉 quit; give up [stop] (drinking, smoking); abstain [refrain] from (drinking, smoking); cut (smoking) altogether
♦ 버릇을 떼다 overcome [get over] a habit / 젖을 떼다 wean a child
11 〈끝내다〉 finish up
♦ 책을 떼다 read [get] through a book; finish (reading) a book; have done with a book / 일손을 떼다 finish one's work
12 〈장기에서 말을〉 play games with a handicap

♦말을 떼고 두다 play without *mal* [a knight] as a handicap
떼도둑 a group [gang] of robbers; a pack of thieves
떼돈 ♦떼돈 벌다 make money hand over fist; (俗) make a pile [bundle]; make quick money; (口) rake it in
▶ 야, 그거 떼돈 버는 장사구나 What a highly profitable [lucrative] business (it is)!
떼밀다 push; shove; give a push [shove]
♦떼밀고 들어가다 force *one's* way into
▶ 우리는 붐비는 지하철 안에서 거세게 떼밀렸다 We were violently jostled in a crowded subway.
떼보 a fretful child ⇨ 떼쟁이
떼새 1 〈새떼〉 a flock of birds in flight
2 a plover ⇨ 물떼새
떼송장 a lot of corpses [bodies]
떼쓰다 ask for the impossible ⇨ 떼⁴
▶ 그 아이는 어머니한테 사탕을 달라고 떼썼다 The child asked [pressed] his mother for some candy.
▶ 그녀는 아버지에게 옷을 사 달라고 떼썼다 She begged her father to buy her a dress.
떼어내다 tear off; strip off; rip off; bare
♦종이를 떼어내다 tear off the paper / 한 장씩 떼어내는 달력 a tear-off [block] calendar
떼어놓다 1 〈뒤에 처지게 하다〉 get [be] ahead of 〈another〉; have a lead on *sb*; outrun; out-strip; leave 〈another〉 behind (in a race)
♦2등을 3미터나 떼어놓다 run 3 meters ahead of the second runner
2 〈갈라놓다〉 part; separate; draw [pull, set] (persons, things) apart; 〈격리하다〉 isolate; 〈이간하다〉 estrange; 〈저축하다〉 save for
♦맞붙어 싸우는 아이들을 떼어놓다 pull apart the grappling boys / 애인 사이를 떼어놓다 sep-arate the pair of lovers / 부부 사이를 떼어놓다 sever husband and wife / 떼어놓고 가다 leave *sb* behind / 돈을 따로 떼어놓다 set 《a fund》 apart (for)
▶ 그들은 노후를 위해 돈을 떼어놓았다 They saved money for old age.
▶ 권리와 의무는 절대로 떼어놓을 수 없다 Right and duty are inseparable as Siamese twins.
떼어먹다 bilk [jump] 《a bill》; fail to pay 《*one's* debt》; leave 《a bill》 unpaid; (俗) welsh on 《a debt》; eat and beat
♦술값을 떼어먹다 do not pay for *one's* drink; leave *one's* bar bill unpaid / 빚을 떼어먹고 도망치다 bolt without paying *one's* debts / 여관비를 떼어먹다 jump hotel bills; leave an inn without paying *one's* bill
▶ 그들은 이 가게의 술값을 곧잘 떼어먹는다 They often bilk this bar of money.
▶ 그에게 돈을 빌려줄 때는 조심하지 않으면 떼어먹힌다 If you loan him money, be careful as he may not return it.
▶ 그는 노무자의 노임에서 10 퍼센트를 떼어먹었다 He took a cut of ten percent on the laborers' wages.
떼이다 be cheated 《of a debt》; be welshed [welched]; be dishonored

▶ 빚을 떼이었다 A debt was dishonored.
▶ 그 녀석한테 10만원을 떼이었다 He has cheated [bilked] me out of a hundred thousand won.
떼쟁이 a fretful child; an insistant person; a person who always makes impossible [unrea-sonable] demands
떼짓다 crowd (together); group; throng; form groups; 〈새 등이〉 flock (together); 〈곤충 등이〉 swarm; herd together; 〈물고기가〉 school
▶ 비둘기가 떼지어 날아올랐다 Pigeons flew up in crowds.
▶ 공원에는 사람들이 떼지어 있었다 The park was crowded with people.
▶ 봄이 되면 사람들이 떼지어 벚꽃 구경을 간다 In spring people go to see the cherry blos-soms in crowds.
떼치다 1 〈떼어 물리치다〉 tear *oneself* away 《from》; shake *oneself* loose [free] from; 〈떼밀어〉 push away [aside]; brush [force] aside; 〈떼어놓다〉 leave *sb* behind
▶ 그녀는 우는 아이를 떼치고 밖으로 나갔다 She went out pushing aside a crying child.
2 〈거절하다〉 refuse [brush aside] 《a re-quest》; decline; reject; turn down
♦요구를 떼치다 refuse a demand [request]
뗏목 —木— a raft
♦뗏목을 만들다 make a raft 《of logs》 / 뗏목으로 나르다 raft *sth* 《to》; carry *sth* on a raft / 뗏목을 타고 강을 내려가다 go down the river on a raft; raft down the river
▶ 그들은 뗏목을 타고 태평양을 건넜다 They crossed the Pacific on a raft.
뗏장 a sod; a turf; a piece of sod [turf]
♦뗏장을 새로 입힌 무덤 a newly sodded grave / 뗏장을 뜨다 cut [tear] turfs 《from a field》
또 1 〈다시 더〉 too; not only... but (also); (both)... and; 〈게다가〉 more; moreover; besides; further (more); another
♦또 한 마디 one more word / 그와 또 한 사람 he and one other person
▶ 그는 의사요 또 대학 교수이기도 하다 He is a doctor and university professor.
▶ 그 책은 재미있고 또 교훈적이기도 했다 The book was interesting and instructive (as well).
▶ 그것은 경제적이고 또 건강에도 좋다 It is not only economical but (also) good for the health.
▶ 전 날에는 편지를, 또 어제는 전화를 해주시니 너무 감사합니다 Thank you for your letter the other day, and also for the phone call yesterday.
▶ 나는 부자가 아니고 또 되고 싶지도 않다 I am not rich, neither do I wish to be.
▶ 대구에 또 불이 났다 There was another fire in Taegu.
▶ 그에게는 아들이 또 하나 있다 He has another son.
▶ 그는 대학자요 또 강의도 잘 한다 He is a great scholar, and what is better, a good teacher. ⇌ He is a good teacher as well as a good scholar.
▶ 그는 수완도 좋고 또 돈도 많다 He has abil-

ity and plenty of money to go with it.
▶〈장사꾼이〉 또 무엇을 드릴까요? Anything else?
2 〈다시〉 again; once more [again]
▶또 뵙겠습니다 I'll see you again.
▶또 놀러 오시오 Come and see me again.
▶어제 읽었던 편지를 또 읽고 있어요 I'm reading again the letter I read yesterday.
▶중동에서 또 전쟁이 일어났다 Another war has broken out in the Middle East.
▶오늘 밤에 또 눈이 왔다 It snowed again this evening.
▶또 전화하겠습니다 I'll call you later.
▶그와 같은 사람이 또 있을까? Shall we ever see the like of him again?
▶그는 한 입을 먹고 또 한 입을 베풀었다 He ate one bite, and then another.
▶그는 또 실패했다 He failed a second time [again]. ⇒ He had another failure.
3 〈한편〉 while; on the other hand; 〈뜻밖에〉 contrary to 《expectations》
▶난 또 누구라고 Well, it is you! (I thought it was somebody else.)
▶형은 언제나 게으른데 동생은 또 그렇게 열심이다 The elder brother is always idle, while the younger one is such a hardworking man.

또그르르 ♦또그르르 구르다 roll over and over

또는 or; 〈바꾸어 말하면〉 in other words
▶내일은 비나 또는 눈이 내릴거다 There will be rain or snow tomorrow.
▶당신 또는 내가 집에 있어야 한다 You or I am to stay home.
▶그가 틀렸던가 또는 내가 틀렸다 Either he or I am in the wrong.
▶또는 이렇게도 말할 수 있다 In other words, it can be said like this.
▶나는 영어나 또는 프랑스어를 공부하려고 생각하고 있습니다 I am going to study English or French.

또다시 〈한번 더〉 once more [again]; 〈재차〉(over) again; twice; 〈새로이〉 afresh
▶한번 거짓말을 하면 또다시 하게 된다 One lie leads to another.
▶그는 또다시 시험에 낙제했다 He failed the examination again.
▶또다시 나는 죽음을 면할 수가 있었다 Again I was able to escape death.
▶그녀는 또다시 지각했다 She was late once again.
▶또다시 폐를 끼치게 되어 죄송합니다 I am sorry to put you to repeated troubles.

또닥거리다 tap; pat; rap; knock gently
♦등을 또닥거리다 pat [clap] sb on the back / 애기를 또닥거려 주다 pat a baby

또닥또닥 tap-tap; rat-tat-tat
—**또닥또닥하다** 또닥거리다

또랑또랑하다 very clear; distinct; vivid; plain; explicit ♦또랑또랑한 목소리로 in a clear [distinct] voice [tone]
▶그녀는 그 사나이를 또랑또랑한 눈으로 바라봤다 She looked at the man with a clear eye.
▶아이들의 또랑또랑한 목소리가 들렸다 I heard the clear, vivid voices of children.

또래 〈나이의〉 (of) the age; 〈사물의〉 (of) the size ♦내가 너희 또래였을 때는 when I was your age
▶모두 그 또래다 All of them are of the same age [size].
▶그 또래의 아이들이 날 찾아왔었다 A group of boys of that age had been here to see me.
▶그 사람도 꼭 네 또래다 He is just about your age.
▶그 또래의 것을 몇 개 더 보여주시오 Show me a few more of that size.

또렷또렷 all clearly [vividly, distinctly]
♦또렷또렷 설명하다 explain explicitly / 글씨를 또렷또렷 쓰다 write a clear hand
—**또렷또렷하다** all clear [distinct, vivid, plain, explicit]
♦또렷또렷한 이목구비 clear-cut feature / 또렷또렷한 목소리 crisp voice / 정신이 또렷또렷하다 be wide awake; look alive

또렷이 clearly ⇨ 뚜렷이 ▶옛 추억이 또렷이 생각난다 Old memory come vividly to mind.

또렷하다 clear ⇨ 뚜렷하다

또르르 rolling ⇨ 도르르

또바기 〈한결같이〉 always; regularly; punctually; without fail ♦또바기 인사를 잘하다 greet [salute] whenever to see [meet]
▶나는 식전에 또바기 한 시간씩 산책을 한다 I make it a rule to take an hour's walk before breakfast.

또박또박 1 〈정확히〉 exactly; correctly; accurately; punctually
♦시간을 또박또박 지키다 be punctual (to the moment) / 갯수를 또박또박 세서 받다 count the number exactly and then take them / 또박또박 발음하다 pronounce correctly / 글씨를 또박또박 쓰다 write a letter exactly [correctly]
2 〈거르지 않고〉 regularly; with regularity ♦이자를 또박또박 지불하다 be regular [punctual] in one's payment of interest 《on a loan》 / 모임에 또박또박 출석하다 never miss [fail to attend] a meeting

또아리 a head pad ⇨ 따리

또한 〈역시〉 also; too; and; 〈게다가〉 besides; moreover; as well (as); both... and; 〈부정구문에서〉 neither; nor; not... either
▶그의 강의는 재미도 있고 또한 교훈적이다 His lecture is both [at once] interesting and instructive.
▶그는 영어회화도 잘 하거니와 또한 작문도 잘 한다 He speaks English and writes it as well.
▶그도 또한 가지 않았다 He didn't go there either.
▶그것도 또한 문제다 That is also a problem.
▶이것도 또한 쉽지 않다 This isn't easy either.
▶그 여자는 아름답고 또한 총명하다 She is bright as well as beautiful. ⇒ She is as clever as she is gorgeous.
▶그도 또한 진정한 모험가이다 He is a real adventurer, too.
▶그도 또한 숙제를 하지 않았다 He didn't do his homework, either.

똑[1] 〈틀림없이〉 exactly; just; right; precisely;

〈완전히〉 completely
▶ 형제가 똑 같다 The brothers are exactly alike.
▶ 돈이 똑 떨어졌다 We have run out of money completely.

똑² **1** 〈가볍게 떨어지는 소리〉 drop; plop; with a tap [rap, flop]
♦ 똑 떨어지다 fall flop; flop down
▶ 똑하는 소리가 들린다 A light tap is heard.
▶ 동전이 손에서 똑 떨어졌다 A coin slipped from my hand.
2 〈부러지는 소리〉 with a snap; snappingly
♦ 똑 부러지다 break with a snap / 막대기를 똑 부러뜨리다 snap a stick in two
3 〈때리는 소리〉 a light tap; a clink
♦ 똑 때리다 tap; rap

똑같다 just [exactly] alike; uniform; absolutely identical 《with》; exactly the same 《as》; 〈닮아서〉 be the exact image [likeness] 《of》
▶ 똑같은 날에 on the very same day / 높이가 똑같다 be of the same height
▶ 아버지는 똑같은 말을 몇번이고 되풀이하셨다 My father said the same thing again and again.
▶ 쌍둥이는 똑같은 옷을 입고 있었다 The twins wore the same dress.
▶ 상자의 크기는 똑같지는 않다 The boxes are not uniform in size [of the same size].
▶ 어제 들은 이야기와 똑같다 It is the same story that I heard yesterday.
▶ 나도 당신과 똑같은 생각입니다 Your thoughts echo mine.
▶ 그녀의 얼굴은 어머니와 똑같다 Her face is her mother's to a T.

똑같이 equally; 〈한결같이〉 evenly; 〈공평하게〉 impartially; 〈차별 없이〉 indiscriminately; alike; likewise
♦ 똑같이 분배하다 divide 《money》 equally [into equal parts] / 높이를 똑같이 하다 make all of uniform height / 비용을 똑같이 부담하다 share the expenses equally with sb
▶ 그들은 똑같이 취급되는 것을 싫어하는 사람들이다 They are men who do not want to be treated equally [all alike].
▶ 그들은 모두 똑같이 검은 옷을 입고 있었다 They were all uniformly dressed in black.
▶ 그들은 모두 똑같이 찬성했다 They all agreed. ⇌ They agreed unanimously.
▶ 그들은 똑같이 심리학에 관계하고 있었다 They were all alike concerned in psychology.
▶ 5년만에 그들의 지위가 똑같이 되었다 Five years evened up their positions.

똑딱거리다 〈시계가〉 ticktack; ticktock; tick; 〈딱딱한 물건이〉 click; clack; clatter; patter
♦ 똑딱거리는 타이프라이터 소리 clacking typewriters
▶ 시계가 똑딱거리는 소리에 귀를 기울이고 있었다 We were listening to the clock ticking.
▶ 똑딱선이 똑딱거리며 지나가고 있었다 The motorboat was chugging along.
▶ 그 여자의 여행 가방이 똑딱거리며 잠겼다 Her suitcase clicked shut.

똑딱단추 a snap fastener ♦ 똑딱단추를 채우다 close a snap fastener; fasten a snap

똑딱똑딱 ticktock; ticking; ticktack; clickclack
▶ 시계가 똑딱똑딱 소리를 내고 있다 The clock is ticking [going ticktack]. ⇌ The clock is making a clicking noise.
▶ 방이 조용해서 시계의 똑딱똑딱하는 소리를 잘 들을 수 있었다 I could hear the ticktock of the clock well in the quiet room.
▶ 공항의 공안원이 여행 가방에서 무엇인가 똑딱똑딱 소리를 내는 것을 발견했다 An airport security officer detected something ticking in a suitcase.

똑딱선 一船 a motorboat; a motor ship; a motor-powered boat

똑똑 **1** 〈물이 떨어지는 모양〉 dripping one by one; trickling; drop by drop
♦ 똑똑 떨어지다 drip; dribble; trickle; fall in drops / 똑똑 떨어지는 빗방울 소리 the drip-drip of the rain
▶ 지붕에서 물이 똑똑 떨어졌다 Water fell in drops from the roof.
▶ 내 이마에서 땀이 똑똑 떨어지고 있었다 The sweat was dripping off my brow.
2 〈두드리는 소리〉 a knock; a tap; a rap
♦ 문을 똑똑 두드리다 knock [tap, rap] on [at] the door / 책상을 똑똑 두드리다 rap [beat a tattoo] on a desk
▶ 그녀는 똑똑 구둣소리를 내면서 걷고 있었다 She was walking with a click of heels.
▶ 창문을 똑똑 두드리는 소리가 들렸다 There was a rap on the window.
▶ 나는 누군가 문을 똑똑 두드리는 소리를 들었다 I heard someone knocking on the door.
3 〈부러지는 소리〉 with a snap; snappingly
▶ 나뭇가지가 똑똑 부러진다 The branches are broken with snaps.

똑똑하다 **1** 〈분명하다〉 clear; distinct; plain; definite; vivid; sharp
♦ 똑똑한 발음 distinct pronunciation / 〈텔레비전의〉 똑똑한 화면 distinct pictures
▶ 그녀는 똑똑한 목소리로 외쳤다 She shouted in a clear [distinct] voice.
2 〈영리하다〉 clever; bright; wise; brainy; 〈빈틈없다〉 shrewd; smart
♦ 똑똑한 아이 a bright child; a clever boy [girl] / 똑똑한 체하는 사람 a knowing chap / 똑똑한 체하다 try to appear smart; pretend to be wise / 똑똑해 보이다 look brainy [intelligent]
▶ 그가 똑똑한지 바보인지는 하는 일을 보면 알게 된다 His wisdom will be shown by his way of doing things.

똑똑히 **1** 〈분명히〉 clearly; distinctly; vividly; plainly
♦ 똑똑히 말하다 [읽다] speak [read] distinctly / 똑똑히 들리다 be heard distinctly
▶ 전화로는 그녀의 목소리가 똑똑히 들리지 않았다 Her voice was not clear over the phone.
▶ 사진 속의 인물들은 모두 똑똑히 나왔다 All the figures in the photograph are very plain.
▶ 그것은 똑똑히 보였다 It was in plain sight.
▶ 그들이 호텔에 들어가는 것을 나는 이 눈으로 똑똑히 보았다 I saw them go into that hotel

with my own eyes.
▶ 나는 그 사건을 똑똑히 기억하고 있다 I remember the event clearly [vividly].
2 〈영리하게〉 wisely; cleverly; brightly; 〈빈틈없게〉 shrewdly; smartly
♦ 똑똑히 행동하다 act wisely [sensibly] / 일처리를 똑똑히 하다 dispose of a matter intelligently

똑 바 로 1 〈곧게〉 straight; in a straight line; 〈곧추〉 upright; erect
♦ 똑바로 앉다 sit upright [erect, square] / 똑바로 서다 stand [sit] upright [erect] / 똑바로 가다 go [keep] straight on; make straight (toward, for) / 똑바로 놓다 set *sth* upright
▶ 방과 후 똑바로 집으로 가거라 Go straight [right] home after school.
▶ 똑바로 앞을 보거라 Look straight ahead.
▶ 줄을 똑바로 그어라 Draw a straight line.
▶ 화살은 표적을 향해 똑바로 날아갔다 The arrow went right to the mark.
▶ 바람이 불지 않아서 연기가 똑바로 올라가고 있다 There is no wind blowing and the smoke is rising straight up.
▶ 그는 우리들 쪽으로 똑바로 다가왔다 He came directly toward us.
▶ 이 길을 똑바로 100미터쯤 가면 교차로가 나옵니다 If you go straight along this road about a hundred meters, there is an intersection.
2 〈솔직히〉 honestly; frankly; straightforwardly; 〈옳게〉 right(ly); 〈틀리지 않게〉 correctly; exactly
♦ 똑바로 말하자면 to tell the truth; to be frank [honest] with you / 똑바로 대다 make an honest [frank] confession (of) / 똑바로 처신하다 act on the square; behave properly [correctly]
▶ 그는 똑바로 말하는 사람이기 때문에 이따금 적을 만든다 He is such an outspoken [a frank] person (that) he sometimes makes enemies.
▶ 이 세상에서 똑바로 살아가기란 어렵다 It is difficult to live honestly in this world.
▶ 땅에 말뚝을 똑바로 박아라 Thrust a stick upright in the earth.

똑 바르다 1 〈곧다〉 (dead) straight; (as) straight as an arrow; straight; direct; 〈직립하다〉 upright; erect
♦ 똑바른 줄 a straight line / 똑바른 자세로 in a correct posture; sitting [standing] erect
2 〈올바르다〉 right; righteous; just; right as nails
♦ 똑바른 행동 right conduct / 행실이 똑바르다 behave properly [correctly]

똘똘이 a bright child; a clever boy [girl]
똘똘하다 clever; bright; smart
♦ 똘똘한 아이 a bright [clever] boy [girl]

똥 excrement(s); feces; ordure; (俗) shit; 〈짐승의〉 dung; 〈조류의〉 droppings; 〈바닷새의〉 guano
♦ 똥 누다 evacuate [move] the bowels; ease [relieve] nature; relieve *oneself*; 〈짐승이〉 dung; (俗) shit / 똥 마렵다 feel a motion; feel *one's* bowels urge / 똥 싸다 〈매우 혼나다〉 have a hard [bad] time; have a hell of time

■ —개 a mongrel (dog) —배짱 foolhardiness; daredevil(t)ry; reckless courage [bravery] —오줌 feces and urine; human waste —줄: 똥줄 빠지다 get frightened out of *one's* sense; be scared to death —통 〈큰 통〉 a manure tub; 〈수거용〉 a manure pail

똥값 a nominal price; a dirt-cheap [dog-cheap] price
♦ 똥값이다 be dirt-cheap [dog-cheap] / 똥값으로 팔다 sell dirt-cheaply; sell for almost nothing
▶ 그런 것은 팔아봐야 똥값이다 That would fetch only a small price.

똥거름 night soil; dung(-manure)
♦ 똥거름을 주다 apply dung-manure to (land); dung [manure] the ground

똥구멍 the anus; the anal passage [orifice]
똥구멍이 찢어지게 가난하다 (속담) be as poor as a church mouse
똥기다 〈귀띔하다〉 give hint; awaken; inform
똥끝 the tip(s) of excrement / 똥끝이 타다 feel anxious [uneasy] very much; be fidgeted (about); worry *oneself* (sick)

똥 누러 갈 적 마음 다르고 올 적 마음 다르다 (속담) Once on shore, we pray no more. ⇌ The danger past and God forgotten.

똥똥하다 fat ⇨ 뚱뚱하다

똥 묻은 개가 겨 묻은 개 나무란다 (속담) That's a case of the pot calling the kettle black.

똥싸개 a child who is too young to control his bowel movements

똥이 무서워 피하나, 더러워서 피하지 (속담) Shun bad people as you would filth

똥집 1 〈대장(大腸)〉 a large intestine **2** 〈체중〉 *one's* body weight **3** 〈위(胃)〉 stomach; 〈사냥〉 a gizzard

똥차 —車 〈분뇨차〉 a night soil wagon [car]; 〈고장 잘 나는 차〉 a rattletrap; (美口) 〈싸구려 차〉 a jalop(p)y

똥칠하다 smear dung; disgrace
♦ 얼굴[이름]에 똥칠하다 disgrace [stain] *one's* name; bring disgrace on *sb*
▶ 그는 부모 얼굴에 똥칠했다 He disgraced his parents.

똥파리 a bottle-green fly; a dung fly

똬리 a headload pad; a ring-shaped [coiled] pad (put on the head by women to ease the weight of a headload)
▶ 뱀이 똬리를 틀었다 A snake coiled itself.

뙈기 1 〈논·밭의 작은 한 구획〉 a patch; a plot; a lot; a section
♦ 밭[논] 한 뙈기 a patch of field [paddy] / 한 뙈기의 땅 a patch [piece, plot] of land [ground]
▶ 그는 논밭 뙈기나 가지고 있다 He has a few fields. ⇌ He has a few patches of rice paddy. ⇌ He is an owner of some farmland.
2 〈한 조각, 한장〉 a piece; a mat; a sheet

뙤약볕 the scorching [blazing] sun; dazzling [broiling, burning] sunshine
♦ 한 여름 뙤약볕 the burning sun in midsummer / 뙤약볕을 쬐다 expose *oneself* to strong [scorching] sunshine / 뙤약볕 속을 걷다 walk

under the burning [blazing] sun
뙤창문 —窓門 a door with a small window in it
뚜껑 〈덮개〉 a cover; 〈상자·솥 등의〉 a lid; 〈병·만년필 등의〉 a cap; 〈호주머니의〉 a flap; 〈시계의〉 a case
♦ 뚜껑이 있는[달린] covered; lidded / 뚜껑이 있는 그릇 a covered vessel; a dish with a lid / 뚜껑이 없는 lidless; open; 〈시계 등의〉 open-faced; 《a saucepan》 without a top / 뚜껑을 덮다 put on the lid; cover up; close / 뚜껑을 열다 open; uncover; take off [lift, undo] the lid [cover]; 〈발표하다〉 make public; lay *sth* before the public / 뚜껑을 닫아두다 keep *sth* covered
▶ 이 하수구에는 뚜껑이 없다 This sewer is open to the air.
▶ 뚜껑을 꼭 덮어라 Screw the cap on tightly.
▶ 뚜껑을 열어보기까지는 아무도 모른다 No one can predict the result. ⇌ No one can make any prediction before it becomes an actuality.
뚜뚜 toot-toot; hoot-hoot ♦ 뚜뚜 기적을 울리다 be hooting a steam whistle / (자동차가) 뚜뚜 경적을 울리다 toot a horn; give off its 'honk-honk' / 뚜뚜 나팔을 불다 toot a bugle
뚜렷이 distinctly; vividly; clearly; in bold [strong] relief; with crystal clarity
♦ 뚜렷이 인쇄하다 print clearly
▶ 사람의 모습이 뚜렷이 보였다 You could see human figure clearly.
▶ 통로에 사람의 발자국이 뚜렷이 남아 있다 You can see distinctly human footsteps left on the passage.
▶ 눈 덮인 봉우리가 푸른 하늘에 뚜렷이 떠올라 있다 The snowcapped peaks stand clearly outlined against the blue sky.
▶ 돌아가신 어머니의 모습이 뚜렷이 떠올랐다 I saw a vivid image of my dead mother.
▶ 그녀의 고뇌가 얼굴에 뚜렷이 나타났다 Her sufferings markedly showed on her face.
▶ 내 방법과 그의 방법은 뚜렷이 다르다 My approach is substantially different from his.
▶ 알프스의 봉우리들이 푸른 하늘을 배경으로 뚜렷이 드러나 있다 The peaks of the Alps stand out sharp [are clearly outlined] against the blue sky.
▶ 그의 사인(死因)은 뚜렷하지 않다 He died from some unknown cause.
뚜렷하다 clear; plain; distinct; vivid; definite
♦ 뚜렷한 증거 clear [positive] evidence; an evident proof / 뚜렷한 이유 a definite reason / 뚜렷한 구별[윤곽] a sharp distinction [outline] / 뚜렷한 위법 행위 a flagrant violation of the law / 뚜렷하게 distinctly; clearly
▶ 이 사진은 뚜렷하지 못하다 This photograph has not come out clear.
뚜벅뚜벅 struttingly; with a strutting gait
♦ 뚜벅뚜벅 걷다 strut; swagger
▶ 거리를 뚜벅뚜벅 걷는 사람의 발소리가 들렸다 I heard the footsteps of somebody walking on [in] the street.
뚜쟁이 a pimp; a pander; a procurer
♦ 뚜쟁이질하다 pimp; pander; procure; act as a pander

뚝 **1** 〈갑자기 그치는 모양〉 suddenly; abruptly; unexpectedly
♦ 뚝 그치다 come to a dead stop; break short; 〈엔진 등이〉 go dead
▶ 〈울음을〉 뚝 그쳐라 Stop crying !
▶ 그는 담배를 뚝 끊었다 He gave up smoking once and for all.
▶ 나는 그와의 인연을 뚝 끊었다 I broke up with him utterly.
▶ 그녀는 나와의 서신을 뚝 끊었다 She dropped her correspondence with me.
2 〈떨어지는 소리〉 with a thump [thud, whack]
▶ 접시가 땅에 뚝 떨어졌다 A dish dropped with a thud on the ground.
▶ 경기가 뚝 떨어졌다 Business suddenly dropped off.
▶ 이번 학기에는 내 성적이 뚝 떨어졌다 My grades this term have really gone down.
3 〈부러지는 소리〉 (with a) snap
♦ 뚝 부러지다 snap [break] short
뚝뚝 〈액체가 떨어지는 모양〉 dripping; in drops; trickling
♦ 뚝뚝 떨어지다 drip; trickle down / 눈물이 뚝뚝 떨어지다 tears fall in drops
▶ 물이 수도꼭지에서 뚝뚝 떨어졌다 The water trickled from the faucet.
▶ 소녀는 닭똥같은 눈물을 뚝뚝 떨어뜨렸다 The little girl shed large tear drops.
▶ 나뭇가지에서 물이 뚝뚝 떨어졌다 Water trickled down in drops from the branches.
▶ 빗방울이 처마에서 뚝뚝 떨어졌다 The rain was dripping from the eaves.
▶ 그의 오른팔에서 피가 뚝뚝 떨어지고 있었다 His right arm was dripping blood.
뚝뚝하다 **1** 〈거세고 단단하다〉 rough and hard; tough; strong
2 〈인정미가 없다〉 harsh; rough; tough; unaffable
♦ 뚝뚝한 사람 [성질] an unsociable person [nature] / 뚝뚝하게 대답하다 give a blunt [curt] answer / 뚝뚝하게 말하다 speak with asperity
▶ 그는 사람이 뚝뚝해서 남에게 좋은 인상을 주지 못한다 He is so rough that he usually gives people a bad impression.
▶ 그는 사람이 뚝뚝해서 다루기가 힘든다 He is stiff and very hard to deal with.
뚝배기 an earthen(ware) bowl
뚝배기보다 장맛이 좋다 (속담) You can't tell a book by its cover.
뚝별나다 hot[quick, short]-tempered; testy; touchy
▶ 그 여자는 나이 얘기만 나오면 아주 뚝별나게 군다 She is most touchy on the subject of age.
뚝별씨 〈불뚝불뚝하는 성질〉 quick [hot] temper; touchiness; testiness; 〈불뚝불뚝하는 사람〉 a testy person
뚝심 great physical power [strength]; brute force; 〈버티는 힘〉 staying power; endurance
♦ 뚝심이 센 사람 a man of mighty sinews / 뚝심이 있다 be endowed with brute force; be persevering
▶ 그는 뚝심이 있다 He is very resolute [firm,

뚤뚤 =둘둘
뚫다 1 〈구멍을 내다〉 bore (a hole); punch; perforate; 〈관통하다〉 penetrate; pierce (through); go through; break through
♦ 바위를 뚫다 pierce a rock / 터널을 뚫다 excavate [bore] a tunnel (through a hill) / 총알이 뚫지 못하는 be bulletproof; be impenetrable to bullets
▶ 열차는 터널을 차례로 뚫고 지나갔다 The train passed [went, ran] through tunnel after tunnel.
▶ 탄환이 두꺼운 널빤지를 뚫었다 The bullet pierced the thick board (through).
▶ 그들은 언덕을 뚫어 터널을 냈다 They drove a tunnel through the hill.
▶ 그 아이는 얼음에 구멍을 뚫었다 The boy cut a hole in the ice.
2 〈굀을 알아내다〉 find a way
♦ 돈구멍을 뚫다 find a way to get money / 일자리를 뚫다 look for a job; seek a job
3 〈법망·감시 등을 벗어나다〉 evade; elude (the law)
♦ 감시망을 뚫다 elude the vigilance of the guard / 포위망을 뚫다 break [cut one's way] through the besieging enemy / 폭풍우를 뚫고 나아가다 ride out [weather] a storm / 어려움 [곤경]을 뚫고 나아가다 get through [tide over, cut one's way through] a difficulty
▶ 나는 감시의 눈을 뚫고 그와 연락을 취했다 Avoiding the watchful eye of the guard, I managed to make contact with him.
▶ 범인은 비상선을 뚫고 달아났다 The guilty man slipped through the police cordon and escaped.
▶ 그는 법망을 뚫고 국외로 도주했다 He gave the police the slip and fled across the border.
▶ 그들은 적의 포화를 뚫고 전진했다 They advanced under the enemy's fire.
▶ 그녀는 그가 인파를 뚫고 나아가는 것을 보았다 She saw him elbowing his way through the crowd.
▶ 어둠을 뚫고 번갯불이 번쩍 빛났다 Lightning flashed through the darkness.
▶ 나는 수많은 난관을 뚫고 나왔다 I have come through [overcome] all kinds of hardships.
▶ 그들은 빽빽한 덤불을 뚫고 길을 냈다 They cut [cleared, opened] a path through the thick undergrowth.
뚫리다 〈구멍이 뚫어지다〉 be pierced [bored, drilled, penetrated]; get opened up
▶ 구멍이 뚫리다 A hole is made.
▶ 터널이 뚫리다 A tunnel is bored.
▶ 길이 뚫리다 A road [path] is made [open]. ⇒ A way is found.
▶ 이 터널이 뚫리기까지는 아직 1년쯤 더 남았다 It will be one year or so before this tunnel is driven through.
뚫어지게보다 watch; gaze (intently) (at); stare fixedly [look hard] at sb; bore sb with one's eyes
♦ 아무의 얼굴을 뚫어지게 보다 stare hard at sb; bore sb with one's eyes; stare sb in the face; scrutinize sb's face

▶ 그녀는 방 안의 여러 종류의 난초를 뚫어지게 보고 있었다 She was gazing intently at the various kinds of orchids in the room.
뚫어지다 be bored [drilled, pierced]
▶ 험한 산에 긴 터널이 겨우 뚫어졌다 A long tunnel in a steep mountain has been laboriously excavated.
▶ 이 송곳은 도무지 뚫어지지 않는다 This drill won't bore.
▶ 네 양말에 구멍이 뚫어져 있다 There is a hole in your sock.
뚬기다 1 〈퉁겨지게 하다〉 let spring back; make sth spring [snap back]
2 〈귀띔하다〉 bring one to one's senses
뚬딴지 1 〈사람〉 a blunt and dull person; a dunce; a blockhead
♦ 뚬딴지같은 preposterous; absurd; foolish; laughable; unexpected / 뚬딴지같은 생각 a wild idea; a fantastic notion / 뚬딴지같은 말을 하다 make a preposterous [an absurd] remark; say extraordinary things
▶ 뚬딴지같은 소리 하지 마라 Don't talk rot ! ⇒ Nonsense !
2 〈애자(碍子)〉 an insulator
3 〔植〕 a Jerusalem artichoke
뚬땅거리다 keep drumming and twanging [twangling] ♦ 뚬땅거리며 놀다 make merry; have a hilarious time; hold high jinks; go on a spree; (美) whoop it up
뚬땅뚬땅 drumming and twanging
뚬뚬보 a fat person ⇒ 뚬뚬이
뚬뚬이 a fat [plump] person; a corpulent [stout] person; a fatty; 〈어린이의〉 a roly-poly
뚬뚬하다 plump; fat; stout; corpulent; fatty; fleshy; (美口) corn-fed
♦ 뚬뚬한 부인 a stout lady [matron] / 뚬뚬한 남자 a man with a lot of fat on him / 뚬뚬한 애기 a chubby baby / 뚬뚬해지다 fatten; grow [get] stout [fat]; grow corpulent; become fat; fat (up) / 배가 뚬뚬하다 be potbellied; have a full stomach; 〈임신하여〉 be big with child
▶ 나는 뚬뚬해졌다 I have grown stouter.
뚬보 1 〈뚬한 사람〉 a sulky [sullen, glum] person 2 ⇒ 뚬뚬이
뚬하다 1 〈성질이〉 taciturn; reticent; incommunicative
♦ 성질이 뚬한 사람 a taciturn person; a man of few words
2 〈시무룩하다〉 moody; sullen; sulky; sour; glum
♦ 뚬하고 말이 적다 be reserved and taciturn
▶ 그녀는 그의 말을 듣고 뚬하니 입을 다물고 말았다 Upon hearing his words, she fell into a moody silence.
뛰놀다 romp (about); frisk about; frolic; kid around; rollick
▶ 아이들이 눈 속에서 뛰논다 The children are frolicking in the snow.
▶ 새끼양이 들에서 뛰놀고 있다 Lambs are skipping about in the field.
뛰는 놈 위에 나는 놈이 있다 (俗談) Talent above talent.
뛰다¹ 1 〈물방울·진흙 등이〉 spatter; splash
♦ 옷에 기름이 뛰다 have splashes of grease on

one's clothes
▶내 바지에 진흙이 뛰었다 My trousers are splashed with dirt.
2 〈달아나다〉 run away; flee
3 〈가슴 등이 두근거리다〉 beat; throb; thump; palpitate; pound; go pit-a-pat
♦맥박[가슴]이 뛰다 *one's* pulse [heart] beats; pulsate
▶내 이름을 부르는 소리를 듣고 가슴이 뛰었다 When I heard my name called, my heart went pit-a-pat.
▶그녀는 뛰는 가슴으로 그가 도착하기를 기다리고 있었다 She was waiting for his arrival with a fluttering heart [in a flutter].
▶그 소식을 듣고 내 가슴은 뛰었다 My heart beat quick at the news.
4 〈물가가 오르다〉 rise; advance 《in price》; run [go] up; shoot up
▶이 달에는 물가가 뛰었다 This month prices have gone up.
5 〈거르다〉 skip; jump
♦3등에서 1등으로 뛰다 jump from the third place to the top / 10페이지에서 15페이지로 건너 뛰다 skip [jump] from page 10 to 15 / 《책의》 어려운 대목을 건너뛰다 jump [skip] (over) difficult passages
6 〈단호한 태도를 보이다〉 be firm [decisive]
♦펄쩍 뛰며 부인하다 deny 《it》 emphatically [flatly, hotly]
7 〈일하다〉 work
▶그는 열심히 뛰었다 He worked hard.
▶그는 결코 생계를 위해서 뛸 필요가 없었다 He never had to work for a living.
▶우리는 주당 40시간을 뛴다 We generally work 40 hours a week.

뛰다² **1** 〈도약하다〉 jump; leap; spring; bound; 〈한발로〉 hop
♦펄쩍 뛰다 jump to *one's* feet; jump [leap] out of *one's* skin
▶나는 펄쩍 뛰어 일어났다 I sprang to my feet.
▶그는 멀리뛰기에서 6미터를 뛰었다 He jumped six meters in the broad jump.
2 〈뛰어넘다〉 jump [vault, skip] over
♦도랑을 뛰어 건너다 jump over a ditch
3 〈달리다〉 run; dash; rush
♦뛰어 가다 run 《to, for》; go running / 뛰기 시작하다 begin to run; start running / break into a run / 언덕을 뛰어 올라가다 run up a hill; 〈계단을〉 run [dash] upstairs
▶역까지는 뛰어서 10분이다 It is ten minutes' [a ten-minute] run to the station.
▶그는 뛰어서 녹초가 되었다 He ran himself ragged.
▶그는 매일 아침 2킬로미터를 뛴다 He runs two kilometers every morning.
▶그녀는 뛰어서 돌아왔다 She came back running.

뛰다³ **1** 〈그네를〉 swing 《on a swing》; rock back and forth; propel 《a swing》; have a swing
♦그네를 뛰다 get on [sit in] a swing
2 〈널을〉 seesaw; play seesaw [teeter-totter]
▶아이들이 널을 뛰며 놀고 있다 The children are playing on a seesaw.

뛰어가다 go running; run 《to》; rush 《for》; dash
♦단숨에 뛰어가다 dash in a breath [with *one* breath]
▶그는 교회까지 줄곧 뛰어갔다 He ran all the way to church.
▶뛰어가지 않으면 열차를 놓칠거다 Make a run, or you'll miss the train. ⇌ You'll not be in time for the train unless you run.
뛰어나가다 〈밖으로〉 run out [outside]; dash [rush, burst] out; barrel out; start forward [out]
♦거리로 [밖으로] 뛰어나가다 rush out into the street / 집을 뛰어나가다 dash out of the house; 〈가출하다〉 run away from home; fly from *one's* home
▶나는 밥도 먹지 않고 집을 뛰어나갔다 I flew out of the house without eating.
▶사자가 우리에서 뛰어나갔다 The lion jumped out of the cage.
▶한 사람이 뛰어나가자 뒤에 있던 사람들도 모두 뛰어나갔다 When a person began to run, the people behind him did the same.
뛰어나다 excel; surpass; be superior to; 〈우수하다〉 be excellent; 〈유명하다〉 be noted; 〈탁월하다〉 distinguish *oneself*; come out on top 《of》
♦뛰어난 superior; best; surpassing; 〈훌륭하다〉 excellent; outstanding; 〈탁월한〉 prominent; eminent; choicest; outstanding; conspicuous / 뛰어난 재능 a distinguished talent / 뛰어난 업적 an outstanding [a brilliant] achievement / 뛰어나게 prominently; conspicuously / 뛰어나게 좋은 물건 an article far superior to others; an extra-fine article / 뛰어난 솜씨를 보이다 show [display] *one's* skill 《in》 / 남보다 역량이 뛰어나다 surpass [excel] others in ability / 뛰어나게 아름답다 be strikingly beautiful / 영어에 뛰어나다 excel others in English
▶그는 글 솜씨가 뛰어나다 He is a good writer.
▶그는 언변이 뛰어나다 He speaks eloquently.
▶그는 재간이 뛰어나다 He is a man of ability.
▶그는 뛰어나게 키가 크다 He is uncommonly tall.
▶그는 반에서 수학을 뛰어나게 잘한다 He is far ahead of his class in mathematics. ⇌ He outshines the others in his class in math.
▶침팬지는 다른 동물보다 지능이 뛰어나다 The chimpanzee is superior in intelligence to other animals.
뛰어내리다 jump [leap, spring] down [off]
▶그는 창문에서 뛰어내렸다 He jumped [leaped] out of the window.
▶그는 달리는 열차[말]에서 뛰어내렸다 He jumped off [out of] a moving train [the running horse].
뛰어넘다 **1** 〈장애물 등을〉 jump [spring] over; clear 《a fence》; vault over 《a gate》
♦담을 뛰어넘다 jump over a fence / 장애물을 뛰어넘다 clear [take] a hurdle / 6피트를 섭사리 뛰어넘다 clear six feet with an easy jump

뛰어다니다

▶그들은 개천을 뛰어넘었다 They jumped across a brook.
2〈순서를 거르다〉 skip [jump] (over)
◆12페이지에서 15페이지로 뛰어넘다 skip from page 12 to 15
▶그녀는 내 자리를 뛰어넘어 과장에게 문제를 가져갔다 She took the matter over my head to the section chief.
▶오늘은 가을을 뛰어넘어 겨울이 온 듯한 추위다 It's so cold today (that) it feels as if we've skipped autumn and gone directly into winter.

뛰어다니다 1〈껑충껑충〉 jump about; frisk; skip
▶개가 정원을 뛰어다니고 있다 A dog is jumping about in the garden.
2〈바삐 돌아다니다〉 run about [round]; bustle [hurry, fly] about
▶그는 일자리를 찾아 매일 뛰어다녔다 He bustled about every day looking for employment.
▶그는 돈을 마련하려고 이곳저곳을 뛰어다녔다 He busied himself to raise money here and there.

뛰어들다 1〈몸을 던져〉 spring [jump] in [into]
◆강물에 뛰어들다 throw *oneself* into a river / 별안간 방안으로 뛰어들다 make a sudden rush into a room
▶그는 수영장에 풍덩하고 뛰어들었다 He jumped into the swimming pool with a splash.
▶사나이는 다리에서 강으로 뛰어들었다 The man dived [jumped] off the bridge into the river.
2〈갑자기 들어오다〉▶트럭이 우리 집으로 뛰어들었다 A truck crashed into my house.
3〈참견하다〉thrust *oneself* into《a quarrel》; thrust *one's* nose in; butt into; 〈참여하다〉 take part [participate] in (a game) from the outside
▶불청객이 뛰어들었다 An unwanted fellow butted in.

뛰어들어오다 jump [dash, rush] in [into]; burst into
▶강아지가 갑자기 내 방에 뛰어들어왔다 A puppy made a sudden rush into my room.
▶학생들이 기세 좋게 교실로 뛰어들어왔다 The students rushed into the classroom.

뛰어오다 come running; come at a run
▶아이들은 우리가 서 있는데로 뛰어왔다 The children came running to where we were standing.
▶집에서 여기까지 줄곧 뛰어왔다 I have run here all the way from home.

뛰어오르다 1〈위로〉 spring up; jump up; start [leap, jump] to *one's* feet
▶그의 아들은 막 떠나가는 기차에 뛰어올랐다 His son jumped into a train just as it was starting.
▶개구리가 공중으로 뛰어올랐다 The frog leaped into the air.
▶그 소년은 안장 없는 말에 뛰어올라 탔다 The boy leaped bareback onto the horse.
▶달리는 열차에 뛰어오르는 것은 위험하다 It is dangerous to jump onto a moving train.
▶선거에서 무명의 신인이 선두로 뛰어올랐다 An unknown new figure suddenly became the frontrunner in the election campaign.
2〈가격·지위 등이〉 rise suddenly; jump; rise; go up
▶물가가 뛰어올랐다 Prices took a jump.

뜀 1 ⇨ 달리기 **2**〈도약〉 jumping; leaping; a bound; a vault

뜀뛰기 jumping
■─선수 a jumper ─운동 a jumping exercise ─종목 a jumping event ─판 a springboard; a leaping board

뜀박질 1 ⇨ 달음박질 **2** ⇨ 뜀뛰기

뜀틀 a vaulting horse; a buck ◆뜀틀을 뛰어넘다 vault over a horse; vault a (long) horse

뜨개실 knitting yarn

뜨개질 knitting;〈코바늘의〉 crochet; knitwork
◆뜨개질을 시작하다 take up *one's* knitting ─뜨개질하다 knit; do knitting; crochet
◆뜨개질한 스웨터 a hand-knit sweater / 뜨개질하는 사람 a knitter / 뜨개질하는 손을 쉬다 lay down *one's* knitting
▶이 장갑은 뜨개질한 것이다 These gloves are hand-knitted.
■─바늘 a knitting needle;〈코바늘〉 a crochet hook

뜨거운 감자 〈성가신 일〉 a hot potato
▶인종차별 문제는 정치적인 뜨거운 감자다 The racial discrimination issue is a political hot potato.

뜨거워지다 become hot; grow [get] warm
▶모터가 너무 뜨거워졌다 The motor is overheated.

뜨겁다 1〈열이 높다〉 hot; heated; burning
◆뜨거운 물로 접시를 닦다 wash plates in boiling water
▶음식이 너무 뜨거워서 못 먹겠다 The food is too hot to eat.
▶국은 뜨거울 때 들어야 한다 Soup should be eaten while it's hot.
▶태양이 뜨겁게 내 얼굴을 내리쬐었다 The sun shone hot on my face.
▶부끄러워 얼굴이 뜨겁다 My face burns with shame.
2〈열렬하다〉 hot; passionate; ardent; fervent; burning
◆뜨거운 사랑 a passionate [burning] love / 나라를 사랑하는 뜨거운 마음 deep love for *one's* country / 뜨거운 박수를 보내다 give a big hand《to》; clap and shout《to》 / 뜨거운 눈물을 흘리다 shed hot tears
▶두 사람은 뜨거운 사이인 것 같다 They seem to be deeply [passionately] in love with each other.

-뜨기 guy; person; thing; fellow
◆시골뜨기 a (country) bumpkin / 얼뜨기 a half-wit / 칠뜨기 a moron; an idiot

뜨끈뜨끈하다 burning hot

뜨끈하다 fairly hot

뜨끈히 hotly

뜨끔하다 1〈아프다〉 prickly; stinging; painful
◆뜨끔하게 아프다 have a prick

2 〈양심에 거리끼다〉 smart
뜨내기 〈사람〉 a wanderer; a vagabond; a vagrant; 〈일꾼〉 a casual workman; 〈일〉 an odd job ■—**손님** a chance [casual] customer; a chance comer; a stray visitor
뜨내기장사 a business done off and on; a casual [temporary] business
▶ 그는 뜨내기장사로 돈을 꽤 모았다 He has amassed quite a sum of money by doing casual business.
—뜨내기장사하다 do business temporarily [off and on]

뜨다¹ **1** 〈가라앉았거나 떨어지지 않다〉 float; buoy; 〈비행기가〉 fly ♦하늘 높이 떠 있는 기구 a balloon floating on high
▶ 돌은 물 위에 뜨지 않는다 The stone does not float on the water.
▶ 호수 위에 배가 떠 있다 A boat is on the lake.
▶ 햇빛 속에 먼지가 떠 있다 Specks of dust swim in the sunbeams.
▶ 달이 중천에 떠 있다 The moon is riding high in the sky.
▶ 하늘에 연이 하나 떠 있었다 A kite was flying in the air.
2 〈솟아오르다〉 rise; come up
▶ 해는 동쪽에서 뜬다 The sun rises in the east.
▶ 오늘밤에 달이 7시경에 뜬다 The moon will come out around 7 o'clock tonight.
▶ 나는 잠시 몸이 공중에 뜨는 것을 느꼈다 I felt my body rise into the air for a moment.
3 〈관계가 멀어지다〉 be estranged
▶ 오해로 말미암아 두 친구는 사이가 뜨게 되었다 A misunderstanding between the two friends had caused their estrangement.
▶ 그 부부는 사이가 뜬지 오래다 The man and wife have long been estranged from each other.
4 〈틈이 생기다〉 come off [apart]; get [become] loose
♦장판이 뜨다 floor paper comes off the floor / 잇새가 뜨다 have a gap between the teeth; one's teeth are loose
5 〈시간·공간이 벌어지다〉 have an interval 《of time, of space》; be [get] separated; be distant [apart] 《from》 ♦마을에서 멀리 뜬 곳 the place far from the town
6 〈준 것을 받지 못하다〉 be lost for good; go up in smoke
▶ 그에게 빌려 주었던 돈이 떴다 The money I lent him is gone.

뜨다² **1** 〈발효하다〉 ferment; undergo fermentation; 〈썩다〉 become stale; grow moldy; turn bad 《from heat》
▶ 날이 더워 창고의 쌀이 떴다 The rice in the granary has become stale due to hot weather.
2 〈얼굴이 누렇게 붓다〉 become sallow and bloated
♦누렇게 뜬 얼굴 a sallow face

뜨다³ 〈떠나다〉 leave; quit; go away 《from》; depart 《from》; 〈옮기다〉 move 《out of a place》; 〈비우다〉 clear out
♦고향을 뜨다 leave one's hometown / 서울을 뜨다 leave Seoul / 세상을 뜨다 depart (from) this world 《to the eternity》; pass away; die / 자리를 뜨다 leave one's seat 《to go out》; slip out of one's office / 자리를 뜨지 않고 있다 keep one's seat
▶ 나는 자리를 뜨려고 막 일어서는 참이었다 I half rose to my feet to leave my seat.

뜨다⁴ **1** 〈눈을 벌리다〉 open 《one's eyes》
♦눈을 뜨다 open one's eyes; wake up; awake / 사실[시대]에 눈을 뜨다 be awakened to a fact [the times] / 눈을 크게 뜨고 보다 look at with one's eyes wide open
▶ 졸려서 눈을 뜰 수가 없다 I'm so sleepy that I can't keep my eyes open.
▶ 나는 거의 눈을 뜨고 있을 수가 없었다 I could hardly keep my eyes open.
2 〈처음으로 듣다〉 open; prick up 《one's ears》
♦음악에 귀를 뜨다 become to appreciate music / 아기가 귀를 뜨다 a baby begins to hear

뜨다⁵ **1** 〈일부를 떼어내다〉 cut off [out]; shovel off ♦뗏장을 뜨다 cut sod 《from a field》; tear turf / 석재를 뜨다 cut out [quarry] stone
2 〈떠내다〉 scoop [dip] up; ladle out; spoon up [out] ♦국자로 국을 뜨다 ladle soup; dip up soup / 숟가락으로 뜨다 spoon out [up] / 저녁을 한 숟갈 뜨다 have a bite of supper
▶ 그는 우물 물을 두 손으로 떠서 마셨다 He scooped up some water from the well in his hands and drank it.
3 〈덩이로 만들어 내다〉 poach 《eggs》
4 〈해체하다〉 cut up ♦소를 잡아 각을 뜨다 cut up a slaughtered cow
5 〈얇게 저미다〉 slice 《meat》; cut into slices ♦고기를 포 뜨다 cut meat into slices 《to be dried》
6 〈피륙에서 끊어 내다〉 buy 《a piece of cloth》
▶ 장에 가거든 옷감을 한 감 떠다 주시오 When you go to the market place, get me a piece of cloth for making my dress, please.
7 〈종이를 만들어 내다〉 make; shape
♦종이를[김을] 뜨다 make paper [laver]

뜨다⁶ 〔韓醫〕 〈약쑥을 태우다〉 cauterize 《the skin》 with wormwood; burn wormwood 《on the skin》; give wormwood treatment
♦머리에 뜸을 뜨다 cauterize the top of one's head 《with wormwood》

뜨다⁷ **1** 〈짜다〉 net; weave; knit; crochet
♦그물을 뜨다 make [knit, weave] a net; net / 털실로 양말을 뜨다 knit stockings out of wool; knit wool into stockings
2 〈한땀씩 바느질하다〉 stitch; sew
▶ 터진 데를 한두 바늘 뜨다 put one or two stitches in a rip / 손수건에 이름의 머릿글자를 뜨다 work one's initials on a handkerchief

뜨다⁸ **1** 〈따라가다〉 follow suit; model 《oneself》
2 〈똑같게 하다〉 make; take
♦지형을 뜨다 make a paper mold; take a papier-mâché mold 《of》
3 〈본을 떠내다〉 copy; trace; draw; facsimile
♦버선본을 뜨다 copy a pattern of socks from the original model / 사본을 뜨다 copy; make a

뜨다⁹ 〈뿔로 들이받다〉 horn up; toss (up); butt ▶ 소가 사람을 떴다 A cow tossed a man with its horns.

뜨다¹⁰ **1** 〈느리다〉 slow; 〈완만하다〉 easy; gentle ♦ 템포가 뜬 음악 music in a slow tempo / 물매가 뜬 지붕 a gently sloping roof; a roof which has an easy slope / 걸음이 뜨다 be slow-paced; be slow of foot
2 〈둔하다〉 dull; slow-witted; dull-witted ♦ 깨우침이 뜨다 be slow at understanding lessons / 눈치가 뜨다 be slow [dull] in catching a situation
3 〈입이 무겁다〉 taciturn; reticent; tight-lipped ♦ 입이 뜬 사람 a man of few words
4 〈연장이 무디다〉 dull; blunt ♦ 칼날이 뜨다 the edge of a knife is blunt

뜨뜻미지근하다 lukewarm; tepid; disagreeably warm ♦ 뜨뜻미지근한 박수 tepid applause / 뜨뜻미지근한 대접을 받다 get a lukewarm reception
▶ 그녀의 사랑은 뜨뜻미지근해졌다 Her love has grown lukewarm.

뜨뜻하다 warm ⇨ 따뜻하다

뜨락 a garden ⇨ 뜰

뜨물 (turbid) water in which rice has been washed

뜨악하다 unwilling; reluctant ♦ 대답이 뜨악하다 give a cold answer; make a halfhearted reply / 그는 이 일을 하기가 뜨악한 모양이다 He seems indisposed to do this job.

뜨음하다 infrequent; 〈서술적〉 have a rather long interval
♦ (비·바람 등이) 뜨음한 사이 a lull [break] (in the rain) / 발길이 뜨음하다 come [visit] less frequently (than before) / 집 소식이 뜨음하다 have not heard from home for quite a long time
▶ 비가 뜨음해졌다 The rain is letting up a little.
▶ 졸업하고 나면 학교 가는 일이 뜨음해지게 마련이다 People visit their school less often after their graduation.

뜨이다 **1** 〈눈이 열리다〉 be opened; awake; 〈귀가 들리다〉 prick up; 〈깨닫게 되다〉 come to know [understand]
♦ 아침 일찍 눈이 뜨이다 awake early in the morning / 성에 눈이 뜨이다 be awakened to sex; be sexually awakened / 그림에 눈이 뜨이다 begin to appreciate painting / 눈이 번쩍 뜨이다 awake suddenly; be wide awake / 귀가 번쩍 뜨이다 strike [catch] *one's* ears / 음악에 귀가 뜨이다 begin to understand music
2 〈보이다〉 be seen; be in sight [view]; 〈발견되다〉 be found; catch the eye; 〈돋보이다〉 be remarkable; be prominent; be conspicuous
♦ 눈에 뜨이는 prominent; conspicuous; attractive / 눈에 뜨이지 않는 inconspicuous; unnoticeable; unattractive / 눈에 뜨이는 특징 conspicuous characteristics / 눈에 뜨이는 대로 at [on] sight / 눈에 뜨이지 않게 in a quiet way; so as not to attract attention
▶ 그들은 눈에 뜨이는 곳에 게시했다 They put up a notice in a conspicuous place.
▶ 그는 눈에 뜨이게 향상했다 He has made remarkable progress.
▶ 그는 눈에 뜨이게 건강이 쇠약해졌다 His health has declined noticeably.

뜨임 〔冶〕 tempering

뜬구름 〈떠다니는 구름〉 a floating [drifting] cloud; a cloud drift
2 〈덧없음〉 transience; transitoriness; evanescence ♦ 뜬구름 같은 인생 transient life
▶ 인생은 뜬구름에 지나지 않는다 Life is but an empty dream.

뜬눈 unsleeping eyes ♦ 뜬눈으로 밤을 새우다 sit up all night; pass a sleepless [wakeful] night; do not sleep a wink; do not get a wink of sleep

뜬세상 —世上 the (transitory) world; transient [fleeting] life; the earth ♦ 뜬세상을 버리다 forsake [retire from] the world

뜬소문 —所聞 a groundless rumor; an unfounded report; a canard
▶ 그가 죽었다는 뜬소문이 돌았다 An unfounded rumor was going round that he had died.
▶ 그것은 뜬소문이다 There is no foundation for the rumor.

뜬숯 used charcoal; cinders

뜬주낙 a floating long line

뜯게 worn-out clothes to be unsewn

뜯게질하다 unsew 《a dress》; undo a seam

뜯기다 〈물리다〉 be bitten ♦ 벼룩한테 뜯긴 자리 a fleabite / 모기한테 뜯기다 be bitten by a mosquito
2 〈빼앗기다〉 have *sth* bitten off; be plucked [fleeced] 《of》; be exacted [squeezed] 《by》 ♦ 돈을 뜯기다 be fleeced 《of money》 《by sharpers》; be squeezed out of *one's* money / 낚시 미끼를 뜯기다 have a bait bitten off; lose *one's* bait
3 〈내기에서 잃다〉 lose; forfeit ♦ 노름으로 재산을 뜯기다 gamble away *one's* fortune
4 〈머리털 등을 뽑히다〉 be plucked; be pulled out; be torn out [off]
▶ 그 공작은 깃을 뜯겼다 The peacock was plucked of his feathers.
5 〈풀을 뜯어 먹게 하다〉 put 《cattle》 to grass; graze 《cattle》; pasture ♦ 소에게 풀을 뜯기다 put a cow to feed on growing grass

뜯다 **1** 〈떼어 내다〉 pluck [pick, pull, tear] (off); 〈뜯어내다〉 tear off [up, down]; tear [take] apart; take off; remove; disassemble; break up; 〈붙인 것을 열다〉 open 《a letter》; 〈솔기를 풀다〉 unsew; unstitch
♦ 풀을 뜯다 pluck grass; weed 《a garden》 / 닭의 털을 뜯다 pluck [pick] a chicken; pick feathers from a chicken / 담요의 보풀을 뜯다 pick at the blanket / 기계를 뜯다 take a machine apart [to pieces]; break up a machine / 봉투를 뜯다 open [break open] an envelope; cut 《a letter》 open / 봉함을 뜯다 break [take off] the seal / 솔기를 뜯다 undo a seam; unsew
2 〈노름판에서 돈을 얻다〉 gain; get
♦ (노름판에서) 개평을 뜯다 take a (free) cut of the winnings; pick up tidbits of the win-

nings
3 〈돈을 우려내다〉 pluck [fleece] 《sb of his money》; extort 《money from sb》
♦백성들한테 돈을 뜯다 extort money from the people
4 〈현악기의 줄을 퉁기다〉 play (on); pluck [touch] (the strings of); pick 《a guitar》
♦가야금을 뜯다 play on the Korean harp
5 〈이로 물어 떼다〉 bite; graze; pasture
♦불갈비를 뜯다 eat roast ribs of beef / 소가 풀을 뜯다 let the cattle graze [pasture]
뜯어고치다 **1** 〈해체하여 고치다〉 tear [take] apart and mend [repair]; 〈개조하다〉 reconstruct; rebuild; remodel
♦옷을 뜯어고치다 remake one's clothes / 집을 뜯어고치다 alter a house / 방을 뜯어고치다 remodel a room
2 〈검토하여 시정하다〉 look over and change [alter]; examine and improve; revise
♦법령을 뜯어고치다 revise an ordinance / 원고를 뜯어고치다 revise a manuscript / 행실을 뜯어고치다 mend one's ways
뜯어내다 **1** 〈떼어 내다〉 tear off [away]; take off [away, down]; pick [pluck] (off)
♦달력을 한 장 뜯어내다 tear off a leaf from a calendar / 옷의 안쪽을 뜯어내다 rip off [out] the lining / 옷에서 실밥을 뜯어내다 remove waste thread from clothes / 뼈에서 고기를 뜯어내다 take [tear] off the meat from a bone / 물어서 뜯어내다 bit [eat] off
▶그는 게시판에서 포스터를 뜯어냈다 He tore the poster down from the bulletin board.
2 〈분해하다〉 take [pull] sth to pieces; take 《a machine》 apart [down]
▶동생은 자명종을 뜯었다 My brother took his alarm clock apart.
3 〈돈을〉 extort; pluck; fleece
♦남편한테서 돈을 뜯어내다 pluck one's husband of his money; tease [importune, press] one's husband for money
뜯어말리다 pull [draw] 《fighters》 apart; stop 《a fight》 ♦싸움을 뜯어말리다 draw [pull] combatants [quarreling persons] apart; put down a fight
뜯어먹다 **1** 〈마소가 풀을〉 graze; pasture
▶소들이 목장에서 풀을 뜯어먹고 있다 The cattle are grazing [feeding on grass] in the pasture.
2 〈이로 떼어먹다〉 eat on [at]; nibble (on, at); gnaw (at) ♦닭고기를 뜯어먹다 nibble on a chicken / 뼈에 붙은 고기를 뜯어먹다 gnaw the meat of a bone
3 〈손으로 떼어먹다〉 take sth off and eat it
4 〈졸라서 얻어먹다〉 pinch; squeeze; sponge 《off sb》; hang on sb; act like a leech on sb
♦남을 뜯어먹고 살다 live [prey] on sb; victimize sb
뜯어보다 **1** 〈열어서 살펴보다〉 open [tear] sth and look at it
♦편지를 뜯어보다 open [unseal, cut open] a letter and read it
▶남이 뜯어볼 수 없도록 봉투를 단단히 붙이시오 Seal (up) the envelope in order to make it confidential.

2 〈자세히 살피다〉 scrutinize; scan; study; look closely 《at》; take a good look 《at》; examine sth closely; inspect [examine] carefully [in detail]
♦사람됨을 뜯어보다 scrutinize the caliber [quality] of sb / 얼굴을 뜯어보다 scrutinize [study] sb's face; get a good look into sb's face / 집을 이모저모로 뜯어보다 look a house over thoroughly
3 〈겨우 읽다·해독하다〉 read [construe] with difficulty; falter (in reading) ♦고문서를 뜯어보다 decipher an old manuscript
뜰 a yard; a garden; a courtyard

> **解說** (1) 《美》에서는 꽃·나무의 조경 유무나 포장·비포장에 관계 없이 집 주변의 뜰이나 안뜰을 **yard**라 하고, **garden**은 「정원」「화원」의 뜻으로 쓰는 것이 보통이다.
> (2) 《英》에서는 **yard**는 포장된 뜰을 말하고, 잔디·꽃·나무가 심겨져 있으면 **garden**이라고 한다.

♦앞뜰 a front garden [yard] / 뒤뜰 a backyard / 뜰에 심은 나무 a garden tree / 뜰에 나무를 심다 plant a garden (with trees) / 뜰을 손질하다 trim (up) a garden
뜰아래채 an outhouse (separated by a garden from the main building)
뜰아랫방 a room in an outhouse
뜰채 a landing net
뜸¹ a cattail [rush] mat
뜸² 【韓醫】 wormwood cautery
♦뜸 자국 a mark made by wormwood cautery / 뜸 자리 a spot cauterized with wormwood; an effective spot for applying wormwood / 뜸(을) 뜨다 ⇨ 뜨다⁶
뜸³ ♦ 뜸(이) 들다 be steamed to a proper degree; be well steamed ▶밥이 뜸이 잘 들었다 The rice has been properly steamed.
뜸들이다 **1** 〈음식을 푹 익게 하다〉 steam sth to settle; cook thoroughly
♦밥을 뜸들이다 allow boiled rice to settle by its own heat
2 〈한 동안 멈추다〉 give a necessary pause [interval of time]; give time (enough)
♦일을 뜸들여 하다 allow enough time to get a job done
뜸부기 【鳥】 a water cock; a mud [marsh] hen
뜸직뜸직 gravely; solemnly; in a dignified manner
♦뜸직뜸직 말하다 speak solemn words; measure one's words / 뜸직뜸직 걷다 walk with dignified [measured] steps
뜸직하다 dignified; composed; measured; imposing; self-possessed; weighty
♦뜸직한 사람 a man of composure / 뜸직하게 gravely; solemnly
뜸질 cauterizing with wormwood; wormwood cautery
　—**뜸질하다** cauterize 《the skin》 with wormwood; burn wormwood 《on the skin》
뜸집 a thatched hut [shack]
뜸하다 infrequent ⇨ 뜨음하다
뜻 **1** 〈마음〉 a [one's] mind; 〈의지〉 (a) will;

⟨의향⟩ (an) intention; (a) motive; (a) design; ⟨목적⟩ an objective; an aim; a purpose; ⟨야망⟩ (an) ambition; (an) aspiration; ⟨희망⟩ a wish; (a) hope

▶우리가 만난 것은 하늘의 뜻이다 It is divine will that has brought us together.

⟨뜻이[은]⟩ 뜻이 큰 사람 a man of great ambition; an ambitious man / 뜻이 서로 통하다 come to [arrive at] an understanding; understand each other / …할 뜻이 있다 have an intention 《of》; be inclined to 《do》/ 뜻이 있다면 if you wish [want]; if you are inclined [disposed] to

▶뜻이 있는 곳에 길이 있다 (속담) Where there's a will, there's a way.

▶나는 장사할 뜻은 조금도 없다 I haven't the slightest intention of going into business.

⟨뜻을⟩ 뜻을 세우다 set an aim in life; set an object before one / 높은 뜻을 품다 aim high; have a high [lofty] aim / …의 뜻을 떠보다 sound sb's views / 뜻을 밝히다 reveal [express] one's intention; speak one's mind / …의 뜻을 거역하다 act against sb's will / 뜻을 이루다 attain one's aim; realize one's aspiration / 결과에 대하여 만족의 뜻을 표하다 express one's satisfaction at [with] the result

▶그는 아버지의 뜻을 어기고 상경했다 He came up to Seoul against his father's will.

▶연작이 어찌 홍곡의 뜻을 알리오 A man must be a hero to understand a hero.

▶그는 마침내 뜻을 이루었다 He finally achieved [accomplished] his object [purpose].

▶부모의 뜻을 거스르면 안된다 You shouldn't do anything against your parents' wishes.

▶그는 부모의 뜻을 거스르고 그녀와 결혼했다 He married her against the will of his parents.

▶그는 뜻을 이루지 못하고 죽었다 He died before he could realize his dream.

▶나는 그의 유족에게 애도의 뜻을 표했다 I expressed my condolences to his bereaved family.

⟨뜻에⟩ 남의 뜻에 따르다 yield to another's wishes / 뜻에 맞다 meet one's wish; suit one's fancy; be to one's liking

▶그것은 내 뜻에 맞는다 It is to my liking.

▶당신의 의견은 내 뜻에 부합됩니다 Your opinion agrees with mine.

▶나는 그의 뜻에 따라 그녀를 방문했다 I called on her in compliance with his will.

▶나는 아버님의 뜻에 따라 가업을 이었다 In obedience to [Following] my father's wishes, I took over the family business.

2 ⟨의미⟩ (a) meaning; (a) sense; significance; ⟨취지⟩ the import; the purport; the effect; a point; ⟨함축⟩ implication

♦깊은 뜻 a deep [profound] meaning / 숨은 뜻 a latent [hidden] meaning / 애매한 뜻 an ambiguous [obscure] meaning / 글자 그대로의 뜻 literal meaning

▶그것은 무슨 뜻이오? What do you mean by that? ⇌ What does that mean?

▶그것은 뜻있는 계획이다 That's a meaningful [sensible] project.

▶그는 뜻없는 말을 중얼거리고 있다 He is muttering meaningless sounds.

⟨뜻의⟩ 뜻의 미묘한 차이 a delicate shade of meaning

▶내가 그런 뜻의 말을 했을지도 모른다 I may have said something to that effect.

▶나는 그가 잘 있다는 뜻의 편지를 받았다 I received a letter to the effect that he is getting along well.

⟨뜻이⟩ 뜻이 없다 be meaningless / 뜻이 모호하다 have an ambiguous [obscure] meaning; be vague [ambiguous] / 뜻이 깊다 have deep [profound] meaning; be meaningful [full of meaning]

▶네가 참석하지 않으면 모임은 뜻이 없다 The meeting will mean little without your attendance.

▶그다지 깊은 뜻이 있어서 그렇게 말한 것은 아니다 I did not mean anything serious when I said so.

▶그 모임에 정치적 뜻은 없다 The meeting has no political significance.

▶이 단어에는 약간 속어적인 뜻이 있다 This word has some slangy senses.

⟨뜻을⟩ 뜻을 이해하다 understand [comprehend] the meaning 《of》; follow the sense 《of》 / 뜻을 파악하다 grasp [catch] the meaning / 뜻을 전하다 convey one's meaning / 뜻을 곡해하다 pervert [twist] the meaning / 뜻을 잘못 알다 mistake the meaning; misunderstand

▶전보의 뜻을 모르겠다 I can make nothing of the telegram.

▶그의 말 뜻을 모르겠다 I don't understand him. ⇌ I don't understand what his remarks mean. ⇌ I can't make out what he means.

▶이 의식의 진정한 뜻을 아는 사람은 적다 Few people can understand the true meaning of this ceremony.

▶그 뜻을 그에게 전화로 알리겠소 I shall telephone him to that effect.

⟨뜻으로⟩ 일반적인[막연한] 뜻으로 in a general [vague] sense / 넓은[좁은] 뜻으로 in a broad [narrow] sense / 다른 뜻으로 in another meaning / 좋은[나쁜] 뜻으로 해석하다 take 《it》 in a favorable [bad] sense; take 《it》 well [ill]

▶나쁜 뜻으로 말한 것은 아니다 I meant no ill will.

▶내 말을 그런 뜻으로 받아들여서는 곤란하다 You must not take my words that way.

▶이 구절은 여러 가지 뜻으로 해석된다 This passage may be read in various ways.

뜻대로 (in) one's own way; as one likes [pleases, desires, wishes]; just as wished [hoped, intended, meant]; at one's pleasure

♦뜻대로 되다 come up to one's expectations; turn out satisfactory [just as one wishes] / 뜻대로 되지 않다 fall short of one's expectations

▶그녀는 만사를 자기 뜻대로 하려고 했다 She wanted to have everything her own way.

▶세상 만사 자기 뜻대로는 안된다 (속담) If wishes were horses, beggars would [might]

ride. ⇒ Things will not turn out as you wish. ⇒ You cannot have your own way in everything [everything your own way].

뜻맞다 1 〈뜻이 맞다〉 agree 《with sb》; be congenial; be like-minded; be of congenial temper; be in [of] a mind 《with》 ♦ 뜻맞는 친구 a congenial friend; a like-minded company
▶ 그들은 뜻맞는 사이다 They are like-minded. ⇒ They are congenial spirits [souls].
2 〈마음에 들다〉 be satisfactory; be acceptable; 〈서술적〉 be to *one's* taste [liking]; 〈사물이 주어〉 suit [please, catch, capture] *one's* fancy
▶ 좀처럼 뜻맞는 사람을 구할 수가 없다 It's hard to find a man to suit me.

뜻밖 unexpectedness; a surprise
♦ 뜻밖의 결과 an unexpected result / 뜻밖의 선물 a surprise gift / 뜻밖의 소식 surprising news / 뜻밖의 손님 an unexpected guest / 뜻밖의 수입 an unexpected income / 뜻밖의 승리 an accidental victory / 뜻밖의 일 an unlooked-for event; an unexpected happening; an unforeseen occurrence
▶ 그가 오다니 참 뜻밖이다 He is the last man I expected to see.
▶ 그것은 천만 뜻밖이다 That is a great surprise. ⇒ That is a bolt from the blue.
▶ 그의 결혼은 아주 뜻밖이었다 His marriage was utterly unexpected.
▶ 그것은 전혀 뜻밖의 사태였다 It was a totally unexpected development.
▶ 나는 뜻밖의 장소에서 그를 만났다 We met where I had least expected to see him.
▶ 나는 그의 뜻밖의 제의에 깜짝 놀랐다 I was surprised at his completely unexpected offer.
▶ 이거 정말 뜻밖의 말씀을 하시는 군요 What you say is the last thing I expected.

뜻밖에 beyond [contrary to] *one's* expectations; by accident [chance]; unexpectedly; accidently; suddenly; surprisingly
♦ 뜻밖에 빨리 earlier than (was) expected / 뜻밖에 이기다 score an upset victory 《over》; bring off an unexpected win 《over》
▶ 뜻밖에 손님이 찾아왔다 I had an unexpected visitor.
▶ 역에서 뜻밖에 그를 만났다 I happened to meet [bumped into] him at the station.
▶ 뜻밖에 날씨가 좋아졌다 To our pleasant surprise, the weather has turned out fine.
▶ 뜻밖에 좋은 성적이었다 The results were better than we had expected.

뜻있다 〈의미있다〉 significant; 〈함축성있다〉 meaningful; 〈가치있다〉 worthwhile
♦ 뜻있는 생애 a life worth living; a well-spent life / 뜻있는 미소를 띠고 with a meaningful smile / 뜻있게 사용하다 put *sth* to a good use
▶ 그것은 매우 뜻있는 강연이었다 It was a very meaningful lecture.
▶ 대학을 졸업하면 뭔가 뜻있는 일을 하고 싶다 I hope to do something significant when I graduate from college.
▶ 뜻있는 시민은 모두 우리나라의 현상을 개탄하고 있다 All concerned citizens deplore the present situation in our country.

뜻하다 1 〈의도하다〉 plan; intend 《to do》; aim at; aspire to [after] 《fame, honor》; have *sth* in view
♦ 뜻하는 바 something aimed at; the end in view / 뜻하지 않은 선물 a surprise gift / 뜻하지 않은 성공 an unlooked-for success / 뜻하지 않은 손님 an unexpected visitor / 뜻하지 않은 일 an unforeseen event / 뜻하지 않게 casually; by chance [accident]; accidentally
▶ 그것은 뜻하지 않은 횡재다 It is a windfall [godsend].
▶ 나는 그가 뜻하고 있는 바를 모르겠다 I cannot guess what he is driving at.
▶ 뜻하지 않게 서울역에서 은사를 만났다 I met my former teacher unexpectedly [by chance, by accident] at Seoul Station.
2 〈의미하다〉 mean; imply; signify
▶ 침묵은 승낙을 뜻한다 Silence implies consent.
▶ 그것은 무엇을 뜻하느냐? What does it mean [signify]?
▶ 그녀의 미소는 우리를 용서했음을 뜻했다 Her smile implied that she had forgiven us.

띄다 1 be opened
▶ 책상 위의 편지가 그의 눈에 띄었다 He noticed a letter on the desk. ⇒ A letter on the desk caught his eyes.
2 let fly

띄어쓰기 spacing words

띄어쓰다 write with a space between each words; space 《words, letters》
♦ 한자 한자 띄어쓰다 space out words

띄엄띄엄 1 〈드문드문〉 sparsely; thinly; scatteredly; 〈사이를 두고〉 at intervals; intermittently
♦ 띄엄띄엄 읽다 skip (in reading); read skippingly; read at random [desultorily] / 띄엄띄엄 이야기하다 speak in broken accents [phrases]; chop *one's* sentences [words] / 나무를 띄엄띄엄 심다 plant trees at considerable intervals / 인가가 띄엄띄엄 있다 be sparsely dotted with houses
2 〈느릿느릿〉 slowly; sluggishly

띄엄띄엄 걸어도 황소 걸음 (속담) Slow and [but] sure [steady] wins the race.

띄우다[1] 1 〈공중에 뜨게 하다〉 fly; let [make] fly; send up ♦ 연을 띄우다 fly a kite / 풍선을 띄우다 fly [float, send up] a balloon
2 〈물 위에 뜨게 하다〉 float; set 《a ship》 afloat; sail 《a toy boat》 / 뗏목을 띄우다 float timber [a raft] 《down a river》
▶ 아이는 연못에 장난감 배를 띄웠다 The child set a toy boat afloat on the pond.
3 〈나타나게 하다〉 express; let show
♦ 얼굴에 근심의 빛을 띄우고 with a gloomy brow; with a worried look / 입가에 미소를 띄우고 with a smile (playing) about *one's* lips / 눈에 기쁜 빛을 띄우고 with *one's* eyes beaming with joy
▶ 그녀는 만면에 웃음을 띄우고 나를 맞았다 She was all smiles, when she received me. ⇒ She received me, smiling all over her face.

띄우다[2] 〈발효시키다〉 ferment; leaven; mold
♦ 누룩을[메주를] 띄우다 ferment malt [boiled

띄우다³

soybean lumps]
▶쌀을 창고에 오래 두어 띄워버렸다 The rice was kept in the warehouse so long that it got stale from the heat.

띄우다³ 〈사이를〉 space; leave space 《between》; leave an interval
♦사이를 띄워서 at intervals; sparsely / 단어 사이를 띄우다 space out words / 행과 행 사이를 띄우다 leave space between the lines
▶우리는 10 미터씩 띄워서 나무를 심었다 We planted trees with the space of 10 meters.
▶한 줄씩 띄워서 쓰시오 Write on every other [second] line.
▶활자의 행간을 좀더 띄우시오 Space out the type more.

띄우다⁴ 〈보내다〉 send; dispatch
♦편지를 띄우다 send [address] a letter 《to sb》; mail [(英) post] a letter / 파발마를 띄우다 dispatch a messenger on a post horse / 전국에 격문을 띄우다 make a nationwide appeal in writing

띠¹ **1** 〈허리띠〉 a belt; a (waist) band; a girdle; 〈장식띠〉 a sash
♦띠를 매다 tie a belt [girdle] / 띠를 죄다 tighten [adjust, fix] one's belt / 띠를 풀다 untie [undo] the belt; ungird [unbelt] oneself
2 〈아기를 업는 띠〉 a baby-carrying band [strap]
3 〈짐띠〉 a (drawing) string; a tape
■가죽— a leather belt [girdle]

띠² 〈활터에서의〉 a sub-team in archery

띠³ 〔植〕 a cogon; an alang-alang; an alang grass

띠 그래프 a band graph

띠다 **1** 〈두르다〉 wear; tie; put on
2 〈지니다〉 wear; bear; carry; be armed with
♦몸에 비수를 띠다 be armed with a dagger
3 〈맡다〉 be charged with 《a duty》; be entrusted with; be invested [vested, clothed] with 《authority》
♦공무를 띠고 on official affairs [business] / 중요한 사명을 띠다 be charged [entrusted] with some important mission
▶그는 극비의 임무를 띠고 중동에 파견되었다 He was sent to the Middle East on a top secret mission.
▶그녀는 중요한 사명을 띠고 워싱턴으로 향했다 She left for Washington on some important mission.
4 〈빛깔을 조금 가지다〉 have; wear; assume; put on; take on 《the character of》; 〈기색을 보이다〉 be tinged with; partake [smack, reek] of; present 《an appearance》; offer 《a prospect》; show 《a tendency》; exhibit
♦붉은 빛을 띤 reddish; tinged with red / 붉은 빛을 띤 자주색 purple tinged with red; purple with a dash of red / 노기를 띤 말 sharp [angry] words / 걱정하는 빛을 띠고 with an expression of worry; with a worried look / 걱정하는 빛을 띠다 look worried; have a worried look / 주기를 띠다 be under the influence of liquor; be tipsy / 활기를 띠다 present an animated appearance; display [show] activity
▶그 소식을 듣고 그들은 슬픈 빛을 띠었다 They looked sad at the news.
▶그 운동은 점차 반정부적 성격을 띠어 갔다 The movement has gradually assumed [taken on] an antigovernment character.

띠앗머리 fraternal [sororal] love; sibling [brotherly, sisterly] affection
♦띠앗머리가 없다 lack affection for one's brothers [sisters]; lack in brotherly affection

띠종이 a strip of paper; 〈돈다발을 묶는〉 a money band

띠톱 〔機〕 a band [belt] saw

띵띵하다 **1** 〈팽팽하다〉 tense; taut; swollen
▶배가 불러 띵띵하다 I have my stomach full.
▶젖이 불어 띵띵하다 The breasts are swollen with milk.
2 〈튼튼하다〉 stable; secure; solid
♦살림이 띵띵하다 be well off.

띵하다 〈머리가 아프다〉 dull; obtuse; 〈정신이 흐릿하다〉 muddled ♦띵한 머리 a muddled head / 머리가 띵하다 have a dull headache; feel heavy in the head; feel one's head muddled
▶나는 수면 부족으로 머리가 띵하다 I feel my brains muddled owing to want of sleep.

-ㄹ 〈…할〉 ◆할 일 things to do / 잘 시간 the time to go to bed

-ㄹ걸 〈추측〉 perhaps; probably; may; might; possibly
▶네가 그녀와 결혼했더라면 좋았을걸 Perhaps you should marry her.
▶그는 아마도 출석할걸 He will probably attend.
▶사실인지도 모를걸 It might be true.
▶어쩌면 그가 말하는 대로일지도 모를걸 Possibly it is as he says.

-ㄹ것같다 ▶내가 6시에 거기 갈 것 같다 I think I will be there at six o'clock.
▶폭탄은 지금이라도 폭발할 것 같다 The bomb seems to go off any minute.

-ㄹ게 〈자기 의사〉 ▶다시는 안 그럴게 I will never do such a thing again.
▶네가 원하면 뭔든지 할게 I will do anything if you wish.

-ㄹ까 1〈의문·추측〉▶이건 누가 잊은 걸까? I wonder who forgot this.
▶어떻게 말해야 좋을까? I wonder how to say it.
▶그는 어떻게 될까? What will become of him?
▶이 시간에 누굴까? Who can it be at this hour?
▶어떻게 하면 좋을까? What shall I do?
▶비가 오지 않을까? I'm afraid (that) it's going to rain.
▶내가 시간내에 도착할까? Shall I get there in time?
2〈제의·권유〉▶장기 한 판 둘까? What do you say to a game of chess? ⇌ What [How] about (having) a game of chess?
▶한 잔 할까요? How about a drink? ⇌ What do you say to having a drink?
▶산책할까? What do you say to taking a walk?
3〈부탁·허락〉▶그 버터 좀 이리 건네주실까요? May I trouble you to pass the butter? ⇌ May I trouble you for the butter?
▶길을 안내해 주실까요? Would you mind showing me the way?
▶내일 방문해도 괜찮을까요? May I visit you tomorrow?

-ㄹ까말까 1〈주저〉▶그녀는 편지를 썼으나 부칠까말까 망설였다 She wrote a letter, but she hesitated over mailing it.
▶나는 해외여행을 갈까말까 망설였다 I was balancing in my choice whether I should go abroad or not.
2〈미달〉 less than; barely; scarcely
▶1마일이 될까말까한 거리다 It's less than a mile.
▶그녀는 16세가 될까말까한 나이다 She is barely sixteen.
▶출석자가 20명이 될까말까였다 Scarcely twenty people were present.

-ㄹ까보다 1〈…것 같다〉 look; seem; appear; seem likely 《to do》
▶폭풍우가 일까보다 It looks as though we should have a storm.
▶그렇게 하는 것이 좋을까 보다 It seems good to do so.
▶비가 올까 보다 It seems likely to rain.
2〈욕망·의사〉 feel like 《doing》
▶커피나 한잔 마실까보다 I feel like (having) a cup of coffee.

-ㄹ까봐 1〈우려〉 fear 《that》
◆…할까봐 염려하다 be afraid of
▶우리는 너무 늦었을까봐 우려된다 I fear (that) we are too late.
▶그는 죽을까봐 염려했다 He was afraid of dying.
2〈욕망·의사〉 ⇨ -ㄹ까보다 2

-ㄹ까하다 1〈의향〉 think 《that, of doing》; have a mind to
▶나는 해외 여행을 갈까한다 I think of travelling abroad.
▶나는 그것을 할까한다 I have a mind to do it.
2〈기대〉 expect
▶우리는 용서받지 않을까 한다 We expect to be forgiven.

-ㄹ꼬 ▶그것이 무엇일꼬 what could it be?

-ㄹ는지 ▶그녀가 언제 올는지 모르겠다 I don't know when she will come.
▶그가 올는지 안 올는지 확실치 않다 I am not sure whether he will come or not.
▶맥주 한 잔 어떨는지요? How about a glass of beer?
▶지금 일을 중지하는 것이 어떨는지요? What about stopping work now?

-ㄹ는지도모르다 〈가능성·예측〉 may [might] 《be, do》; maybe; perhaps
▶나도 갈는지도 모른다 Maybe I will go, too.

-ㄹ듯이 〈…할 것처럼〉 as if [though]
▶그는 미칠듯이 슬퍼했다 He was nearly mad with grief.

-ㄹ듯하다 ▶그는 성공할 듯하다 He bids fair to succeed.
▶날씨가 좋아질 듯하다 The weather bids fair to be fine.
▶그는 안 올 듯하다 He is not likely to come.

-ㄹ라 〈염려〉▶과로하지 마라, 건강을 해칠라 Don't overwork, or you will ruin your health.
▶내 전화번호를 적어두어라, 잊어버릴라 Write my telephone number down lest you forget it.

-ㄹ라치면 when(ever); if
▶그를 방문할라치면 그는 옛날 이야기를 했다 Whenever I visit him, he talked about old times.

- ㄹ락말락 〈간신히〉 narrowly; dimly; barely; slightly
  ♦잠이 들락말락하다 be half asleep
  ▶그 차는 벽에 닿을락말락 지나갔다 The car narrowly avoided touching the wall.
  ▶옆방의 목소리가 들릴락말락한다 You can slightly hear a voice from the next room.
  ▶그 섬이 보일락말락했다 We could see the island dimly.
- ㄹ망정 although; though; even if [though]; however; nevertheless
  ♦가난할망정 though (he is) poor / 나이가 아주 많을망정 although (he is) very old; even though very old
  ▶그는 찬성할망정 참가는 안할지도 모른다 Even if he agrees, he may not participate.
  ▶그는 찬성 안할망정 나는 찬성하겠다 Even though he disagrees, I'll agree.
- ㄹ모양이다 〈상황 예측〉▶그는 안 올 모양이다 He is not likely to come. ⇌ It is not likely that he will come.
  ▶태풍이 올 모양이다 It threatens a storm.
- ㄹ바에는 〈어떤 경우·입장·상황이라면〉▶이왕 할 바에는 철저히 해라 If you do it at all, do it thoroughly.
  ▶어차피 살아날 가망이 없을 바에는 먹고 싶어하는 대로 먹여라 Let him eat whatever he likes, if there is no hope for his life.
  ▶나쁜 짓으로 돈을 벌 바에는 차라리 가난뱅이가 되겠다 I would rather be poor than get money by dishonest means.
- ㄹ밖에 ▶나는 계획을 포기할 밖에 없었다 I was compelled [was forced] to give up my plan.
  ▶그는 사직할 밖에 다른 대안이 없었다 He had no other choice than resignation.
  ▶걸을 밖에 다른 대안이 없었다 There was no alternative but to walk.
- ㄹ뿐더러 not only [merely]... but (also); as well as
  ♦재미있을뿐더러 교훈적이다 be both [at once] interesting and instructive
  ▶그는 근면할뿐더러 정직하다 He is honest as well as diligent.
  ▶그것은 경제적일뿐더러 건강에도 좋다 It is not only economical but also good for the health.
  ▶그녀는 대학교수일뿐더러 소설가이기도 하다 She is both [at once] a university professor and a novelist.
- ㄹ세라 lest (should); for fear (that)
  ▶그녀는 비를 만날세라 우산을 가지고 갔다 She took her umbrella for fear of being caught in a rain.
- ㄹ수록 the more [less]... the more [less]
  ▶사람은 많이 가지면 가질수록 더 갖고 싶어한다 The more one has, the more one wants.
  ▶빠르면 빠를수록 좋다 The sooner, the better.
  ▶미루면 미룰수록 하기 싫어진다 The longer you put it off, the less inclined you will be to do it.
  ▶말은 적을수록 좋다 〈속담〉 (The) least said, (the) soonest mended.
  ▶이 문제는 생각하면 할수록 모르겠다 This question becomes more puzzling, the more I think about it.
- ㄹ수없다 cannot (do); be unable to (do); be incapable of (doing); fail to (do); cannot afford to (do); 〈사물이 주어〉 be impossible; be too much for
  ▶나는 그 문제를 풀 수 없었다 I could not solve the problem.
  ▶이 책은 너무 어려워 1주일에 읽을 수 없었다 This book was too difficult for me to read in a week.
  ▶급한 일로 어제는 올 수 없었다 Urgent business kept me from coming yesterday.
  ▶우리는 그 값으로는 그것을 살 수 없다 We cannot afford to buy it at that price.
- ㄹ수있다 can (do); be able to (do); be capable of (doing); be equal [up] to (the task); have sth in one's power; 〈사물이 주어〉 be possible
  ♦할 수 있다고 생각하다 feel it in one's power to (do); feel fit to (do)
  ▶그것은 공짜로 얻을 수 있다 It can be had for nothing.
  ▶그는 수입이 넉넉해서 안락한 생활을 할 수 있었다 His income enabled him to live in comfort.
  ▶이 문제에 대하여 누구나 자기 의견을 말 할 수 있다 Everyone is entitled to give his opinion on this subject.
- ㄹ양으로 with a view to (doing); with the intention [idea] of (doing); for the purpose of (doing)
  ♦죽일 양으로 with intent to murder sb / 교사가 될 양으로 with the idea of becoming a teacher
  ▶그는 여생을 부인과 함께 보낼 양으로 영국에 돌아왔다 He had come back to England purposing to live with his wife for the rest of his life.
- ㄹ양이면 if one is going to (do); if one has the intention of (doing)
  ▶걸어서 갈 양이면 하루 종일 걸릴 게다 It will take a whole day (if you are going) to go on foot.
  ▶기차로 갈 양이면 지금 표를 사 두어라 Get a ticket now (if you are going) to go by train.
- ㄹ이만큼 enough to (do); so... that; so much as to (do)
  ▶그는 천장에 닿을이만큼 키가 크다 He is tall enough to reach the ceiling.
  ▶그는 일어설 수 없을이만큼 취해 있었다 He was so drunk that he could not stand up. ⇌ He was too drunk to stand up.
- ㄹ줄 1 〈능력〉 ♦…할 줄 알다 can (do); know how to (do); be able to (do); be capable of (doing)
  ▶그는 거짓말을 할 줄 모르는 사람이다 He is incapable of telling a lie.
  2 〈예상〉 ▶설마 여기에 네가 있을 줄은 아무도 몰랐다 This is about the last place where anyone will look for you.
  ▶그 사람이 도둑일 줄이야 To hear that he is

[That he should be] a robber!
- ㄹ지 when... will; what may; if
▶ 회의가 언제 끝날지 모르겠다 I don't know when the meeting will be over.
▶ 무슨 일이 있을지 누가 알아 No one can say what may happen.
▶ 그가 집에 있을지 모르겠다 I wonder if he is at home.
▶ 우리가 그것을 파는 것이 현명할지 어떨지 생각 중이다 I am wondering if we are wise to sell it.
- ㄹ지도모르다 may [might] 《be, do》; perhaps; maybe; possibly
▶ 우리가 늦을지도 모르겠다 We may be late.
▶ 그렇지 않을지도 몰라 I am afraid not.
▶ 그녀가 올지도 모른다 She may come. ⇌ Maybe she will come.
▶ 그렇지 않았으면 그는 목숨을 잃었을지도 모른다 Otherwise he might possibly have lost his life.
▶ 그가 혹시 내일 올지도 모른다 It is possible that he may come tomorrow.
- ㄹ지라도 though; even if [though]; no matter 《who, what, when, where, how》
♦ 아무리 부자랄지라도 however [no matter how] rich one may be / 무슨 일이 일어날지라도 whatever may happen; come what may / 설령 그렇다할지라도 granting [admitting] that it is so; even if it were so
▶ 네가 아무리 힘이 세다할지라도 조심해야 한다 However strong you may be, you must be careful.
▶ 내일 비가 올지라도 나는 가겠다 Even if it rains tomorrow, I will go.
▶ 어린애일지라도 그쯤은 할 수 있을 게다 Even a child could do that.
- ㄹ지언정 even if [though]; rather [sooner] than
▶ 굶어 죽을지언정 도둑질은 안 하겠다 I would rather [sooner] starve than steal.
▶ 실패를 할지언정 한번 해 보겠다 Though I might fail, I will attempt it.
- ㄹ진대 〈조건〉 if; in case; suppose; supposing; provided; judging from
♦ 그러할진대 if it be so; if so; in that case; then
▶ 자네 충고가 없을진대 내가 어찌 그것을 해 보겠나 If it were not for your advice, I should not try it.
▶ 내가 볼진대 그는 사업에 성공할 사람이 아니다 In my opinion he is not a man who will succeed in business.
- ㄹ터이다 〈예정・의지〉 intend to 《do》; will 《do》; have a mind to 《do》; mean to 《do》; have the intention of 《doing》; be going to 《do》
▶ 그는 3시까지는 돌아올 터이다 He will come back by three.
▶ 내일 갈 터이니 그리 알게 You may expect me to call on you tomorrow.
▶ 한 번 해볼 테야? Are you going to try?
라 [樂] 1 〈제 6계명〉 la 2 〈음명〉 D; re
■─단조[장조] D minor [major]
-라 1 〈서술적 연결 어미〉 ▶ 그는 아직 어린애라 그 말을 이해할 수 없었다 He was too young to understand it.
▶ 하는 짓이 그 따위라 누구나 그를 싫어했다 His behavior was such that everyone disliked him.
▶ 그는 내 아들이 아니라 내 조카다 He is not my son but my nephew.
2 〈명령〉 ▶ 조심해라 Be careful!
▶ 신사답게 행동해라 Do like a gentleman.
▶ 그에게 오지 말라 해라 Tell him not to come.
▶ 책을 제자리에 갖다 놓아라 Put back the book where you found it.
라고 ♦ 존이라고 하는 사람 a man named [called] John / 학교라고 하는 학교는 다 every school / 누가 뭐라고 하든 no matter what one says / …라고 신문에 나왔다 the paper said 《that》… / 아무를 신사라고 부르다 call sb a gentleman
▶ 그는 사직할 거라고 한다 People say he will resign.
▶ 나는 취미라고 할 만한 것이 없다 I have no hobby to speak of.
▶ 그는 선량한 사람이라고 알려져 있다 He is known as a good man.
-라고 ▶ 도와달라고 외치다 cry for help / 그러지 말라고 경고하다 warn sb not to do that
▶ 그에게 잠깐 기다리라고 말해라 Tell him to wait a minute.
라고는 ▶ 우리는 보수라고는 아무 것도 받지 않았다 We have received nothing as for [in the way of] recompense.
▶ 내 소유라고는 거의 없다 I have few things I can call my own.
라고도 ▶ 탁구는 핑퐁이라고도 한다 Table tennis is also known as ping-pong.
라고스 〈나이지리아의 수도〉 Lagos
라고해서 ▶ 반짝이는 것이라고 해서 모두 금은 아니다 《속담》 All is not gold that glitters.
▶ 부자라고 해서 꼭 행복한 것은 아니다 The rich are not always happy.
라기보다 more of... [rather] 《than》 ▶ 그는 학자라기보다 기자다 He is more of a journalist than a scholar. ⇌ He is a journalist rather than a scholar.
라놀린 [化] lanolin(e)
라는 ▶ 어제 화이트라는 사람이 당신을 찾아 왔었습니다 A Mr. White called on you yesterday.
▶ 서울의 다리라는 다리는 거의 다 건너보았다 I crossed almost every bridge in Seoul.
▶ 나는 그 소년이 음악의 천재라는 것을 알았다 I found the boy a musical prodigy.
-라는 ▶ 하지말라는 충고 an advice not to do
▶ 하라는 대로 해라 Do as you are told.
▶ 그녀는 그들이 각각 다른 차로 올거라는 말을 했다 She said 《that》 they would come in separate cars.
-라니 1 〈의문・의외〉 ▶ 의사라니, 어느 의사 말인가? Doctor? Which doctor do you mean?
2 〈…고 하니〉 ▶ 그 일을 중지하라니 중지하겠소 I will stop that work as you told me to.
-라니까 1 〈강조하여〉 ▶ 정말이라니까 I mean it. ⇌ I tell you. ⇌ I'm telling you. ⇌ I'm not kidding.
▶ 빨리 가라니까 Go quick, I tell you.

2 〈…라고 하니까〉 ▶내가 들어오라니까 그가 들어왔다 I asked him to come in and he came in.
▶집에 가라니까 그가 가더라 I told him to go home and he did.

라도 〈…조차(도)〉 even (if)
♦어떤 경우라도 in any case / 언제라도 (at) any time; anytime
▶언제라도 좋습니다 Any time will do.
▶어린애라도 그건 안다 Even a child can understand it.
▶가장 빠른 차라도 그것을 따라잡지 못한다 The fastest car cannot overtake it. (▶최상급에는 even의 뜻이 있음)
▶그건 내일이라도 할 수 있다 〈꼭 오늘 안해도 된다〉 You can do it tomorrow just as well. ⇌ Tomorrow will do.
▶어느 것이라도 맘에 드는 것을 가져라 Pick whichever you like.

라돈 〔化〕 radon
라듐 〔化〕 radium ■─요법 radiumtherapy; radiotherapy ─천(泉) a radium spring
라드 〈정제 돼지 기름〉 lard
라든지 and; or
♦사과라든지 배라든지 하는 과실 fruit such as apples and pears
▶칼이라든지 냄비라든지 하는 부엌 용품을 가져오는 것을 잊지 말게 Don't forget to bring kitchen utensils such as knives and cooking-pots.

-라든지 〔연결 어미〕 ▶그에게 그 일을 하라든지 말라든지 하는 결정을 내려 주어야 한다 We must decide whether to make him do the work or not.

라디에이터 a radiator
라디오 (美) radio; (英古) wireless;〈수신기〉 a radio (receiving) set (▶set는 보통 생략함); a radio 《pl. ~s》
♦트랜지스터 라디오 a transistor radio / 포터블 라디오 a portable radio / 라디오 뉴스를 듣다 listen to the radio news
▶요즘은 라디오 음악을 들으면서 공부하는 학생들이 많다 These days many students study listening to music on the radio.
▶라디오 소리를 높이[낮추]시오 Turn up [down] the radio.
▶이 시합은 라디오로 중계됩니다 This game will be broadcast over [on] the radio.
▶라디오를 켜[끄]시오 Turn on [off] the radio, please.
▶그는 가끔 라디오를 켠채로 잠든다 He sometimes falls asleep with the radio on.
▶라디오를 KBS에 맞추세요 Tune the radio to KBS, please.
■─녹음 radio transcription ─뉴스 the news on the radio; radio news ─드라마[코미디] a radio drama [comedy] ─방송 radio broadcasting; 〈1회의〉 a radio broadcast ─방송국 a radio (broadcasting) station ─방송망 a radio network ─부(속)품 radio parts ─송신기 a radio transmitter ─아나운서 a radio announcer ─영어강좌 a radio English course [program] ─전국 중계 a nationwide radio hookup ─전파 radio waves ─좌담회 a radio forum ─청취자 a radio listener ─체조 radio (gymnastic) exercises; radio gymnastics [calisthenics] ─프로그램 a radio program ─해설자 a radio commentator

라디오존데 〔氣〕 a radiosonde
라디오카세트리코더 a radio cassette recorder
라르고 〔樂〕 largo
라마¹ 〈라마교의 고승(高僧)〉 a lama
■─교 Lamaism ─교도 a Lamaist; a Lamaite ─사원(寺院) a lamasery
라마² 〔動〕 a llama
라마르크설 ─說 〔生〕 Lamarckism
■─신─ Neo-Lamarckism

-라면 1 〈가정·조건〉 if; supposing; provided
▶내가 너라면 직업을 바꾸겠다 If I were [was] you, I would change my job.
▶그런 경우라면 내가 하겠다 If that is the case, I will do it.
▶검은 색이라면 어떤 옷도 좋다 Any dress will do, provided it is black.
2 〈…에 관해서는〉 for
♦그 일이라면 as for that matter
▶경치라면 뉴질랜드만한 나라가 없다 For scenery, there is no country like New Zealand.
3 ♦가라면 If you are told to go / 읽으라면 If you are told to read / …하라면 if you are told to do
▶하라면 해 Do as you are told. ⇌ Do as I tell you.

라벤더 〔植〕 lavender
■─향수 lavender water
라벨 label
♦라벨을 붙이다 put a label on
▶나는 잼 병에 라벨을 붙였다 I labeled jars of jam.
라서 〈감히〉 dare ▶뉘라서 이런 말을 할까? Who dare say such a thing?
▶뉘라서 그것을 생각이나 했겠는가? Who would have thought of it?
-라서 〈때문에〉 because, since
▶밤이라서 그것을 찾을 수가 없었다 I couldn't search it because it was night.
▶내돈이 아니라서 줄 수 없다 Since it is not my money, I can not give it to you.
라셀 〈이상호흡음〉 (독)〔醫〕 Rasselgeräusch; a rale; a rhonchus
라스트 〈최후〉 the last
■─러너 〈최종 주자〉 the last runner ─배터 the last batter ─스퍼트 the last spurt ─신 the last scene ─이닝 the last inning
라야 〈지정·강조하는 말〉 only; alone; just
▶너라야 그 일을 할 수 있다 You alone [Nobody but you] can do the work.
▶은행은 9시반이라야 연다 The bank does not open until 9:30.
라오스 Laos; 〈공식명〉 the Lao People's Democratic Republic ♦라오스의 Lao; Laotian
■─어(語) Lao; Laotian ─사람 a Laotian; a Lao 《pl. ~(s)》
라우드스피커 a loudspeaker ⇨ 확성기
라운드 〈권투 등의 …회〉 a round
♦10라운드의 권투 시합 a boxing match of ten rounds

▶ 우리는 골프를 1라운드 쳤다 We played one round of golf.
▶ 그는 5라운드 2분 5초만에 녹아웃이 되었다 He was knocked out at 2:5 in the fifth round.
라운지 a lounge
라이너 〈야구의 타구〉 a liner
◆ 라이너를 치다 hit a liner / 1루 라이너를 치다 line out [hit a liner] to first
라이노타이프 〈활자 제작·제판기〉 〈商標〉 Linotype ◆ 라이노타이프 조판공 a linotyper; a linotypist
라이닝 〈일〉 〈옷의 안감〉 lining
라이덴병 —甁 〔物〕 a Leyden jar
라이벌 〈경쟁 상대〉 a rival
◆ 사랑의 라이벌 a rival in love / 라이벌 회사 a rival company
▶ 그는 그 지위를 둘러싼 나의 라이벌이었다 He was my rival for the post.
— 의식 a sense of rivalry
라이베리아 〈나라 이름〉 Liberia; 〈공식명〉 the Republic of Liberia ◆ 라이베리아의 Liberian ■ — 사람 a Liberian
라이브 〈녹화[녹음]한 것이 아닌 실황〉 live ■ —콘서트 a live concert
라이브러리 a library ■ 시청각— an audio-visual library 필름— a film library
라이선스 〈면허〉 a license ■ 의사개업— a license to practice medicine ■ —료 a license fee
라이스 〈쌀〉 rice ■ 카레— curry and rice; curried rice
라이온스인터내셔널 〈국제 라이온스 협회〉 Lions International
라이온스클럽 the Lions Club
라이카 〈독일제 카메라〉 〈商標〉 a Leica
라이터 a (cigarette) lighter
◆ 라이터를 켜다 strike [light] a lighter; snap [click] a lighter into [to] flame
▶ 이 라이터는 안 켜진다 This lighter doesn't work.
▶ 그는 라이터로 담뱃불을 붙였다 He lit his cigarette with a lighter.
■ 가스— a gas lighter ■ —기름 lighter oil [fluid] ■ —돌 a lighter flint
라이트¹ **1** 〈빛〉 light; 〈전등〉 a light
◆ 자동차 라이트 the headlights [headlamps] of a car
▶ 전시품은 라이트가 효과적으로 비추어져 있었다 The display was lighted very effectively.
2 〔體〕 lightweight
■ —급 선수 a lightweight (boxer) —헤비[웰터]급 선수 a light heavyweight [welterweight]
라이트² **1** 〔野〕 〈우익〉 right field; 〈우익수〉 a right fielder
◆ 라이트를 수비하다 play right field / 라이트에 안타를 치다 make a hit to right field
▶ 그는 라이트에 라이너를 쳤다 He drove a liner to right field.
2 〔拳〕 a right (to the jaw)
■ —스트레이트 a right straight
라이프 〈생명·인생〉 (a) life
■ —보트 a lifeboat —사이언스 life sciences —사이클 the life cycle —스타일 one's life-style —워크 one's lifework; one's life's work : 나는 아직 라이프워크를 찾지 못했다 I have not yet found a job to devote my life to [my true career].
라이플 〈소총〉 a rifle
라인 a line
라인강 —江 the Rhine (River)
라인업 〔蹴·野〕 〈출전 선수의 진용〉 a lineup
라일락 〔植〕 a lilac
라켓 〈테니스·배드민턴·탁구의〉 a racket; a racquet; 〈탁구의〉 a bat; 〈美〉 paddle

— 라켓 —

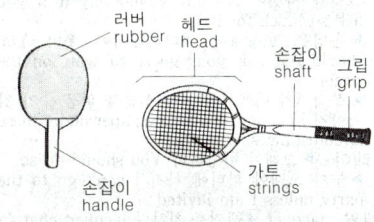

라크깍지벌레 〔昆〕 a lac insect
라텍스 〈고무나무의 수액〉 latex
라트비아 〈나라 이름〉 Latvia; 〈공식명〉 the Republic of Latvia ◆ 라트비아의 Latvian ■ —사람 a Latvian
라틴 Latin ■ —문학 Latin literature —민족 the Latin races [peoples] —어 Latin : 라틴어학자 a Latinist; a Latin scholar —음악 Latin music
라틴아메리카 Latin America
◆ 라틴아메리카(인)의 Latin-American
라파스 〈볼리비아의 수도〉 La Paz
락타아제 〔化〕 lactase
락토오스 〔化〕 lactose; milk sugar
란 ▶ 진리란 무엇인가? What is truth?
▶ 그의 글쓰는 솜씨란 참 놀랍다 The way he writes is wonderful.
▶ 친구란 누구말인가? Who do you mean by a friend? ⇒ What do you mean, a friend?
-란 〈어미〉 ▶ 날보고 어떻게 하란 말이냐? What do you want me to do?
▶ 날 보고 가란 말이냐? Do you mean that I should go?
-란 —欄 ▶ 가정란 the domestic affairs section [columns] / 광고란 the ad-column / 문예란 the literary column
-람 ▶ 도대체 내가 해야할 이유가 뭐람? Why should I do of all things?
랑 and; or...; and so on [forth]; etc.; 〈함께〉 (together) with ◆ 너랑 나랑 you and me / 친구랑 놀다 play with a friend
랑데부 〈밀회〉 a rendezvous; (口) a date; 〈우주선의〉 a rendezvous
— 랑데부하다 have a rendezvous 《with》; (口) date [have a date] 《with》
▶ 그 두 우주선은 우주에서 랑데부에 성공했다 The two spaceships effected a successful rendezvous in space.
▶ 나는 오늘 밤에 아가씨와 랑데부한다 I have a

-래 date with a girl tonight.
-래 they say; I hear
▶그 사람 동생은 장교래 I hear that his brother is an officer.
▶그 사람이 뭐래? What did he say?
▶그들은 올봄에 결혼할 거래 I hear [people say] (that) they will get married this spring.
래글런 〈외투〉〈服〉a raglan
■―슬리브 raglan sleeves
-래서 ▶하래서 했습니다 I did it as I was told.
▶그래서 어쨌다구? So what?
-래서야 ▶그렇게 턱없이 많이 달래서야 누가 그것을 사겠어 Nobody would buy it if you ask so much for it.
▶손님을 노상에서 기다리래서야 쓰나 You should not ask your guest to wait on the street.
▶분위기가 이래서야 어디 신문을 읽을 수가 있어야지 I cannot read a newspaper under these circumstances.
-래야 ▶그래야 마땅하다 You should do so.
▶누가 오래야 파티에 가지 I can't go to the party unless I am invited.
래커 lacquer ◆래커를 칠하다 lacquer; coat (a thing) with lacquer
락 lac; lac resin ―칠 shellac
랜 〈근거리·기업내 정보 통신망〉LAN [〈local area network〉]
랜덤샘플링 random sampling
랜싯 〈外科〉a lancet
랜턴 〈각등〉a lantern
랠리 1〈테니스 등의 치고 받기〉a rally
2〈자동차의 장거리 경주〉a (car) rally
램 〈임의 접근 기억 장치〉RAM [〈random access memory〉]
램프¹ 〈등〉a lamp
▶램프의 갓 a lamp shade / 램프의 심지 a lampwick
■석유― an oil lamp : 그는 석유 램프를 켰다 [껐다] He lit [put out] an oil lamp. 알코올― an alcohol [a spirit] lamp
램프² 〈고속도로 등의 진입로〉a ramp
랩 〈연구실·실험실〉a laboratory; (口) a lab
▶랭귀지 랩 a language lab
랩 〈경주로의 일주〉a lap
■―타임 the lap time
랩소디 〈樂〉a rhapsody
랩톱 〈휴대용 퍼스널 컴퓨터〉a laptop
랭크 〈지위〉(a) rank ◆제 1위에 랭크되다 be ranked No. 1; be given the first rank
랭킹 〈서열〉ranking
◆국내[국제] 랭킹 national [international] ranking / 랭킹 상위의 테니스 선수 a top-ranking tennis player
▶그는 매년 랭킹의 상위에 든다 He ranks near the top every year.
-랴 1〈반어적〉▶내가 왜 가랴? Why in the world should I go?
▶어찌 우리가 그처럼 잔인한 짓을 할 수 있으랴? How can we be so cruel?
▶그녀가 설마 그런 말을 했으랴? She can not have said that.
2〈문의〉▶들어가랴? May I come in?
▶무얼 어떻게 해주랴? Tell me what you want.

-량 ―量 volume; quantity; (an) amount
◆교통량 traffic volume / 생산량 an output (of a factory) / 일정량 a fixed amount
-러 ◆낚시하러 가다 go fishing / 스케이트를 타러 가다 go skating / 친구를 만나러 나가다 go out to meet a friend
러거 〈럭비〉rugger; rugby; 〈럭비선수〉a rugby [rugger] player
러너 〈주자〉〈野〉a (base) runner
◆러너를 (내)보내다 send a runner
■펀치― a pinch runner
러닝 running; 〈러닝셔츠〉(美) an athletic (-style) shirt; (英) vest; 〈스포츠용〉an athletic shirt; 〈러닝 홈런〉an inside-the-park home-run ―메이트 a running mate
러버 〈고무〉rubber
■―슈즈 rubber shoes [boots]
러브 〈사랑〉love; 〈테니스〉〈무득점〉love
■―게임[테니스] a love game ―레터 a love letter ―스토리 a love story ―신 a love scene
러브호텔 an inn for couples
러스크 〈얇게 썬 빵을 구운 것〉a rusk
러시 〈제작중의 편집용 프린트〉〈映〉rushes; 〈돌진〉rush
러시아 Russia ◆러시아의 Russian
―어 Russian; the Russian language ―사람 a Russian ―황제 a Czar; a Tsar; a Russian emperor
러시아연방 Russian Federation
러시아워 the rush hour(s)
◆아침 저녁의 러시 아워 the morning and evening rush hours / 러시 아워의 혼잡 rush-hour congestion
러키 〈행운의〉lucky
■―세븐 〈野〉the lucky seventh inning (▶7회에 그 내용과는 관계없이 lucky를 붙이는 습관은 (美)에는 없음) ―존〈野〉the lucky zone
러프 〈거친〉rough; 〈골프〉the rough
◆러프한 경기 a rough play
럭비 Rugby (football); (英俗) rugger
■―공[볼] a Rugby ball; (口) an oval ―선수 [시합] a rugby player [match]
럭스 〈物〉a lux (pl. ~es, luces) (略 lx)
런치 〈점심〉lunch ―타임 (at) lunchtime ―파티 a luncheon (party)
럼(주) ―(酒) rum
레 〈樂〉re [rei, ri:]; ray [rei]
레가타 〈보트 경주〉a regatta; (英) a boat race
레귤러 regular; 〈정규 선수〉a regular player
―멤버 a regular member : 그는 이 팀의 레귤러 멤버다 He is a regular member [a regular] of this team. ⇌ He plays regularly for this team.
레그혼 〈닭의 품종〉a Leghorn
◆백색 레그혼 a white Leghorn
레늄 〈化〉rhenium
레더 〈무두질한 가죽〉leather; 〈모조 피혁〉imitation leather; 〈레더클로스〉leathercloth
레디메이드 〈기성품〉◆레디메이드의 ready-to-wear; ready-made / 레디메이드의 양복 ready-made clothes; 〈기성복〉 store-bought clothes
레모네이드 〈청량 음료〉lemonade

레몬 〔植〕 a lemon ■—껍질[즙] lemon rind [juice] —수 lemonade —스쿼시 lemon squash —차[티] tea with lemon; lemon tea
레버 〈지렛대〉 a lever; 〈자동차의〉 a gearshift ♦레버를 당기다 pull a lever / 레버를 앞으로 밀다 throw [push] a lever forward
레벨 a level ⇨ 수준(水準)
레뷰 〔劇〕 a revue; 〈논평〉 a review ■—북— a book review —댄서 a revue dancer
레스비언 〈여성 동성애자〉a lesbian; a female homosexual; (俗) a les
레스토랑 〈음식점〉 a restaurant
레슨 a lesson ♦피아노 레슨을 하다[받다] give [have, take] a piano lesson [a lesson in piano] ▶올해는 바이올린 레슨을 받고 싶다 I want to take violin lessons this year.
레슬러 〈레슬링 선수〉a wrestler
레슬링 wrestling ■—선수 a wrestler; (美俗) a matman —시합 a wrestling match [tournament]: 텔레비전으로 레슬링 시합을 보았다 I saw a wrestling match on television.
레위기 —記 〔聖〕 (The Book of) Leviticus (略 Lev.)
레이 〈하와이의 화환〉 a lei ▶그녀는 그의 목에 레이를 걸어주었다 She put on a lei around his neck.
레이더 〈전파탐지기〉 (a) radar [<*r*adio *d*etecting *and r*anging] ▶레이더에 무언가 비치고 있다 There's [I see] something on the radar screen. ■—기지 a radar base [site, station] —망 a radar fence [screen, network] —시설[장치]a radar installation [device, set]
레이디 a lady ■퍼스트— 〈대통령·수상의 부인〉 the First Lady —퍼스트 Ladies first
레이디얼 타이어 a radial tire
레이서 〈경주자〉a racer; 〈경주용 자동차〉a racer; a racing car
레이스¹ 〈수예품〉 lace; lacework ♦레이스 커튼 a lace curtain / 레이스를 달다 trim with lace ▶그 소녀의 드레스는 레이스로 가장자리가 장식되어 있다 The girl's dress is trimmed with lace. ■—실 cotton thread —장식 enlacement; lacing
레이스² 〔競〕 a race ♦보트 레이스 a boat race / 요트 레이스 a yacht race ▶그는 그 레이스에서 이겼다[졌다] He has won [lost] the race.
레이싱카 〈경주용 자동차〉a racing car; a racer
레이아웃 〈인쇄·도안의〉 (a) layout ▶이 책은 사진 레이아웃에 세심한 주의를 기울였다 Great care is taken of the layout of pictures in this book.
레이온 rayon; artificial silk ♦레이온 셔츠 a rayon shirt ■—펄프 rayon pulp
레이저 〔物〕〈빛의 증폭 장치〉 (a) laser [<*l*ight *a*mplification by *s*timulated *e*mission of *r*adiation]
■—광선 laser beams —디스크 a laser disk —통신 (a) laser communication
레인슈즈 rain shoes ⇨ 우화
레인저 〈유격대원〉a ranger ■—부대 rangers
레인지 a (kitchen) range; a cooking stove ■가스— a gas range 전자— a microwave oven
레인코트 a raincoat; 〈벨트 달린〉 a trench coat; a waterproof; 〈고무 입힌〉 a mackintosh
레일 〈한 가닥의〉 a rail; a (railway) line; (美) a (railroad) track ♦레일을 깔다[떼다] lay [rip up] rails ▶저 도시들 사이에 레일을 부설하는 데 며칠 걸립니까? How many days will it take to lay rails between those towns? ■가드— a guardrail
레저 leisure ▶레저를 즐기는 법을 모르는 사람들도 있다 Some people don't know how to enjoy their leisure. ■—붐 a leisure boom —산업 the leisure industry —시설 leisure facilities —용품 equipment for leisure time amusement
레종데트르 〈존재 이유〉 (프) a raison d'être
레지스탕스 resistance (activity) ♦프랑스 레지스탕스의 일원 a member of the French Resistance ■—운동 a resistance movement
레지옹도뇌르 〈프랑스의 최고 훈장〉the order of the Legion of Honor [(프) la Légion d'Honneur]
레치타티보 〔樂〕〈서창(敍唱)〉 recitativo
레커차 —車 〈견인용 트럭〉(美) a wrecker; (美) a tow car (truck); (英) a breakdown lorry [van]
레코드 **1** 〈음반〉 a (phonograph, gramophone) record; a disk; a disc ♦레코드를 내놓다 release a record / 레코드를 틀다 put a record on a player; play a record / 레코드에 녹음하다 cut a record / 레코드에 취입하다 disc (*one's* singing); record (*one's* speech) on a disk ▶어느 레코드를 틀[들을] 까요? Which record shall we put on [hear, listen to]? ■어학— a Linguaphone 엘피— an LP [a long-playing] record ♦—수집가 a discophile —음악 record [disk] music; recorded music —콘서트 a record concert —팬 a discophile; a phonophile —플레이어 a record player; a phonoplayer —회사 a record company **2** ⇨ 기록
레크리에이션 a recreation ♦레크리에이션 시설 recreational facilities ▶그는 가끔 레크리에이션으로 골프를 친다 He sometimes plays golf for recreation. ■—센터 a recreation center
레터링 〈글자의 도안화〉 lettering
레테르 〈표찰·라벨·상표〉 a label; (美) a sticker ♦병에 「독약」의 레테르를 붙이다 label a bottle "Poison"; put a label of poison on a bottle; attach a label of poison to a bottle ▶그는 거짓말쟁이라는 레테르가 붙였다 He was labeled [was branded] (as) a liar.

레토르트 〔化〕〈화학 실험용 증류기〉 a retort

레퍼리 〔심판〕 a referee
♦ 레퍼리를 맡아보다 act referee (for a match); referee (a match)
■ —스톱 the referee stop : 이 시합은 부득이 레퍼리 스톱이 되었다 The referee had to stop the match.

레퍼토리 a repertory; a repertoire
♦ 레퍼토리가 많다 have a large [a wide] repertoire (of songs)
▶ 그 노래는 내 레퍼토리에는 없습니다 That song is not in my repertoire.

레프트 〈야구의 좌익〉 left field; 〈야구의 좌익수〉 a left fielder; 〔拳〕 a left (to the jaw)
♦ 레프트를 수비하다 play left field / 레프트에 2루타를 치다 hit a double to left field

렌즈 a lens (pl. ~es)
♦ 렌즈의 중심 the optical center / 렌즈를 맞추다 train the lens (on) / 렌즈를 죄다 stop down a lens / 렌즈를 …에 향하게 하다 direct the lens to
■ 광각— a wide-angle lens 대물— an objective lens; an objective 망원— a telephoto lens 볼록[오목]— a convex [concave] lens 어안(魚眼)— a fisheye lens 접안— an eyepiece; an ocular lens 합성— a compound lens 확대— a magnifying lens; a magnifier

렌치 〈틀거나 죄는 공구〉 a wrench

렌터카 a rent-a-car; a rental car
♦ 렌터카를 빌리다 rent a car
■ —업자 a car-rental agent

-려 1 〔막 …하려 하다〕 be ready to ((do)); be about to ((do)); (be) on the point [verge] of ((doing))
♦ 막 쓰러지려 하는 나무 a tree ready to fall / 히스테리를 일으키려 하다 be on the point of hysteria
▶ 콘서트가 막 시작하려 하고 있다 The concert is just about to start.
2 ⇨ -려고

-려고 with the intention of ((doing)); with a view to ((doing)); 〈목적〉 in order to ((do)); for the purpose of ((doing))
♦ 대학에 갈 학자금을 모으려고 in order to save money for college / 모욕하려고 하다 intend to insult sb / 죽이려고 들다 make an attempt on sb's life
▶ 그는 노부모에게 드리려고 아담한 집을 지었다 He has built a snug little house for his old parents.
▶ 그는 그것을 하려고 마음먹었다 He made up his mind that it should be done.
▶ 그는 내주에 오려고 하고 있다 He purposes to come [coming] next week.

-려나 ▶ 누가 오려나 I wonder who will come.
▶ 만원으로 족하려나 I doubt whether ten thousand won will be enough (or not). (▶ …if …or not 은 불가)
▶ 내일 비가 오려나 I wonder if it will rain tomorrow.

-려네 I will ((do)); I intend [mean, purpose] to ((do)); I am going to ((do))
▶ 나는 내년에 영국에 가려네 I'm going to go [I'm going] to Britain next year.
▶ 오늘 저녁에는 외식을 하려네 I'm going to eat [I'm eating] out this evening.
▶ 그런 짓을 다시는 안하려네 I will never do such a thing again.

-려느냐 ▶ 무엇을 하려느냐? What do you intend to do?
▶ 커피를 좀 더 마시려느냐? Do you care for some more coffee?

-려는가 ▶ 어디로 가려는가? Where are you going (to)?
▶ 넌 커서 무엇이 되려는가? What are you going to be when you grow up [are grown up]?

-려는데 ▶ 내가 막 나가려는데 그가 왔다 He came just as [just when] I was going out. (▶ just as는 단순히 시간적 우연의 일치를 나타내지만 just when은 「하필 그때에」와 같이 곤란함을 암시하는 경우가 있음)
▶ 가게에서 나가려는데 소년이 말을 걸어왔다 I was about to leave the store, when a boy spoke to me.

-려는지 1 〔종결 어미〕 ▶ 이 다리는 언제 완성하려는지 I wonder when this bridge will be completed.
2 〔연결 어미〕 ▶ 그가 오려는지 안 오려는지 확실하지 않다 It is uncertain whether he will come or not.
▶ 그녀가 왜 너를 만나려는지 말해 봐라 Tell me why she wants to see you.

-려니 ▶ 그를 만나려니 생각하고 있었는데 (못 만났다) I expected to have seen him. ⇒ I had expected to see him.
▶ 나는 네가 오려니 생각했다 I thought you would come. ⇒ I expected you (to come).
▶ 무슨 일이 일어나려니하고 서성거리며 기다렸다 We waited about for something to happen.

-려니와 not only… but; as well as; and; moreover; besides
▶ 그의 근저(近著)는 재미있기도 하려니와 또한 학구적이기도 하다 His last work is an entertaining and scholarly book.
▶ 그녀는 시를 읽기도 하려니와 짓기도 한다 She not only reads but also writes poetry.
▶ 나는 그를 알지도 못하려니와 그의 모친도 아는 바 없다 I remember neither him nor his mother.

-려다가 ▶ 낚시하러 가려다가 바람이 몹시 불어서 그만두었다 It was so windy that I gave up an attempt to go fishing.
▶ 그는 사표를 내려다가 생각을 고쳐 그만두었다 He was going to hand in his resignation, but he thought better of it.

-려도 〈…려고 하여도〉 ▶ 함께 가려도 이런 사정으로 못간다 Such being the case [Under the circumstances], I can't come with you.
▶ 어떤 방법으로 하려도 어렵다는 것을 알 것이다 However you do it, you will find it difficult.

-려면 ▶ 내가 하려면 할 수 있었는데 (하지 않았다) I could have done it if I had wished to.
▶ 이 집을 지으려면 많은 시간과 돈이 든다 This house costs [takes] a lot of time and money to build.

-려면야 ▶ 하려면야 할 수 있지 I could do it if I would.

-려무나 ▶ 좋을대로[마음대로] 하려무나 Do as you please [like].
▶ 곧 시작하려무나 You may (just) as well begin at once (as not).
▶ 오늘은 집에서 쉬려무나 You had better rest indoors today.

-려야 ▶ 그래도 그녀에게 감탄하지 않으려야 않을 수 없다 Still, I cannot help but admire her.
▶ 가려야 사정이 허락하지 않는다 Circumstances do not permit (of) my going.

-려오 will 《do》; intend to 《do》
▶ 당신이 무슨 소리를 해도 나는 떠나려오 I will start, no matter what you say.
▶ 내일 그를 만나려오 I'm going to see him tomorrow.
▶ 내일 서울로 떠나려오 I'm going to go to Seoul tomorrow.

-력 -力 〈힘〉 power; force; strength; 〈능력〉 ability; competence; capability; capacity
♦구동력 driving force / 구매력 purchasing power / 구심력 centripetal force / 노동력 manpower; labor power [force] / 영도력 the capacity as a leader; leadership / 접착력 adhesive strength / 폭발력 explosive power

-력 -曆 a calendar ♦달력 ▶태양력 the solar calendar / 태음력 the lunar calendar

-련 ⇨ -려느냐 ▶이것을 가지련? Will you take this?
▶맥주 한 잔 더 하련? Won't you take one more mug of beer?

-련다 ▶한번 더 해보련다 I'll try again. ⇌ I'll have another try.
▶다시는 그런 무모한 짓은 안하련다 I will never do such a reckless thing again.

-련마는, -련만 1 〈연결 어미〉 ▶그것이 실현되면 좋으련마는 하고 생각했다 I hoped it might come true.
2 〈종결 어미〉 ▶말해줄 수 있으면 좋으련만 (유감스러우나 말할 수 없다) I wish I might tell you.
▶가도 좋으면 가련만 I would go if I might.

-렴 ⇨ -려무나 ▶보고 싶거든 보렴 You may see if you like.

-렵니까 ▶오후 4시에 사무실에 계시렵니까? Will you be in your office at four (o'clock) in the afternoon?
▶이곳에서 얼마나 계시렵니까? How long will you stay here?
▶고속버스로 가시렵니까? Are you going by express bus?

-렵니다 ⇨ -려오, -련다 ▶나는 과학자가 되렵니다 I purpose to become a scientist.

-렷다 〈당연한 추측·다짐·명령〉 ▶내일쯤은 눈이 오렷다 I expect [suspect] it will snow by tomorrow.
▶너는 그 일을 알고 있으렷다? You must be aware of it. ⇌ You know it, don't you?
▶10시에 떠났으니 이제 도착했으렷다 They left at ten, so they must have arrived by now.

-령 -領 a dominion; a domain; a territory
♦아프리카의 프랑스령 the French possessions in Africa

로 1 〈수단·방법〉 by; by means of; through; on; in; 〈도구〉 with

♦연필로 쓰다 write with a pencil [in pencil] / 편지[전보]로 알리다 inform by letter [telegram]
▶부산에는 비행기로 갑니까, 아니면 배로 갑니까? Will you go to Pusan by plane [air] or by ship [sea]?
▶그는 도보로 통학하고 있다 He goes to school on foot.
▶전화나 편지로 알려드리겠습니다 I'll let you know either by telephone or by letter.
▶그 뉴스는 라디오로 들었다 I heard the news on the radio.

2 〈방향·목적지〉 for; to; toward; into; in
♦서울에서 제주로 떠나다 leave Seoul for Cheju
▶모든 길은 로마로 통한다 All roads lead to Rome.
▶3시까지 이리로 와야 해 You must come here by three (o'clock).
▶그는 풀로 뛰어들었다 He jumped into [in] the pool.
▶강은 바다로 흘러든다 Rivers run [flow down] into the sea.

3 〈원료〉 from; 〈재료〉 of; out of
▶이 집은 나무로 지어져 있다 This house is built [made] of wood.
▶빵은 밀가루로 만든다 Bread is made from flour.
▶우리는 종이로 많은 유용한 것을 만든다 We make a lot of useful things out of paper. ⇌ We make paper into a lot of useful things.

4 〈원인·동기〉 because of; owing to; of; at; with; from; through
▶그는 과로로 죽었다 He died from overwork.
▶우리 엄마는 감기로 고생하고 계시다 My mother is suffering from a cold.
▶그 사고는 그의 부주의로 일어났다 The accident happened through his carelessness [because he was careless].

5 〈형식〉 in ♦한국어로 쓰다 write in Korean / 수표로 지불하다 pay by check

6 〈지위·신분〉 as; for
♦비서로 고용하다 engage *sb* as a secretary / 지도자로 선출하다 choose *sb* for 《their》 leader

7 〈척도·단위·기준〉 by ♦다스로 팔다 sell by the dozen / 월급제[주급제, 일당제]로 일하다 work by the month [the week, the day] / 8을 2로 나누다 divide eight by two
▶고기는 그램 단위로 판다 Meat is sold by the gram.

8 〈근거〉 by; on; from ♦내 시계로 5시 five o'clock by my watch / 이런 사실로 미루어 보아 judging from these facts / 겉보기로 판단하다 judge from appearances
▶목소리로 그라는 것을 알았다 I recognized him by the voice.
▶무슨 근거로? On what ground?

9 〈내용〉 of; with ♦자동차로 꽉 차 있는 거리 streets jam-packed with cars / 물로 가득차다 be full of water / 자기 일로 분주하다 be full of *one's* own affairs

10 〈구성·성립〉 of ♦목조로 된 집 a house of

wood / 3개의 침실로 된 아파트 an apartment of three bedrooms
▶이 책은 5부로 되어 있다 This book consists of five parts.
11 〈변화·결과〉 into; to ◆물을 수증기로 변하게 하다 turn water into vapor / 우리말을 영어로 번역하다 put Korean into English / 장을 5절로 나누다 divide the chapter into five sections
▶폭풍이 폭우로 변했다 The storm developed into a heavy rain.
12 〈상태·정도〉 with; in; at ◆시속 40마일로 at a speed of 40 miles an hour / 전속력으로 at full speed / 편한 자세로 앉다 sit in a comfortable position
▶그 도시는 폐허로 변해 있었다 The town lay in ruins.
▶안개로 남의 눈에 띌 위험도 없었다 With the fog to help me, there wasn't any danger of being seen.
13 〈시간·경과〉 by; at ◆때때로 from time to time / 밤낮으로 by day and (by) night / 수시로 at any time
14 〈통과·경로〉 through; by ◆시베리아 경유로 여행하다 travel by (way of) Siberia / 육로〔항로〕로 여행하다 travel by land [sea, water] / 제일 가까운 길로 가다 go by the nearest road
▶소년은 눈물어린 눈시울로 나를 보았다 The boy looked at me through his tears.
-로 **-路** a route; a street; a road; (美) an avenue ◆교차로 a crossroads / 교통로 a traffic route
-로고 ▶창피한 일이로고 What a disgrace it is!
▶알수 없는 일이로고 What a mystery it is!
▶참으로 한심한 놈이로고 How wretched he is!
로고스 〔哲〕 logos
-로구나, -로군 ▶이것 근사한 책이로구나 It's a good book, isn't it?
▶그녀는 정말 재능이 풍부한 여자로구나 What talent she has! ⇌ What a talent she is!
▶오늘밤은 별들이 참으로 장관이로구나 The stars make a fine spectacle tonight.
▶해수욕할 만한 날씨가 아니로구나 It's no weather for swimming in the sea.
▶만사휴의(萬事休矣)로구나 The game is up.
로그 〔數〕 a logarithm (略 log)
로는 **1** 〈…을 가지고는〉 ▶영어로는 「안녕히 가세요」를 뭐라고 하지? How do you say 'annyŏnghi kaseyo' in English?
2 〈…에 있어서는〉 ▶풍경이 아름답기로는 설악산이 으뜸이다 For scenic beauty, Sŏraksan is the best place in the country.
▶어떤 의미로는 그녀는 내가 알고 있는 사람 중에서 가장 멋있는 사람이라고 할 수 있다 In a way, she's the nicest person I know.
3 〈…에 의하면〉 ▶내가 알기로는 그것은 뛰어난 작품이다 It is an excellent piece of work, as far as I can tell.
▶내 시계로는 정각 6시다 It's exactly six o'clock by my watch.
4 〈…에는〉 ▶그후로는 그를 보지 못했다 I haven't seen him since (then). ⇌ I didn't see him after that.
5 〈…로서는〉 ▶그 손실은 성공의 대가로는 너무 비싼 것이었다 Such losses were too high a price to pay a success.
-로다 ▶이것은 웃을 일이 아니로다 This is no laughing matter.
▶그야말로 천재로다 What a genius he is!
로데오 a rodeo (pl. ~s)
로도 ▶이것은 우리말로도 잘 표현할 수 없다 I can't express this well even in Korean.
▶그는 어학자로도 이름이 나 있다 He is noted as a linguist also.
-로되 ▶정말, 그는 젊은이로되 아주 박학하다 True, he is young, but he is well read.
로듐 〔化〕 rhodium
로드게임 〈원정 시합〉 a road game; an away game [match]
로드레이스 〈자전거의〉 a road race; road racing
로드쇼 (美) a road show; a (special) first-run showing (of a film) ◆로드쇼 극장 a road-show [first-run] theater [(英) cinema]
로드워크 〈트레이닝을 위한〉 a roadwork
로르샤흐테스트 〔心〕 a Rorschach [ró:rʃɑːk] test
로마 〈이탈리아의 수도〉 Rome
◆신성로마제국 the Holy Roman Empire / 로마의 Roman / 로마화하다 Romanize
▶로마는 하루 아침에 이루어지지 않았다 (속담) Rome was not built in a day.
▶모든 길은 로마로 통한다 (속담) All roads lead to Rome.
■—교황 the Pope; the Holy Father —교황청 the Vatican (Palace) —법 the Roman law —사람 a Roman —서〔聖〕 (The Epistle of Paul the Apostle to the) Romans —숫자 Roman numerals —제국 the Roman Empire —클럽 the Club of Rome
로마가톨릭(교) —(敎) Roman Catholicism ■—교도 a Roman Catholic —교회 the Roman Catholic Church
로마네스크 Romanesque ■—건축[양식] Romanesque architecture [style]
로마자 —字 Roman characters [letters]; the Roman [Latin] alphabet
◆로마자로 철자하다 spell in Roman letters / 한글을 로마자로 표기하다 Romanize Korean
■—표기 the Romanization; writing Korean in Roman characters
로망스어 —語 a Romance language
로맨스 a romance; a love affair; an affair; a love story
◆로맨스 그레이 a fine elderly gentleman with gray hair / 멋있는 남성과의 로맨스 (have) a romance [a love affair] with a handsome man / 로맨스가 많은 romantic; full of romance / 로맨스가 싹트다 fall in love with each other
▶그는 젊은 시절에 로맨스가 많았다 He had many romantic affairs in his younger days.
로맨티시스트 〈낭만주의자〉 a romanticist; 〈공상가〉 a daydreamer
로맨티시즘 〈낭만주의〉 romanticism

로맨틱하다 〈공상적〉 romantic ◆로맨틱한 생애 a romantic [checkered] career / 로맨틱한 생각에 잠기다 indulge in romantics
▶그녀는 로맨틱한 소녀다 She is a romantic girl.
▶그녀는 로맨틱한 기분이 되었다 A romantic mood came over her.
로봇 〈인조 인간〉 a robot; 〈허수아비 같은 사람〉 a figurehead ◆로봇 장관 a figurehead minister / 산업용 로봇 an industrial robot / 로봇화하다 robotize ■—공학 robotics —학 robotology
로부터 from; out of ◆아버지로부터 재산을 물려받다 inherit [succeed to] a fortune from one's father
▶이것은 친구로부터 받은 선물이다 This is a present from a friend of mine.
로비 a lobby; a lounge ■—활동 lobbyism: 로비활동을 하다 lobby 《in UN》 —활동가 a lobbyist
로빙 〔테니스〕 lobbing —로빙하다 lob 《a ball》
로서 〈지위·신분·자격〉 as; for; in the capacity of; in [under] the character of
◆부부로서 어울리지 않는 쌍 an ill-mated pair / 교사로서의 책임 one's duty as a teacher / 어버이로서의 의무 one's duty as a parent / 작가로서 유명하다 be famous as a writer / 증인으로서 소환하다 call sb in evidence
▶내가 어떡하면 좋을지 친구로서 조언해주지 않겠니? As a friend what would you advise me to do?
▶그는 지사로서 발언했다 He spoke (in his capacity) as a governor.
▶당신은 장관으로서 그것을 말하고 있는 것입니까? Are you saying that in your capacity as a minister?
로서는 for; considering ◆나로서는 as for me; for my part; as far as I am concerned
▶나로서는 그런 비겁한 짓은 할 수 없었네 For my own part [Personally], I couldn't act the coward like that.
로션 〈화장수〉 (a) lotion ◆스킨 로션 skin lotion / 애프터 셰이브 로션 after-shave lotion / 핸드 로션 hand lotion / 헤어 로션 hair lotion
로스트 〈불고기〉 roast (meat) ■—비프[치킨] roast beef [chicken]
로써 〈도구〉 with; 〈수단〉 by; by means of; through
◆문필로써 생활하다 write for living / 서면으로써 통지하다 inform sb by letter
▶사상은 말로써 표현된다 Thoughts are expressed by means of words.
▶두 사람은 늘 눈으로써 의사를 전한다 They communicate constantly with their eyes.
로열젤리 royal jelly
로이드 ■—감정서 a Lloyd's survey report —감정인 a Lloyd's surveyor —대리인 a Lloyd's agent —선급 증명서 a Lloyd's list
로이터 ■—전보 a Reuters dispatch —통신사 Reuters; Reuter's Ltd.; the Reuter's News Agency —특파원 a Reuters' correspondent 《in Washington》

로저 〔通信〕 roger
▶로저, 목하 확인중 "Roger, identifying."
로제타석 —石 the Rosetta stone
로진백 〔野〕 〈투수용의 송진가루가 든 주머니〉 a rosin bag
로카 ROKA 〔*Republic of Korea Army*〕
로커 a locker ■—룸 〈선수 등의〉 a locker room
로커빌리 〔樂〕 rockabilly ◆로커빌리 가수 a rockabilly singer
로컬 〈지방의〉 local 《▶general 〈전국〉에 대한 말로 「시골」의 뜻은 없음》
■—뉴스 local news —컬러 local color —판(版) 〈신문〉 the local edition 《of a newspaper》; 〈로컬란〉 the local section —프로그램 [방송] a local program [broadcast]
로케이션 〔映〕 a location ◆신작을 위해 속초로 로케이션을 가다 go on [out for] location in Sokch'o for a new film
▶그 영화는 파리에서 로케이션 중이다 The (shooting for the) movie is now on location in Paris.
▶그 장면은 로케이션으로 촬영되었다 The scene was filmed [was shot] on location.
■—팀 a location unit; a unit on location —헌팅 location hunting
로켓¹ 〈장신구〉 a locket
로켓² 〈비행체〉 a rocket
◆로켓 추진식의 rocket-powered [-propelled] / 우주 로켓을 쏘아 올리다 launch a space rocket
▶내가 로켓을 타고 달까지 날아갈 수 있으면 좋으련만 I wish I could take a rocket to the moon.
■감속— a retarding [deceleration, braking] rocket 달[우주]— a moon [space] rocket 3단[다단]식— a three-stage [multistage] rocket 역추진— a retro-rocket 행성— an interplanetary rocket ■—공학 rocketry —발사장치[대] a rocket launcher [launching pad] —비행기 a rocket plane —시험 발사장 a rocket range —실험장 a rocket field —엔진 a rocket engine —연료 rocket fuel —전문가 a rocketeer —탄 a rocket bomb —포 a rocket gun; 〈보병용〉 a rocket launcher
로코코 〔建·美〕 rococo ◆—식 건축 rococo architecture —식 회화 양식 a rococo style of painting
로큰롤 〈춤·곡〉 rock-'n'-roll; rock and roll
로터리 〈환상 교차로〉 《美》 a rotary; a traffic circle; 《英》 a roundabout
로터리클럽 the Rotary Club ◆국제— the Rotary International ■—회원 a Rotarian
로테이션 rotation
◆5명의 로테이션에 들어있다 be in the five-man rotation
▶그는 로테이션에서 빠졌다 He was dropped [demoted] from the (starting) rotation.
로틴 〈시기〉 one's early teens; 《美口》 low-teen ages; 〈사람〉 a low teen; a subteen
◆로틴의 소년[소녀] a boy [girl] in his [her] early teens
로프 (a) rope; (a) cord; (a) cable
■—웨이 a ropeway; a [an aerial] cableway: 로프웨이로 by ropeway

로하여금 ♦―로 하여금 하게 하다 〈강제〉 make *sb* do; force [compel] *sb* to do; get *sb* to do; 〈허락·방임〉 let *sb* do; allow *sb* to do ▶나는 그들로 하여금 그 방을 청소하게 했다 I made [had] them clean the room. ⇌ I got them to clean the room. ⇌ I had [got] the room cleaned by them.
▶그의 자살은 나로 하여금 생각에 잠기게 했다 His suicide made me (stop and) think.

로힐 low-heeled [flat] shoes; shoes with low heels; (口) flats
♦로힐을 신은 여자 a woman in low heels

록 〔樂〕 rock (music)

록클라이밍 〈암벽 등반〉 rock-climbing
♦록클라이밍을 하는 사람 a rock-climber / 록클라이밍을 하다 go rock-climbing

록펠러재단 ―財團 the Rockefeller Foundation

-론 ―論 1 〈논의〉 (an) argument; (a) discussion ♦추상론 an abstract argument
2 〈이론〉 a theory; a doctrine
♦진화론 the theory [doctrine] of evolution
▶그의 교육론은 흥미롭다 His theory on education is interesting.
3 〈논설·논문〉 an essay; a treatise; 〈평론〉 (a) comment ♦문학론 an essay on literature
4 〈문제〉 a question; a problem
♦한자(漢字) 제한론 the question of limiting the use of Chinese characters

론 〈대출금〉 a loan

론도 〔樂〕 a rondo (*pl.* ~s)
―형식 a rondo form

론코트 a grass court; a lawn-tennis court

론테니스 lawn tennis ⇨ 테니스

롤러 a roller; a roll; a runner; 〈땅을 고르는〉 a (road) roller; 〔寫〕 a squeegee ♦롤러로 지면을 고르다 level the ground with a roller
■―베어링 a roller bearing ―코스터 a roller coaster

롤러스케이트 〈구두〉 (a pair of) roller skates; 〈놀이〉 rollerskating ♦롤러스케이트를 타는 사람 a roller skater / 롤러스케이트를 타다 roller-skate; skate on wheels
■―장 a roller-skating rink

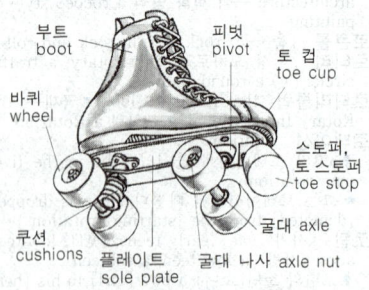

――――― 롤러스케이트 ―――――
부트 boot
피벗 pivot
토 컵 toe cup
바퀴 wheel
스토퍼, 토 스토퍼 toe stop
쿠션 cushions
플레이트 sole plate
굴대 axle
굴대 나사 axle nut

롤링 〈좌우 동요〉 rolling; a roll ―롤링하다 roll (from side to side) ▶배가 롤링하기 시작했다 The ship started rolling [to roll].

롤백 a rollback ■―작전 a rollback operation ―전술 rollback (tactics) ―정책 〈구소련에 대한 미국의〉 a rollback policy

롤빵 a roll (of bread); (美) a bun

롤스로이스 〈자동차〉 〈商標〉 a Rolls-Royce

롤오버 〈높이뛰기 자세〉 a rollover (jump); a Western roll

롬퍼스 〈어린이 옷〉 rompers

롱 〈긴〉 long ■―숏 〔映〕 a long [full] shot (of a scene)

롱런 〔映·劇〕 〈장기 흥행〉 a long run
▶그 연극은 500회의 롱런을 했다 The play had a long run of 500 performances.

롱스커트 a long skirt

롱플레잉레코드 a long-playing record (略 LP)

뢴트겐 〈뢴트겐선(線)〉 Roentgen [Röntgen] rays; X-rays; 〈뢴트겐 사진〉 an X-ray (photograph); a roentgenograph; a roentgenogram
♦뢴트겐 사진을 찍다 take an X-ray (photograph) (of); roentgenograph / 뢴트겐 사진을 판독하다 examine [read, interpret] an X-ray (photograph)
▶뢴트겐의 결과는 이상이 없었다 The X-ray showed nothing wrong. ⇌ The X-ray was clear.
■―검사 an X-ray examination: 뢴트겐 검사를 받다 have an X-ray (examination); have an X-ray taken; be X-rayed ―기사 a radiologist; (英) a radiographer ―사진술 radiography ―요법 roentgenotherapy; X-ray treatment ―조사(照射) roentgen irradiation; X-raying ―촬영 장치 an X-ray apparatus ―투시(법) roentgenoscopy; fluoroscopy

-료 ―料 〈요금〉 a charge; a rate; a fee
♦배달료 delivery charge / 진찰료 a (doctor's) consultation fee / 통화료 〈1회의〉 a telephone charge

루골액 〔藥〕 Lugol's solution

루르 〈독일 서부 탄광지역〉 the Ruhr

루미놀 〔化〕 luminol
■―반응 the luminol reaction

루브르 〈파리의 박물관〉 the Louvre (Museum)

루블 〈러시아의 화폐 단위〉 a r(o)uble

루비 1 〈보석〉 a ruby ♦루비 반지 a ruby ring; a ring set with a ruby / 루비색의 ruby 2 〈7호 활자〉 〔印〕 (美) an agate [ǽgət]; (英) a ruby

루스리프 a loose-leaf (book)

루스하다 loose; sloppy; slovenly; careless; unpunctual ♦루스한 생각 a loose mind / 루스한 여자 a loose woman / 루스한 생활을 하다 lead a slovenly life

루안다 〈앙골라의 수도〉 Luanda

루오 〈프랑스 화가〉 Rouault, Georges (1871-1958)

루이스 〈미국 소설가〉 Lewis, Sinclair (1885-1951)

루이지애나 〈미국의 주〉 Louisiana (略 La.)

루주 〈연지〉 〔프〕 rouge
♦루주를 짙게 바른 입술 thickly rouged [painted] lips / 루주를 바르다 rouge

루키 〈신인〉 a rookie; rookey; rooky

루터 〈독일의 종교 개혁자〉 Luther, Martin (1483-1546) ♦루터파 교리 Luther's doctrine

■—주의 Lutheranism —파 the Lutheran Church —파 교회 the Lutheran church —파 신자 a Lutheran

루트¹ 〔數〕 a root ◆제곱루트 a square [second] root (sign) / 세제곱루트 a cubic root (sign) ▶ 루트 4는 2다 Root 4 is 2.

루트² 〈경로〉a route; a channel ▶ 나는 공식[비밀, 외교] 루트를 통해 그 정보를 얻었다 I have got the information through official [secret, diplomatic] channels.

루프 a loop ■—선 a loop line —안테나 a loop antenna

루피 〈인도·파키스탄의 화폐단위〉 a rupee (略 R, Re)

루피아 〈인도네시아의 화폐단위〉 rupiah (pl. ~(s)) (略 Rp)

룩셈부르크 〈나라 이름〉Luxemburg; 〈공식명〉the Grand Duchy of Luxemburg ■—사람 a Luxemburger

룰 a rule ◆야구의 룰 the rules of baseball / 룰대로 하다 do what the rules prescribe / 룰을 어기다 be against the rules

룰렛 1〈도박〉roulette; 〈도구〉a roulette ◆룰렛(게임)을 하다 play roulette 2 〈양재용〉a roulette

룸 a room ■리빙— a living [sitting] room —메이트 a roommate —서비스 room service

룸바 〈춤〉r(h)umba ◆룸바를 추다 rumba; dance the [a] rumba

룸펜 [〈獨〉 Lumpen] 〈부랑자〉a tramp; a loafer; a hobo (pl. ~(e)s); a vagabond; a vagrant; an unemployed man

룻기 —記 〔聖〕 The Book of Ruth (略 Ruth)

-류¹ -流 1〈모양·방식〉a style; a type; a fashion; a mode; a form; a way ▶ 자기류를 고집하면 바르게 배울 수 없다 You can't learn it correctly if you stick to your own way.
2 〈유파〉a school; a system ◆추사류 서체의 *Ch'usa* school of calligraphy / 플라톤류 철학 the Platonic school of philosophy
3 〈등급〉a class; a rate; a rank ◆상류 계급 the upper classes / 일류의 first-class; first-rate; leading

-류² -類 1〈종류〉a sort; a kind; a genus; a type; a species ◆거미류 a genus of spider / 채소류 vegetables
2 〔生〕〈강(綱)〉a class; 〈목(目)〉an order

류머티즘 〔醫〕rheumatism; (俗) the rheumatics ◆류머티즘을 앓다 suffer from rheumatism
■ 관절— articular rheumatism 근육— muscular rheumatism 급성[만성]— acute [chronic] rheumatism —치료약 an antirheumatic —환자 a rheumatic

류트 〈악기〉a lute ■—연주자 a lutanist; a lutenist; a lutist

륙색 〈배낭〉a rucksack; a knapsack

> 解說 「륙색」은 〈獨〉Rucksack에서 온 것인데 영어에서도 *rucksack* [rʌ́ksæk]이라고 한다. 미국에서는 *knapsack*도 자주 쓴다.

▶ 그는 륙색을 (등에) 지고 있다 He is carrying a rucksack (on his back).

-륜 -輪 -wheel; -wheeled ◆2륜차 a two-wheeled vehicle; a two-wheeler / 4륜 구동차 a four-wheel drive vehicle

르나르 〈프랑스 소설가·극작가〉Renard, Jules (1864-1910)

르네상스 the Renaissance; the Renascence ◆르네상스 화가[건축] Renaissance painters [architecture] ■—양식 Renaissance style

르누아르 〈프랑스 화가〉Renoir, Pierre Auguste(1822-1919)

르완다 〈나라 이름〉Rwanda; 〈공식명〉the Republic of Rwanda

르코르뷔지에 〈스위스 태생의 프랑스 건축가〉Le Corbusier, Charles Edouard Jeanneret (1887-1965)

르포(르타주) 〈현지 보고〉《do, write》 reportage; a report 《on》

를 ⇨ 을 ◆나무를 베다 cut a tree / 벽시계를 쳐다보다 look up at the wall clock / 자전거를 타다 ride a bicycle / 폭풍우를 만나다 get caught in a storm

리 理 〈까닭·이치〉reason; possibility ▶ 그럴 리가 없다 It cannot be true.
▶ 그가 그런 일을 했을 리가 없다 He cannot have done such a thing.
▶ 그가 그렇게 바쁠 리가 없다 He can't be so busy.

-리 -裡 〈가운데·속〉◆성공리에 successfully / 암암리에 secretly

리그 〈연맹〉a league ◆고교 야구— the High School Baseball League 메이저[마이너]— the Major [Minor] League ■—전 a league game [match]; (총칭) the league series

-리까 〈문의〉 ▶ 무얼 도와드리까? What can I do for you? ▶ 지금 당장 가리까? Shall I go right now?

리넨 linen ■ 리넨제의 블라우스 linen blouse

리놀륨 〈마루 깔개〉linoleum

리니어모터 a linear motor ■—카 a linear motor car

-리다 1〈…하겠소〉 ▶ 곧 돌아오리다 I will return soon.
2 〈경고·추측〉 ▶ 서둘러요, 지각하리다 Hurry up, or you will not be in time.
▶ 오늘은 아마 파도가 세리다 I fear the waves will be high today.

리더¹ 〈지도자〉a leader ◆리더 노릇을 하다 lead others; take the lead; act as a leader ▶ 그는 조합 리더다 He is the leader of the union.

리더² 〈독본·독자〉a reader

리더십 leadership ◆리더십을 발휘하다 take the leadership [initiative]

리드¹ 〈앞섬·선두〉a lead ◆리드를 빼앗다 gain [take] the lead
—하다 lead ◆클럽을 리드하다 lead a club
▶ 우리 팀이 5대 3으로 리드하고 있다 Our team leads by 5 to 3.

리드² 〈악기의 떨림판〉a reed ■—악기 a reed instrument —오르간 a reed organ

리드³ 〈영국 시인·평론가〉Read, Sir Herbert

리드미컬하다 rhythmical
♦리드미컬하게 rhythmically
리듬 (a) rhythm ♦리듬있는 rhythmic(al) / 리듬에 맞추어 to the rhythm; (sing) in rhythm [time] with (the piano) / 빠른 리듬으로 (dance) in quick rhythm
■—감(感) rhythmical sense —체조 rhythm calisthenics
리딩히터 〔野〕a leading hitter
리라 〈이탈리아의 화폐단위〉a lira (pl.~s, lire) (略 L)
-리라 〈추측〉may [might] (be, do); must; I hope...; I think [suppose]
▶아마 그러리라 It may be so. ⇌ I suppose so.
▶틀림없이 그는 알고 있으리라 He must be aware of this.
▶그는 틀림없이 성공하리라 He will certainly succeed.
-리라고 that... ▶그가 반드시 성공하리라고 믿는다 I am sure (that) he will succeed.
▶그가 오리라고는 생각하지 않는다 I don't expect [think] he will come.
-리라는 ▶네가 그녀와 결혼하리라는 소식을 그에게서 들었다 He told me that you would marry her.
리리시즘 〈서정미〉lyricism
리릭 〈서정시〉a lyric ■—테너 a lyric tenor
리마 〈페루의 수도〉Lima
리모트컨트롤 〔電〕remote control ♦리모트컨트롤로 조종하다 remote-control (a robot)
■—장치 a remote-controlled device
리무진 〈자동차〉a limousine
리바이벌 〈재생·부흥〉revival ♦바로크 음악의 리바이벌 revival of baroque music
리버럴리스트 〈자유주의자〉a liberalist
리버럴리즘 〈자유주의〉liberalism
리버럴아트 liberal arts
리버럴하다 liberal
▶나는 이 대학의 리버럴한 전통에 마음이 끌렸다 I was attracted by the liberal tradition of this university.
리버풀 〈영국의 도시〉Liverpool
■—시민 a Liverpoolian
리베이트 a rebate; (美口) kickback; a rake-off

解說 우리말의 「리베이트」는 「(몰래 받는) 수수료」라는 나쁜 뜻으로 쓰는 경우가 많으나 rebate 본래의 뜻은 「(지불금 일부의) 환불」이다. 나쁜 뜻의 「리베이트」에 해당하는 말로는 kickback이나 rake-off를 쓰는데 특히 rake-off는 「정가의 할인」이란 뜻으로 쓰는 경우도 있다.

리벳 a rivet ♦리벳을 박다 rivet; fasten with rivets ■—공(工) a riveter —용접 rivet welding —해머 a rivet hammer
리보플라빈 〔生化〕riboflavin
리보핵산 —核酸 〔生化〕ribonucleic acid (略 RNA)
리본 a ribbon; 〈모자의〉a band
♦리본으로 매다 tie [bind] sth with a ribbon
▶그녀는 머리에 푸른 리본을 맸다 She wore a blue ribbon in her hair.
▶그는 선물을 빨간 리본으로 묶었다 He tied the present with a red ribbon.
리볼버 〈연발 권총〉a revolver
리뷰 〈평론〉a review ■—북 a book review
리비도 〔心〕〈성(性)본능〉libido
리비아 Libya; 〈공식명〉the Socialist People's Libyan Arab Jamahiriya ♦리비아의 Libyan
■—사람 a Libyan
리빙스턴 〈스코틀랜드 선교사·아프리카 탐험가〉Livingstone, David (1813-73)
리빙키친 〈주방·식당·거실을 겸한 방〉a living room with a kitchen in it
리사이클 〈재활용(품)〉a recycle ⇨ 재활용
리사이틀 〔樂〕a recital ♦피아노 리사이틀을 열다 give [have] a piano recital
리서스인자 —因子 〔生化〕a Rhesus factor (略 Rh factor)
리센코 〈러시아의 생물학자〉Lysenko, Trofim Denisovich (1898-1976) ■—학설 Lysenkoism
리셉션 a reception ♦…를 위해 리셉션을 열다 hold [give] a reception in honor of sb
리슐리외 〈프랑스 추기경·재상〉Richelieu, Armand Jean du Plessis (1585-1642)
리스 〈임대〉lease
리스본 〈포르투갈의 수도〉Lisbon
리스트 〈목록〉a list
♦리스트를 작성하다 make a list (of); list / 리스트에 올리다 put sb on the list
▶그 여자는 구입하고자 하는 물건의 리스트를 만들었다 She made a list of the articles she was going to buy.
리스트 〈헝가리 작곡가·피아니스트〉Liszt, Franz (1811-86)
리시브 〔球〕receiving ♦리시브를 잘하다 be a good receiver ■—리시브하다 receive (the served ball)
리시트 a receipt ⇨ 영수증
리아스식해안 —式海岸 〔地〕a ria coast; rias
리야드 〈사우디아라비아의 수도〉Riyadh
리얼 〈현실〉real —리얼하다 real; realistic
♦인생의 리얼한 묘사 a realistic depiction of life
▶그 소설 속의 인물들은 실제 인물들처럼 아주 리얼하게 묘사되었다 The characters in the novel seem quite real.
■—타임 〔電算〕real time
리얼리스트 〈사실주의자〉a realist
리얼리즘 〈사실주의〉realism
-리요 ▶내가 왜 너를 원망하리요? Why should I blame you?
▶낸들 어찌 하리요? What am I to do now? ⇌ What shall I do?
▶이 고마움을 무슨 말로 다 표현하리요 I do not know how to express my thanks.
리우데자네이루 〈브라질의 항구 도시〉Rio de Janeiro
리조트 〈행락지〉resort ♦서머[윈터] 리조트 a summer [winter] resort ■—웨어 resort wear; casual wear [clothing] —호텔 a resort hotel
리치 〔拳〕reach ♦리치가 길다 have a long reach
리카도 〈영국의 경제학자〉Ricardo, David (1772-1823)

리케차 〔菌〕 a rickettsia 《*pl.* ~s, -ae》
리코더 〈기록 장치〉 a recorder ■ 타임 — a time recorder 테이프 — a tape recorder
리코딩 〈녹음〉 recording
리콜 〈소환·해임·결함 상품의 회수〉 (a) recall ♦리콜제(制) the recall system / 우리 나라 대사의 리콜 the recall of our ambassador / 결함 제품의 리콜 작전 the recall operation of faulty products ─리콜하다 recall
리퀘스트 a request ─곡 a request tune [song] ─프로그램〔放〕 a request program
리큐어 〈술〉 liqueur ─브랜디 liqueur brandy ─잔 a liqueur glass
리터 〈용량 단위〉 a liter (略 l., lit.)
리턴매치 〔拳〕 a return match
리투아니아 〈나라 이름〉 Lithuania; 〈공식명〉 the Republic of Lithuania
리튬 〔化〕 lithium
리트 〔樂〕 〈독일 가곡〉 a lied 《*pl.* lieder》
리트머스 〔化〕 litmus ─시험 litmus test ─시험지 litmus paper ─액(液) litmus solution
리포터 〈기자〉 a reporter
리포트 〈보고〉 a report; 〈학교의〉 a term [research] paper
리프트 〈스키장의〉 a (ski) lift
리플레이션 〔經〕 reflation
리허빌리테이션 〈갱생·재건〉 rehabilitation ■ ─센터 a rehabilitation center
리허설 a rehearsal ♦연극의 리허설을 하다 rehearse a play ▶ 햄릿은 지금 리허설 중이다 Hamlet is in rehearsal now.
리히터지진계 ─地震計 the Richter scale
리히텐슈타인 Liechtenstein ■ ─공국 the Principality of Liechtenstein
린네 〈스웨덴의 식물학자〉 Linnaeus, Carolus (1707-78)

린드버그 〈미국 비행가〉 Lindbergh, Charles Augustus(1902-74)
린스 〈화장품〉 (a) rinse ─린스하다 rinse ▶ 그녀는 머리를 린스했다 She rinsed her hair. ⇌ She gave her hair a rinse.
린치 〈사형(私刑)〉 lynch law; lynching ♦린치를 가하다 lynch ▶ 그들은 배신자에게 린치를 가했다 They lynched the traitor.
릴 a reel ■ ─낚싯줄을 릴에 감다[릴에서 풀어내다] reel in [out] a fishing line
■ ─낚싯대 a spinning rod
릴레이 a relay ▶ 우리는 400미터 릴레이에 참가하였다 We took part in a 400-meter relay.
릴리프[1] 〈양각〉 relief
■ ─맵 a relief map
릴리프[2] 〔野〕 relief
■ ─피처 a relief pitcher
릴케 〈독일 시인〉 Rilke, Rainer Maria(1875-1926)
립스틱 a lipstick
링 1 〈권투 등의〉 the ring 2 〔體操〕 (the) flying rings; the rings 3 〈피임용〉 an intrauterine (contraceptive) device IU(C)D
■ ─사이드 (sit at) the ringside ─사이드석(席) a ringsideseat
링거액 〔醫〕 Ringer's solution [fluid]
■ ─주사 an injection of Ringer's solution: 환자는 링거액 주사를 맞았다 The patient was given an injection of Ringer's solution.
링거폰 (商標) Linguaphone
링컨 〈미국 제16대 대통령〉 Lincoln, Abraham (1809-65)
링크[1] 〔經〕 link ♦링크제(도) 〔經〕 a link system
링크[2] 〈스케이트장〉 a (skating, roller-skating) rink
링크스 〈골프장〉 (golf) links

ㅁ

-ㅁ세 〈하겠네〉 ▶ 자네와 같이 갈세 I'll be glad [I'd be happy, I'd be pleased, I'm willing, I'm ready, I'd love] to go with you. ▶ 내 할 수 있다면 무엇이든지 도와줌세 I shall be glad to do what I can.

마¹ 〈남쪽〉 the south (▶뱃사람들의 말)
♦ 마파람 the south wind; a souther

마² 〔植〕 a yam

마³ 〈도레미파 창법의〉 〔樂〕 mi
♦ 마음 E / 내림[올림] 마 E flat [sharp] / 마장조[단조] (a symphony in) E major [minor]

마 魔 〈악마〉 a demon; a devil; an evil spirit; 〈행악·불운〉 ill [bad] luck
♦ 마의 금요일 an unlucky Friday / 마가 끼다 be possessed by a devil; be tempted by a devil; come under the influence of an evil spirit
▶ 마가 끼었지, 글쎄 그 여자가 은행에서 1천만 원을 횡령했다니까 I wonder what could have possessed her to have embezzled ten million won from the bank.
▶ 마가 낀건지, 제정신 가지고야 그런 말을 할 수 있나 That's the devil talking, not you.

마 碼 a yard (略 yd.) ♦ 천을 마로 재어 팔다 sell a fabric by the yard

-마 -魔 a devil of a man; a (human) fiend
♦ 살인마 a devilish murderer / 색마 a male flirt; a brute (of a man)

마가린 margarine; (美) oleo; (英口) marge
♦ 식물성 마가린 nut margarine / 빵에 마가린을 바르다 spread margarine on bread

마가목 〔植〕 a mountain ash; a rowan tree

마가복음 —福音 〔聖〕 The Gospel according to St. Mark (略 Mark)

마각 馬脚 〈본성〉 one's true character [colors]
▶ 결국 그는 마각을 드러냈다 In the end he revealed his true character.
▶ 예상대로 그녀는 마각을 드러냈다 She gave herself away [betrayed herself], just as I had expected.

마갈궁 磨羯宮 〔天〕 the Goat; Capricorn; Capricornus

마감 a deadline (for); closing; an end; a finish
♦ 오후 5시 마감까지 by the 5 p.m. deadline / 편집 마감 editorial deadline
▶ 금일 마감 (揭示) Closed today.
▶ 신청 마감은 언제지요? When does the time for application end?
▶ 신청 마감은 2월 말입니다 The closing date [The deadline] for application is the end of February.
▶ 리포트 제출 마감은 언제입니까? When is the deadline for (turning in) the paper?
—마감하다 close; end
♦ 계산을 마감하다 close the account / 원고를 마감하다 accept no more manuscripts
■ 원고— the deadline for the manuscript 장부— the closing of books ■—기입 〔商〕 closing entry —날 the closing day; the final day (for); (美) the deadline (for) ■—시간 a closing time; 〈신문 기사의〉 the time limit for a copy : 마감시간에 대다 make [meet] the deadline

마개 〈병 등의〉 a stopper; a stop; 〈통의〉 a tap; a bung; a stopple; 〈코르크의〉 a cork; 〈수도·가스관 등의〉 a stopcock; 〈금속제의〉 a crown cap
♦ 맥주병의 마개를 따다 uncap a bottle of beer; remove the cap of a beer bottle / 병의 코르크 마개를 막다[뽑다] cork [uncork] a bottle / 병에 단단하게[느슨하게] 마개를 하다 cork a bottle tightly [loosely]
■ 귀— an earplug (소음방지용) ■—뽑이 a bottle opener; 〈코르크 마개의〉 a corkscrew; 〈맥주병 등의〉 a cap opener

마거리트 〔植〕 a marguerite; a Paris daisy

마고자 a Korean jacket worn over one's upper garment; *magoja*

마구 〈분별없이〉 recklessly; rashly; 〈지나치게〉 excessively; too much; 〈부당하게〉 unreasonably; 〈무차별하게〉 indiscriminately; 〈닥치는 대로〉 at random; 〈아낌없이〉 freely
♦ 마구 속도를 내다 speed recklessly / 마구 행동하다 act blindfold [recklessly]
▶ 그 갱은 마구 총을 쏴댔다 The gangster fired his gun at random [blindly].
▶ 돈을 마구 쓰지 말아라 You shouldn't spend your money like water [foolishly, lavishly].
▶ 그는 마구 술을 마신다 He drinks too much [to excess, excessively].
▶ 그는 주를 마구 사들였다 He bought stocks blindly.
▶ 그녀는 마구 지껄여댔다 She kept rattling away [on].

마구 馬具 harness; horse gear [equipment]; 〈장식한 것〉 trappings
♦ 마구 한 벌 a set of harness / 마구를 단 말 a harnessed horse / 마구를 달다 harness (a horse); put harness on (a horse) / 마구를 벗기다 remove the harness from (a horse)
■ —류 harnessry —상 〈상인〉 a harness maker; a saddler; 〈상점〉 a harnessry; a saddler's shop; a saddlery

마구간 馬廐間 a stable; (美) a (horse) barn
♦ 말을 마구간에 넣다 stable a horse; put [lodge] in a stable
■ —지기 a stabler

마구리 〈물건의 양쪽면〉 end pieces; an end face; both sides; 〈덮어끼우는 쇠붙이 등〉 caps on both ends
■ 베개— wooden end pieces on a Korean pillow ■—판 a device for squaring wooden end pieces

마구리쌓기 〖工〗 header bond
마구잡이 careless [haphazard, random] behavior; a reckless act
♦ 마구잡이로 blindly; senselessly; at random / 마구잡이로 일하다 do *one's* work carelessly; do a slapdash job of it / 책을 마구잡이로 읽다 read 《books》 at random [desultorily]
마굴 魔窟 〈마귀의 소굴〉 a lair of devils
2 〈악한들의 소굴〉 a den; an underworld hangout
3 〈사창굴〉 a brothel; a house of ill fame; (美口) a good-time house; 〈홍등가〉 a red-light district; 〈아편굴〉 an opium den
마권 馬券 a pari-mutuel ticket
♦ 5번 마의 마권을 사다 buy a ticket on horse No. 5 / 마권을 사다 buy a ticket [betting ticket]
■ —세 the pari-mutuel tax; the horserace tax —업자 a bookmaker
마귀 魔鬼 〖基〗 the Devil; 〈마왕〉 Satan; 〈사람에게 들린〉 a demon; a devil; 〈악령〉 an evil spirit
♦ 마귀와 같은 devilish; demoniac; fiendish / 마귀를 쫓다 drive out [exorcise] evil spirits
▶ 그는 마귀에 씌운 듯 갑자기 떨기 시작했다 Suddenly, he shook as if he had been possessed by an evil spirit [a demon, the devil, Satan].
■ —할멈 a witch; a hag; a harridan; an ogress
마그나카르타 〖史〗 the Magna C(h)arta
마그네슘 〖化〗 magnesium, 〈사진의〉 flash powder
■ —산화— oxide of magnesium; magnesia 수산화— magnesium hydroxide 염화— magnesium chloride 탄산— magnesium carbonate —광 〖寫〗 magnesium light
마그네시아 〖化〗 magnesia
■ —황산— sulphate of magnesia
마그네트론 〖工〗 magnetron
마그네틱 magnetic ■ —테이프 a magnetic tape
마그니튜드 〖地質〗〈지진의 규모〉 magnitude
▶ 마그니튜드 6의 지진이 있었다 There was an earthquake registering [reading] six on the Richter scale.
마그데부르크반구 半球 〖物〗 Magdeburg hemispheres
마그레오드진공계 —眞空計 〖水産〗 Magreod vacuum gauge
마그마 〖地質〗 magma (*pl.* ~s, -mata)
■ —굄 magma chamber —분화작용〖分化作用〗 magmatic differentiation —수〖水〗 magmatic water —주머니 magma pocket
마나과 〈니카라과의 수도〉 Managua
마나님 〈나이 많은 여자〉 an elderly lady; an old woman; 〈호칭〉 madam; ma'am; Mrs...; your good lady
마나슬루 〈히말라야산 가운데 여덟번째의 고봉〉 Manaslu
마냥 **1** 〈끊임없이〉 continuously; always; all the time; without a break; incessantly
▶ 그는 마냥 불평이다 He is always [continually, constantly] making complaints. ≠ He is grumbling all the time.
▶ 마냥 비가 내렸다 It rained without a break [continuously, incessantly].
▶ 나는 마냥 눈물이 흘렀다 Tears streamed down my face incessantly. ≠ I could not hold back my tears.
2 〈실컷〉 as much as *one* wants; to *one's* content; to the full
♦ 마냥 놀다 enjoy *oneself* to the full / 마냥 먹다 eat as much as *one* likes [wants]; eat to *one's* content; eat *one's* fill / 마냥 울다 have a good cry; have a cry out; 〈가슴이 터지도록〉 cry *one's* heart out
3 〈늑장을 부리며〉 slowly; draggingly ♦ 마냥 걷다 walk slowly / 마냥 끌다 drag on
마네 〈프랑스의 화가〉 Manet, Edouard (1832-83)
마네킹 〈인형〉 a mannequin; a manikin; a manakin; a tailor's dummy ■ —걸 a manikin girl —인형 (美) a window dummy
마녀 魔女 a witch; a sorceress; 〈여자 악마〉 a she-devil; a she-demon ■ —재판 a witch trial
마노 瑪瑙 〖鑛〗 agate [ǽgət]
마논트로포 〈그러나 지나치지 않게〉 〖樂〗 ma non troppo
마누라 **1** 〈자기 아내〉 *one's* wife; *one's* better half ♦ 마누라를 얻다 get [take] a wife; take 《a woman》 to wife; get married
▶ 그 사내는 마누라 없이는 하루도 못 살아 His wife is everything to him.
▶ 그는 마누라 손에 쥐어 산다 He is a henpecked husband.
2 〈노파〉 an old woman
마는 but; though; although; (and) yet; while; only
▶ 난 가난하지마는 행복하다 I am poor but happy. ≠ I am happy though poor.
▶ 미안하지마는 잠깐 기다려 주세요 I'm sorry, but please wait for a moment.
▶ 기호는 머리가 좋지마는 동생은 그렇지 않다 Ki-ho is bright, while his brother isn't.
▶ 가고는 싶지마는 시간이 없어 I would go, if I had time.
마늘 〖植〗 a garlic; 〈향료의〉 garlic
■ —장아찌 pickled garlics —종 the stalk [stem] of a garlic —쪽 a clove of a garlic
마니교 摩尼敎 Manich(a)eanism; Manich(a)eism ■ —도 a Manich(a)ean; a Manichee
마니아 〈열광〉 a mania; a craze 《for》; 〈열중하는 사람〉 a (dance) maniac; a (baseball) fan; (美口) a (camera) buff ■ 재즈— 〈상태〉 jazz mania; 〈사람〉 a jazz maniac
마닐라 〈필리핀의 수도〉 Manila
■ —로프 Manila rope —삼[마] Manila hemp —지〖紙〗 Manila paper; manila —코펄〈천연수지〉〖工〗 Manila copal
마님 madam; 〈호칭〉 ma'am; Milady [miléidi, mai-]; My Lady ♦ 안방 마님 the mistress 《of a house》
—마님 Your [His] Excellency
♦ 대감[영감] 마님 My Lord
마다 〈낱낱이〉 every; each; all
♦ 날마다 everyday; each day; daily; day by day / 밤마다 every evening; every night / 10분마다 every ten minutes / 해마다 year by

[after] year; yearly; every [each] year / 5년마다 (once) every five years; (in) every fifth year / 집집마다 at every door; from door to door / 매 페이지마다 page after page; every page / …할 때마다 every [each] time; as often as [whenever]
▶비가 올 때마다 서늘해지고 있다 It's getting cooler with every rainfall.
▶나는 가는 곳마다 대환영을 받았다 I was warmly welcomed everywhere I went.
▶주차료는 30분마다 1,000원입니다 The parking rate is 1,000 won per every 30 minutes.
▶이 약을 세 시간마다 드세요 Take this medicine every three hours.
▶내가 전화할 때마다 그는 외출중이었다 Every time I phoned [called] him, he was out.

마다가스카르 〈나라 이름〉 Madagascar; 〈공식명〉 the Democratic Republic of Madagascar
■―사람 a Madagascan

마다하다 〈싫어·거절·사양하다〉 hate; dislike; mind; refuse; decline
▶그는 부엌일도 마다하지 않았다 He didn't mind doing kitchen work.
▶그는 불편도 마다하지 않고 내 아들을 마중하러 역까지 나갔다 He took trouble to see my son at the station.
▶그의 제의를 마다할 수 없었다 I could not refuse [decline] his offer.

마담 a madam (▶호칭·칭호의 경우 복수형은 mesdames [meidɑ́ːm]이 됨); 〈요정·다방 등의〉 a proprietress

解說 *madam*은 일반적으로 여성에 대한 정중한 호칭으로 쓰인다: Excuse me, madam. / Thank you ma'dm. / Yes, ma'am. / Yes'm. 또 (Dear) madam 이라고 하여 미지의 여성에게 보내는 편지의 서두에도 사용한다.

■유한― a leisured lady; an idle rich woman
마당 1〈뜰〉 a garden; a yard; a courtyard
♦안마당 a courtyard / 앞[뒷]마당 a front [rear] garden
▶마당에서 참새가 짹짹 울고 있다 There are some sparrows chirping in the garden.
▶마당이 워낙 넓어서 청소하는 것도 큰 일이다 It's hard work to clean such a big yard.
2〈곳〉 a place; a ground
3〈타작마당〉 a threshing ground; the yard for threshing
♦볏마당질 threshing rice
4〈경우〉 an instance; a case; an occasion; 〈때〉 the moment
♦이 마당에 on this occasion; at this time [juncture]/ 떠나는 마당에 at the time [on the occasion] of *one's* departure
▶궁한 마당에 무엇을 가리랴 Beggars should not be choosers.
▶이 급한 마당에 뭘하고 있니? What a hell are you doing at this emergency?
5〈판소리 등의〉 an episode
♦봉산탈춤 일곱 마당 the seven episodes of the Pongsan mask dance.
■―맥질 leveling the threshing ground by ramming and daubing it with clay ―발 a flatfoot 《*pl*. -feet》; a wide-sized foot ―비 a yard broom ―질 threshing in the yard: 마당질하다 thresh 《rough rice》 in the yard

마대 麻袋 a gunny sack; a burlap bag
마도로스 [〈네〉 matroos] a sailor; a seaman
――파이프 a (tobacco) pipe
마도요 〔鳥〕 an Indian curlew; a sabre-[〈美〉 saber-]bill
마돈나 〈성모〉 the Madonna
―상[그림] a Madonna
마드리갈 〔樂〕 a madrigal
마드리드 〈스페인의 수도〉 Madrid
마드무아젤 (프) a mademoiselle 《*pl*. mesdemoisells》 《略 Mlle.; *pl*. Mlles.》; a young lady; 〈양〉 Miss
마디 1〈관절〉 a joint; 〈손가락·무릎 등의〉 a knuckle
2 〈결절(結節)〉 〔物〕 a node; a knot; a joint; a knob; 〈나무의〉 a knar; a gnarl
♦대나무 마디 a bamboo joint / 실의 마디 a knot; a burl / 마디가 없는 재목 clean [clear] timber; timber without a knot / 마디투성이의 널 a board full of knots; a knotty board
3 〈체절(體節)〉 a ringlike segment; a segment; 〈곤충 등의〉 an annulus
4 〈말의〉 a word; a phrase; 〈노래의〉 a snatch; a tune; a melody; 〈소절〉 a bar; a measure
♦〈노래의〉 첫째 마디 the first measure; measure 1 / 몇 마디 말하고 나서 after making a brief remark / 한 마디 부르다 sing a tune / 한두 마디 인사말을 나누다 exchange a word or two of greeting 《with》
▶한 마디 하겠나 I'll say a word. = I have a word to say.
―선(線) 〔物〕 nodal line
마디다 〈오래가다〉 durable; long-lasting; enduring; long-wearing
♦마디게 쓰다 make [keep] long
▶이런 셔츠는 예쁘지만 마디지 못하다 This kind of shirts are pretty but not very durable.
마디마디 1〈식물의〉 all the joints [nodes]; every joint [node]
2〈뼈의〉 the joints; every joints (of a body)
♦마디마디가 쑤시다 *one's* joints hurt; feel pain in *one's* joints
▶겨울이 되면 나는 마디마디가 쑤신다 In winter my joints ache.
3〈말〉 (all) the words [phrases]; every word [phrase]
♦의심스러운 마디마디를 지적하다 point out doubtful points
마디지다 1〈마디가 있다〉 gnarled 《trees》; bony; knuckly [strong-jointed] 《finger》; knotty 《hand》
2〈마디가 생기다〉 form a knot [gnarl, joint]
마디충 ―蟲 〔昆〕 a rice borer; a pear; a pearl moth
마디풀 〔植〕 a knotgrass; a knotweed
마따나 〈말한대로〉 according to *sb*; as; like; just as *sb* say
♦네 말따나 as you say / 그의 말따나 as he says
마땅하다 1〈적합하다〉 becoming; due; proper; fit; suitable; right; appropriate; 〈상당하다〉

마땅 a competent person / 마땅한 값에 사다 buy at a reasonable price
▶ 그는 그 자리에 마땅한 사람이다 He is just the one for the place. ⇌ He is the right man for that position.
2 〈당연하다〉 justifiable; warrantable; rational
♦ 죽어 마땅한 죄 a serious crime deserving of death
▶ 그것이 마땅한 처사다 That is the usual way of doing it.
▶ 빚진 이상 갚는게 마땅하다 One ought to pay what one owes.
3 〈마음에 들다〉 good; satisfactory; pleased; gratifying
▶ 이 옷이 가장 마땅하다 This suits my taste best.

마땅히 1 〈의당·당연히〉 justly; properly; naturally; as a matter of course
♦ 마땅히 …해야 하다 ought to 《do》; it is (just and) proper that 《one》 should 《do》
▶ 너는 마땅히 부모님의 말씀에 순종해야 한다 You ought to obey your parents.
▶ 너는 마땅히 더 좋은 대우를 받아야 한다 You deserve a better treatment.
▶ 마땅히 그래야 한다 That's the natural thing to be expected.
▶ 아침 일찍 떠났으면 그는 지금쯤은 마땅히 여기에 도착했어야 한다 He ought to be here by now, if he left early in the morning.
2 〈적당히〉 suitably; adequately; appropriately; properly; reasonably
▶ 아이들이 마땅히 놀 장소가 있어야 한다 We need a suitable place for our children to play.

마뜩찮다 dissatisfactory; offensive
▶ 그 식당의 음식은 모두가 마뜩찮다 None of the foods and dishes at the restaurant can be served to my taste and satisfaction.

마뜩하다 satisfactory; agreeable; acceptable
▶ 이런 옷감이 마뜩하다 These patterns suits my fancy.

마라톤 〔體〕 a marathon (race)
♦ 마라톤을 하다 take part in a marathon race
▶ 학생들은 한 달에 한 번 마라톤을 한다 The students run a marathon (race) once a month.
■ —경주 a marathon race —선수 a marathon runner; a marathoner

마래미 〔魚〕 a young yellowtail
마량 馬糧 fodder; forage; hay; provender
마력 魔力 〈이상한 힘〉 magical powers; supernatural powers; spell; 〈매력〉 the power to charm; fascinating power; charm
♦ 마력을 지닌 charming; fascinating; bewitching / 마력에 걸리다 fall under [be bound by] a magic spell
▶ 그것은 숫자의 마력이다 It's the magic of numbers.
▶ 그는 그 여자의 마력에 매혹되었다 He fell under the spell of her charms.

마력 馬力 〔物〕 horsepower (略 HP, h.p., hp)
♦ 50 마력의 모터 a motor of 50 HP; a 50-horsepower [50 h.p.] motor / 마력을 올리다 push the power up
▶ 이 차는 150마력이다 This car has 150 horsepower.
■ 공칭— nominal horsepower 실— actual horsepower 유효— effective horsepower 정격 (定格)— rated horsepower 축— brake horsepower ■ —시 horsepower hour (略 h. p. h.)

마련¹ 1 〈준비·장만〉 preparation; provision
—**마련하다** 〈준비하다〉 prepare; 〈미리 갖추다〉 provide; arrange; build; construct
♦ 도로를 마련하다 build a road / 땅을 마련하다 buy 《a piece of》 land; buy a plot [a lot] / 집을 마련하다 get a house / 아침을 마련하다 prepare [fix] breakfast; get breakfast ready / 방에 가구를 마련하다 furnish a room; put furniture into a room / 옷을 새로 마련하다 have a new suit made; buy a new suit / 육교를 마련하다 build [construct] an overpass / 아이들이 앉을 자리를 마련하다 prepare [provide] seats for children / 연회를 마련하다 give a feast
▶ 그 빌딩에 그의 새 사무실이 마련되었다 His new office was established in the building.
▶ 그 회의는 이 점에 관하여 특별 규정을 마련했다 The meeting laid down a special rule on this point.
2 〈변통·조달·융통〉 management; contrivance; makeshift
—**마련하다** manage 《to do》; get *sth* ready; arrange; contrive; make shift
♦ 돈을 마련하다 〈준비하다〉 get money ready; 〈조달하다〉 raise money / 어떻게 해서 돈을 마련하다 find the money somehow / 일자리를 마련하다 find a job
▶ 여비를 마련할 수 없는데 I cannot raise the money for the trip.
▶ 여비는 마련해 두었다 I have some money put aside for a trip.
▶ 가까스로 마련해서 수업료를 냈다 I managed somehow to pay the tuition.
▶ 나는 구실을 마련하여 그 모임에 불참했다 I made an excuse and absented myself from the meeting.
▶ 그 사업을 시작하기 위해서는 적어도 2,000만원이 마련돼야 한다 At least twenty million won must be raised to start the enterprise.
▶ 그 손님들 자리를 마련해 놓았다 The seats were arranged for the guests.

마련² 〈당연함〉 ▶ 살아있는 것은 언젠가는 죽게 마련이다 The living must die some time or other.
▶ 겨울은 춥게 마련이다 Winter is naturally cold time.
▶ 그런 짓을 하면 손해를 보게 마련이다 If you do that, you are bound [sure] to lose.

마렵다 ♦ 똥이 마렵다 have to defecate; feel like going to stool / 오줌이 마렵다 have a desire to urinate [pass water]; feel an urge to urinate; have a call of nature / (변이) 마렵지 않다 don't feel any urge to ease nature
▶ 엄마, 오줌 [똥] 마려워 (口) Mammy, I want to do my needs.

마령서 馬鈴薯 a potato ⇨ 감자

마로니에 [〈프〉 marronnier] 〔植〕 a horse chestnut tree
▶ 우리는 마로니에가 늘어선 가로수 길을 걸었다 We walked along a street lined with horse chestnut trees.

마루[1] 〈집안의〉 a wooden floor; a flooring
◆ 집에 마루를 놓다 floor a house; board the floor; cover the floor with boards / 마루를 뜯다 break open the floor
▶ 그는 떡갈나무 널로 방에 마루를 깔았다 He floored the room with oak. ⇌ He put down an oak floor.
▶ 이 집은 낡아서 마루가 꺼져가고 있다 This house is old and the floor is starting to fall through.
■ —방 a room with a wooden floor; a floored room —운동〔體操〕 floor exercise —청 a floorboard; a flooring 마룻귀틀〔建〕a joist 마룻대〔建〕a ridge piece

마루[2] 〈산·지붕의〉 a ridge; 〔物〕 crest
— 산 — the ridge of a mountain

마루터기 the top; the summit; a peak; a ridge
— 고갯 — the summit of a pass 산 — the peak of a mountain 지붕 — the top of a roof

마루턱 the top ⇨ 마루터기

마룻바닥 the floor ◆ 마룻바닥에 앉다 sit on the floor

마르 〔地〕 Maar; maar

마르다[1] **1** 〈건조하다〉 dry up; get [become] dry; 〈목재가〉 be seasoned; 〈초목이〉 wither; be withered
◆ (물이) 마른 우물 a dry [an exhausted] well
▶ 세탁물이 빨리[잘] 마른다 The laundry dries fast [well].
▶ 오랜 가뭄이 강물을 말라붙게 했다 A prolonged drought dried up the river.
2 〈목·입술이〉 be thirsty; parch; be parched (up)
◆ 바싹 마른 입술 parched lips / 목이 마르다 be thirsty; have a dry throat
▶ 그녀는 목이 말라 죽을 지경이었다 She was parched with thirst.
3 〈몸이〉 become [grow, get] thin; grow gaunt [slim]; 〈목재가〉 lose weight; 〈병으로〉 lose flesh; 〈절식 등으로〉 reduce; 〈사랑·근심으로〉 pine away
◆ 마르고 키가 큰 사람 a tall and lanky person / 빼빼 마른 사람 a drybones / 걱정으로 마르다 worry *oneself* to a frazzle
▶ 나는 이전보다도 말랐다 I have got thinner than I was.
▶ 여러 가지 걱정이 끊이지 않아 나는 2킬로그램이나 줄어 말랐다 I have been under a lot of stress and I lost two kilograms.
▶ 그는 병 때문에 빼빼 말랐다 He lost much weight because of illness. ⇌ His illness reduced him to nothing.
4 〈고갈되다〉 run out; become exhausted; be used up
◆ 돈이 마르다 have no money left; be cleaned out / 호주머니가 마르다 have a cold purse; (英俗) feel the draught; be low in (*one's*) pocket
▶ 그의 상상력은 마르는 일이 없다 His imagination is never exhausted.
▶ 너무 울어서 눈물이 말라버렸다 The tears have dried up from crying too much.
▶ 그녀는 이제 돈이 말랐다 Her money came to an end.

마르다[2] 〈옷감 등을〉 cut out; make by cutting; 〈마름질하다〉 design setting [cutting]
◆ 옷을 마르다 cut out clothes / 재목을 마르다 cut lumber to measurement

마르세예즈 〈프랑스 국가(國歌)〉 La Marseillaise

마르세유 〈프랑스 남동부의 항구도시〉 Marseilles ■ —시민 a Marseillaise

마르카토 〔樂〕 marcato

마르코니 〈이탈리아의 전기 학자〉 Marconi, Guglielmo (1874-1937)

마르코폴로 〈이탈리아의 여행가〉 Marco Polo (1254?-1324)

마르크 〈독일의 화폐 단위〉 a mark

마르크스 〈독일의 경제학자·철학자〉 Marx, Karl (1818-83) / —레닌주의 Marxism-Leninism —주의 Marxism —주의자 a Marxist

마르탱뒤가르 〈프랑스의 작가〉 Martin du Gard, Roger (1881-1958)

마른간법 —法 〔工〕 dry salting; 〔農〕 dry cure method; dry salting

마른갈이 〔農〕 plowing a rice field while it is dry; tillage of a dry rice field
— 마른갈이하다 plow a dry rice paddy

마른걸레 a dry cloth [duster]; a dry mop
◆ 마른 걸레질하다 wipe [clean up] (the floor) with a dry mop [cloth]; rub (the table) with a dry cloth

마른기침 a dry cough; 〈짧은 헛기침〉 a hack
— 마른기침하다 make a dry [hacking] cough

마른날 a fine [clear] day

마른논 〔農〕 dry paddy

마른반찬 —飯饌 dried meat [fish] as a subsidiary food

마른밥 〈국없는 밥〉 boiled-rice eaten without soup; 〈주먹밥〉 balled rice

마른버짐 〔醫〕 psoriasis, a kind of ringworm

마른번개 lightning in a clear blue sky

마른빨래 1 〈흙묻은 옷을 말려 비빔〉 drying muddy clothes and then scraping the dirt off
2 〈드라이클리닝〉 dry cleaning
— 마른빨래하다 rub the dirt off the clothes

마른안주 —按酒 dried meat or fish tidbits to eat as a snack while drinking

마른옴 〔醫〕 the itch; scabies

마른일 housewife's chores done without wetting her hands
— 마른일하다 do *one's* dry-handed housework

마른입 1 〈국물을 마시지 않은 입〉 a thirsty mouth after a soupless meal
2 ⇨ 잔입

마른장마 a dry rainy season
▶ 신문에 의하면 금년은 마른 장마가 될거래 According to the newspaper, we shall have a dry rainy season this year.

마른천둥 thunder in the clear blue sky

마른침 ▶ 나는 마른침을 삼키고 발표를 기다렸다 I waited for the announcement holding my breath.

마른하늘 the clear (blue) sky; the cloudless

sky ♦마른하늘에 생벼락 a bolt from the blue; a thunderbolt
마른행주 a dry dish towel
마름¹ 〈이엉을 말아놓은 단〉 a roll of thatch
마름² 〈소작 관리인〉 the supervisor of a tenant farm; the manager of tenant farms; an estate agent
마름³ 〔植〕 a water chestnut; a caltrop
마름돌쌓기 〔工〕 ashlar masonry
마름모(꼴) 〔數〕 a rhombus; a lozenge; a diamond ♦마름모(꼴)의 lozenge-shaped; rhombic ■—꼴교차 〔鐵〕 a diamond crossing —꼴무늬 diaper; lozenge pattern
마름자 a tailor's yardstick
마름질 〈재단〉 cutting (out) 《clothes》; conversion of timber
—**마름질하다** cut out
♦옷을 마름질하다 cut out a dress
마리 a head (▶단수·복수 동형); the number (of animals) ♦두 마리의 개 a couple [two head] of dogs / 소 50 마리 50 head of cows / 세 마리의 물고기[곤충] three fishes [insects] / 마릿수를 세다 count the number (of animals); count noses (of sheep)
마리네티 〔工〕 Marinetti
마리노니 〔工〕 Marinoni
마리아 Maria ■성모— the Blessed Virgin (Mary) (略 B.V.(M.)); the Virgin Mary; the Holy Mother
마리아나제도 —諸島 the Mariana Islands; the Marianas
마리아테레지아 〈오스트리아 여황제〉 Maria Theresia (1717-80)
마리앙투아네트 〈프랑스의 왕비〉 Marie Antoinette (1755-93)
마리오네트 〈망석중이·인형〉 a marionette; a puppet
마리화나 〈환각제〉 marihuana; marijuana; 《美俗》 grass ♦마리화나 흡연 marijuana smoking
마림바 〈악기〉 a marimba
♦마림바를 연주하다 play the marimba
마마¹ 媽媽 Your [His, Her] Majesty [Highness] ⇨ 폐하, 전하
—**대전[상감]—** His Majesty; the King 동궁— His (Royal) Highness; the Crown Prince; Your Highness 중전— Her [Your] Majesty; the Queen [the Empress]
마마² 媽媽 〔韓醫〕 (the) smallpox; variola
♦마마에 걸리다 have smallpox; suffer from smallpox; be taken ill of smallpox
■**자반성**(紫斑性)— black smallpox ■—**균** a smallpox germ [virus] —**꽃** pox pustules —**환자** a case of smallpox **마맛자국** a pockmark; a pit: 그는 얼굴에 마맛자국이 있다 His face is marked by smallpox.
마말레이드 〈잼〉 marmalade
마멋 〔動〕 a marmot
마멸 磨滅 wear (and tear); defacement; abrasion
▶타이어의 마멸을 막을 방책이 있다 There are some devices to save wear and tear on the tire.
—**마멸하다** wear out [away]; be worn out [away, down]; be defaced

♦마멸시키다 wear away; deface
▶물은 돌을 마멸한다 Water wears away a stone.
▶그 기계는 마멸되고 있다 I am afraid the machine is wearing out.
■—**제**(劑) abrasive
마모 磨耗 wear (and tear); abrasion
—**마모하다** be worn away
▶이 기계는 상당히 마모되어 있다 This machine is badly worn.
▶이 돌에 새긴 글씨는 퍽 마모되었다 The inscription on the stone had been worn smooth [defaced completely].
마무르다 **1**〈끝손질하다〉 finish; give the final touch; put [add] the finishing touches (on); finish up; touch up finally
♦바느질을 마무르다 make [sew] the final stitches
2〈일을 끝맺다〉 settle; complete; conclude; bring (a matter) to a finish; get through with
♦문장을 마무르다 round off a sentence / 일을 마무르다 finish one's work; finish up one's job / 분쟁을 원만히 마무르다 settle a dispute peacefully
마무리 〈완성〉 finish; completion; elaboration; 〈끝손질〉 finishing touches [strokes]; finishing up; 〈벽 시멘트 칠의〉 a setting [finishing] coat
♦마무리가 엉성한 roughly finished / 마무리 단계에 이르다 come to the finish
▶만사는 마무리가 중요하다 All's well that ends well.
—**마무리하다** finish ⇨ 마무르다
♦사건을 마무리하다 settle a case
▶서둘러서 일을 마무리하자 Let's hurry up and finish the job.
▶1주일 안에 마무리해 주시오 I want (to have) it finished [ready] within a week.
▶이번 일을 마무리하고 나서 여행을 떠나야겠다 After I finish this job, I am going to take a trip.
■—**공**(工) a finisher —**공장**(工場) a fitting [fitter's] shop —**기계** a finishing machine; 〈세탁의〉 a mangle —**대패** a finishing [smoothing] plane —**줄** a smooth file
마물 魔物 a devil; a demon; an evil spirit; malignant spirits; a thing of evil
마바리 〈짐〉 a horse load; a horse carrying a burden; a pack; 〈말〉 a packhorse
■—**꾼** a packhorse man [driver]
마방 馬房 〈마구간〉 a horse stable; a livery stable; 〈마구간을 갖춘 주막집〉 an inn [a pub] with stable facilities
마방진 魔方陣 〔數〕 a magic-square
마법 魔法 magic; the black art; witchcraft; sorcery ⇨ 마술(魔術)

> 解說 *magic*은 자연의 힘이나 초자연의 힘을 부리는 방법으로서의 주술이나 마법, *witchcraft*는 여자 마법사가 부리는 간계를, *wizardry*는 남자 마법사가 부리는 비범한 재주나 교묘함 등을 포함하는 마법을 말한다.

♦마법의 융단 a magic carpet / 마법을 걸다

마부

cast a spell 《on sb》/ 마법에 걸리다 be bound by a spell / 마법을 풀다 break a spell
▶ 내게는 무엇이든 원하는 것이 나오는 마법의 가방이 있다 I have a magic case from which you can take out anything you want.
▶ 약하고 마법이 풀려 백조는 왕자로 돌아왔다 The spell was broken at last and the swan turned back into the prince.
■ ―사 a magician; a wizard; 〈남자〉 a sorcerer; 〈여자〉 a sorceress; a witch: 소설가는 말의 마법사다 The story writers are word magicians.

마부 馬夫 〈역마차의〉 a driver; a cabman; a coachman; 〈짐마차의〉 a carter; a wagoner; 〈경마 잡는〉 a packhorse driver
■ ―석 the driver's seat; the coach box

마분 馬糞 horse dung [manure]
■ ―지 strawboard; pasteboard; millboard

마블 〈대리석〉 marble

마비 痲痺 paralysis; palsy; numbness; 〔醫〕 monoplegia; 〈정신의〉 stupor; an(a)esthesia (약물로 인한)
◆ 교통 마비 a traffic jam [tie-up] / 도의심의 마비 moral paralysis
▶ 갑자기 조깅을 시작하면 심장마비를 일으킬 수 있다 If you begin jogging suddenly, you might get a heart attack.
―마비되다[시키다] be paralyzed; be benumbed; go numb; be palsied; be an(a)esthetized

〔解說〕 ***benumb, numb***는 특히 추위로 감각을 느끼지 못한다는 뜻: Her feet were benumbed by [with] the cold. 그녀의 발은 추위로 마비되었다. ***paralyze***는 신체의 마비, 또는 비유적으로 활동할 수 없다는 뜻: The city is paralyzed by the snowstorm. 눈보라로 도시의 기능이 마비돼 있다

◆ 국회의 기능을 마비시키다 hamstring the National Assembly / 양심을 마비시키다 atrophy sb's conscience
▶ 그는 정의감이 완전히 마비되어 있다 He has no sense of justice at all.
▶ 스트라이크로 산업이 마비되었다 The strike paralyzed the industry.
▶ 나는 뇌혈전증으로 왼쪽 다리가 마비되어 있다 My left leg has been paralyzed since I was afflicted with cerebral thrombosis.
▶ 그의 손과 발의 감각은 추위로 완전히 마비되어 있다 His hands and legs are completely numb with cold.
■ 급성― 〔醫〕 foudroyant paralysis 뇌성― cerebral palsy 소아― infantile paralysis; polio 심장― heart failure 안면― facial paralysis 전신[국부]― general [local] paralysis 진행성― progressive paralysis ■ ―성패류독(貝類毒) paralytic shellfish poisoning ―약 an an(a)esthetic ―어법(語法) stupefying method

마사 麻絲 hemp yarn [thread]; linen thread

마사지 a massage; a rubdown
―마사지하다 massage [rub down] sb; give sb a massage
▶ 그녀는 매일 밤 얼굴을 마사지한다 She massages her face every night.
▶ 나는 어깨를 마사지했다 I was massaged on my shoulders.
■ 근육― a massage of the muscles 얼굴― a face massage 전기― electromassage ■ ―사 〈남자〉 a masseur; 〈여자〉 a masseuse; 〈남녀 공통〉 a massager; a massagist ―요법 massotherapy

마사회 馬事會 ◆ 한국마사회 the Korean Horse Affairs Association

마상 馬上 horseback
◆ 마상의 상(像) a equestrian statue / 마상에서 소리치다 call out 《to another》 from on *one's* horse

마상이 〈작은 배〉 a skiff; a small boat; 〈통나무배〉 a canoe
■ ―운임 boatage

마성 魔性 devilishness
◆ 마성의 devilish / 마성을 지닌 사람[것] an evil spirit / 마성을 지닌 여자 a temptress; an enchantress

마세 〔撞球〕 a massé (shot)

마셜제도 ―諸島 the Marshall Islands

마셜플랜 the Marshall Plan

마소 horses and cattle [oxen]
◆ 마소처럼 부리다 work sb hard; sweat *one's* workers; work like a beast of burden

마손 磨損 wear and tear; friction loss; 〈기계 등의〉 abrasion
―마손하다 wear; be worn (away)
■ ―위험하주부담(保險) the owner's risk of chafing (略 ORC) ―학 tribology

마수 魔手 an evil hand; evil influence
◆ 마수를 뻗치다 make a victim of sb / 마수에 걸리다 fall a victim to sb; be made a victim of sb

마수(걸이) the first break of the day's business; the first sale of the day; 〈개점의 첫거래〉 the first transaction of a new business
▶ 오늘 아침 마수걸이 손님이니 싸게 드립니다 We'll give you a good price since [(英) as] you are the first customer this morning.
―마수하다 make the first sale of the day; break the ice in the day's business

마술 馬術 horseback riding; horsemanship; the art of riding; 〈곡마술〉 equestrian art
◆ 마술에 능하다 be at home in the saddle; be a good horseman [horsewoman] / 마술을 배우다[가르치다] take [give] lessons in horsemanship
■ 고등― high school: (프) haute école 종합― 〈올림픽의〉 the three-day events ■ ―경기 an equestrian [riding] event ―경마장 (프) dressage ―교사 a riding master ―연습 riding practice [lessons]; equestrian exercise

마술 魔術 〈마법〉 magic (arts); a conjuring [conjurer's] trick art; sorcery; witchcraft; 〈요기〉 jugglery
◆ 말의 마술 the spell of words / 마술을 부리다 use [practice] magic; play a conjurer's trick; conjure
▶ 원주민들은 차가 마술로 움직인다고 생각했다 The natives thought the car was driven by magic.
■ ―사 a magician; a conjurer; 〈여자〉 a sor-

마스카라 〈화장품〉 mascara
마스코트 a (good-luck) mascot
마스크 1 〈탈〉 a mask; 〈보호구〉 a face guard
♦마스크를 쓰다 wear a mask
▶그는 감기가 들어서 마스크를 하고 있다 He is wearing a face [gauze] mask because he has a cold.
2 〈용모〉 looks; features
▶저 가수는 마스크가 좋다 The singer has good [pleasant, attractive] feature.
■감기— a flu mask 방독— a gas mask; (英) a respirator 산소— 〈空〉 an oxygen mask
마스크피롬 〔電算〕 MPROM [*mask programmed ROM*]
마스킹색분해 —色分解 〔印〕 color separation masking
마스터 〈주인〉 a master; 〈경영자〉 the proprietor
—마스터하다 〈숙달하다〉 master
♦완전히 마스터하다 achieve a complete mastery 《of》
▶나는 영어를 2년 안에 마스터하고 싶어 I'd like to master English within two years.
■—컴퍼스 〈주(主) 나침반〉 〔航〕 master compass —코스 〈석사 과정〉 a master's course 《in》 —키 a master key —플랜 a master plan
마스터베이션 〈자위〉 masturbation
마스트 〈돛대〉 a mast
♦마스트가 셋인 배 a three-masted ship; a three-master / 마스트를 세우다 mast
마시다 1 〈액체를〉 drink; take; have; get a drink

〔解説〕 *drink*는 액체를 입에서 목으로 넘기는 것으로서 자동사로는 주로 「술을 마시다」의 뜻으로 쓰인다. *take*는 액체·기체·물체를 체내에 넣는 것이고 *have*는 「먹다(eat), 마시다(drink), (담배를) 피우다(smoke)」라는 뜻의 구어적인 말이다.

♦먹지도 마시지도 않고 with no food to eat and no water to drink; without bite or drop / 물을 마시다 drink water / 차를 마시다 take tea / 물을 한 모금 마시다 have [take] a swallow of water / 술을 한 잔 마시다 drink a glass of wine / 먹고 마시다 eat and drink / 마셔서 시름을 잊다 drink away one's worries / 한 잔 마시고 싶어 못 견디다 be thirsty for a drink / 홀짝홀짝 마시다 drink in little sips
▶나는 마음껏 마셨다 I drank to my heart's content.
▶우리는 일을 중단하고 커피를 마셨다 We took time out for a cup of coffee.
▶그는 콜라를 병채로 마셨다 He drank the coke straight from the bottle.
▶많은 젊은 샐러리맨들이 아침에 우유나 커피 한 잔만 마시고 출근한다 A lot of young salaried workers have only a glass of milk or a cup of coffee in the morning before going to work.
▶술을 마시고 운전하는 것은 교통 법규 위반이다 Driving under the influence of alcohol is a violation of the traffic rules.
▶아버지는 버는 돈을 전부 마셔서 없앤다 My father drinks all he earns [his earnings].
▶뭐 좀 마시지 않겠니? Won't you have something to drink?
▶오늘은 하루 종일 먹지도 마시지도 못했다 I have tasted neither bite nor sup all day.
▶〔會話〕「뭘 마실래?」「커피 마실게」"What do you want to drink?" "I'll have coffee."
2 〈기체를〉 breathe 《in》; inhale
♦독기를 마시다 inhale poisonous fumes / 신선한 공기를 마시다 breathe 《in》 [inhale] fresh air
마시멜로 〈과자〉 a marshmallow
마식 磨蝕 〔地質〕 corrasion
마신 魔神 a malevolent deity; a devil
마야 Maya ♦마야의 Mayan ■—문명 Mayan civilization [culture] —사람 a Maya —어 Maya —족 the Maya(s)
마약 痲藥 a drug; a narcotic; (口) junk; (俗) dope
♦마약을 밀매하다 peddle [traffic] drug / 마약을 상용하다 be on dope / 마약을 쓰다 administer *sb* an anesthetic; put *sb* on dope / 마약을 한대 놓다 inject a unit of narcotic / 마약에 중독되다 become addicted to (the use of) narcotics; (美俗) be [go] hooked (by the morphine habit)
■—남용 drug abuse —남용자 a drug abuser —단속관 a narcotic agent; (美) a buster; (美俗) a nark —단속반 a narcotic squad —단속법 〔法〕 the Narcotic Control Law [Act] —밀매 drug traffic; (口) dope peddling —밀매자 a narcotic trafficker; a drug [dope] peddler; (美口) a (dope) pusher —상용자 a drug [narcotic, dope] addict [fiend]; a narcotic; (俗) a hophead; a junkie —중독 narcotics [drug] addiction
마에스토소 〔樂〕〈장엄하게〉 maestoso
마오쩌뚱 毛澤東 〈중국의 공산혁명지도자〉 Mao Tse-tung (1893-1976)
마왕 魔王 Satan; the Prince of Darkness; 〔佛敎〕 an evil spirit
마요네즈 mayonnaise
▶그녀는 야채 샐러드에 마요네즈를 쳤다 She dressed the vegetable salad with mayonnaise.
마우리아왕조 —王朝 〈고대 인도의 왕조〉 the Maurya
마우스피스 a mouthpiece
마운드 〔野〕 the mound
♦마운드에 서다 take [be on] the mound / 마운드에서 내려오다 leave the mound; (口) get knocked out
▶누가 마운드에 오를까? I wonder who is going to be on the mound. ⇒ Who's taking the mound? ⇒ Who's pitching?
마을 1 〈동네〉 a village; a hamlet; a rural community

〔解説〕 영국에서는 *village*와 *town*을 구별하지만 미국에서는 명확한 구별이 없다. 미국에서는 village를 고풍스러운 분위기를 낼때, 예를 들면 가게 이름 등에 쓰는 경우가 많다. 우리나라의 「마을」은 village로 나타내면 되지만 편지의 주소 등에서는 -maul로 표기하는 것이 좋다.

♦이웃 마을 a neighboring village / 외딴 마을 an isolated village; a remote village [hamlet] **2** 〈이웃 나들이〉 a visit to *one's* neighborhood; an outing (for a chat with *one's* neighborhood)
♦늘 마을만 다니다 be always (going) out for a chat with *one's* neighborhood
3 〈옛 관청〉 a government office ■—금고 a village fund —문고 a village library —사람 〈한 사람〉 a villager; (총칭) village folk [people]

마음 mind; heart; soul; spirit; 〈감정〉 feelings; 〈생각〉 an idea; (a) thought, 〈심성〉 mentality; 〈의지〉 (a) will

解說 ***mind***는 「물질(matter)」에 대비되는 말로 사고·기억하는 이성적인 마음. ***heart***는 「지력(知力) (head)」에 대비되는 말로 사랑이나 슬픔을 느끼는 감정적인 마음. ***soul***은 「육체(body)」에 대비되는 말로서 「영혼, 넋」을 의미하며 때로는 spirit으로 바꿔 쓸 수 있으나 spirit보다 감정·감성의 깊이가 크고 도덕적 성질을 띤다. ***spirit***는 「육체(flesh)」에 대비되는 말로서, 육체를 갖지 않은 정신을 의미한다. 그러나 우리말의 「마음」은 영어로 그대로 나타낼 수 없는 경우가 있음을 알아야 한다.

♦감사하는 마음 (a sense of) gratitude; a feeling of thankfulness / 따뜻한 마음 a warm heart / 불순한 마음 an impure heart / 어리석은 마음 (*one's*) foolish idea / 어린 마음 young ideas; a juvenile mind / 어머니의 마음 a mother's love [feeling]; maternal affection / 여자의 마음 a woman's heart
〈마음의〉 마음의 벗 *one's* bosom friend; a cordial friend / 마음의 양식 food for thought; mental [spiritual] food / 마음의 평화 peace of mind
▶눈은 마음의 창이라고 한다 They say the eyes are the windows of the soul.
▶나는 마음의 준비가 되어 있지 않다 I'm not mentally prepared for it.
〈마음이[은]〉 마음이 맞는 친구 a like-minded company / 마음이 젊은 사람 a man of youthful spirit(s) / 마음(이) 훈훈한 이야기 a heart-warming story / 마음이 넓은[큰] large-minded; broad-minded; big-hearted; liberal; generous / 마음이 좁은[옹졸한] narrow-minded; small-minded; ungenerous / 마음이 고운 tender-hearted / 마음이 곧은[바른] right-minded; right-hearted / 마음이 더러운 dirty-minded / 마음이 가라앉다 recover *one's* presence of mind / 마음이 들뜨다 be in a buoyant spirit / 마음이 변하다 have *one's* mind changed / 마음이 부풀다 feel excited [encouraged] / 마음이 상하다 *one's* heart breaks / 마음이 쓰이다 be worried [concerned, anxious] about / 마음이 아프다 be sorry; be grieved; be agonized / 마음이 울적하다 be in a low mood; be low-spirited; feel blue / 마음이 움직이다 be (easily) moved [touched, affected, influenced] (by) / 마음이 커지다 become emboldened; lose *one's* timidity / 마음이 편하다 feel easy; find *oneself* more at ease / 마음이 편치 않다 feel ill at ease; feel constrained [awkward]
▶그는 입은 험해도 마음은 착한 녀석이다 He has a foul tongue, but is, at heart, a good fellow.
▶내 장래를 생각하니 마음이 무겁다 My heart is heavy when I think of my future.
▶그 노래를 들으니 마음이 가벼워진다 The song makes me feel light-hearted [happy].
▶오늘은 도무지 일할 마음이 나지 않는다 I don't feel like working today. ⇌ I'm in no mood [humor] for working today.
▶아들의 장래를 생각하니 마음이 아프다 It pains [upsets] me to think of my son's future.
▶내일 그를 만난다 생각하니 마음이 설렌다 My heart starts thumping [pounds] when I think of seeing him tomorrow.
▶그들 두 사람은 마음이 통한다 They understand each other. ⇌ (口) They're on the same wavelength.
▶그의 마음은 멀리 그리운 고국을 향해 있었다 His heart was far away in his dear fatherland.
▶그는 그녀에게 마음이 끌렸다 He was [felt himself] drawn to her. ⇌ He found himself attracted to her.
▶그 사업에 마음이 없는 것도 아니다 I am not without interest in that enterprise.
▶어떻게 그런 힘든 일을 떠맡을 마음이 들었니? What induced you to undertake such hard work?
▶도대체 너는 뭘 할 마음이 있는 거냐? Do you ever have the will to do something?
〈마음을〉 마음을 합하여 with one accord; in concert (with); in one mind / 마음을 가다듬다 brace *oneself* up; brace *one's* energies / 마음을 가라앉히다 calm [compose, collect] *oneself*; collect *one's* scattered mind / 마음을 고쳐 먹다 change *one's* mind; turn over a new leaf; reform *oneself* / 마음을 기울이다 direct *one's* attention 《to》 / 마음을 끌다 attract *one's* attention; appeal to *one's* curiosity / 마음을 두다 put *one's* mind 《on》 / 마음을 떠보다 probe [try to find out] *sb's* intention; sound *sb's* mind / 마음을 모질게 먹다 harden [steel] *one's* heart [*oneself*] 《against pity》 / 마음을 빼앗다 charm; bewitch; captivate; fascinate / 마음을 빼앗기다 be fascinated [captivated] 《by》 / 마음을 쏟다 give *one's* whole mind 《to》 / 마음을 쓰다 be kind to *sb*; 〈인정을〉 show *sb* sympathy; 〈신경을〉 take care; be careful; mind; be mindful 《of》 / (남의) 마음을 움직이다 move *sb*; touch *sb's* heart / (…하려고) 마음을 정하다 make up *one's* mind (to do *sth*); have *one's* heart [mind] set (on doing *sth*) / 마음을 태우다 pine for love / 마음을 터놓고 이야기하다 speak frankly; be frank with *sb*; talk heart to heart 《with》 / 마음을 합하다 be united; act in concert 《with》; cooperate in harmony / (남의) 마음을 헤아리다 read *sb's* mind [idea, thoughts] / 여자에게 마음을 주다 give *oneself* up to a woman
▶그의 마음을 알 수가 없다 I can't understand [see through] him. ⇌ I can't understand what

he is thinking.
▶ 그는 마음을 고쳐 먹고 열심히 일했다 He turned over a new leaf and worked hard.
▶ 전원이 마음을 합하여 그 일에 대처했다 All the staff acted in concert on the issue.
▶ 저에게 마음을 써주셔서 고맙습니다 Thank you for considering me, sir.
▶ 이제 제 마음을 아셨지요 Now you understand what I mean.
▶ 나는 네 마음을 알고 있었다 I knew what was working in your mind.
〈마음에〉 마음에 드는 그림 a picture which strikes *one's* fancy / 마음에 드는 집 a house to *one's* mind [fancy]; a house after *one's* heart [fancy] / 마음에 드는 favorite; pet; darling; after *one's* heart [heart]; to *one's* taste [liking] / 마음에 거리끼다 have an uneasy conscience; be smitten with compunction / 마음에 거리낄 것이 없다 have a clean conscience / 마음에 걸리다 weigh on [upon] *one's* mind / 마음에 떠오르다 occur to *one*; come across [to] *one's* mind / 마음에 사무치다 go to *one's* heart / 마음에 그리다 picture *sth* in *one's* mind; imagine / 마음에 두다 take *sth* to *one's* heart; bear *sth* in mind; be mindful of / 마음에 두지 않다 do not mind; do not care (about [for]) / 마음에 새기다 engrave (an image) on *one's* memory; take *sb's* remark to heart / 마음에 품다 cherish; harbor; entertain / 마음에 없는 소리를 하다 say what one does not mean; say what is not in *one's* mind
▶ 그의 충고가 내 마음에 와 닿았다 His advice struck me to the heart [touched my heart].
▶ 이것이 가장 내 마음에 든다 This suits me [my taste] best. ≒ I like this best.
▶ 이 물건은 아무래도 마음에 안 든다 These goods are by no means satisfactory.
▶ 어느 응모자도 그의 마음에 차지 않는 것 같았다 No applicant seemed to come up to his requirements.
▶ 새로 온 점원이 마음에 드십니까? How do you like your new clerk?
▶ 모든 사람의 마음에 든다는 것은 전혀 불가능하다 It's quite impossible to please everybody.
▶ 그 말이 내 마음에 들었다 The remark appealed to me.
▶ 그는 그녀를 마음에 두고 있다 He takes a fancy to the girl.
▶ 마음에 있는 것이 입밖으로 나오게 마련이다 What the heart thinks, the mouth speaks.
▶ 시험 결과가 마음에 걸린다 I am anxious about the result of the examination.
▶ 일을 중단한다는 것이 무척 마음에 걸린다 I feel most reluctant to leave the work unfinished.
▶ 그는 마음에도 없는 칭찬을 했다 He made empty compliments.
▶ 〔會話〕「마음에도 없는 말은 하지도 마세요」「아녜요, 진정으로 그렇게 생각하고 있어요」 "Don't say what you don't mean." "But, at the bottom of heart, that's what I am thinking."
▶ 그가 하는 말을 마음에 두지 마라 Don't mind what he says.
▶ 그녀는 행복한 결혼 생활을 마음에 그렸다 She has pictured to herself [imagined] a happy married life.
▶ 그 광경이 그의 마음에 깊이 새겨졌다 The scene was deeply etched in his mind.
〈기타〉 마음으로부터의 감사 warm [cordial, heartfelt] thanks; thanks from the bottom of *one's* heart / 마음 편히 살다 live in peace and comfort
▶ 나는 가고 싶은 마음도 없지 않다 I have (just) half a mind to go.
▶ 마음만 굳게 먹으면 안되는 일이 없다 Nothing is impossible to a determined mind.
▶ 나는 가벼운 마음으로 집을 나섰다 I left home with a light heart.

마음가짐 a mental attitude; *one's* attitude of mind; 〈각오〉 preparation

|解說| 영어에는 이에 딱 들어맞는 대응어가 없기 때문에 상황에 따라 「마음의 준비」, 「노력하는 자세」 등으로 의역한다.

▶ 너는 마음가짐이 나와 다르구나 Your attitude is not the same as mine.

마음결 a cast [turn] of mind; disposition; nature; grain; temper
♦ 마음결이 곱다 be tender-hearted; have a sweet temper; be sweet-tempered; be of gentle disposition / 마음결이 사납다 be ill-natured; be bad-tempered; be cross(-minded)

마음껏 〈실컷·진탕·만족할 만큼〉 to *one's* heart's content; to *one's* satisfaction; as much as *one* likes [wants, wishes]; to the full; heartily; fully
♦ 마음껏 먹다[마시다] eat [drink] *one's* fill / 마음껏 울다 weep *oneself* out; weep *one's* fill; cry *one's* heart out / 마음껏 즐기다 enjoy *oneself* to the full / 재능을 마음껏 발휘하다 give full play [free scope] to *one's* talent / 휴일을 마음껏 즐기다 enjoy the holiday to *one's* heart's content
▶ 바닷가로 가서 마음껏 수영을 하고 싶다 I want to go to the seaside and swim to my heart's content.
▶ 그 녀석을 마음껏 때려주었다 I hit him as hard as I could.

마음내키다 feel inclined (to do); feel like (doing); be in the mood (for doing, to do); be willing (to do)
♦ 마음내키는 대로 as *one* feels inclined; as fancy dictates [leads] *one*; as the humor takes *one* / 마음내킬 때 when the humor takes *one*; when *one* feels like (it) / 마음내키는 일을 하다 follow *one's* own bent / 마음내키지 않다 have no inclination (to do); be in no humor (for); be in no mood (to do)
▶ 나는 마음내키는 대로 여행했다 I traveled as fancy led me.
▶ 네 마음내키는 대로 하는 편이 좋다 You had better do as you like.
▶ 마음내키면 아무 때라도 전화 주십시오 Please call me up whenever you like it.
▶ 그들은 이 기획에 대해 별로 마음내켜 하는 것

같지 않다 They don't seem very enthusiastic about [interested in] this project.

마음놓다 1〈안심하다〉set *one's* mind [heart] at ease [rest]; take it easy; relax
▶ 이제 나는 마음놓고 살고 있다 I have [lead] a carefree life now.
▶ 그 점은 마음놓으십시오 Set your heart at ease about that.
▶ 그는 마음놓고 여행을 떠났다 He set out on a journey without anxiety.
▶ 우리는 밤잠도 마음놓고 잘수 없다 We can't even get [enjoy] a good night's sleep.
▶ 나는 마음놓고 일에 전념할 수 있었다 I was able to devote myself to my work free from worries.
▶ 나는 처음으로 그녀와 마음놓고 이야기를 나누었다 I talked with her without any reserve for the first time.
▶ 시험에 합격했으니 이제 다시 마음놓고 숨 좀 쉴 수 있겠다 I can breathe freely again now that I've passed the exam.
▶ 會話「어머니께서는 차차 차도가 있으십니다」「정말 마음놓이네요」 "My mother is getting better." "What a relief."
2 〈방심하다〉relax *one's* attention [guard]; slacken [let up in] *one's* effort; be off *one's* guard; be inattentive; be negligent
◆ 마음놓지 않다 be on (*one's*) guard; be wide awake
▶ 일이 좀 잘됐다고 마음놓아서는 안된다 Don't relax your attention because of a small success or two.

마음대로 〈하고싶은 대로〉as *one* pleases [likes, wishes]; at *one's* pleasure; 〈자유의사로〉at (*one's* own sweet) will; of *one's* own accord; freely; 〈독단으로〉at *one's* (own) discretion; 〈무단으로〉without leave
◆ 마음대로 쓰다 make free use of 《*sb's* books》/ 마음대로 행동하다 have *one's* (own) way 《in everything》/ 권력을 마음대로 휘두르다 abuse *one's* authority; usurp power / 남을 마음대로 주무르다 get *sb* under *one's* thumb; have *sb* at *one's* beck and call
▶ 마음대로 하시오 Do as you please. ⇒ Take [Have] your own way. ⇒ 〈편잔하는 투로〉Please yourself. ⇒ 〈화를 내어〉Go to Hell [the Devil].
▶ 과자를 마음대로 드십시오 Please help yourself to the cookies.
▶ 내 장서를 마음대로 이용하시오 You are welcome to the use of my library.
▶ 이 방은 네 마음대로 쓰면 안된다 You should not use this room without permission.
▶ 내 마음대로 하게 내버려두시오 Let me do my own way.
▶ 이제 무엇이건 내 마음대로 할 수 있게 되었구나 Now, I'm quite free to do anything I like.
▶ 나는 그녀를 자기 마음대로 하게 내버려 두었다 I let her have her own way. ⇒ I allowed her to do as she pleased.
▶ 그것은 네 마음대로다 That's up to you.
▶ 만사가 내 마음대로 되었다 Everything went just as I'd hoped [I wanted].
▶ 그 아이는 자기 마음대로 안되면 울어버린다 If that child doesn't get his way, he breaks into tears.
▶ 일생은 우리 마음대로 되는 것이 아니다 Life doesn't go the way we want it to.

마음든든하다 feel secure [safe, reassured]
▶ 나는 그와 함께 있으면 마음든든하다 I feel secure [safe] when I'm with him.
▶ 네가 같이 있으니 마음든든해 I feel encouraged by your presence.

마음먹다 1〈의도하다〉intend to 《do》; have a mind to 《do》; have the intention of 《doing》; 〈대망을 품다〉have an ambition to 《do》; 〈예정하다〉be going to 《do》; plan [want] to 《do》
▶ 그는 외교관이 되려고 마음먹고 있다 He intends to become a diplomat.
▶ 나는 아들을 대학에 보내려고 마음먹고 있다 I am going to send my son to college.
▶ 만사가 내가 마음먹은대로 되었다 Everything turned out as I (had) wished.
2 〈결심하다〉decide [determine] 《on doing, to do》; make up *one's* mind 《to (do) *sth*》; be determined [resolved] 《to do》
◆ 하려고 단단히 마음먹고 with a full [firm] determination to 《do》/ 굳게 마음먹다 be firmly determined / 마음먹은대로 하다 act up to *one's* resolution
▶ 나는 크게 마음먹고 1억원을 기부했다 I've overcome my scruples and made a donation of one hundred million won.
▶ 그는 대학자가 되려고 굳게 마음먹고 있다 He is firmly determined to become a great scholar.
▶ 그는 한번 마음먹으면 여간해서 번복하지 않는다 Nothing could dissuade him from his resolution.
▶ 하려고 마음먹으면 못할 일이 없다 Nothing is impossible to a determined mind. ⇒ There is nothing we cannot do, once we set our mind on it. ⇒ A resolute will makes the gods give way. ⇒ Where there is a will, there is a way.

마음보 nature; disposition; spirit; mind; temper; a cast of mind
◆ 마음보가 나쁜 녀석 an ill-natured fellow / 마음보가 사나운 여자 a scratch cat; a she-devil / 마음보가 비뚤어진 사람 a crooked person; a crosspatch / 마음보가 고약하다 be ill-natured [evil-minded, ill-tempered, ill-disposed]/ 마음보 사납게 굴다 behave with evil intention; behave maliciously [crossly, ill-naturedly]

마음속 〈가슴속〉*one's* heart; the bottom of *one's* heart; *one's* inmost feelings; *one's* innermost thoughts; *one's* bosom
◆ 마음속에서 우러나오는 말 words flowing out of *one's* heart / 마음속으로 at heart; in *one's* mind [heart]; inwardly / 마음속 깊이 deep down in *one's* heart / 마음속을 꿰뚫어보다 read *sb's* inmost thoughts; see through *sb's* intention [heart]; see *sb* inside and out / 마음속을 털어놓다 speak [tell] *one's* mind; speak [tell, lay bare] *one's* inmost thoughts [feelings]/ 마음속에 묻어두다 keep *sth* to *oneself* / 마음속에 사무치다 sink deep into *one's* heart;

go to *one's* heart / 마음속에 새기다 bear [keep] *sth* in mind; have *sth* stamped [engraved] on *one's* mind / 마음속에 품다 cherish; harbor
▶ 그것을 듣고 그는 마음속이 편치 않았다 Hearing it upset him.
▶ 그는 그녀에게 마음속을 털어놓았다 He opened up his heart to her.
▶ 그는 마음속으로 웃고 있었다 He was laughing in [up] his sleeve.

마음쓰다 1 〈유의하다〉 give heed to; pay attention to; mind; care; worry
▶ 사소한 일에 마음쓰지 마라 Don't worry (yourself) about trifles.
▶ 그녀는 모든 일에 지나치게 마음쓴다 She takes everything too seriously. ⇒ She is nervous by nature.
▶ 나는 무슨 일이 일어나건 마음쓰지 않는다 I don't care what happens.
2 〈생각·연구하다〉 use *one's* mind [head]; work *one's* brain
3 〈생각해 주다〉 be thoughtful of [for]; think of; 〈동정하다〉 sympathize with

마음씨 disposition; nature; temper
♦ 마음씨가 좋은 사람 a man of good nature / 마음씨가 나쁜 ill-natured; bad-tempered / 마음씨가 좋은 good-natured; kind-hearted / 마음씨가 더러운 [비루한] mean; dirty; base
▶ 그녀는 마음씨는 곱지만 별로 영리하지는 못하다 She has a good heart, but not much sense. ⇒ She is naturally sweet-tempered, but hasn't much sense.

마음자리 nature ⇨ 심지(心地)

마음잡다 settle (down); calm *oneself*; keep the presence of mind; recover *one's* composure
♦ 마음잡고 일을 시작하다 settle (down) to work / 마음잡고 올바르게 살다 amend *one's* way of living

마음졸이다 worry *oneself* (about); trouble *oneself* (with); be anxious [nervous, uneasy] (about)
♦ 마음졸이게 하다 worry *sb*; keep [hold] *sb* in suspense / 실패할까봐 마음졸이다 be nervous at the possibility that *one* might fail
▶ 네가 늦어서 몹시 마음졸였어 I was irritated at your delay.
▶ 그런 사소한 일로 마음졸이지 마라 Don't get so worried over such a little thing.

마음죄이다 be worried; be anxious [concerned, nervous] (about); be upset; fret; stew
♦ 마음죄이는 판국 a tense [jittery] situation / 전에 없이 마음죄이는 분위기 an unusually tense atmosphere
▶ 그가 무사히 돌아올지 마음 죄인다 I am worried whether he will get back safely.
▶ 시험 결과가 어떻게 될지 몹시 마음 죄인다 I am very anxious about the result of examination.

마의 麻衣 〈베옷〉 hemp clothes

마이너리그 〈미국 프로야구의〉 a minor [bush] league
♦ 마이너리그의 선수 a minor leaguer

마이너스 1 〈뺄셈 기호·음수〉 〔數〕 minus
▶ 6 마이너스 4는 2 Six minus four is [leaves, equals] two.
2 〈결점〉 a defect; 〈불리한 점〉 a disadvantage; a handicap; 〈결손〉 a deficit
♦ 마이너스가 되다 be disadvantageous ((to)); handicap *sb*; be a minus ((for))
▶ 너의 매명 행위는 네 경력에 마이너스가 될 거야 Your publicity seeking will be a minus for your career.
■ ─기호 a minus (sign) ─성장 negative growth ─성장률 a negative growth rate ─전기 a negative charge of electricity; a negative electric charge

마이동풍 馬耳東風 (속담) Talking to the wall. ⇒ Like water off a duck's back. ⇒ In one ear and out the other.
▶ 내가 무슨 충고를 해도 그녀에게는 마이동풍이었다 All my advice was lost [wasted] on her.
▶ 그는 그녀의 충고를 마이동풍으로 흘려버린다 He turns a deaf ear [pays no attention] to her advice.

마이신 〔藥〕 -mycin ⇨ 스트렙토마이신

마이오세 ─世 〔地質〕 Miocene Epoch

마이카 a privately-owned car
■ ─족 people who drive their own cars; owner-drivers

마이크로- 〔物〕 micro-·
♦ 마이크로마이크로 micromicro-; pico-
■ ─볼트 〔電〕 a microvolt (略 μV)

마이크로리더 a microreader; a microfilm reader; a microfilm viewing machine

마이크로미터 a micrometer; micrometer calipers

마이크로버스 a microbus

마이크로스피어 〔生〕 a microsphere

마이크로웨이브 〔物〕 a microwave

마이크로컴퓨터 〔電算〕 a microcomputer

마이크로파 ─波 a microwave

마이크(로폰) a microphone; (口) a mike
♦ 무선 마이크 a wireless microphone / 비밀 마이크 a concealed mike / 마이크 앞에 서다 speak at the microphone; stand before [at] a microphone / 마이크 앞에서 얼다 suffer mike fright / 마이크(로폰)으로 이야기하다 speak over [through] a microphone
▶ 그는 마이크로 청중에게 연설을 했다 He addressed his audience through a mike.
■ ─공포증 mike fright ─스탠드 a microphone stand ─이동장치 〔映〕 〈촬영용 음향 조절용〉 a sound boom

마이크로필름 a microfilm
♦ 옛 사료를 마이크로필름에 담다 microfilm old historical records

마일 a mile
♦ 시속 60마일로 달리다 run at sixty miles per hour; run 60 mph [m.p.h.]
▶ 집에서 학교까지 3마일 반이다 It's three and a half miles [three miles and a half] from home to my school.
▶ 지금 이 열차는 시속 80마일로 달리고 있다 This train is going at 80 miles an [per] hour now.

마임 〔劇〕 a mime

마작 麻雀, 마장 mah-jong(g) ◆마작의 패 a tile —**마작하다** play mah-jong ■—꾼 a mah-jong player

마저¹ 〈전부·남김없이〉 with everything else; with all the rest; without leaving any
◆이야기를 마저 듣다 hear the last [rest] of the story / 일을 마저 해치우다 finish all the rest of work / 재고품을 마저 팔아치우다 sell off all the stock left over
▶이것까지 마저 드십시오 Please take [eat] this last one up, too.

마저² 〈까지·조차〉 even; also; besides; to the length [extent, extreme] of; on top of; into the bargain; in addition (to); so far as
◆빚마저 내어 even going to the extent of incurring debt / 도둑질마저 하다 go to the length [extent] of committing theft; go so far as to commit theft / 집마저 팔다 go so far as to sell *one's* house
▶그는 이제 늙어 걸음마저 제대로 걷지 못한다 He is now too old even to walk properly.
▶하인들마저 그를 업신여긴다 Even his servants despise him.
▶밤에는 비마저 내리기 시작했다 On top of that, it began to rain at night.

마적 馬賊 mounted bandits
마전¹ 〈표백〉 bleaching —**마전하다** bleach
마전² 〈곡식을 되는·곳〉 a grain-measuring place (in the market)
마젤란운 —雲 〔天〕 the Magellanic clouds
마젤란은하 —銀河 〔天〕 Magellanic galaxies
마젤란해협 —海峽 the Strait of Magellan
마조히즘 〔醫〕 masochism (↔ sadist)
마주 (right, just, directly) opposite; face to face; facing each other; vis-à-vis; tête-à-tête; just across (from each other)
◆마주 바라보다 face [confront] each other; look each other in the face
마주놓다 set (things) opposite each other
마주르카 〔舞蹈〕 mazurka
마주보다 〈마주 대하다〉 be opposite (to); face each other; confront; 〈눈으로〉 look at each other; exchange glances
◆마주보고 앉다 sit face to face [vis-à-vis, tête-à-tête] with sb / 놀라서 〔난처하여〕 서로 마주보다 exchange looks of astonishment [embarrassment]
▶그녀와 나는 테이블을 사이에 두고 마주보고 앉았다 She and I sat facing each other with a table between us.
▶그들은 서로 마주본 채 침묵에 잠겼다 They fell into silence, facing each other.
▶그 소식을 듣고 그들은 안도하며 서로 마주보았다 At the news, they looked at each other in relief.
▶은행과 우체국은 마주보고 있다 The bank and the post office stand opposite to each other.
마주서다 stand face to face; stand right opposite; confront
마주앉다 sit face to face [vis-à-vis] with sb; sit facing each other (across a table); take a seat opposite to sb
◆마주앉아 이야기하다 talk face to face with sb; have a tête-à-tête with sb
▶마주앉아 허심탄회하게 이야기합시다 Let's sit face to face and talk frankly.
▶나는 테이블을 사이에 두고 그와 마주앉았다 I sat facing him across the table.
▶우리는 마주앉아 두 시간이나 술을 마셨다 We enjoyed drinking for two hours, sitting face to face.

마주잡다 1 〈서로 잡다〉 take each other; take [hold] together
◆손에 손을 마주잡다 hand in hand (with) / 손을 마주잡고 울다 take each other's hands and weep / 책상을 미주잡아 들다 lift a table together
▶부부는 손을 마주잡고 울었다 The couple took each other's hand and wept.
2 〈제휴하다〉 go hand in hand with; join hands with; join together; cooperate (with)
◆…와 손을 마주잡고 in concert [cooperation] with sb
▶그들은 서로 손을 마주잡고 사업을 한다 They do a business in cooperation with each other.

마주치다 1 〈충돌하다〉 run against [into] sth; collide [clash] with (each other); knock [dash] against
2 〈우연히 만나다〉 meet (with); happen to meet; come [run, fall] across; knock against; fall [drop] in with
◆딱 마주치다 come [be brought] face to face with sb / 학교 가는 도중에 친구와 마주치다 meet (up with) a friend on *one's* way to school / 막다른 골목에서 원수와 마주치다 confront an enemy in a blind alley
▶도서관에 가다가 선생님과 마주쳤다 I came across [happened to meet] my teacher on the way to the library.
▶두 사람은 시선이 마주쳤다 Their eyes met.

마중 meeting; reception —**마중하다** meet; greet; receive; go [come] out to meet sb on arrival
▶공항에는 아내가 마중나와 있으리라고 생각한다 I expect my wife to be waiting to meet me at the airport.
▶자동차가 역으로 우리를 마중나오게 되어 있다 A car is to meet us at the station.
▶마중나온 차가 당신을 기다리고 있습니다 There is a car waiting for you.
▶나는 역에서 많은 사람의 마중을 받았다 I was met by a lot of people at the station.
▶삼촌을 마중하러 역에 가는 길이다 I'm going to the railway station to meet my uncle.

마중물 pump priming; priming
◆펌프에 마중물을 붓다 prime [fetch, fang] the pump

마지기 〈두락〉 a patch of field requiring one *mal* of seed; 〈논밭의 넓이의 단위〉 a *majigi*
◆논 한 마지기 a patch of rice paddy / 밭 두 마지기 two *majigi* of fields

마지노선 —線 the Maginot line

마지막 1 〈맨 끝〉 the last; 〈결말〉 the end; the conclusion
◆마지막 기회 *one's* last chance / 마지막 날 the last [final] day; the closing day / 마지막 수단 the last resort / 마지막 승리 the final

[ultimate] victory / 마지막 싸움 the last battle; a final struggle / 마지막으로 lastly; finally; for the last time; in conclusion / 마지막까지 싸우다 fight to the last [end]; fight it out
▶ 나는 여행의 마지막 이틀을 싱가포르에서 지냈다 I spent the last two days of my journey in Singapore.
▶ 학교에 오는 것도 오늘이 마지막이구나 This is the last day for me to come to school.
▶ 그것이 내가 그를 본 마지막이 되었다 That was the last I saw him.
▶ 그를 마지막으로 본 것이 작년 여름이었다 It was last summer that I saw him last.
▶ 마지막으로 그의 어머니가 왔다 His mother came last.
▶ 마지막으로 우리는 모두 만세 삼창을 했다 At the end we all gave three cheers together.
2 〈죽음·임종〉 one's last moment; one's death; one's end
♦ 마지막 말 one's dying words / 마지막을 지켜보다 watch sb die; be present at sb's deathbed / 마지막 길을 가다 go on one's last journey

마지못하다 be compelled [forced, obliged] to 《do》; cannot help [but]
♦ 마지못할 사정 compelling [unavoidable] circumstances; dire [sheer] necessity / 마지못해 reluctantly; unwillingly; against one's will [wish]; out of necessity / 마지못해 승낙하다 give an unwilling [a reluctant] consent / 마지못해 수락[양보]하다 accept [yield] with a bad grace
▶ 나는 마지못해 음악회에 갔다 I went to the concert unwillingly.
▶ 사정이 사정인 만큼 나는 마지못해 거짓말을 했다 Circumstances compelled me to tell a lie.
▶ 그렇게 한 것은 좋아서가 아니라 마지못해서였다 I did it out of necessity, not of choice.

마지아니하다, 마지않다 ♦ 감사해 마지아니하다 can never thank sb enough; offer one's heart-felt thanks / 축하해 마지않다 offer one's sincerest congratulations
▶ 호의에 감사해 마지 않는 바입니다 I heartily appreciate your kindness. ⇒ A thousand thanks for your kindness.
▶ 시험에 합격한 것을 축하해 마지않는 바입니다 Let me [I] offer my heartiest congratulations to you on your success in the examination.

마직물 麻織物 hemp cloth
마진 〔商〕 a margin 《of profit》
♦ 마진 폭이 크다 [작다] leave a large [slim] margin of profit
━제(制) the margin system

마차 馬車 a carriage; a coach; a cab; 〈짐마차〉 a cart; a wagon
♦ 사륜 마차 a four-wheeler; a wagon / 쌍두 마차 a carriage and pair / 포장 마차 a covered wagon / 말 한 필이 끄는 마차 a one-horse carriage / 마차를 몰다 drive (in) a carriage / 마차를 타다 ride in [(美) on] a carriage / 마차로 가다 go by carriage; drive in a carriage to 《a place》
━길 a drive(way); a carriage drive ━삯 a carriage fare; cartage

마차부자리 馬車夫━ 〔天〕 the Charioteer; the Wagoner; Auriga

마찬가지 sameness; the (very) same; the self-same; one and the same; 〈유사〉 likeness; similarity
♦ 마찬가지의 the same; like; similar; equal; equivalent; of the same kind [sort] / 마찬가지로 similarly; likewise; equally; in like manner; in the same way [manner] 《as》 / [위와] 마찬가지로 like the preceding; ditto / 마찬가지가 되다 come to the same thing
▶ 그것은 날더러 죽으라는거나 마찬가지다 It's just like telling me to die.
▶ 이 점에 관해서 내 의견은 당신과 마찬가지요 I have the same opinion as you on this point.
▶ 나[당신]도 마찬가지입니다 I am [You are] another. ⇒ So am I [are you].
▶ 둘 다 마찬가지다 There is nothing to choose between the two. ⇒ The two are much the same.
▶ 이 증서는 휴지나 마찬가지다 This bond is little [no] better than waste paper.
▶ 이제 우리의 조사는 끝난 것이나 마찬가지다 Our research is now practically over.
▶ 휴식은 일과 마찬가지로 필요한 것이다 Rest is as much a necessity as work.
▶ 그는 나를 자기 아들과 마찬가지로 사랑한다 He loves me just like his own son.
▶ 나도 마찬가지로 그 계획에 반대한다 I am against the plan, too.

마찰 摩擦 **1** 〈문지르기〉 rubbing; chafing; 〔物〕 friction
♦ 공기 마찰 air friction / 금속과 나무의 마찰 friction between metal and wood / 마찰이 없는 frictionless / 마찰을 막다 prevent friction; minimize the effect of friction / 마찰을 줄이다 reduce [diminish] friction
━마찰하다 〈문지르다〉 rub 《against, with》; chafe 《the skin》
▶ 전선과 나뭇가지가 마찰하면 위험하다 It is dangerous for the electric wire to rub against the branch.
2 〈불화·알력〉 friction; feud; (a) discord; (a) trouble
♦ 마찰을 일으키다 produce friction; raise [make] trouble / 마찰을 피하다 [없애다] avoid [remove] friction
▶ 항상 일부 학생이 학교에서 말썽을 일으킨다 Some students always cause troubles [friction] on campus.
■ 건포[냉수]━ a rubdown with a dry [cold water] towel 무역━ trade friction [dispute, conflict] ━각 the angle of friction; a frictional angle ━계수 the coefficient of friction ━력 the frictional force ━브레이크 a friction brake ━손실 〔物〕 friction loss ━열 frictional heat ━음 a frictional sound; 〔音聲〕 a fricative sound [consonant]; a fricative ━적 실업 frictional unemployment ━전기[저항] frictional electricity [resistance]

마천루 摩天樓 a skyscraper

마초 馬草 horse pasturage
마취 痲醉 anesthesia; narcotism
♦ 마취에서 깨어나다 come [wake up] out of the ether
—**마취하다** anesthetize
▶ 수술은 클로로포름[에테르]으로 마취하고서 행한다 The operation is performed under chloroform [ether].
■**국부[국소]**— local anesthesia **전신[척수]**— general [spinal] anesthesia ■**—법** a method of anesthesia; narcosis **—상태** narcosis **—요법** narcothcraphy **—의(醫)** an anesthetist **—작용** narcosism; narcotic influence **—학** anesthesiology

마취약[제] 痲醉藥[劑] an anesthetic; a narcotic; a (narcotic) drug
♦ 국소[전신] 마취약 a local [general] anesthetic / 마취약을 탄 술 drugged wine

마치¹ a hammer ⇨ 장도리
마치² 〈흡사〉 (just) like [as]; as if [though]; as it were

[解說] (1) *as if* [*though*] 절(clause)에서는 보통 가정법을 쓰지만 주절이 현재형인 경우 as if [though] 절에는 직설법 현재형을 쓰기도 한다. 이 경우 현재의 사실 또는 미래의 실현성을 강조하고 있는 사실에 주의해야 한다 : He talks as if he is suspicious of me. (그는 마치 나를 의심하고 있는 듯한 말투다) / He looks as if he is going to cry. (그는 마치 금방 울음을 터뜨릴 것 같다)
(2) 〈美〉에서는 as if [though] 절 대신에 *like*를 쓰는 경우가 있다. 이 경우 like절은 보통 직설법을 쓴다 : She acts like she is a queen. ⇌ She acts (just) like a queen. (그녀는 마치 여왕인 것처럼 행동한다)

♦ 마치 나가라는 듯이 as if to say "get out" / 마치 죽은 것 같다 look as if dead; be more dead than alive
▶ 그는 마치 해골 같다 He looks (just) like a skeleton.
▶ 그는 마치 무엇이나 다 아는 것처럼 이야기한다 He talks as if [though] he knew everything.
▶ 여기서 보면 자동차가 마치 개미 같다 Seen from here, the automobiles look like so many ants.
▶ 나는 마치 천둥소리 같은 굉음을 들었다 I heard a roaring sound like that of thunder.
▶ 마치 한대 얻어맞은 것처럼 머리가 띵했다 I felt as if I had been hit on the head.

마치³ 〈행진곡〉 a march
♦ 웨딩 마치 the wedding march

마치다¹ **1** 〈부딪다〉 hit; be obstructed; be struck; be stuck
▶ 말뚝이 바위에 마치어 더는 들어가지 않는다 The stake has hit a rock and won't drive in any deeper.
2 〈결리다〉 pinch; feel an acute pain; have a pain [stitch]
♦ 옆구리가 마치다 have a stitch in the side

마치다² 〈끝내다〉 finish; end; complete; conclude; get [be] through 《with》; make an end of; put an end to; 〈수행하다〉 accomplish; 〈졸업하다〉 graduate 《from》
♦ 하루의 일과를 마치고 after a day's work / 일을 마치다 finish [be through with] *one's* work; get *one's* work done / 불일을 마치다 make an end of *one's* business / 대학 과정을 마치다 complete [pass through] a [*one's*] university course; complete college
▶ 우리는 수업을 마치고 테니스를 쳤다 We played tennis after school.
▶ 너 숙제 다 마쳤니? Are [Have] you done with your homework?
▶ 그는 셰익스피어의 한 구절을 인용하는 것으로 연설을 마쳤다 He concluded his speech by quoting a passage from Shakespeare.

마침 〈꼭 알맞게〉 just (in time); fortunately; luckily; opportunely; as good luck would have it; in the (very) nick of time; 〈공교롭게〉 accidentally
▶ 마침 잘 왔다 You have come at just the right moment.
▶ 마침 민 교수는 집에 있었다 Fortunately, Professor Min was at home. ⇌ I was fortunate to find Prof. Min at home.
▶ 마침 버스가 바로 왔다 Luckily, the bus came right away.
▶ 그가 마침 그곳에 있었다 He happened to be there.
▶ 마침 그날은 비가 왔었다 The day happened to be rainy.
▶ 미안합니다만, 그 물건은 마침 떨어졌습니다 I'm sorry but we don't have the goods in stock [the goods are out of stock].

마침내 at (long) last; at length; finally; in the end; after all; in the long run

[解說] (1) *at* (*long*) *last*와 *finally*는 긍정문에만 쓰고 부정문에는 쓰지 않는다. at (long) last은「여러 가지 경과를 거쳐 장기간의 노력 뒤에」의 뜻으로 long이 있으면 보다 강한 뜻이 된다.
(2) *in the end*는「결말로서는, 최종적으로는」의 뜻으로 긍정문에 쓴다.
(3) *after all*은 at (long) last와 같은 뜻으로 긍정문·부정문의 양쪽에 쓰이지만「그예, 드디어, 결국」의 뜻으로 어느 정도 부정문이나 부정적 뉘앙스가 강한 문장에서 쓴다.

▶ 그 일도 마침내 끝나가고 있다 We are finally nearing the end of the work.
▶ 마침내 긴 여름 방학이 끝났다 At last the long summer vacation is over.
▶ 마침내 그는 그것을 이해하게 되었다 At length he came to understand it.
▶ 마침내 전쟁이 터졌다 A war broke out at last.
▶ 마침내 결단을 내려야 할 때가 왔다 There comes a time when I must make a decision.
▶ 많은 실패를 거듭했지만 마침내 그는 성공했다 He failed so many times, but finally succeeded.

마침표 —標 〈종지부〉 a period (.); 〈英〉 a full stop
♦ 마침표를 찍다 put a period 《to》

마카로니 〈서양식 국수〉 macaroni
마카오 〈중국 남동부에 있는 포르투갈령의 도시〉 Macao; Macau
◆ 마카오의 Macanese ■ ―사람 a Macanese
마케도니아 Macedonia ◆ 마케도니아의 Macedonian
마케팅 〔經〕 marketing
■ ―리서치 marketing research
마켓 a market ◆ 슈퍼마켓 a supermarket
마크 〈기호〉 a mark; 〈상표〉 a trademark; 〈표〉 a label; 〈표장〉 a badge
◆ 마크를 붙이다 mark; put a mark 《on》
마크하다 〈구기에서〉 guard [check, (英) mark] 《a certain player》
마키아벨리 〈이탈리아의 정치가〉 Machiavelli, Niccolò di Bernardo(1469-1527)
■ ―주의[즘] Machiavellism; Machiavellianism: 마키아벨리즘의 Machiavellian ―주의자 Machiavellist
마태복음 ―福音 〔聖〕 the Gospel according to St. Matthew; Matthew (略 Matt.)
마티네 a matinee
마티니 〈칵테일〉 a martini [Martini] (cocktail)
마티스 〈프랑스의 화가〉 Matisse, Henri (1869-1954)
마파람 〈남풍〉 the south wind; a souther
마파람에 게눈 감추듯 〈속담〉〈음식을 순식간에 먹어치우다〉 eat up in a moment [in no time]
마편초 馬鞭草 〔植〕 verbena
마포 麻布 flax ⇨ 삼베
마피아 〈미국 등의 범죄 조직〉 the Maf(f)ia
■ ―단원 a Mafioso 《pl. -si, ~s》
마필 馬匹 horses
마하 〔物〕 Mach (略 M)
▶ 이 신예기는 마하 2로 비행한다 This new and powerful plane flies at (the speed of) Mach 2.
■ ―계(計) a Machmeter
마호가니 mahogany
▶ 이 테이블은 마호가니로 마무리되어 있다 This table is finished in mahogany.
마호메트 〈이슬람교의 교조〉 Mohammed; Muhammad; Muhammed; Mahomet; Mahomed; (570-632) ■ ―교 Islam; Islamism; Mohammedanism ―교도 a Muslim; a Muslem; a Moslem; a Mohammedan
마흔 forty
막 recklessly ⇨ 마구
막² 〈방금〉 just (now); just [right] at the moment
◆ 막 …하려던 참이다 be about to 《do》; be ready to 《do》; be on the point [edge, verge] of 《doing》
▶ 막 도착했다 I have just arrived.
▶ 그는 이제 막 나갔습니다 He went out just a moment ago [just now].
▶ 꽃봉오리가 막 피어나려 하고 있다 The buds are just ready to burst.
▶ 막 떠나려던 참에 민 선생이 찾아왔다 I was just going out, when Mr. Min came to see me.
▶ 어, 마침 잘 왔다. 내가 막 전화하려던 참이었어 Oh, you've come at just the right time. I was about to call [telephone] you.

막 幕 1 〈임시로 지은 집〉 a temporary shed [shelter]; a booth; a shack; a shanty; a hut; a cabin; a cottage
◆ 막을 짓다 put up a booth [shed]
2 〈장막〉 a curtain; a hanging screen; hangings; 〈천막〉 a tent
◆ 막을 내리다 let down [draw down, drop, lower] a curtain / 막을 당겨 가리다 draw a curtain over / 막을 올리다 raise [draw up] a curtain; lift a curtain / 막을 치다 pull the curtains across; stretch a curtain
▶ 이별하는 장면으로 막이 내린다 The curtain falls [drops, closes] on a parting scene.
▶ 바야흐로 막이 오르는[내리는] 참이었다 The drop curtain was just going up [down].
▶ 조금 늦게 막이 올랐다 The curtain rose a little late.
3 〈연극의〉 an act
◆ 3막 5장의 연극 a play in three acts and five scenes / 햄릿 제1막 제1장 Hamlet, Act I, Scene I
▶ 그것은 1[3]막 짜리 연극이었다 It was a one-act [three-act] play.
▶ 방금 제2막이 시작되었다 The second act has just begun.
▶ 그녀는 제1막에 출연합니까? Does she perform in the first act?
4 〈끝장〉 an end; a close; a conclusion
▶ 전쟁은 막을 내렸다 The war has come to an end.
▶ 장기간에 걸친 노동쟁의도 마침내 막을 내렸다 The prolonged labor dispute at last drew to a close.
막 膜 〈점막〉 a membrane; 〈물갈퀴의〉 webbing; 〈얇은 껍질〉 a film
◆ 막 모양의 membran(e)ous; filmy
막가다 behave rudely [recklessly]; misbehave *oneself*
막간 幕間 an intermission [(英) interval] (between the acts [scenes])
◆ 10분간의 막간에 during a ten-minute intermission / 막간에 가벼운 식사를 하다 take a snack in the intermission
■ ―극 an interlude
막강하다 莫强― mighty; very strong; enormously powerful
◆ 막강한 군사력 great military strength / 막강한 전함 a mighty battleship
막걸리 makkŏlli; raw [unrefined] rice wine
막깎다 have *one's* hair close-cropped[-cut]; cut 《*one's* hair》 short
◆ 막깎은 머리 a close-cropped head
막내 the youngest child
■ ―딸 the last [youngest] daughter ―며느리 the wife of *one's* last [youngest] son ―아들 the last [youngest] son ―아우 *one's* youngest brother 막냇누이 *one's* youngest sister 막냇동생 *one's* youngest brother 막냇사위 the husband of *one's* last [youngest] daughter 막냇삼촌 *one's* youngest uncle 막냇자식 the youngest child; the baby of the family
막내둥이 the youngest of the family; the youngest child ◆ 막내둥이 응석받듯 하다 humor *sb* indulgently

막노동—勞動 manual work ⇨ 막일

막다 1 〈구멍·갈라진 틈 등을〉 stop up; stuff up 《a hole》; fill up 《a crevice》; clog 《a pipe》

♦귀를 막다 wad [fill, stop, stuff] one's ears 《with cotton》; 〈손으로〉 place one's hand over one's ears / (쥐)구멍을 막다 block [stop up] a (rat)hole / 병 아가리를 막다 stop (up) [seal] a bottle

▶우리는 흙으로 큰 구멍을 막았다 We filled the big hole with earth.

▶그는 샛바람이 들어오지 못하게 틈을 종이로 막았다 He closed up the openings with paper to keep out the drafts.

2 〈가로막다〉 bar; block (up);〈저지하다〉 stop; check; interrupt (the progress); hold in check; 〈방해하다〉 obstruct; hinder; 〈흐름을 막다〉 dam up 《a river》; 〈차단하다〉 cut off

♦가는 길을 막다 block the way; bar [obstruct, blockade] sb's way; 〈훼방하다〉 stand [get] in sb's way / 발언을 막다 prohibit sb from speaking / 바람을 막다 shut out the wind; screen 《a house》 from the wind / 빛[시야]을 막다 block (off) the light [obstruct the view] / 소문을 막다 hush up a rumor / 인플레이션을 막다 check [hold back, stem the tide of] inflation / 산업의 발전을 막다 deter the growth of the industry / 입을 막다 〈자기의〉 hold a hand over one's mouth; 〈남의〉 cover sb's mouth; forbid sb to mention; gag sb; silence sb; 〈돈을 주어〉 buy sb's silence

▶쓰러진 나무가 길을 막았다 A fallen tree obstructed [blocked] the road.

▶생활고가 내 대학 진학을 막았다 The difficulty of living hindered me from entering the university.

▶경찰이 군중을 막았다 The police headed off the crowd.

▶큰 나무들이 햇빛을 막고 있었다 The large trees shut out the sunlight.

▶입구가 좁으니까 막고 있지 마십시오 The entrance is narrow, so don't block it, please.

▶두꺼운 벽은 소리를 막아준다 Thick walls exclude sound.

▶마을 사람들은 그 개울을 막아 연못을 만들었다 The villagers dammed up that stream and made a pond.

▶정부는 인플레이션을 막기 위한 조치를 취했다 The government has taken measures to hold back inflation.

▶빨리 출혈을 막지 않으면 그 사람은 죽을지도 모른다 He may die if we don't stop the bleeding quickly.

▶아무 것도 나의 결심을 막을 수는 없다 Nothing can deter me from my determination.

▶현재의 추세는 아무도 막을 수 없다 Nobody can check the present tendency.

3 〈둘러 막다〉 enclose; wall (up); fence (round); rail off (가로대로); rope off (줄로)

♦정원[집]을 울타리[돌담]로 막다 enclose a garden [house] with a fence [stone wall]

4 〈칸을 치다〉 screen off; partition (off); compart

♦방의 칸을 막다 partition a room / 휘장으로 칸을 막다 screen off part of a room

5 〈방어하다〉 defend oneself 《against the enemy》; protect 《against, from》; 〈얻씬 못하게 하다〉 keep off; ward off; 〈방지하다〉 keep away [out, off, back]; check [guard against, provide against] 《accidents》; 〈예방하다〉 prevent 《sth [sb] from doing》

♦도난을 막다 prevent theft / 오해를 막다 avoid misunderstandings / 요동을 막다 check rolling / 전염을 막다 prevent infection / 위험을 막다 stave off a danger / 적을 막다 hold off the enemy; keep [hold] the enemy at bay / 추위를 막다 protect oneself from the cold / 파리[모기]를 막다 keep off flies [mosquitoes]/ 강물의 범람을 막다 keep the river from overflowing / 적의 공격을 막다 stop the enemy's attack / 적의 침략을 막다 defend 《one's country》 against the aggressors [invaders] / 어린 아이가 불에 가까이 가지 못하게 막다 keep a child away from the fire / 도둑을 막기 위해 문단속을 단단히 하다 fasten the doors securely to protect the house against [from] burglars / 청소년의 비행을 미리 막다 prevent juvenile delinquency

▶그들은 단결하여 적을 막았다 Together they kept off [guarded against] the enemy.

▶소방관들은 불길이 마을 전체로 퍼지지 못하게 막았다 The firemen prevented the fire from spreading through the town.

▶추위를 막는 데는 난로가 제일이다 A stove is the best protection against the cold.

▶이 음식이 상하는 것을 막는 방법을 혹시 아세요? Do you know any means of preserving this food from decay?

▶그들에게는 비바람을 막아 줄 것이 아무 것도 없었다 There was nothing to protect [shield] them from the wind and rain.

▶시 당국은 콜레라가 퍼지는 것을 막기 위해 전력을 다했다 The municipal authorities did their best to check the spread of cholera.

막다르다 blind (alley); closed at one end; dead-end 《street》; 〈비유적〉 final; 〈정체된〉 deadlocked; 〈옴짝 못하는〉 stalemated

♦막다른 집 a house at the end of a blind alley [dead-end street] / 막다른 길 the dead end of a road / 막다른 지경에 at the last moment; at the eleventh hour

▶나는 이 길의 막다른 집에 삽니다 I live in the house at the end of this street.

▶똑바로 쭉 가시면 막다른 길에 그 은행이 나옵니다 Keep straight on, and you will find the bank at the end of the road.

막다른골(목) 〈막힌 골목〉 a blind alley [lane]; a dead-end street; a dead end; the end of a road [street]; an impasse; (프) a cul-de-sac 《pl. -sacs, culs-》; 〈교착상태〉 a deadlock; a standstill; an impasse; a stalemate; a (tight) corner

♦막다른 골목에 다다르다 come to the end of a road; reach [come to, be at] a dead end; reach [come to] a deadlock [a stalemate, an impasse]; be stalemated [deadlocked]; be at the end of one's tether / 막다른 골목에 몰아넣다 drive sb into a corner / 막다른 골목에 몰리다 be driven into a corner [to the last extrem-

막무가내

ity]; be cornered; be brought to a standstill; come to a deadlock / 막다른 골목에 이른 국면을 타개하다 bring a deadlock to an end; break the deadlock [stalemate]; find a way out of the deadlock [impasse]
▶ 길은 거기서 막다른 골목이 되었다 The road came to a dead end there.
▶ 그 연구는 막다른 골목에 부딪혔다 The research has reached a dead end.
▶ 우리 사업은 자금 부족으로 막다른 골목에 다다랐다 Our business came to a standstill due to lack of money. ⇌ Our enterprise has got completely bogged down for want of funds.
▶ 두 사람의 관계는 결국 막다른 골목에 이르렀다 Their relationship finally reached a dead end.
▶ 미·중 협상은 곧 막다른 골목에 다다랐다 The U.S.-Chinese negotiations soon came to a deadlock.

막달라 마리아 〔聖〕 Mary Magdalene; Mary of Magdala

막대기 a stick; a bar; a rod; 〈장대〉 a pole; 〈지휘봉〉 a baton
♦ 커튼 거는 막대기 a curtain rod
▶ 나는 막대기로 묘목을 받쳐 주었다 I propped up the young tree with a pole.
▶ 그는 막대기로 개를 때렸다 He beat the dog with a stick.
■ 금속[쇠]— a metal [an iron] bar 대— a bamboo stick

막대나선은하 —螺旋銀河 〔天〕 a barred spiral galaxy

막대자석 —磁石 〖物〗 a bar magnet

막대패 a fore plane; a jack plane
♦ 막대패질하다 use a fore plane (after a saw); plane roughly

막 대 하 다 莫大— vast; huge; enormous; immense; tremendous; colossal; fabulous; stupendous
♦ 막대한 금액 a vast [a huge, an immense, a fabulous] sum (of money) / 막대한 재산 an immense wealth [fortune] / 막대한 비용 enormous [immense] expense; considerable [stupendous] cost / 막대한 빚에 시달리다 suffer from a vast [mammoth] debt
▶ 그는 주식으로 막대한 손실을 입었다 He suffered heavy losses on the stock market.
▶ 그의 갑작스런 죽음은 국가적으로 막대한 손실이다 His sudden death is an immeasurable loss to the nation.
▶ 벼 농사에 막대한 피해가 발생했다 A vast damage was done to the rice crop.
▶ 그는 아버지에게서 막대한 재산을 물려받았다 He inherited an enormous fortune from his father.

막도장 —圖章 a private seal; an unregistered personal seal
▶ 여기다 막도장을 찍으세요 Please stamp your private seal here.

막 되 다 ill-mannered[-bred]; rude; boorish; wild; outrageous; lawless
♦ 막된 놈 an ill-bred[-mannered] fellow; a wild guy; (口) a roughneck / 막된 말씨 rude language; a rude way of speaking / 막된 여자 a loose woman / 막되게 굴다 behave rudely; be rude to sb
▶ 이 아이들은 막돼 먹었구나 These children have no manners.
▶ 그렇게 막되게 굴지 마라 Don't act so roughly. ⇌ Stop that coarse behavior.

막둥이 1 youngest of the family ⇨ 막내둥이 **2** 〈잔심부름꾼〉 a boy servant; a page; a handy boy

막둥이 씨름하듯 (속담) be all of more or less the same average ability

막론하다 莫論— go without question; be needless to say; be a matter of course; there is no need to speak of
♦ …을 막론하고 without distinction of…; irrespective of…/ 날씨 여하를 막론하고 rain or shine; in all weathers; regardless of the weather / 남녀 노소를 막론하고 regardless [irrespective] of sex or age; without distinction of age or sex / 때와 장소를 막론하고 in all times and places; any time and anywhere / 지위 고하를 막론하고 irrespective of rank; without distinction of rank; high and low alike
▶ 이유 여하를 막론하고 폭력은 허용될 수 없다 No matter what the reason, violence cannot be allowed.
▶ 결과 여하를 막론하고 우리는 그 일을 시작해야만 한다 We must begin it, no matter what the consequence may be.
▶ 누구를 막론하고 불법 침입자는 사살함 (게시) Anyone who trespasses be shot.

막료 幕僚 (총칭) the staff; 〈개인〉 a staff officer; a member of one's staff
♦ 사령관과 그 막료 a commander and his staff
▶ 그는 총사령관의 막료로 복무했다 He served on the staff of the commander-in-chief.

막막하다 寞寞— 〈쓸쓸하다〉 desolate; dreary; deserted; 〈외롭다〉 lonely; lonesome; 〈의지가 지 없다〉 forlorn; helpless
♦ 막막한 밤 a dreary [hushed] night / 막막한 생활 a desolate life / 막막한 장래 a gloomy future / 살 길이 막막하다 do not know how to maintain life / 어쩌해야 좋을지 막막하다 be at a loss what to do

막막하다 漠漠— vast; extensive; boundless
♦ 막막한 벌판 a vast plain / 막막한 초원[바다] a vast expanse of grass [water]; a boundless grassland [ocean] / 막막한 황야 a vast [boundless] wilderness

막말 〈막된 말〉 rude [rough] talk; harsh [vulgar, foul] language; 〈잘라서 하는 말〉 a blunt remark [speech]
♦ 막말로 to put it bluntly [roughly]; 〈상말로〉 in foul [bad] language
▶ 그 친구는 툭하면 막말을 한다 He is apt to be rough of speech.
▶ 막말로 그건 순 헛소리 아니냐? To put it bluntly, that is utter nonsense, isn't it?
—**막말하다** 〈되는 대로 말하다〉 speak roughly [impolitely]; talk wild [at random]; utter wild words; 〈잘라서 말하다〉 put it bluntly

막매듭 〖海〗 a sheet bend knot

막무가내 莫無可奈 ♦ 막무가내로 obstinately;

막바지

stubbornly; doggedly; resolutely; firmly / 막무가내로 듣지 않다 refuse flatly; turn a deaf ear to; will not listen to
▶내가 아무리 사정을 해도 그 양반은 막무가내였다 I tried very hard to persuade him, but he won't listen.
▶그렇게 막무가내로 굴지 마라 Don't be so obstinate.

막바지 1 〈끝〉 the end [bottom] 《of a street》; the very [dead] end
▶우리집은 그 골목 막바지에 있어 My house is at the end of the alley.
2 〈고비〉 the last moment; the final stage; 〈극한〉 (the last) extremity; 〈절정〉 a climax
♦일의 막바지 the final stage of an affair / 막바지에 몰리다 be driven to the last extremity [moment] / 막바지에 몰아넣다 drive [bring] sb to bay
▶일이 막바지에 이르렀을 때 갑자기 사태가 어수선해졌다 When it all came to the final stage, things suddenly began to move.
▶선거운동도 막바지에 이르렀다 The election campaign has reached [gone into] its last [final] stage.
■길— the dead end of a road 언덕— the top of a hill

막벌다 earn wages as a day laborer; earn by doing rough work

막벌이 earning wages as a day [physical, manual] laborer
—**막벌이하다** earn wages as a day [physical, manual] laborer
—**꾼** a day laborer

막사 幕舍 〈군대가 거주하는〉 a barracks; a camp; quarters
▶서둘러 막사가 세워졌다 A barracks was hastily erected.

막살다 lead [live] a rough [haphazard, careless] (sort of) life; lead a nondescript life; rough it
▶산골에 있을 때 나는 한동안 막살았다 I roughed it for a while in the mountain village.
▶그 녀석은 막살고 있다 He lives in a happy-go-lucky fashion.

막상 〈급기야〉 ultimately; in the last analysis; after all; 〈실제로〉 really; actually; in reality
♦막상 때가 닥치면 if the time comes; when the moment arrives / 막상 일이 닥치면 〈다급해지면〉 at a push; at a pinch; when one is put to the push; 〈만부득이하면〉 if compelled [forced]; when occasion demands
▶막상 해보면 알 거다 You will see what it is once you have done it in practice.
▶막상 하려면 일은 꽤 어려운 법이다 When one comes to doing it, one finds it rather difficult.
▶막상 당해 보니 듣던 것과는 아주 달랐다 I found the reality quite different from what I had heard.

막상막하 莫上莫下 nothing better and nothing worse
♦막상막하의 열전 an evenly-matched contest; a nip and tuck [neck and neck] race / 막상막하로 equally (well); (美口) nip and tuck; 〈경주 등에서〉 (run) neck and neck
—**막상막하다** equally-[evenly-]matched; well-balanced[-matched]; equal (to); be on a par (with); stand even
▶그 두 팀은 기량이 막상막하다 The two teams are equally-matched in skill.
▶김군은 박군과 실력이 막상막하다 Kim is a match for [equal to] Park in ability.
▶그 두 사람은 힘에서는 막상막하다 The two men are well-balanced in strength [equally strong].

막새(기와) 〈建〉 a round eaves tile; 〈수키와〉 convex tiles at the edge of eaves; 〈처마끝의 암·수기와〉 (both concave and convex) tiles at the edge of eaves

막서다 〈대들다〉 defy; face; rise (against); flash out (at [against] sb); lift a [one's] hand against; turn [fall] upon sb
▶그 얘기를 듣자 그는 주인에게 막섰다 Hearing that, he turned [fell] upon his master.
▶그 여자도 마주 노려보며 막섰다 Her eyes flashed back defiance.

막심하다 莫甚— immense; enormous; tremendous; extreme; severe; heavy
♦막심한 손해 a tremendous [heavy] loss; serious damage / 막심한 타격을 받다 suffer a hard blow / 고생이 막심하다 have tremendous difficulties
▶나는 후회가 막심하다 I regret it very much.
▶두뇌유출은 국가적으로 막심한 손실이다 The brain drain is a heavy loss to the nation.
▶화물은 막심한 피해를 입었다 The freights are heavily damaged.

막아내다 keep away [out, off]; ward [hold] off (danger); (hold [keep] in) check; prevent; 〈방어하다〉 defend (against); protect (against, from); shield (from)
♦적 (군)을 막아내다 keep off [guard against] the enemy (troops); hold the enemy (troops) in check / 전염병을 막아내다 check the spread of an infectious disease / 추위를 막아내다 protect oneself from the cold / 화살을 막아내다 ward [fend] off an arrow / 공격을 정면으로 막아내다 bear [take] the brunt of an attack / 불길이 번지는 것을 막아내다 arrest the spread of fire
▶경찰은 시위대의 행진을 막아내려 했다 The police tried to check the demonstration parade.

막역하다 莫逆— intimate; close; familiar
♦막역한 사이 intimate relations / 막역한 친구 a close [an intimate] friend; a steadfast and trusted friend; a devoted [bosom] friend / 막역한 사이다 be on intimate terms (with); be David and Jonathan [Damon and Pythias] / 막역하게 지내다 be intimate (with); be on good [intimate, friendly] terms (with)
▶그 두 사람은 막역한 친구다 They are good [great] friends. ⇌ They are David and Jonathan [Damon and Pythias]. ⇌ They are hand and glove with each other.

막연하다 漠然— 〈어렴풋하다〉 vague (idea); obscure (meaning); hazy (notion); misty

(conception); nebulous 《idea》; indefinable 《word》; 〈목적없는〉 aimless; random
♦ 막연한 대답 a vague [an obscure] answer / 막연한 말을 하다 speak in general terms / 막연한 불안에 사로잡히다 be overcome with a nameless fear / 막연한 생활을 하다 live without an aim
▶ 그것에 대해서는 나는 막연한 인상밖에 없다 I have only a vague [an indistinct] impression of it.
▶ 그녀에게서는 막연한 대답이 왔다 An indefinite reply came from her.
▶ 군중들 사이에 막연한 불안감이 일어났다 A vague unrest prevailed among the masses.
▶ 이 문장은 의미가 너무 막연하다 The meaning of this sentence is too obscure.
▶ 그의 생각은 막연하고 요령부득이다 His ideas are vague and pointless.
—막연히[하게] 〈어렴풋이〉 vaguely; obscurely; hazily; 〈목적없이〉 aimlessly; at random
♦ 막연히만 알다 have only a vague idea of / 책상 앞에 막연히 앉아 있다 sit aimlessly at one's desk
▶ 나는 가난하다는 것이 어떤 것인지 막연히 알고 있다 I know vaguely what it is to be poor.
▶ 요즘에는 막연하게 대학에 가는 젊은이들이 많다 Today a lot of young people go to college aimlessly.
▶ 나는 그가 무슨 말을 하고 있는지 막연하게만 분간할 수 있다 I have only a remote conception of what he is saying.

막 이 〈보호〉 protection 《against》; 〈엄호〉 sheltering; 〈독쌓기〉 damming [banking] up; 〈칸막이〉 a screen
■ 동— embankment [embanking]; building up levees 바람— a windbreak; a shelter from the wind 방패— warding off; defending 보— banking up (a pool for) paddy 서리— a frost shelter; a shelter against [protection from] frost 액— warding off evil

막 일 manual labor; hard [heavy] work [labor]; rough work; toil; a muscle job; (口) a roughneck job
▶ 자네는 막일에는 적합하지 않은 사람일세 You are not fit for hard labor.
—막일하다 be engaged in [do] rough work
■ —꾼 a manual [physical] laborer; a handyman

막자 a pestle ■—사발 a mortar

막잡이 1 〈막쓰는 물건〉 a crude [rough] article for careless use; a coarse article; 〈잡동사니〉 odds and ends; sundries
2 careless behavior ⇨ 마구잡이

막장 1 〈鑛〉〈채벽〉 a blind end [front] in a mine gallery; 〈채굴 현장〉 a (working) face
2 〈막장일〉 mining; digging; exploitation (work)
—막장하다 mine; work [exploit] a mine; engage in mine exploitation [mining operations]
■ —꾼 a pitman; a miner; a digger —일 mining; digging —지주(支柱) a (working) face support

막중하다 莫重— 〈귀중하다〉 extremely [very] precious; priceless; invaluable; 〈중요하다〉 very important; serious; grave; of great account
♦ 막중한 시간 priceless time / 막중한 인명과 재산 invaluable life and property / 막중한 책임 a weighty [heavy] responsibility / 막중한 사명을 띠다 be charged with very important mission
▶ 그는 회사에서 막중한 지위에 있다 He holds an important position in the company.
▶ 이번 임무는 대단히 막중하다 This mission involves very heavy responsibilities.

막지르다 1 〈앞길을〉 block; bar; stand in one's way; 〈말을〉 interrupt
♦ 길을 막지르다 block [bar] one's way [passage]; cross sb's path / 말을 막지르다 interrupt sb; cut sb short
2 〈냅다 지르다〉 thrust [stab, jab, push, kick] wildly [with force]; 〈소리를〉 shout loudly; yell out; shout and yell

막질리다 1 〈앞길을〉 be blocked [barred]; 〈말을〉 be interrupted
2 〈냅다 질리다〉 get thrust [stabbed, kicked] wildly [with force]

막차 —車 the last bus [train]
▶ 서둘러라, 막차 놓칠라 Hurry up, or you will miss the last train [bus].

막 초 —草 coarse [poor-quality, cheap] tobacco; tobacco of inferior quality

막치 a coarse [crude] article; a low grade article; poor stuff; (口) junk

막판 1 〈마지막 판〉 the last round; the final scene [stage]; 〈위기〉 the last [critical] moment; the eleventh hour
♦ 막판에 (가서) at the last moment; at the eleventh hour / 막판에 접어들다 be on the last stage of 《doing》 / 막판으로 몰아넣다 drive sb into a corner
▶ 그는 마침내 막판에 몰렸다 He was driven to bay at last.
▶ 우리는 막판에 역전승했다 We turned the tables at the last moment and won the game.
2 〈뒤범벅판〉 a haphazard [chaotic] scene; a mess

막후 幕後 ♦ 막후에서 behind the scenes; backstage / 막후에서 조종[공작]하다 maneuver behind the scenes; pull (the) wires [strings] 《from behind》 / 막후에서 활약하다 take an active part in the background
▶ 누군가가 막후에서 획책하고 있는 듯하다 It seems that someone is working behind the scenes. ⇌ Someone is maneuvering behind the scenes.
■ —인물 a man behind the curtain [scenes]; a wire-puller —협상[접촉, 회담] a behind-the-scenes [backstage] negotiation [contact, conference]

막후거래 幕後去來 a backdoor dealing
▶ 그는 그 사람들과 막후 거래를 했다 He had a backdoor dealing with them.

막히다 1 〈구멍 등이〉 be stopped [plugged] up; be [get] clogged; be choked [obstructed]
♦ 소변이 막히다 have trouble (in) urinating / 숨이 막히다 be choked; be suffocated

막힘없이

▶ 개수대는 주방 쓰레기로 자주 막힌다 The sink often gets stopped [becomes clogged] (up) with kitchen waste.
▶ 나는 감기로 코가 막혔다 My nose is stuffed up with [because of] a cold.
▶ 병 주둥이가 막혔다 The mouth of the bottle is clogged [stopped up].
▶ 방이 작아서 숨이 꽉 막혔다 The small room was quite suffocating.
▶ 그 파이프는 진흙으로 막혀 있다 That pipe is clogged with mud.
▶ 굴뚝[하수도]이 검댕[오물]으로 막혀 있다 The chimney [drain] is choked up with soot [dirt].

2 ⟨길 등이⟩ be blocked (up); be barred; be obstructed

♦ 앞길이 막힌 골목 a blind [dead] alley / 앞길이 막히다 have no way out; be at the end of a road; be stalled; have no opportunity / 통행이 막히다 be held up 《for a few minutes》
▶ 이 길은 차량들로 꽉 막혔다 This road is clogged [jammed] with cars.
▶ 눈[쓰러진 나무] 때문에 도로가 막혀 있었다 The road was blocked [obstructed] by snow [a fallen tree].
▶ 그들의 퇴로는 적군에게 막혀 버렸다 Their retreat was cut off [blocked] by enemy troops.
▶ 우리는 교통이 막혀 늦었다 We were late because we got caught in a traffic jam.

3 ⟨말·생각 등이⟩ be stuck 《in one's speech》; get tongue-tied; be at a loss for 《an answer》; be driven to one's wit's end

♦ 막힌 사람 a blockhead; a thickhead / 말문이 막히다 be stuck for a word; be at a loss for words
▶ 그 소녀는 너무 감동하여 말문이 막혔다 The girl was so moved (that) she found no words to express herself.
▶ 그 연사는 연설 도중에 말이 막혔다 The speaker broke off in the middle of his speech.
▶ 나는 대답할 말이 막혀버렸다 I was at a loss for an answer.

4 ⟨구획되다⟩ be partitioned [compartmented]; ⟨가로놓이다⟩ lie across

♦ 벽으로 막히다 be partitioned with a wall / 방이 각 칸마다 막히다 the rooms are partitioned [compartmented] 《with screens》 / 앞길이 강으로 막히다 have a river ahead; a river lies across the path ahead / 앞[뒤]이 산으로 막히다 have a mountain ahead [behind]; a mountain obstructs [blocks] one's way ahead [be walled in from behind by a mountain]
▶ 우리 정원은 옆집 정원과 담으로 막혀 있다 Our garden is separated from our neighbor's by a fence.

막힘없이 smoothly; fluently; easily

▶ 그 학생은 그 난제를 막힘없이 풀었다 The student solved the difficult question easily [effortlessly, with hardly any effort].
▶ 그 여자는 프랑스어를 막힘없이 한다 She speaks French fluently.
▶ 계획은 막힘없이 진행되고 있다 The project is going ahead smoothly.

만¹ ⟨시간의 경과⟩ lapse; interval ♦ 3년 만에 after the lapse [an interval] of three years / 열흘 만에 목욕하다 take a bath after ten days / 5년 만에 친구를 만나다 meet [see] a friend after an interval of five years [five years' separation] / 2년 만에 어머니께 편지를 하다 write to one's mother after two years' silence

▶ 이것은 10년 만의 추위다 This is the coldest winter in ten years.
▶ 10년 만에 뵙는군요 It has been [is] ten years since I saw you last.
▶ 형님은 5년 만에 고향에 돌아왔다 My brother came home for the first time in five years. ⇌ After an absence of five years my brother returned home.
▶ 그가 태어난지 7년 만에 그의 어머니가 돌아가셨다 His mother died seven years after he was born.
▶ 오래간 만입니다 It's a long time since I saw you last.

만² **1** ⟨다만·뿐⟩ only; just (▶ 보통 한정하는 어구 앞에 위치하며, 후자가 구어적); alone (▶ 보통 한정하는 말 뒤에 위치); merely; ⟨단지⟩ simply; ⟨한도·범위⟩ as many [much] as; as [so] far as

♦ 한국어만 하는 사회 a society that talks only Korean / 나만은 as for me / 한 번만 just [only] once / 이번 한 번만 (for) just this once / 한 번만 더 just once again / 오전 중에만 just for the morning / 이번[그때]만은 (just) for this [that] once; on this [that] particular occasion
▶ 나는 이것만 있으면 족하다 I want nothing else. ⇌ That's all I want.
▶ 하나만 주세요 Give me just one.
▶ 나만 잘못했습니까? Am I the only one to blame?
▶ 잠깐만 기다리세요 Just a moment.
▶ 그 여자는 유명 상표 제품만 산다 She buys nothing but [only] brand-name merchandise.
▶ 필요한 것만 가지시고 나머지는 반환해 주세요 Take only what you need, and please return the rest.
▶ 언제 우리 둘이만 만날 수 있을까요? When can I see you alone?
▶ 會話 「어디 가니?」「그냥 편지만 한 통 부치러」 "Where are you going?" "Just to mail a letter."
▶ 그 사람은 이름만 화가다 He is an artist in name only.
▶ 그는 겨우 목숨만 붙어 있어 He is all but [as good as] dead.
▶ 이 서식에는 성명만 기입할 것 Nothing should be written but your name on this form.(▶but은 except의 뜻)
▶ 會話 「아가씨, 무엇을 드시겠습니까?」「커피만 주세요」 "What would you like, miss?" "Just coffee, please."
▶ 나만 집에 남겨놓고 식구들은 모두 외출했다 Everybody went out, leaving me home all alone.
▶ 그는 자기 일만 생각한다 He thinks of nothing but his work.

▶ 會話 「엄마, 나 사탕 좀 먹어도 돼요?」「그래, 하지만 하나만 먹어라」 "May I have some candy, Mom?" "All right, but only one."
▶ 그 소년만이 정확한 대답을 했다 Only the boy gave the right answer.
▶ 그녀만이 그날이 내 생일이라는 것을 기억하고 있었다 Only she remembered that it was my birthday.
▶ 그 사람만이 그 사실을 알고[그 일을 할 수] 있다 He alone knows the fact [can do it].
▶ 돈만이 인생의 목적은 아니다 Money is not the only thing in life.
▶ 이것만은 확실히 말할 수 있습니다 I can say this much for certain.
▶ 會話 「저보고 가라는 얘깁니까?」「그것만은 못하겠습니다」 "You mean I have to go?" "I will do anything but that."
▶ 사회적 지위만으로 저 사람을 평가해서는 안 된다 That person should not be judged only by his social status.
▶ 인간이 빵만으로 살 수 있나요? Can man live by bread alone?
▶ 네가 있어 주는 것만으로 족해 Your very presence will be enough.
▶ 나 혼자만으로는 그것을 할 수가 없습니다 I can't do it alone.
▶ 이 버스는 주말에만 운행한다 This bus runs only on weekends.
▶ 이것은 너에게만 하는 말이다 This is for your private ear.
▶ 중국에서만도 그런 사건이 10건이나 있었다 There were ten such cases in China alone.
▶ 그녀는 피아노뿐만 아니라 바이올린도 켤 줄 안다 She can play the violin as well as the piano.
▶ 너뿐만 아니라 그 사람도 옳다 Not only you but (also) he is right.
▶ 물가는 오르기만 한다 Prices keep on [never stop] rising.
▶ 과식만 하지 않으면 아무거나 먹어도 된다 You may eat anything, so long as you don't eat too much.
▶ 그것은 보기만[생각만] 해도 몸서리가 쳐진다 The mere sight [thought] of it makes me shudder.
▶ 자네가 주의만 했더라면 이런 일은 생기지 않았을 걸세 This would not have happened if only you had been careful.
▶ 그들은 만나기만 하면 싸운다 They never meet without quarreling.
2 〈적어도〉 at least
▶ 한번만 외국에 가봤으면 좋겠다 I wish I could go abroad at least once.
▶ 나는 월 10만원씩만은 저축하고 싶다 I wish to save a minimum of one hundred thousand won a month.
3 〈-만큼[쯤]〉 by
♦ 반만 줄이다 reduce by half
▶ 고기 1킬로그램만 주세요 Just give me one kilogram of meat.
▶ 이만하면 카메라를 살 수 있겠다 The amount will be enough to buy a camera.
4 〈겨우 그 정도〉 ▶ 그만 빚에 무슨 걱정이냐? Don't worry about such a nominal debt.

▶ 그만 일로 화낼 것은 없네 Don't be offended at such a trifle. ⇒ Don't let so slight a thing put you out [ruffle your temper].
▶ 그만 돈이 없다니 웬일이냐? How comes it that you don't have that little amount of money?

만 卍 〈표지〉【佛敎】 the Buddhist cross [emblem]; 〈글자〉 a fylfot; a gammadion 《pl. -dia》; a swastika

만 滿 just; full; fully; complete, whole; to a day
♦ 만 한 시간 (for) a full [good] hour; (for) one solid hour / 만 3일간 for fully three days; for three whole [full, clear] days; for three days solid / 만 20세에서 몇 개월 모자라다 want some months of twenty / 만으로 나이를 세다 count *sb's* age in full
▶ 이제 만 3년이다 It is now three years to a day.
▶ 그 여자 아이는 만 다섯 살이 되었다 The girl is five years old.
▶ 내가 한국에 온지 오늘로 만 1년[2년]이 되었다 It has been a full year [exactly two years] today since I came to Korea.
▶ 울릉도에 가는 데는 만 이틀이 걸린다 It takes fully two days to go to Ullŭngdo.
▶ 그의 아내가 죽은지 만 5년이 된다 It's been five full years since his wife died.

만 灣 〈작은〉 a bay; 〈큰〉 a gulf; 〈입구〉 an inlet ♦ 울산만 Ulsan Bay; the Bay of Ulsan / 멕시코 만 the Gulf of Mexico / 페르시아 만 Persian Gulf / 만을 이루다 form a gulf [bay]

만 萬 ten thousand; 〈다수〉 a myriad

> 解說 영어에는 '만'에 해당하는 말이 없으므로 1000의 10배」로 생각하고 ***ten thousand*** 라고 말한다. '2만'은 ***twenty thousand***이라고 한다.

♦ 몇만 tens of thousands 《of crowd》 / 만인 a myriad of people; all the people / 만분의 일 a ten-thousandth / 만에 하나(라도) one in a thousand; very rarely; by any chance
▶ 그들은 은행에서 1만 달러를 훔쳤다 They stole ten thousand dollars [《俗》 ten grand] from the bank.
▶ 만에 하나라도 네가 성공하리라고 생각하니? Do you think you will succeed by any chance?
▶ 선생님의 은혜는 만분의 일이라도 갚겠습니다 I would dearly wish to pay back even an infinitesimal part of your kindness to me.
▶ 이것은 축척 2만분의 1짜리 한국 지도다 This is a Korean map on the scale of 1 to 20,000.

만 〈독일의 소설가・평론가〉 Mann, Thomas (1875-1955)

만가 挽歌 〈애가〉 an elegy; a dirge; 〈장례의〉 a funeral song

만감 萬感 a crowd [flood] of emotions; all sorts of thoughts
▶ 나는 만감이 가슴에 북받쳤다 A thousand emotions filled my heart [crowded in on me]. ⇌ I was overwhelmed with a flood of emotions.

만강 萬康 peace ⇨ 만안(萬安)
만강 滿腔 full-heartedness; whole-heartedness
♦ 만강의 hearty; heartfelt; whole-hearted / 만강의 경의를 표하다 express one's whole-hearted [most sincere] respect(for, to) / 만강의 사의를 표하다 tender [express] one's heartfelt thanks; express (one's) deep gratitude
▶ 도와주신 데 대해 만강의 사의를 표하는 바입니다 I express my heartfelt thanks [deep gratitude] for your help.
만개 滿開 (in) full bloom
♦ 만개하다 be in [come into] full bloom
▶ 정원의 라일락이 머지 않아 만개할 것이다 The lilacs in the garden will soon be in full bloom [at their best].
만경 萬頃 a vast extent; an expanse (of water); a wide spread (of prairies); vastness; boundlessness; extensiveness
━창파 the boundless expanse of water
만고 萬古 〈옛날〉 remote [all] antiquity; time immemorial; 〈영원〉 eternity; perpetuity
♦ 만고의 진리 an eternal truth / 만고에 유례 없는 unique for all generations
━불멸 immortality; imperishability; eternity; everlastingness ━불변[불역(不易)] immutability; everlastingness; unchangeability : 만고 불변의 진리 immutable [eternal] truths [laws] ━불후(不朽) imperishability; remaining intact [undecayed] forever : 만고 불후의 명작 an immortal masterpiece [work] ━절담(絶談) an immortal saying; an unchangeable maxim ━절색 a matchless [peerless] beauty; the fairest of the fair; an unsurpassed beauty ━절창(絶唱) an unparalleled singer
만고풍상 萬古風霜 all kinds of hardships and privations
♦ 만고풍상을 다 겪다 undergo [suffer, experience] all kinds [sorts] of hardships (and privations); taste all bitters of life; go through the ups and downs of life
만곡 彎曲 a curve; a crook; a bend; a bow; curvature; flection
━만곡하다 curved; crooked; bent; bowed; sinuous; 〈무릎이〉 bandy; 〔數〕 tortuous
♦ 도로가 급히 만곡한 곳 a sharp curve [bend] in the road
■ ━척추━ the curvature of the spine; spinal curvature ━부 〈무릎 등의〉 a genu [dʒíːnjuː] (pl. genua); 〈강의〉 a bend; 〈밑바닥의〉 a bilge : 만곡부 용골 a bilge keel ━성 근시 〔醫〕 curvature myopia [maióupiə] ━수(手) 〔醫〕 a clubhand ━제어 〔電〕 bulge control
만구 灣口 the mouth [entrance] of a bay; a baymouth ━사주(砂洲) a baymouth bar
만국 萬國 all countries (on earth); world nations; all nations; the (whole) world
♦ 만국의 universal; international
▶ 이 기호는 만국 공통이다 This symbol is common to all nations [universal].
■ ━공통어 an international language ━미터동맹 the *International Meter Group* (略 IMG) ━박람회 an international exposition; a world('s) fair ━신호 the international code signals ━우편연합 the *Universal Postal Union* (略 UPU) ━우편조약 the Universal Postal Convention ━음성기호 the *international phonetic alphabet* (略 IPA) ━저작권조약 the Universal Copyright Convention ━전신부호 *International Code* ━평화회의 the International Peace Conference ━표준시 *universal (standard) time* (略 UT)
만국기 萬國旗 the flags of all nations; (총칭) 〈장식용〉 bunting ♦ 만국기를 매단 운동장 the playground decked with bunting
만금 萬金 an immense sum of money
♦ 만금을 투자하다 invest an immense sum (in) / 만금으로도 비꿀 수 없다 be invaluable; be priceless
만기 滿期 expiration (of a term); expiry (of a contract); 〈어음의〉 maturity (略 mat.)
♦ 만기가 되다 〈어음 등의〉 mature; fall [be, become] due; 〈임기의〉 expire; 〈복무의〉 complete one's term of service; serve (out) one's time / 만기 전에 prior to the expiration of the period; before the full term is up
▶ 그 계약은 이달 말로 만기가 된다 The contract runs out at the end of this month.
▶ 선생님의 생명보험(계약)은 3월 말에 만기가 됩니다 The term of your life insurance (contract) expires on the last day of March.
▶ 이 채권은 5년 있으면 만기가 된다 This bond matures in five years.
▶ 임대차 계약이 만기가 되었다 The lease has expired.
▶ 그는 형기가 만기가 되었다 He served out his sentence.
■ ━배당 〔保險〕 a maturity dividend ━병(兵) a time-expired soldier ━상환 redemption at [on] maturity ━석방 release (of a prisoner) on the expiration of the prison term [period of punishment] ━어음 a matured bill ━일 the expiration date; 〈어음의〉 the day [date] of maturity; the due date ━제대 an honorable discharge; discharge on expiration of term of service
만끽하다 滿喫 〈마음껏 먹다[마시다]〉 have [eat, drink] enough [one's fill] (of); eat [drink] to one's heart's content; 〈충분히 즐기다〉 enjoy fully [to the full]
▶ 지난 일요일 나는 시골에 가서 봄을 만끽했다 Last Sunday I enjoyed spring in the countryside to the full.
▶ 저 음식점에서는 본바닥 중국 음식을 만끽할 수 있다 We can have our fill of genuine Chinese food at that restaurant.
만나다 1 〈사람을 대하다〉 see; meet; 〈마주치다〉 meet (with); come across [upon]; encounter; 〈손님을 맞다〉 receive

---

解說 meet는 처음 만나알다는 의미 말고도, 약속하고 만나는 경우나 우연히 만나는 경우에 다 쓰인다. see는 꼭 시간·장소를 정하지 않고 우연히 잠깐 만나는 것을 의미하는 때가 많다. meet는 대화를 하는 것을 암시하며, see는 실제로 대화를 하는 경우와 단순히 보기만 하는 경우에 모두 쓰인다. 오래간만에 만나는 경우에는 meet 보다는 see를 쓴다.

♦만난 적도 없는 사람 a complete [total] stranger / 애인을 만나다 have a rendezvous with *one's* sweetheart / 두 사람을 만나게 해주다 arrange a meeting between the two [two persons]/ 만나러 가다[오다] go [come] to see [meet] *sb*; go [come] (and) see *sb* (▶go [come] (and) see의 표현은 go나 come이 원형일 경우에만 씀)/ 다시 만나다 meet again / 우연히 만나다 come [run, fall] across *sb*; meet up with *sb*; happen to meet
▶만나서 반갑습니다 Glad [Pleased, Nice] to meet you. (▶두번째 만날 때부터는 see를 씀)
▶나중에[내일] 또 만납시다 See you later [again tomorrow].
▶얼마나 만나고 싶었는지 모르겠습니다 I have missed you very badly.
▶나는 그를 역에서 만나기로 했다 I've arranged to meet him at the station.
▶요즘 그를 통 만나지 못했다 I have seen nothing of him lately.
▶나는 내일 친구를 만난다 I'm seeing [meeting] a friend tomorrow. (▶이 표현은 미리 약속을 한 경우이며, I'm going to see [meet]...는 단순한 현재의 의도를 나타냄)
▶이 공원은 젊은 두 사람이 늘 만나던 곳이었다 This park was the young couple's usual rendezvous [where the young couple always met].
▶그 사람과 어제 커피숍에서 만났다 I met him at a coffee shop yesterday.
▶사람은 만나면 헤어지는 법 To meet is to part. ⇌ We meet only to part.
▶[會話]「안녕하세요, 김선생?」「박선생, 여기서 만나다니요!」 "Hello, Mr. Kim." "Fancy meeting you here, Mr. Park!"
▶나는 길에서 우연히 친구를 만났다 I came across [happen to meet] a friend of mine on the street.
▶나는 오늘 아침 엘리베이터에서 네 동생을 만났어 I met your brother in the elevator this morning.
▶손님들을 응접실에서 만나겠다 I'll receive my guests in the parlor.
2 〈회견하다〉 interview; have an interview 《with》
▶우리 회사 기자가 국무총리를 만났다 Our reporter interviewed the Prime Minister.
▶나는 내일 기자들을 만나겠다 I will give an interview to the pressmen tomorrow.
3 〈회합하다〉 meet 《with》; get together 《with》; gather
▶동급생들이 10년만에 만났다 Our classmates met (together) for the first time in ten years.
▶그 클럽 회원들은 한 달에 한 번씩 만난다 The club members meet [get together] once a month.
▶우리 다섯 사람은 박여사 댁에서 만나 서예 연습을 했다 Five of us gathered at Mrs. Park's to practice calligraphy.
4 〈알게 되다〉 become [get] acquainted 《with》; get [come] to know; come in contact 《with》
▶그녀와 나는 만난지 오래 되었다 She and I have been long acquainted (with each other).
▶나는 우연히 그녀를 만나 결국 결혼했다 I picked an acquaintance with her and succeeded in marriage.
▶그녀석과 만난 것이 내 불운의 시초였다 Getting acquainted with him was the beginning of my bad luck.
5 〈부딪치다·당하다〉 meet (with) (▶with는 좋지 않은 일을 만날 경우에 씀); come upon [across]; encounter
♦장애[적군]를 만나다 encounter an obstacle [the enemy (troops)] / 폭풍우를 만나다 〈사람이〉 be caught in a storm; 〈장소가〉 be visited [struck, hit, swept] by a storm
▶나는 집에 돌아오는 길에 소나기를 만났다 I was caught in a shower on my way home.
▶교통 체증을 만났다 I was stuck in a traffic jam. (▶회화체에서는 was 대신에 got이 쓰이기도 함)
▶우리는 예상치 못한 난관을 만났다 We ran up against an unforeseen difficulty.
6 〈얻어걸리다〉 find
♦하숙[호텔]을 잘 만나다 find a good boarding house [hotel]
▶나는 좋은 일거리를 만났다 I have found a good job. ⇌ A nice job has fallen [come] my way.
7 〈교차하다〉 cross; intersect; 〈합쳐지다〉 join
♦두 선이 만나는 점 the junction of two lines; the point of intersection
▶미주리 강은 미시시피 강과 만난다 The Missouri meets the Mississippi.
▶그 마을은 그 두 길이 만나는 지점에 있다 The village is situated at the junction of the two roads.
▶거기서 본류와 지류가 만난다 The main stream and a branch converge there.
만난 萬難 thousand and one difficulties; all obstacles [hindrances]
♦만난을 무릅쓰고 at any cost; at all costs [risks, hazards]; through thick and thin; in the face of all difficulties; come hell and high water / 만난을 무릅쓰다 surmount [overcome] all difficulties
▶나는 만난을 무릅쓰고 그 일을 해내겠다 I will carry it out at any cost [all costs].
만날 all the time; always; constantly; every day ♦만날 서로 싸우다 quarrel with each other all the time
▶만날 비가 온다 It rains continuously.
▶그 친구는 만날 허풍만 떤다 He always talks big.
▶그 사람은 만날 지각이다 He always comes late.
▶이런 일은 만날 있는 것이 아니다 Such things do not occur every day.
만남 〈회합〉 a meeting; 〈조우〉 an encounter; 〈면회〉 an interview; 〈밀회〉 a date
♦운명적인 만남 a fateful encounter
▶그이와의 만남이 내 운명을 결정지었다 The encounter with him decided my fate.
만년 晩年 *one's* later [last, declining] years; the latter part of *one's* life; the close [evening] of *one's* life [days]; *one's* closing days
♦만년의 김 교수 Professor Kim in his later

만년 years / 만년에 late in life; in the evening of one's life; in one's latter [later, last] days; in the sunset of one's life / 만년을 불우하게 보내다 live the rest of one's life in obscurity / 만년에 접어들다 enter the twilight of one's life ▶이 그림은 그의 만년의 작품이다 He painted this picture in his later years. ▶그 여인은 만년을 행복하게 보냈다 She was happy in her last years. ▶그는 만년에 가서야 성공했다 It was only late in life that he achieved success.

만년 萬年 〈1만년〉 ten thousand years; 〈영구〉 eternity; perpetuity
♦만년지계(萬年之計) a plan for the ages / 만년저택(宅) a substantial building; a strongly-built house
▶그는 만년 평사원이다 He is a permanent [eternal] clerk.
▶그는 만년 조교수로 끝날 것이다 He'll be an assistant professor forever.
■—강사 a (university) instructor who never gets promoted to professorship —야당 the perennial opposition —조수 an assistant never promoted —처녀 a fadeless beauty; a perennially youthful woman —청년 a man of perennial [ageless] youth —후보 a candidate who always fails of election; an ever unsuccessful candidate

만년빙 萬年氷 〔地〕 polar icecaps
만년설 萬年雪 perpetual [eternal, permanent] snow (field); 〈높은 산의〉 an icecap
♦극지(極地)의 만년설 polar icecaps
▶이 지방에는 꼭대기가 만년설로 뒤덮여 있는 높은 산이 많다 In this district there are many high mountains with perpetual snow on their tops.

만년필 萬年筆 a fountain pen
♦만년필에 잉크를 넣다 fill [refill] a fountain pen
▶그 만년필은 잉크가 샌다 The fountain pen has a bad leak.
▶이 만년필은 잘 써진다 This fountain pen writes smoothly.
▶만년필 뚜껑을 꼭 닫아 두어라 Don't forget to cap the fountain pen.

만능 萬能 omnipotence; almightiness
♦만능의 all-powerful; omnipotent; almighty; 〈다재다능한〉 all-round; (美) all-around / 황금만능의 mammonish / 기계 만능의 시대 the age of machinery
▶그 사람은 만능이다 He can manage everything.
▶지금은 황금만능의 세상이다 Money is everything [rules the world] nowadays.
▶돈이 만능이 아니다 Wealth is not everything.
■—공(工) an all-round mechanic —공구 an all-purpose tool —밀링 장치 universal milling attachment —선수 an all-round [(美) all-around] player [athlete] —약 a cure-all ⇨ 만병 (~통치약) —연삭기 (硏削機) a universal grinding machine —재료 시험기 a universal material testing machine —코일 a universal coil

만다라 曼陀羅 〔佛敎〕 Mandala [<Skt]
만단 萬端 everything; all; all sorts of affairs; 〈방법〉 every possible means
♦만단의 준비를 갖추다 make every preparation; get everything ready
▶만단의 준비가 다 갖추어졌다 Every preparation is made. ⇒ Every detail is carefully arranged. ⇒ Everything is ready [(美) O.K.]

만담 漫談 a gag; a joke; a comic dialog [chat] —만담하다 gag; tell a comic story; give [deliver] a comic monologue; have a comic chat
■—가 a gagster; a gagman; a professional comic storyteller [chat artiste]

만당 滿堂 the whole house [hall, company]; all the audience [assemblage]
만대 萬代 all ages [generations]; eternity
♦만대에 for all ages; forever; everlastingly; eternally / 〈위업이〉 만대에 전해지다 be remembered for ages to come; live forever on the lips of people
▶그의 이름은 만대에 전해질 것이다 His name shall endure for ages.

만돌린 〔樂〕 a mandolin(e)
♦만돌린을 타다 play (on) the mandolin
■—연주자 a mandolinist

만두 饅頭 a dumpling; a bun stuffed with seasoned meat and vegetables
♦만두를 빚다 make a stuffed bun
■—고기— a meat bun; a bun with meat stuffing 군— a fried dumpling 물— a boiled meat dumpling 찐— a steamed dumpling 팥— a bean-jam bun —가게 a bun shop —국 dumpling soup —소 (a) bun filling [stuffing]

만두사주 灣頭砂洲 〔地〕 a bayhead bar
만득 晚得 〈만년에 자식을 낳음〉 begetting a child in one's later years; 〈만년에 낳은 자식〉 a child begotten in one's later years
—만득하다 beget [procreate] a child in one's later years

만들다 1 〈창작·창조하다〉 make; create; invent
♦노래를 만들다 compose a song / 신어[새로운 표현]를 만들다 coin [invent] a new word [expression] / 영화를 만들다 make [produce] a film / 점토상(像)을 만들다 mold a clay figure
▶신이 인간[세상]을 만드셨다 God made man [created the world].
▶그는 새로운 형식의 텔레비전 드라마를 만들었다 He created [originated] a new style in television dramas.
▶그는 이런 형태의 열쇠를 처음 만든 사람이다 He was the first to make this type of key.
2 〈제조·가공하다〉 make; manufacture; produce

> 解說 *make*는 꽤짝, 의자, 책상, 가구 등 이동 가능한 정도의 물건을 만든다는 의미의 가장 일반적인 말. *manufacture*는 기계를 사용하여 제품을 대규모로 제조하는 것을 의미하며 *produce*는 판매를 목적으로 상품을 대량 생산하는 것을 의미한다.

♦ 공들여 만들다 make *sth* carefully; elaborate / 자동차를 만들다 produce [manufacture] automobiles / 나무로 책상을 만들다 make [fashion] a desk of wood / 달걀로 케이크를 만들다 make a cake with eggs (▶ with is 재료의 일부분을 나타냄) / 플라스틱으로 여러 가지 그릇을 만들다 make plastic into various kinds of containers / 딸에게 드레스를 만들어 주다 make a dress for *one's* daughter
▶ 저 회사에서는 무엇을 만듭니까? What does that company produce [manufacture]?
▶ 책은 종이[유리]로 만든다 Books are made of paper [Glass is made from sand]. (▶ 원칙상 재료의 질이 변하는 경우는 from, 변하지 않는 경우는 of를 씀)
▶ 어머니가 내게 스커트를 만들어 주셨다 Mother made me a skirt. ⇌ Mother made a skirt for me.
▶ 그 서랍장은 잘 만들었다 This chest of drawers is well made.
▶ 會話「손잡이는 무엇으로 만드실 겁니까?」「나무로요」 "What are you going to make the handle of?" "Of wood."
3 〈건설·건조하다〉 make; build; erect; put up; construct
♦ 도로를 만들다 build [construct] a road / 배를 만들다 build a ship / 보금자리를 만들다 build a nest / 정원[공원]을 만들다 lay out a garden [park]
▶ 새 고속도로를 만드는 중이다 A new expressway is now under construction.
▶ 우리는 지금 대형 유조선을 만들고 있다 We are building a supertanker right now.
4 〈양조하다〉 make; brew; distill
♦ 맥주를 만들다 brew beer / 쌀로 술을 만들다 make wine from rice
▶ 원유를 정제하여 가솔린으로 만든다 Crude oil distilled into gasoline.
▶ 위스키는 곡식을 증류하여 만든다 Whiskey is distilled from grain.
5 【작성하다】 make; draw up; 〈청구서·표 등을〉 make out
♦ 예산안[예정표]을 만들다 draw up a budget [prepare a schedule] / 연설 초고를 만들다 make [prepare] a draft of the speech / 청구서[지원자 명단]를 만들다 make out the bill [a list of applicants] / 프로그램을 만들다 prepare a program 《for》
▶ 우리는 계약서를 만들어야 합니다 We must make [draw up] a contract.
6 〈주조하다〉 cast; strike; mint
♦ 주화를 만들다 strike [mint] coins; coin money / 청동으로 동상을 만들다 cast a statue in bronze
7 〈형성하다〉 form; make; shape
▶ 스포츠는 젊은이들의 인격을 만들어 준다 Sports form [shape] the character of young people.
▶ 좋은 선생님은 어린아이의 성격을 만드는 데 도움을 준다 A good teacher helps (to) build up a child's character.
8 〈조직·구성하다〉 organize; form; set up
♦ 조합을 만들다 form a union / 새 가정을 만들다 make a new home / 협회를 만들다 organize a society [an association] / 야구팀을 만들다 organize [form] a baseball team 《of twenty members》 / 4열(列)을 만들다 form fours / 두세 명씩 그룹을 만들다 form groups of two or three
▶ 인간은 사회를 만든다 Men form a society.
▶ 그들 네 사람은 새 회사를 만들었다 The four of them established a new company.
9 〈양성하다〉 foster; cultivate; build (up)
♦ 좋은 후계자를 만들다 train a good successor / 인물[선량한 시민]을 만들다 build up [train] a man of talent [good citizens]
10 〈장만·마련하다〉 make; get
♦ 규칙을 만들다 make [lay down] a rule / 일정 기준을 만들다 establish a standard / 선례를 만들다 set [create] a precedent / 돈[운동자금]을 만들다 raise money [funds for a campaign] / 재산을 만들다 make a fortune / 친구[적]를 만들다 make a friend [an enemy] / 시간을 만들다 manage to find time; make time 《to do》
▶ 나는 다음 주까지 500만원을 만들어야 한다 I have to raise five million won by next week.
▶ 자네들이 (그를) 만날 기회를 만들어 주겠네 I will make an opportunity for you to meet (him).
11 〈상처 등을 내다〉 wound; injure
♦ 예쁜 얼굴에 흠집을 만들다 disfigure [mar] the beautiful face
12 〈조작하다〉 make up; invent; fabricate
♦ 그럴 듯한 구실을 만들다 make up [concoct, invent] a good [convincing] excuse
▶ 그거 그녀석이 만들어낸 이야기 아냐? Isn't that a story invented by him?
▶ 會話「정당한 이유가 없는데」「그럼 하나 만들어」 "I have no real excuse." "Invent one, then."
13 〈조리하다〉 prepare 《food》; fix; cook (▶ cook은 열을 가해서 요리할 경우에만 씀)
♦ 샐러드를 만들다 make [fix] salad / 스튜를 만들다 make stew
▶ 우리 어머니는 케이크를 잘 만드신다 My mother is good at baking cakes.
▶ 맛있는 것을 만들어 드리지요 I'll prepare something nice for you [get you something nice].
14 〈…이 되게 하다〉 make; 〈…으로 바꾸다〉 change [turn, convert] 《into》
♦ 소년을 선원[사나이]으로 만들다 make a sailor [man] (out) of a boy ⇌ make a boy a sailor [man] / 아들을 가르쳐 변호사를 만들다 train *one's* son to be a lawyer / 황무지를 개간하여 밀밭을 만들다 turn barren land into wheat fields / 밥으로 죽을 만들다 turn rice into gruel / 사람을 행복하게[부자로] 만들다 make *sb* happy [rich] / 사람을 불구로 만들다 cripple [deform] *sb* / 사람을 바보로 만들다 make a fool of *sb* / 물건을 돈으로 만들다 turn [convert] goods into money
▶ 열은 물을 수증기로 만든다 Heat turns water into vapor.
▶ 그는 아들을 시인으로 만들었다 He made his son a poet [made a poet of his son].
▶ 이 대답이 그를 노하게 만들었다 This answer

made him angry.
15 〈…하게 하다〉 make [have] 《sb do》; get [induce, cause, force] 《sb to do》
♦ 가게[믿게] 만들다 make sb go [believe (in)] / 서명하게 만들다 force sb to sign 《the paper》
▶ 그 여자는 그를 그곳에 가게 만들었다 She made him go there.
▶ 그들은 그에게 강제로 그 일을 하게 만들었다 They forced him to do the work.

만듦새 〈만들어진 본새〉 make; workmanship; craft(s)manship
♦ 만듦새가 좋은 가구 furniture of good make / 만듦새가 최고급인 옷 a coat of (a) first-class make / 만듦새가 좋은 of fine [exquisite] workmanship / 만듦새가 좋은 beautifully made 《brooches》 / 만듦새가 나쁜 of poor workmanship
▶ 만듦새가 좋지 않군 The make is poor. ⇌ It is of poor make.

만료 滿了 expiration 《of a term》; termination 《of office》
♦ 계약[임기]의 만료 the termination of an agreement [one's office] / 기한 만료일 the expiration date / 임기 만료일 the date of termination of one's office
▶ 그는 임기 만료 전에 사망했다 He died before the term was up.
▶ 계약 만료시에 지급해 드리겠습니다 I will pay you at the end of the contract.
—**만료하다** expire; fall [become] due; complete
▶ 그의 대통령 임기는 내년 1월에 만료된다 His term of office as President will expire [come to an end] next January.

만루 滿壘 a full [loaded] base
♦ 만루에서 〔野〕 with the bases loaded / 만루를 만들다 fill the bases; (俗) load the sacks
▶ (2사) 만루다 The bases are full [loaded] (with two outs).
▶ 무사 만루에서 그가 홈런을 쳤다 He hit [swatted] a home run with the bases full [loaded] and none out.
■ —홈런 a homer [home run] with the bases full [loaded]; a grand slam(mer) [slam homer] / 역전 만루 홈런을 치다 hit a grand slam to win the losing game

만류 灣流 〈멕시코만류〉 the Gulf Stream
만류하다 挽留— detain; keep [hold] back 《sb from doing》; check; dissuade 《sb from doing》
♦ 타일러 만류하다 talk sb out of 《doing》 / 싸우지 말라고 만류하다 hold [dissuade] sb from fighting [wrangling] / 소매를 잡고 만류하다 detain sb by the sleeve / 사임을 만류하다 persuade sb not to resign; persuade [induce] sb to stay [remain] in office; dissuade sb from resigning
▶ 더는 만류하지 않겠습니다 I won't keep you any longer.
▶ 그녀는 어머니가 만류하는 것도 듣지 않고 집을 뛰쳐나갔다 She rushed out of the house in spite of her mother's efforts to dissuade her.

만리 萬里 a (very) long distance [way]
♦ 만릿길 a journey of ten thousand miles; 《have》 a long way to go / 만리 창파를 건너 오다 come from afar over the sea
▶ 그분들은 만릿길을 마다 않고 모두 와 주셨다 They all came despite the long [great] distance.
■ —장서(長書) a very long letter —장성(長城) the Great Wall 《of China》 —장천(長天) the (very) high (and vast) heavens

만만하다 滿滿— full of 《ambition》; filled with 《courage》; brimming with 《vigor》
♦ 불평만만하다 be thoroughly discontented / 야심만만하다 be full of [bubbling over with] ambition; be highly ambitious / 자신만만하다 be full of self-confidence / 패기만만하다 be highly ambitious; be full of go [(口) pep]; be brimming with enterprise
▶ 그는 자신만만했다 He was full of [brimming with] self-confidence.
▶ 그는 투지만만하게 시합에 임했다 He took part in the match in full [full of] fighting spirit.
▶ 나는 아주 자신만만하게 시험을 보았다 I took the examination with all the self-confidence in the world.

만만하다 1 〈연하다〉 soft; tender; pliable; supple
2 〈다루기 쉽다〉 easy to deal with; docile; tactable; easily manageable
♦ 만만한 사람 a person easy to deal with; 《美口》 an easy mark; (口) a pushover / 만만한 일 an easy job / 만만찮은 문제 no easy matter / 만만찮은 적수 a formidable adversary / 만만찮은 상대를 만나다 catch a Tartar
▶ 그 녀석은 만만치가 않아 He is a hard [tough] fellow. = He is hard to deal with. ⇌ He is a tough [an ugly] customer.
▶ 내가 만만하게 보이니? Do you see [Is there] any green in my eye?
3 〈대수롭지 않다〉 insignificant; slight; of no account [importance]; negligible; trivial
♦ 만만찮은 적 no common enemy / 만만하게 보다[여기다] 〈사람을〉 hold sb cheap; make little [light] of sb; 〈일을〉 treat sth as of little account
▶ 그 사람을 만만하게 보지 마라 Don't underestimate him.
▶ 그분은 만만한 학자가 아니다 He is no mean scholar.
▶ 그것은 만만하게 여길 일이 아니다 That is not a matter to be slighted [taken light of].

만면 滿面 the whole face
♦ 만면에 웃음을 띠고 with a broad smile; smiling all over one's face
▶ 그는 만면에 붉게 노기를 띠었다 He was red with indignation. ⇌ His face was flushed with anger.
▶ 그 학생은 만면에 웃음을 띠고 시험장에서 나왔다 The student came out of the examination hall all smiles.
—**만면하다** ♦ 희색이 만면하여 with one's face beaming with joy
▶ 그는 희색이 만면했다 He was all smiles. ⇌ His pleasure showed clearly on his face.

▶ 그는 희색이 만면해서 돌아왔다 He came back beaming with joy [smiling all over].
■ —수색(愁色) a face full of anxiety : 만면 수색이다 be full of anxiety [worry] —수참(羞慚) a face filled with shame : 만면수참하다 be filled with shame
만목 蔓木 〔植〕〈덩굴나무〉a winder; a liana; a liane
만무하다 萬無— cannot be; be impossible [unbelievable]; it is utterly impossible [not likely at all] that...; it is out of the question that...; there is no reason why...
▶ 그것은 사실일 리가 만무하다 It cannot be true.
▶ 그녀가 그런 짓을 했을 리 만무하다 She cannot have done such a thing.
▶ 그 사람이 기차를 놓쳤을 리가 만무하다 It is impossible that he should have missed the train.
▶ 그 여자가 그것을 썼을 리는 만무하다 It is not likely at all that she should have written it.
▶ 그것이 저절로 깨질 리가 만무하다 It cannot break of itself.
만문 漫文 〈수필〉a desultory essay; 〈만필〉jottings
만물 萬物 all things (under the sun);〈피조물〉all creation
▶ 천지[우주] 만물 all things in the universe; the whole creation
▶ 인간은 만물의 영장이다 Man is lord of creation.
▶ 만물은 유전(流轉)한다 All things change.
■ —박사 a well-informed person; a walking dictionary; a pantologist —상(商) a general [convenience] shop [store]
만민 萬民 all the people
만반 萬般 all things [affairs]; everything; all sorts (of matters)
♦ 만반의 all; every / 만반의 준비[태세]를 갖추다 make full [thorough] preparations; get everything in readiness 《for》
▶ 만반의 채비가 갖춰졌다 Arrangements are fully made in every respect.
만반진수 滿盤珍羞 a groaning table [board]; rich and dainty food
▶ 상다리가 휘도록 만반진수가 차려져 있다 The table literally groaned with food.
만발 滿發 full bloom
—만발하다 be in full bloom [blossom, flower]; bloom all over
♦ 꽃이 만발한 초원 a meadow spread with flowers
▶ 식물원에는 각종 꽃들이 온통 만발해 있다 A variety of flowers are in their glory [are in full bloom, have bloomed fully] all over the botanical garden.
만방 萬方 all directions; every way; all possible means
▶ 만방으로 진력하다 make every effort; exert *oneself* to the utmost / 만방으로 손을 쓰다 try all [every] means possible [available]
▶ 그 사상은 만방으로 전파되었다 The idea spread in all directions.

만방 萬邦 all the countries of the world; all nations [(the) countries] on earth
▶ 그 작품으로 그는 만방에 명성을 떨쳤다 That piece made his name known all over the world.
만백성 萬百姓 all the people; the whole nation
만병 萬病 all (kinds of) diseases [maladies]
▶ 감기는 만병의 근원이다 A cold may lead to [develop into] all kinds of diseases [illness].
만병초 萬病草 〔植〕a rhododendron; an alpine rose
만병통치약 萬病通治藥 a cure-all; a heal-all; a (universal) panacea; a universal remedy
▶ 이 세상에 만병통치약이란 없다 There is no cure-all in the world.
만복 萬福 blessedness; all kinds of good luck
▶ 만복을 빕니다 I wish you every happiness in the world.
▶ 귀댁의 만복을 기원합니다 I pray for all blessings on your family.
▶ 소문만복래(笑門萬福來) (속담) Fortune comes in by a merry gate. ⇒ Fortune comes to a merry home. ⇒ Laugh and be [grow] fat.
만복 滿腹 a full stomach [belly]; satiety
♦ 만복이 되게 먹다 eat *one's* fill; eat heartily
▶ 만복시에는 뛰지[심한 운동은 하지] 않는 것이 You had better not run [do heavy exercise] on [with] a full stomach.
■ —감 a feeling of fullness 《after a meal》: 만복감을 주는 식사 a filling meal
만부득이 萬不得已 unavoidably ⇨ 부득이(不得已)
만분지일 萬分之一 〈아주 조금〉▶ 은혜의 만분지일이라도 보답하겠습니다 I will do my bit, however little, to repay your kindness.
▶ 은혜를 만분지일이라도 갚을 수 있었으면 좋겠습니다 I wish I could do even a little to repay your kindness.
만사 萬事 all; everything (in the world); all (sort of) things [affairs, matters]
♦ 만사에 in all things / 〈세상〉만사가 뜻대로 된다면 if ifs and ans were pots and pans
▶ 만사 오케이다 All is well. ⇒ Everything is all right [O.K.].
▶ 만사가 잘[잘못]되었다 Everything went well [badly].
▶ 만사 잘 부탁합니다 I will leave everything to you. ⇒ See that all is well.
▶ 만사 형통하시기를 빕니다 I wish everything goes well with you. ⇒ May fortune attend you!
▶ 인간 만사 새옹지마(塞翁之馬)다 Inscrutable are the ways of Heaven.
▶ 그는 만사 태평이다 He is perfectly carefree. ⇒ It looks as if there were nothing to trouble him.
▶ 만사 제쳐놓고 참석해 주시기 바랍니다 I beg you will kindly favor us with your company.
▶ 만사에 조심해라 You must be careful in every respect.
만삭 滿朔 〈해산달이 참〉parturiency; completion of time for childbirth;〈해산 달〉the last

month of pregnancy; the month of parturition
♦ 만삭이 된 여자 a parturient woman; a woman near her time / 만삭이 되다 come to one's time (of parturition)
▶ 그 여자는 지금 만삭이다 Her time (of childbirth) is near. ⇌ She is near her time (of childbirth).

만산 滿山 the whole hill [mountain]; all the hills
▶ 만산에 신록이 우거져 있다 All the mountains are robed in fresh verdure.
▶ 만산이 단풍으로 덮여 있다 The whole hill is covered [dressed up] with red leaves.
—**만산하다** (blossoms) cover the whole hill [mountain]

만석꾼 萬石— a wealthy [millionaire, many-acred] landlord

만성 晩成 slow to mature [develop]; maturing late; being slow in maturing
▶ 대기만성(大器晩成) Great talents mature late.
—**만성하다** mature late; be slow in maturing

만성 慢性 chronicity; (being) chronic
♦ 만성의[적] chronic; confirmed; inveterate / 만성적 실업 chronic unemployment / 만성이 되다 become chronic
▶ 내 콧병은 만성이 되었다 My nose trouble has become chronic.
▶ 불경기가 만성이 되어가고 있다 The recession [business slump] is becoming chronic.
▶ 그는 만성 조울증 환자다 He is a chronic manic-depressive.
■ —위장병 inveterate [confirmed] dyspepsia —인플레이션 chronic inflation —전염병 a chronic infectious disease —중독 chronicity poisoning —환자 a chronic [an established] invalid

만성병 慢性病 a chronic disease
▶ 그는 만성병을 앓고 있다 He is suffering from a chronic disease.
■ —환자 a chronic [an established] invalid

만세 萬歲 1 〈만년〉 ten thousand years; all ages; eternity
2 〈외침 소리〉 cheers; hurrah; hurray; rah
♦ 만세 삼창을 하다 give three cheers ((for)); give cheers three times (▶ Hip, hip, hurray!를 세번 반복함)/ 만세를 부르다 hurrah ((for)); cry [shout] hurrah; give cheers ((for))
▶ 만세! 우리가 이겼다 We won, hurray!
▶ 국왕 만세! Long live [reign] the King!
▶ 대한민국[프랑스] 만세! Vive la Korea [France]!
■ —력 a perpetual calendar

만수 滿水 ♦ 만수가 되다 be filled (to the brim) with water
▶ 저수지가 만수(가 되었)다 The reservoir is filled to capacity. ⇌ The dam is now full of water.

만수무강 萬壽無疆 a long life; longevity
▶ 만수무강하시기를 빕니다 Long life to you!
—**만수무강하다** live long; enjoy longevity; live to a great age

만시지탄 晩時之歎 repenting of one's missing a chance ♦ 만시지탄은 있지만 though it is rather too late

만신 滿身 the whole body ♦ 만신에 all over (the body); from head to foot
▶ 그는 만신에 햇빛을 쬐며 바닷가 모래밭에 누워 있었다 He was lying on the sandy beach exposing his whole body to the sunshine.

만신창이 滿身瘡痍 being covered all over with wounds
▶ 그는 만신창이가 되었다 He had wounds all over his body. ⇌ He was wound all over.

만심 慢心 self-conceit; pride
♦ 만심을 갖다 be [get] proud; be self-conceited; (口) have a swelled head; be puffed up / 작은 성공으로 만심을 갖다 conceit oneself over minor successes
▶ 성공에 만심을 갖지 마라 Don't be too proud of your success.
▶ 그는 자신의 재능에 만심을 갖고 있다 He is too proud of his talent.
▶ 그들은 승리로 만심을 품고 있다 They are puffed up with victory.

만안 萬安 peace; tranquil(l)ity; security; health ▶ 댁내의 만안을 빕니다 I wish you and your family every peace and prosperity. ⇌ I offer prayers for peace and prosperity to your family.

만약 萬若 if ⇨ 만일

만연 蔓延 spread(ing); prevalence; diffusion
♦ 질병의 만연을 막다 prevent [check] the spread of a disease
▶ 위생 당국은 콜레라의 만연을 막기 위해 전력을 다했다 The sanitary authorities did their utmost to prevent the spread of cholera.
▶ 그 항구 도시에는 독감 만연의 징후가 있다 There are signs of influenza spreading in the port town.
—**만연하다** spread; prevail; diffuse; be widespread [prevalent]
▶ 악[오염]이 만연하다 vice [pollution] thrives [is widespread] (in)
▶ 유행병과 기근이 그 지방에 만연하고 있다 Pestilence and famine stalk the area.
▶ 수원 일대에 독감이 만연하고 있다 Influenza [The flu] is sweeping (over) [running riot in] Suwon.

만용 蠻勇 brute courage; foolhardiness; savage valor; barbaric vigor; recklessness
♦ 만용을 부리다 show reckless valor; display a reckless courage
▶ 그들은 만용을 부려 적진으로 쳐들어갔다[적지로 뛰어들었다] With brute courage [reckless valor] they charged on the enemy camp [marched into enemy territory].

만우절 萬愚節 April [All] Fools' Day
♦ 만우절 바보 an April fool
▶ 나는 만우절에 속았다 I was made an April fool.

만원 滿員 no vacancy; 〈극장의〉 a full [capacity] house; 〈교도소 등의〉 congestion
▶ 만원 지하철[버스] a crowded [packed, jam-packed, jammed, full] subway train [bus] (▶ packed, jam-packed, jammed는 crowded 보다 붐비는 정도가 더 심한 표현)/ 초만원이 되다[을 이루다] be overcrowded; be crowded beyond

capacity; be filled to bursting; be packed to (its) fullest capacity / 만원 사례의 성황을 이루다 bring in [play to] a capacity audience
▶ 만원사례 (게시) 〈극장의〉 Full house; 〈매진〉 Sold out; 〈열차·엘리베이터 등의〉 Car full; 〈호텔 등의〉 No vacancy
▶ 좌석은 만원이었다 All the seats were taken. ⇒ There were no seat left.
▶ 그 영화관은 한달 동안 계속 만원이다 The movie theater has drawn great crowds for one month.
▶ 경기장은 관중으로 만원이었다 The stadium was filled to capacity with spectators.
▶ 열람실은 언제나 만원이다 The reading room is always well patronized.
▶ 호텔에 갔더니 만원이라고 들어오지 못하게 하더군 I went to the hotel, but they turned me away saying they had no vacancies.
■ㅡ청중[관객] a capacity [full] audience
ㅡ팻말 a sold-out [full-up] notice; a full-house notice; (美) an SRO sign (▶SRO는 standing room only (입석만 매진)의 약어) : 만원 팻말을 달다 put up a "Full up" notice

만월 滿月 a full moon
♦만월의 밤에 on a night with a full moon
▶오늘 밤은 만월이다 The moon is (at its) full tonight. ⇒ We have a full moon tonight.

만유 漫遊 a (leisurely) tour; a (pleasure) trip
♦세계 만유자 a globe trotter
▶일행은 세계 만유 여행을 떠났다 The party started on a (leisurely) tour of [pleasure trip around] the world.
ㅡ만유하다 make a tour 《of, through》; tour 《a country》
♦세계를 만유하다 make [go on] a (leisurely) tour of the world; tour the world (at leisure)
▶나는 작년에 미국을 만유했다 I made a leisurely tour of America last year.

만유신론 萬有神論 〔哲〕 pantheism ⇨ 범신론
만유인력 萬有引力 〔物〕 universal gravitation
♦만유인력의 법칙 the law of universal gravitation / 만유인력의 상수 the universal gravitational constant

만인 萬人 all (the) people; all sorts of people [men]; all men; everybody
♦만인이 인정하는 진리 (a) universal truth / 만인에게 알맞다 suit [satisfy, meet] all tastes; be suitable for every taste
▶그 여자는 만인의 사랑을 받는다 She is loved by [beloved of, beloved by] everybody.
▶그분이 위대한 정치가라는 것은 만인이 인정하는 일이다 It is known by everybody that he is a great statesman.
▶이 소설은 만인에게 맞는다 This novel satisfies all tastes.

만일 萬一 1 〈만약〉 if; 〈…의 경우에는〉 in case 《of》; 〈…조건으로〉 provided [supposing] 《that》; 〈어쩌다가〉 by any chance
2 〈현재·미래의 불확실한 사실을 나타냄〉
▶만일 내일 비가 오면 나는 외출하지 않겠다 If it rains tomorrow, I'll not go out. (▶단지 조건을 나타내므로 가정법은 쓰지 않음)
▶만일 그 사람이 오거든 기다리라고 해 주세요 If he comes, please have him wait.
▶만일 시간이 나면 거기에 가겠다 If I have any [some] free time, I'm going to go there. (▶some을 쓰는 경우는 여가 시간이 날 것을 예상하고 있음을 암시함)
▶만일 내가 늦으면 먼저 가세요 If I'm late, please go (on) ahead [without me].
▶만일 파업만 없으면 내일 돌아오겠습니다 I'll be back tomorrow unless there's [if there's not] a strike. (▶unless는 「…아닌 한」이라는 제외의 의미를 함축하여 if...not 보다 강조적임)
3 〈현재의 사실과 반대되는 가정을 나타냄〉
▶만일 돈이 넉넉하다면 그 컴퓨터를 살 수 있을 텐데 If I had enough money, I could buy the computer.
▶만일 그 친구가 여기 있다면 내가 도와줄텐데 If he were [Were he] here, I would help him.
▶내가 만일 너라면 그 일은 하지 않을 거다 If I were you, I wouldn't do that. (▶충고의 표현으로 직접 Don't do that.라고 하는 것보다 정중한 의미)
▶만일 내가 바쁘지 않으면 당신과 함께 가겠는데 If I was not busy, I'd come with you. (▶가정법 과거형에서 be동사는 were를 쓰지만 주어가 단수인 경우 일상회화에서는 was를 쓰는 수가 많음. 그러나 If I were you...와 같은 관용적 표현에서는 was는 비표준적이며, 또 Were I...의 형식에서도 was는 쓰이지 않음)
▶만일 공기가 없다면 우리는 살 수 없을 것이다 If it were not for [But for, Without, Were it not for] air, we could not live.
4 〈과거의 사실과 반대되는 가정을 나타냄〉
▶만일 내가 좀더 열심히 공부했더라면 시험에 합격했을 것이다 If you had studied [Had you studied] harder, you would have passed the examination.
▶만일 당신이 도와주지 않았더라면 나는 성공하지 못했을 겁니다 If it had not been for [But for, Without, Had it not been for] your help, I could not have succeeded.
▶만일 네가 온다는 것을 알았더라면 내가 집에 있었을텐데 If I had known [I'd have known] you came over, I'd have stayed (at) home.
5 〈실현성이 희박한 가정을 나타냄〉
▶만일 그녀를 만나게 되거든 내게 전화해 달라고 전해 주세요 If you should run into her, tell her to call me up. (▶가능성이 낮음을 특별히 나타내려고 할 때 외에는 간단히 If you run into her...와 같이 하는 것이 보통임)
▶만일 자네가 우리보다 먼저 거기에 도착하거든 밖에서 기다려라 If you should get there ahead of us, wait outside.
▶만일 내가 죽는다면 우리 가족은 어떻게 될까? If I were to [Were I to] die, what would become of my family? (▶were to를 쓰는 것이 should보다 불확실성을 나타내는 뜻이 강함)
6 〈확실히 하기〉 for confirmation; just to be [make] sure; 〈주의·대비를 위해〉 (just) in case; by way of (pre)caution
▶만일을 위해 우리는 서면으로 계약했다 We put the contract in writing for confirmation.
▶만일을 위해 나는 보험에 들었다 I am insured just in case.
▶만일을 위해 우산을 가지고 가거라 Take an umbrella with you just in case. (▶「비가 오면

안되니까)는 (just) in case it rains [should rain]와 같이 함)
▶ 만일을 위해 다시 한 번 말씀드립니다 Allow me to repeat it by way of precaution [for caution's sake].
▶ 會話 「의자는 40개면 충분하지 않을까요?」 「만일을 위해 한두 개 더 가져가시오」 "Won't forty chairs be enough?" "To be on the safe side, take one or two more."

7 〈긴급한·어려운 때[일]〉 (an) emergency; the worst; a rainy day; 〈뜻하지 않은 일〉 an unlikely event
♦ 만일의 경우에 in an emergency / 만일을 대하다 hope against hope; trust to luck / 만일에 대비하다 prepare for the worst; provide for a rainy day
▶ 만일의 경우에는 이 붉은 단추를 누르시오 Push this red button in an emergency.
▶ 내게 만일의 사태가 발생하면 내 돈은 모두 네 것이다 If the worst were to happen to me, all my money would be yours.
▶ 만일의 경우에는 즉시 내게 전화하시오 Call me immediately if anything (unexpected) should happen.
▶ 그는 만일을 믿고 큰 사업을 시작했다 Trusting to luck, he embarked on a great undertaking.
▶ 만일에 대비해서 나는 저축을 약간 하고 있다 I am saving a little money against a rainy day.
▶ 우리는 만일에 대비하지 않으면 안된다 We must provide for a rainy day [an emergency]. ⇒ We must prepare for the worst.

> 解說 *if*절은 미래를 표시하는 경우에도 미래시제는 쓰지 않지만 주어의 의지를 나타낼 때는 will, would를 쓴다: If you will [would] do so, I would be much obliged. 만일 그렇게 해 주신다면 대단히 감사하겠습니다 (※would는 정중한 표현임) 또 if절이 주절의 행위의 결과에 대해 말할 때는 will도 가능하다: If it will make you happier (as a result), I'll stay here. 그래서 당신이 행복하다면 내가 여기 머물겠소

만입 灣入 〔地〕 embayment; 〈해안선의〉 an indentation ─**만입하다** curve in; push a bay (into the land)
♦ 만입한 해안 an embayed shore
▶ 해안선이 만입해 있다 The coastline curves inward.

만자 卍字 a fylfot; a gammadion; 〔佛教〕 a swastika
■ ─기 the swastika flag ─무늬 a fylfot pattern ─창 a window with a swastika-shaped frame

만장 萬丈 〈길이의 만 길[발]〉 ten thousand *kil*[*pal*]; 〈아주 높음〉 unfathomable height
♦ 파란만장한 eventful; stormy; full of ups and downs
■ ─봉(峰) a lofty peak; an alp

만장 輓章·挽章 a funeral ode; an elegy; a funeral streamer

만장 滿場 the whole house [hall]; the whole company [assembly]; all the audience
♦ 만장하신 여러분 Ladies and Gentlemen
▶ 음악회는 만장의 갈채를 받았다 The concert brought down the (whole) house.
▶ 그의 연설에 만장의 청중이 깊은 감동을 받았다 The entire audience was deeply moved by his speech.

만장일치 滿場一致 unanimity (of the whole assembly)
♦ 만장일치로 unanimously; by a unanimous vote; by common [universal] consent; without a dissenting voice; with one accord
▶ 그 법안은 만장일치로 가결되었다 The bill passed unanimously [by common consent].
▶ 그 제안에는 만장일치의 찬성표가 모였다 There was a solid [unanimous] vote in favor of the proposal.
▶ 우리는 만장일치로 그 계획을 승인했다 We were unanimous in our approval of the plan.

만재 滿載 full load; the loaded condition
─**만재하다** 〈한계까지 짐을 싣다〉 be loaded to capacity 〈가득 짐을 싣다〉 be fully loaded (with); 〈짐을 가득 나르다〉 carry a full load [cargo] (of); 〈신문·잡지가 기사 등을 가뜩 기재하다〉 be full of...; be filled with...
▶ 싱싱한 물고기를 만재하고 트럭이 하나하나 떠나갔다 One truck after another went out, loaded to capacity with fresh fish.
▶ 열차가 석탄을 만재하고 달려가고 있다 A train carrying [with] a full cargo of coal on board is running past.
▶ 이 잡지에는 모터사이클에 관한 기사가 만재해 있다 This magazine is full of articles about motorcycles.
■ ─흘수(吃水) full [load] draft ─흘수선(吃水線) a load draft line ─흘수선표 the Plimsoll line [mark]

만적거리다 fumble (with) ⇨ 만지작거리다

만전 萬全 perfectness; perfection
♦ 만전의 sure; secure / 만전을 기하다 make perfection more perfect; make assurance doubly sure; see that all is right
▶ 우리는 만전을 기하여 A루트를 따랐다 In order to make assurance doubly sure, we took route A.

만전지책 a carefully thought-out plan [measure]; the best possible measure; a prudent policy
♦ 만전지책을 취하다 adopt a prudent policy; use [play] a sure card
▶ 태풍에 대비하여 만전지책을 강구했다 All possible measure were taken against the typhoon.

만점 滿點 **1** 〈꽉 찬 점수〉 perfect score; the top grade; (英) full marks
♦ 만점을 따다[받다] get [obtain, gain, secure, attain] full marks; achieve a perfect score / 만점을 주다 give full marks (to) / 백점 만점으로 답안을 채점하다 mark examination papers on the basis [a maximum] of 100 points
▶ 그는 수학에서 백점 만점중 90점을 땄다 He got ninety (points) out of a hundred in mathematics.
▶ 나는 역사에서 만점을 받았다 I got [gained]

a hundred percent [full marks] in history.
2 〈흠이 없음〉 ♦ 만점이다 be perfect; be quite satisfactory
▶ 우유는 영양 만점이다 Milk is very nutritious.
▶ 이 호텔은 서비스 만점이다 They give excellent service at this hotel.
▶ 그 약효는 만점이었다 The medicine proved completely effective. ⇌ The medicine had a satisfactory effect.

만조 滿潮 (a) high [full] tide; the flood tide; the high water
♦ 만조 때에 at high tide [water]; when the tide is high
▶ 지금 만조다 It's high tide now.
▶ 오늘은 아침 4시에 만조가 되었다 High tide was at four this morning.
▶ 이 바위들은 만조 때에 자취를 감춰 버린다 These rocks disappear at full [flood, high] tide.
▶ 會話 「만조는 몇시입니까?」 「4시 입니다」 "What time is it high tide?" "At four."

만조백관 滿朝百官 all the (civil and military) officials of the court

만족 滿足 satisfaction; contentment
▶ 행복은 만족에 있다 Happiness lies in contentment.
▶ 그는 직업에서 상당한 만족을 얻고 있다 He derives considerable satisfaction from his work.
—**만족하다[스럽다]** satisfactory; contented; pleased; happy; satisfied; gratified
♦ 그 방정식을 만족시키는 x의 값 the value of x that satisfies the equation / …에 만족하고 있다 be satisfied with; 〈반갑다〉 be pleased with; be content(ed) with; content *oneself* with; 〈만족을 느끼다〉 feel satisfaction [contentment] (in); 〈기쁘다〉 be happy about 《with》/ 호기심을 만족시키다 satisfy *one's* curiosity / 야심을 만족시키다 gratify *one's* ambition / 미각을 만족시키다 tickle *one's* palate
▶ 이번 시험의 결과는 만족스럽지 못했다 The result was not satisfactory this time.
▶ 나는 남편에게 만족하고 있다 I am quite content(ed) with my husband.
▶ 나는 현재 급료에 전적으로 만족하고 있다 I am quite satisfied [content(ed)] with my present salary.
▶ 총리는 선거 결과에 만족했다 The prime minister was gratified with [at] the result of the election.
▶ 우리는 작으나마 가지고 있는 것에 만족해야 한다 We must be content [pleased] with what little we have.
▶ 이 물건이라면 너는 꼭 만족할 거야 I am sure you will find it satisfactory.
▶ 우승을 하여 나는 대단히 만족했다 I was greatly satisfied [very happy, very pleased] to win the championship. ⇌ 〈만족을 느꼈다〉 I felt great satisfaction at winning the championship. ⇌ 〈만족을 얻었다〉 I got [received] great satisfaction from winning the championship. ⇌ 〈사물이 주어〉 Winning the championship gave me great satisfaction [was a great satisfaction to me].
▶ 그는 만족스럽게 고개를 끄덕였다 He nodded with satisfaction.
▶ 그의 플레이는 코치를 만족시키지 못했다 His playing didn't satisfied the coach.
▶ 그녀는 외아들의 소망을 모두 만족시켜 주었다 She gratified her only son's every wish.
■ —자기 self-complacency; self-contentment
■ —감 a sense [feeling] of satisfaction [contentment]

만족 蠻族 a savage tribe

만종 晚鐘 an evening bell; a curfew (bell); a bell at sunset

만좌 滿座 the whole company [assembly] ⇨ 만장(滿場)
▶ 나는 만좌 앞에서 노래를 부르게 되었다 I was made to sing before the whole company [in public].

만주 滿洲 Manchuria
♦ 만주의 Manchurian
■ —말 Manchu ―사람 a Manchu; a Manchurian ―사변 the Manchurian Incident ―족 the Manchus

만지 蠻地 savage land; a barbaric region

만지다 1 〈손대다〉 touch; feel; 〈美〉 feel of; 〈쓰다듬다〉 pat; 〈스치다〉 brush
♦ 손으로 만지다 touch *sth* with the hand / 손가락으로 만지다 feel *sth* with *one's* fingers; finger
▶ 그것은 만지면 차갑다 〔뜨겁다, 단단하다, 말랑하다〕 It is cold [hot, hard, soft].
▶ 맹인들은 물건을 만져보고 식별한다 Blind people recognize things by feeling [touching] them.
▶ 젖은 손으로 전구를 만지면 위험하다 It is dangerous to touch an electric bulb with a wet hand.
▶ 몸을 굽혀서 손가락으로 발끝을 만질 수 있니? Can you bend down to touch your toes with your fingers?
▶ 만지지 마시오 (게시) Hands off. ⇌ Do not touch.
2 〈다루다·손질하다〉 handle; mend; take care of; tend
▶ 정원을 만지다 tend a garden

만지작거리다 〈손가락으로〉 finger; 〈더듬다〉 fumble 《with》; 〈건드리다〉 touch; 〈가지고 놀다〉 play 《with》; meddle 《with》
▶ 그녀는 안절부절 못하고 손수건을 만지작거렸다 She nervously fumbled with her handkerchief. ⇌ She was playing with a handkerchief because she was nervous.
▶ 아이들은 장난감을 만지작거리며 놀고 있었다 The children were playing with toys.

만찬 晩餐 dinner; supper
♦ (그리스도의) 최후의 만찬 Last Supper / 만찬회를 열다 give [hold] a dinner (party) / 아무를 만찬에 초대하다 ask [invite] *sb* to dinner
▶ 그는 나를 만찬에 초대해 주었다 He invited me to dinner.
■ —회 a dinner (party); a banquet : 대통령은 그 대사를 위해 만찬회를 베풀었다 The President gave a dinner party for the am-

만천하 滿天下 〈전세계〉 the whole world; 〈전국〉 the whole country; 〈세상〉 the public
♦ 만천하에 in the whole world; throughout the country; under the sun / 만천하에 이름을 날리다 become world-famous; be well-known all over the world [country] / 만천하를 손아귀에 넣다 〈정권을 잡다〉 come into power; be in power; 〈전국을 정복하다〉 conquer the whole country
▶ 그의 용감한 행동은 만천하에 알려졌다 His bravery was known to the whole world.
▶ 그의 비극적인 죽음은 만천하의 동정을 자아냈다 His tragic death aroused the sympathy of the public in general.

만초 蔓草 〈덩굴풀〉 a vine; a creeper; a climber; a trailing [climbing] plant

만추 晚秋 〈늦가을〉 late fall [autumn]
♦ 만추의 어느 날 one day in late fall / 만추에 in late fall; late in fall; towards the end of fall

만춘 晚春 〈늦봄〉 late spring ♦ 만춘에 late in spring; towards the end of spring

만취 滿醉 dead drunkenness; intoxication
―만취하다 get dead [beastly, blind] drunk; 《美俗》 be boozed (up); be zonked (out); be boozy

만큼 1 〈비교〉 like; as; as...as; so...as; 〈부정〉 not so [as]...as; less...than
▶ 시간만큼 귀중한 것은 없다 Nothing is more precious than time.
▶ 누나는 나만큼 키가 크지 않다 My sister is not as [so] tall as me.
▶ 그의 병은 생각했던 것만큼 심하지 않다 His illness is not as [so] serious as I thought.
▶ 그것은 내가 걱정했던 것만큼 나쁘지는 않아 It is not as bad as I expected.
▶ 그 영화는 기대했던 만큼 재미있지는 않았다 That movie wasn't as interesting as I expected.
▶ 나는 그 사람만큼 책을 가지고 있다 I have as many books as he (has).
▶ 그는 부자라고 할 만큼은 못된다 He is not so rich as to be called a wealthy man.
2 〈정도〉 so...that; so...as to; enough...to
▶ 그는 먹고 살 만큼의 돈을 번다 He earns just enough money to live on.
▶ 지붕이 날아갈 만큼의 강풍이었다 The wind was so strong (that) the roof was almost blown off.
▶ 그녀는 지금은 여행을 할 수 있을 만큼 건강하다 She is now well enough to travel.
▶ 그 방은 글씨를 읽지 못할 만큼 어두웠다 The room was so dark (that) I couldn't read.
▶ 그것은 말로 표현할 수 없을 만큼 멋지다 It's too wonderful for words. ⇒ It's beyond description.
▶ 사태는 걱정할 만큼 심각하지는 않다 It is not serious enough to grieve.
▶ 오늘은 견딜 수 없을 만큼 덥다 It is unbearably hot. ⇒ It is too hot for me to stand.
▶ 그녀는 말을 못할 만큼 지쳐 있었다 She was so tired (that) she could not speak.
3 〈이유·근거〉 in as much as; since
▶ 시험 직전이니 만큼 감기에 걸리지 않도록 조심해야 한다 Be careful that you do not catch a cold just before the test.
▶ 그는 학자이니 만큼 매사에 정통하다 Like the scholar (that) he is, he is well versed in everything.

만판 1 〈마음껏·실컷〉 to one's heart's content; to one's satisfaction; to the full; as much as one wants to; until one gets tired of it
♦ 만판 먹다[마시다] eat [drink] one's fill; eat [drink] as much as one likes / 인생을 만판 즐기다 enjoy life to the full
▶ 우리 만판 마시자 Let's drink to our heart's content. ⇒ Let's drink up.
▶ 그는 휴일을 만판 즐겼다 He enjoyed the holiday to his heart's content.
2 〈마냥·줄곧〉 entirely; solely; only; always
♦ 만판 놀기만 하다 do nothing but idle [play]; spend one's time (in) doing nothing; be always playing [idle]

만평 漫評 a rambling criticism; literary gossip; a satire; 〈만화로 그린〉 a caricature
―만평하다 criticize ramblingly; gossip; 〈만화로〉 satirize; caricature

만풍 蠻風 barbarous customs [habits]

만필 漫筆 stray [random, rambling] notes; random jottings; 〈신문·잡지의〉 causeries

만하 晚夏 〈늦여름〉 late summer
♦ 만하에 in late summer; near [toward] the end of summer

만하다 1 〈가치가 있는〉 worth; worthy (of, to be done); deserving; meritorious; claimed
♦ 칭찬할 만하다 merit [deserve] praise; be praiseworthy; be worthy of praise / 상을 받을 만하다 deserve a reward
▶ 그는 믿을 만하다 He is worthy of trust. ⇒ He is reliable [trustworthy].
▶ 그의 행위는 칭찬받을 만하다 His deed is worthy of praise [deserves to be praised].
▶ 이것은 다시 읽을 만한 책이다 This book is worth reading twice [or a second reading]. ⇒ This book deserves to be read twice.
▶ 그의 업적은 감탄할 만하다 His achievement entitles him to our admiration.
2 〈가능한〉 likely (to do); 〈알맞은〉 suitable (for); fitted (to)
♦ 쓸 만하다 be fit for use; can be used / 먹을 만하다 be good to eat; be fit for eating; be eatable [edible]
▶ 그가 있을 만한 곳은 모조리 가봤다 I looked for him in every likely place.

-만하다 1 〈같은 정도〉 be as...as
♦ 새알만하다 be the size of a bird egg; be as small as a bird egg
▶ 그는 키가 나만하다 He is as tall as I [me].
2 〈…보다 더하지 않다〉 be not more (than)
▶ 그의 병세는 그저 그만하다 His condition is getting neither better nor worse.

만학 晚學 learning late in life; a late education
▶ 그는 만학이다 He took up [began] learning late in life.
▶ 그는 만학이면서도 대학자가 되었다 Although he started learning late in life, he

became a great scholar.
—만학하다 get a late education; study late in life ■ —자 a late learner

만함식 滿艦飾 **1** 〈군함의 깃발 장식〉 full dressing
♦ 만함식을 하다 dress a ship (with flags)
▶ 군함은 모두 만함식을 하고 있었다 All the ships were in full regalia.
2 〈성장〉 a full dress; gala dress

만행 蠻行 a savage deed; an act of barbarity; a barbarous act; a barbarism; an outrage; a brutality; savagery

만혼 晚婚 (a) late marriage; (a) marriage late in life —만혼하다 get married late; marry late in life
▶ 그는 만혼하였다 He got married late in life.

만화 漫畵 〈만화책〉 a comics; (美) a comic book; 〈시사 풍자〉 a cartoon (보통 한컷); 〈인물 풍자〉 a caricature (보통 한컷); 〈네컷짜리〉 a comic strip; (美) comics; (英) a strip cartoon
♦ 만화적인 funny / 만화를 그리다 draw a cartoon / 텔레비전 만화[만화영화]를 보다 watch a cartoon on TV [a TV cartoon] / 만화화하다 make a caricature of; caricature; cartoon
▶ 신문에 총리의 풍자 만화가 실려 있다 There is a cartoon of prime minister in the newspaper.
▶ 그는 만화를 그려서 먹고 산다 He makes his living drawing cartoons.
■ 불량— substandard comic books 연재— (美) a comic strip; serial comics ■ —가 〈인물 풍자의〉 a cartoonist; a caricaturist; a comic artist; 〈애니메이션의〉 an animator —란(欄) a comic section 《of a newspaper》; (美) a funny column; (美口) funnies —영화 a cartoon; (美) movie [(英) film]; an animation; an animated cartoon —제작 cartooning —책[잡지] a comic book [magazine]; the comic; a funny book

만화경 萬華鏡 a kaleidoscope
♦ 만화경 같은 kaleidoscopic 《scenery》.

만회 挽回 〈회복〉 recovery; restoration; revival; 〈부활〉 revival; rehabilitation; 〈명예 등의〉 retrieval
♦ 명예의 만회 restoration of *one's* honor; recovery of *one's* reputation / 퇴세의 만회를 꾀하다 try to restore [retrieve] *one's* declining fortune
—만회하다 recover; take [get] back; regain; retrieve; redeem
♦ 세력을 만회하다 regain *one's* power / 시간의 지체를 만회하다 make up for lost time
▶ 그는 명성을 만회했다 He recovered his reputation.
▶ 그는 인기를 만회하려고 필사적이었다 He made a desperate attempt to regain his popularity.
▶ 적은 세력을 만회했다 The enemy regained their strength.
■ —책(策) a measure for retrieving 《*one's* lost credit》

많다 **1** 〈수가〉 a lot of; (口) lots of; many; large; a good many; a large [great] number of; 〈풍부하다〉 abundant
▶ 네 작문에는 틀린 데가 많다 There are quite a few mistakes in your compositions.
▶ 그렇게 생각하는 사람이 많다 A lot of people think so. ⇒ There are a lot of people who think so.
▶ 그날 밤에는 대단히 많은 사람들이 몰려 나왔다 There was a big crowd that night. ⇒ Very many people turned out that night.
▶ 그는 식구가 많다 He has a large family. ⇒ His family is large.
▶ 이 연못에는 물고기가 많다 There are a lot of fish in this pond. ⇒ This pond is rich [abundant] in fish. ⇒ Fish are abundant in this pond.
▶ 누나는 나보다 두살 많다 My sister is two years older than I.
2 〈양이〉 a lot of; (口) lots of; much; large; a good [great] deal of
▶ 그는 나보다 수입이 많다 His income is larger than mine. ⇒ He earns more than I (do).
▶ 아직 시간이 많으니까 서두르지 않아도 돼 We still have lots of time, so there is no need to hurry.
3 〈빈도가 잦다〉 frequent
▶ 그는 학교에 지각할 때가 많다 He is often late for school.
▶ 사람이란 실수할 때가 많다 Man is apt to make mistakes.
▶ 나는 일요일에는 집에 있을 때가 많다 [대개는 집에 있다] I usually stay (at) home on Sundays.
▶ 이 병은 어린이에게 많다 This disease often attacks children.

많이 **1** 〈다수〉 in large [great] numbers; innumerably; in quantity; in abundance; abundantly; amply
▶ 그것에 관해서 많이 알지는 못한다 I don't know much about it.
▶ 그 아이는 피를 많이 흘리고 있었다 The child was bleeding profusely.
▶ 금년에는 작년보다 눈이 많이 온다 We have more snow than last year.
▶ 그는 담배를 너무 많이 피운다 He smokes heavily [too much, to excess].
2 〈빈도가 잦은〉 frequently; very often; at short [frequent] intervals
♦ 많이 일어나는 사건 a common event; a matter of frequent occurrent
▶ 최근 비행기 사고가 (전보다) 많이 일어난다 Airplane accidents are occuring (more) frequently these days.

맏- eldest; firstborn
♦ 맏누이 the eldest [oldest] sister / 맏딸 the eldest daughter; the first daughter / 맏며느리 the wife of *one's* eldest son / 맏동서 the eldest brother-in-law (남자); the eldest sister-in-law (여자) / 맏사위 the husband of *one's* eldest daughter; *one's* eldest son-in-law / 맏상제 the chief mourner; the eldest son of the deceased / 맏손녀 the eldest granddaughter; *one's* first granddaughter / 맏손자 the eldest grandchild [grandson]; the first grandchild [grandson] /

맏물

맏아들 the eldest [oldest] son / 맏형수 one's eldest brother's wife; one's eldest sister-in-law

맏물 〈첫물〉 the first of the season; the earliest produce (crop, fruits) of the season; the first supply (of peaches); 〈채소·벼 등〉 the first cut
♦ 맏물 과일 early fruits / 맏물 사과 apples from the first crop; the first apples of the season; early apples
▶ 이 복숭아는 맏물이다 These peaches are the first of the season.
▶ 나는 맏물 포도를 먹었다 I ate the first grapes of the season.

맏배 〈첫번째 새끼〉 the first delivery of an animal; the firstborn of an animal; the first litter
■ 一돼지 the first litter of pigs

맏이 1 〈형제·자매 중의 맨 손위〉 the firstborn [eldest] (child [son])
♦ 맏이로 태어나다 be born first; be the eldest
2 〈손위〉 seniority; 〈손윗사람〉 one's elder; a senior
▶ 두 사람 중 누가 맏이세요? Which is the elder of the two?

말¹ 〖動〗 a horse; 〈간지의 오(午)〉 (the Year of) the Horse

[解說] 말은 암·수·나이·용도에 따라 다음과 같이 나눈다. 3~5살까지의 수말 a colt; 암망아지 a filly; 암말 a mare; 종마 a stallion; 군마 a steed; 조랑말 a pony; 거세마 a gelding; 1살 미만의 망아지 a foal.

♦ (아이에게) 말이 되어 주다 give (him) a ride on one's back; ride (him) on one's back / 말을 타다 ride (a horse); mount [get on] a horse / 말을 길들이다 train a horse; 〈야생마를〉 break (in) a horse / 말을 기르다 keep a horse / 말을 매다 hitch a horse (to a post) / (고삐를 당겨) 말을 세우다 pull [rein] up a horse; rein back a horse / 말을 달리다 gallop a horse / 말을 타고 가다 ride (on) a horse; ride horseback / 말을 익숙하게 타다 ride a horse well / 말을 타고 있다 be on a horse / 말에게 물을 먹이다 water a horse / 말에게 안장[멍에]을 메우다 saddle [harness] a horse / 말에게 편자를 박다 shoe a horse / 말에서 내리다 get off [down from] a horse; dismount (from) a horse / 말에서 떨어지다 fall off [from] a horse; be thrown off a horse
▶ 말이 울다 Horses neigh.
▶ 말이 나직이 울다 〈기분 좋은 듯이〉 Horses whinny.
▶ 이 말은 타기 쉽다 This horse is easy to ride.
▶ 자, 말을 타 주십시오 Now please mount the horse.
▶ 너는 말을 타본 적이 있니? Have you ridden (on) a horse?
▶ 말에서 내려 주십시오 Please get off the horse. ⇌ Please dismount.
■경마 a racehorse [racer] ■一똥 horse dung [manure, droppings] 一채찍 a horsewhip 一총 horsehair

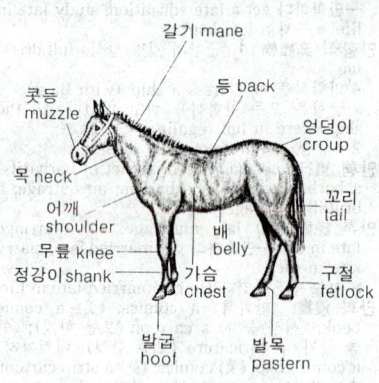

말: 갈기 mane / 등 back / 엉덩이 croup / 콧등 muzzle / 꼬리 tail / 목 neck / 배 belly / 어깨 shoulder / 무릎 knee / 가슴 chest / 정강이 shank / 구절 fetlock / 발굽 hoof / 발목 pastern

말² 〈용량의 단위〉 a mal; 〈용기〉 a mal; a measure containing about 18 liters
♦ 말로 되다 measure (grain) with a mal

말³ 〈장기의〉 a chessman; a piece; a man; 〈체커〉 a checker ♦ 말을 쓰다 move; make a move; move a piece

말⁴ 〖植〗 a pondweed

말⁵ 1 〈언어〉 language; speech; 〈국어〉 a language; a tongue; 〈단어〉 a word; 〈용어〉 a term; 〈관용구〉 a phrase; 〈방언·사투리〉 a dialect; 〈표현〉 an expression; 〈이야기〉 a talk; a conversation; a chat; 〈발언〉 a remark; a statement; (an) utterance; 〈속담〉 a proverb
♦ 우리[한국] 말 Korean; the Korean language / 말을 걸다 speak [talk] to one / 아무와 말을 주고 받다 have a word [a few words] with sb; talk to sb / 말을 꺼내다 bring up; begin to speak; break the ice / 말을 덧붙이다 add
▶ 쉬운 말로 설명해 주게 Explain it in plain [simple] words [terms].
▶ 나는 「보도관제」라는 말의 뜻을 알 수 없었다 I didn't know the meaning of the word "blackout".
▶ 내 말이 영어로 통하지 않았다 I couldn't make myself understood in English. ⇌ People didn't understand my English.
▶ 지금 내 기분을 말로 표현하기는 어렵다 It's difficult to express [put] how I feel in words.
▶ 다른 말로 하자면 그는 게으름뱅이다 In other words, he is lazy.
▶ 그 아픔은 말로는 표현할 수 없다 The pain is beyond words [description]. ⇌ The pain is unspeakable.
▶ 나는 말이 막혔다 I didn't know what to say. ⇌ I was at a loss for words.
2 〈말씨·말투〉 language; one's speech
♦ 세련된[야한] 말 refined [vulgar] language / 멋진 말 a clever expression / 달콤한[거친] 말 a polite [rough] speech; a polite [rough] way of talking
▶ 그는 말이 거칠다 He uses vulgar [violent] language. ⇌ He is rough of speech.

▶ 그녀는 말이 서투르다 She is a poor speaker. ⇌ She is poor at talking.
▶ 그는 세련된 말을 쓴다 He uses refined words.
▶ 그의 말을 들어보면 그가 부산 사람임을 알 수 있다 You can tell [I know from] his speech that he comes from Pusan.
3 〈잔소리·불평·꾸중〉 (a) scolding; a telling-off; (口) a talking-to; a lecture; a complaint
♦ 말에 가시가 있다 be ironical in expression; sound ironical; say spiteful things
▶ 넌 어떻게 그런 말을 할 수 있니? How dare you say such a thing?
▶ 나는 네 말을 그대로 받아들였어 I took you at your word.
4 〈소문〉 (a) rumor; (a) report; a story; common talk; gossip; hearsay
5 〈전갈·전언〉 a message
♦ 말을 전하다 give [deliver] a (verbal) message; send word [a message] (to)
6 〈주장·할 말〉 one's say; what one has to say; what one says [said]
♦ 말[화제]을 돌리다 change the subject [topic]; switch the conversation; divert the talk
▶ 말을 조심하시오 Be careful in your speech.
▶ 호락호락 남의 말을 믿지 말게 Don't believe what people say.
▶ 그녀의 말을 기억하니? Do you remember what she said [her words]?
▶ 그는 그 문제에 관해서는 늘 말을 흐린다 He always equivocates on that issue.
7 〈명분·이름〉 ♦ 말뿐인 요금 a nominal fee / 말뿐인 nominal; token; 〈아주 적은〉 only a little; very small
▶ 그는 그녀의 말뿐인 변명을 꿰뚫어 보았다 He saw through her specious excuse.
8 〈이성〉 reason; (a) cause; ground
▶ 말도 안되는 소리 마라 Don't be so unseasonable.
▶ 그의 제의는 말이 안된다 His proposal is not worth talking about. ⇌ His proposal is out of the question.
9 〈뜻〉 meaning; a sense
▶ 그게 무슨 말이오? What do you mean by that?
▶ 나 말입니까? Do you mean me?
10 〈명령·지시〉 commands; orders; directions
♦ 말을 잘 듣지 않는 아이 a disobedient child / 말을 듣지 않다 disobey sb; 〈손·발이〉 refuse to work / 아무의 말을 따르다 obey [follow] sb's directions; listen to sb; obey sb; 〈조언을〉 take sb's advice
11 〈말을 다시 잇거나 꺼낼 때〉 저어, 말이야 Well; Listen; Look here; I say
말[6] 〈받치는 나무토막〉 a sawhorse
말 末 1 〈끝〉 the end [close] (of)
♦ 6월 말경에 toward [about] the end of July; in late July
2 〈야구 등의〉 the second [lower, last] half; the bottom
♦ 5회 말 the second half of the fifth inning
-**말** -末 〈가루〉 powder
말갈기 a (horse's) mane

말갈다 clear; clean; pure; limpid
말개지다 〈물 등이〉 become clear; clear up; get clean; 〈기분이〉 be refreshed
말거머리 〔動〕 a horseleech
말고 〈대신에〉 not...but...; instead of...; 〈밖에〉 except; but
▶ 이것 말고 저것을 주시오 Give me that one instead of this one.
▶ 그 사람 말고 제가 가겠습니다 I will go instead of [in place of] him. ⇌ I will go in his place.
▶ 그 사람 말고는 그런 짓을 할 사람이 없다 Nobody except [but] him would do such a thing. ⇌ Nobody would do such a thing except [but] him.
▶ 그 사람 말고는 내겐 친구가 없다 He is my only friend. ⇌ I have no close friends except [besides] him.
말고기 horsemeat; horseflesh
■ ―자반 〈술취한 얼굴〉 a red-faced drunk
말고삐 reins; a bridle; ribbons
♦ 말고삐를 잡다 hold [lead] a horse by the bridle; handle the reins
▶ 그는 말고삐를 당겼다 He tightend [pulled up] the reins.
▶ 그는 말고삐를 늦췄다 He loosened his reins. ⇌ He gave his horse his reins.
▶ 그는 말고삐를 당겨 말을 세웠다 He reined back his horse. ⇌ He drew his reins.
말곰 〔動〕 a Manchurian bear
말공대 ―恭待 addressing in honorifics
―말공대하다 be polite; use polite expressions; use respectful terms; use honorifics; address respectfully [in honorifics]
▶ 어른하고 애기할 때는 말공대하거라 You should be polite [use respectful terms, use honorifics] in speaking to your seniors.
말괄량이 a tomboy; (口) a filly
♦ 말괄량이 같은 tomboyish; saucy; forward; unladylike
▶ 저 말괄량이는 어찌할 도리가 없어 That tomboy [naughty girl] is completely out of hand [control].
말구유 a manger; 〈가로장이 있는〉 a crib; a horse trough
말구종 ―驅從 a groom; a footman; an ostler; (英) a horseboy
말굳다 〈말을 더듬다〉 stammer; falter; stutter; (be) stammering
말굴레 a headstall; a headgear; a bridle; a halter
말굽 a horse's hoof; 〈편자〉 a horseshoe
♦ 말굽 소리 the beat [clack, clatter] of a horse's hoofs / 말굽 모양의 horseshoe-shaped; U-shaped
말굽자석 ―磁石 a horseshoe magnet
말귀 〈말뜻〉 the meaning [import] of a word; 〈알아듣는 총기〉 hearing; understanding; an ear (for words)
♦ 말귀가 밝다 be quick of hearing; have quick [sharp] ears; be quick-eared; have long ears; distinguish delicate shades of meaning / 말귀가 어둡다 be dull [weak] of hearing; have a bad ear; be slow in understanding what sb

말기 says / 말귀를 못 알아듣다 cannot make out what *sb* says / 말귀를 알아듣다 understand the meaning; make sense (of)
▶ 그는 말귀가 밝아 말을 빨리 배웠다 He had a good ear and (so) picked up languages quickly.

말기 末期 the end (of); the close; 〈명확한 시대 구분의〉 the last period; 〈병의〉 the last [terminal] stage
♦ 전쟁 말기 the last stage of the war / 19세기 말기에 at the close of the 19th century
▶ 세계는 말기적 징조를 보이고 있다 It seems that the world shows signs of a downfall [decadence].
━암 terminal cancer ━암환자 a terminal (cancer) patient

말꼬리 the end of *one's* words ⇨ 말끝

말꼬투리 a slip of the tongue
▶ 그는 늘 내 말꼬투리를 잡는다 He always trips me up. ⇌ He always catches me up on a slip of the tongue.

말꼴 fodder; provender; forage; hay
♦ 말꼴을 주다 feed [fodder] a horse

말꾸러기 1 〈잔말이 많은 사람〉 a constant [confirmed] grumbler; a malcontent 2 〈말썽꾼〉 a troublemaker; a troublesome person

말끔 all; completely; entirely; clean; totally; thoroughly
▶ 나는 그것을 말끔 잊어 버렸다 I forgot all about it.
▶ 그는 빚을 말끔 갚았다 He paid [cleared, wiped] off his debts.

말끔하다 clean; clear; tidy; comely; pure
▶ 그녀는 말끔한 것을 좋아한다 She is very tidy. ⇌ She has neat habits.
▶ 그녀는 말끔한 옷차림을 하고 있었다 She was dressed neatly.

말끔히 clear(ly); neatly; tidily; beautifully
♦ 방을 말끔히 치우다 make a room tidy [neat]; tidy up a room; put a room in order / 방을 말끔히 청소하다 clean up a room
▶ 네 책상을 말끔히 치워라 Clear up your desk.
▶ 접시를 더 말끔히 닦아라 Wash the dishes more cleanly.
▶ 이를 늘 말끔히 닦아라 Always keep your teeth clean.
▶ 그는 방을 말끔히 해두라는 분부를 받았다 He was told to keep his room in (good) order.
▶ 그녀는 머리를 말끔히 매만졌다 She arranged her hair neatly.

말끝 the end of *one's* words [speech]; 〈어미〉 the ending of a word
♦ 말끝을 흐리다 slur the end of *one's* words; leave *one's* statement vague; evade the point; give a vague answer / 아무의 말끝을 잡고 늘어지다 pick [cavil] at *sb's* words; trip *sb* up; find fault with *sb's* remark

말나다 1 〈화제에 오르다·소문나다〉 be talked about; be gossiped about; become the talk (of); be in everybody's mouth
♦ 말난 김에 by the way; in passing; incidentally; in the course of conversation
▶ 같이 있는게 남의 눈에 띄지 않는 것이 좋소. 말날테니까 We'd better not to be seen together. People might talk.
▶ 말난 김에 그는 자기 가족 얘기를 비쳤다 He mentioned his family (only) in passing.
▶ 말난 김에 말인데 너 영어 할 수 있니? By the way, can you speak English?
2 〈비밀이 새다〉 come [be] out; leak out; be heard outside; be revealed; come [be brought] to light
▶ 이 비밀이 외부에 말나면 큰일 나 If this secret should leak [slip] out, it will bring serious consequences.

말내다 1 〈화제에 올리다·소문 내다〉 talk about; gossip about, start [spread] rumor; bring up (a topic); broach (a topic); begin to talk about; mention; refer to
▶ 누가 말냈는지 모르지만 그것은 낭설이야 I don't know who started the story, but it is entirely groundless.
2 〈비밀을 폭로하다〉 tell (to other); expose; reveal; let out; disclose; betray
▶ 이것은 비밀이니 말내지 않도록 해라 Don't let out [disclose] this secret. ⇌ Keep this secret to yourself.
▶ 그는 그녀의 과거에 관해서 결코 말내지 않았다 He never said anything about her past.

말년 末年 1 〈늘그막〉 *one's* later years
♦ 말년에 late in life; in the evening of *one's* life / 말년을 행복하게 지내다 live the rest of *one's* life happily / 말년에 접어들다 enter the twilight of *one's* life
▶ 그녀는 말년이 행복했다 She was happy in her last years.
2 〈말기〉 the end (of)

말다¹ 〈감다〉 roll (paper); roll *sth* up (in paper) ♦ 지도를 말다 roll (up) a map / 카펫을 말다 roll up a carpet

말다² 〈국물에 밥 등을〉 put (boiled rice) into soup [water]; mix (food) with soup [water]
♦ 국수를 말다 put noodles into soup; prepare noodles

말다³ 〈그만두다〉 stop; cease; 〈직장 등을〉 resign; retire; leave; quit; discontinue; drop; 〈단념하다〉 give up; throw up; abandon; 〈일시적으로〉 suspend; 〈예정된 일을〉 cancel; call off
▶ 쓰다 만 편지 an unfinished letter / 쓰다 만 원고 a half-finished manuscript
▶ 비가 오다가 말았다 It started to rain and then stopped.

말다⁴ 1 〈금지·명령〉 don't; cease; stop; keep from (doing); be careful not to
▶ 떠들지 마라 Don't be noisy. ⇌ Be quiet.
▶ 끝까지 단념하지 말아라 Never give up to the very end.
▶ 거짓말을 하지 마라 Never tell a lie.
▶ 들어가지 마시오 (게시) Keep out [off].
▶ 일 없는 사람은 들어오지 마시오 (게시) No Trespassing.
2 〈필경·결국〉 end up (doing); get around to (doing)
▶ 그는 죽고 말았다 He died in the end.
▶ 그는 꿈을 실현하고야 말았다 His dreams came true.

말다툼 a quarrel; a dispute; 〈논쟁〉 (an) argu-

ment; (口) a row; 〈사소한〉 a squabble
—**말다툼하다** argue 《with》; have an argument; have words 《with sb over...》
▶ 나는 돈 때문에 그와 말다툼했다 I quarreled [argued] with him over money.
▶ 그녀는 아이들 때문에 남편과 말다툼했다 She quarreled with her husband about their children.

말단 末端 the end; the tip
▶ 지배인의 명령이 말단까지 전달됐다 The manager's order reached the rank and file.
■ —**가격** 〈소매 가격〉 a retail price; 〈마약 등의〉 a street price —**공무원** a petty [minor, subordinate] official; an understrapper; (英) a humble placeman —**관절** 〔解〕 terminal joints —**기관** terminal offices [organs] —**기구** a terminal organization; the smallest unit 《of an organization》 —**비대** 〔醫〕 hyperpituitarism —**사원** a minor clerk; an underling

말대꾸 a back talk; a retort
—**말대꾸하다** talk [answer] back; give sb a retort; make a retort 《to》
▶ 그녀는 말대꾸한다고 아이를 야단쳤다 She told her child off for talking back.
▶ 부모님께 그렇게 말대꾸해서는 못써 You shouldn't talk [answer] back to your parents like that.

말대답 —對答 a retort ⇨ 말대꾸

말더듬다 stammer; 〈특히 습관적으로〉 stutter; falter ◆ 말더듬으며 대답하다 answer stammeringly [stutteringly] / 말더듬으며 사과하다 stammer (out) an apology

말더듬이 a stammerer; a stutterer ▶ 그는 심한 말더듬이다 He has a bad stammer. ≒ He stammers badly. ■—**교정기** an articulator

말동무 a companion (⇨ 말벗) ▶ 그는 말동무가 없다 He has no one to talk to. ▶ 말동무가 있었으면 좋겠다 I want someone to talk to [with].

말되다 〈이치에 맞다〉 be reasonable; be logical; be convincing; be natural; stand to reason; make sense ◆ 말도 되지 않는 소리를 하다 talk nonsense
▶ 그의 제안은 말도 되지 않는다 His proposal is not worth talking about. ≒ His proposal is quite out of the question.

말똥가리 〔鳥〕 a buzzard

말똥말똥 ◆ 말똥말똥 쳐다보다 stare 《at》; watch; look hard at sb; look up and down; look sb full in the face
▶ 남을 말똥말똥 쳐다보는 것은 결례다 It is rude to stare at others.
—**말똥말똥하다** 〈잠이 안오다〉 be wakeful; be wide-awake

말뚝 a stake; a post; a picket; 〔建〕 a pile
◆ 말뚝을 박다[뽑다] drive (in) [pull up] a stake [a pile] / 말뚝을 세우다 put up a post

말뜨다 falter; hesitate (to say); be slow of speech; be slow in one's speech

말뜻 the meaning (of a word); a sense

말라게냐 (에) 〔樂〕 a malaguena

말라기 〔聖〕 Malachi (略 Mal.)

말라깽이 a skinny person; a (living [walking]) skeleton

말라르메 〈프랑스의 시인〉 Mallarmé, Stéphane (1842-98)

말라리아 〔醫〕 malaria ◆ 말라리아의[에 걸린] malarial; malarian; malarious / 말라리아에 걸리다 contract malaria; be stricken with malaria
▶ 그는 말라리아에 걸려 있다 He is suffering from [sick with] malaria.
■ **3일[4일]열—** vivax [malignant] malaria
■ —**열** malarial fever —**요법** a malaria fever treatment —**원충** a malaria(l) parasite —**전염지구** a malarious area; a malaria-stricken area —**환자** a malarial patient

말라붙다 dry up; be dried up
◆ 말라붙은 우유 a shriveled milk
▶ 오랜 가뭄으로 강이 말라붙었다 The river ran dry by a long drought.

말라빠지다 become [get] thin [lean, skinny]
◆ 말라빠진 lean; emaciated / 말라빠진 사람 a skinny person; a living [walking] skeleton

말라위 〈나라이름〉 Malawi; 〈공식명〉 the Republic of Malawi ■—**사람** a Malawian

말라죽다 〈초목이〉 wither; die; dry up; be blighted ◆ 말라죽은 나무 a blighted [withered] tree

말라카해협 —海峽 the Strait of Malacca

말랑거리다 be soft; be tender

말랑말랑하다 soft ◆ 말랑하다

말랑하다 〈빵 등이〉 soft; spongy; tender; 〈사람이〉 easy to control [deal with] ◆ 말랑한 사람 a person easy to deal with
▶ 이 토마토는 감촉도 말랑하다 This tomato is soft to the touch [feels soft].
▶ 빵이 말랑하게 구워졌다 The bread has been baked nice and soft.

말레이 Malay ■—**곰** 〔動〕 a Malay(an) bear; a sun bear —**군도** the Malay Archipelago —**말** Malay —**반도** the Malay Peninsula —**사람** a Malay(an)

말레이시아 Malaysia; 〈공식명〉 the Federation of Malaysia; the Malaysia(n) Federation —**사람** a Malaysian

말려들다 1 〈감겨 들어가다〉 be [get] caught in 《a machine》
▶ 그의 손가락이 롤러에 말려들어갔다 His fingers were caught in a roller. ≒ He got his fingers caught in a roller.
▶ 기계에 끈이 말려들었다 A rope was entangled [caught] in the machinery.
▶ 그 소년은 소용돌이에 말려들었다 The boy was caught in a whirlpool.
2 〈관계에 끼여들다〉 be involved 《in》; be dragged 《into》
▶ 그는 범죄에 말려들었다 He got involved [got caught (up)] in a crime.
▶ 이 나라는 전쟁에 말려들었다 This country was dragged into the war.
▶ 그는 음모에 말려들었다 He was involved in the conspiracy.
▶ 그는 그 사건에 말려들어 있다 He has been involved [has been entangled] in that case.

말로 末路 one's last days; the end ◆ 유명한 야구선수의 말로 the wreck of a noted ballplayer
▶ 그의 말로는 비참했다 His last days were

miserable.
▶ 그의 말로가 안쓰럽다 I feel pity for his last days.

말로 〈프랑스의 소설가·정치가〉 Malraux, André (1901-76)

말리 茉莉 〔植〕 a jasmin(e); a jessamine

말리 〈나라 이름〉 Mali; 〈공식명〉 the Republic of Mali ■―사람 a Malian

말리다¹ 〈감겨서〉 be rolled [curled] (up)
◆ 치맛자락이 말리다 the end of a skirt is rolled

말리다² 〈만류하다〉 stop; dissuade; get *sb* not to; 〈금지하다〉 prohibit; forbid ◆ 싸움을 말리다 stop a quarrel / 사표 내려는 것을 말리다 dissuade *sb* from tendering (his) resignation / 나무를 못 베게 말리다 prohibit (people from) cutting the forest trees
▶ 나는 그들의 싸움을 말렸다 I stopped their quarrel.
▶ 그녀는 어머니가 말리는 것도 듣지 않고 뛰쳐나갔다 She rushed out of the house inspite of her mother's efforts to dissuade her.
▶ 일단 그녀가 결심한 이상 말려 봤자 소용없어 Once she is determined, it is no use trying to talk her out of it.

말리다³ 〈젖은 것을〉 dry; make [let] dry; 〈초목을〉 blight; let (the grass) wither; 〈목재를〉 season
◆ 말린 물고기 dried fish / 볕에 말리다 dry *sth* in the sun / 담요를 (밖에) 널어 말리다 air (out) a blanket
▶ 그는 젖은 셔츠를 볕에 말렸다 He dried his wet shirt in the sun.
▶ 그는 손수건을 히터에 말렸다 He dried his handkerchief over the heater.

말림 conservancy [protection, reservation] (of forest, pasture)
■―갓 a reserved forest; a forest reserve

말마디 a piece [bit] of speech; a phrase; a clause; a speech; a talk ◆ 말마디나 하다 have a ready [fluent] tongue; be eloquent
▶ 그는 말마디나 할 줄 안다 He is a smooth talker.
▶ 그녀는 페인트공에게 일이 서툴다고 말마디나 했다 She complained to the painter about doing such a poor job.

말막음 an excuse; hushing up; shutting up; avoiding *sb's* words
▶ 그녀는 말막음을 잘한다 She is good at making [cooking up] excuses.
▶ 그것은 말막음에 불과하다 That's a mere excuse.
―**말막음하다** hush up; shut *sb* up; make an excuse ((for)); allay
▶ 그는 질문 공세를 받자 요령껏 말막음했다 He talked himself out of a cross-examination.

말머리 〈말의 시작〉 the beginning [opening] words; introductory remarks; 〈화제〉 a topic [subject] (of conversation) ◆ 말머리를 돌리다 change the subject

말먹이 fodder; hay; forage (grass)

말못하다 ▶ 그가 옳다고는 말못하겠다 I dare not say he is right. ▶ 뭐라고 말못하겠소 I don't know what to say.

말문 ―門 ▶ 나는 말문이 막혔다 I was dumbfounded. ⇌ I was at a loss for an answer.
▶ 뜻밖의 소식을 듣고 나는 말문이 막혔다 The unexpected news struck me dumb.
▶ 나는 어처구니가 없어 말문이 막혔다 I was speechless with amazement.
▶ 그는 말문을 열었다 He opened conversation. ⇌ He began to speak.

말미 〈휴가〉 leave (of absence); (*one's*) vacation ◆ 말미를 주다 give [grant] leave
▶ 그녀는 말미를 얻었다 She took her leave.
▶ 그는 10일간의 말미를 얻었다 He took ten days leave [days off].
▶ 사흘의 말미를 주십시오 I should [would] like to get a three-days' leave [leave for three days].

말미 末尾 〈끝〉 the end; the close ◆ 말미의 last; final / 보고서의 말미에 at the end of a report / 나는 편지 말미에 사인을 했다 I signed at the end of my letter.

말미암다 be due to...; be caused by; be owing to ◆ 말미암아 because of; on account of; owing to; due to
▶ 그 사고는 부주의한 운전으로 말미암은 것이었다 The accident was due to [was caused by] careless driving.
▶ 어제 그는 병으로 말미암아 오지 못했다 He couldn't come yesterday because he was ill [because of illness].

말미잘 〔動〕 a sea anemone

말발굽 a horse's hoof ⇨ 말굽

말방울 a horse bell

말버릇 *one's* manner of speaking; *one's* way of talking
▶ 그는 말버릇이 거칠다[고약하다] He is rough in speech [has a spiteful tongue].
▶ 무슨 말버릇이 그러냐? How dare you talk to me like that?

말버짐 〔韓醫〕 ringworm

말벌 〔昆〕 a wasp; a (yellow) hornet

말벗 a companion ▶ 그녀는 우리 할머니의 좋은 말벗이다 She makes a good companion for my grandmother.

말복 末伏 the last phase of the dog days; the late dog days

말본 grammar ⇨ 문법(文法)

말사 末寺 a branch [subordinate] temple

말살 抹殺 cancel; erasure; deletion; obliteration; a blot-out
―**말살하다** cancel; erase; strike [cross] out [off]; rub [blot] out; obliterate; efface
▶ 프랑스 혁명은 귀족 계급을 말살했다 The French Revolution liquidated the nobility.

말상 ―相 a horseface; an extremely long face
▶ 그는 말상이다 He is horsefaced.

말상대 ―相對 someone to talk to; a conversational partner
◆ 말상대가 없다[필요하다] have no one [want someone] to talk to / 말상대를 하다 have a chat ((with))
▶ 그녀는 1주일에 한 번 우리 할아버지의 말상대가 되어 드리려고 찾아온다 She comes to have a chat with my grandfather once a week.

말석 末席 the lowest seat; the bottom ◆ 말석

을 차지하다 have the honor of being present at 《a meeting》
▶ 그는 언제나 학급의 말석이다 He is always at the bottom of the class.
▶ 나도 이사회의 말석을 차지하고 있는 사람이다 I am one of the members of the board of directors.
▶ 하급자는 말석에 앉기로 되어 있다 Inferiors are supposed to take lower seats.

말세 末世 the end of the world; 〈타락한 세상〉 a corrupt [degenerate] age
◆ 세상 말세로다 The world is going to the dogs. ⇌ It is indeed an age of decadence we live in.
▶ 말세에 살아서 무슨 낙이 있겠는가? What pleasure can I find, living in such a degenerate world?

말소 抹消 erasure; deletion ◆ 등기의 말소 cancellation of registration
—**말소하다** delete 《from》; strike [cross] out [off]; write off
▶ 그의 이름이 명단에서 말소되었다 His name was deleted from the list.
■ —**키** 〔電算〕 the delete [deletion] key

말소리 a voice ◆ 뚜렷한[높은, 부드러운] 말소리 a clear [high-pitched, soft] voice / 말소리를 높이다[낮추다] raise [drop, lower] one's voice
▶ 옆방에서 그들의 말소리가 들렸다 I heard their voices in the next room. ⇌ I heard them talking in the next room.
▶ 덤불 속에서 사람들의 말소리가 들려왔다 I heard voices [some people talking] in the thicket.

말솜씨 one's way of speaking; one's speech
◆ 말솜씨가 좋은 사람 a good talker; a conversationalist; a good speaker / 말솜씨가 없는 사람 a poor talker; an inarticulate person / 말솜씨가 좋다[없다] be good [poor] at speaking [talking]
▶ 그는 말솜씨가 없어서 곧잘 오해를 받는다 He speaks so poorly [is so awkward with words] that he is often misunderstood.

말수 —數 the words one speaks
◆ 말수가 적은 남자 a man of few words; a quiet man; a reticent man
▶ 그녀는 말수가 많다 She is talkative. ⇌ She talks a great deal [too much].
▶ 그는 말수는 적지만 적절한 말만 한다 He is spare of speech, but his words are to the point.

말승냥이 〔動〕 wolf 《pl. wolves》

말실수 —失手 〈실언〉 a slip of the tongue; 〈부적절한 말〉 an improper remark
▶ 장관은 말실수를 사과했다 The Minister apologized for his slip of the tongue.
—**말실수하다** make a mistake in speaking; make a slip of the tongue; say sth one should not

말썽 (a) trouble; complaint; a dispute
◆ 말썽 없이 〈불평 없이〉 without making complaints; 〈이의 없이〉 without any objection / 말썽이 나 있다 be in trouble 《with》
▶ 오해가 흔히 말썽을 일으킨다 Misunderstandings often cause trouble.
▶ 그녀는 이웃과 항상 말썽을 일으키고 있다 She is constantly picking quarrels [causing trouble] with her neighbors.
▶ 아이들은 말썽을 부리기 일쑤다 Children can be a nuisance.

말썽거리 a cause [source] of trouble; trouble; a burden ◆ 말썽거리가 되다 become a source of trouble / 말썽거리를 만들다 sow the seeds of discord
▶ 저 집에는 말썽거리가 끊이지 않는다 There is constant trouble in the family.

말썽꾸러기 a burden; a nuisance; a troublemaker; a black sheep ◆ 말썽꾸러기 아이 a troublesome child
▶ 그의 집에서는 그를 말썽꾸러기로 친다 His family treats [regards] him as a burden [nuisance].
▶ 넌 정말 말썽꾸러기로구나 You really are a complete nuisance.

말썽꾼 a burden ⇨ 말썽꾸러기

말쑥하다 neat; neat and tidy; clean; smart
◆ 말쑥하게 neatly; tidily; cleanly / 말쑥하게 차려 입다 tidy [smarten] oneself up / 방을 말쑥하게 치우다 make a room tidy [neat]; tidy up a room; put a room in order; clean up a room
▶ 그는 언제 보아도 차림이 말쑥하다 He is always neat and clean.
▶ 이발하고 보니 말쑥하구나 You look sharp after a haircut.

말씀 speech; saying; a remark; a word
◆ 전에 말씀 드린대로 as I mentioned before / 말씀 드리다 say; talk; tell; mention; state / 삼가 말씀 드립니다 I wish to [beg to] inform you《that...》
▶ 당신에 대해 사장님께 이미 말씀 드렸습니다 I have informed the president about you.
▶ 여러분들께 말씀 드립니다 〈장내 방송 등에서〉 May I have your attention, please?
▶ 지당한 말씀입니다 Yes, indeed. ⇌ You are quite [absolutely] right.
—**말씀하다** 말씀하시는 그대로입니다 You [You've] said it! ⇌ You are quite right.
▶ 무어라고 말씀하셨습니까? I beg your pardon? ⇌ Pardon? ⇌ 《英》 Sorry? ⇌ What did you say?
▶ 제가 할 수 있는 일이라면 무엇이든지 말씀하세요 If there is anything I can do (for you), just let me know.
▶ 말씀하세요 〈전화에서〉 Go ahead, please.

말씨 one's way [manner] of speaking; mode of expression; use of words; wording; speech; language; an accent
◆ 경상도 말씨 a Kyŏngsang-do accent / 강경한 말씨로 in strong language / 말씨가 공손하다 speak politely; be polite in speaking / 조용한 말씨로 말하다 talk in a calm [quiet] tone
▶ 그는 말씨가 야비하다[거칠다] He uses vulgar [indecent] language.
▶ 그의 말씨에는 빈정거리는 데가 있다 He talks sarcastically.
▶ 그것은 상관에게 할 말씨가 아니다 That is no way to talk to your superiors. ⇌ You should

말아니다

not use that kind of language with your superiors.
▶ 그의 말씨로 이 고장 사람이 아닌 것을 알았다 I knew he was an out-of-towner by his accent [from the way he spoke].
말아니다 1 〈이치에 맞지 않다〉 nonsensical; unreasonable; absurd
♦ 말 아닌 값 an unreasonable price / 말아닌 말을 하다 say awful things 《about》 / 말아닌 요구를 하다 make an unjustified [exorbitant] demand
2 〈형편이 딱하다〉 horrible; miserable; wretched; 〈서술적〉 be in very bad shape
♦ 형편이 말(이) 아니다 live a wretched [dog's] life; lead a miserable existence
▶ 그녀는 말아닌 고생을 했다 She suffered unspeakable hardships.
▶ 그 거리의 교통 체증은 말(이) 아니다 There is terrible traffic congestion in the street.
말안되다 unreasonable; illogical; absurd; nonsense
♦ 말 안되는 소리 Nonsense, nonsense!
▶ 저렇게 어린 소년을 일하게 하다니 말 안된다 It is unreasonable [outrageous] to make such a little boy work.
▶ 그가 학자라고? 말 안돼 Him a scholar? Don't be silly.
말없이 〈잠자코〉 in silence; silently; without a word; 〈항의없이〉 without protest; 〈무단으로〉 without (previous) notice
♦ 말없이 착실하게 일하다 work steadily in silence / 말없이 보고 있다 be looking in silence / 말없이 앉아 있다 be sitting in silence / 말없이 방을 나가다 leave the room in silence [without (saying) a word, without saying anything] / 말없이 학교에 가지 않다 stay away from school without (previous) notice
▶ 그는 말없이 결근했다 He absented himself without notice.
▶ 그 부부는 말없이 잘 산다 The couple are getting along well without any trouble between them.
▶ 누가 말없이 내 차를 썼지? Who used my car without (my) permission?
말엽 末葉 the end; the close of an age
♦ 19세기 말엽에 in the last years [toward(s) the end] of the nineteenth century
말오줌나무 〔植〕 an elder (tree); an elderberry
말일 末日 the last day 《of a month》
▶ 9월 말일에 지불하겠소 I'll pay on the last day of September.
말잡이 a person who measures grain with a *mal*
말장난 a play upon words; a wordplay; a pun; a repartee; a word game; a verbal wit
♦ 어설픈 말장난 a poor pun
—**말장난하다** play on words; pun; make puns
말재간 —才幹 a talent for words ⇨ 말재주
말재주 a talent for words [language]; the gift of gab; eloquence
♦ 말재주가 없는 사람 a poor talker; an inarticulate person / 말재주가 있다[좋다] be gifted with eloquence; have a talent for speaking / 말재주가 없다 be awkward in speaking; be a poor speaker
▶ 그는 말재주는 있지만 남의 말을 잘 듣지 않는다 He is a good talker, but a poor listener.
■—꾼 a sweet talker; a glib [facile] talker
말전주 〈이간질〉 talebearing; taletelling; mischief-making —**말전주하다** tell tales; make mischief; spread gossip ■—꾼 a telltale; a talebearer; a tale-teller
말조심 —操心 carefulness in speech
—**말조심하다** be careful about *one's* language [what *one* says]
▶ 말조심해라 Watch your words.
▶ 그는 언제나 말조심하고 있다 He always tries to be careful of what he says. ⇌ He tries to be discreet [prudent] in speech.
말주변 tactfulness in speech; talkativeness
♦ 말주변이 없는 사람 a poor talker / 말주변이 좋은 사람 a glib [facile] talker / 말주변이 없는 poor at talking; clumsy in the use of words / 말주변이 좋은 tactful in speech; eloquent; fluent; talkative
▶ 그는 말주변이 없다 He is a poor talker [speaker]. ⇌ He is poor [not very good] at expressing himself.
말죽 boiled forage [feed] for horses
■—통 a forage tub; a manger
말즘 〔植〕 a curly pondweed; a watercaltrop
말직 末職 the lowest post; a petty office ♦ 말직에 있는 사람 a petty official; an underling; a subordinate official
말질 〈말다툼〉 a quarrel; an argument 《with, about》; 〈험담〉 slander; abuse
▶ 그는 뒷전에서 남의 말질을 한다 He speaks ill of [says bad things about] others behind their backs.
—**말질하다** dispute; quarrel with *sb* 《about》
▶ 그는 하찮은 일로 아내와 말질했다 He had an argument [had a quarrel, quarreled] with his wife about a little thing. ⇌ (口) He had word with his wife about a little thing.
말짜 末— 〈나쁜 물건〉 trash; rubbish; junk; 〈버릇없는 사람〉 a good-for-nothing (fellow); a brute ♦ 인간 말짜 the dregs of humanity
말짱하다 1 〈온전하다〉 complete; intact; unhurt; 〈깨끗하다〉 clean; tidy; 〈흠없다〉 faultless; flawless
♦ 말짱한 옷 spotless clothes / 말짱하게 completely; cleanly; faultlessly / 방을 말짱하게 치우다 make a room tidy [neat]; tidy up a room; put a room in order
▶ 그것은 말짱한 거짓말이다 It's an outright [an out-and-out, a downright] lie.
▶ 이 그림들은 말짱하게 보존되었다 These paintings have been preserved in perfect condition.
▶ 과거의 일은 말짱하게 잊어버리시오 Forget all about the past.
2 〈정신이 또렷하다〉 sane; sound; (be) in *one's* right mind; 〈의식이〉 (be) conscious; sober
▶ 그는 정신이 말짱하다 He is sane. ⇌ He is in his right mind.
말째 末— 〈맨끝의 차례〉 the last; the bottom

▶그는 경주에서 말째였다 He came in [was] last in the race.
▶그녀는 학급에서 말째다 She is at the very bottom [tail end] of her class.

말참견 ―**参見** interference; meddling
―**말참견하다** put in a word; cut into the conversation; intervene in; interfere in [meddle with] 《*sb's* business》
▶남의 일에 말참견하지 마라 Don't interfere in [(口) poke your nose into] other's affairs.
▶쓸데없는 말참견 마라 Mind your own business.

말채찍 a horsewhip ■―**질** whipping [lashing] a horse : **말채찍질하다** whip [lash] a horse

말초 **末梢** 〈나뭇가지의 끝〉 the tip of a twig; 〈말단〉 a tip; 〔解〕 the periphery
♦**말초적인** insignificant; trivial; nonessential; peripheral / **말초부의** 〔解〕 peripheral; distal
▶그는 말초적인 일에 구애 받는다 He sticks at trifles.
■―**신경** 〔解〕 a peripheral nerve; the nerve ending ―**신경계** the peripheral nervous system

말총 horsehair ■―**체** a horsehair sieve
말치레 (a) flattery; a compliment; a lip service
▶결코 말치레가 아니다 It's no compliment.
▶그는 말치레를 잘한다 He has a flattering tongue. ⇒ He is a smooth talker.
―**말치레하다** pay compliment; flatter; use sweet words; pay [give] lip service
▶그는 마음에도 없는 말치레를 한다 He makes insincere compliments.
▶그녀의 그 말은 말치레였다 Her remarks on it were complimentary. ⇒ She said it in [as a] compliment.

말캉하다 soft ⇨ 물컹하다
말코지 〈거는 갈고리〉 a branched wooden hanger

말 타면 경마잡히고 싶다 (속담) The more one has, the more one wants. ⇒ Give him an inch and he'll take an ell. ⇒ Set a beggar on horseback, and he'll ride a gallop.

말투 ―**套** *one's* manner [way] of talking [speaking]; *one's* speech; delivery
♦**야비한 말투** a mean expression / **효과 있는 말투** a telling delivery / **말투를 바꿔서** in an altered tone
▶그녀의 말투로 부산 출신인 것을 알았다 I could tell by [from] her speech that she was from Pusan.
▶그녀는 선생님의 말투를 흉내내어 모두를 웃겼다 She made everyone laugh by impersonating their teacher.
▶그녀의 말투로 보아 아직 결심하지 않은 것 같다 Judging from the way she talks, she doesn't seem to have made up her mind yet.
▶그는 마치 큰 부자같은 말투다 He talks as if he were a millionaire.
▶그는 마치 결혼하겠다는 말투였다 He talked as if he would get married.

말파리 〔昆〕 a horsefly; a horse botfly
말판 〈체스〉 a chessboard; 〈주사위〉 a dice board; 〈윷판〉 a *yut* board

말편자 a horseshoe ♦**말편자꼴의** horseshoe-shaped; U-shaped / **말편자를 대다[박다]** shoe a horse

말피기 〈이탈리아의 해부학자〉 Malpighi, Marcello (1628-94)
■―**관** 〔動〕 the Malpighian tubes ―**소체** 〔解〕 the Malpighian corpuscles [bodies]

말하다 **1** 〈이야기하다〉 speak; talk; 〈말로 나타내다〉 say; 〈전하다〉 tell

|解説| *speak*와 *talk*는 말하는 활동에 중점을 두고, 양자를 바꿔 쓸 수 있는 경우가 많다. speak는 한 사람이 여러 사람에게 말하는 것을 암시하고, talk는 둘 이상이 서로 말을 주고 받는 것을 암시한다. *say*와 *tell*은 말하는 내용에 중점을 둔다. say는 말하는 내용을 그대로 표현하고, tell은 요약된 말을 전한다. 따라서 say yes는 쓸 수 있지만, tell me yes라고는 쓸수 없다. 우리말로 「…하여 말하다」 「…처럼 말하다」라고 할 경우 영어에서는 한 단어로 쓸 수 있는 경우가 많다.

강조하여 말하다	stress, emphasize
되풀이해서 말하다	repeat
과장해서 말하다	exaggerate
지적해서 말하다	point
넌지시 말하다	hint, suggest

♦**일반적으로[솔직히] 말하면** generally [frankly] speaking / **진실을 말하면** to tell (you) [speak] the truth / **거짓을 말하다** tell a lie [lies] / **크게 말하다** speak [talk] loudly; speak [talk] up / **영어로 말하다** speak in English / **전화로 말하다** speak [talk] on [over] the telephone / **좋게[나쁘게] 말하다** praise [criticize]; speak well [ill] of *sb*
▶시험중에는 말하지 마라 Don't talk during examination.
▶〖會話〗「난 그녀석이 싫어」「그에게 그렇게 말해 주지 그래」 "I hate him." "Why not tell him so [that]?"
▶다시 말해 주십시오 Could you say that again? ⇒ I beg your pardon.
▶말하기는 쉬워도 행하기는 어렵다 Saying and doing are two things. ⇒ Easier said than done.
▶네게 말할 것이 있어 I have something to tell [say to] you.
▶어제 무슨 일이 있었는지 내게 말해라 Tell me what happened yesterday.
▶그는 그 문제에 대해서는 아무것도 말하지 않았다 He didn't say [speak] a word about the matter. ⇒ He said [told me] nothing about the matter. ⇒ He made no remark [comment] on the matter.
▶메리는 「톰과 오늘 수영갔다」고 말했다 Mary said, "Tom and I went swimming today."
▶「담배를 끊으시오」라고 의사는 그에게 말했다 "You'd better give up smoking," the doctor said to me. ⇒ The doctor advised [recommended] me to give up smoking.
▶그녀는 「거기에 가고 싶지 않다」고 말했다 She said, "I don't want to go there." ⇒ She said (that) she didn't want to go there.

말하자면

▶ 그는 우리 나라가 낳은 최고의 과학자라고 말할 수 있다 You could say that he is the greatest scientist (that) our country has ever produced.
▶ 그는 이 도시에서 제일 가는 부자라고 사람들은 말한다 People say [They say, It is said] that he is the richest man in this town.
2 〈나타내다〉 express; describe; set [put] forth
♦ 간단히 말하면 to put it briefly
▶ 나는 말 못한 고생을 했다 I can't express how much I have suffered.
▶ 나는 그것을 한국어로 이렇게 말하는지 모른다 I don't know how to put [say] it in Korean.
▶ 잃어버린 카메라의 특징을 말하시오 Describe your lost camera.
3 〈이름을 부르다〉 call; name
▶ 이 꽃은 영어로 무어라고 말합니까? What do you call this flower in English? ⇒ What is the English (word) for this flower?
4 〈의견을 말하다〉 express [give] one's opinion; remark; comment (on); 〈주장하다〉 insist; claim
▶ 그 건에 대하여 그는 무어라고 말하디까? What was his opinion about the matter?
▶ 말할 것이 없소 〈보도진의 질문에〉 No comment.
5 〈뜻하다〉 mean; 〈언급하다〉 mention; refer to ▶ 너는 무엇을 말하려고 하니? What do you mean (by that)? ⇒ What are you trying to say?
▶ 이것이 내가 어제 말한 사전이다 This is the dictionary I told you about yesterday.
6 〈명령하다〉 order; tell; 〈충고하다〉 advise; 〈권하다〉 recommend
▶ 내가 말하는대로 해라 Do as I say [tell you].
▶ 그에게는 아무리 말해도 소용없다 It is no use giving him any advice.
▶ 나는 무어라고 말할 수 없어. 네 책임이니까 I can't advise you. It's your own responsibility.
7 〈부탁하다〉 ask; request; demand
▶ 그는 나에게 도와달라고 말했다 He asked me for help [to help him].
8 〈제의하다〉 suggest
▶ 그는 나에게 다시 한 번 생각해 보라고 말했다 He suggested to me that I (should) give it a second thought.
9 〈인정하다〉 admit; acknowledge
▶ 그는 자기가 잘못했다고 말했다 He admitted [acknowledged] that he was wrong.
▶ 그녀는 그를 만난 적이 없다고 말했다 She denied ever having [that she had ever] met him.
10 〈불평하다〉 complain; 〈꾸짖다〉 scold
▶ 그녀는 이웃의 피아노가 성가시다고 말한다 She is complaining of her neighbor's annoying piano.
11 〈기타의 표현〉
▶ 말해서 좋은 것 있고 나쁜 것 있다 There are some things which should not be said.
▶ 내가 그렇게 말했지 I told you so. ⇒ Didn't I tell you?

말하자면 so to speak; as it were; 〈실질적으로〉 virtually ♦ 다시 말하자면 that is (to say); in other words
▶ 그녀는 말하자면 공주다 She is, so to speak [as it were], a princess. ⇒ She is a princess, so to speak [as it were].
▶ 탄생은 말하자면 죽음의 시작이다 Birth is, in a sense [manner], the beginning of death.
▶ 그것은 말하자면 사기다 It amounts to fraud, as a matter of fact. ⇒ It is virtually a fraud.

말할 것도 없다 ♦ 말할 것도 없이 not to mention; not to speak of; to say nothing of
▶ 그가 훌륭한 예술가임은[매우 기뻐한 것은] 말할 것도 없다 It is needless to say [It goes without saying] that he is an excellent artist [he was very delighted].
▶ 그녀는 독일어는 말할 것도 없고 영어도 못한다 She can't speak English, let alone German.
▶ 나는 미국은 말할 것도 없고 유럽에도 간 적이 있다 I have been to Europe, to say nothing of the United States.

말할 수 없다 unspeakable; beyond expression [description]
♦ 말할 수 없는 기쁨 unspeakable joy / 말할 수 없는 슬픔 inexpressible sorrow
▶ 나는 이 시점에서 뭐라고 말할 수 없다 I can't say anything at this moment.
▶ 내일 일은 뭐라고 말할 수 없다 There is no saying [telling] what may happen tomorrow.
▶ 그 경치는 말할 수 없이 아름답다 The scenery was beautiful beyond description [indescribably beautiful].

말향 抹香 〈가루향〉 incense (powder) ♦ 이 방에서는 말향 내가 난다 This room smells of incense.

말향고래 抹香— 〔動〕 a cachalot; a sperm whale = 향유고래

맑다 1 〈물·공기 등이〉 clear; clean; pure; lucid; transparent; crystal
♦ 맑은 공기 clean air / 맑은 물 clear [crystal] water / 맑은 눈 a limpid eyes / 맑은 음색 a clear note / 맑은 하늘 clear [serene] sky / 맑아지다 become clear; clear up
▶ 여기는 공기가 맑다 The air is clear here.
2 〈날씨가〉 fine; fair
♦ 맑은 날씨 fine [fair] weather / 어느 맑은 아침 one fine morning
▶ 이 달은 맑은 날씨가 오래 계속되고 있다 We have had a long spell of fine weather this month.
▶ 아침에는 비가 왔지만 후에 맑아졌다 It rained in the morning but it cleared up later.
3 〈마음·생활이〉 맑은 마음 a pure heart [soul] / 맑은 생활 a pure [an honest] life
▶ 산책을 하고 나니 기분이 맑아졌다 After a walk, I felt refreshed.
▶ 나는 맑은 심경이다 I am in a serene state of mind.

맑디맑다 very clear; as clear as can be [as crystal]; transparent

맑으그레하다 rather clear; somewhat clear

맑은 물에 고기 안 논다 (속담) Clear water doesn't breed fish. ⇒ Strict integrity leaves one isolated.

맑은술 refined rice wine = 청주

맑은장국 ―膓― clear (meat) soup
맘보 (the) mambo
▶ 젊은 남녀는 강렬한 맘보 리듬에 맞춰 춤추기 시작했다 The young boys and girls began to dance to a violent mambo rhythm.
■―바지 drainpipes; drainpipe trousers
맙소사 Oh no!; God forbid!; My [Good, Oh] God!
맛¹ **1** 〈음식의〉 (a) taste; (a) flavor; (a) savor
♦ 맛이 있다[좋다] taste good [nice, delicious]; have a good taste / 맛이 없다[나쁘다] taste bad [poor]; be unpalatable / 맛이 …하다 〈사물이 주어〉 taste; have a…taste [flavor, savor]; 〈사람이 주어〉 (can) taste
▶ 저 가게는 여러가지 맛의 아이스크림을 판다 They sell a lot of flavors of ice cream [ice creams in a lot of flavors] at that shop.
▶ 이것은 맛이 좋다[이상하다, 달다, 시다] This tastes good [strange, sweet, sour]. ⇌ This has a good [strange, sweet, sour] taste.
▶ 그 음식은 마늘 맛이 조금 난다 The food tastes slightly of garlic. ⇌ The food has a slight flavor [savor] of garlic.
▶ 会話「그 수프는 맛이 어떠니?」「스튜 맛같은 데요[우리 어머니 손맛인데요]」 "What does the soup taste like?" "It tastes like stew [like it is made by my mother]."
〈맛을〉 맛을 내다 season 《beef with ginger》; flavor; give a taste to 《a drink》 / 맛을 보다 taste; have [take] a taste 《of》
▶ 그녀는 간을 맞추려고 수프 맛을 보았다 She tasted [had a taste of] the soup to see if it needed more salt.
▶ 감기 때문에 맛을 모르겠다 I am unable to taste on account of my cold.
▶ 그 아이는 맥주 맛을 알았다 The boy has acquired a taste for beer.
▶ 너무 배가 고파 음식맛을 모르겠더라 I was too hungry to pay attention to the taste.
2 〈묘미〉 (a) taste; (a) savor
♦ 원문의 맛을 전하다 convey the charm of the original
▶ 노래의 맛을 모르는 사람도 있다 Some people cannot appreciate songs. ⇌ Some people don't enjoy songs.
▶ 나는 골프의 맛을 모른다 I cannot understand why golf is such fun.
3 〈재미〉 ▶ 그녀는 무슨 맛으로 사는지 몰라 I wonder what she lives for.
▶ 꼭 오늘이어야 맛이니? Why should it be today?
▶ 네가 남들 앞에서 내 욕을 해야만 맛이니? Why do you abuse me [call me names] in public?
4 〈경험〉 (an) experience; a taste
♦ 쓴맛 단맛 다 알다 have had the bitter with the sweet; have been through the mill
▶ 그는 한번 성공의 맛을 알고 나서 많은 돈을 주식에 투자했다 He got a taste of success and invested a lot of money in stocks.
▶ 그는 가난의 맛을 모른다 He has no experience [taste] of poverty. ⇌ He doesn't really know what it is to be poor.
▶ 그에게 고생의 맛을 가르쳐주겠다 I will give him a taste of hardship. ⇌ I'll teach him what hardship is like.
5 〈혼내기〉 ♦ 맛을 보여주다 teach *sb* a lesson
▶ 그 녀석 맛 좀 보여주어야겠다 I'll tell him what's what. ⇌ I'll tell him a thing or two.
맛² 〔貝〕 a razor clam [shell]; a solen
맛김 seasoned laver
맛깔스럽다 1 〈입에 맞다〉 delicious; tasty; palatable; 〈서술적〉 be nice to the palate
♦ 맛깔스런 요리 an appetizing meal
2 〈마음에 들다〉 pleasant; agreeable to *one's* taste; satisfactory ♦ 맛깔스런 디자인 a smart design / 맛깔스러운 집 a house to *one's* taste
맛나다 delicious ⇨ 맛있다
맛난이 1 〈조미료〉 (a) seasoning; (a) spice; artificial flavoring [seasoning] (화학 조미료); 〈맛있는 음식〉 delicious food; (美口) good eats
맛 들다 become tasty [delicious]; become good to eat [drink]; 〈익다〉 ripen
맛들이다 1 〈음식을〉 season; flavor; give a flavor 《to》; add seasoning to
♦ 김치를 맛들이다 get the *kimchi* well pickled / 소금으로 맛들이다 season with salt
2 〈재미를 붙이다〉 get [acquire] a taste for; find pleasure 《in》
▶ 한 번 도박에 맛들이면 그만두기 어렵다 Once one is successful in gambling, it's hard to give it up.
맛대로 according to *one's* taste [pleasure]
♦ 맛맛으로 골라 먹다 pick up what *one* eats
맛보기 tasting; sampling; foretaste
맛보다 1 〈음식을〉 taste; have [take] a taste 《of》; try; sample
♦ 음식을 맛보다 taste the food / 특별한 요리를 맛보다 enjoy [relish] a special dish / 포도주를 맛보다 sample [try the flavor of the wine / 케이크를 한 입 맛보다 have a (small) taste of cake
▶ 포도주를 한 모금 맛 보시지 않겠어요 Won't you have a taste of this wine?
2 〈경험하다〉 experience; go through
♦ 사랑의 단맛과 쓴맛을 맛보다 experience [know] the sweet and bitter aspects of love / 자유를 맛보다 enjoy [taste] *one's* freedom / 큰 슬픔을 맛보다 experience [taste] a great sorrow
▶ 그는 인생의 괴로움을 맛보았다 He went through [experienced] the hardships of life.
맛살 the flesh of a razor clam
맛없다 〈음식이〉 unsavory; tasteless; flavorless; ill-tasting; unpalatable; 〈서술적〉 taste bad untasty; undelicious
♦ 맛없는 맥주 bad [flat] beer / 맛없는 수프 tasteless [flat] soup / 맛없어 보이는 요리 an unappetizing [uninviting] dish
▶ 이 고기는 맛없다 This meat is [tastes] bad.
▶ 그런 말을 하면 식사가 맛없어진다 Such talk spoils my dinner.
2 〈재미가 없다〉 insipid; dull; dry; flat
♦ 맛없는 생활을 하다 lead an insipid [an unhappy, a dull] life
맛있다 1 〈맛나다〉 delicious; tasty; nice
♦ 맛있는 스테이크 a tasty [delicious] steak / 맛있어 보이는 요리 a delicious-looking dish

맛의 표현

혀로 느끼는 맛을 나타내는 말에는 「달다」 「쓰다」「시다」「맵다」「떫다」 등이 있다. 이것은 영어의 경우에도 마찬가지다. 영어로는 어떻게 번역하면 되는지 다음에 열거한다.

1. **달콤한·단(맛) sweet; sugary**
   ▶ 새콤달콤한 탕수육 sweet and sour pork / 단맛이 나다 be [taste] sweet; have a sweet taste / 달콤하고 매콤한 맛이 나다 be [taste] sweetly tangy [pepperish, hot]
   ▶ 나는 쌉쌀한 와인보다는 단맛이 도는 와인을 좋아한다 I prefer sweet wine to dry wine.
   ▶ 이 드레싱은 새콤달콤하다 This dressing is [tastes] sweet and sour.

2. **쌉쌀한·쓴(맛) bitter**
   ▶ 쓴 약 a bitter medicine / 쓴맛이 나다 be [taste] bitter; have a bitter taste / 쌉쌀한 맛이 나다 be [taste] slightly bitter / 달콤쌉쌀하다 bittersweet
   ▶ 블랙커피는 나한테는 너무 쓰다 Black coffee is too bitter for me.
   ▶ 나는 맥주의 쌉쌀한 맛이 좋다 I like the slight bitterness of beer.

3. **시큼한·신(맛) sour; acid; tart**
   ▶ 신 포도 a sour grape / 신 사과 a tart apple / 신 자두 a sour plum / 신 레몬 an acid lemon / 신 드레싱 sour dressing / 시큼한 맛이 나다 be [taste] sour [acid]; have a sour [an acid] taste
   ▶ 이 우유는 시어졌다 This milk has turned [gone] sour.
   ▶ 이 귤은 좀 시큼하다 This orange is [tastes] rather acid.

4. **알알한·매운(맛)〈톡 쏘다〉hot;〈향신료 등의 매운 맛〉pungent**
   ▶ 매운맛이 나다 be [taste] hot [tangy, pepperish, pungent]; have a hot [tangy, pepperish, pungent, sharp] taste (▶sharp는 치즈 등의 얼얼하고 강한 맛) / 알알하고 톡 쏘는 소스 a rich and pungent sause / 매운 겨자[후추] hot mustard [pepper]
   ▶ 이 카레는 너무 맵다 This curry is too hot.

5. **짠(맛) salty; salted**
   ▶ 짠 음식 salty food / 짠 연어 salted salmon / 간이 부족하다 be not salty [salted] enough / 짠맛이 나다 be [taste] salty; have a salty taste
   ▶ 이 수프는 좀 짜다 This soup is a little too salty.

6. **떫은(맛) astringent; a puckery taste**
   ▶ 떫은 감 an astringent persimmon / 떫은 와인 rough [harsh] wine (▶harsh는 역겨운 맛)

7. **부드러운(맛) smooth** (▶음식물·담배 등이 자극성이 없는); mellow; mild
   ▶ 이 위스키는 부드럽다 This whiskey is smooth.

8. **산뜻한(맛)〈담백한 맛〉plain;〈소화가 잘되는 음식〉light**
   ▶ 그녀는 산뜻한 음식을 좋아한다 She likes plain [light] meals.

9. **짙은[기름진](맛) heavy (food)**
   ▶ 기름진 요리는 소화가 잘 되지 않는다 Heavy food is not easily digested.

▶ 이 파이는 참 맛있다 This pie is very good [very nice, delicious]. ⇌ This pie tastes very good [nice].
▶ 이런 맛있는 요리를 먹어본 적이 없다 I've never had such a delicious meal.
▶ 저녁을 맛있게 먹었습니다 I enjoyed the nice dinner.
▶ 야외에서 먹으면 훨씬 맛있다 Food tastes better outdoors.
▶ 저 호텔 요리는 맛있다 That hotel serves very good food. ⇌ I like the food in that hotel very much.
▶ 〖會話〗「음식맛이 어때요?」「음, 맛있어요. 당신 것은요?」「아주 맛있어요」"How's your food?" "Mm, delicious. And yours?" "Mm, very good."

2〈재미있다〉interesting; pleasant

망望 (a) watch; lookout; guard
♦ 망보는 사람 a watch; a watchman; a guard; a lookout / 망을 보다 watch; keep (a) watch (on)/ 망을 세우다 place a watch [guard, lookout] (for)
▶ 밖에서 망 좀 봐주겠나? Would you keep watch outside?

망 網 1〈그물〉a net; (총칭) netting ♦ 망을 뜨다 make a net / 망을 치다 lay [spread] a net / 망에 걸리다 be trapped [caught] in a net
2〈조직〉a network ♦ 수사망을 치다 spread a dragnet ((around him)) / 법망을 뚫다 escape the meshes [clutches] of the law; evade the law
■ 라디오[텔레비전] 방송— a radio [television] network 어— a fishing net 정보— an intelligence network 철도— a network of railroads 통신— a communication network 투— a cast net ■—구조 network structure

망가뜨리다〈부수다〉break (down); destroy;〈손상하다〉damage; ruin;〈고장내다〉put[get] (a watch) out of order ♦ 장난감[창문]을 망가뜨리다 break a toy [window]
▶ 그들은 미술품을 거칠게 다뤄 망가뜨렸다 They damaged the art object by rough handling.
▶ 그는 너무 마셔서 몸을 망가뜨렸다 Excessive drinking ruined his health.
▶ 그들은 소나무를 베어서 아름다운 경치를 망가뜨렸다 They destroyed the beautiful scenery by cutting down the pine trees.

망가지다 be broken ⇨ 망그러지다

망각 忘却 forgetting; oblivion
—**망각하다** forget; be forgetful of; be oblivious of ((duty))
▶ 그는 공무원으로서의 본분을 망각했다 He neglected his duty as a public servant.
▶ 그 사건은 오랫동안 망각되었다 The event had been forgotten [consigned to oblivion]

망간 (化) manganese ♦ 망간의 manganic
■ —강(鋼) manganese steel —산 manganic acid —석류석 a spessartite; a spessartine
망건 網巾 a headband made of horsehair
망건 쓰고 세수한다 (속담) The order is reversed.
망건 쓰자 파장 (속담) It is for late now.
망고 (植) a mango 《pl. ~ (e)s》
망고스틴 (植) a mangosteen
망국 亡國 〈망한 나라〉 a ruined country; 〈나라의 멸망〉 national ruin; 〈나라를 망침〉 ruining one's country
♦ 망국적인 ruinous to one's country / 망국적 재정 finances ruinous to the state
—망국하다 ruin [destroy] one's country
■ —민 people without a country; homeless people —지본(之本) the causes of national ruin —지탄(之歎) lamentation [grief] over the national ruin
망그러뜨리다 break ⇨ 망가뜨리다
망그러지다 be broken; be damaged; be destroyed
♦ 크게 망그러진 차 a badly damaged car / 장난감이 망그러지다 a toy gets broken
▶ 카메라가 망그러졌다 My camera got out of order.
▶ 이 세탁기가 또 망그러졌다 This washing machine broke down again.
망극 罔極 —망극하다 1 〈은혜가 그지없다〉 immeasurable; inestimable; great
♦ 망극한 은혜 a great favor[love]; immeasurable great benefit
▶ 성은이 망극하옵니다 Inscrutable are the king's favors.
2 〈슬픔이 한없다〉 the greatest grief beyond expression 《at the death of one's parents》
▶ 얼마나 망극하십니까? Please let me offer my condolence to you on this sad event.
■ —지통(之痛) the greatest grief [lament]; grief beyond expression
망나니 1〈참수인〉 an executioner; a headcutter 2〈못된 놈〉 a hooligan; a rowdy; a gangster ♦ 망나니 짓을 하다 play the gangster
망녀 亡女 1〈죽은 딸〉 one's deceased daughter 2〈주책없고 고약한 여자〉 an ill-mannered woman; a bad woman
망년회 忘年會 a New Year's Eve Party; a year-end (dinner) party ♦ 망년회를 열다 hold a year-end party; give a party to see the year out
망녕그물 a net to catching rabbits or pheasants
망단 忘斷 a rash [reckless, hasty] conclusion —망단하다 conclude recklessly[hastily]; make a hasty conclusion
망대 望臺 a watchtower; an observation tower ▶ 그는 망대에서 화재를 발견했다 He spotted a fire from the watchtower.
망동 妄動 a rash act —망동을 삼가다 refrain from rash action —망동하다 act blindly; behave rashly
망둥이 (魚) a goby
망라하다 網羅— 〈모든 것을 포함하다〉 include [comprehend, contain] all…; 〈남김없이 모으다〉 collect all…
♦ 모든 것을 망라한 exhaustive; comprehensive; all-inclusive; thorough
▶ 그의 연구는 영문학의 전분야를 망라하고 있다 His studies cover the whole field of English literature.
▶ 그 목록에는 그 책에 있는 모든 단어가 망라되어 있다 The list contains all the words in that book.
망령 亡靈 〈죽은이의 혼〉 a departed spirit [soul]; 〈유령〉 an apparition; a ghost; a specter ▶ 햄릿은 아버지의 망령을 보았다 Hamlet saw the ghost of his father.
망령 妄靈 senility; dotage
♦ 망령든 노인 a senile old man; a dotard / 망령들다 grow senile; become senile / 망령이 나 있다 be in one's dotage
▶ 그는 망령이 들기 시작했다 He has recently begun to show signs of senility.
▶ 그는 나이가 들어 망령이 들어버렸다 He has grown senile with age.
망령되다 妄靈— absurd 《remark》; foolish; unreasonable
▶ 이 무슨 망령된 짓이냐? How can you behave so foolishly [be so silly]?
망루 望樓 a watchtower ⇨ 망대
망륙 望六 fifty-one years of age ♦ 망륙의 나이가 되다 reach one's 51st year of age.
망막 網膜 (解) the retina 《pl. ~s, -nae》
■ —검영기 (眼科) retinoscope; a skiascope —검영법 (眼科) retinoscopy; skiascopy —박리 detachment of the retina —상 a retinal image —세포 a retinal cell; a retinula 《pl. ~s, -lae》 —열(화)상 a retinal burn —염 retinitis —출혈 a retinal hemorrhage
망막하다 茫漠— 1〈넓고 아득하다〉 vast; extensive; boundless ♦ 망막한 평원 a vast stretch of plain
2〈막연하다〉 vague; obscure
♦ 망막한 장래의 기대 vague prospects
망망 茫茫 —망망하다 vast; boundless
■ —대해 a vast expanse [stretch] of sea; a boundless ocean ♦ 우리는 망망대해를 조망할 수가 있었다 We could command a view of a boundless expanse [stretch] of water.
망망하다 忙忙— 〈서술적〉 be very busy; have much to do
망명 亡命 flight from one's own country; exile; 〈적국으로 도피하는〉 defection
♦ 망명중인 국왕 a king in exile / 정치적 망명을 허용하다 grant political asylum
▶ 그는 미국에 정치적 망명을 요청했다 He asked for political asylum in the United States.
▶ 그는 여러 해 동안 미국에서 망명생활을 보냈다 He lived in exile in America for many years.
—망명하다 flee from one's own country 《for political reasons》; exile oneself; defect 《to》; 〈피난하다〉 seek refuge 《in》
♦ 스위스로 망명하다 take [seek] refuge in Switzerland / 망명하여 외국에서 살다 live in exile

▶ 많은 과학자들이 제2차 세계대전 중 미국으로 망명했다 Many scientists obtained [sought] political asylum in the United States during World War Ⅱ.
▶ 그는 독일에 망명할 것이다 He will seek refuge in Germany.
■—객 a political exile —생활 (a) life in exile —자 a refugee; a defector; an exile —작가[문학자] a writer in exile —정권 an exiled regime —정부 a government in exile; a refugee government

망모 亡母 one's deceased [late] mother
망민 罔民 〈백성을 속임〉 deceiving [deluding] the public —망민하다 deceive [delude] the public; commit a fraud upon the public
망발 妄發 a silly talk; a reckless remark; an absurd [unreasonable] speech
▶ 그 말은 망발이었다 That remark was a bad slip of the tongue.
—망발하다 talk nonsense; say silly things; make reckless [thoughtless] remarks
—풀이 a treat given to make excuse oneself for one's reckless remarks
망배 望拜 worshiping from a distance [far] —망배하다 worship from a distance; bow to the direction of (one's ancestral graveyard)
망보다 望— watch; keep (a) watch (on)
▶ 여기서 망보고 있어라 Keep a lookout here.
▶ 그들은 적의 동정을 망보고 있다 They are now watching [on the lookout for] enemy movements.
망부 亡父 one's deceased [late] father
망부 亡夫 one's deceased [late] husband
망부석 望夫石 the stone on which a faithful wife stood waiting for her husband until she perished
망사 網紗 gauze
망상 妄想 〈어림없는 공상〉 a wild fancy; a fantastic idea; a fantasy; a delusion
♦ 망상을 품다 nurse delusions / 망상에 빠지다 be lost in wild fancies; be obsessed by delusions / 망상으로 괴로워하다 suffer from delusion
▶ 그는 자기가 영웅이라는 망상을 품고 있다 He is under the delusion that he is a hero.
▶ 그녀의 모습을 보았다고 생각한 것은 망상에 지나지 않았다 It was only my imagination when I thought I saw her.
■—과대— delusions of grandeur; megalomania: 과대망상(증) 환자 a megalomaniac 피해— delusions of persecution: 피해망상증 a persecution complex; persecution mania / 피해망상에 빠지다 suffer from a persecution complex —광 [醫] paranoia
망상 網狀 net shape; reticulation ♦ 망상의 netlike; reticular; reticulate / 망상을 이루(게하)다 reticulate
■—섬유 a reticulum —조직 [解] a retiform tissue; a reticulum (pl. -la)
망상스럽다 〈요망하고 깜찍하다〉 crafty; tricky; wicked; 〈경솔하다〉 frivolous; flippant
망새 [建] a ridge end tile; a decorative ridge [roof] tile
망석중이 1 〈꼭두각시〉a marionette; a puppet
♦ 망석중이를 놀리는 사람 a puppeteer; a marionette man **2** 〈사람〉 a puppet; a dummy
■—놀이 a puppet show[play]
망설망설 hesitatingly; hesitantly; waveringly; lingeringly
▶ 그녀는 수업이 끝났는데도 망설망설 남아 있다 She lingers on even after class is over.
망설이다 〈주저하다〉hesitate (about, to do); be hesitant (about); 〈머뭇거리다〉 waver (between); hover
♦ 망설이지 않고 without any [with no] hesitation / 확실한 대답을 망설이다 hesitate to give a definite answer / 갈까 말까 망설이다 can't make up one's mind whether to go or not / 나아갈까 돌아설까 망설이다 hesitate [waver] between going on and turning back
▶ 그는 아직도 승낙을 망설이고 있다 He is still hesitating [hesitant] about accepting it. ⇌ He is still hesitating (about) whether to accept it [whether he should accept it].
망성어 望星魚 〔魚〕 a surf fish; a surfperch
망신 亡身 disgrace; dishonor; shame; humiliation; loss of reputation
▶ 그것은 우리집안 망신이다 That is a disgrace [a shame] to my family.
—망신하다 bring shame on oneself; disgrace oneself (in public); humiliate oneself
♦ 망신시키다 put sb to shame; humiliate; make sb lose face
—망신스럽다 disgraceful; dishonorable
▶ 퇴학은 실로 망신스러운 일이다 It is really shameful [a disgrace] to be expelled from the school.
■—살 bad luck [misfortune] to bring disgrace on oneself : 망신살이 뻗치다 have a run [stroke] of disgrace
망실 亡失 loss; disappearance ♦ 망실 재산 lost property —망실하다 lose; miss
망아 忘我 self-oblivion; (an) ecstasy; (a) trance ▶ 그는 망아지경을 헤매고 있었다 He was hovering in ecstasies.
망아지 〈총칭〉 a foal; 〈수컷〉 a colt; 〈암컷〉 a filly
망양지탄 望洋之歎 grief for one's inability; lamenting over one's lack of resourcefulness
♦ 망양지탄이 있다 feel one's object to be unattainable
망언 妄言 〈당치 않은 말〉 an absurd remark; 〈실언〉 thoughtless words; a blunder; 〈못된 말〉 an ill-considered remark; irresponsible remarks
—망언하다 make irresponsible [indiscreet] remarks
■—다사 (多謝) 〈편지에서〉 I hope you will forgive my brashness (in making the above suggestion). ⇌ Please excuse me for expressing myself candidly.
망연자실 茫然自失 abstraction; stupefaction
—망연자실하다 be abstracted [stupefied] (with grief); be dazed (by the news)
♦ 망연자실하여 absentmindedly; with an air of complete abstraction
▶ 그는 불탄 자기집 옆에 망연자실하여 서 있었다 He stood by the charred ruins of his house

in a state of shock.
▶ 그 남자는 망연자실하여 나를 바라보았다 He looked at me with an air of abstraction.
▶ 그녀는 망연자실하여 어찌할 바를 몰랐다 She was quite at a loss as to what to do.

망연하다 茫然— **1** 〈넓고 아득하다〉 extensive; boundless; vast; wide
2 〈멍하다〉 vacant; abstracted; stupefied
♦ 망연히 vacantly; blankly / 망연히 서 있다 stand 《there》 vacantly
▶ 그는 그녀가 죽었다는 소식에 망연할 따름이었다 He was stunned by [at, to hear] the news of her death.

망 외 望外 ♦ 망외의 unexpected; unlooked-for / 망외의 성공 an unlooked-for success
▶ 이것은 망외의 영예입니다 It is an unexpected [unlooked-for] honor.

망운 亡運 evil luck which will bring ruin
♦ 망운이 들다 one's star is on the wane

망울 1 〈덩어리〉 a lump; a ball; a mass
♦ 망울이 지다 have a lump; get lumpy
2 〈꽃망울〉 a (flower) bud ♦ 망울진 장미 a swollen rose bud / 망울지다 put forth buds
▶ 꽃이 망울지기 시작했다 The flowers are budding [putting out buds].
3 〈임 파 선 종〉 an induration; 〔醫〕 lymphadenoma ♦ 젖 망울 a lump in the breast / 망울서다 have a swollen (lymph) glands; have lymphadenoma

망원경 望遠鏡 a telescope; 〈소형의〉 a spyglass; 〈쌍안경〉 binoculars; field glasses
♦ 망원경으로만 보이는 물체[별] a telescopic object [star] / 망원경으로 보다 look through a telescope
▶ 망원경으로 멀리 있는 배를 보았다 I looked at a distant ship through a telescope.
■ 감마선— a gamma-ray telescope 광학— an optical telescope 굴절— a refracting telescope 반사— a reflecting telescope; a reflector 전파— a radio telescope 조준— a sighting telescope 지상— a terrestial telescope 천체— an astronomical telescope 태양 관측— a helioscope

망원렌즈 望遠— a telephoto(graphic) lens; a telephoto ♦ 망원렌즈로 새를 촬영하다 telephotograph a bird
▶ 그는 멀리 솟아 있는 산을 망원렌즈로 촬영했다 He telephotographed a heightening mountain in the distance.

망원사진 望遠寫眞 a telephoto(graph) ■ —기 a telephotographic camera —술 telephotography

망은 忘恩 ingratitude; unthankfulness ♦ 망은 행위 an act of ingratitude —망은하다 be ungrateful; lose one's gratitude

망인 亡人 the deceased (person); the dead (person)

망조 亡兆 an omen of a downfall; an ominous sign; an ill omen ♦ 망조가 들다 show an evil sign; be ominous of ruin

망종 亡種 〈행실이 못된 사람〉 a rogue; a rascal [villain]; a worthless scamp

망종 芒種 **1** 〈까끄라기가 있는 곡식〉 awned [bearded] grain **2** 〈24절기의 하나〉 one of the 24 seasonal divisions (around 5 June)

망주석 望柱石 a pair of stone posts in front of a tomb

망중한 忙中閑 a moment of leisure from pressure of business ▶ 누구나 망중한은 있다 One can find moments of leisure even on the busiest of days.

망집 妄執 obsession; a deep-rooted delusion

망처 亡妻 one's deceased wife

망측하다 罔測— 〈해괴하다〉 absurd; inordinate; 〈추잡하다〉 nasty; vicious; ugly; 〈상스럽다〉 indecent; low; 〈꼴사납다〉 bad-looking; unsightly
▶ 그는 울어대고 소리지르며 망측하게 굴었다 He screamed and shouted and behaved in a most unseemly way.

망치 〈쇠망치〉 a hammer; 〈나무 망치〉 a mallet; a maul (큰); 〈대장간의〉 a sledge(hammer)
▶ 망치로 나무에 못을 박았다 I drove a nail into the wood with a hammer. ⇒ I hammered a nail into the wood.
■ —자루 the handle of a hammer —질 hammering: 망치질하다 hammer

망치다 destroy; lay waste; ruin; spoil; mar
♦ 계획을 망치다 frustrate [upset] a plan; throw a wet blanket over a project
▶ 그는 수학을 망쳤다 He failed in math. ⇒ He has done badly in math.
▶ 금년에는 벼농사를 망쳤다 The rice crop has failed [is poor] this year.
▶ 그 실언으로 그는 일생을 망쳤다 The slip of the tongue ruined his life.
▶ 그는 술로 몸을 망쳤다 He ruined himself [美口] did himself in] by drinking too much. ⇒ Drink was his ruin.
▶ 그는 노름으로 신세를 망쳤다 He went wrong through gambling. ⇒ He ruined himself by gambling.
▶ 저 흉물스러운 광고탑이 거리의 미관을 망치고 있다 The ugly advertisement tower mars the beauty of the city street.
▶ 저런 여자 때문에 일생을 망치고 싶지 않다 I don't want to ruin my life for such a girl.

망태기 網— a mesh [net] bag

망토 a manteau; a mantle; a cloak; a cape
♦ 망토를 걸치다 put on [draw] one's cloak; throw a cloak over one's shoulders

망토비비 〔動〕 a sacred baboon; a hamadryad

망투 —反應 〔醫〕 〈결핵 검사의〉 Mantoux reaction —시험 a Mantoux test

망판 網版 〔印·寫〕 a halftone; a halftone plate [block] ■ —제판 a halftone process

망하다 亡— **1** 〈멸망하다〉 fall; perish; die (out); 〈파멸하다〉 be ruined; ruin oneself; 〈파산하다〉 go bankrupt
♦ 나라가 망하다 a country perishes / 집안이 망하다 a family goes down / 함께 망하다 fall together; be ruined together
▶ 그는 망했다 He came down in the world. ⇒ He was down and out.
▶ 그는 술로 망했다 He ruined himself by drinking too much. ⇒ Alcohol was his ruin.
▶ 인류는 언젠가는 핵전쟁으로 망할 것이다

The human race will be ruined [destroyed] by nuclear war someday.
▶ 많은 중소기업이 속속 망했다 Many small-and-medium firms went bankrupt [went out of business, failed] one after another.
2 〈고약하다〉 wretched; hard to deal with; 〈꼴사납다〉 very ugly; 〈다루기 힘들다〉 hard to deal with; difficult
♦ 보기가 망하다 look ugly
▶ 그 책은 읽기 망하다 The book is hard [difficult] to read.
▶ 망할 놈의 날씨다 What foul [wretched] weather!

망향 望鄕 homesickness; nostalgia
망형 亡兄 *one's* dead [deceased] (elder) brother
망혼 亡魂 the spirit [soul] of the dead ♦ 망혼을 위로하다 solace [pacify] the departed soul
맞- opposite; face-to-face; equal; mutual; reciprocal; together; jointly ♦ 맞대면 a face-to-face meeting / 맞바람 a head wind
맞갖다 pleasant; agreeable 《to》; satisfactory; palatable; 〈서슴히〉 suit [please] *sb* fancy
♦ 맞갖은 요리[음식] an appetizing [agreeable] meal [food] / 맞갖은 집 a house to *one's* taste
맞갖잖다 unpleasant; disagreeable 《to》; unsatisfactory; offensive; disgusting
♦ 맞갖잖은 소리 an unpleasant [a weird] sound / 맞갖잖은 음식 an unappetizing food / 맞갖잖은 일[사람] a disagreeable job [person]
▶ 무슨 맞갖잖은 일이라도 있습니까? Is there something that gets on your nerves [offends you]?
맞걸다 **1** 〈마주 걸다〉 lock [link] with another; interlock **2** 〈노름판에서〉 bet [stake] the same amount against the opposite party
맞걸리다 **1** 〈물건이〉 be linked together; be coupled
▶ 차량 연결기가 맞걸려 있다 The couplers of the cars are engaged [joined].
2 〈사람이〉 be pitted against each other
▶ 둘이 결승전에서 맞걸려 있다 The two are pitted against each other in the final match.
맞고소 —告訴 a counterclaim; a claim made to offset another claim in law; a cross action; a countersuit
▶ 그는 명예훼손으로 맞고소를 했다 He brought a cross action [countersuit] for libel.
—맞고소하다 claim so as to offset a previous claim; counterclaim; bring a cross action
■ —인 a counterclaimant
맞구멍 a hole on the opposite side
맞꼭지각 —角 〔數〕 vertically opposite angles; vertical angles
맞다¹ **1** 〈정확하다〉 be right; be correct; keep good time 〈시계가〉
♦ 맞는 답 a right answer
▶ 맞는 답에 동그라미를 치시오 Circle the correct answer.
▶ 아무래도 계산이 맞지 않는다 These figures don't add up.
▶ 내 시계는 떨어뜨린 다음부터 맞지 않는다 My watch has not kept good time since I dropped it.
2 〈적합하다〉 suit 《*one's* taste》; answer [serve] 《the purpose》; meet 《*one's* wishes》
♦ 마음에 맞는 여자 a woman after *one's* heart / 입에 맞는[맞지 않는] 음식 an agreeable [a disagreeable] food / 체질에 맞는 음식 food suitable to *one's* constitution
▶ 그는 장사꾼으로는 맞지 않는다 He is not of a business turn. ⇌ He isn't cut out for business [a trader]. ⇌ He won't do for [isn't suited to be] a businessman.
3 〈일치하다〉 agree 《with, on》; correspond 《with》; 〈부합히다〉 coincide 《with》; ally 《with》
▶ 팀 전원은 마음이 딱 맞는다 The whole team plays in perfect harmony.
▶ 우리의 의견은 늘 맞지 않는다 Our opinions always differ.
▶ 그녀는 이상에 맞게 살려고 한다 She tries to live up to her ideals.
4 〈알맞다〉 go well with; fit; suit; agree with
▶ 살이 쪄서 이 옷은 내게 맞지 않는다 This dress doesn't fit me any more. I'm getting fat.
▶ 거기 기후는 당신에게 맞습니까? Does the climate there suit you [suit your health, agree with you]?
▶ 적포도주는 고기에 맞는다 Red wine goes with meat.
5 〈어울리다〉 go 《with》; match 《with》; be in harmony 《with》; become
♦ 장단이 맞다 be in tune
▶ 그의 사상은 오늘날의 세상에는 맞지 않는다 His ideas are not in [are out of] tune with the modern world.
▶ 그런 짓은 네게 맞지 않는다 It is not like you to do such a thing. ⇌ It does not become you to do such a thing.
6 〈적중하다〉 hit; strike 《against, on》
▶ 일기 예보가 맞았다[맞지 않았다] The weather forecast proved right [wrong].
▶ 그 예언이 맞을까? I don't think the prediction will come true.
7 〈제비·복권 등이〉 win; draw
▶ 복권에서 백만원이 맞았다 I won a million won in a lottery.
▶ 제비뽑기에서 냄비가 맞았다 A pan fell to me in the lottery.
8 〈수지가〉 pay; 《美》 pay off
♦ 수지 맞는 장사 a profitable [paying] business
▶ 이 장사는 수지가 맞지 않는다 This business yields no profit. ⇌ This business doesn't pay [make money].
▶ 3천부 팔아야 겨우 수지가 맞으야 If we sell three thousand copies, we will just about break even.
맞다² **1** 〈영접하다〉 meet; go to meet; 〈접대하다〉 receive; 〈차로 맞으러 가다〉 pick...up; 〈환영하다〉 welcome
▶ 그는 현관에서 손님을 맞았다 He welcomed [greeted, received] his guest at the (front) door.
▶ 집주인은 그를 따뜻하게 맞았다 He was well received by the host.

2 〈맞아들이다〉 invite; engage
♦ 전문가를 맞다 invite [call] a specialist / 사위로 맞다 take a son-in-law into *one's* family / 양자로 맞다 adopt as *one's* son
▶ 그들은 그를 강사로 맞았다 They invited him to give them a lecture.
▶ 그는 유명한 여배우를 아내로 맞았다 He married a famous actress.
3 〈어떤 시기·상태가 되다〉 ♦ 새해를 맞다 greet the New Year / 새 국면을 맞다 enter a new phase
▶ 그는 금년에 환갑을 맞았다 He reached the age of sixty this year.
▶ 그는 20살의 생일을 맞았다 His twentieth birthday came around.
4 〈적 등을 상대하다〉 meet [confront] 《the enemy》
♦ 적을 맞아 싸우다 fight to repulse the attack of the enemy
5 〈비바람을〉 be exposed to; expose *oneself* to
♦ 밤이슬을 맞다 be exposed [expose *oneself*] to the night dew / 비를 맞다 be exposed to rain
▶ 집에 가는 길에 비를 맞았다 I was caught in the rain [in a shower] on my way home.
6 〈어떤 일을 당하다〉 meet 《with》; encounter
♦ 위기를 맞다 face a crisis [an emergency]; arrive at [reach] a critical point / 야단맞다 be scolded for / 퇴짜맞다 meet with a rebuff; get rejected
7 〈매·총 등을〉 get a blow; be shot
♦ 매를 맞다 be beaten; be struck; get a blow / 벼락을 맞다 be struck by lightning
▶ 그 돌은 그의 이마에 맞았다 The stone hit him on the forehead.
▶ 그는 총에 맞아 죽었다 He was shot dead.
8 〈주사를〉 get [have] 《an injection》; 〈도장을〉 receive 《a seal [stamp] of approval》
▶ 나는 독감 예방주사를 맞았다 I had myself vaccinated against the flu.
9 〈점수를〉 get; receive
♦ 만점을 맞다 《美》 get a perfect score; 《英》 gain [win] full marks / 좋은[나쁜] 점수를 맞다 get good [poor] marks [grades]; get high [low] marks
▶ 《會話》「영어 시험에서 몇 점 맞았니?」「80점」 "What mark [What, How much] did you get in the English test?" "I got a mark of 80 [《英》 80 marks] in it."

맞닥뜨리다 meet with; 《美口》 meet up with; come across; encounter 《the enemy》
♦ 난관에 맞닥뜨리다 face [be brought face to face with] a difficulty / 외나무 다리에서 원수와 맞닥뜨리다 encounter an enemy on a log bridge
▶ 우리는 뜻하지 않은 난관에 맞닥뜨렸다 We met with [were confronted with] an unforeseen difficulty.

맞닥치다 face; encounter; be faced [confronted] 《with》; come [be brought] face to face 《with》; meet with
♦ 위험에 맞닥치다 face 《a》 danger / 난관에 맞닥치다 be confronted with a difficult problem
▶ 우리는 새로운 문제에 맞닥쳐 있다 We are faced [are confronted] with a new problem.
▶ 그는 죽음에 맞닥쳐도 태연했다 He remained calm in the face of (imminent) death.

맞담배 ♦ 맞담배피우다, 맞담배질하다 smoke to *sb's* face; smoke in the presence of *one's* superior [elder]

맞당기다 pull [draw, drag, haul] from both sides ▶ 줄이 맞당겨 끊어졌다 A rope was pulled apart.

맞닿다 come in contact [touch] 《with》; touch with each other
▶ 두 원이 맞닿는 점 the point where two circles come in contact with each other
▶ 하늘과 바다가 서로 맞닿아 있다 Sky and water merge into each other.
▶ 선 A가 그 원에 맞닿아 있다 Line A touches the circle.

맞대다 **1** 〈마주 대다〉 put into contact with each other; apply 《*sth* to *sth*》; face each other
♦ 무릎을 맞대다 sit opposite each other / 이마를 맞대다 bring brows together / 이마를 맞대고 의논하다 put 《their》 heads together
▶ 두 사람은 얼굴을 맞대고 테이블에 앉았다 The two sat at the table facing each other. ≒ The two sat across the table from each other.
▶ 네가 나를 맞대어 놓고 어떻게 그런 말을 할 수 있니? How dare you say such a thing to my face?
2 〈대면시키다〉 confront *sb* to 《another》
♦ 피고와 원고를 맞대다 bring the accused face to face with the accuser
▶ 우리는 두 당사자들을 맞대어 놓고 의견을 물었다 We brought the two parties concerned together face to face and asked their opinions.
3 〈비교하다〉 compare 《with》; match; be equal to
▶ 그와 맞댈 사람은 없다 He has no equal [rival].
▶ 우리는 견본과 물건을 맞대어 보았다 We compared the article with the sample.

맞대면 —對面 a face-to-face meeting
—맞대면하다 confront face to face
▶ 나는 그와 3년만에 맞대면했다 I met him for the first time in three years.
▶ 나는 동생과 10년만에 다시 맞대면할 수 있었다 I was able to meet my brother again after ten years' seperation.

맞대하다 —對— face [confront] each other
♦ …과 맞대하고 앉다 sit face to face with
▶ 그 건물은 호수와 맞대하고 있다 The building faces [looks out on] the lake.

맞돈 cash; ready money
♦ 맞돈으로 거래하다 deal in cash
▶ 자동차를 맞돈으로 샀다 I bought a car for [in] cash. ≒ I paid (in) cash for a car.
▶ 지불은 맞돈도 좋고 월부도 좋습니다 You may pay [Payment may be made] either by cash or monthly installments.

맞들다 **1** 〈마주들다〉 lift (up) together; hold up together ♦ 책상을 맞들다 lift a desk together **2** 〈협력하다〉 join forces 《with》; co-operate 《with》

맞뚫다 bore [drill] 《a hole》 from both sides

맞먹다 1 〈상당하다〉 be worth; correspond to; be equal to
♦ 석달치 봉급에 맞먹는 보너스 a bonus equivalent to three month's pay
▶ 1달러는 한국돈 9백원에 맞먹는다 One dollar is equivalent to nine hundred won in Korea.
2 〈필적하다〉 equal; match; compare 《with》
▶ 이 대학은 미국의 일류대학과 맞먹는다 This university ranks with the best university in the U.S.
▶ 테니스에서 그와 맞먹을 자는 없다 No one can equal [match, compare with] him at tennis. ⇌ He has no equal [match] at tennis. ⇌ He is second to none at tennis.

맞물다 〈서로 물다〉 bite each other; 〈톱니바퀴〉 mesh

맞물리다 〈톱니바퀴가〉 go in gear 《with》; mesh [engage] 《with》; gear 《into》; 〈아래윗니가〉 occlude
▶ 이 톱니바퀴는 맞물리지 않는다 The teeth of the gear don't mesh.

맞바꾸다 exchange 《a thing for another》; barter; trade; swap
▶ 나는 그와 자리를 맞바꾸었다 I exchanged seats with him.
▶ 딕은 자전거를 빌의 새 시계와 맞바꾸었다 Dick swapped his bike for Bill's new watch.
▶ 그들은 무기를 현지인의 식량과 맞바꾸었다 They bartered weapons for food with the natives.

맞바둑 an unhandicapped *paduk* match
♦ 맞바둑을 두다 play *paduk* on an even basis

맞바람 a head wind; an adverse [contrary] wind
♦ 맞바람을 안고 달리다 run against a head wind; run in the teeth of the wind
▶ 자전거를 타는 동안 내내 맞바람이 불었다 While I was cycling, the wind was against me all the time.

맞받다 1 〈정면으로〉 receive directly [to one's face]
▶ 이 곳은 북서풍을 맞받고 있다 This place is hit directly by the northwesterly wind.
2 〈마주 들이받다〉 crash head on; crash into each other
♦ 이마를 맞받다 bump [knock] heads together
3 〈응수하다〉 retort; answer; respond to
♦ 상대의 말을 맞받다 talk back to *one's* opponent

맞받이 an opposite side [spot]
♦ 길 건너 맞받이 집 a house right across the street

맞발기 commercial records kept by buyer and seller alike

맞배지기 〔씨름〕 *matpaejigi*; counter-lifting

맞배지붕 a gable roof

맞벌이 working together for a living; working in double harness
▶ 아이가 태어날 때까지 그들은 맞벌이를 했다 Both of them were working (to make a living) before the baby was born.
▶ 그들 부부는 맞벌이를 하는데도 살림이 어려웠다 The couple had difficulty making both ends meet even though they both worked.
—**맞벌이하다** work together for a living; work in double harness
■—**가정** a two-bread-winner house [family]; a dual-income family —**부부** a working couple; a two-paycheck couple [family] —**생활** dual-income living

맞벽 —**壁** the outer part of a double wall

맞보다 look at each other ⇨ 마주보다

맞부딪치다 bump [hit, dash] against; run into; collide with
▶ 덤프트럭이 열차와 맞부딪쳤다 A dump truck collided with a train.
▶ 거리에서 낯선 사람과 맞부딪쳤다 I ran [bumped] into a stranger in [(美) on] the street.
▶ 예기치 않은 어려움에 맞부딪쳤다 We met [ran into] unforeseen difficulties.

맞불 1 〈마주 놓는 불〉 a backfire; opposite fires
▶ 산불을 잡으려고 맞불을 놓았다 We started a backfire to check the forest fire.
2 〈담뱃불〉 lighting a cigarette on *sb's* cigarette

맞붙다 1 〈마주 붙다〉 stick [cling] together; stick close together
▶ 두 개의 판자가 접착제로 맞붙어 있었다 The two boards were glued tightly together.
▶ 그 두 건물은 맞붙어 있다 The two buildings stand close to each other.
2 〈격투하다〉 wrestle [grapple] 《with》; come to grips [grapples] 《with》; 〈대적하다〉 compete 《with》
♦ 맞붙어 싸우다 fight hand to hand
▶ 그는 우승 후보와 1회전에서 맞붙었다 He ran up against the top candidate in the first match.
▶ 두 아이가 맞붙어 싸우고 있다 The two children are fighting [grappling 《with each other》].

맞붙들다 grapple [wrestle] 《with》; catch [hold] each other
♦ 맞붙들고 있다 〈레슬링 등에서〉 be in holds; be at grips
▶ 두 아이는 서로 맞붙들었다 The two children grappled with each other.

맞붙이다 1 〈물건을〉 stick [fix, glue] *sth* together
♦ 깨진 조각을 접착제로 맞붙이다 glue broken pieces; stick broken pieces together with glue
2 〈사람을〉 bring 《them》 into contact; match one against another 〈경기 등에서〉

맞붙잡다 grasp [seize] each other; hold together

맞비겨떨어지다 balance; offset each other; come out even ♦ 셈이 맞비겨떨어지다 the accounts balance

맞상대 —**相對** 〈사람〉 an opponent; a competitor; a match 《for》; the other person [party]; a confrontation; a man-to-man fight

맞서다 1 〈마주 서다〉 stand face to face 《with》; face each other
2 〈대항하다〉 confront; stand up to; fight against; 〈필적하다〉 match; compare 《with》

◆여론에 맞서다 defy public opinion
◆세상의 비난에 용감하게 맞서는 그가 참 존경스럽다 I admire his ability to face public censures bravely.
▶그는 감연히 위험에 맞섰다 He boldly confronted the danger.
▶그들은 용감하게 적과 맞섰다 They fought bravely against the enemy.
▶그에 맞서는 권투선수는 한국에 없다 No boxer in Korea matches him.

맞선 marriage introduction; an interview [arranged meeting] with a view to marriage
▶나는 내일 숙모 소개로 맞선을 본다 I'll meet a prospective marriage partner through my aunt's arrangement tomorrow.

맞소송 —訴訟 a countersuit; a counterclaim
맞수 —手 a match ⇨ 맞적수
맞아들이다 receive; welcome; invite [ask] sb in ◆외국인 관광객을 맞아들이다 receive foreign tourists
▶주인은 손님을 방으로 맞아들였다 The host showed his guest into the room.

맞아떨어지다 agree (with, on); be correct
▶네 계산은 내 계산과 맞아떨어진다 Your figures agree with mine.
▶그의 이야기는 사실과 전혀 맞아떨어지지 않는다 What he says doesn't correspond in the least with the facts.

맞아죽다 be beaten to death; be killed by blows
맞욕 —辱 counter-abuse; answering back with abusive language —**맞욕하다** abuse back; call names back
맞은바래기 the opposite side [place]; the other side
맞은편 —便 〈반대쪽〉 the opposite side; the other side; 〈상대편〉 the opposite party
▶그녀는 내 맞은편에 앉았다 She sat across from me.
▶길 맞은편에 병원이 있다 There is a hospital on the other side of [across, over] the street.

-맞이 meeting; reception; welcoming
◆달맞이 moon viewing; enjoying the moon
▶손님맞이 때문에 바쁘다 I'm busy receiving visitors.

맞이하다 go to meet; receive; greet; invite; welcome
◆새해를 맞이하다 greet the New Year / 아내를 맞이하다 get married; take a wife / 따뜻하게 맞이하다 give sb a warm welcome; greet sb with a smile / 역으로 아무를 맞이하러 가다 [오다] go [come] to the station to meet sb; go [come] to meet sb at the station
▶그는 문에서 손님을 맞이했다 He welcomed [greeted, received] his guest at the (front) door.
▶형이 공항으로 나를 맞이하러 왔다 My brother came to meet me at the airport.
▶그들은 그를 회장으로 맞이했다 They made him president.
▶이제 우리는 새 시대[새 국면]를 맞이하고 있다 We are entering [going into] a new era [phase].

맞잡다 hold together ⇨ 마주잡다

맞잡이 a (good) match [rival]; an equal; a peer
◆장기의 맞잡이 a match in changgi
맞장구치다 give responses (to make the conversation go smoothly); throw in words of agreement [encouragement] (while sb is speaking); chime in
▶"물론이지요"라고 그는 맞장구쳤다 "Of course," he broke in.
▶그는 내 말에 맞장구쳤다 He chimed in with my remarks.

맞장기 —將棋 even-match changgi; an unhandicapped changgi-game ◆맞장기를 두다 play changgi on even terms

맞적수 —敵手 a (good) match (for); a worthy opponent
◆바둑의 맞적수 paduk players of equal skill; well-matched paduk players / 맞적수를 만나다 meet one's rival

맞절 simultaneous exchange of bows
—**맞절하다** bow to each other; exchange bows
◆공손하게 맞절하다 bow deeply at each other
맞접다 fold in half; fold on itself; fold together

맞추다 1 〈대조하다〉 compare (with); check (with)
◆번역문과 원문을 맞추어 보다 check a translation against the original; compare a translation with the original
▶사본을 원본과 면밀히 맞추어 보았다 The copies have been checked precisely with [against] the original.
2 〈조립하다〉 assemble; fix up; put [fit] together
◆모형비행기를 맞추다 build a model airplane / 엔진을 맞추다 assemble an engine
3 〈맞게 하다〉 set [fit, adjust, adapt] (one thing to another); tune sth (to the purpose); bring sth into line (with another)
◆박자를 맞추다 keep (good) time with [to] (the music) / 말을 맞추다 get together with one's story / 라디오의 다이얼을 맞추다 tune in the radio (to (the frequency of) a station) / 아무에게 카메라의 초점을 맞추다 focus one's camera on sb / 피아노에 맞추어 노래하다 sing to the piano
▶음악에 스텝을 맞춰라 Keep step to the music.
4 〈적응시키다〉 fit; accommodate; meet
◆비위를 맞추다 curry favor with sb / 넥타이를 양복에 맞추다 make a match to tie with one's suit
5 〈주문하다〉 order; give an order
◆새로 맞춘 옷 a brand-new [newly-made] suit
▶나는 새 양복을 맞췄다 I had a new suit ordered.
6 〈갖다 대다〉 touch
◆입을 맞추다 kiss (a girl on the mouth)

맞춤법 —法 〈철자법〉 orthography; the rules of spelling; 〈한글 맞춤법〉 the spelling system of Hangŭl; the rules of Korean spelling [orthography]
■—통일안 a draft for unified [standardized]

맞장구치는 법

1. 긍정·찬성의 표현
- 예 Yes.
- 좋고 말고요 Yes, certainly. ⇌ Sure. ⇌ Surely. (▶Sure.가 흔히 쓰임)
- 물론이조 Of course. (▶상대방의 부정하는 내용에 대하여도 동조를 표시할 때에는「물론 틀립니다」「물론 그런 일은 없습니다」라는 뜻으로 Of course not.을 씀)
- 그래 맞아 Right. ⇌ That's true [right]. ⇌ Exactly.
- 응, 그거야 Yes, that's it.
- 저도 그렇게 생각합니다 I think so, too.
- 동감입니다 I agree (with you).
- 알았습니다 All right. ⇌ OK.
- 부디 그리 해주십시오 By all means.
- 기꺼이 (하겠습니다) With pleasure.
- 물론 좋지 Why not? (▶「그래서 안될 이유는 없다」는 수사(修辭) 의문으로 기꺼이 찬성한다는 эти 스스럼없는 표현)
- 좋습니다 Fine! ⇌ Good.

2. 부정·반대의 표현
- 아니오 No.
- 그런 일은 없습니다 Certainly not! ⇌ I'm afraid not. (▶상대방의 말에 반대할 때에는 어조를 부드럽게 하는 의미에서 I'm afraid를 부정문의 앞에 붙임)
- 절대로 안됩니다 By no means.
- 전혀 틀립니다 Not at all.
- 당신이 잘못 생각한 겁니다 You are mistaken [wrong].
- 동의할 수 없는데요 I don't agree [disagree] (with you).
- 그렇게는 생각지 않습니다 I don't think so.
- 괜찮습니다 It doesn't matter.

3. 가벼운 응답
(1) 반문하는 형식
- 그렇습니까? Is that so?
- 정말입니까? Really? ⇌ Is that true [right]?

(2) 상대방의 말에 반응하여 상대방 말의 첫머리를 의문형으로 하든가, 아니면 그대로 되풀이하여 맞장구치는 일이 많다.
- [會話]「나는 너의 누님을 잘 알고 있어」「그래?」 "I know your sister very well." "Do you?" ⇌ "You do?"
- [會話]「정호는 외국에 간대」「그래?」 "Chŏng-ho is going abroad." "Is he?" ⇌ "He is?"
- [會話]「그는 어제 인천에 갔어」「그랬구나」 "He went to Inch'ŏn yesterday." "Did he?" ⇌ "He did?"

4. 불확실·의심의 표현
- 아마 그럴거야 (美) Maybe. ⇌ Perhaps. ⇌ Probably.
- 그럴겁니다 I think [suppose] so.
- 있을법한 일이군요 It's quite probable. ⇌ That's very likely.
- 경우에 따라서지요 That [It] depends.
- 글쎄 어떨까요 I'm not quite sure.
- 믿어지지 않는데요 That's very doubtful.
- 그럴리가 없습니다 It cannot be true.

5. 놀라움의 표현
- 어머 Oh! ⇌ Dear me! (▶후자는 특히 여성용어)
- 뭐라고 What!
- 아, 이런 Well, well.
- 아이 가엾어라 What a pity!
- 거 이상하다 That's very strange! ⇌ That's very odd!
- 거 재미있다 That's funny!
- 멋지다 Wonderful! ⇌ Great!
- 설마 You don't say!
- 농담이겠지 You're joking! ⇌ You must be joking! ⇌ You're kidding (me)! ⇌ No kidding! (▶뒤의 둘은 구어적인 표현)
- 그거 안됐다 That's too bad.

---

spelling system

맞흔인 —婚姻 〈양가가 혼비를 똑같이 부담하는〉 a marriage with equal share of marriage expenses between the two families

맞흥정 〈소비자와 상인간의 직거래〉 a buyer-to-seller deal; face-to-face bargaining
—**맞흥정하다** make a direct bargain; make a deal without a broker

맞히다 1 〈알아맞히다〉 guess right; make a good guess [hit]; take [have] a guess (at); hit the truth
▶[會話]「이 꽃은 누가 준거니?」「(누군지) 맞혀보렴」 "Who are the flowers from?" "Guess (who)."
▶네가 바로 맞혔다 You hit the mark. ⇌ You have guessed right.
2 〈명중시키다〉 hit (the mark)
▶화살은 과녁 한복판을 맞혔다 The arrow hit the target right in the center [the bull's-eye].
3 〈비 등을〉 expose 《to》; subject 《to》
◆비를 맞히다 expose *sth* to the rain / 비를 맞히지 않도록 하다 protect *sth* from the rain
4 〈주사 등을〉 ◆아이에게 주사를 맞히다 have a child get an injection

맡기다 1 〈보관시키다〉 entrust [trust] 《*sb* with *sth*, *sth* to *sb*》; deposit [leave] 《*sth* with *sb* [in a bank]》; place [leave] *sth* in *sb's* charge [hands]; put *sth* in charge of *sb*
◆짐을 맡기다 (美) check *one's* baggage; (英) book *one's* luggage
▶그녀는 많은 돈을 은행에 맡겼다 She deposited [put] a large amount of money in the bank.
▶그렇게 큰 돈은 그에게 맡기지 마라 Don't trust him with such a large sum of money.
2 〈위임하다〉 entrust *sth* to *sb*; entrust *sb* with (a task); leave *sth* (up) to *sb*
◆임무를 맡기다 charge *sb* with a duty; assign *sb* to a task [job] / 아무에게 책임을 맡기다 place [put] the responsibility for *sth* on *sb*
▶나는 재산 관리를 아내에게 맡기고 있다 I

have left my property to [placed my property under] the care of my wife.
▶ 우리는 이 일을 그에게 맡겼다 We left this work up to him. ≒ We entrusted this work to him [him with this work].
▶ 남에게 맡기지 말고 네 자신이 해라 Don't leave it to others. Do it yourself.
▶ 이 문제는 경찰에 맡기십시오 Let the police take care of this problem.
▶ 내가 그의 학비를 맡겠다 I'll take care of his education.
3 〈사람을〉 leave 《a child》 in the care of *sb*; give *sb* charge of 《a child》
▶ 그는 목숨을 의사에게 맡겼다 He put his life in the hands of the physician.
▶ 외출할 때마다 이웃 사람에게 아이들을 맡긴다 Every time we go out, we leave our children with our neighbor.
▶ 아이들은 가정부에게 맡기고 있다 My children are under their maid's care.
▶ 우리가 그 아이들을 맡기로 했다 We have decided to take charge [care] of the children.
4 〈방임하다〉 leave 《*sb* to do *sth*》; let 《*sb* do *sth*》
▶ 운을 하늘에 맡기는 수밖에 없다 There is no choice but to leave everything to the fate.

맡다¹ 1 〈보관하다〉 keep; receive in trust [custody]; take charge of *sth*; be entrusted with *sth*
▶ 그는 학교 열쇠를 맡아가지고 있다 He has charge of the school keys.
▶ 나는 그에게 우산을 맡아달라고 했다 I asked him to keep my umbrella for me.
2 〈담당·감독하다〉 undertake; take [have] charge of; be in charge of 《a class》; assume the care of 《children》; take *sb* in charge
♦ 중책을 맡다 assume a heavy responsibility / 직책을 맡다 take office; be installed in an office / 교섭의 책임을 맡다 take [it] upon *oneself* to conduct negotiations
▶ 어제 난 큰 불은 소방서장이 직접 지휘를 맡았다 During the big fire yesterday, the fire chief took charge himself.
3 〈허가를 받다〉 get; obtain; receive; take out 《a license》
♦ 면허를 맡다 get [obtain] a license / 허가를 맡다 be permitted; get a permit
▶ 여기서 사진을 찍으려면 당국의 허가를 맡아야 한다 You must apply to the authorities for permission to take a photograph here.

맡다² 1 〈냄새를〉 smell; scent; 〈개가〉 sniff 《at》

[解說] 가장 일반적인 말은 ***smell***, 후각을 동원하여 미미한 냄새나 흔적 등을 맡으려고 하는 동작은 ***scent***, 쿵쿵 소리를 내거나 소리가 날 만큼 숨을 들이쉬는 것은 ***sniff***다.

♦ 냄새를 맡다 smell 《at》 《a flower》; take a smell 《at》; have a smell 《of》
▶ 이 꽃 냄새를 맡아 봐 Smell this flower.
▶ 개는 바닥에 있는 손수건의 냄새를 맡았다 The dog sniffed at the handkerchief on the floor.
▶ 그는 감기가 들어서 냄새를 잘 맡지 못했다 He felt hard to smell because he had a cold.
2 〈낌새채다〉 scent; get wind of; smell out 《a secret》; 《俗》 smoke out
♦ 계략의 낌새를 맡다 sniff out [get wind of] a trick [plot]
▶ 그녀는 돈 있는 것을 냄새 맡고 나를 찾아 왔다 She sensed that I had money and came to see me.

매¹ 1 〈때리는〉 a whip; a rod; a cane
♦ 매를 때리다 lash; flog; whip; give *sb* the rod; castigate / 매를 맞다 be whipped; be lashed; get the cane
2 〈매질〉 whipping; lashing; flogging; flagellation
▶ 그들은 매를 휘둘러 노예를 부렸다 They whipped their slaves to make them work.
매² 1 〈맷돌〉 a millstone; a (stone) hand mill; a quern
2 ⇨ 매통
매³ 〔鳥〕 a hawk; 〈매사냥용의〉 a falcon
♦ 매의 발톱 a hawk's talons
매⁴ 〈염소 등의 울음소리〉 baa; bleat
▶ 염소가 매하고 울었다 The goat bleated.

매 毎 every; each
♦ 매 초[분] per second [minute] / 매달 every [each] month / 매 페이지마다 page after page; every page
▶ 어머니는 매주 월요일 병원에 가십니다 My mother goes to the hospital every Monday.
▶ 매 식사후에 약을 두 알씩 드십시오 Take two tablets after each meal.

매- quite; absolutely
♦ 매일반[매한가지]이다 come to the same thing
▶ 오늘 가나 내일 가나 매한가지다 It makes little difference whether I go today or tomorrow.

-매 〈모양〉 a shape; a form; 〈외양〉 appearance; 〈모습〉 figure
♦ 눈매 an expression of the eyes / 몸매 *one's* figure [shape]
▶ 그는 몸매에 상관하지 않는다 He doesn't care how he looks. ≒ He is quite careless about his appearance.

매가 買價 〈사는 값〉 a purchase [buying] price; 〔證〕 a bid price
매가 賣家 〈파는 집〉 a house for sale; selling a house
매가 賣價 〈파는 값〉 a sale [selling, labeled] price
▶ 소매점의 매가는 500원이다 The retail price is five hundred won.
매가오리 〔魚〕 an eagle ray
매각 賣却 sale; disposal (by sale)
—**매각하다** sell (off); dispose of (by sale)
▶ 그는 집을 매각했다 He sold his house.
■ —**계정** sales account —**공고** a public notice of sale —**대금** proceeds from sale —**물** an article for [on] sale; offerings —**인** a seller; a vendor —**조건** terms of sale —**처분** disposal [disposition] by sale —**통지** a notice of sale
매갈이 〈벼껍질벗기기〉 removing the hulls from rice; hulling rice

매개

—**매갈이하다** hull [husk] rice; remove the hulls from rice
■—**기계** a husker —**꾼** a husker **매갈잇간** a rice-hulling mill

매개 每個 each piece [one]; apiece; every piece
▶ 이 사과는 매개 500원이다 These apples are five hundred won apiece.

매개 媒介 agency; intermediation; mediation
▶ 소리는 공기를 매개로 하여 전해진다 Sound travels through the medium [agency] of air.
—**매개하다** 〈중개하다〉 mediate; act as (an) intermediatry (between); 〈전염병을〉 carry 《germs》
▶ 파리는 병균을 매개한다 Flies carry infectious diseases.
■—**동물** 〈병균의〉 a vector; a carrier —**물** 〈매체〉 a medium 《pl. ~s, media》; 〈전달수단〉 a vehicle; 〈병균의〉 a carrier : 전염병의 매개물 a vehicle of infection —**변수** 〔電算·數〕 parameter —**변수표** 〔電算〕 PT 〔*parameter table*〕 —**변수함수** 〔數〕 parametric function —**자** a mediator; an agent; a go-between; 〈거래의〉 a middleman

매개념 媒概念 〔論〕 the middle concept [term]; the mean term

매거진 1 〈잡지〉 a magazine
2 〈필름을 넣는 금속제 용기〉〔寫〕 a magazine; a cartridge

매거하다 枚擧— enumerate; list
▶ 이런 유의 사례는 일일이 매거할 수 없다 There are too many cases of this nature to enumerate [count].
▶ 매일의 교통 사고는 일일이 매거할 수 없다 There are too many traffic accidents every day to mention them all [every one of them].

매관매직 賣官賣職 the sale of offices; trafficking of official posts
—**매관매직하다** traffic in government positions

매국 賣國 selling one's country; betrayal of [treachery to] one's country
◆ **매국적인** unpatriotic; traitorous
—**매국하다** sell [betray] one's country
■—**노** a traitor (to one's country); a betrayer (of one's country) —**외교** sellout diplomacy —**행위** an unpatriotic act

매기 每期 〈기간〉 each period; every term; 〈회기〉 each session; every sitting

매기 買氣 a desire to buy; an interest in buying; 〔證〕 a bullish sentiment; buying enthusiasm
◆ **매기가 있다** be in the buying mood
▶ 매기가 없다 There is a lock of interest in buying.

매기다 decide; set; put; fix
◆ 만원의 값을 매기다 offer [bid] ten thousand won (for a thing) / 값을 비싸게 매기다 put the price high (on an article) / 등급을 매기다 classify; grade / 접수를 매기다 give marks; score / 주류에 관세를 매기다 impose duties on alcoholic beverages

매끄럽다 1 〈물건의 표면이〉 smooth; 〈감촉이〉 soft; 〈미끄럽게〉 slippery; greasy
◆ 비단처럼 매끄러운 피부 skin as smooth [soft] as silk; velvet skin
▶ 이 종이는 감촉이 매끄럽다 This paper is smooth to the touch.
▶ 그녀의 매끄러운 말투에 놀랐다 I was surprised at her smooth manner of speaking. ⇒ Her smooth way of speaking surprised me.
▶ 목재의 표면을 매끄럽게 하기 위해 사포로 닦 았다 We sandpapered the wood smooth.
2 〈움직임 등이〉 smooth; 〈유창한〉 fluent
◆ 매끄러운 손놀림 smooth movement of sb's arms
▶ 그는 프랑스어를 매끄럽게 말했다 He spoke French fluently. ⇒ He spoke fluent French. ⇒ He was fluent in French.

매끈거리다 be slimy ⇨ 미끈거리다

매 끝에 정든다 (속담) Spare the rod and spoil the child.

매끼 〈곡식못 등을 묶는 새끼〉 a strip of straw rope (for binding sheaves, fagots); a binding rope

매나니 1 〈맨손〉 an empty hand
◆ **매나니로** with empty hands
2 〈맨밥〉 a meal without side dishes; a simple fare [diet]

매너 manners

[解說] 예의·예절을 말하는 「매너」는 영어에서는 ***manners***로 항상 복수형으로 쓰인다. 「테이블 매너」도 table manners로 나타낸다. 야구에서 말하는 「그라운드 매너」나 테니스 등의 「코트 매너」는 sense of fairplay(페어 플레이 정신)라고 하거나 show good sportsmanship(스포츠맨으로서 훌륭한 태도를 보이 다)처럼 말하여 매너가 좋은 것을 표현할 수 밖에 없다.

▶ 그녀는 매너가 좋다[나쁘다] She has good [bad] manners.

매너리즘 a stereotype; mannerism
◆ **매너리즘에 빠지다** become stereotyped; fall in mannerism
▶ 그 운동은 오랜 세월이 흐르는 동안에 매너리 즘에 빠졌다 That movement became stereotyped after so many years.

매년 每年 every [each] year; yearly; annually
◆ **매년의 행사** an annual [a yearly] event
▶ 매년 이맘 때는 비가 많이 온다 We have a lot of rain about this time every year [about this time of (the) year].
▶ 이 지방에는 매년 홍수가 진다 Flood is practically an annual occurrence in this district.
▶ 나는 매년[매년 여름 휴가에는, 매년 한 번은] 고향에 간다 I go home every year [every summer vacation, at least once a year].

매니저 〈연예인 등의〉 a manager; 〈프로 권투 등의〉 a handler; 〈스포츠 팀의〉 the team caretaker (▶ 이 경우 manager는 감독); 〈흥행의〉 an impresario (*pl.* -rios); a proprietor
▶ 그는 매니저로 취임했다 He was installed as a manager.

매니지먼트 〈경영관리〉 management

매니큐어 (a) manicure; (美) nail polish; (英)

nail varnish
♦손톱에 매니큐어를 하다 〈자기가〉 manicure; do manicuring; 〈남을 시켜서〉 have [get] a manicure
▶그녀는 1주일에 한 번 매니큐어를 한다 She has a manicure once a week.

매다[1] **1** 〈묶다〉 tie (up); fasten (together)
♦구두끈을 매다 tie *one's* shoes; lace (up) *one's* boots / 허리띠를 매다 fasten [put on] a belt / 밧줄로 단단히 매다 tie fast with a rope
▶우리 아이는 아직 구두끈도 매지 못한다 My son still can't even tie his shoelaces.
2 〈잡아매다〉 tie; fasten; chain; leash
♦A를 B에 매다 make fast A to B; leash [chain] A to B
▶우리는 배를 부두에 맸다 We moored a ship [made a ship fast] to the wharf.
▶그는 말을 나무에 맸다 He fastened [hitched] his horse to a tree.
3 〈묶어 만들다〉 bind; make
♦선반을 매다 make a shelf; fix a shelf (to the wall) / 책을 매다 bind a book
4 〈치다〉 stretch; extend; string
♦그네를 매다 put up a swing / 빨랫줄을 매다 stretch a clothesline
5 〈구속하다〉 bind; fetter; tie

매다[2] 〈풀을 뽑다〉 weed (out)
♦김을 매다 sweep off weeds; weed out / 논을 매다 sweep off [weed out] a rice paddy

매달 每－ every [each] month
♦매달 지불 monthly payment / 매달 두 번 twice a month / 매달의 monthly
▶그는 매달 수입에서 얼마씩 저축한다 He saves portion of his income every month.

매달다 〈달아매다〉 bind up; hang; suspend
♦고양이 목에 방울을 매달다 attach a bell to a cat / 천장에 등을 매달다 hang a lamp from the ceiling

매달리다 1 〈달려 늘어지다〉 hang down (from); be hung (down)
♦철봉에 매달리다 hang down from the horizontal bar
▶귤나무에 귤이 주렁주렁 매달려 있다 Oranges are dangling all over the orange tree.
▶쇠사슬이 트럭 뒤에 길게 매달려 있었다 A long chain dangled from the back of the truck.
2 〈붙잡다〉 cling to; hang on; hold on to *sb*
♦손잡이에 매달리다 〈전철 등의〉 hang on [hold on to] a strap
▶그 아이는 그의 외투에 매달렸다 The child held on to his coat.
3 〈달라붙다〉 hold on to; stick (fast) to; cling to
♦일에 매달리다 stick at a job [*one's* work] / 지위에 매달리다 cling to *one's* post
▶그는 온종일 일에 매달려 있다 He sticks at his works all day.
▶이 아이는 어머니한테 매달려 떨어지지 않는다 This child is holding on to his mother and won't let her go.
4 〈말리다〉 depend [rely, lean] on [upon]; place [put] reliance on [in]
♦매달린 식구 family dependents / 자식한테 매달리다 depend upon *one's* son for support
▶내게는 매달린 식구가 많다 I have a big family to support.
5 〈애원하다〉 appeal to; entreat [implore] 《*sb* to do》
♦아무의 자비심에 매달리다 appeal to *sb* for mercy

매대기 smearing [daubing] all over 《with》; besmearing
♦매대기치다 daub all over; besmear / 벽에 진흙을 매대기치다 daub a wall all over with mud / 분을 얼굴에 매대기치다 powder *one's* face thick; wear a heavy make-up

매도 罵倒 abuse; denunciation; condemnation
♦매도의 말 words of abuse; abusive language —**매도하다** denounce; condemn; vilify; abuse; disparage; rail 《at》
▶그는 나를 내 친구들 앞에서 매도했다 He abused me [called me names] in front of my friends.
▶그는 언제나 정부 시책을 매도한다 He always denounces [rails against] the government's policy.

매도 賣渡 sale and delivery
—**매도하다** sell over to *sb*; negotiate 《a bill》; sell *sth* to *sb*; delivery
■**—가격** a selling quotation [rate of exchange] **—계약** a contract for selling **—인** a seller; 《法》 a vendor **—증서** a bill of sale; a sales note **—청약** 《法》 selling offer **—품 목록** a bill of parcels

매도 먼저 맞는 것이 낫다 《속담》 The devil takes the hindmost.

매독 梅毒 《醫》 syphilis [sífələs]; 《美俗》 a secret disease
♦매독성의 syphilitic 《retinitis》; luetic / 매독에 걸리다 contract [get] syphilis
■**선천성—** congenital syphilis **양성—** florid syphilis **유전성—** hereditary syphilis **음성—** latent syphilis **제1〔2, 3〕기—** primary [secondary, tertiary] syphilis ■**—검사** an examination of syphilis **—학** syphililogy **—환자** a syphilitic (person)

매듭 1 〈끈의〉 a knot (in a rope); a tie
♦매듭을 맺다 knot; make [tie] a knot / 매듭을 풀다 unknot; untie [undo] a knot
▶너 이 매듭 풀 수 있니? Can you untie [undo] this knot?
▶그는 로프에 두 개의 매듭을 지었다 He made [tied] two knots in the rope.
▶매듭이 단단해서 푸는 데 시간이 걸렸다 It took me some time to undo the hard knot.
▶끈의 매듭이 느슨해졌다 The knot in the string loosened.
2 〈일의 해결〉 a settlement; 〈결말〉 a conclusion; an end
▶그 분쟁은 원만하게 매듭이 지어졌다 The dispute has been settled [solved] peacefully.

매듭짓다 1 〈끈 등을〉 knot; make [tie] a knot
2 〈결말짓다〉 settle; fix (up); bring 《a matter》 to an end; put an end 《to》; finish *one's* work
♦교섭을 매듭짓다 bring the negotiations to a successful close [conclusion] / 일을 매듭짓다

conclude a stage of *one's* work
▶ 이번주 안에 빌린 돈을 매듭짓겠습니다 I'll pay back the debt by the end of this week.
▶ 나는 이제 이 문제를 매듭지었으면 한다 I'd like to put the matter to rest [bring the matter to a conclusion] now.
▶ 그는 세계 평화를 기원한다는 말로 연설을 매듭지었다 He concluded his speech by expressing his wish for world peace.

매력 魅力 (a) charm; (a) fascination; (an) appeal
◆ 인간적 매력 personal magnetism / 매력 있는 제안 an attractive [inviting] offer / 성적 매력 sex appeal / 매력이 있는[매력적인] charming; fascinating / 매력이 없는 unappeal; unattractive / 매력이 있다 appeal (to); have an appeal / 매력을 느끼다 feel attracted to *sb* / 아무의 매력에 사로잡히다 be captivated with [be a captive of, be bewitched by] *sb's* charms
▶ 오늘날 고전은 젊은이들에게 별로 매력이 없다 Today classics have almost no appeal to [attraction for] young people. ⇌ Today classics hardly appeal to the young.
▶ 그 분양 맨션의 가장 큰 매력은 교통편이 좋다는 거다 One of the biggest attractions of the condominium is [lies in] its convenience of transportation.
▶ 푸른 옷을 입으니 아주 매력적이다 You are very attractive in blue.
▶ 아름다운 눈은 그녀의 큰 매력의 하나다 Her beautiful eyes are among her greatest charms.

매료하다 魅了— charm; attract; fascinate; captivate
▶ 그 연극은 관객을 매료했다 The play fascinated [cast a spell over] the audience.
▶ 그녀의 우아함은 파티에 참석한 모든 사람들을 매료했다 Her graciousness charmed everyone at the party.
▶ 그 마술사의 속임수는 아이들을 매료했다 The magician's tricks fascinated the children.

매립 埋立 (land) reclamation; filling up
◆ 해안의 매립 reclamation of the foreshore —매립하다 fill in (a moat); fill up (a pond with earth)
◆ 바다를 매립하다 reclaim a tract (from the sea); recover land from the sea / 호수의 일부를 매립하다 reclaim part of the lake
■—공사 reclamation work —지 a reclaimed land

매만지다 adjust; trim; smooth down
◆ 옷을 매만지다 adjust *one's* clothes / 정원을 매만지다 tend trees and plants in the garden
▶ 그는 쑥스러움을 감추려고 머리를 매만졌다 He smoothed down his hair to hide his embarrassment.
▶ 그는 헝클어진 머리를 빗으로 매만졌다 He ran a comb through his disheveled hair.

매맛 the bitters of a whip
◆ 매맛을 보이다 lash; whip; switch (a boy) with a cane
▶ 매맛을 알아야 넌 게으름을 피우지 않을거다 I'll flog laziness out of you.

매맞다 be whipped [lashed, thrashed]; get flogged; get the cane
▶ 그런 짓하면 매맞는다 If you do such a thing, you will get licked.
▶ 또 매맞고 싶니? Do you want another thrashing?

매매 賣買 buying and selling (▶우리말의 어순과 반대인 점에 주의); 〈거래〉 trade; traffic; transaction; purchase and sale

解說 *trade*는 장사, 거래 등을 뜻하는 일반적인 말. *traffic*은 무역, 교환 등의 뜻을 가지며 *transaction*은 거래(업무)를 뜻하는 격식 차린 말이다.

◆ 인신매매 traffic in human beings
▶ 나는 주식 매매로 큰 돈을 벌었다 I made a lot of money on the stock market.
—매매하다 buy and sell; 〈취급하다〉 deal [trade] (in); traffic (in)
◆ 토지를 매매하다 deal in land
▶ 그는 주식을 매매하고 있다 He deals in stocks and shares.
▶ 저 사람은 부동산을 매매하고 있다 He deals in real estate.
■—가격 the sale price —결혼 a marriage purchase —계약 a sale contract : 매매 계약을 하다[맺다] make [strike] a bargain [contract] (with) —계약서 a contract note —계약자 a bargainer —계정 a trading account —당사자 parties to a sale —보고서 [證] a bought and sold note —수수료 a brokerage commission —절차 transaction procedure —조건 sales terms; terms of sale [bargaining] —조직 a market organization —증권 a sales warrant —증서 a bill of sale; a contract note —차익금 a margin —통제 marketing control

매머드 〈빙하시대의 거상〉[動] a mammoth; 〈거대한 것〉 a mammoth
◆ 매머드화하다 become huge [gigantic, mammoth]
■—건물 a massive [colossal] building —기업 a mammoth enterprise

매명 賣名 〈자기 선전〉 self-advertisement; 〈지명도를 얻기〉 publicity
◆ 매명을 위해 for publicity's sake / 매명을 꾀하다 court [seek] publicity
▶ 그는 매명을 위해서는 무슨 짓이든 한다 He would do anything for the sake of publicity. ⇌ He will do anything to advertise himself [for publicity, to seek publicity].
▶ 그는 매명을 위해 사회사업에 많은 돈을 기부했다 He contributed a large sum of money to charity to advertise himself.
—매명하다 〈자기 선전을 하다〉 sell *oneself*; advertise *oneself*; 〈유명해지고자 하다〉 seek publicity
■—가 a publicity seeker; a self-advertiser —행위 publicity stunts

매명사 媒名辭 [論] the middle term
매목 埋木 lignite; fossil wood; bogwood (▶주로 장식품으로 쓰임)
■—세공 bogwood work; mosaic
매몰 埋沒 burying

—**매몰하다** bury (in, under)
♦ **매몰되다** lie [be] buried in
▶ 길이 눈으로 매몰되었다 The road is buried in snow.
▶ 산사태로 집이 매몰되었다 The house was buried under the landslide.
매몰스럽다 〈무정한〉 cold-hearted; 〈동정심이 없이 차가운〉 heartless; pitiless; hard
♦ **매몰스런 사람** a cold-hearted person / **매몰스럽게** cold-heartedly / **매몰스럽게 굴다** behave coldly toward *sb*; treat *sb* coldly [in a cold way] / **매몰스럽게 거절하다** give a point-blank refusal
▶ 그는 내게 매몰스런 짓을 했다 He did something very cold-hearted to me.
매몰차다 very unkind [cold]; harsh; heartless
▶ 그녀는 매몰찬 사람이다 She is as cold as ice.
매몰하다 cold-hearted; cold; heartless
매무새 the appearance of *one's* dress
♦ **매무새가 단정하다[단정치 못하다]** be neatly [slovenly] dressed / **매무새를 고치다** adjust *one's* dress
▶ 그녀는 언제나 매무새가 깔끔하다 She always looks neat and tidy.
▶ 그녀는 흐트러진 매무새를 하고 있었다 She was dressed untidily [disorderly, slovenly].
매무시 〈몸치장하다〉 primping [adjusting] of the attire —**매무시하다** primp *oneself*; make *one's* toilet
♦ **단정히 매무시하다** be careful [attentive] about *one's* outward appearance
매문 賣文 literary hackwork; selling of writing
♦ **매문을 업으로 하다** do literary hackwork —**매문하다** be engaged in literary journeywork; sell *one's* writing
■ —**업자** a literary hack; a hack writer : 나는 일개 매문업자에 지나지 않는다 I am nothing but a literary hack.
매물 賣物 an article for [on] sale; offerings
♦ **매물차** a car for [on] sale / **매물로 내놓다** put (it) [offer (it)] market; offer 《a thing》 for sale
▶ 시장에는 지금 매물이 많이 나돌고 있다 The market is now flooded with sales.
▶ **매물 (게시)** For [On] sale. (↔ Not for sale. (비매품)) (▶On sale.의 경우 (美)에서는「특가 매물」을 뜻함. 또 for는 흔히 개인의 경우에, on 은 상점의 경우에 씀)
매미 〔昆〕 a cicada 《*pl.* ~, -dae》; (美) a locust
♦ **매미의 허물** the cast-off shell of a cicada
♦ **매미가 울고 있다** Cicadas are singing [chirping].
매발톱꽃 〔植〕 a columbine; an aquilegia
매발톱나무 〔植〕 a barberry
매번 每番 〈번번이〉 every [each] time; 〈자주〉 very often; 〈늘〉 always
▶ 그는 매번 같은 말을 한다 He says the same thing every time.
▶ 매번 들러주셔서 감사합니다 〈손님에게〉 Thank you for your patronage. ≈ Thank you very much for your constant patronage.
▶ 〔會話〕 「그는 또 잔소리를 하고 있어」 「매번 하

는 일이야」 "He is complaining again." "It's the same old thing."
매복 埋伏 ambush; 〔軍〕 ambuscade
—**매복하다** ambush; lie in wait 《for》; hide in ambush 《for》
♦ **매복하여 적을 습격하다** attack enemy from ambush / **매복하여 행인을 습격하다** waylay a passerby / (맹수가) **매복하여 먹이를 잡다** take prey by ambush
▶ 우리는 매복하여 적을 붙잡았다 We trapped the enemy by ambush.
■ —**치** (齒) an impacted tooth
매부 妹夫 the husband of *one's* sister; *one's* brother-in-law
매부리¹ 〈매부리는 사람〉 a falconer; a hawker
매부리² 〈매의 부리〉 a hawk's beak [bill]
■ —**징** 〈구두의〉 a kind of hobnail —**코** a hawk nose; a hooked nose; a Roman nose : 매부리코 hawk-nosed
매사 每事 〈일〉 each affair; every matter; 〈사업〉 every business; 〈상황〉 every circumstance
♦ **매사에 in everything [every way]
▶ 그는 매사에 내게 반대했다 He opposed me in every way.
▶ 그녀는 내가 하는 매사에 흠을 잡는다 She finds fault with everything I do.
■ —**불성** failing in every undertaking
매사 媒辭 〔論〕 the middle term=매명사
매사냥 hawking; falconry
—**매사냥하다** go hawking; hawk; hunt with a hawk
■ —**꾼** a falconer; a hawker
매사추세츠 〈미국의 주〉 Massachusetts (略 Mass.)
매상 買上 buying; 〈구입〉 a purchase
♦ **정부의 쌀 매상 가격** the Government's purchasing price of rice
—**매상하다** buy up; purchase
매상 賣上 selling; sale
♦ **매상을 늘리다** increase [boost] sales / **매상을 크게 올리다** realize a large turnover
▶ 오늘 매상은 30만원이었다 The sales of today totaled three hundred thousand won.
▶ 오전 중에는 매상이 없었다 There were no sales during [in] the morning.
▶ 이 달의 매상은 목표에 이르지 못했다 The sale target has not been attained this month.
■ —**계정** sales account —**계정서** account sales (略 A/S) —**금** the sales; the amount sold; the proceeds (of sales) —**장부** a sales book —**전표** a sales slip [check] —**총액** the total sales
매상고 賣上高 the sales; the proceeds (of sales); the amount sold; the takings
▶ 금주에는 매상고가 올랐다[내려갔다] Sales were up [down] this week.
▶ 하루의 매상고가 500만원에 달했다 The day's receipts [The sales for the day] came to five million won.
■ —**당기** the sales for this term —**순** the net sales —**연간** the annual sales —**총** the gross sales —**평균** the average sales
매석 賣惜 an indisposition to sell; holding back

—매석하다 hold back 《goods》 from the market; restrict sales; be unwilling to sell *sth* (in expectation of better prices)
▶그들은 사과를 매석했다 They were unwilling [indisposed] to sell the apples. ≒ They restricted the sale of the apples.
▶그들이 물건을 매석하고 있는 동안에 값이 급속히 떨어져요 While they were holding back their commodities, prices went down rapidly.

매설 埋設 laying
—매설하다 〈지하에〉 lay 《a cable》 under the ground
♦수도관을 매설하다 lay water pipes under the ground
■—선 underground wiring —케이블 a buried cable

매섭다 fierce; severe; sharp; stern
♦매서운 눈초리 fierce eyes / 매섭게 노려보다 glare fiercely 《at》
▶그는 등에서 매서운 통증을 느꼈다 He felt a sharp pain [was in acute pain] in the back.
▶신문은 정부에 대해 매섭게 공격했다 The papers attacked the government bitterly.

매수 枚數 the number of leaves [sheets] ⇨ 장수(張數)
♦엽서의 매수를 세다 count the number postcards
▶시험이 끝나서 회수한 답안지의 매수를 확인해 주세요 When the exam is over, please check how many answer sheets you've collected.

매수 買收 **1** 〈사들임〉 purchase; buying up [off]; 〈회사 등의 탈취〉 a take-over
—매수하다 buy up; purchase; take over
♦정부가 매수한 건물 a building taken over by the government / 상점을 매수하다 〈탈취하다〉 take over *sb's* business; 〈사들이다〉 buy out *sb's* business
2 〈뇌물을 줌〉bribery; corruption
—매수하다 buy over [off]; corrupt
♦매수할 수 있는 corruptible; accessible to bribery / 아무를 매수해 침묵케 하다 bribe *sb* to be silent [into silence]
▶업자에게 매수된 관리가 있었다 Some officials were bribed by business interested.
▶그는 돈으로 유권자를 매수했다 He bribed voters with money.
▶저 경찰은 매수할 수 없다 That policeman cannot be bought.
■—가격 a purchase price —계획 a purchasing plan —공작 a scheme of bribing —운동 an agitation for buying *sb* off —자 a fixer —행위 〈선거의〉 corrupt practices

매수 買受 (a) purchase
—매수하다 buy [take] over; acquire 《a thing》 by purchase
■—대금 the price for goods purchased —인 a buyer; a purchaser

매스게임 《體》 a mass game; mass calisthenics

매스미디어 〈대중 매체〉 the mass (communication) media (▶본래는 복수형이지만 오늘날에는 혼히 단수형으로 취급함); the means [media] of communication

매스커뮤니케이션 〈대중전달〉 mass communications; 〈대중전달기관〉 the mass media (▶단수·복수 취급); journalism
♦매스커뮤니케이션 시대 the age of mass communications / 매스커뮤니케이션[매스컴]을 떠들어대다[떠들어대지 않다] receive much [little] publicity from the press
▶그는[그 사건은] 매스커뮤니케이션을 떠들썩하게 했다 He [The incident] got a lot of attention from the mass media.
▶나는 매스커뮤니케이션 쪽에서 활동하고 싶다 I would like to work in the field of mass communications.

매스프로덕션 〈대량 생산〉 mass production
▶현대는 매스프로덕션 시대라 불러도 좋을 것이다 The present day might be called the age of mass production [the mass production age].
▶오늘날 의류품이나 구두 등의 상품은 매스프로덕션화되어 있다 Today goods such as clothing and shoes are mass-produced.

매시 每時 every hour; per hour
▶매시 정각에 시계가 울린다 The clock strikes every hour on the hour.
▶그 열차는 매시 240킬로미터(의 속도)로 달린다 That train runs (at [at a speed of]) 240 kilometers an [per] hour. (▶드물게 240kph [KPH]로 생략해 쓰기도 함)
▶열차는 매시 0분[30분]에 발차한다 Trains leave every hour on the hour [on the half hour].

매시근하다 tired; languid; weary; listless; languish

> 解說 피로를 나타내는 일반적인 말이 ***tired***. 지쳐서 힘이나 원기를 잃은 것을 표현하는 말이 ***languid***. 장시간의 일 등으로 느른한 것이 ***weary***다.

▶오늘은 몸이 매시근하다 I feel tired today.
▶몸이 매시근해서 일하기가 싫다 I feel too lazy to work.

매시트포테이토 〈으깬 감자〉 mashed potatoes; (口) mash

매식 買食 〈사먹는 식사〉 a paid meal; 〈사먹는 행위〉 eating at a restaurant
♦한국인의 매식 습관 the eating at a restaurant habits on the Korean
—매식하다 take [have] a meal at a restaurant; eat at a restaurant

매씨 妹氏 **1** 〈남의 누이〉 your [his] sister
2 〈손윗 누이〉 one's elder sister

매암돌다 turn [go] round [in circular]; spin *oneself* round; whirl; twirl
▶암운이 매암돌고 있다 Dark clouds are hanging low.

매암돌리다 〈제자리에서〉 spin [turn] *sb* round; make *sb* turn round [in circular]; 〈이곳저곳으로〉 lead *sb* a chase [dance]; send *sb* on a wild-goose chase; pull about

매약 賣約 a contract for sale
▶매약필 (게시) Sold.
—매약하다 make [conclude] a sale contract 《with》; make a bargain 《with》

매약 賣藥 a patent medicine; a drug
—**매약하다** sell a patent medicine
■ —**상** (美) a druggist; (英) a chemist —**행상인** a nostrum vendor; a medicine peddler

매양 每— 〈언제든지〉 always; all the time; 〈번번이〉 often; frequently; 〈매번〉 every time
► 그는 매양 놀고만 있다 He is always playing [idle]. ⇌ He does nothing but play.
► 그는 매양 같은 말을 한다 He says the same thing every time.

매연 煤煙 〈연기〉 sooty smoke; soot and smoke; 〈자동차의 배기 가스〉 automobile exhaust fumes; exhaust gas
♦ 매연이 많은[없는] 연료 smoky [smokeless] fuel / 매연으로 더럽혀진 건물 a smutty [smoke-blackened] building / 매연을 내뿜다 fume out exhaust gas
■ —**공해** smoke pollution —**차량** a vehicle [car, bus] that discharges exhaust fumes: 경찰은 매연 차량을 엄중 단속했다 Police exercised strict control over vehicles with faulty exhausts that produce harmful fume.

매염 媒染 mordanting; color-fixing by means of a mordant
—**매염하다** mordant *sth*; treat *sth* with a mordant
■ —**성** mordancy : 매염성의 mordant —**염료** 〔工〕 mordant dyes [dyestuffs] —**제[료]** 〔工・化〕 a mordant; a fixative

매우 very; greatly; (very) much; so; 〈꿩히〉 awfully; terribly; exceedingly; 〈대단히〉 extremely; excessively
♦ 매우 놀랍게도 to *one's* great surprise / 매우 크다 be extremely large / 매우 피곤하다 be very tired
► 그는 그것을 매우 좋아한다 He likes it very [so] much. ⇌ He is very fond of it. ⇌ He is very [very much, greatly] pleased with it.
► 나는 매우 건강하다 I am very well. ⇌ I am in high spirits.
► 나는 그 소식을 듣고 매우 놀랐다 I was very surprised at [to hear] the news.
► 그날 밤은 바람이 매우 거세었다 It was very windy that night.
► 나는 매우 기쁘다 I am very glad.

매운맛 ♦ 매운맛을 내다 〈요리 등에〉 give a pungent flavor (to)

매운바람 a sharp [biting, piercing, cutting] wind

매월 每月 〈매달〉 every [each] month; 〈달마다〉 month after month; monthly
♦ 매월의 수업료 a monthly school [tuition] fee / 매월 한 번의 회의 a monthly meeting / 매월 한 번 once a month / 매월 두번 twice a month / 매월의 monthly

매음 賣淫 〈매춘〉 prostitution; harlotry
—**매음하다** prostitute; sell *oneself* for money; prostitute *oneself*; walk the streets; (美口) work as a hooker
■ —**굴** a brothel; a whorehouse; a house of prostitution; a bawdy house —**녀[부]** a prostitute; a harlot —**반대운동** an anti-vice campaign —**방지법** the Anti-Prostitution Act —**행위** (an act of) prostitution: 매음 행위를 하다 practice prostitution

매이다 1 〈끈 등으로〉 be tied; be bound; be fastened
♦ 소가 나무에 매이다 a cow is tied to a tree
► 연이 실에 매여 있다 The kite is on a string.
► 그 말은 말뚝에 매여 있다 The horse is tied to a stake.
2 〈일에 구속되다〉 be bound [tied, fettered, restricted]
♦ 규칙에 매이다 be bound by a rule / 시간에 매이다 be restricted by time / 일에 매이다 be chained [tied down, fettered] to *one's* work [business]
► 나는 일에 매여 있다 My work ties me (down). ⇌ I am tied (down) to my work.
► 나는 시간에 매이는 것이 싫다 I hate to be bound [restricted] by time.

매인 每人 each [every] person
♦ 매인당 for each person; per head [capital]/ 매인당 세개씩 배당하다 distribute three pieces for each person

매인목숨 ♦ 매인 목숨이다 be not *one's* own master
► 나는 직장에 매인 목숨이라 오늘 오후에는 틈을 낼 수가 없다 I have no time to spare this afternoon as I am busy with my office work.

매일 每日 every [each] day; 〈날마다〉 daily
♦ 매일의 사건 everyday occurrences [events]; what happens every day / 매일 밤 every night [evening]; nightly; night after night / 매일 하는 일 *one's* daily work [duties] / 매일의 everyday 《use》; daily 《life》 / 매일매일 〈되풀이하여〉 day after day; day in day out; 〈나날이〉 day by day; from day to day / 매일 오전 중에 every morning
► 매일 비가 오고 있다 It's been raining for (the past) several days.
► 나는 매일 1킬로미터를 달린다 I run one kilometer every day. ⇌ I jog a kilometer a day.

매일반 ——般 sameness ⇨ 매한가지
♦ 매일반인 all the same; much the same
► 지금 지불해 주거나 나중에 지불해 주거나 나에게는 매일반이다 You can pay now or later, it is all the same.
► 둘러치나 메치나 매일반이다 It's six of one and half-a-dozen of the other.

매입 買入 buying; purchase
—**매입하다** purchase; obtain *sth* by purchase; buy (in) 《books, sundries》
♦ 돈을 딴 토지를 매입하는데 돌리다 apply the money to purchase the other lands
► 나는 쌀을 대량으로 매입했다 I made a large purchase of rice.
► 나는 헌 피아노를 싸게 매입했다 I bought an old piano cheap.
■ —**매출환(賣出換)** 〔商〕 selling and buying exchange —**세액** 〔商〕 buying tax —**원가[가격]** the purchase[purchasing] price; the buying cost

매자기 〔植〕 a bulrush
매자나무 〔植〕 the Korean barberry
매자목 賣子木 〔植〕 a snowbell; a storax
매장 賣場 the place where *sth* is sold; 〈판매 장

소〉 a counter; a sale(s) room; 〈점포〉 a store; a shop
♦ 문방구[장난감] 매장 the stationery [toy] counter / 바겐 상품 매장 a bargain floor / 신사화 매장 the men's shoe department / 매장의 여자 판매원 a girl behind the counter
▶ 그녀는 화장품 매장의 판매원으로 일한다 She clerks behind the cosmetic counter.
■ —감독[주임] (美) a floorwalker; a floor [section] manager; (英) a shopwalker

매장 埋葬 1 〈시체를 땅에 묻다〉 burial; interment
▶ 매장은 열시에 치루어졌다 The burial (service) took place at ten o'clock.
—매장하다 bury; inter; lay [consign] 《sb's body》 to rest 《the grave》; entomb
▶ 그들은 방금 아버지를 매장했다 They have just buried their father.
▶ 그들은 그 죽은 이를 정성껏 매장했다 They buried the deceased with heartfelt sympathy.
2 〈사회적으로 추방하다〉 social ostracism
—매장하다 ostracize; oust [expel] sb from society
♦ 세상에서 매장되다 be ostracized; 〈잊혀지다〉 be sunk [lost] in oblivion; be buried alive
▶ 그런 인간은 사회에서 매장되어야 한다 He ought to be ostracized from society.
■ —비 cost of burial —식 (perform) the burial service [rites] —신고 the report of a burial —지 a burial place; 〈묘지〉 a graveyard; 〈공동묘지〉 a cemetery —허가증 a burial certificate [permit]

매장 埋藏 1 〈묻어 감춤〉 burying underground
—매장하다 bury [hide] sth underground [in the ground]
2 〈광물이 땅속에 묻히어 있음〉 deposits 《of mineral》
—매장하다 have 《oil》 deposits underground
♦ 매장되다 be deposited; lie underground
■ —량 reserves; an estimated amount 《of》: 석유의 매장량 oil reserves; an estimated amount of oil —물 buried property —탄량 coal reserves

매저키즘 masochism ⇨ 마조히즘
매절 賣切 being sold out ⇨ 매진
매점 買占 〈사재기〉 buying up; 〈주식 등의〉 a corner; cornering; coemption
♦ 시장 매점 market cornering / 주식 매점 a bull corner
▶ 무역상사의 매점으로 콩값이 올랐다 The trading company's heavy buying has sent the price of beans up.
—매점하다 〈몽땅 몰아 사다〉 buy up; 〈주식 등을〉 corner; make [establish] a corner in
▶ 외국 회사가 밀을 매점했다 The foreign firm cornered the market in wheat.
▶ 그는 그 회사의 주식을 매점했다 He bought up shares in the company.
■ —매석 cornering and hoarding: 매점매석을 단속하다 crack down on practices of cornering and hoarding —인[자] a corner man; a cornerer
매점 賣店 a stand; a stall; a booth; 〈공원·역 등의〉 a kiosk

♦ 역의 매점 a station kiosk [stall] / 신문 매점 a newsstand; (英) a bookstall / 학교 매점 a school store; 〈대학의〉 (美) a campus store / 매점을 내다 install a booth; set up a stand [stall]
매점스럽다 heartless; pitiless ⇨ 매정하다
매정하다 〈무정한〉 heartless; merciless; pitiless; 〈사려없는〉 thoughtless; 〈무책임한〉 irresponsible
♦ 매정한 말 an inconsiderate remark / 매정하게 거절하다 give a point-blank refusal / 매정하게 굴다 treat sb coldly; behave coldly toward sb
▶ 그는 참으로 매정한 사람이로구나 How heartless he is!
▶ 네가 그렇게 하다니 참으로 매정하구나 How thoughtless of you to do that!
매제 妹弟 one's younger sister's husband; a brother-in-law
메조미쌀 —糙米— unpolished rice ⇨ 현미
매조이 sharpening the teeth of a mill
—매조이하다 sharpen the mill(stone) teeth
매조지 the finish; finishing; 〈최후의〉 the finishing touches [strokes]
매주 每週 every [each] week; weekly
♦ 매주 토요일에 every Saturday / 매주 목요일 밤에 every Thursday night
▶ 나는 매주 고향의 어머님께 편지를 쓴다 I write back home to my mother every week.
매주 買主 〈사는 사람〉 a buyer; a customer; a purchaser; 〔法〕 a vendee (↔ vendor); 〔證〕 a bull; a bull operator
▶ 이 신제품에는 곧 매주가 나타날 것이다 You'll find ready buyers for these new products.
▶ 그의 집은 수년간 매주가 없었다 His house remained unsold for some years.
■ —시장 a [the] buyers' market
매주 賣主 〈파는 사람〉 a seller; a bargainer; a vendor; 〔證〕 a bear; 〔法〕 bargainor
♦ 그림의 매주 the seller of a picture / 중고차의 매주 the seller of a used car
■ —시장 a sellers' market
매지구름 a rain cloud
매직 〈마술〉 magic
■ —거울 a one-way mirror —아이 (商標) 〈라디오 등의〉 a Magic Eye; a tuning indicator [eye] —유리 one-way glass —잉크 (a kind of) marking ink; (商標) Magic ink —펜 (商標) a felt tip(ped) pen; a Magic Marker —핸드 〔電子〕 a magic hand; a manipulator
매진 賣盡 being sold out; a sellout
▶ 금일 매진 (게시) All sold out for today.
—매진하다 sell [clear] out; run out of 《merchandise》
♦ 매진되다 be sold out; 〈품절되다〉 be [go] out of stock
▶ 그 사전의 초판은 매진되었다 The first edition of the dictionary is sold out.
▶ (철도에서) 금일 예약은 매진되었다 All the reserved seats for today have been sold.
매진 邁進 pushing on; dash
—매진하다 push on; dash forward; struggle on; dash on; 〈노력하다〉 strive 《for》
♦ 일에 매진하다 push forward with one's

work / 진리 탐구에 매진하다 strive for the truth
► 너의 목표를 달성하기 위해 일로 매진하라 Strive on strenuously to carry out your aim. ⇌ Push forward along the path you have chosen until you achieve your goal.

매질 whipping; flogging; lashing; flagellation —**매질하다** whip; lash; flog; use the rod 《on》
♦ 매질하여 말을 가게 하다 whip a horse on / 죄인에게 매질하다 flog a criminal

매질 媒質 〈물리적 작용의 매개물〉 〖物〗 a medium 《pl. ~s, -dia》 ♦ 음을 전하는 매질 a medium that carries [conveys] sound

매체 媒體 〈매질 물체〉 〖物〗 a medium
♦ 텔레비전을 매체로 하여 through the medium of television
► 공기는 소리를 전달하는 매체다 Air is the medium that conveys sound.
■ 광고— a medium of advertisement 대중— the mass media; the mass media (of communication) 인쇄[전파]— printed [wave] media

매초 每秒 every second; per second
♦ 매초 10미터의 속도로 at a speed [velocity] of 10 meters a [per] second

매초롬하다 possess a healthy beauty; healthy and beautiful

매축 埋築 (land) reclamation —**매축하다** fill up 《a pond with earth》
■—공사 reclamation work —지 a reclaimed land; 〈간척지〉 a polder

매춘 賣春 prostitution ⇨ 매음 —**매춘하다** sell *oneself* for money; walk the street
► 그녀는 돈을 벌기 위해 매춘했다 She sold herself [turned to prostitution] to get money.
■—부 a prostitute; 〈美俗〉 a hooker; a whore; a streetwalker —생활 a life of prostitution; streetwalker —업자 a vice racketeer

매출 賣出 (a) sale; selling
♦ 여름용 상품 매출 the opening sale of summer goods; a summer sale
—**매출하다** sell; put [place] *sth* on sale; offer 《articles》 for sale
► 신간서적을 이달 말부터 매출할 예정이다 The new books will be put on sale late this month.
■—연말(대)— a special year-end sale 염가 대— a bargain sale 재고정리 대— a clearance sale ■—가격 a selling [an offering] price —가격 환원법 〖商〗 retail inventory method —세액 〖商〗 sales tax —환(換) 〖商〗 selling exchange

매치 1 〈시합〉 a match
♦ 타이틀[리턴] 매치 a title [return] match
► 타이틀 매치는 내주에 할 예정이다 The title match will be held next week.
2 〈어울림〉 a match
► 그녀의 모자는 옷과 잘 매치한다 Her hat matches [goes with] her dress well.
► 이 넥타이는 그 신사복과 매치하지 않는다 This tie doesn't match (with) the suit.
■—포인트 〖體〗 a match point : 시합은 매치 포인트가 되었다 The game has reached match points. —플레이 〈골프의〉 a match play

매캐하다 1 〈연기내가 나다〉 smoky

♦ 매캐한 냄새 a smoky smell
♦ 방에서 매캐한 냄새가 난다 The room is smoky.
2 〈곰팡내가 나다〉 musty; fusty; moldy
♦ 이 책에서 매캐한 냄새가 난다 This book smells musty.

매켄지 〈캐나다 북서부의 강〉 the Mackenzie

매콜리 〈영국의 역사가·저술가·정치가〉 Macaulay, Thomas Babington(1800-59)

매콤하다 hot; peppery; pungent
♦ 매콤한 요리 hot [spicy, pungent] food
♦ 겨자는 매콤한 맛이 난다 Mustard has a hot taste.

매크로 〈거시적인〉 macro (↔ micro)
■—경제학 macroeconomics (► 단수 취급) —명령 〖電算〗 macroinstruction —이름 〖電算〗 macroname —이름표 〖電算〗 MNT 〔〈*macro-name table*〕 —정의〈정의〉 〖電算〗 macrodefinition —편석(偏析) 〖工〗 macro segregation —호출 〖電算〗 macrocall

매큼하다 pungent ⇨ 매콤하다

매킨리 〈알래스카주의 산〉 Mount McKinley

매킨토시 Mackintosh
■—블랭킷 〖工〗 Mackintosh blanket

매탄 煤炭 coal ⇨ 석탄(石炭)

매통 〈목매〉 a wooden hand mill for hulling rice

매트 〖體〗 〈깔개〉 a 《floor》 mat
♦ 마루에 매트를 깔다 spread a mat on the floor
► 그는 상대를 일격으로 매트위에 쓰러뜨렸다 He floored his opponent with one blow.
► 현관의 매트에서 신을 닦으시오 Please wipe [clean] your shoes on the doormat.
■—도어[현관]— a doormat 욕실— a bath mat —운동 a mat exercise

매트리스 a mattress

매파 —派 〈강경파〉 the hawks; a hardliner
♦ 매파 사람 a hawk / 의회의 비둘기파와 매파 the doves and the hawks of the congress

매파 媒婆 an old woman go-between

매판 〈맷방석〉 an under mat (for a handmill)

매판자본 買辦資本 comprador capital

매팔자 —八字 easy circumstances
♦ 매팔자다 lead an easy life; be in easy circumstances

매표 賣票 selling of tickets
► 매표 시간 09 : 00-17 : 00 (게시) Ticket sales hours 9 : 00 am-17 : 00 pm.
—**매표하다** sell tickets
■—구 a ticket window —기 a ticket vending machine —소 a ticket office; 〈英〉〈극장의〉 a booking office —원 〈美〉 a ticket agent [girl]; 〈극장의〉 a box office girl; 〈英〉 a booking clerk

매품 賣品 an article for sale
► 매품으로 내놓다 offer for sale
► 매품 (게시) For Sale.
► 비매품 (게시) Not for sale.

매한가지 sameness
♦ 매한가지다 be the same; all the same
► 어느 것을 선택하든 결국은 매한가지다 It makes no difference which we choose.
► 행복해지기를 원하는 것은 누구나 매한가지다

The desire to be happy is common to all of us.

매형 妹兄 one's elder sister's husband; one's brother-in-law

매호 每戶 each [every] house [household]

매호 每號 every number; each issue
▶이 잡지는 매호 특집을 꾸미고 있다 Each issue of this magazine contains a special feature.

매혹 魅惑 (a) charm; (a) fascination; glamor
♦매혹적인 charming; fascinating; captivating; attractive; bewitching / 매혹적인 미소 a killing [bewitching] smile / 매혹적인 여배우 a glamorous actress
―**매혹하다** charm; fascinate; bewitch; enchant; captivate

[해설] **charm, fascinate**는 다 같이 마법처럼 신비한 힘으로「매혹하다」라는 뜻으로 쓰이는데 fascinate 쪽이 뜻이 강하다.

♦청중을 매혹하다 charm the audience
▶나는 그의 웅변에 매혹되었다 I was charmed with his eloquence. ⇌ His eloquence charmed me.
▶우리는 그 웅장한 경치에 매혹되어 서 있었다 We stood by the magnificent sight.

매회 每回 each [every] time; 〔野〕 every inning; 〔拳〕 each [every] round
▶매회의 득점을 계산해 주십시오 Please add up the score each time.

매흙 〈토벽재〉(a fine) gray loam (for plastering)
♦매흙질하다 face [plaster] a wall with gray loam

맥 脈 1 ⇨ 맥박
♦맥이 없는 puleseless / 맥이 고르다[고르지 않다] the pulse is regular [irregular]/ 맥이 뛰다 pulsate / 맥을 재다 count sb's pulse
▶당신의 맥은 빠릅니다 [느리닙다] Your pulse is quick [slow].
▶그는 아직 맥이 있다 His pulse is still beating. ⇌ We can feel his pulse. ⇌ **(비유)** There is still some [a ray of] hope.
▶의사는 그의 맥을 짚었다 The doctor took [felt] his pulse.
2 〈광맥〉 a vein (of ore); lode; 〈광상〉 deposits
♦맥을 뚫다 open up a vein of ore /〈금〉맥을 찾아내다 strike a vein (of gold)
3 〈생기〉 spirit; vigor
♦맥이 빠지다 be disappointed; be discouraged; be disheartened
▶그는 권력 앞에서는 맥도 못췄다 He bowed [yielded] to authority.
■결체(結滯)― intermitten pulse 부정(不整) ― an irregular pulse 평(平)― a regular [normal] pulse

맥각 麥角 〔植〕 ergot ■―균〔植〕 Claviceps purpurea ―소(素) ergotine ―중독 ergotism

맥고 麥藁 〈밀짚·보리짚〉 straw of barley [wheat] ■―모자 (美) a sailor (hat); (英) a (boating) straw hat; a stiff straw hat (for men); a boater

맥노 麥奴 〔植〕〈보리의 깜부기〉 The black ear (of barley)

맥놀이 脈― 〔物〕 beat
■―주파수 〔工〕 beat frequency

맥농 麥農 barley [wheat] farming; cultivation of barley [wheat]

맥도 脈度 a pulse [heart] rate; (a) pulse frequency

맥도널드 〈영국의 정치가〉 McDonald, James Ramsay (1866-1937)

맥동 脈動 pulsatory motion; pulsation
■―변광성(變光星) 〔天〕 a pulsating variable star ―설〔地〕 the pulsation theory ―성〔天〕 a pulsating star ―전류〔物·工〕 a pulsating current ―전압 a pulsating voltage

맥락 脈絡 1 〈혈맥〉〔解·生〕 the veins; the system of veins
2 〈기맥〉 interconnection; intricacies ; 〈연계〉 a thread [line] of connection; a chain of reasoning; 〈조리〉 logical connection; coherence; 〈문맥〉 the context
▶그는 그때까지말해 왔던 것과 전혀 맥락이 닿지 않는 내용을 말하고 있었다 He was speaking on a subject that had no connection with what he had been saying.
■―막(膜)〔解〕 the choroid

맥량 麥凉 the cool weather at the barley ripening season

맥량 麥糧 barley of summer at the provisions

맥류 脈流 a ripple
■―백분율(百分率)〔物〕 ripple percentage

맥류 麥類 barley, wheat, oats, rye, etc.

맥리 脈理 1 〈문맥〉 the context; coherence; logical connection
2 〈진맥〉 the diagnostic theory of the pulse

맥망 麥芒 〈보리·밀의 수염〉 a wheat beard; an awn (of barley)

맥맥이 脈脈― continuously; ceaselessly
♦맥맥이 이어온 전통 an unbroken tradition
▶우리 회사에는 지금도 창업자의 정신이 맥맥이 흐르고 있다 The spirit of the founder still permeates our company.
▶평화운동의 정신은 맥맥이 이어질 것이다 The spirit of peace movement will live on.

맥맥하다 1 〈코가 막혀 답답하다〉 stuffy; bunged-up
▶내 코가 맥맥하다 I have a stuffy nose.
2 〈생각이 잘 돌지 않다〉 be stuck (for an idea); be at a loss (for); be at one's wit's end
♦생각이 맥맥하다 can't form any idea
▶어떻게 대답해야 할지 나는 맥맥하다 I am at a loss [at my wit's end] how to answer.

맥박 脈搏 〔生理〕 the pulse; pulsation; the stroke of the pulse; sphygmus
▶평상시 내 맥박은 74이다 My normal pulse rate is 74.
■―계 a pulsimeter; a sphygmometer ―도〔醫〕 a sphygmogram ―수 a pulse [heart] rate ―촉진 sphygmopalpation ―학 sphygmology

맥박치다 脈搏― 1 〈맥박이 뛰다〉 pulsate; pulse; beat
▶내 심장은 빠르게 맥박쳤다 My heart pulsed fast.
2 〈약동하다〉 ▶그의 몸 안에는 자유의 정신이

맥박치고 있다 He has a strong spirit of liberty throbbing [beating] within him.
맥분 麥粉 wheat flour=밀가루
맥빠지다 脈— 1〈피곤하다〉be tired [exhausted]; be worn out
▶밤이 깊어지면서 얘기는 맥빠져 갔다 It grew late, and the conversation began to flag.
▶그는 맥빠진 것처럼 허공을 응시할 뿐이었다 He simply gazed into space absent-mindedly [with a blank look on his face].
2〈낙심하다〉be disappointed; be dispirited; be discouraged; be let down
▶그는 아직 맥빠진 상태이다 He is still in a state of apathy.
맥석 脈石〔鑛〕gangue; veinstone
맥스웰〈영국의 물리학자〉Maxwell, James Clerk (1831-79)
맥시〔服〕a maxi
◆—스커트 a maxiskirt —코트 a maxicoat
맥시류 脈翅類〔昆〕Neuroptera
◆맥시류의 neuropteran
◆—곤충 a neuropteron
맥아 麥芽〔植〕malt ■—당 maltose; malt sugar —물엿 malt syrup —박 (粕) malt cake
맥아더〈미국의 육군 원수〉MacArthur, Douglas (1880-1964)
맥암 脈岩〔地質〕a dike rock
맥압 脈壓〔醫〕〈맥폭〉a pulsatile pressure
◆—계 a sphygmomanometer
맥없다 脈— 〈기운이 없다〉weak; feeble; feel tired;〈풀이 죽다〉dispirited; dejected; be in low spirits
▶너 맥없어 보인다 You look gloomy.
맥없이 脈— 1〈기운 없이〉weakly; dejectedly; feebly; easily
◆맥없이 쓰러지다 fall down helplessly / 맥없이 앉아 있다 sit exhausted [dejected]
▶적은 맥없이 패했다 The enemy was beaten without much resistance.
▶그는 맥없이 방에서 나갔다 He left the room looking depressed.
2〈공연히〉without any reason for nothing
◆맥없이 벌받다 be punished for nothing [without cause]/ 맥없이 울다 start crying at the least little thing
맥작 麥作〈재배〉wheat [barley] cultivation;〈수확〉barley [wheat] harvest
맥주 麥酒 beer; ale (▶ale은 (英)에서는 홉이 들어 있지 않은 순한 맥주);〈저장 맥주〉lager

〔解說〕(1)「맥주 한 병」은 *a bottle of beer*,「맥주 한 잔」은 *a glass of beer*라고 한다.
(2)「맥주 홀」같은 데서 jug로 맥주를 주문할 때는 One [A] beer, please! 또는 Two beers, please!라고 말한다.
(3) 맥주라고 하면 보통 lager(beer)를 말하는데 이 밖에 홉 맛이 강한 ale, 흑맥주 porter, 이보다 알코올 도수가 더 높은 흑맥주 stout, 쓴맛이 강한 bitter 등 많은 종류가 있다.

◆맥주의 거품 froth [bubbles] on beer; the head on beer / 맥주 한 잔[병] a jug [bottle] of beer / 거품이 잘 이는 맥주 grassy beer / 맥주를 한 잔 마시다 have a glass of beer; have a beer
▶그 맥주는 김이 빠졌다 The beer was flat.
▶맥주 한 잔 하시겠어요? Would you like a (glass of) beer?
▶맥주에 취했군 You're drunk on beer, aren't you?
■깡통— canned beer 냉— cooled beer 병— bottled beer 생— draft〔(英) draught〕beer; beer on tap [draft] 흑— dark [black] beer; stout (▶dark beer 보다 높은 도수) ■—공장 a beer brewery —병 a beer bottle —양조 beer brewing —통 a beer barrel 맥줏집 (美) a beer hall; (英) a beerhouse; a beer parlor [saloon]
맥줄 脈— an artery
맥쩍다 1〈무료하다〉tiresome; bored; wearisome
▶할 일이 없어 맥쩍다 With nothing to do, I am bored to death.
2〈면목없다〉shameful;〈서술적〉be ashamed of *oneself*
▶그를 다시 만나기에는 너무 맥쩍다 I am too ashamed of myself (ever) to see him again.
맥추 麥秋 the harvest time for barley; the barley harvest season
맥파 脈波 a pulse wave
■—계〔醫〕a sphygmograph —곡선 a pulse curve; sphygmogram
맥풀리다 脈— be tired; be disappointed ⇨ 맥빠지다
맨[1]〈오직〉exclusively; nothing but [else]; just
▶이 좌석들은 맨 금연자 전용이다 These seats are for nonsmokers exclusively.
▶구경거리는 없고 맨 사람뿐이다 There is nothing to see but a crowd of people.
맨[2]〈가장〉extreme; most
◆맨 끝 a (tail) end; the tip;〈뒤끝〉the rear / 맨 앞 the head; the lead / 맨 앞의 foremost; headmost / 맨 뒤의 hindmost / 맨 왼쪽의 leftmost / 맨 위의 at the top; uppermost; highest / 맨 안쪽의 innermost / 맨 먼저 in the first place; first of all; to begin with; above all / 맨 나중에 behind all others; last of all; hindmost / 맨 꼭대기에 on (the) top《of》; uppermost / 맨 꼴찌다 be at the very bottom [tail end] 《of a class》
맨-〈접두사〉bare; naked; just; nothing but; unadulterated
맨꽁무니〈무일푼〉a bare [an empty] hand; without resources; empty-handed; empty-headed business
◆맨꽁무니로 장사를 시작하다 start a business with practically no capital
맨끝 the (very) last [end]
◆맨 끝의 last; final; concluding; closing / 편지의 맨 끝에 at the close of a letter; in closing *one's* letter / 맨 끝까지 영화를 보다 watch a movie to the end
▶편지의 맨 끝에 그는 나의 성공을 기원한다고 썼다 He closed his letter by wishing me my success.
맨나중 the very last [end]
◆맨 나중의 last; ultimate; final / 맨 나중에 in conclusion;〈끝에〉finally;〈맨 마지막에〉last-

맨둥맨둥하다 ly / 맨 나중까지 to the end [last] / 맨 나중에 나가다 go out 《of a theater》 after all the others
▶ 그는 맨 나중에 왔다 He arrived last.

맨둥맨둥하다 treeless; bald; bare
◆ 맨둥맨둥한 산 a bald mountain

맨뒤 the very last [end]; the tail (end)
◆ 행렬의 맨 뒤에 서 있다 be at the end (tail) of a procession

맨드라미 〔植〕 a cockscomb

맨드리 1 〈옷맵시〉 a style of dressing
2 〈만듦새〉 workmanship; make

맨드릴 〔機〕〈선반의〉 mandrel

맨땅 bare ground ◆ 맨땅에 쭈그리고 앉다 squat on the bare ground

맨머리 a bare head
◆ 맨머리로 밖에 나가다 go out bareheaded [with no hat on]; go out with *one's* head bare [uncovered]

맨머신 시스템 〔電算〕 man-machine system

맨먼저 〈최초의〉 at the very first [beginning]; 〈무엇보다 먼저〉 first of all; the beginning
◆ 맨 먼저 first; foremost
▶ 맨 먼저 뭘 할까? What shall we do first?
▶ 내가 병이 들었을 때 맨 먼저 그가 문병하러 왔다 When I got sick he was the first to come and see me.
▶ 아침에는 어머니가 맨 먼저 일어나신다 Mother gets up earliest of all in the morning.
▶ 중요한 일은 맨 먼저 끝마쳐라 Finish the most important things first (of all).

맨몸 1 〈벌거벗은 몸〉 a naked body; nudity; nakedness; a nude
◆ 맨몸의 아기 a baby with nothing on / 맨몸에 옷을 입다 wear [put on] clothes without any underwear / 맨몸이 되다 become naked; strip; strip *oneself* naked / 맨몸으로 헤엄치다 swim in the nude [(口) in the raw]
2 〈무일푼〉 pennilessness
◆ 맨몸이 되다 become penniless; (俗) go (clean) broke

맨밑 the very bottom
◆ 맨 밑의 the lowest; the bottommost
▶ 그의 이름이 맨 밑에 있었다 His name was the bottom of the list.

맨바닥 the bare floor [ground]

맨발 a bare [naked] foot
◆ 맨발의 barefooted; unshoed / 맨발의 소년 a barefoot(ed) boy / 맨발이 되다 become barefooted / 맨발로 잔디 위를 걷다 walk on the lawn in bare feet; walk barefooted on the lawn
▶ 그들은 언제나 맨발로 다닌다 They always go barefoot(ed).

맨밥 (boiled) rice without any side dishes
◆ 맨밥을 먹다 eat rice alone; eat rice without any side dishes at all

맨션 (美) 〈고급분양주택〉 a condominium; (口) a condo (*pl.* ~s); (英) a flat; 〈건물 전체의 임대 맨션〉 (美) an apartment building [house, complex]; (英) a block of flats; 〈한 세대분〉 (美) an apartment; (英) a flat (▶ mansion은 「대 저택」의 뜻. 공동주택의 한세대분을 가리켜 mansion이라고 하지는 않음)

◆ 고급 맨션 a luxury apartment (house); (英) a luxury flat

맨손 〈맨주먹〉 empty hands; a bare hand; 〈비무장〉 unarmed
◆ 맨손으로 with *one's* bare hands / 맨손으로 사업을 시작하다 start a business with no capital ⇌ open a business on a shoestring / 맨손으로 무장 강도와 싸우다 fight unarmed with an armed robber
▶ 그는 맨손으로 공을 잡았다 He caught the ball with his bare hands.
■ ━ 체조 free exercise; free gymnastics

맨송맨송하나 1 〈몸에 딜이 없다〉 hairless; bare; bald
◆ 턱이 맨송맨송하다 be beardless; have no beard; have a bald chin
2 〈산에 나무가 없다〉 treeless; bare; bald
3 〈술취하지 않다〉 sober; not drunk [tipsy]; unintoxicated
▶ 나는 술을 많이 마셨는데도 아직 맨송맨송하다 I have so much drunk, but yet I seem none the worse for it.

맨숭맨숭하다 hairless; bare ⇨ 맨송맨송하다

맨스필드 〈영국의 여류작가〉 Mansfield, Katherine (1888-1923)

맨아래 the very bottom
◆ 맨 아래의 the lowest; the undermost

맨앞 the forefront; the van; the foremost
◆ 맨 앞의 차 the foremost car / 맨 앞에서서 가다 go at the head of 《a party》
▶ 그의 이름이 맨 앞에 나와 있다 His name leads the list.
▶ 내 자리는 맨 앞 오른쪽에서 네번째이다 My seat is the fourth from the right in the front.

맨위 the top; the peak; the summit; the apex
◆ 맨 위의 topmost; highest; uppermost / 맨 위의 선반 the top shelf / 맨 위에 on (the) top (of)

맨입 an empty stomach [mouth] ◆ 맨입에 술을 마시다 drink on an empty stomach
▶ 맨입으로 학교에 갔다 I went to school without eating.

맨주먹 a naked fist; an empty fist; a bare hand ⇨ 맨손
◆ 맨주먹으로 barehanded; barefisted; empty-handed / 맨주먹으로 싸우다 fight with naked fists [unarmed] / 거의 맨주먹으로 장사를 시작하다 start a business with practically no capital [(口) from scratch, (口) from the ground up]
▶ 그는 맨주먹으로 막대한 재산을 모았다 Though he had nothing to start with, he had made a colossal fortune.

맨처음 (at) the very beginning; the first; the outset
◆ 맨 처음부터 from the beginning [start] / 맨 처음에 at first; at [in] the beginning
▶ 그가 맨 처음에 왔다 He was the first to come.
▶ 내일 아침 맨 처음으로 그걸 하겠다 I'll do it first thing tomorrow morning.

맨체스터 〈영국의 상공업도시〉 Manchester

맨 투 맨 〈구기에서〉 man-to-man (defense); one-to-one

▶그는 맨투맨으로 발음 훈련을 받고 있다 He receives pronunciation drill on a one-to-one basis.
■—방어[공격] 〔籠・蹴〕 a man-to-[for-]man defense [offense]
맨틀 1〈지구의〉 a mantle
2〈가스 등의〉 a (gas) mantle
맨틀대류설 —對流說 〔地球物〕 mantle convection theory
맨틀피스 a mantelpiece; a mantel
▶그는 맨틀피스 앞에 있는 의자에 앉아 있었다 He was sitting on a chair before the mantelpiece.
맨해튼 1〈미국 뉴욕시의 1구〉 Manhattan
2〈칵테일〉 manhattan (cocktail)
맨홀 a manhole ■—뚜껑 a manhole cover
맬서스 〈영국의 경제학자〉 Malthus, Thomas Robert (1766-1834) ■—주의[학설]〈맬서스의 인구론〉 Malthusianism
맴돌다 turn round ⇨ 매암돌다
맴돌이 1〈맴도는 일〉 a spin *oneself* round; turning round and round
2〔數〕〈회전체(回轉體)〉 a body of rotation
3〔物〕〈소용돌이〉 an eddy; a whirl
■—전류〔物・工〕 eddy current —전류감속기 (減速器)〔工〕 eddy current retarder —전류식 회전계〔工〕 eddy-current type tachometer —전류제어〔工〕 eddy current control
맴맴 〈매미의 울음소리〉 chirpingly
▶매미가 맴맴 울고 있다 Cicadas [Locusts] are chirping [singing].
맵다 1〈맛이〉 hot; spicy; pungent; sharp
♦매운 맛 a sharp taste / 매운 양념 pungent condiments; a pungent seasoning / 매운 소스 a hot sauce / 작지만 매운 piquant though small
▶멕시코 요리는 매운 것이 많다 Most Mexican foods are spicy [hot].
▶이 고추가 나에게는 너무 맵다 This pepper is too hot for me.
2〈추위 등이〉 intense; severe; inclement
♦겨울의 매운 추위 the intense [severe] cold of winter
▶추위가 참 맵군요 How intense the cold is!
맵시 stylishness; shapeliness; smartness; figure; form; appearance; a style
♦맵시있는 몸매 a handsome [graceful] figure / 맵시있는 상의 a stylish coat; a smart [wellcut] coat / 맵시있는 smart; stylish; chic; shapely; wellcut; fashionable / 맵시있는 illshaped[-formed]; awkward; ungainly; clumsy; gangling; shapeless / 맵시 내다 dress [smarten, doll] *oneself* up; be dressed up / 맵시가 있다 be nicely turned out; look smart [stylish]
▶그녀는 모자를 맵시있게 쓰고 있다 She is wearing her hat at a rakish angle.
▶맵시있게 차리고 어딜 가니? Where are you going all dressed up?
▶그녀는 맵시있게 옷을 입고 있다 She is stylishly dressed.
■—몸— *one's* figure [carriage] 옷— a style of dressing; the cut of *one's* clothes
맷돌 a hand mill; a quern; a millstone

■—중쇠 the pivot and gudgeon of a millstone —질 grinding grain in a stone mill: 맷돌질하다 grind corn in a hand mill; mill (corn)
맷방석 —方席 a round straw mat 《for a hand mill》
맹— 猛— hard; intensive; heavy
♦맹반격 a severe counterattack / 맹연습 hard training; intensive practice
맹격 猛擊 a fierce attack ⇨ 맹공격
맹견 猛犬 a fierce [ferocious] dog
▶맹견 주의 《게시》 Beware of the Dog. ⇌ Beware — Fierce Dog.
맹곡 盲谷 〔地質〕 a blind valley
맹공격 猛攻擊 vehement [víːəmənt] attack; a fierce [violent] attack
♦맹공격을 받다 come under heavy attack —맹공격하다 make a vigorous attack 《on》
▶우리는 적을 맹공격했다 We fiercely [violently] attacked the enemy. ⇌ We assaulted the enemy.
▶친구들은 나의 의견에 대해 맹공격했다 My friends criticized me severely for my opinions.
맹그로브 〔植〕 a mangrove
맹근하다 slightly warm; lukewarm; tepid
맹글〈압착 롤러〉 a mangle
맹글링 mangling; lustering
맹금 猛禽 a bird of prey; a predatory [raptorial] bird
맹꽁맹꽁 croakily
♦맹꽁맹꽁 울다 croak
맹꽁이 1〔動〕 a small round frog
2〈맹추〉 a fool; an idiot; a bird-brain; a diehard; a bigot; a simpleton; a blockhead; 〈땅딸막한 사람〉 a potbelly; a humpty-dumpty
♦맹꽁이 결박한 것 같다 be a humpty-dumpty
■—자물쇠 a padlock
맹도견 盲導犬 a guide dog; a Seeing Eye dog
맹독 猛毒 (a) deadly [virulent] poison; 〈동물의〉 deadly venom
♦맹독의 뱀 a highly poisonous [venomous] snake / 맹독이 있다 be virulently poisonous
맹랑하다 孟浪— 1〈허망하다〉 false; groundless; unreliable; 〈믿을 수 없다〉 unbelievable; incredible; 〈터무니없다〉 absurd; unreasonable; 〈무책임하다〉 irresponsible
♦맹랑한 사람 an irresponsible [unbelievable] man / 맹랑한 소문을 퍼뜨리다 set wild rumors afloat / 맹랑한 이야기를 하다 have a silly conversation; talk idly
▶누가 그런 맹랑한 소리를 하던? Whoever told you such a nonsense?
2〈허술히 볼 수 없다〉 not negligible; shrewd; tough; clever; difficult
▶이 문제는 맹랑하다 The problem is difficult [hard] to solve. ⇌ It's a knotty [troublesome] problem.
맹렬하다 猛烈— furious (anger); violent (storm); vehement 《wind》; fierce 《hatred》; keen 《competition》
♦맹렬한 경쟁 fierce [keen] competition / 맹렬한 반대 strong opposition / 맹렬한 훈련 heavy [intensive, hard, rigorous] training / …을 위한 맹렬한 운동을 수행하다 carry on [conduct]

active [intensive] campaign ((for)) / 소아마비를 퇴치하는 맹렬한 운동을 개시하다 start [launch] a vigorous campaign against polio

맹렬히 猛烈— violently; furiously; vehemently; fiercely; intensely

♦ 맹렬히 공부하다 study hard [intently] / 맹렬히 꾸짖다 score *sb* like anything / 맹렬히 공격하다 make a fierce [furious, vigorous] attack ((on)); attack *sb* ferociously / 맹렬히 싸우다 fight desperately [hotly]

▶ 그는 시험전 한 달 동안 맹렬히 공부했다 He studied like mad [crazy] for a month before the examination.

▶ 그들은 연사에게 야유를 맹렬히 퍼부었다 They interrupted the speaker with scathing hoots.

맹모삼천지교 孟母三遷之敎 Mencius' mother changed houses three times for the sake of her son's education. ⇌ Change of pasture makes fat calves.

맹목 盲目 blindness

♦ 맹목의 blind ⇨ 맹목적
■ —구간 blind sector landing

맹목적 盲目的 blind; reckless

♦ 맹목적인 사랑 blind love; dotage / 맹목적으로 recklessly / 맹목적으로 사랑하다 love blindly; dote on ((*one's* grandchild))

▶ 그는 그녀를 맹목적으로 사랑하고 있다 He is infatuated with her.

▶ 그녀는 외아들을 맹목적으로 사랑했다 She doted on [upon] her only son.

맹문 〈사정〉 the circumstances; the situation; the state of things; 〈상세〉 particulars; details

♦ 맹문 모르다 have no grasp of the situation; do not understand the matter [circumstances] at all / 맹문도 모르고 일에 덤벼들다 rush [plunge] into *sth* without knowing anything about it

맹문이 a person who doesn't know how the wind blows; a person who has no sense; a person who doesn't understand the situation at all

맹물 1 〈물〉 plain [tasteless] water

♦ 맹물같은 술[스튜] watery [washy] liquor [stew] / 맹물같은 커피[차] weak [watery] coffee [tea]

▶ 이 수프는 맹물같다 This soup is mere wash.

2 〈사람〉 a dull [tiresome, boring] person

맹반격 猛反擊 ((make)) a severe counterattack ((on))

맹방 盟邦 a friendly nation; an ally; an allied power; a confederate (state); a league (of allies)

맹성 猛省 〈깊은 반성〉 grave [serious] reflection [reconsideration]; penitence ((for *one's* wrongdoing))

♦ 맹성을 촉구하다 urge *sb* to reflect seriously ((on *one's* conduct))

—맹성하다 reflect seriously on *oneself*

맹세 〈신에 대한〉 an oath; 〈서약〉 a pledge; a vow; 〈약속〉 a promise; a plight

♦ 맹세를 어기다 break *one's* vow [oath, pledge] / 맹세를 지키다 keep *one's* vow [oath, pledge]

—맹세하다 swear; take [swear, make] an oath; vow; pledge; give *one's* word [honor, pledge]; promise ((to do)); pledge *oneself* ((to do))

解說 ***swear***와 ***take an oath***는 정식으로 또는 선서하고 맹세하다. ***vow***는 공적으로 또는 엄숙히 맹세하다. ***pledge***는 딱딱한 말로 남과 굳게 약속(promise)한다는 말임.

♦ 금주를 맹세하다 vow abstinence; swear off drinking / 명예를 걸고 맹세하다 swear on *one's* honor / 영원한 우정[신의]을 맹세하다 swear eternal friendship [fidelity] / 충성을 맹세하다 pledge allegiance ((to)) / 신 앞에 맹세하다 swear by God [Heaven]; swear before [to] God / 마음속으로 맹세하다 swear within *oneself*

▶ 신혼 부부는 영원한 사랑을 맹세했다 The newly married couple vowed eternal devotion to each other.

▶ 나는 금연하기로 맹세했다 I am under a vow to give up smoking.

▶ 그는 앞으로 행실을 고치기로 맹세했다 He took a pledge to mend his ways in the future.

맹세지거리 a curse; a bad language; swearing in vulgar [coarse] language

—맹세지거리하다 swear profanely; utter curses; curse

맹세코 on *one's* oath; on *one's* honor; upon my word; by God

▶ 맹세코 나는 그것을 하지 않았다 I will give you my word that I have never done it.

▶ 맹세코 거짓말은 하지 않겠다 On my honor, I'll never tell a lie.

맹수 猛獸 a fierce [ferocious] animal; a savage beast; a predatory animal; a beast of prey

■ —사냥 big game hunting : 맹수 사냥을 하다 shoot big game; go big game hunting —조련사 a tamer [trainer] of wild animals

맹습 猛襲 a violent assault; a vigorous [fierce, heavy] attack

—맹습하다 make a fierce [savage, ferocious] attack ((on the enemy)); attack fiercely [furiously]

맹신 盲信 a blind belief [faith]; credulity

—맹신하다 be credulous; believe blindly

▶ 그 마을 사람들은 옛 미신을 맹신하고 있다 The villagers are credulous about [have blind faith in] the old superstition.

맹아 盲啞 ((총칭)) the blind and mute

■ —교육 education for the blind and mute —학교 a blind and mute school; a school for the blind and mute

맹아 萌芽 a bud; a sprout; a shoot

맹약 盟約 〈서약〉 a pledge; a pact; 〈동맹〉 an alliance; confederacy; a league

♦ 맹약을 맺다 conclude a pact; enter into a covenant

■ —국 a pact member; an ally; a confederate state

맹연습 猛練習 hard [intensive] training; heavy [vigorous] practice

—맹연습하다 do hard training; carry out vigorous practice [exercises]
▶그는 그 시합에 대비해서 2개월간 맹연습했다 He has trained hard for two months for that fight.
맹우 盟友 a sworn friend; an ally
맹위 猛威 ferocity; fierceness; violence
♦태풍의 맹위 the rage of a typhoon
▶어젯밤 태풍이 맹위를 떨쳐 많은 피해를 초래했다 A typhoon raged last night and caused a lot of damage.
▶독감이 맹위를 떨치고 있다 Influenza is now raging.
맹인 盲人 a blind [sightless] person; (총칭) the blind ♦맹인이 되다 become [go] blind; lose [be deprived of] *one's* sight
■—교육 blind education; education of the blind
맹자 孟子 〈사람〉 Mencius (372-289 B.C.); *the Works* [*Discourses*] *of Mencius*
맹장 盲腸 〖解〗 the c(a)ecum (*pl.* -ca); the blind gut
맹장 猛將 a strong [valiant] general; a dauntless leader; a veteran fighter
맹장염 盲腸炎 〖醫〗 cecitis
맹점 盲點 〖解〗 a blind spot [point]; 〈망막의〉 a scotoma (*pl.* ~s, -mata); 〈법 등의〉 a blind spot
♦법의 맹점 a blind spot in the law / 법의 맹점을 이용하다 take advantage of a loophole in the law; make an illicit use of law
▶그 이론에는 맹점이 있다는 것을 나는 알았다 I have found that there is a blind spot in the theory.
▶그는 법의 맹점을 이용해서 막대한 돈을 벌었다 He made a huge sum of money by taking advantage of a blind spot of law [imposing on a loophole in the law].
맹종 盲從 blind [unquestioning] obedience
—맹종하다 follow [obey] *sb* blindly
▶그가 너의 상사라고 해서 맹종할 필요는 없어 You need not follow him blindly because he is your superiors.
맹주 盟主 the leader of confederate states [confederacy, league]; the leading power
♦…의 맹주가 되다 become the leader of…; hold sway over…
▶그는 그 운동의 맹주가 되었다 He became the leader of the movement.
맹진 猛進 a dash; a drive; a thrust
—맹진하다 advance furiously; dash [make a bold dash] forward; push forward vigorously
맹추 a fool; a dunce; a simpleton; a blockhead
맹추 孟秋 〈초가을〉 early fall [autumn]; 〈음력 7월〉 July of the lunar calendar
맹타 猛打 a heavy blow; a hammerblow; 〖野〗 a heavy hit; slugging
♦맹타를 퍼붓다 〖野〗 hit hard; give heavy hit; pump out hits; hammer 《a pitcher》; 〖拳〗 make a punching bag out of 《*one's* opponent》
■—자 a heavy batter [hitter]; a slogger; (美口) a slugger
맹탕 〈국물〉 insipid [watery, washy] soup; 〈사람〉 a dull [boring] person

▶이 수프는 맹탕이다 This soup is mere wash.
⇌ This soup needs a bit of salt.
맹폭 盲爆 unscrupulous [blind] bombing
—맹폭하다 bomb blindly
맹폭 猛爆 heavy bombing [bombardment]; 〈공중 폭격〉 a heavy air raid; 〈융단 폭격〉 carpet bombing
—맹폭하다 bomb 《enemy positions》 heavily
맹학교 盲學校 a school for the blind; a blind school
맹호 猛虎 a fierce [ferocious] tiger
맹화 猛火 〈타는 불〉 raging flames; a roaring [devastating] fire; 〈큰불〉 a big fire; a raging fire; a conflagration
♦맹화 속으로 뛰어들다 rush into raging flames
▶그 불타고 있는 건물은 삽시간에 맹화에 휩싸였다 The burning building was soon a mass of raging flames.
맹활동 盲活動 vigorous activity [action]
—맹활동하다 take [play] a very active part 《in》; be in full activity [swing]
▶그는 20년간 화단의 중요 인물로 맹활동하고 있다 He has been very active in the front rank of painters for twenty years.
맹훈련 猛訓練 hard [intensive] training [exercise, practice]; —맹훈련하다 carry out intensive training; train hard
맹휴 盟休 a strike; a walkout; 〈동맹 휴학〉 a school strike
—맹휴하다 strike; go on (a) strike
▶학생들이 맹휴했다 The students went on strike.
맺다 1 〈열매를〉 bear; produce
♦열매를 맺다 produce [bear] fruit; (비유) produce a result; go to seed; come [be brought] to fruition
▶그들의 노력은 열매를 맺었다 Their efforts bore fruit.
▶너의 수년 동안의 노력을 맺을 날도 멀지 않을 것이다 It will not be long before your long years of work bear fruit.
▶이 자두나무는 열매를 많이 맺는다 This plum tree produces a lot of fruit.
2 〈끈·매듭을〉 tie (up); knot; bind
3 〈끝내다〉 close; finish; conclude; end (off); wind up
♦토론을 끝맺다 close a debate / …이라고 말하면서 끝을 맺다 conclude by saying…
▶그는 감사하다는 말로써 연설을 맺었다 He concluded [wound up] his speech with a few words of thanks.
4 〈원한을〉 cherish [harbor, bear, nurse] a grudge 《against》
♦원한을 맺다 bear *sb* a grudge; harbor an enmity 《toward》
5 〈인연·관계를〉 enter [come] into 《relation with》; form a relationship 《with》
♦백년가약을 맺다 exchange the vows of marriage; get married
▶우리는 모두 우정으로 맺어져 있다 We're all linked in friendship.
6 〈계약·조건을〉 make 《a contract》; close 《a bargain》; conclude 《a treaty》; strike up 《a bargain》

♦계약을 맺다 contract; make [enter into] a contract / 협정을 맺다 conclude an agreement (with)
▶ 우리 회사는 브라운 형제사와 판매계약을 맺었다 We've signed a sales contract with the Brown Brother's.
맺음말 a conclusion; a peroration; a concluding [closing] remark
맺히다 1 〈열매가〉 fruit; come into bearing; go [run] to seed
2 〈매듭이〉 be knotted; be tied; get tied into knot
3 〈원한이〉 be pent up; smolder
♦가슴에 맺힌 원한 a grudge smoldered in one's heart / 맺힌 원한 pent-up rancor; a deep grudge / 원한이 맺히다 have a long-smoldering grudge
4 〈눈물·이슬이〉 form
♦눈물이 맺힌 눈 bedewed eyes; eyes filled with tears / 이슬이 맺힌 moist [sprinkled] with dew; dewy / 피가 맺히다 blood gathers; 〈피부에〉 be bruised
▶ 풀잎에 이슬이 맺혔다 Dewdrops formed on the blades [grass].
맺힌데 〈상처〉 a bruised [contused] spot; 〈원한〉 a deep-set rancor
머금다 1 〈입에 물다〉 keep [hold] sth in one's mouth
♦음식을 입에 가득 머금고 with one's mouth full of food
2 〈마음에 품다〉 hold; have; bear in mind; entertain; harbor
3 〈간직하다〉 contain; hold; comprise; have
♦물을 흠뻑 머금은 땅 water-logged ground / 눈물을 머금다 have tears in one's eyes / 이슬을 머금다 be wet with dew; have dew on (it) / 웃음을 머금다 have a smile on one's lips; wear a smile
▶ 그녀는 눈에 눈물을 머금고 거기에 서 있었다 She stood there with tears in her eyes.
▶ 서쪽 하늘의 구름은 비를 잔뜩 머금고 있었다 The western clouds were big with rain.
머나멀다 1 〈거리가〉 far; far-off; faraway; very far [distant]
♦머나먼 곳 a faraway place / 머나먼 길 a long long road [distance]
▶ 머나먼 산꼭대기에는 눈이 덮여 있다 The faraway [distant] mountains are capped with snow.
2 〈시간〉 remote ♦머나먼 옛날 the remote ages; the far-off days
▶ 그것은 머나먼 옛날에 일어났다 It happened a long time ago.
머다랗다 rather far [distant, long]
머독 〈영국의 여류 소설가〉 Murdoch, Iris (1919-)
머루 〖植〗 〈열매〉 wild grape; 〈나무〉 a wild grapevine
머리 1 〈두부(頭部)〉 a head (▶얼굴도 포함한 목 위 전체)

解説 「머리」에 대한 영어 표현이 반드시 **head**가 되는 것은 아니다. 예를 들면 「네가 머리에 떠올랐다」라는 말은 You came across my mind. 「골머리 아픈 문제」는 a tricky problem, 「머리가 나쁜 학생」은 students without any brains 등이 된다.

〈**머리가**〉 머리가 아프다 have a headache; suffer from headache / 머리가 지끈지끈 아프다 be racked with a headache; have a splitting headache / 머리가 어질어질하다 have a giddy head; feel dizzy [giddy]
▶ 오늘은 머리가 무겁다 My head feels heavy [depressed] today.
▶ 머리가 떵하다 My head hums.
〈**머리를**〉 머리를 들다 raise [lift up] one's head / 머리를 수그리다 hang (down) one's head; bow [lower] one's head; but [get] one's head down / 머리를 부딪치다 butt heads with (another) / 양손으로 머리를 감싸다 bury [hold] one's head in one's hands [arms] / 머리를 맞대고 의논하다 lay [put] (their) heads together / 머리를 가우뚱하다 put one's head on one side / 머리를 쓰다듬다 pat sb on the head; stroke sb's head / 머리를 끄덕이다 nod (one's head); 〈동의하다〉 nod one's agreement (to); agree (to); give one's assent (to)
2 〈머리털〉 hair (of the head)

解説 두발 전체를 가리킬 때는 총칭적이어서 머리털이지만 한올 한올의 털을 말할 때는 머리카락이 된다. 예컨대 He has gray hair [hairs]. 에서 **hair**라고 하면 전체적 인상으로서 반백의 머리임을 말하며 **hairs**의 경우는 흰 머리카락이 몇 있다는 뜻이 된다.

♦곱슬곱슬한 머리 kinky hair / 부드러운[뻣뻣한] 머리 soft [bristly] hair / 머리 손질 a hairdo (pl. ~s); hairdressing / 머리를 깎다 have [get] one's hair cut [trimmed]; get [have] a haircut / 머리를 손질하다 dress [do up] one's hair; hairdress / 머리를 풀다 let [take] down one's hair
▶ 그의 머리는 까맣고 숱이 많다 He has a full head of black hair.
▶ 그는 머리가 길었다 His hair grew (long).
▶ 가을에는 머리가 빠진다 In the fall the hair comes out.
3 〈두뇌〉 a brain; a head; mind; 〈지력〉 intelligence
♦명석한 머리 a clear head / 머리 회전이 빠른 사람 a quick-witted person; a quick thinker / 머리 회전이 느리다 be slow-witted; have a slow mind
〈**머리가**〉 머리가 모자라다 lack [want] brains / 머리가 필요하다 need [require] brains / 수학적인 머리가 있다 have a head for mathematics
▶ 그는 머리가 좋다 He is clever [bright, (美) smart]. ⇒ He has a clear head [(good) brains, a brilliant mind].
▶ 그는 머리가 나쁘다 He is weak in the head. ⇒ He has no brains. ⇒ He is stupid [dull, thick].
▶ 놈은 머리가 돌았어 That fellow is out of his head [mind]. ⇒ That guy is crazy [mad].
▶ 그 문제를 해결하는 데는 머리가 있어야 한다 It

requires brains [intelligence] to settle the problem.
▶ 나는 머리가 혼란스러워 잘 생각할 수가 없었다 My thoughts were chaotic and I couldn't think clearly.
▶ 〖會話〗「부모님은 내가 대학에 가기를 바라서」「넌 머리가 좋으니까 갈거야」 "Mom and dad want me to go to university." "Well, you're clever enough to get there."
〈머리를〉 머리를 쓰는 일 mental work; brainwork / 머리를 쓰다 be sensible 《enough to do》; use *one's* head [brain(s)]; work [use] *one's* wit; exercise *one's* wits; set *one's* wits at work / 머리를 짜내다 think hard 《of, about》/ 그 문제에 관해 머리를 짜내다 bother *one's* head about the problem; rack *one's* head about the problem; puzzle 《*one's* brains [mind]》 over the problem
▶ 그는 그 문제를 풀려고 머리를 짜냈다 He racked his brains trying to solve the problem.
▶ 머리를 좀 써라 Use your brains if you can.
4 〈고려〉 consideration; 〈생각〉 an idea
♦ 머리에 두다 have [keep] *sth* in mind / 머리에 두지 않다 leave *sth* out of consideration; take no notice [account] of *sth*
〈머리는〉 내 머리는 그녀 생각으로 가득 차 있었다 The thought of her had usurped my mind.
〈머리에(서)〉 그런 생각은 머리에 떠오르지도 않았다 The idea never occurred to me. ≒ I never hit on the idea.
▶ 그것이 그의 머리에서 떠나지 않았다 He could not get it out of his mind [head]. ≒ It was always on his mind.
5 〈우두머리〉 the head; a chief; a leader; a boss
6 〈끝·첨단·최초〉 the beginning; the top [head, tip] 《of》
♦ 말머리 introductory remarks / (첫)머리에서 세번째 the third from the head

머리글자 —字 an initial
♦ 머리글자로 서명하다 initial 《a paper》
▶ 손수건에 「Y.K.」의 머리글자를 넣어 주십시오 Please initial the handkerchief with "Y.K."
머리끄덩이 the clump [lock] of *one's* hair
♦ 남의 머리끄덩이를 잡다 grab *sb* by the hair / 머리끄덩이를 잡고 싸우다 have a hair-pulling fight
머리끝 〈머리털의 끝〉 the ends of *one's* hair
♦ 머리끝에서 발끝까지 from head to foot [heel, toe] / 머리끝까지 부아가 치밀다 (美) get mad with anger; be in hot anger [a fume]
머리대고물구나무서기 〖體〗 a head stand
머리띠 a headband; 〈여자용〉 a hairlace
머리말 a preface; a foreword; introductory remarks; an introduction
▶ 그 교수님이 친절하게도 내 신간에 머리말을 써주셨다 The professor was kind enough to write a preface to my new book.
머리맡 *one's* bedside
♦ 머리맡에(서) at the head of *one's* bed; at [by] *one's* bedside; by *one's* pillow / 머리맡에 붙어 있다 be [watch] at [by] *sb's* bedside
머리모양 —模樣 a hair style; 〈여성의〉 a coiffure; (口) a hairdo; 〈남성의〉 a haircut
♦ 머리모양이 매력적이다 have a nice [an attractive] hairdo; *one's* hair looks very nice
머리소리 a head voice
머리쓰개 headgear; a headpiece; a kerchief; a hood; a veil
머리얹다 1 〈머리를 틀어 얹다〉 turn [put] up *one's* hair; 〈쪽지다〉 do *one's* hair in a chignon; 〈시집가다〉 become a woman; attain womanhood; get married
2 〈기생이〉 lose *one's* virginity; be deflowered
머리염색 —染色 hair dyeing ▶ 나는 까맣게 머리염색을 했다 I dyed my hair black.
■ **—약** hairdye
머리채 a long tress of hair
머리치장 —治粧 a hair ornament; hairdo; hairdressing **—머리치장하다** do up *one's* hair; dress *one's* hair
머리카락 a hair (of *one's* head)
♦ 굵은 머리카락 a coarse [thick] hair / 흰 머리카락 a white hair / 머리카락을 뽑다 pull out a hair
머리칼 a hair ⇨ 머리카락
머리털 hair
♦ 뻣뻣한[부드러운] 머리털 bristly [soft] hair / 흐트러진 머리털 untidy hair / 헝클어진 머리털 tousled hair / 머리털이 쭈뼛하다 have *one's* hair stand on end 《at a sight》
▶ 그 무시무시한 광경에 내 머리털이 곤두섰다 My hair bristled up at the frightful sight.
■ **—자리** 〖天〗 the Berenice's Hair; Coma Berenices
머리통 the bulk of *one's* head
♦ 머리통이 크다 have a big head
머리핀 a hairpin
머릿골 the brain; brains; gray matter
▶ 머릿골이 좀 아프다 I have a slight headache. ≒ My head aches a little.
머릿기름 hair oil; hair cream; brilliantine; 〈포마드〉 pomade
♦ 머릿기름을 바르다 apply hair oil to *one's* hair; pomade *one's* hair
머릿니 a head louse; vermin in the hair
머릿살 nerves of the head
♦ 머릿살이 아프다[어지럽다] have headache; be troublesome [burdensome, annoying]
머릿수 —數 the number of persons; a head count
♦ 머릿수대로 per head; per capita / 이익을 머릿수 대로 나누다 share the profits equally; (英) go shares in the profits / 머릿수가 많다 [적다] there are a large [small] number 《of》; be large [small] in number / 머릿수를 늘리다 [줄이다] increase [decrease] the number / 머릿수를 세다 count the number of people present; count head
머무르다 1 ⇨ 멈추다
2 〈묵다·남아 있다〉 stay; remain
♦ 집에 머무르다 remain [stay] at home
▶ 나는 이 도시에서 머무르고 싶지 않다 I don't want to stay in this city.
▶ 나는 삼촌댁에 머무르고 있다 I am staying with my uncle.
▶ 그는 현직에 머무르기로 결심했다 He has decided to remain in his present office.

머무적거리다 hesitate 〈about, in, to do〉; waver 〈between〉; falter; be irresolute; shilly-shally
♦ 말을 머무적거리다 hesitate to say; hum and haw
▶ 그는 얼른 대답을 못하고 머무적거렸다 He was tardy in his response.
▶ 그는 아직도 갈 것인가 가지 않을 것인가를 놓고 머무적거리고 있다 He is still hesitating about going [whether he should go].
▶ 그는 어느쪽 의견을 들을 것인가에 대해 머무적거렸다 He wavered [vacillated] between the two opinions.

머무적머무적 hesitantly; irresolutely; diffidently; in a hesitant [diffident] manner
—머무적머무적하다 hesitate; be hesitant
▶ 머무적머무적하면서 그는 이야기를 끄집어냈다 Hesitantly, he broached the subject.

머뭇거리다 hesitate ⇨ 머무적거리다

머서(화)가공 —(化)加工 mercerization (▶무명류에 광택을 내기 위해 진한 수산화나트륨으로 처리하는 법)

머스캣 〔植〕 muscat

머스크멜론 〔植〕 a muskmelon

머슴 a farmhand; a farm worker [laborer]; a (male) servant; a manservant 《pl. menservants》
♦ 머슴을 살다 become [serve as] a farmhand / 머슴을 두다 keep a farmhand
■ —방 a farmhand's room —살이 working [serving] as a farmhand : 머슴살이하다 work [hire on] as a farmhand —애 a boy farm servant; a boy farmhand; 〈사내아이〉 a boy; a lad

머시 some(thing); any(thing); somebody
♦ 톰 머시라는 사람 Tom Somebody [What's-His-Name] / 송 머시라는 사람 a (certain) Mr. Song
▶ 그 머시라는 절은 어디에 있나? Where is the temple you mentioned?
▶ 어제 네가 보여준 것 말야 그것이 머시더라? What do you call it — the thing you showed me yesterday, I mean?

머쓱하다 1 〈키가크다〉 lank(y); gangling; spindly; rangy
♦ 머쓱한 소년 a lanky boy
2 〈풀죽은〉 disheartened; dispirited; depressed; 〈풀죽어 있다〉 feel small
▶ 너는 왜 그렇게 머쓱해져 있니? Why are you looking so dejected [depressed, dispirited, disheartened, down]?

머위 〔植〕 a butterbur

머저리 〈바보〉 a fool; an ass; a blockhead; a simpleton; 〈백치〉 an idiot

머천다이징 merchandising

머츰하다 (it) stop for a while; break; lull; hold up; let up

머캐덤 도로 —道路 a macadam

머큐로크롬 〔藥〕 Mercurochrome
♦ 다리에 머큐로크롬을 바르다 apply Mercurochrome to one's leg

머큐리 〔로神〕 Mercury

머플러 〈목도리〉 a muffler; a scarf; 〈내연 기관 등의 소음기〉 (美) a muffler; (英) a silencer

解說 「목도리」의 뜻인 「머플러」는 **muffler**에서 온 말이지만 최근에는 이 말도 구식이 되어 **scarf**가 대신 「머플러」의 뜻으로 쓰이게 되었다. 〈내연기관 등의〉 소음기의 뜻으로는 지금도 muffler라고 한다. 다만 (英)에서는 silencer가 일반적이다.

▶ 그는 흰 머플러를 목에 두르고 있었다 He wore [had] a white muffler around his neck.

머핀 a muffin

먹 〈먹물〉 India(n) [Chinese] ink; 〈고체의〉 an India(n) ink stick; a cake ink
♦ 먹을 갈다 rub down an ink stick / 붓에 먹을 묻히다 dip a brush in ink; 〈손 등에〉 smear [stain] with ink / 먹으로 쓰다 write in India ink

먹고살다 〈생활하다〉 live 〈on, by〉; subsist 〈on〉; feed on 〈grass〉; earn [gain] one's bread
♦ 월 80만원으로 먹고살다 live on eight hundred thousand won a month / 먹고살기 어렵다 find it hard to make a living; be badly off
▶ 그 집안은 먹고살기가 어렵다 His family is badly off.
▶ 그는 겨우 먹고산다 He can barely stay alive.
▶ 내 월급으로는 나 혼자서 먹고살기도 어렵다 My salary is too small for my life style. ⇌ I cannot live on my small salary.
▶ 이 수입으로는 6인 가족이 먹고살기 어렵다 With this income, I cannot support my family of six.
▶ 그는 뭘 해서 먹고사니? What does he live on?

먹구름 a dark [black] cloud; black clouds; a brewing
♦ 먹구름이 하늘을 덮었다 The sky is overspread with dark clouds.
▶ 먹구름은 흔히 폭풍우의 전조가 된다 A dark cloud often betokens [portends, presages] a storm.
▶ 동부 유럽에 먹구름이 덮이기 시작했다 Ominous clouds have begun to gather over Eastern Europe.

먹다[1] 〈톱·대패 등이〉 saw; cut (well); bite
▶ 이 대패는 잘 먹지 않는다 This plane doesn't bite [cut] well. ⇌ This plane is blunt.
2 〈씨아가〉 gin; 〈맷돌이〉 grind
▶ 씨아가 잘 먹는다 The cotton gin gins well.
▶ 맷돌이 잘 먹는다 The millstone grinds well.
3 〈물감·풀 등이〉 be dyed; dye; take (up) color; soak in
♦ 풀이 잘 먹은 셔츠 a well-starched shirt / 〈물감이〉 잘 먹다[먹지 않다] dye [take dye] well [badly]
▶ 이 분은 아주 잘 먹는다 This powder spreads very well.
▶ 이 종이는 잉크가 잘 먹지 않는다 This paper is not good for writing on with ink.
4 〈소요되다〉 cost; consume; spend
▶ 이 낡은 차는 기름을 많이 먹는다 This old car consumes much oil.

먹다[2] 〈귀가〉 become [go] deaf; lose one's

hearing
▶ 그는 아주 귀가 먹었다 He is stone-deaf. ⇌ He is as deaf as door. ⇌ He is deaf as a post [a stone].
▶ 그는 병이 나서 귀가 먹었다 He lost his hearing because of an illness.

먹다³ **1**【음식물】eat; take; 〈상식하다〉live on 《rice》; 〈동물이〉feed on

解說 일반어 *eat* 외에 여러가지 먹는 모습을 나타내는 동사는 다음과 같다.

급히[걸신들린듯] 먹다	***gobble***
게걸스럽게 먹다	***devour***
우적우적 먹다	***munch***
아삭아삭 먹다	***crunch***
소리내며 먹다	***slurp***
조금씩 씹어서 먹다	***nibble***
꿀꺽 삼키다	***swallow***

♦ 먹을 것 something to eat; eatables / 먹느냐 먹히느냐의 싸움 a life-and-death struggle; a struggle without quarter given or taken / 먹을 수 있는 eatable; fit to eat; edible; good to eat / 먹을 수 없는 not good to eat; inedible; uneatable / 먹고 살다 manage to live; get along / 한입 먹다 have [take] a bite [munch]《of》/ 한입에 먹다 eat at a [in one] mouthful / 먹기 위해 일하다 work for *one's* bread / 맛있게 먹다 eat with relish / 급히 먹다 take a hasty snack 《of cold meat and bread》/ 남김없이 먹어치우다 eat to the last morsel / 와작와작 먹다 eat like a horse / 겨우 먹고 지내다 stretch a living; eke out a precarious living; barely manage to keep body and soul together / 먹다 남기다 leave 《a dish》unfinished; leave 《food》half-eaten
▶ 어제는 배부르게 먹고 마셨다 I ate and drank my fill yesterday.
▶ 우리는 한솥밥을 먹는 사이다 We ate at the same table. ⇌ We lived under the same roof.
▶ 우리는 보통 하루에 세끼를 먹는다 We usually have [eat] three meals a day.
▶ 대부분의 한국 사람들은 쌀을 먹고 산다 Most Koreans live on rice.
▶ 일하지 않는 자는 먹지도 말지어다 No work, no grub. ⇌ The idle gets no bread.
▶ 좋아하는 것은 무엇이든 마음대로 먹어라 Please help yourself to anything you like.
▶ 이 버섯은 먹을 수 있다 This mushroom is good to eat [edible].
▶ 이 생선은 날것으로 먹을 수 있다 You can eat this fish raw.
▶ 먹지도 못하면서 욕심만 낸다 He wants more than he can eat. ⇌ His eyes are bigger than his belly.
▶ 오늘은 아무것도 먹지 않았다 I haven't had a morsel of food today. ⇌ I didn't touch food [taste anything] all day.
▶ 이 요리는 먹고 나면 속이 든든하다 This dish is really substantial.
▶ 잘 먹었습니다 I have enjoyed my dinner very much. ⇌ Thank you for your hospitable entertainment.
▶ 오늘 저녁은 집에서[밖에서] 먹을 작정이다 I am going to eat in [out] this evening.
▶ 그는 밤새껏 먹고 마시면서 지냈다 He spent the whole night eating and drinking [stuffing himself with food and drink].
▶ 소는 풀을 먹는다 Cows feed on grass.

2 〈피우다·복용하다·마시다〉drink; take; have
♦ 담배를 먹다 smoke cigarettes / 술을 먹다 drink 《wine》/ 〈아이가〉젖을 먹다 suck milk; suck the breast / 약을 먹다 take medicine / 우물을 먹다 drink [get a drink] at [from] a well
▶ 술을 먹으면 취하는 것이 당연하다 If we drink, we are drunk, no wonder.

3 〈벌레가〉be worm-eaten; eat into; be moth-eaten; be decayed
♦ 벌레먹은 이 a decayed tooth / 좀먹은 책 a moth-eaten book

4 〈남의 것·재물을〉embezzle; pocket; appropriate (to *oneself*); seize upon
♦ 공금을 먹다 embezzle [misappropriate] public money [funds] / 은행[남]의 돈을 먹다 embezzle money from a bank [person] /〈장기에서〉졸을 먹다 take pawn
▶ 그는 그 돈의 반 이상을 먹었다 More than half of the money stuck to his fingers.
▶ 그는 내 재산을 먹었다 He had taken liberties with my property.

5 〈이문·구문을〉receive; get; have
♦ 매상에 대해 6퍼센트의 구문을 먹기로 하고 at [for] a commission of 6% on sales / 이문을 먹다 take [get, receive] a commission 《on the sale of...》/ 2만원의 이문을 먹다 make [gain] a profit of 20,000 won

6 〈욕·겁을〉undergo; get; receive; suffer
♦ 겁을 먹다 be struck with awe; get into [be in] a funk / 욕을 먹다 〈꾸지람을 듣다〉be scolded [reproved, rebuked]; (口) catch [get] it 《from dad》; 〈비난을 받다〉be blamed [criticized]

7 〈나이를〉grow older; get on [up] in years; (口) get on
♦ 나이를 먹다 be an old man; be at an advanced age
▶ 그는 꽤 나이를 먹었다 He is well on in years.
▶ 그는 나이를 먹어감에 따라 원숙해졌다 He mellowed with age [as he grew older].

8 〈더위를〉be affected 《by the heat》
♦ 더위를 먹다 be affected by the (summer) heat; suffer from hot weather

9 〈판돈·상금을〉win 《bear away》《a prize, a wager》
▶ 5만원의 상금은 그 사람이 먹었다 The 50,000 won prize went to him.

10 〈녹(祿) 등을〉receive; be given
♦ 녹을 먹다 receive [hold] a stipend 《of 200 *suk* of rice》

11 〈마음을〉decide; fix (up); determine; make
♦ 마음을 먹다 be determined 《to do》; make up *one's* mind; put *one's* heart (into); set [keep] *one's* mind (on)
▶ 그는 의학 연구에 일생을 바치려고 마음먹었다 He made up his mind [decided, resolved] to devote his (whole) life to the study of

먹똥 1 〈말라붙은 먹물〉 dried sediment of India(n) [Chinese] ink
2 〈먹물 자국〉 a black ink spot

먹먹하다 〈귀〉 deaf; deafened; earsplitting; stunned; piercing
▶ 귀가 먹먹해질 정도의 새된 소리가 들렸다 A piercing [an earsplitting] shriek was heard.

먹물 India(n) [Chinese] ink; 〈오징어 등의〉 ink [sepia] 《of a cuttlefish》
♦ 먹물이 들다 be stained with Chinese ink / 먹물로 쓰다 write in India ink

먹빛 a shade of India, an ink(y) black
▶ 하늘은 먹빛이 되었다 The sky turned as black as ink.

먹새 cooking ⇨ 먹음새

먹성 appetite; how to eat; 〈먹는 양〉 one's eating capacity
♦ 먹성이 좋다 have a good appetite; have a large stomach; be omnivorous

먹실 1 〈실〉 a carpenter's inking string; a string dyed black; a string stained with ink
2 ⇨ 문신(文身)

먹은금 the cost price; cost ♦ 먹은금에 팔다 sell [offer] at cost [(the) cost price] / 먹은금 이하로 팔다 sell below cost

먹음새 1 〈음식 만드는 범절〉 cooking; cookery; cuisine
▶ 그 집의 먹음새는 매우 좋다[신통치 않다] The cuisine of that house is very good [poor]. ⇌ Cooking there is very good [bad].
2 〈음식 먹는 태도〉 the way of eating; table manners; 〈식욕〉 appetite
♦ 먹음새가 좋은 사람 (口) a heavy [big] eater; a trencherman / 먹음새가 좋다 be a hearty eater

먹음직스럽다 delicious-looking; appetizing; tempting
♦ 먹음직스러운 냄새 an appetizing smell / 먹음직스럽게 양념한 스튜 a stew seasoned nicely / 먹음직스러워 보이다 look delicious; be tempting [appetizing]

먹음직하다 delicious-looking ⇨ 먹음직스럽다

먹이 feed; food; 〈맹수의〉 a prey; 〈낚시의〉 bait; 〈개의〉 meat; 〈유혹물〉(비유) a lure; a bait
♦ (동물에게) 먹이를 주는 시간 feeding time / …의 먹이가 되다 become the prey of…; become the victim of… / 먹이를 주다 feed (hens) / 먹이로 하다 prey upon… / make a prey (of…)
▶ 그는 먹이를 노리는 사자처럼 적을 기다리고 있었다 He was waiting for the enemy like a lion eying its prey.
▶ 호랑이는 죽인 먹이를 밀림으로 끌고 갔다 The tiger dragged its kill into the jungle.
▶ ―그물 〔生〕 food web ―연쇄 〔生·水産〕 food chain ―회유 〔水産〕 feeding migration

먹이다¹ 1 〖먹게 하다〗 〈음식을〉 let sb eat; treat 《sb to beefsteak》; serve 《sb with a hamburger》; entertain sb with; 〈먹이를〉 feed 《an animal on oats》; feed (oats) to (an animal)
♦ 배불리 먹이다 let sb have (his) fill / 억지로 먹이다 force food upon sb; force sb to eat
▶ 그녀는 아이들을 배불리 먹였다 She let the children eat their fill.
2 〈부양하다〉 support; feed; keep; provide for; maintain
♦ 대가족을 먹여 살리다 support [feed, keep] a large family
▶ 대가족을 먹여 살리는 일은 쉽지 않다 It is not easy to feed [support] a large family.
3 〈사육하다〉 raise (sheep, hogs, etc.); rear (silkworms); keep (a cat); feed (cattle on hay)
▶ 그 땅은 100마리의 양을 먹이기에 충분할 것이다 The land will depasture 100 sheep.
4 〈뇌물을〉 offer [give] a bribe to sb; bribe sb; grease sb's palm
♦ 남에게 뇌물을 먹여 입을 다물게 하다 bribe sb into silence [to say nothing]
▶ 그는 관리에게 뇌물을 먹여 그것을 하게 했다 He bribed the official into doing it.
▶ 먹인 보람이 있다 The bribe has worked.
5 〈욕을〉 put sb to shame; humiliate
♦ 남을 욕 먹이다 let sb get a scolding
6 〈음료를〉 make [let] sb drink; 〈술을〉 give sb a drink; entertain sb with 《wine》; 〈약을〉 give sb (a medicine); administer 《a does of medicine》 to sb; 〈마소에게 물을〉 water (cattle); 〈아기에게 젖을〉 feed; give a baby milk
♦ 억지로 먹이다 force [compel] sb to drink (wine); force (water) down sb's throat
7 〈겁을 주다〉 frighten; give sb a fright; scare; terrify; intimidate
♦ 겁을 먹여 승낙케 하다 terrify sb into agreeing; intimidate [threaten] sb into compliance; browbeat sb into accepting 《the proposal》

먹이다² 1 〈물감·풀·기름·물 등을〉 soak 《sth with water》; apply (dye, starch, oil)
♦ 풀먹인 종이 wax paper / 풀을 너무 먹인 셔츠 a stiffly starched shirt / 줄에 밀랍을 먹이다 wax a string / 장판에 기름을 먹이다 oil floor paper
2 〈기계에〉 put sth in; feed sth at [with]
♦ 인쇄기에 종이를 먹이다 feed paper to a printing press
3 〈돈을 들이다〉 put 《money》 in; spend (money) on; consume
▶ 그는 돈을 많이 먹인 집을 지었다 He put a lot of money into building a house.
4 〈때리다〉 deal; give; administer
♦ 한 방 먹이다 give [deal] sb a blow / 따귀를 한 방 먹이다 give sb a box on the ear; box sb's ear
▶ 녀석에게 주먹을 한 대 먹였다 I punched the guy.

먹자 a carpenter's square (for drawing ink line)

먹자판 1 〈향락주의적 생각〉 hedonism; epicurism; a pleasure-loving way of life
2 〈먹고 마시는 자리〉 a spree; a frolic; a scene of riotous eating
▶ 오늘의 모임은 먹자판이다 At today's party you can eat as much as you want.

먹장 a piece [stick] of Chinese ink
♦ 먹장 같아부는 듯하다 be as black [dark] as ink [pitch]

먹―구름 a dark cloud; an inky cloud: 먹장구름이 하늘을 뒤덮었다 The sky is overspread with dark clouds.

먹줄 1〈먹통줄〉a string attached to an inkpot and stained with ink for drawing lines 2〈먹통줄로 친 금〉a carpenter's inking line ♦먹줄을 치다[띠다] stretch out an inking line / 먹줄 친 듯하다 be straight and even / 곧기는 먹줄 같다 be straight as a carpenter's inking line; *one* looks honest but is wicked at heart

■―꼭지 the tip of an inking line

먹지 ―紙 carbon paper; copying paper

먹칠 1 coating [smearing] with Chinese ink ―먹칠하다 smear [coat] with Chinese ink 2〈명예를 더럽힘〉disgrace; discredit; dishonor ―먹칠하다 injure; disgrace; spoil ♦가문에 먹칠하다 bring disgrace on *one's* family / 명성에 먹칠하다 sully [tarnish] *one's* reputation; cast slur on *one's* fame / 조상의 이름에 먹칠하다 disgrace the good name of *one's* ancestors

먹칼 an inking spatula 《of a carpenter》

먹통 〈바보〉a fool

먹통 ―桶 〈목수의〉an [a carpenter's] ink pad;〈먹물 그릇〉an inkpot; an inkbottle

먹투성이 a thing smeared all over with ink ♦먹투성이의 covered with Chinese ink; smeared all over with Chinese ink ▶손이 먹투성이가 되었다 My hands are all smeared with ink.

먹황새 〔鳥〕a black-headed stork

먹히다 1〈먹음을 당하다〉be eaten up 《by》;〈맹수 등에〉be devoured 《by》;〈삼켜지다〉be swallowed up 《by》

♦먹느냐 먹히느냐의 싸움 a life-and-death [life-or-death] struggle; a struggle without quarter given or taken

▶개구리가 뱀한테 먹혀 버렸다 A frog was swallowed by the snake.

2〈먹어지다〉can be eaten [drunk]

♦밥이 많이 먹히다 have a keen [hearty] appetite / 술이 먹히지 않다 do not feel like having a drink

▶나는 요새 밥이 잘 먹히지 않는다 I have little [a poor] appetite these days.

3〈돈이〉take; cost; require

♦돈이 많이 먹히다 cost 《one》 much money; be expensive

▶이것은 5천원 가량 먹혔다 This cost me a little less than 5,000 won.

▶이 일은 돈이 많이 먹힌다 This job will take much money. ⇌ This is a very costly enterprise.

4〈빼앗기다〉be cheated [swindled] of; be taken for; lose

♦돈을 먹히다 be cheated [fooled] out of *one's* money

▶그에게 돈을 주었다간 먹히기 쉽다 You will probably never see the money again if you lend it him.

5〈화장품이 얼굴에〉♦이 분은 (얼굴에) 잘 먹힌다 This face powder sticks well.

먼길 a long way;〈긴 여행〉a long journey;〈장거리〉a long distance

♦먼길을 가다 go a long way; make a long journey

▶먼길을 오시게 해서 죄송합니다 I'm sorry to have made you come so far.

먼나라 a remote [faraway] country; a distant land

먼눈[1] 〈시각장애인의〉a blind eye

먼눈[2] 〈먼 곳을 보는〉eyes looking into the distance

♦먼눈이 밝다 be able to see a long way [far into the distance] / 먼눈을 팔다 look into the distance; look into (vacant) space; gaze blankly (at); look vacantly

먼데 〈먼거리〉a great [long] distance; a long way;〈먼곳〉a distance [far-off] place

♦먼데의 distant; faraway; far; remote / 먼데에 far away [off]; a long way off; in the distance / 먼데서 보면 seen from a distance / 먼데서 오다 come a long way 《from》; come from afar / 먼데에 가 있다 be [have] gone far away / 먼데서 오는 손님을 접대하다 entertain a guest (coming) from a distance

▶그렇게 먼데까지 그를 만나러 갈 수는 없다 I can't go all that way to see him.

먼동 the eastern sky of an early morning; the dawning sky

♦먼동이 틀 때 at dawn [daybreak]; at break of dawn / 먼동이 트기 전에 before dawn [daybreak]; before it is morning [light]

▶먼동이 튼다 Day dawns [breaks, cracks]. ⇌ It dawns.

▶먼동이 틀 때[트기 전에] 그는 집에 왔다 He came home at [before] dawn [daybreak].

먼로 〈미국 제5대 대통령〉Monroe, James (1758-1831) ■―主義 the Monroe Doctrine; Monroeism

먼바다 〈외양〉the high seas;〈공해〉the open sea

먼발치 a spot far off; a somewhat distant place

♦먼발치에 at some [a] distance / 먼발치에서 보면 in a distant view; (when) seen at [from] a distance / 먼발치에서 보다 have a distant view 《of》

먼빛으로 from far away; from afar ♦먼빛으로 보아 when viewed from a distance; in a distant view; to a gaze at a distance

먼산 ―山 a distant mountain [hill] ■―바라기 a person with a faraway look in the eyes [with a vacant stare]

먼셀색채체계 ―色彩體系 〔美術〕Munsell color system

먼일 distant [future] events; events to come ♦먼일을 생각하다 think of the future; look into the future 《of》/ 먼일을 예측하다 foretell [predict] the future

먼저 1〈우선〉first of all; first; above all; before anything else; in the first place; to begin with

▶당신이 일을 끝내시면, 제가 먼저 시내를 안내하겠습니다 When you have finished your business, I would like to take you around the city first.

▶ 먼저 이것을 해야 한다 First of all I must do this.
▶ 무엇을 먼저 할까요? What shall we do first?
2 〈앞서〉 earlier than; before; ahead of; prior to; in advance of
♦ 먼저 가다 go first; go before *sb*
▶ 그것보다 이것을 먼저 해야 한다 You must do this before that.
▶ 먼저 실례합니다 Would you mind my leaving now? ⇒ Please excuse my going first.
▶ 숙녀부터 먼저 Ladies first.
▶ 나는 누구보다도 먼저 왔다 I came earlier than anybody else. ⇒ I came earliest of all.
▶ 일행은 예정보다 1시간 먼저 출발했다 The party started an hour earlier than scheduled.
3 〈전에〉 previously; formerly; before
♦ 먼저 말한 바와 같이 as has been pointed out; as previously stated; as above-mentioned
4 〈미리〉 in advance; beforehand; previously; ahead of time
▶ 나는 짐을 먼저 보냈다 I sent my baggage beforehand.
▶ 이 식당에서는 식대를 먼저 지불해야 한다 We have to pay in advance for a meal at this restaurant.
▶ 집세는 먼저 지불해야 한다 The rent is to be paid in advance.

먼저께 the other day; some time [a little while] ago; some [a few] days ago; recently; not long ago

먼지 dust; 〈티끌〉 a mote; (美) trash; (英) rubbish
♦ 미세한 먼지 fine dust / 먼지투성이의 책 a dusty book / 먼지 하나 없는 방 a spotless room; a room free of dust / 뿌옇게 이는 먼지 a cloud of dust / 먼지투성이의 dusty 《room》; covered with dust; full of dust / 먼지가 나다 [끼다] be [become] dust; be covered with dust / 먼지를 가라앉히다 lay the dust / 먼지를 일으키다 raise [stir up] dust / 먼지를 털다 brush away [beat off] dust; dust 《one's coat》; shake off the dust
▶ 그녀의 방에는 먼지 하나 없다 There is never a speck of dust in her room.
▶ 이 도로는 먼지가 많다 This is a dusty road.
▶ 먼지가 뿌옇게 일고 있다 The dust is rising in clouds.
▶ 먼지가 가라앉았다 The dust has settled.
▶ 바람이 부는 날에는 먼지가 인다 On a windy day dust rises.
▶ 방구석에는 먼지가 쌓이기 쉽다 Dust's apt to collect in the corners of a room.
■ ─떨이 a duster ─보라 〔地〕 a dust [sand] storm ─잼 rain just enough to settle the dust

멀거니 absentmindedly; blankly; vacantly; with an abstracted air; with a blank look
♦ 멀거니 바라보다 look vacantly [blankly] 《at》; moon 《about, around》 / 멀거니 앉아 있 be sitting absentmindedly
▶ 그는 멀거니 구름을 바라보고 있었다 He was gazing vacantly [blankly] at the clouds.
▶ 그녀는 문 옆에 멀거니 서 있었다 She was standing absentmindedly by the door.

멀건이 an absentminded person; (美俗) a goofer; a blockhead; a dunce

멀겋다 1 〈흐릿하게 맑다〉 dim; dull; leaden
♦ 멀건 눈 glassy [glazed] eyes; clouded [fishy] eyes / 멀건 하늘 a gray [leaden] sky; a gloomy [an overcast] sky
2 〈액체 등이 묽다〉 thin 《coffee, porridge, paste》; weak [watery] 《tea, beer》; (wishy-) washy 《milk》; sloppy
♦ 멀건 술 watery [washy] liquor
▶ 이 수프는 너무 멀겋다 This soup is mere wash.

멀게지다 〈흐릿하게 맑아지다〉 become dull; 〈묽어지다〉 become weak; become watery [thin]

멀구슬나무 〔植〕 a chinaberry; a bead tree

멀다¹ 〈눈이〉 become [go] blind; lose [be deprived of] *one's* (eye)sight; become sightless
♦ 눈이 먼 blind; sightless / 한쪽 눈이 멀다 be [become] blind of [in] one eye / 돈에 눈이 멀다 be blind by gold [money]
▶ 그는 탐욕에 눈이 멀어 살인했다 Avarice [Greed] drove him to murder.

멀다² **1** 〈거리가〉 far 《from》; a long way 《off》; distant 《from》; faraway; far-off; remote

> **[解説]** *far*는 막연하게 멀리 떨어져 있음을 나타내며, 보통 부정문·의문문에 쓰인다. 긍정문에서는 ***a long way (off)*** 등을 쓴다. 다만 far도 too, so, as, very, away, off 등이 붙을 때는 긍정문에서도 쓰인다. ***distant***는 간단히 도달할 수 없는 아주 먼 곳을 뜻한다. 그러나 I live [My house is] two kilometers distant from here.와 같이 특정한 거리를 표시하는 어구 뒤에 쓸 때는 그냥 떨어져 있다는 것을 나타낸다. ***faraway, far-off***는 far를 강화한 어법으로 다소 딱딱한 표현이고, ***remote***는 궁벽함과 불편함을 암시하여 도착하기 곤란함을 나타낸다.

♦ 먼 나라 a faraway [far-off, distant, remote] country; a country a long way off [far away] / 먼 곳에 far away [off]; a long way off; afar; in the distance / 멀지 않은 곳에 not far off [away]; a little way from 《the station》; at a short distance / 먼길을 떠나다 go a long way; make a long journey
▶ 그녀의 집은 여기서 멀다 Her house is far from here. ⇒ She lives a long way from here.
▶ 사무실은 여기서 멉니까? Is the office far from here?
▶ 먼 길을 오시느라 수고하셨습니다 It is very kind of you to come all the way to see me. ⇒ Thank you for coming all this way.
2 〈시간적으로〉 distant; remote
♦ 먼 조상 a remote ancestor / 먼 과거에 in the distant [far, remote] past; far in the past / 먼 옛날에 in the far-off days; long ago / 먼 장래에 in the remote [far-off] future
▶ 그 전설은 먼 옛날부터 전해져오고 있다 The legend has been handed down from ancient times [the remote past].
▶ 봄은 멀지 않았다 Spring is not far away. ⇒

Spring is just around the corner.
▶ 그 빌딩이 완공되려면 아직 멀었다 The building is far from being completed.
▶ 머지않아 벚꽃이 필 것이다 It will not be long before the cherry blossoms are out.
3 〈관계가〉 distant; remote
◆ 먼 친척 a distant [remote] relative
▶ 그녀는 내 먼 친척이다 She is a distant [remote] relation of mine.
▶ 멀고도 가까운 것이 남녀 사이다 Distant yet so close is the relationship between man and woman.
4 〈정도가〉 be no match; be far inferior (to)
▶ 그는 행복과는 거리가 멀다 He is far from (being) happy. ⇒ He is not happy at all.
▶ 그의 설명은 진실과는 아주 멀다 His explanation is a long way from the truth.

멀떠구니 〈새의 모이주머니〉 a crop; a craw; 〈새의 모래주머니〉 a gizzard

멀뚱멀뚱 1 〈멀거니〉 blankly; vacantly; absentmindedly; with a stupid [vacant] look; with a look of amazement; with a blank look
◆ 멀뚱멀뚱 바라보다 look blankly [vacantly] (at)
—**멀뚱멀뚱하다** absentminded; vacant; blank; moony
◆ 멀뚱멀뚱한 눈 vacant [glassy] eyes / 멀뚱멀뚱한 표정 a vacant [blank] look; a moony face
▶ 그녀는 멀뚱멀뚱한 표정을 하고 있었다 She looked stupefied [dazed].
2 〈국물이〉 —**멀뚱멀뚱하다** watery; (wishy-)washy; thin; sloppy
◆ 멀뚱멀뚱한 국 washy soup / 멀뚱멀뚱한 차 watery tea

멀리 far; far off [away]; in the distance; (from) afar; a long way off; at [to] a distance
◆ 멀리서 오다 come from afar [a great distance, remote parts, from a distance] / 멀리 여행하다 make [go on] a long journey
▶ 그의 농장은 마을에서 멀리 떨어져 있다 His farm is a long way from the town.
▶ 소리는 멀리 사라졌다 The sound died away in the distance.
▶ 멀리서 보면 무엇이나 아름답게 보이는 법이다 Distance lends enchantment to all views. ⇒ Things look beautiful at a distance.
■ —**뛰기** (英) a long jump; (美) a broad jump: 제자리 멀리뛰기 a standing long [broad] jump

멀리하다 〈경원하다〉 keep sb at a (respectful) distance; keep sb at an arm's length; give a wide berth (to); keep away from sb; shun sb; eschew; alienate; 〈절제하다〉 abstain (from); keep off
◆ 못된 친구를 멀리하다 avoid [keep away from] bad company; avoid evil companions / 여자를 멀리하다 eschew women; keep away from women
▶ 그녀는 요즈음 그를 멀리하고 있다 She keeps him at arm's length these days.
▶ 저런 녀석은 멀리하는 편이 좋다 It is wiser for you to keep your distance from [(口) give a wide berth to] that kind of person.
▶ 그의 오만한 태도 때문에 친구들은 그를 멀리했다 His arrogance alienated his friends.

멀미 1 〈메스꺼운 증세〉 (motion) sickness; queasiness; nausea
◆ 뱃멀미 seasickness / 비행기 멀미 airsickness / 차멀미 carsickness
▶ 나는 뱃멀미를 하지 않는다[한다] I am a good [poor, bad] sailor.
—**멀미하다** feel [be] sick
◆ 뱃멀미하다 get seasick / 차멀미하다 get carsick
▶ 내 딸은 버스를 탈 때마다 멀미한다 My daughter gets sick every time she rides on a bus. ⇒ Bus rides always make my daughter sick.
▶ 뱃멀미할 때는 어떻게 하면 제일 좋으냐? What is the best thing if I get seasick?
2 〈싫증〉 dislike; an aversion; disgust
◆ 멀미가 나다 be sick and tired (of); get sick of…; be tired of…; (口) be fed up with…
▶ 날마다 똑같은 보리밥에 멀미가 난다 I'm sick and tired of eating boiled barley every day.

멀쑥하다 1 〈키가〉 lean and tall; lank; lanky; gangling ◆ 키가 멀쑥한 사내 a lanky [spindly] man **2** 〈묽다〉 (wishy-)washy; watery; thin (porridge) ◆ 멀쑥한 국 water soup

멀어지다 1 〈거리가〉 become more distant; 〈멀리 사라지다〉 become far off [distant]; recede; get [fall] away; 〈소리가〉 die away (in the distance); fade away; grow faint
▶ 북소리는 멀어졌다 The drum faded away.
▶ 천둥소리가 멀어져서 들리지 않게 되었다 The thunder died away in the distance.
2 〈가까이 하지 않다〉 keep away from; keep at a distance
◆ 발길이 멀어지다 come [visit] less frequently (than before)
▶ 그의 발길이 근래 멀어졌다 His visits have become less frequent recently.
3 〈관계가〉 be estranged (from); become alienated from; fall away (from)
▶ 그들은 서로 멀어졌다 They become estranged from each other.

멀쩡하다 1 〈온전하다〉 faultless; flawless; spotless; free from blemish; perfect; sound; 〈다친 데가 없다〉 unhurt; unwounded; uninjured; 〈정신이〉 sane; 〈취하지 않다〉 sober
◆ 멀쩡한 옷 clean [spotless] clothes / 정신이 멀쩡하다 be in one's right mind; be in one's (right, sober) senses
▶ 그는 정신이 멀쩡하다 He is sane enough. ⇒ He's quite sober.
2 〈뻔뻔스럽다〉 impudent; brazen; brazen-faced; shameless; bold; cheeky
◆ 멀쩡한 놈 a brazen-faced fellow; a guy as bold as brass / 멀쩡한 거짓말을 하다 tell a barefaced lie; tell a transparent [shameless] lie

멀찍막하다 rather distant; pretty [fairly] far
멀찍멀찍 far apart; at distant intervals (between); some distance apart; at a good distance
◆ 멀찍멀찍 떨어져 앉다 take seats some dis-

멀찍이 tance apart / 나무를 멀찍멀찍 심다 plant trees at a good distance from each other ▶ 집들이 산허리에 멀찍멀찍 흩어져 있었다 Houses dotted the hillside at a good distance from each other

멀찍이 pretty far; far apart; rather distant
◆ 멀찍이 보이는 산 a mountain in the distance; a distant mountain / 멀찍이 사이를 두다 leave a pretty long interval (between)
▶ 나의 집은 길에서 멀찍이 떨어져 있다 My house is quite a way off the street.

멀찍하다 rather distant; far off; pretty far; some distance away [apart]

멈추다 1 〈멎다〉 stop; cease; come to an end; 〈폭풍 등이〉 calm [die] down; subside
▶ 비가 멈추었다 It has stopped raining. ⇌ The rain has let up.
▶ 딸꾹질은 멈추지 않았다 The hiccups would not stop.
▶ 그 소리를 듣고 그는 딱 멈춰 섰다 The sound made him stop short [dead].
2 〈멎게 하다〉 stop; cease; bring sth to a stop [an end]; put a stop to
◆ 발을 멈추다 stop; make a stop; stand still / 이야기를 멈추다 cease [stop, leave off] talking; drop the subject / 일을 멈추다 lay aside [cease] one's work; leave [knock] off work / 엔진을 멈추다 stop [kill] an engine / 출혈을 멈추다 stop [arrest, stanch] bleeding [the flow of blood] / 시선을 멈추다 let one's eyes rest (on); look 〈at〉
▶ 그들은 그 건물 앞에서 차를 멈추었다 They pulled their car in front of the building.
▶ 기수는 고삐를 세게 당겨 말을 멈추었다 The horseman held his horse tightly reined in.
▶ 그는 웃음을 멈출 수 없었다 He was unable to resist [stop] laughing.

멈칫거리다 hesitate; waver; falter; dally; hang [hold] back; linger; dawdle
◆ 분명한 대답을 못하고 멈칫거리다 hesitate to give a definite answer / 멈칫거리다가 기회를 놓치다 dally away one's opportunity / 멈칫거리지 않다 do not hesitate to do; have no hesitation about [in] doing
▶ 멈칫거리지 말고 말하시오 Don't hesitate to speak out.
▶ 그는 방문 앞에서 멈칫거리다가 곧 나가버렸다 He hesitated in front of the door, but soon ran out of the room.
▶ 그녀는 들어갈지 말지 결정을 못해 멈칫거렸다 She hesitated as she couldn't decide whether to come in or not.

멈칫멈칫 hesitatingly; hesitantly; lingeringly; waveringly
◆ 멈칫멈칫 말하다 speak hesitatingly; speak in a halting way; drawl / 멈칫멈칫 자리에서 일어나지 않다 be slow to leave one's seat; 〈잠자리에서〉 dally in bed
▶ 그는 멈칫멈칫 이야기를 끄집어냈다 Hesitantly, he broached the subject.
▶ 그녀는 멈칫멈칫 그에게 비밀을 털어 놓았다 She confessed her secret to him hesitatingly.

멈칫하다 stop abruptly [suddenly]; stop for a moment; 〈주춤하다〉 draw [shrink] back; flinch 《from》; fall [hold] back; falter; waver 《in》; recoil 《from》
▶ 소름끼치는 광경에 그는 멈칫했다 He shrank back [recoiled] from the horrifying spectacle.
▶ 나는 치과의사의 드릴 소리를 들을 때면 멈칫하지 않을 수 없다 I cannot help flinching when I hear the dentist's drill.

멋 1 〈풍치·운치〉 relish; elegance; taste; gusto; zest; aroma; savor; flavor; interest; delight; pleasure
◆ 멋(이) 있는 tasty / 멋(이) 없는 tasteless / 농담의 맛을 알다 relish a joke / 시의 멋을 알다 appreciate [take a delight in] poetry / 세상 멋을 알다 have been around; have been through the mill; have seen the world / 노래의 멋을 모르다 fail to appreciate the song; don't get the song at all
▶ 서울의 야경은 멋이 있다 The night view of Seoul has special beauty [a beauty all its own].
▶ 황량한 겨울 풍경에도 그 나름의 멋이 있다 A desolate winter scene has a charm of its own.
▶ 낡은 물방아 하나가 그 정원의 멋을 더해 주었다 An old water wheel graced the garden.
2 〈맵시〉 dandyism; dudism; foppery; 〈과시〉 show
◆ 멋(을) 부리다 smarten oneself up / 안경을 멋으로 쓰다 wear spectacles [glasses] for show
▶ 그는 멋과는 거리가 먼 사람이다 He is quite free from dandyism.
▶ 나는 멋으로 카메라를 메고 다니는 것이 아니다 I am not carrying a camera about with me merely [just] for show.

멋내다 dress oneself up ⇨ 멋부리다

멋대로 as one pleases [likes, wishes]; 〈자유의 사로〉 freely; of one's own accord; of one's (own) free will; 〈독단적으로〉 at one's (own) discretion; arbitrarily; 〈무단히〉 without leave [permission]
◆ 멋대로 굴다 have one's (own) way 《in everything》; do as one pleases / 멋대로 하게 내버려 두다 allow sb to go 《his》 way; let sb have 《his》 own way
▶ 무엇이든 멋대로 하려고 하지 마라 Don't try to have everything your way.
▶ 그들은 멋대로 행동했다 They acted as they liked.
▶ 이 방을 멋대로 사용하면 안됩니다 You should not use this room without permission.

멋들어지다 splendid; wonderful; grand; excellent; capital; exciting; delightful; captivating; dashing; fascinating; (口) great; (口) swell
◆ 멋들어진 노래 a fascinating song; a song full of gusto / 멋들어진 생각 a capital [good] idea / 멋들어진 연주 a swell [tiptop, topping] performance / 멋들어지게 fascinatingly; wonderfully; with gusto [zest]
▶ 그는 노래를 멋들어지게 불렀다 He sang wonderfully [tremendously well].

멋모르다 have no idea [conception] 《of》; be ignorant [innocent] 《of》; be quite unconscious [unaware] 《of》

♦멋모르고 unknowingly; unawares / 멋모르는 사이에 without one's knowledge (of it); before one is aware (of it) / 멋모르고 달려들다 try to go at sb [sth] without knowing anything about (him) [it]

멋부리다 dress oneself up; dress [be dressed] smartly [stylishly]; smarten oneself up; be decked out
▶여자아이는 사내아이보다 멋부리기를 더 좋아한다 A girl thinks more of looking nice than a boy.
▶그 사람 좀 만난다고 그렇게 멋부릴 필요는 없잖아 You don't have to dress up like that just because you are going to see him.

멋없다 tasteless; inelegant; plain; insipid; dull; uninteresting; flat; unrefined; unromantic; rustic; senseless; vulgar
♦멋없는 생활 a prosaic [cut-and-dried] life / 멋없이 굴다 act awkwardly; be ungainly; be unseemly
▶그녀의 제의를 거절했다니 당신 참 멋없는 사람이구만 It was stupid of you to refuse her offer.
▶내가 그런 말을 할 정도로 멋없이 굴지는 않을 거야 I wouldn't be so inelegant as to say such a thing.
▶그 소년은 멋없이 키만 크다 The boy has height but that's about all.

멋있다 〈풍치있다〉 tasty; tasteful; elegant; refined; fine; chic; 〈맵시있다〉 stylish; smart; fashionable; smartish; (美) groovy; gallant; attractive
♦멋있는 노래 a song full of gusto [life] / 멋있는 농담 a clever [witty] joke / 멋있는 모자 a fanciful hat / 멋있는 생각 a bright [an ingenious] idea / 멋있는 옷 smart clothes / 멋있는 인품 an interesting personality / 멋있는 정원 an elegant garden; a tasteful garden / 멋있는 춤 a dance full of zest [grace] / 멋있는 표현 an apt expression; a nice turn of phrases
▶검은 옷을 입으니 그녀는 더욱 멋있게 보였다 She looked all the more chic in black.
▶그 여자는 어딘지 멋있다 There is something chic about her.

멋쟁이 a dandy; a gallant; a fop; (美俗) a dude; a beau (pl. ~s, -x)

멋지다 〈근사하다〉 fairly good; very smart [cute]; 〈훌륭하다〉 fine; splendid; beautiful; nice; excellent; wonderful; 〈풍치있다〉 tasty; tasteful; elegant; 〈솜씨가〉 skillful; dexterous; 〈맵시·옷차림 등이〉 smart; stylish; chic; refined
♦멋진 드레스 a lovely dress / 멋진 물건 a spanker; a stunner / 멋진 생각 a smart [good, capital] idea / 멋진 솜씨 skillful [excellent] workmanship / 멋진 집 a stylish [tasteful] house / 멋진 플레이 a fine play / 멋지게 성공하다 achieve brilliant success / 멋지게 차려 입다 be dressed in style; be smartly dressed / 멋져 보이다 look chic
▶거기서 바라본 한라산은 멋지다 Hallasan viewed from there is wonderful.
▶참으로 멋진 생각이로구나 What a splendid idea!
▶그는 멋진 말을 했다 He made witty [smart] remarks.
▶그는 멋진 집에 살고 있다 He lives in a fancy house.
▶그는 멋진 소녀를 데려 왔다 He brought a cute girl.
▶빛깔이 정말 멋지게 나왔다 The color is really beautifully brought out.

멋쩍다 1 ⇨ 멋없다
2 〈거북하다〉 awkward; embarrassing; embarrassed
♦멋쩍은 듯이, 멋쩍게 awkwardly; embarrassedly; bashfully / 멋쩍은 침묵을 지키다 keep awkward silence
▶대중 앞에서 연설하기가 멋쩍다 It is embarrassing [I am embarrassed] to make a speech in public.
▶혼자 가기가 좀 멋쩍다 It is sort of awkward to go there all alone.
▶사람들 앞에 나서자니 어쩐지 멋쩍다 I feel kind of shy to be seen in public.

멍 〈피부의〉 a bruise; a contusion; 〈눈 언저리의〉 a black eye
♦멍이 들다 become black(ish); blacken / 멍이 들도록 때리다 beat sb black and blue
▶그는 전신이 멍투성이었다 He had bruises all over his body.
▶그는 싸우고 나서 온 몸에 멍이 들었다 He was black and blue all over after the fight.

멍게 [動] a sea squirt

멍군 a defensive move against a check
▶멍군 장군[멍이야 장이야] It is hard to tell which of the two is wrong.

—멍군하다 get out of a check; make a defensive move against a check

멍들다 1 〈몸이〉 be bruised (all over); bruise; get [sustain] a bruise; be contused; 〈마음 등이〉 be hurt [ruined, marred, spoiled]
♦멍든 눈 a black eye / 멍든 마음[가슴] a wounded heart / 맞아서[꼬집혀서] 멍들다 be bruised by a blow [pinch] / 아무의 감정을 멍들게 하다 hurt [bruise] sb's feelings; hurt sb
▶그는 맞아서 팔이 멍들었다 The blow bruised his arm.
2 〈일이 탈이 생기다〉 go wrong (with); be spoiled; develop trouble; suffer a hitch [setback]; run into a real snag
▶난 이제 멍들었다 I am done for. ⇌ It's all up [over] with me.

멍멍 〈개짖는 소리〉 bowwow ♦멍멍 짖다 bow-wow; bark (at)
▶개가 나를 보고 멍멍 짖기 시작했다 The dog started barking at me.

멍멍개 (兒) a bowwow; a doggie

멍멍하다 deafened (by the din); stunned; dazed ▶꼬박 밤을 새웠더니 머리가 아주 멍멍하다 I feel really muddle-headed from staying up all night.

멍멍히 absentmindedly ⇨ 멍하니

멍석 a mat; (총칭) a matting
♦멍석을 깔다 spread a mat (on the floor)

멍석딸기 [植] a white-flowering raspberry

멍에 a yoke
♦멍에를 메우다 put (oxen) to the yoke; put a

yoke on 《oxen》 / 멍에를 벗다 throw [cast, shake] off the yoke (of); (비유) free *oneself* from restraint / 멍에를 짊어지다 come under a yoke

멍울 a lump; lymphadenoma ⇨ 망울

멍청이 a blockhead; a fool; a dunce; an ass; a dolt; a fathead; a half-wit; (美俗) a goofer; 〈부주의한 사람〉 a careless [thoughtless] person

멍청하다 silly; stupid; foolish; idiotic; dull-witted[halfwitted, slowwitted]; (美俗) goofy
♦멍청한 얼굴로 with a stupid face [look] / 멍청한 짓을 하다 act foolishly [sillily]; do a stupid thing; make an ass of *oneself* / 멍청해 보이다 look stupid [foolish] / 멍청한 소리를 하다 talk nonsense [rot, rubbish]
▶멍청하게 길을 막고 서 있지 마라 Don't stand there in the way like a dummy.
▶멍청한 말로 흥을 깨지 마라 Don't spoil the fun.
▶그녀에게 그런 것을 묻다니 참 멍청하구나 It is thoughtless [silly] of you to ask her such a question.

멍텅구리 a stupid fellow; a good-for-nothing (fellow); a simpleton; a blockhead ⇨ 멍청이

멍하니 blankly; absently; vacantly; with a blank look; absentmindedly; idly; as if stunned
♦멍하니 바라보다 look [gaze] blankly [vacantly] 《at》 / 멍하니 보고만 있다 remain an idle spectator / 멍하니 서[앉아] 있다 stand [sit] idle / 멍하니 세월을 보내다 idle *one's* time away
▶나는 멍하니 있다가 엉뚱한 버스를 탔다 I was so absentminded (that) I took the wrong bus.
▶저 학생은 수업 중에 멍하니 창 밖을 내다보고 있다 That student is looking vacantly out (of) the window during class.
▶그는 그것을 어떻게 해야할지 몰라 멍하니 있었던 것 뿐이다 He didn't know how to do it and so he was just standing idly by.
▶나는 어제 일요일을 하루종일 멍하니 보냈다 I spent all Sunday yesterday loafing.

멍하다 vacant; blank; absentminded; abstracted; (美俗) moony; 〈귀가〉 deafened
▶그는 멍한 표정을 짓고 있었다 He had a distant [vacant] look on his face.
▶그는 큰 쇼크를 받아 멍해 있었다 He was in a daze from a great shock.
▶그녀는 그 소식을 듣고 너무 기뻐 멍해졌다 She was entranced with joy to hear the news.

메¹ 〈제삿밥〉 boiled rice offered to a deceased spirit

메² 〔植〕 (the root of) a convolvulus [bindweed]

메³ 〈나무망치〉 a maul; a beetle; a (sledge) hammer; a large mallet

메- 〈차지지 않은〉 nonglutinous; not sticky

메가바이트 〔電算〕 megabyte

메가사이클 〔物〕 a megacycle (略 mc, mc., m.c.) (▶지금은 megahertz를 씀)

메가톤 〈핵무기의 폭발력의 단위〉 a megaton
♦메가톤급의 수소폭탄 a hydrogen bomb in the megaton range

메가폰 〈확성기〉 a megaphone ♦메가폰을 잡다 〔映〕 direct the production of a movie / 메가폰으로 알리다 announce by (a) megaphone

메가헤르츠 〈주파수의 단위〉 a megahertz (略 MHz, Mhz) (▶단수·복수동형)

메갈로폴리스 〈거대도시〉 a megalopolis

메공이 a hammer-shaped pounder

메귀리 〔植〕 oats

메기 〔魚〕 a catfish; a bullhead; a horned pout
■—수염 a slender drooping moustache —입 (a person with) a large [wide] mouth

메기다¹ 〈소리를〉 lead (a song, chorus, cheer, a chant) 2 〈톱질에서〉 take the lead (on a two-man saw)

메기다² 1 〈화살을〉 fix; put
♦화살을 메기다 fix [put] an arrow (to the string); notch an arrow (upon the bow) 2 〈윷놀이에서〉 move 《a *yut* marker》

메꽃 〔植〕 a bindweed ⇨ 메²

메뉴 a menu; a (menu) card; a bill of fare
♦오늘의 메뉴 the menu for today / 메뉴를 만들다 make out a menu / 메뉴를 보다 consult [look out] a menu / 메뉴에 있다 be on the menu [card, bill]
▶저녁식사 메뉴는 무엇입니까? 〈가정에서〉 What's for dinner tonight? ⇌ 〈레스토랑에서〉 What's on the menu tonight?
▶메뉴 좀 보여 주시겠어요? May I see the menu, please?

메다¹ 1 〈막히다〉 be choked [filled, stifled, smothered] 《with, by》; be [get] blocked; get clogged; be obstructed; be glutted
♦목메어 울다 sob; be choked with tears
▶그녀는 감동하여 목메어 울었다 She was moved, and sobbed.
▶코가 메었다 I have a stopped-up [stuffy] nose. ⇌ My nose is bunged [stuffed] up.
▶굴뚝은 검댕으로 메었다 The chimney is choked (up) with soot.
2 fill in 《a moat》 ⇨ 메우다¹

메다² 〈어깨에 지다〉 carry [take, bear] *sth* on *one's* shoulder; shoulder
♦무거운 짐을 메고 with a heavy burden on *one's* shoulder
▶이 상자를 2층으로 메다 다오 Carry this box upstairs.

메달 a medal; 〈대형의〉 a medallion
♦메달을 획득하다 win [be awarded] a medal (in the 100-meter dash) / 메달권에 들다 enter the range of winning a medal / 메달권에서 탈락하다 drop out of the range of winning a medal
■금[은, 동]— a gold [silver, bronze] medal

메달리스트 〈금—〉 a gold medalist; a gold medal winner

메들리 1 〔樂〕 〈접속곡〉 a medley 2 〔競〕 a medley ■—릴레이 〈수영·육상〉 a medley relay: 개인 메들리 릴레이 the individual medley relay[race]

메디치가 一家 the Medici (▶이탈리아 르네상스 시대의 명문)

메떡 cakes made from nonglutinous grain

메뚜기 〔昆〕 a grasshopper; 〈벼메뚜기〉 a locust
▶메뚜기도 오뉴월이 한철이라 (속담) Grass-

hoppers enjoy their days in May and Jane.

메레디스 〈영국의 소설가·시인〉 Meredith, George (1828-1909)

메르카토르도법 —圖法 Mercator's projection

메리고라운드 〈회전목마〉 a merry-go-round; (英) a roundabout

메리노 〈양모〉 merino; 〈직물〉 a merino (*pl.* ~s) —양 a merino (sheep)

메리메 〈프랑스의 소설가〉 Mérimée, Prosper (1803-70)

메리야스 knitted [knit] goods; knitwork ■—공장 a knitting mill —셔츠 a knit shirt [undershirt] —의류 knitwear; (英) hosiery

메리트 〈가치〉 a merit; 〈이점〉 a plus
▶그런 일을 해 봤자 대단한 메리트는 없다 There isn't much merit in doing so.

메릴랜드 〈미국 대서양 연안의 주〉 Maryland (略 Md., Md) ■—주민 a Marylander

메마르다 1 〈땅이〉 dried-up; very dry; arid; parched; sterile; barren; infertile
◆메마른 땅 sterile [barren] land; dry soil; arid land; wasteland; unproductive soil
2 〈피부 등이〉 dried-up; shriveled; rough; withered
◆메마른 살갗 a dry skin
3 〈마음이〉 heartless; unfeeling; hard-hearted; cold-hearted; harsh; severe
◆메마른 마음 a heart of stone; a cold [a hard, an unfeeling] heart

메모 〈비망록〉 a memorandum (*pl.* -dums, -da); (口) a memo (*pl.* ~s); a note

> [解說] 「메모」는 *memorandum*의 단축형인데 주로「비공식적인 기록 또는 연락 사항」,「기억하기 위해 기재하는 것, 또는 주의해야 할 것을 써서 남에게 넘겨주는 것」의 뜻으로 쓰인다. 우리말에서 말하는「메모」는 *note*에 해당하며「메모하다」는 *make [take] a note*라고 한다.

◆메모를 남기다 leave a note [letter, message] behind
▶그는 메모없이 이야기했다 He spoke without notes.
—하다 make a note [memo] ((of, on); note; take notes (of a lecture); jot down
▶나는 그의 주소를 메모했다 I took a note of his address.
■—용지 memo paper —장 a memo (note, scratch) pad; a memorandum pad

메모리 〔電算〕 a memory

메밀 〔植〕 (common) buckwheat
■—가루 buckwheat powder —국수 buckwheat noodles —국수집 a buckwheat-noodle shop —나깨 buckwheat chaff [husks] —묵 buckwheat curd

메부수수하다 rusticated; rustic; boorish; countrified

메사 〔地質〕 mesa

메소포타미아 〈서남아시아의 고대 지명〉 Mesopotamia ◆메소포타미아의 Mesopotamian ■—문명 Mesopotamian civilization

메스 [〈(네) mes] a scalpel; a (surgical [surgeon's]) knife
◆메스를 가하다 (비유) plunge a scalpel [make a searching inquiry] into (a graft case)
▶검찰당국은 그 독직사건에 메스를 가하기로 결정했다 The prosecution authorities have decided to conduct a thorough probe [investigation] into the political scandal.

메스껍다 〈아주 불쾌하다〉 nauseating; sickening; nauseous; disgusting; loathsome; abominable; offensive; revolting
◆메스꺼운 냄새 a sickening smell / 메스꺼운 녀석 a repugnant character; a disgusting fellow / 속이 메스껍다 be sick at the stomach; feel like vomiting; feel sick [nausea, queasy] / 메스껍게 굴다 act [behave] disgustingly
▶그 냄새 때문에 그는 속이 메스꺼웠다 The smell turned his stomach.
▶그의 얼굴을 보게 된다는 생각만 해도 메스꺼워진다 The very thought of seeing him makes me sick.

메스실린더 〔化〕 measuring cylinder

메스티소 〈중남미의 에스파냐계 백인과 토착 인디언의 혼혈 인종〉 mestizo

메슥거리다 feel like vomiting [throwing up]; feel sick [queasy] ◆속이 좀 메슥거리다 get sickish

메슥메슥하다 feel sick [nausea]; be sick at the stomach; feel like vomiting ▶보기만 해도 메슥메슥해진다 The mere sight of it makes me sick.

메시아 〈구세주〉 the Messiah ■—사상[신앙] Messianism

메시지 〈전할 말〉 a message ◆축하 메시지를 보내다 send a congratulatory message

메신저 〈심부름꾼〉 a messenger

메아리 an echo (*pl.* ~es)
◆메아리치다 echo; resound; be echoed; reverberate
▶우리가 소리치자 골짜기에서 메아리가 울려왔다 The valley echoed as we shouted.
▶숲은 그들의 웃음소리로 메아리쳤다 The woods echoed [resounded] with their laughter.
▶여자의 비명이 긴 통로에 메아리쳤다 A woman's scream echoed through the long passage.

메어치다 throw *sb* over *one's* shoulder; get [knock] *sb* down; throw *sb* to the ground
▶그는 유도에서 대전 상대를 메어쳤다 He threw his judo opponent (down).

메역취 〔植〕 a goldenrod

메우다 1 〈움푹 팬 땅을〉 fill in (a moat); fill up (a pond); 〈바다·늪 등을〉 recover; reclaim; plug (up); stop (up)
◆바다를 메우다 recover land from sea; reclaim a foreshore / 여백을 메우다 fill space; fill (in) a blank / 쥐구멍을 메우다 plug up a rathole / 틈을 메우다 fill [make] up a gap; stop a gap
▶그 공업단지는 바다를 메워서 된 것이었다 The industrial park was formed by reclaiming from the sea.

메우다²

2 〈결핍을〉 make up for; supply; repair; 〈결함을〉 stop [fill up] 《a gap》; offset 《a fault》
♦결원을 메우다 fill up a vacancy; fill a vacant place
3 〈메워 넣다〉 make up for; compensate for; make good; 〈보충하다〉 supplement 《one's income by doing a side job》; complement
♦결손을 메우다 make good the loss / 부족액을 메우다 replenish a shortage; make up [supply] the deficit
▶ 군중이 거리를 메웠다 The crowd jammed the street.
▶ 여백을 삽화로 메워야겠다 I'll fill in the blank spaces with illustrations.
▶ 부족액을 메우기 위해 반지를 팔았다 I sold my ring to make up for the deficit.

메우다² **1** 〈끼우다〉 ♦통에 테를 메우다 put a hoop on a tub; bind a tub with hoops; hoop a tub / 쳇바퀴에 쳇불을 메우다 fix a sieve net [screen] on its frame; make a sieve
2 〈씌우다〉 ♦북통에 가죽을 메우다 put a skin [drumhead, cloth] on a drum; make a drum
3 〈얹다〉 ♦소에 멍에를 메우다 put a yoke on an ox; yoke an ox; put an ox to the yoke

메이다 ♦북테를 메이다 get *sb* to put a drumhead [skin, cloth] on a drum; get *sb* to make a drum / 통에 테를 메이다 make *sb* hoop [put a hoop on] a tub / 채를 메이다 have *sb* fix a sieve net on its frame; have *sb* make a sieve

메이데이 May Day

메이저¹ 〔電子〕 a maser [<*m*icrowave *a*mplification by *s*timulated *e*mission of *r*adiation]

메이저² 〈국제 석유 자본〉 an oil major

메이저³ 〔樂〕 major

메이저리그 the Major Leagues; (美俗) the Majors ♦메이저리그 선수 a major-leaguer; (口) a big-leaguer

메이커 a maker; a manufacturer
♦일류 메이커의 제품 articles manufactured by well-known makers; name brands

메이크업 (a) makeup ♦메이크업을 한 채로 with *one's* makeup on / 메이크업을 잘[못] 하다 be good [poor] at making up
—메이크업하다 make *oneself* up ♦메이크업한 madeup 《complexion》

메인¹ 〈주요한〉 main
■—마스트 the mainmast —빌딩 the main building —스탠드 the grandstand —스트리트 the main [(英) high] street —이벤트 the main event —타이틀 the main title —테이블 the main table —폴 the main flagpole

메인² 〈미국 북동부의 주〉 Maine (略 Me.)
■—사람 a Mainer

메조 nonglutinous [regular] millet

메조소프라노 〔樂〕 mezzo-soprano
■—가수 a mezzo-soprano (*pl.* ~s, -ni)

메주 fermented soybeans [soybean malt] molded in shape of a block or a ball (for making soy sauce and soybean paste)
♦메주를 쑤다 boil soybeans
♦콩으로 메주를 쑨대도 곧이 듣지 않는다 (속담) do not accept a story at the face value; do not believe a story to be true
■—콩 soybeans for preparation of soy sauce and soybean paste 메줏덩이 a lump of fermented soybeans

메지다 nonglutinous (rice); not sticky

메질 hammering —메질하다 hammer; pound

메추라기 〔鳥〕 a quail / 메추라기 떼 a bevy of quails / 메추라기 알 a quail's egg

메치기 〈유도의〉 a standing throw

메카 Mecca ▶이 전람회는 우표 수집가들의 메카다 This exhibition is a mecca for stamp collectors.

메커니즘 (a) mechanism
▶현대사회의 메커니즘은 복잡하다 The structure of present society is complicated.

메케하다 smoky ⇨ 매캐하다 1

메콩강 —江 the Mekong River

메타포 metaphor

메탄(가스) 〔化〕 methane; marsh gas

메탄올 〔化〕 methanol; methyl 〔wood〕 alcohol

메트로 〈파리의 지하철〉 the Metro

메트로놈 〔樂〕 a metronome

메트로폴리스 a metropolis

메탈알코올 =메탄올

메피스토펠레스 Mephistopheles

멕시코 Mexico; 〈공식명〉 the United Mexican States ♦멕시코의 Mexican / 멕시코계 미국인 a Mexican-American; a Chicano
■—사람 a Mexican

멕시코만 —灣 the Gulf of Mexico
■—류 the Gulf Stream

멘델 〈오스트리아의 생물학자〉 Mendel, Gregor Johann (1822-84) ■—법칙 Mendel's [Mendelian] laws (of heredity); Mendelism

멘셰비키 a Menshevik (*pl.* ~s, -viki)

멘스 the menses; menstruation

멘탈테스트 a mental test [examination]
♦멘탈테스트를 하다 hold [give, conduct] a mental test

멘톨 〔化〕 menthol

멘히르 〔考古〕 a menhir

멜대 a pole (for shouldering); a carrying pole [stick] ♦멜대로 메다 carry *sth* on a pole; pole *sth*

멜라네시아 Melanesia ■—사람 a Melanesian

멜라닌 〔生化〕 melanin

멜랑콜리 melancholy

멜로드라마 a melodrama ♦멜로드라마조의 melodramatic ■—작가 a melodramatist

멜로디 a melody; a tune

멜론 a melon

멜빵 〈짐의〉 a shoulder strap [belt]; 〈총의〉 a sling; 〈바지의〉 (美) suspenders; (英) braces
■—붕대 a sling; a suspensor; a suspensory (bandage); 팔에 멜빵 붕대를 메고 있다 have [carry] *one's* arm in a sling

멤버 a member

解説 「출장 선수의 면면」의 뜻으로는 ***lineup***을 쓴다. 그러나 「(…팀의) 멤버」, 예를 들어 「나는 그 팀의 멤버다」는 "I'm a member of the team."이라고 할 수도 있지만 "I'm on the team."이라고 표현하는 것이 영어로는 더 자연스럽다.

♦베스트 멤버 the best members [players] (of

a team》/ 정규 멤버 a regular member
멥새 =멧새 2
멥쌀 nonglutinous rice
멧누에 a wild silkworm
멧닭 〔鳥〕a black grouse; 〈수컷〉a blackcock; 〈암컷〉a gray hen
멧대추 a jujube ■—나무 a jujube tree
멧돼지 a (wild) boar
멧새 1 〈산새〉a mountain bird [fowl]
2 〔鳥〕a meadow bunting
멧종다리 〔鳥〕a mountain hedge sparrow
며 and ⇨ 이며
♦나무며 돌이며 trees and stones / 사자며 호랑이며 코끼리 등등 lions, tigers, elephants and so forth
▶가게에는 사과며 포도며 기타 여러 가지 과일이 있었다 There were apples, grapes and many other fruits in the shop.
-며 1 〈열거〉and; or
▶그 책은 유익하기도 하며 재미도 있다 The book is both useful and amusing.
2 〈면서〉while; as; between; during; over; with; at the same time (that)…
♦울며 세월을 보내다 spend *one's* days in tears; live in sorrow / 한잔 하며 이야기하다 talk over a bottle of wine
▶산책하며 이야기합시다 Let's talk as we walk.
▶나는 파란 하늘을 바라보며 풀밭에 누워 있었다 I lay on the grass looking at the blue sky.
▶그녀는 울며불며 법석을 떨었다 She made a scene, crying and screaming.
며느리 a daughter-in-law; *one's* son's wife
♦며느리를 맞다[보다] take a daughter-in-law into *one's* family; get *one's* son a bride
▶댁의 따님을 우리 며느리로 삼고 싶습니다 I wish to have your daughter for my son's wife.
며느리가 미우면 손자까지 밉다 〈속담〉He who hates Peter harms his dog.
며느리발톱 a spur; a cockspur; a calcar 《*pl.* calcaria》
며느리밥풀 〔植〕a cowwheat
며칟날 what day (of the month); the date
▶오늘이 며칟날이죠? What day of the month is it today? ⇌ What's the date today? ⇌ 《美》What date (is it) today?
▶그녀는 며칟날 돌아오지? When will she be back?
며칠 1 〈일수〉how many days; how long; 〈수일〉a few days; several days
♦며칠 동안 for (a few) days / 며칠 전 a few days ago; the other day
▶금년도 이제 며칠 안 남았다 There are only a few days left this year.
▶이곳에 며칠이고 묵어도 좋습니다 You may stay here as long as you like.
▶며칠이고 기다리겠습니다 I'll wait any number of days.
▶며칠 동안 좋은 날씨가 계속되었다 We have had a spell of fine weather.
▶그것을 마치는데 며칠이나 걸리겠습니까? How many days will it take you to finish it?
▶한국에서 호주까지 배로 며칠이나 걸립니까? How many days does it take to get to Australia from Korea by ship?
2 〈며칟날〉what day (of the month)
멱¹ 〔목〕a throat; a gullet ♦돼지 멱따는 소리 a squealing sound; a squeal; a squeak / 멱을 따다 cut 《a fowl's》 gullet
멱² 〔장기〕the path of a horse's or an elephant's move (in Korean chess)
■—부지(不知) a beginner of chess
멱³ 〔植〕a brown seaweed ⇨ 미역¹
멱⁴ 〔목욕〕bathing ⇨ 미역²
멱 冪 〔數〕power ♦2[3]승 멱 the second [third] power ■—지수 an exponent
멱살 the flesh of the throat; 〈옷깃〉a collar; lapels ♦멱살을 잡다 seize *sb* by the front of 《his》 coat; grab [seize] *sb* by the collar [lapels]
멱통 the throat
-면 if; when
▶일단 시작하면 그렇게 어렵지 않을 거요 It won't be so difficult once you get started.
▶내일까지 기다려 보면 어떨까 Suppose we wait till tomorrow.
▶이 책을 깨끗이 본다면, 빌려줄 수 있지 You can [may] borrow this book provided you keep it clean.
▶다들 모이면 사진을 찍자 When everyone gets here, we will take a picture.
면¹ 面 1 〈표면〉the surface; the face
♦거울면 같이 잔잔한 바다 a sea as smooth as a glass [as placid as a mirror] / 호수면을 달리는 요트 yachts sailing on the surface of the lake / 산의 북면을 오르다 climb the north face of the mountain
2 〈측면〉a side; 〈다면체의〉a facet; a face; 〈활자의〉the face
♦동전의 뒷면 the reverse (side) of a coin; 《俗》tails / 면대칭 plane symmetry
▶정육면체는 6면이 있다 A cube has six sides [faces].
3 〈방면・국면〉an aspect; a phase; a respect; a side; a front
♦모든 면에서 in every respect [aspect] / 이런 면에서는 in this respect / 재정면에서 in the financial aspect / 다른 면에서 보면 viewed from a different angle [point of view]
▶그녀는 사물의 밝은[어두운] 면만을 본다 She looks only on the bright [dark] side of things.
▶사생활면에서 그는 결코 좋은 사람이라고 할 수 없다 You cannot say that he is a good man in his private life.
▶어느 면으로 보나 자네가 틀린 것 같은데 I think you are wrong in every respect.
4 〈지면〉a page
♦제1면 the first [front] page / (신문의) 사회면 the local [city] news page [section]
5 〈검도・야구 등의〉a face guard [protector, mask] ♦면을 쓰다[벗다] put on [take off] *one's* face guard
면² 面 〈행정 구역〉*myŏn* (as a subdivision of a *gun*); a township
■—소재지 the seat of a *myŏn* [township]
■—의회 a *myŏn* [township] council
면 綿 cotton ♦면 100%의 셔츠 a pure-cotton

shirt; an all-cotton shirt
▶ 이것은 면제품이다 This is made of cotton.

면각 面角 〔數〕 a face angle

면경 面鏡 a hand mirror; a small looking glass

면관하다 免官— dismiss *sb* from a government [an official] post
◆ 〈장교가〉 면관되다 lose *one's* commission
▶ 그는 의원 면관되었다 He was relieved of his official post at his own request.

면구스럽다 面灸— shamefaced; abashed; 〈서술직〉 feel awkward [embarrassed]; be self-conscious
▶ 나는 모든 사람한테 칭찬받기가 면구스러웠다 I was shy about being praised by everybody.

면나다 面— 〈체면이 서다〉 win [gain] honor; get credit (for); be honored; be glorified

면내다 面— save (*one's*) face [*one's* honor]; 〈면나게 하다〉 save *sb's* face [honor]; do [bring] *sb* credit

면담 面談 an interview; a face-to-face talk
▶ 상세한 것은 면담 후 결정 (광고) Particulars to be arranged personally.
—**면담하다** have an interview (with); talk personally (with); meet and talk (with)
▶ 내일 사장과 면담하기로 되어 있다 I'll have an interview [a talk] with the president tomorrow.
▶ 주인과 면담하고 싶소 I wish to speak to your master.

면대 面對 (a) confrontation; facing
—**면대하다** confront *sb*; meet face to face (with); face ◆ 면대하여 face to face; to *sb's* face; 면대하여 꾸짖다 reprove *sb* vis-à-vis / 면대하여 꾸짖다 reprove *sb* to his face [in *his* teeth]
▶ 사장을 면대하여 불평할 수 있겠는가? Can you make any complaints to the president's face?

면도 面刀 1 〈면도질〉 a shave; shaving
▶ 칼이 잘 들면 면도가 잘 된다 A sharp razor gives you a close shave.
▶ 면도만 해주시오 I want only a shave.
—**면도하다** shave *oneself*; 〈남을 시켜서〉 get [have] a shave; get *oneself* shaved (by)
◆ 갓[깨끗이] 면도한 얼굴 a fresh(ly)-shaven [clean-shaven] face
2 〈면도칼〉 a razor ◆ 안전 면도 a safety razor / 전기 면도 an electric razor
—**로션** an after-shaving[-shave] lotion —**용거울** a shaving mirror —**용 솔** a shaving brush —**용 크림** shaving [shave] cream

면도날 面刀— a razor's edge; 〈안전면도기의〉 a razor blade
◆ 면도날 같은 사내 a very shrewd man; an acute fellow / 면도날을 세우다 sharpen [strop, strap] a razor / 면도날처럼 잘 들다 be razor-sharp
▶ 그 젊은 교수는 면도날처럼 예리하다 The young professor is (as) sharp as a razor.

면도칼 面刀— a razor ◆ 면도칼을 갈다 sharpen a razor; whet [hone] a razor

면려 勉勵 industry; diligence; assiduity
—**면려하다** be industrious; be diligent; work hard; apply *oneself* closely to (*one's* studies);

attend diligently to (*one's* duties)

면류 麵類 〈국수〉 noodles; vermicelli

면류관 冕旒冠 a (royal) crown; a diadem
◆ 가시 면류관 the crown of thorns

면마 綿馬 〔植〕 a male fern; an aspidium (*pl*. -ia)

면면히 綿綿— continuously; unceasingly; without a break; at (great) length
▶ 이 기술은 오늘날까지 면면히 이어지고 있다 This art has come down unbroken to this day.

면모 面貌 〈얼굴〉 a countenance; looks; features; 〈사물의〉 (an) appearance; an aspect; a phase
◆ 면모를 새롭게 하다 put on quite a new aspect; be completely changed [transformed]; become quite a new person [thing]
▶ 체육관은 재건되면서 면모가 완전히 달라졌다 The gym was rebuilt and looked completely different.
▶ 철도가 놓여서 마을의 면모가 새로워졌다 The village entered upon a new phase because a railway was constructed.

면목 面目 1 〈체면〉 face; countenance; honor; reputation; prestige; dignity
◆ 신사의 면목 a gentleman's honor / 집안의 면목 an honor [a credit] to the family / 면목에서는 타협 a face-saving compromise / 면목을 세우다 save *one's* honor [face]; win [gain] *one's* honor / 면목을 유지하다 preserve *one's* honor / 면목을 잃다 lose (*one's*) face; be put out of countenance; disgrace [humiliate] *oneself*
▶ 그렇게 하시면 면목이 설 겁니다 If you do so, you will save face.
▶ 그는 시합에 이겨 면목이 섰다 He won the game and saved face. ⇒ His victory did him credit.
▶ 그는 면목없이 고개를 떨어뜨렸다 He hung his head shamefully.
▶ 이런 실수를 하다니 정말 면목없게 되었습니다 I've disgraced myself with this mistake. ⇒ I'm very ashamed of this mistake.
2 〈양상〉 an appearance; an aspect
◆ 면목을 일신하다 undergo a renewal [complete change]; change the appearance
▶ 그 차는 이제 면목을 일신했다 It is quite a new car now.

면밀하다 綿密— minute; detailed; close; thorough; careful; attentive; scrupulous; elaborate
◆ 면밀한 검사 a close [thorough] examination / 면밀한 계산 accurate calculation / 면밀한 계획 a careful [an elaborate] plan / 면밀한 관찰 minute observation / 면밀히 minutely; in detail; closely
▶ 당초에 면밀한 계획을 세우고 나서 실행해 나가세요 Make plans carefully first, and then carry them out.
▶ 당국은 사건의 진상을 면밀히 조사하고 있다 The authorities are thoroughly inquiring into the truth of the accident.

면바르다 面— smooth; even; level

면박 面駁 refutation to *sb's* face —**면박하다** refute [confute] *sb* to (*his*) face; cast [throw]

the fault in sb's teeth
▶ 남편은 사람들 앞에서 아내를 면박했다 The husband abused his wife to her face in public.
면방(적) 綿紡(績) cotton spinning
면병 麵餠 [가톨릭] holy bread [loaf]
면봉 綿棒 〚醫〛a swab (fixed to a stick); (俗) a cotton bud
면분 面分 a nodding acquaintance ♦면분이 있다 be a nodding acquaintance; be on nodding terms; know by sight
면사 綿絲 cotton yarn [thread]
면사무소 面事務所 a *myŏn* [township] office
면사포 面紗布 a bridal [wedding] veil
면상 面上 the face ♦면상을 때리다 strike *sb* in the face / 면상에 흉터가 있다 have a scar on the face
면상 面相·面像 a countenance; features; looks; physiognomy
-면서 1 〈동시에〉as; while; over; between; with

> [解說] *as*는 두 가지 동작이 병행하여 행해지고 있는 느낌이 강하고 *while*은 비교적 오래 계속되는 시간을 나타낸다. *over*는 전치사로서 동작을 나타내는 명사를 목적어로 취하여「…하면서」라는 뜻을 나타낸다

♦웃으면서 with a smile; smiling / 노래하면서 일하다 sing over *one's* work / 먹으면서 이야기하다 talk while eating / 울면서 이야기하다 tell (a story) between sobs [with tears]
▶ 그녀는 걸으면서 노래하기를 좋아한다 She likes singing while walking.
▶ 두 대의 차는 늘 일정한 거리를 유지하면서 주행했다 The two cars always drove maintaining [keeping] a fixed distance (between them).
▶ 우리는 옛날 이야기를 하면서 늦게까지 자지 않았다 We stayed up late, talking about bygone days.
▶ 한잔 하면서 그 이야기를 합시다 Let's talk about it over a drink.
▶ 그녀는 함빡 웃으면서 손님들을 맞이했다 Smiling heartily, she welcomed the guests.
2〈불구하고〉though; but; yet; still; in spite of; notwithstanding; for [with] all

♦가난하면서(도) though he is poor; poor as he is / 싫어하면서(도) against *one's* will; reluctantly / 재산이 그토록 많으면서 for all *one's* wealth
▶ 그는 나쁜 줄 알면서 거짓말을 했다 He told a lie, though he knew it was wrong.
▶ 잘못인 줄 알면서 나는 일을 저질렀다 I did it, knowing [though I knew] that it was wrong.
▶ 그 학생은 공부는 열심히 하면서 성적은 나쁘다 He is a poor student in spite of his hard work.
▶ 그는 중병이면서 그 회합에 출석했다 Though [Although] he was seriously ill, he went the meeting. ⇒ He was seriously ill, but [yet] he went to the meeting ⇒ He went to the meeting in spite of his serious illness.
면서기 面書記 a *myŏn* official; an official of a township office

면세 免稅 exemption from taxation; tax [duty] exemption; remission of taxes; immunity from taxes
▶ 그들은 20년간 면세를 받고 있다 They are let off taxes for 20 years.
▶ 위스키를 면세로 살 수 있습니까? Can I get the whisky tax-free?
▶ 시계는 공항에서 면세로 살 수 있습니다 You can buy a watch duty-free at the airport.
―**면세하다** exempt (*one*, *land*) from taxation; 〈관세를〉free 《goods》from 《customs》duties
▶ 이 물품들은 관세가 면세되어 있다 These articles are exempt from customs duty.
■―**기간** a period of tax exemption; a tax holiday ―**수입품** (duty-)free imports; free goods ―**점**(店) a duty-free shop ―**표** (美) a free list ―**품** articles free [exempt] from taxes; free goods; tax[duty]-free goods [articles]
면세점 免稅點 the tax exemption limit
♦면세점을 올리다[내리다] raise [lower] the tax exemption limit [point]
면소 免訴 dismissal 《of a case》; acquittal 《discharge, release》《of a prisoner》
―**면소하다** dismiss 《a case》; discharge 《acquit, release》《a prisoner》
▶ 그 사건은 증거불충분으로 면소되었다 The case was dismissed for lack of evidence.
면수 面數 the number of pages
면식 面識 acquaintance
♦면식이 있는 사람 an acquaintance
▶ 나는 저 신사와 면식이 있다 I am (personally) acquainted with that gentleman.
▶ 그 사람과는 전연 면식이 없다 I am quite a stranger to him. ⇒ I am not acquainted with him. ⇒ He is an utter stranger to me.
면실 棉實 cottonseed ■―**유** cottonseed oil
면양 綿羊 [動] a sheep (▶단수·복수 동형)
면업 綿業 the cotton industry
면역 免役 〈부역〉exemption from public labor; 〈병역의〉exemption [immunity] from military service; 〈징역의〉discharge from penal servitude
―**면역하다** 〈부역을〉be exempted [relieved, spared] from public labor; 〈병역을〉be exempted from military service; 〈징역을〉be released [discharged] from prison; be set free
면역 免疫 immunity
♦면역이 되다 become [be rendered] immune 《to, against, from》/ 면역이 되어 있다 be immune 《to, against, from》; (비유) be callous [impervious] to 《public censure》; be not affected by 《adverse criticism》
▶ 나는 예방주사를 맞았기 때문에 독감에 면역이 되었다 Thanks to an injection, I am immune to influenza.
▶ 나는 그의 혹평에 면역이 되어 있다 I am impervious [immune] to his scathing criticism.
▶ 우두는 천연두에 대한 면역을 준다 Vaccination immunizes us against smallpox.
■―**기간** a period of immunity ―**기구** 《the body's》immune mechanism ―**반응** an immune reaction [response] ―**유전학** im-

munogenetics —주사 (a protective) inoculation —체 〔醫〕 an immune body; an antibody: 자가(自家)면역체 an auto-immune body —학 immunology —학자 an immunologist —혈청 an immune serum; an antiserum

면역성 免疫性 immunity
♦면역성이 없는 nonimmune / 면역성을 얻다 gain [secure] immunity / 면역성을 주다 confer immunity 《on the patient》; immunize 《sb against a disease》

면작 棉作 cotton growing [cultivation, culture]; cultivation of cotton

면장 免狀 〈면허장〉 a license; a certificate; a permit; a charter; 〈사면장〉 a letter of pardon

면장 面長 the head [chief] of a *myŏn* [township]

면적 面積 (an) area; 〈건물의〉 floor space; 〔幾〕 superficial content(s)
♦경작 면적 the area under cultivation; arable acreage / 총면적 the gross area
▶이 정원은 면적이 500 제곱미터다 The area of this garden is 500 square meters. ⇌ This garden is 500 square meters in area. ⇌ This garden has an area of 500 square meters.
▶이 공장의 총면적은 얼마나 됩니까? What is the total floor space of this factory?
▶이 방은 면적에 비해 커 보인다 This room looks big for its size.
■—계 a planimeter —속도 〔物〕 areal velocity

면전 面前 presence
♦…의 면전에서 in the presence of *sb*; under *one's* eyes; before [in front of] *sb*
▶그는 내 면전에서 내 아버지를 모욕했다 He insulted my father in my presence.
▶그는 사람들 면전에서 꾸중을 들었다 He was scolded in the presence of people.

면접 面接 an interview —면접하다 interview; have an interview 《with》 ■—시간 hours for interviews —실 a reception room

면접시험 面接試驗 an oral test [examination]; an interview ♦면접시험을 보다 give an oral test [examination] 《to an applicant》 / 면접시험을 치르다 undergo an oral test

면정 面疔 〔醫〕 a carbuncle on the face

면제 免除 (an) exemption; remission; release; discharge; excuse; impunity
▶교회 자산은 고정자산세의 면제를 받고 있다 Church property is exempt from real estate taxes.
▶그들은 세금 면제 혜택을 받고 있다 They are exempt from (paying) taxes. ⇌ They are free of taxes.
—면제하다 exempt *sb* from 《taxation》; release [relieve] *sb* from 《obligation》; excuse [remit] *sb* from 《a task》; discharge *sb* from 《a debt》
▶어린이는 입장료를 면제한다 Children are admitted free.
▶이 달에 입학하는 자는 입학금을 면제한다 Applicants are admitted free of entrance fees this month.

면제품 綿製品 cotton goods [stuff]

면종 面從 eye-service; pretended [disguised] obedience —면종하다 pay eye-service 《to one's master》; pretend obedience ■—복배(腹背) treacherous obedience; (a) Judas kiss

면종 面腫 a carbuncle on the face; a facial furuncle [boil]

면죄 免罪 acquittal; remission of sin; freedom from punishment for sin; pardon; 〈교황의〉 papal indulgence
▶새로운 증거로 그의 무죄가 밝혀진 후 그는 면죄를 받았다 He was granted a pardon after new evidence had proved his innocence.
—면죄하다 acquit
▶그들은 증거불충분으로 면죄되었다 Lack of evidence resulted in their acquittal.
■—부(符) an indulgence

면지 面紙 〔印〕 a flyleaf; an end paper; an end leaf; the inside [back] of the cover

면직 免職 dismissal [discharge] from office; deprivation of office; discharge
♦의원(依願) 면직 dismissal at *one's* own request / 징계 면직 disciplinary dismissal [discharge]
—면직하다 dismiss [discharge] *sb* from office; relieve *sb* of his office [post]
♦직무태만으로 면직되다 lose *one's* position [place] through neglect of duty
▶그는 뇌물을 받았기 때문에 면직되었다 He was dismissed [discharged] from office for accepting bribes.

면직물 綿織物 cotton fabrics [textiles, cloth]; cotton; cotton stuff; cotton piece goods
■—업자 cotton weavers

면책 免責 exemption [immunity, discharge] from responsibility [obligation, duty]
—면책하다 be exempted [discharged] from responsibility
♦면책되다 receive immunity from responsibility; become immune from obligation
■—조항 an escape [exemption] clause; 〔海保〕 a negligence clause —특권 〈국회의원의〉 the privilege of exemption from liability for *one's* speech in the National Assembly; 〈외교관의〉 diplomatic immunity

면책 面責 personal reproof —면책하다 reprove *sb* to his face; reprimand *sb*

면추하다 免醜— be (born) not so [quite] ugly

면치레 面— face-saving ♦면치레의 행동[변명] a face-saving action [excuse]
—면치레하다 save 《one's》 face; save [keep up] appearances; put up a good front
▶그녀는 실직했으면서도 스스로 그만 두었다는 말로 면치레했다 Though she'd lost her job, she saved face by saying she'd left it willingly.

면포 綿布 cotton (cloth); cotton stuff [tissue]
■—류 cotton piece goods —상 a dealer in cotton stuff

면하다 免— 1 〈피하다·벗어나다〉 escape 《danger》; be spared of 《a lot of trouble》; be saved [rescued] from 《drowning》; be relieved of 《pain》; miss
♦굶주림을 면하다 stave [keep] off hunger / 부상을 면하다 escape [get off] unhurt / 위기를 면하다 get through a crisis; get [tide] over

a crisis
▶ 그는 처벌을 면했다 He escaped punishment [being punished].
▶ 그는 가까스로 죽음을 면했다 He narrowly [barely] escaped being killed. ⇌ He escaped death by a hairbreadth. ⇌ He had a narrow [hairbreadth] escape from death.
▶ 그사람 덕분에 나는 퇴학을 면했다 Thanks to him, I was saved from being kicked out of school.
▶ 다행히 내 차는 사고를 면했다 Fortunately my car missed being involved in the accident.
▶ 그들의 행동은 비난을 면할 수 없다 Their conduct is not safe from criticism.
▶ 사람은 죽음을 면할 수 없다 Man is mortal. ⇌ Man's inevitable end is death.
2 〈회피하다〉 escape (responsibility); evade 《one's duty》; elude (taxation); get round 《the law》
▶ 자기의 책임을 면하려고 하면 안된다 You ought not to try to evade [avoid taking] your responsibilities.
3 〈면제되다〉 be exempt(ed) from 《taxation》; be immune from 《draft》
♦ 성가신 일을 면하다 get rid of a nuisance / 병역[징집]을 면하다 be exempted from military service [draft]

면하다 面— face; front on; look out on [onto, into]
♦ 바다에 면해 있는 건물 a building facing the sea / 한길에 면한 집 a house standing on a street / 호수에 면한 호텔 a hotel on the lake; a lakeside hotel
▶ 한국은 동쪽으로 태평양에 면해 있다 To the east Korea faces the Pacific.
▶ 그 건물은 바다에 면해 있다 The building faces [fronts on, looks out on] the sea.
▶ 사무실은 골목에 면해 있었다 The office was on an alley.
▶ 그의 방은 뜰에 면해 있었다 His room looked out onto [into] the garden.

면학 勉學 study; academic pursuit; pursuit of knowledge
—면학하다 study; pursue
■—분위기 the studious atmosphere on campus; 《create》 an academic atmosphere

면허 免許 permission; license
♦ 제조 면허 manufacturing license / 면허가 있는 licensed / 면허가 없는 unlicensed / 면허를 취득하다 get [obtain] a license / 면허 정지[취소] 당하다 have one's license suspended [canceled] / 무면허로 운전하다 drive without a license
—면허하다 permit; license; authorize
■—기간 a term of license —날짜 the date of license —료 a license fee —세(稅) taxation on a licensed business; a license fee —영업 a licensed business —제(도) a licensing system

면허장[증] 免許狀[證] a license; 〈증명서〉 a certificate; 〈허가증〉 a permit; 〈특허장〉 a charter
♦ 임시 면허증 a temporary license / 운전 면허증 a driver's [英 driving] license; a chauffeur's license / 면허장을 가지고 있다 hold a license / 운전 면허증을 갱신하다 renew one's driving license / 면허증을 교부하다 award a license; grant [issue] a license [certificate]
▶ 그 의사는 면허증이 없다 He is practicing medicine without a license.
▶ 운전 면허증을 보여 주시오 Let me see your driver's license.
■—소유자 a license holder; a licensee

면화 棉花 〔植〕 a cotton plant ⇨ 목화(木花)

면화약 棉火藥 guncotton ⇨ 솜화약

면회 面會 an interview; a meeting
♦ 면회를 청하다 ask sb to see one; ask for [request, seek] an interview 《with》 / 면회를 거절하다 refuse an interview 《with》; decline to see; excuse [deny] oneself to 《a caller》
▶ 면회입니다 Someone wants to see you.
▶ 오늘은 누구에게도 면회를 사절해 주시오 Excuse me to callers today. ⇌ I am not at home to callers today. ⇌ I'm seeing no one today.
▶ 면회 사절 (게시) No visitors (allowed).
▶ 작업중 면회 사절 (게시) Interviews declined during working hours.
—면회하다 see; receive; meet; have an interview 《with》
▶ 사장님을 면회하고 싶은데요 I should like to see the president.
▶ 아버지는 선생님을 면회하고 내 문제를 상의했다 My father had an interview with the teacher about me.
■—시간 the visiting hour(s) —실 〈교도소 등의〉 an interview room —인 a visitor; a caller —일 a receiving [reception, visiting] day; an at-home day

멸공 滅共 rooting up [uprooting] communists; eradication of communism
■—정신 the anti-Communist spirit; the "Defeat Communism" spirit

멸구 〔昆〕 a green leafhopper

멸균 滅菌 sterilization; pasteurization ⇨ 살균
■—거즈 sterilized gauze —작용 sterilizing action [power]

멸망 滅亡 a downfall; a fall; ruin; collapse; destruction; undoing
♦ 로마제국[마야족]의 멸망 the fall of the Roman Empire [the Maya] / 멸망의 길을 걷다 be on the road to collapse [ruin, doom] / 멸망 직전에 있다 be on the brink [verge] of ruin
▶ 핵무기는 인류를 멸망으로 이끌 수도 있다 Nuclear weapons may lead to the ruin of mankind.
—멸망하다 fall; be ruined; go to ruin; collapse; be destroyed; cease to exist
♦ 멸망시키다 ruin; destroy; overthrow; exterminate; annihilate
▶ 이 제국은 13세기에 멸망했다 This empire was ruined in the 13th century.

멸사봉공 滅私奉公 selfless devotion to one's country; self-annihilation for the sake of one's country

멸시 蔑視 contempt; scorn; disdain
▶ 그의 눈에는 멸시의 빛이 가득했다 His eyes were full of scorn.

—멸시하다 despise; disdain; hold sb in contempt; have a contempt for; look down upon; make light [little] of
♦ 멸시당하다 be despised; be looked down upon; be held in contempt
▶ 그녀는 나를 멸시하는 눈으로 바라보았다 She gave me a contemptuous look.
▶ 그런 짓을 하면 사람들한테 멸시당하게 마련이다 Such behavior will make you contemptible. ⇒ That will lower you in public estimation.

멸족 滅族 extermination of a tribe [family]
—멸족하다 〈멸망시키다〉 exterminate sb's whole family [kinsfolk]; wipe [put, blot] a tribe out of existence; 〈멸망하다〉《a family, a tribe》 be exterminated

멸종 滅種 extermination of a stock [race]
—멸종하다 〈멸망시키다〉 exterminate a stock [race]; 〈멸망하다〉《a stock》 be exterminated

멸치 〔魚〕 an anchovy
■—젓 salted [pickled] anchovies

멸하다 滅— 〈멸망시키다〉 ruin; destroy; overthrow; exterminate; 〈멸망하다〉 go to ruin; perish ♦ 나라를 멸하다 ruin [destroy] a nation / 적을 멸하다 destroy [conquer] an enemy

명 命 1 〈목숨〉 life ♦ 명이 길다 live long; last long; have a long life / 제 명에 죽다 die a natural death / 명을 다하다 live out a natural life
▶ 그는 명이 긴 녀석이다 He has nine lives like a cat.
▶ 이래서는 제 명에 못살겠다 This will make me die before my time. ⇒ This will bring me to an early grave.
2 ⇨ 운명(運命)
3 〈명령〉 an order; a command
♦ 당국의 명에 의하여 by order (of the authorities) / 명을 따르다[거역하다] obey [disobey] sb's orders / 명을 받다 receive orders 《from sb》; be ordered 《by sb》

명 明 〔史〕 the Ming dynasty ⇨ 명조

명 銘 1 〈기념비의〉 an inscription; 〈묘의〉 an epitaph **2** 〈경계의 말〉 a precept; a motto; a maxim ♦ 좌우명(座右銘) one's motto

명 名 〈사람수〉 number of persons ♦ 여러 명 several people / 30명 thirty persons [people] / 모두 열명 ten in all / 도합 40명 forty persons all told [in all]
▶ 이 버스에는 50명이 탈 수 있다 The capacity of this bus is fifty people.

명- 名- noted; celebrated; distinguished; great
♦ 명연설 a fine speech / 명재판 a judicious judgment / 명탐정 a great detective / 명판사 an able judge; a Daniel

명가 名家 1 ⇨ 명문(名門) **2** 〈사람〉 a celebrated person; a celebrity; a notable

명가 名歌 a fine [famous] song [ballad]; an excellent song
■—집 a collection of specially chosen songs [ballads]

명가수 名歌手 a famous [renowned, reputable, distinguished] singer; a great singer

명검 名劍 an excellent [a fine] blade; a noted [famous] sword

명견 名犬 a good [fine] dog

명곡 名曲 an excellent piece of music; a famous work of music; a famous [well-known] tune; (총칭) famous music
♦ 명곡을 감상하다 appreciate an excellent piece of music

명과 銘菓 a cake of an established [a well-known] name; an excellent cake

명관 名官 a renowned [famous, celebrated] magistrate [governor]

명구 名句 a famous phrase; a beautiful passage; 〈명언〉 a wise saying; an epigram; 〈시가(詩歌)의〉 a beautiful verse
■—집 a collection of choice passages [famous sayings]; a golden treasury of thoughts; an anthology of fine expressions [splendid remarks]

명군 名君 a good king; a wise ruler

명금 鳴禽 〔鳥〕 a songbird; a singing bird; a songster

명기 名妓 a famous [celebrated] kisaeng

명기 名器 〈진귀한 물건〉 a novel vessel

명기 明記 writing clearly [expressly]
—명기하다 write expressly; write [put down] clearly; specify
▶ 그것은 규칙에 명기되어 있다 It is specified [defined clearly] in the regulations.

명년 明年 next year; the coming year ⇨ 내년

명단 名單 a list of names; a roll ⇨ 명부

명단 明斷 a clear [definite] judgment
—명단하다 pass [make] a clear judgment 《on》

명담 名談 a wise [golden] saying; a witty [felicitous, famous] remark
▶ 그것 참 명담인걸 That's well [wisely] said.

명답 名答 a correct [right] answer; an excellent [a clever] answer ▶ 명답이오 You said it. ⇒ You've hit it.

명당 明堂 1 〈정전(正殿)〉 the king's audience [presence] hall **2** 〈무덤 앞의 평지〉 the graveyard lawn; the front yard of a grave **3** ⇨ 명당자리

명당자리 明堂— a propitious site for a grave; 〈썩 좋은 자리〉 a very good place; an excellent [ideal] spot ♦ 붕어 낚시의 명당자리 a superfine spot for crucian (carp) fishing

명도 名刀 a fine blade ⇨ 명검(名劍)

명도 明度 〈색의 밝기〉 lightness

명도 明渡 evacuation; surrender; delivery ⇨ 인도
♦ 세든 사람에게 명도를 요구하다 ask a tenant to vacate the house; give a tenant a notice to quit [move] / 건물의 명도 통고를 하다[받다] serve [receive] a notice to evacuate a building
—명도하다 vacate 《a house》; clear out of; evacuate 《a town》; surrender 《a castle to the enemy》
■—소송 an eviction suit; dispossession proceedings —신청 ⇨ 인도(~청구)

명도 冥途 〔그俗〕 Hades; the underworld; the other [nether] world; the region beyond the grave

명동 鳴動 rumbling —명동하다 rumble

명란 明卵 spawn [roe] of a (walleye) pollack
- 一젓 salted pollack roe

명랑하다 明朗— bright; clear; cheerful; gay; merry; sunny; sunshiny

♦ 명랑한 가정 a cheerful [merry] home / 명랑한 기분 a happy [light] heart / 명랑한 목소리 a clear [sonorous, gay] voice / 명랑한 사람 a sunshiny [bright and cheerful] person; a man of sunny disposition / 명랑한 성격 an open character / 명랑한 아이[처녀] a cheerful child [girl] / 명랑하게 cheerfully; merrily; with a light heart; in a gay spirit / 명랑하게 살다 lead [live] a merry life; live merrily [gaily] / 가정을 명랑하게 하다 fill *one's* home with happiness / 사람을 명랑하게 하다 make *sb* cheerful [merry]; enliven *sb*

▶ 그녀는 아주 명랑한 모습으로 나타났다 She appeared with a radiant face.
▶ 그는 애써 명랑한 태도를 취해 보였다 He tried to behave as cheerfully as possible.

명령 命令 1〈분부〉 an order; a command; a direction; an instruction; a fiat; bidding

> [解說] *order*와 *command*는「명령」이란 뜻으로는 같지만 command는 권위자에 의한 공식 명령을 가리키는 딱딱한 말이다. *direction, instruction*은 모두 해야 할 일을 가르치는 것인데 direction 쪽이 명령의 정도가 강하다. instruction은 direction 보다 작은 지시를 말한다.

♦ 명령적으로 imperatively; peremptorily / 명

명령의 표현

명령문은 명령·요구·의뢰·금지 등을 나타내는 글로서 보통 주어 없이 동사의 원형으로 시작된다.

1. 직접 명령
(1) …하시오, …해라
▶ 유미, 일어나기라 Wake up, Yu-mi.
▶ 조용히 해라 Be quiet.
▶ (시험 등에서) 다음 논설을 요약하라 Summarize the following essay.
▶ (선생님이 수업시간에) 교과서 15페이지를 펴시오 Open your (text)book to [at] page 15.
▶ 소금을 좀 집어 주세요 Pass me the salt, please.
▶ 잘 생각해 봐요, 네? Think it over, won't you? (▶첫머리나 끝머리에 please를 붙이거나 끝머리에 won't you?를 붙이면 공손한 말투가 된다)

(2) …하지 마라
보통은 Don't를, 강하게 말할 때는 Never를 동사 앞에 붙인다.
▶ 걱정 마라 Don't worry.
▶ 이제 다시는 나한테 거짓말을 하지 마라 Never lie to me again.
▶ 그를 방문할 때는 미리 전화하는 것을 잊지 마세요 Please don't forget to call him (up) in advance when you visit him.

(3) 꼭 …하시오
긍정의 명령문 앞에 do를 붙이면 「부디 …하시오」라는 강한 뜻이 된다.
▶ 조용히 하라니까, 몇 번이나 말해야 알겠니? Do be quiet! How many times do I have to tell you that?
▶ 꼭 편지를 해주세요 Do write me a letter.

(4) …하시오, 그러면 [그렇지 않으면] ~
「명령문 + and」는 「…하시오, 그러면 ~」, 「명령문 + or」는 「…하시오, 그렇지 않으면 ~」의 뜻이 된다.
▶ 이것을 읽으시오, 그러면 그 문제를 잘 알게 될거요 Read this, and you will understand the problem better.
▶ 서두르시오, 그렇지 않으면 8시 기차를 놓치게 돼요 Hurry up, or you'll miss the 8:00 train.

(5) …하여 ~하시오
「동사의 원형 + (and) + 동사의 원형」은 「…하여 ~하시오」의 뜻이 된다.
▶ 현관에 누가 왔는지 보고 오시오 Go (and) see who's at the door.
▶ 안달하지 말고 경과를 지켜보시오, 지금은 그것이 제일 좋소 Wait and see. That's the best thing to do now.

(6) 너는 …해라
상대에 대한 초조감이나 분노를 나타내거나 복수의 인간 가운데 특정한 자에게 명령을 전달할 때는 주어를 붙인다.
▶ 자, 무슨 일이 있었는지 얘기 해 Come on, you tell me what has happened.
▶ 영희야, 너는 방에서 좀 쉬어라. 일남이는 이리로 와 Yŏng-hŭi, you go to your room and get some sleep. Il-nam, you come here.

2. 간접 명령
「나에게 …하게 해주세요」「~에게 …시켜 주세요」란 뜻의 명령문은 「let + 목적어 + 동사의 원형」으로 만든다.
▶ 대구에 올 때에는 알려주세요 Please let me know when you come to Taegu.
▶ [會話]「이봐, 나비를 잡았어」「놓아줘」 "Look, I caught a butterfly!" "Let it go."
▶ 이 귀중한 교훈을 잊어서는 안된다 Don't let this important lesson be forgotten. ⇌ Don't forget this important lesson.

3. 명령문의 형식을 취하지 않는 명령문
▶ 도서관에는 음식물을 가지고 들어갈 수 없게 되어 있다 You are not supposed to bring food or beverages into the library.
▶ 우리는 학교에서 집으로 가는 도중에 오락실에 들러서는 안된다는 주의를 받고 있다 We've been told not to hang around the game house on the way home from school.
▶ 답안은 볼펜이나 만년필로 쓸 것 You are to write the answers either in ball-point or fountain pen.
▶ 경찰관은 우리더러 「차를 옮기시오」라고 명령했다 The policeman ordered us to move the car.

령대로 하다 do as *one* is ordered; act on sb's order; do sb's bidding / 명령조로 말하다 speak in a commanding [an authoritative] tone
▶ 명령이 내리면 언제라도 출발할 준비가 되어 있다 I am ready to leave anytime the order comes.
▶ 우리는 당신의 명령은 듣지 않겠소 We will not be dictated [ordered about] by you.
▶ 군중은 거듭된 경찰의 명령을 무시했다 The crowd ignored the repeated injunctions of the police.
▶ 그들은 귀국 명령을 받고 있다 They have [are under] orders to return home.
▶ 그는 일을 중지하라는 명령을 내렸다 He gave orders [a command, instructions] that the work (should) be stopped.
▶ 우리는 명령에 따라 그 방을 나갔다 We obeyed the order and left the room.
▶ 명령에 따르지 않는 자는 처벌 받는다 The ones who do not obey the order will be punished.
▶ 명령에 불복하면 어찌 되는지 아는가? Do you know what will become of you when you disobey an order?
▶ 법원의 명령으로 나는 목요일에 출두해야만 한다 I have to appear on Thursday by order of the court.
—**명령하다** command; order; give [issue] orders [a command]
▶ 그는 명령하고 우리는 순순히 따랐다 He commanded and we obeyed.
▶ 대장은 병사들에게 퇴각을 명령했다 The captain commanded his men to retreat.
▶ 그는 자기가 명령한대로 하지 않았다고 나한테 화를 냈다 He got angry with me for not having done just as he ordered [told] me to do.
2 〈법령〉 an ordinance; a decree; a public injunction
■—**계통** a line [chain] of command : 명령계통이 확실히 서 있는지 나는 의심스럽다 I doubt if the line [chain] of command is clearly defined. —**문**〔文法〕an imperative sentence —**법**〔文法〕the imperative mood —**서** a warrant; a precept —**위반** violation of an order —**자** a commander; a dictator; an orderer

명론 名論 a sound argument; an excellent opinion ■—**탁설** excellent arguments and opinions

명료하다 明瞭— clear; plain; distinct; evident
▶ 그는 사건을 명료하게 설명했다 He gave a clear description of what happened.
▶ 그 편지에는 사건의 진상이 명료하게 기술되어 있었다 The letter described the truth of the case in plain words.

명리 名利 fame and profit [wealth]; name and fortune; riches and honor
♦ 명리에 급급하다 be constantly hankering [striving] after fame and gain; be bent on gaining wealth and fame / 명리에 뜻이 없다 be over [indifferent to] riches and honor

명마 名馬 a fine [an excellent] horse

명망 名望 (high) reputation; repute; renown; 〈인기〉 popularity
♦ 명망이 있는 reputed; renowned; popular / 명망을 얻다 gain [win] fame [popularity] / 명망을 잃다 lose *one's* reputation [popularity]
▶—**가** a man of high repute [renown]

명매기 〔鳥〕 a white-rumped swift ⇨ 칼새

명맥 命脈 life; the thread of life
♦ 명맥이 끊어지다 die (out); come to an end; expire; go out / 명맥을 유지하다 〈사람이〉 keep [remain] alive; maintain life; 〈풍습 등이〉 stay [remain] in existence
▶ 회사는 가까스로 명맥을 유지하고 있다 The company is barely keeping its head above water.

명멸 明滅 glimmering; blinking —**명멸하다** flicker; glimmer; appear and vanish
▶ 네온등이 명멸하고 있다 A neon light is flickering.
▶ 청신호가 명멸하기 시작했다 The green light [signal] began to blink.
■—**신호** a blinking signal

명명 命名 naming; 〈세례명의〉 christening —**명명하다** give a name (to); name; call; christen; style; denominate; designate
▶ 그는 할아버지의 이름을 따서 헨리로 명명되었다 He was named 'Henry' for [(英) after] his grandfather.
▶ 그 배는 퀸 메리호로 명명되었다 The ship was named [christened] the Queen Mary. ⇨ They named [christened] the ship the Queen Mary.
■—**법** the nomenclature 《of chemistry》 —**식** a christening ceremony

명명백백하다 明明白白— as clear as day [daylight]; as plain as a pikestaff ▶ 그의 부정은 명명백백하다 His injustice is as clear [plain] as day.

명모 明眸 bright eyes —**호치**(皓齒) starry eyes and pearly teeth; (personal) beauty: 명모호치의 여인 a beautiful woman

명목 名目 〈명칭〉 a title; a name; an appellation; 〈구실〉 a pretext
♦ 명목상의[뿐인] nominal / 무슨 명목이든 만들어 on [upon] some pretext or other / 명목에 지나지 않다 be just nominal; be in name only
▶ 영국 여왕은 명목상의 통치자다 The queen of England is a nominal ruler.
▶ 그는 명목뿐인 사장이다 He is a nominal president of the company.
■—**론**〔哲〕nominalism; terminism —**임금** nominal wages —**자본** nominal capital

명문 名文 〈유명한 글〉 a noted composition; a literary gem; 〈우수한 글〉 a beautiful [superb] passage; an excellent composition; a fine piece of prose
♦ 명문이다 be well written; be high in literary merit / 명문을 쓰다 write a fine style
■—**가** a fine writer; a stylist —**집** a choice collection of prose [writings]; an anthology of prose

명문 名門 a distinguished [famous, noble] family
♦ 사학(私學)의 명문 one of the leading private schools / 명문 출신이다 come [be

born] of a noble [distinguished] family; be high-born; be born of good ancestry
▶ 그는 명문 출신이다 He comes from a noble [distinguished] family.
■ —거족 mighty [powerful] clans —교 a school of high (academic) reputation; a prestigious [prestige] school; a big-name school [university]

명문 明文 1〈조문〉 an express provision [statement]; a specific proviso 2〈증서〉 a written contract; a deed ■ —규정 substantive enactment

명문화 明文化 stipulation
—명문화하다 stipulate expressly in the text; provide for in the law; stipulate
▶ 그 조건은 입국관리법에 명문화되어 있다 That condition is stipulated in the immigration law.
▶ 이 문제에 관해서는 법률에 명문화되어 있지 않다 This subject is not provided for in the law. ⇒ There is no provision in the law on this subject.

명물 名物 1〈명산물〉 a special [noted] product; a specialty; (英) a speciality
▶ 이 지방의 명물은 무엇입니까? What is this locality noted for?
▶ 나는 숙모한테서 대구의 명물인 사과를 받았다 My aunt brought me some famous apples from Taegu.
2〈인기있는 사람〉 a popular figure; (口) an institution
▶ 그는 우리 클럽의 명물이다 He is a popular member of our club.
3〈이름난 사물〉 a feature; an attraction
▶ 이 식당은 샐러드가 명물이다 This restaurant features salad.
▶ 그 축제는 티베트의 명물 가운데 하나다 The festival is one of the attractions of Tibet.

명민 明敏 intelligence; sagacity
—명민하다 intelligent; sagacious; clear
♦ 명민한 두뇌의 소유자 a sagacious [an intelligent] person; a clever [clearheaded] person
▶ 그는 두뇌가 명민하다 He has a clear head.

명반 明礬 alum ■ —석(石) alumstone; alunite

명반응 明反應 〔生〕 light reaction (↔ dark reaction)

명배우 名俳優 a great [an excellent] actor [actress]; a famous actor [actress]; a star

명백하다 明白— clear; distinct; plain; evident; obvious; apparent

> [解説] *clear*가 가장 일반적인 말로 「애매한 점이 없는」의 뜻이다. *evident*와 *obvious* 모두 「논의할 여지가 없을 정도로 명백한」의 뜻이지만 *obvious*가 명백성의 정도가 강하다. *apparent*는 「보기에 명백한」의 뜻으로 흔히 눈에 보이는 경우 등에 쓰인다.

♦ 명백한 구별 a clear distinction / 명백한 사실 an obvious [evident, apparent] fact / 명백한 증거 (a piece of) clear [definite, positive] evidence / 명백히 clearly; plainly; distinctly / 명백히 진술하다 state clearly [plainly] / 입장을 명백히 하다 define [clarify] *one's* position / 태도를 명백히 하다 make *one's* attitude clear / 명백해지다 become clear [plain]; be (made) known; come [be brought] to light
▶ 그의 의도는 누가 보아도 명백하다 His intention is clear [plain] to everyone.

명복 冥福 happiness in the other world; heavenly bliss ♦ 명복을 빌다 pray for the repose of *sb's* soul ▶ 그의 명복을 빕니다 God have mercy on him! ⇒ May he [his soul] rest in peace!

명부 名簿 a list; a register; a roll
▶ 형의 이름이 명부에 올라 있다 My brother's name is on the list.
■ 선거인— a pollbook; a voting [voter] roll; a voters' list 승객— the passenger list 직원— a register of the staff; a staff list 학생— a register of students 회원— a list of members; a membership list: 그들은 회원 명부를 작성했다 They made a membership list.

명부 冥府 the other world ⇨ 저승

명분 名分 *one's* moral duty [obligations];〈정당성〉 (moral) justification; justice;〈이유〉 a just cause
♦ 명분이 서지 않는 unjustifiable / 명분이 서지 않는 행동 an unjustifiable act / 명분을 밝히다 clearly define *one's* moral obligations / 명분을 세우다 justify *oneself* [*one's* conduct]
▶ 그래서는 명분이 서지 않는다 Justice will not approve of it.
▶ 전혀 명분이 서지 않는 것은 아니다 It is not altogether without justice.

명사 名士 a man of note [distinction]; a noted [distinguished] person; a celebrity; a notable; a VIP
♦ 각계의 명사 notables of all spheres of social activity / 경제계의 명사 a prominent figure in business circles; a noted businessman / 당대의 명사 prominent men of the time / 문단의 명사 notabilities in literary circles; a famous [noted] writer / 지방의 명사 local celebrities [worthies] / 학계의 명사 a distinguished scholar; a prominent figure in the academic world

명사 名詞 〔文法〕 a noun; a name word; a substantive
♦ 명사의 변화 inflexion of nouns
■ 물질[추상]— a material [an abstract] noun 보통[고유]— a common [proper] noun —구[절] a noun phrase [clause] —화 nominalization : 명사화하다 nominalize

명사 名辭 〔論〕 a term; a name
♦ 명사의 terminal / 대[소]명사 the major [minor] term

명산 名山 a noted [celebrated] mountain
■ —대찰 noted mountains and large Buddhist temples

명산(물) 名產(物) a special [noted] product; a specialty; (英) a speciality
▶ 강원도의 명산(물)은 감자다 Kang-won-do is famous for its potatoes.
▶ 사과는 대구의 명산(물)이다 Apples are one of Taegu's well-known products.

명상 瞑想 meditation; contemplation
♦ 명상적인 meditative; contemplative / 명상

에 잠기다 be lost [sunk] in meditation
▶그는 깊은 명상에 잠겨 있다 He is deep in thought [meditation].
—명상하다 meditate 《on》; contemplate
■—가 a meditator; a contemplator —록 meditations

명색 名色 a name; a title
◆명색 뿐인 사장 a president in name only / 명색 뿐인 자유 the shadow of freedom
▶명색이 사내라면 그런 짓이 어울릴 리가 없다 It cannot be becoming in any man worthy of the name.
▶명색이 학생이면 학생답게 행동해라 If you are anything of a student, behave like one [as such].

명석하다 明晳— clear; bright; distinct; lucid
◆명석하지 못한 indistinct; vague
▶그는 두뇌가 명석하다 He has a clear head. ⇒ He is a clearheaded man.

명성 名聲 fame; reputation; renown
◆명성이 자자하다 command admiration [renown]; have *one's* fame in everybody's mouth / 명성을 더럽히다 tarnish *one's* reputation; put a slur on *one's* fame [reputation] / 명성을 얻다 win [earn, gain, acquire] fame / 명성을 잃다[유지하다] lose [maintain] *one's* reputation
▶그는 의학계에서 명성이 높다 His reputation stands high in medical circles.
▶그는 세계적인 명성이 있는 물리학자다 He is a physicist of world-wide fame.
▶화가로서 그의 명성이 국내외에 자자하다 His name as a painter is known both at home and abroad.
▶그는 홈런타자로서 명성을 얻었다 He gained fame [became famous, made a name for himself] as a home-run hitter.
▶그 작가는 참신한 작품으로 명성을 얻었다 The writer gained fame with his original style.

명성 明星 1〈별〉Venus ⇨ 샛별
2〈뛰어난 사람〉a (shining) star
◆문단의 명성 a literary star [talent]

명세 明細 details; particulars
◆지출 명세를 보고하다 render an account of payments [all money spent]
▶합계 300만원이며 그 명세는 다음과 같다 It totals 3,000,000 won, made up as follows.
—명세하다 detailed; minute; particular
◆명세하게 설명하다 set forth *sth* in detail; go [enter] into details
■—표 an itemized account

명세서 明細書 a detailed account [statement]; a minute description; specifications
◆선적 명세서 shipping specifications / 지출 명세서 a bill of expenditures / 별첨 명세서와 같이 as per specifications attached

명소 名所 a place of interest; a noted place; a beauty spot
◆관광 명소 a tourist attraction; a sight spot / 서울의 명소 중 하나 one of the show places of Seoul / 경주의 명소를 구경하다 see [do] the sights of Kyŏngju
▶내일 런던의 명소를 돌아보고 싶다 I'd like to make a tour of famous sites in London tomorrow.
▶로마의 명승 고적의 명소를 안내해 주시오 Please show me places of scenic and historic interest in Rome.
■—안내서 a guide to the (principal) sights

명수 名手 a master-hand; an expert
◆사격의 명수 a first-rate [crack, dead] shot 《with rifle》/ 서양 장기의 명수 a masterful player of chess
▶그는 피아노의 명수다 He is a very good pianist. ⇒ He is a highly-talented piano player.

명수 名數 1〈인원수〉the number of persons
2〔數〕a concrete number

명수법 命數法 〔數〕numeration

명승 名勝 scenic beauty; noted [picturesque] scenery ■—지 a beauty [scenic] spot; a place of scenic beauty

명승 名僧 a distinguished Buddhist monk

명승고적 名勝古蹟 scenic spots and places of historic interest
◆명승고적이 많다 be rich in scenic and historic interest / 명승고적을 돌아보다 visit [pay visits to] places of natural beauty and historic interest

명시 明示 clear statement; elucidation
—명시하다 state plainly; indicate clearly; point out specifically; elucidate; specify
▶비용은 청구서에 명시되어 있다 The expenses are specified on the bill.

명시 明視 clear vision —명시하다 see *sth* clearly; see in a clear light ■—거리〔物〕the distance of distinct vision —도(度)〔物〕luminance

명신 名臣 a celebrated subject [retainer]

명실 名實 name and deed [reality]
◆명실 상부한 대정치가 a great statesman worthy of his reputation [the name] / 명실 공히 both nominally and virtually [really]; both in name and deed [reality]/ 명실상부하다 be true to *one's* [the] name
▶그는 명실 공히 생존해 있는 가장 위대한 배우다 In both name and deed, he is the greatest actor alive.
▶그는 명실 상부한 대과학자다 He is a great scientist both in name and reality [in fact as well as in name].

명심하다 銘心— bear [keep] *sth* in mind; take 《sb's advice》to heart; have *sth* branded [stamped, engraved] on *one's* mind
▶내 말을 명심해라 Keep my words in mind.
▶댁의 말씀을 명심하겠습니다 I'll treasure up your words. ⇒ I'll keep [bear] your words in mind.
▶고마우신 충고 평생 명심하겠습니다 I will remember your kind advice in mind all my life.

명아주〔植〕wild spinach; a goosefoot; a pigweed

명안 名案 a good [brilliant, splendid, capital] idea [plan]; a well-devised scheme
▶무슨 명안이 있느냐? Can you think of anything better? ⇒ Have you got a better idea?

▶명안이 떠올랐다 A good idea came [occurred] to me. ⇒ I hit upon [came up with] a good idea.
▶그것 참 명안이다 That's an [a good] idea.
명암 明暗 light and shade [darkness]
▶우리는 인생의 명암 양면을 보아야 한다 We should look on the bright and dark sides [phases] of life.
■—등 an occulting light —법〔美術〕shading; chiaroscuro; clear obscure
명약관화하다 明若觀火— as clear [plain] as day [daylight]; as plain as a pikestaff
명언 名言 a wise [golden] saying; a witty remark
▶거 명언이군 (That's) well said! ⇒ (口) You said it!
명언 明言 (a) declaration; a definite statement
▶그는 그 점에 관해 명언을 피했다 He avoided saying anything definite on the point.
—명언하다 declare; say [state] positively [definitely]
명역 名譯 an apt [a fine, an excellent] translation
명연기 名演技 a fine [an excellent] performance
명예 名譽 〈영예〉honor; credit; (a) distinction; glory; 〈명성〉fame; (a) reputation; a good name; 〈체면〉dignity; prestige
♦명예를 얻다 gain [win, attain] honor / 명예를 더럽히다 bring [invite] disgrace on *sb* / 명예를 존중하다 value [prize] honor / 명예를 회복하다 retrieve [vindicate] *one's* (lost) honor; rehabilitate [right] *oneself*; redeem *one's* reputation
▶우리는 조국의 명예를 위해 싸웠다 We fought for the honor of our country.
▶그의 행위가 일가의 명예를 더럽혔다 His deeds brought disgrace [dishonor, shame] on his family.
▶나는 명예를 회복하고 싶다 I want to redeem my reputation.
▶그것은 나의 명예에 관계되는 문제다 It's a point of honor with me.
▶그들은 우리 학교의 명예다 They are an honor [a credit] to our school. ⇒ They are the pride of our school.
▶의장에 선출된 것은 나로서는 굉장한 명예다 It is a great honor for me to have been elected chairman.
■—교수 an emeritus [honorary] professor; a professor emeritus —박사 an honorary doctor —시민 an honorary citizen 《of Seoul》 —제도 〈사관학교의〉the honor system —직 an honorary post [office] —총장 an honorary president; a president-emeritus 《of Korea University》 —학위 an honorary degree —회복 regaining *one's* impaired reputation —회장 [원] an honorary president [member]
명예심[욕] 名譽心[慾] (a) desire for fame
♦명예욕에 불타다 burn with the desire for fame
명예훼손 名譽毁損 defamation of character; 〈구두의〉slander; 〈문서에 의한〉libel

▶그는 명예훼손으로 출판사를 고소했다 He sued the publisher for libel [slander].
명왕성 冥王星 〔天〕Pluto
명우 名優 a great [an excellent] actor [actress] ⇨ 명배우
명월 明月 a bright moon ♦중추명월 the harvest moon
명의 名義 a person's name
♦명의뿐이 당수 the nominal head of a party
▶명의상으로는 그가 책임자다 He is nominally the person in charge.
▶재산은 아들 명의로 되어있다 My property is in [under] my son's name. ⇒ My property is (registered) in my son's name [in the name of my son].
▶그는 토지의 상당 부분을 처의 명의로 이전했다 He transferred a large part of the land to his wife.
■—도용 an illegal use of other's name —인 (人) 〈주(株)의〉a registered stockholder; 〈임대의〉a lessee; a leaseholder
명의 名醫 a skilled physician [doctor]; a famous [well-known] doctor
명의변경 名義變更 transfer (of name)
♦〈증권 등의〉명의변경 대장 a transfer book / 주식의 명의변경을 정지하다 close the transfer books; suspend transfers of stocks
▶나는 땅을 아들 앞으로 명의변경했다 I transferred my land to my son.
명인 名人 a master; an expert; (口) a wizard
♦조각의 명인 a master [an expert, a wizard] at carving
▶그는 카드 놀이에 있어서는 가히 명인이다 He is a real master [an expert] at card playing.
▶그의 민요창은 명인으로 불리기에 부족함이 없는 절창이었다 His chanting [singing] of Korean folk songs was a performance worthy of a master.
명일 名日 a festive [gala] day; a national holiday
명일 明日 tomorrow ⇨ 내일
명일 命日 the anniversary of *sb's* death
명작 名作 a masterpiece; a great work (▶구체적으로 a great novel, a famous story 등으로 써도 됨)
▶저 미술관에서는 근대화가의 명작이 전시되고 있다 Masterpieces by modern artists are being exhibited [on show] at that art museum.
명장 名匠 a master craftsman; a skilled [skillful] workman [artisan, artist]
명장 名將 a great commander; a renowned general [admiral]
명재상 名宰相 a great prime minister
명저 名著 a great [fine] book [work]; a masterpiece; a famous book
♦고금의 명저 ancient and modern classics
명절 名節 1 a festive day [season]; a gala [fete] day; a national holiday
▶크리스마스는 서양에서는 중요한 명절이다 Christmas is an important festival [feast] in the West.
▶온 마을이 명절 기분이었다 The whole town was in a festive mood.

2 〈명예와 절조〉 honor and integrity
3 〈명분과 절의〉 moral obligation and justice
명정 酩酊 drunkenness; intoxication —**명정하다** be intoxicated; be in drunken condition; get drunk
명정 銘旌 a flag with an inscription of the name and the rank of the dead
명제 命題 〔論〕 a proposition
■가언(假言)[정언(定言)]— a hypothetical [categorical] proposition 긍정[부정]— an affirmative [a negative] proposition ■—함수 a propositional function
명조 明朝 〔史〕 the Ming dynasty; 〈활자〉 Ming(-style) type
명주 明紬 silk; 〈견직물〉 silk fabrics ◆명주로 만든 물건 silk goods; silks ■—실 silk thread; 〈직물용〉 silk yarn —옷 a silk dress
명주 銘酒 nice wine [liquor] of a superior brand
명주잠자리 明紬— 〔昆〕 an ant lion
명중 命中 a hit —**명중하다** hit the mark
◆세 번 명중하다 make three hits / 명중하지 못하다 miss (the mark); go wide (of the mark)
▶화살은 과녁의 한복판에 명중했다 The arrow hit the target right in the center [(口) hit the bull's eye].
▶눈덩이가 그의 눈[머리]에 명중했다 The snowball hit him in the eye [head].
■—률 the rate of hit —탄 a hit; a dead shot
명찰 名札 〈몸에 다는〉 a name card [tag]; 〈표찰〉 a nameplate; 〈미아의〉 an identification tag
◆명찰을 달다 attach [affix] a name tag (to)
▶그는 웃깃에 명찰을 달고 있다 He has a name card on his lapel.
명찰 名刹 a famous [noted] temple (with a long history)
명찰 明察 discernment; perception; insight —**명찰하다** discern; recognize [apprehend] clearly
명창 名唱 〈노래〉 excellent singing; 〈사람〉 a great singer
명철 明哲 wisdom; sagacity ▶명철은 꾀와는 달리 나이와 더불어 늘 수가 있다 Sagacity, unlike cleverness, may increase with age. —**명철하다** wise; sagacious
명추 明秋 next autumn [fall]; the coming autumn [fall]
명춘 明春 next spring; the coming spring
명충 螟蟲 〔昆〕 a rice borer ⇨ 이화명충
명치 the pit of the stomach; (口) the solar plexus
명칭 名稱 a name; a title; a term; a designation
◆법률상의 명칭 a legal name / 명칭을 바꾸다 change the name; rename
▶이 협회의 명칭은 무엇이냐? What is the name of [What do you call] this society?
명쾌하다 明快— clear; lucid; explicit; clear-cut
◆명쾌한 발언 a clear statement / 명쾌한 지시 explicit directions / 명쾌한 주장 a clear-cut argument / 명쾌하게 clearly; explicitly
▶그 설명은 아주 명쾌하다 The explanation is quite clear [lucid, to the point].
▶질문에 명쾌하게 대답해라 Give a clear answer to the question.
명태 明太 〔魚〕 a walleye pollack
명패 名牌 a nameplate; 〈문패〉 a doorplate; 〈자리의〉 a place card
명필 名筆 〈서법〉 (a) superb [masterful] (piece of) calligraphy; 〈사람〉 a master [famous] calligrapher; a master of calligraphy ▶그는 명필이다 He writes a good hand.
명하다 命— **1** 〈명령하다〉 order; give orders [instructions]; command; tell
◆사장이 명하는 바에 따라 at [on] the president's order(s); under [on] the order(s) of the president
▶심판은 그 선수에게 퇴장을 명했다 The referee ordered the player off the field.
▶누구나 법이 명하는 대로 따라야 한다 Everyone is subject to the dictates of law.
2 〈임명하다〉 appoint; nominate
명함 名銜 a card; 〈방문용의〉 (美) a calling card; (英) a visiting card; 〈업무용의〉 a business card (▶a name card는 「명찰」, 「명패」의 뜻)
◆명함을 내놓다 give [hand, present] one's card (to) / 명함을 두고 오다 leave one's card
▶한국에서는 초면에 흔히 명함을 서로 교환한다 In Korea people often exchange their cards at their first meeting.
■—곽 a card case —받이 a card tray
명함판 名銜判 〔크〕 8.3 × 5.4cm photograph size ■—사진 (프) a carte de visite; a card-size photograph
명화 名花 〈꽃〉 a celebrated flower; 〈미인〉 a renowned beauty; a celebrated beauty
▶그녀는 파리 사교계의 명화라는 말을 들었다 She was said to be the flower [belle] of Paris society.
명화 名畫 〈그림〉 a great picture [painting]; a masterpiece; a famous picture; 〈영화〉 an excellent film; a film classic
명확하다 明確— clear; definite; precise; distinct
◆명확한 대답 a definite answer / 명확한 설명 a clear explanation / 불명확한 unclear; indistinct / 명확하게 clearly; definitely; distinctly / 공과 사를 명확하게 구별하다 draw a distinct line [make a clear distinction] between public and private matters / 권한과 책임의 한계를 명확히 하다 establish clear-cut lines of authority and responsibility
▶이 점을 명확히 할 필요가 있다 It is necessary to make this point clear.
▶그는 그 문제에 대하여 자신의 태도를 명확히 하였다 He clarified his stand on the matter. ⇒ He made his attitude clear about the matter.
명후년 明後年 the year after next
명후일 明後日 the day after tomorrow
몇 1 【의문문에서】 〈수〉 how many (people, days); 〈양·금액〉 how much; 〈연령〉 how old; 〈시일〉 how long; 〈시간〉 at what time
▶의자가 몇 개나 더 필요하냐? How many

more chairs do you need?
▶ 이 방에 몇 사람이나 있니? How many people are there in this room?
▶ 지금 몇 시지? What time is it now?
▶ 그의 강의를 이해할 수 있는 학생이 몇이나 됐는지 모르겠다 How many students were able to understand his lecture, I wonder?
▶ 이곳에서 몇 해나 사셨나요? How long have you lived here?
▶ 서울에서 올림픽이 열린 게 몇 년도였지? What year was it when we had the Olympic Games in Seoul?
▶ 이 선생은 당신보다 몇 살 위입니까? How much older is Mr. Lee than you are?
2 【평서문에서】 some; a few; several
▶ 그는 친구가 몇 안된다 He has only a few friends.
▶ 질문이 몇 가지 있어요 I have some [several] questions.
▶ 이 마을에는 영어를 구사할 만한 사람이 몇 없다 There are not many people who [Only a very few people] can speak English in this town.
▶ 몇 개던 가지고 싶은대로 가지시오 Please take as many as you like.
▶ 그의 영어편지에는 철자가 몇 군데 틀려 있었다 There were a few spelling mistakes in his English letter.
▶ 열차는 5시 몇 분인가에 떠난다 The train leaves at five something.
▶ 그는 20 몇 년 전에 세상을 떠났다 He died twenty-some[-odd] years ago.
▶ 야, 이게 몇 년 만이야! Hello! I haven't seen you for ages.

몇몇 several; a few; some

> 解說 **several**은 보통 4개 이상의 수를 가리키며 「약간 많다」라는 말하는 기분을 나타낸다. **a few**는 「적지만 없는 것은 아니다」라는 느낌에 중점을 둔다. **some**은 불특정한 수량을 막연하게 가리킨다. 다만 이 모두가 상대적인 표현으로서 말하는 사람의 느낌이나 문맥에 따라서는 같은 수량을 가리키기도 한다.

♦ 몇몇 사람 some [several] persons
▶ 몇몇은 죽고 몇몇은 부상당했다 Some people were killed, others wounded.
▶ 몇몇은 그런 식으로 생각한다 A few people think that way.
▶ 그들 중의 몇몇은 이성을 잃었다 Some of them lost their heads.

몇번 —番 how often; how many times; several times
▶ 나는 빚을 몇 번에 나누어 갚았다 I paid the debt in [by] installments.
▶ 〔會話〕 「파리에 몇번 가봤니?」「세번」 "How many times [How often] have you been to Paris?" "Three times."
▶ 그를 몇번 만난 적이 있다 I've met him several times.
▶ 몇번 해봐도 허사였다 I tried again and again, but couldn't succeed.

모[1] **1** 〈벼의 싹〉 rice sprouts; sprouts of rice; a rice seedling
♦ 모를 내다[심다] transplant rice seedlings; set [bed] out rice plants
2 a seedling ⇨ 모종
♦ 一판 a seedbed; a nursery

모[2] **1** 〈각도〉 an angle
♦ 세모꼴 a triangle / 네모꼴 a square; a quadrangle / 당근을 네모로 자르다 cut a carrot into (small) cubes
2 〈각진 모서리〉 an angle; an edge
♦ 모가 난 돌 an angular stone / 나무의 모를 다듬다 round off the corners of a piece of wood
3 〈성품〉 ♦ 모가 난 stiff; difficult; abrasive ⇨ 모나다
4 〈측면〉 the side
♦ 어느 모로 보아도 to all appearance; every inch / 여러 모로 관찰하다 look at (it) from various angles / 여러 모로 논하다 discuss (it) in many aspects [from many sides]

모[3] 〈두부를 세는 말〉 a cake; a piece ♦ 두부 세 모 three pieces [cakes] of bean curd

모 母 one's mother
♦ 모비행기 〈유도탄 발사의〉 a parent plane / 모선 〈우주선의〉 a command module / 모함(母艦) a mother ship / 모회사 a holding company

모 某 〈밝히지 않는〉 certain; one
♦ 모씨 a certain person / 모 선생 Mr. X; Mr. So-and-so / 김모씨 a certain (Mr.) Kim; a man called Kim; a [one] Mr. Kim / 작년 4월 모일에 one day [on a certain day] in April last year
▶ 나는 서울 모처에서 모박사와 비밀리에 만났다 I secretly met Dr. So-and-so at a certain place in Seoul.

모 毛 1 〈털〉 hair; wool **2** 〈십진 급수의 하나〉 a *mo* (=one-tenth of a *ri*)

모가디슈 〈소말리아의 수도〉 Mogadishu

모가지 the neck; 〈해고〉 (a) dismissal
♦ 모가지가 잘리다 〈해고당하다〉 lose one's job; (口) be fired [sacked] / 모가지를 자르다 〈해고하다〉 (口) fire; sack; give *sb* the sack; dismiss
▶ 그는 게을러서 모가지가 잘렸다 He was fired [sacked] from his job because he was lazy.
▶ 넌 모가지야 You're fired. ≒ I'll fire you.

모가치 one's share ⇨ 몫

모감주나무 〔植〕 a goldenrain (tree); a Chinese bladdernut

모개로 all together; the whole lot; in the lump; collectively
♦ 모개로 사다 buy in (the) mass / 모개로 흥정하다 make a package deal
▶ 여기 있는 것은 모개로 백만원에 드립니다 I'll let you have the whole lot for a million won.

모계 母系 the maternal line; the mother's side
♦ 모계의 maternal; on the mother's side / 모계의 친척 relatives on the maternal side
▶ 그의 모계에는 미술가가 많다 There are many artists on his mother's side of the family.
■ —가족 a maternal [matrilineal] family
—제도 matriarchy

모골 毛骨 hair and bone
♦ 모골이 송연한 이야기 a hair-raising [blood-

curdling, horrifying] story / 모골이 송연하다 shudder; feel one's hair stand on end; get terribly soared; be scared to death; lose one's nerve; (口) have[get] cold feet

모공 毛孔 pores (of the skin); the skin pores

모과나무 〔植〕 a Chinese quince

모관 毛管 a capillary tube ⇨ 모세관 ■—수 〔生〕 capillary water —현상 ⇨ 모세관(~현상)

모교 母校 one's (old) school; (라) one's alma mater (▶주로 대학의)
▶ 당신의 모교는 어디입니까? Which school did you graduate from?
▶ 우리 모교가 텔레비전에 나왔다 Our alma mater appeared on TV.
■—애(愛) almamaterism

모국 母國 one's homeland; one's mother country ▶ 그는 마침내 모국인 한국으로 돌아왔다 He has finally come home to Korea.

모국어 母國語 one's native language [mother tongue]
♦ 외국어를 모국어로 하는 사람에게서 배우다 learn a foreign language from a native speaker
▶ 그는 영어를 모국어처럼 말한다 He speaks English like a native.

모권 母權 maternal rights; mother's authority
♦ 모권을 신장하다 raise [promote] the status of motherhood
■—사회 a matriarchal society —설 the theory of matronymy —제 matriarchy: 모권제 시대 the matriarchal stage

모근 毛根 the root of hair; a hair root
■—이식 hair implantation

모금 〈美〉a draft; 〈英〉a draught; 〈차 등의〉a sip; 〈물·술 등의〉a gulp; a swallow; 〈담배의〉a puff
물 한 모금 a draft of water / 궐련을 한 모금 피우다 puff at one's cigar / 차를 한 모금 마시다 take a sip of the tea
▶ 그는 술을 한 모금도 안 한다 He is a teetotaler. ⇌ He totally abstains from wine.

모금 募金 〈기부인으로 부터의〉a collection; 〈자금 조달〉fund raising
—모금하다 collect contributions; raise money
▶ 우리는 태풍 이재민을 위해 모금했다 We collected some money for the refugees from the typhoon.
■—가두— a street collection of contributions
이웃 돕기—〈美〉community chest ■—운동 a fund-raising compaign [drive]; a drive for [to raise] funds

모기 〔昆〕a mosquito
♦ 모기 떼 a swarm of mosquitoes; (a column of) swarming mosquitoes / 모기가 많은 곳 a mosquito-ridden place / 모기한테 물린 자국 a mosquito bite / 모기를 때려잡다 swat [slap] a mosquito / 모기를 부채[연기]로 쫓다 fan [smoke] out mosquitoes
▶ 모기가 귓가에서 앵앵거리고 있다 A mosquito is whining around my ear.
▶ 거기서는 낮에도 모기에 물렸다 We were bitten by mosquitoes there even in the daytime.
▶ 소녀는 모기 소리처럼 가냘프게 대답했다 The girl answered in a very faint voice.
▶ 늪에는 모기가 우글거렸다 The marshes were swarming with mosquitoes.

모기 보고 칼 빼기 〈속담〉break a butterfly on the wheel

모기장 —帳 a mosquito net ♦ 모기장을 걷다 take down a mosquito net / 모기장을 치다 hang [put, set] up a mosquito net / 모기장을 치고 자다 sleep under a mosquito net

모기향 —香 a mosquito-repellent[-incense]; a mosquito coil ♦ 모기향을 피우다 burn a mosquito coil

모깃불 a smudge fire; a smoky fire to drive away mosquitoes ♦ 모깃불을 피우다 make a smudge to keep mosquitoes away; smoke mosquitoes away; smoke out mosquitoes

모나다 1 〈물체가〉be pointed; be angled; be sharp
♦ 모난 바위 끝 the sharp edges of a rock / 모난 돌 an angular stone / 모난 병 a square bottle / 모난 턱 a square jaw
2 〈인품이〉difficult; abrasive
♦ 모난 사람 a harsh [an abrasive] person
▶ 그렇게 모나게 말할 게 뭐니? Why should you speak so harshly?
▶ 그는 결혼하더니 모난 데가 없어졌다 The rough edges of his character have been rounded off since he got married.
3 〈쓸쓸이가 값지다〉be useful; be effective
♦ 돈을 모나게 쓰다 put money to a good use; spend money well [to good cause]

모나리자 the Mona Lisa (▶Leonardo da Vinci가 그린 초상화로 La Gioconda라고도 함)

모나즈석 —石 〔鑛〕monazite

모나코 〈나라 이름〉Monaco; 〈공식명〉the principality of Monaco ♦ 모나코의 Monacan
■—사람 a Monacan

모난 돌이 정 맞는다 〈속담〉A tall tree catches much wind. ⇌ The highest branch is not the safest roost.

모내기 rice-planting; transplanting of the rice seedlings from the rice nursery to the paddy field
—모내기하다[모내다] plant rice; plant [transplant] rice seedlings
■—철 the rice-planting season

모네 〈프랑스의 화가〉Monet, Claude (1840-1926)

모녀 母女 mother and daughter ▶ 그들은 모녀 간이다 They are mother and daughter.

모년 某年 a certain year

모노드라마 〔劇〕a monodrama

모노레일 〈궤도〉a monorail; 〈차량〉a monorail car; 〈열차〉a monorail train
♦ 모노레일로[을 타고] by [on a] monorail

모노크롬 (a) monochrome

모노타이프 〔印〕a monotype

모놀로그 a monologue; a soliloquy

모눈종이 〈美〉graph paper; 〈英〉section paper

모니터 〈감시장치〉a monitor; a monitor screen; 〈의견 제공자〉a test viewer (TV의); a test listener (라디오의); a (consumer) tester (상품의)
♦ 방송국의 모니터 a monitor to a broadcast-

ing company / TV프로그램을 모니터하다 monitor a TV program
■ —방식 [電算] a monitor mode —사진식자기 a monitor photocomposing machine

모닝코트 〈남자 예복〉 a morning coat
모닥불 a fire in the open air; an open-air fire; a bonfire; a campfire ▶ 우리는 낙엽을 모아 모닥불을 피웠다 We collected fallen leaves and made [built up] a fire.
모더니스트 a modernist
모더니즘 modernism
모던 modern ■ —발레 modern ballet —아트 modern art —재즈 modern jazz
모데라토 [樂] moderato
모델 1 〈모범〉 a model 《of honesty》 2 〈그림·소설의〉 a model; a sitter ▶ 이 소설에 나오는 의사는 그의 부친이 모델이다 The doctor in that novel was modeled on his father. ▶ 그녀는 화가의 모델을 하고 있다 She works as an artist's model [sitter]. ⇒ She models [sits] for an artist.
■ 패션— a fashion model ■ —도시 a model city —소설 a novel based on real people and events; (프) a roman à clef —스쿨 a model school —케이스 a model [typical] case —하우스 a model house
모뎀 〈변복조 장치〉 a modem (▶modulator와 demodulator의 합성어)
모독 冒瀆 blasphemy; profanity; disrespect
◆ 모독적인 blasphemous; profane ▶ 그것은 인간성 모독이다 That is disrespect of humanity. ▶ 그는 모독적인 말을 서슴지 않고 한다 He does not hesitate to use profane [blasphemous] language.
—모독하다 profane; desecrate; blaspheme
◆ 신을 모독하다 blaspheme against God; profane the name of God / 존엄성을 모독하다 debase *sb's* dignity
모두 1 〈명사〉 all; 〈사람〉 everyone; everybody; 〈물건〉 everything
〈모두(가)〉 모두 가면 나도 가겠어 If everybody else is going, I'll go too. ▶ 모두가 행복한 것은 아니다 Not all men are happy. ▶ 모두(가) 같이 가자 Let's all go together. ▶ [會話]「그녀가 한 말은 모두(가) 정말이냐?」 「그래, 맞아」 "Is everything she said true?" "Yes, it is." ▶ 모두(가) 지쳐 있었다 Everyone was tired. ▶ 그들은 모두(가) 부산 출신이다 They are all from Pusan. ▶ 학생들은 모두(가) 각자 사전을 가지고 있다 All (of) the students have their own dictionaries. ⇒ Every student has his [their] own dictionary. ▶ 이 도시 사람들은 모두(가) 차를 가지고 있다 Everybody in this town has a car. ▶ 그들은 모두(가) 그 계획에 반대다 They are all against the plan. ▶ 사과는 모두 썩어 버렸다 All (of) the apples have gone bad. ▶ 가족들은 모두 일찍 일어났다 The whole family got up very early. ▶ 500명 모두가 참석했다 A total of 500 people were present.
〈모두(를)〉 나는 하루 저녁에 그 책 모두를[그 책을 모두] 읽었다 I read the whole book [read through the book, read the book from cover to cover] in one evening. ▶ 나는 그것들 모두를[그것들을 모두] 샀다 I bought all of them. ▶ 나는 하디의 작품 모두를 가지고 있다 I have a complete set of Hardy's works. ▶ 그는 우리 모두를 초대했다 He invited all of us [us all].
〈모두에게〉 여러분 모두에게 부탁이 있습니다 We have something to ask everyone of you. ▶ 모이신 여러분 모두에게 소개하겠습니다 Let me introduce you to everyone of the party.
2 〈부사〉 entirely; completely; all; without exception; unanimously; in all ▶ 그가 모두 나쁜 것은 아니다 He is not entirely to blame. ▶ 그의 생활을 모두 음악에 바치고 있다 His life is entirely given up to music. ⇒ His whole life [All his life] is given up to music. ▶ 내 말을 모두 듣기 전에 가면 안돼요 You may not leave until you have heard me out [to the end]. ▶ 그건 모두 네 잘못이야 It's all your fault. ▶ 하는 족족 모두 실패했다 Whatever I tried was a failure. ▶ 그 사건은 모두 세상에서 잊혀졌다 The event was entirely [completely] forgotten by the public. ▶ 그가 하는 일은 모두 잘된다 Everything he does goes well. ▶ [會話]「모두 해서 7만원입니다」「6만원으로 깎아주시지요?」 "Seventy thousand won in all." "Could you come down to sixty thousand?"
모두 冒頭 the beginning; the opening; the head
◆ 연설의 모두에 at the opening [beginning] of *one's* speech / 편지의 모두에 at the head of the letter / 모두부터 from the beginning [start] ▶ 그는 강연의 모두에 셰익스피어의 말을 인용했다 He quoted Shakespeare at the beginning of his lecture. ⇒ He opened his lecture by quoting Shakespeare.
■ —진술 an opening statement
모듈 a module ■ 루너— a lunar module
모드 a mode ◆ 금년의 모드 this year's fashion; the style of this year / 파리의 새 모드 new modes from Paris
모든 all; every; the whole; each (and every)
◆ 모든 것 all; everything / 모든 기억 the whole of *one's* memory / 모든 사람 all the people; everybody / 모든 종류의 물건 all kinds [sorts] of things / 모든 경우에 있어서 in all cases; on every [any] occasion / 모든 점에서 in all respects; in every respect / 문제를 모든 각도에서 검토하다 study a problem from all angles ▶ 그는 하룻밤 사이에 모든 재산을 잃었다 He lost all his fortune overnight.

▶ 모든 학생이 시험에 합격한 것은 아니다 Not all the students [Not every student] passed the exam.(▶부분부정임. All the students did not pass....하면 전체부정인지 부분부정인지 분명하지 않으므로 쓰지 않는 것이 좋음)
▶ 그는 모든 것을 잃었다 He lost everything [all] he had.
▶ 모든 길은 로마로 통한다 (속담) All roads lead to Rome.
▶ 그에게는 그녀가 모든 것이었다 She was everything to him. ⇒ She was his all.
▪ 그것으로 모든 것이 명백해졌다 That tells the whole story.

모듬냄비 〈요리〉 a chowder; a hotchpotch; a mixed stew (of chicken, fish and shellfish, vegetables and soybean curd)

모딜리아니 〈이탈리아의 화가〉 Modigliani, Amedeo (1884-1920)

모라토리엄 〈지급 유예〉 a moratorium (*pl.* ~s, -ria)

모락모락 rapidly ⇨ 무럭무럭

모란 牡丹 〔植〕a (tree) peony ▪—꽃 a peony flower —정원 a peony garden

모란병 牡丹餅 a rice dumpling shaped like a peony flower

모란채 牡丹菜 〔植〕broccoli

모랄 〈도덕〉 morals (▶복수형으로 씀)
♦ 모랄을 향상시키다[어지럽히다] improve [contaminate] the public morals

모랄리스트 〈도덕가〉 a moralist

모래 sand
♦ 모래(투성이)의 sandy / 고운 모래 ⇨ 모새 / 한 알의 모래 a grain of sand / 모래 자루 a bag filled with sand / 모래 (섞인) 바람 a gritty wind / (바닷가의) 모래 알처럼 수많은 (as) numberless [numerous] as the sand(s) (on the seashore) / 모래를 씹은 듯한 tasteless (food) / 도로에 모래를 뿌리다 sand a road; sprinkle sand over a road; sprinkle a road with sand / 모래로 닦다 sand /모래 장난을 하다 play with [on] the sand / 모래 속으로 스며들다 sink into the sand
▶ 내 눈에 모래가 들어갔다 I have got (a grain of) sand in my eye. ⇒ Some sand got in my eye.
▶ 그 항구는 조류에 밀려온 모래로 얕아졌다 The harbor is sanded up by the current.
▶ 그 얼룩때는 모래로 문질러 닦아내야 한다 The stain has to be sanded out.
▪—강변 river beach; a sandy riverside —땅 a sandy place; sandy soil; the sands —밭 a sandy-soil field; the sands; 〈놀이터〉 (美) a sandbox; (英) a sandpit —사막 a erg —사장 a sandbank —시계 a sandglass; an hourglass —알 a grain of sand —언덕 a sand hill; 〈바닷가의〉 a (sand) dune —채취장 a sandpit —폭풍 〈사막의〉 a sandstorm —흙 sandy soil —홈 a sand mark

모래무지 〔魚〕a false goby minnow

모래주머니 〈주머니〉 a sandbag; 〈새의 위〉 a gizzard

모래집 〈양막〉〔解〕the amnion (*pl.* ~s, -nia) ▪—물 ⇨ 양수(羊水) —유착 amniotic adhesion

모래찜(질) a (hot) sand bath
—모래찜질하다 take a sand bath
▪—요법 sand treatment [psammotherapy]

모래톱 a sand spit

모랫길 a sandy road; a path on the sand

모랫발스크린 grained screen

모략 謀略 〈음모〉 a plot; an intrigue; 〈책략〉 a stratagem
♦ 모략을 꾸미다 form [hatch] a plot (to do, against); plan a stratagem
▶ 그는 적의 모략에 빠졌다 He fell into the snare set up by his opponents.
—가 a schemer; a plotter; a conspirator
—선전 tricky propaganda

모레 (the) day after tomorrow ♦ 모레 아침 [밤] the morning [night] after next

모렌도 〔樂〕morendo

모로 〈옆쪽으로〉 sideways; 〈비스듬히〉 diagonally; obliquely
♦ 모로 구르다 turn over and lie on its side; roll sideways / 모로 눕다 lie on *one*'s side / 모로 자르다 cut *sth* diagonally
▶ 게는 모로 걷는다 A crab walks sideways.
▶ 열차가 탈선해서 모로 쓰러졌다 A train derailed and fell on its side.

모로 가도 서울만 가면 된다 (속담) The end justifies the means.

모로아 〈프랑스의 소설가〉 Maurois, André (1885-1967)

모로코 〈나라이름〉 Morocco; 〈공식명〉 the Kingdom of Morocco ♦ 모로코의 Moroccan
▪—가죽 morocco —사람 a Moroccan

모롱이 a spur of a mountain [hill]

모루 〈철침〉 an anvil ▪—받침 an anvil block —채 〈쇠메〉 a hammer; a sledge (hammer)

모르다 1 〈알지 못하다〉 do not know; be ignorant of
♦ 글을 모르다 be uneducated; be illiterate; be ignorant / 답을 모르다 don't know the (correct) answer / 전혀 모르다 know nothing (about); have no idea (of, how) / 어쩔 줄 모르다 do not know what to do; be quite at a loss; be at *one*'s wit's [wits'] end / 하나만 알고 둘은 모르다 know only one side (of)
▶ 나는 법률은 모른다 I am ignorant of [about] law. ⇒ I don't know anything about law. ⇒ I have no knowledge of law.
▶ 〔회話〕「그는 몇살입니까?」「모릅니다」 "How old is he?" "(I'm) sorry but I don't know." ⇒ "I've no idea." (▶대답에서 (I'm) sorry는 빼고 I don't know.로만 하면 무뚝뚝한 어감. I've no idea.는 「알게 뭐요」라는 느낌을 줌)
▶ 저는 그가 시험에 합격했는지 어쩐지 모릅니다 I don't know whether he passed the examination.
▶ 그것을 나는 오늘 아침까지 몰랐다 I did not hear of it until this morning. ⇒ I heard of it only this morning.
▶ 모르는게 약 Ignorance is bliss.
▶ 모르는 것이 부처 He that knows nothing doubts nothing.
2 〈이해하지 못하다〉 do not understand; have no idea of
▶ 나는 그가 무슨 말을 하는지 모르겠다 I can't

make him out.
▶ 그의 행동은 정말 모르겠어 I can't make any sense out of his behavior.
▶ 난 그가 왜 그런 어리석은 짓을 했는지 모르겠어 I just can't understand why he did such a foolish thing.
▶ 【會話】「내 말을 알아듣겠소?」「모르겠어요」 "Do you understand me?" "No, I don't." ⇒ "Do you see what I mean?" "No, I don't." (▶앞의 질문은 상대방의 이해를 다짐하는 말투. 뒤의 질문은 요점을 알겠느냐는 말투.「안다」고 할 때는 모두 "Yes, I do.")
3 〈인식하지 못하다〉 do not recognize [appreciate]; ignore; disregard 《of》; slight
♦돈을 모르다 do not appreciate the value of money; be indifferent to money / 어른을 모르다 do not recognize the prestige of *one's* elders; slight [be disrespectful to] *one's* superiors / 중요성을 모르다 do not recognize the importance 《of》
▶우리는 그 납치범의 신원을 아직도 모르고 있다 The hijackers have not yet been identified. ⇒ The identities of the hijackers are not yet known.
▶ 그의 턱수염 때문에 나는 그가 누군지 몰랐다 I hardly recognized him, with his beard.
▶ 나는 골동품에 대해서는 잘 모른다 I don't truly appreciate antiques. ⇒ I am not a good judge of antiques.
4 〈안면이 없다〉 be unfamiliar; be not acquainted with; be a stranger
♦모르는 얼굴 an unfamiliar face; a stranger / 잘 모르는 곳 an unfamiliar [a strange] place
▶ 나는 이 근방을 전혀 모른다 I am a complete stranger here.
5 〈경험이 없다〉 have no experience; be ignorant of
♦가난을 모르다 be ignorant of poverty; be free from poverty / 여자를 모르다 have had no experience with women; be indifferent to women
▶ 그는 세상을 모른다 He knows nothing of real life [the world]. ⇒ He is ignorant of the real life [world].
▶ 나는 등산은 모른다 I know nothing about [I have no experience in] mountain climbing.
6 〈깨닫지 못하다〉 be unaware 《of》; be unconscious 《of》
▶ 우리는 자기도 모르게 잘못을 저지를 수 있다 We sometimes make unconscious mistakes.
▶ 그는 자기도 모르게 소리를 질렀다 He cried in spite of himself.
▶ 나는 나도 모르게 소리 질러 도움을 청하고 있었다 I was crying out for help before I knew it.
▶ 차가 부딪치려고 하자 나도 모르게 눈을 감았다 I shut my eyes instinctively just as the car was about to crash.
▶ 그것은 내가 모르는 사이에 일어났다 It came about without my knowing [before I knew] it.
▶ 그는 도중에 그 역을 통과했다는 것을 몰랐다 He didn't notice that he had passed the station on the way.

7 〈느끼지 못하다〉 be insensible 《of, to》; do not feel; be dead 《to》
♦은혜를 모르는 학생 an ungrateful student / 부끄럼을 모르다 be shameless
▶ 여기는 더위를 모르는 곳이다 It's never hot here. ⇒ The heat doesn't affect us here.
▶ 그는 인정을 모르는 사람이다 He is heartless [cold-hearted]. ⇒ He has no heart.
▶ 그는 두려움을 모르는 사람이다 He is a daredevil. ⇒ He doesn't understand the meaning of fear.
8 〈추측하지 못하다〉 cannot tell; do not know
▶ 무슨 일이 생길지 아무도 모른다 Nobody knows [can tell] what will happen. ⇒ Who can tell what will happen? (▶반어적 말투) ⇒ There is no knowing what will happen.
▶ 여기 누가 있는지 넌 절대로 모를거야 You'll never guess who's here.
▶ 나는 어찌해야 할지 모르겠다 I don't know what to do.
▶ 이 계획이 잘 될지 아직 모른다 It remains [is yet] to be seen whether this plan will work or not.
▶ 우리는 그렇게 많은 사람이 파티에 올 줄 몰랐다 We hardly expected so many people to come to party.
9 〈기억하지 못하다〉 do not remember; forget
▶ 나는 그 당시의 일은 전혀 모르겠다 I cannot remember anything of those days at all.
10 〈관계가 없다〉 have no relation 《with》; have nothing to do 《with》; be not concerned 《with》
▶ 그런 건 난 몰라요 It's none of my business. ⇒ I have nothing to do with it. ⇒ It's no concern of mine.
11 〈기타〉 그것은 정말일지도 모른다 Who knows but (that) it may be so?
▶ 꼭 가야 한다면 모르지만 그렇지 않으면 좀더 계십시오 Unless you must (needs) go, you might stay here a little longer.
▶ 【會話】「언제 한국을 떠나요?」「아직 몰라요」 "When are you leaving Korea?" "I haven't decided yet." (▶I don't know [understand]. 는 쓸 수 없음. 자기가 결정하지 않았으니까)

모르면 모르되 most likely [probably]; If I guess right; If my guess is right; It may be wrong but I think
▶ 모르면 모르되 그는 쉰 살이 넘었을 것이다 If my guess is right, he must be over fifty.

모르면 약이요 아는 게 병 《속담》 Where ignorance is bliss, 'tis folly to be wise.

모르모트 〖動〗 a guinea pig (▶marmot은 전혀 다른 동물)
▶ 그는 자기 환자를 신약의 모르모트(실험 재료)로 이용하고 있다 He is using his patients as quinea pigs for a new medicine.

모르몬교 —教 〖宗〗 Mormonism
■—도 a Mormon

모르쇠 〈불가지론〉 know-nothingism; feigned ignorance; 〈벙어리 행세〉 playing dumb ♦모르쇠 잡다 play dumb; feign ignorance; pretend not to know

모르타르 mortar ♦모르타르를 칠한 집 a mortared [stucco] house / 외벽에 모르타르를 칠하

다 mortar [plaster, stucco] the outside of a house
모르핀 〔藥〕 morphine ♦모르핀을 주사하다 give a morphine injection
━─중독 morphinism ━─중독자 a morphinist
모른체하다 〈관계없는 체 하다〉 be indifferent; 〈시치미떼다〉 pretend not to know; play innocent
♦모른 체하고 unconcernedly; as if *one* knew nothing of
▶ 모른 체하지 마라 Don't pretend you don't know. ⇒ Don't play innocent.
▶ 무슨 말을 해도 그녀는 모른 체했다 She feigned ignorance of whatever I told her.
▶ 소년은 그 사고에 대해서 모른 체했으나 허사였다 The boy tried to pretend not to know [feign ignorance of] the accident, but failed.
모름지기 〈마땅히〉 It is essential [proper] that *one* should (do); One ought to...; rightly; no doubt; of course
▶ 우리는 모름지기 인명을 존중해야 한다 It is essential that we (should) have respect for human life.
▶ 우리는 모름지기 부모에게 순종해야 한다 We [You] should obey our [your] parents.
▶ 약속은 모름지기 지켜야 한다 You must keep your word.
모름하다 stale; bad
모리 謀利 profiteering
♦모리를 단속하다 crack down profiteering
━─하다 profiteer; make unfair [excessive] profits ■─간상배 a profiteering scoundrel
모리배 a profiteer ♦전쟁 모리배 a war profiteer
모리셔스 〈나라이름〉 Mauritius; 〈공식명〉 Republic of Mauritius ♦모리셔스의 Mauritian
■─사람 a Mauritian
모리아크 〈프랑스의 소설가〉 Mauriac, Francois (1885-1970)
모리타니 〈나라이름〉 Mauritanie; 〈공식명〉 the Islamic Republic of Mauritanie ♦모리타니의 Mauritanian ━─사람 a Mauritanian
모멘트 〔物〕 moment ♦모멘트의 momental / 힘의 모멘트 the moment of a force; torque ━─관성— moment of inertia
모면 謀免 evasion; elusion; escape
━─모면하다 evade; shirk; avoid; escape; be saved from
▶ 그는 내 질문에는 대답하지 않고 책임을 모면하려고 했다 He tried to avoid [evade taking] his responsibilities without answering my questions.
▶ 그는 큰 위험을 모면했다 He escaped a great danger.
▶ 그는 가까스로 죽음을 모면했다 He narrowly escaped being killed.
▶ 파손된 배는 침몰을 모면했다 The damaged ship was saved [rescued] from sinking.
모멸 侮蔑 contempt ⇨ 경멸
♦모멸적인 말 a word of contempt
▶ 그녀는 모멸적인 눈빛으로 나를 바라보았다 She looked at me contemptuously. ⇒ She gave me a contemptuous look.
━─모멸하다 despise; scorn

모모 某某 such and such persons ⇨ 아무아무
♦모모인 Messrs. So-and-sos [so's]
모모한 某某— worthy of mentioning; notable; celebrated; well-known
♦모모한 인사 a big name; a celebrity
모밀잣밤나무 〔植〕 a pasania
모반 母斑 〔醫〕 a birthmark; a n(a)evus ■─신경성— naevus organomatosus
모반 謀叛 (a) rebellion; (a) revolt; (an) insurrection; treason
♦모반을 일으키다 rise in revolt (against); start an insurrection (against) / 국왕에 대하여 모반을 꾀하다 plot treason against the king
━─모반하다 rebel [revolt, conspire] (against); rise in revolt [rebellion] (against)
■─자[인] a rebel; an insurgent; a mutineer
━─죄 (high) treason: 그는 모반죄로 사형에 처해졌다 He was put to death for treason.
모발 毛髮 hair ⇨ 머리털
■─습도계 a hair hygrometer ━─영양제 (a) hair tonic : 모발 영양제를 바르다 apply hair tonic to *one's* hair
모방 模倣 imitation; copying
♦모방으로 영어발음을 배우다 learn English pronunciation by [through] imitation
━─모방하다 imitate; copy; follow *sb's* example
▶ 그들은 서양문화를 모방하는 데 급급하였다 They were busy copying Western culture.
▶ 그는 포크너의 문체를 모방해 소설을 쓰려고 했다 He tried to write a novel after Faulkner's style.
━─무용 imitation dance ━─문명 imitated civilization ━─본능 mimicking [imitative] instinct ━─설 the imitation theory ━─성 imitative nature ━─예술 imitative arts ━─자 an imitator; (口) a copycat
모범 模範 a model; an example; a pattern
♦모범적인 남편[아내] a model husband [wife] / 모범적인 태도 model behavior / 모범적인 행위 an exemplary deed
▶ 상급생은 신입생에게 모범을 보여야 한다 Seniors should give [set] a good example to freshmen.
▶ 그는 아버지를 모범으로 삼았다 He followed the example of his father. ⇒ He made his father his model. ⇒ He modeled [patterned] himself after [on] his father.
▶ 그의 용감한 행위는 타의 모범이 되었다 His brave deed served as a pattern for others.
■─경기 an exhibition match ━─공무원[용사, 운전자] an exemplary official [soldier, driver] ━─답안 a model paper ━─림 a model forest ━─부락 a model village ━─생 a model [an exemplary] student ━─소년 a model boy ━─수(囚) a well-behaved [model] prisoner
모법 母法 〔法〕 a mother [parent] law
모병 募兵 recruiting; conscription; enlistment of soldiers; (美) drafting
▶ 많은 젊은이가 모병에 응했다 Many young men enlisted in the army.
━─모병하다 recruit; (美) draft
━─관 a recruiting officer
모본단 模本緞 damask (silk); satin damask
모비율 母比率 population ratio

모빌 〔美術〕 a mobile
모빌유 —油 mobile oil; lubrication oil
모사 毛絲 woolen yarn [thread] ⇨ 털실
모사 模寫 copying; 〈사본〉 a copy; exact copy 〈복제〉 a reproduction; facsimile
◆ 성대(聲帶) 모사 vocal mimicry / 라파엘의 모사 a copy from Raphael
▶ 이것은 고흐의 모사다 This is a reproduction of Gogh.
—모사하다 copy; make a copy; reproduce
◆ 모사한 그림 a copy of a picture
■ —전송(電送) facsimile telegraphy
모사 謀士 〈나쁜 뜻으로〉 a schemer; a crafty [wily] person; 〈좋은 뜻으로〉 a resourceful person; a tactician
▶ 저자들은 모사들이니 무슨 일을 할지 모르지 As they are Machiavellians one never knows what they will do.
모사 謀事 planning; plotting ▶ 그는 무언가 모사 중이다 He is up to something.
—모사하다 plot; devise a plot; make a plan; scheme
—꾼 a schemer
모사는 재인이요, 성사는 재천이라 〈속담〉 Man proposes, God disposes.
모사탕 —砂糖 lump [cube] sugar ⇨ 각설탕
모살 謀殺 (a) premeditated [deliberate] murder
▶ 모살은 고의적인 살인행위다 Murder is intentional homicide.
—모살하다 murder; kill *sb* of malice prepense [with malice of forethought]
▶ 그는 동업자를 모살했다 He murdered his partner.
■ —범 a murderer —사건 a murder case —죄 (the crime of) murder
모살미수 謀殺未遂 (an) attempted murder; a murder attempt ■ —범 an attempted murderer; a would-be murderer
모상 母喪 the death of *one's* mother ⇨ 모친(~상)
모새 fine sand
모색 摸索 groping
—모색하다 grope (for); fumble (about, around, for)
▶ 그는 문제의 해결책을 모색하고 있다 He is groping for a solution to the problem.
◆ 암중 — groping in the dark: 나는 암중모색하는 느낌이었다 I felt as if I were groping about [for something] in the dark.
모색 暮色 evening twilight; dusk
▶ 모색이 짙어가고 있다 Dusk is gathering.
▶ 마을은 모색에 싸여 있었다 The village was veiled in dusk [twilight].
모서리 an edge; an angle; a corner ◆ 뾰족한 바위 모서리 the sharp edges of a rock / 책상 모서리 the corners of a desk
■ —각 〔數〕 edge angle —이음 corner joint
모선 母船 a mother ship; 〈우주선의〉 a command module
■ —포경 — a (whaling) factory ship
모선 母線 〔數〕 generator
모성 母性 motherhood; maternity
■ —보호 the protection of mothers [(the state of) motherhood] —본능 (a) maternal [(a) mother] instinct —유전 maternal inheritance
모성애 mothering; maternal [motherly, mother's] love [affection]
▶ 그녀의 모성애가 솟아났다 Her motherly [maternal] love was raised. ⇌ The mother in her was stirred.
▶ 그녀는 그에게 모성애같은 감정을 가졌다 She felt something like maternal love [a kind of motherly love] for him.
모세 Moses ◆ 모세의 율법 the Law of Moses; the Mosaic Law / 모세의 십계명 Moses' Ten Commandments
모세관 毛細管 1 〔物〕 〈가는 관〉 a capillary tube 2 ⇨ 모세혈관 ■ —벽 a capillary wall —작용 a capillary action —현상 capillarity
모세포 母細胞 〔生〕 a mother cell
모세혈관 母細血管 〔解〕 a capillary (vessel)
모션 〈동작〉 (a) motion
▶ 그는 나에게 앉으라는 모션을 취했다 He motioned (to) me to sit down.
▶ 투수가 제1구의 모션을 취한다 The pitcher winds up for the first pitch.
모손 耗損 〈닳아 없어짐〉 wear; friction loss
◆ 기름을 쳐서 기계의 모손을 방지하다 lubricate the machine to protect it against wear
—모손하다 be worn out; wear (out)
모수 母數 〔統〕 parameter
모수 母樹 〈어미 나무〉〔農〕 a mother tree
모순 矛盾 (a) contradiction; a conflict; (an) inconsistency; (a) discrepancy
▶ 그의 말은 모순투성이다 What he says is full of inconsistencies.
▶ 그녀는 항상 모순된 말을 한다 She always makes contradictory statements.
▶ 두 증인은 서로 모순된 증언을 했다 The two witnesses gave contradictory testimony.
▶ 네가 하고 있는 것은 네가 한 말과 모순된다 What you're doing contradicts [is inconsistent with] what you said.
▶ 그런 행동은 자치 정신과 모순된 것이다 Such an action is inconsistent [imcompatible] with the spirit of self-government.
▶ 논문을 쓸 때는 모순된 말을 하지 않도록 주의해야 한다 You must be careful not to contradict yourself when you write your paper.
■ —개념 〔論〕 a contradictory concept —명제 〔數〕 contradiction —율 〔論〕 the law [principle] of contradiction
모숨 a handful (of grass); a lock (of straw)
모스크 a mosque
모스크바 〈러시아의 수도〉 Moscow ◆ 모스크바의 Moscow; Muscovite ■ —시민 a Muscovite
모슬린 〔織〕 muslin; 〈프〉 mousseline; delaine [dəléin]
모습 1 〈사람의 생김새〉 (a) shape; an image; 〈풍채〉 a figure; a form; 〈용모〉 features; (outward) looks
◆ 걷는 모습 the walking figure (of *sb*) / 뒷모습 *one's* appearance from the back / 옛모습 *one's* former self / 초라한 모습 a shabby appearance / 잘 균형잡힌 모습 a well-proportioned figure [form] / 천사의 모습을 새긴 상 a statue in the shape [form] of an angel

▶ 저 소년을 보면 그의 아버지 모습이 떠오른다 That boy reminds me of his father.
▶ 그의 모습이 아직도 눈에 선하다 His image is still vivid in my mind.
▶ 그는 자기 아버지의 모습 그대로다 He is the very image [picture] of his father.
▶ 그녀는 거울에 제 모습을 비춰보기 좋아한다 She likes to look at her image [look at herself] in the mirror.
▶ 하나님은 사람을 그의 모습대로 지으셨다 God created man in his own image.
2 〈형체〉 a shape; a form; 〈자취·흔적〉 a vestige; a trace; 〈몸〉 oneself
▶ 아직도 그 마을에는 옛 영화를 간직한 모습이 남아 있다 The town still retains some vestige of its former glory.
▶ 그의 목소리는 들려도 모습은 보이지 않는다 He can be heard but not seen. ⇌ We can hear him, but we can't see him.
▶ 이내 호수가 모습을 드러냈다 Soon the lake came into view [sight].
▶ 그런 짓을 해놓고 내가 어떻게 남 앞에 모습을 나타낼 수 있겠는가 How can I appear [show myself] in public after having done such a thing.
▶ 그 이후로 그는 모습을 감추어 버렸다 We have seen nothing of him since. ⇌ That was the last we saw of him.
3 〈양상〉 an aspect; a phase; 〈상태〉 a state; a condition
▶ 우리는 그 나라의 실제 모습을 모른다 We don't know the actual state of the country.
▶ 그 영화는 자연의 모습을 그대로 보여준다 The movie gives us a true picture of nature. ⇌ The movie shows nature as it is.
▶ 그것이 민주국가의 참모습이다 That is what a democratic country should be like.

모시 〈옷감〉 ramie(e) fabric [cloth]
■—방적 ramie spinning —실 ramie yarn —옷 ramie goods [stuff]

모시 某時 a certain hour [time]
♦ 모일 모시에 at a certain day and hour

모시다 1 〈공경하다〉 serve; attend [wait] (upon); respect
♦ 부모를 모시다 have *one's* parents with him; serve [support] *one's* parents
▶ 어른을 잘 모셔야 한다 You should respect your elders.
▶ 그녀는 시어머니를 극진히 모신다 She does not spare herself in taking good care of her mother-in-law. ⇌ She is faithful to her mother-in-law.
▶ 저 아들은 아버지를 모시기 위해 할 수 있는 일이라면 무엇이든 한다 That son does whatever he can for his father.
2 〈받들다〉 deify; enshrine; worship as a god
♦ 사당을 세우고 모시다 set up a shrine; enshrine / 제사를 모시다 hold a ceremony for *one's* ancestors
▶ 이 사당은 임경업 장군을 모시고 있다 This shrine is dedicated to general Im Kyŏng-ŏp.
3 〈안내하다〉 show [usher] in [into]; receive; send in; call in; 〈초빙하다〉 invite; ask
♦ 모시고 가다 accompany; attend an important person (on) / 손님을 집으로 모시다 invite [show] a guest into the house / 의사를 모시러 가다 send for [call in] a doctor
4 〈추대하다〉 have 《*one* as the president of》
▶ 우리는 그를 고문으로 모셨다 We called him in as an adviser.
▶ 우리 협회는 김교수를 총재로 모시고 있다 Our society has the honor of having professor Kim as president.

모시조개 〔貝〕 a short neck clam
모시풀 a ramie; a ramee; a China grass
모시항라 —亢羅 loosely woven ramie(e) stuff [cloth]
모식 模式 a type
모심기 rice-planting; transplanting of rice seedlings to the paddy field ⇨ 모내기
모씨 某氏 a certain person; Mr. X
모악동물 毛顎動物 chaetognath
모암 母岩 〔鑛〕 ground; a matrix 《*pl.* ~es, -trices》; 〔地質〕 a mother rock
모액 母液 〔工〕 a pregnant solutions; 〔化〕 a mother liquor
모양 模樣·貌樣 1 〈외견〉 a look; (an) appearance; 〈형상〉 (a) shape; (a) form; figure

> [解說] **shape**는 구체적이고 입체적인 모양을 나타낸다. **form**은 낱낱으로 이루어진 전체의 모양·형태를 말하며 추상적인 의미로도 쓰인다. **figure**는 선으로 둘러싸인 도형 등 윤곽에 중점을 두는 말이다.

♦ 구름의 모양 the appearance of a cloud / 괴상한 모양의 바위 a curious-looking rock
▶ 도시는 그 회담 때문에 모양이 일신되었다 The city put on a new face for the convention.
▶ 그 산의 모양은 참 매력적이다 The mount has a very charming shape.
▶ 그는 내용보다 모양을 중시한다 He is more concerned with form than substance.
▶ 건물 모양으로 보아 그것은 교회 같았다 By the appearance [look] of the building, it seemed to be a church.
2 〈형편〉 the state of things; a situation; (a) condition
▶ 잠시 기다리며 일이 되어가는 모양을 보자 Let's wait and see the run of events. ⇌ Let's see which way the wind blows [the cat jumps].
▶ 이 모양으로는 그 문제는 당분간 해결되지 않을 것 같다 Under the present situation [conditions] the problem is unlikely to be solved for the time being.
3 〈체면〉 honor; prestige
▶ 그는 모양이 말이 아니다 He lost face completely. ⇌ He suffered total loss of face.
▶ 이 실수로 내 모양이 구겨졌다 I've disgraced myself with this mistake.
▶ 그런 짓을 하면 내 모양이 이상하게 되지 Such conduct would affect my honor.
4 〈짐작〉 ▶ 내가 잘못한 모양이었다 Maybe I was wrong.
▶ 그녀는 그것을 몰랐던 모양이다 She doesn't seem to have known it. ⇌ It doesn't seem (that) she knew it.

▶오늘 밤에는 눈이 올 모양이다 It looks like snow tonight.
▶물가가 오를 모양이다 There is a sign of [There seems to be] a price rise. ⇌ Prices seem to go up.
모양새 〈됨됨이〉 (a) shape; (a) figure; a form; an appearance; 〈체면〉 face; honor
◆겉 모양새의 outward appearance / 모양새가 나쁘다 be bad-looking; be ugly; be misshapen / 모양새가 예쁘다 be nice-looking; be well-shaped; be shapely; look nice [pretty]
▶네 덕분에 내 모양새가 유지됐어 You kept up my prestige [appearances]. ⇌ You saved my face.
▶그녀는 그 보석을 모양새를 보고 샀다 She bought the jewel for appearance's [prestige's] sake.
▶그는 자기의 모양새에 개의치 않는다 He is indifferent to his appearance.
모양체 毛樣體 〈눈의〉〔解〕a ciliary body
◆모양체의 ciliary ■ —근(筋) a ciliary muscle —염〔醫〕cyclitis
모어 母語 〔言〕mother tongue; a parent language ⇨ 모국어
모어 〈영국의 정치가·저술가〉 More, Sir Thomas (1478-1535)
모여들다 gather [flock] (together); come [get] together; crowd; assemble
◆둘레에 모여들다 gather [crowd, flock, swarm] about [around] / 사방에서 모여들다 flock from all quarters
▶개미떼가 설탕에 모여들었다 Ants swarmed upon the sugar.
▶사고 현장에 사람들이 모여들었다 People flocked to the scene of the accident.
▶아이들은 이야기를 들으려고 선생님 주위로 모여들었다 The children gathered [grouped] around the teacher to hear his story.
▶뉴스센터에는 전세계에서 뉴스가 모여든다 News comes to the news center from all over the world.
모욕 侮辱 (an) insult; 〈경멸〉 contempt
◆모욕적인 말 insulting remarks / 모욕을 당하다 be insulted; suffer an insult / 모욕을 참다 swallow an insult [an affront]
▶난 이런 모욕은 참을 수 없다 I cannot put up with such an insult.
▶내가 그에게 모욕을 당하리라고는 생각지도 못했다 I had no idea I would be insulted [slighted] by him.
▶그의 발언은 우리에 대한 모욕이다 His words are an insult to us.
—모욕하다 insult
▶그는 나를 천치라며 모욕했다 He insulted me by calling me [saying that I was] an idiot.
■ —죄 contempt : 그는 법정 모욕죄로 고소되었다 He was charged with contempt of court.
모월 某月 a certain month ◆모월 모일 a certain day of a certain month
모유 母乳 mother's milk; breast milk
◆아기를 모유로 키우다 feed a baby on mother's milk; breast-feed a baby
▶모유를 완전히 대신할 만한 것은 없다 There is no perfect substitute for a mother's milk.
▶모유로 키운 아이는 우유로 키운 아이보다 건강하다고 한다 It is said that breast-fed babies are healthier than bottle-fed babies.
■ —영양 breast-feeding
모으다 **1** 〈한곳으로〉 gather (together); bring [get, put] together; 〈수집하다〉 collect; make a collection of; 〈모집하다〉 recruit 《factory hands》; raise 《a fund》
◆골동품을 모으다 collect curios / 기금을 모으다 raise [collect] funds / 사람들을 모으다 gather people; bring people together / 일꾼을 모으다 recruit workmen / 자료[정보]를 모으다 gather [collect] data [information] / 회원을 모으다 invite people to join (a club)
2 〈집중시키다〉 focus 《on》; concentrate
◆정신을 모으다 concentrate [focus] one's attention 《on》
▶전원이 힘을 모아 노력했기에 대성공이었다 It was a great success through the combined efforts of all the members.
3 〈끌다〉 draw; attract
▶그 사건이 세인의 관심을 모았다 The incident drew [attracted] public attention.
▶그 연사는 항상 많은 청중을 모은다 That lecturer always draws a large audience.
▶그 가수는 최근에 젊은이들의 인기를 모으고 있다 The singer is becoming popular [enjoying popularity] among young people these days.
4 〈축적하다〉 accumulate; store [save] (up)
◆어렵게 모은 돈 one's hard-saved money / 재산을 모으다 accumulate [amass] a fortune / 만일에 대비하여 돈을 모으다 save (up) [put aside, lay aside] money for a rainy day
▶나는 새 차를 사려고 돈을 모으고 있다 I am saving (up) to buy a new car.
▶원주민들은 빗물을 모아서 식수로 쓴다 The natives collect and store rainwater to drink.
▶여기에 헌 신문을 모아 두지 마시오 Don't heap [pile] up old newspapers here.
모음 母音 〔音聲〕a vowel (sound)
■ 단— a monophthong 반— a semivowel 이중— a diphthong 중성— a neutral vowel ■ —변화 (vowel) mutation —자 a vowel (letter) —조화 vowel harmony —화 vowelization : 모음화하다 vowelize
모음곡 —曲 〔樂〕suite; partita
모음악보 —樂譜 〔樂〕full score; score; Partitur; spartito
모의 模擬 imitation ◆모의의 sham; mock
■ —국회 a mock assembly —법정 a moot court —시험 a trial examination; a mock exam —재판 a mock trial —전 a sham fight; a mock-fighting —점(店) a refreshment stand [booth]; 〈파티의〉 a buffet —투표 (美) a straw vote [poll]
모의 謀議 conference; 〈음모〉 conspiracy
◆공동모의 (a) joint conspiracy
▶정부를 전복하려는 모의가 발각되었다 A plot to overthrow the government was uncovered.
▶그들은 대통령 암살모의를 했다 They conspired [plotted] to assassinate the President. ⇌ They plotted the assassination of the President.

─**모의하다** consult together 《about》; plot [conspire] together

모이 feed; food
♦가축의 모이 feed [food] for cattle / 닭모이 chicken feed / 새모이 bird feed; birdseed (씨) / 암탉에게 모이를 주다 feed hens
▶동물에게 모이를 주지 마시오 (게시) Please don't feed the animals.
■─**주머니** 〈새 등의〉 a crop ─**통** a feeder

모이다 1 〈집합·회합하다〉 gather [flock] (together); come [get] together; assemble; meet
▶모두 모였나? Is everybody here?
▶모인 사람은 모두 서른 명이었다 Those present were thirty in all.
▶그의 주위에 모인 사람은 모두 뜻을 같이 하는 사람들이었다 Those who gathered around him had the same mind.
▶서울역에 오전 일곱시까지 모이시기 바랍니다 I want all of you to meet [assemble] at Seoul Station by seven o'clock in the morning.
▶모두 모여 상의합시다 Let's gather together and talk about it.
▶여름과 겨울 1년에 두번 모이자 Let's get together twice a year, in (the) summer and in (the) winter.
▶위원회는 매주 금요일에 모인다 The committee meets every Friday.
2 〈모아지다〉 be collected; be saved
▶지금까지 약 백만원이 모였다 About a million won was collected so far.
▶아마 이 입후보자에게 과반수의 표가 모일 것이다 This candidate will probably get a majority of the votes.
3 〈집중되다〉 focus on; center on
▶모든 사람의 시선이 그에게 모였다 Everyone's gaze was focused on him.

모인 某人 a certain person; Mr. [Miss, Mrs.] So-and-so ♦모인의 말에 따르면 according to a certain person

모일 某日 a certain day; one day

모임 〈집회〉 a meeting; 〈비공식의〉 a gathering; 〈친목적인〉 a get-together; 〈집단〉 a group
♦송별[환영] 모임 a farewell [welcome] party / 종교적인 모임 a religious meeting [gathering]
▶참가자의 모임이 어제 있었다 The meeting of the participants took place yesterday.
▶우리는 어제 작은 모임을 가졌다 We had a little get-together yesterday.
▶내주 이 홀에서 음악 모임이 있습니다 There will be a musical entertainment in this hall next week.
▶너는 다음 모임에는 출석[결석]하는 것이 좋겠어 You had better be present at [absent from] the next meeting.

모자 母子 mother and child (▶보통 관사를 쓰지 않으나 (美)에서는 때로 붙이기도 함)
▶모자가 다 건강하다 Mother and child are both doing well.
■─**가정** a home of (a) mother and child; a fatherless home [family] ─**보건법** the Mother and Child Health Law ─**보건센터** a mother-child health center ─**원** a mother's home

모자 帽子 〈테없는〉 a hat; 〈챙달린〉 a cap; 〈테없는 부인모〉 a bonnet; 〈수렵모〉 a hunting cap; a sporting cap; 〈중산모(中山帽)〉 (美) a derby; (英) a bowler; 〈중절모〉 a soft [felt] hat; 〈베레모〉 a beret; 〈실크해트〉 a silk hat; 〈맥고모자〉 a straw hat; 〈햇빛 가리개용 헬멧〉 a topee; 〈총칭〉 headgear
♦모자의 띠 a hatband / 모자의 산 the crown of a hat / 모자의 챙 the visor [shade, peak] of a cap / 모자의 테 the brim of a hat / 모자를 손에 들고 hat in hand / 모자를 젖혀 쓰다 have *one's* hat on the back of *one's* head / 모자를 깊이 눌러쓰다 pull *one's* hat over *one's* eyes
▶그는 모자를 쓰고 있었다 He was wearing a hat. ⇌ He had a hat on.
▶그녀는 모자를 쓴 채 방안에 들어왔다 She came into the room with her hat on.
▶소년은 모자를 쓰지 않고 밖에 나갔다 The boy went out bareheaded [without a hat].
▶멀리서 모자를 흔들고 있는 사람이 보이니? Can you see the person in the distance waving his hat at us?
▶그는 모자를 벗고 내게 인사했다 He raised his hat to me.
■─**걸이** 〈벽의〉 a hat rack; a hatrail; 〈대의〉 a hatstand; a hat tree ─**상** 〈사람〉 a hatter; 〈부인용의〉 a milliner; 〈가게〉 a hat shop ─**상자** a hat case; a hat box ─**솔** a hatbrush ─**제조업자** a hat maker

모자

단추 button
운두 crown
장식 decoration
차양 visor
구멍 eyelet
차양 brim
리본 hatband

모자라다 1 〈부족하다〉 lack; want; be not enough; be short (of); be insufficient
♦역량이 모자라다 be wanting in ability / 지식이 모자라다 have only a poor knowledge (of) / 키가 모자라다 be short of stature
▶그 옷을 사기에는 돈이 모자란다 I don't have enough money to buy the dress.
▶ 會話 「네게 여섯 상자를 남겨뒀어」「그걸론 모자라」 "I've left you six boxes." "That's not enough."
▶우리 가게에는 일손이 모자란다 We are shorthanded at our store.
▶가솔린이 모자란다 I'm low on gas.
▶그에게는 아무리 감사해도 모자란다 I cannot be too thankful to him.
▶이 책은 10페이지 분이 모자란다 Ten pages

are missing in this book.
2 〈머리가 나쁘다〉 be stupid; be dull; be simpleminded
▶그녀는 머리가 좀 모자란다 She isn't very bright. ⇒ She is a little stupid. ⇒ (口) She's a bit short on brains. ⇒ She is a bit weak-headed [half-witted].

모자반 〔植〕 a gulfweed; a sargasso
모자이크 〔美術〕(a) mosaic; (프) mosaïque
♦모자이크식 마루 a mosaic floor
■—결정 a mosaic crystal —란(卵) 〔生〕 mosaic egg —무늬 mosaic —병(病) a mosaic disease —세공 mosaic work —식 포장도로 a mosaic [tessellated] pavement
모작 模作 an imitation (work) ♦피카소의 모작 an imitation of Picasso [Picasso's work]
모잘록병 —病 damping-off
모잠비크 〈나라 이름〉 Mozambique; 〈공식명〉 the People's Republic of Mozambique
♦모잠비크의 Mozambican
■—사람 Mozambican
모재 母材 〔工〕 base metal
모쟁이 〔魚〕 a young gray 〔英〕 grey] mullet
모정 母情 maternal affection [love]; a mother's love
모정 慕情 love; longing (for); affection
♦모정을 품다 have a longing for
▶이 영화에는 어머니와 아들의 모정이 아름답게 묘사되어 있다 The affection of mother and child is prettily expressed in this movie.
모제르총 —銃 (商標) a Mauser
모조 模造 imitation
♦모조 가죽 an imitation [artificial] leather / 모조의 imitation; artificial
▶이 항아리는 모조다 This jar is an imitation.
▶이 다이아몬드 반지는 모조다 This diamond ring is a fake.
—모조하다 imitate; fake; counterfeit
▶그들은 수정으로 다이아몬드를 모조했다 They made an imitation diamond out of crystal.
■—금 imitation gold; gilt —보석 imitation jewelry; fake(d) stones —자 an imitator —지(紙) imitation vellum; vellum (paper) —진주 an imitation pearl —품 an imitation; a sham; a counterfeit; a fake; a replica
모조리 all; without exception; thoroughly; completely; wholly; all the way; from the beginning to the end
♦모조리 가져가다 take away everything (one can lay hands on) / 모조리 털어놓다 make a clean breast of 《a matter》/ 가지고 있던 돈을 모조리 쓰다 spend all (of) one's money / 세간을 모조리 태우다 lose every stick of furniture in a fire
▶값나가는 것은 모조리 도난당했다 Everything of value was stolen.
▶나는 그 시를 모조리 암기하고 있다 I can recite the whole poem by heart. ⇒ I have memorized the entire poem.
▶사과가 모조리 썩어 버렸다 All (of) the apples have gone bad.
▶그 사건은 세상에서 모조리 잊혀졌다 The event was entirely [completely] forgotten by the public.
▶나는 내 서재에 있는 책은 모조리 읽었다 I have read every book in my study.
▶그는 생각하고 있던 것을 모조리 이야기했다 He told everything he had been thinking.
▶나는 할 수 있는 일은 모조리 해봤다 I have tried every possible [conceivable] means.
▶꽃은 어제 내린 비 때문에 모조리 져버렸다 Every one of the flowers was knocked down by the rain yesterday.
모종 a seedling; 〈묘목〉 a young plant [tree]; a sapling ♦고구마 모종 a sweet potato cutting / 볏모종 young rice plants / 토마토 모종 a tomato seedling
▶서리로 모종이 말라 죽었다 The frost has killed the seedlings.
—모종하다[내다] plant [transplant] seedlings; plant out
♦팬지를 모종하다 plant pansy seedling
■—삽 a (garden) trowel
모종 某種 a certain kind ♦모종의 이유로 for a certain reason / 모종의 혐의를 받다 be [lie] under some suspicion
모주 a drunkard ⇨ 모주망태
모주 母酒 〈밑술〉 crude [raw] liquor; 〈재강〉 lees; dregs ■모줏집 a cheap liquor seller's [(美) store]
모주꾼 a tippler ⇨ 모주망태
모주망태 a (confirmed) drunkard; a heavy [hard] drinker; a tippler; (口) a boozer; (美俗) a boozehound
모지 拇指 a thumb=무지(拇指)
모지 某地 (at) a certain place
모지다 1 〈모양 등이〉 angular **2** ⇨ 모질다 1
모지랑붓 a worn-out writing brush
모지랑비 a worn-out broom
모지랑이 something worn to a stump; a stump
모직 毛織 1 woolen fabric [cloth]; worsted fabric ♦모직 넥타이 a woolen tie
2 ⇨ 모직물
모직물 毛織物 woolen fabrics [cloth]
■—공업 the woolen textile [manufacturing] industry —공장 a woolen mill —상 (美) a woolen dry goods dealer; (英) a woollen draper —업 the woolen textile industry —제조업자 a woolen manufacturer
모질다 1 〈잔인하다〉 brutal; cruel; merciless; cold-blooded; ruthless; atrocious; harsh
♦모진 사람 a brute; a hard-hearted person / 모진 성격 (have, be of) a brutal [cruel] nature / 모질게 굴다 act ruthlessly
▶계모는 그녀를 모질게 대했다 Her stepmother treated her cruelly [unkindly].
2 〈배겨내다〉 patient; persevering; bear
♦모진 목숨 one's contemptible [miserable, wretched] life
▶그녀는 슬픔을 모질게 참아냈다 She patiently bore [endured] her sorrow.
3 〈바람·날씨 등이〉 사납고 매섭다〉 violent; fierce; strong; bitter
♦모진 비바람 a violent storm / 모진 추위[더위, 날씨] a severe cold [heat, weather]
모질물 母質物 〔地〕 parent material

모집 募集 1 〈군인·노무자 등의〉 levy; recruitment; enlistment; 〈지원자 등의〉 invitation; 〈학생의〉 registration
♦모집에 응하다 apply (for)
▶새 회원 모집 (광고) New members asked [invited] to join.
▶사원 모집 (광고) Clerks wanted. ⇒ Wanted clerks. (▶Clerks are wanted. 에서)
▶현상논문 모집은 내일 시작된다[마감된다] They will open [close] the essay contest tomorrow.
▶그는 사병 모집에 응했다 He enlisted as a soldier.
▶아르바이트 모집에 응모자가 많았다 There were many responses to our advertisement for part-time help.
―**모집하다** 〈사원 등을〉 look for; seek; 〈사병·회원 등을〉 levy; recruit; invite; 〈광고 등에서〉 advertise
♦학생을 모집하다 recruit students / 신문에서 사원을 모집하다 advertise for partners in the newspaper
▶그 공장은 종업원을 모집하고 있다 The factory is looking for [seeking] workers.
▶우리 학교에서는 입학 지원자를 모집하고 있다 Our school is accepting applications for admission.
2 〈기부금 의〉 collection; raising (funds); subscription; an appeal; 〈공채의〉 flotation (of a public loan)
♦기금 모집을 시작하다 start a fund [(for)] / 공채 모집에 응하다 take up a loan; apply [subscribe] for a loan / 주식 모집에 응하다 subscribe for shares [stocks]
―**모집하다** collect; 〈대규모로〉 raise; float
♦공채를 모집하다 raise [float] a loan / 자선 사업을 위한 기부금을 모집하다 collect contribution [money] for charities; make [take up] a collection for charities / 학교 신설 자금을 모집하다 raise a fund [money] for a new school (▶money는 관사 없음)
―**광고** advertisement; 〈개개의〉 a want ad : 점원모집광고 an advertisement for shop clerks [英] assistants] —**인원** the number to be admitted [accepted]
모집단 母集團 〔統〕 a population
모찌기하다 remove rice seedlings from the seedbed for transplanting
모차르트 〈오스트리아의 작곡가〉 Mozart, Wolfgang Amadeus (1756-91)
모채 募債 loan flotation; the flotation of a loan ♦비모채주의 a non-loan policy
―**모채하다** float [raise, issue] a loan
■―**가격** the issue price ―**액** the amount of a loan ―**인수** underwriting ―**정책** a loan policy ―**조건** the terms of loan flotation
모처 某處 a certain place; an undisclosed spot; somewhere
모처럼 1 〈오래간만에〉 after a long time [interval, silence, absence, separation]; 〈고대했던〉 long-awaited; much-awaited
♦모처럼 좋은 날씨 fine weather after a long spell (of rain) / 모처럼의 휴일 the first holiday in a long time; a long-awaited holiday / 모처럼 찾아오다 take the trouble to pay a visit after a long interval
▶그들은 모처럼 서로 만나 무척 기뻐했다 They were very pleased to see each other after a long separation.
▶모처럼의 기회니 함께 사진 한장 찍지 않으시겠습니까? This is a valuable opportunity, so why don't we have a photograph (taken) of everyone together?
2 〈애써서〉 with (much) trouble; at great pains; 〈각별히〉 specially; 〈일부러〉 on purpose
▶모처럼 우중에 만나러 갔더니 그녀는 외출했다 Though I went to see her all the way in the rain, she was out.
3 〈친절하게도〉 (so) kindly; with special kindness
▶모처럼의 후의입니다만 그렇게 값비싼 물건은 받을 수가 없습니다 It is very kind of you, but I cannot accept such an expensive present.
모체 母體 〈어머니의 신체〉 the mother's body; the mother; 〈바탕이 되는 것〉 the parent body; 〈기초〉 the basis; 〈이끼·균류의〉 a matrix
♦저항운동의 모체 the basis of the resistance / 모체를 보호하기 위해 for the health of the mother
▶모체를 보호하기 위해 과로는 금물이다 Overwork should be avoided for the health of the mother.
▶프랑스어는 라틴어를 모체로 하여 발달했다 French has developed from Latin.
―**발아** 〔植〕 viviparity ―**전염** hereditary transmission
모춤 〔農〕 a bunch of rice seedlings; bundled rice seedlings
모충 毛蟲 〔動〕 a (hairy) caterpillar
모친 母親 a mother ▶모친께서는 안녕하십니까? How is your mother?
―**상** mourning for one's mother; one's mother's death : 모친상을 당하다 have one's mother die; lose one's mother; be bereaved of one's mother
모카 커피 mocha
모탕 1 〈장작 팰 때의〉 a wooden block on which wood is cut; 〈톱질용의〉 a sawhorse
2 〈굄목〉 wooden blocks on which things are piled up
■―**세(貰)** storage charges
모태 母胎 〔解〕 the mother's womb; 〈생성의〉 the matrix
♦서민 문화의 모태 the matrix [wellspring, cradle] of popular culture
모택동 毛澤東 Mao Tse-tung ⇨ 마오쩌둥
모터 〈원동기〉 a motor; 〈엔진〉 an engine
♦모터를 끄다 turn off [cut off, stop] a motor / 모터를 돌리다 start a motor
▶모터가 돌고 있다 The motor is running.
■―**보트** a motorboat ―**사이클** a motorcycle; a motorbike ―**스쿠터** a motor scooter ―**크로스** a motorcross ―**풀** a parking lot [area]; a motor pool; (英) a car park
모텔 〈자동차 여행자용 숙박소〉 a motel; a motor [an auto] court
모토 〈신조·표어〉 a motto (pl. ~ (e)s) ♦…을 모토로 하다 make it one's motto to do

▶「정직이 최선책」이라는 것이 내 모토다 "Honesty is the best policy" is my motto.

모퉁이 a corner; a turn
♦ 길모퉁이에서 at a street corner; at the corner of the street / 모퉁이를 돌다 turn [go around] a corner
▶ 모퉁이에 있는 가게에서 모자를 샀다 I bought a hat at a store at [on] the corner.
▶ 모퉁이에 서점이 있다 There is a book store on the corner.
▶ 두번째 모퉁이에서 왼쪽으로 도십시오 Turn (to the) left at the second corner. ⇌ Take the second turn to the left.
▶ 모퉁이에서 세번째가 우리 집입니다 My house is the third from the corner.

모퉁잇돌 〔建〕 a corner [an angle] stone
모티브 a motive ⇨ 모티프
모티프 〔樂·美術·文〕 a motif; a motive
모파상 〈프랑스의 소설가〉 Maupassant, Guy de (1850-93)
모판 一板 〔農〕 a nursery; (an individual) seedbed; a rice seedbed
■ 一흙 〔農〕 bed soil; nursery soil
모평균 母平均 〔數〕 population mean
모포 毛布 a blanket; a rug ⇨ 담요
모표 帽標 a cap badge; a badge on a cap
모표준편차 母標準偏差 〔數〕 population standard deviation
모피 毛皮 (a) fur; a fell; 〈생가죽〉 a pelt
♦ 밍크 모피 (제품) a mink fur / 모피 코트[목도리] a fur coat [wrap]; a coat [boa] made of fur / 안에 모피를 댄 외투 a fur-lined overcoat
▶ 그녀는 모피를 입고 있다 She is wearing a fur. ⇌ She is wrapped in furs.
■ 一상 a furrier ─제품 a fur piece; (총칭) furs
모필 毛筆 a (writing) brush
♦ 모필 편지 a letter written with a brush
■ 一화 a hair-pencil picture
모함 母艦 ■ 잠수─ a submarine tender [depot ship] 항공─ an aircraft carrier
모함 謀陷 slander; false incrimination; a plot to entrap sb / 모함에 빠지다 fall into a snare [trap]; be caught in a trap
─**모함하다** intrigue against sb; ensnare
▶ 그는 기회 있을 때마다 나를 모함하려 했다 He never lost an opportunity to set a trap for me.
모항 母港 the (ship's) home port
모핵 母核 〔生〕 mother nucleus
모험 冒險 (an) adventure; a venture; a risk
♦ 모험을 좋아하는 사람 an adventurous person; a lover of adventure / 무모한 모험을 하다 tempt providence; leap in the dark / 수많은 모험을 하다[경험하다] have [experience] a lot of adventures / 모험적인 adventurous; hazardous; risky / 모험삼아 해보다 take [try] one's chance; venture in 《an enterprise》/ 연속 모험물 a cliff-hanger
▶ 그는 목숨을 건 모험을 했다 He risked his life.
▶ 무엇 때문에 그런 모험을 하려고 하니? Why do you choose to run such a risk?
▶ 그는 모험을 좋아하는 사람이다 He is an adventurous person.
▶ 그는 모험을 하기로 결심했다 He decided to take a chance [run the risk].
▶ 그것은 모험적인 사업이다 It is a hazardous enterprise.
▶ 때로는 다소 모험도 필요하다 Sometimes it is necessary to take [run] some risks.
▶ 그것은 조금도 모험이 아니다 There is no risk in this.
▶ 나는 그건 좀 모험이 아닐까 염려된다 I'm afraid that is rather risky [hazardous].
▶ 내 남편은 그런 모험은 절대 하지 않는다 My husband never takes such a risk.
■ 一가 an adventurer ─담 a tale of adventure; an adventure story : 모험담을 들려주다 tell sb about one's adventures ─대(隊) a body of adventurers ─소설 an adventure story [novel] ─심 an adventurous spirit; the spirit of adventure [enterprise] : 그는 모험심이 있다 He is adventurous [ambitious].
모헤어 〈앙고라염소 털로 짠 피륙〉 mohair
모형 母型 〈활자의〉 a matrix 《pl. -trices》
모형 模型 a model; 〈기계의〉 a pattern; 〈주형(鑄型)의〉 a mold
♦ 실물 크기의 모형 a full-[life-]size model; a mock-up / 인체의 모형 a model of the human body / 배[비행기]의 모형을 만들다 make [build] a model of a ship [plane]
▶ 학생들은 협력하여 한라산과 그 일대의 모형을 만들었다 The pupils cooperated in making a model of Mt. Halla and its whole neighborhood.
■ 소형─ a miniature 축적─ a scale model
■ 一도 a model picture ─번호 a model number ─비행기 a model (air)plane ─시험 a model test ─제작자 a patternmaker ─지도 a relief map; a 《three-dimensional》 model map ─화 〔電算〕 modeling
모호로비치치 불연속면─不連續面 〔地質〕〈지각과 그 아래쪽 맨틀 사이의 불연속면〉 Mohorovičič discontinuity
모호하다 模糊─ dim; faint; vague; obscure; ambiguous; equivocal
♦ 모호하게 dimly; obscurely; in a haze / 모호하게 대답하다 give a vague [dubious] answer / 모호한 태도를 취하다 take an dubious [equivocal] attitude
▶ 그는 언제나 모호한 말만 한다 He never commits himself to anything definite.
모홀계획 ─計劃 〔地球物〕〈미국 과학아카데미의 지구내부구조 구명계획〉 Mohole project
모회사 母會社 a parent company; 〔商〕〈지주(持株)회사〉 a holding company [corporation]

목 1 〈모가지〉 a neck
♦ 길고 가느다란 목 a long, slender neck / 목이 굵은[가는] thick-[thin-]necked / 목이 뻣뻣하다 have a stiff neck / 목을 끌어안다 throw both arms round sb's neck / 목을 비틀다 wring the neck 《of a chicken》; wring (off) 《a chicken's》 neck / 목을 빼고 보다 crane one's neck [make a long neck] to get 《a better view》; rubberneck / 목을 조르다 strangle sb; grip sb's throat / 목을 졸라 죽이다 strangle sb

to death / 목에 매달리다 hang on *sb's* neck / 목에 붕대를 감다 tie a bandage around *one's* neck
▶ 그는 목이 짧다 He has a short neck. ⇌ He is bull-necked.
▶ 그는 고양이 새끼의 목을 잡았다 He seized a kitten by the neck.
▶ 그녀는 목에 스카프를 하고 있다 She wears a scarf around her neck.
2 〈머리〉 a head
♦ 목을 매다 hang *oneself* 《on a tree》; strangle *oneself* 《with a cord》/ 목을 자르다 cut off *sb's* head; behead *sb*
3 〈비유〉 ♦ 목이 잘리다 be sacked; 《美口》 be fired; 《口》 get dismissed; 《口》 get [have] the sack / 목을 자르다 《美口》 fire; 《口》 sack; dismiss; give *sb* the sack
▶ 그녀는 태만했기 때문에 목이 잘렸다 She was fired [sacked] from her job for being lazy.
4 〈목구멍〉 a throat; 〈식도〉 a gullet; a food passage; 〈기관〉 a windpipe; a trachea
♦ 목이 마르다 be [feel] thirsty ⇨ 목마르다 / 목이 메다 be choked 《with》/ 목이 쉬다 get [become] husky [hoarse, harsh]/ 목이 아프다 have a sore throat/목이 메어 울다 lose *one's* voice in tears; be choked with tears / 목놓아 울다 weep bitterly; wail / 맥주로 목을 축이다 relieve [quench] *one's* thirst with beer; 《口》 wet *one's* whistle [lips] with beer / 목에 걸리다 〈말이〉 stick in *one's* throat
▶ 목(이) 말라죽겠다 I am 《as》 dry as a bone. ⇌ I am dying of thirst.
▶ 감기 때문에 목이 아프다 I have a sore throat from a cold.
▶ 가시가 목에 걸렸다 A fishbone stuck [I got a fishbone stuck] in my throat.
5 〈요소〉 an important [a key] point [place]; 〈좁은 통로〉 a bottleneck 《in a way》; 〈요충〉 a strategic point
▶ 목이 좋아야 장사가 잘 된다 The locality brings a great deal of business.
6 〈물건의〉 the narrow part; the neck; the throat
■ 발— the ankle 버선— the ankle of a sock 병— the neck on a bottle; the bottleneck 손— the wrist 여울— the throat of a stream

목 目 **1** 〈항목〉 an item; a division; a class; 〈생물의 분류〉 an order
♦ 같은 목에 속하는 co-ordinal 《animals, plants》
2 〈바둑 돌〉 a stone; a piece; 〈바둑의 집〉 a point; a cross; an eye
♦ 다섯 목 이기다[지다] win [lose] by five points [eyes]/ 네 목 놓다[놓게 하다] take [give] odds of four crosses; give *sb* [have] a four-stone handicap

목가 牧歌 a pastoral song [poem]
♦ 목가적인 pastoral; bucolic

목각 木刻 〈새김〉 wood carving [sculpture, engraving]
—**목각하다** carve [engrave] wood; make a wood carving [woodcut]
■ —술 woodcraft —인형 a wooden doll; a doll carved in wood —화 a woodcut; a wood engraving —활자 a block letter

목간 沐浴간 〈목욕간〉 a bathroom; 〈목욕〉 a bath

목걸이 a necklace; 〈작은〉 a necklet; 〈장식품〉 a rivière; 〈개의〉 a collar
♦ 목걸이를 목에 걸다 wear a necklace / 목걸이를 달다 put a collar on 《a dog》
▶ 그녀는 진주 목걸이를 하고 있다 She wears a pearl necklace.

목검 木劍 a wooden sword; a singlestick

목격 目擊 observation; sighting
—**목격하다** witness; observe; see 《with *one's* own eyes》
♦ 목격되다 come under *one's* eyes [notice, observation]
▶ 나는 그 사고를 목격했다 I witnessed the accident. ⇌ I saw the accident with my own eyes.
▶ 그의 이웃 사람이 도둑이 도망치는 것을 목격했다 One of his neighbors observed a thief run away.
▶ 나는 끔찍한 광경을 목격했다 I witnessed [was a witness to] a horrible scene.

목격자 目擊者 a witness; an eyewitness; an observer
♦ 목격자의 말 an eyewitness report [account]; a firsthand account
▶ 그 사고는 목격자가 없었다 There were no (eye)witnesses to the accident.

목곧다 〈완고하다〉 stiff-necked

목공 木工 〈세공〉 woodworking; 〈목세공인〉 a woodworker; 〈목수〉 a carpenter
■ —기계[공구] a woodworking machine [tool] —선반 a woodworking lathe; a wood lathe —소 a woodworking shop [plant] —술 carpentry; woodcraft —일 woodwork(ing)

목관 木棺 a wooden coffin

목관악기 木管樂器 a woodwind 《instrument》; (총칭) the wood

목구멍 a throat; 〈식도〉 a gullet; 〈기관〉 a windpipe
♦ 목구멍이 막히다 be choked 《with》
▶ 아들 걱정 때문에 밥이 목구멍을 넘어가지 않았다 I was so worried about my son (that) I lost my appetite.
▶ 생선가시가 목구멍에 걸리지 않도록 조심해라 Be careful not to get the fishbone stuck in your throat.
▶ 그 말이 거의 목구멍까지 나오려 했지만 그에게는 차마 말하지 못했다 I almost blurted it out, but I couldn't bring myself to tell him.

목구멍이 포도청 (속담) Hunger makes any man a criminal. ⇌ The hungry belly has no ears. ⇌ Hunger breaks stone wall.

목금 木琴 a xylophone ■ —주자 a xylophonist

목기 木器 a wooden vessel [container]; (총칭) woodenware

목다리 木— 《a pair of》 crutches
♦ 목다리를 짚고 걷다 walk [go] on crutches

목대잡다 supervise; superintend; control; direct; 《口》 boss

목대잡이 a supervisor; a superintendent; a foreman; boss

목덜미 the nape [scruff] 《of the neck》

♦아무의 목덜미를 잡다 take [seize] *sb* by the scruff of neck [by the collar]; collar *sb*
▶그녀는 목덜미가 길다[아름답다] She has a long [charming] nape.
▶그는 아이의 목덜미를 잡았다 He seized [took] a child by the collar.

목도 〈일〉 carrying 《a weight》 with a pole [poles] jointly shouldered by two [four] persons; 〈몽둥이〉 a carrying [shouldering] pole
—**목도하다** shoulder 《a weight》 by the use of poles
■—꾼 polebearers

목도 木刀 a wooden sword ⇨ 목검(木劍)

목도 目睹 observation ⇨ 목격(目擊)

목도리 a muffler; a neckerchief; 《英》 a comfortable; 《英》 〈긴 털실제의〉 a comforter; a scarf; a 《neck》 wrap; a boa; 〈여성용 모피의〉 a neckpiece
♦목도리를 두르고 with a muffler (a)round *one's* neck / 목도리를 하다 wear a muffler [(neck) scarf]

목돈 a sizable [tidy] sum [amount] of money; a (good) round sum
♦목돈을 좀 만들다 scrape together some money

목동 牧童 a herder; a herdsman; 〈양의〉 a shepherd; 〈소의〉 a cowboy; 《美口》 a cowpuncher
▶목동이 소를 몬다 A cowboy drives cattle.
▶목동이 양떼를 지키고 있다 A shepherd tends a flock.

목련 木蓮 [植] a magnolia; a cucumber tree
■백— a white magnolia ; ■—화 a magnolia flower

목례 目禮 a nod; nodding
♦목례를 주고 받다 exchange nods 《with》
—**목례하다** nod 《to》; give *sb* a nod; greet with *one's* eyes
▶복도에서 만났을 때 그녀는 내게 목례했다 She greeted me with her eyes when we met in the corridor.

목로 木壚 a long and narrow table in a public house; a bar
■—(술)집 a bar; 《英》 a public house; 《美》 a saloon; 《口》 a pub

목록 目錄 1〈상품·장서의〉《美》 a catalog; 《英》 a catalogue; a checklist; 〈재산·재고의〉 an inventory
♦목록을 만들다 make a list [an inventory] 《of articles》; list; catalog / 장서 목록을 만들다 catalog a library / 목록에 싣다 catalog 《articles》; put [place] 《an item》 on [in] the catalog / 목록에 올라있다 be (listed) in the catalog
▶그 상점에서 상품 목록을 보내왔다 The store sent us a catalog of their merchandise.
▶나는 요새 장서의 목록을 만드느라 바빴다 I have been busy making a list of my library of late.
2〈차례〉 〈a table of〉 contents; 〈인명 등의 표〉 a list; 〈연주 등의〉 a program
■물품— a list of articles 신간 서적— a list [catalog] of new books [publications]

목리 木理 〈나뭇결〉 the grain (of wood)

목마 木馬 〈목제의〉 a wooden horse; 〈회전목마의〉 a rocking horse; a hobbyhorse ■회전— a merry-go-round; 《英》 a roundabout

목마르다 1〈갈증나다〉 be [feel, get] thirsty; *one's* throat is dry; be dry; have a dry throat
♦탈듯이 목마르다 be parched with thirst
▶목말라도 도천(盜泉)의 물은 아니 마신다 《속담》 Honest poverty is preferable to ill-gotten wealth.
2〈갈망하다〉 be thirsty for 《knowledge》; be eager for; have a strong desire (for); have a thirst for 《money, knowledge》; thirst [yearn, crave] for 《money》; desire *sth* eagerly; hunger for 《knowledge, affection》
♦목마르게 기다렸던 비 long-awaited rain / 목마르게 기다리다 be on tiptoe of expectation 《for》; wait for 《news》 on tiptoe

목말 a piggyback; a pickaback ♦목말 타다 ride on *sb's* shoulders; ride pickaback [piggyback] on *sb* / 목말 태우다 mount [have, hold] 《a child》 on *one's* shoulders; have 《a child》 pickaback / 목말 태우고 가다 carry 《a child》 on *one's* shoulders; ride [carry] 《a child》 pickaback [piggyback]
▶아버지는 내가 어렸을 때 나를 목말 태워 주곤 했다 My father would give me a ride on his shoulders, when I was a child.

목매다 hang *sb* ⇨ 목매달다

목매달다 〈남을〉 hang *sb*; 〈스스로〉 hang *oneself*
♦나무에 목매달다 hang *oneself* on a tree [down from a tree branch]/ 벨트로 목매달아 죽다 hang *oneself* with *one's* belt / 대들보에 목매달아 죽다 hang *oneself* from a beam of *one's* house
▶그는 목매달아 자살했다 He committed suicide by hanging himself.

목매아지 a tethered colt

목메다 be choked [stifled, suffocated, smothered] 《by, with》
♦목메어 우는 어머니 a sobbing motherhood [mother]; a mother [motherhood] choked with tears / 목메어 울다 sob; be choked with [drowned in] tears
▶그는 설움에 목메어 말이 나오지 않았다 His voice was choked with sorrow.

목면 木棉 1〈무명〉 cotton cloth
2〔植〕 ⇨ 목화

목물 〈물로 씻는 일〉 a bust bath —**목물하다** 〈물로 씻다〉 take a bust bath

목민 牧民 government (of people); governing the people
■—관 a governor; a magistrate

목발 木— 《俗》 〈목다리〉 〈a pair of〉 crutches

목본 木本 〔植〕 an arbor 《pl. -bores》; a woody plant

목부용 木芙蓉 〔植〕 a hibiscus; a cotton rose-mallow

목불인견 目不忍見 ♦목불인견이다 be unable to bear [stand] the sight of; cannot bear [endure] to see; be extremely pitiful
▶그 참상은 목불인견이었다 The tragic sight was simply appalling.
▶그 일가의 참상이라니 실로 목불인견이었다 I

목사 牧師 a minister 《of the Gospel》; a clergyman; a pastor; a churchman; a cleric; 〈교구의〉 the parson; a rector; a vicar; the Reverend;〈종군의〉 a chaplain

> |解說| (美)에서는 ***minister***가 일반적인 말이다. ***clergyman***도 「목사」의 뜻으로 쓰이나 본래는 널리 각 종교·종파의 성직자를 가리킨다. (英)에서는 영국 국교회파의 목사를 clergyman이라 하고 그 외의 목사는 minister라고 한다. 교회·교구를 맡은 목사는 ***pastor***이지만 영국 국교회파에서는 ***parson***, 미국 성공회에서는 ***rector***라고 한다. 「…씨」라고 하는 경우에는 ***the Reverend*** [the Rev.]로서 모두가 글말로는 정식표현이지만 회화체로는 the Rev.를 쓰는 것이 스스럼없는 표현이다.

◆김목사(님) the Reverend Kim; the Rev. Kim / 목사가 되다 become a clergyman; be ordained; enter the ministry; go into [enter] the church; take (holy) orders
■―관(館) a rectory; a vicarage ―직 orders; ministry

목상 木像 〈조각〉 a wooden image [statue, idol];〈나무로 만든 사람 형상〉 a wooden figure [doll]; a dummy

목새 fine sand washed in by waves

목석 木石 〈나무와 돌〉 trees and stones; 〈무감각한 것〉 stocks and stones; inanimate objects
◆목석같은 사람 an insensible person; stocks and stones / 목석같은 insensible; unimpressionable; unsusceptible / 목석이 아니다 be sentient; be a sentient being
▶나는 목석이 아니다 I am not a stock nor a stone. ⇌ I am made of flesh and blood.
▶그는 마치 목석처럼 무표정하다 He is as apathetic as a stone.

목선 木船 a wooden vessel [ship]

목성 木星 〔天〕 Jupiter
■―형행성 Jovian planets

목소리 a tone (of voice); a voice
◆가는[가냘픈] 목소리 a thin voice / 굵은 목소리 a deep [full] voice / 날카로운[카랑카랑한] 목소리가 shrill [high-pitched] voice / 낭랑한 목소리 a resonant [sonorous] voice / 낮은 목소리 a low voice; a whisper; a murmur / 다정한 목소리 a soft [gentle] voice / 아름다운 목소리 a sweet [beautiful] voice / 맑은 목소리 a clear voice / 성난 목소리 an angry voice [tone] / 큰 목소리 a loud voice / 탁한 목소리 a gruff [thick] voice / 듣기 싫은 목소리 an ugly [a discordant] voice / 감기로 쉰 목소리 a voice hoarse [husky] from a cold
〈목소리가〉 목소리가 들리는[들리지 않는] 곳에 within [out of, beyond] hearing [earshot] / 목소리가 변하다 one's voice changes [breaks, cracks] / 목소리가 나오지 않다 lose one's voice / 목소리가 좋다 have a sweet [fine, musical] voice
▶옆방에서 그들의 목소리가 들렸다 I heard their voices in the next room. ⇌ I heard them talking in the next room.
〈목소리를〉 목소리를 낮추다[죽이다] lower [sink, drop] one's voice / 목소리를 높이다 raise [lift] one's voice; raise one's pitch / 목소리를 짜내다 strain one's voice / 목소리를 삼키다 swallow one's voice / 아무의 목소리를 알아듣다 recognize sb's voice
〈목소리로〉 떨리는 목소리로 in a faltering [quivering, trembling] voice / 우레와 같은 목소리로 in a voice of thunder / 작은[낮은] 목소리로 in a low voice; in whispers [a whisper]; in a quiet tone; 《talk》 low; in an undertone / 큰 목소리로 in [with] a loud voice; loudly; loud / 한 목소리로 with one voice; in chorus [unison]

목수 木手 a carpenter
◆목수일을 하다 carpenter

목수 木髓 〔植〕 the pith ⇨ 고갱이

목숨 life ⇨ 생명
◆귀한 목숨 one's most precious life; one's dear(est) life / 초로(草露)와 같은 목숨 a dewdrop-like [transitory] life [existence] / a life as tenuous as the dew on the grass; a frail life / 목숨보다도 소중하다 be dearer [more precious] (to one) than life itself
〈목숨이[은]〉 목숨이 있는 living; live; alive / 목숨이 없는 lifeless / 목숨이 붙어 있는 한 as [so] long as one lives [life lasts] / 목숨이 위태롭다 one's life is in danger; be in peril of one's life / 목숨이 다할 때까지 싸우다 fight to the last drop of one's blood
▶목숨이 있는 동안은 희망이 있다 While there is life, there is hope.
▶사람의 목숨은 이슬처럼 덧없다 Man's life is as transient as dew.
〈목숨을〉 목숨을 건 사랑 love at the risk of one's life / 목숨을 건 《a matter》 of life and death; 〈필사의〉 desperate 《efforts》; deadly 《combat》 / 목숨을 걸고 at the risk [hazard] of one's life; neck or nothing [naught]; desperately / 목숨을 걸다 risk [stake] one's life; risk one's neck / 목숨을 걸고 맹세하다 swear on [upon] one's life / 간신히 목숨을 건지다 have a narrow [hairbreadth] escape; have [be] a close shave (of it) / 아무의 목숨을 구하다 save sb from death; save sb's life / 목숨을 가볍게 여기다 slight one's life / 목숨을 노리다 seek sb's life; plot sb's death / 목숨을 돌보지 않다 disregard one's life; set one's life at naught / 목숨을 버리다 give (up) one's life 《for》; throw away [lay down] one's life; die 《for》 / 나라를 위해서 목숨을 바치다 die for one's country; offer [sacrifice] one's life for one's country / 목숨을 부지하다 sustain [maintain] life / 목숨을 빼앗다 take sb's life; kill / 목숨을 소중히 여기다 hold one's life dear; value one's life / 목숨을 이어가다 support oneself; manage to; keep body and soul together; subsist 《on》 / 목숨을 잃다 die; lose one's life
▶그녀는 인류의 행복을 위해 목숨을 바쳤다 She offered [sacrificed] her life for the good of humanity.
▶그는 교통사고로 목숨을 잃을 뻔했다 He was

almost killed in a traffic accident.
▶ 그 사고로 50명이나 목숨을 잃었다 Fifty lives were lost [Fifty people were killed] in that accident.
▶ 그는 술 때문에 목숨을 잃었다 Drinking was the cause of his death. ⇒ He lost his life because of drinking.
▶ 그들은 빵과 물로 목숨을 부지했다 They sustained themselves [kept themselves alive] on bread and water.
▶ 그는 나의 목숨을 구해 준 은인이다 I owe him my life. ⇒ He saved my life.
▶ 쌀은 우리가 목숨을 이어가는 데 필수 불가결한 것이다 Rice is indispensable to our life.

목쉬다 become [get, grow] hoarse [husky, harsh]
◆ 목쉰 소리로 in a hoarse [husky] voice; throatily; hoarsely / 목쉬도록 소리치다 scream [shout] *oneself* hoarse 《for help》
▶ 그녀는 목쉬도록 지껄였다[외쳤다] She talked [shouted] herself hoarse.

목양 牧羊 sheep breeding [raising, farming]
■ ─견 a sheep dog; a shepherd dog ─자 a sheep raiser; a shepherd; 《美》a sheepman; 《英》a sheep farmer

목양말 木洋襪 cotton socks [stockings]

목요일 木曜日 Thursday 《略 Thur(s).》 (▶보통 관사 없음)

목욕 沐浴 a bath; bathing; ablution
─목욕하다 have [take] a bath; bathe; wash [tub] *oneself*; clean up; 《英》bath; have [take] a (hot) tub
◆ 목욕하기를 좋아하다 be fond of bath /《목욕탕에》목욕하러 가다 go to the public bath; go to a bathhouse; go to take a bath / 자주 목욕하다 enjoy frequent baths / 목욕시키다 give 《a baby》a bath; give a bath 《to a baby》; bathe 《《英》bath》《a baby》
▶ 나는 날마다 목욕한다 I take [have] a bath every day.
▶ 목욕한 후에 맥주를 한 잔 하자 Let's have a mug of beer after a bath.
■ ─비[료, 값] a bath fee; a bath(-house) charge ─비누 bath [toilet] soap ─실[간] a bath(room)

목욕물 沐浴─ water for bath; bath (water)
◆ 목욕물을 데우다 heat the bath; prepare a bath; get a bath ready
▶ 목욕물이 데워졌습니다 The bath is ready.

목욕재계 沐浴齋戒 ablutions; a purification ceremony ─목욕재계하다 perform [make] *one's* ablutions

목욕탕 沐浴湯 a bath; a bathhouse ◆ 공중─ a public bath [bathhouse] ■ ─주인 a bathkeeper

목욕통 沐浴桶 a (bath)tub ◆ 목욕통에 들어가다 soak in a bathtub; sink into a (hot) bath

목우 牧牛 pasturing cattle; cattle at pasture

목운동 ─運動 a neck exercise

목이버섯 木耳─ 【植】a Jew's-ear

목자 牧者 1 〈목축업자〉a stock farmer [raiser]; a cattle breeder; a rancher; a herdsman; a herder; a shepherd
2 〔가톨릭〕a pastor; 〈목사〉〔聖〕a shepherd (of souls)

목잠기다 get [become, grow] hoarse [harsh, husky]; hoarsen

목장 牧場 a ranch; a stock farm; 〈방목장〉a pasture (ground); a pasturage; 〈초원지대〉a meadow
◆ 목장의 일꾼 a ranch hand; a cowhand / 목장을 경영하다 run [conduct] cowhand / 목장에 풀어놓다 put [send, turn] (out) 《cattle》to pasture / 목장에서 일하다 work on a stock farm; ranch
▶ 목장에서 소가 풀을 뜯고 있다 Cattle are grazing [at grass] in the pasture [meadow].
▶ 그는 양을 마을의 목장으로 끌고갔다 He took his sheep to the village pasture.
■ ─주 the owner of a stock farm; a cattleman; a 《sheep, cattle》farmer; a cattleman; a (cattle) rancher; a ranchman

목재 木材 wood; 〈건축용의〉《美》lumber; 《英》timber; 《총칭》timbering
■ ─건류(乾溜) wood distillation ─공업 the lumber industry ─벌채업 a timbering ─벌채인부 a lumberman ─상 a lumberman; a timber merchant ─소 a sawmill; a timber mill; a lumbermill ─운반선 a lumber [timber] carrier ─운반용 트럭 a logging truck ─저장소 a timber basin; 《美》a lumberyard; 《英》timberyard ─펄프 wood pulp

목적 目的 a purpose; an aim; an end (in view); an object; an objective; 〈목표〉a goal; 〈의도〉a design; an intention

> 解說 **purpose**는 가장 일반적인 말로서 결과보다도 확고한 결심에 의한 과정에 중점을 둔다. **aim**은 달성하고자 하는 소원을 나타내며 노력의 방향을 암시한다. **end**는 약간 딱딱한 말로 수단(means)에 대한 목적으로서 멀리 있는 최종적인 것을 암시한다. **object**는 딱딱한 말로서 개인의 소원·필요·의도 등에 따라서 정해진 최종 목적을 가리킨다. **objective**는 좀 더 딱딱한 말로서 장기에 걸쳐 달성할 수 있는 원대한 목표를 가리킨다. **goal**은 경기의 골을 연상시키는 것으로 노력·인내를 필요로 하고 달성한 후에는 보답이 있음을 암시한다.

◆ 인생의 목적 one's aim [goal] in life / 공동의 목적 a common cause / 목적이 없는 인생 a life without aim [purpose]; a life with no object; an aimless [a purposeless] life / 목적이 있는 purposive 《action》; purposeful / 목적 없이 for no purpose; without aim
〈목적은〉그의 목적은 아인슈타인과 같은 위대한 물리학자가 되는 것이다 His purpose [aim, goal, objective] was to be a great physicist like an Einstein.
▶ 교육의 주된 목적은 선량한 시민을 양성하는 데 있다 The chief aim of education is to bring up good citizens.
▶ 목적은 수단을 정당화한다고 생각하는 사람이 있다 Some think that the end justifies the means.
▶ 그의 사임 목적은 무엇입니까? What is the purpose of his resignation [his purpose in resignation]? ⇒ What has he resigned for?

목적의 표현

1. …하기 위하여; …하러; …하도록 (동사를 수식)
(1) 부정사
▶ 우리는 살기 위하여 먹는다 We eat to live.
▶ 그녀는 영어를 공부하러 미국에 갔다 She went to the United States to study English.
▶ 나는 그녀를 기쁘게 해주려고 그렇게 말했다 I said that to please her.
▶ 우리는 시대에 뒤떨어지지 않도록 신문을 읽어야 한다 We should read the newspaper to keep abreast of the times.
[어법]
부정에는 not to do를 쓰지 않고 so as not to do를 쓴다.
(2) so as to do; in order to do
▶ 우리는 9시 30분 열차에 댈 수 있도록 서둘렀다 We hurried so as to be in time for the 9:30 train.
▶ 그는 신문을 보려고 불을 켰다 He turned on the light in order to see the newspaper.
[어법]
① 「…하지 않도록」이라는 부정의 목적을 나타내는 데는 (2)의 구문을 쓴다.
② in order to는 부정사보다도 약간 격식을 차린 말투다. 또 so as to에는 결과의 뜻도 포함된다.
③ 술어동사의 목적어가 사람을 나타내는 말일 때 문장의 주어가 부정사의 동작을 하고 있는 경우에는 so as to를 쓴다.
[보기] He sent his children into the garden so as to take an afternoon nap. (그는 낮잠을 자려고 아이들을 정원으로 내보냈다)

2. …이 ~하기 위하여 [~하러, ~하도록] (주어와 함께 동사를 수식)
(1) for sb to do
▶ 그에게 서명을 받으려고 비서는 서류를 가져왔다 The secretary has brought the papers for him to sign. ⇌ …so that he may sign them.
▶ 동물원은 누구나 구경할 수 있도록 일요일에도 개방해 놓고 있다 The zoo is open even on Sunday for everyone to see. ⇌ …so that everyone may see it.
(2) so that…can [will]; in order that…may (격식차린 말투)
▶ 그의 부모는 그를 대학에 보내기 위하여 저금하고 있다 His parents are saving money so that he can [will] go to college.
▶ 버스가 서도록 그는 손을 들었다 He raised his hand so that the bus would stop.
▶ 좋은 자리를 잡기 위하여 그들은 일찍 도착했다 They arrived early in order that they might get a good seat.
[어법]
① 현재의 일이나 습관 등을 나타낼 때는 can, will 대신에 동사의 현재형을 쓴다.
[보기] He always starts early so that he doesn't have to run. (서두르지 않아도 되도록 그는 언제나 일찍 떠난다)
② 과거일 때는 could, would 외에 should도 쓴다.
[보기] The boy hid behind the door so that no one should see him. (아무한테도 들키지 않도록 그 소년은 문 뒤에 숨었다)
③ so that…clause에는 이 밖의 조동사가 쓰일 때도 있으나 보통 현재인 경우에는 so that…can [will]을, 과거일 때는 so that…could [would]를 쓰는 것으로 알고 있으면 된다.
④ in order that…may는 격식을 차린 딱딱한 말투므로 목적을 나타내는 데는 so that을 쓰는 것이 좋다.

3. …이 ~하지 않도록 (동사를 수식)
(1) so as not to do
▶ 그녀는 갓난아기가 깨지 않도록 조용히 들어왔다 She came in quietly so as not to wake the baby. (▶그냥 not to wake라고는 하지 않음)
▶ 나는 모임에 늦지 않도록 서둘렀다 I hurried so as not to be late for the meeting. (▶그냥 I hurried not to 라고는 하지 않음)
(2) so that…can't [won't]
▶ 그녀는 어린애가 감기 들지 않도록 창문을 닫았다 She closed the window so that her child wouldn't catch cold.
▶ 그는 아무도 보지 못하도록 그 편지를 조심해서 감추었다 He hid the letter carefully so that no one would [could] see it.
▶ 그들은 마지막 버스를 놓치지 않으려고 서두르고 있다 They are hurrying so that they won't miss the last bus.
[어법]
종속절의 주어와 주절의 주어가 같을 때에는 so as not to do를 흔히 쓴다. 또 과거형에서는 so that…should not의 형식도 쓰인다.
(3) 기타
▶ 김선생 부인은 이웃 사람들을 만나지 않도록 언제나 다른 동네에서 쇼핑을 한다 Mrs. Kim always shops in another street to avoid meeting her own neighbors. ⇌ …so that she won't meet her own neighbors.
▶ 그는 우리가 보지 못하도록 서둘러 지나가 버렸다 He hurried past to prevent us from seeing him. ⇌ He hurried past to avoid being seen. (=…so that we shouldn't see him.)

4. …하기 위한; … 할 만한
(1) 부정사
▶ 뭔가 먹을 것을 주시오 Give me something to eat.
▶ 그것을 열기 위한 연장이 필요하다 I want a tool to open it with.
(2) for sb to do
▶ 당신이 서명해 주셔야 할 편지가 몇 통 있습니다 There are several letters for you to sign.
▶ 당신은 서둘러야 할 필요가 있습니까? Is there any need for you to hurry?

〈목적을〉 목적을 가지고 있다 have an object; have an end in view / 목적을 달성하다 accomplish [attain, gain, achieve, succeed in] *one's* object [purpose, end]; achieve [carry out] *one's* aim / 목적을 바꾸다[바꾸지 않다] change [stick to] *one's* purpose / 목적을 정하다 set up a purpose; erect an aim 《for *oneself*》/ 목적을 이루지 못하다 miss *one's* object [purpose]
▶ 그는 목적을 위해서는 수단방법을 가리지 않았다 He would use any means [do anything] to achieve his end.
▶ 나는 어떤 희생을 치르더라도 나의 목적을 달성할 작정이다 I will accomplish my purpose at any cost.
▶ 내년에는 어떤 일이 있더라도 대학에 들어가기로 한 목적을 달성하고 싶다 By all means I wish to achieve my goal of entering the university next year.
〈목적에〉 목적에 맞다 answer [fit, be fit for] the purpose; suit *one's* end [purpose]; serve *one's* purpose / 목적에 맞지 않다 be unfit for [inappoite to] the purpose
〈목적으로〉 나는 야생동물의 연구를 주된 목적으로 하고 있다 Wildlife is the main object [subject] of my study.
▶ 그는 한국의 역사를 연구할 목적으로 한국에 왔다 He came to Korea with the intention [with the aim, for the purpose] of studying Korean history.
▶ 국제 협력은 국가간의 상호 이해를 증진시키는 것을 목적으로 한다 International cooperation is aimed at increasing mutual understanding among nations.
▶ 너는 무슨 목적으로 이런 짓을 했니? What is your purpose in doing this?
─목적하다 aim at; have *sth* as [for] *one's* object
▶ 내가 목적한 마을에 도착하기 전에 날이 저물었다 Night had fallen before I reached the village which was my destination.
■ 주― the [*one's*] central aim ■―격《文法》the objective case ■―론 《哲》teleology ―물 the object; the objective; the aim; the goal; the game ―세 an object tax ―어 an object (to a verb)

목적의식 目的意識 a sense of purpose
▶ 그는 뚜렷한 목적의식도 없이 그 운동에 가담했다 He joined the movement without any clear sense of purpose [reason for doing so].

목적지 目的地 *one's* destination; the end of *one's* journey
◆ 목적지에 도달하다 arrive at *one's* destination; reach the end of *one's* journey

목전 目前 ◆ 목전의 before [under] *one's* eyes; immediate / 목전의 위험 an imminent [impending] danger / 목전의 이익만을 꾀하다 be after immediate profit [quick profits]; seek [look to] immediate gain; take a short-sighted policy / 목전의 이익에 눈이 멀다 be blinded by the desire for immediate gain
〈목전에〉 목전에 before [under] *one's* eyes; in *one's* presence / 목전에 닥치다 be close [near] at hand; be imminent; be just ahead /

시험[선거]을 목전에 두고 with the examination [election] close at hand
▶ 크리스마스가 목전에 다가왔다 Christmas is near [close] at hand. ⇒ Christmas is just around the corner.
▶ 그의 죽음이 목전에 닥쳐왔다 Death stared him in the face.
〈목전에서〉 목전에서 일어난 사건 an event which took place [happened] under *one's* eyes / …의 목전에서 in (the) face of…; in the presence of…
▶ 사고는 그의 목전에서 일어났다 The accident took place under his (very) nose [right before his eyes].
▶ 그는 그것을 내 목전에서 했다 He did it under my very eyes [nose].

목정 木精 methanol ⇨ 메탄올
목젖 the uvula 《*pl.* ~s, -lae》
목제 木製 wooden structure
◆ 목제의 wooden; made of wood
▶ 이것은 목제 책상이다 This desk is made of wood. ─품 wooden articles; wood products; woodwork

목조 木造 wooden construction [structure]
◆ 목조의 wooden; 《a house》 built of wood
▶ 그의 집은 목조로 지었다 His house is built [made] of wood
■ ―가옥[건물] a wooden house [building]; a frame house ―선 a wooden vessel ―인형 a wooden doll

목조르기 〔레슬링〕 《have》 a stranglehold 《on an opponent》
목줄 〔낚시〕 a snell; a leader
목질 木質 ◆ 목질의 woody; ligneous
■ ―부 the woody parts 《of a plant》 ―섬유 wood(y) fiber ―조직 woody tissue ―화 lignification : 목질화하다 lignify
목찌르다 stab *sb* in the throat; jab [pierce] *sb's* neck 《with a knife》
▶ 그녀를 목찌른 사람은 그녀의 전남편이었다 Her ex-husband stabbed her in the throat.
목차 目次 (a table of) contents
▶ 이 책에는 목차가 없다 This book has no table of contents.
목책 木柵 a wooden barricade [fence]
목청 1〈성대〉 the vocal c(h)ords [bands]
◆ 목청을 울리다 vibrate the vocal chords
2〈목소리〉a (tone of) voice
◆ 목청껏 at the top of *one's* voice [lungs]; at the pitch of *one's* voice / 목청이 나쁘다 have a poor voice / 목청을 돋우다 raise [lift up] *one's* voice; raise *one's* pitch / 목청이 좋다 have a sweet [pleasant, lovely] voice
▶ 그는 목청껏 그녀의 이름을 불렀다 He called her name at the top of his lungs.
▶ 그녀는 자기의 목청을 자랑한다 She is proud of her voice. ⇒ She boasts of her singing voice.

목초 牧草 grass; pasture; pasturage
목축 牧畜 cattle breeding; stockbreeding; stock farming; livestock farming; raising animals; ranching
─목축하다 raise [rear] cattle; ranch
■ ―시대 the pastoral age [stage] ―지대 cat-

목축업 牧畜業 stock raising; (live)stock farming; cattle breeding
♦목축업을 하다 raise cattle; engage in stock farming; practice cattle breeding; (美) run a ranch
▶이 지방은 목축업이 성하다 Cattle breeding is a big business in this area.
━업자 a stock farmer [raiser]; a cattle breeder; (美) a rancher; a cattleman; a stockman

목측 目測 eye measurement
━목측하다 measure with the eye [by (the) eye]
▶우리는 건물과 건물 사이의 거리를 목측했다 We measured the distance between those buildings with the eye.
━━거리 distance measured with the eye

목침 木枕 a wooden pillow

목탁 木鐸 1〔佛敎〕a temple block; a (Buddhist monk's) wooden gong [drum]
♦목탁을 두드리다 strike a wooden drum (used in a Buddhist temple); sound [beat] a temple block
2 〈사람이나 기관〉 a guide of the public; a leader
♦사회의 목탁인 신문 the press that should lead the public / 사회의 목탁이 되는 사람들 leaders of public opinion

목탄 木炭 〈숯〉charcoal;〈데생용의〉(a pencil of) charcoal; fusain
■━가스 charcoal gas ━지 charcoal paper ━화 a charcoal drawing; a fusain

목판 木板 〈그릇〉a wooden platter [tray]; a trencher;〈널조각〉a board; a plank

목판 木版 a (printing) block; a wood (printing) plate; an engraving block
♦목판 인쇄의 block-printed 《cards》 / 목판으로 인쇄하다 make a print from a wood block
━본 a block [xylographic] book ━술 (wood-)block printing; xylography; wood engraving ━화 a (wood)cut; a (wood-)block print

목표 目標 1〈표지〉a mark; a sign; a landmark;〈길잡이〉a guide
▶우체국을 목표로 하여 이 거리를 똑바로 가시오 Go straight on this street with the post office for your guide.
▶그 근처에 뭔가 목표로 삼을 만한 것이 있느냐? Is there any landmark near there?
▶우리는 남극을 목표로 하여 항해했다 We sailed toward the Antarctic.
2 〈표적〉a target; a mark
♦쉬운 공격 목표 an easy target for attack; (口) a sitting duck / 좋은 목표가 되다 present a fine target 《for》
3 〈목적〉a goal, a target; an aim; an object; an objective;〈표준〉(a) standard
♦학습의 목표 the aim of a lesson / 살아가는 목표가 되는 것 have sth to live for / 인생의 목표를 정하다 set one's goal in life / 목표를 높게 세우다 aim high; set one's sight high / 목표에 도달하다 reach the goal / 목표에 미달하다 be short of the goal
▶우리 팀은 우승을 목표로 하고 있다 Our team aims to win the championship.
▶나는 1년간 500만원을 목표로 하여 저금하고 있다 I am saving with the goal of putting aside five million won a year.
━목표하다 aim at; have sth as [for] one's object
━군사━ a military target ━연도 the goal year ━일〈계획 등의〉a target date [day] ━지점〔軍〕the target spot; the objective point ━탑〈비행장의〉a pylon

목표액 目標額 a target figure
♦목표액에 달하다 reach the targeted level; realize [hit] the target / 목표액을 돌파하다 pass [exceed] the target [targeted level]
▶기부금은 2백만원의 목표액에 달하지 않았다 Contributions did not reach the target of [come up to the targeted] two million won.
━수출━ an export target 월생산━ the target for monthly output

목하 目下 now; at present; currently; presently
▶그렇게 하는 것이 목하의 급선무다 It is an urgent necessity of the day [a pressing need of the hour] to do so.
▶목하의 상태로는 우리는 성공할 수 없을 것이다 We shall not be able to succeed in the present condition [under these circumstances, as things stand now].
▶목하 그것의 수요는 많다 There is a great demand for it at present [now].

목향 木香 〔植〕an elecampane

목형 木型 a wooden model; a wooden pattern
♦구두의 목형 a (shoemaker's) last / 모자의 목형 a block

목화 木花 〔植〕a cotton plant; raw cotton; cotton wool
♦목화 따는 사람 a cotton picker / 목화를 따다 pick cotton (from a cotton plant) / 목화를 틀다 gin cotton
■━꽃 a cotton flower ━다래 a cotton boll ━씨 a cottonseed ━재배 cotton growing ━지대 a cotton belt

몫 a portion; a share;〈할당〉an allotment;〈할당액〉a quota; (俗) a whack; (美口) a cut; (美俗) a split;〔數〕the quotient 《略 q.》
♦자기 몫 one's share; one's winnings / 자기의 몫을 받다 get one's share; receive one's quota / 자기의 몫을 요구하다 claim one's share (in the profit) / 자기의 몫을 치르다 pay one's share / 세 몫으로 나누다 divide [split] into three portions / A의 몫으로 남겨두다 reserve [leave aside] (sth) for A / 한 몫 끼다 have [take] a (one's) share (in); come in for a share (of) / 남의 몫까지 먹다 eat another's part [portion] as well as one's own
▶재산 중에서 그의 몫은 많았다[적었다] His portion [share] of the property was large [small]. ⇌ He received a large [small] share of the estate.
▶그 몫이 적다면 좀더 생각해 드리겠습니다 If you are not satisfied with your share, I'll make it a bit more attractive.
▶나에게도 내 몫을 주시오 Please give me my

share, too.
▶각자 제몫을 받았다 A share was allotted to each.
▶이것이 네 몫이다 This is your share (of it).
▶당연히 나도 이익 배당에 한 몫 끼기로 되어 있다 Naturally I'll have [take] a share in the profits, too.

몫몫이 into shares [portions]; each [every] share [portion]
♦(공평하게) 몫몫이 나누다 divide 《the profits》 into (equal) shares [portions]; allot shares (equally) / 몫몫이 차지하다 take each *one's* own share; take *one's* respective shares
▶우리는 그 돈을 몫몫이 나누었다 We divided the money equally [into equal parts]. ⇌ We got even shares of the money.

몬로비아 〈라이베리아의 수도〉 Monrovia
몬순 〔氣〕 a monsoon
━━지대 a monsoon climate
몬태나주 ━州 〈미국 북서부의〉 Montana (略 Mont.); 〈속칭〉 the Treasure State
몬테비데오 〈우루과이의 수도〉 Montevideo
몬트리올 〈캐나다 남동부에 있는 최대도시〉 Montreal
━━시민 a Montrealer

몰¹ 〔化〕 a mol(e); a gram molecule
몰² 〔《포》 mogol〕 lace; lacing; braid
♦금[은]몰 gold [silver] lace [braid] / 금몰이 달린 상의 a coat braided with gold lace [braid]

몰각 沒却 〈무시〉 disregard; ignoring; 〈없애 버림〉 effacement
━━몰각하다 〈무시하다〉 disregard; ignore; forget; 〈없애버리다〉 efface
♦개성을 몰각하다 suppress *one's* individuality / 당초의 목적을 몰각하다 forget [lose sight of] *one's* original object
▶나는 자아를 몰각하려고 애썼다 I tried to efface my (concept of) self.
▶법의 정신이 몰각되어 있다 The spirit of the law is ignored.

몰골 unshapely figure [features]
♦몰골 사나운 차림새 unsightly appearance; a shabby dress / 몰골 사나운, 몰골스러운 unshapely; unseemly; unsightly; shapeless; ungainly; clumsy; ugly; offensive to the eye / 몰골이 초라하다 cut [make] a poor [sorry] figure / 몰골 사나운 복장을 하다 be shabbily dressed (in)
▶나는 이런 몰골로는 남 앞에 나설 수가 없다 I am not fit to be seen.

몰교섭 沒交涉 **1** 〈무관계〉 lack of relations
▶그는 사회와는 몰교섭이다 He stands [keeps, holds] aloof from the world.
▶그의 인생은 예술하고는 몰교섭이었다 His life had nothing to do with art.
▶국민 감정과는 몰교섭으로 정치 공작이 이루어지고 있다 Political maneuvering is being carried on regardless [quite independently] of the people's feelings.
━━몰교섭하다 have nothing to do (with); have no relation [connection] 《with》
2 〈불간섭〉 noninterference; nonintervention
━━몰교섭하다 do not interfere [intervene]

(in); do not meddle 《in, with》

몰년 沒年 〈나이〉 *one's* age at death; 〈해〉 the year of *sb's* death
▶그의 몰년은 1990년이었다 He died in 1990.

몰다 1 〈마소·차 등을〉 drive; spur
♦말을 몰다 drive [urge] a horse forward [on]; spur a horse (on) / 차를 몰다 drive a car / 소를 시장으로 몰고가다 drive the cattle to market / 차를 몰고 현장으로 급히 가다 rush [hasten] in a car to the scene 《of the murder》 / 차를 몰고 시내를 돌아다니다 ride about the city (streets) in a motorcar; drive about the town
2 〈쫓다〉 chase [pursue] (after); give chase to; run after; hunt out
♦여우를 몰다 run [chase, hunt out] a fox / 물고기떼를 그물로 몰다 chase a school of fish into a net
3 〈내쫓다〉 drive away; hunt away [out]
4 〈궁지로〉 drive [chase] (into); corner
♦궁지로 몰다 corner *sb*; drive *sb* into a corner ⇨ 몰아넣다 2
▶그는 친구를 궁지로 몰았다 He drove his friend into a corner [to the wall].
5 〈죄인 등으로〉 impute (to); accuse (of); charge 《with》; lay (on); brand (as); call
♦사람을 역적으로 몰다 denounce [brand] *sb* as a traitor / 살인죄로 몰다 accuse *sb* of murder; charge *sb* with murder / 도둑으로 몰다 call *sb* a thief

몰두 沒頭 devotion (to); absorption (in); immersion (in)
━━몰두하다 devote *oneself* (to); be devoted (to); be immersed (in); immerse *oneself* [be absorbed [lost, engrossed] (in); give *oneself* up [over] entirely 《to》; bury *oneself* [be buried] 《in *one's* work》
♦독서에 몰두하다 spend all *one's* time reading; devote all *one's* time to reading
▶지금은 이 일에 몰두하고 있습니다 I am wholly immersed in this business at present.
▶그는 바이러스 생태 연구에 몰두했다 He devoted himself to the research of the virus behavior.
▶그는 무서운 열의로 그 일에 몰두했다 He plunged into the work with a dreadful zest.
▶그는 자극적인 얘기에 몰두했었다 He was engrossed in the exciting story.

몰디브 〈나라 이름〉 Maldives; 〈공식명〉 the Republic of Maldives
♦몰디브의 Maldivian ━━사람 a Maldivian

몰라보다 cannot [fail to] recognize; show no appreciation of 《the kindness》; fail to appreciate
♦친구를 몰라보다 fail to recognize *one's* friend; neglect [disregard] *one's* friend / 노고를 몰라보다 fail to appreciate *sb's* trouble
▶그녀는 몰라볼 만큼 우아해졌다 She has become elegant beyond recognition.
▶할머니는 몰라볼 만큼 야위었다 My grandmother had become so thin (that) I could hardly recognize her.
▶그는 내가 첫눈에 몰라볼 만큼 컸다 He had grown so tall that I could hardly recognize

몰락

▶ 너 몰라볼 만큼 변했구나 You have changed almost beyond recognition. ⇌ You have changed so much that I hardly recognized [knew] you.

▶ 오랫동안 뵙지 못했기 때문에 몰라보았습니다 I haven't seen you for so long (that) I can hardly recognize you.

몰락 沒落 〈파멸〉 fall; ruin; collapse; downfall; wreck; 〈파산〉 bankruptcy
♦ 로마 제국의 몰락 the fall of the Roman Empire / 탄광업의 몰락 the decline of the coal-mining industry

▶ 그 사건은 그의 가족의 몰락을 초래했다 The incident brought about the ruin of his family.
—하다 fall; be ruined; go to ruin; be wrecked; 〈파산하다〉 become [go] bankrupt
♦ 몰락한 귀족 ruined peers / 몰락시키다 bring [reduce] to ruin; put the skids under [on]

▶ 그는 몰락하여 거지꼴이 되었다 He was reduced to no better than beggary.

▶ 혁명 후 귀족계급은 몰락했다 After the revolution, the aristocracy lost their status.

▶ 그렇게 번영을 누린 왕국도 결국 몰락했다 Even the prosperous kingdom eventually collapsed [fell].

몰래 stealthily; secretly; by stealth; on the quiet [sly]; in secret; quietly; privately
♦ 몰래 도망치다[떠나다] sneak away (from) / 몰래 만나다 meet sb in secret; have a clandestine meeting; meet secretly / 몰래 방에 들어가다 slip into the room / 몰래 뒤를 밟다 shadow sb stealthily / 몰래 보다 cast stealthy glances (on); steal a look [a glance] (at) / 몰래 빠져나가다 sneak out; slip away / 몰래 알려주다 tell sb secretly (about sth); (口) tip sb off (that..., about sth) / 몰래 조사하다 spy out (the land) / 몰래 결혼식을 올리다 have a quiet wedding / 몰래 좋은 일을 하다 do [perform] good deeds anonymously

▶ 그는 수업중에 몰래 소설을 읽고 있었다 He was secretly reading a novel in class.

▶ 그 소년은 부모 몰래 담배를 피웠다 The boy had a smoke when his parents were out of sight.

▶ 그는 창문으로 몰래 빠져 나갔다 He stole out through the window.

몰려가다 1 〈쫓겨가다〉 be driven [pursued, chased]
♦ 구석으로 몰려가다 be driven into a corner
2 〈떼지어가다〉 throng (into) (a place); storm (a theater); go in groups

▶ 휴가가 시작되면 사람들은 산과 바다로 몰려간다 People flock to mountains and beaches when vacation starts.

▶ 승객들은 문으로 몰려갔다 The passengers thronged toward the doors.

몰려나다 1 〈쫓겨나다〉 be driven [turned, put, sent, expelled] out; (俗) be booted out; 〈직장에서〉 be ousted [dislodged] (from a position); 〈셋집 등에서〉 be ejected [evicted] (from a rented house)
♦ 동네에서 몰려나다 be driven out of one's village / 클럽에서 몰려나다 be expelled from the club
2 〈떼지어 나가다〉 go out in groups [crowds, flocks, swarms]; turn out en masse; sally forth

▶ 사람들이 홀에서 몰려났다 People swarmed out of the hall.

몰려다니다 1 〈쫓겨다니다〉 be chased about; be driven round [about]
2 〈떼지어 다니다〉 walk in groups [crowds, flocks, swarms]; throng about [round]

▶ 아이들이 몰려다니며 놀고 있었다 Children were playing about in groups.

▶ 호랑이는 몰려다니지 않는다 Tigers do not herd together.

▶ 이리는 먹이를 찾아 몰려다닌다 Wolves hunt in large packs.

몰려들다 1 〈쫓겨 들어오다〉 be driven [pursued, chased] into
2 〈떼지어 들어들다〉 come in groups; storm (a store); crowd; swarm (about in the park); cluster; throng (into a room, to see a play); gather (around a campfire); pile into (a house); flock (together)
♦ 극장으로 몰려들다 flock in a theater / 해안으로 몰려들다 flock to the seaside

▶ 행진을 보기 위해 많은 사람이 몰려들었다 A crowd of people flocked to see the parade.

▶ 소녀들은 그 영화배우 주위로 서명을 받으려고 몰려들었다 The girls crowded [swarmed] around the movie star (asking) for autographs.

▶ 군중은 교회로 몰려들어 갔다 The crowd poured into the church.

▶ 그곳에는 여름에 많은 사람들이 몰려든다 In summer the place attracts many visitors.

몰려오다 1 〈쫓겨오다〉 come driven [chased, pursued] (back)
2 〈떼지어 오다〉 come in groups [crowds, flocks]; come en masse
♦ 몰려오는 the surging enemy / 개미떼처럼 몰려오다 come on in great [overwhelming] numbers / 우르르 몰려오다 storm [stampede] (a place); come swarming about / 주말에 시골로 몰려오다 flock to [pour into] the country for the weekend

▶ 소녀들이 극장에 많이 몰려왔다 There was a great rush of girls into [Girls crowded] the theater.

▶ 최근에 철새들이 시베리아에서 몰려오기 시작했다 Flocks [Flights] of migratory birds from Siberia began to reach here recently.

▶ 경주로 관광객이 몰려왔다 Kyŏngju was deluged with tourists.

몰로토프 칵테일 (俗) a Molotov cocktail

몰리다 1 〈쫓기다〉 be chased [pursued] (after); be trailed [hunted up]

▶ 몹시 몰리다 be heavily pursued

▶ 도둑이 몰려서 방으로 뛰어들었다 The hunted robber rushed into a room.
2 〈한 곳으로〉 come [get] together; gather [flock] (together); crowd; swarm; cluster; throng
♦ 난로 주위에 몰리다 draw (together) around fireplace

▶ 청중은 방 한쪽에 몰려 앉아있었다 The audience had clustered on one side of the room.
3 〈일 등에〉 be pressed; be driven; be pushed
♦ 일과에 몰리다 be overtasked [too busy] with one's daily work / 〈바둑에서〉 초읽기에 몰리다 be pressed by countdown
▶ 그는 일에 몰리고 있다 He is pressed with work. ⇌ He is very busy with work.
4 〈궁지에〉 be driven into a corner; be cornered; be pushed to the wall; be placed in a fix; be [stand] at bay; 〈궁해지다〉 be hard up; be pressed for 《money》; 〈난처해지다〉 be at a loss for; be driven to one's wit's end
♦ 대답에 몰리다 be embarrassed [be at a loss] for an answer / 돈에 몰리다 be pinched [pressed, hard up] for money
▶ 그는 궁지에 몰렸다 He was driven into a corner [to the wall]. ⇌ He was in a fix.
5 〈죄인 등으로〉 be charged with; be accused of; be blamed for
♦ 살인죄로 몰리어 on a charge of murder / 간통죄로 몰리다 be charged with adultery / 역적으로 몰리다 be accused of [charged with] treason; be arraigned for treason

몰리브덴 〈〈(독) Molybdän〉 [化] molybdenum ■—강(鋼) molybdenum steel —광 molybdenite
몰리에르 〈프랑스의 극작가〉 Molière (1622-73)
몰매 beating in a group ⇨ 뭇매
몰바이데도법 —圖法 [地] Mollweide projection
몰부피 [化] molar volume
몰분율 —分率 [化] mole fraction
몰비열 —比熱 [物] molar (specific) heat
몰사 沒死 extinction; annihilation; dying out
—몰사하다 become extinct; be annihilated; wipe out; die to the last man
▶ 전염병으로 마을 주민들이 몰사했다 The plague wiped out all the villagers [annihilated the whole (population of the) village].
몰살 沒殺 〈대학살〉 annihilation; (a) massacre; extermination; 〈무차별 학살〉 (a) total slaughter; a wholesale murder
—몰살하다 kill to a man; kill out; massacre; exterminate; annihilate; wipe out
♦ 온 가족을 몰살하다 kill [murder] the whole family / 적을 몰살하다 annihilate the enemy
▶ 그 부락민은 몰살당했다 The whole villager was massacred.
몰상식 沒常識 lack of common sense; senselessness; thoughtlessness; absurdity
—몰상식하다 senseless; absurd; thoughtless; have no [lack] common sense
♦ 아주 몰상식한 utterly absurd; ridiculous
▶ 그 사람은 몰상식하다 He has no common sense. ⇌ He is wanting in [lacks] common sense.
▶ 그런 행동은 몰상식한 짓이다 It is senseless to behave like that.
▶ 그런 이야기를 하다니 몰상식하구나 It is absurd of you to say such a thing.
몰수 沒收 confiscation; 〈벌로서의〉 forfeiture; 〈압수〉 seizure
—몰수하다 confiscate; impound; seize; 〈징발하다〉 commandeer; requisition
♦ 몰수당하다 be confiscated; forfeit
▶ 세금을 내지 않아서 당국은 그의 집을 몰수했다 The authorities confiscated his house because he had not paid the tax.
▶ 보건 당국은 그 식품을 몰수했다 The health authorities seized the food.
■—게임 a forfeited game —자 a seizor; a confiscator —품 a confiscated article [property]; a forfeit; a forfeiture
몰식자 沒食子 a gall; a gallnut
몰씬하다 soft ⇨ 물씬하다
몰아 one and all; in a body; (all) in all; all together; en masse; in a lump; in the aggregate; collectively ♦ 몰아 사다 buy up all; buy in bulk / (돈을) 몰아 지급하다 pay in a lump sum [in one sum]
▶ 나는 두 달치 월급을 몰아 받았다 I received two-months' pay in a lump.
▶ 그들을 몰아서 비난할 수는 없다 You cannot blame them indiscriminately.
몰아 沒我 selflessness; self-effacement; self-renunciation; self-oblivion
♦ 몰아적(인) self-effacing; disinterested; selfless / 몰아의 경지에 이르다 rise above self
▶ 그는 몰아의 경지에 이른 사람이다 He has got to the self-effacing way of living.
몰아가다 1 〈몰고 가다〉 drive (away)
♦ 소를 풀밭으로 몰아가다 drive cattle (out) to the pasture
▶ 바람이 구름을 몰아갔다 The wind drove clouds along [along].
2 〈휩쓸어 가다〉 take away in a lump [in bulk, by the gross, in one lot, en masse]; buy (things) in a mass [lot]; buy up; sweep away
♦ 시장의 밀을 몰아가다 corner the stock of wheat on the market
▶ 그들은 오늘 공연 입장권을 다 몰아갔다 They have bought up all the tickets for today's performance.
몰아내다 1 〈내쫓다〉 put [get, turn, drive] sb out; kick [throw] sb out; 〈지위에서〉 oust [expel] 《sb from a position》; 〈해고하다〉 fire; dismiss; discharge; (口) sack; (口) give sb the sack; 〈셋집 등에서〉 eject [evict] 《a tenant》 from 《the house》 (▶eject는 힘으로, evict는 법적 수단으로)
♦ 왕위에서 몰아내다 dethrone (a king) / 적군을 나라에서 몰아내다 expel the enemy from the country / 집에서 몰아내다 turn sb out of doors; show the door / 마음에서 나쁜 생각을 몰아내다 purge the mind of false notions
▶ 경찰은 시위 학생들을 몰아냈다 The policeman drove the demonstrating students away.
▶ 그는 집세를 내지 않았다는 이유로 세든 사람을 몰아냈다 He evicted his tenant for not paying the rent.
2 〈사냥에서〉 hunt out [up]; chase (out) 《a fox》; run (a hare) (down)
♦ 여우를 굴에서 몰아내다 draw a fox from its lair
▶ 사냥개가 숲에서 사슴을 몰아냈다 The hound chased a deer out of the bush.
몰아넣다 1 〈안으로〉 drive [chase, push] in

몰아대다

[into]
♦ 양을 우리 안으로 몰아넣다 drive the sheep into an enclosure / 여우를 굴 속으로 몰아넣다 pursue a fox into it's earth / 죄수를 노역장으로 몰아넣다 drive [push] prisoners into a workhouse [labor house]
▶ 나는 소를 우리에 몰아넣었다 I drove the cattle into a corral.
▶ 경찰관은 용의자를 막다른 골목으로 몰아넣었다 The policeman drove the suspect into a blind alley.
2 〈궁지에〉 corner *sb*; get [drive] *sb* into a (tight) corner; drive [push, put] into a corner; (口) put *sb* in a fix [hole]
♦ 그녀는 그를 궁지에 몰아넣었다 She cornered him. ⇒ She drove him into a corner.
3 〈휩쓸어〉 put [push, press] all into (a place)
♦ 가방에 옷가지를 몰아넣다 cram [squeeze] all the clothes into a suitcase / 국민을 전쟁으로 몰아넣다 drive [urge] the nation to war
▶ 작은 교실에 학생 50명을 몰아넣었다 Fifty students were crammed [jammed, packed] into the small classroom.

몰아대다 1 〈막 해대다〉 take [call, bring] *sb* to task; give *sb* a setdown; press *sb* close; denounce; blame; criticize
♦ 직무태만으로 몰아대다 reproach [denounce, scold] *sb* for neglect of duty
▶ 그녀는 내가 저녁 식사에 늦었다고 몰아댔다 She reproached me for being late for dinner.
▶ 그들은 즉각적인 답변을 요구하며 나를 몰아댔다 They drew closer [nearer] to me, demanding my immediate answer.
2 〈재촉하다〉 hasten; hurry (up); press; urge on ♦ 일을 몰아대다 press *sb* with work [to speed up the work]/ 꾼 돈을 갚으라고 몰아대다 press *sb* to repay a loan
▶ 사냥꾼은 말을 몰아댔다 The hunter urged his horse on.
▶ 좀 몰아대지 마라 Stop pushing me!

몰아들이다 1 〈안으로〉 drive in [into]
♦ 목장의 소를 몰아들이다 round up the cattle on the range
2 〈휩쓸어〉 take all in a mass [in bulk]; buy up in a lot [mass]
♦ 시장의 쌀[장작]을 몰아들이다 buy up all the rice [firewood] on the market

몰아붙이다 1 〈한쪽으로 몰다〉 push [press, thrust] all to one side
♦ 책상을 방 구석으로 몰아붙이다 move the desk into the corner of the room
▶ 나는 장난감들을 옆으로 몰아붙이고 그에게 앉을 자리를 마련해 줬다 I moved the toys aside and made room for him to sit down.
2 〈한 군데에 붙이다〉 stick [put] all in one place ♦ 그림을 벽 오른쪽에 몰아붙이다 hang all pictures on the right side of a wall

몰아세우다 censure [reproach] *sb* severely [roundly]; scold away; rate *sb* roundly; take *sb* roundly to task; (口) blow up; 〈재촉하다〉 urge [press] (*sb* to do)
♦ 몰아세워 고백하게 하다 squeeze [extort] a confession from *sb* / 대답하라고 몰아세우다 press *sb* for an answer / 빚을 갚으라고 몰아세우다 storm at *sb* for the payment of a debt / 약속을 어겼다고 몰아세우다 call *sb* to account for breaking his promise
▶ 주위 사람들은 여러가지 날카로운 질문으로 그를 몰아세웠다 He was tortured with a lot of sharp questions from those around him.

몰아오다 1 〈자동사적〉 〈한꺼번에 오다〉 come all at once [one time]; come all together
▶ 오랜 가뭄 끝에 폭우가 몰아왔다 We had a downpour [There was a heavy rain] all at one time after a long spell of dry weather.
2 【타동사적】 〈끌고 오다〉 drive [pursue, chase] along; 〈휩쓸어 오다〉 bring [take] the whole lot
▶ 폭풍이 마을에 소나기를 몰아왔다 The storm brought a shower along to the village.
▶ 그는 헌책방의 만화책을 모두 몰아왔다 He bought up all the comic books in a secondhand bookstore.

몰아치다 1 〈몰려 닥치다〉 rush [make] for; 〈비바람이〉 storm; 〈파도가〉 surge [beat, rush] (on)
▶ 눈이 몰아쳤다 It was snowing thick and fast.
▶ 어제는 온종일 비바람이 몰아쳤다 It stormed all day yesterday.
▶ 바람이 몰아쳐 눈이 흩날려 쌓이고 있다 The wind is so strong that it is drifting the snow.
2 〈한 곳으로 몰다〉 drive [chase] to (a place); 〈궁지에 빠뜨리다〉 drive [push, thrust] *sb* to the wall; press 《a criminal》 hard [close]
3 〈한꺼번에 하다〉 do at [with] a (single) swoop; do [work] all at once; do at one sweep [try]
♦ 밀린 일을 몰아쳐서 해치우다 dispose of a backlog of work in a big push / 시험 공부를 몰아치서 하다 cram [get crammed] for an examination
▶ 학생들은 학기말 시험 공부를 몰아쳐서 하고 있다 The students are cramming for the terminal examination.
▶ 질문을 너무 이것저것 몰아쳐서 하지 마라 Don't ask too many questions at a time.

몰액화열 —液化熱 〔化〕 molar heat of liquefaction

몰염치 沒廉恥 shamelessness
—**몰염치하다** shameless; impudent; have no shame ♦ **몰염치하게도** …하다 have the impudence to do

몰융해열 —融解熱 〔化〕 molar heat of fusion
몰응고열 —凝固熱 〔化〕 molar heat of solidification

몰이 〈사냥의〉 chasing; running; hunting
♦ 멧돼지 몰이를 하다 hunt down [out] wild boars
—**몰이하다** chase; beat; run 《a hare》 (down); hunt out [down]
■ —**꾼** a beater; a chaser —**포수** a chaser; a hunter

몰이해 沒理解 lack of understanding [sympathy]; nonunderstanding
▶ 장애자에 대한 사회의 몰이해는 시정되지 않

으면 안된다 Society's lack of understanding [sympathy] toward(s) the handicapped must be corrected.
▶ 양국민 간의 상호 몰이해가 전쟁을 유발했다 Lack of mutual understanding between the two nations caused the war.
―몰이해하다 lacking in understanding; unsympathetic; unfeeling

몰인정 沒人情 want of sympathy; unkindness; inhumanity; heartlessness
―몰인정하다 〈불친절한〉 unkind; 〈냉담한〉 coldhearted; 〈무정한〉 heartless; 〈동정심이 없는〉 unsympathetic; stonyhearted; inhuman; pitiless
♦ 몰인정한 사람 a hard-hearted [an unsympathetic] person; a heartless [an unfeeling] person; a man cold as a stone / 몰인정한 짓을 하다 do a cruel thing; behave callously
▶ 그 사람은 몰인정해 He has no sympathy for us.
▶ 그것은 참으로 몰인정한 처사로구나 What an unkind treatment it is!
▶ 나는 그런 몰인정한 짓은 할 수가 없다 I'm not heartless enough to do that.
▶ 그런 몰인정한 소리 하지 마라 Don't talk so cruelly.
▶ 몰인정하게 굴지 않도록 해라 I advise you not to behave in a heartless manner.

몰입 沒入 1 〈몰두〉 immersion; absorption; devotion
―몰입하다 be immersed [absorbed] in 《one's work》; get oneself absorbed in 《one's study》
▶ 그는 자기 일[그 신나는 이야기]에 몰입해 있었다 He was engrossed [absorbed, immersed] in his work [the exciting story].
▶ 나는 사색에 몰입해 있었다 I was lost in thought.
2 〈몰수〉 confiscation; seizure
―몰입하다 confiscate; seize; forfeit

몰잇그물 어법 ―漁法 〔水産〕 drive-in net method

몰증발열 ―蒸發熱 〔化〕 molar heat of evaporation

몰지각 沒知覺 indiscretion; thoughtlessness
―몰지각하다 indiscreet; thoughtless; senseless; ill-advised
▶ 몰지각하게도 그는 그 돈을 받았다 He had the indiscretion to accept the money.

몰취미 沒趣味 lack of taste; tastelessness
―몰취미하다 tasteless; out of taste; uninteresting; prosaic; dry (as dust)
♦ 몰취미한 사람 a man of no taste; a man who has no interests; a prosaic man / 몰취미한 생활 a commonplace [vapid] life; a prosaic life
▶ 그는 몰취미한 사람이다 He has no particular hobbies. ⇌ He is a man of no tastes.

몰타 〈나라이름〉 Malta; 〈공식명〉 the Republic of Malta ♦ 몰타의 Maltese
■ ―사람 a Maltese

몰토 〔樂〕 molto

몰하다 歿― 〈죽다〉 die; pass away; perish
▶ 나폴레옹은 1821년에 몰했다 Napoleon died in 1821.

몰후 歿後 after *one's* death ⇨ 사후(死後)
▶ 베토벤 몰후 약 170년이 되었다 Some 170 years have passed since Beethoven died.

몸 1 〈신체〉 the body (▶ 넓은 의미로는 몸 전체를, 좁은 의미로는 머리와 수족을 제외한 몸통을 뜻하며 종종 정신·혼과 대비해서 씀); 〈몸집·체격〉 build (▶ 남녀 모두에 씀); physique (▶ 주로 남성에 씀); a figure (▶ 주로 여성의 체형에 씀); 〈골격〉 frame; 〈체질〉 constitution; 〈신장〉 stature; 〈크기〉 size
♦ 좋은 몸 a robust [fine] physique / 허약한 몸 a delicate constitution
〈몸의〉 bodily; physical (▶ bodily는 직접적으로 육체를 가리킴)
♦ 몸의 결함 a bodily [physical] defect / 몸의 구조 the bodily structure / 몸의 발달 physical development
▶ 그녀는 몸의 선이 아름답다 She is built with beautiful curves.
▶ 나는 지금 몸의 상태가 좋다[좋지 않다] I am in good [bad, poor] shape [health].
〈몸이〉 몸이 딱 벌어진 남자 a man of [with a] sturdy build (▶ with를 쓰는 것이 구어적); a sturdy man / 몸이 큰 남자 a man of large build / 몸이 건장한 남자 a man of robust build; a well-built man / 몸이 약한 사람 a person with a weak constitution / 몸이 가냘픈 slim-figured; thin; slender 《girl》 / 몸이 작은 small(-sized); short / 몸이 큰 large(-sized); big-bodied; of imposing [large] figure / 몸이 튼튼하다[약하다] have a strong [weak] constitution / 몸이 나다[수척해지다] gain [lose] weight; put on [lose] flesh
▶ 그는 몸이 우람하다 He is (a man) of sturdy build. ⇌ He has a sturdy physique.
▶ 그 여자는 몸이 호리호리하다[뼈만 앙상하다] She has a slender figure [an angular frame].
▶ 그는 몸이 튼튼하고 건강하다 He has a strong and healthy body.
▶ 나는 몸이 나른하다 I feel tired and languid.
▶ 그 학생은 축구를 하기에는 몸이 너무 왜소하다 The student's build [physique] is too small for playing football.
▶ 그는 가족을 부양하기 위해 몸이 부서져라 일했다 He worked very hard [himself to the bone] to support his family.
▶ 나는 운동 후에는 온몸이 아프다 I ache all over after the exercises. ⇌ My whole body aches after the exercises.
▶ 몸이 두 개라도 모자랄 정도다 I am too busy even if I had two bodies. ⇌ If I cut myself into four quarters, they would not be sufficient.
▶ 적당한 운동을 하면 몸이 튼튼해질 것이다 Moderate exercise will give you a strong constitution.
▶ 몸이 나서 이젠 옷이 맞지 않는다 Since I gained weight, my clothing does not fit my body anymore.
▶ 그녀는 몸이 가냘퍼 그런 중노동에는 맞지 않았다 Her tender frame was not suited to the heavy work.
▶ 그 애는 몸이 어른이지만 생각하는 것은 아직 어린애 같다 Although he is physically grown

〈몸을〉 몸을 굽히다 〈앞쪽으로〉 lean forward; 〈창밖 등으로〉 lean out of 《the window》 / 몸을 꼿꼿이 세우다 hold *oneself* erect / 의자에 몸을 기대고 앉다 lean back in a chair / 몸을 씻다 wash *oneself* / 몸을 팔다 sell *oneself* 《into slavery》; 〈여자가〉 give *oneself* 《for money》; prostitute *oneself* 《for living》 / 몸을 편하게 하다 make *oneself* comfortable; ease *oneself* / 〈여자가〉 남자에게 몸을 허락하다 give *herself* to a man / 분노에 몸을 떨다 shake with anger
▶ 젊을 때 몸을 단련해라 Build up your body while young.
▶ 그 남자는 잔디밭에 몸을 쭉 펴고 누웠다 He stretched himself out on the lawn.
▶ 그들은 바위 뒤에 몸을 숨겼다 They hid (themselves) behind the rock.
▶ 전쟁 때 그는 나라를 지키기 위해 몸을 바쳤다 During the war he devoted himself to the defence of the country.
▶ 그녀는 몸을 던지듯이 침대에 누웠다 She threw herself down on the bed.
▶ 그녀는 그에게 몸을 허락하지 않았다 She refused to give herself to him [didn't let him sleep with her].
〈몸에〉 몸에 맞는 옷 well-fitting clothes / 온몸에 on all over (the body); from head to foot / 비싼 옷을 몸에 걸치다 wear expensive clothes; have [put] expensive clothes on
▶ 이 드레스는 그녀의 몸에 맞지 않는다 This dress doesn't fit her.
▶ 경찰은 근무 중에는 권총을 몸에 지니고 있어야 한다 A policeman on duty must carry a revolver (with him).
▶ 전화 벨이 울릴 때 그는 아무 것도[속옷 밖에는] 몸에 걸치고 있지 않았다 He had nothing [nothing but his underwear] on when the phone rang.
〈몸과〉 몸과 마음이 건전한 사람 a man of sound mind and body
▶ 그는 그 일에 몸과 마음을 바치고 있다 He devotes himself [his body and soul] to the work. ⇌ He is devoted to the work body and soul. (▶뒷 문장의 body and soul은 부사적)
2 〈몸통〉 the body; the trunk (of the body); 〈조각상 등의〉 the torso
♦ 여자 머리에 사자 몸을 가진 스핑크스 the sphinx with a woman's head and a lion's body
▶ 닥스훈트라는 개는 다리가 짧고 몸이 길다 The dog known as the dachshund has short legs and a long body.
3 〈건강〉 health; 〈몸의 상태〉 shape
〈몸이〉 몸이 튼튼한[허약한, 병약한] 아이 a healthy [delicate, sickly] child / 몸이 나빠지다 break down in health / 몸이 약해지다 become weak; be run down / 몸이 튼튼하다 be in robust health / 몸이 허약하다 be weak [poor] in health; have poor health / 몸이 좋아지다 get well; improve in health / 몸이 회복되다 be well [all right] again; be restored to health
▶ 그는 태어날 때부터 몸이 병약하다[허약하다] He has been sickly [in delicate health] from birth.
▶ 그 사고 후부터 그는 몸이 좋지 않다 He's not been (feeling) well since the accident.
▶ 하루 바삐 내 몸이 회복되었으면 좋겠다 I want to get better [recover my health] as soon as possible.
▶ 수면 부족으로 내 몸이 상하지 않을지 모르겠다 I'm afraid my health will break down from lack of sleep.
▶ 그래도 몸이 감당할 수 있겠니? Can you stand the strain?
〈몸을〉 몸을 조심하다 take (good) care of *oneself*; be careful about *one's* health / 몸을 상하다 injure [lose] *one's* health / 몸을 해치다 undermine *one's* constitution
▶ 그 남자는 과로로[과음으로] 몸을 망쳤다 He ruined [damaged, injured] his health from overwork [by drinking too much].
▶ 나는 더 이상 몸을 지탱할 수 없을 것 같다 I'm afraid I can't keep this up any longer.
〈몸에〉 몸에 나쁘다 be bad for the health; be unhealthful [unwholesome] / 몸에 좋다 be good for the [benefit *one's*] health; do *sb* good; be healthful [healthy, wholesome] / 몸에 해롭다 hurt [affect, ruin] *one's* health; do *sb* harm
▶ 적당한 운동은 몸에 좋다 Doing some exercise is good for the [our, your] health.
▶ 신선한 공기는 몸에 이롭다 The fresh air benefits you.
▶ 담배는 몸에 아주 해롭다 Smoking is fatal to the health.
▶ 밤샘은 몸에 해롭다 Staying up late is harmful to your health.
4 〈일신·자신〉 *oneself*; self; *one's* self
♦ 자유로운 몸이다 be a free man [woman]; be *one's* own master [mistress]
▶ 요즘엔 잠시도 몸이 편할 틈이 없다 I have not a minute to call my own these days.
▶ 나는 지진의 공포를 몸으로 체험했다 I experienced the terror of an earthquake personally.
〈몸을〉 몸을 담다 be employed in; work for / 몸을 던지다 throw *oneself* 《into a river》 / 몸을 두다 find shelter with ⇨ 몸두다 / 몸을 맡기다 give *oneself* up (to); place *oneself* at [put *oneself* into] *sb's* disposal / 몸을 숨기다 conceal [hide] *oneself*; tuck *oneself* away 《somewhere》 / 몸을 아끼다[사리다] spare *oneself* (the trouble) / 정계에 몸을 던지다 throw *oneself* [enter] into politics / 위험으로부터 몸을 지키다 protect *oneself* from [against] the danger
▶ 나는 삼촌 댁에 잠시 몸을 의탁했다 I stayed with my uncle for a while.
▶ 그는 도박으로 몸을 망쳤다 He ruined himself by gambling. ⇌ Gambling brought him to ruin [ruined him].
▶ 나는 몸을 아끼지 않고 일했다 I worked without sparing myself.
5 〈습관〉 ♦ 아직 몸에 배지 않은 기술 a half-learned skill / 몸에 익다[배다] be [get] used (to); grow [become] accustomed to 《a job, work》; grow familiar 《with》 / 교양을 몸에 익

히다 acquire culture / 기예를 몸에 익히다 master an art
▶ 외국어는 쉽사리 몸에 익혀지지 않는다 A foreign language is not easy to learn [master].
▶ 먹고 살 기술을 몸에 익혀 두어야 한다 You ought to acquire some art [skill] useful in making a living.
6 〈신분〉 one's social status; standing; 〈처지〉 one's circumstances; 〈자리〉 one's position [place]
◆ 귀하신 몸 a person of high rank; a distinguished [an important] figure / 노예[종]의 몸 the status as a slave / 천한 몸 a person of humble condition [birth, social standing] / 미천한 몸으로 출세하다 rise from obscurity into fame
▶ 예술가의 몸으로 생계를 이어가기는 쉽지 않다 It is not easy to make a living as an artist.
7 〈월경〉 menstruation; the menses
—몸하다 menstruate; have the menses [monthlies]; have one's periods
8 〈도자기의〉 unglazed pottery; bisque; biscuit (ware)
몸 〈영국의 작가〉 Maugham, William Somerset (1874-1965)
몸가짐 〈품행〉 behavior; conduct; morals; 〈거동〉 demeanor; a manner; movements; 《polite》 bearing; 〈태도〉 an attitude
◆ 몸가짐이 나쁜 남자[여자] a man [woman] of loose morals / 몸가짐이 나쁘다 misconduct [misbehave] oneself; be loose in one's behavior / 몸가짐이 바르다 live a straight [moral] life / 몸가짐이 얌전하다 be well behaved [conducted]; behave well [oneself] / 몸가짐이 점잖다 behave like a gentleman; have gentlemanly behavior / 몸가짐에 주의하다 be careful [prudent] in one's conduct
▶ 그녀는 몸가짐이 우아하다 She has a graceful [an elegant] carriage [manners].
▶ 그 숙녀는 몸가짐이 차분하다 The lady has a quiet demeanor.
▶ 그 여자는 숙녀다운 몸가짐을 갖는데는 도무지 관심이 없다 She cares nothing about being ladylike.
몸값 the money [price] for flesh traffic [for a slave]; 〈인질·포로 등의〉 (a) ransom; price of redemption
◆ 몸값을 받다[요구하다] exact [demand] a ransom (for a prisoner, from sb) / 몸값을 노리고 감금하다 hold sb for [《英》to] ransom / 몸값을 내고 목숨[생명]을 건지다 redeem oneself [one's life]
▶ 그 비행기 납치범은 승객을 인질로 잡고 몸값을 요구했다 The hijacker held the passengers for [to] ransom.
▶ 그는 몸값을 6천만원이나 내고 아들을 되찾아 왔다 He paid a ransom of sixty million won to get his son back.
몸나다 gain [put on] weight; get [grow] fat (▶fat은 흔히 경멸적으로 보기 싫게 살이 찌는 것을 뜻하는 경우가 많으므로 여성에게는 피하는 것이 좋음. stout는 흔히 fat의 완곡한 표현으로 쓰임); fatten; grow [get] stout [fleshy, plump]; fat (up)
◆ 몸난 중년 여인 a stout middle-aged woman / 몸나기 시작하다 run to fat
▶ 그는 약간 몸이 났다 He has gained a little weight.
몸단장 —丹粧 decorating oneself; dressing up
—몸단장하다 ornament [adorn, deck] oneself; smarten [spruce] oneself up
▶ 그녀는 몸단장을 빨리 한다 She dresses herself quickly.
▶ 그녀는 몸단장에 너무 소홀하다 She is too careless about her appearance.
몸달다 fidget 《about》; be all hot and bothered; fret 《about》; be [get] eager [anxious] 《for, to do》; get impatient
◆ 애인을 못 만나서 [영화 구경을 가고 싶어] 몸달다 be all hot and bothered to be kept from seeing one's sweetheart [because one wants to go to the movies] / 몸달게 하다 give sb the fidgets
▶ 그렇게 몸달아 하지 마라 Don't fret like that!
▶ 그 회사는 새로운 시장을 개척하려고 몸달아 있다 That firm is very eager to open new markets.
몸두다 stay [live] in [with]; find [take] shelter with 《a relative》; stay with 《one's aunt》
◆ 몸둘 곳이 없다 have no place for one; have no place to live [stay] in / 몸둘 바를 모르다 do not know where to put oneself; do not know what to do with oneself
▶ 이 세상에 몸둘 곳이 없구나 There is no place in the world for me.
▶ 몸둘 바를 모르겠습니다 I am deeply ashamed of myself.
▶ 나는 창피해서 몸둘 바를 몰랐다 I was so ashamed that I didn't know what to do with myself.
몸뒤로굽히기 〈體〉 trunk backward bending
몸뚱이 the body ⇨ 몸
몸매 one's figure [shape]; one's form
◆ 균형잡힌 몸매 a well-proportioned figure [form] / 날씬한 몸매 a slender figure
▶ 그 여자는 몸매가 좋다[예쁘다] She has a nice [good, lovely] figure. (▶「몸매가 나쁘다」라고 할 때는 She has a poor figure. 보다는 She is fat and short. 등과 같이 구체적으로 표현하는 것이 보통임)
▶ 적당한 운동을 하면 몸매가 좋아진다 Moderate exercise improves one's figure.
▶ 내 여동생은 옷을 입으면 말라 보이는 몸매다 My sister has the type of build that makes her look thinner (than she really is) when she's dressed.
몸보신 —補身 nurturing ⇨ 보신〈補身〉
몸부림 1 〈버둥거림〉 writhing; squirming; a (violent) struggle
—몸부림하다 writhe ⇨ 몸부림치다 1
2 〈잠자리에서의〉 tossing about in sleep; turning over in bed
—몸부림하다 toss about in bed ⇨ 몸부림치다 2
몸부림치다 1 〈버둥거리다〉 writhe; flounce; flounder; struggle; squirm
◆ 자유를 얻으려고 몸부림치다 struggle to get

free
▶ 그는 너무나 괴로워서 몸부림쳤다 He has writhed in agony. ≒ He has been in dire distress.
▶ 나는 심한 복통으로 밤새껏 몸부림쳤다 I writhed with a severe stomachache all night long.
▶ 그는 비참한 처지에서 벗어나려고 몸부림쳤다 He struggled [strove] to break out of the miserable circumstances he was in.
▶ 나는 속박에서 벗어나려고 몸부림쳤다 I struggled to free myself from my bonds.
▶ 아무리 몸부림쳐 봐야 소용없다 It's no use struggling and wriggling
2 〈잠자리에서〉 toss [roll] about in bed; turn [heave] (over, round) in sleep

몸살 illness from fatigue; general [great] fatigue
♦ 몸살이 나다 suffer from fatigue; 〈…하고 싶어 못견디다〉 be anxious [eager] to do; be dying for [to do] / 몸살로 눕다 take to one's bed from fatigue
▶ 그는 결과를 알고 싶어 몸살이 났다 He is anxious to know the result.
▶ 그녀가 보고 싶어 몸살이 나겠다 I am dying to see her.

몸서리 1 〈공포 등으로 진저리가 남〉 a shudder; a shiver; a thrill; trembling; quivering
—**몸서리나다[치다]** shudder; tremble; shiver; quiver
♦ 몸서리나는 terrible; terrifying; hair-raising / 무서워서 몸서리치다 tremble with [for] fear / 생각만 해도 몸서리나다 shudder [be shocked] at the mere thought [bare idea] of 《it》
▶ 그 여자는 눈앞의 광경에[뱀을 보고] 몸서리쳤다 The woman shuddered at the sight before her [of the snake].
▶ 그는 공포에 몸서리쳤다 He trembled for fear.
▶ 그는 그 생각에 몸서리쳤다 He shuddered at the thought of it.
▶ 그것은 몸서리나는 광경이었다 It was a frightful [terrible, shocking] scene.
2 〈지긋지긋하게 싫증이 남〉 weariness; tiresomeness; being sick 《of》; being fed up 《with》
—**몸서리나다[치다]** be sick [quite tired] 《of》; be sickened 《of》; be fed up 《with》
♦ 몸서리 나는 일 an abominable thing / 학교에 가기가 몸서리나다 be sickened of going to school
▶ 그 사람의 장황한 이야기에는 몸서리난다 I am sick of [fed up with] his endless talk.
▶ 나는 가난한 살림에 몸서리난다 I am tired of my humble life.
▶ 나는 이 일에는 이제 몸서리난다 I've become utterly disgusted with this work.
▶ 서비스가 엉망인 그 호텔에 묵어야 하다니 생각만 해도 그는 몸서리가 났다 He shuddered just to think he had to stay at the hotel with terrible service.
▶ 나는 그 여자의 잔소리에 몸서리난다 I am fed up with her complaints [carping].
▶ 난 너의 말도 안 되는 소리에는 몸서리난다 I've had enough of your nonsense.

몸소 personally; in person; for oneself
♦ 몸소 방문하다 make a personal call 《on, at》/ 몸소 시찰하다 make a personal inspection 《of》/ 몸소 지휘하다 take [assume] personal command 《of》; be in personal command 《of》
▶ 관장님이 몸소 박물관을 두루 내게 안내해 주셨다 The curator took me personally through the museum.
▶ 그는 몸소 부하들에게 모범을 보였다 He personally set an example to his inferiors.
▶ 당신이 몸소 갈 필요는 없습니다 You don't have to go yourself [in person].

몸수색 —**搜索** a body searching; 〈옷 위로 하는〉 a frisk
▶ 경찰은 그가 권총을 가지고 있는지 몸수색을 했다 The policeman searched him to see if he had a pistol.
—**몸수색하다** search [frisk] 《sb for concealed weapons》

몸앞굽혀뛰기 〔體〕 trunk bending vault
몸앞으로눕히기 〔體〕 trunk forward leaning
몸엣것 〈월경〉 menstruation; the menses; menstrual blood

몸져눕다 be laid up with [by] (an) illness; be bedridden; lie in one's sickbed
♦ 몸져누워 있는 노인 an old bedridden [a bedridden aged] person / 독감으로 몸져눕다 come down with (the) flu
▶ 그는 오랫동안 몸져누워 있다 He has been sick in bed for a long time.
▶ 우리 어머니는 몸져누워 계신다 My mother is bedridden.

몸조리 —**調理** care of health; 〈병후의〉 recuperation
♦ 산후 몸조리 postpartum care / 몸조리를 안 하다 neglect [be careless of] one's health
▶ 그는 병후 몸조리를 위해 해변에 가 있다 He has gone to the seaside to recuperate [for (his) recuperation].
—**몸조리하다** take good care of oneself [one's health]; 〈병후에〉 recuperate 《oneself》; convalesce; recruit 《oneself》
♦ 몸조리하기 위해 to recuperate / 몸조리하여 감기를 낫게 하다 nurse a cold
▶ 몸조리하기 위해 나는 고원으로 전지요양을 갔다 I moved to the highlands to improve my health.

몸조심 —**操心** 1 〈건강을 위함〉 care of one's health
▶ 너는 좀더 몸조심을 해야겠다 You should take more care of yourself.
▶ 출산 때까지는 몸조심을 해야 한다 You must take good care of yourself until the baby is born.
—**몸조심하다** take (good) care of oneself; be careful of one's health
▶ 부디 몸조심하세요 Please take (good, great) care of yourself [your health]. 《▶가까운 사이에서는 간단히 Take care. 라고 함》
▶ 병나지 않게 몸조심해라 Take care not to make yourself ill.

2 〈언행을 삼감〉 prudence; discretion; being cautious about *one's* behavior
▶ 그는 일거일동에 몸조심을 했다 He was cautious in all his movements.
―**몸조심하다** behave *oneself* prudently; be prudent in action; be cautious
▶ 그 사건 이후 나는 아주 몸조심하고 있다 The accident has rendered me very cautious.
▶ 이런 일에는 몸조심하는 것이 제일이다 One must observe caution in these matters.

몸종 a lady's maid; a handmaid [slave girl] (to Mrs. ...); a body maid; a parlormaid

몸집 the body; 〈체격〉 physique; build; frame
♦ 작은[큰] 몸집 small [large] stature [build] / 몸집이 작은 남자 a little man; a short man; (俗) a shortie / 몸집이 큰 여자 a big woman; a woman of large build / 몸집이 당당한 사람 a man with a magnificent build; a magnificently built man; a man of stout build / 몸집이 호리호리한 소녀 a girl of slender frame / 몸집이 작다 be of small stature [build] / 몸집이 통통하다 be pudgy
▶ 그 녀석은 몸집이 크다 He is a bulky fellow.

몸짓 a gesture; (a) gesticulation; a motion; (an) action
♦ 몸짓으로 하는 의사 전달 gestural communication / 화난 몸짓을 하다 make an angry gesture; make a gesture of anger / 몸짓으로 나타내다 express 《*oneself*》 by gesture; gesture 《the size of a box》; indicate in dumb show / 몸짓으로 부르다 motion *sb* toward *one* / 몸짓으로 흉내내다 imitate by [mimic with] gesture
▶ 그는 몸짓으로 방으로 들어오라고[앉으라고] 했다 He motioned me (to come) into the room [to sit down].(▶「motion+사람」다음에는 방향을 나타내는 어구가 옴)
▶ 그녀는 과장된 몸짓으로 그때의 상황을 설명했다 She explained how it happened with exaggerated [a lot of] gestures.
▶ 경찰관은 몸짓으로 그 차를 멈추라고 신호했다 The policeman signaled the car to stop.
▶ 아이들은 몸짓으로 이야기하고 있었다 Children were talking in sign language [speaking by gesture].
▶ 선생님은 나에게 몸짓으로 나가라고 하셨다 The teacher motioned me out of the room.
▶ 〔會話〕「당신들 두 사람은 어떻게 의사소통을 했습니까?」「몸짓으로 했습니다」 "How did you understand each other?" "We communicated with signs and gestures."
―**몸짓하다** make gestures; gesticulate; motion
♦ 몸짓해 가며 말하다 accompany *one's* speech with gesture
▶ 나는 그들에게 조용히 하라고 몸짓했다 I motioned them to be silent.

몸차림 〈차림새〉 attire; (口) a getup; 〈입기〉 dressing 《*oneself*》 up
♦ 몸차림이 소박하다[화려하다] be simply [gorgeously] attired / 몸차림을 단정히 하다 dress neatly; tidy *oneself* up
▶ 그 학생은 몸차림이 늘 단정하다 The student always looks neat and tidy.
▶ 그 여자는 몸차림에 신경을 쓰지 않는다 She doesn't care how she looks.
―**몸차림하다** dress [attire, equip] *oneself*; get dressed

몸채 the main house [building]; the main building house in the premises

몸치장 -治粧 dressing 《*oneself*》 up
▶ 그녀는 서둘러 몸치장을 했다 She dressed up [got dressed up] in a hurry.
▶ 그 여자는 진주로 몸치장을 했다 She adorned herself with pearls.
▶ 내 여동생은 몸치장에 신경을 쓴다[통 무관심하다] My sister is careful [quite careless] about her appearance.
―**몸치장하다** 〈옷으로〉 dress 《*oneself*》 up; be dressed up; be gaily dressed; 〈장식물로〉 ornament [deck, adorn] *oneself* 《with》
♦ 화려하게[야하게] 몸치장하다 be gaudily dressed; overdress 《*oneself*》 / 보석으로 몸치장하다 deck *oneself* up with jewels; bejewel *oneself*
▶ 그 여자는 단정하게 몸치장했다 She trimmed herself up.

몸통 the trunk (of the body); the (bulk of *one's*) body
♦ 남자의 몸통과 수족 a man's trunk and limbs / 몸통이 절구통 같다 be fat as a mortar barrel
▶ 그 사람은 몸통이 굵다[길다] He has a thick [long] trunk.

몸풀다 〈해산하다〉 give birth to 《a baby》; be delivered of 《a baby》; 〈피로를 풀다〉 take [have] a rest; relieve [banish] *one's* fatigue
▶ 나는 아내를 몸풀러 친정에 보냈다 I have sent my wife to her parents' home to give birth to her baby.

몹 〈자루 달린 걸레〉 a mop

몹시 **1** 〈대단히〉 very (much); greatly; 〈굉장히〉 awfully; terribly; 〈극도로〉 excessively; extremely
♦ 몹시 가난하다 be awfully poor / 몹시 기뻐하다 be highly [much] pleased / 몹시 바쁘다 be very busy with 《work》; be pressed with business; have *one's* hands full / 몹시 차다 be keenly cold / 몹시 화를 내다 be furious 《with, at》; be mad with anger
▶ 그녀는 그것을 몹시 갖고 싶어한다 She badly wants it.
▶ 그는 회의 결과가 몹시 궁금했다 He felt quite anxious about the result of the conference.
▶ 내 동생은 여행 준비를 하느라고 몹시 바쁘다 My brother is very busy preparing for the tour.
▶ 너는 몹시 기분이 좋구나 You are in an unusually merry mood.
▶ 오늘은 네 누나가 몹시 예뻐 보이지? Today your sister looks very pretty, doesn't she?
▶ 그녀는 오늘 몹시 서두르고 있다 She is in a great [in such a] hurry today.
▶ 나는 몹시 배가 고프다 I'm very hungry. ⇌ I'm simply starving.
▶ 그이가 없어서 몹시 쓸쓸하다 I miss him very [so] much.

몹쓸

▶ 그녀는 음악을 몹시 좋아한다 She is excessively fond of music.
▶ 나는 몹시 운이 좋았다 I had capital luck.
▶ 오늘은 몹시 춥다 It's awfully [bitterly, icy, freezing] cold today.
▶ 오늘은 몹시 피곤하다 I'm very [dead] tired today.
2 〈심하게〉 severely; violently; intensely; badly; hard; 〈모질게〉 harshly; cruelly; severely
♦ 몹시 꾸짖다 scold severely / 몹시 때리다 beat *sb* too hard / 몹시 부려먹다 drive *sb* hard; sweat 《a servant》/ 몹시 아프다 feel [suffer] a severe pain / 몹시 울다 cry bitterly / 피를 몹시 흘리다 bleed badly / 돈이 없어서 몹시 곤란을 겪다 be badly in want of [hard up for] money
▶ 아침부터 눈이 몹시 내린다 It has been snowing hard since this morning.
▶ 머리가 몹시 아프다 I have a bad [severe, terrible] headache.
▶ 내 동생은 독감을 몹시 앓고 있다 My brother is suffering from a severe attack of influenza.
▶ 그는 자동차 사고로 몹시 다쳤다 He was badly [severely, seriously] injured in the car accident.
▶ 인수는 지각했다고 몹시 꾸중을 들었다 In-su was severely told off [scolded] for being late.
▶ 그것을 보고 그녀는 몹시 불쾌했다 The sight excited strong disgust in her.
▶ 그는 몹시 취해 있었다 He was heavily [dead] drunk.

몹쓸 **1** 〈나쁜〉 bad; evil; ill; immoral; 〈사악한〉 wicked; malicious; ill-natured
♦ 몹쓸 놈 a wicked guy; a rascal [crook] / 몹쓸 짓 an evil deed; a misdeed /〈아무에게〉 몹쓸 짓을 하다 do *sb* harm [an ill turn]; do a cruel thing to *sb* / 몹쓸 패들과 어울리다 keep bad company; associate with bad fellows
▶ 그런 말을 하다니 그자들도 몹쓸 녀석들이다 It's wicked of them to say such things.
▶ 그렇게 순진한 처녀를 속이다니 너도 참 몹쓸 놈이구나 How wicked you are to deceive such an innocent girl.
▶ 어렸을 때 나는 온갖 몹쓸 장난을 다 했었다 As a boy I used to play all sorts of pranks.
2 〈악성의〉 virulent 《disease》; malignant 《influenza》; nasty
♦ 몹쓸 형벌 《inflict》 a cruel punishment / 몹쓸 병에 걸리다 suffer from a virulent disease

못¹ 〈연못〉 a pond; 〈작은 물웅덩이〉 a pool; 〈저수지〉 a reservoir
♦ 연못 속 a lotus pond / 못가에서 by a pond [the pondside] / 못의 물을 빼다 drain a pond / 못을 파다[처내다, 메우다] dig [drag, fill up] a pond / 못에서 낚시질하다 fish in a pond / 못에서 스케이트를 타다 skate on a pond / 못에서 헤엄치다 swim in a pond
▶ 못 주위를 산책합시다 Let's have a walk around the pond.
▶ 못에 얼음이 두껍게 얼었다 Ice was thick on the pond.

못² a nail; 〈침목용〉 a spike; 〈나무못〉 a peg
♦ 쇠못 an iron nail / 장식못 an ornamental stud / 둥근 못 《보통 쓰는 것》 a wire nail / 못 대가리 a nailhead / 못박는 기계 a riveting [nailing] machine / 못 제조소 a nailery / 못통 a nail keg / 못을 박다 nail; drive [hammer] a nail 《into》/ 판자의 못을 뽑다 pull [draw] a nail out of a board; unnail a board / 못에 발을 찔리다 run a nail into *one's* feet / 가슴에 못을 박다 ⇨ 못박다 3
▶ 못이 단단히[헐겁게] 박혀 있다 The nail is fast [loose].
▶ 기둥에 못을 박아라 Drive [Hammer] a nail into the pillar.
▶ 그는 모자를 못에 걸었다 He caught his hat on the nail.
▶ 그녀의 소맷자락이 못에 걸렸다 The nail caught her sleeve.
▶ 나는 현관에 못으로 문패를 달았다 I nailed a (name) plate on [to] the door.

못³ 〈손발 등의〉 a callosity; a callus; 〈주로 발가락의〉 a corn
♦ 못이 박인 발가락 a toe with a callosity / 못이 여러 개 박인 손 a hand with callous places / 못이 박이다[생기다] become [get] callous [callused]; thicken into callus; have [get] a corn / 귀에 못이 박이도록 듣다 hear more than enough of *sth*; be sick (and tired) of hearing *sth* / 귀에 못이 박이도록 타이르다 drum a lesson into *sb's* head
▶ 나는 왼쪽 발에 못이 박였다 I have a corn [A corn has formed] on my left foot.
▶ 내 가운뎃손가락에 (글씨를 많이 써서) 못이 박혔다 A callus has formed on my middle finger (from writing so much).
▶ 당신의 잔소리는 귀에 못이 박이도록 들었습니다 I'm tired of hearing [I've heard more than enough of] your scolding.
▶ 그만큼 얘기했으면 됐어 귀에 못이 박이겠다 You are constantly dinning it in my ears. I am sick of hearing it.

못⁴ 〈불능〉 cannot 《do》; unable 《to do》; incapable 《of doing》; 〈불가〉 (definitely) not; won't
▶ 어두워서 못 읽겠다 It is too dark to read.
▶ 우리는 그와 함께 못 간다 We can't go with him.
▶ 우리는 비 때문에 소풍을 못 갔다 The rain prevented us from going on a picnic.
▶ 교내에서는 담배를 못 피우게 되어 있다 Smoking is prohibited within the school bounds.

못갖춘마디 〖樂〗 an incomplete bar
못갖춘마침 〖樂〗 imperfect cadence
못걸이 a pegboard; a hook; a hatpeg; a clothes rack
못나다 **1** 〈못생기다〉 ugly; plain; plain-[ugly-]looking; 《美》 homely (-looking)
♦ 못난 얼굴 an ugly face / 못난 여자 a plain [homely] girl [woman]
▶ 그녀는 얼굴이 못났다 She looks plain.
2 〈어리석다〉 foolish; stupid; dull (▶dull은 이해력·사고력이 둔한 것을, stupid는 지능이 낮은 것을 뜻함)
♦ 못나게도 foolishly enough / 못난 짓을 하다 do a foolish [stupid] thing; act foolishly;

commit a folly
▶ 이 못난 놈아 You big fool!
▶ 그런 거짓말을 하다니 그 녀석도 못났군 It's stupid of him to tell such a lie.
▶ 그는 곧 그런 짓이 못난 짓이라는 것을 알았다 He soon saw the folly of such a course.

못난이 〈바보〉 a fool; a simpleton; a blockhead; a goose; a booby; 〈못생긴 사람〉 an ugly fellow; 〈겁쟁이〉 a coward

못내 〈그지없이〉 immeasurably; incalculably; 〈몹시〉 deeply; greatly; ever so much; 〈잊지 않고〉 unforgettably; 〈늘〉 always; ever
♦ 못내 서러워하다 be in constant sorrow / 못내 잊지 못하다 never forget; hold sb's memory ever dear / 이별을 못내 아쉬워하다 be deeply sorry to part from sb
▶ 그 아이는 돌아가신 어머니를 못내 그리워했다 The child yearned much toward [solely missed] his dead mother.
▶ 그녀는 못내 아쉬운 듯 몇 번이고 뒤를 돌아보며 떠나갔다 She went her way, looking back wistfully again and again.

못되다 1 〈미달하다〉 less than; short [inside] of; not up to
♦ 1만원이 못되는 돈 a sum less than two thousand won / 1마일이 좀 못되다 a little short of a mile / 60이 못되어 죽다 die before sixty
▶ 역까지는 1킬로미터가 못되다 It is less than a kilometer to the station.
2 〈여위다〉 worn-out; emaciated; worn; haggard ♦ 앓고 나서 얼굴이 못되다 look thin after an illness
▶ 오래 앓더니 그는 얼굴이 아주 못되었다 He is emaciated by his long illness.
▶ 그는 얼굴이 못되어 보인다 He looks thin in the face.
3 〈나쁘다〉 evil; bad; wrong; 〈사악하다〉 ill-natured; wicked; malicious
♦ 못된 놈 a wicked [an evil] man; a rascal / 못된 아이 a bad [naughty] child (▶이 경우 wicked나 evil은 쓰지 않음) / 못된 장난 mischief / 못된 짓 an evil deed; a wrong; a misdeed; a vice / 못된 생각을 품다 harbor evil intentions / 못된 장난을 치다가 들키다 be caught in mischief / 못된 짓을 꾸미다 plot evil / 못되게 굴다 misbehave *oneself*
▶ 못된 장난[농담]은 그만 두어라 Don't be so naughty. ⇌ Don't make such nasty jokes.
▶ 그는 못된 짓을 해서 처벌을 받았다 He was punished because he did something bad.
▶ 그 사람은 술만 마시면 못되게 군다 He turns vicious when he drinks.
4 〈기울다〉 sinking; declining; waney ♦ 못되어 가다 be on the decline [wane]; be on the downgrade
▶ 그들은 형편이 전보다 더 못되었다 They are worse off than before.
5 〈아니다〉 unworthy; not worth; below 《notice》
♦ 논할 바가 못되다 be too trifling to take up for discussion; be unworthy of comment / 상종할 사람이 못되다 be not worthy of *one's* friendship

못된 송아지 엉덩이에서 뿔이 난다 (속담) The lean weed lifts it's head high. ⇌ An ill-bred boy behaves rudely. ⇌ A no-good person is acting up [putting on airs].

못마땅하다 〈마음에 들지 않다〉 disagreeable 《to》; unacceptable; unsatisfactory; distasteful; not to sb's liking; 〈불만이다〉 not pleased 《with》; dissatisfied 《with》
♦ 못마땅한 듯이 with a displeased look / 못마땅한 말을 하다 say *sth* disagreeable [unpleasant] / 못마땅한 얼굴을 하다 scowl; look displeased / 못마땅해 하다 be displeased [dissatisfied] with *sth*
▶ 그의 사내답지 못한 태도가 못마땅하다 His sissy attitude gets on my nerves.
▶ 내가 민호를 초대한 것을 못마땅했니? Did you mind my inviting Min-ho?
▶ 무엇이 그렇게 못마땅한가? What are you so annoyed [upset] about? ⇌ What makes you so unhappy?
▶ 뭔가 못마땅한 일이 있나 보죠? Is there something that offends you [gets on your nerves]?
▶ 그는 그 나라의 대외정책이 못마땅했다 He was impatient with the country's foreign policy.

못박다 1 〈못을 박다〉 nail; drive a nail
♦ 십자가에 못박힌 예수의 상 a crucifix / 못박아 붙이다[고정하다] nail *sth* to 《the door》; fasten with nails / 십자가에 못박다 crucify *sb*
▶ 그들은 문을 못박아 폐쇄했다 They nailed the door shut.
2 〈고정시키다〉 set; fix; peg; stabilize
♦ 가격을 8백원으로 못박다 peg the price at eight hundred won / 회합 장소를 못박다 fix the place for the meeting
3 〈가슴에〉 hurt [lacerate] *sb's* feelings; hurt *sb* ♦ 남에 대한 원한이 깊이 못박히다 bear *sb* a deep grudge; have [hold, carry] a deep grudge against *sb*
▶ 그의 그 말이 그녀의 가슴에 못박았다 That remark of his was a great hurt [injury] to her feeling. ⇌ He deeply hurt [injured] her feelings with that remark.
4 〈다짐하다〉 assure; pledge; make sure
▶ 나는 그에게 다시는 그런 바보짓을 하지 않도록 (단단히) 못박았다 I gave him a (strong) warning not to do such a foolish thing again.
▶ 그는 다음 달까지 그 일을 끝내겠다고 못박았다 He gave his word that he would finish the work by next month.
5 〈꼼짝 못하게 하다〉 rivet; transfix
▶ 그는 공포에 질려 그 자리에 못박힌 듯 서 있었다 He was riveted [stood transfixed] to the spot with terror. ⇌ Terror nailed him to the spot.
▶ 그는 텔레비전에 눈을 못박고 게임을 구경했다 He was [kept his eyes] glued to the TV 《set》 watching the game.

못박이다 〈손발에〉 be callused; become callous

못보다 pass by [over]; overlook; fail to notice; 〈놓치다〉 miss 《seeing》

못본체하다 〈보고도〉 pretend [affect] not to see [to have seen]; 〈관대하게〉 look over;

못비 a (timely) sufficient rain for rice transplantation

못뽑이 (a pair of) pincers [nippers]; a nail puller [extractor]; a claw hammer

못살게굴다 〈학대하다〉 treat *sb* harshly; abuse; persecute; bully(약자를); oppress; ill-treat; torment; be cruel to (a dog);〈집적거리다〉 annoy; tease; peck at *sb*
♦ 고양이를 못살게 굴다 torment a cat / 며느리를 못살게 굴다 be cruel to [hard on] *one's* daughter-in-law
▶ 그는 어린아이들을 종종 못살게 군다 He often bullies little children.
▶ 동물을 못살게 굴면 안된다 You shouldn't pester animals.
▶ 그 아이는 종종 어리석은 질문으로 형을 못살게 군다 The child often torments his brother with silly questions.

못생기다 1 〈얼굴이〉 ugly; plain; uncomely; bad-[ugly-]looking; (美) homely (▶ 여성에게는 ugly 보다는 plain, homely를 씀)
♦ 못생긴 여자 a plain [(美) homely] woman / 못생긴 코 an unshapely nose / 얼굴이 못생기다 have an ugly [unattractive] face; be plain-looking
▶ 그 여자는 얼굴은 못생겼지만 마음씨는 곱다 She is [looks] plain, but sweet-tempered [has a kind heart].
2 〈어리석다〉 stupid; foolish; dull; thick-headed

못쓰다 〈금지〉 must [shall] not (do) (▶ 2, 3인칭에); ought not to (do); should not (do);〈사용 불능〉 be useless [no good, past use]
♦ 못쓰게 되다 〈사람이〉 get bad [worse] /〈병으로〉 become poor in health;〈물건이〉 become worthless; be spoiled uselessly
▶ 그런 말하면 못쓴다 You should not [ought not to] say such a thing.
▶ 너 그러면 못쓴다 You shouldn't do that. ⇌ It's improper for you to do that.
▶ 어머니는 나보고 그런 짓을 하면 못쓴다고 하신다 Mother says I can't do that sort of thing.
▶ 이 상자는 너무 커서 못쓰겠다 This box won't do because it's too big.

못자리 a rice seedbed [seed-plot, nursery]
♦ 못자리를 내다 prepare a rice nursery [seed-bed] —**못자리하다** sow rice; seed on the beds

못주다 〈못을 박다〉 drive a nail (into the wall); nail (up) (a box); nail down (a lid); fasten with nails

못줄 a guideline for rice planting

못지않다 no less (than); just as good (as); not inferior (to); equal (to)
♦ 남 못지않게 like the common run; like others [other people]; like most people
♦ 암산에 있어서는 나는 누구 못지않았다 I was second to none in calculating in my head.
▶ 그녀는 언니 못지않게 예쁘다 She is no less beautiful than her sister.
▶ 그 여자애는 배짱이 어떤 사내아이 못지않다 The girl is as bold as any boy.
▶ 오락은 일 못지않게 필요하다 Recreation is no less necessary than work.
▶ 오늘도 어제 못지않게 춥다 Today is just as cold as yesterday was.

못질 nailing; riveting; tacking
—**못질하다** nail (up) (a box); drive (in) a nail; nail down (a lid)
♦ 상자 뚜껑을 덮고 못질하다 nail the box shut; nail a cover on the box
▶ 창문을 단단히 못질해 두어라 Nail down the window.

못하다[1] 1〈할 수 없다〉 cannot (do); be unable (to do); be incapable (of doing);〈…할 여유가 없다〉 cannot afford (to do)
▶ 그는 새 차를 사지 못한다 He can't afford to buy a new car.
▶ 그놈들은 못할 짓이 없다 They dare to do anything. ⇌ They will go to any extreme.
▶ 그 사고로 그는 평생 동안 일을 하지 못하게 되었다 The accident incapacitated him for work for the rest of his life.
▶ 그것은 어려워서 못하겠다 It is too difficult for me to do.
2 〈하지 못하다〉 fail to (do); miss (doing)
♦ 승진하지 못하다 fail to be promoted / 알아맞히지 못하다 guess wrong [amiss] / 기차를 타지 못하다 miss *one's* train
▶ 비 때문에 우리는 소풍을 가지 못했다 The rain prevented us from going on a picnic.
▶ 그는 그 뜻을 전혀 이해하지 못했다 He utterly failed to understand the meaning.
▶ 나는 하려고 생각한 것을 반밖에 이루지 못했다 I've achieved only half of what I hoped to do.
▶ 나는 아직 이 책을 다 읽지 못했다 I'm not yet through with this book.
▶ 너무 바빠 연락을 드리지 못해 죄송합니다 I am sorry I was so busy that I failed to get in touch with you.
3 〈서투르다〉 be poor [bad, weak]
♦ 공부를 못하는 학생 a dull [poor] scholar; a backward student / 계산을 못하다 be bad [lousy, rotten] at figures / 영어를 못하다 be not good at English
▶ 그는 노래를 못한다 He is a poor singer. ⇌ (口) His singing is awful.
▶ 우리 아이는 수학을 못합니다 My son is poor at [weak in] mathematics.
4 〈술・담배를〉 be unaccustomed (to drinks)
♦ 술[담배]을 못하는 사람 a nondrinker [nonsmoker]
▶ 그 사람은 독한 술은 못한다 He can't drink hard liquor.
5 〈금지〉 ♦ …을 못하게 하다 stop [discour-

age] *sb* from 《doing》
▶개는 버스에 데리고 타지 못합니다 Dogs are not allowed in the bus.
▶가져가지 못함 《게시》 Not to be taken out [removed from the premises].

못하다² 〈뒤떨어지다〉 inferior to; worse than; below; unequal to; not as good as
♦약간 못하다 fall a little behind 《another》; be a cut below *sb* / 훨씬 못하다 be far beneath 《another》 / …보다 못한 보이다 compare unfavorably [poorly] 《with》; cannot stand [bear] comparison 《with》
▶나는 학교 성적이 형만 못하다 My school records are inferior to [not so good as] my brother's.
▶네 그림은 그녀 것만 못하다 Your picture is not as [so] good as hers.
▶지능면에서 그는 그 소녀보다 훨씬 못하다 He is far below [inferior to] her in intelligence.
▶그 살인범은 짐승만도 못한 놈이다 The murderer is worse than a beast.

못하다³ 〈아니다·않다〉 not
▶물이 맑지 못하다 The water is not clear.
▶빛깔이 곱지 못하다 The color is not fine.
▶그는 유능하지 못하다 He is lacking in ability.

몽고 蒙古 Mongolia ⇨ 몽골
—반(斑) a Mongolian spot

몽골 〈나라 이름〉 Mongolia; 〈공식명〉 the Mongolian People's Republic
♦몽골의 Mongolian; Mongol; Mongolic
■내[외]— Inner [Outer] Mongolia ■—말 Mongolian; Mongol —말(馬) a Mongolian pony —문자 Mongolian script [literature] —민족 the Mongolian people —사람 a Mongolian; a Mongol —족 the Mongolian race

몽구스 [動] a mongoos(e)《*pl.* -ses, -geese》
몽근벼 awnless [beardless] rice grains
몽근짐 a heavy [weighty] load for its bulk
몽글거리다 be clotty; be lumpy
몽글다 clean; beardless; fine 《flour》
몽글리다 1 〈곡식을〉 take away [remove] awns from 《grain》
♦벼를 몽글리다 strip an ear of rice; strip rice of awns
2 〈단련시키다〉 habituate; accustom; inure
♦추위에 몸을 몽글리다 inure *oneself* to cold
3 〈옷맵시를〉 dress [smarten] *oneself* up; spruce 《*oneself*》 up

몽깃돌 a killick; 〈낚싯봉〉 a sinker
몽니 greed; rapacity; avarice
♦몽니 사납다 be greedy; be rapacious / 몽니 부리다 act greedy; show *one's* greed
—쟁이 a greedy fellow; (口) a hog

몽달귀 —鬼 the ghost of a dead bachelor
몽당붓 a worn-out writing brush
몽당비 a worn-out broom; a stumpy broom
몽당연필 —鉛筆 a stubby pencil
몽당이 a stump; 〈실뭉치〉 a ball of thread
몽둥이 a stick; a club; a cudgel
♦몽둥이를 휘두르다 brandish a club / 몽둥이로 때리다 beat [hit, strike] *sb* with a club; club; cudgel / 몽둥이로 때려 죽이다 club 《a dog》 to death / 몽둥이로 얻어맞다 get beaten with a club; be clubbed [cudgeled]
—맛 an experience of being clubbed

몽둥이세례 —洗禮 beating with a stick; clubbing; cudgeling ♦몽둥이세례를 받다 get beaten with a stick; be clubbed / 몽둥이세례를 주다 beat with a stick; club; cudgel

몽둥이찜 clubbing ⇨ 몽둥이세례 —몽둥이찜 하다 beat with a stick; club; cudgel

몽땅 all; entirely; completely; wholly; in a body
♦있는 대로 몽땅 all that *one* has [that there is] / 몽땅 가져가다 take everything away / 돈을 몽땅 써버리다 spend all the money *one* has / 투기로 돈을 몽땅 잃다 lose the whole of *one's* money in speculation / 옷을 몽땅 저당잡히다 pawn *one's* clothes to the last rag / 재산을 몽땅 사업에 투자하다 invest all *one* has in an enterprise / 뼈까지 몽땅 먹어 치우다 eat 《a fish》 bone and all
▶나는 돈을 몽땅 도둑맞았다 I had all my money stolen.
▶그는 가지고 있던 것을 몽땅 털렸다 He was robbed of all he had.
▶나는 그것들을 몽땅 샀다 I bought all of them.
▶몸에 지닌 것을 몽땅 두고 가라고 하더라 I was told to leave there everything I had on.

몽똑하다 stumpy ⇨ 뭉뚝하다
몽롱하다 朦朧— dim; indistinct; vague; faint; dizzy; delirious; fuzzy
♦의식이 몽롱하다 have a dim consciousness / 의식이 몽롱해지다 get fuzzy / 몽롱하게 나타나다 loom; appear indistinctly
▶지금은 머리가 몽롱하다 My head is not clear now.
▶그는 고열로 인해 의식이 몽롱해 있다 He is delirious with a high fever.

몽매 蒙昧 ignorance —몽매하다 ignorant; unenlightened; uncivilized
▶그의 말은 자신의 몽매함을 드러내고 있다 His remark displays [reveals] his ignorance.

몽매 夢寐 sleeping and dreaming
♦몽매(간)에도 잊지 못하다 do not forget *sth* even in sleep [even while *one* is asleep]

몽상 蒙喪 mourning ♦몽상중이다 be in mourning —몽상하다 observe [go into, take to] mourning (for *one's* mother)

몽상 夢想 a dream; a vision; a daydream
♦몽상에 잠기다 be given to daydreaming; indulge in idle fancies; be lost in [fall into] (a) reverie
▶그는 역사 시간에 몽상에 잠겼다 He daydreamt during his history class.
▶그것은 몽상적인 계획이다 It's nothing but a Utopian scheme.
—몽상하다 dream 《of》; daydream; fancy; indulge in reveries
—가 a dreamer; a visionary; an idealist

몽설 夢泄 a nocturnal pollution [emission]; a wet dream —몽설하다 have a nocturnal pollution [emission]; have a wet dream

몽실몽실 〈통통함〉 plumply; fleshily ♦몽실몽실 살찐 아기 a chubby baby / 몽실몽실 살이 찌다 be [grow] plump —몽실몽실하다 lumpy;

plump ◆몽실몽실한 몸 a fleshy body
몽유병 夢遊病 sleepwalking; somnambulism ■─자 a sleepwalker; a somnambulist
몽정 夢精 a nocturnal pollution ⇨ 몽설
몽치 a cudgel; a club; a truncheon ◆쇠몽치 an iron cudgel / 몽치로 치다 beat *sb* with a club; cudgel; club
몽키다 lump ⇨ 뭉키다
몽타주 (a) montage ■─사진 (make) a composite picture; (compose) a montage picture [photo]; a photomontage
몽혼 矇昏 anesthesia ⇨ 마취(痲醉)
몽환 夢幻 dreams and phantasms; (a) fantasy; visions ◆몽환적인 dreamlike; fantastic ■─경 a visionary world; a dreamland: 나는 마치 몽환경을 헤매고 있는 기분이었다 I felt as if I were in a dreamland. ─곡〈야상곡〉a nocturne ─극 a dream play
뫼 1〈무덤〉a grave; a tomb ◆선산에 뫼를 쓰다 bury in the family graveyard **2**〈산〉a hill; a mountain
묏자리 a grave site; a burial [burying] site ◆묏자리를 잡다 select [choose] a grave site; determine a burial site
묘 卯〈십이지의〉the Sign of the Hare
묘 妙〈현묘(玄妙)〉a mystery; a wonder; a miracle;〈교묘〉adroitness ◆조화의 묘 the mystery [wonder] of nature [creation]; the wisdom of the creator
묘 墓 a grave; a tomb ⇨ 무덤
묘 廟〈능〉a mausoleum (*pl.* -lea);〈사당〉a shrine
묘계 妙計 a clever scheme ⇨ 묘책(妙策)
묘구도적 墓丘盜賊〈도굴범〉a grave robber; a looter [plunderer] of a grave;〈송장 도둑〉a body snatcher
묘기 妙技〈솜씨〉an exquisite skill;〈연예 등의〉a wonderful performance;〈곡예 등의〉a feat; a stunt;〈야구 등의〉a fine play ◆공중 묘기 an aerial stunt / 묘기를 보이다 exhibit [display] *one's* prowess; perform a feat; give a wonderful performance
▶ 그 선수는 놀라운 묘기를 연출했다 The player performed a wonderful feat.
묘령 妙齡 (the prime of) youth; (in) young [early] womanhood ◆묘령의 young; blooming; in the flower of maidenhood;(a woman) of marriageable age / 묘령에 이르다 attain budding womanhood; reach [arrive at] a marriageable age
▶ 묘령의 여성이 찾아왔습니다 A young lady came to see you.
묘리 妙理 an abstruse principle; a profound law;〈비결〉the secret ◆묘리를 터득하다 apprehend the profound principle [law] (of); get the knack (of); know the secret (of)
묘망하다 渺茫 vast; boundless; limitless
묘목 苗木 a young tree [plant]; a nursery tree; a sapling; a seedling ◆묘목을 심다 plant a seedling ■─상자 a flat
묘미 妙味 (a) subtle charm; beauty; exquisiteness; a nice point
▶ 그녀의 문제에는 뭐라고 표현할 수 없는 묘미가 있다 There is an indescribable charm in her style.
▶ 거기에 등산의 묘미가 있다 That's the attraction of mountain climbing.
▶ 그의 시의 묘미를 알겠습니까? Can you appreciate the exquisite flavor [beauty] of his poems?
묘박 錨泊 anchoring; anchorage ─**묘박하다** anchor
묘방 妙方 1〈처방〉a secret [an excellent] prescription **2** ⇨ 묘법(妙法) 1
묘법 妙法 1〈방법〉an excellent method; a clever way [means] **2**〈불법〉the supreme [marvelous] law of Buddha
묘비 墓碑 a tombstone; a gravestone
▶ 그들은 항구가 내려다보이는 묘에 묘비를 세웠다 They set up [erected] a tombstone over the grave overlooking the harbor.
■─명(銘) an epitaph; an inscription on a tombstone
묘사 描寫 (a) description; (a) depiction;〈그림에서의〉representation; portrayal
─**묘사하다** describe; depict; represent; portray ◆빈민가의 생활을 묘사한 소설 a novel depicting slum life / 인물을 묘사하다 describe [portray] a character
▶ 작가는 그 장면을 생생하게 묘사했다 The author described the scene vividly.
▶ 이 작품 속에 당시의 풍습이 잘 묘사되어 있다 The manners and customs of the day are well represented in this work.
■감각적[사실적]─ a sensational [realistic] description 성격─ characterization; character portrayal 실물─ model drawing 심리[자연]─ psychological [naturalistic] description
묘상 苗床 a nursery; a seedbed; a seed-plot;〈못자리〉a rice seedbed
묘석 墓石 a gravestone; a tombstone; a headstone
묘성 昴星〔天〕the Pleiades
묘소 墓所 a graveyard; a burial ground
묘수 妙手〈솜씨〉excellent skill;〈명수〉a master hand; an expert; an adept;〈바둑·장기의〉a good [capital] move
묘안 妙案 a happy [bright] idea; an excellent [ingenious] plan [scheme]
▶ 도무지 묘안이 떠오르지 않는다 Bright ideas never occur to me.
▶ 갑자기 묘안이 떠올랐다 Suddenly I hit on a happy idea.
묘안석 猫眼石〔鑛〕(a) cat's-eye
묘약 妙藥 a specific; an excellent [a golden] remedy; a wonder [miracle] drug
▶ 인플레이션 방지의 묘약이 없다 We have no remedy for inflation.
묘역 墓域 the boundaries of a grave
묘연하다 杳然─〈거리가〉faraway; remote;〈기억이〉dim; vague; indistinct;〈소식이〉unknown; missing
▶ 그의 행방이 묘연하다 No one knows his whereabouts. ⇌ His whereabouts is completely unknown.
묘지 墓地 a graveyard; a burial [burying] ground; a cemetery;〈교회의〉a churchyard

■공동— a cemetery 공원— a cemetery park 국립— the National Cemetery 무연(無緣)— a potter's field 외국인— a foreigners' cemetery 유엔— the U.N. Memorial Cemetery

묘지 墓誌 an epitaph; an inscription on a tomb ■—명(銘) an epitaph; an inscription on a tombstone

묘지기 墓— a grave keeper

묘책 妙策 a clever [an ingenious] scheme; a capital plan

묘판 苗板 a nursery ⇨ 못자리, 모판

묘포 苗圃 a nursery (garden); a seedbed

묘표 苗表 a gravepost; a headstone

묘하다 妙— 1 〈이상야릇하다〉 strange; queer; odd; curious; enigmatic; mysterious
▶ 그것은 묘한 이야기다 It is a strange [curious] story.
▶ 그는 묘한 녀석이다 He is an odd fellow.
▶ 그녀에게는 뭔가 묘한 데가 있다 There is something strange about her.
▶ 옛날엔 우리 마을에 묘한 풍습이 있었다 There used to be curious customs in my town.
▶ 나는 어제 묘한 일을 겪었다 A curious thing happened to me yesterday.
▶ 그녀는 때로 말을 묘하게 한다 She often speaks in riddles.
▶ 너는 묘하게 연필을 쥐는구나 You have a queer way of holding your pencil.
2 〈썩 잘되다〉 exquisite; subtle; marvelous; wonderful; excellent ♦ 묘하게 되다 be exquisitely made

묘혈 墓穴 a grave ♦ 스스로 묘혈을 파는 짓 a self-destroying [suicidal] act
▶ 그는 스스로 묘혈을 팠다 He dug his own grave. ⇌ He brought a calamity upon himself. ⇌ He worked [brought about] his own ruin.

무¹ 〈의복의〉 a gusset; a gore

무² 〔植〕 a radish; an icicle radish
♦ 무쪽 같다 be ugly [homely]; look plain ■—김치 radish *kimchi* [pickles]; pickled radish —다리 〈여자의〉 fat legs; beer-barrel legs —장아찌 sliced radish soaked in soybean paste —즙 grated radish —진디 〔昆〕 a cabbage aphis [aphid] —짠지 salted (whole) radish —채 radish shreds [strips]; shredded radish —청 the green part of a radish; radish tops [leaves]

무 無 nothing; naught; nil; nihility; zero
♦ 무가 되다 come [be brought] to naught [nothing]; go for nothing
▶ 무에서 유(有)는 생기지 않는다 Nothing comes of [from] nothing. ⇌ You cannot make something out of nothing.
▶ 당신의 친절을 무로 돌리고 싶지 않습니다 I do not want your kindness to come to nothing.

무 武 〈군사〉 military affairs; 〈무예〉 military arts ♦ 무를 닦다 train *oneself* in warlike arts / 무를 숭상하다 pursue the policy of militarism; glorify the military power

무- 無— no; none; un-; in- ♦ 무관심 indifference; unconcern

무가 武家 a military family

무가내(하) 無可奈(何) having no alternative; inevitability
♦ 무가내(하)다 there is no alternative; be at *one's* wit's end; be helpless / 무가내로 듣지 않다 will not listen to; turn a deaf ear to
▶ 아무리 타일러도 듣지 않으니 무가내하다 All my efforts to persuade him are helpless.

무가당 無加糖 ♦ 무가당의 sugar-free; sugarless; unsweetened / 무가당 오렌지 주스 sugarless orange juice

무가치 無價値 worthlessness; valuelessness
—무가치하다 worthless; valueless; useless; of no value

무간섭 無干涉 nonintervention ⇨ 불간섭

무간하다 無間— intimate; familiar; friendly; close 《to *one's* bosom》
♦ 무간한 친구 a bosom [close] friend / 무간하게 지내다 be on an intimate footing 《with》; be thick 《with》; associate on friendly [cordial] terms 《with》

무감각 無感覺 insensibility; senselessness; 〈무신경〉 apathy; impassiveness; callousness
—무감각하다 insensible; senseless; numb; anesthetic; apathetic; callous
♦ 무감각해지다 become numbed [insensible, senseless] 《with cold》; be benumbed / 남의 고충에 무감각하다 be callous [apathetic] to the sufferings of others
▶ 내 손가락이 추위로 무감각해졌다 My fingers have gone numb with cold.
▶ 그는 세상의 비난에 전연 무감각하다 He is quite callous to public criticism.
▶ 그녀는 유행에 전연 무감각하다 She is utterly indifferent to the fashion.

무감사 無鑑査 (being) not subject to a panel of judges ♦ 무감사의 그림 a painting not submitted to the selecting committee
▶ 무감사 입선 (게시) Not submitted to the jury.

무감찰 無鑑札 ♦ 무감찰의 unlicensed / 무감찰로 without a license

무개 無蓋 ♦ 무개의 open; uncovered
■—자동차 an open car —화차(貨車) (美) an open freight car; a gondola car; (英) an open goods wagon

무거리 coarse flour; tailings; screenings
—고추장 hot-pepper paste mixed with coarse soybean-malt flour

무겁다 1 〈무게가〉 heavy; weighty
♦ 무거운 돌 a heavy stone / 무거운 짐 a heavy [weighty] burden [load] / 무거워지다 get [become, grow] heavy [heavier]; increase in weight / 무겁게 하다 make *sth* heavier
▶ 이 상자는 너한테는 너무 무겁다 This box is too heavy for you.
▶ 그들은 무거운 다리를 끌며 계속 걸어갔다 They kept on walking wearily.
2 〈언행이〉 grave; serious; quiet
♦ 입이 무거운 사람 a close-mouthed person / 사람이 무겁고 조용하다 be grave and quiet / 입이 무겁다 be taciturn; be a man of few words
3 〈기분이〉 heavy; depressed; dull; languid
♦ 무거운 분위기 an oppressive atmosphere /

무게의 표현

1. 무게에 관한 질문법·표현법
남의 체중을 물을 때는 동사 weigh (무게가…나가다)를 써서 How much do you weigh?라고 한다. 또는 weigh의 명사형 weight를 써서 What is your weight?라고 말할 수도 있다. 이에 대한 대답은 I weigh 60 kilograms. ⇌ I am 60 kilograms.라고 한다. 물건의 무게를 물을 때는 보통 How heavy is it?이라고 하면 된다.

2. 체중에 관한 표현
▶ 會話 「나는 체중이 55킬로그램인데 파운드로 하면 얼마나 되나요?」「미안하지만 파운드로 환산하는 방법을 모르는데요」 "I weigh 55 kilograms and I wonder how much it would be in pounds." "Sorry, but I don't know how to convert it to pounds."
▶ 저 씨름 선수는 족히 100킬로그램은 넘겠다 That wrestler weighs well over 100 kilograms.
▶ 요사이 체중이 늘었다. 다이어트를 해야겠어 I've gained weight recently. I've got to go on a diet.
▶ 나는 뚱뚱해져서 체중계에 올라가기가 겁이 난다 Since I got fat, I'm scared to step on the scales.
▶ 어머니는 체중을 줄이기 위해 헬스클럽 회원이 되셨다 My mother has become a member of a fitness club to lose weight.
▶ 우리 아버지는 바짝 마르셔서 뼈만 남으셨다. 살이 좀 쪄셨으면 좋으련만 My father is so skinny that he looks like a skeleton. I wish he were a little heavier.
▶ 그는 유도의 무제한급에서 우승했다 He won the championship in the open category at the judo tournament.

3. 물건의 무게에 관한 표현
▶ 會話 「금과 쇠는 어느 쪽이 무겁습니까?」 「금입니다」 "Which is heavier, gold or iron?" "Gold is."
▶ 會話 「자네가 낚은 고기는 무게가 얼마나 나갔지?」「어린애 만한 무게였어」 "How heavy was the fish you caught?" "It was as heavy as a child."
▶ 會話 「이 차의 중량이 얼마나 됩니까?」「1,500킬로그램 남짓 됩니다」 "What's the weight of this car?" "It's a little more than 1,500 kilograms."
▶ 會話 「이 엘리베이터는 몇 사람까지 탈 수 있습니까?」「최대 적재량이 1,400킬로그램이니까, 어른이 약 20명까지 탈 수 있습니다」 "How many people can this elevator hold?" "The maximum load is 1,400 kilograms, so it can hold up to approximately twenty adults."
▶ 그 새 가구는 아주 가벼워서 손쉽게 옮길 수가 있다 The new furniture is so light that it can be easily moved.
▶ 우주 비행사들은 무중력 상태에서 몇 가지 실험을 할 예정이다 The astronauts are expected to do some experiments under zero gravity conditions.

4. 비유적인 표현
(1) 중요성
▶ 선생님의 충고에는 무게가 있다 Our teacher's advice carries weight with us.
▶ 우리 학교에서는 예절 교육에 중점을 두고 있다 We put emphasis on the importance of discipline in our school.
▶ 그는 우리 회사의 중요 인물이다 He is a VIP in our company. (▶VIP는 very important person의 약어)
▶ 나는 양복을 고를 때 품질을 중시한다 I give priority to quality when choosing clothes.

(2) 정도·부담
▶ 그 사고에서는 세 명이 사망, 수십 명이 중상을 입었다 Three people were killed and several dozens were seriously injured in the accident.
▶ 사람들은 범인에게 중벌이 내릴 것을 기대하고 있다 The people expect that severe punishment will be inflicted on the criminal.
▶ 병든 부모님의 시중을 드는 것이 그녀에게는 너무 무거운 부담이었다 Taking care of sick parents was too heavy a burden for her.
▶ 그는 입이 무겁다 He talks very little.
▶ 그녀는 그 까다로운 문제를 거뜬히 풀었다 She answered the difficult question easily.

마음이 무겁다 have a heavy heart; be depressed in spirits / 머리가 무겁다 feel heavy in the head / 발걸음이 무겁다 walk with leaden foot; tread heavily / 어깨가 무겁다 have a heavy feeling in the shoulders
▶ 이 실패로 나는 마음이 무거워졌다 This failure weighed heavily upon my mind.
4 〈중하다〉 serious; critical; severe; grave; grievous
◆무거운 벌 a heavy [severe] punishment / 무거운 죄 a grave crime; (a) felony / 무거운 병에 걸리다 get seriously [critically] ill / 병이 무거워지다 become worse [serious]; take a turn for the worse
5 〈중대하다〉 important; weighty; grave
◆무거운 사명[직책] an important mission [position] / 무거운 책임을 맡기다 place [trust] sb with a heavy [grave] responsibility
▶ 이번 임무는 대단히 무겁다 This mission involves very heavy responsibilities.

무게 1 〈중량〉 weight; (美) heft
◆무게가 넘다[모자라다] be over [under] weight / 무게가 늘다 gain [pick up] (in) weight; put on weight / 무게가 있다 be heavy [weighty] / 무게를 달다 weigh (a stone) / 무게를 지탱하다 bear the weight / 무게로 팔다 sell by weight
▶ 그것은 무게가 많이[적게] 나간다 It is heavy [light] in weight. ⇌ It weighs heavy [light].

▶ 그녀는 무게가 3킬로그램 늘었다[줄었다] She has gained [lost] three kilograms.
▶ 저 가게는 항상 무게를 속인다 They always falsify the weight at that store.
▶ 목조 다리가 트럭의 무게로 허물어졌다 The wooden bridge collapsed under the weight of the truck.
2 〈중요성〉 importance; weight; 〈관록〉 dignity; prestige
♦ 무게 있는 말 a remark carrying weight [authority, conviction]/ 무게 있는 사람 a man of dignified presence; a person of dignity / 무게가 없는 unimposing; undignified; 《an opinion》 of no weight
▶ 그는 무게가 없다 He is lacking in dignity.
▶ 그는 학자로서 무게가 있다 He is held in high respect as a scholar.
▶ 그 사람 말은 무게가 있다 What he says carries weight [authority, conviction].
■ —중심 〔物〕 the center of gravity; the centroid

무결근 無缺勤 perfect attendance ⇨ 무결석
무결석 無缺席 perfect [regular] attendance ⇨ 개근(皆勤)
무경험 無經驗 lack of experience; inexperience ♦ 무경험의 inexperienced; green; untrained
■ —자 an inexperienced person; a green hand; (口) a greenhorn: 무경험자 환영 《광고》 Help wanted. Experience not necessary.
무계획 無計劃 being planless —무계획하다 planless; unplanned; haphazard; reckless
▶ 그런 무계획한 행동으로는 아무것도 되지 않는다 You would not realize anything by such a rash act.
무고 無故 〈무사〉 being without mishap —무고하다 safe and sound; well; 《be》 all right
♦ 무고하게 지내다 get along well [all right]
▶ 댁내 두루 무고하신지요? Have all of you been well?
무고 無辜 innocence —무고하다 innocent; guiltless ♦ 무고한 백성 innocent people / 무고함이 밝혀지다 have one's innocence established; be cleared from the charge
무고 誣告 〔法〕 a false charge [accusation]; 〈문서상의〉 a libel; 〈구두상의〉 a slander; a calumny ♦ 절도를 했다는 무고 a false accusation of theft aganist sb
—무고하다 make a false charge [accusation] 《against sb》; accuse sb falsely 《of theft》
■ —자 a false accuser; a calumniator —죄 a calumny; a false accusation [charge]: 무고죄로 고소당하다 be sued on charges of making a false accusation
무곡 舞曲 〈음악과 춤〉 dancing and music; 〈무용곡〉 dance music
무골충 無骨蟲 〈벌레〉 a boneless worm; 〈사람〉 a spineless person; a spiritless fellow
▶ 그는 무골충이다 He has no backbone.
무골호인 無骨好人 an excessively good-natured person
무공 武功 military exploits [merits, feats]; distinguished military services ♦ 무공을 세우다 distinguish oneself in war [battle]; render distinguished military services
■ —훈장 the Order of Military Merit: 화랑 무공훈장을 받다 be awarded the Order of Military Merit Hwarang
무공해식품 無公害食品 pollution-free food
무공해차 無公害車 a non-polluting car; an anti-pollution car; a pollution-free [low-emission] car
무과 武科 the military service examination
무관 武官 an officer; a military officer
■ 시종(侍從)— an aide-de-camp to His [Her] Majesty 대사관부(附)육군[해군, 공군]— a military [a naval, an air] attaché to an embassy
무관 無官 ♦ 무관으로 without office
무관 無冠 ♦ 무관의 제왕 a king without a crown; an uncrowned king [monarch]
무관(계) 無關(係) no connection; irrelevance; impertinence
—무관(계)하다 unconcerned; unrelated; unconnected; 〈서술적〉 have no connection [relation] 《with》; have nothing to do 《with》; have no bearing 《on》; be irrelevant 《to》
▶ 그것은 나와는 무관(계)하다 That has nothing to do with me.
▶ 당신의 의견은 이 문제와 무관하다 Your opinion has no bearing on this matter.
▶ 누가 이기든 나와는 무관하다 It does not matter to me who wins.
▶ 당신의 제안은 의제와 무관(계)합니다 Your proposal is extraneous [irrelevant] to the subject under discussion.
▶ 그가 그 사건과 전연 무관한 것은 아니다 He is involved in the case a little.
무관심 無關心 indifference; unconcern; apathy; nonchalance; callousness
♦ 정치적 무관심 political apathy / 교육에 대한 일반의 무관심 the indifference of the general public toward education
—무관심하다 indifferent 《to》; disinterested; uninterested 《in》; callous [apathetic] 《to》; careless [unconcerned, incurious] 《about》; unmindful 《of》
♦ 남의 감정에 무관심하다 have no regard for the feelings of others / 복장에 무관심하다 be careless about one's personal appearance
▶ 남들은 당신의 의견에 무관심합니다 Others are unconcerned about your opinion.
▶ 그는 영문학에 전연 무관심했다 He was not at all [in the least] interested in English literature.
▶ 회담의 성패에 내가 무관심할 수 없다 The success of the conference cannot be a matter of indifference to me.
▶ 정치에 무관심한 사람이 많네요 There are a lot of people who don't show any interest in [are quite indifferent to] politics, aren't there?
▶ 그는 세속적인 이득에 무관심하다 He has no interest in worldly gain. ⇒ He is indifferent to worldly gain.
무교육 無敎育 lack [want] of education
♦ 무교육의 uneducated; uncultured; illiterate
■ —자 an uneducated person

무교회주의 無敎會主義 the non-church movement

무구 武具 arms ⇨ 무기

무구 無垢 purity; immaculacy; innocence
—무구하다 pure; spotless; immaculate; innocent; unspoiled
♦ 무구한 농민 an innocent farmer / 무구한 처녀 an innocent [immaculate] virgin

무국적 無國籍 —자 a stateless [denationalized] person; a person of no nationality

무굴제국 —帝國 〔史〕 the Mogul [Moghul, Mughal] Empire

무궁 無窮 eternity; infinitude
—무궁하다 eternal; infinite; everlasting; endless; boundless

무궁무진하다 無窮無盡 infinite; endless; boundless; limitless; inexhaustible

무궁화 無窮花 〔植〕 a rose of Sharon
—대훈장 the Grand Order of *Mugunghwa*
—동산 the beautiful land of Korea

무궤도 無軌道 ♦ 무궤도의 railless; trackless
—무궤도하다 aberrant; extravagant; eccentric; unprincipled; wild
♦ 무궤도한 생활 a loose [reckless, dissipated] life / 무궤도한 행동 unprincipled behavior
—전차 a trolley bus; a trackless tram [trolley car]

무균 無菌 〔醫〕 asepsis
♦ 무균의 aseptic; germless; without bacilli [germs]; 〈살균한〉 sterilized
—배양 aseptic culture —법 〔醫〕 an asepsis (*pl.* -ses) —상태 an aseptic [a germ-free] condition; an asepsis 《*pl.* -ses》 —수술 aseptic surgery —우유 sterilized [pasteurized] milk

무극 無極 〈무한〉 endlessness; limitlessness; 〔物〕 without poles 〈무극(성)의〉 nonpolar
—결합 nonpolar union —분자 a nonpolar molecule

무근 無根 ♦ 무근한 소문 a groundless [wild] rumor; a canard / 무근의 groundless; unfounded; baseless; false
▶ 그 소문은 전연 사실무근이었다 The rumor turned out to be completely false [groundless]. ⇌ There was not a bit of truth in the rumor.

무급 無給 ♦ 무급의 unpaid; unsalaried; non-salaried / 무급으로 without pay; for nothing
▶ 그 직책은 무급이다 The post carries no pay.

무기 武技 military arts ⇨ 무예(武藝)

무기 武器 a weapon; arms
♦ 무기의 불법 소지 illegal possession of arms / 무기를 들고 일어서다 take up [rise in] arms (against) / 무기를 버리다 give up [lay down] one's arms / 무기를 빼앗다 disarm sb of (his) weapons
▶ 무기를 들어라 To arms!
▶ 무기를 버려라 Surrender your weapons!
▶ 무기를 버리고 나와라 Lay [Throw] down your weapons [arms] and come out.
▶ 눈물이 그녀의 유일한 무기였다 Tears were her only weapon.
▶ 그녀의 여동생은 미모라는 무기를 가지고 있었다 Her younger sister was armed with beauty.
■ 궁극— an ultimate weapon 재래식— conventional weapons 핵— a nuclear weapon
■ —경쟁 arms race : 갈수록 치열해지는 무기경쟁 the ever-mounting arms race —고 an armory; an arsenal —구입 arms purchase —원조 arms aid —제조 arms production; weaponry; weaponeering

무기 無期 ♦ 무기의 unlimited; indefinite / 무기 휴회가 되다 be adjourned for an indefinite period
—공채 a perpetual public loan —수(囚) a lifer —정학 suspension from school for an indefinite period : 그는 무기정학 처분을 받았다 He was suspended from school for an indefinite period. —형 imprisonment for life

무기 無機 ♦ 토양의 무기 성분 the mineral content of the soil / 무기의 inorganic; unorganized; mineral
■ —계(界) the inorganic world —물 inorganic matter; an inorganic substance; 〈광물질〉 a mineral —산 a mineral [an inorganic] acid —염류 inorganic salts —영양 mineral nutrition —질 〈무기물〉 inorganic matter; 〈광물질〉 mineral matter: 무기질 비료 inorganic fertilizer —호흡 an aerobic respiration —화학 inorganic chemistry; abiochemistry —화합물 an inorganic compound

무기대여 武器貸與 lend-lease; lease-lend
—법 〈미국의〉 the Lend-Lease [Lease-Lend] Act : 무기대여법에 의한 공급 물자〔원조〕 lend-lease materials [aid]

무기력 無氣力 enervation; lethargy; languor
—무기력하다 spiritless; inactive; nerveless; lethargic; languid; tame; weak-kneed; feeble
♦ 무기력한 남편 a tame husband / 무기력한 모습 a watery style / 사람을 무기력하게 하는 풍토 an enervating climate
▶ 그는 점잖고 선하지만 어딘가 무기력하다 He is gentle and good, but a rather spiritless person.

무기명 無記名 ♦ 무기명의 unregistered; unsigned; uninscribed; blank / 설문지에 무기명으로 답하다 answer a questionnaire unsigned
■ —공채 an unregistered [a bearer] bond —식 이서 (a) blank [general] endorsement —어음 a blank bill —주권(株券) a bearer stock; a stock certificate issued to a bearer —투표 a secret [an unsigned] vote [ballot]; secret voting : 무기명투표로 선출하다 elect by a secret vote [ballot]

무기연기 無期延期 (an) indefinite postponement
▶ 공식 방문은 무기연기되었다 The state visit was postponed [put off] indefinitely.
▶ 재판은 무기연기되었다 The court was adjourned for an indefinite period.

무기음 無氣音 〔音聲〕 an unaspirated sound

무기징역 無期懲役 penal servitude for life; life imprisonment ▶ 그는 무기징역형을 받았다 He was given penal servitude for life [sentenced to life imprisonment].

무기한 無期限 ♦ 무기한의 indefinite; limitless
▶ 이 조약은 무기한으로 유효하다 This treaty will be effective indefinitely.

▶이 표는 무기한으로 유효하다 This ticket is valid [good] at any time.
■─대부금 an advance without a fixed date for settlement; a dead loan ─파업 a no-time-limit strike; an indefinite strike

무꾸리 a shaman's divination [fortune-telling] ─무꾸리하다 consult a shaman; have one's fortune told by a shaman

무난하다 無難── 1〈수월하다〉easy
♦무난히 easily; with ease; without difficulty [trouble] / 무난히 이기다 win an easy victory 《over》; win hands down
▶그는 그 문제를 무난히 풀 수 있었다 He found no difficulty in solving the problem.
2〈안전하다〉safe; free from danger
▶너는 그렇게 하는 것이 무난하다 It's safe for you to do so.
▶그날 밤은 무난하게 지나갔다 The night passed uneventfully [without accident].
▶나는 하루하루를 무난히 보낼 수 있으면 그것으로 족하다 I'm happy if I can live safely from day to day.
3〈무던하다〉fairly good; moderate; passable; acceptable; free from fault
▶이 정도면 그저 무난하다 This may pass [be acceptable].
▶그녀의 창법은 무난한 편이다 There is no particular flaw in her singing.

무남독녀 無男獨女 an [the] only daughter; a daughter and only child 《of》

무너뜨리다 pull [tear, break] down; destroy; demolish
♦건물을 무너뜨리다 demolish [tear down, pull down, destroy] a building / 돌담을 무너뜨리다 tear [pull] down a stone wall
▶여기 쌓여 있던 책을 누가 무너뜨렸니? Who knocked over the books that were piled up here?

무너지다 collapse; crumble; fall [come] down; go [fall] to pieces; give way; be destroyed
♦무너져가는 성 a moldering castle / 무너져가는 판잣집 a tumble-down [beat-up] shack
▶대홍수로 제방이 무너졌다 The bank gave way [broke down] under the deluge.
▶저 콘크리트 블록벽이 무너지면 위험하겠네 Think of the danger if that concrete-block wall collapses.
▶건물이 요란한 소리를 내며 무너졌다 The building fell down with a crash.

무녀 巫女 a shaman ⇨ 무당

무너리 〈첫새끼〉the first-born of a litter;〈사람〉a simpleton; a dunce

무념무상 無念無想〔佛敎〕freedom from all ideas and thoughts
─무념무상하다 be free from all worldly [distracting] thoughts; be in a frame of mind void of all ideas and thoughts

무능 無能 lack of ability; inability; incompetency; inefficiency; incapacity
▶야당은 정부의 물가 정책의 무능을 공격했다 The opposition party attacked the government for its inefficiency over price policies.
─무능하다 incapable; incompetent; inefficient; good-for-nothing; lacking in ability
♦무능한 사람 a man of inability; an incompetent (man); a good-for-nothing (fellow) / 무능한 정권 an inefficient regime
▶그는 무능하여 파면되었다 He was dismissed for incompetency [lack of ability].
▶그는 의사로서 무능하다 He is no good as a doctor.

무능력 無能力 inability; lack of ability;〔法〕incompetence; incapacity
─무능력하다 incompetent; incapable
■─자 an incompetent [incapable] person; a person without legal capacity

무늬 a pattern; a design; a figure
♦기하학적 무늬 geometric patterns / 줄무늬 a linear design; stripes / 벽지의 무늬 wallpaper patterns; a design on wallpaper / 새의 깃털 무늬 the marking of a bird's plumage / 꽃무늬가 있는 드레스 a dress with flower patterns [designs]; a flower-patterned dress / 무늬를 넣다 figure; pattern; decorate with [put on] a pattern; make designs [patterns]
▶이 줄무늬는 참으로 아름답다 This striped pattern is so beautiful.
▶무늬가 고상하다 The pattern is in good taste.
▶그는 무늬있는 셔츠를 좋아한다 He likes patterned shirts.

무단 武斷 militarism ■─정치 military government [rule]; government by the bayonet

무단 無斷 ♦무단히 without leave [permission]; without notice; without warning / 무단히 차용하다 borrow sth without the owner's permission / 남의 것을 무단으로 쓰다 make free use of another's possessions / 무단으로 학교를 결석하다 stay away from school without notice
▶그는 무단으로 내 방에 들어왔다 He entered my room without permission.
▶무단으로 외박해서는 안된다 You are not allowed to stay out overnight without notice.
▶무단출입금지 (게시) No trespassing.
▶무단 흥행을 금함 All rights of performance reserved.

무단결근 無斷缺勤 absence without due notice
─무단결근하다 be absent [absent oneself]《from one's office》without leave [due notice]

무단결석 無斷缺席 (school) truancy
─무단결석하다 play truant; stay away《from school》without leave; (美) play hookey; skip school

무단외출 無斷外出 absence without leave
─무단외출하다 be absent without leave; (美軍俗) go AWOL ■─병 a soldier who is absent without leave; (美軍俗) an AWOL

무담보 ♦무담보의 unsecured; naked; without collateral [security] / 무담보로 대부하다 grant sb a loan without collateral
■─대부금 an unsecured loan ─사채 (社債) an unsecured [英] a naked] debenture ─신용장〔商〕a clean L/C

무당 a (female) shaman; an exorcist; a sorceress

무당개구리 〔動〕 a red-bellied frog
무당벌레 〔昆〕 a ladybird; (美) a ladybug
무대¹ 〈해류〉 〔地〕 a (marine) current; an ocean current ◆더운-[찬] 무대 a warm [cold] current
무대² 〈못난이〉 an ass; a fool; a goose
무대 舞臺 1 〈연극의〉 the stage
◆처음으로 무대를 밟다 make one's debut; make one's first appearance on the stage / 무대에 서다 appear on the stage [before the footlights]; 〈배우가 되다〉 go on [come on, follow] the stage; tread the boards / 각본을 무대에 올리다 stage a play; present [produce] a play; put a play on the stage / 무대에서 얼다 have stage fright / 무대에서 물러나다 go [come] offstage
▶그는 무대를 떠났다 He retired from the stage.
▶네가 무대에 섰었다는 것이 아무래도 믿어지지 않는다 I can't believe you used to appear on the stage.
▶그녀는 5년 후 무대로 복귀했다 She came back to the stage after five years' absence [for the first time in five years].
2 〈활동의〉 the arena; the theater; the sphere; the scene; a field
◆국제 무대에서 활약하다 take an active part in the international arena
▶이 소설의 무대는 금세기로 접어들 무렵의 뉴욕이다 The scene [setting] of this story is (laid) in New York around the turn of this century.
▶그는 세계 외교 무대에서 활약하고 있다 He is active on the world diplomatic scene.
▶무대가 바뀌었다 The scene (has) changed.
■활동— one's sphere [arena] of activity; one's field of action: 그의 활동무대는 점점 더 넓어지고 있다 His sphere of activity is getting larger and larger. 회전— a revolving stage
■—감독 〈사람〉 a stage director; 〈일〉 stage management —경험 a stage experience —극 a stage drama [play]; the speaking stage —기교 stagecraft —뒤 the backstage; behind the scenes; a greenroom —배우 a stage actor [actress, player] —생활 a stage [theatrical] career: 무대생활을 시작하다 follow [enter upon] a stage career —연습 (have) a dress rehearsal —예술 theatrical art —의상 stage costume: 무대 의상을 입은 배우 an actor in stage costume —장치 a setting; the set(s); a set scene; scenery: 무대장치를 하다 set the stage —장치가 a scenic designer —조명 stage lighting —효과 stage effect; scenic effects
무더기 a pile; a heap; a deposit; a lot
◆돌 무더기 a pile [heap] of stones / 한 무더기 천원 1,000 won a lot / 무더기로 팔다[사다] sell [buy] by the lot
▶사과[바나나]가 무더기로 쌓여 있다 Apples [Bananas] lie in heaps.
▶그는 책상 위에 책을 무더기로 쌓았다 He piled books on his desk.
▶돈을 무더기로 준다고 해도 이것은 팔지 않겠다 I wouldn't sell this for all the money in the world.

무더위 sultriness; hot and humid weather; sweltering heat
◆대단한 무더위다 be oppressively [unbearably] hot and humid; be awfully sultry [sweltering]
무덕 無德 lack of virtue ⇨ 부덕(不德)
무던하다 1 〈마음씨가〉 generous; liberal; broad-minded; magnanimous; quite good [nice]
◆무던한 마음씨 generosity; magnanimity / 무던한 사람 a good-natured man / 성질이 무던하다 be moderate in temper
▶그는 사람됨이 무던하다 His personality is gentle and sincere. ⇌ He is quite a nice man. ⇌ He is broad-minded [good-natured].
2 〈정도가〉 enough; sufficient; satisfactory; quite good
▶그에게는 그만하면 무던하다 I think that will be enough for him. ⇌ I am sure that will satisfy him.
무던히 1 〈너그럽게〉 kindly; generously; warmly; satisfactorily
▶그는 우리 아이들에게 무던히 잘해 주었다 He was quite nice to our children.
2 〈꽤〉 pretty; fairly; considerably; quite
◆무던히 많다 be quite a lot / 무던히 애쓰다 make considerable efforts
▶오늘은 무던히도 추운 날씨다 It's awfully cold today.
▶그 사람 키가 무던히도 크군 What a tall man he is!
무덤 a grave; a tomb; a sepulcher
◆연고자 없는 무덤 a neglected grave / 무덤 파는 사람 a gravedigger; a sexton / 무덤을 파다 dig a grave / 무덤을 파헤치다 dig open a grave / 스스로 무덤을 파다 dig one's own grave; bring about one's own ruin / 무덤에 묻다 bury (the body) to the grave / 무덤에 묻히다 lie in one's grave; be under the sod
▶나는 선조의 무덤 앞에서 맹세했다 I swore in front of the family tomb.
▶그것은 스스로 무덤을 파는 짓이다 It is suicidal [tantamount to digging your own grave] to do such a thing.
무덥다 sultry; muggy; sweltering; oppressively hot; (hot and) stuffy
▶어젯밤에는 무더워서 잠을 제대로 못잤다 Last night I could not sleep well on account of the oppressive heat.
▶어제는 무더웠는데, 오늘은 좀 선선하다 It was stifling yesterday, but it is cooler today.
무도 武道 〈무예〉 military arts [science]; 〈무사도〉 chivalry; knighthood
무도 舞蹈 〈춤〉 a dance; dancing
◆무도를 하다 dance; perform a dance
■—곡 the dance music —병 〔醫〕 St. Vitus's dance; chorea —장 a dancing hall; (美) a dance hall —화 dancing shoes
무도하다 無道— inhuman; brutal; cruel; outrageous ◆무도한 짓 a cruel deed; an inhuman act / 무도한 짓을 하다 act brutally [cruelly] toward sb
무도회 舞蹈會 a ball; a dancing party; a dance ◆무도회를 열다 give a ball
■—가면[가장]— a masked [fancy dress] ball,

a masquerade

무독하다 無毒— 〈독이 없다〉 nonpoisonous; harmless; innoxious; nonvenomous 《snake》; 〈성질이 순하다〉 gentle; mild
▶ 이 뱀은 무독하다 This snake is harmless [not venomous].

무두장이 a tanner

무두질 1〈모피의〉 tanning; tannage
—**무두질하다** tan; dress
♦ 무두질한 가죽 tanned leather / 무두질하지 않은 untanned; raw 《hide》 / 가죽을 무두질하다 tan leather; dress skin
2 〈고통〉 a grinding [pricking, piercing, gnawing, stabbing] pain
♦ 뱃속에서 무두질하다 have a gnawing pain in one's stomach

무드 〈기분·분위기〉 a mood; an atmosphere
♦ 무드 있는 찻집 a coffee shop with atmosphere / 가정적인 무드가 있는 레스토랑 a restaurant with a homely atmosphere / 무드를 조성하다 create [set] a mood
—**음악** mood music

무득점 無得點 ♦ 무안타 무득점의 시합 a no-hit and no-run game / 무득점의 scoreless; 〔野〕 runless / 무득점으로 끝나다 end scoreless
▶ 우리는 그들을 8회까지 무득점으로 막아냈다 We held them runless for eight innings.

무디다 1〈날이〉 dull; blunt
♦ 무딘 칼 a blunt [dull] knife / 무딘 면도날 a blunt razor blade
▶ 그 연필은 끝이 무디다 The pencil has a dull point.
▶ 가위가 무디어졌다 The scissors have become dull [blunt]. ⇌ The scissors don't cut well any more.
2 〈머리·감각 등이 둔하다〉 dull; slow-witted; dim
♦ 머리가 무딘 사람 a dull [slow-witted] person / 감각이 무디어지다 get dull of one's sense
▶ 그는 무디어서 상황을 모르고 있다 He doesn't realize the situation because he is not very bright.
3 ⇨ 무뚝뚝하다

무뚝뚝하다 blunt; brusque; abrupt; curt; short
♦ 무뚝뚝한 사람 a blunt [brusque] person; a gruffish [short-spoken] man; a bad mixer / 무뚝뚝하게 대답하다 reply in a monosyllable; answer shortly; give a curt [blunt] answer / 무뚝뚝하게 말하다 talk bluntly [shortly]; speak stiffly

무량 無量 immensity —**무량하다** infinite; inestimable; immeasurable
▶ 그 사건을 생각하면 감개가 무량하다 When I call that event to mind, I am filled with deep emotion [my heart is too full for words].
■ —**대복**(大福) infinite happiness; immeasurable bliss —**수**(壽) constant life

무럭무럭 1〈자라는 모양〉 rapidly; quickly; healthily; well
♦ 무럭무럭 자라다 grow healthily; grow up quickly [rapidly]; grow fast
▶ 벼가 무럭무럭 자라고 있다 The rice is growing very well.

2〈냄새·김·연기 등이〉 thickly; densely
♦ 김이 무럭무럭 나는 요리 a steaming dish / 김이 무럭무럭 나다 puff steam / 연기를 무럭무럭 내뿜다 send up volumes of smoke
▶ 굴뚝에서 연기가 무럭무럭 났다 Plumes of smoke rolled lavishly from the chimney.

무려 無慮 as many [much] as; no less than; 〈약〉 about
▶ 무려 3만원을 주고 이 책을 샀다 This book cost as much as thirty thousand won.
▶ 야구장에는 무려 35,000명의 관중이 모였다 No less than 35,000 spectators were present at the baseball field.

무력 武力 military force [power]; force of arms; armed force
♦ 무력에 호소하다 resort [appeal] to arms; use force / 무력으로 굴복시키다 keep 《people》 in submission by the sword
▶ 우리는 국제간의 분쟁을 결코 무력으로 해결하지 않을 것이다 We will never settle international disputes by force [resorting to military power].
■ —**개입** armed interference [intervention] —**도발** an armed provocation —**외교** power diplomacy; diplomacy backed by force —**충돌** an armed conflict : 그들 사이에 무력 충돌이 있었던 것같다 There seemed to be an armed conflict between them. —**행사** the use of armed force —**혁명** an armed revolution

무력 無力 〈힘없음〉 powerlessness; 〈무능〉 incompetence; 〈환자·유아 등〉 helplessness; 〈재력이 없음〉 lack of funds
—**무력하다** powerless; helpless; impotent; 〈무능하다〉 incompetent
♦ 적의 공격에 대하여 무력하다 be helpless against the enemy's attack / 무력하게 하다 incapacitate; neutralize 《enemy defenses》
▶ 그가 없으면 나는 정말 무력할 것이다 I would be quite helpless without him.
■ —**감** an impotent feeling; a feeling of helplessness

무렵 〈특정한 때〉 time; 〈쯤〉 about; around; toward; 〈…할 때〉 when...; while...
♦ 그 무렵에 in those days; at that time; then / 날이 밝을 무렵에 toward daybreak / 20세기가 끝날 무렵에 toward the end of the twentieth century
▶ 그녀는 해마다 이 무렵이면 감기에 걸린다 She always catches cold about this time of the year.
▶ 네가 귀가할 무렵까지는 끝내 놓겠다 I will get it finished by the time you get home.

무례 無禮 〈예의에 벗어남〉 impoliteness; discourtesy; 〈거칠고 모욕적임〉 rudeness
▶ 무례를 용서하시기 바랍니다 I humbly apologize for my lack of courtesy. ⇌ Please forgive my rudeness [bad manners].
—**무례하다** 〈거칠고 모욕적인〉 rude; 〈예의에 벗어나는〉 impolite; insolent; discourteous; disrespectful
♦ 무례한 짓 rude behavior / 무례한 짓을 하다 behave [act] rude(ly) 《to sb》
▶ 그렇게 무례한 녀석은 처음 봤다 I've never met such an impolite man like him. ⇌ He is

무뢰한

the rudest man I've ever met.
▶ 그는 무례하게도 나의 제의를 거절했다 He rudely [impolitely] rejected my offer.
▶ 무례하구나 Don't be rude to me. ⇒ How rude of you!

무뢰한 無賴漢 a rogue; a villain; a scoundrel; a rascal; a hooligan; a ruffian; a hoodlum; (美俗) a hood; 〈무리〉 a gang of rogues

무료 無料 free of charge; no charge
♦ 무료의 free (of charge); gratuitous / 무료로 배달하다 deliver *sth* free of charge / 무료로 보내다 send *sth* free / 무료로 봉사하다 serve for nothing; work without pay / 무료로 제공되다 be offered free [without cost]
▶ 그것은 무료입니다 You can get it free. ⇒ It is free (of charge).
▶ 이 팜플렛은 무료입니다 There is no charge for this pamphlet.
▶ 여기서 산 물건은 무료로 배달해 드립니다 Articles bought here will be delivered free of charge.
▶ 견본은 청구하시는 대로 무료로 보내드립니다 The sample is sent gratis on request.
▶ 입장 무료 (게시) Admission (is) free. ⇒ No charge for admission.
▶ 운임 무료 (게시) Freight free.
▶ 6세 미만 무료 (게시) Admission free for children under six.
—무료 달 delivery (略 FD) —수화물 허용량 free baggage allowance —승차권 a free pass 《over a subway》 —입장 free admission —입장[관람]권 a free pass 《to a show》; (美俗) an (Annie) Oakley —입장[관람]자 a free visitor; (美口) a deadhead —진료소 a free clinic; a dispensary

무료 無聊 〈심심하고 따분함〉 boredom; ennui; tedium; 〈열적음〉 awkwardness
▶ 음악을 들으며 무료를 달랬다 I relieved my ennui [tedium, boredom] by listening to music.
—무료하다 〈재미가 없어서〉 boring; 〈지루한〉 tedious; 〈신선미가 없는〉 dull; 〈단조로운〉 monotonous; 〈서술하게〉 get bored; be weary
♦ 무료한 시간 a dull time; dull [tedious] hours / 무료하여 for want of occupation; because *one* has nothing to do / 무료함을 달래다 kill time; while away the time; beguile the tedium
▶ 담배를 끊고 나니 남과 이야기할 때 어쩐지 무료하다 I feel rather awkward in talking with people, now that I've given up smoking.

무룡태 a soft-headed person

무루 無漏 without omission [exception]; in full; one and all

무르녹다 1 〈과일이〉 get [become] fully ripe; become overripe; attain full maturity
♦ 무르녹은 감 a fully ripened persimmon
2 〈기회 등이〉 be ripe; mature
▶ 혁명의 기운이 무르녹았다 The time was ripe for a revolution.
3 〈녹음이〉 deepen; become deeper [verdurous] ♦ 신록이 무르녹는 5월 the month of May with its fresh verdure

무르다[1] 〈녹실녹실해지다〉 soften; get soft;

become tender; be well done [cooked]
♦ 무른 감자 well-cooked potatoes / 알맞게[적당히] 무르다 be done to a turn / 너무 무르다 be overdone; be boiled to a pulp
▶ 복숭아가 물렀다 The peach has got soft.
▶ 고기가 잘 물렀다 The meat has become tender enough.
▶ 이것은 아직 안 물렀다 This is only half boiled [half done]. ⇒ This is underdone.

무르다[2] **1** 〈산 것을〉 take back [redeem] money canceling a purchase; get a refund; 〈판 것을〉 give back [return] money canceling a sale; give a refund
♦ 대금을 무르다 refund the price paid / 샀던 라디오를 무르다 return the radio *one* (has) bought and get the money back
2 〈상쇄하다〉 cancel [offset] each other's accounts
♦ 빌려준 돈과 구전을 무르다 set off a loan against the commission
3 〈장기·바둑에서〉 retract a move

무르다[3] **1** 〈연하다〉 soft; tender; flabby; flaccid
♦ 무른 감 a soft [squashy] persimmon / 무른 고기 tender meat / 무른 살 flabby [flaccid] flesh / 무르게 하다 soften; make soft
2 〈마음·힘이 약하다〉 weak; feeble; infirm; delicate; submissive; pliant; yielding
♦ 아내에게 무른 남편 an uxorious [a doting] husband / 자식에게 무른 아버지 an indulgent [a doting] father / 정에 무르다 be easily moved; be sentimental [tenderhearted] / 여자에게 무르다 have a weakness [soft spot] for girls; be spoon(e)y on [over] a woman

무르익다 1 〈술·과일 등이〉 ripen; be [grow] ripe; mellow; mature
♦ 무르익은 술 mellow [well-mellowed] wine / 무르익은 멜론 ripe (and soft) melon
▶ 사과가 따도 좋을 만큼 무르익었다 The apples are ripe enough to be picked.
2 〈때가〉 be ripe for 《action》
♦ 기회가 무르익기를 기다리다 wait till the time is ripe; wait for a ripe opportunity [moment]
▶ 정상회담의 시기가 무르익었다 The time is now ripe for a summit conference.

무릅쓰다 〈위험 등을〉 risk; face; brave; defy; dare; venture
♦ 곤란을 무릅쓰다 overcome difficulties / 위험을 무릅쓰다 run a risk [risks]; take a risk [risks] / 폭풍우를 무릅쓰다 brave a storm
▶ 그것이 죽음을 무릅쓰고까지 할 만한 가치가 있는 것이냐? Is it worth doing at the risk of your life?
▶ 구조대는 폭풍을 무릅쓰고 출발했다 Braving the storm, the rescue party set out. ⇒ The rescue party set out in the face of the storm.

무릇[1] 〈植〉 a squill

무릇[2] 〈대체로〉 generally (speaking); as a rule; in general; on the whole
▶ 무릇 부모란 자식을 사랑하게 마련이다 Parents generally [usually] love children.
▶ 무릇 역사는 되풀이되는 것이다 As a whole history repeats itself.

무릉도원 武陵桃源 an Arcadia; a Utopia; the Happy Valley ◆ 무릉도원의 꿈 a Utopian dream

무릎 a knee; a lap
◆ 무릎 깊이의 knee-deep / 무릎 위에 앉다 sit on *sb's* lap / 아이를 무릎에 앉히다 hold a child on *one's* lap
〈무릎이〉 무릎이 떨렸다 My knees were knocking.
▶ 그의 바지는 무릎이 불룩하다 His pants are baggy at the knees.
▶ 내 진 바지는 무릎이 해졌다 My jeans are worn out at the knees.
〈무릎을〉 무릎을 굽히다[세우다] bend [draw up] *one's* knees / 무릎을 꿇다 fall [go down] on a knee / 무릎을 꿇고 기도하다 kneel in prayer; pray on *one's* knees / 무릎을 맞대고 담판하다 have direct negotiations 《with》 / 무릎을 맞대고 정담을 나누다 have a friendly talk with *sb*
▶ 그는 무릎을 치며 큰 소리로 웃었다 He slapped his knees and burst into laughter.
▶ 도랑에 빠져 무릎을 다쳤다 Falling into a ditch, I was wounded in the knee.
〈무릎에〉 그녀는 무릎(위)에 아기를 앉히고 있었다 She held her baby on her knees [lap].
▶ 그는 무릎(위)에 서류 가방을 놓고 앉아 있었다 He sat with an attaché case across his knees [lap].
〈무릎까지〉 무릎까지 올라오는 장화 knee-high boots / 무릎까지 물에 잠기다 stand knee-deep in the water
▶ 눈이 무릎까지 쌓였다 The snow lay knee-deep.
▶ 나는 무릎까지 물에 잠겼다 I was up to my knees in the water.
▶ 초원은 무릎까지 닿는 풀로 덮여 있었다 The meadow was covered with knee-high grass.
■ ―마디 a knee joint ―맞š음 a confrontation; a face-to-face meeting ―반사〈生〉knee-jerk reflex ―받이 a kneecap; a kneepad ―뼈〈슬개골〉 the kneepan; the kneecap

무리[1] **1** 【사람의】〈집단〉a group; a company; a party; 〈군중의〉a crowd; a throng; 〈도적의〉a band; 〈악한의〉a gang; 〈폭도의〉a mob
◆ 사람의 무리 a crowd of people / 이민의 무리 a group of immigrants / 한 무리의 도적 a band of thieves / 무리를 짓다 form a group; band together; gang up
▶ 광장에는 3천명이나 되는 학생이 무리를 지어 모였다 A huge throng of 3,000 students came together in the square.
2 【짐승의】〈대형 동물의〉a herd 《of cattle》; a drove; 〈새·양 등의〉a flock 《of pigeons》; 〈사냥개·이리 등의〉a pack; 〈물고기의〉a shoal; a school
◆ 한 무리의 연어 a shoal of salmon / 무리를 이루다 group [herd, flock] together / 무리를 지어 살다 live in herds [flocks]
▶ 한 무리의 양이 몰려오고 있다 A flock of sheep is coming.
▶ 그 물고기는 혼자 헤엄쳐 다니기도 하고 무리를 지어 다니기도 한다 Those fish swim either singly or in schools.

무리[2] 〈생산물의 성수기〉the season ▶ 조기가 한창 잡힐 무리다 It is the yellow corbina season.

무리[3] 〈앙금〉the settlings of rice-flour

무리[4] 〈해·달의〉a halo 《*pl.* ~(e)s》; a ring
■ 달[햇]— the halo of the moon [sun]

무리 無理 1 〈이치에 맞지 않음〉unreasonableness
―무리하다 〈도리에 반한〉unreasonable; 〈부당한〉unjustifiable; 〈부자연스런〉unnatural
◆ 무리한[과도한, 부당한] 요구를 하다 make an unreasonable [excessive, unfair] demand 《of *sb*》 / 무리하게 요구[기대]하다 ask [expect] too much 《of *sb*》
▶ 그것은 무리한 주문이다 Your demands are unreasonable. ⇌ You're asking [expecting] too much. ⇌ (口) That's a tall order.
▶ 무리한 요구를 해서는 안된다 You cannot make unreasonable demands.
▶ 무리한 소리 하지 마라 Be reasonable.
2 〈불가능〉―무리하다 impossible; beyond *one's* power
▶ 그 일을 전부하다는 건 무리한 일이야 I can't [It is impossible for me to, I am unable to] do all that job.
▶ 그건 그에게는 무리한 일이다 The task is beyond his power.
3 〈강제〉compulsion
―무리하다 〈강제·의무적인〉compulsory; 〈우격다짐의〉forcible; 〈강제된〉forced
◆ 무리하게 by force; forcibly; compulsorily; 〈뜻에 반하여〉against *one's* will / 아이에게 약을 무리하게 먹이다 make the child take the pill; force [compel] the child to take the pill
▶ 나는 가고 싶지 않았는데 그가 무리하게 나를 가게 했다 I didn't want to go, but he forced me (to) [made me go].
4 〈과도〉excess; excessiveness; 〈과로〉overwork; overstrain
◆ 무리를 하다 〈일을 너무 많이 하다〉work too much; overwork; 〈혹사하다〉strain *oneself*
▶ 그는 무리를 해서 병이 났다 He became sick because he worked too much [from overwork]. ⇌ Overwork made him sick.
▶ 무리를 하지 마라 Don't work too hard.
■ ―방정식 〈數〉an irrational equation ―수 (數) an irrational number; a surd ―식 (式) an irrational expression ―함수 an irrational function

무 마 하 다 撫摩― 〈어루만지다〉stroke; pat; 〈달래다〉soothe; appease; calm; quiet; pacify
◆ 싸움을 무마하다 smooth down a quarrel / 성난 사람을 무마하다 calm [soothe] an angry person / 소동을 무마시키다 pour oil on [upon] troubled waters

무말랭이 dried strips of radish

무면허 無免許 ◆ 무면허의 unlicensed; unregistered 《driver》 / 무면허로 운전하다 drive 《a car》 without a license
■ ―운전사[의사] an unlicensed driver [medical practitioner]

무명 cotton; cotton cloth ■ ―베 cotton cloth; muslin ―실 cotton thread [yarn] ―옷 cotton clothes [garments]

무명 武名 military fame [distinction]; renown in arms ◆무명을 떨치다 win [gain] military fame

무명 無名 ◆무명의 nameless; unnamed; 〈알려지지 않은〉 obscure; unknown; 〈익명의〉 anonymous
▶ 당시 그는 아직 무명이었다 At that time he was not known to us.
■—수(數) 〔數〕 an absolute number —씨(氏) an anonym; an anonymous person : 이 답안지는 무명씨의 것이구나 This examination paper is Mr. Unknown's [has no name on it]. —인(人) an obscure individual —작가 an obscure [a nameless] writer : 그는 죽을 때까지 무명작가였다 He was an obscure writer until he died. —지(指) the ring finger

무명용사 無名勇士 an unknown soldier
◆무명용사의 묘〈미국 워싱턴의 알링턴 묘지〉the Tomb of the Unknown Soldier(s)

무모 無毛 ◆무모의 hairless; glabrous
■—증〔醫〕 atrichia; atrichosis (*pl.* -ses)

무모하다 無謀— reckless; rash; thoughtless; imprudent; inconsiderate; daredevil
◆무모한 시도 a reckless attempt; a wild [mad] scheme / 무모한 운전 reckless driving / 무모한 짓을 하다 do reckless things; behave recklessly; take a leap in the dark
▶ 무모한 짓은 하지 마라 Look before you leap.
▶ 내 동생은 무모한 녀석이야 My brother is a reckless fellow [doesn't care about anything].
▶ 그런 비 오는 날에 등산을 하다니 무모한 짓이었다 It was imprudent of them to climb the mountain on such a rainy day.
◆무모하게 마시면 사고를 일으키게 돼 Reckless drinking will cause accident.

무문근 無紋筋 〔解〕 an unstriated muscle

무미 無味 ◆무미 무취의 of no taste or scent / 무미 무취의 액체 a tasteless, odorless liquid
—무미하다 tasteless; flavorless; vapid; flat; insipid

무미건조하다 無味乾燥— dry (as a chip); dry-as-dust; dusty; insipid; dull; flat
◆무미건조한 생활 a prosaic [cut-and-dried] life / 무미건조한 이야기 a dry and tasteless story
▶ 그의 연설은 무미건조했다 His speech was insipid [dull].

무미류 無尾類 〔動〕 Anura; Salientia
◆무미류의 동물 a salientian; an anuran

무미익기 無尾翼機 a tailless airplane

무반 武班 〔史〕 the military nobility

무반동 無反動 ◆무반동 포(砲) a recoilless cannon [gun]

무반주 無伴奏 ◆무반주의 unaccompanied / 무반주로 노래하다 sing without accompaniment

무방비 無防備 ◆무방비의 defenseless; open; unfortified; naked 《to》
▶ 그 도시는 지금 무방비 상태다 The town is now in a defenseless state.
■—도시 an open city; a naked city

무방하다 無妨— do no harm; be harmless; 〈이의 없다〉 have no objection 《to》; 〈상관없다〉 do not matter; make no difference; 〈해도 좋다〉 may; can; be all right
▶ 그건 없어도 무방하다 We can do without it.
▶ 약간의 산책 정도는 무방하다 A little walk will do you no harm.
▶ 술이나 담배는 조금 해도 무방하다 A little wine or tabacco will do you no harm.

무배당 無配當 ◆무배당의 without paying a dividend; non-dividend paying / 무배당으로 하다 suspend payment of dividends; declare no dividend
■—주(株) a non-dividend stock [payer]: 그 우량주는 무배당주가 되었다 That blue chip stock became a non-dividend payer.

무법 無法 〈불법〉 injustice; lawlessness; unlawfulness; outlawry; outrage; violence
—무법하다 unjust; unlawful; lawless; outrageous; violent
◆무법한 짓을 하다 act unlawfully; do *sb* wrong; commit an outrage [an unlawful act] —자 a lawless man; an outlaw; a rascal —지대 a lawless area [district]; a disturbed area —천지 a lawless world; a state of extreme disorder

무변 無邊 **1** 〈무한〉 infinity; limitlessness; boundlessness
—무변하다 infinite; limitless; boundless; endless
◆광대무변한 하늘 vast and boundless sky
2 〈무이자〉 free of interest; no interest
■—대해(大海) a boundless ocean; a vast expanse of water

무변화 無變化 changelessness; 〈단조로움〉 monotony ◆무변화의 unchanging; unchanged; monotonous

무병 無病 freedom from ailment [illness]
—무병하다 sound; healthy; 〈서술적〉 be in sound [good] health; be quite well

무보수 無報酬 ◆무보수의 일 an unpaid work; a voluntary task / 무보수의 gratuitous; unsalaried / 무보수로 일하다 work for nothing [without pay]
▶ 그는 무보수로 영어를 가르치고 있다 He teaches English free [without a fee].
▶ 나는 무보수로 이 일을 하고 있다 I am not paid for this job.

무복 巫卜 shamans and fortunetellers; sorceresses and soothsayers

무복친 無服親 a distant relative (for whom *one* wears no mourning)

무분별 無分別 indiscretion; 〈생각이 모자람〉 thoughtlessness; 〈경솔〉 imprudence; recklessness; rashness
◆아무의 무분별을 나무라다 reprove *sb* for (his) indiscretion
—무분별하다 indiscreet; imprudent; thoughtless; reckless; rash; ill-advised
◆무분별하게도 indiscreetly; imprudently; thoughtlessly; recklessly / 무분별한 짓을 하다 commit a rash act; act rashly
▶ 환자에게 그런 말을 하다니 무분별했구나 It was thoughtless of you to say such a thing to a sick person.

▶무분별하게도 그는 폭풍 속에 배를 저어 나갔다 He rashly rowed out in the storm.
▶혼잡한 거리에서 그런 속력으로 차를 몰다니 참으로 무분별한 사내로구나 How reckless of him to drive at such a speed in crowded streets!

무불간섭 無不干涉 indiscreet [unnecessary] meddling in everything
—**무불간섭하다** poke one's nose into everything; never fail to meddle with [in]; always nose into; interfere in everything

무불통지 無不通知 being well informed; broad and extensive knowledge
—**무불통지하다** well-informed; erudite

무비하다 無比— matchless; peerless; unrivaled; unequaled; unique ♦당대 무비한 unparalleled by one's contemporaries
▶그는 중국 미술에 관해서 당대 무비한 지식을 가지고 있다 He has an unrivaled knowledge of Chinese art.

무비판 無批判 ♦무비판적(으로) uncritical(ly); indiscriminate(ly)
▶그는 남의 의견을 무비판적으로 받아들인다 He accepts others' opinions without due reflection [uncritically].

무빙 霧氷 hoarfrost; rime

무사 武士 a warrior; a soldier; 〈기사〉 a knight
■**—도** chivalry; knighthood

무사 無私 selflessness; unselfishness —**무사하다** unselfish; selfless; disinterested; impartial ♦공평무사한 fair and disinterested

무사 無事 1〈안전〉 safety —**무사하다** safe ♦무사하기를 빌다 pray for one's safety
▶네가 무사해서 다행이다 Thank God [Heaven], you're safe.
2〈평온〉 peace —**무사하다** peaceful; uneventful
3〈건강·탈없음〉 good health —**무사하다** well; doing well [nicely] ▶나는 무사합니다 Nothing is wrong with me.

무사 無死 〔野〕 no out [down]; none out
▶무사 만루다 The bases are full [loaded] with no outs.
▶그들은 무사 만루의 위기를 벗어났다 They got out of a bases-loaded no-out jam.

무사고 無事故 ♦무사고로 without a trouble [an accident] ▶나는 10년간 무사고다 I have had no accidents in the ten years. ■**—비행** accident-free flying; flying without an accident

무사마귀 a wart
♦무사마귀 투성이의 warty / 무사마귀가 생기다 have a wart; a wart forms [grows] 《on one's finger》

무사분열 無絲分裂 〔生〕 amitosis

무사분주하다 無事奔走— very busy about nothing; busy with nothing to mention in particular

무사(안일)주의 無事(安逸)主義 a peace-at-any-price principle; the policy of safety first
▶그는 무사(안일)주의로 나가고 있다 He is playing it safe.

무사태평 無事泰平 〈평안〉 (perfect) peace; tranquility; 〈태평〉 easiness; optimism
—**무사태평하다** peaceful; tranquil; easy; easy-going; happy-go-lucky; free from care; optimistic ♦무사태평한 치세 a reign of peace and happiness / 무사태평한 세상에 살다 live in a peaceful world
▶그는 워낙 무사태평한 성격이라 그 일을 별로 걱정하지 않을거요 He is such a happy-go-lucky man (that) he probably won't worry much about that.

무사히 無事— 1〈안전하게〉 safely; safe; in safety; 〈사고없이〉 without accident; all right; 〈성공적으로〉 successfully
▶비행기는 무사히 착륙했다 The airplane landed safely.
▶무사히 다녀오십시오 I hope you get back safe (and sound) [in safety].
▶내 딸은 무사히 돌아왔다 My daughter came back safe [whole].
2〈평온하게〉 ♦무사히 지내다 live in peace [peacefully]
▶그 달은 무사히 지나갔다 That month passed without accident.
3〈탈없이〉 well; all right
♦무사히 지내다 get along well [all right]; live in good health
▶부모님은 고향에서 무사히 지내고 계신다 My parents live in good health in my hometown.

무산 無産 ♦무산의 without property
■**—계급** the proletariat(e); proletarians; the propertyless class **—자** a proletarian; (口) have-nots; a man without property **—정당** a proletarian party

무산 霧散 dispersion; dissipation; dissipating like the mist —**무산하다** disperse; dissipate; be dispersed; be dispelled; vanish

무삶이 〔農〕 〈고르기〉 softening a rice field with water; 〈갈기〉 plowing [(英) ploughing] a rice field wet

무상 無上 ♦무상의 기쁨 the greatest [supreme] pleasure; the greatest [sweetest] joy 《of life》 / 무상의 highest; the greatest; supreme; the best
▶이 상을 받게 된 것을 무상의 영광으로 생각합니다 I feel it the highest honor to be awarded this prize.
■**—명령** 〔論〕 the categorical imperative

무상 無常 mutability; uncertainty; transiency; evanescence ♦인생 무상을 느끼다 realize the vanity [evanescence] of life
—**무상하다** uncertain; mutable; transient; transitory; vain
▶인생은 무상하다 Nothing remains the same in this world. ⇒ All is vanity in life. ⇒ Life is but an empty dream.
■**—관** a sense of the evanescence [vanity] of life

무상 無償 ♦무상으로 gratuitously; for nothing; without charge; without compensation [pay]; gratis; free of charge
▶초등학교의 교과서는 무상으로 학생들에게 배포된다 Elementary school textbooks are distributed (to children) free of charge [gratis].
■**—계약** a gratuitous contract; a naked pact

[contract] —교부 delivery without compensation [charge] —기술 수출 unpaid technique exports —대출 a free [an interest-free] loan —배급 free distribution [issue] —양도 gratuitous [voluntary] conveyance —원조 a grant; grant-type aid —주(株) a stock dividend —행위 a gratuitous act

무상출입하다 無常出入～ go in and out constantly; visit freely; have free access to 《sb's house》; frequent

무색 無色 **1** 〈빛깔 없음〉 colorlessness; lack of color ◆무색 렌즈 an untinted lens / 무색의 colorless; achromatic / 무색으로 하나 make sth colorless; achromatize
▶물은 무색 투명하다 Water is colorless and transparent.
2 〈무안〉 shame; disgrace
—무색하다 feel shame; ashamed
◆무색할 만한 미인 a paragon of beauty / 무색케 하다 put sb to shame; cast [put, throw] sb in [into] the shade; outshine [eclipse, overshadow] sb / 무색해지다 be put into the shade; be outshone
▶그의 작품은 대가를 무색케 할 정도다 His work would put the masters to shame.

무색옷 —色— colored clothes; a dyed dress
무생대 無生代 〔地質〕 the Azoic Era [Age]
무생물 無生物 an inanimate object [being]; a nonliving [lifeless] thing; inanimate matter ■—계 inanimate [inorganic] nature [world]
무서리 the first frost of the year [season]; light frost ▶지난밤에 무서리가 내렸다 We had the first frost of the year last night.
무서움 fear; fearfulness; terror; dreadfulness; horror ◆무서움 때문에 for [from, out of] fear / 무서움을 모르다 feel no fear / 무서움을 타다 be easily frightened / 무서움을 참다 bear one's fear
▶나는 암의 무서움을 처음으로 알았다 I realized for the first time how dreadful cancer is.
무서워하다 fear; dread; be 《much》 afraid of; be frightened 《at, by》; have a fear [horror] 《of》; be in a fright; be scared 《at》; be timid 《of》; be nervous 《about》
◆…을 무서워하여 for fear of / 뱀을 몹시 무서워하다 fear [dread] snakes very much
▶그녀는 죽음을 무척 무서워한다 She is very much afraid that she is going to die.
▶너는 아무것도 무서워할 것 없다 You have nothing to fear.
▶실패를 무서워하면 큰 일을 할 수 없다 You'll never be able to do anything great if you are afraid of failure.
무석인 武石人 a stone statue of a warrior (standing) in front of a royal tomb
무선 無線 radio; (英) wireless ◆…와 무선으로 연락을 하다 be in radio contact with… / 무선으로 송신하다 send a message by radio; radio a message
▶긴급한 연락이 무선으로 들어왔다 An urgent message was received on the radio.
■—검파기 a radiodetector; a detector —공학 radio engineering —국 a radio [wireless] station —기사 a radio operator; a radioman —방송 radio broadcasting; radiocasting —방향탐지기 radio direction finder (略 RDF) —부표 radio buoy —사진 전송 radiophotography —송신 radio transmission —송신기 a radio transmitter —수신기 a radio receiver; a radio receiving set —실 a radio-room; a wireless room —장치 a wireless installation —주파수 radio frequency —표지 a radio beacon —항로표지 〔空〕 a radio range beacon —항법[항행] radio navigation —항행업무 radio navigation service

무선 舞扇 a dancing fan; a dancer's fan
무선전보 無線電報 a radiogram; a telegram; a wireless (telegram); a radiotelegram
◆무선전보를 치다 radio [wireless] a message; send [dispatch] a radio [wireless]
무선전송 無線電送 —무선전송하다 radio-photo 《a picture》 ■—사진 a radiophoto; radiophotograph
무선전신 無線電信 wireless telegraph; radio telegraph
◆무선전신으로 (美) by radio; (英) by wireless / 무선전신을 치다 telegraph by wireless; radio / 무선전신을 가로채어 받다 pick up a wireless message / 《배가》 무선전신을 갖추다 carry radio [wireless] / 무선전신으로 송신하다 send a message by radio; radio a message / 무선전신으로 교신하다 communicate by radio
▶F국은 조난신으로부터 구조를 청하는 무선전신을 받았다 The F Station picked up wireless calls for help from a wrecked ship.
▶통신은 무선전신으로 보냈다 I have sent the message by radio [wireless].
■—국 a radio [wireless] station —기 a radio [wireless] apparatus; a wireless [radio] set —기사 a radio-telegraphist; a radio [wireless] operator; a radioman
무선전화 無線電話 〈전화기〉 a wireless telephone [set]; a radiotelephoty; 〈내용〉 a radiophoney; wireless telephony
◆무선전화기 a radiotelephony; a radiophone / 휴대용 무선전화기 a walkie-talkie / 무선전화를 걸다 telephone by radio [wireless]; radiotelephone 《to》; wireless; radio / 무선전화로 말하다 talk over the radiophone [by wireless]; have a wireless talk 《with》
▶이 섬에 무선전화가 개통되었다 A radiophone service has been inaugurated on this island.
■—국 a radio station
무선조종 無線操縱 radio [wireless] control —무선조종하다 control 《a plane》 by radio [wireless]; radio-control
■—기 a radio-controlled airplane; a drone —법 telemechanics
무선중계 無線中繼 radio relay ■—국 a radio relay station —방식 a radio relay system
무선통신 無線通信 radio [wireless] communication
■—국 a radio communication station —규칙 a radio regulation —로 a radio channel —방해 jamming (of wireless) —사 a radio operator; a radioman

무섭다 1 〈끔찍하다〉 frightening; frightful; fearful; dreadful; terrible; horrible; (口) scary; 〈으스스하다〉 uncanny; 〈섬뜩하다〉 grim; 〈흉악하다〉 ferocious; 〈사납다〉 fierce; savage

♦무서운 광경 a frightening sight / 무서운 독 a dreadful poison / 무서운 병 a horrible disease / 무서운 동물 a fierce animal / 무서운 영화 a horrible [scary] film / 무서운 무기 a formidable weapon / 무서운 폭풍우 a terrific [fearful] storm / 무서워서 도망치다 run away through fear / 무서운 나머지 기절하다 faint with horror / 무서워서 말이 막히다 be struck dumb with fright / 무서워서 큰소리를 지르다 cry out for fear; shriek in fear [terror]/ 무서워지다 be [get, become] frightened [scared] 《at》; be seized with fear / 무섭지 않게 되다 lose *one's* fear

▶나는 무서운 꿈을 꾸었다 I had a terrible dream.
▶무서워 혼났어 I was scared to death.
▶나는 개가 무섭다 I am afraid of dogs.
▶그는 무서운 태도로 나를 노려봤다 He glared at me with a threatening attitude.
▶무서워서 소리도 안 나왔다 My voice was frozen with horror.
▶그는 화가 나면 무섭다 He is terrible in anger.

2 〈지독하다〉 awful; terrific; terrible; tremendous; frightful

♦무서운 정력 prodigious energy / 무서운 속도로 at a terrific speed / 무섭게 awfully; terribly; horribly; frightfully; extremely / 무섭게 서두르다 be in an awful rush

▶그는 무서운 구두쇠다 He is an awful miser.
▶불은 무서운 기세로 번져갔다 The flames spread with terrible force.
▶그 방은 무섭게 더웠다 The room was awfully hot.
▶서울에서는 생활비가 무섭게 든다 In Seoul the cost of living is awfully heavy.
▶습관이란 무섭다 A habit is something not to be lightly treated.

무성 無性 ♦무성의 nonsexual; sexless; 〔植〕 neutral (flowers); neuter; asexual; agamic; 〈무배우자의〉 agamous; 〔文法〕 genderless
■ㅡ생식 〔生〕 asexual reproduction; monogeny; agamogenesis; 〔植〕 blastogenesis ㅡ세대 〔生〕 a asexual generation; a sexless generation ㅡ식물 a neuter (plant) ㅡ아(芽) a gemma (*pl.* -mae) ㅡ화(花) a neuter [an asexual] flower ㅡ화(化) desexualization

무성 無聲 ♦무성의 silent; noiseless; dumb; voiceless
■ㅡ방전(放電) silent discharge ㅡ영화 a silent film [(motion) picture, movie] ㅡ영화시대 the silent picture days ㅡ자음〔音聲〕a voiceless consonant ㅡ총 a noiseless firearm [rifle]

무성음 無聲音 〔音聲〕 a voiceless [an unvoiced] sound; a breath(ed) sound

♦무성음의 voiceless; unvoiced; breathed / 무성음으로 발음하다 unvoice / 유성음을 무성음으로 발음하다 devoice [unvoice] a voiced sound

무성의 無誠意 insincerity —무성의하다 insincere; lacking in sincerity

♦무성의한 답변[정책] a haphazard reply [policy]/ 무성의한 짓을 하다 act in bad faith
▶그의 말은 무성의하다 You can't put any faith in what he says. ⇌ There is not a scrap of sincerity [good faith] in what he says.
▶네 행위는 무성의하다 Your conduct betrays want of sincerity.

무성하다 茂盛— thick; dense; luxuriant; exuberant; profuse

♦나무가 무성한 산 a thickly-[heavily-] wooded hill / 잎이 무성한 나무 a leaf-heavy tree; a tree thick of leaves / 잡초가 무성한 정원 a garden overgrown with weeds / 무성하게 자라다 〈초목이 주어〉 grow thick(ly) [luxuriantly]; grow rank; become dense; 〈장소가 주어〉 be thickly covered with 《trees》; be overgrown [rank] with 《weeds》
▶정원에는 풀이 무성하다 The garden is overgrown with grass. ⇌ The grass grows thick in the garden.

무세 無稅 〈세금이 없음〉 ♦무세의 free; tax-free; duty-free; untaxed; tax-exempt / 무세로 free of duty [tax]; tax-free; duty-free / 무세 수입을 허가하다 allow the free entry 《of goods》; admit 《goods》 free of duty [custom free]
■ㅡ수입품 (duty-)free imports; articles on the free list ㅡ품 duty-free goods; goods free of duty [tax]; nondutiable goods

무소 〔動〕 a rhinoceros; (口) a rhino 《*pl.* ~s》

무소 誣訴 〈없는 일을 꾸며 관청에 고소함〉〔法〕 false accusation; a trumped-up charge
—무소하다 accuse *sb* falsely; make a false accusation 《against *sb*》

무소권 無訴權 〈소권이 없음〉〔法〕 no right to bring an article in court

무소기탄하다 無所忌憚— 〈아무것도 꺼려하는 바가 없다〉 afraid of nothing; outspoken; unreserved ▶무소기탄하고 내 생각을 말하겠다 I will give my opinion without reserve.

무소득 無所得 no gain [income, benefit]
—무소득하다 〈서술적〉 get no benefit 《from》; gain [get] nothing 《from, by》; be little benefited 《by》

무소르크스키 〈러시아의 작곡가〉 Musorgskii, Modest Petrovich (1835-81)

무소부재 無所不在 omnipresence; ubiquity
—무소부재하다 omnipresent; ubiquitous
▶하느님은 무소부재하다 God is omnipresent.

무소부지 無所不知 omniscience; infinite [universal] knowledge
—무소부지하다 omniscient; know everything

무소불능 無所不能 omnipotence; almightiness
—무소불능하다 omnipotent; almighty

무소불위 無所不爲 omnipotence ⇨ 무소불능

무소속 無所屬 ♦무소속의 independent; unattached; 〈중립의〉 neutral; 〈정당에 속하지 않음〉 nonpartisan; affiliated with no party / 무소속 입후보자 an independent (candidate) / 무소속이다 be independent; (美俗) be not a party man
▶그는 무소속으로 입후보했다 He ran as an

무소식

independent candidate.
—의원 an independent (member); a nonaffiliated representative [member]; a nonpartisan representative —자 a free lance; a freelancer —정치인 an independent (politician)

무소식 無消息 no news 《from》
♦(감감)무소식이다 hear nothing from *sb*; receive no words from; have no news from
▶그 후로 그는 감감 무소식이다 Nothing has been heard from him since.

무소식이 희소식 (속담) No news is good news.

무손하다 無損— 〈서술적〉 be without any loss; be undamaged

무솔다 〈푸성귀가〉 decay from the dampness

무솔리니 〈이탈리아의 독재 정치가, 파시스트 당수〉 Mussolini, Benito (1883-1945)

무쇠 cast iron; iron ♦무쇠같은 근육 muscles of iron

무수 無水 〔化〕 ♦무수의 anhydrous
■—규산 ⇨ 이산화(~규소) —물(物) an anhydride —알코올 absolute alcohol; pure alcohol —화합물 an anhydrous compound

무 수 無 數 an infinite [untold] number; immensities
—무수하다 countless; numberless; incalculable; innumerable
♦무수한 별 countless stars; stars beyond [without] number / 무수한 곤란에 직면하다 face innumerable difficulties / 무수한 예를 들다 give no end of examples
▶하늘에는 무수한 별들이 반짝이고 있었다 The myriads of stars were twinkling in the sky.

무수기 〈썰물과 밀물의 차〉 the difference in water level between ebb and flood tides

무수다 〈닥치는 대로 때리거나 부수다〉 destroy whatever [anything that] *one* can lay hands on; beat relentlessly [without mercy]

무수리 〔鳥〕 an adjutant (bird); an adjutant crane [stork]

무수정 無修正 ♦무수정으로 without revision [amendment] / 예산안을 무수정 통과시키다 pass the budget with no revision

무수히 無數— innumerably; countlessly; infinitely; without [out of] number
▶해결되지 않는 문제가 무수히 있다 There are innumerable problems to be solved.

무숙자 無宿者 a homeless wanderer; a vagabond; a tramp

무순 無順 ♦무순의[으로] without order; in no particular [special] order; in random [unalphabetical] order

무술 巫術 shamanism ♦무술을 하다 practice shamanism

무술 武術 military [martial] arts ♦무술에 다소 조예가 있다 have some military accomplishments —사범 a fencing master

무쉬 the 9th and 24th days of the lunar month, when the spring tide sets in [begins after the neap tide]

무슨 〈의문〉 what; what kind [sort] of; 〈어떤〉 some kind of; some
♦무슨 일 〈의문〉 what; 〈어떤 일〉 something; 〈만사〉 everything / 무슨 일로 on what business / 무슨 일이나 in everything; in all matters [things]/ 무슨 일이 있으면 in case of emergency [need]/ if anything [the unexpected] should happen 《to *sb*》/ 무슨 일이 있어도 at any cost [price, risk]; by all means; at all costs [hazards]/ 무슨 일이 일어나더라도 whatever may happen / 무슨 까닭에 what... for; why; for what reason
▶이게 무슨 꽃이니? What (kind of) flower is this? ⇌ What's the name of this flower?
▶무슨 일로 오셨습니까? What have you come here for?
▶무슨 일로 거기에 갔습니까? What did you go there for?
▶지금 무슨 얘기를 하고 있니? What are you talking about now?
▶무슨 죄로 내가 이런 고통을 당하는지 모르겠다 I don't know what I have done to deserve such misery.
▶그것은 무슨 뜻인가? What do you mean by that?
▶그것을 해서 무슨 소용이 있느냐? What is the use [good] of doing such a thing?
▶(안색이 나쁜데) 무슨 일이냐? What's the matter (with you)?
▶무슨 일이 일어나든 나는 각오가 돼 있다 I am prepared for the worst.
▶무슨 일이 일어나든 나는 내 알 바 아니다 I don't care what happens [may happen].
▶너는 지금 무슨 공부를 하고 있니? What [What subject, Which subject] are you studying now?
▶무슨 방법을 써서라도 나는 성공하고 싶다 I want to succeed no matter what means I have to use.
▶오늘은 무슨 시험이 있느냐? What examination do you have today?
▶무슨 일이 일어났음에 틀림없다 Something must have happened.
▶언제 무슨 일이 일어날지 모른다 Anything can happen any time. ⇌ You can never tell what will happen.
▶그것에 대해서 그가 네게 무슨 말을 했니? Did he say anything to you about it?
▶나는 그것에 대해 무슨 조치를 해야 한다 I have to do something about it. ⇌ Something must be done about it.
▶다음에 무슨 일이 일어날지 아무도 모른다 No one knows what may follow.
▶무슨 일인가 하고 뛰어나가 보았다 I ran out to see what the matter was.
▶무슨 말로 사과드려야 할지 모르겠습니다 I don't know how to apologize to you for it.
▶무슨 말로 당신의 친절에 감사드려야 할지 모르겠습니다 I can hardly thank you enough for your kindness. ⇌ I have no words to thank you.
▶인내하지 않으면 무슨 일에나 성공하지 못한다 You cannot succeed in anything unless you persevere.
▶그에게 무슨 충고라도 해 주어라 Give him some advice.
▶무슨 일이 있어도 그것을 마쳐라 Finish it by

무승부 無勝負 a drawn game [match]; a draw 《in a game》; a tie (game)
♦ 무승부로 끝나다 end in a tie [draw]; be drawn; tie 《with》
▶ 그 야구 시합은 무승부로 끝났다 The baseball game ended in a draw [tie].

무시 無視 disregard; neglect
—**무시하다** ignore; disregard; discount; neglect; take [make] no account of
♦ 개인의 의사를 완전히 무시하고 in total disregard of [with complete disregard for] the wishes of the individual / 규칙을 무시하다 disregard the rules / 문법을 무시하다 do violence to grammar / 남의 충고를 무시하다 set another's advice at defiance [naught] / 소수 의견을 무시하다 ignore [disregard] a minority opinion / 민의(民意)를 무시하다 override the wishes of the people / 무시당했다고 생각하다 feel slighted
▶ 그는 나를 완전히 무시했다 He turned up his nose at me.
▶ 그는 그녀의 제안을 무시했다 He scorned [pooh-poohed] her proposal.
▶ 그 사고는 운전자가 교통신호를 무시했기 때문에 일어났다 The accident occurred because the driver ignored the traffic lights.
▶ 그것은 그가 내 경고를 무시했기 때문이다 It was entirely due to his disregard of my warning.
▶ 그들이 너에 대해 뭐라고 말하든 무시해 버려라 Pay no attention to whatever they say about you.

무시근하다 〈게으른〉 lazy; idle; 〈쓸모없는〉 good-for-nothing; slovenly; spiritless; sloppy
♦ 무시근한 생활을 하다 lead an idle life

무시로 無時— 〈수시로〉 (at) any time; 〈언제나〉 all the time; at all times [hours]; always
▶ 본교는 무시로 학생의 입학을 허가한다 Students are admitted at any time into this school.
▶ 누구나 무시로 신청할 수 있다 Anyone can apply at any time.

무시류 無翅類 〔昆〕 Aptera

무시무시하다 ghastly 《face》; dismal; uncanny; weird; fearsome 《monster》; terrible; horrible; frightful; dreadful
♦ 무시무시한 광경 a frightful [gruesome] sight / 무시무시한 얼굴 a terrible [ghastly] look / 무시무시한 폭발 a terrific explosion
▶ 그것은 무시무시한 영화였다 That was a very weird film.
▶ 그는 무시무시한 얼굴로 그녀를 보았다 He gave her a fierce look.

무시험 無試驗 ♦ 무시험의 free of examination / 무시험 입학 자격이 있다 be entitled to admission without taking an examination
▶ 그는 무시험으로 그 대학에 입학했다 He was admitted to the college without examination.
■ —검정 getting a certificate without examination —진학 admission to a school without examination

무식 無識 ignorance; illiteracy
♦ 무식을 드러내다 betray [expose] one's ignorance; display one's lack of knowledge
—**무식하다** ignorant; illiterate; unlettered; uneducated
♦ 무식한 탓으로 due to ignorance
▶ 무식하다고 해서 기죽을 것은 없다 You need not feel small because you are uneducated.
■ —꾼[쟁이] an ignorant [illiterate] person

무신경 無神經 insensitivity; insensibility; apathy; indifference; callousness
—**무신경하다** insensitive; insensible; indifferent; apathetic; thick-skinned; callous; stolid
▶ 그는 남이 뭐라고 하든 무신경하다 He is too thick-skinned to mind what others say about him.
▶ 너는 그녀의 슬픔에 대해 무신경하다 You are insensible to her grief.

무신고 無申告 ♦ 무신고의 without (previous) notice; without leave
▶ 그는 무신고로 회의에 결석했다 He stayed away from the meeting without giving any advance notice.
■ —집회 a meeting held without previous notice to the authorities [without notifying the authorities beforehand]

무신론 無神論 atheism ♦ 무신론적(인) atheistic ■ —자 an atheist; an unbeliever

무실 無實 falsehood; untruth —**무실하다** false; untrue; unfounded ♦ 무실한 죄로 on a false charge / 무실함을 주장하다 protest one's innocence

무실점 無失點 ♦ 무실점으로 without losing a point / 무실점을 기록하다 record no losing point [score]

무심 無心 1 〈생각없음〉 detachment; 〈천진함〉 innocence
—**무심하다** innocent; casual; 〈관심없다〉 unconcerned; 〈인정없다〉 insentient; heartless; inconsiderate; hard
♦ 무심한 어린이 an innocent child
—**무심히** unintentionally; 〈문득〉 casually; 〈부주의하게〉 unguardedly; carelessly
♦ 무심히 놀고 있다 be innocently at (one's) play; be absorbed in (one's) play / 무심히 창 밖을 보다 look casually out of the window
▶ 아기가 무심히 젖을 빨고 있었다 The baby innocently sucked the breast.
▶ 그 어린 소녀는 무심히 그림을 그리고 있었다 The little girl was absorbed in drawing a picture.
2 〔佛敎〕 absence of the worldly desires

무심결 無心— ♦ 무심결에 unintentionally

무심코 無心— 〈아무 생각없이〉 involuntarily; unintentionally; thoughtlessly; 〈문득〉 by chance; casually; accidentally; 〈부주의하게〉 carelessly; inadvertently; 〈제도 모르게〉 unconsciously; in spite of oneself
♦ 무심코 한 말 a casual remark; an inadvertent remark / 무심코 말하다 〈실언하다〉 make a slip of the tongue; 〈비밀 등을〉 blurt out 《a secret》; let 《the truth》 slip out / 무심코 시계를 보다 glance casually at one's watch
▶ 나는 무심코 뒤를 돌아다 보았다 I chanced [happened] to look behind.
▶ 나는 무심코 형의 책을 가지고 왔다 I brought

my brother's book by mistake.
▶ 무심코 그 말을 하고 말았다 The word slipped out of my mouth before my throat.
▶ 무심코 한 말이 그의 기분을 상하게 한 것 같다 My unwitting remark seem to have hurt him.
▶ 무심코 다른 방면의 열차를 탔다 I took the wrong train by mistake.
▶ 그녀는 무심코 비밀을 털어 놓았다 She revealed the secret in an unguarded moment.

무쌍 無雙 matchlessness
—**무쌍하다** matchless; peerless; unparalleled; incomparable; unrivaled; unequaled
◆ 대담 무쌍한 dauntless; fearless; daredevil; death-defying / 변화 무쌍한 인생 the kaleidoscope of life; the shifts and changes of life / 용감 무쌍한 사람 a man of great prowess

무아 無我 self-effacement; self-renunciation; annihilation of self; selflessness
◆ 무아의 경지에 이르다 attain a spiritual state of perfect selflessness; go into an impersonal state; rise above self
▶ 그 승려는 명상을 통해 무아의 경지에 이르렀다 The priest attained the state of selflessness through meditation.
■ —애 selfless love; absolute altruism

무아경 無我境 ecstasy; transport

무악 舞樂 (樂) dancing and music; 〈궁정의〉 court dance music

무안 無顔 shame; disgrace; dishonor
◆ 무안을 주다 put *sb* to shame [the blush]; put *sb* out of countenance / 무안을 당하다 be put to shame; disgrace *oneself*; be humiliated; bring disgrace upon *oneself* / 무안을 참다 endure *one's* disgrace; bear up under *one's* shame; pocket *one's* pride
—**무안하다** feel ashamed at; be ashamed 《of *oneself*》; lose face ◆ 무안해서 고개를 떨구다 hang *one's* head with shame
▶ 여러 사람 앞에서 그가 그런 말을 하는 바람에 나는 무안했다 I was ashamed to hear him say such a thing about me in public.
▶ 시험에서 0점을 받아서 무안했다 I was ashamed when I got zero on the test.
▶ 모두가 나를 보고 웃었기 때문에 무안했다 Everyone laughed at me and I was humiliated.
▶ 그 소년의 나쁜 행실은 어머니를 무안케 했다 The boy's bad behavior embarrassed his mother.

무안타 無安打 〔野〕 ◆ 무안타 시합 a no-hitter / 무안타의 no hit
▶ 톰은 상대팀을 무안타로 막았다 Tom held the other team hitless. ⇒ Tom threw a no-hit game against our opponents.

무양무양하다 inflexible 《in personality》; unadaptable; hidebound; rigid

무어 1 〈무엇〉 what; which; something
◆ 무어 먹을[마실] 것 something to eat [drink]
▶ 무어 잘못된 게 있소? Did I do anything wrong?
▶ 이 상자 속에 무어 중요한 것이 있습니까? Is there anything important in this box?
▶ 무어 쓸 도구를 빌려 주십시오 May I borrow something to write with?
▶ 무어 하러 왔어? What have you come for?
▶ 무어 먹을 것을 주십시오 Please give me something to eat.
2 〈감탄・놀람〉 what!; huh!; why!
▶ 무어라고 말했지? What [Huh]! What did you say?
▶ 무어, 또 지각했니? What! Were you late again?
▶ 무어, 내가 미쳤다고? What! I am mad [crazy]?
▶ 무어야, 그러면 그렇다고 진자 말할 것이지 Why, you ought to have said it before.
3 〈어리광・강조〉 but; but anyway; somehow or other
▶ 세상이란 무어 그런 거지 Such is the way of the world.
▶ 무어 그렇게 화낼 것 없다 You have no reason whatever to be so angry.
▶ 누워서 떡 먹이기지 무어 Why, nothing is easier.
▶ 무어, 괜찮다 Why, it's all right. ⇒ Why, never mind. ⇒ Never mind. ⇒ I don't care.

무어니무어니해도 when all is said and done; after all; all things taken together
▶ 무어니무어니해도 그는 네 동생이다 After all, he is your brother.
▶ 무어니무어니해도 가난처럼 견디기 어려운 것은 없다 Indeed there is nothing so hard to bear as poverty.
▶ 무어니무어니해도 세상을 움직이는 것은 돈이야 After all is said and done, it's money that makes the world go round.

무어라 남이 무어라 하든 whatever others [people] may say 《about, of》/ 무어라 해도 when all is said and done; all things taken together; after all / 무어라 말할 수 없는 unspeakable 《sorrow》; nameless 《horror》; indescribable [inexpressible] 《beauty》; indefinable 《longing》/ 무어라 말할 수 없다 who knows?; God knows; nobody can tell
▶ 무어라 사과해야 할지 모르겠습니다 I don't know how I can apologize to you.
▶ 무어라 대답해야 할지 몰랐다 I was at a loss what answer to make.
▶ 무어라 감사의 말을 드려야 할지 모르겠습니다 I don't know how I can express my thanks. ⇒ I cannot find words to thank you.
▶ 세상 사람들이 무어라 하든 개의치 않는다 I don't mind [care] what people say of me.

무언 無言 silence; taciturnity; muteness; reticence
◆ 무언의 고행 the ascetic practice of silence / 무언의 반항 silent resistance / 무언의 silent; speechless; mute; dumb; tacit / 무언으로 in silence; silently; mutely; speechlessly; without (uttering [saying]) a word
▶ 두 사람 사이에 무언의 양해가 있었다 There was a tacit understanding between the two.
▶ 그는 그 문제에 대해 함구 무언이었다 He was silent on that matter.
■ —가 〔樂〕 a song without words —극 a

무얼 〈무엇을〉 ▶무얼 달라고? What do you want? ⇌ What did you say [What was it] you wanted?
▶그걸 알아서 무얼 해? What is that to you?

무엄 無嚴 impertinence; impudence; insolence ━**무엄하다** impertinent; impudent; insolent; 〈버릇없다〉 impolite, rude
◆무엄한 놈 an outrageous [insolent] fellow / 무엄한 소리[말] an impudent utterance / 무엄하게도 …하다 have the impertinence [impudence] to ⟪do⟫; be impertinent enough to ⟪do⟫
▶나는 그런 무엄한 질문에는 대답할 수 없다 I can't answer such impertinent questions.

무엇 what; which; something; anything
▶무엇을 도와드릴까요? 〈점원이〉 What can I do for you?
▶그는 무엇 하는 사람입니까? What does he do? ⇌ What is he?
▶무엇을 숨기랴, 주모자는 나였다 To tell the truth [To be frank with you], I was the ringleader.
▶그의 말은 무엇이 무엇인지 전혀 모르겠다 I can't make either head or tail of what he says.
▶무엇부터 시작해야[말해야] 좋을지 모르겠다 I don't know where to begin.
▶너는 무엇 하러 여기까지 왔니? What did you come here for? ⇌ Why did you come here?
▶무엇을 하거나 우선 건강해야 한다 Health is the first thing [consideration] in doing anything.
▶무엇을 하거나 두뇌가 첫째다 Brains are everything in this world.
▶방 안에는 무엇 하나 남아 있지 않았다 There was nothing left in the room.
▶그는 취미라곤 무엇 하나 없다 He doesn't have any hobbies at all.

무엇보다 above all (things); before everything (else); first of all; most of all; of all things
▶무엇보다 건강이 중요하다 Health is more important than anything else.
▶나는 아이스크림을 무엇보다도 좋아한다 I like ice cream better than anything else.
▶영어를 배우려는 사람은 무엇보다 발음에 주의해야 한다 If you want to learn English, you must, first of all, be careful about pronunciation.
▶무사히 도착하셨다니 무엇보다도 기쁩니다 I am so happy that you have arrived safely.
▶너는 무엇보다도 우선 그 이를 치료해야 한다 You ought to get that tooth treated first of all [before you do anything else].

무엇이든 whatever; any; whatever [anything] you like; 〈무엇이든 하나〉 anything; 〈이것저것 모두〉 everything; 〈모두〉 all
◆무엇이든 좋아하는 것 anything one likes
▶무엇이든 좋다 Anything will do.
▶모르는 것은 무엇이든 물어 봐라 Any question will do [be OK].
▶좋아하는 것이라면 무엇이든 사 주겠다 I'll buy you anything [whatever] you like.
▶재미있는 책이라면 무엇이든 좋다 Any book will do, if [so long as] it is interesting.
▶원하는 것은 무엇이든 가져라 You can [may] have anything [whatever] you like.
▶나는 음악이라면 무엇이든 관심이 있다 I am interested in all [any] music.
▶그밖의 일이라면 무엇이든 하겠다 I will do anything but that.
▶⟪회화⟫ 「무슨 영화 좋아하니?」 「무엇이든 좋아, 그러나 특히 서부극을 좋아해」 "What kind of movies do you like?" "All kinds, but especially westerns."

무엇하다 〈부적절하다〉 incongruous; improper; unbecoming; 〈어색하다〉 awkward; embarrassing; 〈불만스럽다〉 unsatisfactory
◆그렇게 말하면 무엇하지만 if I may be permitted to say so; it may be rude to say so, but…; though I say it who shouldn't…
▶그것을 남들 앞에서 논하기는 무엇한 것 같다 That seems too delicate [awkward] to discuss in public.
▶그런 것을 그에게 물어보기란 좀 무엇하지 않을까? Would it be quite proper for me to ask him such a question?
▶그것을 내가 직접 하기가 좀 무엇하다 It is awkward for me to do that myself.
▶무엇하면 그만둬도 괜찮네 You can give it up, if you don't like it.

무역 貿易 trade; commerce
◆무역의 자유화 liberalization of trade / 무역 확대 trade expansion / 무역을 시작하다 open (up) trade ⟪with⟫; establish trade ⟪with⟫ / 무역을 자유화하다 liberalize (external) trade / 무역을 증진하다 increase foreign trade / 무역을 진흥하다 promote foreign trade
▶한국은 미국과 무역이 활발하다 Korea does [has] a lot of trade with America. ⇌ Korea trades a lot with America.
▶한·중 무역은 최근 확대되었다 Sino-Korean trade [Trade between Korea and China] has expanded recently.
▶그 나라의 무역은 해마다 신장하고 있다 The trade of that country grows larger year after year.
▶우리 회사는 외국 무역에 관계하고 있다 Our company is engaged in foreign trade.
▶한국은 그 나라와 무역 관계가 없다 Korea has no trade relations with that country.
━**무역하다** trade ⟪with⟫; carry on commerce ⟪with⟫; conduct trade

■ 가공— processing trade 구상— compensation [barter] trade; trade on a barter system 국내— domestic [home] trade 국제[세계]— international [world] trade 다각— multilateral trade 대미— Korea's trade with America; commerce between Korea and America 대일— Korea's trade with Japan 보세가공— bonded processing trade 보호— protective trade (policies) : 보호 무역주의 protectionism 삼각— triangular trade 상호— two-way trade 수출— export trade 자유— free trade 중계— transit trade 해상— floating trade

■ —경쟁국 a trade rival —과(科) the trade

department (of a college) —관리 (foreign) trade control —국 a trading country [nation] —금융 trade financing —량 the volume of trade —마찰 a trade friction —박람회 a trade fair —불균형 trade imbalance —사절단 a trade mission —상 a trader; a trading merchant —상대국 a trade partner —선 a merchant ship [vessel]; a trader —수지 trade balance; balance of trade —어음 a trade bill [paper] —업 trade [trading] business —업계 trading circles —역조 adverse balance of trade; adverse [unfavorable] trade balance —연보(年報) annual trade returns —외 수입 earnings on [income from] invisibles —외 수지 balance except foreign trade; invisible trade balance —자금[기금] a foreign trade fund; a commercial fund —장벽 a trade barrier —적자 a trade deficit [gap] —전쟁 a trade war —정책 a trade policy —조건 terms of trade; trade terms —통계 foreign trade statistics —품 trade goods; imports (수입품); exports (수출품) —풍 the trade wind; the trades —항 a trading port —허가장 a permit for trading —협력기구 the Organization for Trade Cooperation (略 O.T.C.) —협정 a trade agreement —회사 a trading firm [company, concern] —흑자 a trade surplus

무연 無煙 ♦ 무연의 smokeless ■ —연료 smokeless fuel —탄 anthracite (coal); (美) hard coal; smokeless [stone] coal —화약 smokeless powder

무연(고) 無緣(故) ♦ 무연(고)의 〈무관계의〉 indifferent; unrelated; 〈연고자가 없는〉 having no surviving relatives; without relations ■ —묘지 a cemetery for those who left no relatives behind —분묘 an unknown person's grave; a neglected [deserted, forlorn] grave

무연하다 憮然— gloomy; discontented; 〈낙담하다〉 disappointed; dejected; disheartened; 〈놀랍다〉 surprised; startled; astonishing
♦ 무연히 gloomily; discontentedly; 〈낙담하여〉 disappointedly; dejectedly; 〈놀라서〉 in surprise; 〈탄식하여〉 with a sigh; with dismay
▶ 그는 그 사고를 생각할 때마다 무연해졌다 He became depressed whenever he thought of the accident.
▶ 그는 그것을 무연히 바라보고 있었다 He was looking at it surprisedly.

무염 無鹽 ♦ 무염의 saltless; salt-free; unsalted ■ —버터 unsalted [salt-free] butter —식 a salt-free diet

무영등 無影燈 〈외과용〉 an astral lamp

무예 武藝 military [martial] arts; feats of arms
♦ 무예의 달인 a master of martial arts; a man of martial accomplishments / 무예를 닦다 practice military arts / 무예에 능하다 be skilled in the military arts

무욕 無慾 freedom from avarice
—무욕하다 〈이기적이 아닌〉 unselfish; disinterested; unavaricious; free from avarice; 〈무관심한〉 indifferent to gain
♦ 지나치게 무욕하다 be disinterested to a fault

무용 武勇 bravery; valo(u)r; military prowess
♦ 무용으로 평판이 자자한 군인 a soldier famed [celebrated] for his valor
■ —담 a tale of heroism [bravery] : 무용담을 늘어놓다 fight one's battle over again (in one's talk)

무용 無用 〈쓸모 없음〉 uselessness; 〈필요 없음〉 needlessness
▶ 무용자 출입 금지 (게시) No admittance except on business.
—무용하다 〈쓸모없다〉 of no use [avail, good]; useless; 〈필요없다〉 unnecessary; needless; 〈불일없다〉 without business
■ —지물 a useless and obstructive thing [person]; deadwood; a good-for-nothing

무용 舞踊 〈춤추기〉 dancing; 〈춤〉 a dance
♦ 무용을 배우다 take lesson in dancing
▶ 그녀는 무용을 잘 한다 She dances well. ⇌ She is a good dancer.
—무용하다 dance; perform a dance
■ 민속— a folk dance 한국— Korean dance —가 a dancer —교사 a dancing master —극 a dance drama [play] —단 (프) a corps de ballet; (a troupe of) ballet dancers —학원 a dancing school

무운 武運 the fortune(s) of war ♦ 무운이 없다 be unfortunate in war
▶ 무운을 빕니다 I pray for your victory in war. ⇌ May you be victorious!
▶ 그는 무운이 없어서 전사했다 Fortune being against him, and he was killed in action.

무운 無韻 ♦ 무운의 unrhymed; blank
■ —시 a blank verse; an unrhymed poem

무위 無爲 doing nothing; idleness; inactivity; inaction; faineancy
♦ 무위의 생활 an idle life / 무위 무책의 do-nothing 《government》 / 무위로 끝나다 come to nothing
■ —도식(徒食) an idle life : 무위도식하다 idle one's time away; live an idle life; eat the bread of idleness

무유증 無乳症 (醫) agalactia

무의무신 無義無信 lack of integrity and trust
—무의무신하다 be unfaithful and untrustworthy

무의무탁 無依無托 having no place to turn to; having no one to depend on
—무의무탁하다 forlorn; helpless; homeless; 〈서술적〉 have no one to turn [look] to (for help); have no place to go; be (left) stranded (in a foreign country)
♦ 무의무탁한 고아 a lonely [helpless] orphan / 무의무탁한 노인들 old people with no relatives to look after them [to turn to]

무의미하다 無意味— 〈뜻없다〉 insignificant; meaningless; 〈무익하다〉 purposeless; 〈어리석다〉 senseless; absurd; nonsensical
♦ 무의미한 논의 a meaningless [pointless] argument / 무의미한 생활 an insignificant life / 무의미한 전쟁 a meaningless war / 무의미한 생활을 하다 live to no purpose
▶ 그런 시험을 보다니 무의미하다 There's no point [sense] in giving tests of that sort.
▶ 너의 노력은 무의미하지 않았다 You have

not gone to all this trouble for nothing. ⇒ Your efforts were not in vain.
▶ 그런 것은 논의해 봤자 무의미하다 There is no point in arguing about it. ⇒ It is meaningless [nonsense] to argue about it.

무의식 無意識 unconsciousness; 〔精神分析〕 the unconscious
◆무의식적인 동작 spontaneous movement / 무의식적인 involuntary; unconscious; 〈기계적인〉 mechanical; automatic / 무의식적으로 involuntarily; unconsciously; mechanically; automatically
▶ 나는 그것을 무의식중에 했다 I did it unconsciously [involuntarily].
▶ 그 남자는 거의 무의식적으로 뛰기 시작했다 Scarcely witting, he began to run.
▶ 나는 무의식중에 브레이크를 걸었다 I applied the brakes unconsciously.
▶ 그는 전방의 신호가 녹색으로 바뀌자 무의식중에 뛰기 시작했다 When the signal in front turned green, he started to run without giving it a second thought.
■—상태 an unconscious state [condition]; (lapse into) unconsciousness

무의촌 無醫村 a doctorless village; a village without a doctor

무이자 無利子 no interest
◆무이자의 bearing no interest; free of interest; 〔法・經〕 passive / 무이자로 without interest; interest-free / 무이자로 돈을 빌리다 borrow money without interest / 무이자로 돈을 빌려주다 lend money without taking interest
■—공채(公債) passive bonds —채무 a passive debt

무익 無益 uselessness; futility —**무익하다** unprofitable; futile; useless; unavailing
◆무익한 노력 a futile effort / 무익한 책 a useless book / 무익한 논쟁 a futile argument / 무익한 살생을 하다 kill 《animals》 wantonly / 무익한 시도를 하다 make a futile [useless] attempt
▶ 그것은 백해무익하다 It does more harm than good.
▶ 인기 있는 많은 만화들이 유해무익하다 Many popular comics do more harm than good.
▶ 이런 무익한 논쟁은 그만두자 Let's stop this futile argument.
▶ 그에게 충고해도 무익하다 It's useless [of no use] to advise him. ⇒ It's no good [use] giving him advice.

무인 戊寅 〔民俗〕 the 15th binary term of the sexagenary cycle

무인 武人 a soldier; a military man; a warrior

무인 拇印 a thumbmark; a thumb impression; a thumbprint
◆무인을 찍다 seal 《a document》 with one's thumb
▶ 나는 서류에 무인을 찍었다 I affixed my thumbprint to the papers. ⇒ I put my thumbmark on the papers.
▶ 혹시 인감을 가지고 계시지 않다면 그 서류에 무인을 찍어주십시오 If you don't have your seal with you, please imprint a thumbmark on the papers.

무인 無人 ◆무인의 manless; unmanned; 〈사람이 살지 않는〉 uninhabited; 〈인적이 없는〉 deserted
■—건 널 목 an unattended [unguarded] (railroad) crossing —공장 a fully automated factory —도 an uninhabited [a desert] island —로켓 an unmanned rocket —비행기 a pilotless [radio-controlled] airplane —열차 a driverless [motormanless, crewless] train —우주선 an unmanned spacecraft —위성 an unmanned satelite —자동차 a driverless car —지대 (a) no-man's-land: 무인지대를 가다 step into an untrodden [uninhabited] region (▶ untrodden은 「인적미답의」의 뜻임) —판매대 a self-service stand

무인지경 無人之境 no-man's land; an uninhabited [a vacant] region
◆무인지경을 가다 step into an untrodden [uninhabited] region; 〈경쟁상대가 없는〉 (비유) be [do sth] unrivaled

무일물 無一物 having nothing; being penniless
▶ 그는 무일물이다 He has got practically nothing in the house to claim for his own. ⇒ He is as poor as a church mouse.

무일푼 無一— pennilessness
◆무일푼의 penniless; (口) broke / 무일푼으로 without a penny / (美) a cent / 무일푼이 되다 become penniless; (俗) go clean [flat] broke; be cleaned out
▶ 나는 무일푼이야 I am broke.
▶ 그는 무일푼이 되고 말았다 He has become penniless. ⇒ He has spent the [his] last penny. ⇒ He became penniless.
▶ 나는 지금 완전히 무일푼이다 I'm utterly broke now.
▶ 그는 서울에서 무일푼이 되어 부산으로 갔다 He became penniless in Seoul and went to Pusan.

무임 無賃 ◆무임으로 free; free of charge; charge-free; 〈화물이〉 carriage-free
■—승객 a free passenger; 〈우대권을 가진〉 (口) a deadhead —화물 free baggage 〔(英) luggage〕

무임소 無任所 ◆무임소의 unattached; unassigned; without portfolio
■—장관 a minister without portfolio

무임승차 無賃乘車 a free ride: 무임승차하다 ride free; 〈부정으로〉 cheat (the railway); (美口) steal a ride; pinch a free ride
—권 a free pass

무자 戊子 〔民俗〕 the 25th binary term of the sexagenary cycle

무자각하다 無自覺— 〈알아차리지 못하다〉 unaware 《of》; insensible 《of》; unconscious 《of one's responsibility》; 〈마음에 두지 않다〉 unmindful 《of》; 〈이해력이 없다〉 blind 《to》
▶ 그는 무자각한 행동을 취했다 He rushed blindly into an irresponsible act.
▶ 많은 사람이 자기 책임에 대해 무자각한다 A lot of people are unconscious of their own responsibilities.

무자격 無資格 disqualification; 〔法〕 incapacity; incompetence

무자격 간호사 [의사] an unlicensed nurse [doctor] / **무자격의** disqualified; incompetent; 〈무면허의〉 unlicensed; uncertified
■ **─교사** an unlicensed teacher; a teacher without qualification **─자** an unqualified [unlicensed] person; 〔法〕 an incompetent **─진료** unlicensed medical practice : 무자격 진료를 하다 practice medicine without a license

무자력 無資力 want [lack] of funds; 〈지불 불능〉 insolvency
─무자력하다 be without funds
■ **─자** a person of no resources [means]; an insolvent (person)

무자맥질 〈잠수〉 diving; ducking
─무자맥질하다 dive 《into, in, under》 water; duck 《down》; dip into 《the river》

무자본 無資本 ◆**무자본으로** without capital; with nothing to start with

무자비 無慈悲 mercilessness; cruelty
─무자비하다 merciless; pitiless; heartless; 〈잔혹한〉 ruthless; cruel
◆**무자비한 마음** a hard heart / **무자비하게** mercilessly; heartlessly; cruelly; pitilessly
▶그것은 너무나 무자비하다 That's too cruel.
▶그런 무자비한 짓은 할 수 없다 I have not the heart to do such a cruel thing.
▶그는 그들의 탄원을 무자비하게 거절했다 He pitilessly [coldly] rejected their plea.

무자식 無子息 **─무자식하다** childless; heirless; 〈서술적〉 have no children [issue]

무자식상팔자 《속담》 Love of children is an eternal encumbrance.

무자위 〈양수기〉 a water pump ◆**무자위로 물을 푸다** pump up water 《from》

무작위 無作爲 〔統〕 random
◆**무작위의** unintentional; unintended / **무작위로** unintentionally; 〈임의로〉 at random
■ **─추출[표본]** a random sample **─추출법** random sampling

무작정 無酌定 〈명사적〉 lack of any definite plan; 〈부사적〉 without a plan; with no particular plan; at haphazard; aimlessly; rashly; recklessly
◆**무작정 아무가 하는 대로 하다** follow [imitate] sb blindly
▶나는 남과 무작정 약속하지 않는다 I do not make rash promise.
▶그는 무작정 상경했다 He went up to Seoul with no definite object in view.
─무작정하다 unplanned; planless; haphazard; rash; reckless; aimless

무장 武將 a general; a military commander; a warlord
▶유감스럽게도 그는 무장감이 아니다 I regret to say that he is no general.

무장 武裝 〈국가의〉 armament; 〈병사의〉 equipment
◆**비무장 지대** a demilitarized zone 《略 DMZ》 / **무장을 해제하다** disarm 《a troop》; demilitarize 《a nation》; dismantle 《a ship》
─무장하다 arm sb; equip 《an army》; 〈스스로〉 equip [arm] oneself 《with a rifle》; bear [take up] arms
◆**무장한** armed; under [with] arms / **무장하고 있다** be armed 《with》; be under arms
▶그들은 총으로 무장했다 They armed themselves with rifles.
▶거기에는 약 30명의 무장한 군인이 있었다 We found about thirty armed soldiers [soldiers under arms] there.
■ **완전─** 〈in〉 full kit ■ **─간첩** an armed spy [agent] **─간첩선** an armed espionage boat **─경찰[경관]** an armed policeman; 〈총칭〉 armed police **─공비** an armed Red bandit; an armed communist guerilla **─봉기** rising in arms; an armed uprising **─상선** an armed merchantman **─중립** armed neutrality **─평화** armed peace **─해제** disarmament; demilitarization **─화** militarization

무장지졸 無將之卒 a leaderless army

무재 無才 lack of ability; incompetence
─무재하다 lacking in ability; untalented; talentless; incompetent
■ **─인** an untalented person

무저항 無抵抗 nonresistance
◆**무저항의** unresistant; nonresistant / **무저항으로** without resistance; without making [offering] any resistance
▶그들은 무저항의 주민에게 총격을 가했다 They fired at the unresisting people.
▶그들은 무저항으로 항복했다 They surrendered without (offering any) resistance.
■ **─주의** a principle of nonresistance **─주의자** a nonresistant

무적 無敵 invincibility
◆**무적의 용사** a man of matchless valor / **무적의** unrivaled; matchless; invincible; unequaled
▶그 팀은 무적이다 The team is invincible [unrivaled].
▶내구성에서 이 차는 무적이다 In durability, this car cannot be matched.
■ **─함대** 〈스페인의〉 〔史〕 the Invincible Armada

무적 無籍 absence of a registered domicile; lack of a record
◆**무적의** without a registered domicile
■ **─자** a person without a registered domicile; 〈부랑자〉 a vagabond; a vagrant

무적 霧笛 〈고동〉 a foghorn; a fog siren [whistle]
◆**무적을 울리다** sound a foghorn

무전 無電 radio; wireless
◆**무전기를 갖춘 자동차** a radio car; a telecar / **무전설비를 한 배** a ship equipped [fitted] with a wireless installation / **무전으로** by radio; by wireless / **무전으로 유도하다** talk down 《a plane》 / **무전을 치다** telegraph by wireless; send a message by wireless [radio]; send a radio [wireless message] to
▶그 배는 무전으로 구조를 요청했다 The ship radioed for help.
■ **─국** a wireless station **─기사** a wireless operator; a radioman **─실** a radio room; a wireless room **─장치** radio [wireless] apparatus **─탑** a radio tower

무전 無錢 being moneyless [penniless]
◆**무전의** moneyless; penniless

—여행 a penniless trip; a vagabond journey : 무전여행하다 travel without money; go on penniless journey; (美俗) hitchhike —여행가 a hitchhiker —취식 jumping a restaurant bill : 무전취식하다 jump [(英) skip out] a restaurant bill; defraud [bilk] a restaurant

무절제 無節制 immoderation; incontinence; intemperance; excesses —무절제하다 immoderate; incontinent; intemperate
♦ 무절제한 생활을 하다 lead an intemperate life
▶ 그는 무절제해지는 경향이 있었다 He was apt to fall into careless ways.

무절조 無節操 inconstancy; unchastity
—무절조하다 〈생각이 자주 바뀌는〉 inconstant; wanton (woman); 〈정견이 없는〉 unprincipled (politician); unchaste
♦ 무절조한 정치인 an unprinciple politician
▶ 그는 무절조한 사람이다 He is an unprincipled [inconstant] man.

무정 無情 heartlessness; cruelty; hardness of heart
—무정하다 cold; heartless; hard-hearted; cold-hearted; 〈잔혹한〉 cruel; harsh; inhuman; 〈무자비한〉 merciless; pitiless
♦ 무정한 마음 a cold [stony] heart; a heart of stone / 무정한 세월 fleeting [transient] time / 무정하게도 mercilessly; heartlessly; pitilessly; cruelly
▶ 당신은 참 무정한 사람이구려 What a cold man you are!
▶ 그 가련한 모습을 보면 아무리 무정한 사람이라도 눈물을 흘리지 않을 수 없을 것이다 The sad appearance will wring tears from the hardest heart.
▶ 그는 무정하게도 앤을 무시했다 He heartlessly ignored Ann.

무정견 無定見 a lack of fixed principles; fickleness; inconstancy
—무정견하다 lacking a fixed principle; inconstant; vacillating; wavering; fickle
▶ 정부는 무정견한 농업정책을 수정해야 한다 The government should rectify the lack of a fixed policy for agriculture.

무정란 無精卵 〈生〉〈달걀〉 a wind egg; 〈미수정란〉 an unfertilized egg

무정부 無政府 anarchy
♦ 무정부의 anarchic
—상태 anarchy : 무정부상태의 anarchic; anarchical / 무정부상태에 있다 be in a state of anarchy; be in a chaotic condition —주의 anarchism —주의자 an anarchist

무정위 無定位 〔物〕 astaticism ♦ 무정위의 〔物〕 astatic
—검류계 an astatic galvanometer —조속기(調速機) an astatic governor —침 an astatic needle

무정형 無定形 shapelessness; amorphousness
♦ 무정형의 shapeless; formless; 〈비결정체인〉 amorphous
—무정형하다 formless; shapeless; amorphous
—금속 amorphous metal —물질 an amorphous substance —상태 amorphous state —수정(水晶) massive quartz

무정형 無定型 —무정형하다 formless; shapeless
—시 formless verse; 〈무각운의〉 blank verse

무제 無題 no title ♦ 무제의 titleless; untitled; without a title
▶ 무제 〈그림 등의〉 No title.

무제한 無制限 ♦ 무제한의 unlimited; unrestricted; free; limitless / 무제한으로 without any restriction; freely; without reserve [limitation] / 무제한으로 입장을 허가하다 admit people without any restriction
—급 〔레슬링·柔道〕 the open-weight division —법화(法貨) unlimited legal tender —입국 unrestricted admission (of immigrants) —통화 〈자유 발행의〉 free currency

무조건 無條件 ♦ 무조건의 unconditional; unconditioned; unqualified; absolute / 무조건으로 unconditionally; absolutely; unqualifiedly; without condition [reservation] / 무조건 받아들이다 accept (another's statement) without reserve / 무조건 승낙하다 give an unqualified [unconditional] contest (to) / 무조건 조약에 조인하다 sign a treaty without any conditions
▶ 그들은 내 제안을 무조건 받아들였다 They accepted my proposal without any conditions.
▶ 나는 무조건 찬성한다 I agree with you absolutely [unconditionally].
—반사 〔生·心〕 an unconditioned reflex —사면 a free pardon —항복 unconditional surrender : 무조건 항복하다 surrender unconditionally —협상 unconditional negotiations

무조지 無租地 〔法〕 tax-[duty-]free land

무족 無足 ♦ 무족의 apodal; apodous
—류 〔動〕 Apoda; Apodes; Apodia —류 동물 an apod

무좀 〔醫〕 athlete's foot; dermatophytosis
♦ 무좀에 걸리다 have athlete's foot

무종교 無宗敎 lack of religion; irreligion
♦ 무종교의 irreligious; atheistic
▶ 그는 무종교인이다 He doesn't believe in any particular religion. ⇒ He is an irreligious man.
—자 a man without religion; an atheist

무종아리 the lower part of the calf

무죄 無罪 〔法〕 innocence; being not guilty; guiltlessness
♦ 무죄의 not guilty; guiltless; innocent / 무죄가 되다 be found innocent [not guilty]; be acquitted (of) / 무죄를 언도하다 declare sb not guilty; acquit / 무죄를 주장하다 assert one's innocence [that one is innocent]
▶ 그는 고소당했으나 무죄가 되었다 He was innocent of the charge.
▶ 배심원은 그 남자를 무죄로 판정하였다 The jury acquitted the man of the crime.
—무죄하다 not guilty; guiltless; innocent
—판결 a judgment of acquittal; a decision of "not guilty"

무죄석방 無罪釋放 〔法〕 acquittal (and discharge)
♦ 무죄석방이 되다 be found innocent and acquitted

무주 無主 being ownerless
■—고혼 a forlorn wandering spirit (that has no posterity to perform the memorial service) —공당(空堂) an ownerless house; an unoccupied house —공처(空處) a deserted lot; an unowned land: 그 주(州)의 광대한 지역은 무주공처다 A large extent of the state is uninhabited. / 그 마을은 무주공처가 되었다 The village was deserted. —물 an ownerless thing
무주의 無主義 ◆무주의의 without any principle; unprincipled
■—자 a person without definite principle
무주정 無酒精 ◆무주정의 nonalcoholic
■—음료 a nonalcoholic beverage; a soft drink
무주택자 無住宅者 people who don't have their own houses
무중력 無重力 zero gravity; gravity-free; weightlessness; nongravitation
■—비행 a zero-gravity [weightless] flight —상태 a state of weightlessness [nongravitation]; a gravity-free state; a weightless state: 무중력 상태에서[로] in a weightless state; under weightless conditions / 무중력 상태가 되다 become [go] weightless; at [in] zero G
무지 〈한 섬이 못되는 곡식〉 not quite enough grain to fill a *sŏm*; a short *sŏm* of grain
무지 拇指 a thumb ⇨ 엄지
무지 無地 solid color
◆무지 스커트 a plain-colored skirt / 밤색 무지 커튼 a curtain of [in] solid brown / 무지의 plain; 〈무늬가 없는〉 unfigured; solid 〈black〉; self-colored; of solid color
▶ 그의 넥타이는 무지의 검은 빛깔이었다 His tie was solid black.
■—천 plain [solid-color] cloth; cloth without a pattern
무지 無知 1〈모름〉 ignorance 《about》; 〈문맹〉 illiteracy; 〈어리석음〉 stupidity
◆무지로 인하여 out of [from, through] ignorance / 무지를 깨우치다 enlighten 《a sb's mind》 / 자신의 무지를 드러내다 display one's lack of knowledge; betray one's ignorance / 자신의 무지를 부끄러워하다 be ashamed of one's ignorance [lack of knowledge] 《of, about》
—무지하다 ignorant 《of》; 〈무식하다〉 illiterate; 〈어리석다〉 stupid; silly
▶ 나는 컴퓨터에 관해서는 아주 무지하다 I'm quite ignorant about the computer.
▶ 나는 법률에 관해서는 무지하다 I'm ignorant of [about] law. ⇌ I don't know anything about law.
2〈우악스러움〉 roughness; violence; rudeness
—무지하다 rough; rude; wild; violent
◆무지한 행동 rude [rough] behavior / 무지한 짓을 하다 act outrageously; commit an outrage / 무지하게 굴다 behave rudely; play it rough
무지각 無知覺 insensibility; indiscretion —무지각하다 insensible; senseless
◆무지각한 짓을 하다 act indiscreetly; commit an imprudence
무지개 a rainbow ◆무지개의 일곱가지 빛깔 the seven colors of rainbow
▶ 무지개가 하늘에 떴다 A rainbow appeared [formed] in the sky. ⇌ A rainbow arched across the sky.
■쌍— a couple [double] rainbow ■무지갯빛 iridescence; rainbow [spectral] colors: 무지갯빛의 rainbow-colored; iridescent
무지개송어 〔魚〕 a rainbow trout
무지근하다 〈서술적〉 feel heavy [dull]
◆머리가 무지근하다 feel heavy in the head
▶ 뒤가 무지근하다 My bowels are stuffy [constipated].
무지기 〈치마 속에 입는 짧은 통치마〉 an underwear skirt; a slip
무지러지다 wear down to a stump; get stumpy [blunt]; wear out [away]; wear to a stump
◆무지러진 비 a stumpy broom
▶ 붓이 무지러졌다 The writing brush is worn to a stump.
무지렁이 a stupid [blunt] person; a rustic; a lout; a dunce; a moron
무지르다 cut off [away]; break (off); snap
◆나뭇가지를 무지르다 cut branches off a tree; cut away branches from a tree
무지막지하다 無知莫知— ignorant and uncouth
◆무지막지한 행동을 하다 act rudely; be wild; commit an outrage
무지몰각 無知沒覺 ignorance and lack of understanding —무지몰각하다〈서술적〉utterly ignorant; know nothing
무지몽매 無知蒙昧 lack of enlightenment —무지몽매하다 unenlightened; ignorant
▶ 그 외딴 섬 사람들은 무지몽매하다 The solitary islanders are in the darkest ignorance.
무지향성마이크로폰 無指向性— 〔工〕 non-directional microphone
무지향성무선표지 無指向性無線標識 〔工·水産〕 non-directional radio beacon
무지향성신호 無指向性信號 〔水産〕 non-directional call
무지향성안테나 無指向性— non-directional antenna
무직 無職 ◆무직의 without [having no] occupation; 〈실직한〉 out of work [employment]; unemployed; jobless
▶ 그는 지금 무직이다 He is jobless [out of work] now.
■—자 a person without occupation; 〈실업자〉 a person out of work; the unemployed (▶복수 취급): 무직자 수가 늘어나고 있다 The number of jobless [unemployed] people is on the increase.
무진 戊辰 〔民俗〕 the 5th binary term of the sexagenary cycle
무진 無盡 1〈무궁무진〉 infinite
—무진하다 unending; unlimited
2〈상호신용계〉 a mutual loan [financing] association
무진동 —銅 copper containing over 50% iron sulfide
무진장하다 無盡藏 inexhaustible; limitless; unlimited; infinite; unfailing

▶ 사람들은 천연자원이 무진장하다고 믿고 있다 People believe that there is no limit to our natural resources.
▶ 그 지방에는 철광석이 무진장하다 The region has inexhaustible deposits of iron ore.
▶ 그는 돈이 무진장하다 He has a mint [no end] of money.
▶ 그는 에너지가 무진장하다 He has a great deal of energy.

무질리다 be cut off [out, away]; be broken off ▶ 바람에 나뭇가지가 무질렸다 Branches were cut out from the tree by the wind.

무질서 無秩序 disorder; chaos; confusion; disorderliness
▶ 교실 안은 무질서 상태였다 The classroom was in (a state of) disorder.
—**무질서하다** disordered; confused; 〈혼란한〉 chaotic; 〈무법의〉 lawless
♦ 무질서하게 without any order [system]; randomly

무집게 a pair of pincers; nippers
무쩍 all at once; in a sweep [push]
▶ 일을 한꺼번에 무쩍 해버렸다 I did my work in one sweep.

무찌르다 1 〈공격하다〉 attack; assault; 〈격파하다〉 defeat; crush; destroy; 〈유린하다〉 devastate; overrun; conquer
♦ 적을 무찌르다 conquer [defeat] the enemy
▶ 우리는 적을 무찔렀다 We crushed our enemy.
2 〈마구 죽이다〉 wipe out; kill off; mow [cut] down
♦ 수천의 적군을 무찌르다 mow down thousands of the enemy

무찔리다 1 〈살육당하다〉 be mowed down; get killed off; be mopped [cleaned] up; be wiped out
2 〈격파되다〉 be defeated; 〈짓밟히다〉 be overrun; be devastated
▶ 적의 부대는 무찔렸다 The enemy forces were stamped [cleared] out.
▶ 성은 적군에게 무찔렸다 The castle was devastated by the enemy.

무차별 無差別 indiscrimination; nondiscrimination
♦ 무차별의 indiscriminate; equal / 무차별로 indiscriminately; without distinction; with impartiality; equally / 남녀 무차별로 without distinction of sex / 무차별로 취급하다 treat equally; be impartial 《to》
—**무차별하다** indiscriminate; equal
■—**폭격** indiscriminate [nonselective, carpet] bombing

무착륙 無着陸 ♦ 무착륙의 nonstop; without alighting
■—**비행** a nonstop flight : 무착륙 비행을 하다 make a nonstop flight 《to》; nonstop 《to》

무찰 無札 ♦ 무찰 입장하다 enter [sneak in] without a ticket
■—**승객** a passenger without a ticket; 〈우대권을 가진〉 《美口》 a deadhead —**승차** riding 《a train》 without a ticket; a free ride —**입장자** a person who paid no admission

무참 無慚 shame; disgrace
—**무참하다** 〈서술적〉 feel [be] ashamed 《of, for》; be overwhelmed with shame
♦ 무참히 shamefully; disgracefully; shyly

무참하다 無慘 〈잔인한〉 cruel; atrocious; pitiless; ruthless; merciless; 〈비참한〉 tragic; pitiful
♦ 무참한 광경 a horrible scene [sight] / 무참한 재해 a horrible disaster / 무참한 처사 a cruel deed / 무참히 without pity [mercy]; mercilessly; cruelly / 무참한 최후를 마치다 meet with a tragic end [death]
▶ 그들은 무참히 그를 죽였다 They murdered the man in cold blood.

무채색 無彩色 an achromatic color
무책 無策 lack of policy; resourcelessness
♦ 속수무책 resourcelessness; helplessness / 무책의 resourceless; shiftless / 무책이다 have no [lack] policy
▶ 정부는 그 사태에 대해 전혀 무책이었다 The Government was utterly unable to devise any appropriate measures to cope with the situation.

무책임 無責任 irresponsibility; lack of a sense of responsibility
—**무책임하다** irresponsible
♦ 무책임한 사람들 irresponsibles / 무책임하게 irresponsibly; without a due sense of responsibility / 무책임한 말을 하다 make an irresponsible statement [remark]
▶ 나는 무책임한 사람은 좋아하지 않는다 I don't like an irresponsible person.
▶ 무책임한 말은 하지 마라 Don't talk at random [wildly].
▶ 그런 곳에 어린아이를 혼자 놔두다니 무책임하다 It is irresponsible to leave a small child alone in such a place.

무척 greatly; very (much); highly; extremely; exceedingly
♦ 무척 따뜻해지다 become very warm / 무척 야위다 lose much flesh [weight]
▶ 그 소식을 듣고 우리는 무척 놀랐습니다 We were greatly surprised to hear the news.
▶ 네가 무척 보고 싶었다 I wanted to see you very badly.
▶ 나는 그에게 무척 화가 났다 I got so angry with him.
▶ 나는 골프를 잘 치지 못하지만 무척 좋아한다 I am very fond of playing golf though a poor hand at it [not a good player].

무척추동물 無脊椎動物 〔動〕 an invertebrate (animal)

무체 無體 ♦ 무체의 incorporeal; intangible
■—**동산** a chose in action —**물** intangibles; an immaterial being —**재산** 〔法〕 intangible property

무춤하다 halt; stop short; hold back *one's* steps
♦ 뱀을 보고 무춤하다 stop short at the sight of a snake

무취 無臭 ♦ 무취의 scentless; unscented; 《美》 odorless; 《英》 odourless / 무색 무취의 colorless and odorless
—**무취하다** scentless; odorless; inodorous

무취미 無趣味 tastelessness ➪ 몰취미

무치 無恥 shamelessness; impudicity
—**무치하다** shameless; brazen(-faced)
♦후안무치한 사람 a shameless rascal; a brazen-faced man

무치다 season; dress 〈vegetables〉 with 〈vinegar, soy sauce, etc.〉; mix 〈bean sprouts〉 with seasonings

무크 a mook [〈magazine book〉]

무턱대고 〈무분별하게〉 recklessly; 〈닥치는대로〉 haphazardly; at random; 〈준비〉[까닭〉 없이〉 without any preparation [reason]; 〈무차별하게〉 indiscriminately; blindly
♦무턱대고 나무라다 scold sb for no good reason / 무턱대고 남을 믿다 trust others too much; trust everybody indiscriminately / 무턱대고 돈을 쓰다 spend (one's) money recklessly [like water]; be lavish with one's money
▶범인은 무턱대고 발포했다 The criminal fired his gun blindly [at random].
▶그는 무턱대고 믿어서 탈이다 It is no good of him to believe hastily [to give ready credence].
▶그녀는 무턱대고 시험을 쳤다 She took an examination without any preparation.
▶무엇이든 무턱대고 시작하면 성공할 가망이 없다 You have little chance of success in anything, if you start it rashly [haphazardly].

무텅이 planting a newly-developed field with 〈rice, barley, wheat, corn, etc.〉

무테 無— ♦무테의 rimless; frameless; unframed
■—안경 (a pair of) rimless spectacles; rimless glasses

무통 無痛 painlessness; 〔醫〕 indolence
♦무통의 painless; free from pain
■—분만 (a) painless delivery; 〈마취를 한〉 delivery in twilight sleep

무투표 無投票 ♦무투표로 without vote [voting]
▶그는 무투표로 시장에 선출되었다 He was elected mayor without voting.
■—당선 being elected without voting

무트로 〈한 목에 많이〉 plentifully at a time; amply [in a lump] at one time

무판화 無瓣花 〔植〕 an apetalous flower

무패 無敗 no defeat; a clean record
♦무패의 undefeated / 무패의 기록을 유지하다 maintain one's undefeated record
▶이 팀은 그때까지 무패의 전적이었다 So far the team had a clean record.

무표정 無表情 absence [lack] of expression
—**무표정하다** expressionless; impassive; blank (look); wooden (stares); (口) poker-faced
♦무표정한 얼굴 an expressionless [wooden, poker] face; (美口) a deadpan / 무표정하게 expressionlessly; impassively; without showing one's emotions [feelings]; woodenly
▶그 배우는 아주 무표정하게 연기를 했다 The actor played his part completely deadpan.

무풍 無風 1 〈바람이 없음〉 ♦무풍의 windless; calm
2 〈평온함〉 ♦노사관계는 지금 무풍상태다 At present there is no dispute between labor and management.

무풍대 無風帶 the calm belt [latitudes]
♦정치적 무풍대 political doldrums
■온대— 〈아열대의〉 the horse latitudes 적도— the equatorial calm; the doldrums

무학 無學 illiteracy; a lack of education; illiterateness; ignorance ♦무학의 unlettered; 〈교육받지 않은〉 uneducated; 〈문맹의〉 illiterate; 〈무지한〉 ignorant
▶그는 무학이지만 사람의 도리는 알고 있다 Though he is ignorant, he is a man of virtue.
▶나는 무학이기 때문에 그런 어려운 말은 이해하지 못한다 I am so uneducated (that) I cannot understand such a difficult remark.

무한 無限 infinity; 〈영원〉 eternity; infinitude
—**무한하다** unlimited; limitless; boundless; 〈영원한〉 eternal; 〈무진장의〉 inexhaustible; endless; interminable; infinite
♦무한한 가능성 infinite [limitless] possibilities / 무한한 천연자원 inexhaustible natural resources / 무한한 보고 an inexhaustible mine of wealth [treasure] / 무한한 욕망 unbounded desire / 무한한 활력 boundless energy / 무한히 infinitely; limitlessly; boundlessly; endlessly / 무한한 즐거움을 주다 give no end of pleasure
▶우리의 시간은 무한하지는 않다 Our time is not unlimited.
▶그의 힘은 무한하다 His strength is boundless.
▶우주는 무한히 넓다 The universe is immeasurably vast.
▶수요는 무한히 증대할 것이다 The demand will increase to an unlimited extent.
■—공간 infinite space —궤도 a caterpillar; an endless track —궤도차 a caterpillar tractor —급수(級數) 〔數〕 infinite series —대infinity; an infinite magnitude —등비급수 〔數〕 infinite geometrical series —등비수열 〔數〕 an infinite geometrical sequence —량 (an) infinite quantity —소 the infinitesimal: 무한소의 infinitesimal; infinitely small —소수 〔數〕 an infinite decimal —집합 an infinite set

무한정 無限定 〈명사적〉 infinity; unlimitedness; 〈부사적〉 boundlessly; unlimitedly; without limit [end]; endlessly
▶무한정 기다릴 수는 없다 I can't wait (for him) indefinitely [forever].
▶그는 나를 호텔 로비에서 무한정 기다리게 했다 He kept me cooling my heels in the hotel lobby.

무한책임 無限責任 〔商〕 unlimited liability
■—사원 a general partner; a partner with unlimited liability —회사 an unlimited (liability) company

무함 誣陷 slander; backbiting
—**무함하다** slander; calumniate; bring a false charge (against)

무항산 無恒産 ♦무항산이면 무항심(無恒心)이다 A real property, a real purpose. ⇌ Competency is for constancy of mind.

무해 無害 harmlessness; inoffensiveness; innocence
▶인축(人畜) 무해 〈살충제 등의 표시〉 No harm [Harmless] to men and beasts.

—무해하다 harmless ((to)); innocent; innoxious; innocuous; inoffensive; 〈서술적〉 do *sb* no harm
▶ 이 나무의 열매는 먹어도 무해하다 Even if you eat it, this nut will do you no harm.
▶ 약간의 술은 무해하다 A little alcohol will do you no harm.

무해무득 無害無得 no gain no loss
—무해무득하다 〈서술적〉 be neither gain nor loss; be neither harmful nor useful

무허가 無許可 no permit
♦ 무허가로 영업하다 engage in business without a license [permit]
▶ 그는 무허가로 약을 팔고 있다 He sells medicine without a license.
■ —건물 an unauthorized house; an unlicensed building —판매[제조] nonlicensed sale [production]

무혈 無血 ♦ 무혈의 승리 a bloodless victory / 무혈의 bloodless; without bloodshed
■ —전쟁 a white war ((of propaganda))—점령 a bloodless occupation —혁명 a bloodless revolution; [史] the Glorious Revolution

무혐의하다 無嫌疑— clear ((of suspicion)); unsuspected

무협 武俠 chivalry; gallantry; heroism
♦ 무협적(인) gallant; chivalrous; chivalric; heroic

무형 無形 ♦ 무형의 원조[이익] moral support [gains] / 무형의 〈형체가 없는〉 formless; 〈보이지 않는〉 invisible; 〈추상적〉 abstract; 〈비물질적〉 immaterial; incorporeal; 〈정신적〉 moral; spiritual; 〈만질 수 없는〉 intangible
▶ 사기는 전쟁에서 무형의 요소다 Morale is the intangible factor in war.
▶ 지식은 무형의 재산이다 Knowledge is an intangible asset.
▶ 아이들은 부모에게서 유형 무형의 원조를 받고 자란다 Children grow with assistance, both material and moral, rendered by parents.
■ —고정자산 〔商〕 intangible fixed assets —무역 〔商〕 invisible trade —문화재 intangible cultural assets —물 an immaterial thing; an incorporeal entity —재산[자산] immaterial [intangible] property; invisible assets

무호동중이작호 無虎洞中狸作虎 When the cat's away, the mice will play. ⇌ In the land of the blind a one-eyed man is king.

무화과 無花果 1 ⇨ 무화과 나무
2 〈열매〉 a fig

무화과 나무 無花果— 〔植〕 a fig (tree)
무환수입 無換輸入 〔經〕 no-draft import
무환수출 無換輸出 〔經〕 no-draft export
무환자나무 無患者— 〔植〕 a soapberry (tree)
무효 無效 invalidity; nullity; 〈통용되지 않음〉 unavailability; 〈효과가 없음〉 futility; ineffectiveness
♦ 무효의 〈실효적〉 invalid ((act)); of no force; void ((contract)); 〈효력이 없는〉 unavailable ((ticket)); 〈효과가 없는〉 of no effect; ineffective / 무효가 되다 become null [void, ineffective]; be no longer good; be of no use [avail]; lose effect; 〔法〕 lapse; prove futile / 무효로 하다 void; invalidate; annul; make ((null and)) void; nullify ((a law))
▶ 돈을 치르지 않으면 그 계약은 무효가 된다 If you don't pay the money, the agreement will become invalid.
▶ 그 유언은 법정에서 무효라고 선언되었다 The will was declared void by the court.
▶ 네 여권은 기한이 지났으므로 무효다 Your passport is out of date and invalid.
■ —계약 a void [an invalid] contract —심리 (審理) 〔法〕 a mistrial —전력 reactive power —조항 〔法〕 an irritant clause; an irritancy —차표 an invalid [unavailable] ticket —투표 〈행위〉 invalid voting; 〈그 표〉 an invalid vote —화 invalidation; 〔法〕 defeasance

무후하다 無後— childless; heirless
무훈 武勳 military merits ⇨ 무공
무휴 無休 ((having)) no holiday
▶ 그는 연중무휴로 일했다 He has been working without a holiday throughout the year.
▶ 이 가게는 연중무휴다 This store has no vacation.
▶ 연중 무휴 (게시) Open throughout the year.

무흠 無欠 〈흠이 없음〉 flawlessness; faultlessness **—무흠하다** flawless; faultless; free from blemish

무희 舞姫 a dancer; a dancing girl (▶ dancing 에 악센트를 둠. 양쪽에 악센트를 두면「춤추고 있는 소녀」의 뜻)

묵 curd ♦ 도토리— acorn curd 메밀— buckwheat curd

묵계 默契 a tacit understanding [agreement, promise]; a secret understanding
♦ 묵계하에 on a tacit understanding
▶ 그 두 사람 사이에는 묵계가 있다 There is a tacit understanding between the two of them. ⇌ A tacit understanding exists between the two of them.
—묵계하다 agree tacitly [implicitly]; make a tacit agreement ((with))

묵고 默考 meditation; a silent thought
—묵고하다 meditate ((on)); contemplate; muse ((on))
▶ 그는 죽음의 신비에 대해 묵고해 보았다 He mused on the mystery of death.

묵과 默過 connivance [kənáivəns]
—묵과하다 overlook; pass [look] over; connive [wink] ((at))
♦ 묵과할 수 없는 모욕 an intolerable insult / 과실을 묵과하다 overlook [slur ((over))] *sb*'s fault
▶ 나는 그런 부정은 묵과할 수 없다 I cannot put up with such an injustice.
▶ 이건 정말 묵과할 수 없다 I can't overlook it.

묵낙 默諾 tacit consent [understanding]; acquiescence
—묵낙하다 consent tacitly ((to)); give tacit consent [a silent assent] ((to))
♦ 제안을 묵낙하다 give tacit consent to a proposal

묵념 默念 1 ⇨ 묵상(默想)
2 ⇨ 묵도
—묵념하다 pray silently; offer a silent prayer ((to))

묵다¹

♦순국선열에 대하여 1분간 묵념하다 pay one minute's silent tribute to the patriotic martyr

묵다¹ 〈숙박하다〉 stay 〔at 〔in〕 a place〕; put up; stop 〔at, with〕; lodge 〔at〕

> [解說] *stay*는 일반적으로 개인집이나 아파트, 호텔 등에 두루 쓰인다. *put up*은 보통 호텔이나 가정에서 손님으로 머무는 것을 나타낸다. *stop*은 특히 단기간일 경우에 쓰인다. *lodge*는 단기간이나 일정 기간 동안 방값을 지불하고 묵는 것을 나타낸다.

♦하룻밤 묵다 stay overnight, stop 〔for〕 the night / 묵게 하다 lodge *sb*; give *sb* a bed / 하룻밤 묵어 가기를 청하다 ask for a night's lodging
▶우리는 그날 밤 제주의 한 해변 호텔에서 묵었다 We put up at a seaside hotel in Cheju for the night.
▶그는 숙부님 댁에 묵고 있다 He stays at his uncle's.
▶나는 호텔에 묵으면서 논문을 썼다 I stayed in a hotel to write my thesis.
▶우리는 그를 하룻밤 묵게 했다 We lodged him overnight.
▶나를 오늘밤 묵게 해주시겠어요? Will you put me up for the night?

묵다² **1** 〈오래되다〉 become 〔get〕 old; become antiquated 〔outdated〕
♦묵은 관습 an old 〔a worm-eaten〕 custom / 묵은 병 an old ailment / 묵은 빚 an old debt; a debt of long standing / 묵은 빵 stale bread / 묵은 상처 an old wound / 묵은 쌀 old 〔long-stored〕 rice / 케케 묵다 be hackneyed
▶그건 묵은 학설이다 That theory is dated.
2 〈낙제하다〉 be off 〔school〕; lead a life away from 《school》; 〈유급하다〉 stay back (in the same class); remain (in the original class)
▶내 동생은 대학에 들어가려고 2년 묵었다 My brother spent two years preparing for the college entrance examination.
▶그는 입학 시험에 떨어져 1년 묵었다 He was off school for one year because of a failure entrance exam.
3 【사용되지 않다】〈토지・자본이〉 be not in use; lie idle; 〈상품이〉 remain unsold 《on the shelf》

묵도 默禱 a silent prayer
—묵도하다 offer a silent prayer; pray silently 〔in silence〕

묵독 默讀 silent reading; reading to *oneself*
—묵독하다 read silently 〔to *oneself*〕
▶교과서 12쪽을 세번 묵독하세요 Read page twelve of your textbook three times to yourselves.

묵례 默禮 a silent bow; a nod
♦묵례를 나누다 exchange bows 〔nods〕
▶그녀는 들어올 때 내게 묵례를 했다 She gave me a nod 〔nodded to me〕 when she came in.
—묵례하다 bow in silence; make a bow 〔to〕; nod 〔to〕
▶학생들은 선생님께 묵례했다 The students bowed to their teacher in silence.

묵묵하다 默默— silent; mute; tacit
묵묵히 默默— silently; in silence; mutely
♦묵묵히 산을 오르다 climb a mountain silently / 묵묵히 있다 keep silent
▶그들은 묵묵히 일하고 있었다 They were working in silence 〔silently〕.
▶그녀는 그의 제안에 묵묵히 따랐다 She acquiesced in his proposal.
▶그는 묵묵히 일을 잘해주었다 He served me well without uttering any complaints.

묵비권 默祕權 the right to keep silent
♦묵비권을 행사하다 〔法〕 stand mute; use 〔exercise〕 the right of silence; **(美)** take the Fifth (Amendment)
▶용의자는 묵비권을 행사했다 The suspect used the right of silence 〔exercised the right to refuse to answer about it〕.

묵살하다 默殺— take no notice of; ignore (by keeping silence); pass 〔over〕 《a matter》 in silence
♦묵살되다〔당하다〕 be ignored; meet with disregard / 제안을 묵살하다 ignore *sb's* proposal / 탄원을 묵살하다 turn a deaf ear to *sb's* entreaty
▶학계는 그의 연구를 묵살했다 The academic world took no notice of his research.
▶그 사실을 함부로 묵살할 수는 없을 것이다 You will be unable to ignore the fact deliberately.

묵상 默想 (a) meditation; contemplation
▶그는 가끔 묵상에 잠긴다 He is sometimes buried 〔absorbed〕 in deep meditation. ⇌ He is sometimes lost in thought 〔contemplation〕.
—묵상하다 meditate 〔on, upon〕; muse 〔on〕
▶나는 인생의 의미에 대해 조용히 묵상했다 I meditated on the meaning of life.

묵새기다 make a long stay (without doing much)

묵수 墨守 adherence 〔to〕 —묵수하다 adhere to; stick 〔cling, keep〕 to
♦옛 관습을 묵수하는 사람들 people who cling to old customs; adherents to old customs

묵시 默示 1 〈계시〉 revelation —묵시하다 reveal
2 〈은연중 나타내 보임〉 implication
♦묵시적인 tacit; implied
■—록 ⇨ 계시록 (요한 ~)

묵시하다 默視— watch in silence; remain a passive spectator
▶내가 어찌 그들의 참상을 묵시할 수 있겠는가? How can I remain indifferent 〔shut my eyes〕 to their miserable state?

묵약 默約 a tacit agreement ⇨ 묵계

묵은세배 —歲拜 New Year's Eve greetings (to *one's* elders) bidding the old year out; bowing *one's* greeting to elders on New Year's Eve

묵은해 the old 〔past〕 year; the year gone by
♦묵은 해가 가는 것을 지켜보다 see the old year out / 묵은 해를 보내고 새해를 맞이하다 ring out the old year and ring in the new year

묵음 默音 ♦묵음의 silent; 〔音聲〕 mute

묵이 an old thing 〔matter〕; old stuff

묵인 默認 tacit admission 〔permission〕; silent

approval [consent]; 〈잘못·죄 등의〉 connivance 《at, with》; toleration
◆ 묵인하에 with sb's connivance; with the connivance of sb
━묵인하다 permit [admit] tacitly; overlook; connive [wink] at
▶ 나는 그런 부정은 묵인하지 못한다 I can't connive at such an injustice.
▶ 나는 그의 잘못을 묵인할 수가 없다 I can't overlook [pass over] his fault.
▶ 선생님은 학생들이 시간제로 일하는 것을 묵인해 주고 계시다 The teacher gives tacit consent to his students working part-time.
▶ 경찰 당국이 그것을 묵인하고 있다 The police authorities simply pass it over [connive at it].

묵자 默字 a silent letter; 〔音聲〕 a mute (letter)

묵정밭 an abandoned field; weed-grown fallow; a fallow field that has gone to waste

묵정이 an old thing; old stuff; stuff that has been laid aside for a long time

묵종 默從 acquiescence; passive [silent] obedience
━묵종하다 acquiesce [ækwiés] (in); obey passively; submit unprotestingly [tamely] 《to》
◆ 계획에 묵종하다 acquiesce [give acquiescence] in a plan

묵좌하다 默坐— sit in silence

묵주 默珠 〈로사리오〉〔가톨릭〕 a rosary

묵주머니 1 〈묵물 짜는 주머니〉 a curd bag 2 〈망쳐놓은 일〉 a mess; a wreck
◆ 일을 묵주머니로 만들다 spoil; mess up; make a mess of

묵즙 墨汁 〈먹물〉 India [Chinese] ink
■ 一낭 〈고락〉 an ink bag

묵지 墨紙 carbon paper; copying paper ⇨ 먹지
◆ 묵지를 대고 쓰다 take a carbon copy

묵직이 〈무겁게〉 heavily; 〈언행이〉 seriously; gravely; solemnly

묵직하다 1 〈무게가〉 rather heavy [massive, weighty]
◆ 묵직한 지갑 a filled-up purse
▶ 그의 지갑은 묵직하다 He has plenty of money [(口) a nice fat wallet].
2 〈태도가〉 rather serious [grave]
◆ 입이 묵직하다 be rather reserved [taciturn]

묵허 默許 tacit approval [permission, consent]; connivance ⇨ 묵인
◆ 묵허를 얻다 get sb's tacit consent
━묵허하다 give tacit permission 《to》; connive [wink] 《at》; pass over

묵화 墨畵 〈화법〉 monochromatic ink painting; 〈그림〉 an India(n)-ink picture [drawing]; a monochrome [black-and-white] painting
◆ 묵화를 그리다 paint an India-ink drawing

묵흔 墨痕 ink marks; 〔필적〕 handwriting
▶ 그는 묵흔도 선명하게 글씨를 썼다 He wrote in bold, beautiful strokes.

묵히다 leave unused [wasted]; keep idle in stock; let sth lie idle; keep 《money》 idle
◆ 땅을 묵히다 lay land fallow; keep a land idle / 위스키를 묵히다 age whiskey / 쌀을 묵히다 leave rice unused
▶ 묵히는 돈이 있으면 좀 빌려 주십시오 If you have some extra money, would you lend me some?
▶ 돈을 묵혀 두지 말고 활용해라 Don't keep your money idle, but make good use of it.
▶ 물건을 묵히느니 차라리 값을 내려서 파는 게 낫겠다 We would rather sell our merchandise at reduced prices than let them lie idle.
▶ 묵혀 썩이느니 써서 없애는 편이 낫다 Better wear out than rust out.

묶다 1 〈매다〉 bind; tie up; fasten; 〈사슬로〉 chain
◆ 볏단을 묶다 sheave rice; bind rice into sheaves / 짚단을 묶다 bundle straws / 꽁꽁 묶다 bind [fasten] tightly; bind [tie] up / 개를 기둥에 묶다 tie [chain] a dog to a post / 상자를 끈으로 묶다 cord (up) a box / 짐을 끈으로 묶다 tie [bind] a package with a string / 포로의 손발을 밧줄로 묶다 bind [tie] a captive hand and foot with (a) rope / 묶어서 다발짓다 tie up in a bundle; bundle up / 죄인을 묶어 가다 arrest a criminal; take a criminal away all tied up
▶ 농부는 볏단을 새끼로 묶었다 The farmer tied up the sheaves of rice with a straw rope.
▶ 그는 책들을 끈으로 묶었다 He bound the books with a piece of string.
▶ 나는 잔가지들을 단으로 묶었다 I bound twigs in [into] faggots [bundles].
▶ 강도는 그의 손을 묶고 눈을 가렸다 The robber tied his hands together and blindfolded him.
▶ 엄마, 리본으로 내 머리 좀 묶어 주실래요? Mom, will you tie my hair with a ribbon?
2 〈일괄하다〉 collect; put [bring] together; get together
◆ 잡지에 게재한 글을 한 권의 책으로 묶다 collect one's magazine articles under one cover
▶ 그 문장을 괄호로 묶으시오 Put [Enclose] the sentence in brackets [parentheses.]
3 〈속박하다〉 bind; tie; restrict; restrain
◆ 낮은 수준으로 묶어놓은 임금 wages pegged at a low level / 규칙으로 묶다 restrict sb by rule

묶음 a bundle; a bunch; 〈철사 등의〉 a coil; 〈볏단 등의〉 a sheaf 《pl. sheaves》; 〈장작 등의〉 a faggot; 〈건초 등의〉 a truss

> 解說 **bundle**은 몇개의 물건을 되는대로 묶거나 싼 것을, **bunch**는 같은 종류의 물건을 모아 특히 깔끔하게 묶은 것을 가리킨다.

◆ 서류 한 묶음 a sheaf of papers / 편지 한 묶음 a batch of letters / 2천원 두 묶음으로 만들다 make [pack into] a bundle; tie [do] up in bundles; bundle up / 묶음으로 팔다 sell by the bundle
▶ 나는 헌책들을 여러 묶음으로 묶어 쌓아올렸다 I tied the used books in bundles and piled them up.

묶이다 1 〈사람·물건이〉 be bound [tied]; be

trussed; be chained
♦ 손발이 묶이어 with *one's* hands and feet are tied up / 꽁꽁 묶이다 be tightly [securely] bound
▶ 우리는 튼튼한 줄로 손발이 묶였다 Our legs and arms were bound with stout cord.
▶ 그 개는 묶여 있으니까 겁내실 필요없습니다 You need not fear the dog, it is on a leash.
2 〈속박되다〉 be bound [tied, fettered] by; be restricted by
♦ 규칙에 묶이다 be bound by rules / 시간에 묶이다 〈제한받다〉 be restricted by time; 〈시간이 없어 곤란하다〉 be pressed for time / 의무에 묶이다 be fettered by the bonds of obligation
▶ 나는 시간에 묶여 마음껏 이야기할 수가 없었다 I could not talk to my heart's content because of the time limit.
▶ 나는 일에 묶여 있다 I am chained (down) to my work.
▶ 그는 계약에 묶여 있다 He was bound by his contract.
▶ 그 파업으로 인해 수십만 통근자들의 발이 묶였다 The strike prevented hundreds of thousands of commuters from getting to work.
▶ 많은 여성들이 가정에 묶여 있다 Many women have home ties.

문 文 1 〈글〉 writings; 〈작문〉 composition; 〈문법상의〉 a sentence; 〈문학〉 literature; letters
♦ 명문 a beautiful passage; a fine piece of writing / 결문(結文) a closing sentence / 본문 the text / 단[복, 중, 혼합]문 a simple [complex, compound, mixed] sentence / 평서[의문, 명령, 감탄]문 a declarative [an interrogative, an imperative, an exclamatory] sentence
▶ 문 중에 불분명한 점이 있다 There is an obscure point in the text.
▶ 이 구절은 명문이다 This passage is well composed [written].
▶ 이 책에 대한 감상문을 써라 Write down your impressions of this book.
2 〈무(武)에 대해〉 the pen
▶ 문은 무보다 강하다 The pen is mightier than the sword.
3 〈신발의 크기〉 footgear [shoe] size
♦ 10문짜리 고무신 size 10 rubber shoes

문 門 1 〈대문〉 a gate; 〈방문〉 a door; 〈장지문·미닫이〉 a sliding door

> 解說 *gate*는 통용문·성문·개찰구 등 출입구를 총칭하는 말로 양쪽으로 열리는 경우에는 흔히 gates라고 한다. *door*는 일반적으로 건물·방·탈것·가구 등의 문을 가리키지만, 넓은 뜻으로는 「문간·현관 출입구(doorway)」를 포함하며 보통 the를 붙여 쓴다.

♦ 두짝 문 a two-leaved door / 앞[뒷]문 the front [back] door [gate] / 쪽문 a wicket / 좁은 문 the strait gate 《to Heaven》 / 차[찬장]문 a car [closet] door / 회전문 a revolving door / 문 손잡이 a doorknob
〈문이[은]〉 문이 조금 열려 있었다 The door stood ajar [was slightly open].
▶ 문이 저절로 닫혔다 The door closed [shut] by itself.
▶ 학교 정문은 낮에는 열어 둔다 The main gate to [of] the school is (kept) open during the day.
▶ 그 문은 밖으로[안으로] 열린다 The door opens outward [inward].
〈문을〉 문을 열다 open a door; 〈밀어서〉 push a door open; 〈열쇠로〉 unlock a door / 문을 닫다 shut [close] a door [gate] / 문을 두드리다 knock on [at] the door / 문을 빠져나가다 go [pass] through a gate / 문을 잠그다 lock the door
▶ 문을 열어[닫아]주십시오 Open [Shut] the door, please.
▶ 그는 문을 닫고 나갔다[들어왔다] He closed the door after he got out of [got into] the room. ⇌ He closed the door behind him. 《behind him은 나갈 때나 들어올 때나 다 쓰임》
▶ 형은 문을 쾅 닫았다 My brother slammed [banged] the door.
▶ 누가 문을 두드리고 있다 There's a knock on [at] the door.
▶ 문을 열어놓지 마라 Don't leave the door open.
〈문에〉 그녀는 문 앞에 서서 내게 손을 흔들었다 She stood and waved at me from the door.
〈문으로〉 문으로 들어가다 enter at the gate / 문으로 나가다 go out of the gate
▶ 좁은 문으로 들어가라 Enter at the strait gate!
2 〈생물 분류상의〉〔動〕 a phylum 《*pl.* -la》; 〔植〕 a division ♦ 문의 phyletic
3 〔解〕 hilum 《*pl.* -la》
4 〈대포 수를 세는 단위〉 a cannon
♦ 수백 문의 대포 hundreds of guns [cannons]; hundreds of pieces of ordnance

― 문 ―

노커 knocker
초인종 doorbell
손잡이 knob
문패 doorplate
신발흙털개 doorscraper
문간 층대 doorstep
도어 매트 doormat

문 紋 a pattern ⇨ 무늬
문 問 〈물음·문제〉 a question (in a test); a problem
♦ 제1문 the first question / 문1 the question one
문간 門間 the (front) door; the entrance; the gateway; 〈현관 앞〉 the doorway
▶ 문간에 누군가가 있다 Someone is at the

gate.
▶ 그 여자는 그를 문간까지 바래다 주었다 She saw him out as far as the gate.
▶ 나는 그 여자를 배웅하러 문간까지 나갔었다 I have been to the gateway to see her off.
■ —방 a room beside the entrance [gate]

문갑 文匣 a box [case] for papers [letters]; a stationery chest (of drawers)

문견 聞見 〈견문〉 knowledge; experience

문경지교 刎頸之交 〈생사를 같이 할만한 벗〉 inseparable [sworn, devoted] friendship
♦ 문경지교를 맺다 pledge [swear] eternal [lifelong] friendship
▶ 그와 나는 문경지교다 He and I are sworn friends. ⇌ He is a friend who would die with me.

문고 文庫 〈서고・총서〉 a library; 〈장서〉 a collection of books; a library
■ 마을— a village library 학급— a class library ■ —판 pocketbook size

문고리 門— an iron-ring handle (attached to a door); a doorpull; 〈미닫이의〉 a catch; 〈걸쇠〉 the ring and staple (of a door) ♦ 문고리를 걸다 lock [latch, fasten] a door

문고본 文庫本 a pocket edition; a paperback
♦ 문고본으로 읽다 read 《a novel》in paperback
▶ 그 소설은 문고본으로 나와 있다 The novel is available in paperback.

문과 文科 **1** 〈이과에 대하여〉 the department of liberal arts; 〈문학의〉 the literary course
♦ 문과 학생 a student in the school of liberal arts; (美) a liberal arts major
▶ 우리 아들은 문과가 적성에 맞아요 Our son is better suited for liberal arts, isn't he?
2 〈과거(科擧)〉 the civil service examination under the dynasty
♦ 문과 급제하다 pass the civil service examination
■ —대학 a college of literature; a college of liberal arts

문관 文官 〈개인〉 a civil servant [officer]; a public official; a civilian; 〈총칭〉 the civil service [authorities]

문구 文句 〈어구〉 words; a phrase; 〈표현〉 an expression; wording; 〈문장〉 a sentence; 〈인용구〉 a passage
♦ 명문구 a famous quotation / 선전 문구 a catchphrase; promotional lines; 〈책 표지 등의〉 a blurb expression; a cliché [kliʃéi] / 편지의 문구 the wording of a letter
▶ 이런 문구로 수필을 시작하는게 어때? How about beginning your essay with these words?

문구 文具 stationery ⇨ 문방구

문구 門— a peephole; a rip in a door [window]

문단 文段 a paragraph

문단 文壇 〈문학계〉 the literary world [circles]; the world of letters
♦ 기성 문단 existing literary circles / 한국의 문단 the Korean literary circles [scene] / 문단의 거성 a literary magnate; the most prominent figure in the literary world / 문단의 경향 literary trends / 문단의 총아 a popular writer / 문단에 데뷔하다 start a literary career; make *one's* debut in letters [as a writer]/ 문단에서 명성을 얻다 win literary fame; become a famous writer
▶ 그는 문단에서 지위를 굳혔다 He established himself in the literary world.
▶ 그는 30대 중반에 문단에서 명성을 떨쳤다 He won literary fame in his mid-thirties.

문단속 門團束 fastening [locking] the doors [a gate]; securing the doors
♦ 밤에 문단속을 하다 lock up for the night / 문단속을 단단히 하다 fasten the doors securely
▶ 외출할 때는 반드시 문단속을 해라 Don't forget to lock the doors when you go out. ⇌ Make sure (that) you lock (the house) up when you go out.
—**문단속하다** lock (the house) up; lock [fasten, secure] the doors; make the doors fast

문답 問答 questions and answers; 〈대화〉 a dialog; 〈교리 문답〉 catechism [kǽtəkizəm]
♦ 소크라테스의 문답법 the catechetic(al) [kæ̀təkétik(əl)] method of Socrates / 문답식으로 catechetically; in the form of questions and answers
▶ 이 역사책은 문답식으로 되어 있다 This history book is written in question and answer form.
—**문답하다** exchange questions and answers 《with》; hold a dialogue [discussion]
■ —식 교수법 the interrogatory method of teaching

문대다 rub ⇨ 문지르다

문덕(문덕) in lumps; into pieces —**문덕(문덕)하다** fall apart 《from deterioration [decomposition]》

문도 門徒 〈제자〉 a disciple [disáipəl]; a follower; 〈신자〉 a believer 《in》; 〈신봉자〉 an adherent 《of》

문두 文頭 ♦ 문두에 at the beginning of a sentence
▶ 명령문에서는 동사를 문두에 놓으시오 Put the verb at the beginning of a sentence in an imperative sentence.

문둥병 —病 leprosy ⇨ 나병(癩病)

문둥이 a leper

문드러지다 〈썩어서〉 rot; decay; decompose; 〈익어서〉 be overripe; 〈상처・피부가〉 be sore; be inflamed; 〈곪다〉 fester; ulcerate
♦ 문드러진 잇몸 an ulcerated gum / 썩어 문드러진 시체 a decomposed body / 문드러진 토마토 an overripe tomato / 살이 썩어 문드러지다 flesh rots off / 문둥병으로 얼굴이 문드러지다 have *one's* face disfigured by leprosy
▶ 통나무는 썩어 문드러져 가고 있었다 The log was rotting away.
▶ 빨리 익으면 빨리 문드러진다 《속담》 Soon ripe, soon rotten.

문득 〈갑자기〉 suddenly; 〈우연히〉 by chance [accident]; casually; 〈생각지 않게〉 unexpectedly
♦ 문득 생각나다 occur to *one*; cross [come across, flash across] *one's* mind

문득
▶나는 문득 여행을 하고 싶은 생각이 들었다 I suddenly got a notion to travel. ⇌ I had [felt] a sudden urge to travel.
▶나는 문득 좋은 생각이 떠올랐다 A good [bright] idea suddenly occurred to me [came across my mind, struck me, came to my head]. ⇌ I hit on a good idea.
▶노인은 문득 멈춰서서 뒤를 돌아다 보았다 The old man stopped suddenly and looked back.
▶문득 그들이 사기꾼이 아닌가 하는 의심이 들었다 The suspicion flashed across his mind that they were impostors.

문뜩 suddenly ⇨ 문득

문란 紊亂 disorder; confusion; derangement
▶교육의 혼란은 정치의 문란에서 온다 Disruption of education results from government disorganization.
—**문란하다** disordered; confused; corrupt; loose; lax
♦문란한 가정 a disorderly household / 문란한 풍기를 바로잡다 correct the deplorable state of public morals / 문란하게 하다 derange 《social order》; corrupt 《public morals》
▶국가 재정이 극도로 문란해져 있다 The national finances are in extreme confusion [at sixes and sevens].
▶풍기가 몹시 문란하다 Public morals are very lax [sadly decayed].
■**풍기**— an offense against public decency

문례 文例 an example 《for writing》; a model sentence
♦편지 문례집 a collection of model sentences for letterwriting / 문례를 들다 give an example / 문례가 풍부하다 be full of illustrative examples / 문례에 따라 쓰다 model *one's* writing on an example; use a sentence as an example
▶그는 많은 문례를 들어 가며 설명했다 He explained it, giving many examples.

문루 門樓 a gatehouse; a gate tower

문리 文理 1 ⟨문맥⟩ the context; the construction [style] of classical Chinese; ⟨조리⟩ the line of thought **2** ⟨문과와 이과⟩ liberal arts and science(s)

문리과대학 文理科大學 the College of Liberal Arts and Science(s)

문망 文望 literary fame [reputation]

문맥 文脈 the context 《of a passage》
♦문맥상의 contextual / 이 문맥에서는 in this context / 문맥으로 단어의 의미를 알다[파악하다] learn [grasp] the meaning of a word from the context
▶나는 문맥으로 그 단어의 의미를 알 수 있었다 I understood the meaning of the word from the context.

문맹 文盲 illiteracy
♦문맹의 unlettered; illiterate; uneducated

문맹률 文盲率 the illiteracy rate
♦문맹률을 낮추다 lower the illiteracy rate
▶그 나라는 문맹률이 낮다 The illiteracy rate is low in the country.

문맹자 文盲者 an unlettered person; an illiterate (person)

문맹퇴치 文盲退治 the eradication of illiteracy
♦문맹 퇴치 운동 a crusade against illiteracy; a campaign to abolish illiteracy

문면 文面 ⟨서면⟩ the contents [wording] of a letter
♦문면에 의하면 according to what the letter says / 그 서류의 문면상으로는 on the face of the document
▶편지의 문면은 다음과 같다 The letter reads as follows.
▶편지의 문면에 의하면 그는 다음 달에 귀국할 모양이다 According to his letter, he will come home next month.

문명 文名 literary fame [reputation]
♦문명을 날리다 win literary fame; establish *oneself* as a writer [an author]
▶이 작품으로 그는 문명을 얻었다 This work made him a famous writer.

문명 文明 civilization; ⟨문화⟩ culture; ⟨개화⟩ enlightenment
♦고대 문명 ancient civilization / 서구 문명 Western civilization / 문명의 이기(利器) a modern convenience (▶modern conveniences 는 「현대적[최신식] 설비」의 뜻임) / 근대 문명의 산물 a gift [product] of modern civilization / 고대 문명의 발상지 the birthplace [cradle] of ancient civilization / 문명이 발달함에 따라 with the advance of civilization / 문명이 발달하다 civilization advances [progresses] / 외래 문명을 받아들이다 adopt [introduce] the foreign civilization
▶이집트 문명은 나일강 유역에서 발생했다고 한다 It is said that Egyptian civilization started in the valley of the Nile.
▶지금과 같은 문명 시대에도 불치병은 있다 Even in this civilized age [age of civilization] there are incurable diseases.
■**기계[물질]**— mechanical [material] civilization —**개화** civilization and enlightenment —**국** a civilized country [nation] —**병** disease incidental to civilization —**비평** criticism on civilization —**비평가** a critic of civilization —**사** the history of civilization (▶저서를 말할 때는 부정관사 a) a) —**사회** (a) civilized society

문묘 文廟 a shrine [temple] of Confucius; a Confucian shrine

문무 文武 literary [civil] and military arts; the pen and the sword; civil and military affairs
♦문무를 겸비하다 have literary and military accomplishments
▶그 사람은 문무를 겸비한 인물로 알려져 있다 He is known as a man of literary and military accomplishments [endowed with civil and military virtues].
■—**백관** civil and military officials

문문하다 1 ⟨무르다·부드럽다⟩ soft; tender; supple / 문문한 가죽 soft leather / 문문한 고기 tender meat **2** ⟨우습게 보이다⟩ easy to deal with

문물 文物 the products of civilization
♦한국의 문물 the Korean culture; things Ko-

rean / 서구 문물을 받아들이다 adopt the products of Western civilization / 한국의 문물을 외국에 소개하다 introduce things Korean to (the people of) foreign countries

문미 文尾 ♦문미에 오는 말에 강세를 두다 stress the word at the end of a sentence ▶영문을 쓸 때는 마침표를 문미에 찍으시오 When you write in English, put a period at the end of a sentence.

문미 門楣 the lintel (of a door)

문민 文民 a civilian
♦문민의 civilian (↔ military)
■—정부 a civilian government —지배[통제] civilian control

문밖 門— 1 〈문의 바깥〉 the outside of a house
♦문밖 출입을 하지 않다 keep [remain] indoors / 문밖에서 놀다 play outside near the door
2 〈성문 밖〉 the suburbs [outskirts] of a city
♦서울 문밖에서 살다 live in the suburbs of Seoul

문발 門— a screen; a blind

문방구 文房具 〈필기구〉 writing materials; (총칭) stationery
■—상 〈사람〉 a stationer —점 a stationery shop [store]; a stationer's

문벌 門閥 lineage [líniidʒ]; pedigree; 〈명문〉 high birth; good [noble] lineage; a distinguished family
♦문벌있는 집안에 태어나다 come of a good family; be of noble [high] birth
▶이 사람은 문벌이 좋다 He is of high birth. ≒ He was born of a distinguished family.
▶그는 문벌도 돈도 없다 He has neither birth nor money.

문범 文範 model composition; a model sentence

문법 文法 grammar; rules of composition
♦국어문법 Korean grammar / 영문법 English grammar / 문법상[적인] grammatical / 문법적으로 grammatically / 문법에 맞추다 grammatize / 문법에 맞는[맞지 않는] 어법을 쓰다 use good [bad, poor] grammar / 문법상 오류를 범하다 make a grammatical mistake; make a mistake in grammar
▶그 문장은 문법적으로 맞는다[틀린다] The sentence is grammatical [ungrammatical]. ≒ The sentence is grammatically correct [incorrect].
▶그의 글에는 문법상의 오류가 많다 His writing has a lot of grammatical errors.
■ 규범[기술]— prescriptive [descriptive] grammar 비교— comparative grammar 학교— school grammar ■—책 a grammar (book) —학자 a grammarian

문병 問病 a visit to a sick person
—문병하다 inquire [ask] after a sick person; visit sb in (his) sickbed; visit [go to see] sb in (the) hospital
▶나는 그 환자를 문병했다 I called on the patient.
▶우리는 다함께 병원으로 선생님을 문병하러 갔다 We went together to visit our teacher in the hospital.

문복하다 問卜— have one's fortune told; consult a fortune-teller

문빗장 門— a (door) latch; a (gate) bar; a bolt
♦문빗장을 걸다[벗기다] bar [unbar] a gate; bolt [unbolt] a gate

문사 文士 a literary man; a writer; a man of letters ♦얼치기[삼문]문사 a literary hack; a hack writer
▶그는 훌륭한 문사로 널리 인정받고 있다 He is universally recognized as a fine literary man.

문살 門— the ribs of a lattice door

문상 問喪 a call [visit] of condolence; a condolatory call ♦문상을 받다 receive callers for condolence [who (have) come to express their sympathy]
—문상하다 make a call of condolence; call on sb to express one's condolences
▶나는 그의 유가족을 문상했다 I made a call of condolence on his bereaved family.
■—객(客) a condoler; a condolence caller

문서 文書 〈서류〉 papers; 〈자료·증거로서의〉 a document; 〈기록〉 a record; 〈공문서〉 archives [áːrkaivz]; a missive
♦문서(형식)으로 in written form; in [by] writing / 문서로 작성해두다 keep a written record 《of》; have sth down in black and white / 문서로 지령을 내리다 issue written instructions / 문서로 회답하다 answer in writing / 문서화하다 put sth down in writing; commit sth to writing
▶훗날을 위해 그들한테서 문서를 받아두는 것이 좋다 You'd better get their signed [written] statement for future reference.
▶문서로 신청해 주십시오 Please send in your application in writing [written form].
▶노사간의 합의 사항은 문서화해놓지 않으면 무효가 된다 The agreement between labor and management will be invalid unless it is specified in written terms.
■ 공[사]— official [private] documents 극비— a top-secret document 불온[inflammatory] literature 외교— diplomatic correspondence ■—과 〈관청의〉 the archives and documents section; 〈회사의〉 the correspondence department —관리 documents control —변조 (法) spoliation —보관함 a file cabinet —위조 forgery of documents; falsification —철 file

문선 文選 1 〈시문집〉 a selection of literary works; an anthology —문선하다 select literary works
2 〔印〕 type picking
—문선하다 pick types
■—공(工) a type picker

문설주 門— a gatepost; a doorpost

문소리 門— a sound [noise] made by opening or shutting a door; 〈hear〉 a sound [noise] of the door opening or closing

문수 文數 shoe size ⇨ 문(文) 3

문수보살 文殊菩薩 〔佛教〕 the god [(산) bodhisattva] of wisdom and intellect

문신 文臣 a civil minister [vassal]

문신 文身
a tattoo (*pl.* ~s); tattoo marks
♦장미꽃 문신 a tattoo picture of roses / 등에 용의 문신이 있다 have a dragon tattooed on *one's* back
▶그 선원은 팔에 뱀의 문신이 있었다 A snake was tattooed on the sailor's arm. ⇒ The sailor had a snake tattooed on his arm.
—문신하다 tattoo
♦등에 문신하다 〈남을 시켜서〉 have *one's* back tattooed / 팔에 문신해 주다 tattoo *sb's* arm

문안 門—
1 〈문의 안〉♦문안에 within [inside] the gate [door]; indoors 2 〈성내〉♦문안 사람 a city dweller; townsfolk / 문안에 살다 live in the city limits (of)

문안 文案
a draft; 〈초안〉 a sketch
♦광고 문안을 작성하다 draft [prepare a draft of] an advertisement
▶나는 간단한 연설 문안을 만들었다 I have drawn up a rough draft for a speech.
■—작성자 a drafter; a draftsman

문안 問安
an inquiry [asking] after *sb's* health; sending kind regards
♦병문안을 가다 go to visit *sb* in the hospital
▶우리는 은사님께 문안을 드리러 댁으로 찾아갔다 We called on our old teacher at his home to see how he was doing.
—문안하다 inquire [ask] after *sb's* health; send *one's* kind [best] regards to *sb*
♦문안하러 가다 visit [call on] *sb* to inquire after (his) health
■—편지 a letter of inquiry: 문안편지를 보내다 write a letter to *sb* to inquire after (his) health

문약 文弱
effeminacy; literary indulgence to the neglect of military arts
♦문약에 빠지다 become effeminate; sink into effeminacy / 문약에 흐르다 tend to scholarly [artistic] pursuits
▶그 집 사내 아이들은 모두 문약에 흐르는 경향이 있다 All the boys in that family are of a delicate scholarly [artistic] type.
—문약하다 effeminate
▶아버지는 내가 너무 문약하다고 걱정하셨다 My father was worried because he thought I was too much of an effeminate bookworm.

문어 文魚 〈動〉
an octopus; a devilfish
♦문어 통발[단지] an octopus trap [pot] / 문어발식으로 배선하다 put many loads on one electrical outlet; use a multiple outlet extension plug [cord] / 문어발식으로 기업을 확장하다 expand *one's* business lines as an octopus spread its arms
▶그 회사는 문어발식 기업 확장을 꾀하고 있다 The firm is going to extend its relations with various kinds of business.

문어 文語
〈문장어〉 written language (↔ spoken language); literary (↔ colloquial) language; 〈표현·단어〉 a literary expression [word]; a book word
▶이 말은 문어로밖에는 쓰이지 않는다 This word is used only in literary writing.
■—체 a literary [book] style: 문어체 영어 literary English

문예 文藝
literary arts; 〈문학과 예술〉 art and literature; 〈문학〉 literature
♦한국문예진흥원 the Korean Culture and Arts Foundation / 문예에 종사하는 사람들 those involved in literary and artistic pursuits
▶그 사람은 전혀 문예의 소양이 없다 He has no literary knowledge.
▶그는 문예에 조예가 깊다 He has a profound knowledge of [is well versed in] art and literature.
■—가 a literary man; a man of letters: 문예가 협회 a writers' association —기자 a literary writer —독본 literary selections; a literary reader —란 a literary column [page, section]; a column on literature and the arts —비평[평론] literary criticism —비평가 a literary critic —사조 literary thoughts; trends in literary theory —영화 a literary picture [film]; a film based on a literary classic —작품 a literary work [production] —잡지 a literary magazine —학 the study of literature —학부 the department [faculty] of liberal arts —활동 literary activity

문예부흥 文藝復興
the Revival of Learning; 〈유럽의〉 the Renaissance ♦문예부흥기 the Renaissance period; the period of the Renaissance

문외한 門外漢
an outsider; a layman; an amateur; the man in the street
♦문외한의 의견 a lay [layman's] opinion; an outsider's opinion
▶나는 음악에는 문외한이다 I am an amateur in music.
▶이 업계에서 나를 모른다고 하면 당신은 문외한이오 You are a stranger in this trade if you say you don't know me.

문우 文友
a literary friend [associate]; a fellow writer

문의 文義·文意
the meaning (of a passage); the purport (of a letter [writing, phrase])
▶문의가 명확해질 때까지 반복해서 읽어 보아라 Read it again and again until the meaning becomes clear.
▶이 문장은 문의가 모호하다 The meaning of this sentence is ambiguous.

문의 問議
(an) inquiry; request for information; 〈조회〉 (a) reference
♦냉장고에 관한 거래 문의를 받다 receive inquiries about [request for] refrigerators (from)
▶전화 문의가 많다 There are many telephone inquiries.
▶문의는 001-2114번으로 하시기 바랍니다 For inquiries please call us on 001-2114. ⇒ Call [Dial] double o one-two one one four for information. ⇒ Inquiries should be directed to 001-2114.
▶전화 문의는 삼가해 주십시오 Please refrain from making inquiries by telephone.
—문의하다 inquire (of *sb* about *sth*); make inquiries (about); refer (to *sb* for information); ask (about); make reference
♦안내소에 항공 운임을 문의하다 ask [inquire,

make inquiries] at the information counter about the air fare / 다른 권위자에게 문제를 문의하다 relegate a question to another authority
▶ 우리는 여행사에 기차 시간표를 문의했다 We inquired of the travel agency about the train schedule.
▶ 우리는 마감 날짜를 문의했다 We inquired [made an inquiry] about the deadline.
▶ 상세한 것은 총무부[인사과]에 문의하십시오 For particulars [further information], apply [I refer you] to the general affairs department [personnel (affairs) section].
■—서 a letter of inquiry —처 a reference
문인 文人 a literary man; a man of letters; a writer; (총칭) the literati [lìtərάːtiː]
■—극 a theatrical performance [theatricals] by literary men —사회 literary circles; the literati —협회 the Literary Men's Association —화 a painting in the literary artist's style; literati painting
문인 門人 a pupil [student]; a disciple
문자 文字 1〈알파벳 등〉a letter; an alphabet; 〈한자 등〉a character
♦그리스 문자 Greek letters / 문자의 배열의 arrangement of letters [characters] / 문자를 아는[모르는] 사람들 literate [illiterate] people / 문자에 구애되다 adhere to the letter 《of the law》 / 문자 그대로 해석하다 interpret 《a passage》 literally [to the letter, word for word]; take a word in its literal sense
▶ 이 그림은 문자가 없던 시절에 그린 것이다 This picture was drawn when there were no letters.
▶ 서울역은 문자 그대로 서울의 현관이다 Seoul Station is literally the front door of Seoul.
▶ 문자 그대로 해석하면 이것은 거절 편지다 If you take this just as it is, it's a letter of refusal.
▶ 나는 그가 한 말을 문자 그대로 받아들였다 I took what he said literally [in a literal sense].
2〈글귀〉a maxim [(idiomatic) phrase] from the Chinese classics; a pedantic expression
♦문자를 잘 쓰다 be much given to using [quoting] idiomatic phrases from the Chinese classics; talk like a book
■대[소]— a capital [small] letter
■—반(盤)〈시계 등의〉a dial (plate); the face 《of a clock》; the clockface
문자다중방송 文字多重放送 teletext
문자새 門— 〔建〕 doors and windows
문자판독장치 文字判讀裝置 character reader
문장 文章 1〈글월〉a composition; a writing; 〈문체〉a style; 〈소론〉an article [essay]
♦뛰어난 문장 master writings / 테니슨의 문장 Tennyson's style / 문장을 다듬다 polish (up) one's style / 문장을 짓다 write [make] a composition
▶ 그는 문장이 능하다[서투르다] He is good [poor] at writing. ⇒ He writes well [poorly]. ⇒ He is a good [poor] writer.
▶ 문장이 능하다는 것은 유익하다 It pays to be a good writer.
▶ 그것은 훌륭한 문장이다 It is well written.
2〈글〉a sentence
♦간결한[복잡한] 문장 a crisp [complicated] sentence / 세련된[서투른] 문장 a polished [clumsy, poor] sentence / 완전한 문장 a complete sentence / 그 이야기의 첫 문장 the first sentence of the story / 문장을 고치다[고쳐 쓰다] correct [rewrite] a sentence / 문장을 분석하다 analyze a sentence
▶ 명료하고 정확한 문장을 쓰시오 Write a clear and correct sentence.
▶ 다음 문장을 우리말로 옮기시오[수동태로 고치시오] Translate [Rewrite] the following sentence into Korean [a passive sentence].
■—강세 a sentence stress [accent] —구조 the sentence structure —론〈文法〉syntax —분석 a sentence analysis —어 literary [written] language —중심 교수법 sentence method
문장 紋章 a crest; a coat of arms; family insignia ▶ 깃발에는 공작가의 문장이 새겨 있었다 The banner bore the arms of the Duke.
문장가 文章家 a good [fine, clever] writer; a stylist ▶ 그 사람은 문장가다 He writes a good style. ⇒ He is quite a writer.
문장부 門— a door pivot
문재 文才〈글재주〉literary talent [ability]
♦문재가 있는 여성 a woman of [gifted with] literary ability
▶ 그는 문재가 있다 He has a talent [an aptitude] for writing. ⇒ He is a man of literary attainment.
문전 文典 a grammar; a grammar book
문전 門前 ♦문전에(서) before [in front of] a gate; at the gate [door] / 문전을 지나가다 pass sb's door
▶ 그 여자는 그를 문전박대했다 She shut [slammed] the door in his face. ⇒ She turned him away from her door.
문전걸식하다 門前乞食 beg one's bread from door to door ▶ 그 남자는 문전걸식(을) 하고 다녔다 The man went begging from door to door.
문전성시 門前成市 ♦문전성시를 이루다 be crowded [thronged] with callers; have many [a constant stream of] visitors
▶ 그 점쟁이의 집은 항상 문전성시다 There is always a line of visitors before the fortuneteller's door.
▶ 그의 집은 문전성시를 이룬다 His home has a constant stream of visitors.
문제 問題 1〈설문〉a question;〈수학 등의〉a problem;〈프린트 등 전체로서의〉a paper
♦ 시험 문제 an examination question [paper] / 애먹이는 문제 a puzzling question [problem] / 주어진 문제 a given question [problem] / 시험 문제지 a question [test] sheet [paper] / 문제를 내다 set [give] a question; set sb a paper / 수학 문제를 풀다 solve a problem in math(ematics); solve a math problem / 연습문제를 하다[풀다] do an exercise (in) / 문제에 답하다 answer a question / 문제와 씨름하다 attack [tackle, grapple with] a problem
▶ 선생님은 숙제로 어려운 문제를 내 주셨다

문제

The teacher gave [set] us difficult questions [problems] for homework.
► 나는 그 시험 문제를 푸는데 약 두 시간이 걸렸다 It took me about two hours to answer the questions [to solve the problems] in the test.
► 나는 영어 시험에서 세 문제밖에 풀지 못했다 I was able to solve only three problems on the English exam.
2 〈해결해야 할 사항〉 a question; a problem; 〈쟁점〉 an issue; 〈과제·주제〉 a subject
♦가장 중요한[부차적인] 문제 a matter of prime [secondary] importance / 공해 문제 a pollution problem / 긴급한 문제 an urgent problem / 당면 문제 the question [point] at issue / 미해결 문제 an open question; an unsolved problem / 아무도 손대지 않은 문제 an untouched subject / 중대한 문제 a matter of grave concern / 해결해야 할 문제 a problem awaiting solution / 문제의 발단은… The question was posed when…/ 그 문제는 제쳐두고 putting aside the question
► 세금 인상은 우리에게는 사활의 문제다 A tax increase is a matter of life and death to us.
〈문제가[는]〉 문제가 되다 become an issue [a subject of discussion]; be at issue; come into question / 문제가 되지 않다 be out of the question; 〈대수롭지 않다〉 do not matter [figure]; matter little; 〈하찮다〉 be insignificant; be negligible; count for nothing
► 어떻게 노동력을 절감하느냐 하는 문제가 제기되었다 The problem of how to save labor was raised.
► 주택 문제보다 빵 문제가 급선무다 The question of food precedes that of housing.
► 그것이 사실이냐 아니냐는 문제가 안된다 It doesn't matter whether it is true or not.
► 실업 문제가 세계 각국에서 심각해지고 있다 The problem of unemployment is becoming serious in every country of the world.
► 그 문제는 미해결상태다 The problem remains unsolved.
► 다음 문제는 학교 폭력 문제입니다 The next subject is the problem of the school violence.
► 문제는 누가 그것을 다룰 것이냐[어떻게 그것을 확보하느냐]다 The question is who will deal with [how to secure] it.
〈문제를〉 문제를 다루다 handle [treat] a problem [question] / 문제를 의식하다 be aware of the issue / 문제를 제기하다 pose a problem (to) / 식량 문제를 해결하다 solve [settle] the food problem / 흥미있는 문제를 토론하다 discuss an interesting subject
► 그 사건이 청소년법에 새로운 문제를 야기했다 The incident raised new questions about the law on juveniles.
► 우리는 그 계획의 기술적 문제를 논의했다 We discussed [argued] the technical points of the plan.
〈문제에〉 문제에 봉착하다 meet [confront] a problem
► 그 여자는 이 문제에 커다란 흥미를 갖고 있다 She has a great interest in this subject.
〈기타〉 능력을 문제삼다 call *sb's* ability into question
► 경찰은 그의 동기를 문제시했다 The police regarded his motives as questionable.
► 그가 그것을 제일 처음 문제삼았다 He was the first to make an issue out of it.
► 會話「막차를 놓칠지도 모르겠네」「문제 없어. 내가 차로 집까지 바래다 줄게」 "I'm afraid I won't be in time for the last train." "That's no problem. I'll see you home in my car."
3 〈의문〉 question
► 그 여자가 우리 의견에 동의할지 어떨지 문제다 It is a question whether she will agree with us or not.
► 그가 회의에 출석할지가 문제다 It is doubtful whether he will come to the meeting.
► 그는 선거에 문제 없이 당선될 것이다 There is no doubt that he will win the election. ≒ His success in the election is beyond question.
4 〈논쟁거리·물의〉 public discussion [comment]
♦문제의 영화[인물] the film [person] in question / 문제가 많은 작품 a controversial work / 문제를 일으키다 cause [give rise to] public discussion
► 이것이 문제의 영수증이다 This is the receipt in question.
► 그의 발언은 문제가 있다고 생각합니다 I think his remarks are controversial ones.
► 그 사람의 지도력은 약간 문제가 있다[없다] There is some [no] question about his leadership.
5 〈말썽·곤란한 일〉 trouble; a problem
♦문제아 a problem child; a child who needs special care / 문제를 일으키다 cause (some) trouble
► 그 사람의 교수 방법에는 문제가 있다 There is something wrong [Something is wrong] with his way of teaching.
► 제일 큰 문제는 자금 부족이다 The main trouble [The biggest problem] is lack of funds.
► 그는 또 여자 일로 문제를 일으켰다 He has caused a problem [some trouble] with a girl again.
► 會話「이 세제는 모직물에 써도 됩니까?」「모직물은 괜찮습니다. 아무 문제 없어요」 "Can this detergent be used with wool?" "Wool's fine. No trouble at all."
6 〈관계된 일〉 a matter; a question
♦금전 문제 money matter / 양심의 문제 a case [point] of conscience / 인도적인 문제 a humanitarian question; a question touching humanity
► 그것은 옳으냐 그르냐의 문제가 아니라 취향의 문제다 It's a matter of taste. (►matter를 부정문에 써서 It is not a matter of… 처럼 말하지는 않음)
► 네 거짓말이 탄로나는 것은 다만 시간 문제다 It's just a matter of time before your lie is discovered.
► 성공은 단지 시간 문제다 Success is only a question [matter] of time.
■ 경제[사회]— an economic [a social] question [problem] 연구— a subject for inquiry

[study] 정치— a political issue ■ —극[소설] a problem play [novel]; a controversial play [novel]; a play [novel] which causes a furor [raises an uproar] —은 an item pool —의식 a critical mind: 문제의식이 있다 have a critical mind —집 a collection of questions [problems]

문제점 問題點 the point at issue; a controversial point
▶ 문제점으로 돌아갑시다 Let's return to the point at issue.
▶ 이 논설은 현대사회의 몇 가지 문제점을 지적하고 있다 This article points out several problems concerning modern society.

문제화하다 問題化— 〈문제가 되다〉 become an issue; come into question; 〈문제삼다〉 call *sth* to account; put *sth* in question
♦ 사회문제화하다 become a social problem / 정치문제화하다 make a political issue of *sth*

문조 文鳥 〔鳥〕a Java sparrow; a paddybird

문죄 問罪 (an) accusation; indictment; arraignment —문죄하다 accuse (*sb* of a crime); indict [indáit] *sb* for [on a charge of]

문주란 文珠蘭 〔植〕a crinum

문중 門中 a family; a clan; one's kinsfolk; one's relatives

문지기 門— a gatekeeper; a gateman; a doorkeeper; a doorman; a janitor; a guard; (프) a concierge ■ —방 a lodge; a gatehouse

문지도리 門— a hinge; a pivot (of a door)

문지르다 rub; scrub; 〈문질러 닦아내다〉scour (of); scrape (off, away); 〈솔로〉brush
♦ 솔로 보트를 문지르다 scrub the boat with a brush / 광내는 가루로 주전자를 문지르다 scour a kettle with polishing powder / 문질러 없애다 scrape off / 접시를 문질러 닦다 scrub out a dish / 막대기 두 개를 서로 문질러 불을 일으키다 start a fire by rubbing two sticks together / 마룻바닥을 깨끗이 문지르다 scrub the floor clean
▶ 그들은 뱃바닥을 문질러 닦아냈다 They scraped the ship's bottom.

문지방 門地枋 a doorsill; 〈입구〉the threshold
♦ 문지방을 넘다 cross [pass] the threshold / 문지방이 닳도록 찾아가다 make frequent visits to *sb*
▶ 다시는 이 집 문지방을 넘지 마라 Never set foot in this house again.
▶ 다시는 네가 내 집 문지방을 넘지 못하게 하겠다 I shall never let you cross the threshold of my house again.

문직 紋織 figured textile

문진 文鎭 a (paper)weight

문집 文集 a collection of works; an anthology
♦ 포크너 문집 a collection of Faulkner's works

문짝 門— a door; a leaf of a door ♦ 문짝을 열어젖히다 push [pull] a door open

문책 問責 (a) reproof; reprimand; censure —문책하다 reprimand; reprove [rebuke]; censure ♦ 아무의 실수를 문책하다 censure *sb* for his blunder
▶ 그는 직무태만으로[실수 때문에] 문책당했다 He was called to account [reprimanded] for neglect of duty [his mistake].
▶ 수상은 그 장관의 실언을 문책했다 The Prime Minister censured [reprimanded] the minister for his slip of the tongue.

문책 文責 ▶ 문책 재기자(在記者) The editor is responsible for the wording of this article. ⇌ The responsibility for the wording of this article lies with the editor.

문체 文體 (a) style; language
♦ 간결한 문체 a pithy [concise] style / 명쾌한 문체 a clear style / 세련된[거친] 문체 a polished [rough] style / 짜임새 없는[있는] 문체 a slovenly [crisp] style / 화려한 문체 a flowery [florid] style; fine language / 힘찬 문체 a vigorous [powerful] style / 독자적인 문체를 만들어내다 make [cultivate, develop] a style of one's own / 쉬운[평이한] 문체로 쓰여 있다 be written in an easy [a plain] style
▶ 그는 헤밍웨이의 문체를 모방해서 쓰고 있다 He is writing in the style of E. Hemingway.
▶ 그의 문체는 좀 딱딱한 데가 있다 His style (of writing) is somewhat stiff. ⇌ He writes in a rather formal style.
■ —론 stylistics

문초 問招 questioning ((a criminal); (an) interrogation; an examination; an inquiry
♦ 문초를 받고 있다 be under examination / 심한 문초를 받다 be subjected to [be put through] a severe examination
▶ 용의자는 경찰의 엄한 문초를 받았다 The suspect was severely questioned [was grilled] by the police.
—문초하다 question ((a criminal); examine; interrogate ♦ 엄중 문초하다 subject *sb* to a close examination

문치 文治 civil administration
■ —정책 a policy of civilian government —주의 the principles of civilian government

문치 門齒 〔解〕〈앞니〉an incisor (tooth); a foretooth

문턱 門— a threshold; a doorsill
♦ 문턱을 넘다 cross [step over] the threshold / 문턱에 걸터앉다 sit on a doorsill / 문턱에 서서 (집안을) 들여다보다 stand on the threshold and look inside
▶ 그는 살아서 이 집 문턱을 다시 넘을 수 있을까 생각하며 전선으로 나갔다 He went to the front doubting that he would ever come home alive.

문투 文套 a (literary) style [form] ⇨ 문체
♦ 자기 나름의 문투로 in a style of one's own
▶ 그 편지는 비난조의 문투였다 The letter was written [couched] in critical language.

문틀 門— the framework of a door; a doorframe

문틈 門— a chink [crack] in a door [gate]; a chink between doors
♦ 문틈으로 들여다보다 peep [look] in through a chink in the door / 문틈으로 들어오는 바람을 막다 cut off the drafts [(英) draughts]

문패 門牌 a doorplate; a nameplate ♦ 문에 문패를 달다 put up a nameplate on [at] the door; peg one's nameplate at the door
▶ 집집마다 문패가 달려 있다 There is a name-

plate on every door.

문풍지 門風紙 a weather strip
♦ 문풍지를 달다 seal up [weatherstrip] ((a window)) / 문풍지로 찬바람을 막다 paper out the cold wind

문필 文筆 literary work; writing
♦ 문필로 먹고 살다 live by *one's* pen; make a profession of literature
▶ 그는 문필에 재능이 있다 He has a talent for writing.
▶ 그는 문필에 종사하고 있다 He is doing literary work [following a literary career].
▶ 그 여자는 문필로 생활한다 She writes for a living.

문필가 文筆家 a writer; a literary man; a man of letters ▶ 그는 직업이 문필가다 He is a writer by profession. ⇌ His profession is writing.

문필노동 文筆勞動 literary work
■ —자 a literary worker; a writer
♦ 문필업에 종사하다 follow [engage in] the profession of letters

문하 門下 ♦ 문하의 under *sb's* tutelage; trained by *sb* / …의 문하에 들어가다 become a tutee of... / A씨의 문하에서 배우다 study under (the tutorship of) Mr. A
▶ 그 사람의 문하에서 노벨상을 수상한 물리학자가 두 명 나왔다 Among his former students are two Nobel Prize-winning physicist.

문하생 門下生 a student; a tutee [disciple, follower]; (총칭) a following ▶ 그는 김선생의 문하생이다 He is a tutee [disciple] of Mr. Kim. ⇌ He studies under Mr. Kim.

문학 文學 literature; letters
♦ 낭만[자연]주의 문학 romantic [naturalistic] literature / 한국[미국] 문학 Korean [American] literature / 문학적 표현 an elegant expression / 문학적으로 literarily / 문학적(인) literary / 문학을 논하다 discuss literature; 〈학문적으로〉 talk on literature; 〈동료로서〉 talk about literature / 문학에 취미가 있다 have a taste for literature / 문학적 소양[재능]이 있다 have a knowledge of literature [literary talent]
▶ 그는 문학에 뜻을 두고 상경했다 He came to Seoul with aspirations of becoming a writer.
■ 고전[근대]— classic [modern] literature 국— Korean literature 국민[기록, 대중]— national [documentary, popular] literature 비교— comparative literature 순— pure [polite] literature; (프) belles lettres 아동— juvenile [children's] literature 영[독, 불]— English [German, French] literature / 나는 대학에서 영문학을 전공했다 I majored in English literature at the university. ■ —가 a writer ⇨ 문학자 —개론 an introduction to literature; a literary survey; a survey of literature —계 the literary world; literary circles; the world of letters —과(科) the literary course ((of a college)); a literature department; a department of literature —론 a literary theory; a theory of literature; comment on (theories of) literature —박사 〈사람〉 a doctor of literature; 〈학위〉 Doctor of Literature [Letters] (略 Lit(t). D.) —사(士) 〈사람〉 a bachelor of arts; 〈학위〉 Bachelor of Arts (略 B.A.) —사(史) the history of literature: 국문학사 the [a] history of Korean literature —상(賞) a literary award —서(書) a literary work [book] —석사 〈사람〉 a master of arts; 〈학위〉 Master of Arts (略 M.A.) —소녀 a young lady of literary interests —예술 literary art —운동 a literary movement —작품 a literary work [production, writing]; (총칭) literary works —잡지 a literary magazine —청년 a young lover of literature; a literary [lettered] youth; a youthful literary enthusiast [aspirant] —취미 (a) taste for literature —회 a literary meeting [society]

문학부 文學部 a college [(英) faculty] of literature ■ —장 the dean [head] of the faculty of literature —학생 (美俗) a lit student [boy, girl]

문학애호가 文學愛好家 a lover of literature
▶ 그는 문학 애호가다 He has a taste for literature [a literary taste]. ⇌ He likes reading [is a lover of reading].

문학자 文學者 〈작가〉 a writer; an author; 〈저술가〉 a man of letters; 〈문학 연구가〉 a literary man —영[불]— a scholar of English [French] literature

문함수 文函數 a statement function

문헌 文獻 〈학술 연구 자료〉 literature; 〈서적〉 a book; 〈기록 자료〉 documents (▶ 보통 복수형으로 씀); 〈전거〉 an authority
♦ 지진에 관한 최초의 문헌 the first mention of [reference to] earthquakes in literature / 의학 문헌을 참고하다 refer to medical literature / 그 문제에 관한 많은 문헌을 수집하다 collect much [a large] literature on the subject
▶ 그는 그 주제에 관한 문헌을 모두 조사했다 He researched all the literature on the subject.
▶ 이 연구에 필요한 문헌은 많이 있다[문헌이 풍부하다] There is abundant literature for this research.
■ 참고— references; literature cited; books for reference; 〈목록〉 bibliography ■ —학 philology; bibliography —학자 a philologist

문형 文型 a sentence pattern
♦ 기본 문형 a basic sentence pattern

문호 文豪 a great [an eminent] writer; a great man of letters; a literary master [magnate]
▶ 한국에서 문호라고 할 만한 사람이 누구일까 I wonder who would deserve to be called a great writer in Korea.

문호 門戶 the door
♦ 문호를 개방하여 with open doors / 외국에 문호를 개방[폐쇄]하다 open [close] the door to foreign countries
▶ 우리는 군축협정에 문호를 닫아버릴 수는 없다 We can not close the door [turn our backs] on a disarmament agreement.
■ —개방주의 the open-door principle [policy]

문화 文化 (a) culture (▶ 구체적인 개개의 문화를 말할 때 이외에는 보통 무관사); 〈문명〉 (a) civilization

[解說] *culture*는 어떤 민족, 인간 집단이 창출하고 습득·전달해가는 생활양식·풍속·언어·사상·예술 등의 정신적인 총체를 가리킨다. *civilization*은 미개 상태가 개화되거나 과학·기술 등 사회가 물질적인면에서 고도의 발전을 이룩해가는 상태를 이르는 말이다.

♦ 고대 그리스 문화 ancient Greek culture / 고도의 문화 a high level culture; a high cultural level [standard] / 서양 문화 Western [Occidental] culture / 문화의 발달 advance of culture / 문화의 전파 culture diffusion / 한국 문화의 전통 Korean cultural tradition / 문화적인 cultural / 문화가 발달하다 advance [make progress] in culture / 문화가 뒤떨어져 있다 be backward in civilization; be at a low level of culture / 스스로의 문화를 창조하다 create a culture of *one's* own / 비교문화 문제를 연구하다 study cross-cultural [intercultural] problems

▶ 그 나라는 문화가 뒤떨어졌다[발달했다] That nation is behind [advanced] in civilization.

▶ 고대 그리스인들은 고도의 문화를 가지고 있었다 The ancient Greek had high level of culture.

■—공로자 a person who has contributed to culture —국가 a cultured [civilized] nation; a nation with a high level of culture —국민 a cultured nation; a nation of culture; civilized citizens —권(圈) a cultural [culture] area [zone]; a cultural sphere —단체 a cultural organization —마찰 cultural friction; cultural conflict —복합체 a culture complex —부〈신문사의〉 the culture desk —사(史) cultural history —사업 a cultural enterprise; cultural work —사절 a cultural envoy [ambassador] —시설 cultural facilities [institutions] —양식 (樣) a culture pattern —영화 a cultural [an educational] film —자산 cultural assets [wealth] —제(祭) a cultural festival;〈학교의〉 a school [college] festival —주택 a new-type residence; a modern [an up-to-date] (dwelling) house —지리학 cultural geography —집단〔社〕 a culture —체육부 the Ministry of Culture and Sports —촌 a model village —협정 a cultural agreement —회관 a cultural center; (美) a lyceum [láisí(ː)əm]: 세종문화회관 the Sejong Cultural Center —훈장 an Order of Cultural Merits; a Cultural Medal

문화 교류 文化交流 cultural exchange; an exchange of culture ♦ 국가간의 문화교류를 촉진하다 promote cultural exchange [interchange] between [among] nations

문화대혁명 文化大革命〔史〕〈중국의〉 the (Great Proletarian) Cultural Revolution

문화생활 文化生活 a civilized life
♦ 문화생활을 하다 lead a civilized life; enjoy modern living

문화수준 文化水準 a cultural level; a level [standard] of culture
♦ 문화수준이 높은[낮은] 나라 a nation of high [low] cultural level; a nation with an advanced [a primitive] culture / 문화수준을 높이다 uplift the cultural level 《of Africa》
▶ 이 나라는 문화수준이 높다[낮다] This nation has a high [low] level of culture.

문화유산 文化遺産 cultural inheritance [heritage] ▶ 그들은 고대 그리스의 문화유산을 이어받았다 They are the heirs to the cultural heritage of ancient Greece.

문화인 文化人 a cultured [cultivated] man; a man of culture;〈학문·예술 종사자〉 a person in an academic or artistic career

문화재 文化財 cultural assets [properties]
♦ 문화재 보호[보존] protection [preservation] of cultural properties / 중요 문화재로 지정되다 be designated as important cultural properties
■ 무형— intangible cultural properties 인간— human cultural assets ■—관리국 the Cultural Property Preservation Bureau —보존위원회 the Cultural Properties Protection Committee —보호법 the Cultural Properties Protection Law

묻다¹ 〈들러붙다〉 stick 《to》; adhere 《to》; be stuck; be covered 《with》;〈기름 등이 얼룩지다〉 be smeared [stained] 《with》

♦ 검댕이 묻은 얼굴 a face smudged with soot / 핏자국이 묻어 있는 셔츠 a shirt stained [smeared] with blood; a bloodstained shirt / 잉크가 묻어 있다 be stained with ink

▶ 옷깃에 묻은 때가 지워지지 않는다 The dirt clinging to the collar can't be washed out.

▶ 내 손가락에 페인트가 묻었다 Paint got on my fingers.

▶ 내 구두에 진흙이 묻어 있다 My shoes are muddy. ⇌ There's some mud on my shoes.

▶ 자네 코트에 기름 얼룩이 묻어 있네 Your coat is stained with an oily mark.

▶ 용의자의 셔츠에 혈흔이 묻어 있었다 The suspect's shirt was bloodstained.

묻다² **1** 〈파묻다〉 bury *sth* 《in the ground》; inter

♦ 시체를 묻다 bury *sb's* corpse [body] / 죽은 새를 뜰에 묻다 bury a dead bird in the yard / 머플러에 얼굴을 반쯤 묻다 bury half *one's* face in a muffler / 숯불을 잿속에 묻다 cover charcoal with ash

▶ 일꾼들은 도관을 묻었다 The workmen sank a pipeline.

▶ 그녀는 그의 가슴에 자기의 얼굴을 묻었다 She buried her face against his chest.

▶ 아버지는 김칫독을 땅에 묻으셨다 Father buried a *kimchi* jar in the ground.

▶ 내 미국인 동료는 한국에 뼈를 묻을 작정이라고 말한다 My American colleague says that he intends to be buried here in Korea.

2 〈숨기다〉 cover [hush] up; keep *sth* secret 《from》; conceal [hide] 《*sth* from *sb*》
♦ 부정[독직] 사건을 묻어 두다 cover [hush] up the corruption scandal / 살인 사건을 비밀로 묻어 두다 keep a case of murder (a) secret
▶ 나는 그것을 내 마음 속에만 묻어 두었다 I have kept it to myself.

묻다³ **1** 〈질문하다〉 ask 《*sb* a question [a question of *sb*]》;〈문의·조사하다〉 inquire; interro-

gate
♦값을 묻다 ask the price / 길을 묻다 ask sb the way to 《a place》 / 이유를 묻다 inquire [ask for] the reason / 아무의 의도를 묻다 ask sb's intention; ask sb what he intends to do / 그 제안의 찬반을 묻다 put the proposal to the vote / 안내소를 묻다 ask [inquire] at the information desk / 여론에 묻다 ask the public for judgment on sth / 그 일에 관해 묻다 ask [inquire of] sb about the matter
▶그들은 내 이름을 물었다 They asked my name. ⇒ They inquired [wanted to know] what my name was.
▶그녀는 나에게 시간을 물었다 She asked me the time. ⇒ She inquired the time of me.
▶그는 나에게 사전 사용법을 물었다 He asked [inquired of] me how to use a dictionary.
▶어머니는 내게 방 청소를 했느냐고 물으셨다 My mother asked me [inquired of me] if I had cleaned my room.
▶그녀는 내게 파티에 갈 생각이냐고 물었다 She asked me if I was going to the party.
▶판사는 증인에게 물었다 The judge asked [inquired of, questioned] the witness.
▶나는 경찰관에게 올림픽 공원으로 가는 길을 물어 보았다 I asked a policeman the way to the Olympic Park.
▶나는 많은 사람들의 의향을 물어 보았다 I sounded out a lot of different people.
▶그 일에 대해서는 전문가에게 물어 보는게 좋겠다 We had better consult an expert on the matter.
▶말씀 좀 묻겠습니다 May I ask you a question?
2 〈추궁하다〉 accuse 《sb of a crime》; charge 《sb with a crime》
♦절도 죄를 묻다 call [bring] the minister concerned to account
▶그들은 그에게 사고의 책임을 물었다 They accused him of causing the accident.
3 〈문제삼다〉 care 《about》; mind (▶보통 의문문·부정문으로)
♦연령·성별을 묻지 않고 regardless [irrespective] of age or sex / 날씨 여하를 묻지 않고 rain or shine
▶값의 고하를 묻지 않고 그 책을 사고 싶으 I want to buy that book at any cost [no matter what the price is].
▶나는 일의 성패는 묻지 않는다 I don't care about success or failure. ⇒ It doesn't matter [I don't care] whether you will succeed or fail.
4 〈안부를 전하다〉 ask [inquire] after [about]
♦안부를 묻다 inquire after sb's health [well-being]; ask after sb
▶그녀는 우리의 건강을 물었다 She asked [inquired] about our health. ⇒ She asked [inquired] after us [our health]. (▶만일 She asked about us. 라고 하면 건강을 포함한 근황을 물었다는 의미) ⇒ She asked how we were.
▶나는 그들의 소식을 물었다 I asked what had become of them. ⇒ I asked for new about them.

묻히다¹ 〈들러붙게 하다〉 smear; stain; cover

♦구두에 진흙을 묻히다 get mud on one's shoes / 떡에 콩고물을 묻히다 cover a rice cake with bean flour / 손가락에 잉크를 묻히다 stain one's fingers with ink / 얼굴에 검댕을 묻히다 get [have] one's face smudged with soot / 옷에 흙을 묻히다 soil one's clothes / 우표에 물[침]을 묻히다 moisten a stamp
▶너 앞치마에 육수를 묻혔구나 You have stained your apron with gravy, haven't you?
▶나는 바지에 페인트를 묻혔다 I got paint on my pants.

묻히다² 〈매장되다〉 be buried 《in, under》; 〈감춰지다〉 be kept secret 《from》; be concealed [hidden] 《from sb》
♦무덤에 묻혀 있다 be buried in the ground; lie beneath a grave / 시골에 묻혀 살다 bury oneself in the country
▶그는 국립 묘지에 묻혔다 He was buried [was laid to rest] in National Cemetery.(▶완곡호 속의 완곡한 표현)
▶오래지않아 그는 망각 속으로 묻혀 버렸다 In time he sank into [was buried in] oblivion.
▶이 불상은 어느 시골 고찰에 오랫동안 묻혀 있었다고 한다 This statue of Buddha is said to have been sitting obscurely in some old country temple for a long time.
▶그 일은 곧 과거 속에 묻힐 것이다 The event will soon be buried in the past.

물¹ **1** 〈일반적인〉 water
♦바닷물 sea water / 맑은 물 clear [crystal] water / 수돗물 the tap water / 찬[더운] 물 cold [hot] water
〈물이[은]〉 물이 새지 않다 be watertight [waterproof]
▶이 물은 마실 수 없다 This water is not good to drink.
▶우물[강]물이 말랐다 The well [The river] has dried up.
▶여름에는 물이 모자란다 We have a short supply of water in (the) summer. ⇒ We are short of water in (the) summer.
▶물은 낮은 곳으로 흐른다 It is the nature of water to run downhill.
〈물을〉 물을 붓다 pour water into 《a kettle》 / 물을 빼다 drain off 《a pool》 / 거리에 물을 뿌리다 sprinkle water on the dusty street / (수도의) 물을 틀다[잠그다] turn on [off] the water
▶물을 틀어놓지 마십시오 Don't leave the water running, please.
▶그녀는 꽃에 물을 주었다 She poured water on [watered] the flowers.
▶법정은 물을 끼얹은 듯이 조용했다 The court was so quiet (that) you could have heard a pin drop.
〈물에[로]〉 물에 적시다[잠그다] dip [soak] in water / 물에 빠져 죽다 be drowned; find a watery grave / 물로 회석하다 water down / 물로 헹구다 rinse with water
▶기름은 물에 뜬다 Oil floats on water.
▶통나무가 물에 떠 있었다 There was a log floating on the water.
〈그 밖의 표현〉 물샐틈 없는 경계를 펴다 keep airtight water 《on, over》

▶ 두 사람 사이는 물과 기름같이 어울리지 않는다 The two can't mix like [are like mixing] oil and water.
2 〈홍수〉 a flood; an inundation
▶ 물이 났다 The river has flooded.
▶ 호우로 각지에 물이 났다 The heavy rain caused floods in many places.
▶ 논이 물에 잠겼다 The rice field is flooded [under water, inundated].
3 〈액체·즙〉 liquid; 〈유동체〉 fluid; 〈과실의〉 juice; 〈초목의〉 sap; soup
▶ 나무에 물이 오르기 시작한다 The sap begins to flow in a tree.
■ —당량(當量) 〔物〕 water equivalent

물² 〈빛깔〉 dyed color; dye
◆ 물이 들다 dye / 검정물을 들이다 dye black / 물을 빼다 bleach; take the color out / 물이 날다 the color fades / 물이 잘 들다[잘 들지 않다] dye [take dye] well [badly]

물³ 1 〈빨래〉 a period between one wash and another; a wash; the number of times clothes have been washed ◆ 첫[새]물 옷 new clothes that have yet to be laundered / 한물 빤 옷 clothes that have been washed once
2 〈과일·해산물〉 the season; a crop
◆ 만물 사과 the first (crop of) apples in its season / 끝물 조기 yellow corvina caught in the last of its season
▶ 수박이 한물 갔다 Watermelon have passed the season.
3 〈누에〉 a batch of silkworms
◆ 첫물 누에 the first [earliest] batch of silkworms

물가 the water's edge; the brink of the water; the beach ◆ 물가에 to the beach; ashore / 물가에서 on the shore

물가 物價 (commodity) prices; 〈시가〉 the market price
◆ 도매[소비자] 물가 지수 a wholesale [consumer] price index / 저물가 정책 a low prices policy
〈물가의〉 물가의 안정 price stability / 물가의 하락 a fall in prices / 물가의 현실화 price rationalization / 물가의 변동이 크다 prices fluctuate widely
▶ 정부는 물가의 상승을 연 5%로 억제하려 하고 있다 The Government is trying to limit price increases to five percent a year [to an annual rate of five percent].
〈물가가〉 이 달에는 물가가 올랐다[내렸다] Prices have gone up [down] this month.
▶ 이 근처는 물가가 비싸다[싸다] Prices are high [low] in this neighborhood.
▶ 언제나 물가가 내릴지 걱정이다 I wonder when prices will come down.
▶ 요 3년 동안은 물가가 안정되어 있다 Prices have been stable for the past three years.
〈물가를〉 물가를 내리다 lower [bring down] prices / 물가를 안정시키다 stabilize prices / 물가를 올리다 raise [advance] prices / 물가를 현실화하다 rationalize the price structure
■ 소비자— the cost of living; the consumer(s)' price: 소비자물가에 맞는 승급 a cost-of-living adjustment (in wages) 저— low prices 주요— prices of staple commodities ■ —고 high prices of commodities —대책[정책] a (commodity) price policy —동결 pegging [freezing] of prices —등귀[하락] a rise [fall] in prices; a price rise [fall] —변동[파동] price fluctuation —수당 (commodity) price allowance; an allowance for price increase —수준 the price level —안정 a price stabilization —인하 a price reduction —인하운동 a cut-price drive; a cut-the-price campaign —조절 regulation of prices —체계 a price structure [system] —통제 price control(s): 정부는 물가 통제에 착수했다 The Government has decided to introduce price controls. —표 a price list

물갈이 〔農〕 plowing a paddy with water in it
—물갈이하다 plow a paddy with water in it

물갈퀴 〔動〕〈물오리·개구리의〉 a web; 〈물갈퀴 있는 발〉 a webfoot; a webbed foot
◆ 반물갈퀴의 semipalmate(d)

물감 1 〈염료〉 dyestuffs; dyes; colors; stain
◆ 물감의 3원색 three primary colors / 물감을 들이다 dye / 물감을 잘 먹다 dye well; dye fast **2** 〈그림물감〉 colors; 〈유화의〉 oil colors; oils
■ 합성[인조]— synthetic [artificial] dyes —제조 dye making [manufacture]

물개 1 〔動〕 a fur seal ◆ 물개 가죽 a sealskin / 물개 번식지 a seal rookery **2** 〈수달〉 an otter

물거름 〈액체 거름〉 liquid fertilizer [manure]
■ —통 a night soil bucket; **(**美俗**)** a honey bucket

물거리 〈땔감〉 sticks (used as fuel); brushwood; dead twigs

물거리 —距離 navigable distance at high tide

물거미 1 〔動〕 a water spider **2** 〔昆〕 a water strider

물거품 1 〈물의 거품〉 a bubble (▶ 보통 복수형); a foam; froth
◆ 물거품같은 foamy; frothy / 물거품처럼 사라지다 burst like a bubble; end [go up] in smoke
2 〈덧없음〉 transience
◆ 물거품같은 명성 a bubble reputation / 물거품같은 vain
▶ 지금까지의 노력이 모두 물거품이 되었다 All my efforts came to nothing [were in vain, were wasted, **(**口**)** went down the drain].

물건 物件 1 〈물체〉 a thing; stuff; an object; 〈물품〉 an article; goods; 〈물질〉 substance; 〈재료〉 material; 〈소유물〉 possession

> 解說 **thing**은 「물건」이란 뜻의 가장 일반적인 말. **stuff**는 구어적인 말로 막연하게 물질·물체·재료 등을 가리킨다. **object**는 지각의 대상이 되는 물건임을 강조하며, **substance**는 물건을 구성하는 물질로서 특히 화학성분의 물질을 가리킨다.

◆ 온갖 물건 all sorts of goods / 물건을 탐내다 lust for [after] a thing
▶ 이런 종류의 물건은 품절입니다 Articles of this kind are out of stock.
▶ 화재시에 가지고 나온 물건은 단지 책 한 권뿐이었다 The only object rescued from the fire was a book.

2 〈품질〉 quality; 〈품종〉 a brand
◆물건이 좋다[나쁘다] be of good [bad, poor] quality
▶ 이 차는 지난 주에 사신 물건보다 더 좋은 상품입니다 This tea is better than that (which) you bought last week.
▶ 이 종이는 물건이 좋다 This paper is of good quality.

물걸레 a wet floorcloth
◆물걸레질하다 wipe with a damp cloth [wet duster]

물것 biting insects

물결 1 〈수면의 움직임〉 a wave
◆거친 물결 wild waves; a rough sea / 잔물결 하나 없는 수면 the rippleless surface of the water / 물결이 일다 waves rise / 물결에 휩쓸리다 be washed away by the waves
▶ 어린 아이가 밀려온 물결에 휩쓸려 갔다 A child has been washed away [carried away] by the surging waves.
2 〈물결처럼 움직이는 것〉 (a) flow; a stream; a current
◆시대의 물결을 타다[거스르다] go with [against] the tide of the times / 인기의 물결을 타다 ride on the wave of popularity / 호경기의 물결을 타다 ride the crest of the boom
▶ 사람의 물결에 떠밀려 갔다 I was pushed along by the stream of people.
■—표 a swung dash

물결치다 1 〈물결이 일다〉 move in waves; wave; roll; undulate
◆물결치는 바다 a rolling sea / 물결치는대로 at the mercy of the waves / 파도가 바람에 물결치다 waves rise in the wind
▶ 파도는 크게 물결치면서 배를 밀어 올렸다 The waves surged high and lifted the ship.
2 〈물결치듯 움직이다〉 wave; heave
▶ 벼이삭이 물결치고 있다 The ears of rice are waving in the field.
▶ 그녀는 물결치는 듯한 금발이 자랑이었다 She was proud of her wavy blonde hair.

물경 勿驚 surprisingly (enough); startlingly; shockingly ▶ 그는 물경 만 권의 책을 수집했다 He made a marvelous collection of ten thousand volumes.
▶ 쌓인 빚이 물경천만 원이었다 The debt went on increasing, reaching at last a surprising amount of ten million won.

물고 物故 1 〈저명 인사의 죽음〉 death of an eminent person [a celebrity]
2 〈죄인의 죽음〉 death of a notorious person; being put to death
◆물고를 내다 kill *sb*; put (a criminal) to death / 물고가 나다 die; be dead

물고기 a fish (*pl.*~, ~es); 〈총칭〉 fish
◆물고기 떼 a school [shoal] of fish / 물고기 뼈 a fish bone / 강으로 물고기를 낚으러 가다 go fishing in the river (▶in 대신에 to를 쓸 수 있음)
▶ 이 강에는 물고기가 많다 This river abounds [teems] with fish.
▶ 이 강에서는 이 시기에 물고기가 잘 잡힌다 The river is well fished this time of the year.
■—자리 〔天〕 the Pisces; the Fishes

물고기
첫째 등지느러미 spinous dorsal fin
둘째 등지느러미 soft dorsal fin
주둥이 snout
센 줄기 spiny rays
콧구멍 nostril
여린 줄기 soft rays
비늘 scales
꼬리지느러미 tail fin
아감딱지 gill cover
측선, 옆줄 lateral line
뒷지느러미 anal fin
가슴지느러미 pectoral fin
배지느러미 pelvic fin

물고늘어지다 1 〈이빨로〉 bite at *sb* [*sth*] and hang on to it
▶ 개는 여우의 목을 물고늘어졌다 The dog latched onto the throat of the fox.
2 〈들러붙다〉 stick to; hang on to; get a firm grip on; hold out for
◆아무의 말꼬리를 물고늘어지다 catch *sb* in (his) own words; cavil at *sb's* words
▶ 기자들은 날카로운 질문으로 수상을 물고늘어졌다 The reporters kept after [harassed] the prime minister with shrewd questions.

물고동 〈수도꼭지〉 a faucet; (美) a spigot ◆물고동을 틀다[잠그다] turn on [off] a faucet

물곰팡이 〔植〕〈수생균〉 aquatic mold

물관(부) —管(部) 〔植〕 xylem

물구나무서다 stand on *one's* hands; do a handstand ◆물구나무서기 a handstand; handstanding / 물구나무서서 걷다 walk on *one's* hands ◆물구나무 설 줄 아니? Can you stand on your hands?

물구덩이 a puddle; a (stagnant) pool; a plash
◆물구덩이가 생기다 a pool forms
▶ 비가 온 뒤에 군데군데 물구덩이가 생겼다 There came out muddy pools here and there after the rain.

물굽이 a bend [curve] in a river [stream]
▶ 강이 물굽이진다 The river has a bend. = The river meanders.

물권 物權 〔法〕 a real right ◆물권의 설정[이전] the creation [transfer] of a real right
■—법 The Law of Reality —증권 reality securities —행위 reality right action

물귀신 —鬼神 a water demon [spirit]
◆물귀신이 되다 be drowned; drown

물기 —氣 moisture; wetness; dampness
◆물기가 많은 오렌지 a juicy [succulent] orange / 물기가 있는 moist; damp / 물기가 없는 dry; husky / 두부의 물기를 빼다 drain (the water off) the bean curd
▶ 이 배는 물기가 적다 This pear is too dry.

물기둥 a column of water; a water spout; a water column
▶ 비행기가 바다에 추락하자 커다란 물기둥이 솟구쳐 올랐다 The plane crashed into the sea,

sending up a huge column of water.
물기름 hair oil
물길 a waterway; a watercourse; a water route; a canal
♦ 두 도시 사이에 물길을 열다 cut [dig] a canal between the two cities / 물길을 따라 항해하다 sail along a waterway
물까치 〔鳥〕 an azure-winged magpie
물꼬 an irrigation gate; a sluice gate
♦ 물꼬를 트다 sluice; irrigate
물끄러미 with a blank look
♦ 물끄러미 쳐다보다 stare *sb* in the face; gaze at *sb's* face
▶ 그는 그 그림을 물끄러미 바라봤다 He gazed [looked intently] at the painting.
물난리 —亂離 1〈수해〉a flood disaster
♦ 물난리가 나다 have a flood disaster
▶ 이번 물난리에 많은 사람이 죽었다 Many people lost their lives in the recent flood.
2〈물부족〉a water famine; the shortage of water supply
▶ 이 지방은 여름만 되면 많든 적든 물난리가 난다 This district suffers more or less from a water famine every summer.
물납 物納 payment in kind [goods] ─**물납하다** pay 《taxes》 in kind ─**세금**─ tax payment in kind ─**세** a tax in kind
물놀이 1〈잔물결이 일어남〉rippling; wrinkling of water ─**물놀이하다** wrinkle; ripple
2〈물장난〉dabbling in water ─**물놀이하다** dabble in water; play with water
3〈물가로의 행락〉a waterside excursion;〈뱃놀이〉a boating excursion
♦ 물놀이 가다 go on a waterside excursion; go to a summer resort; go swimming 《to the seaside》
물다¹〈상하다〉rot; go bad; spoil ♦ 문 생선 a stale fish ▶ 이 귤들은 물기 시작하고 있다 These oranges are beginning to go bad.
물다² 1〈돈을 치르다〉pay; repay
♦ 벌금을 물다 pay a fine; pay *one's* penalty / 책값을 물다 pay for books
▶ 주차 위반으로 벌금을 물었다 I was fined for illegal parking.
▶ 매달 방세로 20만원을 물어야 한다 I have to pay 200 thousand won a month for rent.
2〈배상·보상하다〉compensate; make good; make up for
♦ 손해배상을 물다 make good [make up for] the loss
물다³ 1〈개 등이〉bite 《at》; snap 《at》; have a bite at
♦ 물어 뜯다 bite off; gnaw [cut] off with the teeth
▶ 나는 개에게 다리를 물렸다 I was bitten on the leg by a dog.
▶ 개는 고기를 물어 뜯었다 The dog took [made] a snap at the meat.
2〈물것이〉bite; sting
▶ 모기가 문다 Mosquitoes bite.
▶ 벼룩이 문 데가 가렵다 The fleabite itches.
3〈물고기가〉bite [nibble] at; take a bait
▶ 물고기가 미끼를 물었다 The fish snapped at the bait. ⇌ A fish took the bait.

▶ 오늘은 물고기가 잘 문다 The fish are taking [biting] well today.
4〈입에〉take [hold] *sth* in *one's* mouth; hold [have] *sth* between *one's* teeth
▶ 아버지는 파이프를 입에 물고 의자에 앉아 계셨다 Father sat on the chair with a pipe in his mouth.
▶ 저 아기는 손가락을 무는 버릇이 있다 The baby has a habit of putting his finger in his mouth.
5〈얻어 차지하다〉get; catch; find
6〈톱니바퀴 등이〉gear 《with, into》; be in gear 《with》
물독 a water jar [jug]
물동 〔鑛山〕a prop [support] used to hold the puddle in a mine
물동 物動 mobilization of materials = 물자 (~동원)
물동이 a water jar
물두부 ─豆腐 bean curd boiled in water; boiled bean curds
물들다 1〈빛깔이 들다〉dye; be dyed; be stained
♦ 붉게 물들다 be dyed red
▶ 이 옷감은 물이 잘 든다[들지 않는다] This cloth dyes [doesn't dye] well.
▶ 손수건이 피로 물들어 있었다 The handkerchief was stained with blood.
2〈초록이 빛깔을 띠다〉color; become colored;〈단풍 등이〉turn crimson [red]
▶ 봄에는 초록이 초록색으로 물든다 In spring plants put on fresh green colors.
3〈감염되다〉be imbued; be influenced by
♦ 악에 물들다 be affected by evil influence; be steeped in [tainted with] vice
▶ 혼자 도시에서 사는 동안에 그녀는 악에 물들었다 She became corrupted while living alone in the city.
▶ 그는 사회주의에 물들어 있다 He is imbued with socialism.
물들이다 1〈물들게 하다〉dye
♦ 머리를 검게 물들이다 dye *one's* hair (in) black
▶ 지는 해가 하늘을 붉게 물들였다 Sunset dyed [tinged] the sky red.
▶ 그녀는 볼을 붉게 물들였다 She blushed [turned red].
2〈채색하다〉color; paint
♦ 손을 피로 물들이다 stain *one's* hand with blood / 손톱을 빨갛게 물들이다 paint *one's* nails red
물딱총 ─銃 a water pistol [gun]; a squirt (gun) ♦ 아무에게 물딱총을 놓다 shoot *sb* with a water pistol
▶ 그 아이는 물딱총으로 새를 쐈다 The child shot a bird with his water pistol.
물라토 〈제1대 흑백 혼혈아〉〔人類〕mulatto 《*pl.* ~s, -es》
물때¹〈간만 시간〉tide time; the tidal hour;〈밀물 때〉the time when the tide begins to rise [flow in]
♦ 물때를 기다리다 wait for the high tide 《to set sail》 / 물때를 놓치다 miss the high [full, flood] tide

물때²

▶ 어부는 물때를 기다려 낚시를 한다 A fisherman waits for a favorable tide to fish with rod and line.

물때² 〈물로 생긴 때〉 scale; fur; incrustation
◆ 물때가 낀 쇠주전자 a furred iron kettle / 물때가 끼다 fur; scale / 주전자의 물때를 벗기다 remove scale from a kettle
▶ 물때가 끼었다 Fur has formed.
▶ 이 주전자는 물때가 꽤 많이 끼어 있다 This kettle is covered with a great deal of scale.

물떼새 〔鳥〕 a plover

물똥싸움 a splashing water on each other; a water fight

물량 物量 the amount [quantity] of materials [resources]
◆ 물량의 우세 material odds / 적은 물량으로 압도하다 overwhelm the enemy with material superiority
▶ 적은 물량을 과시하며 공격을 개시했다 The enemy opened an attack on us on the strength of their material superiority [advantage].
▶ 우리는 물량으로는 저들을 도저히 당해낼 수 없다 We are no match for them in material resources.

물러가다 1 〈뒷걸음질쳐 가다〉 move backward; draw [step] back; back
◆ 한 걸음 뒤로 물러가다 take a step backward
2 〈어른 앞에서〉 retire; leave; withdraw
◆ 아버지 앞에서 물러가다 withdraw from the presence of one's father
▶ 수행원들은 옆 방으로 물러갔다 The attendents retired to the next room.
▶ 그만 물러가겠습니다 I think I must be off [be going now].
3 〈사임·은퇴하다〉 retire (from); resign from (a post)
◆ 공직에서 물러가다 resign [withdraw] from public office
4 〈더위 등이〉 be over; be gone ▶ 더위가 물러갔다 The hot weather is over [gone].
5 〈연기되다〉 be put off; be postponed; be delayed

물러나다 1 〈후퇴하다〉 retreat; recede; leave; withdraw (from)
◆ 급히 물러나다 beat a hurried retreat / 남의 면전에서 물러나다 withdraw from sb's presence / 옆으로 물러나다 step [move] aside
▶ 그는 한 걸음도 물러나지 않았다 He did not yield an inch.
2 〈사임하다〉 withdraw; retire ◆ 직위에서 물러나다 resign one's post in an office
▶ 그는 금년 안으로 정계에서 물러날 거라고 한다 I hear that he is going to retire from [leave] the political world.
3 〈벗어지다〉 come loose [out]
▶ 책상다리가 물러났다 A leg of the table came loose.

물러서다 1 〈뒤로 나서다〉 step back; retreat; recede; 〈길을 내어주다〉 make way (for sb)
◆ 아무가 지나가게 물러서다 make way for sb
▶ 그는 한 걸음 뒤로 물러섰다 He took a step backward.
▶ 여러분, 뒤로 물러서 주십시오, 구급차가 옵니다 Everybody, stand back! Here comes the ambulance!
▶ 나는 좀더 잘 보려고 뒤로 물러섰다 I backed up to get a better view.
▶ 뒤로 물러서라 Stand back! ⇒ Get away!
2 〈사임하다〉 withdraw; retire ◆ 관직에서 물러서다 retire from government service

물러앉다 1 〈물러나 앉다〉 draw one's seat back; sit back
▶ 이 애가 앉게 좀 물러앉아라 Would you mind sitting back a bit so that this child may have a seat?
2 〈은퇴하다〉 retire; withdraw
◆ 정계에서 물러앉다 retire from political life; withdraw from the political arena

물러지다 1 〈무르게 되다〉 soften; become tender ▶ 밀랍은 열을 가하면 물러진다 Wax softens in heat. 2 ⇨ 누그러지다

물렁하다 1 〈물건이〉 soft; tender; squashy
◆ 물렁한 감 a ripe and squashy persimmon
2 〈성질이〉 soft; yielding; compliant

물레 a spinning wheel
■ —바퀴 the wheel of a spinning wheel —방아 a water mill; a waterwheel —질 spinning; making yarn: 물레질하다 spin yarn 물렛가락 a spindle 물렛돌 a stone put on the base of a spinning-wheel (to keep it stable) 물렛줄 a spinning-wheel belt

물려받다 〈재산 등을〉 inherit (sth from sb); 〈지위 등을〉 succeed to; take over (another's duty, a task)
◆ 아버지의 사업을 물려받다 succeed to [take over] one's father's business
▶ 형과 나는 아버지의 재산을 물려받았다 My brother and I inherited our father's property.
▶ 그의 어학적 재능은 부모에게서 물려받았다 He inherited his language ability from his parents. ⇒ His aptitude for language comes [is an inheritance] from his parents.
▶ 우리는 물려받은 재산으로 유복하게 살았다 We lived quite comfortably on our family property.
▶ 그녀의 우아함은 어머니한테서 물려받았다 Her elegance comes from her mother. ⇒ She inherited her mother's elegance.

물려주다 hand [turn, make] over; transfer; 〈남겨주다〉 leave; 〈왕위를〉 abdicate; 〈동산을〉 bequeath; 〈부동산을〉 devise
▶ 그 도예가는 기술을 아들에게 물려주었다 The potter taught the art to his son.
▶ 그는 회사 소유권을 아들에게 물려주었다 He handed over [transferred] ownership of the company to his son.
▶ 나는 증권을 조카에게 물려주었다 I transferred my securities to my nephew.

물려지내다 be in sb's clutch; be under sb's thumb; act [move, work] at sb's back and call ▶ 그는 아내에게 물려지낸다 He is under his wife's thumb.

물력 物力 1 〈물건의 힘〉 material power
2 〈재료와 노력〉 materials and efforts; 〈건축재료〉 building [construction] materials
▶ 그 집을 짓는데 많은 물력이 들었다 It took a

물론 勿論 (as a matter) of course; 〈당연〉 naturally; 〈말할 것도 없이〉 needless to say; 〈확실히〉 certainly; surely
▶물론, 자네의 파티에 가겠네 Of course, I'll come to [attend] your party. (▶여기서는 go to는 쓰지 않음)
▶[話]「그게 정말 네것이냐?」「물론」 "Is that really yours?" "Of course!" ⇒ Why, yes!" (▶ of course는「알고 있지 않니」라는 뜻으로 때로 무례한 느낌을 줌)
▶[話]「화난 게 아니지?」「물론이지」 "You're not angry?" "Of course [Certainly] not."
▶물론 그는 그 제안을 거절할 것이다 Naturally(,) he will refuse the proposal.
▶네가 곤란하다면 물론 도와 줄께 If you're in trouble, I'll certainly help you.
▶[話]「네 차 좀 빌려주겠니?」「물론이지」 "Will you lend me your car?" "Sure [Of course, Certainly], I will. ⇒ (口) I sure will. ⇒ (口) OK. ⇒ (口) Why not? ⇒ By all means."

> [解説] (美)에서는 ***sure***, (英)에서는 ***certainly***, ***of course***가 일반적이며 ***by all means***는 정중한 답변. 또 정중한 말로는 Sure [Certainly], I'd be glad [happy] to.라고도 한다.

▶그는 영국에는 물론 아프리카에도 가본 적이 있다 He has been to Africa, not to mention England.
▶그는 영어는 물론 프랑스어도 할줄 안다 He speaks French as well as English. ⇒ He can speak not only English but (also) French.

물리 物理 1 〈사물의 이치〉 the law of nature; physical laws 2 ⇨ 물리학
■—광학(光學) physical optics —량 physical quantity —상수(常數) physical constant —요법 physical therapy [treatment] —탐사 geophysical survey —화학 physical chemistry; 〈물리와 화학〉 physics and chemistry —흡착 physical absorption

물리다¹ 〈싫증나다〉 get [grow] tired ((of)); feel [be] satiated; (口) be fed up ((with)); get sick ((of)); 〈음식에〉 be tired of eating
▶떡을 물리도록 먹었다 I was satiated with rice cake.
▶나는 영화에 물렸다 I have lost interest in movies.
▶이 노래는 물리도록 들었다 The song has been sung to death.

물리다² 1 〈연기하다〉 put off; postpone; defer
♦기한을 물리다 extend the term ((from...to...))
♦소풍을 비 때문에 하루 물렸다 The excursion was postponed until the following day because of rain.
2 〈옮겨놓다〉 shift; transfer; move
♦의자를 뒤로 물리다 push back a chair

물리다³ 〈치우다〉 take away sth; clear off
♦상을 물리다 take away the table

물리다⁴ 1 〈동물·벌레 등에〉 be [get] bitten
▶개에 다리를 물렸다 I was bitten in the leg by a dog.
▶모기에 물렸다 I was bitten by mosquitoes.
2 〈물게 하다〉 make sb hold sth in the mouth
▶나는 그의 입에 아스피린 두 알을 물렸다 I made him hold two aspirin tablets in his mouth.
▶그녀는 아기한테 젖꼭지를 물렸다 She gave the breast to her baby. ⇒ She suckled her baby.

물리다⁵ 〈보상케 하다〉 make sb compensate
♦아무에게 깨뜨린 그릇값을 물리다 make sb pay for a broken dish / 엄청난 서비스 요금을 물리다 charge exorbitantly [unreasonably] for a service

물리적 物理的 physical
▶그런 계획을 실행에 옮기는 것은 물리적으로 불가능하다 It is physically impossible to carry out such a plan.
■—레코드 〔電算〕 physical record —모형 physical model —변화[법칙, 현상] a physical change [law, phenomenon] —성질 physical property —자극 〔生〕 physical stimulus

물리치다 1 〈거절하다〉 refuse ((a request)); reject ((a demand)); spurn ((an offer)); repulse ((advice)); turn down ((an offer))
♦제안을 물리치다 turn down [wave away] a proposal
2 〈격퇴하다〉 drive [turn, send] away; repel; expel
♦적의 공격을 물리치다 repulse an attack by the enemy / 사람을 물리치고 밀담하다 have a closed-door conference ((with))
3 〈지우다〉 defeat; beat
♦연거푸 5명을 물리치다 beat five opponents in succession

물리학 物理學 〔物〕 physics (▶단수취급); physical science ♦물리학적 physical / 물리학적으로 physically
■—실험 experimental physics 응용[이론]— applied [theoretical] physics 정신— psychophysics 지구— geophysics 핵— nuclear physics: 그의 전공은 핵물리학이다 He is majoring in [His major (subject) is] nuclear physics. ■—기구 physical instrument —자 a physicist; a natural philosopher

물림 〔建〕 an extra space of half a kan added to a regular room as a kind of porch

물림쇠 a staple; a metal band; a clamp

물마 flood on the ground (caused by rain); an overflow

물마개 〈병 등의〉 a stopper; 〈코르크로 만든〉 cork; 〈수도 등의〉 a stopcock; 〈배 밑바닥의〉 a bung

물마루 the crest of a wave; a wave crest

물만두 —饅頭 a stuffed bun served in water; boiled ravioli

물말이 1 〈물만밥〉 cooked rice served in water 2 〈젖은 것〉 a thing drenched with water

물맛 the taste of water
▶물맛이 짜다 The water tastes salty.

물망 物望 popular prospects [favor]
♦물망에 오르다 win popular support; be popularly [widely] expected
▶그는 국무장관 물망에 올라 있다 He is expected to be nominated as Secretary of

State.
물망초 勿忘草 〔植〕 a forget-me-not
물맞이 drinking [bathing in] mineral water
—물맞이하다 drink [bath in] mineral water
물매¹ 〔工·建〕〈경사〉 a slope; a slant;〈지붕의〉 a pitch
▶ 지붕의 물매가 싸다 The roof has a steep slant.
▶ 지붕의 물매가 뜨다 The roof is not steep enough.
물매² a slingshot; a sling (for throwing stones)
◆ 물매로 과일을 따다 knock off fruits with a slingshot
물매³ 〈매질〉 hard whipping [flogging] ◆ 물매 맞다 be whipped hard / 물매치다 punish sb with a good sound flogging
물매암이 〔昆〕 a water [whirligig] beetle
물매화풀 —梅花— 〔植〕 a grass-of-parnassus
물멀미 dizziness [vertigo] caused by looking at a vast expanse of water; seasickness
—물멀미하다 feel dizzy [seasick]
물명 物名 the names of a thing [an article]
물목 1 〈물어귀〉 the point at which the water flows in or out; the fork of a river [stream]
◆ 물목을 지키다 stand watch at the fork of a river
2 〈사광에서〉 〔鑛〕 the spot where gold dust pans thickest
물목 物目 a catalog of goods
물몽둥이 a kind of hammer used by blacksmiths and masons; a maul; a sledgehammer
물문 —門 a sluice; a floodgate
물물교환 物物交換 barter ◆ 물물교환으로 barter; on the barter system
—물물교환하다 barter (A for B); (美) trade
▶ 그들은 식량과 총을 물물교환했다 They bartered food for guns.
물미 a ferrule; a spike ■ —작대기 a spiked prop on an A-frame
물밀다 〈조수가〉 rise; flow; come in
◆ 물밀 때 the time of the flowing tide; tide time; high tide / 물밀 때에 at high tide
물밑 the bottom of the water [sea, river]
◆ 물밑에 가라앉다 sink [go down] to the bottom of the water [sea]
▶ 침몰선은 물밑에 가로 누워 있었다 The sunken ship lay on her side at the bottom of the sea [on the ocean floor, on the sea bottom].
물바가지 a gourd for dipping water
물바다 ▶ 강이 범람하여 밭이 물바다가 되었다 The river overflowed and submerged [inundated] the field.
물받이 a waterspout; a drainspout; a gutter
물방개 〔昆〕 a diving beetle
물방아 1 ⇨ 물레(~방아)
◆ 물방아를 돌리다 operate a water mill / 물방아에 곡식을 찧다 grind grain in a water mill
2 〈방아두레박〉 water wheel buckets
물방울 a drop of water; a drop; a trickle
◆ 물방울이 떨어지다 drip; trickle; fall in drops
▶ 처마에서 물방울이 떨어지고 있다 The trickles are dripping from the eaves.

—무늬 polka dots: 물방울 무늬의 스커트 / 그 소녀는 물방울 무늬의 여름 옷을 입고 있었다 The little girl wore a polka-dotted summer dress.
물뱀 〔動〕 a sea snake [serpent]; a water snake [moccasin]
■ —자리 〔天〕 the Water Snake; Hydrus
물벌레 a water insect; a water beetle
물베개 a (rubber) water pillow [cushion]
물벼락 dashing [splashing] water on sb suddenly; dousing sb with water
◆ 물벼락(을) 맞다 get doused; be suddenly poured over with water
물벼룩 〔動〕 a water flea
물병 —甁 a water jar; a jug
■ —자리 〔天〕 the Water Bearer; Aquarius
물보라 a spray (of water); a splash
◆ 물보라를 일으키다 raise [throw up] spray; send up clouds of spray
▶ 파도가 방파제에 부딪쳐 물보라를 일으켰다 Waves dashed against the wharf sending up spray.
물볼기 whipping [flogging] a woman wearing drenched underwear as a punishment
◆ 물볼기를 치다 give a woman a wet flogging
물부리 〈담뱃대의〉 a mouthpiece; 〈궐련의〉 a cigarette holder ◆ 물부리 달린 궐련 a filter-tipped cigarette; a filter tip
물분 —粉 a liquid face-paint; a face-powder fluid; a liquid makeup [face-paint]
물불 water and fire ▶ 그는 주인을 위해서는 물불을 가리지 않는다 He is willing to go through fire and water for his master.
물비누 liquid soap; soft soap
물비린내 a fishy smell of water
물빛 1 〈물 같은 빛깔〉 the color of water
2 〈남색〉 aquamarine; light blue
◆ 물빛 드레스 a light blue dress
3 〈물감의〉 a dye color; a dyed color
물산 物産 a product; (총칭) produce ◆ 물산의 집산지 a produce distributing center
물살 the flow [current] of water ▶ 이 강은 물살이 세다[약하다] This river has a swift [gentle] current.
물상 物象 〈사물〉 an object; 〈현상〉 a material phenomenon (pl. ~s, -na); 〈학과〉 the science of inanimate nature
물새 1 a waterfowl; a water bird; a swimming bird 2 ⇨ 물총새
물색 物色 1 〈물건의 빛깔〉 the color of a thing
2 〈물들인 빛〉 a dyed color
3 〈풍경〉 scenery; nature; a landscape
4 〈찾음〉 looking for; 〈고름〉 selecting
—물색하다 〈찾다〉 look for; search for; 〈고르다〉 select; pick out
▶ 그는 후계자를 물색하고 있다 He is looking for his successor.
물색없다 物色— unreasonable; irrational; illogical; absurd ◆ 물색 없이 irrationally; unreasonably; illogically
물샐틈없다 1 〈꼭 막히다〉 watertight
2 〈완벽하다〉 watertight; strict; rigorous
◆ 물샐틈없는 경계 closed guard / 물샐틈없는 경계망을 펴다 throw a tight cordon [net]

물성 物性 〖物〗 properties of matter; physical properties

물세 物稅 a real tax; a tax on goods and possessions

물세례 —洗禮 1 〖基〗 baptism (by immersion) 2 ⇨ 물벼락

물소 〖動〗 a (water) buffalo

물소리 the sound of flowing [running] water; murmurs of a stream ▶조금 떨어진 곳에서 개울의 물소리가 들렸다 I heard the sound of a stream in the distance.

물속 ◆물속의 underwater / 물속에 in the water; under water; below the surface of the water / 물속에 가라앉다 sink under water / 물속에 빠지다 〈실수로〉 get a ducking

물수건 —手巾 a wet [moist] towel; a steaming hot hand towel

물수란 —水卵 a poached egg

물수리 〖鳥〗 an osprey; a fish hawk; an ossifrage

물수제비 duck(s) and drake(s)
◆물수제비를 뜨다 skip a stone (on the surface of the water); play ducks and drakes

물시계 —時計 1 〈시계〉 a water clock; an hourglass 2 〈수도 계량기〉 a water gauge

물신 物神 a fetish
■—숭배 fetishism; fetishistic religion

물실호기하다 勿失好機— do not miss [lose, let slip] a chance

물심 物心 matter and mind

물심양면 物心兩面 ▶난 너를 물심 양면으로 돕고 싶어 I'd like to help you both materially and spiritually [morally].

물싸움 1 〈논물의〉 an irrigation [a water-right] dispute ◆물싸움하다 dispute over [about] the water-rights 2 ⇨ 물둥싸움

물써다 〈조수가 빠지다〉 ebb; go out; be on the ebb ◆물썰 때(에) (at) low tide
▶물이 썰고 있다 The tide is ebbing [at its ebb]. ≒ The tide is going out.

물썽하다 〈만만하다〉 gullible; unstubborn; feeble

물쑥 〖植〗 a kind of wormwood; an artemisia

물쓰듯하다 spend money unsparingly [like water]; be a free spender ▶돈을 물쓰듯하다 He is quite a spendthrift. ≒ He plays ducks and drakes with his money.

물씬거리다 1 〈물체가〉 be soft; become tender 2 〈냄새가〉 smell nice

물씬물씬하다 〈물링물링 하다〉 soft; tender; 〈냄새가〉 smell strongly [prodigally]; 〈악취가〉 reek (of); stink (of fish)
▶그에게서는 언제나 술냄새가 물씬물씬한다 He always reeks of wine.
▶그녀가 지나갈 때 향수냄새가 물씬물씬했다 She passed along, leaving a strong scent behind her.

물씬하다 1 〈부드럽다〉 soft; tender
◆물씬한 고기 meat cooked tender
2 〈냄새가〉 nicely [strongly] scented

물아 物我 〖哲〗 (external) object and self; the ego and the non-ego; 〈물질계와 정신계〉 the material world and the spiritual world

물아래 a down-river area; 〈하류〉 the lower part of a river ◆물아래로 헤엄처 가다 swim downstream / 물아래로 재목을 띄우다 float lumber [timber] downstream

물안개 a wet fog; a rain-fog

물안경 —眼鏡 a pair of (diver's) goggles

물알 soft unripe grain ◆물알 들다 develop into soft unripe grain

물앵두 a fruit of the honeysuckle
■—나무 〖植〗 a honeysuckle

물약 —藥 1 〈액체약〉 a liquid medicine; (美) liquor 2 〖鑛山〗 a shot of dynamite

물어내다 1 〈변상하다〉 pay for; compensate 2 〈퍼뜨리다〉 air [let out] family secrets; 〈누설하다〉 leak out (a family secret); 〈짐승이 밖으로 내다〉 carry off in the mouth; 〈몰래〉 smuggle sth out of (the house)
▶쥐가 밤을 물어내고 있다 A rat is carrying off chestnuts in its mouth.

물어넣다 repay; refund; pay back; compensate for ▶그는 유용한 회사 돈을 물어넣었다 He repayed misappropriated company funds.

물어떼다 bite off; gnaw off [away]; cut off with the teeth
◆떡을 한 입 물어떼다 bite off a mouthful of rice cake

물어뜯다 bite (hard); gnaw on; bite off
◆줄을 물어뜯다 bite off [through] the leash
▶그 곰은 밧줄을 물어뜯고 도망쳤다 The bear chewed the rope off and escaped.
▶그녀는 실을 물어뜯었다 She bit a thread in two.

물어보다 ask (sb about sth); inquire (of sb about sth); question; 〈조회 하다〉 make inquiries (about)
◆길을 물어보다 ask the way to; inquire for the way / 안부를 물어보다 ask [inquire] after sb
▶나는 그에게 그것을 물어봤어야 했다 I should [ought to] have asked him about it.

물어주다 pay for; compensate
◆비용을 물어주다 compensate sb for (the) cost [expenses] / 아들의 빚을 물어주다 pay [settle] one's son's debt

물억새 〖植〗 a common reed

물에 빠지면 지푸라기라도 움켜 쥔다 〈속담〉 A drowning man will grasp at a straw.

물역 物役 1 〈건축자재〉 building [construction] materials
2 〈품과 비용〉 labor or expenses in construction work
▶집을 짓는 데 많은 물역이 들었다 It took a lot of labor and materials to build the house.

물엿 starch syrup; glucose

물오르다 1 〈나무에〉 《sap》 rise; be up
▶봄이 되니 나무에 물오르기 시작한다 Spring has come and the sap of trees begin to rise.
2 〈사람이〉 get rich; make money; get ahead (in life); rise

물오리 〖鳥〗 a wild duck; a mallard duck; 〈수컷〉 a greenhead

물오리나무 〖植〗 a Siberian alder

물외 a (water) cucumber

물욕 物慾 worldly desire; a desire for material gain(s) ▶ 그녀는 물욕에 사로잡혀 있다 She is worldly-minded.

물위 1 〈수면〉 the surface of the water
♦ 물위에 떠오르다 come up to the surface (of the water)
▶ 배는 물위에 뜬다 A boat floats on the water.
2 〈상류〉 the upper reaches of a river; an upper stream [course]

물유리 —琉璃 〔化〕 water [liquid, soluble] glass

물은 건너 보아야 알고 사람은 지내 보아야 안다 〈속담〉 The proof of the pudding is in the eating.

물음 a question; an inquiry; an interrogation
▶ 다음 물음에 답하시오 Answer the following question(s) ■—꼴 the question form (of a verb) —표 a question mark

물의 物議 public criticism [censure]; public discussion
▶ 그의 에세이는 젊은 여성층에 상당한 물의를 일으켰다 His essay excited considerable criticism among young women.
▶ 장관의 수뢰행위는 큰 물의를 일으켰다 The minister's corruption raised a storm of public protests.

물이끼 〔植〕 (a) sphagnum; bog moss

물자 物資 〈물품〉 goods; 〈상품〉 commodities; 〈공급물〉 supplies; 〈원료〉 raw materials; 〈자원〉 resources; materials
♦ 물자의 부족 a scarcity of materials / 물자 공급을 받다 get a supply of commodities / 물자를 확보하다 secure the supply of goods
▶ 그 나라는 물자가 부족하다 The country is poor in resources.
▶ 쿠웨이트의 가장 중요한 물자는 석유다 Oil is Kuwait's most important material.
■—구호— relief goods 생활— subsistence goods; the necessities of life; basic necessities 필수— essentials; necessities —동원 mobilization of materials —수급 supply and demand of goods —활용 utilization of materials

물자동차 —自動車 〈살수차〉 a water [street] sprinkler; a sprinkler truck; 〈급수용차〉 a water supply wagon

물자체 物自體 〔哲〕 the thing-in-itself; (독) Ding an sich

물잠자리 〔昆〕 a damselfly

물잡다 draw water into (a paddy); supply (a paddy) with water; irrigate (a paddy)

물장구 1 〈장단〉 drumming on gourd vessels turned over on the water 2 〈헤엄칠 때〉 the beating; the flutter kick; the thrash ♦ 물장구 치다 make flutters; swim with the thrash

물장난 playing [dabbling] in water; playing with water —물장난하다 play [dabble] in water; play with water

물장사 〈물 판매업〉 water-seller; 〈술집 영업〉 a gay trade ♦ 물장사하는 여자 a gay lady; a woman of the gay world
▶ 그는 물장사하던 여자와 혼인했다 He married a woman who worked in a bar.
▶ 그녀는 물장사로 재산을 모았다 She made a fortune following a liquor and entertainment trade.

물장수 1 〈물을 길어다 파는 사람〉 a water-seller; a water-carrier
2 〈술집 경영인〉 a liquor and entertainment trade.

물 재배 —栽培 〈수경재배〉 water culture; hydroponics; aquiculture

물적 物的 〈물질적〉 material; 〈감지할 수 있는〉 physical
■—손해 physical damage —원조 material help [aid, support] —유통 physical distribution —유통기능 physical distribution function —자원 material resources —증거 real [material, physical] evidence

물정 物情 1 〈사물의 정상〉 the condition of things; the state of affairs
▶ 그녀는 아무런 물정도 모른다 She is as innocent as a lamb.
2 〈세상 형편〉 the condition of the world; worldly matters; public feelings
♦ 세상 물정에 밝은 worldly-wise; experienced in worldly affairs
▶ 그는 세상 물정에 어둡다 He is unaccustomed [unused] to the way of the world. ⇌ He is ignorant of the world.
▶ 넌 세상 물정을 모르는게 문제야 Your inexperience is a problem [inconvenient, trying].
▶ 그는 세상 물정에 밝은 사람이다 He is a man of the world [experience].

물주 物主 〈장사 밑천을 대는 전주〉 a financier; a financial supporter; 〈노름판의〉 a banker

물줄기 1 〈물의 흐름〉 a stream of water; a water current; a watercourse; a flow
▶ 물줄기는 두 갈래로 갈라진다 The water branches off into two streams.
2 〈내뻗는〉 a spout [gust] of water
▶ 물줄기가 세차게 뻗쳐 나왔다 Water spouted [gushed] out.
▶ 고래가 물줄기를 내뿜었다 The whale spouted water. ⇌ The whale blew.

물중탕 —重湯 water bath

물증 物證 〔法〕 real [material] evidence

물지게 a water-carrying yoke

물질 物質 matter; material; substance
♦ 물질불멸의 법칙 〔物〕 the law of conservation of matter ▶ 얼음과 눈은 같은 물질이다 Ice and snow are the same substance.
■—반(反)— 〔物〕 antimatter 화학적— a chemical substance ■—계 the material [physical] world —대사(代謝) 〔生〕 metabolism —명사 〔文法〕 a material noun —문명 material civilization —수송 〔生〕 transportation of material —순환 〔生〕 cycle of material —욕 a desire of material gain —의시대 〔地〕 matter era —전달계수 〔工〕 material transfer coefficient —주의 materialism —주의자 a materialist —파(波) 〔物〕 material wave; matter wave

물질적 物質的 material; physical; objective
♦ 물질적인 material; physical / 물질적으로 materially; physically
▶ 그 가정은 물질적으로 부유하다[곤란받고 있다] The family is materially well [badly] off.

▶그의 생각은 너무 물질적이다 He is very materialistic in his ideas.
■—번영 material prosperity —우주 the material universe —원조 material aid [help] —이익 a material gain —존재 materiality —쾌락 physical comfort

물집¹ 〈염색집〉 a dye house; a dye shop
물집² 〈피부의〉 a (water) blister
♦피가 섞인 물집 a blood blister
▶내 발에 물집이 생겼다 I got a blister on my feet.
▶그는 전신이 물집투성이가 되었다 He was all covered with blisters.
▶내 피부는 물집이 잘 생긴다 My skin blisters easily.

물쩍지근하다 〈일하는 태도가 느리다〉 stagnant; dull; tedious; stalemated

물쩡하다 〈성질이 무르다〉 soft; weak-willed; 〈서술적〉 be a milksop; have no spirit

물찌똥 1 〈묽은 똥〉 watery [loose] feces
♦물찌똥을 싸다 have loose bowels
2 〈물덩이〉 splashing waterdrops

물 차 —車 〈살수차〉 a street sprinkler; 〈급수차〉 a water wagon

물참 〈만조〉 the high tide
물참나무 〔植〕 a kind of oak
물체 物體 〔物〕 a body; 〈물건의 형체〉 an object; 〈고체〉 a solid (body); 〔法〕 a material object
♦미확인 비행 물체 UFO [⟨an *u*nidentified *f*lying *o*bject]
▶나는 멀리 이상한 물체를 보았다 I saw a strange object in the distance.
■—거리〔寫〕the object distance —심도〔寫〕the depth of field

물초 getting wet all over; dripping wet
■—물초하다 get wet through [all over]; get dripping wet; get [be] drenched [wet] to the skin

물총 —銃 a squirt (gun) ⇨ 물딱총
물총새 —銃— 〔鳥〕 a kingfisher; a halcyon
물치 〔魚〕 a frigate mackerel
물컥(물컥) with a strong stench; stinking(ly)
▶소독약 냄새가 물컥 코를 찔렀다 The smell of disinfectant stung [assailed] my nose.
▶썩은 생선 냄새가 물컥 풍겼다 The rotten fish really stank.

물컹거리다 be very mushy [pulpy, squash]
▶고기가 상해서 물컹거린다 The meat has gone bad and lost its texture.

물컹이 〈물건〉 soft [overripe] stuff; something squashy [mushy]; 〈사람〉 a weakling; a softy; a milksop; a sissy

물컹하다 pulpy; squashy; mushy
▶어둠 속에서 무엇인가 물컹한 것이 밟혔다 I stepped on something mushy in the dark.

물크러지다 〈과일이〉 spoil; be reduced to pulp; 〈궤양·종기가〉 ulcerate
▶야채가 삶아지자 물크러졌다 The vegetables were overcooked and soggy.

물큰(물큰) with a strong smell [stench]
▶그 약품 냄새가 물큰 난다 The medicine smells pungent [bad].
▶그곳은 생선 썩은 냄새가 물큰 났다 The place reeked of rotten fish.

물통 —桶 a (water) pail; a (wooden) bucket; 〈수조〉 a water tank; a cistern
▶그 소는 한 번에 물을 물통으로 한 통씩이나 마신다 The cow drinks a bucketful of water at a time.

물퍼붓듯 fluently; eloquently; with great fluency —물퍼붓듯하다 speak very fluently; speak glibly [volubly] ♦물퍼붓듯하는 말 an eloquent speech; a torrent of eloquence / 물퍼붓듯하는 욕설 a torrent of abuse

물표 物標 a (baggage) check; a tally; a tag
▶여기 당신이 맡긴 여행 가방의 물표가 있습니다 Here's a check for your suitcase.

물푸레나무 〔植〕 an ash
물품 物品 〈상품〉 an article; goods; things; wares; stuff; a commodity
♦물품의 종류 items of merchandise / 물품이 많다[적다] 〈수량〉 have a large [small] stock of goods; 〈종류〉 have a rich [limited] assortment of goods
▶저 가게에서는 각종 물품을 다 취급한다 That store carries things [articles] of all kinds.
▶나는 그것을 물품으로 지불하겠소 I'll pay for it in kind.

물품목록 物品目錄 a list of goods; a catalog(ue); 〈재고 조사의〉 an inventory ♦물품목록을 작성하다 itemize; make a list of goods
▶이것은 물품목록에 올라 있다 This article is on the list [is listed (on the catalog(ue))].

물품세 物品稅 a commodity tax; an excise tax ♦물품세를 부과하다 impose an excise tax (on everything)
■—법〔法〕 the Commodity Tax Law

물행주 〈식기용〉 (美) a wet dish towel; (英) a wet tea towel [cloth]; 〈식탁용〉 a wet dishcloth

물화 物貨 goods; merchandise; commodities
물활론 物活論 animism; hylozoism
■—자 an animist; a hylozoist

묽다 1 〈농도가〉 watery 〈stew〉; washy; thin 《coffee, porridge, paste》; sloppy 《food》
♦묽은 수프 thin soup / 묽은 우유[죽] watery [thin] milk [gruel] / 고깃국물을 묽게 하다 dilute the broth / 물을 타서 풀을 묽게 하다 thin (down) paste with water
▶수프가 너무 묽다 This soup is mere wash.
▶이 페인트는 좀 묽게 하는 게 좋다 You'd better thin this paint down.
2 〈사람이〉 weak; feeble; weak-spirited; fainthearted ♦묽은 사람 a softy

묽디묽다 〈액체가〉 very watery [thin]; very wishy-washy; 〈사람이〉 very weak; very feeble ♦묽디묽은 스튜 very watery stew

뭇¹ 〈큰 작살〉 a large harpoon [fish spear]; a gig
뭇² 〈묶음〉 a bundle; a bunch; a sheaf 《*pl.* sheaves》 ♦볏집 한 뭇 a sheaf of rice straw / 생선 두 뭇 twenty fish / 장작 두 뭇 two bundles of firewood
뭇³ 〈여러〉 many; all; numerous; all kinds [sorts] of; every; every sort [kind] of ♦뭇사내 all sorts [kinds] of men
뭇매 beating in a group [all at one time]

뭇매를 때리다 gang up on [against] sb and beat (him) up [to a pulp]; join in giving sb a drubbing [sound thrashing] / **뭇매를 맞다** get a drubbing; be under [subjected to] a pelting rain of (kicks and) blows
▶ 그들은 깡패한테 뭇매를 때렸다 They ganged up on the bully and gave him a good beating.

뭇발길 1 〈발길질〉 kicking in a group [from all sides] ♦ **뭇발길에 채다** get [be under, be subjected to] a pelting rain of kicks (by a gang) 2 〈공박〉 attacks from all quarters

뭇사람 people of all sorts and conditions; 〈여러 사람〉 the public; company; society
♦ **뭇사람 앞에서** in public; in the presence of others; in company / **뭇사람 앞에 나서다** appear in public; go into society / **뭇사람 앞에 나서지 않다** keep to oneself; keep one's own company
▶ 뭇사람이 거기 다 모여 있었다 All sorts of people were gathered there.
▶ 그는 뭇사람 앞에 나서면 당황한다 He is embarrassed in society.
▶ 뭇사람이 다 그녀를 칭찬한다 All the people praise her.

뭇시선 ―視線 everyone's eyes [gaze]; public gaze
♦ **등에 뭇시선이 쏠리는 것을 느끼다** feel public gaze [eyes] on one's back / **뭇시선을 모으다** attract public gaze / **뭇시선을 피하다** avoid everyone's eyes [gaze]
▶ 뭇시선이 그에게 집중되었다 Everyone's eyes were focused on him.

뭉개다 1 〈으스러뜨리다〉 crush; smash; squash; mash (potatoes)
♦ **밟아 뭉개다** smash [crush] sth by treading on; flatten sth under one's feet; trample sth underfoot / **모자를 깔고 뭉개다** sit on a hat (and mash it in) / **꽃을 구두 뒤축으로 뭉개다** squash the flower under one's heel
2 〈쩔쩔매다〉 do not know what to do with [how to deal with]; make a mess of; be confused (by); be bewildered; be embarrassed (by, at); be at a loss; be at one's wits' end
3 〈꾸물거리다〉 dally; linger; dawdle ((over)); idle about; dally away ((one's time))
♦ **이불 속에서 뭉개다** dally in bed / **뭉개고 앉아서 시간을 보내다** dally [putter] away one's time

뭉게구름 [氣] a cumulus

뭉게뭉게 in (thick) clouds; massively; thickly; densely
♦ **뭉게뭉게 피어오르는 김[증기]** thick vapors; bursts of white steam / **뭉게뭉게 피어오르는 연기** volumes [billows] of smoke / **여름에 뭉게뭉게 피어오르는 구름** massively rising summer clouds
▶ 구름이 뭉게뭉게 피어오른다 Thick clouds are gathering.
▶ 공장 굴뚝에서 연기가 뭉게뭉게 뿜어져 나왔다 Volumes of smoke poured from the chimneys of the factory.

뭉구리 1 〈까까머리〉 a close-cropped head; a shaven [tonsured] head 2 〈중〉 a Buddhist monk

뭉그러뜨리다 〈허물어뜨리다〉 demolish; destroy; pull down; 〈찌부러뜨리다〉 level (down)
♦ **돌담을 뭉그러뜨리다** tear [pull] down a stone wall / **벼랑[언덕]을 뭉그러뜨리다** level a cliff [hill] / **쌓아 놓은 과일을 뭉그러뜨리다** throw [knock] down piled-up fruits

뭉그러지다 〈부서지다〉 crumble; fall to pieces; 〈무너지다〉 collapse; break; give away; 〈파괴되다〉 be destroyed
♦ **비바람을 맞아서 뭉그러지다** collapse [fall down] as the result of exposure to wind and rain
▶ 화물 더미가 뭉그러졌다 The piles of cargo collapsed.

뭉그적거리다 linger; dawdle over ((one's breakfast)); dally away ((one's time)); dillydally; idle about
♦ **면회 시간이 지났는데도 뭉그적거리다** linger on past visiting hours / **모임이 끝났는데도 뭉그적거리다** dawdle after a meeting
▶ 다른 사람은 모두 갔는데도 그는 뭉그적거렸다 He lingered about after everyone else had left.
▶ 일을 꽤 뭉그적거리며 하는구나 You are dawdling [lingering] over your work.

뭉그적뭉그적 slowly; sluggishly; tardily; lazily; idly ♦ **뭉그적뭉그적 나아가다** proceed [go] at a snail's pace [gallop]; crawl; drag one's feet [heels]

뭉근하다 low but steady; simmering; slow
♦ **뭉근한 불** a low [slow] fire; a simmering fire / **뭉근한 불에 삶다** simmer (the meat); boil slowly; cook sth over a gentle heat

뭉긋이 gently; slightly; smoothly ♦ **뭉긋이 경사진** gently-sloping
▶ 그 탑은 왼쪽으로 뭉긋이 기울어져 있다 The tower inclines slightly to the left.

뭉긋하다 1 gently-sloping; easy; gentle
♦ **뭉긋한 고개** an easy [a gentle] slope
▶ 우리는 뭉긋한 언덕을 내려갔다 We went down a gentle slope.
▶ 이 마룻바닥은 뭉긋하다 This floor slants [slopes] a little.
2 〈휘우듬하다〉 slightly bent; gently curved
▶ 눈이 쌓여 나뭇가지가 뭉긋하게 휘어져 있다 The branches of the tree are slightly bending under the (weight of the) snow.

뭉기다 pull down; demolish; destroy

뭉떵뭉떵 lump after lump; chunk after chunk; in chunks; in big lumps
♦ **떡을 뭉떵뭉떵 자르다** cut a rice cake into big chunks / **돈을 뭉떵뭉떵 잘리다** lose great chunks of money repeatedly
▶ 그 신임 시장은 예산을 뭉떵뭉떵 삭감했다 The new mayor reduced [cut (down)] the budget drastically.

뭉뚝하다 stumpy; blunt; stubby ♦ **뭉뚝한 끝** a blunt point / **뭉뚝한 손가락** stubby fingers
▶ 연필이 뭉뚝하다 This pencil is blunt.
▶ 도래송곳 끝이 뭉뚝해졌다 The point of the gimlet is blunted [damaged].

뭉뚱그리다 〈대강 뭉쳐 싸다〉 wrap [pack, do] up (a parcel) in a slipshod way; bundle up

뭉실뭉실 plumply; fleshly
♦ 뭉실뭉실 살찐 돼지 a plump pig
─**뭉실뭉실하다** plump (like a dumpling); rotund; portly ♦ 뭉실뭉실한 뺨 full [plump] cheeks / 뭉실뭉실한 중년 남자 a portly middle-aged man / 뭉실뭉실한 팔뚝 a round arm
▶ 그는 뭉실뭉실하다 He has rolls of fat on him.

뭉치 1 〈덩이〉 a bundle; a roll; a lump; a ball
♦ 눈뭉치 a snowball / 솜뭉치 a wad of cotton / 실뭉치 a ball of string / 자필 원고 한 뭉치 a sheaf of autographs / 지폐 한 뭉치 a bundle [roll, wad] of bills; a roll of (paper) money / 신문 한 뭉치 a wad of newspaper
2 〈쇠고기의 뭉치사태살〉 round

뭉치다 1 〈단결하다〉 unite; stand [band, hold, hang] together; be leagued [banded] together
♦ 뭉쳐서 in a body; in union; in one united body / 굳게 뭉치다 have a strong solidarity; be strongly united / 뭉쳐서 …에 대항하다 be united against... / 뭉쳐서 일어서다 rise in unity 《against》/ 뭉쳐서 행동하다 act in a body
▶ 그들은 뭉쳐서 공동의 적에 대항했다 They united against their common enemy.
▶ 그 사건은 그들을 굳게 뭉치게 했다 The incident served to strengthen their solidarity.
▶ 뭉치면 살고 흩어지면 죽는다 United, we stand; divided, we fall.
2 〈덩이지다〉 lump; mass; conglomerate
♦ 풀이 뭉친다 Paste lumps [forms a mass].
▶ 구름이 서쪽에 뭉쳐 있었다 The clouds had massed in the west.
3 〈덩이짓다〉 lump; make a lump; mass; conglomerate; press together
♦ 눈을 뭉치다 make a snowball; press snow into a lump / 종이를 뭉치다 crumple paper into a ball / 진흙을 뭉치다 harden the clay into a mass
▶ 나는 편지를 둘둘 뭉쳐서 내던졌다 I crumpled the letter into a ball and threw it away.

뭉클하다 1 〈가슴이〉 be filled 《with emotion》; be choked 《with grief》; feel a lump in one's throat
▶ 그것은 가슴 뭉클한 이야기였다 It was a moving [touching] story.
▶ 그것은 가슴이 뭉클해지는 광경이었다 The sight gave me a twist in my heart.
2 〈먹은 음식이〉 be heavy; sit [lie] heavy 《on one's stomach》; remain undigested 《in one's stomach》; be not easily digested
♦ 뱃속이 뭉클하다 sit [lie] heavy on the stomach; remain undigested in the stomach

뭉키다 〈덩어리지다〉 lump; mass; conglomerate; 〈몰리다〉 gather together; crowd; cluster
♦ 눈이 뭉키어 단단해지다 snow lumps into a hard mass / 풀이 뭉키어 덩이가 되다 paste masses into a lump
▶ 사과가 한 가지에 뭉키어 달렸다 Apples have hung on a branch in clusters.
▶ 그렇게 뭉키어 오지 말고 한 사람씩 오시오 Come one by one instead of in a group.

뭉텅뭉텅 lump after lump ⇨ 뭉덩뭉떵
뭉텅이 a lump; a bundle; a package; a wad
♦ 헝겊[솜, 머리카락] 뭉텅이 a wad of cloth [cotton, hair]

뭉툭하다 stumpy ⇨ 뭉뚝하다

뭍 1 〈육지〉 land; 〈배에서 본〉 the shore
♦ 뭍에 닿다 come to [reach] land; 〖海〗 make (the) land / 뭍에 살다 live on land / 뭍으로 오르다 go ashore [on shore]
▶ 뭍이 시야에 들어왔다 We came in sight of land.
▶ 배가 뭍을 떠났다 The ship cleared the land.
▶ 그는 뭍에 오른 물고기 같다 He is like a fish out of water.
2 〈섬 사람들이 본 본토〉 the mainland; the country proper
■─바람 a land wind [breeze] ─사람 〈육지 생활자〉 a landlubber; a landsman; 〈본토인〉 mainlanders ─짐승 a land animal

뭍살이 ♦ 뭍살이의 terrestrial ■─동물 a land [terrestrial] animal ─생물 land [terrestrial] life ─식물 a land [terrestrial] plant

뭐 1 〈무엇〉 ▶ 뭐 맛있는 것 없니? Have you not anything nice to eat?
▶ 너 뭐 좀 먹어야지 Surely you have to eat something, don't you?
2 〈의문〉 what
▶ 뭐라구요? What? ⇌ I beg your pardon? ⇌ What did you say?
▶ 뭐하러 시내에 갔다 왔니? What have you been to town for?
3 〈무슨 이유로〉 why
▶ 뭐 그렇게 화낼 것 없잖아 You have no reason whatever to be so angry.
▶ 뭐 그렇게 할 필요 있을까? Why should I do it?
4 〈감탄사적으로〉 what!; why!; well
▶ 뭐, 벌써 자정 아냐 Why, it's midnight.
▶ 뭐, 상관없어 Oh, I don't care a bit!

뭐니뭐니해도 no matter what one says; all things taken together; after all
▶ 뭐니뭐니해도 그는 네 동생이다 After all, he is your brother.
▶ 뭐니뭐니해도 집만큼 좋은 곳은 없다 Whatever you may say, there's no place like home.

뭐라고 1 〈의문〉 what
♦ 뭐라고 할 수 없이 기묘한 표정 an unspeakably weird look / 남들이 뭐라고 하든 whatever others may say 《about, of》
▶ 뭐라고 사과의 말씀을 드려야 할지 모르겠습니다 I have no words to apologize to you enough.
▶ 뭐라고 위로를 드려야 할지 모르겠습니다 I don't know how to console you.
▶ 그것에 대해 아직은 내가 뭐라고 명확히 말할 수 없다 I can't say anything definite about it yet.
▶ 그것은 뭐라고 형용할 수 없이 아름다웠다 It was beautiful beyond description.
2 〈불확실〉 some(thing); any(thing)
♦ 그 뭐라고 하는 사람 Mr. So-and-so; Mr. What's-his-name; Mr. Thingummy / 뭐라고 하는 것 a whatchamacallit; a thingamajig

▶저 그 뭐라고 하는 것을 가져 오너라 Bring me that, uh, whatchamacallit.

뭐야 what ⇨ 무엇
▶이것은 도대체 뭐야? Whatever is this? ≠ What's all this?
▶다음은 또 뭐야? What next?

뭣하다 awkward ⇨ 무엇하다

뭣하면 if you (don't) like [wish, please, prefer]; if necessary; if (it is) convenient (for you)
▶뭣하면 올 필요 없다 You don't have to come if it's inconvenient.
▶뭣하면 내달에 지불해도 좋습니다 You can pay for it next month if you prefer [wish].
▶뭣하면 내일 다시 전화해 주십시오 Please call again tomorrow if necessary.

뭣하지만 ◆내가 이렇게 말하는 것은 뭣하지만 if I may be permitted to say so; it may be rude to say so, but...; excuse me for my frankness, but...
▶내 입으로 이렇게 말하는 것은 뭣하지만 내 아들은 참 착하다 My son is a very good boy, though I say it who shouldn't.
▶이런 말하기는 뭣하지만 너도 나이를 먹었구나 I hate to say this, but you have aged, haven't you?

뮌헨 〈독일의 도시〉 Munich ■—조약 the Munich Pact

뮤즈 〈시신(詩神)〉《one's》 Muse [the muse]

뮤지컬 a musical —드라마 a musical drama —쇼 a musical show —영화 a musical (film) —코미디 a musical comedy; a comic opera

뮤직 music ■—홀 a music hall

-므로 〈까닭에〉 as; because (of); on account of; owing to
▶비가 오기 시작했으므로 나는 외출하지 않았다 I didn't go out, because it began to rain.
▶그는 아버지의 재산을 물려받았으므로 지금 매우 부자다 Because [Since, As] he inherited his father's fortune, he is now very rich.
▶그는 너무 피곤했으므로 더 이상 걸을 수가 없었다 He was too tired to walk any further.

미¹ 美 beauty; the beautiful
◆자연의 미 the beauty of the natural scenery; natural beauty / 남성미 masculine [manly] beauty / 여성미 womanly [female, feminine] charms / 육체미 physical beauty / 진선미 truth, goodness and beauty / 미적 감각 a sense of beauty; an aesthetic [esθetik] sense

미² 美 〈미국〉 (the United States of) America

미- 未- un-; in-; not yet ◆미발표 작품 an unpublished work; a work not yet published

미 〔樂〕 mi

미가 米價 〈쌀값〉 the price of rice
◆미가를 동결하다 leave the price of rice at its current level; freeze the price of rice
▶농민들은 미가 인상을 요구했다 The farmers demanded the higher price of rice.
■—정책 the rice price policy —조절 control [regulation] of the rice market [price]

미가공 未加工 ◆미가공의 raw; crude; unprocessed; (diamonds) in the rough / 미가공의 직물 greige; gray goods

미가서 —書 〔聖〕 (The Book of) Micah

미각 味覺 the taste sense; the palate; the gustation
◆미각의 계절인 가을 autumn, the season of the pleasures of the table / 미각을 돋우는 음식 appetizing [tempting, inviting] food / 미각이 발달되어 있다 have a keen sense of taste; have a delicate palate / 미각을 돋우다 tempt the appetite; tickle one's palate; make one's mouth water / 미각을 만족시키다 please [suit] one's palate; be to one's taste
▶미각을 돋우는 냄새로군요 It is a tempting smell [aroma], isn't it?
▶그는 감기로 미각이 둔해졌다 His cold impaired his sense of taste.
■—기관 a gustatory organ —세포 a taste [gustatory] cell —신경 a gustatory nerve

미간 未刊 ◆미간의 unpublished; as-yet-unissued (numbers of the journal); not yet published

미간 眉間 〔解〕 a glabella (pl. -lae); the middle of the forehead
◆미간의 상처 a scar between the eyebrows / 미간을 찌푸리다 knit [gather] the brows; bend one's brows; frown
▶그는 싸워서 미간이 찢어졌다 He got a cut across the forehead in a fight.

미감아 未感兒 〈나병의〉 a child uninfected with leprosy [lepra]

미개 未開 1 〈야만의〉 ◆반미개의 semibarbarous; semicivilized —미개하다 〈원시적〉 primitive; uncivilized; benighted; savage; 〈야만의〉 barbaric; barbarous; wild
▶그 지역은 아직 미개한 채로 있다 The area is still undeveloped.
2 〈꽃 등이〉 —미개하다 be not in blossom; be unbloomed [unblossomed]
■—국 an uncivilized [a savage] country —사회 (a) primitive society —인 a barbarian; a savage; 〈종족〉 a savage [primitive] people [race] —지 a savage [barbaric] land; a backward [an uncivilized] region

미개간 未開墾 ◆미개간의 uncultivated; wild
■—지 uncultivated land; land in grass; wilds; virgin soil

미개발 未開發 ◆미개발의 undeveloped (region); wild (land); unexploited (district); untapped (resources)
■—국 an underdeveloped country; a backward country —지역 an undeveloped area

미개척 未開拓 ◆미개척의 〈개발되지 않은〉 undeveloped; untapped; 〈연구되지 않은〉 unexplored; 〈개간되지 않은〉 uncultivated; unreclaimed; unexploited; wild / 미개척 삼림 (a) virgin forest / 미개척 자원 untapped resources
▶이것은 미개척 연구 분야다 This is an unexplored field of research.
■—분야 an unexplored field —시장 a potential market —지 undeveloped [unreclaimed, waste] land; untapped territory; virgin [maiden] soil

미거하다 未擧— 〈생각이 없다〉 thoughtless; imprudent; indiscreet; 〈몽매하다〉 unenlightened; 〈아둔하다〉 stupid; unwise; silly ◆미거한 사람 an inexperienced [a thoughtless] person

▶ 미거하나마 전력을 다하겠습니다 Unwise as I am, I will do all I can.

미결 未決 pendency
◆미결의 〈미결정의〉 undecided; unsettled; 〈미해결의〉 pending; open; 〈판결이 내려지지 않은〉 unconvicted / 미결대로 be left unsettled; be in abeyance [the balance]
▶ 그것은 아직 미결이다 We haven't solved it yet. ⇌ It remains unsolved.
▶ 그 문제는 몇 년씩이나 미결 상태로 있다 The question has been left unsettled for years.
▶ 그는 미결로 10일 동안 구류를 살고 있다 He has been in detention for ten days pending trial.
■ ―구류 detention pending trial; unconvicted detention ―구류일수 the number of the days of unconvicted detention ―문제 a pending [a moot, an open] question; an unsettled problem ―사항 arrearage; matters yet to be settled ―서류 pending documents ―서류함 a pending tray ―수 an unconvicted [undertrial] prisoner; a prisoner under trial ―안 an undecided matter; a pending case

미결산 未決算 ◆미결산의 unsettled 《debt》; outstanding; unpaid ■―계산서 an unsettled bill ―계정 an unbalanced account

미결제 未決濟 ◆미결제의 unsettled 《debts》; outstanding 《accounts》; 〈미불의〉 unpaid
■―거래 an incomplete transaction

미경과 未經過 ◆미경과의 prepaid; prereceived
■―보험료 a prepaid [prereceived] premium; an unearned premium ―비용 prepaid expenses; expenses paid in advance ―이자 prepaid interest

미경토 未耕土 〔農〕 uncultivated soil

미경험 未經驗 inexperience ◆미경험의 inexperienced (in); unexperienced; new; green
▶ 그는 이 방면의 일에는 미경험이다 He is new to this job [inexperienced in this line of business].

미경험자 未經驗者 an inexperienced person; a novice; (口) a greenhorn; a green hand; a person new to the job
▶ 미경험자 환영 Welcome the inexperienced.

미곡 米穀 rice; 〈곡물〉 grain
■―도매상 a rice factor; (美) a rice commission merchant ―비축량 rice in stock; rice stocks ―상 a rice dealer [merchant] ―시장 the rice market ―연도 the rice (crop) year ―중매인 a rice broker

미골 尾骨 〔解〕 the coccyx [kǽksiks]

미공인 未公認 ◆미공인의 unauthorized; not yet officially recognized; unofficial ■―기록 an unofficial [a pending] record

미관 美觀 a fine [beautiful] sight; a fine [pretty, lovely] view; a charming [beautiful] spectacle
◆미관을 더하다 add to the beauty 《of》/ 미관을 해치다 spoil [injure] the beauty 《of》/ 거리의 미관을 해치다 spoil [mar] the appearance of the streets / 자연의 미관을 해치다 damage the beauties of nature
▶ 벽에 포스터를 붙여 놓으면 실내 미관을 해친다 Putting up a poster on the wall spoils [mars] the beauty of the room.
■―지구(地區) an aesthetic [esθétik] area

미관 微官 a petty [minor] official ■―말직 the lowest position 《of the Government》

미광 微光 a faint light; a glimmer ▶ 어둠 속에서 뭔가 미광을 발하는 것을 보았다 We saw something glimmering in the darkness.

미구 未久 ◆미구에 soon; shortly; before long; in the near future
▶ 미구에 좋은 소식이 올 것입니다 You will hear good news soon [shortly].
▶ 새 간선도로가 미구에 완성될 것이다 The new highway will be completed soon [in the near future].

미국 美國 〈미합중국〉 the United States (of America) (略 U.S., U.S.A.); America; (口) the States
◆미국의 American; U.S. / 미국산 밀 American grown wheat / 미국식 파티 an American-style party / 미국제의 완구 a toy made in the U.S.A.; an American-made toy
▶ 나는 미국에 가본 적이 없다 I've never been to America [the United States].
■―국기 the American flag; 〈속칭〉 the Star-Spangled Banner; 〈성조기〉 the Stars and Stripes ―군인 an American soldier; a GI ―령 American territory; an American possession ―말[어] the American language; American ―문학 American literature ―문화원 the U.S. [American] Cultural Center ―본토 the continental U.S. ―시민 an American citizen ―어법 an Americanism ―영어 American English ―의 소리 the Voice of America (略 V.O.A.) ―정부 the U.S. Government; (口) the White House ―중앙정보국 the Central Intelligence Agency (略 CIA; C.I.A.)

미국독립전쟁 美國獨立戰爭 〔史〕 the American Revolution

미국인 美國人 an American; (총칭) American people; the Americans; (俗) a Yankee; 〈전형적인〉 Uncle Sam ◆영국계 미국인 an Anglo-American; an Anglo 《pl. ~s》 / 미국인 기질 [정신] Americanism
▶ 그 사람은 미국인이다 He is (an) American. (⇒관사 없이 쓰는 것이 보통임)

미국화 美國化 Americanization ―미국화하다 Americanize

미군 美軍 the United States [U.S.] Armed Forces; the U.S. Army [Navy, Air Force]; American forces; 〈병사〉 an American soldier [sailor, airman]; a GI
■주한― the U.S. Forces (stationed) in Korea ―점령지역 the American-occupied area

미궁 迷宮 a labyrinth; a maze; mystery
◆미궁에 빠진 살인 사건 an unsolved murder case [mystery] / 〈사건 등이〉 미궁에 빠지다 become shrouded [be wrapped] in mystery; go unsolved; become [prove] impossible of solution
▶ 그 사건은 여전히 미궁에 빠져 있다 The case is still shrouded in mystery [unsolved]. ⇌ The authorities are still in the dark about the

미그 〈제트 전투기〉 a MIG; a Mig [MIG] jet fighter

미급하다 未及— be attainable; do not reach; do not amount (to); fall short (of); fall behind; be beyond *one's* tether
♦훨씬 미급하다 be far behind 《another》; be not nearly so good as 《another》
▶생각이 거기까지는 미급했다 I was not far-sighted enough to think of it.

미기 美妓 a beautiful *kisaeng*

미기 美技 〈훌륭한 연기〉 a beautiful [brilliant, neat] performance; a stunt; 〈스포츠의〉 《make》 a fine play

미기입 未記入 ♦미기입의 unentered 《item》
■—장부 a blank book

미기후 微氣候 〖氣〗 microclimate

미꾸라지, 미꾸리 〖魚〗 a loach; a mudfish
♦미꾸라지 같은 놈 a slippery [an eely] fellow
▶그 사람은 아주 미꾸라지 같은 인물이다 He is an elusive person.

미꾸라지 한 마리가 온 웅덩이를 흐려 놓는다 (속담) The rotten apple injures its neighbor. ⇌ One ill weed mars a whole pot of pottage.

미끄러뜨리다 let *sth* slip; slide; glide
▶그는 마루에 상자를 미끄러뜨려서 나에게 보냈다 He slid the box across the floor to me.

미끄러지다 1 〈표면에 접촉해서〉 slide; 〈매끄럽게〉 glide; 〈잘못해서〉 slip; 〈차 등이〉 skid; 〈수면 등을〉 skim
♦바나나 껍질에 미끄러지다 slip on a banana peel / 얼음에서 미끄러지다 slide on the ice / 비탈을 미끄러져 내려가다 slide down a slope / 미끄러져 넘어지다 slip and fall / 계단에서 미끄러져 떨어지다 slip [slither] down the stairs / 스키로 비탈을 미끄러져 내려가다 go [slide] down a slope on skis
▶차가 젖은 도로에서 미끄러졌다 The car skidded on the wet road.
▶그 여자애는 빙판길에서 미끄러져 넘어졌다 The girl slipped on the icy road and fell.
▶보트가 호수 위를 미끄러지듯 나아갔다 The boat skimmed over the lake.
2 〈낙제하다〉 fail (in) an examination
▶나는 대학 입학 시험에 미끄러졌다 I failed in my university entrance exam(ination).

미끄럼 a slide; sliding; a slip; slipping; 〖機〗 slippage
♦차바퀴의 미끄럼을 방지하다 prevent a wheel from slipping / 미끄럼을 타다 〈눈 위에서〉 slide over the snow 《in a sleigh》; 〈얼음판에서〉 slide [skate] on the ice; 〈미끄럼틀에서〉 slide [play] on a 《playground》 slide; take a slide
▶미끄럼 주의 (게시) Slippery.
■—마찰 (摩擦) a sliding friction —마찰력 sliding frictional force —물림식 변속기 a sliding mesh type transmission —방지 타이어 a nonskid [skid-proof] tire —저항기 a slide rheostat

미끄럼틀 〈놀이용의〉 a slide; 〈진수대 식의〉 a sliding way; a slipway; a launching platform
▶그녀의 아이들은 미끄럼틀에서 놀고 있다 Her children are playing on a slide.

미끄럽다 slippery; 〈미끈미끈하다〉 slithery; greasy; 〈반드럽다〉 (feel) smooth; slick; sleek 《skin, paper》
♦미끄러운 길 a slippery road [hallway] / 몹시 미끄럽다 be as slippery as an eel
▶미끄러우니 조심하시오 Watch your steps so as not to slip.
▶비가 와서 길이 미끄러웠다 The path was slippery with the rain.

미끈거리다 be slimy; be slippery; 〈기름으로〉 be greasy; 〈반들거리다〉 feel smooth ♦미끈거리는 액체[물고기] slimy liquid [fish]
▶기름 때문에 손이 미끈거린다 My hands are greasy with oil.
▶무언가 미끈거리는 것이 발에 닿았다 Something slimy touched my feet.

미끈미끈하다 slimy; greasy; oily; slippery; slick
▶연못 바닥이 미끈미끈하다 The bottom of the pond is slimy.
▶지면이 이끼 때문에 미끈미끈했다 The ground was slippery with moss.

미끈하다 1 〈사물이〉 smooth; streamlined; sleek; slick ♦미끈한 자동차 a streamlined car / 미끈하고 번쩍번쩍하는 스포츠카 a sleek, shiny sports-car
2 〈사람이〉 sleek; smart 《figure》; 〈옷맵시가〉 neat; gay; flashy; well-dressed
♦미끈한 얼굴 a good-looking [sleek] face / 미끈한 여자 a tall beautiful girl / 미끈하게 생기다 be good-looking [handsome]; have nice features / 미끈하게 차리다 be flashily dressed; be well-dressed

미끼 1 〈낚시의〉 a bait
♦산 미끼 a live bait / 인공 미끼 〈제물낚시〉 a fly / 낚싯바늘에 미끼를 꿰다 bait [put a bait on] an angling hook; bait up / 낚시의 미끼를 떼이다 lose the bait to the fish / 미끼를 물다 take a bait / 작은 새우를 미끼로 쓰다 use shrimps for bait
▶미끼 없이는 고기를 낚을 수 없다 Without bait no fish can be caught.
2 〈유혹〉 a bait; a decoy; a lure; an enticement; an allurement
♦미끼에 걸려들다 be lured; get decoyed / 미끼로 쓰다 〈사람을〉 use [employ] *sb* as a decoy / 경품을 미끼로 물건을 사게 하다[손님을 끌다] use presents to tempt *sb* to buy a thing [attract customers by offering a present] / 돈을 미끼로 여자를 낚다 decoy [lure] a woman with money / 여자를 미끼로 돈을 옭아내다 get money from *sb* using a woman as a bait
▶그는 돈을 미끼로 그녀를 유혹하려 했다 He tried to entice her by offering her money. ⇌ He tempted her with money.
■—통 a feeder

미나리 〖植〗 a dropwort ■—꽝 a dropwort field

미나리아재비 〖植〗 a buttercup; a goldcup

미나마타병 —病 Minamata disease; a disease caused by mercury poisoning

미남 美男 a handsome man ⇨ 미남자(美男子)

미남자 美男子 a handsome [good-looking] man; an Adonis; a beau 《pl. ~s, ·x》

미납 未納 《make》 default in payment; non-payment ◆ 미납의 unpaid; outstanding / 수업료 미납 학생 students who have not yet paid their tuition fees
▶ 그는 수업료가 미납이다 He is in arrears with his tuition fees. ⇌ He has not yet paid his tuition fees.
▶ 그는 세금 미납으로 처벌을 받았다 He was penalized for defaulting on his taxes.
—**미납하다** leave *sth* unpaid; be in arrears
▶ 그는 세금을 미납했다 He has not yet paid his taxes.
■ —세 unpaid taxes; arrears of taxes —액[금] the amount in arrears; arrearages —자 a person in arrears; a 《tax》defaulter

미네랄 〈광물〉 a mineral ■ —워터 mineral water; 《英》 minerals

미네소타 〈미국 중북부의 주〉 Minnesota (略 Minn.) ■ —사람 a Minnesotan

미녀 美女 a beauty; a belle; a good-looking [pretty] girl; a beautiful [an attractive] woman; 《口》 a peach [bombshell]
◆ 절세의 미녀 a woman of peerless [matchless] beauty; the fairest of the fair
▶ 그 여자는 대단한 미녀다 She is a great [stunning] beauty.

미노스 〔그神〕 Minos
미노타우로스 〔그神〕 the Minotaur
미농지 美濃紙 (a kind of) rice paper
미뉴에트 〔樂〕 a minuet
미늘 〈낚시 등의〉 a barb (of a fishhook); 〈갑옷의〉 metal scales (on a coat of armor)
■ —창 a halberd; a forked spear

미니 a mini ■ —스커트 a miniskirt; a mini —카 a minicar —카메라 a miniature camera; a minicamera

미니멀 아트 〔美術〕 minimal art
미니멈 〈최소한〉 minimum
미니바이크 a minibike; a moped; a mobilette
미니어처 〈소형 모형〉 a miniature ◆ 서브 미니어처 관 a subminiature tube ■ —세트 a miniature set —(진공)관 a miniature tube

미다¹ 〈털이 빠지다〉 become [go, grow] bald
◆ 정수리가 민 with a bald patch on the crown of *one's* head
▶ 그는 이마가 꽤 미었다 He has a receding forehead.
▶ 나는 앞머리[뒷머리]가 미기 시작한다 I am going bald in front [at the back].

미다² 〈구멍을 내다〉 tear [make] a hole in 《paper》; get torn; rip (open)
◆ 장지를 미다 tear a hole in a paper screen / 잘못해서 천을 미다 tear a hole in the cloth by mistake

미다³ 〈따돌리다〉 keep clear of *sb*; avoid [shun] *sb's* company; treat with scorn; give *sb* the cold shoulder

미닫이 a sliding door [screen] ■ —창 a sliding window

미달 未達 insufficiency; shortage; deficiency
◆ 연령 미달의 underage / 체중 미달인 아기 an underweight baby / 정족수 미달로 for want [in the absence] of a quorum
▶ 아직 정원 미달이다 The number limit has not been reached.
▶ 투표 결과 과반수에서 10표 미달이다 The vote lacks ten of being a majority.
—**미달하다** be short 《of》; be deficient 《in》; be under; be less than
◆ 정족수에 미달하다 lack [want] a quorum
▶ 출석자가 정족수에 미달했다 There were not enough people present for a quorum. ⇌ The number of those present did not reach a quorum.

미담 美談 a moving [beautiful] story; an impressive tale; an admirable story; a praiseworthy [laudable, fine, commendable] anecdote [episode]
▶ 그가 미담의 주인공이었다 He was the hero of the moving tale.
▶ 그 이야기는 지금까지 미담으로 전해지고 있다 The story is told down to this day with undiminished admiration.

미답 未踏 ◆ 미답의 untrodden; unexplored / 전인 미답의 분야를 연구하다 study an unexplored field
▶ 탐험대는 전인 미답의 밀림 속으로 헤치고 들어갔다 The explorers forced their way into the virgin forest.

미덕 美德 a virtue; a noble attribute; 〈선행〉 a good deed
◆ 미덕과 악덕 virtue and vice / 미덕을 쌓다 accumulate virtues / 겸양의 미덕을 발휘하다 display [show] the virtue of humility
▶ 정직[친절]은 미덕이다 Honesty [Kindness] is a virtue.

미덥다 reliable; trustworthy; 〈장래가 유망하다〉 promising; hopeful
◆ 미더운 사람 a reliable person / 장래가 미더운 사람 a promising person, a person (full) of promise / 미덥지 못한 unreliable; undependable; untrustworthy; unpromising
▶ 그 사람은 미더워 보인다 He seems (to be) trustworthy.
▶ 미더운 아드님을 두셨군요 You have a promising son.

미동 美童 1 〈미소년〉 a handsome [good-looking] boy 2 〈남색 상대〉 a catamite

미동 微動 a slight movement; a stir; a quiver
◆ 미동도 않다 do not budge [stir, move] an inch; stand as firm as a rock
▶ 아무리 밀어도 문은 미동도 하지 않았다 No matter how hard I pushed, the door would not move an inch [budge].
▶ 그의 표정은 미동도 없었다 His expression remained (quite) unchanged.
■ —계(計) a tromometer —기압계 a statoscope —측정기 a microdetector

미두 米豆 bucket-shop operations in rice; speculation in rice ◆ 미두에 손을 대다 speculate in rice
▶ 그는 미두로 많은 돈을 벌었다 He made a lot of money speculating in rice.
■ —장(場) the rice exchange

미드필드 〔競〕 a midfield
미들급 —級 〈체급 경기의〉 the middleweight

(division) ♦미들급의 middleweight 《boxer》 ■—선수 a middleweight —챔피언 a middle-weight champion

미등 尾燈 〈자동차의〉 a taillight; a tail lamp; a rear light

미등 微騰 a fractional advance —미등하다 inch up

미디 〈미니와 맥시의 중간〉 a midi; a midiskirt

미라 〈〈포〉 mirra〉 a mummy ♦미라로 만들다 mummify; embalm

미락 徵落 a fractional [marginal] decline ▶주가가 미락 중이다 Stock prices are slipping [eroding].

미란 糜爛 〈썩어 문드러짐〉 decomposition; 〈진무름〉 fester; a sore; 〈궤양〉 ulceration; erosion —미란하다 be decomposed; ulcerate; fester ■—성 가스 irritating poisonous gas; mustard gas; lewisite

미래 未來 **1** 〈장래〉 (the) future; time [days] to come
♦미래의 future; coming; prospective / 미래의 남편[아내] one's future husband [wife] / 미래의 스타 a future star / 미래가 있는 promising; full of promise / 미래의 계획을 세우다 form a plan for one's future / 미래를 예측하다 foretell [predict] the future / 미래에 살다 live in the future
▶그는 미래가 있는 젊은이다 He is a promising young man.
▶이 나라의 미래는 자네들의 양 어깨에 달려 있네 The future of this country rests on your shoulders.
▶한국의 미래를 어떻게 생각하십니까? What do you think the future of Korea will be?
▶우리는 미래에 대해 희망을 가져야 한다 We should keep hope for the future.
2 〈내세〉 (the) afterlife; the future life [existence]; the next [other] world; the world to come
3 〔文法〕 the future tense
■—상(像) an image of the future —완료(시제) the future perfect tense —의 man of the future world —파 futurism; 〈사람〉 a futurist —학 futurism; futurology

미량 徵量 a very small amount [quantity] 《of》; extremely small quantities
▶미량의 독물이 검출되었다 A very small amount [A trace] of poison was detected.
■—분석 〔化〕 microanalysis —영양소 micronutrient —원소 〔動·植〕 a trace element; a microelement —천칭[저울] a microbalance —측정기 a microdetector —화학 microchemistry

미레자 a T square
미레질 〈대패질〉 reverse [backhand] planing
미려하다 美麗 pretty; beautiful; fine; lovely; graceful; elegant
미력 徵力 〈능력〉 small [poor] ability; the little one can do; 〈자력(資力)〉 slender means; 〈세력〉 little influence; 〈노력〉 one's pygmy effort
♦미력이나마 in spite of one's poor ability / 미력을 다하다 do one's bit; do what (the little) one can; contribute one's mite 《to》

▶미력이나마 도와 드리겠습니다 I'll do what little I can to help you.
—미력하다 helpless; uninfluential

미련 stupidity; imbecility; silliness; asininity —미련하다[스럽다] stupid (as an owl); imbecile; thickheaded; silly; soft-[dull-]witted
▶그는 미련하기가 곰 같다 He is stupid as an owl.

미련 未練 lingering attachment [affection]; reluctance to give 《it》 up; 〈후회〉 regret
♦미련이 〈남아〉 있다 be still attached 《to》; have a lingering regret 《for the past》; have a lingering affection [love] 《for》 / 미련이 없다 have nothing to look back on with regret
▶그는 여전히 그 여자에게 미련이 있었다 He was still attached to the woman. ⇒ Still he couldn't give her up.
▶이젠 서울에는 미련이 없다 I am no longer interested in Seoul.
▶미련이 많이 있었지만 그 제안을 거절했다 I turned down the offer with much regret.
▶그녀는 아직도 무대에 미련이 있다 Her heart is still on the stage.
▶지금 집필을 그만두기에는 미련이 남는다 I feel reluctant to give up writing now.
▶그는 미련을 남기고 고향을 떠났다 He left his hometown with lingering regrets.

미련쟁이 a senseless fellow ⇨ 미련퉁이
미련퉁이 a senseless fellow; a soft-[dull-]witted person; a dullard; a stupid; an ass; a slow-coach; a blockhead

미로 迷路 a maze; a labyrinth
♦미로같은 labyrinthine; labyrinthian / 미로같은 좁은 거리 a labyrinth [maze] of narrow streets; labyrinthine streets / 미로를 빠져나가다 go through a labyrinth; thread a maze / 미로에 빠지다 be lost in a maze; be at a loss
■—학습 〔心〕 maze learning

미로 〈스페인의 화가〉 Miro, Joan (1893-1983)
미뢰 味蕾 〔解〕 a taste [gustatory] bud [bulb]
미료 未了 ♦미료의 unfinished; unfulfilled
미루나무 〔植〕 a popular

미루다 **1** 〈연기하다〉 adjourn; put off; defer; 〈기한을 연장하다〉 prolong; extend; protract; 〈지연시키다〉 delay; hold off
♦기한을 미루다 extend the term 《from... to...》 / 결정[판단]을 미루다 stay [suspend] judgment 《till》 / 사흘 〈뒤로〉 미루다 shift three days back; defer (the date) by three days / 하루하루 미루다 put off from day to day / 출발을 월요일까지 [1주일간] 미루다 postpone [put off] one's departure till Monday [for a week]
▶그것은 뒤로 미루고 이 문제를 먼저 토의하자 Let us discuss this matter first, leaving that till later on.
▶시합은 비 때문에 미루어졌다 The game was put off [postponed] because of (the) rain.
▶나는 일을 너무 미루어 놓았다 I have too much work left unfinished.
▶오늘 할 수 있는 일을 내일로 미루지 마라 Never put off till tomorrow what you can do today.
2 〈전가하다〉 lay [throw] 《the blame》 on sb;

shift [shuffle off] 《the responsibility on sb's shoulders》; impute [ascribe] 《the failure》 to sb
◆일을 남에게 미루다 shift one's work on 《another》; thrust [force] a task on sb / 책임을 남에게 미루다 shift [shuffle] the responsibility 《for sth》 on to sb
▶ 그녀는 그 일을 내게 미루었다 She thrust the work on me.
▶ 남에게 책임을 미루지 마라 Don't shift responsibility to someone else.
3 〈추측하다〉 infer [deduce, gather] 《from》; judge 《from, by》; 〈억측하다〉 guess; surmise; conjecture; suppose
◆그의 말로 미루어 (보면) from what he says; I gather from what he says; judging from his statement
▶ 여러 가지 정황으로 미루어 보건대 그는 사임하지 않을 수 없을 것 같다 Considering the circumstances, I assume he'll have to resign.
▶ 결과는 미루어 짐작할 수 있다 The outcome can easily be guessed.
▶ 나머지는 미루어 알 수 있다 From this one may judge the rest. ⇒ The rest you can easily imagine.

미루적거리다 delay; prolong; draw [drag] out ◆일을 미루적거리다 delay one's work / 미루적거리다가 기회를 놓치다 dally away one's opportunity

미류나무 美柳— a popular ⇨ 미루나무

미륵(보살) 彌勒(菩薩) Maitreya (-bodhisattva); 〈돌부처〉 a stone image of Buddha; a stone Buddhist image

미리 beforehand; in advance; previously; ahead of time; in anticipation
◆미리 손을 쓰다 make early preparations / 미리 계획을 세우다 plan ahead / 미리 써두다 write in advance / 미리 알려주다 let sb know beforehand / 미리 준비하다 have sth ready beforehand; make preparations in advance / 미리 주의를 주다 give warning / 미리 통지하다 give previous notice
▶ 늦을 것 같으면 미리 전화로 연락해 주시오 Call ahead if you're delayed.
▶ 모든 일이 미리 타협된 방향에 따라 진행되었다 Everything proceeded by a preconcerted arrangement.
▶ 그걸 내가 미리 알았어야 하는 건데 I should have known it beforehand.

미립자 微粒子 a minute [tiny] particle; a fine grain; 〔物〕 a corpuscle [kɔ́ːrpʌsl]
■ —설 the corpuscular theory of light —전류 a corpuscular current —필름 a fine-grained film —현상 a corpuscular phenomenon

미립체 微粒體 〔生〕〈세포 내의〉 a microsome

미만 未滿 ◆미만의 below; under; less than / 3세 미만의 소아 children under three (years of age)
▶ 여기서는 2세 미만의 아이는 받지 않습니다 Here we do not accept children under two years of age.
▶ 18세 미만은 입장 사절 No one under eighteen is [will be] admitted.

미만 彌滿 pervasion; permeation; diffusion
—미만하다 pervade; permeate; prevail; spread (out); extend all around
▶ 당시는 반전 사상이 전국에 미만해 있었다 The antiwar sentiment pervaded the whole country in those days.

미망 迷妄 an illusion; a delusion; a fallacy
◆미망을 깨우치다 dispel [shatter] an illusion; disillusion sb / 미망에서 깨어나다 be disillusioned; come [be brought] to one's senses; awake [wake up] from a delusion [an illusion]
▶ 그것은 순전히 미망이었다 That was all a delusion [an illusion].
▶ 그를 미망에서 깨어나게 해야겠다 I'll disillusion him. ⇒ I'll bring him to his senses.

미망인 未亡人 a widow (↔ widower); a widowed woman; 〈귀족의〉 a dowager
◆김선생의 미망인 the wife of the late Mr. Kim; the widowed wife of Mr. Kim
▶ 그녀는 미망인이 되었다 She lost her husband.
■ 전쟁— a war widow; a war-bereaved wife

미명 未明 early dawn; the gray of the morning ◆미명에 before dawn [daylight, daybreak]; before it is light; in the early dawn; in the gray of the morning
▶ 그 배는 15일 미명에 인천에서 샌프란시스코를 향해 출항했다 The ship sailed [set sail] from Inch'ŏn for San Francisco before dawn [daybreak] on the 15th.

미명 美名 a good [fair] name
◆ …의 미명 아래 in the name of…; under the name of…; under the cloak [veil] of
▶ 애국심이라는 미명 아래 온갖 살인이 자행되었다 Various murders have been committed under cover [the mask] of patriotism.
▶ 공익이라는 미명 아래 그들의 인권은 유린되고 있다 Under the name of public benefit, their human rights are trampled.

미모 美貌 a beautiful [fair, handsome] face; good [attractive] looks; beauty; pretty features; personal beauty
◆미모의 good-looking; beautiful; pretty; handsome; comely / 미모를 자랑하다 boast of one's good looks
▶ 그녀는 보기 드문 미모의 여인이다 She is a woman of rare beauty.
▶ 그는 그녀의 미모에 사로잡혔다 He was attracted [captivated, fascinated] by her beauty.

미모사 〔植〕〈함수초〉 a mimosa

미목 眉目 looks; features; a face
◆미목이 수려한 청년 a handsome youth [young man] / 미목이 수려하다 have a handsome face [cleancut features]

미몽 迷夢 an illusion; a delusion; a fallacy
◆미몽에서 깨어나다 be disillusioned; come to oneself [one's senses] / 미몽에서 깨어나게 하다 dispel sb's illusions; bring sb to his senses; open sb's eyes
▶ 그 정치가는 대중의 미몽을 깨우쳐 주었다 The statesman disillusioned the common people.

미묘 微妙 subtlety; delicacy; nicety
—미묘하다 subtle; delicate; nice; fine

미묘한 문제 a tender [delicate, ticklish] subject / **미묘한 뜻의 차이** delicate [nice] shades of meaning
▶나는 아주 미묘한 처지에 있다 I'm in a delicate [an awkward] position [situation].
▶그들의 의견에는 미묘한 차이가 있다 There is a subtle difference between their opinions.
▶국제 정세가 미묘해졌다 The world situation has become delicate.

미문 美文 flowery language; a literary composition full of flowery rhetoric; elegant prose; fine writing ━체 a flowery [an ornate] style; a florid prose style ━학 polite literature [letters]; (프) belles lettres

미물 微物 a lower animal; a minute form of life; 〈미생물〉 a microorganism; microbe; 〈하찮은 것〉 a trifle ━학 micrology

미미 美味 deliciousness; relish; a good flavor; 〈진미〉 a delicacy; a dainty; a rich diet; epicurean dishes ◆미미의 tasty; sweet; dainty; delicious; palatable; pleasing to the palate

미미하다 微微 slight; small; little; tiny; petty; trifling; insignificant
◆미미한 문제 a matter of small importance / 미미한 수입 a meager income / 미미한 증가[감소] an immaterial increase [decrease]
▶그런 사건은 그에게는 미미한 일로 보였다 Such an event seemed insignificant [of little importance] to him.
▶손해는 미미했다 We've had only a small loss.

미발견 未發見 ◆미발견의 (as yet) undiscovered; unexplored

미발달 未發達 ◆미발달의 not yet developed; ill-developed; undeveloped; 〈발달이 아직 불충분한〉 underdeveloped; of [at] an early stage of development / 미발달 근육 underdeveloped muscles / 미발달 문화 an undeveloped civilization

미발표 未發表 ◆미발표의 unpublished; not yet made public / 미발표 작품 an unpublished work ▶응모작은 미발표 작품에 한함 Works already published elsewhere are not accepted.

미발행 未發行 ◆미발행의 not yet issued; unissued 《stocks》; unpublished

미복 微服 disguise in dress ◆미복으로 in disguise; incognito / 미복 잠행하다 go [travel] incognito [in disguise]; make a secret visit (to); visit (a place) incognito

미봉 彌縫 patching up; temporizing; timeserving ━미봉하다 patch things up for the moment; temporize; make (a) shift

미봉책 彌縫策 a makeshift; a temporary [timeserving] remedy; temporizing measures; a stopgap measure [policy]
◆미봉책을 쓰다 adopt a stopgap measure; resort to a temporary expedient
▶정부는 미봉책으로 이 난국을 벗어나려 하고 있다 The Government is determined to tide over the present critical situation by taking a temporizing measure [by resorting to a makeshift].

미부 尾部 the tail (section)

미분 微分 〔數〕 differential; differentiation ━미분하다 differentiate
■━계수(係數) a differential coefficient [quotient] ━방정식 a differential equation ━적분학 differential and integral calculus ━학 differential calculus ━함수 a differential function

미분음 微分音 〔樂〕 a microtone

미분자 微分子 an atom; a molecule; a particle; a corpuscle

미불 未拂 nonpayment; 〈체납〉 default; arrears; arrearage
◆미불의 unsettled; unpaid; outstanding / 아직 미불인 채이다 be still unpaid / 미불로 남아 있다 remain unsettled [unpaid, outstanding]
▶노동자들은 미불 임금에 대하여 불평하고 있다 The workers are complaining of unpaid wages.
▶그 청구서는 아직 미불이다 The bill hasn't been paid [settled] yet.
■━계정 an outstanding [unpaid] account; 〈지급할〉 an account payable; 〈받을〉 an account receivable ━금 an account not yet paid; arrears; arrearages ━배당금 accumulated dividends ━봉급 back pay [salary]; pay [salary] in arrears ━액 an unpaid [outstanding] amount; (the amount in) arrears ━이자 interest accrued [in arrears]; accrued [outstanding] interest (payable) ━잔고 an outstanding balance

미불 美弗 the U.S. dollar ⇨ 미화(美貨)

미불입 未拂入 ◆미불입의 unpaid; outstanding; unsettled; not yet paid
■━주[자본금] unpaid stocks [capital]

미비 未備 defectiveness; imperfection; insufficiency; inadequacy; 〈미비점〉 a fault; a defect; an omission; an imperfection; a flaw; 〈법률 등의〉 a loophole; 〈부족〉 deficiency; lack
◆하수도 시설의 미비 lack of an adequate sewage system
▶그는 법의 미비를 악용하여 큰 부자가 되었다 He abused legal loopholes and became very rich.
━미비하다 defective; faulty; deficient; imperfect; incomplete
▶서류가 미비하여 각하되었다 The papers were incomplete and were rejected.
▶미비한 점이 있으면 용서하십시오 Please forgive any oversight on our part.

미쁘다 〈믿음직하다〉 reliable; trustworthy; dependable; sincere; faithful

미사 美辭 flowery [pretty] words; flowery language; rhetorical flourishes [expressions]
◆미사여구가 많은 연설 a speech full of flourishes; a flowery speech / 미사여구를 늘어놓다 use all sorts of flowery words

미사 〔가톨릭〕 (a) Mass 《▶ mass로도 씀. 우리말 「미사」는 라틴어 missa에서 유래》
◆미사를 올리다 read [say] mass / 미사에 나가다 attend [go to] mass
■━장엄— Solemn Mass 진혼— a requiem mass 추도— a mass for the dead ━곡 a mass

미사일 a missile
◆미사일을 발사하다[쏘아올리다] fire [launch a missile

■공대지(空對地)— an air-to-surface missile (略 ASM) 다핵탄두— a multiple independently targeted reentry vehicle (略 MIRV) 대공— an antiaircraft missile 대륙간— an intercontinental missile 대전차— an antitank missile 순항— a cruise missile 요격— an interceptor missile 유도— a guided missile (略 GM) 장[단]거리— a long [short] range missile 전략— a strategic missile (略 SM) 전술— a tactical missile: 전술 미사일부대 a tactical missile forces 지대공— a surface-to-air missile 핵— a nuclear missile ■—경쟁 a missile race —기지 a missile (launching) base [site, station] —발사대 a missile launching ramp [pad] —발사장치 a missile launcher —실험 a test-firing of a missile

미삼 尾蔘 rootlets [root hairs] of ginseng
미상 未詳 ♦미상의 unknown; unidentified / 작자미상의 anonymous / 원인미상의 unaccounted-for; (a fire) of an unknown origin / 신원미상의 시체 an unidentified corpse
▶그 사고로 인한 부상자들의 신원은 미상이다 Those injured in the accident have not yet been identified.
미상불 未嘗不 〈아닌게아니라〉as a matter of fact; really; indeed
▶그는 괴짜라더니 미상불 그렇구나 He is said to be eccentric and he really is.
미상환 未償還 unpaid; unsettled; outstanding / 미상환금 unpaid loans
미색 米色 〈쌀 빛깔〉pale yellow
미색 美色 〈빛깔〉a beautiful color; 〈미모〉good looks; beauty; 〈미인〉a beautiful woman
♦미색을 자랑하다 boast of *one's* beauty / 미색에 빠지다 be captured by a woman's beauty; fall a victim to the charms of a woman
미색류 尾索類 〔生〕Urochorda; Tunicata
미생물 微生物 a microbe; a microorganism
♦미생물의 microbic; microbial ■—분해성 biodegradability —학 microbiology: 미생물학자 a microbiologist —화석 〔地質〕fossils of microbe
미성 美聲 a sweet [beautiful] voice
미성년 未成年 a minority (▶법적으로는 (美) 21살, (英) 18살 미만); nonage ♦미성년의 minor; underage
▶미성년자의 음주는 금지되어 있다 Minors are forbidden to drink alcohol.
▶그는 아직 미성년자다 He is still a minor [in his minority]. ≒ He is still underage. ≒ He is not yet of age.
■—노동 child labor —범죄 juvenile delinquency —범죄자 a juvenile delinquent —자 a minor
미성숙 未成熟 immaturity; unripeness
♦미성숙의 immature; unripe
■—재(材) immature wood —토(土) 〔地質〕unmatured soil
미성품 未成品 an unfinished product
미세 微細 minuteness; fineness —미세하다 minute; detailed; fine
♦미세한 사항 the minor details / 미세한 점까지 down to the minute details / 미세하게 minutely; in full detail
■—구조 〔物〕fine structure —혈관 microvessel

미세기 a horizontally sliding door [window]
미세스 Mrs. 《*pl.* Mrs, Mesdames》⇨ 미시즈
미션스쿨 a missionary [mission] school
미소 微소 minuteness
—미소하다 minute; microscopic
▶인간은 우주에서 미소한 존재에 지나지 않는다 Man is but an insignificant being in the universe.
■—돌기 〔生〕microvilli —식물 a microphyte —전류 〔電〕minute current —체 〔生〕a microcyte
미소 微少 —미소하다 very small in amount
♦미소한 양 a very small [slight] amount; extremely small quantities
▶피살자의 위에서 미소한 독물이 검출되었다 A trace of a poisonous substance was detected in the victim's stomach.
미소 微笑 a smile ♦미소띤 얼굴 a smiling face; a face beaming with smiles / 미소를 띠고 with a smile; smilingly / 입가에 미소를 띠고 with a smile on *one's* lips
—미소하다 〈미소짓다〉smile
▶그 여자는 상냥하게 미소했다 She smiled tenderly.
▶그는 미소하며 사의를 표했다 He smiled and said, "Thank you."
▶그녀는 천사처럼 미소했다 She smiled an angelic smile.
▶그는 미소하며 찬성했다 He smiled approval.
▶스튜어디스가 미소하며 말을 걸어왔다 A stewardess spoke to me with a smile.
미소년 美少年 a handsome [good-looking] boy [young man, youth]
미속 美俗 a good custom ⇨ 미풍(美風)
미송 美松 an Oregon [a Douglas] fir [pine]
미수 未收 uncollected; outstanding; receivable
■—금 an uncollected [outstanding] sum —금계정 accounts receivable —수익 uncollected [accrued] revenue —요금 an outstanding fee
미수 未遂 〔法〕attempt ♦미수의 attempted; unconsummated / 미수로 끝난 쿠데타 an abortive coup d'état
▶그녀는 자살하려 했으나 미수에 그쳤다 She attempted suicide but survived.
■—방화 attempted arson 살인— attempted murder; murder attempt: 그는 살인미수로 체포되었다 He was arrested on charge of attempted murder. ■—범 a would-be criminal —죄 an attempted [uncommitted, unconsummated] offense [crime]; an attempt to commit a crime
미수 米壽 〈여든여덟 살〉eighty-eight years of age
▶그들은 부친의 미수 잔치를 열었다 They celebrated their father's eighty-eighth birthday.
미숙 未熟 immaturity; inexperience —미숙하다 〈익지 않다〉unripe; immature; green; 〈서투르다〉unskilled; inexperienced

▶그는 이 일에 아직 미숙하다 He is still green in this job.
▶그는 운전이 미숙하다 He is an inexperienced driver. ⇒ He is a poor driver. ⇒ He is poor at driving.
■—아 a premature baby: 아기는 미숙아로 태어났다 The baby was born prematurely. —자 an inexperienced person; a greenhorn

미숙련 未熟練 unskillfulness; inexpertness
♦미숙련의 unskillful; inexperienced
—공 an unskilled worker [laborer]

미술 美術 art (▶한 분야를 말할 때는 an art); the fine arts (▶이상 모두 회화·조각·건축 등을 말함. art는 음악·문학·연극·무용 등을 포함하는 「예술」의 뜻으로도 씀)
♦미술의 artistic / 미술적인 artistic(al) / 미술적으로 artistically / 미술을 감상하다 appreciate art / 미술에 흥미가 있다 be interested in art [the fine arts]
▶미술은 선택 과목이다 Art is an elective subject.
▶나의 취미는 미술 감상이다 My hobby is viewing works of art.
■ 공업[상업]— industrial [commercial] art 근대— modern art 동양[서양]— Oriental [Western] art: 대학에서 동양[서양] 미술을 전공하다 study the Oriental [Western] art at college 응용— applied art 조형[장식]— plastic [decorative] art ■—가 an artist —감독 an art director —감정가 a connoisseur of art —공예품 industrial art works —관 an art gallery [museum]: 근대미술관 a museum of modern art —상 an art dealer —전(시회) an art exhibition: 서양미술 전시회 an exhibition of Western art —전공학생 an art student; a student majoring in art —학교 an art school

미술품 美術品 a work of art; an art object; (총칭) (fine) art
♦동양 미술품 objects of Oriental art
■—애호가 a curioso (*pl.* ~s)

미숫가루 roasted grain [rice, barley] powder

미스 〈미혼 여성의 호칭〉 Miss; 〈미혼 여성〉 an unmarried woman (▶김씨 집안의 여러 미혼 여성일 때는 the Misses Kim; the Miss Kims)
♦1997년도 미스 코리아[유니버스] Miss Korea [Universe] (for) 1997
▶그녀는 아직도 미스다 She is yet unmarried. ⇒ She is still single.

미스캐스팅 〈부적당한 배역〉 miscasting

미스터 Mr. (*pl.* Messrs); Mister ♦미스터 김 Mr. Kim / 미스터라고 부르다 mister *sb*

미스터리 (a) mystery ▶그것은 여전히 미스터리다 It's still a mystery.

미스테리오소 〔樂〕〈신비스럽게〉 misterioso

미스테이크 〈잘못〉 a mistake

미스프린트 a misprint; a printer's error ⇨ 오식(誤植) ♦미스프린트를 고치다 correct errors in printing

미시 微視 ♦미시적인 microscopic(al) ■—경제학 microeconomics

미시간 〈미국의 주〉 Michigan (略 Mich., MI)
■—사람 a Michigander; a Michiganite; a Michiganian —호 Lake Michigan

미시시피 〈미국의 주〉 Mississippi (略 Miss., MS) ■—강 the Mississippi (River) —사람 a Mississippian

미시즈 〈호칭〉 Mrs.; 〈기혼 여성〉 a married woman

미식 米食 a rice-based diet; a rice-centered diet ▶한국 사람은 미식을 한다 The Korean diet is based on rice [is rice-based].
—미식하다 eat rice; live on rice

미식 美式 the American way [fashion, style]; Americanism ♦미식의 생활 the American way [style] of living / 미식으로 환영하다 welcome *sb* in the American way [fashion]
■—영어 American English —축구 American football

미식 美食 delicious food; gourmet meals; 〈영양식〉 a nourishing diet —미식하다 live on rich [good] food; be an epicure
■—가 a gourmet; 〈식도락가〉 an epicure —주의 epicurism

미신 迷信 (a) superstition
♦미신적인 superstitious / 미신을 믿다 believe in a superstition / 미신을 타파하다 break down [do away with] superstitions
▶4가 불길한 숫자라는 것은 미신이다[라는 미신이 있다] It's [There's] a superstition that four is an unlucky number.
▶검은 고양이를 보면 불길한 징조라는 미신이 있다 There is a superstition that those who see a black cat will have bad luck.
■—가 a superstitious person; a superstitionist

미심하다, 미심쩍다, 미심스럽다 未審— doubtful; dubious; suspicious
♦미심한 점 a doubtful [suspicious] point / 미심쩍은 사나이 a suspicious [doubtful, dubious] man / 미심스러운 이야기 a fishy story / 미심쩍은 근거 an unreliable source / 미심쩍어 하다 doubt 《that》; suspect 《that》; be doubtful (of); be suspicious (of)
▶그가 미심스럽다 I suspect him. ⇒ I am suspicious of him.
▶그녀는 여느때와 달리 친절해서 미심쩍었다 She was unusually friendly and I was suspicious.

미아 迷兒 a lost [stray] child; a missing child
♦미아를 찾다 search for a lost [missing] child
▶그 아이는 숲에서 미아가 되었다 The child got lost [lost his way] in the woods.
▶사람들은 미아가 된 소년을 수색했다 The people searched for the lost [missing] boy.
■—보호소 a home for missing children

미안 美顔 a beautiful face; good looks
■—수 a beauty lotion; a skin lotion —술 facial care; beauty treatment for a face; 〈미용술〉 beauty culture; cosmetology

미안스럽다 未安— regrettable ⇨ 미안하다
미안쩍다 未安— regrettable ⇨ 미안하다
미안하다 未安— regrettable; regretted; sorry; 〈외설적〉 be to be apologized (for); regret; apologize
▶미안합니다, 괜찮습니까? I'm sorry. Are you all right?
▶시끄럽게 해서 미안합니다 Excuse me for

being so noisy. ⇒ I'm sorry for [about] this noise.
▶오래 기다리게 해서 미안합니다 I'm sorry to have kept you waiting for a long time. ⇒ I hope I haven't kept you waiting long.
▶미안합니다만, 문을 닫아주세요 Please close the door. ⇒ Would [Could] you please close the door? ⇒ Would you mind closing the door, please?
▶차를 망가뜨려서 미안합니다 I must apologize to you for damaging your car. ⇒ Please forgive me for damaging your car.
▶폐를 끼쳐서 미안합니다 I'm sorry to trouble [have troubled] you.
▶ 会話 「실례합니다, 가까운 은행은 어디입니까?」「미안합니다, 모르겠어요」「어떻든 감사합니다」"Excuse me. Where's the nearest bank, please?" "I'm sorry I don't know." "Thank you anyway."

解説 (1) 실례되는 행동을 했을 때 (美)에서는 *Excuse me*, (英)에서는 (*I'm*) *sorry*가 일반적이며 *Pardon me*.는 더 공손한 말이다. 더 정중한 표현은 *I beg your pardon*.이며 이에 대한 대답으로는 (*It's*) *all right*. ⇒ (口) *OK*. ⇒ *Never mind*. ⇒ *Don't worry* (*about it*). ⇒ *Forget it*. 등이 있다.
(2) 자기 잘못을 인정할 때는 *I'm sorry*.지만 이 경우는 때로 보상이나 책임이 뒤따르므로 주의해야 한다. 강조할 때는 *I'm really* [*so, awfully, terribly*] *sorry*. 더욱 중대할 때는 *I apologize*. ⇒ *Forgive me*. 등이 있다.

미약 媚藥 an aphrodisiac; a love-potion; a love-philter; a philter
미약하다 微弱— faint; feeble ◆미약한 맥박 a feeble pulse / 미약한 반응을 보이다 react slightly; make a faint [feeble] response
미얀마 〈나라 이름〉 Myanmar; 〈공식명〉 the Union of Myanmar
미양 微恙 〈대수롭지 않은 병〉 a slight illness; an indisposition
미어 美語 American English; 〈미식 어법〉 an Americanism
미어뜨리다 tear a hole in 《paper, leather》; rend; rip
미어지다 be [get] torn; tear; rip 《open》; wear out ◆가슴이 미어지는 듯한 heartbreaking; heartrending 《sorrow》
▶갑자스런 어머니의 죽음으로 그는 가슴이 미어지는 듯 했다 His heart almost burst with grief at the sudden death of his mother.
미역¹ 〔植〕 Undaria pinnatifida; a brown seaweed
미역² 〈목욕〉 bathing; 〈수영〉 a swimming; a dip; (英) a bathe
▶아이들이 강에서 미역을 감고 있다 The children are swimming in the river.
미역국 ▶미역국 먹다 〈시험에 실패하다〉 fail in [flunk] an examination; 〈해고당하다〉 be dismissed; get fired
▶그는 입학시험에서 미역국 먹었다 He failed (in) [flunked] the entrance exam.
▶그들은 하나같이 미역국을 먹었다 All of them flunked [failed] without exception.
미연 未然 ◆미연에 beforehand; previously; before *sth* happens / 교통 사고를 미연에 방지하다 prevent traffic accidents
▶그녀의 재빠른 행동이 사고를 미연에 방지했다 Her quick action prevented an accident.
▶우리는 소문이 퍼지는 것을 미연에 방지했다 We stopped the rumor before it spread.
미열 微熱 a slight fever
▶그녀는 미열이 있다 She has a slight fever.
▶나는 저녁이 되면 미열이 난다 I get [run, develop] a slight fever in the evenings.
미오글로빈 〔化〕 myoglobin
미오신 〔化〕 myosin
미온 微溫 tepidity; lukewarmness
■—계〔計〕〔物〕 a micropyrometer —수 tepid water —욕 a tepid bath
미온적 微溫的 〈소극적인〉 lukewarm; lax; tepid; 〈마지못하는〉 indifferent; halfhearted
◆미온적인 단속 lax controls; indifferent restraints / 미온적인 수단[정책, 태도] a lukewarm measure [policy, attitude]
▶지금까지 취한 대책은 너무 미온적이었다 The measures we have taken have been too lukewarm.
미완 未完 incompletion ⇨ 미완성 ◆미완의 incomplete; unfinished; unaccomplished / 미완의 작품 an unfinished work
▶그의 미완의 시가 방 안에 전시돼 있었다 His unfinished poems were exhibited in the room.
미완성 未完成 incompletion
◆미완성의 incomplete; unfinished / 미완성의 대작 an incomplete masterpiece / 미완성인 채로 두다 leave off half-finished
▶내 논문은 아직 미완성이다 My paper is still incomplete. ⇒ I haven't finished my paper yet.
▶그 남자는 연구를 미완성으로 남긴 채 죽었다 Leaving his research uncompleted, he died [passed away].
■—교향곡 The Unfinished Symphony
미용 美容 (a) beauty treatment [culture]
◆미용과 건강에 좋다 be good for *one's* health and beauty
▶미용과 건강을 위해 매일 아침 체조를 한다 I practice gymnastics every morning for my beauty and health.
■—사 a beauty artist; a cosmetician; (美口) a beautician; a hairdresser —성형 cosmetic surgery —술 cosmetology; beauty culture —식 food for beauty —원[실] ⇨ 미장(~원) —체조 calisthenics; aesthetic gymnastics —학교 a beauty school
미욱하다 〈어리석고 미련하다〉 stupid (as an owl); silly; dull; thickheaded
◆미욱한 짓을 하다 do a stupid [an absurd] thing; play [act] the fool
▶그녀가 그런 짓을 하다니 정말 미욱하군 It is very silly of her to do such a thing.
미움 hate; hatred; enmity; hatefulness
◆미움을 사다[받다] incur *sb's* hatred [disfavor]; become an object of hatred
▶나는 그에 대한 미움도 이제는 사라졌다 My resentment against him is now gone.

미워하다 hate; detest; abhor

▶ 소설은 대개 사랑과 미움이 주제다 Novels mainly deal with love and hate [hatred].

♦미워할 만한 hateful; detestable; cursed; damned / 서로 미워하다 hate each other; be hateful to one another

▶ 넌 아직도 그를 미워하고 있니? Do you still hate [feel a hatred for] him?

▶ 그녀는 무슨 일을 해도 미워할 수가 없어 No matter what she does, it's hard to hate her.

▶ 그는 약속을 어겼다는 이유로 나를 미워하고 있다 He hates me for having broken my promise.

▶ 죄는 미워하되 사람은 미워하지 말라 (속담) You must hate the offense [sin], but not the offender [sinner]. ⇒ Condemn the offense, but pity the offender.

미음 米飮 thin rice gruel; water gruel

♦미음을 먹이다[먹다] give [take] one's rice gruel / 미음을 쑤다 prepare thin rice gruel

미의식 美意識 a sense of beauty; an aesthetic sense

미이다 get torn ⇨ 미어지다

미익 尾翼 〈비행기의 꼬리 날개〉 the empennage (of an aircraft); the tail; a tail unit ■수직— a vertical tail (plane) 수평— a (horizontal) tail plane ■—각 the tail angle

미인[1] 美人 〈미국 사람〉 an American; (총칭) the Americans

미인[2] 美人 〈미녀〉 a beauty; a beautiful woman; a belle; (口) a pinup (girl)

♦굉장한 미인 a stunning beauty; (口) a knockout; a bombshell / 요염한 미인 (美) a glamor girl / 절세의 미인 a woman of unsurpassed beauty

▶ 그녀는 절세의 미인이다 I have never seen such a beautiful woman as she. ⇒ She is a woman of matchless [peerless] beauty. ⇒ She is unequal in beauty.

▶ 그녀는 참 미인인 걸 She's good looking [pretty], isn't she?

■—계(計) a badger game: 미인계를 쓰다 pull a badger game ■—대회 a beauty contest

미인박명 美人薄命 Those whom the gods love die young. ⇒ Beauty and good fortune seldom go hand in hand.

미작 米作 〈벼 농사〉 rice cultivation [growing]; 〈벼 수확〉 a rice crop [harvest]

▶ 올해의 미작은 전망이 좋다 The prospects for this year's rice crop are favorable. ⇒ A good rice crop is expected this year.

■—예상 수확량 the estimated rice crop —지대 a rice-producing district

미장 〔韓醫〕 a deconstipating [laxative] suppository; a purgative suppository

♦미장을 넣다 insert a laxative suppository

■—질 deconstipating oneself: 미장질하다 deconstipate oneself; loosen [relieve] the bowels

미장 美匠 a decorative [an artistic] design

미장 美粧 beauty culture [art]; beauty treatment; cosmetology ■—원 a beauty salon; a beauty parlor [shop]

미장이 〈土工〉 a plasterer ■—일 plastering; plaster work

미적 美的 (a)esthetic(al) ♦미적으로 (a)esthetically ▶ 그것은 미적인 관점에서는 아무런 가치도 없다 From an aesthetic point of view, it has no value.

■—가치 aesthetic value —감각 (an) aesthetic sense; a sense of beauty: 그에게는 미적 감각이 없다 He has no eye for the beautiful [beauty]. —교육 aesthetic education —생활 an aesthetic existence [life] —쾌감 aesthetic pleasure

미적거리다 1 〈내밀다〉 push forward little by little [inch by inch] 2 ⇨ 미루적거리다

미적분 微積分 〔數〕 differential and integral calculus; infinitesimal calculus ■—학 calculus

미적지근하다 1 〈미지근하다〉 tepid; barely warm; lukewarm ♦미적지근한 물 tepid water

▶ 거기 나온 수프는 미적지근했다 The soup served there was lukewarm.

2 〈소극적이고 흐리멍덩하다〉 indecisive; vague; lukewarm; irresolute; mild; lenient; halfway

♦미적지근한 대답 a dubious [vague] reply / 미적지근한 태도 an indecisive [a lukewarm] attitude

▶ 그런 미적지근한 방법은 효과가 없다 That's too mild a method to have any effect.

▶ 그의 미적지근한 성격에 짜증이 난다 He is so wishy-washy that he always irritates me.

미전 美展 an art exhibition ⇨ 미술(~전(시회))

미점 美點 〈장점〉 a good point; 〈가치〉 a merit; 〈미덕〉 a virtue ▶ 누구나 미점과 결점을 가지고 있는 법이다 Everybody has his good points and bad points.

미정 未定 suspense; pendency ♦미정의 undecided; unfixed; 〈확실치 않은〉 uncertain

♦미정의 문제 an open question / 미정이다 remain unsettled; be in abeyance

▶ 다음 모임의 일시와 장소는 미정이다 The date and place of the next meeting is not fixed [decided] yet.

▶ 여정(旅程)은 아직 미정임 The itinerary is still unsettled. ⇒ The itinerary has yet to be decided.

▶ 연제(演題) 미정 (게시) Subject undecided.

■—계수법 〔數〕 method of undetermined coefficients —고(稿) an unfinished manuscript

미제 未濟 ♦미제의 pending; unsettled; 〈미지급의〉 unpaid; outstanding; 〈미완성의〉 unfinished

미제 美製 ♦미제의 American made; made in USA ■—품 American-made goods; articles of American make

미조 美爪 manicure ■—사 a manicurist —술 〈손톱〉 manicure; 〈발톱〉 pedicure —원 (院) a manicure parlor

미조직 未組織 ♦미조직의 unorganized ■—근로자 unorganized workers [labor]

미죄 微罪 a minor [petty] offense

미주 美洲 the Americas ■—기구 the Organization of American States (略 O.A.S.) —대륙 the American Continent(s) —회의 the Inter-American Conference

미주 美酒 a delicious [tasty] wine; (a) good

drink
미주리 〈미국의 주〉 Missouri (略 Mo., MO) ■―사람 a Missourian
미주신경 迷走神經 〔解〕 a vagus 《pl. -gi》; a vagus nerve; the pneumogastric (nerve)
미주알 the anal sphincter; 《라》 the sphincter ani ⇨ 항문(―괄약근)
미주알고주알 〈속속들이 캐묻는 모양〉 inquisitively; overcuriously
▶ 그렇게 미주알고주알 캐묻지 마라 Don't be so inquisitive (about it).
▶ 그는 우리 계획에 대해서 미주알고주알 캐물었다 Out of curiosity he asked many questions about own plan(s). ⇒ He was very eager [curious] to know the details of our plan.
▶ 이웃들은 우리 일을 미주알고주알 알고 싶어한다 Our neighbors are very inquisitive about what we do.
미증유 未曾有 ◆ 미증유의 unprecedented; unheard-of; record-breaking / 미증유의 대사업 the greatest enterprise which has ever been made (and probably will never be attempted)
▶ 그 해 세계무역은 미증유의 성장을 기록했다 World trade registered an unprecedented growth that year.
▶ 그것은 역사상 미증유의 지진이었다 It was the greatest earthquake in history [on record].
미지 未知 ◆ 미지의 unknown; strange / 미지의 땅 a strange land / 미지의 세계를 탐험하다 explore the unknown world
▶ 미지의 사람들을 만나는 것은 여행의 즐거움 가운데 하나다 Meeting strangers is one of the pleasures of a trip.
▶ 그것은 많은 사람들에게 미지의 일이다 It's a closed book to most people.
미지근하다 1 〈미적지근하다〉 lukewarm; tepid; not warm enough
◆ 미지근한 물 tepid [lukewarm] water
▶ 커피를 미지근한 물로 타지 마라 Don't use tepid [lukewarm] water to make coffee.
▶ 차가 미지근해서 못마시겠다 The tea is too tepid to drink.
2 〈소극적이다〉 not strict [severe] enough; mild; lenient
◆ 미지근한 대답 an unenthusiastic answer / 미지근한 태도 one's lukewarm attitude
▶ 그들에게는 그런 미지근한 조치는 통하지 않는다 Such halfway measures won't have any effect on them.
미지수 未知數 the unknown (thing); 〔數〕 an unknown (quantity)
▶ 승패는 전혀 미지수다 The match is a very open one.
▶ 그 회의에 몇 사람이나 참석할지는 아직 미지수다 We don't know yet how many people will take part in the convention.
미진 微塵 an atom; a particle; a mite; a bit
미진 微震 a slight [weak] earthquake; an earth tremor ■―계(計) tromometer
미진하다 未盡― 〈다하지 못하다〉 unfinished, incomplete; 〈만족하지 못하다〉 unsatisfied
◆ 마음에 미진한 데가 있다 have an unsatisfied feeling; miss something
▶ 그의 설명만으로는 아무래도 미진하다 I'm not quite satisfied with his explanation. ⇒ His explanation is not satisfactory to me.
미착 未着 ◆ 미착의 unarrived; undelivered
▶ 그 소포는 미착이다 The parcel hasn't been delivered yet.
■―상품 〔商〕 goods in transit ―신용장 a letter of credit en route
미착수 未着手 ◆ 미착수의 not yet started [begun] ■―공사 construction work not yet started
미채 迷彩 〈위장 채색〉 〔空〕 camouflage; 〔海〕 dazzle paint
◆ 미채를 한 전차 a camouflaged tank / 미채를 하다 camouflage 《a ship》
미처 〈아직〉 yet; before; 〈지금까지〉 as yet; up to now; so far ◆ 미처 생각하지 못한 beyond one's imagination; unimaginable / 미처 손도 쓰기 전에 《die》 before we [a doctor] come to one's aid
▶ 나는 미처 그걸 몰랐다 I didn't know that before.
▶ 그것까지는 미처 생각지 못했어 I hadn't thought of that. ⇒ It did not occur to me.
▶ 그렇게 하면 된다는 걸 미처 알지 못했다 I never imagined that it was possible to do it that way.
▶ 네가 거기 있는 줄 미처 몰랐어 I didn't notice [wasn't aware] that you were there.
미처리 未處理 ◆ 미처리의 outstanding; 《business》 yet unattended; 《paper》 yet to be dealt with
▶ 그에게는 미처리된 일이 있다 He has some unattended business.
▶ 미처리된 서류가 몇 장 있다 There are some papers still to be dealt with.
미처분 未處分 ◆ 미처분의 not yet disposed of; undisposed 《articles》
미천하다 微賤― lowly; humble; ignoble ◆ 미천한 몸[신분] a man of obscure birth; a person in humble station / 미천하게 태어나다 be baseborn; be of humble origin / 미천한 신분에서 출세하다 rise from obscurity [the gutter]
▶ 그는 미천하게 살다 갔다 He lived and died in obscurity.
미첼 〈미국의 여류작가〉 Mitchell, Margaret (1900-49)
미쳐날뛰다 rage; rave; rush about furiously
미추 美醜 beauty or ugliness
미추룸하다 healthy and fair [handsome]; youthful and fresh
미취 微醉 slight intoxication; mellowness ―미취하다 be slightly intoxicated; be in a cheerful mood with drink
미취학 未就學 ◆ 미취학의 not yet attending school; preschool ■―아동 a preschool child; a preschooler; a child not attending school
미치광이 1 〈미친 사람〉 a madman; a madwoman (여자); a crazy person; a lunatic; an insane person
◆ 미치광이처럼 like mad; madly; frantically / 미치광이가 되다 go [become] mad [insane]; lose one's mind / 미치광이 짓을 하다 behave

미치다¹

like a madman; act crazy
▶그런 짓을 하다니 미치광이짓이다 You must be insane [It is madness] to do such a thing.
2 〈열광자〉 a maniac; a fan; a fanatic
◆경마 미치광이 a race maniac; a horse racing nut [enthusiast]

미치다¹ 1 〈정신이상이 되다〉 go mad [crazy]; go insane; (口) go nuts; lose *one's* mind [head, senses]; go out of *one's* mind; go off *one's* head
◆미친 mad; crazy; insane; out of *one's* mind / 미친듯이 madly; frantically; (口) like mad [crazy] / …하고 싶어서 미치다 be unable to contain *oneself*; be dying (to do, for) / 미치게 하다 drive *sb* mad
▶그녀는 슬픈 나머지 미쳐버렸다 Grief drove her mad. ⇒ She was driven mad by grief. ⇒ She went out of her mind with grief.
▶그녀는 실연해서 미쳐버렸다 Losing his love drove her mad.
▶그녀가 보고 싶어 미치겠다 I'm impatient to see her. ⇒ I'm dying to see her. ⇒ I have a wild urge to see her.
▶그런 짓을 하다니 너 미쳤구나 You are mad [crazy] to do such a thing. ⇒ It is mad [crazy] of you to do such a thing.
▶그녀는 미친듯이 소리를 질러댔다 She yelled and screamed like mad [frantically].
▶그는 화가 나서 미칠 것만 같았다 He was beside himself with rage.
2 〈열중하다〉 become enthusiastic; go mad; go crazy 《about》; get very excited 《at, by》; 〈열중하다〉 be absorbed 《in》; be devoted 《to》
▶그는 경마에 미쳐 있다 He is mad about horse racing.
▶그는 그녀에게 미쳐 있었다 He was madly in love with her. ⇒ He was nearly out of his mind with love for her.

미치다² 1 〈이르다〉 reach; amount to; come up to; 〈걸치다〉 extend 《to, over》; stretch; range over; 〈언급하다〉 refer to
◆생각이 미치다 be clever enough to think of / 생각이 미치지 못하다 miss; overlook; be not clever [alert] enough to think of / 품질 등이) 표준에 미치다 come up to standard / 기대에 미치지 못하다 do not come up to *one's* expectations
▶그는 키가 커서 천장까지 손이 미친다 He is so tall that he can reach the ceiling.
▶약은 아이들의 손이 미치지 않는 곳에 두시오 Keep the medicine out of the reach of the children. ⇒ Keep the medicine where the children can't get at it.
▶수해가 이웃 마을에까지 미쳤다 The flood damage spread [extended] to the next village.
▶대기오염은 시골까지 미치고 있다 Air pollution is already spreading into the countryside.
▶그의 충고는 소년들에게 좋은 영향을 미쳤다 His advice exerted a favorable influence upon [had a good influence on] the boys.
▶내 생각이 거기까지는 미치지 못했다 Such an idea never occurred to me. ⇒ I should [ought to] have known better.

▶그녀의 영향력은 동시대의 시인들에게까지 미치고 있다 Her influence has extended even to contemporary poets.
▶삼각관계의 갈등이 유혈의 참사로까지 미쳤다 The love triangle ended in bloodshed.
2 〈닥치다〉 visit; befall *sb*; happen to *sb*
▶그에게 재난이 미쳤다 A misfortune befell him. ⇒ An accident happened to him.
3 〈견주다〉 match; equal; be a match for; rival 《another》 in
◆…에 미치지 못하다 be no match for; fall behind; be inferior to
▶그 일에는 내 힘이 미치지 못한다 I'm not equal to the task. ⇒ The task is beyond my power [ability].
▶약삭빠르기로는 나는 그에게 도저히 미치지 못한다 I am no match for him in shrewdness.
▶그는 회사를 위해서 힘이 미치는데까지 노력했다 He did all he could [He did his best] for his company.
▶아무도 그의 역량에 미치지 못한다 No one can even remotely rival him. ⇒ Nobody can in any way equal him.

미칭 美稱 〈아름답게 일컫는 말〉 a euphemism
미케네 〔史〕 Mycenae ◆미케네의 Mycenaean; Mycenian ■—문명 the Mycenaean civilization
미켈란젤로 〈이탈리아의 화가〉 Michelangelo, Buonarroti (1475-1564)
미크로네시아 〈나라 이름〉 Micronesia; 〈공식명〉 Federated States of Micronesia
◆미크로네시아의 Micronesian ■—사람 a Micronesian
미크론 a micron (*pl.* ~s, micra)
■밀리— a millimicron; a micromillimeter; a nanometer
미터 1 〈길이의 단위〉 a meter; (英) a metre
▶이 판자는 길이가 3미터, 폭이 1미터다 This board is three meters long and one meter wide.
2 〈자동계량기〉 a meter; a gauge
◆미터에 나온 숫자 the meter reading / 미터를 달다 install a meter / 미터를 검사하다 〈이상 유무를〉 examine a meter; 〈검침하다〉 inspect [read] a (gas) meter / 미터를 속이다 tamper with a meter
▶그들은 한 달에 한 번 집에 가스미터를 조사하러 온다 They come to my house to read the gasmeter once a month.
■—검침원 a meter inspector [reader, man] —글래스 a graduated [measuring] glass; 〔化〕 a graduate —법 the metric system —사용량 meterage —사용료 meterage —자 a meter rule —톤 a metric ton
미토콘드리아 〔生〕 mitochondria
미투리 hemp-cord sandals [shoes]
미트 〔野〕 a (padded) mitt ◆캐처 미트 a catcher's mitt
미팅 〈회합〉 a meeting; 〈남녀의〉 a date
▶우리는 주 1회 미팅을 한다 We have [hold] a meeting once a week.
▶ 話 「미팅을 한 번 해야지」「언제로 할까?」 "We must have a meeting." "Well, when exactly?" (▶when만으로도 좋으나 exactly (정

미풍 美風 a good [fine, laudable] custom ■—양속(良俗) a long-established good custom; time-honored social morals: 한국에서는 웃어른의 의견을 따르는 것이 미풍양속으로 되어 있다 In Korea it is considered proper to go along with the ideas of *one's* superiors.

미풍 微風 a gentle [light] wind; a breeze; a breath of air
◆ 봄의 미풍 a spring breeze
▶ 상쾌한 미풍이 불고 있다 There is a refreshing breeze [gentle wind] blowing.
▶ 미풍조차 없다 There is not a breath of wind.

미필 未畢 〈아직 끝내지 못함〉 incompletion
◆ 미필의 unfinished; incomplete; unfulfilled / 심의 미필의 의안 a pending bill / 병역 미필자 a person who has not completed his military duty
—미필하다 have not finished [fulfilled]

미필적고의 未必的故意 〔法〕 willful [conscious] negligence

미학 美學 aesthetics ◆ 미학적 a esthetic / 미학적 견지에서 보면 from an aesthetic point of view ■—자 an aesthetician

미합중국 美合衆國 the United States of America (略 the USA) ⇨ 미국

미해결 未解決 ◆ 미해결의 unsolved; unsettled; pending; outstanding / 미해결의 문제 an unsolved problem; an unsettled [a pending] matter / 미해결인 채로 있다 remain unsolved [unsettled]
▶ 오래된 미해결 문제가 산더미처럼 많다 There is a pile of long-pending problems.
▶ 미해결 사건을 남겨 놓은채 그 형사는 정년퇴직했다 The police detective retired with some cases left unsettled.
▶ 그것은 양국간 미해결 문제의 하나다 That is one of the pending [unsolved, outstanding] problems between the two countries.

미행 尾行 shadowing; following
▶ 그는 미행을 따돌렸다 He shook off the shadow.
—미행하다 shadow; trail; tail after *sb*; follow; put a shadow [tail] on *sb*
▶ 경찰은 용의자를 미행시켰다 The police put a tail [shadow] on the suspect.
▶ 그는 형사에게 미행당했다 He was shadowed [trailed, followed] by a police detective.
■—자 a shadow; a tail: 그는 미행자가 있음을 알고 있었다 He was aware that he was wearing a tail.

미행 美行 a good deed; good conduct

미행 微行 incognito traveling / 미행으로 방문하다 pay an incognito visit to
—미행하다 go [travel] incognito; make a secret visit 《to》; pay a private visit to

미혹 迷惑 〈홀림〉delusion; (an) illusion;〈갈팡질팡함〉 perplexity; bewilderment
◆ 미혹에서 깨어나다 awake from an illusion; be disillusioned
—미혹하다 be deluded; be infatuated; be at a loss ◆ 헛소문에 미혹되다 be carried away by rumors

미혼 未婚 ◆ 미혼의 unmarried; unwed; single
▶ 그는 평생 미혼으로 지냈다 He remained [stayed] single all his life.
▶ 그는 마흔 살이지만 미혼이다 He is unmarried [single] though he is forty.
■—남자 a bachelor —모 an unmarried [unwed] mother —여성[녀] a maiden lady [woman]; an unmarried woman; (口) a bachelor girl —자 an unmarried person

미화 美化 beautification; idealization
—미화하다 〈장식하다〉 beautify; make 《the look of the town》 beautiful; 〈조경하다〉 landscape
▶ 젊은이는 죽음을 미화하는 경향이 있다 Young people are apt to romanticize death.
■—운동 a beautification drive; a cleanup campaign: 도시 미화 운동 a city beautification movement

미화 美貨 American currency [money]; the U.S. dollar; the American dollar
◆ 미화 1달러 당 880원 880 won per a U.S. dollar / 미화로 지불하다 pay in U.S. dollars
■—공채 a dollar bond [loan] —어음 a dollar bill —지급 payable in dollars —환 dollar exchange

미확인 未確認 ◆ 미확인의 unconfirmed; not yet confirmed ■—보도 news from an unconfirmed source —비행물체 an unidentified flying object (略 UFO) —신용장 an unconfirmed letter of credit —정보 unconfirmed information; an unconfirmed report

미흡 未洽 insufficiency; inadequacy
—미흡하다 insufficient; inadequate; unsatisfied 《with》; unsatisfactory
◆ 미흡한 감이 들다 feel not quite satisfied / 미흡한 점이 있다[없다] leave something [nothing] to be desired
▶ 그의 수입은 가족을 부양하기에 미흡하다 His income is not enough [sufficient] to support his family.
▶ 그는 아직도 기술이 미흡하다 His technique still leaves much to be desired.
▶ 저희가 미흡해서 폐를 끼쳐드려 죄송합니다 We are sorry to have troubled you through our error [blunder].

미희 美姬 a beautiful girl; a beauty

믹서 〈혼합기〉 a mixer; an electric mixer; a blender; (英) a liquidizer ◆ 콘크리트 믹서 a concrete mixer

믹스 〈혼합〉 mixture —믹스하다 mix

-민 -民 유랑민 a wandering race; a gypsy / 유목민 a nomadic race / 이재민 the sufferers 《from》; the afflicted people

민가 民家 a private house; a commoner's house

민간 民間 ◆ 민간의 〈공(公)에 대하여〉 private; nongovernmental; nonofficial; 〈군(軍)에 대하여〉 civil; civilian; nonmilitary / 민간측 the unofficial side / 민간에서 among the people / 민간에 맡기다 leave *sth* to private hands
▶ 이것은 민간에 뿌리를 두고 있는 신앙이다 This is a belief rooted in the people.
■—단체 a private [nongovernmental] organization —대표 〈위원〉 nongovernmental dele-

민감 968

gates —무역 private foreign trade; privately-based trade; trade on commercial basis —방송 commercial [sponsored] broadcasting —방송국 a commercial radio [TV] station —사업 a private enterprise [business] —설화 a folktale; a folk story —신앙 a popular [folk] belief —약 a folk medicine —외교 non-governmental [people-to-people] diplomacy —요법 a folk [popular] remedy —인 a private citizen; a nongovernmental person; 〈군인에 대하여〉 a civilian —자본 private capital —전승 folklore; a legend —항공 civil aviation

민감 敏感 sensitiveness; sensitivity; sensibility; susceptibility
—민감하다 sensitive; susceptible; touchy
▶나는 더위와 추위에 민감하다 I am sensitive to heat and cold.
▶그들은 유행에 민감하다 They are susceptible to changes in fashion.
▶정치가는 여론에 민감하다 A politician is easily swayed [influenced] by public opinion.
▶신체 가운데서 가장 민감한 것이 혀 끝이라고 들 하더라 I hear that the tip of the tongue is the most sensitive part of the body.

민국 民國 a republic; a democratic country
민권 民權 civil rights; the people's rights
♦민권을 신장[옹호, 주장]하다 extend [defend, assert] the people's rights / 민권을 유린하다 trample on the people's rights
■—(수호)운동 a civil rights movement; a movement for the protection [defense] of civil rights —운동가 (美口) a civil righter

민단 民團 a settlement corporation ⇨ 거류민 (〜단)
민도 民度 the living [cultural] standard of the people ▶민도가 매우 높다[낮다] The people's standard of living is very high [low].
민둥민둥하다 bald; bare; deforested; treeless
민둥산 —山 a bald [bare, treeless] mountain
민들레 〔植〕 a dandelion
민란 民亂 a riot [revolt] of people
민력 民力 national resources; national power [strength]
민망하다 憫惘— embarrassed; sorry; sad
▶가진 돈이 적어서 민망했다 I felt awkward to find myself short of cash.
▶거 참 민망하구 That's very embarrassing.
▶내가 방에 혼자 남게 되었을 때 얼마나 민망했 겠는가 생각해 보시오. Imagine my embarrassment upon being left alone in the room.
민머리 1 〈대머리〉 a bald head **2** 〈쪽 안찐 머리〉 undone hair **3** 〈백두〉 a person holding no office
민며느리 a young girl taken into *one's* family as a future daughter-in-law
민무늬근 —筋 〔解〕 a smooth muscle; an unstriated muscle
민물 fresh water
▶소금물을 민물로 바꾸는 데는 비용이 너무 든다 It is too expensive to turn salt water into fresh water.
■—고기 a freshwater fish —낚시 freshwater fishing

민박하다 民泊— lodge at a private residence
민방위 民防衛 civil defense
■—대 the Civil Defense Corps —대원 a Civil Defense Corps member —체제 the Civil Defense system
민방위훈련 民防衛訓練 Civil Defense training
♦민방위 훈련의 날 the day designated for Civil Defense training
민법 民法 (총칭) civil law; 〈협의의〉 the Civil Law Act; 〈법전〉 the Civil Code
■—학자 a scholar of the civil law; an authority on the civil law
민병 民兵 〈부대〉 a militia; 〈개인〉 a militiaman ■—대[단] a militia corps
민복 民福 national welfare; well-being [welfare] of the people
민본주의 民本主義 democracy
민사 民事 civil affairs; 〔法〕 a civil case
■—범 a civil offender —법원 a civil court —사건 a civil case —원고 a plaintiff —책임 civil liability —피고 a defendant
민사소송 民事訴訟 a civil suit [action]
▶그는 가해자에 대해 민사소송을 제기했다 He brought a civil suit against the assailant.
■—법 〔法〕 the Code of Civil Procedure; the Civil Proceedings Act
민사재판 民事裁判 a civil trial ■—권 civil jurisdiction
민생 民生 public welfare; the livelihood of the people; the people's livelihood
♦민생 안정 stabilization of the people's livelihood
■—고 the people's economic difficulties [plight]; economic distress of the people; impoverished life of the people —문제 public welfare problems; problems concerning public welfare
민선 民選 popular election ♦민선의 elected [chosen] by the people [by popular vote]
■—의원 a representative [an assemblyman] elected by the people [by popular vote]
민성 民聲 the voice of the people; the people's voice; public opinion
민속 民俗 folkways; folk customs; manners and customs of the people
■—공예 folkcraft; folk handicraft; folk [native] art : 민속공예품 a folkcraft article [object] —극 a folk drama [play] —무용 a folk dance : 국립 민속무용단 the National Folk Ballet Troupe —문학 folk literature —박물관 a folklore museum —예술 folk art : 전국 민속 예술 경연 대회 the National Folk Arts Festival; the Folk Arts Contest —음악 folk music —자료 (collection of) folk material; folklore data —촌 the Folk Village —학 folklore —학자 a folklorist
민속 敏速 quickness; promptness; alacrity; agility —민속하다 quick; agile; prompt; swift
민수 民需 private [civilian] demands [requirements] —산업 civilian industry —품 civilian [consumer's] goods; goods for civil use
민수기 民數記 〔聖〕 (The Book of) Numbers (略 Num., Numb.)
민숭민숭하다 bare ⇨ 맨숭맨숭하다

민심 民心 popular feelings; public [popular] sentiment; the mind of the people
♦민심의 동요 popular unrest / 민심을 선동하다 inflame [stir up] the popular passion / 민심을 얻다 win the confidence of the people / 민심에 역행하다 go against public sentiment
▶민심이 동요하고 있다 Restlessness prevails among the people.
▶민심이 천심이다 The people's voice is the voice of God.
▶그 정당은 점차 민심을 잃었다 The political party gradually lost the support of the people.
▶정치가는 반드시 민심을 파악해야 한다 It is absolutely necessary for a politician to grasp how people feel.

민약설 民約說 〔社〕 the theory of social contract

민어 民魚 〔魚〕 a sciaenoid fish; a croaker

민영 民營 private management [operation]
♦민영의 privately-managed[-operated]; private; nongovernment(al) / 민영이다 be under private management; be run by private concerns / 민영으로 하다 place under private management; commit (an enterprise) to private hands / 민영으로 되다 fall into private hands; come under private management
▶이 유스 호스텔은 민영이다 This is a youth hostel under private management.
━사업 a private enterprise [undertaking, business] ━화 privatization

민예 民藝 folk arts; folkcrafts ━품 a folk-art article; a folkcraft

민완 敏腕 ability; capability; capacity; finesse; shrewdness
♦민완의 shrewd; sharp; astute / 민완을 발휘하다 show [give full play to] one's ability; display one's (uncommon) shrewdness (in)
━가 a shrewd man; an able person; a man of ability [resources]; (美口) a go-getter ━형사 a competent detective

민요 民謠 a folk song; a (folk [popular]) ballad ━가수 a folk singer

민원 民怨 public resentment [hatred]; popular enmity [complaints]
♦민원의 대상이 되다 become a target of public grievance / 민원을 사다 incur the enmity of the people; provoke the hatred of the people

민원 民願 a civil appeal [petition]; a civil application ♦각종 민원 사항을 처리하다 deal with various civil petitions
━공무원 a civil affairs official ━봉사 speedy processing of civil petitions ━비서 a secretary in charge of civil affairs ━사무[업무] civil affairs administration ━상담소 a civil affairs office ━서류 civil affair documents : 민원서류의 간소화 simplification of civil affair documents ━실 the public service center ━창구 a window for civil petitions ━처리 기관 a grievance organization [machinery]

민유 民有 private ownership ━림 a forest under private ownership ━지 private land

민의 民意 the will of the people; the popular will; public opinion [sentiment]; a public consensus
♦민의의 표시 a manifestation of the popular will / 민의를 묻다 seek the judgment of the people; consult the will of the people / 민의를 반영[존중, 무시]하다 reflect [respect, disregard] the will of the people

민의원 民議院 〈하원〉 the Lower House; (美·日) the House of Representatives; (英) the House of Commons; (프) the Chamber of Deputies
━선거 the election of the House of Representatives ━의원(議員) (美) a Representative; (英) a member of the House of Commons ━의장 (美) the Speaker of the House

민적 民籍 〈등록〉 census registration; 〈등본〉 a census [family] register
♦민적에 올리다 have [get] sb's name entered in the family register / 민적에서 빼다 have sb's name deleted [removed] from the family register

민정 民政 civil administration [government]
♦민정을 실시하다 establish a civil government
━이양 transfer of power to civil government ━장관 a civil administrator [governor]

민정 民情 the condition [state] of the people; the realities of the people's life
♦민정을 살피다 see how the people live; observe the conditions of the people
▶국무총리는 민정을 시찰했다 The Prime Minister traveled about to observe how people lived.
▶저 정치가는 민정에 밝다 That statesman is well acquainted with the actual living conditions of the people.

민족 民族 a race; a people; a nation; 〔社〕 an ethnos; an ethnic group
♦소수 민족 a minority race / 지배 민족 a master race / 한(국)민족 the Korean race / 민족의 national; racial
▶영국민은 다수의 이민족과 접촉했다 The English people came into contact with many alien races.
━감정 a national sentiment 《toward》 ━국가 a nation-state : 다민족 국가 a multiracial [multinational] country / 단일 민족국가 a racially homogeneous nation ━기원론 〔人類〕 ethnogeny ━문제 a racial problem ━문화 national culture ━성 national [racial] characteristics [traits] ━심리학 folk [ethnic] psychology; ethnopsychology ━애 love for [of] one's own race ━언어학 ethnolinguistics ━운동 a national movement 《for independence》 ━의식 national [racial] consciousness ━이동 a racial migration; 〔史〕 the migration of nations ━자본 national [native] capital ━적 긍지 a national pride ━적 편견 a national prejudice ━전선 a people's [racial] front ━정신 the national spirit ━주체성 national identity ━진영 the nationalist bloc [camp] ━차별주의 racism ━해방 national liberation ━해방전선 〈아랍의〉 the National

Liberation Front (略 NLF)

민족자결 民族自決 self-determination of peoples ■ —주의 the principle of self-determination of peoples

민족주의 民族主義 〈국민주의〉 nationalism; 〈인종주의〉 racialism ■ —자 a nationalist; a racialist

민족학 民族學 ethnology ■ —자 an ethnologist

민주 民主 democracy
♦ 민주적(인) democratic / 비민주적(인) undemocratic / 반민주적(인) antidemocratic / 민주적으로 democratically
▶ 우리는 회의를 민주적으로 진행했다 We chaired the meeting democratically [in a democratic way].
■ —공화국 a democratic republic —사상 democratic ideas —사회주의 democratic socialism —전선 a democratic front —정당 a democratic party —정체 democracy —정치 a democratic form of government; democratic government —평화통일 자문위원회 the Advisory Council on Democratic and Peaceful Unification (略 ACDPU)

민주국(가) 民主國(家) a democratic state; a democracy ▶ 한국은 민주국가다 Korea is a democracy.

민주당 民主黨 (美) the Democratic Party; the Democrats ■ —원 a Democrat

민주제도 民主制度 a democratic system; democracy ♦ 대의(代議) 민주제도 representative democracy / 절대 민주제도 absolute democracy

민주주의 民主主義 democracy; democratism; democratic principles
♦ 의회[사회] 민주주의 parliamentary [social] democracy / 직접[간접] 민주주의 direct [indirect] democracy
■ —자 a democrat; a democratist —혁명 a democratic revolution

민주화 民主化 democratization ♦ 교육의 민주화 democratization of education —민주화하다 democratize

민중 民衆 the people; the masses; the multitude; people in general; the populace
♦ 민중의 지혜 the wisdom of the people; folk wisdom / 민중적인 popular; democratic
▶ 그는 항상 민중의 편이었다 He was always on the people's side.
■ —대회 a mass meeting; a people's rally; a (protest) rally —심리 the psychology of the common people; popular psychology —예술 popular arts —오락 popular amusements —운동 a popular movement —정치 popular government

민중화 民衆化 popularization —민중화하다 popularize

민짜 a plain thing ⇨ 민패

민첩 敏捷 agility; alacrity; quickness; nimbleness; promptness; smartness
—민첩하다 quick; prompt; nimble; agile; smart ♦ 민첩하게 quickly; promptly; nimbly; briskly
▶ 그는 동작이 민첩하다 He is quick [nimble] in action. ⇌ He moves with alacrity.
▶ 저 노인은 발걸음이 민첩하다 That old man walks with a brisk step.
▶ 그녀는 민첩하게 대답했다 She replied promptly.

민틋하다 even and slant; gently-sloping; smoothly-sloping

민패 a plain [simple] thing; an artless [undecorated] article

민폐 民弊 public harm [damage]; an abuse suffered by the public; 〈대중 상대의〉 a public nuisance; 〈개인 상대의〉 a private nuisance
♦ 민폐를 끼치다 cause a nuisance to the people; cause inconvenience to the general public

민하다 senseless; thoughtless; stupid; foolish; slow-[dull-]witted

민화 民話 a folktale; a folk story

민활 敏活 agility ⇨ 민첩(敏捷)

믿는 도끼에 발등 찍힌다 (속담) have one's hand bitten by his own dog; be double-crossed [betrayed] by one's trusted follower

믿다 1 〈의심치 않다〉 believe; give credit [credence] to; put [place] credit [credence] in; accept sth as true; be convinced of (a fact); be persuaded (of, that...)
♦ 믿을 만한 credible; believable / 믿을 수 없는 incredible; unbelievable
▶ 나는 그의 말을 곧이곧대로 믿었다 I took him at his word seriously. ⇌ I took his word(s) at face value. ⇌ I believed his word(s) [him].
▶ 그는 그 여자의 거짓말을 전적으로 믿었다 He swallowed the lie the woman told him.
▶ 나는 그녀의 말을 믿는다 I believe what she says. ⇌ I believe her.
▶ 그녀는 남의 말을 너무 쉽게 믿는다 She is very credulous. ⇌ She readily takes people at their word.
▶ 그들은 자신들의 승리를 굳게 믿고 있었다 People were confident of their victory [that they would win].
▶ 요즈음 아이들은 유령의 존재를 믿지 않는다 Nowadays children don't believe in ghosts.
▶ 나는 정직이 최선책임을 믿고 있다 It is my belief [My belief is] that honesty is the best policy.
▶ 그것은 도저히 믿어지지 않는다 It is quite beyond credibility.
▶ 도대체 누가 그런 말을 믿으리라고 생각하느냐? Who on earth do you expect to believe such a story?
2 〈신용・신뢰하다〉 trust; put [have] trust in; put [place] confidence (in); put [have] faith in; 〈의지하다〉 rely [depend, count] (up)on; look [turn] to sb for help; lean [reckon, calculate] on
♦ 믿을 곳 one's resort; a person one can turn to for help / 믿을 수 없는 사람 an unreliable [untrustworthy] person; a dishonest person / 믿을 수 없는 직업 a fly-by-night occupation / 믿을 만한 reliable; trustworthy; dependable; authentic / 요행을 믿다 rely on chance / 자기 힘을 믿다 have confidence in [rely on] one's strength / 다수의 힘을 믿다 rely on [trust to]

numbers / 아들을 집안의 기둥으로 믿다 rely on *one's* son as the prop and stay of the family / 믿지 못할 것을 믿다 lean on [turn to] a broken reed; hope against hope
▶ 나는 너를 믿는다 I believe in you.
▶ 믿을 사람이라고는 너 하나 밖에 없다 You are the only person I can trust. ⇌ I have no one but you to turn to for help.
▶ 그는 친구 하나만 믿고 상경했다 He came up to Seoul, counting on his only friend for help.
▶ 그 사람은 믿을 수 없다 He is not reliable. ⇌ He cannot be depended upon.
▶ 당신을 믿고 이 일을 맡깁니다 I will trust to you for the performance of the task.
▶ 나를 너무 믿지 마라 Don't expect too much of me.
▶ 그들은 다수의 힘을 믿고 행패를 부렸다 They behaved in an unruly way on the strength of their numbers.
▶ 어머니는 그의 편지를 믿고 기다리고 있었다 His mother waited in reliance on his letter.
3 〈신앙하다〉 believe (in); have belief [faith] (in); embrace; profess
♦ 믿는 사람 a believer; an adherent; a religious-minded person / 불교를 믿다 profess [believe in] Buddhism / 하느님을 믿다 believe in God / 아무 종교도 믿지 않다 profess no religion
▶ 그는 신불을 믿지 않게 되었다 He lost faith in gods.

믿음 1 〈신뢰〉 credit; trust; confidence; reliance
♦ 믿음을 배반하다 betray *sb's* trust [confidence]/ 믿음을 얻다 be trusted by *sb*; get *sb's* credit [trust]/ 믿음을 잃다 lose credit 《with》; lose the confidence (of)
2 〈신앙〉 faith; belief
♦ 믿음이 없는 사람 an impious person; an infidel / 믿음이 두텁다 be (deeply) religious; be devout [pious]; have a strong [deep] faith / 믿음이 약하다 be weak in faith / 믿음을 갖게 되다 get religion; become pious / 믿음을 버리다 forsake [give up] *one's* faith

믿음성 —性 reliability; trustworthiness
♦ 믿음성이 있다 be reliable [trustworthy]/ 믿음성이 없다 be unreliable [untrustworthy]

믿음직하다 reliable; trustworthy; dependable; 〈유망하다〉 promising; hopeful
♦ 믿음직한 사람 a promising man; a person of promise / 믿음직한 솜씨 dependable workmanship / 믿음직한 친구 a steadfast friend / 아무를 믿음직하게 여기다 place great trust in *sb*; hope [expect] much from *sb*

밀 wheat; (英) corn ♦ 봄[겨울]밀 spring [winter] wheat ■ —밭 a wheat field

밀가루 wheat flour ♦ 밀가루 반죽을 만들다 knead dough

밀감 蜜柑 〔植〕 a mandarin orange; a tangerine ♦ 밀감 껍질을 벗기다 peel an orange

밀계 密計 a secret plan [design, plot]; an intrigue ♦ 밀계를 꾸미다 plot secretly; frame [weave] a secret plot

밀계 密啓 a secret [confidential] report to the throne [king] —**밀계하다** submit a confidential report to the king; report secretly to the king

밀고 密告 (secret) information 《against》; an anonymous report; betrayal
♦ 밀고를 받다 receive secret information [an anonymous notice] 《from》
—**밀고하다** inform 《against》; give secret information; betray
▶ 그는 동료 밀수업자들을 밀고했다 He informed on his fellow smugglers.
▶ 공범자가 경찰에 밀고했다 The accomplice squealed to the cops.
■ —자 an informant; a betrayer

밀교 密教 〔佛教〕 Esoteric [Tantric] Buddhism

밀국수 wheat vermicelli; noodles

밀기울 wheat bran

밀깜부기 a smut ball [ear] of wheat

밀다 1 〈떠밀다〉 push; thrust; shove
♦ 문을 밀어 열다[닫다] push the door open [shut]/ 수레를 밀다 push [wheel] a cart / 밀고 가다 shove along / 밀고 들어가다 force *oneself* [*one's* way] into / 밀어 내다[올리다] push out [up]/ 밀어 넘어뜨리다 push down [over]/ 밑에서) 밀어주다 give *sb* a hoist [boost]/ 열차[벼랑]에서 밀어 떨어뜨리다 push *sb* off the train [over the cliff]/ (파도가) 물가로 밀어 올리다 throw [cast, wash] up 《a boat》 on the shore; wash 《seaweeds》 ashore / 밀고 밀리는 대혼잡이다 be packed to overflowing; be overflowing with people / 자기의 생각을 밀고 나가다 persist in *one's* opinion; adhere [hold on] to *one's* belief
▶ 내 차 좀 밀어주시겠습니까 ? Will you give my car a push?
▶ 문은 아무리 밀고 당겨도 열리지 않았다 I couldn't open the door [The door would not open] no matter how much I pushed and pulled.
▶ (만원 버스 등에서) 너무 밀지 마시오 Don't push me so much!
▶ 사자는 새끼를 골짜기로 밀어 떨어뜨린다고 한다 Lions are said to push their cubs down into a valley.
▶ 그는 반대를 무릅쓰고 자기의 계획을 밀고 나갔다 He carried his plans through in the face of opposition.
▶ 그는 잘못된 생각을 끝까지 밀고 나갔다 He persisted in his wrong idea to the last.
2 〈깎다〉 shave; plane; 〈문지르다〉 rub; scrub
♦ 등을 밀다 wash [rub] down *one's* back; scrub *one's* back / 때를 밀다 wash [rub] off the dirt / 수염을 밀다 shave *oneself* [*one's* face]; have [get] a shave / 대패로 판자를 밀다 plane a board (smooth)
3 〈추천하다〉 recommend; 〈지지하다〉 support; back (up); (美) boost
♦ 후진을 밀다 help *one's* juniors to get ahead
▶ 우리는 그를 회장으로 밀었다 We recommended [backed, nominated] him for the post of chairman.
4 〈밀대로 눌러 펴다〉 press; roll
♦ 파이 반죽을 밀다 roll out pie dough

밀담 密談 a secret [private] conversation; a

밀대

confidential talk
▶ 우리는 밀담을 가졌다 We had a private talk. ⇌ We talked behind closed doors.
—**밀담하다** talk secretly [behind closed doors] 《with》; have a confidential talk 《with》

밀대 1 〈막대〉 a push stick 2 〈총의〉 the recoil mechanism

밀도 密度 density
♦ 인구 밀도 population density; the density of the population / 밀도가 높은 dense 《metal》; of high density
▶ 인구 밀도가 가장 높은 대륙은 유럽이고 가장 낮은 대륙은 오스트레일리아다 The most densely populated continent is Europe and the least Australia.
■ —계 a densimeter; a densitometer —류 〔海〕 a density current —측정 densimetry

밀도살 密屠殺 illegal butchery; secret [clandestine] slaughter 《of cattle》 —**밀도살하다** slaughter [butcher] 《cattle》 clandestinely [unlawfully, in secret]

밀떡 wheat plaster [paste] 《to be applied to a wound》

밀뜨리다 push [shove] (off); thrust; give a push [thrust]

밀라노 〈이탈리아의 도시〉 Milan ♦ 밀라노의 Milanese ■ —시민 a Milanese

밀랍 蜜蠟 beeswax; (yellow) wax

밀려나다 be pushed [thrust, forced] out
♦ 회사에서 밀려나다 get shoved [pushed] out of one's job with the company / 사장 자리에서 밀려나다 be squeezed out of the president's seat / 시대의 흐름에 밀려나다 be swept under by the current of the times
▶ 그녀는 들어가려고 했으나 사람이 많아서 밀려났다 She tried to get in but was crowded out.

밀려오다 advance [come, press] on 《a castle》; make [rush] for 《the door》; 〈파도가〉 dash against; break on 《the rocks》; surge in 《from the Pacific》
♦ 밀려오는 적 the surging [advancing] enemy / 밀려오는 파도 advancing [surging, incoming] waves
▶ 조수가 밀려오기 시작했다 The tide has begun to rise. ⇌ The tide is flowing [on the flow].
▶ 높은 파도가 해안으로 밀려왔다 The waves came surging against the shore. ⇌ The high waves broke against the shore.
▶ 수십만의 적군이 밀려왔다 Hundreds of thousands of enemy troop rushed us.

밀렵 密獵 poaching —**밀렵하다** poach (for) (pheasants); steal game ■ —선(船) a poaching boat [vessel] —자 a poacher

밀리- milli-
■ —그램 a milligram(me) (略 mg) —리터 a milliliter (略 ml) —미크론 a millimicron (略 mμ) (pl. ~s, -cra) —미터 a millimeter (略 mm): 눈이 10밀리미터 내렸다 The snow is ten millimeters thick. —바 a millibar (略 mb)

밀리다 1 〈일 등이〉 be left undone; be delayed [retarded]; be piled up; be accumulated
♦ 밀린 일 piled-up work / 일이 밀리다 get behind in one's work / 주문이 밀리다 orders pile up
▶ 지금 일이 많이 밀려 있다 I have a lot of work on my hands [left unfinished].
▶ 나는 밀린 일을 해치워야 한다 I have some unfinished work to dispose of.
▶ 러시아워에는 차량이 밀린다 Traffic piles up at rush hour. ⇌ Traffic jams develop during rush hour.
2 〈지불이〉 fall into arrears; be overdue; be outstanding; be left unpaid
♦ 밀린 이자 an interest on arrears / 밀린 임금 back pay / 밀린 집세 back rent; rent in arrears / 빚이 밀리다 get behind in one's debts / 집세가 밀리다 fail to pay [meet] one's rent promptly; get into arrears with one's rent
▶ 그는 집세가 밀려 있다 He is in arrears with his rent.
▶ 그는 집세가 두 달 분이나 밀려 있었다 He was two months behind [in arrears] with the rent.
3 〈떠밀리다〉 be pushed; be shoved [thrust]
♦ 밀고 밀리는 경쟁[싸움] a dingdong race [fight]; a seesaw struggle [battle] / 인파에 밀리다 be jostled in the crowd / 물결에 이리저리 밀리다 be tossed about by the waves; be at the mercy of the waves; drift on the waves / 파도에 밀려 바닷가에 닿다 be cast ashore; be washed up on the beach
▶ 군중은 강당으로 밀려 들어갔다 The crowd pushed into the auditorium.
▶ 출구가 혼잡하여 밀고 밀리는 통에 많은 사람이 다쳤다 There was a jam at the exit, and many were injured.
4 〈깎이다〉 get shaved; shave; 〈대패로〉 get planed; plane
▶ 이 연장은 잘 밀린다 This tool planes well.

밀림 密林 a thick [dense] forest; a jungle
■ —지대 a jungle area

밀막다 〈핑계대고 거절하다〉 refuse under a pretense; decline on the pretext 《of》

밀매 密賣 an illicit sale [trade] 《of》; illicit traffic 《in》; smuggling
—**밀매하다** sell secretly; deal secretly 《in》; smuggle; practice smuggling
■ —자 an illicit dealer; a secret trader; a smuggler —품 smuggled goods

밀매음 密賣淫 illegal [unlicensed] prostitution —**밀매음하다** prostitute illegally

밀모 密謀 a plot; an (underhand) intrigue; 〈공모〉 a conspiracy —**밀모하다** plot; conspire

밀무역 密貿易 smuggling ⇨ 밀수(密輸)
—**밀무역하다** smuggle (in [out])
■ —자 a smuggler

밀물 〈조수가 들어옴〉 the inflow [rising] of the tide; 〈조수〉 the rising [incoming] tide; (a) flood tide; high tide ♦ 밀물을 기다리다 wait for the tide to come [flow] in
▶ 밀물이 들어온다 The tide is rising.

밀방망이 〈밀대〉 a rolling pin

밀보리 〈밀과 보리〉 wheat and barley; 〈쌀보리〉 rye

밀봉 密封 tight sealing —**밀봉하다** seal up; seal tightly ♦병을 밀봉하다 bottle up [in] ▶편지를 밀봉하여 우체통에 넣었다 I sealed and mailed the letter.
■—교육 secret training (for a spy)

밀사 密使 a secret messenger [envoy]; an emissary; a confidential agent ♦아무를 밀사로 보내다 send *sb* on a secret mission

밀살 密殺 illegal butchery ⇨ 밀도살(密屠殺)

밀생 密生 thick [dense] growth (of grass) —**밀생하다** grow thick [luxuriantly] ▶이 섬에는 수목이 밀생해 있다 The island is thickly wooded [grown with trees]. ≒ The island is covered by dense stands of trees.

밀서 密書 a secret [confidential] letter [message] ♦밀서를 지니다 carry [bear] a secret message

밀선 密船 a smuggling vessel [boat]; a smuggler

밀송 密送 sending secretly —**밀송하다** send [dispatch] secretly [in secret]

밀수 密輸 smuggling; contraband (trade) ▶정부는 마약 밀수를 방지하기 위해 애썼다 The government tried to prevent the smuggling of drugs.
—**밀수하다** 〈수입하다〉 smuggle *sth* in [into] (the country); import through illegal channels; (美) run 《guns》 ▶그들은 대마를 밀수하다 잡혔다 They were caught smuggling in hemp [importing hemp illegally into the country].
■—감시선 a contraband control vessel —**단** a gang of smugglers; a smuggling ring [gang] —**선** a boat for smuggling; a smuggler —**업자** a smuggler; a contraband trader; a contrabandist —**품** contraband 《goods》; smuggled goods [articles]

밀수제비 wheat flakes boiled in soup

밀수출 密輸出 smuggling abroad —**밀수출하다** smuggle *sth* abroad [out of the country]; export *sth* unlawfully ▶그 일당은 시계를 밀수출했다 The gang smuggled watches abroad [out of the country]. ≒ The gang exported watches illegally.

밀실 密室 a secret room [chamber]; a closet ♦밀실에서 behind closed doors / 밀실에 감금하다 keep *sb* in solitary [close] confinement / 밀실에서 이야기하다 closet *oneself* with *sb*; be closeted together
■—정치 closed-door politics

밀약 密約 〈약속〉 a secret promise [understanding]; 〈조약〉 a secret treaty; 〈협약〉 a secret agreement ♦밀약을 맺다 make a secret promise; conclude [enter into] a secret treaty [agreement] 《with》 ▶그들 사이에는 밀약이 맺어져 있었다 There was a secret agreement [understanding] between them.

밀어 密語 a secret conversation ⇨ 밀담(密談)

밀어 密漁 poaching —**밀어하다** poach (for) 《salmon》 ■—선 a poaching boat [vessel] —**자** a poacher

밀어내기 pushing [pressing, squeezing] out ♦〈야구에서〉 밀어내기 1득점 a point given by forcing ▶밀어내기로 1점을 얻었다 They forced in a run with a bases-loaded walk.

밀어내다 push [press, thrust, force, squeeze, crowd, elbow] out ♦링 밖으로 밀어내다 thrust [push] 《*one's* antagonist》 out of the ring ▶선생님은 그를 교실 밖으로 밀어냈다 Our teacher pushed him out of the classroom. ▶나는 남을 밀어내고 승진할 생각은 추호도 없다 I'd never want promotion at the expense of others.

밀어닥치다 close [swarm] in 《on *sb*》; crowd 《to a place》; rush for 《the door》; 〈파도가〉 surge [beat, rush] 《on》

밀어붙이다 push [drive] *sb* to; push [thrust] against; pin against; press hard ♦벽 쪽으로 밀어붙이다 drive *sb* to the wall / 끝까지 밀어붙이다 keep pushing to the end

밀어젖히다 push away [aside]; force [thrust] aside [out of the way]; 〈팔꿈치로〉 elbow *sb* out [aside, to one side] ▶그는 나를 밀어젖히려고 했다 He tried to push me aside. ▶그는 워낙 급해서 사람들을 밀어젖히고 나아갔다 He was in such a hurry that he pushed his way through the crowd.

밀어치기 〔撞球〕 a follow shot

밀월 密月 a honeymoon ♦양국간의 밀월 시대 a honeymoon (period) between the two countries
■—여행 ⇨ 신혼여행

밀의 密議 a secret conference; a private consultation; a conclave ▶그 정객들은 호텔에서 밀의를 가졌다 The politicians held a secret conference at a hotel.
—**밀의하다** confer in secret [private] 《with》; hold a secret conference 《with》 ♦장시간 밀의하다 have long discussions behind closed doors

밀입국 密入國 illegal entry into a country —**밀입국하다** smuggle *oneself* into a country ▶그들은 어선으로 밀입국하려 하고 있었다 They were trying to smuggle themselves into the country on a fishing boat.

밀장지 —障 a sliding door [partition]

밀접하다 密接— close; intimate ♦밀접한 관계 a close relationship [connection] / 수요와 공급의 밀접한 관계 the intimate relationship between supply and demand ▶그는 그 사건과 밀접한 관계가 있다 He has a close connection [is closely connected] with the event. ▶기후와 농작물 사이에는 서로 밀접한 관계가 있다 There is a close correlation between climate and crops. ▶양국 관계는 더욱 밀접해졌다 The two countries have come even closer together.

밀정 密偵 a spy; a secret [confidential] agent

밀조 密造 illicit manufacture; 〈술의〉 unlawful brewing; (美俗) moonshining —**밀조하다** manufacture clandestinely; 〈술을〉 brew illicitly; (美俗) moonshine

밀주 密酒 home brew; (美俗) moonshine

밀집

■—제조소 an illicit distillery; (美俗) a bootlegging distillery —제조자 an illicit distiller; (美俗) a moonshiner

밀집 密集 ♦건물 밀집 지대 a (densely) built-up area / 인구 밀집 지역 a densely populated district
—밀집하다 crowd; swarm; close up [together]; be in close order
♦밀집해 있는 close; massed; crowded; thick; congested; compact; close-packed
▶ 그 지역에는 아파트가 밀집해 있다 The apartments stand close together in that area.
■—대형(隊形) 〔軍〕 a close order; (a) close [compact] formation —화성(和聲) 〔樂〕 close harmony —훈련 close-order drill

밀짚 (a) wheat straw ■—모자 a straw hat —세공 strawwork

밀착 密着 close adhesion [adherence]
♦밀착 취재 close reporting —밀착하다 stick (fast) (to); adhere closely (to)
▶ 붕대가 상처에 밀착해서 떨어지지 않는다 The bandage is stuck to the wound and will not come loose.
■—법(寫) contact printing —인화 a contact print [copy] —(인화)지 contact paper

밀초 a wax candle

밀치다 push; thrust; give a push [thrust]
♦서로 밀치다 jostle [push, hustle] one another / 군중을 밀치고 나아가다 push [force, elbow] one's way through the crowd

밀치락달치락하다 hustle and jostle; push and shove; push one another

밀칙 密勅 a king's secret instruction [order]

밀크 milk ■—셰이크 milk shake —커피 white coffee; (프) café au lait

밀타승 密陀僧 〔化〕 litharge; lead monoxide

밀탐 密探 〈몰래 살핌〉 spying, espionage; secret investigation
—밀탐하다 spy (on sb, into a secret); make secret inquiries into sth; investigate secretly
♦적의 동정을 밀탐하다 spy upon the enemy's movement / 회사의 내정을 밀탐하다 investigate the inside affairs of a company

밀턴 〈영국의 시인〉 Milton, John (1608-74)
♦밀턴(의 시풍)의 Miltonic; Miltonian

밀통 密通 1 〈간통〉 an illicit intercourse [amour]; adultery
—밀통하다 misconduct oneself (with); make an illicit love (to); commit adultery (with)
2 ⇨ 내통(內通)
■—자 〈남자〉 an adulterer; 〈여자〉 an adulteress

밀폐 密閉 tight closing
—밀폐하다 shut tight(ly); cover [close] up tight; seal up; make airtight
♦밀폐된 상자 an airtight box / 뚜껑을 덮어 밀폐하다 cover tightly with the lid
▶ 용기를 밀폐하면 내용물이 꽤 오래 갑니다 If the receptacle is made airtight, the contents will keep for quite a long time.
■—용기 an airtight container

밀항 密航 a secret passage; stowing away; smuggling oneself
▶ 그는 밀항을 꾀하다가 걸렸다 He plotted to stow away [escape the country], but was caught.
—밀항하다 stow away (on a steamer); smuggle oneself (into America)
■—선 a smuggler —자 a stowaway

밀행 密行 going secretly; a prowl —밀행하다 prowl (about); go secretly [stealthily] (to)

밀회 密會 a secret [clandestine] meeting; a rendezvous
—밀회하다 meet secretly; have a secret [clandestine] meeting (with); rendezvous
■—장소 a place of secret meeting

밉다 hateful; detestable; odious; disgusting; abominable; cursed; spiteful
♦밉지 않은 innocent; artless; naive / 밉게 굴다 behave [act] detestably [abominably]
▶ 미운 일곱 살이라는 말에 틀림이 없구나 A boy of six or seven is really mischievous.
▶ 왠지 저 사내는 주는 것 없이 밉다 I don't know why, but that man rubs me (up) the wrong way.

밉살맞다 hateful ⇨ 밉살스럽다

밉살스럽다 hateful; detestable; disgusting; abominable; cursed; horrible; spiteful
♦밉살스러운 말투 an insolent [a malicious] tone / 밉살스러운 얼굴 a repulsive countenance; a hateful look / 밉살스러운 태도 a hateful [detestable] manner / 밉살스럽게 웃다 smile a malicious smile
▶ 그녀는 내 앞에서는 항상 밉살스럽게 말한다 She always speaks spitefully in my presence.
▶ 그는 밉살스러울 정도로 침착했다 He remained provokingly cool [calm].
▶ 정말 밉살스러운 놈이로구나 What a repulsive [an odious] wretch he is!

밉상 —相 a repulsive [disgusting] countenance [face]

밋밋이 long and slender [upright]; straight and smooth; plainly
♦밋밋이 자란 나무 a tree grown straight and tall / 턱수염을 밋밋이 밀다 shave one's beard off cleanly; shave one's chin clean

밋밋하다 〈곧고 길다〉 long and slender; 〈반반하다〉 straight and smooth; smooth and flat
♦밋밋한 나무 a slender and upright tree / 밋밋한 다리 long and slender legs / 밋밋한 언덕 a soft [gently-sloping] hill; 〈벌거숭이 산〉 a bare hill / 밋밋한 턱 a beardless chin

밍근하다 lukewarm; tepid

밍밍하다 tasteless; weak [watery] (tea); thin (porridge); washy (milk); flat (beer); mild (tobacco); light (liquor)
♦밍밍한 국 thin soup / 밍밍한 술 flat wine; washy liquor; sloppy drink

밍크 〔動〕 a mink (pl. ~(s)) ■—코트 (wear) a mink (coat)

및 and (also); both...and; as well as; in addition to ▶성명, 생년월일 및 직업을 쓰시오 Write your name, date of birth, and occupation, please.

밑 1 〈아래(쪽)〉 the bottom; the foot; the base; the lower part
♦책상 오른쪽 밑 서랍 the lower right drawer of a desk / 밑의 under; lower / 바로 밑의

directly [just, right] under
〈밑이〉 무릎 밑이 썰렁하다 I feel chilly below the knees.
〈밑을〉 지하철이 이 길 밑을 지나 다닌다 The subway runs under this street.
▶ 말하면서 밑을 보지 마라 Don't look down while talking.
〈밑에〉 밑에; under; beneath; below; underneath / 계단 밑에 at the foot [bottom] of the stairs / 나무 밑에 under a tree / 눈 밑에 under the eye / 밑에 놓다 put [lay, set] down
▶ 교회는 언덕 밑에 세워져 있었다 The church stood under [at the foot of] a hill.
▶ 다리 밑에 배가 한 척 있다 There is a boat under [beneath] the bridge.
▶ 그것은 이 돌 밑에 묻혀 있다 It is buried beneath this stone.
〈밑에서〉 밑에서 세번째 줄을 읽으시오 Read the third line from the bottom.
▶ 한 쌍의 교각이 밑에서 다리를 떠받치고 있다 A pair of piers support the bridge from below.
▶ 그가 테이블 밑에서 나왔다 He came out from under the table.
▶ 그가 밑에서 너를 기다리고 있다 He is downstairs waiting for you.
〈밑으로〉 밑으로 down(ward) / 밑으로 내려가다 go [come] down; /〈아래층으로〉 go [come] downstairs / 밑으로 떨어지다 fall down;〈지상으로〉 fall to the ground / 지평선 밑으로 지다〈the sun〉 sink below the horizon

2 〈바닥〉 the bottom 《of a bottle》; the bed 《of a river》
▶ 양동이 밑이 빠졌다 The bottom fell out of the bucket.
▶ 수조 밑에 물고기가 보인다 I see a fish at the bottom of the tank.
▶ 그것은 바다 밑으로 가라앉았다 It sank to the bottom of the ocean.

3 〈하위〉 ◆밑의 lower; subordinate; 〈이하의〉 below; under / 밑에서 두번째 아이 the second youngest of one's children / 남의 밑에 있다 be subordinate to sb / 남의 밑에서 일하다 work under sb
▶ 대위는 소령보다 한 계급 밑이다 A captain is one rank below a major.
▶ 그녀는 오빠보다 다섯 살 밑이다 She is five years younger than her brother. ⇌ She is younger than her brother by five years.

4 〈근본〉 the root; the source; the origin; the foundation ◆밑도 끝도 없는 소문 a groundless rumor; an unfounded gossip

5 〈조건·환경〉 ◆부모 밑을 떠나다 leave [bid farewell to] one's parental roof / 민 선생 밑에서 피아노를 배우다 take piano lessons from Mr. Min
▶ 그는 홍박사 밑에서 법률 공부를 했다 He studied law under Dr. Hong.

6 〈궁둥이·밑구멍〉 the buttocks; 《口》 the bottom; the anus ◆제 밑 들어 남 보이기 wash one's dirty linen in public

7 〈뿌리〉 the root; the base
◆나무 밑 the base of a tree / 귀밑까지 빨갛지다 blush to the roots of one's hair

8 〖數〗 a base; a radix

밑각 —角 〖幾〗 a base angle
밑감 〈원료〉 raw materials
밑거름 manure given at sowing [planting] time; initial [base] manure
▶ 그는 조국 재건의 밑거름이 되기로 결심했다 He decided to sacrifice himself for the reconstruction of his homeland.
밑구멍 a bottom hole; 〈항문〉 the anus
밑그림 a rough sketch; a draft; a design
◆자수의 밑그림 a design for embroidery / 밑그림을 그리다 make a rough sketch 《of》; make a design 《of》; design / 밑그림에 따라 조각하다 carve on a design
밑넓이 〖幾〗 the area of base; the base area
밑돈 a nest egg
밑돌다 do not amount 《to》; fall short 《of》; be less [lower] than; be worse than; be [fall] below 《the average》
▶ 금년에는 악천후로 인해 쌀 수확이 평년작을 밑돌았다 The rice crop was worse than usual this year due to the bad weather.
▶ 관객수는 예상을 훨씬 밑돌았다 The number of spectators fell far short of our expectations.
밑동 the bottom; the base 《of a tree》
◆기둥의 밑동 the base of a pillar / 벌목한 큰 나무의 밑동 the stump of a large felled tree
▶ 강풍으로 나무의 밑동이 부러졌다 The tree broke at the base [near the root] because of the strong wind.
밑면 —面 〖幾〗 the base
밑면적 —面積 〖幾〗 the base area ⇨ 밑넓이
밑바닥 1 〈물건의〉 the bottom; the base; the bed 《of a river》
◆구두의 밑바닥 the sole of a shoe / 냄비의 밑바닥 the under surface of a saucepan / 밑바닥이 빠진 bottomless / 밑바닥이 이중으로 된 double-bottomed 《ship》
▶ 내 트렁크는 더미의 밑바닥에 깔려 있었다 My trunk was at the bottom of the heap.
2 〈환경 등의〉 the bottom; the nadir 《of one's fortune》
◆사회의 밑바닥 the bottom of the social scale; the lowest social stratum / 밑바닥 생활 a life of penury [extreme poverty]; a life in the slums / 밑바닥 생활을 하는 사람들 the submerged tenth; people at the bottom of the social scale
▶ 그는 밑바닥 인생을 살고 있다 He is at the bottom of the pecking order.
밑바탕 1 〈근저〉 the foundation; the base; the ground; the groundwork
▶ 이 주의가 그 학설의 밑바탕이 되어 있다 This doctrine underlies the theory.
2 〈본성〉 (real) nature; one's true character [colors]
◆밑바탕이 드러나다 reveal [show] one's true character [colors]; unmask oneself / 밑바탕이 좋다[나쁘다] be good [bad] by nature
밑받침 1 〈밑에 까는 것〉 an underlay; 〈책받침〉 a celluloid board [cardboard]
2 〈버팀〉 a support; a prop; a stay ◆기둥의 밑받침 a stay at the base of a pillar

밑밥 〈낚시의〉 a ground bait
밑변 —邊 〔幾〕 the base
밑 빠진 가마에 물붓기 〈속담〉 It will be like throwing water on thirsty soil.
밑씨 〔植〕 an ovule
밑씻개 toilet paper; (英俗) bumf
밑알 a nest egg
밑줄 an underline ♦ 밑줄친 부분 an underlined [underscored] part / 밑줄을 긋다[치다] underline 《a word》; draw an underline; underscore 《a line》
▶ 나는 어려운 단어에는 모두 붉은 색으로 밑줄을 그었다 I underlined all the difficult [big] words in red.
밑줄기 the lower part of a stalk [stem]
밑지다 lose on the cost price; lose 《over》; suffer [incur] a loss
♦ 밑지는 장사 a losing [an unprofitable] business / 밑지고 팔다 sell with loss on cost; sell below cost (price)
▶ 그러면 밑집니다 Then I shall be unable to cover the cost.
▶ 밑져야 본전 (속담) I am none the worse for it. ⇒ I can cover the cost.
밑질기다 stay (too) long; overstay *one's* time; make a long visit ♦ 밑질긴 손님 a sticker / 밑질겨서 남이 싫어하다 outstay [wear out] *one's* welcome
밑창 the outsole 《of a shoe》
밑천 **1** 〈자본〉 capital; fund; 〈원금〉 the principal; 〈도박의〉 a stake
♦ 장사 밑천 business funds / 밑천이 떨어지다 run out of funds / 장사 밑천을 대다 provide capital 《for》; provide [supply] *sb* with capital [funds]; finance / 밑천을 건지다 recover *one's* investment / 밑천을 들이다 lay out money 《on》; put [sink] money 《in》 / 한 밑천을 잡다 amass [pile up] a fortune / 밑천을 건지지 못하다 fail to return the original investment / 적은 밑천으로 사업을 시작하다 start business on a small capital / 밑천까지 다 날리다 lose both principal and interest; run through all that *one* has
▶ 그것은 밑천이 많이 드는 장사였다 That business required a large amount of capital.
▶ 이 기계는 5년 쓰면 밑천이 빠진다 This machine will pay for itself in five years.
▶ 무엇을 하든 밑천을 들여야 한다 You must sow [give] before you can reap [take].
▶ 그녀는 5천만원의 밑천으로 상점을 열었다 She opened a store with capital of fifty million won.
2 〈성기〉 *one's* penis; *one's* equipment
밑층 —層 the downstairs ⇨ 아래층

-ㅂ니까 Are 《you, they》…?; Is 《he, she, it》…?; Do 《you》…? ▶ 얼마 동안 여기에 계실 겁니까? How long will you be here?
-ㅂ니다 be; do ♦ 나는 학생입니다 I am a student. ▶ 비가 옵니다 It rains.
-ㅂ디까 Be it known that…?; Did you hear [notice] that…?; Have you been told that…?; Have you found that…?
▶ 그는 몇시에 온다고 합디까? What time did he say he would come?
▶ 이 사건에 대해 무슨 말이 있습디까? Have you heard anything about this incident?
-ㅂ디다 they say; it is said [known] that; as it is found; I hear [am told] that
▶ 브라운씨가 여름 휴가 동안에 우리를 방문한다고 합디다 I am told Mr. Brown is going to visit us during summer vacation.
-ㅂ시다 Let us 《do》; Let's 《do》; we will 《do》
▶ 밖에 나가서 야구를 합시다 Let's go out and play baseball.
바¹ 〈줄〉 a rope; 〈마소용의 고삐〉 a tether
♦ 바를 치다 stretch a rope; rope off / 범행 현장에 바를 쳐서 들어가지 못하게 하다 rope off the scene of the crime
바² 〔樂〕 fa(h); F ♦ 올림 바음 F sharp / 내림 바음 F flat ■—단조[장조] F minor [major] —음자리표 an F clef
바³ 1 〈일〉 a thing; what
♦ 위에서 말한 바와 같이 as mentioned [stated] above
▶ 그것은 네가 알 바 아니다 That is none of your business. ⇌ Mind your own business.
▶ 그것은 내가 예상했던 바이다 It is what I expected.
▶ 전술한 바와 같이 필자는 그 의견에 동의할 수 없다 As stated [mentioned] above, the writer cannot agree with that view.
2 〈방법〉 a means; a way; how to 《do》; 〈범위〉 extent
♦ 내가 말하는 바 what I say / 어찌할 바를 모르다 be at a loss what to do
▶ 그녀를 만났을 때 나는 어찌할 바를 몰랐다 When I met her, I was at a loss what to do.
3 〈…하였더니〉 and then; and; but
바⁴ 1 〈술집〉 a bar; a tavern; (美) a saloon; (英) a public house; (口) a pub
♦ 바의 주인 a barkeeper / 바의 여급 (英) a barmaid; (美俗) a B-girl
2 〈가로장〉 a bar; a crossbar
♦ 바를 뛰어 넘다 clear a bar
▶ 현재 바의 높이는 2미터다 The bar is at 2 meters.
3 〈막대기〉 a bar
4 〔物〕 a bar
■ 밀리— a millibar
바가지 1 〈그릇〉 a gourd (dipper)

♦ 바가지로 물을 푸다 scoop [dip] water with a gourd
2 〈터무니없는 요금 등〉 extortionate [exorbitant] prices [fees]; overcharge
■ —요금 an exorbitant price [fare]
바가지긁다 nag [(俗) yap] 《at one's husband》; speak crossly 《to one's husband》; grumble 《at》
♦ 밤늦게 돌아온다고 바가지긁다 yap at 《him》 for being late at night / 바가지긁는 아내 a nagging wife [woman]; a shrew; a Xanthippe
▶ 그녀는 언제나 남편이 늦게 돌아오면 바가지 긁었다 She kept nagging at her husband for coming home late.
바가지쓰다 be overcharged; (be made to) pay through the nose
▶ 나는 엄청나게 바가지 썼다 They rushed me shockingly.
바가지씌우다 overcharge; demand extortionate prices; make unjust [undue] profits; charge an unreasonable price
▶ 제게 너무 바가지 씌우는 건 아닙니까? I'm afraid you've charged me a bit too much.
바각 with a scrape [scraping, scratch]
바각거리다 scrape (harshly); keep a scraping noise
바각바각 scraping and scraping
바겐세일 a bargain sale ▶ 이 상점은 매주 토요일에 바겐세일을 한다 This shop sells things cheap [at a bargain] on Saturdays.
바곳¹ 〈송곳〉 an awl [a gimlet] with a side-handle ♦ 바곳으로 구멍을 뚫다 bore a hole in sth with a gimlet
바곳² 〔植〕 a wolfsbane; a monkshood
바구니 a basket; a crate
♦ 과일 한 바구니 a basket(ful) of fruit
■ 대— a bamboo basket 장— a shopping basket ■ —세공품 basketry; basketwork
바구미 〔昆〕 a rice [black, grain] weevil [insect]
바그너 〈독일의 작곡가〉 Wagner, Wilhelm Richard (1813-1883) ♦ 바그너풍[작]의 Wagnerian
바그다드 〈이라크의 수도〉 Bag(h)dad
■ —조약 the Bagdad Pact
바그르르 〈물 등이〉 (boil) simmering; 〈거품이〉 bubbling; foaming
♦ 냄비에서 바그르르 끓고 있는 스튜 stew simmering in a pot / 물이 바그르르 끓다 water simmers / 비누거품이 바그르르 일다 suds bubble up
바글거리다 〈물이〉 simmer; seethe; boil; 〈거품이〉 bubble; 〈우글거리다〉 swarm 《with》
바글바글 〈물이〉 seethingly; on [at] the simmer; 〈거품이〉 bubblingly; 〈우글우글〉 in a swarm

♦ 물을 바글바글 끓이다 boil water; bring water to a simmer
▶ 거기에는 개미가 바글바글하다 You will find ants there in swarms.
▶ 쓰레기통에는 구더기가 바글바글했다 The garbage can was crawling with maggots.

바깥 〈집밖〉 the open (air); the outdoors; 〈바깥쪽〉 the outside; 〈표면〉 the exterior ⇨ 밖 1 ♦ 바깥의 〈외부의〉 outer; outside; external; exterior; 〈옥외의〉 outdoor / 바깥에서 in the open; outdoors; out of doors / 바깥에서 운동하다 get some outdoor exercise / 바깥이 덥다[춥다] be hot [cold] outside / 바깥을 내다보다 〈창문에서〉 look out (of) the window; 〈창 너머로〉 look out through the window / 바깥에서 식사하다 dine [eat] out / 바깥에서 놀다 play outside [outdoors, in the open] / 바깥에서 문을 잠그다 fasten [lock] the door from outside / 바깥에서 기다리다 wait outside [without] / 바깥으로 나가다 go out (of doors); go out into the open air [the street]
▶ 바깥의 온도는 어느 정도냐? What is the outdoor temperature?
▶ 바깥은 매우 춥다 It is very cold outside.
▶ 아이들은 바깥을 좋아한다 Children are creatures of the outdoors.
▶ 바깥에서 놀아라 Play outdoors [out of doors].
▶ 그는 좀처럼 바깥 출입을 하지 않는다 He is a stay-at-home [homekeeping] man.
■ ―공기 outdoor air ―뜰 an outer yard [garden] ―문 〈앞쪽의〉 the front [street] door; 〈대문〉 the outer gate ―부모 one's father ―사돈 the father of one's son-in-law [daughter-in-law] ―소문 a rumor; a report; the talk of the town ―식구 male members of a family ―양반 your master [husband] ―채 an outhouse; an outbuilding; an annex

바깥소식 ―消息 news; the news of the town
♦ 바깥소식에 어둡다 be unfamiliar with what is going on in the world; do not know [has not seen] much of the world; be inexperienced in [ignorant of] the ways of the world

바깥일 outdoor work ♦ 바깥일을 하다 work in the yard [field]

바깥쪽 the outside; the outer side; the exterior
♦ 바깥쪽의 outer; outside; exterior; external / 바깥쪽으로 outward; to the outside / 바깥쪽에서 from the outside; from without
▶ 그녀는 담 바깥쪽에 서서 기다리고 있었다 She stood waiting outside the wall.

바꾸다 1 〈변경하다〉 change; vary; alter; shift; remodel; convert
♦ 계획을 바꾸다 vary one's plans / 진로를 바꾸다 alter the course / 직업을 바꾸다 change one's occupation [job] / (무대) 장면을 바꾸다 shift the scenes / 당구를 바꾸다 change sides / 주의를 바꾸다 depart from one's principle / 말투를 바꾸다 speak in a different way / 화제를 바꾸다 change the subject; switch the conversation 《to another subject》 / 사고방식을 바꾸다 change one's way of thinking
▶ 신념을 바꾸지 마라 Stick to your principle.
▶ 성공의 비결은 뜻을 바꾸지 않는 데 있다 The secret of success is constancy to purpose.
▶ 시대가 변했으니 사고방식을 바꾸는 편이 좋다 Since times have changed, you'd better change your way of thinking.
▶ 이번에 가게의 실내장식을 바꿀 것이다 We will remodel [do over] the shop interior now.

2 〈교환하다〉 change; exchange [barter] 《one thing for another》; 〈변형하다〉 change 《the shape of》; transform 《a barn into a garage》; 〈전환하다〉 change [switch] over 《to》
♦ 수표를 현금으로 바꾸다 cash a check / 만원짜리를 백원짜리 동전으로 바꾸다 change [break] a 10,000-won note into 100-won coins / 달러를 원화로 바꾸다 convert dollars into won
▶ 건강은 돈과 바꿀 수 없다 You can't buy good health.
▶ 옆 사람과 자리를 바꾸시오 Change seats with the person sitting next to you.

3 〈고치다〉 reform 《a system》; revise 《a law》; remold 《a rule》; amend 《a regulation》; 〈갱신하다〉 renew

4 〈대체하다〉 substitute 《A for B》; replace 《an old thing with a new one》
♦ 꽃병의 꽃을 바꾸다 change the flowers [put new flowers] in a vase / 새 프로그램으로 바꾸다 replace 《an old program》 by a new one
▶ 3월부터 새 교과서로 바꿀 것이다 We're going to replace an old textbook with a new one in March.
▶ 헌 타이어를 새 것과 바꿨다 I replaced a worn tire with a new one.
▶ 이 그림하고 저 꽃병을 바꿔 놓아라 Replace this painting with that vase.

5 ⇨ 사다

6 〈전화를 대주다〉 ▶ 김선생을 바꿔주십시오 Please connect me with [get me through to, (英) put me through to] Mr. Kim.

바꿈질 (an) exchange; barter; swap(ping)
―바꿈질하다 exchange; change; make an exchange 《with another》; swap [swop, exchange] 《one thing》 for 《another》

바꿔말하다 say [express] sth in other [different] words; put (it) (in) another way
♦ 바꿔말하면 (to put it) in other words; to put it (in) another way; that is (to say); namely

바꿔치다 substitute 《one thing for another》 fraudulently; change 《one thing for another》 secretly
▶ 누군가가 역의 벤치에서 내 여행가방을 바꿔치기 틀림없다 Someone must have replaced my suitcase on the station bench.

바뀌다 〈변하다〉 change; be changed; alter; be altered; be modified; shift; turn
♦ 주소가 바뀌다 have one's address changed / 화제가 바뀌다 pass (on) to another subject
▶ 보초는 정오에 바뀌었다 Sentinels were relieved at noon.
▶ 집주인은 두 번 바뀌었다 This house has changed hands twice.
▶ 해가 바뀌었다 A new year began.
▶ 늙은 선생님에서 젊은 선생님으로 바뀌었다

The old teacher gave place to [was succeeded by] a young teacher.
▶ 이 물질은 가열하면 기체로 바뀐다 When heated, this substance changes [turns] into gas.

바나나 a banana ♦ 바나나 나무 a banana (tree) / 바나나 껍질을 벗기다 peel (off the skin of) a banana

바나듐 〔化〕 vanadium ■―산 vanadic acid

바느질 needlework; sewing
♦ 바느질로 생계를 꾸리다 earn *one's* living [make a living] by needlework
▶ 그녀는 바느질을 잘한다[못한다] She is good [poor] at needlework.
▶ 이 바느질감을 내일까지 손님에게 전해 주어야 한다 I have to deliver this needlework to the customer by tomorrow.
▶ 주문하신 웨딩드레스는 10일 후에 바느질이 끝납니다 Your wedding dress will be finished in ten days.
―**바느질하다** sew; stitch; do needlework

> 〖解說〗 *sew*는 천 등을 꿰매거나 의복 같은 것을 바느질해서 짓는 것이고 ***stitch***는 한 땀 한 땀 바늘로 꿰매는 것. up을 붙이면 완전히 꿰매기를 마친다는 뜻이 된다.

♦ 손[재봉틀]으로 바느질하다 sew by hand [on a (sewing) machine]
▶ 그녀는 의자에 앉아 바느질하고 있었다 She was sewing on the chair. ⇌ She sat on the chair doing her needlework.
■―**거리** sewing; a dress to be made ―**삯** sewing charges ―**자** a ruler [measure] for sewing ―**품** needlework (as a means of living)

바늘 1 〈재봉용〉 a (sewing) needle
♦ 작은[큰] 바늘 a short [large] needle / 실 꿴 바늘 a needle and thread / 바늘에 실을 꿰다 pass a thread through the eye of a needle; thread a needle
▶ 바늘 떨어지는 소리가 들릴 정도로 조용했다 It was so quiet (that) you could almost hear a pin drop.
2 〈핀〉 a pin; 〈시계바늘〉 a hand 《on the clock》; 〈축음기·주사기의〉 a needle; 〈축음기의〉 a stylus; 〈낚시의〉 a (fish)hook
■―**겨레** a pincushion; a needle pad ―**구멍** a hole made by a needle; a pinhole; a pinprick ―**귀** the eye of a neelde; a needle eye ―**끝** the point of a needle; a needlepoint ―**쌈** a packet of needles

바늘 가는 데 실 간다 《속담》 be inseparably related 《to each other》

바늘 구멍으로 황소바람 들어온다 《속담》 The small hole made with a needle lets in a big blow.

바늘도둑이 소도둑 된다 《속담》 He who steals a pin will steal an ox. ⇌ Once a use, forever a custom.

바늘방석 ―**方席** a pincushion
▶ 나는 줄곧 바늘방석에 앉은 것 같았다 I was sitting on thorns the whole time.

바니시 varnish ⇨ 니스

바닐라 〔植〕 a vanilla

바닐린 vanillin

바다 the sea; 〈대양〉 the ocean
♦ 거울같은 바다 a sea as smooth as glass; a glassy sea / 고요한 바다 a calm [peaceful, placid] sea / 바다의 사나이 a sailor; a seaman; a mariner / 넓고 넓은 바다 a vast expanse of waters / 바다의 생활 a sea life; life on the sea; seafaring [marine] life / 바다의 생물 a sea creature; 《총칭》 marine [sea] life / 바다에 면하다 face [front] the sea / 바다에 떨어지다 fall into the sea; 〈배에서〉 fall overboard / 바다로 나아가다 go [sail] out to sea; put (out) to sea / 〈배에서〉 바다로 뛰어들다 leap [jump] overboard / 〈피서 등으로〉 바다로 가다 go to the seaside / 바다를 건너다 cross the sea / 바다를 건너 중국으로 가다 go over to China
▶ 오늘은 바다가 거칠다[고요하다] The sea is rough [calm] today.
▶ 나는 바다에서 헤엄치기를 좋아한다 I like to swim in the sea [ocean].
▶ 여름에는 가족과 함께 바다로 간다 In summer I go to the seaside with my family.
■―**낚시** sea fishing; offshore fishing ―**밑** the bottom [bed] of the sea; the sea bottom; the seabed **바닷길** a sea [water] route; a seaway **바닷바람** a sea breeze; a breeze from the sea; briny air

바다거북 〔動〕 a sea [marine] turtle; a turtle
▶ 바다거북을 잡다 turtle

바다뱀 〔動〕 a sea snake [serpent] ■―**자리** 〔天〕 the Water Snake; Hydra

바다비오리 〔鳥〕 a merganser

바다사자 ―**獅子** 〔動〕 a sea lion

바다삵 〔動〕 a beaver ⇨ 비버

바다새 a seabird; a seafowl

바다쇠오리 〔鳥〕 an auk

바다오리 〔鳥〕 a (common) murre; a (Bering Island) guillemot

바다제비 〔鳥〕 a storm(y) petrel; a petrel

바다조름 〔動〕 a sea pen

바다짐승 a marine [sea] animal

바다표범 ―**豹**― 〔動〕 a seal; an earless [a true] seal; a sea leopard ―**가죽** a sealskin

바닥 1 〈평면〉 the broad; the flat; the floor
♦ 손바닥 the palm [flat] of a hand / 방바닥 the floor / 땅바닥에 앉다 sit down on the (bare) ground / 마룻바닥에 눕다 lie on the bare floor
2 〈밑부분〉 the bottom 《of a bottle》; 〈신의〉 the sole; 〈강·바다·호수의〉 the bed
♦ 강바닥 the bottom [bed] of a river; a riverbed / 바닥이 두꺼운 냄비 a thick-bottom pan / 이중 바닥 a double bottom; 〈구두의〉 a double sole / 바닥이 없는 unfathomable; bottomless / 헌 신의 바닥을 고치다 repair the soles of old shoes / 바닥에 쌓다 stow 《goods》 in [at] the bottom 《of》
▶ 나무상자의 바닥이 빠졌다 The bottom of the wooden box fell [came] out.
▶ 그 보트는 강바닥에 가라앉았다고 한다 They say that the boat sank to the bottom of the river.
▶ 컵 바닥에 홍차가 조금 남아 있다 There is some tea left at the bottom of the cup.

▶냄비 바닥에 구멍이 났다 There is a hole in the bottom of the pan.
3 〈직물의〉 texture; weave
♦바닥이 고운[거친] of fine [coarse] texture
4 〈고장〉 an area; a district; a place
♦서울[종로] 바닥 the Seoul [the Chongno] area / 장바닥 a marketplace

바닥나다 be exhausted [used up, consumed]; be gone; run out [short] of; be out of 《stock》 ▶우리는 식량이 바닥났다 Our food has run out. ⇌ We have run out of the food.
▶그 물건은 이제 바닥났다 The article is out of stock.
▶자금이 바닥났다 We have run out of funds.
▶그 나라의 경제는 바닥났다 The economy of that country has reached its nadir.

바닥내다 allow *sth* to run out; run out of 《sugar》 ♦식량을 바닥내다 let provisions out of stock; run [be] out of provisions

바닥(시)세 —(時)勢 the (rock-)bottom price; the bedrock price ♦바닥시세에 달하다 reach [strike] (the) bottom

바닥짐 ballast ♦바닥짐을 싣다 ballast a ship; take on ballast ▶배가 바닥짐만으로 항해한다 The ship sails unloaded [light, in ballast].

바닷가 the beach; the seashore; the seaside ♦바닷가에(서) by the sea [seaside]; on the beach / 바닷가를 산책하다 walk along the seashore [beach]
▶바닷가의 냄새가 난다 We can smell the sea. ⇌ There is a smell of the sea in the air.

바닷게 a sea crab
바닷말 seaweed(s); marine algae [plants] ⇨ 해조(海藻)
바닷물 seawater; the brine; salt water
♦바닷물이 들어오는 강 a tidal river
바닷물고기 a sea fish; a saltwater fish
바닷바람 a wind blowing from the sea; a sea breeze

바대 〈덧대는 헝겊조각〉 a patch
♦바대 투성이의 full of patches; patchy / 팔꿈치에 바대를 댄 상의 a coat with patches on the elbows / 바대를 대다 patch
▶그는 언제나 바대를 댄 바지를 입고 있다 He is always wearing patched trousers.

바동거리다 struggle ⇨ 버둥거리다
바둑 *paduk*
♦바둑을 두다 play *paduk*; have a game of *paduk* / 바둑의 명수 a master of *paduk* / 바둑의 사범 a professor of the art of *paduk*
■접— a game of *paduk* with a handicap ■—돌 a *paduk* stone [piece] —무늬 a pattern [design] with black and white spots —점 spots; specks; patches; mottles

바둑말 〔動〕 a piebald (horse)
바둑이 a black and white dog; a dog spotted with black and white
바둑판 —板 a *paduk* board ■—무늬 checks; checkers; a check [checkered] pattern: 바둑판 무늬의 checked; checkered
바드득 with a grating [rasping, creaking] sound; creakingly
▶그는 분해서 이를 바드득 갈았다 He gnashed [grated, ground] his teeth in chagrin.

—**바드득하다** grate; rasp; make a creaking sound; creak; be creaky
바들바들 tremblingly ⇨ 부들부들
바디 〈베틀의〉 a reed; 〈삼을 훑는〉 a hackle
바라 哱囉 〈소라〉 a small gong; 〈자바라〉 small cymbals

바라다 **1** 〈원하다〉 desire; be desirous of; wish (to do); want; wish [long, crave] for; 〈큰 목적의 달성을〉 aspire to [after]; hanker after [for]; be anxious 《that…》; yearn for; 〈부정·의문구문에서〉 care for
▶부귀를 바라다 be ambitious after wealth / 성공을 바라다 wish for success; desire to be successful / 명성을 바라다 aspire after fame; crave [hanker] for fame
▶우리는 그의 성공을 바라고 있다 We wish for [hope for, desire] his success.
▶그녀는 선생님이 되기를 바란다 She wishes to be a teacher.
▶그것이야말로 바로 내가 바라는 바다 That is just the thing. ⇌ That is just what I wish.
▶그는 다시 한 번 그녀를 만나기를 바랐다 He yearned for a sight of her again.
▶그 이상 바랄 것이 없다 I can hope for nothing better than that. ⇌ Nothing suits me better than that.
2 〈기대하다〉 expect; hope (for); look for; look forward to *sth*
♦…을 바라고 in hopes [the hope] 《of doing, that…》; hoping 《that…》; in anticipation of *sth* / 보다 나은 생활을 바라다 hope for a better life / 요행을 바라다 trust to luck [chance] / 바랄 수 없는 것을 바라다 hope against hope 《that…》
▶당신이 정각에 그곳에 도착해 있기를 바란다 I expect [want, wish] you'll be there on time. ⇌ I hope you'll be there on time.
3 〈부탁하다〉 hope; 〈간절히 원하다〉 beg; entreat; request; implore; make an appeal; ask; want
▶더 큰 소리로 말씀해 주시기 바랍니다 Please speak a little louder [more loudly].
▶진열품에 손대지 마시기를 바랍니다 Visitors are requested not to touch the exhibits.
4 〈선택하다〉 like; care for; prefer; choose
▶나는 부보다 건강을 바란다 I prefer health to wealth.

바라문 婆羅門 a Brahman ⇨ 브라만
바라보다 **1** 〈보다〉 see; look at; have a look at; 〈멀리〉 take [get] a view 《of》; look out across; take an extensive view of 《a town》; 〈응시하다〉 watch; stare at; gaze at [on]; 〈전망하다〉 view
♦하늘을 바라보다 look up at the sky / 우두커니 바라보다 look absent-mindedly / 경치를 바라보다 command a view / 뚫어지게 바라보다 look hard [fixedly] at / 찬찬히 바라보다 give *sb* a long look; study 《*sb's* face》
▶나는 차창 밖을 바라보았다 I looked out (of) the train window.
▶그는 길가에 핀 꽃들을 우두커니 바라보았다 He turned his eyes vacantly toward the flowers by the roadside.
2 〈방관하다〉 look on; sit [stand] by and

watch
▶ 그는 싸움을 바라보고만 있었다 He remained a spectator [an idle onlooker] to the quarrel.
3 〈기대하다〉 expect; hope [look] for; count [calculate, reckon] on [upon]
♦ 장래를 바라보다 look forward to the future
▶ 우리는 그의 성공을 바라보고 있다 We expect him to [that he will] succeed.
▶ 그는 승진을 바라보고 열심히 일했다 He worked hard in expectation of promotion.
바라보이다 be looked over; come into view; come in sight; command; overlook
▶ 그는 경기장 전체가 바라보이는 자리에 앉았다 He took his seat overlooking the whole ground.
▶ 이 창문에서 바다가 바라보인다 This window overlooks [looks out on] the sea. ⇒ This window commands a view of the sea.
▶ 이 방에서 아름다운 야경이 바라보인다 You can have a fine night view from this room.
▶ 그 집은 바다가 바라보이는 언덕 위에 서 있다 The house stands on a hill commanding the sea.
바라지 care; looking after
—**바라지하다** take care [charge] of; care for; look after; attend to
♦ 환자를 바라지하다 take care of a patient; attend to [look after] a sick person
▶ 그 기관에서는 어머니가 없는 아이 5명을 바라지하고 있다 The institution has the care of five motherless children.
바라지다[1] **1** 〈몸이〉 short and fat; thickset; stumpy; have a stocky build
▶ 그는 어깨가 딱 바라졌다 He is broad-shouldered. ⇒ He has broad shoulders.
2 〈그릇이〉 shallow
♦ 바라진 냄비 a shallow pan
3 ⇨ 되바라지다
바라지다[2] 〈벌어지다〉 widen; open; be wide open; 〈틈나다〉 be cracked; 〈갈라지다〉 split off [away] (from); be separated
▶ 그의 이는 틈이 바라졌다 His teeth gapped.
바라크 〈판잣집〉 a shanty; a shack; a makeshift hut; a temporary shelter; a barrack
♦ 바라크를 짓다 build a shack
바락 (all) of a sudden; suddenly ⇨ 버럭
바락바락 desperately; frantically; **(口)** like hell
♦ 바락바락 덤비다 turn upon *sb* desperately / 바락바락 기를 쓰다 make desperate efforts; struggle [strive] frantically
▶ 그는 바락바락 내게 대들었다 He turned upon me.
바람[1] **1** 〈공기의 유동〉 a wind; a breath of air; 〈미풍〉 a breeze; 〈선풍기 등의〉 a current

解說 ***wind***는 가장 일반적인 말로서 선풍기 등에 의한 인공적인 바람도 포함한다. much, no 등을 써서 정도를 나타낼 때는 불가산명사로, 종류를 말할 때는 가산명사로 취급한다. wind에는 종종 불쾌한 뜻도 포함되어 있으나 ***breeze***는 주로 가볍고 상쾌한 바람을 가리킨다. ***gale***은 강하고 파괴적인 힘을 가진 바람. ***gust***는 갑자기 부는 강한 바람. ***blast***는 gust

보다도 강하고 오래 지속되는 바람이다.
참고로 보퍼트의 풍력 계급표를 소개한다.

계급	명칭		초속 (m/s)
0	고요	*calm*	0.0~0.2
1	실바람	*light air*	0.3~1.5
2	남실바람	*light breeze*	1.6~3.3
3	산들바람	*gentle breeze*	3.4~5.4
4	건들바람	*moderate breeze*	5.5~7.9
5	흔들바람	*fresh breeze*	8.0~10.7
6	된바람	*strong breeze*	10.8~13.8
7	센바람	*near gale*	13.9~17.1
8	큰바람	*gale*	17.2~20.7
9	큰센바람	*strong gale*	20.8~24.4
10	노대바람	*storm*	24.5~28.4
11	왕바람	*violent storm*	28.5~32.6
12	싹쓸바람	*hurricane*	32.7 이상

♦ 회오리 바람 a whirlwind / 변덕스러운 바람 a fitful [choppy, fickle, fluky] wind; 〈방향이 자주 바뀌는〉 a fishtail wind / 선선한 바람 a cool [refreshing] breeze / 찬 바람 a cold wind; a chill wind / 맞바람 an adverse [a contrary, a foul] wind; a head wind / 살을 에는 듯한 바람 a cutting [piercing, biting, nipping] wind / 얼어붙는 듯한 바람 a freezing wind / 모진 바람 a violent [raging, high] wind / 윙윙대는 바람 a piping [whistling] wind / 바람의 방향이 바뀌다 《the wind》 shift [veer, change] / 바람이 세다 〈바람이 주어〉 blow hard; 〈장소가 주어〉 be windswept; be windy [rough] / 바람에 나부끼다 flutter [flow] in the wind / 바람에 펄럭이다 flap in the wind / 바람을 안고[거슬러] 가다 go [sail] against the wind [in the wind's eye, in the teeth of the wind] / 바람을 등지고 가다 go before the wind; 〈범선이〉 sail [run] before [with] the wind / 선풍기 바람을 쐬다 sit in front of the (electric) fan
▶ 바람이 불고 있었다 It [The wind] was blowing.
▶ 바람이 일기[자기] 시작하고 있다 The wind is getting up [going down].
▶ 바람이 불다가 그쳤다가 한다 The wind [It] blows fitfully.
▶ 바람이 거세어졌다 It began to blow hard. ⇒ The wind hardened [grew stronger].
▶ 바람이 그쳤다 The wind died away [went down, died down, fell, dropped, let up].
▶ 바람이 윙윙거리고 있다 The wind howls [moans, roars, rages].

바람이 북쪽에서 불어오고 있다 The wind is blowing from the north.
▶ 바람이 잠잠해진다 The wind lulls [abates, subsides].
▶ 바람이 동쪽에서 서쪽으로 방향을 바꿨다 The wind has shifted [veered, changed] from the east to the west.
▶ 탄알이 바람을 가르고 날아갔다 The bullet whizzed through the air.
▶ 밖에서 바람을 쐬고 오겠다 I'm going outside to get some fresh air.
▶ 그는 밖에 나가서 시원한 바람을 쐬었다 He was out of doors enjoying the cool air.
▶ 배가 바람을 거슬러 항해하고 있다 The ship is sailing against the wind [in the teeth of the wind].
▶ 모자가 바람에 날렸다 I had my hat blown off.
▶ 가지가 바람에 흔들리고 있다 The branches are swaying about in the wind.
▶ 바람에 등불이 꺼졌다 The wind blew out the light.
▶ 한 차례 비가 올 듯한 바람이다 There is a threat of rain in the wind.
2 〈외기〉 air
♦바람이 잘 통하는 well-ventilated; airy / 바람이 잘 통하지 않는 ill-[poorly-]ventilated; stuffy / 바람에 쐬다 expose *sth* to the air; give an airing to (clothes) / 바람을 들이다 [통하게 하다] admit[let] fresh air (into); ventilate; air 《a room》/ 찬 바람을 못 들어오게 하다 keep out cold air
▶ 바람에 쐬면 옷은 곧 마를 것이다 The clothes will soon dry in the wind.
3 〈외풍〉 《美》 a draft; 《英》 a draught
♦바람을 막다 cut off the drafts
▶ 이 집은 틈새기 바람이 들어온다 This house is drafty. ⇌ There is a draft in this house.
4 〈공・타이어 등의〉 air
♦바람이 나가다 leak; escape; get [find] vent; be [have gone] flat / 바람을 넣다 fill 《a football》 with air; pump up [air into] 《a tire》 / 바람을 빼다 deflate 《a tire》
5 〈들뜬 마음〉 inconstancy; fickleness
♦바람난 fickle; wanton; flirtatious 《woman》; unchaste; inconstant / 바람을 피우다 play with love; be an unfaithful wife [husband]; be unfaithful in love; take to amours / 무슨 바람이 불어서인지 by a curious turn of events; for some reason or other
▶ 그녀는 남편이 바람을 피워 속상해 한다 She is worried over her husband's fickleness.
▶ 그녀의 남편은 젊은 여자와 바람을 피웠다 Her husband had an affair with a young woman.
6 〈풍병〉 palsy; paralysis 《*pl.* -ses》
7 〈허풍〉 gas; a big [tall] talk; a whopping lie; 《美俗》 hot air
♦바람이 센 친구 a braggart; a gasbag; a boaster; 《口》 a blowhard
8 〈유행〉 (the) fashion; fad; vogue; a craze
▶ 젊은 여자들 사이에 미니스커트 바람이 불고 있다 Miniskirts are in vogue with girls.
9 〈어수선한 분위기〉 ♦ 정치 바람 a political storm / 재계에 새 바람을 불어 넣다 send a breath of fresh air through economic circles

바람² **1** 〈결〉 (a) momentum; an impetus; a motive; 〈결과〉 a consequence; a result; 〈영향〉 influence; effect; 〈과정〉 process
♦…바람에 in conjunction (with); in the process of; as a result [consequence] of; under the influence of; on account of; owing to
▶ 철야 작업하는 바람에 수면이 부족했다 I wanted [lacked] sleep on account of night-long work.
▶ 넘어지는 바람에 지갑을 떨어뜨렸다 I dropped my wallet when I fell down.
2 〈차림〉 ♦ 셔츠 바람으로 in *one's* shirt-sleeves; without *one's* coat on / 파자마 바람으로 in pajamas only
▶ 그녀는 에이프런 바람으로 나타났다 She appeared with an apron on.
▶ 나는 셔츠 바람으로 산책하러 나갔다 I went out for a walk in my shirt-sleeves.

바람³ 〈길이〉 an arm-span (about six feet or two yards); 몇 바람의 새끼 several arm-spans of rope

바람개비 **1** 〈풍향계〉 a (weather [wind]) vane; a wind indicator; 〈수탉 모양의〉 a weather-cock
▶ 바람개비는 바람을 따라 돈다 The vane turns with the wind.
2 〈팔랑개비〉 a pinwheel; a windmill

바람결 **1** 〈바람의 움직임〉 ♦ 바람결에 《be carried, come》 on the wind
2 〈풍문〉 a rumor; hearsay
♦바람결에 들으니 I heard say that…; it has come to my ears that…; the wind brought the news that…; a little bird told me that…
▶ 바람결에 들으니 그녀가 결혼했다더군 Rumor has it that she has gotten married.
▶ 그 소식은 바람결에 들었다 A little bird told me about it.

바람구멍 a wind-vent; a wind hole; an air hole; a ventilation hole; a vent

바람기 —氣 **1** 〈바람이 불 듯한 기운〉 the force [feel] of wind
2 〈들뜬 마음〉 inconstancy; fickleness; wantonness; capriciousness
♦바람기가 있는 inconstant; unfaithful; fickle; flighty; wanton / 바람기 있는 여자 a woman of loose morals [easy virtue]; a wanton woman; a flirt / 바람기 있는 남자 a playboy

바람나다 **1** 〈들뜨다〉 become fickle [flippant]; take to fast living; take to amours; lead a loose [fast] life; be unfaithful (with); 《美口》 play around; keep fast company; have an affair (with)
2 〈능률이 오르다〉 warm up; get warmed up; be keyed up; hit [get into] *one's* stride; really get started

바람둥이 **1** 〈바람피우는〉 a licentious man; a playboy; a Don Juan; an inconstant lover; a philanderer; 〈여자〉 a flirt; a fickle [wanton] woman; an unfaithful woman; a woman of easy virtue; a light-o'-love
2 〈허풍선이〉 a braggart; a gasbag; a boaster;

바람들다 1 〈무 등이〉 get porous [spongy, full of pores]
♦ 바람든 무 a porous radish
2 〈바람나다〉 become flirtatious; take to amours; play with love
3 〈방해가 생기다〉 be hindered [impeded, interrupted, disturbed, balked]; meet with a setback; go wrong

바람막이 a windbreak; a shelter from the wind; a protection from [against] the wind; an air screen; 〈자동차·모터사이클 등의 앞유리〉 (美) a windshield; (英) a windscreen
▶ 이 나무들이 교정의 바람막이가 되어 있다 These trees help to protect the school yard from the wind.

바람맞다 1 〈중풍에 걸리다〉 be paralyzed; be stricken [smitten] with paralysis; have a stroke of paralysis
♦ 바람맞은 apoplectic; paralytic; palsied
▶ 그는 바람맞아 오른발을 못쓴다 He is paralyzed on his right leg.
2 〈바람들다〉 become flippant [frivolous]; become fickle [flirtatious]; play with love
3 〈속다〉 be fooled [cheated, deceived, swindled]; be taken in; 〈퇴짜맞다〉 be rejected [refused, rebuffed]; get a snub; meet with a rebuff; get the cold shoulder 《from》; (俗) get the (frozen) mitten
▶ 나는 그녀에게 바람맞았다 She gave me a rebuff. ⇌ She gave me the cold shoulder.
4 〈헛되이 기다리다〉 be kept waiting for sb in vain
▶ 나는 그녀에게 한 시간이나 바람맞았다 I wasted a whole hour waiting for her in vain.

바람맞히다 1 〈퇴짜놓다〉 reject; rebuff; refuse; snub; give [show, turn] the cold shoulder to sb; give sb a rebuff [setdown]; give [send] 《a suitor》 the (frozen) mitten; kick 《sb's proposal》
2 〈헛기다리게 하다〉 keep sb waiting in vain; break [fail to keep] an appointment; (口) stand sb up
▶ 그녀는 나를 바람맞혔다 She stood me up. ⇌ I was stood up by her.

바람받이 a place exposed to the wind; a windy [bleak] place; a windswept place
♦ 바람받이에 있는 산허리 a windswept mountainside / 바람받이에 있는 집 a house in an exposed position
▶ 이 집의 북쪽은 바람받이에 있다 The wind blows strongly against the north side of this house.

바람벽 —壁 a wall; 〈칸막이의〉 a partition [party] wall

바람잡다 1 〈들떠서〉 be fickle [flippant]; take to amours; lead a fast [dissolute] life; take up a wild [fast] life; burn [light] one's candle at both ends
2 〈허황되게〉 conceive a wild hope [scheme]; be lost in wild fancies; nurse delusions; build castles in the air; spin a daydream

바람잡이 1 ⇨ 바람둥이
2 〈허풍선이〉 a braggart; a boaster; (口) a gasbag; (美口) a blowhard
3 〈소매치기의〉 an assistant

바람직하다 desirable; welcome; satisfactory; suitable; nice; fine; agreeable; advisable
♦ 바람직한 일 a matter to be desired / 바람직한[바람직하지 않은] 인물 a desirable [an undesirable] person
▶ 가는 것이 바람직하다고 생각하십니까? Do you think it advisable to go?
▶ 그는 면접에서 바람직하지 않은 인상을 주었다 He gave a bad impression in [at] the interview.
▶ 그는 바람직한 동업자가 아니다 He is not a desirable partner.

바랑 〈배낭〉 a knapsack; a shoulder pack; backpack; a rucksack; (美) a packsack; a wallet; a sack; a holdall; a scrip

바래다¹ 1 〈빛깔이 주어〉 fade (away); come [go] off; 〈물건이 주어〉 lose color; discolor
♦ 바랜 빛깔 a faded color / 바래지 않는 빛깔 a fast [a fadeless, an unfading, a standing] color / 잘 바래는 빛깔 a fugitive [fading] color / 색깔이 바랜 faded / 햇볕에 바래다 bleach sth in the sun
▶ 그 빛깔은 바래기 쉽다 The color comes off easily.
▶ 이 빛깔은 빨아도 바래지 않는다 This color will stand washing.
▶ 이 넥타이는 햇볕에 색이 바랬다 This tie has been discolored by the sun.
▶ 이 천은 강렬한 햇빛에도 바래지 않는다 This material does not discolor in strong sunlight.
2 〈표백하다〉 bleach; blanch; wash out (dye)

바래다² 〈배웅하다〉 see [take] 《sb to a place》 ⇨ 바래(다)주다

바래(다)주다 see [take] 《sb to a place》; escort; see sb off
♦ 집까지 바래다주다 see sb home; 〈자동차로〉 take sb home 《in one's car》/ 집밖[현관]까지 바래다주다 see sb out [to the door]
▶ 집[역]까지 내가 차로 바래다 주겠다 I'll drive you home [to the station]. ⇌ Let me take you home [to the station] in my car.

바레인 〈나라 이름〉 the Bahrain

바로¹ 1 〈정당하게〉 justly; rightly; properly; duly; 〈정확하게〉 correctly; accurately; 〈참되게〉 honestly; truly; straightforwardly; 〈굽지 않고〉 straight; upright
♦ 바로 말하면 properly [strictly] speaking; frankly speaking; to tell the truth / 바로 발음하다 pronounce correctly / 바로 대답하다 give a correct answer; answer right
▶ 의자에 바로 앉아라 Sit up (straight) in the chair.
▶ 자세를 바로 가져라 Hold yourself straight.
▶ 마음을 바로 가져라 Be honest. ⇌ Be upright at heart.
2 〈꼭〉 just; right; precisely; 〈확실히〉 surely; certainly; undoubtedly; 〈분명히〉 evidently; 〈정말로〉 really; truly; duly; 〈불과〉 only; but
♦ 바로 코 앞에 right before one's nose; under one's (very) nose / 바로 가까이에 hard [close, near] by; close at hand; quite near 《the house》; in the immediate neighborhood 《of》 /

바로 위[아래]에 right above [under] / 바로 뒤에 right [just] behind; just at the back of / 바로 머리 위에 just above one's head; right overhead / 바로 그때에 just then; just at that moment / 바로 어젯밤에 only [just] last night
▶ 그의 집은 역 바로 가까이에 있었다 His house was just a stone's throw from the station.
▶ 그는 바로 내 뒤에 있었다 He was just [right, directly] behind me.
▶ 나는 바로 2,3일 전에 그를 만났다 I met him only two or three days ago.
▶ 내가 바라는 것이 바로 그거다 That's just what I want.
▶ 다리의 바로 아래에 무언가 하얀 것이 떠 있다 There is something white floating just [right] under the bridge.
▶ 그 남자 바로 옆에 앉아 있는 사람은 누구냐? Who is that sitting next to him?
▶ 달은 우리의 바로 위에 있었다 The moon was right [just] over us.
▶ 그는 바로 우리 이웃 사람이다 He is an immediate neighbor.
▶ 이것이 바로 일석이조다 This is a typical case of killing two birds with one stone.
3 〈곧〉 at once; directly; on the spot; instantly; swiftly; immediately; promptly; without delay [hesitation]; right away; (口) straight away [off]
▶ 그것을 바로 우리 집에 보내 주십시오 I want you to send it to my home right away.
▶ 이 신약은 한 번 복용하면 효과가 바로 나타난다 A dose of this new medicine will work right away.
4 〈곧장〉 straight; directly
▶ 집으로 바로 가거라 Go straight home.
5 〈마치〉 just like [as]; (just) as if [though]; as it were
▶ 그는 바로 억만장자같은 말을 한다 He talks as if he were a billionaire.
6 (口슈) As you were!
▶ 會話 「겨누어 총」 「바로」 "Present!" "Recover arms!"
▶ 會話 「우로 봐」 「바로」 "Eyes right!" "Eyes front!"
7 〈다름아닌〉 the very...; (just) the same; in itself
♦ 바로 그날에 on the very same day
▶ 그녀는 작년에 반에서 내 옆자리에 앉았던 바로 그 소녀다 She is the same girl I sat next to in class last year.
▶ 그것 내가 잃어버린 바로 그 시계다 It is the same [very] watch that I lost.

바로² 〈부근〉 (right) in the neighborhood [vicinity] / 그 바로에 우체국이 있습니다 Right about there you'll find the post office.
바로미터 〈기압계·청우계〉 a barometer; 〈척도〉 a barometer; an index; an indicator
▶ 신문이 여론의 바로미터가 되는 일이 종종 있다 Newspapers are often barometers of public opinion.
▶ 안색은 흔히 건강의 바로미터 역할을 한다 Complexion often serves as a barometer of health.

▶ 식욕은 건강의 바로미터다 Appetite is a barometer of health.
바로잡다 1 〈굽은 것을〉 straighten; make straight [right]
♦ 자세를 바로잡다 straighten oneself / 굽은 등뼈를 바로잡다 straighten one's bent backbone
▶ 그는 서둘러 앉은 자세를 바로잡았다 He sat up straight in a hurry.
2 〈잘못을〉 correct (a mistake); redress; reform (evil practices); remedy; rectify (an error); cure; set right; set [put, bring] (people) to rights; straighten
♦ 행실을 바로잡다 mend one's ways; amend one's conduct; correct one's behavior / 아무의 잘못을 바로잡다 set [put, bring] sb to rights; set sb right / 문장 속의 틀린 데를 바로잡다 correct mistakes [errors] in the (following) sentence
▶ 잘못이 있으면 지체없이 바로잡아 주십시오 Please correct me immediately if I make a mistake.
▶ 자네는 투구하는 폼을 바로잡아야겠어 You should correct your pitching form.
바로크 baroque ♦ 바로크식의 baroque (architecture) / 바로크식 대저택 a baroque mansion ■ ―미술[음악] baroque art [music]
바륨 〔化〕 barium
바르다¹ 1 〈곧다〉 straight; erect; upright
♦ 바른 길 a straight road / 바른 자세로 in an erect [upright] position [posture]
▶ 자세를 바르게 하여라 Hold yourself straight [erect]. = Straighten yourself.
2 〈참되다〉 honest; upright; true; straight; 〈솔직하다〉 straightforward; frank; 〈옳다〉 right; rightful; righteous; true; just; proper; 〈정확하다〉 correct; accurate; precise; exact
♦ 바른 행위 right conduct / 바른 사람 a righteous [an honest] man; (총칭) the righteous / 바른 정보 correct [accurate] information / 바른 대답 a correct [the right] answer / 숟가락을 사용하는 바른 방법 the proper way to use spoon / 바른 일을 하다 do right / 바른 대로 털어놓다 confess straightforwardly [frankly]; make a frank confession
▶ 그의 행동은 법률적으로 바르다 His action is legal [lawful].
▶ 바른 행동만 한다면 겁날 것이 없다 If you are upright in all your actions, you need not fear anything.
▶ 너의 판단은 바르다 You are right in your judgment.
▶ 바른 대로 말해라 Be honest and tell me. ⇒ Tell me the truth.
▶ 그는 바른 영어를 구사한다 He speaks correct English.
3 〈햇볕이〉 sunny
♦ 양지바른 곳 a sunny place
바르다² 1 〔붙이다〕 stick; paste; plaster; affix; put; post; 〈장지문을〉 paper (a sliding door)
♦ 창문에 종이를 바르다 paste the window with paper / 벽지를 바르다 wallpaper; paper a wall
▶ 나는 벽에 고급 벽지를 바르겠다 I'll have the

walls covered with good wallpaper.
2【문지르다】 put on; apply 《one thing to another》; 〈칠을〉 paint; spread 《on》; 〈회반죽 등을〉 plaster; smear; daub; 〈페인트 등을〉 coat; 〈니스를〉 varnish; 〈옻칠을〉 lacquer; 〈문질러서〉 rub (in)
♦ 바르는 약 (an) ointment / 입술에 연지를 바르다 put on lipstick; rouge 《one's lips》 / 벽을 바르다 plaster a wall / 머리에 포마드를 바르다 put pomade on *one's* hair; dress *one's* hair with pomade; pomade *one's* hair / 얼굴에 크림을 바르다 spread cream on [apply cream to] *one's* face / 빵에 버터를 바르다 spread butter on bread; spread bread with butter / 종이에 풀을 바르다 put paste on a sheet of paper
▶ 간호사는 상처에 연고를 발랐다 The nurse applied ointment to the wound.
▶ 그 소년은 얼굴에 흙탕물을 발랐다 The boy smeared his face with mud.
▶ 그녀는 얼굴에 더덕더덕 분을 바르고 나갔다 Putting on thick make-up, the woman went out.
▶ 그는 팔에 연고를 문질러 발랐다 He rubbed the ointment on [into] his arm.
바르다³ tear off ⇨ 발라내다
바르르 1 〈물이 끓는 소리〉 seething; in bubbles; boiling; hiss
♦ 바르르 끓기 시작하다 come to a bubbling boil
2 〈성내는 모양〉 in a fit of anger; in hot blood; in a huff
♦ 바르르 성내다 get into a huff; fly into a rage; (口) blow *one's* top; (口) hit the ceiling; flare up; boil over
3 〈타오르는 모양〉 in a (sudden) burst of flame
♦ 바르르 타오르다 burst into flames; flare up (into flames)
4 〈떠는 모양〉 tremblingly; shiveringly; quiveringly
♦ 추워서 바르르 떨다 shiver with cold
▶ 그는 무서워서[화가 나서] 바르르 떨고 있었다 He was trembling with fear [anger].
바르샤바 〈폴란드의 수도〉 Warsaw
바르셀로나 〈스페인의 도시〉 Barcelona
바른길 1 〈곧은 길〉 a straight way [road]
2 〈옳은 길〉 the right path [track]; the path of righteousness [virtue]; the straight path; the right track
♦ 바른길을 걷다 tread the path of righteousness; (口) keep on the straight and narrow; follow the path of virtue; pursue an honest career; be just; keep to the right path / 바른길에서 벗어나다 stray [deviate] from the right track [the path of righteousness] / 바른길로 되돌리다 guide *sb* back to the right path / 바른길로 되돌아가다 get back on the right track
바른말 〈옳은 말〉 a right [proper, reasonable] word; 〈직언〉 plain speaking; a straight talk; a straightforward [candid, frank] remark; outspoken advice
▶ 바른말은 귀에 거슬린다 (속담) Outspoken advice is [sounds] harsh to the ear. ⇨ A good medicine tastes bitter [is bitter to the taste].
—**바른말하다** 〈옳은 말을 하다〉 speak reasonably [properly]; tell the truth; 〈직언하다〉 speak plainly [frankly]; speak without reserve; speak straightforwardly [candidly]
♦ 바른말하는 사람 an outspoken [a plainspoken] person / 상사에게 바른말하다 speak plainly [frankly, without reserve] to *one's* boss
바리¹ **1** 〈밥그릇〉 a woman's brass rice bowl
2 ⇨ 바리때
바리² 〈짐을 세는 단위〉 a pack 《of firewood》; a load 《of radishes》
▶ 무를 한 바리로 꾸려라 Make a load of the green radishes.
▶ 그는 짐수레에 나무 한 바리를 실었다 He put a load of wood in the cart. ⇨ He loaded the cart with wood.
바리나무 firewood loaded on a horse [an ox]
바리때 a wooden rice bowl (used by temple priests)
바리에이션 〈변주곡〉 《樂》 a variation 《on》
바리케이드 a barricade
♦ 바리케이드를 치다 make [set up] a barricade; barricade 《a place》
▶ 그 입구는 바리케이드로 막혀 있었다 The entrance was blocked with [by] a barricade.
▶ 그들은 바리케이드를 둘러치고 건물 속에 들어가 있었다 They barricaded themselves in the building.
바리톤 《樂》 barytone; baritone; 〈가수〉 a baritone
바림 《美術》 gradation; shading off
—**바림하다** shade off; gradate
♦ 빨간색을 핑크색으로 바림하다 shade off red into pink
■—**사진** a vignette
바바리(코트) (商標) a Burberry
바베이도스 〈나라이름〉 Barbados; 〈공식명〉 Barbados
■—**사람** a Barbadian
바벨 《聖》 Babel
■—**탑** the Tower of Babel
바보 a fool; a simpleton; an ass; a donkey; a goose; a dunce; a blockhead; a thickhead; a fathead; (俗) a dumbbell; a nut; 〈백치〉 an idiot; an imbecile
♦ 바보같은 생각 a stupid [an absurd, a ridiculous] idea / 바보같은 소리 nonsense; silly talk / 바보같은 소리를 하다 talk nonsense [rubbish] / 바보 취급을 하다 make a fool [an ass] of *sb*
▶ 이 바보야 You fool [stupid thing]! ⇨ You idiot! ⇨ You silly ass!
▶ 바보같은 소리 마라 Nonsense! ⇨ Don't be silly! ⇨ (美俗) Nuts!
▶ 그 사람은 그런 짓을 할 바보는 아니다 He knows better than to do such a thing.
▶ 그런 짓을 하다니 바보로구나 What a foolish man you are to do such a thing.
▶ 나는 그런 하찮은 일에 돈을 낭비하는 바보가 아니야 I am not so foolish as [I know better than] to waste my money on such trifles.

바보짓 a foolish act; a folly; a foolery ◆ 바보짓을 하다 do a foolish [stupid, silly] thing; commit a folly; play [act] the fool; make an ass [a fool] of *oneself*
▶ 그는 당황한 것을 눈치채이지 않으려고 바보짓을 했다 He played the fool to cover his confusion [hide his embarrassment].

바비큐 〈통구이〉 a barbecue
◆ 바비큐로 하다 barbecue (meat)
▶ 우리는 뜰에서 바비큐를 먹었다 We enjoyed a barbecue in the yard.

바빌로니아 Babylonia
◆ 바빌로니아 (사람)의 Babylonian
—말 Babylonian —사람 a Babylonian

바빌론 Babylon ■ —유수(幽囚) Babylonian captivity

바쁘다 1 〈틈없다〉 busy; 〈서술적〉 be occupied; be engaged; be not free; have much to do
◆ 바쁜 사람[몸] a busy person / 바쁜 생활[하루] a busy life [day] / 바쁜 일정 a crowded [heavy, crammed] schedule / 바쁘기 때문에 owing to pressure of business [work] / 바쁜 듯이 with an air of busyness / 일 때문에 바쁘다 be busy with *one's* work / 시험 준비로 바쁘다 be busy (in) preparing for the examination / 가사에 바쁘다 be busily occupied with household duties / 눈이 핑핑 돌 정도로 바쁘다 live in a whirl of business; be in a rush
▶ 나는 하는 일 없이 바쁘다 I am busy with nothing to mention in particular.
▶ 그는 장사로 바쁘다 He has his hands full with his business.
▶ 오늘은 매우 바빴다 I've had a hectic time today.
▶ 바쁘신데 와 주셔서 감사합니다 Thank you very much for coming right in the middle of your day.
▶ 바쁘실 때 폐를 끼쳐 죄송합니다 I'm sorry to trouble you when you're busy.
▶ 죄송합니다만 지금은 바쁩니다 I'm sorry, but I am busy [engaged] just now.
▶ 일이 바빠서 찾아뵙지 못했습니다 I've been too busy with my work to pay you a visit.
2 〈급하다〉 pressing; urgent; hurried; hasty
◆ 바쁜 걸음으로 at a quick [brisk] pace; with hurried [hasty] steps / 바쁜 경우에는 in an emergency / 바쁜 볼일로 on urgent [pressing] business / …하기가 바쁘게 no sooner…than; hardly [scarcely]…when [before]
▶ 행인들의 발걸음이 바쁘다 People in the street are walking at a hurried pace.
▶ 아버지는 바쁜 볼일로 시내에 가셨다 My father has gone to town on urgent [pressing] business.

바삐 1 〈분주하게〉 busily; like a busy bee
◆ 바삐 지내다 lead [live] a busy life
2 〈급히〉 in a hurry; in haste; hastily; hurriedly; in a rush; 〈즉시〉 at once; without delay [loss of time]; immediately
◆ 한시 바삐 without a moment's delay; as soon as possible / 바삐 걷다 walk hurriedly / 바삐 가다[들어오다, 내려가다] hurry along [in, down] / 일을 바삐 하다 hurry (up) a job; rush a job (through)

▶ 왜 그리 바삐 구니? What's the hurry? ⇒ Why (are you in) such a hurry?
▶ 바삐 서두를 필요는 없다 There's no hurry.
▶ 그는 현장으로 바삐 갔다 He hastened [hurried] to the scene.
▶ 우리는 바삐 점심을 먹었다 We had lunch in a hurry.
▶ 우리는 그를 바삐 병원으로 보냈다 We hurried [rushed] him to the hospital.

바삭 〈가랑잎 등이 스치는 소리〉 with a rustle; rustlingly; 〈깨물 때의 소리〉 with a crunch
—바삭하다 give a rustle; rustle; crunch

바삭거리다 rustle; crinkle; crunch
◆ 바삭거리는 나뭇잎 rustling leaves
▶ 나뭇잎이 밤바람에 바삭거렸다 The leaves rustled in the night breeze.
▶ 미풍에 갈대가 바삭거렸다 The gentle wind rustled in the reeds.

바삭바삭 rustlingly; with a rustling sound; with a rustle [crinkle, crisp sound]
◆ 쿠키를 바삭바삭 씹다 munch on a cookie / 눈을 바삭바삭 밟으며 가다 crunch through the snow
▶ 이 포테이토 칩은 바삭바삭 씹힌다 These potato chips are crisp to eat.
▶ 아이들은 크래커를 바삭바삭 소리내며 먹기 시작했다 The children began to munch (at) crackers.
—바삭바삭하다 be crisp
◆ 바삭바삭한 쿠키 crisp cookies
▶ 이 과자는 바삭바삭하다 This cake eats short. ⇒ This cookie is crisp to eat.

바서만 〈독일의 세균학자〉 Wassermann, August von (1866–1925) ■ —검사 〔醫〕 Wassermann test —반응 〔醫〕 Wassermann reaction

바셀린 〔商標〕 Vaseline

바소 〈랜싯〉 a lancet

바소쿠리 a wicker basket

바수다 break ⇨ 부수다

바순 a bassoon ■ —연주자 a bassoonist

바스 〔樂〕 bass ⇨ 베이스

바스대다 stir [move] restlessly; be [grow] restless; be fidgety; fidget; be nervous
▶ 바스대지 말고 좀 가만히 있어라 Be still and don't fidget!
▶ 그 아이는 잠시도 가만 있지 못하고 바스대었다 The child couldn't keep still even for one minute.

바스라기 a broken piece ⇨ 부스러기

바스락 with a rustle [rustling sound]
—바스락하다 rustle ⇨ 바스락거리다

바스락거리다 rustle; make a rustling sound
◆ 바스락거리는 나뭇잎 rustling leaves
▶ 가랑잎이 바람에 바스락거린다 The fallen leaves are rustling in the wind.

바스락바스락 rustlingly; with a rustling sound —바스락바스락하다 rustle

바스러뜨리다 smash; shatter; break (into pieces); crush
▶ 그는 그 비싼 꽃병을 왕창 바스러뜨렸다 With one blow, he smashed [shattered, broke] the valuable vase to [into] pieces.

바스러지다 1 〈조각나다〉 break; be broken [smashed, crushed, shattered]; go [fall] to

pieces; go smash; crumble
♦바스러진 접시 a broken plate / 빵이 바스러지다 bread crumbles
▶ 흙이 바스러진다 Earth breaks loose.
▶ 꽃병이 바스러졌다 The vase broke [was smashed] into pieces.
▶ 빵은 바싹 말라 바스러졌다 The bread was dry and crumbling [dried up crisp].
2 〈얼굴이 쇠하다〉 get thin [lean, haggard] (for *one's* age); get emaciated; be worn out

바스스 1 〈머리털 등이〉 untidily
—바스스하다 shaggy; disheveled; unkempt; tousled; untidy
♦바스스한 머리 disheveled hairs
▶ 그는 언제나 머리가 바스스하다 He always has unkempt hairs.
2 〈부스러기 등이〉 crumblingly
▶ 빵 부스러기가 바스스 테이블에 떨어졌다 Bread crumbs fell onto the table.
3 〈조용히〉 quietly; gently; softly; lightly
▶ 그녀는 잠자리에서 바스스 일어나 앉았다 She quietly sat up in her bed.

바스켓 a basket ■—볼 〈농구〉 basketball; 〈공〉 a basketball

바슬바슬 crumblingly —바슬바슬하다 crumbly

바심¹ harvesting unripe grain ⇨ 풋바심
바심² trimming lumber ⇨ 바심질
바심질 trimming lumber; smothing the surface of lumber —바심질하다 trim [dress, shape, smooth] lumber

바싹 1 〈물기 없게〉 (dry) as a bone; (dried up) completely; in a parched manner
♦바싹 마른 dried-up; bone-dry / 바싹 마른 입술 parched lips / 바싹 마른 공기 dry air / 바싹 말라붙은 지면 parched ground / 바싹 마르다 dry up; be dried up; be parched; 〈우물 등이〉 run dry / 바싹 튀기다 fry [frizzle] crisp
▶ 지난 여름에 그 저수지는 바싹 말랐다 The reservoir ran dry last summer.
▶ 나는 목이 바싹 말랐다 I was parched with thirst. ⇌ My throat was as dry as dust.
▶ 논은 물이 바싹 말랐다 The rice fields are [have been] entirely dried up.
▶ 입안이 바싹 말라붙는 기분이었다 My mouth felt parched.
2 〈밀착하여〉 closely; close to; side by side; hard (by)
♦바싹 붙어앉다 sit closely together; sit close to each other / 바싹 다가가다 draw near; edge [sidle] up to; nestle close [up] to / 땅에 바싹 엎드리다 keep close to the ground; (美俗) hug the ground / 벽에 바싹 붙어서다 stand close to the wall; (美俗) hug the wall / 아무의 뒤를 바싹 따라가다 follow close(ly) on the heels of *sb*; dog the heels of *sb*
▶ 그렇게 말하면서 그녀는 남자친구에게 바싹 다가갔다 Saying so, she drew closer to her boy friend.
▶ 개가 주인에게 바싹 다가갔다 The dog nestled close to its owner.
3 〈짧게〉 short; close; 〈최소한으로〉 to the minimum
♦손톱을 바싹 깎다 cut *one's* nails close; trim *one's* fingernails close; cut a nail to the quick / 비용을 바싹 줄이다 reduce [cut down, retrench] expenses to the bone
▶ 그는 비용을 바싹 줄여서 그럭저럭 그것을 했다 He managed to do it at minimum cost.
4 〈단단히〉 firmly; tightly; 〈완강히〉 stubbornly; doggedly; resolutely; obstinately; stiffly
♦바싹 껴안다 hug (a child) to *one's* breast / 바싹 동여매다[묶다] bind fast; tie securely; fasten tight / 바싹 우기다 persist stubbornly; stick to it
5 〈홀쭉하게〉 leanly; haggardly; gauntly
♦바싹 마른 사람 a skinny person; a bag of bones / 바싹 마른 얼굴 a haggard [worn, emaciated] face / 몸이 바싹 마르다 become [get, grow] emaciated; be reduced to a mere skeleton; be worn to a shadow
▶ 어머니는 오랜 병으로 바싹 여위셨다 My mother has lost a lot of weight [is emaciated] because of her long illness.
6 〈깨물 때의 소리〉 with a crunch
♦한번 바싹 깨물어보다 at one crunch

바야흐로 1 〈한창〉 in full swing [operation]; at the height (of); 〈바로〉 just; really; truly
▶ 바야흐로 봄이다 Spring is really here. ⇌ We are now in the midst of spring.
▶ 가보니 바야흐로 싸움이 한창이었다 I found them at the height of quarrel.
▶ 지금이 바야흐로 진달래철이다 The azaleas are in full bloom [at their best] now.
2 〈이제 곧〉 (be) going [about] to (do); on the point [brink, verge] of (doing); almost; nearly; (come, be) near (doing)
▶ 해가 바야흐로 지려고 하고 있다 The sun is about to sink [set]. ⇌ The sun is near setting [sinking].
▶ 배가 바야흐로 침몰하려 하고 있었다 The boat was on the point [verge] of sinking.
▶ 기차가 바야흐로 떠나려 하고 있었다 The train was just about to leave [on the point of leaving].
▶ 그는 바야흐로 점프하려는 참이었다 He was in the very act of jumping.

바와같이 as; like
♦아시는 바와같이 as you know [see] / 약속한 바와같이 in accordance with [true to] *one's* promise; as promised / 예정한 바와같이 as scheduled; according to schedule
▶ 우리는 계획한 바와같이 그것을 했다 We did it as planned [according to (the) plan].

바운드 〈공 등의〉 bounce; bound
♦공을 원[투] 바운드로 잡다 catch a ball on the first [second] bounce
—바운드하다 bounce; bound
▶ 공은 유격수 앞에서 불규칙 바운드했다 The ball took a bad bounce in front of the shortstop.
▶ 공이 벽에 맞고 바운드했다 The ball hit the wall and bounced back [rebounded].

바위 a rock; a crag
♦바위 한 덩어리 a block of rock / 바위투성이의 rocky; cragged; craggy / 바위가 많은 곳 a craggy place / 자연 그대로의 바위에 조각한 불상 an image of Buddha carved in the

surface of a living rock / 바위가 널려 있는 비탈 a rock-strewn slope
▶ 그 배는 바위에 부딪쳐 침몰했다 The ship struck a rock and sank.
▶ 우리는 바위투성이인 산을 기어올랐다 We climbed a rocky mountain.
 ■ 흔들― a rocking stone; a log(g)an stone ―굴 a rock cave; 〈큰 것〉 a rock cavern ―너설 a projection [sharp edge] of a rock ―타기 rock-climbing
바위옷 〔植〕 rock moss
바위종다리 〔鳥〕 a hedge sparrow; a hedge warbler
바위취 〔植〕 a saxifrage
바윗돌 a (block of) rock; a rock block
바음자리표 ―音―標 〈낮은 음자리표〉〔樂〕 an F clef
바이러스 a virus ♦바이러스성의 viral
 ■ 감기― the common cold virus ―병 a virus [viral] disease ―학 virology ―학자 a virologist
바이런 〈영국의 시인〉 Byron, Lord George Gordon (1788-1824)
바이마르 Weimar ■―헌법 the Weimar Constitution
바이블 〈성경〉 the Bible; 〈명저〉 a bible
♦바이블에 맹세하다 swear on the Bible
▶ 이 책은 경제학의 바이블이라고 일컬어진다 This book is called the bible of economics.
바이스 (美) a vise; (英) a vice
바이어 a buyer; a buying agent from abroad
바이없다 1 〈전혀없다〉 not at all; not by any means; not in the least; utterly [absolutely] not
▶ 나로서는 방법이 바이없다 I am quite at a loss [I simply do not know] how to do it.
▶ 이 궁지에서 벗어날 방법이 바이없다 There is no way out of this dilemma.
2 〈도리없다〉 there is no way 《to》; cannot help 《it》; 《it》 cannot be helped; cannot be avoided
♦바이없다고 체념하다 abide by the inevitable; accept the situation; resign *oneself* to fate
▶ 그것은 운명이니 바이없다 We have to accept our fate. ⇌ We must resign ourselves to fate.
3 〈비할데 없다〉 be incomparable; 〈한량없다〉 be unlimited [boundless]; be limitless; be endless.
▶ 슬프기 바이없다 I cannot control my grief. ⇌ I am overwhelmed [overcome] with sorrow [grief].
▶ 그는 바이없이 행복했다 He was extremely happy.
▶ 다시 그를 만나는 것은 바이없는 기쁨이다 Nothing will give me more pleasure than to see him again.
바이올리니스트 a violinist
바이올린 a violin; (口) a fiddle
♦바이올린을 켜다 play the violin
 ■ 제1[2]― the first [second] violin ―독주 a solo on the violin; a violin solo ―연주자 a violinist

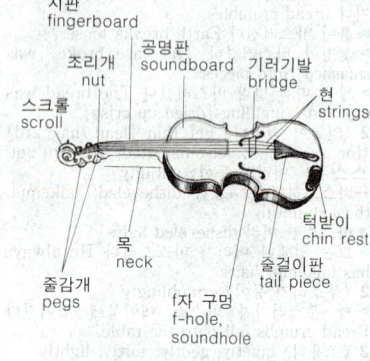

바이올린
지판 fingerboard
공명판 soundboard
조리개 nut
기러기발 bridge
스크롤 scroll
현 strings
목 neck
턱받이 chin rest
줄감개 pegs
f자 구멍 f-hole, soundhole
줄걸이판 tail piece

바이칼호 ―湖 Lake Baikal
바이킹 〔史〕 a Viking
바일병 ―病 〔醫〕 Weil's disease
바자 〈자선시〉 a baz(a)ar
♦바자에 의류를 출품하다 contribute clothes to a bazaar / 바자에서 물건을 사다 buy things at a bazaar / 바자를 열다 open [hold] a bazaar
 ■ 자선― a charity bazaar; a rummage sale
바작바작 1 〈타는 소리〉 crack; cracklingly; 〈빻는 소리〉 crunchily
♦바작바작 소리내다 crack; crackle / 바작바작 타다 burn crackling
▶ 불이 바작바작 타고 있었다 The fire was crackling.
▶ 콩을 묶자 바작바작 튀었다 The beans crackled and popped as I parched them.
2 〈초조하게〉 fretfully; nervously; anxiously; in (great) anxiety
♦하찮은 일로 바작바작 속을 태우다 fret (and fume) over [about] trifles / 마음을 바작바작 죄다 be held in suspense; (口) stew 《over, about》
▶ 그는 병이 낫지 않아 바작바작 속을 태우고 있다 He is fretting because he does not get better.
▶ 어머니는 아들이 돌아오기를 바작바작 속을 태우며 기다렸다 The mother waited for her son in great anxiety.
바장이다 ramble; stroll aimlessly
바제도병 ―病 〔醫〕 Basedow's disease
바조 ―調 〔樂〕 the note F
♦바조장조 F major / 바단조 F minor
바주카포 ―砲 a bazooka
바지 (a pair of) throusers; (口) pants
♦바지의 단 (美) the cuffs [(英) the turnups] on *one*'s trousers / 바지의 단을 접다 turn up the trousers at the bottom / 바지의 단추를 채우다 button up *one*'s trousers / 바지를 입다 put on trousers / 바지를 벗다 take off trousers / 바지에 주름을 세우다 crease *one*'s trousers
▶ 바지 앞이 열려 있네요 Your stable door is

open. ⇌ **(俗)** Your fly is undone.
▶ 그는 언제나 주름이 잘 잡힌 바지를 입는다 He always wears neatly pressed [creased] pants.
■ 반— breeches; shorts; 〈아동용〉 short pants; knee pants 속— drawers; underpants; **(英)** pants 승마용— riding breeches; jodhpurs 여자— slacks 작업— overalls ■—멜빵 **(美)** suspenders; **(英)** braces —주머니 a trouser pocket 바짓가랑이 a trouser [pant] leg

바지게 1 〈지게〉 an A-frame with a clamshell-shaped receptacle on it 2 ⇨ 발채

바지락(조개) 〔貝〕 a short neck clam

바지랑대 a clothes pole; a clothesline [laundry] pole; a drying pole

바지런하다 〈부지런하다〉 diligent

바지저고리 trousers and coat; 〈비유〉 a man of no guts; a good-for-nothing 《fellow》; **(口)** a no-good; 〈무실권자〉 a figurehead; a dummy
▶ 그는 명색이 사장이지만 바지저고리나 다름없다 He is a dummy [nominal] president. ⇌ He is a president in name only.

바지지 with a sizzle [hiss, fizzle]; with a hissing sound
▶ 프라이 팬에서 기름이 바지지 끓고 있다 The oil is sizzling in the frying pan.
▶ 뜨거운 냄비를 젖은 행주 위에 놓았더니 바지지 소리가 났다 There was a hiss when I put the hot pan on a wet cloth.
—**바지지하다** hiss; give [let out] a hiss

바지직 with a (sharp) hiss [sizzle, fizzle, rip]; sputteringly
♦ 바지직바지직 with a hissing [ripping] sound; sputteringly / 바지직바지직 타는 도화선 a sputtering fuse
▶ 전선에서 바지직 불꽃이 튀었다 A shower of sparks shot from the electric wire.
—**바지직하다** give [let out] a hiss; sizzle; fizzle; sputter

바짝 as a bone ⇨ 바싹

-바치 a maker; a worker; an artisan; a mechanic ♦ 갖바치 a maker of leather shoes; a shoemaker

바치다¹ 1 〈드리다〉 give 《to a superior》; present; make a present 《of》; dedicate; offer 《to a god》; make an offering 《to》; consecrate 《to》
♦ 영전에 꽃을 바치다 offer flowers to the spirit of a dead person / 신께 제물을 바치다 offer a sacrifice to the god; present the god with a sacrifice / 신께 평화를 위한 기도를 바치다 pray [offer a prayer] to God for peace
▶ 돌아가신 어머님께 바칩니다 〈저서의 헌사〉 Dedicated to the memory of my late mother.
2 〈헌신하다〉 devote; sacrifice
♦ 일신을 바치다 devote [dedicate, give] oneself to 《a cause》 / 목숨을 바치다 sacrifice [immolate] oneself 《for the country》; give [lay down] one's life 《for one's country》; die 《for the cause》 / 예술에 일생을 바치다 devote one's life to art
▶ 그는 모든 시간과 정력을 저술에 바쳤다 He devoted all his time and energy to writing.
▶ 그는 교육에 일생을 바쳤다 He devoted his life to education.
3 〈납입하다〉 pay; 〈납품하다〉 supply; serve; deliver; purvey
♦ 수업료를 바치다 pay one's school fee [tuition] / 세금을 바치다 pay one's taxes / 뇌물을 바치다 bribe [corrupt] sb; offer [give] a bribe to sb; grease [cross, oil] sb's palm; tickle sb in the palm; tickle the palm of sb

바치다² 〈추잡할 정도로 즐기다〉 be overly fond of; be preoccupied with; be addicted to; have an excessive liking for; be crazy [mad, wild] about

바캉스 〈프〉 vacances; **(美)** (a) vacation; **(英)** one's holidays

바커스 〈주신(酒神)〉 Bacchus

바퀴¹ 1 〈수레의〉 a wheel; a rundle; 〈가구에 달린〉 a caster
♦ 앞[뒷]바퀴 the front [rear] wheel / 바퀴를 달다 fix a wheel / 바퀴를 멈추게 하다 brake; apply [put on] the brake / 바퀴에 기름을 치다 grease the wheels / 바퀴에 깔려 죽다 be killed by being run over
▶ 앞 바퀴가 빠졌다 The front wheel came off.
▶ 냉장고 아래에 바퀴가 달려있다 The refrigerator has casters under it.
▶ 그 두 사람은 수레의 양 바퀴와 같다 Those two are inseparable (from each other).
2 〈도는 횟수〉 a round; a turn; 〈회전〉 a revolution; a rotation
♦ 공원을 한 바퀴 돌다 take a walk through the park / 박물관 내를 한 바퀴 돌다 go [look] around [round] the museum / 섬을 한 바퀴 돌다 go round the island; make a tour of the island / 세계[지구]를 한 바퀴 돌다 travel round the world
▶ 그는 아들을 데리고 시내를 한 바퀴 돌았다 He took his son around the town.
▶ 정원을 한 바퀴 돌아볼까요? Let's take a walk around the garden, shall we?
▶ 지구가 태양을 한 바퀴 도는 데 1년이 걸린다 It takes a year for the earth to make its circuit of the sun.
▶ 그 경비원은 빌딩내를 한 바퀴 돌았다 The (security) guard made his rounds of the building.
■ 톱니— a toothed wheel ■—살 a spoke 《of a wheel》 —자국 a rut; wheel marks; a (wheel) track; the print of a wheel: 도로에 깊은 바퀴자국이 났다 The road was rutted deeply. —통 the hub 《of a wheel》; a nave

바퀴² 〔昆〕 a cockroach; a roach
♦ 바퀴가 득실거리는 부엌 a cockroach-ridden kitchen

바탕¹ 1 〈성질〉 nature; (a) disposition; temperament; temper; character; 〈재질〉 endowments; gifts; talent; 〈소지·소질〉 an inclination; the making; 〈체질〉 (physical) constitution
♦ 바탕이 좋은 사람 a man of good disposition; a good-natured person
▶ 그는 작가가 될 바탕이다 He has the making of a writer.
▶ 그녀는 일류 배우가 될 바탕이다 She has the making of a first-rate actress.

바탕² 2 〈그림·무늬·글씨 등이 실리는 면〉 ground; field; 〈직물의〉 texture; weave; fabric; material; stuff; 〈품질〉 quality; 〈뼈대·틀〉 the body; the frame
♦ 바탕이 흰 천 white cloth / 검은 바탕에 흰 a black ground / 흰 바탕에 적십자 a red cross on a white field; a white field with a red cross / 흰 바탕에 붉은 무늬 a red design [pattern] on a white ground / 〈벽에〉 바탕칠을 하다 give [apply] the wall the first coat
▶ 그 옷감은 바탕이 곱다[거칠다] The cloth is of fine [coarse] texture.
▶ 그는 흰 바탕에 아름다운 꽃을 그렸다 He drew beautiful flowers on the white background.
3 〈기초·근본〉 foundation; groundwork; basis (*pl*. bases)
♦ …에 바탕을 두다 be based [founded] on…
▶ 우리는 그 앙케트[질문표]에 바탕을 두고 새 계획을 세웠다 We developed our new plan on the basis of the questionnaire.

바탕² 1 〈동안〉 (for) a time [while]; 《for》 a (short) spell; a bout; a turn; a round; a scene
♦ 한 바탕 부는 바람 a gust [blast] of wind / 한 바탕 기침을 하다 have a spell of coughing / 아무와 한 바탕 싸우다 have a hard fight with *sb* / 한 바탕 울다 cry for a spell / 한 바탕 야단 치다 give *sb* a good scolding [sound rating]
▶ 그녀는 하찮은 일로 한 바탕 소동을 벌였다 She made a great fuss about nothing for a while.
▶ 한 바탕 비가 온 후 개였다 After a short shower it cleared up.
2 〈활의 사정거리〉 a bowshot

바터 barter ■—무역 barter trade —제 the barter system [basis]

바텐더 a barman; 《美》 a bartender; a barkeeper

바통 1 ⇨ 배턴
2 (프) bâton ♦ 바통을 물려받다 《비유》 succeed to; take over a task

바투 near [close] (by); closely; close at hand
▶ 좀더 바투 앉어 주십시오 Please sit [squeeze up] a little closer (together).
▶ 그렇게 바투 쓰면 읽기 어렵다 It is hard to read if you write so closely.

바특이 〈바투〉 a little close(ly); 〈국물 등이〉 thick ♦ 바특이 쓰다 write close(ly) / 국을 바 특이 끓이다 make the soup a bit thick(er)

바특하다 〈국물이 적다〉 thick; not watery; rather dense

바티칸 〈로마 교황청〉 the Vatican

바티칸시국 —市國 〈나라이름〉 Vatican City; 〈공식명〉 the State of the City of Vatican

바하마 〈나라이름〉 the Bahamas; 〈공식명〉 the Commonwealth of Bahamas

박¹ 〈植〉 a gourd; a calabash; 〈바가지〉 a (dried) gourd dipper [bowl] ♦ 박을 타다 split a gourd in two ■쪽— a small gourd (dipper) —꽃 a gourd flower

박² 〈소리〉 with a scrape [grind, rip]
♦ 통을 박 긁다 rub a tub hard / 박 찢다 rip up; tear off [up]

박 拍 〔樂〕〈박자〉 a beat

박 箔 〈두꺼운〉 (metal) foil; 〈얇은〉 leaf; 〈칠한〉 gilt ♦ 금[은]박 gold [silver] leaf / 금속으로 박을 만들다 beat metal into foil [leaf]

박 泊 stay ♦ 4박 5일의 여행 a trip of five days and four nights / 1박 2식(食)에 2만원 twenty thousand won a night including two meals / 1박하다 stay [《美》 stop] overnight

박격포 迫擊砲 a trench mortar [gun]; a mine thrower
■—대 a mortar corps —탄 a mortar shell

박고지 dried gourd shavings

박공 博栱 〔建〕〈널〉 a gable ■—널 a bargeboard; a gableboard —지붕 a gable roof —창 a gable window

박구기 a small (dried) gourd dipper [ladle]

박다 1 〈말뚝 등을〉 drive [strike, knock] in [into]; hammer; 〈쐐기 등을〉 wedge in
♦ 판자에 못을 박다 drive [hammer, strike] a nail into a plank / 말뚝을 땅속에 3피트 깊이로 박다 drive [sink] a post three feet into the ground / 통나무에 쐐기를 박다 drive a wedge into a log
▶ 널빤지에 못을 박아 고정시켜라 Drive a nail into the board and fix it in place.
2 〈촬영하다〉 take (a photograph); 〈인쇄하 다〉 print; put (a book) in print
♦ 명함을 박다 have *one's* business cards printed / 사진을 박다 take a picture [photograph] / 2만부를 박다 print [strike] off twenty thousand copies
3 〈재봉하다〉 sew (by backstitch)
♦ 재봉틀로 커튼의 가장자리를 박다 stitch the edge of a curtain on *one's* sewing machine
4 〈소를 넣다〉 fill (rice cake) with 《savory matter》; stuff with
♦ 만두에 소를 박다 stuff a dumpling 《with bean jam》; fill a dumpling with stuffing; put stuffing [fillings] in a dumpling
5 〈찍어내다〉 make [cut out] 《cookies》 in a shape; shape; mold
♦ 동전을 박아내다 mint [strike] coins
6 〈상감하다〉 inlay; set; fix; stud; enchase; mount
♦ 진주를 박은 브로치 a brooch studded with pearls / 금은을 박다 inlay with gold and silver / 반지에 다이아몬드를 박다 set a ring with a diamond
7 〈식물이〉 ♦ 뿌리를 박다 take root
▶ 장미는 곧 뿌리를 박았다 The roses rooted easily. ≒ The roses took [struck] root easily.

박다위 a hemp shoulder strap

박대 薄待 (a) cold treatment; ill-treatment; a cold reception; inhospitality
▶ 그는 가는 곳마다 박대를 받았다 He was given [met with] a cold reception wherever he went.
—박대하다 treat coldly

박덕 薄德 (a) lack of virtue
—박덕하다 have little virtue
▶ 모두 제가 박덕한 탓입니다 All is due to my lack of discretion. ≒ I have no one to blame but myself.

박두하다 迫頭— come [get] near; draw near; come up; be near [close] at hand; be immi-

nent ◆박두한 문제 a pressing [an urgent] problem
▶시험이 박두해 있다 The examinations are close at hand [are getting near, are approaching].

박람회 博覽會 an exhibition; (口) an expo [Expo]; an exposition; a fair
■만국— an international exhibition; (美) a world('s) fair ■—장 exhibition [fair] grounds —출품자 an exhibitor

박력 迫力 force; power; drive
◆박력 없는 문체 an enervated [a washy] style / 박력이 있다 be powerful; be impressive; be of strong appeal (to)
▶대통령의 연설은 박력이 있었다 The president's address was very appealing.

박리 薄利 small profits; a narrow margin (of profit) ◆박리로 팔다 sell at small profits
■—다매 small profits and quick returns (略 S.P.Q.R.); quick sales at small profits; making profits by selling in large quantities —다매주의 a small-profits and quick-returns policy

박멸 撲滅 eradication; extermination; annihilation ◆결핵 박멸 운동 a movement [crusade] against tuberculosis
—박멸하다 eradicate; exterminate; annihilate; wipe out (of existence); stamp out
◆해충을 박멸하다 exterminate vermin
▶보건소는 전염병을 박멸하기 위해 모든 수단을 다했다 The health center has taken every possible measure to stamp out the epidemics.

박명 薄命 〈불운〉 unhappiness; bad luck; misfortune; 〈단명〉 a short life
▶미인 박명 Beauty and luck [good fortune] seldom go hand in hand.

박물 博物 1 〈넓은 견문〉 wide knowledge
2 ⇨ 박물학
■—표본 a specimen of natural history

박물관 博物館 a museum
▶그것은 박물관 감이다 That's quite a museum piece.
■과학— a science museum 국립— a national museum 대영— the British Museum

박물학 博物學 natural history; the study of nature ■—자 a naturalist

박박[1] 〈긁는·찢는 소리〉 with a scratching [scraping, grating, ripping] sound
◆이를 박박 갈다 gnash [grate, grind] one's teeth furiously / 다리를 박박 긁다 scratch one's legs briskly / 수건으로 몸을 박박 문지르다 scrub oneself with a towel
▶그녀는 벽에서 낡은 페인트를 박박 긁어냈다 She scraped roughly the old paint from the wall.
▶비누를 칠해 박박 문지르면 얼룩이 곧 진다 Rub briskly with soap, and the stain will soon wash off.
▶그녀는 남편에 바가지를 박박 긁었다 She nagged at her husband with a vengeance.

박박[2] 1 〈얽은 모양〉 (pockmarked) all over 〈the face〉; solid 〈with pockmarks〉
▶그녀의 얼굴은 박박 얽었다 Her face is pitted with the ravages of smallpoxes.
2 〈바짝 깎은 모양〉 close; short
◆머리를 박박 깎다 have one's hair closely cropped [cropped short]
3 〈우기는 모양〉 stubbornly
▶그는 그녀를 만나지 않았다고 박박 우겼다 He obstinately [stubbornly] insisted that he had not seen her.

박복 薄福 misfortune; ill luck; unhappiness
—박복하다 unfortunate; unlucky; unhappy
◆박복함을 한탄하다 lament one's bad fortune / 박복하게 태어나다 be born under an unlucky star

박봉 薄俸 a small [slender, meager, scanty, low] salary; low wages
◆박봉으로 일하다[생활하다] work at [live on] small pay [salary] / 박봉을 받다 draw a poor pay
▶그는 박봉에도 불평을 하지 않았다 He was content(ed) with his small salary.

박사 博士 a doctor; 〈칭호〉 Doctor 《略 Dr.》; 〈정통한 사람〉 an expert; 〈식자〉 a learned [well-informed] man
■만물— a well-informed person; a walking [living] dictionary ■—과정 the doctoral course 《in law》: 박사 과정에 등록하다 be enrolled in a doctoral course [(美) program] —논문 a thesis for a doctorate; a doctoral thesis [dissertation] —학위 a doctor's degree; a doctorate: 박사 학위를 따다[받다] get [receive, obtain] a doctorate [a doctor's degree] 《in economics》 / 박사 학위를 수여하다 confer a doctorate on sb

박살 〈산산이 부서짐〉 ◆박살나다 be shattered; go to smash [pieces] / 박살내다 shatter; smash; crush; knock sth to pieces; break sth up / 꽃병을 박살내다 smash a vase to pieces
▶충돌로 차 앞유리가 박살났다 The windshield was shattered by the collision.

박살 撲殺 clubbing [beating] sb to death
—박살하다 club [beat, knock, strike] sb to death; slaughter

박새 〔鳥〕 a great tit

박색 薄色 an ugly look [face]; a plain [homely(-looking), bad-looking] woman
▶그녀는 천하에 없는 박색이다 She is ugly enough to stop the clock.

박수 〈남자 무당〉 a male shaman; a sorcerer; a medium; an exorcist

박수 拍手 hand clapping; (a) clapping of hands; a handclap
◆우레와같은 박수 속에 amidst a thunderous clapping of hands [a storm of applause] / 박수를 보내다 give sb a clap; clap sb / 박수로 맞이하다 receive [greet] sb with applause
▶그가 강연을 끝내자 일제히 박수가 터졌다 There was a round of applause as he ended his speech.
▶그들에게 큰 박수를 보냅시다 Let's give them a big hand.
—박수하다 clap (one's hands in applause); applaud
▶관객은 열광적으로 박수했다 The audience applauded [clapped] enthusiastically.
■—부대 claque; 〈한 사람〉 a claquer

박수갈채 拍手喝采 cheering and clapping; cheers; applause
▶ 연주가 끝나자 그 바이올리니스트는 큰 박수갈채를 받았다 The violinist got a big round of applause [a standing ovation] at the end of his performance.
―**박수갈채하다** clap *one*'s hands in applause [joy]; applaud *sb*《an act》with hands [hand clapping]

박스 〈상자〉a box; a case; 〈자리〉a box; 〈야구의〉 the box; 〈술집 등의〉 a booth
♦ 전화 박스 (美) a telephone booth; (英) a telephone [call] box

박식 博識 wide [extensive] knowledge; encyclop(a)edic knowledge; erudition
―**박식하다** learned; well-informed; knowledgeable; erudite
♦ 박식한 사람 a well-informed person; a man of great knowledge [wide information]; a know-all; 〈학자〉 a learned person
▶ 그는 모든 면에 대단히 박식하다 He has a remarkable knowledge of everything.

박신거리다 〈바글거리다〉 flock together; crowd; throng; swarm
▶ 그 가게에는 손님들이 박신거리고 있었다 The store was very crowded with shoppers.
▶ 그 늪에는 모기가 박신거린다 The marsh is swarming with mosquitoes.

박신박신 in swarms; in crowds
▶ 쓰레기통에는 파리가 박신박신 들끓고 있다 There are swarms of flies in the garbage can.
⇌ The garbage can is swarming with flies.

박애 博愛 love of mankind; philanthropy; charity; benevolence
■―**사업** philanthropic work ―**주의** philanthropism ―**주의자** a philanthropist

박약 薄弱 infirmity; weakness; insufficiency
―**박약하다** feeble; weak; infirm; 〈근거가〉 unsound; insufficient
♦ 심신 박약, 정신 feeble-mindedness / 정신 박약의 weak-minded / 의지가 박약하다 have a weak will; be weak-willed.
▶ 네 주장은 근거가 박약하다 Your argument is based on weak [filmy] grounds.

박음질 a backstitch ―**박음질하다** backstitch

박이다¹ 1 〈속에〉 get stuck in
2 〈마음에〉 come home to 《*one*'s heart》; remain deep in 《*one*'s heart》; 〈습관이 되다〉 become a habit; get used to
♦ 마음속 깊이 박인 원한 an inveterate grudge; deep-rooted rancor
▶ 아버지의 마지막 말씀이 뇌리에 박혀 떠나지 않는다 My father's last words have always stuck in my memory.
▶ 일단 커피에 인이 박이면 끊기 어렵다 Once coffee drinking became a habit, you can hardly give it up.
3 〈죽히다〉 ⇨ 틀어박히다

박이다² 〈인쇄물을〉 let [put into] print; 〈사진을〉 have *one*'s picture taken
♦ 명함을 2백장 박이다 have two hundred namecards printed

박자 拍子 time; (a) rhythm; measure; timing; 〔樂〕 a musical time pattern
♦ 2[3,4,6]박자 duple [triple, quadruple, sextuple] time / 4분의 2박자의 곡 a melody of two-four time [meter] / 박자를 맞추어 in measured time / 메트로놈에 박자를 맞추다 keep time with the metronome
▶ 그녀는 발로 박자를 맞추고 있었다 She was keeping time with her feet.
▶ 그들은 음악에 박자를 맞추어 춤을 추었다 They danced to the tune of the music.
■―**표** a time signature

박자기 拍子器 〔樂〕 a metronome

박작거리다 bustle ⇨ 북적거리다

박작박작 in a bustle

박장 拍掌 (hand) clapping
―**박장하다** clap *one*'s hands (in applause)

박장대소하다 拍掌大笑― laugh aloud clapping *one*'s hands; engage in applause mingled with laughter; cheer and applaud

박절 迫切 heartlessness; coldheartedness; harshness
―**박절하다** heartless; cold; hardhearted; indifferent; unkind
♦ 박절한 사람 a heartless person / 박절한 처사 cold treatment / 박절하게 거절하다 give a point-blank [flat] refusal
▶ 그렇게 박절하게 내치지 마십시오 Please don't refuse flatly [bluntly] like that.

박정 薄情 coldheartedness; hardheartedness; heartlessness; coolness (of heart); cruelty
―**박정하다** heartless; coldhearted; hardhearted; stonehearted; cruel
♦ 박정하게 굴다 be hard on *sb*; treat *sb* pitilessly

박제 剝製 〈일〉 stuffing; mounting; 〈박제한 것〉 a stuffed [mounted] thing
♦ 동물의 박제 a stuffed animal
―**박제하다** stuff [mount]《a bird》
♦ 박제한 새 a stuffed [mounted] bird
■―**사(師)** a taxidermist ―**술** taxidermy ―**표본** a stuffed [mounted] specimen

박쥐 〔動〕 a bat; a flittermouse
▶ 박쥐는 야간 비행성 포유동물이다 A bat is a nocturnal flying mammal.

박지 薄紙 〈엷은 종이〉 thin paper

박진감 迫眞感 truthfulness to life; verisimilitude
▶ 그의 박진감이 있는 연기 his (compellingly) realistic acting / 박진감이 있는 true to life [nature]; realistic; lifelike
▶ 이 그림은 박진감이 있다 This picture is drawn to life.

박차 拍車 〈말의〉 a spur; a rowel spur; 〈촉진〉 speedup; acceleration
♦ 박차 달린 승마화 spurred riding boots / 박차를 가하다 〈비유적〉 spur [urge] *sb* 《to do, on to activity, into action》; accelerate / 말에 박차를 가하다 spur [put spurs to] *one*'s horse
▶ 공업화가 농업의 쇠퇴에 박차를 가했다 Industrialization prompted the decline [aggravated the condition] of agriculture.

박차다 kick away [off]; give a vigorous kick
▶ 그는 자리를 박차고 가버렸다 He left the place indignantly.
▶ 온갖 어려움을 박차고 그 계획은 실행되었다

The plan was put into practice in spite of [in the face of, despite] all difficulties.

박치기 butting; 〈서로의〉 bumping of heads
♦ 아무에게 박치기하다 give sb a butt with one's head; butt sb / 서로 박치기하다 bump against [into] each other

박탈 剝奪 〈권리 등의〉 deprivation; forfeit; forfeiture; 〈관직의〉 divestiture; 〈명예 등의〉 deplumation ♦ 시민권의 박탈 the deprivation [forfeit] of civil rights
—**박탈하다** deprive [strip] sb of sth; divest sb of 〈his rank〉
♦ 박탈당하다 be deprived of 〈one's rank〉; be stripped of 〈all one's party posts〉 / 특권을 박탈당하다 be shorn of one's privileges
▶ 그는 변호사 자격을 박탈당했다 He was disqualified as a lawyer.

박테리아 bacteria (▶단수는 a bacterium이지만 거의 쓰지 않음) ⇨ 세균

박토 薄土 〈메마른 땅〉 barren [poor] soil; sterile [infertile] land

박판 薄板 a thin plate [board]; a sheet
♦ 강철 박판 a thin sheet of stainless steel

박편 薄片 a thin leaf [layer]; a scale
♦ 박편으로 떨어지다 come off in scales

박피 剝皮 peeling, paring —**박피하다** peel; pare; bark ♦ 나무〈바나나〉를 박피하다 bark a tree [banana]

박피 薄皮 a thin skin; 〈피막〉 a membrane; 〈표면의〉 a film; a filmy covering; a scum

박하 薄荷 〔植〕 mint; peppermint
■—**껌** peppermint [spearmint] gum —**뇌** menthol —**담배** a menthol cigarette —**사탕** (a) peppermint; peppermint candy [drops] —**수** a peppermint solution —**유** peppermint oil

박하다 薄— 1 〈인색하다〉 stingy; mean; 〈인정이〉 heartless; hardhearted
♦ 인심이 박한 세상 a hard world to live in / 점수가 박하다 be strict [severe] in marking
▶ 우리 선생님은 평점이 박하다 Our teacher is a hard grader [marker].
2 〈적다〉 scanty; meager; little
▶ 그 사업은 이문이 박했다 The business yielded only small profits.

박학 博學 extensive learning; wide [encyclop(a)edic] knowledge; erudition
—**박학하다** learned; well-read; well [widely] informed
♦ 박학한 사람 a man of extensive knowledge; a widely-read man
▶ 그는 박학 다재(多才)하다 He is very learned and talented. ⇌ He has profound learning and great ability.

박해 迫害 persecution; oppression
♦ 종교상의 박해 religious persecution
▶ 많은 신자가 박해를 당했다 Many believers were persecuted [suffered persecution].
—**박해하다** persecute; torment
—**자** a persecutor; an oppressor

박히다 1 〈꽂이다〉 stick; be [get] stuck
♦ 다리에 박힌 총알 a bullet embedded in the leg
▶ 손가락에 가시가 박혔다 A thorn stuck [got stuck] in my finger.
▶ 생선 가시가 목에 박혔다 A fish bone has stuck [got caught] in my throat.
2 【찍히다】 be taken; 〈인쇄물이〉 be printed; 〈점 등이〉 be placed
♦ 얼굴에 박힌 사마귀 a mole in the face / 주근깨가 박힌 얼굴 a freckled face

밖 1 〈바깥쪽〉 the outside; 〈겉〉 the exterior; 〈옥외〉 the open (air)
♦ 밖의 outer; outside; external; exterior; outward; outdoor / 밖에 outside; outside the house / 창밖을 보다 look out (of) the window / 밖에 나가다 go out of doors; take the air / 밖에 나가 있다 be away from home / 밖에서 문을 잠그다 lock the doors from the outside
▶ 밖은 몹시 춥고 바람이 분다 It is very cold and windy outside.
▶ 그는 감정을 좀체로 밖으로 내보이지 않는다 He hardly ever [seldom] shows his feelings.
▶ 밖에 나가 놀아라 Go and play outdoors.
▶ 오늘 저녁은 밖에서 식사하자 Let's eat [dine] out this evening.
▶ 문밖에서 기다릴께요 I'll be waiting for you outside of the gate.
▶ 밖으로 나가자 Let us go into the open.
▶ 그의 셔츠 자락이 바지 밖으로 나와 있었다 His shirttail was sticking out of his pants.
2 〈이외〉 other; another; the other; any other; the rest
♦ 그 밖의 많은 것들 many other things / 그 밖의 사람들 other people; others; the rest / 하나밖에 없는 몸 the only body we have / 그[이] 밖의 other; another; different; else / 그 밖에도 in addition to; besides / 문제 밖이다 be beside [aside from] the question [subject]
▶ 그 밖의 것은 미루어 짐작할 수 있다 The rest may be inferred.
▶ 남은 방법은 하나 밖에 없다 There is only one way left.
▶ 그 밖에 질문 있습니까? Do you have any other questions?
▶ 〔會話〕「그 밖에 필요한 것이 있으십니까?」「이거면 됐어요」 〈가게에서〉 "Anything else, sir [ma'am]?" "That's all for now."
▶ 나는 만원밖에 없다 I have only [no more than] ten thousand won with me.
▶ 그 밖에 내가 할만한 일이 또 있습니까? Is there anything else I can do?
▶ 나는 그것 밖에 모른다 I know no more than that.
▶ 나는 그렇게 밖에 해석할 수 없다 I cannot interpret it in any other way.
▶ 우리는 그의 도움을 요청할 수밖에 없다 We had no alternative [choice] but to ask for his help.
▶ 젊은 시절은 한번밖에 없다 We are young only once.
▶ 그 뉴스를 듣고 우리는 놀랄 수밖에 없었다 We could not help being [but be] surprised at the news.

반 半 1 〈절반〉 (a) half
♦ 8시 반 half past eight / 한 배 반 one and a half times; half as much [many] again as… /

한[두] 시간 반 one [two] and a half hours; 《英》 an hour [two hours] and a half / 반 마일 a half mile; 《英》 half a mile / 반 시간 half an hour
▶한 달 반이 지났다 One month and a half has passed. ⇌ One and a half months have passed.
▶배는 반이 썩어 있었다 Half of the pears were rotten.
▶극장은 반이 비어 있었다 The theater was half empty.
▶4의 반은 2다 The half of four is two.
▶그녀는 남편의 1배 반을 번다 She earns half as much again as her husband.
▶경비를 반으로 줄여라 Cut down the expenditure by half.
▶반씩 나누자 Let's share it equally.
▶그 책을 아직 반밖에는 읽지 못했다 I have read only half the book.
▶공사는 반 이상 완성되었다 The work is more than half finished.
2 〈중간 부분〉 the middle; the center; 〈중도〉 halfway
♦인생의 반을 지나다 pass the middle milepost of life
▶우리는 이미 반은 왔다 We have already covered half the distance.
▶그 도시는 서울과 부산간의 반쯤 되는 곳에 있다 The town is located about halfway between Seoul and Pusan.
3 〈일부분〉 partial; half; incomplete
♦반은 partly; in part; partially / 반 기계적[무의식적]으로 half mechanically [unconsciously]/ 반 농담으로 half in jest; partly for fun [jest]
▶그는 반은 병 때문에 그 계획을 포기했다 He gave up his plan partly through illness.
▶그의 성공은 반은 요행이다 His success is partly due to luck.

반 班 1 〈집단〉 a group; a team; a unit; a party; a company; 〈학급〉 a class; [軍] a section; a squad
♦구급반 a rescue squad / 상급[하급]반 the senior [junior] class / 합동 조사반 a joint investigation party / 영어 회화반 an English conversation class
▶우리는 소년들을 4개 반으로 나누었다 We divided the boys into four groups.
2 〈행정 구역〉 *pan*; a neighborhood association ♦반상회 a (monthly) meeting of a neighborhood association

반- 反- anti- ♦반사회적 행위 an antisocial act / 반정부 시위 an antigovernment demonstration

반- 半- half; semi-; hemi- ♦반장화 (a pair of) half boots / 반코트 a half-length coat

반가공품 半加工品 half-processed articles; semi-manufactured [semi-processed] goods

반가부좌 半跏趺坐 sitting cross-legged with one leg put under the other

반가워하다 rejoice [be rejoiced] (in, over); be [look] glad [pleased, delighted] about (meeting); take pleasure in
♦소식을 듣고 반가워하다 be overjoyed at (hearing) the news / 옛 친구를 만나 반가워하다 be glad to meet *one's* old friend; rejoice to see *one's* old friend

반가이 gladly; delightedly; joyfully; with pleasure; with [for] joy; happily; cheerfully
♦반가이 맞이하다 welcome *sb*; give *sb* a warm [hearty] welcome; receive *sb* with great joy 《with open arms》

반감 反感 (an) antipathy; animosity; ill feeling; hostility; a feeling of revolt
♦두 사람 사이의 반감 a mutual antipathy between two persons / 반감을 사다 rouse [provoke] *sb's* antipathy [hostility]; incur 《another's》 ill feeling
▶그는 나에게 반감을 가지고 있는 것 같다 He seems to have ill feeling [an antipathy] toward me.
▶그녀의 주제넘은 태도가 급우들의 반감을 샀다 Her obtrusive manner aroused [provoked] her classmates' hostility [antagonism].
▶나는 그에게 반감을 품을 아무런 이유가 없다 I have got nothing against him.

반감 半減 a reduction [cut] by half; a fifty percent reduction
—**반감하다** 〈줄다〉 be halved; be cut in half; be reduced by half; decrease to half; 〈줄이다〉 reduce [cut] by half [50 percent]; halve; 〈가격을〉 take off half the price
▶새 법규가 시행되면서 교통사망자 수가 반감했다 The number of traffic deaths has been reduced by [to] half since the new regulation went into effect.
▶그 기계로 일이 반감된다 The machine halves the work.

반감기 半減期 〈방사능의〉 a half-life (period); a half life period ♦생물학적 반감기 a biologic half-life

반갑다 glad; happy; joyful; joyous; welcome; delightful; pleasant 《to see》
♦반가운 소식 glad [welcome, happy, joyful] news [tidings]/ 반가운[반갑지 않은] 손님 a welcome [an unwelcome] guest
▶만나뵈어 반갑습니다 I'm glad to see you. ⇌ It is a pleasure to see you.
▶그 소식을 듣고 반가웠다 I was glad [happy, pleased] at the news.
▶오늘 반가운 소식을 들었다 I heard joyful [good] news today.
▶그가 돌아왔다는 반가운 소식이 왔다 We received the joyful news of his return.

반값 半— half the price; half price
♦반값으로 at half-price; at half the (usual) price; half-price; at fifty percent off the regular price / 반값으로 깎아주다 take off half the price; give a 50% discount
▶그 옷은 반값에 팔렸다 The dress was sold at half price.

반개 半個 half a piece; half ♦사과 반 개 half (an) apple

반개 半開 〈문의〉 being half [partly] open; being ajar; 〈꽃의〉 being half out [in bloom]
—**반개하다** be partly [half] open [ajar]; be half in bloom; be half out

반거들충이 半— a smatterer; a dilettante 《pl.

~es, ·ti); a man of half [superficial] knowledge

반격 反擊 a counterattack; a counteroffensive; a counterdrive; a counterblow
► 그 팀은 1라운드에서 졌으나 2라운드에서 반격에 나섰다 The team was defeated in the first round, but launched a counterattack in the second.
—**반격하다** counterattack; make a counterattack; strike [fight, beat, hit] back
■ —기지 a retaliation base —작전 counterattack operations

반경 半徑 a radius; a semidiameter
♦ 반경 3마일 이내[밖]에 within [outside] the radius of three miles (of) ► 반경 50센티의 원을 그려라 Draw a circle with a radius of fifty centimeters.
■ —행동—a radius of action [operation]

반고리관 半一管 〔解〕 semicircular canals
반고체 半固體 a semisolid (substance)
반골 反骨 an uncompromising [unyielding] attitude of mind
♦ 반골의 작가 an antiestablishment writer
■ —정신 a rebellious spirit

반공 反共 anti-Communism
♦ 반공의 anti-communist / 반공 사상을 고취하다 infuse [instill] strong anti-communist idea [sprits] (into the mind of the public) / 반공의 보루를 구축하다 build a bulwark against communism
■ —법 the Anti-Communist Law —운동[정책, 태세] an anti-communist movement [policy, stand] —주의자 an anti-communist —포로 the anti-communist prisoners of war

반공 反攻 a counteroffensive ⇨ 반격
반공일 半空日 〈반 휴일〉 a half-holiday; 〈토요일〉 Saturday
► 토요일은 매주마다 반공일이다 We have Saturday afternoons off every week. ≒ We work a half day on every Saturday.

반공중 半空中 midair; the sky; the air
♦ 반공중에 in midair; in the air [sky]/ 반공중을 날다 fly through the air

반과거 半過去 〔文法〕 the imperfect tense
반관반민 半官半民 semi-governmental management ♦ 반관 반민의 통신사[항공회사] a semi-governmental news agency [airline] / 반관 반민의 semiofficial; semi-governmental
■ —회사 a semi-government [semi-public] corporation

반구 半球 a hemisphere
■ 동[서]— the Eastern [Western] Hemisphere 북[남]— the Northern [Southern] Hemisphere

반국가적 反國家的 antinational; antistate 〈activities〉
반군 叛軍 a rebel army ⇨ 반란(~군)
반금속 半金屬 〔化〕 metalloid ⇨ 준금속
반기 半期 a half term [year]; a semester
♦ 상[하]반기 the first [latter] half of the year / 전[후]반기 the first [second] half year / 반기의 semiannual; half-yearly / 반기마다 semiannually; half-yearly; every six months
► 이자는 반기마다 지불된다 Interest is paid semiannually.

반기 反旗・叛旗 a standard [banner] of revolt [rebellion]
♦ 반기를 들다 rise (up) in revolt [rebellion] (against); take up arms (against); be up in arms (against); revolt; rebel
► 육군의 일부가 대통령에게 반기를 들었다 Part of the army mutinied [revolted] against the President.

반기 半旗 a flag at half-mast [half-staff] ⇨ 조기(弔旗)
♦ 반기를 게양하다 fly [hoist, hang out] a flag at half-mast [half-staff]; half-mast a flag
► 집집마다 반기가 걸려 있었다 Flags were hung out at half-mast [half-mast high] at every door.

반기다 be [look] glad (about); be pleased [delighted] (at, with); rejoice [be rejoiced] (in, at, over, to do); 〈환영하다〉 greet; welcome
► 입원해 있는 동안 그녀는 문병객을 무척 반겼다 While in the hospital, she looked extremely happy [was overjoyed] when visitors came.

반기생 半寄生 〔生〕 semiparasitism; hemiparasitism ♦ 반기생의 hemiparasitic; semiparasitic
■ —생물 a hemiparasite; a semiparasite

반나절 半— a quarter of the daytime
♦ 오전의 반나절 half the morning / 독서로 반나절을 보내다 spend a quarter of the daytime in reading

반나체 半裸體 a half-naked body; seminudity
♦ 반나체의 half-naked; seminude; seminaked
■ —화 a seminude (picture)

반날 半— 〈한나절〉 half a day; half the daytime; a half day ► 어제는 반날을 자 버렸다 I slept away half the daytime yesterday.

반납 返納 return; restoration
—**반납하다** return; give [send] back
► 이 책은 다음주까지 반납해야 한다 This book is due [to be returned] next week.

반년 半年 half a year; a half year
♦ 반년마다의 semiannual; half-yearly / 반년마다 half-yearly; semiannually; every half year ► 이 잡지는 반년마다 간행된다 This magazine is published semiannually [every six months, twice a year].

반다이크 〈플랑드르의 화가〉 Van Dyck, Sir Anthony (1599-1641)

반달 半— 1 〈달〉 a half moon; a dichotomy
♦ 반달꼴 a semicircle
2 〈한달의 반〉 a half month
♦ 반달마다 나오는 정기 간행물 a semimonthly (publication) / 반 달 치[분]의 semimonthly (pay)
3 〈속손톱〉 a lunula (*pl.* lunulae)

반당 反黨 〈행위〉 antiparty activities; 〈무리〉 traitors
♦ 반당행위를 하다 engage in antiparty activities; rebel against *one's* own party
■ —분자 antiparty elements

반 대 反 對 1 〈반 항〉 opposition; resistance;

antagonism; 〈적대 행위〉 hostility; 〈반론〉 objection; dissension; (口) kick
♦반대의 opposite ((to)) ; contrary ((to)); hostile ((to))/반대 의사를 표명하다 declare *oneself* (to be) against ((a policy))/반대에 부딪치다 meet with [run into] opposition; be opposed ((by))/반대를 위한 반대를 하다 oppose for opposition's sake; oppose for the sake of opposition
▶그들은 부모의 반대를 무릅쓰고 결혼했다 They got married against their parents' wishes. ⇌ They got married in defiance of their parents' opposition.
▶그의 완강한 반대로 우리의 계획은 무산되었다 His stubborn resistance killed our plan.
▶[會話]「너는 그것에 찬성이냐 반대냐?」「난 절대 반대야」 "Are you for or against it?" "You'll have to do it over my dead body."
▶투표 결과는 찬성 20표, 반대 15표였다 This vote stood at twenty ayes and fifteen nays.
─반대하다 oppose; be opposed ((to)); object ((to)); take exception ((to)); raise [make, have] an objection ((to))
♦…에 반대하여 in opposition to…; in defiance of…; against…/끝까지 반대하다 stubbornly [tenaciously] oppose ((a plan)); hold out ((against *sb's* order))
▶그는 그 계획에 반대하고 있다 He is against the plan.
▶그는 내 아이디어가 비현실적이라고 반대했다 He objected that my idea was impractical.
▶이 계획에 반대하는 사람은 손을 들어 주세요 Those who are against this plan, please indicate by a show of hands.
2 〈역(逆)〉 the opposite; the contrary; the reverse
♦반대의 증거 evidence to the contrary / 반대의 opposite; contrary; reverse; adverse / 반대로 conversely; reversely; the other [wrong] way (around); on the contrary
▶「white」의 반대는「black」이다 The opposite of "white" is "black." ⇌ "White" and "black" are opposites.
▶순서가 반대다 They are in contrary [reverse] order.
▶사실은 그 반대다 The reverse [(very) contrary] is the case.
▶표결했더니 예상과는 반대의 결과가 나왔다 The decision by vote brought about a result contrary to our expectations.
■─개념 a contrary concept ─급부 a quid pro quo; 〈대가〉 a consideration ─당 an opposition (party) ─동의(動議) a countermotion ─론 an opposite opinion; a counterargument ─명제 a contrary (proposition); an opposite ─방향 the opposite direction: 차는 갑자기 반대 방향으로 달리기 시작했다 The car began to move suddenly in the opposite direction. ─설 an opposite view [opinion]; a counterview ─세력 counterforce; counterpressure ((to cold war)) ─어 an antonym ─운동 (start) a movement [campaign] against *sth*; an opposition movement ─자 an opponent; an opposer; (美口) a kicker ─파 the opposing party; a dissident group; *one's* rival faction ─표 a dissenting vote

반대신문 反對訊問 〔法〕 a cross-examination ♦반대신문을 하다 cross-examine; cross-question
▶피고측 변호사가 검찰측 증인에 대해 반대신문을 했다 The defense counsel cross-examined the witness for the prosecution.
■─자 a cross-examiner

반대투표 反對投票 a negative [an adverse] vote ▶반대투표가 다수입니다 〈의장의 발표〉 The noes have it. ─반대투표하다 vote against ((a measure)); blackball ((an applicant))

반도 半島 a peninsula ♦반도의 peninsular
▶이탈리아는 장화 모양의 반도다 Italy is a peninsula shaped like a boot.
■─사람 a peninsular

반도 叛徒 rebels; insurgents ♦반도를 소탕하다 mop up [clean up] the rebels

반도체 半導體 〔物〕 a semiconductor

반독립 半獨立 halfway [part] independence; quasi-independence ─국 a quasi-[semi-]independent state [country]

반동 反動 (a) reaction; (a) counteraction; 〈총 등의〉 a kick; a recoil; 〈탄력체의〉 resilience ♦혁명에 대한 반동 a counterrevolution / 반동적(인) reactionary / 반동으로서 as a reaction
▶이 총은 반동이 거의 없다 This gun kicks only slightly.
▶그들은 보수 반동이다 They are right-wing reactionaries.
─반동하다 react; 〈총 등이〉 kick; recoil; rebound; 〈탄력체가〉 resile; spring back
■─사상 a reactionary thought [idea] ─정부 a reactionary government ─주의자 a reactionary

반두 〈그물〉 a scoop net
반둥 〈인도네시아의 도시〉 Bandung
반드럽다 1 〈매끄럽다〉 smooth and shiny; glossy
♦반드러운 대리석 smooth marble / 반드러운 빰 a smooth cheek / 마루를 반드럽게 청소하다 make the floor shiny clean
2 〈약빠르다〉 shrewd; smart; sharp; alert

반드르르 smoothly; glossily; lustrously
─반드르르하다 smooth; glossy; sleek
♦반드르르한 머리 glossy [lustrous] hair
▶그녀의 살갗은 반드르르하다 Her skin is velvety [smooth and soft].

반드시 1 〈꼭〉 certainly; surely; positively; without fail; by all means; at any cost
▶그는 반드시 성공할 것이다 He'll surely succeed. ⇌ It is certain that he'll succeed.
▶반드시 내게 그 결과를 알려줘 Don't fail to let me know the result.
▶이 돈은 열흘 안으로 반드시 갚아야 한다 This money has to be returned [paid back] without fail within ten days.
▶식사 전에는 반드시 손을 씻어라 Be sure to wash your hands before a meal.
2 〈항상〉 always; invariably; 〈필연적으로〉 necessarily; inevitably
♦반드시 …하다[하기로 되어 있다] make it a rule to ((do))

▶그는 아침 식사 전에 반드시 한 시간동안 산책을 한다 He makes it a rule to take an hour's walk before breakfast.
▶그런 짓을 하면 반드시 천벌을 받는다 It will bring with it inevitable retribution.
▶덩치가 크다고 반드시 튼튼한 것은 아니다 A big man is not necessarily robust. ⇌ Not all big men are robust.
▶부자라고 해서 반드시 행복한 것은 아니다 A rich man is not always [necessarily] happy.

반들거리다 have a gloss; get glossy [lustrous]; shine; glitter ♦반들거리는 구두 well-polished shoes / 은수저를 반들거리게 닦다 give silver spoons a good shine

반들반들 smoothly; glossily; shiningly
—**반들반들하다** smooth; glossy; shiny
♦반들반들한 대머리 a head as bald as an egg
▶새 차는 반들반들하다 The new car is bright and shiny.

반듯이 straight; in a straight line; in a beeline; upright; erect; squarely; orderly; in good order [shape]
▶반듯이 서다 stand straight [upright] / 반듯이 눕다 lie on one's back / 못을 반듯이 박다 hammer a nail in straight
▶그는 기둥을 반듯이 세웠다 He set the post upright.
▶자세를 반듯이 해라 Hold yourself upright. ⇌ Straighten yourself.

반듯하다 1 〈곧다〉 straight; upright; erect; 〈고르다〉 even; square and level
♦반듯한 길 a straight road / 네모 반듯한 종이 a perfectly square sheet of paper
▶반듯하게 줄을 그어라 Draw a straight line.
2 〈흠없다〉 flawless; decent; 〈정연하다〉 orderly; in good order [shape]
♦반듯한 집안 a decent [respectable] family
3 〈반반하다〉 handsome; well-shaped; clear-cut; nice-looking
♦반듯한 용모 finely-chiseled features

반등 反騰 〔證〕 a reactionary rise [advance]; a rebound; a rally ♦주가의 급반등 a sharp rebound in stock prices
—**반등하다** rally; rise in reaction; rebound

반디 a firefly ⇨ 개똥벌레

반딧불 the glow [glimmer, gleam] of a firefly; glowfly light ♦수많은 반딧불이 풀밭에서 반짝이고 있었다 Numerous fireflies [glow-bugs] glowed in the grass.

반뜻하다 straight ⇨ 반듯하다

반락 反落 〔證〕 a reactionary fall (in stock prices); a fall in reaction
—**반락하다** fall [drop] in reaction; fall back

반란 叛亂 a rebellion; a revolt; an insurrection; 〈봉기〉 a rising; an uprising
♦반란을 일으키다 rise in revolt [rebellion, insurrection]; revolt [rise, rebel] 《against》 / 반란을 진압하다 put down [suppress] a revolt [rebellion]
▶반란이 일어났다 A revolt broke out.
■—군 a rebel army; the rebel forces —부대 insurgent troops —자 an insurgent; a rebel

반려 伴侶 a companion; a comrade; a partner
♦일생의 반려 a companion for life; a life partner; 〈배우자〉 one's spouse / 여행의 반려자 one's traveling companion

반려 返戾 giving back; return —**반려하다** give back; return 《to》 ■—품 returned goods

반론 反論 a counterargument; a refutation; an antagonistic argument
▶이 논의에는 반론의 여지가 없다 This argument admits of no refutation.
—**반론하다** make an objection 《to》; bring forth [build up] a counterargument; refute

반만년 半萬年 five millenniums [millennia]; five thousand years ♦반만년의 역사 a five thousand year-old history

반말 半— the low forms of speech
♦반말로 대답하다 give a rough [rude] reply
—**반말하다** use the low forms of speech 《to》; practice familiarism; talk in an easy [a familiar] manner

반 맹 半 盲 half blindness ■—증 〔醫〕 hemianopsia; hemiopia

반면 反面 the other side [hand]
▶그 반면에 on the other hand; while
▶그녀는 강인한 반면 소극적인 면도 있다 She is aggressive, but on the other hand she is reserved.
▶이 천은 물에 강한 반면 열에 약하다 While this cloth is impervious to water, it does not tolerate heat.

반면 半面 1 〈얼굴의〉 half the face; a half face; 〈옆 얼굴〉 a profile
2 〈사물의〉 one side; 〈다른면〉 the other side
♦생활의 반면 one side of one's living / 문제의 반면만을 보다 look on [upon] only one side of a question
▶너는 그의 성격의 반면을 모르고 있다 You don't know the other side of his character.
■—상(像) a profile; a silhouette

반면 盤面 〈바둑·장기판의 겉면〉 the face of a board; 〈바둑·장기의 형세〉 the stage of a game ♦반면이 내게 유리[불리]하다 The game is favorable [unfavorable] to me.

반모음 半母音 〔音聲〕 a semivowel

반목 反目 antagonism; hostility; enmity; feud
♦두 정당간의 반목 antagonism between the two political parties
▶그들의 반목의 원인은 돈이다 Money set them against each other.
—**반목하다** be antagonistic [hostile] 《to》; be at odds [feud, enmity] 《with》
▶그들은 서로 공공연히 반목하고 있다 They are at open defiance with each other.

반문 反問 a return question
—**반문하다** ask in return; 〈반대신문에서〉 cross-question; cross-examine
▶「누구 잘못이니?」라고 그녀는 그에게 즉각 반문했다 "Well, whose fault is it?" she shot back at him.

반문 斑文 a spot; a speck; a speckle

반미 反美 ♦반미의 anti-American[-U.S.] / 점증하는 반미 감정 growing [increasing] anti-American sentiment
■—운동[활동] anti-U.S. movement [activities] —주의 anti-Americanism; anti-Yankeeism

반미개 半未開 semibarbarism ■ —국 a semi-civilized country —인 semibarbarous people; a semibarbarian

반미치광이 半— a half-mad [half-insane] person; a slightly mad [crazy] person

반바지 半— knee pants [trousers]; shorts; knee [short] breeches

반박 反駁 refutation; confutation; retort; 〔法〕〈원고의〉 rebuttal; 〈피고의〉 rebutter
▶ 그의 주장은 반박의 여지가 없다 His statement is irrefutable. ⇌ There's no denying what he says.
—반박하다 refute; retort; rebut
▶ 내 말이 끝나자마자 그들은 반박하기 시작했다 As soon as I concluded my speech, they started refuting me.
■ —(성명)서 a written refutation [retort]

반반 半半 1 〈반과 반〉 half-and-half; fifty-fifty
♦ 반반씩 half-and-half; in half [halves] / 반반씩 나누다 halve; go halves; split [go] fifty-fifty / 설탕과 소금을 반반씩 섞다 put in sugar and salt half-and-half; mix equal amounts of sugar and salt
▶ 승산은 반반이다 The chances stand even.
▶ 환자의 회복 가능성은 반반이다 The patient has a fifty-fifty chance of recovery.
▶ 찬성과 반대 의견이 반반이었다 There were an equal number of assenting and dissenting opinions.
▶ 두 형제는 유산을 반반씩 나누었다 The two brothers divided the legacy equally [evenly].
2 ⇨ 반의반

반반하다 1 〈반듯하다〉 smooth; even; flat; level
♦ 반반한 길 a level road / 반반한 표면 a smooth surface / 땅[길]을 반반하게 고르다 level the ground [a road]
2 〈예쁘장하다〉 nice-looking; pretty; handsome; attractive; charming
♦ 반반한 여자 a nice-looking woman / 반반하게 생기다 be good-looking; have regular [clear-cut] features
3 〈지체가 상당하다〉 decent; respectable
♦ 집안[출신]이 반반하다 be of high [noble] birth; come of [from] a good family

반발 反撥 1 〈되받아서 퉁김〉 repulsion; a backlash
—반발하다 repel; repulse
▶ 자석의 두 음극은 반발한다 The negative poles of two magnets repel each other.
2 〈반항〉 opposition; resistance
—반발하다 oppose; resist; defy
▶ 부친이 엄격하여 아들들이 반발했다 As their father was strict with them, the boys rebelled.
■ —력 force of restitution; repulsive [repelling] power —작용 repulsion

반백 半白 ♦ 반백의 half-white; gray; 〈머리가〉 gray-haired; grayish; grizzled ■ —노인 a grizzled [gray-haired] old man

반벙어리 半— a half-mute; a man of inarticulate pronunciation; a stammerer; a stutterer

반병신 半病身 1 〈반불구자〉 a half-cripple; a partially handicapped person **2** 〈반편이〉 a half-wit

반보 半步 a half step ♦ 반보를 내딛다[물러서다] take a half step forward [back]

반복 反復 (a) repetition; a repeat; reiteration
▶ 어학 학습에는 반복이 중요하다 Repetition is important in language learning.
—반복하다 repeat; reiterate; do over again
♦ 반복하여 repeatedly; over and over (again); again and again / 반복하여 말하다 say over again; repeat *oneself*
■ —기호 〔樂〕 a repeat mark; a sign of repetition —설 〔生〕 the recapitulation theory —시험 a repeat test

반복 反覆 〈언 행 의〉 fickleness; inconstancy; 〈생각의〉 repeated switching 《of *one's* opinion [decision]》
—반복하다 switch [shift] again and again
■ —무상 inconstancy; instability : 반복 무상한 inconstant; fickle

반봉건 半封建 semi-feudalism ■ —사상[사회] a semi-feudalistic idea [society]

반분 半分 halving; an equal division
—반분하다 cut in [into] halves; halve; go halves [fifty-fifty]; divide *sth* into equal shares [halves]
♦ 이익을 반분하다 share the profits equally; go fifty-fifty on the profit / 재산을 반분하다 divide the fortune into equal shares

반비례 反比例 inverse proportion
—반비례하다 be in inverse proportion [ratio] 《to》; be inversely proportional 《to》
▶ A는 B에 반비례한다 A is in inverse proportion to B. ⇌ A is inversely proportional to B.

반사 反射 reflection; reverberation; **(英)** reflexion
♦ 반사적 reflecting; reflective; reflexive / 반사적으로 reflectively; reflexively; by a reflex action
▶ 어떤 신경을 자극하면 반사적으로 어떤 운동이 일어난다 If you stimulate a certain nerve, a certain movement takes place reflexively.
—반사하다 reflect; throw [flash, strike] back (light); reverberate; 〈비추다〉 image; mirror (in)
▶ 거울은 빛을 반사한다 A mirror reflects light.
▶ 소리는 벽에 반사하여 울린다 The sound reverberates [echoes] on the wall.
▶ 달은 태양의 빛이 반사되어 빛난다 The moon shines by the reflected light of the sun.
■ 난(亂)— diffused reflection 전(全)— total reflection 조건— a conditioned reflex ■ —각 an angle of reflection —경 a reflex [reflecting] mirror; a reflector —광[열] reflected light [heat] —광선 reflected ray —광학 catoptrics —기(器) a reflector —등(燈) a reverberator —로(爐) a reverberating furnace [kiln]; a reverberatory furnace —망원경 a reflecting telescope; a reflector —면 a specular surface —상(像) a reflected image —신호 a heliogram —운동 a reflex (movement) —율 reflectance —작용 a reflex (action) —체 a reflector —카메라 a reflex camera —현미경 a reflecting microscope

반사회적 反社會的 antisocial ♦반사회적 행위 antisocial action

반삭 半朔 half a month; a half month

반상회 班常會 a monthly meeting of a neighborhood association [group]

반색하다 show great joy; rejoice 《in, at》; be delighted 《in》; smile a welcome 《to》
▶그 소식을 듣고 그녀는 아주 반색했다 She was very happy [glad] to hear the news. ⇌ She danced [jumped] for [with] joy at [to hear] the news.

반생 半生 half one's life; half a lifetime
♦반생을 보내다 spend half a lifetime
▶그는 반생을 고고학 연구에 바쳤다 He devoted half his life to research in archeology.
■전[후]— the former [latter] half of one's life

반석 盤石 〈큰 돌〉a huge rock; 〈견고함〉firmness; steadfastness
♦반석같은 as firm [steadfast] as a rock; adamant / 국기(國基)를 반석같이 튼튼히 하다 place one's country on a stable foundation

반성 反省 〈자성〉self-examination; reflection; introspection; 〈재고〉reconsideration
♦반성을 촉구하다 ask [urge] sb to reconsider 《the matter》; call for grave reflection / 정부의 반성을 촉구하다 demand the government's reconsideration; urge the government to reconsider
—**반성하다** examine oneself; reflect 《on》; introspect; reconsider
♦반성해 보면 on second thought(s); on reflection / 스스로의 행위를 반성하다 reflect on one's conduct; reexamine one's behavior

반성유전 伴性遺傳 〔生〕 sex-linked inheritance; sex-linkage

반세기 半世紀 half a century ♦반세기 전에 in the half century previous to / 4 반세기 a quarter of a century

반소 反訴 〔法〕 a cross action; a counteraction; a counterclaim; a countersuit
♦반소를 제기하다 counterclaim
—**반소하다** counterclaim 《for, against》; plead a counterclaim; bring a cross action
■—인 a counterclaimant —장(狀) a crossbill

반소 半燒 partial destruction 《by fire》
—**반소하다** be partially destroyed 《by fire》
▶집이 반소되었다 The house was half destroyed by fire.

반소경 半— a half-blind person; a person of purblind eyes; 〈문맹자〉an illiterate [ignorant, unlettered] person

반소매 半— a half-sleeve; a half-length sleeve
■—셔츠 a shirt with half-length [short] sleeves

반송 返送 sending back; return
—**반송하다** return; send back
▶배편으로 반송하다 ship back / 소포를 발송자에게 반송하다 return a package [send a package back] to the sender
■—화물[운임] return cargo [freight]

반송 搬送 conveyance —**반송하다** convey; carry ■—파〔通信〕a carrier wave

반송 半— a person half-dead 《from age and infirmity》; a person who has one foot in the grave ▶그는 반송장이나 다름없다 He is as good as dead.

반수 半數 half the number; half 《of the members》
♦학생[종업원]의 반수 half 《of》 the students [employees] / 위원의 반수 the reelection of half the committee / 반수를 넘다 be more than half the number; show a majority

반숙 半熟 ♦반숙의 half-boiled; soft-boiled; half-cooked; half-done —**반숙하다** boil 《an egg》 soft [lightly] ■—란 a half-done egg; a half-[soft-]boiled egg; a soft-cooked egg

반시간 半時間 half an hour; a half hour
♦반시간의 half hour(ly) / 반시간마다 every half hour

반시류 半翅類 〔昆〕 Hemiptera

반식민지 半植民地 a semicolony ■—국가 a semicolonial state —상태 semicolonialism

반신 半身 half the body; 〈좌우의 한쪽〉one side of the body
♦왼쪽 반신이 마비되다 be paralyzed on the left side of the body
■—상[—] the upper [lower] half of the body
■—사진 a half-length photograph —상 〈회화의〉a portrait of a person from the waist up; 〈조각의〉a half figure; a bust

반신 返信 a reply; an answer; 〈전보의〉a reply telegram
—**반신하다** reply to a letter; answer a letter; send a reply 《telegram》
■—용 봉투 a stamped self-addressed envelope : 반신용 봉투를 동봉하시오 Please enclose a stamped, self-addressed envelope —용 엽서 a reply [return] postcard [postal card]

반신료 返信料 return postage ⇨ 회신료

반신반의 半信半疑 ♦반신반의의 incredulous; dubious; half in doubt
—**반신반의하다** be half in doubt; do not quite believe; be doubtful [suspicious] of
▶나는 그녀의 이야기를 반신반의하며 들었다 I listened to her story dubiously [doubtfully].

반신불수 半身不隨 paralysis of one side [one lateral half] of the body; hemiplegia
▶그는 오른쪽이 반신불수다 He is paralyzed on his right side.

반암 斑岩 〔鑛〕 porphyry

반액 半額 half amount [sum]; half the amount [sum, price, fare]
♦반액으로 at half the price [fare]; at half price / 반액으로 하다 cut [reduce] the price by half / 반액을 할인하다 discount half the sum
▶어린이는 반액임 〈버스·입장료 등이〉 Half fare [price] for children.
▶반액으로 드리겠습니다 You can have it for [at] half price. ⇌ I'll sell it to you at a fifty percent discount.

반양성자 反陽性子 〔物〕 an antiproton

반양식 半洋式 a semi-Western style ▶우리는 반양식의 집에 산다 We live in a semi-Western styled house.

반어 反語 an irony; a word in reverse; 〈수사의문〉 a rhetorical question
♦ 반어적 표현 an ironic expression / 반어적 ironic / 반어를 쓰다 speak ironically [sarcastically]

반역 反逆·叛逆 (high) treason; (an) insurrection; (a) rebellion; (a) revolt; insurgency; mutiny
♦ 반역적 treasonous; treacherous; rebellious / 반역을 꾀하다 plot treason (against); conspire (against)
—**반역하다** turn traitor (to *one's* country); revolt [rebel] (against); rise in revolt [mutiny] (against)
■ —심 a rebellious spirit; a treasonous intention —자 a traitor; an insurgent; a rebel —죄 (high) treason : 그는 반역죄로 처형되었다 He was executed for treason.

반열 班列 (a) rank; order ♦ 반열이 높은 사람 a man of high rank / …의 반열에 서다 rank [be ranked] among…; take *one's* place among…

반영 反映 reflection
—**반영하다** reflect; be reflected; be reflective of
▶ 여론은 국회에 반영된다 Public opinion is reflected in the National Assembly.
▶ 주가는 경기를 반영한다 Stock prices reflect [mirror] business. ⇌ Business is reflected [mirrored] in stock prices.
▶ 신문은 사회를 반영하는 거울이다 The press is the mirror of society.

반영구적 半永久的 semipermanent
▶ 이 욕조는 반영구적이다 This bathtub will last (almost) indefinitely.

반올림 半— rounding to the nearest whole number
—**반올림하다** round off; count fractions of .5 and over as a unit and cut away [disregard] the rest
▶ 소숫점 다섯자리 이하를 반올림하시오 Round off the fractions to five decimal places.
▶ 6.115를 소숫점 셋째 자리에서 반올림하시오 Round off 6.115 to the second decimal place.
▶ 반올림하면 6.12가 된다 We have 6.12 in round figures.

반원 半圓 a semicircle; a half circle
♦ 반원(형)의 semicircular; half-round / 반원을 그리다 make a half circle; describe a semicircle
■ —주(周) a semicircumference —형 a semicircle; a hemicycle : 반원형으로 앉다 sit in a semicircle

반월 半月 a half moon; a half month ⇨ 반달

반유대주의 反—主義 anti-Semitism ♦ 반유대주의의 anti-Semite ■ —자 an anti-Semite

반유동체 半流動體 〔化〕 a semifluid; a semiliquid

반음 半音 〔樂〕 a semitone
■ —계 a chromatic scale —기호 a chromatic sign —정 a halftone

반응 反應 〈反響〉 a response; 〈효과〉 an effect; 〔化〕 (a) reaction
♦ 반응이 없는 irresponsive; ineffectual / 반응이 있다 react 《to》; take [have] effect 《on》 / 반응이 없다 show no reactions; have no effect 《on》 / 반응을 일으키다 act on [upon] / 반응을 타진하다 tap *sb's* reaction
▶ 그 액체는 알칼리성[산성] 반응을 나타냈다 The fluid showed an alkaline [acidic] reaction.
▶ 그의 제안에 큰 반응이 있었다 There was a lot of response to his proposal.
▶ 그 아이는 꾸짖어도 전혀 반응이 없었다 Scolding had no effect on the child. ⇌ I scolded the child to no effect [in vain].
—**반응하다** react 《to, on》; act 《upon, on》; respond 《to》; effect
▶ 금속은 산에 반응한다 Metals react on acid.
■ —양성[음성]— a positive [negative] reaction 연쇄— a chain reaction 투베르쿨린— a tuberculin reaction; a tuberculin test 핵— a nuclear reaction —속도 reaction velocity [rate] —시간 reaction time —실험 a reaction experiment —열 heat of reaction

반의반 半—半 a half of a half; a quarter; one fourth ▶ 난 숙제를 반의반도 못하고 있다 My homework is less than half of the half done.

반의식 半意識 〔心〕 subconsciousness
♦ 반의식적 subconscious; half-conscious

반의어 反義語·反意語 an antonym 「down」의 반의어는 「up」이다 "Up" is the antonym of "down."

반일 半— 〈하루 일의 절반〉 half of a daywork; a half day('s) work; 〈어떤 일의 절반〉 half of a work

반일 反日 ♦ 반일의 anti-Japanese
■ —감정 anti-Japanese sentiment [feeling] —정책 an anti-Japanese policy

반일 半日 half a day; half day

반입 搬入 carrying [taking, bringing] in [into] —**반입하다** carry [bring, take] into
▶ 그들은 그림을 전시장에 반입했다 They brought in the pictures for an exhibition.

반자 〔建〕 ceiling ♦ 반자를 들이다 ceil; board a ceiling ■ —널 a ceiling board [panel] —지 the ceiling paper —틀 a ceiling joist

반자성 反磁性 〔物〕 diamagnetism ♦ 반자성의 diamagnetic ■ —체 a diamagnetic (substance)

반작용 反作用 〔物〕 (a) reaction; (a) counteraction
♦ 작용과 반작용 action and reaction / 반작용을 일으키다 cause a reaction
▶ 그 반작용으로 이 일이 일어났다 This came to happen as a reaction of that.
▶ 작용에는 언제나 반작용이 따르게 마련이다 Action is inevitably [always] followed by reaction.

반장 班長 a squad [section, team, party, group] leader; 〈학급의〉 a monitor; the head of a class; a class president; 〈직공의 감독〉 a foreman; 〈행정 구획 동(洞)의〉 the head of a neighborhood association
■ —제도 the monitorial system

반장화 半長靴 half boots; short boots

반전 反戰 opposition to war; renunciation of war ♦ 반전의 antiwar / 반전을 부르짖다 cry

against war
■—데모 an antiwar demonstration —론 (an) antiwar argument; (美) pacifism; pacificism : 반전론을 부르짖다 advocate peace —론자 a pacifist; a dove —사상 an antiwar idea [sentiment] —운동 an antiwar movement; antiwar protests —주의 pacifism —파 an antiwar faction [party, elements]; the dove

반전 反轉 1 〈반대로 구름〉 revolution in the opposite direction; 〈機〉 reverse
—반전하다 〈반대로 구르다〉 turn [revolve] in the opposite direction; reverse
2 〈뒤바뀜〉 turning over; 〈뒤집힘〉 reversal
—반전하다 turn reversely [the other way round]; reverse its [one's] course
▶ 이 단추를 누르면 바퀴가 반전한다 Press this button and the wheel will turn the other way.
▶ 그때 그의 태도는 반전했다 Then he reversed himself [changed his attitude 180 degrees]. ⇒ Then he did an about-face.
▶ 적기는 기수를 갑자기 반전하여 우리 쪽으로 향했다 The enemy's plane suddenly turned toward us.
3 〔物·化〕 inversion
■—음〔普聲〕a retroflex —증폭기 an inverting amplifier —필 름 a reversal film —현 상〔寫〕reversal; solarization

반절 半— 〈여자가 하는〉 a half bow

반절 半切 cutting in half [into two]; 〈종이의〉 a half sheet of paper; half size
▶ 그 책임의 반절은 나에게 있다 I am partly [partially] responsible for that.
—반절하다 cut in half [into two]; divide into halves

반절 半折 〈접음〉 folding in half —반절하다 fold in half [into two] ■—지 a piece of paper folded in half

반점 斑點 a spot; a speck; a speckle; 〈얼굴의〉 dapples; mottles; a dot; a fleck
♦ 둥근 반점 무늬 a spotted pattern / 반점이 있는 개 a spotted dog / 반점이 있는 spotted; specked; dappled; speckled
▶ 깔개에 진흙 반점이 붙어 있었다 The mud spotted the rug.
▶ 저 반점이 있는 말을 봐라 Look at the dapple horse.
▶ 붉은 반점이 내 피부에 남아 있었다 Some red patches remained on my skin.

반정부 反政府 ♦ 반정부의 antigovernment; antiministerial ♦ —당 an opposition party —신문 an antigovernment [antiministerial] newspaper

반제 反帝 〈반제국주의〉 anti-imperialism
■—사상 anti-imperialist ideas [thought] —운 동 the anti-imperialist movement —투쟁 the struggle against imperialism

반제 返濟 return; 〈돈의〉 payment; repayment; reimbursement; refundment; redemption
♦ 빚이 반제 기일이 되다 the debt falls due
▶ 나는 그에게 그 돈의 반제를 졸랐다 I pressed him for repayment of the money.
—반제하다 〈돈을〉 pay (back, off); return; repay; refund; redeem
▶ 나는 빚을 반제하여 안심했다 I am relieved

to repay a debt.
▶ 나는 그에게 빚을 전부 반제했다 I repaid him in full.
■—기한 the term of repayment [redemption]: 빚의 반제 기한이 지났다 The debt is overdue.

반제국주의 反帝國主義 anti-imperialism ⇒ 반제(反帝)

반제품 半製品 half-finished goods; semimanufactured [semiprocessed] goods [articles]; semimanufactures

반주 半周 a semicircle; a hemicycle
—반주하다 go half round 《the globe》
▶ 나는 연못 둘레를 걸어서 반주했다 I walked half around the pond.

반주 伴奏 an accompaniment
♦ 무반주 바이올린독주 an unaccompanied violin solo / 반주에 맞추어 to the accompaniment of... / 악기 반주없이 노래하다 sing without instrumental accompaniment / 피아노 반주로 노래하다 sing to a piano (accompaniment); sing accompanied by piano
—반주하다 play sb's accompaniment 《on the piano》; accompany sb
♦ 피아노로 그녀의 노래를 반주하다 accompany her singing on the piano
♦ 관현악— an orchestral accompaniment
■—부 the accompaniment —자 an accompanist

반주 飯酒 liquor taken at a meal

반죽 dough; paste 《of bread》
♦ 밀가루와 물을 섞어 반죽을 만들다 mix flour and water and knead into dough
—반죽하다 knead 《dough, flour》; mold 《clay》
♦ 되게 반죽하다 harden by kneading
▶ 아이가 진흙을 반죽하며 놀고 있었다 A child was enjoying squeezing the mud through his fingers.

반죽음 半— half death
♦ 반죽음이 되어 있다 be more dead than alive; be half dead
▶ 그는 반죽음이 되어 거기에 누워 있었다 He was lying there nearly [half] dead.
▶ 그들은 그를 반죽음시켰다 They nearly [half] killed him.

반줄 〈감비아의 수도〉 Banjul

반증 反證 (a) proof to the contrary; contrary evidence; disproof; counterevidence
♦ 반증을 들다 prove the contrary; produce counterevidence [contrary evidence]; disprove / 알리바이에 대해 반증을 들다 disprove sb's alibi / 진술의 반증으로 증거를 제시하다 offer evidence against a statement
▶ 이 증언에 대한 반증을 들어주기 바랍니다 I would like you to produce evidence against [which contradicts] this testimony.
▶ 그것에 대한 반증은 없다 There is no evidence to disprove it.
—반증하다 disprove; prove against

반지 斑指 a (finger) ring
▶ 반지를 끼다 put [slip] a ring on one's finger / 반지를 끼고 있다 have [wear] a ring on one's finger / 반지를 빼다 slip a ring off one's finger

반지르르

▶그녀는 반지를 끼었다[뺐다] She put the ring [took the ring off] her finger.
■결혼[약혼]— a wedding [an engagement] ring 금[다이아몬드]— a gold [diamond] ring: 그녀는 다이아몬드 반지를 끼고 있었다 She wore [had] a diamond ring on her finger. 루비— a ring gemmed with rubies 보석— a ring set with a jewel; a jewel ring ■—자국 a ring mark (on the finger)

반지르르 1〈윤이 나는 모양〉glossily; sleekly; lustrously; lubricously
—반지르르하다 lubricous; glossy; sleek; lustrous
♦반지르르한 마루 a glistening floor / 반지르르한 피부 lustrous skin / 반지르르한 명주 glossy silk / 머리에 기름을 반지르르하게 바르다 oil one's hair till it shines
2〈겉만 그럴듯한 모양〉showily; tawdrily
—반지르르하다 showy; deceptive
♦겉보기만 반지르르하다 be not so good as it looks; be deceptive

반지름 半— 〈數〉 a radius; a semidiameter

반직업적 半職業的 semiprofessional ♦반직업적인 운동선수 a semiprofessional athlete [player]

반짇고리 a workbasket; a sewing box; a workbox; a workbag; a needle case; a housewife [házif]; a hussy

반질거리다 1〈매끈거리다〉be slippery; be smooth; be glossy; be sleek; be oily
♦반질거리는 마루 a slippery floor / 반질거리는 머리 sleeky hair
▶이 종이는 감촉이 반질거린다 This paper is smooth to the touch.
▶새로 니스칠한 마룻바닥이 반질거린다 The newly varnished floor shows glossy surface.
2〈교활하다〉be sly [cunning, crafty]

반질반질 1〈매끈하게〉sleekly; glossily; smoothly; in an oily [slippery] fashion
—반질반질하다 sleek; glossy; smooth; slippery
♦반질반질한 머리 sleek [glossy, lustrous] hair
▶그녀는 언제나 마루를 반질반질하게 깨끗이 한다 She always makes the floor shining clean.
▶그녀의 피부는 아주 반질반질하다 Her skin is very smooth.
2〈교활하게〉slyly; craftily; artfully; cunningly
—반질반질하다 sly; sneaky; crafty; cunning; foxy

반짝 1〈빛나는 모양〉with a flash [sparkle, shine]
▶그의 눈이 반짝 빛났다 His eyes glittered.
▶멀리서 무엇인가 반짝 빛나는 것이 보였다 I saw something glitter far away.
2〈쉽게 들어올리는 모양〉〈lift〉easily; lightly
▶그는 바위를 반짝 들어 올렸다 He lifted the rock easily [without effort].
3〈갑자기 정신이 드는 모양〉suddenly; strongly
♦정신이 반짝 들다 come to oneself with a start

반짝거리다 shine ⇨ 반짝이다

반짝반짝 glitteringly; brilliantly; dazzlingly
▶하늘에는 별이 반짝반짝 빛나고 있었다 The stars were twinkling in the sky.
—반짝반짝하다 glitter; twinkle; sparkle; shine; flash; glisten; wink
♦반짝반짝하는 보석 a glittering jewel / 반짝반짝하는 다이아몬드 dazzling diamonds / 반짝반짝하는 glittering; sparkling; shining; shiny; spangly
▶해가 뜨자 풀은 이슬로 반짝반짝했다 The grass sparkled with dew as the sun rose.
▶반짝반짝한다고 모두가 금은 아니다 (속담) All is not gold that glitters.

반짝이다 shine; glitter; sparkle; glimmer; glisten; twinkle; be bright [brilliant]; 〈순간적으로〉flash; wink
♦기쁨에 반짝이는 눈 eyes sparkling with joy / 반짝이는 별처럼 like the twinkling stars / 햇빛에 반짝이다 glitter in the sun
▶멀리서 등불이 반짝이고 있다 A light is glimmering from afar.

반쪽 半— (a) half; one side (of the body)
♦생선 반쪽 a sliced side of a fish
▶반쪽이라도 없는 것보다 낫다 (속담) Half a loaf is better than no bread.

반쯤 半— (about) half; halfway
♦눈을 반쯤 뜨고 with one's eyes slightly open / 두 지점 사이의 반쯤되는 곳에 있다 be somewhere in between
▶그는 반쯤 단념하고 있었다 He had half [nearly] given up.
▶교회는 우리 집과 너의 집의 반쯤되는 곳에 있다 The church stands halfway between my house and yours.

반찬 飯饌 subsidiary articles of diet; 〈곁들이는 요리〉a side dish
♦고기 반찬 a meat dish / 맛없는 반찬 tasteless side dish / …을 반찬삼아 밥을 먹다 eat rice with...as an accompanying dish
▶오늘 저녁 반찬은 무엇일까? I wonder what we're having for dinner this evening.
▶점심도시락 반찬은 무엇이 좋으냐? What would you like in your box lunch?
■—가게 a grocery (store); a grocer's (shop) —거리 groceries; materials for making side dishes

반창고 絆瘡膏 a sticking plaster; an adhesive plaster; 〈테이프 모양의〉an adhesive tape
♦상처에 반창고를 붙이다 apply a sticking plaster to the wound
▶등에 반창고 좀 붙여 주시겠어요? Will you apply plasters to my back?

반체제 反體制 ♦반체제의 antiestablishment
■—운동 an antiestablishment movement —인사 a dissident —작가 an antiestablishment writer; a dissident writer

반추 反芻 rumination
—반추하다 ruminate; chew the cud
▶소가 반추하고 있다 The cow is ruminating [chews its cud].
■—동물 a ruminant —위 the ruminant stomach

반출하다 搬出— carry [take] (rice) out of 《a district》

반취 半醉 half-drunkenness; slight intoxication ―**반취하다** be half-drunk[-tipsy]; be mellow; be slightly drunk

반칙 反則 〈법규의〉 (an) infringement [violation] of rules; an irregularity; 〈스포츠의〉 (a) foul play; a foul; 〈투수의〉 a balk
♦반칙의 foul; against the rules; contrary to the regulations
▶그것은 반칙이다 It is against the rules.
―**반칙하다** violate [act against] the rules; play foul; commit a foul
▶반칙하면 퇴장 당한다 If you play foul, you'll be ordered away from the ground.
▶시합 전반에 그는 계속해서 반칙했다 He fouled repeatedly during the first half of the game.
■―**구역** 〈축구의〉 a penalty area ―**자** an offender

반침 半寢 (美) a closet; an alcove; (英) a store cupboard

반코트 半― a half-coat

반 타 작 半打作 tenancy on half-and-half shares; a half crop
―**반타작하다** share the crop equally

반토 礬土 〔化〕 aluminum oxide ⇨ 산화 (~알루미늄)

반투명 半透明 semitransparency; translucency
♦반투명 유리 semitransparent [translucent] glass
―**반투명하다** semitransparent; translucent
■―**체** a translucent [semitransparent] body

반파 半破 partial destruction
―**반파되다** be partially [partly] destroyed

반편 半偏 1 〈반쪽〉 a half
2 ⇨ 반편이

반편스럽다 半偏― half-witted; dull; stupid; slowwitted; foolish; silly ♦반편스럽게 웃다 smile a fatuous smile

반편이 半偏― a half-wit; a simpleton; a ninny; (口) a dimwit
♦반편이의 foolish; stupid; half-witted; slow-witted / 반편이같은 짓을 하다 do a stupid [foolish] thing
■―**짓** a foolish act; foolery

반평생 半平生 half *one's* life ▶그는 그 연구에 반평생을 바쳤다 He devoted half his life to the research.

반 포 頒 布 〈공포〉 proclamation; promulgation; (a) public announcement; 〈발표〉 publication; distribution; circulation
―**반포하다** proclaim; promulgate; announce publicly; make public [known]; publish

반푼 半― a farthing ♦반푼어치의 값어치도 없다 be not worth a farthing [penny]

반품 返品 returned goods; an article sent back; returns
▶반품 사절 〈게시〉 All Sales Final.
―**반품하다** return goods; send back articles [goods] 《to the manufacturer》
▶불황으로 많은 서적과 잡지가 반품된다 A lot of books and magazines return unsold from the market because of a business depression.

반하다 1 〈연모하다〉 fall in love 《with》; be enamored 《of》; be attached 《to》; take a fancy 《to》; lose *one's* heart 《to》; (口) be taken 《with her, by her beauty》; (口) be keen 《on》
♦서로 반하다 be in love with each other / 첫눈에 반하다 fall in love [come to love] with her at first sight; take a fancy 《to *sb*》 at first meeting
▶톰은 케이트에게 반했다 Tom is infatuated with Kate.
▶녀석은 그녀에게 얼마 동안 반했는가 했더니 벌써 열이 식어버렸다 He was head over heels in love with her some time ago, but the flame has burned itself out now.
▶그녀는 그의 사람됨됨이가 아니라 재산에 반했다 She loves him not for what he is but for what he has.
▶그는 그녀의 아름다움에 완전히 반해 버렸다 Her beauty fetched him completely.
2 〈감탄하다〉 admire; be charmed [attracted] 《by》; 〈넋을 잃다〉 forget *oneself*; be entranced [enraptured] 《by, with》
♦아름다운 목소리에 반하다 be entranced with *sb's* sweet voice / 인품에 반하다 be attracted [charmed, taken] by *sb's* personality
▶그는 음악에 반했다 He was absorbed in the music.
▶나는 그가 피아노 치는 것을 듣고 반했다 I forgot myself as I listened to him playing the piano. ⇌ I was entranced by his performance on the piano.

반하다 反― go against; be contrary to; be opposed to; be contradictory to
♦이에 반해서 〈한편으로〉 on the other hand
▶그는 자기의 의지[희망]에 반해서 그 학교에 입학했다 He was forced to enter that school against his will [wishes].
▶규칙에 반하는 짓은 하지 마라 Don't break the rules!
▶그것은 나의 주의에 반한다 It goes against my principles.
▶그 조치는 우리의 이익에 반한다 The measure is adverse to our interests.
▶너의 말은 사실에 반하고 있다 Your statement is opposed to the fact. ⇌ You're not telling the truth.

반합 飯盒 a messtin; 〈군인용〉 a mess kit; a (soldier's) canteen

반항 反抗 〈저항〉 resistance; insubordination; opposition; 〈도전〉 defiance; 〈대항〉 opposition; 〈적대〉 hostility; antagonism; 〈반역〉 rebellion; revolt; 〈상관에 대한 저항〉 mutiny
♦반항적인 아이 a rebellious child
―**반항하다** 〈저항하다〉 oppose; resist; offer resistance 《to》; 〈불복종하다〉 disobey; revolt 《against》; be insubordinate 《to》; 〈권위를 무시하다〉 defy; bid defiance 《to》; 〈적대하다〉 antagonize; mutiny; be antagonistic 《to》; rebel 《against》; stand against; turn on [upon]
♦···에 반항하여 in opposition to...; in defiance of... / 단호하게 반항하다 set *one's* face against / 주인에게 반항하다 lift a hand against *one's* master; turn on *one's* master
▶요즘 그는 부모에게 반항한다 These days he disobeys his parents.

▶ 병사들은 상관에게 반항했다 The soldiers mutinied against their superiors.
▶ 민중들은 침략군에 반항했다 The people put up [offered] resistance to the invaders.
━━-기 a rebellious age; the period of contrariness; the negative phase ━━-심 a spirit of insubordination [contradiction]; a rebellious spirit [mind]

반항적 反抗的 rebellious; defiant; hostile
◆ 반항적 태도를 취하다 take [assume] a defiant [hostile] attitude (toward)

반향 反響 1 〈메아리〉〔物〕 an echo (*pl*. ~es); reverberation; 〈음향〉 acoustics
━━반향하다 echo; reecho; resound; reverberate
2〔영향〕〈사건 등의〉 repercussions; influence; an effect; 〈반응〉 reflection; an echo, a response; (a) reaction; 〈신문 등의〉 a comment; a sensation
◆ 반향이 없다 have no response (to) / 반향이 있다 have [receive, find] a response [an echo] (in); be echoed (abroad); be reflected (on)
▶ 그 사건은 세계적인 반향을 불러일으켰다 The incident caused global [worldwide] repercussions.
▶ 우리의 제안은 신문에서 좋은 반향을 얻었다 Our proposal received favorable comments in the newspapers.
▶ 그 책은 커다란 반향을 일으켰다 The book created a great sensation.
▶ 그의 제안에 대해 아무도 반향이 없었다 No one responded [There was no response] to his proposal.

반혁명 反革命 a counterrevolution ◆ 반혁명의 counterrevolutionary

반환 返還 return; restoration; 〈돈·부채의〉 repayment; 〈토지·사람의〉 rendition; 〈정당한 소유주의〉 restitution
◆ 영토의 반환 retrocession of a territory
▶ 우리는 우리 영토의 반환을 요구한다 We demand the return [restoration] of our territory.
━━반환하다 return; restore; retrocede; give back; send back; replace; repay
◆ 우승기를 반환하다 return [restore] the championship flag (to)
▶ 정부는 소유주에게 그 집을 반환했다 The government returned [restored] the house to its owner.
━━-점 〈마라톤의〉 the turn; the turning point

받다¹ 1 〈오는 것·주는 것을〉 get; have; receive; take; be given; be awarded
◆ 나는 생일 선물로 시계를 받았다 I got [received] a watch as my birthday present.
▶ 그는 노벨 평화상을 받았다 He received [was awarded] the Nobel Peace Prize.
▶ 나는 어제 친구의 편지를 받았다 I got [received] a letter from a friend yesterday.
▶ 그녀는 장학금을 받았다 She was given [awarded] a scholarship.
2 〈받을 것을〉 receive; get; accept; take
▶ 그는 중고 자전거 대금으로 50,000원을 받았다 He took five thousand won for the second-hand bicycle.
▶ 너 얼마 받았니? How much did they give you?
▶ 월세로 한 달에 200,000원을 받습니다 I'll take [collect] 200,000 won a month for the room rent.
▶ 會話「너는 월급을 얼마나 받지?」「100만원 받아」 "What [How much] salary do you get?" "I get one million won."
3 〈허가를〉 get; have; obtain
◆ 허가를 받다 get [have, obtain] permission
▶ 그는 선생님에게 조퇴 허가를 받았다 He get his teacher's permission to leave school early.
4 〈치료·수술 등을〉 have; undergo
◆ 우리는 1년에 한번 건강 진단을 받는게 좋다 We'd better have [undergo] an annual checkup.
▶ 그는 위암 수술을 받았다 He had an operation on his stomach for cancer.
5 〈당하다〉 suffer (a blow); 〈벌을〉 be punished
◆ 모욕을 받다 be insulted; suffer an insult
▶ 돈을 훔치면 벌을 받는다 If you steal money, you will be punished [take punishment].
▶ 그 화재로 그의 사업은 큰 타격을 받았다 His business suffered a great blow from the fire.
6 〈공·물 등을〉 catch (a ball, the rainwater)
◆ 공을 받다 catch [stop] a ball / 빗물을 물통에 받다 catch the rainwater in the bucket / 물을 한 통 받다 get water in a bucket
7 〈사들이다〉 buy; get
◆ 받아서 팔다 〈소매로 팔다〉 retail / 물건을 (팔기 위해) 대량으로 받다 buy things in a mass
8 〈서류·신청 등을〉 accept; receive
◆ 신청을 받다 accept applications / 청혼을 받다 [받아들이다] receive [accept] a proposal (of marriage)
9 〈우산 등을 펴서 들다〉 hold (an umbrella) over *one*'s head; carry; put up
◆ 양산을 받다 hold a parasol over *one*'s head
10 〈전화를〉 answer ◆ 전화를 받다 answer the phone; come to the phone
11 〈손님 등을〉 admit; show in
▶ 오늘은 손님을 받지 않습니다 (게시) Closed today.
12 〈아기를 낳다〉 deliver (of a child)
13 〈혈통·재질 등을〉 inherit; succeed; follow; get
◆ 아버지의 재질을 받다 inherit *one*'s father's talent
14 〈햇볕·바람 등을〉 be exposed (to); bask; be bathed (in sunshine); shine upon
▶ 물은 햇볕을 받아 따뜻했다 The water was warm from the sun.
15 〈뿔·머리로〉 butt; gore; 〔蹴〕 〈헤딩하다〉 head
◆ 황소에 받히다 be gored by a bull / 염소가 다리를 받다 a goat butts *sb* in the leg / 머리로 전주를 받다 bump *one*'s head on the pole

받다² 〈입에 맞다〉 agree with *sb*; suit *one*'s palate [taste]
◆ 음식이 잘 받다 〈입맛이 당기다〉 eat well; have a good appetite / 음식이 받지 않다 〈입맛이 없다〉 have a poor appetite; 〈속이 거북하다〉 *one*'s stomach revolts against food

받들다 1 〈받쳐 들다〉 lift up; hold up; uphold 2 〈지지하다〉 support; 〈보좌하다〉 aid; assist; help; 〈따르다〉 obey; 〈믿다〉 believe in; 〈추대하다〉 have sb over
3 〈공경하다, 모시다〉 treat sb with deference; 〈존경하다〉 look up to; hold sb in reverence; esteem

받들어총 —銃 받들어총을 하고 (stand) at the present (arms)
▶ 받들어총 (口令) Present arms!
▶ 병사들은 받들어총을 했다 The soldiers presented arms.
—**받들어총하다** present arms

받아넘기다 parry; fend off; turn; aside; 〈씨름에서〉 dodge ♦질문을 능숙하게 받아넘기다 take the edge off sb's questions with skillful [flexible] answers

받아쓰기 (a) dictation; writing to dictation ♦반 학생에게 받아쓰기를 시키다 give dictation to the class
▶ 오늘 오후에 받아쓰기 시험이 있다 We have an examination in dictation this afternoon.
—**받아쓰기하다** take dictation ⇨ 받아쓰다

받아쓰다 write [take, put, note] down; 〈구술을〉 take dictation; take down from dictation ♦구술(口述)을 속기로 정확히 받아쓰다 take sb's dictation accurately by shorthand / 받아쓰게 하다 dictate (a passage to the class)
▶ 나는 그들의 이름을 받아썼다 I took down their names.
▶ 그녀는 환자의 말을 받아썼다 She took down what the sick man said.
▶ 그는 비서에게 편지를 받아쓰게 했다 He dictated a letter to his secretary.

받아치다 hit [strike] back; return a blow (to); receive and give back; 〔拳〕 counter; give a counterblow (to)

받을어음 a bill receivable (略 b.r., B.R., B/R)

받치다 1 〈배기다〉 be hard; pinch; squeeze
▶ 의자가 궁둥이에 받친다 The seat is hard under my buttocks.
2 〈치밀다〉 surge; feel a surge [gush] (of anger); well up (in one); 〈사물이 주어〉 fill one's heart
3 〈밀어대다〉 sit [lie] heavy on one's stomach; remain undigested in the stomach
4 〈괴다〉 prop [bolster, shore] (up); support (with a prop); underpin; hold up
♦벽을 기둥으로 받치다 support a wall with a post
▶ 글 쓰는 데 받칠 것 좀 주시오 Give me something to lay under writing paper.
5 〈펴서 받쳐들다〉 hold up (an umbrella); hold (an umbrella) over one's head; put up [raise] (an umbrella)
▶ 그 사람은 나에게 우산을 받쳐 주었다 The man held an umbrella over me.
6 〈닿소리를 달다〉 place a consonant [consonants]

받침 1 〈괴는 것〉 a support; a prop; a fulcrum (pl. ~s, -cra)
♦받침을 괴다 put a support (under); underpin / 책상다리에 받침을 괴다 put a support under a desk leg

2 〔言〕 〈한글의 종성[종자음]〉 a final (consonants) on the end of a Korean orthographic syllable
■ 책— a celluloid board [cardboard] (laid under writing paper)

받침대 a prop; a stay; a support; a strut; a shore; underpinnings; a crosspiece; a beam; 〔木工〕 a block

받히다 〈부딪히다〉 be butted; be gored; be struck; be hit; be bumped ♦황소에 받히다 be gored by a bull / 트럭에 받히다 be run [struck] against by a truck

발¹ 1 〈일반적으로〉 a foot 《pl. feet》; 〈고양이 등의〉 a paw; 〈문어 등의〉 a tentacle; an arm ♦발이 아프다 be footsore; have a sore foot / 발이 저리다 one's feet have gone to sleep; one's foot is asleep; one has pins and needles in one's foot / 발을 걸다 trip sb up / 발을 다치다 get hurt in the foot; injure one's foot / 발을 삐다 sprain [twist] one's foot; have one's ankle sprained / 발을 잘못 디디다 miss [lose] one's footing; slip / 발을 밟다 step [tread] on (another's) foot [toes]
▶ 발을 밟지 마라 Get off my feet.
▶ 그녀는 발이 작다 She has small feet.
▶ 나는 발을 헛딛여 계단에서 떨어졌다 I lost [missed] my footing and fell downstairs.
▶ 나는 혼잡한 차내에서 오른발을 밟혔다 My right foot was stepped on in a crowded car.
▶ 그는 화가 나서 발을 동동 굴렀다 He stamped his feet in [with] anger.
▶ 다시는 우리 집에 발을 들여놓지 마라 Never [Don't] darken my door [cross the threshold of my house] again.
2 〈기물의〉 a foot; a leg; 〈글래스의〉 the stem ♦발이 셋인 탁자 a three-legged table
3 〈걸음〉 walking; walk; 〈보조〉 a step; 〈걷는 속도〉 pace; speed
♦ 발 가는 대로 걷다 walk as one's legs lead [carry] one; walk at random; go wherever one's fancy takes one / 발이 빠르다[재다] be quick on one's feet; be light-[quick-]footed; be a fast walker [runner] / 발이 느리다 be slow on one's feet; be a slow walker [runner] / 발을 멈추다 stop; halt; stay
▶ 자네 발로는 거기 당도하기 전에 해가 지겠네 At your pace it will be dark before you get there.
4 〈발짝〉 a step; a stride
♦한 발 나서다[물러서다] take a step forward [backward] / 한 발 늦다 fall a step behind sb; miss sb by a second [little]
▶ 우리는 그들보다 한 발 앞서 떠나기로 결정했다 We decided to leave [start] a little before them.
5 〈비유〉 발길다 be (just) in time for a treat; be lucky enough to come by a treat / 발 짧다 come too late for a treat / 발이 넓다 have a wide [large circle of] acquaintances; be widely acquainted; (美口) get around /〈운행 정지 등으로〉 발이 묶이다 be deprived of (means of) transport; be stranded; be tied up / 발을 끊다 cease to visit / 발을 빼다 wash one's hands of (an affair); be through with;

clear out / 제 발로 서다 stand alone; stand on one's legs; be independent; live on one's own / 제 발로 서게 하다 make sb independent; set sb on 《his》 legs
▶통근자들은 철도 노동자들의 파업으로 발이 묶였다 The commuters had no transportation because of the railroad workers' strike.
▶그는 저 폭력단에서 발을 뺐다 He washed his hands of that gang of racketeers.
▶그는 도둑질에서 발을 빼고 정직한 생활을 시작했다 He quit being a robber and started on an honest life.

발² 〈가리는 것〉 a bamboo [rattan] blind [curtain]
◆발을 치다[내리다, 말아 올리다] hang [let down, roll up] a bamboo blind / 남쪽 창에 발을 치다 hang a bamboo blind over the south window

발³ 〈길이〉 a fathom; a span; the length of outstretched arms ◆밧줄 두 발 two fathoms of rope

발⁴ 〈날·씨의 굵기〉 texture; weave
◆발이 성기다[촘촘하다] be loose [close] in weave / 발이 곱다[거칠다] be fine [rough, coarse] in texture

발 發 〈탄환 수〉 a round; a shot; a cartridge; 〈포탄 수〉 a shell; 〈발사 횟수〉 a round; a shot
◆열 발의 탄환 ten rounds of ball cartridge / 다섯 발 쏘다 fire five rounds [shots]
▶두 발의 총성이 들렸다 I heard two shots.
▶그는 기러기를 한 발에 떨어뜨렸다 He dropped a goose with a shot.
▶그는 두 발로 멧돼지를 죽였다 He killed a wild boar with two shots.
▶그들은 폭탄을 여러 발 투하했다 They dropped several bombs.
2 〈발동기 수〉 a motor; an engine
◆쌍발의 bimotor(ed); twin-engine(d); twin-motor(ed)

-발 發 1 〈출발〉 departure
◆다섯시 십분 발 열차 the 5:10 [five-ten] train / 브라질 발 화물선 a freighter from Brazil / 부산 발 급행열차 an express 《train》 from Pusan / 3월 1일 뉴욕 발 기선으로 by steamer leaving New York on March 1
2 〈발신〉 sending
◆2월 4일 발 전보 the cable dated February 4 / 4월 6일 발 편지 a letter of [dated] April 6 [《英》 6th April] / 파리 발(의) 보도 a news report under a Paris dateline

발가락 a toe ◆발가락이 보이는 (디자인의) 구두 peeptoe(d) shoes / 발가락을 구부리다 curl one's toes

발가벗기다 strip sb bare [to the skin]; strip sb (down) naked; denude; 〈몽땅 뺏다〉 strip [rob] sb of all he has
◆어린아이를 발가벗기다 undress a young child / 산을 발가벗기다 denude a hill; deforest a mountain

발가벗다 strip oneself of all one's clothes; strip oneself bare [stark-naked]
◆발가벗은 아이들 naked children / 발가벗고 with nothing on; stark-naked; in the nude; in one's bare skin
▶아이들은 발가벗고 수영하러 갔다 The children went swimming naked.

발가숭이 a naked body ⇨ 벌거숭이

발각 發覺 detection; revelation; discovery; disclosure; exposure
◆독직 사건의 발각 the discovery of graft / 발각이 두려워 for fear that it might come to light; lest it should be found out / 발각되다 be detected [revealed, discovered, disclosed, exposed]; be found out; come [be brought] to light
▶그는 들치기를 하다 발각이 되었다 He was caught [detected] in the act of shoplifting.
▶음모가 사전에 발각되었다 The plot was detected before it was carried out.

발간 發刊 publication; issue —**발간하다** publish; bring out; issue; 〈창간하다〉 start 《a magazine》; launch 《a newspaper》 ◆발간되다 be published; come out

발강이 [魚] a young carp

발갛다 bright [light] red; scarlet ◆뺨이 발갛다 have red cheeks ▶나는 발강게 빛나는 낙조를 보았다 I saw a bright red sunset.

발걸음 a step; a pace; a tread
◆무거운[가벼운] 발걸음으로 (walk) with a heavy [light] step; (walk) with heavy [light] feet / 급한 발걸음으로 at a quick [brisk] pace; at a trot / 발걸음을 재촉하다 [늦추다] quicken [slack(en)] one's pace [steps] / …쪽으로 발걸음을 돌리다 direct [turn, bend] one's steps toward 《a place》
▶그의 발걸음은 안정되어 있었다 His step was steady.
▶그는 묘지 쪽으로 발걸음을 돌렸다 He turned his steps to a cemetery.

발걸이 〈발 놓는 데〉 a foothold; a footrest; 〈책상 등의 가로대〉 a foot rail; 〈의자 등의 가로장〉 a rung; 〈자전거 등의 발판〉 a pedal

발견 發見 discovery; revelation; 〈발각〉 detection
◆신대륙의 발견 the discovery of a new continent
▶그는 과학상의 대발견을 했다 He made a great discovery in science.
▶그것은 내게는 큰 발견이었다 That was quite a revelation to me.
—**발견하다** discover; make a discovery; find; detect; spot; chance upon sth; light upon 《a fact》; strike out 《a theory》
◆잘못을 발견하다 find out a mistake [an error]
▶나는 신문에서 우연히 그의 이름을 발견했다 I struck (out) his name in the newspaper.
▶조사 결과 놀랄 만한 사실이 발견되었다 The inquiry has revealed a surprising fact.
▶그는 숲에서 시체로 발견되었다 He was found dead in the woods.
■—물 a discovery; a find —자 a discoverer; a finder; a detector

발광 發光 luminescence; radiation; emitting light
◆발광성의 luminous; photogenic; radiant
—**발광하다** radiate; emit [give out] light
▶이 물질은 발광한다 This substance emits

light [gives off light, is luminescent].
■—균 luminous [photogenic] bacteria —도료 ⇨ 야광(~도료) —동물[식물] a luminous [photogenic] animal [plant] —신호 a flashing caution signal —지 luminous paper —체 a luminous body; a luminary; an illuminant; a radiant; [電] a glower —탄 a luminous projectile; a light ball

발광 發狂 1 〈미침〉 madness; craziness; distraction; insanity; lunacy; mental derangement; (mental) alienation
—**발광하다** go [run] mad; become insane [lunatic, crazy]; become mentally deranged; lose *one's* head [mind, reason, senses]; go out of *one's* mind [head, senses]
♦ 발광한 mad; insane; crazy; lunatic / 발광한 사람 an insane [mentally deranged] person / 발광하게 하다 drive *sb* mad [crazy]; craze; derange
▶ 그는 절망한 나머지 발광했다 In an excess of despair he lost his reason.
2 〈지랄〉 a crazy act; a wild action; an insanity
—**발광하다** be beside *oneself*; act [behave] like mad

발군 拔群 ♦ 발군의 preeminent; conspicuous; distinguished; outstanding / 발군의 공을 세우다 serve with distinction; distinguish *oneself* by extraordinary exploits / 발군의 성적으로 졸업하다 graduate from 《school》 with honors
▶ 그는 언어 연구에 발군의 업적을 올렸다 He distinguished himself in linguistic research.

발굴 發掘 (an) excavation; unearthing; 〈시체의〉 exhumation
♦ 발굴 작업에 참가하다 take part in an excavations; attend an exhumation
—**발굴하다** dig (out [up]); excavate; unearth; turn up;〈시체를〉exhume; disentomb; untomb; disinter
유적을 발굴하다 unearth [dig up] the ruins / 탤런트를 발굴하다 scout for talent; pick out 《young》talent
▶ 그들은 공사 현장에서 많은 옛 금화를 발굴했다 They came upon lots of old coins at the construction side.
■—자 an excavator —지 the digs; 〈발굴품이 발견된〉 a findspot; a find place —品[物] an excavation; a find

발굽 a hoof (*pl*. hooves, ~s)
♦ 발굽 자국 a hoofprint / 말발굽 소리 the sound of a horse's hoofs; the clatter of hoofs; hoofbeats
▶ 말발굽 소리가 들렸다 The clatter of hoofs was heard.

발권 發券 the issue of banknotes; note issuing
■—액 the amount of notes issued —은행 a bank of issue

발그레하다 reddish; tinged with red; 〈안색이〉 ruddy; (be) aglow; reddened; flushed
♦ 발그레한 뺨 ruddy cheeks
▶ 그녀는 얼굴이 발그레했다 Her face was aglow 《with delight》.

발그림자 a trace; a shadow; a footmark
♦ 발그림자도 얼씬 않다 cease to visit; never come; do not appear

발그스름하다 reddish; somewhat red

발급하다 發給— issue ♦ 여권을 발급하다 issue a passport

발기 勃起 erection
♦ 발기성의 erectile / 발기력 감퇴 impotence; impotency —**발기하다** stand erect; rise up; become rigid [stiff] ■—근(筋) an erector (muscle)

발기 發起 〈계획〉 projection; 〈제의〉 a proposal; a suggestion; instance; a proposition; 〈설립〉 promotion; 〈솔선〉 initiation; 〈주최〉 auspices
♦ …의 발기로 at the proposition [proposal, suggestion, instance] of…; under the auspices [sponsorship] of…
—**발기하다** propose; project; suggest; promote; initiate
♦ 회사 설립을 발기하다 promote an organization of a company
■—설립 (독) Übernahmegrundung —이득 benefit of initiators

발기 cut *sth* open; open (up); crack (open) 《a chestnut》; split (open); shell 《peas》; tear 《away, off, out》

발기발기 in [to] pieces; 《tear》 into [in, to] shreds ♦ 발기발기 찢다 tear 《a letter》 up [to pieces]; pick [pull] to pieces

발기인 發起人 〈계획자〉 a projector; an originator; a sponsor; 〈후원자〉 a promoter; 〈제안자〉 a proposer
■—주(株) promoters' shares; management shares —회 a meeting of promoters

발길 1 〈차는 힘〉 (the force of) a kick
♦ 발길에 채다 be given a kick; get kicked 《by a horse》
2 〈걸음〉 a step; a pace
♦ 발길 닿는 대로 가다 go wherever *one's* feet [steps] lead *one*; go wherever humor [fancy] dictates *one*; walk at random / 발길이 잦다 frequent 《a place》; make frequent calls 《on *sb*, at a place》 / 발길을 돌리다 turn [bend] *one's* steps [heel]; turn [go] back / 발길을 재촉하다 quicken *one's* pace [steps]
▶ 나는 차마 친구에게서 발길이 떨어지지 않았다 I could hardly tear myself 《away》 from my friend.
▶ 그는 항상 발길 닿는대로 여행하고 있다 He is always on the move as the mood [spirit, fancy] takes him.
▶ 졸업 후 우리는 서로 발길이 끊어졌다 After leaving school we stopped seeing each other.

발길질 kicking —**발길질하다** give *sb* a kick; kick ♦ 신을 발길질하듯 하여 벗다 kick off *one's* shoes

발깍 1 〈성내거나 힘쓰는 모양〉 all of a sudden; in a sudden outburst
♦ 발깍 성내다 fall [get, fly] into a passion; flare up (in anger)
▶ 그는 문을 발깍 열었다 He jerked open the door.
2 〈소동이 일어나는 모양〉 topsy-turvy; in a great bustle; in a turmoil [hubbub, mess]; in utter confusion
▶ 온 집안이 발깍 뒤집혀 있다 All is confusion

발깍거리다

in the house. ⇌ The house is all torn up.
▶ 시 전체가 발깍 뒤집혔다 The entire city fell [was thrown] into great confusion [disorder].

발깍거리다 1 〈괴어오르다〉 bubble up; rise in bubbles
▶ 술이 발깍거린다 The wine is in bubbling ferment [brewing hubble-bubble].
▶ 물이 발깍거렸다 The water bubbled up [was foaming].
2 〈비어져 나오게 하다〉 knead 《dough, mud》 to squash [squish]
◆ 진흙을 짓밟아 발깍시리다 make mud squash [squish] underfoot

발끈 (get angry) on a sudden (at [about] trifles); with a burst; in a fit of passion; in a (fit of) rage
—**발끈하다** fly [fall] into a passion [rage]; flare [flash] up (in anger); (口) blow one's top; (口) hit the ceiling
◆ 발끈해지기 쉬운 성질 《a man with》 an explosive temper / 발끈해서 소리를 지르다 yell out in anger
▶ 그는 발끈해지는 것을 참았다 He checked the leap of his anger.
▶ 그녀는 발끈해서 일어섰다 She sprang to her feet in a rage.

발끈거리다 be roused to anger easily (at trifles); be irascible [irritable]; be quick to flare [flame, flash, burn] up; easily fall [fly, burst] into a passion

발끝 the tip of a toe; tiptoe; 〈구두 코〉 a toe
◆ 머리끝에서 발끝까지 from top to toe; from head to foot / 발끝으로 서다 stand on tiptoe / 발끝으로 걷다 tiptoe; walk on tiptoe(s)
▶ 이 구두는 발끝이 아프다 These shoes pinch my toes.
▶ 그는 발끝으로 서서 선반 위의 앨범을 꺼냈다 He stood on tiptoe to reach the album on the shelf.

발놀림 footwork

발단 發端 the origin; the opening; the start; the beginning; the commencement; the outset
◆ 사건의 발단 the origin of an affair / 발단부터 이야기하다 tell (a story) from the (very) beginning
—**발단하다** originate 《from, in, with》; be originated; start 《from》; begin; commence; stem 《from》
▶ 우리의 싸움은 어떤 오해에서 발단했다 Our quarreling started from a misunderstanding.

발 달 發達 〈성장·발육〉 development; growth; 〈진보〉 progress; advance; advancement
◆ 심신의 발달 mental and physical development / 지식[학문, 과학, 예술]의 발달 the advancement of knowledge [learning, science, art] / 인지(人智)의 발달 the advancement of human knowledge; intellectual progress / 도시의 급속한 발달 rapid growth of cities / …의 발달을 돕다[늦추다, 저해하다] promote [retard, arrest] the development [growth] of...
▶ 한국의 산업은 근년에 괄목할 만한 발달을 했다 Korea's industries have made remarkable progress in recent years.
—**발달하다** develop; grow (up); progress; make progress; advance
◆ …에서 발달하다 grow [develop] out of... / 크게[잘] 발달한 highly-[well-]developed / 발달하여 …으로 되다 develop [grow] into...
▶ 그것은 우주과학이 발달한 결과다 It is the result of the advancement of space science.
▶ 수영은 몸의 여러 근육을 발달시킨다 Swimming will develop many different muscles.

발돋움 standing on tiptoe; 〈발판〉 something to stand on —**발돋움하다** stand on tiptoe; straighten one's back; stretch oneself

발동 發動 motion; activity; 〈권력의〉 exercise; operation
◆ 사법권의 발동 operation of the judicial power
—**발동하다** move; put 《a machine》 in motion; 〈행사하다〉 exercise; invoke; put in action; put 《a law》 into operation
◆ 강권을 발동하다 take strong measures; appeal to legal action / 거부권을 발동하다 exercise one's veto (against)
▶ 대통령은 강권을 발동하여 파업을 중지시켰다 The president took legal action to stop the strike.
▶ 특별 조례가 발동되었다 A special ordinance was put into effect.
■—력 motive power

발동기 發動機 a motor; an engine
기름 [가솔린, 가스, 증기, 석유]— an oil [a gasoline, a gas, a steam, a petroleum] engine 수력— a water [hydraulic] motor ■—선 a motorboat; a motor ship

발뒤꿈치 the heel
▶ 발뒤꿈치가 높은[낮은] 신 high-[low-]heeled shoes; shoes with high [low] heels
▶ 나같은 건 그의 발뒤꿈치에도 못 미친다 I am no match for him. ⇌ I cannot stand comparison with him.

발등 the instep (of a foot) ◆ 발등을 밟다 tread on sb's foot ▶ 발등에 불이 떨어졌다 I am pressed by urgent business.

발라내다 tear [peel, take] off; pare; shuck; shell; husk; hull; crack; remove
◆ 닭고기의 뼈를 발라내다 bone a chicken / 생선 가시를 발라내다 clean [bone] a fish / 복숭아씨를 발라내다 remove the stone [pit] from a peach; pit a peach

발라드 a ballade

발라맞추다 〈아랑거리다〉 flatter; adulate; coax; butter sb up; curry favor 《with one's superior》; (俗) suck up to sb; play up to sb; court sb's favor
▶ 그는 언제나 상사에게 발라맞추고 있다 He is always flattering [trying to curry favor with] his superiors.

발라먹다 〈알맹이만 빼어 먹다〉 shell and eat 《nuts》; bone and eat 《a fish》; (비유) cajole [wheedle] sb out of sth

발랄라이카 〈악기〉 a balalaika

발랄하다 潑剌— lively; sprightly; vigorous; animated; brisk; smart; fresh; vivid
◆ 발랄한 젊은이 a lively [sprightly] youth /

발랄한 소녀 a perky [jaunty] girl / 발랄한 재기 keen intellect; acumen / 생기 발랄하다 be full of vigor [go, vitality, animation]; be vivid with life; 《美俗》 be peppy; be full of pep

발레 ballet
◆발레를 가르치다[배우다] give [take] ballet lessons
■—단 (프) a corps de ballet —댄서 a ballet dancer; a ballerina —학교 a ballet school

발레리 〈프랑스의 시인·비평가〉 Valery, Paul (1872-1945)

발레리나 a ballerina 《pl. ~s, -rine》; a female ballet dancer

발렌시아 〈스페인의 항구도시〉 Valencia

발렌타인데이 Saint [St.] Valentine's Day 《▶ 2월 14일》

발령 發令 〈명령〉 giving (an) official order; 〈사령〉 (an) official announcement (of appointment)
▶ 4월 1일자 발령으로 그는 부산으로 전근되었다 According to the assignments announced officially on April 1, he has been transferred to Pusan.
▶ 파랑 주의보가 발령중이다 A high wave warning has been issued.
—발령하다 give an (official) order; announce 《sb's appointment》 officially; issue 《regulations, a warning》
▶ 그의 새 직책의 임명이 오늘 발령된다 His appointment to a new post will be announced today.

발로 發露 (an) expression; a sign; (a) manifestation; exhibition
◆애국심의 발로 an expression [a manifestation] of patriotism
—발로하다 express [manifest, reveal] itself; become manifest

발론 發論 a motion; a proposal; a suggestion
—발론하다 move; propose; suggest
◆발론할 것이 있다 have a proposal to make
■—자 a mover; a proposer

발름하다 partly open; half-open ◆입을 발름하게 벌리고 with one's mouth half-opened

발리 (a) volley

발리볼 volleyball ⇨ 배구(排球)

발맞다 fall into step; be in step
◆발맞지 않다 be [get, walk] out of step; break step
▶ 그는 나머지 사람들과 발맞지 않는다 He is out of [is not in] step with the rest.

발맞추다 keep pace 《with》; fall [get] into step 《with》; 〈행동상〉 act in concert 《with》
◆발맞추어 걷다 walk [march] in step [line] 《with》; walk with measured steps
▶ 이 일에서는 그와 발맞추는 것이 최상책이다 In this matter, the best thing is to act [work] in concert with him.

발매 發賣 sale
◆발매중이다 be on sale / 발매를 금하다 suppress 《a book》; place 《a book》 under the ban
▶ 그 기계는 이미 발매중이다 The machine is already on the market [on sale].
—발매하다 sell; put 《books》 on the market [on sale]; release 《a new CD》

▶ 새 사전은 내달 발매된다 The new dictionary will be [come] out next month.
■—부수 circulation —일[시기] the date of issue —처 a sales [selling] agent

발매금지 發賣禁止 prohibition of sale; suppression 《of a book》 ▶ 내 책이 발매 금지 되었다 My book was prohibited [banned].

발명 發明 1 〈고안〉 invention; contrivance
◆발명의 재능이 있는 사람 a man of ingenuity
▶ 그에게는 발명의 재능이 있다 He has an inventive mind.
▶ 그의 발명이 최근에 실용화되었다 His invention has lately been put to practical use.
▶ 필요는 발명의 어머니 (속담) Necessity is the mother of invention.
—발명하다 invent; devise; contrive
◆문자를 발명하다 originate [invent] a system of writing
▶ 이 장치는 그가 발명한 것이다 This device is his invention.
2 an excuse ⇨ 변명
■—가[자] an inventor —품 an invention; 〈신고안품〉 a contrivance; a device

발목 an ankle ▶ 나는 발목을 삐었다 I sprained my ankle.

발목잡히다 1 〈벗어날 수 없게 되다〉 be tied to 《a steady job》; be chained [fettered] to 《one's business》; be pressed with
2 〈약점 잡히다〉 have one's sore spot found; give a handle to the enemy

발문 跋文 an epilogue; a postscript [an afterword] 《to a book》

발밑 ◆발밑에 at one's feet; close to one's feet / 발밑에도 미치지 못하다 be far inferior 《to》; be no match 《for》; cannot hold a candle 《to》
▶ 발밑을 주의하시오 Watch [Mind] your step.
▶ 깜깜해서 발밑도 보이지 않는다 It is too dark to see where I am treading.

발바닥 the sole of a foot

발바리 [動] a lap [pug] dog; a Pekin(g)ese 《dog》

발발¹ tremblingly ⇨ 벌벌

발발² 《tear, rip》 easily [asunder]
—발발하다 tear [rend] easily

발발 勃發 outbreak; outburst; sudden occurrence
—발발하다 break [burst] out; flare up; occur suddenly
▶ 내란이 발발했다 A civil war broke out.
▶ 그 관례는 전쟁이 발발할 때까지 계속되었다 The custom continued till the outbreak of the war [until the war broke out].

발버둥이치다 flutter one's feet; kick and struggle; squirm; writhe; wiggle; make vain effort; make a useless struggle
▶ 기린은 일어나려고 발버둥이쳤다 The giraffe struggled to its feet.
▶ 그는 발버둥이치면 칠수록 깊은 곳으로 빠졌다 He struggled only to fall into a depth.
▶ 이제 와서 발버둥이쳐야 소용없다 It's no use struggling now.

발버둥질 fluttering one's feet; wriggling; useless [fruitless] struggling —발버둥질하다

flutter one's feet; kick and struggle; 《헛해를 쓰다》 make a fruitless struggle 《against》

발벗다 1〈맨발이다〉 be barefoot(ed); have bare [naked] feet
♦ 발벗고 잔디 위를 걷다 walk on the lawn in bare feet; walk barefoot(ed) on the lawn
2〈적극성을 띠다〉♦ 발벗고 나서다 take up a positive attitude 《toward》; throw oneself into 《a matter》 with eagerness / 계획에 발벗고 나서다 take an active part in a project
▶그는 그 문제에 발벗고 달려들었다 He attacked the problem actively.
▶그는 지역사회의 일에 발빗고 나섰다 He was active in community affairs.

발병 —病 a foot disease [trouble]; footsoreness; a pain in the foot ♦ 발병나다 have a sore foot; one's foot gets sore; be footsore

발병 發病 falling [becoming] sick [ill]; coming down with a disease; the outbreak of one's illness
—발병하다 be attacked with [contract] a disease; be taken ill; become [get, fall] sick [ill]; show [present] the symptoms 《of a disease》
▶그는 귀국 후 곧 발병했다 Soon after he came home, he fell [was taken] ill.
▶감염되었어도 발병하지 않은 사람이 있었다 Not everyone who was exposed became ill.

발본 拔本 〈근원을 뽑음〉 eradication
♦ 발본적 개혁 a radical [drastic] reform
▶그들은 발본적인 대책을 제안했다 They proposed drastic measures.
—발본하다 eradicate; root up [out]; uproot

발본색원하다 拔本塞源— 〈폐단의 근원을 제거하다〉 eradicate sources of 《evil》; lay the ax to the root of 《evil》

발부리 the tip of a toe; tiptoe; 〈신발 등의〉 toe ♦ 돌에 발부리를 채다 trip on [against] a stone / 발부리로 걷다 tiptoe; walk on tiptoe / 발부리로 서다 stand on tiptoe

발붙이다 〈의지하다〉 depend [lean, rely] 《on, upon》; put reliance 《on, in》 ♦ 발붙일 곳 없는 lonely; helpless

발빼다 wash one's hands of; sever connection with; break away from; withdraw oneself 《from》
▶그는 암흑가에서 발빼기로 작정했다 He decided to sever his connections with [wash his hands of] the underworld and go straight.
▶그는 마약에서 발뺐다 He kicked drug habit.

발뺌 〈변명〉 an excuse; a pretext; a pretense; (口) an alibi
▶그런 발뺌은 통하지 않는다 Such an excuse won't do.
—발뺌하다 make [find, invent] an excuse [a pretext] 《of》; excuse oneself; talk oneself out of 《difficulty》; evade
▶그는 자기 과실을 비서의 탓으로 돌리고 발뺌했다 He made an excuse for [explained away] his fault by blaming his secretary.
▶그는 추궁받았지만 용케 발뺌했다 He talked himself out of a cross-examination.

발사 發射 〈총포의〉 discharge; firing; shooting; 〈로켓·미사일의〉 launching 《a moon rocket》; blast-off; lift-off
—발사하다 fire off; shoot; let off; discharge; 〈로켓·미사일 등을〉 launch; blast off
♦ 총을 발사하다 fire a gun / 인공위성을 발사하다 launch [blast off, put up] a [an artificial] satellite / 일제히 발사하다 fire a volley; fire by volley
▶그 우주선은 내일 발사될 예정이다 The spacecraft is to be launched tomorrow.
■ —각 the angle of fire —관 〈어뢰의〉 a torpedo [launching] tube —단계 the launch phase —대 〈로켓 등의〉 a launch(ing) ramp [pad]; a launch platform —물[체] 〈총탄 등의〉 a projectile —속도 rapidity of fire —시간 the lift-off time; T-time —시험 proof firing —약 propellant —용로켓 〈우주선 등의〉 a booster (rocket); a launch vehicle (a launcher (of a guided missile)) —지점[장, 기지] a launching site —탑 a launch tower

발산 發散 1〈방사능·냄새 등의〉 exhalation; emanation; 〈기체·액체 등의〉 diffusion
—발산하다 give forth [out, off]; send forth; emit; exhale 《from》
♦ 매력을 발산하다 display one's charms / 악취를 발산하다 emit a foul odor
▶이 동물은 강한 냄새를 발산한다 This animal emits [gives off] a strong scent.
2〈복사〉 radiation; 〈빛·열의〉 irradiation
—발산하다 radiate; irradiate
▶이 물체에서 광선이 발산되고 있다 Light radiates from this object.
3〈증발〉 evaporation; volatilization; transpiration; 〈삼출(渗出)〉 exudation 《of moisture》
—발산하다 evaporate; volatilize; transpire
4 [數·氣·物] divergence; divergency
■ —광속(光束) a divergent pencil of rays —급수 a divergent series —기류 diffusion current of air —렌즈 a diverging [divergent] lens

발상 發想 〈착상〉 idea; 〈구상〉 conception; [樂] expression ♦ 발상이 풍부하다 be full of ideas
▶그것은 재미있는 발상이다 That's an interesting idea [conception].

발상 發祥 birth; beginning —발상하다 begin; rise; start

발상지 發祥地 the place of origin; (비유) the cradle; the birthplace 《of jazz music, where sth started》
♦ 고대 문명의 발상지 the birthplace [cradle] of ancient civilization / 서양 문명의 발상지 the cradle of Western culture
▶중국은 문화의 발상지다 China is the cradle of culture.

발상하다 發喪— set up cries of lamentation

발샅 the space between toes

발색제 發色劑 a color former

발생 發生 〈일어남·생김〉 occurrence; (an) outbreak; 〈출현함〉 appearance; 〈비롯됨〉 origination; genesis; birth; creation; 〈열·전기 등의〉 generation; production; 〈자람〉 growth; [生] development

♦사건의 발생 the occurrence of an event / 지진의 발생 the occurrence of an earthquake / 콜레라의 발생 an outbreak of cholera / 파리의 발생을 막다 prevent [stop] the growth of flies
▶이 약은 해충의 발생을 막아준다 This chemical prevents the appearance of harmful insects.
─**발생하다** occur; happen; take place; 〈갑자기〉 break out; come into existence [being]; appear; 〈전기 등의〉 be generated; be produced; originate 《from》; 〈자라다〉 grow; 〈번식하다〉 breed; 〔生〕 develop
▶인플루엔자가 발생하였다 Influenza has broken out.
▶어젯밤 큰 열차 사고가 발생했다 A terrible train accident happened [occurred] last night.
▶이 근처에 나쁜 병이 발생하고 있다 There has been some serious illness going around here.
▶장차 무슨 일이 발생할지 모른다 One cannot tell what may happen in the future.
발생로 發生爐 〈가스의〉 a gas generator [producer] ■─가스 air gas; producer gas
발생학 發生學 〔生〕 embryology ♦발생학적 embryological ■─자 an embryologist
발설 發說 disclosure; revelation; announcement; divulgence; publication
─**발설하다** tell; mention; reveal; disclose; betray; divulge; leak 《a secret to》
♦비밀을 발설하다 let out [divulge] a secret / 비밀을 발설하지 않다 keep a secret; keep 《it》 a secret; keep mum about 《a matter》
발성 發聲 utterance; vocalization; phonation; exclamation; ejaculation
▶너는 발성이 좋지 않다 You vocalize poorly [have poor vocalization].
─**발성하다** produce [utter] a speech sound; vocalize; make voice; speak; exclaim; ejaculate
■─기 a vocal organ; a talking apparatus 《pl. ~, ~es》 ─기관 the vocal organs ─법 〔樂〕 vocalization; 〈화법〉 enunciation ─연습 vocal exercises ─영화 a talking picture [film]; a talkie; a sound picture [film] ─장치 a mechanism of voice production
발소리 the sound of footsteps [feet]; a footstep; a footfall; a step; a tread
♦시끄러운[조용한, 경쾌한, 무거운] 발소리 noisy [soft, light, heavy] footsteps / 아이들의 발소리 the sound of children's feet / 발소리를 내고 with noisy footsteps / 발소리를 죽이고 with stealthy steps; stealthily; 《move》 on cat's feet / 발소리가 들리다 hear 《the sound of》 *sb's* footsteps
▶사람의 발소리가 났다 Footsteps were heard. ⇌ Steps sounded.
▶발소리가 사라졌다 The footsteps died away.
▶저것은 아버지의 발소리다 That's Father's step.
▶밖에서 발소리가 들렸다 We heard footsteps outside. ⇌ We heard someone walking outside.
발송 發送 sending; 〔商〕 forwarding; 〈신속한〉 dispatch; 〈화물 등의〉 shipping
─**발송하다** send out [forth, off] 《a package》; forward; dispatch; ship; 〈우편물을〉 《美》 mail out; 《英》 post
♦화물을 철도편으로 발송하다 ship goods by rail
▶주문하신 물품은 2,3일 내에 발송하겠습니다 Your order will be dispatched within the next few days.
■─담당(원) a forwarding clerk; a shipping clerk; 《美》 〈우편물의〉 a mail clerk ─문서 dispatched documents ─역 a forwarding [an initial] station ─인 a sender; a consignor; 〈송금자〉 a remitter : 발송인 불명의 편지 an anonymous letter ─항 a port of dispatch
발신 發信 〈편지의〉 dispatch of a message [letter]; 〈전신의〉 sending [dispatch of] a telegram
─**발신하다** send 《a letter, a telegram》 (↔ receive); 〈전보 등을〉 dispatch 《a message》; telegraph; 〈해외로〉 cable
▶우리는 본토에 조난신호를 발신했다 We sent an SOS to the mainland.
▶이 뉴스는 로마에서 발신되었다 This news was telegraphed from Rome.
■─국(局) the sending office [station]; the office of origin 《of dispatch》 ─기(器) a transmitter; a transmitting set ─번호 sending number ─신호〔電信〕 a transmitting signal [circuit] ─음 〈전화의〉 a dial tone; 〈무전 등의〉 a signal ─인 〈편지의〉 an addresser; 〈전신 등의〉 the sender 《of a telegram》 ─지 the place of dispatch
발심 發心 1 〈마음먹음〉 resolution
─**발심하다** intend to 《do》; make up *one's* mind to 《do》; decide [resolve] 《to do》
2 〔佛教〕 religious awakening; conversion
─**발심하다** become religious [pious]; have a spiritual [religious] awakening; be converted; get religion
■─자 a convert
발싸개 feet wraps ▶이 거지 발싸개같은 놈아 You filthy [nasty] scum!
발씨름 leg-wrestling; shin [ankle] wrestling
발아 發芽 budding; gemmation; 〈씨앗의〉 germination; sprouting
─**발아하다** sprout 《out》; bud 《out》; pullulate; put out [forth] buds; germinate
▶봄비로 씨가 발아했다 The spring rain germinated [sprouted] the seeds.
발악 發惡 〈버둥댐〉 struggle; wriggle; 〈욕설〉 abusive language; revilement
♦최후의 발악 the last-ditch fight [struggle, effort]
─**발악하다** use abusive language; revile; rail 《at》; rave; inveigh 《against》; do infernal things; kick and struggle
▶탈주범들은 경찰 포위망을 뚫으려고 발악했다 The escaped convicts struggled desperately to cut their way through the besieging police.
발암 發癌 〔醫〕 carcinogenesis; the production of cancer
♦발암성의 carcinogenic 《chemicals》; cancerogenic; cancer-causing; cancer-forming;

cancer-producing ■—물질 a carcinogenic [cancerogenic] substance; a carcinogen

발언 發言 (an) utterance; speaking; 〈의견을 말함〉(a) speech; 〈제언〉 a proposal
♦ 발언의 기회를 잃다 lose the opportunity of speaking / 발언을 금지하다 prohibit sb from speaking / 발언을 취소하다 retract one's words / 발언이 허용되다 be allowed to speak; 〈회의에서〉 be recognized
▶ 그는 손을 들어 발언을 요청했다 He raised his hand and asked permission to speak.
—발언하다 speak; utter; open one's mouth; take the floor
▶ 그는 한 마디도 발언하지 않았다 He did not utter a single word.
■—자 a speaker; a utterer

발언권 發言權 the right to speak [of speaking]; (the right to) a voice; a say; the right to say
♦ 발언권이 있다[없다] have a [no] voice (in a matter) / 발언권을 얻다 have [hold, get, take] the floor; 〈의회에서〉 catch the Speaker's eye
▶ 회사에서 그는 발언권이 커지고 있다 He is strengthening his voice in the firm.

발 없는 말이 천리 간다 〈속담〉 Words have wings and cannot be recalled. ⇌ Words and feathers the wind carries away. ⇌ Bad news travels quickly.

발연 發煙 emitting smoke; fume
—발연하다 emit; smoke; fume ■—무기 smoke arms —제 a fumigant; a smoke generating agent —탄 a smoke shell [bomb]

발열 發熱 1〈물체의〉 generation of heat; calorification ♦ 발열의 exothermic; exothermal; exoergic
—발열하다 emit [generate] heat
2 〈신체의〉(an attack of) fever; pyrexia; febrility
—발열하다 become feverish; be attacked with fever; have [develop] (a) fever; run a temperature
▶ 그는 갑자기 발열했다 He had a sudden attack of fever. ⇌ He suddenly became feverish [developed a fever].
■—기(期) a pyrogenetic [hot] stage —량 calorific value [power] —물질[인자] a pyrogen —반응 〔化〕 exothermic reaction —요법 fever therapy —체 a heating element

발염 拔染 discharge printing
■—제 a discharging agent

발원 發源 1〈물의〉 the source; the fountainhead
—발원하다 rise [flow, come] 《from a lake [spring]》; take (its) rise [source] 《from a mountain》
▶ 그 강은 소양호에서 발원한다 The river has its source in Soyangho.
2〈사물의〉 the origin; the root; 〈시작〉 the beginning
—발원하다 originate (in); have (its) origin

발원하다 發願— offer a prayer (to a god); make a petition [vow] (to a deity)

발육 發育 growth; development; progress
♦ 발육중인 아이 a growing child / 발육이 늦은 아이 a physically [mentally] retarded child / 발육이 빠르다[늦다] grow [develop] rapidly [slowly] / 발육이 좋다[나쁘다] be well grown [undergrown] / 발육을 돕다 promote the growth (of)
▶ 이런 종류의 놀이는 아이의 발육을 촉진시킨다 This sort of play will promote the growth [development] of a child.
—발육하다 grow; develop
♦ 완전히 발육한 full-grown; fully-developed / 발육하지 않다 fail to develop; abort
▶ 벼는 더할나위없이 잘 발육하고 있다 The rice is doing well [growing quite nicely].
■—기(期) the period of development —기관 a development organ —부전 incomplete development; 〔生〕 abortion; underdevelopment; undergrowth; 발육 부전의 underdeveloped; undergrown

발음 發音 1〔言〕 pronunciation; enunciation; articulation
♦ 영어의 발음 English pronunciation; the pronunciation of English / 또렷한[정확한] 발음 clear [correct] pronunciation / 틀린 발음 mispronunciation / 발음이 명확한 사람 an articulator / 발음이 좋다[나쁘다] have a good [bad] pronunciation; one's pronunciation is good [bad]
—발음하다 pronounce; enunciate; articulate
♦ 발음하기 어려운 말 a sound difficult to pronounce / 올바로 발음하다 pronounce correctly / 강하게 발음하다 stress [accent] (the word) / 잘못 발음하다 pronounce (a word) wrongly; mispronounce (a word)
▶ 이 단어는 어떻게 발음합니까? How do you pronounce this word? ⇌ What is the pronunciation of this word?
2〔物·生〕 production of sound; sound production
■—기관 a speech [vocal] organ; a sound-producing organ —기호 a phonetic symbol [sign, alphabet] —사전 a pronouncing [phonetic] dictionary —연습 drills in pronunciation

발음학 發音學 〈음성학〉 phonetics ■—자 a phonetician; a phonologist

발의 發議 〈제안〉 a proposal; a suggestion; 〈동의〉 a motion
♦ 김 의원의 발의로 at the instance of [on the motion] Rep. Kim; at Rep. Kim's suggestion [proposal]
▶ 그녀의 발의로 우리는 바자를 열기로 했다 At her suggestion, we decided to hold a bazaar.
—발의하다 propose; suggest; move
■—권 〔政〕 the initiative —자 a proposer; a mover; an introducer

발인 發靷 the departure of a funeral (from home for the burial place); the starting of a funeral procession (toward a graveyard)
—발인하다 carry out a bier for burial; leave for a cemetery
▶ 일곱 시에 발인할 예정이다 The hearse is to leave the house at seven o'clock.

발자국 a footprint; a footmark; a spoor; 〈종적〉 a trace; tracks; 〈발짝〉 a step
♦ 눈 위에 뚜렷이 남은 발자국 footmarks printed off distinctly in the snow / 발자국 소리가 들리다 hear *sb's* footsteps / 발자국을 남기다 leave *one's* footprints; track 《a floor》
▶ 길에 큰 발자국이 남아 있었다 There were large footprints [footmarks, tracks] on the path.
▶ 우리는 사냥개의 발자국을 따라갔다 We followed the tracks left by the hounds.
▶ 경찰은 강도의 발자국을 뒤쫓고 있다 The police are on the trail [track] of the robber.

발자취 1 〈발자국〉 a footprint; a footmark
♦ 발전의 발자취 signs [traces] of progress / 역사에 발자취를 남기다 leave *one's* mark on history / 과학 분야에 위대한 발자취를 남기다 make a great contribution to science
2 〈인생길〉 a course; *one's* walk of life
♦ 10년간의 발자취를 회고하다 think of [recollect] the course *one* has followed for ten years

발자크 〈프랑스의 소설가〉 Balzac, Honoré de (1799-1850)

발작 發作 a fit; a spasm; a paroxysm; an ictus
♦ 격렬한[가벼운] 발작 a violent [mild] fit [stroke] 《of apoplexy》/ 간질 발작을 일으키다 have a fit of epilepsy
―**발작하다** have a fit [spasm, paroxysm]; throw a fit
▶ 그는 위경련이 발작했다 He was seized with [had] a fit of gastralgia.

발작적 發作的 spasmodic; paroxysmal; fitful
♦ 발작적 정신 이상 a temporary derangement of the mind / 발작적으로 spasmodically; paroxysmally; by [in] fits (and starts)
▶ 그녀는 발작적으로 웃음을 터뜨렸다 She burst into a fit of laughter.
▶ 그는 발작적으로 화를 냈다 He exploded with anger.

발장구 the beating; the kick
♦ 발장구치다 〈발길질하다〉 kick; flutter *one's* feet; 〈태평하게 지내다〉 lead an easy life; pass *one's* days in indolence

발장단 ―長短 ♦ 발장단을 치다 beat [mark] time 《to the music》 with *one's* foot
▶ 그녀는 코러스를 지휘할 때 언제나 발장단을 친다 She always beats time with her foot when she directs the chorus.

발적 發赤 〈醫〉 flare; rubefaction ■―**제(劑)** a rubefacient

발전 發展 1 〈뻗어나감〉 extension; enlargement; 〈성장〉 growth; 〈진보〉 progress; advance; development
♦ 공업의 발전 industrial growth / 나라의 발전 the progress of the nation / 발전을 저해하다 hamper the growth 《of trade》/ 산업의 발전을 꾀하다 foster (the growth of) industry
―**발전하다** develop; make progress; grow
♦ 발전하는 도시 a developing city [town] / 교외로 발전하다 〈도시가〉 expand over the surrounding country area / 해외로 발전하다 expand overseas; make overseas expansion
2 〈번영〉 prosperity

―**발전하다** prosper; flourish; be prosperous
▶ 이 마을은 점차 발전하고 있다 This town has developed gradually.
▶ 그 마을은 대도시로 발전하였다 The town developed [grew] into a large city.
■―**도상국** a developing country [nation]

발전 發電 1 〈전기의〉 the generation (of electricity); the production of electric power
―**발전하다** generate electricity; produce electric power ♦ 100만 킬로와트를 발전하다 generate one million kilowatts of power
2 ⇨ 타전(打電)
■―**수력[화력, 원자력]―** hydroelectric [thermal, nuclear] power generation **자가―** home generation of electricity

발전기 發電機 a [an electric] dynamo; a (power) generator; an electric generator
■―**교류[직류]―** an alternating [a direct] current dynamo; an A.C. [a D.C.] generator **수력[화력]―** a hydro [thermal] generator **열핵―** a thermonuclear generator

발전성 發展性 possibility of future growth; possibilities; 〈잠재 능력〉 potential
♦ 발전성이 있는 산업 promising industries; industries with futures

발전소 發電所 a power plant [station]; a powerhouse; a generating plant [station]
■―**수력[화력]―** a hydroelectric [thermoelectric] power plant [station] **자가―** an isolated [a home] power plant

발전적 發展的 expansive; developmental; growing ♦ 발전적 해체 the dissolution of several sections into a new organization / 발전적으로 해체하다 be dissolved into 《a new organization》

발정 發情 sexual excitement; 〈動〉 (o)estrus; 〈암컷의〉 heat; 〈수컷의〉 rut
―**발정하다** come into heat; get on heat; rut; go to rut
♦ 발정한 개 a dog at [《美》 in, 《英》 on] heat
■―**기** puberty; estrus; heat; rutting season; 〈새의〉 the mating season ―**주기** an estrous cycle ―**호르몬** estrous [estrogenic] hormone; estrogen

발족 發足 〈출발〉 starting; 〈사업 등의〉 inauguration
―**발족하다** begin; set...up; start; make a start; be inaugurated
♦ 새로 발족하다 start afresh; make a new start / 새 사업을 발족시키다 start [launch] a new enterprise
▶ 새 협회는 3월에 발족하기로 되어 있다 The new association is to start functioning in March.
▶ 특별 위원회가 발족되었다 The special committee has been set up [established].

발주 發注 〈주문〉 ordering; an order
―**발주하다** give an order; order 《an article from Korea》; place [send out] an order 《for the articles》
▶ 나는 새로운 가구를 제조업체에 발주했다 I have ordered new furniture from the manufacturer.

발진 發疹 〈醫〉 (an) eruption; (an) efflores-

cence; 〈부스럼〉 a rash; an exanthem(a)
♦발진성의 eruptive
▶나는 얼굴에 발진이 생겼다 A rash has appeared on my face.
─발진하다 break out (in a rash); come out in a rash; erupt; effloresce
■─티푸스 typhus (fever); eruptive [spotted] fever

발진 發進 〈비행기의〉 departure; takeoff; 〈로켓의〉 launching; blast-off; lift-off
─발진하다 depart 《from》; launch; 〈이륙하다〉 take off

발진기 發振器 〔通信〕 an oscillator

발짝 a step; a pace
♦한 발짝 한 발짝 step by step
▶나는 놀라서 한 발짝 뒤로 물러섰다 I took a step backward in astonishment.
▶여기서 가게까지는 한 발짝밖에 안된다 It is only a step from here to the store.

발쭉거리다 keep on slightly opening and shutting 《one's mouth》

발쭉하다 〈입을 발쭉이 벌리다 open one's mouth slightly

발쭉하다 half open; slightly parted

발차 發車 the starting; (a) departure
─발차하다 start 《from》; leave 《from the station》; depart 《from》; 〈역을 나가다〉 pull out 《of》
▶열차는 7번선에서 발차한다 The train start from track [platform] No. 7.
▶발차합니다! 〈안내 방송〉 All aboard!
▶부산행 열차는 당역에서 15분마다 발차합니다 The train for Pusan leaves [pulls out of] this station every fifteen minutes.
■─담당(원) a starter ─시간 the time for departure ─신호 a starting signal ─플랫폼 a departure platform

발착 發着 departure and arrival [coming and going] 《of trains》
♦비행기의 발착시간 departure and arrival time for airplanes
─발착하다 come and go; arrive and depart
▶이 플랫폼에서 여수행 열차가 발착한다 The train for Yŏsu depart from and arrive at this platform.

발초 拔抄 〈발췌〉 an extract; an excerpt
─발초하다 extract ♦책에서 발초하다 make excerpts [extract passages] from a book

발췌 拔萃 excerption; selection; 〈뽑아낸 것〉 an extract; an excerpt; 〈적요〉 an abstract; a summary
♦신문의 발췌 newspaper cuttings [《美》 clippings]
─발췌하다 〈중요한 부분만을 뽑아내다〉 extract [select] 《from》; take out 《from》; pick up; make an abstract [extract] 《of》
♦논문의 개요를 발췌하다 make an abstract of a treatise / 책에서 한 구절을 발췌하다 extract a passage from a book
■─개헌안의 선택된 수정안 the selected amendment bill to the Constitution ─곡 a (musical) selection

발치 the area where the feet lie; the foot 《of one's bed》
♦발치에(서) at one's feet; close to one's feet

발칙하다 〈버릇없다〉 ill-bred; ill-mannered; impolite; impertinent; impudent; insolent; rude; 〈괘씸하다〉 audacious; outrageous
♦발칙한 언사 an impertinent [insolent] remark / 발칙한 젊은이 an ill-bred young man / 발칙하게 굴다 behave rudely; act improperly
▶이 아이들은 발칙하구나 These children have no manners.

발칵 all of a sudden ⇨ 발깍

발칸 ■─반도 the Balkan Peninsula ─전쟁 the Balkan War ─제국 the Balkan States; the Balkans

발코니 a balcony
♦발코니로 나가다 go out on the balcony

발탁 拔擢 〈여럿중에서 뽑음〉 selection; 〈등용〉 promotion; choice
♦인재 발탁의 길을 열다 open up opportunities for the talented
─발탁하다 select [choose, pick out] sb 《from among many》; draw 《from》
♦열명 중에서 한명을 발탁하다 choose one out of ten / 많은 사람 가운데서 발탁되다 be picked out from among many others
▶그는 이사로 발탁되었다 He was selected [chosen, singled out] for a directorship.

발톱 〈사람의〉 a toenail; 〈짐승의〉 a claw; 〈맹금의〉 a talon
♦발톱이 빠지다 have one's toenail off [peeled] / 발톱으로 할퀴다 claw; scratch with the claws
▶고양이가 발톱으로 나를[내 얼굴을] 할퀴었다 The cat scratched me [my face].

발트해 ─海 the Baltic Sea

발틀 〈재봉틀〉 a pedal-operated [treadle, foot] sewing machine

발파 發破 〈바위 등의〉 blasting
─발파하다 set dynamite; blast 《a rock》; blow 《it》 up with dynamite
♦바위를 발파하다 blast [dynamite] a rock; 〈다이너마이트로〉 blow up a rock with dynamite
■─공 a blaster ─약 a bursting charge ─쇼 a shot ─점화장치 a portfire

발판 ─板 1 〈건축 공사용〉 scaffolding; a scaffold; 〈발받침〉 a foothold; footstool; a stepladder; a footboard; a footing
♦발판용 판자 a footing board / 발판을 놓다 set up scaffolding
▶소년은 발판에 올라서서 선반 위의 과자를 집었다 The boy stood on a footstool to reach for the cakes on the shelf.
2 〈목적 달성의 수단〉 a step; a stepping-stone; a springboard
♦장래의 발판이 되다 serve as a stepping-stone for future success / 남을 발판으로 삼다 make a stepping-stone of sb
▶남을 발판으로 하여 출세하려는 것은 매우 좋지 못한 짓이다 It is quite wrong to gain success by stepping on another [using another as a stepping-stone].

발포 發布 promulgation; proclamation; issue
─발포하다 promulgate; proclaim; make sth public; publish; announce officially

▶새 헌법이 발포되었다 A new constitution was promulgated.
발포 發泡 〈거품이 남〉 foaming; foamy effluence; effervescence —**발포하다** 〈거품나다〉 foam; froth; effervesce
■—정 a foam tablet —제 a blowing [foam, foaming] agent
발포 發砲 〈발사〉 firing; the discharge (of a gun); shot
—**발포하다** 〈총포를 쏘다〉 fire 《upon》; open fire 《on》; discharge [fire off] a gun
◆병사들은 도주하는 적에게 발포했다 The soldiers fired [shot] at the fleeing enemy.
▶어느 쪽이 먼저 발포했나? Which side fired [opened fire] first?
■—사건 a shooting case [incident]
발표 發表 (an) announcement; publication; 〈성명〉 a statement; a communiqué
◆결과의 발표 an announcement of the results / 뉴스의 발표 a news release / 미발표 작품 an unpublished work
—**발표하다** announce; make public; 〈공표하다〉 publish; lay 《a matter》 before the public; issue 《a statement》; present 《the results of study》; 〈뉴스 등을〉 release; express 《one's opinion》
◆약혼을 발표하다 announce one's engagement / 정견을 발표하다 air [make a declaration of, set forth] one's political views
▶그는 잡지에 수필을 발표했다 He wrote an essay for a magazine.
▶외무부 장관이 성명을 발표했다 The Foreign Minister issued a statement.
▶시험 성적이 발표되었다 The results of the examination have been announced.
■정식— a formal announcement
발풀무 (a pair of) foot bellows
발하다 發— **1** 〈발산하다〉 issue forth [out]; 〈빛 등을〉 emit; emanate; radiate; give out [forth]
◆신음소리를 발하다 fetch [give] a groan / 소리를 발하다 utter [give] a cry / 향기를 발하다 give out [emit] a fragrant smell
▶장미꽃은 향기를 발한다 Roses give off a sweet smell.
2 〈명령 등을〉 issue; give; send [give] out
◆경고를 발하다 issue a warning 《to them》; give 《them》 a warning
3 〈보내다〉 send (out [forth]) 《a troop》; dispatch
발한 發汗 〈땀을 흘림〉 sweating; perspiration; hidrosis; diaphoresis
—**발한하다** perspire; sweat
◆발한시키다 sweat 《a patient》; perspire; induce perspiration; throw sb into a sweat
■—작용 perspiration —제 a diaphoretic; a sudorific; a sudatory
발해만 渤海灣 the Bo Hai [Po Hai]; the Gulf of Zhili [Chihli]
발행 發行 **1** 〈책의〉 publication; issue
◆책의 발행을 중지[금지]하다 cancel [prohibit] the publication of a book
—**발행하다** publish; issue; bring out; put into circulation

◆책[잡지, 신문]을 발행하다 publish [issue] a book [magazine, newspaper]
2 〈지폐·채권의〉 issue; flotation
◆우표[화폐]의 발행 the issue of stamps [currency]
—**발행하다** issue 《bank notes》; float 《a loan》
◆새 동전을 발행하다 put new coins in circulation / 채권[증명서]을 발행하다 issue a bond [certificate]
3 〈어음·수표 등의〉 drawing; issue; draft
—**발행하다** draw; issue
◆어음을 발행하다 draw a bill [draft] 《upon sb for a sum》 / 은행 앞으로 10만원의 어음[수표]을 발행하다 draw a bill [check] on a bank for one hundred thousand won
▶나는 그에게 50만원의 수표를 발행하였다 I wrote a check for five hundred thousand won for him.
■—가격 an issue price; 〈증권 등의〉 an issue par —고 〈지폐·증권 등의〉 the amount of issue —권(權) the right of publication —금지 suspension [prohibition] of publication —소[처] a publishing office; the publishers —인 a publisher; a drawer 《of a bill》; a remitter 《of a money order》; an issuer 《of a check》 —일 the date of issue [publication] —정지 prohibition [suppression, suspension] of publication —지 〈어음 등의〉 a place of drawing [issue]
발행부수 發行部數 the circulation 《of a magazine》
◆발행 부수 100만부의 잡지 a magazine with a circulation of one million (copies)
▶이 신문은 발행 부수가 많다 This newspaper has a large circulation.
발현 發現·發顯 revelation; manifestation
—**발현하다** reveal; manifest ◆**발현되다** be revealed [manifested]; manifest itself
발호 跋扈 〈날뜀〉 rampancy; prevalence; domination; predominance
—**발호하다** 〈날뛰다〉 be [run] rampant 《among people》; prevail; dominate; domineer over
◆해적이 발호하는 연안 a coast infested with pirates
▶여러 종류의 악덕이 발호하고 있었다 Vice of all kinds was rampant.
발화 發火 〈점화〉 the production of fire; 〈인화〉 ignition; 〈연소〉 combustion; 〈화재〉 an outbreak of fire
◆발화의 원인 the cause [origin] of a fire
—**발화하다** ignite; catch [take] fire; a fire break out
◆발화하기 쉬운 〈인화성의〉 inflammable; combustible; ignitable
▶기차의 맨 앞칸에서 발화하였다 The fire originated in the first car of the train.
▶그것은 발화하기 쉽다 It catches fire easily.
■자연— spontaneous combustion : 그 불은 자연 발화로 인한 것이었다 The fire began by spontaneous combustion. ■—점 the ignition [combustion] point
발효 發效 coming into effect; effectuation; effectuality
◆휴전 조약의 발효에 따라 with the effectua-

발효

tion of the cease-fire agreement
━발효하다 become effective; take effect; 〈시행되다〉 come [go] into effect [force, operation]
▶이 조례는 아직 발효되지 않았다 The ordinance has not taken effect yet.

발효 醱酵 ferment; fermentation; zymosis
♦발효성의 fermentative; fermentable; zymotic / 발효중이다 be fermenting; be in ferment
━발효하다 ferment; undergo fermentation
♦발효시키다 ferment; leaven; sweat
━━균(菌) a ferment bacillus [fungus]; a zymogen ━력 fermentability ━소(素)〔生化〕 ferment; yeast; leaven ━유 fermented milk ━음료 fermented drinks [beverages] ━작용 fermentation; zymosis; zymolysis ━학 zymology; fermentology; zymurgy

발휘 發揮 〈드러냄〉 display; exhibition; manifestation; demonstration
━발휘하다 〈드러내다〉 display; exhibit; show; demonstrate; manifest
♦능력을 발휘하다 bring one's ability into full play / 상상력을 한껏 발휘하다 give free play to imagination
▶그 선수는 그 시합에서 진짜 실력을 발휘했다 The player showed his real ability during the game.
▶그는 그림에 비상한 재능을 발휘했다 He showed [displayed, exhibited] great talent for painting.

발흥 勃興 a sudden rise; a sudden increase in the power (of)
━발흥하다 rise suddenly; rise into power
▶그때쯤 중산계급이 발흥하기 시작했다 At about that time, the middle class began its rise to power.

밝기 brightness

밝다¹ 1 〈빛이〉 light; bright
♦밝은 방 a well-lighted room / 집안에서 제일 밝은 방 the room with the most light / 달 밝은 밤 a bright moonlit night / 밝은 햇빛 bright sunlight / 밝게 brightly; bright; brilliantly; with brightness / 아주 밝은 곳에서 in good light / 밝은 동안에 while it is light; during daylight; before dark [nightfall] / 대 낮처럼 밝다 be as bright as day / 밝아오다 〈새벽녘의 하늘이〉 brighten; grow [get] light; dawn
▶이 전구는 밝다 This bulb gives a good [bright] light.
▶여섯시 반인데도 밖은 아직 밝다 It is now six-thirty, but it is still light outside.
▶아침 일찍 떠나면 밝은 동안에 거기에 도착할 수 있다 If you start early in the morning, you can get there before dark.
▶해가 밝게 비치고 있었다 The sun was shining bright(ly).

2 〈성격 등이〉 cheerful; sunny; sunshiny; bright; happy
♦밝은 가정 a happy home [family] / 밝은 성격 a sunny disposition / 밝은 전망 a bright prospect / 밝은 마음 (with) a happy [light] heart; (in) a cheerful mood / 밝은 미래 a bright [rosy] future / 밝은 표정 a cheerful [bright] look [expression]
▶시험 성적이 좋아서 그녀는 표정이 밝아 보였다 She looked cheerful because she did well on [(英) in] the exam.
▶그에게는 밝은 미래가 있다 He has a bright future.

3 〈공명하다〉 clean; clear
▶국민은 언제나 밝은 정치를 요구한다 The people always demand clean politics.

4 〈잘 알다〉 well versed [informed] (in); well learned (in); familiar (with); well acquainted (with)
♦미국 문학에 밝다 be well read in American literature / 사무에 밝다 be well versed in business methods / 세계 사정에 밝다 be well informed on [about] world events
▶그 정치가는 중국 문제에 밝다 The statesman is familiar with [well up in] Chinese affairs.
▶그 학자는 언어학에 밝다 That scholar is an expert in linguistics.

5 〈눈·귀가〉 sharp; acute; keen; quick
♦밝은 눈[귀] acute vision [hearing]; sharp eyes [ears] / 귀가 밝다 have a sharp [quick] ears; be quick-eared
▶그는 눈이 밝아서 작은 오자(誤字)도 곧 찾아낸다 His sharp eyes are quick to spot any small spelling mistakes.

밝다² 〈날이〉 dawn; (day) break
♦밝아오는 하늘 the dawning sky / 날이 밝기 전에 before light
▶다섯시에 날이 밝는다 The day breaks [dawns] at five.
▶날이 밝았다 Day [Morning, Dawn] broke [has broken].
▶새해가 밝았다 The New Year has begun.

밝을녘 dawn; daybreak; the break of day

밝히다¹ 1 〈밝게 하다〉 brighten; lighten; light up ♦등불을 밝히다 turn up the light
▶그 탐조등이 해상을 밝혔다 The searchlight flashed over the sea.

2 〈분명하게 하다〉 make (a matter) clear [plain]; clear (up) (the cause); clarify [define] (one's attitude); 〈공개하다〉 bring (a matter) to light; make (a matter) public; 〈뚜렷이 하다〉 throw [cast, shed] light on (the meaning); 〈확인하다〉 ascertain (a matter); verify
♦계획[의중]을 밝히다 reveal [lay bare] a scheme [one's intentions] to sb / 동기를 밝히다 clarify sb's motives / 사고의 원인을 밝히다 determine the cause of an accident / 이름[신분]을 밝히다 reveal [disclose] one's name [identity] / 태도를 밝히다 define [clarify] one's attitude / 밝혀지다 become clear [plain]; be ascertained; come [be brought] to light; prove [turn out] (to be)
▶그녀는 나에게 비밀을 밝혔다 She revealed [disclosed] the secret to me.
▶장교는 그 계획을 부하들에게 밝히려 하지 않았다 The officer would not reveal the plan to his men.
▶방문객은 이름을 밝히지 않고 가버렸다 The caller left without leaving his name.

▶ 새로운 사실이 몇가지 밝혀졌다 Some new facts came to light.
▶ 그는 죄상이 밝혀져 교도소에 수감되었다 His guilt becoming clear, he was taken to prison.

밝히다² 〈밤을 새우다〉 sit [stay] up all [the whole] night; keep [remain] awake all night; keep vigil; see the dawn in; pass [spend] a night
♦ 독서로 밤을 밝히다 sit up all night reading [over a book] / 하룻밤을 눈물로 밝히다 pass a whole night in tears; weep [cry] all night
▶ 그날 밤 우리는 이야기로 밤을 밝혔다 We spent the night (in) [passed the night (by)] talking. ⇒ We sat [stayed] up all night talking. ⇒ We talked the night away. ⇒ We talked all night (long) [all the night through].

밟다 1 〈디디다〉 step on; tread (up)on (with the feet); 〈짓밟다〉 trample (up)on; stamp
♦ 아무의 발을 밟다 tread [step] on sb's toes [foot] / 미국 땅을 처음 밟다 place one's foot on the soil of America / 첫 무대를 밟다 make one's [a] début; make one's first appearance on the stage / 페달을 밟다 pedal / 눈을 밟아 다지다 stamp down the snow
▶ 그는 브레이크를 밟았다 He put on [applied] the brakes.
▶ 이 산길은 잘 밟아 다져져 있다 This mountain path is well-trodden [well-beaten].
▶ 나는 지금까지 프랑스 땅을 밟아본 적이 없다 I have never set foot in France [on French soil] before. ⇒ I've never visited France.
▶ 잔디를 밟지 마시오 《게시》 Keep off the grass. ⇒ Don't tread [step] on the grass.
2 〈수속 등을〉 go through; carry out; undergo; 〈마치다〉 finish; complete
♦ 절차를 밟다 go through 《formalities》; take proceedings / 정규 과정을 밟다 complete a regular course
3 〈추적하다〉 follow sb secretly; track; shadow; tail
♦ 형사로 하여금 뒤를 밟게 하다 set [put] a detective on sb's track
▶ 누군가가 우리 뒤를 밟고 있는 것 같다 I think someone is following us. ⇒ I think we are being shadowed [tailed].

밟히다 be stepped on; be [get] trampled on; be [get] trod(den) (up)on

밤¹ 1 〈야간〉 (a) night; nighttime; 〈저녁〉 (an) evening
♦ 내일 밤 tomorrow night / 어젯밤 last night; yesterday evening / 오늘밤 tonight; this evening / 전날 밤 the previous night / 밤이나 낮이나 night and day
〈밤의〉 밤의 nocturnal; nightly / 밤의 고요 stillness of the night / 밤의 서울 Seoul by [at] night
〈밤이[은]〉 밤이 되면 when night comes [falls] / 밤이 되기 전에 before dark; before night [evening] / 밤이 깊도록 《work》 till late at night; late into the night
▶ 밤이 깊어졌다 The night is far [advanced, gone].
▶ 나는 그날 밤은 그와 함께[호텔에서] 잤다 I stayed with him [at a hotel] for the night.
▶ 밤은 독서에 가장 좋다 Night is the best time for reading.
〈밤을〉 밤을 밝히다[새우다] pass a night without sleep; sit [stay] up all (through the) night / 이야기로 밤을 새우다 talk the night away
▶ 우리는 그 나무 아래서 밤을 보냈다 We spent the night under the tree.
〈밤에〉 밤(사이)에 during the night
▶ 그는 9월 16일 밤에 자동차 사고가 났다 He had a car accident on the night of September 16.
▶ 우리는 토요일 밤에 영화보러 갈거다 We're going to the movies (on) Saturday night.
▶ 밤에만 나타나는 동물도 많다 Many animals come out only at night [by night].
2 〈행사〉 an evening
♦ 음악의 밤 a musical evening [soiree] / 모차르트의 밤 Mozart evening / 자선의 밤 a charity evening

밤² 〈열매〉 a chestnut ♦ 밤 따러 가다 go chestnut-gathering / 밤을 까다 crack a chestnut / 밤을 줍다 pick up [gather] chestnuts

밤길 a night journey [walk, trip]
♦ 밤길을 가다 go [travel] by night [after dark]; go out at night; make a night journey
▶ 혼자 밤길을 가는 것은 위험하다 Walking alone at night is dangerous.

밤나무 〔植〕 a chestnut (tree)

밤낚시 fishing at night; night fishing [angling] ―**밤낚시하다** angle at night; go fishing by night ―꾼 a night angler

밤낮 night and day; day and night
♦ 밤낮없이 night and day; all day and night; always; all the time / 밤낮 영어공부에 몰두하다 work at one's study of English day and night
▶ 공사는 밤낮으로 진행되고 있다 The (construction) work continues day and night.
▶ 그들은 밤낮 교대로 일했다 They worked in night and day shifts.

밤눈 night vision
♦ 밤눈이 밝다 have good sight in the dark; have the eyes of a cat / 밤눈이 어둡다 be blind at night; be night-blind [moon-blind]

밤늦다 (be) late at night
♦ 밤늦게 late at night / 밤늦게까지 일어나 있다 sit [stay] up late / 밤늦도록 공부하다 work far into the night; burn the midnight oil
▶ 그 밤늦은 거리에는 사람이라곤 한명도 없었다 At that late hour of the night there was no one in the streets.

밤도둑 a burglar; a night thief
♦ 밤도둑질하다 commit burglary

밤도와 all night through; all through [throughout] the night ♦ 밤도와 일하다 work the whole night through; work the night away
▶ 그녀는 밤도와 환자 곁을 지켰다 She kept an all-night vigil by the side of the patient.

밤마다 every night; night after night; nightly; at nights ♦ 밤마다 외출하다 go out every evening [every night, nightly]

밤바람 the night wind [breeze]
▶ (차가운) 밤바람을 맞으며 감기가 들었다 Being exposed to the (chilly) evening breeze, I caught a cold.

밤비 the evening [night] rain; nightly rain

밤사이 the nighttime ♦밤사이에 during the night; overnight / 밤사이의 폭우로 owing to the heavy rain that has fallen during the night.

밤새 the nighttime ⇨ 밤사이

밤새껏 all night (long) ⇨ 밤새도록

밤새도록 all night (long); all the night through; through [throughout, all through] the night
♦밤새도록 울다 keep crying all night; weep all night / 밤새도록 마시다 drink all night long; (口) make a night of it
▶ 개가 밤새도록 짖어 한 잠도 못잤다 The dog howled and kept me awake all night.
▶ 우리는 밤새도록 이야기했다 We spent the night [stayed up all night] talking.
▶ 우리는 밤새도록 토론했다 We had an all-night discussing about it. ⇒ We spent the whole night discussing it. ⇌ We had discussed it through [throughout] the night.

밤새(우)다 be [stay] up all (through the) night; pass a night without sleep; keep [stay] awake all night
♦공부로 밤새(우)다 study all night; stay [sit] up all night studying / 회의로 밤새우다 have an all night [an overnight] conference

밤새움 sitting up all night ⇨ 밤샘

밤색 —色 ♦밤색의 chestnut(-colored); nut-brown; maroon / 밤색털의 말 a bay [sorrel] (horse)

밤샘 sitting [staying] up all night; an all-night vigil [sitting]; 〈초상집의〉 a death-watch
—**밤샘하다** ⇨ 밤새(우)다
♦초상집에서 밤샘하다 keep an all-night watch over a dead body
▶ 그녀는 앓는 아들 때문에 밤샘했다 She kept all night over her sick son.

밤소경 a night-blind [moon-blind] person

밤손님 a night thief [prowler]; a burglar; (俗) a night bird

밤송이 a chestnut bur

밤안개 a night fog [mist]
▶ 골짜기에는 밤안개가 깔려 있었다 The valley lay hidden in a night fog. ⇌ A night fog hung over the valley.

밤알 a chestnut

밤이슬 the evening [night] dew; nightly dew
♦밤이슬을 맞다 be exposed to the night dew; be washed in the night dew [air]

밤일 night work; 〈야간 근무〉 a night shift
—**밤일하다** work at night; do night work; work (on) the night shift

밤잠 night sleep; sleeping at night
▶ 어제는 밤잠을 설쳤다 I didn't get enough sleep last night.

밤중 —中 midnight; the middle of the night
♦밤중의 midnight / 밤중에 at midnight; in the middle of the night

▶ 밤중에 지진이 났다 There was an earthquake during the night.
▶ 이 밤중에 무슨 일이오? What do you want of me at this time of night?

밤차 —車 〈야간열차〉 a night train; 〈밤 버스〉 a night bus

밤참 —站 a nighttime meal; a night snack
♦밤참을 먹다 have a night snack / 밤참으로 국수를 먹다 have noodles for a midnight snack

밤톨 〈밤의 알〉 a chestnut

밤하늘 a night [nocturnal] sky ▶ 우리는 밤하늘에 반짝이는 별을 쳐다보았다 We looked up at the stars shining in the night sky.

밥¹ 1 〈쌀밥〉 boiled [cooked] rice; rice served in a bowl ♦ 밥 세 그릇 three bowls of (boiled) rice / 밥을 짓다 boil [cook] rice
2 〈식사〉 meal; food ♦밥을 먹다 have [take, eat] one's meal; dine; sit [be] at table
▶ 나는 오늘 아침 밥으로 빵을 먹었다 I had [took] bread this morning.
▶ 아침밥이 다 됐어요 Breakfast is ready! ⇌ Time to eat!
3 〈생계〉 one's living; one's livelihood
▶ 그것으로는 밥을 먹고 살 수 없다 I can't make a living out of it.
▶ 그는 자동차 외판원으로 밥 먹고 산다 He makes his living as a car salesman.
4 〈동물의 먹이〉 food; feed; a bait; 〈희생물〉 a prey; a victim ♦돼지 밥 hog feed / 물고기 밥이 되다 become food for fishes
▶ 사슴은 가엾게도 호랑이 밥이 되었다 The poor deer became the tiger's prey.

밥² 〈부스러기〉 (a) waste; chips ■가윗— scraps of cloth by scissoring 대팻— (wood) shavings 톱— sawdust

밥값 〈식비〉 the price for a meal; food expenses; 〈하숙의〉 (the charge for) board

밥그릇 a rice bowl ♦밥을 밥그릇에 담아내다 serve [put] rice in a bowl

밥맛 〈식욕〉 (an) appetite; 〈밥의 맛〉 the taste of boiled rice ♦밥맛이 떨어지다 lose one's appetite / 밥맛을 떨어뜨리다 spoil one's appetite

밥물 〈밥짓는 물〉 water for boiling rice

밥벌레 a useless mouth; a good-for-nothing (fellow); an idler; a drone ▶ 그는 밥벌레다 He is not worth his salt. ⇌ He is a useless good-for-nothing.

밥벌이 (a means of) living; breadwinning; livelihood
♦밥벌이를 못하다 be unable to earn one's bread; cannot make a living / 밥벌이가 시원찮다 have a small income; earn little
▶ 요즈음 컴퓨터 프로그래머는 밥벌이가 좋다 A computer programmer can make [earn] good money these days.
—**밥벌이하다** earn one's daily bread; earn one's livelihood; make [get, earn] one's [a] living

밥상 —床 〈소반〉 a low dining table; 〈식탁〉 a table
♦밥상에 앉다 sit down to the meal [to din-

밥상 ner, to table / 밥상을 올리다[차리다] set [lay] a meal before *sb* / 밥상을 치우다 clear the table; remove [take away] the table

밥솥 an iron pot for cooking [boiling] rice ▶ 우리는 한 밥솥의 밥을 먹은 사이다 We lived under the same roof. ⇌ We have shared many things.
■ 전기— an electric rice cooker

밥알 a grain of boiled rice

밥장사 restaurant business; running a restaurant —밥장사하다 run a restaurant; serve meals to customers

밥장수 an eating house [place] keeper; an owner of a restaurant

밥주걱 a rice scoop [spatula]

밥줄 〈생계〉 a means of livelihood; a source of income; 〈직업〉 one's occupation; one's job ▶ 그런 짓을 하면 네 밥줄이 끊어져 If you do such a thing, you will lose your means of livelihood.

밥집 an eating house; a chophouse; a cheap restaurant

밥통 -桶 1〈그릇〉 a (boiled) rice tub [container] **2**〈위〉 the stomach; 《俗》 the breadbasket **3**〈무능력자〉 a good-for-nothing (fellow); an idler
■ 전기— an electric rice tub

밥투정하다 grumble at [about, over] *one's* food; complain about *one's* food ▶ 우리 아이는 늘 밥투정을 한다 My boy is always complaining about his food.

밥풀 rice paste; grains of boiled rice (used as paste) ♦ 밥풀로 붙이다 stick *sth* with rice paste; put rice paste on ■ —강정 a rice-coated fried cake —과자 popped-rice cake

밧줄 a rope; a cord; a line

解說 *rope*는 밧줄이나 새끼를 의미하는 일반적인 말로서 *cord*보다 굵다. 「한 가닥의 밧줄」이라고 하면 a (piece of) rope [cord]라고 한다. *line*은 thread (실), cord, rope 등 노끈 모양의 것을 모두 가리키는 넓은 의미의 말이다.

♦ 세 가닥으로 꼰 밧줄 a three-ply rope / 밧줄을 잡아당기다 pull at a rope ▶ 나는 그것을 밧줄로 묶었다 I tied it with a rope. ▶ 그는 기둥 사이에 밧줄을 팽팽하게 쳤다 He stretched a rope tight between the poles.

방 房 a room; a chamber ♦ 빈 방 a vacant [an unoccupied] room / 아이들 방 a children's room / 햇볕이 잘 드는 방 a sunny room / 남향 방 a southward room; a room with a southern aspect / 방이 5개 있는 집 a five-room(ed) house / 방을 세내다 rent a room / 방을 세놓다 《美》 rent 《英》 let) a room (to *sb*) / 〈호텔의〉 방을 잡다 reserve a room 《at a hotel》 / 한 방을 같이 쓰다 share a room 《with》 ▶ 우리 집은 방이 많다[적다] My house has a large number of rooms [has only a few rooms].

방 榜 an official notice ⇨ 방문(榜文) ♦ 방을 내걸다 issue [put out] an official notice

방 放 〈총포를 쏘는 횟수〉 a round; a shot; a shell ♦ 총을 여섯 방 쏘다 fire six rounds [shots]

-방 -房 《美》 a store; 《英》 a shop ■ 금은— a gold and silversmith's shop 복덕— a real estate agent 약— a pharmacy; 《美》 a drugstore; 《英》 a chemist's shop

방갈로 〈建〉 a bungalow

방값 房— 〈방세〉 room rent; (a) rent (for a room); 〈호텔 등의〉 room charge ▶ 너는 이 방값으로 매달 얼마를 내니? How much do you pay for this room each month?

방계 傍系 a collateral family [line] ♦ 방계의 collateral; 〈부차적인〉 subsidiary; side / 방계의 자손 an oblique descendant ■ —비속[존속] a collateral descendant [ascendant] —인족(姻族) collateral relatives-in-law —친족 a collateral relative [relation] —혈족 a collateral relation by blood —회사 a subsidiary company; a subsidiary 《of a company》; an affiliated company

방 고 래 房— the flue of an *ondol* [a hypocaust] ♦ 방고래를 놓다 lay [set] the flue system under an *ondol* room

방공 防共 defense against communism ♦ 방공의 anti-communist(ic) —방공하다 fight [defend against] communism ■ —전선 a defense line against the spread of communism —정책 an anticommunist policy —협정 an anticommunist treaty

방공 防空 air defense; antiaircraft defense ■ —감시원 an air-raid warden; 《美》 an air warden —대책 air-raid precautions —시설 antiair-raid establishments; air defense facilities —연습[훈련] 〈민간의〉 an air-raid drill; 〈군의〉 air defense maneuvers [exercises] —체제 an air defense setup

방공호 防空壕 an air-raid shelter; a bomb shelter; a dugout ♦ 방공호에 들어가다 shelter *oneself* in a dugout

방과 放課 dismissal of a class ♦ 방과후 after school (is over) ▶ 방과 후까지 기다려라! Wait until school is over [out]. ▶ 우리는 방과 후 테니스를 쳤다 We played tennis after school. —방과하다 be dismissed; (school) be over

방관 傍觀 onlooking; standing by; remaining [looking on] as a spectator ♦ 방관적 태도를 취하다 assume the attitude of an onlooker; assume an indifferent attitude —방관하다 look on (in idleness); remain indifferent [impassive]; remain an unconcerned [a mere] spectator; stand by (idly); be on the hedge ♦ 수수 방관하다 look on with folded arms ▶ 그는 그저 방관할 따름이었다 He just looked on without doing anything. ▶ 이대로 방관만 하고 있을 수는 없지 않은가 You can't get away with sitting on the fence forever. ■ —자 an onlooker; a looker-on 《*pl.* lookers-

on); a bystander; an idle spectator
방광 膀胱 〔解〕 the bladder; the urinary cyst [bladder]; the vesica
　■—결석 a bladder stone; 〔醫〕 a cystolith; a urinary calculus —염 〔醫〕 cystitis; inflammation of the bladder
방구석 房— 〈방의 구석〉 a corner of a room; 〈방 속〉 the interior of a room
　◆온종일 방구석에 틀어박혀 있다 keep (in) one's room all day long
　▶방구석이 이게 뭐냐? What a devil of a mess the room is in?
방귀 breaking wind; 《卑》 a fart ◆방귀를 뀌다 break wind; 《卑》 fart; let a fart
방귀가 잦으면 똥싸기 쉽다 《속담》 Coming events cast their shadows before.
방귀 뀐 놈이 성낸다 《속담》 get angry at others for one's own mistakes
방그레 smilingly ⇨ 방글방글 ◆방그레 웃다 smile sweetly 《at sb》; smile a sweet smile; beam 《upon sb》
　▶낯선 부인이 방그레 웃으면서 내게 다가왔다 A strange woman came smiling toward(s) me. = A strange woman came toward(s) me with a smile on her face.
방글거리다 smile radiantly; beam; look happy [radiant, cheerful] ▶그녀는 좋아서 방글거렸다 She beamed with delight.
방글라데시 〈나라 이름〉 Bangladesh; 〈공식명〉 the People's Republic of Bangladesh
　—사람 Bangladeshi
방글방글 smilingly; beamingly; with a smiling face; with a bright [sweet] smile
　◆방글방글 웃는 얼굴 a smiling [beaming] face; a radiant look / 방글방글 웃다 smile radiantly 《at》; smile a sweet smile; beam 《upon sb》
　▶그녀는 항상 방글방글 웃는 얼굴이다 She always seems to have a smile on her face.
방금 方今 right now; just now
　◆방금 말씀드린대로 as I have just said
　▶나는 방금 돌아왔다 I have just come home.
　▶아버지는 방금 떠나셨어요 Father left just now.
　▶방금 은행에 갔다 온 길이다 I have just been to the bank.
　▶방금 내가 본 사람은 누구지요? Who is the man I saw just now?
　▶어머니는 방금 나가셨어요 Mother went out just a moment ago [just now].
방긋 〈웃는 모양〉 smilingly; beamingly; with a (bland) smile
　◆방긋 웃다 smile sweetly 《at sb》; beam 《upon sb》; break into a smile / 방긋 웃으며 인사하다 greet sb with a smile
　▶그녀는 좋아서 방긋 웃었다 She beamed with satisfaction.
방긋이 1 ⇨ 방긋 2 〈약간 열린 모양〉 gently ajar; half-opened
　▶꽃이 방긋이 피어 있다 The flower is half out [open]. = The flower is in half bloom.
　▶창문이 방긋이 열려 있다 The window is opened a crack [little].
　▶배꽃이 방긋이 피기 시작했다 The pear blossoms have begun to open [bloom].
방긋하다 〈꽃이〉 half in bloom; 〈문 등이〉 ajar; slightly open
방년 芳年 the sweet age 《of a young girl》
　◆방년 17세의 처녀 a girl of sweet seventeen [seventeen summers]; a girl in her seventeenth year
방 놓다 房— 〈구들을〉 fix a hypocaust [ondol] floor in a room; 〈다시 놓다〉 renovate [refurbish] a room; 〈늘리다〉 add a room
방뇨 放尿 urination; 《俗》 pissing
　—방뇨하다 urinate; make [pass, discharge] urine [water]; relieve oneself; 《俗》 piss
방담 放談 a random talk; a free [freewheeling] talk; a frank, informal talk
　◆K씨의 시사 방담 Mr. K's at-random commentary on current events
방대하다 尨大— enormous; vast; extensive; voluminous; copious; massive; colossal; fabulous; mammoth
　◆방대한 우주비행 계획 a colossal space flight project / 방대한 예산 a budget of staggering proportions / 방대한 자료 massive material / 방대한 저술 a voluminous work
　▶그 나라는 방대한 자연자원을 가지고 있다 That country is blessed with vast natural resources.
방도 方道·方途 a way; a method; a means
　▶그것을 할 어떤 방도를 찾아야 한다 We must find some way [find out how] to do it.
　▶그것 말고는 달리 방도가 없다 There is no alternative for it. = There is nothing for it but to do so.
　▶이 궁지에서 벗어날 방도가 없다 There is no way out of this dilemma.
방독 防毒 keeping away poisonous substances; protection against poison
　—방독하다 protect oneself from poison; keep away poisonous substances
　■—마스크[면] a gas mask [helmet]; an antigas mask; 《英》 a respirator —실 a gastight shelter
방둥이 the rump; the buttock 《of a quadruped》
방랑 放浪 wandering; roaming; roving; a Bohemian life
　◆방랑길에 오르다 start [set out] on a wandering journey
　—방랑하다 wander about; roam; ramble; tramp (abroad); 《美》 be on the bum; bum (around); lead a Bohemian life
　◆나는 온 유럽을 여러 달 동안 방랑했다 I wandered all over Europe for many months.
　■—객[자] a vagabond; a wanderer; 〈유랑자〉 a drifter; 〈부랑자〉 a tramp; 《美口》 a hobo —벽 vagrant habits; vagabondism: 방랑벽이 있다 be of a rambling disposition
방랑생활 放浪生活 a roaming [an unsettled] life ◆방랑생활을 하다 live a roaming life; live the life of a wanderer; lead a vagabond [wandering] life
방략 方略 〈정책〉 a policy; 〈방책〉 a plan; a scheme; a means; 〈군략〉 a strategy
　◆방략을 세우다 establish [make, draw up] a

방류 放流 discharge
━**방류하다** 〈물을〉 discharge; 〈물고기를〉 release (fish) into 《a river》; stock [plant] 《a river》 with 《fish》
♦호수에 잉어를 방류하다 stock a lake with carp(s)
▶그들은 수문을 열고 물을 방류했다 They opened the floodgate and discharged water.

방만하다 放漫━ lax; loose; random; careless; reckless
♦방만한 재정 a lax [an irresponsible] financial policy
▶그는 방만한 경영 때문에 사업에 실패했다 He failed (in) his enterprise through reckless [careless] management.

방망이 a club; 〈무기로 쓰는〉 a cudgel; 〈경찰관의〉 (美) a billy (club); a truncheon
♦방망이로 치다 hit [beat, strike] *sb* with a heavy stick; club; cudgel / 방망이질하다 〈빨래하다〉 beat (laundries) with a stick to wash; 〈심장을〉 palpitate; throb; pound
■국수━ a rolling pin 다듬잇━ (a pair of) round fulling sticks 빨랫━ a laundry stick 야구━ a (baseball) bat 요술━ a mallet of luck

방매 放賣 selling; sale ━**방매하다** sell; 〈정리하기 위해〉 sell off; dispose of; offer for sale; put [set] *sth* on sale ■━가(家) a house for [on] sale

방면 方面 1〈방향〉 a direction; 〈지역〉 quarter; a district
♦목포 방면으로 in the direction of Mokp'o / 각 방면으로 in all directions [quarters] / 각 방면으로부터 from various places; from all [various] directions [quarters]
▶그는 수원 방면 출신이다 He comes from Suwon or somewhere near there.
▶태풍이 북쪽 방면으로 향하고 있다 The typhoon is going toward [in the direction of] the northern part.
▶원주 방면으로 여행갑니다 I shall go on a trip to Wonju and its neighborhood.
2〈분야〉 a field; a sphere; a line; 〈국면〉 an aspect; a phase; 〈각도〉 an angle; 〈출처〉 a source
▶넌 장래 어떤 방면으로 나가려고 하느냐? In what line are you going to work in the future?
▶그는 전자 공학 방면에서 매우 유명한 학자다 He is quite a famous scientist in the field of electronics.
▶우리는 그 문제를 가능한 모든 방면에서 검토했다 We examined the problem in all its conceivable aspects [from all possible angles].

방면 放免 〈석방〉 release; discharge; acquittal ━**방면하다** release; discharge; liberate; acquit 《*sb* of the charge》; let go
♦무죄 판결이 내려진 사람을 방면하다 release an acquitted person from custody / 형기를 마친 복역수를 방면하다 release a convict who has completed his sentence [served his time]
■무죄━ acquittal (and discharge): 무죄 방면이 되다 be found innocent and acquitted 훈계━ release after admonition

방명 芳名 〈명성〉 a good [fair] name; *one's* good reputation; 〈경칭〉 your (honored) name
▶댁의 방명은 종종 들은 적이 있습니다 I have often heard of you [your name].
■━록 〈방문객의〉 a visitors' list; a list of names; 〈명사의〉 a Who's Who

방모 紡毛 spinning wool ■━사 woolen (yarn)

방목 放牧 pasturage; grazing ━**방목하다** graze 《cattle》; put [send, turn out] 《cattle》 to grass; pasture
▶그들은 이 들에 양을 방목하고 있다 They pasture their sheep [put their sheep to graze] in these fields.
▶여름에는 소를 산허리에 방목한다 In (the) summer they leave the cattle to graze on the hillsides. ■━권 herbage ━장[지] a grazing land; a pasture

방문 房門 a chamber-door; a room-door

방문 訪問 a call; a visit; an interview
♦첫 방문 the first visit / 방문을 받다 receive [get] a call [visit] 《from *sb*》
▶국무총리는 지금 미국을 방문중이다 The Prime Minister is now on a visit to America.
━**방문하다** visit; call on *sb*; call at 《a house》; make [pay] a call 《on》; pay [make, give] a visit 《to》; (go to) see *sb*; 〈기자가〉 interview

> **解說** *visit*는 문어·구어의 어느 쪽에도 쓰인다. *call on* [*upon*], *call at*는 (美)에서는 딱딱한 문장어에서, (英)에서는 사업[사무] 등의 격식을 차린 회화에서 쓰인다. 「사람을 불쑥 방문하다」에는 *drop by*를, 「(지도 등을 의지해서) 사람을 방문하다」에는 *look sb up*을 쓴다.

♦호별 방문하다 make a house-to-house visit
▶나는 김 선생님을 회사로 방문했다 I visited [called on] Mr. Kim at his company.
▶선생님들은 1년에 한 번 가정 방문을 한다 Teachers make a home call once a year.
▶언제 방문할까요? When shall I call on you [at your house]?
▶내일 당신을 방문하겠습니다 I'll come and see you tomorrow. (▶상대방에게 갈 경우는 go를 쓰지 않고 come을 씀)
■공식━ a formal visit; an official call; 〈국가원수의〉 a state visit ■━기사 an interview ━기자 a reporter; an interviewer ━외교 diplomacy through personal visitation

방문 榜文 a public [an official] notice; a proclamation

방문객 訪問客 a caller; a visitor; a guest
♦방문객을 접하다 receive a caller [visitor, guest] / 방문객을 사절하다 deny *oneself* to a caller; refuse to see a caller / 방문객이 많다 have many callers

방문단 訪問團 a group [team] of visitors
♦재미동포 모국 방문단 a group of Korean residents in America who are visiting their fatherland

방물 fancy goods; (美) notions; (英) haberdashery; (英) smallwares; knickknacks
■━장사 selling [peddling] knickknacks [fancy goods] ━장수 a fancy goods dealer;

방미 訪美 a visit to the United States ◆방미 길에 오르다 leave for the United States

방바닥 房— the floor of a room ▶방바닥이 눅눅하다 The floor is damp [wet].

방방곡곡 坊坊曲曲 everywhere throughout the country; every nook and corner of the country [area]
◆방방곡곡에 all over the country; in all parts of the country; throughout the country; in every nook and cranny of the land / 방방곡곡에서 from every quarters; from every nook and corner of the country / 방방곡곡에 알려지다 be [become] known far and wide [all over the country] / 방방곡곡을 여행하다 travel all over [to the far corners of] the country
▶그의 학자로서의 명성은 대번에 방방곡곡에 퍼졌다 His high reputation as a scholar spread rapidly far and wide [all over the country].

방백 傍白 [劇] an aside; a stage aside
◆방백으로 말하다 say [mutter] in an aside; speak aside

방범 防犯 crime prevention; prevention of crimes —**방범하다** prevent crimes; take preventive measures against crimes ■—대책 anticrime measures —주간 Crime Prevention Week

방법 方法 〈방식〉 a method; a way; fashion; a plan; a system; 〈방침〉 a course; 〈책략〉 a device; a scheme; 〈수단〉 a means; 〈과정〉 a process; 〈조치〉 a measure; a step; 〈절차〉 a procedure; a proceeding; 〈처방〉 a recipe; a formula (pl. ~s, -lae)
▶그녀를 도와줄 방법을 모른다 I don't know how to help her.
▶나는 스웨터를 짜는 방법을 배웠다 I was taught how to knit a sweater.
▶그는 독자적인 방법으로 그것을 했다 He did it in his own way.
▶이런 방법으로는 성공을 못한다 This is not the (proper) way to obtain success.
▶그런 방법으로는 안된다 That is not the way to do it.
▶그것은 현명한 방법이 못된다 That's not a wise course to take [follow].
▶그는 부정한 방법으로 시합을 이겼다 He won the game by unfair means.
■—론 methodology

방벽 防壁 a protective [defensive] wall; a barrier; a bulwark

방부 防腐 preservation from [against] decay; antisepsis; prevention against putrefaction; 〈시체의〉 embalmment
◆방부(성)의 antiseptic / 목재의 방부 보존 preservation of timber against decay / …에 방부 처리를 하다 apply antiseptic treatment to; preserve; 〈시체에〉 embalm
▶식품의 방부에는 여러 가지 방법이 있다 There are many methods of preserving food [keeping food from going bad].
—**방부하다** preserve from decay; prevent putrefaction; 〈시체를〉 embalm

방부제 防腐劑 an antiseptic (substance [solution]); a (rot-)preservative; a resist
◆방부제 처리를 하다 apply antiseptic treatment (to); 〈시체에〉 embalm; preserve
■ 목재— a wood preservative

방불 彷彿 close resemblance
—**방불하다** 〈서술적〉 resemble closely; be very like; bear a close resemblance (to)
◆…을 방불케 하다 remind sb of sth
▶이 기동 작전은 실전을 방불케 한다 The maneuvers remind the spectators of actual warfare.

방비 房— a broom for indoor use; an indoor broom

방비 防備 〈방어〉 protection; defense; defensive preparations; 〈방어 공사〉 defense works; fortifications
◆방비가 없는 defenseless; unguarded; unfortified / 무방비 도시 an open city / 방비를 공고히 하다 reinforce [strengthen] the defense 《of a town》
▶우리 도시는 방비를 공고히 할 필요가 있다 It is necessary to reinforce [strengthen] the defense of our town.
▶그 섬은 무방비 상태다 The island is defenseless.
—**방비하다** protect; make defensive preparations; fortify; secure; defend; guard

방사 房事 〈성교〉 (have) sexual intercourse; what occurs in the privacy of the bedroom
◆방사를 삼가다 abstain from sexual intercourse; practice continence / 방사에 탐닉하다 indulge in sexual pleasure
■—과도 sexual excess [indulgence, intemperance]

방사 放射 〈빛・열 등의〉 emission; 〈복사〉 radiation; 〈라듐 등의〉 emanation
—**방사하다** radiate; emit; emanate
◆방사하는 radiant 《rays》 / 열을 사방으로 방사하다 radiate heat on all sides
▶태양은 빛과 열을 방사한다 The sun emits [sends out] light and heat.
■—계 a radiometer —기 an ejector —물 an emission

방사능 放射能 radioactivity
◆방사능의 radioactive / 방사능이 있는 radioactive 《rain》 / 방사능이 없는 inactive
▶어제 내린 비에서 70만 카운트의 방사능이 검출되었다 A count of 700,000 of radioactivity was detected in yesterday's rain.
▶그 야채는 방사능 낙진에 오염되어 있었다 The vegetables were contaminated by radioactive fallout.
■—검사 radioactivity check —구름 a radioactive cloud —멀미 a radiation sickness —비[눈] radioactive rain [snow] —시험 radioscopy —연구자 a radiologist —오염 radioactive contamination —이론 the theory of radioactivity —전(쟁) radioactive [radiological] warfare (略 R.W.) —조사 a radiological survey —진(塵) radioactive dust [ashes]; radiodust; radioactive fallout —측정 radiological monitering —측정기 a radiation detector —투시 radioscopy —허용한도 the maximum permissible exposure

방사림 防沙林 shifting sand prevention for-

방사상 放射狀 ◆방사상 도로 roads radiating [branching off] in all directions; radial roads / 방사상의 radial; radiate; radiated / 방사상으로 radiately; radially; in a radial manner
▶ 몇 개의 좁은 도로가 도시의 중앙 광장으로부터 방사상으로 뻗어 있었다 Several narrow streets radiated from the town's main square.

방사선 放射線 radiation; radial [radiant] rays; 〈방사능 광선〉 radioactive rays
◆방사선의 강도 radiation intensity / 방사선에 민감한 radiosensitive / 방사선을 쐬다 〈폭격으로〉 be exposed to radiation / 방사선 치료를 받다 undergo radiological treatment
■ —계수기 a radiation counter —과 the department of radiology —누출 a radiation leak —사진 a radio(auto)graph; an autoradiograph; a skiagraph —요법 radiotherapy —의학 radiotherapeutics —치료의사 a radiotherapist —학 radiology —화학 radiation chemistry; radiochemistry

방사성 放射性 radioactivity; radiative
◆의약용 방사성 물질 atomic cocktail / 방사성 탄소 연대 측정법 radiocarbon dating
■ —동위원소 [化] a radioactive isotope; a radioisotope —물질 a radioactive substance; (俗) radioactive waste —원소 a radioactive element; a radioelement —폐기물 radioactive waste

방사하다 放飼— 〈방목하—〉 pasture [graze] (cattle); 〈놓아기르다〉 leave (a dog) at large; keep (a pig) loose
◆방사하는 닭 a free-range chicken / 개를 방사하다 let a dog run loose
▶ 소를 방사하다 Those cows are at pasture.

방사하다 倣似— 〈비슷하다〉 look like; be like; be (very) similar; be akin (to); resemble (closely)

방생 放生 setting free [the release] of captive birds or animals

방석 方席 a cushion
◆방석에 앉다 sit [seat oneself, be seated] on a cushion / 바늘 방석에 앉은 것 같다 sit [stand] on thorns
▶ 방석에 앉으세요 Please sit on the cushion.
▶ 나는 손님들에게 방석을 권했다 I offered cushions to the guests.

방선 傍線 a sideline (▶영문의 경우는 밑줄 underline) ▶중요한 구절에 방선을 그어라 Draw sidelines along important passages. ⇌ 〈영문의 경우는〉 Underline important passages.

방설 防雪 protection from [against] snow
—방설하다 protect sth from [against] snow
■ —공사 snow protection work —림 a snowbreak —벽 a snowwall; a snowbreak wall

방세 房貰 a room rent
◆방세를 올리다 raise the (room) rent / 방세를 10만원 내다 pay 100,000 won for one's room [lodging]
▶ 방세는 얼맙니까? What is the rent for the room?

방세간 房— (room) furniture; furnishings

방송 放送 〈라디오・텔레비전의〉(radio, TV) broadcasting; 〈한 회의〉 a (radio, television) broadcast; a telecast; television broadcast
◆방송중이다(아니다) be on [off] the air / 라디오 방송을 듣다 listen to the radio broadcast / (방송국이) 방송을 끝내다 sign off
▶ 나는 그 콘서트를 라디오 방송에서 들었다 I heard the concert on the radio.
—방송하다 〈방송국이〉 broadcast; put [send] (the news) on the air; (美) aircast; 〈사람이〉 speak through [over] the radio; give a broadcast (about); go on radio
▶ 이 노래자랑은 전국적인 중계로 방송된다 This amateur singing contest is to be broadcast over a nationwide hookup.
▶ 이 시합은 텔레비전으로 방송된다 There will be TV coverage of this game.
■ 뉴스— newscasting; a newscast 민간[상업]— commercial broadcasting 생— a live broadcast [program] 시험— an experimental broadcast 유선텔레비전— cable television broadcasting 전국— a nationwide broadcast 재— rebroadcast 중계— (a) relay (broadcast); a broadcast; (口) (a) hookup ■ —극 a broadcast play; a radio [television] drama; a radio [television] play —기사 a radio [television] engineer —기자 a radio [TV] reporter [newsman] —망 a (radio, television) network; a (radio, TV) circuit —방해 jamming —사업 the broadcasting industry —시간 〈시각〉 the time (for); 〈길이〉 the length (of a program); 〈방송국의〉 broadcasting hours —시청자 a (TV) viewer; a televiewer —실 a (radio, television) studio (pl. ~s) —연설 a radio [TV] speech [address] —위성 a broadcasting satellite —종료 sign-off —주파수 radio frequency —중단 (俗) dead spot —청취자 a (radio) listener; a radio subscriber —프로그램 a broadcasting program; a radio [TV] program

방송국 放送局 a broadcasting station; a radio [TV] station ■ 중앙[지방]— a key [local] station

방송통신대학 the University of the Air; the Air and Correspondence College

방수 防水 1 〈넘치는 물의〉 flood control, prevention of flood
—방수하다 control [prevent] flood
2 〈스며드는 물의〉 waterproofing
◆방수의 〈물이 스며들지 않는〉 waterproof; 〈물이 새지 않는〉 watertight
—방수하다 waterproof; make (cloth) waterproof; make (a box) watertight
▶ 그의 시계는 방수되어 있다 His watch is waterproof.
■ —가공 a waterproofing —모(帽) a waterproof hat; 〈선원의 방수모・방수외투〉 a tarpaulin; (美俗) a tarp —설비 flood protection —시계 a waterproof watch —외투 a waterproof (overcoat) —제(劑) a waterproof agent; waterproof stuff —처리 waterproofing —포(布) waterproof cloth; 〈범포〉 tarpaulin; oil-

skin —화 rainshoes; rubbers; 〈고무를 입힌 덧신〉 galoshes; overshoes
방수 放水 〈물의 배출〉 discharge; drainage
—방수하다 drain water off
■—관 a drainpipe —구(口) an outlet —로 diversion channel; tail race; 〈저수지 등의〉 a spillway —문 a flood [drainage] gate —펌프 a drain pump
방순 芳醇 mellow wine
방술 方術 1 〈방법과 기술〉 method(s) and technique(s) 2 〈신선의 술법〉 necromancy; Taoist magic (arts)
방습 防濕 ♦방습 외 dampproof; moistureproof ▶그 상자는 방습이 되어 있다 The box is dampproof. ■—공사 dampproofing work —제 a desiccant; a desiccating agent
방시레 beamingly; blandly
방식 方式 〈공식〉 a formula (*pl.* ~s, ·lae); 〈방법〉 a way; a method; 〈형식〉 a form; 〈양식〉 a mode; a manner; process; a system; 〈절차〉 formalities; procedures; 〈관례〉 usage
♦교통정리의 새 방식 a new system of traffic control / 일정한 방식으로 in an established [a regular] form / 그런 방식으로 in that way [method]/ 자기 방식대로 하다 do *sth* in *one's* own way / 방식에 따르다[따르지 않다] follow [run counter to] the established form [usage]/ 올바른 방식을 취하다 adopt a correct form
▶나는 내 방식대로 하겠다 I'll do it my way [in my own way].
▶우리는 그것을 하는 방식이 각각 다르다 Each of us has a different way of doing it.
방식 防蝕 corrosion protection ♦방식의 corrosion-proof; corrosion-resistant
■—제(劑) 〔化〕 an anticorrosive —페인트 anticorrosive paint
방실거리다 smile sweetly [radiantly]; beam with a smile
▶아이는 그녀를 보고 방실거렸다 The child smiled at her.
▶그 소녀는 기뻐서 방실거렸다 The girl beamed with delight.
방심 放心 1 〈정신 차리지 않음〉 absence of mind; absentmindedness; abstraction
▶그녀는 방심 상태에 있다 She is in an abstracted state of mind.
—방심하다 be absentminded; be abstracted
♦방심하여 absentmindedly; with an air of abstraction; abstractedly
▶그는 방심한 얼굴로 거기에 앉아 있었다 He just sat there with a blank look on his face. 2 〈부주의〉 inattention; carelessness; 〈대비 없음〉 unpreparedness
—방심하다 be careless; be inattentive; be off *one's* guard; let *one's* guard down; be guardless
♦방심하지 않고 있다 be on *one's* guard; be alert [attentive]; have *one's* eyes wide open; keep sharp watch / 방심한 틈을 찔리다 be taken off *one's* guard; be caught asleep
▶너희는 방심했기 때문에 시합에 졌다 You lost the game because you were careless.
3 〈안심〉 freedom from care; relief

—방심하다 feel easy 《about》; feel at rest [ease]; feel [be] relieved
▶요즈음은 방심할 수 없는 세상이다 We can't be too careful in this world these days.
방아 a mortar; a mill
♦방아를 찧다 mill; grain; pound [beat] 《rice》 in a mortar
■—디딜— a treadmill 물— a water mill ■—굴대 the wheel shaft of a mill —꾼 a miller —두레박 a sweep-well bucket —확 the mortar (of a mill)
방아깨비 〔昆〕 an Oriental longheaded locust
방아빌레 〔昆〕 a click beetle; a skipjack; a snapping beetle
방아쇠 the trigger (of a gun) ♦방아쇠를 당기다 pull [press] the trigger 《at, on》; trigger 《a riffle》
방아타령 —打令 a miller's song
방안 方案 a plan; a device; project; a scheme; a program ♦방안을 세우다 draw up a plan; lay out [frame] a scheme
방안지 方眼紙 graph paper ⇨ 모눈종이
방앗간 a mill
방앗공이 a pestle
방약무인 傍若無人 〈뻐김〉 overbearance; arrogance; 〈뻔뻔스러움〉 insolence; audacity; impudence; defiance
—방약무인하다 overbearing; arrogant; shameless; unrestrained; reckless; outrageous; insolent; defiant
♦방약무인하게 행동하다 behave outrageously [audaciously]; conduct *oneself* recklessly; act as if *one* owns the place; be [make] free 《with *sb*》; ride roughshod over 《others》
▶참으로 방약무인한 녀석이구나! What an impudent guy [fellow] he is!
방어 防禦 defense; safeguard; protection
♦방어용 무기 defensive weapons / 방어가 튼튼한[안된] well-defended [unprotected]; well-fortified [defenseless]/ 방어 위치에 있다 be [stand, act] on the defensive
▶공격은 최상의 방어다 The most effective defense is offense. ⇒ Offense is the best defense.
—방어하다 defend 《against, from》; protect 《against, from》; safeguard 《against》; shield; bulwark
♦타이틀을 방어하다 defend the title
■—공세[수세]— an offensive [a passive] defense 밀집— tight defense 지역— zone defense ■—갑판 a protective deck —공사 defense works —구역 a sector of defense —동맹 a defense alliance —력 defensive strength —물 a shield; a protector —선 a line of defenses —수단 defensive measures —율 〔野〕 〈투수의〉 an earned run average (略 ERA) —자세 〔劍道·拳〕 guard : 방어 자세를 취하다 guard; be on guard —전 a defensive fight [war, battle, struggle] —진지 a defensive position —포화 defensive fire
방어 魴魚 〔魚〕 a yellowtail
방언 方言 〈사투리〉 a dialect; a provincialism
♦방언적[의] dialectal
▶스코플랜드어는 영어의 한 방언이다 Scottish

■개인— an idiolect 계급— class dialect 지역— a regional [local] dialect ■—지도 a dialect map [atlas] —지리학 dialect geography —학[연구] dialectology —학자 a dialectologist

방역 防疫 prevention of epidemics [infectious diseases]; communicable diseases control; disinfection; quarantine
—방역하다 take preventive measures against epidemics; prevent an epidemic of
■—관 a quarantine officer —대책 anti-epidemic measure : 방역 대책을 강구하다 take preventive measures against epidemics / 콜레라가 발생하자 관계 당국은 즉시 방역 대책을 강구했다 As cholera broke out, the authorities concerned immediately took preventive measures against it. —선(線) a (sanitary) cordon; (프) cordon sanitaire

방연광 方鉛鑛 〔鑛〕 galena

방열 防熱 heat resistance; protection against heat ♦방열의 heat-resisting; heat-resistant ■—복 heatproof clothes

방열 放熱 〈발산되는 열〉 radiant heat; 〈열의 발산〉 radiation of heat —방열하다 radiate heat ■—기 a radiator

방염제 防染劑 a resist; resistant

방영 放映 televising 《a movie》; telecasting
▶ 특별 프로그램이 지금 방영중이다 A feature program is on the air now.
—방영하다 televise 《a concert》; telecast
♦우주 왕복선의 착륙 광경이 전세계에 방영되었다 The landing of the space shuttle was televised [seen on television] all over the world.

방울 1 〈종〉 a (small) bell
♦방울을 달다 attach a bell 《to》; bell 《a cat》/ 방울을 흔들다 shake a bell / 방울을 울리다 ring [jingle, tinkle] a bell
▶ 방울이 울린다 The bell is ringing. ⇒ There goes the bell.
▶ 누군가가 방울을 울리고 있다 Someone is ringing the bell [buzzer].
2 〈액체의〉 a drop
♦눈물 방울 a teardrop / 물방울 a drop of water / 빗방울 a raindrop / 땀방울 drops of perspiration / 이슬 방울 a dewdrop
▶ 그는 술은 한 방울도 안 마신다 He does not drink even a drop of wine [liquor].
▶ 그의 모자와 레인코트에서 빗방울이 떨어지고 있었다 His hat and raincoat were dripping wet.
3 〈모자 등의〉 a pompon
♦털실 방울 a ball of wool

방울방울 drop by drop; in drops; dripping; dribbling
▶ 수도꼭지에서 물방울이 방울방울 떨어지고 있다 Water is dripping from the faucet. ⇒ The faucet is dripping.
▶ 그녀의 수영복에서 물방울이 방울방울 떨어지고 있었다 Her bathing suit was dripping with water.

방울뱀 〔動〕 a rattlesnake

방울벌레 〔昆〕 a 'bell-ring' insect

방울새 〔鳥〕 a goldfinch; a greenfinch

방울지다 form a drop ♦방울져 떨어지다 drip; drop; trickle; dribble; fall in drops ▶ 물이 방울져 떨어졌다 The water trickled [dribbled] down in drops.

방위 方位 a direction; a point of the compass; a compass direction [bearing]; a course; 〔天·海〕 an azimuth
♦나침반의 방위 the points of the compass / 방위를 정하다 find *one's* bearings [position] / 방위를 알 수 없게 되다 lose *one's* bearings
▶ 그는 태양을 보고 방위를 정했다 He got his bearings from the sun.
■—기본— the cardinal points 진(眞)— the true bearing [heading] ■—각 an azimuth angle; 〈편각〉 a declination —계기 orientation instruments —권(圈) an azimuth circle —기선[기점] the lubber's line [mark, point] —나침반[안정기] an azimuth compass [stabilizer] —의(儀) 〔海〕 a pelorus —차(差) an azimuthal error —측정기 〈비행기의〉 an azimuth finder —표 〈배의〉 a traverse table

방위 防衛 defense; safeguard; protection
♦방위를 강화하다 build up [strengthen] defenses / 방위 자세를 취하다 put *oneself* in the posture of defense / 방위를 분담하다 share the defense load / 방위 수단을 강구하다 adopt some measures to defend *oneself* against 《pollution》
—방위하다 defend 《from, against》; protect 《from, against》; safeguard 《against》; shield
♦국토를 방위하다 defend *one's* country
■민간— ⇨ 민방위 자위[자주]— self-defense 정당— legal defense 지상— ground defense
■—계획 a defense plan [program] —군 a defense corps —동맹 a defensive alliance —력 defense capabilities; defensive strength —비 defense expenses [costs];〈예산〉 the defense budget —산업 the defense industry —소집 the defense call-up; the defensive mobilization —조약 a defense treaty —체제 a defense set-up [system] —협정 a defense [defensive] agreement; a (mutual) defense pact

방음 防音 sound isolation [insulation]; sound-proofing
♦방음의 soundproof; soundproofed
—방음하다 soundproof; arrest [absorb] sound
▶ 나는 방음한 방에서 매일 피아노를 연습한다 I practice the piano in a soundproof room every day.
■—실 a soundproof chamber [room] —유리 soundproof glass —재(료) soundproof materials

방음장치 防音裝置 soundproofing; soundproof equipment; a sound arrester; an antinoise device; 〈내연기관의〉 a silencer
♦방음장치가 된 벽 a soundproofed wall / 방음장치를 하다 soundproof; make 《a room》 soundproof / 방음장치가 되어 있다 be soundproofed

방일 放逸 impudence ⇨ 방자(放恣)

방임 放任 〈외교의〉 noninterference; nonintervention; 〈경제의〉 (프) laissez-faire; go-as-you-please

―방임하다 leave *sb* alone; 〈일을〉 leave 《a matter》 to take [run] its own course; leave *sb* to *oneself*; give [leave] *sb* a free hand
▶ 당국은 사건을 방임했다 The authorities let the matter run [take] its course.
▶ 부모는 아들을 방임했다 The parents let their son do what he liked.

방임주의 放任主義 a noninterference [let-alone] policy; a hands-off policy; 〈경제적〉 a laissez-faire policy [principle]
▶ 나는 아이에 대해서는 방임주의다 I do not, on principle, interfere with my children.

방자 放恣 impudence; self-indulgence; impertinence; dissoluteness; rudeness
―**방자하다** rude; uncontrolled; willful; impudent; licentious; self-indulgent; dissolute; unrestrained
♦ 방자한 여자 a woman of loose morals / 방자하게 굴다 behave as *one* pleases
▶ 그는 방자하게도 선생님께 말대꾸를 했다 He had the impudence to answer his teacher back.
▶ 그는 방자한 생활을 하고 있다 He lives an unrestrained [unruly] life.

방장 房帳 1 〈방에 친 커튼〉 a room curtain; hangings **2** 〈모기장〉 a mosquito net [curtain] ♦ 방장을 치다 put [hang] up a mosquito net

방재 防災 prevention of [against] (natural) disasters [calamities]
▶ 이 도시는 방재에 노력을 기울이고 있다 This city is making an effort to protect itself from natural disasters.
―**방재하다** prevent [fend off] disasters
■―**계획** a plan for preventing disasters ―**대책** a countermeasure against [for preventing] disaster ―**용품** emergency supplies; requisites for use in the event of a disaster ―**훈련** antidisaster drills

방재 防材 a boom; 〈교각 등의〉 a fender

방적 紡績 spinning; cottonspinning
■―**견사** spun silk ―**공** 〈여자〉 a spinner; cotton spinner; a cotton-mill hand ―**공장** a cotton [spinning] mill; a spinnery ―**기(계)** a spinning jenny [machine]; (총칭) spinning machinery ―**사 (絲)** cotton yarn ―**업** the spinning industry ―**업자** a cotton spinner ―**인견** rayon yarn; spun rayon ―**회사** a spinning [cottonspinning] company

방전 放電 [物] discharge
―**방전하다** discharge electricity
♦ 방전시키다 discharge 《a Leyden jar》
■―**공중[진공, 불꽃]―** atmospheric [vacuum, spark] discharge ―**관[등, 구]** a discharge tube [lamp, ball] ―**율[수, 전압]** discharge rate [number, potential] ―**전류** discharge current

방점 傍點 a side dot [mark] ♦ 〈국·한문에〉 방점을 찍다 mark with a side dot / 강조할 말에 방점을 찍다 put dots [marks] alongside the words to show emphasis

방정 frivolity; levity; flippancy ⇨ 방정떨다, 방정맞다 ■―**꾼** a light-minded [giddy] person; a frivolous [flippant] person; a scatter-brain; a rash [an imprudent, hasty] fellow

방정 方正 goodness; uprightness; irreproachableness
―**방정하다** good; upright; irreproachable
♦ 품행이 방정한 사람 a man of irreproachable conduct; an upright person

방정떨다 act imprudently [thoughtlessly, carelessly, frivolously, rashly]; behave in a giddy way
▶ 이제부턴 방정떨지 마라 Be serious from now on.
▶ 그녀는 방정떤다 She is careless. ⇒ She is a careless girl. ⇒ She behaves carelessly.

방정맞다 1 〈경망스럽다〉 rash; imprudent; flippant; frivolous; unstable; giddy; flighty
♦ 방정맞은 여자 a flighty woman
2 〈불길하다〉 ill-omened; inauspicious; ominous; unlucky
♦ 방정맞은 소리를 하다 croak; forebode evil
▶ 그가 머지않아 죽지나 않을까 하는 방정맞은 예감이 든다 I have a premonition [an uneasy feeling] that he will die before long.
▶ 내 꿈은 방정맞은 전조로 밖에 생각할 수 없다 I cannot help regarding my dream as ominous [an ill-omen].

방정식 方程式 〈數〉 an equation
♦ 방정식을 세우다 set up an equation; equate one term to [with] another / 방정식을 풀다 solve an equation
■ **고차―** an equation of higher degree **대수[기하]―** an algebraic [a geometric] equation **미분―** a differential equation **연립―** system of equations **이항―** a binomial equation **일차[이차, 삼차]―** a linear [quadratic, cubic] equation

방제 防除 〈해충 등의〉 prevention of the breeding and extermination 《of flies》; control 《of insect pests》
▶ 이 약은 초목의 병충해 방제에 좋다 This chemical helps prevent disease in plants.

방조 幇助 aid; assistance; help; backing 〈범죄의〉 aiding and abetting
―**방조하다** aid; assist; help; back up; 〈범죄를〉 aid and abet
♦ 범죄를 방조하다 abet *sb* in a crime
▶ 그녀는 남편의 문서 위조를 방조했다 She abetted her husband in committing [helped her husband commit] forgery.
■―**자** a backer; a supporter; 〈범죄의〉 an abettor; an abetter; a backer

방조문 防潮門 a tide gate
방조제 防潮堤 a coastal; a seawall
방종 放縱 self-indulgence; license; dissoluteness; dissolution; wanton; looseness; 〈방탕〉 debauchery
▶ 방종을 자유로 착각하지 마라 Don't take the license for the liberty.
▶ 젊은이들은 방종에 흐르기 쉽다 The young men are given to self-indulgence.
―**방종하다** self-indulgent; licentious; unbridled; unrestrained; dissolute; fast; free; loose
▶ 그녀는 방종한 여인이다 She is a wanton woman.
▶ 그는 방종한 생활을 했다 He led a fast

방주 方舟 an ark ♦ 노아의 방주 Noah's Ark

방주 旁註 marginal [side] notes; marginalia
♦ 책에 방주를 달다 add [append] marginal notes to the text

방죽 防— a bank; an embankment; a dike; a dyke; (美) a levee; a causeway
♦ 방죽을 쌓다 construct [build] a bank (for); embank; put up a (confining) levee
▶ 방죽이 무너졌다 The dike has broken. ≒ The embankment has collapsed.

방증 傍證 (indirect) evidence supporting ((an opinion, a judgment)); supporting evidence; circumstantial evidence; corroboration
♦ 방증을 굳히다 corroborate ((one's case))
▶ 피고측은 방증수집을 끝냈다 The defense has finished collecting supporting [collateral] evidence.

방지 防止 prevention; 〈억제〉 check
♦ 소음 방지 prevention of street noises / 범죄 방지 crime prevention
▶ 그 학교에는 화재 방지용 설비가 갖추어져 있다 That school has very good facilities for fire prevention.
—방지하다 prevent ((from)); stop; check; keep off; hold in check; preserve ((sth from decay)); 〈미연에 막다〉 nip... in the bud
♦ 사고를 방지하다 prevent an accident / 청소년의 비행을 미연에 방지하다 nip juvenile delinquency in the bud / 물가 상승을 방지하다 check the rise in prices
▶ 그런 범죄는 방지하지 않으면 안된다 We must prevent such crimes.

방직 紡織 spinning and weaving
—방직하다 spin and weave
■ **—공** a weaver; a textile plant worker **—공장** a textile factory [mill] **—기** spinning and weaving machinery; spindles and looms; a (power) loom **—업** the spinning and weaving industry; the textile industry **—업자** a textile manufacturer

방진 方陣 a square formation; a square; 〈그리스의〉 a phalanx ♦ 방진을 치다 form a square / 방진을 풀다 break a square

방진 防塵 protection against dust ♦ 방진 장치 a dust laying / 방진의 dustproof; dusttight

방책 方策 〈방안〉 a plan; 〈책략〉 a scheme; 〈방침〉 a policy; 〈수단〉 a means; measures
▶ 그들이 세운 방책은 성공적이었다 The policy they formulated proved successful [worked out well].
▶ 돈을 버는 방책이 달리 있을지도 모른다 There may be some other means [way] of making money.
▶ 기금을 모을 방책을 세우고 있다 They are working on a plan to raise funds.

방책 防柵 a fence; a palisade; a paling; a railing; a stockade; a barrier ♦ 집 주위에 방책을 치다 put (up) a fence around a house

방첩 防諜 counterespionage; counterintelligence ■ **—기관** an anti-espionage organization **—(부)대** Counterintelligence Corps(略 C. I. C.)

방청 傍聽 hearing
▶ 방청 무료 (게시) Admission Free.
▶ 그 공판은 방청이 허용되었다 The trial was open to the public.
▶ 청문회는 방청 금지로 진행되었다 The hearing was held behind closed doors.
—방청하다 hear; listen to
♦ 국회를 방청하다 visit the National Assembly in session; attend a session of the National Assembly
▶ 나는 그 재판을 방청했다 I attended the trial.
▶ 그 회의는 자유로이 방청할 수 있다[없다] The meeting is open [closed] to the public.
■ **—객** a hearer; an auditor; (총칭) an audience; the public **—권** an admission ticket; 〈의회의〉 an order **—료** the admission fee **—석** seats for visitors; public galleries; 〈법정·의회 등의〉 an observers' gallery

방추 紡錘 a spindle ♦ 방추형의 spindle shaped
방추형 方錘形 a square pyramid ♦ 방추형의 pyramidal

방축 防築 a bank ⇨ 방죽

방축 防縮 ♦ 방축의 shrink-proof [resistant]
■ **—가공 (처리)** non-shrink treatment; shrink resistant finish : 방축 가공한 shrunk; pre-shrunk; (商標) Sanforized ((cloth))

방출 放出 1 〈물자의〉 release ((of government-stocked rice)) **—방출하다** release
2 〈배출〉 discharge; 〈폐수의〉 effluence; 〈열·빛 등의〉 emission; radiation
—방출하다 discharge; exhaust; emit; radiate
■ **—물자** released goods [commodities]

방충망 防蟲網 an insect net
방충제 防蟲劑 an insecticide; 〈예방의〉 an repellent insect; 〈가루의〉 insect powder; a vermicide; 〈좀약〉 a mothball

방취 防臭 deodorization **—방취하다** deodorize
♦ 다락을 방취하다 deodorize a closet
■ **—제(劑)** a deodorizer; a deodorant **—판** a stink [stench] trap; a gas trap; 〈하수구의〉 a water seal

방치하다 放置— let sth [sb] alone; leave sth as it is [stands]; leave sth to chance [to take its own course]; 〈등한히 하다〉 neglect
♦ 병을 방치하다 leave the disease untreated / 환자를 방치하다 leave a patient unattended
▶ 그 문제는 그대로 방치되어 있다 The problem remains unsettled.
▶ 자전거를 집 밖에 방치해 두지 마라 Don't leave your bicycle out-of-doors.
▶ 우리는 이 문제를 방치해 둘 수는 없다 We cannot leave the matter unsettled [let the matter go].

방침 方針 〈방향〉 one's course ((of action)); a line; a tack; a guideline; 〈정책〉 a (line of) policy; 〈계획〉 a plan; 〈주의〉 a principle; 〈목적〉 an aim; an object (in view); a purpose
♦ 국가의 방침 a national policy / …의 방침에 따르다 follow the policy of... / 방침을 세우다 frame [make] a plan; map out one's course; formulate [decide on] one's policy / 방침을 변경하다 change [shift] one's course [plan, policy]

▶그들은 너와 같은 방침에 따랐다 They acted on the same lines as you (did).
▶나는 아직 장래의 방침을 정하지 않고 있다 I have not yet shaped my course for the future.
▶시험을 보지 않는 것이 이 학교의 방침이다 It is the policy of this school not to give the students any examinations.
■—교육— an educational policy 근본— a fundamental policy 영업— a business plan 외교— a foreign policy

방콕 〈타이의 수도〉Bangkok

방탄 防彈 protection against bullets
◆방탄의 bulletproof; bombproof; shellproof
—방탄하다 protect against shells [bombs]
■—복[조끼] a bulletproof jacket [vest] —실 a bombproof room —유리 bulletproof glass —차 a bulletproof car —창 a bullet-resistant window

방탕 放蕩 dissipation; prodigality; debauchery; dissoluteness
◆방탕에 빠지다 abandon *oneself* to dissipation [wild ways]; give *oneself* up to dissolute habits; indulge *oneself* in debauchery / 방탕으로 자멸하다 be ruined *oneself* by dissipation
—방탕하다 dissipated; dissolute; prodigal
◆방탕한 여자 a loose woman / 방탕한 자식 a prodigal son / 방탕한 생활을 청산하다 give up *one's* fast living
▶그는 젊었을 때는 방탕했다 He has sown his wild oats.
■—생활 a fast [dissipated] life; fast living —아 a fast liver; a libertine; a prodigal; (口) a loose fish

방파제 防波堤 a breakwater; 〈배의〉bulwarks (▶보통 복수형); a mole; a seawall
◆방파제를 쌓다 build a breakwater

방패 防牌 a shield; 〈작고 둥근〉a buckler; 〔天〕〈방패자리〉Scutum
◆방패 모양의 shield-shaped / …을 방패로 삼다 use *sth* as a shield 《against bullets》; screen *oneself* behind; shield [cover] *oneself* behind *sth*; hide [shelter] (*oneself*) behind *sth*
▶그가 갑자기 강도의 습격을 받았을 때 그는 여행 가방을 방패삼아 막았다 He shielded himself with his suitcase when he was suddenly attacked by a mugger.

방편 方便 〈수단〉a means; 〈편법〉an expedient; expediency; a shift; 〈도구〉an instrument
◆생활의 방편 a means of living / 일시적 방편 a temporary expedient; a makeshift; a stopgap (measure) / 임시 방편으로 하는 일 temporary work; a stopgap [makeshift] job
▶일시적인 방편으로서 그 조치를 취했다 We adopted the measure as a temporary expedient [means].
▶거짓말도 하나의 방편이다 (속담) Circumstances may justify a lie. ⇌ The end justifies the means.

방풍 防風 protection against wind ■—림 a windbreak forest; a shelterbelt forest; shelter forest : 방풍림을 조성하다 plant trees for protection against the wind —유리 〈자동차의〉a windshield

방학 放學 the school vacation [holidays]
▶나는 산에서 여름 방학을 보냈다 I spent my summer holidays in the mountains.
▶우리는 지금 방학중이다 We are on vacation.
▶초등 학교는 내일부터 방학이다 Vacation begins tomorrow for elementary school pupils.
—방학하다 close [break up] the school 《for a vacation》; go on vacation; have holidays
■겨울— the winter vacation

방한 防寒 protection against cold
—방한하다 protect against cold; keep out cold
■—구(具) an outfit for cold weather —모 a winter cap —복 winter [arctic] clothes; clothes for cold weather : 우리들은 방한복을 입고 있었다 We were [dressed] for cold weather. —설비 (make) provisions against the cold : 우리의 방한 설비는 완전하다 We are fully equipped against the cold [for cold weather]. —화 arctic boots [shoes]; arctics

방한 訪韓 a visit to Korea
◆방한중인 미국대통령 Mr. President of U.S.A. who is on a visit to [in] Korea
—방한하다 visit Korea
▶방한하는 미국 사절단은 내일 이 공장을 시찰할 것이다 The American mission to Korea will visit this factory tomorrow.

방해 妨害 〈훼방〉disturbance; 〈통행·진행 등의〉obstruction; hindrance; 〈중단〉interruption; 〈간섭〉interference; check; 〈전파의〉jamming
◆방해없이 진행되다 proceed unhindered [without hindrance] / 방해를 받다 meet with a check
▶방해가 안 되는지 모르겠군요 I hope I am not disturbing you [intruding (on you)].
—방해하다 〈진행을 막다〉block; 〈교란하다〉disturb; 〈중단시키다〉interrupt; 〈간섭하다〉interfere with; hinder; obstruct; hamper; be [get] in the way; prevent; check; clog (up); 〈전파를〉jam

解說 *disturb*는 「정상적이고 평온한 상태를 흐트러놓다」이고 *interrupt*는 「이야기를 중단시키다」, *interfere*는 「간섭하다, 대립함으로써 방해하다」, *hinder*는 「일의 진행을 (일시적으로) 지연시키다, 멈추다」, *obstruct*는 「장애물을 놓아서 통행·진행을 막다」란 뜻이다. 또 *be* [*get*] *in the way*는 「앞길을 막다」란 뜻인데 비유적으로도 쓰인다.

▶소음이 수면을 방해했다 The noise disturbed my sleep.
▶그들은 광고지를 돌려 내 영업을 방해했다 They interrupted my business by distributing handbills.
▶우리 꼬마가 내 작업을 방해했다 My child hindered me in my work.
▶방청인의 한 사람이 큰 소리를 질러 의사진행을 방해했다 One of the visitors [hearers] cried out to obstruct the proceedings.
▶통행을 방해하지 마시오 Get out of the way.
■공무집행— interference with a government official in the execution of his duty 수비—

〔競〕 interference ■ —방송 〔通信〕 jamming —자 an obstructor; an obstructionist; 〈의사진행 등의〉 a filibuster(er) —행위 holding; block; interference

방해물 妨害物 an obstacle; a hindrance; an impediment; a check; a drag
♦성공의 방해물 an obstacle to success / 방해물을 만나다 encounter [meet with] obstacles / 방해물이 되다 become a drag 《on sb》 / 방해물을 제거하다 remove [get rid of] an obstacle; get obstacles out of the way

방해석 方解石 〔鑛〕 calcite

방향 方向 1 〈방위〉 a direction; bearings; 〈진로〉 a course; a line
♦방향이 바뀌다 turn; shift 《to the west》 / 방향이 맞다[틀리다] have the right [wrong] course / 방향을 바꾸다 change direction; change [shift] *one's* course / 방향을 잡다[유지하다] take [hold] *one's* course / 방향을 잘못 잡다 go in the wrong direction; 〈배가〉 take the wrong course
▶강이 흐르는 방향은 남쪽이었다 The trend of the river was to the south.
▶바람의 방향이 남쪽으로 바뀌었다 The wind shifted to the south.
▶물고기가 강의 흐름과 반대 방향으로 헤엄치고 있다 The fish are swimming against the flow of the river.
▶바람이 바다 방향으로 불고 있다 The wind is blowing toward [in the direction of] the sea.
▶나도 그 방향으로 갑니다 I'm going that way, too.
2 〈방침〉 *one's* course [aim, objective]
♦방향을 그르치다 err from the right path; make an error in choosing *one's* course of life / 방향을 바꾸다 change *one's* object [course]
▶그는 처음에 관리가 되었으나 방향을 바꿔 작가가 되었다 He became a government official at first, but changed his career to become a writer.
■ —지시기 〈자동차의〉 a direction indicator; blinkers; 〈美俗〉 a winker —키 〈방향타〉 a (vertical) rudder —탐지기 (a) radar; a direction finder

방향 芳香 a sweet smell; 〈향수 등의〉 perfume; 〈꽃 등의〉 (a) fragrance (↔ stench, stink); 〈풍미가 있는 냄새〉 (an) aroma
♦방향이 있는 꽃 a fragrant flower / 방향이 있는 fragrant; aromatic; sweet-smelling / 방향을 풍기다 give out [emit] fragrance; smell sweet; diffuse aroma; spread fragrance
■ —유 a fragrant oil —제 an aromatic —족 (族) 화합물 〔化〕 aromatic compounds

방향감각 方向感覺 a sense of direction
♦방향감각이 없다 have no sense of direction
▶그는 방향감각이 예민하다[둔하다] He has a good [poor] sense of direction.

방향전환 方向轉換 a turn; a change of direction [course]; a turnabout; 〈방침 바꾸기〉 a change of *one's* object
♦방향전환을 하다 change [shift] *one's* course (in life) / 차를 방향전환시키다 turn a car around / 180도 방향전환하다 do an about-face

(on); do an about-turn

방형 方形 a square ♦방형의 square; square-shaped

방호 防護 protection (against, from); custody; guard
♦방호용 마스크 a protective mask —방호하다 protect; guard; have custody of ■ —자 a protector; a custodian

방화 放火 〈죄〉 arson; fire-raising; incendiarism; 〈화재〉 an incendiary fire
▶어젯밤의 화재는 방화로 단정되었다 The fire that broke out last night was judged to be caused by arson.
—방화하다 set fire to 《a house》; set 《a house》 on fire; commit incendiarism [arson]
▶그는 학교 건물에 방화했다 He set fire to the school building.
■ —광 〈증세〉 incendiary mania; pyromaniac; a pyromania; 〈사람〉 an incendiary maniac; a pyromaniac —범 an incendiary; an arsonist —죄 arson

방화 邦貨 〈한국 화폐〉 Korean money [currency]; won; 〈한국 상품〉 Korean goods

방화 邦畫 〈한국 영화〉 a Korean film [movie, motion picture]

방화 防火 fire prevention; prevention of fires; protection against fire
♦방화의 fireproof / 방화에 힘쓰다 try to prevent the spread of a fire
▶방화문 — 열지마시오 《게시》 Fire door — keep door closed.
■ —구조물[건물] a fireproof construction [building] —대 a fire belt; a firebreak; fireguard —도료 a fireproof paint —벽 a fire-protection wall —선 a firebreak; a fire-arresting line —설비[장치] fire prevention; a safeguard against fire; fire protection: 이 미술관은 방화 설비가 되어 있다 This museum is equipped with a fire prevention system. —용수 fire fighting water —전(栓) a fireplug (略 F.P.); a hydrant —천장 a counter-ceiling —훈련 a fire drill: 우리는 어제 방화 훈련을 했다 We had a fire drill [practice] yesterday.

방황 彷徨 wandering; roaming
—방황하다 wander about; roam (about); rove; loiter; knock about; hang about [around]; prowl 《about, around》; be [go] on the prowl; take a prowl
♦방황하는 사람 a wanderer; a vagabond / 이곳저곳 방황하다 wander from place to place; wander up and down
▶나는 밤새 산속에서 방황했다 I was roaming over the mountains all 《through the》 night.

밭 ordinary field; a farm; non-paddy fields; a dry field; an upland field
♦감자밭 a potato plot / 배추밭 a Korean cabbage patch / 귤밭 a tangerine grove / 딸기밭 a strawberry field [patch] / 밀밭 a field; a field of rye / 사과밭 an apple orchard / 야채밭 a vegetable patch / 대밭 a bamboo thicket [grove] / 솔밭 a pine grove; a pinery / 커피밭 a coffee plantation / 포도밭 a vineyard / 밭작물 farm products [produce] / 밭을 일구다 crop a field; place the fields under crops / 밭

밭갈이 을 갈다 cultivate [plow, till] a field [the soil]/ 밭에 씨를 뿌리다 sow seeds in a field
밭갈이 plowing [cultivation] (of a field)
—**밭갈이하다** plow [till] a field; farm
밭고랑 a furrow ◆ 밭고랑을 일구다 make furrows (in); furrow
밭곡식─穀食 dry crops; a field crop; crops (grown in non-paddy fields) ◆ 밭곡식이 잘 [안]되다 have a good [bad] dry crop
밭농사─農事 dry-field farming (done in non-paddy fields)
—**밭농사하다** do dry-field farming
밭다¹ 〈체로 거르다〉 filter; sift; filtrate; sieve (out); strain; percolate
◆ 술을 밭다 strain rice wine / 불순물을 받아내다 filter out impurities / 커피 찌꺼기를 받아내다 strain coffee to remove the grounds
밭다² **1** 〈시간·공간이 가깝다〉 very [too] close [near]; tight; urgent
▶ 시간이 밭다 Time is pressing. ⇌ There is (very) little time left
▶ 의자 사이가 밭으니 좀 떼어라 The chairs are too close together, leave some more space between them [keep them apart].
2 〈알뜰하다〉 thrifty; frugal; saving; 〈인색하다〉 stingy; mean
3 〈기침이〉 dry (cough); hacking
◆ 밭은 기침을 하다 give a dry [hacking] cough; cough dryly [drily]
밭도랑 a drain [ditch] in a dry [non-paddy] field ◆ 밭도랑을 내다 make drains [ditches] in a dry field
밭두둑 a ridge in a dry [non-paddy] field
밭둑 an embankment around the end of field
밭매기 weeding a dry field
—**밭매기하다** weed a dry field [farm]
밭머리 an end of a dry field [patch]
밭벼 dry-field rice; rice grown in a dry [non-paddy] field
밭보리 barley grown in a non-paddy field
밭은기침 a dry cough; a hack; a hacking cough ◆ 밭은 기침을 하다 give [have] a dry [hacking] cough; cough dryly
밭이다 〈거르다〉 be strained [filtered]; be sieved (through)
밭이랑 a row in a dry [non-paddy] field; a ridge; a rib ◆ 밭이랑을 만들다 ridge; rib; form ridges
밭일 farming (done in non-paddy fields); farm work [labor]; field labor
—**밭일하다** do farm work; work on the farm; work out in the field
밭장다리 a out-toed person
◆ 밭장다리로 걷다 toe out; walk with the toes turned out [outward]
밭치다 filter ⇨ 밭다¹
배¹ 〈선박〉 a ship; a boat (ship 보다 작은); a vessel (ship 보다 큰); 〈기선〉 a steamer; 〈정기선〉 a liner; 〈짐배〉 a barge; (총칭) shipping; (water)craft
◆ 나룻배 a ferryboat / 낚싯배 a fishing boat / 오징어잡이 배 a boat used in cuttlefish angling [fishing] / 바닥이 평평한 배 a flatboat / 두 사람이 젓는 배 a two-oared boat / 동남아로 가는 배 a ship (bound) for southeast Asia / 다섯 척의 배 five ships [boats]
〈배가[는]〉 배가 (항구를) 떠나다 sail; leave (a) port; take off 《from》; clear a port / 배가 항구에 도착하다 arrive in port; enter [make] (a) port
▶ 배는 강을 따라 내려갔다 The boat sailed down the river.
▶ 배는 해안선을 따라 항해했다 The ship sailed along the coast.
▶ 그 배는 7월 9일 동해에서 출항할 예정이다 The ship is scheduled to leave Tonghae on July 9.
〈배를〉 배를 타다 go on a ship; go [get] on board (a ship); get [go] aboard a ship / 배를 출범[출항]시키다 put to sea; set sail; put out 《for》 / 배를 젓다 row a boat
▶ 배를 타본 적이 있니? Have you ever traveled on board a ship?
〈배에(서)〉 배에서 내리다 leave a ship; disembark; land 《at Inch'ŏn》
▶ 그 배에는 500명의 승객이 타고 있었다 There were five hundred passengers on board [aboard] the ship.
▶ 나는 그 배에서 브라운 부부를 만났다 I saw the Browns on board the ship.
〈배로〉 배로 by ship; on board [aboard] a ship; by water / 배로 제주도에 가다 go to Cheju-do by ship [on a ship]; go by [boat]; take a ship [(口) (a) boat] to Cheju-do
배² 〈열매〉 a pear ◆ 서양배 a (Western) pear
—나무 a pear tree —밭 a pear orchard
배³ **1** 〈生〉 the stomach (▶가장 일반적인 말. 배·위 등을 통틀어 말함); 〈복부〉 the abdomen; (口) the belly; 〈장(腸)〉 the bowels
◆ 빈 배 an empty stomach
〈배가〉 배가 나오다 develop a potbelly / 배가 고프다 be [get] hungry; feel hungry / 배가 거북하다 feel heavy in the stomach / 배가 아프다 have a stomachache; have a pain in the stomach; one's stomach aches
▶ 그는 요즘 배가 나왔다 He has grown a potbelly lately.
▶ 나는 지금 배가 몹시 고프다 I'm awfully [terribly] hungry now.
▶ 배가 고파 죽을 지경이다 I am dying of hunger. ⇌ I'm starving to death.
〈배를〉 배를 굶다 go hungry / 배를 채우다 [불리다] satisfy one's appetite; stuff out the belly / 아무의 배를 치다 hit sb in the stomach / 닭의 배를 가르다 clean a chicken; take out the inside of a chicken
▶ 나는 감자로 배를 채웠다 I satisfied my appetite on potatoes.
▶ 식구들의 배를 곯릴 수야 없지 My family must not be left hungry. ⇌ How can I let my family go hungry?
2 〈모태〉 the womb
◆ 뱃속의 아이 the coming [expected] baby / 배가 부르다 〈임신하여〉 be pregnant; be big [large] with child / 배가 다르다 be born of a different mother
3 〈시샘〉 envy; jealousy
◆ 배 아파하다 〈남의 성공, 행운에〉 be jealous

[envious] 《of sb's success》; envy 《sb's good fortune》
▶ 그녀의 명성에 그는 배가 아팠다 Her reputation made him jealous. ⇌ Her reputation aroused his jealousy.
4 〈불룩한 부분〉 the belly 《of》; the bulge; the swelling ♦ 통의 배 the belly of a cask
5 〈새끼낳는 회수〉 one birth; a litter
♦ 한 배에 at one birth [a litter]/ 한 배에 낳은 강아지 [돼지 새끼] a litter of puppies [pigs] / 한 배의 다섯 마리 돼지새끼 five piglets in a birth

배 胚 〔動·植〕 an embryo 《pl. ~s》;〈포유류의〉 a fetus;〔發生〕 a germ
■―발생[형성] an embryonic growth [formation] ―분화 embryonic differentiation ―이식 (移植) (an) embryo transfer

배 倍 1 〈갑절〉 two times; twice; double; twofold
♦ 배의 double; twice; twofold / 두 배되는 양 [수] twice as much [many] as...; twice [double] the quantity [number] of... / 남보다 배 일하다 do double work; work twice as hard as others
▶ 6의 배는 12다 Twice [Two times] six is [equals] twelve.
▶ 그녀의 방은 넓이가 내 사무실의 배다 Her room is twice as large as [twice the size of] my office.
2 〈곱〉 times; -fold
♦ 1배 once; one time / 한배 반 one and a half times [time and a half] 《as...as》/ 두배 double; twice; twofold / 세배 three times; treble; thrice; threefold / 네배 quadruple / 다섯배 quintuple / 여섯배 sextuple / 일곱배 septuple / 여덟배 octuple / 아홉배 nonuple / 열배 decuple / 백배 centuple
▶ 5의 여섯배는 30이다 Six times five is thirty.
▶ 會話「런던 인구는 파리의 몇배인가?」「약 세배다」"How many times is the population of London larger [more] than that of Paris?" "It's about three times as large."
▶ 물가가 두배, 세배로 올라서 여러 가정이 요금을 지불하기 어려운 지경이었다 Prices doubled and then tripled and many families couldn't pay their bills.

배가 倍加 doubling ―배가하다 double; double *itself*; be doubled; increase double [twofold]
♦ 노력을 배가하다 redouble *one's* efforts
▶ 인구가 30년 동안에 배가되었다 The population was doubled in thirty years.
▶ 수송 능력이 배가되었다 Transport capacity was doubled.

배가리개 a belly [waist] band
배갈 〈고량주〉 Chinese kaoliang liquor [spirit]
배겨나다 endure; overcome; bear up; stand up to; put up with; 〈지탱하다〉 hold (out); keep (up)
♦ 배겨날 수 있는 bearable; endurable
▶ 그때는 일이 힘들어 나는 배겨날 수가 없었다 I couldn't stand the strain of the work at that time.
▶ 그는 많은 난관을 배겨났다 He overcame [surmounted] various difficulties.

배겨내다 ride out; withstand; weather; endure; stand up to; bear up ▶ 우리는 간신히 위기를 배겨냈다 We managed to weather [ride out] the crisis.

배격 排擊 rejection; denunciation
―배격하다 drive out; denounce; reject; show strong disapproval of; boycott
▶ 그 나라에서는 전체주의가 배격되었다 Totalitarianism was rejected in that country.

배경 背景 1 〈배후〉 a background; a backdrop
▶ 우리는 폭포를 배경으로 사진을 찍었다 We had our picture taken with the waterfall for a background.
▶ 남산이 푸른 하늘을 배경으로 우뚝 솟아 있다 Mt. Namsan stands out clear against the blue sky.
2 〈무대의〉 scenery; a setting; a scene
♦ 배경을 바꾸다 shift the scenes; change the scenes [setting]/ 호수를 나타내는 배경을 그리다 paint scenery representing a lake
3 〈배후 세력〉 backing; (美俗) pull; a background
♦ 정치적 배경 political backing [support, pull]/ 그 사건의 사회적 배경 the social background of the affair
▶ 그의 배경에는 유력한 정치가가 있다 He has an influential politician backing him.
▶ 그녀는 재정적 배경이 든든하다 She has secure [sound] financial backing.
■―막 a backdrop ―음악 background music ―화 scene painting; a set scene ―화가 a scene painter

배고프다 hungry; sharp-set; 〈서술적〉 feel [be] hungry
♦ 배고파서 죽을 지경이다 be starving; be dying with hunger / 배고파하다 complain of hunger
▶ 나는 아주 배고프다 I'm simply starving.
▶ 배고파지면 이것을 드십시오 Please have this when you get [become] hungry.
▶ 너는 배고플 때는 술을 마시지 말아야 한다 You'd better not drink alcohol when you are hungry [on an empty stomach].
▶ 배고픈 놈이 이밥 조밥 가리랴 (속담) A hungry man will not be particular about the quality of the food he eats. ⇌ Any port in a storm. ⇌ Beggars must not be choosers.

배고픈 놈더러 요기시키란다 (속담) beg (favor) from those worse off than *oneself*

배곯다 starve; be famished; be hungry; have an empty stomach
♦ 배곯리다 leave *sb* to starve
▶ 우리는 배곯고 일할 수는 없다 We cannot work on an empty stomach.
▶ 전쟁 중에는 많은 사람이 배를 곯았다 Many people starved during the war.

배관 配管 pipe arrangement [laying]; (총칭) piping;〈배관 공사〉 plumbing; piping work
―배관하다 lay [arrange] pipes
■―공 a plumber ―도 (圖) a piping diagram
배광성 背光性 〔生〕 negative phototropism
배교 背敎 renegation; apostasy; the renunciation of *one's* (religious) beliefs ―배교하다 renegade; apostatize; renounce *one's* religion

배구 ■—자 a renegade; an apostate; a backslider
배구 排球 volleyball ♦배구를 하다 play volleyball ■—공 a volleyball —선수 a volleyballer —시합 a volleyball game —코트 a volleyball court

──── 배구 ────

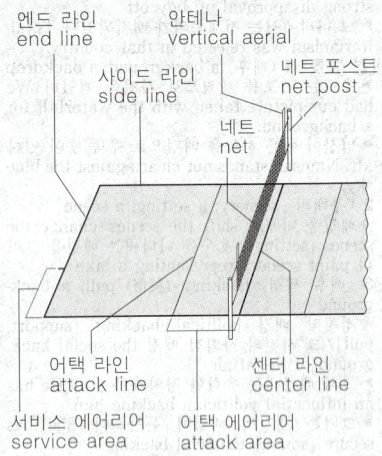

엔드 라인 end line / 안테나 vertical aerial / 사이드 라인 side line / 네트 포스트 net post / 네트 net / 어택 라인 attack line / 센터 라인 center line / 서비스 에어리어 service area / 어택 에어리어 attack area

배금 拜金 the worship of money; money worship; mammon ■—주의 mammonism —주의자 a mammonist; a money worship(p)er
배급 配給 distribution; supply; 〈할당〉 rationing ♦배급을 타다 draw one's rations —배급하다 distribute; supply; deal out; 〈식량을〉 ration
배기 排氣 exhaust; exhaustion; 〈기체〉 exhaust 《steam, gas》; 〈통풍〉 ventilation ■—가스 waste [exhaust] gas; exhaust fumes; (engine) exhaust —갱(坑) an exhaust gallery —관《파이프》 an exhaust pipe —구 an exhaust port —규제 exhaust emission control —량 (piston) displacement: 배기량 1,000cc의 차 a one-thousand cubic centimeter displacement car —장치 an air exhauster [escape] —판(밸브) 〈엔진의〉 an exhaust [eduction] valve; 〈내연기관의〉 a cutout
배기다¹ be hard on; pinch; squeeze; press so as to hurt ♦등이[엉덩이가] 배기다 feel [be] hard on one's back [hips, bottoms]
배기다² 〈견디다〉 bear up (under); withstand; endure; suffer; put up with; persevere
♦배길 수 없는 unbearable; unendurable; beyond one's perseverance / …하지 않고는 못 배기다 …cannot help [keep from] 《doing》; cannot but 《do》
▶그녀는 어려운 생활을 배겨냈다 She endured a hard life.
▶고통은 심했으나 배겨낼 만했다 The pain was severe but tolerable.
▶그녀의 불평을 나는 배겨낼 수가 없다 I can't put up with [tolerate] her grumbling.

배꼽 1 the navel; (俗) the belly button
♦움푹 들어간 배꼽 a deep [sunken] navel / 내민[불거진] 배꼽 a protruding navel / 배꼽이 빠지게 웃다 hold [split] one's sides with [for] laughter ; laugh oneself into convulsions
2 〈열매의〉 the basin 《of an apple, of a navel orange》
■—노리 parts around the navel —쟁이 a person with a protruding navel —점(占) fortunetelling by dominoes —참외 a melon with a navellike formation at the top
배낭 胚囊 〔植〕 an embryo sac
배낭 背囊 〈등산용〉 a rucksack, a knapsack; 〈여행용〉 a packsack
♦배낭을 꾸리다 pack 《things》 in a knapsack; pack a knapsack with 《things》 / 배낭을 벗다 take off a knapsack / 배낭을 메다 carry [shoulder] a rucksack on one's back
▶그는 큰 배낭을 메고 산에 올랐다 He climbed the mountain with a big rucksack.
배내- 1 〈타고난〉 existing at [from] birth; by birth; by nature; natural; congenital
♦배냇병 a connate disease / 배냇소경 a born blind
2 〈갓난아기의〉 of a newborn baby; a baby's
♦배냇냄새 the smell of a newborn baby
배내똥 〈갓난아기가〉 the first faecal discharges of a newborn baby; 〈죽을 때〉 the last excrement of a dying person
배내밀다 〈남의 요구에〉 reject [turn down] 《sb's offer》 haughtily; snub [spurn] 《sb's offer》; turn up one's nose 《at》 ; sneer 《at》
배내옷 baby clothes; clothes for a newborn baby
♦배내옷 세 벌 three sets of baby clothes
배냇니 a milk [baby] tooth ⇨ 젖니
배냇머리 downy [fine soft] hair 《of a baby》; 〔生〕 lanugo 《pl. ~s》
배냇병신 —病身 〈바보〉 a born idiot; a fool by nature; 〈불구자〉 a congenital cripple; deformity by birth
배냇짓 (an) infant's sleeping spasms
배뇨 排尿 〔醫〕 urination; excretion of urine —배뇨하다 pass urine [one's water]; urinate ■—장애 〔醫〕 urination trouble
배니싱크림 vanishing cream
배다¹ 1 〈물기 등이〉 soak 《through, into》; permeate
♦…이 배어 있다 be saturated with / 배어 나오다 ooze (out)
▶비는 마른 땅에 바로 배어 들었다 The dry ground soaked up [absorbed] the rain in an instant.
▶셔츠에 땀이 배어 있다 My shirt is wet with sweat.
▶그 색깔이 셔츠에 배었다 The color has soaked into the shirt.
▶그 편지에는 그녀의 향수 냄새가 은은히 배어 있었다 The letter had a lingering scent of her perfume.
2 〈버릇·일이〉 get [fall into] the habit; be [get] accustomed to; be [become] habituated to
♦몸에 밴 일 a familiar work; one's accus-

tomed work / 몸에 밴 음주 습성 habitual drinking / 규칙적인 생활이 몸에 배게 하다 accustom *oneself* to a regular life

배다² 〈아이를〉 conceive; become pregnant
♦아이를 배고 있다 be (big) with child; be pregnant; be in the family way; 〈동물이〉 be (big) with young
▶그녀는 아이를 배고 있다 She is pregnant. ⇌ She is expecting.
▶암소가 새끼를 뱄다 The cow is heavy with calf.

배다³ 1 〈촘촘하다〉 close; compact; tight; 〈조밀하다〉 dense; thick
♦올이 밴 옷감 cloth of a close texture; closely woven fabric / 나무를 배게 심다 〈간격이〉 plant trees closely together; 〈빽빽이〉 plant trees densely
2 〈속이 차다〉 be full; be packed to the full; be close-packed; be filled up

배다르다 (born) of a different mother; half-blood(ed)
♦배다른 형제[자매] a half brother [sister]; a brother [sister] by a different mother [of the half-blood]; 〈계부·계모의 아들딸인 경우〉 a stepbrother [stepsister]

배다리 a pontoon bridge
♦배다리를 놓다 build a pontoon [floating] bridge 《across [over] a river》

배달 配達 delivery 《service》; distribution
▶신속 배달 《게시》 Quick delivery.
—**배달하다** deliver; distribute
♦신문[우유]을 배달하다 deliver [carry] newspapers [milk] to 《houses》
▶우편은 하루 두번 배달된다 Mail is delivered twice a day.
▶그 편지는 잘못 배달되었다 The letter was delivered at the wrong address.
■무료— free delivery : 시내는 무료 배달합니다 The goods are delivered free within the city limits. ⇌ The delivery is free within the city limits. 시내[특별]— local [special, express] delivery ■—구역 a (postal) delivery zone 〔area〕 —료 a delivery charge —불능 편지 〈주소 불명으로〉 a dead letter; a blind letter —원 [부] a delivery man [boy]; a distributor; 〈신문의〉 a newspaper (delivery) boy [man]; 〈우유의〉 a milkman —증명서 a delivery certificate [receipt] —증명우편 certified mail —차 a delivery wagon [van]

배달 倍達 (the earliest name for) Korea
■—민족 the Korean people [race]

배당 配當 (an) apportionment; (an) allotment; 〈자기몫〉 a share; 〈보험의〉 a disbursement 《to a policyholder》; 〈주식의〉 a dividend; 〈인원 등의〉 a quota; distribution
♦이익 없는 배당 a bogus dividend (paid out of fictitious profits)
—**배당하다** apportion 《to》; allot 《to》; divide; share; 〈배당금을〉 pay a dividend
♦5퍼센트를 배당하다 pay a dividend of 5 per cent / 각각의 일에 시간을 배당하다 allot [apportion] time for each work / 이익을 배당 받다 share [participate] in the profits; get a share in profits
■무— non dividend (略 non div.) : 무배당으로 하다 pass [suspend] a dividend / 이 주는 무배당이다 This stock pays no dividends. 우선— a preferred dividend 주식— a stock dividend; a dividend 《on shares》 특별— an extra dividend 《on stocks》 —공제 a tax credit for dividends received —락(落) ex dividend (略 ex div.); less [minus] dividend; (美) dividend off —률 a dividend rate —부(附) cum dividend (略 cum div.) —소득 income from (stock) dividends —주 a dividend yielding stock —통지서 a dividend notice

배당금 配當金 a dividend ■특별— an extra dividend 《on stocks》; a bonus 《on stocks》

배당체 配糖體 〔化〕 glycoside; glucoside; saponin

배덕 背德 immorality; corruption; a lapse from virtue ■—자 an immoral [a corrupt] man —행위 immoral conduct; an immoral act

배두렁이 a stomach [health] band [wrapper] for a baby; swaddling bands
♦아이에게 배두렁이를 둘러 주다 have a baby wear a stomach band [wrapper]

배드민턴 badminton ♦배드민턴을 치다 play badminton ■—공 a shuttlecock; (口) a birdie

배때기³ 《俗》 the belly; the abdomen
▶움직이면 배때기에 총알 구멍이 날 줄 알아! One move and I'll shoot right through your damned side!

배 란 排卵 〔動·醫〕 ovulation —**배란하다** ovulate ■—기 an ovulatory phase —연령 an ovulation age —유발제 an ovulation induction drug; an ovulation inducer

배럴 〈용량 단위〉 a barrel ♦석유는 지금 배럴 당 얼마인가? How much is oil per barrel now?

배려 配慮 consideration; care; concern; 〈수고〉 trouble; 〈알선, 주선〉 effort; good offices
♦세심한 배려 thoughtful consideration; scrupulous care / …의 배려로 through the good offices of…
▶그녀에게는 남에 대한 배려가 없다 She has no consideration [regard] for others.
—**배려하다** take care; give consideration 《to》; take the trouble; consider
▶여러 가지로 배려해주셔서 감사합니다 I am obliged to you for your kind consideration [good offices]. ⇌ Thank you very much for your trouble [concern].

배 리 背理 irrationality; unreasonableness; absurdity ♦배리의 irrational; unreasonable; contrary to reason; absurd

배릿하다 somewhat fishy ⇨ 비릿하다

배막 胚膜 〔動〕 a germinal [an embryonic] membrane

배맞다 1 〈남녀가〉 commit adultery 《with》; have illicit intercourse 《with》
2 〈나쁜 짓에〉 conspire 《with》; be in cahoots [conspiracy] 《with》

배먹고 이닦기 《속담》 Killing two birds with one stone.

배메기 〔農〕 tenancy on a half-and-half share basis ⇨ 병작

배면 背面 the back; the rear ♦배면의 back;

배문자

rear ■-공격 a rear attack -뛰기 〈높이뛰기에서〉 a backward jump [dive]; the "Fosbury Flop" -비행 an inverted flight

배문자 背文字 〈책의〉 letters on the spine (of a book)

배미 a plot [patch] of rice paddy ⇨ 논배미
♦논 두 배미 two small lots [strips] of (rice) paddy

배밀이하다 〈아기가〉《a baby》creep [crawl] on (its) stomach; crawl on all fours [on its hands and knees]

배반 背反・背叛 **1** 〈저버림〉(a) betrayal; (a) perfidy; treachery
—**배반하다** betray; (口) go back on; (口) cheat on; 〈변절하다〉change front; turn one's coat; double-cross; play sb false [foul]
▶그는 나를 배반하지 않을 것이다 He won't betray [be unfaithful to] me.
▶친구를 배반하는 자는 믿을 수 없다 We cannot trust a man who betrays [goes back on] his friends.
▶그는 아내에게 배반당해 자포자기상태에 빠졌다 He was in a desperate mood, having been betrayed by his wife.
2 〈반역〉rebellion; revolt; treason
—**배반하다** commit treason; revolt [rebel] 《against》
■-이율- 〔哲〕antinomy ■-자 a betrayer; 〈변절자〉a turncoat; 〈밀고자〉an informer; 〈반역자〉a traitor; 〈파업의〉a strikebreaker

배반 胚盤 〔生〕the germinal disk; the blastodisc

배배 windingly; twistingly; coilingly

배번 背番 a player's [uniform] number
♦배번 9번의 선수 the player wearing uniform number nine

배변 排便 evacuation; excretion; the action [movement] of the bowels
▶나는 오늘 아직 배변을 보지 않았다 I haven't had a bowel movement today.
—**배변하다** empty [evacuate] the bowels
■-곤란증 dyschezia -약 a laxative

배 보다 배 꼽이 크다 〈속 담〉Incidental expenses surpass the original outlay

배본 配本 〈구매자에게〉distribution of books to subscribers; 〈소매점에〉delivery of (new) books to (retail) bookstores
♦『세계백과사전』의 최종 배본(예정) the last volume of the "World Encyclopedia" (to be) distributed
—**배본하다** distribute [deliver] books

배부 配付 distribution —**배부하다** distribute 《among, to》; pass out; deal out
▶통지서가 집집마다 배부되었다 A notice was distributed to each household.

배부르다 1 〈양이 차다〉full; satiated; 〈서술적〉have a full stomach; have the stomach full
♦배부르게 먹다 eat heartily / eat one's fill / have enongh [plenty]
▶나는 배부르다 I'm full. ⇌ I've eaten my fill [have had enough].

2 〈배가 뚱뚱하다〉big-bellied; potbellied; paunchy; 〈임 신 하 여〉big (with child); pregnant
♦배부른 여자 a woman big with child
▶그녀는 배불러 있었다 She was expecting a baby [big with child, pregnant].
3 〈지내기가 넉넉하다〉rich; affluent; well-off; well-fixed
▶신세지는 주제에 무슨 배부른 소리냐? A beggar must not be a chooser.

배부른흥정 a bargain one may close at will
♦배부른 흥정을 하다 make a take-it-or-leave-it deal 《with》; make onesided [lopsided] dealings

배분 配分 distribution; apportionment; allotment; division —**배분하다** distribute 《to, among》; share; portion out; divide; apportion 《to》; allot 《to》
♦의제의 각 항목에 시간을 배분하다 allot time for each of the items on the agenda
▶이익은 둘이서 배분했다 The profits were shared [divided] between the two.

배불뚝이 a potbelly; a potbellied [paunchy] person; a person with a potbelly

배불리 heartily; to one's heart's content
♦배불리 먹다 eat [have, take] one's fill [to one's heart's content]; eat heartily

배불리다 fill one's stomach; satisfy one's appetite [the inner man]; 〈사복을 채우다〉stuff [fill] one's (own) pocket [purse]; feather one's (own) nest; enrich oneself

배사 背斜 〔地質〕an anticline
♦배사의 anticlinal
■-구조 anticline structures -축[습곡] an anticlinal axis [fold]

배상 拜上 〈편지의 끝맺음〉Yours sincerely [truly, respectfully, faithfully]; Sincerely [Truly, Respectfully] yours

배상 賠償 reparation; compensation
♦…의 배상으로서 in reparation of…; in compensation for…
▶우리는 정부에 피해 배상을 요구했다 We demanded that the government (should) make compensation [reparation] for our loss. ⇌ We claimed damages from the government.
▶그는 부상에 대한 배상으로 많은 돈을 받았다 He received a large sum of money in [by way of] compensation for his injury.
—**배상하다** compensate 《for》; recompense 《for》; give compensation 《for》; make up for 《a loss》
▶이 손실은 제가 배상하겠습니다 I will compensate [pay] you for this loss.
■금전[현물]— reparation in cash [kind] 손해— compensation for the damages [loss] -요구 a claim for compensation -자 a compensator; an indemnitor -주의 (the theory of punishment as) social reparation -책임[의무] a liability for reparation -청구권 the right to demand compensation -협정 a reparations treaty

배상금 賠償金 (a) compensation; indemnities; 〈전쟁의〉reparations; 〈손해에 대한〉damages

배색 配色 a color scheme [arrangement]; coloring; coloration ─**배색하다** match colors; arrange colors ▶배색이 좋다[나쁘다] The colors match well [badly].

배서 背書 (an) endorsement (written on the back of a document) ◆배서가 있는[없는] endorsed [unendorsed]
─**배서하다** endorse 《a bill》◆어음에 배서하다 endorse 《one's name on》a bill

배서양도 背書讓渡 a transfer 《of a bill》 by endorsement ─**배서양도하다** endorse over 《a bill》

배서인 背書人 an endorser ─**피**─ an endorsee

배석 陪席 sitting 《with one's superior》
◆강선생님의 배석하에 with Mr. Kang attending [in attendance]
─**배석하다** sit with 《one's superior》
▶회의에 나도 배석하는 영광을 얻었다 I had the honor of attending the conference.
■─**자** an attendant ─**판사** an associate judge

배선 配線〈공사〉wiring;〈전선〉distributing wires;〈총칭〉wiring
▶전화기의 배선이 끝나지 않았다 The telephone wiring has not been completed yet.
▶이 낡은 배선을 바꾸어야 한다 We must have this old wiring replaced.
─**배선하다** wire 《a building》
■─**도** a wiring diagram ─**반** a distributing board; a control panel;〈전자계산기의〉a circuit board

배설 排泄 (an) excretion; (a) discharge; (an) evacuation
◆배설을 촉진하는 evacuant
─**배설하다** excrete; discharge 《bodily wastes》
▶신장은 신진대사에 의한 노폐물을 배설한다 Kidneys excrete the waste products of metabolism.
■─**강(腔)** a cloaca 《pl. -cae》; an atrium 《pl. atria》─**관** an emunctory; a nephridium 《pl. -dia》─**기관** an excretive [excretory] organ ─**로** an excretory passage ─**물** excrement; discharges; evacuated matter; bodily wastes ─**선(腺)** an excretory gland ─**작용** the excretory process

배소 焙燒 calcination; torrefaction
─**배소하다** calcinate; calcine; roast; torrefy
■─**로(爐)** a calcinating furnace; a calciner

배속 配屬 assignment; attachment
─**배속하다** assign; attach 《an officer》
◆배속되다 be attached 《to》; get posted
▶그는 그 연구소에 배속되었다 He was assigned to the research center.

배수 配水 supply [distribution] of water; water supply [service]
─**배수하다** distribute [supply] water 《to》
■─**공사** laying water pipes; construction of a water system ─**관** a water [conduit] pipe; a conduit ─**본관** a water [service] main ─**탑** standpipe; a water tower

배수 倍數 1〔數〕a multiple
◆최소 공배수 the least [lowest, smallest] common multiple
▶10은 5의 배수다 Ten is a multiple of five.
2〈갑절〉a double number
■─**비례** multiple proportion ─**성**〔生〕polyploidy ─**염색체** a diploid

배수 排水 1〈물 빼내기〉draining; drainage; pumping out; bailing
▶이 운동장은 배수가 잘 된다[안 된다] This playground drains [does not drain] well.
▶이 택지는 배수장치가 불완전하다 The sewage [sewerage] arrangements at this housing site are incomplete [inadequate].
─**배수하다** drain 《off》;〈도랑으로〉dike;〈펌프로〉pump 《the water》out;〈배에 괸 물을〉bail
2〈선박의〉displacement
─**배수하다** displace 《20,000 tons of water》
■─**거(渠)** a drain; a culvert ─**공사** drainage works ─**관**〈건물의〉a drainpipe;〈지표수·하수의〉a drain ─**구(口)** an outlet ─**구(溝)[로]** an overflow; a drain; a drainage 《ditch, canal》─**기(器)** a drainer ─**작업** draining 《work》; pumping out ─**지역** a catchment area [basin] ─**톤수(船)** displacement 《tonnage》─**펌프** a drain《ing》pump; a sump pump

배수량 排水量 a displacement
▶이 배는 배수량이 2만톤이다 This ship has a displacement of twenty thousand tons.
■─**수상[수중]**─ a surface [submerged] displacement

배수성 倍水性〔植〕negative hydrotropism

배수진 背水陣 ◆배수진을 치다〈목숨을 걸고 싸우다〉burn one's boats [ships]; burn one's bridges 《behind one》; fight with one's back to the wall [sea]; fight desperately [for one's life]
▶이번 파업은 배수진을 친 격이다 This strike is a do-or-die effort.

배신 背信 betrayal; infidelity
▶그것은 국가에 대한 배신이다 That's the act of treason against the nation.
─**배신하다** betray sb's confidence [trust]; break faith with 《one's friend》
■─**자** a betrayer;〈변절자〉a turncoat ─**행위** (a) breach of faith ; (an) abuse of confidence

배심 陪審 (a) jury
▶배심이 유죄 평결을 내렸다 The jury brought in a verdict of guilty.
─**배심하다** hold (a) jury; participate in a trial as a jury member; serve [sit, be] on a jury; do jury duty
■─**재판** trial by jury; a jury trial ─**제도** the jury system

배심원 陪審員 〈총칭〉the jury; 〈한 사람〉a juryman; jurywoman; a juror; a jury member
◆배심원을 선임하다 impanel a jury / 배심원이 되다 serve [sit, be] on a jury
▶배심원들의 평결이 나왔다 The jury has reached a verdict.
▶배심원은 피고의 유죄[무죄]를 인정했다 The jury found the accused guilty [not guilty].
■─**대**─ a grand juror ─**보결**─ a talesman ─**소**─ a petty juror ─**석** the jury box

배아 胚芽 〔植〕an embryo bud; a germ

배아미 胚芽米 whole rice; rice with the germ

배수의 표현

1. …의 O배 (크기, 길이 등)
(1) O times as + 형용사 + as…
▶ 그의 집은 우리 집의 2배 크기다 His house is twice as large as mine.
▶ 이 다리는 저 다리의 3배 길이다 This bridge is three times as long as that one.
(2) O times as + 부사 + as…
▶ 그녀는 나보다 3배나 빨리 영어를 읽을 수 있다 She can read English three times as fast as I can.
▶ 그는 줄잡아 내 갑절은 공부한다 He studies at least twice as hard as I do.
(3) O times the + 명사 + of…; O times + 인칭대명사의 소유격 + 명사
▶ 그 나라는 한국의 3배 크기다 The country is three times the size of Korea. ⇌ The country is three times as large as Korea.
▶ 중국의 인구는 한국의 약 20배이다 China has about twenty times the population of Korea. ⇌ The population of China is about twenty times as large as that of Korea.
▶ 그 비행기의 속도는 음속의 배다 The plane has twice the speed of sound. ⇌ The plane travels twice as fast as sound.
▶ 그는 자네의 갑절되는 급료를 받고 있네 He gets twice your salary. ⇌ His salary is twice as large as yours.
[어법]
① 「2배」의 뜻으로는 two times가 아니라 twice를 쓴다.
② (3)의 경우에는 twice 대신에 double을 쓰기도 한다.
[보기] The airplane has double the speed of sound. / He gets double your salary.
③ (3)의 구문에서 쓰이는 명사는 population, speed, size, weight 등과 같이 양적인 관념을 갖는 것이 많다.

2. …의 O배의 (책, 돈)
O times as many + 복수명사 + as… (수를 나타냄); O times as much + 단수 명사 + as… (양을 나타냄)
▶ 그는 내 배가 되는 책을 가지고 있다 He has twice as many books as I do.
▶ 우리 학교에는 남자의 3배나 되는 여자가 있다 There are three times as many girls as boys in our school. ⇌ Our school has three times as many girls as boys.
▶ 저 사람은 적어도 내 갑절 돈을 가지고 있다 He has at least twice as much money as I do.
▶ 그들은 예전에 비해 3배 가까운 석유를 생산하고 있다 They are producing nearly three times as much oil as they used to.

3. …의 몇 배[몇 십배]나 (빠르다 등); …의 몇 배[몇 십배]나 되는 (돈, 석유 등)
many times [dozens of times] as + 형용사 [부사] + as…
▶ 그는 나의 몇 배나 빨리 헤엄칠 수가 있다 He can swim many times as fast as I can.
▶ 이 빌딩은 저 빌딩보다 몇 배나 높다 This building is many times as high as that one.
▶ 한국은 지금 30년 전의 몇 십배나 석유를 소비하고 있다 Korea consumes dozens of times as much oil as she did 30 years ago.
[어법]
이상 기술한 것 외에 다음과 같은 표현이 있다.
▶ 수백 배의 hundreds of times / 수천 배의 thousands of times / 수만 배의 tens of thousands of times / 수십만 배의 hundreds of thousands of times / 수백만 배의 millions of times

4. …의 절반의 (크기, 길이 등); …의 절반인 (책, 돈 등) half as + 형용사[부사] + as…; half as many + 복수 명사 + as…; half as much + 단수 명사 + as…
▶ 이 정원은 저 정원의 약 반 정도의 넓이다 This garden is about half as large as that one.
▶ 나는 넥타이를 아버지의 반밖에 가지고 있지 않다 I have only half as many neckties as my father does.
▶ 그녀는 옷치레에 동생의 반밖에 돈을 쓰지 않는다 She spends only half as much money on clothes as her sister does.

5. …의 O분의 ~
분수 + as + 형용사[부사] + as…
▶ 캐나다의 인구는 한국의 약 3분의 1이다 The population of Canada is about one-third as large as that of Korea.
▶ 나는 그의 3분의 1 정도 밖에 돈을 쓰지 않는다 I spend only about one-third as much money as he does.
▶ 내 장서는 그의 3분의 2다 I have two-thirds as many books as he does.

6. …의 1배반(의)
half as + 형용사 [부사] + again as…
▶ 이 터널은 저 터널의 1.5배 길이다 This tunnel is half as long again as that one.
▶ 이 차의 가격은 저 차의 약 1.5배다 This car is about half as expensive again as that one. ⇌ This car costs about half as much again as that one.

7. … 몇 배입니까?
How many times as + 형용사[부사] + as… + 동사 + 주어?
▶ 브라질은 한국의 몇 배 크기입니까? How many times as large as Korea is Brazil?
▶ 에베레스트의 높이는 백두산의 몇 배입니까? How many times as high as Paekdusan is Mt. Everest?
▶ 제트기는 음속의 몇 배 속도로 날 수 있습니까? How many times as fast as sound can a jet plane travel?
[어법]
형용사의 원급을 쓰는 대신 비교급을 쓰는 말투도 있다.
[보기] How many times larger is Brazil than Korea? ⇌ How many times higher is Mt. Everest than Paekdusan?

(but not with the bran)
배알 1 〈창자〉 the bowels; the intestines; 〈동물의〉 the guts
2 〈부아〉 anger; rage; indignation
▶ 그의 방자함에 배알이 꼴린다 I can't stomach his rudeness. ⇌ I can't put up with his rude manner.
배알 拜謁 an audience 《with the king》; seeing a superior
▶ 그는 국왕의 배알을 청하여 허락받았다 He begged [sought] and was granted an audience with the King.
—배알하다 have audience of 《the king》
▶ 나는 여왕을 배알할 수가 있었다 I was admitted to the Queen's presence.
배앓이 a stomachache; (口) a bellyache; 〈격심한〉 colic; (口) the gripes
♦ 배앓이를 하다 suffer from [have] a stomachache; have a pain in the stomach
배액 倍額 double the price [amount, charge, fee]; a double sum
♦ 통상 요금의 배액을 지불하다 pay double the usual fare
▶ 초과 근무로 배액의 수당을 지급받았다 I was given double pay for overtime work.
배양 培養 cultivation; nurture; culture
♦ 이 과일 나무에는 특수 배양으로 이런 큰 과실이 열리게 되었다 Special cultivation has made this tree yield such big fruit.
—배양하다 cultivate; culture; nurture; breed; raise
♦ 세균[장티푸스균]을 배양하다 culture [cultivate] bacteria [typhoid bacilli]
■ 세균— germiculture; cultivation of bacteria 순수— pure culture 인공— artificial culture 조직— tissue culture ●—균 cultured bacteria; cultures —기(基) a culture medium ; a medium —법 a method of cultivation; 〈세균의〉 a method of culture —소 a farm; a nursery; a culture ground —액 a culture fluid [solution] —자 a cultivator; a culturist —토 culture soil; compost
배어나오다 ooze (out); exude; seep ▶ 물이 벽에서 배어나오고 있었다 Water oozed [seeped] from the walls.
배역 配役 〈역〉 the cast 《of a play》 (▶집합적으로 쓰며 단수·복수 용법 모두 가능); 〈배역을 정하기〉 casting
♦ 연극의 배역을 정하다 decide the cast of a play; cast a play
▶ 배역진이 프로그램에 나와 있다 The cast is [are] listed on the program.
배열 排列·配列 (an) arrangement; array
♦ 책상의 배열을 바꾸다 change the arrangement of desks
—배열하다 arrange; dispose; put [place, set] in order; array
♦ 단어를 ABC 순으로 배열하다 arrange words alphabetically [in alphabetical order]
▶ 진열품은 연대순으로 분류, 알파벳순으로 배열되어 있었다 The exhibits were divided [grouped] according to historical period and arranged in alphabetical order.
배엽 胚葉 〈植〉 a germinal [germ] layer; a blastoderm
배영 背泳 the backstroke
—배영하다 swim on *one's* back [with the backstroke]; do the backstroke
—선수 a backstroke swimmer
배외 排外 anti-foreign; anti-alien ♦ 배외의[적인] anti-foreign
▶ 배외적 풍조가 퍼져나갔다 A nationalistic [An anti-foreign] mood prevailed.
—사상 anti-alienism; anti-foreign spirit
배우 俳優 a player; a performer; 〈남자〉 an actor; 〈여자〉 an actress; 〈총칭〉 people of the stage
♦ 순회 공연 배우 a strolling actor / 연기가 서툰 배우 a poor actor / 배우가 되다 become an actor [actress]; go on [take to] the stage; appear before the footlights
▶ 그는 상당한 배우다 He is no mean showman.
▶ 그는 배우가 되려고[배우를 그만두려고] 결심했다 He made up his mind to go on [retire from] the stage.
—무대[연극]— a stage actor [actress] 아마추어— an amateur actor 인기— a star (player [actor, actress]) ■—학교 a school of acting —학교 학생 a student of acting
배우다 〈익히다〉 learn; be taught 《history by Mr. Min》; 〈가르침을 받다〉 take lessons 《in》; 〈연구하다〉 study 《chemistry under Prof. Kim》; 〈연습하다〉 practice; 〈교훈을 얻다〉 draw a lesson 《from》
▶ 너는 대학에서 무엇을 전공으로 배우고 있지? What are you majoring in at college?
▶ 그 목수는 경험으로 많은 것을 배웠다 The carpenter has learned a great deal by experience.
▶ 그녀는 성악을 홍여사에게 배우고 있다 She is taking singing lessons from Mrs. Hong.
▶ 이 책을 읽고 배운바 컸다 I have gained a great deal of information [enlightenment] from this book.
▶ 여름 방학에 자동차 운전을 배울 작정이다 I'm going to learn how to drive during the summer vacation.
▶ 우리는 브라운 선생님에게서 영어를 배웠다 We were taught English by Mr. Brown. ⇌ We learned English from Mr. Brown.
▶ 나는 주말에 그에게서 피아노를 배우고 있다 I take piano lessons from him on weekends.
▶ 배우기보다 스스로 익혀라 **(속담)** Practice makes perfect. ⇌ Custom makes all things easy.
▶ 세상에는 책으로 배울 수 없는 일이 많다 There are many things in this world that cannot be learned from books.
▶ 그들한테서는 아무것도 배울 것이 없다 There is nothing to be learned [We have nothing to learn] from them.
배우자 配偶子 〈生〉 a gamete
배우자 配偶者 *one's* spouse; *one's* mate; a consort; a life partner; a companion for life; a partner in life; 〈남편〉 a husband; 〈아내〉 a wife; 〈서류란 등에서 배우자의 유무〉 *one's* marital status

♦ 배우자가 없는 spouseless; mateless / 적당한 배우자를 고르다 choose a suitable match 《for one》

배운 도둑질같다 《속담》 be like second nature 《to sb》

배움 learning; study ▶ 배움의 길은 멀다 The path of learning is long.

배웅 seeing sb off; a send-off ♦ 역까지 배웅 나가다 go to the station to see sb off ▶ 우리는 따뜻한 배웅을 받았다 We were given a hearty send-off.
—**배웅하다** see sb off; send sb off; give sb a send-off ♦ 손님을 대문까지 배웅하다 accompany a visitor to the gate; see the visitor to the gate / 공항에서 성대히 배웅하다 give sb a royal send-off at the airport ▶ 아내는 내가 외출할 때 현관까지 배웅한다 My wife comes to the door to see me off. ▶ 많은 사람이 송선생님을 배웅하러 나왔다 Many people came to give Mr. Song a send-off.

배유 胚乳 〔植〕 an albumen; an endosperm ⇨ 배젖

배율 倍率 〔光〕 〈확대율〉 magnification; magnifying power ♦ 배율이 높은[낮은] 망원경 a high-[low-]powered telescope

배은망덕 背恩忘德 ingratitude 《to》; ungratefulness
—**배은망덕하다** be ungrateful; lose one's gratitude 《to》; forget kindness [benefits] received ♦ 배은망덕한 놈 an ingrate; an ungrateful person / 배은망덕한 짓을 하다 act ungratefully ▶ 참으로 배은망덕한 놈이로구나 What an ungrateful man!

배음 倍音 〔物〕 harmonics; 〔樂〕 an overtone; a harmonic (overtone)

배일성 背日性 〔植〕 negative heliotropism; apheliotropism

배임 背任 breach of trust [faith]; 〈의사·변호사 등의〉 malpractice; 〈특히 공무원의〉 malfeasance; 〈부정 유용〉 misappropriation ♦ 배임죄로 기소되다 be charged with malfeasance [breach of trust]
■ —**행위** an act in violation of one's duty

배자 褙子 a woman's waistcoat

배전 倍前 ♦ 배전의 more than ever; all the more / 배전의 노력을 하다 redouble one's exertions; make redoubled efforts ▶ 배전의 애호를 바랍니다 We solicit your further patronage.

배전 配電 supply [distribution] of electric power [electricity]; electric [power] supply; power distribution ▶ 벼락으로 배전이 정지되었다 The electric supply was cut off on account of lightning.
—**배전하다** supply electricity [electric power]
■ —**기** a (power) distributor —**반** a distributing board [panel]; a switchboard —**선** a service wire; a power (distribution) line —**소** [회사] a power distribution station [company]

배점 配點 distribution [allotting] of marks ▶ 문제에는 배점이 기입되어 있었다 The allotment [distribution] of points was indicated on the examination paper.
—**배점하다** allot 《10 points》 to 《a question》 ▶ 이 문제에는 30점을 배점합시다 Let's allot thirty points to this question.

배정 配定 assignment; allotment; allocation; quota; apportionment
—**배정하다** assign; allot; allocate; apportion ▶ 그 방은 소녀들에게 배정되었다 The room was assigned to the girls. ▶ 우리는 각 연사에게 한 시간씩 배정했다 We allotted an hour to each speaker. ▶ 나는 그 반에 배정되었다 I was assigned to the class. ▶ 웅변대회에서는 각자에게 10분이 배정됩니다 In a speech contest each of you will be allotted ten minutes.

배젖 胚— 〔植〕 an albumen; an endosperm ♦ 배젖이 있는 albuminous

배제 排除 exclusion; removal; elimination; 〔法〕 abatement ♦ 몇몇 직업에서의 여성 배제 the exclusion of women from some jobs
—**배제하다** exclude; remove; eliminate; make [do] away with ♦ …을 배제하고 to the exclusion of… / 정실을 배제하다 eliminate favoritism ▶ 의심을 살만한 조항은 모두 배제합시다 Let's remove [eliminate] all articles that may cause doubt.

배종 胚種 〔動·植〕 a germ; a germinal vesicle ■ —**세포** a germinal [germ] cell

배주 胚珠 〔植〕 an ovule ⇨ 밑씨

배증 倍增 redoubling; doubling
—**배증하다** redouble; double ♦ 소득을 배증하다 double one's income ▶ 회원수가 3년 사이에 배증했다 The membership doubled in three years.

배지 a badge ♦ 경찰관[학교] 배지 a police [school] badge / 배지를 달다 wear [carry] a badge

배지기 〔씨름〕 a belly grab; a belly throw

배지느러미 〔魚〕 the ventral fin

배지성 背地性 〔植〕 negative geotropism; apogeotropism

배진 配陣 battle array [formation, disposition]; a lineup —**배진하다** dispose [deploy] troops in battle array

배짱 1 〈마음〉 one's inmost thought(s); one's real intention ♦ 배짱이 맞다 get along with sb / 배짱이 맞지 않다 cannot get along [on] 《with sb》
2 〈뱃심〉 self-confidence; boldness; audacity; assurance; nerve; cheek; 〔俗〕 guts ♦ 배짱이 센 남자 a man with plenty of guts ▶ 그는 배짱이 두둑하다 He has iron nerves [nerves of steel]. ⇒ He is not troubled by little things. ▶ 배짱을 부리는 수밖에 없다 There is no other way than to push forward. ▶ 그렇게 배짱이 약해서는 안된다 Don't be so weak-kneed [timid].

배차 配車 allocation of cars; operation of cars —**배차하다** operate [run] cars; allocate

[dispatch, send out] cars
—담당[원] a 《train》 dispatcher
배척 排斥 rejection; expulsion; exclusion
—배척하다 drive out; reject; exclude; expel
▶그는 간사해서 모두 그를 배척하고 있다 He's crafty, so everyone shuns him.
▶그 나라에서 전체주의는 배척되었다 Totalitarianism was rejected in that country.
배추 a Chinese [white] cabbage
■—김치 cabbage *kimchi*; pickled cabbage —꼬랑이 a cabbage-root —속대 cabbage heart —찜 cabbage stew
배추벌레 a green caterpillar
배추흰나비 [昆] a small [cabbage] white; a cabbage butterfly
배출 排出 discharge; exhaust; 〈배설〉 excretion
◆이산화탄소의 배출 carbon dioxide emissions
◆이 효소는 노폐물의 체외 배출을 돕는다 This enzyme helps eject waste matter from the system.
—배출하다 excrete; evacuate; exhaust; issue
◆노폐물을 체외로 배출하다 eliminate waste matter from the system
▶오수는 하수구로 배출된다 The filthy water is discharged into the sewers.
■—관 a discharge [an exhaust] pipe
배출 輩出 appearing one after another
—배출하다 appear one after another [in succession, in large numbers]; produce a large number of
▶그 대학은 다수의 우수한 학자를 배출했다 That university has produced many great scholars.
배출구 排出口 a vent; an outlet ◆여분의 물의 배출구 an outlet for the surplus water / 욕구 불만의 배출구 an outlet for *one*'s frustrations
배치 背馳 contrariety; inconsistency; contradiction —배치하다 be contrary 《to》; run counter 《to》; contradict 《each other》; interfere 《with》
▶그의 말은 행동과 배치된다 His words are inconsistent [at variance] with his conduct. ⇒ His words contradict his behavior.
▶그것은 법의 정신에 배치된다 It would run counter to the spirit of the law.
배치 配置 arrangement; disposition; stationing; posting; placement; [軍] deployment
▶식탁 배치는 자네한테 맡기겠네 I will leave the arrangement of the tables to you.
▶가구 배치 좀 바꿉시다 Let's change the arrangement of our furniture a little.
—배치하다 arrange; dispose; [軍] deploy; 〈부서에〉 post; station; put 《missiles》 in position
◆의자를 반원형으로 배치하다 dispose chairs in a semicircle / 진열창에 상품을 보기좋게 배치하다 arrange articles nicely in the show window
▶십여명의 경찰관이 요소에 배치되었다 More than ten policemen were stationed [posted] at important positions.
■—공격[방어]— offensive [defensive] disposition —인원— disposition of men ■—계획 〈도시계획 등의〉 block planning; [建] plot planning

—도 [機] an arrangement plan; [建] a plot plan; a block plan
배타 排他 exclusion ◆배타적(인) exclusive; exclusionary; clannish; cliquish
▶그의 태도는 배타적이다 He's quite cold [unfriendly] to outsiders.
—배타하다 exclude; expel
■—론자 an exclusionist —주의 exclusivism; exclusionism; cliquism
배탈 a stomach disorder [trouble, upset]
◆배탈이 나다 have [suffer] from a stomach trouble
배태 胚胎 〈임신〉 pregnancy; germination; 〈기원〉 origin; germ ◆민주주의의 배태 the germination of democratic principles
—배태하다 〈임신하다〉 become pregnant; 〈…에서 기원하다〉 originate 《in》; have 《its》 origin [genesis] 《in》; arise 《from》; result 《from》
▶뒤의 재난은 거기에서 배태했다 That was the source of later evils. ≒ It was there that many later ills originated.
배터 [野] a batter ⇒ 타자(打者)
배터리 1 〈전지〉 a battery ◆자동차의 배터리 a car battery / 배터리를 충전하다 charge a battery 2 [野] 〈투수와 포수〉 the battery
▶나는 그와 배터리를 이루었다 I formed a battery with him.
배터박스 [野] a batter's box ⇒ 타석(打席)
배턴 a baton ◆다음 주자에게 배턴을 넘기다 hand over [pass] the baton to the next runner / 배턴을 물려받다 receive [accept] the baton 《from the starting runner》; 《비유》 succeed to; take over 《a task》
■—터치 (a) baton pass
배통기다 turn up *one*'s nose 《at》
배트 [野] a (baseball) bat ◆배트를 휘두르다 swing *one*'s bat / 배트를 길게[짧게] 잡다 hold *one*'s bat long [short]

―― 배트 ――

손잡이 handle, grip
몸통 barrel
그립엔드 knob
라벨(상표명) label
헤드 head

배팅 [野] batting ■—오더 the batting order
배편 —便 shipping sevice
◆배편으로 by ship [steamer, water, sea] / 배편으로 보내다 send *sth* by ship [vessel] / 다음 배편을 기다리다 wait for the next boat
▶그 섬으로 가는 배편이 있습니까? Is there (a) steamer service to the island?
▶그 섬에는 배편이 하루 한 번 있다 There is steamer [ferry] service to the island once a day.
▶이 소포는 배편으로 보내겠다 I will send this parcel by sea.

배포 配布 (wide) distribution; division
─**배포하다** distribute 《among, to》; deal out; divide 《among》
▶ 통지서가 집집마다 배포되었다 A notice was distributed to each household.
■─망 a network of distribution

배포 排布·排鋪 〈계획〉 mapping out [drawing up] a plan; scheming; 〈속셈〉 a plan [scheme] (in one's mind)
♦ 배포가 크다 think on a large scale; have a big idea; be magnanimous / 배포가 유하다 do not care about trifles; be hard to ruffle / 가슴에 띤 배포가 들이 있다 have some plot in one's mind; have an axe to grind

배필 配匹 a spouse; a consort; a mate; a wife [husband]; one's better half ♦ 적당한 배필을 고르다 choose a suitable match
▶ 그의 딸은 좋은 배필을 만났다 His daughter has made a good match [married a good man].
■─천생 a well-matched couple [pair]

배합 配合 1 〈조화〉 harmony; match
♦ 색의 배합 the combination [arrangement] of colors; a color scheme [harmony] / 과일의 배합 an assortment of fruit / 배합이 잘된[안된] well-[ill-]matched
▶ 이 색갈들은 배합이 잘[안]된다 These colors match well [do not match].
▶ 색깔과 모양의 배합이 잘 배합된 것이 사람들의 눈길을 끌었다 A happy combination of colors and forms fascinated the viewers.
2 〈혼합〉 mixture; blending
─**배합하다** mix; blend
■─비료 compound fertilizer ─사료 assorted feed

배혁 背革 〈제본의〉 quarter binding ■─본 a quarter-bound book

배화교 拜火敎 fire worship; Zoroastrianism; Parsiism ─**도** a fire worshipper; a Zoroastrian; a Parsi

배회 徘徊 loitering; sauntering
─**배회하다** loiter (about [along]); saunter; hover (about); (美) hang around [about]; wander [roam, ramble, knock] about; 〈도둑이〉 prowl (about)
♦ 밤에 유흥가를 배회하다 hang around [loiter about] the amusement quarters at night / 거리를 정처없이 배회하다 stray aimlessly through the street

배후 背後 the back; the rear
♦ 적의 배후를 찌르다 attack the enemy in the rear [from behind] / 배후에서 조종하다 pull (the) wires [strings] from behind; maneuver from behind the scenes [in the background]
▶ 사건의 배후 관계를 조사중입니다 We are inquiring into the background of the case.
■─인물[조종자] a wire-puller; a man behind the scenes: 배후인물이 누구냐? Who is behind the affair?

백 白 1 〈백색〉 white ♦ 백을 흑이라고 하다 call white black 2 〈흰 바둑돌〉 a white (paduk) stone ♦ 백을 쥐다 〈바둑에서〉 occupy the superior side of board

백 百 a [one] hundred

解說 *one hundred*는 특히 숫자를 강조하는 경우나 구어에서 많이 쓰인다. *hundred*는 *hundreds of...* (수백의, 몇백의)와 같은 연어(連語)일 때가 아니면 단수형으로 쓴다.

♦ 수백명 hundreds of men / 백번째(의) the (one) hundredth / 수백을 헤아리다 be counted by (the) hundreds [by the hundred]
▶ 수백명의 사람이 거리에 모여 있다 There are hundreds of people on (英) in the street.
▶ 그 사고로 수백명의 승객이 부상됐다 Hundreds of passengers were injured in the accident.

백 〈뒤〉 back; 〈후원〉 backing; support; 〈후원자〉 a backer; a supporter; 〈후위〉 a back
♦ 백이 든든하다 have a good backing

백건 白鍵 〈건반의〉 a white key; a natural

백계 百計 〈모든 수단〉 all [every] means; 〈갖은 꾀〉 all resources
♦ 백계무책이다 exhaust all resources [means]; be at one's wit's [wits'] end; be at the end of one's resources

백계노인 白系露人 a (White) Russian émigré

백곡 百穀 all kind(s) of grain (英) corn

백골 白骨 a bleached [white] bone; a skeleton ♦ 은혜는 백골 난망입니다 I shall never forget your kindness.

백곰 白─ [動] a white [polar] bear

백과 百科 all branches of knowledge; all sciences

백과사전 百科事典 an encycl(a)edia
♦ 백과 사전적 encyclopedic 《knowledge》
▶ 나는 백과 사전을 찾아 보았다 I consulted an encyclopedia.
▶ 그가 알고 있는 것은 백과사전적인 지식에 불과하다 He has only encyclopedic knowledge.

백과전서 百科全書 an encycl(a)edia; 〈18세기 프랑스의〉 the Encycl(a)edia

백관 百官 all the government officials
■─문무─ civil and military officials; all the officials of both services

백구 白鷗 [鳥] a gull ⇨ 갈매기

백군 白軍 1 [史] the White Russian Army (at the time of the Russian Revolution)
2 〈경기의〉 the white team; the white(s)

백귀야행 百鬼夜行 pandemonium ▶ 그것은 백귀야행의 광경이었다 It was a hell of a sight.
─**백귀야행하다** be a veritable pandemonium; present a most scandalous scene [sight]

백그라운드 [劇] the background

백금 白金 white gold; 〔化〕 platinum

백기 白旗 a white flag; 〈항복을 나타내는 기〉 a flag of truce [surrender] ▶ 우리는 백기를 들었다 We raised a white flag. ≒ We signaled that we were surrendering.

백날 百─ 1 a hundred days ⇨ 백일 2 〈많은 날〉 a long time ▶ 백날 해 봤자 그 타령이다 It is no use making any efforts.

백납 〔韓醫〕 leucoderma; vitiligo 《pl. ~s》
♦ 백납 먹다 have leucoderma

백내장 白內障 〔醫〕 cataract

백넘버 〈잡지의〉 a back number; a back volume [copy, issue] 《of a magazine》; 〈운동선수

의〉 a uniform number

백네트 〔野〕 the backstop

백년 百年 a [one] hundred years; a century; 〈한평생〉 one's whole life
■—대계 a farsighted program [plan]: 국가의 백년대계를 세우다 draw up a long-range plan for the nation —제(祭) a centenary; a centennial (anniversary)

백년가약 百年佳約 a conjugal [matrimonial] tie; a marriage bond ♦백년가약을 맺다 exchange marriage vows; tie the nuptial knot; become man and wife for weal and woe

백년하청 百年河淸 ▶백년하청격이다 It's like waiting for pigs to fly. ⇌ If the sky falls, we shall catch larks.

백년해로 百年偕老 —백년해로하다 live together in happy union till parted by death

백단향 白檀香 〔植〕 (Indian) sandalwood

백대 百代 one hundred generations; 〈오랜 동안〉 a very long time

백대(하) 白帶(下) 〔醫〕 leukorrhea; (口) (the) whites

백도 白桃 a white peach

백랍 白蠟 white [refined] wax; 〔藥〕 tree [insect] wax

백랍 白鑞 pewter; solder ⇨ 땜납

백로 白露 1〈이슬〉 white dew; a white dewdrop 2〈절기〉 the 15th of the 24 seasonal divisions of a year

백로 白鷺 〔鳥〕 a snowy heron; 〈큰 해오라기〉 an egret (유럽·미국산) ▶그것은 마치 백로를 까마귀라고 우기는 것과 같다 It seems as though you talked black into white.

백리 白痢 〔韓醫〕 diarrhea alba

백마 白馬 a white horse

백만 百萬 a [one] million
♦백만번 a million times / 백만원 one million won / 백만인 one million persons / 백만분의 1 one millionth; one part per million; 1 ppm / 백만대(代)에 이르다 〈숫자·액수 등이〉 reach the seven-figure mark
▶그는 한 달에 수백만원의 돈을 쓴다 He spends millions of won a month.
▶나는 백만의 지지자를 얻은 것 같다 I feel as if I had a great many supporters.
—장자 a millionaire

백면서생 白面書生 a pallid student of books; a callow student; a novice

백모 伯母 an aunt who is the wife of one's father's elder brother

백목련 白木蓮 〔植〕 a yulan

백묵 白墨 chalk ♦백묵 한 자루 a piece of chalk / 백묵으로 칠판에 글을 쓰다 write letters with chalk on the blackboard

백문 百聞 ▶백문이 불여일견 (속담) Seeing is believing. ⇌ The proof of the pudding is in the eating.

백미 白米 polished [cleaned, faced, hulled] rice ▶백미에 뉘 섞이듯 (속담) be very rare

백미 白眉 the finest example (of); the best [pick] (of)
♦한국 단편소설 중의 백미 one of the best Korean short stories / 그의 작품 중의 백미 his masterpiece; one of his best works

백반 白斑 1〈흰점〉 a white spot 2 ⇨ 백납

백반 白飯 boiled [cooked] rice

백반 白礬 〔化〕 alum

백발 白髮 gray [(英) grey] hair; white [silvery] hair; snowy [snow-white, hoary] hair
♦백발의 white-haired; white-headed; hoary; with white hair / 백발이 섞인 grizzled / 백발이 되다 〈머리가 주어〉 turn gray; 〈사람이 주어〉 grow gray
▶나이가 들자 나의 머리는 급속히 백발이 되었다 My hair has rapidly turned gray with age.
▶그녀는 백발을 갈색으로 염색했다 She has her white hair dyed brown.
■—노인 a gray-headed[-haired] old man

백발백중 百發百中 hitting [making] the bull's-eye one [a] hundred percent
▶그는 백발백중의 명사수다 He never misses the mark.
▶그의 예언은 백발백중이다 He never fails in his prophecies.
▶저 의사의 진단은 백발백중이다 That doctor never makes a wrong diagnosis.
—백발백중하다 never miss the target
▶(총알이) 백발백중했다 Every shot told.

백방 百方 〈온갖 방법〉 all means; various ways; 〈여러 방면〉 every direction; all sides
♦백방으로 in every way; by all means; in all directions [quarters] / 백방으로 힘쓰다 make every effort; exert oneself to the utmost / 백방으로 사람을 물색하다 look all around [over] for a person
▶백방으로 손을 썼으나 허사였다 I tried every means possible but in vain.

백배 百拜 many times of bowing
♦백배 사례하다 bow one's thanks a hundred times; offer a thousand thanks / 백배 사죄하다 bow a hundred apologies; make a humble apology
—백배하다 bow a hundred times; bow many times

백배 百倍 one [a] hundred times; one [a] hundredfold
♦백배의 centuple; one [a] hundredfold
▶이 도시의 인구는 우리 도시의 백배다 The population of this city is a [one] hundred times as large as that of ours.
—백배하다 increase (a number) a hundredfold [a hundred times]; multiply (a number) by one hundred
♦5를 백배하다 increase 5 a hundred times; multiply 5 by 100
▶그 소식에 우리는 용기 백배했다 We perked up at the news.

백병전 白兵戰 close combat; hand-to-hand fighting; fighting at close quarters; fighting with swords and bayonets
♦백병전을 벌이다 fight hand to hand (with)

백부 伯父 an uncle (who is one's father's elder brother)

백부장 百夫長 〔로史〕 a centurion

백분 白粉 white powder; flour; 〈화장분〉 (face) powder ♦백분을 얼굴에 바르다 powder one's face; put powder on one's face

백분 百分 ♦ 백분의 percent; centesimal / 백분

의 1 one percent; one hundredth / 백분의 30 30 percent; thirty hundredths
―백분하다 divide (it) into a hundred parts ■―도표 a centesimal scale ―율[비] (a) percentage

백사 白沙 white sand ■―기(器) white earthenware ―장 a white sandy plain; a white (sandy) beach

백사 百事 all matters ⇨ 만사(萬事)

백삼 白蔘 white ginseng

백색 白色 1 〈색깔〉 white (color) ◆백색의 white; of white color; white-colored 2 〈우익〉 the white [right] wing ■―인종 the white race; Caucasians ―테러 a white terror

백서 白書 a white paper (on); a white book (on) ―경제― (publish, issue) an economic white paper

백선 白癬 〔醫〕 a ringworm (in the groin); 〔醫〕 the tinea; 〈두부의〉 favus

백설 白雪 (white) snow
◆백설로 덮인 산 a snow-capped mountain / 백설같은 snowy; snow-white; white as snow ◆산정은 백설로 하얗게 덮여 있었다 The top of the mountain was pure white with snow. ◆산정의 백설은 햇빛을 받아 빛나고 있었다 The snow on the summit was glistening in the sunshine.
▶그녀의 피부는 백설처럼 희다 Her skin is (as) white as snow.

백설탕 白雪糖 white [refined] sugar

백성 百姓 〈서민〉 the people; the populace; 〈국민〉 the nation ◆온 백성 all people; the entire people

백세 百世 one hundred generations; all ages

백세 百歲 〈백년〉 a hundred years; 〈백살〉 a hundred years of age

백수 百獸 all (kinds of) animals ◆백수의 왕 the king of beasts ▶사자는 백수의 왕이라고 일컬어진다 The lion is said to be the king of beasts.

백수건달 白手乾達 a penniless bum; a good-for-nothing

백숙 白熟 meat [fish] boiled in water ■영계― chicken boiled with rice

백스트로크 〈배영〉《swim with》a backstroke

백신 〔醫〕 vaccine

백씨 伯氏 your [his] elder brother

백악 白堊 chalk; chalkstone; 〈흰벽〉 a white wall ■―관 the White House ―기(紀) 〔地質〕 the Cretaceous (period) ―질 〈치아의〉 cement ―층 a chalk bed [layer] ―토 malm

백안시 白眼視 ―백안시하다 look coldly upon sb; have a prejudiced view (of); affect a detached irony
▶그녀는 언제나 나를 백안시한다 She always looks coldly upon me.
▶그의 행위는 동료 학자로부터 백안시되었다 His fellow scholars frowned on his behavior.

백야 白夜 nights with the midnight sun

백약 百藥 sundry medicines [remedies]; all sorts of medicines ▶백약 무효하다 All medicines prove useless.

백양 白羊 a white sheep ―자리 〔天〕 the Ram; Aries

백양 白楊 〔植〕 a (white) poplar; a white asp [aspen]

백업 backup ―백업하다 back up

백연 白鉛 white lead; ceruse; flake white

백열 白熱 1 〈높은 열〉 white heat; incandescence; white glow
◆백열화하다[되다] become white-hot; be [become] incandescent; glow white
2 〈최고조〉 the climax; enthusiasm
◆백열화된 토론[논쟁] a heated discussion [controversy] / 백열화하다[되다] grow [get] excited; 〈토론 등이〉 become heated
■―광 incandescent light ―등 an incandescent electric lamp [light]; a glow lamp ―전 hot fighting; a close contest [game]; a dead heat : 백열전을 벌이다 put on a blistering race [game]

백엽상 百葉箱 〔氣〕 an instrument screen [shelter]; a box housing for outdoor meteorological instruments

백옥 白玉 a white gem

백운 白雲 a white cloud

백운모 白雲母 〔鑛〕 white [common] mica; muscovite

백운석 白雲石 〔鑛〕 dolomite

백의 白衣 a white robe [dress]; 〈간호사 등의〉 a white overall; a white gown [coat]; 〔宗〕 an alb; 〈포의(布衣)〉 a commoner
◆백의를 입고 있다 be dressed in white / 백의 종군하다 serve in a war as a commoner
■―민족 the white-clad[-robed] race; the Korean people ―용사 a hero in white; a wounded soldier in a white robe ―천사 an angel in white; a ministering angel [nurse]; a white-clad[-robed] nurse

백인 白人 a white man; a Caucasian; (俗) a white ◆백인에 의한 지배 white domination / 백인으로 통하다 pass off as [for] white
―여자 a European woman [lady]; a white woman ―종 the white race; the whites

백일 白日 〈백주〉 broad daylight; the daytime; 〈태양〉 the bright sun [sunshine]
◆백일하에 드러나다 be exposed to the light of day [to the public eye]/ 청천 백일의 몸이 되다 be cleared from [of] the charge
▶모든 것이 백일하에 드러날 것이다 Everything will be brought to light [exposed to the public eye].
■―몽 a daydream; a waking dream; daydreaming ―장 a composition [literary] contest

백일 百日 a [one] hundred days; the hundredth day of one's child
■―기도 prayer for a hundred days ―잔치 a party given to a hundred-day-old baby ―천하 a hundred-day reign; a very brief reign ―해 whooping cough; 〔醫〕 pertussis

백일초 百日草 〔植〕 a garden zinnia

백일홍 百日紅 〔植〕 a crape [crepe] myrtle; an Indian lilac

백작 伯爵 a count; (英) an earl ―부인 a countess

백장 〈도살자〉 a butcher; (美口) a meatman;

〈고리장이〉 a wicker worker; 〈최하층민〉 a member of the lowest class
■—개 a dogcatcher; a dog killer
백장이 버덩잎을 물고 죽는다 (속담) The leopard cannot change its spots.
백전노장 百戰老將 a veteran; an old-timer ▶ 그는 백전노장이다 He is an old veteran.
백전백승 百戰百勝 an ever-victorious record; invincibility
◆ 백전백승의 군대 an invincible army / 백전백승의 ever-victorious; unbeaten; invincible
—백전백승하다 win every battle (that is fought); be ever-victorious
▶ 아군은 백전백승했다 Our army was unbeaten [victorious in every battle].
백절불굴 百折不屈 ◆ 백절불굴의 젊은이 an unyielding [indomitable] youth / 백절불굴의 unyielding; indefatigable; indomitable
백점 百點 one [a] hundred points; 〈만점〉a perfect score; a full mark; full marks
◆ 백점 만점으로 성적을 매기다 grade 《the students' achievement》on a scale [the basis] of one hundred (points)/ 백점 만점에서 80점을 받다 obtain 80 points out of a possible 100
▶ 나는 수학시험에서 백점을 받았다 I got 100 points on the math test.
▶ 그것은 백점 만점이다 It's quite perfect.
백정 白丁 a butcher ⇨ 백장
백조 白鳥 〈고니〉a swan; a cob (swan) (수컷); a pen (암컷); a cygnet (새끼); 〈해오라기〉a white heron ◆ 백조의 노래 a swan song
—자리 〔天〕 the Swan; Cygnus
백주 白晝 broad [full] daylight; the daytime
◆ 백주에 in broad [open] daylight; in [during] the daytime / 백주에 당당히 openly [unshamedly] in broad daylight
백중 伯仲 1 〈맏형과 둘째 형〉 one's eldest and second eldest brothers
2 〈실력 등이〉 being equal; being even (with)
—백중하다 match (each other); be equal (to); be even (with); be on a par (with); be evenly matched; be equally balanced
▶ 두 사람은 능력 면에서 백중했다 The two were nearly equal in their ability.
▶ 양팀의 실력은 백중했다 The opposing teams were equally matched in skill. ≒ The two teams were equally balanced.
■—숙계(叔季) the first, second, third, and fourth of brothers
백지 白紙 1 〈흰 종이〉 white paper
◆ 얼굴이 백지장 같다 look pale; look as white as a sheet
2 〈기입하지 않은〉 a blank sheet of paper
◆ 백지의 blank / 백지 답안을 내다 give [hand] in a blank paper
▶ 그의 답안지는 완전 백지였다 His examination paper was completely blank.
3 〈백지 상태〉 a clean state
◆ 백지로 돌리다 call off; nullify; cancel; make a fresh start
▶ 모두 백지로 돌리고 다시 합시다 Let's begin all over again [make a fresh start, start afresh].
■—위임장 a blank power of attorney —투표

(cast) a blank vote
백지도 白地圖 a blank [an outline] map
백지장도 맞들면 낫다 (속담) Many hands make light [quick, slight] work. ≒ Two heads are better than one. ≒ Four eyes see more than two.
백차 白車 a (police) patrol car; a squad [cruise, prowl] car; (美口) a cruiser
백척간두 百尺竿頭 the last [critical] extremity; the eleventh hour ◆ 백척간두에 서다 be driven [brought] to bay; be driven [reduced] to the last extremity
백철광 白鐵鑛 〔鑛〕 marcasite; white iron pyrites
백청 白淸 white honey of fine quality
백출하다 百出— arise in great numbers
▶ 그 문제로 의론이 백출했다 The matter became the subject of heated discussion.
백치 白痴 〈상태〉 idiocy; imbecility; 〈사람〉 an idiot; an imbecile ◆ 백치의 [같은] idiotic
▶ 그녀는 예쁘지만 백치다 She is a beautiful fool. ≒ She is only a (pretty) doll.
백탄 白炭 〈참숯〉 hard charcoal; 〈석탄의 일종〉 white coal
백탕 白湯 (plain) hot water
백태 白苔 〔醫〕〈혀의〉the fur [coat] 《on the tongue》; 〈눈의〉a cloudy film 《on the lens of the eye》 ▶ 내 혀에 백태가 끼었다 My tongue is furred [coated].
백태 百態 various phases
▶ 이 만화는 월급쟁이들의 백태를 묘사하고 있다 These comic strips depict white-collar workers in various situations.
■—인생— various phases of life
백토 白土 white earth; China clay
백통 白— nickel; white brass; cupronickel
■—전 a nickel (coin)
백팔십도 百八十度 one hundred and eighty degrees; a full half circle ◆ 백팔십도 전환하다 make a complete about-face [turnabout]; reverse one's course [opinion] (completely)
백퍼센트 百— a [one] hundred percent
◆ 효과м 백퍼센트다 be 100 percent efficacious; be most effective
◆ 그것은 백퍼센트 틀림없다 It is a hundred percent right.
▶ 백퍼센트 자신이 있다 I am one hundred percent sure of myself.
▶ 출석률은 백퍼센트였다 The attendance was one hundred percent.
백포도주 白葡萄酒 white wine; 〈라인산의〉 Rhine wine; hock; 〈스페인산〉 sherry
백합 百合 〔植〕 a lily ■—뿌리 a lily bulb —화 [꽃] a lily flower
백해 百害 all (sorts of) evils
▶ 백해 무익하다 It does more harm than good. ≒ It produces all evil and no good.
백핸드 〔테니스〕 a backhand (drive)
◆ 백핸드로 on backhand
백혈구 白血球 a white (blood) corpuscle; a leukocyte ◆ 백혈구의 leukocytic
■—감소증 leukopenia —수 leukocyte count —증가증 leukocytosis
백혈병 白血病 〔醫〕 leuk(a)emia; leukosis

백형 伯兄 one's eldest [(美) oldest] brother
백호주의 白濠主義 the "White Australia" principle
백화 百花 all sorts [varieties] of flowers
▶그곳은 지금 백화가 만발해 있다 The place is now alive [bright] with all sorts of flowers. ■—제방 운동 the "Hundred Flowers" Campaign
백화 白話 colloquial [spoken] Chinese ■—문학 literature in colloquial Chinese
백화점 百貨店 (美) a department store; (英) the stores
백화현상 白化現象 〔植〕 chlorosis; 〔動〕 albinism
밴 〈부가 가치 통신망〉 VAN; the value-added network
밴드¹ 〈악대〉 a (musical) band ■—재즈— a jazz band ■—마스터 a bandmaster
밴드² 〈띠〉 the band; a strap;〈혁대〉 a (leather) belt ♦ 밴드를 죄다〔늦추다〕 tighten [loosen] one's belt
밴들거리다 idle one's time away ⇨ 빈둥거리다
밴앨런대 —帶 the Van Allen (radiation) belt
밴조 〈악기〉 a banjo 《pl. ~(e)s》 ■—연주자 a banjoist
밴쿠버 〈캐나다의 항구도시〉 Vancouver
밴텀급 —級 〔拳〕 the bantamweight class ■—선수 a bantamweight
밸러스트 〔海〕〈바닥짐〉 ballast;〈자갈〉 gravel
밸런스 balance ⇨ 균형
♦ 밸런스가 잡힌〔잡히지 않은〕 well-[ill-]balanced / 한 발로 밸런스를 잡다 balance oneself on one leg
▶그 아이는 담 위에서 몸의 밸런스를 잡았다〔잃었다〕 The child kept [lost] his balance on the wall. ■—시트 〈대차 대조표〉 a balance sheet
밸류 value ♦ 네임 밸류가 있는 작가 a writer of established reputation; a name [well-known] writer
밸브 a valve ■—장치 valve gear ■—콕 a valve cock
뱀 a snake;〈구렁이〉 a serpent
♦ 뱀 껍질 (a) snakeskin / 뱀의 허물 the slough [cast skin] of a snake / 뱀 같은 serpentine; snakelike; snaky / 뱀처럼 성질이 독하다 be as spiteful as a viper / 뱀에 물려 죽다 die from a snake bite; die of the bite of a snake
■—자리 〔天〕 the Serpent
뱀딸기 〔植〕 an Indian strawberry
뱀밥 〔植〕 a field horsetail
뱀뱀이 〈예의〉 courtesy; etiquette; (good) manners;〈교양〉 culture; cultivation
♦ 뱀뱀이가 좋은〔나쁜〕 well-[ill-]cultivated; well-[ill-]mannered; well-[ill-]bred
▶그는 뱀뱀이가 있다 He has good manners.
뱀잠자리 〔昆〕 a dobsonfly
뱀장어 —長魚 〔魚〕 an eel
뱁새 〔鳥〕 a Korean crow-tit ■—눈이 a person with small, narrow eyes
뱁새가 황새를 따라가면 다리가 찢어진다 (속담) People ruin themselves by trying to ape their betters. ⇒ Tailor your ambitions to the measure of your abilities.
뱃고동 a boat whistle; a gong
뱃길 a waterway;〈항로〉 a sea route; a seaway;〈항구 등의〉 a fairway
♦ 1주일 걸리는 뱃길 a week's passage [crossing] / 뱃길로 가다 go by ship [water]
뱃노래 a sailor's [boatman's] song; a boat [boating] song; a chant(e)y ♦ 뱃노래를 부르다 sing a boating song
뱃놀이 a boating (excursion); (美) a boat ride; sailing;〈요트의〉 yachting
—뱃놀이하다 enjoy boating [a boat ride]
♦ 호수에서 뱃놀이하다 enjoy boating on a lake / 뱃놀이하러 가다 go boating [rowing, sailing]; (美) go for a boat ride
뱃대끈 1 〈여자의〉 a woman's bloomer sash **2** 〈마소의〉 a bellyband; a (saddle) girth; a cinch
뱃머리 〈이물〉 the bow(s); the prow; the head (of a ship) ♦ 뱃머리 쪽으로 fore; forward / 뱃머리를 돌리다 veer (a ship) / 뱃머리부터 가라앉다 sink bow first; sink by the head
뱃멀미 (qualms of) seasickness; nausea
—뱃멀미하다 get [become] seasick
♦ 뱃멀미하는 사람 a bad [poor] sailor / 뱃멀미하지 않는 사람 a good sailor
▶나는 뱃멀미를 잘한다〔하지 않는다〕 I easily get [never get] seasick.
뱃밥 oakum; caulking ♦ 뱃밥으로 메우다 caulk (a seam, a boat); stop up (seams) with oakum
뱃사공 —沙工 a boatman;〈나룻배의〉 a ferryman ⇨ 사공
뱃사람 a sailor; a crewman; a mariner; a seaman ♦ 노련한 뱃사람 an old sailor [salt] / 뱃사람의 생활 a sailor's life; seafaring life / 뱃사람이 되다 become a sailor; go to sea / 뱃사람의 노릇을 하다 take to the sea (as a career); follow the sea
뱃삯 〈승선료〉 passage (fare); boat fare;〈도선료〉 ferryboat charge; ferriage;〈화물 운임〉 freight (rates) ▶제주도까지는 뱃삯이 얼마입니까? What is the fare to Cheju-do?
뱃살 the skin [flesh] of the belly [abdomen]; abdominal muscle ♦ 뱃살을 잡다 be convulsed with laughter; split one's sides
뱃속 1 〈배의 속〉 (the inside of) the stomach
♦ 뱃속이 비다 have an empty stomach / 뱃속이 좋지 않다 one's bowels are out of order;〈위가〉 have (a) stomach trouble
2 〈마음속〉 one's heart; one's mind;〈의도〉 one's intention
♦ 뱃속이 검은 evil-hearted; wicked; crafty; scheming / 뱃속을 알 수 없다 cannot read sb's thoughts [mind] / 뱃속을 떠보다 sound sb
뱃심 〈버티는 힘〉 push;〈배짱〉 nerve; pluck; mettle; brazen effrontery; impudence
♦ 뱃심(이) 좋은 사람 a man of push and go / 뱃심 좋게 밀고 나아가다 push on to the front / 뱃심(이) 좋다 have a lot of nerve; be brazenfaced; be cheeky
뱃일 work on board (a ship) —뱃일하다 work on board
뱃전 the side of a boat [ship]; boat sides; the

gunwale [gʌnl]; the gunnel
♦ 뱃전에서 몸을 내밀다 lean over the side of a boat / 뱃전에서 떨어지다 fall overboard
► 뱃전이 기울어진다 The boat tips [lists] to one side.
뱃짐 a (ship's) cargo; a freight; a freightage; a lading; load ♦ 뱃짐을 싣다 load a ship (with); lade (a ship) with cargo / 뱃짐을 부리다 discharge cargo; unload a ship
뱅그르르 《turn》 around smoothly ⇨ 빙그르르
뱅글뱅글 round and round ⇨ 빙글빙글
뱅어 —魚 〔魚〕 a whitebait
　■ —젓 salted whitebait —포 dried slices of seasoned whitebait
-뱅이 a person; a man; a fellow ♦ 가난뱅이 a poor man; a pauper / 게으름뱅이 a lazy fellow; a sluggard / 비렁뱅이 a beggar / 주정뱅이 a drunkard; a boozer
뱅충맞다 dull; clumsy; 〈어리석다〉 stupid; half-witted; slow-witted
뱅충(맞)이 a fool; a clumsy fellow; 〈바보〉 a simpleton; a dunce; a dimwit
뱉다 spit [spew] 《at》; throw up; belch out; 〈기침하여〉 cough up [out]; (비유) give up 〈stolen goods〉; surrender; disgorge
♦ 침을 뱉다 spit 《on》; expectorate / 길에 침을 뱉다 spit on the road / 손바닥에 침을 뱉다 spit on one's palms; wet one's hand with saliva [spit] / 가래를 뱉다 cough out [bring up] phlegm / (내)뱉듯이 말하다 snap [rap] out
► 그는 껌을 바닥에 뱉었다 He spat chewing-gum on the floor.
► 굴뚝이 검은 연기를 뱉어내고 있었다 The chimney was belching (out) black smoke.
► (바닥에) 침을 뱉지 마시오 (게시) No spitting (on the floor).
► 그는 착복한 돈을 뱉어 놓았다 He surrendered the embezzled money.
반죽거리다 act flippantly
버그러지다 split apart; come loose; separate; cleave; widen; be warped
버글거리다 1 〈물이 끓다〉 boil; seethe; simmer
► 가마솥의 물이 버글거리고 있다 The cauldron is boiling hard.
2 〈거품이 일다〉 bubble up; rise in bubbles
► 비누 거품이 버글거린다 Suds are bubbling up.
► 강물이 세제 때문에 버글거리고 있었다 The water of the river was foamy on account of detergents.
3 〈많이 모여〉 teem; swarm; squirm [wriggle about] in swarm
버글버글 〈끓어서〉 boiling (briskly [furiously]); 〈거품이〉 bubbling; 〈많이 모여서〉 in swarms; in crowds
► 화분 밑에는 벌레들이 버글버글했다 Under the flowerpots a lot of worms were wriggling.
버금 the second (in order); the next
♦ 뉴욕에 버금 가는 대도시 the greatest city next [second only] to New York / 버금가다 be second to; be in the second place
버너 a burner ■ 가스[석유]— a gas [an oil] burner
버둥거리다 (kick and) struggle; wriggle; flutter; flounder
♦ 손발을 버둥거리며 fluttering one's hands and feet
► 그는 물에 빠지지 않으려고 팔다리를 버둥거렸다 He floundered in the water with arms and legs to keep himself afloat.
► 아기는 어머니의 품에서 벗어나려고 버둥거렸다 The baby struggled to get free from its mother.
버둥버둥 struggling; floundering
버드나무 a willow ♦ 휘늘어진 버드나무 가지 long drooping branches of a willow tree
버들 〔植〕 a willow; an osier ■ —개지 a pussy; a cattail; a catkin —고리 a wicker [an osier] trunk —눈 a willow bud
버라이어티 variety ■ —쇼 a variety show; (美) a vaudeville; (英) a variety
버럭 suddenly; abruptly; on a sudden
♦ 버럭 소리를 지르다 cry [shout] suddenly; burst out / 버럭 화를 내다 be roused to anger; get [be] furious
버럭¹ 〈광산의〉 muck; gob; debris ♦ 감돌과 버럭 ore and muck ■ —t 더미 a dump (of muck)
버럭² 〈천벌〉 Heaven's vengeance; the wrath of Heaven; divine punishment ♦ 버럭 입다 be punished by Heaven; incur the wrath of Heaven
버르르 seething ⇨ 바르르
버르적거리다 struggle; writhe; wriggle; flounder ♦ 배가 아파서 몸을 버르적거리다 writhe in agony with a stomachache
버르적버르적 struggling; writhing; wriggling; floundering
버르집다 1 〈벌려서 펴다〉 open up; spread
2 〈일을 크게 만들다〉 make more serious [troublesome]; aggravate ♦ 일을 버르집어 놓다 make too much of the matter
3 〈들추어내다〉 expose; disclose [let out] 《a secret》; lay bare
버름하다 loosely fitted; slightly [partly] open
버릇 1 〈습관〉 a (personal) habit; one's way; a habitual practice; 〈특징〉 a peculiarity; 〈성벽〉 a propensity
♦ 고질적인 버릇 an inveterate [a deeply ingrained] habit / 말 버릇 one's peculiar way of speaking; one's peculiarity in speech / 아침 일찍 일어나는 버릇 the habit of early rising 〈버릇이[은]〉 버릇이 고쳐지다 be cured of a habit; get out of a habit / 버릇이 되다 grow into a habit with one; 〈선례가 되다〉 become a precedent / 버릇이 생기다 get [fall] into a habit 《of》; develop [form, acquire, contract] a habit 《of》 / …하는 버릇이 있다 have [be in] the habit of 《doing》
► 일단 버릇이 붙으면 여간해서 고쳐지지 않는다 Once you get a habit, it will stay with you [it is difficult to shake it off].
► 버릇은 천성이 된다 Custom is another nature.
► 나쁜 버릇은 붙기는 쉬워도 떼기는 어렵다 Bad habits are easy to get [tumble] into and hard to get rid of.
► 자기 전에 책을 읽는 버릇이 있다 It is a habit with me to read some books before

버릇없다

falling asleep.
▶ 또 그의 투덜대는 버릇이 시작되었다 He's started on his usual grumbling again.
▶ 내버려둬, 그의 버릇이 그러니 Never mind. It's just his way.
〈버릇을〉 버릇을 고치다 〈남의〉 cure sb of a habit; get sb out of a habit; 〈자기의〉 get rid [break oneself] of a habit; overcome a habit / 버릇을 들이다 form [cultivate] a habit (of); be [get] accustomed [used] to 《sth, doing》
♦ 식사 전에 손을 씻는 버릇을 들여라 You must make a habit of washing your hands before each meal.
▶ 이 버릇을 고치는 데 3개월 걸렸다 It took me three months to break (myself of) the habits.
▶ 그녀는 아기의 손가락 빠는 버릇을 고쳐놓았다 She cured the child of (the habit of) sucking his fingers.
2 〈예의〉 (good) manners; etiquette; 〈행실〉 behavior
♦ 버릇이 나쁘다 be ill-mannered [ill-behaved]; be of bad behavior / 버릇이 없어지다 be spoilt / 버릇을 가르치다 teach how to behave; give sb lessons in manners [etiquette]; teach sb manners
▶ 이 아이들은 버릇이 없다 These children have no manners.
▶ 그는 부모가 너무 귀여워해서 버릇이 없어졌다 He is spoilt by his fond parents.

버릇없다 ill-mannered; ill-behaved; ill-bred; impertinent; rude
♦ 버릇없는 아이 a spoilt child; an ill-bred boy / 버릇없이 말을 하다 say a rude thing / 버릇없이 굴다 behave rudely
▶ 그건 버릇없는 짓이다 It is bad manners to do such a thing.

버릇하다 be [get, grow] accustomed [used] to; be experienced in
♦ 내가 먹어 버릇하지 않은 음식 what I've never tried [eaten] before / 써 버릇하다 be accustomed to use [to the use of] sth / 밤 아홉시에 자 버릇하다 be in the habit of going to bed at nine
▶ 나는 가 버릇한 길로 갔겠다 I'll take this familiar road.

버릇다 scratch; dig out; 〈헤뜨리다〉 scatter

버리다¹ **1** 〈내던지다〉 throw [fling, cast] away; get rid of; discard; dump
♦ 쓰레기를 버리다 dump refuse / 쓸 만큼 쓰고 버리다 get all the use out of sth and then discard it / 한 번 쓰고 버리다 use sth only once and then throw it away / 헌 신짝처럼 버리다 throw away [cast aside] sth like an old shoe [hat]
▶ 그것은 돈을 버리는 것이나 다름없다 It is a mere waste of money.
▶ 담배 꽁초를 길에 버리지 마라 Don't throw cigarette butts out on the street. ⇒ Don't litter (up) the street with cigarette butts.
▶ 쓰레기를 버리지 마시오 《게시》 No litter please. ⇒ No dumping here.
2 〈돌보지 않다〉 abandon; leave; desert; discard; forsake; 〈포기하다〉 give up

♦ 대학 진학의 꿈을 버리다 give up [abandon] the hope of going to [for entering] a university / 낡은 생각을 버리다 dismiss [scrap] old ideas / …할 생각을 버리다 give up the idea of (doing) / 신앙을 버리다 abjure [renounce] one's faith / 처자를 버리다 desert one's wife and children [one's family] / 편견을 버리다 get rid of one's prejudice / 희망을 버리다 give up [relinquish] (all) hope (of)
▶ 많은 젊은이가 나라를 위해 목숨을 버렸다 Many young men laid down their lives for their country.
▶ 그는 속세를 버리고 은둔 생활을 했다 He renounced the world and lived in seclusion.
▶ 그녀는 자기 목숨을 버려 자식을 구했다 She saved her child at the price [cost] of her own life.
3 〈못쓰게 만들다〉 spoil; mar; ruin; impair; 〈더럽히다〉 soil; stain
♦ 건강을 버리다 injure [ruin, destroy] one's health; be broken [affected] in health / 아이를 버리다 spoil a child / 옷을 버리다 soil one's clothes
▶ 과음하면 몸을 버린다 Too much drinking is bad for [harmful to] your health.
▶ 매를 아끼면 아이를 버린다 《속담》 Spare the rod, and spoil the child.
▶ 눈에 거슬리는 많은 건물들이 거리의 미관을 버려놓았다 A lot of eyesore buildings soiled [marred] the beauty of the streets.
4 〈생략하다〉 omit; discard
♦ 소숫점 두 자리 이하를 버리다 omit the figures below the second place of decimals / 우수리를 버리다 ignore [discard, cut off] fractions

버리다² 〈끝내다〉 finish; end; (美) get [be] through (with); do completely
♦ 다 마셔 버리다 drink up [off]; drink to the dregs / 다 먹어 버리다 eat up (the food) / 다 써 버리다 be used up; be exhausted; spend out / 잊어 버리다 completely forget about (a matter) / 타 버리다 be burnt to ashes
▶ 돈을 다 써버렸다 I have spent all my money.
▶ 그녀는 가 버렸다 She has gone away.
▶ 나는 그 책을 3시간만에 읽어 버렸다 I read through the book in three hours.
▶ 이곳의 석탄은 바닥이 나 버렸다 The coal in this area has been exhausted.

버림받다 be abandoned; be deserted; be left behind; 〈망각되다〉 be forgotten
▶ 그는 세상에서 버림받았다 He died from the memory of the public.
▶ 그녀는 남편에게서 버림받았다 She was deserted [left] by her husband.
▶ 그는 친구들한테 완전히 버림받았다 He was completely ignored [disregarded] by his friends.

버림치 waste articles; useless stuff; garbage; refuse; junk; trash

버마재비 〖昆〗 a (praying) mantis ⇨ 사마귀²

버몬트 〈미국의 주〉 Vermont (略 Verm.)

버무리다 mix together [up] ♦ 나물을 양념에 버무리다 mix the potherbs with dressings

[seasonings]/ 모래와 시멘트를 버무리다 mix sand and [with] cement
버무리떡 rice cake with beans
버물리다 〈버무려지다〉 be mixed up; be admixed; 〈버무리게 하다〉 have sb mix [dress]
버뮤다 〈섬 이름〉 Bermuda
버새 〔動〕 a hinny
버석거리다 rustle ⇨ 바삭거리다
버석버석 rustlingly ⇨ 바삭바삭
버선 (Korean) socks
♦버선 한 켤레 a pair of socks / 버선을 신다 [벗다] put on [take off] one's socks
■겹[홑]— lined [unlined] socks 솜— wadded [padded] socks
—목 the ankle of a sock —본 a (paper) pattern for socks —볼 〈넓이〉 the width [breadth] of a sock; 〈헝겊 조각〉 a piece of cloth [a patch] for mending socks
버선발 feet in socks ♦〈반가워서〉 버선발로 뛰어나가 손님을 맞다 dash [rush] out of the room (in one's socks) to greet [welcome] a visitor
버섯 a mushroom; a fungus (pl. -gi)
♦버섯을 따다 gather [pick (up)] mushrooms / 버섯 따러 가다 go mushroom gathering; (美) go (out) mushrooming
■독— a toadstool; a poisonous mushroom —구름 〈핵폭발시의〉 a mushroom cloud —재배자 a mushroom grower
버성기다 1〈틈이 있다〉 loose; loose-fitting; loosely fitted; creviced 2〈두 사람 사이가〉 awkward; estranged; unharmonious; not getting along well with
버스 a bus (pl. ~es, (美) busses)
▶여기는 버스편이 좋다 There's a good bus service here. ⇌ This place is convenient for taking bus.
〈버스가[는]〉 자, 버스가 왔다 Here's the bus. ⇌ Here comes our bus.
▶ 〔會話〕「이 버스는 어디로 갑니까?」「서울역이오」 "Where is this bus for?" "It's for Seoul Station."
▶ 〔會話〕「다음 버스는 언제 옵니까?」「15분쯤 후에요」 "How soon will the next bus be here?" "It'll be along in about fifteen minutes."
▶이 버스는 목동 갑니까? Does this bus go to Mok-dong? ⇌ (口) Is this the Mok-dong bus?
〈버스를〉 버스를 놓치다 miss [be late for] one's bus / 버스를 타다[내리다] get on [off] a bus (at) / 버스를 잘못 타다 take [be on] the wrong bus / 9시 30분 버스를 잡아타다 catch [be in time for, (口) make] the 9:30 bus
〈버스로〉 버스로 학교에 가다 go to school by [on a] bus
▶여기서 그 마을까지는 버스로 두 시간 걸립니다 It takes two hours to go to the town from here by bus. ⇌ It is a two-hour bus ride from here to the town.
■공항— an airport limousine 관광— a sightseeing [tour] bus; (美俗) a rubbernecker bus 마이크로— a microbus 미니— a minibus 시내— a city bus 이층— (英) a double-decker 장거리— a long-distance bus 통근— a commuter [commuting] bus 통학[스쿨]— a school bus ■—노선 a bus route [line] —사고 a bus accident —요금 a bus fare —정류장 a bus stop; 〈장거리버스의〉 a coach station —카드 a bus card —터미널 a bus terminal —토큰 a (bus) token
버스러지다 1〈표면이〉 come [fall] off; be worn off; peel [scale] off
▶래커 칠이 버스러지고 말았다 The lacquer coating has worn away.
▶벽이 버스러지고 있다 The wall is peeling off.
2〈벗나가다〉 miss; be not up to…; unsatisfactory
▶그의 일은 우리 기대에 버스러진다 His work didn't come up to [fall short of] our expectations.
버스럭 with a rustle ⇨ 바스락
버스트 the bust
▶그녀는 버스트가 큰[작은] 편이다 She has a rather large [small] bust.
▶그녀의 버스트는 35인치다 Her bust measures 35 inches.
버저 a buzzer
▶버저가 울리고 있다 There goes the buzzer.
▶누가 버저를 눌렀지? Who sounded [rang, pushed, pressed] the buzzer?
버젓하다 respectable; decent; honorable
♦버젓한 신사 a real gentleman / 버젓한 집안 a respectable [respected] family / 버젓한 태도 a stately manner
▶이 그림은 버젓한 예술품이다 This painting is a work of art in its own right.
버정이다 walk idly back and forth [up and down]; stroll [saunter] aimlessly [at a leisurely pace]
버지니아 〈미국의 주〉 Virginia (略 Va.)
버짐 ringworm; favus; tinea
■마른— psoriasis 진— pityriasis
버찌 a cherry; 〈두개가 맞붙은 송이〉 a cherry bob —술 kirsch(wasser); cherry wine —씨 a cherrystone
버캐 scum; an incrustation; (a) crust
■소금[오줌]— salt [urine] incrustations
버클 (a belt) buckle ♦혁대의 버클을 끄르다 unbuckle [unfasten the buckle of] one's belt
버킹엄궁전 —宮殿 〈런던의〉 the Buckingham Palace
버터 butter
♦버터를 바른 빵 bread and butter / 빵에 버터를 바르다 butter the bread; spread butter on bread / 쇠고기 저민 것을 버터에 튀기다 fry slices of beef in butter
■땅콩— peanut butter ■—나이프 a butter knife [spreader]
버터플라이 〈접영〉 the butterfly (stroke)
♦버터플라이로 헤엄치다 swim the butterfly (stroke)
버튼 a button ⇨ 단추
버티다 1〈참고 배기다〉 bear up 《well》; endure; stand out [firm, fast]; hold out [firm]; 〈고집하다〉 persist in; insist on; 〈저항하다〉 resist; oppose

♦끝까지 버티다 stand it out; hold out to the last; 《口》 stick it out / 버티어 나가다 endure through; persevere / 버티지 못하다 cannot hold out any longer
▶그들은 증원 부대가 올 때까지 버텼다 They held out [hung on] until reinforcements arrived.
▶그는 거짓말을 안했다고 버텼다 He insisted that he had not lied.
▶포기하지 말고 끝까지 버텨라 Don't give up, but stick to it to the last! ⇒ 《口》 Hang in there!
▶승리는 끝까지 버티는 자의 것이다 Victory is to him who fights the longest.
2 〈괴다〉 prop (up); support; hold up; bolster up
♦기둥으로 벽을 버티다 support a wall with a post / 다리를 버티고 서다 brace one's legs; stand firm
▶두 개의 까치발이 선반을 버티고 있다 Two brackets support the shelf.
▶입구에 사복 경찰들이 버티고 서 있어서 나는 들어가지 못했다 I could not get in because plainclothesmen were watching the door.

버팀목 —木 a prop [support]; a strut; a stay
♦버팀목으로 받치다 prop (up) 《a wall》; support 《with a post》; stick
▶이 가지에는 버팀목이 필요합니다 This branch needs a support.

버팅 〈拳〉 a butt; butting
벅벅 with a scratching ⇨ 박박[1,2]
벅차다 **1** 〈힘에 겹다〉 too much for one; beyond one's power [capacity]; above one's ability
♦벅찬 일 work beyond [that surpasses] one's power; a stiff [formidable] task
▶이것은 내게 벅차다 This is more than I can handle.
▶그건 나 혼자서는 벅차다 I cannot manage it alone.
▶그 일은 내게 너무 벅차다 The job is too hard [much] for me.
2 〈넘치다〉 full; overflowing
♦나는 기쁨으로 가슴이 벅찼다 My heart throbbed [was overflowing] with joy.
▶가슴이 벅차 그녀는 울 뻔했다 She was so touched that she was almost crying.
▶나는 가슴이 벅차서 말도 나오지 않았다 My heart was too full for words. ⇒ Words stuck in my heart with emotion.

번 番 **1** 〈갈마들기〉 (a) shift; (a) change
♦번(을) 갈다 relieve sb; alternate 《with another》
2 〈당번〉 duty; one's turn
♦든[난]번 on [off] duty
3 〈횟수〉 a time
♦한 번 once / 두 번 twice / 세 번 three times / 한두 번 once or twice / 두세 번 two or three times / 몇 번이고 many times; time [again] and again; many a time; so many times
▶나는 미국에 한 번도 가보지 못했다 I've never been to America.
▶그런 짓은 두 번 다시 하지 않겠다 I will never do that again.

4 〈번호〉 a number
♦1번[2번] number one [two]; No. 1 [2]
▶몇 번입니까? What number, please? ⇒ What number are you calling?
▶1번 문제부터 시작하자 Let's begin [start] with question (number) one [the first question]!
▶열차가 2번 플랫폼에 도착합니다 The train will arrive at platform [《美》 Track] (No.) 2.
▶3번 창구로 가십시오 〈은행 등에서〉 Please go to wicket No. 3.
5 〈때·경우〉 time; occasion
♦지난 번 last time; the other day / 이번에는 this time; on this occasion

번가루 flour thickener; extra flour in kneading dough properly

번각 飜刻 reprinting; 〈복제〉 reproduction
—번각하다 reprint ■—물[본] a reprint —판 a reprinted edition

번갈아 番— by turns; in turn; alternately; in rotation 《with》 ♦번갈아 근무하다 be on duty in turn [by turns]
▶그들은 번갈아 일한다 They work in shifts.
▶그들은 번갈아 차를 운전했다 They drove the car by taking turns. ⇒ They took turns (at) driving the car.

번개 (a flash [streak] of) lightning
♦번개같은 lightning / 번개처럼 like (a flash of) lightning; in a flash; at [with] lightning speed
▶번개가 쳤다 There was a flash of lightning.
▶그것은 번개처럼 빠르다 It goes as fast [quickly] as lightning.

번개가 잦으면 천둥을 한다 〈속담〉 Coming events cast their shadows before.

번갯불 a bolt; a flash [streak] of lightning
번갯불에 솜 구워 먹겠다 〈속담〉 tell all sorts of lies; lie right and left
번갯불에 콩 볶아 먹겠다 〈속담〉 be quick [nimble] in action

번거롭다 **1** 〈복잡하다〉 complicated; complex; intricate; 〈어수선하다〉 confused; entangled
♦도시의 번거로운 생활 the complex life of a city; the wear and tear of city life
▶이들 규정은 번거로워서 알기 어렵다 These bylaws are too complicated to understand.
2 〈귀찮다〉 troublesome; 〈성가시다〉 annoying; cumbersome
♦번거로운 일 a troublesome [bothersome] task / 법률상의 번거로운 절차 the cumbersome processes of the law
▶번거로우시겠지만 이것 좀 봐 주세요 I'm sorry to trouble [bother] you, but could you have a look at this?

번견 番犬 a watchdog; a house dog
번뇌 煩惱 anguish; agony; worries; 【佛教】 earthly [worldly] desires [passions]; carnal desires
♦번뇌를 씻다 rarefy one's earthly desires
▶인생에는 많은 번뇌가 따른다 Life is full of troubles [worries].
—번뇌하다 agonize oneself; be in anguish; be harassed by passions

번답하다 反畓— convert a dry field into a

paddy; cultivate land for the growing of rice
번데기 〔昆〕 a pupa 《*pl.* ~s, -pae》; a chrysalis 《*pl.* ~es, -lides》
♦ 번데기가 되다 become a pupa; pupate
―시기[상태] the pupal stage
번둥거리다 idle *one's* time away
번드르르 smoothly ⇨ 반드르르
번득이다 flash; fulgurate; glitter; 〈재치 등이〉 sparkle
▶ 빛이 번득이더니 다시 어둠이 우리를 감쌌다 After a flash of light, there was again darkness all around us.
▶ 그 여자의 이야기에는 재치가 번득였다 Her conversation was brilliant. ⇌ Her words revealed her brilliant mind.
번들거리다 get glossy ⇨ 반들거리다
번들번들 glossily ⇨ 반들반들
번듯하다 straight ⇨ 반듯하다
번롱하다 飜弄 trifle [play, sport, toy] 《with》; make fun [a fool] of; make sport of; play fast and loose 《with》; 〈파도가〉 toss about 《a ship》
▶ 배는 풍파에 번롱되었다 The boat was tossed about by the wind and waves.
▶ 그 여자의 마음을 번롱하지 마라 Don't trifle with the woman's feelings.
번망 煩忙 〈바쁨〉 pressure of business [work]
―번망하다 busy; 《be》 pressed [occupied] with business
번문욕례 繁文縟禮 red tape; red-tapism; officialism
♦ 번문욕례의 red-tape
번민 煩悶 anguish; (mental) agony; (a) worry; (an) affliction
♦ 번민을 잊으려고 술을 마시다 drown *one's* agony in drink
▶ 그는 나에게 자기 일에 대한 번민을 털어놓았다 He confided his anxiety about his job to me.
―번민하다 be in agony [anguish]; be agonized; be worried; worry [fret] *oneself* 《about》
▶ 그는 번민하던 끝에 병이 났다 He worried himself into illness.
▶ 그녀는 양심의 가책에 번민하고 있다 She is tormented by a guilty conscience.
▶ 그는 사업의 실패로 몹시 번민하고 있다 He is terribly distressed by [in anguish over] the failure of his business.
번번이 番番― each [every] time; as often as; each occasion; whenever; many times; repeatedly ▶ 번번이 폐를 끼쳐 죄송합니다 I am sorry to have troubled you so often.
번복 飜覆 〈뒤엎음〉 (a) change; reversal
―번복하다 reverse; change 《*one's* mind》; retract
▶ 그는 자기가 한 말을 번복했다 He took back his words.
♦ 용의자는 자백을 번복했다 The suspect retracted his confession.
번분수 繁分數 〔數〕 a complex fraction; a compound fraction

번성 蕃盛 〈자손의〉 prosperity; 〈초목의〉 luxuriance; rankness ―**번성하다** prosper; flourish; thrive; grow vigorously
♦ 잡초가 번성한 정원 a garden overgrown [rank] with weeds
▶ 그 집안은 그가 가장일 때 번성했다 The family prospered [thrived, flourished] while he was at its head.
번성 繁盛 prosperity ⇨ 번창(繁昌)
번식 繁殖·蕃殖 propagation; breeding; reproduction; 〈증식〉 increase; 〈배양〉 culture
♦ 세균의 번식 the propagation of bacteria
▶ 쥐는 번식이 빠르다 Mice breed [propagate, multiply] rapidly.
―번식하다 breed; propagate [reproduce] *oneself*; 〈동물이〉 proliferate
♦ 번식시키다 breed / 식물[가축]의 신종을 번식시키다 propagate a new variety of plant [breed of cattle]
▶ 괸 물이 모기를 번식시킨다 Stagnant water breeds mosquitoes.
■ 동종― narrow [close] breeding; inbreeding 이종― broad breeding; crossbreeding; outbreeding 인공― artificial fecundation [spawning] ■ ―기 a breeding season ―력 propagation [procreative] power; fertility : 번식력이 있는 fertile; prolific ―률 a breeding coefficient ―지 a breeding place
번안 飜案 **1** 〈작품의〉 an adaptation; an modification ―번안하다 adapt; modify
▶ 그는 「로미오와 줄리엣」을 번안하여 연애소설을 썼다 He modified "Romeo and Juliet" to write a love story.
▶ 그 이야기는 영화[연극]로 번안되었다 The story was adapted for the movies [stage].
2 〈안건을 뒤집음〉 change ―번안하다 change [reverse] a former original plan
■ ―소설 an adapted story
번역 飜譯 (a) translation; a version; rendering
♦ 서투른 번역 a poor translation / 잘못된[틀린] 번역 (a) mistranslation / 원문에 충실한 번역 a translation faithful to the original / 번역을 잘하다 be clever at translation
▶ 나는 헤밍웨이의 소설을 한국어 번역판으로 읽곤 했다 I would often read Hemingway's novels in Korean translation.
▶ 나는 조이스를 번역이 아닌 원문으로 읽었다 I read Joyce not in translation but in the original.
―번역하다 translate; put into; 〈암호 등을 해독하다〉 decipher; decode
♦ 번역하기 어려운 untranslatable; (a phrase) difficult [hard] to translate / 영어로 번역하다 translate 《Korean》 into English
▶ 다음의 우리말을 영문으로 번역하라 Translate [Put] the following Korean into English.
▶ 이 우리말 속담은 영어로 번역할 수 없다 This Korean proverb does not translate [does not bear translation] into English.
▶ 그의 시는 다른 나라 말로 번역할만한 가치가 있다 His poetry is worthy enough to be rendered in other languages.
■ ―가[자] a translator ―권(權) the right to

translate; translation rights ━료 a charge [fee] for translation ━물[판] a translation; a 《Korean》 version: 프랑스 소설을 번역판으로 읽다 read French novels in translation / 성경의 한국어 번역본 the Korean version [translation] of the Bible

번연히 飜然― suddenly; all of a sudden
♦번연히 깨닫다 realize suddenly; 〈사물이 주어〉 suddenly become clear to *one*
▶그는 번연히 그의 잘못을 깨달았다 It suddenly dawned upon him that he was in the wrong.

번영 繁榮 prosperity
♦국가의 번영 the prosperity of a country; national prosperity
▶이 지방의 번영은 눈부시다 The prosperity of this area is amazing.
▶귀사의 번영을 빕니다 〈편지의 맺음말〉 With best wishes for your prosperity.
━번영하다 prosper; flourish; thrive

번의하다 飜意― change *one's* mind [decision]; reverse *one's* will; go back on *one's* resolution
♦잘 이야기하여 번의시키다 talk *one* out of *one's* resolution

번잡 煩雜 〈번거로움〉 troublesomeness; 〈혼잡〉 confusion; 〈복잡함〉 complexity
━번잡하다 troublesome; complicated; complex; crowded
♦번잡한 절차[서식] complicated procedure [forms, formats]
▶번잡한 도시 생활에서 벗어나고 싶다 I want to escape from the wear and tear of city life.

번전하다 反田― 〈논을 밭으로〉 convert a paddy (field) into a (dry) field

번제 燔祭 [基] a sacrificial offering consumed by fire; a burnt offering; 〈유대교의〉 a holocaust

번지 〔農〕 a soil-leveling board with a handle

번지 番地 a lot number; 〈집의〉 a house number; 〈거리의〉 a street number; an address
♦같은 번지에 살다 live at the same number
▶이 편지는 번지가 잘못되어 있다 This letter is wrongly addressed.
▶우리집 번지는 종로 5가 30번지다 I live at 30, Chongno 5-ga.
▶나는 그녀의 집 번지를 모른다 I don't know her address.
▶댁은 몇 번지입니까? What is the street number of your house?

번지다 1 〈잉크 등이〉 blot; spread; pass; run
♦피가 번져 있는 붕대 a blood-stained bandage
▶번지지 않는 종이가 필요해 I want the kind of paper that does not blot.
▶잉크가 번져서 글씨가 알아볼 수 없게 되었다 The ink ran [spread] and the letters became indistinct.
2 〈질병·불 등이〉 spread; prevail; diffuse; be prevalent
▶콜레라가 전국으로 번졌다 Cholera spread throughout the country.
▶독이 그의 몸에 번졌다 The poison got into his circulation.
▶산불이 사방으로 번졌다 The forest fire spread in all directions.
▶불은 크게 번지기 전에 잡혔다 The fire was put out before it got serious.
3 〈일이〉 expand; spread
▶전쟁이 크게 번져갔다 The war was expanded.
▶전쟁이 반도 전역으로 번졌다 The war has spread through the peninsula.

번지럽다 greasy and smooth; slippery; sleek; sodden

번지르르 glossily ⇨ 반지르르
━번지르르하다 〈번지럽다〉 greasy and smooth; slippery; slimy; 〈겉만 그럴듯하다〉 deceptive; showy; tawdry; gaudy
♦번지르르한 그의 얼굴 his oily [greasy] face / 말이 번지르르한 glib; smooth-tongued; honey-tongued / 겉보기만 번지르르하다 seemingly impressive; be deceptive
▶말이 번지르르한 사람치고 실속있는 자는 별로 없다 He who gives fair words feeds you with an empty spoon.

번지질하다 〔農〕 level the soil with a soil-leveling board

번질거리다 be glossy ⇨ 반질거리다

번질번질 glossily ⇨ 반질반질

-번째 ♦첫[두]번째 the first [second] / 왼쪽에서 세번째 책 the third book from the left
▶구로역은 서울역에서 몇번째 역입니까? How many stops are there between Seoul Station and Kuro (Station)? ⇌ How many stops is Kuro from Seoul?
▶그는 두번째로 왔다 He was the second to come [that came].
▶한국에서 네번째로 큰 도시는 어디입니까? What's the fourth largest city in Korea?
▶그녀는 오른쪽에서 세번째다 The third (woman) from the right is she.

번쩍 1 〈빛나는 모양〉 with a flash
♦번쩍 빛나다 give out a flash; flash / 눈에서 불이 번쩍 나다 see stars
▶어둠속에서 번쩍 빛이 났다 A light flashed in the dark.
━번쩍하다 flash; give out a flash
▶그는 동에 번쩍 서에 번쩍한다 He appears in one place and then in another like a flash of lightning.
2 〈쉽게 들어올리는 모양〉 lightly; easily; without (any) effort; 〈높이〉 aloft; high
♦두 손을 번쩍 들고 with *one's* hands high up; 《stand》 with upraised hands / 큰 돌을 번쩍 들어올리다 lift a huge stone lightly [easily]/ 상대를 번쩍 들어올리다 〔競〕 hold *one's* opponent high
▶그는 얼굴을 번쩍 들어 나를 보았다 He popped his head up to look at me.
3 〈관심이 쏠리는 모양〉 suddenly; strongly
♦눈이 번쩍 뜨이는 (美口) eye-catching / 귀가 번쩍 뜨이다 〈사물이 주어〉 catch *one's* ear; be attracted strongly 《by》; take a vivid interest 《in》 / 눈이 번쩍 뜨이다 〈정신이 들다〉 become wide awake; 〈사물이 주어〉 catch *one's* eye; attract *one's* attention

번쩍이다 shine; glitter; sparkle; glisten; flash

⇨ 반짝이다
♦번쩍이는 눈 piercing [fiery] eyes
▶하늘에는 수많은 별들이 번쩍이고 있었다 Countless stars were twinkling in the sky.
▶경고등이 멀리서 번쩍였다 Warning lights flashed in the distance.

번차례 番—〈순서〉a turn; an order
♦번차례로 by turns; in turn; alternately / 번차례로 파수 보다 keep watch by turns / 번차례로 노래하다 take turns at singing

번창 繁昌 prosperity; success; flourishing
—**번창하다** prosper; flourish; thrive; do well
♦번창한 가게 a prospering [flourishing] shop / 사업이 크게 번창하다 drive a prosperous [thriving] trade / 날로 번창하다 enjoy increasing prosperity as time goes on
▶그는 장사가 번창하고 있다 He's doing good [prosperous] business. ⇌ His business is prosperous. ⇌ He has a very successful [a thriving] business.

번트〔野〕a bunt; bunting
♦번트가 성공[실패]하다 bunt successfully [unsuccessfully]/ 번트로 주자를 보내다 advance the runner(s) with [on] a bunt
—**번트하다** bunt (the ball); lay a bunt
♦1루 쪽에 번트하다 beat out a bunt to first
■드래그— a drag bunt 희생— a sacrifice bunt ■—히트 a bunt hit

번호 番號 a number
♦큰[작은] 번호 a high [low] number / 번호가 없는 unnumbered; numberless / 번호가 낮은 [높은] low-[high-]numbered / 번호를 찍다[매기다] number; assign [give] a number 《to》/ 번호를 부르다 call out sb's number / 좌석에 1부터 50까지 번호를 붙이다 number [give numbers to] the seats (from) 1 to 50 / 번호순으로 늘어서다 line up in numberical order
▶번호 (口令) Number [Count] off!
▶모든 제품에는 번호가 붙어 있다 The products are all numbered.
▶번호가 틀렸습니다 You've got the wrong number.
■등록— a registration number 신청— an application number 일련— serial number 자동차— the license number of a car 제조— the manufacture's serial number 좌석— a seat number 허가— a license number ■—판 a license [number] plate; a registration number plate —표 a number ticket [check]

번화 繁華〈번창〉prosperity; 〈북적댐〉bustle; gaiety
—**번화하다** prosperous; flourishing; thriving 《town》; bustling 《street》; busy 《quarters》
♦번화한 거리 a busy [crowded] street / 번화해지다 grow prosperous; prosper; thrive; flourish
▶우리는 번화한 거리를 지나갔다 We went along a busy [bustling] street.
▶이 일대는 주말에는 번화하다 This neighborhood is alive with people on [《英》at] weekends.
■—가〈상점가〉a busy shopping area; business [shopping] quarters; 〈오락가〉an amusement quarter

벋가다 go astray [wild]; go away [deviate] from the right path [way]
▶이 나이 또래의 소년은 벋가기 쉽다 A boy at this age is apt to go astray [to become a delinquent].

벋나다 grow outward; stick out; stretch outwards; protrude

벋다 protruding 《tooth》; sticking out; projecting

벋정다리 a stiff leg; 〈사람〉a stiff-legged person

벌[1]〈들〉a field; 〈초원〉the green; 〈평야〉a plain; 〈황무지〉the wilds
♦김제 벌 the Kimje Plain(s)

벌[2]〈짝〉a set (of cups); a suit (of clothes); a deck [《英》pack] (of cards)
♦정찬 식기 한 벌 a set of dinner dishes / 새 가구 한 벌 a set [suite] of new furniture / 네개 한 벌의 찻잔 a four-piece tea set

벌[3]〔昆〕〈꿀벌〉a (honey)bee; 〈말벌〉a hornet; a wasp; 〈땅벌〉a ground wasp; 〈떠호박벌〉a bumblebee
♦벌침 a wasp's [bee's] sting / 벌에 쏘이다 be stung by bees [wasps]
▶벌들이 꽃 주변에서 윙윙거린다 Bees are buzzing [humming] around the flowers.
■여왕— a queen (bee) 일— a worker (bee)

벌 罰 (a) punishment; a penalty; 〈천벌〉divine punishment
♦가벼운[무거운] 벌 a light [heavy] punishment / 어리석은 짓을 한 벌 the harvest of one's follies / 벌을 면하다 escape punishment; go unpunished / 벌을 받을만하다 deserve punishment
▶그는 엄한 벌을 받았다 He was [got] punished severely. ⇌ He suffered a severe punishment.
▶살인[살인자들]은 법에 의해 벌을 받는다 Murder is [Murderers are] punished by the law.
▶이 규칙을 어기면 벌을 받는다 A violation of this regulation is liable to punishment.
▶이것은 불효에 대한 벌이다 This is a punishment for my want of filial piety.
—**벌하다** punish; inflict (a) punishment 《on sb, for sth》; 〈징계〉discipline; 〈경기 등에서〉penalize ♦아무의 죄를 벌하다 punish sb for (his) crime
▶그는 거짓말한 아들을 벌했다 He punished [disciplined] his son for telling a lie.

벌거벗다 strip oneself bare ⇨ 발가벗다

벌거숭이 a naked body; a nude; 〈상태〉nakedness; nudity
♦벌거숭이의 naked; bare; undressed; unclothed; 〈알몸의〉stark-naked; nude / 벌거숭이가 되다 become (stark-)naked; take off one's clothes; undress; strip oneself naked
▶그 산은 겨울에는 벌거숭이였다 The mountain was completely bare in winter.
■—산 a bare [bald] mountain [hill]

벌겋다 bright red ⇨ 발갛다

벌게지다 turn red; redden

벌금 罰金〈과태료〉a fine; 〈범칙금・위약금〉a (monetary) penalty

♦5만원 이하의 벌금 a fine not exceeding fifty thousand won / 벌금으로 매우다 get off [be let off] with a fine / 벌금을 과하다 fine *sb*; punish *sb* with a fine; impose [inflict] a fine on *sb* / 벌금을 물다 pay a fine; pay *one's* penalty / 벌금을 징수하다 collect a fine
▶ 그는 주차위반으로 3만원의 벌금을 물었다 He was fined 30,000 won for illegal parking.
▶ 늦게 오면 천원의 벌금을 내야 해 The penalty for being late is a thousand won.
■—형 punishment with [by] a fine; a monetary [pecuniary] penalty : 이 규칙위반은 5만원의 벌금형이다 Any violation of this regulation is punishable with a fine of 50,000 won.

벌꿀 honey

벌다¹ 1 〈틈이 생기다〉 become wider; spread
▶ 사이가 벌었다 The crack spreads.
2 〈맞닿은 자리가 벌어지다〉 split open

벌다² 1 〈돈을〉 make money; earn; gain money; 〈이익을 얻다〉 profit (by); make [get, obtain] a profit (from)
♦애써 번 돈 hard-earned money / 정직하게 벌다 turn [earn] an honest penny / 하루에 5만원 벌다 make [earn] fifty thousand won a day / 쉽게 벌다 make easy money / 점심값을 벌다 earn [pick up] some lunch money / 용돈을 벌다 earn [make] *one's* pocket money
▶ 그는 아내가 번 돈으로 먹고 산다 He lives on his wife's earnings.
▶ 그녀는 한 달에 100만원을 번다 She makes [earns] one million won a month.
▶ 너는 하루에 얼마나 버니? How much do you earn a day?
▶ 그는 그 투자로 100만원 벌었다 The investment brought him in a million won.
2 〈자초하다〉 bring upon (*oneself*); incur; invite
♦매를 벌다 incur whipping

벌떡 suddenly; quickly
▶ 그는 벌떡 일어났다 He sprang [jumped] to his feet.

벌떡거리다 1 〈마시다〉 quaff; guzzle; swig; swill 2 〈심장·맥박이〉 throb; beat; go pitpat; palpitate

벌떡벌떡 1 〈마시는 모양〉 ♦벌떡벌떡 마시다 drink freely [heavily]; swill; guzzle; quaff / 맥주를 벌떡벌떡 들이켜다 guzzle beer; take a swig at beer
2 〈심장 등이 뛰는 모양〉 pit-a-pit
▶ 내 가슴이 벌떡벌떡 띈다 My heart is pounding [beating]. ⇒ 〈걱정으로〉 (口) I have butterflies in my stomach.

벌떼 a swarm of bees
♦벌떼같은 swarms of (insects); multitudinous / 벌떼같이 밀어 닥치다 come on in swarms; surge (round)

벌렁 on *one's* back
♦벌렁 드러눕다 lie down on *one's* back; throw *oneself* down / 벌렁 나가자빠지다 fall [be thrown] on *one's* back
▶ 그는 정신을 잃고 벌렁 나가자빠졌다 He fainted and fell to the ground.

벌렁코 a flat nose with flared nostrils

벌레 an insect; a bug; a worm; 〈땅딱 벌레〉 a beetle; 〈나방〉 a moth; 〈송충이〉 a caterpillar; 〈애벌레〉 a larva (*pl.* -vae); 〈해충〉 (총칭) vermin
♦벌레 우는 소리 the singing [chirping] of insects / 우는 벌레 a singing insect / 벌레 먹이 a carious [decayed] tooth / 벌레가 꾄 나무 a tree infested with insects; an insect-infested tree / 벌레 먹은 사과 a wormy apple / 벌레 먹은 worm-eaten; wormy; moth-eaten / 벌레 먹다 be eaten by worms / 벌레가 꾀다 be infested with (noxious) insects [vermin] / 벌레에 물리다[쏘이다] be bitten by vermin; get stung by an insect
▶ 들에서 벌레가 많이 울고 있다 A lot of insects are chirping [singing] in the field.
▶ 농약 때문에 벌레가 적어졌다 Bugs have decreased in number because of insecticides.
▶ 벌레에 물려 온몸이 가렵다 I itch all over because I was bitten by insects.
■책— a great booklover; a bookworm
■—집 a cocoon

벌룩거리다, 벌룽거리다 inflate and deflate alternately

벌름거리다 inflate and deflate alternately; quiver; wriggle ♦코를 벌름거리다 quiver [twitch] *one's* nostrils

벌리다¹ 〈돈벌이가 되다〉 be profitable [gainful]; pay; be paying ♦벌리는 장사 a profitable [lucrative, paying] business
▶ 벌리는 장사라면 그는 무엇이든지 한다 He would do anything for money.

벌리다² 1 〈넓히다〉 leave (space); widen; 〈열다〉 open 〈입을 딱 벌리고 with *one's* mouth open; agape / 두물건 사이를 벌리다 widen the space between two things / 입을 벌리다 open *one's* mouth
▶ 의사는 내게 입을 크게 벌리라고 말했다 The doctor told me to open my mouth wide.
2 〈펴다〉 stretch; outstretch; spread
▶ 팔을 벌리다 open [spread] *one's* arms / 다리를 벌리고 앉다 sit with *one's* legs stretched out [stretched apart]
▶ 새가 날개를 벌렸다 The bird spread its wings.

벌린춤 ♦이왕에 벌린춤이다 We have gone too far to go back. ⇒ There is no turning back.

벌모 young rice plants growing outside the nursery

벌목 伐木 felling; logging
—**벌목하다** cut down [fell, hew] trees; lumber; log
▶ 지나치게 벌목하면 홍수가 난다 Too much deforestation causes floods.

벌물 〈넘치는 물〉 overflowing water; spillage

벌물 罰— 〈들이켜는〉 water that is swilled
♦벌물 켜듯 하다 drink heavily [in great drafts]; guzzle

벌받다 罰— be punished; undergo punishment
♦벌받지 않고 넘어가다 escape punishment; go unpunished
▶ 그런 짓을 하면 반드시 벌받는다 You cannot do such a thing without being punished.

벌벌 tremblingly; shiveringly; shakingly

♦ 무서워서 벌벌 떨다 shake [tremble] for fear; shiver [tremble] with fear / 추워서 벌벌 떨다 shiver with [from] (the) cold; quiver from (the) cold
▶ 그 무서운 소리에 그들은 벌벌 떨었다 The horrible voice struck terror into them.
▶ 손이 벌벌 떨려서 글씨를 잘 쓸 수 없었다 My hands were shivering so badly that I could not write well.

벌서다 罰— stand in the corner
▶ 나는 숙제를 안해 가서 복도에서 벌섰다 I was made to stand in the hall as a punishment for forgetting my homework.

벌세우다 罰— put [stand] 《a boy》 in the corner

벌써 already; long ago [since]; 〈의문문에서〉 yet; 〈어느새〉 so soon
▶ 벌써 3시가 지났다 It is well [already] past three o'clock.
▶ 역에 가니 기차는 벌써 떠난 뒤였다 The train had already left when I arrived at the station.
▶ 그녀는 벌써 떠났니? Has she left already?
▶ 會話 「숙제부터 먼저 해라」「벌써 끝냈어요」 "You must do your homework first of all." "I already have."
▶ 벌써 갈 시간이 되었습니다 It is high time that I must be going.
▶ 그들은 벌써 아이가 둘이나 된다 They now have two children.

벌쏘이다 be [get] stung by a bee [wasp]

벌쏜 사람 같다 make a hurried departure; hurry away [off]; leave hastely

벌쓰다 罰— suffer punishment; get punished

벌어먹다 earn one's livelihood [bread]; make [earn] one's living; support [maintain] oneself ♦ 번역으로 벌어먹다 make a living translating; make a living by doing translation work / 정직하게 벌어먹고 살다 eat one's honest bread / 가족을 벌어먹이다 support [maintain] one's family
▶ 그는 하루 하루를 겨우 벌어먹고 산다 He just manages to earn enough money for his day-to-day [daily] needs.

벌어지다 1〈갈라지다〉crack (apart); become open; 〈넓어지다〉widen; become wider; 〈밤송이 등이〉split [burst] open
♦ 반쯤 벌어진 꽃봉오리 a half-opened bud
▶ 만사가 잘 되어가니 그는 입이 딱 벌어졌다 He could not stop exulting over his luck.
▶ 어쩌다가 그와의 사이가 벌어졌다 Somehow he and I drifted apart.
2〈사건이〉arise; happen; take place
♦ (일이) 크게 벌어지다 get serious; assume serious proportions
▶ 미국과 일본간에 무역전쟁이 벌어졌다 A trade war has broken out [has started] between America and Japan.
▶ 무슨 일이 벌어질 것만 같다 Something is likely to happen.
3〈차이가〉have a (wide) margin; differ (from) ♦ (차이가) 크게 벌어지다 differ greatly [a great deal] (from); 〔競〕have a long lead (on)
▶ 주자들 간에 거리가 벌어졌다 The distance between the runners widened.
4〈몸이〉♦ 어깨가 딱 벌어지다 be broad-shouldered; have broad shoulders

벌이 〈수입〉moneymaking; income; 〈이익〉 (a) profit; gain(s); earnings; gainings; pay ♦ 벌이가 좋다[시원찮다] earn a good [poor] income; be profitable [unprofitable]; pay well [badly] / 큰 벌이를 하다 make a large profit
▶ 불경기로 좋은 벌이가 없다 With the current recession good jobs are scarce.
▶ 그는 적은 벌이로 만족하고 있다 He is satisfied with a small margin of profit.

—**벌이하다** work for one's living; earn one's bread [living]; 〈돈을〉earn [make] 《money》 ♦ 객지로 벌이하러 가다 work away from home / 벌이하러 나가다 go to work; go for work

벌이다 1〈차리다〉open; start; begin; 〈착수하다〉set up; embark in [on, upon] 《a new business》
♦ 가게를 벌이다 open [start] a store / 사업을 벌이다 start [get launched on] an enterprise / 전투를 벌이다 engage in a battle 《with》
▶ 그녀는 가게를 벌이고 있다 She keeps [runs] a store.
2〈베풀다〉hold; give ♦ 술잔치[파티]를 벌이다 hold [give] a banquet [party]
3〈늘어놓다〉display; show; arrange 《goods》 ♦ 물건을 진열장에 벌여 놓다 arrange goods in a show window

벌잇줄 〈수입원〉a source of income; a means of making a living; one's job ♦ 벌잇줄이 끊기다 lose sources of income; lose one's job; be out of a job

벌점 罰點 a black mark; a demerit (mark); 〈낙제점〉a failing mark
♦ 벌점을 주다 give black marks
▶ 그는 이것 때문에 벌점을 또 하나 받을 것이다 He'll get another demerit for this.

벌주 罰酒 a penalty cup (of wine); liquor one is forced to drink as a penalty

벌주다 罰— punish; inflict (a) punishment 《on sb, for sth》

벌집 a (honey)comb; a beehive; a hive
♦ 벌집을 건드리다 stir up [arouse] a hornet's nest [a nest of hornets] / 벌집을 쑤신 듯이 소동이 벌어지다 be thrown into utter confusion; (口) turn into a madhouse
■ —위 〔動〕the reticulum 《pl. -la》

벌창 overflow ⇨ 범람

벌채 伐採 felling; deforestation; logging; (美) lumbering —**벌채하다** cut down [fell] trees; lumber; log
♦ 벌채한 산림(지) a cleared section of forest (land) / 산림을 벌채하다 exploit [cut down] a forest
■ —량 a fall —면적 a cut; a cutting area —시기 the felling season

벌초하다 伐草— weed [tidy up] one's family graveyard

벌충 amends; (a) compensation; reparation; a supplement
—**벌충하다** make up for 《a loss》; make

amends; make good; cover; compensate
♦부족액을 벌충하다 replenish a shortage; make up a deficit / 손실을 벌충하다 compensate for loss / 낭비한 시간을 벌충하다 recover [make up for, make good] lost time
▶그는 장부상의 결손을 벌충하려고 주식에 손을 댔다 He dabbled in stocks to make up the deficit in the accounts.

벌칙 罰則 penal regulations [clauses]; punitive provisions; a penal code
♦벌칙을 적용하다 apply [enforce] the penal regulations / 벌칙에 따라 처벌하다 punish sb according to the penal regulations

벌컥 with a burst; all of a sudden ⇨ 발깍

벌통 —桶 a beehive; a hive

벌판 〈들판〉 a field; a plain; (美) a prairie; 〈황야〉 a wilderness ♦황량한 벌판 a desolate [bleak] field

범 a tiger; 〈암컷〉 a tigress
♦새끼 범 a tiger kitten [cub] / 범을 길러 화를 입다 nourish a serpent in one's bosom

범- 汎- pan- ♦범아랍주의 Pan-Arabism / 범태평양회의 the Pan-Pacific Conference

-범 -犯 〈범행〉 an offense; 〈사람〉 an offender ♦초범 the first offense / 방화범 an arsonist / 살인범 a (convicted) murderer / 소년범 a juvenile delinquent

범국민 汎國民 ♦범국민의[적인] pan-national; nationwide / 범국민적 환경 보호 운동 a nationwide campaign for the protection of the environment
■—운동 a nationwide campaign [movement, drive]: 범국민운동을 벌이다 conduct [carry on] a nationwide campaign [drive]

범굴에 들어가야 범을 잡는다 (속담) Nothing venture, nothing gain [win].

범나비 〔昆〕 a swallowtail (butterfly)

범도 제 소리하면 온다 (속담) Talk [Speak] of the devil, and he is sure to appear.

범람 氾濫 overflowing; flood; inundation; a deluge
—범람하다 flood; overflow; flow [run] over (the banks); be inundated
▶태풍으로 강이 범람했다 The typhoon caused the river to flood.
▶압록강이 호우로 범람했다 The Yalu River flooded [overflowed its banks] after the heavy rain(s).
▶외제 물건이 시장에 범람하고 있다 There is an oversupply [a flood] of foreign goods on the market.
▶강이 범람해서 온 마을이 물에 잠겼다 The river flooded the whole village.

범례 凡例 〈일러두기〉 introductory remarks; explanatory notes; general explanations; 〈지도·도표의〉 a legend

범미 汎美 ♦범미의 Pan-American
■—주의 Pan-Americanism —주의자 a Pan-Americanist —회의 Pan-American Congress

범벅 1 〈음식〉 mixed-grain porridge
2 〈뒤죽박죽〉 (utter) confusion; a muddle; a jumble; a mess; a pell-mell
♦범벅이 되다 get [be] mixed up; be jumbled together; be confused / 범벅이 되게 하다 jumble (up) together; mix up
▶이것 저것이 범벅이 되어 있다 All sorts of things are jumbled up together.

범법 犯法 lawbreaking; violation of the law; an offense 《against》
—범법하다 break [violate] the law; commit an offense [a crime]; go against the law
■—자 a lawbreaker; an offender (against the law); a violator —행위 an illegal [unlawful] act; 〈공무원 등의〉 a malfeasance

범부 凡夫 〈보통 사람〉 an ordinary man; a mediocre person
▶그는 범부가 아니다 He is no ordinary man.

범사 凡事 〈모든 일〉 all matters [things]; everything; 〈평범한 일〉 an ordinary matter
▶범사에 신중하라 Be careful [prudent] with everything.

범상 凡常 mediocrity; ordinariness —범상하다 ordinary; usual; common; commonplace
♦범상한 사람 an ordinary [average] person; the common run of men / 범상한 일 an everyday happening / 범상치 않다 be out of the common
▶그에게는 범상치 않은 데가 있다 There is something extraordinary about him.

범서 梵書 1 〈산스크리트어로 된〉 a book written in Sanskrit [Pali]
2 〈불경〉 Buddhist scriptures

범선 帆船 〈돛단배〉 a sailing boat [ship, vessel]; a sailboat; a sailer

범속 凡俗 commonness; commonplaceness; banality; mediocrity; vulgarity
♦범속을 초탈하다 stand aloof from the world; rise above the rest of mankind
—범속하다 common; ordinary; commonplace; mediocre; vulgar
♦범속한 사람 a common [an ordinary, a mediocre] person / 범속한 생각 a commonplace idea

범신론 汎神論 〔哲〕 pantheism ♦범신론적 pantheistic
■—자 a pantheist

범아랍 汎— ♦범아랍의 Pan-Arabic
■—주의 Pan-Arabism

범아시아 汎— ♦범아시아의 Pan-Asiatic
■—주의 Pan-Asianism

범어 梵語 〈산스크리트〉 Sanscrit; Sanskrit
♦범어의 Sanskrit; Sanscrit
■—학자 a Sanscrit scholar; a Sanscristist

범 없는 골에는 토끼가 스승이다 (속담) In the kingdom of blindmen the one-eyed is the king.

범에 날개 (속담) a double advantage

범용 凡庸 mediocrity; banality —범용하다 mediocre; common; ordinary; banal
♦범용한 재주를 가진 화가 a painter of mediocre [indifferent] ability

범위 範圍 a range; an extent; a scope; a sphere; 〈한계〉 limits
♦대통령 권한의 범위 the extent of a president's powers / …의 범위 안에 within the limits [scope, range, sphere] of…/ 200해리 영해의 범위 내에서 within [inside] the 200-mile territorial waters [seas, sea limits]/ …의 범

위 밖에 beyond the limits [scope] of.../ 조사 범위를 넓히다[한정하다] extend [limit] the scope of the inquiry
▶ 그녀는 교제 범위가 넓다[좁다] She has a large [small] circle of friends (acquaintances).
▶ 시험 범위는 20쪽에서 60쪽까지다 The examination covers pages twenty to [through] sixty.
▶ 그것은 인간 지식의 범위를 넘어서는 것이다 It's beyond the boundary [limits] of human knowledge.
▶ 검사 결과는 모두 정상치의 범위내에 있다 The results are all in the normal range.
▶ 온도는 10℃에서 25℃ 범위에서 오르내렸다 The temperature ranged from 10℃ to 25℃.
■ 세력― the sphere [circle] of influence; the domain 활동― one's scope [sphere] of activity

범유럽 汎― ◆ 범유럽의 Pan-European
■ ―주의 Pan-Europeanism
범의 犯意 a criminal intent; malice
▶ 피고는 범의가 있었음을 인정했다 The accused admitted that his crime was premeditated.
범의귀 〔植〕 a creeping [strawberry] saxifrage
범인 凡人 〈보통 사람〉an ordinary person; (총칭) the common [ordinary] run of men; 〈범용한 사람〉 a (man of) mediocrity; a mediocre person
▶ 그것은 범인이 할 수 있는 일이 아니다 That would be beyond the power of an ordinary person.
범인 犯人 a criminal; 〈미결의〉 a culprit; 〈기결의〉 a convict; 〈위반자〉 an offender; 〈용의자〉 a suspect
◆ 범인을 은닉하다 harbor a criminal / 범인을 쫓다 track down a criminal / 범인을 체포하다 arrest the man [suspect]
▶ 범인은 아직 잡히지 않고 있다 The criminal is still at large.
▶ 범인은 자수했다 The criminal turned himself in.
▶ 과자를 먹은 범인이 누구냐? Who is guilty of eating the cake?
▶ 이 강을 오염시킨 범인은 저 공장이다 It is that factory that polluted this river.
■ ―인도협정 an extradition agreement
범자 梵字 Sanskrit characters
범작 凡作 a poor work; a mediocre work
▶ 이 소설은 범작이야 This novel is mere trash.
범재 凡才 〈재주〉ordinary ability; mediocrity; 〈사람〉a person of average ability; a mediocre person
범절 凡節 etiquette; manners
범종 梵鐘 the bell of a Buddhist temple; a (Buddhist) temple bell
범죄 犯罪 (a) crime; an offense
◆ 범죄의 소추(訴追) criminal prosecution / 범죄의 예방 the prevention of crimes; crime prevention / 범죄의 현장 the scene of crime / 범죄(상)의 criminal / 범죄를 감식하다 identify a crime / 범죄를 구성하다 constitute a crime / 범죄를 저지르다 commit a crime
▶ 절도는 범죄다 Theft is a crime.
▶ 음주 운전은 범죄가 된다 Drunken driving constitutes a crime [an offense].
▶ 범죄가 증가하고 있다 Crime is on the increase.
■ ―경― a minor offense [crime]; a misdemeanor 중― a major [serious] crime [offense]; (a) felony 청소년― juvenile delinquency ■ ―감식 criminal identification ―감식 자료 materials [data] for criminal identification ―건 수 the number of offenses [crimes] committed ―과학 criminalistics ―발생률 a crime rate ―사실 constituting an offense [a crime] ―수사 (a) criminal investigation ―심리학 criminal psychology ―용의자 a suspect; a suspected [an alleged] criminal ―조직 a criminal syndicate ―통계 criminal [crime] statistics ―학 criminology ―행위 a criminal act [offense] ―형 a crime type
범죄자 犯罪者 an offender; a criminal; 〈미결의〉 a culprit; 〈기결의〉 a convict
■ 상습― a habitual criminal; a repeated offender 전쟁― a war criminal
범주 帆走 sailing
―범주하다 sail; go by sail
범주 範疇 a category ◆ …의 범주에 넣다 place sth under the category of... / …의 범주에 속하다 belong to the category of...
▶ 그것은 심리학의 범주에 들어간다 It falls under the category of psychology.
범천(왕) 梵天(王) 〔佛敎〕 Deva
범칙 犯則 violation of regulations
▶ 교통 범칙은 엄히 단속해야 한다 We must exercise strict control over any violation of traffic regulations.
―범칙하다 violate [infringe] the regulations; transgress
■ ―금 a fine; a penalty ―물자 illegal goods; 〈밀수품〉 a smuggled article ―자 an offender; a transgressor
범타 凡打 〔野〕 an easy fly [grounder]; poor batting
◆ 범타에 그치다 prove poor at bat
▶ 2번 타자는 범타로 끝났다 The second batter was put out easily.
범태평양 汎太平洋 ◆ 범태평양의 Pan-Pacific
■ ―회의 the Pan-Pacific Conference
범퇴 凡退 〔野〕 ▶ 삼자 범퇴가 되었다 The three batters went out in quick order.
―범퇴하다 be easily put out
범퍼 〈자동차의〉 a bumper
범포 帆布 sailcloth; (a piece of) canvas
범하다 犯― 1 〈저지르다〉 commit; sin against 《morality》 ◆ 과오를 범하다 commit [make] a fault; err / 죄를 범하다 commit a crime; violate [break] the law
▶ 나는 돌이킬 수 없는 오류를 범했다 I have made an irreparable error.
▶ 저 자는 살인죄를 범했다 That man committed a murder.
2 〈위반하다〉 violate; break; offend against;

범행

transgress; trespass against ♦교칙을 범하다 break the school regulations
3 〈무시하다〉 defy; disregard
▶ 그는 어딘지 범하기 어려운 데가 있다 He has something that commands respect.
4 〈부녀자를〉 abuse; violate; rape

범행 犯行 a criminal act; a crime; an offense ♦잔인한[대담한] 범행 an atrocious [a bold] crime / 범행이 발각되다 have one's offense detected / 범행을 부인하다 deny one's (having committed the) crime / 범행을 시인하다 plead guilty / 범행을 자백하다 confess one's crime
▶ 그 자는 체포될 때까지 세번이나 같은 범행을 저질렀다 He had repeated the same offense three times before being arrested.
■—현장 the scene of an offense : 형사들이 범행 현장으로 달려갔다 Detectives rushed to the scene of the crime.

법 法 1 〈법률〉the law; an act; 〈법칙〉a law; a rule; 〈조례〉a regulation; 〈법전〉a code (of laws); 〈사법〉justice
♦법과 질서 law and order / 법의 정신 the spirit of the law / 법의 효력 the force of the law / 법의 적용을 받다 be under the application of the law
▶ 만인은 법 앞에 평등하다 All men are equal before [in the eye(s) of] the law.
〈법이[은]〉 버스 안에서의 흡연을 금지하는 법이 있다[법은 없다] There is a law [no law] against smoking in buses.
▶ 법은 엄정해야 한다 Hard cases make good law.
〈법을〉법을 고치다[개정하다] revise [alter] the law / 법을 시행하다 enforce a law; put a law in force / 법을 어기다 infringe [break, violate] the law; go against the law / 법을 지키다 observe [keep, obey] the law
〈법에〉법에 맞는 lawful; legal / 법에 어긋난 unlawful; illegal / 법에 따라 according to [in obedience to] the state law / 법에 맞다[합치하다] conform to the law / 법에 저촉되지 않도록 하다 stay on the right side of the law / 법에 호소하다 appeal to the law
▶ 그것은 법에 어긋나는 행동이다 That act is against the law. ⇌ It is an unlawful act. ⇌ It is an illegal action.
▶ 그 분쟁은 법에 호소하지 않고 해결되었다 The dispute was settled without recourse to the law.
2 〈방법〉a method; a way; a means; 〈과정〉a process; 〈기술〉an art; 〈기법〉technique
♦영어 교수법 a method of teaching English / 요리법을 가르치다 teach sb how to cook
▶ 그것이 사물을 바르게 보는 법이지요 That's a good way of looking at things.
▶ 이 단어를 발음하는 법을 가르쳐 주세요 Please tell me how to pronounce this word.
▶ 그는 내게 골프를 잘 치는 법을 가르쳐 주었다 He taught me how to improve my golf.
3 〈도리〉reason; 〈예법〉etiquette; manners
▶ 우는 아이에게는 못 당하는 법이다 There's no arguing with a crying child.
▶ 아무리 노력해도 한계가 있는 법이다 However [No matter how] hard we (may) try, there is a limit to what we can do.
▶ 그런 법이 어디 있니? That's against reason. ⇌ That's unreasonable [outrageous].
▶ 어른한테 그렇게 말하는 법이 아니다 You shouldn't speak like that to your elders.
4 〖佛敎〗 ⇨ 불법(佛法)
5 〈제수(除數)〉〖數〗a divisor ♦법과 실(實) divisor and dividend
6 〖文法〗the mood 《of a verb》 ♦직설[명령, 가정]법 the indicative [imperative, subjunctive] mood

법계 法系 a legal system; a code of law
■로마— Roman law 중국— Chinese law; the Chinese legal system

법계 法界 1 〖佛敎〗the universe; 〈불교도 사회〉the world [society] of Buddhists
2 〈법조계〉judicial circles; the judicial world

법과 法科 〈학과〉the law department; the faculty of law; 〈과정〉a law course
▶ 그는 법과를 나왔다 He has a law degree [a degree in law]. ⇌ 〈대학원〉(美) He graduated from law school.
■—대학 a law college; a college [school] of jurisprudence —대학생 a law student —출신 a graduate of a law school [college]

법관 法官 a judge; a judicial officer; (총칭) the judiciary; the bench; the court

법권 法權 a legal right

법규 法規 the law; laws and regulations; (a) statute; (총칭) legislation
♦교통 관계 법규 traffic regulations / 상거래 관계 법규 regulations concerning [regarding] business transactions / 법규상 legally / 법규의 legal / 법규의 불비로 owing to a defect [fault] in legislation / 교통 법규를 지키다 obey [observe] traffic regulations / 법규상의 절차를 밟다 go through the legal formalities / 법규에 따라 처벌하다 punish sb according to the law [regulations]
■현행—(observe) the law in force : 현행 법규를 무시할 수는 없다 We cannot reglect the law in force. ■—집 the statute book

법당 法堂 a building that contains a statue of Buddha; a main hall at a temple

법도 法度 〈법률〉a law; regulations; 〈예의 범절〉manners; etiquette; courtesy
♦법도를 배우다 learn good manners / 법도를 어기다 violate [infringe] the law; have no manners; go against etiquette

법등 法燈 〖佛敎〗〈등불〉a light offered to the Buddhist altar; 〈불법〉the light of Buddhism; 〈전통〉Buddhistic heritage [tradition]
▶ 법등을 지키다 defend and maintain the Buddhist tradition

법랑 琺瑯 (porcelain) enamel
♦법랑을 칠한[입힌] enameled / 법랑을 입히다 enamel; cover with enamel
■—질 〈치아의〉enamel

법령 法令 a law; an ordinance; laws and ordinances; (총칭) statute
♦법령에 의하여 by law
▶ 누구나 6년간은 학교에 다니도록 법령에 정해져 있다 It is stipulated by law that everybody should go to school for six years.

■—양식 legal forms —집 a complete collection of laws and regulations; the statute book; statutes at large

법례 法例 rules concerning [for] the application of the law

법률 法律 a law; legislation; (총칭) (the) law
♦법률 지식이 있는 사람 a person who has legal knowledge / 법률의 legal; juridical / 법률상 legally; from a legal point of view / 법률의 맹점을 이용하다 outwit [circumvent] the law
▶만인은 법률 앞에 평등하다 All men are equal before the law.
〈법률이[은]〉 그것은 법률이 정하는 바다 It is provided [ordained, prescribed] by law.
▶환경오염을 규제하는 새 법률이 만들어졌다 A new law to control [against] environmental pollution has been made.
▶세금을 내는 것은 법률이 명하는 바다 The law requires us to pay taxes.
▶법률은 미성년자의 흡연을 금하고 있다 The law prohibits minors from smoking. ⇒ The law forbids minors to smoke.
〈법률을〉 법률을 공부하다 study law; 〈법관이 되려고〉 read law / 법률을 만들다[제정하다] enact [make] a law; legislate / 법률을 시행하다 put a law in force; put a law into effect / 법률을 어기다 break [violate] the law / 법률을 지키다 keep [observe, obey, abide by] the law / 법률을 집행하다 administer [deal out] justice / 법률을 폐지하다 repeal [abrogate] a law
▶나는 대학에서 법률을 공부하고 있다 I am studying law at college.
▶법률을 몰랐다고 해서 용서받을 수는 없다 Ignorance of the law excuses no one. ⇒ You cannot be excused if you plead ignorance of the law.
〈법률에〉 법률에 규정되어 있다 be provided for [specified] in the law / 법률에 호소하다 have recourse to law
▶그는 법률에 밝다 He is learned in the law. ⇒ He is a good lawyer. ⇒ He is an expert in legal matters.
■—가 a lawyer; a jurist —고문 a legal adviser [counsel] —문제 a legal question [problem] —사무 law [legal] business —사무소 a law office [firm] —상담 legal advice —상담소 a legal center —서 a lawbook —안 a legislative bill; a draft of a proposed law —용어 a legal [law] term —위반 a breach [violation] of the law —제도 the legal system —제정자 a legislator; a lawgiver —학 jurisprudence; the science of law —학자 a jurist; a jurisprudent

법리 法理 a principle of law; legal principles
■—학 jurisprudence; the science [philosophy] of law —학자 a jurist; a jurisprudent

법망 法網 the net [grip, clutches, meshes] of the law; justice
♦법망을 피하다[빠져나가다] evade [avoid, dodge, elude] the law; escape the grip [long arm] of the law
▶그 사기꾼은 마침내 법망에 걸려들었다 The swindler at last fell into the clutches of the law [was brought to justice].

법명 法名 〔佛敎〕〈승명〉 a Buddhist name; 〈계명〉 posthumous Buddhist name

법무 法務 〔法〕 judicial affairs
■—관 a law officer; a judiciary; 〔軍〕 a judge advocate —국 〈검찰청의〉 the Legal Affairs Bureau —부 the Ministry of Justice; (美) the Justice Department —부 장관 the Minister of Justice; (美) the Attorney General

법문 法文 1 〈법조문의 글귀〉 the text [letter, wording] of the law
♦법문에 명시[규정]되어 있다 be specified [provided for] in the law / 법문화하다 enact a law; make a law
2 〔佛敎〕〈불경의 글귀〉 Buddhist writings

법문 法門 〔佛敎〕 (the gate to) Buddhism
♦법문에 들어가다 embrace Buddhism; become a Buddhist

법복 法服 1 〈법관의 정복〉 a judge's robe [gown]
2 〈승려의 법의〉 a priest's [clerical] robe; priestly vestment

법사 法師 a Buddhist priest [monk]; a bonze

법사위원회 法司委員會 the Legislation and Judiciary Committee ⇨ 법제(∼사법 위원회)

법석 an uproar; a hubbub; a clamor; fuss; bustle
—법석하다[떨다] make a fuss 《about》; fuss 《about》; raise an uproar; make much ado
♦하찮은 일로 법석떨다 make a big fuss [get all upset] over nothing
▶그녀는 첫 해외 나들이를 준비 하느라고 법석 떨고 있다 She is extremely busy preparing for her first trip abroad.
■—판 a clamorous scene

법선 法線 〔數〕 a normal (line)

법수 法數 〔數〕 a divisor ⇨ 제수(除數)

법식 法式 〈법도·양식〉 a rule; a law; a regulation; 〈방식〉 a method; 〈절차·격식〉 procedures; formalities
♦일정한 법식 a regular [proper] form / 법식에 따르다[어긋나다] follow [run counter to] the formalities / 소정의 법식대로 하다 follow the accepted [standard] form

법안 法案 a bill ♦법안을 제출하다 introduce [propose, bring in] a bill / 법안을 가결[부결]하다 pass [reject, shelve] a bill
▶법안은 국회를 통과하면 법률이 된다 A bill becomes law when it has passed the National Assembly.

법어 法語 Buddhistic terms; 〈설교〉 a Buddhist sermon [lecture]

법 열 法悅 〈법희〉 religious exultation [ecstasy]; 〈환희·도취〉 (a) rapture; (an) ecstasy ♦법열에 잠기다 be in ecstasies 《over》

법왕 法王 〈로마 교황〉 the Pope ⇨ 교황

법요 法要 〔佛敎〕〈법회〉 a Buddhist service

법원 法院 〈법정〉 a court of justice [law]; a law court; 〈건물〉 a courthouse
♦법원에 출두하다 appear in court
■—가정— a family court; (美) a domestic relations court 간이— a summary court 고등— a high court 대— the Supreme Court 민사— a civil court 지방— a district court 항고[상

고]— a court of complaint [appeal] 형사― a criminal court ■―서기 a court clerk ―장 the president of a court

법은 멀고 주먹은 가깝다 〈속담〉 When might is right, then (of) justice there is none. ⇒ Where drums beat, laws are silent.

법의 法衣 a priest's [monk's] robe ⇨ 법복

법의학 法醫學 medical jurisprudence; legal [forensic] medicine ♦ 법의학의 medicolegal ■―강의실 a legal medicine lecture room ―자 a doctor of forensic medicine

법인 法人 〔法〕 a juridical [juristic, legal] person; a corporate body; a corporation; a body corporate ♦ 법인의 corporative ■―공개― a public corporation 단독― a corporation sole 사단― a corporate juridical person; a corporation aggregate 재단― a (juridical [judicial]) foundation; (美) a nonprofit corporation 학교― an educational foundation ■―과세 taxation on juridical persons ―단체 a body corporate ―명의 a corporate name ―설정 the creating of a juridical person; incorporation ―세 the corporation tax ―소득 the income of a corporation ―소득세 the corporation profit tax ―자산[재산] corporate assets [property] ―조직 a corporate organization: 법인 조직으로 하다 incorporate 《a firm》 ―주주 an institutional stockholder

법적 法的 legal; legalistic ♦ 법적 근거 a legal basis / 법적으로는 legally (speaking); in the eye of the law / 법적 수단 을 취하다 take an (legal) action; institute legal proceedings
▶ 당신의 요구에는 법적 근거가 없습니다 Your demand has no legal basis.
▶ 그것은 법적으로는 옳을지 모르나 도덕적으로는 옳지 않다고 생각한다 That may be legally right, but I think it's morally wrong.
▶ 안락사는 법적으로 인정되지 않고 있다 Euthanasia is not legally recognized.

법전 法典 〔法〕 a code (of laws); a statute; 〔宗〕 a canon ♦ 현행 법전 the code in force / 법전을 제정하다 establish a code / 법전을 편찬[집성]하다 codify laws ■―함무라비― the Code of Hammurabie

법정 法廷 a (law) court; a court of justice [law]; a courtroom; a tribunal; the bar ♦ 법정을 개정(開廷)하다 hold a court / 범인을 법정에 끌어내다 drag a criminal into court / 법정에 출두하다 appear in court / 〈사건을〉 법 정으로 끌고 가다 bring 《a matter》 before the court [to court]
▶ 오늘은 법정이 열리지 않는다 The court will not sit today.
▶ 법정은 이틀 후에 열린다 The court will be held [in session] two days from now.
▶ 우리는 그와 법정에서 소송을 벌였다 We took him to court. ⇌ We brought a suit [an action] against him.
▶ 법정에서는 진실을 말해야 한다 You have to tell the truth in court.
▶ 그들은 그 사건을 법정으로 끌고 가지 않고 해 결했다 They settled the affair out of court.
■―군사― a military court; a court-martial 대― the grand courtroom ■―모욕죄 contempt of court ―투쟁 a court battle; 〈소송〉 a suit; litigation; 〔勞〕 a litigating struggle

법정 法定 ♦ 법정의 legal; designated by law; statutory 《age》; provided [stipulated] by law ■―가격 a legal price ―권한 legal authority ―금리 the legal interest rate ―기간 a legal term [period] ―대리권 the right of legal representation ―대리인 a legal representative ―득표수 the minimum number of votes set by law ―보호자[후견인] a legal [statutory] guardian ―상속인 a legal heir ―세율 the statutory tariff ―소독약 legal disinfectant ―수[정족수] a (prescribed) quorum ―유예기 간 legal delay; days of grace ―재산제 the legal property system ―전염병 legal communicable disease ―준비금 legal reserve(s) ―화폐[통화] legal tender ―휴일 a legal holiday

법제 法制 〈입법〉 legislation; laws ■―사(史) annals of legislation; a history of laws ―사법위원회 〈국회의〉 the Legislation and Judiciary Committee ―처 the Ministry of Legislation; the Office of Legislation; the Legislative Office ―처장 the Administrator of the Office of Legislation

법조 法曹 a judicial officer ⇨ 법조인

법조계 法曹界 legal circles; the judicial world; (英) the bench and bar ♦ 법조계의 원로들 leaders of the legal circles

법조인 法曹人 a judicial officer [official]; 〈변호사〉 a lawer; (美) an attorney

법치 法治 constitutional government ■―국가 a constitutional state; a law-governed country; a country under the rule of law ―주의 legalism; constitutionalism ―주의 자 a legalist; a constitutionalist

법칙 法則 a law; a rule ♦ 경제 법칙 economic laws
▶ 〈만유〉인력의 법칙은 왜 모든 물체는 땅으로 떨어지는지 설명해 준다 The law of gravity explains why things fall to earth.
▶ 물가는 수요 공급의 법칙을 따른다 Prices follow the law of supply and demand.
■―자연― a law of nature; a natural law ―론 〔哲〕 nomology

법통 法統 〔佛教〕 a religious tradition; the Buddhist tradition ♦ 법통을 잇다 maintain [uphold] the Buddhist tradition

법하다 1 〈당연하다〉 have a good reason to be [do]; It is natural [proper] 《that》
▶ 그가 네게 성을 낼 법도 하지 It is (only) natural for him to get angry with you.
▶ 그가 그것을 요구할 법도 하다 It is reasonable that he (should) demand it.
2 〈기대·추측〉 It seems reasonable 《that》; There is reason to expect 《that》; ought [be supposed] to be
▶ 넌 영어 공부를 했으니까 영어를 알 법한데 You ought to know English, since you have studied it.
▶ 그가 적어도 작별 인사쯤은 하러 왔을 법한데 He ought at least to have come to me to say

goodbye.
3 〈가능성〉 It seems likely 《that》; be likely 《to》; be probable
▶그녀의 말은 그럴 법하다 Her story sounds true.
▶비가 올 법하다 It looks like rain.
▶그건 그럴 법한 일이다 That may well be. ⇌ That is very likely.

법학 法學 〈법률학〉 law; jurisprudence
◆법학을 공부하다 〈학문으로〉 study law [jurisprudence]; 〈법조인이〉 read law
■—개론[통론] an outline of law; an introduction to law —도 a law student —박사〈사람〉 a doctor of laws; 〈학위〉 Doctor of Laws —사〈사람〉 a bachelor of laws; 〈학위〉 Bachelor of Laws —석사〈사람〉 a master of laws; 〈학위〉 Master of Laws —자 a jurist; a lawyer; a legal scholar

법호 法號 〈아호〉 a Buddhist name
법화 法貨 legal tender ⇨ 법정(~화폐)
법화 法話 〔佛敎〕〈불법의 설교〉 a Buddhist sermon [lecture, homily]
법화경 法華經 〈묘법 연화경〉 the Lotus Sutra
법회 法會 〔佛敎〕〈재(齋)〉 a Buddhist mass [service]; 〈설법회〉 a Buddhist lecture meeting
◆법회를 열다 hold a Buddhist service [mass]

벗 〈친구〉 a friend; a companion; a comrade; 〔口〕 a pal
◆믿을 수 없는 벗 a fair-weather friend / 신앙의 벗 a brother [sister] in faith / 참다운 벗 a true [tried] friend / 평생의 벗 a lifelong friend / 벗이 없는 friendless
▶그와 나는 오랜 벗이다 He and I have been friends for a long time.
▶우리는 학문상의 벗이었다 We were fellows in our studies.
▶좋은 벗을 사귀는 것이 중요하다 It is important to keep good company [to choose your company well].
▶어려울 때 벗이 참된 벗이다 《속담》 A friend in need is a friend indeed.

벗개다 〈날이 개다〉 clear up
벗겨지다 1 come off; be taken off
▶구두는 너무 크면 잘 벗겨진다 Shoes will come [slip] off if they are too big.
2 〈칠·비늘 등이〉 fall [come] off; 〈껍질 등이〉 get stripped off; peel off
▶바나나 껍질은 잘 벗겨진다 Bananas peel easily.
▶등의 살갗이 벗겨지기 시작했다 The skin on my back has begun to peel (off).
▶회벽이 군데군데 벗겨져 내리고 있었다 The plaster was coming loose and falling here and there.
3 〈덮인 것이〉 get removed; be taken off
▶그의 가면이 마침내 벗겨졌다 He was at last unmasked. ⇌ His mask was at last ripped away. ⇌ At last he revealed his true nature.

벗기다 1 〈옷 등을〉 strip *sb* of 《his clothes》; take off 《*sb's* clothes》
◆옷을 벗기다 unclothe [undress, disrobe] *sb*; strip [divest] *sb* of 《his》 clothes
▶그녀는 아이의 젖은 옷을 벗겼다 She took off the child's wet dress.
2 〈껍질 등을〉 chip [slice, flake] off; peel; 〈가죽을〉 skin (off); 〈곡식을〉 husk
◆감자를 벗기다 peel [pare] potatoes / 나무 껍질을 벗기다 take the bark from a tree; strip a tree of its bark / 귤 껍질을 벗기다 peel a tangerine / 때를 벗기다 wash off the dirt / 칠을 벗기다 peel the paint off / 옥수수를 벗기다 husk Indian corn / 콩깍지를 벗기다 shell peas
▶나는 사과를 껍질을 벗기지 않고 먹는 것이 좋다 I like to eat an apple, skin and all.
3 〈떼어내다〉 remove; take off; 〈덮인 것을〉 uncover
◆위선자의 가면을 벗기다 unmask a hypocrite / 지붕에서 기와를 벗기다 remove tiles from the roof / 상자의 뚜껑을 벗기다 take off the lid from a box
▶대문 빗장을 벗겨라 Unbolt [Unlatch] the gate.

벗나가다 deviate 《from》 ⇨ 빗나가다

벗다¹ 〈몸에 걸친 것을〉 take off; strip [divest] *oneself* of; remove; 〈스르르〉 slip off; 〈잡아 당겨서〉 pull off
◆모자[신발]를 벗다 take off *one's* hat [shoes] / 안경을 벗다 remove [take off] the glasses / 옷을 벗다 get undressed; undress *oneself* / 모자와 외투를 벗지 않고 있다 keep *one's* hat and overcoat on
▶나는 옷을 벗고 파자마를 입었다 I took off my clothes [I got undressed] and put on my pajamas.
▶그는 옷도 벗지 않고 곯아 떨어졌다 He fell asleep with his clothes on [without undressing].
2 〈짐을〉 unburden; be relieved [ease *oneself*] of a burden
◆마음의 짐을 벗다 take a load off *one's* mind; lift a load from *one's* mind
▶그는 빚을 모두 갚아 마침내 큰 짐을 벗었다 When he repaid his loan full, he was finally relieved of a heavy burden.
3 〈누명·책임 등을〉 be freed from; get rid of
◆누명을 벗다 clear [divest] *oneself* of a false charge / 오명을 벗다 clear *one's* name; cleanse *one's* dishonor / 책임을 벗다 be relieved of *one's* responsibility
4 〈티 등을〉 get rid of; get refined [polished]
◆때를 벗다 get sophisticated [polished]; get smart / 촌 티를 벗다 get citified / 어린 티를 벗다 grow out of childhood
5 〈허물을〉 slip out of 《its skin》; cast [slough] (off) 《the skin》; 〈곤충이〉 leave the cocoon
▶뱀이 허물을 벗었다 A snake sloughed its skin.
6 〈갚다〉 pay off [up]; clear off 《*one's* debts》
◆빚을 벗다 free *oneself* from debts; clear up *one's* debts

벗다² 〈벗어지다〉 come [peel] off ◆칠이 벗다 the paint comes off

벗삼다 make friends with; associate with; keep company with
◆자연을 벗삼다 take nature for a friend; make a friend of nature
▶그는 책을 벗삼아 인생을 즐기고 있다 He is

벗어나다 1 〈빠져나오다〉 come out of; leave; emerge from; slip out of; get out of; be relieved of; escape from; free *oneself* of [from]
♦ 벗어날 수 없는 unavoidable; inescapable / 가난에서 벗어나다 overcome poverty / 나쁜 버릇에서 벗어나다 break *oneself* [get rid] of a bad habit / 속박에서 벗어나다 free *oneself* from fetters / 슬럼프에서 벗어나다 recover from *one's* slump / 위험[위급한 상태]에서 벗어나다 escape a danger / 죽음에서 벗어나다 be saved from death; escape unkilled; be snatched from the jaws of death
▶ 그 환자는 이제 위급한 상태에서 벗어났다 The patient is now out of danger.
▶ 나는 마침내 추적자들에게서 벗어났다 I finally eluded my pursuers.
▶ 시내 중심가에서 벗어나자 널따란 논이 펼쳐졌다 Once we left the center of the town, we came upon an expanse of paddy fields.
▶ 터널을 벗어나자 바다가 보였다 When we came out of [emerged from] the tunnel, the sea came into view.
2 〈어긋나다〉 deviate [swerve] from; be against; be contrary to; depart from
♦ 도리에 벗어난 행동 immoral behavior / 이치에 벗어나다 be contrary to reason / 정도(正道)에서 벗어나다 stray from the right path; take a wrong step
▶ 그것은 규칙에 벗어난다 That is against the rules.
▶ 그 정책은 인도주의 원칙에 벗어나는 것이었다 The policy was inhuman. ⇌ The policy was out of line with humanitarian principles.
3 〈눈밖에 나다〉 be out of [lose] *sb's* favor; incur [fall under] *sb's* displeasure
▶ 그녀는 하는 일마다 어머니 눈에 벗어났다 Everything she did displeased her mother.
▶ 왜 그가 그녀의 눈에 벗어났는지 모르겠다 I wonder why he lost her favor.
4 〈빗나가다〉 miss the mark; go wide; stray (from); deviate (from a course) ♦ (배가) 침로를 벗어나다 swerve from the course; sheer (off)
▶ 화살이 과녁을 벗어났다 The arrow missed the mark.
▶ 기상 위성이 지구 궤도에서 벗어났다 The weather satellite strayed out of its orbit around the earth.
▶ 그 질문은 핵심을 벗어난 것이다 The question is beside the point.
▶ 비행기는 진로를 벗어나 날았다 The plane flew off course.
벗어버리다 1 〈몸에 착용한 것을〉 take [cast, throw, fling] off 《*one's* coat》; shed 《*one's* clothes》
▶ 그는 구두[슬리퍼]를 벗어버렸다 He kicked off his shoes [slippers].
▶ 그녀는 옷을 바닥에 벗어버렸다 She pulled [yanked] her dress off and threw [flung] it to the floor.
▶ 그는 옷을 벗어버리고 강에 뛰어들었다 He plunged into the river throwing off his clothes.
2 〈책임·누명 등을〉 shift off *one's* duty [responsibility]; take off *one's* burden; clear *oneself* completely of... ⇨ 벗다 3
벗어부치다 slip off *one's* clothes
▶ 그는 웃통을 벗어부치고 일에 달려들었다 He took off his coat and tackled the work squarely.
벗어지다 1 〈몸에 착용한 것이〉 come off; slip off [down]
▶ 이 모자는 곧잘 벗어진다 This hat often falls [comes] off.
▶ 구두가 벗어지지 않는다 My shoes won't come off.
2 〈표면 등이 깎이다〉 peel (off); come [strip] off;〈살갗이〉 get [be] skinned
▶ 나는 무릎이 벗어졌다 My knees got skinned. ⇌ I skinned my knees.
3 〈대머리가 되다〉 become [go, grow] bald; be [get] bald
▶ 요즈음 내 머리가 많이 벗어진다 I lose a lot of hair these days.
▶ 그는 이마가 많이 벗어졌다 His hair retreated way back leaving forehead bald.
4 〈덮인 것이 들추어지다〉 be taken off; get removed; 〈이탈하다〉 come off; come apart; get out of place; get loose
벗하다 1 〈벗삼다〉 associate (with); make a friend (with); make friends (with)
♦ 벗하고 지내다 be friends (with); be on friendly terms (with); 〈너나 하고〉 be on a first-name basis with each other
2 (비유) make a companion of; have *sth* for a companion; live with
♦ 자연을 벗하다 take nature for a friend; make a friend of nature; live with nature / 책과 벗하다 have books for companions; make companions of books
벙거지 〈모자〉 a hat; 〈옛 군인의〉 a soldier's (felt) hat [helmet]
벙그레 smilingly ⇨ 방그레
벙글거리다 smile (radiantly) 《at》; be all smiles; wear a smile 《on *one's* face》
▶ 그는 만족해서 벙글거렸다 He beamed with satisfaction.
벙글벙글, 벙굿벙굿 with a broad [bland] smile; cheerfully; smilingly
♦ 벙글벙글 웃는 얼굴 a smiling [beaming] face; a radiant look
▶ 그는 행복에 겨워 벙글벙글했다 There was a happy smile on his face.
벙벙하다 〈얼떨떨하다〉 stunned; tongue-tied; dumbfounded; stupefied; (口) flabbergasted
♦ 어안이 벙벙하다 be stunned [dumbfounded]
▶ 그녀는 어안이 벙벙한 채 그를 바라보았다 She stared at him in dumb [blank] surprise.
▶ 나는 벙벙하여 말이 안 나왔다 I was (struck) dumb with astonishment.
벙실거리다 smile beamingly ⇨ 방실거리다
벙어리[1] a mute; a dumb person; 〈농아〉 a deaf-mute ♦ 벙어리의 dumb; mute
▶ 그녀는 갑자기 입을 다물고 벙어리가 되었다 She shut up like a clam. ⇌ She fell silent [dumb] suddenly.

■—장갑 (a pair of) mittens
벙어리² 〈저금통〉 a saving box; 〈돼지 저금통〉 a (piggy) bank
벙커 〔軍〕〈지하 엄폐호〉 a bunker; 〔골프〕〈코스의 장애〉 a bunker; a sand trap/〈배의 석탄 창고〉 a bunker
벙커시유 —油 bunker C oil
벚꽃 cherry blossoms [flowers] ■—놀이 a cherry-blossom viewing; 〈행락〉 a picnic [party] under the cherry blossoms
벚나무 〔植〕 a cherry tree
베 〈삼베〉 hemp cloth; 〈무명베〉 cotton cloth ♦ 베 짜는 사람 a weaver / 베를 짜다 weave ■—실 hemp thread —옷 hempen clothes
베개 a pillow; 〈긴 덧베개〉 a bolster ♦ 베개를 베다 lay [rest] one's head on the pillow / 베개를 베고 자다 sleep with one's head on a pillow / 책을 베개삼아 pillow one's head on the book ■ 공기— an air cushion 물— a water pillow ■ 베갯모 a sidepiece of a pillow 베갯속 the stuffing of a pillow 베갯잇 a pillowcase; a pillow slip [sham]
베갯머리 〈머리맡〉 one's bedside ♦ 베갯머리에 앉아 시종을 들다 sit up by [at] sb's bedside ▶ 그의 베갯머리에는 책이 몇 권 있었다 There were some books at his bedside. ■—송사(訟事) one's wife's private advice; a curtain lecture: 베갯머리 송사에 넘어가지 않는 남자 없다 No one can fail to comply with his wife's private entreaties.
베갯밑공사 —公事 a curtain lecture ⇨ 베갯머리(～송사)
베고니아 〔植〕 a begonia
베끼다 **1** 〈옮겨쓰다〉 copy; take [make] a copy (duplicate) (of); transcribe; 〈복사하다〉 trace over ♦ 새 단어들을 노트에 베끼다 copy the new words into a notebook / 통째로 베끼다 copy (a passage) entirely [verbatim] **2** 〈모사하다〉 imitate; copy; trace ♦ …을 그대로 베끼다 make an exact copy of…
베니어 veneer (▶합판[플라이우드]에 붙인 얇은 장을 말함) ■—톱 a veneer saw
베다¹ 〈베개를〉 rest [lay] one's head on 〈a pillow〉/ 팔베개를 베고 with one's head (pillowed) on one's arm
베다² 〔자르다〕 cut; 〈얇게〉 slice; 〈가위로〉 shear; clip; 〈톱으로〉 saw; 〈풀을〉 mow ♦ 나무를 베다 fell [cut] a tree; cut wood / 낫으로 벼를 베다 reap [gather (in)] rice with a sickle ▶ 나는 유리 조각에 손가락을 베었다 I cut my finger on the broken glass. ▶ 그는 손가락에서 피가 났다 He (had) cut his finger and it was bleeding. ⇌ His finger was bleeding where he had cut it. ▶ 고기를 조금 베어주시오 Cut [Slice, Carve] me some meat [some meat for me]. ▶ 이 나무는 잘 베어지지 않는다 This tree doesn't cut easily [won't cut at all].
베다³ 〔佛敎〕 the Veda(s) ■—문학 Vedic literature

베델른 〔스키〕 wedeln —베델른하다 wedel
베도라치 〔魚〕 a gunnel
베드 〈침대〉 a bed ♦ 편한[딱딱한] 베드 a comfortable [hard] bed ■ 더블— a double bed 싱글— a single bed 이단— a bunk bed ■—커버 a bedcover; a bedspread
베란다 a veranda(h); 〔美〕〈현관 앞의〉 a porch
베레(모) —(帽) 〔〈프〉béret〕 a beret
베르가모트 〔植〕〈불수감나무〉 a bergamot orange
베르무트 〈백포도주〉 vermouth
베르사유 Versailles ■—궁전 the Versailles Palace; the Palace of Versailles —조약 the Treaty Versailles
베를린 〈독일의 수도〉 Berlin
베릴륨 〔化〕 beryllium
베물다 cut off with one's teeth; bite off; gnaw off [away]
베서머 —강(鋼)〔工〕 Bessemer steel
베셀 ■—함수〔數·天〕 Bessel function
베스트셀러 a best-seller; a best-selling book ▶ 그의 책이 금주의 베스트셀러 수위를 차지했다 His book was at the top of the best-seller list this week. —작가 a best-selling author [writer]
베슥거리다 be reluctant 〈unwilling〉 (to do); be unenthusiastic 〈about〉; take little interest 〈in〉
베어내다 cut off [down]; cut out [away]; 〈풀 등을〉 mow (a field) ♦ (나뭇)가지를 베어내다 cut off [prune] a branch / 고기를 한 점 베어내다 cut off a slice of meat / 산에서 목재를 베어내다 bring down logs from a mountain
베어링 〔機〕 a bearing ■—롤러— a roller bearing 볼— a ball bearing ■—공업 the (ball and roller) bearing industry
베어먹다 bite [take a slice] and eat it ♦ 배를 한 입 베어먹다 take a bite out of a pear
베어버리다 cut away [off]; cut down; chop [chip] off
베이다 be cut; get (it) cut; get a cut (on) ♦ 칼에 손가락을 베이다 get a cut on the finger with a knife ▶ 그는 오른손을 깊게 베였다 He received a deep cut on his right hand. ▶ 나는 면도하다가 (얼굴을) 베였다 I cut myself while I was shaving.
베이비붐 baby boom
베이스¹ **1** 〈기초·기준〉 base; basis ♦ 임금 베이스 the wage base; the basic wage rate **2** 〔野〕〈누(壘)〉 a base; a base bag ♦ 베이스를 밟다 step on a base; 〈도달하다〉 reach a base / 베이스에 나가다 go to first / 〈주자가〉 베이스에 있다 be on the base; hold the base ▶ 주자 풀베이스다 The bases are loaded [full].
베이스² 〔樂〕 bass ■—가수 a bass (singer) —기타 a bass guitar
베이스볼 baseball (game) ⇨ 야구
베이스업 a raise of the basic wage rate ♦ 베이스업을 요구하다 demand a higher basic wage; ask [demand] 《the company》 for a

raise of the basic wage
—베이스업하다 raise the basic wage rate 《by 20 percent》
베이스온볼 〔野〕 a base on balls
베이스캠프 〔登山〕 a base camp
베이식 〔電算〕 BASIC; Basic (▶규격화된 일상어를 사용하는 초급 단계의 프로그래밍 언어) 〔《Beginner's All-purpose Symbolic Instruction Code》〕
베이지 beige ◆베이지 색 정장 a beige suit
베이커리 〈빵집〉 a bakery
베이컨 bacon ■—에그 bacon and eggs —조각 a slice of bacon
베이클라이트 〈商標〉〈합성수지의 일종〉 bakelite ◆베이클라이트 제품 bakelite goods
베이킹파우더 baking powder
베일 a veil
◆신부의 베일 a bridal veil / 베일을 벗다 unveil; reveal *oneself* / 베일을 쓰다[베일로 얼굴을 가리다] veil *one's* face; muffle *one's* face in a veil / 베일을 쓰고 있다 wear a veil; be in a veil
▶그 사건은 아직 신비의 베일에 싸여 있다 The incident is still hidden in a veil of mystery.
베짱이 〔昆〕 a long-horned grasshopper; a katydid
베타 *B*; beta ■—선 *B*-rays; beta rays —입자 beta particles
베테랑 a veteran; 〈전문가〉 an expert; 〈노련한 사람〉 an old hand
◆중동 문제의 베테랑 an expert on Middle East problems
베토벤 〈독일의 작곡가〉 Beethoven, Ludwig van (1770-1827)
베트남 〈나라이름〉 Vietnam; 〈공식명〉 Socialist Republic of Vietnam
베틀 a loom ◆베틀로 짜다 weave; weave 《fabric》 on a loom
베풀다 1 〈벌이다〉 give 〔have, 《口》 throw〕 《a party》; hold 《a banquet [meeting]》
▶우리는 지난 주 그에게 생일 잔치를 베풀어 주었다 We gave a birthday party for him last week.
▶그의 수상 축하연이 베풀어졌다 A party was held [given] to celebrate his receiving the prize.
2 〈주다·펴다〉 give 《money, things》 in charity [alms]; bestow 《a favor on *sb*》; render 《services to mankind》
◆선정(善政)을 베풀다 govern wisely / 은혜를 베풀다 do *sb* a favor / 자비를 베풀다 have mercy 《on》; show *sb* mercy / 자선을 베풀다 practice charity
▶그는 남에게 친절을 베풀 사람이 아니다 He isn't a man who does others favors.
벡터 〔數·物〕 a vector ■—공간 vector space —함수 a vector function
벤자리 〔魚〕 a grunt(er)
벤젠 〔化〕 benzene ■—환[핵] a benzene ring [nucleus]
벤졸 〔化〕 benzol
벤진 〔化〕 benzine; benzoline
벤치 a bench; 〈야구의〉 a dugout; 〈선수 대기소〉 the bench ◆공원의 벤치 a park bench / 벤치에 앉다 sit on a bench
벨 a bell; 〈문간의〉 a doorbell
◆벨을 울리다 ring the bell; ring at the bell / 벨을 울려 사람을 부르다 ring 《the bell》 for *sb* / 전화 벨이 울렸다 The telephone rang [went off]. (▶go off는 「갑자기 울리다」의 뜻이 강함)
▶현관의 벨이 울리고 있다 There's a ring at the door. ⇒ There goes the doorbell.
■비상— an emergency bell; an alarm bell
벨기에 〈나라이름〉 Belgïe; 〈공식명〉 kingdom of Belgium
벨벳 velvet ◆벨벳 같은 감촉 velvety touch
벨트 〈허리띠〉 a belt; a waist belt; 〔機〕 a belt; belting
◆그린— a green belt 안전— a safety [seat] belt : 안전 벨트를 매십시오 Please fasten your seat belt. ■—컨베이어 a belt conveyor
벰베르크 〈商標〉〈인견사〉 Bemberg
벼 〈식물〉 a rice plant; a paddy; 〈열매〉 (unhulled [rough]) rice; 〈낟알〉 a grain of (unhusked) rice
◆벼를 베다 cut [mow] rice (plants); harvest [reap] rice / 벼를 심다 plant rice seedlings / 벼를 타작하다 thrash [thresh] rice (plants)
▶벼가 잘 자란다 The rice is doing well.
▶벼는 논에 심는다 Rice is planted in a rice paddy. (▶rice는 「벼·쌀·밥」에 모두 쓸 수 있으며 특별한 경우 외에는 구태여 rice plant로 할 필요가 없음)
▶벼는 익을수록 고개를 숙인다 The more noble the more humble. ⇒ Manners maketh man.
■—베기 rice reaping; harvesting [mowing] of the rice (plants) —이삭 an ear of a rice plant —타작 rice threshing
벼농사 —農事 〈농사〉 rice farming; rice growing; 〈작황〉 a rice crop ◆벼농사를 짓다 do [engage in] rice farming
▶올해는 벼농사가 잘[안]되었다 This year's rice crop is good [poor].
벼락 a thunderstroke; a thunder(bolt)
◆벼락 치는 소리 a clap 《crack, crash, peal》 of thunder / 벼락 맞은 thunderstruck; thunderstricken / 벼락 같은 소리를 지르다 thunder out; cry in a thunderous voice / 〈상사에게서〉 get [receive] a (good) scolding / 벼락을 맞다 be struck [hit] by lightning
▶그의 집에 벼락이 떨어졌다 His house was hit [struck] by lightning.
▶등산객이 벼락을 맞아 죽었다 A mountain climber was hit dead [was struck dead, was killed] by 《a stroke of》 lightning.
벼락감투 a post of an upstart; an upstart's post ◆벼락감투를 쓰다 become an upstart (government) official
벼락공부 —工夫 cramming 《for an examination》
—벼락공부하다 cram 《up》; grind 《away》 《at examination subjects》; 《美口》 bone up 《on a subject》; 《英口》 swot 《a subject》 up
▶그는 영어 시험 때문에 벼락공부하기 시작했다 He began to cram for an English examination.

벼락맞다 1 be struck by lightning
2 (비유) meet with an unexpected accident; 〈야단맞다〉 be scolded severely
▶ 너 그런 짓 하면 벼락 맞는다 If you do that, there will be hell to pay.
▶ 이 벼락맞을 놈아 The deuce [devil] take you! ⇌ Go to the devil [deuce]!

벼락부자 —富者 a new-rich; an upstart; (총칭) the new-rich
♦ 전쟁 경기를 탄 벼락부자 a war profiteer; a war-made millionaire / 벼락부자의 악취미 the bad taste typical of the new-rich / 벼락부자가 되다 gain quick riches; get [become] rich suddenly
▶ 그는 땅으로 벼락부자가 되었다 Land made him an upstart.

벼락불 〈번갯불〉 a flash [bolt] of lightning; 〈사나운 명령〉 a tyrannical [stern, rigid] order
♦ 벼락불치다 thunder at

벼락치기 hasty work; cramming
▶ 벼락치기 공부는 실제로 쓸모가 없다 A hastily crammed [acquired] knowledge is of no practical use.
▶ 그는 시험 때문에 벼락치기 공부를 하고 있다 He is cramming for an examination.

벼락치다 a thunderbolt falls; lightning hits [strikes]

벼랑 a cliff; a precipice; 〈바다에 접한〉 a bluff
▶ 그녀는 급한 벼랑을 기어올랐다 She climbed a steep cliff.
▶ 자동차가 벼랑에서 바다로 떨어졌다 A car fell over the precipice into the sea.
▶ 그 나무는 벼랑 끝에 서 있다 The tree stands on the edge of a cliff.

벼루 an inkstone; an ink slab
♦ 벼루에 먹을 갈다 rub an ink stick back and forth on an inkstone
■ **벼룻돌** an inkstone **벼룻집** 〈연갑〉 an inkstone case; a case for an inkstone; 〈연상〉 a stationery cabinet

벼룩 a flea
♦ 벼룩에 물린 자국 a fleabite / 벼룩에 물린 팔 a flea-bitten arm / 벼룩의 간을 내어 먹다 skin a flea for its hide (and tallow) / 벼룩을 잡다 catch fleas; hunt fleas / 벼룩에 물리다 be [get] bitten by a flea
▶ 엊저녁엔 벼룩 등살에 잠을 잘 못잤다 I could not sleep well last night because I was tormented by fleas.
■ —**시장** a flea market [fair]

벼르다 〈마음먹다〉 intend (to do); design; plan; be intent [bent] 《on》; have sth in mind
♦ 원수를 갚으려고 벼르다 burn with the desire for revenge [with the vengeful thoughts] / 죽이려고 벼르다 have designs upon sb's life
▶ 그녀는 케임브리지 유학을 벼르고 있다 She is eager [anxious] to study in Cambridge.
▶ 내가 오래 벼르던 것이 마침내 이루어졌다 My long-cherished desire has been fulfilled [realized] at last.
▶ 그는 오랫동안 벼르던 금주를 결행했다 He resolutely gave up drinking, which had been his yearlong intention.

벼리 〈그물의〉 a head rope; 〈책의 줄거리〉 a general plan; the skeleton 《of a poem》

벼리다 forge [temper] the blade 《of an old knife》 ♦ 식칼을 벼리다 forge the blade of a kitchen knife

벼슬 〈관직〉 a government [public] post [position]; official rank
♦ 벼슬이 높은 a high(-ranking) official [officer] / 벼슬이 높다[낮다] be high [low] in official rank; be of high [low] government position / 벼슬을 내놓다 resign from [leave] one's government post / 벼슬을 얻다[잃다] obtain [lose] a government position
—**벼슬하다** become a public [government] official; take up a public office; enter into government service; hold an office under [in the] government

벼슬길 government service [employ] ♦ 벼슬길에 오르다 enter (the) government service; start one's official career

벼슬살이 an [one's] official [public] life [career] —**벼슬살이하다** lead an official life; serve as [become] a government official

벼슬아치 a government [public] official ♦ 벼슬아치 티 officialism; bureaucratic spirit / 벼슬아치가 되다 enter (into) the government service; get employment in a government office

벼훑이 a rice-thresher

벽 壁 〈바람벽〉 a wall; 〈칸막이〉 a partition [party] wall
♦ 벽이 있는 walled / 벽을 사이에 두고 (live) with a wall between (us) / 벽을 바르다 plaster a wall / 벽을 하얗게 칠하다 paint a wall white / 벽에 기대다 lean against the wall / 벽에 그림을 걸다 hang a picture on the wall / 벽에 그림을 붙이다 fix a picture to the wall / 벽에 부딪치다 run [come up] against a wall; 〈교착상태에 빠지다〉 be deadlocked; be at a deadlock / 10초의 벽을 깨뜨리다 crack the 10-second barrier (for 100 meters)
▶ 벽에 그림이 걸려 있다 There is a picture on the wall. ⇌ A picture is (hanging) on the wall.
▶ 벽에도 귀가 있다 (속담) Walls have ears.
▶ 연구는 벽에 부딪쳐 전혀 진전이 없다 The research has run into a brick wall and isn't progressing at all.

벽 癖 1 〈버릇〉 a (personal) habit; a (peculiar) way; a peculiarity; 〈습관〉 a habitual practice
2 〈광(狂)〉 a craze 《for》; a mania 《for》
■ 도— thievish habits; a tendency to steal 수집— a mania for collecting 주— drinking habits

벽개 劈開 〔鑛〕 cleavage —**벽개하다** cleave
—**선[면]** a line [plane] of cleavage

벽걸이 壁— (a wall) tapestry; wall hangings [decorations]

벽난로 壁煖爐 a fireplace

벽돌 甓— (a) brick
♦ 붉은 벽돌 (a) red brick / 벽돌로 지은 집 brick houses / 벽돌을 굽다 bake [burn, make] bricks / 벽돌을 쌓다 lay bricks / 벽돌로 짓다

build (a house) of brick [with bricks]
▶그 길에는 벽돌을 깔아놓았다 The road is paved with bricks.
■내화— (a) firebrick; (a) fireproof brick 장식— dressed brick ■—공 a bricklayer; a mason; 〈제조공〉 a brick maker [burner] —공장 a brickyard; brick works —담 a brick wall —점토 brick clay —조각 a brickbat —집 a brick house; a brick building

벽두 劈頭 〈글의〉 the opening [beginning] (of a writing [composition]); 〈일의〉 the first; the start; the outset
◆벽두에 at the (very) outset [beginning]; in the first place; to begin [start] with; first of all / 벽두부터 from the (very) start [outset]
▶그는 회의 벽두에 다음과 같이 말했다 At the beginning of the meeting he addressed as follows.
▶전당대회는 개회 벽두부터 험악해질 듯했다 The national convention of the party showed many signs of rough going at the very outset.

벽력 霹靂 a thunderstroke ⇨ 벼락 ◆벽력같이 소리치다 roar [thunder] (at)
▶우리 담임 선생님은 벽력같이 소리쳤다 My homeroom teacher shouted in a thunderous voice.
■청천— a bolt from the blue: 그것은 나로서는 청천벽력이었다 For me it was a veritable bolt from the blue. ⇌ I was thunderstruck.

벽면 壁面 the surface [face] of a wall

벽보 壁報 a wall newspaper; a poster; a bill
◆벽보를 붙이다 stick [paste up] a bill; put up a poster
▶벽보 금지 (게시) Stick [Post] no bills here. ⇌ Do not stick any bills.

벽성 僻姓 an uncommon [a rare] surname

벽시계 壁時計 a wall clock

벽신문 壁新聞 a wall newspaper [poster]

벽안 碧眼 blue eyes
◆벽안의 blue-eyed / 금발 벽안의 미녀 a blond (blue-eyed) beauty; a blue-eyed (beautiful) blonde

벽옥 碧玉 〔鑛〕 jasper

벽자 僻字 a rare [an odd] (Chinese) character; an uncommon (Chinese) letter

벽장 壁欌 a (wall) closet; a built-in closet; a wall cupboard

벽장코 a broad, squat nose

벽제 辟除 traffic blocking; road blockade for a dignitary's passage (in the old times)

벽지 僻地 a secluded [remote] area; an out-of-the-way place; a (remote) corner of the country; (口) a backwoods area; (美) the back-country
◆벽지에서 살다 live in a remote country place; live in an out-of-the-way place; live far away from a city
▶그녀는 벽지에서 교육에 일생을 바쳤다 She devoted all her life to education in remote places [regions].
■—교육 (school) education in remote (rural) areas

벽지 壁紙 wallpaper ◆녹색 벽지를 바르다 (wall)paper a room in green; cover the walls of a room with green wallpaper

벽창호 碧昌— an obstinate [a stubborn, a headstrong, a pigheaded] person; a diehard; a hardhead; a bigot
▶저런 벽창호한테는 무슨 말을 해도 소용없다 It's of no use telling such a stubborn man anything.

벽촌 僻村 a remote village; an out-of-the-way place; a remote (rural) area
▶그는 영남 지방의 벽촌에서 태어났다 He was born in a secluded village in the Yŏngnam district.

벽토 壁土 wall mud; 〈회벽〉 plaster; 〈치장용〉 stucco

벽해 碧海 the blue sea

벽화 壁畫 〈벽에 그린〉 a wall [mural] painting; a mural; 〈프레스코〉 a fresco (pl. ~(e)s)
■—가 a muralist; a mural painter

변 便 〈대소변〉 excreta; excrement; 〈대변〉 feces; stool(s); a bowel movement
◆묽은 변 soft [loose] stool
▶오늘 아침에 변을 봤나요? Did you have a bowel movement [Did your bowels move] this morning?
■—검사 an examination of the feces

변[1] 邊 〈한자의〉 a side; a left-hand [left-side] radical (of a Chinese character)
◆나무목 변 the "wood" radical of Chinese characters

변[2] 邊 〈변리〉 interest (on a loan) ◆비싼[싼] 변으로 at high [low] interest / 2푼 변으로 돈을 꾸다 borrow money at 2 percent interest

변[3] 邊 **1** 〈가장자리〉 an edge; a side
2 〔數〕 〈다각형의〉 a side; 〈입체의〉 an edge; 〈등식·부등식에서〉 a member ◆삼각형의 한 [세] 변 a side [the three sides] of a triangle
3 〈바둑판의〉 the side area
4 〈과녁의〉 the fringe [periphery] of the bull's-eye of a target

변 變 〈돌발사〉 a sudden happening; an unexpected incident [event]; 〈사고〉 an accident; 〈재앙〉 a mishap; a calamity; a disaster; a misfortune; 〈난리〉 a disturbance; a change (for the worse)
◆변이 나다 an accident [incident] happens [occurs] / 변을 당하다 have a mishap; have bad luck; meet with an accident [a disaster] / 변을 모면하다 escape a disaster
▶외국 여행 중 그가 무슨 변을 당했을지도 모른다 Something may have happened to him during his trip abroad.
▶그에게 무슨 변이라도 났습니까? Has anything gone wrong with him?
▶이런 변을 봤나! Oh, what a tremendous mishap! ⇌ What an awful luck!

변격 變格 **1** 〈변칙〉 (an) irregularity
2 〔文法〕 〈변exchange 활용〉 irregular conjugation

변경 邊境 a remote region; outlying [frontier] districts; the border(land); a fringe [border] area
◆변경의 도시 a frontier town; a town on the frontier / 변경의 수비를 견고히 하다 fortify (the defense of) the frontier / 변경을 침범하다 violate a frontier

■—개척자《美》a frontiersman —개척정신 the frontier spirit [mind]

변경 變更 (a) change;〈일부의〉(an) alteration;〈일부 수정〉(a) modification;〈수정〉(an) amendment
♦ 열차 운행 시간의 변경 a change of a train schedule / 외교 정책의 변경 reorientation of a foreign policy / 항로의 변경 deviation
▶ 예정에는 변경이 없습니다 The schedule remains unaltered [unchanged].
—**변경하다** change; alter; modify; shift; amend; initiate a change
♦ 변경할 수 있는[없는] alterable [unalterable] / 날짜를 변경하다 change the date (of) / 명의를 변경하다 transfer 《the title》 to 《another》 / 예정을 변경하다 change [alter] one's schedule; make a change [make alterations] in one's schedule / 주소를 변경하다 change one's address
▶ 명세는 예고 없이 변경될 수가 있습니다〈안내문 등〉The specifications are subject to change without prior notice.

변고 變故〈사고〉an accident; a mishap; an emergency;〈재난〉a disastrous event; a misfortune
♦ 변고없이 지내다 get along without any trouble / 변고를 당하다 meet with trouble; fall on a disastrous event; have a mishap
▶ 그녀가 너무 늦는군. 무슨 변고가 생긴게 아닐까 She is too late. I am afraid something might have happened to her.

변광성 變光星〔天〕a variable star

변괴 變怪〈재변〉something unusual; an extraordinary disaster [event];〈못된 짓〉an outrageous deed; an extraordinary misdeed

변기 便器〈변소의〉a (toilet) stool;〈침실의〉a chamber pot; a nightstool; a bedpan

변놀이 邊— moneylending; usury
—**변놀이하다** lend one's money at interest; run moneylending business

변덕 變德 a whim; a whims(e)y; whimsicality; a caprice; volatility
♦ 변덕스러운, 변덕맞은 capricious; whimsical; full of whims (and fancies); casual; fickle; changeable / 변덕스러운 가을 날씨 changeable autumn weather / 변덕스러운 마음 a fickle [faithless] heart / 변덕을 부리다 behave capriciously
▶ 그것은 일시적인 변덕이었다 It was a caprice of the moment.
▶ 그는 아주 변덕스러운 사람이다 He is a very casual sort of person.
■—**꾸러기**[**쟁이**] a man of (incalculable) moods; a capricious [whimsical] person; a man with a fickle mind

변돈 邊— money lent [put out] at interest; a loan

변동 變動 (a) change; (an) alteration;〈상하의〉fluctuation(s)
♦ 계절적 변동 seasonal fluctuation / 사회의 대변동 social upheaval [cataclysm] / 주가의 끊임없는 변동 a constant fluctuation in stock prices / 변동이 심한 fluctuating 《market, prices》 / 변동이 없는 unchanged; unaltered; firm / 변동이 전혀 없다 show no change;〔證〕be pegged / 변동 / 정책의 대변동을 초래하다 bring about a great change in policy
▶ 생선은 가격의 변동이 심하다 The prices of fish fluctuate very widely.
▶ 그들은 사회의 급속한 변동을 따라갈 수 없었다 They could not keep up with the rapid changes in society.
—**변동하다** change; undergo a change; alter; fluctuate
▶ 주식은 날마다 시세가 변동한다 Stock prices vary [fluctuate] from day to day.
▶ 세계 정세가 변동하고 있다 The world situation is changing.
■—**기** uncertain times —**소득** fluctuating income —**폭** the range of fluctuation《in prices》—**환율** the floating exchange rate《for the won》

변두리 邊— 1〈교외〉the outskirts [environs]《of a town》;〈근교〉the suburbs
♦ 서울 변두리에 on [in, at] the suburbs [outskirts] of Seoul / 전주와 그 변두리에 in and around Chŏnju
▶ 그들은 시 변두리의 모텔에서 1박했다 They stayed at a motel on the outskirts of the town for one night.
2〈가장자리〉the outer edge; the rim; the brim; the fringe

변란 變亂〈사변〉a (social) disturbance; an upheaval;〈반란〉an uprising; a rebellion;〈전란〉a war ♦ 변란을 일으키다 create [make, cause, raise] a disturbance; revolt against
▶ 변란이 일어났다 An uprising broke out [arose].

변론 辯論 1〈법정의〉(oral) proceedings; pleading
♦ 변론에 들어가다 open the (oral) proceedings
—**변론하다** proceed (orally); plead (at the bar, before the court)
♦ 피고를 위하여 변론하다〈형사상〉argue on behalf of the accused;〈민사상〉argue the case for the defendant
▶ 변호인이 피고를 위해 변론했다 The defense attorney [counsel] pleaded [argued] for the accused.
2〈토론〉debate;〈논쟁〉discussion; argument; controversy; disputation
—**변론하다** debate; hold (a) debate; discuss; argue; have [hold] (a) discussion
■—**구두**— oral proceedings [pleadings] **최종**— final [concluding] arguments ■—**가** a debater; an orator —**기일** the date for pleading —**인** a pleader

변류기 變流器〔電〕a converter; a current transformer

변리 辨理 management; disposition —**변리하다** manage [dispose of]《a matter》; conduct《business》■—**공사** a minister resident

변리 邊利 interest《on a loan》⇨ 변(邊)²

변리사 辨理士 a patent lawyer [attorney, agent]

변말 a secret language; a cant phrase; a jargon; a slang; a lingo《pl. ～(e)s》♦ 변말을 쓰다 speak the jargon of one's society [clique]

변명 辨明 an excuse; a plea; a pretext; explanation; vindication; exculpation; justification
♦ 궁색한 변명 a lame [sorry, poor] excuse / 어색한 변명 an awkward excuse
▶ 그런 잘못을 저지른 것에 대해선 변명의 여지가 없습니다 I have no excuse to offer for making such mistakes.
▶ 그런 행동은 어떤 변명으로도 정당화될 수 없다 Nothing can justify such behavior.
▶ 그 남자는 내 변명을 들으려 하지 않았다 He wouldn't listen to my excuses.
—**변명하다** explain; explain *oneself* (for); vindicate (*oneself*, *one's* honor); defend *oneself*; excuse *oneself* (for doing *sth*)
♦ 그는 몰라서[아파서] 그랬다고 변명했다 He pleaded ignorance [illness] as an excuse [in excuse]
▶ 그는 자기가 한 일에 아무런 변명도 하지 않았다 He said nothing whatsoever in explanation of what he had done. ⇒ He did not try to justify what he had done.
▶ 나한테 확실히 변명할 수 있겠니? Can you give me a convincing explanation?
■ —**서** a letter of explanation; a written plea [explanation] —**자** a vindicator

변명 變名 an assumed name ⇨ 변성명

변모 變貌 (a) transfiguration; (a) transformation; a change in *one's* looks [appearance]
—**변모하다** be transformed; change; come to look different (from what it used to be)
♦ 완전히 변모하다 undergo a complete transfiguration [change]
▶ 마을이 완전히 변모해서 나는 깜짝 놀랐다 I was astonished to see how entirely different [changed, transformed] the village was.

변발 辮髮 a pigtail; (the Chinese) queue —**발하다** plait *one's* hair into a pigtail ♦ 변발한 pigtailed / 변발하고 있다 wear a pigtail

변방 邊方 a remote region ⇨ 변경(邊境)

변변치않다 1 〈생김새가〉 plain; homely; unattractive
♦ 용모가 변변치 않은 소녀 an unattractive [plain] girl
2 〈사람·사물이〉 unbecoming; unfitting; ungainly; coarse; poor (workmanship); simple

[解說] 우리 나라 사람은 선물을 줄 경우「변변치않습니다」라고 말하지만 영미인은 그렇게 자기를 낮추지 않는다. 「당신에게 드리는 변변치 않은 선물입니다」란 뜻으로 *Here's something for you.*라고 말하고 난 뒤에 I hope you'll like it.(마음에 드시기를 바랍니다)라고 덧붙여 말하는 경우가 많다. 선물 등을 가벼운 마음으로 받도록 하기 위해 *This is a little something* [*a small gift*].라고 말하는 경우도 있다.

♦ 제 변변치 않은 글 my modest writing / 변변치 않은 사람 a good-for-nothing (fellow) / 변변치 않은 음식 coarse [plain] food
▶ 변변치 않은 것이지만 받아주십시오 I have a small present for you. ⇒ I hope you will accept this as a small token of my gratitude.
3 〈규모·수량이〉 trifling; tiny; small
♦ 변변치 않은 수입 a small income / 변변치 않은 장사 business on a small scale

변변하다 〈생김새가〉 good-looking; handsome; 〈사람·사물이〉 good; fair; decent; respectable; proper
▶ 이 도시에는 변변한 호텔이 하나도 없다 There is not a decent hotel in this town.
▶ 그는 영어로 변변한 편지 한 장 못 쓴다 He can't even write a good letter in English.

변변히 〈잘〉 well; 〈충분히〉 enough; sufficiently; 〈알맞게〉 properly; decently; adequately
♦ 변변히 생각해 보지도 않고 without due [careful, serious] consideration
▶ 어젯밤엔 변변히 자지도 못했다 I couldn't [didn't] sleep very well last night. ⇒ I didn't have a good sleep last night.
▶ 그 아이는 불쌍하게도 변변히 먹을 것도 없었다 The poor boy did not have sufficient food.
▶ 그녀는 편지 한장 변변히 쓸 줄 모른다 She does not even know how to write a letter properly.

변별 辨別 distinction; discrimination

변복 變服 (a) disguise ⇨ 변장

변비 便秘 constipation; costiveness ♦ 변비를 고치다 relieve constipation / 변비에 걸리다 be constipated; suffer from constipation
▶ 나는 일주일 째 변비다 I have been constipated for a week.
▶ 변비약을 주세요 I want some medicine good for constipation.
▶ 운동을 하지 않으면 변비가 된다 Lack of exercise will constipate you [will bind your bowels].
▶ 변비가 좀처럼 낫지 않는다 My constipation is obstinate.

변사 辯士 1 〈말을 잘하는 사람〉 an eloquent speaker; an orator; 〈연사〉 a speaker; a talker 2 〈무성 영화의〉 a silent film narrator; a movie talker

변사 變死 an unnatural [accidental] death; a violent death
—**변사하다** die [meet (with)] an unnatural [a violent] death; be accidentally killed; be killed by [in] an accident
■ —**자** a person who has met [died] an unnatural death; a person accidentally killed

변상 辨償 reimbursement; 〈배상〉 compensation; indemnification; reparation; 〈변제〉 payment ♦ 변상을 요구하다 demand [claim] compensation (for)
▶ 그는 손실에 대한 변상으로 그 회사에서 약간의 돈을 받았다 He accepted from the company a small sum of money in compensation for the loss.
—**변상하다** compensate 《*sb* for loss》; indemnify 《*sb* for losses》; reimburse 《*sb* for the losses》; repair 《the damage》; make good 《a loss》
▶ 당신에게 끼친 피해를 변상하겠습니다 I will pay for [make good] your loss I have caused you.
▶ 그 손해에 대해 변상할 의무가 우리에게는 없다고 생각합니다 We don't think we ought to compensate [pay for] the loss [damage].

■一금 a compensation; an indemnity

변색 變色 change of color; 〈퇴색〉 discoloration; fading
—변색하다 change color; become discolored; discolor; fade; 〈광택이〉 lose (its) luster
♦변색하지 않는 unfading; fast (color)
▶이 천은 변색하지 않는 색으로 염색되어 있다 This cloth is dyed with fast [unfading] color.

변설 辯舌 eloquence; speech; tongue
♦유창한 변설 fluent speech; an eloquent tongue / 변설이 좋다 have a fluent tongue; be fluent in speech
▶그의 변설은 청중을 매료했다 His eloquent speech charmed his audience.

변성 變成 (a) regeneration; (a) metamorphosis —변성하다 regenerate; metamorphose
■—암 a metamorphic rock —작용 metamorphism

변성 變性 degeneration; denaturation
—변성하다 〈바뀌다〉 be denatured; degenerate; 〈바꾸다〉 denaturalize; denature
■—알코올 denatured alcohol —제 a denaturant

변성 變聲 the change [breaking, cracking] of voice —변성하다 one's voice changes [breaks, cracks]
▶아들 녀석이 변성하기 시작했다 My boy's voice has begun to change [break].
▶소년은 사춘기에 이르면 변성하여 목소리가 굵어진다 A boy's voice changes and becomes deeper at puberty.
■—기 the age of the change of voice

변성명 變姓名 1 〈가명〉 an assumed [a fictitious] name; a false name; an alias
—변성명하다 assume another [a false] name
♦변성명하고 under an assumed [a false] name
2 〈개명〉 changing one's name
—변성명하다 change one's name

변소 便所 a rest room; a toilet (room); a bathroom; (美) a lavatory; a water closet (略 W.C.); a washroom; 〈막사·공장 등의〉 a latrine; (美) 〈남자용〉 a men's room; (英) the Gentlemen; Men; 〈여자용〉 a ladies' (powder) room; (英) Ladies; Women; 〈선박의〉 the head; (口) the john; (美俗) the jane; the can
♦변소에 가다 go to the toilet [bathroom, closet]
▶변소에 사람이 있다[없다] The bathroom is occupied [vacant].
▶변소는 어디 있습니까? 〈가정에서〉 May I use your bathroom? ≒ Where can I wash my hands? / 〈공공장소에서〉 Where [Which way] is the rest [men's, ladies'] room?
■공중[공동]— a public toilet [lavatory]; (美) a comfort station [room]; (英) a (public) convenience 수세식— a flush toilet; a water closet 옥외— (美) an outhouse; a privy

변속 變速 a change of speed
▶이 차는 4단 변속이다 This car has a four-speed transmission. ≒ This car is a four speed.
—변속하다 change speed; change [shift] gears
■—기[장치] a gearbox; a transmission

변수 變數 〔數〕 a variable

변신 變身 1 ⇨ 변장
2 〈변태〉 transformation; metamorphosis
—변신하다 change 《into》; turn 《into》; transform oneself 《into》; be transformed [metamorphosed] 《into》

변심 變心 〈마음이 변하기〉 a change of mind [heart]; infidelity; 〈변덕〉 fickleness, inconstancy; 〈변질〉 treachery; betrayal
—변심하다 change one's mind; undergo [have] a change of heart; be inconstant; prove unfaithful 《to》; betray sb
▶여자는 변심하기 쉽다 Women are fickle.
▶쉽게 변심하는 자를 믿지 마라 Don't believe [trust] a man who can easily change his mind.

변압 變壓 〔電〕 voltage transformation —변압하다 transform 《a current》 (in voltage)
■—기 a transformer: 강압 변압기 a step-down transformer / 승압변압기 a step-up transformer

변온동물 變溫動物 〔動〕 a cold-blooded [poikilothermic] animal; a poikilotherm

변용 變容 a transfiguration ⇨ 변모

변위 變位 〔物〕 displacement; 〔醫〕 〈태아의〉 malposition ■—전류 a displacement current

변이 變異 〔生〕 (a) variation; 〈열등한〉 a rogue ■—돌연— (a) mutation ■—설 the variation theory —성 variability —종 a variable species

변장 變裝 (a) disguise
—변장하다 put on a makeup; disguise oneself 《as》; make up 《as》; 〈가장하다〉 masquerade 《as》
♦…으로 변장하여 in [under] the disguise [guise] of... / 여자로 변장하다 disguise oneself as a woman
▶그 왕자는 거지로 변장했다 The prince disguised himself as a beggar.
▶그는 안경과 가짜 콧수염으로 변장했다 He put on glasses and a false mustache for disguise.
▶그는 경찰관으로 변장하고 도망쳤다 He got away dressed like a policeman.
■—술 the art of disguise [camouflage]

변재 邊材 sapwood

변재 辯才 oratorical talent [skill]; 〈능변〉 eloquence; the gift of the gab
♦변재가 있는 사람 an eloquent [a gifted] speaker / 변재가 없다 be awkward in speaking; be a poor speaker
▶그는 변재가 대단하다 He is a really good speaker.

변전 變轉 (a) change; vicissitude; mutation
—변전하다 change; mutate

변전소 變電所 a (transformer) substation

변절 變節 〈주장〉 defection; apostasy; (a) betrayal; (a) treachery
—변절하다 change sides [front]; desert [abandon] one's cause [principles]; go over to 《the other party》; change [turn] one's coat; turn (a)round
■—자 a traitor; a renegade; a turncoat; an apostate

변제 辨濟 repayment; liquidation ─**변제하다** repay; pay (off); liquidate ◆빚을 변제하다 repay *one's* debt; pay off what *one* owes
■─기 the time appointed for payment; maturity: 변제기가 되다[지나다] be due [overdue]

변조 變造 alteration; falsification; forgery ─**변조하다** alter; falsify; forge
◆공문서를 변조하다 alter official documents / 수표를 변조하다 (美) raise a check
■─수표 an altered [a falsified, a forged, a raised] check ─자 a forger; a falsifier ─화폐[지폐] a counterfeit [false] coin [note]

변조 變調 〔樂〕 a change of tone; 〔物〕 modulation; 〈언행의〉 abnormality
─**변조하다** change keys; modulate
■─주파수─ frequency modulation (略 FM, F.M.) 진폭─ amplitude modulation(略 AM, A.M.) ■─관 a modulation tube ─기 a modulator

변종 變種 〔生〕 a variety
◆인공 변종 an artificial [a man-made] variety / 풍토적 변종 a climatic variety / 장미의 새 변종 a new variety of rose

변주 變奏 〔樂〕 playing a variation ─**변주하다** play a variation 《on a tune, on a theme》
─**곡** a variation

변죽 邊─ 〈가장자리〉 a rim; a brim; an edge
변죽울리다 hint; imply; suggest

변증 辨證 demonstration ─**변증하다** demonstrate

변증법 辨證法 〔哲〕 dialectic ◆변증법적(인) dialectic / 변증법적으로 dialectically
─**론자** a dialectician ─**적 유물론** dialectical materialism

변질 變質 change in quality; degeneration; deterioration ◆식품의 변질을 막다 prevent spoilage of food
─**변질하다** change in quality; degenerate; deteriorate; 〈음식물이〉 go bad; spoil
▶더울 때는 음식이 쉽게 변질한다 Food goes bad [spoils] quickly in hot weather.
■─자 a pervert : 그것은 변질자의 소행일 것이다 It must have been done by a pervert.

변천 變遷 〈변화〉 changes; 〈추이〉 (a) transition; 〈성쇠〉 vicissitudes; 〈부침〉 ups and downs (of life)
◆시대의 변천 the changes of times; the changing times / 사태의 급속한 변천에 따라 as a result of the quick changes in the situation / 인생의 변천을 겪어내다 bear up under the vicissitudes of life
─**변천하다** change; undergo [go through] changes; shift ◆변천하는 세태 changing [passing] phases of the world
▶풍속과 습관은 시대에 따라 변천해 왔다 Our manners and customs have changed with the times.

변칙 變則 (an) irregularity; (an) anomaly
◆변칙적인교육 an irregular education / 변칙적인 절차 (an) irregular procedure; an irregular way of doing things / 변칙적인 irregular; anomalous; abnormal / 변칙적으로 by an irregular [an unnatural] method [way]
■─동사 ⇨ 불규칙(~동사)

변태 變態 〔生〕 (a) metamorphosis (*pl.* -ses); (a) transformation; 〈이상〉 (an) abnormality; anomaly ◆변태의[적인] metamorphic; abnormal; perverted
▶올챙이는 개구리로 변태를 한다 Tadpoles are metamorphosed into frogs.
■─성욕 abnormal sexuality [sexual desire]; sexual perversion

변태심리 變態心理 abnormal mentality
─**학** abnormal psychology

변통 便通 the movement [action] of the bowels; a bowel movement
◆하루 한번의 변통 a bowel action every day / 정상적인 변통 regular stools
▶이 약은 변통을 좋게 한다 This medicine keeps the bowels active [quickens the action of the bowels].
▶나는 4일 동안 변통이 없다 I haven't had a bowel movement for four days.

변통 變通 〈융통〉 versatility; adaptability; 〈처리〉 contrivance; management; makeshift; arrangement
─**변통하다** contrive; manage 《with》; make shift; make do; arrange
◆돈을 변통하다 make shift [out] to raise money / 자금을 변통하다 finance 《an enterprise》
▶나는 가까스로 건축 자금을 변통했다 I have managed to raise the money to meet the building expenses.
▶가지고 있는 것으로 어떻게 변통해 보겠습니다 I will make shift with what I have.
■─임시─ a temporary [rough] makeshift ■─수 contrivances; makeshift measures; an expedient

변통성 變通性 〈주변성〉 versatility; adaptability; flexibility; resourcefulness ◆변통성 있는 versatile; adaptable; flexible; resourceful
▶그는 변통성이 없다 He lacks flexibility. ≠ He's incapable of adapting to changing circumstances.

변하다 變─ 〈변화하다〉 change; undergo a change; 〈달라지다〉 become different; be altered; turn; 〈갖가지로〉 vary; 〈바람이〉 come round [about]; shift 《to the east》; 〈변형되다〉 change [turn] (into); be turned (into)
◆변하기 쉬운 changeable; variable; unsettled; 〈변덕스러운〉 capricious; fickle / 변하지 않는 unchangeable; constant; steady / 영원히 변하지 않는 eternal; perpetual; everlasting / 안색이 변하다 change color; change *one's* countenance; turn pale; 〈화가 나서〉 go black in the face / 마음이 변하다 change *one's* mind / 맛이 변하다 turn sour [stale]; 〈육류가〉 get high / 변하지 않다 be [remain] unchanged; be [remain] the same (as before); be constant
▶여름에는 날씨가 잘 변한다 The weather is changeable [inconstant] in summer.
▶보통 사내 아이는 10대에 목소리가 변한다 Usually a boy's voice breaks [changes] when he is in his teens.
▶그의 태도가 지난 1년 사이에 많이 변했다 His attitude has changed [altered] a lot in the past year.

▶지진으로 이 마을은 완전히 변했다 This town has undergone a complete change owing to the damage caused by the earthquake.
▶그는 몰라보게 변해버렸다 He has been completely changed beyond recognition.
▶세상도 이젠 변했다 We are now in a different world. ⇌ How the world has changed!
▶나에 대한 그의 태도가 변했다 His attitude toward me underwent a change.
▶가격은 수요에 따라 변한다 The price varies with demand.
▶사랑은 미움으로 변할 수 있다 Love can turn to hate. ⇌ Love can give way to hate.
▶신호가 빨강으로 변했다 The lights turned red.
▶바람이 남풍에서 서풍으로 변했다 The wind has shifted from south to west.

변함없다 變— unchanging ♦변함없는 우정 constant [steady] friendship / 변함없이 without a change; constantly; as ever; as always
▶나의 의견은 변함없다 I am still of the same opinion.
▶그의 재주는 변함없었다 His skill remained the same.
▶지난 10년 동안 이 도시의 인구는 변함없다 There has been no change in the population of this city these ten years.
▶《會話》「그녀의 병세는 차도가 있습니까?」「별로 변함없습니다」 "Is she feeling better?" "She's about the same."

변혁 變革 〈변화〉 a change; 〈개혁〉 a reform; a reformation; 〈혁명〉 a revolution; an upheaval ♦기술상의 변혁 a technical innovation
▶전기기구의 보급이 가사에 대변혁을 가져왔다 The wide use of electrical appliances has revolutionized housework.
—**변혁하다** change; reform; revolutionize
▶원자력의 이용은 우리의 생활 양식을 변혁할 것이다 The use of atomic energy will revolutionize our way of life.

변형 變形 〈모양의〉 transformation; metamorphosis; modification; variation; deformation; 〈변형된 모양〉 a modification; a variety; a deformity
▶선인장의 가시는 잎의 변형이다 Cactus thorns are metamorphosed leaves.
—**변형하다** 〈바꾸다〉 change (the shape of) sth; transform; metamorphose; 〈바뀌다〉 change [turn] 《into》; be transformed [metamorphosed] 《into》
■—**생성문법** transformational generative grammar

변호 辯護 1 〈변명〉 defense; vindication; 〈정당화〉 justification; 〈해명〉 explanation
▶그의 행동은 변호의 여지가 없었다 There was no justification for his behavior. ⇌ What he did was indefensible.
—**변호하다** defend; vindicate; justify; speak in defense of sb; speak for [in favor of] sb
♦친구를 변호하다 say in justification of one's friend
▶지사는 새 제안을 변호했다 The governor spoke in defense of the new proposal.
2 〈재판정에서의〉 (a) defense 《피고의》; pleading 《원고·피고의》
♦피고의 변호에 나서다 plead for the defendant; hold a brief for the defendant / 변호를 의뢰하다 employ [approach] a lawyer
▶아무도 그의 변호를 맡지 않았다 Nobody undertook his defense.
—**변호하다** defend; plead for [in favor of] 《the accused》; argue [plead] the case 《for the defendant》
▶법정에서는 경험이 많은 변호사가 그를 변호했다 A lawyer of vast experience defended him in court.
■—**자기** self-justification; self-defense —**권** the right of defense —**료** a lawyer's [an attorney's] fee —**의뢰인** a client

변호사 辯護士 a lawyer; 《美》 an attorney(-at-law); 〈법정 변호사〉 《英》 a barrister; 〈사무 변호사〉 《英》 a solicitor 《▶미국에서는 법정변호사와 사무변호사의 자격 구분이 없음》
♦변호사를 (개업)하고 있다 practice law; be in a law practice / 변호사를 대다 get [retain, employ] a lawyer
▶나는 변호사에게 사건의 변호를 맡겼다 I got a lawyer to plead my case.
■—**개업** a practicing lawyer —**고문** a legal adviser —**악덕** 《美口》 a shyster (lawyer) —**형사[민사]** a criminal [civil] lawyer ■—**법[法]** the Attorneys-at-Law Act —**사무소** a law office; a lawyer's office —**시험** the bar examination —**회** a lawyer's association; a bar association; the bar [Bar]

변호인 辯護人 a counsel; a pleader; a defender; an advocate; a defense lawyer
♦원고측— the plaintiff's lawyer 피고측— the defense counsel ■—**단** the (defense) counsel —**측 증인** a defense witness

변화 變化 1 〈바뀜〉 (a) change; 〈부분적〉 (an) alteration; 〈변동〉 (a) variation; 〈변이〉 (a) mutation
♦날씨의 변화 a change in the weather / 온도의 변화 a variation of temperature / 그의 태도의 변화 his change of attitude / 정세[환경]의 변화 a change in situation [of circumstances] / 변화있는 changeful; inconstant / 변화없는 changeless; unchanging; constant / 변화가 없다 remain unchanged
▶나는 변화가 없는 시골 생활에 싫증이 난다 I am tired of the monotonous life in the country.
▶시대의 변화에 맞추어 살아가야 한다 You have to live keeping pace with the change of the times.
—**변화하다** change; undergo a change; turn 《into, to》; shift 《into》; alter; vary
♦변화하기 쉬운 changeable; variable; liable to variation / 변화하기 쉬운 날씨 changeable [variable] weather
▶상황은 계속 변화하고 있다 Circumstances are constantly changing.
2 〈변성·변태〉 (a) transformation; (a) transfiguration
—**변화하다** transform (itself) 《into》; transfigure
3 〈다양〉 variety; diversity

♦ 변화가 많은 full of variety; varied / 변화가 많은 생활을 하다 have a life full of variety; lead a varied [an eventful] life
─변화하다 vary
▶ 차창의 경치는 시시각각 변화했다 The view from the train window varied every minute [from one minute to the next].
4 〖文法〗〈격(格)의〉declension;〈동사의〉conjugation;〈어미·어형의〉inflection
─변화하다 decline; conjugate; inflect
▶ 다음 동사를 변화시키시오 Conjugate the following verbs.

변화구 變化球 〖野〗〈커브〉a curve (ball);〈스크루볼〉a screwball ♦ 변화구를 던지다 throw a breaking pitch

변환 變換 change; conversion;〈물길 등의〉diversion;〖數〗transformation ─**변환하다** change; convert; divert;〖數〗transform
♦ 변환할 수 있는 convertible / 변환할 수 없는 inconvertible / 열을 일로 변환하다 convert heat into work / 열에너지로 변환되다 be transformed into heat energy

변환기 變換器 〖電〗a converter; an inverter; a transducer

별 1 〈천체〉a star;〈총칭〉the stars
♦ 망원경으로 별을 관측하다 observe the stars through a telescope
▶ 별이 빛나는 밤이었다 It was a starlit night.
▶ 하늘에는 별이 총총 빛나고 있다 Stars are [There are stars] twinkling in the sky. ⇒ The sky is starry.
▶ 그것은 하늘의 별 따기다 It is a prize beyond my reach [ability]. ⇒ It is an unattainable object.
2 〈별표〉a mark; an asterisk;〈장성 등의 계급장의〉a star
♦ 별 둘의 장군 a two-star general; a major general / (군인이) 별을 달다 become a general

-별 -別 classified by ♦ 도(道)별 인구 population by the provinces / 성(性)[국적]별로 분류하다 classify by sex [nationality]
▶ 직업별 전화번호부가 있습니까? Do you have a classified (tele)phone book?

별갑 鱉甲 tortoiseshell ♦ 별갑테의 안경 a pair of tortoiseshell-rimmed glasses
■ ─세공 tortoiseshell work

별개 別個 a different thing; another thing; a separate [distinct] one;〈예외〉an exception; a special case
♦ 별개의 〈개개의〉several; separate; discrete;〈다른〉different; another / 별개로 separately; severally
▶ 이것은 별개의 문제다 This is another [a separate] problem [question].
▶ 그의 수법은 내 것과는 아주 별개다 His technique is quite different from mine.
▶ 학문과 상식은 별개다 Learning is one thing, and common sense another.

별거 別居 separation;〈법률적인〉legal [judicial] separation
▶ 그녀는 남편과의 별거를 원하고 있다 She wants a separation [wants to separate] from her husband.
▶ 그들은 지금 별거 중이다 They are now living separately.
─**별거하다** live separately;〈생활형편상〉live away [apart] (from one's family [husband, wife]); live in separate houses
■ ─**수당** a separate allowance [maintenance];〖法〗alimony;〈회사가 주는〉an allowance for maintaining two households

별건 別件 〈별개의 사건〉another incident
■ ─**체포** an arrest on a separate charge

별것 別 1 〈진기한 물건〉a rare article; a rarity; a peculiar thing
▶ 그것은 별것 아니다 That does not matter much. ⇒ It's nothing to speak of.
▶ 감기는 들었지만 별것 아냐 I have a cold, but it's nothing serious.
▶ 그는 재산이라고 해야 별것 아니다 He has no property to speak of [worth mentioning].
▶ 참 별것이 다 있군 How strange [weird]!
2 〈다른 것〉another thing; a different item

별견 瞥見 a glance; a glimpse
─**별견하다** glance ⟨at⟩; have [take] a glance ⟨at⟩; catch [get] a glimpse ⟨of⟩; cast a glance ⟨over, upon⟩; glance through

별고 別故 1 〈사고〉an accident; a mishap; an untoward event; a hitch
♦ 별고 없이 〈건강하게〉quite [very] well;〈무사히〉safe(ly); without mishap [accident] / 별고 없이 지내다 get along well [all right]
▶ 그날 밤은 별고 없이 지나갔다 The night passed quietly [without incident].
▶ 별고 없으신지요? How are you? ⇒ How are you getting along?
▶ 별고 없으셨지요? I hope you have been well.
2 〈까닭〉a particular reason

별관 別館 an annex(e) (to a hotel); (美) an extension; an outhouse; an outbuilding
♦ 박물관의 별관 an annex to the museum; the museum annex

별기 別記 ♦ 별기와 같이 as stated [noted, mentioned] in a separate paragraph; as stated elsewhere
─**별기하다** state [write] in a separate paragraph; make a separate notation [mention] (of)

별꼴 別 ─ an eyesore; an offensive figure [person, thing, sight]; a disgusting behavior
▶ 별꼴 다 보겠네 What an eyesore! ⇒ What a sight [spectacle]! ⇒ What a disgusting sight!

별꽃 〖植〗a chickweed

별나다 別─ eccentric; queer; unusual; odd; singular
♦ 별난 사람 an eccentric [a strange, a peculiar] man; a queer fish [card, customer] / 별난 취미 a taste for odd things; a bizarre taste / 별나게 굴다 behave eccentrically [extraordinarily, uncommonly]
▶ 그는 좀 별난 데가 있다 There is something odd about him.

별나라 the land of the stars; the stellar world
별납 別納 separate payment [delivery]
♦ 요금 별납 charges separately paid / 요금 별납 우편의 [으로] (美) postpaid; (英) post-free

—**별납하다** pay [deliver] separately

별다르다 別— particular; special; exceptional; extraordinary
♦별다른 일 something particular
▶별다른 일 없이 잘 지냅니다 I'm getting along as usual with nothing particular happening.
▶댁에 별다른 일 없으시지요? Are your people doing well [all right]?
▶그녀가 보여준 것은 별다를 것 없는 그림이었다 It was an ordinary [a featureless] picture that she showed me.
▶그는 별다른 이유 없이 회의에 참석하지 않았다 He didn't attend the meeting without any particular reason.

별당 別堂 an annex; an outbuilding; a detached building

별도 別途 〈딴 방면〉 a separate way; another way; 〈딴 용도〉 a separate [special] use
♦별도의 separate; special / 별도로 〈별개로〉 separately; apart; for a special purpose [use]; 〈추가로〉 extra; additionally; in addition
▶그에게는 별도의 수입이 있다 He has a special [casual] income.
▶값은 5만원이며, 포장비·운송료는 별도(입니다) 《표시》 Price 50,000 won, packing and postage extra.

별도리 別道理 another way [means]; a better way [measure]; an alternative; a choice
♦별도리 없이 unavoidably; inevitably
▶그가 혼자 간다고 하면 별도리가 없는 일이지 We cannot help it if he wants to go alone.
▶그렇게 할 수 밖에 별도리가 없다 There is no alternative [We have no choice] but to do so.
▶운명이라면 별도리 없지 We have to accept our fate. ⇌ We must resign ourselves to fate.

별동 別棟 an outbuilding; a house [building] separate from the main building

별동대 別動隊 a detached force; a flying column

별똥별 a meteor ⇨ 유성(流星)

별로 別— particularly; in particular; specially; 〈그다지〉 《not》 very; 《not》 much
♦별로 좋지 않다 be not particularly good
▶그녀는 돈이 별로 없다 She doesn't have (very) much money. ⇌ She is not very rich.
▶그것은 별로 중요하지 않다 It is of no great importance.
▶【會話】「요즘 바쁘셨지요?」「별로 그렇지도 않았습니다」 "Have you been busy recently?" "No, not very much."
▶【會話】「다치지 않았니?」「별로」 "Weren't you hurt?" "No, I'm all right."
▶별로 이야기할 것도 없다 I have nothing particular to tell you.
▶별로 이렇다 할 이유는 없다 I have no particular reason for it.

별리 別離 parting ⇨ 이별

별말 別— an extraordinary [unexpected] remark; an absurd [unreasonable] remark
—**별말하다** make an unexpected [extraordinary] remark; make an absurd [a preposterous] remark
▶별말 다 한다 What a thing to say! ⇌ Nonsense! ⇌ Don't say such ridiculous things!
▶《감사하다는 말에 대한》 별말씀 다 하십니다 Oh no, not at all. ⇌ Oh, don't mention it.

별명 別名 another name; a byname; a nickname; an alias; also known as 《略 a.k.a.》
♦별명을 …이라고 하는 also called…; otherwise known as; a.k.a./ 별명을 붙이다 give *sb* a nickname; nickname *sb* / 별명으로 부르다 call *sb* by 《his》 nickname
▶그는 「꼬마 잭」이란 별명으로도 불린다 He is often called "Tiny Jack," too.
▶고수머리라서 그의 별명은 「컬리」다 His nickname is "Curly" because he has curly hair.

별명 別命 another order; a special mission
▶별명이 있을 때까지 기다리는 게 좋다 You had better wait for another order.

별무늬 a star [star-shaped, starry] pattern

별문제 別問題 another [a different] question [problem]; another thing; a different story [case] ♦…은 별문제로 하고 apart [aside] from…; separately from…
▶그것과 이것은 별문제다 They are two different things. ⇌ They must be dealt with separately.
▶이런 사정에서는 우리가 성공하느냐 못하느냐는 별문제다 Under the circumstances, it is irrelevant [it doesn't matter] whether we succeed or not.

별미 別味 〈맛〉 delicate [exquisite] flavor [taste]; 〈음식〉 a (choice) delicacy; a gourmet delight; dainty foods

별반 別般 particularly ⇨ 별로
▶정세에는 별반 변화가 없다 There has been no particular change in the situation.

별별 別別 〈온갖〉 of various [different] and unusual sorts; all kinds of
♦별별 나무들 various kinds of trees; trees of various kinds / 별별 물건 unusual things of every sort (and kind)/ 별별 사람 all sorts of people (in all conditions of life)/ 별별 수단을 다 쓰다 try every means available; try every possible [imaginable] method
▶별별 의견이 다나와서 결론에 이르지 못했다 With various opinions presented, we couldn't reach a conclusion.

별봉 別封 (a letter [package] under) separate cover; an accompanying letter [package] ♦별봉으로 보내다 send under separate [another] cover

별빛 starlight ♦별빛이 밝은 밤 a clear [bright] starry night; a starlit night / 별빛에 [아래] in (the) starlight ▶별빛에 사람 모습이 보였다 A figure was visible in the starlight.

별사람 別— a queer (kind of) person; an oddity; an eccentric (person); 《口》 a crank; an oddball
▶별사람 다 보겠군 I have never seen such a mess of a man.
▶그도 별사람 아니다 He too is a mediocre [an ordinary] man.

별세 別世 death; decease; demise; passing away —**별세하다** die; decease; pass away; depart this world

별세계 別世界 〈딴 세상〉 another world; a different world; a world of its own
♦ 별세계의 of another world
▶ 그녀는 별세계 사람처럼 아름답다 She is as beautiful as if she had come from another world.
▶ 그곳은 실로 별세계다 The place makes a world of its own. ⇌ It is a world in itself.

별소리 別— an extraordinary remark ⇨ 별말

별송 別送 —별송하다 send by separate mail [under separate cover] ■—소포 a package sent by separate mail [post]

별쇄 別刷 〔印〕 an offprint

별수 別數 **1** 〈행운〉 good luck [fortune]; special luck
♦ 별수가 나다 come upon [run into] unexpected good fortune; make a big [smash] hit; strike a bonanza
▶ 어딜 가나 별수 없을 거다 Wherever you may go, you will not have any better luck.
2 〈묘책〉 a special means; a clever scheme; a secret formula (*pl.* ~s, -lae); a magical formula; measures
▶ 그건 바람직하지 않지만 별수가 없다 It's not a desirable thing, but it can't be helped.
▶ 이젠 별수 없다 Now we are at the end of our tether [resources]. ⇌ Now there is no help for it.
3 〈여러 방법〉 every means; all resources
♦ 별수를 다 쓰다 try every means available; try every possible method

별스럽다 別— eccentric ⇨ 별나다

별식 別食 a special [rare] dish; a special menu

별실 別室 a separate room; another [a different] room; 〈특실〉 a special room

별안간 瞥眼間 〈갑자기〉 suddenly; all of a sudden; all at once; 〈느닷없이〉 unexpectedly; abruptly
♦ 별안간 나타나다 burst on the scene / 별안간 유명해지다 become famous overnight; spring into fame / 별안간 죽다 die suddenly
▶ 차가 별안간 섰다 The car stopped suddenly [abruptly]. ⇌ The car came to a sudden [an abrupt] stop.
▶ 날씨가 별안간 변했다 There was a sudden change in the weather.

별일 別— 〈특별한 일〉 a particular thing [event]; an unusual event; 〈이상한 일〉 an odd thing; a strange thing; 〈변고〉 an accident
♦ 별일없이 without any accident [mishap]; safely; peacefully
▶ 그날은 별일없이 지나갔다 The day passed without incident.
▶ 별일없이 잘 지내실 줄 압니다 I hope you are getting along all right. ⇌ I hope you have been well.
▶ 별일 다 보겠네 Ridiculous!
▶ 거 참 별일일세 How can a thing like that happen, I wonder?

별자리 〔天〕 a constellation

별장 別莊 a villa; a country house; (美) a cottage
♦ 여름 별장 a summer house [cottage] / 해변 가의 별장 a seaside villa / 청평의 별장 *one's* cottage at Ch'ŏngp'yŏng; *one's* Ch'ŏngp'yŏng house
■—지기 a villa keeper

별정직 別定職 privileged [special] government positions ■—공무원 officials in special government service

별종 別種 〈다른 종류〉 a different kind; 〔生〕 〈변종〉 a variety
♦ 별종의 different; another

별지 別紙 a separate sheet of paper; an annexed [attached] paper; an accompanying sheet; an annex; an enclosure
♦ 별지의 annexed hereto / 별지와 같이 as per enclosure [separate papers] / 별지에 기재된 바와 같이 as stated in the accompanying sheet [document]
▶ 해답은 별지에 쓰시오 Write your answers on another [a separate] sheet.

별책 別冊 a separate volume; an independent volume; a separately bound volume; 〈잡지 등의〉 an extra number [issue]
▶ 지도가 별책으로 되어 있다 The maps come in a separate volume [are bound separately].
■—부록 a separate-volume supplement ■—색인 a separate [loose] index

별천지 別天地 another world ⇨ 별세계
▶ 여기는 별천지 같습니다 I feel as if I were in a different world [paradise]. ⇌ This is something like another world.

별칭 別稱 another name ⇨ 별명(別名)

별편 別便 separate post; (美) separate mail; another post ♦ 별편으로 보내다 send under separate cover; send by separate mail [post]

별표 —標 a star (mark); an asterisk(*); a pentagram (★) ♦ 별표가 붙은 단어 a word (marked) with an asterisk; an asterisked word

별표 別表 an attached list [chart]; an annexed table ♦ …에 관해서는 별표 참조 refer to [see] the attached table [chart] for...
■—양식 an attached form

별항 別項 a separate paragraph; 〈조문의〉 another clause [provision, section]
♦ 별항에 기재된 바와 같이 as mentioned [stated, shown] in another section
▶ 이 사항은 별항에 있다 This matter comes under a different [separate] heading.

별행 別行 another line ♦ 별행을 잡다 begin a new line ▶ 이름을 별행에 쓰시오 Write your name on a separate line.

별호 別號 〈호〉 a pen name; 〈별명〉 a nickname

볍씨 rice seed

볏[1] 〈닭의〉 a cockscomb; a comb; a crest 〈of a fowl〉 ♦ 볏이 있는 crested

볏[2] 〈보습의〉 a moldboard

볏가리 a rick; a stack of rice straw

볏단 a sheaf [bundle] of rice

볏모 rice seedlings [sprouts]; young rice plants

볏섬 a straw rice-bag; a sack of rice

볏짚 rice straw ♦ 볏짚을 단으로 묶다 make bundles of rice straw; bundle rice straw; tie up rice straw into bundles / 볏짚을 엮다 plait rice straw / 볏짚을 깔다 spread rice straw

병 丙 **1** 〈등급의〉 the third class [grade]; C; 〈제3자〉 a third party [person] ♦ 병종이 되다 be put under Class C **2** 〈천간의〉 the 3rd of the 10 Heaven's Stems

병 病 **1** 〈일반적〉 《美》 sickness; 《英》 illness; 〈특정한 이름이 붙는〉 a disease; 〈만성의〉 a malady; an affection; 〈가벼운〉 an indisposition; an ailment; 〈국부적인〉 a trouble; a complaint; a disorder
♦ 마음의 병 mental illness / 가슴의 병 a chest trouble [disease] / 중병 a serious [severe] illness [disease] / 가벼운 병 a slight [minor] illness; a minor ailment / 오래 끄는 병 a protracted [lingering] sickness, a disease of long duration / 위[심]장병 a stomach [heart] disease [trouble] / 불치병 an incurable [a fatal] illness / 잘 낫지 않는 병 an obstinate disease / 병원에 친구 병문안을 가다 go to the hospital to see *one's* sick friend; visit *one's* sick friend in the hospital
〈병이[은]〉 병이 나다 get sick [ill] / 병이 낫다 a disease is cured; 〈사람이 주어〉 recover from *one's* sickness; be cured of a disease; get well of an illness / 병이 위중하다 *one's* illness is serious; 〈사람이 주어〉 be very [seriously, critically] ill
▶ 아버지 병은 어떠시냐? How is your father?
〈병을〉 병을 앓다 suffer from a disease / 병을 고치다 cure a disease [an illness]; cure *sb* of a disease [an illness] / 병을 치료하다 treat a disease / 병을 치료받다 undergo [receive] medical treatment / 병을 예방하다 prevent [stave off] a disease / 병을 옮기다 transmit [communicate] *one's* illness [disease] to 《another》; infect 《another》
▶ 그는 아직 한번도 병을 앓은 적이 없다 He's never had [known] a day's illness.
〈병에〉 병에 걸리다 get [become, fall] ill [sick]; be taken ill; contract a disease; take a disease; be attacked [affected] by a disease; 〈전염성의 병〉 catch a disease / 병에 듣다 〈효험이 있다〉 be of medicinal value
▶ 저 아이는 병에 잘 걸린다 The boy gets ill easily.
▶ 병에 걸렸지만 곧 나았다 I got [was taken] sick, but got well [recovered] soon.
▶ 아이들은 여러가지 병에 걸리기 쉽다 Children are susceptible to various illness.
▶ 특히 아기들이 이 병에 걸리기 쉽다 Infants particularly are subject to this disease.
〈병으로〉 병으로 인한 결석 absence on account of [due to] illness / 병으로 누워 있다 be ill [sick] in bed / 병으로 고생하다 be afflicted [troubled] with a disease / 병으로 죽다 die of sickness [illness]; die of [from] a disease (▶ 죽음의 직접적인 원인을 나타낼 경우는 from이 아니고 of)
▶ 나는 병으로 1주일간 휴가를 받았다 I was on sick leave for a week.
▶ 나는 병으로 학교를 결석했다 I was absent from school because I was sick.
▶ 할머니는 80세 때 병으로 돌아가셨다 My grandmother died of a disease at eighty.
2 〈약점・나쁜 버릇〉 a fault; an infirmity
▶ 게으른 것이 그의 병이다 Idleness is his fault.
▶ 그 병이 다시 도졌다 He's got that habit again.
3 ⇨ 고장(故障)

병 瓶 a bottle; 〈꽃병〉 a vase
♦ 작은 약병 a phial; a vial / 병마개를 하다 cap a bottle / 병마개를 뽑다 uncap a bottle / 물을 병에 채우다 put water into a bottle; fill a bottle with water; bottle water
▶ 식초는 병으로 판다 They sell vinegar by the bottle.
▶ 이 위스키는 한 병에 20,000원이다 This whisky is 20,000 won a bottle.
▶ 그는 위스키 한 병 비웠다 He emptied a bottle of whisky.
▶ 이 병은 얼마나 들어갑니까? How much does this bottle hold?
■ —맥주 bottled beer

병가 兵家 〈군인〉 a man of arms; a military man; 〈병법가〉 a tactician; a strategist

병가 病暇 sick leave ▶ 그는 병가 중이다 He is on sick leave.

병결 病缺 absence due to [on account of] illness ♦ 병결 중이다 be [go] on the sick list
▶ 그는 오늘 병결이다 He is absent today due to sickness.
—병결하다 go [report] sick

병고 病苦 the pain [torment] of sickness; suffering from illness
♦ 병고에 시달리다 suffer acutely from *one's* illness / 병고를 덜다 relieve *one's* suffering from illness
▶ 그는 병고와 빈곤에 쪼들리고 있다 He is suffering from illness and poverty.
▶ 그는 병고를 견디지 못해 자살했다 Unable to bear the pain of sickness, he killed himself.

병골 病骨 a sickly person; a weak [delicate] person ▶ 그 소년은 날 때부터 병골이었다 The boy was born weak [sickly from birth].

병과 兵科 an arm [of the army]; a branch of the service ■ 보— the infantry (arm [branch]) 포— the artillery (arm) ■ —장교 a combatant officer

병구 病軀 a sick body; a sickly constitution
♦ 병구를 이끌고[무릅쓰고] in spite of *one's* failing health ▶ 그는 병구를 무릅쓰고 외출했다 He went out in spite of his poor health.

병구완 病— 〈간호〉 nursing; tending 《a sick person》; care 《for the sick》
♦ 극진한 병구완 careful nursing
▶ 첫째로 병구완, 둘째로 약 Nursing first, medicine next. ⇌ Nursing before medicine.
▶ 그녀는 남편의 오랜 병구완으로 쓰러졌다 She broke down from the fatigue caused by nursing her husband for such a long time.
—병구완하다 nurse; tend; care for; attend on
♦ 밤새도록 병구완하다 sit up with 《a patient》; attend on [nurse] 《a sick person》 all through the night

병권 兵權 military power [authority] ♦ 병권을 잡다 possess [assume, seize, grasp, hold] military power

병균 病菌 a germ ⇨ 병원(病原) (~균)
　■─보유자 a germ carrier
병근 病根 the cause [origin] of a disease; a morbific agent; 〈화근〉 the root [cause] of an evil ◆병근을 없애다 〈병원(病原)을〉 stamp out a disease; 〈화근을〉 root out an evil
병기 兵器 arms; a weapon (of war); 〈총칭〉 ordnance; weaponry
　■공격[방어]— an offensive [a defensive] weapon 화학— a chemical weapon ■—고(庫) an armory; an arsenal —공업 armament industry —장교 an ordnance officer —제조 weaponry; manufacture of arms (and ammunition) —창(廠) an arsenal; an ordnance depot; 《美》 an armory; an arms factory —학 ordnance science
병나다 病— 1 〈병들다〉 fall [get, be taken] ill [sick]; suffer from a disease; take a disease; be affected by a disease
◆과식[과음]하여 병나다 make *oneself* ill by overeating [overdrinking]
▶그는 병났다 He is sick [ill].
▶그는 병나서 결근했다 He was on sick leave.
2 〈고장나다〉 get [be] out of order; *sth* go wrong 《with》
병나발 瓶— ◆병나발 불다 drink from a bottle; take a swig
병내다 病— 1 〈병을〉 cause [bring on] illness; make *sb* sick 2 〈고장을〉 put [get] *sth* out of order; make *sth* go wrong [break down]
병독 病毒 a virus; a disease germ; taint
◆병독에 감염되다 be infected 《with》 / 병독을 퍼뜨리다 disseminate [spread] infection
　■—매개 동물 a vector —보유자 a germ carrier; a reservoir (host)
병동 病棟 a ward —격리— an isolation [isolated] ward 일반— a general ward
병들다 病— 〈병나다〉 fall [get, be taken] ill [sick]; take a disease; suffer from a disease; be attacked [affected] by a disease
◆병든 ill; sick; in ill [bad] health; diseased / 병들기 쉬운 liable to illness [a disease] / 병들어 눕다 lie on a sickbed; be ill in bed
▶어머니는 병들어 한 달 동안 누워 계신다 My mother has been ill [sick] in bed for a month.
▶그는 로마에서 병들었다 He fell [was taken] ill in Rome.
병란 兵亂 a war; a military disturbance
병력 兵力 〈전투력〉 military strength; force of arms; 〈군인수〉 the (numerical) strength of an army
◆100만의 병력 a force 1,000,000 strong; an army of 1,000,000 effectives / 병력 200명의 중대 a company 200 strong; a company of the strength of 200
▶병력에 있어서는 아군이 적군보다 우세하다 Our army is superior to the enemy in strength [number].
▶그들은 병력을 증강했다 They reinforced in their troops.
병력 病歷 the history of a case; *one's* medical history; *one's* past illness; a case [clinical] history; an anamnesis ◆아무의 병력을 조사하다 check *sb's* medical history
병렬 並列 arranging in a row [line]; parallel
◆병렬의 parallel
—하다 〈…이〉 stand [be] in a row [rows]; 〈…을〉 draw up in a line; arrange in a row; line up
　■—접속[연결] parallel connection —회로 [電] a parallel circuit
병리 病理 pathology ■—해부학 morbid [pathologic(al)] anatomy
병리학 病理學 pathology ◆병리학(상)의 pathological / 병리학상으로 pathologically
　■—교실 a pathology classroom —자 a pathologist
병립 並立 standing side by side; compatibility
　■—개념 [論] a coordinate concept
병마 兵馬 〈병기와 군마〉 arms and (war-) horses; 〈병사와 군마〉 soldiers and (war-) horses; 〈군대〉 an army; troops
병마 病魔 a disease; the demon of ill health; the curse of a disease
◆병마가 덮치다 be seized [afflicted] with an illness; be attacked by a disease / 병마에 시달리다 suffer from illness; labor under *one's* disease / 병마에 쓰러지다 succumb to a disease; come down with an illness
▶귀국 후 곧 그에게 병마가 덮쳤다 He fell ill soon after he returned from abroad.
병마개 瓶— a bottle cap [top, stopper, cork]; a metallic cap; a crown cap [cork]; a cork; a stopper
◆병마개를 뽑다 〈코르크 마개를〉 uncork a bottle; pull out a stopper / 맥주병마개를 따다 uncap a bottle of beer / 병마개를 하다 cap [cork] a bottle
병명 病名 the name of a disease
◆병명을 알 수 없는 병 an unidentified disease [case] / 병명을 밝히다 diagnose [identify] a disease
▶그는 병명을 알 수 없는 병에 걸려 있다 He is suffering from an unidentified disease.
병목 瓶— the neck of a bottle; 〈장애〉 the bottleneck ▶이 지점이 자동차 흐름의 병목이다 This point is a bottleneck in road traffic.
병무 兵務 conscription affairs
　■—국 the Military Service Bureau —청 the Office of Military Manpower Administration —행정 conscription administration
병발 並發 1 〈병의 동시 발생〉 complication
—병발하다 〈병이〉 have a complication; be complicated by 《another disease》
▶나는 맹장염에서 복막염을 병발하였다 I suffered [was suffering] from appendicitis complicated with peritonitis.
▶다른 병이 병발했다 A complication set in.
2 〈일이 동시에 발생함〉 concurrence; synchronization; coincidence ◆두 사건의 병발 the coincidence of two events —병발하다 concur; synchronize; coincide 《with》; break out at the same time
　■—반응 simultaneous reaction
병법 兵法 〈전술〉 tactics; 〈전략〉 strategy
　■—가(家) a tactician; a strategist
병사 兵士 a soldier; a private; a warrior; a

병사 兵舍 (a) barracks ⇨ 병영(兵營)
병사 兵事 military affairs ■—계 an official in charge of military affairs —과 a military affairs section
병사 病死 death of [from] a disease [an illness, a sickness]; dying of sickness
—병사하다 die of an illness [a sickness]; die from a disease
▶ 병사한 사람이 많았다 There were many deaths due to sickness.
▶ 그 배우는 23세에 병사했다 The actor died of a disease at the age of twenty-three.
병살 倂殺 〔野〕 a double play
—병살하다 make [execute, pull off] a double play
♦ 병살당하다 be doubled up; have [be victims of] a double play
병상 病床 a sickbed ♦ 병상에 눕다 lie in *one's* sickbed; be ill in bed
▶ 그녀는 아이의 병상 곁에서 간병했다 She watched at her child's bedside.
▶ 그의 아내는 병상에 누워있다 His wife is sick [ill] in bed.
■—일지 〈병원의〉 a clinical report [diary]; 〈환자의〉 a sickbed record; a nurse's report
병상병 病傷兵 the sick and wounded (soldiers); the invalid (soldiers)
병색 病色 a sickly complexion; sickly appearance
병서 兵書 〈전략〉 a book on military strategy; 〈전술〉 a book on military tactics; 〈군사학〉 a book on military science
병석 病席 a sickbed ♦ 병석에 눕다 be ill in bed; lie in *one's* sickbed / 병석에서 일어나다 leave *one's* sickbed; rise from a sickbed
병설 竝設 establishment as an annex; juxtaposition
—병설하다 establish 《a research center》 as an annex 《to the college》
▶ 그들은 그 대학에 연구소를 병설했다 They built a research institute in juxtaposition with the university.
병세 病勢 the condition [state] of a disease [patient]
♦ 병세가 악화되다 grow worse; take a turn for the worse / 병세가 호전되다 grow better; take a turn for the better
▶ 그의 병세가 상당히 진행되어 있다 His illness is in its advanced stage. ⇌ He is far gone in his sickness.
▶ 그의 병세는 일진일퇴하고 있다 His condition fluctuates between better and worse.
병소 病巢 〔醫〕 a focus 《*pl*. ~es, foci》; a lesion; a nidus 《*pl*. ~es, nidi》 ♦ 병소를 적출하다 extract a focus
병술 瓶— bottled liquor; liquor sold by the bottle
병신 病身 1 〈장애자〉 a deformed [maimed] person; a deformity; a cripple
2 〈병든 몸〉 a sick body; a sickly person; a sickly constitution
3 〈바보〉 a fool; a stupid (person)
♦ 병신같은 소리 a silly talk; nonsense / 병신같은 짓을 하다 do a foolish [stupid] thing; act foolishly
4 〈온전치 못한 물건〉 a defective thing; an odd set
♦ 병신으로 만들다 damage [spoil] *sth*; make *sth* defective
병신구실 病身— a folly; foolery; a foolish move [act] —병신구실하다 act foolishly [like a fool]; do *sth* foolish [stupid, silly]; make a fool of *oneself*; play [act] the fool
병실 病室 a sickroom; 〈병원의〉 a (sick) ward; a hospital room; a (hospital) ward; 〈함선내의〉 a sick bay [berth]; 〈학교·공장의〉 an infirmary
♦ 외과 병동 제3병실의 환자 the patient in Room No. 3 of the surgical ward
■개인— a private room
병아리 a chicken; a chick ♦ 한 배의 병아리 a brood of chickens / 병아리를 까다 hatch chickens ■—감별사 a chicken sexer
병약 病弱 (constitutional) infirmity; delicate [sickly, weak] constitution
—병약하다 weak; sickly; invalid; infirm; 〈서술적〉 have a weak [delicate] constitution
♦ 병약한 아이 a sickly child
▶ 그녀는 병약하다 She is rather sickly.
▶ 그는 날 때부터 병약했다 He was born weak [sickly from birth].
병어 〔魚〕 a pomfret
병역 兵役 〈군복무〉 military service; service in the army
♦ 병역을 필한 자 a person who fulfilled *one's* military service / 병역에 복무하다 do military service; serve (*one's* time) in the army / 병역을 면제받다 be exempted from military service / 병역을 기피하다 dodge [evade] *one's* military service
▶ 모든 남성은 병역의 의무가 있다 Every male citizen is liable to military service [to serve in the army].
■—기피 evasion of military service —기피자 a shirker of military service —면제 exemption [immunity] from military service —법 the military service law —연한 the term of military service
병영 兵營 〈병사(兵舍)〉 a barracks 《▶ 보통 복수형으로 단수·복수 취급》; a camp ■—생활 a barrack [an army] life
병용 竝用·倂用 —병용하다 use [make use of] together; use jointly [in combination] 《with》; use 《two things》 at the same time
♦ 가루약과 물약을 병용하다 take a powder medicine with a liquid one
▶ 이 약은 다른 어떤 약과 병용해서도 안된다 Don't take this medicine together with any other medicine.
▶ 전력회사는 석탄과 석유를 병용하고 있다 The electric power company uses oil with coal.
병원 兵員 〔軍〕 military personnel; strength of an army [troops]
병원 病院 a hospital; 〈사무실〉 an infirmary
♦ 병원에 입원하다 enter [go into] (the) hospital; be hospitalized (▶ 입원·퇴원 등의 경우

(美)에서는 관사 the를 붙이지만 (英)에서는 붙이지 않음) / 병원에 입원시키다 send *sb* to (the) hospital; hospitalize / 병원에 다니다 attend a hospital (as an outpatient); go to (the) hospital / 병원에 입원해 있다 be in (the) hospital / 병원으로 병문안 가다 visit [call on] *sb* in (the) hospital; go to ask after ((a friend)) in hospital
▶ 그는 구급차로 병원에 실려갔다 He was carried to the hospital by ambulance.
▶ 곧 병원에 (의사의 진찰을 받으러) 가는 게 좋겠어 You'd better go and see your doctor [go to the doctor's (office)] right away. (▶ go to (the) hospital은 입원이 필요한 중병을 암시하므로 이 예문으로는 부적합함)
■개인— a private hospital; (英) a clinic 구급— an emergency [receiving] hospital 소아과— a children's hospital 종합— a general hospital ■—선 a hospital ship —장 the director [head, superintendent] of a hospital

병원 病原 (醫) the cause [origin] of a disease [an illness]; an etiological cause
◆병원 불명의 병 a disease of unknown etiology / 병원의 pathogenic
■—균 pathogenic bacteria; a (disease) germ; a bacillus (*pl.* -li) —체(體) a pathogen; a pathogenic organ [microbe]

병인 病因 the cause of a disease; an etiological cause [factor] ■—론[학] etiology

병자 病者 〈환자〉 a sick person (▶ an ill person이라고는 하지 않음. ill을 쓰면 「악인」의 뜻); a patient; (총칭) the sick; 〈만성적인 병약자〉 an invalid
◆병자용의 식사 a diet for the sick; an invalid diet / 병자같다 look sickly
▶ 간밤에는 밤새도록 병자를 간호했다 Last night I stayed up all night nursing the sick person.
▶ 홍수가 난 뒤에 병자가 속출했다 After the flood, people fell ill one after another. ⇌ After the flood, disease was prevalent.

병작 並作 tenancy on half-and-half shares [basis] —병작하다 tenant ((a farm)) on half-and-half shares

병장 兵長 〔陸軍·海兵〕 a sergeant; 〔海軍〕 a petty officer second class; 〔空軍〕 a staff sergeant

병적 兵籍 1 ⇨ 병적부 2 〈군인의 신분〉 one's military status
◆병적에 올리다 enlist [enroll *oneself*] in the army; enter [join] the army

병적 病的 unsound; morbid; diseased; 〈변태적〉 abnormal
◆병적인 안색 an unsound complexion / 병적 소질 diathesis / 병적일 정도의 호기심 morbid curiosity / 병적으로 morbidly; abnormally / 병적으로 좋아하다 have a morbid liking for; have a weakness [passion] for
▶ 그의 호기심은 병적이다 His curiosity is morbid.
▶ 그녀는 병적으로 뚱뚱하다 She is unhealthily fat.
▶ 그녀는 탐정소설에 병적이라 할 정도의 흥미를 가지고 있다 She has a morbid interest in detective stories.

병적부 兵籍簿 a muster roll

병정 兵丁 a soldier
◆병정놀이를 하다 play (at) soldiers
■—개미 〔動〕 a soldier (ant); a dinergate

병조림 甁— bottling —병조림하다 bottle *sth*; seal *sth* in a bottle
◆병조림한 피클[식품] bottled pickles [food]

병존 並存 coexistence —병존하다 coexist ((with)); be coexistent ((with)); exist together

병졸 兵卒 〈사병〉 a private (soldier); a (common) soldier; (美) an enlisted man; (총칭) the ranks, the rank and file ◆병졸로 강등되다 be degraded [demoted] to the rank of private

병종 丙種 the third class [grade]
◆병종이 되다 〈징병 검사에서〉 be put under Class C

병종 兵種 an arm ((of the army)) ⇨ 병과(兵科)

병중 病中 ◆병중임에도 불구하고 in spite of *one's* illness; though *one* is ill [sick] / 병중이다 be ill in bed
▶ 그의 병중에 어머니가 별세했다 His mother died while he was ill [during his illness].

병증 病症 the nature of a disease

병진 並進 —병진하다 keep abreast of *sb*; keep pace with *sb*; advance side by side
■—운동 〔物〕 translational motion

병참 兵站 〔軍〕 communications; impedimenta; supply
■—감 the quartermaster general (略 QMG) —기지 a supply [commissary, logistics] base; a base for supplies —보급창 (美) a quartermaster depot —부 the commissariat; a supply department —부대 (美) the quartermaster corps —사령부 the Logistic Support Command —선 a line of communications [supply]; a supply line —장교 (美) a quartermaster; a commissary —학 logistics

병충해 病蟲害 damage from disease and harmful insects

병치 並置 juxtaposition —병치하다 put [place] ((two things)) side by side ((with)); juxtapose ((with, to)); place in juxtaposition ((with))

병칭 並稱 —병칭하다 rank [class] *sb* with ((another)) ◆병칭되다 be ranked [classed] ((with))

병탄 倂呑 annexation; absorption; (a) merger —병탄하다 annex ((to)); absorb; merge; swallow up; devour

병폐 病弊 ills; evils (⇨ 폐해(弊害)) ◆사회적 병폐 social ills / 물질문명의 병폐를 없애다 get rid of the evils of material civilization

병풍 屛風 a folding screen
◆여덟폭 병풍 a eight-fold screen; a folding screen of eight panels / 병풍을 치다 set up a screen / 병풍으로 칸막이하다 screen off
▶ 그 방은 병풍으로 칸막이가 되어 있었다 The room was screened off.
■—바위 a sheer [perpendicular] cliff

병합 倂合 〈영토 등의〉 (an) annexation; 〈회사 등의〉 (an) amalgamation; 〈흡수〉 absorption; consolidation; (a) merger; 〔電算〕 coalescence —병합하다 annex; amalgamate; unite; merge;

consolidate; 〔電算〕 coalesce
♦병합되다 be annexed 《to》; be amalgamated [merged] 《into》
▶우리 회사는 머지않아 그 회사를 병합할 것이다 Our company will amalgamate with that company in the near future.
▶로마는 많은 영토를 병합했다 Rome annexed many territories.

병해 病害 〈작물의〉 blight; crop damage (due to disease)

병행하다 並行— 1 〈나란히 가다〉 go side by side 《with》; go abreast 《of》; keep pace 《with》; run parallel 《to, with》
2 〈동시에 행하다〉 do 《two things》 simultaneously; perform [practice] at the same time
▶두 가지 일이 병행해서 진행되고 있다 The two jobs [projects] are going on at the same time.
▶권리와 의무는 병행한다 Rights and duties go hand in hand.

병화 兵火 a fire caused by war ⇨ 전화(戰火)
♦병화로 황폐해지다 be laid waste by a fire caused by warfare

병환 病患 〈어른의 병〉 a disease; sickness; illness ▶아버님의 병환은 좀 어떻습니까? How is your (sick) father?

병후 病後 〈회복기〉 convalescence
♦병후의 몸조리 aftercare / 병후 요양중인 사람 a convalescent / 병후의 convalescent / 병후에 after an illness / 병후가 양호하다 convalesce favorably
▶그는 온천에서 병후의 요양을 하고 있다 He is recuperating at a hot spring.
▶그는 병후에 체력이 쇠약해지고 있다 He is weak after his sickness [illness].

별 the sun; sunshine; sunlight; the rays of the sun
♦별이 잘 드는 방 a sunny room / 별이 잘 안드는 unsunned; shadowy / 별이 잘 들다 be sunny; admit ample sunshine / 별에 말리다 dry sth in the sun / 별에 쬐다[쏘이다] expose sth to the sun / 별에 타다 get sunburnt; be tanned with the sun / 별을 쬐다 take the sun; bask [bathe] in the sun
▶그는 그것을 별에서[별이 안 드는 데서] 말렸다 He dried it in the sun [shade].
▶별이 따갑다 The sun is burning-hot.
▶내 방은 별이 잘 든다 My room gets a lot of sunshine [is very sunny].

보 〈들보〉 a beam; 〈대들보〉 a girder

보 步 1 〈걸음〉 a step; a pace
♦제1보 the first [initial] step / 2보 전진[후퇴]하다 take [make] two steps forward(s) [backward(s)]
2 〈단위〉 one step; a step
♦3보 떨어져 있다 be three steps away
▶오십보 백보다 There is little [not much] difference between the two.

보 洑 1 〈저수지〉 a dam; a dammed pool for irrigation; a reservoir; 〈작고 낮은 댐〉 a weir; 〈갑문·수문〉 lock
2 ⇨ 봇물

보 褓 〈덮개〉 a cloth-covering (for a table); a cloth cover; 〈보자기 등〉 a (cloth) wrapper; a square cloth for wrapping; a wrapping cloth
♦상보 a tablecloth / 책보 a cloth for wrapping books / 보에 싼 꾸러미 a parcel wrapped in a cloth; a cloth-wrapped bundle

-보 -補 〈보좌관〉 an assistant; 〈견습·후보〉 a probationer
♦서기보 an assistant clerk / 외교관보 a probationary diplomat / 차관보 an assistant vice-minister [under secretary]

보각 補角 〔數〕 a supplementary angle; a supplement

보간법 補間法 〔數〕 interpolation

보감 寶鑑 1 〈책〉 a handbook; a manual; a thesaurus 《*pl.* ~es, -ri》
2 〈모범〉 a model 《of》; (an) example 《of》; a paragon; a mirror; an exemplar

보강 補強 reinforcement
▶이 담은 보강이 필요하다 This wall needs to be reinforced.
▶수상은 내각을 보강 조치했다 The Prime Minister took steps to strengthen the Cabinet.
—보강하다 reinforce; strengthen
■—공사 reinforcement work —재 a stiffener —제 a reinforcing agent —증거 〔法〕 a corroboration —철근 additional bar

보강 補講 a supplementary lecture
—보강하다 give a supplementary lecture; make up for a missing lecture
▶그녀는 수학을 보강하고 있다 She is taking supplementary lessons in mathematics.

보건 保健 preservation of health; 〈위생〉 hygiene; sanitation
♦국립 보건원 the National Health Institute / 세계보건기구 the World Health Organization (略 WHO)
■—물리학 health physics —복지부 the Ministry of Health and Welfare —소 a (public) health center —식량 sanitary [healthful] food —원 a hygienist; 〈여자〉 a (public) health nurse —음료 a hygienic drink —제도 the health system —지도 a health guidance —체육 health and physical education —행정 public health administration

보검 寶劍 a precious [treasured, famous] sword; 〈의장용〉 the sword of state [honor]

보결 補缺 〈채움〉 filling a vacancy; supply of deficiency; supplementation; 〈사람〉 a substitute; a alternate
♦보결의 supplementary; substituted / 보결로 입학하다 be admitted into a school to fill (up) a vacancy
■—모집 invitation 《of students》 for filling vacancies: 보결 모집하다 invite 《students》 to fill vacancies —생 a student for filling a vacancy; a supplementary student; a standby student —선수 a substitute (player); a reserve —시험 a special entrance examination for standby students

보고 報告 a report; an account; (a) briefing; information; a statement; 〈통계표〉 returns
—보고하다 report; make [submit] a report 《of, on》; inform *sb* of 《an event》; give an account of 《an affair》; brief *sb* on 《a matter》; 〈학회 등에서〉 read a paper 《on》

♦보고 받다 be briefed (on); get a briefing (from *sb* on a matter)
▶그는 그 사고를 경찰에 보고했다 He reported the accident to the police.
▶나는 그 문제에 대해 아무런 보고를 받지 못했다 I have received no report on that matter.
▶보고는 다음과 같다 The report runs as follows.
■연차[연례]— an annual report 중간— an interim report 최종— the final report ■—문학 reportage —자 a reporter; an informer; an informant —회 a briefing session

보고 寶庫 a treasure-house; a treasury
♦지식의 보고 a treasure-house [storehouse] of knowledge [information]
▶이 지역은 지하 자원의 보고다 This region is a treasure-house of underground resources.
▶바다는 광물과 식량의 보고다 The sea is a treasure-house of minerals and food.

보고 to *sb* ⇨ 더러²

보고서 報告書 a (written) report (on); 〈학회의〉 a paper; 〈회고의〉 a memoir; 〈통계표〉 returns; 〈협회 등의〉 a journal; transactions
♦그 사고의 보고서 a written report on the accident / 보고서를 작성하다[쓰다] make a report (on) / 보고서를 제출하다 send in [file] a report

보고타 〈콜롬비아의 수도〉 Bogotá

보관 保管 safekeeping; custody; keeping; a diposit; 〈창고의〉 storage
—보관하다 keep; have *sth* in one's keeping; have the custody (of); take charge (of); keep *sth*; hold (money) on deposit
♦보관시키다 ask *sb* to keep *sth* for (one); give *sth* in the custody of *sb* / deposit (money) with *sb* / 보관되어 있다 be in custody (of); be in one's safekeeping
▶서류는 김선생이 보관하고 있다 The papers are in the custody of Mr. Kim.
▶너의 화물은 역에 보관되어 있다 Your packages are being held at the station.
▶그녀가 내 시계를 보관하고 있다 She keeps my watch. ⇒ My watch is in her keeping.
▶귀중품은 접수처에 보관하십시오 The receptionist will take custody of your valuables.
■—료 charges for custody; 〈창고의〉 storage fee —물 an article in custody; a thing on deposit —소 a depository: 휴대품 보관소 (美) a checkroom; a cloakroom; (英) left-luggage office —인[자] a custodian; a keeper; a depository —증 a certificate of custody; a deposit receipt; 〈수화물의〉 a claim check

보국 報國 patriotism; service(s) to one's country
—보국하다 serve one's country; place oneself in the service of one's country; render services to the state

보국안민 輔國安民 building up the nation and providing for the welfare of the people
—보국안민하다 promote the interests of the nation and provide for the people

보국훈장 報國勳章 the Order of National Security Merit

보굿 1 〈나무의〉 a piece of bark 2 〈그물의〉 a net float (usually made of bark)

보궐 補闕 filling a vacancy ⇨ 보결

보궐선거 補闕選擧 an election to fill a vacancy; (英) a by-election

보균 保菌 —보균하다 carry germs [bacteria]; be infected; carry a disease
■—자 a germ [bacteria, bacillus] carrier; an infected person: 보건소는 보균자를 격리했다 The health center isolated the germ carrier from others.

보그르르 simmeringly ⇨ 바그르르

보글보글 bubblingly; burblingly; simmeringly
▶물이 보글보글 끓었다 The water bubbled up.
—보글보글하다 bubble up; rise in bubbles

보금자리 a nest; a roost; a home
♦사랑의 보금자리 a love nest / 보금자리로 돌아가다 return to its nest; fly home to roost; return home / 보금자리에 들다 settle in the nest; nest / 보금자리를 짓다 build (and settle in) a nest; nest (in a tree)
▶새가 보금자리에 들어 있다 The birds are at roost [in their nests].

보급 普及 distribution; diffusion; spread; propagation; 〈확장〉 extension; 〈대중화〉 popularization
♦학문[교육]의 보급 the spread of learning [education]
▶불교는 한자 보급에 도움이 되었다 Buddhism helped the spread of Chinese characters.
—보급하다 distribute; spread; diffuse; extend; propagate; popularize
♦보급되다 pervade; permeate; come into wide [general] use / 지식을 보급하다 spread [diffuse] knowledge
♦컴퓨터는 널리 보급되어 있다 Computers have come into wide use.
▶그 기계는 전세계에 보급되어 있다 The machine is widespread all over the world.
■—소 a distributing agency —판 a popular [cheap] edition

보급 補給 supply; replenishment
♦보급이 끊어지다 go [run] out of supplies; become short of supplies
▶비상 식량의 보급이 재해 지역에 공수됐다 An emergency food supply was airlifted to the disaster area.
—보급하다 supply (*sth* to *sb*, *sb* with *sth*)
♦배에 연료를 보급하다 supply the ship with fuel; refuel the ship / 영양을 보급하다 take furnishing of nutrition
▶배는 식량과 연료를 보급하기 위해 항구에 들어왔다 The ship came to port to replenish its food and fuel supplies.
■—관 a supply officer; a quartermaster —기지 a supply base [depot] —로 a supply route [road] —선 a supply ship

보기 〈예〉 an instance; a case; an example; 〈선례〉 a precedent ♦보기를 들다 draw [quote] an instance (from)
▶이것이 좋은 보기다 This is a good example.

보기 [골프] a bogey; a bogy; a bogie
■더블— a double bogey

보깨다 〈뱃속이〉 suffer indigestion; sit heavy

on the stomach; be not easily digested; remain undigested in the stomach
▶ 이 음식은 속이 보깬다 This food sits [lies] heavy on the stomach.
보나마나 needless to say; to be sure; undoubtedly
▶ 그녀석 보나마나 거짓말일 거야 He is certainly telling a lie. ⇌ No doubt he is telling a lie.
▶ 너는 보나마나 이 책을 읽었겠지 I'm sure [No doubt] you've read this book.
보내기 狀 — making irrigation ditches
보내다 1 〈물건·사람 등을〉 send; 〈파견하다〉 dispatch; 〈물품을〉 forward; 〈배나 화차로〉 ship; 〈송금하다〉 remit; 〈일방적으로〉 send *sth* to
♦ 편지를 보내다 send a letter / 심부름 보내다 send *sb* on an errand / 소포 우편으로 보내다 send *sth* by parcel post / 우편환으로 돈을 보내다 remit money by money order / 편지를 써 보내다 write (a letter) to *sb* / 기사를 보내다 〈기자 등이〉 file a story
▶ 나는 해마다 그녀에게 크리스마스 카드를 보낸다 I send a Christmas card to her every year.
▶ 그의 조부는 그가 보내는 돈으로 생활하고 있다 His grandfather lives on an allowance from him.
▶ 아버지는 나에게 매달 학비를 보내신다 My father supplies me with my school expenses every month.
2 〈배웅하다〉 see off; send off
♦ 손님[친구]을 보내다 see a guest [a friend] off
3 〈시간·세월을〉 pass (time); pass away (*one's* time); kill time; spend (*one's* time)
♦ 할일없이 시간을 보내다 live in idleness; idle *one's* time away / 독서로 시간을 보내다 spend *one's* time (in) reading / 만년을 즐겁게 보내다 live the last years [rest] of *one's* life happily / 외로운 세월을 보내다 lead a lonesome life
▶ 나는 오늘 오전에 텔레비전을 보면서 시간을 보냈다 I wasted my time watching TV this morning.
▶ 지난 일요일에는 잠으로 하루를 보냈다 I dozed away the day last Sunday.
4 〈그냥 가게 하다〉 let (it) go / 투수의 공을 그대로 보내다 let a pitch go by
보너스 a bonus 〈⇨ 상여금〉 ▶ 오늘 월급 2개월분에 상당하는 보너스를 받았다 We got a bonus equivalent for two months' pay.
보늬 〈밤의 속껍질〉 an astringent coat
보닛 〈여성 모자〉 a bonnet; 〈자동차의〉 《美》 a hood; 《英》 a bonnet
보다¹ 1 〈눈으로〉 see; look at; take [have] a look (at); get (a) sight (of); witness
▶ 어디 좀 봅시다 Let me have a look at it.
▶ 좀더 자세히 보자 Let's take a better look [have a closer look] at it.
▶ 무얼 보고 있습니까? What are you looking at?
▶ 그는 하늘을 보고 있었다 He was looking (up) at the sky.

▶ 모두 여기를 봐 주세요 Look this way, everybody.
▶ 이것 좀 보렴 Just look at this.
▶ 우[좌]로 봐 **(口슈)** Eyes right [left]!
▶ 누군지 가 보아라 〈문앞에 손님이 왔을 때〉 Go and see who it is.
▶ 경찰관을 보자 그는 도망쳤다 He ran away at the sight of a policeman.
▶ 보는 것 듣는 것이 모두 신기했다 Everything I saw and heard was new to me.
▶ 그 여자는 보면 볼수록 아름답다 The more closely I look at her, the more beautiful she becomes.
▶ 나는 저런 짐승을 본 적이 없다 I've never seen an animal like that.
▶ 이 그림을 잘 보시오 Have [Take] a good look at this picture. ⇌ Look at this picture carefully.
▶ 그녀는 창문 쪽을 보았다 She looked toward the window.
▶ 얼핏 보기에는 쉬운 일 같았다 It seemed an easy task at first sight.
▶ 사람의 얼굴을 말똥말똥 보는 것은 실례다 It is impolite of you to stare at people.
▶ 나는 그녀가 털실로 양말을 뜨고 있는 것을 보았다 I saw her knitting wool stockings.
▶ 그는 똑바로 그녀의 눈을 보며 「사랑합니다」 라고 말했다 He looked her (straight) in the eye(s) and said, "I love you."
2 〈관찰하다〉 observe; view; look at; see; 〈시찰하다〉 inspect; visit
▶ 사장은 내일 공장을 보러 온다 The president is inspecting [visiting] the factory tomorrow.
▶ 어떻게 그가 헤엄치는지 잘 보아라 Observe how he swims.
▶ 그는 미국의 교육상황을 보러 갔다 He has gone to America to observe educational conditions.
▶ 이 책을 읽어보면 외국인이 본 한국을 알 수가 있다 In this book we can find Korea as seen by foreigners.
3 〈돌보다〉 look [see] after; take charge of; take care of
▶ 우리 아기를 봐 주시겠습니까? Will you look after [take care of] our baby?
▶ 누가 이 집을 보고 있나요? Who is taking care of this house?
▶ 나는 그에게 집을 비운 동안 봐 달라고 청했다 I asked him to look after my house while I was out [while I was away, during my absence].
4 〈구경하다〉 see [do] the sights ((of a place)); do [visit] ((a place)); visit ((a museum)); tour; go to see ((the movies))
♦ 볼 만하다 be worth seeing [visiting]; be visitable
▶ 경주는 고도이므로 절 등 볼만한 곳이 많다 Kyŏngju is an old city so there are a lot of temples and other places to see.
▶ 그녀는 한 달에 한 번 연극을 보러 간다 She visits theater once a month.
▶ 그는 야구[영화]를 보러 갔다 He went to see the baseball game [the movies].
5 〈읽다〉 read; see; 〈훑어보다〉 look through;

보다²

look over; 〈구독하다〉 take (in) 《a newspaper》
▶ 나는 아침에 신문을 보고 저녁에 잡지를 읽는다 I look through the newspapers in the morning and read magazines in the evening.
6 〈헤아리다〉 consider; deliberate; think over
▶ 나를 봐서 그를 용서해 주시지 않겠어요? Won't you please forgive him for my sake?
▶ 이전의 행동을 보아 이번만은 용서하겠다 I will excuse you this once out of consideration for your previous conduct.
7 〈조사·검사하다〉 look over [into]; examine; check; see; 〈찾아보다〉 refer to 《a dictionary》; consult 《a dictionary》
▶ 거실에 있는 난로를 껐는지 보고 올게 I'll go and see if I turned off the stove in the living room.
▶ 그녀는 물건을 사기 전에 잘 본다 She examines an article before buying it.
▶ 나는 그 여자에게 수프 맛을 봐 달라고 했다 I asked her to taste the soup.
▶ 문을 잠갔는지 봐 주십시오 Please see if the door is locked. ⇌ Please check the door to see if it is locked.
8 〈점치다〉 read; tell
♦ 손금을 보다 read *sb's* hand [palm]; have *one's* fortune told 《by a palm reader》 / 신수를 보다 tell [forecast] *sb's* fortune
▶ 나는 사주를 보았다 I had my fortune told by a fortune-teller.
9 〈여기다〉 take 《for》; look upon 《as》; regard 《as》
▶ 그렇게 보는 사람도 있습니다 Some people think [take it] that way.
▶ 나는 그를 친구로 보지 않는다 I don't look on [regard] him as a friend.
▶ 많은 사람들이 이 소설을 애거서 크리스티의 대표작으로 보고 있다 A lot of people regard [look upon] this novel as Agatha Christie's most important work.
10 〈판단하다〉 judge; 〈추정하다〉 presume; 〈산정하다〉 calculate; 〈간주하다〉 regard 《as》
▶ 나는 그를 잘못 봤다 I misjudged him.
▶ 내가 보는 눈이 틀림없다 My judgment never errs.
▶ 나는 그녀를 양가 출신으로 보았다 I judged her to be from a respectable family.
▶ 조난자의 대부분은 사망한 것으로 보인다 It is presumed that most of the victims are dead.
▶ 그는 그것을 쓸모없는 것으로 보았다 He regarded it as useless.
▶ 겉보기에는 그들은 친한 사이 같다 Seemingly [Apparently] they are close friends. ⇌ They seem [appear] to be close friends.
▶ 어떻게 보아도 그녀는 40이 넘어 보인다 She is over 40 (years old) in every respect [way].
11 〈겪다·입다〉 encounter; suffer; experience; undergo; go through; enjoy
♦ 손해를 보다 suffer a loss; lose (money) 《over》 / 이익을 보다 make a profit / 재미를 보다 have a good time (of it); have fun; enjoy prosperity
▶ 재미 보십시오 Have a good time. ⇌ Have fun. ⇌ 〈장사꾼에게〉 I wish you a lot of business.
▶ 너석에게 따끔한 맛을 보여주겠다 I'll show [teach] him a thing or two.
▶ 휴강이 되어 덕을 좀 보았다 I was a bit of luck that the lecture was canceled.
12 〈치르다〉 take; undergo
♦ 시험을 보다 take [undergo] an examination; sit (for) an examination
▶ 그는 시험을 보지 않고 대학에 입학했다 He was admitted into a university [college] without examination.
13 〈똥·오줌을 누다〉 relieve *oneself*; relieve nature; go to stool
♦ 대변을 보다 have a bowel movement; have a motion / 소변을 보다 urinate; make [pass] water; pass [discharge] (*one's*) urine
▶ 소변을 보고 싶었다 I needed to go to the bathroom. ⇌ I felt the need to urinate.
14 〈장에서 물건을 사거나 팔다〉 ♦ 장을 보다 buy [sell] in the market; do *one's* [the] marketing / 장보러 가다 go shopping; go marketing
15 〈값을 평가하다〉 price; name [bid] a price (for)
▶ 5천원 보면 잘 본거죠 Five thousand won should be enough.
16 〈새식구를 얻거나 맞다〉 get; have
♦ 며느리[사위]를 보다 get a daughter-[son-]in-law / 손자를 보다 have [get] a grandson [grandchild] / 자식을 보다 get [have] a child; beget [father] a child
17 〈몰래 사귀다〉 have a secret (love) affair 《with》
18 〈참고 기다리다〉 bear; stand; wait for
▶ 보자보자 하니까 너무 거만하구나 I can no longer put up with his arrogance. ⇌ His arrogance has almost exhausted my stock of patience.
19 〈맡아보다〉 take [have] charge of; deal with; undertake; act as
♦ 사회를 보다 preside at [over] 《a meeting》; take the leadership 《of a meeting》; 《美口》 emcee 《a show》 / 사무를 보다 do [carry on] business
▶ 그 여자는 저 은행에서 사무를 보고 있다 She works in that bank.

보다² 〈시도하다〉 try; test; attempt
▶ 할테면 해봐라 Try and do it. ⇌ Go ahead, if you dare.
▶ 맞혀 보아라 Try to guess.
▶ 날 한번 시켜 봐라 Give me a chance.
▶ 한 번 더 해봐 Try and do it again.
▶ 시험적으로 그 신제품을 써 보자 Let's give the new product a try.
▶ 이 비디오카메라를 시험적으로 써 보겠다 I'll take this video camera on trial.
▶ 그는 새 옷을 입어 보았다 He tried on a new coat.

보다³ 〈추측〉 it seems (to *one*) 《that》; I guess
▶ 그런가 보다 I guess [suppose] so.
▶ 비가 오려나 보다 It looks like rain.
▶ 그는 친구가 많은가 보다 He appears to have a lot of friends.

보다⁴

1 〈비교〉 than; to
▶ 그는 나이보다 늙어 보인다 He looks older than he really is.
▶ 그는 나보다 빨리 헤엄칠 수 있다 He can swim faster than I [(口) me].
▶ 항복하느니보다 죽는 편이 낫다 I would rather die than surrender.
▶ 나는 저것보다 이것이 좋다 I like this better than that. ⇌ I prefer this to that.
▶ 나는 그보다 그녀를 더 좋아한다 I love her more than (I love) him.
▶ 그는 나보다 일을 빨리 한다 He is a quicker worker than I (am). ⇌ He works more quickly than I (do).
▶ 한국의 기후는 영국보다 쾌적하다 The climate of Korea is more pleasant than that of England.
▶ 이보다 큰 행운은 없다 There can be no greater fortune than this.
▶ 붓은 칼보다 강하다 〈속담〉 The pen is mightier than the sword.
▶ 그는 누구보다 열심히 공부했다 He studied [worked] harder than anyone else.
▶ 혼자 가기보다 가이드를 고용하는 편이 안전할 것이다 It will be safer to get a guide than (to) go alone.
▶ 그는 나보다 세 살 아래다 He is three years younger than I (am). ⇌ He is younger than I by three years.

2 〈한층 더〉 more; still [much] more
▶ 톰도 나이가 들었지만 존은 보다 더 나이가 들었다 Tom is old but John is still older [older still].

보다못해 being unable to stand by (any longer); being more than one can bear to see

보답 報答 repayment of a kindness; (a) recompense; a return
◆ …의 보답으로서 in recompense [return] for / 충분한 보답을 받다 be amply rewarded [recompensed]
▶ 이것이 고인에 대한 최소한의 보답입니다 This is the least I can do to show my gratitude to the deceased.
— **보답하다** recompense 《sb for》; show one's gratitude; repay sb's kindness [favor]
◆ 친절에 보답하다 repay sb for 《(his) kindness》; repay sb's kindness / 친절을 악으로 보답하다 pay kindness with evil
▶ 남에게 친절하면 언젠가 보답받는다 Be kind to people, and you will someday be rewarded.
▶ 선생의 도움에 보답할 길이 없습니다 I will never be able to repay you for your help.
▶ 회사는 그의 손실에 충분히 보답해 주었다 The company amply recompensed him for the loss.
▶ 나는 어머니의 사랑에 보답할 수 있을는지 모르겠다 I wonder if I will be able to return my mother's love.

보도 步道 《美》 a sidewalk; 《英》 a pavement; a footpath; a footway ■ 횡단— 《英》 a pedestrian crossing; 《美》 a crosswalk ■육교 a pedestrian overpass; 《英》 a pedestrian bridge

보도 報道 news; a report 《of, on》; coverage; information; 〈방송〉 newscast; intelligence (▶news, information, intelligence는 셀 수 없는 명사. 셀 때는 a piece of news 등으로 씀)
◆ 보도의 자유 freedom of the press / 그 사고의 보도 a report of the accident / 신문 보도에 따르면 according to a newspaper report / 보도의 자유를 위협하다 threaten freedom of the press / 보도에 접하다 receive the news 《(of)》 / 그 살인사건에 관해 단편적인 보도를 하다 make a fragmentary report of the murder case
▶ 신문의 보도는 정확하지 않았다 The report in that newspaper was not accurate.
— **보도하다** report; cover (▶보통「기자」가 주어); inform sb of 《an event》; notify sb of sth
◆ 이미 보도한 대로 as previously reported / 크게[큰 표제로] 보도하다 give prominent coverage 《to》; headline / 신문에 자세히 보도되다 get full coverage in the press
▶ 신문은 그 사고를 보도할 것이다 The newspaper will report 《on》 that accident.
▶ 그 사건을 신문에서는 어떻게 보도하고 있습니까? How is the accident reported [handled] by (the) press [in the newspapers]?
▶ 신문은 나날의 사건을 보도한다 The newspaper informs us of daily events.
▶ 모든 신문이 한보 사건을 상세히 보도했다 Every paper covered the Hanbo scandal in detail. ⇌ Every paper gave detailed coverage to the Hanbo scandal.
■ 신문— a press report ■ 가치 news value —관제 〈보도금지〉 a news blackout; 〈검열 통과분만을 보도〉 news censorship; a press ban —기관 an information [a news] medium 《pl. ~s, -dia [-diə]》; the press —반 a press corps 《pl. ~ [kɔ́ːrz]》 —사진 a news photo(graph) —원 a reporter; a newsman —전(戰) a reportorial warfare —진 the press; reporters; a news front; the newsmen; 《英》 the pressmen

보도 輔導 guidance; direction
◆ 청소년의 보도 the protection and guidance of youth [young people] — **보도하다** guide; direct; lead — 직업[학생]— vocational [student] guidance

보라 violet ⇨ 보랏빛

보라매 a young hawk (tamed for hawking)

보람 **1** 〈좋은 결과〉 (an) effect; (a) result; 〈가치〉 worth; 〈이익〉 use; avail; fruit; benefit
◆ 보람없이 to no avail; without avail / 노력한 보람도 없이 in spite of [for all] one's efforts / 치료한 보람도 없이 all medical care proving of no avail / 보람(이) 있다 be worthwhile; be worth doing / 보람있는 생활을 하다 live a useful life; lead a worthwhile life; live to some purpose / 사는 보람이 있다[없다] have something [nothing] to live for; be [be not] worth living / 사는 보람을 느끼다 find one's life worth living; find this world worth living
▶ 아이들은 내가 사는 보람이다 Children are what I live for.
▶ 노력한 보람도 없이 그의 외아들은 죽었다 In spite of every medical effort his only son died.
▶ 이것은 보람있는 일이다 This is a rewarding job. ⇌ This is a job worth doing.

▶애 쓴 보람이 있었다 I have not labored in vain.
▶노력한 보람으로 그는 시험에 합격했다 Thanks to his efforts [hard study], he passed the examination. ⇒ His efforts were rewarded with success on [(英) in] the examination.
▶열심히 일했지만 보람이 없었다 I worked hard only to fail. ⇒ I labored, but in vain.
▶이런 책을 읽어봤자 무슨 보람이 있겠는가? What is the use [good] of reading a book like this?
▶그것은 할 만한 보람이 없는 일이다 It is not worthwhile doing [to do] it. ⇒ It is not worth doing.
▶그 노인에게는 사는 보람이 없었다 The old man had nothing to live for.
2 〈표적〉 an indication; a sign; a mark; a symptom ♦보람 뵈다 give indications 《of》; show signs of
3 〈구별하기 위한 표〉 a mark; a sign; a note

보랏빛 violet; purple ♦연보랏빛 light purple; lavender; orchid / 진보랏빛 deep purple
▶그녀는 보랏빛 옷을 입고 있었다 She was dressed in purple.

보로통하다 〈부어서〉 swollen; bloated; bulging; 〈불만으로〉 sullen; sulky; sour ⇨ 부루퉁하다 ♦보로통한 얼굴을 하다 look cross [displeased, sullen]

보료 a decorated pouf; a fancy matress used as cushion

보루 堡壘 a fort; a fortification; a fortress; a stronghold ♦보루를 구축하다 construct [raise] a fort; construct defense works

보류 保留 〈유보〉 reservation; 〈연기〉 deferment; 〈일시적 정지〉 suspension; 〈법안 등의〉 pigeonholing
—보류하다 reserve; defer; postpone; withhold; shelve; delay; put...off
♦태도를 보류하다 do not commit *oneself* / 발표를 보류하다 withhold an announcement / 계획을 보류하다 hold a plan in abeyance / 구매를 보류하다 hold off buying / 잠깐 동안 판단을 보류하다 defer [suspend, reserve] judgment in the meantime
▶그 계획은 보류되었다 The plan was tabled [shelved]. ⇒ They tabled [shelved] the plan.
▶이 문제는 잠시 보류합니다 We'll keep the matter on ice for a while.
▶당국은 발표를 보류하기로 했다 The authorities decided to withhold an announcement.
▶그들은 가사용품 구매를 보류했다 They held off from buying household commodities.
■—조건 a reservation: 보류 조건을 붙이다 make a reservation —조항〈法〉a reddendum (*pl.* -da)

보르네오 〈섬 이름〉 Borneo I. ♦보르네오의 Bornean
■—사람 a Bornean

보르도 〈포도주〉 Bordeaux [bɔːrdóu]

보름 1 〈15일 동안〉 fifteen days; a half month
♦보름 안에 within fifteen days; within half a month; within a fortnight / 보름만에 돌아오다 come home after a fortnight's absence
2 ⇨ 보름날

■—달 a full moon (on the fifteenth night) —밤 a full-moon night —사리 〈조수〉 tidal bulge on the 15th of the lunar month; 〈조기〉 a corbina caught around the 15th of the lunar month

보름날 the fifteenth day of the (lunar) month
♦정월 보름날 the 15th of the first lunar month [of January] / 보름날께 about [(美) around, toward] the middle of the month

보리 〈대맥〉 barley; 〈라이보리〉 rye
♦볶은 보리 parched barley / 꾸어다 놓은 보릿자루처럼 (美口) like a cat in a strange garret
—걷이 barley harvest; mowing barley —고추장 hot pepper mash made with barley —깜부기(병) a smutted barley ear —논 a paddy where barley is grown as a second crop —농사 the barley raising [farming]; a barley crop —누름 the ripening time of barley —바둑 a game of *paduk* (played) by poor players: 그는 보리 바둑이다 He is a poor player of *paduk*. —밟기 treading barley [wheat] plant —밭 a barley field; (英) a cornfield —수확 a wheat [barley] crop —쌀 polished barley —죽 porridge made with barley; barley gruel —차 barley tea [water]; ptisan —타작 barley threshing —파종 sowing barley [wheat] —풀 grass or leaves gathered for barleyfield manure 보릿가루 barley flour 보릿가을 the time of barley harvest 보릿겨 barley bran 보릿고개 spring famine (before the barley harvest): 보릿고개를 넘기다 overcome spring famine 보릿짚 (a) barley straw

보리 菩提 〈佛〉 Bodhi; the Supreme enlightenment [wisdom]

보리멸 〔魚〕 a sillaginoid (fish); a sillago

보리밥 boiled barley (and rice); boiled rice with barley

보리밥에는 고추장이 제격이다 〈속담〉 Like goes well with like. ⇒ Like matches (with) like.

보리새우 〔動〕 a prawn

보리수 菩提樹 〔植〕 〈인도의〉 a bo tree; a pipal (tree); a sacred fig; 〈유럽의〉 a linden; a lime (tree)

보링 〈천공〉 boring; drilling ■—머신 a boring machine

보막이 洑— building a dammed pool (of water) —보막이하다 build a dammed pool

보매 〈언뜻 보기에〉 apparently; in appearance; seemingly; outwardly; on the surface; to the eye; judging from the appearance
▶보매 그는 학자같았다 The man was apparently a scholar. ⇒ He looked like a scholar.
▶그 요리는 보매 맛있어 보이지만 실은 맛 없다 The dish looks appetizing but it tastes awful.
▶그는 보매 약은 것 같지만 실은 그렇지 않다 He looks [appears] intelligent, but in fact he isn't.
▶보매 그는 낙제한 듯하다 He appears [seems] to have failed in the examination.

보모 保姆 a (dry) nurse; a nursery governess
♦유치원 보모 a kindergarten teacher; a kindergartener; a kindergartner

보무 步武 (lively) steps; marching steps

♦보무당당하게 걷다 march [advance] in fine array; go on proudly

보무라지 〈잔 부스러기〉 scraps [bits] 《of paper, cloth》

보물 寶物 (a) treasure; 〈귀중한 것〉 a precious [valuable] thing; 〈재보〉 riches; 〈중요한 것〉 a jewel; a highly prized article; valuables; 〈가보〉 an heirloom

♦집안의 보물 a family treasure / 〈놀이에서〉 감춘 보물을 찾다 look for a buried treasure
▶ 그는 진정 우리 회사의 보물이다 He is a real treasure to our company.
▶ 그 섬에는 보물이 묻혀 있었다 There was treasure buried in the island.
▶ 이런 보물을 보기는 흔치 않다 One seldom has a chance to see such treasures as these.
■ —상자 a treasure chest —선 a treasure ship —섬 a treasure island —찾기 treasure-hunting; a treasure hunt

보배 a treasure; a jewel; a precious [valuable] thing; valuables

♦집안의 보배 an [a family] heirloom / 나라의 보배 a national asset; a treasure of the country / 발굴한 보배 treasure trove
▶ 이 아이가 내 유일한 보배다 This child is my only treasure [all I have].
▶ 자식보다 더 귀한 보배는 없다 There are no treasures more precious than one's children.

보배롭다 very precious; valuable

보병 步兵 〈부대〉 the infantry ; 〈병사〉 an infantryman; a foot soldier; 《美》 a dogface
■ —과(科) the infantry arm —부대 an infantry corps —사단[연대] an infantry division [regiment] —전(戰) an infantry action [engagement] —진지 an infantry position —학교 an infantry school

보병궁 寶甁宮 Aquarius ⇨ 물병(~자리)

보복 報復 (a) revenge; retaliation; (a) reprisal; retorsion; retribution

♦보복적인 retaliatory; revengeful; vindictive / …의 보복으로 in retaliation [revenge] for…; in [by way of] reprisal for… / 보복 조치를 취하다 take a retaliatory measures
▶ 나는 보복의 기회를 노렸다 I sought revenge.
▶ 그는 그들에게 모욕받은 보복을 했다 He was avenged [avenged himself] on them for the insult.
—보복하다 retaliate; make [carry out] reprisal(s) 《on》; revenge oneself 《on》; have one's revenge 《on》; avenge oneself 《an injury, a wrong》

♦상대가 한 대로 똑같이 보복하다 repay sb 《back》 in one's own coin
■ 대량— a massive retaliation ■ —관세 a retaliatory tariff —병기 a retaliatory weapon —정책 a policy of revenge —정치 the politics of retaliation —조치 reprisal measures —폭격 (make) a reprisal [retaliatory] bombing 《on》

보부상 褓負商 a peddler; 《英》 a pedlar; a packman ♦보부상을 하다 peddle; hawk

보부아르 〈프랑스의 여류 소설가〉 Beauvoir, Simone de(1908-86)

보비위 補脾胃 〈위의 원기를 도움〉 strengthening of one's stomach and spleen; 〈남의 비위를 맞춤〉 flattery; adulation
—보비위하다 strengthen one's stomach and spleen; aid digestion; flatter; act obsequiously; curry favor with sb; toady 《to》; humor

보빙 堡氷 〔地〕 barrier ice; the (Antarctic) barrier

보살 菩薩 1 〈산〉 〈보리살타〉 a bodhisattva; a Buddhist saint **2** 〈보살승〉 the Bodhisattva vehicle **3** 〈나이 든 여자 불교도〉 an old she-Buddhist ■ —할미 a Buddhist nun with an unshaved head

보살 補殺 〔野〕 an assist

보살피다 take care of; look [see] after sb; see to; 〈간호하다〉 attend to; 〈후원하다〉 back up; support

♦노후의 양친을 보살피다 attend to one's parents in their old age
▶ 우리는 그를 전적으로 보살펴 주었다 We backed him up one hundred percent.
▶ 나는 그가 집을 비운 동안 개를 보살펴 주었다 I took care of the dog while he was away from home.
▶ 외출할 때는 옆집 부인에게 애기를 보살펴 달라고 부탁합니다 We ask the woman next door to sit with our baby when we go out.
▶ 그는 오늘의 번영이 있기까지 회사를 보살폈다 He brought the company up to its present prosperity.

보상 報償 compensation; recompense; indemnity; 〈죄 의〉 atonement; consideration; remuneration

▶ 그는 나에게 손실에 대한 보상으로 돈을 주었다 He gave me money in compensation for my loss.
▶ 사고의 피해자들은 충분한 보상을 받지 못했다 The victims of the accident did not receive sufficient compensation.
▶ 내 노력은 충분한 보상을 받았다고 생각한다 I feel more than recompensed for my efforts.
—보상하다 compensate [make up, make amends, atone] for; recompense; remunerate; reward

▶ 나는 너에게 그것을 보상해 주겠다 I will make it up to you.
▶ 회사는 그의 상해를 보상해 주었다 The company compensated him for his injury.
▶ 그들은 우리에게 손실분은 보상하겠다고 제의했다 They offered to indemnify us for our losses.
■ 수출— export compensation 전면— 《덴마크》 full [complete] compensation ■ —가격 amount of the indemnity —금 an indemnity; compensation payment; a remuneration: 보상금을 받다 receive the compensation money 《from》 / 보상금을 지급하다 pay compensation to 《sb for》 —링크제 〔經〕 compensation link —안 a compensation bill —작용(心) compensation —조치 a compensation measure; compensation

보색 補色 a complementary color

보석 保釋 〔法〕 bail; bailment
▶ 그는 보석중이다 He is free on bail.
▶ 재판관은 보석을 허락하지 않았다 The judge

보석

refused bail.
▶ 판사는 일금 1,000달러를 지불케 하고 보석을 허락했다 The judge allowed bail on the payment of one thousand dollars.
―보석하다 bail; let 《a prisoner》 (out) on bail
▶ 그는 보석되었다 He was released on bail. ⇒ He was freed on bail.
■병― sick bail ■―금 bail (money) ―보증인 a bail; a bailsman: 보석 보증인이 되다 go bail for sb ―신청 an application for bail

보석 寶石 a jewel (▶ 장신구의 의미로는 복수형); 〈원석을 가공·연마한 것〉 a gem; (총칭) jewelry; 〈원석〉 a precious stone
◆ 반지에 보석을 박다 set gems in a ring; set a ring with gems
▶ 하늘에는 별이 보석처럼 총총히 박혀 있었다 The sky was jeweled with stars.
▶ 그녀는 보석이 박힌 브로치를 달고 있었다 She was wearing a brooch studded with jewels.
▶ 그녀는 많은 보석을 몸에 걸치고 있었다 She wore a lot of jewels.
■―공〔세공사〕 a lapidary ―류 jewelry ―반지 a ring set with jewels [a jewel]; a jeweled ring ―상 〈장수〉 a jeweler; a gem dealer; 〈가게〉 a jeweler's (store) ―상자 a jewel box; a jewelry case ―세공 jewelry; (英) jewellery

보선 保線 〔鐵〕 maintenance of way; permanent of way
―보선하다 keep [maintain] the tracks in good condition
■―공〔요원〕 a lineman; (美) a tracklayer; (英) a platelayer ―공사 maintenance [track] work ―구〔區〕 a track maintenance section; a railroad section ―사무소 a track [railroad] maintenance office

보세 保稅 ◆ 보세의 in bond; bonded
■―가공 bonded processing ―가공 수출[무역] bonded processing exports [trade] ―공장 a bonded factory ―구역 a bonded area ―화물 bonded goods; goods in bond

보세창고 保稅倉庫 a bonded warehouse
◆ 물품을 보세창고에 맡기다〔넣다〕 bond; store goods in bond / 물품을 보세창고에서 꺼내다 take goods out of bond

보송보송하다 1 〈물기가 없다〉 dry; dried up [out]; parched
◆ 보송보송해지다 lose all moisture; dry up / 말라서 보송보송하다 be dried up; be parched
2 〈곱고 보드랍다〉 ◆ 보송보송한 살결 soft and moistureless skin

보수 步數 〈걸음의 수〉 the number of steps taken ◆ 보수를 세다 count one's steps ■―계 a pedometer

보수 保守 〈전통을 지킴〉 conservatism; conservativeness
◆ 보수적(인) conservative / 보수적으로 conservatively
▶ 그의 생각은 보수적이다 He is conservative in idea. ⇒ His opinions are conservative.
▶ 영국국민은 보수적이다 The British are a conservative people.
▶ 결혼에 대한 그녀의 생각은 무척 보수적이다 Her attitude toward marriage is very conser-

vative. ⇒ She is very conservative in her attitude toward marriage.
■―당 〈영국의〉 the Conservative Party ―당원 a Conservative; (英) a Tory ―세력[파] the conservatives; the old-liners ―주의 conservatism; Toryism ―주의자 a conservative (person); a Tory ―중도세력 the conservative-centrist force ―진영 a conservative camp

보수 補修 repair; mending
―보수하다 repair; (美口) fix
▶ 공장의 일부를 보수했다 A part of the factory was repaired.
▶ 그 다리는 보수하는 중이다 The bridge is under repair.
■―공사 repair [maintenance] work

보수 報酬 a reward; remuneration; a recompense; a consideration; (a) return; an honorarium 《pl. ~s, -ia [-iə]》; 〈의사·변호사 등의〉 a fee; 〈급료〉 emoluments; pay
◆ 무보수로 without consideration [pay]; for nothing / 보수를 주다 reward [recompense] sb 《for his work》 / 보수를 요구하다 claim a reward
▶ 변호사의 보수는 무척 높다 The lawyer's fee is very high.
▶ 그는 수고에 대한 보수로 돈을 받았다 He was given money in reward [as a reward] for his services. ⇒ He was rewarded with money for his services.

보스 a boss; a chief; a head ◆ 재계의 보스 the boss of the business world ■―정치 oligarchy; boss-ridden [machine] politics; bossdom

보스턴 〈미국의 도시〉 Boston ―백 a Boston bag; (美) an overnight bag ―시민 a Bostonian ―차 사건 〔史〕 the Boston Tea Party

보슬보슬 gently; softly ▶ 비가 보슬보슬 내리고 있다 It is drizzling. ⇒ The rain is gently falling.

보슬비 a drizzling rain; a fine rain; a drizzle; a misty rain. ▶ 보슬비가 내린다 It drizzles. ⇒ It is drizzling.

보습 a plowshare; a share

보습 補習 supplementary lessons; refresher training ―보습하다 supplement (education)

보시 布施 〈일〉 almsgiving; charity; 〈물건〉 alms; a (monetary) offering 《to a temple》
◆ 절에 보시를 바치다 make an [a monetary] offering to a temple / 보시를 청하다 beg [ask] sb for (an) alms
―보시하다 give alms 《to》

보시기 a small bowl of porcelain [brass]

보신 保身 self-protection
▶ 그는 보신에 급급한다 He thinks only of defending his own interests [self-preservation].
―보신하다 protect oneself; protect one's life
■―술 the art of self-protection ―책 the ways [techniques] of self-protection

보신 補身 nurturing; tonicing ◆ 보신이 되는 tonic; roborant ―보신하다 build oneself up by taking tonics; improve [build up] one's health by taking tonics

보쌈김치 褓― wrapped-up kimchi; kimchi wrapped in a large cabbage leaf like a bundle

보아 〈큰 뱀〉〖動〗 a boa (constrictor)
보아란듯이 showily; for show [display]; demonstratively; ostentatiously
▶ 이웃집 꼬마는 장난감을 보아란듯이 친구에게 자랑했다 The neighbor's child showed off a toy to his friend.
▶ 그녀는 보아란듯이 반지를 낀 왼손을 흔들었다 She waved her left hand about to show off her ring.
▶ 젊은 연인들이 보아란듯이 팔짱을 끼고 간다 The young lovers are walking arm in arm as if to attract others' attention [to show themselves off].
보아주다 1 〈돌보아 주다〉 give a helping hand (to); deliver *sb* out of 《difficulty》
▶ 내가 없는 동안 집의 아이를 좀 보아주십시오 Would you take care of my child while I am away? ⇒ Please look after [watch (over)] my little son in my absence.
2 〈눈감아주다〉 over look; turn a blind eye to
♦ 부정행위를 보아주다 turn a blind eye over to [wink at] dishonest acts
▶ 제발 이번 한 번만 보아주십시오 Please let it pass [go] just this once.
보아하니 apparently; so far as my observation goes; so far as the appearances go; to all appearances
▶ 보아하니 그는 우리 약속을 잊은 것 같다 He has apparently forgotten our engagement.
▶ 보아하니 점잖은 분이 왜 이러시오 You look like a gentleman — you should behave yourself better.
보안 保安 the preservation [maintenance] of public peace [security] ♦ 국가보안법 the National Security Law
■ ─경찰 the public-security police ─관 (美) a sheriff; a marshal; a peace officer ─등 a security light ─림 a reserved [protection] forest ─사범 national security violators; a public security offender
보암직하다 charming; eye-catching; attractive; (well) worth seeing
-보았자 (even) if [though]...; granting [supposing] that... ▶ 그것을 해보았자 실패할 것이다 Even if you do it, you will fail.
보약 補藥 a restorative; a tonic (medicine); an invigorant
보양 保養 health seeking; preservation of health; 〈병후의〉 recuperation; 〈기분 전환〉 recreation; relaxation
─보양하다 take care of *one's* health; recruit [recuperate] *oneself* [*one's* health]; convalesce
보양제 補陽劑 medicine to aid [strengthen] virility; aphrodisiacs
보양하다 補陽─ 〈韓醫〉 aid [strengthen] virility; invigorate [vitalize, stimulate] *oneself*; take a tonic
보얗다 1 〈빛깔이〉 milk-white; pearly; frosty; cream-colored; opaque
▶ 그 여자는 살결이 보얗다 She has a pearly skin.
2 〈안개·연기 등으로〉 hazy; misty; heavy (in the air) ♦ 보얀 하늘 a hazy sky
3 〈희미하다〉 blurred; dim; indistinct; blurry

보어 補語 〖文法〗 a complement
▶ 불완전자동사는 보어를 취한다 An incomplete intransitive verb requires a complement. ■ 주격[목적(격)]─ a subjective [an objective] complement
보옥 寶玉 a gem ⇨ 보석 (寶石)
보온 保溫 keeping warmth; keeping heat; heating; heat [thermal] insulation
♦ 보온이 잘 되는 속옷 warm [heat-trapping, heat-retaining] underwear
■ ─병 a thermos (bottle [flask, jug]); a vacuum bottle ─장치 〈자동 조절식의〉 a thermostat ─재(材) lagging (materials); lags
보우 保佑 protection; help; assistance
♦ 하느님의 보우 providential help; Divine help [aid] ─보우하다 protect; guard; assist; help
보위 寶位 〈제왕의 자리〉 the throne; the crown
♦ 보위에 오르다 take [accede to] the throne; ascend [amount, come to] the throne / 보위를 잇다 succeed to the throne
보유 保有 possession; retention; maintenance
♦ 영토의 보유 the maintenance of territory / 보유 의석 a party's seats; the seats held by a party; a party's current strength 《in the National Assembly》 / 보유 자재 materials on [at] hand / 보유 병력 current military [troop] strength / 기록보유자 a record holder / 정부 보유미 the government's rice holdings; the government-stocked [-owned] rice (holding) / 핵 보유국 a nuclear state
─보유하다 possess; hold; keep; retain; maintain
▶ 우리 회사는 현재 트럭 30대를 보유하고 있다 Our company now owns 30 trucks.
▶ 아버지는 어떤 회사의 주식을 보유하고 계시다 My father holds shares [stocks] in a company.
■ ─고 holdings: 금(金)보유고 gold holdings ─량 holding amount [volume]; capacity ─물 tenements; holdings; stock ─자 a possessor; a holder
보유 補遺 〈부록〉 a supplement (to a dictionary); 〈추가물〉 an addendum 《*pl.* -da [-də]》; an appendix 《*pl.* ~es, -dices [-dəsì:z]》 (▶ supplement는 보통 별책, appendix는 권말에 붙음)
♦ 보유의 supplementary ─보유하다 add a supplement to 《a main work》
보육 保育 upbringing; nurture
─보육하다 nurse 《a baby》; nurture; bring up; rear; foster
■ 아동─ childcare; the bringing up [care] of children; 〈유아 교육〉 children's education
■ ─기(器) 〈미숙아의〉 an incubator ─료 a fee for day care ─원 (美) a day nursery; a day-care center; (英) a nursery school ─학교 a training school for kindergarten workers
보은 報恩 repayment of a favor [kindness]; gratitude
♦ 보은으로 …하다 do in return for *sb's* kindness; do out of gratitude to *sb*
─보은하다 repay an obligation; repay kindness
▶ 그는 보은하는 뜻으로 모교에 많은 책을 기증했다 He contributed a lot of books to his

보음제 alma mater out of gratitude.
▶ 그녀는 그에게 보은하는 뜻으로 아이를 돌보고 있다 She feels morally indebted to him and takes care of his children.

보음제 補陰劑 a medicine for counterbalancing one's virile powers

보음하다 補陰— 【韓醫】 aid [strengthen] the negative principle in one's nature; counterbalance one's virile powers

보이 〈소년〉 a boy; 〈식당의〉 a waiter; 〈호텔·클럽 등의〉 (美) a bellboy; a page; 〈역·호텔에서 짐을 나르는〉 a porter; 〈열차의〉 a carriage boy; 〈기선의〉 a steward [cabin boy]; 〈사무실의〉 an office boy ━장(長) a headwaiter [porter]; 〈호텔의〉 (美) a bell captain

보이다¹ 1 〈눈에 띄다〉 see; 〈사물이 주어〉 be seen; be visible; show; be in sight [view]
▶ 저 높은 건물이 보이니? Can you see that tall building over there?
▶ 무엇이 보이니? What do you see?
▶ 여기서는 잘 보인다 It is easy to see from here.
▶ 내 방에서는 성이 잘 보인다 My room has a good view of the castle.
▶ 그가 저기 걸어가는 것이 보인다 I can see him walking away.
▶ 비행기는 곧 보이지 않았다 The plane passed out of view [disappeared from view] soon.
▶ 그 마을은 짙은 안개로 보이지 않았다 The town was blotted out by a thick fog.
▶ 저 모퉁이를 돌면 오른쪽으로 병원이 보입니다 Turn that corner, and you will find the hospital on your right.
▶ 달이 구름 사이로 보였다 The moon peeped through the scattered clouds.
▶ 그녀는 군중 속에 섞여 보이지 않게 되었다 She was lost in the crowd.
▶ 그것을 잘 보이는 곳에 진열해 주시오 Display it in a conspicuous [prominent] place.
▶ 보이지 않을 때까지 그를 전송했다 We watched him (until he was) out of sight.
2 〈시력이 있다〉 be able to see; can see
♦ 보이지 않는 눈 a sightless eye
▶ 그 별은 육안으로는 보이지 않는다 The star is invisible in the naked eye.
▶ 고양이는 어둠 속에서도 보이다 Cats can see in the dark.
3 〈보기에 …인 듯하다〉 look (like); seem; appear
▶ 그녀는 피곤해 보인다 She looks tired.
▶ 이 문제는 언뜻 보아 간단해 보인다 This problem seems easy at one sight.
▶ 그는 실제보다 훨씬 늙어보인다 He looks much older than he really is.
▶ 나는 영국인으로 보이는 사람을 만났다 I met a man, who looked like an Englishman.
4 〈발견되다〉 ▶ 지갑이 보이지 않는다 I cannot find my purse. ⇌ My purse is missing.
▶ 그것을 찾아봤으나 보이지 않았다 I looked for it in vain.
5 〈오다〉 ▶ 손님은 아직 보이지 않았다 The guest has not come yet.
▶ 목사님이 보이면 곧 차를 내오도록 하십시오 Please serve tea as soon as the pastor arrives [gets here].

보이다² 〈보여주다〉 show; let sb see [look at] sth; 〈진열하여〉 exhibit; display
▶ 다른 것을 보이다 show sb another kind / 모범[표준]을 보이다 set sb an example [the standard] / 실력을 보이다 show [display] one's ability
▶ 그 책을 좀 보여주세요 Let me have a look at the book.
▶ 의사에게 보이는 게 좋겠어 You should see [consult] your doctor.
▶ 아기를 의사에게 보이는 게 좋겠다 You had better have your baby examined by the doctor.
▶ 선배는 후배에게 모범을 보여야 한다 Seniors must set a good example for juniors.
▶ 이 다음번에는 꼭 100점을 따 보이겠습니다 I'll get a 100 next time, I will.
▶ 그 엽서를 좀 보여 다오 Let me see that postcard.
▶ 입국카드를 보여주십시오 Show me your disembarkation card.
▶ 넥타이를 좀 보여주시오 I want to see [should like to have a look at] some ties.

보이스카우트 〈단체〉 the Boy Scouts
■━대원 a boy scout ━대장 a Scout Leader; a scoutmaster ━대회 a boy scout rally; 〈전국적·국제적인〉 a jamboree; 〈지방에서의〉 (美) camporee

보이콧 〈불매 동맹〉 a boycott; boycotting ━**보이콧하다** boycott; stage a boycott
▶ 소비자들은 그 가게를 보이콧했다 Consumers boycotted the store.
▶ 우리는 그 잡지를 보이콧하기로 결정했다 We decided to put the magazine under a boycott.
▶ 그들은 그 회사의 제품을 한 달 동안 보이콧했다 They boycotted the firm's products for a month.

보이프렌드 a boyfriend; a boy friend (↔ girlfriend)

보일 〈영국의 화학자〉 Boyle, Robert (1627-91)

보일러 〈기관〉 a boiler ♦ 보일러를 때다 stoke (up) the boiler ■━석유━ an oil-burning boiler 석탄━ a coal-fired boiler ■━맨 a boiler operater [man] ━실 a boiler room

보자기 a cloth wrapper; a wrapping cloth; a kerchief ♦ 보자기로[에] 싸다 wrap sth in a kerchief ━━꾸러미 a bundle; a parcel in a wrapper

보잘것없다 beneath notice; trifling; trivial; worthless; of no use; useless
♦ 보잘것없는 너석 a nobody; a man of straw / 보잘것없는 물건[일] a trifle; a triviality / 보잘것없는 작품 a work of low [small] merit
▶ 보잘것없는 것이지만 받아주십시오 Kindly accept this little trifle.
▶ 저의 작품은 보잘것 없습니다 My work is insignificant.

보장 保障 〈보증〉 guarantee; 〈확보〉 security
♦ 평화의 보장 security of peace; peace guarantee / 〈유엔의〉 안전보장이사회 the Security Council (略 S.C.)
━**보장하다** guarantee; secure; ensure
♦ 생활을 보장하다 guarantee sb's living

▶ 네 장래는 보장되어 있다 Your future is assured.
▶ 헌법은 언론의 자유를 보장하고 있다 The constitution guarantees freedom of speech.
▶ 기본권은 헌법으로 보장되고 있다 The fundamental human rights are guaranteed under the constitution.
■ 사회— social security 집단안전— collective security ■ —제도 a security system

보쟁기 〈쟁기〉 a plow [(英) plough] with a metal blade; 〈겨리〉 a plow pulled [drawn] by two oxen

보전 保全 integrity; preservation; conservation; maintenance
—**보전하다** preserve [safeguard] the integrity (of); keep (a machine) in good condition; preserve [keep] (*one's country*) intact
♦ 재산을 보전하다 keep *one's* property intact
■ 국토— conservation of national land 영토— territorial integrity 증거— perpetuation of evidence 환경— preservation of environment —처분 a preservative measure

보전 寶典 1〈법전〉 an important [a highly prized] code; a treasury (of words and phrases) **2**〈귀중한 책〉 a thesaurus (*pl.* ~es, -ri); a precious book

보전하다 補塡— make up for [make good] (a loss); cover ▶ 우리는 그 결손을 보전하기 위해 빚을 졌다 We borrowed money to cover the deficit.

보정 補正 revision; 〔機〕 compensation; 〔數·物〕 correction —**보정하다** revise; make revisions; correct; compensate (a pendulum)
■ —기 a compensator —예산 a revised [supplementary] budget

보제 補劑 a restorative ⇨ 보약

보조 步調 (a) pace; (a) step
♦ 빠른[느린] 보조로 at a fast [slow] pace / 보조를 맞추다 keep [mark] step / 보조를 흐뜨리다 break step; walk out of step / 보조를 빨리 [느리게] 하다 quicken [slacken] *one's* pace / ⋯과 보조를 맞추다 keep in (perfect) step with...; 〈발걸음을〉 keep in (perfect) step with...; 〈일 등의 속도를〉 keep pace [up] with...; 〈협력하다〉 act [work] in concert with...
▶ 그는 딴 사람들과는 보조가 맞지 않는다 He is out of [not in] step with the rest [the others].

보조 補助 help; assistance; support; aid
♦ 보조적인 accessory; supplementary; auxiliary / 보조를 받다 be assisted (by); 〈금전의〉 be subsidized (by)
▶ 이 단체는 정부의 재정 보조를 일체 받지 않고 있다 This organization does not receive any financial aid [support] from the government.
▶ 그는 아무 보조도 받지 않고 이 계획을 완수했다 He carried out this project entirely on his own.
—**보조하다** help; assist; aid; subsidize
♦ 생활비를 보조하다 furnish *sb* with money for (his) support; help *sb* with (his) living expenses
▶ 수동 브레이크는 주 제동장치의 기능을 보조한다 The hand brake supplements the function of the main braking system.
■ —과학 an ancillary [auxiliary] science —기관(機關)〈엔진〉 an auxiliary [a donkey] engine; a subsidiary organ —날개〈비행기의〉 an aileron —어간 a stem supplement; a non-final suffix added to the stem of an inflectional word —원 an assistant; a helper —의자 〈예비의〉 a spare [an extra] chair; 〈버스 등의〉 an auxiliary seat; a jump seat —화폐 subsidiary [auxiliary] coins

보조개 a dimple ♦ 보조개가 있는 얼굴 a dimpled face ▶ 그녀는 웃으면 보조개가 진다 Her cheek dimples with a smile. ⇌ She has dimples in her cheeks when she smiles.

보조금 補助金 a subsidy; a grant of money; a grant-in-aid (*pl.* grants-)
♦ 보조금을 내다 subsidize (an industry); make grants for (a research)
▶ 이 연구[계획]는 정부의 보조금을 받고 있다 This research [project] is subsidized by the government.
■ 생활— a supplementary living allowance

보족 補足 supplementation; (a) complement
♦ 보족적(인) complementary; supplementary; additional / 보족적 설명을 하다 give supplementary explanation
—**보족하다** complement; supplement; supply
♦ 거기에 또 하나의 예를 보족하다 add another example to it; supplement it with another example

보존 保存 preservation; conservation; storage; maintenance ♦ 사적의 보존 preservation [conservation] of historic spots —**보존하다** preserve; conserve; keep; maintain
♦ 잘 보존되어 있다 be well preserved; be in fair [fine] preservation / 잘못 보존되어 있다 be in poor preservation / 천연자원을 보존하다 conserve natural resources
▶ 이 우유는 장기간 보존된다 This milk can be kept [preserved] for a long time.
▶ 좋은 전통은 보존되어야 한다 Good traditions should be preserved.
■ —림(林) a forest reserve [preserve] —비용 the expense of preservation —식품 nonperishables; preserved food —제 a preservative —혈액 stored blood

보좌 補佐 aid; assistance ♦ 보좌 역할을 하다 act as (an) adviser (to) —**보좌하다** aid; assist; help; (口) backstop; counsel; advise
▶ 그는 회장을 보좌하고 있다 He is an adviser [an assistant, a councelor] to the president.
■ —관 an aide : 대통령 보좌관 a presidential aide —인 an assistant; a counselor; an advisor

보주 補註 a supplementary note

보증 保證 (a) guarantee; a guaranty; 〈담보〉 (a) security; 〈확약〉 (an) assurance; 〈품질〉 (a) warranty
♦ 보증을 서다 go [give, stand] security (for); stand [go] surety (for) / 보증을 세우다 find [give] security [surety] (for)
▶ 그가 성공한다는 보증은 없다 There is no guarantee that he will succeed.
▶ 품질 보증(표시) Quality guaranteed.
—**보증하다** guarantee; warrant; 〈확언하다〉 assure; ensure; answer for; 〈진실성·인격 등

을〉 vouch for; certify; endorse
♦신원을 보증하다 guarantee *sb's* character; stand [go] surety for *sb* / 기계의 품질을 보증하다 guarantee [warrant] the quality of the machine / 상품의 파손에 대하여 보증하다 guarantee goods against breakage
▶노력은 해보겠지만 성공은 보증하지 못합니다 I'll try, but I can't guarantee success.
▶그것은 내가 보증한다 I give you my word for it.
▶그것이 사실인지는 보증할 수 없다 I cannot vouch for its truth.
■신원— fidelity guarantee 연대— joint liability on guarantee 품질[수량, 중량]— guarantee of quality [quantity, weight] —수표 a certified check —채무 surety obligations —책임 the responsibility of a surety

보증금 保證金 security [guaranty] money; a deposit; (英) 〈세드는 사람의〉 key money
♦보증금 없이 without a deposit / 보증금을 걸다 deposit money as security / 보증금을 몰수당하다 forfeit the deposit

보증서 保證書 a letter of guarantee; a written guarantee; 〈상품의〉 a warranty (card)
■신원— a fidelity guarantee 재정— an affidavit of support

보증인 保證人 〔法〕 a guarantor; a guaranty; 〈채무의〉 a surety; 〈신원의〉 a reference
♦보증인을 세우다 give [find] surety [security] (for)
▶숙부님이 내 빚의 보증인이 되어주셨다 My uncle stood guarantee [security, surety] for my debts. = My uncle guaranteed my debts.
▶국회의원이 그의 보증인이다 He has a National Assemblyman as his guarantor [a reference].

보지 〔解〕 the vulva (*pl.* ~s, -vae)

보지 保持 maintenance; preservation; retention ⇨ 보유 보지자 a record holder —보지하다 maintain; preserve; sustain; retain; hold (a world record)

보직 補職 assignment to a position; appointment —보직하다 assign [appoint] (*sb* to the post of) ▶그는 교장에 보직되었다 He was appointed (to be) school principal.

보짱 boldness ⇨ 배쩡

보채다 cry for *sth*; beg; whine; tease; be fretful for *sth*; try to get *one's* own way; be peevish; 〈아이가〉 grizzle ♦보채는 아이를 달래다 soothe a fretful child
▶그 애가 보채는 것은 졸립기 때문이다 He is so fretful because he is sleepy.

보철 補綴 〔齒〕 prosthetic dentistry; dental prosthesis

보청기 補聽器 a hearing aid ▶나는 보청기를 끼면 잘 들립니다 I can hear all right with [if I wear] a hearing aid.

보초 步哨 a sentry; a sentinel; 〔軍〕 a guard
♦보초를 서다 stand [keep] sentry; be on sentry (duty) / 보초를 세우다 post a guard on sentry; stand guard / 보초를 교대시키다 relieve a guard [sentry]
■—근무 sentry [guard] duty —선 (線) a sentry line; a cordon

보충 補充 〈추가〉 supplementation; (a) supplement; replenishment; 〈교체〉 replacement —보충하다 supplement; replenish; replace; fill up; supply
♦결원을 보충하다 fill (up) a vacancy / 식량을 보충하다 replenish food / 탱크에 석유를 보충하다 replenish a tank with oil
▶그는 부족분을 빚으로 보충했다 He made up the deficit with a loan.
▶부서진 의자는 새것으로 보충했다 The broken chairs were replaced by new ones.
■—계획 a replacement program —문제 a supplementary question —병 a reservist; a recruit; (총칭) reserve conscripts —수업 supplementary lessons —역 reservist duty —증거 〔法〕 adminicle —질문 〔法〕 a supplementary question —판결 a supplementary judgment

보츠와나 〈나라 이름〉 Botswana; 〈공식명〉 the Republic of Botswana
■—사람 a Botswanan; a Botswanian

보측 步測 pacing —보측하다 pace (off) 《the distance》; measure 《the distance》 by pace
▶나는 그 땅이 얼마나 되는지 보측했다 I paced off [out] the lot. = I measured the lot by pacing it off.

보칙 補則 supplementary rules

보카치오 〈이탈리아의 작가·시인〉 Boccaccio, Giovanni (1313-75)

보컬 a vocal (performance) ♦남성[여성] 보컬 male [female] vocals ■—그룹 a vocal group —뮤직 vocal music

보크 〔野〕 a ba(u)lk ♦보크를 범하다 make [commit] a ba(u)lk; ba(u)lk

보크사이트 〔鑛〕 bauxite

보태다 1 〈가산하다〉 add 《one number to another》; add up ♦보태어 말하다 exaggerate a story; make *one's* story tall [high]
▶4에 5를 보태면 9다 Four and five make(s) [is, are] nine. = Four plus five is [equals] nine. = Add 4 and 5, and you get 9.
▶당신을 보태면 모두 8명이 됩니다 We are eight in all, including you.
2 〈보충하다〉 make up (for); make good; supply; supplement ♦모자라는 것을 보태다 make [fill] up the deficit
▶그녀는 가정교사로 일해서 생활비를 보탰다 She supplemented her regular income by working as a tutor.
▶이것을 네 용돈에 보태 써라 Here's something for you. = Keep this for your own use.

보탬 〈도움〉 help; aid ♦보탬이 되다 be an aid to; help; do much to help; be useful / 실용에 아무 보탬이 되지 않다 be of no practical use
▶그것이 혹시 보탬이 될지도 모르지 It may come in handy for something.
▶만원으로는 아무 보탬이 되지 않아요 Only ten thousand won is of no help.

보통 普通 commonness; normality
♦보통(의) 사람 an average [ordinary] man [person]; a common being [man] / 보통의 normal; ordinary; common; usual; general; universal; 〈평균의〉 average; medium / 보통이 아닌 uncommon; unusual; extraordinary / 보통 이상의 out of the common [ordinary];

above the average; uncommon; extraordinary / 보통으로 usually; ordinarily; commonly; in common; normally; generally; as a general thing [rule]/ 보통 이상으로 uncommonly; extraordinarily
▶ 나는 보통 10시에 잔다 I usually go to bed at ten.
▶ 우리는 보통 하루에 8시간 일한다 We generally work eight hours a day.
▶ 그런 표현은 보통 쓰지 않는다 That is not the usual way of expression.
▶ 검정옷은 보통 장례식 때 입는다 Black is generally worn at funerals.
▶ 그것은 보통으로 일어나는 사고가 아니다 That is no everyday accident.
▶ 그의 학업성적은 보통 이상[이하]이다 His school record is above [below] the average.
▶ 지금은 여성이 결혼 후 일을 계속하는 것이 보통이다 It is now quite common for women to continue their work after marriage.
▶ 이것은 보통 더위가 아니다 This hot weather is rather abnormal.
■一개념 [論] an ordinary concept 一교육 a general [common] education; elementary [primary] education 一급행(열차) an ordinary express (train) 一명사(名詞)〔文法〕 a common noun 一명사(名辭)〔論〕 a common term 一법 common law 一석 an ordinary seat 一선거 a popular election; universal suffrage 一열차 a slow [local] train 一예금 an ordinary deposit 一요금 an ordinary rate; a normal fare 一우편 an ordinary mail [post] 一은행 a commercial [city] bank 一주(株) (美) a common stock; (英) an ordinary (share)

보통내기 普通— an ordinary man ⇨ 행내기
▶ 그는 보통내기가 아니다 He is a knowing fellow. ⇌ He knows a thing [move, trick] or two.
▶ 나는 그가 보통내기가 아니라고 여겼다 I saw that he was no ordinary man. ⇌ I took him to be someone out of the ordinary.

보툴리누스균 —菌 a botulinus

보퉁이 褓— a bundle; a package
♦ 옷 한 보퉁이 a bundle of clothes / 보퉁이를 싸다[꾸리다] make (up) a bundle [package]; bundle (clothes) / 보퉁이를 풀다 unpack; undo [untie, open] a package [bundle]

보트 a boat; (美) a rowboat; (英) a rowing boat
♦ 고무 보트 a rubber boat / 보트를 젓다 row a boat / 보트를 타다 take [get on] a boat / 보트를 내리다 lower a boat / 보트를 2시간 빌리다 rent a boat for two hours
▶ 우리는 보트로 강을 건넜다 We crossed the river by boat [in a boat].
■一경기 a boat race; 〈대회〉 a regatta 一선수 an oarsman; 〈전원〉 the crew

보티첼리 〈이탈리아의 화가〉 Botticelli, Sandro (1444?-1510)

보편 普遍 universality; generality; 〈편재(遍在)〉 ubiquity
♦ 보편적 진리 universal truth / 보편적(인) universal; omnipresent; ubiquitous / 보편적으로 universally; ubiquitously; generally
▶ 그것은 보편적으로 인정된 진리다 That is a universally acknowledged truth.
■一개념 universal [general] concept 一성 universality 一주의 universalism 一타당성 universal validity

보폭 步幅 a step ⇨ 걸음나비

보표 譜表 〔樂〕 a staff (pl. staves); a score; a stave ■一기법 staff notation

보푸라기 nap ⇨ 보풀

보풀 nap; shag; fuzz; fluff; 〈옷단 등의〉 pile
♦ 보풀이 인 nappy; fluffy / 보풀을 일게 하다 raise a nap 《on a fabric》; nap; fluff

보풀다 be nappy [fluffy]; have a slight nap (on a fabric); become fuzzy [piled]; have fuzz (on the surface of paper)

보풀리다 raise a nap on; make fluffy; nap; fluff

보풀보풀 with a (rough) nap; with fuzz 一보풀보풀하다 nappy; fluffy; pily

보필 輔弼 assistance to the throne 一보필하다 help; assist; advise; give advice [counsel] (to); counsel; support
▶ 그는 대통령을 잘 보필했다 He assisted the president very capably. ⇌ He was a good assistant to the president.

보하다 補— 1 〈원기(元氣)를 돕다〉 strengthen 《one's body》; tone up; build up 《one's health》; invigorate
2 〈관직을 주다〉 appoint; assign
▶ 그는 교장에 보해졌다 He was appointed (to be) principal.

보합 步合 〈비율〉 rate; ratio; percentage

보합 保合 [證] steadiness; no change
♦ 보합세를 보이다 《the prices of stocks》 show a steady tone
▶ 시세는 보합상태다 Prices are steady [stationary]. ⇌ The market hold [remain] steady. ⇌ Prices remain on the same level.
▶ 주가가 강[약] 보합상태다 Stock [Share] prices are steady with an upward [a downward] tendency.

보행 步行 (a) walk; walking; ambulation
♦ 보행이 곤란하다 find it hard to walk; have difficulty in walking
▶ 그는 병을 앓은후 보행이 불편했다 He had trouble walking after his illness.
■一기(器) 〈유아의〉 a baby walker 一동물 an ambulatory animal 一위반 traffic violation by a pedestrian 一위반자 a jaywalker 一인[자] a walker; a pedestrian : 보행자가 우선한다 Pedestrians [Walkers] have the right of way.

보험 保險 insurance; assurance
♦ 보험 든 insured; (英) assured
〈보험을〉 보험을 권유하다 canvass for insurance / 보험을 계약하다 effect an insurance contract; contract insurance / 보험을 해약하다 cancel insurance; surrender one's insurance policy / 보험을 신청하다 apply for an insurance policy; open an insurance
〈보험에〉 보험에 들다 insure oneself; take out (a policy of) insurance 《on goods》 / 보험에 들어 있다 have insurance; be insured

▶그는 1억원의 생명보험에 들어 있다 He carries a hundred million won insurance policy on his life.
▶보석상은 항상 충분히 보험에 들어 있다 Jewellers are always well insured.
▶그 집은 5천만원의 화재 보험에 들어 있다 The house is insured against fire for 50 million won.
▶보험에 들어 있어서 수술에는 큰 돈이 들지 않았다 Since I had insurance, the operation didn't cost me very much.
〈보험으로〉그 손해는 보험으로 보상된다 The damage is covered by insurance (money).
▶이 보험으로 지진에 의한 피해는 보상되지 않는다 Damage caused by earthquake is not covered by this insurance.
■간이(생명)― postal (life) insurance 강제[임의]― obligatory [voluntary] insurance 건강― health insurance 재― reinsurance ■―가격[가액] insurance [insurable] value ―감독원 the Insurance Inspection Board ―계약 an insurance contract ―계약자 a policyholder ―금액 an insured [insurance] amount ―기간 the term insured ―료 an insurance premium; a premium ―률 a premium rate ―물 property [a thing] insured; insured goods ―업 insurance business [industry]; underwriting ―업자 an underwriter; an insurer ―증권 an insurance policy; a policy ―회사 an insurance company

보험금 保險金 insurance money ▶그들은 가옥의 화재로 많은 보험금을 받았다 They received a large insurance for a house burnt. ■―수령인 a beneficiary

보헤미아 Bohemia

보헤미안 〈보헤미아 사람〉 a Bohemian
◆보헤미안 기질 Bohemianism

보혈 寶血 〔基〕 the precious blood (of Jesus)

보혈제 補血劑 〔藥〕 a hematic; a hematinic; an antianemic (agent)

보호 保護 protection; guardianship; safeguard; harborage; 〈돌봄〉 care; 〈보존〉 preservation; conservation
◆문화재의 보호 (the) preservation of cultural assets / …의 보호 아래 under the protection [care, guardianship] of.../ 보호를 받다 be protected 〈by〉; be under sb's protection; shelter *oneself* under *sb* / 생활 보호를 받다 be on relief [welfare]/ 경찰에 보호를 요청하다 apply to [ask] the police for protection / 정치적 망명자로서 보호를 요청하다[받다] request [receive] (political) asylum
―보호하다 protect; shelter; safeguard; shield; 〈돌보다〉 take care of; look after; patronize; 〈보존하다〉 preserve; reserve; conserve; provide protection for *sb*; provide shelter
◆국내 산업을 보호하다 protect home [domestic] industries / 야생 동식물을 보호하다 preserve wildlife
▶선글라스는 햇빛으로부터 눈을 보호한다 Sunglasses protect the eyes from [against] the sunlight. ⇒ Sunglasses are a protection for the eyes against the sunlight.
■―관세 a protective tariff ―림 a reserved forest; a forest reserve ―무역 protective [protected] trade ―무역주의 protectionism ―자 a protector; a guardian; a patron; 〈여자〉 a patroness ―조(鳥) a protected bird ―지(역) 〈야생 동식물의〉 wildlife preserves; 〈수렵의〉 game preserves; 〈새의〉 a bird sanctuary

보호관찰 保護觀察 〔法〕 probation ◆소년 범죄자를 보호관찰에 부치다 place [put] a juvenile delinquent on [under] probation ■―제도 the probation system

보호색 保護色 protective coloring [coloration]; cryptic coloration; a protective color
▶그것들은 이른바 보호색으로 자기를 지킨다 They protect themselves by what is called protective coloring.

보호조치 保護措置 (an) arrest for protection; protective custody ―보호조치하다 arrest *sb* for protection; hold *sb* in protective custody

보화 寶貨 a treasure ⇨ 보물(寶物)

복 〔魚〕 a blowfish; a swellfish; a globefish; a puffer (fish)
◆복의 독 swellfish poison; tetrodotoxin / 복치듯 하다 〈속담〉 strike [beat, pound] *sth* roughly [at random]/ 복의 이 갈듯 한다 〈속담〉 gnash *one's* teeth with resentment
■―요리 a blowfish dish; blowfish prepared in various ways ―중독 blowfish poisoning

복 伏 the dog days ⇨ 복날

복 福 (good) fortune; blessing; bliss; good luck; happiness
◆복 받은[된] blessed; happy / 복이 있다 be fortunate; be in luck / 복이 없다 be out of luck; have no luck; be unfortunate / 복을 주다 [받다] bless [be blessed] (with a good thing)
▶마음이 가난한 자는 복이 있나니 〔聖〕 Blessed are the poor in spirit.
▶누구나 자기 먹을 복은 타고난다 The Lord never sends a mouth into the world without providing meat for it.
▶새해 복 많이 받으십시오 Happy New Year!
▶넌 참 복도 많다 How lucky [fortunate] you are! ⇌ What a lucky [fortunate] person you are!

복- 複- double; bi-; compound; composite; multiple

복각 伏角 〔物〕 a dip (of the compass); an inclination ◆무복각선 〈지자기(地磁氣)의〉 the aclinic line ■―계 an inclinometer ―측원기 a depression range finder

복각 覆刻 reproduction; reprint ◆원본을 복각하다 reproduce [reprint] the original text
■―판 a reprinted edition

복간 復刊 reissue; revived publication ◆복간 잡지 제1호 the first number of a revived magazine ―복간하다 reissue; revive the publication
▶그 책은 복간되었다 That book was reissued [published again].

복강 腹腔 〔解〕 the abdominal [peritoneal] cavity ■―임신 abdominal pregnancy

복고 復古 restoration; revival (of the ancient regime); 〈반동〉 reaction
■―왕정― the restoration of the monarchy;

복교 復校 return to school
  ◆ 복교를 허락하다 allow (a boy) to return to school; readmit (a boy) into school / 복교를 허가받다 be readmitted into school; be allowed to return to school
  ─복교하다 return to school; come back to school; be at school again

복구 復舊 reconstruction; restoration; repair; recovery
  ▶ 그것은 복구의 전망이 전혀 없다 There is no hope for its restoration.
  ▶ 노선 복구의 전망은 불투명하다 The prospect of reopening the line is still uncertain.
  ─복구하다 restore; be restored (to the original state); reconstruct
  ◆ 복구시키다 restore (to the original state); bring (it) back to (its) former condition / 평상 상태로 복구되다 return [be restored] to normal(cy)
  ▶ 다리가 마침내 복구되었다 The bridge was restored at last.

복구공사 復舊工事 restoration [repair] work
  ◆ 복구공사중이다 be under repair / 복구공사에 착수하다 get [set] to repair work
  ▶ 그들은 교량의 복구공사를 하고 있다 They are now repairing [reconstructing] the bridge.

복굴절 複屈折 〔物〕 double refraction; birefringence

복권 復權 restoration of rights; reinstatement
  ─복권하다 be rehabilitated; be reinstated; regain one's (civil) rights ◆ 복권시키다 reinstate sb to (his) lost privileges

복권 福券 a lottery ticket
  ◆ 복권 추첨 a lottery / 복권부 채권 a lottery bond / 복권이 당첨되다 win (a prize) in a lottery [raffle]; draw [have, get] the winning ticket [number] in a lottery / 복권을 하나 사보다 (美) take a chance on a raffle
  ▶ 복권이 당첨되었다 The lot fell on me. ⇌ I drew [got] the winning number in a lottery.

복귀 復歸 (a) return; (口) a comeback
  ─복귀하다 return (to); be restored (to); come back; 〔法〕 revert (to)
  ◆ 이전 직위로 복귀하다 be reinstated in one's former position / 평상 상태로 복귀하다 return to normal(cy)
  ▶ 노동자는 전원 직장으로 복귀했다 All workers returned [went back] to work.
  ▶ 그녀는 일단 은퇴했으나 5년후 무대에 복귀했다 She retired from the stage once, but made a comeback five years later.

복근 腹筋 an abdominal muscle ■ ─운동 exercises to strengthen the abdominal muscles; sit-up

복날 伏─ 〈초·중·말복〉 the dog days; 〈복중〉 the hottest period of summer; midsummer

복날 개 패듯 한다 〈속담〉 beat [strike, hit] sb mercilessly as if he were a dog; give a good licking [sound thrashing]

복닥거리다 bustle ⇨ 북적거리다 1

복당 復黨 rejoining the party ─복당하다 〈스스로〉 rejoin [return to] the party; 〈허가 받아〉 be reinstated in the party
  ▶ 그는 민주당에 복당했다 He rejoined the Democratic Party.

복대 腹帶 a health [belly] band; 〈임부의〉 a maternity belt; a binder; 〈말의〉 a (saddle) girth

복대기다 1 〈여럿이 떠들다〉 be noisy; make a great fuss (about); bustle; be in a bustle
  ◆ 복대기는 교실 a noisy classroom
  ▶ 특매장은 몹시 복대겼다 There was a terrible crush at the clearance sale.
  2 〈몰리다〉 push and shove; be tossed about; be jostled around
  ▶ 사람들 틈에 복대기다가 그를 시야에서 놓쳐 버렸다 Jostled in the crowd, I lost sight of him.

복대기치다 bustle ⇨ 복대기다

복더위 伏─ the heat of the dog days; the midsummer heat ⇨ 삼복(~더위)

복덕방 福德房 a house [real estate] agent; (美) a Realtor; (英) an estate agent; a house-finding agency

복도 複道 a corridor; (美) a hallway; a passageway; 〈극장 등의〉 a lobby
  ▶ 우리는 복도로 해서 방으로 갔다 We went to the room through the corridor [hallway].

복되다 福─ 〈용모가〉 happy-looking; plump and well-looking; 〈축복받은〉 blessed; happy
  ▶ 앞길이 복되기를 기원합니다 I wish you the best of luck [a successful future].

복리 福利 welfare ⇨ 복지(福祉)

복리 複利 compound interest
  ◆ 복리로 계산하다 calculate [reckon] at compound interest
  ■ ─법 the compound interest method ─표 a table of compound interest

복마 卜馬 〈짐싣는 말〉 a draft [cart] horse; a packhorse

복마전 伏魔殿 an abode of demons; a pandemonium; 〈부패·독직 등의〉 a hotbed of corruption
  ◆ 정계의 복마전 a hotbed of political corruption [iniquity]

복막 腹膜 〔解〕 the peritoneum (pl. -nea)
  ■ ─염 peritonitis

복망하다 伏望─ beg earnestly [humbly, ardently]; entreat; desire [hope] earnestly
  ▶ 선처하여 주시기를 복망하나이다 I sincerely hope [hope very much] that you will take good care of the matter [deal with the matter prudently].

복면 覆面 a mask; a veil; a vizard
  ◆ 복면의 masked; vizarded / 복면을 벗은 unmask oneself
  ▶ 강도는 복면을 쓰고 있었다 The burglar wore a mask [was masked].
  ─복면하다 mask oneself; muffle (up) [cover] one's face; have one's face masked
  ■ ─강도 a masked burglar [robber]

복명 復命 a report
  ─복명하다 report to (sb on one's work); report to (one's superior) on the mission one

복명어음 has carried out ━━서 a (written) report (of a mission, on a commission); a finding

복명어음 複名━ 〔商〕 a double-name paper [note]; a two-name paper [note]

복모음 複母音 〔音聲〕 a diphthong
▶ 단어 boy에서 oy는 복모음이다 Oy in the word boy is a diphthong.

복무 服務 (public) service
♦ 육군[해군]에 복무중이다 be in the army [navy]
▶ 그는 복무중에 그 사고를 당했다 He met with the accident while on duty.
━복무하다 serve; 〈복무중〉 be in (public) service
▶ 그는 경찰관으로 30년간 복무했다 He served as a policeman for thirty years.
━━규정 the office (service) regulations; 〔軍〕 standing orders ━기간 the period of (active) service ━연한 the term of (public) service; the tenure of office

복문 複文 〔文法〕 a complex sentence

복받치다 〈솟아오르다〉 rise to; come to; well up; gush out [forth]; 〈치밀어오르다〉 be filled [seized] (with); have a fit (of)
♦ 뭉클한 것이 가슴에 복받치다 feel a lump rise in one's [the] throat
▶ 그녀는 눈물이 복받쳤다 Tears came into her eyes. ⇌ Tears welled up in her eyes.
▶ 나는 그 광경을 보고 분노가 복받쳤다 Anger welled up in me at the sight. ⇌ I was filled with anger at the sight. ⇌ A feeling of anger surged up in me.

복벗다 服━ 〈탈상하다〉 go out of [leave off] mourning; the period of mourning is over

복벽 腹壁 〔解〕 the abdominal wall
━━반사 abdominal wall reflex━절개(수술) laparotomy

복병 伏兵 an ambush; troops [men] in ambush; an ambuscade
♦ 복병을 만나다 fall into an ambush / 복병을 배치하다 lay [make, plant] an ambush
▶ 적은 복병을 배치해 놓고 있었다 The enemy lay [was waiting] in ambush.

복복선 複複線 〔鐵〕 a four-track line; a quadruple track

복본위(제) 複本位(制) 〔經〕 the double [bimetallic] standard
━금은━ gold and silver bimetallism

복부 腹部 the abdomen; the abdominal region; the belly
▶ 그는 복부의 압박감을 호소하고 있었다 He complained of an oppressive sensation about his abdomen.
━━수술 an abdominal operation; abdominal surgery; ventrotomy ━팽만 abdominal distention [swelling]

복부호 複符號 〔數〕 a double sign

복분수 複分數 〔數〕 a compound [complex] fraction

복분열 複分裂 〔動〕 multiple division

복분해 複分解 〔化〕 double decomposition; metathesis (pl. -ses)

복비 複比 〔數〕 compound ratio

복비례 複比例 〔數〕 compound proportion

복빙 複氷 〔物〕 regelation

복사 伏射 prone shooting [firing]; firing from a prone position ━━경기 a prone shooting [firing] event ━자세 a prone firing position

복사 複寫 copying; reproduction; duplication; 〈복사물〉 a reproduction; a duplicate; a copy; a facsimile
♦ 피카소 그림의 복사(물) a copy from Picasso
▶ 복사본은 두고 원본을 송부합니다 I'm sending you the original, keeping a copy [photocopy, duplicate] (with me [myself]).
━복사하다 copy; reproduce; duplicate; manifold; take [produce] a copy of; make a duplicate [copy] of; facsimile; reprint
♦ 사진을 복사하다 reproduce [take copies of] a photograph / 원고를 복사하다 copy [manifold] a manuscript
▶ 이 다섯 페이지를 복사해 주세요 Please copy [make copies] of these five pages.
▶ 이 사진을 다섯 장만 더 복사해 주세요 Please make five more copies of this picture.
━━사진 photocopy: 사진 복사기 a photocopier ━━기 a copying machine; a duplicating [reproduction] machine; a duplicator ━물 a copy; a reproduction ━사진 a photostat; a photocopy ━잉크 copying ink ━지(紙) copying paper; carbon paper ━카메라 a reproduction camera ━필(筆) a copying pen

복사 輻射 〔物〕 radiation ♦ 복사의 radiant
━복사하다 radiate; be radiative
━━가열기 a radiation superheater ━각 an angle of radiation ━광[파] radiant light [wave] ━난방 panel [radiant] heating ━등급 bolometric magnitude ━선 a radiation ━에너지 radiant energy ━열 radiant heat ━체 a radiator

복사뼈 the anklebone; 〔解〕 the malleolus (pl. -li); the talus (pl. -li); the astragalus (pl. -li)
♦ 복사뼈를 삐다 sprain [wrench] one's ankle / 복사뼈까지 물이 차다 be ankle-deep in water

복상 服喪 mourning ━복상하다 put on [wear] mourning; go into [take to] mourning (for sb); be in mourning

복상 福相 a happy look [physiognomy]

복상 複像 〔電〕 a multiple image; 〔TV〕 a ghost (image)

복서 a boxer ⇨ 권투(~선수)

복선 伏線 preparation; foreshadowing
♦ 복선을 깔다 〈뒷일의 준비로 두는 것〉 take (precautionary) measures beforehand; 〈소설 작법〉 lay an underplot; give [provide] a hint which is to be developed later

복선 複線 〔鐵〕 a double track; a two-track line; double-tracking; 〈겹줄〉 double lines
♦ 복선의 double-track(ed) / 복선으로 하다 double-track 〈a railway line〉
▶ 이 선로는 복선이 아니다[단선으로만 되어 있다] This line is not double-tracked [has only a single track].
━━공사 double-tracking

복성 複姓 a two-Chinese-character surname

복성 複星 〔天〕 a multiple star
복성스럽다 happy-looking; fat and well-looking ◆복성스러운 얼굴 a fat and happy-looking face; a happy look
복소수 複素數 〔數〕 a complex number ■—체 complex number field
복수 復水 〔化〕〈증기를 액체로 복원시키기〉 condensation; 〈복원된 물〉 condensed water ■—기(器) a condenser —기관[판(瓣), 펌프] a condensing engine [valve, pump]
복수 復讐 revenge; vengeance; 〈보복〉 retaliation; reprisal (▶행위일 때는 a를 취하나 복수형은 없음)
◆복수적 revengeful; vindictive / …에 대한 복수로 in revenge for [of]…; in revenge against 《one's father》 / 복수를 꾀하다 seek vengeance 《upon》 / 복수를 맹세하다 swear revenge 《on, against》
▶그는 적에게 복수의 기회를 노렸으나 허사였다 He looked for a chance to take revenge [vengeance] upon his enemy, but in vain.
—**복수하다** take revenge; revenge [avenge] oneself; be [get] revenged [avenged] on [upon]; revenge; avenge; retaliate for 《an injury》
▶그는 배반자에게 복수했다 He revenged [avenged] himself on the betrayer. ⇌ He was revenged on the betrayer.
—극 a revenge tragedy —수단 a retaliatory measure —심 (burn with) revengeful thought —자 a revenger; an avenger —전 a vengeful war; a war of vengeance; a battle of revenge; 〈경기의〉 a return match
복수 腹水 〔醫〕 abdominal dropsy; ascites
복수 複數 the plural (number)
◆복수의 plural / 복수로 하다 pluralize
▶복수의 사람들이 그것을 보았다 More than one person saw it.
▶"fish"의 복수는 뭐지? What is the plural (form) of "fish"?
■—명사 a plural noun —형 〔文法〕 the plural
복수초 福壽草 〔植〕 a pheasant's-eye; an adonis (plant)
복술 卜術 〈점술〉 the art of divination; the mantic [prophetic] art; fortune-telling
복숭아 a peach ■—꽃 a peach blossom : 곧 복숭아꽃이 필 것이다 Peach blossoms will soon bloom —나무 a peach (tree) —털 fuzz on a peach
복스럽다 福— happy-looking; fat [plump] and well-looking
◆아기의 복스러운 뺨 a baby's plump cheeks
복슬복슬하다 shaggy; bushy
◆복슬복슬한 개 a shaggy dog
복습 復習 a review; a rehearsal
—**복습하다** review 《one's lesson》; go over [through] 《one's lesson》
▶그녀는 매일 영어를 복습한다 She reviews her English lessons every day.
■—시간 review hours —용 연습문제 review exercises
복시 複視 double vision; 〔醫〕 diplopia
복식 服飾 dress and its ornaments
■—여성용— ladies' trimmings ■—디자이너 a fashion designer; a dress [an accessory] designer —잡지 a fashion magazine —품 accessories (to a dress)
복식 複式 multiple forms [formulae]; 〔數〕 a compound expression [formula]; 〔競〕 doubles; a doubles match
■—기관 a compound [double-acting] engine —부기 bookkeeping by double entry; the double-entry bookkeeping —테니스 tennis doubles —투표 a plural vote; plural voting —화산 a composite volcano
복식호흡 腹式呼吸 abdominal breathing [respiration]
◆복식 호흡을 하다 breathe from the abdomen; practice abdominal breathing
복신 福神 the God of Wealth; Billiken
복싱 boxing ⇨ 권투 ■새도— shadowboxing —경기 a boxing match
복안 腹案 a plan [scheme] (in one's mind); an idea ◆복안이 다 서 있다 have a plan ready (in one's mind) / 복안을 세우다 map out [draw up, formulate] a plan
▶네 복안을 들어보자 Tell me your plan.
복안 複眼 〔動〕 compound eyes
복약 服藥 taking medicine ⇨ 복용(服用) 1
복어 —魚 a blowfish; a globefish; a swellfish; a puffer (fish) ◆복어 중독에 걸리다 be poisoned by a swellfish / 복어를 요리 a blowfish dish —중독 blowfish poisoning
복역 服役 penal servitude; military service
◆복역 중이다 be serving [doing] one's sentence [time]; be in prison
—**복역하다** serve one's time [a sentence]; serve a prison [jail] term; serve 《one's time [term]》 in the army
◆만기 복역하다 serve one's full time / 5년간 복역하다 serve a five-year sentence [serve five years] in prison
■—기간 〈징역의〉 the term of penal servitude [imprisonment] —연한 〈병역의〉 the term [period] of military service
복엽 複葉 a compound leaf ■—(비행)기 a biplane
복용 服用 1 〈약을 먹음〉 taking medicine; internal use [application]
—**복용하다** take (a dose of) medicine
◆복용시키다 administer medicine
▶주의, 한 번에 세 알 이상 복용하지 마시오 Warning: Do not take more than three tablets at a time.
▶1일 3회 식후에 복용하시오 To be taken three times a day after meals.
2 〈옷을 입음〉 wearing 《clothes》
■—량 dosage : 최대 복용량 the maximum dose; dose —자 a taker
복원 復元 restoration (to the original state); restitution; 〈건조식품의〉 rehydration ◆벽화의 복원 the restoration of a wall painting —복원하다 restore to the original state
■—도 〈건물의〉 a diagram of a restored building —력 〔物〕 force of restoration; restoring force; 〈선박 등의〉 stability —성 stability —작용 reintegration

복원 復員 〈소집 해제〉 demobilization; bemob; disbanding; deactivation
―**복원하다** demobilize; disband; deactivate
♦ 복원되다 be demobilized and sent home
―군인 an ex-soldier; a demobilized soldier; a demob; an ex-serviceman ―령 a demobilization order

복위 復位 restoration; rehabilitation; reinstatement; reinstallment
―**복위하다** be restored [rehabilitated, reinstated, reinstalled]
▶ 왕이 복위했다 The king was restored to the throne.

복음 福音 〈희소식〉 good [welcome] news; glad tidings; 〈그리스도의 가르침〉 the (Christian) gospel ♦ 복음을 전하다 preach the gospel; evangelize
▶ 그 소식은 우리에게 복음이었다 The information [news] was (like) sweet music to us.
■―공관(共觀)― 〔基〕 the synoptic Gospels
■―교회 the Evangelical Church ―서 the (four) Gospels : 신약 성경의 최초의 4편을 복음서라고 한다 The first four books of the New Testament are called the Gospels. ―전도 evangelism

복음 複音 〔音聲〕 a compound sound
복인수 複因數 〔數〕 compound factors
복자 福者 a fortunate [blissful] man; 〔가톨릭〕 Blessed...; 〈총칭〉 the Blessed
복자 覆字・伏字 〈해당하는 활자가 없는 경우〉 〔印〕 a turn (in set type)

복작거리다 1〈많은 사람이〉 be crowded; be congested; be thronged
♦ 복작거리는 세밑 거리 the crowded streets of December / 복작거리는 저녁 시간에 in the evening rush hour
▶ 가게는 손님으로 복작거리고 있었다 The store was alive with customers.
2 〈술 등이 괴어오르다〉 boil (over); come to a boil

복잡 複雜 complexity; complication; intricacy
♦ 복잡 기괴한 complicated and inscrutable
―**복잡하다** complex; complicated; intricate; involved; mixed; labyrinthine; tangled
♦ 복잡한 기계 an intricate piece of machinery / 복잡한 문제 a knotty problem / 복잡한 장치 a complicated device / 복잡한 절차 a long and involved [complicated] process / 복잡하게 되다[되어 있다] be [become] complicated [intricate]; be in a tangle
▶ 이 기계는 구조가 복잡하다 This machine is complicated in structure.
▶ 그것에 관해서는 내 심경이 복잡하다 I have mixed feelings about it.
▶ 이 소설은 줄거리가 복잡하다 The plot of this story is very intricate.
▶ 그것은 사태를 더욱 복잡하게 만들 뿐이다 It will just further complicate the situation. ⇌ It will only make the situation more complicated.

복장 1〈가슴의 한복판〉 the center of the chest
2 〈속마음〉 (a) heart
♦ 복장이 검다 be blackhearted / 복장이 타다 be nervous 《about》; be anxious [worried] 《about, for》

복장 服裝 (the style of) dress; clothes; costume; attire; habiliment; clothing
♦ 중국식 복장 Chinese-style clothes / 조선 시대의 복장 the costumes of the Chosŏn Dynasty (period) / 복장을 단정히 하다 dress up (oneself); tidy up (oneself) / 근무에 맞는 [히피처럼, 나이에 걸맞는] 복장을 하고 있다 be dressed for one's work [like a hippie, for one's age]
▶ 복장은 자유 〈초대장의 후기〉 "Dress optional." ⇌ "Informal dress."
▶ 그는 복장에 대해서 개의치 않는다 He does not care about his dress.
▶ 제 아내는 복장에 까다롭습니다 My wife is particular about her clothes.
▶ 오늘 파티에는 무슨 복장으로 갈까? What should I wear to today's party?
■―검사 a dress inspection; 〈군인의〉 a kit inspection

복적 復籍 return to one's original domicile [family]
♦ 복적 수속을 하다 go through the formalities of one's return to the original domicile
―**복적하다** return to one's original domicile; be reinstated in one's original family

복제 服制 1 〈복장의 규정〉 dress regulation; a dress code; costume ♦ 복제를 정하다 adopt a definite [special] uniform
2 〈상복의 제도〉 the traditional system of mourning clothes

복제 複製 duplication; reproduction; reprinting; 〈복제품〉 a reproduction; a facsimile (복사판); a duplicate; a replica
♦ 2분의 1 크기의 복제 a half-size replica
▶ 이 그림은 원본이요 복제요? Is this picture an original or a reproduction?
▶ 복제 불허 All rights reserved. ⇌ Reprinting prohibited.
―**복제하다** reproduce 《a picture》; reprint
♦ 원본을 복제한 삽화 illustrations reproduced from originals / 명화를 복제하다 reproduce [duplicate] a famous picture
■―사진 a photocopy ―인간 a human clone ―품 a reproduction ―화(畫) a reproduced picture

복족류 腹足類 〔動〕 Gastropoda
복종 服從 obedience; submission; subordination
♦ 맹목적인 복종 blind obedience / 자발적인 복종 active [willing] obedience / 복종적인 obedient; submissive; yielding
▶ 누구나 국법에 복종해야 한다 We are subject to the laws of our country.
―**복종하다** obey; be obedient 《to》; submit (oneself) 《to》; yield (obedience) 《to》
♦ 명령에 복종하다 obey sb's orders / 상사에게 복종하다 be obedient [deferential] to one's superiors / 복종시키다 subordinate; subdue; subjugate; hold sb in subjection / 명령에 복종시키다 submit sb to one's orders / 위협하여 복종케 하다 frighten sb into submission
▶ 자식은 부모에게 복종해야 한다 Children should obey their parents.

▶ 그는 권력에 복종하지 않았다 He did not submit to authority.
▶ 나는 이런 사람에게는 복종하지 않겠다 I am not going to bow down to people of this sort.
■ 절대- absolute obedience; complete submission : 명령에 절대 복종하겠습니다 I will be all obedience to your commands. ■ —심 obedience; a submissive spirit

복죄 服罪 acceptance of one's sentence —복죄하다 submit to [accept] a sentence

복중 伏中 (the period) of the dog days; midsummer

복지 服地 cloth; suiting ⇨ 양복(~지)

복지 福祉 (public) welfare; well-being; prosperity
♦ 국민의 복지를 증진하다 promote [improve] a nation's welfare
■ —국가 a welfare state —사업 welfare work; a welfare project : 아동 복지 사업 child welfare work —사회 a welfare society —시설 welfare facilities —정책 social welfare measure —제도 welfare system

복직 復職 resumption of office; reinstatement; reinstallation; reappointment
▶ 학생들은 그 교수의 복직을 요구하며 동맹휴학 중이다 The student are on strike for the return of the professor.
—복직하다 resume one's office; be restored [come back] to one's former position; be reappointed
▶ 그는 병이 나으면 복직될 것이다 He will be reinstated (in his former position) when he recovers.

복창 復唱 repetition —복창하다 repeat 《an order》 ♦ 상관의 명령을 복창하다 repeat one's senior officer's order

복채 卜債 a fortune-teller's fee

복통 腹痛 (a) stomachache; (a) bellyache; an abdominal pain; 〔醫〕 gastralgia; 〈급성의〉 colic; 〈간헐적인〉 the(s)
♦ 복통이 있다 have a pain in the stomache; suffer from stomachache / 복통을 호소하다 complain of a stomachache / 복통이 가라앉다 be cured of stomachache

복판 1〈한가운데〉 the (very) middle; the center; the heart
♦ 복판의 middle; central / 복판에 right [just] in the middle [center] 《of》; in the midst; midmost《of》 / 상가 복판에 in the heart of; the business district / 과녁의 복판을 맞히다 hit the target right in the center / 길 복판에 서다 stand in the middle of the road
2 〈소고기〉 beef attached to the ribs [groin, knee bone]

복학 復學 returning to school
▶ 이 대학에서는 휴학 후 3년이 지나면 복학이 허가되지 않는다 At this university students are not allowed to return after three years' absence.
—복학하다 return to school; be reenrolled in school
■ —생 a returnee; a reenrolled student

복합 複合 composition; compositeness; complex
♦ 복합의 compound; composite; complex
—복합하다 compound; mix; be mixed
■ —개념 a complex concept —국가 a union of states; a federation; united states —기업 a conglomerate (company) —명사 〔文法〕 a compound noun —비료 composite [compound, complex] fertilizer —비타민 B vitamin B complex —사회 a mixed society —어 〔文法〕 a compound (word) —영농 〔農〕 combined agriculture —오염 multiple contamination; combined pollution —이온 a cluster ion —체 a complex (body) —핵(核) 〔物〕 a compound nucleus

복화술 腹話術 ventriloquism; ventriloquy
♦ 복화술로 말하다 use ventriloquism; ventriloquize ■ —사 a ventriloquist

복활차 複滑車 〈겹도르래〉 a tackle; a compound pulley

볶다 1〈불에 익히다〉parch; broil dry [down]; panbroil; roast
♦ 볶은 콩 parched beans [peas] / 차를 볶다 roast [toast] tea; heat tea leaves / 기름에 볶다 fry in oil / 콩을 알맞게 볶다 roast the beans brown
▶ 커피콩을 볶으면 향기로운 냄새가 난다 When we roast coffee beans, it smells fragrant.
2 〈못살게 굴다〉 tease; annoy ⇨ 들볶다

볶아대다 keep bothering [pestering]; pester [bother, annoy] sb excessively [persistently]; press; nag; hound
♦ 차를 사달라고 볶아대다 pester [badger, (口) keep after] sb to buy a car
▶ 그는 용돈을 달라고 어머니를 볶아댔다 He pressed [pestered] his mother for pocket money.

볶아치다 hurry (up); press [urge, push] on; rush about; dash off ♦ 일은 볶아친다고 되는게 아니다 It's no good rushing things.

볶음 〈음식〉 panbroiled [roasted] food; a roast; a broil —닭— chopped roast chicken
■ —밥 frizzled (boiled) rice —질 panbroiling; roasting; toasting; parching

본 本 1 〈모범〉 a model; a form; an example
♦ 여성의 본 a model of womanhood / 영국의 본을 딴 의회제도 a parliamentary system modeled on [after] that of Britain / 본을 보이다 set an example to sb; set sb a good example / …을 본으로 삼다 take (an) example from…
2 〈형지(型紙)〉 a (paper) pattern 《for a dress》 ♦ 종이로 본을 뜨다 make a pattern out of paper
3 〈본관(本貫)〉 family origin ▶ 본이 어디십니까? Where did your family originate?
4 the principal

본 〈독일의 도시〉 Bonn

본- 本- 1 〈주된〉 head; main; chief; principal
♦ 본선(線) a main line / 본예산 a main budget / 본점 a head office
2 〈실제의〉 real; 〈정식의〉 regular; normal; proper ♦ 본명 sb's real name / 본회의 a plenary session [meeting]; a regular [full-dress] debate
3 〈이〉 this; 〈그〉 the

♦본교 this [our] school / 본협약 the [this] agreement

본가 本家 1 〈본집〉 the head [main] family; the head house 2 ⇨ 친정(親庭) 3 〈본채〉 the main house

본거 本據 the base; one's stronghold; headquarters
♦생활의 본거 the principal place of one's living; the base and center of one's life / 종파의 본거 the headquarters of a religious sect
▶그들은 생활의 본거를 그 마을에 정했다 They settled down in the village.
▶우리는 적의 본거를 공격했다 We attacked the stronghold of the enemy.

본거지 本據地 a base (of operations)＝근거지
♦…을 본거지로 하여 with...as the base of operations

본건 本件 this case [affair, matter]; the case in question [at issue]; the case (lying) before us
♦본건에 관하여 as to this matter; concerning this matter
▶본건은 현재 심의중이다 This case is now under consideration.

본격 本格 regular form; fundamental rules; a regular style ♦본격화하다 become serious; get into (its) stride ■一소설 a serious [realistic] novel 一파 the orthodox school

본격적 本格的 full-scale; full-dress; regular; genuine; real; earnest; serious; standard
♦본격적인 여름[겨울] a real summer [winter] / 본격적인 오페라 a full-length opera / 본격적인 토의 a full-dress debate / 본격적으로 in earnest; on a full scale / 본격적으로 하다 go about 《work》 in earnest; get down to one's job
▶본격적인 겨울이 닥쳐 왔다 Winter has really come. ⇌ Winter is really here.
▶본격적인 전쟁이 시작되었다 A full-scale war has begun.
▶그는 본격적으로 법률 공부를 시작했다 He began studying law in good earnest.
▶비가 본격적으로 내리기 시작했다 It began to rain in earnest.

본견 本絹 pure silk

본계약 本契約 a formal contract [agreement]

본고사 本考査 the final examination (of a university)

본고장 本— 1 〈본고향〉 one's native place; one's home town
♦본고장으로 돌아가다 go [return] home
2 〈본바다〉 the home 《of grapes》; the habitat; the (best) place (for); 〈중심지〉 the center
♦귤의 본고장 the home of the tangerine
▶나는 본고장의 독일어를 들은 적이 없다 I have never heard German spoken by native speakers.
▶한국의 대구는 유명한 사과 재배의 본고장이다 Taegu is one of the famous apple-growing centers of Korea.

본고향 本故鄕 one's native place [area]; one's home town

본과 本科 the regular course
♦본과를 수료하다 finish the regular course
■一생 a regular(-course) student

본관 本官 1 〈본디의 관직〉 one's principal official post 2 〈관리의 자칭〉 the present official; I; me
▶그것은 본관이 알 바가 아니다 That is not my business.

본관 本貫 one's ancestral home; family origin

본관 本管 a main (pipe) ■一가스[수도]— a gas [water] main : 가스의 본관이 어제 파열되었다 The gas main burst yesterday.

본관 本館 the main building

본교 本校 〈분교에 대하여〉 the principal school; 〈이 학교〉 this [our] school

본국 本局 〈분국에 대하여〉 the head [main, principal] office; 〈방송국〉 a key station; 〈전화국〉 (美) the central (office); (英) the exchange

본국 本國 1 〈자기 나라〉 one's own country; one's home [native] country; home
♦본국으로 돌아가다 go home / 본국으로 송환하다 send sb back to 《his》 home country; repatriate sb
▶전쟁 포로의 본국 송환이 결정되었다 It was decided to repatriate the prisoners of war.
▶그는 임기를 끝내고 본국으로 돌아갔다 Finishing up his tenure of office, he returned home.
2 〈보호국〉 the mother country
▶식민지는 본국에 대하여 반기를 들었다 The colonies rose against their mother country.
■一법 (法) the law of the domicile 一송환 repatriation 一정부 the home government

본남편 本男便 〈전 남편〉 one's ex-husband; 〈본디의 남편〉 one's (real) husband; one's legal [lawful] husband

본능 本能 (an) instinct
♦본능을 만족시키다 satisfy one's instinct / 본능에 따라 행동하다 act on instinct
▶기어 오르는 것은 원숭이의 본능이다 Climbing is instinctive in monkeys.
▶인간은 본능이 아니라 이성으로 행동한다 Human beings act not on instinct but on reason.
■귀소— homing instinct 자기보존— the instinct of self-preservation 一주의 instinctivism

본능적 本能的 instinctive; instinctual by [form] instinct
♦본능적으로 instinctively; instinctually / 본능적으로 좋아[싫어]하다 have an instinctive taste for [horror of] sth
▶동물은 본능적으로 먹을 수 있는 식물과 먹지 못할 식물을 식별한다 Animals instinctively distinguish plants that can be eaten from those that cannot.

본당 本堂 〔佛敎〕 the main [inner] temple; the main hall 《of a temple》; 〔가톨릭〕 a parish church

본대 本隊 〈본부의〉 the main body (of an army); the main force; 〈자기 소속의〉 the main body to which one belongs; one's regular outfit

본댁 本宅 one's principal residence; one's home ■一네 one's legal [lawful] wife

본데 (good) manners; propriety; discipline; experience ♦본데없다 be ill-mannered [bred]; be inexperienced; be rude; have no manners

본도 本島 〈주된 섬〉 the main island; 〈이 섬〉 this island

본도 本道 **1** 〈큰 길〉 a main road; a highway **2** ⇨ 정도(正道) **3** 〈이 도(道)〉 this province

본드 (商標) bond (glue)

본디 本— originally; by nature; in itself; at first; from the first [beginning] ♦본디대로 as before [usual]; as it was before ▶개는 본디 육식 동물이다 Dogs are carnivorous by nature. ▶그는 본디 머리가 나쁘다 His head is constitutionally weak. ▶본디는 유독할지라도 적절하게 쓰면 치유 효과가 있는 약도 있다 A medicine, though poisonous in itself, may have a medicinal effect if used properly.

본때 〈본보기〉 a model; a pattern; an example; 〈교훈〉 a lesson; a warning ♦본때를 보이다 teach *sb* a lesson; make an example [a lesson] 《of》 ▶그녀는 본때가 없다 She's got no figure. ⇌ Hers is not much of figure. ▶그에게 한 번 본때를 보여줘야겠다 He must be taught a lesson.

본때있다 〈본받을 만하다〉 exemplary; typical; 〈멋있다〉 stylish; smart; splendid ♦본때있게 잘하다 do a splendid job of it ▶그녀는 옷을 본때있게 입는다 She wears stylish clothes.

본뜨다 本— follow; model 《on, after》; copy 《from》; imitate; pattern 《after》 ♦…을 본떠 after the model [manner] of… / 토끼 모양을 본뜬 병따개 a cap opener in the shape of a rabbit / 미국의 제도를 본뜨다 be modeled on [after] the American system / 디자인을 본떠서 물건을 만들다 pattern a thing after [upon] a design ▶그 건물은 버킹엄 궁전을 본떠서 지은 것이다 The building was modeled after Buckingham Palace. ▶네 형을 좀 본떠 봐라 You may well pattern yourself upon your brother.

본뜻 本— **1** 〈본래의 의미〉 the original [primary] meaning; the original idea; the true [basic, literal] meaning ♦헌법의 본뜻 the basic principle of constitutional government ▶그 말의 본뜻을 모르겠다 I can't make out the original meaning of the word. **2** 〈의도〉 *one's* original purpose; *one's* (real) intention [will, mind, heart, motive] ▶그렇게 하는 것은 내 본뜻이 아니다 It goes against my heart to do so. ▶내 본뜻은 아니지만 부득이 그렇게 했다 I was obliged to do so against my will. ▶그것은 내 본뜻과는 전혀 달랐다 It was far from my true intention. ▶그것이 네 본뜻은 아니겠지? You don't really mean that, do you?

본래 本來 〈본디〉 originally; primarily; from the first; 〈본질적으로〉 essentially; fundamentally; in itself; intrinsically; 〈자연적으로〉 naturally; by nature ♦본래의 original; primary; essential; natural ▶그들은 본래 평화를 사랑하는 국민이다 They are essentially a peace-loving people. ▶그는 본래 매우 온순한 사람이었다 By nature he was very gentle. ▶본래는 내가 그 재산을 상속해야 마땅하다 Legally speaking, I ought to succeed to the property. ▶본래는 좋은 것도 쓰기에 따라서는 해롭게 된다 A thing good in itself may become harmful in use.

본령 本領 〈본분〉 the proper province [function]; *one's* duty; 〈전문영역〉 *one's* specialty [line]; 〈본성〉 the original nature; the real [essential] character ♦문학의 본령 the proper function of literature ▶섭외사무는 그의 본령이 아니다 Public relations is outside his province.

본론 本論 the main discourse [issue, subject] ♦본론으로 돌아가서 to return (to the subject)/ 본론으로 들어가기 전에 before getting in touch with [taking up] the main subject / 본론으로 들어가다 proceed to the main issue ▶그의 말은 본론에서 조금 빗나가는 것 같았다 His statement seemed to deviate slightly from the main theme. ▶선생님의 강의는 본론에서 종종 벗어나곤 했다 The teacher's lecture would often deviate from the main subject. ▶이야기의 본론으로 돌아갑시다 Let's pick up the original thread of our talk.

본루 本壘 〈野〉 the home base [plate] ♦본루를 밟다 get home; cross home base [the plate]/ 본루를 향해 돌진하다 rush home ━타 ⇨ 홈런

본류 本流 the main course 《of a river》; the mainstream; a main current ▶비가 오지 않아서 본류마저도 고갈되었다 For lack of rain, even the main stream dried up.

본말 本末 cause and effect; the means and the end; root and branch; the substance and the shadow ♦본말을 전도하다 confuse the order of things; put the cart before the horse; fail to put first things first; mistake the means for the end

본맛 本— the original taste [flavor, savor]

본명 本名 *one's* real name; 〈필명에 대해〉 *one's* autonym; 〈가톨릭〉 *one's* Christian [baptismal] name ♦본명으로 under *one's* real name / 본명을 말하다 give *one's* real name

본무 本務 **1** 〈본분〉 *one's* duty; the proper function ♦본무를 소홀히 하다 neglect *one's* duty **2** 〈업무〉 *one's* regular [main] work [job] ▶우선 본무에 힘쓰시오 Attend to your business first. ⇌ Sweep before your own door.

본문 本文 the text 《of a treaty》; the body 《of a letter》 ▶국민의 총의가 조약의 본문에 구현되어 있다 The general will of the nation is incorporated in the text of the treaty.

본문제 本問題 1 〈본래의 문제〉 the original problem [question] 2 〈이 문제〉 this problem [question] 3 〈기본 문제〉 the fundamental [main] problem

본밑천 本— capital ⇨ 밑천 ♦본밑천을 건지다 recover the principal (investment)

본바닥 本— the home; the (best) place (for); a habitat; a native place; the place of origin ♦커피의 본바닥 the home of the coffee / 서울 본바닥 사람 a native of Seoul; an indigenous Seoulite / 본바닥 영어 English as it is spoken by its native speakers / 외국어를 본바닥에서 배우다 learn a foreign language in the country where it is spoken (by its native speakers)
▶우리는 서산에서 직송된 본바닥 굴을 먹었다 We ate [had] oysters directly sent from Sŏsan, the home of oysters.
▶본바닥의 스카치 위스키를 마셔본 적이 있습니까? Have you ever tasted a genuine Scotch whisky?
▶그는 독일어를 본바닥에서 배웠다 He learned German in Germany.

본바탕 本— essence; (real) substance; intrinsic [true] nature; essential quality; disposition; *one's* true color
♦온화한 본바탕 a mild disposition / 본바탕이 예술적인 사람 a man with an artistic temperament / 본바탕이 정직한 naturally honest; honest by nature / 본바탕은 at bottom [heart]
▶사람은 취하면 본바탕이 드러난다 Wine reveals one's real nature.
▶그는 본바탕은 썩 좋은 사람이다 He is a very good fellow at heart [bottom].

본받다 本— follow; model *oneself* 《on, after》; make *sb one's* model; take pattern by 《another》; imitate
♦본받을 만한 행위 an exemplary conduct / …을 본받아 after; after the manner [model, example, style] of…; in imitation of… / 남의 덕목을 본받다 imitate [emulate] another's virtues
▶그를 좀 본받아라 You may well follow his example.

본보기 本— an example; a model; a lesson; a pattern
♦훌륭한 애국심의 본보기 a fine example of patriotism / 본보기로 as an example / 본보기가 되다 serve as a lesson 《to *sb*》 / 본보기를 보이다 set [give, offer] an example 《to》 / 아무를 본보기로 삼다 make an example of *sb*; follow the example [model] of *sb*
▶이것은 부주의한 실수의 좋은 본보기다 This is a good sample of a careless mistake.
▶이것을 본보기로 삼아라 Let this be a lesson to you.
▶그의 실패를 본보기로 삼아라 Take warning from his failure.

본봉 本俸 the regular salary [pay]; the basic salary ▶그는 본봉 월 2,000 달러로 고용되었다 He was engaged at a regular salary of two thousand dollars a month.

본부 本部 the head [main] office; the headquarters; 〈대학 등의〉 the administrative [administration] building; 〈연맹의〉 the seat
▶대학 본부 건물은 교내의 중앙에 있다 The administrative department of the university stands in the center of the campus.
▶국제연맹의 본부는 제네바에 있었다 The seat of the League of Nations was in Geneva.
■—중대[대대] a headquarters company [battalion]

본분 本分 *one's* duty [part, role]
♦본분을 게을리하다 neglect [fail in] *one's* duty / 본분을 다하다 do [perform, fulfill] *one's* duty / 공무원으로서의 본분을 잊다 neglect *one's* duty as a public servant
▶학생으로서의 본분을 염두에 두고 행동하여라 Conduct yourself bearing in mind your duty as a student.
▶그는 교육자로서의 본분에 합당하지 않은 행동을 했다 He has committed deeds unworthy of a school teacher.
▶그런 짓을 하면 학생의 본분에 어긋난다 It is not proper for a student to do such a thing.

본사 本社 〈지사에 대해〉 the head office 《of a firm》; a main office; 〈당사〉 our firm [company]
♦본사 근무가 되다 be assigned to the head office
▶그는 서울 본사로 전근되었다 He was transferred to the head office in Seoul.

본산 本山 1 〈중심 사찰〉 the head temple of a Buddhist sect; a Buddhist cathedral 2 〈중심지〉 headquarters
▶런던은 한때 상아 거래의 본산이라고 일컬어졌다 London was once called the headquarters of the ivory trades.

본새 本— 1 〈생김새〉 appearance; looks; features ♦본새가 곱다 be nice-looking; have good features
2 〈됨됨이〉 nature; quality; character
♦본새가 사납다 have a rude nature

본색 本色 〈정체〉 *one's* real character; 〈색깔〉 *one's* true [natural] colors; *one's* original colors
♦본색을 드러내다 show *one's* true [natural] colors; reveal *one's* true character; betray [unmask] *oneself* / 본색을 숨기다 wear [put on] a mask; disguise *oneself*
▶이 한 마디에 그의 본색이 드러난다 This remark is very characteristic of him.
▶마침내 그는 본색을 드러냈다 At last he showed [revealed, disclosed] his true character.

본서 本書 this book; this volume

본서 本署 the principal office; 〈경찰서의〉 police headquarters; the chief police station; 〈이 서〉 this office [station]
▶그는 살인 용의자로 본서에 연행되었다 He was taken to the chief police station as a suspected murderer.

본서방 本書房 *one's* legal husband ⇨ 본남편

본선 本船 〈모선〉 a mother ship [vessel]; 〈이 배〉 this [our] ship
■—수취증(受取證) a mate's receipt (略 M/R) —인도가격 free on board (略 FOB)

본선 本線 〔鐵〕 the main line [track]; 〈간선〉

the trunk (line) ♦경인 본선 the Kyŏngin Main Line

본선 本選 the final selection ▶본선에 오른 사람은 여덟명이었다 There were eight entries in the final contest [competition].

본성 本性 〈천성〉 one's true character [colors]; one's real nature
▶아이를 사랑하는 것이 어머니의 본성이다 It is in the nature of mothers to love their children.
▶취중에 본성이 나타난다 Wine reveals one's real nature.
▶인간의 본성은 선이다 Man is good by nature.
▶그녀는 마침내 본성을 드러냈다 She revealed her true character [showed her true colors] at last. ⇌ She betrayed herself at last.

본숭만숭하다 〈건성으로 보다〉 glance over; run one's eyes over 《a letter》; take a cursory view of; skim over [through] 《a newspaper》

본시 本是 originally ⇨ 본래

본심 本心 〈본마음〉 one's right mind; one's conscience; 〈진심〉 one's real [true] intention; one's true [real] motive
♦본심은 at heart [bottom]/ 본심이 아니다 be not in one's right mind / 본심으로 돌아오다 come to one's senses / 본심을 밝히다 reveal [confess] one's real intention; unbosom oneself / 본심으로 말하다 speak from one's heart
▶그의 본심을 알 수가 없다 I don't know what he's really thinking.
▶그는 언제나 본심을 털어놓지 않는다 He always does not speak his mind.
▶그는 마침내 본심을 드러냈다 He has finally revealed his real intention.
▶그것으로 그의 본심을 알 수 있었다 He betrayed himself by that.
▶이것이 과연 그의 본심에서 나온 말일까? I wonder if he really meant what he said.

본안 本案 1 〈원안〉 the original bill [draft]; the original plan; 〈이 안건〉 this bill [matter, item, proposal]
▶본안은 찬성 300표, 반대 50표로 가결되었다 The bill was passed by three hundred in favor to fifty opposed.
2 〈法〉 〈소송의〉 the merits

본얼굴 本— one's original [unpainted] face; a face without makeup
▶그녀는 사진보다 본얼굴이 낫다 The picture does not do her justice.

본업 本業 〈본직〉 one's principal [main] business [occupation]; one's regular business [work, trade]
♦본업 외의 일 a side business [job, line] / 본업에 힘쓰다 attend to one's business
▶그의 본업은 축산이다 Livestock breeding is his main occupation.
▶그는 본업을 열심히 하지 않고 아르바이트에 힘쓰고 있다 He works hard not at his main business but at his side one.

본연 本然 ♦본연의 natural; inborn; innate; inherent / 본연의 자세 the way that one [it] should be / 정당 본연의 자세 what a political party should be

본원 本源 a source; an origin; the root 《of》 ⇨ 근본

본위 本位 1 〈기본〉 a standard; 〈기초〉 a basis 《pl. bases》; 〈제1주의〉 principle; first; 〈중심의〉 -centered; -oriented
♦영리 본위의 학교 a school run for profit / 자기 본위의 사람 a self-centered person; an egoistic person / …본위로 하다 make it one's principle 《to do》 / 현금 본위로 장사하다 do a business on a cash basis
▶우리는 품질 본위입니다 Quality first is our motto.
▶우리는 고객 본위 주의입니다 We make it our principle to serve customers' interests.
2 〈화폐의〉 a (monetary) standard
♦금[은]— the gold [silver] standard: 금본위의 국가 a gold-using country / 금본위를 정지[이탈]하다 suspend [go off] the gold standard 단[복]— a single [double] standard ■—기호 《樂》 a natural (sign) —화폐 a standard coin; standard money; legal tender

본의 本意 one's original purpose; one's real intention [will, motive]
♦본의 아닌 reluctant; unwilling / 본의 아니게 against one's will; reluctantly; unwillingly / 본의를 오해하다 misjudge sb's motive
▶그 돈을 받은 것은 내 본의가 아니었다 I was unwilling to accept the money.
▶그것은 나의 본의가 아니다 It is not my real intention. ⇌ It goes against my intention.
▶이 일을 그만두는 것은 내 본의가 아닙니다 I am reluctant to leave this job.
▶본의 아니게 거짓말을 했다 Circumstances compelled me to tell a lie.
▶나는 본의 아니게 모임에 참석했다 I went to the meeting reluctantly.

본의 本義 〈참뜻〉 the true [real] meaning; 〈본지(本旨)〉 the basic principle
▶민주주의의 본의는 무엇인가? What is the basic principle of democracy?

본이름 本— one's real [original] name ⇨ 본명

본인 本人 1 〈자기, 나〉 I, me, myself 2 〈바로 그 사람〉 the person himself [herself]; the subject; 〈당사자〉 the said person; the person in question
♦본인의 사진 one's own photograph / 본인 자신이 in person; personally
▶그는 본인이 직접 갔다 He went himself.
▶본인 자신이 신청할 것 Apply in person.
▶그녀 본인이 대답했다 She answered me personally.
▶(마침 얘기를 하고 있을 때) 이크, 본인이 나타나셨네 Here he is, as large [big] as life!
▶나는 그 본인을 만났다 I saw the man himself.
▶본인에게서 들은 말이므로 사실임에 틀림없다 I have the news at first hand, so it must be true.
▶본인임을 밝힐 수 있는 증명서를 지참할 것 Bring some identification (papers) with you.
2 〈대리인에 대해〉 the principal; the constituent ♦본인이 출두하다 present oneself 《at a court》

본임자 本— the original owner
본적 本籍 one's original [permanent] domicile; 〈본적지〉 one's domicile of origin

> [解說] 영국이나 미국에서는 호적 제도가 없기 때문에 「본적(지)」에 해당하는 단어는 없다. 한국의 「본적(지)」은 one's permanent domicile; one's legally recognized permanent address 등으로 표현하면 된다.

♦본적은 서울이다 be legally domiciled in Seoul / 본적을 옮기다 transfer one's domicile ((to))
▶그는 본적이 서울 마포구다 He is legally domiciled in Map'o-gu, Seoul.

본전 本殿 〈중심 전당〉 the inner [main] shrine [temple] ⇨ 본당(本堂)
본전 本錢 〈밑천〉 capital; fund; 〈노름의〉 a stake; 〈원금〉 the principal (sum)
♦밑져야 본전이다 be none the worse for the loss / 본전을 건지다 recover the cost [one's investment]
▶이 장사는 본전도 못 건진다 This business doesn't pay.

본점 本店 1 〈지점에 대해〉 the head [main] office [shop]
♦본점 근무가 되다 be assigned [transferred] to the head office
▶그 회사는 서울에 본점이 있다 The firm has its head office in Seoul.
2 〈이 업소〉 this store; this (branch) office

본제 本題 1 〈중심 제목[과제]〉 the main subject; the original topic [subject]
♦본제로 돌아가서 returning to the main subject / 본제로 들어가다 enter into the main question
▶자, 교육이란 본제로 돌아갑시다 Now, let's return to the main problem of education.
2 〈이 제목〉 this subject

본존 本尊 〔佛敎〕 〈주불(主佛)〉 the principal image of Buddha; 〈석가모니불〉 Buddha (as the principal image)
본죄 本罪 〔가톨릭〕 〈자의적인〉 an actual [a personal] sin
본 주인 本主人 the original proprietor [owner]
본줄기 本— 〈간선〉 the main line; 〈식물의〉 trunk; stalk; 〈흐름의〉 stream; 〈산맥의〉 range
본지 本旨 〈근본 취지〉 the main [principal] object; 〈본목적〉 the true aim
▶그의 의견은 교육의 본지에 반하는 것이다 His opinion is contrary to the true aim of education.
본지 本紙 〈부록에 대한〉 the main section [sheet]; 〈자사 신문〉 our paper
♦본지의 애독자 our readers
▶그는 본지의 논설을 쓰고 있다 He writes editorials [leading articles] for our newspaper.
본지 本誌 〈자사 잡지〉 our magazine [journal]; 〈부록에 대해〉 the main section
▶본지에는 늘 두세 가지 긴 정치기사가 실린다 Our magazine always carries a couple of long political articles.

본직 本職 〈본업〉 one's (regular) occupation [profession]; one's principal [main] business; one's regular work [job]
♦본직을 소홀히 하다 neglect one's regular [main] work
▶그는 본직이 제화공이다 He is a shoemaker by profession [trade].
본질 本質 essence; (real) substance; true nature; essential [intrinsic] qualities
♦본질적 substantial / 본질적 속성 an intrinsic attribute / 본질적인 essential / 본질적으로 essentially; in essence; in itself; in substance; intrinsically
▶중요한 것은 그 본질이다 What is important is its true nature.
▶너는 문제의 본질을 모르고 있다 You don't understand the essence of the problem.
▶그는 게으름뱅이로 보이나 본질적으로는 다르다 He seems lazy, but basically [essentially] he is not.
본집 本— 〈제집〉 one's principal residence; one's (own) house [home]
본채 the main building (of a house)
본처 本妻 one's lawful [legal] wife; one's wedded wife; one's first wife
본척만척하다 pretend not to see ⇨ 본체만체하다
본체 本體 1 〈본바탕〉 ture nature; 〈참모습〉 a true form
▶아무튼 사물의 본체를 파악하는 것이 중요하다 It is essential to get at the heart of the matter, no matter what they are.
2 〔哲〕 〈실체〉 the substance; the noumenon (pl. -na); the entity; the thing in itself; 〔佛敎〕 〈실상〉 reality
■—론 〔哲〕 ontology; substantialism
본체만체하다 pretend not to see [to have seen]; 〈경시하다〉 neglect; show indifference to; be indifferent to
▶그는 내가 곤란을 당하고 있었건만 본체만체 했다 He looked the other way when I was in trouble. ⇌ He was indifferent to my distress.
▶그는 길에서 나를 본체만체했다 He gave [showed, turned] me the cold shoulder in the street. ⇌ He cut me (dead) in the street.
본초 本初 the origin
■—자오선 the prime [first] meridian
본초 本草 〈한약재〉 medicinal herbs
♦본초를 채집하다 botanize; herborize
■—가(家) a herb doctor; a herbalist —강목(綱目) a botanical list; a flora (pl. ~s, -rae) —서(書) a herbal —학 botany; phytology
본칙 本則 〈원칙〉 principles; 〔法〕 〈부칙에 대해〉 the main rules
본토 本土 the mainland; the country proper
♦본토에서 멀리 떨어진 섬 an island far from the mainland; a remote island
■영국— England proper: 영국 본토는 웨일스를 포함하지 않는다 England proper does not include Wales. 중국— The Chinese mainland; China proper ■—인 natives; mainlanders
본토박이 a native; an aborigine
♦본토박이의 nativeborn, trueborn, born and bred / 서울 본토박이 a Seoulite born and bred

본포 本鋪 the head shop ⇨ 본점(本店)
본헤드 〔野〕 〈실수〉 a bonehead play
  ▶그 선수는 또 본헤드(플레이)를 했다 The player pulled a boner again.
본형 本刑 a regular penalty
본회담 本會談 a full-dress [full-scale] talk; the main conference
본회의 本會議 〈국회의〉 a plenary session 《of Congress》; a full meeting [session]; a fulldress meeting [debate]
  ▶그 법안은 본회의에 상정되었다 The bill was submitted to a plenary session [sent to the floor].
볼¹ 〈뺨〉 a cheek
  ◆볼이 붉은 건강한 아이 a healthy [red-rosy] cheeked child / 볼이 훔쭉하다 have hollow [sunken] cheeks; one's cheeks are hollow [sunken] / (음식을) 볼이 미어지게 처넣다 cram [stuff, fill] one's mouth with (food); cram (food) into one's mouth / 볼을 (맞대고) 비비다 press [nestle] one's cheek against another's / 볼을 싸매다 cover [wrap] one's cheeks 《with a towel》
  ▶그녀는 부끄러워 볼이 붉어졌다 She blushed with [for] shame.
볼² 〈너비〉 the width (of a long and narrow object); 〈버선의〉 a patch ◆볼이 넓은 발 a broad foot / 버선에 볼을 대다[받다] put patches on the sole of a Korean sock
볼³ 1 ⇨ 공
  2 〔野〕〈스트라이크가 아닌 투구〉 a ball
  ▶심판은 볼을 선언했다 The umpire called it a ball.
  ▶볼에 배트를 휘두르지 마라 Don't swing at a ball.
  —카운트 〔野〕 the count; ball count: 그는 볼 카운트 투 스트라이크 노볼이다 He had no ball and two strikes on the batter.
볼가심 a bite; a snack; sth to chew on
  ▶볼가심으로 한 입 드시겠습니까? Would you like one of these to tide you over?
  —볼가심하다 have [eat] just a bite of food (to appease one's hunger)
  ◆볼가심할 것도 없다 do not have a bite to eat
볼가지다 protrude ⇨ 불거지다
볼강거리다 be chewy [leathery, lumpy]; take a lot of chewing
볼강볼강 chewy; leathery; lumpy; hard to chew
볼거리 〔韓醫〕 (get) (the) parotitis; mumps
  ◆볼거리가 나다 [서다] have (the) mumps
볼그대대하다 reddish; ruddy
볼그레하다 reddish; tinged with red
볼기 buttocks; (口) the hips; (口) the bottom; the rear; (口) the behind; (美口) one's butt; (英俗) one's bum
  ▶볼기가 크다 be big in the hips, have a big butt / 볼기를 때리다 flog [beat] sb on the buttocks (as a punishment); give a child spanking; spank (a child) / 볼기를 맞다 get spanked; be flogged on the buttocks [hip]
  ■볼기살 〈소의〉 rump
볼꼴 〈모양새〉 outward appearance; show; look ◆볼꼴 사납게 unseemly; shabbily; in an awkward [a clumsy] manner / 볼꼴 사납다 be unsightly [shabby, ugly, unshapely, unseemly, mean]
  ▶참 볼꼴 사납다! What a sight!
  ▶모임에서의 그는 사나웠다 He made a poor appearance at the meeting.
  ▶한밤중에 깨어나서 그녀는 볼꼴 사나운 모습으로 문간에 나타났다 Awakened in the middle of the night, she appeared at the door looking disheveled.
  ▶그는 볼꼴 사나운 걸음걸이로 걸어갔다 He walked away with an awkward gait.
  ▶볼꼴 사나우니 그만두게 Stop it for decency's sake.
  ▶그는 볼꼴 사납게 나뒹굴어졌다 He tumbled [fell] to the ground in an ungainly [unseemly] sprawl.
볼끈 with a burst ⇨ 불끈
볼락 〔魚〕 a gopher (rock cod); a rockfish
볼러 〔球〕〈볼링 선수〉 a bowler
볼레로 〈여성용 재킷〉 a bolero 《pl. ~s》;〈스페인의 민속무용〉 bolero 《pl. ~s》
볼록거리다 palpitate; swell and subside
볼록거울 a convex mirror
볼록렌즈 a convex lens [glass]; a convex
볼록면 —面 a convex surface; a convexity
볼록하다 baggy; bulgy ⇨ 불룩하다
볼륨 1 〈분량·양감〉 volume ◆볼륨이 있는 책 [사전] a thick book (dictionary)
  ▶그 여자는 볼륨이 대단하다 She has some [quite a] build.
  2 〈음량〉 volume ◆볼륨이 있는 목소리 a very powerful [loud] voice / 스테레오[라디오]의 볼륨을 높이다[낮추다] turn up [turn down] the volume on the stereo [radio]
  ▶볼륨을 낮춰주세요 Please turn the volume down.
볼리비아 〈나라 이름〉 Bolivia; 〈공식명〉 the Republic of Bolivia ◆볼리비아의 Bolivian
  ■—사람 a Bolivian
볼링 〔球〕 bowling ▶그녀는 볼링에서 200점을 냈다 She bowled a two hundred game.
  ■—장 bowling alleys
볼만하다 worthy of seeing [notice]; worth seeing; sightsworthy
  ◆볼만한 것 a sight; a spectacle; a feature; a highlight
  ▶그 프로그램은 참으로 볼만했다 That program was really worth seeing.
  ▶그것은 참 볼만했다 It was something to see [watch]. ⇌ It was a thing worthy of seeing.
  ▶이것은 꽤 볼만한 연극이다 This play is quite enjoyable [impressive].
  ▶박람회에서는 실물 크기의 우주선 모형이 볼만했다 The exhibition was highlighted [featured] by life-size models of spaceships.
볼멘소리 〈성난 말투〉 sullen [sulky, grouchy] words ◆볼멘 소리로 in angry tone / 볼멘소리로 대답하다 give a sullen answer
  ▶그녀는 볼멘소리로 말대답했다 She answered back sulkily.
볼모 〈담보〉 a pawn; a pledge; (a) security; a mortgage; a guarantee; 〈인질〉 a hostage
  ◆볼모가 되다[볼모로 잡히다] be taken [held]

볼베어링 (機) ball bearing(s)
볼세비즘 Bolshevism
볼세비키 a Bolshevik 《pl. ~s, -viki》; a Bolshevist
볼썽 appearances; show; look
♦볼썽 사납다 indecent; shabby; mean; unseemly; ungainly; unsightly
볼일 〈업무〉 affairs; business; 〈할일〉 an engagement; work; things to do
♦급한 볼일 urgent [pressing] business / 부득이한 볼일이 있어서 owing to an unavoidable engagement / 볼일이 있다[없다] have *sth* [nothing] to do; be [be not] engaged / 볼일이 남아 있다 have *sth* more to do / 볼일을 마치다 finish [do, settle] *one's* business; have done with *sth*
▶ 그분은 볼일로 나가 지금 자리에 없습니다 He is out now on (some) business.
▶ 어머니는 이웃에 볼일 보러 가셨다 My mother went to see a neighbor on business.
▶ 내게 무슨 볼일이냐? What do you want with [of] me?
▶ 볼일이 있을 때는 언제라도 불러 주십시오 Please call me any time you want me.
▶ 그녀에게 볼일이 좀 있습니다만 I'd like to speak to her.
▶ 나는 오늘은 볼일이 없다 I am free today. ⇒ I have nothing to do today.
▶ 오늘 저녁에 볼일이 있니? Are you busy this evening?
▶ 볼일이 있어서 가지 못했습니다 Business prevented me from going there.
▶ 난 이제 볼일은 다 봤다 I have done all the work assigned to me.
▶ 무슨 볼일로 여기 왔느냐? What brings you here?
볼장다보다 〈끝장나다〉 have done with *sth* / 〈실패하다〉 be ruined
▶ 나는 이제 볼장 다 봤다 It is all up with [over for] me. ⇒ (口) I'm done for.
볼타미터 〈전량계(電量計)〉 a voltameter
볼타전지 —電池 a voltaic battery [cell]; a Volta's cell
볼테르 〈프랑스의 계몽사상가·철학자·문필가〉 Voltaire, François-Marie Arouet (1694-1778)
볼트[1] 〈나사못〉 a bolt; a screw bolt
♦볼트를 죄다 tighten a bolt / 볼트로 죄다 fasten with a bolt; bolt (up)
▶ 볼트를 더 단단히 죄어라 Fasten the bolt tighter.
▶ 나는 창의 격자를 볼트로 죄었다 I bolted a grating over the window.
볼트[2] 〈전압〉【電】a volt; 〈볼트수〉 voltage
♦220볼트의 전류 a 220-volt current
볼트미터 〈전압계〉 a voltmeter
볼티모어 〈미국 메릴랜드 주의 항구〉 Baltimore
볼펜 a ball-point(pen); a ball pen; (英)(商標) a biro[báiərou]《pl. ~s》
볼품 (outward) appearance; looks; show
♦볼품없는 복장 an indecent [a shabby] dress / 볼품이 있다 look nice; make a fine show; be of a good style / 볼품이 없다[사납다] look poor; have a bad appearance; make a poor show; be unattractive [vulgar] / 방을 볼품있게 꾸미다 make a room look nice
▶ 너는 언제나 볼품없는 옷만 입는구나 You are always poorly dressed, aren't you?
▶ 그녀의 외모는 볼품이 없다 She is unattractive in appearance.
▶ 이 책은 얼개가 볼품이 있다 This book is well got up. ⇒ This book is of elegant format.
▶ 이쪽이 훨씬 볼품이 있다 This looks better. ⇒ This is more pleasing in appearance.
▶ 볼품은 아무래도 좋으니 튼튼하게만 만들어 주시오 I don't care how it looks, only I want it made solid.
봄 spring; springtime; springtide
♦인생의 봄 the springtime of life; the flower [prime] of youth / 봄의 따뜻한 햇살 a soft, warm spring sun(shine) / 봄 같은 날씨 spring-like weather
▶ 봄에는 나무에 새 잎이 움튼다 Trees put forth new leaves [buds] in (the) spring.
▶ 점점 봄다워지고 있다 It is getting spring-like all over.
■—기운 a feel [an air] of spring —농사 a spring crop —옷 (a suit for) spring wear; spring clothes; a spring dress
봄가물 spring drought [dry spell]
봄갈이 tilling [cultivating] 《a paddy field》 in the spring; spring plowing; turning over 《the soil》 in the spring
—봄갈이하다 do the spring plowing
봄나물 young greens [herbs] ♦봄나물을 캐다 pick [gather] young herbs
봄날 a spring day; spring weather
♦화창한 봄날 the mild days of spring
봄눈 spring snow ♦봄눈 녹듯하다 melt like spring snow; disappear [vanish] into thin air
봄바람 a spring wind [breeze]
봄베 [《(독) Bombe》a bomb; a cylinder
■ 가스[산소]— a gas [an oxygen] cylinder
봄베이 〈인도의 향구·상공업 도시〉 Bombay
봄볕 the spring sun(shine)
♦따뜻한 봄볕 the warm spring sunshine
▶ 나는 눈부시게 내리쬐는 봄볕 속을 걸었다 I walked in the gentle spring sunlight.
봄비 spring rain [drizzle]; rain in springtime
▶ 봄비 속에 산들이 흐릿하게 보였다 The hills looked hazy in the spring rain.
봄빛 〈봄경치〉 spring scenery; the scenery in spring; the vernal aspect of nature
봄안개 spring haze
▶ 봄안개가 벌판에 자욱이 끼어 있다 A spring haze is hanging over the fields.
봄철 spring; the spring season; springtime
봄타다 suffer from spring fever; get peevish in spring
봅슬레이 〈썰매〉 a bobsled; a bobsleigh; 〈경기〉 bobsledding; bobsleighing
봇논 洑— a paddy backed by a reservoir

봇도랑 洑— a reservoir channel; an irrigation ditch

봇돌 〈아궁이의〉 a support stone on either side of the fireplace; fireplace jambs; 〈지붕의〉 stone weights over a roof

봇돌 洑— a reservoir channel ⇨ 봇도랑

봇둑 洑— a dam; banks of a reservoir

봇물 洑— water of a reservoir; dam (water); irrigation water
▶ 그 아이는 봇물이 터진듯이 떠들어 댔다 The child burst out speaking.

봇줄 〈말·소에 쟁기 등을 매는 줄〉 a trace (tug); a tug ◆봇줄에 매여 in the traces / 〈말이〉 봇줄을 차내다 kick over the traces

봇짐 褓— a bundle; a backpack
◆봇짐을 짊어지다 carry a bundle on one's back; shoulder a bundle / 봇짐을 풀다 undo one's backpack
■一장수 a peddler with a backpack of wares

봉¹ a weight ⇨ 봉돌

봉² 〈땜질의〉 a solder patch; 〈치아 충전재〉 filling; 〈충치 구멍의〉 stopping; a plug; plugging
◆이에 봉을 해박다 fill [plug, stop] a tooth

봉 封 a paper package; 〈약의〉 a dose
◆약 한 봉 a packet of medicine
◆이 약을 식후 한 봉씩 드세요 Take [Have] a dose of this medicine after each meal.

봉 鳳 1 ⇨ 봉황
2 〈만만한 사람〉 a dupe; an easy mark; a gull; a pigeon; a prey; a victim
◆봉이 되다 fall an easy prey to sb's trick / 봉으로 삼다 make a sucker out of sb

봉건 封建 〈봉건제도〉 feudalism ◆봉건적(인) feudal; feudalistic; 〈중세적〉 medieval; 〈인습적〉 conventional; 〈전제적〉 despotic
▶ 우리 아버지는 봉건적이다 My father's ideas are feudalistic.
■一국가 a feudal state 一군주 a feudal lord 一사상 feudal ideas 一사회 the feudal society 一시대 the feudal age [days, times]; the era of feudalism 一제도 feudalism; the feudal system 一주의 feudalism; feudality

봉고도 棒高跳 pole vault ⇨ 장대높이뛰기

봉급 俸給 (a) salary; pay; wages; 〈전체의〉 (美) the payroll
◆많은[적은] 봉급 high [low, small] salary; high [small] pay / 쥐꼬리만한 봉급 a slender salary / 지난달 봉급 one's salary for last month / 봉급으로 생활하다 live on one's salary / 봉급이 오르는 have one's salary raised; get a raise in one's salary / 봉급을 깎다 cut sb's salary / 봉급을 올리다[내리다] raise [lower] sb's salary / 봉급을 지불하다 pay a salary / 봉급을 타다[받다] receive a salary; draw [get] one's salary / 월 백만원의 봉급을 받다 draw a monthly salary [pay] of a million won 《from a firm》; get 1,000,000 won a month
▶ 나는 봉급이 10만원 올랐다 My salary has been raised by one hundred thousand won.
▶ 그는 봉급이 얼마입니까? What is his salary? ≒ How much [What] salary does he get [draw]?
▶ 그 회사가 직원들에게 지불하는 봉급은 총액 1억원에 달한다 The monthly payroll of the firm amounts to 100 million won.
▶ 그는 시에서 봉급을 받고 있다 He is on the city payroll.
▶ 그는 고용인들에게 봉급을 후하게 주기로 했다 He decided to pay his employees well.
■一규정 the salary schedule regulation 一날 a payday 一봉투 a pay [salary] envelope 一생활자 a salaried man; a salary earner; (美俗) a white-collar worker; 〈총칭〉 the salaried class; the salariat(e): 나는 평범한 봉급생활자다 I'm just a run-of-the-mill salaried man.

봉기 蜂起 an uprising; (an) insurrection; (an) insurgency
一봉기하다 rise in revolt [rebellion, arms] (against); rise [revolt] (against)
▶ 전국 각지에서 농민이 봉기했다 The peasants rose up [revolted] against the government throughout the country.

봉납 奉納 dedication; offering; presentation 《to a deity》; oblation 一봉납하다 offer; make an offering; dedicate; present
■一물 an offering; a votive offering 一자 an offerer; a dedicator

봉당 封堂 an unfloored [a dirt-floored] space between two rooms

봉당을 빌려주니 안방까지 달란다 《속담》 Give him an inch and he'll take an ell.

봉돌 a weight (of stone [lead]) on a fishline); a sinker ◆봉돌을 달다 weight a fishing line; tie a weight on a fishing line; put a sinker to a line

봉두난발 蓬頭亂髮 an unkempt head of hair; shaggy [disheveled] hair

봉랍 封蠟 (sealing) wax ◆편지를 봉랍으로 봉하다 seal a letter with wax; wax 《an envelope》

봉랍 蜂蠟 propolis; beeswax

봉밀 蜂蜜 honey ⇨ 벌꿀

봉변 逢變 〈욕을 당함〉 having bitter experiences; receiving insult; being humiliated; 〈변을 당함〉 encountering a mishap; meeting with an accident
一봉변하다 〈망신당하다〉 have bitter experiences; be insulted [humiliated]; encounter a mishap; get a by-blow; have a hard time of it

봉봉 〈과자〉 (프) a bonbon

봉분 封墳 a (grave) mound 一봉분하다 mound 《a grave》; build a mound over a grave

봉사 奉仕 service; attendance
◆봉사 정신이 희박하다 be wanting in public spirit / 봉사 가격으로 팔다 sell at a (large, great) sacrifice; offer at a bargain price
一봉사하다 serve; be in the service of; render service(s) 《to》; attend [wait] on sb
◆나라에 봉사하다 place oneself at the service of one's country / 인류에 봉사하다 serve mankind
▶ 그녀는 그 집에서 5년 동안 봉사했다 She was in the service of that family for five years.
▶ 그는 30년간 외교관으로서 조국에 봉사했다 He served his country as a diplomat for thirty years.
▶ 친절 봉사하오니 많은 이용 바랍니다 We'll

do whatever we can to please you, so please favor us with your patronage.
■ 근로— labor service 사회— social service ■—자 a person who serves 《the public at large》; a servant 《of the people》 —활동 voluntary service

봉사 奉事 〈소경〉 a blind person
봉살 封殺 〈野〉 a force-out —**봉살하다** force 《a runner》 out
봉서 封書 a sealed letter [document]
♦ 봉서로 under cover; in sealed covers
봉선화 鳳仙花 〔植〕 a 《garden》 balsam; a touch-me-not 《pl. -nots》
봉소위 蜂巢胃 〈반추동물의〉 a reticulum 《pl. -la》; a honeycomb
봉쇄 封鎖 a blockade; blocking 《up》; containment ♦ 봉쇄를 뚫다 break [run] a blockade / 봉쇄를 풀다 raise [lift] a blockade
—**봉쇄하다** block; blockade 《a port》; block [bottle] up; seal off
♦ 바리케이드로 통로를 봉쇄하다 block 《up》 a passage with a barricade / 항구를 봉쇄하다 blockade the harbor entrance
▶ 출입구를 봉쇄하지 않으면 안된다 The doorway must be blocked up.
▶ 퍼레이드 때문에 도로는 모두 봉쇄되었다 The streets were all blocked off because of the parade.
■ 경제— an economic blockade [boycott] 해상— a naval [sea] blockade —구역 a blockade zone [line] —선《船》 a blocking ship; a blockader —작전 containment tactics [operations] —정책 a containment policy —함대 a blockading squadron [fleet] —항 a blockaded port —화폐 blocked currency
봉수 烽燧 a signal fire ⇨ 봉화《烽火》
봉숭아 a 《garden》 balsam ⇨ 봉선화《鳳仙花》
봉안 奉安 enshrinement —**봉안하다** enshrine
봉양 奉養 supporting [serving] one's parents —**봉양하다** support [provide for] one's parents; serve one's parents faithfully
▶ 나에게는 봉양해야 할 노부모가 계신다 I have aged parents to support.
봉오리 a flower bud ⇨ 꽃봉오리
♦ 피어나는 봉오리 bursting buds / 봉오리마다 all the buds / 봉오리가 맺혀 있다 be in bud / 봉오리가 피다 open its buds / 봉오리를 맺다 put forth [send out, shoot out] 《the》 buds
봉우리 a peak; a summit; a top ♦ 산봉우리 a mountain top [peak]; the peak of a mountain / 높이 솟은 봉우리 a towering peak
봉인 封印 a seal; sealing
♦ 봉인된 편지 a sealed letter; a letter under seal / 봉인을 떼다 unseal 《a letter》 / 봉인을 뜯다 break [take off] a seal
—**봉인하다** seal; put the seal 《up》on; put 《a letter》 under seal
▶ 그 서류는 단단히 봉인되어 있었다 The document was kept tightly sealed.
봉작 封爵 investiture [investment] with the titles of nobility; ennoblement —**봉작하다** invest with the titles of nobility; ennoble
봉정 奉呈 〈바침〉 dedication; presentation —**봉정하다** dedicate; present; offer

봉제 縫製 sewing; needlework; dressmaking —공[사] a needleworker; a dressmaker; a worker in a sewing factory —공장 a sewing factory
봉죽 〈보조〉 assistance; help; aid ■—꾼 an assistant; a helper; an aide
봉지 封紙 a paper bag [sack]; 〈세는 단위〉 a pack《age》 《of》
♦ 약 한 봉지 a packet of medicine / 봉지 붙이기 paper-bag making
▶ 그것을 봉지에 넣어 주시오 Put it in a paper bag for me.
봉직하다 奉職— be in office; hold an office 《at, in》; serve 《at, in》; 〈재직하다〉 be in the service 《of》 ♦ 외무부에 봉직하다 be 《serving》 in the Foreign Office
▶ 본교에 봉직한지 10년이 된다 I have been teaching at this school for ten years.
▶ 그녀는 교사로 봉직했다 She had a job [got a position] as a teacher.
봉착하다 逢着— encounter; face; meet with; be confronted [faced] with
♦ 예기치 못한 난관에 봉착하다 be confronted with [encounter] an unforeseen difficulty
▶ 그는 생사의 문제에 봉착했다 He confronted with the problem of life and death.
봉창 封窓 〈봉하기〉 sealing 《up》 a window; 〈봉한 창〉 a sealed window; a small blind window
봉축 奉祝 celebration 《of an occasion》
♦ …을 봉축하여 in honor [celebration] of... —**봉축하다** celebrate 《the birth of Buddha》
봉토 封土 1 〈흙을 쌓아 올린 것〉 an earthen mound 2 〈제후의 영지〉 a feud; a feudal estate [land, territory]
봉투 封套 an envelope
♦ 봉투를 봉하다 seal 《up》 [close up] an envelope / 봉투를 뜯다 open [break open, cut open] an envelope / 봉투에 주소를 쓰다 address an envelope / 봉투에 편지를 넣다 put a letter in an envelope
▶ 나는 봉투에 사진 넣는 것을 잊었다 I forgot to put the picture in the envelope.
■ 각— a side-opening envelope 반신용— a return envelope 편지— a letter envelope
봉하다 封— 1 〈봉투·문 등을〉 seal 《a letter》; seal up 《a window》; glue up; fasten
♦ 봉한[봉하지 않은] 편지 a sealed [an unsealed] letter / 창을 봉하다 seal up a window / 편지를 봉하다 seal a letter / 봉해 보내다 send sth under seal / 봉하지 않은 채 부치다 send 《a letter》 unsealed
▶ 남이 뜯어볼 수 없도록 봉투를 단단히 봉하시오 Seal 《up》 the envelope in order to make it confidential.
2 〈입을〉 shut; close; seal
♦ 입을 봉하고 말하지 않다 shut one's mouth and remain silent; keep silent; hold one's tongue
▶ 그들은 그의 입을 봉하려고 애썼다 They tried to seal his lips.
3 〈구멍을〉 close [stop] up 《a hole》
♦ 창구멍을 봉하다 cover a hole in a paper window

4 〈작위를〉 confer a peerage; 〈봉토를〉 invest *sb* with a fief; enfeoff

봉함 封函 a sealed letter

봉함 封緘 a seal; sealing ♦봉함을 뜯다 break the seal; unseal 《a letter》
—**봉함하다** seal ♦봉함한 sealed / 단단히 봉함하여 in a tight cover / 봉함하지 않고 with [under] a flying seal
■—엽서 a letter card

봉합 縫合 stitch; seam; suture —**봉합하다** stitch (up) 《a wound》; seam; suture
▶그 의사는 상처를 봉합했다 The doctor stitched [sewed] up the wound.
■—사(絲) 【外科】 a suture; a stitching fiber —선 a suture; a seam

봉행하다 奉行— do in obedience to 《a superior's order》; carry out 《an order》

봉헌 奉獻 dedication; presentation; consecration —**봉헌하다** dedicate [consecrate] *sth* to 《a shrine》
▶교회는 예배 장소로 봉헌된 곳이다 A church is consecrated to worship.
■—물 votive offerings —자 a dedicator; a consecrator

봉화 烽火 a signal fire; a beacon; a rocket
♦봉화(를) 들다 raise a beacon fire / 봉화를 올리다 send up a rocket as a signal; light a signal fire
▶그들은 반핵운동의 봉화를 올렸다 They started [launched] a campaign against nuclear weapons.
▶그들은 봉화를 올려 자신의 위치를 알렸다 They made known their position by lighting a beacon [signal fire].
■—대 a beacon mound

봉황 鳳凰 a Chinese phoenix

봐하니 so far as my observation goes ⇨ 보아하니

뵈다¹ have the honor of seeing *sb* ⇨ 뵙다
▶어디서 한 번 뵌 것 같습니다 I remember seeing [having seen] you once somewhere.

뵈다² see ⇨ 보이다

뵙다 see; meet; have the honor [pleasure] of seeing *sb*
▶처음 뵙겠습니다 How do you do?
▶그럼 내일 또 뵙겠습니다 Well then, I (shall) come tomorrow.
▶여기서 뵙게 되어 반갑습니다 It's good [nice] to see you here. ⇌ I'm glad I've met you here.
▶오늘 저녁 뵙고자 합니다만 I'd like to meet you this evening.
▶오랫동안 뵙지 못했습니다 It's a long time since I saw you last.

부 父 a father

부 否 no; nay; negation ♦가부(可否) aye and no; pro and con
▶부쪽이 다수였다 The noes had it.

부 部 1 〈부분〉 (a) part; a portion; a section
♦시의 중심부 the center [central part] of a town / 제1부 Section [Part] I / 2부로 된 소설 a novel in two parts / 3부 합창으로 노래하다 sing in three parts
▶그 보고서는 4부로 되어 있다 The report is in four parts.
2 〈부서〉 a department; a section; a division
♦백화점의 식품부 the foodstuffs section of a department store / 회사의 영업부 the sales department [division] of a company / 신문의 편집부 the editorial department [staff] of a newspaper / 몇 개의 부로 나뉘어 있다 be divided into several bureaus [departments]
3 〈책을 셀 때〉 a copy; a volume
♦한 부에 5,000원 five thousand won per copy
▶그 책을 한꺼번에 열 부 샀다 I bought ten copies of the book at a time.
▶이 잡지는 한 부에 얼마입니까? How much is a copy of this magazine?

부 富 riches; wealth; a fortune
♦부의 분배 the distribution of wealth / 부를 쌓다 pile up [amass, build up] a fortune
▶그의 부는 야심과 근면의 결과였다 His wealth was a product of ambition and hard work.

부 賦 〈시〉 an ode 《to》; a prose poem; poetical prose

부- 副- vice-; deputy; sub-; assistant; 〈부본〉 a copy

┌─────────────────────────────────┐
│ 解說「부(副)-」에 해당하는 영어에는 *vice-*, │
│ *deputy*, *sub-* 등이 있다. 그 가운데서 *vice*와 │
│ *deputy*는 관직·공직명 앞에 붙인다. *sub-* 는 │
│ 「다음 차례의, 하위의」의 뜻. *assistant*를 쓰 │
│ 는 경우도 있다.   │
└─────────────────────────────────┘

♦부사령관 the deputy commander-in-chief / 부지배인 an assistant manager [director]
▶부사장은 서류를 원본과 사본으로 두 통 만들었다 The vice-president made an original and a copy of the documents.

-부 -附 1 〈날짜〉 dated; under the date of
▶귀하의 4월 1일부 편지를 받았습니다 I received your letter dated [under the date of] April 1.
▶그는 10월 15일부로 부장으로 승진했다 He was promoted to department head as of [effective] October 15.
2 〈소속〉 attached to 《the headquarters》
♦대사관부 무관 a military attaché to an embassy

부가 附加 addition; supplement; annexation
♦부가적인 일[정보] additional work [information]
—**부가하다** add (to); make addition(s); 〈보충〉 supplement; 〈첨부〉 annex; append; 〈추가〉 subjoin
■—물 an addition, an annex; an appendage; an affix; an appendix —세 (美) a surtax; a supertax; an additional tax —형(刑) an accessory [an additional, a supplementary] penalty —화합물 an addition product; an additive compound

부가가치 附加價値 value added; added value
♦부가가치가 높은 제품의 생산 the production of high value-added products
■—세 a tax on value added; a value-added tax (略 VAT) —통신망 a value-added network (略 VAN)

부각 俯角 〔數〕〈내려본 각〉 a dip; an angle of depression [declination]

부각 浮刻 relief; relievo; embossed carving ―부각하다 emboss; carve in relief ◆부각시키다 bring sth into relief / 부각되다 be embossed; stand out in (bold) relief ▶주화에는 문자와 숫자가 부각되어 있다 Coins are embossed with letters and figures.

부감 俯瞰 overlooking; looking down 《upon》 ―부감하다 overlook; look down upon; command [get] a bird's-eye [an air] view 《of》 ▶이것은 비행기에서 부감하여 찍은 사진이다 This is a bird's-eye view photo taken from an airplane. ―도 〈조감도〉 a bird's-eye view 《of》; an air [overhead] view 《of》

부갑상선 副甲狀腺 〔解〕 the parathyroid (glands) ■―호르몬 parathormone

부강 富强 wealth [prosperity] and power ◆국가의 부강 the wealth [prosperity] and power of a nation; national wealth and power ―부강하다 rich and powerful ◆부강한 나라를 세우다 found a rich and powerful country [nation]

부글거리다 bubble; pop (in fermenting)

부결 否決 voting down; rejection ―부결하다 reject; vote [decide] against; vote down ◆부결되다 be rejected; be voted down; be killed / 의안을 부결하다 reject [vote down] a bill ▶제안은 51 대 49표로 부결되었다 The proposal was rejected by a vote of 51 to 49.

부계 父系 the paternal line [side]; the patrilineage ◆부계의 paternal; patrilineal; on the paternal [father's] side ■―가족 a paternal [patriarchal] family ―사회 a patrilineal society ―친족 a relative on the father's [paternal] side; an agnate

부고 訃告 an announcement of sb's death; an obituary (notice); 〈부고장〉 a mourning card ◆부고를 받다 receive a notice of sb's death ―부고하다 send (out) a notice of sb's death

부고환 副睾丸 〔解〕 the epididymis 《pl. -mides》

부골 富骨 physiognomy denoting wealth

부과 賦課 levy; imposition ◆자동 부과제 taxation-by-schedule system ―부과하다 levy 《on》; impose 《on》; lay (a tax on an article) ◆소득세를 부과하다 levy an income tax 《on》 ▶토지에는 고정자산세가 부과된다 A fixed assets tax is imposed on land. ▶수입 주정(酒精) 음료에는 관세가 부과된다 The customs duties are imposed on imported alcoholic drinks. ■―금 〈세관 등의〉 dues; a levy ―액 the amount imposed; assessment

부관 副官 an adjutant; an aid(e)-de-camp 《pl. aid(e)s-de-camp》 ■―전속― an aide; an aid(e)-de-camp 《pl. aid(e)s-de-camp》 (略 A.D.C.); 〈연락장교〉 a galloper ■―참모 an adjutant general

부광 富鑛 a rich ore; a rich mine ■―대 a bonanza

부교 浮橋 a floating [pontoon] bridge

부교감신경 副交感神經 〔解〕 a parasympathetic (nerve)

부교수 副敎授 an associate professor

부교재 副敎材 an auxiliary textbook

부국 富國 a rich [wealthy, prosperous] country; national enrichment

부국강병 富國强兵 wealth and military strength [power] of a nation ◆부국 강병을 꾀하다 promote the national prosperity and military strength policy ■―책 a measure to enrich and strengthen a country

부군 夫君 a [one's] husband; one's man

부권 父權 paternal rights [authority]; 〈가장권〉 patriarchal right ■―사회 a patriarchal society ―시대 the patriarchal age ―제도 patriarchy

부권 夫權 the husband's rights; marital authority

부권 婦權 women's rights ⇨ 여권(女權)

부귀 富貴 riches and honors; wealth and rank [honor, fame] ◆부귀를 타고나다 be born rich; be born with a silver [gold] spoon in one's mouth ―부귀하다 rich [wealthy] and noble ◆부귀한 사람들 the wealthy and noble ■―공명 wealth, rank and fame

부귀영화 富貴榮華 wealth and prosperity ◆부귀영화를 누리다 live in splendor [wealth and honor]; be at the height [zenith] of one's prosperity

부그르르 boiling briskly ⇨ 부글부글

부근 附近 〈근처〉 the neighborhood; the vicinity; environs ◆부근의 neighboring; nearby; 〈인접한〉 adjacent / 부근에 near; around; in the neighborhood of / 이 부근에 somewhere around [about, near] here ▶형은 부근의 농가에서 일하고 있습니다 My brother is working on a nearby [neighboring] farm. ▶서울 부근에 눈이 왔다 They had snow in and around Seoul [in Seoul and its vicinity]. ▶이 부근에 우체국이 있습니까? Is there a post office in this vicinity [neighborhood]? ▶내가 살고 있는 부근에는 절이 많다 There are a lot of temples in my neighborhood.

부글거리다 1 〈물이〉 boil (over); simmer; seethe ▶주전자의 물이 불 위에서 부글거리고 있었다 The kettle was singing on the fire. 2 〈거품이〉 bubble (up); rise in bubbles ▶거품이 부글거리며 흘러 넘쳤다 Bubbles oozed and foamed along. 3 〈마음이〉 be fretful; fret

부글부글 1 〈끓는 모양〉 boiling briskly; with a sizzling sound ◆부글부글 끓다 boil over [briskly]; simmer ▶이윽고 물이 부글부글 끓었다 The water eventually came to a rolling boil. 2 〈거품이〉 bubblingly; foamily ◆부글부글 가라앉다 sink leaving a trail of bubbles / 거품이 부글부글 일다 bubble up; rise

in bubbles
3 〈마음이〉 ◆화가 나서 속이 부글부글 끓다 boil with rage
부금 賦金 an instal(l)ment; 〈보험의〉 a premium
◆이달치 부금 this month's instal(l)ment / 부금을 붓다 pay in [by] instal(l)ments; 〈계 등의〉 pay *one's* share 《in a mutual aid society》 by instal(l)ments
▶나는 생명보험에 들어 매달 5만원의 부금을 붓고 있다 I pay the premium of fifty thousand won on life insurance every month.
부기 〈어리석은 사람〉 a foolish person; a dolt; a simpleton; a blockhead; a ninny
부기 附記 an additional remark; a supplementary note; a postscript (略 P.S., p.s.)
—**부기하다** add; write in addition; append 《a note》; add a postscript 《to a letter》
부기 浮氣 (a) swelling (of the skin)
▶다리의 부기가 내렸다[가라앉았다] The swelling in the leg has gone down [subsided].
부기 簿記 bookkeeping
◆부기를 하다 keep books; keep accounts
◆가계[공장]— domestic [factory] bookkeeping 단식[복식]— bookkeeping by single [double] entry 상업[공업, 은행]— commercial [industrial, bank] bookkeeping ─장(帳) an account book ─학 (the art of) bookkeeping
부기우기 〔樂〕 boogie-woogie; boogie
부꾸미 a kind of fried cake made by various flours
부끄러움 1〈수줍음〉 (feeling of) shyness; bashfulness; coyness
◆부끄러움을 잘 타는 사람 a shy [bashful] person / 부끄러움을 타다 feel shy; be bashful [coy]
▶민호는 부끄러움을 잘 타는 아이다 Min-ho is a shy boy.
2 〈창피〉 shame; disgrace; dishonor; humiliation
◆부끄러움을 모르는 여자 brazen [shameless] hussy / 부끄러움을 당하다 disgrace *oneself*; humiliate *oneself*; be put to shame / 부끄러움을 알다 be sensible to shame; have a sense of shame [dishonor]/ 부끄러움을 무릅쓰고 …하다 bear shame to 《do》; stoop to 《do》
▶나는 이제 부끄러움이고 뭐고 없다 I am now beyond [past] all sense of shame [decency].
▶나는 부끄러움을 무릅쓰고 그에게 부탁을 했다 I stooped to ask a favor of him.
부끄러워하다 1〈수줍어하다〉 be [feel] shy; be bashful; be coy
◆부끄러워하여 shyly; bashfully
▶그녀는 의사에게 진찰 받는 것을 몹시 부끄러워했다 She was very shy of consulting a doctor.
▶부끄러워하지 마라 Don't be bashful [shy].
2 〈창피해하다〉 be [feel] ashamed 《of》; feel shame 《at》
◆부끄러워하는 얼굴 an ashamed look / 가난을 부끄러워하다 be ashamed of *one's* being poor
▶그는 자기가 한 짓을 부끄러워하고 있다 He is ashamed of what he did.
부끄럼 shyness ⇨ 부끄러움
부끄럽다 1 〈수줍다〉 shy; bashful; coy
◆부끄러운 듯이 shyly; bashfully; coyly; sheepishly / 어쩐지 부끄럽다 be [feel] ashamed somehow or other / 부끄러운 표정이다 look shy [abashed]/ 부끄러워 말을 못하다 be coy of speech; be too shy to talk
▶나는 남이 나를 쳐다보면 부끄럽다 I am [feel] shy when people are watching me.
▶그 소녀는 부끄러워서 두 손으로 얼굴을 가렸다 The little girl covered her face with her hands from bashfulness.
2 〈창피하다〉 shameful; disgraceful
◆신사로서 부끄러운 행위 an act unworthy of a gentleman / 부끄러워서 고개를 숙이다 hang *one's* head in shame / 부끄러워서 얼굴을 붉히다 blush with shame / 부끄러워서 얼굴이 화끈거리다 burn with shame / 신사로서 부끄럽지 않은 행동을 하다 act as a gentleman; do *sth* worthy of a gentleman / 부끄럽지 않게 살다 live respectably [decently]; make a decent living
▶그는 어처구니없는 실수를 저질러 부끄러웠다 He felt ashamed that he had made an outrageous mistake.
▶부끄럽습니다만 그것은 사실입니다 I blush to own it.
▶부끄러워 몸둘 바를 모르겠습니다 I am really ashamed of myself.
▶나는 부끄러워 고개를 들 수가 없었다 I could hardly hold up my head for shame.
▶그들은 노동을 부끄러운 일로 여기고 있다 They think it a shame to work.
▶남자라면 그것을 부끄럽게 여겨야 한다 A man must be ashamed of it.
부나비 〔昆〕〈불나방〉 a tiger moth
부낭 浮囊 1〈구명용〉 a float; a life preserver; a life belt; 〈수영용〉 a (tire) tube; (英) a tyre 2 〈물고기의 부레〉 an air bladder; a swimming bladder
부내 部內 circles; the department ◆부내의 inside (the department)/ 부내 사람 an insider
부녀 父女 father and daughter
부녀(자) 婦女(子) a woman; (총칭) womenfolk(s); the fair [weaker] sex
◆부녀자 같은 womanish; feminine; effeminate / 부녀자를 괴롭히다 bully the fair sex
부농 富農 a prosperous [rich, wealthy] farmer
부닥치다 confront; encounter; face; be faced [confronted] with; meet with
◆난관에 부닥치다 be confronted with a difficult problem / 벽에 부닥치다 be up against a wall; run into a blank wall; (비유) reach a deadlock / 부닥쳐 보다 have a try; face up 《to》
▶그는 마침내 생사의 문제에 부닥쳤다 He was finally confronted with the problem of life and death.
▶이런 장애는 아직까지 부닥쳐 본 적이 없다 Such obstacles have never been encountered before.
부단하다 不斷— constant; continual; ceaseless; incessant; persistent; perpetual
◆부단한 노력 constant efforts; incessant

labor / 부단한 주의 constant attention / 부단히 constantly; continually; ceaselessly / 부단히 노력하다 make a ceaseless effort; continue one's unremitting exertions

부담 負擔 a burden; a charge; a load; 〈경비의〉 defrayment; 〈조세의〉 incidence; 〈책임〉 a responsibility; 〈의무〉 obligation; 〈채무〉 liability

♦ 부담이 되다 be a burden [strain] 《on》; weigh 《on》 / 부담이 많다 have too many things on one's hands / 부담을 주다 burden sb 《with》; impose burden on sb / 부담을 줄이다 lighten a burden / 마음의 부담을 덜어주다 take a load off one's mind / 각자 부담으로 하다 split the account; (口) go Dutch

▶ 덕분에 마음의 부담을 덜었습니다 You have taken a load off my mind.

▶ 그는 회사 부담으로 유럽을 여행했다 He took a trip to Europe at the expense of the company.

—부담하다 bear; stand; shoulder 《a burden》; take upon oneself

♦ 비용을 부담하다 bear [shoulder, stand] the expense / 부담시키다 charge 《expenses》 to sb; make sb bear [pay] 《the expenses》

▶ 비용은 각자 부담하기로 결정되었다 It was decided that we would each pay our own expenses.

■ —액 an amount to be borne; one's share 《in expenses》; an allotment; a share

부담스럽다 負擔— burdensome; bothersome

♦ 부담스럽게 여기다 regard sth as a bother / 이 일은 나에게 너무 부담스럽다 This work is too much for me.

▶ 그 비용은 그의 재력으로는 부담스러웠다 The expense was a strain on his resources.

부당 不當 injustice; unreasonableness; wrongfulness; exorbitance; impropriety

—부당한 unjust; unreasonable; wrongful; unfair; improper; 〈지나치다〉 undue; excessive; exorbitant; unmerited; undeserved

♦ 부당한 가격 an exorbitant [unreasonable] price / 부당한 요구 a bad claim; an exorbitant [unjustified] demand / 부당하게 unreasonably; unjustly; unlawfully; lawlessly / 요구가 부당하다 be extortionate in one's demands

▶ 그의 비난은 부당하다 His criticism isn't justified.

▶ 사장의 처사는 부당했다 The president has done wrong.

▶ 우리는 부당한 요구는 받아들일 수 없다 We will not accept your excessive demands.

—가정(假定) an unreasonable hypothesis —거래 an unfair [unconscionable] bargain —과세 unreasonable taxation —노동행위 unfair labor practice —이득 an undue [unreasonable, excessive] profit; (法) unjust enrichment; 〈행위〉 profiteering —지출 an unjust disbursement; a misappropriation of funds —해고 unfair [wrongful] dismissal

부대 附帶 ♦ 부대적인 appendant; collateral; incident; incidental; accessory; secondary

—부대하다 accompany; be incidental [accessory, appendant] 《to》; be attached [annexed] 《to》

■ —가치 extrinsic value —결의 an additional [a supplementary] resolution; an incidental [a contingent] vote —계약 an accessory contract —공사 〔土〕 appurtenant work —권리 〈토지 등에 대한〉 〔法〕 an appendant (right) —사건 a side issue —사업 a subsidiary enterprise —사정 collateral circumstance —사항 a supplementary item —설비 incidental facilities [equipment] —업무 business incidental to 《a railway enterprise》 —조건 a collateral [an incidental] condition —증서 a collateral bond —친구 an attendant [accessory] claim

부대 負袋 a sack; a burlap bag; a gunny sack [bag] ♦ 밀가루 한 부대 a sack of flour / 밭에서 감자를 부대에 담다 sack potatoes in the field; put potatoes into a sack in the field

부대 部隊 a (military) unit; a corps; a party; a detachment; 〈분대〉 a squad; troops

■ 기갑— armored forces [troops]; an armored unit [column] 기계화— a mechanized unit 외인— a foreign legion 전투— a fighting unit 지상— ground troops 후방— rear guards ■—기 a guidon; a squad flag —명 unit designation —장 an officer commanding; (美) a commanding officer (略 C.O.) —행진 a march in columns

부대끼다 〈시달리다〉 be pestered 《by》; be harassed 《by, with》; be annoyed 《by》; 〈고통을 받다〉 suffer 《from》; be troubled 《with》; be afflicted 《with》

♦ 빚쟁이에게 부대끼다 be tormented [hounded] by creditors / 속이 부대끼다 feel uncomfortable with one's stomach loaded with heavy food / 아이한테 부대끼다 be pestered by one's child

▶ 나는 만원버스에서 사람들에게 부대끼는 데 이골이 났다 I got used to being jostled in a crowded bus.

▶ 그는 소싯적부터 거친 세파에 부대껴 왔다 He has gone through many hardships of life ever since he was a boy.

부덕 不德 lack [want] of virtue

▶ 모두 제 부덕의 소치입니다 I am solely to blame for it. ⇌ It's all my fault.

—부덕하다 short [lacking] of virtue

부덕 婦德 womanly [female] virtues

♦ 부덕의 귀감 a model of female virtues; a mirror [paragon] womanhood / 부덕을 갖추다 possess womanly virtues; be invested with womanly [female] virtues

부도 不渡 dishonor; nonpayment

♦ 부도가 나다 be dishonored

▶ 그들은 사업 실패로 어음[수표]을 부도냈다 Their business has collapsed to the point where they have dishonored a bill [check].

■ —수표 a dishonored [bad] check; a rubber check —어음 a dishonored [bad] bill

부도 附圖 an attached [appended] map [plan, graph, figure]

부도 婦道 womanhood; the duty of a woman

부도덕 不道德 (an) immorality; lack of morality; bad morals; vice

—부도덕하다 immoral; unvirtuous; wicked;

vicious; dissolute; licentious; profligate
♦부도덕한 행동 immoral conduct / 부도덕한 짓을 하다 act immorally; commit an immoral act
▶부도덕하기 짝이 없는 일이다 It is a flagrant breach of morality.

부도심 副都心 a subcenter of a metropolis; a newly emerging [developed] city center

부도체 不導體 〔物〕 a nonconductor; a non-conducting substance ♦열[전기]의 부도체 a nonconductor of heat [electricity]

부독본 副讀本 a supplementary reader

부동 不同 dissimilarity; inequality; lack of uniformity ━**부동하다** unequal; uneven; dissimilar; lacking in uniformity
♦표리가 부동한 double-dealing; double-faced; treacherous / 표리가 부동하다 carry two faces under one hood; play a double game

부동 不動 immobility; immovability; firmness
♦부동의 immovable; immobile; firm / 부동의 지위 an indisputable [unshakable] position
▶나의 결심은 부동이다 My resolution is unshakable.
■━자세 an immobile posture; 〔軍〕 the position at attention : 국기가 게양되자 사람들은 모두 부동 자세를 취했다 All the people stood at attention as the flag was raised.

부동 浮動 floating; wafting ━**부동하다** float; be afloat; 〈시세 등이〉 fluctuate
♦부동하는 물가 fluctuating prices / 부동하는 시황 an unsteady market
■━구매력 floating purchasing power ━性 instability; unstableness ━시세 unsteady quotations ━인구 the floating [transient] population ━주 floating stocks ━표[투표자] floating votes [voters]

부동 不凍 nonfreezing
■━액 an antifreezing solution ━제 an antifreeze (agent) ━항 an ice-free port

부동산 不動産 real [fixed, immovable] property; immovables; real estate; realty; a landed estate
♦부동산을 매매하다 deal in real estate
▶그는 1억원 상당의 부동산을 가지고 있다 He has real estate worth one hundred million won. ⇌ He has one hundred million won in real estate.
▶그는 부모에게서 많은 부동산을 물려받았다 He inherited from his parents extensive real estate holdings.
■━감정사 a real estate appraiser ━거래 a real estate transaction ━권리증 a title deed; a land certificate; muniments ━대출 a loan on real property ━등기 real-estate registration ━등기법〔法〕 the Real Property Registration Act ━보험 property insurance ━소득 an income from immovables [real property] ━시가[과세]표준액 the standard value of real estate based on the current prices [computed for tax imposition] ━양도세 real estate sale [transfer] tax ━중개업자 a realty dealer; a real estate agent [broker]; (美) a realtor ━취득세 real estate acquisition tax ━투기 speculative investment in real estate ━투기억제세 a tax aimed at curbing speculation on real estate ━투자 investment in real estate

부두 埠頭 a quay; a wharf 《pl. ~s, wharves》; a pier; a jetty
♦부두에 배를 대다 bring [moor] 《a steamer》 alongside the quay
■━노동조합 a stevedores union; a longshoreman union ━세 wharf dues; quayage; jettage ━인도〔商〕 ex wharf; free on wharf; ex quay ━인부[노동자] a longshoreman; a stevedore; a dock laborer

부둑부둑하다 damp-dry; pretty well dry
▶빨래가 다리기 알맞게 부둑부둑하게 말랐다 The wash is dry enough to iron [for ironing].

부둣가 埠頭━ the wharfside; the quayside
♦보트를 부둣가에 매어 두다 tie up a boat alongside the quay

부둥키다 embrace [hug] sb; hold [take] sb in one's arms; grasp
♦아기를 부둥켜 안다 give a baby a hug; hold a baby in one's arms / 어깨를 부둥켜 안다 take [hold] sb round the shoulders / 인형을 부둥켜 안다 clutch one's doll to one's breast
▶두 사람은 공원의 벤치에서 서로 부둥켜 안고 있었다 The two were embracing each other on the bench in the park.
▶자매는 서로 부둥켜 안고 울었다 The sisters wept in each other's arms.

부드득 with a grating sound ⇨ 바드득

부드럽다 1 〈촉감이〉 soft; tender; 〈빛 등이〉 mellow; subdued; gentle
♦부드러운 가죽 soft [pliable] leather / 부드러운 감촉 a soft touch / 비단처럼 부드러운 살결 skin soft as silk / 감촉이 부드럽다 feel soft; be soft to the touch
▶열을 가하니 고무가 부드러워졌다 Heat softened the rubber.
2 〈성질·태도가〉 gentle; tender; soft; meek; smooth; suave; mild(-mannered)
♦부드러운 미소[목소리] a gentle [soft] smile [voice] / 목소리를 부드럽게 하다 soften one's voice; modify one's tone (of voice) / 남한테 부드럽게 대하다 behave gently toward others / 부드럽게 이야기하다 speak in a familiar tone
▶나는 그녀의 부드러운 말씨에 마음이 놓였다 I was relieved at her gentle way of speaking.

부드레하다 very soft [tender]; very gentle [mild]

부득부득 〈고집스레〉 stubbornly; obstinately; persistently; importunately; tenaciously
♦부득부득 우기다 persist in [stick to] one's opinion(s) / 돈을 달라고 부득부득 조르다 importunate sb for money; ask sb importunately for money
▶그녀는 부득부득 영화 구경을 가겠다고 고집을 부렸다 She insisted on going to the movies.

부득불 不得不 inevitably; unavoidably; necessarily; from [out of] sheer necessity
♦부득불 …하다 be compelled [forced, obliged] to 《do》; be hard put to it to 《do》; be driven by dire [sheer] necessity to 《do》 / 부득불 최후의 수단을 쓰다 be driven [impelled] to extreme measures
▶나는 부득불 거짓말을 했다 I lied out of

necessity.
▶ 그는 부득불 그런 조치를 취하지 않을 수 없었다 Necessity obliged him to that action.

부득이 不得已 unavoidably; inevitably; necessarily; unwillingly; from [through, out of] necessity
♦ 만부득이 from [out] of sheer necessity
▶ 나는 부득이 출발을 연기했다 I had no choice but to postpone my departure.
▶ 아버지가 파산하는 바람에 부득이 나는 대학을 중퇴했다 Father went bankrupt, so I was obliged [forced] to drop out of college.
—**부득이하다** unavoidable; inevitable; necessary; obligatory; compelling; pressing
♦ 부득이한 사정으로 owing to circumstances beyond *one's* control
▶ 사소한 혼란은 부득이하다 A little confusion can't be helped.
▶ 부득이한 경우를 제외하고는 이것을 처분해선 안된다 You must not dispose of this except when there is no other choice [it is absolutely unavoidable].
▶ 나는 부득이한 사정으로 결석했다 I was absent due to [because of] unavoidable circumstance.
▶ 그가 그렇게 한 데는 부득이한 사연이 있었을 것이다 There must have been some compelling reasons for his having done so.

부들 〔植〕 a cattail; a reed mace
부들부들 tremblingly; shiveringly; quiveringly
♦ 부들부들 떨다 tremble like an aspen leaf; shiver like a jelly / 공포[분노]로 부들부들 떨다 tremble with fear [anger] / 추위서 몸을 부들부들 떨다 shiver with [from] cold
▶ 그녀는 전신을 부들부들 떨고 있었다 She was trembling all over. ⇒ She was all of a tremble.
▶ 나는 입술이 부들부들 떨렸다 My lips quivered.
▶ 손이 부들부들 떨려 글씨를 쓸 수가 없다 I cannot write because my hands shake.
▶ 두려움으로 그녀의 무릎은 부들부들 떨리기 시작했다 Her knees began to knock together from fear.

부들부들하다 soft; tender; smooth
♦ 부들부들한 감촉 a smooth touch

부등 不等 inequality; disparity
■—식 〔數〕 an inequality —호 〔數〕 a sign of inequality
부등가리 an improvised fire shovel
부등변 不等邊 ♦ 부등변의 unequal-sided; inequilateral; scalene ■—삼각형 an inequilateral triangle; a scalene (triangle)
부등속운동 不等速運動 〔物〕 ununiform [accelerated] motion

부디 〈아무쪼록〉 kindly; I pray you; (if you) please; I beg; 〈꼭〉 by all means; without fail; in any case
▶ 부디 한 번 들러 주십시오 Please drop in by all means.
▶ 부디 몸조심하십시오 Take good care of yourself.
▶ 부디 집회에 참석해 주십시오 By all means, please arrange to come to the meeting. ⇒ Your presence at the meeting is respectfully requested.
▶ 부디 행복하게 사십시오 I wish you will live a happy life.
▶ 부디 그렇게 해주십시오 I hope you will do so.

부딪다 collide with ⇨ 부딪치다 1
부딪뜨리다 crash [smash, bump] 《into, against, together》; knock [dash] 《against》
♦ 몸을 문에 부딪뜨리다 dash [throw] *oneself* against the door / 자동차를 벽에 부딪뜨리다 crash a car into a wall
▶ 그 유조선은 짙은 안개 속에서 어선 한 척을 부딪뜨려 침몰시켰다 The oil tanker ran down a fishing boat in thick fog.

부딪치다 1〈충돌하다〉collide with; crash into [against, together]; bump against [into]; hit; run against [into]
▶ 서두르다가 다른 사람과 부딪쳤다 In my hurry I bumped into a man.
▶ 자동차 두 대가 서로 부딪쳤다 The two cars collided with [ran into] each other.
▶ 그 제안은 강경한 반대에 부딪쳤다 The proposal met with a strong objection.
▶ 배가 암초에 부딪쳤다 The boat struck [ran on] a sunken rock.
▶ 내 차가 전봇대에 부딪쳤다 I ran my car into a telegraph pole.
▶ 나는 넘어지면서 머리를 마루에 세게 부딪쳤다 I fell and hit my head hard on the floor.
▶ 파도가 바위에 부딪쳐 부쉬진다 The waves break on the rocks.
2〈당면하다〉face; face up to; be confronted by
♦ 난관에 부딪치다 face [run up against] a difficulty; be confronted by a difficulty
3〈해보다〉try; risk; chance
♦ 운에 맡기고 부딪쳐 보다 run [take] a risk [chance]; risk it; (口) chance it

부딪히다 be run [crashed, bumped] 《against》; be collided 《with》
♦ 자동차에 부딪히다 be hit [run over] by a car
▶ 나는 한 어린이한테 부딪혔다 I was run into by a child.
▶ 그 배는 빙산에 부딪혀 산산조각이 났다 The ship was dashed to pieces by an iceberg.

부뚜막 a cooking fireplace; a kitchen range; a cooking range
부뚜막의 소금도 집어넣어야 짜다 《속담》 Everything demands some work. ⇒ No mill, no meal.

부라리다 glare 《at》; look with glaring eyes; 〈화나서〉 look angrily [fiercely, sharply]
▶ 그가 늦게 들어오자 사장은 그에게 눈을 부라렸다 The boss glared at him when he came in late.
▶ 그는 눈을 부라리고 나를 쏘아보았다 He pressed hard on me with a fierce [glaring] look in his eyes.

부라질하다 rock a baby; rock
부라퀴 〈암팡스러운〉 a harsh tough person; a tenacious person; 〈이익에 악착같은〉 an eager

beaver

부락 部落 a village; a hamlet; a community; a settlement ■산간— a village among the mountains —민 people of the community, villagers —회의 a village meeting

부란 孵卵 〈부화〉 incubation —부란하다 hatch (out) 《an egg》; incubate ■—기 an (artificial) incubator —기간 incubation time

부란 腐爛 〈썩음〉 ulceration; 〈시체의〉 decomposition —부란하다 decompose; ulcerate; putrefy ■—시체 a decomposed [putrefied] body

부랑 浮浪 〈떠돎〉 vagrancy; vagabondage —부랑하다 wander about; roam about; tramp; vagabondize; lead a vagrant life
■—배 a vagrant tribe; the scum of the street —생활 vagrancy; hoboism —아 a juvenile vagrant; a waif; a young loafer —자 a wanderer; a vagabond; a loafer; an outcast; a vagrant; a tramp; a hobo

부랴부랴 〈급히〉 hastily; hurriedly; in a (great) hurry
♦부랴부랴 떠나다 make a hurried departure / 부랴부랴 일을 해치우다 hurry through *one's* work / 부랴부랴 집에 돌아오다 hurry [hasten] home
▶ 그는 부랴부랴 아래층으로 내려갔다 He hastened downstairs.
▶ 그 소식을 듣고 그는 부랴부랴 귀가했다 Receiving the news, he speeded homeward [hurried home].

부러 purposely ⇨ 일부러
♦부러 거짓말을 하다 lie deliberately

부러뜨리다 break (off); 〈딱 하고〉 snap; 〈뼈를〉 fracture
♦나뭇가지를 부러뜨리다 break a branch from a tree / 팔을 부러뜨리다 have *one's* 《right》 arm broken; break *one's* arm / 막대기를 무릎에 대고 부러뜨리다 break a stick over *one's* knee / 이를 하나 부러뜨리다 have a tooth knocked out / 막대기를 딱하고 부러뜨리다 break a stick with a snap

부러워하다 envy; be envious of; feel envy of
♦남이 부러워할 만한 학업 성적 an enviable school record / 남의 건강을 부러워하다 be [feel] envious of another's health; envy *sb* 《his》 health
▶ 그의 행운을 부러워하지 않는 사람이 없다 Everybody envies him his good fortune.

부러지다 break; be broken; give way; 〈딱 하고〉 snap; 〈뼈가〉 fracture
▶ 이 심은 잘 부러진다 This lead is easy to break. ⇌ This lead breaks easily.
▶ 이 막대기는 잘 부러지지 않는다 This stick won't break.
▶ 가지는 눈의 무게를 견디지 못하고 부러졌다 The branch gave way under the weight of the snow.

부럼 nuts eaten on the 15th day of the first lunar month

부럽다 enviable
♦부러운 듯이 enviously; with envy; with envious eyes / 부럽지 않다 be not to be envied / 부럽게 여기지 않다 feel no envy 《at》 / 부러운 눈으로 보다 regard *sb* [*sth*] with envy [envious eyes]; eye *sth* enviously
▶ 네가 정말 부러워 How I envy you!
▶ 저 부부를 봐. 부럽지 않니? Look at the couple. Doesn't it make you envious?

부레 an air [a swimming] bladder; a fish bladder; a float
■—풀 isinglass; fish glue

부려먹다 work [drive] *sb* hard; sweat 《*one's* employees》
♦남을 마음대로 부려먹다 have *sb* at *one's* beck / 소나 말처럼 부려먹다 work [drive] *sb* hard like a beast of burden; make *sb* drudge / 싼 임금으로 부려먹다 underpay and sweat *one's* workers

부력 浮力 〔物〕 buoyancy; flotage; 〈비행선 등의〉 lifting power; lift ♦부력의 중심 the center of buoyancy / 부력이 있는 buoyant
■—계 a buoyancy gauge

부령 部令 a ministerial ordinance
♦국방부령 제2호 Ordinance No. 2 of the Defense Ministry

부록 附錄 a supplement; 〈본문 끝의〉 an appendix 《*pl.*~es, -dices》; extra; an addendum 《*pl.* -da》
♦책[잡지]의 부록 a supplement [an appendix] to a book [magazine] / 부록을 붙이다 add an appendix to 《a book》
▶ 이달 호에는 여행 특집 부록이 있다 This month's issue has a travel supplement.
■별책— a separate-volume supplement

부루퉁하다 1 〈부어서〉 swollen; bloated; bulging ♦얼굴이 부루퉁하다 have a swollen [bloated] face
2 〈불만으로〉 sulky; sour; sullen; pouty
♦부루퉁한 얼굴 a sulky look [face] / 부루퉁하여 말을 안하다 maintain a sulky silence
▶ 그는 부루퉁해 있다 He is [looks] sullen [sulky]. ⇌ He is making a sour face.

부룩 intercrop(ping); catch cropping
♦부룩받다[치다] plant in the space between the rows of another crop; grow 《beans》 as a catch crop; intercrop

부룬디 〈나라이름〉 Burundi; 〈공식명〉 the Republic of Burundi

부류 部類 〈종류〉 a class; a heading; a group; 〈범주〉 a category; an order; a division
♦…의 부류에 넣다 classify [group] *sth* with [as]...; place *sth* in the category of... / …의 부류에 들다 come [fall] under the group [category] of... / 같은[다른] 부류에 속하다 belong to the same [different] class
▶ 그의 노래는 민요의 부류에 속한다 His song comes [falls] under the head [heading] of folk music.
▶ 그것들은 세 부류로 나누어진다 They can be classified into three kinds.

부르걷다 〈걷어올리다〉 roll up [back]; tuck [turn, pull] up
♦팔을 부르걷고 with bare arms; with *one's* sleeves tucked up / 셔츠 소매를 부르걷다 roll up *one's* shirt sleeves

부르다[1] 1 〈소리쳐〉 call; call out 《to》; hail
♦아무의 이름을 큰소리로 부르다 call out *sb*'s

부르다²

name / 택시를 부르다 hail a taxi
▶ 거리에서 모르는 사람이 내 이름을 불렀다 A stranger called me (by name) on the street.
▶ 누가 너를 부르고 있다 Somebody is calling you.
▶ 엄마가 지금 나를 부르셔. 그럼 안녕 Oh, there's my mom calling me. Bye!
▶ 네 이름을 부르면 「네」하고 대답해라 Say "Present," when your name is called.
▶ 학교에 가는 길에 나를 불러줘 Call for me on your way to school.
2 〈청하다・호출하다〉 send for; send after; summon; 〈전화로〉 call; 〈연예인 등을〉 engage; hire
◆ 전문가를 부르다 engage the service of an expert / 의사를 부르러 보내다[가다] send [go] for a doctor / 택시를 부르러 가다 go to find a taxi
▶ 구급차[경찰]를 불러라 Call an ambulance [the police]!
▶ 사장님 부르셨습니까? Did you want me, sir [boss]?
▶ 〖會話〗「교장선생님이 부르셔요」「곧 갑니다」 "The principal wants you." "I'll be right there."
▶ 스미스씨를 전화로 불러주십시오 Please get Mr. Smith on the phone.
3 〈초대하다〉 invite; ask
◆ 잔치에 손님을 부르다 invite guests to a feast / 저녁 식사에 친구를 몇명 부르다 invite [ask] some friends to dinner
▶ 우리 학교는 졸업식에 학부모를 부른다 My school ask the students' parents to attend the graduation ceremony.
4 〈일컫다〉 call; name; address; designate
▶ 이 꽃을 무슨 꽃이라고 부릅니까? What do you call this flower?
▶ 우리는 그를 영시의 아버지라고 부른다 We call him the father of English poetry.
▶ 학생들은 그를 「교수님」이라고 부른다 The students address him as "Professor".
▶ 우리는 친구들을 별명으로 부른다 We call our friends by their nicknames.
5 〈호가하다〉 quote; 〈경매에서〉 bid 《for an article》; make a bid 《for》
◆ 값을 부르다 make [quote] a price / 만원을 부르다 be quoted at 10,000 won / 부르는 값에 사다 buy 《an article》 at the first price asked
▶ 이 물건은 부르는 게 값이다 This article is beyond pricing. ⇌ This article is above [without] price.
▶ 그는 터무니없이 비싼 값을 불렀다 He asked [named] an unreasonable [extravagant, exorbitant] price.
6 〈외치다〉 cry; shout
◆ 만세를 부르다 cry "Hurrah"
7 〈노래를〉 sing; chant; recite; 〈콧노래를〉 hum
◆ 노래를 부르다 sing a song / 피아노에 맞춰 노래를 부르다 sing to the piano / 노래를 부르기 시작하다 break into song
8 〈일으키다〉 cause; bring about
▶ 음주 운전은 사고를 부른다 Drunk(en) driving leads to [causes] accidents.

▶ 높은 임금은 물가고를 부른다 Higher wages bring about [result in] higher prices.

부르다² **1** 〈배가〉 full
◆ 배가 부르도록 먹다 eat one's fill [bellyful]; 〈실컷〉 eat heartily [to one's heart's content]
▶ 난 배가 부르다 I'm full. ⇌ I've eaten my fill. ⇌ I have had enough.
▶ 아무리 먹어도 나는 배가 부르지 않다 However much I eat, I don't feel full.
▶ 배가 불러서 졸리다 I have eaten enough [my fill] and feel sleepy. ⇌ I feel heavy in the stomach and am sleepy.
▶ 배가 부를 때는 심한 운동을 하지 않는 것이 좋다 You had better not do heavy exercise on a full stomach.
2 〈임신하여〉 big with 《child》; pregnant ◆ 배가 잔뜩 부른 암소 a cow big in [with] calf
▶ 그녀는 배가 많이 불러 있다 She is big with child.
3 〈중배가〉 swollen; bulging; bulged
▶ 그 병은 배가 부르다 The bottle swells in the middle.

부르르 ▶ 그 물에 젖은 개는 몸을 부르르 떨었다 The wet dog shook itself.
▶ 그 남자는 무서워서[추워서, 흥분하여] 몸을 부르르 떨었다 He trembled with fear [cold, excitement].

부르릉 with a burr [vroom]
━부르릉하다, 부르릉거리다 burr; roar; splutter
▶ 엔진이 부르릉거리며 시동이 걸렸다 The engine started with a vroom.

부르주아 〈중산층 시민〉 a bourgeois; a man of means; 《총칭》 the bourgeoisie.

> 〖解說〗 ***bourgeois***는 ***proletarian*** (무산 계급)에 반대말로, 우리말의 「부자」란 뜻은 없으나 물질주의를 신봉하는 중산계급에 대한 뉘앙스가 있다.

▶ 그게 소위 부르주아 근성이라는 것이다 That is what we (would) call the bourgeois mentality.

부르쥐다 hold firmly; 〈주먹을〉 clench [tighten] 《one's fists》
◆ 주먹을 부르쥐고 with one's hand closed in a tense fist

부르짖다 **1** 〈주장하다〉 cry 《for》; clamor 《for》; advocate
◆ 개혁을 부르짖다 cry (loudly) for reform / 남북 통일을 부르짖다 cry out for the unification of Korea / 핵무장 금지를 부르짖다 appeal for a nuclear ban
2 〈소리치다〉 cry; shout; shriek; scream
◆ 목이 터져라 부르짖다 shout oneself hoarse / 아파서 부르짖다 cry [shout, scream] of pain
▶ 한 밤중에 여자의 부르짖는 소리가 들렸다 I heard a woman's scream at midnight.

부르짖음 a shout; a cry; an outcry; an exclamation; a clamor; 〈비명〉 a shriek; a scream; 〈노호〉 a roar; a howl
▶ 거리에서 살려달라는 부르짖음이 들렸다 A cry for help was heard outside in the street.

부르키나파소 〈나라 이름〉 Burkina Faso; 〈공

식명〉 Burkina Faso
부르트다 blister; rise in blisters; get [have] a blister (on); swell up
♦ 발이 부르트다 get [have] a blister [blisters] on *one's* foot
▶ 엄지손가락이 부르텄다 A blister formed on my thumb.
▶ 새 구두를 신었더니 발뒤꿈치가 부르텄다 My new shoes have made blisters on my heels.
부릅뜨다 〈눈을〉 make *one's* eyes glare; glare fiercely; goggle
♦ 눈을 부릅뜨고 보다 look with glaring eyes (at); stare with bulging eyes (at)
▶ 그는 두 눈을 부릅뜨고 나를 노려보았다 He stared at me with angry [glaring] eyes.
부리[1] 1 【새의】 a bill (좁고 납작한); a beak (맹금의 날카로운)
▶ 딱따구리는 긴 부리로 나무에 구멍을 뚫는다 A woodpecker makes holes in the wood of trees with its long beak.
2 〈끝〉 the tip; the end; the nozzle
♦ 총부리 the muzzle (of a gun) / 총부리로 협박하다 threaten *sb* at gunpoint
부리[2] 【民俗】 a tutelary spirit
부리나케 〈바삐〉 hurriedly; in a (great) hurry; in (great) haste; hastily; speedily
♦ 부리나케 역으로 가다 hurry [rush] to the station
▶ 그는 한번도 뒤돌아보지 않고 부리나케 그 자리에서 도망쳤다 He fled from there in all haste without looking back once.
▶ 그는 부리나케 돌아왔다 He came back hotfoot [with flying feet].
부리다[1] 1 〈일시키다〉 keep *sb* at work; work *sb*; 〈고용하다〉 employ; manage; handle
♦ 하인을 부리다 keep a servant; work a servant
▶ 그는 부하를 잘 부린다 He is good at handling [managing] his men.
2 〈동물을〉 manage; use
▶ 나는 말을 부릴 줄 안다 I know how to handle [control, manage] a horse.
3 〈꾀·재주를〉 play; practice; do
♦ 꼭두각시를 부리다 manipulate [work] a puppet (by strings) / 요술을 부리다 do conjuring tricks / 재주를 부리다 exercise *one's* talent; perform a trick
▶ 그는 갖은 수단을 부려 겨우 돈을 융통했다 Using every possible means, he managed to borrow money.
4 〈조종하다〉 manage; work; operate; handle; control
♦ 기계를 부리다 operate [handle, work] a machine / 배를 부리다 steer a ship / 차를 부리다 drive a car
5 〈행사하다〉 wield; exercise
♦ 고집을 부리다 persist; be wil(l)ful / 권세를 부리다 exercise *one's* power / 허세를 부리다 make a display [show]
▶ 그는 언제나 이것저것 말썽을 부린다 He is always in one kind of trouble or another.
▶ 저 아이는 늘 신경질을 부리고 있어 That child is always fretting.
부리다[2] 〈짐을〉 unload [discharge] (a ship)

▶ 배에서 화물을 부리다 unload cargo from a ship / 트럭에서 짐을 부리다 unload a truck; unload goods from a truck
부리망 —網 a muzzle (for a cow)
♦ 소에 부리망을 씌우다 muzzle a cow; put a muzzle on a cow
부리부리하다 〈눈이〉 big and bright; glaring; flaring ♦ 부리부리한 눈 big, glaring eyes
부마(도위) 駙馬(都尉) 〈왕의 사위〉 a royal son-in-law
부모 父母 〈양친〉 parents (▶ 단수형은 부모의 어느 한 사람만을 가리킴); *one's* father and mother
♦ 부모의 마음 parental affection [feeling, love]; a parent's heart / 부모의 사랑 parent's [parental] love for their children / 부모가 없는 parentless; orphaned / 부모의 말을 듣다 obey [be obedient to] *one's* parents / 부모의 말을 거스르다 disobey *one's* parents / 부모를 공경하다 respect *one's* parents / 부모를 봉양하다 support [look after, care for] *one's* parents / 부모를 여의다 have *one's* parents die; lose *one's* parents; be left an orphan
▶ 아이들에게 버릇을 가르치는 것은 부모의 책임이다 It's the parents' responsibility to discipline their children.
▶ 그는 부모의 사랑을 모르고 자랐다 He grew up without knowing parental love.
▶ 그녀는 부모를 모르는 아이를 길렀다 She raised a foundling.
▶ 아이들은 부모의 은혜를 모른다 Children do not know how indebted they are to their parents.
■ —형제 *one's* parents, brothers and sisters; *one's* nearest relatives
부목 副木 【外科】 a splint ♦ 부목을 대다 splint (an arm); apply a splint (to an arm, on)
▶ 내 부러진 팔에 부목을 댔다 My broken arm was put in splints.
부문 部門 〈조직의〉 a division; a department; 〈범주〉 a category; 〈방면〉 a branch; a line; a field; 〈종류〉 a genus; an order; a type
♦ 생활의 모든 부문 every phase of life / 홍보부문 the public relations department / A부문에 넣다 classify *sth* under A / …의 부문에 들다 fall [come] under the head of...; belong to [in] the classification [category] of...
▶ 업계의 여러 부문에서 최고의 사람들이 모였다 The top people assembled from various branches [fields] of industry.
▶ 그는 청소년 부문에서 1등상을 탔다 He won (the) first prize in the junior class [category].
▶ 이 학문 분야는 3개 부문으로 나누어진다 This field of study is divided into three areas.
부보 訃報 an announcement of *sb's* death ⇨ 부고(訃告)
부복하다 俯伏— fall prostrate (on the ground); prostrate *oneself* (before)
▶ 그 남자는 왕의 발 아래 부복하여 용서를 빌었다 He threw himself at the king's feet and begged his pardon.
▶ 그 노인은 제단 앞에 부복했다 The old man prostrated himself before the altar.

부본 副本 〈사본〉 a duplicate (copy); a counterpart; an extra [additional] copy

부부 夫婦 a (married) couple; husband and wife (▶보통 관사없이 씀); man and wife [woman]

♦박선생 부부 Mr. and Mrs. Park; Mr. Park and his wife / 어울리는[어울리지 않는] 부부 a well-matched [an ill-matched] pair [couple] / 젊은[노] 부부 a young [an old] couple / 부부의 애정 love between (a) husband and wife; married love / 부부의 conjugal; connubial; matrimonial / 부부동반으로 with *one's* wife [husband] / 부부가 되다 become man and wife; be [get] married

▶ 그들은 부부다 They are husband and wife.
▶ 그들은 좋은 부부가 될 거야 I hope they'll make a nice couple.
▶ 부부는 한 몸이다 Man and wife are one flesh.
▶ 그 부부는 금실이 좋다[좋지 않다] The couple are happy together [don't get on well (with each other)].

■ 맞벌이— a working couple: 우리는 맞벌이 부부입니다 My wife and I are both working [both have jobs]. 신혼— a newly married [a newlywed] couple; (口) newlyweds

부부생활 夫婦生活 married life; wedlock
♦부부생활을 하다 live together as husband and wife; live a married life

부부싸움 夫婦— a quarrel [squabble] between husband and wife; a marital quarrel; a domestic scene —**부부싸움하다** quarrel with *one's* husband [wife]
▶ 우리는 어젯밤 부부싸움을 했다 I had a fight [row] with my wife [husband] last night.

부부 싸움은 칼로 물 베기 (속담) Nothing is so unpalatable as a lover's quarrel.

부부유별 夫婦有別 A distinction should exist between husband and wife.

부분 部分 (a) part (▶단수의 경우 부정관사가 흔히 생략됨); a section; a portion; a piece
♦그 책의 최초의 부분 the first part [portion] of the book / 부분적(인) partial; sectional; divisional / 부분적으로 partially; partly; locally
▶ 이것이 이야기의 가장 중요한 부분이다 This is the part and parcel of the story.
▶ 그의 팔의 어느 부분이 부러졌니? What part of his arm is broken?
▶ 밑줄 친 부분을 우리말로 옮겨라 Put the underlined parts [portions] into Korean.

■ —부정 〔文法〕 partial negation —분수 〔數〕 partial fraction —색맹 partial color blindness —수열 subsequence —월식 partial lunar eclipse —일식 partial solar eclipse —적분 integration by parts —집합 〔數〕 a subset —품 ⇨ 부품(部品)

부빙 浮氷 drift [floating] ice; an ice floe; 〈합쳐진〉 pack ice

부사 副詞 〔文法〕 an adverb ♦양태 (樣態)의 부사 adverbs of manner / 부사적으로 adverbially —구 an adverbial phrase —절 an adverb(ial) clause

부사령관 副司令官 a deputy commander-in-chief

부사장 副社長 a vice president

부산물 副産物 a by-product; 〈사업·연구 결과의〉 (a) spin-off ♦그 책 번역의 부산물로 용어집이 생겨났다 A glossary was obtained as a by-product of the translation of the book.

부산하다 1 〈바쁘다〉 busy; restless; bustling
♦부산한 거리 a busy street / 부산한 사람 a restless [busy] person / 잔치 준비로 부산하다 bustle up preparing for the feast
▶ 그녀는 부엌에서 언제나 부산하게 일하고 있다 She is always bustling about in the kitchen.

2 〈시끌벅적하다〉 noisy; boisterous; clamorous ♦부산하게 굴다 be noisy [boisterous]; make a noise

부삽 —鍤 a fire shovel; (英) a firepan

부상 負傷 a wound; an injury; a hurt; 〈벤 상처〉 a cut; 〈타박상〉 a bruise
♦가벼운 부상 a slight injury / 심한 부상 a serious injury / 팔에 부상을 입다 be injured in the arm; have *one's* arm wounded
▶ 그는 머리의 부상이 치명상이 되었다 The injury to his head proved fatal.
▶ 그 아이는 교통 사고로 심하게 부상을 입었다 The boy was seriously injured in the traffic accident.

—**부상하다** be wounded; get [be] injured; sustain [suffer] an injury; get hurt
♦부상시키다 wound; injure; hurt
▶ 그녀는 화재로 부상당했다 She got [was] injured in a fire.
▶ 그는 계단에서 떨어져 팔[양다리]를 크게 부상당했다 He fell down the floors and (he) was badly hurt [injured] in the arm [both legs].

■ —자 a wounded [an injured] person; a casualty

부상하다 浮上— rise [come up] (to the surface); 〈잠수함이〉 surface ▶ 무명의 화가가 일약 부상했다 An unknown painter suddenly leaped into prominence.

부상 副賞 a supplementary prize

부서 部署 *one's* post [station]; *one's* place of duty; 〈함선 내의〉 *one's* quarters
♦부서를 지키다 keep [hold, remain at] *one's* post [station] / 부서를 이탈하다 desert [quit] *one's* post / 자기 부서에 가다 be at *one's* post; take up *one's* (appointed) station; 〈함선에서〉 go to *one's* quarters
▶ 전경 기동대원은 각자의 부서에 배치되었다 The riot policemen took up their stations.
▶ 전원 부서로 (口令) All hands to stations!

부서 副署 (a) countersignature —**부서하다** countersign; endorse; witness 《*sb's* signature》

부서뜨리다 break (down [into pieces]); crush; shatter; smash
♦산산이 부서뜨리다 smash *sth* into fine pieces [to atoms]; break [smash, shatter] *sth* into pieces / 차를 부서뜨리다 wreck a car

부서지다 break; be [get] broken; crack; be cracked; smash; be smashed; 〈파손되다〉 be destroyed; be demolished
♦부서진 broken; destroyed / 부서진 자동차 a

damaged [disabled] car / 부서지기 쉬운 easy to break; fragile; frail / 산산이 부서지다 be shattered; smash up; break into pieces / 부서져라 문을 두드리다 thunder at a door
▶ 마른 흙은 잘 부서진다 Dry soil is friable.
▶ 그 차는 사고로 크게 부서졌다 The car was badly damaged [wrecked] in the accident.
▶ 접시는 바닥에 떨어져 산산이 부서졌다 The plate broke [was broken] into pieces when it fell on the floor.

부석 浮石 pumice (stone); floatstone

부석부석하다 (slightly) swollen [bloated]
♦부석부석한 얼굴로 with a swollen [bloated] face

부선거 浮船渠 a floating dock ■—사용료 the charge for transportation via floating dock

부설 附設 attachment; annexation —**부설하다** attach [annex] 《sth to another》
♦대학에 연구소를 부설하다 establish [set up] a research institute attached to a university
■—기관 an auxiliary organ; an attached [affiliated] organization —도서관 a library attached [affiliated] ⟪to⟫; a library in affiliation

부설 敷設 laying; construction; building —**부설하다** lay (down); construct; build
♦기뢰를 부설하다 lay [place] a mine / 철도를 부설하다 lay [build, construct] a railroad / 해저 전선을 부설하다 lay a submarine cable
▶ 양국을 연결하는 해저전선을 부설했다 They laid a submarine cable between the two countries.
■—권 a right of construction: 철도부설권 a concession to lay a railway; a railway concession

부성 父性 paternity; fatherhood; the father ⟪in sb⟫ ♦부성의 paternal

부성분 副成分 an accessory ingredient

부성애 父性愛 paternal love
▶ 그는 차차 부성애에 눈을 떴다 The father gradually came into his heart.

부셸 ⟨곡물의 계량 단위⟩ a bushel (of wheat)

부속 附屬 ♦부속의 attached [annexed, affiliated, belonging] to; associated with; adjunctive; accessory; subordinate; dependent
▶ 이 병원은 서울대학교 부속이다 This hospital is attached [affiliated] to Seoul National University.
—**부속하다** be attached [annexed; affiliated] to; belong to
■—건(축)물 an annex; an accessory [attached] building —기관 a subsidiary agency; an auxiliary organ; an affiliated organization —병원 a hospital in affiliation —시설 attached [affiliated] facilities; accessory structures —초등학교 an attached elementary [primary] school; an elementary [a primary] school affiliated to ⟪a university⟫

부속물 附屬物 a thing attached ⟪to⟫; belongings; attachments; adjuncts; accessories (▶ 이 상은 주로 복수로 씀)
♦집과 일체의 부속물 a house and all its appurtenances / 교실의 책상 및 기타 부속물 desks and other appurtenances of a classroom

부속품 附屬品 accessories; fittings
♦자동차 부속품 the accessories of a car; car accessories / 진공 청소기의 부속품 attachments for a vacuum cleaner

부수 附隨 —**부수하다** be annexed ⟪to⟫; ⟨수반하다⟩ accompany; go with; follow; attend [be attendant] ⟪on, upon⟫; be incident(al) ⟪to⟫
♦전쟁에 부수되는 여러 죄악 various crimes incidental [attendant] to a war/ 그 장사에 부수되는 위험 risks contingent to the trade / 부수되는 accompanying; accessory; annexed; incidental; attendant
▶ 위험이나 어려움은 우리 일상생활에 부수되는 것이다 Dangers and difficulties are incidental to our daily life.
■—사건 a dependent event —사실 a collateral fact —음악 incidental music —정황 attendant circumstances

부수 負數 ⟪數⟫ a negative (number) ⇨ 음수 (陰數)

부수 部數 ⟨권수⟩ the number of copies; ⟨발행 부수⟩ circulation ♦발행 부수가 많다[적다] have a large [small] circulation
▶ 그 월간지는 발행 부수가 1만 5천이다 The monthly (magazine) has a circulation of fifteen thousand.
▶ 초판은 발행 부수가 1만부였다 The first edition consisted of 10,000 copies.

부수다 break (down); ⟨완전히⟩ destroy; ⟨건물 등을⟩ demolish; smash
♦집을 부수다 tear down [demolish] a house/ 산산이 부수다 shatter ⟪a window⟫; break sth to pieces; smash sth to bits / 금고를 부수다 break [crack] a safe / 창문을 부수고 집에 들어가다 break the window into [to enter] the house
▶ 실수로 마룻 바닥에 시계를 떨어뜨려 부쉈다 I dropped my watch on the floor by accident and broke [damaged] it.
▶ 그 남자는 종이 상자를 발로 밟아 부쉈다 He crushed the cardboard box under his feet.

부수상 副首相 a deputy prime minister; a vice-premier

부수수하다 untidy; disorderly; disheveled

부수입 副收入 a side income; ⟨가외 수입⟩ an additional income; an extra profit [gain]
▶ 그는 부수입이 꽤 있다 He enjoys various benefits.

부숭부숭하다 dry ⇨ 보송보송하다

부스대다 stir restlessly ⇨ 바스대다

부스러기 a broken piece; a fragment; scraps; crumbs; chips; ends
♦종이 부스러기 wastepaper / 빵 부스러기 breadcrumbs / 나무 부스러기 chips of wood
▶ 식사때 빵 부스러기를 흘뜨리지 마라 Don't scatter bits of bread about when you eat.
▶ 많은 토기 부스러기가 건설현장에서 나왔다 A lot of fragments [shards] of earthenware were dug up in the construction site.

부스러뜨리다 break ⇨ 부서뜨리다

부스러지다 crumble; break; be - broken [smashed, crushed] into pieces [bits]; be destroyed; be wrecked; come [go] to smash; go

부스럭 with a rustle ⇨ 바스락
부스럼 a boil; a tumor; a swelling; a swell; an abscess
♦부스럼이 나다 have a boil 《on》
▶긁어 부스럼 《속담》 It is as if asking for trouble. ⇌ Let sleeping dogs lie. ⇌ Wake not a sleeping lion.
▶나는 목에 부스럼이 났다 I have got a swelling on my neck.
▶그녀의 얼굴에 부스럼이 났다 A boil developed on her face.

부스스 1 〈조용히〉 slowly; quietly; gently
♦잠자리에서 부스스 일어나다 sit up leisurely in *one's* bed
▶그는 부스스 일어났다 He stood up without haste.
2 〈머리털 등이〉 disheveledly ─부스스하다 disheveled; unkempt; untidy
♦부스스한 머리 disheveled [tousled] hair

부슬부슬[1] 〈눈비가〉 sprinklingly; drizzly; gently ♦부슬부슬 내리는 비 a drizzling rain; a drizzle

부슬부슬[2] crumblingly ⇨ 바슬바슬

부슬비 a sprinkling rain; a sprinkle; a drizzle
▶하루 종일[오후 내내] 부슬비가 내렸다 It drizzled all day [all afternoon].

부시 (a) steel for striking sparks from flint; a spark-producing alloy (steel)
♦부시를 치다 strike fire [sparks] with [out of] flint and steel; make sparks with steel on flint

부시다[1] 〈씻다〉 rinse (out); wash (lightly); clean out ♦깨끗한 물로 그릇을 부시다 rinse dishes in clear water / 병을 부시다 rinse out a bottle

부시다[2] 〈눈이〉 dazzling; glaring; blinding 《flash》; radiant
♦눈이 부신 바다[햇빛] the glaring [dazzling] sea [sunshine] / 눈이 부시게 아름다운 여자 a woman of dazzling beauty / 눈이 부시게 빛나다 dazzle; glare; 〈전등 등이〉 flare
▶빛에 눈이 부셔서 뜨고 있을 수가 없다 The light is so bright that I cannot keep my eyes open.
▶바깥의 빛에 눈이 부셔서 나는 일순간 앞이 보이지 않았다 I was blinded for a moment by the dazzling light from outside.

부시장 副市長 a deputy mayor

부식 扶植 implantation ─부식하다 plant; implant; establish ♦세력을 부식하다 establish [extend] *one's* influence

부식 腐蝕 corrosion; 〈산에 의한〉 erosion; 〈썩음〉 decay; 〈녹에 의한〉 rust
♦부식성의 corrosive
─부식하다 corrode; erode; rot; 〈녹슬다〉 rust; 〈녹슬어 들어가다〉 bite in; 〈산 등이〉 eat (away) 《into》 ♦부식되지 않는 incorrodible; rustless; anticorrosive
▶이 금속은 부식되기 쉽다 This metal is apt to corrode quickly.
▶소금기 때문에 철주가 부식했다 Salt corroded [ate into] the iron pillar.
■─성[력] corrosiveness; causticity ─작용 corrosive [erosive] action; corrosion; erosion ─제 a corrosive (agent); a corroder; 〔醫〕 a caustic

부식(물) 副食(物) a side dish; a subsidiary food; dishes other than staple food

부식토 腐植土 humus (soil); mold ▶알뿌리는 부식토가 많은 땅에 심으시오 Plant the bulbs in soil rich in humus.

부신 副腎 〔解〕 a renal gland [capsule]; an adrenal (body, gland); a paranephros 《*pl.* -roi》

부신피질 副腎皮質 〔解〕 the adrenal cortex
■─호르몬 an adrenocortical hormone

부실 不實 1 〈허약〉 weakness ─부실하다 weak; sickly; feeble; not strong
▶그는 몸이 부실하다 He is in poor health. ⇌ He has a weak [delicate] constitution.
2 〈불성실〉 faithlessness ─부실하다 faithless; unfaithful; insincere; 〈거짓의〉 false
▶그는 일하는 것이 부실하다 He is not a conscientious worker.
3 〈불신〉 ─부실하다 unreliable; untrustworthy; undependable; shaky
♦부실한 언행 the insincerity in *one's* speech and actions
▶그의 말은 부실해서 믿을 수가 없다 I cannot depend on what he says because he is unreliable.
4 〈부족〉 (a) lack; deficiency; insufficient ─부실하다 wanting; lacking; deficient; short
♦식량이 부실하다 be scant [short] of food
■─경영 insolvent operation ─기업 an insolvent enterprise; an improperly-run enterprise ─기재 〈장부의〉 false [fake] entries

부심 副審 《競》 a sub-umpire; sub-referee; an assistant umpire [judge]

부심하다 腐心─ take (great) pains; be at (great) pains 《to do》; be bent [intent] on
♦해결책을 찾으려고 부심하다 rack [cudgel] *one's* brains trying to find a solution
▶그는 아들의 교육에 부심하고 있다 He is taking great pains [a great deal of trouble] over his son's education.

부싯깃 tinder

부싯돌 (a) flint; (a) firestone

부아 1 〈허파〉 the lungs
2 〈분함〉 anger; resentment; indignation; rage; wrath ♦부앗김에 in a fit of temper [anger] / 부아통 터지다 burn [flash, be furious] with anger / 부아통 터지게 하다 get on *sb's* nerves; give *sb* the nerves
▶그것은 생각만 해도 부아가 난다 The mere thought of that irritates me [makes me angry].
▶그의 말에 부아가 치민다 I'm outraged by his remarks. ⇌ His remarks are provoking.

부양 扶養 support; maintenance ─부양하다 keep up; support; maintain
▶그녀는 16명의 고아를 부양하고 있다 She is fostering sixteen orphans.
▶내 적은 수입으로 가족을 부양하는 것은 쉽지 않다 It's not easy to maintain my family on

부엌과 조리기구

1. 조리 기구
▶ 개수대[싱크대] a sink / 수조 2개[3개]식 싱크대 a double [triple] sink / 싱크대용 매트 a sink mat / 음식 찌꺼기 처리기 (food waste) disposer / 수도꼭지 a faucet; (英) a tap / (수도꼭지의) 포말기 an aerator / 물기 빼는 기구 a dish drainer / 식기 세척기 a dishwasher / 환기장치 a ventilator; a range hood / 가스레인지 a gas stove; a gas range; 〈전기용〉 an electric range (▶점화구 a burner, 버너가 있는 부분 전체 a cooktop, 오븐 an oven, 고기 굽는 기구 a broiler, 생선 등을 굽는 철판[번철] a griddle)
▶ 냉장고 a refrigerator; (口) a fridge; 〈좌우로 열리는 형〉 a side-by-side refrigerator (▶냉동실 a freezer compartment; a frozen food section, 제빙실 an icemaker, 계란 보관 선반 an egg rack, 야채 보관실 a vegetable [fresh food] crisper, 고기·생선 케이스 a meat pan)
▶ 믹서 a blender (▶a mixer는 전동 믹서를 가리킴) / 과즙 짜는 기구 a juicer / 토스터 [빵 굽는 기구] a toaster / 오븐 토스터 an oven toaster / 커피 끓이개 a coffee maker (▶드립식 a drip coffee maker, 여과기가 달린 a percolator) / 자동 팝콘 제조기 an electric corn popper
▶ 냄비류 pots and pans (▶운두가 높은 냄비를 a pot라 하고 얕은 것을 a pan이라고 함) / 수프 냄비 a stockpot; a stewpot / 소스 냄비 a saucepan / 프라이팬 a frying pan; 〈유리나 도자기로 된〉 a skillet / 찜용 냄비 a casserole / 압력솥 a pressure cooker / 밥솥 a rice cooker / 시루[찜통] a steamer
▶ 조리기구류 kitchen helpers / 교반기 a whisk; an egg beater / 국자 a ladle / 강판 a grater / 깡통 따개 a can opener / 계량컵 a measuring cup / 계량 스푼 a measuring spoon / 껍질 벗기는 기구 a peeler (▶감자용은 a potato parer) / 여과기[체] a strainer / 차 여과기 a tea strainer / 감자 으깨는 기구 a potato masher / 밥주걱 a rice scoop / 제분기 a grinder / 마개[코르크] 뽑이 a corkscrew / 체 a sifter / 튀김 건져놓는 소쿠리 a deep frying basket / 주걱 a spatula; 〈긁어내는 주걱〉 a scraper / 도마 a cutting board / 밀방망이 a rolling pin / 레몬 짜는 기구 a lemon sqeezer / (포장용) 랩 clear-plastic wrap / 은박지 aluminum foil
▶ 부엌칼 kitchen knives; cook's knives / 고기 써는 칼 a carving knife; a carver / 생선 칼 a filleting knife; a fish knife / 뼈 발라내는 칼 a boning knife / 빵 써는 칼 a bread knife / 껍질 벗기는 칼 a paring knife

2. 조리 용어

(1) 굽다

굽다	직접 불에	석쇠를 써서	grill; (美) broil
		산적이나 통구이로 하다	barbecue
		철판에 기름을 두르고	fry
	오븐에	야채·빵·케이크를	bake
		고기를	roast
		얇게 썬 빵을	toast

(2) 끓이다·삶다·데치다

끓이다	cook	삶다·끓이다·데치다	boil
		일단 기름에 볶아	braise
		여러 가지 재료를 장시간에 걸쳐	stew
		부글부글 끓이다	simmer

(3) 튀기다·볶다

튀기다	fry	일반적으로	deep-fat fry; deep-fry
		「튀김옷을 안입히고 튀기다」 특히	French-fry
볶다		일반적으로	shallow-fry; pan-fry; (프) sauté
		휘저어 뒤섞어가며	stir-fry
		황갈색이 될 때까지	brown

my small income.
■—공제 an allowance [a tax exemption] for dependents —비 a sustenance allowance; alimony —수당 a dependency allowance —의무 the duty of supporting 《one's family》 —자 a supporter; a breadwinner
부양 浮揚 floating; flo(a)tage; flo(a)tation —**부양하다** float (in the water [air]); be buoyant ◆침몰선을 부양시키다 refloat a sunken vessel [ship]
■—력 buoyancy
부양가족 扶養家族 a (family) dependent
▶ 나는 부양 가족이 넷이다 I have four people to support.
▶ 부양 가족이 몇이나 됩니까? How many dependents do you have?
■—수당 a family allowance
부언 附言 an additional remark —**부언하다** add 《that...》; say in addition; make an additional remark

▶ 그는 이 건에 대해 몇마디 부언했다 He added a few remarks upon this matter.
부업 副業 a side job; a by-job; a sideline; a side business; a subsidiary occupation ◆벌이가 좋은 부업 a remunerative sideline / 부업으로 닭을 기르다 raise chickens as a sideline
▶ 그는 부업으로 야간 경비를 했다 He moonlighted as a night watchman.
▶ 아내는 부업으로 영어를 가르친다 My wife is teaching English on the side.
부엉이 tu-whit tu-whoo
◆부엉부엉 울다 hoot; whoop; ululate
▶ 부엉이가 부엉부엉 울었다 An owl hooted.
부엉이 〈鳥〉 a horned [an eared] owl
▶ 부엉이 우는소리에 잠이 깼다 The hoot of a horned owl awakened me.
부엉이 소리도 제가 듣기에는 좋다고 〈俗談〉 be blind to *one's* own defects
부엌 a kitchen ◆부엌 겸 식당 a kitchen with a dining area; a kitchen-dining room

■ㅡ데기 a kitchenmaid ㅡ바닥 the kitchen floor ㅡ설비〈싱크대 등의〉《英》a kitchen unit ㅡ용품〔살림〕 kitchen utensils [appliances]; kitchenware;《총칭》kitchen equipment ㅡ일 kitchen work; cooking : 부엌일을 하다 do kitchen work

부에노스아이레스 〈아르헨티나의 수도〉Buenos Aires

부여 附與 grant; bestowal; allowance ㅡ부여하다 give; grant; bestow 《with》; confer 《a degree》on; vest
◆전권을 부여하다 vest sb with full powers
▶공로자에게는 연금이 부여된다 A distinguished person is granted a pension.

부여 賦與 endowment ㅡ부여하다 endow [bless] sb with
◆하늘이 부여한 재능 innate [natural, inborn] talent
▶그녀는 훌륭한 음악적 재능을 부여받았다 She was endowed [blessed] with splendid musical talent.

부여잡다 take [catch] (fast [firm]) hold of; grasp
▶그는 내 손을 부여잡고 만나서 반갑다고 말했다 He clasped my hands and said he was glad to see me.

부역 附逆 ◆부역 행위 a sympathetic act to the rebel's cause ㅡ부역하다 take sides with the rebels

부역 賦役 compulsory [statute] labor; compulsory service; (a) corvée ◆부역을 시키다 put sb to statute labor; exact statute labor [corvée] from 《people》

부연 附椽 〔建〕 flying rafter; extended eaves

부연 敷衍 expatiation; dilatation ㅡ부연하다 expatiate [dilate, dwell, elaborate] on
▶나는 그 주제를 부연하여 설명했다 I dilated upon [dwelt on] the theme.

부엽토 腐葉土 leaf mold

부영사 副領事 a vice-consul ◆한국 주재 독일 부영사 a German vice-consul in Korea

부옇다 opaque ⇨ 보얗다

부예지다 1〈사물이〉get misty; become hazy
▶하늘이 부예졌다 The sky turned hazy.
▶하늘이 부예지며 날이 밝았다 The sky was starting to get [grow] light.
2〈눈이〉become dim; be blurred [dimmed]
▶눈물로 부예진 눈 eyes dim with tears

부용 芙蓉 〔植〕a cotton rose; a Confederate rose;〈연꽃〉a lotus

부운 浮雲 〈뜬 구름〉floating [drifting] clouds

부원 部員 〈전원〉the staff;〈개인〉a person on the staff; a member 《of a department [club]》; a staff member
◆영업부원 (a member of) the staff of the sales department / 테니스부원 a member of a tennis club /편집부원 (a person on) the editorial staff

부위 部位 a region; a part
◆폐〔심장〕 부위 the part [region] of the lung [heart]

부유 浮遊 floating;〈고체 입자의〉〔物〕suspension ㅡ부유하다 waft; float; drift ◆공중에 부유하는 먼지 dust floating in the air

■ㅡ기뢰 a floating [surface] mine ㅡ물 floating [suspended] matter [particles];〈난파선의〉flotsam ㅡ생물 ⇨ 플랑크톤 ㅡ선광〔鑛〕flo(a)tation ㅡ식물 floating plants

부유 富裕 wealth; richness; affluence ㅡ부유하다 rich; wealthy; affluent
◆부유한 사람 a wealthy person; a well-to-do person / 부유한 집안에 태어나다 be born rich; be born into a rich family
▶그들이 사는 모습을 보니 꽤 부유한 것 같다 From the way they live, they seem to be quite well-off [well-to-do].
■ㅡ층 the rich; the high income bracket

부뉴스름하다 somewhat milky [hazy, misty]; milk-white

부음 訃音 an obituary ⇨ 부고(訃告)

부응하다 副應ㅡ meet; satisfy; comply with; fulfill; answer ◆기대에 부응하다 meet [satisfy, carry out] sb's expectations / 목적에 부응하다 answer the purpose / 수요〔시대 요구〕에 부응하다 meet [satisfy] a demand [the demands of the age]
▶신임에 부응하도록 노력하겠습니다 I will try to be worthy of your trust.

부의 附議 submitting for discussion ㅡ부의하다 bring 《a matter》before 《a conference》; place 《a bill》on the agenda; submit [present] 《to》
◆의안을 위원회에 부의하다 refer [submit] a bill to a committee

부의 賻儀 (offering) condolence money; a monetary token of condolence ㅡ부의하다 offer condolence money [goods]

부의장 副議長 a vice-president; a vice-chairman; a deputy chairman

부이 〈부표〉a buoy;〈구명대〉a life buoy [preserver]

부인 夫人 〈아내〉a wife;〈기혼자〉a married lady;〈경칭〉Mrs.; Madam; Lady
◆한 선생 부인 Mrs. Han
▶존슨 씨는 부인 동반이었다 Mr. Johnson was accompanied by his wife.
▶부인께 안부 전해 주십시오 Give my best regards to your wife.
▶그는 부인을 동반하고 파티에 참석했다 He attended the party with his wife.

부인 否認 denial; repudiation ◆사실의 부인 denial of the truth ㅡ부인하다 deny; refuse to admit; say nay [no] 《to》; disaffirm ◆부인할 수 없는 사실 an indisputable [undeniable] fact
▶그는 기소 사실을 모두 부인했다 He denied all the indicted facts.
▶그녀는 그에게 뭔가를 주었다는 사실을 부인했다 She denied that she had passed anything to him.
▶그 사실을 부인할 순 없다 The fact cannot be denied. ⇌ There is no denying the fact.

부인 婦人 a (married) woman;〈신분·교양이 있는〉a lady; (총칭) womankind ◆중년 부인 a middle-aged [an elderly] woman
▶그의 모친은 인품이 남다른 부인이다 His mother is a woman of remarkable personality.

부인 ■—병 a women's disease; a female disorder
부인과 婦人科 gynecology
■—병원 a gynecological clinic —의사 a gynecologist
부인용 婦人用 ◆ 부인용 시계 a lady's watch / 부인용 장신구 women's accessories
■—모자 a lady's hat; (총칭) millinery
부인회 婦人會 a women's [ladies'] society [association]; a women's club [group, organization]
부임 赴任 leaving for *one's* new post ◆ 부임길에 오르다 leave [start] for *one's* new post —**부임하다** leave [start, go] for *one's* new post; proceed to *one's* new post
▶ 다음주에 새 선생님이 부임하신다 A new teacher is to arrive here next week.
▶ 새로 부임하신 김선생님을 소개합니다 I'll introduce you to Mr. Kim, a newly appointed teacher.
▶ 주한 미대사는 어제 부임했다 The American Ambassador to Korea arrived at his post yesterday.
▶ 내가 맨처음 부임한 곳은 목포 지점이었다 My first assignment was the branch office in Mokp'o.
■—지 the place of *one's* assignment; *one's* new post
부자 父子 father and son
부자 富者 a rich [wealthy] person; a man of wealth; (총칭) the rich
◆ 큰 부자 a very rich [wealthy] man; a millionaire; a billionaire; a multimillionaire / 부자가 되다 become rich; make a fortune
▶ 그는 사업에 성공해서 부자가 되었다 His successful business made him rich.
▶ 부자가 하늘나라에 들기보다는 낙타가 바늘구멍을 지나가기가 더 쉽다 [聖] It is easier for a camel to go through the eye of a needle, than for a rich man to enter into the kingdom of God.
▶ 부자라고 반드시 행복한 것은 아니다 The rich are not always happy.
부자연 不自然 unnaturalness; artificiality —**부자연하다** ⇨ 부자연스럽다
부자연스럽다 不自然— unnatural; against nature; 〈인위적〉 artificial; 〈무리한〉 forced; strained; affected ◆ 부자연스러운 웃음[문제] a forced smile [style]/ 부자연스러운 태도 affected manners ◆ 부부가 따로 사는 것은 부자연스럽다 It is unnatural for a married couple to live separately.
부자유 不自由 lack of freedom; 〈불편〉 inconvenience; 〈구속〉 restraint; restriction
◆ 빈곤의 부자유에서 벗어나다 break loose from the restraints of poverty
—**부자유하다** not free; restricted; inconvenient; 〈몸이〉 disabled; handicapped
◆ 팔[다리]이 부자유하다 have lost the use of *one's* arms [legs]
▶ 그는 몸이 부자유하다 He is physically handicapped. ≒ He is disabled.
부자유스럽다 不自由— inconvenient
▶ 시골에서 사는 것은 부자유스럽다 It is inconvenient to live in the country.

부자재 副資材 subsidiary [ancillary] materials
부작용 副作用 a side [secondary] effect 《on》
◆ 부작용이 없다 have no side effects; be free from [produce no] harmful side effects / 부작용을 일으키다 produce unfavorable side effects; cause harmful side effects
▶ 항생물질의 부작용으로 식욕을 잃었다 I reacted badly to an antibiotic and lost my appetite.
부작위 不作爲 〔法〕 forbearance; nonperformance; omission ■—범 〔法〕 a crime of omission
부작위추출법 不作爲抽出法 random sampling ⇨ 임의(∼추출법)
부잣집 富者— a rich [wealthy] family
◆ 부잣집에 태어나다 be born rich; be born into a rich [wealthy] family; be born with a silver spoon in *one's* mouth
▶ 그녀는 부잣집으로 시집갔다 She married a wealthy man.
부장 部長 the general manager; the head [chief, director] of a department [division]; a department manager [head, chief]
◆ 부장급의 사람들 those at the managerial level
■ 경리[인사]— the chief of the accountants' [the personnel (affairs)] department ■—검사 a superintendent public prosecutor —대리 the acting manager [director]
부장품 副葬品 grave goods; burial accessories; the possessions of a dead person which were [are to be] buried with him
부재 不在 absence ◆ 부재 중에 in [during] *one's* absence; while *one* is [has been] away / 부재 중이다 be absent; be out [away]; be not at home
▶ 그는 출장으로 2주간 부재 중입니다 He is away on a business trip for two weeks.
▶ 부재 중에 무슨 일이 있으면 그녀에게 전화하시오 If anything happens in [during] my absence, please call [phone] her.
■—자 an absentee —지주 an absentee [a nonresident, a noncultivating] landowner [landlord, landlady] —투표자 an absentee voter
부재자투표 不在者投票 absentee voting; voting by an absentee; voting by mail ■—용지 an absentee ballot
부재증명 不在證明 an alibi
◆ 부재증명이 있다 have an alibi / 부재증명을 하다 establish [prove, set up] an alibi
부적 符籍 a charm; an amulet; a talisman
◆ 액막이 부적 an amulet to avert evils; a charm against bad luck
▶ 이 부적을 몸에 지니고 있으면 안전할 것이다 You'll be safe if you wear this talisman.
▶ 그는 항상 질병을 막아주는 부적을 지니고 다닌다 He always wears a charm to ward off disease.
부적격 不適格 disqualification; unfitness
◆ 부적격의 disqualified 《for》; unqualified 《for》; unfit 《for》
■—자 a person disqualified for [unaccepta-

부적당 不適當 unsuitableness; unfitness ―**부적당하다** unsuitable; unfit (for); inappropriate (to); inadequate; out of place; inapplicable ◆야외 운동을 하기에 부적당한 날씨 unfavorable weather for outdoor sports ▶이 책은 학교에서 사용할 책으로서는 부적당하다 This book is unfit for school use. ▶그런 복장은 이런 자리에는 부적당하다 That dress is out of place on this occasion. ▶그녀는 그 일을 하기에 부적당합니다 She is not the right person to undertake the job. ⇌ She is not fit for the job.

부적응 不適應 maladjustment (to one's social environment) ―**-아**〔心〕 a maladjusted child

부적임 不適任 unfitness; unsuitableness; inadequacy ◆부적임의 unfit (for); unsuitable (to); inadequate; unqualified ▶그녀는 비서로서는 부적임이다 She is unfit [unsuitable] for a secretary. ▶그런 영어 실력이라면 그는 영어 교사로서 부적임이다 With that sort of English, he is not qualified to be an English teacher. ―**-자** an unqualified [incompetent] person : 그는 그 자리에는 부적임자다 He is not the right man for the place.

부적절 不適切 unsuitableness; inappropriateness; inadequacy; infelicity ◆표현의 부적절 the infelicity of expressions ―**부적절하다** unsuitable; unfit; inappropriate; impertinent ◆부적절한 예〔행동〕 an inappropriate example [behavior] ▶그의 연설은 그 자리에서는 부적절한 것이었다 His speech wasn't suitable [good, fit, appropriate, proper] for the occasion.

부적합 不適合 incongruity ―**부적합하다** incongruent; 〈서술적〉 do not match; be out of proportion

부전 不全 imperfection ◆발육 부전의 개 an undergrown dog / 부전의 〈불완전한〉 incomplete; imperfect; 〈부분적인〉 partial

부전 不戰 renunciation of war ―**조약** an antiwar pact; a peace [no-war] treaty : 부전 조약을 맺다 conclude an antiwar pact (with)

부전 附箋 〈쪽지〉 a tag, a slip; a label ◆부전을 달다 tag; label; put a tag on ▶그 편지는「거주지 부재」라는 부전이 붙어 되돌아왔다 The letter was returned with a tag which said, "Not at this address."

부전승 不戰勝 an unearned win; a win by default ◆부전승이 되다 〈추첨으로〉 draw a bye ―**부전승하다** win by default; win without playing

부전자전 父傳子傳 transmission from father to son ◆부전자전의 handed down from father to son ▶부전자전이다 Like father, like son. ―**부전자전하다** transmit from father to son

부절 符節 a tally

부절제 不節制 intemperance ⇨ 무절제

부점 附點 〔樂〕 a dot =점(點) 7

부점음표 附點音標 〔樂〕 a dotted note =점음표

부접못하다 1〈가까이 하지 못하다〉 cannot approach [come near to]; be kept from approaching; be denied access (to) ◆부접 못하게 하다 keep *oneself* inaccessible [unapproachable]; keep *sb* away from *one* [*sth*] 2〈배기지 못하다〉 cannot [be unable to] stay long; cannot bear [stand, endure] ▶그의 집에는 가정부가 부접못한다 Kitchenmaids do not stay long in his house.

부젓가락 ―箸 (a pair of) fire tongs; metal chopsticks for handling charcoals ◆벌겋게 단 부젓가락 (a pair of) red-hot tongs

부정 不正 〈불공정〉 injustice; unfairness; iniquity; 〈비행〉 wrong; unrighteousness; 〈부정직〉 dishonesty; 〈위법〉 illegality; unlawfulness; 〈부당〉 impropriety ◆부정을 바로잡다 redress [remedy] injustice / 대학에 부정 입학하다 enter a university fraudulently [by improper means]; bribe *one's* way into a university ▶조사 결과 부정이 드러났다 The investigation has brought the corruption [graft] to light. ▶이 부정은 비난 받아 마땅하다 This unjust act should naturally be blamed. ▶나는 아무 부정도 저지르지 않았다 I have done nothing wrong. ⇌ Everything I did was fair and square. ―**부정하다** wrong; unjust; unfair; foul; unrighteous; iniquitous; 〈위법인〉 illegitimate; unlawful; illegal; 〈부당한〉 improper; 〈허위의〉 false; fraudulent ◆부정한 거래 unfair dealings [trade]; (口) a queer transaction / 부정한 돈 dirty [tainted] money; ill-gotten money; illicit funds / 부정한 방법으로 이기다 win unfairly / 부정한 짓을 하다 do a dishonest thing [act]; commit irregularities; do wrong; 〈경기에서〉 play foul; 〈시험에서〉 cheat [crib] (in an examination) ▶그의 방법은 부정하고 불공평하다 His method is unjust and unfair. ▶부정하여서 번 돈은 오래가지 못한다 (속담) Ill got, ill spent. ■**―공무원** a corrupt(ed) official ―**대부**〔대출〕 an unlawful accommodation of money; an illegal loan [advance] ―**부패** illegality and corruption; 〈공무원 등의〉 abuse of power and graft ―**사건** a scandal; a bribery [(美) graft] case; a case of (official) corruption ―**선거** a rigged election ―**이득**〔소득〕 illicit [ill-gotten] gains; illegal profits; 〈공무원 등의〉 graft ―**저울** a false balance; a tampered weighing machine ―**품** a fraudulent article; an adulterated article

부정 不定 uncertainty; indefiniteness; incertitude; indeterminateness ◆주소 부정인 사람 a homeless man; a person with no fixed address; the homeless / 부정의 uncertain; indefinite; unsettled; unfixed; undetermined; undecided; indeterminate; 〈불규칙의〉 irregular; 〔文法〕 indefinite; 〈변하기 쉬운〉 inconstant; variable; changeful; changeable ■**―관사**〔대명사〕〔文法〕 an indefinite article [pronoun] ―**기간** an uncertain duration; an

부정의 표현

1. not, no, nobody, nothing 등
▶나는 클래식 음악에는 흥미가 없다 I'm not interested in classical music.
▶내일 비는 오지 않을것으로 생각한다 I don't think it will rain tomorrow. (▶영어에서는 이런 경우 「…할 것이라고는 생각지 않는다」라는 표현을 쓰는 것이 보통)
▶아무도 그가 학교를 그만둔 것을 모른다 No one [Nobody] knows he has quit school.
▶이들 잡지는 모두가 재미없다 None of these magazines is [are] interesting. (▶one of + 복수 명사의 경우 구어체에서는 동사를 복수로 씀)
▶그는 그 사건과는 아무 관계도 없다 He has nothing to do with the incident.

2. 강한 부정
▶그녀는 결코 학교에 지각하지 않는다 She never comes late for school.
▶이 부근에는 비디오 가게 같은 건 하나도 없다 There's not a single rental video shop in this neighborhood.
▶이건 농담이 아니다 This is no joke.
▶물상 시험에 만점을 맞으리라고는 꿈에도 생각지 못했다 I never dreamed [Never did I dream] that I'd get a hundred [〔英〕full marks] in the physics test. (▶강조하는 뜻으로 never나 little 등 부정어를 첫머리에 내세우는 형식은 문어체의 표현이다. 이 때에는 어순이 바뀜)

3. 약한 부정
▶나는 선생님 말씀을 거의 알아듣지 못했다 I could hardly hear what the teacher was saying.
▶아버지는 차를 가지고 계시긴 하지만 좀처럼 타지 않으신다 My father hardly ever [seldom] drives, though he has a car.
▶우리 반에서 해외에 가본 적이 있는 사람은 거의 없다 Very few students in our class have been abroad.
▶나는 상대성 이론에 관해서는 거의 모른다 I know very little about the theory of relativity.

4. 부분 부정・이중 부정
부분 부정: no와 all [both, everything, always, necessarily 등]이 함께 쓰여서 「전부 [쌍방, 모두, 항상, 반드시] …하지는 않다」의 뜻으로 쓰인다.
▶우리들 모두가 네 생각에 찬성하는 것은 아니다 Not all of us are for your plan.
▶돈으로 모든 것을 살 수 있는 것은 아니다 You cannot buy everything with money.
▶암에 걸리는 것이 반드시 죽음을 의미하는 것은 아니다 Getting cancer does not necessarily mean death.
이중 부정: 한 문장에 2개의 부정이 겹쳤을 때가 이중 부정으로 「부정」을 「부정」함으로써 「긍정」을 나타내는 완곡한 표현이다.
▶예외 없는 규칙이란 없다 There is no rule without an exception.
▶아버지가 밤늦게 귀가하시는 것은 드문 일이 아니다 It is not uncommon for my father to come home late at night.
▶화학약품을 혼합할 때는 아무리 주의를 해도 지나치지 않는다 You cannot be too careful in mixing chemicals.

5. 부정어를 사용한 관용 표현
▶그들은 정치에 전혀 관심이 없다 They are not in the least interested in politics.
▶외국어를 마스터하는 것은 결코 쉬운 일이 아니다 A foreign language is by no means easy to master.
▶이 학교가 교복을 폐지할 날도 그리 멀지 않을 것이다 It will not be long before this school does away with uniforms.
▶그녀는 첫시간이 끝날 때까지 나타나지 않았다 She didn't turn up until the first period was over.
▶소음은 더 이상 참을 수 없다 I can't stand the noise any longer.

6. 부정어를 쓰지 않는 부정 표현
▶이 책은 너무 어려워서 읽을 수가 없다 This book is too difficult for me (to read).
▶이 미분 문제는 내 실력으로는 풀 수 없다 This differential calculus problem is beyond my ability.
▶그는 남을 속이는 그런 사람이 아니다 He is the last person to deceive others.
▶그 섬에는 환경 오염 같은 건 없다 That island is free from environmental pollution.
▶내일 무슨 일이 일어날 것인지를 누가 알랴? (아무도 모른다) Who knows what will happen tomorrow? (▶이 문장은 반어적인 표현으로서 No one knows...를 의문문으로 강하게 표현한 것)

---

indefinite period of time —방정식 〔數〕 an indefinite [indeterminate] equation —법 〔文法〕 the infinitive mood —수 an indefinite number —수입 an irregular [incidental] income —적분 〔數〕 an indefinite integral —형 an indeterminate form
부정 不貞 unchastity; unfaithfulness; 〈간통〉 adultery ◆부정을 저지르다 deceive [be unfaithful to] one's husband
—**부정하다** unchaste; unfaithful; faithless; false (to one's husband)
◆부정한 여자 an unfaithful wife

부정 不淨 1 〈불결〉 uncleanliness; dirtiness; filthiness; 〈불순〉 impurity; defilement
—**부정하다** unclean; dirty; filthy; 〈종교적으로〉 unholy; impure
2 〈기휘(忌諱)의〉 happening of an evil event (during one's unlucky day)
◆부정 타다 suffer an evil [a bad luck]; have [meet with] a misfortune

부정 否定 denial; negation ◆부정적 판단 a negative judgment / 부정의 negative
—**부정하다** deny; negate; say no (to); answer in the negative; disown ◆부정할 수 없는

undeniable; incontestable; indisputable
▶ 당국은 단연코 사실을 부정하고 있다 The authorities are positive in denying the fact.
▶ 그는 내 말을 부정했다 He denied what I said.
▶ 그 사실은 부정할 수 없다 The fact is undeniable. ⇌ It is an undeniable fact.
▶ 그가 정직하다는 것은 부정할 수가 없다 There is no denying his honesty. ⇌ It is impossible to deny his honesty.
■이중— 〔文法〕 a double negative [negation] ■—명제(命題) a negative —문 〔文法〕 a negative sentence —어 〔文法〕 a negative

부정기 不定期 ♦부정기의 irregular; unfixed; indeterminate ▶ 이 잡지는 부정기적으로 간행된다 This magazine is published irregularly.
—선 a tramp (steamer); a nonregular liner —열차 an unscheduled [extra] train —예금 an irregular deposit —항공편 a nonscheduled flight; (美口) a nonsked —항로 a tramp route —형(刑) penal servitude [imprisonment] for an indeterminate term

부정맥 不整脈 〔醫〕 arrhythmia; an irregular pulse

부정사 不定詞 〔文法〕 an infinitive ■분리— a split infinitive

부정수단 不正手段 a dishonest [an improper, an unlawful, an unfair, an illegal, an illicit] means; a fraud ♦ 부정 수단으로 by a dishonest means; dishonestly; wrongfully
▶ 그는 부정 수단을 써서 그 땅을 차지했다 He acquired the land by dishonest [unlawful] means.

부정유출 不正流出 illegal disposition; sale through illegal channels ♦ 관용품을 부정유출하다 sell [dispose] government supplies by illegal channels

부정직 不正直 dishonesty —부정직하다 dishonest; untruthful
♦ 부정직한 신고 an untruthful [a dishonest] statement / 부정직한 행위[사람] a dishonest act [person]

부정축재 不正蓄財 accumulation of wealth by illicit means —부정축재하다 accumulate [amass] wealth by unlawful [illicit] means; make a fortune by illegal means
■—자 an illicit fortune maker; an illegal profiteer

부정행위 不正行爲 an unfair [a corrupt] practice; an illegal [a dishonest, an improper, a wrongful] act; irregularities; 〈시험 중의〉 cheating; 〈경기 중의〉 foul play
♦ 경기에서 부정 행위를 하다 play foul; hit below the belt / 시험에서 부정 행위를 하다 cheat [play] foul in an examination
▶ 부정 행위는 엄벌에 처한다 Severe punishment is imposed for unlawful behavior.

부정형시 不定型詩 free verse

부정확 不正確 inaccuracy; incorrectness; inexactness —부정확하다 inaccurate; incorrect; inexact
♦ 부정확한 번역 a loose translation / 부정확한 추론 inexact reasoning
▶ 그녀의 계산은 부정확하다 Her calculations are inaccurate.
▶ 비용의 계산이 부정확해서 여행 도중에 돈이 바닥났다 We miscalculated our expenses and ran out of money halfway through the trip.

부제 副題 a subtitle; a subhead(ing)

부조 父祖 father and grandfather; 〈선조〉 ancestors; forefathers
♦ 부조 전래의 patrimonial; hereditary / 부조 전래의 토지를 상속받다 inherit the land passed down from *one's* ancestors; inherit the ancestral lands

부조 不調 〈건강 등의〉 a bad condition; a disorder; a slump; 〈날씨 등의〉 unseasonableness; unfavorableness; irregularity

부조 扶助 〈도와줌〉 aid; help; assistance; 〈부양〉 support; 〈구조〉 relief; 〈잔칫집에의〉 a wedding (congratulatory) gift; contribution to the expenses of a wedding; 〈상가(喪家)에의〉 condolence money [goods]; a donation to help out a bereaved family
—부조하다 offer goods [money] to help *sb* (to) perform a marriage [funeral] service; aid; help; render *sb* assistance; support; sustain; give relief to
■상호— mutual aid [assistance, help] ■—금 〈축의금〉 congratulatory money; 〈조위금〉 a solatium [condolence money]; an allowance in aid

부조 浮彫 〈돋을새김〉 〔美術〕 relief; relievo; embossed carving
♦ 얕은[높은] 부조상 a sculpture in low [high] relief; a sculpture in bas-relief [alto-relievo]
—부조하다 emboss; carve [sculpture] in relief
▶ 그는 아버지의 옆모습을 부조했다 He carved a relief of his father's profile. ⇌ He carved his father's profile in relief.
■—세공 raised [relief] work

부조리 不條理 absurdity; irrationality; unreasonableness; (프) 〔哲〕 absurde
♦ 부조리를 제거하다 eliminate unreasonableness [(social) absurdities]; put 《things》 straight
■—극 the theater of the absurd

부조화 不調和 lack of harmony; inharmony; disharmony; 〈불화〉 discord, discordance; incongruity; 〈불균형〉 disparity; 〈의견차〉 disagreement; dissonance; dissonancy
♦ 색의 부조화 inharmoniousness of colors
—부조화하다 be inharmonious [disharmonious, discordant, incongruous, ill-sorted, (樂)] inharmonic]; do not harmonize [match] 《with》; be out of harmony 《with》

부족 不足 1 〈모자람〉 shortage; deficiency; 〈특히 금전이〉 deficit; 〈불충분〉 insufficiency; 〈결핍·고갈〉 want; lack; scantiness; scarcity; dearth; famine 《of oil [water]》
♦ 아이디어의 부족 a paucity of ideas / 운동의 부족 lack of exercise / 중량의 부족 short weight; shortage of weight / 자금 부족으로 for [from, through] want [lack] of funds / 부족을 메우다 make good [make up (for)] a deficiency; supply [meet, cover, fill up, remedy] the shortage [deficiency] / 〈구멍을〉 메우다〉 supply [stop] a gap

▶ 문제는 식량부족이다 The trouble is a shortage [want, deficiency] of food.
▶ 아무리 비용을 줄여도 부족이 생긴다 However much I cut down the cost, I can't make both ends meet.
▶ 주택 부족은 오늘날 가장 심각한 문제의 하나다 The housing shortage is one of the most serious problems today.
▶ 그는 수면 부족으로 중대한 실수를 저질렀다 He made a serious mistake for lack of sleep.
—부족하다 insufficient; short; deficient; wanting; lacking; scanty; 〈사물이 주어〉 be in short supply; fail; 〈사람이 주어〉 be [come, drop, fall, run] short 《of》; want; lack; be in want [need] 《of》
♦ 경험[시간, 지혜]이 부족하다 be short on experience [time, brains] / 만원이 부족하다 be ten thousand won short; be short by ten thousand won / 일손이 부족하다 be short-handed; be short of hands / 생각이 부족하다 lack thought; be thoughtless [imprudent] / 식량[돈]이 부족하다 be scant [short] of food [money] / 부족해지다 run short of / 연료가 부족해지다 run low of fuel
▶ 우리에게 부족한 점이 있다면 일깨워 주세요 Please remind us if there is anything amiss on our part.
▶ 그는 경험이 부족해서 고용되지 못했다 He was not hired because he lacked experience.
2 〈궁핍〉 indigence; need; want
▶ 아무 부족 없이 살다 live in comfort [plenty]; be well off; want [lack] for nothing
—부족하다 indigent; needy; wanting
♦ 살림이 부족하다 be in needy [narrow, straitened] circumstances; be badly [poorly] off
▶ 그 가족은 무엇 하나 부족한 것 없이 살고 있다 The family live in affluence [are in affluent circumstances, want for nothing].
3 〈불만족〉 dissatisfaction 《about, with》; discontent 《about, at, with》
—부족하다 dissatisfied; discontented; 〈불완전하다〉 imperfect; 〈부적당하다〉 inadequate
♦ 아무것도 부족한 점이 없다 leave nothing to be desired
▶ 그래도 부족한가? Are you still dissatisfied?
▶ 그 사람이라면 내 상대로서 부족하지 않다 He is a good match for me. ⇒ I find a worthy opponent in him. ⇒ He is worthy of my steel [metal].
■ 공급— failure in supply; shortage in [of] supply; short supply 석유— a shortage [a dearth] of oil; an oil shortage [dearth] 세입— a deficit in revenue 식량— a scarcity [shortage] of food; insufficiency of provisions 인식— ignorance ■ —액 shortage; a deficiency; a deficit; the balance due —품 a missing item

부족 部族 a tribe ♦ 부족의 tribal
■ 인디언— Indian tribes

부종 浮腫 dropsy ⇨ 부증(浮症)

부주의 不注意 〈조심성 없음〉 carelessness; heedlessness; incautiousness; want of care [attention]; inattention; 〈태만〉 negligence
♦ 운전 부주의로 인한 사고 an accident due to [caused by] careless driving / 부주의로 인한 실수 a careless mistake / 부주의로 생기다 arise from carelessness
▶ 그는 부주의로 비밀을 누설하고 말았다 He revealed a secret out of carelessness [because he was careless]. ⇌ He carelessly revealed a secret [(口) spilled the beans].
—부주의하다 be careless [negligent]; lack care [attention]
♦ 부주의한 careless 《mistake》; heedless; inattentive; unmindful 《of one's duty》; inadvertent; incautious; negligent / 부주의하게 carelessly; heedlessly; imprudently; inadvertently; with inattention
▶ 그 사람을 믿다니 나도 부주의했다 I was imprudent [careless] enough to trust him.
▶ 부주의하게도 그곳을 지나쳐 버렸다 I carelessly passed it by. ⇌ I was so careless that I passed it by.

부주제 副主題 〖樂〗the subsidiary

부즉불리 不卽不離 두 사람 사이에는 여전히 부즉 불리다 The two keep in touch with each other from a careful distance.
▶ 나는 그 사람과는 부즉 불리로 해나가고 있다 My relationship is neither too close nor too remote with him.

부증 浮症 〖韓醫〗dropsy; dropsical swelling; anasarca; edema 《pl. -mata》
▶ 나는 다리에 심한 부증이 있다 I have a nasty swelling on my leg.

부지 不知 ignorance —부지하다 do not know; be ignorant of; (口) be innocent of
■ —거처 missing; whereabouts unknown —기수 (其數) being numberless [innumerable, countless]

부지 敷地 a (building) site; (a plot of) ground; a lot
♦ 부지를 물색하다 look for a site (for) / 부지를 확보하다 secure the location (for)
▶ 우리집 부지는 150제곱미터입니다 My plot of land is 150 square meters.
■ 건축— a building site [lot] 학교— a site for a school 후보— the site proposed (for) —면적 plottage —선정 the selection of site

부지깽이 a poker

부지런 ♦ 부지런을 떨다 display diligence; work hard [diligently, like a bee]
—부지런하다 diligent; industrious; assiduous; hardworking
♦ 부지런한 사람 a diligent [an industrious] person; a hard worker; a laborious man; (口) a wheelhorse

부지런히 〈열심히〉 diligently; assiduously; with assiduity; hard; industriously; 〈자주〉 frequently
♦ 부지런히 다니다 frequent; visit 《a place》 frequently / 부지런히 일하다 work diligently (for money [one's living]); work like a bee [beaver] / 부지런히 공부하다 work hard; apply oneself closely to one's studies

부지배인 副支配人 an assistant manager

부지불식간 不知不識間 ♦ 부지불식간에 uncon-

sciously; unknowingly; unwittingly; without knowing it; before *one* knows (it)
▶ 그는 부지불식간에 악의 길로 들어섰다 He slip [drifted] into evil way [course].

부지중 不知中 ♦부지중에 〈자기도 모르게〉 unconsciously; unwittingly; unknowingly; unawares; in spite of *oneself*; before *one* knows (it); 〈본능적으로〉 instinctively; 〈뜻하지 않게〉 unintentionally
▶ 우리는 부지중에 잘못을 저지르는 수가 있다 We sometimes make unconscious mistakes. ⇌ We sometimes make mistakes unconsciously [unawares, without knowing it].

부지지 with a sizzle ⇨ 바지지
부지하다 扶支— 〈배겨내다〉 hold (out, on, up); last; endure; bear; maintain; keep up
♦ 목숨을 부지하다 sustain [maintain] *one's* life
▶ 그녀석 목숨을 잘도 부지하고 있군 It is a wonder that he is still alive.

부지하세월 不知何歲月 ♦부지하세월이다 do not know when a thing will be completed
▶ 다리가 언제 완공될지 부지하세월이다 Nobody knows [can tell] when the bridge will be completed.

부직 副職 an additional post; a side job
부직포 不織布 (a) nonwoven fabric
부 진 不振 dullness; depression; inactivity; stagnation; a slump
♦ 경제 부진 an economic depression [slump]/ 사업 부진 business depression; stagnation of trade; a slump [slack] in business/ 석유 업계의 부진 the oil industry slump
▶ 그는 회사의 영업 부진에 대한 책임을 졌다 He assumed responsibility for the firm's poor business.
—**부진하다** be dull [inactive, depressed, stagnant, flat, slack]; be at a low ebb; be in (a) bad shape; be in a bad condition; be in a poor way; be in a slump; be in out of form
▶ 식욕이 통 부진하다 I've completely lost my appetite.
▶ 거래가 부진하다 Business is dull [slack, slow]. ⇌ Trade is depressed [at a low ebb].
▶ 어제의 주식 시장은 다소 부진했다 The stock market was rather dull [not very active] yesterday.
▶ 우리 야구팀은 올 봄에 부진했다 Our baseball team made [gave] a poor showing this spring.

부진 不盡 inexhaustibleness —**부진하다** inexhaustible; unfailing; endless; never-ending
부진하다 不進— make no [little, poor] progress
▶ 지지부진하다 make very slow progress; progress at a snail's pace
▶ 그의 영어 실력 향상은 아주 지지부진하다 He is making hardly any [almost no, (very) little] progress in English. ⇌ His progress in English is discouragingly slow.

부질없다 〈쓸데없다〉 useless; vain; unprofitable; idle; futile
♦ 부질없는 반대 a trivial objection / 부질없는 시도 a futile attempt / 부질없는 생각 an idle [a useless] thought / 부질없는 이야기 a useless [silly] talk; idle gossip
▶ 어쩌면 이토록 부질없는 짓을 했는지 What a foolish [silly] thing you have done!

부질없이 uselessly; fruitlessly; to no purpose; in vain; idly
♦ 부질없이 시간을 보내다 idle *one's* time away / 부질없이 돈을 쓰다 trifle away *one's* money
▶ 그녀는 자신의 일생을 부질없이 보내버렸다 She has trifled her life away.

부집게 fire [charcoal] nippers
부차 副次 ♦부차적(인) secondary
▶ 그것은 부차적인 중요성밖에 없다 It is only of secondary [minor] importance.

부 착 附着 sticking; adhesion; bond(ing); agglutination; conglutination
—**부착하다** adhere [stick, attach, cling] to; agglutinate; conglutinate
—**—근(根)** an adhesive root; a holdfast —**력** adhesive [cohesive] power; adhesion —**어** ⇨ 교착(~어)

부창부수 夫唱婦隨 conjugal harmony
▶ 그 내외는 부창부수다 They lead and follow as husband and wife.

부채 a fan; 〈쥘부채〉 a folding fan
♦ 부채를 부치다 fan *oneself*; use a fan
▶ 그녀는 부채를 부쳐 타다 남은 불을 되살렸다 She fanned the embers to a flame.
—**꼭지** the pivot of a folding fan **부챗살** the ribs of a fan

부채 負債 a debt; liabilities; dues
♦ 장부상의 부채 a book debt / 부채가 생기다 [를 지다] get [run, fall] into [in] debt; put *oneself* in debt / 부채가 없다 be clear [free] from debts; be out of debts / 부채를 갚다 repay [clear off, pay off] a debt; liquidate *one's* liabilities / 부채를 면제하다 cancel [release *sb* from, forgive *sb*] a debt
▶ 당신은 부채가 얼마나 됩니까? How much do you owe? ⇌ What is the extent of your liabilities?
▶ 그는 부채가 산더미 같다 He is heavily in debt. ⇌ He has a large [heavy] debt.
▶ 그의 부친은 부채를 남기고 돌아가셨다 His father left debts behind.
—**고정[유동]—** fixed [floating] liabilities —**상각준비금** a sinking fund —**상환** debt redemption —**액** the amount of debts; indebtedness; liabilities

부채꼴 1 〈부채처럼 생긴〉 fan shape
♦ 부채꼴로 펼치다 fan out
▶ 그들은 부채꼴로 흩어져서 행방불명된 아이를 찾았다 They fanned out to look for the lost child.
2 〈數〉 a sector

부채질하다 1 〈부채로〉 fan; use a fan; fan *oneself*
▶ 강풍이 부채질하여 불길이 숲을 삼켜버렸다 Fanned by strong winds, flames licked up the woods.
2 〈선동〉 instigate; incite; stimulate; stir [whip] up; agitate; 〈감정 등을〉 kindle; inflame

부처 〈불타〉 Buddha; Gautama [Gotama] Buddha; 〈성자〉 a Buddhist saint; (비유) a saint of a man; a saintly person; 〈불상〉 an image of Buddha; the Buddha
♦ 지옥에서 부처님을 만난 것 같았다 I felt as if I had found a true friend.
▶ 부처님한테 설법한다 (속담) Teach your grandmother to suck eggs. ⇌ Don't try to teach your grandmother to suck eggs.

부처 夫妻 husband [man] and wife
♦ 김씨 부처 Mr. and Mrs. Kim; the Kims
♦ 김교수 부처는 하와이 대학에 초빙되었다 Prof. Kim and his wife were invited to the University of Hawaii.

부척 副尺 a vernier ⇨ 아들자
부촌 富村 a rich [wealthy] village
부총리 副總理 a deputy prime minister
부총재 副總裁 a vice president
부추 〈植〉 a leek; a scallion
부추기다 stir up; instigate; incite; egg on; abet; 〈개 등을〉 set (a dog) on [at] sb; set on (a dog)
♦ 국민을 부추겨서 반란을 일으키게 하다 instigate the people to revolt / 부추겨서 싸움을 시키다 egg [spur] sb on to fight with (another) / 부추겨서 파업을 시키다 instigate a strike
▶ 석유 값의 등귀가 인플레이션을 부추겼다 The rise in oil prices fanned inflation.

부축하다 support (by the armpits); assist; help
♦ 부축하여 일으키다 help sb to (his) feet; help sb up / 부축하여 집에 데리고 가다 support sb home / 부축하여 내려주다 help sb down
▶ 그는 부인을 차에서 부축해 내렸다 He helped a lady off a car [assisted a lady out from a car].
▶ 그는 노파를 부축하여 계단을 올라가게 했다 He helped the old woman up the stairs.

부츠 (a pair of) boots
♦ 부츠를 신은 booted / 부츠를 신다[벗다] pull on [off] one's boots

부치다¹ 〈힘이 모자라다〉 be beyond [out of] one's capacity [power, strength]; be too much for one
♦ 힘에 부치는 일 work beyond one's power [capacity, ability, skill]
▶ 그 일은 내게 힘에 부치다 The work is beyond [above] me. ⇌ The work is beyond my ability. ⇌ I am not equal to the task.
▶ 이 아이는 내게 힘에 부치다 This child is beyond my control.
▶ 계획한 사업이 내 힘에 부친다는 것을 알았다 I find myself unequal to what I have undertaken.

부치다² ♦ 부채를 부치다 use a fan; fan oneself / 불을 부치다 fan a fire / 모닥불을 부치어 타오르게 하다 fan an open-air fire into a blaze

부치다³ 〈경작하다〉 cultivate; farm; grow
♦ 논[밭]을 부치다 cultivate a paddy [a field] / 옥수수를 부치다 grow corn
▶ 개척자들은 밭을 부치는 데 고생했다 The pioneers had a hard time cultivating the field.

부치다⁴ 〈번철에〉 griddle; fry; cook [bake] in a greased pan
♦ 달걀을 부치다 fry eggs / 빈대떡을 부치다 cook mung-bean pancakes

부치다⁵ 〈보내다〉 send; forward; transmit; ship (배・차로); 〈송금하다〉 remit; 〈우송하다〉 send [forward] sth by post [mail]; (美) mail; (英) post
♦ 기차로 상품을 부치다 ship goods by rail / 편지를 항공편으로 부치다 send a letter by airmail; airmail a letter / 우편환으로 돈을 부치다 remit money by money order
▶ 상품을 즉시 차편[철도편, 우편, 항공편]으로 부치겠습니다 We will dispatch the goods by car [rail, mail, airmail] immediately.
▶ 곧 돈을 부치다오 Remit [Send] the money at once.

부치다⁶ 1 〈회부하다〉 refer; put; commit; hand over [submit] to
♦ 의안을 위원회의 심의에 부치다 commit a bill / 인쇄에 부치다 commit (it) to print / 사건을 재판에 부치다 commit a case for trial / 동의를 표결에 부치다 put the motion to a vote
▶ 이 문제는 다음 회의에 부쳐질 것이다 This question will be submitted to the next conference.
2 〈대우를 하기로 하다〉 overlook; pass over
▶ 미성년자여서 그의 범행은 불문에 부쳐졌다 As he was a minor [was under age], his offense was overlooked.
3 〈심정을 의탁하다〉 say metaphorically; liken [compare] (one thing) to (another)

부칙 附則 additional [supplementary] rules; an additional clause [provision]; 〈의안・계약서의〉 a rider

부친 父親 one's father

부침 浮沈 sinking and floating; rise and fall; ebb and flow; 〈성쇠〉 ups and downs (of life); vicissitudes (of life [fortune]); prosperity and adversity
♦ 부침이 많은 운명 a checkered lot [fortune] / 일생의 부침에 관계되다 affect the whole course of one's life
▶ 인생에는 부침이 있게 마련이다 Life has its ups and downs [rise and fall].
▶ 나는 인생의 온갖 부침을 경험했다 I have gone through all sorts of ups and downs in life.

부침개 panfried food; a fry

부칭 浮秤 〈액체 비중계〉 an areometer; a hydrostatic balance; a hydrometer

부탁 付託 1 〈당부〉 a request; a favor; a solicitation
♦ 친구의 모처럼의 부탁 (at) the pressing request of a friend / 아무의 부탁으로 at the request of sb; at sb's request; by a request from sb / 부탁이 있다 have a favor to ask of sb; wish to make sb a request; wish to ask a favor of sb / 부탁을 거절하다 turn down [refuse, decline] another's request; refuse sb a favor / 부탁을 들어주다 comply with [accede to] another's request; grant a re-

quest; do *sb* a favor; oblige *sb*
▶ 제발 부탁이니 혼자 있게 해 다오 Please leave [let] me alone, for a favor.
▶ 모처럼의 부탁이니 자네를 채용하겠네 I will take you to oblige you.
▶ 부탁이 하나 있네 I have a favor to ask of you. ⇌ Would you do me a favor?
▶ 그의 부탁으로 모두 자리를 떴다 At his request, they left.
━**부탁하다** ask 《*sb* to do》; ask for *sth*; ask a favor 《of *sb*》; request; beg; implore; beseech; solicit

|解說| **ask**는 남에게 어떤 일을 부탁하는 데 쓰는 가장 일반적인 말이다. ***request***는 공손한 또는 격식을 차린 부탁인데 ask보다도 강한 부탁이다. ***beg***는 허리를 굽히고 비는 부탁이고 ***implore***는 감정을 담은 필사적이며 간절한 부탁을 나타낸다.

♦ 아무에게 부탁하여 through (the courtesy of) *sb* / 도움[설명, 연설]을 부탁하다 ask [call upon] *sb* for help [an explanation, a speech] / 무릎 꿇고 부탁하다 beg on *one's* knees
▶ 자네가 부탁한다면 뭐든지 해야지 I can refuse you nothing.
2 〈위탁〉 charge; trust; entrusting; committal; commitment
━**부탁하다** entrust *sth* to *sb* [*sb* with *sth*]; trust 《*sb* with *sth*》; charge 《*sb* to do》; place *sth* under *sb's* charge [care]; commit 《a child》 to *sb's* care
♦ 일을 부탁하다 give *sb* a commission; charge [entrust] *sb* with a commission; commission *sb* to 《do》 / 남에게 모든 일을 부탁하다 leave everything in another's hands / 부탁받은 일을 하다 do what *one* has been asked to do; execute *sb's* commission
▶ 수화물은 포터에게 부탁하게 Give the baggage to the porter.
▶ 이 수화물 좀 부탁합니다 Please look after the baggage.
▶ 시내에 가신다면 두어 가지 부탁할 게 있는데요. I have a few things for you if you are going to town.

부탄¹ 〈나라 이름〉 Bhutan; 〈공식명〉 the Kingdom of Bhutan
■ ━사람 a Bhutanese
부탄² 〔化〕 butane
부터 **1** 〔시간〕 from; at; on; in; 〈이래〉 since; 〈이후〉 after; 〈어느 날 이후〉 on and after
▶ 학교는 8시부터[3월 1일부터, 3월부터] 시작한다 School begins at eight [on March 1, in March].
▶ 회의는 2시부터 3시까지다 The meeting is from two to [through] three.
▶ 이 조례는 12월 1일부터 시행된다 This regulation will come into effect on and after December 1.
▶ 나는 어릴때부터 그녀를 알고 있다 I have known her since childhood. ⇌ I have known her from a child.
▶ 3시부터는 모임에 참석할 수 있다 I can go to the meeting after three o'clock.
▶ 나는 아침부터 쭉 텔레비전을 보고 있다 I have been watching television since morning.
2 〈장소〉 from; out of; off; through; by; with; at; in
♦ 서울부터 부산까지 from Seoul to Pusan / 10미터 떨어진 곳에서부터 from a distance of ten meters / 5쪽부터 시작하다 begin at page 5 / 제1장부터 시작하다 begin with the first chapter
▶ 그 사무실은 역으로부터 차로[걸어서] 20분 이내의 곳에 있다 The office is (situated) within a twenty-minute ride [walk] of the station.
▶ 〔會話〕「어디서부터 기차를 탔어요?」「대구부터요」 "Where did you get on the train?" "At Taegu."
3 〈사람에게서〉 from; of; through; with
♦ 멀리 있는 친구로부터 온 편지 a letter from a friend far away / 아무로부터 돈을 받다 receive money from *sb*
▶ 누구로부터 들었는가? Who told you?
4 〈순서〉 first; beginning with; starting from
♦ 영어 공부부터 하다 study English first; study beginning with English
▶ 무엇부터 시작할까요? What shall I begin with?
▶ 이것부터 시작합시다 Let's do this first.
▶ 방 청소부터 합시다 Let's start by getting the room cleaned up.
▶ 너부터 시작해라 You begin first. ⇌ 〔口〕 You kick off!
▶ 해는 동쪽으로부터 떠서 서쪽으로 진다 The sun rises in the east and sets in the west.
5 〈범위〉 처음부터 끝까지 from beginning to end / 15세부터 25세까지의 젊은 여성 young women from 15 to 25
▶ 초임은 50만원부터 60만원까지다 The commencing salary ranges from 500,000 to 600,000 won.

부통령 副統領 a vice president 《略 V.P.》
부티크 a boutique
부패 腐敗 1 〈썩음〉 decomposition; spoiling; rottenness; putrefaction; decay; 〔醫〕 sepsis
♦ 부패를 막다 preserve [keep] *sth* from decay [rotting]
━**부패하다** rot; become rotten; putrefy; be decomposed; decay; go bad; be spoilt
♦ 잘 부패하는 음식 perishables / 부패 한 rotten; spoiled; putrid; decomposed; decayed; addled 《egg》; tainted 《meat》; turned 《milk》 / 부패하기 쉬운 corruptible; perishable; putrescible
▶ 이 생선[고기]은 부패했다 This fish [meat] spoiled [is rotten].
▶ 계란은 부패하기 쉽다 Eggs are apt to addle.
▶ 여름에는 음식이 부패하기 쉽다 Foods are apt to spoil in summer.
2 〈타락〉 corruption; degeneration; deterioration; depravity; taint
♦ 공무원[공직자]의 부패 corruption of government officials / 도덕의 부패 moral taint [corruption]; gangrene
▶ 공직자의 부패는 도저히 묵과할 수 없다 We

can't afford to overlook the corruption of government officials.
―**부패하다** corrupt; degenerate; deteriorate
♦ 부패한 corrupt(ed); degenerate; vitiated 《mind》
▶ 국민이 무관심하면 정치는 부패한다 Public apathy causes corruption in government.
▶ 금전욕은 정계를 부패하게 한다 The love of money is the corruption of the political world.
■ ―**균** putrefying [seprogenic] bacteria ―**물** decomposing matter; septic (matter) ―**방지제** an antiseptic; a preservative ―**산(酸)** putrid acid ―**성** septicity ―**열** surgical [septic] fever

부평초 浮萍草 〈개구리밥〉〔植〕a duckweed
부표 否票 a negative vote [ballot]; a "nay" vote; a vote "no"
♦ 부표를 던지다 vote against [in opposition to]...
▶ 법안에 부표를 던진 사람은 소수에 불과했다 Only a few voted against the bill.
부표 浮標 a (marker) buoy [bɔ́i]
■ 계선(繫船)― a mooring buoy ■ ―**설치** buoyage
부풀다 〈살가죽 등이〉swell; become swollen
♦ 살가죽이 부풀다 the skin swells (up)
2 ⇨ 보풀다
3 〈물체가〉swell out; get big; 〈팽창하다〉expand; be inflated; 〈빵 등이〉rise
▶ 떡은 구우면 부푼다 When you heat rice cake, it rises [swells up].
▶ 풍선이 부풀었다 The balloon has swelled [swollen].
▶ 꽃망울이 부풀기 시작했다 The buds began to swell [expand].
▶ 빵이 잘 부풀지 않는다 The bread will not rise.
4 〈희망 등으로〉be buoyant; be lighthearted; be cheered up
▶ 우리는 기쁜 소식을 듣고 가슴이 부풀었다 We are buoyed up by good news.
▶ 그들의 가슴은 새로운 희망으로 부풀었다 Hope sprang afresh in their hearts.
▶ 신입생들은 모두 희망에 부풀어 있었다 All the freshmen were full of hope.
부풀리다 1 〈사물을〉swell (out); fill out; bulge; expand; puff; 〈공기·가스 등으로〉inflate 《with gas》; 〈불어서〉blow up; 〈효모로〉raise
♦ 공기 베개를 부풀리다 plump up a pillow / 빵을 부풀리다 raise bread / 풍선을 부풀리다 inflate a toy balloon
▶ 바람이 배의 돛을 부풀렸다 The wind swelled [puffed out] the ship's sails.
▶ 반죽을 부풀리는 데 효모가 쓰인다 Yeast is used to make dough rise.
2 ⇨ 보풀리다
부풀부풀 with fuzz ⇨ 보풀보풀
부풀어오르다 swell (out, up); bulge; dilate; expand; become inflated
▶ 타이어에 공기를 넣으면 부풀어 오른다 If you put air into a tire, it swells up.
부품 部品 〈기계 등의〉parts; 〈구성 요소〉a components 《of, for》
♦ 부품을 조립하다 put together [assemble] the parts 《into》
■ **예비**― spare parts **자동차**― (美) automobile parts; (英) motorcar parts
부프다 1 〈부피가〉bulky; voluminous
♦ 부픈 물건[짐] a bulky article [package]
2 〈성질이〉hasty; rash; impatient; restless
▶ 그는 천성이 부프다 He is hasty by nature.
부픗하다 1 〈부피가〉somewhat bulky [voluminous]
♦ 부픗한 꾸러미 a bulky package
▶ 이것은 부픗해서 우편으로 못보낸다 This is too bulky [voluminous] to send by mail.
2 〈말이〉exaggerated; magnified
▶ 그녀는 항상 부픗하게 말하는 사람이다 She always exaggerates.
부피 bulk; volume; size
♦ 부피가 큰 물건 an article of bulky / 부피는 있지만 가벼운 상자 a bulky but light box / 부피가 큰 bulky; voluminous; unwieldy
▶ 우리는 그것을 부피가 아니고 무게로 판다 We sell it by the weight instead of volume.
부하 負荷 1 〈짐〉a burden; a load; 〈짐을 짐〉carrying [bearing] a burden [load]
―**부하하다** carry [bear] a burden [load]; be loaded
2 〔電〕load
■ **최대**― peak load ■ ―**손(損)** load loss ―**시험** a load test ―**율** a load factor ―**전동기** a loaded motor
부하 部下 a subordinate; a follower; (총칭) one's people [men, staff]; one's inferiors; a [one's] following

┌───┐
│ 解說 「부하」는 총칭적으로는 one's **people**인데 (美)에서는 one's assistants라고도 하고 (英)에서는 one's junior라고도 한다. 개개인을 말할 때는 He is one of my people [assistants, juniors]. (그는 내 부하 중의 하나다)라는 식으로 말하지만 일반적으로는 He works for me.와 같이 말하는 경우가 많다. │
└───┘

♦ 믿을 수 있는 부하 a henchman / 부하 병사 men under one's command / 많은 부하를 거느린 지도자 a leader with a large following / 부하가 되다 place oneself under sb's orders / 부하로 삼다 place sb under one's orders / 부하가 많다 have a large following / …의 부하로서 일하다 serve [work] under sb; serve sb as one of (his) followers
▶ 그에게는 유능한 부하가 많다 He has a lot of able assistants.
▶ 그는 남의 부하가 되기를 좋아하지 않는다 He does not like to be in a subordinate position.
▶ 그는 부하를 몇 명 데리고 갔다 He took some of his men with him.
부하다 富― 〈살림이〉rich; wealthy; 〈몸이〉fat; fatty; corpulent; fleshy
부합 符合 coincidence; correspondence; conformity; agreement; tally(ing)
―**부합하다** 〈들이 들어맞다〉coincide [correspond, conform] with; accord [agree, tally] with; (美) check (up) with

▶이 사실은 목격자의 증언과 부합한다 This fact is coincident with the testimony of the witness of the scene.
▶그의 얼굴 생김새가 인상서와 부합한다 His features answer (to) the description.
▶그의 이야기는 사실과 부합했다 His story corresponded [agreed, tallied] with the facts.
▶그의 정보는 이 보고서에 기술되어 있는 내용과 부합하지 않는다 His information does not agree with what this report states.

부형 父兄 〈아버지와 형〉 one's father and older [elder] brothers
부호 負號 〔數〕 the minus sign ⇨ 뺄셈(~표)
부호 符號 a mark; a sign; a symbol; 〈전신부호〉 a (telegraphic) code
♦부호를 붙이다 mark; affix a mark / 부호를 읽다 interpret the signs [marks]
▶이 부호는 무슨 의미입니까? What does this sign [mark] stand for?
▶강세— 〔言〕 a graphic accent 모스— the Morse code [alphabet] ■—표 a table of signs —화 〔電算〕 encoding; encodement
부호 富豪 a rich [wealthy] man; a man of wealth; 〈백만장자〉 a millionaire; 〈억만장자〉 a billionaire ⇨ 부자(富者)
부화 孵化 hatching; incubation —부화하다 hatch; incubate; brood; sit on 《eggs》 ♦병아리를 부화하다 hatch [incubate] chickens
▶알이 부화했다 The eggs have hatched.
▶오늘 아침에는 병아리가 몇 마리 부화되었습니까? How many chickens have hatched this morning?
▶병아리가 부화되었다 The chickens are out [have hatched].
▶인공— artificial incubation ■—기 an artificial incubator —용계란 a hatching egg —장 a hatchery
부화뇌동 附和雷同 blind following —부화뇌동하다 follow others blindly (and uncritically); follow suit without (due) reflection; echo 《sb's view》
부활 復活 〈소생·재생〉 (a) revival; rebirth; resurrection; 〈회복〉 restoration 《of》; 〈그리스도의〉 the Resurrection (of Christ)
♦구제도의 부활 the revival [return] of the old system
—부활하다 come to life again; come back to life; revive; rise again; be restored 《to the original state》
♦스러진 관습을 부활시키다 resurrect obsolete customs
▶그리스도는 죽은 자 가운데서 부활했다 Christ rose [raised] from the dead.
부활절 復活節 Easter
■—계절 Eastertide —날 Easter Day [Sunday] —다음날 Easter Monday —전야 the Easter eve [even] —주간 Easter week
부회장 副會長 a vice-chairman; a vice-president
부흥 復興 (a) revival; restoration; rehabilitation; 〈재건〉 reconstruction
♦전후의 부흥 《Korea's》 postwar rehabilitation
—부흥하다 revive; be revived; reconstruct; be reconstructed; rehabilitate; restore 《to》; make a comeback
▶우리 나라는 완전히 부흥했다 Our country has been completely reconstructed.
▶서울은 잿더미 속에서 부흥했다 Seoul rose from the [its] ashes.
▶황폐한 시가가 부흥되어 가고 있다 The devastated town is undergoing reconstruction.
■경제— economic revival; an economic comeback 문예— the Revival (of Learning [Letters, Literature]); the Renaissance —목사 a revivalist (preacher) —사업 reconstruction work; the work of rebuilding and rehabilitation —회 〈교회의〉 a revival (service)

북¹ 〈악기〉 a drum
♦북소리 a drumbeat; the sound of a drum / 북치는 사람 a drummer / 북을 울려 아이들을 모으다 drum up children / 북을 치다 beat a drum; drum
▶북은 칠수록 소리가 난다 〈속담〉 Don't waste argument on such a person.
■작은— a high drum; 〈오케스트라용〉 a side [snare] drum 큰— a big drum; 〈오케스트라용〉 a low [bass] drum
북² 〈재봉틀의 밑실이 든〉 a shuttle; 〈베틀의〉 a spindle
북³ 〈흙〉 soil that covers roots; a hill (over [around] roots) ♦북(을) 주다 heap soil around 《a plant》; earth up; hill 《potatoes》
북⁴ 〈긁는 소리〉 with a scratching sound; 〈찢는 소리〉 with a rip ♦딱성냥을 북 긋다 strike a friction match / 헝겊을 북 찢다 rip a piece of cloth / 포대를 북 찢어 열다 rip open a sack
북 北 (the) north (略 N) ⇨ 북쪽
북경 北京 Peking
■—원인(原人) 〔人類〕 a Sinanthropus; the Peking man
북구 北歐 North [Northern] Europe
♦북구의 Scandinavian ■—사람 a Scandinavian; a Northman —신화 Norse mythology
북국 北國 a northern country ■—사람 a northerner
북극 北極 the North [Arctic] Pole
♦북극의 arctic; polar
—곰 a polar [white] bear —광 ⇨ 극광(極光) —권(圈) the Arctic Circle —대(帶) the Arctic Zone —지방 the Arctic region —탐험대 a polar [an Arctic] expedition (team) —항로 the polar route —해 the Arctic Ocean
북극성 北極星 〔天〕 the polar star; the polestar; Polaris; the North Star; the lodestar
북녘 北— the north(ward); the northern part
북단 北端 the northern end [tip, extremity]
북대서양 北大西洋 the North Atlantic Ocean
—조약 the North Atlantic Treaty —조약기구 the North Atlantic Treaty Organization (略 NATO)
북데기 waste straw
북도 北道 1 〈남·북도의〉 the North (part of a split) Province ♦경상북도 North Kyŏngsang Province; Kyŏngsangbuk-do

2 ⟨경기도 북쪽의⟩ the northern provinces; the provinces north of Kyŏnggi-do

북돋다 earth up ⇨ 북돋우다

북돋우다 **1** ⟨북주다⟩ earth up ⟨a tree⟩; heap soil around ⟨a plant⟩; hill (up) ⟨potatoes⟩ **2** ⟨용기 등을⟩ encourage; stimulate; invigorate; cheer up; stir up
♦ 사기를 북돋우다 raise [stiffen, stir up] the morale / 용기를 북돋우다 encourage; give *sb* courage; hearten [cheer] up
▶ 그런 노래가 우리의 투지를 북돋운다 Such songs stir up our fighting spirit.
▶ 풍선들이 축제 분위기를 더욱 북돋우었다 The balloons added to the festive atmosphere.

북동 北東 the northeast (略 NE)
♦ 북동의 northeast; northeastern / 북동으로 northeast(ward) ■ ―풍 a northeast [northeastern, northeasterly] wind; a northeaster

북두칠성 北斗七星 〖天〗 the (Great [Big]) Dipper; the Great Bear; the Plow; Ursa Major

북면 北面 ⟨북향⟩ facing (the) north; ⟨왕을 섬김⟩ serving the king as a subject; allegiance ―**북면하다** face (the) north; ⟨왕을 섬기다⟩ serve the king as a subject

북미 北美 North America ♦ 북미의 North American ■ ―대륙 the North American Continent

북미동 北微東 north by east (略 NbE)

북미서 北微西 north by west (略 NbW)

북미주 北美洲 North America

북바늘 a guard pin inside a shuttle

북반구 北半球 the Northern Hemisphere

북받치다 rise to ⇨ 복받치다

북방 北方 ⟨북쪽 방향⟩ the north(ward); the northern direction; ⟨북쪽 지방⟩ a northern district ♦ 북방의 northern; northerly ■ ―민족 a northern race ―영토 the northern territories ―정책 a northward policy

북벌 北伐 an expedition to conquer the north; the subjugation [conquest] of the northern areas ―**북벌하다** send an expedition to conquer the north

북부 北部 the north; the northern part

북북 ⟨긁는 소리⟩ with a scraping sound; ⟨찢는 소리⟩ ⟨rip⟩ to pieces
♦ 이를 북북 갈다 gnash [grind] *one's* teeth furiously / 다리를 북북 긁다 scratch *one's* leg roughly / 북북 문지르다 scrub [rub] hard

북북동 北北東 north-northeast (略 NNE)

북북서 北北西 north-northwest (略 NNW)

북빙양 北氷洋 the Arctic Ocean ⇨ 북극(~해)

북상 北上 going north ▶ 태풍이 북상중이다 The typhoon is moving northward.
―**북상하다** go up north; proceed northward

북새 ⟨법석⟩ hustle; bustle; hubbub; commotion; ⟨방해⟩ disturbance
♦ 북새 놓다 hustle and bustle; stir up a riot; make [put up] a fuss ⟨about, over⟩; ⟨방해놓다⟩ raise [create, cause] a disturbance

북새통 〚화재 북새통에 도둑질하다 commit theft in the confusion of a fire / 북새통에 아이를 잃다 lose *one's* child in the hustle and bustle / 북새통에 잠입하다 sneak in during the confusion

북새판 a confusion; the scene [site] of a commotion

북서 北西 the northwest (略 NW)
♦ 북서의 northwest; northwestern / 북서로 northwest(ward) ■ ―풍 a northwest [northwestern, northwesterly] wind; a northwester ―항로 the Northwest Passage

북송 北送 repatriation to the north ―**북송하다** repatriate to the north

북슬개 a big hairy [shaggy] dog

북슬북슬하다 plump and hairy [shaggy]

북아메리카 北― North America ⇨ 북미

북안 北岸 the north(ern) shore [coast]

북양 北洋 the north ocean [sea]; the northern waters ■ ―어업 the northern-sea fishery

북어 北魚 a dried pollack
■ ―찜 (a seasoned and) steamed pollack

북위 北緯 the north latitude (略 N.L.)
♦ 북위 38도 38 degrees [38°] North Latitude / 북위 28도 55분에 at twenty-eight degrees fifty-five minutes of north latitude (▶ Lat. 28°55′N. 으로 줄여 씀)
▶ 당시 그 비행기는 북위 43도 18분, 서경 91도 20분 지점을 날아가고 있었다 The plane was flying in Lat. 43°18′N. and in Long. 91°20′W. at that time.

북유럽 北― Northern Europe ⇨ 북구(北歐)

북적거리다 **1** ⟨사람이⟩ bustle; crowd; jostle; throng; be crowded [thronged] ⟨with people⟩; be bustling; be in a bustle
♦ 북적거리는 인파 a thick, jostling crowd; a seething mass of people
▶ 거리는 물건 사려는 사람들로 북적거렸다 The streets were thronged with shoppers.
▶ 야구장 입구에 관객들이 북적거리고 있었다 The spectators were thronging [jostling] in front of the ball park gate.
2 ⟨술·식혜 등이⟩ boil (over); come to a boil; bubble up

북적북적 ⟨사람이⟩ in a bustle; bustlingly; uproariously; tumultuously
―**북적북적하다** ⇨ 북적거리다
▶ 극장은 사람들로 북적북적했다 The theater was jammed with people.

북주다 earth up ⇨ 북³

북지 北地 the northern region [lands, districts]

북진하다 北進― go [march] north; sail northward

북쪽 北― the north(ward)
♦ 북쪽의 north(ward); northern; northerly / 북쪽에 to the north; in the direction of north / 시(市)의 북쪽 10 마일 지점에 10 miles (to the) north of the city / 북쪽으로 northward(s); north; toward the north / 북쪽으로 가다 go [head] north; go toward the north; proceed northward
▶ 어디가 북쪽이냐? Which way is north?
▶ 한국은 북쪽으로 만주와 접한다 On the north Korea borders on Manchuria.

북창 北窓 a north window [light]

북채 a drumstick
북천 北天 the northern sky
북춤 a drum dance ♦ 북춤을 추다 perform a drum dance
북측 北側 the north(ward) ⇨ 북쪽
북통 —筒 the (wooden) body of a drum; a drum frame
북풍 北風 a north [northerly] wind; a wind from the north
  ♦ 차디찬 북풍 a freezing [biting, piercing] north wind
  ▶ 북풍이 분다 The wind is blowing from the north.
  ▶ 북풍이 살을 에는듯이 차갑다 The north wind cuts like a blade.
북한 北韓 North Korea ■—문제전문가 an expert on North Korea affairs
북해 北海 〈영국 북쪽의〉 the North Sea; 〈북쪽의〉 a northern sea
  ■—유전 the oil field in the North Sea
북행하다 北行— go north; go toward the north; proceed northward
북향 北向 a northern aspect [exposure]
  ■—북향하다 face (the) north; have a north aspect
  ■—집 a house facing (the) north [with a northern exposure]
북회귀선 北回歸線 the Tropic of Cancer
분 ♦ 이[저] 분 this [that] gentleman [lady] / 여러분 ladies and gentlemen; everybody; all of you / 손님 두 분 two customers [guests] / 민선생이라는 분 a gentleman named Min; a (certain) Mr. Min
  ▶ 저 분은 누굽니까? Who is that gentleman?
  ▶ 오늘 몇 분이나 오십니까? How many people [guests] are you expecting today?

분 分 **1** 〈10분의 1〉 one-tenth; a tenth; ten percent ♦ 칠팔분의 가망이 있다 have seven or eight chances out of ten
  2 〈시간·각도 등〉 a minute
  ♦ 10분 ten minutes / 15분 a quarter (of an hour [a degree]); fifteen minutes / 30분 half an hour; a half hour; thirty minutes / 45분 three quarters (of an hour) / 2시 15분 a quarter past two / 북위 35도 15분 35 degrees 15 minutes north latitude (▶ Lat. 35°15′N. 으로 줄여 씀)
  ▶ 3시 15분 발 열차를 타겠습니다 I'll get on the 3:15 train. (▶ 3:15는 three fifteen으로 읽음)
  ▶ 5시 5분[5분전]입니다 It is five minutes past [to] five.
  ▶ 역까지는 걸어서 10분입니다 It takes ten minutes to walk to the station.
  ▶ 3시 몇 분엔가 출발하는 기차가 있다 There is a train due out at something past [after] three.
  3 〈분수·신분〉 one's lot [status, place]; one's social station [position, standing]
  ♦ 분에 맞게 살다 live within one's means; live up to one's income
  ▶ 선생의 말씀 분에 넘칩니다 Your words are more than I deserve.
  4 〈본분·의무〉 one's duty; one's part
분 憤·忿 indignation; wrath; anger; rage
  ♦ 분을 돋우다 fan sb's anger; add insult to injury / 분을 참지 못하다 lose one's temper; get out of patience; be angry / 분을 풀다 vent one's anger [spite] 《on》
  ▶ 나는 참았던 분이 폭발했다 My repressed anger [indignation] exploded.
분 盆 a flowerpot ⇨ 화분(花盆)
분 粉 〈화장분〉 toilet [face] powder; powder
  ♦ 분도 안 바르는 여자 a woman wearing no makeup at all / 얼굴에 분을 바르다 powder one's face; put powder on one's face
  ▶ 너는 분이 잘 먹는구나 Your skin takes powder well, doesn't it?
  ▶ 그녀는 분을 처덕처덕 발랐다 Her face was thickly powdered.
-분 -分 **1** 〈부분〉 a part; 〈나눔〉 division
  ♦ 2분의 1 one-half; a half / 4분의 1 one-fourth (part); a quarter / 5분의 2 two-fifths / 100분의 1 one-hundredth / 5와 7분의 6 five and six-sevenths / 234분의 123 a hundred and twenty-three over two hundred and thirty-four / 5만분의 1 지도 a map on the scale of 1:50,000 (▶ one-fifty thousands로 읽음)
  ▶ 참가자의 3분의 1이 여성이었다 One-third of the participants were women.
  ▶ 내 월급은 그 사람의 3분의 2다 My salary is two-thirds of his.
  ▶ 줄섰던 사람 중 4분의 3이 표를 살 수 있었다 Three quarters of those who were standing in line were able to buy the tickets.
  2 〈몫〉 a share; a portion; 〈분량〉 an amount; quantity; a ration
  ▶ 의사는 3일분의 약을 주었다 The doctor gave (enough) medicine for three days.
  ▶ 그들은 가을에 한 겨울분의 연료를 구입한다 In autumn they buy enough fuel for the whole winter.
  ▶ 식량은 아직 3일분이 남아 있었다 Rations for three days were still left.
  ▶ 5인분의 점심을 주문해 주시오 Please order lunch for five.
  3 〈함유량〉 content; percentage
  ▶ 이 과자는 당분이 많다 This cake contains a lot of sugar.
  ▶ 이 술은 알코올분이 적다 This liquor has a small percentage of alcohol in it. ⇌ The alcoholic strength of this liquor is weak.
분가 分家 a branch family [house]; a cadet family [branch]; a branch; an offshoot
  —**분가하다** create a new family; set up a branch family; separate a family
분간 分揀 distinction; discrimination
  —**분간하다** distinguish [discriminate] 《A from B, between A and B》; know [tell] 《A from B》
  ♦ 분간하기 어려운 indistinguishable / 분간할 수 없을 정도로 beyond [out of] recognition; indistinguishably
  ▶ 그와 그의 형은 분간하기 어렵다 It is hard to distinguish him from his brother.
  ▶ 그는 선악을 분간하기에는 아직 어리다 He is still too young to know right from wrong.
  ♦ 영국인과 미국인을 분간할 수 있는가? Can you tell an Englishman from an American?

▶ 나는 하늘과 바다를 분간할 수가 없었다 I couldn't tell where the sky and the sea met.
분갑 粉匣 a (powder) compact; a puff case [box]
분개 分介 〔簿〕 journalizing ━**분개하다** journalize ■ ━**장** a journal: 분개장에 기입하다 enter in a journal
분개 憤慨 anger; indignation; resentment
━**분개하다** resent; be indignant 《at, over》; be enraged 《at [against] *sth*, with *sb*》; be [get] angry [mad] 《with, at》; burn with anger
♦ **분개하여** in a rage; in resentment [indignation]/ 부당한 처사에 분개하다 smart under an injustice
▶ 그는 그 잔혹 행위에 분개했다 He resented [was indignant over] the cruelty.
▶ 그러면 누구라도 분개하겠다 Anybody would get mad at it. ⇌ It is enough to provoke a saint.
▶ 그런 모욕을 받으면 분개하는 것이 당연하다 It's natural that one should get indignant at such insult.
▶ 그는 분개하여 방에서 뛰쳐나갔다 He rushed [flung] out of the room in indignation.
분격 憤激 exasperation; resentment; wrath
━**분격하다** be exasperated 《at [by] *sth*, against *sb*》; get enraged; be infuriated 《at》
▶ 그들의 심한 냉대에 그는 극도로 분격했다 He was just beside himself with indignation over their coldest treatment.
분견 分遣 detachment; detail ━**분견하다** detach; detail; draft; tell off ━**대** a detachment; a detached force; a contingent ━**소** an outstation ━**함대** a detached fleet
분경 分境 the border ⇨ 분계(分界)
분계 分界 the boundary; the border
분계선 分界線 a boundary line; a line of demarcation
♦ 군사 분계선 the Military Demarcation Line 《on the Korean Peninsula》/ 분계선을 긋다 draw a line between 《the two》
분골쇄신하다 粉骨碎身━ 〈노력하다〉 do everything in one's power; exert *oneself* to the utmost; do *one's* best
분공장 分工場 a branch factory [workshop, plant, mill]
분과 分科 a section; a division; a department; a branch ▶ 물리학은 과학의 한 분과다 Physics is a branch of science. ■━**위원회** a subcommittee; a sectional meeting
분관 分館 an annex; a detached building; 〈도서관의〉 a branch library
분광 分光 a spectrum 《*pl*. ~s, -tra》
■━**계** 〔物〕 a spectrometer ━**기** 〔物〕 a spectroscope; a spectral apparatus ━**분석** spectroscopic [spectrum] analysis; (a) spectral analysis; 〔物〕 spectrometry ━**사진** a spectrogram; a spectrograph ━**사진기** a spectrograph
분교 分校 a branch school
분국 分局 a branch office; a branch bureau
분권 分權 decentralization (of authority)
━**분권하다** decentralize power [authority]
■ 지방━ decentralization ■━**주의** decentralism

분규 紛糾 complication; entanglement; a trouble; confusion; disorder; a tangle
♦ 학원 분규 a campus dispute [strife]/ 분규를 일으키다 cause [stir up] trouble; arouse a complication
▶ 그 부정 사건이 있은 후로 그 회사는 분규가 끊이지 않는다 There's been nothing but trouble in that corporation since the scandal.
▶ 그 분규에 말려들지 않도록 주의하시오 Be careful not to be involved in that complication.
분극 分極 〔電〕 polarization ♦ 분극화하다 polarize
분근 分根 〈나누기〉 division of roots; root division; 〈뿌리〉 a divided root
━**분근하다** part [divide] the roots 《of a plant》 for transplanting
분기 分岐 〈갈라짐〉 divergence; ramification; forking
━**분기하다** diverge 《from》; branch 《off, out》; turn off; fork; ramify
▶ 강은 그 지점에서 두 갈래의 지류로 분기한다 The river forks into two branches there.
■━**선** 〈지선〉 a branch (line); a spur track; a turnout track
분기 分期 a quarter year; a quarter of a year; three months (of a year)
♦ 1[2] /4분기 the first [second] quater of the year / 3[4]/ 4분기에 in [during] the third [fourth] quarter of the year
분기 噴氣 ejection; spouting (of gas)
━**분기하다** eject; spout; emit
분기 奮起 stirring up; bestirring *oneself*
━**분기하다** be stirred up; be inspired 《by》; brace *oneself* up 《for》; rouse *oneself* 《to》
♦ 분기시키다 stir (up); brace up; rouse *sb* into activity; put [set] *sb* on [to] his mettle
▶ 모두가 분기하지 않으면 만회는 불가능하다 Unless everyone is stirred up [exerts himself, does what he can], there will be no restoration.
분기공 噴氣孔 〔地質〕 a fumarole; 〔機〕 a steam valve; a gas escape; 〈고래의〉 a fistula 《*pl*. ~s, -lae》; a spout (hole)
분기점 分岐點 a diverging [turning] point; 〈길의〉 a fork; a crossroad; 〈철도의〉 a junction
▶ 여기가 성패의 분기점이다 Success depends on this point.
▶ 그것은 내 인생의 분기점이었다 It was the turning point of my life.
분김 忿━ ·**憤**━ ♦ 분김에 from [out of] spite; out of vexation [chagrin]; in (a fit of) anger [rage]; in (*one's*) resentment [indignation, mortification]
▶ 그는 분김에 편지를 갈기갈기 찢었다 He tore the letter into pieces in a fit of anger.
분꽃 粉━ 〔植〕 a marvel-of-Peru; a four-o'clock; an afternoon lady
분납 分納 installment payment; payment by [in] installments; 〈상품의〉 installment delivery
▶ 수업료의 분납은 허용되지 않는다 The payment of school fees by installments is not

—**분납하다** pay by [in] installments; deliver 《goods》 in parts [installments]
▶ 수업료는 2회에 분납하도록 되어 있다 We are supposed to pay school fees in two installments.

분내 粉— the smell of face powder

분노 忿怒·憤怒 anger; fury; rage; wrath; indignation; resentment
◆ 분노를 가라앉히다 calm [quell, appease] one's anger / 분노를 억제하다 restrain [hold in, contain] one's anger [wrath] / 분노를 터뜨리다 open the floodgates of wrath; vent [wreak] one's anger 《on》; take it out 《on》
▶ 그의 눈은 분노의 빛을 띠고 있었다 There was an angry look in his eyes.
▶ 그 정치가의 부정은 세인의 분노를 샀다 The politician's injustice aroused public indignation.
▶ 그의 음성은 분노로 떨리고 있었다 His voice was trembling with rage.
—**분노하다** get [become] angry; get into rage; flare [fire] up; be exasperated [enraged]
▶ 나는 마음 속으로 분노했다 I felt resentment in my heart.

분뇨 糞尿 excreta; excretions; feces and urine; human waste; wastes; night soil
■ —관 a soil pipe —소각장치 a night-soil incinerator —수거인 a night-soil man —운반차 a dung cart; a night-soil wagon; 《美俗》 a honey wagon

분단 分團 a branch; a (local) chapter

분단 分斷 dividing into sections; division; partition
◆ 한반도의 분단 the partition of the Korean Peninsula
—**분단하다** divide (into sections); partition
■ 국토— division of territory; national division; division [partitioning] of the country
■ —국 a divided [partitioned] country [nation, state]

분담 分擔 partial charge; taking [having] a [one's] share (in)
—**분담하다** bear [take] one's share of 《the responsibility》; take partial charge of 《business》; bear part of 《the expenses》
▶ 같은 비율로 비용을 분담합시다 Let's bear an equal share of the expenses.
▶ 그는 나와 비용을 분담했다 He shared the expense with me.
■ —금 a share of expenses; allotted charges —분 (分) a share; a portion —액 an allotment; an allotted amount —자 a sharer; a partaker

분당 分黨 〈가름〉 splitting a (political) party; 〈갈라진 당〉 a party split; a splinter party
—**분당하다** split [secede] a (political) party
■ —파 the seceders; the separatists

분대 分隊 〈軍〉〈육군〉 a squad; 〈해군〉 a division; 〈지대〉 a detachment; 〈분견대〉 a party
■ —장 〈육군〉 a squad leader; 〈해군〉 a divisional officer

분대꾼 a troublemaker; a meddler; a nuisance

분대질 〈말썽〉 trouble-making; making [raising] trouble; 〈소란〉 disturbance; botheration; 〈폐끼침〉 nuisance
—**분대질치다[하다]** make [raise] trouble; make a nuisance of oneself; (口) kick up a dust [row, fuss, shine, shindy]; meddle; bother; upset; disturb

분도기 分度器 a protractor ⇨ 각도기(角度器)

분동 分銅 a (balance) weight; a counterbalance; a counterweight; a counterpoise ■ —저울 a balance

분란 紛亂 disorder; confusion; trouble(s)
▶ 그는 어딜 가나 분란을 일으키기로 유명하다 He is known for getting into trouble wherever he goes.

분량 分量 a quantity; an amount; a measure; volume; 〈약의〉 a dose
◆ 많은[적은] 분량 a large [small] quantity / 정확한 분량 the exact quantity / 일정 분량의 연어 a fixed quantity of salmon / 분량이 늘다[줄다] gain [diminish] in quantity / 분량을 재다 measure [calculate] the quantity 《of》 / 분량을 배가시키다 double the quantity 《of》
▶ 나는 매일 밤 분량을 정해 놓고 술을 마신다 I drink in fixed quantities every evening.

분력 分力 〖物〗 a component (of a force); a component force

분류 分流 〈지류〉 a distributary; a (river) branch; a tributary (river) —**분류하다** branch from

분류 分溜 〖化〗 fractional distillation; fraction
—**분류하다** fractionate; crack ■ —관(管) a fractionating column —장치 a fractionator —휘발유 cracked gasoline

분류 分類 〈유별〉 classification; assortment; division; grouping
◆ 제목에 의한 책의 분류 classification of books by subjects
—**분류하다** classify; divide into classes; sort; assort
▶ 경찰은 작년의 교통사고를 원인별로 분류했다 The police classified last year's traffic accidents by cause.
▶ 이 책들은 제목별로 분류된다 These books are classified by subjects.
▶ 자료는 세세히 분류되었다 The data have been broken down minutely.
▶ 카드는 알파벳 순으로 분류되어 있었다 The cards were (classified) in alphabetical order.
■ —목록 a classified catalog(ue) —번호 〖圖書〗 a class number —법 a system of classification; a classification system : 인위[자연] 분류법 artificial [natural] classification —표 a classified table [list] —학 taxology; taxonomy —학자 a taxonomist; a systematist

분류 奔流 〈세찬 흐름〉 a rapid [rushing] stream; an onrush (of water); a torrent; rapids —**분류하다** rush; flush; run with rapidity; dash along

분리 分離 〈떨어 짐〉 separation; division; detachment; disunion; disjunction; severance; secession; 〈흑·백인의〉 segregation
◆ 종교와 과학의 분리 the divorce between religion and science / (고속도로의) 중앙 분리대 a median strip; (英) a central reserve

—분리하다 〈떼어놓다〉 separate; secede; disjoin; disconnect; split; detach; sever; 〈떨어지다〉 be separated 《from》; be divided 《from》; secede [sever] *oneself* 《from》

♦분리할 수 없는 inseparable; indivisible / 우유에서 크림을 분리하다 separate cream from milk

■—재산 separation of property 정경— separation of political and economic affairs ■—계수법 〔數〕 a method of detached coefficients —기〔器〕 a separator : 원심 분리기 a centrifugal separator —론 secessionism —론자 a secessionist —법 a method of chemical separation —수거 〈쓰레기의〉 collection of garbage by type —운동 a separatist movement —주의 separatism —주의자 a separatist; 〈흑·백인의〉 a segregationist —파 seceders; secessionists; separatists

분립 分立 〈따로 섬〉 separation; segregation; independence

♦입법, 행정, 사법권의 분립 the independence of the powers of legislation, administration and judicature; the independence of legislative, executive, and judicial authority

—분립하다 set up independently; become independent 《of》; separate [segregate, secede] 《from》

분만 分娩 childbirth; delivery; parturition

♦분만중이다 be in labor

—분만하다 be delivered of; give birth to

▶그녀는 어제 사내아이를 분만했다 She gave birth to [was delivered of] a boy yesterday.

■—무통 a painless delivery ■—비 childbirth [delivery] expenses —실 a delivery [labor] room —휴가 maternity leave

분말 粉末 powder; dust ♦분말의 powdered; powdery / 분말로 만들다 powder; reduce to [grind into] powder; pulverize

■—주스 powdered juice —차(茶) powdered [dust] tea

분망 奔忙 pressure [press] of business; busyness —분망하다 busy; bustling; 〈서술적〉 be occupied 《with business》; be heavily engaged 《in》 ▶나는 회의 준비로 분망했다 I was very busy preparing for a conference.

분매 分賣 selling separately

—분매하다 sell 《things》 separately [singly]

▶지주는 땅을 분매했다 The landowner sold his [the] land in lots.

분명하다 分明— clear; evident; plain; obvious; distinct; definite; certain

♦분명한 기억 a vivid recollection / 분명한 대답 a definite answer / 분명한 사실 a plain [an obvious] fact / 분명한 증거 clear [indisputable] evidence; an evident proof / 분명치 않은 indistinct; vague; unclear; inarticulate 《pronunciation》 / 분명해지다 become clear [plain]

▶그 뜻은 아주 분명하다 The meaning is quite clear.

▶그가 거짓말을 하고 있는 것이 아주 분명하다 It is quite obvious that he is lying.

▶이제는 모든 것이 분명해졌다 Everything is now quite clear to me.

▶이유는 분명치 않다 The reason is not clear.

▶그 돈이 어떻게 쓰여졌는지 분명치 않다 How the money was spent is not accounted for.

분명히 分明— clearly; evidently; plainly; distinctly; obviously; definitely; certainly

♦분명히 하다 make clear [plain]; clear 《the cause》; clarify [define] 《*one's* attitude》 / 분명히 대답하다 answer definitely; give a definite answer

▶분명히 말해 두겠다 I say that once and for all.

▶이 정도는 분명히 말할 수 있다 I can say this much clearly.

▶우리 두 사람의 관계를 분명히 해 둡시다 Let's make clear the relation between you and myself.

분모 分母 〔數〕 a denominator

♦분모를 없애다 cancel a denominator

■공통— a common denominator: 최소 공통분모 the least [lowest] common denominator

분묘 墳墓 a grave; a tomb

분무 噴霧 spray; spraying; 〈향수 등의〉 atomizing —분무하다 spray; atomize

♦농작물에 농약을 분무하고 있는 농부 a farmer spraying his crops with pesticide

—도장(塗裝) spraying; spray painting

분무기 噴霧器 a spray(er); a spray gun; a vaporizer; a pulverizer; 〈향수용〉 an atomizer; 〈의료용〉 a nebulizer

♦분무기로 천에 물을 뿌리다 spray water on cloth with a sprayer / 식물에 분무기로 살충제를 뿌리다 spray plants with insecticide; spray insecticide over plants

분문 噴門 〔解〕 the cardia; the cardiac orifice

분받침 盆— a flowerpot saucer

분발 奮發 strenuous efforts; a spurt; exertion(s)

—분발하다 use [make, put forth] 《strenuous》 exertions [efforts]; brace *oneself* 《up》; stir up *oneself* [*one's* fighting spirit]; spurt; pluck up *one's* spirits [heart, courage]

♦남을 분발시키다 inspire *sb* with courage; rouse *sb* 《into activity》

▶우리는 좀 더 분발해야 한다 We must try a little harder.

▶그 팀은 이기려고 분발했다 The team strove to win.

■—심 the spirit of exertion; a strenuous spirit

분방하다 奔放— 〈제멋대로인〉 wild; extravagant; unrestrained; free(-spirited)

▶그는 자유 분방한 생활을 하고 있다 He lives a free and unrestrained life.

▶그는 자유 분방하게 행동했다 He conducted himself without any reserve whatsoever.

분배 分配 distribution; allotment; sharing; division

♦부의 분배 the distribution of wealth

▶그들은 이익의 분배를 요구했다 They claimed a share in [of] the profits.

▶우리는 이익의 분배를 받을 자격이 있다 We are entitled to share [have a share] in the profits.

—분배하다 distribute 《to, among》; share

(with, between); divide 《between, among》; give out; apportion 《to, between, among》; portion (out)

> [解說] ***distribute***는 수량이 한정되어 있는 물건을 대체로 똑같이 나누어 준다는 뜻으로, 배분자는 분배에 끼지 않는다는 뜻을 내포한다. ***share***는 물건을 나누어 주거나 사용케 한다는 뜻이지만, 경험·수고·기쁨 등의 추상적인 것도 분담함을 뜻하며 배분자도 분배에 참여한다는 뜻을 내포한다. ***divide***는 distribute와 share 양자의 의미를 포함하지만, 목적이나 계획에 따라 (별도의 약정이 없는 한) 똑같이 나눈다는 뜻을 내포한다. ***give out***은 distribute의 구어 표현이다.

▶ 그들은 이익을 어떻게 분배했나요? How did they divide the profits up?
▶ 그는 재산을 세 아들에게 균등하게 분배했다 He divided his property equally among his three sons.
▶ 나는 그들에게 각각 응분의 몫을 분배했다 I apportioned a fair amount to each of them.
▶ 이익은 주주들에게 분배된다 Profits are divided among the shareholders.
■ 이익— division of profit; profit sharing —금 a dividend —액 a share —자 a portioner; a distributor

분별 分別 **1**〈사물의 구분〉division;〈구별〉distinction; discrimination;〈분류〉classification; assortment;〈분리〉separation; 〔化〕 fractionation
—**분별하다**〈구별하다〉separate; distinguish; discriminate;〈구분하다〉divide;〈분류하다〉classify; assort; 〔化〕 fractionate
♦ 목소리를 분별하다 recognize *sb's* voice / 방향을 분별하지 못하다 cannot tell the direction
▶ 그는 선악을 분별하지 못한다 He does not know good from evil. ⇒ He cannot discriminate [tell] good from evil.
2〈사려〉discretion; prudence;〈양식〉wisdom; good sense; common sense
♦ 분별이 없는 indiscreet; imprudent; ill-advised; thoughtless; rash / 분별이 있는 discreet; prudent; thoughtful; sensible; wise / 분별 없는 짓을 하다 commit a rash act; act rashly / 분별이 생기다 attain *one's* years of discretion; cut *one's* wisdom teeth / 나이는 어리지만 분별이 있다 have an old head on young shoulders / 분별을 잃다 lose *one's* wits [mind]; lose control of *oneself*
▶ 분별이 있는 사람이라면 그런 짓은 안 한다 A sensible man wouldn't do such a thing
▶ 그와 다투지 않을 정도의 분별은 있었다 I had more sense than to quarrel with him.
—**분별하다** judge; know (better); use [exercise] discretion
▶ 그 정도는 분별할 줄 알아야지 You should know better than that.
■ —결정(結晶) 〔化〕 fractional crystallization —법 〔化〕 fractionation —증류 ⇨ 분류(分溜)

분복 分福 *one's* lot [portion] in life
분봉 分蜂 hiving off; splitting the hive; swarming —**분봉하다** hive off; split the hive; swarm

분부 分付·吩咐 an order; a bidding; a command;〈지시〉directions; instructions
♦ 분부를 받다 be told [ordered] 《to do》 / 분부를 어김없이 거행하다 carry out [follow] instructions to the letter / 분부대로 하다 do as *one* is told; follow *sb's* [the] instructions; act according to orders [commands]
▶ 선생님을 역으로 마중 나가라는 부친의 분부를 받고 I was ordered by my father to meet you at the station.
—**분부하다** tell [order, command, direct, instruct]《*sb to do sth*》; give orders; bid《*sb do sth*》
▶ 일이 있으면 언제라도 분부하십시오 Whenever you want me, I am at your service.

분분하다 紛紛—〈의견 등이〉diverse; divergent; various;〈어수선하다〉complicated; scattered; pell-mell;〈시끄럽다〉tumultuous
♦ 분분한 소문 contradictory rumors / 분분하게 confusedly; in confusion; pell-mell / 의견이 분분하다 vary [be divergent] in opinion《as to》
▶ 이 문제에 관해서는 이견이 분분하다 There are conflicting opinions on this question.
▶ 같은 사건에 관한 보도가 신문마다 분분하다 The same event is reported differently [in different ways] in a variety of papers.

분비 分泌 〔生〕 secretion
♦ 분비를 촉진하는 secretive; secernent
—**분비하다** secrete; secern
▶ 몇몇 선(腺)은 호르몬을 분비한다 Some glands secrete hormones.
■ 내— internal secretion —관 a secretory vessel —기관 a secernent; a secretory organ —물 a secretion —선(腺)[세포] a secreting gland [cell] —액 a secreting fluid; juice —작용 secretion —조직 secretory tissue

분사 分詞 〔文法〕 a participle ■ 현재[과거, 완료]— a present [past, perfect] participle —구[절] a participial phrase [clause] —구문 a participial construction —형 a participial form

분사 憤死 dying of indignation
—**분사하다** die of indignation [resentment]; die [destroy *oneself*] in a fury

분사 噴射 jet; spray; injection
—**분사하다** jet (out)
♦ 엔진이 화염을 분사한다 The engine jets (out) flames.
■ 연료— fuel injection ■ —관[노즐] an injection pipe [nozzle] —식추진기 a jet propeller —총〈우주 유영에 쓰는〉a jet gun

분사추진 噴射推進 jet propulsion (略 JP) ■ —기관 a jet-propelled engine —식비행기 a jet(-engined, -propelled, -powered) plane —식전투기 a jet fighter

분산 分散 (a) breakup; scattering; dispersion; decentralization
♦ 빛의 분산 dispersion of light / 인구 분산책 the population decentralization policies / 공해의 분산을 방지하다 prevent the dispersion of pollution
—**분산하다** break up; scatter; disperse

▶그들은 분산하여 목적지로 향했다 They dispersed and headed for their destination.
▶프리즘은 빛을 분산시킨다 A prism breaks up [disperse] light.
▶대도시의 공장을 지방으로 분산시키는 것이 시급한 일이었다 It was an urgent need to decentralize factories in cities into the country.
■ー계 〔化〕 a dispersion system ―도 degree of dispersion ―매 〔化〕 dispersion media ―상 〔化〕 dispersed phase ―성 dispersibility ―율 the index of dispersion ―질 〔生〕 dispersoid

분서 焚書 book burning ―분서하다 burn books ―갱유(坑儒) 〔史〕 burning books on the Chinese classics and burying Confucian scholars alive

분석 分析 analysis; 〈광석의〉 assay; assaying
▶분석 결과 물에 철분이 많은 것으로 밝혀졌다 Analysis showed that the water was strongly impregnated with iron.
―분석하다 analyze; make an analysis; reduce 〈it〉 to its elements; resolve; assay 〈a drug, an alloy〉
♦광석의 견본을 분석하다 assay an ore sample / 논문의 내용을 분석하다 analyze the contents of the thesis / 행위의 동기를 분석하다 analyze the motives of *sb's* conduct
▶그들은 이 샘의 물을 분석했다 They analyzed the water of this well.
■정량[정성(定性)]― quantitative [qualitative] analysis 정신― psychoanalysis ■―자 an analyst; an assayer ―적 사고 analytic thinking ―표 an analysis table ―학 analytics ―학자 an analyst ―화학 analytical chemistry

분설 分設 establishment of a branch
―분설하다 establish [set up] a branch

분손 分損 〔海保〕 partial loss

분쇄 粉碎 pulverization; 〔土〕 grinding
―분쇄하다 〈부스러뜨리다〉 reduce to powder; pulverize; shatter [smash] to pieces; break into fragments [atoms]; pulverize; 〈쳐부수다〉 defeat; beat
♦적군을 분쇄하다 crush [annihilate] the enemy / 적의 기도를 분쇄하다 frustrate an opponent's plan / 음모를 분쇄하다 crush [smash] a plot / 아무의 주장을 분쇄하다 tear *sb's* argument to pieces
■―기 a pulverizer; a grinder; a crusher; a muller; a mill

분수 分水 the diversion [shedding] of water
■―계[선] ⇨ 분수령 ―로 a flood-control [a diversion] channel ―산맥 ⇨ 분수령 ―장치 a diversion device ―전(栓) 〈수도의〉 a corporation cock [stop]

분수[1] 分數 1 〈분별심〉 discretion; propriety; good sense; discrimination
♦분수 있는 사람 a prudent man; a man of discretion [good sense] / 분수 없는 imprudent; undiscerning; indiscreet
▶그는 분수 없이 말을 한다 He does not know when to shut up.
▶농담도 분수가 있지 You carry your joke too far.
2 〈분한(分限)〉 one's place [status]; one's social standing [station]
♦분수를 모르다 fail to know *oneself* [*one's* place]; be self-conceited / 분수는 알다 know *one's* place [station in life] / 분수를 잊다 forget *oneself*; get above *oneself* / 분수에 넘치는 짓을 하다 do *sth* out of *one's* line [element] / 분수에 맞게 기부하다 give *one's* bit / 분수를 지키다 keep *one's* place; keep within *one's* bounds [own province] / 분수에 맞게[맞지 않게] 살다 live within [above] *one's* means
▶그는 자기 분수를 모르고 있다 He does not know his place.
▶그에게 제 분수를 알게 해주겠다 I will put him in his place.

분수[2] 分數 〔數〕 a fraction; a fractional number ♦분수의 fractional; fractionary
■ 가[진]― an improper [a proper] fraction 기약― an irreducible fraction; a fraction reduced to its lowest terms 대(帶)― a mixed fraction 번[복]― a compound [complex] fraction 부분― partial fractions ■―방정식 a fractional equation ―식 a fractional expression

분수 噴水 〈설비〉 a fountain; 〈물〉 a jet of water ▶분수가 물을 뿜고 있는 것이 보인다 The fountain can be seen playing.
■―(孔) a jet; a spout ―기(器) a water-spout ―식 음료기 a drinking fountain

분수령 分水嶺 a dividing ridge; (美) a divide; (英) a watershed ▶이 산맥은 분수령의 역할을 하고 있다 This mountain range plays the part of a divide [watershed].

분승하다 分乘― ride separately
▶우리는 다섯 대의 버스에 분승해서 출발했다 We started [set out] in five buses.

분식 粉食 powdered [pulverized] food; flour-based meals ♦분식을 장려하다 encourage the use of flour for food ―분식하다 eat flour [ground grain]

분식 粉飾 〈겉만 꾸밈〉 embellishment; adornment; decoration; gilding ―분식하다 adorn; decorate; embellish ■―예금 a sham deposit

분신 分身 〈제2의 나〉 the other self; *one's* alter ego; 〔佛教〕 an incarnation of the Buddha
▶이 소설의 여주인공은 작가의 분신인 것 같다 The heroine of this novel seems to be the other self of the writer.
▶그는 그 소년에게서 자신의 분신을 발견했다 He found his alter ego in the boy.

분신 焚身 burning *oneself* to death; self-burning; suicide [self-immolation] by fire
♦분신을 기도하다 make an attempt to burn *oneself* to death
―분신하다 burn *oneself* to death; commit suicide [self-immolation] by fire
■―자살 suicide by burning *oneself*

분실 分室 a branch [detached] office
분실 紛失 loss ♦분실 신고를 하다 report the loss of an article 〈to〉 ―분실하다 lose ♦분실한 편지 a missing letter
▶가방을 분실한 사람이 나타났다 The man who lost the briefcase has shown up.
▶도장을 분실하여 은행에 신고했다 I reported

분야

the loss of my seal to the bank.
▶ 그 편지는 분실된게 틀림없다 The letter must have got lost.
■ ―물 a lost [missing] article; lost property ―물 취급소 the Lost and Found ―자 the owner of a lost article

분야 分野 a sphere; a field; a realm; a branch; a division; a department
♦ 산업의 각 분야 various fields of industry / 학문의 한 분야 a branch of learning / 새로운 분야를 개척하다 open up a new field / 다른 분야로 진출하다 move in another sphere
▶ 많은 과학자들이 같은 분야를 연구하고 있다 Many scientists are working in the same field.
▶ 그들의 과학적 연구는 폭넓은 분야에 걸쳐 있다 Their scientific investigations cover a wide territory [field].
▶ 나는 분야가 다르다 I work in a different field [line].
▶ 그는 음악 분야에서는 중요한 존재다 He is very important in the field of music.
■ 연구― a field [an area] of study 전공― a major field of study; one's specialty

분양 分讓 sale (of land) in lots [parcels]; lotting-out; parceling-out ▶ 그 땅은 지금 분양 중이다 The land is being sold in lots.
―분양하다 sell (land) in lots [parcels]; lot out; parcel out
■ ―아파트 a lot-sold apartment; (美) a condominium ―주택 a house on its own lot; a house in a development project ―지 land for sale by the lot; plots of land for sale

분업 分業 division of labor [work]
―분업하다 divide work 《among》
▶ 그들은 그 일을 분업했다 They divided the work among themselves.
■ 국제― international division of labor 의약 (醫藥)― separation of dispensary from medical practice

분연히 忿然― indignantly; in indignation; in anger; in a rage; in a fit of passion
♦ 분연히 일어서다 spring up [get to one's feet] in a rage
▶ 그는 분연히 자리를 떴다 He went away [walked off] in indignation [in a rage].
▶ 대표단은 자리를 차고 분연히 방에서 나왔다 The delegates walked out of the room in indignation.

분연히 奮然― resolutely; courageously; boldly; plucking up one's spirits [heart]
♦ 분연히 난국에 맞서다 rise to a crisis; take the bull by the horns
▶ 중과부적이었지만 우리는 분연히 적에 대항했다 Although greatly outnumbered, we courageously [boldly] faced the enemy.

분열 分列 filing off ♦ 분열 행진하다 march in file ―분열하다 file off

분열 分裂 〈갈라짐〉 division; disunion; 〈나라의〉 disruption; a split; breakup; 〈세포의〉 disorganization; 〈종파의〉 schism
♦ 급진파와 보수파의 분열 a schism between radicals and conservatives / 사상적 분열 an ideological division / 의식[인격]의 분열 dissociation of consciousness [personality]
▶ 그 사건으로 인해 당내 분열이 일어났다 The affair brought about a split in the party.
―분열하다 be disrupted [divided, disunited]; break up; split ♦ 분열시키다 break up; disturb
▶ 그 문제를 둘러싸고 평의회는 여러 파로 분열했다 The council split [divided] into several factions over the question.
▶ 그 문제가 여당을 분열시킬 것이다 The issue will split the ruling party.
■ 감수― 〔生〕 meiosis; reduction division 다수― 〔生〕 multiple division 세포― cell division 원자핵― nuclear [atomic] fission ■ ―생식 reproduction by fission [through division]; schizogenesis ―식물 a schizophyte ―조직 〔植〕 meristematic tissue; meristem ―편(片) a segment

분열식 分列式 a march-past 《pl. march-pasts》; 〈항공기의〉 a flypast; an air review
♦ 분열식을 하다 march past 《the Presidential stand》; have a march-past; 〈비행기가〉 fly past

분외 分外 ♦ 분외의 undeserved; beyond one's lot [status]; unmerited; undue; inordinate
▶ 분외의 바람 같은 것은 없습니다 I have no inordinate desires.
▶ 분외의 영광인 줄 압니다 I am afraid I do not deserve this great honor. ⇌ It is an honor I hardly deserve.

분원 分院 a branch (of a hospital [an institute])

분위기 雰圍氣 an atmosphere; an ambience
♦ 긴장된 분위기 a tense atmosphere / 딱딱한 [어색한] 분위기 an uncomfortable atmosphere / 자유로운 분위기 an atmosphere of freedom / 분위기를 잘 살린 소설 a novel rich in atmosphere / 분위기를 망치다 destroy [mar] the atmosphere / 문학적인 분위기를 자아내다 produce [create] a literary atmosphere
▶ 그는 종교적인 분위기 속에서 자랐다 He was born and bred in a religious atmosphere.
▶ 저 레스토랑의 가정적인 분위기가 마음에 든다 I like the family atmosphere in that restaurant.
▶ 그녀는 자유롭고 개방된 분위기 속에서 소녀 시절을 보냈다 She spent her girlhood in a free and open atmosphere.
▶ 나는 이 호텔의 분위기가 마음에 들지 않는다 The atmosphere of this hotel is not to my liking.
▶ 회의장에는 긴장된 분위기가 감돌았다 The atmosphere of the conference was very tense.

분유 粉乳 powdered milk; dry [dried] milk

분자 分子 1 〈구성원〉 an element; a faction
♦ 당내의 부패 분자를 일소하다 clear the party of its corrupt elements
2 〔數〕 a numerator; 〔化〕 a molecule
■ ―그램 ―〔化〕 a gram molecule; a mole 반동― reactionary elements 불온― a disturbing element 불평― malcontent [discontented] elements ■ ―구조 molecular structure ―량 molecular weight ―력 molecular force ―생물학 molecular biology ―선[살] a molecular

beam; molecular rays —설 the molecular theory —식 a molecular formula 《pl. ~s, -lae》 —인력 molecular attraction

분잡 紛雜 confusion; crowdedness
—**분잡하다** confused; crowded; bustling

분장 分掌 〈나눠 맡음〉 division of duties
—**분장하다** divide [allot] 《office duties》; take partial charge 《of business》

분장 扮裝 〈배우 등의〉 (a) makeup; impersonation; 〈변장〉 disguise —**분장하다** make up; put on a makeup; impersonate 《Hamlet》; 〈변장하다〉 disguise *oneself* 《as》
◆ 분장한 채로 in stage costume [makeup]/ 여자로 분장하다 disguise *oneself* as a woman / 왕자로 분장하다 dress (up) as a prince
■ —실 a dressing room; the backstage —자 an impersonator

분재 盆栽 growing 《a plant》 in a pot ◆ 분재 소나무 a dwarf(ed) pine tree —**분재하다** plant [grow] 《a tree》 in a pot; pot (up) 《a plant》 ■ —식 a potted plant

분쟁 紛爭 a trouble; a dispute; a strife
◆ 분쟁의 씨 the apple of dispute [discord]/ 분쟁의 초점 the focus of (a) trouble / 분쟁의 평화적인 해결 peaceful settlement of the dispute / 분쟁 중이다 be in conflict [a dispute] 《with》/ 분쟁을 일으키다 raise a trouble [dust] / 분쟁을 중재하다 mediate a dispute
▶ 중동에서는 분쟁이 끊이지 않는다 There is no end of troubles in the Middle East.
—**분쟁하다** have [get into] trouble 《with》; have a dispute 《with》
■ 국제— an international dispute: 국제 분쟁을 야기하다 lead to an international trouble 노사(勞使)— conflicts between labor and management 학원— a campus dispute [strife] ■ —조정 grievance mediation [settlement] —처리 기관 grievance machinery

분전 奮戰 a plucky [desperate] fight; (a) hard fighting
—**분전하다** fight hard [desperately, furiously] 《끝까지 분전하다 fight to the finish [to the bitter end]; fight it out / 끝까지 분전하다가 죽다 die in the last ditch
▶ 한국 팀은 분전한 결과 그 시합에서 승리했다 The Korean team won the hard-fought game.

분점 分店 a branch store [shop]; a branch firm [office] ◆ 신촌 분점 the Shinch'on branch 《of a store》 / 마포에 분점을 차리다 open a branch shop at Map'o

분점 分點 〔天〕 equinoctial points; equinoxes
■ 평균[진(眞)]— the mean [true] equinox
■ —월 a tropical month

분젠등 —燈 a Bunsen burner

분주하다 奔走— busy
◆ 분주한 생활 a busy [stirring, bustling] life / 분주한 일정 *one's* tight [heavy] schedule / 분주한 하루를 보내다 pass a busy day / 분주하게 쏘다니다 bustle about; be on the run
▶ 대도시의 생활은 분주하다 In a large city, life moves with a rush.
▶ 이제는 도회의 분주한 생활에 익숙해졌다 I am now accustomed to a busy life in the city.

▶ 금년도 분주하게 지나갔다 This year passed all too quickly.

분지 盆地 〔地〕 a basin; a (round) valley
▶ 이 산간 분지는 피서지로 조성하고 있다 This basin among the mountains forms a summer resort.
▶ 하천 분지에는 대개 농지가 비옥하다 The basin of a river usually has rich farmland.
▶ 이 일대는 분지로 되어 있다 This district forms a basin.

-분지 -分之 a part; a fraction ⇨ -분 1

분책 分冊 a separate volume; a fascicle
▶ 그 소설은 분책으로 출판되었다 The novel was published in separate volumes.
▶ 이 백과사전은 분책으로 팝니까? Do you sell volumes of this encyclopedia separately [singly]?

분첩 粉貼 〈화장용〉 a (powder) puff; 〈습자용〉 a writing slate

분초 分秒 a minute and a second; 〈짧은 시간〉 a moment; an instant ▶ 이것은 분초를 다루는 일이다 It's a matter of great urgency. ⇌ It admits of no delay. ⇌ It's urgent.

분출 噴出 spouting; (a) gush; a violent outflow —**분출하다** 〈액체를〉 spout; gush out; spurt; 〈가스 등을〉 belch up; shoot up
▶ 이 바위 밑에서 찬 물이 분출한다 Cold water spouts [gushes out] from under this rock.
▶ 화산은 용암을 분출한다 Volcanoes vomit lava.
▶ 플라스틱 건축 자재는 화재시에 유독 가스를 분출한다 Plastic building material shoots up poisonous gas when it catches fire.
▶ 그의 상처에서 피가 분출했다 Blood spurted out of his wound.
■ —구 a jet; an exhaust nozzle —물 jet; ejecta; eruptions —암 an eruptive rock

분침 分針 the minute [long] hand

분탄 粉炭 slack; dust [fine, slack] coal; coal dust; powdered coal

분통 憤痛 resentment; vexation; fury; indignation ◆ 분통(이) 터지다 be greatly vexed 《at》; get furious 《at》 / 분통을 터뜨리다 blow *one's* top; give vent to *one's* anger
▶ 그 생각을 하면 분통이 터진다 The thought of it makes my blood boil.

분투 奮鬪 a struggle; hard fighting; a strenuous effort
▶ 그의 성공은 그의 분투 노력에 힘입은 것이다 He owes his success to his strenuous efforts.
—**분투하다** fight; struggle [strive] 《for》; make strenuous efforts; exert *oneself*
◆ 선전 분투하다 put up a good fight / 분투하여 성공하다 fight *one's* way to success
▶ 우리는 자유를 위해 최후까지 분투할 결심이다 We are resolved to fight for liberty to the last.
■ —정신 a fighting spirit; gameness; pluck

분파 分派 a branch; an offshoot; 〈종교의〉 a sect; 〈당내의〉 a faction ◆ 새 분파를 이루다 form a new sect ■ —주의 factionalism —활동 factional activities

분패 憤敗 a regrettable defeat ⇨ 석패

분포 分布 distribution ◆ 동식물의 지리적 분포

분풀이

the geographical distribution of plants and animals / 분포가 넓은 widely distributed; of wide distribution
—분포하다 be distributed; range 《from one place to another》
▶이 식물은 캐나다에서 멕시코에 걸쳐 분포하고 있다 This plant ranges from Canada to Mexico.
▶이 종의 꽃은 제주도 전체에 널리 분포하고 있다 This species of flower is widely distributed [has a wide distribution] throughout Chejudo.
■수직[수평]— vertical [horizontal] distribution 인구— the spread of population
■—도 a distribution chart [map]

분풀이 憤— revenge; retaliation; (a) reprisal
♦분풀이로 by way of revenge; in retaliation 《for》; out of spite
▶그래서 분풀이가 된다면 나를 실컷 때려라 Beat me as much as you like, if it makes you feel better.
▶그것으로 다소 분풀이가 됐다 That is some consolation to me.
—분풀이하다 give vent to *one's* indignation; vent *one's* anger [spite] 《on》; revenge *oneself*; retaliate
▶그는 우리한테 분풀이했다 He worked off his anger on us.

분필 粉筆 chalk ♦분필 한 자루 a piece of chalk / 분필로 쓰다 write with [in] chalk; chalk (down) ■—색 colored chalk

분하다 扮— 〈분장하다〉 dress (up) 《as》; 〈배우가 《…의 역으로》〉 impersonate 《a character》 ⇨ 분장(~하다)

분하다 憤— 1〈원통하다〉 vexatious; vexing; mortifying
♦분한 나머지 눈물을 흘리다 shed tears in *one's* mortification [chagrin] / 분해서 이를 갈다 grind [gnash] *one's* teeth with resentment / 분하게 여기다[분해 하다] be [feel] mortified [chagrined, vexed] 《at, on》
▶아아 분하다 How vexatious [disappointing]!
▶그는 실패한 것을 분해 했다 He was vexed at his failure.
▶그는 옛 친구의 냉대를 분하게 여겼다 He felt mortified at his former friend's neglect.
▶그는 분해서 미칠 지경이었다 He nearly went mad with vexation.
▶분하게도 그는 그 경주에서 꼴찌를 했다 Much to his chagrin, he came last in the race.
2〈아깝다〉 regrettable; regretful; sorry; distressed
▶그 기회를 놓친 것이 분하다 It is a pity that I failed to grasp that opportunity.
▶나는 입시에 떨어진 것이 분했다 I was distressed at failing the entrance examination.
▶다 이겼던 시합을 분하게 놓쳤다 I lost the game I had nearly won.

분한 分限 1〈분수〉 *one's* social status [standing] 2〈실용 한도〉 utility; usefulness; 〈경제적 가치〉 economical [good] use
♦분한이 있다 be economical/ 분한이 없다 be uneconomical; be wasteful ▶분한있게 돈을 써라 Put your money to good use.

분할 分割 division; partition ♦토지[국토]의 분할 the partition of land [a country]
—분할하다 divide (up); partition; cut up
♦분할할 수 없는 indivisible; impartible / 땅을 분할하여 팔다 sell *one's* land in lots
▶좁은 길이 그 목초지를 분할하고 있다 A narrow path divides the pasture.
▶독일은 한때 동과 서로 분할되어 있었다 Germany was once divided into East and West.
■—법 〔論〕 partition —상속(제) divided succession; division of succession —소유권 divided [mixed] ownership —인도 installment delivery —주문 split order —지배(책) divide and rule

분할불 分割拂 payment in [by] installments; an installment plan [system]; (美) an easy payment plan ♦분할불로 팔다[사다] sell [buy] on the installment [easy payment] plan

분해 分解 1〈해체〉 dismantling; disassembly; disintegration —분해하다 dismantle; disassemble; disintegrate; break down; take (a machine) apart [to pieces]
♦라디오[시계]를 분해하다 dismantle [disassemble] a radio [watch]/ 엔진을 분해하다 take the engine apart [to pieces]
▶비행기가 공중 분해했다 The airplane disintegrated [broke into pieces] in midair.
2〔化〕 analysis; 〈성분・요소로〉 decomposition; resolution; dissolution
—분해하다 analyze; decompose; resolve (into); dissolve (into)
♦분해할 수 있는 resolvable; decomposable / 분해할 수 없는 irresoluble; irresolvable; indecomposable / 속력을 그 구성 요소로 분해하다 resolve a velocity into its components / 화합물을 원소로 분해하다 reduce [dissolve, resolve] a chemical compound into its constituent elements
▶프리즘은 햇빛을 여러 가지 색깔로 분해한다 A prism decomposes sunlight into its various colors.
▶물을 화학적으로 분해하면 산소와 수소가 된다 Water can be chemically resolved into oxygen and hydrogen.
▶이 물질은 더 이상 분해되지 않는다 This matter can't be analyzed any further.
▶단백질은 아미노산으로 분해된다 Proteins are broken down into amino acids.
■—가스 cracking gas —검사 an overhaul: 자동차 엔진을 분해 검사하지 않으면 안되겠다 I must have the car's engine overhauled. —능(能)〔物〕 resolving power —도〔建〕 a deal drawing —사진〔TV〕 a photographic playback —성 resolvability —수리 a thorough overhaul: 분해 수리를 하다 overhaul (an engine) thoroughly —작용 disintegration —점〔化〕 decomposition point

분향 焚香 incense burning ♦합동 분향소 a joint (memorial) altar —분향하다 burn [offer] incense

분홍색 粉紅色 pink

분화 分化
differentiation; 〈특수화〉 specialization —**분화하다** differentiate; specialize ♦ 분화되지 않은 unspecialized; undifferentiated
▶ 이 (신체) 기관은 적으로부터 몸을 지키기 위해 분화했다 This organ became specialized for defense against enemies.

분화 噴火
an eruption (of fire); volcanic activity ♦ 화산의 분화 a volcanic eruption
▶ 그 산은 지금도 분화 중이다 The mountain is still active.
▶ 그들은 무모하게도 분화 중인 화산에 오르려 하고 있다 They are reckless enough to plan to climb a volcano that is in eruption.
—**분화하다** erupt; become active; burst into eruption; emit [belch] fire
♦ 맹렬히 분화하다 go into violent eruption / 분화하고 있다 be in eruption [activity]
■ —구 a crater —산 an erupting volcano

분회 分會
a branch; a (local) chapter

붇다
1 〈물에〉 become soaked [bloated]; grow [become] sodden; swell ♦ 물에 붙은 손 a hand sodden [swollen] with water
▶ 국수가 통통 붙었다 The noodles have gone soft.
▶ 밤새 물에 담가두었더니 콩이 붙었다 Soaked in water overnight, the beans swelled up.
▶ 젖이 통통 붙었다 The breasts swelled.
2 〈많아지다〉 increase; swell; rise; grow
♦ 물이 붙은 강 a swollen river
▶ 식구가 자꾸 붙고 있다 The family grows larger.
▶ 눈이 녹아 강물이 붙었다 The river was swollen with melted snow.

불
1 〈일반적인〉 fire; 〈화염〉 flame; blaze; 〈난로 등의〉 a fire ♦ 불같은 burning; blazing / 불바다가 되다 become a sheet of fire / 불 장난을 하다 play with fire
〈불이〉 불이 붙다 be ignited; catch (on) [take] fire
▶ 휘발유는 불이 붙기 쉽다 Gasoline is highly inflammable.
▶ 이 나무는 젖어서 불이 잘 붙지 않는다 This wood is so wet (that) it is not quick to catch fire.
〈불을〉 불을 붙이다 burn; set 《a piece of paper》 alight; ignite; light [kindle] a fire / 담배에 불을 붙이다 light (up) a cigarette / 불을 끄다 put out the fire /〈부채의〉 불을 부치다 fan the fire / 불을 지피다 put fuel on fire; feed a fire 《with wood》/ 불(기운)을 줄이다 turn the fire low; 〈가스 등의〉 lower the flame / 불을 피우다 make a fire
▶ 대부분의 동물은 불을 두려워한다 Most animals dread [are afraid of] fire.
▶ 그는 불을 발로 밟아 껐다 He stamped out the fire.
▶ 이리 와서 불을 쬐시오 Come over here and warm yourself by [at] the fire.
▶ 불 좀 빌려 주십시오 Please give me a light. ⇌ May I have a light, please?
▶ 그는 시가를 꺼내 불을 붙였다 He took out a cigar and lighted it up.
〈불에〉 냄비를 불에 얹다 put a pan over a fire / 불에 타다 burn; be burnt; be destroyed [consumed] by fire / 불에 태우다 burn; put [throw] sth into a fire; commit to the flames
▶ 종이는 불에 잘 탄다 Paper catches [takes] fire easily.
2 〈화재〉 a fire
♦ 원인 불명의 불 a fire of unknown origin / 큰 불 a big [large] fire / 불이 (옮겨) 붙다 catch (on) [take] fire; the fire catches / 불을 내다 cause [start] a fire / 불을 끄다 put out [extinguish] a fire; get a fire under control / 집에 불을 지르다 set fire to a house; set a house afire [on fire]
▶ 불조심해라 Be careful with fire!
▶ 불이야 Fire!
▶ 불의 원인은 난방기기의 과열이었다 Overheating of the heater was the cause of fire.
▶ 불은 부엌에서 났다 The fire started [broke out] in the kitchen.
▶ 집이 불타고 있었다 The house was afire.
▶ 불이 이집 저집 급속히 번져 갔다 The fire spread [ran] rapidly from house to house.
3 〈등불〉 a light; a lamp
♦ 전깃불 electric light / 불을 켜다 light a lamp [light]; light up 《a room》;〈전등의〉 turn on the light / 불을 끄다 put out the light [lamp]; 〈전등의〉 turn [switch] off the light / 불을 켜놓은 채 잠들다 fall into sleep with the light on
▶ 불이 너무 어둡다 The light is too dim.
▶ 불이 켜져 있는 것을 보니 그가 돌아와 있나 보다 His lights are on, so I suppose he's back.
▶ 실험실은 불이 밝게 켜져 있었다 The laboratory was brightly lit up.
▶ 불이 나갔다 The light is out.
▶ 불이 하나씩 꺼졌다 The light went out one by one.
4 (비유) burning passion; flame; fire
♦ 정열의 불 flame [fire] of passion / 불같은 연정 passionate love
▶ 그는 그 소식을 듣고 불같이 화가 나 있다 He is burning with anger at the news.
▶ 기둥에 부딪치자 눈에서 불이 번쩍였다 I saw stars when I ran into the pillar.

불 佛
〈프랑스〉 France ♦ 한불 Korea and France; Franco-Korean / 불한 사전 a French-Korean dictionary

불 弗
a dollar; (美俗) a buck ♦ 20불 twenty dollars / 10불짜리 지폐 a ten-dollar bill

불- 不-
not; non-; un-; in-; dis- ♦ 불공평 unfairness / 불신임 nonconfidence

불가 不可
wrongness; badness; impropriety; 〈투표의〉 a nay ♦ 가도 아니고 불가도 아니다 be neither good nor bad
▶ 가가 5명이고 불가가 3명이었다 The ayes [yeas] were five against three nays [noes].⇌ Five were in favor of it, while three were against it.
—**불가하다** wrong; bad; improper
▶ 그는 내 계획을 불가하다고 했다 He disapproved my plan.
■ —**가** right or wrong; good or bad

불가 佛家
〈불교신자〉 a Buddhist; 〈불문〉 Buddhism;〈절〉 a Buddhist temple

불가결 不可缺
indispensability; essential

불가능

―**불가결하다** indispensable; essential; vital
▶물은 인간 생활에 불가결하다 Water is indispensable [essential] for [to] human life.
▶이 계획의 성공에는 당신의 조력이 불가결합니다 Your assistance is vital to the success of this project.

불가능 不可能 impossibility ◆불가능을 가능하게 하다 turn an impossibility into a possibility; make the impossibe possible
▶그것은 불가능에 가깝다 It's almost [(口) next to] impossible.
―**불가능하다** impossible; unattainable; impracticable
◆실현 불가능한 계획 an impracticable plan / 불가능한 일을 꾀하다 try the impossible
▶이 단어는 번역이 불가능하다 This word is impossible to translate. ⇌ It is impossible to [We can't] translate this word. ⇌ This word can't be translated.
▶나폴레옹은 자신에게 불가능한 것은 없다고 했다 Napoleon said that nothing was impossible for him.

불가래 a wooden fire shovel

불가리아 〈나라 이름〉 Bulgaria; 〈공식명〉 the Republic of Bulgaria ◆불가리아의 Bulgarian ―**사람** a Bulgarian; a Bulgar

불가물 〈심한 가물〉 a severe [serious] drought; a long drought

불가분 不可分 indivisibility; inseparability
◆불가분의 indivisible; undetachable; inseparable
▶자애와 명예심은 불가분이다 Self-love is inseparable from the desire for fame.
▶그 두 문제는 불가분의 관계에 있다 The two issues are inseparable [can't be separated] (from each other).

불가불 不可不 〈도리없이〉 inevitably; unavoidably; by force of circumstances
▶불가불 그 일을 해야 한다 There is nothing for it [We have no choice, There is no other way] but to do that.
▶그 일은 불가불 오늘 안으로 마쳐야 한다 I must finish it today by all means [no matter what].

불가사리 [動] a starfish; an asteroid

불가사의 不可思議 a mystery; a wonder; 〈기적〉 a miracle; 〈수수께끼〉 a riddle
◆세계의 7대 불가사의 the Seven Wonders of the World / 불가사의 중의 불가사의 the mystery of mysteries; the wonder of wonders / 우주의 불가사의를 해명하다 solve the mysteries of the universe
―**불가사의하다** 〈불가해하다〉 incomprehensible; mysterious; 〈이상하다〉 wonderful; miraculous; marvelous
▶이 우주에는 불가사의한 일이 많다 The universe is full of wonders.

불가시 不可視 invisibility ■―**광선** an invisible ray

불가지 不可知 〈알 수 없음〉 unknowableness; inconceivability ―**불가지하다** unknowable; inconceivable; mysterious
■―**론** [哲] agnosticism; nescience; knownothingism ―**론자** an agnostic; a nescient ―**물** the Unknowable

불가측 不可測 unpredictability

불가침 不可侵 inviolability; nonaggression
◆불가침의 inviolable; 〈신성한〉 sacred
■―**권** an inviolable right: 영토 불가침권 the inviolability of territory ―**조약** a nonaggression pact [treaty]: 그 두 나라는 불가침 조약을 맺었다 The two countries concluded nonaggression treaty.

불가피하다 不可避― unescapable; unavoidable; inevitable ◆불가피한 사정으로 owing to [through] unavoidable circumstances; under unavoidable situations / 불가피하게 unavoidably; inevitably
▶전쟁은 불가피한 것으로 생각되었다 War seemed inevitable [unavoidable]. ⇌ It seemed impossible to avoid war.
▶이혼은 불가피했다 It was an unavoidable divorce.

불가항력 不可抗力 inevitability; an irresistible force; (프) force majeure
◆불가항력의 사고 an inevitable accident; an accident beyond (human) control / 불가항력의 uncontrollable; beyond control
▶천재는 불가항력이다 Natural disasters are beyond human control.
▶그 참사는 불가항력이었다고 한다 The disaster is said to have been inevitable [unavoidable].

불가해하다 不可解― mysterious; incomprehensible; inscrutable
◆불가해한 인물 a mystery man; a sphinx; an enigma
▶네 행동은 내겐 불가해하다 I cannot understand your behavior [why you did such a thing].
▶인생은 불가해하다 Life is a mystery.
▶그의 자살은 불가해한 면이 있다 There's something incomprehensible about his suicide.

불간섭 不干涉 nonintervention; noninterference ■―**정책** a nonintervention policy; a laissez-faire [hands-off] policy

불감증 不感症 [醫] frigidity
◆불감증인 여자 a frigid woman / 불감증이 되다 grow insensible (to)
▶그는 그런 비평에는 불감증이 되어 있다 He is immune to such criticism.
▶주민들 중에는 공해에 불감증이 된 사람들도 있다 Some of the inhabitants are indifferent to pollution.

불감청 不敢請 ▶불감청이언정 고소원(固所願)이라 That is just what I wanted. ⇌ Nothing would make me happier than that.

불개미 [昆] a red ant

불개입 不介入 noninvolvement; nonintervention ◆불개입주의를 견지하다 maintain a policy of nonintervention ■―**방침[정책]** a noninvolvement [nonintervention] policy

불거지다 〈튀어 나오다〉 protrude; project; jut out; 〈부어오르다〉 bulge [swell] out
◆툭 불거진 개구리 눈알 the protruding [protuberant] eyeballs of a frog

불걱거리다 1 〈계속 씹다〉 chew away **2** 〈주물

불건전 不健全 unsoundness ―**불건전하다** unsound; unwholesome; 〈병적이다〉 morbid; sick
◆ 불건전한 놀이 an unwholesome game / 불건전한 생각 unhealthy [unwholesome] ideas / 불건전한 오락 unhealthy amusements
▶ 그의 정신은 불건전하다 He has an unsound mind. ⇒ He is unsound of mind.

불겅거리다 be chewy ⇨ 물겅거리다

불결 不潔 uncleanliness; dirtiness; filthiness
▶ 불결은 질병의 원인이다 Dirt breeds disease.
―**불결하다** unclean; dirty; nasty; foul; filthy
◆ 불결한 거리 a dirty [squalid] street / 불결한 물 foul [impure] water / 불결한 음식 bad [tainted] food
▶ 불결한 손으로 먹지 마라 Don't eat with dirty [unclean] hands.
▶ 그녀는 부엌을 절대로 불결하게 내버려두지 않는다 She never keeps the kitchen in an unsanitary condition.

불경 不敬 disrespect; want of respect; irreverence; impiety; blasphemy ―**불경하다** disrespectful; impious; blasphemous ◆ 불경한 말을 하다 blaspheme (against); swear
■ ―사건 a lèse-majesté affair ―죄 lese majesty; (프) lèse-majesté ―행위 an act of insulting and disrespectful nature

불경 佛經 the Buddhist script; the sutras
◆ 불경을 외다 chant [recite, read] a sutra; intone the service

불경기 不景氣 bad [hard] times; depression; dull market [trade]; recession; 〈침체〉 dullness; a slump
◆ 불경기의 dull; inactive; depressed; stagnant / 불경기가 되다 grow dull [flat]; slacken; 〈가게 등이 주어〉 fall on hard times / 불경기를 모르다 be always prosperous
▶ 지금은 불경기다 Times are bad [hard]. ⇒ We are having a hard time.
▶ 이번 불경기는 매우 심각하다 The current business slump is very serious.
▶ 최근 콜레라 발병으로 어시장이 불경기다 Owing to the recent outbreak of cholera, the fish market is inactive [quiet].
▶ 그 가게는 불경기 때문에 문을 닫았다 The store was closed due to hard times.

불경제 不經濟 being uneconomical; bad [poor] economy; 〈낭비〉 waste
▶ 싸구려 물건을 사는 것이 불경제일 수 있다 It can be uneconomical [poor economy] to buy cheap goods.
▶ 그런 일을 하는 것은 시간의 불경제다 It is (a) waste of time to do such a thing.

불계 不計 〔바둑〕 ◆ 불계로 이기다[지다] win [lose] (a game) by a wide margin
■ ―승 a victory by a wide margin; a one-sided game

불고 不顧 disregard; negligence; indifference ―**불고하다** disregard; ignore; neglect; pay no attention
◆ 체면을 불고하다 have no regard to one's honor; do not care about appearances / 염치 불고하고 …하다 bear shame to 《do》; stoop to 《do》
▶ 염치 불고하고 나는 그에게 돈을 달라고 했다 I swallowed my pride and asked him for money.

불고기 *pulgogi*; roast beef; grilled [broiled] meat

불곰 〔動〕 a brown bear; an American black bear

불공 不恭 disrespect; imprudence; irreverence
―**불공하다** disrespectful; imprudent; irreverent

불공 佛供 a Buddhist prayer [mass, service]
◆ 불공 드리다 offer [hold] a Buddhist prayer [service]

불공대천 不共戴天 ◆ 불공대천의 원수 an irreconcilable [a mortal, a sworn] enemy
▶ 두 사람은 불공대천의 사이다 There is a deadly feud between them. ⇒ The two can't live together under the canopy of heaven.

불공정 不公正 unfairness; injustice; inequity
―**불공정하다** unfair; inequitable; partial
◆ 불공정한 거래 unfair trade [transactions, dealing] / 불공정한 경쟁 unfair competition

불공평 不公平 partiality; inequity; injustice
―**불공평하다** partial; inequitable; biased; discriminating
◆ 불공평한 처사 unfair treatment [dealing] / 불공평하게 다루다 treat *sb* unfairly; discriminate against *sb*
▶ 그는 나에게 불공평하다 He is unfair to me. ⇒ He treats me unfairly.
▶ 지금의 불공평한 세제를 개정하는 것이 급선무다 The present unfair tax system should be revised first.
▶ 법은 누구에게나 불공평해서는 안된다 Laws must not be discriminatory [unfair to anyone].

불과 不過 only; just; merely; no more than
◆ 불과 5백원 only [no more than] five hundred won; a petty [paltry] sum of five hundred won
▶ 학교까지는 걸어서 불과 10분이다 It is only ten minutes' walk from here to our school.
―**불과하다** be nothing but; be no more than
▶ 이것은 흔해빠진 물건에 불과하다 This is nothing but a common article.
▶ 나는 일개 은행원에 불과하다 I'm no more [better] than a bank clerk.
▶ 그것은 핑계[구실]에 불과하다 It is a mere excuse. ⇒ That is an excuse, and nothing more.
▶ 이것은 한 예에 불과하다 This is only one example [instance] out of many.
▶ 청중은 50명에 불과했다 The audience consisted of only fifty people. ⇒ There were no more than fifty people in the audience.

불교 佛敎 Buddhism ◆ 불교의 Buddhist; Buddhistic / 불교를 믿다 believe in Buddhism
■ ―건축[문학, 미술, 음악] Buddhist architecture [literature, art, music] ―도[신자] a Buddhist; a believer in Buddhism ―문화 Buddhist culture [civilization]

불구 不具 1 〈신체의〉 deformity; malformation; disablement ◆ 불구의 (physically) handicapped; deformed; disabled; crippled; lame / 불구로 태어나다 be born deformed

▶ 그는 전쟁으로 불구가 되었다 He was crippled [disabled] in the war.
2 〈편지 끝에〉 Yours truly; Sincerely yours
■ —자 〈신체 장애자〉 a (physically) handicapped person; a disabled person; a deformed [maimed] person; a cripple; (총칭) the disabled; the (physically) handicapped

불구 佛具 Buddhist alter fittings; articles used in a Buddhist service

불구대천 不俱戴天 (⇨ 불공대천) ♦ 불구대천의 원수 an irreconcilable enemy

불구속 不拘束 nonrestraint ♦ 불구속으로 without physical restraint [detention]
■ —입건 booking without detention (by the police)

불구하고 不拘— in spite of; despite (of); disregarding; in disregard of; notwithstanding; no matter (how, what); for all; with all; although
♦ 그럼에도 불구하고 nevertheless; none the less; for all that / 아무의 충고에도 불구하고 in disregard of [after all] *sb's* advice
▶ 그는 고난에도 불구하고 언제나 명랑하다 He has such trouble, but he is cheerful all the time. ⇌ For [With] all his trouble, he is cheerful all the time.
▶ 그는 아주 부자임에도 불구하고 행복하지는 않다 With all his riches [wealth], he is not happy. ⇌ Though he is very rich, he is not happy.
▶ 유능한 인재라면 성별, 연령, 국적에 불구하고 채용합니다 We will employ a person who is able irrespective of sex, age, nationality.

불굴 不屈 indomitability; fortitude
♦ 불굴의 의지 a will of iron; an unyielding will / 불굴의 indomitable; unyielding; invincible / 불굴의 정신으로 with an indomitable [unconquerable] spirit
▶ 스포츠에는 불굴의 투지가 반드시 필요하다 An unyielding [indomitable] spirit is essential in sports.

불귀객 不歸客 the dead [deceased] person
♦ 불귀객이 되다 pass away; die; go on *one's* last journey; depart (from) this life

불규칙 不規則 irregularity; unsteadiness
—**불규칙하다** irregular; unmethodical; unsystematic ♦ 불규칙하게 irregularly; by fits and starts; off and on
▶ 불규칙한 생활은 건강에 나쁘다 Living an irregular life [Keeping irregular hours] is not good for the [one's] health.
▶ 그 환자는 호흡이 거칠고 불규칙했다 The patient's breathing was hard and irregular. ⇌ The patient was breathing hard at irregular intervals.
■ —동사〔文法〕irregular verbs —변화〔文法〕irregular conjugation

불균형 不均衡 imbalance; unbalance; disproportion; inequality
♦ 생활 수준의 불균형 (an) inequality of living standards / 무역의 불균형을 시정하다 redress [correct] trade imbalance
—**불균형하다** ill-balanced; unbalanced; out of balance; out of proportion (to); disproportionate; unequal; lopsided

불그데데하다 dull red; reddish
불그레하다 reddish; tinged with red
♦ 불그레한 얼굴 a ruddy face
▶ 그는 술을 마셔서 얼굴이 약간 불그레하다 His face is slightly flushed with wine.

불그스름하다 reddish; ruddy

불근신 不謹愼 indiscretion; imprudence
♦ 불근신한 태도 imprudent manners

불급하다 不急— not urgent; not pressing
♦ 불급한 문제 a problem that can wait

불긋불긋 with red dots ▶ 바닥에는 불긋불긋 핏자국이 있었다 The floor was spotted with blood.

불기 —氣 the heat of a fire ▶ 그녀의 방은 불기가 없었다 Her room was unheated.
▶ 난로에는 불기라곤 없었다 There was no sign of fire in the stove.

불기 佛紀 Buddhist Era (略 B.E.)

불기둥 a column [pillar] of fire [flames]; a fiery [blazing] column ▶ 폭탄이 떨어진 곳에서 불기둥이 솟았다 A column of fire rose where the bomb fell.

불기소 不起訴 non-prosecution ♦ 불기소로 하다 drop (a case); do not prosecute *sb*
▶ 그 사건은 불기소되었다 The case was dropped.
▶ 그녀는 불기소되었다 She was not indicted [prosecuted]. ⇌ She was acquitted.
■ —처분 a disposition not to insititute a public action

불기운 the force of fire [flames]; the heat of a fire
♦ 불기운이 세지다 the fire gathers strength [grows violent] / 불기운이 약해지다 the fire goes down
▶ 소방차가 도착하자 곧 불기운이 수그러졌다 The fire engines arrived and the fire soon burned down.

불길 blazes; the force of the fire; the flames
♦ 사나운 불길 raging flames [blazes] / 불길이 솟다 burst [break] into flame(s); flame out [up] / 불길이 burn low [down] / 불길을 잡다 get [put] the fire under control / 불길에 싸이다 be enveloped in flames
▶ 그 낡은 건물은 불길에 휩싸였다 The old building was in flames [burst into flames].
▶ 그것은 불길에 뛰어드는 나방 꼴이다 It's like a moth flying into the flame.
▶ 그것은 불길에 기름을 붓는 격이다 It is like adding [putting] oil to the flame [fire].

불길 不吉 an ill omen; inauspiciousness
—**불길하다** unlucky; ill-omened; inauspicious; ominous
♦ 불길한 꿈 an ominous dream / 불길한 날 a dark [an evil, an unlucky] day / 불길한 예감 an ominous presentiment / 불길한 징조〔조짐〕 an unlucky [evil, ill] omen
▶ 뭔가 불길한 일이 일어날 것같은 생각이 든다 I have the feeling that something evil is going to happen.

불김 the heat of a fire ⇨ 불기운
불까다 castrate; emasculate; geld; alter
♦ 불깐 돼지 a castrated pig / 불깐 소〔말〕 a

bullock [gelding]/ 말을 불까다 geld a horse

불꽃 1 〈화염〉 a flame; a blaze
♦불꽃이 타오르다 flame [flare] up; blaze (up)/ 불꽃에 싸이다 be enveloped [wrapped] in flames
2 〈석화·방전〉 a spark
♦작은 불꽃 a sparklet / 불꽃이 튀다 spark; sparkle; sparks fly
▶그 법안에 대하여 불꽃 튀는 논전이 있었다 They had a heated [hot] argument about the bill.
▶끊어진 전선에서 불꽃이 튀었다 The broken wire sent out sparks.
3 〈폭죽〉 fireworks; a firecracker
♦불꽃을 쏘아 올리다 set off [let off, shoot] fireworks
━━반응 flame reaction ━방전 spark discharge ━전압 spark voltage

불꽃놀이 a fireworks display; an exhibition of fireworks ━불꽃놀이하다 display fireworks; do a fireworks display

불끈 1 〈성을 내어〉 with a burst (of anger)
━불끈하다 flare up (in anger); flame out; lose *one's* temper; fly into a rage; be stirred into passionate anger
♦불끈하여 in a fit of passion; in a (fit of) rage
▶그는 불끈하는 성미다 He is hot-tempered [quick-tempered].
2 〈주먹을〉 ▶그는 분노로 주먹을 불끈 쥐었다 He clenched his fist(s) in anger.

불끈거리다, 불끈대다 be hot-tempered [quick-tempered, short-tempered, ill-tempered]; be liable to get angry [lose *one's* temper]; be easily offended 《by》; be furious; rage

불나다 a fire breaks out ♦불난 집 〈타고 있는〉 a house on fire; 〈탄〉 a burnt house / 불난 집에 부채질하다 add [put] oil to the fire [flames]; pour oil on the flame; add fuel to 《the disturbance》
▶어젯밤 근처에서 크게 불났었다 There was a big fire in the neighborhood last night.
▶불난 곳이 어디냐? Where is the fire?

불나방 〔昆〕 a tiger moth

불난리 ━亂離 the confusion of a fire
▶불난리통에 여러 사람이 다쳤다 Many people were injured in the confusion of the fire.

불내다 1 〈실수로〉 cause [start] a fire 2 ⇨ 불놓다 1

불놀이 1 ⇨ 불꽃놀이 2 〈불장난〉 playing with fire

불놓다 1 〈방화하다〉 set fire to 《a house》; 《a building》 on fire; raise a fire
▶그는 헛간에다 불놓았다 He set fire to the barn. ⇌ He set the barn on fire.
2 〈광산에서〉 light a fuse; detonate

불능 不能 incapability; incompetency; 〈불가능〉 impossibility
▶폭설 때문에 도로는 통행 불능이 되었다 The road was impassable because of the heavy snow.
━불능하다 incapable; incompetent; unable; impossible; 〈성적으로〉 impotent

━성적(性的)━ impotence : 성적불능자 an impotent (person) 지급━ 〔法〕 insolvency ━━문제 〔數〕 an impossible problem ━방정식 〔數〕 inconsistent equation ━범 an impossible crime

불다¹ 〈바람이〉 blow ♦바람이 세차게 불다 blow hard; blow a gale / 바람이 솔솔 불다 breeze
▶오늘은 바람이 세게 분다 The wind is blowing hard today. ⇌ It is windy today. ⇌ The wind is strong today.
▶바람이 북쪽에서 불고 있다 The wind is blowing from the north.
▶서풍이 불면 비가 온다 The west wind brings rain.

불다² 1 〈입으로〉 blow (up); breathe out
♦손을 불다 blow on *one's* hands / 풍선을 불다 blow up [inflate] a toy balloon / 휘파람을 불다 whistle / 뜨거운 차[음식]를 불어서 식히다 blow on hot tea to cool it [*one's* food to make it cool]
▶나는 촛불을 불어서 껐다 I blew out the candle.
2 〈악기를〉 play (on); blow [sound] 《a bugle》
♦플루트를 불다 play 《a tune》 on the flute; play (on) a flute
▶그는 트럼펫을 불었다 He blew the trumpet.
▶호루라기를 불면 경기를 그쳐라 Stop the game when I blow the whistle.
3 〈자백하다〉 confess
♦모조리 불다 make a clean breast of everything / 사실대로 불다 confess the truth [the facts as they are]/ 죄를 모조리 불다 confess *one's* guilt; confess to a crime [an offense]/ 협박하여 불게 하다 threaten *sb* into confession
▶그 사람은 자기 죄를 불었다 The man confessed himself (to be) guilty.
▶죄다 불어 Spit it out! ⇌ Own up! ⇌ Out with it! ⇌ Come clean!

불단 佛壇 a Buddhist altar

불당 佛堂 a Buddhist temple [shrine, sanctum]; a temple building enshrining a Buddhist statue

불덩이 a mass [ball] of flames [fire]; a fireball ♦몸이 불덩이가 되다 〈열이 나서〉 have [get] high fever; 〈불길에 휩싸여〉 be covered with flames
▶한 여자가 불덩이가 되어 그 집에서 뛰쳐 나왔다 A woman came rushing out of the house, her body ablaze.

불도 佛徒 a Buddhist; a believer in Buddhism

불도 佛道 the teachings of (the) Buddha; Buddhism; Buddhist doctrines ━━수행 the practice of Buddhistic austerities

불도저 a bulldozer ♦불도저로 땅을 고르다 bulldoze land; level (the) land with a bulldozer

불독 a bulldog ♦불독 같은 강인성 bulldog tenacity

불돋우개 a wick-raiser ⇨ 심돋우개

불등걸 〈숯의〉 pieces of glowing charcoal

불때다 fire 《a furnace》; make a fire ♦방에 불

불똥 **1** 〈심지의〉 a charred wick
2 〈작은 불덩이〉 sparks (of fire) ◆불똥을 뒤집어 쓰다 be covered with sparks
▶불똥이 튀다 Sparks shoot up in the air.
▶불똥이 튀어서 또 불이 났다 The flying sparks started another fire.
▶얻어맞았을 때 눈에서 불똥이 튀었다 I saw stars when I was hit.

불뚝 in a fit of passion; in a (fit) of rage; with a flare of temper ◆불뚝 화를 내다 explode with anger; flare up in anger; fly into a (great) rage

불란서 佛蘭西 France ⇨ 프랑스

불량 不良 1 〈질의〉 badness; inferiority
—**불량하다** 〈질이〉 bad; poor; inferior; faulty; defective; 〈건강이〉 unwholesome
◆발육이 불량한 아이 an underdeveloped child / 날씨가 불량하여 owing to bad [inclement] weather / 학교 성적이 불량하다 do badly at school; have a poor school record
▶품질이 불량하다 The quality is poor.
▶작년에는 벼 수확이 불량했다 We had a poor rice crop last year.
2 〈품성의〉 delinquency
—**불량하다** wicked; delinquent
◆불량한 짓을 하다 indulge in delinquent behavior / 불량해지다 go into bad way; become delinquent; be degraded
▶청소년이 불량해지는 것을 방지해야 한다 We should prevent juvenile delinquency.
─소화— indigestion 정비— poor maintenance ■—도체(導體) 〔電〕 a bad conductor —소년 a delinquent [bad, naughty] boy; a juvenile delinquent ─식품 adulterated food ─품 inferior goods; a defective article; an imperfect product; an item of defective merchandise

불량배 不良輩 〈무리〉 a gang [group] of hoodlums [hooligans]; 〈개인〉 a rascal; a scoundrel

불러내다 ask [tell] sb to come; call sb out; call sb to; 〈소환하여〉 summon
◆전화로 불러내다 call [ring] sb up on the phone; call sb to the telephone
▶밤 늦게 불러내어 참 미안하구나 I'm very sorry to have troubled you to come so late at night.

불러들이다 call sb in [into]; have sb in
▶그가 나를 그의 방으로 불러들였다 He called me into his room.

불러모으다 call people together; assemble; summon
▶아버지가 가족을 전부 불러모았다 Father called together all the members of the family.
▶그는 전화로 회원 전원을 불러모았다 He summoned all the members by telephone.

불러세우다 call sb to stop
▶경찰관이 나를 불러세웠다 The policeman called me to stop.
▶비가 오기 시작해서 택시를 불러세웠다 As it began to rain, I hailed a taxi.

불러오다 call [get] sb to come; ask [tell] sb to come; 〈사람을 보내서〉 send for sb
◆의사를 불러오다 send for a doctor; call (in) a doctor
▶제가 지배인을 불러오지요 I'll get [go and get] the manager for you.

불러일으키다 〈일깨우다〉 rouse [gather] up; arouse; call forth; stir up; remind; recall
▶그의 소설은 큰 화제를 불러일으켰다 His novel caused [created] a great sensation.
▶그것이 그에게 의심을 불러일으켰다 It raised doubts in his mind.
▶달력의 그 산들이 그녀의 유럽 여행의 추억을 불러일으켰다 Those mountains on the calendar reminded her of her trip to Europe.

불려가다 〈상사 등에게〉 be asked [told] to come; be summoned to (the police)
◆선생님에게 불려가다 be called before a teacher
▶그는 법정에 증인으로 불려갔다 He was summoned to appear as a witness in court.

불로 不老 eternal [perennial] youth
◆불로불사의 나라 a land of perennial youth and immortality; Elysium / 불로의 비결 the secret of perpetual youth / 불로의 샘 a fountain of ageless youth / 불로의 ever-young; unfading; ageless

불로소득 不勞所得 unearned income; windfall income [profits] ■—생활자 a person living on unearned income

불로장생 不老長生 eternal [perennial] youth and long life [longevity] ◆불로장생의 비결 the secret of perennial youth and long life
—**불로장생하다** live ever-young; enjoy eternal youth

불로초 不老草 a herb of eternal youth; an elixir of life

불룩하다 swollen; baggy; bulging; bulky; 〈똥뚱하다〉 fat; protuberant; inflated
◆불룩한 가슴 the rich [well-fleshed] breasts / 배가 불룩한 남자 a man with a potbelly [paunch] / 배가 불룩하다 have a big paunch; be potbellied; 〈아기를 배어〉 be big with child; be pregnant; 〈새끼를 배어〉 be big with young

불륜 不倫 immorality; 〈간통〉 adultery
◆불륜의 사랑 illicit love / 불륜의 immoral; illicit; illegal; adulterous / 불륜 관계를 갖다 commit adultery

불리 不利 disadvantage; a handicap; a drawback —**불리하다** disadvantageous; unfavorable; adverse
◆불리한 증거 evidence against sb / 불리한 조건을 극복하다 overcome one's handicap / 남에게 불리한 증언을 하다 testify against sb / 원고에게 불리한 판결을 내리다 give a decision unfavorable to [decide against] the plaintiff / 불리한 처지에 있다[놓이다] be at a disadvantage; be in [stand at] a disadvantageous position; be handicapped
▶그가 영어를 하지 못하는 것은 불리하다 It is to his disadvantage that he cannot speak English. ⇌ His inability to speak English puts him at a disadvantage.
▶형세가 우리에게 불리하다 The chances [odds] are against us.

▶진실을 말한다고해서 네게 불리할 건 없다 You'll lose nothing by speaking the truth.

불리다[1] ◆배를 불리다 fill one's stomach; stuff out the belly; 〈사복을 채우다〉 enrich oneself / 공금으로 자기 배를 불리다 enrich oneself [line one's own pocket] with public money [funds]

불리다[2] 1 〈금속을〉 temper; anneal ◆쇠를 불리다 temper iron
2 〈곡식을〉 fan (rice husks from the grain)

불리다[3] 1 〈액체에〉 steep; soak ◆보리를 물에 불리다 soak barley in water ▶콩은 삶기 전에 물에 불리는 게 좋다 It is better to soak [steep] beans in water before boiling them.
2 〈과장하다〉 exaggerate; magnify; stretch (the fact) ◆불려서 말하다 exaggerate (a story); talk big
3 〈증가시키다〉 increase; add to ◆재산을 불리다 increase [add to] one's fortune

불리다[4] 1 〈부름을 받다〉 be called; 〈소환되다〉 be summoned; 〈초대받다〉 be invited
2 〈이름붙다〉 be named [called] ▶그는 어렸을 때 신동이라고 불리었다 When he was little he was called a child prodigy.

불리다[5] 〈바람에〉 be blown; blow ◆바람에 불리어 오다 come on the wind; be blown in ▶기가 바람에 불리어 펄럭이고 있다 The flag is fluttering in the wind.

불리다[6] 〈악기 등을〉 make sb blow (a trumpet); 〈자백시키다〉 make sb admit himself guilty ◆죄상을 강제로 불리다 force [compel] a confession from sb; force sb into confession ▶우리는 그에게 나팔을 불렸다 We made him blow a trumpet.

불림 〈금속을〉 annealing; tempering

불만 不滿 dissatisfaction; discontent; discontentment; complaint ◆성적 불만 sexual dissatisfaction / 현재상태에 대한 불만의 소리 expressions of discontent with the present state of things / 불만이 있다 〈사람이 주어〉 be dissatisfied (with); be unhappy; 〈사물이 주어〉 leave sth to be desired / 불만이 없다 〈사람이 주어〉 be satisfied [content] (with); be happy; have nothing to complain of; 〈사물이 주어〉 leave nothing to be desired ▶나는 지금의 내 일에 불만이다 I am not happy [am discontented] with my job. ▶저임금에 근로자들의 불만이 고조되었다 A lot of discontent grew among the workers because of low wages. ▶시민들은 시장의 결정에 불만을 표시했다 The citizens expressed their disapproval of the mayor's decision. ▶그들은 퇴장함으로써 불만을 나타냈다 They showed their displeasure by leaving the room.
—**불만스럽다** unhappy; dissatisfied; discontented; displeased; unsatisfied (desires); 〈사물·결과 등이〉 unsatisfactory; indifferent ◆불만스러운 결과 an unsatisfactory result / 불만스럽게 생각하다 be displeased [dissatisfied] (with, at); feel discontented (with)
▶그는 불만스러운 눈으로 나를 보았다 He gave me a discontented look.

불만족 不滿足 dissatisfaction ⇨ 불만

불매동맹 不買同盟 a (trade [commercial]) boycott ◆외국 차의 불매동맹을 맺다 form an alliance to boycott foreign cars [to put foreign cars under boycott] ■소비자— a consumers' boycott; a buyers' strike

불매운동 不買運動 boycotting; a boycott; a consumer strike ▶주부들은 쇠고기 불매운동을 펴기로 합의했다 The housewives agreed to boycott [refuse to buy] beef.

불면불휴 不眠不休 ▶그는 불면불휴로 일하였다 He worked hard night and day. ▶그는 불면불휴로 그 작품을 완성했다 He finished his work with no sleep and rest.

불면증 不眠症 insomnia; sleeplessness ◆불면증에 걸리다 suffer from [be troubled with] insomnia ▶나는 요새 불면증이 좀 있어 I have been sleeping badly [suffering from a little insomnia] lately. ■피로성— insomnia of exhaustion ■—환자 an insomniac

불멸 不滅 immortality; indestructibility; imperishability; athanasia ◆불멸의 예술작품 an immortal work of art / 불멸의 명성 immortal fame / 불멸의 사랑 undying love / 불멸의 영광 undying glory / 불멸의 immortal; indestructible; undying; imperishable; permanent; eternal ▶바하의 음악은 불멸이다 Bach's music is immortal.

불명 不明 1 〈불분명〉 indistinctness; obscurity; ambiguity; 〈불가해〉 incomprehensibility ◆국적 불명의 비행기 a plane of unknown nationality / 신원 불명의 사체 an unidentified body / 원인 불명의 사고 an accident of unknown origin [cause] / 행방 불명이 된 아이 a missing child ▶그의 생사는 아직 불명이다 It is not yet confirmed whether he is still alive or not.
—**불명하다** unknown; unclear; indistinct; obscure; vague; ambiguous; incomprehensible ◆불명한 태도 an indefinite [a dubious, a noncommittal] attitude
2 〈사리에 어두움〉 lack of sagacity [insight]; 〈무지〉 ignorance
—**불명하다** unwise; ignorant

불명 佛名 〈부처의 이름〉 the name of Buddha; the name of a Buddhist saint; 〈신도 이름〉 one's Buddhist name

불명료 不明瞭 unclearness ⇨ 불분명

불명예 不名譽 dishonor; disgrace; discredit; shame ▶그런 짓을 하면 네게 불명예가 된다 That would bring disgrace upon your good name. ▶이것은 학교의 불명예가 될 것이다 This will disgrace the school. = This will bring disgrace on (the good name of) the school.
—**불명예스럽다** dishonorable; disgraceful; shameful ◆불명예스러운 사건 a dishonorable

[shameful] incident
■—제대 a dishonorable discharge

불명확하다 不明確— unclear; indefinite; indistinct; vague; obscure; ambiguous
▶그의 발음은 불명확하다 His pronunciation is not clear [distinct, articulate].
◆양자의 경계선이 불명확하다 The line of demarcation between the two is not well-defined.

불모 不毛 〈땅의〉 sterility; barrenness
◆불모의 barren; sterile; infertile; lean; waste; unproductive / 불모의 땅을 개척하다 open [develop] wasteland
■—지 barren [arid] land; sterile soil; wasteland

불목하니 a temple servant; a sexton

불문 不問 ◆불문에 부치다 disregard; let go; lay aside; overlook; leave *sth* out of consideration; take no notice of
▶그는 미성년자여서 범행을 불문에 부쳤다 As he was a minor [an infant], his offense was overlooked.
▶이 문제는 불문에 부칠 수 없다 We should not pass this [let this pass] without protest. ⇌ This should not be passed unmentioned.
—**불문하다** ◆남녀 노소를 불문하고 irrespective [regardless] of age or sex / 다소를 불문하고 however small [little] it may be; regardless of quantity / 시간과 장소를 불문하고 in all times and places; any time and anywhere
▶그것은 연령을 불문하고 누구든지 할 수 있는 스포츠다 It is a sport anyone can play regardless [irrespective] of age.
▶이유 여하를 불문하고 폭력은 안 된다 No matter what the reason, violence cannot be allowed.

불문 佛文 〈글〉 a French sentence; 〈문학〉 French literature
▶그 편지는 불문이었다 The letter was written in French.
■—과 〈대학의〉 the department of French literature —학 French literature

불문 佛門 Buddhism; Buddhist
◆불문에 들어가다 enter the Buddhist priesthood; become a Buddhist priest [monk]

불문가지 不問可知 ▶그것은 불문가지다 You can easily understand it without asking. ⇌ It goes without saying. ⇌ The facts speak for themselves. ⇌ It's self-evident [obvious].

불문곡직 不問曲直 ◆불문곡직하고 whether right or wrong; without inquiring into the rights and wrongs (of the case)
▶나는 불문곡직하고 이곳에 연행되었다 I have been forced [compelled] to come here.
▶불문곡직하고 그에게 이 약을 먹이시오 Let him take this medicine whether he likes it or not.

불문법 不文法 an unwritten law ⇨ 불문율

불문율 不文律 an unwritten law [rule]; a consuetudinary law; (英) common law

불문헌법 不文憲法 an unwritten constitution

불미하다, 불미스럽다 不美— bad; unfavorable; unsavory; nasty; shameful; scandalous; disgraceful
◆불미스러운 사건 an ugly [a scandalous] case; a scandal / 불미스러운 행동 an indecent act
▶그에 대한 불미스러운 소문을 들었다 I heard an unfavorable rumor about him.

불바다 a sheet [sea] of flames [fire]
▶방 안은 불바다였다 The room was in flames [was a sea of flame].
▶상점가는 불바다로 변했다 The shopping district turned into a blazing inferno.

불발 不發 〈총포의〉 misfire
▶그 계획은 불발로 끝났다 The plan fell through [failed to go off].
—**불발하다** misfire; fail to go off; do not go off; fail to explode ▶그 포탄은 불발했다 The shell did not go off.

불법 不法 〈위법〉 unlawfulness; illegality; illegitimacy; 〈부정〉 wrong; wrong fulness; injustice; iniquity
◆불법으로 illegally; unlawfully; wrongfully
—**불법하다** unlawful; illegal; unjust; illegitimate
◆불법한 수단을 쓰다 take illegal means [steps] / 불법한 짓을 하다 act unlawfully [outrageously]; do *sb* a wrong [an injustice]
■—감금 illegal confinement —소지 illegal possession —점거 illegal occupation —점거자 〈건물·토지 등의〉 a squatter —주차 illegal parking —집회 (英) unlawful assembly —체포 an illegal arrest —출판 illegal publication

불법 佛法 〈불교〉 Buddhism; 〈교리〉 the law [teachings] of Buddha

불법입국 不法入國 illegal entry; unlawful immigration ■—자 an illegal entrant; (美) an illegal alien

불법침입 不法侵入 illegal entry; intrusion; forcible [unlawful] entry; 〈토지 등에의〉 trespass
—**불법침입하다** intrude (into); trespass (on, upon) ■—자 an intruder; a trespasser

불법행위 不法行爲 an unlawful [illegal] act; a wrongful act; a delict; a malfeasance; a misfeasance; [法] a tort
■—자 a wrongdoer; an offender

불벼락 1 〈번갯불〉 a bolt of lightning
2 〈비유〉 a dressing down; a talking-to; yelling
◆불벼락을 내리다 give *sb* hell; thunder at; bawl out / 불벼락을 맞다 get a talking-to; catch [get] hell (from)

불변 不變 constancy; unchangeability; eternity; permanence
◆불변의 법칙 invariable [unchangeable] laws / 불변의 진리 eternal [everlasting] truth / 불변의 unchangeable; invariable; inalterable; immutable; constant; eternal; everlasting; permanent
▶그의 생각은 불변이었다 His views remained unchanged. ⇌ He was immovable in his views.
—**불변하다** do not change; be unchangeable [invariable, inalterable, immutable, constant, permanent]
■—색 a permanent [lasting] color

불벌 the burning [scorching, blazing] sun
불벌더위 intense heat
▶ 오늘은 불벌 더위다 It is scorching [broiling, smoking] hot today.
불복 不服 1〈불복종〉 disobedience 《to an order》; insubordination 《to》
—**불복하다** disobey; be disobedient
▶ 상관의 지시에 불복했다 He disobeyed the senior's instruction.
2〈복죄(服罪) 않음〉 denial of one's guilt; pleading not guilty;〈이의〉 a protest; an objection;〈불평〉 a complaint
—**불복하다** plead not guilty; be dissatisfied; protest against; object to
■—**상고**〔法〕 an appeal [institution] of dissatisfaction to the Supreme Court —**신청**〔法〕 an appeal [institution] of dissatisfaction —**항소**〔法〕 an appeal of dissatisfaction to a higher court : 그는 일심 판결에 불복 항소했다 He appealed from the finding of the court of the first instance.
불복종 不服從 disobedience ⇨ 불복(不服) 1
불분명 不分明 unclearness; vagueness; obscurity; ambiguity; indistinctness
—**불분명하다** unclear; obscure; dim; indistinct; ambiguous; inexplicit; vague
♦ 불분명한 발음 inarticulate [indistinctive] pronunciation / 불분명한 태도 an unclear attitude; an indistinctive course of action / 불분명하게 indistinctly; obscurely / 불분명하게 대답하다 give a vague [an equivocal] answer
▶ 그 전보의 뜻이 불분명하다 The meaning of the telegram is not clear.
불붙다 catch [take] fire; catch on fire; light up; kindle; ignite
▶ 휘발유는 잘 불붙는다 Gasoline is flammable.
▶ 잠시 중단한 후에 그들의 논쟁이 다시 불붙었다 After a brief interruption, the argument flared up again.
▶ 종이는 잘 불붙는다 Paper catches fire easily.
불붙이다 set on fire; fire; light (up); kindle; ignite; (비유) touch off《a quarrel》
♦ 담배에 불붙이다 light (up) a cigarette / 장작에 불붙이다 light the firewood / 폭약에 불붙이다 fire [set off] a charge of dynamite
불비 不備 imperfection; defectiveness; inadequacy; deficiency
♦ 교통 수단의 불비 lack of means of conveyance; imperfect [defective] means of transportation / 하수도의 불비 lack of an adequate sewage system
▶ 그는 법의 불비를 악용하여 큰 부자가 되었다 He abused legal loopholes and became very rich.
—**불비하다** defective; faulty; deficient; imperfect; incomplete
♦ 불비한 점 a defect; an imperfection; an omission / 불비한 점을 시정하다 correct [remedy] a defect
▶ 서류가 불비하여 반려되었다 The papers were incomplete and were rejected.
불빛 1〈화광(火光)〉 firelight;〈등불〉 a light

▶ 불빛이 밝다 The light is bright.
▶ 바다 위에 어선들의 불빛이 가물거린다 The lights from the fishing boats glimmer on the waves.
▶ 그들은 야음을 타고 다가오는 불빛을 보았다 They saw a light approaching in the darkness of the night.
2〈타는 불의 빛깔〉 the color of a flame; flame color; red;〈광선〉 rays of light
불사 不死 immortality; eternal life
♦ 불사의 영약 an elixir of life / 불사의 deathless; undying; immortal; imperishable
불사르다 burn; set sth on fire; put sth into the flames
♦ 정원에서 낙엽을 불사르다 burn the fallen leaves in the garden / 연구에 정열을 불사르다 burn with passion [enthusiasm] for one's research
▶ 그녀는 사랑을 불살랐다 She gave herself to flames [a flame] of love.
불사리 佛舍利 relics of Buddha ⇨ 사리(舍利)
불사신 不死身 an invulnerable body; invulnerability; immortality
♦ 불사신이다 be immortal; be invulnerable
▶ 고대 그리스의 신들은 불사신이라고 믿어졌다 The gods of ancient Greece were believed to be immortal.
불사조 不死鳥 the phoenix ▶ 그는 불사조처럼 다시 일어날 것이다 He will rise again like the phoenix from the ashes.
불사하다 不辭— 〈사양치 않다〉dare [venture, presume]《to do》; be ready [willing]《to do》
▶ 피해자는 소송도 불사할 것 같았다 The victim appeared ready to take the matter to court.
불상 佛像 a Buddhist image [statue]; an image [a statue] of Buddha
불상놈 —常— a base [mean] fellow
불상사 不祥事 an unhappy [ill] event; an accident; a mishap; a scandal
▶ 그들은 그 불상사를 덮어버리려고 애썼다 They tried to blanket the scandal. ⇌ They tried to keep the scandal quiet.
불상정 不上程 deferment of the introduction of a bill [proposal]
■—**안** a motion to defer the deliberation on a bill [proposal]
불서 佛書 〈불교 서적〉 the Buddhist scriptures; Buddhist literature;〈프랑스어 책〉 a French book
불선명하다 不鮮明— indistinct; unclear; obscure; dim; blurred
▶ 인쇄가 약간 불선명하다 The printing is somewhat blurred.
불성 佛性 the nature of Buddha
불성립 不成立 failure; miscarriage
—**불성립하다** fail; fall through
불성실 不誠實 insincerity; unfaithfulness; dishonesty —**불성실하다** insincere; unfaithful; dishonest; untruthful; untrustworthy; be not serious-minded; lack sincerity
▶ 불성실한 답장을 하느니보다 답장을 내지 않는 것이 낫다 It is better not to reply than to say things you don't mean.

불세출 不世出 ♦불세출의 대정치가 a great statesman of unequaled ability / 불세출의 영웅 a great man without a parallel in history; the hero of the century / 불세출의 extraordinary; unparalleled; unequaled; peerless

불소 弗素 fluorine ⇨ 플루오르

불소하다 不少- 〈수〉 not a few; quite many; 〈양〉 not a little

불속 ♦불속으로 몸을 던지다 throw [plunge] oneself into the flames / 불속으로 편지를 던지다 throw a letter into the fire

불손 不遜 arrogance; impudence; haughtiness; insolence
—**불손하다** arrogant; haughty; insolent; presumptuous; impudent; rude
♦불손하게 insolently; rudely; high-handedly; arrogantly / 불손한 말을 하다 talk insolently / 불손하게 굴다 behave haughtily / 불손한 태도를 취하다 assume an arrogant attitude

불수 不隨 paralysis; palsy ⇨ 반신불수
▶그는 반신불수가 되었다 He was paralyzed on one side.

불수의 不隨意 ▶심장의 박동은 불수의다 The beating of the heart is involuntary.
■—근(筋) 〈解〉 an involuntary muscle —운동(生) involuntary motion [movement] —작용 an involuntary action

불순 不純 impurity
—**불순하다** impure; foul; mixed
♦불순한 마음 an impure [a dishonest] mind [heart]
▶그는 불순한 동기에서 그녀를 도왔을 것이다 He must have helped her from some impure [selfish] motives.
■—분자 an impure element : 당내의 불순분자 rebellious elements of a party

불순 不順 1 〈성질이〉 disobedience
—**불순하다** disobedient; rebellious
2 〈날씨가〉 unseasonableness; irregularity
—**불순하다** unseasonable; unsettled; changeable; unfavorable; 〈불규칙한〉 irregular
♦불순한 날씨 unsettled [changeable] weather / 날씨가 불순하여 on account of the unseasonable weather
▶요즈음은 날씨가 불순하다 The weather is changeable these days. ⇌ We are having unsettled weather these days.
■월경— menstrual irregularity; irregular menstruation

불순물 不純物 a impurity; 〔醫〕 foreign matter
♦불순물을 제거하다 remove impurities
▶이 물에는 불순물이 있다 There is something impure [some impurity] in this water.

불승인 不承認 disapproval; dissent; 〈거부〉 veto; 〈불인정〉 nonrecognition
—**불승인하다** disapprove; veto; dissent

불시 不時 ♦불시의 공격[검사] a surprise attack [inspection] / 불시의 〈때아닌〉 untimely; 〈예측 못한〉 unexpected; unforeseen; 〈돌발적인〉 accidental; incidental / 불시에 unexpectedly; untimely; abruptly; by surprise / 불시에 덤벼들다 take sb by surprise
▶그는 불시의 사고를 당해 오른손을 잃었다 He had an accident and lost his right hand.
▶어젯밤 불시에 손님이 왔었다 I had an unexpected visitor last night.
▶항상 불시에 닥칠 사태에 대비해라 Don't forget to provide against emergency [contingencies, a rainy day].

불시착 不時着 a forced [an emergency] landing; a crash landing
—**불시착하다** make [attempt] a forced [an emergency] landing 《at》; crash-land
▶그 비행기는 짙은 안개로 불시착했다 The airplane was forced down by a dense fog.

불식 佛式 the Buddhist ritual; Buddhist rites
♦불식에 의하여 in Buddhist rites
▶장례는 불식으로 거행되었다 The funeral was held according to Buddhist rites.

불식하다 拂拭- 〈말끔히 없애다〉 wipe out; eradicate ♦있을지도 모를 오해를 대화로 불식하다 get rid of possible misunderstandings through dialogs

불신 不信 distrust; mistrust; disbelief; discredit; lack [want] of confidence 《in》
♦남의 불신을 사다 lose sb's credit
▶젊은이들의 정치 불신이 해마다 늘고 있다 Young people's distrust of politics is increasing year by year. ⇌ Young people have less and less faith in politics every year.
▶그녀가 불신을 해소하는 데는 오랜 시일이 걸릴 것이다 It will take a long time to dispel her mistrust.
—**불신하다** do not trust; distrust; mistrust

불신감 不信感 (a) distrust; a feeling of distrust; (a) suspicion
♦불신감을 품다 be distrustful of; have a 《deep》 distrust
▶그의 행동이 사람들에게 불신감을 일으켰다 His action incurred people's distrust. ⇌ His action caused everyone to distrust him.

불신용 不信用 mistrust; lack of confidence

불신임 不信任 nonconfidence; want [lack] of confidence 《in》
♦야당이 추진한 내각 총사퇴 불신임 동의 nonconfidence motion calling for the resignation of all Cabinet members en masse pushed by oppositionists
—**불신임하다** distrust; have no confidence in
■—결의 a nonconfidence resolution —투표 a vote of nonconfidence; a nonconfidence vote

불신임안 不信任案 a nonconfidence [no-confidence] motion ♦정부 불신임안을 상정[결의]하다 propose [pass] a vote of nonconfidence in the Government

불실 不實 infirmness ⇨ 부실(不實)

불심 佛心 the merciful heart of Buddha; Buddha's love [mercy]

불심검문 不審檢問 questioning of a suspicious person by a patrolman
▶나는 형사에게 불심검문을 당했다 I was stopped and questioned by a police detective.
—**불심검문하다** question sb

불쌍하다 〈가엾다〉 poor; pitiable; pitiful; unfortunate; 〈비참하다〉 miserable; wretched; 〈동정이 가다〉 pathetic; touching
♦불쌍한 고아 a poor orphan / 불쌍한 노인 a poor old man / 불쌍한 형편 a miserable [sad,

wretched, pitiful] plight [situation]/불쌍해서 out of pity [sympathy]/불쌍히 여기다 take [have] pity [compassion, mercy] on; feel pity for; pity
▶ 그 여자는 그 고아를 불쌍하게 여겼다 She felt sorry [sympathy, compassion, pity] for the orphan.
▶ 불쌍(도)해라 What a pity! ⇌ Poor thing! ⇌ I'm so sorry!
▶ 불쌍한 것은 어린 자매였다 It was the little sisters who aroused our compassion.
▶ 나는 아이들이 불쌍해서 그녀를 도와주었다 I helped her out of pity for her children.

불쏘시개 a lighter; a kindler; kindling wood; (美) kindling(s) ◆ 신문지를[나무 토막을] 불쏘시개로 쓰다 use newspaper [chips of wood] as kindling [to light a fire]

불쑥 〈돌연〉 suddenly; unexpectedly; abruptly; unusually; 〈예고없이〉 without (previous) notice [warning]; 〈생각 없이〉 carelessly; bluntly
◆ 창밖으로 머리를 불쑥 내밀다 pop one's head out of the window / 불쑥 나타나다 make an abrupt appearance; appear unexpectedly; pop in [up]; bob up / 불쑥 들르다[찾아오다] make a sudden call 《on》; pay a surprise visit 《to》; pop in / 불쑥 말하다 blurt out a remark; speak [talk] bluntly
▶ 그는 옆에서 손을 불쑥 내밀었다 He abruptly thrust [stuck] out his hand from the side.
▶ 덩치 큰 녀석이 불쑥 들어왔다 A big fellow suddenly came in.
▶ 그는 무슨 말이든 불쑥 내뱉으니 탈이야 He is a nuisance because he blurts everything out.

불쑥불쑥 〈여기저기〉 here and there; 〈잇달아〉 one after another ◆ 우후죽순처럼 불쑥불쑥 솟아나오다 come out like so many bamboo shoots
▶ 도심에 고층 건물이 불쑥불쑥 치솟기 시작했다 High-rise buildings are going up one after another in the heart of the city.
─**불쑥불쑥하다** bulge out here and there; be full of projections, large or small

불쑥하다 projecting; protruding; jutting out; 〈볼록하다〉 bulgy; swelling
▶ 거기는 땅이 불쑥하게 솟아 있다 There the earth rises into a little hill.

불씨 〈불덩이〉 a live coal (to make a fire); 〈꼬투리〉 a cause; a factor; the origin ◆ 분쟁의 불씨 an apple of discord; the cause of quarrel; a tinderbox
▶ 영토 문제가 불씨가 되어 전쟁이 일어났다 The territorial dispute led to a war.

불안 不安 1〈마음의〉 uneasiness; anxiety; apprehension; fear; restlessness
◆ 일말의 불안을 느끼다 feel a touch of anxiety [uneasiness]; be under some uneasiness 《at》 / 건강에 불안을 느끼다 have [feel] misgivings about one's health / 불안에 사로잡히다 be overcome with apprehensions
▶ 갑자기 알 수 없는 불안이 그를 엄습했다 Suddenly he was attacked by an inexplicable disquiet.
─**불안하다** uneasy; ill at ease; restless; anxious; worried
◆ 불안한 느낌 a feeling of unrest [restlessness]; an uneasy feeling / 불안한 표정 an anxious look; an uneasy look / 표정이 불안하다 look anxious [concerned]/ 불안하게 생각하다 feel uneasy [ill at ease] 《about》; be anxious 《about》
▶ 내 아들 때문에 나는 언제나 불안하다 I always feel nervous [uneasy] about my son.
▶ 나는 다치지 않을까 불안하다 I am afraid I shall be injured.
▶ 그녀의 얼굴에는 불안한 빛이 감돌고 있었다 There was an air of anxiety in her look.
▶ 결과가 어떻게 될지 불안해서 견딜 수가 없다 I tremble to think [feel anxious] how it will end.

2 〈정세 등의〉 insecurity; instability; unrest; uncertainty ◆ 사회 불안을 조성하다 cause social unrest
▶ 정계[사회]의 불안이 주가의 대폭락을 야기했다 Political [Social] unrest caused a drastic fall in stock prices.
─**불안하다** uncertain; insecure
◆ 불안한 정세 the unsettled political world / 불안한 걸음걸이로 with unsteady [uncertain] steps [gait]
─■**─감** a feeling of uneasiness [unrest, restlessness]

불 안 땐 굴뚝에 연기 날까 (속담) Where there is smoke, there is fire. ⇌ There is no smoke without fire.

불안정 不安定 instability ◆ 생활의 불안정 insecurity of living / 정서적 불안정 an uneasy feeling [emotion]/ 통화의 불안정 currency instability
─**불안정하다** unstable; shaky; 〈변하기 쉬운〉 changeable ◆ 불안정한 정국 an unstable situation in politics / 불안정한 자리 an insecure [a precarious, an untenable] position
▶ 정국은 불안정하다 The political situation is out of joint.

불알 the testicles; the testes 《sing. -tis》; the stones; 《俗》 the balls ◆ 불알을 까다 castrate / 불알을 긁어 주다 (비유) curry favor with sb; get into sb's good grace

불야성 不夜城 a city that never sleeps; an all-night city; nightless [gay] quarters; a nightless city
▶ 밤이면 온 도시가 불야성을 이룬다 At night the whole city is brilliantly illuminated.

불어 佛語 〈프랑스어〉 French; the French language

불어나다 increase (in number [volume]); grow; 〈금액이〉 run [go, mount] up (to a large sum); 〈강물이〉 rise; swell
◆ 물이 불은 강 a swollen river / 강물이 불어나다 the river rises / 빚이 불어나다 get deeper in debt / 살림[재산]이 불어나다 one's fortune is prospering [increasing]
▶ 나는 체중이 5킬로그램 불어났다 I've gained [put on] five kilograms.
▶ 원가가 불어날 것이다 The cost will run [pile] up.

불어넣다 〈숨을〉 breathe into; 〈사상·의식 등

을〉 inspire 《*sb* with a spirit》; indoctrinate; inoculate; inform
♦새로운 생명을 불어넣다 breathe new life into *sb* / 자신감을 불어넣다 inspire confidence in *sb* / 위험한[새로운] 사상을 불어넣다 inoculate [inspire] *sb* with a dangerous [new] idea / 학생들에게 학습열을 불어넣다 inspire students with eagerness to learn

불어대다 1 〈바람이〉 blow ceaselessly; keep blowing ▶바람이 하루종일 불어댔다 The wind blew all day through.
2 〈호각 등을〉 keep blowing 《a whistle》; 〈피리 등을〉 keep playing on 《a trumpet》

불에 놀란 놈이 부지깽이 보고 놀란다 《속담》 Once bitten, twice shy. ⇌ A scalded cat [dog] fears cold water.

불여우 〔動〕 a red fox ♦불여우 같다 be foxy

불여의하다 不如意 〈여의치 않다〉 go contrary to *one's* wishes; go wrong [amiss]
▶매사가 불여의하다 Everything goes wrong (with me).

불연성 不燃性 noninflammability; nonflammability ♦불연성의 fireproof; incombustible; nonflammable; uninflammable
■―물질 incombustibles; noninflammables ―재료 noncombustible [incombustible] material

불연속 不連續 discontinuity ♦불연속의 discontinuous ―변이[분포]〔生〕a discontinuous variation [distribution] ―선〔氣〕 a line [front] of discontinuity; a gap in the isobaric line

불온 不穩 unrest; disquiet
―불온하다 disquieting; 〈의견 등이〉 alarming; turbulent; 〈형세 등이〉 threatening; 〈언행이〉 improper; riotous
♦불온한 공기 a charged atmosphere / 불온한 언사 (use) improper words; strong [violent, disquieting, sensational] language / 불온한 행동 improper [riotous] behavior
▶형세가 불온하다 The situation looks threatening. ⇌ Things are assuming a serious aspect.
■―문서 seditious [subversive] documents [literature] ―분자 a disturbing element; riotous [turbulent] people

불완전 不完全 imperfection; incompleteness ―불완전하다 imperfect; incomplete; faulty; defective
♦불완전한 점 a defect; a fault; an imperfection / 불완전한 지식 an imperfect knowledge / 불완전하게 imperfectly; incompletely; defectively; by halves / 다소 불완전한 데가 있다 lack [want] something of perfection; be somewhat defective
▶인간은 불완전한 존재다 Man is imperfect.
▶자네의 영어 발음은 아직 불완전하다 Your English pronunciation is still imperfect [far from perfect].
■―고용〔經〕 underemployment ―연소 imperfect combustion ―타[자]동사〔文法〕 an incomplete transitive [intransitive] verb

불요불굴 不撓不屈 ♦불요불굴의 노력 untired [persistent] industry / 불요불굴의 indomi-table; inflexible; dauntless; unyielding; unflinching; resolute; tenacious
▶그는 불요불굴의 정신을 가지고 있다 He has an indomitable spirit.

불요불급하다 不要不急― nonessential; nonurgent; not pressing
♦불요불급한 물건 a nonurgent thing / 불요불급한 지출 nonessential expenses

불용성 不溶性 insolubility
♦불용성의 insoluble

불용품 不用品 a disused [discarded] article; useless things

불우 不遇 〈불운〉 misfortune; ill fortune [luck, fate]; 〈역경〉 adversity
♦불우 이웃돕기 운동을 벌이다 launch a campaign to help unfortunate [needy] neighbors
―불우하다 unfortunate; ill-fated; unfavored; adverse
♦불우한 청소년 unfortunate youths / 불우한 처지에 있다 be in adverse circumstances; be in obscurity
▶그 시인은 불우한 가운데 죽었다 The poet died in obscurity.

불운 不運 (a) misfortune; ill luck [fortune]
♦이번 달은 불운의 연속이다 I have had a run of bad luck this month.
▶그는 자신의 불운을 한탄했다 He lamented his hard lot [fate].
―불운하다 unfortunate; unlucky; luckless
♦불운하게 (도) unfortunately; unluckily; as ill luck would have it
▶그는 평생 불운했다 He was hapless to the end of his life.

불원 不遠 〈거리상으로〉 not far (from); not so distant; not a long way; 〈시간적으로〉 soon; shortly; before long; in the near future
♦불원 천리하고 찾아오다 come a long way; come from a very long distance
▶불원간 희소식이 올 것이다 It will not be long before the good news arrives.

불유쾌 不愉快 unpleasantness ⇨ 불쾌

불응 不應 nonacceptance; declination; disobedience; 〈거절〉 refusal; rejection
―불응하다 do not answer; do not accept; decline; disobey; refuse; reject; turn down
♦소환에 불응하다 disobey a summons / 초대에 불응하다 decline an invitation
▶경영자측은 근로자측의 요구에 불응했다 The management turned down the request of the labor.

불의 不意 〈의외〉 suddenness; unexpectedness
♦불의의 만남 a chance meeting / 불의의 방문 a surprise visit [call] / 불의의 사건 an unexpected event / 불의의 〈예상밖의〉 unexpected; unforeseen; 〈돌연한〉 sudden; abrupt; 〈우연의〉 casual / 불의에 suddenly; abruptly; (all) of a sudden; 〈뜻밖에〉 unexpectedly; 〈우연히〉 by chance; 〈허를 절려〉 by surprise
▶우리는 모든 불의의 사고에 대비해야 한다 We must be prepared for every contingency.
▶그의 불의의 질문에 나는 당황했다 I was put out [confused, embarrassed] at his abrupt question.

불의 不義 〈옳지않음〉 injustice; unrighteous-

ness; impropriety; 〈밀통〉 illicitness; misconduct; adultery
♦ 불의의 씨 a child born in sin; a bastard / 불의의 unjust; unrighteous; illicit

불이익 不利益 disadvantage; a handicap; a drawback
♦ …에게 불이익이 되다 be against [detrimental to] sb's interests; compromise sb's interests [reputation]
▶ 그 조약은 한국 농민들에게 불이익으로 작용할 수도 있다 The treaty could work to the disadvantage of Korean farmers.

불이행 不履行 nonfulfillment; nonperformance; nonobservance; failure; breach
♦ 계약 불이행 nonfulfillment of a contract / 약속 불이행 failure to keep one's promise / 의무 불이행 failure in duty / 조약 불이행 nonobservance of a treaty / 채무 불이행 failure to pay one's financial debt; 〔法〕 default
▶ 그는 계약 불이행으로 고소당했다 He was sued for breach of contract.
ー불이행하다 fail to fulfill [perform, observe, carry out]; break 《one's promise》
ー자 a defaulter

불인가 不認可 disapproval; disallowance; 〈기각〉 rejection; refusal ー불인가하다 reject; refuse; turn down

불일간 不日間 before long ⇨ 불일내(不日內)

불일내 不日內 before long; in a few days; shortly; soon; one of these days
▶ 그는 자기가 얼마나 바보였는가를 불일내에 알게 될 것이다 One of these days he'll realize what a fool he has been.

불일듯이 lively; actively; successfully
♦ 장사가 불일듯이 잘 되다 one's business is thriving

불일듯하다 prosperous; flourishing; thriving
♦ 사업이 불일듯하다 one's business is thriving [growing like wildfire]; 〈사람이 주어〉 drive a prosperous [roaring, booming, thriving] trade

불일치 不一致 discord; discordance; discordancy; disagreement; 〈모순〉 inconsistency; 〔文法〕 false concord
♦ 언행의 불일치 discordance between one's words and actions
ー불일치하다 inharmonious; discordant; 《be》 in discord 《with》

불임 不姙 ♦ 불임의 sterile; barren
■ー수술 sterilization

불임증 不姙症 sterility; infertility; infecundity
♦ 불임증의 sterile; barren / 불임증이 되다 become sterile; lose one's reproductive power / 불임증을 고치다 cure 《her》 sterility
▶ 그녀는 불임증이 있는 것 같다 She seems to be sterile.

불입 拂入 (a) payment ⇨ 납입(納入)
ー불입하다 pay in; pay up 《stocks》
▶ 나는 매달 3만원씩 은행에 불입했다 I paid thirty thousand won into the bank every month.
▶ 매월 회비를 불입하기만 하면 회원이 될 수 있다 Anyone can be a member if only he pays his due every month.

■ー금 ⇨ 납입(~금)

불자 佛子 1 〈부처의 제자〉 a Buddha's disciple
2 〈보살〉 a Buddha saint
3 〈불교 신자〉 a believer in Buddhism

불자 佛者 〈불교 신자〉 a Buddhist; a believer in Buddhism

불자동차 —自動車 a fire engine [truck]

불장 佛葬 a Buddhistic funeral
♦ 불장으로 하다 conduct a funeral according to Buddhist rites

불장난 1 〈장난〉 playing with fire [matches]
ー불장난하다 play with fire [matches]
2 〈남녀간의〉 an idle love affair; an amatory escapade ♦ 사랑의 불장난 an amorous adventure
ー불장난하다 have an idle love affair

불전 佛典 the Buddhist scriptures [sutras]

불전 佛前 ♦ 불전에 바치다 place sth before the Buddhist altar

불전 佛殿 a Buddhist sanctum

불제 祓除 〈악귀를 물리침〉 exorcism; purification; 〈의식〉 a purification ceremony

불제자 佛弟子 a Buddhist; a believer in Buddhism

불조심 —操心 precautions against fire ▶ 불조심 (게시) Beware of fire. ー불조심하다 be careful with fire; take precautions against fire; look out for fire

불종 —鐘 a fire alarm [bell]
♦ 불종을 치다[울리다] sound a fire bell

불지르다 burn; set fire to 《a house》; set 《a house》 afire [on fire]; fire 《a house》
▶ 그는 광에 불질렀다 He set fire to the barn. ⇌ He set the barn on fire.

불지피다 〈불때다〉 make [build (up)] a fire; fix a fire; get a fire going ♦ 아궁이에 불지피다 make a fire in the fireplace

불집 a (fire) hazard; a hornet's nest
♦ 불집을 건드리다 stir up a hornet's nest; cause a troublesome situation

불쬐다 〈사람이〉 warm oneself at the fire; 〈물건을〉 put sth over a fire
♦ 손을 불쬐다 warm one's hands at the fire
♦ 불쬐세요 Please warm yourself at the fire.

불착 不着 nonarrival; nondelivery

불찬성 不贊成 disapproval; disagreement; dissent; disfavor; dissension
▶ 그래서 나는 불찬성이다 That is why I would not consent.
ー불찬성하다 disapprove 《of》; disagree 《with sb to a proposal》; dissent 《from》
■ー자 a disapprover; a dissenter

불찰 不察 〈부주의〉 carelessness; lack of attention; negligence; thoughtlessness; an oversight; 〈실수〉 a blunder; a mistake
▶ 제 불찰을 용서하십시오 Forgive me for my carelessness.
▶ 그런 사람을 신용한 것은 나의 불찰이었다 I made a mistake in trusting such a fellow.

불참 不參 absence; nonattendance; a failure in attendance; nonappearance
ー불참하다 be absent 《from》; absent oneself 《from》; fail to attend; stay away 《from》
■ー자 an absentee ー통고 a notice of absence

불철주야 不撤晝夜 day and night; night and day; around [round] the clock
♦불철주야(로) 일하다 work around the clock; work double tides [shifts]
─불철주야하다 never relax day and night; persevere in one's efforts night and day

불청객 不請客 a self-invited [an uninvited] guest; 《美》 a gate-crasher
▶나는 그의 집에 불청객이었다 I entered his house uninvited.

불체포특권 不逮捕特權 privilege of exemption from apprehension; nonapprehension privilege

불초 不肖 〈아버지만 못함〉 being unworthy of one's father; 〈자칭〉 I; myself
♦불초 자식 an unworthy son / 불초 제자 a pupil unworthy of his teacher

불출 不出 1 〈못난 사람〉 a stupid person; a good-for-nothing 2 〈외출하지 않음〉 confining oneself at home ♦두문 불출하다 keep [stay] indoors; confine oneself at home

불충 不忠 disloyalty; infidelity; failure in one's duty (to the state); 〈반역〉 treason
─불충하다 disloyal; unfaithful; undutiful; treacherous; false (to one's country)
─불효 disloyalty and filial impiety

불충분 不充分 insufficiency; 〈불완전〉 imperfection; 〈부적당〉 inadequacy
▶피고는 증거 불충분으로 석방되었다 The accused was set free on the ground of insufficient evidence.
─불충분하다 insufficient; not enough; unsatisfactory; imperfect; incomplete; defective; inadequate; not up to the mark
♦불충분한 일광 insufficient daylight / 자금이 불충분하다 be short of capital
♦제 영어 지식은 불충분합니다 My knowledge of English is quite imperfect.
▶그것은 내 질문에 대한 답변으로는 불충분하다 That is an unsatisfactory answer to my question.
▶보수는 수고에 비해 불충분하다 The remuneration is inadequate to the labor.

불충실 不忠實 disloyalty; faithlessness; infidelity ─불충실하다 disloyal; faithless; unfaithful ♦남편[아내]에게 불충실한 행동을 하다 be unfaithful to one's husband [wife]

불치 a shot down animal [bird]; game; a bag
♦많은 불치 a good [big] bag / 불치 넣는 부대 a gamebag

불치 不治 incurability; malignity
♦불치의 병 an incurable [a remediless, a fatal] disease / 불치의 incurable; immedicable; malignant; fatal; irremediable

불치하문하다 不恥下問 — be not ashamed to inquire of those beneath one

불친절 不親切 unkindness; unfriendliness
─불친절하다 unkind; unfriendly; 〈무뚝뚝하다〉 inhospitable ♦불친절하게 unkindly; in an unkind manner
▶저 여점원은 손님에게 불친절하다 The salesgirl is very inattentive to customers.
▶그녀는 그에게 불친절했다 She was not kind to him.

불침번 不寢番 all-night watch; sleepless [all night] vigil; 〈사람〉 a night watchman
♦불침번을 서다 keep a [go on the] night watch; keep vigil [watch]; be on duty as night watchman

불켜다 light (up) (a lamp); set (a lamp) alight; turn [switch] on (an electric lamp); burn (gas) ♦초에 불켜다 burn [light] a candle / 밤새도록 불켜 두다 keep a light burning all night
▶그의 방은 불켜져 있다 A light is on [burning] in his room.

불콰하다 ruddy; 〈서술적〉 wear the very blossom of health ♦얼굴이 불콰한 사람 a person with a ruddy complexion

불쾌 不快 1 〈기분의〉 displeasure; discomfort; unpleasantness ♦불쾌감을 느끼다[보이다] feel [show] displeasure
─불쾌하다 unpleasant; disagreeable; uncomfortable; displeased; ill-humored
♦불쾌한 냄새 an unpleasant [an offensive, a disgusting] smell / 불쾌한 사람 a disagreeable person / 불쾌한 소리 a jarring sound / 불쾌한 표정 a displeased [an offended] look / 불쾌한 듯이 with a displeased look; in ill humor / 불쾌하게 unpleasantly; disagreeably; displeasedly / 불쾌한 느낌을 주다 give (others) an unpleasant feeling / 불쾌하게 생각하다 feel uncomfortable; feel hurt; be displeased (with, at, by); take offense (at)
▶나는 저 사람이 나타나기만 하면 불쾌하다 I revolt at his mere presence.
▶그의 건방진 말에 그녀는 불쾌했다 His arrogant words hurt her feelings [offended her].
▶남에게 불쾌한 말을 하지 마라 Don't say things that get on others' nerves.
▶나는 불쾌한 소식을 그녀에게 전하지 않는다 I don't pass objectionable news on to her.
2 〈몸의〉 (an) indisposition; an ailment
─불쾌하다 be not well; be indisposed; be out of sorts; be in bad shape
■─지수 a discomfort index (略 DI); a temperature-humidity index (略 THI)

불타 佛陀 Buddha ⇨ 부처

불타다 1 〈타다〉 burn; blaze; be in flames
♦불타는 (듯한) 저녁놀 a fiery [a flaming] sunset / 불타는 집 a burning [blazing] house; a house on fire [in raging flames] / 석양에 불타는 하늘 the sky aglow with the setting sun / 활활 불타다 burn briskly [vigorously, furiously]/불타기 쉽다 be easy to burn; catch fire easily; be combustible [inflammable, flammable] / 불탄 자리를 뒷수습하다 clean up the debris after a fire
▶그 집은 불타고 있었다 The house was burning [on fire, in flames].
▶목조 가옥은 불타기 쉽다 Wooden houses burn [catch fire] easily.
▶산허리는 새빨간 단풍으로 불타는 듯 하다 The hillside glows [flames] with red maples.
2 〈정열·의욕이〉 burn; glow; be aflame
♦불타는 사랑 an ardent love; flaming love / 불타는 정열 a burning [consuming, fiery] passion / 복수심에 불타다 be thirsty for revenge /

청춘의 정열에 불타다 burn with youthful ardor
▶ 그녀는 질투심에 불탔다 She burned with jealousy.
▶ 그는 야심에 불타고 있다 He is burning with ambition.
▶ 그들은 애국심에 불타고 있다 Their hearts burn [glow] with patriotism.
▶ 그녀는 음악에 불타는 정열이 있었다 She had a burning passion for music.

불탑 佛塔 a pagoda
불통 不通 1 〈교통·통신의〉 suspension; interruption 《of telephone service》; stoppage; tie-up 《of traffic》
♦ 열차[전신]의 불통 the interruption of train service [telegraphic communication] / 통신 불통인 지방 a telegraphically isolated district
▶ 전화가 불통이다 The phone [wire] is dead. ⇌ The line is out.
—**불통하다** be suspended; be stopped; be blocked; be interrupted; be paralyzed; be cut off; be tied up
▶ 산사태로 철도가 여러 시간 불통되었다 The landslide tied up railroad service for several hours.
▶ 시 전체의 전화가 불통되었다 All the telephones in the city were cut off [disrupted].
2 〈교제·연락의〉 no association; lack of contact; no communication; 〈익숙하지 못함〉 unfamiliarity; ignorance
♦ 세상 일에 불통이다 know [have seen] but little of the world; be ignorant of [inexperienced in] the ways of the world / 의사가 서로 불통이다 do not understand each other
▶ 그녀와는 2년 동안 소식이 불통이다 I have heard nothing from her these two years.
—**불통하다** lack contact; be not communicated; be ill informed 《on》; be unfamiliar 《with》; be ignorant 《of》

불통일 不統一 disunity; lack of unity [coordination]; inconstancy; disorganization; 〈내부적인〉 disunion; disharmony
♦ 여론의 불통일 lack of (a) public consensus
▶ 그 문제에 대하여 우리는 아직 의견이 불통일이다 Our opinions are divided on the question.

불퇴전 不退轉 unswerving determination; a firm resolve; [佛敎] firm belief in Buddha
♦ 불퇴전의 결의 an indomitable resolve / 불퇴전의 결심으로 with an indomitable spirit; resolved to win [do] or die
▶ 그는 그 조사를 계속하기로 불퇴전의 결의를 했다 He was firmly resolved [determined] to continue the investigation.

불투명 不透明 opacity; opaqueness —**불투명하다** opaque; milky; turbid; cloudy; thick
♦ 불투명한 태도 a vague attitude; an uncertain [a noncommittal] attitude
■ —**도** opacity —**색** an opaque color —**유리** opaque glass; devitrified glass —**체** an opaque; an opaque body [substance]
불퉁불퉁하다 1 〈표면이〉 bumpy; knagged; knaggy; knotty; gnarled; rugged; jagged
♦ 불퉁불퉁한 도로 a bumpy [rough] road / 불퉁불퉁한 바위 a jagged rock / 불퉁불퉁한 해안선 an irregular coastline
2 〈말이〉 brusque; curt; blunt; protruding
불퉁하다 bulgy; protuberant
불특정 不特定 ♦ 불특정의 unspecific; unspecified; general
■ —**기간** an unspecified term —**다수인** many and unspecified persons: 장사란 불특정 다수인을 상대로 하는 것이다 Every trade is for unspecified recipients.
불티 a spark; a sparkle ♦ 불티나다 〈잘 팔리다〉 sell [go] (off) like fun [hot cakes] / 불티가 나다 spark; sparkle; throw sparks ▶ 그것들은 불티나게 팔렸다 They sold like hot cakes.

불패 不敗 invincibility ♦ 불패의 undefeated; unbeatable; 〈무적의〉 invincible / 불패의 기록을 자랑하다 have a proud record of all wins and no defeat

불편 不便 1 〈몸 등의〉 (a) discomfort; an ailment; (an) indisposition; malaise
—**불편하다** be not well; be [feel] unwell [ill]; be indisposed; be [feel] out of sorts [form, condition]; be in bad shape
▶ 나는 몸이 불편하다 I am in poor health. ⇌ I don't feel well.
▶ 속이 뭔가 좀 불편하다 Something is the matter with my stomach.
2 〈편리하지 못함〉 inconvenience
♦ 불편을 끼치다 cause [give] sb inconvenience; inconvenience [incommode] sb / 불편을 느끼다 feel [be put to] inconvenience; be incommoded / 불편을 참다 put up with inconveniences [discomfort]
—**불편하다** inconvenient; unhandy
♦ 장보기에 불편한 곳 a place inconvenient for shopping / 교통이 불편하다 lack traffic facilities / 휴대가 불편하다 be unhandy [bulky] to carry about
▶ 이 집은 살기 불편하다 This house is inconvenient to live in.
▶ 불편하게 해드려서 죄송합니다 I am sorry to have put you to inconvenience. ⇌ I am sorry to have troubled you.

불편부당 不偏不黨 nonpartisanship; impartiality; 〈중립〉 neutrality
▶ 그는 평생 불편부당의 원칙을 관철했다 He continued to have [stuck to] his principle of impartiality all his life.
—**불편부당하다** be impartial [nonpartisan, neutral, fair, unbias(s)ed, unprejudiced]
♦ 불편부당한 신문 an impartial newspaper; a newspaper free from party affiliations

불평 不平 discontent 《with》; dissatisfaction 《with, at》; displeasure; 〈정부에 대한〉 disaffection; 〈불평의 말〉 a grievance; a murmur; a complaint; (俗) a grouse; (美俗) a beef
♦ 불평을 늘어놓다 air one's grievances / 불평을 품다 feel discontented; be disaffected [ill-affected] 《toward》 / 불평이 가득하다 be extremely dissatisfied / 불평이 있다 have complaint to make; have a beef
▶ 그들은 언제나 불평이다 They are always full of complaints.
▶ 그녀는 남편의 일로 좀처럼 불평을 말하지 않

는다 She seldom complains of her husband.
▶ 그는 언제나 정부 정책에 대해 불평을 늘어놓고 있다 He is always sounding off about the government's policies.
▶ 주민들 사이에서는 불평의 소리가 높다 Loud cries of discontent are being voiced among the people. = The residents are voicing their disontent [grievances] loudly.
—**불평하다** complain of; make a complaint; grumble at [about, over]; murmur at [against]; grunt; 《美俗》 gripe; beef
▶ 그는 숙제에 대해 불평했다 He grumbled about his homework.
▶ 그는 우리에게 부당한 대우를 받고 있다고 불평하고 있다 He complains to us that he is unfairly treated.
▶ 불평하지 말고 얼른 심부름이나 가거라 Go on an errand at once without a murmur.
▶ 불평할 이유는 없다 There is no reason for complaint.
■—**꾼** a (chronic) grumbler [complainer]; 《美俗》 a griper; 《英俗》 a grouser; a malcontent —**분자** the malcontents; the discontented [dissatisfied, disaffected] elements

불평등 不平等 inequality 《in, between》; 〈차별〉 discrimination ◆ 인종적 불평등 discrimination by race; racial discrimination
—**불평등하다** unequal; 〈불공평하다〉 unfair
◆ 불평등한 대우 an unfair treatment
■—**조약** an unequal treaty

불포화 不飽和 unsaturation ■—**기(基)** an unsaturated radical —**화합물** an unsaturated compound

불피우다 make [build] a fire 《in a stove》; get a fire going ◆ 방을 따뜻하게 하기 위해 불 피우다 make [build] a fire to warm a room

불필요하다 不必要— unnecessary; needless; unessential; uncalled-for
◆ 불필요한 것 unnecessary things / 불필요하게 unnecessarily; needlessly / 불필요하게 법석 떨다 make an unnecessary fuss 《about》
▶ 여름옷은 이제 불필요하다 Summer clothing is no longer needed.
▶ 이런 것은 불필요하다 We can dispense with this. = We can go [do] without this.

불하 拂下 (a) sale 《of government property》; (a) transfer 《of state property to private ownership》; (a) disposal
—**불하하다** sell; dispose of; transfer
▶ 정부는 국유림의 일부를 불하했다 Government sold off [disposed of] part of the national forest.
■—**품** an article sold [disposed of] by the government

불학무식 不學無識 (utter) ignorance; illiteracy —**불학무식하다** (utterly) ignorant; illiterate; unlettered

불한당 不汗黨 〈강도〉 (a gang of) burglars [robbers, bandits]; 〈깡패〉 a gang of hooligans; (street) gangsters; hoodlums (and racketeers)

불합격 不合格 〈실격〉 disqualification; 〈낙방〉 failure; elimination; 〈퇴짜〉 rejection
◆ 불합격의 unqualified; disqualified; rejected

—**불합격하다[되다]** be disqualified [rejected, eliminated]; come [fall] short of the mark [standard]; be found ineligible [unfit] 《for》; 〈시험에〉 fail (in) [fail to pass] 《an examination》; 《美》 flunk
▶ 나는 연령 미달로 불합격되었다 My lack of age caused disqualification.
▶ 그녀는 입사 시험에 불합격했다 She failed (in) [did not pass] the employment examination.
■—**자** a disqualified [rejected] person; an unsuccessful applicant : 50명의 응모자 중 불합격자는 20명이었다 There were 20 failures among 50 applicants. —**품** a rejected article; off-grade goods

불합리 不合理 irrationality; unreasonableness; absurdity; illogicality; inconsistency
—**불합리하다** irrational; unreasonable; illogical ◆ 불합리한 결론 an illogical conclusion / 불합리한 이론[가격] an unreasonable theory [price] / 불합리하기 짝이 없는 out of all reason
▶ 네 말은 불합리하다 What you say is absurd.
▶ 그의 불합리한 요구에 화가 났다 I was [got] angry at his unreasonable request.

불행 不幸 1 〈불운〉 unhappiness; infelicity; misery; misfortune; ill fortune [luck]; 〈역경〉 adversity
◆ 어떠한 불행을 겪을지라도 no matter what misfortune one may experience / 불행의 밑바닥에 있다 be in the depth of misery / 불행을 당하다 suffer a misfortune; be hit by misfortune
▶ 그에게는 평생 불행이 따라다녔다 He was dogged by misfortune all his life.
▶ 사람의 행 불행은 그 사람의 행동에 달려있다 A man's happiness and unhappiness depends on his deeds.
▶ 불행은 겹치는 법 《속담》 Misfortunes [Troubles] never come single [singly].
—**불행하다** unhappy; unfortunate; unlucky; luckless; miserable; wretched
◆ 불행한 사람 an unhappy [a miserable] person; a wretched mortal / 불행한 소식 ill news / 불행한 집안 an unfortunate family / 불행하게도 unfortunately; unluckily; by misfortune [ill fortune] / 불행한 일생을 보내다 lead [live] an unhappy [a miserable] life
▶ 그녀는 가정적으로 불행했다 Her home life was anything but happy.
▶ 그녀는 부모없는 불행한 아이들을 돌보았다 She looked after unhappy orphans.
2 〈재난〉 a disaster; a calamity; 〈사고〉 an accident; 〈비극〉 a tragedy; 〈재앙〉 woe
3 〈사망〉 a death; a loss; a (sad) bereavement
◆ 불행을 당하다 suffer a loss; be bereaved 《of one's father》
▶ 그의 가족에게 불행이 있었다 There was a death [bereavement] in his family.

불행중다행 不幸中多幸 one consolation in sadness; a stroke of good luck in the midst of misfortune
▶ 중상자는 없다니 불행중 다행이다 It is consoling to know that none was injured seriously.

불허 不許 disapproval; nonpermission
▶불허 복제 All rights reserved. ⇌ Reprint [Reproduction] prohibited.
—**불허하다** disapprove; do not permit [allow, grant, admit]; reject; turn down
▶교실에서는 흡연을 불허한다 Smoking is prohibited [not allowed] in classrooms.
▶허가 없이는 입실을 불허한다 No one is admitted to [allowed to enter] the room without permission.
▶그의 소설은 타의 추종을 불허한다 His novels elude all attempts at imitation.

불현듯(이) suddenly; on [all of] a sudden
♦불현듯이 집 생각이 나다 be overcome with sudden homesickness; suddenly feel homesick / …하려는 생각이 불현듯 일어나다 have a sudden desire to 《do》; be seized with a desire to 《do》; suddenly feel like 《doing》
▶그녀는 불현듯 그가 보고 싶었다 She had a sudden burning desire to see him.

불협화음 不協和音 〔樂〕 a discord; a dissonance; a cacophony ♦불협화음의 dissonant; unconsonant; cacophonous

불호령 —號令 a fiery command; an impetuous order; thunder; a roaring scolding —불호령을 내리다 issue an impetuous [a fiery] order; thunder 《against sb》; storm sb
▶그는 일을 시작하라고 부하들에게 불호령을 했다 He thundered at the men to get to work.

불혹 不惑 〈미혹하지 않음〉 being free from vacillation; 〈나이〉 the age free from vacillation; the age of forty
▶불혹의 나이가 지났는데도 그는 유치하다 He sounds immature for a man past (the age of) forty.

불화 不和 trouble; discord 《among, between》; 〈의견차이〉 differences; disharmony; disagreement; 〈마찰〉 (a) friction
♦부부간의 불화 marital [matrimonial] quarrel / 불화의 원인 the apple of discord / 그룹 내에 불화를 조성하다 cause friction in a group
▶부부간의 불화는 청소년 비행의 원인이다 A quarrel between husband and wife causes juvenile delinquency.
▶양자간에는 당분간 불화 관계가 계속될 것이다 Both of them will remain on bad terms with each other for a while.
—**불화하다** 〈서술적〉 be in discord 《with》; be on bad terms 《with》; be at odds 《with》; (口) be at outs 《with》
■가정— family trouble; family [domestic] discord [dissension]; a family difference [jar]: 가정 불화를 일으키다 cause family trouble [discord]

불화 弗化 〔化〕 fluoridation
■—를 a fluorid(e) —수소[칼슘, 칼륨] hydrogen [calcium, potassium] fluoride

불화 弗貨 dollar; the U.S. dollar

불확대 不擴大 localization
■—방침 a nonexpansion [nonaggravation] policy; a localization policy: 그들은 분쟁의 불확대 방침을 취했다 They adopted a policy localizing the dispute.

불확실 不確實 uncertainty; unreliability
—**불확실하다** uncertain; unreliable; insecure; precarious ♦불확실한 계획 an indefinite plan / 불확실한 기억 an unreliable memory / 불확실한 보도 an unreliable [unauthentic] report / 불확실한 장사 a shaky business

불확정 不確定 indeterminacy; indeterminateness ♦불확정적인 indefinite; indeterminate; uncertain; undecided; unsettled
▶결혼식 날짜는 아직 불확정이다 The date of the wedding is still uncertain [undecided].
—**불확정하다** do not decide upon [settle, confirm]
■—기간 〔法〕 a time uncertain —성 원리 〔物〕 the uncertainty principle; the principle of uncertainty —신용장 an unconfirmed letter of credit —자산 risky assets

불환지폐 不換紙幣 an inconvertible note; (美) flat money

불활성 不活性 〔物·化〕 inactivity; inertness
■—가스 an inert gas

불황 不況 depression; slump; bad [slack] business; 〈정체〉 stagnation; 〈일시적 후퇴〉 recession; the weak tone of market
♦경기 불황 slack business; a (business) slump / 1930년대의 세계적인 불황 the worldwide depression [slump] of the 1930s / 불황의 dull; depressed; weak; slack; stagnant / 불황의 밑바닥에 있다 be at the bottom of the depression / 불황에서 빠져나오다 climb out of the depression / 불황을 극복하다 overcome [get over] the recession
▶불황 때문에 우리 회사는 파산할 지경이다 Our company is almost bankrupt because of [owing to] the depression.
■—기(期) a dull [a dead, an off] season (in trade); a slack time [season] —산업 a depressed industry —시대 depression [bad] days; lean years; hard times

불효 不孝 want [lack] of filial piety; impiety [undutifulness] to one's parents; disobedience
—**불효하다** be undutiful [unfilial, impious, disobedient]
▶넌 참 불효하구나 What a disobedient son you are!
■—자 an undutiful [an unfilial, a thankless] son [daughter]; a bad son [daughter]: 그는 불효자다 He is an undutiful son.

불후 不朽 ♦불후의 명작 an immortal work [book]; an everlasting masterpiece / 불후의 immortal; undying; undecaying; imperishable; everlasting; eternal / 불후의 명성을 남기다 perpetuate [immortalize] one's name; win eternal fame; one's name wins immortality
—**불후하다** never die [decay]; endure; last [live] forever

불휘발 不揮發 ♦불휘발성의 fixed 《oil》; nonvolatile

붉나무 〔植〕 a sumac(h)

붉다 red; 〈심홍〉 crimson; 〈진홍〉 scarlet; 〈사상이〉 communistic
♦붉은 빰 red [ruddy, rosy] cheeks / 붉은 얼굴 a ruddy [rubicund] face; a florid countenance / 붉어지다 turn red [scarlet, crimson]; redden / 화가 나서 붉어지다 be red [flushed]

with anger / 흥분하여 붉어지다 flush with excitement / 부끄러워 붉어지다 blush with [for] shame; color up / 붉게 물들이다 dye red
▶ 그는 술만 마시면 곧 얼굴이 붉어진다 His face gets red as soon as he drinks anything alcoholic.
▶ 나뭇잎이 붉어졌다 The leaves have turned red.
▶ 그녀는 얼굴이 붉어졌다 She blushed.
▶ 화염이 하늘을 붉게 물들였다 The fire reddened the sky.

붉돔 〔魚〕 a crimson sea bream
붉디붉다 very red, deep red; crimson
붉으락푸르락하다 turn alternately pale and red
붉은광장 —廣場 〈모스크바의〉 the Red Square
붉은바다거북 〔動〕 a loggerhead (turtle)
붉은부리갈매기 〔鳥〕 a hooded gull; a black-headed gull
붉은토끼풀 〔植〕 a red clover; a trifolium
붉히다 redden; blush; color up
▶ 그녀는 부끄러워 얼굴을 붉혔다 She turned red [blushed] with shame. ⇌ Shame flushed her face.
▶ 그는 화가 나서 얼굴을 붉혔다 He is flushed with anger.

붐 〈벼락 경기〉 a boom; 〈일시적 유행〉 a craze; (口) a fad ◆ 여행 붐 the travel boom / 붐이 일다 boom / 붐을 타다 ride the crest of the (building) boom
▶ 그들 사이에서는 롤러 스케이팅이 붐이다 Roller skating is a big fad among them.
붐비다 be crowded [thronged] 《with people》; be congested [jampacked]; be full up
◆ 붐비는 버스 a crowded bus / 붐비는 시간 《at, during》 the rush hour(s) [period]
▶ 거리는 쇼핑객들로 붐볐다 The streets were crowded [thronged] with the shoppers.
▶ 차안은 몹시 붐볐다 The car was jammed [jampacked] inside.

붓 〈모필〉 a writing brush; 〈화필〉 a brush; a paintbrush; 〈펜〉 a pen
◆ 붓의 힘 the power of the pen; the pen / 붓이 가는 대로 쓰다 let one's pen wander; write at random / 붓을 던지다 give up (further) writing / 붓을 놓다 lay [put] down one's brush [pen]; cease to write / 붓을 들다 write; put pen to paper / 붓에 먹을 묻히다 dip a writing brush in ink
▶ 명필은 붓을 탓하지 않는다 (속담) A bad workman quarrels with his tools.
붓꽃 〔植〕 a blue flag; an iris (pl. ~ (es), irides)
붓끝 1 〈붓의 끝〉 the point [tip] of a writing brush 2 〈붓놀림〉 wielding of a pen; manipulation of one's pen; one's pen ◆ 붓끝이 날카로운 평론가 a critic who wields [writes with] a sharp pen
붓다¹ 1 〈부풀다〉 swell (up, out); bloat (out); be [become] swollen [bloated]; tumefy
◆ 부은 swollen; bloated; tumid / 울어서 눈이 붓다 have one's eyes swollen with crying; cry one's eyes out / 림프샘이 붓다 develop swollen lymphatic glands
▶ 나는 발목이 부었다 I have a swollen ankle. ⇌ My ankle has swollen.
▶ 그의 얼굴은 벌에 쏘여 붓기 시작했다 His face began to swell [began swelling] from a bee sting.
2 〈성나다〉 get angry 《at》; become sullen; sulk; fret; (口) get sore 《at, on, over》
◆ 부은 angry; cross; sulky; sullen; sour / 부은 얼굴 a sulky look [face]
▶ 그녀는 부어 있다 She's rather put out. ⇌ She is displeased [sullen, irritated]. ⇌ She is in a bad mood.
▶ 무엇 때문에 부어 있니? What makes you (so) sulky?

붓다² 1 〈쏟다〉 pour (in, into)
◆ 주형에 납을 붓다 pour lead into a mold / 독에 물을 붓다 pour water into a pot; fill a jar with water / 물을 더 붓다 pour [add] more water into
▶ 끓고 있는 주전자에 물을 좀더 부었다 I added some water to a boiling kettle.
▶ 포트에 더운 물을 부어라 Pour hot water into the pot.
▶ 이 동상은 청동을 부어 만든 것이다 This statue is cast in bronze.
2 〈뿌리다〉 sow ◆ 밭에 씨앗을 붓다 sow seed in the field; sow the field with seed
3 〈납입금을〉 pay in [by] installments
◆ 월 5만원씩 붓다 pay a installment of 50,000 won
붓대 the shaft of a writing brush
붓두껍 a writing brush protector; a brush cap
붓방아 chewing on one's pen; fingering one's pen while searching ideas ◆ 붓방아를 찧다 chew [bite] on one's pen; finger one's pen
붓순나무 〔植〕 a Chinese anise
붓장난 quill driving; hack writing
—**붓장난하다** drive the quill; be a hack writer
붓질 drawing; painting; a stroke [touch] with a brush —**붓질하다** draw; paint; stroke; make strokes [touches] with a brush
붓통 —筒 a brush vase

붕 1 〈방귀 소리〉 ◆ 방귀를 붕 뀌다 break wind; (卑) let a fart; poop
2 〈벌·비행기 등의〉 humming; buzzing; droning
▶ 벌이 붕 소리를 내며 날고 있다 Bees are buzzing around.
▶ 비행기가 머리 위를 붕 날고 있었다 A plane was droning over head.
3 〈엔진 등의〉 droning; whirring
4 〈허망하게〉 in vain; in smoke; fleetingly
◆ 〈계획 등이〉 붕 뜨다 end [go up] in smoke / 저축(했던 돈)이 도박으로 붕 뜨다 gamble away one's saving

붕괴 崩壞 (a) collapse; (a) breaking; a breakdown; (a) crumbling; a fall; 〈함몰〉 a cave-in; 〔物〕 disintegration
◆ 가정의 붕괴 the ruin [fall] of one's family; 〈이혼 등에 의한〉 the breakup of one's home (▶ 이 결과 생기는 「붕괴된 가정」은 a broken home. (美)에서는 완곡하게 a single parent home 이라고 함) / 제방의 붕괴 the breaking of

an embankment / 증권 시장의 붕괴 the collapse of the securities market
▶그 아파트는 붕괴 직전이었다 The apartment building was on the verge of collapse.
—**붕괴하다** collapse; fall (down); give way; break down; crumble; 〈함몰하다〉 cave [fall] in; 〔物〕 disintegrate
▶터널이 붕괴해 인부 10명이 생매장되었다 Ten workmen were buried alive by a cave-in of the tunnel.
▶그 건물은 붕괴되어 가고 있었다 The building was falling down.
▶그가 죽으면 가정은 붕괴될 것이다 His family will be ruined [break up] if he dies.

붕굿하다 〈언덕 등이〉 swollen; 〈배 등이〉 bulging; bulgy; 〈배접이 들뜨다〉 loose; blistered

붕당 朋黨 a faction; a clique; a coterie ◆붕당을 이루다 form a coterie; clique together ■—심 a cliquish [party] spirit; cliquism

붕대 繃帶 a bandage
◆발에 붕대를 감다 bandage one's foot; put a bandage on [around] one's foot / 다친 손가락에 붕대를 감아 놓다 have a bandage on one's injured finger / 붕대를 풀다 unbandage; undress (a wound); take a bandage off (a wound); remove a bandage
▶간호사는 내 붕대를 갈아주었다 The nurse changed my bandage [renewed dressing].
▶다음 주까지 붕대를 풀수 없을지 모릅니다 I'm afraid the bandages cannot come off until next week.

붕붕 〈나는 소리〉 a hum; a buzz; a whir
▶벌이 꽃 주위를 붕붕 날아다니고 있다 Bees are buzzing [humming] around the flowers.

붕사 硼砂 〔化〕 borax ◆붕사를 함유한 boric; boracic ■천연— native borax; tincal ▶—구슬 반응 a borax bead reaction —땜 soldering with borax

붕산 硼酸 〔化〕 boracic [boric] acid ■—수 a boric acid solution —연고 boric ointment

붕 소 硼素 〔化〕 boron ■ 수 소 화— boron hydride

붕어 〔魚〕 a crucian (carp); a Prussian carp
붕어 崩御 demise; the death of an emperor
▶왕이 붕어했다 The King has passed away.
붕어마름 〔植〕 a hornwort
붕우 朋友 a friend; a companion
▶그는 나의 젊은 시절의 붕우였다 He was a companion of my youth.
▶붕우 유신(有信) Faith should reign over the relation between friends.

붕장어 —長魚 〔魚〕 a conger (eel); a sea eel
붙다 1 〈부착되다〉 stick (to); 〈들러붙다〉 cling (to) ◆착 붙다 stick fast (to)
▶젖은 종이는 유리에 붙는다 The wet paper clings to the glass.
▶접착제가 그의 손가락에 붙었다 Glue had stuck to his fingers.
▶그 이름은 평생 그에게 붙어 다녔다 That name clung to him throughout his life.
▶그 병에는 「독극물」이라는 딱지가 붙어 있었다 The bottle is labeled "Poison."
2 〈맞닿다〉 keep [stand] close (to)
◆벽에 꼭 붙어 서다 stand close to the wall; hug the wall
▶두 집은 서로 붙어 있다 The two houses stand close to each other.
▶그는 옷이 몸에 착 붙어서 기분이 나빴다 His clothes cleaved uncomfortably to his body.
3 〈추종하다〉 be attached to; belong to; join; 〈편들다〉 take sides [a side] with; take the side of; side with
◆반대당에 붙다 join the opposite party / 부자에게 붙다 attach oneself to the rich / 적측에 붙다 go over to the enemy
▶그는 경영자측에 붙었다 He took the side of the management.
▶그는 언제나 가난한 자나 약한 자에게 붙어 있다 He is always on the side of the poor and (the) weak.
▶그 사람에게 붙어 있으면 넌 손해는 없다 Under him you will have nothing to lose.
4 〈딸리다〉 be attached (to); be joined (with); be connected (with); be coupled (with)
▶그 책에는 색인이 붙어 있다 The book has [is provided with] an index.
▶이 열차에는 침대차가 붙어 있다 This train has a sleeping car. ⇌ A sleeping car is attached to this train.
5 〈생기다〉 ◆버릇이 붙다 get [fall] into a habit (of) / 나쁜 버릇이 붙다 form [acquire, develop] a bad habit / 별명이 붙다 be given a nickname; be nicknamed; a nickname sticks to sb / 영어 실력이 붙다 make progress in English; improve one's English
▶이 채권에는 연 1할의 이자가 붙는다 This bond yields [bears] an annual interest of ten percent.
6 〈시중들다〉 attend on; wait on
▶그 중환자에게는 의사가 쭉 붙어 있었다 The doctor was in constant attendance on the dangerous patient.
▶나는 병상의 어머니 곁에 붙어 정성껏 병구완을 했다 I waited on my bed-ridden mother hand and foot.
7 〈오래 머물다〉 stay long; do not leave one's post ◆사무실에 늘 붙어 있다 be constantly at the [one's] office
▶우리 아이들은 집에 좀처럼 붙어 있지를 않는다 Our sons and daughters seldom stay (at) home.
▶그 집에는 가정부가 오래 붙어 있으려하지 않는다 Maids won't stay long (in service) in that family.
▶그가 이 회사에 오래 붙어 있으리라고는 생각되지 않는다 I don't think he will stay long in this company.
8 〈불이〉 catch (fire); be ignited
▶한국의 목조 가옥은 불이 붙기 쉽다 Korean wooden houses easily catch (on) fire.
▶아무래도 불이 붙지 않는다 The fire won't light. / 〈성냥이〉 The match won't strike.
9 〈귀신이〉 be possessed (by, with); be obsessed (by); be haunted (by)
◆귀신이 붙다 be possessed by a devil
10 〈시험에〉 pass (an examination)
◆입학 시험에 붙다 pass an entrance examina-

붙들다

tion / 학교에 붙다 be admitted into a school; obtain [get] admission to a school
11 〈싸움 등이〉 be started
♦싸움이 붙다 start a quarrel; a quarrel is started / 아무와 싸움이 붙다 have a quarrel with *sb*
12 〈정 등이〉 ♦정이 붙다 become [get] intimate (with); become attached to 《a woman》; come to love *sb*
13 〈교미하다〉 link [lock] in copulation; copulate; couple; mate; pair
14 〈일 등이〉 ♦일이 손에 안 붙다 have no mind (to do); be in no mood (to do, for doing)

붙들다 take hold of ⇨ 붙잡다

붙박이 a fixture; a fixed [built-in] article
♦붙박이의 fixed; built-in / 붙박이로 as a fixture; constantly / 붙박이로 하다 fix; build in
▶그것은 붙박이라 떼어낼 수가 없다 It is fixed [built] in, and cannot be taken down.
▶내 서재에는 벽에 서가가 붙박이로 설치되어 있다 The bookshelves are built into the walls of my study.
■ㅡ가구 fittings ㅡ장[책장] a built-in wardrobe [bookcase] ㅡ창 a blind window; a built-in [an immovable] window

붙박이다 be fixed; be fastened firmly [immovably] ♦집에 붙박여 있다 confine *oneself* to [in] *one's* house; be confined in *one's* house; be confined within doors; keep the house; stick at home

붙안다 embrace [hug] *sb* close [tightly, hard]; hold [fold, lock] 《a baby》 in *one's* arms; cuddle *sb*

붙어다니다 follow *sb* about [around]; shadow; (口) tag along
♦그림자처럼 붙어다니다 follow *sb* like a shadow / 여자 꽁무니에 붙어다니다 dangle about [after, round] a girl

-붙이 **1** 〈같은 겨레〉 the same blood; lineage
♦살붙이 kith and kin / 일가붙이 (family) relations; (near) relatives; kinsfolk
2 〈같은 종류〉 things of the same kind [class, group] / 쇠붙이 metals; ironware

붙이다 **1** [부착하다] attach [fix, tag] 《one thing to another》; stick; fasten; post; 〈고약 등을〉plaster; 〈풀로〉paste; 〈아교로〉glue
♦상품마다 가격표를 하나씩 붙이다 attach a price tag to [put a price tag on] each article / 고약을 붙이다 apply a plaster (to skin); plaster 《a sore place》/ 봉투에 우표를 붙이다 put a stamp on an envelope / 소포에 꼬리표를 붙이다 attach a tag to a parcel / 벽에 광고지를 붙이다 stick [paste up] a bill on the wall / 포스터를 붙이다 put up a poster / 깨진 파편을 접착제로 붙이다 glue broken pieces; stick broken pieces together with glue · 책장을 벽에 붙이다 put [set] a bookcase (up) against the wall / 바닥에 타일을 붙이다 tile a floor; floor 《a room》 with tiles
▶풀로 붙였으니까 곧 떨어질 거야 It will soon come off as it is stuck on with paste.
▶광고지를 붙이지 말 것 《게시》 Stick [Post] no bills (here).
2 〈첨부하다〉 add (to); attach (to); affix (to); annex (to); append (to)
♦경품을 붙인 퀴즈 쇼 a giveaway show / 멜로디에 가사를 붙이다 put [set] words to a melody / 조건을 붙이다 attach [annex] a condition (to *one's* proposal); set terms [a condition (on)] / 의견을 붙이다 make an additional comment [opinion]; give [offer, deliver] *one's* opinion (in a debate) / 이자를 붙여서 돈을 갚다 pay back the money with (2%) interest
3 〈불을〉 light; kindle; ignite
♦다이너마이트에 불을 붙이다 fire [set off] a charge of dynamite / 담배[양초]에 불을 붙이다 light a cigarette [candle] / 성냥으로 불을 붙이다 light [kindle] a fire with a match
4 〈이름 등을〉 give 《a name to》
♦이름을 붙이다 name; give a name (to) / 제목을 붙이다 give a title (to a composition)
▶첫아기에게 어떤 이름을 붙였나요? What did you name your first baby?
5 〈흥정·싸움 등을〉 bring two parties for (doing); get two parties to (do); arrange
♦싸움을 붙이다 make (two men) quarrel; kindle a quarrel; set 《dogs》 fighting 《each other》/ 혼담을 붙이다 arrange a match 《between》/ 흥정을 붙이다 get two parties to arrange [strike] a bargain
6 〈사람을〉 have *sb* in attendance; let *sb* be attended [waited upon]
♦피고에게 변호사를 붙이다 provide the defendant with a lawyer [counsel]
▶그들은 그 남자에게 감시자를 붙였다 They set a watch on the man.
▶자네와 동행할 사람으로 그를 붙여 주지 I'll send him with you.
7 〈교미시키다〉 mate; couple; pair
8 〈의지하다〉 rely [depend, lean] on [upon]; look [turn] to *sb* (for help [assistance]); put *oneself* under *sb's* care [wings]; live [hang, sponge] on
▶그녀는 잠시 언니 집에 몸을 붙이고 있다 She is staying with her sister for a while.
▶나는 몸 붙일 곳이 없다 I have no place to go to [no friend to turn to] for help.
9 〈받아 주다〉 admit 《*sb* to membership》; let [allow, take] in; let *sb* join (in *sth*)
♦붙여 주지 않다 keep *sb* out of a group; leave *sb* out [alone]
▶저 애는 붙이지 말자 Let's not let him in.
10 〈내기에 돈을 대다〉 bet [stake, wager, put] 《a thousand won》
♦경마에 돈을 붙이다 bet [make a bet, gamble] on a horse race / 돈을 붙이고 카드놀이를 하다 play cards for money; gamble at cards
11 〈마음에 들게 하다〉 take; have
♦낙을 붙이다 take pleasure [delight] (in) / 재미를 붙이다 take (an) interest (in); find pleasure (in)
▶그는 음악을 듣는 것에 큰 낙을 붙였다 He took great pleasure in listening to music.
▶그는 음악에 취미를 붙이고 있다 He has a taste for music.
▶그는 스포츠에 아주 재미를 붙이고 있다 He has a great interest in sports.

12 〈때리다〉 ◆ 아무의 뺨을 한대 올려 붙이다 give *sb* a slap on the cheek / 아무의 얼굴에 한대 올려 붙이다 slap *sb's* face; slap *sb* on [in] the face

붙임성 ─性 sociability; affability; amiability; companionableness; friendliness
◆ 붙임성 있는 sociable; affable; amiable; suave / 붙임성 없는 unsociable; unaffable; repulsive / 붙임성 있는[없는] 사람 a sociable [an unsociable] person; (美口) a good [bad] mixer / 붙임성 있는 점원 a friendly [pleasant] clerk / 붙임성이 있다 be sociable [affable, amiable, suave]; love company; be easy to approach
▶ 그녀는 내게 붙임성 있게 말을 걸어왔다 She speaks to me amiably [pleasantly].

붙잡다 **1** 〈붙들다〉 catch; seize; take [get, catch] hold of *sth*; hold; clasp; clutch; 〈쥐다〉 grab; grasp
◆ 기회를 붙잡다 seize [catch, take] an opportunity; take the [*one's*] chance 《of》 / 소매를 붙잡다 catch [seize] *sb* by the sleeve
▶ 밧줄을 단단히 붙잡으시오 Keep tight hold of the rope. ⇌ (口) Hang on tight to the rope.
▶ 그는 내 팔을 붙잡았다 He caught [seized, took] my arm. ⇌ He caught [seized, took] me by the arm. (▶앞의 문장은 팔에 중점을 두고 뒤의 것은 「사람」에 중점을 두는 표현임)
2 〈체포하다〉 arrest; capture; take; (口) nab
◆ 현장에서 도둑을 붙잡다 arrest a thief in the act [on the spot]
▶ 저 사람 좀 붙잡아 줘요. 내 지갑을 훔쳐어요. Seize him! He stole my purse!
3 〈일자리를 얻다〉 secure [obtain, get] a job; find employment
4 〈못 가게 말리다〉 detain; hold *sb*
◆ 사람을 붙잡고 긴 이야기를 늘어놓다 buttonhole *sb* / 손님을 오래 붙잡아 두다 detain [keep] a guest long
▶ 김선생이 나를 두 시간이나 붙잡고 있었다 Mr. Kim buttonholed me for two hours.
▶ 그는 나를 붙잡고 놓으려 하지 않았다 He took hold of me and would not let me go.
5 〈잡아 주다〉 help; support; hand; steady
◆ 사다리를 붙잡다 steady a ladder / 일어나도록 붙잡아 주다 help *sb* to his feet / 여성의 손을 붙잡아 자동차에 태우다[에서 내려주다] hand a lady into [out of] a car

붙잡히다 〈잡히다〉 be caught [seized]; be taken hold of; be grasped; 〈체포되다〉 be arrested; 〈만류당하다〉 be detained
◆ 음주 운전으로 붙잡히다 be arrested for drunken driving / 붙잡히지 않도록 하다 keep out of *sb's* clutches
▶ 그는 추적자들에게 붙잡혔다 He was caught by his pursuers.
▶ 그 차는 속도 위반으로 순찰차에 붙잡혔다 The car was stopped by a patrol car for speeding.
▶ 나는 김 선생에게 두 시간이나 붙잡혀 있었다 I was detained by Mr. Kim for two hours.
▶ 범인은 아직도 붙잡히지 않았다 The culprit is still loose [at large].

붙장 ─欌 〈붙박이장〉 a built-in cupboard; a kitchen closet

붙좇다 follow ⇨ 따르다 7

뷔페 a buffet; a refreshment [snack] bar
▶ 파티의 식사는 뷔페식이었다 The food at the party was served buffet style.

뷰티 콘테스트 a beauty contest

브라만 〈인도의 승족〉a Brahman; a Bra(h)min
■ ─교 Brahmanism

브라보 bravo / 브라보를 외치다 bravo

브라스밴드 〈취주 악단〉 a brass band

브라운관 ─管 〔TV〕 a cathode-ray tube (略 CRT); a picture tube

브라질 Brazil; 〈공식명〉 the Federative Republic of Brazil ◆ 브라질의 Brazilian ■ ─사람 a Brazilian

브래지어 a brassiere; (口) a bra ◆ 브래지어를 하다[벗다] wear a [undo *one's*] brassiere
▶ 그녀는 브래지어를 하지 않는다 She doesn't wear a bra.

브랜드 〈상표〉a brand ◆ 유명 브랜드의 brand-name

브랜디 brandy ◆ 한 잔의 브랜디 a snifter of brandy / 소다수[물]를 탄 브랜디 brandy and soda [water] / 브랜디 잔 a brandy glass / 브랜디를 한 잔 마시다 have a brandy
▶ 브랜디 한 잔 주시오 Give me some brandy.

브러시 a brush

브레스트 〈가슴〉 the breast ■ ─스트로크 〈평영〉 the breast stroke

브레이크¹ **1** 〔機〕 〈제동 장치〉 a brake
◆ 브레이크를 걸다 apply [put on] the brakes; brake 《a car》 / 브레이크를 꽉 밟다 step on the brake hard / 브레이크를 늦추다 take off the brakes / 브레이크를 밟아 차를 세우다 brake a car to a stop
▶ 브레이크가 듣지 않는다 The brakes refuse to work [are out of order].
▶ 브레이크를 걸었는데 듣지 않았다 I put on [applied] the brakes, but they did not work.
▶ 급브레이크를 걸어 차를 멈추었다 The car braked hard to a stop.
2 〈억제조치〉 ◆ 물가상승에 브레이크를 걸다 put a brake [the brake(s)] on rising prices
■ 수동[공기, 증기, 비상]─ a hand [an air, a steam, an emergency] brake

브레이크² 〔拳〕 a break

브레인 〈지적 지도자〉 (口) the brains
■ ─드레인 〈두뇌 유출〉 brain drain ─스토밍 〈아이디어 개발 방식〉 brainstorming

브레인 트러스트 〈지능 고문단〉 a brain trust
▶ 그는 대통령의 브레인 트러스트의 일원이다 He is a brain truster behind [an adviser to] the president.

브로마이드 bromide ■ ─사진 a bromide photograph ─인화지 bromide paper

브로치 a brooch; a breastpin; (美) a pin
▶ 그녀는 옷에 멋진 브로치를 달고 있었다 She was wearing a pretty brooch on her dress.

브로커 〈중개인〉a broker; a middleman
◆ 브로커 노릇을 하다 act as a broker [middleman] / 부동산─ a real estate agent [broker]
■ ─수수료 brokerage

브론테 〈영국의 여류 자매 소설가〉 Brontë **1** Charlotte (1816-55) **2** Emily (Jane) (1818-

48) 3 Anne (1820-49)
브롬 〔化〕 bromine
브롬화—化 〔化〕 bromination ■—물 a bromide —은 silver bromide
브루나이 〈나라 이름〉 Brunei
브루넷 ♦브루넷의 brunette / 브루넷의 여자 a brunette
브루크너 〈오스트리아의 작곡가〉 Bruckner, Anton (1824-1896)
브뤼셀 〈벨기에의 수도〉 Brussels
브리지 1〈다리〉 a bridge; an overpass
2 〔齒〕〈가공 의치〉 a (dental) bridge
♦이에 브리지를 하다 fix a bridge (between natural teeth); bridge (a tooth)
3 〈카드놀이〉 bridge
♦브리지 놀이를 하다 play bridge
4 〔레슬링〕 ♦브리지로 폴을 면하다 avoid a fall by bridging; bridge to avoid a fall
브리핑 (a) briefing ♦브리핑을 하다 give a briefing (on); brief ■—차트 a briefing chart
브이아이피 a VIP; a V.I.P. [*v*ery *i*mportant *p*erson]
브이티아르 a VTR [*v*ideo *t*ape *r*ecorder]
블라디보스토크 Vladivostok
블라우스 a blouse ♦긴[반] 소매 블라우스 a long-sleeved [short-sleeved] blouse / 꽃 무늬 블라우스 a blouse with a flower [floral] pattern
블라인드 a (window) blind; 〈美〉 a window shade ♦블라인드를 내리다[올리다] pull down [raise] the blinds [window shades]
블랙 black ▶나는 커피를 항상 블랙으로 마십니다 I always drink my coffee black.
■—커피 black coffee —파워 Black Power —홀 〔天〕 a black hole
블랙리스트 a blacklist; a black book
♦블랙리스트에 올라 있는 자 a man on the blacklist / 블랙리스트에 오르다 be blacklisted; be put on the blacklist / 블랙리스트에 올리다 blacklist sb; put sb on the blacklist
블랭크 a blank; a gap ♦블랭크를 메우다 fill the blank ▶그는 학자로서의 경력에 5년간의 블랭크가 있다 There is the gap of five years in his academic career.
블랭킷 〈담요〉 a blanket
블레이크 〈영국의 시인·화가〉 Blake, William (1757-1827)
블록 1 〔建〕 a concrete [cement] block 2〈시가의 구획〉 a block 3 〈동맹〉 a bloc
—경제— an economic bloc 달러[스털링]— the dollar [sterling] bloc —건물 a concrete-block building —경제 bloc economy
블론드 blond(e) ♦블론드의 여자 a blond(e) woman; a blonde
블루 blue ■—네이비— navy blue ■—칼라 a blue-collar worker ■—필름 a blue film; a porno film
블루스 〔樂〕 (the) blues (▶단수·복수 취급) ♦블루스조의 blue / 블루스를 노래하다 sing a blues —가수 a blues singer
블루진 (blue) jeans ♦블루진을 입은 젊은이 a young man in blue jeans
비[1] 〈내리는〉 rain; 〈한번의〉 a rain; a rainfall; 〈지금 오는〉 the rain; 〈소나기〉 a shower; 〈우기〉 the rains
♦계속 내리는 비 a constant [continuous] rain / 억수 같은 비 a torrential [pouring] rain; a downpour / 오락가락하는 비 an intermittent rain / 이슬비 a misty rain / 지나가는 비 a passing rain; a shower / 비오듯 흘러내리는 땀 a profuse perspiration
〈비가〉 비가 오는 날[밤] a rainy [wet] day [evening]/ 오늘 비가 올 확률 the rainfall probability for today / 비가 갠 뒤의 좋은 날씨 fine weather after a rainfall / 비가 많이 오는 rainy; pluvial / 비가 그친 사이에 between rains; during a lull [break] in the rain / 비가 그치기를 기다리다 wait for the rain to leave off
▶비가 내린다 It rains.
▶비가 축축히 내리고 있다 It's drizzling now.
▶비가 내리기 시작했다 It began to rain. ⇌ It started raining.
▶비가 억수로 왔다 It rained hard [heavily, in torrents]. ⇌ It rained cats and dogs.
▶비가 오기만 하면 억수가 쏟아진다 It never rains but it pours.
▶어젯밤에 비가 심하게 왔다 We had a heavy rain last night.
▶비가 저녁에 심해졌다 The rain became heavier in the evening.
▶비가 오락가락한다 It is raining on and off.
▶비가 올 것 같다 It looks like rain. ⇌ It's going to rain.
▶비가 그칠 것 같지 않았다 The rain showed no sign of stopping [letting up].
▶이 달에는 비가 많이 왔다 We have had many rainy days this month.
〈비를〉 비를 만나다 be caught in a rain [shower]/ 비를 맞으며 걷다 walk in the rain / 비를 피하다 take a shelter [refuge, cover] from the rain
▶그는 비를 맞으며 조깅하고 있었다 He was jogging in [through] the rain.
▶나는 비를 피하여 백화점에 들어갔다 I went into a department store to get out of the rain.
▶나는 나무 밑에서 비를 피했다 I took shelter [sheltered myself] from the rain under a rain.
〈비에[로]〉 비에 젖다 get wet (with rain)
▶나는 비에 젖었다 I got wet in the rain.
▶우리는 비로 일주일간 집에 들어박혀 있었다 We were kept indoors by the rain for a week.
▶경기는 비로 중지되었다 The game was rained out.
비[2] 〈쓸어 내는〉 a broom ▶아버지는 아침마다 비로 마당을 쓰신다 Father sweeps a garden with a broom every morning. ■빗자루 a broomstick
비 比 〔數〕〈비율〉 (a) ratio; 〈비례〉 (a) proportion ♦A와 B의 비 the ratio of A to B; the ratio A:B
▶남녀간의 비는 2대 3이었다 The ratio of men to women [The male-felmale ratio] was two to three.
비 妃 〈왕비〉 a queen; 〈황태자비〉 a Crown Princess
비 碑 〈기념비〉 a monument; 〈묘표〉 a tombstone; a gravestone ♦…을 기념하는 비를 세

우다 erect a tombstone [monument] to the memory of...

비- 非- non-; un-; anti-; in- ♦비위생적인 unsanitary / 비합리적인 irrational

> [解說] 「비(非)-」는 un-, non-, in- 등으로 나타낸다. 그 중 un-은 「반대」, 「역(逆)」을 뜻하는 데 반해 non-은 「(소극적) 부정」을 뜻한다. 또 in-은 라틴어에서 유래한 말에 쓰여 l 앞에서는 il- 로, r 앞에서는 ir- 로, b,m,p앞에서는 im- 으로 변화한다.

-비 -費 expense(s) ⇨ 비용 ♦영업[접대]비 business [entertainment] expenses

비가 悲歌 an elegy; a song of sorrow; a plaintive song

비각 〈양립 못함〉 incompatibles; opposite(s); being (mutually) exclusive; not going together
▶ 물과 불은 비각이다 Fire and water do not mix.

비각 碑閣 a pavilion for a monument

비강 鼻腔 〔解〕 the nasal cavity
—폐쇄(증) nasal atresia

비겁 卑怯 1 〈겁이 많음〉 cowardice
—비겁하다 cowardly; unmanly
♦비겁한 짓을 하다 act in a cowardly way; act [play] the coward
▶ 이제 물러서다니 비겁하구나 It is cowardly of you to pull out now.
▶ 비겁하게도 그는 도망쳤다 He was timid enough to run away.
2 〈비열〉 meanness
—비겁하다 mean; unfair; foul
♦비겁한 짓 〈경기에서〉 a foul play / 비겁한 짓을 하다 play a mean [dirty] trick 《upon sb》; 〈경기 등에서〉 play foul; hit sb below the belt
▶ 상대방의 약점을 이용하는 것은 비겁한 짓이다 It is unfair of you to take advantage of an opponent's weakness.
■ —자 a coward; 《俗》 a chicken; a sneak; a sneaker

비견 鄙見 〈자기의 생각〉 ♦비견으로는 to my (humble) thinking; in my view
▶ 비견을 말씀드리자면 이 계획에는 약간 문제가 있습니다 In my humble opinion [If I may express my opinion], there are some problems with this plan.

비견하다 比肩— rank [range] with; take rank with; equal; bear [stand] comparison with
▶ 발명가로서 그와 비견할 자는 없다 No one can equal [match] him as an inventor. ⇌ He stands alone (unrival(l)ed) as an inventor.

비결 祕訣 a secret; a key 《to》; the mysteries 《of》 ♦성공의 비결 the secret of [a key to] success
▶ 일찍 일어나는 것이 건강의 비결이다 Early rising [Keeping early hours] is a key to good health.
▶ 그는 장사의 비결을 알고 있다 He is familiar with the tricks of the trade.

비결정체 非結晶體 〔物〕 an amorphous body

비경 祕境 an unexplored [untraveled] region; a secluded region ♦히말라야의 비경 the unexplored [untrodden] regions of the Himalayas.

비경 鼻鏡 a nasal speculum; a nasoscope
■ —검사(법) rhinoscopy; rhinoscopia

비계¹ 〔土·建〕〈발판〉 a scaffold; a falsework ♦비계를 설치하다 set up [erect] a scaffold; scaffold 《a house》

비계² fat; fatly meat; 〈돼지 기름〉 lard

비계 祕計 〈비책〉 a secret plan; a secret [underhand] scheme; secret measures; the best card
♦비계를 쓰다 play one's best [trump] card
▶ 그는 비계를 생각해냈다 He devised [worked out] a secret stratagem.

비고 備考 a note; explanatory notes; remarks 《for reference》
■ —란(欄) a remarks [reference] column; (표시) Remarks, Notes

비곡 悲曲 〈슬픈 곡〉 a sad tune; a plaintive melody; a doleful air; an elegy

비골 腓骨 〔解〕〈종아리뼈〉 a fibula 《pl. ~s, -lae [-liː, -lài]》; a splint bone

비골 鼻骨 〔解〕〈코뼈〉 the nasal bone

비공 鼻孔 〔解〕〈콧구멍〉 the nostril

비공개 非公開 ♦비공개의 closed; closed-door; private; secret; not open to the public
▶ 재판은 비공개로 열렸다 The trial was held behind closed doors.
■ —입찰 a closed tender —회의 a closed meeting; a closed-door conference

비공산국 非共産國 a non-Communist country

비공식 非公式 unofficialness; informality
♦비공식 방문 an unofficial visit / 비공식의 unofficial; informal; private / 비공식으로 informally; unofficially
■ —견해 unofficial comments; a private [personal] opinion : 그것은 장관의 비공식 견해이지 공식 견해가 아니었다 It was the minister's private view, (and) not an official one. —회담 〈外交〉 a conversation

비공인 非公認 ♦비공인의 unauthorized; unofficial; unrecognized

비과세 非課稅 〈면세〉 tax exemption
♦비과세의 tax-free; tax-exempt / 비과세 수입품 duty-free imports
▶ 이 예금의 이자는 비과세다 The interest on this deposit is not taxable [is tax-free].
■ —소득 (a) tax-free income —품 a tax-free article

비과학 鼻科學 rhinology

비과학적 非科學的 〈과학적이 아닌〉 unscientific; 〈과학과 관계 없는〉 nonscientific
▶ 비과학적 사고 unscientific thinking / 비과학적으로 unscientifically

비관 悲觀 〈염세〉 pessimism; 〈실망〉 disappointment ♦비관적(인) pessimistic
▶ 그는 비관적인 인생관을 가지고 있다 He has a pessimistic view of life. ⇌ He looks on the dark side of life.
—비관하다 be pessimistic 《about, of》; take a pessimistic [dark] view 《of》; look on the gloomy side 《of》; 〈실망하다〉 be disappointed; lose heart
♦인생을 비관하다 take a gloomy view of life;

lose all hopes of life / 세상을 비관하여 자살하다 kill *oneself* in despair [out of sheer pessimism]
▶ 그는 입학시험에 실패해서 비관하고 있다 He is now in despair, because he has failed in the entrance examination.
▶ 결과에 대해서 그렇게 비관하지 마라 Don't be so pessimistic [so gloomy] about the results.
■ ―론[설] a pessimistic view; pessimism ―론자 a pessimist

비교 比較 (a) comparison; a parallel
◆ 비교도 안 될 만큼 beyond comparison [compare]; 〈훨씬〉 far and away (the best) / 비교가 안 되다 cannot bear [stand] comparison 《with》; cannot compare [be compared] 《with》; be no match 《for》; there is no comparison 《with》
▶ 이 그림은 비교가 안 될 만큼 아름답다 This picture is beautiful beyond comparison.
―비교하다 make a comparison 《between A and B》
◆ …과 비교하여[하면] (as) compared with [to]…; in comparison 《with》…; in contrast to…/ …과 비교하여 더 낫다[못하다] be better [inferior] as compared with…
▶ 네 번역을 원문과 비교해 보아라 Compare your translation with the original.
▶ 나는 무엇에든 그와 비교되기는 싫다 I don't like to be compared to [with] him in anything. (▶수동형에서는 with 보다 to를 많이 사용함)
■ ―급 〔文法〕 the comparative degree ―문법 comparative grammar ―문학 comparative literature ―발생학[생물학] comparative embryology [biology] ―심리학 comparative psychology ―언어학 comparative philology [linguistics]

비교연구 比較研究 a comparative study
―비교연구하다 make a comparative study 《of》; study by the comparative method
■ ―법 the comparative method

비교적 比較的 comparative; relative; 〈부사적〉 comparatively; relatively; rather
▶ 이번 겨울은 비교적 따뜻하다 It is comparatively [relatively] warm this winter.
▶ 이 아이는 비교적 머리가 좋다 This child is rather bright.

비구(승) 比丘(僧) 〈남자 승려〉 〈산〉 a bhikku; a Buddhist priest [monk]

비구 飛球 〔野〕 〈플라이〉 a fly (ball)

비구니 比丘尼 〈산〉 a bhikkuni; a Buddhist priestess [nun]

비구름 a rain cloud; 〔氣〕 a nimbus 《pl. ~es, -bi [-bai, -bi:]》

비굴 卑屈 servility; meanness
―비굴하다 mean-spirited; mean; servile
◆ 비굴한 마음 a servile spirit / 비굴한 사나이 a sneak; a sneaker; an unmanly fellow / 비굴하게 웃다 laugh [give] a servile laugh

비극 悲劇 (a) tragedy; a tragic drama
◆ 가정의 비극 a domestic tragedy / 비극적 사건 a tragic affair [event]; a tragedy / 비극으로 끝나다 end in a tragedy; end tragically / 비극적 죽음을 맞다 die a tragic death; die tragically
▶ 두 사람의 결혼은 비극으로 끝났다 Their marriage ended in a tragedy.
■ ―배우 a tragedian; 〈남자〉 a tragic actor; 〈여자〉 a tragic actress ―작가 a tragic dramatist

비근 卑近 familiar; simple; common; plain
◆ 비근한 예를 들다 give [use, cite] a familiar example

비금속 非金屬 〔化〕 a nonmetal ◆ 비금속의 nonmetallic ■ ―광물 a nonmetallic mineral ―원소 a nonmetallic element

비금속 卑金屬 a base metal ▶ 철[납]은 비금속이다 Iron [Lead] is a base metal.

비기다¹ 1 〈승부가 나지 않다〉 a tie [draw] 《with》; end in a [draw]; come out even
◆ 비긴 경기 a tie [draw]; a drawn game
▶ 우리는 그들과 3대 3으로 비겼다 Our game with them ended in a 3-3 tie.
▶ 고려대와 연세대는 비겼다 Korea (University) tied (with) Yonsei in the game.
2 〈셈을 에끼다〉 offset [cancel] each other; counterbalance

비기다² 〈견주다〉 compare 《A to B》; liken 《A to B》 ◆ 잠을 죽음에 비기다 compare sleep to death / 인생을 연극에 비기다 compare life to a drama
▶ 우리는 흔히 인생을 나그네길에 비긴다 We often campare [liken] life to a journey.
▶ 심장은 펌프에 비길 수 있다 The heart can be compared [You can compare the heart] to a pump.

비길데없다 unrivaled; unequaled; matchless
◆ 비길 데 없는 아름다움 matchless [peerless] beauty
▶ 강제 수용소의 비참한 생활은 비길 데가 없었다 The miserable life in the concentration camp was unspeakable [beyond words].
▶ 이 그림은 비길 데 없이 아름답다 This picture is beautiful beyond comparison.

비김수 ―手 a tying [drawing] move; a draw

비꼬다 1 〈끈을〉 twist (up); entwist ◆ 실을 비꼬아 노끈을 만들다 twist thread into a string
2 〈말을〉 make sarcastic remarks 《on》; give a sarcastic [cynical] twist to *one's* words
◆ 비꼬는 말 cynical words; a sarcastic remark
▶ 그는 때때로 비꼬는 말을 한다 He sometimes makes cynical remarks.
▶ 그녀의 말에는 비꼬는 투가 있었다 There was some [a touch of] irony in her words.
▶ 그렇게 비꼬지 마라 Don't be so cynical [ironical].

비꼬이다 1 〈끈 등이〉 get [be] twisted; 〈사건 등이〉 get [become] entangled; become complicated
2 〈마음이〉 become crooked [distorted]; be perverse
◆ 비꼬인 성질 a crooked disposition
▶ 어린 아이를 너무 야단치면 성격이 비꼬이게 된다 If you scold a child too frequently, he will develop a warped character.

비꼼 an indirect criticism [attack]; sarcasm

비끄러매다 tie (up); tie [fasten] (together)

비교의 표현

1. ~보다(도)…; ~이상…

(1) 비교급(형용사) + than ~
▶그는 너보다 연상이니 연하니? Is he older or younger than you?
▶그는 나이보다도 젊어 보인다 He looks younger than he really is. (▶really의 위치에 주의)
▶이 책은 저 책보다 재미있다고 생각한다 I think this book is more interesting than that one.

(2) 비교급(부사) + than ~
▶그들은 우리보다 먼저 도착하였다 They arrived earlier than we (did).
▶내 아우는 나 이상으로 대식가다 My brother eats more than I (do).
▶그녀는 나보다 영어를 유창하게 말한다 She speaks English more fluently than I (do).

(3) 비교급(형용사) + 명사 + than ~
▶그는 나보다 일을 빨리 한다 He is a quicker worker than I (am). ⇌ He works more quickly than I (do).
▶그녀는 그 사람보다 노래를 잘 부른다 She is a better singer than he (is). ⇌ She sings better than he (does).
▶여성이 남성보다 안전하게 운전한다 Women are safer drivers than men (are). ⇌ Women drive more safely than men (do). (▶단수인 경우는 부정관사가 필요하고 복수인 경우는 필요 없음)

[어법]
than clause에서는 주어 다음에 동사(be, have, do 등)를 넣어도 좋다. 특히 주어가 3인칭 대명사일 때는 보통 동사를 넣는다.

(4) 비교급 + than ~'s; 비교급 + than that [those] of [in] ~
▶내 차는 톰의 것보다 크다 My car is bigger than Tom's.
▶이곳의 날씨는 캘리포니아보다 좋다 The climate here is more pleasant than that of California.
▶그의 생각은 또래들 보다 앞서 있다 His ideas are more advanced than those of the group.
▶힐튼 호텔의 방은 그랜드 호텔보다 좋다 The rooms in the Hilton are more comfortable than those in the Grand Hotel.

[어법]
① 비교는 같은 종류의 것끼리 모아 써야 한다. 따라서 비교되는 것이 소유격일 경우는 than 이하에도 소유격을 써야 한다.
② that은 단수명사 대신에, those는 복수명사 대신에 쓴다. 위 예문에서 that은 the climate 대신에, those는 각각 the ideas와 the rooms 대신에 쓰이고 있다. that 대신에 구어에서는 the one을 쓰기도 한다.
[보기] Our pool is bigger than the one (= the pool) in the Hilton.
③ those 다음의 전치사는 전후 관계에 따라 결정된다.

(5) 부정대명사[명사] + 비교급 + than ~
▶나는 그보다 더 잘생긴 사나이를 보지 못했다 I don't know anyone more handsome than he (is).
▶이 마을에는 박선생보다 더 부자인 사람은 없다 There is no one richer than Mr. Park in this town.
▶나는 토머스 부인만큼 교양있는 사람은 만난 적이 없다 I have never met a woman more educated than Mrs. Thomas.

(6) 비교급(형용사·부사)+than+부사(구)
▶오늘은 어제보다 날씨가 좋다 The weather is better today than yesterday.
▶서울보다 대관령 쪽이 더 춥다 It is colder in Taegwallyŏng than in Seoul.
▶그의 음반 판매는 올해는 작년 이상으로 늘어날 것이다 His records will have bigger sales this year than last year.
▶공원에는 평상시보다[예전에 없이] 많은 사람이 있었다 There were more people in the park than usual [ever].

[어법]
than 이하의 clause가 부사(구)를 제외하고 주절과 공통인 경우에는 비록 시제가 틀리더라도 그 부사(구)만을 남겨둔다. 예컨대 위 예문에서는 …than (it was) yesterday; …than it is (cold) in Seoul.이란 뜻.

2. ~보다 …이 많다; ~보다 …쪽이 많다
more + 명사 + than~
▶나보다도 그 사람이 돈이 많다 He has more money than I (do).
▶예상외로 많은 사람이 왔다 More people came than we had expected.
▶이 학교에는 여자보다도 남자가 많다 This school has more boys than girls. ⇌ There are more boys than girls in this school. (▶more 다음에 양을 나타낼 때는 단수 명사, 수를 나타낼 때는 복수 명사가 각기 쓰인다)

3. ~하는 것보다도 …하는 편이 (좋다, 나쁘다)
it is + 비교급 + to do + than (to) do (▶to는 생략할 수 있음)
▶혼자서 가는 것보다는 가이드를 고용하는 편이 안전할 것입니다 It will be safer to get a guide than (to) go alone.
▶택시를 타는 것보다는 기차를 타는 것이 빠르다 It is quicker to go by train than (to) take a taxi.

4. (다른) 누구 (무엇) 보다도…
비교급(형용사·부사) + than anyone else [any other + 단수명사, anything else]
▶그는 반의 다른 누구보다도 영어를 잘한다 He speaks English better than anyone else in the class. ⇌ He speaks English better than any other student in the class.
▶백두산은 한국의 다른 어떤 산보다도 높다 Paekdusan is higher than any other mountain in Korea.
▶나는 무엇보다도 스키가 좋다 I like skiing better than anything else.
▶그는 가족 중의 다른 누구보다도 일을 많이 한다 He works harder than anyone else in

his family. ⇌ He works harder than any other member of his family.

5. ~보다는 훨씬[월등히]
   much [far] + 비교급 + than ~
   ▶김선생은 우리 아버지보다 훨씬 연상입니다 Mr. Kim is much older than my father.
   ▶작가로서 그 사람이 그의 형보다 훨씬 위다 He is a far [much] better writer than his brother.
   ▶이 차는 저 차보다 훨씬 비싸다 This car is much more expensive than that one. ⇌ This car costs much more than that one.

6. ~보다도 (다섯살 연상, 10미터 높다 등)
   be + (five years, ten meters) + 비교급
   ▶아버지는 숙부보다 다섯살 연상이다 My father is five years older than his brother.
   ▶이 다리는 저 다리보다 10미터 길다 This bridge is ten meters longer than that one.

7. ~보다 훨씬 많은…; ~보다 더 많은…
   much more + 단수명사 (양); many more + 복수명사 (수)
   ▶그녀는 나보다 옷치레에 훨씬 많은 돈을 씁니다 She spends much more money on clothes than I (do).
   ▶나는 그보다 친구가 훨씬 많다 I have many more friends than he (does).
   ▶이 사전은 저 사전보다 용례가 훨씬 많다 This dictionary has many more examples than that one.

8. ~보다도 얼마나 더 …한가?; 앞으로 얼마나 더 …한가?
   (1) **How much + 비교급… than ~?**
   ▶그는 부인보다 몇살 연상입니까? How much older is he than his wife?
   ▶오스트레일리아는 한국보다 얼마나 더 큽니까? How much larger is Australia than Korea?
   ▶비행기는 열차보다 얼마나 더 빠르니까? How much faster can a plane travel than a train?
   (2) **How much more + 단수명사… ? (양); How many more + 복수명사… ? (수)**
   ▶돈은 앞으로 얼마나 더 필요합니까? How much more money do you need?
   ▶한국은 금년도 석유를 앞으로 얼마나 소비합니까? How much more oil will Korea consume this year?
   ▶앞으로 얼마나 더 일손이 모자랍니까? How many more people do you need?

9. 생각했던[예상했던, 희망했던] 것보다
   비교급(형용사・부사) + than one thought [expected, hoped, etc.] (▶시제가 현재일 때는 동사의 현재형을 쓴다)
   ▶그녀는 네가 생각하고 있는 것보다 나이가 많아 She is older than you think (she is).
   ▶그는 기대 이상으로 고기를 많이 낚았다 He caught more fish than he expected (he would).
   ▶그 집은 우리가 바라던 것보다 넓었다 The house was larger than we had hoped (it would).
   ▶그녀는 내가 상상했던 것 이상으로 미인이었다 She was more beautiful than I imagined (she was).
   ▶그는 사람들이 생각하고 있는 것 이상으로 훌륭한 지휘자다 He is a greater conductor than people suppose (he is).
   [어법]
   ( )안은 생략할 수 있다. 또 ( )안은 다음과 같이 생략할 수도 있다. she is (old) / he would (catch) / it would (be) / she was (beautiful)

10. B보다도 A가 좋다
    prefer A to B; like A more [better] than B
    ▶나는 홍차보다 커피가 좋다 I prefer coffee to tea. ⇌ I like coffee more than tea.
    ▶[회화]「수학과 물상 중 어느 쪽이 좋습니까?」「수학이 좋습니다」"Which do you prefer, mathematics or physics?" "I prefer mathematics to phisics." ⇌ "Which do you like more [better], math or physics?" "I like math more [better] than physics."
    ▶나는 도회지보다도 시골에 사는 것이 좋다 I prefer living in the country to living in a city. ⇌ I prefer country life to city life.
    [어법]
    ① to 다음에는 명사・동명사가 온다. 따라서 〈prefer + 명사 + to + 명사〉 / 〈prefer + 동명사 + to + 동명사〉의 구문이 된다.
    ② 부정사를 쓸 때에는 I prefer to stay at home rather than (to) go out.처럼 to 대신에 rather than을 쓴다.
    ③ like를 쓰는 경우, 부사는 more, better 어느 것도 좋다.

11. ~만큼[정도] …한 것은 없다
    nothing is 비교급 than ~; nothing is so… as ~ (▶is 대신에 다른 동사를 쓸 수도 있다)
    ▶야구만큼 즐거운 것은 없다 Nothing is more pleasant than baseball. ⇌ Nothing is so pleasant as baseball.
    ▶등산처럼 즐거운 것은 없다 Nothing is more pleasant than climbing mountains. ⇌ Nothing gives us more pleasure than climbing mountains.
    ▶정직만큼 중요한 것은 없다 Nothing is more important than to be honest (honesty]. ⇌ Nothing is so important as to be honest [honesty].
    ▶밤새 카드놀이를 하는 것만큼 피곤한 것은 없다 Nothing is more tiring than to play cards all night. ⇌ Nothing makes us more tired than to play cards all night.
    [어법]
    than, as의 다음에는 명사 외에 동명사, to가 붙은 부정사가 온다. 이 구문에서는 부정사의 to를 생략할 수가 없다.

비끼다 lie aslant; lie at an angle; be bent; slant; be oblique; lean ◆빛이 비끼다 shine at an angle

비난 非難 criticism; blame; censure; 〈질책〉 (a) reproach; 〈공공연한〉 denunciation ◆비난의 여지가 없다 be irreproachable; be above [beyond] reproach / 비난의 초점이 되다 become the focus [target] of criticism / 비난을 면하다 escape criticism [reproach] / 비난을 면치 못하다 be open to censure [criti-

cism]/ 비난을 초래하다 incur [arouse] a censure; lay *oneself* open to censure
▶그는 나를 비난조의 눈초리로 보았다 He looked at me reproachfully. ⇌ He gave [shot] me a critical look.
▶그 조처에 대해서는 비난의 소리가 높다 The measure is loudly censured.
▶그녀의 행동은 비난을 받아 마땅하다 Her conduct deserves criticism.
—비난하다 criticize unfavorably [adversely]; censure; blame; reproach; denounce; condemn; make a charge against
♦비난할 만한 blamable; reproachable
▶그녀에게는 비난할 데가 없다 I find no fault with her. ⇌ She is beyond [above] reproach.
▶그들은 그를 무능하다고 비난하였다 They criticized him for incompetence [as incompetent].
—자 a critic; a censor; an accuser
비녀 a (rod-like) ornamental hairpin ♦비녀를 꽂다 wear [fasten] an ornamental hairpin
비녀장 a linchpin
비뇨기 泌尿器 the urinary organs
—과 the urology department —과 전문의 a urologist —질환 urinary diseases
비누 soap ♦비누 한 장 a cake [bar] of soap / 비누로 씻다 wash with soap and water
■가루— soap powder 물— liquid soap 세탁[빨래]— (a bar of) washing [laundry] soap 약용— medicated soap 화장[세수]— toilet soap —거품 soapsuds; lather : 면도하기 전에 얼굴에 비누 거품을 칠하다 lather *one's* face before shaving / 센물에서는 비누 거품이 잘 일지 않는다 Soap does not lather well in hard water. —공장 a soap works 비눗물 soapy water; soapsuds; suds 비눗방울 a soap bubble
비누질하다 soap ♦손에 비누질 하다 soap *one's* hands
비늘 a scale; a shard; squama
♦비늘 모양의 scalelike / 비늘이 있는 scaled; scaly; squamate / 비늘로 덮이다 be covered with scales; be scaly
▶요리사는 요리하기전에 생선의 비늘을 벗겼다 The cook scaled the fish before cooking them.
비늘구름 a cirrocumulus ⇨ 권적운
비늘조각 a scale ⇨ 인편(鱗片)
비능률 非能率 inefficiency ♦비능률적인 inefficient / 비능률적인 생산 inefficient production
비닐 vinyl
♦비닐제의 plastic; 〈비닐 수지의〉 vinyl
■염화— vinyl chloride —백 a plastic bag —보자기 a vinyl cloth wrapper —수지 vinyl resin —중합체 vinyl polymers —플라스틱 a vinyl plastic

解說 비닐은 영어의 ***vinyl***에서 온 것으로, 비닐 수지(樹脂)란 뜻의 화학 용어. 영어에서는 비닐 수지를 비롯한 합성수지로 만들어진 것을 일괄하여 plastic이라고 말한다. 따라서 비닐 백은 vinyl bag 보다는 plastic bag이라고 하는 것이 원칙이다.

비닐론 vinylon
비다¹ 1 〈속이〉 empty; vacant; hollow; unoccupied
♦머리가 비다 be empty-headed / 손이 비다 have *one's* hands free
▶나는 주머니가 비어 있다 I have a light [an empty] purse.
▶버스는 대낮에는 빕니다 The buses are not so crowded around midday.
▶그 자리는 비어 있다 The seat is unoccupied.
▶그에게 부탁을 하려면 빈손으로 가면 안 되지 If you want to ask a favor of him, you'd better take a present.
2 〈모자라다〉 be short of
▶100만원에서 1만원이 빈다 It is one million won short of ten thousand won.
▶이 책은 5페이지가 빈다 There are five pages [Five pages are] missing in this book.
비다듬다 arrange; smooth
비단 非但 〈다만〉 merely; simply; only; just
▶이유는 비단 그것 뿐이 아니었다 That was not the only reason.
▶그것은 비단 건강에 해로울 뿐만 아니라 비경제적이다 It is not only unhealthy but also wasteful.
비단 緋緞 silk; silk fabrics; silk goods [stuff]; 〈공단〉 satin ♦비단의 silk; silken / 비단 같은 silky —실 ⇨ 명주(~실) —옷 silk dress [clothes] —이불 silk bedding
비단뱀 緋緞— 〔動〕 a python
비단결 緋緞— the texture of silk; a velvety texture
♦비단결 같은 살결 a soft and velvety skin / 비단결 같다 be silky; be as soft as silk
▶그녀의 마음은 비단결 같다 She has a tender heart. ⇌ She is tenderhearted [kindhearted].
비단벌레 緋緞— 〔昆〕 a buprestid
비단잉어 緋緞— 〔魚〕 a colored carp
비당파적 非黨派的 nonpartisan; nonparty
비대 肥大 fleshiness; corpulence; plumpness; 〔醫〕 hypertrophy
♦심장 비대 〔醫〕 cardiac hypertrophy; cardiomegaly; 〈심한 운동으로 인한 운동 선수의〉 an athletic heart
—비대하다 fat(ty); enlarged; swollen ♦편도선이 비대해지다 have an enlarged tonsils
비대다 assume another's name
비대칭 非對稱 〔數〕 asymmetry; dissymmetry
♦비대칭의 asymmetric(al); dissymmetric(al)
비도덕적 非道德的 immoral
비동맹 非同盟 nonalignment ♦비동맹의 nonaligned ■—국 a nonaligned nation —국 회담 the nonaligned conference —정책 a nonalignment policy
비둘기 a dove; a pigeon
♦비둘기를 기르다 keep [have] pigeons / 비둘기를 날리다 toss [fly, let loose] pigeons (into the air)
▶비둘기가 울고 있다 Pigeons are cooing.
▶비둘기는 평화의 상징이다 The dove is a symbol of peace.
■군용— a military [an army] carrier pigeon 통신용— a carrier [homing] pigeon ■—새끼 a fledgling pigeon; a squab —장 a dovecot(e);

비둘기파 —派 〈온건파〉 the doves; a soft-liner
♦ 비둘기파의 정치가 a dove politician

비듬 dandruff; scurf
♦ 비듬이 많은 머리 a scurfy [dandruffy] head; hair full of dandruff / 비듬이 생기다 become dandruffy / 옷깃에 떨어진 비듬을 털다 remove [brush off] the dandruff off *one's* collar
■ —약 a hair lotion [tonic]; a dandruff remover

비등 沸騰 1 〈액체가 끓어오름〉 boiling; seething
—비등하다 boil; seethe
▶ 물은 섭씨 100도에서 비등한다 Water boils [comes to a boil] at 100°C.
2 〈물끓듯 소란함〉 commotion; excitement; agitation; tumult
—비등하다 become [be] agitated [excited, heated]; be roused
▶ 그 사건으로 논란이 비등했다 The matter gave rise to heated controversies.
▶ 전 국민의 여론이 비등하고 있다 Public opinion is agitated on a nationwide scale.

비등점 沸騰點 〔物〕 the boiling point ⇨ 끓는점

비등하다 比等— about equal; about [nearly] the same; 《be》 on a par with
♦ 비등한 조건으로 on nearly even [equal] terms
▶ 둘이는 실력이 비등하다 The two are equally matched in ability.
▶ 아들 녀석은 나와 키가 비등하다 My son is nearly as tall as I.

비디오 video; videotape; video tape recorder

〔解說〕 *video*는 본래 audio에 대응하는 말로 「텔레비전의 영상」을 가리키는데, 구어에서는 비디오 장치도 의미한다. 다만 의미를 분명히 하기 위해 기계는 ***video tape recorder*** (略 VTR) 또는 ***videocassette recorder*** (略 VCR)라 하고 테이프는 ***videotape*** 라고 할 필요가 있다.

♦ 프로그램을 비디오로 녹화하다 videotape a program; record a program on videotape
■ —게임 a video game —디스크 a video disk —아트 video art —카메라 a video camera; a camcorder —카세트 리코더 a videocassette recorder —테이프 videotape: 비디오테이프에 녹화하다 record on (a) videotape —테이프 리코더 a videotape recorder

비뚜로 askew; aslant; slantwise; at an angle
♦ 베레모자를 비뚜로 쓰다 wear *one's* beret aslant [at a slant]; cock *one's* beret
▶ 그림이 비뚜로 걸려 있다 The picture hangs askew.

비뚤다 crooked; skew; tilted; slanting; aslant; awry ▶ 모자를 비뚤게 쓰지 마라 Don't wear your cap askew.

비뚤비뚤 〈흔들흔들〉 totteringly; ricketily; 〈구불구불〉 windingly; in zigzags ♦ 비뚤비뚤 놓인 책상들이 desks in a zigzag line / 비뚤비뚤 걷다 walk zigzag

비뚤어지다 1 〈사물이〉 be twisted [distorted]; get crooked; become awry [wry]; get out of the straight
♦ 비뚤어진 나무[코] a crooked tree [nose]
2 〈성격·마음이〉 get [become] crooked [perverse, cross-grained, sour]
♦ 비뚤어진 마음 an emotional bias / 성질이 비뚤어진 소녀 a girl with a warped character
▶ 그는 성격이 비뚤어져 있다 He has a crook in his character. ⇒ His disposition is warped.
▶ 그는 만사를 비뚤어진 눈으로 본다 He has a distorted [a twisted] view of everything.

비럭질 begging —비럭질하다 go (about) begging

비렁뱅이 a beggar; 《美口》 a panhandler

비련 悲戀 tragic [disappointed] love ▶ 그들의 사랑은 비련으로 끝났다 Their love ended in tragedy.

비례 比例 (a) proportion; 〈비율〉 (a) ratio
—비례하다 be in proportion (to); be proportioned [proportionate, proportional] (to)
▶ A와 B는 비례한다 A is proportional to B.
▶ 불쾌지수는 습도에 비례하여 높아진다 The discomfort index rises in proportion to a rise in humidity.
■ 단[복]— simple [compound] proportion 정[반, 역]— direct [reciprocal, inverse] proportion ■ —배분 proportional allotment [allocation, distribution] —상수 a proportional factor [constant] —세 regressive taxation —식 a proportional expression (to) —척 a proportional [proportionate] scale —중항(中項) a mean proportional

비례대표 比例代表 proportional representation —제 the system of proportional representation

비로소 〈처음으로〉 for the first time; not... until [till]...
▶ 나는 그때 비로소 부모님의 은혜를 알았다 I realized then for the first time how much I owe my parents.
▶ 나는 어제 비로소 그것을 알았다 I knew it only yesterday. ⇒ Not until yesterday did I know it.
▶ 건강을 잃고서야 비로소 그 가치를 안다 We don't realize the value of health till we lose it. ⇒ It is not until we lose our health that we realize its value.
▶ 선생님이 그만 두시고서야 비로소 그 분의 진가를 알았다 We understood the teacher's worth only when he left.

비록 〈설사〉 if; even if; (even) though; although; admitting [granting, granted] that
♦ 비록 그렇더라도 even if it were so; even so; admitting [granting] that it is so
▶ 비록 농담이라도 그런 말을 하는 법이 아니다 You shouldn't say such a thing even as a joke [in jest].
▶ 비록 사실이라도 증거가 없다 Even granting [granted] that it is true, there is no evidence.
▶ 그 남자는 비록 가난하지만 매우 낙천적이다 Though he is poor, he is very optimistic [cheerful].

비록 祕錄 a confidential document; a secret memoir; secret notes; private papers

♦최근의 대통령 선거전의 비록 confidential notes on the recent presidential election compaign

비롯하다 〈시작되다〉 begin; start; commence; 〈기원하다〉 originate (in); arise (from); date from; date back to
…을 비롯하여 including…; as well as…; beginning with…; headed by…
▶가이드를 비롯하여 여섯 명이 죽었다 Six people were killed, including the guide.
▶문예 부흥은 이탈리아에서 비롯되었다 The Renaissance started in Italy.
▶이 의식은 14세기에 비롯된 것이다 This ceremony dates from [dates back to, goes back to] the eleventh century.

비료 肥料 (a) fertilizer; manure; 〈퇴비〉 compost ♦땅에 비료를 주다 manure [fertilize] the soil; spread fertilizer on land
■배합— mixed fertilizer 인조[합성]— artificial [synthetic] fertilizer 질소[인산, 칼륨]— nitrogenous [phosphate, potash] manure 화학— chemical fertilizer ■—공업 the fertilizer industry —공장 a fertilizer plant —살포기 a fertilizer distributor

비루 〔獸醫〕 〈가축의 피부병〉 mange
♦비루먹다 catch [be affected by] mange

비루스 〔醫〕 a virus ⇨ 바이러스

비루하다 鄙陋— mean; low; base; despicable; vulgar ♦비루한 마음 a mean [base] mind; a sordid spirit
▶그는 그런 비루한 짓은 하지 않는다 He is above such meanness.

비류 比類 ♦비류없는 peerless; matchless; unrivaled; imcomparable

비름 〔植〕 an amaranth

비리 非理 irrationality; unreasonableness; absurdity; 〈불의〉 injustice ♦비리를 저지르다 commit an injustice; do wrong

비리다 〈생선맛이〉 fishy; 〈피냄새가〉 bloody
♦우유의 비린 맛 a cowy taste in milk

비린내 a fish-like [fishy] smell; 〈피의〉 a bloody smell
♦비린내가 나다 smell fishy; stink of fish
▶부엌에서 비린내가 난다 The kitchen smells fishy [stinks of fish].
▶내 손에서 생선 비린내가 나기 시작했다 My hands began to smell of the fish.

비릿하다 〈생선이〉 somewhat fishy; 〈피가〉 a little bloody

비마(자) 萆麻子 〔植〕 a castor bean ⇨ 아주까리, 피마자

비막 飛膜 〈박쥐 등의〉 a flying membrane; a patagium (*pl.* -gia [-dʒiə])

비만 肥滿 overweight; corpulence; fatness; obesity
▶비만은 고혈압을 일으킨다 Overweight causes hypertension [high blood pressure].
—비만하다 too fat; overweight; corpulent; obese; plump; fleshy
♦비만해지다 grow corpulent; become fat; put on weight
—아(兒) an obese child —증〔醫〕 obesity

비말 飛沫 a spray; a splash

비망록 備忘錄 a memorandum (*pl.* ~s, -da); a notebook; (英) a pocketbook; (口) a memo (*pl.* ~s) ♦비망록에 기입하다 make some notes; note on a memorandum [in a memo]

비매품 非賣品 an article not for sale ▶비매품 (게시) Not for sale. ⇌ Not to be sold.

비명 非命 ♦비명에 가다 die an unnatural [untimely, accidental] death; die by violence; 〈모함으로〉 die a victim of foul play

비명 悲鳴 a shriek; a scream; a screech; a shrill voice
♦비명을 지르다 shriek; utter [give] a shriek; scream; screech / 아파서 비명을 지르다 give a cry of pain / 도와달라고 비명을 지르다 scream for help
▶우리는 엄청난 반응에 즐거운 비명을 올렸다 We were both overwhelmed and delighted by the tremendous response.
▶그녀의 비명에 도둑은 놀라 달아났다 Her scream frightened off the burglar [housebreaker].
—비명하다 shriek; scream

비명 碑銘 an inscription (on a monument); an epitaph

비모음 鼻母音 〔音聲〕 nasal vowels

비목 費目 an item of expenditure [expenses]; items of expense ♦경비를 비목별로 나누다 itemize the exenses; list the expense by item

비몽사몽 非夢似夢 ♦비몽사몽간에 half awake and half asleep; dreamily / 비몽사몽간에 듣다 listen ((to a noise)) half asleep

비무장 非武裝 demilitarization
♦비무장의 unarmed; demilitarized
▶런던의 경찰관들은 비무장으로 근무한다 Policemen in London go unarmed [without carrying any weapon].
■—중립 unarmed neutrality —지대 a demilitarized zone (略 DMZ)

비문 碑文 an epitaph; an epigraph; an inscription ♦기념비의 비문 an epitaph on a monument; a monumental inscription

비문명 非文明 ♦비문명의 uncivilized; unenlightened; barbarous ■—국 an uncivilized [a backward] country

비문화적 非文化的 unclutured; uncivilized; unenlightened

비물질적 非物質的 immaterial; nonmaterial

비민주적 非民主的 undemocratic; nondemocratic

비밀 祕密 〈비밀 사항〉 a secret; ; confidentiality; 〈내밀〉 secrecy; 〈수수께끼〉 (a) mystery; 〈사적인 일〉 privacy
♦국가〔업무〕의 비밀 a state [trade] secret / 서신의 비밀 the privacy of (personal) correspondence / 비밀의 secret; classified; confidential; private; clandestine; hidden; undercover ((operation)) / 비밀히 secretly; privately; in secrecy
▶이것은 공공연한 비밀이다 This is an open secret.
▶이것은 당신과 나만의 비밀입니다 This is between you and me.
▶이것은 절대 비밀이다 This is strictly confidential.
▶그 계획은 비밀리에 실행되었다 The plan

was carried out in secret [secretly].
► 비밀히 말씀드릴 것이 있습니다 I have something for your private ear.
〈비밀이[은]〉 비밀이 샜다 The secret leaked [came, got] out.
► 그의 성공의 비밀은 근면에 있다 The secret of [key to] his success lies in his diligence.
► 이 비밀은 절대 밝히지지 않을 것이다 The secret will never come to light.
► 세상에 비밀은 없다 No secret but will come to light.
〈비밀을〉 비밀을 누설하다 leak [let] out a secret; give a secret away / 비밀을 알아내다 find out [get into] the secret / 비밀을 지키다 keep a secret; maintain secrecy / 비밀을 캐다 pry into a secret / 비밀을 털어놓다 confide [reveal] a secret to sb / 비밀을 폭로하다 disclose [reveal] a secret
► 나는 비밀을 지켰는데 그 사람이 누설했다 I kept the secret, but he let it out.
► 그녀는 나에게 비밀을 털어놓았다 She revealed [disclosed] her secret to me. ⇌ She confided her secret to me.
► 나는 그의 비밀을 알고 있다 I hold [have, keep] his secret in my head [memory].
〈비밀로〉 비밀로 하다 keep *sth* secret [private]; (口) keep *sth* under *one*'s hat
► 이것은 비밀로 해두자 Let's keep it a secret.
━━결사 a secret society; an underground organization [society] ━━경찰 the secret police; 〈구 소련의〉 the KGB; 〈나치스의〉 the Gestapo ━━교섭 secret negotiations ━━누설 disclosure of classified information; leakage of a secret ━━마이크 〈도청기〉 a hidden [concealed] microphone; (口) a bug ━━문서 a secret [confidential] document ━━정보 secret [confidential, (美) classified] information ━━조사 a secret [private] investigation; a confidential inquiry ━━조약 a secret treaty ━━주의 secretiveness ━━첩보원 a secret agent; a spy ━━카메라 a hidden camera ━━통로 a secret [concealed] passage [path] ━━투표 secret ballot ━━회의 a closed-door session; a secret meeting

비밀번호 祕密番號 a personal code number
비바람 wind and rain; a rainy wind; 〈폭풍우〉 a (rain)storm
♦비바람에 견디는 weatherproof; weathertight / 비바람을 맞다 be exposed to the weather / 비바람을 무릅쓰고 가다 go in spite [in the teeth] of the storm
► 비바람이 친다 It blows and rains. ⇌ It storms. ⇌ It is stormy.
► 심한 비바람이 쳤다 We had [There was] a heavy storm.
► 그녀는 세찬 비바람을 무릅쓰고 출발했다 She set out in spite of a violent wind and rain.
비발디 〈이탈리아의 작곡가〉 Vivaldi, Antonio (1678-1741)
비방 祕方 **1** 〈약처방〉 a secret recipe [formula]
♦비방을 전하다 initiate *sb* into the secret recipes (of)
2 〈비밀스런 방법〉 ⇨ 비법

비방 誹謗 〈헐뜯음〉 slander; slanderous statements; abuse; defamation
► 그는 비겁하다는 비방을 들었다 He was accused of cowardice.
━비방하다 slander; blame; abuse; criticize; defame; speak ill of
♦뒤에서 아무를 비방하다 backbite; speak ill of *sb* behind (his) back
비버 [動] a beaver ⇨ 해리(海狸)
비번 非番 off duty; 〈경계의〉 off guard
♦비번의[으로] off duty [guard] / 비번인 경찰관 a policeman off duty; an off-duty policeman
► 나는 오늘 비번이다 I'm off duty today.
━━일 a day off; an off day
비범하다 非凡━ extraordinary; uncommon; unusual; rare
♦비범한 솜씨 rare [unusual] ability [skill]
► 그녀는 10살 때 이미 비범한 바이올리니스트였다 She was a violin prodigy at the age of ten.
► 그는 문학에 비범한 재능이 있다 He has an extraordinary talent for literature.
► 우리는 한눈에 그가 비범한 사람임을 알았다 We saw at a glance that he was no ordinary man.
비법 祕法 a secret process [method]; a mystique
♦불로장생의 비법 the secret of longevity / 비법을 터득하다 master the secret (of)
► 건강에 무슨 비법이라도 있으십니까? What is the secret of your good health?
비보 祕寶 a treasure; a treasured article
비보 悲報 (a piece of) sad news; 〈부고〉 a death notice ♦비보에 접하다 receive [hear] the sad news (of)
► 비보를 알리는 그의 목소리는 떨렸다 His voice was trembling as he broke the sad news.
비분 悲憤 indignation; resentment
► 그는 비분의 눈물을 흘렸다 He shed tears of indignation.
━비분하다 resent; be indignant; be resentful
비분강개 悲憤慷慨 sorrowful indignation
━비분강개하다 deplore; be indignant (at, over); resent
► 우리는 사회의 부패상에 비분강개했다 We cannot help deploring the corrupt social conditions.
비브라폰 〈악기〉 a vibraphone ■━연주자 a vibraphonist
비브리오 [菌] a vibrio (*pl.* ~s)
비비 狒狒 [動] baboon; a dog ape
비비 꼬다 1 〈여러번 꼬다〉 twist [entwist, twine] many times; twist over and over again / 몸을 비비 꼬다 twist the body about; writhe / 실을 비비 꼬다 twist [tangle] the threads / 넥타이가 비비 꼬여 있다 have *one*'s tie twisted up
► 사태가 비비 꼬이고 있다 The situation has become quite involved [entangled].
2 〈빈정대다〉 ⇨ 비꼬다
비비다 1 〈문지르다〉 rub; scrub
♦눈을 비비다 rub *one*'s eyes / 손을 비비다 rub

one's hands [palms]《together》/ 눈을 비벼 잠을 쫓다 rub the sleep out of *one's* eyes / 손을 비벼 녹이다 rub *one's* hands warm [to warm them, to get warmth] / 담뱃불을 비벼 끄다 crush [grind, stub] out a cigarette / 옷의 흙을 비벼 털다 scrub the dirt [scrape the mud] off *one's* clothes
▶ 그는 추운 한데서 손을 비벼 녹였다 He chafed his hands in the cold open air.
2 〈버무리다〉 mix
◆밥을 비비다 mix boiled rice with various kinds of side dishes; make (a) hash (with rice)
3 〈송곳 등을〉 drive; drill; twirl《an awl》between the hands
◆송곳을 비벼 판자에 구멍을 뚫다 drill a hole in a board with a gimlet

비비대다 rub repeatedly ▶ 아무리 비벼대도 이 얼룩은 지워지지 않는다 This mark won't rub off.

비비적거리다 chafe [rub] against ▶ 고양이 새끼가 내 다리에 코를 비비적거렸다 The kitten rubbed its nose against my leg.

비비틀다 twist [wrench, screw]《*sb's* arm》hard [repeatedly] ◆비비 틀리다 get twisted [wrenched] hard

비사 祕史 a hidden history; historical secrets; unknown historical facts ◆제2차 세계대전 비사 the secret history of World War Ⅱ

비사교적 非社交的 unsociable
▶ 그는 비사교적인 사람이다 He is an unsociable person. ⇌ He is a bad mixer.

비산 砒酸 〖化〗 arsenic acid ■ ―납 lead arsenate ―염(鹽) arsenate

비상 非常 1〈평범하지 않음〉 uncommonness; unusualness; extraordinariness; excessiveness ―비상하다 unusual; extraordinary;〈비범하다〉 uncommon; prodigious;〈대단하다〉 remarkable; excessive; extreme
◆비상한 인물 a man of no ordinary ability [talent] / 비상한 관심을 가지고 지켜보다 watch with very great concern
▶ 그는 그 제안에 비상한 열의를 보였다 He responded to the proposal with extraordinary enthusiasm.
2〈긴급사태〉 an emergency; a contingency ■ ―경계 emergency [special] guard ―계단 an emergency staircase;〈화재 시의〉 a fire escape ―구 an emergency exit [door]; a fire exit ―금 emergency funds; a nest egg ―소집 an emergency call [summons] ―식량 emergency rations [provisions] ―전화 an emergency call;〈美〉 a hurry call ―조치 an extraordinary step ―직통전화〈국가간의〉 a hot line ―착륙 a forced [an emergency] landing; a crash landing

비상 飛翔〈날아다님〉 a flight; flying; soaring ―비상하다 fly; take a flight; soar (up)
◆비상하는 독수리 a hawk in flight

비상 砒霜〖藥〗 arsenic poison

비상경보 非常警報 an emergency warning; an alarm (signal) ■ ―기 an alarm

비상근 非常勤 (a) part-time service ◆비상근의 part-time / 비상근으로 일하다 work part-time ■ ―강사 a part-time teacher

비상사태 非常事態 a state of emergency
◆비상사태를 선언하다 declare a state of emergency; declare an emergency / 비상사태에 있다 be in a state of emergency / 비상사태에 대비하다 provide against emergencies; prepare for the worst

비상선 非常線 a (police) cordon;〈화재의〉 a fire line
◆비상선을 치다 set up [post, draw] a cordon《around a place》/ 비상선을 돌파하다 break through a cordon
▶ 그 지역에 비상선이 쳐졌다 The area was cordoned off.

비상수단 非常手段 an exceptional measure; an emergency [a drastic] measure
◆비상수단을 쓰다[강구하다] take [resort to] emergency [extreme, exceptional] measures

비상시 非常時 an emergency; a crisis
◆국가 비상시 a national emergency [crisis] / 비상시에 in case of emergency; in an emergency; in case [time, the hour] of need / 비상시에 대비하다 prepare for an emergency

비상식 非常識 lack of common sense

비상용 非常用 for emergency ■ ―사다리 an emergency ladder ―출입구 an emergency door [exit]

비상장주 非上場株 unlisted stocks [shares]

비색 比色 ―계(計) a colorimeter ―분석 (a) colorimetric analysis ―정량(定量) colorimetry

비생산적 非生産的 unproductive; nonproductive; unfruitful ◆비생산적 노동 unproductive labor ▶ 그것은 비생산적 사고다 That is not a productive [constructive] idea.

비서 祕書 a secretary
◆비서의 임무 secretarial work / 사장 비서를 하다 be [act as] secretary to the president ―관 a secretary : 국무총리 비서관 a secretary to the Prime Minister ―직 secretaryship ―학과[학교] a secretarial course [school]

비서실 祕書室 a secretary's office; a secretariat ―장관 the Minister's Secretariat ―장 a chief secretary

비석 碑石 a tombstone; a gravestone;〈기념비〉 a (stone) monument;〖考古〗 a stele
◆…을 기념하여 비석을 세우다 build [erect] a tombstone [stone monument] to the memory of...

비설거지하다 prepare for rain; shelter a thing from rain; put away [clear up] things for rain

비성 鼻聲〈콧소리〉 a nasal voice

비소 砒素〖化〗 arsenic ■ ―제 arsenicals; an arsenic compound ―중독 arsenical poisoning;〈만성의〉 arsenism

비소수 非素數〖數〗 a composite number＝합성(~수)

비속 卑俗 vulgarity ―비속하다 vulgar; coarse; low; broad
◆비속한 취미 vulgar [coarse, unrefined, philistine] taste
▶ 비속한 잡지가 범람하고 있다 There is a flood of vulgar magazines.

▶비속한 영화가 유행하고 있다 Vulgar films are in vogue.
비속 卑屬 〔法〕 a descendant ■**직계—** a lineal descendant
비송사건 非訟事件 a noncontentious [nonlitigation] case
비수 匕首 〈단도〉 a dagger; a dirk
♦비수를 품에 감추고 있다 have a dagger concealed under *one's* clothes / 비수로 찌르다 stab *sb* with a dagger
비수 悲愁 pathos; grief; sorrow
비수기 非需期 a slack season
비술 祕術 a secret art; the mysteries; occult arts ♦쌍방이 서로 비술을 다하여 싸웠다 Both of them fought to the best of their skill.
비스듬하다 slant(ing); sloping; skew; oblique; diagonal ♦비스듬한 선 a slant line / 비스듬한 아치 a skew arch
비스듬히 aslant; askew; obliquely; askance; diagonally
♦줄을 비스듬히 긋다 draw an oblique [diagonal] line; draw a line diagonally / 비스듬히 나아가다 edge [advance] obliquely / 비스듬히 자르다 cut diagonally / 모자를 비스듬히 쓰다 wear a hat tilted to one side; cock *one's* hat ▶나는 그와 비스듬히 마주앉았다 I sat diagonally opposite from him.
비스름하다 rather alike; somewhat similar
▶그들은 성격이 비스름하다 They are somewhat alike in character.
▶그들 사이에는 어딘가 비스름한 데가 있었다 There was a distant [faint] resemblance between them.
비스마르크 〈독일의 정치가〉 Bismarck, Otto von (1815-98)
비스킷 〈英〉 a biscuit; 〈美〉 a cookie [cracker]

〔解說〕 비스킷은 *biscuit*으로 쓰는 데 〈英〉 〈美〉에서는 각각 다른것을 가리킨다. 영국의 biscuit은 우리나라에서 말하는「비스킷」과 같지만, 미국에서는 작고 말랑말랑한 빵을 가리키며, *cookie*나 *cracker*가 우리나라의 비스킷에 해당된다.

비스타비전 〈商標〉〔映〕 VistaVision
비슬거리다 stagger; totter; reel; falter
▶노인은 무거운 짐 때문에 비슬거렸다 The old man tottered [staggered] under a heavy load.
▶그는 두어 발짝 비슬거리가 쓰러졌다 He staggered a few steps and fell.
▶그는 비슬거리면서 걸어갔다 He went on his way with tottering steps.
비슬비슬 staggeringly; totteringly; falteringly; reelingly ♦비슬비슬 걸어가다 dodder along; walk with faltering steps / 비슬비슬 일어서다 stagger [totter] to *one's* feet
비슷비슷하다 much the same; of a [the same] sort
▶그들은 키가 모두 비슷비슷하다 They are all much the same in height.
▶기념품은 어딜 가나 비슷비슷하다 Souvenirs are more or less [almost, pretty much] the same wherever you go.
비슷이[1] 〈조금 비슷하게〉 leaning a bit to one side
♦비슷이 기울어진 벽 a wall with a slight lean
비슷이[2] 〈유사하게〉 alike; similarly; likely; nearly ♦비슷이 닮아 bear some resemblance to *sb* / 비슷이 맞히다 nearly guess right
비슷하다[1] 〈조금 비슷하다〉 lean a bit to one side; have a slight tilt to one side
비슷하다[2] 〈유사하다〉 similar; like; alike; resembling
♦비슷한 사건 a similar case; a case similar to *sth* / 그와 비슷한 이야기 a story like that; a similar tale / 길이가 비슷하다 the length is about the same / 비슷한 데기 있다 there is something that resembles / 서로 비슷한 처지에 있다 be similarly situated / 비슷하지 않다 bear no resemblance [similarity] to; look different
▶이곳 날씨는 런던과 비슷하다 The weather here is like London's.
▶두 소녀는 옷차림이 비슷했다 The two girls dressed similarly [alike].
▶그들은 서로 비슷한 데가 있다[없다] They have something [nothing] in common with each other.
▶두 자매는 생김새는 비슷하지만 성격은 다르다 The two sisters look alike but their personalities are different.
▶나도 비슷한 이야기를 들은 적이 있다 I have also heard a similar story.
비시지 BCG (vaccine) [〈*b*acillus *C*almette-*G*uérin〕 ■**—접종** inoculation of BCG
비신사적 非紳士的 ungentlemanlike; ungentlemanly ♦비신사적인 행위 a conduct unbecoming to a gentleman
비실비실 staggeringly ⇨ 비슬비슬 ♦비실비실 걸어가다 dodder along / 비실비실 다가가다[물러나다] sidle up to [away from] *sb*
비실용적 非實用的 unpractical 《view》; impractical
비아 非我 〔哲〕 nonego
비아냥거리다 〈빈정대다〉 make sarcastic [cutting] remarks; be cynical about
비아냥스럽다 sarcastic; cynical
비아이피 a VIP ⇨ 브이아이피
비애 悲哀 (a) sorrow; (a) grief; sadness; pathos
♦인생의 비애 the sorrows [pathos] of life / 비애로 가득찬 인생 a life full of sorrows / 비애를 느끼다 feel sad / 술로 비애를 달래다 drown grief [sorrow] in drink / 환멸의 비애를 맛보다 have a sad disillusionment
비애국적 非愛國的 unpatriotic
비약 飛躍 〈뛰어오름〉 a leap; a flying jump; 〈진보·향상〉 rapid progress; 〈논리 등의〉 a jump
▶그의 말에는 논리의 비약이 있다 There is a jump of logic [logical jump] in what he says.
▶그의 문체는 비약적이다 He writes in an abrupt style.
▶과학기술이 비약적으로 발전했다 Technology has made rapid progress. ⇌ Technology has advanced by leaps and bounds.
—**비약하다** leap; jump; fly
▶그의 이야기는 어디로 비약할지 모른다 No

비약 祕藥 〈비방〉 a secret medicine [remedy]; 〈묘약〉 a nostrum
비어 卑語 〈천한 말〉 a vulgarism; a slang (word); 〈낮춤말〉 a depreciatory term
비어 蜚語 a wild [flying] rumor
비어지다 1 〈밖으로 내밀다〉 stick [jut] out; protrude; project
▶ 통나무 하나가 목재 적재장에서 비어져 나와 있다 A log protrudes from the lumberyard.
▶ 아이의 다리가 담요 밖으로 비어져 나와 있었다 The child's legs were sticking out from under the blanket.
2 〈드러나다〉 be revealed; come to light; be exposed; be laid bare
비어홀 〈맥주집〉 a beer hall; a beerhouse; an alehouse
비엔나소시지 a Vienna sausage
비엔나왈츠 a Viennese waltz
비엔날레 the Biennale (▶ 2년마다 열리는 국제적 미술 전람회)
비역 sodomy; pederasty
비열 比熱 【物】 specific heat
비열 卑劣 meanness; baseness
―비열하다 mean; base; dirty; sordid; nasty; low(-minded); contemptible
♦ 비열한 놈 a mean bastard; a sneak; a sneaker / 비열한 동기 sordid motivation / 비열한 정신 low spirits / 비열한 행위 a dirty conduct / 비열한 수단을 쓰다 play a mean trick 《on sb》 / 비열한 짓을 하다 play sb foul; hit [strike] below the belt
▶ 저 녀석은 근성이 비열하다 That guy has a mean mind.
▶ 그는 나에게 비열한 수단을 썼다 He played a dirty [mean] trick on me.
▶ 중상 모략은 비열한 짓이다 Backbiting is a mean [contemptible] thing.
▶ 참으로 비열한 녀석이군 What a wretched [mean] fellow he is!
비영리단체 非營利團體 a nonprofit [noncommercial] organization
비영리법인 非營利法人 a nonprofit [noncommercial] corporation
비영리사업 非營利事業 a nonprofit [noncommercial] undertaking
비예술적 非藝術的 inartistic
비오디 〈생물학적 산소 요구량〉 BOD[< *b*iological *o*xygen *d*emand]
비오리 〔鳥〕 a merganser; a goosander
비오큐 〈독신 장교 숙소〉 BOQ [〈*B*achelor *O*fficers' *Q*uarters]
비옥하다 肥沃― fertile; rich; productive; fruitful
♦ 비옥한 땅 fertile [rich, productive] soil / 비옥해지다 grow fertile [rich, productive]
▶ 이곳은 땅이 비옥하다 The soil here is fertile [productive].
▶ 만주에는 비옥한 토지가 많다 Manchuria has a great deal of fertile land.
비온 뒤에 땅이 굳어진다 〈속담〉 Ground packs after a rain. ⇒ After rain comes fair weather. ⇒ After a storm comes a calm.
비올라 〈악기〉 a viola
비옷 a raincoat ♦ 비옷을 입다 put on [wear] a raincoat
비용 費用 expense(s); expenditure; cost(s); 〈재정 지출〉 (an) outlay
♦ 비용이 많이 드는 costly; expensive / 비용이 들지 않는 inexpensive / 막대한 비용을 들여서 at an enormous [a huge] cost / 아무리 비용이 들더라도 at any cost [expense] / 적은 비용으로 at [with] a small outlay / …의 비용으로 at the expense of 《the company》; at a [the] cost of 《100,000 won》 / 비용이 많이 들다 cost a great deal / 비용을 부담하다 bear [defray] the expense; meet *one*'s expenses / 비용을 부담시키다 put sb to expenses / 비용을 절약하다 save expenses / 비용을 줄이다 cut (down) [reduce] expenses / …의 비용에 충당하다 cover the expense of… / 비용을 손해보고 말다 end [result] in a waste of money; do not pay
▶ 차를 굴리자면 비용이 많이 든다 Running a car is a great expense.
▶ 비용은 최소한 10만원은 들 것입니다 The expenses will amount to 100,000 won at least.
▶ 비용은 얼마나 들까요? What will it cost?
▶ 비용은 얼마가 들어도 상관 없다 I don't care how much it may cost.
▶ 우리는 매달 여행 비용을 적립하고 있다 We put aside traveling expenses every month.
▶ 비용에 신경 쓰지 말고 해 보십시오 Try it regardless of the expense.
▶ 이렇게 적은 비용으로 즐길 수 있는 오락은 달리 없다 There is no other amusement that can be obtained at so small a cost.
■ 소송― legal expenses
비우다 1 〈내용물을〉 empty 《a box, a glass》; clear out the contents of
♦ 마음을 비우다 give up *one*'s personal feelings / 상자를 비우다 empty a box / 잔을 비우다 empty *one*'s cup [glass]; drink up [off] / 호주머니를 비우다 empty a pocket of its contents; clear (out) *one*'s pocket
▶ 그는 위스키 한 병을 깨끗이 비웠다 He drank a whole bottle of whisky.
▶ 나는 서류를 찾기 위해 서랍을 다 비워야 했다 I had to empty out the drawer to find the paper.
2【점유지·건물 등을】 leave 《*one*'s house》 empty; stay [stop] away 《from home》; be out; 〈명도하다〉 vacate; evacuate
▶ 그녀는 일요일에는 자주 집을 비운다 She often stays away from home on Sundays.
▶ 이달 말까지 집을 비워 주시오 I request you to evacuate the house by the end of this month.
▶ 1인용 방을 하나 비워 두시오 Reserve a single room for me.
▶ 그 두 페이지는 비워 두시오 Leave the two pages blank.
비우호적 非友好的 unfriendly 《act, nation》
비운 悲運 (a) misfortune; ill [hard] luck
♦ 비운을 만나다 have bad luck; suffer a misfortune / 비운을 한탄하다 complain of *one*'s ill luck
비웅 〔魚〕 〈청어〉 a herring (as food)
비웃다 laugh sb to scorn; laugh scornfully

(at); laugh [sneer, jeer, scoff] at; deride; ridicule
♦남의 성공을 비웃다 deride the success of others / 남의 종교를 비웃다 scoff at others' religion / 비웃는 표정을 짓다 make a face of derision 〈at〉
▶ 사람들은 그가 가난하다고 비웃었다 People laughed at him for being poor.
▶ 그들은 그의 노력을 유치하다고 비웃었다 They derided his efforts as childish.

비웃음 a scornful smile; a mocking laugh; a sneer; ridicule
♦비웃음을 사다 incur ridicule; bring [draw] ridicule upon *oneself*; be scorned
▶ 그는 이웃 사람들의 비웃음거리가 되었다 He became the taunt of his neighbors.

비원 祕苑 1 〈금원(禁苑)〉 a royal [imperial, palace] garden **2** Piwon

비원 悲願 *one's* earnest [pathetic] prayer [wish]; 〔佛敎〕 a merciful prayer 〈to save mankind〉
♦비원을 이루다 attain [achieve] *one's* earnest [dearest] wish; have *one's* earnest [dearest] wish answered [fulfilled]

비위 脾胃 1 〈지라와 위〉 the spleen and the stomach
2 〈기호〉 taste; palate; liking; choice
♦비위가 까다롭다 have a pampered taste [delicate palate] / 비위가 좋다 have a strong stomach / 비위에 맞다 be to *one's* taste; suit to *one's* taste [palate]
▶ 그 음식은 내 비위에 맞지 않는다 The food goes against my stomach.
3 〈기분〉 humor; temper; mood
♦비위가 상하다 be [feel] disgusted 〈at, by, with〉; be nauseated 〈by〉 / 비위가 틀리다 get out of humor; be cross [sour] / 비위를 거스르다[건드리다] offend; hurt *sb's* feeling; put *sb* in a bad humor; rub *sb* the wrong way; get on *sb's* nerves / 비위를 맞추다 put *sb* in good humor; curry favor with *sb*; flatter; please 〈*one's* master〉 / 비위에 거슬리다 be offending [offensive]; be disagreeable to *sb's* feeling
▶ 그의 연설이 당국의 비위를 상하게 했다 His speech incurred the displeasure of the authorities.
▶ 그는 아들의 행실이 비위에 거슬렸다 He was displeased at his son's conduct.
4 〈뻔뻔스러움〉 impudence; audacity; cheekiness
♦비위가 좋다 have a nerve; be impudent

비위생적 非衛生的 unhealthy; unsanitary; insanitary 〈conditions〉; unwholesome 〈food〉
♦비위생적인 생활 an unwholesome way of living / 비위생적인 주거 환경 the unsanitary residential environment / 비위생적이다 be bad for the health; be unhealthy

비유 比喩·譬喩 a figure of speech; 〈비유담〉 a parable; 〈직유〉 a simile; 〈은유〉 a metaphor
♦비유적으로 metaphorical; figurative / 비유로 나타내다 figure; represent by metaphors
▶ 심장을 펌프에 비기는 것은 아주 흔한 비유다 The comparison of the heart to a pump is a very common one.
▶ 비유적으로 말하자면 그녀는 붉은 장미다 To put it figuratively, she is a red rose.
▶ 나는 비유적으로 말했을 뿐이다 I only said it by way of a metaphor.
—**비유하다** liken [compare] 〈one thing〉 to 〈another〉; use a simile [metaphor]; speak figuratively [metaphorically]
♦비유해서 말하자면 figuratively [metaphorically] speaking; to use a simile [metaphor] / 덕을 황금에 비유하다 liken virtue to gold
▶ 그녀를 꽃에 비유한다면 흰 백합이 될것이다 If I were to compare her to a flower, it would be to a white lily.
▶ 책을 친구에 비유하는 사람도 있다 Some people have compared books to friends.
▶ 인생은 종종 항해에 비유된다 Life is often compared to a voyage.

비육 肥育 fatting (up); fattening (up)
—**비육하다** fat [fatten] up 〈cattle〉
■—**우**(牛) a beef; (총칭) beef cattle

비율 比率 〈a〉 ratio; rate; proportion; (a) percentage ♦…의 비율로 〈increase〉 at the rate of 〈ten cars a day〉
▶ 비율이 높다[낮다] The ratio is high [low].
▶ 내 생활비 가운데 집세가 가장 큰 비율을 차지한다 Rent takes up the largest percentage of my living expenses.
▶ 소금과 설탕을 3대 2 비율로 섞으시오 Mix salt and sugar in the ratio of 3 to 2.
■—**구성**—[統] distribution ratio

비음 鼻音 〔音聲〕 〈콧소리〉 nasal sounds; a nasal
■—**화** 〔音聲〕 nasalization

비이론적 非理論的 illogical; absurd

비인간적 非人間的 inhuman; impersonal
♦비인간적인 행동 inhuman behavior / 비인간적인 힘 impersonal forces

비인도적 非人道的 inhumane ♦비인도적인 범죄 a crime against humanity / 비인도적인 취급 inhumane treatment

비인칭 非人稱 ♦비인칭의 〔文法〕 impersonal
■—**동사**[구문] an impersonal verb [construction]

비일비재 非一非再 frequence; occurrence
—**비일비재하다** frequent; repeated; 〈서술적〉 occur often
▶ 그런 일은 비일비재하다 It is just one of those common things. ⇒ It is of frequent occurrence. ⇒ There are no end of such cases.

비자 榧子 a nutmeg apple ■—**나무** 〔植〕 a nutmeg (tree)

비자 a visa ♦비자를 받다 have *one's* passport visaed ▶ 나는 미국 입국 비자를 받았다 I got [was granted] a visa to the U.S.

비잔틴건축 —**建築** Byzantine architecture
비잔틴제국 —**帝國** the Byzantine Empire
비장 祕藏 treasuring; hoarding
♦비장의 그림 a treasured painting / 비장의 수단 (play) *one's* best card; the last resort [resource] / 비장의 treasured; prized
—**비장하다** store in secrecy; treasure; prize; cherish; keep *sth* under lock and key [with great care]

비장 脾臟 〔解〕〈지라〉 the spleen; the melt ■─병 a disease of the spleen; splenopathy ─병 환자 a splenetic (patient)

비장하다 悲壯─ pathetic; touching; tragic ◆비장한 각오[결의] a tragic resolution; a tragic decision in *one's* mind; 〈영웅적인〉 a heroic resolve ▶그는 전쟁터에서 비장한 최후를 마쳤다 He died a tragic [touching, hero's] death in the battlefield. ▶그 비장한 광경은 그를 무척 감동시켰다 The pathetic scene moved him much.

비재 菲才 lack of ability; poor talent; want of talent; incapacity; incompetence ▶비록 비재이오나 전력을 다하겠습니다 Incompetent [Incapable] as I am, I will do all I can.

비적 匪賊 bandits; rebels; insurgents; outlaws

비전 祕傳 secret inheritance; secret transmission ◆비전의 묘약 a proprietary medicine

비전 vision 〈위대한〉 비전을 지닌 정치가 a statesman of (great breadth of) vision

비전략물자 非戰略物資 nonstrategic goods

비전론 非戰論 pacifism ⇨ 반전(反戰)(∼론)

비전투원 非戰鬪員 a noncombatant; 〈민간인〉 a civilian

비전하 妃殿下 Her (Royal) Highness

비점 沸點 the boiling point ⇨ 끓는점

비접 〈전지 요양〉 a change of place (for a sick person); a change of air [climate] ◆비접 나가다 move to another place (for *one's* health); go to 《a place》 for a change of air

비정 非情 〈몰인정〉 inhumanity; 〈무감정〉 insentience ─비정한 〈인정이 없다〉 unfeeling; heartless; cold-hearted; callous; 〈지각이 없다〉 insentient; inanimate ◆비정한 살인 a cold-blooded murder / 비정한 세상 an inanimate world ▶그는 비정한 사람이다 He is a cold-hearted person. ▶그런 비정한 짓은 할 수 없다 I cannot do such a cruel thing.

비정 秕政 〈나쁜 정치〉 misgovernment; maladministration; misrule

비정규 非正規 ◆비정규적인 irregular ■─군 irregulars; irregular troops

비정상 非正常 being abnormal; abnormality; irregularity ◆비정상적인 정신 상태 an abnormal mental condition; an abnormal state of mind / 비정상적인 정서 결핍 abnormal lack of emotion

비제 〈프랑스의 작곡가〉 Bizet, Georges (1838-75)

비조 飛鳥 〈나는 새〉 a flying bird; a bird on the wing ◆비조처럼 빠른 (as) quick as lightning; like a shot

비조 悲調 〈비곡〉 a plaintive melody [note]; a touch of sadness ◆비조를 띤 plaintive; pathetic; sad

비조 鼻祖 the founder ⇨ 시조(始祖)

비조합원 非組合員 a nonunionist; a nonmember

비좁다 cramped; confined; narrow and close 《house》 ▶식구가 늘어 이 아파트로는 비좁다 My family has outgrown this apartment [flat]. ▶그들은 비좁은 곳에서 살고 있었다 They were living in cramped quarters. ▶이 사무실은 비좁아서 운신하기도 힘들다 We have not room enough to swing a cat in this office.

비종교적 非宗敎的 nonreligious ◆비종교적인 단체 a nonreligious organization

비주룩하다 〈삐죽하다〉 《be》 sticking out [protruding, projecting] a bit

비주류 非主流 〈파(派)〉 non(-)mainstreamers; the non(-)mainstream faction [group]

비죽 poutingly; protrudingly; projectingly ◆입을 비죽 내밀다 pout *one's* lips / 창 밖으로 머리를 비죽 내밀다 pop *one's* head out of the window ▶그 남자는 얼굴만 비죽 내밀고 가버렸다 He showed his nose for a moment and disappeared.

비죽거리다 〈입을〉 pout *one's* lips [mouth]; make (up) a lip; make mouths [a mouth] at *sb*; screw up *one's* mouth ◆울려고 비죽거리다 pout [sulk] almost in tears ▶그 소녀는 입을 비죽거리며 대들었다 The girl protested with a pout.

비준 批准 ratification ◆비준이 끝난 ratified / 아직 비준이 안 된 unratified ▶이 조약은 비준을 요한다 The treaty is subject to ratification. ─비준하다 ratify [confirm] 《a treaty》; sanction ▶그 조약은 국회에서 비준되었다 The treaty was confirmed by the National Assembly.

비준서 批准書 an instrument of ratification; a ratification instrument ◆조약의 비준서를 교환하다 exchange ratifications of a treaty

비중 比重 〔物〕 specific gravity; 〈중요성〉 relative importance ◆비중을 재다 measure [find out] the specific gravity 《of》 / 시험 점수보다 출석률에 비중을 더 두다 place more weight on attendance than examination ▶철의 비중은 7.86이다 The specific gravity of iron is 7.86. ▶그 부부의 대화에서는 자녀 문제가 큰 비중을 차지한다 A large proportion of the couple's conversation is occupied by the topic of their children. ▶교육 문제에 더 큰 비중을 두어야 한다 We should give much more weight to the educational problem. ■─계 a gravimeter; a specific gravity balance ─표 a table of specific gravities

비즈니스 business ■─맨 a businessman

비지 residue in the preparation of bean curd

비지땀 beads of sweat; heavy sweat ◆비지땀을 흘리며 all in [of] a sweat; dripping (wet) with sweat; soaked with sweat / 비지땀을 흘리다 get into a profuse [heavy] perspiration; sweat profusely [copiously];

비질 sweeping (with a broom) —비질하다 sweep with a broom

비집다 1 〈틈을 벌리다〉 split open; pull [force] open; spread apart
♦인파 속을 비집고 나아가다 push [thrust] one's way through the crowd; elbow [shoulder] one's way (forward) through the crowd / 비집고 들어가다 wedge oneself in [into]; thrust [squeeze] oneself in [into]/ 상자 뚜껑을 지레로 비집어 열다 pry up the lid of a box; prize off a box
▶ 만원인 극장 안을 가까스로 비집고 들어갔다 I managed to squeeze myself into the crowded theater.
▶ 그는 줄서서 버스를 기다리고 있는 사람들 사이를 비집고 들어갔다 He broke into the bus queue.
2 〈눈을〉 rub one's eyes open

비참하다 悲慘— miserable; wretched; tragic; piteous; pitiable; pathetic
♦비참한 광경 a pitiable scene; a pathetic sight / 비참한 사건 a tragic accident; a tragedy / 비참하기 짝이 없다 be in the depths of misery / 비참한 최후를 당하다 die a miserable [dog's] death; meet with a tragic death [end]
▶ 그의 일생은 비참했다 His whole life was miserable.
▶ 그 광경은 참으로 비참했다 It was a really pitiable sight to see.
▶ 난민들은 비참한 생활을 하고 있었다 The refugees were leading a miserable [wretched] life.
▶ 그는 우리들에게 전쟁이 얼마나 비참한가를 들려주었다 He told us about the misery of the war.

비창 悲愴 pathos; sorrow; sadness —비창하다 sad; pathetic; sorrowful; plaintive
■—교향곡 〈차이코프스키의〉 the Symphonie Pathétique

비책 祕策 a secret plan [scheme]; a subtle stratagem; a secret (of)
♦비책을 가르쳐 주다 give secret measures [tactics]; initiate sb into the secret / 비책을 짜다 work out a secret plan

비척거리다 stagger ⇨ 비틀거리다
비척걸음 a staggering walk ⇨ 비틀걸음
비천 卑賤 humbleness; lowliness; obscurity —비천하다 low; lowly; obscure; humble
♦비천한 몸[사람] a person of humble origin [of low birth]/ 태생이 비천하다 be of humble birth
▶ 그는 비천한 처지에서 출세했다 He has risen from obscurity (into fame). ⇌ He has sprung from a humble origin.

비철금속 非鐵金屬 nonferrous metals
비추다 1 〈밝게 하다〉 shine on; shed [throw] light on; flash (on); light (up)
♦태양은 부자나 가난한 사람이나 똑같이 비춘다 The sun shines on the rich and the poor alike.
▶ 탐조등이 해상을 비추었다 The searchlight flashed over the sea.
▶ 그는 내 얼굴에 호롱불을 비췄다 He flashed a lantern in my face.
▶ 네온 사인이 거리를 환하게 비추고 있다 Neon sign is lighting up the street.
2 〈빛에 대보다〉 hold (up) a thing to [before, against] the light
▶ 나는 지폐를 불빛에 비추어 보았다 I looked at the bill [note] through the light.
3 〈투사·반사하다〉 reflect; mirror; project; cast
▶ 그는 16밀리 영화를 스크린에 비추었다 He projected the 16mm movies on the screen.
▶ 호수가 산 그림자를 비추고 있다 The lake reflects [mirrors] the mountains.
▶ 잔잔한 수면은 강기슭에 있는 나무들의 그림자를 비추고 있었다 The still water mirrored the trees along the bank.
▶ 그녀는 거울에 자기 모습을 비추어 보았다 She looked at herself in the mirror.
4 〈비교·참조하다〉 compare 《with》; refer 《to》; judge by [from]
♦법에 비추어 according to the law / 사실에 비추어 in view [the light] of facts / 오늘날의 세계 정세에 비추어 in the context of the world situation today / 전례에 비추어 in the light of precedents
▶ 그는 그 현상을 최신의 과학적 지식에 비추어 설명했다 He explained the phenomenon in the light of recent scientific knowledge.
▶ 지금까지의 업적에 비추어 이 회사는 크게 발전할 가능성이 있다 Judging from the results so far obtained, this company has great possibilities in the future.
5 〈암시하다〉 ⇨ 비치다

비추이다 be shone; be lighted (up); be reflected [mirrored]

비축 備蓄 storing; stockpiling; saving for [against] emergency
—비축하다 store (up); save for emergency
♦석유를 2개월분 비축하다 keep a two-month stockpile of oil

비취 翡翠 jade; jadeite ■—반지 a jade ring —색 jade green —잠(簪) an ornamental jade hairpin

비치 備置 equipment; provision; furnishing; installation; fitting
♦교수 연구실의 비치 도서 books kept in a professor's office
—비치하다 furnish; provide; equip; fit; install
♦비치된 잡지 periodicals kept on file / 방안에 가구를 비치하다 fit up a room
▶ 그들은 방에 책상과 의자 두 개를 비치했다 They furnished the room with a desk and two chairs.
▶ 이 도서관에는 좋은 책이 많이 비치돼 있다 This library is well stocked with good books.
▶ 방마다 전화가 비치되어 있다 A telephone is installed in each room.

비치다 1 〈빛이〉 shine (in, into, upon)
▶ 구름 사이로 간간이 햇빛이 비친다 The sunlight breaks now and then through the clouds.
▶ 이 방에는 하루 종일 햇빛이 비친다 The sunlight shines into this room in all the daytime.

▶ 달빛이 교교하게 창문으로 비쳐 들어왔다 The moon shone brightly in through the window.
2 〈투영되다〉 be reflected; be imaged; be mirrored; be projected; fall [be thrown] upon
♦ 거울에 비친 그의 얼굴 his face (reflected) on the mirror / 거울[수면]에 비치다 be reflected in a mirror [the water]
▶ 커튼에 사람 그림자가 비쳤다 The shadow of a man fell on the curtain.
▶ 그녀는 물에 비친 자신의 모습을 보고 있었다 She was looking at her figure reflected in the water.
3 〈투시되다〉 show through; be seen through; be transparent
♦ 살이 비치는 블라우스 a see-through blouse
▶ 인쇄가 뒷면에 비친다 The printing shows through on the other side.
▶ 그녀의 옷이 얇아서 등이 비친다 Her back is seen through her thin dress.
4 〈암시하다〉 hint (at, that); suggest; imply; give [drop] a hint (to *sb*) ♦ 불만을 비치다 betray *one's* feeling of discontent
▶ 나는 넌지시 내 의사를 비쳐 보았다 I dropped hints of [hinted at] my intention.
▶ 며칠 전에 그는 내게 사임할 뜻을 비쳤다 The other day he intimated to me his intention to resign.
5 〈인상을 주다〉 impress; strike; appear (to)
♦ 외국인의 눈에 비친 한국 Korea as seen by foreigners; Korea through a foreigner's eye / 좋은 인상으로 비치다 impress (another) favorably; leave a favorable impression on (*sb's* mind); give (another) a favorable impression
▶ 서울이 그 미국인의 눈에 어떻게 비쳤을까 ? I wonder how Seoul struck [impressed] the American.
▶ 그의 눈에 그녀는 천사로 비쳤다 In his eyes, she was an angel. ⇌ She looked like an angel to him.
6 〈나타나다〉 appear; show [turn] up; show *oneself*; drop in 《at》
▶ 스크린에 그의 얼굴이 비쳤다 He appeared on the screen.
▶ 그는 하루 종일 회사에 얼굴도 비치지 않았다 He didn't put in an appearance at the office all day.
비치파라솔 a beach umbrella
비칭 卑稱 (give) a humble [vulgar] title [name, term]
비카타르 鼻― [醫] nasal catarrh
비커 〈실험용 유리그릇〉 a beaker
비컨 a beacon ▶ 라디오― a radio beacon
비켜나다 step [move] aside 《from》; sidestep; step back; get out of the way
비켜서다 stand [move] aside; step back [aside]
♦ 뛰어서 비켜서다 spring [jump] aside
▶ 그는 옆으로 비켜서서 내가 지나가게 해주었다 He stood aside to let me pass.
비키니 〈수영복〉 a bikini
비키다 1 〈길 등에서〉 get out of the way; stand clear of 《the door》; 〈옆으로〉 step [move] aside 《from》; sidestep; 〈뒤로〉 step back; 〈피하다〉 dodge; make a dodge; turn aside
♦ 날쌔게 몸을 비키다 dodge about / 물웅덩이를 비켜서 가다 go stepping aside from the puddle
▶ 비켜라 Make off! ⇌ Get out of my way! ⇌ Clear the way!
▶ 그는 가까스로 왼쪽으로 비켜 목숨을 건졌다 He barely saved himself by dodging to the left.
2 〈물러나다〉 retire; withdraw
▶ 자리를 좀 비켜 주시겠습니까 ? Would you kindly leave me [us] alone?
▶ 나는 그들이 이야기하고 있는 동안 자리를 비켜 주었다 I stayed out while they talked with each other.
3 〈옮기다〉 move *sth* aside
▶ 이것 좀 비켜 주시오 Get this out of the way.
▶ 의자를 조금만 비켜 주시겠습니까 ? Will you please move your chair a little aside?
비타민 vitamin
▶ 당근에는 비타민 A가 많다 Carrots are rich in [contain a lot of] vitamin A.
▶ 각기는 비타민 B_1의 부족으로 생긴다 Beri-beri is caused by lack of vitamin B_1.
▶ 녹차는 비타민 C를 많이 함유하고 있다 Green tea contains a lot of vitamin C.
■ 종합― multivitamin: 종합 비타민제 a multivitamin compound ■ ―결 핍 증 avitaminosis ―과다증 hypervitaminosis ―B 복합체 vitamin B complex ―정 a vitamin solution [tablet, pill] ―제(劑) a vitamin compound [preparation] ―함유량 vitamin content
비타협적 非妥協的 uncompromising; intransigent; unyielding
▶ 그들의 비타협적인 태도 때문에 우리는 합의를 볼 수가 없었다 Owing to their intransigent [uncompromising] attitude we were unable to reach an agreement.
비탄 悲嘆 grief; sorrow; anguish; lamentation
♦ 비탄이 극에 달해서 in the excess of *one's* grief; distracted with grief / 비탄에 잠기다 be grief-stricken 《at》; be plunged into grief; be overwhelmed with grief
▶ 그녀는 부친을 잃고 비탄에 빠져 있다 She has been heartbroken at her father's death. ⇌ She has greatly grieved over her father's death.
▶ 그녀는 비탄 끝에 미쳐 버렸다 She was beside herself with grief.
―비탄하다 grieve; mourn; sorrow 《over, on》; lament; deplore
비탈 a slope; 〈물매〉 an incline; 〈오르막〉 an upward slope; an ascent; an acclivity; 〈내리막〉 a downward slope; a descent; a declivity
♦ 완만한[가파른] 비탈 a gentle [steep] slope / 강 쪽으로 완만한 비탈을 이루고 있는 정원 a garden sloping gently [gradually] towards the river / 비탈지다 slope; 〈오르막으로〉 slope up [upward]; 〈내리막으로〉 slope down [downward]
▶ 나는 비탈을 올라[내려] 갔다 I went up

[down] a slope.
■산— the slope of a mountain; a steep mountain slope ■—길 a sloping road; a slope
비통하다 悲痛— sad; grievous; sorrowful; bitter
♦비통한 표정으로 with a sad look / 비통한 생각에 잠기다 be filled with deep sadness
▶그는 비통한 심정으로 귀향했다 He returned home with bitter grief in his heart.
비트적거리다 stagger ⇨ 비틀거리다
비트족 —族 (총칭) the beat generation; 〈개인〉 a beatnik
비틀 totteringly; staggeringly; reelingly
♦비틀비틀 일어서다 stagger [totter] to one's feet; get shakily to one's feet
▶노인은 거리를 비틀비틀 걸어갔다 The old man went reeling down the street.
—비틀하다 stagger; reel; totter; wobble
♦이리 비틀 저리 비틀하다 reel to and fro
▶그의 걸음걸이는 비틀비틀했다 His steps were faint and faltering.
비틀거리다 stagger; totter; reel; falter; dodder; stumble
♦짐이 무거워 비틀거리다 stagger under a heavy load / 비틀거리며 걷다 reel [stagger] along; walk staggeringly [with tottering steps] / 비틀거리다가 쓰러지다 topple down [over]; stumble and fall
▶나는 돌에 채여 비틀거렸다 I stumbled over a stone and staggered [tottered].
▶그는 밀려서 비틀거렸다 The push made him stagger.
▶나는 일어섰으나 술 취한 사람처럼 비틀거렸다 I got up but reeled like a drunken man.
▶그는 비틀거리며 방으로 들어갔다 He staggered into the room.
비틀걸음 faltering [tottering, unsteady] steps; a tottering gait; a staggering walk ♦비틀걸음으로 걷다 walk staggeringly; walk with tottering steps; reel along
비틀다 twist; give 《a rope》 a twist; wrench; screw; wring; wrest
♦아무의 팔을 비틀다 twist [wrench] sb's arm / 허리를 왼쪽으로 비틀다 twist [turn] one's hip to the left / 과일을 가지에서 비틀어 따다 wrench a fruit off a branch / 아무의 손을 비틀어 권총을 빼앗다 wrench [wrest, twist] a pistol out of sb's hand / 철사를 비틀어 꼬다 twist a wire
▶그는 내 손을 비틀었다 He gave my hand a wring.
▶그는 자물쇠를 비틀어 땄다 He forced the lock open.
▶그는 나무상자의 뚜껑을 비틀어 열었다 He wrenched open the cover of the wooden box.
▶어린 소녀는 인형의 팔을 비틀어 떼어 버렸다 The little girl twisted the arm off her doll.
비틀어지다 1 〈꼬이다〉 get twisted [distorted]; grow warped ♦넥타이가 좀 비틀어져 있다 have one's tie twisted a little
2 ⇨ 틀어지다 2
비틀하다 fishy and savory
비틈하다 〈에두르다〉 indirect; allusive; oblique

비틈히 〈에둘러서〉《say》 indirectly; hintingly; obliquely; in a roundabout way
비파 琵琶 〈악기〉 a Korean mandolin [lute]
비파나무 枇杷 〔植〕 a loquat
비판 批判 (a) criticism; (a) comment; (a) critique
♦칸트의「순수[실천] 이성 비판」Kant's Critique of Pure [Practical] Reason
▶그는 우리의 계획에 통렬한 비판을 가했다 He expressed harsh criticism of our project. ⇌ He criticized our project sharply.
—비판하다 criticize; comment 《on》; sit in judgment 《upon》
▶그는 나를 경솔하다고 비판했다 He criticized me for being careless.
▶남을 비판하기 전에 먼저 자신을 돌아보라 You shouldn't criticize others without first looking at yourself.
■자기— (a) self-criticism ■—력 critical power [ability] —철학 critical philosophy
비판적 批判的 critical
▶어머니는 내가 하는 일에 대해 비판적이었다 My mother was critical of things I did.
▶그녀는 사장에게 비판적인 태도를 취하고 있다 She has taken a critical attitude toward her boss.
비평 批評 (a) criticism; (a) critique; (a) comment; 〈신간 서적 등의〉 a review
▶그는 타임(지)의 신간 비평을 담당하고 있다 He reviews new books for Time.
▶이 소설은 너무 음울하다는 비평을 받았다 This novel was criticized as being too gloomy [for its gloominess].
—비평하다 criticize; comment 《on》; pass criticism 《on》; review 《a book》
▶그녀한테서 신간 서적을 비평해 달라는 요청을 받았다 She asked me to review the new books.
▶그의 신작은 비평할 가치가 없다 His latest work is below criticism.
▶선생님은 내 작품을 비평해 주셨다 The teacher criticized my work.
■문명— criticism on civilization 문예— literary criticism 본문— textual criticism ■—사 the history of criticism
비평가 批評家 a critic; a reviewer
■미술[문예]— an art [a literary] critic
비평안 批評眼 a critical eye
♦비평안이 있다 have a critical [discerning] eye / 비평안을 기르다 cultivate a critical sense
▶그는 예리한 비평안으로 사물을 관찰한다 He observes things with a sharp critical eye.
비폭력 非暴力 ahimsa; nonviolence
비폭력주의 非暴力主義 the doctrine of ahimsa; nonviolence ♦비폭력주의적인 nonviolent
비품 備品 furnishings; fixtures; fittings; 〈설비〉 equipment
♦사무용 비품 office equipment
▶실험실에는 비품 일습이 갖추어져 있었다 The laboratory was equipped with a complete set of fixtures.
■—목록 a list of fixtures; an inventory
비프 beef ■—스테이크 (a) beefsteak; (a)

steak

비하 卑下 〈자신을 낮춤〉 abasement; self-humbling; 〈땅이 낮음〉 low level of ground; 〈지위가 낮음〉 low standing [position]; humbleness
—비하하다 humble [depreciate] *oneself*
▶ 너무 자기를 비하할 필요는 없다 You don't have to humble yourself too much.

비하다 比— 〈비교하다〉 compare 《one thing》 with 《another》
▶ 아버지는 연세에 비해 아주 건강하시다 My father is quite healthy for his age.
▶ 그는 경험이 없는데 비해 잘 한다 He does well, considering that he lacks experience.
▶ 그 경치는 비할 바 없이 아름답다 The scenery is beautiful beyond comparison.

비학술적 非學術的 unacademic; unscientific

비합리 非合理 irrationality ⇨ 불합리(不合理)
■—주의 irrationalism

비합법 非合法 illegality
◆ 비합법적(인) illegal; illicit; unlawful / 비합법화하다 illegalize; outlaw
▶ 그의 활동은 비합법적이다 His conduct is unlawful [out of order].

비핵화 非核化 denuclearization —비핵화하다 denuclearize 《a nation, an area》

비행 非行 misconduct; (a) delinquency; a misdeed; a misdemeanor; an irregularity; wrongdoing
◆ 비행을 저지르다 commit an irregularity; misconduct *oneself* / 비행을 폭로하다 bring [put] *sb's* crime to light; unmask a hypocrite
—소년 a juvenile delinquent

비행 飛行 flying; a flight; 〈항공술〉 aviation; air voyage; aerial navigation
◆ 서울 제주간 왕복 비행 a flight from Seoul to Cheju and back
▶ 비행중 (좌우로) 흔들리는 수도 있으니 주의하시기 바랍니다 Please be careful, as the plane may roll while in flight.
▶ 이런 악천후에는 비행이 불가능하다 We cannot fly [Flying is impossible] in this bad weather.
■고공[저공]— a high(-altitude) [low(-altitude)] flight 곡예[고등]— stunt flying; aerial acrobatics 단독— a solo flight 무사고— accident-free flying; flying without an accident 무착륙— a nonstop flight 선회— a circuitous flight 세계 일주— a round-the-world flight 시험— a test [trial] flight 야간— a night flight 연습— a training [an exercise] flight 정기— a regular air service 정찰— a scouting flight 직선— a straight flight 태평양 횡단— a transpacific flight 편대— a formation flight; flying in formation ■—가 ⇨ 비행사 —갑판 a flight [flying] deck —거리 fly; a flight —기지 an air base —단(團) an air division —대(隊) a flying corps —모(帽) an aviation cap; a flying helmet —복 a flying dress [suit, jacket, clothes]; flying gear; a flight uniform [suit]; an aviation garment —속도 (an) air speed; (a) flying speed —술 aeronautics; the art of flying —시간 〈비행기의〉 flying time; 〈비행사의〉 flight hours —접시 a flying saucer; a UFO —정(艇) a flying boat; an aeroboat; a seaplane —정보구역 the 《Korean》 flight information region (略 F I R) —중대 a squadron —통제구역 the flight restriction area.

비행기 飛行機 1 〈항공기〉 a plane; (美) an airplane; (英) an aeroplane; (총칭) aircraft
◆ 비행기를 타다 board [take] a plane; have a ride in [get aboard] an airplane / 비행기를 내리다 leave [get off] a plane / 비행기를 조종하다 pilot a plane / 비행기로 가다 go [travel] by air [by plane, in an airplane]; fly 《to Moscow》
▶ 나는 아직까지 비행기를 타본 적이 없다 I've never flown [gotten on a plane] yet.
▶ 나는 서울에서 부산까지 비행기로 갔다 I flew [took an airplane] from Seoul to Pusan. ≒ I went to Pusan from Seoul by air [plane].
2 〈추어 올림〉 flattery
◆ 비행기를 태우다 flatter; tickle another's vanity; say nice things 《to》; praise *sb* to the skies
▶ 비행기 좀 그만 태워라 Enough of your flattery [(美) jolly]!
■군용— a military [fighting] plane; a warplane; (총칭) combat aircraft 단엽[복엽]— a monoplane [biplane] 민간— a commercial plane 무인— a pilotless plane 수상— a seaplane; a hydroplane 정찰— a scout plane; a reconnaissance machine —격납고 an aviation [airplane] shed; an airshed —격납고 [aeroshed] a hangar —공장 an airplane [aircraft] factory —구름 condensation trail; contrail —멀미 airsickness: 비행기 멀미를 하다 get airsick —사고 a plane accident [crash] —여행 an air travel —표 an air ticket

비행물체 飛行物體 a flying object
■미확인— an unidentified flying object; a UFO; 〈비행접시〉 a flying saucer

비행사 飛行士 an aviator; a flier; a flyer; an airman; a pilot; (俗) a birdman
◆ 비행사가 되다 take to the air
■민간— a civilian aviator 여류— an aviatress; an aviatrix; a woman aviator [flier]; (俗) a birdwoman

비행선 飛行船 an airship; a dirigible ■경식[연식, 반경식]— a rigid [nonrigid, semi-rigid] dirigible —격납고 an airship shed; a (blimp) hangar —계류탑 a mooring mast

비행장 飛行場 an airfield; a flying field; an air station; (美) an airdrome [air depot]; (英) an aerodrome; 〈공항〉 an airport
■해상— a floating airdrome [aerodrome]

비현실 非現實 비현실적인 계획 an impracticable [unfeasible] plan / 비현실적인 사람 an impractical person / 비현실적인 세계 an unreal world
▶ 그의 생각은 극히 비현실적이다 His idea is far from realistic [very fantastic].
■—성 unreality

비협력적 非協力的 uncooperative

비호 庇護 protection; shelter; patronage
◆ …의 비호하에 under the protection [patronage] of…; under the wing of…

비행기 여행의 상식

1. **체크인(checkin)** — 출발 라운지(a departure lounge)로 가서 항공회사(an airline company) 카운터에서 수화물(baggage, luggage)을 위탁하고 물표(a claim tag)를 받는다. 여권(a passport), 항공권(an air ticket), 출입국 카드(an E/D card; Embarkation/Disembarkation 또는 Entry/Departure의 약어)를 제시하고 탑승권(a boarding card [pass]; a flight coupon)을 받는다. 여기서 좌석 할당(a seat assignment)을 한다. 좌석은 퍼스트 클래스(first class)와 이코노미 클래스(economy class, coach class)가 있고, 다시 돌아 연석(a smoking section), 금연석(a non-smoking section), 통로쪽 좌석(an aisle seat), 창쪽 좌석(a window seat)이 있다. 탑승 게이트(a boarding gate)는 탑승권에 쓰여 있다.

2. **출국 수속(embarkation procedure)**
   (1) **세관(Customs)** — 외국 제품을 가지고 나갈 때는 세관 신고서(a customs declaration form)와 함께 제시한다.
   (2) **출국 심사(Emigration, passport control)** — 여권, 출입국 카드, 탑승권을 제시하고 여권에 출국 스탬프를 받는다.
   (3) **검역(Quarantine)** — 출국 목적지에 따라서는 예방접종 증명서(a vaccination certificate; a Yellow Card [Book])가 필요하다.

3. **수화물 검사** — 하이잭(hijack) 방지를 위해 기내에 들고 들어가는 수화물(carry-on [hand-carry] baggage) 검사(check)를 받는다. 승객은 위험물 검사 통로(a walk-through gate, a security checkpoint)를 통과하고, 공항에 따라서는 보디 체크를 받기도 한다.

4. **탑승(boarding)** — 탑승 대합실(a waiting lounge)에서 출발시간까지 기다린다. 그 사이에 면세점(a duty-free shop)에서 shopping도 할 수 있다.

5. **기내(機內)·승무원**
   (1) **승무원(총칭) aircrew** — 기장 a captain; a chief pilot / 부조종사 a copilot / 항공기관사 a flight engineer / 객실 승무원 a flight [cabin] attendant / 사무장 a purser / 스튜어드 a steward / 스튜어디스 a stewardess; an air hostess
   (2) **기내 방송(an in-flight announcement)** — 기내 방송에는 주로 다음과 같은 것이 있다.
   ▶ 안전벨트를 매고 좌석 등받이를 수직으로 세워주십시오 Please fasten your seat belt and put your seat back in the upright position.
   ▶ 담뱃불을 꺼 주십시오 Please extinguish all cigarettes.
   ▶ 지금부터 약 10분간 난기류에 들어갑니다. 좌석으로 돌아가 안전벨트를 매십시오 We will be encountering a little turbulence for the next ten minutes, so please return to your seats and fasten your seat belts.
   ▶ 샌프란시스코는 기온이 섭씨 25도에 쾌청한 날씨입니다 We are expecting fine weather in San Francisco, and the temperature is 25 degrees centigrade.
   ▶ 승객 여러분, 이 비행기는 곧 로스앤젤레스 국제공항에 착륙합니다 Ladies and Gentlemen, we will be landing at Los Angeles International Airport soon.
   ▶ 엔진이 멎고 게이트에 도착하여 안전벨트의 신호가 꺼질 때까지 좌석에 앉아 계십시오 Please remain seated until the aircraft comes to a complete stop at the terminal gate and the seat belt sign has been turned off.
   (3) **기내 서비스(in-flight service)** — (스튜어디스를 부르는) 콜 버튼 a call button / (개인용) 조명 스위치 a light switch
   ▶ 담요를 갖다 주세요 Could you bring me a blanket?
   ▶ 멀미약 먹게 물 좀 주세요 Could I have a glass of water? I have to take a pill for airsickness.
   ▶ 현지 시간으로 뉴욕은 지금 몇 시입니까? What's the local time in New York?

6. **입국 지점(the port of entry) 도착** — 입국심사대(Immigration)에서 여권과 입국 카드를 제시한다. 이때 직원(an immigration officer)으로부터 예정 체재 기간(intended length of stay)에 관한 질문 How long are you going to stay in the United States? (미국에는 얼마나 있을 예정인가?)와 함께 Are you on sightseeing or on business? (관광입니까? 상용입니까?) 등등 몇가지 질문을 받는다. 다음에 화물 수취소(a baggage claim area)에 가서 턴테이블(a turntable, a carousel)에서 짐을 내린다. 세관에서 화물 체크를 받고 도착 라운지(an arrival lounge)로 나온다. 그리고 갈아탈 손님(a transit passenger)은 갈아타는 라운지(a transit lounge)에서 기다린다.

7. **비행기 예약(reserving a flight)** — 예약확인(하다) confirmation (confirm) / 재 확인(하다) reconfirmation (reconfirm) / 취소하다 cancel / 대기 stand-by / 회사에서 예약을 너무 많이 받아(overbooking) 「그 항공편은 예약이 넘쳐서 손님은 웨이팅 리스트 5번이 됩니다」 (The flight is booked up and you will be the fifth on our waiting list.)라는 말을 듣기도 한다. 예약하고 나타나지 않는 사람을 a no-show passenger라고 한다.

8. **비행기와 비행장**
   (1) **비행기** — 정기 항공편 an airliner / 전세편 a charter flight / 대륙 횡단편 (美) a coast to coast flight / 야간편 (美) a moonlight Special / 에어 버스 an airbus / 초음속 여객기 SST (▶supersonic transport의 뜻) / 점보 제트 a jumbo jet / 대한항공 부산행 120편 Korean Air Lines 120 bound for Pusan
   (2) **비행장** — 활주로 a runway / 이륙하다 take off / 착륙하다 land (▶착륙 순번을 기다리며 상공을 선회하는 것을 holding pattern이라고 한다) / 긴급 착륙 emergency landing / 관제탑 a control tower / 터미널 건물 a terminal building / 송영대 an observation deck / 격납고 a hangar

—비호하다 protect; shelter; shield; take *sb* under *one's* wings
■—자 a guardian; a protector; a patron
비호 飛虎 a flying tiger ♦비호 같다 be as quick as lightning / 비호 같이 달리다 run like a streak (of lightning)
비화 飛火 1 〈튀어 박히는 불똥〉 flying sparks (of a fire); leaping flames; a leap of the flames
—비화하다 flames [sparks] leap 《to another place》
▶화재는 광장 건너쪽으로 비화했다 The fire [flames] leaped across the square.
▶모닥불에서 비화한 것이 그 화재의 원인이었다 Sparks from a bonfire were responsible for the fire.
2 〈후림불〉 an effect felt in unexpected quarters
—비화하다 spread repercussions
▶사건은 의외의 방면으로 비화했다 The effect of the affair was felt in unexpected quarters.
▶그 독직 사건은 정계로 비화했다 The corruption case spread to [had repercussions in] the political world.
비화 祕話 〈숨은〉 a secret story [history]; a behind-the-scenes story; an unknown episode
비화 悲話 〈슬픈〉 a sad [pathetic] story; a tragic tale
비화수소 砒化水素 〔化〕 arseniuretted hydrogen; arsine
비효용 非效用 〖經〗 disutility
빅수 —手 a tying move ⇨ 비김수
빈 〈오스트리아의 수도〉 Vienna; (독) Wien
♦빈의 Viennese
빈개념 賓概念 =빈사(賓辭)
빈객 賓客 a guest (of honor); an honored [a distinguished] guest
빈고 貧苦 hardships [pressure] of poverty; pinching poverty ♦빈고에 시달리다 be poverty-stricken; be in the grip of poverty
빈곤 貧困 poverty; need; want
♦빈곤 속에서 자라다 be brought up amidst destitution / 빈곤에 허덕이다 suffer from poverty / 빈곤에서 벗어나다 emerge from poverty
▶빈곤은 근면의 어머니 (속담) Want is the mother of industry.
▶그의 발언은 상상력의 빈곤을 드러낸 것이다 What he said shows poverty [lack] of imagination.
—빈곤하다 poor; indigent; needy ♦빈곤한 사람들 the poor (and needy) / 빈곤해지다 be reduced to poverty; fall into poverty
빈곳 (a) space ⇨ 빈자리 3
빈광 貧鑛 lean [poor] ore; low-grade ore
빈국 貧國 a poor [needy, have-not] country
빈궁 貧窮 poverty ⇨ 빈곤(貧困)
빈궁 嬪宮 the wife of the crown prince; the crown princess
빈농 貧農 a poor farmer; a needy peasant
빈대 〖昆〗 (美) a bedbug; a housebug
빈대떡 a mung-bean pancake ♦빈대떡을 부치다 make mung-bean pancakes
빈대 미워 집에 불놓는다 (속담) burn the barn down to get rid of the mice

빈대코 a flat nose ⇨ 납작코
빈도 頻度 〈도수(度數)〉 frequency
♦단어의 (사용) 빈도 frequency in use of a word / 빈도(수)가 높은[낮은] 단어 a word of high [low] frequency
▶이 단어는 사용 빈도가 높다 The frequency of use of this word is high. ⇒ This word is very frequently used.
빈둥거리다 loaf [idle, laze] *one's* time away; idle; loiter; lounge
▶빈둥거리며 인생을 보내지 마라 Don't loaf your life away.
▶그는 대학을 나오고도 하는 일 없이 빈둥거리고 있다 Even after graduating from college [Although he has finished college], he is at a loose end.
빈둥빈둥 idly; lazily; doing nothing
♦빈둥빈둥 세월을 보내다 idle [dawdle] *one's* time away; loaf away *one's* time [days]; lead an idle life; live in idleness / 하루 종일 빈둥빈둥 지내다 spend a whole day idly
♦휴일엔 집에서 그저 빈둥빈둥 보냅니다 On holidays I just idle away my time at home.
—빈둥빈둥하다 ⇨ 빈둥거리다
빈들거리다 idle [laze] *one's* time away ⇨ 빈둥거리다
빈들빈들 idly ⇨ 빈둥빈둥
빈랑 檳榔 〈나무〉 a betel palm; 〈열매〉 a betel nut; an areca nut
빈말 (an) idle [empty] talk; empty [hollow] words; an empty [a specious] promise
▶그녀는 그런 빈말에 넘어가지 않아요 She is immune to such insincere flattery [empty compliments].
—빈말하다 talk idly; make empty promises
♦빈말하는 사람 a windy speaker
빈민 貧民 poor men [people]; paupers; poverty-stricken people; the poor; the needy
♦빈민을 구제하다 relieve [give aid to] the poor [needy]
■—가 ⇨ 빈민굴 —구호 the relief of the poor (and) needy; poor relief —구호법 the poor law —복지사업 settlement work —상태 pauperism —생활 a life of poverty
빈민굴 貧民窟 a slum; (총칭) the slum [poor] quarters; the slums ♦빈민굴을 없애다 clear slums; wipe out slums
■—사람들 inhabitants of the slum quarters; slummers
빈발 頻發 frequency; frequent occurrence
♦항공기 사고의 빈발 the high frequency of aviation accidents; frequent airplane accidents
—빈발하다 occur frequently; be frequent
▶그 교차로에서는 사고가 빈발한다 Accidents occur [happen] very frequently [very often] at the intersection.
빈방 —房 〈쓰지 않는〉 a vacant room; an unoccupied [unused] room; 〈사람이 없는〉 an empty room; 〈세놓을〉 a room for rent
빈번하다 頻繁・頻煩— frequent; incessant
♦왕래가 빈번한 거리 a busy [bustling] street; a street with heavy traffic / 빈번히 일어나는 일 a matter of frequent occurrence / 빈번히

빈도의 표현

1. 빈도를 나타내는 부사·부사구의 위치
(1) 부사
a. be동사 뒤
▶그는 자주 학교에 지각한다 He is often late for school.
b. 일반 동사 앞
▶그녀는 내게 자주 편지를 했다 She often wrote to me.
c. 조동사 뒤
▶길을 건널 때는 항상 조심할 것 You should always be careful when you cross a road. (▶빈도를 나타내는 대표적인 부사를 그「빈도」가 높은 순으로 들어보면 always > often > sometimes > seldom > never가 된다)
(2) 부사구
보통은 문장의 끝에 두지만 강조하는 경우 등에는 첫머리에 두기도 한다.
▶나는 매일 적어도 한 시간은 수영을 한다 I swim for at least an hour every day.
▶매일 아침 나는 산책에 개를 데리고 나간다 Every morning, I take my dog out for a walk.

2. 빈도의 표현
(1) 언제나·항상
▶그녀는 언제나 나한테 친절하다 She is always kind to me.
▶주디는 톰에게 「항상 나를 따라다니지 마」라고 말했다 Judy said to Tom, "Don't hang around me all the time."
▶어머니는 언제나 나더러 공부하라고 성화시다 My mother is always telling me to study. (▶「be동사 + always + ~ing」는 「언제나 ~하기만 한다」라는 동작의 반복을 나타냄)
(2) 종종·흔히
▶어머니는 직장에 나가시므로 내가 종종 저녁을 짓지 않으면 안된다 My mother works, so I often have to cook my supper.
▶우리 아버지는 사업상 자주 홍콩에 가신다 My father makes frequent visits to Hong-Kong on business.
▶인호는 수업중에 꽤 자주 존다 In-ho dozes off during classes quite often.
(3) 보통·대개
▶[会話]「토요일 오후는 보통 뭘해?」「별로, 아무것도」 "What do you usually do on Saturday afternoons?" "Nothing in particular."
▶1년중 이 시기는 대개 (날씨가) 맑다 The weather is generally fine at this time of year.
▶비오는 날 이외는 보통 자전거로 통학한다 I normally go to school by bicycle except on rainy days. (▶일반적으로는 normally보다 usually가 많이 쓰인다)
(4) 몇번이고·되풀이하여
▶김선생님은 이 문장을 암기하라고 되풀이해 말씀하셨다 Mr. Kim repeatedly told us to memorize this sentence.
▶시간을 지키라고 몇 번이나 말했지 I've told you again and again to be punctual.
▶네 방을 청소하라고 몇 번이나 말해야 알겠니? How many times do I have to tell you to clean your room?
(5) 때때로·가끔
▶나는 때때로 학교 가는 길에 그녀를 만난다 I sometimes see her on my way to school.
▶나는 가끔 쿠키를 굽는다 I occasionally bake cookies.
▶나는 때때로 누님네 아이를 보아준다 I baby-sit for my sister's child from time to time [once in a while].
(6) 드물게·좀처럼
▶나는 이즈음 좀처럼 부모님과는 외출하지 않는다 I rarely go out with my parents these days.
▶중학생 때에는 영화구경을 가는 따위 일은 좀처럼 없었다 I seldom went to the movies when I was a middle school student.
▶형이 아침 식사를 하는 것은 드문 일입니다 My brother hardly ever has breakfast.
(7) 결코 없다
▶[会話]「너는 괌에 가본 일이 있니?」「아니, 한번도」 "Have you ever been to Guam?" "No, I never have [have never been there]."
▶그와는 두번 다시 말하고 싶지 않다 I'll never speak to him again.

3. 빈도를 묻는 방법과 그 답변
▶[会話]「얼마나 자주 이발소에 가니?」「한달에 한번 가」 "How often do you go to the barber's?" "Once a month."
▶[会話]「병원에는 매일 다니고 있니?」「아니, 하루 걸러 다녀」 "Do you go to the clinic every day?" "No, I go there every other day."
▶[会話]「이 경기장에는 얼마나 자주 왔습니까?」「셀 수 없을 정도로 많이 왔습니다」 "How many times have you been to this stadium?" "I've been here so many times (that) I can't even remember."

---

frequently; very often; at short intervals; incessantly
▶요즈음 교통사고가 빈번하다 These days traffic accidents are frequently reported.
▶겨울에는 화재가 빈번히 일어난다 Fires are frequent in winter.
▶저 음식점에는 정치가들이 빈번히 드나든다 That restaurant is frequented by politicians.
빈병 一瓶 an empty bottle
빈볼 〔野〕 a beanball

빈부 貧富 wealth and poverty; (the) rich and (the) poor
◆빈부의 구별 없이 rich and poor alike; whether they are rich or poor
▶태양은 빈부의 구별 없이 비춘다 The sun shines on the rich and the poor alike.
▶아직도 빈부의 차가 심한 나라들이 있다 The gulf [gap] between rich and poor is still very wide [great] in some countries.
빈사 賓辭 〔論〕 the predicate

빈사 瀕死 ♦빈사 상태의 환자 a dying [moribund] patient; a patient on the verge of death [on the deathbed] / 빈사의 dying / 빈사상태에 있다 be dying; be in a dying condition; be at the point of death
▶ 운전자는 빈사였다 The driver was in a critical condition. ⇌ The driver was near death.

빈상 貧相 a meager face; poor appearance
♦빈상의 poorlooking; seedy; shabby

빈소 殯所 〈관을 두는〉 a mortuary; a lying-in-state room

빈소리 (an) idle [empty] talk ⇨ 빈말

빈소시지 (a) Vienna sausage ⇨ 비엔나소시지

빈속 〈공복〉 an empty stomach ♦빈속에 술을 마시다 drink on an empty stomach
▶ 빈속으로는 일을 할 수가 없다 I can't work on an empty stomach.

빈손 〈맨손〉 empty hands
♦빈손으로 with empty hands; empty-handed; 〈방문할 때 등〉 without taking any present (with one) / 빈손으로 돌아오다 return without attaining one's object
▶ 빈손으로 왔다가 빈손으로 간다 〈공수래 공수거〉 Come empty, return empty.
▶ 그에게 부탁할 일이 있다면 빈손으로 가는 것은 서툰 짓이야 If you want to ask a favor of him, you'd better take a present.
▶ 옛 친구를 빈손으로 찾아갈 수는 없다 I cannot call on my old friend without any present for him.

빈약하다 貧弱— 〈모자라는〉 poor; scanty; 〈불충분한〉 meager; limited
♦빈약한 수입 a limited [scanty, small] income / 빈약한 재능 poor ability / 빈약한 지식 poor [scanty] knowledge (of music) / 몸집이 빈약한 남자 an insignificant-looking man / 빈약한 식사 a meager meal / 빈약한 영어로 in poor [broken] English
▶ 이 책은 내용이 빈약하다 This book is poor in content.
▶ 나는 학생들의 독서력이 빈약한 데 놀랐다 I'm surprised that the pupils don't read well.

빈 왈츠 a Viennese waltz=비엔나 왈츠

빈자 貧者 a poor man; a pauper; 〈총칭〉 the poor [needy]; the destitute
♦빈자 일등(一燈) a widow's mite

빈자리 1 〈빈 좌석〉 a vacant seat; an unoccupied seat; 〈여지〉 room
▶ 이들 두 좌석이 빈자리다 These two seats are vacant [free].
▶ 비행기는 절반이 빈자리다 The plane was half-empty.
▶ 빈자리라고는 하나도 없었다 There was no room left. ⇌ No seat was left unoccupied.
2 〈결원〉 a vacancy; an opening; a vacant post ♦빈자리가 나다 cause a vacancy / 빈자리를 메우다 fill (up) a vacancy
▶ 그 일에 빈자리가 있었는데 곧 채워졌다 There was an opening in the business but it was filled immediately.
3 〈여백〉 a space; a blank ⇨ 빈칸

빈정거리다 〈비꼬다〉 speak ironically; make cynical [caustic] remarks; be cynical [sarcastic] (about); 〈조롱하다〉 make fun of; poke fun at; tease; ridicule
♦정치인들의 언동을 빈정거리다 be cynical about politicians
▶ 그 소녀는 소년의 큰 머리를 가지고 빈정거렸다 The girl teased the boy about his big head.
▶ 그의 빈정거리는 말투가 비위에 거슬렸다 His sarcastic remarks jarred on my nerves.

빈주먹 naked fists ⇨ 맨주먹

빈집 a vacant [an empty] house; an unoccupied [untenanted] house (▶an empty house 는 「가구도 없이 텅빈 집」을 의미함)
▶ 그 집은 빈 집이었다 I found the house vacant.
▶ 그 집은 3개월 전부터 빈 집으로 있다 The house has been vacant [has not been lived in] for the past three months.
■—털이 〈행위〉 sneak-thieving; 〈사람〉 a sneak thief : 요전날 집을 비운 사이 우리 집이 빈집 털이에게 당했다 The other day our house was broken into [burglarized] while we were away.

빈차 —車 an empty car; 〈택시〉 a disengaged taxi ▶ 때마침 운 좋게도 빈차가 있었다 Luckily an empty taxi came along just then. ▶ 빈 차 (게시) Vacant. ⇌ For hire.

빈촌 貧村 a poor village

빈축 嚬蹙 〈눈살을 찌푸림〉 a frown; a scowl; a grimace
♦빈축을 살만한 disdainful; despicable / 〈남의〉 빈축을 사다 be frowned at [on, upon] (by)
▶ 그의 행동은 모든 사람들의 빈축을 샀다 His behavior disgusted everyone. ⇌ Everybody frowned at his bad behavior.
—**빈축하다** frown [scowl] at [on, upon]; look on sth with scorn [disdain]

빈치류 貧齒類 〔動〕 edentate
♦빈치류의 edentate

빈칸 a blank column; a blank (space)
♦빈칸을 메우다 fill (in) a blank; fill up a space; fill a vacancy
▶ 빈 칸에 알맞은 말을 넣으시오 Fill (in) the blanks with appropriate words.

빈탕 1 〈과실의〉 an empty nut 2 〈텅빔〉 emptiness; vacancy ▶ 그 상자는 빈탕이다 The box contains nothing 3 〈제비뽑기의 꽝〉 a blank
♦빈탕을 뽑다 draw a blank (in a lottery)

빈터 unoccupied ground; a vacant lot; a vacancy; 〈공터〉 vacant land; an open space

빈털터리 a penniless person; a man with empty pockets; a man with a flat pocketbook; a man without a farthing [a penny]
♦빈털터리가 되다 become quite penniless; (口) be [go] flat [dead] broke
▶ 그는 빈털터리다 He is penniless. ⇌ (口) He is clean broke. ⇌ He hasn't got a red cent.
▶ 저 녀석은 빈털터리인가봐 He doesn't seem to have a dime in his pocket.
▶ 나는 전쟁통에 빈털터리가 되었다 I lost everything in my possession during the war.

빈틈 1 〈틈새〉 an opening; a gap; a slit; an aperture; 〈균열〉 a crack; 〈틈 새기〉 a chink; 〈여백〉 a space; a blank; 〈여지〉 a room; (a)

빈틈없다

space
♦ 빈틈을 메우다 [막다] fill [stop] a gap; fill in a blank; fill up a space
▶ 내가 끼어들 빈틈이 없었다 I had no room to step in.
▶ 커튼의 빈틈으로 방안이 보였다 We could see the inside of the room through an opening in the curtain.
2 〈미비〉 unpreparedness; 〈허점〉 an unguarded point; a blind side [spot, point]; an opening (for attack); 〈방심〉 a slip; an oversight; inadvertence; 〈부주의〉 inattention; carelessness; imprudence; incautiousness
♦ 빈틈을 노리다 watch for a moment when sb is off his guard / 달아날 빈틈을 엿보다 wait [watch] for a chance to run away
▶ 그는 돈벌이에는 빈틈이 없다 He's very smart at making money [keen on gain].

빈틈없다 〈신중한〉 scrupulous; prudent; 〈주의 깊은〉 attentive (to details); careful; cautious; wide-awake; 〈사려깊은〉 thoughtful; considerate; circumspect; 〈철저한〉 thorough; 〈약삭빠른〉 knowing; clever; shrewd; smart; sharp; alert; canny; cunning; keen; tactful
♦ 빈틈없는 방비 an airtight defense / 빈틈없는 사람 a shrewd [sharp] fellow; knowing man / 빈틈없는 장사꾼 a shrewd merchant; a sharp dealer / 빈틈없이 closely; compactly; leaving no space (between them) / 빈틈없이 들어차 있다 be packed to the full; be chock-full; 〈승객 등이〉 be packed like sardines / 빈틈없이 채워 넣다 pack [crowd] to the full; fill to the utmost (capacity) / 빈틈없이 투자하다 make a very smart investment / 빈틈없이 간호하다 nurse sb with the best of care

빈 한 貧寒 poverty; destitution; pauperism; indigence ━**빈한하다** poor; destitute; poverty-stricken; needy; indigent ♦ 빈한하게 살다 live in poverty; lead an indigent life; be badly off

빈혈 貧血 〖醫〗 anemia [ani:miə]; anematosis
♦ 빈혈(증)이 있는 사람 an anemic person; a person whose blood is poor / 빈혈이 되다 become anemic; be impoverished [drained] of blood / 빈혈증에 걸려 있다 be anemic; suffer from anemia
▶ 빈혈(증)이십니까? Are you anemic?
▶ 그녀는 빈혈을 일으켰다 She had an attack of anemia.
▶ 어머니는 빈혈로 잘 쓰러지신다 My mother often breaks down from anemia.
■ 악성— pernicious anemia 임신— anemia of pregnancy ■—증상 anemic symptom

빌다 **1** 〈구걸하다〉 beg; ask; 〈간청하다〉 solicit; plead (for); appeal (for)
♦ 밥을 빌다 beg one's bread; beg food / 살려 달라고 빌다 ask [plead, appeal] for one's life / 용서를 빌다 implore [beg (for), ask for] forgiveness
▶ 그는 빌다시피 하여 도움을 청했다 He begged [implored] me for help [to help him]. (▶beg는 공손하게, implore는 울다시피 애원하는 것을 의미함)
2 〈기원하다〉 pray (to God); invoke; supplicate
♦ 두 손 모아 빌다 pray with folded [joined] hands / 무릎 꿇고 빌다 pray to God on one's knees / 머리 숙여 빌다 pray to God with a bow / 남편이 무사하기를 빌다 pray to God for the safety of one's husband
▶ 그렇게 되기를 빕니다 I pray it may be so.
3 〈사과하다〉 ask [beg] sb's pardon; apologize (to sb) for; make [beg] an apology (for)
♦ 손이 발이 되도록 빌다 humbly beg sb's pardon; be profuse in one's apologies / 잘못하고 빌다 apologize to sb for one's wrongdoing
▶ 그는 간밤의 일을 빌었지만 진심에서가 아니었다 He apologized [said he was very sorry] for last night, but he wasn't sincere about it.
4 〈바라다〉 wish ▶ 성공을 빕니다 I wish you success. ⇌ May you succeed!
▶ 건강하시기를 빕니다 I wish you good health. ⇌ I pray for your good health.
5 〈남의 물건을〉 borrow ⇨ 빌리다

빌딩 a building; an office building
▶ 불길이 인접한 빌딩으로 번졌다 The flames caught the adjacent building
■ —가(街) a block [street] of large buildings; a street lined with large buildings

빌레몬서 —書 〖聖〗 (The Epistle of St. Paul to) Philemon (略 Philem)

빌려주다 lend; loan ⇨ 빌리다

빌리다 **1** 〈차용하다〉 borrow (sth from sb); have [get, obtain] a loan of (money)
♦ 집을 담보로 돈을 얼마간 빌리다 borrow some money on a house / 옷을 빌려 입다 wear borrowed clothes; be in borrowed clothing [plumes]
▶ 연필 잠깐 빌려주시겠어요? Can I borrow [use] your pencil for a moment?
▶ 전화 잠깐 빌려도 될까요? May I use your telephone? (▶무선 전화인 경우에는 borrow를 써도 됨)
▶ 금융 회사는 높은 이자로 돈을 빌려준다 Finance companies lend [loan] money at high interest (rate).
▶ 3만원만 빌려 주시겠습니까? Would [Could, Can, Will] you lend [spare] me thirty thousand won, please? (▶조동사의 순서대로 공손하지 못함)
▶ 그에게 빌려준 10만원은 영영 못 받았다 The hundred thousand won which I lent him was never paid back.
2 〖임대하다〗〈집·토지를〉 let (one's house for the winter); rent (a house to sb); rent out (a mansion); lease; let out (land) on lease; hire (a boat); engage (a carriage); rent (a house, land); take (a house, a room); lease (land); 〈선박을〉 charter (a vessel); 〈기타를〉〖美〗 rent out; 〖英〗 hire out
▶ 나는 이 집을 장기 계약으로 빌렸다 I have a long lease of this house.
▶ 이 아파트는 싸게 빌릴 수 있다 This apartment rents cheaply.
▶ 나는 여름방학 동안 내 방을 학생에게 빌려주었다 I rented 〖英〗 let (out) my room to a student during the summer vacation.
▶ 그 집이라면 월 50만원에 빌려준다 The house lets [rents] at [for] five hundred thousand

won a month.
3 〈도움 등을 받다〉 employ 《*sb's* assistance》; use; have [get] *sb's* help [aid]
♦ 그의 말을 빌리면 in his phrase; to use [borrow] his words / 돈의 힘을 빌려서 by the power of money / 다수의 힘을 빌려서 on the strength of majority
▶ 신원 보증인으로 존함을 빌리고 싶습니다 May [Could] I use your name as a reference?

빌립보서 —書 〔聖〕 The Epistle of St. Paul (the Apostle) to the Philippians; 〈약칭〉〔略 Phil.〕

빌미 〈불행의 원인〉 the cause [root] of evil [trouble]; a curse ♦ 빌미 잡다 blame 《bad luck》 on

빌붙다 flatter *sb*; fawn upon *sb*; curry favor with *sb*; ingratiate *oneself* with; play up 《to》
♦ 상사에게 빌붙다 play up to [toady to] the boss

빌어먹다 go (about) begging; beg food [*one's* bread]; live as a beggar; (美口) panhandle
♦ 빌어먹는 한이 있더라도 even if *one* would be reduced [brought] to beggary [begging]/ 빌어먹고 살다 live by begging / 빌어먹고 다니다 beg from door to door / 빌어먹는 신세가 되다 be reduced to beggar

빌어먹는 놈이 콩밥을 마다 할까 [이밥 조밥 가리랴] 〈속담〉 Beggars must [should] be no choosers.

빌어먹을 〈욕〉 Damn...; Damn [Hang, Darn, Confound] it!
▶ 빌어먹을 시험 To hell with exams!
▶ 이 빌어먹을 놈아 Confound [Damn] you!
▶ 「빌어먹을, 난 안갈거야」 하고 그는 일정 사납게 말했다 "Damn (it), I won't go!" he swore.

빔 a beam —안테나 a beam antenna —컴퍼스 a beam compass

빗 a comb ♦ 빗으로 빗다 comb (down) 《*one's* hair》; pull [run] a comb through 《*one's* hair》 ■ 얼레[참]— a wide-tooth [fine-tooth] comb

─── 빗 ───

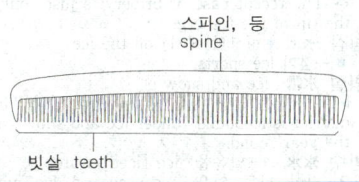

스파인, 등 spine

빗살 teeth

빗각 —角 〔數〕 an oblique angle; a bevel; 〔土〕 an angle of skew

빗금 an oblique line; a slant; a deviant line

빗기다 **1** 〈빗어 주다〉 comb 《*sb's* hair》
2 〈빗게 하다〉 get *sb* to comb 《*one's* hair》
♦ 딸에게 자기 머리를 빗기다 have *one's* daughter comb *one's* hair

빗나가다 **1** 〈표적에서〉 miss; go wild [astray]; miss [fly wide of] the mark; 〈이야기 등이〉 deviate [wander, diverge] 《from》; 〈잘못되다〉 go wrong; miscarry; fail
♦ 〈이야기가〉 딴 데로 빗나가다 wander [digress] from the subject / 예상이 빗나가다 〈사물이 주어〉 fall short of *one's* expectations; 〈사람이 주어〉 be disappointed of *one's* expectations
▶ 화살이 과녁에서 빗나갔다 The arrow missed the target.
▶ 오늘의 일기예보는 빗나갔다 Today's weather forecast proved wrong.
▶ 그녀는 전혀 빗나간 대답을 했다 She gave me an answer quite wide of the point.
2 〈행실이〉 go astray; run wild; stray [depart] from the right path; turn bad
▶ 그는 빗나가기 시작했다 He has lapsed in conduct.
▶ 이 나이 또래의 청소년들은 빗나가기 쉽다 Young people at this age is apt to go astray.

빗다 〈머리털을〉 comb 《*one's* hair》; 〈양털·삼 등을〉 card
♦ 잘 빗은 머리 well-combed hair / 빗지 않은 머리 uncombed [unkempt] hair / 빗어 올리다 〈빗으로〉 comb up 《*one's* hair》; 〈손가락으로〉 run *one's* fingers through 《*one's* hair》

빗대다 **1** 〈넌지시 꼬집다〉 make an insinuating remark 《at》; hint (obliquely) at; give an indirect cut; insinuate; innuendo; satirize
♦ 아무의 경솔함을 빗대다 insinuate [hint at] *sb's* rashness
▶ 그녀는 성실한 여자가 아니라고 그는 나에게 넌지시 빗대었다 He insinuated [hinted] to me that she was dishonest.
▶ 그의 말은 나를 빗대어 하는 말이다 His remark is intended for me.
2 〈틀리게 대다〉 misstate; make a false statement; perjure
♦ 사실을 빗대다 give a false [wrong] fact

빗돌 碑 〈비석〉 a monumental stone; a stone monument

빗맞다 **1** 〈어긋나서 맞다〉 miss the mark; go wide of [fall short of] the mark; glance off
▶ 그들은 연방 쏘아댔으나 모두 빗맞았다 They fired by volley, but all the shots missed
▶ 사냥꾼은 사슴을 빗맞혔다 The hunter missed his shot at a deer.
2 〈어긋나다〉 go wrong [awry]; fail; miscarry; be baffled
▶ 그의 예상이 빗맞았다 He guessed wrong. ⇌ His guess was wrong.

빗물 rainwater ♦ 흐르는 빗물(의 양) runoff / 빗물이 괸 곳 a rainpool

빗발 the density of falling rain ⇨ 빗줄기
▶ 빗발이 아주 굵어졌다 The rain has become quite heavy. ▶ 빗발이 방안으로 들이친다 It rains into the room.

빗발치다 hail; shower like hail; come thick and fast; shower 《arrows》 upon
♦ 빗발치듯 쏟아지는 총탄 a rain [hail, shower] of bullets
▶ 그들은 빗발치듯 질문을 퍼부었다 They put forth a rain of question.
▶ 탄알이 그들 주위에 빗발치듯 떨어졌다 Bullets rained all around them.

빗방울 a raindrop; a drop of rain
♦ 빗방울 소리 pattering of raindrops
▶ 빗방울이 떨어진다 Raindrops fall.

빗변 —邊 〔數〕 〈직각 삼각형의〉 the hypote-

nuse; an oblique side
빗살 the teeth of a comb
빗소리 the sound of raining
빗속 〈in〉 the midst of rain
♦ 빗속을 산책하다 take a walk in the rain
▶ 그는 빗속을 조깅하고 있었다 He was jogging in [through] the rain. (▶through는 「… 속을 무릅쓰고」라는 느낌이 강조됨)
빗장 a (cross)bar; a bolt 《on a door》; a latch
♦ 빗장이 잠겨 있는 [벗겨진] 문 a door on [off] the latch / 빗장을 지르다 bar [bolt] the gate / 빗장을 벗기다 unbar [unbolt] the gate
▶ 이 문은 빗장이 걸리지 않는다 This door won't latch.
빗줄기 1 〈빗발〉 the density of falling rain; (great) streaks [sheets] of rain
▶ 빗줄기가 세차다 It rains hard [heavily]. ⇌ It pours down. ⇌ It rains cats and dogs.
▶ 빗줄기가 가늘어졌다 It is raining less hard.
2 〈소나기의 한 바탕〉 a shower for a while
빗질 combing 《one's hair》 —**빗질하다** comb 《one's hair》; dress [brush] 《one's hair》
빙 1 〈도는 모양〉 round; around
♦ 친지들을 방문해서 한바퀴 빙 돌아보다 go the round of one's friends / 공원을 빙 돌아 산책하다 take a turn in the park / 연못을 한바퀴 빙 돌다 walk around a pond
▶ 그는 아들을 데리고 동네를 한 바퀴 빙 돌았다 He took his son around the whole village.
2 〈둘러싼 모양〉 round; in a circle
♦ 구경꾼에게 빙 둘러싸이다 be surrounded [crowded round] by spectators / 빙 둘러앉다 sit in a circle [ring]
▶ 기자들이 그를 빙 둘러쌌다 The reporters gathered around [surrounded] him.
3 〈아찔해지는 모양〉 ♦ 눈이 빙 돌 것 같은 높이 a dizzy [a giddy] height / 눈이 빙 돌다 get dizzy [giddy]/ 머리가 빙 돌다 one's head swims [spins]/ 〈얼어맞고〉 be stunned
▶ 숙취 탓인지 머리가 빙 돈다 My head is swimming, I think I've got a hangover.
4 〈글썽한 모양〉 ♦ 눈물이 빙 돌다 be moved to tears
▶ 그 비통한 사건에 나는 눈물이 빙 돌았다 I was moved to tears at the sad incident. ⇌ I felt tears coming to my eyes at the sad incident.
빙결 氷結 〈동결〉freezing; congelation
♦ 빙결을 방지하다 keep 《an airplane》 free of ice; 〔空〕 deice
—**빙결하다** freeze; congeal; be frozen 〈over〉; 〈항구 등이〉be icebound
♦ 겨울에도 빙결하지 않다 be ice-free in winter
▶ 호수는 완전히 빙결했다 The lake has completely frozen [iced] over.
■ **—방지 장치** an anti-icer
빙고 氷庫 〔얼음 저장고〕 an icehouse; a storehouse for ice
빙고 〈숫자 카드로 하는 놀이〉 bingo
■ **—게임** a bingo game **—장** a bingo parlor
빙과 氷菓 ices; 〈아이스크림〉 ice cream; an ice-cream cone; 〈아이스캔디〉 a bar of sherbet (on a stick); 〔商標〕 a Popsicle; 《英》 an ice [iced] lolly
빙그레 with a smile; smilingly; beamingly; with a beaming face
♦ 빙그레 웃다 smile; beam 《upon sb》; beam with [break into] a smile; grin
빙그르 (turn, glide, skate) around smoothly
♦ 빙판을 한 바퀴 빙그르르 돌다 take a smooth turn around the ice / 한쪽 발끝으로 빙그르르 돌다 spin on one toe
▶ 돌풍에 그의 모자가 빙그르르 돌며 날아갔다 The gust whirled away his hat.
빙글거리다 smile 《at sb》; beam 《upon sb》
빙글빙글¹ 〈웃는 모양〉 smilingly; beamingly
♦ 빙글빙글 웃는 얼굴 a beaming [smiling] face; a radiant look
—**빙글빙글하다** ⇨ 빙글거리다
빙글빙글² 〈도는〉 (turn) round and round
♦ 걸으면서 우산을 빙글빙글 돌리다 twirl one's umbrella while walking
▶ 비행기는 빙글빙글 돌면서 추락했다 The plane got [went] into a (flat) spin [tailspin] and crashed.
빙긋이 with a smile ⇨ 빙그레
빙낭 氷囊 〔얼음주머니〕 an ice bag [pack]
■ **—걸이** an ice bag suspender
빙모 聘母 one's mother-in-law ⇨ 장모(丈母)
빙벽 氷壁 〈산의〉 an ice ridge; an ice cliff [wall]; a wall of ice
빙부 聘父 one's father-in-law ⇨ 장인(丈人)
빙빙 round and round (about); in circles
♦ 빙빙 돌다 go [turn] round and round; circle (round); whirl; wheel; spin; revolve
▶ 방이 빙빙 도는 것 같았다 I felt as if the room were [(口) was] spinning (around).
▶ 매가 하늘에서 빙빙 돌고 있었다 A hawk was circling in the air.
빙사탕 氷砂糖 〔얼음 사탕〕 sugar candy
빙산 氷山 an iceberg; a floating mass of ice
♦ 빙산의 일각에 지나지 않다 be nothing but the small part of the whole
▶ 이번 수뢰 사건은 빙산의 일각에 지나지 않는다 The recent case of bribery is just [only] the tip of the iceberg.
빙상 氷上 ♦ 빙상의[에서] on the ice
■ **—경기** ice sports
빙설 氷雪 ice and snow
▶ 이 지방은 일년 내내 빙설에 갇혀 있다 This district is icebound [under ice and snow] all the year round.
빙수 氷水 1 〈얼음물〉 ice [iced] water
2 〈갈아 만든 얼음 음료〉 shaved ice with syrup ♦ 빙수 한 그릇 a bowl of shaved ice with syrup
■ **팥—** red bean sherbet
빙어 氷魚 〔魚〕 a pond smelt
빙원 氷原 an ice field; 〈해상의〉 a [an ice] floe
빙자 憑藉 1 〈의지〉 dependence; reliance; leaning 《on》
—**빙자하다** hide behind the authority of; depend [rely] on the strength [authority] of; lean 〈on〉; be dependent 《upon》
♦ 아버지의 세도를 빙자하여 거드럭거리다 give oneself airs under the shelter of one's father's

influence.
2 〈핑계〉 a pretext; a pretense; an excuse; a plea; cloak
―빙자하다 make a pretence [pretext] ; make an excuse [a plea] of; plead; find an excuse
♦…을 빙자하여 under [on] the pretense [pretext] of…; on the plea of [that]…
▶ 그들은 취직 알선을 빙자하여 그에게서 돈을 사취했다 They swindle him out of money under the pretext of finding employment.
▶ 그녀는 일을 빙자하여 그 제의를 거절했다 She refused the offer with the excuse that she had work to do.

빙장 聘丈 the wife's father ⇨ 장인(丈人)
빙장석 氷長石 〔鑛〕 adularia (feldspar)
빙점 氷點 the freezing point
♦빙점하의 기온 a sub-zero [below-zero] temperature; a temperature below the freezing point / 빙점 이하로 내려가다 fall below (the) freezing point / 빙점 이상으로 올라가다 rise above (the) freezing point
▶ 온도는 빙점 이하 (5도)로 내려갔다 The temperature dropped [sank] (to five degree) below (the) freezing point [below zero].
빙정석 氷晶石 〔鑛〕 cryolite
빙초산 氷醋酸 〔化〕 glacial acetic acid
빙충맞다 stupid and timid; clumsy; thickheaded; lumbering
빙충이 a stupid and timid person; a clumsy fellow; a lubber
빙탄 氷炭 1 〈얼음과 숯〉 ice and charcoal
2 〈비유〉〈부조화〉 incompatibility; contradiction; discord
♦빙탄 불상용(不相容) be as irreconcilable as oil and water; be contradictory [antagonistic] to each other
빙판 氷板 〈얼음판〉(on, over) (the) ice; 〈빙판길〉 a frozen road; an icy road [place]
빙하 氷河 1 〈얼어붙은 강〉 a frozen river
2 〔地質〕 a glacier [gléiʃər]
♦빙하의 glacial / 빙하 전기(前期)의 preglacial / 빙하 후기의 postglacial
■ 대륙성[고산성]― a continental [an alpine] glacier ■ ―곡(谷) a glacial valley ―기[시대] a glacial epoch; the ice age ―작용 the action of a glacier; glacier operations; glaciation ―지형 the glacial landform ―호 a glacial lake
빙해 氷海 a frozen sea; icy waters
빚 〈부채〉 a debt; a loan; liabilities; what one owes
♦이자가 붙지 않는 빚 a passive debt / 회수 가망이 없는 빚 a bad debt
▶ 빚 갚을 기한을 조금만 더 연장해 주십시오 Please let me stay a little longer in your debt.
▶ 그는 갚아야 할 빚 때문에 몹시 고통을 겪고 있다 He is greatly distressed with debts to pay back.
〈빚이〉 빚이 있다 be in debt 《to, with》; have a debt to pay; owe sb money / 빚이 없다 be out of debt; be free from [of] debt(s) / 빚이 늘어나다 run up a score
▶ 나는 그에게 빚이 10만원 있다 I owe him one hundred thousand won. ⇌ I owe one hundred thousand to him. (▶ 전자는 금액에, 후자는 사람에게 중점을 둔 표현임)
▶ 나는 아무에게도 빚이 없다 I owe no one. ⇌ I owe nothing to anyone.
▶ 나는 그에게 묵은 빚이 있다 I owe him a debt of long standing.
〈빚을〉 빚을 갚다 pay [repay, discharge] one's debts / 빚을 재촉하다 call up a debt; press sb to pay a debt; dun [press] sb for payment of a debt / 빚을 떼어먹고 달아나다 run away from one's debts; bilk [jump] (a creditor, one's debt) / 빚을 청산하다 clear (up) one's debts; clear [pay] off one's debts; free [clear] oneself from debts
▶ 그는 나에게 빚을 갚으라고 독촉했다 He demanded of me the payment of the debt. ⇌ He demanded that I pay the debt.
▶ 그는 빚을 떼어먹고 행방을 감추었다 He bilked [repudiated] his debts and went into hiding.
〈빚에서〉 나는 빚에서 벗어났다 I got out of debt.
〈빚으로〉 빚으로 꼼짝 못하다 be deeply [over head and ears, up to the ears] in debt; be immersed [sunk deeply] in debt / 빚으로 살아 가다 live on borrowed money
■ 노름― a gambling debt; a debt of honor ■ ―독촉 a dun; a demand for (the) payment of a debt ―문서[증서] an IOU; 《俗》 the three vowels
빚거간 ―居間 〔일〕 agency [brokerage] for moneylending; 〔사람〕 an agent [a broker] for a loan
―빚거간하다 act as an agent [intermediary] for moneylending; act as a loan agent
빚내다 〈꾸다〉 borrow money 《from》; get [obtain] a loan (of money)
▶ 그는 집을 담보로 빚냈다 He raised [borrowed] money on his house.
빚놓다 lend (out) money; 《美》 loan sb money
♦고리로 빚놓다 lend money at a high rate of interest [high interest (rate)]; practice usury
빚다 1 〈술을 담그다〉 brew; ferment; distil
♦술을 빚다 brew (rice) wine
2 〈송편 등을 만들다〉 shape dough for 《rice cakes》 ♦만두[송편]를 빚다 make dumplings [stuffed rice cakes]
3 〈만들어내다〉 bring about [on]; give rise to; cause; engender; breed
♦가난이 빚은 비극 a tragedy resulting from poverty / 분쟁을 빚다 give rise to a dispute
▶ 그가 공청회에서 한 발언이 물의를 빚었다 His speech on the public hearing caused [brought about] trouble.
▶ 그 노골적인 묘사는 크게 물의를 빚었다 The frank description aroused [evoked] much criticism [controversy].
빚쟁이 a creditor; 〈채권자〉 an importunate creditor; a dun; 〈고리대금업자〉 a usurer; 《美俗》 a loan shark
♦빚쟁이에게 시달리다 be hounded by one's creditors; be pressed [tormented] by creditors; be dunned (for payment of a debt)
빚주고 뺨맞는다 《속담》 having good repayed with evil

빚주다 lend (out) money; make a loan
빚지다 1 〈빚돈을 쓰다〉 fall [run, get] into debt; contract [incur] a debt [loan]; owe
♦많이 빚지다 make a lot of debts
▶그는 빚지고 달아났다 He run away leaving his debt unpaid. ⇌ He bilked a his debt [bill].
▶그는 나에게 50만원을 빚졌다 He owes me five hundred thousand won.
2 〈신세지다〉 ▶나는 그 일로 그에게 크게 빚졌다 I put myself under a great obligation to him because of that matter. ⇌ I am much indebted to him because of that matter.
▶친절하게 대해 주신 은인에게 빚진 것을 갚아 야지요 I must repay my benefactor for his kindness.

빛 1 〈광(光)〉 (a) light; 〈광선〉 rays (of light); a ray; a beam; 〈광채〉 the glow《of a firefly》; (a) shine; 〈광택〉 (a) luster (a) gloss
♦밝은 빛 a bright light / 달빛 moonlight / 별빛 starlight; the twinkle of a star / 석양빛 the glow of the sunset / 희미한 빛 dim [feeble, faint] light; glimmer / 빛의 굴절 [반사, 분산, 흡수] refraction [reflection, dispersion, extinction] of light / 빛의 전자설 the electromagnetic theory of light / 빛을 내는 물체 〈발광체〉 a luminous body / 빛을 내다 emit [give out] light; send out rays of light; radiate
▶빛의 속도는 초속 30만 킬로미터다 The velocity of light is [Light travels] three hundred thousand kilometers per second.
2 〈빛깔〉 a color; a hue; a tint; a tinge
♦가을 빛 autumnal tints / 느낌이 좋은 빛 a pleasant [delightful] color / 밝은[어두운] 빛 a bright [dark] color / 부드러운 빛 a delicate [soft] color / 화려한[차분한] 빛 a gay [quiet] color / 빛의 배합 a color scheme / 빛의 조화 color harmony / …한 빛을 띠다 be tinted [tinged] with
▶가을 빛이 짙어졌다 There are fall colors everywhere. ⇌ It has become more like fall.
3 〈기색·안색·태도〉 complexion; color; an air; a sign; a mark; an indication; 〈표정〉 a look
♦실망의 빛 a look of disappointment / 무서워 하는 빛을 (않고) without (showing) any (outward) sign of fear / 피곤한 빛을 보이다 show signs of exhaustion; look tired
▶그녀의 눈에는 실망의 빛이 역력했다 There was plainly a look of disappointment in her eyes.
▶나는 그의 얼굴에서 공포의 빛을 보았다 I observed marks of fear in his face.
4 〈희망〉 light; hope; a bright future [prospect]
♦가문의 빛 the hope of *one's* family / 세상의 빛 〈그리스도〉 the Light of the World
5 〈공인·실현〉 ♦빛을 보지 못하는 작가 an obscure [unacknowledged] writer / (계획 등이) 빛을 보게 되다 be realized
▶그는 빛을 보지 못하고 있다 He has little hope of advancement.
6 〈부류〉 a sort; a class; a group
♦빛이 아주 다른 사람 a person of quite different kind [stripe]
7 (비유) ♦빛을 잃다 go into 《temporary》 eclipse
▶그는 정계에서 빛을 발하고[발하지 못하고] 있다 He makes [cuts] a brilliant figure in the political world.

빛깔 a color; 〈색조〉 a hue; a tint; a tinge; 〈명암〉 a shade; 〈피부색〉 a complexion
♦서로 잘 어울리는 빛깔 harmonizing colors / 빛깔이 짙은[옅은] be deep [light] in color / 빛깔이 변하다 change color; 〈바래다〉 be discolored; fade / 피부 빛깔이 희다[검다] be fair [dark]; have a fair [dark] complexion / 뻴간 빛깔을 띠다 be tinged with red / 빛깔을 칠하다 color; paint
▶「會話」「네 차는 무슨 빛깔이니?」「빨강」 "What color is your car? ⇌ What is the color

빛깔의 이미지

빛깔	좋은 이미지	나쁜 이미지
black	정장(正裝), (재정상의) 흑자, 강력함, 흑인의 혼	죽음, 비애, 실망, 불길, 악성, (표정 등이) 험악함, 흉악함
blue	희망, 성실, 청명, 경신, 영원 불사, 냉정, 심려, 최우수	우울, 음산, 새침떼기, 냉혹
gray	현명, 원숙, 노련	백발, 흐림, 비관, 고난, 우울, 부정, 은폐, 외로움, 쓸쓸함, 노령
green	신실, 기쁨, 불사, 청춘, 젊음, 건강, 호조, 안전, 온난	미숙, 질투, 불길, 공포, 질병, 요괴
pink	젊음, 활력, 신선, 완벽, 희망	좌경, 술취함, 흥분, 분노
purple	정의, 왕후, 귀족, 고상, 화려, 미사여구	격노, 속악
red	정열, 열혈, 사랑, 자선, 순교, 용기, 축하	격노, 위험, 과격, 유혈, 전쟁, 화재, 범죄, 적자, 좌익[혁명]의
white	청순, 고결, 공정, 청결, 진실, 결백, 순수, 순결, 신성	공포, 죽음, 유령, 소심, 항복, 호도
yellow		겁쟁이, 질투, 음침, 선정적, 변덕, 경고, 검역

of your car?" "It's red."
▶ 빨강은 그녀가 아주 좋아하는 빛깔이다 Red is her favorite color. (▶ 빨강에도 온갖 색조의 것이 있는데, 그 중의 특정한 빛깔을 가리킬 경우에는 the를 붙임.)

빛나다 1 〈환하게〉 shine; beam; 〈보석 등이〉 sparkle; glitter; 〈어렴풋이〉 gleam; 〈깜박깜박〉 glimmer; 〈번쩍〉 flash; 〈백열광 등이〉 glow; 〈반짝반짝〉 glisten; 〈별 등이〉 twinkle
♦ 기쁨에 빛나는 눈 eyes sparkling with joy [delight] / 하늘에 빛나는 별 twinkling stars in the sky; stars sparkling in the heavens
▶ 보석이 빛을 받아 빛난다 Jewels shine [sparkle] in the light.
▶ 밤하늘에 별이 빛나고 있다 Stars are twinkling [shining, glittering, gleaming] in the night sky.
2 〈영광스럽다〉 be glorious [splendid]; shine brilliantly
♦ 빛나는 업적 a brilliant [a glorious, an illustrious, a splendid] achievement / 역사에 길이 빛나라 remain long [immortal] in history; go down [shine forth] in history
▶ 너에게는 빛나는 미래가 있다 You have a bright [brilliant] future. ⇌ A bright [brilliant] future lies before you.
3 〈돋보이다〉 look better; be distinguished; shine (in); be outstanding; be prominent; cut a figure (among, with)
♦ 정치가로서 빛나다 shine as a statesman
▶ 그는 작가들 중에서도 빛나는 존재였다 He stood out [was outstanding] among the writers. ⇌ He outshone all the other writers.

빛내다 make sth shine [bright]; 〈광택을 내다〉 luster; 〈닦아서〉 polish; burnish; 〈영광스럽게〉 glorify; bring glory to
♦ 이름을 빛내다 make the name illustrious; win fame / 조국을 빛내다 bring glory to one's fatherland; glorify the name of one's country
▶ 그는 내외에 이름을 빛냈다 He has won fame both at home and abroad.
▶ 그는 천재적인 바이올리니스트로서 그 이름을 세계에 빛냈다 He gained worldwide fame as a highly gifted violinist.

빛 좋은 개살구 〈속담〉 a gimcrack; a gewgaw; a trumpery; be not so good as it looks

빠개다 1 〈쪼개다〉 split; cleave
♦ 통나무를 빠개다 split a log / 둘로 빠개다 split in two
▶ 배는 얼음을 빠개면서 나아갔다 The ship advanced, breaking ice as it went.
2 〈일을 망치다〉 spoil; destroy; ruin

빠개지다 1 〈쪼개지다〉 split (apart); cleave; be smashed
▶ 머리가 빠개질 듯이 아프다 I have a racking [splitting] headache.
▶ 이 통나무는 잘 빠개진다 This log splits nicely.
2 〈일이〉 be [get] spoilt; be ruined

빠그라지다 get broken; be destroyed; be ruined ▶ 그것을 듣고 내 희망은 빠그라졌다 When I heard that, my hopes were shattered [crushed].

-빠듯 a little less than; a little short of; a little under ♦ 3인치 빠듯 a little under three inches / 한 말 빠듯 a short *mal*

빠듯이 1 〈겨우〉 barely; hardly; narrowly; with difficulty
♦ 비행기 시간에 빠듯이 대다 be just [barely] in time for the plane / 빠듯이 살아가다 live up to one's means; live barely within one's income; barely earn a living
2 〈꼭 끼게〉 tightly; closely
▶ 바지 허리가 빠듯이 낀다 The waist of the trousers is [has gotten] too tight for me.

빠듯하다 1 〈꼭 끼다〉 tight; close ♦ 빠듯한 신발 tight shoes
▶ 셔츠의 목이 빠듯하다 I feel the shirt tight about the neck.
▶ 이 구두는 빠듯해서 아프다 These shoes are so tight that they hurt.
2 〈겨우 미치다〉 barely enough; bare; narrow; marginal ♦ 빠듯한 이익 marginal profits / 쉰이 빠듯한 a little under fifty
▶ 월 100만원으로는 먹고 살기에 빠듯하다 We can barely live on one million won a month.

빠뜨리다 1 〈물건을〉 let sth fall into; drop sth in [into] ♦ 병을 우물에 빠뜨리다 drop a bottle into a well / 지갑을 물에 빠뜨리다 let a wallet fall into the water
2 〈함정에〉 entrap; ensnare; 〈유혹에〉 tempt; allure; entice ♦ 남을 함정에 빠뜨리려다가 자기가 빠지다 be caught in one's own trap; be hoist with [by] one's own petard
▶ 그는 나를 함정에 빠뜨렸다 He trapped me. ⇌ I was ensnared by him.
▶ 그들은 그 사람을 곤경에 빠뜨렸다 They plunged the man into a difficult position.
3 〈누락시키다〉 omit; leave out; miss (out, out of); pass [skip, look] over
♦ 명단에서 이름을 빠뜨리다 miss sb's name out of the list / 한 줄 빠뜨리고 읽다 overlook [miss] a line in reading; skip (over) a line
▶ 그는 아무리 사소한 것도 빠뜨리지 않고 철저히 조사했다 He made a thorough investigation down to the minutest detail.
▶ 청중은 그의 말을 한 마디도 빠뜨리지 않고 들으려고 열심히 귀를 기울였다 The audience listened intently [attentively] so that they would not miss a single word of what he said.
4 〈잃어버리다〉 lose; drop; 〈잊고 가다〉 leave sth ▶ 지갑을 이 근처에서 빠뜨렸다 I lost my wallet somewhere around here.

빠르기 rapidness; quickness; tempo

빠르다 1 〈신속하다〉 fast; rapid; quick; speedy; 〈기민하다〉 brisk; smart; prompt
♦ 계산[결단]이 빠르다 be quick at figures [in making decisions] / 눈치가 빠르다 have a quick perception; be a quick judge of situations; size things up fast / 동작이 빠르다 be quick in action; move quickly / 발이 빠르다 be swift of foot; be a good walker; be a fast runner / 이해가 빠르다 be quick to understand [of understanding]; catch on fast / 일손이 빠르다 be quick with [at, about] one's work; be a quick hand [worker] / 진보가 빠르다 make rapid [fast] progress
▶ 택시로 가는 것보다 걷는 것이 빠르다 It is

빠지다¹

quicker (to go) on foot than by taxi.
▶ 대나무는 성장이 빠르다 Bamboos grow rapidly.
▶ 빛은 소리보다 빠르다 Light travels faster than sound.
▶ 그녀는 호흡도 맥박도 빨랐다 Her breathing was fast and her pulse quick.
▶ 그는 빠른 공을 던진다 He throws fast balls.
2 〈이르다〉 early; too soon; 〈때가〉 premature ♦ 빨라야 at the earliest; at (the) soonest
▶ 아직 빠르다 It is still early. ⇌ You've got plenty of time.
▶ 이 시계는 2분 빠르다 This watch is two minutes fast.
▶ 아직 이야기하기에는 빠르다 It is too soon to tell.
▶ 결말은 예상보다 빨랐다 The end came sooner than expected.
▶ 빠르면 빠를수록 좋다 The sooner, the better.
3 〈손쉽다〉 easy; simple; 〈속성의〉 quick; rapid; 〈첨경의〉 shortcut ♦ 영어를 배우는 가장 빠른 길 the shortest way to learn English

빠지다 **1** 〈떨어져 들어가다〉 fall [get] into; run into; be led into; lapse into; 〈물속에〉 drown; be drowned; sink
♦ 궁지에 빠지다 fall into difficulties / 도랑에 빠지다 be mired in a ditch / 물에 빠지다 fall [plunge] into water; drown / 유혹에 빠지다 fall into temptation / 진창에 빠지다 be stuck in the mud; mire / 혼수 상태에 빠지다 lapse [fall] into a state of coma; go into a coma
▶ 물에 빠진 사람은 지푸라기라도 잡는다 (속담) A drowning man will catch at a straw.
▶ 아이가 큰 구멍에 빠졌다 The child fell into a big hole.
▶ 그는 자포자기에 빠졌다 He abandoned himself to despair.
▶ 그는 하마터면 물에 빠질뻔했다 He was nearly [almost] drowned. ⇌ He narrowly escaped drowning.
▶ 차가 진흙속에 빠졌다 The car was mired.
2 〈탈락하다〉 come [fall] out [off]; be taken [broken] off
♦ 머리카락이 빠지다 one's hair falls out [off]; one's hair thins (out) / 이가 빠지다 a tooth comes out; 〈그릇 등의〉 (a cup) chip (off); be chipped; 〈칼날 등이〉 (the edge) be nicked
▶ 나는 이가 하나 빠졌다 I lost a tooth.
▶ 못이 빠져 나왔다 The nail came out.
▶ 바닥이 빠졌다 The bottom dropped off.
▶ 손잡이가 빠져 있다 The handle is off.
▶ 이 코르크 마개는 잘 빠지지 않는다 This cork will not come out.
▶ 이 새는 깃털이 빠지기 시작했다 This bird is starting to lose its feathers.
3 〈탐닉하다〉 indulge (oneself) in; abandon [surrender] oneself to; give oneself (up [over]) to; be absorbed [engrossed] in; be crazy [wild] with [about]
♦ 공상에 빠지다 fall into [indulge in, be lost in] (a) reverie / 도박에 빠지다 be infatuated with gambling / 사랑에 빠지다 be lost [fall] in love (with) / 주색에 빠지다 give oneself up to women and wine; be given to sensual pleasures

▶ 그는 갑자기 그 여자에게 홀딱 빠졌다 He suddenly became infatuated with her.
4 〈누락되다〉 be left out; be omitted; 〈없다〉 be missing; 〈제외되다〉 be excluded (from); be not included ♦ 초대에서 빠지다 be left out of invitation
▶ 몇 페이지가 빠져 있다 There are a few pages missing. ⇌ A few pages are missing.
▶ 내 이름이 명단에서 빠져 있다 My name is missing from the list.
5 〈흘러나가다〉 drain; flow off; run out; 〈새어 나오다〉 leak out; 〈물 등이 줄다〉 subside; abate; fall; go down; sink
▶ 이 땅은 물이 잘 빠진다[빠지지 않는다] This ground drains [does not drain] well.
▶ 홍수가 아직 빠지지 않았다 The floods have not subsided yet.
▶ 이 타이어는 바람이 빠졌다 This tire is [has gone] flat.
6 〈힘·김·냄새 등이〉 be gone; grow weak; be exhausted; get flat; become stale; give out
♦ 김 빠진 이야기 a dull [an insipid] talk / 힘 빠진 목소리 a faint voice
▶ 이 맥주는 김이 빠졌다 This beer has become [drinks] flat.
▶ 나는 힘이 완전히 빠져 버렸다 All my strength is gone.
7 〈여위다〉 get [become] lean [thin]; grow slim; lose (one's) weight; 〈병으로〉 lose flesh
▶ 그녀는 병으로 살이 많이 빠졌다 She lost a lot of weight after becoming ill.
8 〈제거되다〉 be removed; 〈얼룩 등이〉 be taken out; 〈때 등이〉 wash off [out]; 〈염색이〉 run; fade; 〈빛깔이 바래다〉 discolor
♦ 빠지지 않는 색 a standing [fast, fadeproof] color
▶ 색이 다 빠져 버렸다 The colors faded away.
▶ 이 옷감은 색이 빠지지 않는다 This material will never fade.
9 〈탈퇴하다〉 leave; quit; withdraw (from); drop out; secede from; (美) bolt from
▶ 싸움에서 빠지다 pull out of the fight
▶ 이번에 나는 빠지겠다 I will drop out this time.
10 〈통과하다〉 go by [through]; pass [cut, get, run] through; 〈돌파하다〉 break [smash] through; 〈탈출하다〉 escape; slip [steal] out; get away; 〈피하다〉 evade; avoid; 〈핑계를 대고〉 excuse oneself from
♦ 방에서 빠져나가다 slip out of the room / 법망을 빠져나가다 evade [get around] the law / 위험한 곳을 빠져 나오다 escape danger; find one's way out of danger
▶ 여기서 빠져나가자 Let's cut through [across] here.
▶ 그녀는 급히 우리 사이를 빠져나갔다 She slipped through us in haste.
▶ 그는 아무도 모르게 빠져나갔다 He slipped away unseen [unnoticed].
▶ 태풍은 동해로 빠져나갔다 The typhoon blew out into the East Sea.
▶ 그는 용케 빠져나왔다 He managed to wangle out of it.

▶ 강연은 계속되었으나 나는 강당을 빠져나왔다 The lecture was still going on, but I left the auditorium.
▶ 그 모임에는 빠질 수 없다 I can't excuse myself from the meeting.
11 〈뒤떨어지다〉 be [fall] behind; be inferior to; be below
▶ 그는 암산에서는 누구에게도 빠지지 않는다 He is second [next] to none in mental calculation.
▶ 이것들은 타사 제품에 빠지지 않는다 These can easily stand comparison with the products of other companies.
12 〈속다〉 be deceived [cheated]; be taken in; be trapped
▶ 나는 함정에 빠졌다 I fell into [be caught in] a snare [trap].
▶ 그런 속임수에 빠질 내가 아니다 That trick won't do with me.
13 〈잘 생기다〉 ▶ 그녀는 잘빠진 여자다 She is a beautiful [pretty, lovely, good-looking] woman.
빠지다² ♦ 낡아 빠진 사상 a moss-grown [an old-fashioned] idea / 닳아 빠진 구두 a pair of worn-out shoes / 늙어 빠진 말 a decrepit old horse / 게을러 빠지다 be very lazy [indolent, sluggish]
▶ 그것은 흔해 빠진 경우다 There are many such cases. ⇒ There are many numbers of cases like that.
빠짐없이 without omission [exception]; in full; wholly; thoroughly ♦ 빠짐없이 조사하다 make a thorough [an exhaustive] investigation
▶ 전원이 빠짐없이 출석했다 All the members were present. ⇒ Every member was present.
▶ 빈칸을 빠짐없이 채우시오 Please fill in all the blanks (without any omission).
빡빡 hard; roughly; vigorously ♦ 통을 빡빡 문지르다 rub the tub hard; give a tub a hard scrub / 담배를 빡빡 빨다[피우다] puff hard at *one's* pipe; puff away; puff a cigarette [cigar]
빡빡하다 1 〈물기가 적다〉 thick; dry and hard ♦ 빡빡한 밥 hard-boiled rice
2 〈꽉 차다〉 close; compact; full; 〈꼭 끼다〉 pinched; cramped; tight; stiff
♦ 빡빡하게 쓴 편지 a closely written letter / 가방에 물건을 빡빡하게 채우다 cram *one's* bag full of things
▶ 금주는 일정이 빡빡하다 I have a tight [very full] schedule this week. ⇒ My schedule for this week is tight [crowded].
3 〈융통성이 없다〉 rigid; narrow-minded
♦ 빡빡한 규칙 rigid regulations / 빡빡한 사람 an inflexible [an obstinate] person
빡작지근하다 〈뻐근하다〉 stiff; strained ♦ 목이 빡작지근하다 feel stiff in the neck; have a stiff neck
빤하다 1 〈분명하다〉 obvious; evident; plain; self-evident ♦ 빤한 사실 an obvious [a clear, a plain] fact / 빤한 아첨 obvious [clumsy] flattery
▶ 그는 빤한 거짓말을 했다 He told palpable [barefaced, transparent] lies.
▶ 그것은 빤한 일이다 It is self-evident.
2 〈대수롭지 않다〉 trifling; negligible; (very) small
▶ 아버지의 유산이래야 빤하다 My father has left me no property worth mentioning.
▶ 그의 장래란 빤하다 We cannot expect much from his future.
3 〈환하다〉 light; bright
4 〈한가하다〉 free; unoccupied; disengaged
5 〈병세가 좀 낫다〉 get a bit [a little] better
빤히 1 〈분명히〉 plainly; obviously; evidently
♦ 빤히 들여다 보이는 거짓말 a transparent lie / 속이 빤히 들여다 보이는 수를 쓰다 resort to a shallow trick; make a hollow imposture
▶ 우리는 그런 좋은 기회를 빤히 보고 놓칠 수는 없다 We cannot stand idle and miss such a good opportunity.
2 〈환하게〉 bright(ly)
▶ 날이 다시 빤히 들었다 The sky is bright and clear [cleared up] again.
3 〈시선 등〉 fixedly; steadily; intently
♦ 빤히 쳐다보다 gaze [stare fully] at *sb*; look hard [fixedly] at *sb*
▶ 말 한 마디 없이 서서 그녀는 나를 빤히 바라보았다 Without saying a word, she just stood and stared at me.
빨강 red (color); 〈심홍색〉 crimson; 〈진홍색〉 scarlet
빨갛다 red; crimson; scarlet
♦ 빨간 코 a red nose; 〈술꾼의〉 a coppernose; a bottle nose / 빨갛게 단 쇠 red-hot iron / 빨갛게 물들이다[칠하다] dye [paint] red
▶ 서쪽 하늘이 빨갛게 불타고 있었다 The western sky glowed with crimson.
빨개지다 turn red [scarlet, crimson]; redden; 〈부끄러워서〉 blush; 〈흥분하여〉 flush (up)
♦ 부끄러워서 얼굴이 빨개지다 blush for [with] shame
▶ 그녀는 그 말을 듣자 귀뿌리까지 빨개졌다 She flushed to the ears when she heard it.
빨갱이 〈공산주의자〉 a Communist; (俗) a Commie; (총칭) the Reds
빨다¹ 〈입으로〉 suck; suck at; draw; inhale; take a drag at
♦ 사탕을 빨다 suck a candy / 손가락을 빨다 suck *one's* finger [thumb] / 담배를 한 모금 빨다 take a drag at a cigarette [pipe]
▶ 아기가 엄마 젖[젖병]을 빨고 있다 The baby is sucking its mother's breast [a feeding bottle].
▶ 모기는 동물의 피를 빤다 Mosquitos suck animals' blood.
▶ 그녀는 빨대로 레모네이드를 빨고 있었다 She was sucking the lemonade through a straw.
빨다² 〈세탁하다〉 wash; do (the) washing; do the wash; launder; scour
♦ 옷을 빨다 wash (*one's*) clothes; do *one's* wash [washing, laundry] / 빨아도 줄지 않다 do not shrink in the wash; be shrink-proof
▶ 이 얼룩은 빨면 없어질까요? Will this stain wash out [off]?
▶ 이것은 빨면 줄어든다 This shrinks in washing [in the wash].

▶ 이 천은 빨 수 있다 This cloth is washable [stands washing].

빨다³ 〈뾰족하다〉 tapering; pointed
◆ 끝이 빤 pointed; sharp-pointed; tapering (finger) / 하관이 빤 얼굴 a face with a pointed [tapering] jaw

빨대 a (drinking) straw ◆ 빨대로 주스를 빨아먹다 suck juice through a straw

빨 딱 〈일어서는 모양〉 suddenly; abruptly; quickly; with a jerk [spring]; 〈자빠지는 모양〉 on one's back
◆ 빨딱 일어서다 stand up abruptly; spring to one's feet; rise [get up] with jump [a spring] / 의자에서 빨딱 일어서다 bob up from a chair / 빨딱 자빠지다 fall (flat) on one's back; collapse

빨래 1 〈세탁〉 a wash; washing; laundering; cleaning
▶ 이 천은 빨래가 잘 된다 This cloth launders well.
—**빨래하다** wash; launder; clean; do one's washing
◆ 1주일에 세 번 빨래하다 do three washings a week
▶ 나는 직접 빨래 한다 I do my own washing. ⇌ I wash my own things.
2 〈세탁물〉 a [the] wash; the washing; the laundry
◆ 빨래 말리는 곳 a drying place / 빨래가 많다 have a lot of washing to do / 빨래를 말리다 [널다] hang out the washing to dry
▶ 비가 올 것 같다. 빨래를 거두어 들이자 It looks like rain. Let's take in the laundry.
■ —**광주리** a laundry basket; a hamper —**집게** a clothespin; (英) a clothespeg —**터** a wash [washing] place —**통** a washtub; a wash bucket [pail] —**판** a washboard **빨랫감** [the] wash; the washing; the laundry **빨랫돌** a washing stone **빨랫방망이** a laundry stick **빨랫비누** laundry [washing] soap **빨랫솔** a scrub(bing) brush **빨랫줄** a clothesline: 빨랫줄에 빨래를 널다 hang the wash on a clothesline

빨리 〈속히〉 quickly; fast; speedily; swiftly; rapidly; promptly; 〈곧〉 soon; immediately; instantly; at once; without delay; 〈일찍〉 early
◆ 될 수 있는 대로 빨리 as soon as possible [one can]
▶ 겨울 해는 빨리 진다 The winter sun sinks fast.
▶ 빨리 해 Be quick! ⇌ Hurry up!
▶ 빨리 대답해 Answer promptly. ⇌ Give me a prompt answer.
▶ 빨리 와 Come quick! (▶명령문에서는 quickly를 잘 쓰지 않음)
▶ 이 사과는 빨리 먹지 않으면 상한다 This apple should be eaten soon or it will spoil.

빨리다¹ 〈빨아먹히다〉 be sucked; (비유) be squeezed [extorted] (out of)
◆ 돈을 빨리다 be squeezed out of one's money; have one's money squeezed out
▶ 강 위에 떠내려가던 잎은 소용돌이에 빨려 들어갔다 The leaves floating down the stream were swallowed up by the whirlpool.

빨리다² 〈빨게 하다〉 ◆ 젖을 빨리다 give the breast to (a baby); nurse [breast-feed] (a baby); suckle (a baby)
▶ 그녀는 아기에게 젖을 빨리고 있다 She is nursing the baby.

빨빨 profusely ⇨ **뻘뻘**

빨아내다 suck [draw] out
◆ 스펀지로 물을 빨아내다 dry [soak up] water with sponge / 압지로 잉크를 빨아내다 dry [blot (up)] ink with blotting paper

빨아들이다 〈액체를〉 suck in [up]; 〈기체를〉 inhale; breathe [draw, take] in; 〈흡수하다〉 absorb; soak in [up]
▶ 스펀지는 물을 빨아들인다 A sponge sucks in [up] water.
◆ 식물은 뿌리로 땅에서 수분을 빨아들인다 Plants suck (up) moisture from the soil through their roots.

빨아먹다 1 〈음식물을〉 take [eat, drink] by sucking; suck; sip; lick
▶ 그녀는 손가락에 묻은 잼을 빨아먹었다 She licked the jam off her fingers.
2 〈우려내다〉 squeeze; suck; sponge; siphon off; 〈착취하다〉 exploit ◆ 가난한 사람의 피를 빨아먹다 suck the life's blood of the poor

빨아올리다 suck [draw] up
◆ 뿌리는 땅에서 수분을 빨아올린다 Roots suck up water from the soil.

빨치산 a partisan; a partizan

빨판 〔動〕 a sucker; a sucking disk [disc]; an acetabulum (pl. ~s, -la)

빨판상어 〔魚〕 a shark sucker; a remora; a suckling fish

빨펌프 a suction [lift, lifting] pump

빳빳하다 1 〈꿋꿋하다〉 rigid; stiff; stark (and stiff); 〈풀기가 있는〉 starchy
◆ 빳빳한 새 지폐 a crisp bank note / 빳빳하게 풀 먹인 시트 a well-starched sheet / 빳빳하게 stiffly; rigidly; starkly
▶ 이 셔츠는 풀기가 너무 빳빳하다 This shirt is overstarched and stiff.
2 〈고분고분하지 않다〉 strong; firm; tough
◆ 빳빳한 태도 a firm attitude (toward); a strong stand (against)

빵¹ 1 〈터지는 소리〉 pop; bang ◆ 빵 하고 터지다 burst with a bang; go bang; go pop
2 〈구멍난 모양〉 gapingly; with a hole
▶ 울타리에 구멍이 빵 뚫려 있다 There is a hole gaping in the hedge.

빵² 〈음식〉 bread; (총칭) bakery products

> [해설] **bread**에는 베이킹 파우더(baking powder)를 넣어서 만든 leavened bread와 베이킹 파우더를 넣지 않은 flat bread가 있다. 영미의 빵은 주로 leavened wheat bread인데, 흰 빵 (white bread)과 기울이 있는 밀가루로 만든 검은 빵(brown bread), 호밀로 만든 검은 빵 (black bread, rye bread) 등이 있다. **bun**은 (美)에서는 흔히 **hamburger bun**으로 쓰이는 둥글고 갸름한 빵을, (英)에서는 둥글고 조그만 과자빵을 말한다. 빵류의 총칭은 **bakery products**라 하며, 레스토랑의 메뉴에서 빵류는 **breads and griddle cakes**라 쓰여 있다.

♦ 흰 빵 white bread / 롤 빵 a roll (of bread) / 옥수수 빵 corn pone / 크림빵 a cream bun / 프랑스 빵 a French roll / 버터[치즈] 바른 빵 bread and butter [cheese] / 빵 문제 a bread-and-butter question; a question of living [livelihood] / 빵 한 덩어리 a loaf (of bread) / 빵 한 조각 a slice [piece] of bread / 빵을 굽다 bake bread / 빵을 위해 일하다 work for one's bread [living] / 빵에 잼[버터]을 바르다 spread jam [butter] on (the slice of) bread
▶ 사람은 빵만으로는 살 수 없다 〔聖〕 Man doth not live by bread alone.

빵가루 (bread)crumbs

빵나무 〔植〕 a breadfruit (tree); a bread tree
ー**열매** (a) breadfruit

빵빵 1 〈소리〉 bang! bang!(총소리); pop! pop!; crack! crack!(터지는 소리)
♦ 총을 빵빵 쏘다 fire a gun in rapid [quick] succession / (자동차가) 빵빵거리다 honk successively; honk and honk
▶ 나는 빵빵 총소리가 나는 것을 들었다 I heard the cracking [bang·bang] of gunfire.
2 〈구멍이 난 모양〉 with (several) holes
▶ 벽에는 구멍이 빵빵 뚫려 있었다 There were many holes in the wall.

빵집 a bakery; a baker's (shop); 〈판매만 하는〉 a bread shop

빻다 pound; crush; grind; pulverize ♦ 옥수수를 빻다 grind the corn into flour / 가루로 빻다 crush up / 찹쌀을 빻아 떡을 만들다 pound glutinous rice to make rice cake

빼기 〔數〕 subtraction ♦ 빼기를 하다 subtract; take away (A from B)

빼내다 1 〈뽑아내다〉 pull out; draw [pluck, take] out; extract ♦ 손가락의 가시를 빼내다 pick a thorn out of a finger / 판자에서 못을 빼내다 pull a nail out of a board
2 〈골라내다〉 select 《out of many》; pick [single] out; 〈추출하다〉 extract 《from》
♦ 식물에서 독성물질을 빼내다 extract poison from a plant / 불순물을 빼내다 get rid of [extract] impurities / 책에서 중요 대목만 빼내다 make an extract of important points from a book
3 〈훔쳐내다〉 steal; filch; pilfer 《from》
▶ 나는 그에게서 필요한 정보를 빼냈다 I extracted the necessary information from him. ⇌ I wormed the necessary information out of him.
▶ 군중 속에서 누가 내 지갑을 빼내갔다 My wallet was stolen in the crowd. ⇌ I had my pocket picked in the crowd.
4 〈꾀어내다〉 hire (a player) away 《from》; pick out
♦ 고용인을 빼내다 hire an employee away / 다른 팀에서 선수를 빼내다 entice players away from other teams
5 〈얽매인 몸을〉 liberate; set sb free 《from restraint》; help sb get out of 《adversities》
♦ 아무를 교도소에서 빼내다 bail [get] sb out of jail

빼놓다 1 〈제외하다〉 exclude; except 《from》; omit; leave out
▶ 그의 답안은 한 문제만 빼놓고 다 맞았다 His paper was correct except for one answer.
2 〈생략하다〉 omit; skip (over) 《a passage》
♦ 책의 어려운 부분을 빼놓다 skip (over) difficult passages
▶ 맨 앞의 열 쪽은 빼놓아도 좋다 You may omit the first ten pages.
3 〈박힌 것을 뽑아놓다〉 leave sth pulled [drawn, plucked] out ♦ 병마개를 빼놓다 leave [keep] a bottle uncorked
4 〈골라놓다〉 pick [single] out; select ♦ 좋은 것만을 빼놓다 select [pick out] the best

빼다¹ 〈잘 차려입다〉 dress [doll] up; adorn [preen] oneself
▶ 오늘은 쭉 빼셨군요 You are quite dressed up today, aren't you?
▶ 그녀는 쭉 빼 입고 나타났다 She came all dressed up.

빼다² 1 〈뽑다〉 take [draw, pull, put] out; extract
♦ 벽에서 못을 빼다 draw [pull] out a nail from the wall / 논에서 물을 빼다 drain water from a paddy field; drain a rice field / 타이어의 바람을 빼다 let the air out of a tire / 이를 빼다 extract [pull out] a tooth; have a tooth pulled (out) [extracted] / 칼집에서 칼을 빼다 draw [unsheathe] a sword
2 〈덜어내다〉 subtract 《from》; deduct 《from》; take away [off]
♦ 9에서 6을 빼다 subtract 6 from 9 / 급료에서 세금을 빼다 deduct taxes from sb's salary
▶ 10에서 3을 빼면 7이 남는다 Three from ten leaves seven. ⇌ Ten minus three equals [is equal to] seven.
3 〈없애다〉 take out; remove; 〈제외하다〉 exclude; 〈생략하다〉 leave [cut] out; omit; skip; pass over
♦ 셔츠의 얼룩을 빼다 take out [remove] stains out of a shirt; remove stains from a shirt / 때를 빼다 wash off the dirt / 명단에서 이름을 빼다 strike [cross] sb's name from the list / 관계가 없는 항목을 빼다 leave out [exclude] irrelevant items
▶ 그 말은 빼는 편이 낫다 The word had better be left out.
4 〈힘·살 등을〉 cause to lose ♦ 살을 빼다 reduce [lessen] one's weight / 힘을 빼다 weaken; enfeeble
5 〈짐짓 꾸미다〉 make an affected pose; pose for; assume airs; put on airs ♦ 점잔을 빼다 be prudish [genteel]; do the genteel
▶ 어찌된 일인지 그가 오늘은 얌전을 빼고 있다 For some reason, he is strangely well-behaved today.
6 〈회피하다〉 evade; shirk; shrink; 〈손떼다〉 draw back ♦ 빼도 박도 못하다 be in a (pretty [nice]) fix; get bogged down; be put into a helpless position / 공무니를 빼다 shirk [evade] one's responsibility / 수치스러운 생활에서 발을 빼다 quit a life of shame
▶ 그는 지하 조직에서 손을 빼고 정직하게 살기로 결심했다 He decided to wash his hands of the underground and go straight.
▶ 주가가 폭락하여 그는 빼도 박도 못하고 있다 He's in a bind because the stock market

slumped.

빼돌리다 〈물건을〉 hoard secretly; keep secret; conceal; hide; 〈사람을〉 shelter; hide sb away; give refuge to
♦ 빼돌려 둔 돈 pin money; a secret hoard
▶ 범죄자를 빼돌리는 것은 불법이다 It is against the law to hide [harbor] a criminal.

빼먹다 1 〈빠뜨리다〉 omit; leave out; pass over; miss 《out》
▶ 그것을 타자할 때 한 행을 빼먹었다 I left out [missed] one line when I was typing it.
2 〈수업을〉 cut; skip; play truant (from) ♦ 수업을 빼먹다 skip a class; miss one's lessons; cut a class; play truant from school / 수업을 2시간 빼먹다 cut two lessons [classes]
3 〈남의 것을〉 steal; pilfer 《from》; filch
♦ 돈을 빼먹다 pilfer money from

빼물다 〈입(술)을〉 pout one's mouth [lips] haughtily; 〈혀를〉 stick one's tongue out
▶ 개가 혀를 빼물었다 The dog lolled [hung] out his tongue.

빼빼[1] 〈울음소리〉 bawlingly
▶ 아기가 빼빼 운다 The baby is bawling. ⇒ The baby is crying out at the top of his voice.

빼빼[2] 〈여윈 모양〉 ♦ 빼빼 마른 사람 a man of skin and bones / 빼빼 마르다 become very thin; be reduced to a (mere) skeleton
▶ 그는 오래 앓아서 빼빼 말랐다 He has lost a lot of weight because of his long illness.

빼쏘다 〈꼭 닮다〉 be as like as two peas [eggs]; be exactly alike; resemble closely; be a replica [copy] 《of》
▶ 그 아이는 할아버지를 빼쏘았다 The boy is the very picture [the double] of his grandfather.

빼앗기다 1 〈강탈당하다〉 be robbed of sth; have sth stolen; 〈탈취·박탈당하다〉 be deprived [snatched] of sth; be dispossessed; have sth taken [snatched] away
♦ 목숨을 빼앗기다 be deprived of one's life / 자유[권리]를 빼앗기다 be deprived of one's liberty [right]
▶ 그는 어둠 속에서 돈을 빼앗겼다 He was robbed of his money in the dark.
▶ 그녀는 회원 자격을 빼앗겼다 She was deprived of membership.
▶ 그는 재산을 빼앗겼다 He was dispossessed of his estate.
▶ 그 홍수로 수백 명이 목숨을 빼앗겼다 The flood destroyed hundreds of lives.
▶ 그 비행기 추락 사고로 육십명이 목숨을 빼앗겼다 The plane crash killed [took the lives of] sixty people.
2 〈마음을〉 be absorbed [engrossed]; 〈매료당하다〉 be fascinated [charmed, captivated]
♦ 음악에 정신을 빼앗기다 be enraptured [carried away] by music
▶ 나는 그 여자의 뛰어난 연기에 정신을 빼앗겼다 I was fascinated [carried away] by her remarkable performance.

빼앗다 1 〈탈취하다〉 take (by force); snatch sth from sb; deprive [dispossess, strip] sb of sth; rob [fleece] sb of 《his money》; 〈강탈하다〉 plunder; pillage
♦ 목숨을 빼앗다 take sb's life / 무기를 빼앗다 take away a weapon (from); disarm sb of weapons / 정조를 빼앗다 rape a woman; violate the chastity of a woman / 여행자에게 돈을 빼앗다 rob a traveler of his purse
▶ 그녀가 은행을 나서자 사나이가 그녀의 핸드백을 빼앗아 달아났다 When she went out of the bank, a man snatched her handbag and ran away.
▶ 너의 시간을 빼앗지는 않겠다 I shall not take up your time.
▶ 아무도 사람의 자유를 빼앗을 수 없다 No one can deprive people of their freedom.
2 〈마음 등을〉 absorb 《one's》 attention); engross 《one's mind》; carry away; 〈매혹하다〉 fascinate; charm; captivate
♦ 관객의 넋을 빼앗다 enthrall the audience
▶ 그 멜로디는 모든 사람의 마음을 빼앗았다 The melody entranced all the people.

빼어나다 〈서술적〉 be outstanding; be prominent; distinguish oneself; cut a brilliant figure; tower (high) above the rest
♦ 빼어난 연기 an outstanding performance / 빼어난 재능 unusual [rare] ability / 빼어난 정치가 an eminent [a preeminent] statesman
▶ 그녀는 빼어난 가수다 She is by far the best singer.
▶ 그들은 모두 똑똑하지만 그녀는 그중에서도 빼어났다 They are all bright, but she stands out among them.

빽 1 〈목소리〉 eek; yipe ♦ 빽 소리치다 give [utter] a shriek [scream]
▶ 내게 빽 소리지르지 마라 Don't shout at me.
2 〈기적 등〉 toot; hoot ▶ 열차는 기적을 빽 울렸다 The train tooted its whistle.

빽빽 〈새소리〉 peep, peep; 〈신호음〉 bleep, bleep ♦ 빽빽 울다 cheep; peep; chirp; pipe
▶ 너무 아파서 나는 빽빽 소리를 질렀다 It hurts so badly I was yowling with pain.

빽빽이 close(ly); tight(ly); compactly; thickly; densely
♦ 빽빽이 들어차 있다 be closely packed; be jam-packed / 헌옷을 상자에 빽빽이 집어넣다 stuff the old clothes into a box
▶ 스탠드에는 관중이 빽빽이 차 있었다 The stands were crowded [filled solidly] with spectators.
▶ 그 근처에는 집이 빽빽이 들어서 있었다 In the neighborhood houses stood close together there.

빽빽하다 1 〈촘촘하다〉 full; dense; thick; close-packed; jam-packed; compact; crammed; tight and close
♦ 소나무가 빽빽한 산 a mountain dense with pine trees
▶ 주차장은 차들로 빽빽했다 The parking lot was jammed with cars. ⇒ The parking lot was crowded to capacity.
▶ 그의 스케줄은 아침부터 밤까지 빽빽하다 His schedule is jam-packed from morning to night. ⇒ He has a very tight schedule from morning till night.
▶ 그녀의 가방은 책으로 빽빽하다 Her bag is (tightly) packed with books.

2 〈막히다〉 (be) stopped up; (be) blocked [clogged, choked]
▶ 담뱃대가 빽빽하다 The pipe is clogged.
3 〈속이 좁다〉 narrow-minded; ungenerous

뺄셈 subtraction ━**뺄셈하다** subtract; take away 《A from B》 ━**─표** 〔數〕 the negative [minus] sign

뺑 (all) round; 〈美〉 around; in a circle ⇨ 빙
♦ 뺑 돌다 turn around; spin; circle

뺑뺑 round and round ⇨ 빙빙

뺑소니 escape; flight; bolt
♦ 뺑소니치다 run [whip] away 《from》; take (to) flight; break and run; (口) make a hit and run / 돈을 가지고 뺑소니치다 run away [make off] with money; abscond with money
▶ 도둑은 허둥지둥 뺑소니쳤다 The burglar ran away helter-skelter.
━**─사고** a hit-and-run accident ━**─차**〔운전자〕 a hit-and-run car [driver]

뺨 a cheek
♦ 불그레한 뺨 red [rosy] cheeks (▷ 양 뺨이므로 복수형으로 씀) / 뺨이 홀쭉하다 have hollow [sunken] cheeks; be hollow-cheeked / 뺨을 때리다 slap sb in the cheek; hit sb on the cheek / 뺨을 맞다 get slapped in the cheek
▶ 그는 그녀의 뺨에 키스했다 He kissed her on the cheek.

뺨치다 1 〈때리다〉 slap sb in the cheek
2 〈능가하다〉 outdo; outshine; exceed; surpass
♦ 솜씨가 전문가를 뺨치다 (almost) outdo [outshine] a professional
▶ 그는 솜씨가 전문가를 뺨칠 정도다 His ability puts a professional to shame.

뻐근하다 1 〈몸이〉 stiff; feel stiff [a stiffness]; feel a dull pain
♦ 목이 뻐근하다 have a stiff neck
♦ 요즈음 자꾸 어깨가 뻐근하다 These days I often feel stiff in the shoulders.
2 〈힘겹다〉 hard to handle; backbreaking
3 〈가슴이〉 ♦ 감격하여 가슴이 뻐근하다 My heart is full of deep emotion.

뻐기다 〈으스대다〉 act big; be bossy; be proud (of); be haughty; swagger; 〈잘난 체하다〉 put on airs; 〈호언하다〉 boast; talk big [high, tall]
♦ 뻐기는 사람 an arrogant [a haughty, an over-bearing] person / 부하들에게 뻐기다 domineer over one's inferiors; lord it over one's men / 뻐기며 걷다 swagger; strut (about, along); stalk (about); walk tall
▶ 그녀석 뻐기는 꼴은 못 봐주겠어 I cannot stand [bear] his domineering attitude [haughty manner].
▶ 그렇게 뻐기지 마라 Don't be so puffed up.

뻐꾸기 〔鳥〕 a cuckoo ━**─소리** a cuckoo's note [tune]; a cuckoo's song

뻐꾹 〈소리〉 cuckoo ▶ 뻐꾸기가 뻐꾹 하고 울었다 A cuckoo cuckooed.
━**─종**〔시계〕 a cuckoo clock

뻐끔뻐끔 1 〈틈·구멍이〉 with cracks here and there; with many cracks ♦ 총알 구멍이 뻐끔뻐끔 난 벽 a bullet-pocked wall
2 〈담배를〉 with puffs
♦ 담배를 뻐끔뻐끔 피우다 puff (up) a cigarette; puff (away) at one's pipe [cigar, cigarette]
3 〈물고기가〉 ▶ 물고기가 입을 뻐끔뻐끔하고 있다 The fish is puffing its mouth.

뻐끔하다 split open; cleft; cracked; gaping; agape ♦ 입을 뻐끔히 벌리다 gape; open one's mouth wide
▶ 길에 큰 구멍이 뻐끔하게 뚫려 있었다 A big hole had opened up in the road. = There was a gaping hole in the road.

뻐덕뻐덕하다 〈뻣뻣하다〉 hard; tough; (stark and) stiff ♦ 가죽이 뻐덕뻐덕하다 The leather is stiff.

뻐드러지다 1 〈밖으로 벌어지다〉 project; stick out; protrude
♦ 뻐드러진 projecting; protruding
2 〈뻣뻣해지다〉 stiffen; get stiff [tough]; become rigid; 〈죽다〉 die ♦ 뻐드러진 rigid; tough; stiff; stark and stiff

뻐드렁니 projecting [protruding] teeth; buck-teeth

뻐드렁이 a person with buckteeth [protruding teeth]

뻐쭉하다 sticking out; protruding; projecting; outthrust

뻑뻑 〈담배를〉 with puffs ♦ 담배를 뻑뻑 피우다 puff on one's cigarette; 〈파이프를〉 puff away at one's pipe

뻑뻑하다 thick ⇨ 빡빡하다

뻑적지근하다 feel stiff; feel heavy and painful

뻔뻔스럽다 shameless ⇨ 뻔뻔하다

뻔뻔하다 shameless; impudent; brazen-faced; cheeky; pushing
♦ 뻔뻔한 짓을 하다 do shameless things / 뻔뻔하게도 …하다 have the cheek [nerve, impudence] to (do); be shameless [impudent] enough to (do)
▶ 정말 뻔뻔한 놈이로군 What a shameless [cheeky] fellow (he is)!
▶ 그런 짓을 하다니 뻔뻔한 놈이다 What a shameless fellow he is to do that!
▶ 그는 뻔뻔하게 거짓말을 한다 He tells lies without scruple.
▶ 어디서 뻔뻔하게 그런 말이 나오냐? How could you have the face to say so?
▶ 뻔뻔하게도 어떻게 그런 요구를 다 할 수 있을까 I wonder how he has the face to make such a demand.
▶ 그는 뻔뻔하게도 우리 모임에 나타났다 He showed himself shamelessly at our meeting.

뻔질나게 〈빈번〉 very often; frequently
♦ (어떤 곳에) 뻔질나게 드나들다 frequent (a place)
▶ 한 젊은이가 그녀의 집에 뻔질나게 드나들었다 A young man often visited [paid frequent visits to] her house.

뻔하다¹ obvious; plain ⇨ 빤하다

뻔하다² 〈자칫〉 almost [nearly] (do); come near (doing); just barely escape (death)
♦ 물에 빠져 죽을 뻔하다 come near being drowned; be nearly [almost] drowned / 타 죽을 뻔한 것을 구해주다 rescue sb from the flames
▶ 나는 죽을 뻔했다 I very nearly lost my life.

⇒ I came within an inch of being killed.
► 그녀는 차에 치일 뻔했다 She narrowly escaped being run over by a car. ⇌ She was nearly [She came very close to being] knocked down by a car.

뻔히 obviously ⇨ 빤히

뻗다¹ 1 〈가지 등이〉 spread; stretch; extend
♦ 뿌리를 뻗다 put down roots; take roots; become rooted
► 나뭇가지는 해가 비치는 쪽으로 뻗는다 The tree reaches its branches toward the sun.
► 산맥이 동서로 뻗어 있다 The mountains range [run] east and west.
► 바닷가 모래밭이 멀리 뻗어 있다 A sandy beach stretches [extends] far into the distance.
2 〈발전하다〉 make progress; advance; grow; expand ♦ 해외로 뻗어 나가다 make overseas expansion
3 〈죽다〉 die; pass out
♦ 머리를 얻어맞고 뻗다 be stunned by a blow on the head / 싸늘하게 뻗어 있다 be cold and stiff

뻗다² 〈길게 내밀다〉 stick out; stretch (out); hold out
♦ 팔을 뻗다 reach (for, after); reach [stretch] out one's arm (for) (►hand로 하면 「손을 펴다」가 됨) / 팔을 쭉 뻗다 make a long arm (for) / 팔다리를 쭉 뻗다 stretch one's limbs; make oneself comfortable / 다리를 뻗고 자다 (비유) sleep carefree
► 그것은 손을 뻗으면 닿는 데에 있다 It is within (easy) reach of your hand.

뻗대다 resist; oppose; stand against; hold out against; do not give in
► 너무 그렇게 뻗대지 말게나 You shouldn't insist on having your way so stubbornly.

뻗치다 stretch ⇨ 뻗다

뻘 relationship by descent
► 그 아이는 내 조카뻘이다 He is my nephew by descent.

뻘때추니 〈제멋대로 쏘다니는 여자〉 a hoyden; a hussy; a minx; (美俗) a party girl

뻘뻘 flowingly; profusely; copiously; 〈부리나케〉 busily; (very) hard
♦ 땀을 뻘뻘 흘리며 dripping with sweat / 땀을 뻘뻘 흘리다 sweat [perspire] profusely / 뻘뻘 쏘다니다 hurry [bustle] about; run [go] around

뻣뻣하다 stiff; tough; hard ⇨ 빳빳하다
♦ 뻣뻣하게 풀먹인 시트 a stiffly starched sheet / 목이 뻣뻣하다 have a stiff neck / 뻣뻣한 태도로 나오다 take a firm [stiff] attitude (toward, against)
► 소년들은 다리가 뻣뻣해질 때까지 걸었다 The boys walked till their legs were stiff.

뻥¹ 〈거짓말〉 a lie; 〈허풍〉 big talk; brag; a tall tale [story] ♦ 뻥까다 tell a lie; blow off; (美俗) bull

뻥² 1 〈소리〉 with a pop
♦ 샴페인을 뻥 터뜨리다 pop open a champagne bottle / 뻥하고 빠지다 come [draw] with a pop
► 풍선이 뻥 터졌다 The balloon popped [burst with a pop].
► 병마개가 뻥하고 빠졌다 The cork came out plop.
2 〈구멍이〉 ♦ 뻥 뚫어지다 break open; gape

뻥뻥 1 〈소리〉 with pops; pop, pop
♦ 사방에서 샴페인이 뻥뻥 터졌다 Champagne corks were popping on all sides.
2 〈뚫린 모양〉 with (many) holes; full of holes ♦ 나는 판자에 구멍을 뻥뻥 뚫었다 I bored many holes in the board.

뼈 1 〈뼈다귀〉 a bone; 〈골격〉 a skeleton; 〔解〕 an os (pl. ossa)
♦ 갈비뼈 a rib / 생선 뼈 a fish bone / 팔 뼈 the bones of the arm / 뼈가 앙상한 bony; scraggy / 뼈 빠지게 일하다 work one's finger to the bones / 다리 뼈를 삐다 twist [sprain, wrench] one's leg / 부러진 뼈를 맞추다 set a broken bone; ♦ 〈남을 시켜서〉 have a broken bone set / 뼈에 사무치다 penetrate to the bone / 뼈와 가죽만 남다 be reduced to a (mere) skeleton [bag of bones]
► 나는 여러 해 동안 뼈빠지게 일했다 I toiled [slaved] at my work for many years.
► 내 오른팔 뼈가 부러졌다 I broke (a bone) in my right arm. ⇌ I had my right arm broken.
► 그 사고로 그는 왼팔에 뼈까지 상처를 입었다 In the accident his left arm was cut to the bone.
► 그녀는 오랜 병으로 뼈와 가죽만 남았다 She was very thin [skinny] after a long illness. ⇌ She had become all [only, just] skin and bones from a long illness.
2 〈유골〉 remains; ashes; bones
♦ 뼈를 묻다 bury [entomb] sb's ashes / 뼈를 줍다 〈화장한 후에〉 gather sb's ashes
► 나는 이 나라에 뼈를 묻을 작정이다 I wish to die in this country. ⇌ I will make this land my last home.
3 〈속 뜻〉 an implication; (a) hidden meaning
♦ 뼈있는 말 words full of hidden [latent] meaning; suggestive words
4 ⇨ 뼈대 3
5 〈요점〉 the gist; the principal point; 〈핵심〉 the core ♦ 뼈만 추려 이야기하다 give the gist [the main point] of

뼈다귀 a bone; a piece of bone ► 개는 뼈다귀 핥기를 좋아한다 Dogs likes to gnaw [suck] bones.

뼈대 1 〈골격〉 the frame; a skeleton; 〈체격〉 a physique; a build ♦ 뼈대가 튼튼한 사람 a stoutly-built [strongly-built] man
► 그는 뼈대가 튼튼하다[가냘프다] He has a solid [delicate] build [frame].
2 〈구조〉 a framework; a frame; framing; a structure ♦ 건물의 뼈대 the framework [shell] of a building
► 이 다리는 뼈대가 튼튼해서 어떤 홍수에도 무너지지 않는다 This bridge's frame is strong, so it won't break no matter what flood we have.
3 〈기개〉 spirit; grit; (a) backbone; mettle
♦ 뼈대 있는 사람 a man of spirit [mettle]; a staunch fellow / 뼈대 없는 사람 a spineless [(back)boneless] fellow; an invertebrate

▶ 그는 뼈대 있는 집안 출신이다 He is from a respected family.
뼈마디 a joint ◆뼈마디가 굵은 knotty; strong-jointed; large-boned / 온 뼈마디가 쑤시다 feel pain in all one's joints
뼈아프다 bitter; hard (to bear); heartbreaking; trying; painful
◆뼈아픈 경험 a bitter experience / 뼈아프게 번 돈 hard-earned money
▶ 그녀와 이별하는 것은 뼈아픈 일이었다 It was really heartbreaking to part with her.
▶ 그의 책망은 뼈아프게 느껴졌다 His reproof really hit home. ⇒ His reproof really touched me to the quick.
▶ 그의 신랄한 말이 뼈아프게 느껴졌다 His sharp remark stung me to the quick.
뼈오징어 〔動〕 a cuttlefish
뼈저리다 cut [go] deep into one's heart; pierce one's heart; touch the very core of one's heart
◆…이라고 뼈저리게 느끼다 keenly [acutely] realize that…; feel from the bottom of one's heart that… / 뼈저리게 후회하다 repent [regret] bitterly
▶ 나는 마침내 부모님의 사랑을 뼈저리게 느꼈다 I finally realized [It finally came home to me] how much my parents loved me.
▶ 시험에 떨어진 쓰라림은 뼈저리게 느껴졌다 The failure in the examination has sunk deep into my mind.
뼘 a span ◆폭이 세 뼘인 찬장 a cupboard three spans wide / 뼘으로 재다 span; measure sth by spans ▶ 그 물고기는 길이가 한 뼘이었다 The fish was a span long.
뼘다 measure by spans; span
▶ 뼘어 보니 그것은 두 뼘이었다 It was two spans long.
▶ 이 옷장의 길이를 뼘어 보시오 Please measure the length of this wardrobe by spans.
뽀뽀 〔兒〕 a kiss
뽐내다 be haughty; be arrogant; boast of;〈젠체하다〉give oneself airs; show off;〈자랑하다〉take pride in; pride oneself on
◆성공했다고 뽐내다 be proud of [pride oneself on] one's success / 재주를 뽐내다 show off one's talents / 지식을 뽐내다 make a show of one's knowledge / 뽐내며 걷다 swagger; strut 《about, along》; walk tall
▶ 사람이란 조금만 지위가 높아지면 뽐내게 마련이다 People are likely to throw their weight when they get a little authority.
▶ 그는 자기 기술이 한국 제일이라고 뽐내고 있다 He is boasting that his skill is (the) best in Korea.
▶ 그렇게 뽐내지 마라 Don't be so puffed up.
뽑다 1〈잡아 빼다〉draw [pull, pluck, take] out; extract; root up 《a tree》
◆손가락의 가시를 뽑다 pull [draw] a splinter out of one's finger / 닭털을 뽑다 pluck [pick] a chicken / 포도주 병마개를 뽑다 open [uncork] a bottle of wine / 벽에서 못을 뽑다 draw [pull] out a nail from the wall / 무를 뽑다 pull out the radishes / 이를 뽑다 pull out [extract] a tooth;〈치과에서〉have one's

tooth pulled out [extracted]/ (칼집에서) 칼을 뽑다 draw [unsheathe] a sword / 정원의 풀을 뽑다 weed a garden; pull weeds out of a garden / 제비를 뽑다 draw [cast] lots
▶ 의사는 상처에서 총알을 뽑아냈다 The doctor extracted [drew out, pulled out] a bullet from the wound.
2 〈선발하다〉choose; select; single [pick] out;〈선출하다〉elect
◆사람의 인품을 보고 뽑다 choose [pick] a man for his (good) personality / 지원자 5백명 중에서 뽑다 single out of 500 applicants
3 〈근절하다〉root out; exterminate; eradicate
▶ 모든 악의 뿌리를 뽑아버려야 한다 All evil(s) must be rooted out [rooted up].
4 〈모집하다〉enlist; enroll; recruit; raise
◆학생을 뽑다 enroll [admit] students / 회원을 뽑다 invite people to join (a club); issue an invitation for new membership
5 〈본전 등을〉return; recover ◆본전을 뽑다 recover [return] one's investment
▶ 이 사업은 본전도 못 뽑는다 This business doesn't pay.
6 〈발췌하다〉pick out; choose; extract
◆책의 한 구절을 뽑다 quote a passage from a book
-뽑이 a puller [pincer]; an opener
◆마개 뽑이 a corkscrew; a bottle opener / 못뽑이 a nail puller /〈노루발〉the claw of a hammer
뽑히다 1〈뽑아지다〉be taken [pulled] out; (be) come off
▶ 이 못은 잘 뽑히지 않는다 This nail won't come out.
▶ 포도주 병마개가 뽑히지 않는다 I can't uncork the wine bottle.
2 〈선발되다〉be chosen [selected]; be singled out
◆배드민턴 선수로 뽑히다 be singled [picked] out as a badminton player
▶ 그녀는 반 대표로 뽑혔다 She was elected class representative.
뽕 mulberry leaves ⇨ 뽕잎
뽕나무 a mulberry (tree)
◆—밭 a mulberry field [plantation]
뽕빠지다 go [become] bankrupt; suffer a heavy loss; be [go] broke; be brought to ruin; lose all one's money
▶ 그 여자와 그렇게 자주 교제하면 너 뽕빠져 You will go broke if you date her so often.
▶ 나는 혼인을 치르느라고 뽕빠졌다 I am broke after giving the wedding ceremony.
뽕잎 mulberry leaves
◆뽕잎을 따다 pick mulberry leaves
▶ 여름에 농민들은 뽕잎을 따서 누에에 친다 In summer the farmers pick mulberry leaves and feed them to silkworms.
뾰로통하다 pouty; sulky; sullen
◆뾰로통한 얼굴 a sullen [sulky] look / 뾰로통해서 말을 않다 maintain a sulky silence / 뾰로통해지다 be [get] sulky 《at》; become sullen; sulk; pout
▶ 그녀는 걸핏하면 뾰로통한다 She gets sulky [pouts] at the least provocation.

뿌루지 an [a skin] eruption; an abscess; a pimple; a rash ▶등에 뿌루지가 났다 I have got a boil [A boil has formed] on my back.

뽀조록이 slightly projecting [protruding, sticking out]

뽀족하다 protruding [sticking out] slightly [a little bit]

뽀족구두 high-heeled shoes; shoes with pointed toes ◆뽀족구두를 신다 wear high heels [high-heeled shoes]

뾰족뾰족 pointedly ▶죽순이 뾰족뾰족 솟아나고 있다 Bamboo shoots have come out [are shooting up] one after another.
—뾰족뾰족하다 all pointed; equally pointed

뾰족이 slightly protruding ⇨ 뽀조록이

뾰족집 a Western-style building with a steep roof [a pinnacle]; 〈천주교당〉 a Catholic church

뾰족탑 —塔 a spire; a pinnacle; a steeple

뾰족하다 pointed; sharp; peaked
◆뾰족한 끝 a sharp point [end] / 뾰족한 연필 a pencil with a sharp point / 뾰족한 코 a pointed [sharp] nose / 끝이 뾰족하다 be pointed at the end; have a sharp point / 뾰족하게 하다 sharpen; make sharp; point / 연필을 뾰족하게 깎다 sharpen a pencil
▶그 소년은 입을 뾰족하게 내밀고 대들었다 The boy protested with a pout [with his lips protruding].

뿌다구니 a projecting part [corner]
◆뿌다구니가 나다 〈화가 나다〉 take offense (at); feel vexed [annoyed]

뿌드득 with a grating sound

뿌듯하다 1〈꼭 맞다〉 tight; close
2〈벅차다〉 full of; full to the brim
◆가슴이 뿌듯하다 (*one's heart*) be full of deep emotion
▶그녀는 기쁨으로 가슴이 뿌듯했다 Her heart swelled with joy.

뿌리 1〈식물의〉 a root
◆뿌리를 깊이 뻗다 take [spread] deep root; root deep / 뿌리를 뽑다 root up; uproot; pluck [pull] up (a plant) by the roots
▶그 장미는 곧 뿌리가 났다 The roses rooted easily. = The roses took [struck] root easily.
▶이 소나무는 뿌리가 깊이 뻗었다 This pine tree is deep rooted.
2〈근원〉 the origin; the cause; the source; the foundation; genealogy
◆뿌리가 깊다 〈뿌리깊다〉 / 뿌리를 박다 ⇨ 뿌리박다 / 악의 뿌리를 뽑다 eradicate the root of evils; root up the causes of evil
▶나는 족보를 뒤져 나의 뿌리를 찾는 일이 무척 재미있다 I find great amusement in searching from what root I came, investigating my family genealogy.
▶민주주의가 그 나라에 뿌리를 내렸다 Democracy planted its roots in the country.

뿌리깊다 deep-rooted; deep-seated; ingrained; 〈고질적인〉 inveterate; incurable
◆뿌리깊은 습관 a deep-rooted [an inveterate] habit / 뿌리깊은 원한 riveted hatred
▶그 나라에 대한 그들의 반감은 뿌리깊은 것이었다 Their ill feeling against the country is deeply rooted [deep-rooted].
▶이 문제는 뿌리가 깊다 This problem has [results from] a deep cause.

뿌리다 1〈가루・물 등을〉 sprinkle ((on, with)); scatter; strew; spread; spray
◆생선에 소금을 뿌리다 sprinkle salt on fish; sprinkle fish with salt / 땅에 씨를 뿌리다 sow seed in the soil; sow the soil with seed; plant seeds; seed the soil / 빙판길에 연탄재를 뿌리다 scatter briquet ashes on [over] the icy road / 향수를 뿌리다 spray perfume
▶매일 정원에 물을 뿌리십니까? Do you water your garden every day?
▶많은 전단이 뿌려졌다 Great quantities of leaflets were distributed.
▶뿌리지 않는 씨는 싹이 나지 않는다 You cannot make an omelet without breaking eggs.
2〈비가〉 (it) sprinkle; rain in sprinkles
3〈낭비하다〉 squander ((on)); spend wastefully ((in, on)); lavish
◆뇌물을 뿌리다 pass out bribe money here and there / 돈을 뿌리다 lavish money; use [give] money freely; send money recklessly [freely]
▶그 후보자는 표를 매수하려고 많은 돈을 뿌렸다 The candidate scattered around [spend] a great deal of money to buy the votes.

뿌리박다 1〈식물이〉 take [strike] root; root
◆깊이 뿌리박은 deep-rooted; firm-rooted / 깊이 뿌리박다 strike [take] root deep ((into the soil))
▶수집 본능은 인간 본성에 깊이 뿌리박고 있다 The collecting instinct is deeply rooted in human nature.
▶그 식물은 메마른 땅에는 뿌리박지 못한다 The plant will not root in arid soil.
2〈정착하다〉 take hold ((on, upon))
◆깊이 뿌리박힌 편견 deep-rooted [deep-seated] prejudice
▶민주주의가 그 나라에 쉽게 뿌리박았다 Democracy took root easily in that country.

뿌리째 ◆뿌리째 뽑다 pull up [out] by the roots; root out; uproot; eradicate; exterminate
▶그 사건이 정부를 뿌리째 뒤흔들었다 That event shook the government to its foundations.
▶잡초는 뿌리째 뽑지 않으면 곧 다시 자라난다 When you pull out weeds, you have to pull them out by the roots or they'll grow quick back again.

뿌리치다 1〈붙잡은 것을〉 shake off; shake *oneself* loose [free] from ((sb's grasp)); free *oneself* from
◆손목을 뿌리치다 shake off *sb's* hand
▶그 소년은 어머니의 손을 뿌리치고 도망쳤다 The boy shook himself free from his mother's hand and ran off.
2〈물리치다〉 stave [ward] off; 〈퇴짜놓다〉 reject; refuse; turn down ◆유혹을 뿌리치다 thrust temptation away
▶잡념을 뿌리치고 더 열심히 공부해라 Free your mind from worldly thoughts and study harder.

▶동료의 만류를 뿌리치고 그는 회사를 그만두 었다 In spite of his colleagues' efforts to dissuade him from doing so, he quit the company.
▶그는 다른 주자들을 뿌리치고 일등을 했다 He shook off the other runners and cross the finish line first.

뿐 **1** 〈따름〉 nothing but; only; just; simply; merely
▶이젠 결과를 기다릴 뿐이다 There is nothing to do but wait for the result(s).
▶나는 그저 해야 할 일을 했을 뿐이오 I only have done what I ought to (do).
▶나는 신문을 통해 그것을 알았을 뿐이다 I just read it in the newspaper.
2 ⇨ …뿐만 아니라

-뿐 〈단지·다만〉 only; merely; solely; alone; all; nothing but
▶그는 아들이 하나뿐이다 He has only one son.
▶가진 것은 이것뿐입니다 This is all I have.
▶믿을[의논할] 사람은 너뿐이다 I have no one but you to rely upon [to turn to for advice].
▶그 일을 해낼 수 있는 사람은 너뿐이다 You alone [Nobody but you] can do it. ⇌ You are the only one who can do it.
▶하나님은 단 한 분뿐이다 There is but one God.
▶내가 제주에 있는 것도 오늘뿐이다 This is my last day in Cheju.
▶그렇게 생각하는 것은 너뿐이다 Nobody thinks so except yourself.

-뿐더러 not only [merely]...but (also) ⇨ 뿐 만아니라

뿐만아니라 not only...but (also); as well as; besides
▶나뿐만 아니라 너도 나쁘다 You as well as I are to blame.
▶그는 성마를 뿐만 아니라 남을 의심하기까지 한다 He is not only hot-tempered but also suspicious of people.
▶그는 충고뿐만 아니라 돈까지 주었다 He gave me not only some advice but also some money. ⇌ He gave me some money as well as some advice.
▶그녀는 한국뿐만 아니라 미국에서도 유명하다 She is well known not only in Korea but also in America. ⇌ She is famous both in Korea and in America.
▶신문뿐만 아니라 주간지에도 그것이 보도되었 다 It was reported not only in the newspapers but also in the weekly magazines.
▶그는 외과의사일 뿐만 아니라 유명한 작가이 기도 하다 Besides being a surgeon, he is a famous writer.
▶그것은 경제적일 뿐만 아니라 건강에도 좋다 It is not only economical but also good for the health.

뿔 **1** 〈소·양·염소 등의〉 a horn; 〈사슴의 가지 진〉 an antler
♦뿔 세공 hornwork; horn carving / 뿔이 있는 horned; cornute(d) / 뿔이 나다[돋다] grow horns / 뿔로 받다 horn; gore; butt sb with its horns
▶송아지에 뿔이 나기 시작했다 The calf has begun to grow horns.
▶그는 쇠뿔에 받쳐 죽었다 He was gored to death by a bull.
2 〈물건의〉 a projection; a pointed tip ((of))

뿔닭 〔鳥〕 a guinea fowl
뿔매 〔鳥〕 a crested eagle
뿔 뺀 쇠 상이라 〈속담〉 be in a position with no power

뿔뿔이 〈따로따로〉 separately; independently; 〈흩어져〉 scatteringly; dispersedly; in all directions
♦뿔뿔이 흩어지다[헤어지다] disperse [scatter] in all directions; be scattered; get separated ((from each other)); break up
▶그들은 뿔뿔이 도망쳤다 They fled this way and that [in all directions].
▶구경꾼들은 곧 뿔뿔이 흩어졌다 The spectators dispersed by and by.
▶그 가족은 전쟁 때문에 뿔뿔이 흩어졌다 The family got scattered [was broken up] because of the war.

뿔싸움 fighting with the horns
뿔피리 a horn; a bugle; a buglehorn
♦뿔피리를 불다 bugle; blow a horn

뿜다 〈액체를〉 spout ((out)); spurt ((out, up)); gush out; 〈증기·불 등을〉 blow off [up]; emit; 〈연기 등을〉 send out; 〈물보라를〉 spray [sprinkle] ((water)) on [over]
▶고래가 물을 뿜다 A whale blows. ⇌ A whale spouts (water).
▶호스에서 물이 뿜어나왔다 Water spouted [shot, spurted] from the hose.
▶굴뚝이 연기를 뿜고 있다 The chimney is giving off smoke.
▶차가 갑자기 불을 뿜어냈다 The car suddenly burst into flames.
▶그 화산은 지금도 연기를 많이 뿜어내고 있다 The volcano still emits a great deal of smoke.

쀼루퉁하다 sulky; sullen ⇨ 뾰로퉁하다
♦쀼루퉁한 표정을 짓다 make a sour face; look displeased

삐걱 with a creak; with a creaking sound
—**삐걱하다** creak; squeak; grate; make a creaking sound
▶대문이 삐걱하고 열렸다 The gate opened with a creak.

삐걱거리다 creak; squeak; grate; make a creaking sound
♦삐걱거리는 문[계단] a creaking door [stairway]/ 삐걱거리는 소리 a creaking [squeaking] sound; a creak; a squeak
▶걸으면 마루가 삐걱거린다 The floorboards creaks under my feet.
▶경첩이 녹슬어서 삐걱거렸다 The rusty hinges grated [creaked].

삐다[1] 〈물이〉 subside; go down; sink; drain
▶길에 괸 물이 삐고 있다 The puddles along the road are sinking [going down, subsiding].

삐다[2] 〈발목 등을〉 dislocate; sprain
♦다리를 삐다 have a strain [sprain] in a [one's] leg / 목을 삐다 wrick one's neck
▶점프한 후 그는 오른 손목을 뻔 것 같았다

삐딱거리다 After jumping he seemed to sprain his right wrist.
삐딱거리다 sway; wobble; be shaky ◆ 삐딱거리며 걷다 walk with unsteady steps; stagger
삐딱하다 slanting; sloping; leaning; skew ◆ 삐딱하게 기울어진 마루 a slanted floor / 모자를 삐딱하게 쓰다 wear *one's* hat aslant [at a slant]
삐악 with a peep [cheep] ▶ 병아리들이 닭장에서 삐악삐악 울고 있다 The chicks are peeping [chipping] in the cage.
삐죽거리다 pout *one's* lips ⇨ 비죽거리다
삐치다¹ 〈토라지다〉 become [turn, get] sullen; get sulky; be cross ◆ 삐쳐서 말도 않다 maintain a sulky silence
삐치다² 〈글자의 획을〉 draw a downward left-hand stroke (in writing)
삑 1 〈빽빽하게〉 thickly; tightly; densely; squeaking
2 〈새된 소리〉 screaming; shrieking; 〈호각소리〉 whistling; hooting
3 〈전기음〉 beep; 〈삐걱소리〉 creaking; grating; scraping
삥땅 (美俗) skimming; cutting; pocketing ◆ 수입의 일부를 삥땅하다 take [skim] off [take out of] the proceeds

사 〖樂〗 G; (이) sol ♦사음 자리표 a G clef / 올림[내림] 사음 G sharp [flat]

사 死 1 ⇨ 죽음 ♦자연사 a natural death **2** 〔野〕 out ♦2사 만루 bases loaded with two out

사 私 〈공(公)에 대한〉 privateness; privacy; 〈자기〉 self;〈사리〉 self-interest;〈비밀〉 secret; 〈정실〉 favoritism; partiality ♦사를 두다 show favoritism; play favorites / 사를 버리다 sink self; rise above *oneself*
▶ 공과 사의 구별을 분명히 해야 한다 You have to draw a sharp line between public and private affairs.

사 邪 〈악〉 evil; vice; wrong;〈부정〉 injustice; 〈이단〉 heterodoxy

사 社 〈회사〉 a company; (美) a corporation; a firm;〈사무소〉 an office ♦출판사 a publishing company / 사옥 an office building / 사보 a newsletter

사 紗 silk gauze; thin silk; gossamer

사 四 〈넷〉 four;〈네번째의〉 the fourth ♦제 사 the fourth / 사배 four times / 사분의 일 one quarter; one fourth / 사반세기 a quarter [one fourth] of a century / 사배하다 increase fourfold; quadruple

-사 -史 〈역사〉 history;〈연대기〉 the annals; chronicles ♦세계사 world history / 근세[고대]사 modern [ancient] history / 한국사 Korean history; the history of Korea

-사 -寺 〈절〉 a temple

사가 史家 a historian; a historiographer

사각 四角 a square; a rectangular; a quadrilateral; a quadrangular thing ♦사각의 square; four-cornered / 사각으로 만들다 square
■─너트〔工〕a square nut ─모자 a square college cap

사각 死角 a dead angle; dead ground [space]
▶ 그들은 적의 포화의 사각 내로 들어왔다 They came within the dead angle from the enemy fire.

사각 射角 〔砲〕an angle of fire; an elevation

사각 斜角 an oblique angle ⇨ 빗각

사각거리다 crunch; crisp; be crisp; eat crisp

사각사각 with a crunch [crunching sound]; crisply ♦당근을 사각사각 먹다 crunch a carrot / 사과를 사각사각 먹다 munch an apple

사각형 四角形 a quadrilateral; a tetragon; a quadrangle ♦사각형의 quadrilateral; tetragonal; quadrate ─정─ a regular tetragon; a square

사갈 蛇蝎 〈뱀과 전갈〉 snakes and scorpions; 〈사람〉 a malignant person
▶ 그는 그 사내를 사갈처럼 미워했다[사갈시했다] He hated the man like poison.

사감 私憾 a personal resentment [grudge, spite] ♦사감을 품다 bear [have] a private grudge (against); feel resentment at *sb*

사감 舍監 〈기숙사의〉 a dormitory inspector [superintendent, dean]; the supervisor of a dormitory; (英) a housemaster /〈여자감〉 a housemistress; a housemother

사개 1 〈상자·궤 등의〉 the tongues and grooves of dovetail joints; a dovetail
♦사개를 물리다 dovetail
2 〔建〕〈기둥의〉 pillar tenons
■─를 치다 tenoning a pillar ─물림 dovetailing; a dovetail (joint)

사갱 斜坑 〈광산의〉 an inclined shaft

사거 死去 death; decease ─사거하다 〈죽다〉 die; decease; pass away

사거리 射距離 a (shooting) range ⇨ 사정(射程)

사건 事件 〈일어난 일〉 an event; an incident; 〈사고〉 an accident;〈문제〉 a matter; an affair;〈법률상의〉 a case
▶ 그들은 그 사건을 쉬쉬했다 They hushed [covered] up the affair.
▶ 그 경찰관은 그 사건의 윤곽을 설명했다 The policeman outlined the affair.
▶ 그런 사건에 말려들고 싶지 않다 I don't want to be involved in such an affair.
▶ 그 변호사는 많은 사건을 맡고 있다 That lawyer [(英) barrister] has plenty of briefs.
▶ 독립선언의 서명은 역사상 중대 사건이었다 The signing of the Declaration of Independence was an important historical event.
■사기─ a fraud case 살인─ a murder case : 그 살인 사건은 미궁에 빠졌다 The murder case has been wrapped in mystery. 수뢰─ a bribery case 연애─ a love affair

사격 射擊 firing; shooting; fire; gunshot;〈사격술〉 marksmanship ♦사격의 명수 a skillful [good] marksman
▶ 그는 사격을 잘한다[못한다] He shoots well [ill].
▶ 사냥꾼들은 사격을 멈췄다[시작했다] The hunters ceased [opened] fire.
─사격하다 shoot; fire at *sb*; fire upon [on] 《a fortress》
▶ 그는 까마귀를 겨냥해서 사격했다 He made a shot at a crow.
■각개[일제]─ independent [volley] firing 간접─ indirect fire 실탄─ firing [target practice] with live shells [bullets] 유효─ effective fire ■─대회 a shooting match [contest]; a rifle meeting ─술 marksmanship ─신호 a shooting signal ─연습 field firing; (rifle) shooting practice; firing ─장 a firing range; 〈소총의〉 a rifle range [ground];〈옥내의〉 a shooting gallery

사격전 射擊戰 a gun battle; a fire fight

♦ 사격전을 벌이다 fight a gun battle 《with》; exchange fire [shots] 《with》

사견 私見 one's personal [individual, private] views [opinion] ♦ 나의 사견으로는 in my opinion ▶ 제 사견을 말씀드릴까요? Let me give my humble opinion.

사경 死境 a deadly situation; the brink of death; 〈궁경〉 miserable conditions; a sad plight ▶ 그는 수일간 사경을 헤맸다 He hovered between life and death for a few days.

사경제 私經濟 〈공경제에 대하여〉 private [individual] economy

사경회 査經會 [基] a Bible class

사계 四季 〈사시〉 the four seasons; 〈사계삭〉 the last month of each season

사계 射界 a field [zone] of fire

사계 斯界 this circle; this world [field] ▶ 그는 사계의 권위자다 He is an authority on the subject. ⇒ He is an expert in the line.

사고 社告 an announcement [a notice] of a company

사고 事故 1〈사건〉 an accident; an incident; a mischance; a mishap; 〈고장〉 a hindrance; a hitch; trouble ▶ 사고란 나게 마련이다 Accidents will happen. ▶ 사고가 나서 많은 사람이 사망했다 An accident happened and many lives were lost. ▶ 그 비행기 사고로 30명이 죽었다 Thirty people were killed in an airplane accident. ▶ 그가 자동차 사고를 냈게 분명하다 He must have caused a car accident. ▶ 아무 사고 없이 모든 게 끝났다 Everything went [passed] off without a hitch [hindrance]. ▶ 그의 부주의가 사고의 원인이었다 His carelessness caused [brought about] the accident. 2〈사정〉 circumstances; reasons ▶ 부득이한 사고로 결석하였다 Unavoidable circumstances prevented me from attending. ■ 교통[열차]— a traffic [railway] accident 철도건널목— an accident at a railroad crossing ■ —방지 운동 a "Safety First" movement; a movement for accident prevention —빈발지점 a high-accident-frequency location [spot] —사 an accidental death

사고 思考 thought; thinking —사고하다 think ■ —과정[작용] thought process; process of thinking —력 thinking faculty [power]; the power of thought : 독서는 사고력을 키우는데 도움이 된다 Reading is helpful in developing our thinking ability. —방식 one's way of thinking

사고무친하다 四顧無親— 〈외톨이다〉 be orphaned and friendless; have not a relative or a friend to turn to

사공 沙工 a boatman; a waterman; 〈나룻배의〉 a ferryman

사공이 많으면 배가 산으로 간다 (속담) Too many cooks spoil the broth. ⇒ A pot that belongs to many is ill stirred and worse boiled.

사과 沙果 an apple ♦ 풋사과 a green apple / 새빨간[신, 시든] 사과 a redcheeked [sour, withered] apple / 사과씨 the core of an apple / 사과를 깎다 pare an apple ▶ 이 사과는 속이 썩었다 This apple is rotten at the core. ■ —나무 an apple tree —산〔化〕 malic acid —주 apple wine; (sweet) cider

사과 謝過 an apology 《for》 ♦ 사과의 편지 a letter of apology; a written apology / 사과를 받아들이다 accept an apology ▶ 무어라 사과를 드려야 할지 모르겠습니다 I do not know what excuse to offer. ⇒ I have no words to apologize to you. ▶ 거듭 사과 드립니다 I ask you a thousand pardons [apologies]. —사과하다 apologize 《to sb for a mistake》; make an apology 《for》; beg [ask] pardon 《of sb》; ask [beg] sb's pardon; express regret 《for》 ▶ 그는 선생님께 지각한 것을 사과했다 He apologized to his teacher for coming to school late. ▶ 그녀는 아들의 못된 행동에 대해 사과했다 She apologized [made an apology] for her son's behavior. ▶ 사과해야 할 사람은 자네가 아니라 날세 It is not you but I that have to apologize.

사관 士官 an officer —육군[해군]— a military [naval] officer —생도 a cadet (officer); —육군— a military cadet; —공군— an aviation cadet; —해군— a midshipman —학교 a military academy

사관 史觀 a historical view; a view [concept] of history —유물— the materialistic view of history

사광 砂鑛 a placer ■ —권 a placer mining right —업 placer mining

사교 邪敎 a heretical [perverse] religion; heresy; paganism; heathenism ■ —도 a heretic; a pagan; a heathen; an infidel

사교 社交 social intercourse [contact]; society; social life ♦ 사교상의 의무[예의] social duties [etiquette] / 사교 모임 a social gathering [meeting, party] ▶ 그분하고는 사교상 아는 사이인가요? Are you acquainted with him socially? ■ —가 a sociable person; (美口) a good mixer —단체 a social group [organization] —댄스 a social dance; social [ballroom] dancing —술 the art of social intercourse —클럽 a social club

사교계 社交界 society; society circles ♦ 사교계의 사람들 society people; (美) club people / 사교계의 명사 a figure in society / 사교계의 여왕 a society beauty; a belle [queen] of society

사교성 社交性 sociality; sociability; a social nature ♦ 사교성이 있다 be sociable; (美口) be a good mixer / 사교성이 없다 be unsociable; (美口) be a bad mixer

사교적 社交的 social; sociable ♦ 사교적인 모임 a social function / 사교적인 사람 a sociable person; (美口) a good mixer ▶ 그의 아내는 사교적인 사람이다 His wife is

사과의 표현

1. 「실례합니다」「실례지만」

▶ (남과 어깨를 부딪쳤을 때 등) 미안합니다 Excuse me. ⇌ Sorry. ⇌ Pardon me.
▶ (남에게 말을 걸 때 등) 실례지만 Excuse me, but...
▶ (중간에 자리를 뜨거나 남의 앞을 가로지를 때 등) 잠깐 실례합니다 Excuse me (for a moment).
▶ (반문할 때) 미안하지만, 뭐라고 하셨습니까? Pardon me, but what did you say? (▶ I beg your pardon?, Pardon me?도 쓸 수가 있는데 모두 끝을 올려서 발음한다. 내리면 「미안합니다」란 뜻이 된다)
▶ 말씀중에 죄송합니다만 김선생께 전화 왔습니다 Sorry to interrupt you, but there's a (phone) call for you, Mr. Kim.
▶ 저, 미안합니다만, 교무실이 어디지요? Er... Excuse me, but could you tell me where the teachers' room is?
▶ 미안합니다, 저 가방을 보여주시겠습니까? Excuse me, but will you show me that bag?

2. 「용서하십시오」「죄송합니다」

▶ 용서하십시오[미안합니다] I'm sorry! ⇌ I beg your pardon.
▶ 정말 미안합니다[정말로 할 말이 없습니다] I'm very [awfully] sorry.
▶ 참으로 죄송합니다만, 오늘밤에 찾아 뵐 수가 없습니다 I'm terribly sorry, but I cannot come tonight.
▶ 늦어서 죄송합니다 I'm sorry to be late. ⇌ Sorry I'm a bit late.
▶ 방해를 해서 죄송합니다 I'm sorry to disturb you.
▶ 귀찮게 해서 죄송합니다 I'm sorry to trouble you.
▶ 기다리시게 해서 미안합니다 I'm sorry to have kept you waiting.
▶ 죄송합니다. 그것은 지금 재고가 없습니다 Sorry. We are out of stock in those right now.

3. 「…을 사과드립니다」

▶ 나의 부주의를 사과드립니다 Please excuse (me for) my carelessness.
▶ 함부로 편지를 읽은 것을 사죄드립니다 I must apologize (to you) for having read the letter without your permission.
▶ 삼가 사과드립니다 Please accept my sincere apology.
▶ 당신한테 많은 폐를 끼쳐드린 것을 사과드립니다 I am awfully sorry for causing you so much trouble.
▶ 만일 제 말이 마음을 상하게 해드렸다면 사과드립니다 I apologize if I said something that offended you.
▶ 나의 경솔한 발언을 대단히 유감스럽게 생각합니다 I deeply regret my careless remark.
▶ 會話「아, 죄송합니다」「괜찮아요」 "Oh, sorry." "That's all right."
▶ 會話「아, 저런, 다치지 않았습니까?」「아니오, 아무렇지도 않습니다」 "Oh, no! Did I hurt you?" "No, I'm okay."
▶ 會話「방해해서 미안합니다」「아니오, 마침 일을 끝낸 참입니다. 무슨 일이십니까?」 "Sorry to disturb you." "That's all right. I've just finished my work. What can I do for you?"
▶ 會話「여기서 캐치볼을 해서는 안 된다고 몇 번이나 말해야 알겠습니까?」「죄송합니다. 이제 다시는 하지 않을테니 용서해 주십시오」 "How many times do I have to tell you not to play catch here?" "Sorry. Please forgive us. We won't do it anymore."
▶ 會話「아이, 깜짝이야」「아, 대단히 죄송합니다. 여기엔 아무도 없는줄 알고」 "Oh, you scared me." "Oh, I'm terribly sorry. I didn't think there was anyone in here."
▶ 會話「그런 소리를 네게 할 생각은 없었는데」「염려 마, 흔히 있는 일이야」 "I don't mean to say such a thing to you." "Don't worry. That sort of thing happens all the time."
▶ 會話「당신의 충고를 무시하다니 제가 정말 어리석었어요. 대단히 죄송합니다」「사과할 것 없어요. 다시는 같은 실수를 하지 않도록 해요」 "It was really stupid of me to ignore your advice. I'm awfully sorry." "No need for an apology. Just don't make the same mistake again."
▶ 會話「일부러 대구에서 오시게 해서 미안합니다」「천만에요. 언젠가 한번 강릉에 와보고 싶었어요」 "Thank you for coming all the way from Taegu." "Don't mention it. I have wanted to come to Kangnŭng for a long time." (▶ 이 경우의 「미안합니다」는 감사의 뜻. "I'm sorry."가 사죄하는 「미안합니다」 또는 「유감입니다」의 뜻)

---

a social person.

사구 四球 〔野〕 a base on balls
사구 砂丘 a (sand) dune; a sand hill
■ ―림(林) a forest on a sand dune
사구체 絲球體 〔解〕 a glomerulus (*pl*. -li)
사군자 士君子 a gentleman
사군자 四君子 〔美術〕 the Four Gracious Plants (▶ plum, orchid, chrysanthemum and bamboo); the four gentlemanly plants
사권 私權 〔法〕 a private right
사귀다 〈사교로서〉 go [hang] around; go about 《with》; associate 《with》; mix 《with》; 〈남녀간에〉 go 《with》; go steady 《with》; keep company 《with》; keep (him) company
▶ 그는 사귀기 쉽다[어렵다] He's easy [difficult] to get along with.
▶ 그는 이웃과 잘 사귄다 He gets along well with his neighbors.
▶ 그는 친구를 빨리 사귄다 He is quick to make friends.

▶ 그 녀석하고는 사귀지 마라 You should not keep company with that man.
▶ 그는 사귀면 사귈수록 좋은 사람이다 The more I am with him, the more I find out how good a person he is.
▶ 그는 동료들과 대등하게 사귀어왔다 He was on equal terms with his associates.

사귐성 —性 sociability; sociableness; sociality; good-fellowship ♦ 사귐성이 있는[없는] 사람 a sociable [an unsociable] person; (美) a good [bad] mixer

사규 社規 the company regulations
▶ 그는 사규를 어겨서 해고되었다 He was dismissed for breaking the company regulations.
▶ 그는 사규를 지키지 않아서 감봉처분당했다 He had his pay cut because of his disregard of the company regulations.

사그라뜨리다 make *sth* subside; let *sth* wither; make *sth* rust away; resolve

사그라지다 go down; subside; recede; wither; 〈썩어서〉 rot away; 〈녹슬어서〉 rust away; 〈녹아서〉 melt away; 〈종기가〉 resolve
♦ 불이 사그라지다 burn low; sink / 기운이 사그라지다 lose *one's* spirit; get down in the dumps

사극 史劇 a historical play [drama]

사근사근하다 1 〈성품이〉 affable; amiable; agreeable; pleasant; pleasing
♦ 사근사근한 여자 an affable woman / 사근사근히 amiably; affably; with affability; winningly; pleasantly
2 〈입에〉 crisp to the teeth; fresh
▶ 이 사과는 사근사근하다 This apple munches [eats] crisp.

사글세 —貰 monthly rent [rental]
▶ 우리는 집에 5만원의 사글세를 내고 있다 We pay fifty thousand won for the house every month.
▶ 집주인은 사글세를 2만원 올렸다 The landlord has just raised my rent by twenty thousand won a month.
━방 a rented room 사글셋집 a rented house

사금 砂金 gold dust; alluvial [placer] gold
♦ 사금을 채취하다 〈모래를 일어서〉 wash for gold; 〈냄비로 선광하여〉 pan gold
━채취 alluvial [placer] mining ━채취권 a placer mining right ━채취선 a placer (gold) mining boat

사금융 私金融 private loaning [financing, banking]

사금파리 a potsherd; a crock; a broken piece of earthenware

사기 士氣 morale; fighting spirit
♦ 사기 왕성하다 have high morale; be full of fighting spirit / 사기가 죽다[꺾이다] be [become] demoralized / 사기에 영향을 미치다 affect the morale / 사기를 북돋우다 raise the morale

사기 史記 〈역사책〉 a history (book); annals; a chronicle

사기 沙器 〈사기 그릇〉 porcelain; china; earthenware; pottery ■━류 chinaware; earthenware ━접시 a porcelain [china] dish

사기 詐欺 (a) fraud; a swindle; swindling; a trick; (an) imposture
♦ 사기를 치다 commit a fraud / 사기로 돈을 빼앗다 cheat [swindle] *sb* out of money; defraud *sb* of his money
━사기하다 practice a deception 《on *sb*》; swindle; commit a fraud (on); defraud; shark
▶ 그녀는 쉽사리 사기당했다 She was easily swindled.
▶ 그는 그녀의 돈을 사기한 용의를 받고 있다 He has allegedly swindled [cheated] her out of her money.
■결혼━ a marriage fraud 법정━ a legal fraud ■━광고 fraudulent advertising ━꾼 an imposter; a sharper; a swindler; a cheat; a shark; (口) a fraud: 종교를 빙자한 사기꾼 a pious fraud ━행위 (an) imposture; fraudulent practices

사기 社旗 the flag of a company; (海) a house flag (▶배에 닮)

사기업 私企業 〈개인 기업〉 a private enterprise

사나나달 three or four days; four or five days; three [four] days or so; the better part of a week

사나이 〈남자〉 a male; a man; 〈남성〉 the male [sterner, stronger] sex; 〈남자다움〉 manhood; manliness
♦ 사나이 중의 사나이 a man among men / 사나이다운 행동 a manly act / 사나이다운 manly; manlike; manful; masculine / 사나이답게 manfully; like a man; in a manly manner
▶ 사나이답게 굴어라 Be a man! ⇒ Play the man! ⇒ Act like a man!

사날 three or four days; several [a few] days; three days or so

사납다 〈짐승이〉 fierce 《animal》; 〈바다·파도 등이〉 rough [heavy] 《sea》; rude; wild 《waves》; 〈표독한〉 harsh; violent; outrageous; ferocious; 〈운수가〉 unlucky
♦ 사나운 사람 a violent-tempered person / 사나운 짐승 a fierce beast / 사나운 사자 a fierce lion / 사나운 바다 stormy seas; rough seas; a troubled sea; a high sea / 사납게 fiercely; roughly; violently; wildly; harshly / (바람이) 사납게 불다 blow furiously / 운수가 사납다 be unlucky; have bad [ill] luck / 인심이 사납다 be ungenerous [unkind]; be tightfisted [stingy]

사낭 砂囊 1 〈모래주머니〉 a sandbag; 〔軍〕 an earth bag 2 〔鳥〕 a gizzard; the muscular stomach

사내 1 ⇨ 사나이 ♦ 사내 대장부 a man; 〈위인〉 a great man
2 〈남편〉 a husband; *one's* man; 〈정부〉 a lover 3 ⇨ 사내아이

사내 社內 ♦ 사내에서 in *one's* [the] office
▶ 그것은 사내에서는 공공연한 비밀이다 It's an open secret in the office.

사내아이 a boy; a male child; a boy baby
♦ 사내아이가 태어나다 〈부모가 주어〉 become the father [mother] of a boy

사냥 hunting; shooting; a hunt; a chase
▶ 늑대는 떼를 지어 먹이 사냥을 한다 Wolves hunt in packs.

▶오늘 사냥은 어땠습니까? How was the game today?
▶4월부터 10월까지는 사냥이 금지되어 있다 Hunting is not allowed between April and October. ⇌ Game is preserved from April to October.
―사냥하다 hunt; have a hunt; shoot
♦맹수를 사냥하다 hunt big game / 여우를 사냥하다 hunt the fox / 사냥하러 가다 go hunting [shooting]
■―감 a game; a quarry; a bag; spoils of a chase ―꾼 a hunter; a huntsman ―철 the hunting [shooting] season; an open season ―총 a hunting [sporting] gun; a shotgun ―터 a hunting ground [field]

사냥개 a hound, a hunting dog; a gundog; a bird dog ♦사냥개를 풀어 놓다 slip [let loose] a hound ―자리〔天〕the Hunting Dogs; Canes Venatici

사념 邪念 an evil [a wicked] thought; a vicious [an evil] mind ♦사념을 털어버리다 free *oneself* of evil thoughts
▶그녀에게는 사념이 없다 She has no depraved thoughts. ⇌ Her heart is free of evil.
▶사념을 버려야 해 You must free yourself of evil [get rid of wicked] thoughts.

사농공상 士農工商 the scholarly, agricultural, industrial, and mercantile classes; the classes of scholars, farmers, artisans and tradesmen

사다 1〈구매하다〉buy; purchase ♦현금〔외상〕으로 사다 buy *sth* for cash [on credit]
▶나는 이 시계를 30,000원에 샀다 I bought this watch for 30,000 won.
▶그는 그 차를 싸게〔비싸게〕샀다 He bought the car cheap [at a high price].
▶행복은 돈으로 살 수 없다 Money cannot buy happiness.
2〈고용하다〉engage; employ;〈팔다〉sell; dispose of
♦사람을 사다 engage [hire] a person / 쌀을 사다 sell rice
3〈초래하다〉incur; invite; cause
▶나는 그녀의 환심을 사는 데 성공했다 I have contrived to gain [win] her favor.
▶남의 원한 살 짓을 한 기억이 없다 I don't remember giving anyone cause to hate me.
▶남의 노여움을 살 짓은 하지 않는 게 좋다 It is advisable [wise] not to incur anyone's anger.
▶그녀는 무단 결근해서 상사의 노여움을 샀다 Her being absent without permission offended her boss.
4〈인정하다〉set [put]《much, a high》value on [upon]; have a good [high] opinion of *sb*; think highly of *sb*; give *sb* credit for

사다리 a ladder ⇨ 사닥다리 ■―꼴〔數〕《美》a trapezoid;《英》a trapezium

사다새〔鳥〕a pelican

사닥다리 a ladder ♦사닥다리를 올라가다 climb [go up] a ladder / 사닥다리를 내려가다 climb backward down the ladder
■비상― an emergency ladder;〈화재용〉a fire ladder 줄― a rope ladder ■―차〈소방용〉a ladder truck; an aerial ladder truck

사단 事端〈사건의 발단〉the origin [cause] of an affair; the beginning ♦사단을 일으키다 stir up troubles; give rise to complications

사단 師團 a division; an army division
♦사단을 편성하다 organize a division
■기갑― an armored division ―사령부 the division(al) headquarters (略 D.H.Q.) ―장 a division(al) commander

사단법인 社團法人 a corporation; an incorporated body;〔法〕a corporate juridical person

사담 私談 a private conversation;〈비밀의〉a confidential [private] talk ♦사담을 엿듣다 overhear a private talk
―사담하다 talk privately [in private]《with》;〈비밀 얘기를 하다〉have a private [confidential] talk《with》

사당 私黨 a private political association; a private party; a faction

사당 祠堂〈집안의〉an ancestral shrine [tablet hall];〈일반적인〉a shrine; a sanctuary
♦사당에 모시다 enshrine; dedicate a shrine to *sb*

사대 事大 ♦사대적(인) truckling [trusting] to a stronger power ―사대하다〈대국·강자를 섬기다〉submit to the stronger; worship [serve] the powerful; become a toady [flunk(e)y]
■―근성 slavish submission to power

사대부 士大夫（총칭）the gentry;〈고관〉a high official;〈명문가〉a man of high birth

사대사상 事大思想 ▶그들은 사대사상에 사로잡혀 있다 They admire the powerful.

사대주의 事大主義 worship of the powerful; flunkeyism; toadyism ―자 a flunk(e)y; a timeserver

사도 私道 a private road [path]

사도 邪道 1〈못된 길〉an evil course [way]; a wrong course; vice
♦사도로 이끌다 mislead; lead *sb* astray; make *sb* stray from the right path / 사도에 빠지다 be led astray; go astray [wrong]; stray from the right path
2〈사설(邪說)〉a heretical doctrine [teaching]; heresy;〈이단〉heterodoxy

사도 使徒 an apostle ■십이― the Twelve Apostles ■―신경 the Apostles' Creed ―행전〔聖〕The Acts (of the Apostles)

사도 師道 the duty of a teacher; teachers' code

사돈 査頓 a relative [relation] by marriage; a member of the family of *one's* daughter-[son-]in-law;《口》in-laws
♦사돈의 팔촌 a cousin forty times removed; a remote [distant] relative / 사돈간이 되다 get related by marriage《to》
▶사돈과 짐바리는 골아야 좋다（속담）Like blood, like good, and like age, make the happiest marriage.
■―댁〈사람〉the wife of an in-law;〈집〉⇨ 사돈(~집) ―집 the house [family] of *one's* in-laws

사동 使童 an errand [office] boy; a page (boy); a messenger (boy)

사되다 私―〈사사롭다〉selfish; self-interested; partial ♦사되게 쓰다 use *sth* for private pur-

사두마차 四頭馬車 a carriage [coach] and four; a four-horse coach

사들이다 stock; purchase; buy (in); procure; lay in; take in; get in a store of goods
♦많이 사들이다 make a large purchase of 《books》/ 여름 용품들을 사들이다 stock summer goods

사디즘 sadism

사또 a lord; 〈호칭〉 my lord

사또 떠난 뒤에 나팔 분다 〈속담〉 a day after the fair; a day too late for the fair

사뜨기 hole darning ♦구멍난 양말을 사뜨기하다 darn a hole in a sock

사뜨다 〈가장자리를〉 hemstitch; 〈터진 데를〉 sew (up); darn; whip

사라사 [〈포〉 saraça] printed cotton; chintz; (美) calico; (英) print

사라센 ♦사라센(사람)의 Saracen; Saracenic ■―사람 a Saracen

사라지다 〈모습을 감추다〉 vanish; disappear; be gone; 〈증발하다〉 evaporate; fade (away); die away [off, out]; 〈시야에서〉 go out of sight
▶그 서류는 어디로 사라졌니? Where has the document gone?
▶통증이 사라졌다 The pain has gone.
▶구름이 사라지고 해가 다시 빛났다 The clouds broke and the sun shone again.
▶승리의 가능성은 완전히 사라졌다 All hope of winning the game vanished. ⇌ There is no hope of our winning the game.

사람 1 〈인류〉 man; mankind; human beings; the human race; 〈개인〉 a man; a person; an individual; one
♦서울 사람 a Seoulite; (총칭) the people of Seoul
▶사람은 죽게 마련이다 Man is mortal. ⇌ All men must die.
▶젊은 사람들은 원기 왕성하다 Young people are full of vitality.
▶사람의 운명은 알 수 없는 것이다 No one can foretell his or her destiny.
▶사람은 저마다 장점이 있는 법이다 Every man has his own merits.
▶사람은 만물의 영장이다 Man is lord of the creation.
▶너 그 사람 아니? Do you know him [her] that man [woman]?
▶그는 정직한 사람이다 He is an honest man.
▶그는 인천 사람이다 He is [comes, hails] from Inch'ŏn.
2 〈인격·성격·성질·사람됨〉 character; personality; nature; disposition; 〈참된 인간〉 a true man
▶그는 사람 보는 눈이 있다[없다] He is a good [a poor, no] judge of character.
▶그는 어떤 사람입니까? What sort [kind] of man is he?
▶그는 요즈음에 보기 드문 사람이다 He is a kind of man not to be met with these days.
3 〈인재〉 a man of talent; an able [a capable, a fine] man; (총칭) talent; 〈적임자〉 the right man
▶우리 정계에는 사람이 없다 Our political world is suffering from a dearth of talent.
4 〈남·세인〉 another; other people; others
▶그는 사람 다룰 줄 안다 He has an gift of making people at home. ⇌ He knows how to deal with people.
▶사람들이 뭐라고 할까? What will people say?
▶사람들의 입은 막을 수 없다 People will talk.
5 〈손님〉 a visitor; a guest; a caller; (口) company
▶지금 사람이 와 있습니다 We have company [a visitor] now.
▶우리 집에는 좀처럼 사람이 안 온다 We seldom have visitors.
6 〈나〉 I ▶사람 깔보지 마라 Don't look down on me.
7 〈아내〉 one's wife ♦우리 집 사람 my wife
8 〈셀 때〉 one; a person; 〈복수〉 persons; those (who…) ▶3사람이 합격했는데 나도 그 중의 한 사람이었다 Three passed the examination, myself among the number.
9 〈막연히〉 ♦의사를 부르러 사람을 보내다 send for the doctor
▶9시에 사람을 만날 약속이 있다 I have an appointment [engagement] at nine. ⇌ I must meet someone at nine.

사람구실 ▶그는 사람구실을 못한다 He is not worth his salt. ⇌ He doesn't pull his weight.
―**사람구실하다** behave [act] as man should; live up to one's role [name]; do a proper job of it; do everything one can expect

사람답다 worthy of the name of man; decent; modest; human; humane
♦사람다운 사람 a true [decent] man; a man of decent character / 사람답게 행동하다 behave like a man

사람됨 〈성질〉 (a) personal character; (a) personality; 〈타고난 성품〉 one's nature [disposition]
♦홍선생의 사람됨 Mr. Hong the man
▶우리 학장님은 사람됨이 훌륭하다 Our president is a man of noble [good] character.
▶이 사실은 그의 사람됨을 나타낸다 This fact is characteristic of him. ⇌ This fact shows what he is (like).

사람 살 곳은 골골이 있다 〈속담〉 Every bird likes its nest best.

사람 위에 사람 없고 사람 밑에 사람 없다 〈속담〉 All men are equal under the sun.

사람은 겪어봐야 알고 말은 타봐야 안다 〈속담〉 The proof of the pudding is in the eating.

사랑 1 love (for *sb*, of *sth*); 〈애정〉 affection; fondness; 〈애착〉 attachment (to, for); tender passion; 〈기독교적인〉 charity

> 解說 ***love***는 부모·자식·친구·이성·하느님·사물에 대한 사랑 등에 널리 쓰임. ***affection***은 사람에 대한 지속적이며 차분한 사랑. ***attachment***는 사람·물건·주의 등에 대한 애착.

♦부모[형제, 부부]의 사랑 parental [fraternal, conjugal] love / 친구의 사랑 friendly

affection / 하느님의 사랑 divine love / 사랑없는 결혼 a loveless marriage / 사랑의 속삭임 whispers [the cooing] of love / 사랑의 보금자리를 꾸미다 build a love nest; make a lovers' sweet home / 사랑에 눈이 멀다 be blind with love / 사랑에 빠지다 fall in love 《with》 / 사랑을 고백하다 declare [confess] one's love 《to》 / 사랑을 받아들이다 accept sb's love / 사랑을 속삭이다 whisper sweet nothings 《in a girl's ear》 / 사랑을 잃다 lose sb's love / 사랑을 차지하다 win sb's affection; gain sb's heart; earn sb's love
▶ 사랑이란 맹목적인 것 (속담) Love is blind.
▶ 사랑은 수단을 가리지 않는다 All is fair in love.
▶ 사랑에는 국경도 없다 (속담) Love laughs at distance.
▶ 사랑은 가정에서부터 시작된다 Charity begins at home.
2 〈애인〉 one's sweetheart; one's beloved; one's darling; one's lover (남자); one's love (여자)

사랑 舍廊 a guest room for men; the male quarters ■—양반 your husband; the husband —채 the men's part of a house

사랑니 a wisdom tooth ♦ 사랑니가 나다 cut one's wisdom teeth

사랑스럽다 sweet; pretty; lovable; lovely; affable; amiable; charming; attractive
♦ 사랑스러운 여자 a lovely girl

사랑싸움 a lovers' quarrel; a love [matrimonial] quarrel

사랑하다 love; care for; be fond of; like; be attached to; have affection for; have a tender feeling 《toward》
♦ 사랑하는 자녀 one's beloved child / 사랑하는 사람 one's love; one's darling; one's dear one / 사랑하는 아내 one's dear wife / 음악을 사랑하다 love music; like [be fond of] music / 사랑하는 사이가 되다 fall in love with; love each other
▶ 그는 아내를 무척 사랑한다 He loves his wife tenderly [dearly].
▶ 이웃 사랑하기를 네 몸과 같이 하라 〔聖〕 Thou shalt love thy neighbor as thyself.

사례 ♦ 사레 들리다 swallow the wrong way; get sth caught in one's windpipe

사려 思慮 thought; consideration; prudence; discretion; (good) sense
♦ 사려깊은 사람 a prudent man; a man of discretion [good sense] / 사려깊은 thoughtful; prudent; discreet; sensible / 사려없는 thoughtless; indiscreet; imprudent

사력 死力 ♦ 사력을 다하여 desperately; with all the force at command / 사력을 다하다 make frantic [desperate] efforts 《to do》
▶ 그들은 사력을 다하여 싸웠다 They fought a desperate fight. ⇌ They fought to the death.

사련 邪戀 illicit love ♦ 사련을 하다 love someone who belongs to another; fall in love with a married woman [man]

사령 司令 〈통솔〉 command; control; 〈사람〉 a commandant; a commander ■—탑 〈비행장의〉 a control tower; 〈배의〉 a pilothouse; 〈군함의〉 a conning tower

사령 辭令 〈관직의〉 a government order; an official announcement of appointment; 〈장교 임관의〉 a commission
♦ 사령을 내리다 issue a government order / 사령을 받다 receive an official announcement of appointment
■ 외교— diplomatic language; honeyed words 임명[면직]—장(狀) a written appointment; a warrant [writ, letter] of appointment

사령관 司令官 a commander; a commandant; an officer in command; a commanding officer (略 C.O.)

사령부 司令部 the headquarters (略 HQ, H.Q.) ■ 전투— a command post 총— the General Headquarters (略 GHQ, G.H.Q.)

사례 事例 an example; an instance; a case; 〈선례〉 a precedent ■ 연구— a case study

사례 謝禮 〈감사〉 thanks; gratitude; 〈보수〉 a recompense; a reward
♦ 사례(를) 받다 receive [accept, be given] a reward; be rewarded
▶ 그는 자기의 봉사에 대해 어떠한 사례도 기대하지 않는다 He does not expect any reward for his services.
▶ 가이드는 지나친 사례를 요구했다 The guide asked an excessive fee.
▶ 그는 하루의 수고에 대하여 5만원의 사례를 요구했다 He demanded a fee of fifty thousand won for a day's work.
—**사례하다** reward; remunerate; recompense 《sb for his trouble》; give a reward 《for sb's efforts》; pay a fee to sb; fee 《sb for his service》
♦ 듬뿍 사례하다 reward sb generously
▶ 우리는 잃어버린 개를 데려다 주느라고 애쓴 사람에게 사례했다 We recompensed the man for his trouble in bringing [fetching] back our lost dog.
■—금 a reward; a fee; a recompense; a remuneration

사로얀 〈미국의 작가〉 Saroyan, William (1908-81)

사로잡다 〈생포하다〉 catch [take, capture] alive; capture sb; take [make, lead] sb prisoner [captive]; 〈매혹하다〉 captivate; charm; enthrall ♦ 범을 사로잡다 capture a tiger alive
▶ 그의 부드러운 태도가 그녀의 마음을 사로잡았다 His pleasant manner charmed [attracted] her.

사로잡히다 **1** 〈붙잡히다〉 be caught [taken] alive; be captured; be taken prisoner; 〈비유〉 be seized [struck] with; 〈매혹되다〉 be charmed; be enslaved by; be captivated by
♦ 적군에게 사로잡히다 be captured (alive) by the enemy / 망상에 사로잡히다 be possessed by delusions / 여자의 미모에 사로잡히다 be enslaved by a woman's beauty
▶ 그는 갑자기 공포에 사로잡혔다 He was suddenly struck with terror.
▶ 그 사람은 명예심에 사로잡혀 있다 That man is urged by a desire for fame.

사뢰다

2 〈얽매이다〉 be a slave to [stick to] 《a habit, custom》; be shackled by 《convention》

사뢰다 tell; state; relate; inform; report

사료 史料 historical materials; a historic document
■ —편찬 historiography —편찬관[위원] a historiographer; an official historian

사료 飼料 feed; fodder; forage ◆ 건초를 사료로 주다 feed [fodder] 《a horse》 with hay ▶ 닭의 사료는 무엇입니까? What do you feed the chickens? ■ 배합— assorted [mixed] feed

사료하다 思料 think; consider; regard 《as》

사륙배판 四六倍判 〔印〕 a large [royal] octavo

사륙판 四六判 〔印〕 twelvemo; duodecimo

사륜 四輪 ◆ 사륜의 four-wheel(ed) ■ —구동차 a car with four-wheel drive; a four-wheel-drive car —마차 a four-wheel(ed) carriage —차 a four-wheel(ed) vehicle; a four-wheeler

사르다[1] **1** 〈태워 없애다〉 burn (up, away); throw into the fire
◆ 편지를 불에 사르다 throw a letter into the fire
2 〈불을빛다〉 light [make, kindle, build (up)] a fire; make a fire burn
◆ 벽난로에 불을 사르다 make a fire in the fireplace

사르다[2] 〈키질하다〉 winnow

사르르 lightly; gently; softly ◆ 입안에서 사르르 녹다 《candies》 melt easily in the mouth

사르트르 〈프랑스의 실존주의 철학자〉 Sartre, Jean-Paul (1905-1980)

사리[1] the flood [spring] tide ⇨ 한사리

사리[2] 〈새끼 등의 뭉치·세는 단위〉 a coil ◆ 새끼[국수] 한 사리 a coil of rope [noodles]

사리 〈인도의 민족복〉 a sari [saree]

사리 私利 personal profit [gain]; self-interest; *one's* own interests ◆ 사리를 꾀하다 seek personal profit ■ —사욕 self-interest and selfish desire

사리 舍利 〈불사리〉 Buddha's [a Buddhist saint's] bones; relics of Buddha [a Buddhist saint]; 〈경전〉 Buddhist scriptures; the Sutras; 〈사리골〉 ashes
■ —탑 a stupa

사리 事理 〈도리〉 reason; 〈사실〉 facts; 〈적부〉 propriety
◆ 사리에 맞다[닿다] stand to reason; be reasonable; be logical; be justifiable / 사리에 맞지 않다 do not stand [be contrary] to reason / 사리에 밝다 be sensible; have good sense / 사리에 어둡다 be unreasonable
▶ 그는 사리를 안다 He is a man of (good) sense. ⇌ He knows what's what. ⇌ He is sensible.

사리 射利 seeking profit by hook or by crook —**사리하다** seek but profit; aim for gain ■ —심 a mercenary spirit

사리다 1 〈포개어 감다〉 wind
◆ 국수를 사리다 wind noodles into a ball
2 〈몸을 아끼다〉 spare *oneself*; shrink from danger
◆ 몸을 사리지 않다 do not spare *oneself*
3 〈못을 꼬부려 붙이다〉 clinch; clench
◆ 박은 못을 사리다 clinch a driven nail

4 〈뱀 등이 몸을 감다〉 coil ▶ 뱀이 사리고 있다 A snake is lying in a coil.

사리염 瀉利鹽 〔化〕 magnesium sulfate ⇨ 황산(~마그네슘)

사리풀 〔植〕 a (black) henbane

사린 四隣 the whole neighborhood; the surrounding countries

사립 私立 ◆ 사립의 private; nongovernmental ▶ 그 학교는 사립이다 The school is a private institution. ⇌ The school is under private management.
■ —대학 a private college [university] —학교 a private school; a nongovernmental school

사립문 —門 a wicket (made) of branches and twigs; a brushwood [wattle] door

사마귀[1] **1** 〈무사마귀〉 a wart; 〔醫〕 a verruca (*pl*. -cae) ◆ 사마귀가 있는 warty; verrucose
▶ 목에 사마귀가 생겼다 A wart has grown [formed] on my neck. ⇌ I have gotten a wart on my neck.
2 〈흑자〉 a mole (on the skin); a kind of nevus ◆ 사마귀를 떼다 remove a mole

사마귀[2] 〔昆〕 a (praying) mantis [mantid]
◆ 사마귀의 mantid

사마리아 Samaria ■ —사람 〔聖〕 a Samaritan: 선한 사마리아 사람 a good Samaritan

사막 沙漠 a desert ◆ 황량한 사막 a bleak desert / 끝없는 사막 a limitless desert
■ —고비 the Gobi (Desert) 사하라 — the Sahara (Desert) ■ —식물[동물] a desert plant [animal]

사망 死亡 death; decease; demise
◆ 사망의 obituary
—**사망하다** die; pass away; decease
■ —공고 a death notice —기사 an obituary notice —란 an obituary column —보험 《美》 life insurance 《英》 assurance —보험금 a death benefit —신고서 a notice [report] of death: 사망신고서를 내다 send in a notice of *sb's* death —증명서 a certificate of death; a death certificate —통지 an announcement [a notice] of *sb's* death —표 〔保險〕 the mortality table

사망률 死亡率 mortality; death [fatality] rate; the percentage of mortality
◆ 폐암[결핵]에 의한 사망률 the death rate from lung cancer [tuberculosis] / 사망률이 높은 병 a very murderous disease; a decimating illness / 사망률이 높다[낮다] the death rate is high [low]
▶ 이 병은 사망률이 높다 This disease has a high death rate.
■ —유아— infant mortality

사망자 死亡者 the deceased; the dead; 〈사고 등에 의한〉 persons killed; deaths
◆ 교통사고로 인한 사망자 (traffic) fatalities
▶ 그 사고로 많은 사망자가 생겼다 The accident caused many deaths. ⇌ Many lives were lost in the accident.
■ —명단 a death roll —수 the number of deaths; the death toll —통계 statistics of mortality; mortality returns

사면 四面 〈네 면〉 four sides; 〈사방〉 all sides
◆ 사면이 바다로 둘러싸인 나라 a seagirt coun-

try; a country encircled [isolated] by water / 사면 팔방으로 on all sides; in every direction / 사면에서 공격을 받다 be attacked on every side

사면 赦免 (a) pardon; (a) remission; absolution; indulgence; (an) amnesty
―**사면하다** pardon; remit 《a punishment》; absolve 《*sb* from [of]》; grant clemency to 《a prisoner》
▶ 그는 형이 사면되었다 He was set free without being punished.
▶ 그는 벌금만 물고 사면되었다 He was let off with just a fine.
■ 일반― a general pardon 특별― a particular [special] pardon ■―장 a letter of pardon

사면 斜面 a slope; a slant; a slanting [sloping] surface; an inclined [oblique] plane
♦ 완만한 사면 an easy [a gentle] slope
▶ 그는 사면에서 미끄러져 굴렀다 He slipped and fell on the slope.
■ 급― a steep slope ■ ―도(圖) an oblique section

사면발이 a crab; a crab [pubic] louse
사면체 〔數〕 a tetrahedron
♦ 사면체의 tetrahedral

사면초가 四面楚歌 ♦ 사면초가다 find *oneself* betrayed by all of *one's* countrymen; be surrounded by foes on all sides

사멸 死滅 extinction; annihilation; destruction; (a) death
―**사멸하다** die out; perish; become extinct; be annihilated
▶ 인류가 사멸할 날이 멀지 않았다고 예언하는 사람도 있다 Some people predict that the time will not be far away when mankind will perish [die out].

사명 社命 the order of a company ♦ 사명으로 by order of the company ▶ 사명으로 부산에 출장간다 I'll make a business trip to Pusan by order of the company.

사명 使命 a mission; an appointed task; duty
♦ 사명을 띠다 be charged [entrusted] with a mission / 사명을 다하다 accomplish [execute, perform, fulfill, carry out] *one's* mission / 사명을 다하지 못하다 fail in *one's* mission
▶ 그는 중대한 외교상의 사명을 띠고 워싱턴에 파견되었다 He was sent to Washington on an important diplomatic mission.
■ ―감 a sense of duty

사모 思慕 **1** 〈그리워함〉 longing 《for》; yearning 《for》
―**사모하다** burn with love; love dearly; long [pine] for; yearn after [for, toward, to]
♦ 애타게 사모하다 burn with yearning 《after, for》; have a burning love 《for》
2 〈경모〉 love and respect; admiration
―**사모하다** love and respect; admire; adore
♦ 스승의 덕을 사모하다 adore *one's* teacher for his [her] virtue

사모 師母 *one's* teacher's wife
사모바르 〈러시아의 찻주전자〉a samovar
사모아 〈남태평양의 제도〉Samoa ■ ―사람 a Samoan

사무 社務 the affairs [business] of a company [firm]

사무 事務 business; office work; office jobs [labor]; clerical work; desk work; affairs
♦ 사무상의 절차 business [office] routine / 사무에 종사하다 be engaged [engage *oneself*] in business / 사무를 보다 do office work; attend to the duties of an office [to *one's* business] / 사무를 처리하다 transact [manage, execute] business / 사무를 인계하다 transfer [hand over] business / 사무를 인수하다 take over business 《from another》
▶ 나는 그에게서 사무를 인수했다 I took over business from him.
▶ 그는 무역 관계의 사무에 밝다 He is familiar with [experienced in] the office routine of trade.
▶ 일요일에는 사무를 보지 않습니다 (On) Sundays no business is transacted.
■ ―가 a man of business [affairs]; a practical man ―관 an assistant junior official; a subsection-chief-grade official ―관리(管理) office administration [management] ―국 a secretariat; an executive office ―국장 the secretary-general; the director ―규정 regulations for business; office regulations ―당국 the authorities directly in charge; the officials in charge ―복 an office uniform; a working garment; 〔美〕 a duster ―비 office expenses ―소 an office; business premises: 법률사무소 a lawyer's office ―실 an office (room); the clerks' office ―용품 office supplies ―원 a clerk; a clerical worker; an office clerk [man, worker]; 〈여자〉 an office girl ―장 a head official; 〈선박·여객기의〉 a purser ―차장 a vice [deputy] secretary-general; the assistant director-general ―총장 〈국회 등의〉 the secretary-general; the director

사무엘 Samuel ■ ―전서 [聖] The First Book of Samuel; 〈약칭〉 1 Samuel (略 1 Sam.) ―후서 The Second Book of Samuel; 〈약칭〉 2 Samuel (略 2 Sam.)

사무적 事務的 businesslike; practical
♦ 사무적으로 〈handle an affair〉 in a businesslike manner [way]; in a matter-of-fact way
▶ 그는 만사를 사무적으로 처리한다 He takes care of everything in a businesslike manner.

사무치다 touch the heart; pierce; come [go] home to 《one》; strike 《one》 home
♦ 가슴에 사무치다 pierce [come home to] *one's* heart; cut *one* to the heart; sink deep in *one's* mind / 원한이 뼈에 사무치다 resentment has pierced the very marrow; bear *sb* a deep grudge
▶ 추위가 뼈에 사무쳤다 I was chilled to the bone.
▶ 선생님의 말씀이 내 가슴에 사무쳤습니다 My teacher's words came home to my heart.

사문 死文 〈공문〉 a dead letter; a (mere) scrap of paper
♦ 사문화되다 prove [turn out] a dead letter; end in a scrap of paper
▶ 그 조문은 이제 사문화되었다 The contents of the law are virtually dead now.

사문 査問 inquiry; inquisition; hearing

사문하다 interrogate; examine; inquire 《into a matter》
■ —(위원)회 an inquiry [a rogatory] commission: 사문회를 열다 hold an inquiry 《into a matter》; hold an inquest 《on, over》
사문서 私文書 a private document; private papers ■ —위조 forgery of a private document
사문석 蛇紋石 〔鑛〕 serpentine; ophiolite
사물 私物 one's (private) property; one's personal effects
▶ 이것은 내 사물입니다 This is my personal belongings [own property].
사물 事物 things; affairs; a matter
▶ 그는 한국의 사물을 연구하기 위해 내한했다 He came to Korea to study things Korean.
■ —관할 material jurisdiction
사물놀이 四物— samulnori
사뭇 1 〈마구〉 as one pleases [likes, wishes]; willfully; 〈줄곧〉 all through; without break
▶ 술을 마시면 사뭇 시부렁거리게 된다 Wine loosens people's tongues.
▶ 한 주일 동안 사뭇 바빴다 I was busy all through the week.
2 〈매우〉 wholly; utterly; very (much); quite
♦ 사뭇 다르다 be utterly different 《from》
사미 沙彌 〔佛敎〕 a Buddhist acolyte; a young bonze; 〈사미승〉 a novice; (산) a śrāmanera
■ —니 a novice nun; (산) a śrāmanerikā
사민 四民 the four classes; 〈온 백성〉 people of all classes; the whole people [nation]
■ —평등 the equality of the four classes in the country; equality of man
사바나 a savanna(h)
사바사바 bribery
▶ 그들에게는 사바사바가 안 통한다 They are incorruptible. ⇌ They are above [superior to] bribery.
—**사바사바하다** commit bribery; offer a bribe; grease (the hand [palm, fist] of) sb
♦ 사바사바해서 입학하다 obtain [get] admission to 《a college》 by unfair means
사바세계 娑婆世界 〔佛敎〕 this world; here below; (산) Sabha
♦ 사바세계의 earthly; worldly; mundane
▶ 나는 사바세계가 싫어졌다 I am tired of the world.
사박거리다, 사박대다 crunch softly
▶ 사과는 먹을 때 사박거린다 The apple is crisp to eat. ▶ 우리는 사박거리는 눈을 밟으며 역으로 걸어갔다 We crunched through the snow to go to the station.
사박사박 with a soft crunch ♦ 모래밭을 사박사박 걷다 walk across the sand with a soft crunch
사박자 四拍子 〔樂〕 quadruple time [measure, rhythm]
사반 死斑 a death spot; 〔醫〕 a livor
사반기 四半期 a quarter ♦ 금년도의 1사반기 the first quarter of this year
사반세기 四半世紀 a quarter of a century
사발 沙鉢 a (porcelain [china]) bowl; 〈분량〉 a bowlful ■ —밥 a rice bowl ■ —밥 rice served in a bowl —시계 a bowl-shaped clock —통문 a round robin
사방 四方 the four quarters; four sides; all directions
♦ 사방에[으로] on all sides; on every side; in every direction; in all directions; all around / 사방에서 from all quarters; from every quarter [direction] / 사방 10킬로미터 이내에 within a radius of ten kilometers; within ten kilometers around / 사방을 둘러보다 look round
▶ 땅은 사방 15미터의 넓이다 The ground is fiften meters square.
▶ 우리 마을은 사방이 산으로 둘러싸여 있다 Our village is surrounded on all sides by the mountains.
▶ 이 역에서 사방으로 선로가 통하고 있다 The railway lines radiate from this station.
사방 砂防 erosion control; sand arrestation; sandbank fixing
■ —공사 anti-erosion [sand arrestation] work —림 an erosion control forest —조림 afforestation for erosion control
사방정계 斜方晶系 〔鑛〕 the rhombic [orthorhombic, trimetric] system
사방팔방 四方八方 every direction; all directions; all sides; everywhere ⇨ 사방(四方)
▶ 소문이 사방팔방으로 퍼졌다 The rumor spread on all sides.
▶ 그의 연설을 듣기 위해 사방팔방에서 사람들이 모였다 People gathered from all quarters [from every quarter, from every direction] to hear his speech.
사배 四倍 four times; quadruple; fourfold
♦ 사배의 fourfold; quadruple / 사배로 하다 multiply by four; quadruple; quadruplicate
▶ 그는 뭉칫돈을 경마에 걸어 4배로 만들었다 He bet his wad on a race and quadrupled it.
■ —체 〔生〕 a tetraploid
사범 事犯 an illegal act; an offense; a crime; an act subject to punishment ■ 경제— an economic offense 선거— election illegalities 폭력— a crime of violence; a violent crime
사범 師範 〈교사〉 a teacher; a master; a preceptor; an instructor; a coach; 〈모범〉 a model [an example] to others
■ 권투— a boxing instructor [master] 펜싱— a fencing instructor [master] ■ —교육 teacher training; normal [normal-school] education —대학 a college of education
사법 司法 〔法〕 the administration of justice; the judicature
♦ 사법적인 해결 a judicial settlement / 국제사법재판소 the International Court of Justice / 사법의 judicial; judiciary
▶ 근대 국가에서는 행정, 입법, 사법의 삼권이 독립되어 있다 In modern nations the three powers of administration, legislation and jurisdiction are independent of each other.
■ —경찰 the judicial police —경찰관 a judicial police officer —관 a judicial officer; (총칭) judges and prosecutors; the justice —관청 the bureau of judicial affairs —기관 the machinery of the law —당국 the judiciary (authorities) —보호 judicial protection —시

험 a state law examination —연수생 a judicial apprentice —연수원 the Judicial Research and Training Institute —위원(회) the judiciary committee —재판 a judicial trial —제도 the judicial system —행정 judicial administration

사법 私法 [法] private law

사법권 司法權 judicial [judicatory] power; (powers of) jurisdiction; judicature
♦ 사법권의 독립 independence of the judicature / 사법권의 행사[남용] exercise [abuse] of judicial power / 사법권을 발동하다 invoke [exercise] judicial power; exercise jurisdiction
▶ 우리에게 외교관에 대한 사법권은 없다 We have no judicial power [jurisdiction] over diplomats.

사변 四邊 [數] four sides; 〈사방의〉 all sides
♦ 사변에 on all sides; all (a)round ■—형 [數] a quadrilateral; a tetragon

사변 事變 1 〈변고〉 an accident; a mishap; 〈재해〉 a disaster; a calamity
♦ 예기치 못한 사변 an unforeseen accident
2 〈난리〉 an incident; a disturbance; an uprising; 〈급변〉 an emergency; an exigency
■ 만주— the Manchurian Incident: 만주사변은 1931년에 발발했다 The Manchurian Incident broke out in 1931.

사변 思辨 1 [哲] speculation ♦ 사변적 방법 a speculative method / 사변적 speculative
2 〈판별〉 discrimination; distinction
■ —철학 speculative philosophy

사변 斜邊 [數] an oblique side ⇨ 빗변

사별 死別 separation by death; bereavement
—사별하다 be bereaved (of one's husband); be separated from (one's parents) by death
♦ 남편과 사별하여 lose one's husband through death; be parted from one's husband by death
▶ 그녀는 지난 해에 남편과 사별했다 She lost [was bereaved of] her husband last year.

사병 士兵 a private (soldier); (美) an enlisted man; (총칭) the rank and file
♦ 일개 사병에서 입신하여 장군까지 되다 rise from the ranks to be a general

사보타주 sabotage; (美) a slowdown; (英) a go-slow strike
—사보타주하다 go slow; go on a go-slow strike
♦ 사보타주하는 사람 a saboteur
▶ 그들은 1주일이나 사보타주했다 They sabotaged [went on a strike] for a week.

사보텐 [植] a cactus (pl. ~es, -ti)

사복 私服 plain [ordinary] clothes; private [civilian] clothes; (美) civies
♦ 사복으로 in plain clothes; in civilian attire; out of uniform
■ —경찰관 a plainclothes policeman; a policeman in civilian clothes —형사 a plainclothesman

사복 私腹 ♦ 사복을 채우다 stuff [fill, line] one's (own) pockets [purse]; feather one's (own) nest; enrich oneself
▶ 그는 공공 사업에서 사복을 채우려고 했다 He tried to line his pockets from a public enterprise.

사복음 四福音 [聖] the Four Gospels

사본 寫本 a copy; 〈등사물〉 a transcript; 〈부본〉 a duplicate; 〈필사본〉 a (book in) manuscript (略 MS.)
♦ 중세의 사본 a medieval manuscript / 증서의 사본 a copy [duplicate] of a bond / 사본을 첨부하다 subject a copy (of) / 사본을 만들다[뜨다] copy; make a copy [duplicate] of; duplicate (a letter)

사부 師父 〈스승과 아버지〉 one's father and master; 〈스승〉 a (fatherly) master

사부작 四部作 〈희곡·가극 등의〉 a tetralogy; a four-part work

사부합창 四部合唱 ♦ 사부합창의 four-part
■ —곡 a four-part song

사북 1 〈부채 등의〉 the pivot; the rivet; a pivot pin (on a fan)
▶ 부채의 사북이 느슨해졌다 The rivet of the fan is sprung.
2 〈긴요한 부분〉 a main [vital, pivotal] point; a pivot; the key (to)

사분 四分 quartering; dividing in four
♦ 사분의 1 one [a] quarter; one fourth / 사분의 3 three fourths; three quarters
—사분하다 divide in four; separate [divide] into four parts; quarter
■ —기 a quarter: 4 사분기 the last quarter [three months] of the year —면(面) [數] a quadrant —원 [數] a quadrant —음 [樂] a quarter tone —음표 (美) a quarter note; (英) a crotchet —의(儀) a quadrant

사분 私憤 personal grudge [enmity, spite]
♦ 사분을 풀다 vent one's spite

사분거리다 1 〈끈기 있게 조르다〉 tease sb humorously
2 〈가만가만 지껄이다〉 whisper; talk in a low voice

사분오열 四分五裂 disruption; utter disunion [division, breakup]
▶ 위원회는 사분오열의 상태다 The committee is divided against itself.
—사분오열하다 be disrupted; be torn asunder

사비 私費 (at) one's own expense [charge]; (at) private expense
▶ 나는 사비로 유학했다 I studied abroad at my own expense [cost].
■ —유학생 a student studying abroad at his own expense

사비 社費 (at) the company's expenses [charges]; the upkeep of a company; the outlay(s) of a company
▶ 그는 사비로 한달간 미국에 갔다 왔다 He has been to America for a month at the expense of the company.

사뿐 softly; lightly; with a soft step ♦ 땅으로 사뿐 내려서다 jump [leap, hop] down to the ground with a soft [muffled] thud

사뿐사뿐 softly; lightly; with soft steps
♦ 사뿐사뿐 걷다 walk with soft steps; walk with a light tread
▶ 그녀는 젖먹이가 깨지 않도록 방에서 사뿐사뿐 나왔다 She tiptoed out of the room so as not to awaken the baby.

사사 私事 personal affairs ⇨ 사삿일
사사 師事 making sb one's teacher; studying under sb
—**사사하다** study under [with] sb; look up to sb as one's teacher; receive instruction at sb's feet; become sb's pupil
▶나는 김교수에게 사사하여 4년간 회화를 공부했다 I studied paintings under Professor Kim for four years.
사사건건 事事件件 each and every case [matter, affair, event] ▶그는 내게 사사건건 반대했다 He opposed me in every way.
사사기 士師記 〔聖〕 The Book of Judges (略 Jud(g).)
사사로이 私私— personally; privately; in private; informally
▶나는 그녀와 사사로이 이야기하고 싶다 I'd like to have a personal talk with her.
▶너에게 사사로이 할 이야기가 있다 I want to have some private talk with you.
사사롭다 私私— personal; private; informal
♦사사로운 정에 이끌리다 be swayed [influenced] by personal feelings
▶남의 사사로운 일에까지 끼어 들지 않도록 하세요 Please don't go into people's private affairs.
▶사사로운 일이므로 남에게 알리지 않았다 As it was a private affair, we kept it to ourselves.
사사오입 四捨五入 rounding (off) to the nearest whole number ⇨ 반올림
사산 死産 (a) stillbirth —**사산하다** have a stillbirth; have a baby born dead
▶그녀는 사내아이를 사산했다 She gave birth to a stillborn [dead] baby boy.
—**아 a stillborn baby; a stillbirth
사산화삼납 四酸化三— 〔化〕 red lead
사살 射殺 killing by shooting —**사살하다** kill by shooting; shoot sb dead [to death]
▶그는 차 안에서 사살된 시체로 발견되었다 He was found in a car, shot to death.
사삿일 私私— personal affairs; private matters [concerns] ♦남의 사삿일에 참견하다 interfere in sb's private concerns
▶사삿일로 죄송합니다만 잠시 동안 제 말씀을 들어주십시오 Excuse me for being personal, but please listen to me for a while.
사상 史上 in history; on the pages of history
♦사상 최고의 기록 the highest record in history; (美口) 〈hit〉the historical high / 사상 최대의 참사 the greatest disaster in history
▶그것은 사상 유례 없는 사건이었다 That was a case unparalleled [unprecedented] in history.
사상 死相 〈죽을 상〉the seal [sign] of death 《on one's face》; a countenance presaging death; the shadow of death 《on sb's face》; 〈죽은 사람의 얼굴〉a dead person's face
▶그에게는 사상이 나타나 있었다 He had [bore] the appearance of approaching death.
사상 死傷 〈죽음과 상함〉death and injury; 〈사망자와 부상자〉losses; casualties ⇨ 사상자
▶자동차 사고로 인한 사상이 많은 것으로 보도되고 있다 It is reported that automobile casualties are heavy.
■—**병**(兵) the killed and injured [wounded] soldiers; troop casualties
사상 事象 〈현상〉a phenomenon 《pl. -na》; 〈일〉a matter; an event; 〈양상〉an aspect; a phase
사상 思想 thought; an idea; 〈개념〉conception; 〈이데올로기〉an ideology
♦건전한 사상 healthy [sound] thought / 고원한 사상 a lofty thought / 신구 사상의 충돌 a conflict between new and old ideas / 사상이 건전한 sound-thinking 《people》/ 사상을 전달하다 communicate one's thought 《to》/ 위험한 사상을 불어넣다 inoculate sb with dangerous ideas
▶그 지도자는 사상이 풍부[빈약]하다 The leader is rich [poor] in ideas.
■—**과격** a radical [Bolshevik] idea 근대[동양, 서양, 과학, 정치]— modern [Eastern, Western, scientific, political] thought 신[공산주의]— a new [Communist] idea 자유— liberal thought 중심— the central idea ■—**가** a thinker; a man of thought —**계** the world of thought; the thinking world —**극** a problem play —**문제**[운동] a thought problem [movement] —**범** 〈범죄〉a thought offense; 〈사람〉a political offender —**전** ideological warfare; an ideological battle —**투쟁** an ideological strife
사상 絲狀 ♦사상의 filiform; thready
■—**균** 〔植〕 a filamentous fungus; a mold —**균상 효모** moldy yeast —**체** 〔醫〕 a filament —**충** 〔動〕 a heartworm; a filaria 《pl. -ae》
사상누각 砂上樓閣 《build》a castle [castles] in Spain [in the air]; a house of cards
사상자 死傷者 casualties; the killed [dead] and the injured [wounded]; losses
♦다수의[많은] 사상자 heavy [many] casualties; 《take》a heavy toll of lives
▶추락 사고로 123명의 사상자가 났다 One hundred and twenty-three persons were either killed or injured in the crash.
▶열차가 탈선하여 많은 사상자를 냈다 The train was derailed, causing many casualties.
▶다행히 사상자는 한 사람도 없었다 Fortunately there were no casualties.
■—**명단** a casualty list; a list of casualties —**수** losses; (the number of) casualties
사색 四色 1 〈빛깔〉four colors
2 〔史〕 the Four Factions (of the Yi dynasty) —**당쟁** (party) strife [intrigue] among the Four Factions —**판** four-colored printing
사색 死色 deadly [ghastly] pale look
♦얼굴이 사색이 되다 turn deadly [ghastly] pale 《with horror》
▶그 소식을 듣자 그의 얼굴은 사색이 되었다 His face went ashy pale to hear the news. ≒ His face turned deathly ashen at the news.
사색 思索 speculation; thinking; cogitation; contemplation; meditation
♦사색적인 생활 a life of meditation / 사색적인 speculative; meditative
▶그는 사색에 잠겨 있다 He is given to speculation. ⇌ He is lost [absorbed] in meditation

[contemplation].
—사색하다 think; muse [speculate, meditate] on; contemplate (on); cogitate
■—가 a thinking person; a thinker

사생 死生 life and death ■ —관두 (關頭) the brink of life and death: 사생 관두에 서다 lie between life and death; be on the verge of death

사생 寫生 sketching; a sketch; drawing [painting] from nature
—사생하다 sketch; paint [draw, sketch] from nature; draw [paint] from [after] life; make a sketch of 《a view》
▶ 지난 일요일에 우리는 해변으로 사생하러 갔다 Last Sunday we went sketching by the seashore [to the seashore to do sketching].
■—대회 a sketch contest —문 a (literary) sketch —첩 a sketchbook —화 a picture drawn from life [nature]; a sketch

사생결단 死生決斷 desperation; risking [staking] one's life
♦ 사생 결단의 싸움 a life and death struggle
—사생 결단하다 risk [stake] one's life; be desperate [death-defying]; do sth at the risk of one's life
♦ 사생 결단하고 at the risk [peril] of one's life; in desperation

사생아 私生兒 an illegitimate child [son, daughter]; a natural [love] child; a bastard; a child of shame; a child born out of wedlock
♦ 사생아를 인지하다 recognize an illegitimate child as one's issue; legitimate [legitimatize, filiate] a love child / 사생아로 태어나다 be born on the wrong side of the blanket
■ —인지(認知) filiation; affiliation

사생활 私生活 one's private [home] life; one's privacy ♦ 사생활에 간여하다 dig [nose] into sb's private life
▶ 내 사생활을 네게서 간섭받고 싶지 않다 I don't want you to dig into my private life.

사서 〈서적을 맡은 직분〉 a librarian
■ —보(補) an assistant librarian

사서 四書 〈중국 고전 칠서중의 네 가지 책〉 the Four Books; the Four Chinese Classics ■ —삼경 the Four Books and Three Classics; the Seven Chinese Classics

사서 史書 〈역사책〉 a history (book)

사서 a dictionary ⇨ 사전(辭典)

사서오경 四書五經 〔史〕 the Four Books and Five Classics of Confucianism; the Nine Chinese Classics

사서함 私書函 a post-office box (略 P.O.B., POB); 《美》 a call box
▶ 신청서는 서울 중앙 우체국 사서함 100번으로 보내세요 Please send the letter of application to P.O.Box 100, Seoul Central Post Office.

사석 私席 〈사사로운 자리〉 an informal [an unofficial, a private] occasion ♦ 사석에서 informally; unofficially

사선 死線 〈교도소·포로수용소 주위의〉 《美》 a deadline; 〈죽을 고비〉 a life-or-death crisis
♦ 사선을 넘다 cross the deadline; brave death; linger on the brink [verge] of death
▶ 그는 가까스로 사선을 넘어왔다 He narrowly escaped death.

사선 斜線 an oblique line; 〈지도의〉 a shaded portion; a slant(ing) line; 〈and / or의 경우의〉 a slanting stroke; 《美》 a slash (mark)

사설 私設 ♦ 사설의 private —사설하다 establish privately
■ —묘지 a private cemetery —시장 a private market —철도 a private railroad —탐정 a private detective —학원[강습소] a private [《美》 proprietary] school [institute]

사설 社說 〈언론사의 논설〉 《英》 a leader; a leading article; 《美》 an editorial (article)
♦ 강경한 사설 a strong editorial / 사설에서 논하다 discuss 《a matter》 in an editorial; comment editorially (on); editorialize (on)
▶ 그 문제에 관해서는 각 신문사설에서 논평하고 있다 Every paper comments editorially on the subject. ⇌ Every paper editorializes on the subject.
■ —기자 an editorialist; an editorial [a leader] writer —란 the editorial page [column]

사설 辭說 1 〈언사〉 words; speech; 〈노래·연극 사이의〉 narration; description
2 〈잔말〉 tattle; babble; prattle; 〈불평〉 nag; grumble
■ —시조(時調) a form of *shijo* with unlimited length in the middle verse

사설 邪說 〈그릇된 논설〉 a heretical doctrine [teaching]; a heresy

사성 四姓 〈인도의 카스트〉 the four castes (of Brahmans (승려), Kshatriyas (무사·귀족), Vaisyas (평민) and Sudras (천민))

사성 四聖 the four greatest sages of the world (▶ Confucius, Buddha, Jesus and Socrates)

사성 四聲 the four tones (of Chinese characters)

사성하다 賜姓— 〈나라에서 성을 내려주다〉 the king give the right to a family name; the king bestows a surname (on)

사세 事勢 〈일의 형세〉 the situation; the state of things [affairs]; the aspect of affairs; the way things are
♦ 사세 부득이 unavoidably; inevitably; out of sheer necessity; driven by [owing to, through] unavoidable circumstances / 사세 부득이한 경우에는 when circumstances compel [require]; in an unavoidable case / 사세 변화에 대처하다 meet the change of the situation

사세 社勢 ▶ 호경기의 물결을 타고 사세가 번창했다 The company has prospered because of the [a] business boom.

사소설 私小說 a private [real] life novel; an "I"story; 《독》 Ich-Roman; a first-person story; a novel dealing with the author's own life; an autobiographical tale [story]

사소하다 些少— trifling; trivial 《matter》; small; minor 《fault》; petty 《sum》; scanty; slight 《difference》; insignificant
♦ 사소한 일 a trifle; a trifling [trivial] matter / 사소한 잘못 a trifling [minor] error; a light [an insignificant] mistake / 사소한 일에 화내다 get angry at trifles; take offense on the slightest provocation / 사소한 일로 법석떨다 make a fuss about trifles

사수 ▶ 사소한 차이 같은 건 신경쓰지 마라 Don't worry about a slight [little] difference.
▶ 그게 아주 사소합니다만 남아 있습니다 There is only a little of it left.
▶ 손실은 사소하다 The loss is nothing to speak of.

사수 死守 a desperate [stubborn] defense ─**사수하다** defend to the last [to the death]; defend 《a position》 desperately [stubbornly] ♦진지를 사수하다 defend a position [an encampment] to the last
▶ 그들은 도시를 적으로부터 사수했다 They defended the city against the enemy to the last.

사수 射手 a shooter; a marksman; a gunner; a rifleman; 〈활의〉 an archer; a bowman 《pl. -men》 ■**기관총** ─ a machine gunner 명─ a master [crack, dead] shot; a master bowman

사숙 私塾 a private class at *one's* home; a private [home] school

사숙하다 私淑 ─ adore *sb* (in *one's* heart); look up to *sb* as *one's* model; be strongly influenced 《by》
▶ 그녀는 내가 사숙하고 있는 시인의 한 사람이다 She is one of the poets I admire.

사순절 四旬節 〈기독교의〉 Lent ♦ 사순절의 Lenten / 사순절의 금식 the Lenten fast

사술 邪術 〈요사스러운 술법〉 black magic; the black art; sorcery; an evil trick

사슬 〈쇠사슬〉 a chain; 〈매는 줄〉 a tether / 사슬을 풀다 unchain; undo the chain; put 《a dog》 out of chain / 사슬에서 벗어나다 《비유》 free *oneself* from restraint; throw [cast, shake, fling] off the fetters [shackles, yoke] 《of》 / 사슬로 매다 enchain; chain up; put 《men》 in chains
▶ 외출 중엔 개를 사슬에 매어 둔다 I keep the dog on the chain [chained up] while I'm out.
■─**고리** a link ─**망점** a chain dot

사슴 a deer 〈단수·복수 동형〉; 〈수컷〉 a buck; a hart; a stag; 〈암컷〉 a doe; a roe; hind ♦ 사슴의 cervine
■**새끼** ─ a calf; a fawn; a spitter ■─**가죽** deerskin; buckskin ─**고기** venison ─**뿔** an antler ─**사냥** deer hunting; deerstalking ─**사육장** a deer park

사시 史詩 an epic; a historical poem

사시 斜視 〈醫〉 a squint; strabismus; 〈흘겨봄〉 looking askance ♦ 사시의 strabismal; squint; squinting; squint-eyed; cross-eyed
▶ 그는 사시다 He has a squint. ⇌ He has a cast in the eye.
■**내** ─ strabismus convergens **외** ─ strabismus divergens ─**절개술** strabotomy

사시나무 〈植〉 an aspen; a (white) poplar; an abele; a quaking [trembling] aspen ♦ 사시나무 떨 듯하다 tremble like an aspen leaf

사시사철 四時四 ─ 〈부사적〉 at [in] all seasons (of the year); all the year round

사시절 四時節 the four seasons

사식 私食 (prisoner's) private food; private food sent in to a prisoner

사식 寫植 〈사진 식자〉 《美》 photocomposition; 《英》 filmsetting

사신 死神 the god of death; Death
사신 私信 a private [personal] letter
사신 邪神 a malevolent [heathen, false] god; an evil deity; a demon; a devil
사신 使臣 an envoy; 〈대사〉 an ambassador; 〈공사〉 a minister ♦ 각국의 사신 the foreign representatives / 사신을 파견하다 dispatch [send] an envoy 《to》

사실 史實 a historical fact; a matter of history; historical evidence

사실 私室 a private room; 〈내실〉 a boudoir

사실 事實 a fact; an actual fact; 〈현실〉 reality; actuality; 〈진실〉 the truth; the case
♦ 명백한 사실 a broad [an obvious, a palpable] fact / 엄연한 사실 a hard fact / 움직일 수 없는 사실 an established [accomplished] fact; a solid fact / 부정할 수 없는 사실 an undeniable [indisputable] fact / 인정된 사실 a recognized fact / 적나라한[꾸밈없는] 사실 the naked [plain] truth; a straight fact / 사실의 은폐 suppression of the truth / 사실대로 말하다 tell *sth* just as it is; state the naked truth; come clean / 사실대로 고백하다 confess the whole truth; make a clean breast of it / 사실대로 말하면, 사실은 to tell [speak] the truth; the truth (of the matter) is 《that...》; in (point of) fact; in reality [actuality]; really / 사실로 되다 prove a fact; come true; come to pass; be realized; materialize / 사실과 다르다 be contrary to the fact(s) / 사실을 근거로 하다 be grounded [based, founded] on fact; take *one's* stand on fact / 사실을 인정하다[무시하다] admit [ignore] the fact / 사실을 밝히다 reveal the truth / 사실을 왜곡하다 falsify facts; pervert [distort] the truth / 사실을 조사하다 inquire into the facts (of the case)
▶ 그의 말은 사실인 것 같다 He seems to be telling the truth.
▶ 그가 말한 것은 유감이지만 사실이다 What he said is only too true.
▶ 사실의 뒷받침이 없는 추론을 내리는 것은 위험하다 It is dangerous to draw inferences not authorized by facts.
▶ 사실은 다르다 That is not the case.
▶ 사실은 소설보다도 기이하다 《속담》 Fact [Truth] is stranger than fiction.
▶ 그 사실이 밝혀질 때가 올 것이다 Time will come when the truth will come out.
▶ 그 사실은 부정할 수 없다 We cannot deny the fact. ⇌ There is no denying the fact.
▶ 우리는 그 사실을 있는 그대로 인정하지 않으면 안된다 We must admit the fact as it is.
▶ 이 사실을 무시하려는 자도 있었고 왜곡하려는 자도 있었다 Some tried to ignore this fact, others tried to falsify it.
▶ 이것은 사실에 바탕을 둔 이야기다 This is a story grounded [based, founded] on fact.
▶ 소문은 사실로 밝혀졌다 The rumor proved [turned out] to be true.
■**기정** ─ an established [accomplished] fact ─**문제** a matter [question] of fact; 〈당면한〉 the (real) question at issue ─**조사[실태]** fact-finding

사실 寫實 representing things as they really

are; exact, objective description; realism —사실하다 represent things as they really are; describe *sth* exactly and objectively; give a graphic description [representation] 《of》 ■—소설 a realist(ic) novel —파 the realist school

사실무근 事實無根 ♦사실무근의 groundless; unfounded; absurd; entirely contrary to fact ▶그의 비난은 사실무근이다 His accusation is unfounded [groundless, without foundation]. ▶그 보고는 전연 사실무근이다 The report is entirely false [contrary to fact, absurd].

사실상 事實上 actually; in fact; as a matter of fact; really; in reality; virtually ♦사실상의 factual; actual; real; virtual; practical; veritable / 사실상의 정부[승인] a de facto government [recognition] ▶그는 사실상의 당의 지도자다 He is the virtual leader of the party. ▶그해 봄에 전쟁은 사실상 종결되었다 The war was virtually ended in that spring.

사실적 寫實的 realistic; true to life [nature]; objective; graphic ♦사실적으로 realistically; graphically / 사실적으로 묘사하다 describe [depict] realistically; give a graphic description 《of》 ▶그 작가의 사실적인 작품이 독자에게 어필한다 The realistic style of that writer appeals to the readers.

사실주의 寫實主義 realism; literalism ■—자 a realist; a realistic writer; a literalist

사심 私心 selfishness; self-interest ♦사심없는 unselfish; selfless; disinterested; impartial; fair / 사심을 버리고 from unselfish [disinterested] motives; unselfishly; impartially; fairly / 사심을 품다 have an axe to grind

사심 邪心 an evil mind; a wicked [black] heart; a malicious intention; an evil design

사십 四十 forty ♦제 사십 the fortieth / 사십전의 under [on the sunny side of] forty / 사십을 넘은 over forty; on the wrong [other] side of forty ▶우리 아버지는 사십대다 My father is in his [the] forties. ▶우리 선생님은 아마 사십 전후일 것이다 Perhaps our teacher is about forty.

사십에 첫 버선 《속담》 doing *sth* for the first time late in life

사악 邪惡 wickedness; viciousness; vice —사악하다 wicked; vicious; malicious; villainous; sinister ♦사악한 사람 a wicked man; a villain; a godless person

사안 私案 *one's* private plan [scheme, idea, design]

사암 砂岩 〔地質〕 sandstone ■—맥 a sandstone vein

사약 賜藥 (the king's) bestowal of poison ♦사약을 내리다 bestow poison (for an official to kill *sb* with)

사양 斜陽 the setting [declining, slanting, sinking] sun; the evening sun(light) ■—산업 a fading [an eclipsed, a declining] industry; an industry on the decline —족[계급] the new poor; the declining upper-class families; the fallen [impoverished] aristocracy; (口) the has-been (families)

사양 飼養 breeding; raising ⇨ 사육

사양 辭讓 〈양보〉 declining in favor of another; concession; 〈사절〉 courteous refusal [(美) declination, denial]; refusal with appreciation; 〈삼감〉 reserve; restraint; deference; modesty; holding back —사양하다 〈양보하다〉 decline *sth* in favor of another; give way to 《another》; make room for 《another》; concede; make a concession; 〈사절하다〉 refuse courteously; decline with thanks [regrets]; excuse *oneself* 《from》; ask to be excused; 〈삼가다〉 be reserved; be modest; stand on [upon] ceremony; restrain [abstain, keep] from; hold back ♦사양하지 않고 unreservedly; without reserve [ceremony, formality]; freely; without hesitation / 제의를 사양하다 decline an offer / 초대를 사양하다 decline an invitation / …하기를 사양치 않다 be ready [willing] to 《do》 ▶죄송하지만 사양하겠습니다 I am sorry, but I cannot help declining it. ▶사양말고 드십시오 Please help yourself without ceremony. ▶나라를 위해서라면 목숨인들 사양하겠는가? Who would hesitate even to die for his country?

사양토 砂壤土 〔地〕 the sandy loam

사어 死語 〈언어〉 a dead language; 〈폐어〉 an obsolete word

사업 事業 **1** 〈일〉 work; an undertaking; an enterprise; activity; a project; a scheme; operations ♦사업에 실패[성공]하다 fail [succeed] in *one's* undertaking ▶그는 새 사업을 시작했다 He started a new enterprise.

2 〈실업〉 (a line of) business; a business; 〈산업〉 an industry ♦사업이 부진해지다 have a slump in business; business slackens / 사업이 번창해지다 have [do, enjoy] a thriving business / 사업을 확장[축소]하다 extend [reduce] *one's* operations [business] ▶아버지는 무슨 사업을 하십니까? What line of business is your father in?

3 〈업적〉 an achievement; a deed ♦큰사업을 이루다 do [achieve] a great thing ■개척— reclamation [exploitation] work 공공— a public utility enterprise; public works; (public) utilities 공동— a joint enterprise 국가[정부]— a government undertaking 문화[교육]— a cultural [an educational] enterprise; cultural [educational] work 방송— the broadcasting industry ■—가 〈기업가〉 an enterprising man; a man of enterprise; an enterpriser; 〈실업가〉 an industrialist; a businessman —계 the enterprising world; the industrial [business] world; industrial [business] circles —계획 a plan of operation; a business program —공채 an industrial bond —부 an operating division —비 working

사업소득

expenses —세 the enterprise tax —소[장] a place of business; an establishment —연도 a business year [term]; an accounting period —자금 business funds; funds for equipment —자 등록 a registration of enterpriser —주 a business proprietor
사업소득 事業所得 a business income ■—세 the business tax
사업화 事業化 〈공업화〉 industrialization; 〈상업화〉 commercialization —사업화하다 industrialize; commercialize
사에이치클럽 四— a Four-H [4·H] club
사역 使役 employment; work; service; 〔軍〕 a fatigue —사역하다 employ; work; use; set sb to work —동사 〔文法〕 a causative verb
사연 事緣 〈사정〉 circumstances; considerations; the state of things [matters, affairs]; 〈연유〉 the matter; the case; the story
♦ 말 못할 사연이 있어서 for some secret [inexpressible] reasons
▶ 거기엔 복잡한 사연이 있다 There are wheels within wheels.
▶ 사연은 이러합니다 This is how it is. ⇌ Such is the case.
사연 辭緣 〈내용〉 content(s); 〈취지〉 the import; the gist; the point ▶ 편지 사연은 무엇이냐? What is the letter about?
사열 四列 〔軍〕 four rows [lines] ♦ 사열로 서다 〈종대로〉 form fours; line up four abreast; 〈횡대로〉 be drawn up four deep
사열 査閱 (an) inspection; check ♦ 사열을 받다 be inspected (by); undergo inspection —사열하다 inspect; make an inspection (of) ■—관 an inspector —대 a reviewing stand —식 a formal military inspection; a parade
사영 私營 private operation [management]
사영 射影 projection ♦ 사영의 projective —사영하다 project
■—기하학 〔數〕 projective geometry —적 성질 〔數〕 projective property

사역(使役)의 표현

1. [사람·물건]에게 …시키다 (강제를 나타냄) make (sb or sth) do
▶ 그들은 내 의사를 무시하고 내게 일을 시켰다 They made me work against my will.
▶ 김선생은 학생에게 답안을 잉크로 쓰게 한다 Mr. Kim makes his students write their examinations in ink.
▶ 추웠기 때문에 그녀는 딸에게 코트를 입혔다 It was cold, so she made her daughter wear a coat.
▶ 자네는 이 기계를 제대로 작동케 할 수 있는가? Can you make this machine work properly?
[어법]
수동태의 문장에서는 I was made to work against my will. ⇌ The students are made to write their examinations in ink. 에서 처럼 to가 들어간다.

2. [남]에게 …시키다; 부탁해서 …하게 하다
(1) have sb do
▶ 그에게 이 슈트케이스를 2층으로 옮기게 하시오 Have him carry this suitcase upstairs.
▶ 그는 선생님께 부탁해서 작문을 고쳐 달라고 했다 He had his teacher correct his composition.
▶ 나는 그에게 사진을 찍어달라고하고 싶다 I want to have him take my picture.
[어법]
① have는 make와는 달리 강제의 의미가 아니고 남을 시키거나, 고용하거나, 또는 부탁해서 해달라고 할 때에 쓰인다.
② have sb do가 「…하게 하다」의 뜻이 되는지 「…해 달라고 하다」의 뜻이 되는지는 문장의 전후 관계에 따라 정해진다.
③ 행위자에게 관심이 없으면 3의 구문이 된다.
보기 Have him carry this suitcase upstairs.
→ Have this suitcase carried upstairs.

He always has his secretary type his letters.
→ He always has his letters typed (by his secretary).
(2) get sb to do
▶ 나는 그에게 차를 닦게 했다 I got him to wash my car.
▶ 나는 그들에게 내 견해를 받아들이게 할 수가 없었다 I couldn't get them to accept my view.
▶ 그는 모친에게 억지로 차로 배웅을 받았다 He got his mother to drive him to the station. (▶이 구문은 상대를 설득하여 그 어떤 행동을 시킬 때에 쓰임)
(3) have [get] + 목적어 + 과거분사
▶ 나는 시계 수리를 받아야 한다 I must have my watch fixed.
▶ 그는 내일 의사에게 눈을 진찰 받을 생각이다 He is going to have his eyes examined by a doctor tomorrow.
▶ 당신은 한 달에 몇 번 이발을 합니까? How often do you have your hair cut?
▶ 나는 한 달에 한 번 이발을 합니다 I have my hair cut once a month.
▶ 나는 남에게 차를 닦게 하지 않습니다. 내가 직접 닦습니다 I don't have my car washed. I wash it myself.
[어법]
① 이상 어떤 글에도 get을 쓸 수 있는데 get을 쓰는 쪽이 구어적이다.
② 이 구문의 부정·의문에는 do, does, did를 쓴다.
③ 이 구문에서는 특별히 필요한 때를 제외하고는 행위자는 나타내지 않는다.
행위자를 나타내는 1, 2의 구문과의 관계는 다음과 같다.
I have my hair cut. 3→ I have a barber cut my hair. 1 / I get a barber to cut my hair. 2

사옥 社屋 an office building; the building of a company

사외 社外 outside the company

사욕 私慾 a selfish desire; self-interest
♦ 사욕이 없는 unselfish; disinterested / 사욕을 채우다 satisfy [gratify] one's selfish desires / 사욕을 버리다 rise above [put aside] self-interest / 사욕에 사로잡히다 be the slave of [to] self-interest
▶ 그는 사욕에 눈이 멀었다 He is blinded [ruled] by self-interest [his selfishness].

사용 私用 1 〈사사로이 씀〉 private [personal] use; 〈공용물의 유용〉 (an) appropriation; (a) misappropriation
—사용하다 put [turn] *sth* to private use; use *sth* for private [one's own] purposes; misappropriate; appropriate (to *oneself*); embezzle ♦ 공금을 사용하다 misappropriate government funds; put [turn] public funds to private use
2 〈사사로운 용무〉 private business ♦ 사용으로 on private [personal] business

사용 社用 a company business ♦ 사용으로 on company business; on the business of one's firm ■ —족 expense-account spenders

사용 使用 use; employment; 〈응용〉 application; 〈소비〉 consumption; 〈충당〉 appropriation
♦ 사용을 금하다 forbid [ban] the use (of)
▶ 사용 금지 (게시) Not in use.
▶ 사용중 (게시) Engaged. ⇌ Occupied. ⇌ In use.
▶ 그 회의실은 현재 사용중이다 The meeting room is in use now.
▶ 컴퓨터의 사용이 급증하고 있다 The use of electronic computers is growing rapidly.
—사용하다 use; make use of; put to use; employ; apply; consume; appropriate; devote
♦ 사용한 우표 a used stamp / 사용하지 않는 방 an unused room / 사용할 수 있는 usable; practicable; fit for use / 사용할 수 없다 cannot be used; be unfit for use / 사용하게 되다 come into use / 사용하지 않게 되다 go out of use; fall into disuse / 가장 효과적으로 사용하다 make the best (possible) use of / 마음대로 사용하다 have the free use (of); be at liberty to use *sth* / 널리 사용되고 있다 be widely used; be in general use / 일상 사용되다[되지 않다] be in [out of] everyday [daily] use
■ —가치 use [utility] value; the value in use —권 the right of using; the use —량 the amount *sth* used; the quantity *sth* consumed —료 a rental fee; the rental; the rent; the hire —능력 a working force —인 an employe(e) —자 a user; 〈소비자〉 a consumer; 〈고용주〉 an employer

사용법 使用法 the way of using; how to use [handle, operate]; usage; 〈복용법〉 directions (for use)
▶ 나는 이 기계의 사용법을 모른다 I do not know how to work [operate] this machine.

사우 社友 〈회사 동료〉 a colleague; 〈회사 관계자〉 a friend of the firm

사우나 a sauna ■ —실(室) a sauna parlor

사우디아라비아 〈나라 이름〉 Saudi Arabia; 〈공식명〉 the Kingdom of Saudi Arabia
■ —사람 a Saudi Arabian; a Saudi

사우스다코타 〈미국의 주〉 South Dakota (略 S. Dak.); 〈속칭〉 Sunshine State
■ —사람 a South Dakotan

사우스캐롤라이나 〈미국의 주〉 South Carolina (略 S.C.); 〈속칭〉 Palmetto State
■ —사람 a South Carolinian

사우스포 〔野〕 a southpaw (pitcher); 〔拳〕 a southpaw

사운 社運 ♦ 사운을 걸고 at the risk of the future of the company / 사운을 걸다 risk [stake] the future of the company 《on》

사운드 a sound ■ —박스 a sound box —트랙 a sound track

사원 寺院 〔佛教〕 a (Buddhist) temple; 〈수도원〉 a monastery

사원 社員 a member (of the staff); an employee (of a company); a clerk; a worker; a staff member; 〈조합원〉 a partner; (총칭) the staff; the personnel
♦ 사원 일동을 대표하여 on behalf of the staff / 사원이 되다 join the staff; join [enter] the service of a company
▶ 그 회사는 사원을 감원했다[증원했다] The firm has reduced [increased] the staff [personnel].
■ 신입[퇴직]— an incoming [outgoing] partner [employee] 유한[우선]— a limited [predominant] partner 정— a regular member; a staff member 종신— a life member —명부 the roster (of a company)

사원 私怨 personal [private] grudge [spite, enmity, grievances] ▶ 그는 나에게 사원을 품고 있다 He has a private grudge against me.

사월 四月 April (略 Apr.)

사위 a son-in-law (*pl.* sons-in-law)
♦ 큰[맏]사위 the oldest son-in-law / 작은 사위 a younger son-in-law / 사위를 맞다 get [find] a husband for one's daughter; get [take] a son-in-law

사위다 burn (*itself*) out; burn up

사윗감 a suitable match for one's daughter; a likely son-in-law
♦ 사윗감을 고르다 look for a man to marry one's daughter to / 사윗감으로 훌륭하다 [시원찮다] be a good [poor] match for one's daughter

사유 私有 private ownership
♦ 사유의 privately-owned; private / 토지의 사유 private ownership of land
■ —권 the right of private property; private ownership [rights] —림 a private forest —물 private possessions [property] —지 private land

사유 事由 a reason; a cause; a ground; conditions ⇨ 이유(理由)

사유 思惟 thinking; speculation —사유하다 ⇨ 생각하다

사유재산 私有財産 private property
■ —제도 the private ownership system

사육 飼育 breeding [raising] (of cattle); rearing (of silkworms) ♦ 누에의 사육법 the

사육제 method of rearing silkworms
　—사육하다 breed; raise; rear; keep
　▪**—자** a raiser; a breeder; a rearer; a (bird) fancier **—장** a breeding ground: 말의 사육장 a horse-breeding farm; a stud **—학** thremmatology

사육제 謝肉祭 the carnival
사은 謝恩 an expression of gratitude; repayment of a kindness
　—사은하다 repay kindness; express (one's) gratitude; appreciate sb's favors
　▪**—매출** thank-you sales **—회** a dinner [party] given (by the graduates) in honor of (their teachers); a thank-you party (for the teachers); a testimonial dinner

사음 一音 (樂) G ▪**—자리표** a G [treble] clef
사음 邪淫 lasciviousness; lewdness; licentiousness; adultery; fornication
사의 謝意 **1** 〈감사의 뜻〉 gratitude; thanks
　♦**사의를 표하다** express one's gratitude; make a grateful acknowledgement (for); tender one's thanks (to); thank / 미소로써 사의를 표하다 smile one's thanks
　2 〈사과의 뜻〉 apology ♦**사의를 표하다** tender an apology (for); apologize (for)

사의 辭意 one's resolution [intention] to resign ♦**사의를 비치다** hint at resignation / 사의를 밝히다[번복하다] announce [reconsider] one's resignation

사이 **1** 〈공간〉 〈간격〉 an interval; a space; 〈틈〉 a gap; an opening; 〈거리〉 (a) distance; 〈둘 사이〉 between; 〈여럿 사이〉 among(st); 〈한 가운데〉 amid(st); 〈중도〉 halfway; midway; 〈도중〉 on the way
　♦**사이에 든 사람** 〈중개자〉 a go-between; a middleman; 〈조정자〉 a mediator / 일정한 사이를 두고 at regular intervals / 사이에 두다 [끼우다] put between (A and B); interpose; insert / 사이를 벌리다 leave a space; space out / 행과 행 사이를 넓히다 leave space between the lines / 사이를 좁히다 leave no space / 사이를 채우다 fill the space
　▶ 새가 나무 사이에서 지저귀고 있다 Birds are singing in [among] the trees.
　▶ 그 부부 사이에는 자식이 없다 That couple have no children.
　▶ 그들 사이에 끼어서 입장이 난처했다 Placed between them, I found my position awkward.
　2 〔시간〕 〈겨를〉 an interval; time; while; a space; a period; a span; a spell; a pause; a break; a gap; 〈여가〉 leisure; spare time; time to spare; odd moments; (樂) (a) rest
　♦**외출한 사이에** while [when] one is out; in one's absence / 그러는 사이에 in the meantime; meanwhile; in (the) course of time / 눈 깜짝할 사이에 in the twinkling of an eye; in an instant / 어느 사이에 before one knows [is aware]; without one's knowledge; without one's knowing [realizing] it
　▶ 4시에서 5시 사이에 오시오 Come between four and five (o'clock).
　▶ 과거 10년 사이에 로켓은 급속도로 발전됐다 Rockets have made rapid progress during [for] the past ten years.
　▶ 내가 집을 비운 사이에 그녀가 우리집을 찾아왔다 She came to my house while I was out.
　▶ 밥먹을 사이도 없다 I have no time even to take a meal.
　▶ 책을 읽고 있는 사이에 잠이 들었다 While (I was) reading a book, I fell asleep.
　▶ 열차는 5분 사이로 출발한다 Trains leave every five minutes. ⇒ Trains leave at intervals of five minutes.
　3 〈관계〉 relations; relationship; terms
　♦**부부 사이** the relation of [between] man and wife / …과는 만나면 인사하는 사이다 be on nodding terms with... / …과는 너나 하는 사이다 be on thee-and-thou terms with... / 사이가 나쁘다 be on bad terms (with); (美) be at [on] the outs (with) / 사이가 나빠지다 get into bad terms (with); be estranged from each other / 사이를 갈라놓다 keep (them) apart; estrange [alienate] (A from B); come between (A and B)
　▶ 우리 두 사람은 사이가 아주 좋다 We are great [very good] friends.
　▶ 돈이 두 사람 사이를 갈라놓았다 Money came between the two.
　▶ 그는 아내와의 사이가 좋지 않다 He is on unpleasant terms with his wife.

사이공 〈베트남의 도시〉 Saigon ♦**사이공의** Saigon
사이다 〈음료〉 cider; a soda pop

〔解說〕「사이다」는 영어의 *cider*에서 온 것인데 (美)에서는 사과주스 (*sweet cider*라고도 한다), (英)에서는 사과주(酒) (*hard cider*라고도 한다)의 뜻으로 우리나라의「사이다」와는 다르다.

사이드 a side

〔解說〕*side*는 그 본래 가지고 있는「측면의」,「부차적」이라는 뜻의 복합어를 만드는데 우리말을 그대로 바꿔 놓을 수 없는 것이 있으므로 주의해야 한다. 사이드카(sidecar), 사이드테이블 (side table) 등은 그대로 쓸 수 있지만「사이드브레이크」는 hand brake, parking brake, emergency brake라고도 한다.

　▪**—라이트** (a) sidelight **—라인** a sideline **—보드** a sideboard **—스로**(野) a sidearm delivery; throwing sideways **—스텝** a sidestep **—스트로크** a sidestroke **—아웃**(排球) a sideout **—워크** the side work **—테이블** a side table; 〈침대 옆의〉 a night table; nightstand **—플레이어**(映)〈조연〉 a side player; a byplayer

사이렌 a siren; a whistle ♦**사이렌을 울리다** sound [blow] a siren
사이버네틱스 〈인공 두뇌학〉 cybernetics
사이보그 〈인공 인간〉 a cyborg
사이비 似而非 false; fake; would-be; sham; pretended; mock; spurious; pseud(o)-; quasi-
　♦**사이비 군자** a hypocrite; a wolf in sheep's clothing / 사이비 기자 a quasi-reporter / 사이비 신사 a would-be gentleman / 사이비 예술가 a mock artist / 사이비 크리스천 a

pseudo-Christian / 사이비 학자 a pretended scholar; a prig

사이사이 1 〈공간〉 intervals; spaces; gaps
♦ 백합 사이사이에 장미를 꽂다 arrange roses among lilies
2 〈시간〉 intervals 《of, in, between》
♦ 공부하는 시간 사이사이에 in the intervals of study; in spare moments from *one's* study

사이언스 〈과학〉 science ■—픽션 science fiction (略 SF)

사이좋게 on good [friendly, cordial] terms 《with》; in peace [harmony, concord] 《with》
♦ 사이좋게 지내다 get on [along] well 《with》; keep intimate relations 《with》; be on good terms 《with》/ 사이좋게 살다 live together happily; live in peace 《with》
▶ 우리 서로 사이좋게 지냅시다 Let us be good neighbors.
▶ 그 아이하고 사이좋게 지내도록 해라 Try to get on [along] well with the boy.

사이즈 size

[解說] 우리말의 「사이즈」는 신·모자·셔츠·옷 등 그다지 크지 않은 것을 가리켜서 쓰는 경우가 많지만 영어에서의 *size*는 the size of a country [a city, a swimming pool]처럼 우리말에서는 보통 「사이즈」로는 표현하지 않는 큰 것까지도 가리켜 쓴다.

♦ 사이즈를 재다 take the size 《of》/ 사이즈가 맞다[맞지 않다] be [be out of] *one's* size

사이짓기 〔農〕〈간작〉 the intercropping

사 이 참 —站 1 〈휴식〉 a recess 《between working hours》; a break; (a) rest; a respite; time-off; a time-out
2 〈간식〉 a snack between regular meals; between-meals refreshments
♦ 사이참을 먹다 eat (a snack) between meals; have a snack

사이클 〔電〕〈주파〉 a cycle; 〈자전거〉 a cycle; a bicycle; a bike ■—선수 a bicycle racer

사이클로이드 〔數〕 a cycloid

사이클로트론 〔物〕 a cyclotron

사이클링 cycling; bicycling ▶ 작년 여름에 그들은 제주도 일주 사이클링을 했다 Last summer they went on a cycling tour around the Cheju Island.

사이키델릭 〈약물에 의한 환각 상태〉 psychedelic

사이펀 a siphon; a syphon ■자동— an automatic siphon —기압계 a siphon barometer —병 a siphon bottle —작용 siphonage

사인 死因 the cause of *sb's* death
♦ 사인을 조사하다 inquire into the cause of *sb's* death / 사인 불명이다 die from some unknown cause / …의 사인이 되다 be the death of...
▶ 그의 사인은 과로였다 His death was due to overwork.
■—통계 statistics of death causes

사인 私人 a private person [individual, citizen]; 〈개인〉 an individual
♦ 일개 사인의 자격으로 as a private person; in *one's* private [individual] capacity / 사인으로서 행동하다 act as a private individual

사인 私印 a private seal ■—도용 surreptitious use of a private seal —위조 forging [forgery] of a private seal

사인[1] 〈부호·암호〉 a sign
2 〔野〕 a signal ♦ 사인을 보내다 signal; give signals to 《the pitcher》; motion / 사인을 주고 받다 exchange signals
3 〈서명〉 a signature; an autograph
♦ 사인 공세를 받다 be besieged by [plagued with] autograph hunters / 사인을 받다 get *sb's* autograph
—사인하다 sign *one's* name [autograph] 《on》; autograph (a book); sign (a letter)
■—북[첩] an autograph book [album] —수집가 an autograph hunter

사인[2] 〔數〕 a sine (略 sin) ■—곡선 a sine curve —법칙[정리] a sine rule [theorem]

사인교 四人轎 a four-men sedan chair

사인승 四人乘 ♦ 사인승 a four-seater

사인조 四人組 a quartet(te); a foursome

사일구혁명 四一九革命 the Student Revolution on April 19th

사일런트 1 〈묵음자〉 a silent letter
2 〈무성 영화〉 a silent film [picture]

사일로 〈사료 저장고〉 a silo (*pl.* ~s)

사일열 四日熱 〔醫〕 quartan fever ■—말라리아 quarten malaria

사임 辭任 resignation; retirement from office; stepping out [down]; going out of office
—사임하다 resign (from) 《*one's* post》; leave [quit] 《*one's* place》; step out; go out of office
♦ 의원직을 사임하다 vacate [resign] *one's* seat in the National Assembly / 이사직을 사임하다 resign as director; resign *one's* position on the board of director

사자 四者 ♦ 사자(간)의 quadripartite ▶ 시장은 비밀리에 사자 회담을 열었다 The mayor secretly held a quadripartite conference.

사자 死者 a dead person; the deceased; the departed; (총칭) the dead

사자 使者 a messenger; an envoy; 〈밀사〉 an emissary ♦ 사자를 보내다 send a messenger 《to》; dispatch a mission
▶ 개나리는 봄의 사자다 The forsythia is the messenger [harbinger, herald] of spring.

사자 獅子 a lion; 〈암컷〉 a lioness ■새끼 사자 a cub lion; a lionet / 사자같은 leonine; lionlike / 성난 사자처럼 like a lion at bay; with lion-like fury

사자 嗣子 an heir; an heiress(여자); a successor

사자 寫字 copying; transcription ■—생 a copyist; a scribe; an amanuensis (*pl.* -ses)

사자 없는 산에 토끼가 왕 노릇한다 When the cat's away, the mice will play.

사자춤 獅子— a dance with a lion's mask
♦ 사자춤을 추다 do the dance of the lion

사자코 獅子— a pug [snub] nose
♦ 사자코의 pug-nosed; snub-nosed

사자후 獅子吼 1 〔표효〕 the roaring of a lion
2 〈열변〉 an impassioned speech; a harangue
♦ 사자후를 토하다 make an impassioned [a declamatory] speech; make a harangue
3 〈불교의〉 the preaching of Buddha
4 〈질투의〉 the raging of a jealous woman

사장 死藏 hoarding; dead storage
—**사장하다** hoard (up); keep *sth* idle
♦ 재물을 사장하다 keep a fortune as a buried treasure / 책을 사장하다 be a mere book hoarder; coffin books
■ —品 hoarded goods

사장 沙場 the sands; a sandbank; a shoal; a sandy beach

사장 社長 the president; the head 《of a firm》
♦ 사장이 되다 become president of a company; assume the presidency of a corporation —부— a vice president

사장 寫場 a photo studio=사진(~관)

사재 私財 private fortune [funds, means, property] ♦ 사재를 털어 out of *one's* own purse [pocket]; at *one's* own expense / 공공 사업에 사재를 투자하다 expend *one's* funds upon a public undertaking

사재기 hoarding —**사재기하다** lay *sth* in for future use; keep *sth* in reserve

사저 私邸 *one's* private residence [mansion, house]

사적 史蹟 a historic [historical] spot [site]; a place of historic [historical] interest; historic relics [remains]
▶ 그 건조물은 사적으로 지정되었다 The building was designated as a place of historic interest.
▶ 그 지역에는 사적이 풍부하다 The area is rich in historic remains [associations].
▶ 나는 그 지방의 여러 사적을 답사했다 I explored historic spots in the district.
■ —보존회 a society for preservation of historic relics

사적 事績 an achievement; an accomplishment; a deed; services; merits
♦ 위인의 사적 the deeds of a great man

사적 事蹟・事跡 evidence; a vestige; a trace

사적 史的 historical; historic
—고증 historical researches —사실 a historical fact —연구 historical studies 《on》—유물 론 historical materialism

사적 私的 private; individual; unoffical; personal ♦ 사적으로 privately; personally; individually
▶ 나는 내 사적인 문제를 가까운 친구들과 의논 했다 I discussed my private matters with my close friends.
■ —감정 personal feeling —교제 《have》 personal contact 《with》—생활 *one's* private life —제재 〈폭력적인〉 lynching : 사적 제재를 가하 다 lynch *sb*

사전 私田 a private field

사전 私錢 counterfeit [bogus, forged] money
■ —꾼 《美》 a counterfeiter; 《英》 a coiner

사전 事典 a cyclop(a)edia
—백과— an encyclopedia

사전 事前 ♦ 사전에 before the fact; beforehand; in advance / 사전에 준비하다 prepare in advance; arrange 《the schedule》 beforehand / 사전에 통보하다 inform 《*sb* of *sth*》 in advance; give *sb* (a) previous notice 《of》
▶ 한국에 도착하는 날짜를 사전에 알려 주십시 오 Please inform me of the date of your arrival in Korea in advance.
■ —검열 prepublication censorship; pre-censorship —계획 a prearranged plan —공작 preparatory operations; advance work —동의 a prior consent; a consent before the fact —선거운동 preelection campaigning; precandidacy propaganda —수회 acceptance of a bribe before an act —승인 prior approval —준비 advance preparations; preliminary arrangements; prearrangement —통고 an advance notice —행위 an act before the fact —협의 prior consultation

사전 辭典 a dictionary; a wordbook; a lexicon; 〈용어 해설〉 a glossary; 〈전문어 등의〉 a nomenclature; 〈동의어・반의어 등의〉 a thesaurus 《*pl*. ~es, -ri》
♦ 살아 있는 사전 a walking dictionary / 사전 을 찾다 consult [refer to] a dictionary; 《美》 look up 《a word》 in a dictionary / 자주 사전 을 찾다 have frequent recourse to [make frequent use of] a dictionary / 사전과 씨름하다 struggle with [make constant use of] a dictionary
▶ 그런 말은 내 사전에 없다 The word is not found [given] in my dictionary.
■ —편찬법 lexicography —편찬자 a compiler of a dictonary; a lexicographer —학 lexicology

사절 四折 a quarto 《*pl*. ~s》 ■ —판 a quarto (edition)

사절 使節 〈일행〉 a mission; a delegation; 〈개인〉 an envoy; an ambassador; a delegate
♦ 사절로 가다 go on a mission 《to》
■ —교육— an educational mission 군사— a military mission 친선— a goodwill envoy [mission] —단 a mission; a delegation: 캐나다에 문화 사절단을 파견하다 dispatch a cultural mission to Canada

사절 謝絶 refusal; 《美》 declination; denial
▶ 면회 사절 《게시》 No visitors (allowed). ⇌ 〈병실의〉 Appointment only. ⇌ 〈작업장의〉 Interviews [Visits] declined during working hours.
▶ 입장 사절 《게시》 No admission. ⇌ 〈미성년자 에 대한〉 Adults only [No (entrance to) children].
—**사절하다** refuse; decline; deny
♦ 제안을 사절하다 decline an offer / 면회를 사절하다 deny *oneself* to visitors; decline to receive [see] a visitor; be not at home to a visitor / 입장을 사절하다 stop selling tickets; close the box office
▶ 그는 초대를 정중히 사절했다 He politely declined [turned down] the invitation.

사점 死點 〔機〕 a dead point [center]

사정 事情 **1** 〈형편・처지・까닭〉 circumstances; conditions; reasons; 〈정세〉 the situation; the state of things [matters, affairs]
♦ 자세한 사정 the details; the whole circumstances / 복잡한 사정 complicated [divers] circumstances; intricacies / 식량[주택] 사정의 악화 the worsening of the situation of food [housing] supply / 사정이 이러하여 such being the case; under these circumstances / 사

정상 under the [by force of] circumstances / 사정이 허락하면 if circumstances permit [favor] / 어떠한 사정이 있더라도 in any circumstances; in any case; on any account / 사정에 따라서는 according to circumstances; if occasion requires / 일신상 사정으로 for personal reasons / 사정을 참작[고려]하다 make allowance(s) for circumstances
▶아버지는 국제 사정에 밝으시다 [정통하시다] My father is conversant [well-acquainted] with international affairs.
▶집에 안 계실 동안 사정이 크게 변했습니다 During your absence things changed greatly.
▶그녀는 집안 사정으로 직장을 그만두었어 She quit her job for family reasons.
▶부득이한 사정으로 모임에 참석하지 못했습니다 I could not attend the meeting for some unavoidable reasons.
▶사정인즉 이러하다 Such is the case. ⇒ This is how it is.
▶사정이 허락하는 한 요청을 받아들이겠습니다 So [As] far as circumstances permit, I will comply with your requests.
2 〈간청〉 (an) entreaty; solicitation; supplication; an earnest appeal
—**사정하다** entreat; implore; plead 《for help》; beg *sb's* consideration(s); make an earnest appeal 《to *sb* for *sth*》
♦도와 달라고 사정하다 implore aid 《from *sb*》
■가정— *one's* family circumstances [reasons]
교통[호텔]— traffic [hotel] conditions

사정 査定 〈세금의〉 assessment; 〈예산의〉 revision; 〈자격의〉 screening —**사정하다** assess; make an assessment of; value; revise 《a budget》
■세액— the assessment of taxes —가격 an assessed value [price] —기관 an assessing organ —액 an assessed amount

사정 射程 a (shooting) range
♦사정 안[밖]에 within [out of] range / 사정을 정하다 range / 최대 사정 거리로 사격하다 shoot at extreme range
▶이 대포의 사정 거리는 10마일이 넘는다 This cannon ranges over [has a range of more than] ten miles.
■원거리[근거리]— a long [short] range 유효— the effective range (of one mile)

사정 射精 ejaculation; discharge [emission] of semen; seminal emission —**사정하다** ejaculate; emit [discharge] semen
■—관(管) an ejaculatory duct

사정사정 事情事情 pleadingly; imploringly
—**사정사정하다** beg *sb's* consideration(s); plead 《for》; earnestly request [ask for]; implore; solicit; entreat
♦사정사정해서 승낙을 얻다 win over *sb* by entreaties; entreat *sb* into consent

사정없다 事情— merciless; severe; heartless; relentless; ruthless; unsparing
♦(인정)사정 없이 without mercy [pity]; severely; relentlessly; ruthlessly; unsparingly / 사정없이 때리다 beat *sb* unsparingly

사제 司祭 a priest; a pastor; a celebrant
■—관(館) a parsonage

사제 私製 private [illicit] manufacture
♦사제의 private; privately made
■—엽서 (美) a postcard (▶관제 엽서는 a postal card); (英) a postcard (▶관제 엽서도 a postcard) —품 privately made [manufactured] goods [articles]; goods [articles] of private manufacture

사제 師弟 master and pupil; teacher and student ■—간[관계] the relation of [between] teacher and student

사제 瀉劑 a laxative; an aperient; a purgative; an evacuant

사조 —調 〔樂〕 (the key of) G ♦사장[단]조 G major [minor]

사조 思潮 the trend [current] of thought; current thoughts [ideas]
■근대— modernism 문예— the trend of literature; literary thoughts 시대— the spirit of the times [age] 현대— contemporary thought

사족 四足 1 〈네발〉 four feet; 〈사지〉 the limbs **2** 〈비유〉 ♦사족을 못쓰다 be awfully fond of; have a weakness [passion] 《for》; be spellbound; be crazy 《about》
▶그는 여자라면 사족을 못쓴다 He is crazy [mad] about a woman. ⇒ He is gone on a girl.
■—수 (獸) a quadruped; a four-footed animal

사족 蛇足 〈군더더기〉 superfluity; redundancy; padding ♦사족을 달다 make an unnecessary addition 《to》; pad (out) 《a speech, writing》; paint the lily
▶그것은 사족이다 That's superfluous. ⇒ That is (like putting) a fifth wheel to the coach.
▶강사는 강연의 마지막에 사족을 달았다 The lecturer made an unnecessary addition to his lecture in the end.

사죄 死罪 a capital crime [offense]; 〔가톨릭〕 a mortal [deadly] sin

사죄 赦罪 (a) pardon; (a) remission; 〈대사(大赦)〉 (an) amnesty; 〔가톨릭〕 absolution
—**사죄하다** pardon; remit (a punishment); absolve 《*sb* from [of]》

사죄 謝罪 an apology 《for》
♦사죄를 요구하다 demand an apology 《from》 / 사죄를 받아들이다 accept an apology
▶그녀는 그의 사죄를 받아들일 수가 없었다 She could not accept his apology.
—**사죄하다** apologize 《to *sb* for》; beg *sb's* pardon [forgiveness] 《for》; make an apology; express *one's* regret 《for》
▶뭐라고 사죄해야 할지 모르겠습니다 I don't know how to apologize to you. ⇒ I beg your pardon.
■—광고 a notice of apology

사주 四柱 〔民俗〕 the horoscopic data (of a bridegroom); year, month, day, hour of *one's* birth; the "four pillars"
■—팔자 the Four Pillars and Eight Characters; *one's* fate [lot]

사주 私鑄 counterfeit coinage —**사주하다** counterfeit [forge] coins
■—전(錢) a counterfeit [false, bad] coin [copper]

사주 社主 the head of a company; the proprietor of a firm

사주 使嗾 〈부추김〉 instigation; incitement ◆남의 사주를 받고 …하다 do sth at another's instigation ―**사주하다** incite; instigate; entice; abet; egg [edge] sb on ((to)); stir up ◆사주하여 …시키다 incite [instigate] sb to (do) / 사주하여 죄를 범하게 하다 incite [instigate] sb to (commit) a crime; abet sb in a crime ▶그들은 그를 사주하여 나쁜 짓을 하게 했다 They instigated him to the evil deed. ▶그는 백성을 사주해 반란을 일으키려 했다 He tried to incite the people to revolt. ■―**자** an instigator

사주 砂洲 a sandbank; a sandbar

사중 四重 ◆사중의 quadruplex; fourfold / 사중으로 quadruply

사중주 四重奏 〔樂〕 a quartet; (英) a quartette ◆현악― a string quartet / ―단 a quartet

사중창 四重唱 〔樂〕 a quartet

사증 查證 a visa; (프) a visé ⇨ 비자 ◆여권에 사증을 받다 get a visa on one's passport; get one's passport visaed ▶어제 나는 여권에 사증을 받았다 I got a visa on my passport [my passport visaed] yesterday. ―**사증하다** visa (a passport); visé; endorse ■입국[출국]― an entry [exit] visa ■―료 a visa [visé] fee

사지 四肢 the limbs; the legs and arms; the members ◆사지가 멀쩡하다 have no physical defects / 사지를 절단하다 dismember a body; cut off the limbs

사지 死地 the jaws of death; a fatal position [situation] ◆사지에 빠지다 fall into [be in] the jaws of death; be near death / 사지로 들어가다 go [throw oneself] into the jaws of death ▶그는 가까스로 사지를 벗어났다 He managed to make a narrow escape from death.

사지 砂紙 emery paper ⇨ 사포(砂布)

사직 司直 administration of justice; (총칭) the judicial authorities; the court; the bench ▶사직 당국이 그 사건에 손을 댔다 The judicial authorities have taken action on that case. ▶그 사건에 사직의 손길이 미쳤다 The arm of the law has reached the affair.

사직 社稷 〈신〉 the guardian deities of the State; 〈나라〉 sovereignty; the State; 〈조정〉 the Court ◆―단(壇) an altar to the guardian deities of the State

사직 辭職 resignation ◆사직을 권고하다 advise sb to resign / 사직을 만류하다 dissuade sb from resigning ―**사직하다** resign; (美口) check out (of office); give [throw] up one's office; quit office; step out [down] ◆신병을 이유로 사직하다 resign on the ground of illness [for reasons of health] ▶그가 사직한 이유가 무엇이었습니까? What were the reasons behind his resignation? ■―총― a wholesale resignation; a resignation en bloc: 내각의 총사직 the wholesale [general] resignation of the cabinet

사직원 辭職願 one's resignation; a letter of resignation ◆사직원을 내다 tender [submit] one's resignation / 사직원을 수리하다 accept sb's resignation

사진 沙塵 a dust storm; a sandstorm

사진 寫眞 a photograph; (口) a photo (pl. ~s); a picture ◆사진이 잘 받다 be photogenic; photograph well / 사진에 찍히기를 싫어하다 be camera-shy; be shy of camera / 사진을 찍다 〈자기가〉 photograph; take a photograph [picture] ((of)); 〈남을 시켜서〉 have [get] one's photograph taken / 사진을 인화[확대]하다 print [enlarge] a photograph ▶너 사진 잘 나왔다 You look good [nice] in this picture. ▶이 사진에서 날 알아보겠니? Do you recognize me in this picture? ▶이 카메라는 사진이 아주 잘 나온다 This camera works very well. ▶내가 찍은 친구들의 사진이 나오지 않았다 The pictures I took of my friends did not come out. ▶이 사진은 잘 나왔다 This photograph has taken [come out] well. ▶실물보다 사진이 더 잘 나왔다 This picture flatters her. ■광택― a glazed photograph 연속― a picture sequence 전신[반신]― a full-length [half-length] photograph 항공― an air [aerial] photo(graph) 현미경― a microphotograph 흑백― a black and white photograph ■―관 a photo studio ―기 a camera ―기구 photographic [camera] apparatus ―기자 a (newspaper) cameraman ―농도 photographic density ―대지(臺紙) a photograph mount ―사 a photographer; a cameraman ―술 photography ―용전구 a photoflood lamp [bulb] ―작가 a professional photographer [cameraman]; a photo artist ―전보 a photoradiogram ―제판 〔印〕 phototype process; photoengraving ―지도 a photomap ―첩 a photo(graph) album ―촬영대회 a photographic contest ―측량술[법] 〔土〕 photographic surveying; photogrammetry ―틀 a picture [photo] frame ―판 a photo plate; a photostat; 〈철판(凸板)〉 a phototype; 〈요판(凹板)〉 a photogravure ―판정 deciding the winner (in a race) by a photograph ―화보 a pictorial; an illustrated magazine

사진식자 寫眞植字 photocomposition; phototypography ■―기 a phototypographic composing machine; a photocomposer

사진전송 寫眞電送 phototelegraphy; telephotography ―**사진전송하다** send a picture by telegraphy; telephotograph

사질 砂質 ◆사질의 sandy; psammitic ■―암 psammite ―토 sandy soil

사차 四次 〔數〕 ◆사차의 biquadratic; quartic ■―방정식 a biquadratic [quartic] (equation) ―식 a quartic

사차원 四次元 four dimensions
♦사차원의 세계 a four-dimensional world; a world in four dimensions
사찰 寺刹 a Buddhist temple ⇨ 절
사찰 査察 (an) inspection; investigation
—사찰하다 inspect; make [do] an inspection of; investigate
■공중— (conduct) an aerial inspection 세무— tax investigation 학원— inspection on campus activities 현지— an on-site [on-the-spot, on-the-job] inspection ■—관 an inspector —비행 an inspection flight —제도 an inspection system
사창 私娼 a prostitute; a woman of the streets; a streetwalker
■—가 an unlicensed gay [prostitute] quarters —굴 a house of ill fame; a brothel; a bawdy house
사채 私債 a private loan [debt]; a personal liability ♦사채를 주다 make a private loan (to); extend private loans / 사채를 쓰다 use private loans ■—놀이 private loan business; money-lending
사채 社債 a (corporation) debenture; a company [corporation] bond
♦1억원의 사채를 모집[발행]하다 issue debentures amounting to a hundred million won
■담보[무담보]— a secured [an unsecured] debenture 장기[단기]— a long-term [short-term] debenture 전환— a convertible debenture 정리— an adjustment bond ■—권(券) a debenture; a bond —권자 a debenture holder —상환 debenture redemption —시장 the private money market; a curb loan market —업자 a private [curb] money lender; a curb loan dealer —이자 debenture interests —인수자 a debenture underwriter —중개인 a curb loan broker
사채발행 社債發行 flotation of debentures; debenture issue [flotation] ■—액 the debentures issued; the issue amount of debentures
사천왕 四天王 〔佛敎〕 the Four Devas
사철 四— 1 〈네 계절〉 the four seasons (of the year)
♦사철의 변화 a change of seasons
2 〈항상〉 in [through] all seasons; all the year round; throughout the year; always
▶ 경치는 사철 변한다 The scenery varies from season to season.
사철 私鐵 a nongovernmental railroad line; a railroad under private management
사철 砂鐵 iron [magnetic] sand
사철나무 〔植〕 a spindle tree
사체 死體 a (dead) body ⇨ 시체
▶ 어제 경찰은 사체 발굴을 실시했다 Police carried out the exhumation of the body yesterday.
▶ 행방불명된 낚시꾼은 하구에서 사체로 발견되었다 The missing angler was found dead at the mouth of the river.
■—부검 an antopsy; a post-mortem
사체 斜體 (letters in) italics; 〈필기의〉 an oblique hand ♦사체의 italicized
사초 莎草 1 〔植〕 a sedge 2 〈잔디〉 turf; sod
—사초하다 sod [turf] a grave
사촌 四寸 a cousin; a first [full] cousin
▶ 가까운 이웃사촌이 먼 친척보다 낫다 A good neighbor is better than a brother far off.
■외— a cousin on the mother's side ■—간 cousinship; cousinhood —형제[자매] a cousin brother [sister]
사춘기 思春期 (the age of) puberty; adolescence ♦사춘기의 소년 소녀 boys and girls at puberty / 사춘기의 pubescent; adolescent / 사춘기가 되다 arrive at [reach, attain] puberty
▶ 사춘기 소녀의 상처받기 쉬운 마음을 바로 이해하세요 Have the right understanding of the delicate mind of an adolescent girl.
사출 射出 emission; projection
—사출하다 shoot out; emit; project; catapult 《an airplane》; ejaculate; jet; radiate
■—기(機) a catapult —비행 catapulting —성형〔化〕 injection molding —좌석〔空〕 an ejection [ejector] seat
사취 詐取 fraud; a swindle —사취하다 obtain [get] 《money》 by fraud; swindle; defraud
♦돈을 사취하다 swindle *sb* out of money; swindle money out of *sb*; defraud *sb* of 《his》 money; obtain money by false pretenses
▶ 그는 거액의 돈을 사취당했다 He was defrauded of a large sum of money.
사치 奢侈 luxury; extravagance
♦사치성 소비재 luxurious consumer goods / 사치를 좋아하는 luxury-loving 《woman》 / 사치에 대하여 경고하다 warn *sb* against extravagance in living / 사치를 삼가다 abstain from [deny *oneself*] luxuries
▶ 우리의 현재 수입으로 에어컨 구입은 사치다 With our present income, the purchase of an air conditioner would be an extravagance.
▶ 그녀는 분수에 넘치는 사치를 하고 있다 Her style of living is out of keeping with her means.
—사치하다 be extravagant; indulge in luxury; live in luxury ♦옷에 사치하다 indulge in luxurious clothing
■—세 taxes on luxuries; a luxury tax —품 a luxury; a luxurious article
사치스럽다 奢侈— luxurious; extravagant; sumptuous; lavish
♦사치스러운 생활 a luxurious [an extravagant] life; high living / 사치스럽게 살다 live in luxury; live a luxurious [an extravagant] life; live high / 사치스럽게 자라다 be bred in luxury; be brought up in the lap of luxury
▶ 그녀는 옷차림이 사치스럽다 She is extravagant with dress.
▶ 이 물건은 내게는 너무 사치스럽다 This article is too expensive for me.
사칙 四則 〔數〕 the four fundamental rules of arithmetics
사칙 社則 the company regulations
사친회 師親會 a parent-teacher association (略 P.T.A., PTA) ⇨ 육성회
사칭 詐稱 misrepresentation; a false statement —사칭하다 assume another's [a false] name; represent *oneself* as 《an official》; misrepresent

사카린

♦이름을 사칭하여 under a feigned [an assumed] name (of)
▶그는 관직을 사칭했다 He abused [falsely assumed] an official title.
▶그는 학생이라고 사칭했다 He presented himself falsely [as to be] a student.
사카린 〖化〗 saccharin(e) ♦사카린의 saccharic
사커 〈축구〉 soccer; association football
　■—선수 a soccer player
사타구니 the groin ⇨ 샅
사탄 Satan ⇨ 악마
사탑 斜塔 a leaning tower
♦피사의 사탑 the Leaning Tower of Pisa
사탕 砂糖 1 ⇨ 설탕 2 〈과자〉 《美》 candy; 《英》 sweets; sweetmeats
　■얼음— 《美》 rock candy; 《英》 sugar candy
　■—단풍 a sugar maple ■—무 a sugar beet
　■—수수 a sugar cane ■—야자 a gomuti (palm)
　■—옥수수 a sorg(h)o; a (sweet) sorghum
사탕발림 砂糖— sugar-coated [honeyed] words; (비유) soft soap; flattery; cajolery; blarney
♦사탕발림으로 유혹하다 entice [allure] sb with fair words
▶남의 사탕발림에 넘어가지 않도록 해라 Take care not to be deceived by another's honeyed [sugar-coated] words.
　—사탕발림하다 use honeyed [sugar-coated, sweet] words; sweet-talk; sugar up; butter up; (口) soft-soap; curry favor with; say nice things to; cajole; flatter
사태 beef shank (used to make a thick soup)
사태 沙汰 1 〈무너짐〉 a landslide; a landslip; an avalanche [ǽvəlæ̀(ː)ntʃ]
▶폭우로 사태가 났다 There was a landslide owing to the heavy rain.
▶사태로 길이 막혔다 A landslide [landslip] has blocked the road.
　2 〈범람〉 a flood; a deluge; 〈많음〉 lots 《of》
♦사람 사태 an avalanche of people; a surging crowd of people / 주문 사태 an influx of orders
♦시장에 외제 물품 사태가 났다 Foreign goods glutted the market.
▶불경기로 감원 사태가 났다 Depression caused a drastic cut in the staff.
사태 事態 the situation; the state [position] of things [affairs]
♦심상치 않은 사태 a serious situation; the gravity of the situation / 사태를 관망하다 watch [wait and see] (the development of) the situation / 사태를 해결[수습]하다 settle the situation / 사태를 완화[악화]시키다 relieve [aggravate] the situation / 중대한 사태를 초래하다 bring about a remarkable [grave] situation
▶사태는 일변했다 Matters have assumed a different aspect.
▶사태가 호전되고 있는건가 악화되고 있는건가? Are things getting better or worse?
▶사태는 갈수록 악화되고 있다 The situation is becoming more serious.
▶그의 말이 사태를 악화시켰다 His remarks aggravated the situation.
▶너는 최악의 사태에 대비하지 않으면 안된다 You must be prepared for the worst.
사택 私宅 one's home; one's private house
사택 社宅 a company [corporation] house
▶사택에 살고 있기 때문에 집세는 없다 Living in company housing, I don't pay for it. ＝ I live rent-free in company housing.
사토장이 莎土匠— a gravedigger
사통 私通 1 〈편지의〉 private correspondence
　—사통하다 keep a private correspondence 《with sb》
　2 〈밀통〉 illicit intercourse; an illicit liaison; 〈미혼자와의〉 fornication; 〈기혼자와의〉 adultery　—사통하다 have improper relations 《with》; establish illicit liaisons 《with》; fornicate 《with》; commit adultery [misconduct] 《with》
　■—자 a fornicator
사통팔달 四通八達 stretching in all directions
　—사통팔달하다 (roads) stretch in all directions
♦사통팔달한 곳 a place accessible from all directions
▶이 도시는 도로가 사통팔달해 있다 The streets stretch out in all directions in this town.
사퇴 辭退 〈퇴거〉 excusing oneself from a senior's presence; taking one's leave from elders; 〈사직〉 resignations; 〈사양〉 declining; refusing to accept
　—사퇴하다 〈퇴거하다〉 take one's leave of an elder; 〈사직하다〉 resign (one's post); 〈사양하다〉 decline [refuse to accept] (an offer)
♦공직에서 사퇴하다 resign [leave] one's office; resign from public life
　■자진— voluntary resignation
사투 死鬪 a desperate struggle; a mortal combat　—사투하다 fight desperately; engage in a life-and-death [life-or-death] struggle 《with》
사투리 a provincial accent; a dialect; a provincialism
♦시골 사투리 a provincial accent; a local dialect / 사투리를 쓰다 speak with an [a provincial] accent
▶그의 프랑스어에는 사투리가 약간 섞여 있다 He speaks French with a slightly provincial accent.
▶그에게는 사투리가 아직 남아 있다 His provincial accent still hangs on.
사파 娑婆 this world ⇨ 사바세계
사파리 (a) safari
사파이어 〖鑛〗 a sapphire
사팔눈 a squint (eye); a strabismus; 《have》 a cast in the eye ♦사팔눈의 squint-[cross-]eyed
사팔뜨기 a squint-[cross-]eyed person; a squint-eye; a squinter ▶그는 심한 사팔뜨기다 He has a bad [fearful] squint.
사포 砂布 emery cloth; sandpaper ♦사포로 닦다 polish with sandpaper; sandpaper 《the surface of wood》
사표 師表 a model; a pattern; a paragon
♦이 세상의 사표 the salt of the earth; the light of the world / 세상의 사표로 숭앙받다 be looked up to as a man of light and leading
사표 辭表 a (written) resignation; a letter of

resignation
♦ 사표를 제출하다 [내다] give in [tender, send in, hand in, submit] *one's* resignation ((to)) / 사표를 반려하다[수리하다] turn down [accept] *sb's* resignation
▶ 그는 사표를 품에 넣고 사장 앞에 나아갔다 He turned up in front of the boss with a letter of resignation in his pocket.

사풋 with a light-footed step; lightly; softly

사프란 〔植〕 a saffron (crocus)

사필귀정 事必歸正 a corollary
♦ 법원의 판결을 사필귀정으로 환영하다 welcome the court ruling as a corollary
▶ 사필귀정이다 Right will prevail in the end.

사하다 赦— forgive; pardon; excuse; absolve *sb* of ((a sin)); remit; grant clemency to ((a prisoner))

사하다 謝— 1 〈감사하다〉 thank; express *one's* gratitude; tender *one's* thanks
♦ 후의를 사하다 thank *sb* for his kindness
2 〈사과하다〉 apologize ((to *sb* for)); beg *sb's* pardon ((for)); make an apology ((for *one's* rudeness))

사하라사막 —砂漠 the Sahara (Desert)

사하중 死荷重 the deadweight; the dead load ((of a wagon))

사학 史學 history; historical science [studies]
■ —과 〈학부〉 the history department; 〈학과〉 a history course : 사학과 학생 a history student —자 a historian

사학 私學 1 〈사설 교육 기관〉 a private school; a private college [university] ♦ 사학 출신자 a private college graduate 2 〈학설〉 a personal theory [doctrine]

사학 斯學 〈이 학문〉 this study [science, learning, subject, research] ♦ 사학의 대가[권위] an authority on the subject; an expert in the research

사할린 〈러시아의 섬〉 Saghalien; Sakhalin

사항 事項 〈일〉 matters; facts; 〈항목〉 articles; items; particulars
♦ 조사를 요하는 사항 a matter for investigation / 그 이의(異議) 사항에 대하여 upon the subject matter of the complaint / 모든 사항에 관하여 on all matters
■ 관련— relevant [related] facts [matters] 조사— matters for investigation

사해 四海 〈사방의 바다〉 the seven seas; 〈세계〉 the whole world
▶ 사해가 고요하다 The World is at peace.
■ —동포 universal brotherhood [fraternity] —동포주의 cosmopolitanism

사해 死海 〈서남 아시아에 있는 함수호〉 the Dead Sea

사행 射倖 speculation —사행하다 speculate; take the [*one's*] chance ((of)); chance it
■ —심 a speculative spirit : 사행심을 조장하다 stir up [incite] the gambling spirit

사행 蛇行 meandering
—사행하다 snake along; meander

사향 麝香 musk ♦ 사향내가 나는 musky; musk-scented / 사향내가 나다 be musky; be scented with musk
■ —고양이 a musk cat; a civet (cat) —나무 a

musk tree —노루 a musk deer —소 a musk-ox (*pl*. -oxen); musk sheep; ovibos —쥐 a muskrat (beaver)

사혈 瀉血 bloodletting; phlebotomy
—사혈하다 phlebotomize; let [draw] blood ((from a patient))

사형 死刑 death penalty [sentence]; capital punishment
♦ 사형이 되다 be punished with death / 사형에 처하다 put [condemn] *sb* to death; send [bring] *sb* to the scaffold [chair] / 사형에 처해지다 go to [mount] the scaffold / 사형을 집행하다 execute a death sentence; execute / 사형을 선고하다 pass a sentence of death ((on)); condemn [sentence] *sb* to death / 사형을 선고 받다 receive a death sentence / 사형의 폐지를 주창하다 advocate the abolition of capital punishment
▶ 이를 어기는 자는 사형에 처한다 It is forbidden under [on] penalty [pain] of death.
▶ 죄수는 모두 사형을 당했다 The prisoners were all put to death.
▶ 대법원에서 그의 사형이 최종적으로 확정되었다 His capital punishment sentence was finally upheld by the Supreme Court.
—사형하다 condemn [put] *sb* to death
■ 전기— electrocution ■—선고 sentence of death; a capital [death] sentence —실 a death chamber —장 an execution ground —죄 a capital offense [crime] —집행 execution —집행영장 a death warrant —집행유예 a reprieve —집행인 an executioner; a hangman; deathsman

사형 私刑 lynching; private punishment; lynch law ♦ 사형을 가하다 lynch *sb*

사형수 死刑囚 a condemned criminal; a criminal under sentence of death
■ —감방 a death [condemned] cell

사화 史話 a historical story [tale]

사화 私和 (a) reconciliation
—사화하다 become reconciled ((with)); reconcile *oneself* ((with)); make peace ((with))
♦ 사화시키다 reconcile ((A and B)); bring about a reconciliation ((between))
▶ 우리 사화하자 Let us shake hands and be friends again.

사화 詞華 flowery words [language]; flowers of speech

사화산 死火山 an extinct [a dead] volcano

사환 使喚 an attendant; a runner ♦ 사환 아이 an errand boy; an office boy [girl]

사활 死活 life and [or] death
♦ 사활의 문제 a matter [question] of life or death; vital question / 사활의 투쟁 ((engage in)) a life-and-death struggle; a struggle for life or death
▶ 이 사건은 우리 회사의 사활이 걸린 일이다 This incident may affect the fate of our company.

사회 司會 chairmanship; chairing ((a meeting));〈사회자〉 the chairman
▶ 파티는 홍 선생의 사회로 열렸다 The party was opened with Mr. Hong in the chair [as chairman].

▶다음 모임의 사회는 누가 봅니까? Who will be the chairman at the next meeting? ⇌ Who will preside over [at] the next meeting?
▶그는 사회를 잘 본다 He is a good hand at presiding over a meeting.
─**사회하다** preside at [over] 《a meeting》; take the chair; conduct; 〈방송 등의〉 act as master [mistress] of ceremonies 《for》; (口) emcee 《a show》
♦의장으로서 사회하다 officiate as chairman
■─봉 a gavel : 사회봉을 두드리다 rap the gavel

사회 社會 society; 〈세상〉 the world, the public; 〈지역 사회〉 a community
♦사회적 social / 사회 일반의 이익 public interest [welfare]
〈사회의〉 사회의 적 a public enemy; an enemy of society / 사회의 일원 a member of society / 사회의 제재 social sanctions
▶사회의 모진 바람을 맞으면서 한 사람의 사회인이 되는 것이다 By facing the storms of life one becomes a full-fledged citizen.
〈사회를〉 사회를 알다 know the world / 사회를 개량[개선]하다 reform [ameliorate] society
▶우리는 사회를 위해 진력해야 한다 We should do much for [render service to] our society.
〈사회에(서)〉 사회에 나가다 go out into [set out in] the world / 사회에 내보내다 give sb a start in life / 사회에 공헌하다 contribute to social [public] welfare / 사회에 해를 끼치다 be harmful [do harm] to society
▶그는 결코 사회에 해를 끼칠 사람은 아니다 He is the last person to be harmful to society.
■국제─ the world community of nations 문명[상업]─ a civilized [mercantile] community 봉건[시민]─ feudal [civic] society 상[중, 하]류─ the higher [middle, lower] classes [stratum of society] 인간[원시, 혈연]─ human [primitive, blood] society 일반─ the general public; the public in general [at large] ─간접자본 the social overhead capital ─경제 social economy ─계약설 the theory of social contract ─계층 a social stratum ─과 social studies [subjects] ─관 one's view of social life ─관습 social usage(s) ─교육 social education ─구조 social structure ─극 a social drama; a sociodrama ─도덕 social morality ─도태 social selection ─면〈신문의〉 the local news page [section]; the city news page ─민주주의 social democracy ─법칙 a social law ─보험 social insurance ─부〈신문사의〉 the local news section; (美) the city editor's section ─사상 social thought ─상(相) a phase of social life; an aspect of society ─성 sociality; social nature ─소설 a social novel ─심리학 social psychology ─악 a social evil; social ills [abuses]: 각종 사회악을 뿌리뽑다 root up the various social ills ─윤리 social ethics [morals]; social morality ─의식 social consciousness ─정의 social justice ─정책 a social policy ─제도 the social system ─조사 a social survey ─조직 social structure [organization, order] ─집단 a social group [community] ─통념 a socially accepted idea ─풍조 the trend [drift] of public opinion ─혁명 a social revolution ─현상 a social phenomenon ─형태 a social form ─환경 social environment

사회개량 社會改良 social reform ♦사회개량을 하다 reform [improve] society
■─가 a social reformer
사회과학 社會科學 social science
■─대학 a college of social science ─연구소 a social science research institute
사회기강 社會紀綱 social discipline
♦사회기강이 해이해지기 쉬운 여름철 summer season during which social discipline is liable to be slack
사회당 社會黨 the Socialist Party; the Socialists ■─원 a Socialist; a member of the Socialist Party
사회문제 社會問題 a social problem
♦사회문제가 되다 constitute a public [social] problem; become an object of public concern
사회보장 社會保障 social security
♦사회보장을 받다 enjoy the benefits of the social security services
─제도 the social security system [plan]
사회복지 社會福祉 social welfare
♦사회복지를 도모하다 take a measure with a view to [aimed at] social welfare / 사회복지를 증진하다 promote social welfare
■─기관[시설] social welfare organs [facilities]; an organization for social welfare ─사업 social welfare (service)
사회봉사 社會奉仕 social [public] service
♦사회봉사를 하다 do social service; work for the public benefit ■─사업 social service
사회불안 社會不安 social unrest
♦사회불안을 낳다[일으키다] breed [cause] social unrest / 사회불안을 조성하다 ferment social unrest / 사회불안을 제거하다 dispel [remove] social unrest; relieve the public of their sense of insecurity
사회사업 社會事業 social work [service]; public welfare service ♦사회사업을 하다 engage in public welfare service; work for (the) public good ■─가 a social worker
사회생활 社會生活 life in society; social life
♦사회생활을 (영위)하다 live socially
사회운동 社會運動 a social movement; a public campaign ♦사회운동을 일으키다 start a social movement
사회인 社會人 a full-fledged member of society ♦사회인이 되다 go out into the world; start one's adult life
사회자 司會者 the chairman; the president; 〈연회의〉 the toastmaster; 〈방송 등의〉 the master [mistress] of ceremonies (略 m.c., MC); (口) an emcee; 〈토론회 등의〉 the moderator; 〈의식의〉 the officiant
♦퀴즈 프로그램의 사회자 the quizmaster
사회장 社會葬 a public funeral
♦사회장을 지내다 give [accord] sb a public funeral; hold a public funeral 《for》
사회적 社會的 social
▶인간은 사회적 동물이다 Man is a social

animal.
▶사회적인 견지에서 그의 행위는 정당화되지 않을 것이다 His deed will not be justified from the social point of view.
▶사회적으로 그는 상당한 사람이다 He is a somebody in society.
▶그는 사회적으로 매장될 것이다 He will be ruined socially. ⇌ He will lose his social standing.
■반— antisocial —감정 social feeling(s) —긴장 social tension —명사 a society personage; (총칭) the social elite —문제 a social problem; a problem of society —세력 social influence —영향 a social influence; an influence on society —의무 a social [public] duty —제재 social discipline [punishment] —지위 one's social standing [position, status]: 사회적 지위가 높은 사람 a man of high social standing —추방 outlawry; social ostracism —풍토 〔心〕 a social climate —합의 social consensus

사회정세 社會情勢 social conditions; the state of affairs in a community ♦사회정세의 추이[변화] the drift of [a change in] the condition of public life

사회주의 社會主義 socialism
♦사회주의의 socialist; socialistic / 사회주의적(인) socialistic
■국가[공상적, 과학적, 기독교]— state [utopian, scientific, Christian] socialism —경제학 socialist(ic) economics —단체[국가, 정책, 정당, 운동] a socialist organization [state, policy, party, movement] —자 a socialist

사회층 社會層 a social stratum
♦모든 사회층에서 in all stations of life / 모든 사회층의 사람들 people of all social standings

사회학 社會學 sociology ♦사회학의 sociological ■—과 the department of sociology —자 a sociologist

사회화 社會化 socialization
—사회화하다 socialize 《industry》

사후 死後 ♦사후에 after one's death; posthumously / 사후의 posthumous; postmortem / 사후의 명성 posthumous fame [honors]; fame after death / 사후의 세계 the world after death; the world to come / 사후의 일을 생각하다 look beyond the grave / 사후의 일을 부탁하다 give sb the charge of the affairs after one's death
▶경찰은 사후 1개월이 경과한 것으로 추정되는 사체를 발견했다 The police found a body supposed to have been dead a month.
▶이것은 작가의 사후에 발표된 작품이다 This is a posthumous work of the writer.
■—강직 〔醫〕 rigor mortis; cadaveric stiffening [rigidity]

사후 事後 ♦사후에 after the fact; (라) post factum / 사후의 after the fact; (라) ex post facto / 사후의 참고를 위하여 for further reference
▶그들은 사후 처리를 그르쳤다 They made a mistake in dealing with what had happened.
■—검열 ex post censorship —관리 ex post management —대책 ex post facto measures —보고 《make》 an ex post facto report —승낙 an ex post facto approval [consent]

사후 약방문 (속담) After death comes a doctor.

사흗날 the third (day of a month)
♦오월 사흗날 the third of May

사흘 〈3일〉 three days
♦사흘마다 every three days / 사흘 걸러 every fourth day / 사흘이 멀다 않고 almost every other day; very frequently / 사흘에 한 번 once in every three days

사흘 굶어 도둑질 아니 할 놈 없다 (속담) Necessity knows [has] no law.

삭 朔 new moon

삭갈다 〔農〕 plow a paddy before transplanting (rice plants)

삭갈이 〔農〕 a single plowing before transplanting rice plants

삭감 削減 a cut; curtailment; reduction
♦대폭적인 삭감 a drastic reduction [cut]/ 예산의 삭감 cuts in the budget
—삭감하다 〈비용 등을〉 cut (down); curtail; retrench; reduce; pare down; (口) slash; 〈생산·인원 등을〉 cut back
♦경비를 삭감하다 pare [cut, whittle] down expenses / 예산을 대폭 삭감하다 slash [make a drastic curtailment in] the budget
▶시장은 예산을 20퍼센트 삭감하지 않을 수 없었다 The mayor was forced to slash [cut down, reduce] the budget by twenty percent.

삭과 蒴果 〔植〕 a capsule

삭구 索具 rigging; gear ♦배에 삭구를 달다 rig a ship

삭다 1〈옷 등이〉 wear thin [threadbare]; get rotten; decay
♦삭아서 너덜너덜하다 be worn to rags
▶내 바짓자락이 삭았다 The cuffs of my trousers are worn out.
▶구두끈이 삭았다 The shoestrings were worn through.
2〈죽 등이〉 become sloppy [watery]; turn bad; 〈종기가〉 resolve; be resolved
▶그 종기는 곧 삭을 거야 The tumor will soon be resolved.
3〈소화되다〉 be digested; digest
♦잘 삭는 음식 digestible food
▶이 음식은 잘 삭지 않는다 This food digests ill. 4〈분노 등이〉 be alleviated [appeased, mitigated]
♦…에 대한 분이 삭다 relent toward sb
5〈김치 등이〉 acquire [develop] flavor; 〈술이〉 ferment

삭도 索道 a cableway; a ropeway
■—차 a cable car —철도 a cable railway

삭막하다 索莫— 〈기억이 잘 나지 않다〉 dim [vague] (in one's memory); 〈황량하다〉 dreary; bleak; desolate
♦삭막한 풍경 a dreary [bleak] sight

삭망 朔望 1〈음력 초하루와 보름〉 syzygy; the first and fifteenth days of the lunar month
2〈제사〉 sacrfices on the first and fifteenth of the lunar months

삭발 削髮 haircutting; (a) tonsure
—삭발하다 tonsure; shave the head 《of》; have [get] one's hair cut

▶그는 삭발하고 중이 되었다 He took the tonsure and became a monk.

삭신 the sinews and joints
♦삭신이 쑤시다 have an acute pain all over; feel sharp [tingling] pains in the sinews and joints

삭월세 朔月貰 monthly rent ⇨ 사글세

삭이다 1〈음식을〉digest 《food》
♦이 음식은 삭이기 쉽다[어렵다] This food is easy [hard] to digest.
2〈종기를〉resolve
3〈노여움 등을〉mitigate; alleviate; appease; calm down ♦분을 삭이다 mitigate [appease] one's anger

삭정이 dead [withered] branches (on a tree)
♦삭정이를 쳐내다 trim the dead branches off the tree

삭제 削除 deletion; elimination; cancellation; erasure; striking out
♦두 자 삭제 two words crossed out
—**삭제하다** delete; eliminate; cancel; strike out [off]; cross out; erase; 〔印〕 kill
♦단어[구]를 삭제하다 eliminate words [phrases] / 명부에서 삭제하다 strike 《sb's name》 off a list
▶이 항목은 삭제했다 We have deleted this item.
▶그 결의는 의사록에서 삭제되었다 The resolution was struck from the minutes.

삭치다 削— cancel; strike out [off]; write off; cross off [out]; offset
♦셈을 삭치다 cancel [cross] the accounts

삭탈관직 削奪官職 removing [stripping] a government official from office
—**삭탈관직하다** remove *sb* from office; deprive [strip] *sb* of 《his》 office

삭풍 朔風 a north wind; a piercing wind; (詩) Boreas

삭히다〈소화시키다〉digest;〈발효시키다〉ferment;〈익히다〉make *sth* ripe; mellow;〈종기 등을〉resolve

삯 1【요금】a fee; a charge; rate;〈땅[집]세〉(a) rent;〈찻삯〉a fare;〈짐삯〉freight;〈운반비〉carriage
♦기찻삯 a railway fare / 삯을 받다 collect fees [rates, charges]; charge
▶수원까지 찻삯이 얼마입니까? What is the fare to Suwon?
2〈품삯〉wages; pay; hire
♦삯을 올리다 increase [raise] wages / 삯을 내리다 lower [cut down] wages / 하루 5만원의 삯을 받고 일하다 work at a wage [the wages] of fifty thousand won a day
■—꾼 a wage earner; a hired man [hand, laborer] —돈[전] ⇨ 임금(賃金) —말 a horse for hire; (英) a hack —메기 farm work for pay (without meals) —바느질 needlework for pay —빨래 laundry for pay —짐 a load carried for hire; 삯짐(을) 지다 carry a load for hire

삯일 job work; a job (of work); wage labor;〈작업량에 따라 삯을 주는〉piecework; work done by the piece;〈시간제로 삯을 주는〉timework
—**삯일하다** do job work [piecework]; do odd jobs; do work at piece rates
♦삯일하는 사람 a pieceworker

삯팔이 wageworking; wage earning
■—꾼 a wageworker; a wage earner

삯품 wage labor ♦삯품(을) 팔다 work for wages

산 山 1〈산악〉a mountain; a mount;〈봉우리〉a peak;〈구릉〉a hill
♦산이 많은 mountainous 《country》; hilly 《districts》 / 산같이 우뚝 솟다 tower [soar, stand] like a mountain / 산에 오르다 go up [climb (up), ascend] a mountain [hill], make an ascent of a mountain;〈기어오르다〉scale a mountain / 산을 내려가다 come [go, climb] down a mountain; descend a mountain / 산을 넘다 go over [cross] a mountain / 산에 가다 go to the mountains
▶한국은 산이 많은 나라다 Korea is a mountainous country.
▶〔會話〕「미국에서 가장 높은 산은 무슨 산입니까?」「알래스카에 있는 매킨리산인 줄 압니다. 높이가 6,194미터죠」"What's the highest mountain in the America?" "I believe it's Mckinley in Alaska. It's 6,194 meters high."
▶아버지는 건강을 위해 매일 아침 가까운 산에 오르신다 My father climbs the hill near our house every morning for his health.
2〈산소〉a grave(yard)

산 산 酸〔化〕an acid ♦산의 acid / 산을 만드는 acid-forming ■—과다증〔醫〕hyperacidity

산- 山— wild
—**딸기** wild [mountain] berries

-산 -山 Mount; Mt.

〔解說〕(1) 고유명사의 「…산」은 **Mount** 또는 그 약어 **Mt.**을 산 이름 앞에 붙여, Mount [Mt.] Everest 로 한다.
(2)「…산맥」은 Mountains를 고유명사의 뒤에 붙여 the Rocky Mountains처럼 말한다. 정관사가 필요하다.

-산 -産 1〈산물〉a product
♦외국산 밀 foreign-grown wheat / 국산 쌀 homegrown [native] rice
2〈출신〉a native
♦제주산이다 comes from Cheju

산간 山間 ♦산간의[에] in [among] the mountains [hills] ■—벽지 a remote and isolated place in [among] the mountains —벽촌 a remote mountain village [hamlet]

산개 散開〔軍〕(military) deployment; extension; development
—**산개하다** extend; form in open [extended] order; deploy; spread out
▶병사들은 산개하여 횡대를 지었다 The soldiers spread out to form a line.
■—대형 (in) open [extended] order —성단〔天〕an open cluster —운동 an extension movement —전〔戰〕fighting in open [extended] order

산견되다 散見— come across in places; be found here and there ♦여러 서적에서 산견되다 appear [be referred to] in various books

산계 山系 a mountain chain [range, system] ♦ 알프스 산계 the system of the Alps; the Alpine mountain range / 히말라야 산계 the Himalaya Mountains; the Himalayas

산고 産苦 labor (pains); travail; birthpangs; parturient pangs

산골 山— a mountain [mountainous] district; a secluded place ♦ 산골 사람 mountain folks [people]; a mountaineer; (口) a hillbilly / 산골에서 살다 live deep in the mountains

산골짜기 山— hills and valleys; a ravine; a gorge; a glen

산과 産科 obstetrics ♦ 산과의 obstetrical ■—병동 a maternity ward —병원 a maternity (home [hospital]); a lying-in clinic [hospital] —의사 an obstetrician —학 obstetrics; midwifery

산광 散光 〔物〕 scattered [diffused] light

산굴 山窟 a mountain cave

산굽이 山— a mountain bend

산금 産金 goldmining ―산금하다 produce [mine] gold —량 gold output —업 gold-mining industry —지 a gold-producing area —지대 a goldfield

산기 産氣 labor pains; travail; pangs [pains] of childbirth ♦ 산기가 있다 labor starts; 〈사람이 주어〉 begins to labor; have [feel] labor pains ▶ 그녀는 갑자기 산기를 느꼈다 Her labor has suddenly started. ⇌ She has begun to have labor pains suddenly.

산기 産期 the expected time of delivery [parturition]; period [term] of delivery; one's time ♦ 산기가 되다 come to one's time (of parturition)

산기슭 山— the skirts [foot, base, bottom] of a mountain ♦ 산기슭에 있는 마을 a village at the foot of a mountain; a village nestling under a hill

산길 山— a mountain path [trail]; a (mountain) pass ♦ 산길을 걷다 trudge [toil, go] along a mountain path

산꼬대 山— the night chill from a mountain wind —산꼬대하다 grow chill [cold] 《at the mountain top》

산꼭대기 山— the summit [top] of a mountain [hill]; the mountaintop; a peak; a crest ▶ 그 산꼭대기에는 사철 눈이 있다 The mountain is crowned with snow all the year round.

산나물 山— wild edible greens ♦ 산나물을 캐다 pick wild greens

산너머 山— ♦ 산너머에 across [beyond] the mountain / 산너머에서 《come》 from beyond the mountain

산놀이 山— a mountain excursion [picnic, hike]

산누에 〔昆〕 a wild silkworm; a tussah ■—나방 a tussah moth

산달 産— ♦ the month of giving birth

산대 山臺 a stage for a sandi masque ⇨ 산디

산더미 山— a mountain 《of》; a heap [pile]; a great mass; a huge amount; an accumulation ♦ 산더미처럼 많은 a mountain of; lots of; a world of / 산더미같은 숙제 a ton [pile] of homework / 산더미같은 짐 a mountainous load / 산더미같은 빚 a mountainous load of debts / 산더미처럼 쌓다 heap 《a desk with books》; pile 《a cart》 (mountain-)high 《with straw》; make a tall pile 《of》 ▶ 내 책상에는 서류가 산더미처럼 쌓여 있다 My desk is piled high with papers. ⇌ There are vast heaps of papers on my desk. ▶ 일이 산더미처럼 많다 I have lots [a heap] of things to do. ▶ 돈을 산더미같이 준대도 싫다 I would not do it even for all the money in the world.

산도 産道 〔醫〕 the parturient [obstetric, birth] canal

산도 酸度 〔化〕 acidity ■—시험 an acidity test —측정 acidimetry

산독증 酸毒症 〔醫〕 acidosis

산돼지 山— 〔動〕 a wild boar ⇨ 멧돼지

산들거리다 blow gently; breeze; sigh

산들바람 山— a gentle [light]) breeze; a soft wind [breath of air] ♦ 나뭇잎을 스치는 산들바람 a breeze passing through the leaves ▶ 산들바람이 불고 있다 A gentle breeze is blowing.

산들산들 gently; softly; in cool ripples ▶ 바람이 산들산들 분다 The wind blows gently. ⇌ There is a gentle breeze.

산등성이 山— a (mountain) ridge; the ridge [back, spine] of a mountain ♦ 산등성이를 타다[따라서 가다] go along the ridge(s)

산디 〔民俗〕 a (high makeshift) stage for a sandi masque; a masque ■—놀음 a masked drama; a masque

산디탈 a mask (worn by a sandi masker) ■—광대 a masked performer; a sandi masker

산딸기 山— wild berries

산뜻하다 1 〈깨끗하다〉 clean; neat and tidy; 〈선명하다〉 vivid; fresh [bright] 《color》; 〈보기 좋다〉 splendid; beautiful; smart; clear-cut ▶ 그녀는 언제 보아도 옷차림이 산뜻하다 She is always neatly dressed.
2 〈음식 맛이〉 plain; simple; light 《meal》
3 〈상쾌하다〉 cool; fresh; crisp 《weather》 ♦ 기분이 산뜻해지다 feel refreshed [relieved]

산란 産卵 egg-laying; laying eggs; 〈어패류의〉 spawning; 〈곤충의〉 oviposition —산란하다 lay [deposit] eggs; spawn; 〈곤충이〉 oviposit; 〈파리가〉 blow ▶ 바다에 살면서 산란하기 위해 담수로 들어오는 물고기가 많다 A number of fish live in the sea and enter freshwater to spawn. ■—관 〈곤충의〉 an ovipositor —기 the breeding [spawning] season: 연어가 산란기를 맞았다 The breeding season of the salmon has come. —장 〈물고기의〉 a spawning ground

산란 散亂 dispersion; scattering —산란하다 dispersed; scattered about; littered 《with scraps of paper》 ♦ 마음이 산란해지다 be distracted / 산란한 마음을 가라앉히다 calm down the restless mind ▶ 그의 마음은 슬픔으로 산란하다 His mind is

distracted by grief.
▶ 프리즘은 빛을 산란시킨다 A prism disperses light.
■ —광 scattered light

산록 山麓 the foot [base, bottom] of a mountain ⇨ 산기슭 ◆산록의 마을 a village at the foot of a mountain ■ —지대 a piedmont (district)

산류 酸類 〔化〕 acids

산림 山林 〈산과 숲〉 mountains and forests; 〈산중의 숲〉 a forest on the hills
◆산림을 만들다 afforest a mountain; plant a mountain with trees / 산림을 벌채하다 cut down a forest; deforest a mountain
■ —감독 a (government) forester; a forestry officer —남벌 reckless deforestation —법 the Forest Law —보호 forest conservancy —업 the forestry industry —조합 a forest (owner's) association —청 the Office of Forestry —행정 forest administration

산림학 山林學 forestry; dendrology
■ —자 a dendrologist

산마루 the top of a ridge; the ridgetop
■ —터기[턱] ⇨ 산등성이

산마리노 〈나라 이름〉 San Marino; 〈공식명〉 the Republic of San Marino ■ —사람 a San Marinese

산막 山幕 a mountain hut [cottage, shack]; a shanty (for hikers)

산만하다 散漫— diffuse; vague (notion); loose (thinking); vagrant (thought); distracted (attention); discursive (mind); desultory (reading)
◆산만한 문체 a loose [diffuse, rambling] style / 머리가 산만한 사람 a scatterbrained person; a scatterbrain
▶ 그 아이는 주의력이 산만하다 The child has little power of concentration.

산매 散賣 retail sale ⇨ 소매(小賣)

산맥 山脈 a mountain range [chain]; a range [chain, group] of mountains; mountains
■ —록키 the Rocky Mountains; the Rockies 알래스카— the Alaska Range

산모 産母 a woman in childbed [in her confinement, in the state of maternity]
■ —보호 maternity protection

산모퉁이 山— the spur of a hill [mountain]; the corner of a mountain foot

산목숨 one's life ◆산목숨을 이어가다 eke out one's living

산문 山門 1 〈산어귀〉 the entrance to a mountain 2 〈절의 문〉 the main gate of a Buddhist temple; a temple gate 3 〈절〉 a Buddhist temple

산문 散文 prose
◆산문으로 쓰다 write in prose / 운문을 산문으로 바꾸다 turn a verse into prose
■ —시 a prose poem; a poem in prose —작가 a prose writer; a prosaist; a proser —체 (in) prose; prose style

산문적 散文的 prosaic ◆산문적인 사람 a prosaic [matter-of-fact] person / 산문적인 표현 a prosaic expression; a prosaism

산물 産物 1 〈산출물〉 a product; a production; (총칭) produce
▶ 이 지방의 주요 산물은 과일과 차입니다 The staple products around this area are fruit and tea.
2 〈성과〉 a product; a result; a fruit; an outgrowth; an outcome
◆노력의 산물 the fruit [harvest, product] of sheer labor / 두뇌[공상]의 산물 the coinage of the brain [fancy] / 시대의 산물 a creature of the day / 지력의 산물 intellectual products
▶ 인간은 환경의 산물이 아니다 Man is not the product of his environment.

산미 酸味 acidity; sourness; a sour taste
◆산미가 있는 sour; acid / 산미를 띠다 have an acid taste; be sour [sourish]

산밑 山— the foot [bottom, base] of a mountain

산바람 山— a mountain wind [breeze]; a wind from a mountain

산발 散發 sporadic occurrence
◆산발적인 sporadic(al) / 산발적으로 sporadically / 산발 안타 scattered hits
■ —산발하다 occur [break out] sporadically; happen occasionally; 〈안타를〉 scatter (hits)
■ —성 콜레라 sporadic cholera

산발 散髮 disheveled [unkempt] hair
■ —산발하다 make [wear] one's hair disheveled [unkempt]

산법 算法 arithmetic

산병 散兵 〈흩어진 병졸〉 scattered soldiers; skirmishers; 〈흩음〉 dispersion of [scattering] soldiers; 〈산개 대형〉 loose [extended, open] order —산병하다 scatter (troops); deploy in extended order
■ —교련 skirmish drill —선 a skirmish(ing) line —호 a fire [firing, shelter] trench

산보 散步 a walk ⇨ 산책

산복 山腹 a hillside ⇨ 산허리 ■ —공사 hillside work —수로 hillside channel

산봉우리 山— a (mountain) peak; the summit [top] of a mountain

산부 産婦 a woman in childbed ⇨ 산모

산부인과 産婦人科 obstetrics and gynecology
■ —의사 〈산과〉 an obstetrician; 〈부인과〉 a gynecologist

산불 a forest fire; (美) a wood fire

산비둘기 山— a collared dove; a turtledove; a ringdove

산사 山寺 a mountain temple

산사나무 山查— 〔植〕 a (Chinese) hawthorn; a May tree; a May thorn ◆산사나무 꽃 hawthorn blossoms / 산사나무 열매 a haw

산사람 山— a mountain man; a hillman; a wood(s)man; (美) a hillbilly; (총칭) mountain folks [people]; mountaineers

산사태 山沙汰 a landslide; (英) a landslip; a landfall ▶ 산사태로 열차가 불통이 되었다 The landslide blocked the railroad traffic.

산산이 散散 〈조각조각으로〉 to [in] pieces [fragments]; to atoms [smithereens]; 〈흩어져서〉 scatteringly; scatteredly; sporadically; 〈따로따로〉 separately; severally
◆산산이 부수다 break [crush, smash] sth to pieces [atoms, smithereens] / 산산이 부서지다

be broken [smashed] to pieces; be smashed to atoms
▶ 차는 벼랑에 부딪쳐 산산이 부서졌다 The car was dashed to [in] pieces against the cliff.
▶ 우리들의 희망은 산산이 부서졌다 Our hopes have been dashed.

산산조각 散散— broken pieces; bits and pieces; atoms; fragments; smithreens
♦산산조각이 나다 come [fall] asunder; be broken [smashed, crushed] to [into] pieces [fragments, atoms]; break into fragments; go [fall] to pieces
▶ 그 아이는 장난감차를 산산조각 냈다 The child took the toy car to pieces.

산살바도르 〈엘살바도르의 수도〉 San Salvador; 〈브라질 동부의 항구도시〉 São Salvador

산삼 山蔘 〔植〕 a wild [mountain] ginseng

산상 山上 ♦산상의[에] on the hill [mountain]
—수훈(垂訓) the Sermon on the Mount

산새 山— a mountain bird [fowl]

산성 山城 a mountain fortress; a hillfort; walls on a hill

산성 酸性 acidity
♦산성이 되다 become acid; acidify / 산성화하다 acidify
—도(度) acidity —반응 (an) acid reaction —비료 acid fertilizer —산화물 an acidic oxide —시험 an acidity test —식품 acid [acidic] foods —염료 acid dyes —증(症) 〔醫〕 acidosis —토양 acid soil —화 acidification

산성비 酸性— acid rain

산세 山勢 the geographical features of a mountain

산소 山所 a grave; a tomb

산소 酸素 〔化〕 oxygen
♦공기중의 산소 농도 the oxygen content of the air / 생물학적 산소 요구량 the biological oxygen demand (略 BOD) / 산소로 처리하다 treat with oxygen; oxygenate / 산소를 제거하다 deoxidize
■액체— liquid oxygen; lox ■—결핍(증) 〔醫〕 hypoxia; anoxia (특히 심한); anoxemia (특히 혈액의)) : 산소 결핍으로 고통을 받다 suffer from oxygen starvation —땜 [용접] oxyacetylene welding —마스크 an oxygen mask —압축기 an oxygen compressor —요법 oxygen treatment —해리 곡선 oxygen dissociation curve —화합물 an oxygen compound; an oxide

산소흡입 酸素吸入 oxygen inhalation
♦환자에게 산소흡입을 시키다 make a patient inhale oxygen; administer [give] oxygen inhalations to a patient
■—기 an oxygen inhaler [apparatus]

산속 山— the heart [recesses] of a mountain
♦산속의 외딴 집 a solitary cottage among the mountains / 깊은 산속에 deep in the mountains; far up (in) the mountain; in the recesses of a mountain / 산속에 살다 live in the heart of a mountain / 산속에 들어 박히다 shut [seclude] *oneself* in the mountains

산송장 a living corpse; the living dead
▶ 그는 산송장이나 다름없다 He is as good as dead. ⇌ He is be more dead than alive.

산수 山水 1 〈산과 물〉 hills and streams; mountains and water(s); 〈경치〉 a landscape; (natrual) scenery ♦산수의 아름다움 natural [scenic] beauty; beauties of nature
2 a landscape painting

산수 算數 〈계산〉 calculation; reckoning; 〈과목〉 arithmetic ▶ 그는 산수를 잘한다 He is good at arithmetic figures.

산수소 酸水素 〔化〕 oxyhydrogen
■—염 an oxyhydrogen flame —용접 oxyhydrogen welding —취관(吹管) an oxyhydrogen blowpipe —폭발가스 oxyhydrogen detonating gas

산수화 山水畫 〈화법〉 landscape painting; 〈그림〉 a landscape ■—화가 a landscape painter; a landscapist

산술 算術 arithmetic; the science of numbers
♦산술을 하다 do sums; cipher / 산술을 잘하다 [못하다] be good [poor] at sums; have a good [poor] head for figures
■—급수 arithmetic series —문제 an arithmetical problem; a problem in arithmetic; the sum —평균 the arithmetic mean

산스크리트 〈범어〉 Sanskrit (略 Skr., Skt., Sans.) ■—학자 a Sanskritist; a Sanskrit scholar

산식 算式 an arithmetic expression; a (calculating) formula

산신령 山神靈 the spirit of a mountain

산신제 山神祭 a sacrifice to the spirit of a mountain

산실 産室 a maternity room [ward]; a lying-in [labor, delivery] room 《of a hospital》

산아제한 産兒制限 birth [conception] control; birth [family] limitation
♦산아제한을 하다 practice birth control; control conception ■—론자 an advocate of birth control; a birth control proponent —상담소 a birth-control clinic

산악 山岳・山嶽 mountains
■—기압계 an orometer —병 mountain sickness —부 a mountaineering [an alpine] club —지방 a mountainous district; a mountainous [hilly] country —풍경화 a mountainscape —학 orography; orology

산야 山野 fields and moutains; hills and fields; moor and hill
♦산야를 돌아다니다 roam over [range] hills and fields

산양 山羊 1 ⇨ 염소 **2** ⇨ 영양(羚羊) ■—자리 ⇨ 염소자리

산언덕 山— a hillock; a hill; a mound

산업 産業 industry
♦산업의 industrial / 산업의 발달 industrial development / 산업을 장려하다 encourage [promote] industry
▶ 그 나라에서는 산업이 왕성하게 이루어지고 있다 Industry flourishes remarkably in the country.
■—국내— the domestic industry 방위[자동차]— the defense [automobile] industry 수출— the export industry 신흥— the rising industry 정보— the communication [information] industry 주요[기간, 기초]— the chief [key,

basic] industries 철강— the iron and steel industry ■—가[인] an industrialist —개발 industrial development —계(界) industrial circles; the industrial world —공해 industrial pollution —교육 industrial education —구조 industrial structure —국 an industrial country [nation] —단지 an industrial complex —도로 an industrial road —도시 an industrial town —박람회 an industrial exhibition —스파이 an industrial spy —심리학 industrial psychology —예비군 an industrial reserve army [force] —자금 industrial funds —자본 industrial capital —재해 보상 보험 workmen's accident compensation insurance —정책 an industrial policy —조직 industrial organization —조합 an industrial guild [association] —주의 industrialism —지리학 industrial geography —채권 industrial bank debentures —통제 the control of industry —폐기물 industrial wastes —합리화 the rationalization of industry —혁명(史) the Industrial Revolution —화 industrialization: 산업화하다 industrialize —훈장 the Order of Industrial Service Merit

산업별 產業別 ■—(노동)조합 an industrial [a vertical] union —노동조합주의 industrial unionism

산에 가야 범을 잡는다 (속담) Nothing venture, nothing have [win].

산역 山役 tomb work; making a grave —산역하다 make a grave ■—꾼 a grave maker; a graveyard worker

산욕 產褥 childbed; confinement; puerperium —기 a lying-in period; puerperium —부 a lying-in woman —열 puerperal fever; childbed fever

산용숫자 算用數字 Arabic figures [numerals]

산울림 山— a mountain rumbling; an echo (*pl.* ~es)

산울타리 a (quick) hedge; (英) a quickset (hedge); a live [quick] fence ♦ 산울타리를 두르다 enclose (a house) with a hedge; surround (a house) with [by] a hedge; hedge (a garden) / 산울타리를 만들다 plant [lay] a hedge

산월 產月 the month of parturition

산유 產油 oil producing ■—국 an oil producing country

산입 算入 inclusion —산입하다 〈계산에 넣다〉 include in; count [reckon] in; add in; take into account

산자수명 山紫水明 beautiful scenery; scenic beauty —산자수명하다 scenically beautiful ♦ 산자수명한 곳 a place of natural [scenic] beauty; a scenic spot

산장 山莊 a villa in a mountain [hill]; a mountain retreat [villa]

산재 散在 being scattered; lying here and there —산재하다 〈주어가 주어〉 lie [be] scattered; lie sporadically; straggle; be found here and there; 〈장소가 주어〉 be dotted with *sth* ♦ 인가가 산재해 있는 마을 a straggling village / 산재한 scattered; sporadic
▶ 그 언덕 중턱에는 작은 집들이 많이 산재해 있었다 Many small houses were scattered on the hillside.

산재 散財 waste of money; a wasteful use of money; dissipation —산재하다 spend money; waste *one's* money (on); dissipate *one's* fortune (in); throw *one's* money away

산적 山賊 a bandit (*pl.* ~s, -ditti); 〈한사람〉 a brigand; a mountain robber ♦ 산적의 무리 a gang [set] of bandits / 산적의 소굴 a bandits' den / 산적을 만나다 fall among bandits

산적 山積 a mountainous pile (of) —산적하다 form a pile; lie in a heap; lie in piles; pile up; accumulate
▶ 그에게는 일이 산적해 있었다 He had a lot of work to attend to.

산적 散炙 meat with vegetables on a skewer ■—꼬챙이 a skewer; a spit : 산적꼬챙이에 꿰다 spit [skewer]

산전 產前 before childbirth
♦ 산전산후 before and after childbirth [delivery, parturition] / 산전산후 휴가 (a) maternity leave
▶ 그녀는 산전산후 휴가를 얻고 있다 She is on [taking] maternity leave.

산전수전 山戰水戰 fighting all sorts of hardships
♦ 산전수전 다 겪은 사람 a man of the world; an old hand; 〈여자〉 a knowing jade / 산전수전을 다 겪다 go through hell and high water
▶ 그는 산전수전 다 겪은 사람이다 He is an old stager [campaigner]. ⇒ He is an old fox.

산정 山頂 〈산꼭대기〉 the summit [top] of a mountain [hill] ♦ 산정이 눈으로 덮여 있는 산 a snow-capped [snow-covered] mountain

산정 算定 〈계산〉 computation; calculation; 〈평가〉 estimate; assessment ♦ 상환액의 산정 assessment of the amount of redemption —산정하다 compute; calculate; 〈평가하다〉 estimate; assess ♦ 잘못 산정하다 make a mistake in calculation; miscalculate
▶ 피해 총액은 3억원으로 산정되었다 The total amount of the damage was estimated at three hundred million won.
■—가격 estimated value; appraisal

산줄기 山— a mountain range; a chain [line] of mountains

산중 山中 a mountain recess; the heart of a mountain; the bosom of hills
♦ 산중의[에서] among [in] the mountains

산증 疝症 〈韓醫〉 lumbago (*pl.* ~s); lumbar [pelvic] affection; colic ♦ 산증을 앓다 suffer from lumbago

산지 山地 a mountainous [mountain] district [region]; a hilly country; an intermountain area ■—전(戰) mountain warfare

산지 產地 〈물건의〉 a producing center; a place [an area] of producing [origin]; 〈동식물의〉 the home; the habitat; 〈말 등의〉 a breeding center; 〈식물의〉 a growing district; 〈사람의〉 a birthplace; a home
♦ 유명한 말의 산지 a horse-breeding center / 차의 산지 a tea-producing district / 쌀의 산지 a rice-producing district / 산지에서 구입하다 buy at the source
▶ 브라질은 커피 산지로 유명하다 Brazil is a

famous coffee-producing country. ⇌ Brazil is well-known as a coffee-producing country.
산지기 山— 〈산의〉 a (forest) ranger; 〈묘의〉 a grave keeper
산짐승 山— a mountain animal
산채 山菜 〈산나물〉 an edible wild plant [herb] ■—요리 a dish prepared from wild plants
산채 山寨·山砦 a mountain fastness [stronghold]
산책 散策 a walk; a stroll; a lounge; an outing; an airing; a promenade; a turn
♦아침 산책 a morning walk / 한 시간 동안의 산책 an hour's walk / 운동을 위한 산책 a walk for exercise / 산책을 나가다 go for a walk; go out for a walk
▶아버지는 산책을 나가셨다 My father went (out) for a walk.
▶나는 산책 중에 그의 집에 들렀다 I dropped in at his house while taking a walk.
—산책하다 take a walk; have [get] an outing; take the air; take a turn; stroll
♦거리를 산책하다 stroll through a street / 교외를 산책하다 take a walk in the suburbs / 뜰을 산책하다 take a turn in the garden
—로 a walk; 〈포장된〉 a promenade
산천 山川 mountains and streams [rivers]; the country ♦고향 산천 the natural surroundings of one's native place ■—초목 nature; natural scenery
산초어 山椒魚 〈도롱뇽〉〔動〕 a salamander
산촌 山村 a mountain village; a village among the hills
산출 産出 production; output; yield —산출하다 produce; yield; bring forth; turn [put] out
♦그 광산은 양질의 광석을 산출한다 The mine yields good ore.
■—력 producing [productive] power; productivity —률 a yield rate —물 a product; a production; (총칭) produce —액[고] the (amount of) production; the yield (of rice); the output (of gold) —지 ⇨ 산지(産地)
산출 算出 computation; calculation; reckoning —산출하다 compute; calculate; reckon
■—세액 a calculated tax amount
산타마리아 〈이〉 Santa Maria; (英) Saint Mary
산타클로스 Santa Claus; St. Nicholas; (英) Father Christmas
산탄 散彈 a shot (pl. ~(s)); a case shot; (총칭) shot; 〈사슴 사냥용〉 buckshot; slugs
■—총 a shotgun —통 a canister —효과 a shot effect
산턱 山— a shoulder (of a hill [mountain])
산토끼 山— a hare; a wild rabbit; 〈북미의〉 a jackrabbit
산토닌 〔藥〕 santonin(e)
■—정(錠) a santonin tablet
산통 算筒 a case for bamboo fortune slips [for counting-sticks]
♦산통깨(뜨리)다 spoil; ruin; make a mess [muddle] of; mess up
산티아고 〈칠레의 수도〉 Santiago
산파 産婆 a midwife (pl. -wives); a maternity nurse

■—술 midwifery; obstetrics
산파역 産婆役 the job of a midwife; (비유) a sponsor; the originator
♦산파역을 하다 assist 《in the formation of a firm》; act as a go-between
▶우리 클럽을 결성하는 데 그가 산파역을 했다 He assisted in the establishment of our club.
산판 山坂 〈멧갓〉 a forest reserve
산패 酸敗 〔化〕 acidification —산패하다 acidify; turn sour ♦산패한 rancid; sour
—유(乳) sour milk
산포 散布 (a) scattering; dispersion; distribution; spreading
—산포하다 scatter; distribute; sprinkle
—도 〔統〕 a degree of scattering
산포도 山葡萄 〈머루〉〔植〕 wild grapes
산표 散票 scattered votes
산하 山河 mountains and rivers; the country; 〈풍경〉 landscape
산하 傘下 ♦대한 노동 총연맹 산하의 노조 a labor [trade] union under the control of the Federation of Korean Trade Unions / 산하의 under the influence [banner] of / …의 산하에 들다 join; become an affiliate 《of》
■—기업 affiliated enterprises —노조 affiliated [subordinate] (labor) unions —회사 a subsidiary [an affiliated] company; a subsidiary
산학협동체 産學協同體 an educational-industrial complex
산해 山海 mountains and seas; land and sea
산해진미 山海珍味 foods of all lands and seas; rare delicacies of all sorts [descriptions] ♦산해진미를 대접하다 entertain sb with all sorts of delicacies
산허리 山— a hillside; a sidehill; a mountainside; the side of a mountain
♦산허리에 있는 집 a house on a hillside
▶그의 별장은 산허리에 있다 His cottage [(英) villa] is [lies] halfway up the hill.
▶산허리에는 좋은 전망대가 있다 There is a nice observatory on the mountainside.
산협 山峽 a gorge; a ravine; a gap
산호 珊瑚 coral ♦산호 모양의 coralliform / 산호질의 coralline / 산호빛의 coral / 산호를 채집하다 fish for coral
—목걸이 a coral necklace —석 corallite —섬 a coral island —수(樹) a coral —주(珠) coral beads —채취 coral fishing —초(礁) a coral reef; 〈환초(環礁)〉 an atoll; a cay —충 a coral insect [polyp] —해 the Coral Sea
산화 散華 a heroic death in battle [action]
—산화하다 fall as flowers do; die a glorious [heroic] death
산화 酸化 〔化〕 oxidation; oxidization; oxygenation; combustion —산화하다 oxidize; oxidate; be oxidized ♦산화하기 쉬운 금속 an easily oxidizable metal
■—구리 oxidized copper —납 plumbic oxide —망간 manganese oxide —물 an oxide (compound); an oxidized substance —방지제 an antioxidant —수소 oxide of hydrogen —알루미늄 aluminium oxide —염(焰) an oxidizing flame —염료(染料) oxydation dyestuffs —제(劑) an oxidizing agent; an oxidizer —조 〈정

화조의〉 an oxidizing chamber —철 oxidized steel —칼슘 calcium oxide
산회 散會 adjournment; rising —**산회하다** break up; adjourn; disperse; close
▶파티는 오후 다섯시에 산회했다 The party broke up [was over] at 5 p.m.
산후 産後 after childbirth
♦산전산후 before and after childbirth / 산후조리 postpartum care
▶그녀는 산후의 회복이 좋다[좋지 않다] She is doing well [badly] after childbirth [her confinement].

살¹ **1**〈뼈·가죽에 대하여〉 flesh;〈근육〉 muscles;〈과일의〉 flesh
♦단단한[푸석푸석한] 살 hard [loose] flesh / 살이 찐[많은] fleshy; fat; meaty / 살이 없는 [마른] fleshless; thin / 살이 오르다[붙다] put on [gather, get, gain] flesh; get [become] fat; grow fleshy; flesh up [out] / 살이 빠지다 lose flesh; become leaner [thinner]; get thin; flesh falls off
▶자네는 배에 살이 붙은 것 같네 You look fuller in the stomach.
▶음식이 좋아지자 나는 곧 살이 붙기 시작했다 On a better diet I soon began to flesh up.
2【식용 고기】〈짐승의〉 meat;〈생선의〉 fish;〈사냥감의〉 game ♦질긴 살 tough meat / 연한 살 tender meat
▶이 생선은 가시가 많아 살이 적다 There are too many bones and not enough meat on this fish.
3〈호두·게·새우·조개 등의〉 meat
♦새우의 살 the meat of a lobster
4〈살갗〉 the skin ♦살이 곱다 have spotless skin; have a smooth complexion

살² **1**〈뼈대가 되는 부분〉 a rib;〈우산 등의〉 a stretcher;〈바퀴 등의〉 a spoke; a support; a stay; a stick;〈살로 된 뼈대〉 a framework (composed of strips); lattice
♦부챗살 the ribs [stretchers] of a fan / 우산살 the frame [spokes, ribs] of an umbrella / 장지의 살 the ribs of a paper sliding door / 자전거의 바퀴살 the spokes of a bicycle
2〈빗 등의〉 a tooth ♦살이 가는 빗 a fine-toothed comb
3〈어살〉 a (fishing) weir
4〈화살〉 an arrow; a shaft;〈던지는〉 a dart
♦살같이 like an arrow / 살같이 빠르다 be as swift as an arrow / 살을 쏘다 shoot [send] an arrow 《at》
5〈벌의〉 a sting
♦살로 쏘다 sting
6〈광선의〉 a ray; a beam;〈물살〉 a flow; a current;〈다리미의 자국〉 a course; a path
♦다림살 the path of an iron; the ease of ironing / 햇살 a sunbeam / 빠른[센] 물살 a rapid [swift] stream
7〈떡의 무늬〉 a pattern 《pressed on a cake》
살³ 〈나이〉 age; years
♦두 살 난 아이 a two-year-old (child) / 세 살 된 사내아이 a three-year-old boy; a boy of three (years); a boy three years old
▶會話「그는 몇 살이니?」「스무 살은 아직 안 됐을걸」 "How old is he?" ⇒ "What is his age?" "He is as yet on the right [this] side of twenty, I think."
▶그녀는 아흔 살까지 살았다 She lived to be [to the age of] ninety.
▶그는 여든 살에 죽었다 He died at (the age of) eighty.

살 煞 1〈악령〉 an evil spirit; baleful [evil] influence ♦살이 낀 날 a fateful [an ill-starred] day; a day of doom / 살을 풀다 exorcise an evil spirit
▶그 여자는 살이 있다 She is plagued (with the devil). ⇒ She is an ill-starred woman.
2〈나쁜 따앗〉 bad blood; animosity within a family

살가다 煞— be damned [plagued]; be under influence of the devil
살가죽 the skin ♦살가죽이 거칠다 have a rough skin
살갈퀴〈植〉 a tare; a vetch
살강 a kitchen shelf
살갗〈피부〉 the skin (surface)
♦살갗이 잘 트는 사람 a person whose skin is susceptible to chapping
살결 (skin) texture; complexion
♦고운 살결 a smooth [fine, delicate] skin; a smooth complexion / 거친 살결 a rough skin / 흰 살결 a fair skin / 살결이 곱다 have a spotless [clear] skin; have a smooth complexion
▶그녀는 살결이 비단같다 Her skin is (of) a silk-velvety texture.
살구〔植〕 an apricot —꽃 apricot blossoms —나무 an apricot (tree) —빛 apricot (color) —씨 an almond
살균 殺菌 disinfection; sterilization; pasteurization ♦살균성의 disinfectant
—살균하다 sterilize; disinfect; pasteurize
■—기 a sterilizer —력 sterilizing [germicidal] power —법 a pasteurism —시험 a bactericidal test —온도 a thermal death point —유(乳) sterilized [pasteurized] milk —제 a germicidal agent; a bactericide; a germicide; a sterilizer; a disinfectant
살그머니〈몰래〉 stealthily; secretly; in secret
♦살그머니 다가오다 sneak [stalk] (up to) / 살그머니 보다 cast stealthy [furtive] glances (on); steal a look [glance] (at) / 살그머니 방으로 들어가다 steal [sneak] into a room / 동전을 살그머니 손에 쥐어주다 slip a coin into sb's hand
▶그는 살그머니 방 밖으로 나갔다 He left the room stealthily.
살금살금 stealthily; quietly; sneakingly; secretly; on the sly
♦살금살금 돌아다니다 sneak about / 살금살금 나가다[들어오다] steal [slip] out [in] / 살금살금 걷다 walk noiselessly [stealthily] / 살금살금 다가가다 make a stealthy approach; approach sb stealthily
▶그는 살금살금 그녀의 방으로 기어 들어갔다 He stealthily crept into her room.
살기 殺氣 a thirst for blood; blood thirstiness
♦살기에 찬 군중 an excited crowd [mob] / 살기등등하다 be bloodthirsty; be roused to violence

▶거리에는 살기가 가득했다 There was a menacing atmosphere prevailing all over the street.
▶그녀의 눈초리는 살기를 띠고 있었다 She assumed a threatening look.

살길 a means to live; a livelihood
♦살길을 찾다 seek a way to make a living
▶각자가 살길을 찾아나서야 합니다 You must each discover your own way of living.

살날 the rest of *one's* life; *one's* remaining days
▶그녀가 살날도 얼마 남지 않았다 Her days are drawing to their close. ⇌ Her days are numbered.

살내리다 lose *one's* weight; become leaner [thinner]
♦살내리는 식사요법 diet / 살내리기 위해 운동을 하다 take fat-reducing [weight-reducing] exercises

살다¹ **1** 〈생존하다〉 live; exist; be living; be alive; subsist
♦사는 기쁨 the joy of living / 산 물고기 a live [living] fish / 살아 있는 한 so long as *one* lives / 살아 있는 동안에 while *one* lives [is still around, is on earth]; during *one's* life / 오래 살다 live long; enjoy longevity / …보다 오래 살다 outlive; survive / 백살까지 살다 live to (be) a hundred; survive the age of a hundred / 살아 돌아오다 come [return] back alive / 살아 있다 be living; be alive; be still breathing
▶우리는 무슨 목적으로 사는가? What do we live for?
▶사람은 떡으로만 사는 것이 아니다 (聖) Man shall not live by bread alone.
▶거미는 벌레를 먹고 산다 Spiders live on insects.
▶사람은 공기가 없으면 살 수 없다 Man cannot live without air.
▶그들은 죽느냐 사느냐의 문제에 직면해 있다 They are confronted with a matter of life and death.
▶그 곰은 살았니, 죽었니? Is the bear alive [living] or dead?
▶의사는 그녀가 반년밖에 더 살지 못할 거라고 한다 The doctor says that she has only a half year to live.
▶우선 살고 봐야 한다 Life must be the first consideration.
▶사람은 살 권리가 있다 Everyone has a right to live.
2 〈생계를 잇다〉 live; make a [*one's*] living; support *oneself*; earn *one's* livelihood [bread]; 〈기거하다〉 live; get on [along]
♦바쁘게 살다 live [lead] a busy life / 외국에서 살다 live abroad / 사치스럽게 살다 live in luxury; lead a luxurious life / 의좋게 살다 get on [along] very well together / 편안히 살다 live comfortably [in comfort] / 행복하게 살다 live happily [a happy life]
▶이렇게 적은 돈으로는 살 수 없다 We can't get along with so little money.
▶이 사람들은 정직하게 살고 있다 These people live honestly [an honest life].

3 〈거주하다〉 live [dwell, reside] (in, at); inhabit 《a place》
♦혼자 사는 노인 an old man living alone / 사람이 살지 않는 집 an unoccupied [a vacant] house / 살기에 적당한 good [fit] to live in; inhabitable
▶그 노인은 살 집이 없다 The old man is homeless [has no place to live].
▶그 오두막에는 사람이 살았던 것 같았다 The cottage looked (as if it had been) lived in.
▶그 섬에는 사람이 살지 않는다 The island is not inhabited.
▶어디에 살고 계십니까? Where do you live (now)?

4 〈활동하다〉 be enlivened; give life 《to》
▶나는 살아 있는 영어를 배우고 싶다 I want to learn living English.
▶그녀의 소설은 대화가 살아 있다 In her novel the conversations are really alive.

5 [바둑] get permanently secure [free from danger]

6 [野] be safe ♦1루에서 살다 be safe on first base

살다² 〈벼슬·징역을〉 serve 《*one's* term》
♦3년간 징역을 살다 serve a sentence of three years' penal servitude
▶그는 벼슬을 살고 있다 He is in the government service.

살담배 〈한국의〉 shred(ded) tobacco; 〈외국의〉 cut [pipe] tobacco

살덩어리 a lump [chunk] of flesh [meat]

살뜰하다 〈알뜰하다〉 thrifty; frugal; saving
♦살뜰한 주부 a thrifty [an economical] housewife / 살뜰히 frugally; economically; with frugality

살라미 〈이탈리아 소시지〉 salami

살랑거리다 1 〈바람이〉 blow gently [softly]; breeze; 〈소리나다〉 rustle; whisper; 〈흔들리다〉 sway; 〈움직이다〉 flutter; stir; 〈떨다〉 tremble; quiver
▶바람에 살랑거리는 나뭇잎 소리가 들린다 I can hear the leaves of trees rustling in the wind.
2 〈걸음걸이가〉 walk gracefully

살랑살랑 〈바람이〉 with a rustle [whisper]; with a rustling noise; gently; softly; 〈걷는 모양〉 with a mincing gait; briskly
♦살랑살랑 소리를 내다 rustle; whistle

살래살래 ♦고개를 살래살래 흔들다 shake [wag] *one's* head ▶개가 꼬리를 살래살래 흔들며 왔다 The dog came wagging its tail.

살려내다 save; rescue; help *sb* out of; bring back to life
♦물에 빠진 사람을 살려내다 rescue [save] *sb* from drowning
▶그를 살려낸 것은 부인의 정성어린 간호였다 It was his wife's careful nursing that saved his life.

살려주다 save; rescue; (비유) help *sb* in need ♦아무의 목숨을 살려주다 〈죽이지 않고 두다〉 spare *sb's* life; 〈죽는 것을〉 save *sb* from death
▶살려줘 Help me!
▶목숨만 살려 주십시오 Spare me! ⇌ Please

살롱 spare my life!

살롱 1 〈응접실〉 a salon; a saloon; a reception [drawing] room 2 〈파리의 미술전〉the Salon ■―음악 salon music

살리다 1 〈소생시키다〉 bring [restore] *sb* to life; 〈죽이지 않고 두다〉 keep 〈an animal, a fish〉 alive; let *sb* live; 〈죽이지 않다〉 spare 〈*sb, sb's* life〉 ◆살려달라고 간청하다 plead [beg] for *one's* life
▶그 살인자는 살려두지 못한다 We can't let the murderer live [allow the murderer to live]. ⇌ We can't spare the life of the murderer.
2 〈활용하다〉 make the most [the best] of use
▶그 경험을 살리면 당신은 꼭 성공할 것입니다 If you can use your experience, you will surely succeed.
3 〈생기를 주다〉 give life [vividness] 〈to〉; vivify; put vigor [life] 〈into〉
◆그림을 살리다 put life into a painting
4 〈지운 부분을〉 〔印〕 stet (略 st.)

살리실산 ―酸 〔化〕 salicylic acid

살림 〈생계〉 living; (a) livelihood; life; 〈살림 형편〉 circumstances; 〈살림살이〉 a household (establishment); housekeeping
〈살림이[은]〉 살림이 쪼들리다 make a poor living; be badly off; be in needy circumstances / 살림이 풍족하다 make a good living; be well [comfortably] off; be well-to-do
▶그들은 살림이 넉넉한 것 같다 They seem to be fairly well off.
▶그녀는 살림이 어렵다 She is badly off [hard up].
▶그는 실직하여 살림이 어렵다 He is out of job and he's having a hard time.
▶우리 살림은 몇년째 조금도 나아지지 않고 있다 Our living [livelihood] hasn't improved at all for the past few years.
〈살림을〉 살림을 나다 set up a separate household / (딴) 살림을 내다 keep a separate house [establishment]; live separately / 살림을 잘하 다[못하다] be a good [poor] housekeeper [housewife]; be good [bad] at housekeeping / 살림을 줄이다 cut down *one's* living expenses / 호화로운 살림을 하다 lead a luxurious life; live in luxury / 분수에 맞는[맞지 않 는] 살림을 하다 live within [beyond] *one's* means
▶그녀는 결혼하자 자기 직장 근처에 살림을 차 렸다 She married and established a new home near her office.
▶그녀는 살림을 꾸려나갈 줄 몰랐다 She did not know how to manage her household.
―살림하다 make a living; keep house; manage a household; housekeep
▶그녀는 바느질을 하여 살림하고 있다 She earns her living by doing needlework.
■홀아비― 〈미혼자의〉 a bachelor's household; 〈상처자의〉 a widower's household ■―걱정 domestic [household] cares; family concerns ―도구 household goods ―방 living quarters ―집 a private home

살림꾼 a good housewife [manager]
▶그녀는 살림꾼이다 She is a good housewife [housekeeper]. ⇌ She is good at housekeeping.
▶그는 살림꾼이다 He is a family man.

살림맡다 take charge [care] of a household; manage [handle] a household; support [maintain] *one's* family

살림살이 housekeeping; a household (establishment)

살맛 1 〈사는 맛〉 ◆살맛을 느끼다 find *one's* life worth living / 살맛이 있다[없다] have *sth* [nothing]
▶그녀는 노년에 살맛이 나기를 바랐다 She wanted something to live for in her old age.
2 〈육체의〉 the touch of skin; the feel
◆여자의 살맛을 알다 know a woman

살며시 1 〈살그머니〉 stealthily; secretly; in private; furtively
◆살며시 가버리다 go away stealthily; slip away / 살며시 나가다 go out secretly; slip out / 살며시 웃다 laugh inwardly; laugh in *one's* sleeves
2 〈가만히〉 quietly; gently; lightly; cautiously
◆살며시 걷다 walk lightly; walk with soft steps [tread] / 살며시 만지다 feel lightly
▶그녀가 아직 자고 있어서 그는 살며시 화장실 에 갔다 He went quietly to the bathroom because she was still asleep.

살모넬라균 ―菌 〔醫〕 salmonella (*pl.* -lae)

살무사 〔動〕 a (kind of) pit viper; an adder

살바람 1 〈봄철의 찬바람〉a chill spring wind
◆초봄의 살바람 a chill wind in early spring
2 〈틈으로 새어 들어오는 찬바람〉a draft [(英) draught] (of air)
◆살바람을 막다 cut off the drafts
◆살바람이 들어온다 There is a draft here.

살바르산 〔藥〕 salvarsan; arsphenamine
■―신(新)― neosalvarsan; neoarsphenamine ■―주사 a salvarsan injection

살벌하다 殺伐― bloody; bloodthirsty; brutal; savage; violent; fierce; warlike ◆살벌한 분위 기 a brutal [warlike] atmosphere; an air of imminent violence

살별 a comet ⇨ 혜성(彗星)

살붙이 〈친척〉 kin(s)folk; *one's* kith and kin

살빛 the color of (human) flesh; a flesh color [tint]; 〈피부색〉 the color of the skin; complexion ◆살빛의 flesh-colored / 살빛이 검은 dark-skinned / 살빛이 희다[검다] have a fair [dark] skin [complexion]

살빼는약 a (weight) reducing medicine

살살[1] 1 〈가만가만히〉 quietly; stealthily
◆살살 부는 바람 a breeze; a soft [gentle] breeze / 살살 걷다 walk with soft steps / 살살 녹다 〈눈 등이〉 melt imperceptibly
2 〈살그머니 달래는 모양〉 tactfully; cunningly
◆젊은 엄마는 아이를 살살 달래어 약을 먹였다 [재웠다] The young mother coaxed a child to take medicine [into bed].

살살[2] 〈아픈 모양〉 ◆배가 살살 아프다 have a slight pain in the stomach

살살이 a wily [tricky] person; a sneaker; a flatterer

살상 殺傷 killing and wounding; bloodshed
▶다수의 살상자가 났다 Many were killed

—살상하다 kill and wound; shed blood

살생 殺生 destruction of life; butchery; 〈새·물고기의〉 shooting and fishing
♦ 살생을 금하다 prohibit killing animals / 무익한 살생을 자행하다 kill animals needlessly [without any reason]
—살생하다 destroy [take] life; kill animals

살수 撒水 water sprinkling; watering
—살수하다 sprinkle 《the street》 with water; sprinkle [spray] water
■ —기 a sprinkler ―차 a water sprinkler; a sprinkler (truck)

살신성인하다 殺身成仁— sacrifice *oneself* to preserve *one's* integrity; make a martyr of *oneself*

살아가다 1 〈생명을 이어가다〉 live; get along; lead a life; keep on living
♦ 그럭저럭 살아가다 manage to get on [along] / 사이 좋게 살아가다 get along well with; live in peace [harmoniously] with / 정직하게 살아가다 go straight
2 〈살림을 영위하다〉 live; make a [*one's*] living; earn *one's* livelihood [bread] ♦ 분수에 맞게 살아가다 live within *one's* means
▶ 그는 적은 연금으로 살아가고 있다 He lives on a small pension.

살아나다 1 〈소생하다〉 come back to life; revive; be restored to life; return to life
▶ 비가 오자 시든 초목들이 다시 살아났다 The withered plants came back to life again in the rain.
2 〈구조되다〉 be saved [rescued, spared]; survive 《a disaster》; 〈위기에서〉 escape 《from》; 〈곤경에서〉 be relieved 《from》; feel relieved
♦ 기적적으로 살아나다 have a miraculous escape / 간신히 살아나다 have a narrow escape / 살아날 길을 찾다 see [find] *one's* way out
▶ 그는 심장 마사지로 살아났다 He was revived by heart massage.
3 〈불 등이〉 burn [flame up] again; 〈세력이〉 rally; come back; recover
♦ 기세가 살아나다 pick up; rally; regain *one's* strength
▶ 숯불이 다시 살아났다 The charcoal fire grew again.
4 〈형태가〉 be restored to (the original form)

살아남다 survive; outlive; escape death
▶ 그는 그 전쟁에서 살아남았다 He survived the war.
▶ 그 자동차 사고에서 살아남은 사람은 그 사람뿐이다 He is the only one that survived the car accident.

살아생전 —生前 *one's* lifetime ♦ 살아생전에 during [in] *one's* lifetime; before *one's* death

살얼음 thin ice; a thin coat [sheet] of ice
♦ 살얼음을 밟는 것 같다 feel as if (*one* were) treading [skating] on thin ice; feel like treading on eggs
▶ 연못이 살얼음으로 덮여 있다 The pond is thinly coated with ice.
■ —판 a precarious [risky] situation

살육 殺戮 〈무차별의〉 (a) massacre; slaughter; 〈전쟁에 의한〉 carnage; 〈민족·종족의〉 genocide
♦ 대량 살육 mass murder; a great massacre; genocide / 살육을 자행하다 kill recklessly; massacre brutally [cruelly]
—살육하다 massacre; slaughter

살의 殺意 intent to murder; murderous intent; 〔法〕 malice aforethought [prepense]
♦ 살의를 품다 have [conceive] a murderous design; intend to kill *sb*; seek *sb's* life
▶ 그는 마음에 살의를 품었다 He felt a murderous impulse [urge].
▶ 그는 처음부터 그녀에게 살의가 있었던 것은 아니었다 It was not his original intention to kill her.

-살이 living; life ♦ 더부살이 living by relying on others; sponging off / 징역살이 penal servitude

살인 殺人 murder; manslaughter; homicide

解說 법률 용어로 ***murder***는 살의를 품고 범한 계획적인 살인을 말하며 ***manslaughter***는 일시적인 격정으로 사람을 죽였을 때를 말한다. 위의 양자를 다 ***homicide***라고 한다.

▶ 그는 살인 혐의로 체포되었다 He was arrested on suspicion of [on a charge of, for] murder.
▶ 살인은 가장 무거운 죄다 Murder is the greatest crime.
—살인하다 commit murder [homicide]; kill [murder] *sb*
■ —청부 murder by contract ―광선 a death [lethal] ray ―귀[마] a devilish homicide; a killer ―미수 an attempted murder ―미수자 a would-be murderer ―범[자] a homicide; 〈남자〉 a murderer; 〈여자〉 a murderess ―사건 a case of murder; a murder case ―용의자 a murder suspect ―청부업자 a (professional [hired]) killer; a professional gunman [assassin]

살인적 殺人的 ♦ 살인적인 더위 deadly [awful] heat / 살인적 경쟁 cutthroat [murderous] competition / 살인적인 혼잡 a hell of a crush; terrific [horrible] congestion

살인죄 殺人罪 homicide; manslaughter; murder ♦ 살인죄를 범하다 commit murder [homicide] / 살인죄로 체포되다 be arrested on a charge of murder / 살인죄로 기소되다 be accused of murder

살점 —點 a piece of meat [flesh]; a chop; a cut

살집 fleshiness ♦ 살집이 좋은 애기 a plump baby / 살집이 좋아지다 put on flesh; grow fat; become plumpy

살짝 1 〈남모르게〉 quietly; secretly; furtively; stealthily; by stealth ♦ 살짝 보다 cast a stealthy glance (on); steal a look [glance] (at)
▶ 그녀는 나에게 자기 전화번호를 살짝 알려주었다 She told me her phone number in private [privately].
2 〈손쉽게〉 easily; effortlessly; skillfully; deftly; 〈간단히〉 lightly; simply

♦살짝 해치우다 do (a thing) cheap
3 〈가볍게〉 lightly; slightly
♦살짝 때리다 tap lightly
▶그녀는 아기에게 담요를 살짝 덮어 주었다 She gently covered the baby with a blanket.

살짝곰보 a slightly pockmarked face

살쩍 the (tuft of) hair under the temple

살찌다 gain [put on] weight; get plump [stout, fat]

解說 「살찌다」는 *gain* [*put on*] *weight*가 가장 무난한 말투다. *fat*은 직설적으로 들려서 자칫 「뚱뚱이」라는 경멸적인 뉘앙스가 풍기므로 *stout*나 *plump* 등의 완곡한 표현을 쓴다. 특히 *plump*는 여성이나 아이들에 대해 쓰이는 일이 많다.

♦토실토실 살찐 아기 a plump [chubby] baby / 살찐 중년 여성 a stout middle-aged woman
▶난 감자를 먹으면 살찐다 Potatoes make me put on weight.
▶나는 요즈음 5킬로그램이나 살쪘다 I have gained [put on] (weight by) five kilograms recently.
▶그는 해마다 살쪄간다 He get fatter every year.
▶그녀는 좀더 살쪄야 한다 She needs to fill out.

살찌우다 fatten; make fat; fat [feed] up
♦시장에 내려고 돼지를 살찌우다 fatten (up) pigs for market

살차다 1 〈살별이〉 have a long tail **2** 〈성질이〉 cold-hearted; cold and unapproachable

살창 窓 a lattice window

살촉 鏃 an arrowhead

살충 殺蟲 —**살충하다** kill insects; destroy worms; vermifuge ■—등(燈) an insecticidal lamp —**분무기** an insecticide sprayer; a flit-gun

살충제 殺蟲劑 an insecticide; a vermicide; a pesticide; 〈가루〉 an insect powder ♦정원 나무에 살충제를 뿌리다 spray garden trees with insecticide

살치다 cross [mark] out; cancel

살코기 lean meat; the lean (of meat); red meat

살쾡이 〔動〕 a wildcat; a lynx —**자리** 〔天〕 the Lynx

살팍지다 strong and lean; muscular; brawny

살판나다 enjoy good luck; strike it rich; strike a vein

살펴보다 look around [about]; look into; examine; watch for; observe; inspect
♦서류를 살펴보다 examine the papers
♦이 문제를 다른 관점에서 살펴보아라 Consider this problem from another point of view.
▶선생님은 교실을 두루 살펴보았으나 그것은 보이지 않았다 The teacher searched all over the classroom, but he could not find it.

살포 撒布 (a) scattering; (a) sprinkling; (a) spraying —**살포하다** scatter; sprinkle; spray; spread ♦장미꽃에 살충제를 살포하다 spray the roses with insecticide ■—기 a sprinkler —**약** dusting powder

살풀이 煞— exorcism; exorcising an evil spirit —**살풀이하다** exorcise (an evil spirit); have an exorcism rite

살풍경 殺風景 a dreary sight —**살풍경하다** 〈쓸쓸하다〉 dreary; bleak; 〈무미건조하다〉 dull; drab; 〈품위가 없다〉 inelegant; tasteless; unrefined; prosaic; vulgar; boorish
♦살풍경한 경치 rough scenery; a bare landscape; a dreary sight / 살풍경한 해변 a desolate beach
▶방은 탁자와 의자가 하나 있을 뿐으로 살풍경했다 Only with a table and a chair, the room looked bare.
▶홀아비 생활은 살풍경하다 A bachelor's life is drab.

살피다 1 〈관찰하다〉 observe; make observation 《of》; 〈조사하다〉 examine; take a good look at; inspect; study; 〈고찰하다〉 consider; 〈판단하다〉 judge; read
♦사방을 살피다 look around; glance about / 사고의 원인을 살피다 investigate the cause of the incident / 적의 동정을 살피다 spy on the enemy's movements / 민심의 동향을 살피다 watch the trend of popular feelings
▶그녀는 남편의 안색을 살폈다 She studied her husband's facial expression.
2 〈주의하다〉 pay attention 《to》; keep close watch 《on》; 〈경계하다〉 look out
♦교통신호를 살피다 pay attention to traffic signals
▶아이들이 다치지 않도록 잘 살펴라 See [Take care] that the children do not get hurt.
3 〈고려하다〉 take into consideration [account]; sympathize with
▶제 입장을 살펴 주시기 바랍니다 I hope you will kindly take into consideration of my situation.

살해 殺害 killing; 〈살인〉 (a) murder (case)
♦살해 의도를 품고 with murderous intent —**살해하다** murder; kill —**사건** a murder case —**자** a slayer; a murderer; 〈암살자〉 an assassin —**현장** the scene [spot] of murder

삶 life; existence; a living ♦정직하고 바른 삶 an honest and virtuous life / 삶을 위한 투쟁 struggle for life / 삶을 영위하다 lead a life; live

삶다 1 〈끓이다〉 boil; seethe; cook
♦잘 삶아진 well-cooked[-done] / 너무 삶아진 overdone / 달걀을 삶다 boil an egg / 빨래를 삶다 boil clothes / 너무 삶다 overboil; overdo / 딴딴하게 삶아지다 be boiled hard
2 〈구슬리다〉 coax; win *sb* over; 〈매수하다〉 buy *sb* over; bribe
♦아무를 삶아서 …하게 하다 wheedle *sb* into doing...
3 〈흙을〉 ♦흙을 삶다 rake [harrow] the soil smooth

삼[1] 〈태아의〉 the amnion and the placenta
♦삼(을) 가르다 cut the umbilical cord

삼[2] 〔植〕 a hemp (plant); 〈천〉 linen; hemp cloth; 〈섬유〉 hemp

삼 三 〈셋〉 three ♦제 삼 the third / 삼회 three

times; thrice

삼 蔘 〔植〕 ginseng ⇨ 인삼 (人蔘)

삼가 respectfully; sincerely; humbly
▶ 삼가 아룁니다 I have the honor to inform you that....
▶ 삼가 용서를 빕니다 I humbly beg your pardon.
▶ 삼가 애도의 뜻을 표합니다 Let me express my sincere condolences.

삼가다 1 〈절제하다〉 restrain *oneself*; abstain [refrain, keep] from; be moderate [temperate] 《in》
♦ 술[담배]을 삼가다 abstain [refrain] from drinking [smoking]; be temperate
▶ 차내에서는 담배를 삼가주십시오 (게시) Passengers are requested not to smoke.
▶ 당분간 비평은 삼가기로 합니다 I'll refrain from commenting it [I won't make any comments] for the time being.
2 〈조심하다〉 be prudent [careful]; be cautious [discreet]; caution *oneself* 《against》
♦ 말을 삼가다 be careful in what *one* says; mind *one's* language / 언행을 삼가다 be discreet in word and deed

삼각 三角 1 〈세모〉 triangularity ♦ 삼각의 triangular; triangle; three-cornered / 삼각으로 triangularly; in a triangular form
▶ 종이를 삼각으로 잘라라 Cut the paper into a triangle.
2 ⇨ 삼각형
3 ⇨ 삼각법
■ —건 a triangle (bandage) —근(筋) 〔解〕 a deltoid (muscle) —기 a (triangular) pennant —동맹 a triple [triangular] alliance —돛 a jib; a staysail; a leg-of-mutton sail —모 a three-cornered [tricornered] hat —무역 triangular trade —방정식 〔數〕 a trigonometrical equation —뿔 a trigonal [triangular] pyramid —자 a set square; a triangle —점 〔測〕 a triangulation point —주(洲) a delta —지붕 a peaked roof —플라스크 〔化〕 an Erlenmeyer flask —함수 〔數〕 trigonometric function

삼각 三脚 a tripod ■—인— a three-legged race ■—가(架) a tripod mounting —의자 a three-legged stool

삼각관계 三角關係 the eternal triangle; a triangular [triple] love affair
▶ 그들은 삼각관계가 되었다 Their relations developed into a love triangle.

삼각법 三角法 〔數〕 trigonometry ♦ 삼각법의 [에 의한] trigonometric(al) ■평면[구면]— plane [spherical] trigonometry

삼각익 三角翼 〔空〕 a delta wing ♦ 삼각익의 제트기[비행기] a delta-wing(ed) jet [plane]

삼각측량 三角測量 triangulation; triangular surveying; a trigonometrical survey
♦ 삼각측량으로 측량하다 triangulate; survey by triangulation

삼각형 三角形 a triangle
♦ 삼각형의 꼭지점[밑변, 높이] the vertex [base, altitude] of a triangle / 임의의 삼각형 any triangle / 삼각형으로 된 땅 a triangle of land; a triangular plot of land / 삼각형의 triangle; triangular / 삼각형으로 만들다 triangulate; give triangular form 《to》
▶ 파이는 삼각형 조각으로 나누어졌다 The pie was divided into triangular pieces.
■예각[둔각]— an acute-[obtuse-]angled triangle 이등변[직각, 구면]— an isosceles [a right-angled, a spherical] triangle 정— an equilateral [a regular] triangle ■—자리 〔天〕 the Triangle; Triangulum

―――― 삼각형 ――――

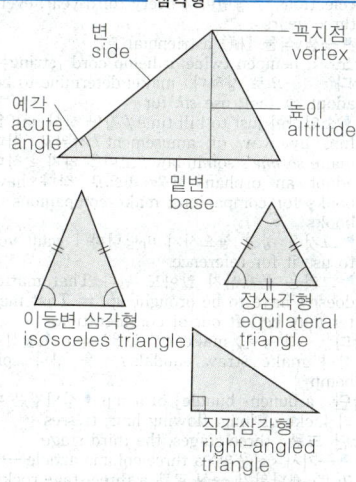

삼강 三綱 the three fundamental principles in human relations; the three bonds
■—오륜 the three fundamental principles and the five moral disciplines in human relations

삼거리 三— a crossing with three corners; a three-forked road

삼경 三經 the Three Chinese Classics
■ 사서— the Four Books and Three Classics (of ancient China); the Seven Chinese Classics

삼관왕 三冠王 〔野〕 a triple crown ♦ 삼관왕이 되다 get [win] a triple crown

삼교 三校 〔印〕 the third proof

삼국 三國 three countries [powers]
■—간섭 〔史〕 the Triple Intervention —동맹 a triple alliance —시대 the period [age, era] of the Three Kingdoms [States] —통일 the unification of the Three Kingdoms [States] —협상 a triple entente —협정 a tripartite agreement

삼군 三軍 〈육해공의〉 three armed services; the three services; the land, sea and air forces; 〈전군〉 the whole army
♦ 삼군을 지휘하다 command all the armed forces
■—의장대 the triservice honor guard —합동작전 joint operations of the three armed services; the triservice operation

삼권분립 三權分立 the separation of the three branches of government; respective independence of the administrative; legislative and judicial branches of government

삼극 三極 ◆삼극의 tripolar ━─(진공)관 〔電〕 a triode

삼나무 杉━ 〔植〕 a cedar; a cryptomeria ■━껍질 cryptomeria barks

삼년 三年 three years ◆삼년마다의 triennial (elections) / 삼년마다 every third year; every three years
■━생 식물 〔植〕 a triennial

삼노 a hempen twine; a hemp cord [string]

삼다¹ 〈…으로 정하다〉 make; determine to be; adopt *sb* (as); use *sth* for
◆소일삼아 just to kill time / 장난 삼아 half in fun; by way of amusement / 사위로 삼다 make *sb one's* son-in-law / 고아를 양자로 삼다 adopt an orphan / 책을 벗으로 삼다 have books for companions; make companions of books
▶그것을 참고 삼으시기 바랍니다 I want you to use it for reference.
▶그것은 문제삼지 않아도 된다 That matter doesn't have to be brought up. ⇒ That matter may be left out of consideration.

삼다² 〈신 등을〉 make; 〈삼 등을〉 spin ◆짚신을 삼다 make straw sandals / 삼을 삼다 spin hemp

삼단 a bunch [bundle] of hemp ◆삼단같은 머리 locks of long, flowing hair; tresses

삼단 三段 three stages; the third stage
■━기사 〈신문의〉 a three-column article ━뛰기 ⇨ 세단뛰기 ━식 로켓 a three-stage rocket

삼단논법 三段論法 〔論〕 a syllogism
◆삼단논법으로 syllogistically / 삼단논법으로 논하다 reason [argue] by (means of) a syllogism
■━생략― an enthymeme

삼대 三代 three generations
▶삼대 가는 부자 없다 Clogs to clogs is only three generations. ⇒ No fortunes of the family last more than three generations.

삼도내 三途━ 〔그艸〕 the Styx ◆삼도내를 건너다 cross the Styx; die

삼동 三冬 〈석달〉 the three winter months; 〈삼년〉 the winters of three years

삼두근 三頭筋 the triceps

삼두정치 三頭政治 〔史〕 triumvirate; triarchy

삼등 三等 〈셋째 등급〉 the third class [rate]; 〈제3위〉 (the) third place
◆삼등이 되다 win the third prize; get (the) third place; 〈경주에서〉 come in third / 삼등으로 여행하다 travel [go] third(-class); 〈배의〉 travel (in the) steerage
■━객[손님] 〈기차 등의〉 a third-class passenger; 〈배의〉 a steerage passenger ━상 (美) third prize ━칸 a third-class compartment ━표[석] a third-class ticket [seat] ━품 a third-rate article

삼등분 三等分 trisection
◆삼등분하다 trisect; cut [divide] into three equal parts
▶그 돈은 너희들끼리 삼등분하여라 Divide the money equally among you three.

삼라만상 森羅萬象 all things [everything] in the universe; all creation

삼루 三壘 〔野〕 third base ◆삼루를 보다 play third base / 삼루에 나가다 go [move, advance] to third; take third ■━수 a third baseman

삼루타 三壘打 〔野〕 a three-base hit; a three-bagger; a triple ◆삼루타를 치다 swat [slam, hit] a triple; triple

삼류 三流 the third rate [grade] ◆삼류 가수 a third-rate singer / 삼류 호텔 a third class hotel / 삼류의 third-rate[-class]; of the third order

삼륜차 三輪車 a tricycle; (口) a three-wheeler; 〈세발자전거〉 a velocipede; 〈엔진 달린〉 an autotricycle; a motor tricycle

삼림 森林 a forest; a wood; woods
▶남미의 삼림에는 여러 야생동물이 살고 있다 Many wild animals live in the forests of South America.
■━공원 a forest park ━관리 forest management ━대 a forest zone ━법 〔法〕 the Forest Act ━보호[애호] conservation [conservancy, protection] of forests; forest conservation ━욕(浴) basking in the wood; a forest bath ━자원 forest [timber] resources ━지대 a wooded region; forest land; woodland; (美) timberland ━학 ⇨ 임학(林學) ━행정 forest administration

삼막극 三幕劇 a three-act play

삼매 三昧 〔佛敎〕 (산) samadhi; concentration; absorption
◆삼매경에 들어가다 enter into a state of perfect spiritual concentration [absorption] / 독서 삼매에 빠지다 be absorbed in reading / 독서 삼매의 나날을 보내다 spend all *one's* time reading books

삼면 三面 1 〈세 방면〉 three sides [faces]
◆삼면에 on three sides
▶그 집은 삼면이 나무로 둘러싸여 있다 The house is surrounded [protected] by trees on three sides.
2 〈신문의〉 the third page 《of a newspaper》; page three
■━각 a trihedral angle ━경(鏡) a three-side [triple] mirror; a dresser with three mirrors ━기사 city news; local (and human-interest) news

삼모작 三毛作 (raise) three crops a year

삼목 杉木 〔植〕 a cedar ⇨ 삼나무

삼문문사 三文文士 a hack writer; a penny-a-liner; a scribbler; (美) a wordmonger ▶그는 지금도 삼문문사다 He still remains to be a hack writer.

삼문소설 三文小說 a cheap novel; (美) a dime novel

삼민주의 三民主義 the (Sun Yat-sen's) Three Principles of the People

삼바 〈춤〉 (a) samba ◆삼바를 추다 dance the samba; samba

삼박거리다 〈눈이〉 feel like blinking; blink lightly

삼박자 三拍子 〔樂〕 three-part time; triple

time [measure]

삼반규관 三半規管 〔解〕 semicircular canals= 반고리관

삼발이 a tripod; a trivet; a three-legged metal stand

삼배 三拜 bowing thrice ♦ 삼배하다 bow three times

삼배 三倍 three times ♦ 삼배의 three-fold; treble; triple / 삼배로 하다[가 되다] treble; triple ▶ 그녀는 너의 약 삼배정도 책을 가지고 있다 She has about three times as many books as you have.
▶ 5의 삼배는 15다 Three times five is fifteen. ⇒ Five (multiplied) by three makes fifteen. —삼배하다 multiply by three; treble; triple

삼베 flax; linen; hemp cloth; 〈흰〉 cambric ♦ 굵은 삼베 crash / 삼베의 hemp; hempen

삼복 三伏 the (three) dog days; the hottest period [the height] of summer; midsummer ■ —더위 the midsummer [canicular] heat

삼부 三部 〈세 부분〉 three parts [sections]; 〈세권〉 three copies (of a book)
■ —곡 〔樂〕 a trilogy —작 a trilogy —합창〔합주〕〔樂〕 a chorus [an ensemble] of three parts; a trio —형식 ⇨ 세도막 형식

삼분 三分 trisection ♦ 삼분의 1 one third; a third / 삼분의 2 two thirds —삼분하다 divide *sth* into three (parts); trisect; 〔數〕 divide by three

삼산화물 三酸化物 〔化〕 a trioxide

삼삼오오 三三五五 by twos and threes; in groups (of twos and threes)
▶ 우리는 삼삼오오 역으로 갔다 We went to the station by twos and threes [in small groups].

삼삼하다 1 〈기억이〉 fresh; vivid
▶ 그것은 지금도 내 기억에 삼삼하다 It is still vivid [fresh] in my memory.
2 〈맛이〉 unsalty and tasty; light; not salty enough

삼색 三色 three colors; tricolor
■ —기 a tricolor (flag); 〈프랑스 국기〉 the Tricolor

삼색판 三色版 〔印〕 tricolor [three-color, trichromatic] printing ■ —법 the three-color process

삼서다 get a corneal ulcer

삼선 三選 election for the third term
♦ 도지사에 삼선되다 be (re)elected provincial governor for the third (consecutive) term

삼성 三聖 the three greatest saints [sages] (of the world)

삼성하다 三省— examine *oneself* over and over again; introspect

삼세 三世 〈삼대〉 three generations; the third generation; …the Third
▶ 재미[재일] 동포 삼세 the grandsons [third generations] of Korean residents in America [Japan] / 리처드 삼세 Richard the Third

삼세번 三—番 exactly [just] three times

삼승 三乘 〔數〕 cube ⇨ 세제곱

삼시 三時 〈세 때〉 three daily meals ♦ 하루 삼시를 먹다 eat three times a day; take three meals a day

삼실 hemp yarn; linen thread

삼십 三十 thirty ♦ 제삼십 the thirtieth / 삼십 대의 사람 a person in the thirties [30's] / 삼십을 조금 넘은 in *one's* early thirties

삼십육계 三十六計 ♦ 삼십육계를 놓다 take to flight; beat a retreat

삼십육계 줄행랑이 제일 (속담) The wisest thing to do is to run away. ⇒ Discretion is the better part of valor.

삼십팔도선 三十八度線 〈위도〉 thirty-eight degrees north latitude; 〈한반도의〉 the thirty-eighth parallel
▶ 한국은 2차대전 직후 삼십팔도선에서 분할되었다 Korea was divided at the 38th parallel of the north latitude soon after the Second World War.

삼엄 森嚴 solemnity —삼엄하다 solemn; awe-inspiring ♦ 삼엄한 분위기 awe-inspiring atmosphere / 삼엄하게 경계하다 keep strict guard [watch] over

삼엽충 三葉蟲 〔古生〕 a trilobite

삼오야 三五夜 〈십오야〉 a full moon night; the fifteenth night (of a lunar month)
♦ 삼오야 밝은 달 the bright full moon on the 15th night

삼원색 三原色 the three primary colors

삼월 三月 March (略 Mar.) ♦ 삼월 초에 in early March

삼위일체 三位一體 〔基〕 the Trinity ♦ 기독교의 삼위 일체의 교리 the Christian doctrine of the Trinity ■ —론 Trinitarianism —론자 a Trinitarian

삼인조 三人組 a trio; a group of three; a triad ♦ 삼인조 강도 a gang of three robbers

삼인칭 三人稱 〔文法〕 the third person
■ —단수[복수] the third person singular [plural]

삼일 三日 1 〈사흘〉 three days
♦ 삼일간 for three days / 삼일 후 after three days
2 〈셋째날〉 the third day of the month; 〈출산·결혼 후의〉 the third day after childbirth [marriage]
♦ 9월 삼일 the third of September
■ —예배 〔基〕 Wednesday evening church service —장〔葬〕 burial on the third day after death

삼일운동 三一運動 the *Samil* Independence Movement (of Korea)

삼일절 三一節 the anniversary of the *Samil* Independence Movement

삼일천하 三日天下 a very brief reign; a short-lived rule

삼자 三者 1 〈세 사람〉 three persons; the three parties ♦ 삼자간의 tripartite 《discussion》; triple 《alliance》
▶ 삼자 범퇴 〔野〕 All the three batters retired [went out] in a one-two-three order. ⇒ Three batters were easily put out.
2 〈제삼자〉 the third party; 〈국외자〉 an outsider
■ —개입 outside interference —회담 a tripartite conference [meeting]

삼재 三災 1 〈운성(運星)〉 one of the unlucky stars 2 〈재난〉 the three disasters [calami-

삼족 三族 the three kindreds-father's, mother's and wife's; *sb's* whole family [clan] ♦ 삼족을 멸하다 exterminate the whole clans of *sb*

삼종 三種 three kinds; 〈제3종〉 the third class ■—우편(물) the third-class mail

삼주기 三周忌 the second anniversary of *sb's* death

삼중 三重 triple ♦ 삼중의 threefold; triple; triplicate / 삼중으로 trebly / 삼중으로 하다 triple; triplicate
■—결합 triple bond —급(품) a triple handicap (of being blind, deaf and dumb); triple distress —목적 a threefold purpose —살(殺) 〔野〕 a triple play —성(星) a triple star —주 (奏)〔樂〕 a trio 《*pl.* ~s》

삼중창 三重唱 〔樂〕 a trio 《*pl.* ~s》 ♦ 삼중창을 하다 sing a trio

삼지사방 —四方 all directions ♦ 삼지사방으로 도주하다 flee [disperse] in all directions

삼진 三振 〔野〕 a strike-out; a three-strike
—삼진하다 be [get] struck out
♦ 타자를 삼진시키다 strike a batter out
▶ 투수는 세 타자를 연속으로 삼진시켰다 The pitcher struck out three batters in a row.

삼짇날 三— the third day of the third lunar month

삼차 三次 the third time ♦ 제삼차 5개년 계획 the third five-year plan / 삼차의〔化〕 tertiary ■—곡선 a cubic (curve) —근수(根數) a cubic root —방정식 a cubic equation; an equation of the third degree —산업 the tertiary industry —생산 tertiary production —식 a cubic expression —함수 a cubic

삼차신경 三叉神經 〔解〕 the trigeminal [trifacial] (nerve); the trigeminus 《*pl.* -ni》
■—통 trigeminal [trifacial] neuralgia

삼차원 三次元 three dimensions
♦ 삼차원의 세계 the world of three dimensions / 삼차원의 three-dimensional; 3-D

삼창 三唱 〈만세의〉 three cheers; 〈노래 등의〉 reciting [singing] three times
—삼창하다 〈만세를〉 give three cheers (for); 〈노래를〉 sing three times

삼척동자 三尺童子 a mere child ▶ 삼척동자도 이건 안다 Even a child knows it.

삼천리 三千里 the whole (land) of Korea; all our country ♦ 삼천리 강산에 all over Korea; throughout Korea

삼촌 三寸 〈숙부〉 an uncle (on the father's side) ■— 외— one's uncle on the mother's side 처— a wife's uncle

삼촌설 三寸舌 〈혀〉 the tongue ♦ 삼촌설로 with one's glib [smooth] talk

삼총사 三銃士 a trio; a group of three comrades

삼추 三秋 〈가을의 석 달〉 the three autumn months; 〈삼년 세월〉 three years; 〈긴 세월〉 many years ▶ 하루가 여삼추다 One day seems like three years.

삼출 滲出 exudation; 〔醫〕 effusion; exosmosis
—삼출하다 exude; ooze (out)
■—액 exudate; percolate

삼층 三層 〈셋째 층〉 the third floor [story]; 〔英〕 the second floor; 〈세층〉 three stories
■—집 a three-story house; a three-storied house; a house of three stories

삼치 〔魚〕 a Spanish mackerel

삼키다 1 〈목구멍으로〉 swallow (up, down); gulp down
♦ 알약을 꿀꺽 삼키다 swallow the pills at one gulp / 통째로 삼키다 swallow whole
▶ 작은 뱀도 개구리를 삼킬 수 있다 Even a small snake can swallow a frog.
▶ 어둠이 모든 것을 삼켜 버렸다 Everything was swallowed up by the darkness.
2 〈참다〉 bear; suppress
♦ 눈물을 삼키다 keep back one's tears
▶ 그 소년은 흐느낌을 꿀꺽 삼켰다 The boy gulped down a sob.
3 〈횡령하다〉 misappropriate; appropriate (for [to] *oneself*); embezzle; take to [for] *oneself*; pocket; peculate
▶ 그는 맡은 돈을 삼켜 버렸다 He appropriated the trusted money for himself.

삼태기 a straw basket

삼투 滲透 〔化・生〕 osmosis —삼투하다 osmose; pass by osmosis ■—계수 an osmotic coefficient —성 osmosis —압 osmotic pressure —작용 (an) osmotic action

삼파전 三巴戰 a three-cornered [three-way] contest [fight] ▶ 이번 대통령선거는 삼파전이 될 것이다 The next presidential election will be a three-way race.

삼판양승 三—兩勝 a three-game match; a contest decided by three rounds; a rubber

삼팔선 三八線 thirty-eight degrees north latitude ⇨ 삼십팔도선

삼포 蔘圃 〈삼밭〉 a ginseng field

삼한 三韓 〔史〕〈마한・변한・진한〉 the Three Han States; the Three Hans

삼한사온 三寒四溫 〔氣〕 a cycle of three cold days and four warm days

삼할타자 三割打者 〔野〕 a .300 [three hundred] hitter

삼항식 三項式 〔數〕 a trinomial (expression)

삽 鍤 a shovel; 〈소형의〉 a scoop; a spade; 〈원예용의〉 trowel

> 解說 우리말의 「삽」은 영어의 ***shovel***, 즉 토사를 옮기는데 쓰는 긴 자루에 폭이 넓고 날이 있는 용구다. 그밖에 이것보다 조금 작은 ***scoop***, 구멍을 파는데 쓰는 ***spade***, 또한 원예용의 작은 ***trowel***을 뜻하는 경우가 있다. 동력삽은 ***power shovel*** 또는 ***mechanical shovel***이라고 한다.

♦ 흙 한 삽 a shovel [shovelful] of earth / 삽으로 모래를 푸다 shovel up sand / 삽으로 땅을 파다 spade (up) the soil
■—동력— a power [mechanical] shovel ■—질 shoveling; spading; spadework; scooping: 삽질하다 shovel; scoop; spade

삽사리 a shaggy dog; a poodle

삽살개 a shaggy dog ⇨ 삽사리

삽상하다 颯爽— (cool and) crisp; fresh; refreshing ♦ 삽상한 가을바람 a crisp autumn breeze

삽시간 霎時間 a moment; an instant; a flash ♦ 삽시간에 in an instant; in a moment [flash] ▶ 유령은 삽시간에 없어졌다 The ghost disappeared in a moment [in an instant, instantly].

삽입 插入 insertion; interpolation
—**삽입하다** insert; put in [between]; interpose; interpolate
▶ 그는 그의 수필에 시 한편을 삽입했다 He inserted [put] a poem into his essay.
■ —**구** a parenthesis 《pl. -ses》; an inserted comment —**물** an insertion —**부** 〔樂〕 an episode —**장면** 〔映〕 an insert

삽지 插紙 〔印〕 paper-feeding —**삽지하다** feed paper —**공**(工.) a feeder

삽화 插話 an episode ♦ 삽화적인 episodic(al)

삽화 插畵 an illustration; a cut ♦ 예쁜 삽화가 실린 잡지 a beautifully illustrated magazine / 삽화를 넣다 illustrate 《a book》; insert [put in] an illustration
■ **원색—** a colored [full-color] illustration —**가** an illustrator

삿갓 a conical bamboo [sedge] hat

삿대 a punt pole ⇨ 상앗대

삿대질 1 ⇨ 상앗대질
2 《달다름 매의》—**삿대질하다** shake one's fist [finger, stick] 《at》
♦ 삿대질하며 비난하다 level [shake] an accusing finger at sb

삿자리 a reed mat ♦ 삿자리를 깔다 spread a reed mat

상 上 **1** 〈상감〉 His Majesty
2 〈위〉 upper ♦ 상부 the upper part
3 〈등급〉 the first (class, grade); the best; the superior; the top (class); A-one
▶ 이 물건은 상에 속한다 This article is one of the best.
4 〈상권〉 the first book [volume]; Book [Volume] One ♦ 상하 2권 a set of two volumes

상 床 a (dining) table; a desk; a tray with legs ♦ 상에 올려놓다 serve sth at sb's table / 상을 차리다 set [lay] a meal before sb; set a dinner table / 상을 치우다 clear the table; remove [take away] the cloth
▶ 상을 차려 놓았습니다 The table [Dinner] is ready. ⇌ Dinner is on the table.

상 相 **1** 〈인상(人相)〉 physiognomy; 〈용모〉 features; 〈표정〉 a look; a face
♦ 울상을 a face ready to cry; a sad face / 천한 상 a low cast of countenance / 상을 찌푸리다 with a grimace; with a wry face / 상을 보다 read [study] sb's physiognomy
▶ 그는 귀인의 상이다 He looks aristocratic. ⇌ He has an aristocratic look about him.
2 〈상태〉 an aspect; a phase; a facet
♦ 사회상 a social phenomenon
3 〔天〕 a phase ♦ 식(蝕)상 a phase of an eclipse / 월(月)상 a phase of the moon
4 〔電·化〕(a) phase ♦ 액상 liquid phase / 단(單)상 single phase / 삼(三)상 three phases
5 〔地質〕 a facies (▶ 단·복수 동형)
6 〔文法〕 (verbal) aspect

상 商 〔數〕 the quotient ⇨ 몫

상 喪 mourning ♦ 상을 입다 go into [take to] mourning for; observe mourning / 상을 벗다 leave off [go out of] mourning / 상중에 있다 be in mourning

상 像 〈조각〉an image; a figure; a statue; 〈그림〉a picture; a portrait; 〈우상〉an idol; 〔物〕an image
♦ 동상 a statue in bronze; a bronze statue / 대리석의 성모 마리아상 a marble image of the Virgin Mary / 자유의 여신상 the Statue of Liberty / 상을 만들다 make [create] an image 《of》; throw an image 《on a screen》
▶ 벽에는 병사들의 상이 조각되어 있었다 There were figures of soldiers carved on [in] the wall.

상 賞 a prize; an award; 〈보수〉a reward
♦ 노벨 평화상 the Nobel Prize for Peace / 퓰리처 상 the Pulitzer Prize / …의 상으로 as a prize for…; in reward for…; in appreciation [recognition] of… / 상을 걸다 offer a prize 《for》/ 상을 주다 award [give] a prize 《to》/ 상을 받다 receive [be awarded] a prize / 상을 타다 win [gain] a prize / 상을 휩쓸다 carry off [away] all the prizes in a contest
▶ 그의 그림이 1등상을 받았다 He won [gained, received] (a [the]) first prize for his painting.

-상 -上 ♦ 교육상 from an educational point of view [educational standpoint] / 역사상의 인물들 historical characters / 편의상 for convenience' sake

-상 -商 〈상인〉a merchant; a dealer; a tradesman; 〈장사〉business; commerce; trade
♦ 도매[소매]상 〈상인〉a wholesale [retail] merchant [dealer]; 〈장사〉wholesale [retail] business [trade]

상가 商街 a business section [quarter]; a shopping district [center] ♦ 상가에 가다 go to a shopping center

상가 喪家 a family in mourning ♦ 상가에 문상 가다 go to offer one's condolences to the family in mourning

상각 償却 (a) repayment; (a) refundment; depreciation; redemption
—**상각하다** repay; refund; pay [clear] off; redeem; amortize; write off
♦ 부채를 상각하다 pay off [repay] a loan
■ **감가**(減價)— depreciation: 감가상각기금 a depreciation fund ■ —**자금**[적립금] a redemption fund; 〈감채〉a sinking fund

상감 上監 His Majesty (the King); the King

상감 象嵌 〈세공〉damascene; inlay; marquetry; 〈상감하기〉inlaying; damaskeening; 〔印〕inlay; mortising —**상감하다** damascene
♦ 은 상감한 담뱃갑 a cigarette case inlaid with silver
■ —**세공** inlaid work —**장**(匠) an inlayer

상갑판 上甲板 〔海〕an upper deck; 〈앞돛대보다 앞의〉the forecastle ♦ 상갑판으로 가다 go topside

상갓집 개 喪家— **1** 〈주인없는 개〉a stray dog
2 (비유) a lean dispirited person ♦ 상갓집 개 같다 be miserable and forlorn (as a dog without a home)

상거래 商去來 a business [commercial] transaction; commercial dealings ◆상거래가 활발한 시장 a brisk market

상거지 上— the most miserable [wretched] of beggars

상견 相見 meeting —**상견하다** meet [see] each other; face each other ■—례(禮) 〈신랑·신부의 맞절〉 the formal exchange of nuptial bows

상경 上京 ◆상경중이다 be in Seoul —**상경하다** come [go] up to the capital; leave for Seoul

상고 上古 ancient times; remote ages ◆상고의 ancient; in [of] remote ages / 상고로부터 from ancient times ■—사 an [the] ancient history

상고 上告 〔法〕 an appeal to a higher court; a final appeal ◆검사의 상고 an appeal filed by the prosecutor / 상고를 기각하다 dismiss [reject] a final appeal —**상고하다** bring [file, make] an appeal; appeal to a higher court ◆대법원에 상고하다 appeal to the Supreme Court ■—기각 dismissal of final appeal —기간 the time limit allowed for making an appeal —법원 a court of appeal; a court of last resort; a final appellate court —심 a hearing of an appeal —이유서 a statement of grounds of the final civil appeal —인 an appellant of final civil appeal

상고 尙古 worship of ancient culture —**상고하다** worship ancient culture; make much of things ancient ■—주의 classicism

상고 詳考 scrutiny; a careful consideration; a careful examination —**상고하다** examine carefully; consider thoroughly

상고대 a heavy frost on plants, (white) frost on trees; silver thaw; 〈英〉 glazed frost ◆상고대 끼다 be frost-covered

상고머리 〈머리 모양〉 square-cut hair; a crew cut; 〈머리〉 a square-cropped [crew-cut] head ◆상고머리로 깎다 have one's hair cut [cropped] square

상공 上空 1 〈하늘〉 the sky; the skies ◆상공으로 날아오르다 fly up into the air ▶ 헬리콥터는 서울 상공을 날았다 The helicopter flew over Seoul. **2** 〈하늘의 높은 곳〉 the upper air [regions] ◆1만 미터의 상공에서 at a height of ten thousand meters; at ten thousand meters (high) in midair ■—비행 high-altitude flying; 〈특정 지역 상공을 통과하는 비행〉 an overflight —파(波) 〔電〕 a sky wave

상공업 商工業 commerce and industry ◆상공업의 commercial and industrial ■—자 merchants and industrialists

상공회의소 商工會議所 The Chamber of Commerce and Industry ◆청년— The Junior Chamber of Commerce and Industry

상과 商科 a department of commerce; a commercial course [department] ■—대학 a college of commerce; a commercial college

상관 上官 a senior officer [official]; an officer of superior rank ◆상관의 명령에 복종하다 obey one's chief's order / 상관을 모욕하다 insult one's senior (in rank) / 상관의 명령을 어기다 disobey one's senior [superior] ▶ 그는 나의 상관이다 He is my superior [boss].

상관 相關 1 correlation; interrelation —**상관하다** be related to; have an interrelation(ship) (with) **2** 〈관련〉 relation; connection; 〈간섭〉 interference; 〈관여〉 involvement; 〈관심〉 concern; care ▶ 그것은 나와는 상관이 없다 I have nothing to do with the matter. ⇒ I am not involved in the matter. —**상관하다** 〈관련있다〉 have sth to do (with); have relations [connections] with; 〈관계하다〉 be concerned in [with]; 〈관여하다〉 take part in (a plot); participate; 〈말려들다〉 be involved in; 〈간섭하다〉 interfere; meddle 《in》 ▶ 내 일에 상관하지 마라 Leave me alone! ▶ 네가 상관할 일이 아니다 That's none of your business. **3** 〈성교〉 connection; (sexual) relations [intercourse] —**상관하다** have connection [relations] 《with》; have sexual intercourse 《with》 ■—계수 〔統〕 a coefficient of correlation; a correlation coefficient —관계 mutual relation; interrelation: 기후와 국민성의 상관관계 an interrelation [a correlation] between climate and national character —성 correlativity; correlation —작용 (a) correlation; (an) interaction —접속사 〔文法〕 a correlative conjunction

상관습 商慣習 business [commercial] usage; a commercial practice

상관없다 相關— 1 〈관계없다〉 have nothing to do 《with》; have no connection [contacts] 《with》; be not concerned 《about》; 〈연루되지 않다〉 be not involved 《in》 ◆…와 상관없이 independent(ly) of; irrespective(ly) of; regardless of... ▶ 유능하기만 하면 남녀, 나이, 국적에 상관없이 채용합니다 We will employ a person who is able irrespective of sex, age or nationality. **2** 〈염려없다〉 do not care [mind]; 〈중요하지 않다〉 do not matter ▶ 그가 뭐라 하든 나는 상관없다 I don't mind [I'm not concerned about] what he may say. ▶ 아무리 먹어도 상관없지만 탈이 나지 않아야 한다 You can eat as much as you want, but don't make yourself sick.

상관적 相關的 interrelative; correlative; mutually related ◆상관적으로 correlatively; interrelatively

상랭이 〔動〕 a porpoise

상궁 尙宮 a court lady

상권 上卷 the first volume [book] (of a work in two or three volumes [books])

상권 商權 〔法〕 commercial rights; 〈힘〉 commercial power [supremacy] ◆상권을 장악하다 dominate the market

상궤 常軌 a normal [common, proper] course

of action; a right way; a beaten track
♦상궤를 벗어나다 be abnormal; be absurd; be eccentric; run [go] off the track; pass [get beyond] the bounds of common sense
▶그의 태도는 상궤를 벗어난 것이었다 His behavior showed a lack of common sense.

상규 常規 〈상례〉 established [conventional] rules; 〈표준〉 a common standard

상극 相剋 incompatibility; (an) antagonism; (an) antipathy to each other; 〈상충〉 (a) conflict ♦신구 세대의 상극 a conflict between old and new generations
♦물과 기름은 상극이다 Oil and water have an antipathy to each other [do not mix].

상금 賞金 prize money; a prize; a reward; 〈장려금〉 a premium
♦천만원의 상금 a prize of ten million won / 논문에 상금을 걸다 offer a prize for an essay / 상금을 주다 award a prize to sb / 상금을 타다 win [get] a prize

상급 上級 an upper grade; a higher level; 〈학급의〉 an upper class; a higher [an advanced] class ♦상급의 upper(-class); higher(-grade); superior; senior / 상급반에 재학중이다 be in a higher class
■—과정 an advanced course —관리 a superior [senior] official —관청 superior offices [authorities] —법원 a higher [superior] court —생 an upper-class student; a senior student; an advanced student; 〈美〉〈고교·대학의〉 an upper-classman —학교 a school of higher grade

상긋거리다 smile gently; smile mildly; beam

상기 上記 the above; the above statement
♦상기의 above-stated; above-mentioned / 상기와 같이 as above-mentioned; as stated above / 상기와 같은 이유로 for the reason mentioned above
▶상기와 상위 없음 〈이력서에서〉 I affirm the above to be true and correct in every particular.

상기 上氣 a rush of blood to the head; 〈홍조〉 flushing; a glow; blush
—상기하다 have a rush of blood to the head; 〈홍조하다〉 flush (up); blush; 〈흥분하다〉 get [be] excited ♦상기된 뺨 flushed cheeks
▶그녀는 귀밑까지 상기되었다 She flushed up to the ears.

상기 想起 recollection; remembrance
—상기하다 remember; recollect; recall; call [bring] to mind
♦상기시키다 remind sb of; recall [call] sth to mind / 상기되다 〈사물이 주어〉 come back into one's mind; come to mind [one's recollection]
▶그때 나는 옛날을 상기했다 Just then, I recalled the old days.
▶낡은 사진 한 장이 나의 어린 시절을 상기시켰다 I was reminded of my childhood by an old photograph.

상길 上— 〈질이 제일 좋은〉 the highest [finest] quality; top-grade [first-class, first-rate] material [goods] ♦상길의 first-class; first-rate; of the highest [finest] / 상길의 종이 paper of the finest quality / 상길의 커피 the best brand of coffee

상납 上納 payment (to the authorities)
—상납하다 pay to the government; 〈뇌물을〉 offer a (regular) bribe (to)
■—금 money paid to the State; 〈뇌물〉 money offered to one's superior —미 rice paid as a tax

상냥하다 kind(hearted); gentle; tender; affectionate; sweet
♦상냥한 목소리 a gentle [sweet] voice / 상냥하게 kindly; tenderly; gently / 아무에게 상냥하게 대하다 be kind [nice, sweet, gentle] to sb; treat sb kindly [nicely] / 상냥하게 말하다 say gently [in a mild way]
▶그는 누구에게나 상냥하다 He is nice to everyone.
▶그녀는 상냥한 여자다 She has a sweet temper. ⇌ She is a kindhearted [tenderhearted] woman.

상년 常— 〈비천한〉 a woman of low birth; 〈상스런〉 a vulgar [mean] woman; 〈음란한〉 a slut; a bitch

상념 想念 a thought; a notion; a conception; an idea

상놈 常— 〈비천한〉 a man of low birth; 〈본데없는〉 a vulgar [mean] fellow; a cur; a cad

상다리 床— table legs ♦상다리가 휘어지게 차리다 serve every kind of delicacies on the table ♦음식을 상다리가 부러지게 차렸다 The table literally groaned with food.

상단 上段 1 〈글의〉 the top [upper] paragraph [division, portion]
2 〈높은 자리〉 a dais; a raised portion of a floor; 〈상좌〉 top seats 《for honor guests》; 〈윗줄〉 the upper row; the highest place
♦열차의 상단 침대 an upper berth of a sleeping car
▶그녀는 좋아하는 책을 책장의 상단에 놓았다 She placed her favorite books on the upper row of the bookshelf.

상단 上端 the upper end; the top

상달 上— the tenth lunar month; October

상달 上達 a report (to a superior [higher official]) —상달하다 report [get through] 《the people's wishes to the ruling class》

상담 相談 (a) talk; (a) consultation; counsel
—상담하다 have a talk (with); consult sb; confer 《with sb about sth》; seek [ask] sb's advice
▶일 때문에 당신과 상담하고자 합니다 I want to ask your advice about my work.
■—란(欄) a personal-advice column; the consulting columns —역(役) an adviser; a counselor

상담 商談 a business talk; 〈교섭〉 negotiations; a deal
♦상담을 중단하다 〈결렬시키다〉 drop [break off] negotiations 《with》 / 상담에 응하다 enter into negotiations 《with》
▶그는 그 건에 관해 미국인과 상담중입니다 He is negotiating with an American for the matter.
▶상담이 끝나면 다시 돌아오겠습니다 I will

come again after I have finished talking business.
—**상담하다** have a business talk 《with》; talk business 《with》; negotiate 《with》

상담소 相談所 an information [a consultation] office ■**결혼**— a matrimonial advice office **법률**— a legal advice office **직업[아동]**— a vocational [child guidance] clinic

상담 上畓 the best paddyfield

상당 相當 ♦상당의 〈알맞은〉 fit; suitable; becoming; appropriate; 〈맞먹는〉 equivalent; corresponding / 1만원 상당의 선물 a present [gift] worth ten thousand won

상당하다 相當— **1** 〈적당하다〉 suitable; proper; 〈걸맞다〉 appropriate; 〈어울리다〉 becoming; befitting; 〈맞먹다〉 corresponding; equivalent to
♦지위에 상당한 수입 an income befitting sb's rank / 신분에 상당한 경의를 표하다 do sb honor due to 《his》 rank
▶ 곤충의 촉수는 인간의 눈에 상당한다 The feelers of insects correspond to the eyes of human beings.
▶ 그 말에 상당하는 영어는 없다 There is no English equivalent for the word.
2 〈마땅하다〉 reasonable; fair; 〈충분하다〉 sufficient; adequate
▶ 그는 자기 일에 상당한 급료를 받고 있다 He gets an adequate pay for his work.
3 〈어지간한〉 considerable; fair; good; passable; decent; respectable
♦상당한 집안 a decent [respectable] family / 상당한 수입 a handsome [tidy] income
▶ 그는 증권에서 상당한 이익을 봤다 He made a considerable sum of money on [in] the stock market.
▶ 그것을 하는데 상당한 용기가 필요했다 It took a lot of courage to do it.

상당히 相當— 〈어지간히〉 pretty; fairly; rather; 〈아주〉 considerably; greatly; much; quite
♦상당히 먼 거리 a good [considerable] distance / 상당히 가파른 경사 a rather [quite, pretty] steep slope / 상당히 잘 살다 be pretty well off; make a decent living
▶ 오늘은 상당히 덥다 It is pretty [rather, fairly] hot today.
▶ 그 일을 마치는데 상당히 오랜 시간이 걸렸다 It took a good long time to finish the work.

상대 相對 **1** 〈서로 대함〉 facing [confronting] each other; being opposite to each other
—**상대하다** face [confront, see] each other; be opposite to each other
2 (美) 〈남녀 교제의〉 a date; 〈짝〉 a partner; a pal; 〈대상〉 an object
♦그의 결혼 상대인 앤 Ann, whom [who] he is going to get married to / 사랑의 경쟁 상대 a rival in love / 의논 상대 a person to consult with; 〈전문적인〉 a counselor; a consultant / 이야기 상대 a talking company; a companion to talk with [to] / 학생 상대의 가게 a shop with students for customers / 주부 상대의 잡지 a magazine for housewives
▶ 그 애는 놀이 상대가 없다 He has no friends to play with.
▶ 나는 상의할 상대가 없다 I have no one to turn to for advice.
▶ 그는 외국인 상대로 장사를 했다 He did business with foreign customers.
—**상대하다** keep company with; deal with; be a companion to; give sb one's company; go [run] with ♦상대하지 않다 ignore; have nothing to do 《with》; take no notice 《of》; do not care 《for》
▶ 그들은 상대하기 좋은 친구들이다 They're good company. ≒ I like their company.
▶ 그는 나를 제대로 상대해 주지 않는다 He gives me little of his company.
▶ 아무도 나를 상대해주지 않는다 Nobody cares about me.
3 〈상대방〉 the other man [person]; the other [opposite] party; 〈적수〉 an opponent; a rival; a competitor; an adversary; an antagonist; 〈호적수〉 a match; an equal
♦춤출 상대 a dancing partner
▶ 상대는 다섯명이었다 It was five against me.
▶ 전화의 상대는 잠시 아무말도 하지 않았다 There was a short silence on the other end of the line.
▶ 그러면 상대로서 괜찮다 He is a good match for me.
▶ 나는 도저히 네 상대가 못 된다 I am no match for you.
▶ 그는 상대를 가리지 않고 말을 마구 한다 He speaks straightforward to anybody.
▶ 나는 그를 상대로 소송을 제기했다 I brought a suit against him.
—**상대하다** contend 《with》; play 《against》 sb; 〈도전을 받고〉 accept the challenge
♦아무를 상대하여 in opposition to sb; in rivalry with sb
▶ 그는 상대하기 벅찬 자다 He is a tough guy to deal with.
4 〈절대의 반대〉 relativity ♦상대적 relative / 상대적으로 relatively
■—**개념[운동, 오차]** a relative concept [motion, error] —**분산도**(分散度) 〔物〕 relative dispersion —**빈도** 〔統〕 relative frequency —**습도[속도]** relative humidity [velocity] —**주의[론]** relativism

상대방 相對方 the other man [party]; 〈경쟁의〉 the opposite party; an opponent; a rival
♦상대방의 주장[말] what the other side [party] has to say
▶ 상대방은 꽤나 완강하였다 The opponents were [The opposite party was] quite tough.

상대성 相對性 relativity; 〔數〕 duality ■—**원리** 〔物〕 the theory [principle] of relativity; the Einstein theory

상대역 相對役 〈연극·영화의〉 the player of an opposite role; 〈춤 등의〉 a partner; 〈동등한 상대〉 a counterpart ♦상대역을 맡다 play (a part) opposite (to) (an actor)
▶ 그녀는 주인공의 상대역으로 선택되었다 She was chosen as a costar.

상대자 相對者 〈상대방〉 the other [opposite] party; a partner; a fellow; a mate
▶ 그것은 당신 상대자 나름입니다 It depends on what kind of person you are dealing with.

상도 常道 an ordinary [a regular] way; a beaten track
♦민주주의의 상도 the fundamentals of democracy / 정치의 상도 (a) common practice in politics / 상도를 걷다 follow the beaten track / 상도로 복귀하다 restore to its regular way [normal course]
▶그 방법은 상도를 벗어나고 있다 That way of doing things is quite unusual.

상도의 商道義 commercial [business, trade] ethics

상동 相同 〔生〕 homology
♦상동의 homologous; homogenous ■—기관(器官) a homologous organ; a homologue —성[관계] homology; homogeny —염색체〔遺〕 a homologous chromosome

상등 上等 superiority; excellence
♦상등의 excellent; first-class; first-rate; of superior grade; superior / 최상등의 포도주 the best wine; wine of the highest quality

상등병 上等兵 〔軍〕〈육군·해병〉a corporal; 〈해군〉a seaman; 〈공군〉an airman first class

상등품 上等品 an article of excellent [superior] quality; first-class articles; the best (articles)

상란 上欄 〈위의〉the top column; 〈앞의〉the preceding column

상량 上樑 〈일〉raising the framework; (美) house-raising; 〈마룻대〉a ridge beam [pole] —상량하다 raise [set up, put up] the framework (of a house)
■—식 a framework-raising [framework completion] ceremony

상련 相憐 mutual sympathy [pity, compassion]
▶동병(同病)상련 Misery [Adversity] makes strange bedfellows. ⇌ Fellow sufferers sympathize with one another [each other].
—상련하다 feel [have] mutual sympathy

상례 常例 a common usage; a custom; established practice; convention
♦상례의 customary; usual; regular / 상례대로 as is customary with sb; as usual / 상례에 따라 in accordance with the usage [custom] / 상례에 따르다 follow [observe] the conventional practice; follow the (common) usage [custom] / 상례에 어긋나다 be against the custom

상례 喪禮 funeral rites

상록 常綠 ♦상록의 evergreen
■—수 an evergreen tree; (총칭) evergreens

상론 詳論 full discussion [treatment]; a detailed explanation —상론하다 treat 《of a subject》in detail; discuss 《a matter》at length

상류 上流 1 〈강의〉the upper stream
♦상류의[로, 에, 에서] upstream; upriver
▶이 강의 상류는 아주 좁다 The upper reaches of this river are very narrow.
▶그 다리의 상류 5킬로미터 지점에 폭포가 있다 There is a waterfall 5 kilometers above the bridge.
2 〈사회의〉♦상류의 사람들 upper-class people; society people
▶상류 출신이다 He is of high birth.
■—계급 high society —사회 the upper society; the higher [upper] classes —생활 high [fashionable] life

상륙 上陸 landing; disembarkation
♦상륙을 허가하다 grant sb shore leave / 상륙을 금지하다 〈선객에게〉forbid disembarkation; 〈선원에게〉withhold shore leave
—상륙하다 land 《in a country, at a port》; get to land; make [effect] a landing; 〈군대가〉disembark; 〈선원이〉go on shore 《at》; 〈태풍이〉strike
▶선장 이외의 전승무원이 상륙하고 있다 All the crew except the captain are on shore [ashore].
▶태풍은 부산에 상륙했다 The typhoon struck [hit] the shore of Pusan.
■—부대 a landing force [party] —용 주정 a landing boat [craft] —작전 landing operations —장[지] a landing place —지점 a point of disembarkation

상리 常理 a matter of course; the nature of things; the natural [proper] course to take

상말 常— a vulgar word [expression]; a vulgarism; vulgar [foul] language; a four-letter word ♦상말을 쓰다 use vulgarisms [vulgar language]

상머리 床— the table side ♦(식사하기 위해) 상머리에 앉다 sit down to table; sit (down) at table

상머슴 上— a seasoned [head] farmhand

상면 上面 the surface [top] 《of a desk》
♦상면에 on the surface of sth

상면 相面 〈대면〉a (face-to-face) meeting; 〈소개〉introduction; 〈면담〉an interview; 〈첫 대면〉the first meeting
—상면하다 see; meet (face-to-face); have an interview; meet for the first time
▶우리는 어제 처음으로 상면했다 We were introduced to each other yesterday.

상모 相貌 〈얼굴 모습〉appearance; looks; countenance ♦상모가 별나다 have a queer appearance

상무 尙武 militarism —상무하다 encourage [exalt] militarism ■—정신 the militaristic [martial] spirit

상무 常務 〈업무〉regular business; routine work [duties]; 〈이사〉a managing [an executive] director ■—위원 a standing committee

상무 商務 commercial [business] affairs
■—관 〈대사관 등의〉a commercial attaché —부[장관] (美) the Department [Secretary] of Commerce

상문 喪門 an evil [a baleful] direction

상미 賞味 appreciation —상미하다 appreciate; relish; taste with relish [gusto, pleasure]

상민 常民 〈평민〉(총칭) the common people

상박 上膊 the brachium 《pl. -chia》; the upper arm ♦상박의 brachial ■—골 a humerus 《pl. -ri》—근 a brachial muscle —동맥 a brachial artery —부 the humeral region

상반 上半 the first [upper] half 《of sth》

상반 相反 ─상반하다 be contrary to 《each other》; run counter to 《each other》; disagree [conflict] with 《each other》
▶ 그의 설명은 사실에 상반된다 His explanation disagrees with the facts.
▶ 우리는 그것에 대해서 상반되는 의견을 갖고 있다 We have conflicting opinions about it.
▶ 이론과 실제는 흔히 상반된다 Theory and practice often conflict.
■ ─곡선 [數] a reciprocal curve ─교배 [生] reciprocal crossing ─잡종 [生] a reciprocal hybrid

상반기 上半期 the first half (of the year); the first half year ▶ 작년 상반기에는 이익이 많았다 A lot of profit was made in the first half of last year.

상반신 上半身 the upper half [part] of the body; the bust ◆ 상반신의 half-length / 상반신을 내밀다 lean forward
▶ 나는 엑스 레이를 찍기 위해 상반신을 드러냈다 I stripped to the waist for an X-ray.
■ ─사진 a photograph of the upper half of the body; a bust shot

상밥 床─ a meal on an individual table; a table d'hôte

상배 賞盃·賞杯 a prize cup; a trophy

상벌 賞罰 reward and punishment [penalty]
▶ 상벌 없음 〈이력서 등에서〉 No reward, no punishment.

상법 商法 commercial [mercantile] law; 〈법전〉 the Commercial Code

상병 上兵 [軍] a corporal ⇨ 상등병

상병 傷兵 a wounded soldier ⇨ 전상(~병)

상보 床褓 a tablecloth; a cloth-covering for a meal ◆ 상보를 덮다 cover the meal on the table with a cloth

상보 詳報 a detailed [full] report; particulars ─상보하다 report in full [detail]; make a full report 《on, of》; give a full account 《of》; give particulars 《of》

상보다 床─ spread [set] the table 《for dinner》

상보다 相─ read sb's physiognomy; tell sb's fortune by physiognomy

상복 喪服 a mourning dress; mourning garments; sables; 《widow's》 weeds ▶ 그 미망인은 상복을 입고 있다 The widow is wearing a mourning dress. ⇌ The widow is in black.

상봉하다 相逢─ meet [see] 《each other》
▶ 그 이산 가족은 20년만에 상봉했다 The dispersed families met after twenty years' separation.

상부 上部 1〈윗부분〉 the upper part; the top [head] 《of》; 〈위쪽〉 the upside; 〈표면〉 the surface ◆ 상부의 upside
2〈상급기관〉 superior offices [authorities]
◆ 상부의 명령 an order from above / 상부의 지시에 따르다 follow the ruling office's directions ─구조 a superstructure

상부상조 相扶相助 mutual dependence; mutual help [aid] ─상부상조하다 help [aid] each other; be interdependent; assist each other

상비 常備 ◆ 상비의 standing; regular; 〈예비의〉 reserve ─상비하다 〈예비하다〉 reserve sth for 《a sudden need》; 〈준비해 두다〉 have sth ready [always available]; 〈갖추어두다〉 be provided with sth
■ ─군 the standing [regular] armed forces ─금 a reserved fund ─약 a household medicine

상사 上士 《美》a master sergeant
상사 上司 a superior officer; a boss; a senior

> 解說 격식을 차리지 않는 일상적인 회화에서는 **boss**라 하고, 격식을 갖춘 회화에서는 《美》 **supervisor**, 《英》 **senior**가 보통 쓰인다. **superior**는 군대나 경찰 등 특정 조직체에서 문어로서 쓰인다.

상사 相似 (a) resemblance; (a) similarity; [生] (an) analogy ─상사하다 similar (to); analogous (to); like
■ ─기관 [生] an analogous organ ─물 an analogue; an analogy ⇨ 닮은꼴

상사 相思 mutual love; loving each other
─상사하다 be deeply in love with each other; be strongly attached to each other

상사 商社 a business [commercial] firm; a trading company [concern] ■ 외국인─ a foreign firm 종합─ a general [an overall] trading company [firm]

상사 商事 commercial matters [affairs]
■ ─계약 a commercial contract ─회사 a commercial company [firm]

상사 喪事 mourning; an occasion for mourning ◆ 상사가 나다 have mourning [a mournful occasion]

상사람 常─ 〈양반에 대해〉 a commoner; a plebeian; (총칭) the common people

상사병 相思病 lovesickness ◆ 상사병으로 죽다 die of love for sb ▶ 그녀는 상사병에 걸려있다 She is lovesick [lovelorn] now.

상상 想像 imagination; 〈공상〉 (a) fancy; 〈가정〉 (a) supposition; 〈추측〉 (a) conjecture; 〈짐작〉 (a) guess; speculation
◆ 상상의 [상상적] imaginary; fancy; fancied; 〈가정적〉 supposed / 상상으로 그리다 see in imagination [with one's mind's eye]; picture to oneself
▶ 나머지는 독자의 상상에 맡기겠다 We'll leave the rest to the readers' imagination.
▶ 너는 상상을 참 잘하는구나 You are very good at giving full play to your imagination.
─상상하다 imagine; fancy; 〈가정하다〉 suppose; 〈추측하다〉 conjecture
▶ 그것은 내가 상상한 대로다 It is just as I imagined.
▶ 네가 화가라고 상상해 보렴 Imagine [Suppose, Fancy] youself as a painter.
▶ 그가 그런 일을 할 수 있으리라고는 아무도 상상하지 못했다 Nobody supposed he could have done such a thing.
▶ 우리는 상상할 수 있는 모든 방법을 검토했다 We have studied every method imaginable [imaginable method].
▶ 그것은 어떤 것인지 상상할 수도 없다 I have no idea [notion] 《of》 what it is like.

■—임신 imaginary [false] pregnancy —화 an imaginary [a fancy] picture
상상력 想像力 imagination; imaginative power [faculty]
♦ 상상력이 풍부하다[부족하다] be imaginative [unimaginative]; have a vigorous [little] imagination / 상상력을 발휘하다 exercise one's imagination
상상봉 上上峰 〈최고봉〉 the highest peak 《of》
상서 上書 (writing) a letter to one's superior —상서하다 write [send] a letter to one's superior
상서롭다 祥瑞— auspicious; lucky; fortunate; happy; of good omen ♦ 상서로운 일 an auspicious [a happy] event
상석 上席 〈윗자리〉 an upper [a higher] seat; the top seat; 〈주빈석〉 the seat [place] of honor ♦ 식탁의 상석에 앉다 sit at [take] the head of the table
상석 床石 〈상돌〉 the stone table [altar] in front of a tomb
상선 商船 a merchant ship [vessel]; a trading vessel; a merchantman (*pl.* -men); (총칭) the merchant marine; merchant shipping
■—기(旗) a merchant flag —대(隊) a merchant fleet; the merchant marine
상설 常設 permanent establishment
♦ 상설의 standing; permanent
—상설하다 establish [create] permanently
♦ 위원회를 상설하다 organize [set up] a committee permanently
■—위원회 a standing committee
상세 詳細 details; particulars
—상세하다 minute; detailed; full
♦ 상세히 in detail; minutely; at length; at large; in full; fully / 상세히 보도하다 report 《on a matter》 in full [at great length]
상소 上疏 〈임금께〉 a memorial to the Throne —상소하다 send up a memorial to the Throne; memorialize the King
상소 上訴 〔法〕 an appeal ♦ 상소를 취하하다 withdraw an appeal —상소하다 appeal 《from a lower court to a higher court》
■—관할권 an appellate jurisdiction —권 the right of appeal —인 an appellant
상소리 常— vulgar language ⇨ 상말
상속 相續 succession; 〔法〕 inheritance; descent
▶ 그는 상속으로 그 집을 받았다 He received the house by inheritance [descent].
—상속하다 succeed to 《sb's estate》; inherit
▶ 그는 아버지의 유산을 상속했다 He inherited [succeeded to] his father's property.
▶ 그는 아버지의 뒤를 상속했다 He succeeded his father. (▶지위·직업 등의 경우는 succeed to 를 쓰지 않음)
■—공동— joint inheritance [succession] 재산— succession to 《sb's property 호주— succession to (the headship of) a house ■—동산— an heirloom —법 the law of inheritance —세— an inheritance [a succession] tax —재산— an inheritance; a heritage; inherited property —쟁의 a dispute about [a quarrel over] the succession
상속권 相續權 (the right of) inheritance; heirship · 공동— joint heirship; (co)parcenary 장자— primogeniture
상속인 相續人 a successor; 〈남자〉 an inheritor; an heir; 〈여자〉 an heiress
■공동— a joint heir; a coheir; a coinheritor 법정— a legal heir; an heir at law 추정— an heir presumptive 《*pl.* heirs presumptive》
상쇄 相殺 an offset; a setoff
—상쇄하다 offset [cancel] each other; countervail; counterbalance each other
▶ 손익이 상쇄된다 The profit and loss are on a par.
■—계정 a offset account —액 the amount of the offset
상수 上手 〈사람〉 a better hand 《at *sth*》; an expert; a veteran; 〈솜씨〉 veteran skill; dexterity
♦ …보다 상수다 be superior (to); be more skillful (than); 〈바둑·장기에서〉 occupy the superior side of the board
상수 常數 〔數〕 a constant; an invariable (number)
상수도 上水道 〈급수〉 water supply; 〈물〉 service water; 〈설비〉 waterworks
■—시설 water supply facilities
상수리 〔植〕 an acorn
■—나무 an (evergreen) oak (tree)
상순 上旬 the first ten days (of a month)
♦ 5월 상순에 at the beginning of May; early in May / 내달 상순에 early next month
상술 上述 —상술하다 say [mention, state] above ♦ 상술한 the above(-stated); the above-mentioned; the said / 상술한 금액 the said amount / 상술한 바와 같이 as stated [mentioned] above
상술 商術 〈장사 수완〉 a trick [knack] of the trade; 〈상재〉 business ability [talent, acumen]; 〈상혼〉 commercialism
♦ 상술이 좋은 사업가 a shrewd businessman; a man of business ability
▶ 그는 상술에 능하다 He has a good sense [head] for business. ⇌ He has a shrewd business acumen.
상술 詳述 a detailed account [description, explanation]; (an) elaboration
—상술하다 explain in full [detail]; make a detailed explanaion (of); give a full account (of); enlarge 《on a subject》
▶ 그는 그 사건에 관해서 상술했다 He gave a detailed account of the incident. ⇌ He described the incident in detail [at length].
상스럽다 常— 〈천하다〉 vulgar; low; 〈외설스럽다〉 lewd; obscene; indecent; bawdy; 〈비열하다〉 mean; base
♦ 상스러운 농담 indecent [bawdy] jokes / 상스러운 말 ribald language; a vulgar expression / 상스러운 말을 하다 talk about indecent things; talk vulgar / 상스러운 짓을 하다 be coarse [unrefined] in manners
▶ 그 말은 상스럽다 That expression is vulgar.
▶ 그런 상스러운 말을 하면 안된다 You should not use such vulgar [unrefined] language.
상습 常習 〈사회의〉 a common practice [cus-

상승 tom]; an established practice; social form [usage]; a convention; 〈개인의〉 a habit
♦마약 상습자 a drug addict / 도박 상습자 a confirmed gambler / 상습적인 customary; habitual; regular; conventional
▶그는 상습(적) 도박꾼이다 He is a confirmed gambler.
■―범(犯) 〈범의〉 a habitual [a confirmed] criminal; a chronic [an old] offender; a jailbird; 〈범죄〉 a habitual crime

상승 上昇 a rise; (a) rising; the ascent; ascension ♦물가의 상승 a rise [an advance] in price / 온도의 상승 a rise in temperature
―상승하다 rise; ascend; go up; climb; 〈급등하다〉 soar
▶물가가 차츰 상승하고 있다 Prices are rising [going up] steadily.
▶기온이 상승하고 있다 The temperature is rising.
▶경기가 상승하고 있다 Business is looking up.
■―급― a sudden rise (of prices); skyrocketing; 〈空〉 zooming; a zoom ■―곡선 a rising curve ―기류 (ride) a rising current of air; an ascending (atmospheric) current ―속도 the rate of climb ―음계 an ascending scale ―한도 〈空〉 a ceiling

상승 相乗 〈數〉 multiplication
―상승하다 involve; multiply
■―법 a multiplication method ―비 a geometrical ratio ―작용 synergy ―적(積) the product of (A) multiplied by (B) ―평균 a geometrical mean

상시 常時 ♦상시의 usual; ordinary; everyday; habitual / 상시에 〈언제나〉 all the time; at all times; around the clock; constantly

상식 上食 the offering of food [food offered] to the deceased

상식 常食 daily food; staple food; a diet
―상식하다 live [diet] on (rice)
▶아시아인은 주로 쌀을 상식하고 있다 Asians live chiefly on rice.
▶양은 풀을 상식한다 Sheep feed on grass.

상식 常識 common sense; practical sense [wisdom]; 〈양식〉 good sense; 〈주지의 사실〉 common knowledge
♦상식적인 practical; sensible; average; ordinary; 〈평범한〉 commonplace; 〈범용한〉 mediocre / 상식이 없는 〈몰상식한〉 lacking common sense; senseless / 상식에서 벗어나다 be eccentric / 상식이 있다 have common sense; be sensible / 상식이 있는 사람 a man of common sense; a person of good sense
▶그는 상식이 있는 남자다 He is a man of common sense.
▶그녀는 상식이 없는 사람이다 She is a senseless person.
▶그가 그 사건과 관계가 있다는 것은 상식이다 It is common knowlege [Everybody knows] that he had a hand in the incident.
▶그런 것은 상식이다 That is a matter of common sense.

상신 上申 a report (to a superior official)
―상신하다 report (to a superior official); submit a report (to one's chief) ■―서 a written report [statement] ―자 a reporter

상실 喪失 loss; forfeiture; lapse
―상실하다 lose; be deprived (of); forfeit
♦기억을 상실하다 lose one's memory / 자격을 상실하다 be disqualified (from, for) / 권리를 상실하다 lose a right
▶그는 시민권을 상실했다 His civil rights were forfeited.
■―권리― the forfeiture [loss, lapse] of one's right 기억― loss of memory 자격― disqualification

상심 傷心 a broken heart; heartbreak; grief; distress; sorrow
―상심하다 grieve; be grieved (at heart); sorrow; be heartbroken; be distressed
♦상심한 brokenhearted; heartbroken; sorrowstricken; dejected; depressed

상아 象牙 an elephant tusk; ivory ♦상아빛의 ivory-white; ivory
■―모조[인조]― imitation [artificial] ivory ―세공 ivory work ―세공사 an ivory worker ―제품 ivory manufactures ―조각 ivory carving ―질 〈치아의〉 dentin(e)

상아탑 象牙塔 a tower of ivory; an ivory tower ♦상아탑에 들어박히다 live in [keep to] an ivory tower

상악 上顎 〔解〕 an upper jaw ■―골 an upper jawbone; a maxillary bone

상앗대 a boat(man's) pole; a punt pole
♦배를 상앗대로 밀다 pole off a boat

상앗대질 〈상앗대로〉 poling; punting
―상앗대질하다 pole (a boat); propel (a boat) with a pole; punt (a boat)

상어 〔魚〕 a shark ■―가죽 sharkskin; shagreen ―기름 shark oil

상업 商業 commerce; trade; business
♦상업의 중심지 the center of commerce; a commercial [business] center / 상업의 commercial; business; mercantile / 상업상 commercially; from the commercial point of view
―상업하다 engage [be engaged] in commerce [trade]; carry on commerce [trade]
■―거래 a commercial [business] transaction ―고등학교 a commercial high school ―구역 [지역] a business section [center, quarter] ―금융 commercial finance ―미술 commercial art ―부기 commercial bookkeeping ―영어 business [commercial] English ―자본 a trading capital ―정책 a commercial policy ―주의 commercialism ―통신 commercial [business] correspondence

상업방송 商業放送 commercial broadcasting; 〈1회의〉 a commercial broadcast ■―국 a commercial radio [TV] station

상업화 商業化 commercialization ―상업화하다 commercialize

상여 喪輿 a hearse; a bier
♦상여를 메다 bear [carry] a bier on the shoulder; shoulder a bier
■―꾼 a bier-carrier; a coffin bearer ―집 a funeral equipment shed

상여금 賞與金 〈보너스〉 a bonus; 〈상금〉 a reward; a prize ♦상여금을 주다 give sb a bonus ▶ 1년에 여섯 번 상여금이 지급된다 The bonus is given six times a year.

상연 上演 dramatic presentation; presentation [staging] 《of a play》; performance —상연하다 put [present] 《a play》 on the stage; stage 《a drama》; play 《a drama》 on the stage ◆ 햄릿을 상연하다 give a performance of *Hamlet*
▶ 이 극장에서는 어떤 연극을 상연하고 있습니까? What's on at this theater?
▶ 그 연극은 한달간 계속 상연되었다 The play ran for [had a run of] one month.
■ —권 performing [acting] rights

상영 上映 screening —상영하다 screen; put on the screen; show; run off; play
◆ 곧 상영할 영화 the forthcoming film
▶ 지금부터 슈퍼맨을 상영하겠습니다 Now *Superman* is going to be shown on the screen.
■ —시간 the running time 《of a movie》

상오 上午 the morning; the forenoon ⇨ 오전
상온 常溫 the normal temperature
상왕 上王 〈선왕〉 the abdicated king; an ex-king
상용 常用 common [habitual, ordinary] use; daily [everyday] use; 〈마약 등의〉 addiction —상용하다 use commonly [habitually]; make habitual use of
▶ 나는 이 수면제를 상용하고 있다 I take this sleeping drug habitually.
■ —로그 common logarithms —어 common [everyday] words; words in common [constant] use —자 a habitual user [drinker]; an addict —한자 Chinese characters in common use

상용 商用 business; engagement ◆ 상용으로 on 《commercial》 business / 상용으로 방문하다 make a business call [visit] 《to》
■ —문 commercial correspondence; a business letter —어 a commercial term

상원 上院 the Upper House; 〈영국의〉 the House of Lords; 〈미국 등의〉 the Senate
■ —의원 a member of the Upper House; 《美》 a senator

상위 上位 a higher rank; a superior rank; precedence
◆ 상위에 있다 be in a higher rank [position]; be high(er) in rank; be above...in rank / 상위를 차지하다 rank high; take [have] (the) precedence 《over [of] others》/ …보다 상위다 rank higher than 《another》
▶ 지금은 여성 상위 시대다 Women are placed above men today.

상위 相違 〈다름〉 (a) difference; disagreement; a gap (⇨ 차이) —상위하다 〈다르다〉 differ 《from》; disagree 《with》; vary 《from》; be different 《from》

상응 相應 1 〈대응〉 correspondence 《to》; answer 《to》
2 〈알맞음〉 suitability; fitness
—상응하다 〈알맞다〉 be suitable 《for, to》; be suited 《to》; suit; 〈어울리다〉 become; befit; be proper 《for》
◆ 노력에 상응하는 보수 reward commensurate with one's efforts

▶ 그는 일에 상응하는 보수를 받고 있다 He gets an adequate pay for his work.

상의 上衣 a coat; an upper garment; a blouse; a jacket ◆ 상의를 입다[벗다] put on [take off] one's coat

상의 相議 (a) consultation; a talk; a discussion; (a) conference; counsel
—상의하다 〈상담하다〉 consult 《sb, with sb about a matter》; have a talk 《with》; discuss 《a matter with sb》; talk 《with sb over a matter》; confer 《with》; 〈조언을 구하다〉 take counsel 《together, with》; ask sb's advice
▶ 부모님과 상의한 후에 확답을 드리겠습니다 I will give you a definite answer after consulting my parents.
▶ 그것에 관해서는 동료와 상의하는 게 좋다 You had better talk over the matter with your colleagues.
▶ 형은 아무하고도 상의하지 않고 갑자기 부산으로 가버렸다 My elder brother suddenly went to Pusan without consulting anybody.

상이군인 傷痍軍人 a wounded soldier; a disabled ex-serviceman; (총칭) the war disabled
■ —회 the Wounded Solders' [Disabled Veterans'] Association

상인 常人 a commoner ⇨ 상사람
상인 商人 a merchant; 〈가게주인·소매상인〉 《美》 a storekeeper; 《英》 a shopkeeper; a trader; a tradesman; a dealer 《in》; (총칭) tradespeople

解說 우리말의 「상인」이나 영어의 ***merchant*** 는 의미가 광범위한데 보통 merchant는 「무역 상인」을 가리킨다. 「소매상인」에 해당하는 것은 ***tradesman[-woman]***이고 「상점경영주·상점주인」에 해당하는 것은 《美》 ***storekeeper***, 《英》 ***shopkeeper***다.

■ —도매 a wholesale merchant [dealer]; a wholesaler 소— a small trader [shopkeeper]
■ —근성 a commercial [mercenary] spirit; commercialism

상인방 上引枋 〔建〕 the upper lintel
상일 〈단순 노동〉 physical work; manual [muscular] labor; rough work ◆ 상일을 하다 do manual labor; labor ■ —꾼 a manual laborer

상임 常任 a permanent post
◆ 상임의 standing; permanent; regular
■ —위원 a member of the standing [permanent] committee —위원회 a standing [permanent] committee —이사 an executive director —이사국 〈유엔의〉 a permanent member of the United Nations Security Council —지휘자 a permanent conductor

상자 箱子 a box; a case; 〈작은〉 a casket; 〈큰〉 a bin; a chest ◆ 상자 뚜껑 the lid of a box; a boxtop / 상자를 열다 unpack a case / 상자에 담다 put [pack] sth in a box [case]

상잔 相殘 —상잔하다 struggle [fight] with each other
■ —동족[골육]— an internal strife [feud]; a dog-eat-dog fight : 동족 상잔하다 engage [be engaged] in an internal feud [war]

상장 上場 〔證〕—상장하다 list 《stocks》
♦상장되다 be listed 《on the Korea Stock Exchange》
■—기업[법인, 회사] an enterprise [a corporation, a company] whose stocks are listed 《on the stock exchange》 —주 listed stocks [shares]

상장 喪章 a mourning badge [band]; a crape 《band》 ♦상장을 달다 〈팔에〉 wear mourning; wear a crape [mourning band] on one's sleeve; 〈가슴에〉 wear a mourning badge on one's breast

상장 賞狀 a certificate [diploma] of merit; a testimonial; honorable mention
♦상장을 타다 obtain honorable mention; receive [be awarded] a certificate of merit
▶그녀는 졸업식에서 상장을 탔다 She was awarded [given] a certificate of merit at the commencement.

상쟁 相争 a struggle [strife, conflict] with each other —상쟁하다 struggle [quarrel, fight] with each other; compete [contend, vie] with each other

상전 上典 〈주인〉 one's master; 〈고용주〉 the employer; 〈상관〉 one's higher [superior] officer ♦상전을 충실히 모시다 serve one's master faithfully

상전 相傳 inheritance; transmission 《from father to son》 —상전하다 inherit; transmit; hand down

상전벽해 桑田碧海 ♦상전벽해가 되다 Naught may endure but mutability

상점 商店 《美》 a store; 《英》 a shop; 〈상회〉 a firm
♦상점을 내다 open [start, set up] a store / 상점을 열다[닫다] open [close] the store
■—가(街) a shopping district [center]; a shopping street —주인 《英》 a shopkeeper; 《美》 a storekeeper; a shop owner

상접 相接 〈맞닿음〉 contact —상접하다 come in [into] contact with each other; touch [be contiguous to] each other
♦피골이 상접하다 〈여위다〉 be reduced to a (mere) skeleton [bag of bones]; be worn to a shadow

상정 上程 —상정하다 〈제출하다〉 introduce [present] 《a bill》 on the agenda; 〈국회에〉 lay a bill before the National Assembly; 〈토의에 부치다〉 bring up 《a bill》 for discussion
▶의안이 상정되었다 The bill came up for debate. ⇒ The bill was on the table.

상정 常情 〈인성〉 human nature; 〈인정〉 human feelings
▶행복을 추구하는 것은 인지 상정이다 The desire to pursue happiness is but natural to the human nature.

상정 想定 〈가정〉 a hypothesis 《pl. -ses》; (a) supposition; (an) assumption; 〈어림짐작〉 (an) estimation
♦상정적인 imaginary; hypothetic
—상정하다 suppose; imagine; assume; 〈어림잡다〉 estimate
▶이렇게 상정하고 토의를 시작합니다 Let's start our discussion with this hypothesis.

■—량 an estimated volume

상제 上帝 God; the Lord; the Creator

상제 喪制 1 〈사람〉 a person in mourning; a mourner ♦만상제 the chief mourner / 상제가 되다 go into [put on, take to] mourning; be bereft of one's parents
2 〈복제〉 the mourning custom [practice]

상조 尙早 prematurity
♦상조의 premature; too early
▶시기상조다 Time is not mature [ripe] for it yet.

상조 相助 mutual dependence; mutual help [aid]; (⇨ 상부상조) ■—회 a mutual friendly [aid, benefit] society; 《美》 a fraternal order [society]

상종 相從 —상종하다 associate 《with》; keep company 《with》; mix [mingle] 《with》
♦좋은 벗과 상종하다 keep good company
▶저 따위들과는 상종하지 마라 Don't keep company with that set.

상좌 上座 the chief [highest, top] seat; 〈방의〉 an upper seat; 〈식탁의〉 the head; 〈주빈석〉 the seat of honor
♦상좌에 앉다 take the top seat; sit at the top [head] 《of a table》 / 남을 상좌에 앉히다 seat sb at the head 《of the table》; give 《a guest》 a seat of honor

상주 上奏 a report [an address] to the Throne —상주하다 report to the Throne; submit 《a matter》 to the Throne
■—문 a memorial to the Throne

상주 常住 —상주하다 reside (habitually) 《in, at》 ■—인구 a settled population —자 (habitual) residents 《in Seoul》

상주 常駐 —상주하다 be permanently stationed 《at》; stay permanently 《at》

상주 喪主 the chief mourner

상중 喪中 (the period of) mourning; being in mourning ▶나는 부친 상중이다 I am in mourning for my father.

상중하 上中下 〈3단계〉 the first, the second, and the third classes [grades]; 〈품질·능력 등의〉 good, better and the best; the three grades of quality [ability]; good, fair, and poor
♦상중하 3권 〈소설〉 a set of three volumes; a three-decker

상지 上肢 〔解〕 the upper limbs; the arms

상지상 上之上 〈최고〉 the best (of the best); the very best

상질 上質 high [excellent] quality ♦상질의 of high quality [grade]; excellent in quality
■—지 paper of fine quality

상징 象徵 a symbol; an emblem
—상징하다 symbolize; be symbolic of
▶까치는 희소식을 상징한다 The magpie is a symbol of a good news.
■—극 a symbolic play [drama] —시 symbolic poetry —파 the symbolist school; the symbolists

상징적 象徵的 symbolic; symbolical ♦상징적으로 symbolically ▶그것은 상징적인 사건이었다 It was a symbolic event.

상징주의 象徵主義 symbolism

■ —자 a symbolist
상찬 賞讚 praise ⇨ 칭찬
상찰 詳察 full [detailed] consideration; minute [close] observation; careful inspection [examination] —**상찰하다** consider in full [detail]; observe closely; examine carefully
상책 上策 a good [capital] plan [idea]; the wisest thing; the best policy ▶ 그것은 상책이 아니다 It is not advisable to do so.
상처 喪妻 loss [bereavement] of one's wife —**상처하다** lose one's wife by death; be bereaved of one's wife; survive one's wife
상처 傷處 〈부상〉 a wound; an injury; a hurt; 〈칼의〉 a cut; 〈깊은〉 a gash; 〈타박상〉 a bruise ◆ **상처를 내다** wound; inflict a wound 《on》; injure; scratch / **상처를 입다** be wounded; get [receive] a wound; (비유) be hurt [ruined, marred, spoiled] / **상처를** 꿰매다 sew up a wound; close a wound with stitches
▶ 아기 이마에 아직 상처가 남아 있다 The scar on the baby's forehead still remains.
▶ 전쟁의 상처가 이제 다 가신 것 같다 It appears that the signs of the war destruction have completely disappeared.
상체 上體 【解】 the upper (part of the) body
상초 上焦 【韓醫】 the upper chest
상추 〔植〕 (a) lettuce —**쌈** boiled rice wrapped in lettuce
상춘 常春 (an) everlasting spring
상춘 賞春 admiring spring scenery; enjoying spring —**객** springtime holidaymakers [merrymakers]; spring picnickers
상층 上層 〈사회의〉 a higher stratum of society [life]; the upper classes; 〈지층 등의〉 the upper layer [stratum]; 〈하늘의〉 the upper air [regions]; 〈건축물의〉 the upper stories [floors]
◆ 정부의 상층부 high official circles
▶ 하늘의 상층에는 공기가 희박하다 The air is rare in the upper regions.
■ —**계급** the upper classes —**공기[기류]** the upper air [air-current] —**운** the upper clouds
상 치 上 — 〈상품〉 an article of superior quality; the best (of its kind)
상치 相値 a conflict; a clash; a collision —**상치하다** conflict [clash] 《with》; be in conflict [discord] 《with》; run counter 《to》; be contrary [contradictory] 《to》; be incompatible 《with》
▶ 아마 너의 이해와 나의 이해가 상치할 것 같다 I am afraid your interests will clash with mine.
상 쾌 하 다 爽 快 — pleasant; comfortable; agreeable; refreshing; exhilarating; invigorating; bracing; crisp 《breeze》
◆ **상쾌한 바람** a refreshing breeze; a bracing wind / **상쾌한 아침** a crisp [nice and cool] morning / **기분이 상쾌해지다** feel [be] refreshed; be enlivened / **심신을 상쾌하게 하다** refresh sb in mind and body
▶ 나는 기분이 상쾌해졌다 I felt refreshed.
▶ 바람이 상쾌하다 The wind is balmy.
상타다 賞— win [obtain, gain, get] a prize; carry away a prize; receive [be awarded] a prize ◆ **상탄 사람** a prize winner
상태 狀態 a state; a condition; 〈모양〉 an appearance; circumstances; 〈국면〉 a situation; 〈양상〉 an aspect; the state of things [affairs]

> 〔解說〕 ***state, condition***은 사람·물건·일의 어떤 상태를 말하는데, condition은 특정의 원인·환경 하에서의 일시적인 상태를 강조하고, 일상생활에서 볼 수 있는 여러가지 상황을 말할 때는 흔히 복수형을 쓴다. ***circumstances***는 사람·물건·일에 영향을 미치는 주위의 상황을 말하며, 보통 복수형으로 쓰인다. 여러가지 circumstances의 집합이 ***situation***이다.

◆ 현 상태로서는 as matters [things] stand (now); in the present state of things [affairs] / 빈사 상태에 있다 be in a dying condition; be dying; be at the point of death; be critically ill / 전쟁 상태를 종결하다 end [terminate] a state of war
▶ 엔진 상태가 이상하다 There is something wrong with the engine.
▶ 저 회사의 재정 상태는 좋다 That company is in good shape financially.
▶ 그녀는 지금 말을 할 수 있는 상태가 아니다 She is in no condition to talk now.
▶ 우리는 지금 세계 각국과 평화 상태에 있다 We are in a state of peace with all nations.
■ **건강**— the state of health; one's condition : 건강 상태가 좋다[나쁘다] be in good [bad] health; be in a good [bad] state of health **경제**— the economic condition [situation] **생활**— a condition of life; living conditions **위험**— a critical condition **재정**— the financial standing [showing] **정신**— a mental state; a state of mind **혼수**— (fall into) a comatose [lethargic] condition [state]
상태 常態 a normal state [condition]; an ordinary [a usual] state; normal; normalcy; normality
상통 相— 〈얼굴의 속어〉 a face; (俗) a phiz; a mug; 〈생김새〉 a look; looks; a countenance
◆ 못난 상통 an ugly face
▶ 저 친구는 아무래도 말썽꾸러기 부릴 상통인걸 That guy looks like a man of uncommon character.
상통 相通 **1** 〈길이 트임〉 communication —**상통하다** communicate 《with》
▶ 그 두 방 사이에는 상통하는 비밀문이 있다 There is a secret door between the two rooms.
2 〈마음 등의〉 mutual understanding —**상통하다** understand each other
▶ 그들은 남몰래 기맥이 상통하고 있었다 There was a secret understanding between them.
3 〈공통〉 commonness; community —**상통하다** have sth in common 《with》
상투 a topknot ◆ **상툿바람으로** (go out) with a bare topknot / **상투를 틀다** wear a topknot; do [wear] one's hair in a knot
상투 常套 conventionality; commonplaceness; staleness ◆ **상투적(인)** conventional; commonplace; worn-out / **상투적인 문구** a hackneyed phrase

상태와 상황의 표현

1. ~하여

(1) ..., ~ing... (현재분사)
▶ 그는 문을 쾅 닫고 나갔다 He went out, slamming the door.
▶ 소년은 애견을 찾아내려고 여기저기 뛰어다녔다 The boy ran everywhere trying to find his dog.

(2) ...~ed ... (과거분사)
▶ 그들은 부인 동반으로 들어왔다 They came in followed by their wives.
▶ 그날 나는 어머니를 모시고 학교에 갔다 That day I went to school accompanied by my mother.
▶ 제인은 한국인 친구들에게 둘러싸여 앉아 있었다 Jane sat surrounded by her Korean friends.

(3) ...with ~ing
▶ 그는 벽에 기대어서 잤다 He fell asleep, with his body resting against the wall.
▶ 차 한 대가 시동을 걸어둔채 길가에 서 있었다 A car was standing at the roadside with the engine running.
▶ 라디오를 틀어 놓고 책을 읽는 사람들도 있다 Some people can read books with the radio playing.
▶ 한 여성이 어깨를 떨면서 벤치에 앉아 있었다 A woman was sitting on a bench with her shoulders quivering.
▶ 그는 눈을 번득이면서 들어왔다 He came in with his eyes shining.
▶ 혜성은 그 꼬리로 빛을 내면서 하늘을 가로지른다 A comet travels across the sky with his tail gleaming.

(4) ...with ~ed
▶ 그는 책상다리를 하고 앉아 있었다 He was sitting with his legs crossed.
▶ 그녀는 눈을 감고 의자에 기대 앉아 있었다 She lay back in the chair with her eyes closed.
▶ 이 문제들은 책을 덮어놓고 해야한다 These exercises should be done with books closed.
▶ 그는 팔짱을 끼고 허공을 바라보고 있었다 He was staring into the space with his arms folded (on his breast).
[어법]
① 현재분사는 능동적인 뜻을, 과거분사는 수동적인 뜻을 나타낸다. 따라서 본래 with ~ing는「~하고 있는 상태로」란 뜻으로 능동적인 상태로, with ~ed는「~되고 있는 상태로」란 뜻으로 수동적인 상태를 나타낸다.
② 명사[대명사]와 분사와의 관계는 주어와 술어 동사의 관계에 해당한다.
③ 위의 글들은 ..., crossing his legs; ..., closing her eyes; ..., closing books; ..., folding his arms 등으로는 쓰지 않는다. 그런 형태로는 상태가 아니고 동작을 나타내어「~하면서」의 뜻이 되기 때문이다.

2. ~하고; ~한채로; ~로

(1) ...with + 명사[대명사] + 형용사[부사]
▶ 입에 음식을 가득 넣고서 이야기하지 마라 Don't speak with your mouth full.
▶ 그들은 창문을 열어 놓고 잔다 They sleep with the windows open.
▶ 그 여자는 남편이 없는 편이 행복해 보인다 She seems happier with her husband away.
▶ 나는 어젯밤에 라디오를 켜놓은 채 잤다 Last night I went to bed with the radio on. (▶with the radio playing 이라고 하면 1.의 (3)의 형식이 된다)
▶ 소년은 옷을 입은 채 잠들어 버렸다 The boy fell asleep with his clothes on.
▶ 그는 블라인드를 반 내리고 책을 읽고 있었다 He was reading a book with the blinds half down.

(2) ...with + 명사[대명사] + 전치사 + 명사[대명사]
▶ 그는 영어책을 겨드랑이에 끼고 귀가를 서둘렀다 He hurried home with an English book under his arm.
▶ 그는 길 모퉁이에서 양손을 주머니에 찔러넣고 서 있었다 He was standing on the corner with his hands in his pockets.
▶ 그는 파이프를 물고서 신문을 보고 있었다 He was reading a newspaper with a pipe in his mouth.
▶ 펜을 집어들고 그는 일을 시작하였다 With a pen in hand, he set to work.
▶ 그는 책상 위에 발을 올려놓고 의자에 깊숙이 앉아 있었다 He was sitting back in his chair with his feet on the desk.
▶ 우리는 테이블을 사이에 두고 앉아 있었다 We sat with a table between us.

▶ 그건 네 상투적인 구실이야 It is your usual excuse.
■—수단 a well-worn device; familiar ways; an old trick; *one's* usual [routine, hackneyed] practice : 상투수단을 쓰다 use *one's* old trick —어 a set [hackneyed] phrase [expression]; (프) a cliché
상판(대기) 相— 〈얼굴의 속어〉 a face; (俗) a phiz; a mug; (俗) a pan; 〈생김새〉 *one's* looks; a cast of countenance; a look
상팔자 上八字 bliss; good fortune; an easy life; a comfortable living ◆ 상팔자다 live in (ease and) comfort / 상팔자로 태어나다 be born under a lucky star
상패 賞牌 a medal; a medallion ■—수령자 a medalist
상편 上篇 the first volume (of a work in two or three volumes [books])
상표 商標 a trademark; a brand
◆ 상표를 붙이다 put [affix] a trademark (on); trademark / 상표를 등록하다 register a trademark; trademark
▶ 상표 등록필 (표시) Registered.
■ 등록— a registered trademark ■—도용 trademark piracy —명 a trade name
상표권 商標權 the trademark right

상품권을 침해하다 infringe upon a trademark
■一침해 piracy of a trademark; a trademark infringement

상품 上品 a first-class [first-grade] article; choice goods; an article of superior quality

상품 商品 goods; merchandise; a commodity; 〈재고품〉 (a) stock

> 解說 *goods*는 이동 가능한 상품을 총칭적으로 일컫는 가장 일반적인 말. 복수취급 하지만 many나 수사와 함께 쓰지는 않음. ***merchandise***도 상품을 총칭적으로 나타내지만 거래를 의식한 딱딱한 말로 쓰이며 셀 때는 a piece of merchandise로 함. ***commodity***는 농산물·광물 등을 상품으로서 대량으로 취급할 때 쓰는 딱딱한 말.

♦상품을 구입[주문]하다 purchase [order] goods from sb / 상품을 사들이다 lay in a stock of goods / 상품을 처분하다 dispose of goods / 각종 상품을 취급하다 deal in various lines of commodities
▶저 가게는 아주 좋은 상품을 취급한다 That store carries really excellent goods.
■중요— staple [major] goods —가치 commercial value —권 a merchandise bond [coupon]; an exchange ticket [check]; a gift certificate; a credit slip —매입[매출] 대장 a purchase [sales] book —목록 a catalog(ue) —시장 a commodity market —이미지 the brand image —재고 the amount of stock —재고대장 a stock book —진열실 a showroom —진열장 a showcase —진열창 a show window —창고 a merchandise warehouse —학 the study of merchandise

상품 賞品 a prize; a trophy; 《俗》 a pot
♦상품을 타다 get [win, gain, obtain, be awarded] a prize / 상품을 수여하다 award sb a prize
■一수여식 a prize-awarding ceremony

상품견본 商品見本 a trade sample; 〈우편물 표기〉 Samples ■一첩 a sample book

상 피 上皮 〔生〕 the epithelium (*pl*. -lia); 〈표피〉 the epidermis ♦상피의 epidermal; epithelial ■一세포 an epithelial cell

상피 相避 incest ♦상피 붙다 commit incest; be incestuous

상피병 象皮病 〔醫〕 elephantiasis (*pl*. -ses)

상하 上下 1〈위와 아래〉 top and bottom; the upper and lower sides [parts]
♦상하의 up-and-down / 상하로 up and down; vertically; upward and downward; 〈높고 낮게〉 high and low / 상하로 움직이다 move [go] up and down; rise and fall; seesaw; 〈배 등이〉 pitch; heave and set
▶배[비행기]가 상하로 흔들렸다 Our ship [plane] pitched. (▶「좌우로 흔들리다」는 roll)
2 〈오르내림〉 rise and fall; fluctuations
♦증권 시세의 상하변동 fluctuations in share quotations
3 〈신분·지위 등의〉 the upper and lower classes; high and low; superiors and inferiors
▶거기에는 상하의 구별 없이 많은 사람이 모였다 A lot of people came there, irrespective of rank.
4 〈책의〉 the first and second volumes
♦상하 2권짜리 사전 a dictionary in two volumes

상하 常夏 (an) everlasting summer ♦상하의 나라 a land of everlasting summer

상하다 傷— 1〈물건이〉 be hurt [injured, damaged]; be impaired; be spoiled; 〈옷 등이〉 be [become] worn out; 〈과일 등이〉 be bruised; have a bad spot; 〈썩다〉 rot; go bad; spoil; 〈우유 등이〉 turn sour; 〈생선이〉 be stale
▶바나나는 쉬 상한다 Bananas bruise [get bruised] easily.
▶너무 오래 두어서 사과가 상했다 The apples spoiled because I kept them too long.
▶나는 상한 오렌지를 싸게 사서 잼으로 만들었다 I bought bruised oranges cheap and made jam out of them.
▶고기는 상하기 전에 빨리 먹어라 Eat the meat as soon as possible before it goes bad.
▶여름에는 음식이 쉬 상한다 Food in summer goes bad quickly [is perishable].
2〈마음이〉 be [get] hurt; be injured; be grieved (at); be worried (about); be distressed (with); be troubled (with)
♦기분이 상하다 take offense (at); get out of humor / 속이 상하다 feel bad; be grieved at heart; be worried [troubled] (about); be pained (by) / 아무의 기분을 상하게 하다 offend sb; hurt sb's feelings; incur the disfavor [displeasure] of sb
3 〈몸이〉 get [become] thin (from); 〈건강이〉 be broken (in health); injure (one's) health; 〈부상하다〉 be [get] injured [wounded, hurt]

상하수도사업 上下水道事業 water supply and drainage

상하이 上海 Shanghai ■一사변 the Shanghai Incident

상학 上學 the beginning of school [lessons]
—상학하다 begin; take up
■一시간 the hour at which school begins

상 학 商學 commercial science ■一과 the department of commercial science

상한 上限 〔數〕 the supremum; the least upper bound; an upper limit; a maximum

상한 象限 quadrant ⇨ 사분(~면) ■一의(儀) ⇨ 사분(~의)

상한선 上限線 the top [highest] limit; a ceiling; the maximum
♦상한선을 두다[정하다] put a ceiling on; set a limit; fix limits

상항 上項 〈항목〉 the above item; 〈조항〉 the above clause [provision]

상항 商港 a mercantile [trading] port; a commercial harbor

상해 上海 Shanghai ⇨ 상하이

상해 傷害 (an) injury; bodily harm
♦상해죄로 on a [the] charge of inflicting (bodily) injury upon sb
—상해하다 injure sb; do sb injury; inflict an injury upon sb
■一보험 〔法〕 accident insurance —치사(죄) 〔法〕 (a) bodily injury resulting in death

상해 詳解 a detailed [minute] explanation 《of》; a full commentary 《on》
　―상해하다 explain minutely [in detail]; make a detailed explanation 《of》; give a full commentary 《on》

상해 霜害 damage by frost; frost damage
　◆ 상해를 입다 suffer from frost

상행 上行 ◆ 상행의 up ―상행하다 go up; go toward Seoul ■―열차[선] an up train [line]

상행위 商行爲 a commercial [business] transaction

상향 上向 ◆ 상향의 upward /〈시세가〉 상향이 되다 have [show] a rising [an upward] tendency; tend upward; look up ▶ 경기는 상향추세다 Business is picking [looking] up.
　■―선(線) an upswing ―시세 an advancing [a bull] market

상현 上弦 〈天〉 the first quarter 《of the moon》 ■―달 a waxing [young] moon; the moon in its first quarter

상형 常衡 avoirdupois (weight)

상형문자 象形文字 a pictograph; a hieroglyph; a hieroglyphic (character)

상호 相互 reciprocity; mutuality
　◆ 상호간의 mutual; reciprocal / 상호간에 mutually; reciprocally; each other; one another / 상호 협조하다 help [aid, offer aid to] each other
　▶ 회원 상호간의 친목과 복지를 도모하는 방법을 토의했다 We talked about how to promote amity and welfare among the members.
　■―감응[유도]〔電〕 mutual induction ―계약 a mutual contract ―교수법 a mutual teaching system ―무역 two-way trade ―방위조약 a mutual defense treaty [pact] ―안전보장조약 a mutual security pact [treaty] ―원조조약 a mutual assistance pact [treaty] ―작용 (a) reciprocal action; (an) interaction ―조직 a cooperative [mutual aid] system ―조합 a cooperative society; a mutual benefit [aid] association ―참조 cross [reciprocal] reference

상호 商號 〈점포명〉 a name of a store; a firm name; 〈회사명〉 a corporate name; 〈품명〉 a trade name

상호관계 相互關係 mutual [reciprocal] relation; correlation; interrelationship
　◆ 상호관계가 있는 interrelated; correlated

상호보험 相互保險 〔經〕 mutual insurance
　■―회사 a mutual insurance company

상호부조 相互扶助 mutual aid [assistance, help] ―상호부조하다 aid [assist, help] mutually ■―론 mutualism

상호의존 相互依存 interdependence; mutual dependence ◆ 상호의존의[적인] interdependent; mutually dependent; correlative ▶ 우리는 상호의존적이다 We are interdependent.

상혼 商魂 a commercial spirit; salesmanship
　▶ 그는 상혼이 악착 같다 He is quite shrewd [aggressive] in business.

상환 相換 exchange; change; 〈태환〉 conversion ◆ 상환급 〈英〉 cash on delivery (略 C.O.D.); 〈美〉 collect on delivery (略 C.O.D.)
　―상환하다 exchange; change; convert

　■―권 an exchange ticket; a coupon

상환 償還 repayment; refundment; redemption; 〈분할에 의한〉 amortization
　◆ 10년 상환의 채권 a bond redeemable in ten years
　―상환하다 repay; refund; redeem; amortize ▶ 공채[외채]를 상환하다 redeem a bond [foreign loan]
　■ 만기전― prior redemption ■―계산서 a recourse account ―금 money repaid; a repayment ―기금 a fund for redemption; a redemption fund ―기한 the term of redemption; 〈만기〉 maturity: 상환기한이 되다 be due for redemption ―만기일 the date of maturity ―의무자 a recourse debtor ―청구권 (the right of) recourse

상황 狀況 a condition; the state of affairs [things]; a situation; circumstances
　◆ 유리한[불리한] 상황 favorable [unfavorable] conditions / 어떤 상황에 있어서도 in [under] any circumstances / 이런 상황에 있어서는 in a state of affairs like this; in [under] these circumstances / 위기적 상황에 있다 be in a critical condition; be at a crisis
　▶ 상황은 호전했다[악화되었다] The situation improved [got worse].
　▶ 그는 상황을 파악하고 재빠르게 행동했다 He sized up the situation and took quick action.
　■―증거 circumstantial [direct] evidence ―판단 circumstantial judgment

상황 商況 trade [business, market] condition; the market situations
　▶ 상황이 부진하다 The market is dull [slack].
　▶ 상황이 활발하다 The market is brisk [active].
　■ 해외― trade [commercial] conditions abroad ■―보고 a market report [bulletin] ―부진 [a slack, an inactive] market; depression (in trade)

상회 商會 a commercial firm [concern]; a trading company

상회하다 上廻― exceed; top; be more than; be in excess of
　▶ 총액은 100만 달러를 훨씬 상회했다 The total was well over one million dollars.
　▶ 수출이 수입을 훨씬 상회했다 Export exceeded import by a great margin.

상훈 賞勳 〈포상함〉 citation of merit

상흔 傷痕 a scar ◆ 상흔을 남기다 leave a scar behind

샅 the inside of the thigh; the crotch; the crutch; 〈서혜부〉 the groin

샅바 〈씨름의〉 a wrestler's thigh band; 〈죄인의〉 a leg-band for a prisoner

샅샅이 all over; throughout; in every nook and corner; all through; thoroughly; everywhere
　◆ 샅샅이 뒤지다[찾다] look in every nook and corner; leave no corner unsearched; search every corner [cranny]; hunt [search] high and low / 집안을 샅샅이 뒤지다 ransack the house (for); search the whole house

새[1] 〈날짐승〉 a bird; a feathered creature; a fowl; 〈물새〉 waterfowl; 〈참새〉 a sparrow

[解說] **bird**는 가장 일반적인 말이며 **fowl**은 닭・오리・칠면조 등 가금을 가리키는데, 수식어가 붙어서 집합적으로 조류의 뜻으로도 쓰인다. 물새는 ***waterfowl***이다.

♦새 가게 a bird shop / 새를 기르다 keep a cage bird / 새를 쫓다 shoo birds away / 새를 잡다 catch a bird / 새에 모이를 주다 feed a bird ((on))

새² an interval ⇨ 사이
새³ 〈새로운〉 new; 〈신기한〉 novel; 〈신선한〉 fresh; 〈최근의〉 recent; latest; hot (news); 〈현대적〉 up-to-date; modern
♦새 차 a new car / 새 사상 an up-to-date idea
▶이 공장에는 새 기기가 설치되어 있다 Up-to-date machines and equipment have been installed in this factory.
새가슴 a chicken [pigeon] breast
♦새가슴의 chicken-[pigeon-]breasted
새것 a new thing [one, brand]
♦새것처럼 보이다 look like new
▶그의 사무실의 헌 냉방 장치가 새것으로 바뀌었다 The old air conditioner in his office was replaced by a new one.
새겨듣다 〈주의해서〉 listen attentively [carefully] to sb; 〈알아듣다〉 catch [get] the meaning of what sb says
▶내 말을 새겨들어라 Please note my words. ⇌ Note what I say. ⇌ Now understand me!
새그물 a fowler's [fowling] net
새근거리다¹ 〈가쁘게 숨쉬다〉 breath quick and hard; puff; pant; breathe roughly
♦화가 나서 새근거리다 breathe hard [roughly] with anger
▶노인은 새근거리면서 계단을 올라갔다 The old man panted up the stairs.
새근거리다² 〈뼈마디가〉 feel [have] a slight pain (in one's joints) ▶뼈 마디마디가 새근거린다 I am aching in my joints.
새근새근 〈sleep〉 calmly; quietly; peacefully
▶젖먹이가 새근새근 자고 있다 The baby is sleeping peacefully [quietly, calmly].
새근하다 feel [have, suffer] a dull pain (in a joint); be slightly painful (in an elbow joint)
▶뼈마디가 새근하여 마음대로 일을 할 수 없다 My joints are slightly painful so that I can't do my work well.

새금하다 ((taste)) a bit sour; sourish; tartish; vinegarish ▶이 사과는 새금하다 This apple tastes sour. ♦레몬은 새금한 맛이 있다 A lemon has an acid taste.
새기다¹ 1 〈조각하다〉 carve (in, on, out of); engrave (▶carve는 나무・상아 등에 새기는 것. engrave는 금속・나무・돌의 표면에 새기는 것); sculpture; cut; 〈끌로〉 chisel; 〈비석・금속에〉 inscribe
♦도장을 새기다 engrave a seal / 나무에 이름을 새기다 carve one's name on a tree
▶대리석에 천사상이 새겨져 있었다 The figure of an angel was engraved [carved] in the marble.
2 〈명심하다〉 impress (deeply); stamp; engrave; inscribe
♦가슴[마음속]에 새기다 bear [keep] sth in mind; take ((the advice)) to heart; have sth stamped [engraved] on one's mind
▶내가 하는 말을 마음속 깊이 새겨 둬라 Keep my words in mind.
새기다² 1 〈풀이하다〉 interpret; explain; construe; paraphrase; elucidate; expound
♦올바로[잘못] 새기다 interpret rightly [falsely]; give [put] a correct [wrong] interpretation (upon)
▶그것은 여러 가지로 새길 수가 있다 It may be interpreted variously.
2 〈번역하다〉 translate (into)
새기다³ 〈반추하다〉 ruminate
새김 1 〈풀이〉 paraphrase; interpretation; 〈번역〉 translation; 〈한자의 뜻〉 the Korean rendering of a Chinese character 2 〈조각〉 carving; engraving; sculpture; cutting
■―칼 a graver; a chisel; a burin
새김질 〈반추〉 rumination; 〈조각〉 carving; sculpture; engraving
▶소가 새김질을 하고 있다 The cow is ruminating [chewing its cud].
새까맣다 deep-black; jet-[coal-]black; raven-[pitch-]black; ((as)) black as coal [ink, pitch, ebony]
♦새까맣게 타다 〈불에〉 be charred; be burnt [scorched] black; 〈햇볕에〉 be deeply tanned; be sunbaked
▶그녀는 머리가 새까맣다 She has raven [jet-black] hair.
▶어부는 햇볕에 그을어 얼굴과 몸이 새까맸다 The face and body of the fisherman were tanned dark brown.
새 까먹은 소리 ((속담)) a groundless rumor; a canard
새끼¹ 〈줄〉 a straw rope
♦새끼 한 사리 a fold of rope / 새끼를 꼬다 make [twist, strand] a rope / 새끼를 치다 stretch a rope ((around a place)); rope off [out] ((a place))
새끼² 1【동물의】 ((총칭)) the young; 〈한 마리〉 a young; a youngling; 〈소의〉 a calf (pl. calves, calfs); 〈고양이의〉 a kitty; a kitten; 〈양의〉 a lamb; 〈염소의〉 a kid; 〈말・사슴 의〉 a colt; 〈개・여우・이리 등의〉 a puppy; a pup; 〈조류의〉 a young bird; a chick(en)
♦호랑이[곰] 새끼 a tiger [bear] cub / 물고기

새끼 fry; the young of fish / 한 배의 새끼 a litter 《of pigs》; a brood 《of chickens》 / 새끼를 배고 있다 be with young; 〈암캐가〉 be in pup / 새끼를 낳다 bring forth 《its》 young; reproduce 《its》 kind; litter; whelp; cub; lamb (양); yean [kid] (염소); pup (개); kitten (고양이); calf (소)
► 고양이가 새끼 다섯 마리를 낳았다 The cat a litter of five kittens.
► 올챙이는 개구리의 새끼다 Tadpoles are baby frogs.
2 〈자식〉 one's son [daughter]; 〈욕하는 말〉 a fellow; a guy; a chap
♦ 저 새끼 that fellow [swine, brute]
♦ 요놈의 새끼야 You rascal!
♦ 이 개새끼야 You son of a bitch!
3 〈이자〉 interest
♦ 새끼를 치다 bear [yield] interest (at 7%)
━발가락[발톱] a little toe [toenail] ―**손가락[손톱]** a little finger [fingernail]; the fifth finger ―**집** the womb (of an animal)
새끼줄 a straw rope ⇨ 새끼[1]
새날 〈새로운 날〉 a new day; 〈새로운 시대〉 a new era [stage, epoch]
새다[1] 〈날이〉 dawn; break
♦ 날이 새기 전에 before dawn [daybreak]; before light / 날이 새기 시작할 무렵에 at the crack [peep] of dawn; at the first break of day
► 날이 샌다 Day dawns [breaks, cracks]. ⇌ It dawns.
► 드디어 날이 샜다 Day broke at last.
► 날이 새고보니 비는 그쳐 있었다 By dawn, the rain had stopped.
새다[2] 1 〈액체·가스 등이〉 leak; escape; get [find] vent; run out
♦ 비가 새는 천장 a leaking ceiling / 새는 곳을 막다 stop [plug] a leak
♦ 파이프에서 가스가 새고 있다 Gas is leaking from the pipe.
► 지붕이 몹시 샌다 The roof leaks badly. ⇌ The roof has a bad leak.
2 〈불빛 등이〉 come [shine, break] through
► 커튼 틈으로 새어 나오는 불빛이 보인다 Light can be seen through the small opening between the curtains.
3 〈말소리·감정 등이〉 be heard outside; get [find] vent; find expression
► 신음소리가 그의 입에서 새어 나왔다 A groan escaped his lips.
► 장례식에 참석한 사람들 사이에서 흐느껴 우는 소리가 새어 나왔다 There were sobbings heard among those present at the funeral.
4 〈비밀이〉 get [slip] out; leak (out); transpire; be disclosed
► 이 비밀이 외부로 새면 큰일난다 If this secret should leak [slip] out, it will bring serious consequences.
5 〈슬쩍 빠져나가다〉 sneak away; slip off [out, away] / 일행 속에서 슬쩍 새다 sneak away from company
새달 next month; the coming month
새댁 ―宅 a bride ⇨ 새색시
새도 가지를 가려 앉는다 (속담) Choose your companions well. ⇌ A bird like the phoenix chooses its tree to alight on.
새되다 high-pitched; shrill; reedy; sharp ♦ 새된 목소리 a shrill voice / 새된 목소리로 말하다 speak in a high-pitched voice
새둥주리 a (bird's) nest; a cage
새득새득 slightly dry
새들 〈안장〉 a saddle
새뜨다 〈간격이 있다〉 separated; scarce; 〈소원하다〉 estranged; alienated
새뜻하다 fresh and bright
새로 new(ly); anew; afresh
♦ 새로 지은 집 a new house; a newly built house / 새로 온 선생 a new teacher / 새로 (들어)온 사람 a newcomer; a freshman / 새로 문을 연 가게 a newly opened shop; a new store / 새로 시작하다 begin afresh / 새로 출발하다 make a fresh [new] start
► 이 분은 우리 회사에 새로 입사한 김 호 씨입니다 This is Mr. Kim Ho, a newcomer in our company. ⇌ This is Mr. Kim Ho who has recently entered our firm.
새로이 newly; anew; afresh (⇨ 새로) ♦ 결의를 새로이 하다 make a fresh determination
► 이 사전은 내용을 새로이 할 필요가 있다 This dictionary needs to be updated [brought up to date].
새롭다 new; 〈신기하다〉 novel; 〈생생하다〉 fresh; 〈최신이다〉 recent; latest; 〈현대적이다〉 up-to-date; modern
♦ 아주 새로운 brand-new; up-to-the-minute; up-to-the-second / 새롭게 newly; freshly; anew; afresh / 새롭게 하다 renew; renovate / 새로워지다 be renewed; be renovated / 아직 기억에 새롭다 be fresh in one's memory
► 뭐 새로운 소식이 있니? Any news?
► 별로 새로운 일이 없다 Nothing fresh has happened.
► 듣고 보는 것치고 새롭지 않은 것이 하나도 없었다 Everything that I saw or heard was new to me.
► 그 사건은 아직 우리의 기억에 새롭다 That incident is still fresh in our memories.
새롱거리다 flirt [sport, fondle, dally] with 《each other》; bill and coo
새마을 *Saemaŭl*; a new community
■ ―공장 [금고, 문고, 사업] a *Saemaŭl* [New Community] factory [fund, library, project] ―운동 the *Saemaŭl* [New Community] Movement ―지도자 a *Saemaŭl* leader
새매 [鳥] a [an Asiatic] sparrow hawk; an accipiter
새물 1 〈과일·생선의〉 the first product of the season; the first supply 《of tomatoes》 ♦ 새물 사과 early apples
► 이 복숭아는 새물이다 These peaches are the first of the season.
2 〈옷의〉 clothes fresh from washing; newly washed clothes
► 그는 새물 셔츠를 입고 있었다 He wore a newly washed shirt.
새벽[1] 〈날이 밝을 녘〉 dawn; daybreak; the break of day; the peep of day; (美) the crack of dawn

♦이른 새벽에 early in the morning; at dawn [daybreak]; at the first light of day; (美) at the crack of day / 새벽부터 해거름까지 from dawn till dusk; (美) from sunup to sundown / 새벽길을 떠나다 start (on *one's* journey) early in the morning / (닭이) 새벽을 알리다 proclaim the dawn / 새벽같이 일어나다 get up at daybreak; rise with the sun
▶우리는 내일 새벽 전에 출발하기로 되어 있다 We will start on the journey before daybreak tomorrow.
■—녘 the peep of dawn [day]; the prime —바람 an early-morning breeze —밥 breakfast at dawn —일 early-morning chores —잠 an early-morning sleep —종 the daybreak [matin] bell —하늘 the dawning sky
새벽² 〔建〕 fine loamy earth; loam; loamy plaster ■—질 plastering
새벽달 the moon at dawn; the morning moon
새봄 〈오는 봄〉 next [the coming] spring; 〈이른 봄〉 early spring
새빨갛다 very red; deep-red; crimson
▶그건 새빨간 거짓말이다 It is a downright [barefaced] lie.
▶지는 해가 서녘 하늘을 새빨갛게 물들였다 The setting sun fired the western sky.
새빨개지다 turn [become] red [crimson]; 〈부끄러워서〉 blush scarlet [crimson] (for shame); color deeply; 〈상기하여〉 flush deeply
▶그녀는 부끄러워서 귀뿌리까지 새빨개졌다 She blushed up to the roots of her hair for shame.
새사냥 fowling ♦새사냥 가다 go fowling [shooting] ■—꾼 a fowler
새사람 **1** 〈신인〉 a newcomer; a new figure; a new face ♦새사람을 구하다 scout for a new talent
2 〈새생활을 하는 사람〉 a new man; a reborn [reformed] person
▶그는 영적으로 새사람이 됐다 He was spiritually reborn.
▶그는 아주 새사람이 되었다 He is quite another man now.
새살 granulation; new skin; proud flesh
♦새살이 나오다 granulate
새살거리다 carry on [behave] flippantly; chatter merrily; talk on smilingly
새살궂다 very light and talkative; dreadfully flippant [frivolous]
새살떨다 frolic; bounce around flippantly
새살림 a new home ♦새살림을 차리다 make a new home
새살스럽다 flippant; frivolous; frolicsome
♦새살스런 여자 a flippant woman
새삼 〔植〕 a dodder; a love vine
새삼스럽다 ♦새삼스러운 말 a remark unnecessary to say anew [again] / 새삼스레 anew; afresh; again; specially; formally
▶새삼스럽게 말할 필요는 없겠지만 늦지 않도록 하세요 I don't have to tell you again [It is hardly necessary to say], but please don't be late.
▶그의 노력에 새삼스럽게 감명을 받았다 I was all the more impressed by his efforts.

▶그런 말은 이제 새삼스럽게 할 필요도 없다 It is too well known to be mentioned here. ⇌ It's an old story.
▶상식의 중요성을 새삼스럽게 느꼈다 I felt all the more keenly the importance of common sense.
▶새삼스럽게 부탁이라니 뭡니까? What do you want me particularly to do? ⇌ What is the particular favor you ask of me?
새색시 a bride; a newly married [wedded] woman
♦새색시 혼숫감으로 in bridal array
새생활 —生活 a new life; a new career
♦새생활에 들어가다 enter (up)on [lead] a new life
새서방 —書房 a new husband; 〈신랑〉 a bridegroom
새소리 a birdcall; a note [song] of a bird; a bird's note; woodnotes
새시 a sash (window) ■알루미늄— an aluminum sash
새싹 a sprout; a bud; a shoot ♦장미의 새싹 a new [young] shoot of a rose / 새싹이 나다 bud; sprout; put forth leaves [buds]
▶온 산의 나무에 새싹이 움트기 시작했다 All the trees in the mountain are budding [sprouting].
새아기 〈며느리〉 one's new daughter-in-law
새알 an egg of a sparrow; a bird's egg
새알심 a small dumpling in red bean gruel
새암 jealousy ⇨ 샘²
새앙 〔植〕 a ginger ⇨ 생강
새앙쥐 a mouse ⇨ 생쥐
새옷 a new suit [dress]; new clothes
새옹지마 塞翁之馬 blessing in disguise
▶인간만사는 새옹지마다 Inscrutable are the ways of Heaven.
새우 〈큰 것〉 a lobster; 〈작은 것〉 a shrimp; 〈보리새우〉 a prawn
♦새우처럼 허리가 굽은 노인 an old man bent almost double with age
■닭— a spring [spiny] lobster ■—젓 salted shrimp
새우다 〈철야하다〉 sit [stay] up all-night; sit the night out
♦공부로 밤을 새우다 study all-night long / 술을 밤새워 마시다 drink all-night long; drink the night away / 이야기로 밤을 새우다 talk the night away; talk all (through) the night / 하룻밤을 꼬박 눈물로 새우다 pass a whole night in tears / 밤을 새워가며 회의하다 have an all-night conference
▶그는 밤을 꼬박 새워 리포트를 썼다 He stayed up all-night writing the report.
새우등 a bent [rounded] back; round [stooped] shoulders; a stoop
♦새우등의 stooped; round-shouldered / 새우등지다 be stooped; have a stoop
새로 잉어를 낚는다 (속담) You must lose a fly to catch a trout. ⇌ Venture a small fish and catch a great one. ⇌ Throw (out) a sprat to catch a whale.
새우잠 ♦새우잠을 자다 curl up; curl *oneself* up (on bed)

새잡이 〈일〉 birdcatching; 〈사람〉 a bird catcher

새장 ─欌 a birdcage; a cage (for birds)
♦새장에 갇힌 새 a caged bird / 새를 새장에 넣다 cage a bird; put a bird in a cage

새장수 a bird dealer; 〈사육자〉 a bird fancier

새조개 〈貝〉 a cockle; a cockle clam

새집¹ 〈신축한 집〉 a newly built house; 〈새로 이사온 집〉 one's new house [home]
♦새집으로 이사하다 move to a new house
▶그는 교외에 새집을 지었다 He built a new house in the suburbs.

새집² 〈새의 둥지〉 a bird's nest; 〈인공새장〉 a birdhouse; a bird box; a nest [nesting] box

새총 ─銃 1 〈공기총〉 an air gun [rifle]; 〈엽총〉 a fowling piece 2 〈고무줄 새총〉 a slingshot; (英) a catapult

새출발 ─出發 a restart ⇨ 재출발

새치 a gray [white] hair in youth; a premature gray hair ♦새치를 뽑다 pull out a gray hair
▶그는 새치가 많다 Though young, he has gray streaks of hair.

새치기하다 break into the line; (英) jump the queue; cut in ▶새치기하지 마시오 In order, please.

새치름하다 1 〈쌀쌀하다〉 standoffish; 〈시치미 떼다〉 play the innocent; assume a prim air
♦새치름한 계집애 a prim young girl / 새치름해져서 demurely
▶그녀는 남 앞에서는 새치름하게 군다 She puts on [assumes] a look of studied composure in public.
2 displeased; disgruntled; not quite happy

새치부리다 behave oneself with reserve

새침데기 〈얌전떠는 사람〉 a person who pretends innocence; 〈새침한 사람〉 a primlooking person; a prim; a prig; a prude
▶그녀는 언제나 새침데기다 She always assumes prim airs.

새침하다 standoffish ⇨ 새치름하다

새카맣다 (be) pitch-dark; jet-black; raven

새커리 〈영국의 작가〉 Thackeray, William Makepeace (1811-63)

새콤하다 somewhat sour; sourish ⇨ 새금하다

새크라멘토 〈미국 California 주의 주도〉 Sacramento

새털 〈깃털〉 a feather; plumage; (총칭) a plume; 〈솜털〉 down ■─구름 〔氣〕 a cirrus (pl. ·ri [·rai])

새퉁스럽다 silly; absurd; ridiculous; 〈갑작스럽다〉 whimsical; sudden; abrupt

새퉁이 〈행동〉 a rash [capricious] act; 〈사람〉 a flippant person ♦새퉁이 부리다 act rashly [flippantly]; be ridiculous

새파랗다 1 〈짙푸르다〉 deep blue; indigo-blue
♦새파란 하늘에 in a deep blue [in an azure] sky
2 〈해쓱하다〉 deadly [ghastly] pale; as white as a sheet
♦새파랗게 질린 얼굴 a pallid face / 무서워서 새파랗게 질리다 turn deadly pale with fright; be scared blue [green]
3 〈썩 젊다〉 young; green

♦새파란 젊은이 a green youth

새하얗다 pure-white; (as) white as snow; snow(y)-white
♦새하얀 드레스 a pure-white dress
▶그녀는 그 소식을 듣고 새하얗게 질렸다 She [Her face] turned pale at the news.

새해 the New Year; a new year ⇨ 신년
♦새해를 축하하다 celebrate the New Year / 새해를 맞다 see the New Year in
▶새해 복 많이 받으십시오 (A) Happy New year! = I wish you a happy New Year.
■─문안[인사] a New Year's greeting ─차례 an ancestor-memorial service on New Year's Day

새호리기 〔鳥〕 a hobby

색 〈자루 등의〉 a sack; 〈피임구〉 a condom; (俗) a rubber

색 色 1 〈색채〉 (a) color; 〈색조〉 a hue; a tint; a tinge

> [解說] 「색」은 일반적으로 color로 나타낸다. 특별한 뉘앙스를 풍길 경우는 shade, tint, hue 등으로 표현한다. shade는 주로 「색의 약간의 차이」를 나타낸다. 색채에 관한 표현은 우리말과 영어 사이에 많은 차이가 있다. 예를 들면 「청신호」 등의 「청」을 영어에서는 항상 green으로 나타낸다. 또 우리말의 「빨강」은 밝은 난색을 총칭하며 영어의 red보다는 뜻이 넓다. 또 대부분 우리나라 사람은 「pink(분홍빛)」나 「외설」과 연관시키나 영미인은 blue를 「외설」과 연관시킨다.

♦무지개의 모든 색 all the colors [hues] of the rainbow / 짙은[엷은] 색 a deep [light] color / 조화가 잘되는 색 harmonizing colors / 여러 색의 기 flags of various colors / 색의 배합 a color scheme / 색이 변하다 change color; discolor
▶그 색은 쉽게 바랜다 The color fades easily.
▶이 색은 세탁을 해도 빠지지 않는다 This color will not come off in the wash. = This color will stand the wash.
▶〔會話〕 「그녀의 차는 무슨 색이지?」 「빨강색이야」 "What color is her car?" "It's red."
▶그녀의 머리는 무슨 색이지? What color hair does she have?
▶개는 색을 식별하지 못한다 Dogs can't see [perceive] colors.
2 〈그림물감의〉 color; tint; tinge
♦색을 내다 bring out the color / 색을 칠하다 color; paint
▶그 아이는 그림에 색을 칠하고 있었다 The child was coloring a picture.
3 〈색욕·호색〉 lust; sexual passion; sensual pleasure
♦색을 좋아하다 be amorous; be lustful
■─감각 〔物·生〕 color sensation ─견본 a color sample; colorings ─분해 〔物〕 color separation ─지수 a color index

색각 色覺 a color sense

색감 色感 ♦색감이 예리하다 have a keen sense of color

색골 色骨 a sex maniac; a lecherous [lewd] man; a lecher; a goat; a Don Juan

색광 色光   colored light
색광 色狂   a sex maniac; 〈남자〉 a sex-crazed person; an erotomaniac; 〈여자〉 a nymphomaniac; 〈광증〉 erotomania
색깔 色—   color ⇨ 빛깔
♦ 정치적 색깔이 없는 사람 a person with no political coloring
색다르다 色—   unusual; uncommon; extraordinary; 〈기묘하다〉 odd; queer; strange; curious; peculiar; 〈갖가지〉 various
♦ 색다른 사나이 a queer fellow [fish]; an eccentric man / 색다른 이름 an odd name / (평소와 다른) 색다른 짓을 하다 break the routine
▶ 그 가게의 장식은 색다르다 The store has an unusual decoration.
▶ 좀 색다른 타이를 보여주세요 Show me a different [another] tie.
▶ 그는 조금 색다른 데가 있다 There is something odd [peculiar] about him.
색대 色—   a trier; a scoop [trier] for grain sampling
색도 色度   chromaticity; 〈조명〉 chroma; color ━측정 colorimetry
색동 色—   striped cloth ━저고리 a child's striped jacket; a child's coat with multicolored sleeves
색마 色魔   a sex maniac ⇨ 색광(色狂)
색맹 色盲   color blindness; achromatopsia
▶ 그는 색맹이다 He is color-blind.
■ 녹[적]— green [red] blindness 부분—dyschromatopsia 선천— daltonism 적록—red-green blindness 전(全)— achromatopsia totalis ━검사표 a color blindness test chart
색사진 色寫眞   a color picture; a color photograph
색상 色相   a hue; the tone of color; a color tone
색상자 色箱子   a varicolored box
색색   with a hissing sound; hissingly ♦ 색색 잠자다 sleep peacefully [soundly]; sleep a peaceful [sound] sleep
색색이 色色—   in [with] various [different] colors
색소 色素   〔生〕 pigment
■ 식용— a food dye ■ —결핍증 〔醫〕 albinism ━세포 〔生〕 a pigment cell ━층 〔解〕 a pigment layer ━침착 a pigment deposit
색소체 色素體   〔生〕 a plastid ━유전 plastid inheritance
색소폰   a saxophone; (口) a sax ■ —주자 a saxophonist
색수차 色收差   〔光〕 chromatic aberration
색스혼   a saxhorn
색시   1 〈처녀〉 a young woman; a girl
2 〈신부〉 a bride ♦ 색시를 얻다 take [get] a wife; get married
3 〈접대부〉 a waitress; a barmaid
■ 촌[시골]— a country girl ■ 색싯감 a likely bride
색시 그루는 다홍치마에 앉혀야 한다 (속담) He is young enough to amend.
색신검사 色神檢査   an examination of the color sense; a color test ♦ 색신검사를 받다 have [undergo] a color test
색실 色—   colored thread
색쓰다 色—   indulge in sexual pleasure; have sexual intercourse; play the coquette
색안경 色眼鏡   (a pair of) colored [tinted] glasses; sunglasses
♦ 색안경을 쓰고 보다 look at sth through colored glasses; look at things with a prejudiced [based] point of view
▶ 해변에서는 색안경을 쓰는 사람이 많다 Many people wear shady glasses [sunglasses] at the seaside.
▶ 그는 색안경을 끼고[쓰고] 그녀를 보았다 He viewed her with prejudice [bias]. ⇌ He took a jaundiced view of her.
색약 色弱   〔醫〕 color weakness; color amblyopia
색연필 色鉛筆   a colored pencil
색욕 色慾   lust; sexual desire; a craving for sex ♦ 색욕을 억누르다 repress one's sexual appetites / 색욕을 만족시키다 gratify one's lust / 색욕에 빠지다 indulge [give into] one's sexual passions
색유리 色琉璃   stained [colored] glass
색인 索引   an index (pl. ~es, -dices [-dəsi:z])
♦ 색인이 있는[없는] 책 an indexed [indexless] book / 책에 색인을 달다 index a book; provide a book with an index; append an index to a book
▶ 이 책은 색인이 잘 되어있다 This book is well-indexed.
■ 자구(字句)— an index verborum 지명— an index locorum
색전증 塞栓症   〔醫〕 embolism
색정 色情   lust; sexual appetite [desire, passion]; carnal desire
♦ 색정이 일어나다 be seized with sexual passion; be roused sexually / 색정을 자극하다 excite [provoke] sexual desire
■ —광(狂) ⇨ 색광(色狂) ━탐닉 sexual indulgence
색조 色調   the tone (of a color); color tone; shade; tonality ♦ 차가운[선명한, 흐릿한] 색조 a cool [vivid, dull] tone
▶ 나는 그 벽에는 엷은 색조의 회색을 칠하기로 했다 I chose a light shade of gray paint for the wall.
색종이 色—   colored paper ▶ 색종이를 접어서 학을 만드세요 Please fold a piece of paper into the figure of a crane.
색주가 色酒家   〈술집〉 a shady bar [saloon]; a bar-whorehouse; 〈작부〉 a whorish barmaid [waitress]
색채 色彩   (a) color; hue; a tint; coloring; coloration
♦ 야한 색채 loud colors / 종교적 색채 a religious tinge / 지방적 색채 local color / 색채가 풍부하다 be colorful; abound in color
▶ 아프리카인의 의상은 색채가 다채롭다 African clothes are fully colored.
▶ 그 풍속에는 종교적인 색채가 있다 The custom has a religious color.
▶ 그 대회는 정치적 색채가 짙다 The rally has a strong political tinge.
■ —감각 color sensation; 〈심미안〉 color sense

색출 索出 ♦부정 공무원의 색출 exposure of corrupt officials
—색출하다 find out; search [ferret] out
▶형사들은 그 도시에 잠복한 살인범을 색출해 내려고 혈안이 되어 있었다 The detectives were all out [working hard] to hunt down the murderer hiding in the town.

색칠 色漆 coloring; painting —색칠하다 paint; color
♦지도에 색칠하다 color a map

샌님 1 〈얌전한 사람〉 a meek-kneed and stubborn person; a milksop; 〈보수적인 사람〉 a conformist
2 ⇨ 생원 (生員)

샌드백 a sandbag

샌드버그 〈미국의 작가〉 Sandburg, Carl (1878-1967)

샌드위치 a sandwich ■햄[치즈]— ham [cheese] sandwich

샌드위치맨 a sandwich man

샌드페이퍼 sandpaper ⇨ 사포 ♦판자를 샌드페이퍼로 문지르다 sandpaper a board

샌들 (a pair of) sandals
♦샌들을 신은 남자 a man in sandals; a sandaled [sandal-footed] man

샌디에이고 〈미국의 도시〉 San Diego

샌안토니오 〈미국의 도시〉 San Antonio

샌퍼라이즈 〈商標〉 ♦샌퍼라이즈 셔츠 a Sanforized shirt / 샌퍼라이즈 가공의 Sanforized

샌프란시스코 San Francisco; 《美俗》 Frisco
♦샌프란시스코 강화회의 the Peace Conference at San Francisco
■—시민 a San Franciscan

샐러드 a salad ♦샐러드를 만들다 mix [prepare] a saiad / 야채— a vegetable salad 햄— ham and salad —용 채소 salad; lettuce —유[기름] salad oil

샐러리 〈급여〉 a salary ▶그녀는 월 100만원의 샐러리를 받고 있다 She is paid [gets a salary of] one million won a month.

샐러리맨 a salaried worker [man, employee]; 《美》 a white-collar [an office] worker

解説 salary man은 영어로서 인정할 수 없다. 「샐러리[월급]를 받고 일하는 사람」의 뜻으로 *salaried man* [*worker, employee*]은 가능하지만 이것들은 뜻으로는 통해도 영·미에서는 쓰이지 않는다. 영어로는 *office worker, company employee, white-collar worker* 등이 무리없이 쓰인다. 우리나라 사람들은 직업에 대해 질문을 받았을 때 I'm a salaried worker for G Company. (G사에 근무하고 있다) 즉 「샐러리맨입니다」 라고 흔히 대답하는데 영미인은 일반적으로 I'm an engineer. 라든가 She works as a secretary. 처럼 구체적으로 직종을 말하는 경우가 많다.

샐비어 〔植〕 a salvia; a scarlet sage; 〈약용 샐비어〉 a sage

샐비지 〈해난 구조〉 salvage ■—선 a salvage boat

샐쭉하다 distort; sullen

샘¹ 〈물의〉 a spring; a fountain; 〈원천〉 a fountainhead; a source
♦지식의 샘 a font [fount] of knowledge / 콸콸 솟는 샘 a gushing [live] spring
▶샘이 말랐다 The spring has run dry.

샘² jealousy; envy
♦샘이 나다 feel [become] jealous / 샘을 내다 show jealousy
—샘하다 envy 《another》; be jealous [envious]; feel envy
■—바리 a jealous person

샘구멍 a fountainhead; a headspring

샘물 spring water ■—줄기 a stream of spring water

샘바르다 (acutely) jealous

샘받이 a paddy field which has a spring in it

샘솟다 spring out; well out; gush out [forth]; spurt
▶그녀의 눈에 눈물이 샘솟았다 Tears welled up in her eyes.
▶내 가슴에 희망이 샘솟아 올랐다 Hope has begun to spring up in my heart.

샘터 a fountain place [site]; washing place watered by a spring ▶샘터가 말라버렸다 The well has gone [run] dry.

샘플 a sample; a specimen ■혈액— a blood sample —케이스 a sample case

샘플링 〈견본〉 sampling ■—추출검사 sampling inspection

샛강 —江 a by-channel of a river enclosing a low islet; a side river; a tributary

샛길 a byway; a byroad; a side road; a bypassage ♦샛길을 가다 take a byway [shortcut] ▶차가 샛길로 들어갔다 The car turned into [onto] a side road.

샛노랗다 bright [golden] yellow

샛문 —門 a side gate [door]

샛바람 an east [easterly] wind

샛별 the morning star; Venus; Lucifer

샛서방 —書房 an adulterer; a secret lover; a paramour

생 生 life ⇨ 생명(生命), 삶

생- 生- 1 〈익지 않은〉 unripe; green; 〈날것의〉 raw; uncooked; 〈설익은〉 underdone; half-boiled[-cooked]; rare; 〈가공하지 않은〉 crude; raw; unprocessed
♦생수 unboiled water / 생고기 raw meat / 생달걀 a raw egg / 생명주 raw-silk fabric / 생밥 half-boiled rice / 생방송 a live broadcast
2 〈살아있는〉 live; living; green
♦생울타리 living hedge
3 〈엉뚱한·공연한〉 irrational; unreasonable; arbitrary ♦생벼락 unreasonable scolding

-생 -生 〈학생〉 a student of...
♦초등학생 a primary school boy [girl] / 의대생 a medical student
2 〈생년생일〉 born in 《1960》; born on 《June 9》
3 〈식물의〉 일년생[다년생] 식물 an annual [a perennial] plant

생가 生家 the house where one was born; the house of one's birth; one's parents' home
▶나는 런던에 있는 디킨즈의 생가를 찾아보았

생각나다

다 I visited Dickens' birthplace in London.
생가죽 生── (a) rawhide; (an) undressed skin; (a) raw pelt
생각 1 〈사고〉 thinking; 〈사상〉 (a) thought; ideas ♦ 생각을 전하다 convey one's thoughts 《to》 / 생각을 고쳐갖다 revise one's thinking / 자기의 생각을 이해시키다 make *oneself* understood 《by》
▶ 그것은 아주 미국적인 생각이다 That's an all [a typical] American way of thinking.
▶ 그는 시대보다 한 걸음 앞선 생각을 갖고 있다 He is ahead of the times in his ideas.
2 〈관념·착상〉 an idea; a notion; a concept; a thought; 〈창의〉 initiative
♦ 잘못된 생각 an erroneous [a false, a wrong] idea / 낡은 생각 an antiquated idea /《떠오른》 생각을 메모해 두다 put one's thoughts [ideas] on paper
▶ 좋은 생각이 떠올랐다 A good idea struck [occurred to] me. ⇌ I hit upon a good idea.
▶ 생각은 좋은데 실행하기가 어렵다 The idea is good but not workable.
▶ 그는 목적을 위해서는 수단을 가리지 않는다는 그릇된 생각을 가지고 있다 He got a wrong idea [notion] that he should accomplish his purpose by fair means or foul.
3 〈의견〉 an opinion; a view; 〈제안〉 a suggestion; 〈신념〉 a belief; one's persuasion; 〈인상〉 an impression
♦ 확고한 생각 a definite opinion / 내 생각으로는 to my mind; in my opinion [view]; to my (way of) thinking / 생각을 말하다 express [give] one's opinion [views]; speak [say, tell, open, disclose] one's mind
▶ 그 점에서는 나는 너와 생각이 다르다 I cannot agree with you on that point.
▶ 그 문제에 대한 자네 생각은 어떤가? What is your opinions [thoughts] about the question? ⇌ Tell me what you think about the question.
▶ 그것 참 좋은 생각이다 That's a good idea. ⇌ That's an idea.
4 〈의도〉 an intention; a purpose; a design; a view; an aim; an idea; 〈동기〉 a motive
♦ 사직할 생각이 없다 have no intention [mind] to resign [no thought of resigning] / 생각을 품다 cherish an intention; conceive an idea / 생각을 실행에 옮기다 carry out one's intention; put one's idea(s) into practice
▶ 그는 도통 공부할 생각이 없다 He doesn't want to study at all.
▶ 나는 아들을 의사로 만들 생각이다 I'm thinking of making my son a doctor. ⇌ I intend (for) my son to be a doctor.
▶ 널 속일 생각은 털끝만큼도 없다 I haven't the slightest intention [the least idea] to cheat you.
5 〈사려분별〉 discretion; prudence; sense; 〈판단〉 judgment
♦ 앞뒤의 생각 없이 recklessly; thoughtlessly; regardless of the consequences
▶ 그는 아직 젊어서 생각이 깊지 않다 He lacks prudence because he is still young.
▶ 네 생각은 틀렸다 You are wrong in your judgment.
▶ 그는 나이는 어리지만 생각은 어른스럽다 He has an old head on young shoulders.
▶ 네 생각대로 결정할 수 없는 것도 있는 법이다 There are some matters you must not decide [in your own judgment, at your own discretion].
6 〈배려〉 consideration; thought; account; regard; 〈참작〉 allowance
♦ 생각이 깊은 thoughtful; considerate / 생각이 없는 inconsiderate; thoughtless
▶ 그녀는 생각이 깊다 She is thoughtful [prudent, sensible].
7 〈숙고〉 deliberation; consideration; 〈사색〉 (a) thought; 〈반성〉 reconsideration; reflection; 〈심사〉 meditation
▶ 그는 생각에 잠겨 식사하는 것도 잊어버렸다 He was so absorbed in thought that he forgot to take his meal.
8 〈각오〉 a resolution; 〈결심〉 decision
♦ 생각을 정하다 decide 《to do》; make up one's mind 《to do》
9 〈기대〉 expectation(s); hope; 〈소망〉 wish; desire; 〈그리움〉 longing
♦ 생각밖의 unexpected; unlooked-for; unforeseen; unanticipated / 생각대로 되다 turn out just as one wished [wanted]
▶ 일이란 종종 생각대로 되지 않는 법이다 Things often doesn't go as you wish.
▶ 결과는 내 생각과는 전혀 딴판이었다 The result was quite contrary to my expectations [what I expected].
10 〈상상〉 imagination; supposition; fancy; 〈추측〉 (a) guess
♦ 생각도 할 수 없는 unimaginable; unconceivable; unthinkable / 생각이 맞다[틀리다] guess right [wrong]
11 〈기억·회상〉 retrospection; recollection; remembrance
♦ 어렸을 때의 생각 a childhood memory
▶ 시간이 지나자 그 일은 사람들의 생각에서 사라졌다 As time passed the event was forgotten [vanished from people's memories].
▶ 그녀를 전에 본 생각이 난다 I remember seeing her once.
▶ 나는 그런 말을 한 생각이 나지 않는다 I have no remembrance [recollection] of having said such a thing.
12 〈느낌〉 a feeling
♦ …하고 싶은 생각이 들다 feel inclined to do *sth*; feel like 《doing》
▶ 노래할 생각이 나지 않는다 I'm not in a mood for singing.
▶ 휴일은 평일보다 짧은 것 같은 생각이 든다 I feel that a holiday is shorter than a weekday.
생각나다 〈사물이 주어〉 come to mind [one's recollection]; occur to one [one's mind]; 〈사람이 주어〉 recall; recollect; remember; think of
♦ 어린 시절이 생각나다 be reminded of one's childhood / 생각나게 하다 remind *sb* of *sth*; recall [call] *sth* to *sb's* mind; bring *sth* to memory
▶ 나는 생각나는대로 적어갔다 I wrote down

whatever came into my mind.
▶너를 보면 내 여동생이 생각난다 You put me in mind [remind me] of my sister.
▶그의 이름이 생각나지 않는다 I cannot remember his name. ⇌ His name does not come to my mind.
▶그의 얼굴은 알지만, 누군지 생각나지 않아요 I know his face, but I can't place him.

생각다못해 at *one's* wit's [wits'] end
▶그의 행동이 하도 이상해서 생각다못해 나는 부모님께 말씀드렸다 He's been acting so strangely, and not knowing what to do, I spoke to my parents.

생각되다 1〈여겨지다〉be thought of 《as》; be supposed; be considered;〈간주되다〉be regarded 《as》
▶그는 명의로 생각되고 있다 He is thought of [regarded as] a skilled physician.
▶그는 남들에게 좋게[나쁘게] 생각되고 있다 He is thought well [ill] of by others.
2〈…처럼 보이다〉seem; appear; look;〈들리다〉sound;〈인상을 주다〉impress *sb* as
▶비가 올 것 같이 생각된다 It looks like rain.
▶네가 잘못이라고 생각된다 It seems to me that you are wrong.
▶그녀가 내일 오리라고는 생각되지 않는다 I doubt if she will come tomorrow.
▶그가 무슨 말을 할 것으로 생각되니? What do you suppose he will say?

생각컨대 in my opinion; I think that…; it seems to me that…
▶생각컨대 인생이란 꿈이다 In my opinion [To my way of thinking, As I see it] life is nothing but a dream.

생각하다 1〈사고하다〉think; think of [on, about, that…]; (俗) consider; suppose; guess; give (a) thought to
◆영어로 생각하다 think in English / 진지하게 생각하다 think seriously of / 마음속으로 생각하다 think to *oneself*
▶나도 그렇게 생각한다 I think so, too.
▶나는 내일 비가 온다고 생각한다 I think [suppose] it will rain tomorrow.
▶무엇을 생각하고 계십니까? What are you thinking about?
▶그것에 대하여 어떻게 생각합니까? What do you think of [about] it?
▶나는 그렇게 생각하지 않는다 I do not think so [that way].
▶나는 그것을 몇 번이나 생각했다 I thought about it over and over again.
▶만사는 생각하기 나름이다 Everything depends upon your way of thinking.
▶인간은 생각하는 동물이라고 한다 Man is said to be a thinking animal.
2〈의견·견해를 갖다〉view; take a view; be of (the) opinion 《that…》
◆깊이 생각하다 have a deep view of things
▶너는 그를 어떻게 생각하니? What is your view of him?
▶나는 그런 제도는 폐지되어야 한다고 생각한다 I think [consider] (that) such a system should be abolished.
3〈의도하다〉intend to 《do》; mean to 《do》; think of 《doing》; plan to do
▶다음 주에 경주로 갈까 생각하고 있다 I'm going to go to Kyŏngju next week.
▶우리는 내년에는 집을 살까 생각하고 있다 We are thinking of buying [are going to buy, intend to buy] a house next year.
4〈믿다〉believe; hold; be convinced;〈느끼다〉feel
▶신이 존재한다고 생각합니까? Do you believe in God?
▶나는 그녀가 무죄라고 생각해 I am convinced that she is innocent.
▶나는 그가 옳다고 생각한다 I feel certain that he is right.
▶나는 그녀가 너무 일하지 않는가 생각한다 I have a feeling [an idea] that she may overwork herself.
▶나는 꿈이 아닐까 생각했다 I felt as if I were in a dream.
5〈예기하다〉expect; hope; anticipate;〈염려하다〉fear; be afraid 《of, that…》
▶그가 곧 오리라 생각한다 I expect him to come soon.
▶그 수학 시험은 생각했던 것보다 더 어려웠다 The math exam was more difficult than I (had) thought [expected].
▶그녀의 병은 생각했던 것처럼 위독하지는 않았다 Her sickness was not as serious as I feared.
6〈판단하다〉judge; conclude;〈오인하다〉take for; mistake for
▶우리는 그를 미국인으로 잘못 생각했다 We took him for an American. ⇌ We mistakenly believed [thought] him to be an American.
7〈상상하다〉think of; imagine;〈추측하다〉suppose; fancy; (美) guess
▶그건 생각하기도 싫다 I hate to think of it.
▶그것을 생각만해도 마음이 설렌다 I feel excited just to think of it [at the mere thought of it].
▶그녀가 없는 생활은 생각할 수도 없다 I can't imagine [fancy] a life without her.
▶이렇게 될 줄은 전혀 생각지도 못했다 I never thought [Little did I dream] that it would come to such a pass.
8〈간주하다〉regard 《*sb* as》; consider 《*sb* to be a fool》; take 《*sth* [*sb*] for [as], *sb* (to be) wealthy》
▶그는 사태를 비관적으로 생각한다 He takes a pessimistic view of the situation.
▶나는 그 돈을 없어진 것으로 생각하고 있다 I regard the money as gone.
▶우리는 그를 바보라고 생각한다 We consider him (to be) a fool.
▶그는 그 일을 너무 심각하게 생각한다 He treats [takes] the matter too seriously.
9〈고려하다〉consider; take 《a matter》into consideration [account];〈걱정하다〉concern *oneself* about; worry 《*oneself*》about
▶비용 문제도 생각해야 한다 We must not leave the expenses out of account.
▶그는 젊다는 것을 생각해 주어야 한다 You must make allowance for his youth.
▶모든 상황을 생각해보니 내가 책임을 져야할

다 In view of all the circumstances, I have to take the responsibility.
10 〈숙고하다〉 consider; think [ponder] over; deliberate [muse, dwell] on; weigh; meditate; 〈반성하다〉 reflect on; reconsider
▶ 결정하기 전에 몇 번이고 생각해 보아라 Think it over and over again before you come to a definite conclusion.
▶ 네가 한 일을 잘 생각해 보아라 Reflect on what you have done.
▶ 생각해보니 전적으로 내 부주의였다 I found on reflection that I had been careless enough.
11 〈기억·추억하다〉 recall; recollect; remember; look back upon 《the past》; think of; call to mind
▶ 그때를 생각하면 격세지감이 있다 When I look back, it seems as if ages have passed since then.
▶ 어디선가 한 번 뵌것처럼 생각됩니다 I remember seeing [having seen] you once somewhere.
12 〈각오·준비하다〉 be ready 《for, to do》; be prepared for; provide against
♦ 만일의 경우를 생각하다 provide against a rainy day; be prepared for the worst
13 〈바라다〉 wish; want; desire
▶ 오후에는 날씨가 갤 것으로 생각합니다 I hope it will clear up in the afternoon.
▶ 함께 갔으면 하고 생각합니다만 I wish I could go with you.
▶ 내가 생각하는 대로 돼 가지 않는다 Things do not turn out [go] as I wish [to my liking].
14 〈염두에 두다〉 think of; be interested in; 〈그리워하다〉 sigh for; yearn after; 〈사랑하다〉 love; care for; take thought for
▶ 세상에 자기 아이를 생각하지 않는 부모가 있을까? Are there any parents in the world who don't love their children?
15 〈의아해하다〉 wonder (if, whether)
▶ 그가 정말 이해할까 하고 나는 생각했다 I wondered if he would really understand.
16 〈의심하다〉 suspect; get suspicious
▶ 나는 그가 거짓말을 하고 있지 않나 생각한다 I suspect (that) he is telling a lie.
생각해내다 1 〈상기하다〉 remember; recall; recollect; think of; call to mind; be reminded of

> [解說] **remember**는 자연히 생각이 나는 것. 노력해서 생각해내는 경우에는 can, try 등을 같이 쓴다. **recall**은 remember보다 딱딱한 말로서 「의식적으로 노력해서 생각해 내다」의 뜻. **recollect**는 다소 딱딱한 말로서 어떤 일을 시간을 두고 조금씩 생각해내는 것. **think of**는 구어적인 표현으로 보통 can, could와 같이 쓴다. **remind**는 물건·일·사람 등이 생각나게 하는 것이다.

♦ 아무의 이름을 생각해내다 recall *sb's* name
2 〈안출하다〉 think out; think of; devise; work out; 《美》 think up; 〈풀다〉 puzzle out; solve
♦ 적당한 대책을 생각해내다 think up a proper measure
▶ 난 좋은 방안을 막 생각해냈다 I've just thought of [hit upon] a good idea.
생간 生肝 a liver (of a living animal)
생강 生薑 〔植〕 a ginger; 〈뿌리〉 a race [root] of ginger; ginger root; race ginger ■ ―나무 a benzoin ━즙 ginger juice ━차 ginger tea
생경하다 生硬― raw; crude; immature; stiff
♦ 생경한 문장 a crude piece of writing; an immature style / 생경한 태도 an awkward manner
생계 生計 a livelihood; a living; 〈직업〉 an occupation ♦ 생계를 유지하다 maintain [keep] *one's* livelihood
▶ 그녀는 부업으로 부모의 생계를 돕고 있다 She helps her parents with their living by working part-time.
■ ―수단 a means of living [livelihood]
생계비 生計費 living expenses; the cost of living ■ ―지수 a cost of living index
생고무 生― raw [crude] rubber
생과부 生寡婦 a neglected [divorced] wife; a grass widow
생과자 生菓子 (a) cake; fresh (and moist) sweets
생굴 生― a raw [fresh] oyster
생글거리다 smile; smile an affable [a beaming] smile ▶ 그녀는 흐뭇해서 생글거렸다 She beamed with satisfaction.
생긋 ♦ 생긋 웃다 smile sweetly; have a happy smile
생기 生氣 energy; liveliness; vivid life; vitality; vigor
♦ 생기 발랄한〔넘치는〕 vigorous; energetic; vivacious; full of life [vitality] / 생기있는 lively; active; vital; spirited; 〈문장이〉 crisp / 생기 없는 lifeless; spiritless; dull / 생기를 주다 invigorate; enliven; vitalize
▶ 그 소식이 그에게 생기를 주었다 The news gave life to him.
생기다 1 〈없던 것이〉 come into being [existence]; form
♦ 섭씨 0도에서 얼음이 생긴다 Ice forms [is formed] at the temperature of 0°C.
▶ 무(無)에서는 아무것도 생기지 않는다 (속담) Nothing comes of nothing.
▶ 우주는 언제 생겼을까? When did the universe come into being?
▶ 그 공화국은 1961년에 생겼다 The republic came into existence in 1961.
▶ 외국인 유학생을 위한 새로운 단체가 생겨났다 A new organization for foreign students has come into being.
2 〈발생하다〉 happen; occur; take place; result (from); come about; come up; come of [from]; arise (from); 〈분쟁·전쟁이〉 break out
▶ 내 신변에 중대한 일이 생겼다 A serious matter happened to me.
▶ 내 얼굴에 두드러기가 생겼다 A rash appears on my face.
▶ 그녀에게 새로운 변화가 생기고 있다 A new change is taking place around her.
▶ 급한 일이 생겨서 나는 즉시 귀가했다 I went home at once because of emergency.
3 〈얻다〉 get; obtain; gain

♦직업이 생기다 get [find] a job / 돈이 좀 생기다 get [earn] some money
4 〈아이가〉 get pregnant; be born; 〈친구가〉 make 《a friend》; 〈애인이〉 have 《a lover》
♦여자 친구가 생기다 have a girl friend
▶두 사람 사이에 아들이 생겼다 A son was born between them.
5 〈모양·얼굴이〉 look 《like》; have looks [appearance]
♦잘[못] 생기다 have good [plain] looks
▶그는 어떻게 생겼나요? What is the man like? ⇌ What does he look like?
6 〈권du 등이〉 spring 《from》; grow; form
♦나쁜 버릇이 생기다 contract [take to] a bad habit
▶용기는 신념에서 생긴다 Courage springs from [is born of] conviction.
▶부(富)는 근면과 절약에서 생긴다 Wealth is born of industry and economy.

생김새 〈형상〉 (a) form; (a) shape; 〈겉모양〉 (an) appearance; 〈용모〉 features; a look; looks; a countenance
♦생김새가 사내답다 look manly / 사람을 생김새로 판단하다 judge sb by 《his》 looks

생나무 生— 〈살아 있는 나무〉 a live tree; 〈갓 베어낸〉 green wood; 〈마르지 않은 목재〉 unseasoned wood [timber]

생남 生男 〈득남〉 the birth of a son
—**생남하다** give birth to a son; beget a son [boy]; be delivered of a (baby) boy; a boy is born to sb
—**례** a celebration of begetting a son

생녀 生女 〈득녀〉 the birth of a daughter; delivery of a daughter [girl]
—**생녀하다** give [have] birth to a daughter; beget a daughter; be delivered of a (baby) girl; a daughter [girl] is born to sb

생년 生年 the year of one's birth ■—**월일** the date of (one's) birth

생니 生— a healthy [good] tooth

생담배 生— a half-smoked cigarette still burning

생도 生徒 a student ⇨ 학생
■**사관—** a cadet; 〈해군의〉 a midshipman

생돈 生— 〈필요없이 쓰는 돈〉 money spent to no purpose ♦생돈을 쓰다[없애다] waste [throw away, fritter away] one's money 《on》

생동 生動 a lively motion; vividness
—**생동하다** move lively; be full of life; be vibrant with life; be vivid lifelike, graphic; be true to life
▶봄에는 만물이 생동한다 In spring everything is fresh and vivid. ⇌ Spring enlivens all nature.
▶이 그림은 생동 하고 있다 This picture looks so lifelike.

생득 生得 ♦생득의 inborn; innate
■—**관념** 〔哲〕 innate ideas —**권** one's birthright —**설**(說) 〔哲〕 nativism

생땅 生— natural ground; untouched [uncultivated] land

생떼 生— unreasonable persistence [adherence]; perverse [insistent] asking; an unreasonable [impossible] demand
♦생떼를 쓰다 stubbornly persist 《in》; stick to 《it》 doggedly; make an unreasonable demand of sb
▶나더러 너에게 경제적인 원조를 하라는 것은 생떼를 쓰는거나 마찬가지다 To ask me to give you financial aid is like asking for the moon.

생략 省略 〈뺌〉 (an) omission; 〔文法〕 (an) ellipsis (pl. -ses); 〈덜어서 줄임〉 (an) abbreviation; (an) abridg(e)ment
—**생략하다** 〈빼다〉 omit; leave out; 〈줄이다〉 abbreviate; abridge; shorten
♦생략할 수 있는 omissible / 생략하지 않고 without abridgment; in full
▶이름과 주소를 생략하지 말고 쓰시오 Write your name and address in full.
▶아메리카합중국은 생략해서 U.S.A.로 부른다 The United States of America is called the U.S.A. for short.
■—**문** an elliptical sentence —**법** ellipsis —**부호** an apostrophe —**어** an abbreviated word; an abbreviation

생령 生靈 〈영혼〉 a fetch; a double; an apparition of a living person; 〈백성〉 people

생리 生理 〈생명 현상〉 physiology; 〈여성의〉 menses ⇨ 월경(月經)
♦생리적 결함 a physiological defect / 생리적 요구 the needs of the body / 생리적 현상 a physiological phenomenon / 생리적(인) physiological
■—**기간** menstruation —**대** a hygienic band; a sanitary belt —**용 냅킨** (美) sanitary napkins; (英) sanitary towels —**위생** physiology and hygienics —**일** one's menstrual [catamenial] period; one's monthly days —**작용** a physiological function —**화학** physiological chemistry —**휴가** a monthly physiological leave; a special monthly leave for women

생리학 生理學 physiology ♦생리학적인[상의] physiological ■정신— psychophysiology
■—**자** a physiologist

생매장 生埋葬 burying alive —**생매장하다** bury sb alive ▶산사태로 남자 세 사람이 생매장되었다 Three men were buried alive in a landslide.

생맥주 生麥酒 draft beer; beer on draft [tap]

생면 生面 〈처음 대함〉 the first meeting [interview] 《with》 ▶그들은 생면 인사를 나누었다 They exchanged formal greetings at the first meeting.
■—**부지**(不知) a total [perfect] stranger; having never seen before : 그때까지 그와는 생면부지였다 Then I met him for the first time.

생명 生命 〈목숨〉 life; 〈가장 소중한 것〉 the life; the soul
♦생명이 없는 lifeless / 생명의 위험을 무릅쓰고 at the risk of one's life / 생명을 구하다 save sb's life / 생명을 빼앗다 take [claim] sb's life; deprive sb of 《his》 life; (비유) devitalize / 생명을 유지하다 maintain one's life / 생명을 노리다 seek sb's life / 생명을 바치다 〈희생하다〉 offer [give, sacrifice] one's life 《for》; lay down one's life / 생명을 잃다 lose one's life; (비유) be devitalized

▶ 그 전쟁에서 수천명이나 되는 생명을 잃었다 Thousands of lives were lost in the war.
▶ 그는 내 생명의 은인이다 I owe him my life.
▶ 그는 생명이 위태롭다 His life is in danger.
▶ 그의 정치 생명은 끝났다 His political life [career] is finished [at an end].
▶ 뉴스는 정확성이 생명이다 Accuracy is the soul [life and soul] of news reporting.
▶ 그의 소설의 생명은 그 해학성에 있다 The soul of his novel lies in its humor
━一과학 life science ━수 life-giving [life-restoring, life-saving] water ━유지장치[시스템] life-support equipment [system] ━표(統) a life table

생명력 生命力 life-force; vital force; vitality
▶ 이 잡초에는 놀라운 생명력이 있다 The weed has an amazing ability to survive.

생명보험 生命保險 life insurance
♦ 생명보험에 들다 insure oneself [one's life]; have one's life insured; take out a policy on one's life / 생명보험에 들어 있다 have a policy in a life insurance company
▶ 나는 1억원의 생명보험에 들었다 I insured myself [my life] for one hundred million won.
━종신— straight [whole] life insurance ━一증권 a life insurance policy ━회사 a life insurance company

생명선 生命線 〈삶과 죽음의 경계선〉 a lifeline; 〈손금의〉 the line of Life; the Lifeline
♦ 생명선을 지키다 guard one's lifeline

생모 生母 one's real [true] mother
생목 生━ 〈되올라오는 음식물〉 regurgitated food
♦ 생목이 오르다 regurgitate; 《undigested food》 come back

생목숨 生━ 1〈살아 있는〉 life; body and soul; breathing and living 2〈죄없는〉 an innocent [a blameless] life

생무지 生━ 〈문외한〉 a novice; a green [an untrained] hand; a greenhorn; an outsider
▶ 그는 장사에는 생무지다 He is a greenhorn [beginner] in business.

생물 生物 a living [an animate] thing; an organism; a creature; (총칭) life
♦ 숲속의 생물 the life of a forest / 생물의 다양성 biodiversity / 바다 생물 sea life / 생물이 없는 행성 a lifeless planet / 생물을 죽이다 destroy life; kill an animal
▶ 달에는 생물이 있습니까? Is there any life on the moon?
▶ 화성에는 생물이 있을까? I wonder if there is any life on Mars.
▶ 모든 생물은 궁극적으로 태양 에너지에 의존하고 있다 All living creatures depend ultimately on the energy of the sun.
━一경제학 bioeconomics ━계 the biological world; the animate nature ━공학 bionics; biotechnology ━물리학 biophysics ━발생설 (the theory of) biogenesis ━분포학 chorology ━상(相) a biota ━생태학 bioecology ━전기 bioelectricity ━진화 biological evolution ━체 a living thing

생물학 生物學 biology ♦ 생물학적[상의] bio-logic(al) / 생물학적으로 biologically
━一자 a biologist ━주의 biologism

생방송 生放送 live broadcasting; live 《TV》 coverage; a live broadcast; a live telecast; a live program
━생방송하다 cover [carry] 《an event》 live 《by television》; broadcast [televise, channel] 《an event》 live 《and unedited》

생배앓이 生━ 〈시기하다〉 be sick with envy; be [feel] jealous

생백신 生━ 〈생균의〉 live-virus vaccine
생벼락 生━ 〈꾸지람〉 an unreasonable scolding; 〈재앙〉 an unexpected disaster; a sudden calamity
♦ 생벼락을 맞다 〈꾸지람을 듣다〉 get an unreasonable scolding; 〈재앙을 당하다〉 meet a sudden calamity [disaster]
▶ 그가 죽었다는 소식은 나에게는 생벼락이었다 The news of his death came to me as a thunderbolt.

생부 生父 one's real [true] father
생부모 生父母 one's real [true] parents; one's parents by blood

생불 生佛 【佛敎】 a living Buddha; an incarnation of Buddha

생사 生絲 raw silk; hackle
♦ 고치에서 생사를 뽑다 reel off raw silk from cocoons
━검사소 a silk conditioning house ━상(商) a raw silk merchant; a dealer in raw silk ━업 the sericultural industry

생사 生死 life and [or] death; 〈안부〉 safety; 〈운명〉 fate
♦ 생사에 관한 문제 a matter of life and [or] death; a vital question / 생사를 같이하다 share one's fate 《with》; be in the same boat / 생사지경을 헤매다 wander [hover] between life and death; linger on the verge of death
▶ 그와는 생사를 함께한 사이다 I shared my fate with him.
▶ 아직 10명의 생사를 모른다 Ten persons are still missing.

생사람 生━ 1〈죄 없는 사람〉 an innocent person [party] ♦ 생사람을 잡다 〈체포하다〉 arrest an innocent person; 〈죽이다〉 kill an innocent person; 〈모함하다〉 inflict injury on an innocent person
2〈아무 관계 없는 사람〉 an unrelated [unconnected] person; an outsider; the third party; a disinterested person
▶ 나는 그 사건과는 아무 관계도 없는 생사람이다 I have nothing to do with the accident.
3〈생때같은 사람〉 a man of strong health

생산 生産 production
♦ …의 기록적 생산 the record production of…/ 생산 설비를 갖추다 tool up 《a plant》 / 생산을 늘리다 increase[step up] production (of) / 생산을 줄이다 curtail production (of)
▶ 생산이 떨어진다 Production declines.
▶ 석탄 생산이 더욱 감소되었다 Coal production dropped further.
▶ 그 공장은 이미 생산을 시작하고 있다 The plant is already in production.
━생산하다 produce; make; turn out; put out

▶ 이 공장에서는 매월 3만대의 자동차를 생산한다 This factory produces 30,000 cars a month. ■ 과잉— overproduction; excessive [surplus] production 국내 총— the gross domestic product (略 GDP) 국민총— the gross national product (略 GNP) 대규모— large-scale production 대량— mass production; high-volume production ■ —가격 ⇨ 생산비 —가치 productive value —계수 a coefficient of production —고(高) ⇨ 생산량 —공장 a manufacturing plant [factory] —공학 production engineering —과잉 overproduction —관리 production control —기간 a period of production —기관 the instruments of production —기술 manufacturing technique [knowhow]; industrial technology —능률 (increase) production efficiency —물 a product; (총칭) produce —방식 a production method —설비 production [productive] facilities; plants and equipment —실적 an actual output [yield] —액 ⇨ 생산량 —업〈생산업〉the manufacturing industry;〈광업·임업·어업 등〉the extractive industries —율 production rate; the rate of production —의욕 the will to produce; zeal [enthusiasm] for industrial production —자본 capital for production; productive capital —재(財) producer's [producer, production, productive] goods —제한 production curtailment; restriction of output [production] —조합 a producer's [an industrial] guild [association] —지수[함수, 곡선] a production index [function, curve] —확장[증가] expansion [increase] of production

생산량 生産量 an output; a turnout; an outturn; production;〈농산물의〉a yield; a crop ♦ 생산량을 높이다 increase [extend] the output (of)
■ 공업— an industrial output 1인당— production per man 총— the total [gross] output [production]

생산력 生産力 productive capacity; producing [manufacturing] power; productivity
♦ 노동[자본]의 생산력 productivity of labor [capital] —확장 expansion of productivity

생산목표 生産目標 a goal of production; a production target; an output goal
♦ 생산목표를 세우다 set up a goal of production / 생산목표를 달성하다 attain [reach, come up to] the goal of production / 생산목표를 달성하지 못하다 fall short of [fail to attain] the goal of production

생산비 生産費 the cost of production; production cost ♦ 생산비를 절감하다 curtail [cut down] the cost of production
■ 평균[한계]— the average [marginal] cost of production

생산성 生産性 productivity ♦ 높은[낮은] 생산성 high [low] productivity / 한국 생산성 본부 Korea Productivity Center (略 KPC) / 생산성을 향상시키다 increase [raise] the productivity (of)
▶ 우리는 생산성 향상에 주력해야 한다 Our energies must be directed [We must direct our energies] toward higher productivity.

생산자 生産者 a producer; a maker
■ —가격 a producer [producer's] price

생산적 生産的 productive ♦ 생산적 노동 productive labor

생산지 生産地 a producing center [district]
♦ 사과의 생산지 an apple-producing center / —증명서 a certificate of origin

생살 生— 〈성한 살〉raw flesh;〈새살〉new flesh

생살 生殺 life and death; sparing life and [or] taking it; letting live and [or] killing ♦ 생살을 마음대로 하다 have an absolute power [the power of life and death] over sb

생살여탈 生殺與奪 (the power of) sparing life and killing ♦ 생살여탈권을 쥐다 hold the power of life and death (over sb)

생색 生色 a demontration of benevolence; patronage ♦ 생색나는 선물 an impressive gift / 생색내다 put on airs; demonstrate benevolence
▶ 그것으로 그는 크게 생색냈다 It reflected great credit on him. ⇌ It did him great credit.
▶ 그렇게 하면 네 생색이 날거야 If you do so, you will save face.

생생하다 生生— fresh; graphic; lively; vivid; lifelike; animated;〈서술적〉be full of life
♦ 생생한 표현 a vivid expression; a graphic description / 생생한 핏자국 a fresh bloodstain / 생생하게 lively; vividly; animatedly; graphically; true to life / 생생하게 그리다 describe [show] vividly [graphically]; draw [paint] true to life; give a graphic [vivid, lifelike] picture [description] (of the scene)
▶ 그 비극은 아직도 우리의 기억에 생생하다 The tragedy is still fresh in our memories.

생석회 生石灰 quicklime ⇨ 산화(~칼슘)

생선 生鮮 a fresh [raw] fish ♦ 생선을 굽다 roast [broil] fish
■ —가게 a fish shop picture —구이 roast [broiled] fish —묵 (boiled) fishpaste —시장 a fish market —장수 (美) a fish dealer; (英) a fishmonger;〈행상〉a fish peddler —회 slices of raw fish; (a dish of) sliced raw fish: 생선회를 치다 slice raw fish

생성 生成 〈창조〉creation;〈형성〉formation;〈생겨남〉generation;〔哲〕becoming
—생성하다 be created; be formed; come into being [existence]; become;〈만들어내다〉create; form; generate; make ■ —문법〔言〕generative grammar —물 a product

생소 生疎 1 〈친하지 않음·낯이 섦〉unfamiliarity; ignorance
—생소하다 unfamiliar 《with》; unacquainted 《with》; uninformed [ignorant] 《of》; new 《to》; strange 《to》
♦ 생소한 사람 a stranger; an unacquainted person / 생소한 고장[땅] an unfamiliar [a strange] place [land];〈외국〉an alien [a foreign] land
▶ 그녀는 세상일에 생소하다 She knows little about the world.
▶ 아버지는 외국사정에 생소하시다 Father is

ignorant of foreign affairs.
2 〈익숙하지 못함〉 inexperience; lack of experience; want of practice
―생소하다 inexperienced; unaccustomed [strange, raw, new] (to)
▶그는 그 일에 생소하다 He is strange [unaccustomed, raw, new] to the work.
생손 (a) paronychia ⇨ 생인손
생수 生水 〈샘물〉 springwater ―받이 a rice field irrigated with springwater
생시 生時 〈난 시각〉 the hour [time] of one's birth; 〈평소〉 one's waking hours; 〈살아있는 동안〉 one's lifetime
생식 生食 eating raw ―생식하다 eat 《a carrot》 raw; eat uncooked food
▶야채를 생식하는 것이 건강에 좋다 It is good for the health to eat vegetables raw.
생식 生殖 reproduction; procreation; generation ―생식하다 reproduce; procreate; generate
■유성[무성]― sexual [asexual] reproduction ■―기(期) a period of reproduction ―력 generative [procreative] power; 〈여성의〉 fecundity; 〈남성의〉 virility ―불능자 an impotent (person) ―선(腺) 〈분비선〉 a genital [sex, sexual] gland; 〈생식소〉 a gonad ―세포 a gamete; a sex [generative, germ] cell ―육 the reproductive urge ―작용[기능] generative [reproductive] function; reproduction
생식기 生殖器 the organs of generation [reproduction]; the genital [reproductive, generative, sexual] organs; genitals; genitalia
■―숭배 phallicism; phallism; phallic worship [cult] ―장애 a genital trouble [disorder]
생신 生辰 one's birthday ⇨ 생일
생쌀 生― uncooked [raw] rice
생약 生藥 〈식물성 초재〉 a herbal medicine; 〈약재〉 a crude drug
생애 生涯 a life; a lifetime; a career
♦생애의 벗 one's lifelong friend / 생애에 한번의 기회 the chance of a lifetime / 행복한[비참한] 생애 a happy [miserable] life
▶그녀는 행복한 생애를 보냈다 She lived [led] a happy life.
▶그는 생애를 독신으로 보냈다 He remained unmarried for life [throughout his life].
▶그는 90세로 생애를 마쳤다 He ended his life of 90 years.
생억지 生― irrational insistence on having one's own way; arbitrariness; stubbornness
♦생억지를 쓰다 demand one's own way; stick to one's unreasonable insistence
▶생억지를 쓰지 마라 Don't be so obstinate [stubborn].
생업 生業 a calling; an occupation; a profession; a trade; a vocation; a business ♦…을 생업으로 하다 make a living by 《doing》
■―자금 a rehabilitation fund; a fund for operating business
생우유 生牛乳 raw milk
생울타리 生― a live fence ⇨ 산울타리
생원 生員 a successful candidate for the minor civil service examination; 〈존칭〉 Mister; Mr.; esquire
생육 生育 〈낳아서 기름〉 birth and breeding; 〈나서 자람〉 growth; development
▶그는 나팔꽃의 생육을 관찰하고 있다 He observes how the morning-glories grow.
―생육하다 〈키우다〉 grow; raise; 〈자라다〉 grow (up); be born and bred [brought up]
■―지〔生〕 the habitat
생으로 生― 1 〈날로〉 raw; fresh; uncooked
▶고기를 생으로 먹기를 좋아하는 사람도 있다 Some people like to eat raw meat.
2 〈무리하게〉 by force; forcibly; compulsorily; willy-nilly; against one's will; 〈부당하게〉 unreasonably; irrationally; unjustly; without any cause [reason]; arbitrarily; wrongfully
생이 〔動〕 a caridean shrimp
생이별 生離別 separation (forced) by circumstances ―생이별하다 part from one's spouse by adverse circumstances
생이지지 生而知之 knowing without being taught ―생이지지하다 know from birth; know intuitively
생인손 a whitlow [felon] in a finger; (a) paronychia
생일 生日 one's birthday; one's natal day
♦생일을 축하하다 celebrate sb's birthday
▶우리는 모친의 90세 생일을 축하했다 We celebrated our mother's ninetieth birthday.
▶생일을 축하합니다 I wish you many happy returns of the day. ⇒ Happy birthday to you!
■―선물 a birthday present [gift] ―잔치 《give》 a birthday party [feast]
생자 生者 〈생명 있는 모든 것〉 living things; animate nature [being]; 〈산 사람〉 a living person; the living
▶생자필멸 All living things must die [are bound to die]. ⇒ No living thing is free from decay [is immortal]. ⇒ Man is mortal.
생장 生長 growth
▶그 식물은 생장이 빠르다[느리다] The plant grows quickly [slowly].
▶그것은 밀의 생장을 촉진할 것이다 It will promote the growth of wheat.
■―점〔植〕 a growing point
생전 生前 1 〈죽기 전〉 one's lifetime
♦생전에 during [in] one's lifetime; while alive [in life]; before one's death / 생전 처음으로 for the first time in one's life
▶그는 생전의 공로로 훈장을 받았다 He was awarded a decoration in recognition of the serivces done in his lifetime.
2 〈아무리 애써도〉 for all one's efforts; on no account; by no means; in no way; never
▶생전 해보렴, 되는가 However hard you may try, you will not be able to do it.
생존 生存 existence; being; life; subsistence; survival ♦생존중에 in life; in one's lifetime ―생존하다 exist; live; survive; outlive
♦생존해 있다 be alive [living]; be in existence
■적자(適者)― the survival of the fittest ■―권 the right to live ―능력 viability ―욕 the desire for existence; the will to live
생존경쟁 生存競爭 a struggle for existence

♦치열한 생존경쟁을 벌이다 have a hard [fierce] struggle for existence
생존자 生存者 a survivor
♦난파선의 유일한 생존자 the sole survivor from [of] the shipwreck
생죽음 生― death by violence; an unnatural death ―**생죽음하다** die [meet] a violent [an unnatural] death; die by violence
생중계 生中繼 live coverage (on TV); a live relay broadcast
생쥐 〔動〕 a (house) mouse 《pl. mice》
♦물에 빠진 생쥐 꼴이다 be like [as wet as] a drowned mouse; be wet [drenched, soaked] to the skin; be dripping wet
생쥐 볼가심할 것도 없다 〈속담〉 haven't a crumb; be (as) poor as a church mouse
생지옥 生地獄 a hell on earth
▶그 광경은 문자 그대로 생지옥이었다 The sight was literally a hell on earth.
생질 甥姪 a nephew; one's sister's son ■―**녀** a niece; one's sister's daughter
생짜 生― 〈날것〉 something raw [fresh]; uncooked stuff
생채 生菜 raw vegetables; a salad ■ 무― a radish salad 오이― a cucumber salad
생채기 a scratch; a brush burn ♦생채기를 입다 get [receive] a scratch (on one's face)
생철 ―鐵 tin; tinplate; latten; white iron ■―**깡통** (英) a tin; (美) a can ―**판** a tinplate (sheet); tinned sheet iron
생청 生淸 raw [unrefined] honey
생체 生體 a living body; an organism ■―**학** somatology ―**현미경 검사** biomicroscopy
생체해부 生體解剖 vivisection
♦동물의 생체해부를 하다 vivisect an animal ―**실험** (make) an experiment on a living body ―**자** a vivisectionist; a vivisector
생태 生態 a mode of life; ecology
♦곤충의 생태 the ecology of an insect / 현대인의 생태 the mode of life of the moderns
▶그는 사자의 생태를 연구하고 있다 He is studying the ecology of lions.
■―**계(系)** an ecosystem ―**변화** ecological adaptation ―**형(型)** an ecotype
생태학 生態學 ecology; biology; ethology; bionomics ♦생태학적인[(상)의] ecological; ethological; bionomic(al)
■**개체**― autecology **군집**― synecology **식물**― ecological botany ■―**자** an ecologist; an ethologist; a bionomist
생텍쥐페리 〈프랑스의 비행사·소설가〉 Saint-Exupéry, Antoine de (1900-44)
생트뵈브 〈프랑스의 문예비평가〉 Sainte-Beuve, Charles Augustin (1804-69)
생트집 生― unreasonable faultfinding; a false charge
♦생트집을 잡다 make a false charge ―**생트집하다** find [pick] fault (with); make a false charge [accusation] 《against》; accuse sb falsely; (口) crab
생파리 〈파리〉 a lively fly; 〈사람〉 a snappish [tart, gruff, crusty, curt] person; a cool and distant person
♦생파리 잡아떼듯 하다 refuse [reject] flatly; give sb a flat refusal
생판 生板 〈전혀〉 wholly [totaly, utterly, entirely, completely] (ignorant of); 〈턱없이〉 unfoundedly; groundlessly; unreasonably; unjustly; outrageously ♦생판 모르는 사람 a total [an utter, a perfect] stranger 《to》
▶나는 집안 살림은 생판 모른다 I am completely ignorant of housekeeping.
생포 生捕 capturing [catching] alive
―**생포하다** catch [take, capture] 《an animal》 alive; take [hold, lead] sb captive; take [make] sb prisoner
▶경찰관들은 달아난 사자를 생포했다 The policemen caught the escaped lion alive.
생피 生― blood of a living animal ⇨ 생혈 (生血)
생핀잔 生― undeserved shame ♦생핀잔(을) 주다 rebuke without any reason [cause]
생필름 生― raw [unexposed] film
생혈 生血 vital blood; lifeblood; blood of a living man [animal]
▶그는 남의 생혈을 빨아 먹는 악인이다 He is a bloodsucker. ⇐ He is a vampire.
생화 生花 a natural [fresh] flower
생화학 生化學 biochemistry; chemicobiology
♦생화학적인 biochemical ■―**자** a biochemist
생환 生還 1 〈살아 돌아옴〉 returning alive ―**생환하다** return alive
▶우주비행사들은 우주선으로 지구를 두 바퀴 돌고나서 무사히 생환했다 The spacemen have returned safely [made a safe return] after two orbits of the earth in the spaceship.
2 〔野〕 reaching the home plate [base] ―**생환하다** cross [reach] the home plate
▶주자를 생환시키다 〈타자가〉 bring home the runner; score the runner / 두 주자를 생환시키다 bring in two runs; bring home two runners
―**자** a survivor
생활 生活 life; existence; 〈생계〉 livelihood; living
♦생활의 안정을 얻다 secure one's living [livelihood] / 생활이 어렵다[윤택하다] be badly [well, comfortably] off; be in needy [easy] circumstances / 생활을 보장하다 guarantee sb's living / 생활을 안정시키다 stabilize one's livelihood [living] / 비참한 생활을 하다 make a wretched [miserable] life; lead a dog's life
▶그는 생활 걱정이 없다 He is free from bread and butter worries.
▶그녀는 생활이 무질서하다 She is leading a disordered life.
▶그는 분수에 맞는[넘치는] 생활을 하고 있다 He lives within [beyond, above] his means. ⇒ He lives up to [beyond] his income.
▶그녀는 남편의 사후에 생활을 위해 일하지 않으면 안되었다 After her husband's death, she had to work for a living.
―**생활하다** live; exist; 〈생계를 세우다〉 make a living; subsist
♦월급으로 생활하다 live on one's salary / 겨우 생활해 가다 pick up a scanty [bare] livelihood; manage to keep body and soul together
▶〖會話〗「무엇으로 생활하십니까?」「월급으로

생활합니다 "What do you live on?" "I live on my salary."
▶ 그녀는 동네 어린이들에게 영어를 가르쳐 생활하고 있다 She makes a living by teaching English to some neighbor's children.
■도시— town [city, urban] life 문화— a cultural [cultured, modern] life 사치— lavish [extravagant] life 사회[일상, 결혼]— social [everyday, married] life 원시— a primitive (form of) life; primeval life 이중— a dual life 전원— rural life; living in the country 최저— a minimum standard of living [life] ■—간소화 the simplification of life —감정 life feeling —고 hardships of life; the grim [stern] realities of life —교육 practical education; education for living —권(權) living rights —권(圈) a zone [sphere] of life —급(給) living wages; a living wage; subsistence wage —기능 vital functions —기록 a life document; an account [a record] of one's life —물자 subsistence goods; daily commodities [necessities, necessaries] —보조[보호] livelihood assistence [protection] —불안 economic insecurity —상태 living conditions —설계 life planning; a design of one's life —안정 the stabilization of livelihood —양식 a mode [manner] of living; a way of life —자금 money to live on —조건 the conditions [terms] of life —필수품 the necessaries [necessities] of life; daily [living] necessaries [necessities] —환경 one's living environment

생활개선 生活改善 the improvement of living conditions ■—운동 a movement for the improvement of living conditions

생활난 生活難 hard life [living]; the difficulty of living [earning a livelihood]; living difficulties; economic distress ♦생활난과 싸우다 struggle against hard living

생활력 生活力 vitality; vital energies; one's capacity for [powers of] living; 〈경제적인 능력〉 one's earning power
▶ 그는 생활력이 강하다 He is full of vitality. ≒ He has high earning power.

생활비 生活費 living expenses; the cost of living ♦높은[낮은] 생활비 the high [low] cost of living / 생활비를 벌기 위해 일하다 work for one's keep
▶ 서울에서는 생활비가 많이 든다 It is expensive to live in Seoul.

생활수준 生活水準 a standard of living; a living standard ♦생활 수준의 저하[향상] a decline [rise] in the standard of living / 생활수준을 높이다 [낮추다] raise [lower] the standard of living

생회 生灰 quicklime ⇨ 생석회
생후 生後 〈부사적〉 after [since] one's birth ♦생후 2개월된 유아 a two-month-old baby
▶ 그녀의 아기는 생후 1주일만에 죽었다 Her baby died a week after his [her] birth.
생흙 fresh soil
샤갈 〈프랑스의 화가〉Chagall, Marc(1887-1985)
샤를의 법칙 —法則 the Charles' law
샤머니즘 shamanism ♦샤머니즘의 shamanistic
샤먼 a shaman (pl.～s) ♦샤먼의 shamanic

샤워 a shower (bath) ♦샤워를 하다 have [take] a shower (bath); shower ■—실 a shower room [box, stall]
샤토브리앙 〈프랑스의 작가・정치가〉Chateaubriand, François René, Vicomte de (1768-1848)
샤프 〔樂〕〈올림표〉 a sharp; the symbol ♯
샤프트 〔機〕a shaft
■크랭크— a crankshaft
샤프펜슬 a propelling [a mechanical, an automatic] pencil

解說 「항상 뾰족하다」란 뜻의 ever sharp를 회사 이름으로 쓴 미국의 Eversharp사가 이 말의 기원이며 sharp pencil은 잘못된 표현. (美)에서는 *mechanical pencil, automatic pencil*, (英)에서는 *propelling pencil*이라고 한다.

샴페인 champagne; (口) fizz ♦샴페인 마개를 평하고 따다 pop open a champagne bottle
■—글라스 a champagne glass
샴푸 〈세발〉a shampoo; 〈세발제〉 shampoo ♦샴푸로 머리를 감다 shampoo (one's hair); have a shampoo
샹들리에 a chandelier
샹송 〔樂〕〈프〉 a chanson; a song
새도복싱 shadowboxing
새도캐비닛 shadow cabinet
새미가죽 chamois; shammy, shamoy
서¹ 〈셋〉 three ♦서 말 three mal / 서 돈 three don
서² **1**〈명사에 붙어〉 ♦서울서 부산까지 from Seoul to Pusan
▶ 그녀는 중국서 왔다 She is from China.
2 〈동사・형용사에 붙어〉 ♦걸어서 가다 go on foot / 추워서 떨다 shiver with [from] cold
▶ 누구인지 가서 보고 오너라 Go and see who it is.
▶ 나는 너무 지쳐서 일을 할 수 없다 I am too tired to work.
서 西 (the) west (略 W) ⇨ 서쪽
♦서로 가다 go west [westward]
서 序 〈서문〉a foreword; a preface
서 書 〈서법・서도〉 calligraphy; penmanship; 〈필적〉 handwriting; 〈서간〉 a note; a letter; an epistle; 〈서적〉 a book
서 署 〈관서〉 an office; a station; 〈경찰서〉 a police station; 〈소방서〉 a firehouse
서가 書架 〈책시렁〉 a bookshelf 《pl. -shelves》; 〈도서관의〉 a bookstack
서간 書簡 〈편지〉 a letter; a note; an epistle; 〈총칭〉 correspondence ■—문 an epistolary style —문학 epistolary literature —집 a collection of letters; collected letters
서간체 書簡體 an epistolary style ■—소설 an epistolary novel
서거 逝去 death; demise ■—서거하다 pass away; die
서걱거리다 crisp ⇨ 사각거리다
서경 西經 west longitude
♦서경 32도 longitude 32° west / 서경 73도 10분에 at seventy-three degrees ten minutes of west longitude (▶at Long. 73°10′ W로 줄여

서경 書經 〈공자가 편찬〉 the *Shu-ching*; the Scripture of Documents
서경 敍景 a description of scenery
서고 書庫 a library; 〈도서관의〉 a stack room; stacks
서고동저 西高東低 〔氣〕 the atmospheric pattern of western high and eastern low
서곡 序曲 〔樂〕 a prelude 《to》; an overture 《to》; 〈특히 가극의〉 a prologue ♦서곡을 연주하다 play an overture; prelude
서광 曙光 the first streak of daylight; dawn ♦평화[문명]의 서광 the dawn of peace [civilization] / 희망의 서광 a flash [gleam] of hope ▶사건 해결의 서광이 보였다 The first ray of hope for the settlement of the affair has arisen.
서구 西歐 〈서유럽〉 Western Europe; 〈유럽〉 Europe; 〈서양〉 the West; the Occident ♦서구의[적인] European; Western ─문명[문화] the Western civilization [culture] ─사람 a European ─사상 Western ideas ─제국 the Western nations [countries]
서구화 西歐化 Europeanization; westernization; Occidentalization ─서구화하다 Europeanize; westernize; Occidentalize
서근서근하다 affable ⇨ 사근사근하다
서글서글하다 generous and gentle; liberal; magnanimous; open-minded ♦서글서글한 사람 a man of magnanimous disposition; an amiable [affable] person
서글프다 sad; sorrowful; plaintive; melancholy; lonesome; lonely; forlorn; cheerless; dreary; inconsolable ♦서글픈 노래 a plaintive [touching] song / 서글프게 말하다 tell [talk] in a lonesome [plaintive] manner ▶오늘밤은 왠지 서글프다 I don't know why, but I feel so sad [melancholy] this evening.
서기 西紀 the year of grace [Christ, our Lord]; the dominical year; the Christian Era; (라) anno Domini (略 A.D.)

〔解說〕 **A.D.**는 라틴어 *anno Domini*의 약어로 특정 연도 앞에 small capitals로 쓴다. 시대·세기에는 붙이지 않는다. **B.C.**는 before Christ(기원전)의 약어로 언제나 연도 뒤에 small capitals로 쓴다. 시대·세기에 써도 된다. B.C.도 A.D.도 써 있지 않을 경우는 기원후라는 뜻이다.

♦서기 1998년에 in A.D. 1998; in the year of our Lord 1998; (美) in 1998 A.D.
서기 書記 〈관직〉a clerk; a secretary; 〈기록자〉 a copyist; a scribe ─법원─ a clerk of a law court ■─보 an assistant clerk; a probationary secretary
서기 瑞氣 an auspicious sign; a good omen
서기관 書記官 a fourth grade official; a section-chief-grade official; a secretary ♦1등 서기관 a first secretary / 영국 대사관의 3등 서기관 the Third Secretary of the British Embassy

서까래 〔建〕 a (common) rafter
서껀 〈함께 다〉 etc., etc.; et cetera and et cetera; and so forth [on]; and what not; and the like; and others; together with
서낭 〔民俗〕 〈신〉 a tutelary [guardian] deity; 〈나무〉 a tree where a tutelary deity dwells ■─단(壇) the altar for a tutelary deity ─당(堂) the shrine for a tutelary deity
서너 three or four; a few; several ♦서너차례 three or four times; several times
서너너덧 (about) four or five; several
서넛 three or four; a few; several
서녘 西─ the west; the western direction
서늘하다 1 〈선선하다〉 cool; refreshing ♦서늘한 날 a cool day / 서늘한 바람 a cool breeze / 서늘한 그늘 a cool shade / 서늘해지다 get [become] cool ▶서늘한 곳에 두시오 (표시) "Keep cool."
2 〈추운 느낌이 있다〉 be [feel] chilled; feel a chill; 〈오싹해지다〉 shudder 《at》; be frightened; have a thrill of horror ▶놀라서 가슴이 서늘했다 I was chilled with fright.
서다 1 〈사람이〉 stand; take a stand 《at》; 〈일어서다〉 stand up; rise; get on [rise to] *one's* feet; draw *oneself* up ♦연단에 서다 take [stand on] the rostrum [platform] / 똑바로 서다 stand erect / 한 줄로 서다 stand in a line / 서서 헤엄치다 tread water / 서서 연극을 보다 see a play standing / 서서 맥주를 마시다 drink beer standing ▶그는 절벽 위에 꼼짝 않고 서 있었다 He was standing still on the cliff. ▶나는 열차에서 줄곧 서 있었다 I stood all the way in the train. ▶그는 두 시간 동안을 꼬박 서 있었다 He was on his feet for two hours on end. ▶서라 Stand up! ⇌ Up with you! ⇌ Get to your feet! ⇌ On your feet!
2 〈물건이〉 stand erect; 〈높은 것이〉 rise; tower; soar ▶언덕 위에 탑이 서 있었다 There was a tower on the top of the hill. ▶그 소나무는 여러 개의 버팀목에 의지해서 서 있다 The pine is barely kept from falling by a number of supports.
3 〈정지하다〉 stop; halt; come to a stop [stand, halt]; make a stop [halt]; 〈말·차 등이〉 draw [pull] up; 〈동력이〉 run down ▶딱 서다 stop dead; come to a dead [full] stop / 갑자기 서다 stop short [dead, suddenly] ▶서라 〈지르는 소리〉 Stop! ⇌ Hold on! ⇌ Pull up! ⇌ Halt! ▶차가 와서 섰다 A car pulled up to a stop. ▶내 손목시계가 섰다 My watch has run down.
4 〈건조물이〉 stand; 〈건립되다〉 be built; be erected; be set up; rise; go up; 〈설립되다〉 be established; be founded ▶그의 기념 동상이 섰다 A bronze statue was erected [set up] to his memory. ▶새 정부가 섰다 A new government was established. ▶이 근처에는 집이 자꾸 들어 선다 Houses are

mushrooming in this neighborhood.
5 〈위치·입장〉 stand
♦ 들러리를 서다 attend the bride [bridegroom]/ 보초를 서다 stand [go on] sentry / 보증 서다 stand surety [guarantee] (for) / 중매 서다 act [serve] as middleman [go-between] (for) / 증인으로 서다 stand [be] witness; be on the witness stand
6 〈칼날 등이〉 ♦ 날이 서다 have a keen [sharp] edge
7 〈조리가〉 hold good; hold water; be made good; 〈이유가〉 pass; be admissible [justifiable, excusable]; 〈계획 등이〉 be formed; be laid; be established; be worked out
♦ 이치[조리]가 서다[서지 않다] stand to [stand to no] reason; be reasonable [unreasonable]
▶ 그것은 전혀 조리가 서지 않는다 That's against all reason.
▶ 계획이 섰다 My plan is formed [laid].
▶ 아직 우리 방침은 서지 않았다 Our policy has not been established yet.
8 〈체면 등이〉 save 《one's face [honor]》
▶ 그렇게 되면 내 체면이 선다 That will save my face [honor].
▶ 그렇게 되면 내 체면이 서지 않는다 That will put me out of countenance.
9 〈규율 등이〉 ♦ 명령이 서다 orders are thoroughly obeyed [followed, carried out]; orders have [carry] authority / 질서가 서 있다 be orderly; be in good [perfect] order
▶ 규율이 서 있지 않다 Discipline is lax [loose, slack].
10 〈결심이〉 ♦ 결심이 서다 make up *one's* mind; make [take] a resolve [resolution]; decide 《to do》; be determined [resolved] 《to do》/ 결심이 서 있지 않다 be hesitating; be in two minds 《about, as to, whether》
11 〈장이〉 open; be opened; be held
♦ 장이 서는 날[마을] a market day [village]
▶ 장이 섰다 A fair was held [opened].
12 〈아이가〉 conceive; become pregnant
♦ 아이가 선 지 6개월이다 be six months gone with child [gone in pregnancy]
13 〈무지개가〉 span [hang in] the sky
▶ 넓은 들판에 무지개가 섰다 A rainbow stood bestriding the wide field.
14 〈볼록한 것이〉 ♦ 핏발이 서다 be bloodshot
▶ 그의 왼쪽 관자놀이에 핏줄이 섰다 Veins stood out at his left temple.
서당 書堂 〈글방〉 a village school for Chinese classics
서당 개 삼년에 풍월한다 《속담》 A saint's maid quotes Latin. ⇌ The sparrows near a school sing the primer.
서대기 〔魚〕 a sole
서덜 〈생선의〉 offal (of fish)
서도 書道 calligraphy; penmanship ⇨ 서예
서두 序頭 the beginning; the inception; 〈연극 등의〉 a prolog(ue); a prolusion; 〈말 등의〉 a preliminary statement
서두르다 hurry (up); hasten; rush; make haste; speed; (美) make time; (口) get a move on

|解說| ***hurry***는 어떤 장소로 한정된 시간까지 가지 않으면 안되는 경우며, 때로는 동요나 긴장감을 나타낸다. ***hasten***은 hurry 보다 딱딱한 말로 긴급한 사태나 어떤 일을 가볍게 생각하거나 준비가 덜된 채 허둥대는 것을 말하며 ***rush***는 몹시 서둘러 내닫는 것을 나타낸다. ***speed***는 단순히 속도를 나타내는 말이다.

♦ 서둘러서 hurriedly; in haste; in a hurry / 서두른 나머지 in *one's* hurry / 길을 서두르다 hurry on *one's* way; hurry along / 일을 서두르다 hurry [speed] up *one's* work / 서두르고 있다 be in haste [in a hurry]; be pressed for time / 몹시 서두르고 있다 be in a great [big, deadly] hurry; be in a big rush
▶ 너무 서두르지 마라 Don't be too hasty. ⇌ Be more cautious.
▶ 전연 서두를 필요가 없다 No need for haste. ⇌ There is no hurry.
▶ 날이 어두워지고 있어서 우리는 길을 서둘렀다 It was getting dark, so we pressed on [forward].
▶ 서두르면 서두를수록 더디다 More haste, less speed.
▶ 서두르면 일을 그르친다 《속담》 Haste makes waste.
▶ 서두르다 보니 사전을 안 가지고 왔다 I left my dictionary behind in my hurry.
서둘다 hurry (up) ⇨ 서두르다
서랍 a drawer ♦ 서랍 깊숙이 in the back of a drawer / 서랍을 빼다 pull [draw] out a drawer / 서랍을 열다[닫다] open [shut] a drawer
서러움 sorrow; grief ⇨ 설움
서러워하다 grieve 《at the news》; be grieved 《at, over》; 〈통탄하다〉 deplore; lament; mourn 《for, over》; regret
♦ 어머니의 죽음을 서러워하다 mourn [lament] *one's* mother's death; grieve [sorrow] over *one's* mother's death
▶ 지금은 서러워만 하고 있을 때가 아니다 This is no time to give way simply to sorrow.
서럽다 sad; sorrowful; mournful; doleful; plaintive; lamentable; deplorable; grievous
♦ 서러운 추억 a sad memory / 서러운 나머지 in *one's* sorrow [grief]
서력 西曆 the Christian Era ⇨ 서기(西紀)
서로 mutually; reciprocally; with each other; with one another
♦ 서로의 mutual; reciprocal; each other's; one another's / 서로의 이익을 도모하다 consult mutual interests / 서로 눈짓하다 exchange glances / 서로 돕다[믿다] help [trust] each other [one another]/ 서로 사랑하다 love each other; love and be loved / 서로 욕하다 call each other names / 서로 헐뜯다 find fault with each other
▶ 어려울 때 서로 돕는 것이 친구다 Friends are people who help each other out in times of need.
서론 序論 an introduction; introductory [prefatory] remarks; a proem
♦ 서론으로 by way of introduction; as an

서론 introduction 《to *one's* story》
서론 緒論 an introduction
서류 書類 a document; a paper
♦서류를 작성하다 draw up [write out] a document / 서류를 정리하다 set the papers in order; file the papers / 서류를 제출하다 submit [send in, hand in] *one's* papers
■ 관계— related [relative] documents; papers relating to 《an affair》 기밀— confidential [《美》classified] papers; secret documents 법률— legal documents 선적— shipping documents 일건— a dossier 《concerning an affair》 중요— important documents ■ —가방 a briefcase; an attaché case —함 a filing cabinet
서류전형 書類銓衡 selection of candidates by examining 《their》 personal histories
▶ 지원자는 서류전형에 의해 입학이 결정된다 Candidates will be admitted by examining the reports on their school records.
—서류전형하다 select candidates by examining 《their》 career papers; select candidates on the basis of 《their》 records
서른 thirty ♦서른살 thirty years of age / 서른 번째 the thirtieth / 서른이 넘다 be over thirty
서름서름하다 1 〈아주 서먹하다〉 quite distant; quite estranged [alienated] 《from》 2 〈아주 익숙하지 못하다〉 quite unacquainted [inconversant, unfamiliar] 《with》; quite uninformed [ignorant] 《of》
서름하다 1 〈서먹하다〉 distant; estranged 《from》; alienated 《from》 2 〈익숙하지 못하다〉 unacquainted [inconversant] 《with》; uninformed [unfamiliar; ignorant 《of》
서리[1] 1 〈가루 얼음〉 frost; hoarfrost; hoary [white] frost; 《詩》 rime
♦서리가 내린 아침 a frosty morning / 서리가 내리다 it frosts; frost falls [forms] / 서리를 맞지 않게 하다 protect [shelter] 《a tree》 from the frost / 냉장고의 서리를 제거하다 defrost a refrigerator
▶ 한낮이 가까워지면서 서리도 녹았다 Toward noon the frost broke [thawed].
2 〈타격·피해〉 a blow; damage; 〈손실〉 a loss ■ 된— a heavy [hard, severe] frost : 그로 인해서 전자공업은 된서리를 맞았다 The electronic industry was hard hit by it. 무— light frost 첫— the first frost of the year [season] : 오늘 아침에 첫서리가 내렸다 This morning we had the first frost of the year. ■ —제거장치 〈냉장고의〉 a defrosting device; a defroster
서리[2] 〈훔치기〉 a mischievous raid; a naughty poaching ♦수박 서리 a mischievous raid on a watermelon patch —서리하다 raid 《sb's orchard》
서리 署理 〈사람〉 a deputy 《official》; a proxy; an acting director; 〈일〉 procuration; attorneyship; subrogation; proxy
—서리하다 act for; stand [be] proxy for; administer as an acting director
■ 교장— an acting principal; a principal [director] in charge 국무총리— an acting prime minister 의장— a deputy chairman
서리다[1] 1 〈김·안개 등이〉 rise; gather; be clouded 《up》 《with》; steam [fog, cloud] up ♦김이 서리다 steam 《up》; get steamed
♦유리창에 김이 서려 있다 The windowpanes are clouded up with steam.
2 〈감정이〉 be kept deep in *one's* heart [mind]; 〈어려 있다〉 be filled [fraught] 《with》 ♦마음 속에 서린 추억 memories enshrined in *one's* heart / 애정이 서린 눈 eyes fraught with affection 3 〈기가 꺾이다〉 lose heart; lose courage; get 《*one's* ego》 deflated
서리다[2] coil ⇨ 사리다 1
서리맞다 be frosted 《over》; 〈식물이〉 be nipped [shriveled, touched] by the frost; 《비유》 be 《hard》 hit; suffer a blow; be socked; be frustrated; receive a setback ▶ 갑작스런 추위로 잎이 모두 서리맞아 떨어졌다 All the leaves were frosted off by the cold snap.
서릿바람 a frosty [chilly, cold] wind; a cold wind on a frosty morning
서릿발 1 frost 《▶ 「서리」와 「서릿발」은 영어에서는 구분하지 않음》
▶ 서릿발이 쳤다 Frost formed on the ground.
2 〈엄함〉 rigor; severity; sternness; relentlessness ♦서릿발같은 논고 《make》 a most relentless argument 《against》
서막 序幕 1 〈가극의〉 the opening [first] act [scene]; 〈단막극의〉 a curtain raiser 2 〈시초〉 a prelude 《to》; a beginning
서머 summer ■ —스쿨 a summer school —타임 daylight saving time 《略 DST》; 《英》 summer time 《略 S.T.》 —하우스 a summer house [cottage]
서머하다 〈서술적〉 be ashamed 《of *oneself*》; be [feel] abashed; feel awkward [nervous, small]
서먹하다 〈낯설다〉 unfamiliar; estranged; alienated; 〈무간하지 않다〉 reserved; formal; 〈서술적〉 feel awkward [nervous, out of place]; feel small 《in company》; feel ill at ease; be not at home
♦서먹하게 대하다 treat *sb* like a stranger
▶ 이 자리가 나에게는 서먹하다 I feel out of place here.
▶ 두 사람 사이가 서먹해졌다 The two became estranged.
▶ 오늘은 왜 이렇게 서먹하게 대하니？ Why all this ceremony today？
서면 書面 〈편지〉 a letter; 〈문서〉 a document; 〈내용〉 contents
♦서면으로 by letter; in writing; in written statement / 본인이 직접 또는 서면으로 personally or through the mail; in person or in writing / 서면 또는 구두로 in writing or orally —결의 a documentary resolution [decision] —심리 《法》 a documentary examination —주문 a written order
서명 書名 the title [name] of a book
서명 署名 a signature; 〈유명인〉 an autograph
♦서명이 없는 편지 an anonymous [unsigned] letter / 서명이 있는 signed 《by the author》; autographed; carrying [bearing] *sb's* signature / …의 서명이 있다 carry the signature of... / 서명날인하다 set *one's* hand and seal 《to an instrument》; add *one's* signature and seal 《to a document》; sign and seal 《a bond》

—서명하다 sign [write (down)] one's name; sign (a treaty); autograph; affix [put] one's signature (to a document); subscribe one's name (to a document)
♦방명록에 서명하다 sign [enter] one's name in the visitors' register [list]
■—운동 a signature-collecting campaign
—자 a signer; a signatory : 아래[위]의 서명자 〈문서 등에서〉 the undersigned [oversigned]

서모 庶母 one's father's concubine
서목 書目 a catalog of books
서무 庶務 general affairs ■—과 the general affairs section
서문 序文 an introduction; a preface; a foreword (▶introduction은 상세하게 주석을 단 본격적인 서문이고 나머지 둘은 간단한 머리말)
♦서문을 쓰다 preface (a book); write a preface to (a book)
서민 庶民 the (common) people; the man on the street; the populace; the commonality; the masses; 〈한 사람〉 a commoner; an ordinary citizen
♦서민적(인) popular; common; democratic
▶물가 상승은 서민 생활에 직접 영향을 미친다 A rise in prices directly affects the lives of the (ordinary) people.
▶신임 사장은 서민적인 사람이다 The new president is a democratic-minded person. ⇌ The new president has the common touch.
■—계급 the mass of (the) people; the populace [masses]; the working classes —금고 a people's bank —금융 petty loans for the people; small-loan finance —사회 popular [common, demotic, democratic] society
서반구 西半球 the western hemisphere
서방 西方 1 〈서쪽〉 the west; 〈지방〉 western districts; 〈나라〉 western countries; 〈동서 양진영의〉 the West
♦서방측 진영 the Western camp [bloc]
2 〖佛教〗〈서방극락〉 the Western Paradise
서방 書房 1 〈남편〉 one's husband [man]; (口) one's hubby
2 〈호칭〉 Mr.; 〈혼히 하인에게〉 Old... ♦김 서방 Mr [Old] Kim
서방질 書房— adultery (of a married woman); cuckolding
—서방질하다 cuckold [deceive] one's husband; commit adultery
서벽돌 a friable [crumbly] stone
서법 書法 penmanship; calligraphy
서부 西部 the west; the western part(s)
♦서부의 western
▶우리 대학은 시의 서부에 있다 Our university is in the western part of the city.
■—극 a Western (film); a cowboy picture; a horse opera —음악 western music —지방 〈미국의〉 the West
서북 西北 1 〈서쪽과 북쪽〉 west and north; 〈방향〉 the northwest (略 NW)
♦서북의 northwestern; northwesterly / 서북으로 northwestward
2 〈한국의 서도와 관북〉 the northwestern districts of Korea
■—서 west-northwest (略 WNW) —풍 a northwestern [northwesterly] wind —항로 a northwest service [line, run] —향 facing the northwest

서브 〈구기의〉 a serve; a service
♦서브가 좋다 [나쁘다] serve well [badly]/ 서브를 넣다 serve a ball; deliver a service / 서브를 받다 receive the serve [service]; receive the served ball / 서브를 정확히 넣다 keep one's service / 서브를 실패하다 lose one's service
▶서브는 어느 쪽이냐? Whose serve [service] is it?
—서브하다 serve (a ball)
▶이번에는 네가 서브할 차례다 It is your turn to serve.
■—권(權) (one's) serve : 서브권을 얻다 get the serve
서브타이틀 a subtitle ♦책에 서브타이틀을 붙이다 subtitle a book
서비스 1 〈봉사〉 service

> 解說 영어에서 **service**는 「접객, 봉사」가 원뜻이며, 「값을 깎아 줌」이나 「무료」의 뜻은 없다. 따라서 「값을 깎아 준다」의 뜻으로는 discount를, 「무료」를 뜻하는 말로는 free를 써야 한다. 즉, 점원들이 말하는 「이것은 서비스입니다」는 This is a complimentary gift. 라든가 This is free. 이다.

▶그 식당은 서비스가 좋다 You get good service at that restaurant. ⇌ The restaurant gives good service.
▶계산서에 서비스 요금이 포함되어 있습니까? Is service charged in the bill?
—서비스하다 give one's services; attend on (a customer)
2 ⇨ 서브
■—라인 the service line —료 a service charge; 〈요리집 등의〉 a cover charge —스테이션 〈주유소〉 a service station; (美) an oil [a filling, a gas] station —코트 the service court
서사 敍事 narration; description ♦서사적이다 descriptive; narrative —서사하다 narrate; describe ■—문 a description; a narrative —체 a narrative style
서사모아 西— Western Samoa ♦서사모아의 Western Samoan
서사시 敍事詩 an epic (poem); (총칭) epos; epic poetry ■—인 an epic poet; an epicist
서산 西山 the western hill [mountain]
서생 書生 1 〈유생〉 a student of Chinese classics; a (young) Confucianist
2 〈남의 집의〉 a student dependent; a student servant [houseboy]
서서히 徐徐— slow(ly); gradually; by slow degrees; little by little ⇨ 천천히
▶온도가 서서히 내려가기 시작했다 The temperature began to go down gradually [by degrees].
▶그녀의 학력은 서서히 향상되고 있다 Little by little she is improving in her studies.
서설 序說 an introduction ⇨ 서론
서설 瑞雪 propitious [auspicious] snow; snow of good omen
서성거리다 walk up and down restlessly;

hang about [around] (a place)
▶ 낯선 사람이 학교 주위를 서성거리고 있었다 A stranger was hanging around the school.
▶ 나는 마음을 가라앉히려고 방안을 서성거렸다 I walked up and down the room trying to compose myself.

서수 序數 〔數〕 an ordinal (number)

서수사 序數詞 〔言〕 the ordinal numerals [numbers]

서술 敍述 description; depiction; delineation; narration; 〔論〕 predication
◆ 서술적인 descriptive; narrative; predicative 서술하다 describe; depict; delineate; narrate ■ ―부[어] the predicate (of a sentence) ―용법 〔文法〕 predicative use ―자 a narrator; a delineator; a depictor ―형용사 〔文法〕 a predicative adjective

서스테이닝프로그램 〈비상업성 프로그램〉 a sustaining program

서스펜디드게임 〔野〕 a suspended game

서스펜스 suspense ◆ 서스펜스로 가득찬 이야기 a very thrilling story; a story full of suspense / 스릴과 서스펜스가 넘치는 영화 a movie full of thrills and suspense

서슬 1 〈날붙이의〉 a sharp [keen-edged] part (of a blade); a burnished blade ◆ 서슬이 시퍼런 칼 a sharp [glittering] sword
▶ 그 칼은 서슬이 시퍼렜다 The knife had a very sharp edge.
▶ 그는 검에 서슬을 세웠다 He gave an edge to [put an edge on] his sword.
2 〈날카로운 기세〉 the brunt (of an attack, argument); sharpness; acuteness; impetuosity
▶ 그는 서슬이 푸른 얼굴로 나를 노려보았다 He looked at me with a fierce look. ⇒ He glared in anger at me.

서슴거리다 hesitate ⇨ 서슴다
◆ 서슴거리며 hesitatingly; with hesitation

서슴다 hesitate; waver; scruple; hang [hold] back; falter
◆ 서슴지 않고 without hesitation [flinching]; unhesitatingly; without scruple [wavering] / …을 서슴지 않다 do not hesitate about [in] doing [to do]…; make no scruple of doing [to do]…; be ready [willing] to do… / 죽음도 서슴지 않다 do not hesitate even to die
▶ 서슴지 말고 대답을 하시오 Don't hesitate to answer.
▶ 그는 어떠한 일도 서슴지 않는다 He will do anything without scruple. ⇒ He'll stick at nothing.
▶ 정직하지 못한 사람은 남을 속이는 일을 서슴지 않는다 A dishonest man does not scruple to deceive others.

서슴없다 unhesitating; 〈서술적〉 be not hesitant; have no scruples about; make no scruple of ◆ 서슴없이 without hesitation [flinching]; unhesitatingly; without scruple [reserve, wavering]; unreservedly
▶ 그녀는 서슴없이 이야기했다 She talked unreservedly.
▶ 원하는 것이 있으면 서슴없이 말하시오 Don't scruple to ask for anything you want.
▶ 그는 나의 제안에 서슴없이 응해 주었다 He was ready and willing to comply with my proposal.

서식 書式 a (fixed [due, prescribed]) form
◆ …의 서식대로 after the form of… / 서식에 기입하다 fill in [out] a form 〔美〕 blank)
▶ 원서는 서식에 따라 써 주시오 The application should be written in due form [according to the form prescribed].
▶ 이것은 서식이 틀렸다 This is not in due [proper] form.

서식 棲息 inhabitation
―서식하다 〈살다〉 inhabit (the earth); live (in the river) ◆ 물속에 서식하다 live in the water / 숲속에 서식하다 inhabit a forest
▶ 바다에는 각종의 물고기가 서식한다 Various kinds of fish inhabit the sea.
▶ 이 산에는 야생의 곰이 서식하고 있다 Wild bears inhabit [live in] this mountain.
■ ―동물 an inhabitant (of the wood) ―지 a habitat; a haunt

서신 書信 〈편지 왕래〉 correspondence; communication; 〈편지〉 a letter; a note
◆ 서신을 내다 write a letter to *sb* / …과 서신 왕래를 계속하다[끊다] maintain [stop, quit] correspondence with…
▶ 그에게 서신을 띄워야겠다 I will write (to) him.
▶ 7월 1일자 귀서신을 배수했습니다 I have received your letter dated [of] July 1.
▶ 미국에 있는 친구와 서신 왕래를 하고 있다 I correspond with a friend of mine in America.
▶ 그는 퇴원했다고 서신으로 알려 왔다 He informed me by letter that he had left the hospital.

서안 西岸 the west coast

서약 誓約 an oath; a vow; a pledge; 〔法〕 a recognizance
◆ 결혼 서약 marriage [lovers'] vows / 서약대로 faithful [true] to *one's* vow; in conformity with *one's* pledge; according to *one's* promise / 서약을 실행하다 put *one's* pledge into effect / 서약을 지키다 keep *one's* pledge [vow] / 서약을 어기다 break *one's* oath [vow]; violate *one's* pledge
―서약하다 swear; vow; pledge; make [take, swear] an oath (that); give *one's* pledge [word] (that); make a vow (to do, that); pledge *oneself* (to do)
◆ 비밀을 지키겠다고 서약하다 take an oath [a vow] of secrecy; pledge *oneself* to secrecy
▶ 명예를 걸고 서약합니다 I pledge (you) my honor.
▶ 그는 전력을 다하겠다고 서약했다 He promised [made a promise] to do his best.
■ ―자 a party to a covenant; a recognizor

서약서 誓約書 a written oath; a written pledge [promise]; a covenant ◆ 서약서를 쓰다 make a written pledge; write a pledge

서양 西洋 the West; the Western countries; the Occident; Europe (and America)
◆ 서양의 Western; European; Occidental / 서양 물이 들다 be touched [imbued] with Occidentalism; be Europeanized; be Westernized; be under Western influence

—문명[사상] Western civilization [ideas] —문학 Western [European] literature —사 Occidental [European] history —요리 ⇨ 양식(洋食) —인 a Westerner; an Occidental; a European —풍 ⇨ 서양식

서양식 西洋式 a European [Western] style [fashion]; Western ways [habits]
♦ 서양식의 건물 a foreign-[Western-]style building / 서양식 사고방식 the Western way of thinking [mode of thought] / 서양식으로 after [in] European fashion; in Western style / 서양식으로 하다 Westernize; Europeanize
▶ 그녀는 서양식 생활을 좋아한다 She likes the Western style of living [life].

서양화 西洋化 Westernization; Europeanization —서양화하다 become westernized; Westernize; Europeanize

서양화 西洋畵 (a) Western [European] painting; 〈유화〉 (an) oil painting ■—가 an artist of Western painting; an oil painter

서언 序言·緖言 a preface; a foreword; an introduction; a prefatory [an introductory] note [remark] ⇨ 서문(序文)

서역 西域 the countries to the west of China

서열 序列 rank; ranking; grade; order
♦ 서열에 따라 in order of importance / 서열이 X의 다음이다 stand next to X in line / 당 서열 제3위를 차지하다 rank No. 3 in the party hierarchy

서열 暑熱 the heat of the summer

서염 暑炎 extremely hot weather; the intense heat of the summer

서예 書藝 calligraphy; penmanship ♦ 서예의 대가 a master [great] calligrapher
■—가 a calligrapher; a penman

서운하다 〈마음이〉 sorry; regrettable; unsatisfied; 〈일·처사 등이〉 unsatisfactory; unfair; displeasing ♦ 서운하게 대하다 treat *sb* in a displeasing way [with unkindness]; behave unfairly toward *sb*
▶ 그가 떠난다니 서운하다 I regret he is leaving.
▶ 네가 오지 않아서 퍽 서운했다 I missed you very much there.
▶ 서운하기 그지없습니다만 여기서 헤어지기로 합시다 How I hate to see you go, but let's say good-bye now.
▶ 그는 아무래도 떠나기가 서운한듯 몇번이나 뒤돌아 보았다 He kept looking back as though he didn't really want to leave.

서운해하다 be sorry [unsatisfied]; miss *sb* [*sth*]; be displeased at ♦ 처사를 서운해하다 consider the treatment unfair

서울 1 〈수도〉 a capital; a metropolis
♦ 미국의 서울 워싱턴 Washington D.C., the capital of the U.S.A.
2 〈한국의 수도〉 Seoul
♦ 서울로 가다 go [come] up to Seoul
■—깍쟁이 a shrewd [canny, grasping] Seoulite —내기 a (native) Seoulite; a (true-)born Seoulite —사람 a Seoulite —시민 a citizen [an inhabitant] of Seoul —시장 the Mayor [Governor] of Seoul (Metropolis)

—시청 the City Hall of Seoul; the Seoul Metropolitan Government (Office) —역 Seoul Station —장안 (in) all Seoul —지방경찰청 the Seoul Metropolitan Police Agency —특별시 〈주소로 쓸때〉 Seoul City; 〈기관 명칭〉 Seoul Metropolitan City

서원 署員 (a member of) the ((police)) staff
♦ 세무서원 a tax office clerk [agent] / 마포서원 a member of the Map'o Police Station

서원 誓願 a vow; an oath; a pledge —서원하다 swear; vow; pledge; take [make] a vow; pledge *oneself* ((to do))

서인도제도 西印度諸島 the West Indies
♦ 서인도제도의 West Indian
—연방 the Federation of the West Indies

서임 敍任 appointment; installation; investiture —서임하다 appoint; install; invest ((*sb* with a position))

서자 庶子 〈첩의〉 a child by a concubine; 〈사생아〉 a child born out of wedlock; an illegitimate child; a love child; a bastard

서작 敍爵 ennoblement; conferment of a peerage —서작하다 raise *sb* to the peerage; ennoble; confer a peerage ((on *sb*))

서장 書狀 〈편지〉 a letter; a note

서장 署長 the head [chief, superintendent] ((of)); 〈경찰서·소방서의〉 a ((town, fire)) marshal ■경찰— ⇨ 경찰서(~장)

서재 書齋 a study; a library ♦ 서재에 틀어박혀 있다 be confined in *one's* study —인(人) a person of the study; an academic person

서적 書籍 books ■—광(狂) a bibliomaniac; a bibliophile —상 〈사람〉 a bookseller; 〈가게〉 a bookstore; (英) a bookshop

서전 緖戰 〈전쟁의〉 the beginning [an early stage] of a war; 〈경기의〉 the first match [game]
♦ 서전을 승리로 장식하다 〈전쟁에서〉 win a victory at the beginning of the war; 〈경기에서〉 win *one's* first match; win the first game

서점 書店 a bookseller's; (美) a bookstore; (英) a bookshop

서정 抒情·敍情 description [expression] of feelings [passions]; lyricism
♦ 서정적인 lyric(al) / 서정적으로 lyrically
■—문 lyric writing —시 a lyric (poem); an ode; (총칭) lyric poetry; lyrical verse —시인 a lyric poet; a lyricist

서정 庶政 civil services ♦ 서정을 쇄신하다 purify officialdom; enforce official discipline
■—쇄신 purification [renovation] of officialdom; enforcement of official discipline

서주 序奏 〖樂〗 an introduction ■—곡 an entree; an overture; a prelude

서지 書誌 a bibliography ■—학 bibliography; bibliology —학자 a bibliographer

서지 ♦ 감색 서지 blue serge / 순모 서지 woolen serge / 서지 옷 a serge suit

서진 書鎭 〈문진〉 a paperweight; a weight

서쪽 西— the west (略 W)
♦ 서쪽의 west; western; westerly / 서쪽에 in [on, to] the west ((of)) / 서쪽으로 west; westward; toward(s) [to] the west / 서쪽으로 가다 go west [westward]

해는 서쪽으로 진다 The sun sets in the west.
그 건물은 공원에서 약 100 미터 서쪽에 있다 The building is about one hundred meters to the west of the park.
콜럼버스 일행은 서쪽에서 서쪽으로 항해를 계속했다 Columbus and his men sailed west and further west.

서천 西天 the western sky

서체 書體 a style of penmanship [handwriting]; a calligraphic style

서출 庶出 a child by a concubine ⇨ 서자(庶子) ♦서출의 born of a concubine; born out of wedlock; illegitimate

서치라이트 a searchlight ♦서치라이트를 비추다 flash [turn, play] a searchlight (on)

서캐 a nit ♦서캐 훑듯하다 leave no stone untouched [unturned] (in a search); look in every nook and corner (of a house for *sth*); comb [scour] (a place for concealed weapons)

서커스 a circus (show) ♦서커스의 곡예사 a circus performer / 서커스를 흥행하다 run [put on] a circus ■—단 a circus troupe —단장 a circus master

서클 a circle; a club
♦서클에 가입하다 join a club (▶join a circle 이라고는 하지 않음); become a member of a (reading) circle (▶circle은 단독으로는 쓰지 않고, 그 앞에 서클인지를 구체적으로 나타내는 말을 붙여, a painting [photography, nature study] circle과 같이 말하는 것이 보통)
■—활동 club [group] activities; extracurricular activities (▶circle activities라고는 하지 않음)

서투르다 1 ⟨익숙지 못하다⟩ unskillful; unskilled; inexpert; poor; awkward; clumsy; unhandy; bungling; bunglesome
♦서투른 그림[번역] a poor picture [translation] / 서투른 목수 an incompetent [unskilled] carpenter / 서투른 변명 a poor excuse / 서투른 솜씨 bad [poor, clumsy, rude] workmanship; botchery / 서투른 직공 a botcher; a tinker / 서투른 솜씨로 with a clumsy hand / 서투르게 unskillfully; clumsily; awkwardly; in a clumsy way; in an awkward manner / 서투른 짓을 하다 make a blunder; make a mess of it; bungle / 계산이 서투르다 be bad [poor] at figures / 글씨가 서투르다 write [be] a poor hand / 바느질이 서투르다 be clumsy [awkward] with the needle; be poor in needlework / 장사에 서투르다 be unskilled in business
▶그는 아직도 젓가락질이 서투르다 He is still awkward with chopsticks.
▶그는 영어 회화가 서투르다 He is a poor speaker of English. ⇌ He is poor [weak] in speaking English. ⇌ He speaks English poorly.
2 ⟨소원하다⟩ unfamiliar (with); unknown; strange; ⟨서술적⟩ feel awkward; feel [be] ill at ease

서투른 무당이 장구만 나무란다 ⟨속담⟩ A bad workman quarrels with his tools.

서퍽 ⟨영국의 주⟩ Suffolk

서평 書評 a book review ♦서평을 하다 review a book
▶그 책의 서평이 이 잡지에 실렸다 There is a review of the book in this magazine.
■—가 a book reviewer —란 the book-review columns: 그 신문의 서평란을 맡고 있다 I review for the newspaper.

서표 書標 a bookmark; a bookmarker
♦책갈피에 서표를 끼워 두다 put [place] a bookmark between the leaves

서푼 ⟨돈⟩ three *p'un*; a farthing; ⟨가치⟩ little value
▶그것은 서푼어치 가치도 없다 It is not worth a penny [farthing, straw, fig, button].

서품 敍品 ⟨가톨릭⟩ ordination ♦서품하다 ordain ■—식 the ceremony of ordination

서풍 西風 a west [westerly] wind; (詩) Zephyr

서풍 書風 a style of penmanship [calligraphy]

서핑 surfing

서한 書翰 a letter ⇨ 편지, 서간(書簡)

서해 西海 the western sea; ⟨한국의 황해⟩ the Yellow Sea

서행 徐行 going slowly
—서행하다 go slow [slowly]; crawl; go [drive] at a crawl [a slow speed]; proceed at reduced speed; ⟨기선이⟩ steam along slowly; ⟨점차로⟩ slow down [up, off]; slack speed
▶열차는 서행하다 멈췄다 The train slowed down and stopped.
▶서행 (게시) Slow down. ⇌ Go slow.
■—속도 (a) slow speed —표지 a slow sign

서향 西向 a western exposure; a western [west] aspect
▶이 집은 서향이다 This house faces west.
■—집 a house facing west; a house with a western exposure; a house open to the west

서향나무 瑞香 〔植〕 a daphne

서혜 鼠蹊 〔解〕 the groin
■—부 the inguinal region —선(腺) inguinal glands

서화 書畫 paintings [pictures] and writings [calligraphic works]; works of pictorial art and calligraphy
■—골동 (deal in) objects of art and curios —상 ⟨사람⟩ a dealer in pictures and writings —전람회 an exhibition of pictures and writings —첩 an album of paintings and calligraphic works

서훈 敍勳 (conferment of a) decoration; bestowal of an order
—서훈하다 confer a decoration (on *sb*); invest *sb* with a decoration; decorate
▶그는 무공으로 서훈되었다 He was decorated for his distinguished war service.

석 three ♦석 달 three months / 석 자 three feet / 석 장 three sheets of paper

석 石 a *sŏk* ⇨ 섬¹

-석 -席 a seat; a place ♦일반석 a general admission seat / 지정석 a reserved seat

석가모니 釋迦牟尼 〔佛教〕 S(h)akyamuni; Buddha
■—여래 S(h)akyamuni Tathagata; the Incarnation of Truth

석가산 石假山 an artificial [a miniature] hill;

a rockery
석각 石刻 stone carving —석각하다 carve stone 《for a statue, into a shape》; carve 《a statue》 out of stone
석간 夕刊 〈석간 신문〉 an evening paper; 〈조간에 대하여〉 the evening edition 《of a paper》; (口) an afternooner
석경 石鏡 a mirror; a (looking) glass
석고 石膏 〔鑛〕 gypsum; gyps; plaster; gesso
—모형 a plaster cast —붕대 a plaster-of-Paris bandage —상(像) a plaster figure; 〈흉상〉 a plaster bust —세공 plastering; plaster work —세공인 a plasterer —조각(술) gypsography
석공 石工 〈석수〉 a (stone)mason; a stonecutter; 〈석공업〉 masonry
석관 石棺 a stone coffin; a sarcophagus 《pl. -gi, ~es》; 〔考古〕 a cist
석교 石橋 a stone bridge
석굴 石窟 a stone cave [cavern]; a grotto 《pl. ~(e)s》
석굴암 石窟庵 〈경주의〉 Sŏkkuram
석권하— 〈휩쓸다〉 carry everything before one; sweep 《over, across》; overwhelm; 〈정복하다〉 conquer; make a conquest of
◆전유럽을 석권하다 sweep [pour] over the whole of Europe
▶외국 자본이 국내 시장을 석권했다 Foreign capital overwhelmed our market(s).
석기 石器 stoneware; stonework; 〔考古〕 a stone implement [tool]
석기시대 石器時代 〔考古〕 the Stone Age —신[구]— the neolithic [palaeolithic] age; the New [Old] Stone Age
석남 石南 〔植〕 a moorwort; a bog rosemary
석녀 石女 a childless [barren, sterile] woman
석뇌유 石腦油 〔化〕 naphtha
석돌 a friable [crumbly, brittle] stone
석등(롱) 石燈(籠) a stone lantern
석랍 石蠟 paraffin
석류 石榴 〔植〕 a pomegranate ■—나무 a pomegranate tree
석류석 石榴石 〔鑛〕 garnet
석면 石綿 〔鑛〕 asbestos; asbestus; amiantus ◆석면의 asbestine ■—사(絲) asbestos fiber —테이프[로프] an asbestos tape [rope]
석명 釋明 (an) explanation; elucidation; explication; making clear —석명하다 explain; elucidate; explicate; make clear; clear up
석묵 石墨 〔鑛〕 graphite ⇨ 흑연
석방 釋放 release; liberation; discharge; (an) acquittal
◆정치범의 석방을 요구하다 demand the release of political prisoners / …의 석방을 교섭하다 negotiate for sb's release
—석방하다 release; let off; set free; turn loose; discharge; liberate; acquit
▶그는 형기를 마치고 어제 석방되었다 He was released [set free] yesterday after serving his term.
■조건부— conditional release
석별 惜別 unwillingness to part 《from》; reluctance to leave; reluctant [regretful] parting; parting with regrets
◆석별의 눈물 tears at parting / 석별의 정 unwillingness to part / 석별의 정을 나누다 express one's sorrow at [on] parting
—석별하다 be unwilling to part 《from one's friend》; be reluctant to leave 《a place》; grudge [regret] parting [to part] 《from sb》; part with regrets
■—연 a farewell party [banquet]; a send-off dinner
석불 石佛 a stone Buddhist image
석비 石碑 〈기념비〉 a (stone) monument; 〈묘석〉 a tombstone; a stone
석빙고 石氷庫 〈서울의〉 an ice storage house (during the Chosŏn dynasty (1392-1910)); an earthen-covered stone construction for ice storage in ancient times.
석사 碩士 〈선비〉 a worthy scholar (holding no office); 〈칭호〉 Mr.; 〈학위〉 Master
■문학— Master of Arts (略 M.A.) 이학— Master of Science (略 M.S., M.Sc.) ■—과정 a master's course : 석사 과정을 밟다 take a master's course —논문 a thesis for master's degree; a master's thesis —학위 a master's degree : 경제학 석사 학위를 취득하다 get [receive] a master's degree in economics 《at Seoul National University》
석산 石山 a stony [rocky] mountain
석산 石蒜 〔植〕 a cluster-amaryllis
석삼년 —三年 nine years; (비유) a long time
석상 石像 a stone image [statue]
석상 席上 ◆회의 석상에서 at the conference [meeting, assembly] / 공개 석상에서 on a public occasion; in public
석송 石松 〔植〕 a club moss; a ground pine; a coral evergreen; a buck grass; a lycopodium
석쇠 a grid; a gridiron; a grill ◆석쇠로 쇠고기를 굽다 grill beef on a gridiron
석수 石手 a (stone)mason; a stonecutter
■—질 masonry (work)
석수 汐水 an evening tide
석순 石筍 〔鑛〕 stalagmite
석순 席順 class standing ⇨ 석차(席次)
석실 石室 a stone chamber
석양 夕陽 the evening [setting] sun; the declining [westering] sun
▶이 방은 석양이 들어 덥다 This room is hot with the evening sun shining in.
▶서쪽 하늘이 석양으로 불타고 있다 The western sky is glowing with the setting sun.
▶석양이 서쪽 하늘을 붉게 물들이며 지고 있다 The evening sun is sinking staining the western sky red.
■—녘 toward sunset —별 the light of the evening [setting] sun —빛 the hue [color] of the sunset
석연하다 釋然— 〈사람이〉 satisfied 《with the explanation》; relieved from doubt; feeling free from doubt; 〈사물이〉 satisfactory; comprehensible; understandable
◆석연치 않은 인물 a doubtful character
▶무언가 석연치 않은 데가 있다 There is something inexplicable in the matter. ⇌ There is something to be clarified.
▶그의 설명은 아무래도 석연치 않다 I am not

quite satisfied with his explanation.
▶ 그에 대한 의심이 석연하게 가신 것은 아니다 My suspicions about him have not really been cleared up.

석영 石英 〔鑛〕 quartz ■녹(綠)— prase 유(乳)— milky quartz ■—반암(斑岩) quartz porphyry —사(砂) quartz sand —암 quartzite —유리 quartz [silica] glass —조면암(粗面岩) quartz trachyte

석유 石油 oil; petroleum; 〈등유〉 《美》 kerosene; 《英》 paraffin; 《美》 coal oil
♦석유를 발견하다 strike [hit] oil / 석유를 연료로 쓰다 use oil for fuel
■—가스 petroleum gas —갱(坑) a petroleum [an oil] well —공업 the petroleum [oil] industry —공장 a petroleum plant —관련제품 petroleum-based products —난로[스토브] an oil stove [heater]; a kerosene heater [stove] —램프[등] an oil [a kerosene] lamp —매장량 (an estimated amount of) oil deposits —버너 an oil burner —비축 oil reserves —수송관 an oil pipe(line) —수출국기구 Organization of Petroleum Exporting Countries (略 OPEC) —업자 an oilman —엔진[발동기] an oil engine; a petroleum motor —위기[파동] an oil crisis [shock, squeeze, pinch] —유제(乳劑) petroleum emulsion —자원 (develop, exploit) petroleum resources —제품 petroleum products —탱크 an oil tank —통 an oil-can; 《英》 a kerosene tin —회사 an oil company

석유화학 石油化學 petrochemistry
■—공업 the petrochemical industry —공장 a petrochemical plant —제품 a petrochemical (product) —콤비나트 a petrochemical complex

석이다 〈눈을〉 thaw; cause (snow) to thaw; make sloppy; 〈술·식혜 등을〉 ferment

석이(버섯) 石耳(—) 〔植〕 a manna lichen

석인 石人 a stone image [figure] of a man

석일 昔日 old [former] times ⇨ 옛날

석자 a ladle with meshes (for dipping up sth fried); an iron scoop net; a skimming spoon; a sieve; a strainer

석재 石材 (building) stone ■—상 〈사람〉 a stone dealer; a dealer in stone; 〈가게〉 a stone dealer's (shop)

석전 石戰 a mock fight with stone missiles

석전제 釋奠祭 the festival (in honor) of Confucius

석조 石造 stone construction ♦석조의 built of stone; stone(-built) ■—가옥 a house built of stone; a stone house [building]

석존 釋尊 Buddha ⇨ 석가모니 ■—제 Buddha's birthday festival

석종유 石鐘乳 〔鑛〕 stalactite

석주 石柱 a stone pillar

석죽 石竹 〔植〕 a pink; a China [rainbow] pink ■—색 pink

석차 席次 the seating order; the order of seats [place, precedence]; 〈학교의〉 class standing
♦석차가 3등 올라가다[떨어지다] gain [lose] in class standing by three places
▶ 그는 학급 석차가 떨어졌다 He lost his standing in the class.
▶ 학기말에는 그의 석차가 뚝 떨어졌다 At the end of the term his name was very low down on the list.
■—졸업 one's graduation standing ■—다툼 a quarrel over precedence; 〈학교에서의〉 a competition for higher class standing

석창포 石菖蒲 〔植〕 a sweet flag [rush]

석축 石築 a reinforcing stone wall ■—제방 a stone embankment

석출 析出 〔化〕 eduction; extraction —석출하다 educe; extract

식탄 石炭 coal
♦석탄을 때다 burn coal / 석탄을 캐다 dig (out) [mine] coal / 석탄을 싣다 bunker [take (in)] coal; ship coal / 석탄을 지피다 put coal on 《the fire》; feed 《a stove》 with coal / 석탄을 연료로 하다 use coal for fuel
■—가루 coal dust —가스 coal gas —갱부 a coal miner; a collier; a pitman —건류(乾溜) coal carbonization —계(系) 〔地質〕 the Carboniferous system —고(庫) a coal cellar [bin]; 〈배의〉 a coal bunker; 〈저탄장〉 a coal depot —광 a coal mine —광업 the coal mining industry —광업권 a coal mining right —기(紀) 〔地質〕 the Carboniferous period —도매상 a coal factor —매장량 coal reserves; (the estimated amount of) coal deposits —보급지 a coal base [depot] —부대[포대] a coal sack —산(化) carbolic acid; phenol —산지 a producing center of coal; a coalfield —액화 liquefaction of coal; coal liquefaction —운반부 〈적재〉 a coal heaver; 〈양륙〉 a coal whipper; 〈海〉 a coal passer —운반선 a coal ship [carrier]; 《英》 a collier —재[찌끼] coal cinders —적탄(~고) —적재 coaling; 〈연료용의〉 bunkering —적재항 a coaling port —차 a coal truck —층 a coal seam [bed] —통 a coal scuttle [bin]; a coalbox

석탑 石塔 a stone pagoda [stupa, tower]

석판 石版 〈석판술〉 lithography; 〈석판화〉 a lithograph
■—용지 lithographic paper —인쇄 lithography; lithographic printing; 〈인쇄물〉 a lithographic print : 석판 인쇄하다 lithograph —화 a lithograph

석판 石板 a slate

석패 惜敗 a defeat by a narrow margin; a regrettable defeat —석패하다 be defeated by a narrow margin; lose a close game
▶ 시합은 연장전으로 들어갔지만 결국 우리는 석패했다 The game extended to extra innings, and we were defeated by a narrow margin.

석필 石筆 a slate pencil

석학 碩學 a great scholar; an erudite scholar; a man of great [profound] learning

석호 潟湖 a lagoon

석화 石火 〈불꽃〉 flint fire; a flint spark; 〈몹시 빠름〉 flash ♦전광 석화와같이 like (a flash of) lightning

석회 石灰 lime ♦석회를 함유하지 않은 limeless / 석회를 뿌리다 sprinkle lime (over); sprinkle sth with lime

■소(消)— slaked [slack, dead] lime ■—가루 lime powder —(동)굴 a lime grotto [cave] —모르타르 lime mortar —비료 lime fertilizer —석[암] limestone —수 limewater —유(乳) milk [cream] of lime —증 calcicosis —질소 lime nitrogen; calcium cyanamide —침착 〔醫〕 calcareous deposit —화(華) flowers of lime; calcareous sinter —화(化) calcification: 석회화하다 calcify; calcine

석회질 石灰質 ♦석회질의 calcareous; calcarious; calcic
■—비료 calcium fertilizer

섞갈리다 get confused [complicated, entangled, tangled]; be mixed up; be confusing
♦계산이 섞갈리다 get confused in calculation
▶이야기가 섞갈린다 The story gets entangled.
▶내 머리가 섞갈린다 I'm getting confused.

섞다 mix; blend; mingle; commingle; adulterate; 〈카드를〉 shuffle
♦물감을 섞다 mix paints / 브랜디에 알코올을 섞다 adulterate brandy with alcohol; add alcohol to brandy / 연설에 재치있는 유머를 섞다 intersperse one's speech with apt humor
▶목욕물이 너무 뜨거워서 나는 찬물을 좀 섞었다 As the bath was too hot, I ran some cold water in it.
▶그들은 시멘트와 자갈을 섞었다 They mingled cement and gravel.
▶물에 기름을 섞기는 어렵다 You can hardly mix oil with water.
▶빨강과 파랑을 섞으면 무슨 빛깔이 됩니까? What color will you get if you mix [blend] the red paint with the blue?
▶나는 카드를 잘 섞어 쳤다 I gave the cards a good shuffle.

섞바꾸다 alternate (with each other); interchange regularly [repeatedly] with *sth*

섞바뀌다 be alternated; alternate; be interchanged regularly with *sth*

섞음질 adulteration; mixing; mixture; admixture —**섞음질하다** adulterate; mix; admix
♦섞음질한 것 a mixture; a compound; an adulteration; impurities / 섞음질하지 않은 unadulterated; pure

섞이다 1〈혼합되다〉 be mixed [mingled, blended] ♦눈과 우박이 섞인 비 rain mixed with snow and sleet / 유머가 섞인 연설 a speech seasoned with humor
▶물과 기름은 섞이지 않는다 Oil and water will not blend.
▶그 소녀에게는 한국인과 미국인의 피가 섞여 있다 The girl is of mixed Korean and American parentage.
▶이 견직물에는 면이 좀 섞여 있다 There is some cotton in this silk cloth.
2〈패거리에 끼이다〉 mix 《with》; join; mingle 《with》 ▶나도 그 중에 섞여 흥청거렸다 I joined in the spree.

섟삭다 〈노여움이〉 be allayed; 〈의심이〉 be resolved; be dissipated; 〈사람이〉 relent 《toward *sb*》

선 an interview [meeting] with a view to marriage ♦선을 보다 see each other with a view to marriage; have an interview with a prospective bride [bridegroom]
▶나 내달에 선보기로 했다 I'll have an interview with a prospective bride [bridegroom] next month.
▶두 사람은 선도 안보고 결혼했다 They were married without even going through the formality of a preliminary interview.

선 先 〈바둑・장기의〉 the first [initial] move; 〈화투・카드놀이의〉 (the) lead; a dealer;〈구기의〉 serve; delivery
♦선을 두다[잡다, 하다] 〈바둑 등에서〉 have [make] the first move; obtain the initiative
▶누가 선이냐? Whose deal [lead] is it?

선 善 the good; goodness; virtue; 〈선행〉 a good deed ♦최고의 선 the highest good / 선과 악 good and evil / 선을 행하다 do (what is) good; practice virtue
▶악을 선으로 갚는 것은 훌륭한 일이다 It is noble to return good for evil.

선 腺 〔解〕 a gland ■내분비— a ductless gland; an endocrine gland 림프— a lymph gland 점액— glandula mucosa ■—폴립 glandular polyp

선 縇 an edge; a frill; a border; trim(ming)
♦선을 두르다 put a border on 《a skirt》; hem 《a handkerchief》; sew on a frill [border]

선 線 1〈줄〉 a line ♦굵은[가는] 선 a thick [thin] line / 선을 긋다 draw a line
2〈기준 한도〉 a level; the limit
♦최후의 선을 넘다 exceed [go beyond, overstep] the limit / 동정과 연민 사이에 명확한 선을 긋다 draw a clear line between sympathy and pity
3〈진로・방침〉 a line
▶이번 계획은 그 선에서 시행합시다 Let's proceed along those lines with our present project.
4〈신경〉 ♦선이 가늘다 sensitive; delicate / 선이 굵다 tough(-minded)
▶그는 선이 굵은 정치가다 He is a broad-minded politician.
▶정말 그는 대담한 것 같지만 실제로는 선이 가는 사람이다 Indeed he looks daring, but in reality he is delicate.
5〈전선〉 a wire; a line ♦집에 전기선을 끌다 wire a house for electricity
6〈철도・선로・항로〉 a line;〈궤도〉 a track; 〈노선〉 a route
▶〔會話〕「열차는 몇 번 선에서 출발합니까?」「2번 선입니다」 "What Track does the train leave from?" "From Track [Platform] (No.) two."
■상행[하행]— an up [a down] line 자오— the meridian

선 選 selection; choice; 〈편집・편찬물〉 compilation; editing ■명작— a selection of masterpieces [famous literary works]

선 禪 〔佛敎〕 Zen (Buddhism); meditation [contemplation] ♦선을 하다 practice Zen
■—도장 a Zen Buddhist seminary —문답 a question-and-answer exchange between Zen Buddhist and their followers —승 a Zen Buddhist

선- 〈덜 된〉 inexperienced; unskilled; un-

trained; poor; clumsy; green; immature; raw
♦ 선머슴 a naughty [mischievous] boy / 선무당 an inexperienced [a new, a green] shaman / 선하품 a forced [feigned] yawn

-선 -船 a ship; a vessel ▶외국선 a foreign ship; a foreigner / 운송선 a transport ship

선가 船價 〈뱃삯〉boat [passage] fare; a (passenger) fare; 〈나룻배의〉ferriage; 〈화물의〉freight (rates); freightage; shipping charges

선각 先覺 seeing [perceiving] in advance
—선각하다 see [perceive] in advance; foresee; foreknow

선각자 先覺者 a pioneer; a forerunner; a leading spirit ▶ 그는 당대의 선각자였다 He was ahead of his times.

선개교 旋開橋 a swivel [swing, turn] bridge
선객 先客 a preceding visitor [customer]
선객 船客 a passenger
♦ 1등 선객 a cabin [first-class] passenger / 2등 선객 a second-class passenger / 3등 선객 a steerage [third-class] passenger; the steerage ■—명부 a passenger list —실 the passenger quarters

선거 船渠 a dock ▪건(乾)— a dry dock 습(濕)— a wet dock

선거 選擧 (an) election
♦ 선거의 예상 an election prediction / 선거의 전망 electoral prospects / 선거의 개표 결과 election returns / 선거를 실시하다 hold [have, conduct] an election / 선거를 참관하다 be witness at polling [the polls]
▶ 선거 결과는 내일 아침 5시까지는 판명된다 The election results will be out by 5 a.m. tomorrow.
▶ 선거는 아주 막상막하였다 The election was very close.
〈선거에(서)〉선거에 출마하다 run [stand, be up] for election / 선거에 간섭하다 intervene in an election / 선거에 지다 be defeated in an election; be beaten at the polls / 선거에 이기다 win in an election; carry an election / 선거에서 최고 득표자가 되다 head the poll
▶ 그는 국회의원[대통령]의 선거에 입후보할 것이다 He will run for Parliament [for President, for (the) Presidency].
▶ 선거에서 노동당의 득표수는 증가했다 The Labor vote increased at the election.
—선거하다 elect; vote for; (英) return
■공명— a fair [clean] election 국회의원— the election of the Assemblymen 대통령— a presidential election 무효— an invalid election 보궐[보결]— a by-election; (美) a special election 예비— a primary election 중간— an off-year [interim] election ▪—간섭《government》intervention in an election —공보 a campaign bulletin; the official gazette for elections —공영(비용) (expenses for) public management of election —대책위원회 an election polling committee —방해 an election obstruction —부정 election malpractice —비용 expenses for an election campaign; (美俗) barrel —사범 election crimes —소송 an election case [lawsuit] —위반 election irregularities [frauds]; an election law violation —일 the day of election; the election [polling] day —자금 an election campaign fund —제도 an election system —참관인 a witness (at the polls); 〈개표의〉a scrutineer —참모 a campaign manager —포스터 a campaign poster

선거관리 選擧管理 election administration
♦ 중앙선거관리위원회 the Central Election Management Committee (略 CEMC) ■—내각 a caretaker government —인 an election judge

선거구 選擧區 an election [an electoral, a voting] district; an electorate; a constituency; (美) a precinct ♦ 대[중, 소] 선거구제 the major [medium, minor] constituency [electorate] system / (의회에서) 선거구를 대표하다 sit for a constituency
▶ 그 선거구에서는 한 사람도 빠짐없이 투표를 했다 The constituency has been polled to the last man.

선거권 選擧權 The suffrage; the (voting, elective) franchise; the right to vote; voting rights
♦ 선거권을 주다 enfranchise; give the franchise (to) / 선거권을 행사하다 exercise one's franchise; exercise the ballot / 선거권을 박탈하다 deprive sb of the right of casting the ballot; disfranchise; disenfranchise
▶미국에서는 1920년에 여자에게 선거권이 부여되었다 In America suffrage was given to women in 1920.
▶지금 우리나라에서는 여자도 선거권이 있다 Women now have the vote in our country.
■—자 an elector; a voter; (총칭) an electorate

선거법 選擧法 election [electoral] law
■—개정 (an) electoral reform —위반 (a) violation of election law; election irregularities

선거사무 選擧事務 election campaign business ■—소 an electioneering [a campaign] office —장 a campaign manager

선거연설 選擧演說 a campaign speech; an election address
■합동— (make) a campaign speech in a joint meeting of candidates

선거운동 選擧運動 an election campaign; canvassing; electioneering
♦ 선거운동을 하다 electioneer; canvass for an election [votes] / 사전 선거운동을 하다 go on a campaign beforehand
▶ 우리는 공화당 후보를 위한 선거운동을 하고 있습니다 We are canvassing for the Republican candidate.
■—비 campaign [electioneering] expenditure —원 an election campaigner; an electioneering agent; an electioneerer; a canvasser —자금 campaign [electioneering] fund

선거위원 選擧委員 an election committeeman ■—장 a campaign chairman —회 an election committee

선거유세 選擧遊說 a canvassing [an electioneering, a speaking] tour; (美) a stumping tour; a campaign tour [trip]
♦ 선거유세를 하다 go canvassing [campaign-

선거인 選擧人 an elector; a voter; a constituent; (총칭) the electorate; the constituency
■—단 (美) the electoral college —자격 electorship; the qualification of an elector

선거인명부 選擧人名簿 a pollbook; a voting register; a voting [voter] roll; a voters' list; (美) a check list ♦선거인 명부에서 누락되다 be left off the voting register

선거전 選擧戰 an election campaign [fight]
■대통령— a presidential race; a race for presidency

선견 先遣 —선견하다 send forward [beforehand, in advance] —대원 an advance man —부대 advance troops; an advance party; the first contingent

선견지명 先見之明 farseeing wisdom [intelligence]; farsightedness; foresight
♦선견지명이 있는 사람 a man of foresight; a farsighted person; a foreseer / 선견지명이 없는 사람 a shortsighted person; a bad prophet / 선견지명이 있다 possess the gift of foresight; have a long head (on); have farseeing wisdom; be wise and farsighted / 선견지명이 없다 lack the gift of foresight; be unable to see afar [far ahead]

선결 先決 a previous decision; prior settlement —선결하다 decide [settle] beforehand

선결문제 先決問題 a previous [prior] question; a preconsideration; a matter calling for prior settlement
▶이것이 선결문제다 This must be settled first. ⇌ This must be decided before anything else.
▶비용이 선결문제다 The question of expenses takes precedence of all others.

선경 仙境 a fairyland; an enchanted [elf] land; beautiful scenery like a fairyland

선고 先考 one's deceased [late] father

선고 宣告 〈공표〉 announcement; pronouncement; 〈판결을 내림〉 a sentence; a verdict; adjudication
♦사형 선고를 내리다 sentence *sb* to death; pass [pronounce] a death sentence (upon *sb*)
▶그는 살인죄로 무기 징역을 선고 받았다 He was sentenced to life imprisonment for murder.
—선고하다 〈공표하다〉 announce; pronounce; 〈판결을 내리다〉 sentence; condemn; adjudge; pass [pronounce] sentence on [upon] *sb*
♦사형을 선고하다 pronounce [pass] the death sentence on *sb*; sentence [condemn] *sb* to death / 파산을 선고하다 adjudicate *sb* to be bankrupt / 무죄를 선고하다 judge *sb* innocent [not guilty]; acquit (a prisoner) of the crime / 유죄를 선고받다 be convicted / 5년 형을 선고받다 be sentenced to penal servitude for five years [to five years' imprisonment with hard labor]
▶재판관은 피고에게 3년 형을 선고했다 The judge condemned the accused to three years in jail.
■유죄— condemnation ■—문 a written sentence —유예 probation

선곡 選曲 selection of music

선공 先攻 〈野〉 batting first ▶상대 팀의 선공으로 게임이 시작되었다 The game began with our opponents batting first.
—선공하다 go to bat first; bat first

선광 選鑛 ore dressing; concentration [dressing, separation] of ore
—선광하다 dress [concentrate] ore
■비중 [부유, 자력]— ore dressing by gravity separation [floatation, magnetic separation]
■—기 an ore separator —소 a dressing plant

선교 宣敎 missionary work —선교하다 preach the gospel; evangelize ■—단 a mission

선교 船橋 1 〈배다리〉 a pontoon [floating, bateau] bridge 2 〈갑판의〉 a bridge

선교사 宣敎師 a missionary ♦선교사로 일하다 be a missionary; engage in mission work / 선교사가 되다 follow the sacred mission

선구 先驅 1 ⇨ 선구자
2 〈앞섬〉 the lead; the initiative; 〈기마(騎馬)의 선도자〉 an outrider
♦선구가 되다 take the lead [initiative] (in); lead the way [van]; get the start

선구 船具 rigging; gearing; tackle; ship's fittings; (총칭) ship chandlery ♦선구를 장비하다 [풀다] rig up [down] a boat ■—상 a ship chandler —일습 a ship's fittings

선구안 選球眼 〈野〉 the batting eye
♦선구안이 없다 have a poor batting eye
▶그는 선구안이 있다 He has a good [sharp] batting eye. ⇌ He doesn't swing at bad pitches.

선구자 先驅者 a pioneer; a forerunner; a pathfinder ♦선구자가 되다 be ahead of *one's* times; take the lead
▶그는 근대 의학의 선구자였다 He was a pioneer of modern medicine. ⇌ He pioneered modern medicine.

선글라스 (a pair of) sunglasses; (wear) dark glasses ♦선글라스를 쓰다 wear sunglasses

선금 先金 money paid in advance; an amount prepaid; an advance (payment); a prepayment
♦선금을 주다[치르다] pay in advance; make an advance; prepay / 선금을 받다 take [receive] money in advance
▶선금이라면 그 일을 하겠습니다 I'll do the work if I'm paid in advance.
▶나는 세탁비를 선금으로 지불했다 I paid the charge for cleaning in advance.

선급 先給 a prepayment; payment in advance

선급 船級 〔商〕 (ship's) classification
■—증서 a classification certificate —협회 a classification society

선남선녀 善男善女 good [virtuous] men and women; 〔佛敎〕 pious people [folk]; religious-minded men and women

선납 先納 prepayment; payment in advance; (an) advance(d) payment
—선납하다 pay in advance; prepay
♦회비를 선납하다 pay the membership fee in advance; prepay *one's* due
▶나는 백만원을 선납했다 I made an advance

payment of one million won. ⇒ I paid one million won in advance.

선내 船內 ♦선내에 on board (a) ship; on shipboard; inboard; aboard / 선내를 수색하다 search the ship

선녀 仙女 a fairy; a nymph; a dryad

선다형 選多型 a multiple choice method ■―테스트[문제] a multiple-choice test [question]

선단 a vertical hem; an up-and-down hem

선단 先端 the foremost tip

선단 船團 a fleet (of ships) ■수송― a convoy of transport ships 출어― a fishing fleet

선대 先代 〈선조〉 a predecessor; a forebear; 〈앞 시대〉 the previous age; 〈앞 세대〉 the previous [last] generation

선대 船隊 a fleet (of ships) ⇨ 선단(船團)

선도 先渡 [商] forward [future] delivery

선도 先導 guidance; leadership ―선도하다 guide; conduct; lead; lead the way; take the lead; precede
♦당신이 선도하는 대로 우리는 따라가겠습니다 You lead (on) and we'll follow.
▶유행에서는 그녀가 언제나 선도해 왔다 In fashion she has always led the way.
■―견(犬) an outrunner ―자 a guide; a leader; 〈기마 행진의〉 an outrider ―차 a leading car; 〈경찰 등의〉 a (police) pilot car

선도 善導 proper [judicious] guidance
♦사상의 선도 proper guidance of public thought; thought guidance; edification ―선도하다 lead [guide] properly; guide aright; instruct; lead (people) to the path of virtue; lead (people) into the right path
■―책(策) measures for proper [judicious] guidance

선도 鮮度 (the degree of) freshness ⇨ 신선도

선돌 [考古] a menhir

선동 煽動 instigation; abetment; (an) incitement; (an) agitation; demagogy; demagoguery
♦선동적(인) incendiary; inflammatory; seditious; agitative; demagogic(al) / 지도자의 선동으로 파업을 하다 go on strike at [by] the instigation of the leader
―선동하다 instigate; abet; incite; stir up; agitate (for, against); set [egg] sb on 《to (do) sth》; fan
♦선동할 목적으로 for agitative purposes / 파업을 선동하다 agitate for [instigate, incite] a strike / 민중을 선동하여 난동을 부리게 하다 instigate [incite, excite, goad] people to violence
▶그들은 군중을 선동해 정부에 대해 반란을 일으키게 했다 They incited the crowd to rise against their government.
▶그는 두 소년을 선동해 싸움을 붙였다 He instigated the two boys to quarrel.
■―연설 an inflammatory harangue; a seditious [an agitating] speech ―연설가 an agitator; a demagog(ue) ―자 an instigator; an agitator; an abetter; a setter(-on); a firebrand; [法] an abettor ―전단 an agitation bill ―정치가 a demagogic politician; a (seditious)

demagog(ue) ―죄 sedition

선두 先頭 the forefront; the front (position); the head; the top; the lead; the van; the first
♦퍼레이드의 선두 집단 the head group of a parade / 마라톤의 선두 그룹 the leading (group of) runners in the marathon / 선두에 세우고 with sb in the lead; led [spearheaded] by 《a band》 / 선두에 서다 be at the head (of); be in the forefront [van] (of a parade); take [gain] the lead (in); take [lead] the van / 선두가 되다 get ahead of 《others in a race》; get [have] the lead (in a race) / 선두에 서서 …하다 take the lead in 《doing》
▶브라스 밴드가 퍼레이드의 선두에 섰다 The brass band led (the way for) the parade.
▶그는 선두에 서서 교육 개혁을 추진했다 He took the lead [initiative] in carrying out the educational reform.
▶그녀는 골인 지점 가까이에서 선두로 나섰다 She gained the lead a little before the goal.
■―주자 a front-running man; a forerunner; 〈선거에서〉 a front runner ―타자 [野] 〈멤버 중의〉 a lead-off man [batter]; 〈그 회(回)의〉 the first batter

선두 船頭 the bow ⇨ 이물

선두르다 fringe; hem; rim; sew on a frill; border; frill; trim ♦드레스에 선두르다 trim a dress 《with frills》

선두리 〈물방개〉 [昆] a water beetle

선둥이 先― 〈쌍둥이 중의〉 the firstborn of twins

선드러지다 lively; buoyant; gay; vivacious; cheerful; lighthearted; sprightly

선득 shudderingly; chillingly ―선득하다 〈추워서〉 chilled; 〈서술적〉 feel [have] a chill; feel [be] chilly; 〈무서워서〉 shudder 《at》; have a thrill of horror
▶그의 얼굴을 보기만 해도 선득했다 Just looking at him gave me the shivers.

선득거리다 〈무서워서〉 shudder 《at》; be horrified; have a thrill of horror; 〈추워서〉 feel chilly; feel a chill ♦…을 보고 선득거리다 shudder at the sight of
♦숲속에 들어가니 (추워서) 선득거렸다 I felt a chill in the air in the wood.

선들거리다 breeze; blow gently; blow cool and gentle

선들바람 a cool breeze ⇨ 산들바람

선떡 〈설 쪄진 떡〉 a half-done [half-boiled] rice cake

선뜻 〈가볍게〉 lightly; lightheartedly; cheerfully; 〈쾌히〉 readily; willingly; 〈서슴없이〉 without hesitation; 〈즉석에서〉 instantly; at once; offhand; (美) right away; 〈거침없이〉 freely; 〈친절히〉 in a friendly manner
♦선뜻 승낙하다 consent readily; give a ready consent / 돈을 선뜻 빌려주다 lend money with a good grace
▶그는 선뜻 그 일을 떠맡았다 He willingly took part in the work.
▶그는 내 부탁을 선뜻 들어주었다 He was ready and willing to comply with my request.
▶그 계획에는 선뜻 동의할 수가 없다 I cannot readily agree upon the plan.

선뜻하다 clean; smart; vivid; bright; splendid ♦ 선뜻해지다 feel refreshed; feel relieved

선량 善良 goodness
—선량하다 good; virtuous; right ♦ 선량한 사람 a good(-natured) man
▶ 세상의 온갖 유혹을 받고 살면서 선량하기란 어렵다 It is difficult to be good amid the temptation of the world.

선량 選良 〈엘리트〉 an elite; the nation's choice; a representative of the people; 〈국회의원〉 a member of the National Assembly

선령 船齡 the age of a vessel ♦ 선령 10년이 넘은 배 ships over ten years old

선례 先例 1 ⇨ 전례(前例) **2** 〔法〕 prejudication

선로 線路 a railroad [railway, rail] track; a track; a roadway; a (railway) line
♦ 선로를 놓다[부설하다] lay a line [track] / 선로를 건너다 cross a line [track]
▶ 선로에 들어가지 마시오 (게시) Keep off the track.
■—공 a track man —공사 〈부설 공사〉 track-laying; 〈보수 공사〉 track maintenance (work) —표지 a track indicator

선룸 〈일광욕실〉 a sunroom; a sun parlor [parlour]; a solarium (*pl.* ~s, ·ia); 〈베란다식의〉 (美) a sun porch

선류 蘚類 〔植〕 moss

선린 善隣 (being) good neighbors; neighborly friendship; a good-neighbor relationship
■—관계 good neighborly relations (with); relationship of neighborly amity —정책 a good neighbor policy

선망 羨望 envy
▶ 그는 나를 선망의 눈길로 바라보았다 He looked at me with envy. ⇒ He looked enviously at me. ≒ He cast envious glances at me.
▶ 그의 성공을 보고 나는 선망의 염을 금할 수 없었다 I was filled with envy at his success.
▶ 그녀의 미모는 급우들의 선망의 대상이었다 Her beauty was the envy of her classmates.
—선망하다 envy; feel envy 〈at〉; be envious 〈of〉; regard *sb* with envy; look enviously 〈at〉

선매 先賣 an advance sale; selling ahead
—선매하다 sell in advance; sell ahead [beforehand] ■ 입도(立稻)— the sale of a standing rice crop

선매권 先買權 (the right of) preemption
♦ 선매권을 얻다 preempt

선머슴 a mischievous [naughty] boy; a little monkey; a little demon of a child; an urchin; an imp

선명 宣明 proclamation; announcement; declaration; promulgation; enunciation.
—선명하다 announce; proclaim; delare

선명 船名 a ship's name —록(錄) a ship's register book

선명 鮮明 clearness; distinctness; lucidity; vividness —선명하다 clear; clear-cut; sharp-cut; distinct; vivid; sharp; plain

♦ 선명한 색 vivid [bright] colors / 선명한 화상 a clear [distinct] picture / 선명하지 않다 lack clearness; 〈인쇄 등이〉 do not come out well; be dim / 선명하게 clearly; distinctly; vividly / 태도를 선명히 하다 assume a definite attitude; make *one's* attitude clear
▶ 나는 그녀의 얼굴을 선명히 기억하고 있다 I remember her face vividly.
■—도(度) definition; visibility; 〈사진의〉 resolution; 〈텔레비전의〉 distinction —야당 a clear-cut opposition party

선모 旋毛 a hair whirl ⇨ 가마²

선모 腺毛 〔生〕 a tentacle; a glandular hair

선묘 線描 line drawing ⇨ 선화(線畫)

선무 宣撫 placation; pacification —선무하다 placate; pacificate; pacify; win over
▶ 그는 격분한 시민을 선무했다 He placated an outraged citizenry.
■—공작 pacification work [activity] —반 a placation [win over] squad; a pacification unit

선무당 —巫堂 a green [novice] shaman
선무당이 사람 죽인다 (속담) A little learning [knowledge] is a dangerous thing.
선무당이 장구 탓한다 (속담) A bad workman always blames his tools.

선물 先物 1 ⇨ 맏물 **2** 〔經〕 futures
♦ 선물로 팔다 sell for futures delivery; sell forward
■—가격 a forward price; futures quotations —거래 ⇨ 선물매매 —매입 forward buying; purchase of futures —시세 futures quotations; the forward rate —시장 a futures market

선물 膳物 a present; a gift; 〈공물·기증품〉 a tribute; 〈기념품〉 a souvenir
♦ 마음에 드는 선물 an acceptable present [gift] / 좋은 선물 a nice [handsome] present / 선물을 주다 give [make, send] *sb* a present; make a gift 《to *sb*》 / 책을 선물로 주다 present *sb* with some books; present books to *sb*; give [offer] *sb* books as a gift [present] / 선물을 받다 take [accept] a gift; receive a gift 《from *sb*》 / 선물을 보내다 send a gift (over) to *sb*
▶ 그녀에게 생일 선물로 루비 반지를 사주었다 I bought her a ruby ring as [for] a birthday present [gift].
▶ 이 물건은 그에게 좋은 선물이 될 것이다 This article would make a nice [handsome] present for him.
▶ 그것은 너에게 줄 선물이었다 The gift was intended for you.
▶ 멋진 성탄절 선물 고맙습니다 Thank you for the wonderful [lovely, beautiful] Christmas present [gift].
—선물하다 give [make] *sb* a present; make *sb* a present of *sth*; present ♦ 반지를 선물하다 make *sb* a present of a ring
▶ 그의 생일에 무엇을 선물할까? What should I give him for his birthday [as a birthday present]?
■ 생일— a birthday gift [present] 신년[크리스마스]— a New Year's [Christmas] gift 연말— a year-end present 축하— a congratulatory present ■—교환 an exchange of presents —판매점 a souvenir store; a gift shop

선물매매 先物賣買 〔經〕 future trading ◆선물매매를 하다 deal in futures
선미 船尾 the stern ⇨ 고물
선민 選民 〔聖〕 the chosen people [race]; the elect ━사상 the idea of God's elect ━의식 elitism
선바람 (one's) present attire; the outfit one has on
◆선바람으로 just as one is
선박 船舶 a vessel; a ship; a bottom; craft; (총칭) shipping
◆선박의 출입 the movements of shipping / 선박에서 육지로의 통신 ship-to-shore communication / 외국 선박으로 in foreign bottoms
━전시 표준━ a wartime standard ship 안내━vessels [shipping] in port ━검사증 a ship inspection certificate ━국적 증명서 the certificate of a ship's nationality ━등급[적재량] ship's classification [burden] ━등기부 the shipping register ━법 (法) the Ships Act ━사용료 charterage ━세 the shipping tax ━소유자 a shipowner ━업 the shipping industry ━업자 a shipping man; (총칭) the shipping interests ━용 기관[기압계] a marine engine [barometer] ━용품 ship's stores ━입항[출항] 신고 a ship's clearance inward [outward]; a ship's entry [clearance] ━주(株) shippings; shipping stocks ━중개인 a ship broker ━해상 보험 hull insurance ━회사 a shipping company
선반 ━盤 a shelf (pl. shelves); 〈그물・격자 모양의〉 a rack
◆선반 위에 두다[얹다] put [place] sth on a shelf; shelve / 선반을 달다 make [put up] a shelf; fix a shelf (to the wall)
■━받이 〈까치발〉 a bracket; a shelf support
선반 旋盤 〔機〕 a lathe; an engine lathe
◆선반으로 가공하다 lathe / 선반에 걸다 lathe / 자동━ an automatic lathe ━공 a turner; a latheman : 선반공으로 일하다 work on the lathe ━공장 a turnery ━대(臺) a lathe bed ━세공 lathe work; turnery
선발 先發 starting [leaving] in advance; getting [taking] a head start
◆이 기종의 선발 메이커 the maker(s) already producing this type of machine
━선발하다 start [go] in advance (of others); go ahead (of); start first
▶ 어느 쪽 열차가 선발합니까? Which train leaves first?
■━대 an advance party [force, element, contingent] ━투수 〔野〕 a starting pitcher; a starter
선발 選拔 selection; choice; picking out
━선발하다 select; choose; mark out (for); pick out; single out; draft
◆선발된 선수들 the very best players / 선발된 picked; selected
▶ 그는 수많은 응모자 중에서 선발되었다 He was selected from among many candidates. ⇒ He was selected out of (the) many applicants.
■━경기 an elimination match; a tryout ━시험 a selective examination; a selection examination [test] ━위원회 a selection committee ━팀 a picked team; selections; an all-star team
선방 善防 a good defense [(英) defence]
━선방하다 put up a good defense; defend well
선배 先輩 a senior; a superior; an elder; a predecessor; (美口) an old-timer

> 解説 우리말의 「선배」는 같은 학교・근무처 등에 먼저 들어갔던 사람이나 모교를 먼저 졸업한 사람 등을 가리키지만 이 말은 연공 서열의 의식이 강하고 혈연주의적 분위기가 중시되는 한국 사회에서 생긴 독특한 개념이다. 따라서 영어에서는 이에 해당하는 한 단어가 없으므로 문맥에 따라 적절하게 그 내용을 영역할 필요가 있다.

◆대선배 a big senior / 선배티를 내다 pose [give oneself airs] as a senior; assume [put on] an air of seniority
▶ 그는 2년 선배입니다 〈나이가〉 He is two years older than I am [(口) than me, than I]. ⇒ He is two years my senior. ⇒ He is senior to me by two years.
▶ 그는 그 일에서는 나보다 훨씬 선배입니다 He has much more experience on the job than I do.
선법 旋法 〔樂〕 a mode ■장[단]━ a major [minor] mode
선변 ━邊 interest paid monthly
선변 先邊 interest paid in advance (on loan)
선별 選別 sorting; selection; 〈광석의〉 concentration; dressing
━선별하다 sort; select; concentrate; dress
▶ 우리는 많은 작품 중에서 최우수작을 선별했다 We selected the best among [(out) of, from] many works.
■━기 a sorter; a grader; a classifier; a selector; a concentrating [dressing] machine; a concentrator: 우편물 선별기 a mail-sorter ━융자 selective lending
선병 腺病 〔醫〕 scrofulosis; strumosis ◆선병의 lymphatic; scrofulous
■━질 the strumous diathesis; the scrofulous diathesis
선보름 先━ the early half of a month
선복 船腹 1 〈바닥〉 the bottom (of a ship); bottoms
2 〈적재량〉 shipping; tonnage; 〈짐 싣는 곳〉 space; freight space
■━과잉 an excess of bottoms ━부족 the scarcity [shortage] of bottoms [space] ━신청서 an application for space ━예약[할당] space booking [allotment]
선봉 先鋒 the vanguard; the van; the advance guard; the spearhead
◆선봉에 서서 in the van (of the attack on...) / 선봉이 되다 lead the van; spearhead (an operation); become the spearhead of an advance [attack] / 운동의 선봉을 맡다 lead [occupy] the van of a movement
▶ 내가 선봉이 되겠소 Let me lead the van.
선분 線分 〔數〕 a segment

선불 〈설맞은 총알〉 a stray bullet
♦선불 걸다[놓ој] aim a clumsy blow [move] at; be hoist with his own petard / 선불 맞은 호랑이 뛰 듯 〈속담〉 hopping mad; furious

선불 先拂 payment in advance; prepayment; cash before delivery (略 C.B.D.)
♦선불 조건으로 on condition of advance payment
─**선불하다** pay [disburse] in advance; advance 《money》; make an advance; prepay
▶집세를 1개월분 선불했다 I paid the one-month rental in advance.
■우편료— postage prepaid 운임— freight prepaid [included]; carriage prepaid: 나는 운임 선불로 짐을 부쳤다 I sent goods freight prepaid. ■—금 money paid in advance; an amount prepaid; an advance (payment); a prepayment

선비[1] 〈학자〉 a (classical) scholar; a learned man; 〈어질고 순한 사람〉 a man of virtue; a gentleman
♦독학(篤學)의 선비 a scholarly man

선비[2] 〈긴 빗자루〉 a long-handled broom

선비 先妣 one's deceased [late] mother

선사 先史 prehistory ─고고학 prehistoric archaeology ─시대 the prehistoric age: 선사 시대 유적 prehistoric remains ─학 prehistory

선사 善事 1 〈착한 일〉a good work [deed]; a virtuous act
2 〈공양〉 an offering; an oblation
─**선사하다** offer
3 〈선물〉 presentation; giving a present
─**선사하다** give [make, send] sb a present; make a gift 《to sb》; present 《sb with sth》
♦모자를 선사하다 present sb with a hat; present a hat to sb / 선사받다 receive a present
■—품 ⇨ 선물

선사 禪師 〖佛教〗 a Zen priest [master]; an esteemed priest

선산 先山 one's family graveyard; one's ancestral burial ground

선상 扇狀 a fan form [shape] ■—삼각주 a fan delta ─지(地) 〖地質〗 a fan; a alluvial fan: 선상지 퇴적층 fan deposit

선상 船上 ♦선상의[에, 에서] on board (a) ship; on shipboard; on a ship aboard
■—난민 boat people ─생활 life on board [shipboard]; a shipboard life

선생 先生 1 〈교사〉 a teacher; a master; an instructor
♦영어 선생 a teacher of English; an English teacher / 스키 선생 a ski instructor; an instructor in ski
▶요즈음 선생과 학생 사이의 대화가 거의 없다 There is little communication between teachers and students these days.
▶선생님, 그 다음 줄의 뜻을 모르겠습니다 Sir [Madam], I can't understand the meaning of the next line.
2 〈의사〉 a doctor
▶선생님, 제 어머니의 용태는 어떻습니까? How is my mother, doctor?
▶[話]「선생님, 어떻게 하면 좋을까요?」「당분간 외출을 삼가세요」 "What do you advice, doctor?" "For the time being, stay indoors."
3 〈당신〉 you; 〈남자의 경칭〉 Mr.; Sir.
▶민선생은 그것에 대해서 어떻게 생각하십니까? What do you think about that, Mr. Min?
4 〈비꼬는 말로〉 sir; mister
♦평론가 선생 sir critic

선서 宣誓 an oath; parole
♦선서를 어기다 break one's parole
▶대통령은 취임 선서를 했다 The president took the oath of office [was sworn into office].
─**선서하다** swear; take [make, swear] an oath; pledge one's word of honor; lift (up) the hand
♦복종을 선서하다 swear allegiance [fidelity] 《to》/ 선서시키다 administer an oath to sb; attest; swear; put sb on [under] oath / 선서하고 증언하다 give evidence under oath
▶법정에서 그는 오른손을 들고 진실을 말하겠다고 선서했고 In court he raised his right hand and swore [took, made] an oath to tell the truth.
■**선수**— a declaration by (a representative of) the athletes [players] ─문 a written oath ─식 administering of an oath ─증언 a deposition; sworn testimony ─증인 a deponent; a person who testifies on [under] oath; a sworn witness

선선하다 1 〈날씨가〉 (nice and) cool; refreshing
♦선선한 바람 a cool [refreshing] breeze / 선선해 보이는 드레스 a cool-looking dress
▶여기는 선선해서 좋다 It is nice and cool here. ⇌ It is pleasantly cool here.
▶무더운 여름이 가고 선선한 가을이 왔다 The hot summer has gone, and the cool autumn has come.
▶아침 저녁으로 제법 선선해졌다 It has got [has become] much cooler mornings and evenings.
2 〈성격·태도가〉 frank; candid; openhearted; unreserved; brisk; spirited ♦말하는 것이 선선하다 be outspoken

선선히 〈기꺼이〉 readily; willingly; with (a) good grace; cheerfully; 〈솔직히〉 candidly; frankly; openly
♦선선히 승낙하다 readily [willingly] consent 《to it》; give a ready consent 《to》; readily accept 《an invitation》/ 선선히 대답하다 answer frankly / 선선히 부탁을 들어주다 comply with (another's) request with good grace / 돈을 선선히 빌려주다 lend money with a good grace / 자기 잘못을 선선히 인정하다 acknowledge one's fault candidly
▶그는 선선히 그리고 객관적으로 자기의 논거를 설명했다 He presented his arguments frankly and objectively.

선세 先貰 〖法〗 advanced payment of rent; prepaid rent ♦세세를 내다 pay rent in advance; prepay the rent

선셈 先— prepayment; settling accounts in advance ─**선셈하다** prepay; settle accounts in advance

선소리 foolish [silly] talk; nonsense; an absurd remark ♦선소리를 하다 talk nonsense; make an absurd remark

선손 先― 〈선수(先手)〉 forestalling; the initiative; the first move ♦선손(을) 걸다 strike [hit] the first blow / 선손(을) 쓰다 forestall; take [obtain] the initiative
▶ 우리는 선손을 써서 적을 공격했다 We forestalled the enemy. ⇒ We made a preemptive attack against the enemy.
▶ 그는 선손을 써서 그 계획을 실행했다 He took the initiative in carrying out the plan.

선손질 先― striking the first blow ―선손질하다 strike the first blow; start a quarrel [fight]

선손질 후방망이 (속담) He who sows the wind shall reap the whirlwind.

선수 先手 1〈바둑〉 placing the first stone; 〈장기〉 moving first; 〈카드놀이〉 lead ♦선수로 두다 have [make] the first [initial] move
2 ⇨ 선손
♦선수를 쓰다[치다] take [seize, obtain] the initiative (from sb in sth); forestall; anticipate / 선수를 빼앗기다 be forestalled
▶ 선수를 친 것은 내가 아니고 그였다 It was he, not I, that took the initiative.

선수 船首 the bow (⇨ 이물) ■―닻 fore anchor ―부 the eyes; the bows ―장식[상] a figurehead ―흘수 fore draft

선수 選手 a player; an athlete
♦테니스[야구] 선수 a tennis [baseball] player / 수영 선수 a swimmer / 스키 선수 a skier / 높이뛰기 선수 a high-jumper
▶ 그는 어느 팀의 선수지요? What team is he [does he play] on?
■단거리― a sprinter 마라톤[장거리]― a marathon [a long-distance] runner 만능― an all-arounder; an all-rounder 후보― a substitute; (口) a sub; 〈야구의〉 a bench polisher [warmer] ■―단 a team; a squad ―서어 an athletes' oath ―촌 an athletic village: 태릉선수촌 the T'aerŭng Training Center / 선수촌 숙박소 the athletes' hostel

선수권 選手權 a championship; a title; the crown
♦선수권을 획득하다 win [gain, capture] the championship / 선수권을 가지고[보유하고] 있다 hold [retain] the championship / (권투 등에서) 선수권을 방어하다 defend the title / 선수권을 빼앗다 wrest the championship (from) / 선수권을 잃다[상실하다] lose the championship [title] / 선수권을 다투다 contend [play] for the championship; play for the title
■세계― a world [an international] championship [title] 전국― a national championship [title] ―보유자 a (world) champion; a championship holder; a titleholder ―시합 a title match; a title bout ―쟁탈전[대회] a championship series; the championships

선술 仙術 magic arts; 〈불로불사의 방술〉 the secret art of immortality

선술집 a tavern; a (stand-up) bar; a public house; (美) a groggery; (英) a grogshop; (口) a pub; (美) a saloon

선승 先勝 winning the first game [match of series] ―선승하다 win the first match [game]; score the first point

선실 船室 a cabin; 〈특실〉 a stateroom; (총칭) the passenger's quarters
♦1등 선실 a first-class cabin / 2등 선실 a second-class cabin / 3등 선실 the steerage / 선실을 예약하다 reserve a passage [berth]; book a berth
▶ 이 배에는 약 3백개의 선실이 있다 There are about 300 cabins in this ship.
■―배당료 a berth list

선심 善心 1〈착한 마음〉 virtuous mind; virtue; conscience; moral sense
2〈자비심·친절〉 a merciful heart; mercy; benevolence; clemency; kindness; 〈너그러운 마음〉 generosity; liberality
♦선심을 쓰다 have mercy on sb; show mercy [clemency] to sb; do a kindness for sb; do something nice for sb; display one's liberality
▶ 그녀는 친구와 이웃들에게 자그마하나마 수없이 많은 선심을 썼다 She has performed countless small kindnesses for [among] her friends and neighbors.
■―공세 pork-barreling; the use of patronage for political advantage

선심 線審 〈테니스·축구 등에서〉 a linesman

선악 善惡 good and evil [bad]; virtue and vice; goodness and badness; 〈정사(正邪)〉 right and wrong
♦선악을 분간하다 know [can tell] good from evil; discern good from bad; distinguish right from wrong; know the difference between right and wrong
▶ 그것은 선악의 문제가 아니다 It's not a matter of right and wrong.
■―과 (聖) the fruit of the Tree of Knowledge (of Good and Evil)

선약 仙藥 a miraculous [wonderful] medicine [remedy]; the elixir of life; 〈만능약〉 a (universal) panacea; a cure-all; (a) medicine with magical (healing) power

선약 先約 a previous [a prior] engagement [appointment]
♦선약이 있다 have a previous engagement / 선약이 없다 have no previous engagement; be disengaged; be free
▶ 會話 "오늘 저녁 식사에 모시고 싶은데요."「죄송합니다. 오늘 저녁 선약이 있어요」"I'd like to invite you to dinner tonight." "I'm sorry. I have a previous [another] engagement appointment (for) this evening."
▶ 선약이 있어서 그는 그 모임에 갈 수 없습니다 He can't go to the meeting because he has a previous engagement. ⇒ He can't attend the meeting because he is already engaged.

선양 宣揚 enhancement; exaltation ―선양하다 enhance; raise; increase; exalt; heighten
♦국위를 선양하다 enhance the prestige of the country; promote the national glory; enhance national prestige

선어 鮮魚 fresh fish ⇨ 생선

선언 宣言 a declaration; a proclamation; a statement; an announcement; a manifesto 《*pl.* ~(e)s》
♦ 폭탄 선언을 하다 drop [throw] a bombshell; make a bombshell announcement
—선언하다 declare; make a declaration 《of》; pronounce; profess; proclaim; announce
♦ (의장이) 개회를 선언하다 call a meeting to order; announce the opening of a meeting / 중립[독립]을 선언하다 declare *one's* neutrality [independence]
▶ 그는 올림픽의 개회를 선언했다 He declared the Olympic Games (to be) open. ⇌ He declared the opening of the Olympic Games. (▶ declared 대신 announced를 쓰는 것은 잘못)
▶ 마침내 종전이 선언되었다 At last the end of war was proclaimed.
■공동— a joint declaration 독립— the declaration of independence 포츠담— the Potsdam Declaration ■—명령 declaration instruction

선언 選言 〔論〕 disjunction ■—명제(命題) a disjunctive proposition; a disjunction

선언서 宣言書 a (written) declaration; a manifesto 《*pl.* ~(e)s》; a statement ♦ 선언서를 작성하다 draw up a declaration / 선언서를 발표하다 issue [give out] a declaration
■독립— the declaration of independence

선열 先烈 patriotic forefathers; previous martyrs ⇨ 순국— martyred patriots

선영 先塋 *one's* family graveyard ⇨ 선산

선왕 先王 the late [preceding] king

선외 選外 ♦ 선외의 left out of selection [choice]/ 선외가 되다 be left out of selection; be rejected; fail to be accepted
▶ 16명이 선외가 되었다 Sixteen entries were left out of selection [not accepted].

선외가작 選外佳作 honorable mentions; good works left out of selection ♦ 선외가작에 들다 receive honorable mention

선용 善用 good use
—선용하다 〈좋은 일에 쓰다〉 put 《money》 to good use; 〈적절히 잘 이용하다〉 make good use [the best] of 《*one's* knowledge》; turn 《spare time》 to good account; employ 《time》 well [wisely, profitably]
♦ 여가를 선용하다 make good use of *one's* spare time

선웃음 a forced [a feigned, an affected] laugh [smile]; a smirk; a (conscious) simper
♦ 선웃음을 치다 force [affect, feign] a laugh [smile]; smile an affected smile; give a forced smile [laugh]; 〈의례적인〉 put on a diplomatic smile

선원 船員 〈총칭〉 the crew; a ship's company; officers and crew; 〈한 사람〉 one [a member] of the crew [the ship's company]; a crew member; a crewman; a seaman; a mariner; a sailor
♦ 노련한 선원 an old sailor [salt]/ 선원이 되다 become a sailor; follow the sea; go to sea / 선원을 그만두다 quit the sea; jump ship
▶ 그 배에는 많은 선원이 타고 있다 The ship has a large crew.

▶ 그는 선원이 되고 싶어한다 He wants to go to sea [be a sailor].
■고급— a ship's officer; an officer; 〈총칭〉 the quarterdeck 보통— ratings 하급— 〈총칭〉 the forecastle /〈한 사람〉 a sailor; a jack-tar; a jacky; 〈화부〉 a stoker ■—법 〔法〕 the Seamen Act ■—보험 seamen's insurance ■—생활 a sailor's life; seafaring life; sailoring ■—수첩 a seaman's pocket ledger ■—숙박소 a seaman's home

선유 船遊 a boating (excursion) ⇨ 뱃놀이

선율 旋律 (a) melody; a tune
♦ 감미로운[슬픈] 선율 a sweet [a melancholy] melody / 아름다운 선율을 만들어내는 작곡가 a fine melodist / 선율적(인) melodious; tuneful
■대위(對位)— 〔樂〕 a countermelody; a counterpoint ■—법 melodics ■—학 melodics

선의 船醫 a ship's doctor

선의 善意 〈좋은 뜻〉 a favorable sense; 〈좋은 의도〉 good intentions; 〈호의〉 good feeling; good will; 〔法〕 good faith
♦ 선의의 제삼자 a third party (acting) in good faith / 선의의 사람 a man of good will / 선의의 조언 well-meant advice / 선의의 well-meaning 《people》; well-intentioned; well-meant

선의권 先議權 the right to prior deliberation [consideration]
▶ 하원이 예산의 선의권을 가지고 있다 The House of Representatives has the right to debate [deliberate on] the budget first [before the Senate].

선의로 善意— in good faith; with good intent [intentions]
♦ 선의로 한 일 a well-meant[-intentioned] attempt; a well-intended act [deed]/ 선의로 해석하다 take 《it》 in a favorable sense; put a good construction upon
▶ 그의 말을 선의로 해석했다 We took his word as well-intentioned.
▶ 선의로 말했지만 그의 말은 오해를 샀다 He meant well but his words were misunderstood.

선인 先人 〈전대의 사람〉 *one's* predecessors; 〈선구자〉 a forerunner; a pioneer
♦ 선인 미답의 untrodden; unexplored / 선인의 발자취를 더듬다 follow in the footsteps of *one's* predecessors [those who have gone before *one*]

선인 善人 a good [virtuous] man; a goody
♦ 선인과 악인 the good people and the bad; the sheep and the goats; the goodies and the baddies
▶ 선인은 요절한다 The good die young.
▶ 선인도 악인도 똑같이 그를 존경한다 Good and bad alike respect him. (▶대구적(對句的) 표현법에서는 the가 생략됨)

선인 善因 〔佛敎〕 a good cause ▶ 선인 선과(善果) Sow virtue, and the harvest will be virtue. ⇌ As you sow, so shall you reap. ⇌ Good deeds bear good fruit.

선인장 仙人掌 〔植〕 a cactus 《*pl.* ~es, -ti》
♦ 선인장 가시 a cactus needle / 부채선인장 an

opuntia

선일 〈서서하는 일〉 a job which requires one to stand; a stand-up task; working on one's feet

선임 先任 〈전임〉 seniority; 〈전임자〉 a elder; a predecessor ◆ 선임의 senior; elder
▶ 승진은 선임순으로 행해진다 Promotion goes by seniority.
■ —권 〔勞〕 the seniority right —자 a senior (member) —장교 a senior officer

선임 船賃 boat fare ⇨ 뱃삯

선임 選任 〈선출〉 election; 〈임용〉 appointment; assignment; 〈지명〉 nomination
◆ 변호인의 선임 designation of counsels —선임하다 select and appoint; elect; assign [nominate] 《sb to a post》 ◆ 의장에 선임되다 be elected (to be) chairman

선입감 先入感 a preconception ⇨ 선입관
선입견 先入見 a preconception ⇨ 선입관
선입관 先入觀 a preconception; a preoccupation; a prepossession; 〈편견〉 a prejudice; a bias
◆ 선입관을 가지다 have a preconceived idea [opinion]; be prepossessed [preoccupied] 《with an idea》; be prejudiced [biased]/ 선입관을 버리다 divest oneself of prejudice; get rid of one's prejudice [preconceived notion] 《against》/ 아무에게 불리한[유리한] 선입관을 가지고 있다 be biased against [in favor of] sb

선잠 a light [short] sleep; a doze; a catnap; a nap; slumber; dogsleep; a drowse ◆ 선잠을 자다 have a light [bad, short] sleep; doze; slumber; drowse
▶ 나는 책을 읽다가 선잠을 잤다 I dozed over a book.
▶ 나는 잠깐 선잠을 자는 사이에 지갑을 도둑 맞았다 I had my wallet stolen while I was dozing for a while.

선장 船長 a (ship's, sea) captain; the master (of a ship); a master mariner; a commander; 〈작은 상선·어선 등의〉 a skipper; 〈연락선의〉 a ferry master
■ —면허증 a master's license —실 a captain's cabin [room] —직 mastership; captaincy

선장 船匠 〈배목수〉 a ship carpenter; a shipwright; a ship builder

선재 船材 (ship-building) timber [lumber]

선저 船底 the bottom of a ship
▶ 선저에는 바닥짐 밖에 없었다 The ship was in ballast.
▶ 선저가 파손되었다 The ship sustained damage to her bottom.
■ —도료 bottom paint

선적 船積 〈발송〉 shipment; shipping; 〈적재〉 loading; lading
—선적하다 ship 《a cargo》; load 《a ship》; lade 《a ship with cargo》; make a shipment; ship goods
▶ 그들은 찰스턴에서 목화를 선적했다 They loaded the ship with cotton at Charleston.
▶ 그 항구에서 대량의 목재가 선적된다 A large amount of timber is shipped (out) from that port.
■ 부분— part [partial] shipment ■ —가격 a free on board price; an F.O.B. price —계약 a shipment [loading] contract —대리인 shipping agent —불 cash on shipment (略 C.O.S.) —비용 shipping expenses [charges] —서류 shipping documents [papers] —송장 (送狀) a shipping invoice —안내서 a shipping note —완료 completion of shipment —요청서 shipping application —인 a shipper —증서 shipping certificate —지시서 a shipping order —통지서 an advice of shipment; a shipping advice —항 a port of loading [lading, shipping, shipment]; a loading [shipping] port —화물 cargo; shipping goods

선적 船籍 the nationality of a ship; a ship's flag
◆ 선적 불명의 선박 a vessel of unknown nationality [identity]/ 한국 선적의 배 a ship of Korean nationality [registry]/ 선적을 등록하다 register a ship
▶ 이 배는 한국 선적을 갖고 있다 This ship flies the Korean flag.
■ —기호 a nationality mark —증명 a certificate of (a ship's) nationality —항 the port of registry; the home port

선전 宣傳 〈정부·단체 등에 의한〉 propaganda (▶ 보통 나쁜 뜻이 따름); 〈널리 알리기 위한〉 publicity; propagation; 〈광고〉 advertisement (▶ 특히 라디오·텔레비전에 의한 선전은 a commercial이라고 함); an advertising campaign; a buildup
◆ 맹렬한 선전 intense propaganda; a propaganda [publicity] barrage / 선전에 넘어가다 swallow the propaganda / 선전을 개시하다 institute [launch] a propaganda / 선전 활동을 하다 carry on a publicity [a propaganda] campaign 《for》
▶ 선전은 대단한 효과가 있었다 The advertisement had a great effect.
▶ 선전이 빈약했기 때문에 극장의 관객이 적었다 Because of poor [bad] publicity, there was a small [poor] attendance at the theater.
▶ 그는 선전을 잘한다 He is good at publicity.
—선전하다 propagate; publicize; give publicity (to); propagandize; conduct [make] propaganda; disseminate; 〈광고하다〉 advertise; give publicity (to); give a (publicity) buildup (to); (口) sell
◆ 야단스럽게 선전하다 make much propaganda (of); propagandize [advertise] extensively; carry on [out] an active [a vigorous] propaganda; publicize insistently; (口) plug / 신인 가수를 선전하여 스타를 만들다 build up a new singer to stardom / 대대적으로 선전하다 carry on propaganda on a large scale; give a big buildup (to)
▶ 우리 회사에서는 신제품을 대대적으로 선전하고 있다 We are advertising our new product heavily.
▶ 이 워드프로세서는 지금 텔레비전에서 한창 선전되고 있다 This word processor is being advertised extensively on television now.
■ 과대— an exaggerated [extravagant] advertisement; a dazzling advertisement; a puff ■ —가치 propaganda [promotional] val-

ue —공세 propaganda offensive; a propaganda [an advertising] onslaught; a propaganda attack —공작 propaganda efforts [maneuvers]; a propaganda buildup —극 a propaganda drama —기관 a propaganda organ [medium]; a propaganda machinery [machine]; a medium of publicity —문구 〈상품의〉 sales message; 〈광고 문안〉 copy —방송 an advertisement broadcast; a commercial —부 the publicity department —부장 the publicity manager —비 advertising [publicity] expenses —사진 a promotion picture —업자 a publicity agent —영화 a propaganda film [picture] —운동 a propaganda [publicity] campaign —원 a public relations man; a publicity man —전 a propaganda war [campaign, battle, contest, struggle]; propaganda warfare; an advertising [a publicity] campaign; a public relations battle —전문가 an expert propagandist —지 〈신문〉 a propagandist sheet —차 an advertising van; a loudspeaker car; a sound truck [car] —포스터 a propaganda [publicity] poster —활동 propaganda activity —효과 (a) propaganda effect; a propaganda impact

선전 善戰 a good fight [battle] —선전하다 〈잘 싸우다〉 fight well [bravely, admirably]; fight a good fight [battle]; put up [make] a good fight
▶ 우리는 선전한 보람도 없이 졌다 Although we fought a very good fight, we were defeated.

선전포고 宣戰布告 a declaration [proclamation] of war —선전포고하다 make a declaration [proclamation] of war 《against》; declare [proclaim] war 《on, against》
◆ 영국과 프랑스는 1939년 9월 독일에 대하여 선전포고했다 Great Britain and France declared war on [against] Germany on September 1939.

선점 先占 prior occupation; occupancy —선점하다 preoccupy ▪ —권자 an occupant —취득 acquisition by occupancy

선정 善政 good [wise] government [administration]; 〈올바른 통치〉 just rule ◆ 선정을 베풀다 govern [rule] the country well [wisely]

선정 煽情 ◆ 선정적인 그림[포스터] a suggestive picture [poster] / 선정적인 inflammatory; voluptuous; sultry; suggestive; lascivious; lustful; lewd; sensational; libidinous
▶ 그 잡지는 선정적인 기사나 소설을 인기물로 하고 있다 The magazine features sensational articles and suggestive novels.
—소설 a sultry novel; a suggestive story

선정 選定 selection; choice —선정하다 〈조직적으로 고르다〉 select; 〈자기 의사대로 고르다〉 choose; make a selection [choice] 《of》
◆ 현명하게 선정하다 make a wise selection

선제 先制 a head start ◆ 선제점을 올리다 score first points [runs]

선제공격 先制攻擊 a containment offensive; 〈권투 등의〉 a leadoff attack; 〈핵전쟁에서의〉 a preemptive strike [unclear attack]
◆ 선제공격을 가하다 strike 《the enemy》 first [before he goes into action]; carry out a preemptive strike against 《the enemy's nuclear installations》; seize [go on] the offensive first

선조 先祖 an ancestor; a forefather; a progenitor; a predecessor

解說 *ancestor*는 보통 조부모보다 이전의 조상. ***forefather***는 먼 조상으로 주로 남성, 또 민족·국가의 선조도 의미한다. 둘 다 보통 복수형으로 쓰인다 : the forefathers of the village 그 부락의 선조

◆ 선조 대대의 집과 터 *one's* ancestral estate / 선조의 묘 a family tomb / 선조 전래의 보물 a (family) heirloom
▶ 선조의 가르침을 잊지 마라 Remember what our forefathers said.

선조 線條 a filament ⇨ 필라멘트
선조총 旋條銃 a rifle
선종 禪宗 the Zen sect; Zen (Buddhism)
◆ 선종의 승려 a Zen priest
선주 船主 a shipowner ▪ —기 a house flag —협회 a shipowners' association
선줄 〔鑛〕〈세로 박힌 광맥〉 a vertical [lengthwise] vein of ore; a lengthwise mineral vein
선지 fresh animal blood; blood from a slaughtered animal
▪ —피 fresh blood : 코에서 선지피가 흐르다 blood gushes from the nose 선짓국 《make》 ox-blood soup 선짓덩이 clotted blood
선지자 先知者 a prophet; 〈여자〉 a prophetess; a predictor
선진 先陣 the van (of an army); the advance guard; the vanguard; 〈선초선〉 a scouting line
◆ 선진을 맡다 lead the van
선진 先進 1 〈선배〉 a senior; a superior; an elder; a predecessor; a progenitor; (ロ) an old-timer; 〈선구자〉 a pioneer; a precursor; a farsighted leader; a pathfinder
2 〈앞서 있는 일〉 advance; advancement
선진국 先進國 an advanced nation [country]; 〈공업선진국〉 an industrialized nation
▪ —수뇌회의 the Summit Conference of the Industrialized Nations
선집 選集 a selection [an anthology] 《of poems》; selected works
◆ 선집으로 엮다 anthologize 《Korean poetry》
▪ 시문— a garland
선착 先着 1 〈먼저 도착함〉 first arrival
◆ 선착순으로 in the order of arrival; 〈신청서 등〉 in the order of receipt; on a first-come-first-served basis
▶ 선착순으로 한 줄로 서 주세요 Please form a line in the order of your arrivals.
▶ 선착순 2,000명에게 초대권을 드립니다 Complimentary tickets will be given to the first two thousand persons.
—선착하다 arrive [come] first [beforehand]
2 〈먼저 착수〉 prior [first] start; undertaking first; taking the first hand
—선착하다 start [undertake] first; set about beforehand [in advance]
3 〈선착편〉 the initiative; getting the first chance

선착장

—**선착하다** take the initiative; forestall
—**자** the first comer; the first to arrive
선착장 船着場 a port; a harbor (➤ port는 인공적, harbor는 자연을 이용한 항구); 〈부두〉 a wharf (*pl.* ~s, wharves)
선창 先唱 leading [the lead] ((in singing)); (비유) advocacy; initiation
▶ 김선생의 선창으로 만세 삼창을 했다 Three cheers were given at the call [instance] of Mr. Kim. ⇌ They gave three cheers led by Mr. Kim.
—**선창하다** beat time; lead the song [chorus, singing]; (비유) play first violin; advance [introduce] ((a new doctrine)); advocate; initiate
♦ 만세를 선창하다 lead a cheer; lead in cheering / 건배를 선창하다 propose [drink] a toast
■ —**자** a chorus leader; 〈주창자〉 a leader; an advocate; 〈파업 등의〉 a ringleader; 〈응원의〉 a head rooter
선창 船窓 a cabin window; a porthole
선창 船艙 a (landing) pier; 〈작은〉 a jetty; 〈부두〉 a wharf (*pl.* ~s, wharves); a quay; 〈부잔교〉 a landing stage; a floating pier
♦ 배를 선창에 대다 bring a ship alongside the pier / 아무를 선창까지 전송하다 see *sb* off at the pier
▶ 배가 선창에 닿았다 The ship docked at the pier.
■ —**사용료** pier dues; pierage; wharfage; quayage
선처 善處 amicable [adequate] management; proper dealing
—**선처하다** make the best of; act with prudence; deal adequately [wisely] with ((an adverse situation)); deal with *sth* as *one* thinks fit
♦ 그 건을 선처하다 〈적당한 조치를 취하다〉 take proper measures about the matter / 문제를 선처하다 〈신중히 대처하다〉 deal with the problem prudently
▶ 선처해 주시기 바랍니다 I beg you will manage it all right.
▶ 여러분의 요청에 대해서는 선처할 생각입니다 We'll give your request due consideration.
▶ 〔會話〕「주문한 것과 다른 물건이 배달되었습니다」「대단히 죄송합니다. 곧 선처하겠습니다」"I received something different from what I ordered." "I'm very sorry. We'll take care of that as soon as we can."
선천론 先天論 〔哲〕 nativism; apriorism
■ —**자** a nativist
선천병 先天病 a congenital [hereditary, connate] disease
선천성 先天性 apriority; inbornness; innateness; inherence ■ —**매독** congenital [hereditary] syphilis
선천적 先天的 native; inborn; 〈본래 갖추어진〉 innate; 〈질환 등이〉 congenital; connate; inherent; 〈타고난〉 natural; 〈유전적〉 hereditary; inherited; 〔哲〕 a priori
♦ 선천적 백치 a congenital idiot; a natural fool / 선천적인 음악의 재능 a natural ability in music; an innate [an inborn] talent for music / 선천적인 장애 a congenital disorder / 선천적으로 심장에 결함이 있는 아이 a child with congenital heart defects / 선천적으로 by nature; naturally; innately; inherently; congenitally
▶ 그는 선천적인 시인이다 He is a born poet. ⇌ He is born a poet.
선철 先哲 an ancient sage [worthy man]; a wise [learned] man of the past; a philosopher of ancient times; (총칭) the sages of old
선철 銑鐵 pig iron
선체 船體 the hull; 〈배〉 a ship; the body of a ship
선출 選出 election; choice
—**선출하다** elect; 〈국회의원을〉 return
♦ 대구에서 선출되다 be elected from [returned for] Taegu
▶ 이 도시의 사람들은 그를 시장으로 선출했다 The townspeople elected him mayor.
▶ 그녀는 위원의 한 사람으로 선출됐다 She was selected as a member of the committee.
선충 線蟲 〔動〕 an eelworm; a nematode
■ —**구제약** a nematocide; nemacide —**류** Nematoda; the nematodes —**학** nematology
선취 先取 taking first; preoccupation; preoccupancy
—**선취하다** take first; preempt; preoccupy
♦ 1점을 선취하다 score the first one point of the game; 〈야구에서〉 score one run first
▶ 우리는 2회초에 3점 선취했다 We were the first to score three runs in the first half of the second inning.
선취점 先取點 the point(s) scored first; 〈야구에서〉 runs scored first
♦ 선취점을 올리다 score first runs [points]
선취 특권 先取特權 a preferential [prior, priority] right; (the right of) priority; priority of claim; a (prior) lien
♦ 선취 특권이 있는 preferential; preferred / 선취 특권을 가지다 have the prior right ((to)); have a priority right ((over)); have a prior lien ((on))
■ —**자[보유자]** a lien holder; a holder of a preferential right
선측 船側 the side of a ship; a ship's side
■ —**인도** 〈적하〉 free alongside (ship) (略 F.A.S.); 〈양륙〉 ex ship
선친 先親 my deceased [late] father
선태 蘚苔 〔植〕 moss(es) ⇨ 이끼¹
■ —**류[식물]** Bryophyta —**학** bryology —**학자** a bryologist
선택 選擇 selection; choice; option; selectivity
♦ 선택의 자유 the liberty [freedom] of choice / 양서의 선택 the choice of good books / 양복에 맞는 넥타이의 선택 the selection of a tie to go with a suit / 직업의 선택을 잘못하다 make a mistake in the choice of *one's* career; make a wrong [a bad] choice of *one's* career
▶ 선택은 너에게 맡긴다 The choice lies with you. ⇌ You have a free choice.
—**선택하다** select; choose; pick up; make a choice
♦ 잘못 선택하다 make a bad choice; choose the wrong thing / 잘 선택하다 make a good

choice / 선택하기가 어렵다 find difficulty in one's choice
▶이 재료 중에서 자유로이 선택할 수 있습니다 You can choose freely from [among, from among, out of] these materials. (▶You have a free choice from... 라고도 함)
■ㅡ스위치 a selective switch ㅡ채널 a selector channel ㅡ투표 preferential voting ㅡ항로 〔海〕 an alternative route

선택과목 選擇科目 〈美〉 an elective (subject); 〈英〉 an optional (subject)

선택권 選擇權 option; the right of choice
◆선택권이 있다 have the right of choice; have the [one's] pick 《of》 / 선택권을 포기하다 waive an option

선팽창 線膨脹 〔物〕 linear expansion ■ㅡ률 〔계수〕 the coefficient of linear expansion; linear expansion cofficient

선편 船便 〈배편〉 shipping service; 〈우편물〉 surface mail ◆선편으로 by ship [steamer, water, sea] / 선편으로 화물을 보내다 send goods by ship [sea, water]

선평 選評 selection and criticism [commentation] ㅡ선평하다 select and criticize [comment on] ◆시를 선평하다 select and comment on [upon] poems

선포 宣布 promulgation; proclamation
ㅡ선포하다 proclaim; promulgate; issue a proclamation; make public; announce; publicize; make promulgation of
◆계엄령을 선포하다 proclaim martial law

선풍 旋風 a whirlwind; 〈口〉 a cyclone; a cyclonic wind; a tornado (*pl*. ~(e)s); 〈美〉 a twister
◆선풍의 중심 the whirlwind center / 선풍에 휘말려 올라가다 be caught up in a whirlwind / 선풍을 일으키다 〈인기면에서〉 create a great sensation; 〈口〉 make [cut] a splash
▶선풍이 일었다 There arose a whirlwind.
ㅡ검거 a wholesale [mass] arrest; a sweeping roundup

선풍기 扇風機 an electric fan; a fan; 〈천장의〉 a ceiling [an overhead] fan; a motor fan
◆선풍기 바람 the draft [breeze] from an electric fan / 선풍기를 틀다 set an electric fan in motion; start [turn on, switch on] an electric fan; have an electric fan going / 선풍기를 끄다 turn [switch] off an electric fan
▶선풍기를 틀어주세요 Please start [turn on] the (electric) fan.
▶그 선풍기를 이 쪽으로 돌려 주세요 Please turn the fan this way.

선하 船荷 a ship's cargo ⇨ 선화(船貨)

선하다 vivid; fresh《before one's eyes》; graphic; distinct
◆눈에 선하다 be fresh in one's memory; live vividly in one's memory
▶그 광경은 지금도 눈에 선하다 I vividly recall the scene. ⇌ I remember the scene distinctly.
▶돌아가신 어머니의 인자한 모습이 아직도 눈에 선하다 My dead mother's benign image is still fresh in my mind.
▶그 교통 사고는 아직도 눈에 선하다 The traffic accident is still vivid in my memory.

선하다 善ㅡ good ⇨ 착하다

선하중 線荷重 lane load

선하품 〈억지의〉 a slight yawn; a forced yawn; 〈체했을 때의〉 a yawn caused by indigestion
▶나는 선하품을 참으려고 했다 I tried to stifle [suppress] a yawn. ⇌ I tried to stop myself from yawning.
ㅡ선하품하다 yawn slightly; force a yawn

선학 禪學 the dogmatics of Zen Buddhism; the doctrine of the Zen sect

선행 先行 precedence; going first; walking ahead 《of》
ㅡ선행하다 precede; go [walk] ahead 《of》; lead
▶선행하던 차가 고장이 났다 The car (which was) ahead of ours broke down.
▶그의 생각은 시대에 선행하고 있다 His ideas are ahead of the times.
■ㅡ권 〈도로 교통의〉《have, yield》 the right of way ㅡ사 〔文法〕 an antecedent ㅡ조건 a condition precedent; an essential prerequisite

선행 善行 good conduct; a good deed
◆선행을 쌓다 keep on doing good (deeds) / 선행을 표창하다 recognize [show appreciation of] sb's good conduct; reward sb in recognition of his good conduct
▶그녀는 선행으로 표창되었다 She was commended for her good deed.
■ㅡ상 a prize for good conduct

선향 線香 a stick of incense; a joss [an incense] stick ◆선향을 피우다 burn incense / 선향을 올리다 offer incense sticks

선험 先驗 ■ㅡ론 〔哲〕 transcendentalism ㅡ철학 transcendental philosophy; transcendentalism; metempirics

선험적 先驗的 〔哲〕 transcendental; (라) a priori ■ㅡ인식 transcendental cognition ㅡ확률 a priori probability

선헤엄 treading water ◆선헤엄을 치다 tread water

선현 先賢 an ancient sage ⇨ 선철(先哲)

선혈 鮮血 fresh blood; lifeblood
▶그 장교는 선혈이 낭자하였다 The officer was dripping with blood. ⇌ The officer's body was covered [drenched] with blood. ⇌ Blood was flowing [trickling down] from his wound.

선형 扇形 〈부채꼴〉 a fan shape; a sector
ㅡ톱니바퀴 a segment [sector] gear

선형 船型 〈배의 형상〉 the type of a ship [vessel]; 〈모형〉 a model of a ship

선형동물 線形動物 a nemathelminth

선호 選好 preference
◆남아 선호 사상 a notion of preferring a son to a daughter
ㅡ선호하다 prefer《A to B》; choose《A rather than B, A over B》
■ㅡ유동성ㅡ 〔經〕 liquidity preference

선홍색 鮮紅色 scarlet

선화 船貨 a (ship's) cargo (*pl*. ~es, ~s); a lading; a loading; a freight; freightage
◆선화를 싣다[부리다] ship [discharge] cargo; load [unload] a ship

선화
■미착— cargo [load] afloat ■—주(主) the shipper
선화 線畫 〈그림〉 a line drawing; 〈그리는 방법〉 line [lineal] drawing; line-work
♦선화로 그린 풍경으로 a line-drawing landscape ■—제판 line engraving; linecut
선화 증권 船貨證券 a bill of lading (略 B/L)
♦선화 증권을 발행하다 issue a bill of lading ■수입[수출]— an import [export] B/L
선화지 仙花紙 reclaimed paper
선회 旋回 revolution; turning; rotation; circling; gyration; gyre; evolution
—선회하다 turn; revolve; rotate; circle round; whirl [swing] round; wheel; gyrate
▶ 새가 언덕 위를 선회하고 있었다 A bird was circling over the hill.
▶ 그 비행기는 비행장 위를 선회하고 있었다 The airplane was circling over the airport.
▶ 우리들 배는 왼쪽으로 선회하였다 Our boat made a turn to the left.
■—비행 (make) a circular [circuitous] flight —운동 a turning movement —축 a pivot —포 a swivel [pivot] gun
선후 先後 〈전후〉 front and rear; 〈시종〉 beginning and end; 〈순서〉 order; sequence
♦선후를 잘 생각하다 be prudent; think of [reflect on] the consequences / 선후를 생각해서 말을 하다 think carefully before one speaks; weigh one's words
▶ 말의 선후가 바뀌었습니다마는 I should have said this first, but....
▶ 선후가 뒤바뀌었다 The order is inverted [reversed].
■—관계 〈글의〉 the context —당착 self-contradiction —도착 reversing the proper order; putting the cart before the horse
선후(지)책 善後(之)策 a remedial [relief] measure; a countermeasure; remedies
♦선후지책을 강구하다 devise [work out] remedial measures; consider the best course [how best] to deal with the situation; resort to an expedient; make the best of a bad bargain
선히 vividly; freshly; graphically
▶ 그녀의 모습이 선히 떠올랐다 I had the memory of her visage recalled with the vividness of real life.
▶ 그의 풀죽은 표정이 다시 눈에 선히 떠올랐다 His dejected expression rose again in my mind.
섣달 the twelfth lunar month; December (略 Dec.) ■—그믐 New Year's Eve; the last day of the year
섣부르다 〈부주의하다〉 careless; thoughtless; 〈경솔하다〉 rash; hasty; (美) brash; 〈어설프다〉 frivolous; awkward; clumsy; unskillful; tactless
▶ 그는 아주 섣부르다 He is so careless. ⇒ (口) He is such a scatterbrain. ⇒ He behaves carelessly.
▶ 섣부른 말 하지 마라 Be careful what you say. ⇒ Don't say anything careless.
섣불리 〈부주의하게〉 tactlessly; carelessly; thoughtlessly; heedlessly; rashly; hastily; 〈어설프게〉 awkwardly; clumsily
▶ 그는 섣불리 남의 이야기를 믿어버렸다 He imprudently believed what they said.
▶ 자네 장래에 대해서 섣불리 결정하지 말게 Don't make a rash decision on your future.
설 〈초하루〉 New Year's Day; the first day of the year; 〈정초〉 the New Year (season)
♦설 음식 the dishes for the New Year / 설 잔치 a New Year banquet [party] / 설 휴가 the New Year holidays [(美) vacation] / 설에 on New Year's Day / 설을 쇠다 observe New Year's Day; celebrate the New Year
■양력— solar New Year's Day 음력— lunar New Year's Day
설 說 1 〈의견〉 an opinion; a view; 〈학설〉 a theory; a doctrine
♦자기 설을 고집하다 adhere [stick] to one's opinion [views]
▶ 그 기원에 대해서는 여러가지 설이 있다 As to its origin, opinions differ.
▶ 거기에는 여러가지 설이 있다 There are a lot of different opinions about it.
2 〈풍설〉 a rumor; a report
▶ 그녀가 이혼했다는 설이 있다 They say [There is a rumor] that she has gotten a divorce.
설- half-done; not enough; insufficient
♦설익은 half-cooked[-done, -boiled]; underdone / 설구운 고기 underdone meat / 설구워진 빵 half-baked bread
설거지 dishwashing; (英) washing-up; kitchen work; washup
—설거지하다 do the dishes [washing-up]; wash the dishes; wash up
■—물 dishwater —통 a washing-up bowl; a (kitchen) sink
설겅거리다 be half-cooked and indigestible
설경 雪景 a snow scene [view]; a snowscape
설계 設計 a plan; a design
♦생활[인생]의 설계 life planning / 차의 설계 the design of a car / 설계가 잘된[잘못된] 집 a well-planned [an ill-planned] house / 설계 중이다 be in the planning [design] stage; be under design; be on the drawing board
▶ 이 호텔은 라이트씨의 설계다 This hotel was designed by Mr. Wright. ⇒ Mr. Wright designed this hotel.
—설계하다 plan; design; project; make a plan 《for》; work out a design 《for》; draw up a plan; 〈배치하다〉 lay out
♦정원을 설계하다 lay out [design] a garden / 교회를 설계하다 plan [make a plan for] a church
■도시— city planning ■—도 a plan (for a building); a blueprint; a design drawing —명세서 design specifications —자 a designer; a planner
설계 雪溪 a snowy [snow-covered] valley [ravine]
설교 說敎 1 〈교회의〉 a sermon; preaching
♦설교를 듣다 hear [listen to] a sermon / 가두 설교를 하다 preach on the streets
—설교하다 〈목사 등이〉 preach; deliver [give] sb a sermon

♦ 청중에게 성경에 대해 설교하다 preach to the audience on [about] the Bible
2 〈훈계〉 a lecture; a moralizing discourse [lecture]; 〈잔소리〉 scolding; a homily
♦ 설교를 듣다 be given [get, receive] a scolding; (口) catch it
▶ 나는 거짓말을 해서 선생님께 호되게 설교를 들었다 I had a severe [long] lecture from my teacher for lying.
—설교하다 lecture; scold; give *sb* a scolding; admonish *sb* 《for *sth*》
▶ 나는 그에게 얌전히 굴라고 설교했다 I gave him a scolding [scolded him, lectured him] on his bad manners.
◆ 순회— a preaching tour ■—단 〈강단〉 a pulpit —자 a preacher

설날 New Year's Day; the first of the year
♦ 설날에 on New Year's Day

설다¹ **1**【덜 익다】〈밥 등이〉 be half-cooked; be half-boiled; be underdone; 〈과일 등이〉 be unripe; 〈술 등이〉 be not thoroughly fermented; 〈김치 등이〉 be not fully pickled
♦ 선 과일 unripe fruits / 선 밥 half-boiled [undercooked] rice
2 〈잠이〉 be insufficient; be short of
▶ 나는 잠이 설어서 몸이 좋지 않았다 I felt unwell from want [lack] of sleep.

설다² **1** 〈서투르다〉 unfamiliar; inexperienced; green ♦ 낯이 선 사람 a stranger / 낯이 설다 be strange; be unfamiliar **2** ⇨ 서럽다

설대 〈담배 설대〉 a bamboo pipestem

설득 persuasion
—설득하다 persuade; prevail on [upon]; talk *sb* into doing; talk *sb* over [round]
▶ 오래 이야기한 끝에 나는 마침내 그를 설득했다 I argued him down finally after a long talk.
▶ 그를 설득하여 내 제안을 받아들이게 했다 I reasoned him into accepting my proposal.
▶ 나는 그를 설득해서 사직하지 않게 했다 I talked him out of resigning.
■—술 persuasive art

설득력 說得力 persuasive [reasoning] power; persuasiveness ♦ 설득력 있게 말하다 speak convincingly ▶ 그의 문장은 매우 설득력이 있다 His writing is very persuasive [convincing].

설렁거리다 blow gently [softly]; breeze
▶ 가을바람이 설렁거리고 있다 An autumn breeze is blowing softly. ⇌ There is a gentle autumn breeze.

설렁설렁 gently; softly

설렁줄 a bell under the eaves with a cord

설렁탕 —湯 *sŏllŏngt'ang*; beef bone and internals soup and rice; meat and rice soup

설레다 1 〈가슴이〉 throb; beat high; pound; be [get, feel] excited; thrilled
▶ 나는 기쁨으로 가슴이 설렜다 I felt my heart beating with joy.
▶ 그녀는 흥분으로 가슴이 설렜다 Her heart pounded [throbbed] with excitement.
▶ 그는 해외여행을 간다는 생각에 가슴이 설렜다 He felt excited at the thought of going abroad.
2 〈서성대다〉 be restless; move about uneasily

설레설레 ♦ 고개를 설레설레 흔들다 shake [wag] *one's* head
▶ 개가 꼬리를 설레설레 흔든다 The dog wags its tail.
▶ 그녀는 머리를 설레설레 흔들며 싫다고 했다 She shook her head and said no.

설령 設令 〈설사〉 even if [though]; though; although; supposing that...; however
♦ 설령 그것이 정말이라 하더라도 granting it to be true; supposing that it is true; granted it is true / 설령 어떠한 일이 생기더라도 whatever may happen; come what may
▶ 설령 비가 와도 간다 I'll go even if [though] it rains.
▶ 설령 그가 아주 좋은 사람일지라도 나는 그를 믿지는 못한다 He looks like a very nice person. Even so I don't really trust him.

설립 設立 establishment; foundation; organization; institution; setting-up
▶ 그 회사는 설립 50년이 된다 The company has been in existence for fifty years.
—설립하다 establish; found; institute; set up; organize; incorporate
♦ 사립학교를 설립하다 found [establish, set up] a private school / 신체장애자 협회를 설립하다 institute a society for the physically handicapped
▶ 광복 후 한국에는 많은 대학이 설립되었다 Many colleges and universities were founded in Korea after the restoration of independence.
■—등기 registration of incorporation —발기인 a promoter —비용 organization expenses —위원회 an establishment committee —자 the founder; the institutor; the organizer —절차 〈회사의〉 formalities of incorporation —취지서 a prospectus

설마 surely (not); (not) really; (not) possibly; (not) by any possibility; it is not [least] likely 《that...》; by no means
▶ 설마 그럴라구 (Not) really! ⇌ You don't say (so)! ⇌ That's impossible! ⇌ You must be joking [kidding]!
▶ 설마 그가 그랬을라구 He can't have done such a thing.
▶ 설마 그런 사람을 믿지는 않으시겠죠? Surely you don't believe such a fellow! ⇌ You don't believe such a fellow, surely.
▶ 會話 「그가 어제 교통사고로 죽었어」「설마 그럴리가」 "He was killed in a traffic accident yesterday." "No kidding!" ⇌ "No joking." ⇌ "I don't believe it!" ⇌ "Oh, no!"

설명 說明 (an) explanation; an account; exposition; illustration; (a) description
♦ 설명을 요구하다 demand an explanation 《of》 / 설명이 필요치 않다 be self-explanatory; be self-evident; need no explanation; tell its own tale / 알기쉬운[충분한, 설득력 있는] 설명을 하다 give an intelligible [a full, a convincing] explanation
—설명하다 explain; give an explanation 《of》; account 《for》; give [render] an account 《of》;

describe; illustrate; tell; 〈대략을〉 outline
♦설명할 수 있는 explainable; explicable / 설명할 수 없는 unexplainable; inexplicable / 대충 설명하다 explain roughly [briefly]; give a brief explanation / 자세히 설명하다 explain at length [at large, in details]; dwell on
▶나는 그에게 그 문장의 뜻을 설명했다 I explained to him the meaning of the sentence. ⇌ I explained to him what the meaning of the sentence was.
▶그는 그것을 도면을 그려서 설명했다 He illustrated it with [by drawing] diagrams.
▶이게 어떻게 된 일인지 설명해 주시오 Can you tell me in brief what this is all about?
■─도 a diagram; an illustration ─의 an explanatory note; an explanation; 〈기계 조작 등의〉 an operating manual; an instruction book; operating instructions ─어 the predicate (of a sentence) ─자 an explainer; an expositor; 〈학설 등의〉 an exponent

설문 設問 a question ⇨ 다음 설문에 답하시오 Answer the following questions.
─설문하다 pose a question

설법 說法 〔佛敎〕 a Buddhist sermon; preaching ─설법하다 preach; preach [deliver] a Buddhist sermon

설복 說伏 persuasion ⇨ 설득(說得)

설봉 舌鋒 ▶그는 날카로운 설봉으로 그 사고에 대한 내 책임을 따졌다 He blamed me sharply for the accident.

설비 設備 〈비품·기계〉 equipment; provision; installation; arrangements; conveniences; 〈시설〉 facilities; 〈숙박·수용 등의〉 accommodation(s)
♦현대적 설비의 공장 a factory with modern equipment / 잘된 사무실 a well-equipped[-furnished] office / 설비가 나쁜 선박 a poorly equipped ship / …의 설비가 되어있다 be equipped [provided, furnished, installed] with…
▶그 빌딩은 자가발전 설비가 되어있다 The building has its own [electric] power plant.
▶우리 공장에는 모든 현대적 설비가 갖추어져 있다 Our factory has all modern systems.
▶이 공항에는 훌륭한 항공관제 설비가 돼 있다 This airport has excellent facilities for flight control.
─설비하다 provide (with); furnish (with); install; arrange; accommodate
♦공장에 기계를 설비하다 equip a factory with machinery
■과잉─ excessive facilities 방화─ fire prevention devices 위생─ sanitary arrangements : 기숙사의 위생설비는 완벽하다 The sanitary arrangements of the dormitory are perfect. ■─비(費) the cost of equipment ─수출 plant export ─투자 investment in plant and equipment; capital investment

설빔 the New Year's best (clothes); a fine [gala] dress worn on the New Year's Day
─설빔하다 wear a gala dress; dress up for New Year's Day

설사 泄瀉 loose bowels; 〔醫〕 diarrhea
♦심한 설사 violent purging / 설사를 멎게 하다 stop [cure] diarrhea / 맹물같은 설사를 하다 have watery movements
─설사하다 have loose bowels; have [suffer from, be attacked by] diarrhea; 《俗》 have the runs
■─약 a medicine for diarrhea; a binding medicine; a laxative

설사 設使 if; even if; (even) though; although; admitting [granting] that…
♦설사 그렇다 치더라도 admitting [granting] that it is so; even if it were so
▶설사 농담이라도 그런 말은 해서는 안된다 You mustn't say such things even in jest [as a joke].
▶설사 사실일지라도 증거가 없다 Even granting [Granted] that it is true, there is no evidence.

설산 雪山 a snow-covered mountain; a mountain covered with snow

설상 舌狀 ♦설상의 lingulate; tongue-shaped
■─기관 a lingua; a tonguelike organ ─돌기 〔解〕 a lingula (pl. -lae) ─편(片) 〔植〕 a ligula; a ligule ─화 〔植〕 a ligulate flower; 〈엉거시 등의〉 a ray (flower) ─화관 〔植〕 a ligulate corolla

설상 雪上 (on) top of the snow

설상가상 雪上加霜 ♦설상가상으로 to add to one's troubles [miseries]; what is worse; to make matters worse; on top of all other misfortunes
▶설상가상으로 눈까지 오기 시작했다 What is worse, it began to snow.
▶그것은 그에겐 설상가상격이었다 It was (a matter of) rubbing salt into his wounds.

설선 雪線 〔地〕 a snow line

설설 1 〈끓는 모양〉 boiling gently
♦물이 설설 끓다 water simmers / 방바닥이 설설 끓다 the floor of the room is comfortably hot
2 〈벌레 등이 기는 모양〉 with a crawl [creep]
▶벌레가 네 등을 설설 기고 있어 A worm is crawling on your back.
▶우리는 설설 기면서 전진했다 We crawled along on all fours [on our hands and knees].
3 〈머리를 젓는 모양〉 with a gentle shake of the head
♦머리를 설설 내젓다 shake one's head
4 〈기를 못 펴는 모양〉 nervously; timidly; gingerly
▶그의 성난 눈초리에 그녀는 설설 기었다 She cowered before his angry look.

설암 舌癌 〔醫〕 cancer of the tongue

설야 雪夜 a snowy night

설왕설래하다 說往說來— argue with; argue (back and forth); cross words; exchange fiery words; have a heated argument
▶그들은 회의에서 설왕설래했다 They argued violently at the meeting.

설욕 雪辱 1 〈부끄러움을 씻음〉 vindication of one's honor ─설욕하다 wipe out a blemish on one's record; vindicate one's honor
2 〈패배를 만회함〉 revenge
─설욕하다 square accounts 《with》; 〈경기에서〉 settle the score; get even 《with》

▶우리는 그들에게 작년의 패배를 설욕했다 We avenged our loss to them in last year's game [match].
　■—전 a return match [game]
설움 sadness; sorrow; grief; mournfulness; misery
　♦아들을 잃은 설움 one's sorrow [grief] at the loss of (his) son / 설움에 겨워 울음을 터뜨리다 burst into tears in (the excess of) one's grief [sorrow]
설원 雪原 a snowy field; a snowfield
설유 說諭 persuasion; admonition; reproof
　—설유하다 persuade; admonish; reprove; advise
설음 舌音 〔音聲〕 a lingual (sound) ♦설음화하다 lingualize
설익다 1 〈음식이〉 get half-cooked; be half-boiled; be half-done ♦설익은 감자 half-cooked [underdone] potatoes
　2 〈과일이〉 be unripe; be partly ripe
　▶이 과일은 설익었다 These fruits are still green [unripe].
설인 雪人 〈히말라야의〉 a [an Abominable] Snowman; a yeti
설전 舌戰 verbal warfare; a war of words; a heated argument; a hot discussion
　▶후보들은 단상에서 설전을 벌였다 The candidates engaged in a verbal battle on the platform.
　—설전하다 have a wordy war 《with》; engage in a heated war of words
설정 設定 establishment; institution; fixation
　—설정하다 establish; institute; set up
　♦장학금을 설정하다 set up a scholarship
　♦저당권— settlement of mortgage
설죽이다 be half-killed; be nearly killed; be half-dead; be nearly dead
설중 雪中 ♦설중의 through the snow; in the snow ▶우리는 설중 등산을 했다 We climbed the mountain in the snow. ■—행군 a march in the snow
설차림 preparing the New Year's festive [special] dishes
설철 屑鐵 scrap iron; iron scraps
설측음 舌側音 〔音聲〕 a lateral (sound)
설치 設置 establishment; installation
　♦전화 설치 공사 telephone installation
　—설치하다 establish; set up; found; institute; install
　▶자문 위원회가 설치될 예정이다 An advisory committee is to be set up [formed].
설치다[1] 〈중도에서 그치다〉 leave sth half-done; stop halfway ♦잠을 설치다 cannot have [enjoy] a good [peaceful] sleep; cannot sleep in peace at night
설치다[2] 〈날뛰다〉 rampage; rave [rage, ramp] about; run [rush] about wildly; (口) act big
　▶깡패들이 시내를 온통 설치고 다녔다 In the town the hoodlums had everything in their own way.
설치류 齧齒類 〔動〕 rodents ♦설치류의 rodential
설탕 雪糖 sugar
　▶나는 커피에 설탕을 타지 않는다 I don't take [have, put] sugar in my coffee. ≒ I drink (my) coffee without sugar.
　▶〖會話〗「홍차에 설탕을 얼만큼 탈까요?」「둘 넣어 주세요」 "How many sugars (do you want) in your tea?" "I want two (sugars)." (▶상황에 따라서는 two spoonfuls [lumps] of sugar 로 할 수 있음)
　■—각— cube [lump] sugar: 각설탕 한 개 a (lump [cube] of) sugar; a sugar cube 백[정제]— refined sugar 흑— raw [unrefined] sugar; muscovado ■—가루 powdered sugar; caster sugar —그릇 〈식탁용의〉 (美) a sugar bowl; (英) a sugar basin —물 sugared water —절임 food preserved in sugar: 설탕절임하다 preserve with [in] sugar
설태 舌苔 fur (on the tongue) ▶그는 설태가 끼었다 His tongue is coated.
설파 說破 〈밝혀 말함〉 elucidation; 〈논파〉 confutation; refutation
　—설파하다 elucidate; expound; express [point out] clearly; 〈논파하다〉 argue [talk] sb down; confute; refute
설핏하다 〈성기다〉 rather loose-woven; gauze-like; coarse; 〈햇빛이〉 dusky; (be) in the gathering dusk
설하선 舌下腺 〔解〕 the sublingual gland
설한 雪寒 the cold following a snowfall
　■—엄동— the bitter [severe, rigorous] cold of winter; a hard winter; the coldest part of the winter
설해 雪害 snow damage; damage by snow
　▶그 지방은 해마다 심한 설해를 입는다 The region suffers serious damage by snow every year.
설형 楔形 ♦설형의 wedge-shaped; arrow-headed; cuneiform; sphenoid(al) ■—문자 a cuneiform (character); a sphenogram
설혹 設或 even though [if] ⇨ 설령(設令)
설화 舌禍 a disastrous slip of the tongue
　▶그는 설화로 일자리를 잃었다 He lost his position through an indiscreet statement [what he said carelessly].
　■—사건 a trouble caused by one's unfortunate utterance (in public)
설화 雪花 〈눈송이〉 snowflakes; 〈나뭇가지에 붙은〉 silver thaw; hoarfrost; snow on the branches ■—석고 alabaster
설화 說話 a tale; a story; a narration; a fable ♦설화적인 narrative ■—문학 narrative [legendary] literature —체 a narrative style: 설화체의 시 a poem in narrative form
섬[1] 1 〈멱서리〉 a straw sack
　♦쌀 섬 a rice bag / 쌀 열 섬 ten bags of rice
　2 〈용량 단위〉 a sŏm
섬[2] 〈도서〉 an island; (詩) an isle; an islet

> 〖解說〗「…섬」은 the Island [Isle] of… 로 표현하는 것이 영어적이다. Isle은 시적인 음감을 갖는 말. 「…제도」는 the… Islands 를 많이 쓴다. 예를들면 마셜제도는 the Marshall Islands, 갈라파고스제도는 the Galápagos Islands 등과 같이 말한다.

　♦섬의 insular
　▶우리는 그 섬을 돌아보았다 We made a tour

of the island.
▶ 그 섬에는 가게가 하나뿐이다 There's only one store on the island.
▶ 그 섬에는 인적이 없었다 I found nobody living on the island.
■ —사람 an islander; a native [an inhabitant] of an island

섬광 閃光 a flash (of light); a glint [gleam] of light; 〔天〕 scintillation
▶ 그것은 섬광을 발하더니 사라졌다 It flashed and (then) disappeared.
— 경보기 a flashlight crossing signal —계(計) a flashmeter —사진 flashlight photography —신호 a flashing light signal —전구 a flash lamp [bulb, tube]

섬기다 serve; be in *sb's* service; work under [for]; wait [attend] on
◆ 신[주인]을 섬기다 serve God [*one's* master]/부모를 잘 섬기다 be good [dutiful] to *one's* parents; look after [care for] *one's* parents well / 남편을 섬기다 be devoted [attentive] to *one's* husband; be [make] a good wife

섬나라 an island country
▶ 영국은 사방이 바다로 둘러싸인 섬나라다 Great Britain is an island country surrounded by sea on all sides.
■ —근성 an island-nation mentality; insularism; insularity

섬누룩 coarse malt
섬돌 stone steps; a stepping-stone; a flight of stone steps; a stone stairway
섬뜩하다 frightened; startled; horrified; horror-stricken; 〈서술적〉 have [get] a fright
◆ 섬뜩하여 with horror; in a fright
▶ 그것은 생각만 해도 섬뜩하다 It makes me shudder to think of it.

섬망 譫妄 〔醫〕 delirium ◆ 섬망 상태에 빠지다 lapse into delirium
섬멸 殲滅 annihilation; extermination
—섬멸하다 annihilate; wipe out; exterminate
■ —전 an exterminatory battle [war]

섬모 纖毛 1 thin hair **2** 〔動〕 a cilium (*pl.* -ia, ~s); (총칭) ciliation ◆ 섬모의 ciliary / 섬모가 있는 ciliate(d); ciliolate **3** ⇨ 섬유
—운동 ciliary movement —충 a ciliate

섬섬옥수 纖纖玉手 a elegant [slender, delicate] hand
섬세 纖細 delicacy; fineness; slenderness
—섬세하다 delicate; fine; subtle; fine and thin; slender
◆ 섬세한 감정 delicate [fine] feeling [sentiment]; delicacy of feeling / 섬세하게 만든 작품 delicately-constructed works
▶ 그녀는 섬세한 미적 감각이 있다 She has an exquisite [a delicate, a fine] sense of beauty.

섬유 纖維 (a) fiber; textiles
■ 단— filament 목질 〔천연〕— (a) wood [natural] fiber 유리— glass fiber; fiber glass 인조 〔화학, 합성〕— (a) man-made [chemical, synthetic] fiber —공장 a textile mill —기계 textile machinery —산업〔공업〕 the fiber [textile] industry —석고 satin gypsum —세포 〔植〕 a fibrous cell —소 〈음식물의〉 roughage; 〔動〕 fibrin; 〔植·化〕 cellulose —속〔束〕 〔解〕 a fascicle; fascicular fibers —작물 a fiber crop —제품 textile products [goods] —조직 〔解〕 fibrous tissue —질 fibroid material: 섬유질의 fibrous / 섬유질 식품 fibroid food —형성 fibrosis

섬지기 paddy land enough to plant one *sŏm* of seed rice
섬화 閃火 a flash; a spark
섭금류 涉禽類 〔鳥〕 wading birds
섭동 攝動 〔天〕 (gravitational) perturbation
섭렵 涉獵 〈책을 많이 읽음〉 extensive reading
—섭렵하다 read extensively; read widely
◆ 관계 문헌을 널리 섭렵하다 range over [dig into] an extensive literature concerning a matter

섭리 攝理 1 〈신의 뜻〉 (divine) providence; dispensation; 〔神學〕 economy
◆ 신의 섭리 divine providence [disposal]; the Providence of God / 하늘의 섭리 the wise providence of Heaven / 자연의 섭리 a happy dispensation of Nature / 신의 섭리에 맡기다 trust in Providence
2 〈병조섭〉 taking care of *one's* ill health
—섭리하다 take care of *one's* ill health

섭새김 emboss; carve in relief
섭생 攝生 care of health; 〔醫〕 regimen
◆ 섭생을 게을리하다 neglect [take little care of] *one's* health; be careless about *one's* health
—섭생하다 take (good) care [be careful] of oneself [*one's* health]; observe the rules of health; 〈병후에〉 recuperate *oneself*
▶ 몸을 건강하게 유지하려면 섭생해야 한다 We must be careful about [of] our health to keep (our bodies) fit.
■ —가 a person careful of his health; 〈음식의〉 a dietarian —법 the rules of health; hygiene

섭섭하다 1 〈서운하다〉 sorry; sad; heartbreaking; heartaching
◆ 섭섭히 여기다 be sorry for; be regretful / 헤어지기 섭섭하다 be sorry [sad] to part from *sb*; be reluctant to leave a place
▶ 친구와 작별하는 것이 섭섭하다 We feel sorry about parting from friends.
▶ 떠나기가 섭섭하지만 이젠 가야합니다 Though I hate to go [leave you], I must say good-bye now.
2 〈유감이다, 애석하다〉 regrettable; sorry
▶ 시간이 없어서 런던 구경을 못해 섭섭하다 I regret that I didn't have enough time to see the sights of London.
▶ 내가 섭섭하게 생각할 것은 아무것도 없다 I have no regrets.
▶ 우리는 네가 없으면 얼마나 섭섭할까 We shall miss you badly.
▶ 섭섭하지만 도와 드릴 수가 없습니다 I am sorry, but I am unable to help you.
3 〈불만이다〉 disappointed; 〈원망스럽〉 rueful
▶ 섭섭하게도 그녀는 오지 않았다 To my disappointment, she did not come.
▶ 이 결정에 대해서 나는 섭섭할 것이 하나도 없

섭씨 攝氏 centigrade (略 C., C); Celsius (略 C., Cels.) ◆섭씨 10도 ten degrees C [centigrade]; 10°C / 섭씨 15도의 물 water at 15°C ■—온도계 a centigrade [Celsius] thermometer

섭외 涉外 〈대외관계〉 public relations; 〈연락〉 liaison (work) ■—과[부] the liaison [public relations] section [division] —담당자 a public relations man; a liaison clerk [officer] —사무 public relations business; liaison work

섭정 攝政 〈직위〉regency; 〈사람〉a regent ◆섭정을 두다 set up regency; appoint a regent —섭정하다 rule as regent ■—직 the office of a regent; regency

섭취 攝取 〈영양 등의〉intake; 〈문화·지식 등의 동화〉assimilation; 〈방침 등의 채택〉adoption; 〈음식물의〉ingestion
◆하루의 음식 섭취량 the daily intake of food / 서양 문화의 섭취 assimilation of the Western civilization / 알코올 섭취량을 억제하다 check *one's* alcohol intake
▶비만은 칼로리의 섭취량과 밀접한 관계가 있다 Obesity is closely linked to caloric intake.
▶알코올 섭취를 제한해라 Limit your alcohol intake.
—섭취하다 take in; ingest; absorb; assimilate; adopt
◆자양분을 섭취하다 take nourishing food; take in nourishments / 외국 문화를 섭취하다 assimilate [take in, adopt] foreign culture ■—물 ingesta

섭호선 攝護腺 〖解〗 the prostate (gland) ⇨ 전립선(前立腺)

성 〈노여움〉anger; (a) rage; (a) fury; a wrath; indignation
◆성을 가라앉히다 calm *one's* [*sb's*] anger; calm down *sb* / 성이 머리끝까지 나다 fly into a rage [fury]; explode in anger

성 姓 (美) *one's* last name; (英) a surname; a family name

〖解說〗 *last name*은 first name (이름)에 대응하는 표현으로 미국인이 즐겨 쓴다. (英)에서는 *surname*을 흔히 쓴다. 우리나라의 경우는 *family name*을 쓰는 것이 좋다.

◆성과 이름을 대다 give *one's* full name
▶당신의 성은 무엇입니까? What is your family [last] name? (▶당돌한 표현) ⇌ May I ask your surname?

성 性 1〈남녀의〉sex
◆성의 자유 sexual freedom / 성의 해방 liberation of sex / 성적 욕구[충동] a sexual desire [impulse] / 성문제 a sex problem / 성범죄 a sex crime; a moral offense / 성본능 the sex instinct [urge] / 성연구 sexology / 성차별 sexual discrimination; sexism / 남녀 양 성 both sexes / 성행위 sex; (sexual) intercourse / 성의 sexual / 성전환 수술을 하다 undergo sex-change surgery / 성에 눈뜨다 be sexually awakened; become conscious [aware] of sex; begin to feel the urge of sex
2 〈본성〉nature; 〈품성〉character
▶인간의 성은 선하다 Man is naturally good. ⇌ All men are born good.
3 〖文法〗 gender
◆남[여, 중]성 the masculine [feminine, neuter] gender / 성,수, 인칭의 일치 an agreement of gender, number and person

성 省 1〈외국의 중앙 관청〉a ministry
◆성의 ministerial / 외무[내무]성 the Foreign [Home] Office
2〈중국의 행정구역〉a province
◆산둥성 Shandong Province

성 城 a castle; 〈성채〉a fortress; 〈성벽〉a wall; the castle walls ◆성을 쌓다 build a castle / 성을 포위하다 besiege a castle / 성을 빼앗다 take [capture] a castle

성 聖 1〈성인〉a sage; a saint ◆성 바울 St. Paul 2〈걸출한 사람〉a great master ◆시성 a master [great] poet 3〈성스러움〉holiness; sanctity

성- 聖- 1〈거룩한〉holy; sacred ◆성지 a sacred place (⇨ 성지) 2〈성자의 이름 앞에 붙여〉◆성 베드로 St. [Saint] Peter

성가하다 成家— 〈가정을 이루다〉establish a family; establish a home of *one's* own; 〈학파를 이루다〉develop [find] a style of *one's* own; establish *oneself* as a master
◆성가한 사람 a master

성가 聖歌 a sacred song; 〈기독교의〉a hymn ■그레고리오— the Gregorian chants 크리스마스— a Christmas carol ■—대 a choir : 성가대에서 노래하다 sing in a choir —대원 a chanter; 〈특히 소년〉a chorister —집 a hymnal; a hymnbook

성가 聲價 (a) reputation; fame and popularity; public reputation
◆성가를 높이다 enhance *one's* reputation; establish *oneself* in public estimation
▶그 사건으로 그의 성가가 높아졌다[떨어졌다] The affair enhanced [lowered, hurt] his reputation.
▶그 공장은 질좋은 제품으로 성가가 높다 The factory has a good reputation for its high-quality products.

성가시다 〈귀찮다〉annoying; troublesome; bothersome; harassing; cumbersome; importunate
◆성가신 아이 a troublesome child / 성가시게 조르다 pester *sb* into (doing); ask importunately for (money) / 성가시게 질문하다 trouble *sb* with questions; be inquisitive
▶성가신 일을 떠맡게 되었다 I'm saddled with a troublesome job [burdensome duties].
▶성가시게 굴지 마라 Don't bother me! ⇌ Stop bothering [(口) bugging] me! ⇌ Leave me alone.
▶그는 내 질문을 성가셔 하지 않고 친절하게 대답해 주었다 He answered my questions kindly without regarding them [me] as a nuisance.
▶그 외판원은 성가시게 내게 전화를 걸어왔다 The salesman plagued me with phone calls.

성가족 聖家族 〈아기 예수, 성모 마리아, 성 요셉을 그린 그림〉the Holy Family

성감 性感 sexual feeling [excitement]
■ —대(帶) a sexually sensitive areas; an erogenous zone

성게 [動] a sea urchin; an echinoid

성격 性格 (a) character; (a) personality; (the) nature
♦ 선천적인[후천적인] 성격 inherited [acquired] character / 성격상의 결점 a flaw [defect] in *one's* character / 성격의 차이 disparity in character / 그 임무의 성격 the nature of the task / 성격이 좋은 사람 a good-natured person; an agreeable character / 강한 성격의 남자 a man with a forceful personality; a forceful character / (어떤 일이) 성격짓다 characterize *sb*
▶ 그녀는 어떤 성격이니? What kind of person is she?
▶ 그건 그의 타고난 성격이야 It is his own nature.
▶ 저 자매는 성격이 제각각이다 The sisters have different characters [personalities]. ⇒ The sisters are different in characters.
▶ 그들은 성격상 맞지 않는다 They aren't cut out for each other.
▶ 사람의 성격은 어릴 때 형성된다 A person's character is formed in childhood.
■ —극 a character drama —묘사 character portrayal [description, sketch]; characterization —배우 〈남자〉 a character actor; 〈여자〉 a character actress —파탄[이상]자 an abnormal character; (俗) a screwball —학 characterology —형성 character formation

성결 性— (a) nature; (a) disposition; (a) temperament
♦ 성결이 곱다[고약하다] be good-natured [ill-natured]; be good-tempered [bad-tempered]; have a sweet [nasty] disposition
▶ 그녀는 성결은 곱지만 별로 영리하지는 못하다 She has a good heart, but not much sense. ⇒ She is naturally sweet-tempered, but has not much sense.

성결 聖潔 holiness and purity
■ —교회 the Holiness Church

성경 聖經 (基) the (Holy) Bible; the (Holy) Scriptures; the Holy [Sacred] Writ
■ 개역— the Revised Version (of the Bible) (略 R.V.) 신약[구약]— the New [Old] Testament 흠정역(欽定譯)— the Authorized [(美) King James] Version (of the Bible) (略 A.V.) ■ —문학 Biblical literature —연구회 a Bible class; a Bible-study group —학자 a Biblical [Bible] scholar; a Biblicist —해석학 hermeneutics

성공 成功 1 〈뜻한 바를 이룸〉 (a) success; 〈흥행 등의〉 a hit; a coup; 〈성취〉 achievement
♦ 성공을 거두다 achieve [win, gain, obtain] success / 성공으로 끝나다 a result [end] in success
▶ 실패는 성공의 어머니 (속담) Failure teaches success.
▶ 그는 사업에서 큰 성공을 거두었다 He was a great success [very successful] in the enterprise. ⇒ He made a great coup in the enterprise.
▶ 성공을 빕니다 I wish you success. ⇒ I hope you (will) succeed. ⇒ Good luck (to you)!
—**성공하다** 〈일이 주어〉 succeed; be [prove] successful; go well; 〈사람 주어〉 succeed (in); do well; be successful (in); win [achieve] success; make good in
♦ 성공시키다 bring *sth* to success; carry *sth* to a successful conclusion
▶ 그는 성공할 가망이 있다 He has a chance of success. ⇒ He is expected to succeed.
▶ 경찰은 인질을 구출하는 데 성공했다 The police succeeded in rescuing the hostage.
▶ 애쓴 보람이 있어 그는 성공했다 His efforts were crowned [rewarded] with success.
▶ 그는 하는 일마다 다 성공했다 Every attempt succeeded with him. ⇒ He succeeded in everything.
▶ 이번에는 성공했지 This time I made [did] it!
2 〈출세〉 success in life [the world]; 〈번영〉 prosperity
▶ 근면이 성공의 비결이다 Diligence is the key to success.
—**성공하다** 〈출세하다〉 succeed [rise] in the world; get on in life; 〈번영하다〉 prosper; thrive
▶ 그는 사업가로서 성공했다 He was a success [succeeded] as a businessman.
■ —대 a great [vast, signal] success; great [gigantic] achievement ■ —담 a success story —률 〈가능성〉 possibility of success; 〈비율〉 a success rate —자 a successful man; a success

성공적 成功的 successful ♦ 성공적으로 successfully; with success / 성공적으로 …하다 succeed [be successful] (in doing)
▶ 그의 수술은 성공적으로 끝났다 His operation was a success [successful].

성공회 聖公會 (美) the Protestant Episcopal Church; (英) the Anglican Church ♦ 대한 성공회 the Episcopal Church of Korea ■ —교인 (美) an Episcopalian; (英) an Anglican

성과 成果 the result(s) (of); a product; (a) fruit; an outcome
♦ 노력의 성과 the fruit of *one's* efforts / 20년간의 연구 성과 the result [outcome, fruits] of 20 years of study / 훌륭한 성과를 거두다 obtain [get, produce] excellent [dazzling] results; achieve (a) brilliant success
▶ 우리는 소기의 성과를 거두지 못했다 We failed to realize the anticipated result. ⇒ The result fell short of our expectations.
▶ 〖會話〗「성과가 있었니?」「별로 없었어」"Have you seen any results?" "Nothing significant."

성과학 性科學 sexology
■ —자 a sexologist

성곽 城郭 〈성〉 a castle; a citadel; 〈성채〉 a fortress; a stronghold; 〈성벽〉 castle walls; ramparts ■ —도시 a walled city

성교 性交 sexual intercourse; 〖醫〗 coitus; lovemaking; (口) sex
—**성교하다** have sexual intercourse 《with》; have sex 《with》; make love 《to》

■—불능 impotence; impotency —불능자 an impotent person

성교육 性敎育 sex education

성구 成句 a set [fixed] phrase;〈숙어〉an idiomatic phrase [expression];〈속담〉a common saying

성군 星群〈天〉a cluster of stars ; an asterism

성극 聖劇 a Biblical play; a scriptural drama

성금 誠金 a gift of money; a contribution; a donation
♦ 기금에 백만원의 성금을 내다 contribute [donate, make a contribution of] one million won to a fund
▶ 아직껏 성금은 별로 많이 들어오지 않고 있다 The donation doesn't amount to much so far.
■불우이웃돕기— a donation for the needy [poor]

성급하게 性急— impetuously; hastily; impatiently
♦ 성급하게 굴면 일을 그르친다 (속담) Haste makes waste.
▶ 성급하게 일을 결정해서는 안된다 You should not decide matters so hastily [impetuously].
▶ 너무 성급하게 굴면 탈이 난다 If you're too hasty, you'll get into trouble.

성급하다 性急— impatient; impetuous; hasty; quick-tempered; hot-tempered; hotheaded; rash
♦ 성급한 사람 an impetuous person; a person of an impetuous disposition; a hot-tempered person

성기 性器 sexual [genital] organs; genitals

성기 聖器〈基〉a holy [sacred, consecrated] vessel

성기다 1〈배지 않다〉sparse; loose; thin; coarse
♦ 성긴 그물 a net with large meshes / 성긴 이 open teeth / 성긴 천 loose fabric; cloth of loose texture / 성긴 체 a wire sieve of large meshes / 성기게 sparsely; thinly; loosely / 머리털이 성기다 have thin hair
▶ 그의 머리털이 성기어져 가고 있다 He's losing his hair. ⇌ His hair is thinning [is getting thin].
2〈서먹하다〉estranged; alienated; not on good terms 《with》

성깃성깃 sparsely; thinly; here and there; scatteredly ♦ 성깃성깃한 머리털 thin hair / 그물을 성깃성깃 쳐서 make a net with large meshes —성깃성깃하다 ⇨ 성깃하다

성깃하다 sparse; thin; sparsely spaced; thinly scattered; separate; a bit separated

성깔 a sharp temper; a fierce temperament; (美口) a conniption (fit) ♦ 성깔이 있는 사람 a man of violent [impetuous] temper / 성깔 부리다 get out of temper; fire up

성나다 1〈화나다〉get [become, grow, be] angry 《with, at》; feel angry 《with,(美)at》; be angered [offended, enraged] 《by》
♦ 성나서 in anger; angrily; in a fit of anger / 성나게 하다 make sb angry; anger [offend] sb; provoke
▶ 그녀는 자기 생일을 그가 잊어버렸다고 성나 있었다 She was angry [offended] that he had forgotten her birthday. ⇌ (口) She was angry [mad] because he forgot her birthday. ⇌ She was angry [mad] with [at] him for forgetting her birthday.
2〈거칠어지다〉become [get] rough; rough (up); rage; rampage;〈덧나다〉get worse
♦ 성난 파도 a rough [high, heavy] sea; wild waves; raging waters
▶ 종기가 성나다 A boil gets worse.

성내 城內 ♦ 성내에 inside the castle [fortress]

성내다 get [become] angry 《at, about, over, with, that》; (口) get mad; become indignant
♦ 발끈 성내다 lose one's temper; blow one's top / 성내어 소리지르다 shout in anger [angrily] / 사소한 일로 성내다 get angry at [about] trifles
▶ 그는 곧잘 성을 낸다 He gets angry [offended] easily. ⇌ He has a short temper.
▶ 그녀는 그걸 알면 몹시 성낼 것이다 She'll be very angry to know it [if she knows it].
▶ 그는 딸에게 아직도 성내고[성이 나] 있다 He's still angry at [about, with] his daughter. (▶at은 직접적으로, about는 간접적으로 자기 기분을 나타내며, with는 성내는 대상을 강조한다)
▶ 네가 성내는 것은 당연하다 You have good reason to be angry.

성냥 a match
♦ 불붙인 성냥 a lighted match / 성냥을 켜다 strike [light] a match / 성냥으로 등잔에 불을 붙이다 light a lamp with a match
▶ 성냥이 젖어서 불이 켜지지 않는다 The matches are damp and won't light [don't catch].
▶ 그는 성냥을 그어 담배에 불을 붙였다 He struck a match to light his cigarette.
▶ 미안합니다만 성냥이 있으면 좀 빌립시다 Excuse me. Do you have a match?
■안전— a safety match 종이—〈떼내는〉a matchfolder; a matchbook;〈한 개비〉a bookmatch ■—개비 a match; a matchstick —불 a match flame

성냥갑 —匣 a matchbox; a box [pack(age)] of matches ♦ 성냥갑 같은 집 a matchbox of a house / 성냥갑 같은 기차 a toy of a train

성 냥 일〈대장일〉forging; blacksmithing; smithery

성냥하다〈쇠를 달구다〉anneal; temper

성녀 聖女 a female saint; a saintly woman

성 년 成 年 full [adult, lawful] age;〔法〕(legal) majority ♦ 성년에 달하다 come of age; attain one's majority; reach full age
▶ 그는 아직 성년이 아니다 He is still underage [a minor]. ⇌ He hasn't come of age yet.
■—식 the celebration of one's coming of age; a coming-of-age ceremony —자 an adult;〔法〕a major; a person of full age

성능 性能 capacity; power; efficiency; performance;〈특질〉a property
♦ 성능이 좋은 기계 a machine of good [high] performance; a highly efficient machine
▶ 이 면도기는 별로 성능이 좋지 않다 This shaver doesn't work very well.

■—계수 quality factor —곡선 a performance curve —시험[검사] a performance [an efficiency] test

성단 星團 a cluster of stars; a star cluster ■ 산개— an open star cluster

성당 聖堂 a church; a Catholic church; a chapel; a sanctuary; a sacred edifice

성대 〔魚〕 a gurnard; a gurnet; a sea robin

성대 聖代 a glorious reign
■ 태평— a peaceful reign [age]

성대 聲帶 〔解〕 the vocal cords [bands]
—모사(模寫) imitation of *sb's* voice; vocal mimicry: 성대모사를 하다 imitate *sb's* voice

성 대 하 다 盛大— prosperous; flourishing; thriving (business); grand; splendid; magnificent; successful
♦ 성대한 환영 a very warm welcome [reception]/ 성대한 모임 an impressive party with a large attendance / 성대하게 splendidly; with splendor; magnificently; 〈대규모로〉 on a large scale
▶ 결혼식 피로연이 어젯밤 성대히 거행되었다 A grand [magnificent] wedding reception was held [given] yesterday evening.

성덕 聖德 〈왕의〉 royal virtues; 〈성자의〉 a saint's virtues; saintly virtues

성도 成道 〔佛敎〕 attainment of Great Wisdom; 〈예술 등의〉 attainment of perfection —성도하다 attain [enter] Buddhahood; attain perfection; be a master

성도 星圖 〈천체도〉〔天〕 a celestial map; a star chart [atlas]

성도 聖徒 〈성인〉 a saint; 〈사도〉 an apostle; a disciple of Christ; 〈기독교인〉 a Christian —전(傳) the lives of saints; hagiology

성도 聖都 the Holy City

성도덕 性道德 sex [sexual] morality ▶ 성도 덕이 아주 문란하다 Sex morality is very lax.

성도착증 性倒錯症 sexual perversion

성량 聲量 the volume of (*one's*) voice
♦ 성량이 풍부하다 have a powerful [rich] voice; have a voice of great volume
▶ 그녀는 성량이 약하다 Her voice is weak [doesn't have much volume].

성령 聖靈 〈聖〉 the Holy Spirit [Ghost]; the Spirit of the Lord ■ 강림절 Whitsuntide; the season of Pentecost —강림제 Whitsunday; Pentecost

성례 成禮 a wedding (ceremony) —성례하다 hold a wedding ceremony; solemnize a marriage

성루 城樓 castle towers [turrets]; parapets

성루 城壘 ramparts; a fort; 〈대규모의〉 a fortress

성립 成立 1 〈생겨남〉 coming into existence [being]; 〈실현〉 realization; materialization
♦ 고대문명의 성립 the birth of an ancient civilization
—성립하다 come [be brought] into existence [being]; materialize; be materialized
♦ 성립시키다 bring [call] into existence [being]; materialize; bring about
▶ 당신의 이론은 성립되지 않는다고 생각합니다 I think your theory does not hold water.

▶ 동의는 14대 3으로 성립되었다 The motion (was) carried by fourteen votes to three.
2 〈결성·조직〉 formation; organization —성립하다 be formed; be organized; 〈이루어 지다〉 be composed [made] of; consist of
♦ 성립시키다 form; organize
▶ 국제 연합은 1945년에 성립되었다 The United Nations was set up [was established] in 1945.
3 〈타결〉 conclusion ♦ 조약의 성립 the conclusion of a treaty —성립하다 be concluded
▶ 양국간에 통상조약이 성립되었다 A treaty of commerce was concluded [effected] between the two nations.
▶ 노사간의 화해가 성립되었다 The workers have reached a settlement with the employer.

성마르다 性— 〈성급하다〉 quick-tempered; impatient; irritable; impetuous
♦ 성마른 사람 a hot-tempered person

성망 聲望 reputation; fame; popularity
▶ 그는 정치가로서 성망을 얻었다 He won [gained] fame and popularity as a politician.

성명 姓名 *one's* (full) name ♦ 성명 미상의 남 자 an unidentified [anonymous] man / 성명을 밝히다 give *one's* name; identify *oneself* / 성 명을 사칭하다 assume a false name
■—판단 onomancy

성명 聲明 a (public) declaration; a statement; an announcement
▶ 우리는 시장에게 항의 성명을 전달했다 We handed the mayor a statement of protest.
—성명하다 announce; declare; proclaim; make [issue] a statement (on)
♦ 반대[지지]를 성명하다 declare *oneself* against [for] *sth*
■ 공동— a joint communiqué [statement] 공식— (deliver, issue) an official statement
■—전 an exchange of charges and countercharges

성명서 聲明書 a (public) statement; a manifesto (*pl.* ~(e)s)
♦ 성명서[공동 성명서]를 내다 issue [make] a statement [a joint communiqué]

성모 聖母 the Holy Mother; the Virgin Mary; Saint Mary; the Madonna
♦ 라파엘로의 성모상 a madonna by Raphael
■ 마리아 the Virgin Mary; the Blessed Mary —무염시태(無染始胎) the Immaculate Conception —승천 the Assumption (of the Virgin Mary) —찬가 〈樂〉 Ave Maria

성묘 省墓 a visit to *one's* ancestral grave —성묘하다 visit [pay a visit to] *one's* ancestor's grave

성문 成文 reducing to writing
■—계약 a written contract —법[율] a statute (law); a written law

성문 城門 a castle gate
♦ 성문을 지키다 guard the castle gate

성문 聲門 〔解〕 the glottis (*pl.* ~es, -tides)
♦ 성문의 glottal

성문 聲紋 a voiceprint

성문화 成文化 codification
—성문화하다 codify; put in statutory form
♦ 규칙을 성문화하다 codify regulations; put

성미 性味 〈성격〉 character; 〈성질〉 nature; a turn of mind; disposition; 〈기질〉 temperament; temper
♦ 성미가 고약한 ill-natured; vicious; wicked / 성미가 까다로운 사람 a man hard to please / 성미가 급하다 be short-tempered; be hot-tempered ; be irritable / 성미에 맞다[맞지 않다] be congenial [uncongenial] to 《one》; agree [disagree] with 《one》
▶ 나는 그와는 성미가 맞지 않는다 I cannot get along [get on well] with him. ⇌ (口) He and I just don't hit it off well.
▶ 나는 그녀의 성미를 잘 알지 I know her disposition [temper, nature, temperament] well.
▶ 그는 지기 싫어하는 성미다 He has an unyielding spirit [nature].
▶ 내 성미에 그런 짓은 못합니다 It is not in my nature to do such a thing.

성범죄 性犯罪 a sex offense [crime]; a sexual offense ♦ 一자 a sex criminal

성벽 性癖 one's (natural) disposition; a natural tendency; inclination; a mental habit; a propensity
▶ 그녀에게는 이상한 성벽이 있다 She has a curious habit [a strange disposition].
▶ 그는 과장하는 성벽이 있다 He has a tendency [propensity] to exaggerate.

성벽 城壁 a castle wall; a rampart; the town walls ♦ 성벽으로 둘러싸인 도시 a walled city / 성벽을 쌓다 build a rampart; wall a castle

성별 性別 the distinction of sex ♦ 병아리의 성별 감정 chick sexing
▶ 성별과 연령에 관계없이 누구나 응모할 수 있다 Anyone may apply regardless [irrespective] of sex or age.

성병 性病 a venereal disease (略 V.D., VD); a sexual disease; (美) a social disease
♦ 성병의 예방 prevention of venereal diseases / 성병에 걸리다 catch (a) venereal disease
■ 一감염 venereal infection 一전문병원 (口) a VD clinic 一학 venereology 一환자 a person venereally infected

성복 成服 wearing mourning 一성복하다 go into [take to] mourning; be in mourning

성부 成否 success and failure ⇨ 성불성(成不成)

성부 聖父 〔聖〕 the (Holy) Father
성부 聲部 〔樂〕 a voice part

성분 成分 an ingredient; a component; an element; a constituent
♦ 합금의 성분을 분석하다 analyze the components [constituent elements] of an alloy
▶ 산소와 수소가 물의 성분이다 Oxygen and hydrogen are the elements of water.
■ 부(副)— an accessory ingredient 주(要)— the main [chief, principal] ingredients (of) ■ 一시험 a chemical experiment [test] 一표(示) an ingredients label

성불 成佛 〔佛教〕 attaining Buddhahood; entering Nirvana 一성불하다 become a Buddha; attain Buddhahood; enter Nirvana; 〈죽다〉 die; pass away; go to heaven

성불성 成不成 success and [or] failure; the result; the issue ♦ 성불성간에 whether successful or not; whatever the result may be

성사 成事 accomplishment; achievement; 〈실현〉 realization; 〈성공〉 success
▶ 모사는 재인(在人)이요 성사는 재천(在天)이라 Man proposes, God disposes. ⇌ Do your best and leave the rest to Providence.
一성사하다 succeed; accomplish 《one's purpose, an undertaking》; achieve; realize
♦ 혼담을 성사시키다 arrange [make up] a marriage

성사 聖事 divine service; 〔가톨릭〕 the sacraments; a sacrament

성산 成算 confidence [hope, chances] of success; prospects of sure success
♦ 성산이 있다 [없다] be confident [have little hope] of success
▶ 성산이 있느냐? Are you quite sure of success?
▶ 성산이 있는 사업이라고 생각한다 I am quite confident of the success of the enterprise.
▶ 성산이 없는 일에는 아예 손을 대지 마라 Never concern yourself with the business that offers little hope of success.

성상 星霜 years; time
▶ 우리가 학교를 졸업한 뒤로 많은 성상이 흘렀다 Many years have passed since we graduated from the school.
▶ 나는 10년의 성상이 지나서야 그녀를 다시 만났다 I met her again after ten years had passed.

성상 聖上 (His Majesty) the King
성생활 性生活 sex [sexual] life
성서 聖書 the Bible ⇨ 성경
성선설 性善說 the ethical doctrine that human nature is originally good
성성이 猩猩— 〔動〕 an orangoutang; a pongo (pl. ~es)
성성하다 星星— hoar(y); gray-haired; gray-headed ♦ 백발이 성성한 머리 gray-white hair; grizzled [frosty] hair; graying hair; hair streaked with gray
성세 盛世 a glorious reign [era]
성소 聖所 〔聖〕 the holy place; sanctum
■ 지(至)— the holy of holies; sanctum sanctorum
성쇠 盛衰 ups and downs; rise and fall; prosperity and decline; vicissitudes
♦ 인생의 성쇠 the vicissitudes [ups and downs, ebb and flow] of life / 로마의 성쇠 the rise and fall of Rome
성수 星宿 〔天〕 the stars; the various constellations
성수 聖水 〔가톨릭〕 holy water
성수기 盛需期 a high-demand season
▶ 그 상품은 성수기를 맞고 있다 The articles are now in great demand.
성숙 成熟 **1** 〈잘 익음〉 ripeness; maturity 一성숙하다 ripen; be [get] ripe
2 〈심신의〉 full [complete] growth; matura-

tion —성숙하다 attain [reach] full growth; grow into adulthood ◆성숙한 처녀 a mature [marriageable] girl / 성숙하여 여자답게 되다 ripen into womanhood
▶요즘 아이들은 빨리 성숙한다 Recently children have begun to mature earlier.
▶그는 심신이 모두 성숙한 청년이다 He is a young man who has matured mentally and physically.
3 〈기회 등의〉 maturity; ripeness —성숙하다 mature; ripen; attain [come to] maturity
▶시기가 성숙하기를 기다립시다 Let us wait till the time is ripe.

성숙기 成熟期 (the period of) maturity; 〈사춘기〉 adolescence; puberty; the age of puberty [adolescence] ◆성숙기에 이르다 arrive at puberty; become adolescent

성스럽다 聖— 〈신성하다〉 holy; sacred; divine; 〈장엄하다〉 solemn; sublime ◆성스러운 장소 a spot of sanctity; a holy [sacred] place

성시 成市 opening a fair [market] —성시하다 open [keep] a fair ◆문전 성시하다 have a constant stream of visitors; be thronged with callers; (a shop) have a crowd of customers

성신 星辰 the stars

성신 聖神 〔聖〕 the Holy Spirit ⇨ 성령

성실 誠實 sincerity; faithfulness; fidelity; honesty; truthfulness; devotion; earnestness —성실하다 sincere; faithful; truthful; honest; earnest
◆성실한 사람 a man of sincerity [integrity] / 성실한 태도 a sincere attitude
▶남에게 성실히 대해야 한다 You should deal honestly with others.
▶나는 지금까지 누구한테나 성실히 대해 왔다 I have always been sincere to [honest with] anybody.
▶일을 좀더 성실하게 해주기 바란다 I would like you to be more conscientious in your work.
■—성 sincerity; faithfulness; fidelity; truth

성심 誠心 sincerity; good faith; a true heart
◆성심껏 sincerely; wholeheartedly; devotedly; heart and soul; from (the bottom of) one's heart / …을 성심껏 하다 deal with sth in all sincerity; go heart and soul into sth; do sth with one's whole heart

성싶다 〈…인듯하다〉 look; seem; appear; be likely (to do)
▶비가 올 성싶다 It looks like rain. ⇌ It is likely to rain. ⇌ It threatens to rain.
▶구름을 보니 벼락이 칠 성싶다 The clouds threaten thunder.
▶비가 그칠 성싶지 않다 There is no sign of rain ceasing.
▶그를 전에 본 성싶다 It seems to me that I have met him before.
▶그는 올 성싶지 않다 It is not likely that he will come. ⇌ He is not likely to come. ⇌ There is little [no] likelihood of his coming.
▶그 집은 빈 집인 성싶다 The house appears deserted.

성씨 姓氏 a family name; a surname

성악 聲樂 vocal music ◆성악을 배우다 take vocal [singing] lessons ■—가 a vocalist

성악설 性惡說 the ethical doctrine that human nature is inherently evil

성안 成案 a definite plan [scheme]; a concrete program ■—성안하다 form a definite plan; map out a concrete program

성애 性愛 sexual love

성어 成魚 a fully-grown fish; an adult fish

성어 成語 a (set) phrase; an idiom; an idiomatic phrase

성업 盛業 a thriving business ◆성업중이다 be doing a flourishing business [trade]; drive a thriving [booming, prosperous] trade

성에 (a layer of) frost; frostwork; frost flowers [ferns] ◆성에가 낀 창문 a frosted window / 냉장고의 성에를 제거하다 defrost a refrigerator
▶유리창에는 온통 성에가 끼어 있었다 The windowpanes were covered with frost [frostwork].

성엣장 floating [drifting] ice; an floe

성역 聖域 sacred [holy] precincts; a consecrated ground; a sanctuary

성역 聲域 a range of voice; 〔樂〕 a register
▶그 가수는 성역이 넓다 The singer has a wide range.

성염색체 性染色體 a sex chromosome

성욕 性慾 sexual [carnal] desire [appetite]; lust ◆성욕이 강한 strongly-sexed / 성욕을 자극하다 stimulate [excite] sexual desire [appetite] / 성욕을 만족시키다 gratify [satisfy] one's carnal desire
▶변태— abnormal sexuality ■—결핍 sexual disinclination [apathy] —도착(倒錯) sexual perversion [inversion] —항진 aphrodisia; morbid sexual excitement —이상 sex mania; erotomania

성우 聲優 a radio actor [actress]

성운 星雲 〔天〕 a nebula (pl. -lae, ~s) ■가스상(狀)— a gaseous nebula 와상(渦狀)— a spiral nebula 환상(環狀)— an annular nebula; a ring nebula ■—설 the nebular hypothesis [theory]

성원 成員 a quorum; a constituent (member); 〈단체의 조직원〉 a member
◆성원을 이루다 constitute [form, make] a quorum / 성원이 미달되다 fail to meet the quorum (required for the session); do not come up to [be short of] the quorum
■—미달 lack of a quorum

성원 聲援 1〈격려〉 cheering; (a shout of) encouragement; 《美俗》 rooting
◆열렬한 성원을 보내다 give enthusiastic encouragement (to); root wildly (for a team); give sb a big yell
▶밖에서도 군중의 성원 소리가 들려 온다 You can hear the cheers of the crowd even outside.
—성원하다 shout encouragement 《for》; cheer 《a team on to victory》; 《美俗》 root 《for a team》
2〈도움〉 support —성원하다 support; give one's support 《to》; patronize
▶앞으로도 계속해서 저희를 성원해 주시기 바

랍니다 We hope you will favor us with your continued patronage.
■ —자 a cheerer; (美俗) a rooter; a supporter
성유 聖油 〈가톨릭〉 holy [consecrated] oil; chrism
성은 聖恩 〈왕의〉 Royal favor [grace, benevolence]; 〈신의〉 divine favor; the goodness of Heaven; heavenly blessings ♦ 성은이 망극하다 Inscrutable are the king's favor.
성음 聲音 a vocal sound ■ —문자 a phonogram —학 phonetics
성의 誠意 sincerity; good faith
▶ 그는 무슨 일에나 성의가 없다 He is insincere [lacks sincerity] in whatever he does.
▶ 너에게 자네의 성의를 보이게 Show her your sincerity.
▶ 나는 성의를 다하여 그녀를 설득했다 I persuaded her in all sincerity.
▶ 그녀는 일을 성의 없이 한다 She does her work by halves. ⇌ She is a sloppy worker.
성인 成人 an adult; a grownup; a grown-up person

解說 *adult*는 법률상 성인인 자. 보통 (美)에서는 21세 이상, (英)에서는 18세 이상. *grownup*은 어린이에 대해 성인이란 말로서 adult의 스스럼없는 말로 쓰인다.

♦ 성인이 되다 grow up; attain [arrive at] manhood [womanhood]; become an adult; come of age
▶ 한국에서는 20세면 성인이 된다 We come of age at twenty in Korea.
▶ 그녀에게는 성인이 된 아들이 둘 있다 She has two grown-up sons.
■ —교육 《give》 adult education —병 diseases of adult people; geriatric diseases —식 a coming-of-age ceremony —영화 an adult [X-rated] movie; a film for adults only
성인 聖人 a saint; a sage; a holy man
♦ 옛 성인 a sage of old / 성인 같은 saintly; saintlike / 성인인 체하다 play the saint; act saintly; set up for a saint
성인도 시속을 따른다 (속담) When in Rome, do as the Romans do.
성자 聖子 〔基・가톨릭〕 the Son
성자 聖者 a saint ⇨ 성인(聖人)
성장 成長 growth
♦ 성장이 빠르다 grow quickly [rapidly] / 성장이 더디다 grow slowly; be of tardy growth / 성장을 돕다 foster [help] the growth 《of》 / 성장을 관찰하다 observe the growth 《of》 / 성장을 촉진하다 promote [stimulate] the growth 《of》 / 아이의 성장을 지켜보다 watch how a child grows up; watch over a growing child
▶ 그것은 암세포의 성장을 저지할 것이다 It will halt the growth of cancer cells.
—성장하다 grow (up); be brought up
▶ 그는 훌륭한 젊은이로 성장했다 He grew up into a fine young man.
▶ 그는 육체적으로 정신적으로 성장했다 He has physically and mentally grown.
▶ 한국 경제는 1970년대에 급속히 성장했다 The Korean economy grew rapidly during the 1970's.
■ 경제— economic growth; growth in economy 고도— rapid growth 안정— 〈경제의〉 stable growth ■ —곡선 a growth curve —기간[과정] a growth period [process] —산업 the growth industry —요인 a growth factor —주 a growth stock —호르몬 growth [somatotrophic] hormone; somatotrop(h)in
성장 盛裝 gala [full] dress; beautiful attire
—성장하다 be dressed up; be finely [richly] dressed; be dressed in one's (Sunday) best; be in gala [full] dress
♦ 성장한 여인들 richly gowned ladies / 성장시키다 dress up [deck out] 《one's daughter》
▶ 그녀는 성장하고 외출했다 She went out in her best (clothes).
▶ 파티 참석자는 모두 성장하고 있었다 Everyone was dressed up at the party.
성장률 成長率 a growth rate; a rate of growth
■ 경제— a rate of economic growth 명목[실질]— the nominal [real] growth rate
성적 成績 a result; a showing; a record; merit; score; grade
▶ 그녀는 학교 성적이 좋다[나쁘다] She does well [poorly] at school.
▶ 그는 성적이 우수했다 His grades were excellent.
▶ 그는 성적이 떨어졌다[좋아졌다] His grades dropped [improved].
▶ 그는 작업 성적이 좋았다 He has made a good showing in his work.
▶ 나는 영어 성적은 좋았지만 수학 성적은 나빴다 I got a good mark in English, but a bad one in mathematics.
▶ 성적은 언제 발표됩니까? When will the results be published?
▶ 이 달의 영업 성적은 어떻습니까? How's business this month?
▶ 그는 새 직장에서 상당한 성적을 올리고 있다 He has been doing fairly well in his new job.
■ —표 a list of students' records; a report card; 〈경기의〉 a scorecard
성적 性的 sexual
▶ 그들은 성적으로 조숙했다[늦되었다] They were sexually precocious [backward].
■ —도착(倒錯) sexual perversion —도착자 a sexual pervert —욕망 sexual appetite [desire] —차별 sexual discrimination —충동 a sex urge [drive]
성적매력 性的魅力 sex appeal; sexual attractiveness; (美俗) "it"
♦ 성적 매력이 있는 여자 a woman with 《strong》 sex appeal; (口) a glamor girl / 성적 매력이 있다 have sex appeal; be sexy; be sexually attractive
성적순 成績順 the order of merit
♦ 성적순으로 앉다 sit in the order of merit
성전 性典 a book on sex; a cyclop(a)edia of sex
성전 聖殿 a sacred shrine; a sanctuary
성전 聖戰 a holy war; a crusade
성전환 性轉換 sex change; the change of sex
■ —수술 a sex-change [transsexual] operation —자 a transsexual

성정 性情 *one's* nature [disposition, character, temper]

성조기 星條旗 〈미국 국기〉 the Stars and Stripes; the Star-Spangled Banner

성좌 星座 〔天〕〈별자리〉 a constellation ◆오리온 성좌 the constellation of Orion ■—도(圖) a star chart; a planisphere

성주 城主 the lord of a castle; a feudal lord; a castellan

성지 城址 the ruins of a castle ⇨ 성터

성지 聖旨 the Royal will [wish]; the King's decree

성지 聖地 a sacred ground; a holy place;〈팔레스타인〉 the Holy Land ■—순례 (make) a pilgrimage to the Holy Land

성지식 性知識 knowledge of sex; sexual information

성직 聖職 a sacred profession; a heaven-sent mission; (holy) orders ◆성직에 취임하다 take orders; be admitted to (holy) orders; be ordained (priest); enter the church
▶그는 성직에 있다 He is in orders.
—자 a churchman; a clergyman; a cleric; a man of the cloth

성질 性質 (a) nature; a disposition; 〈성격〉 (a) character; 〈특성〉 a property; a quality
▶성질이 좋은 사람은 누구에게나 사랑 받는다 A man of good nature is loved by everybody.
▶비누는 때를 빼는 성질이 있다 Soap has the property of removing dirt.
▶해바라기는 태양을 향하는 성질이 있다 The sunflower has the characteristic of turning toward the sun.
▶타고 난 성질은 어찌할 도리가 없다 A man cannot help his own nature.
▶사람의 성질은 가지각색이다 People are of various qualities.
▶그 사건은 국제적인 성질을 띠기 시작했다 The case began to assume an international character.

성찬 盛饌 a capital [grand, sumptuous] dinner; a splendid meal; a feast; a good table ◆진수 성찬 rich viands and sumptuous fare / 성찬을 베풀다 give a capital dinner; set a good table 《for a guest》; feast 《*one's* friends》

성찬 聖餐 〔基〕 the Lord's Supper; Holy Communion; the Eucharist
■—식 the (Holy) Communion; the Sacrament; the Lord's Supper : 성찬식을 거행하다 minister the Sacrament

성찰 省察 reflection; introspection; self-examination —성찰하다 reflect; introspect; examine *oneself*

성채 城砦 a fort; a fortress; a citadel; fortifications; a stronghold; a fastness ◆성채를 쌓다 build a fort; fortify 《a town》

성체 成體 〔生〕 an adult

성체 聖體 1 〈임금의 몸〉 the person of a king; the Royal person 2 〔基•가톨릭〕 the body (of Christ); the holy bread; the (Blessed [Holy]) Sacrament; the Host; 〈성찬〉 the Eucharist ■—영(領)— (Holy) Communion : 영성체하다 receive [take] Communion; commune ■—강복식 〔가톨릭〕 Benediction —공존론 consubstantialism; consubstantiation —봉헌(식) oblation —성사 (the sacrament of) the Eucharist

성충 成蟲 〔昆〕 an imago 《*pl.* ~es, imagines》; an adult ◆성충의 imaginal ■—기(期) the imaginal stage

성취 成就 accomplishment; achievement; completion; realization; fulfil(l)ment
—성취하다 accomplish; achieve; attain; fulfil(l); carry [bring] *sth* to fruition; make 《*one's* wish》 come true; realize 《*one's* wish》
▶나의 오랜 소원이 성취되었다 My long-cherished dream has finally been realized [become a reality].
▶그는 무엇 하나 성취되는 일이 없다 Nothing succeeds with him.

성층 成層 〔地質〕 bedding; stratification
■—암 (a) stratified rock; 〈퇴적암〉 (a) sedimentary rock —화산 a stratovolcano 《*pl.* ~(e)s》; a stratified volcano

성층권 成層圈 the stratosphere
◆성층권의 stratospheric / 성층권을 비행하다 fly through the stratosphere
■—비행 a stratospheric flight; a flight in the stratosphere ■—비행기 a stratoflying plane; a stratoplane; a stratoliner

성큼 with a long step; at [in] a stride
◆시내를 성큼 건너다 stride across a brook / (기일 등이) 성큼 다가오다 draw near [up, on]; be close at hand

성큼성큼 with long steps ◆성큼성큼 걷다 walk briskly; walk with long strides
▶그는 거리를 성큼성큼 걸어갔다 He strode along the street.
▶그는 방에서 성큼성큼 걸어나갔다 He stalked out of the room.

성탄 聖誕 1 〈성인•임금의 탄생〉 the birth of a saint [king] 2 ⇨ 성탄절

성탄절 聖誕節 Christmas Day ; Christmas; Xmas

> 解說 성탄절 기간(Christmastime)은 Christmas Eve (12월 24일)에서 1월 1일 (영국에서는 1월 6일) 까지를 말하며 12월 25일인 성탄일은 ***Christmas Day*** 또는 ***Christmas***라고 한다. Christmas는 광고문 등에서 ***Xmas***라고도 쓰는데 X'mas는 잘못된 표기다.

성터 城— the ruins of a castle; (the site of) a ruined castle; a fortress site

성토 聲討 censure; impeachment; denunciation —성토하다 censure; denounce; impeach
◆굴욕 외교를 성토하다 censure the humiliating diplomacy
■—대회 an indignation meeting; a rally

성패 成敗 success or failure; the result
▶성패는 자네의 노력에 달려 있네 Success depends on your efforts.
▶성패를 떠나서 그것을 해보는 게 어때? How about trying it regardless of the results?

성폭행 性暴行 a sexual assault [violence]; a sexual harassment

성품 性品 〈성질〉 nature; disposition; 〈기질〉 temper; temperament; 〈품격〉 (a) character

♦성품이 좋은 good-natured; kind-hearted / 성품이 좋지 않은 ill-natured; bad-tempered

성하 盛夏 the middle [height] of summer; midsummer

성하 聖下 〈가톨릭〉 His [Your] Holiness ♦바오로 교황 성하 His [Your] Holiness Pope Paul

성하다 1 〈온전하다〉 whole; sound; intact; undamaged; faultless; flawless; spotless
♦성한 과실 sound fruit / 성한 생선 fresh fish / 물건을 성하게 두다 leave [keep] a thing intact
▶성한 접시라고는 하나도 없다 Not a plate is left whole. ⇌ There isn't a whole plate left.
2 〈탈없다〉 healthy; (safe and) sound; (alive and) well; fit; robust
♦성한 몸 a healthy [sound] body / 몸 성히 돌아오다 come back safe [whole] / 몸 성히 지내다 be quite well; be fine; be in good health; get along well [all right]

성하다 盛— 〈초목이〉 thick; luxuriant; dense (forest); exuberant (foliage); leafy (woods); 〈기운·세력이〉 flourishing; prosperous; thriving; active; energetic; lively
▶지금 전염병이 성하다 An epidemic is raging.
▶그 지방에서는 농업이 성하다 Agriculture is extensively carried on in that district.
▶이곳은 그리스도교가 꽤 성하다 Christianity is fairly flourishing here.

성함 姓銜 your [his] (honored) name ⇨ 성명
▶성함이 어떻게 되십니까? May I have your name, please?
▶성함은 익히 들어 알고 있습니다 Your name is very familiar to me.

성행 性行 character and conduct

성행 盛行 prevalence; vogue; a fad; a rage
—성행하다 prevail; be prevalent; be much in fashion [vogue]; be very popular; rage; be rampant
▶투기가 성행하고 있다 Speculation is widely prevalent.
▶학생들 사이에 해외 여행이 성행하고 있다 Traveling abroad is popular among students.
▶정치인들 사이에 골프가 성행하고 있다 Golf is all the rage with politicians.

성행위 性行爲 a sex [sexual] act ♦성행위를 하다 perform a sexual act; have sex (with)

성향 性向 an inclination; a disposition; a propensity; a bent ♦호기심이 강한 성향의 사람 a man of curious disposition
■소비[저축]— the propensity to consume [save]

성현 聖賢 sages; saints and worthy men
♦성현의 가르침 the teaching of the sages; the words of the wise

성혈 聖血 sacred [holy] blood of Jesus

성형 成形 1 〔工〕 molding; forming; shaping **2** 〔醫〕 correction of deformities; 〈얼굴의〉 face-lifting ■—수술 《undergo》 a plastic operation

성형외과 成形外科 plastic surgery; restorative surgery ■미용— cosmetic surgery ■—의사 a plastic surgeon

성호르몬 性— (a) sex hormone

성홍열 猩紅熱 〔醫〕 scarlet fever; scarlatina ■단순 [악성]— scarlatina simplex [maligna]

성화 成火 annoyance; irritation; vexation; worry; (a) bother; (a) trouble; (a) torment
♦성화 나다 be worried [vexed, irritated]; fret; become impatient [nervous]
▶없는 돈을 자꾸 달라니 참 성화구나 You are a pest, the way you keep asking for money I don't have.
■—거리 a source of irritation; a cause of annoyance; a bother; a nuisance

성화 聖火 the sacred fire; 〈올림픽의〉 the Olympic torch [flame, fire]
■—대 a flameholder ■—봉송 the sacred-fire [-torch] relay ■—주자 a flame-bearer : 올림픽 성화 최종 주자 the anchor [last runner] of the Olympic sacred-fire relay

성화같다 星火— urgent; pressing; importunate ♦성화같이 urgently; importunately / 성화같이 독촉[독촉]하다 make an urgent request 《for》; press sb hotly for 《money》; demand sb importunately for 《money》
▶그는 돈을 갚으라고 독촉이 성화같다 He presses me hard for the money.

성황 盛況 prosperity; a boom; a success
♦성황을 이루다 〈모임 등이〉 be a success; be well attended; 〈상점 등이〉 be doing a flourishing business; do thriving business
▶다행히도 그들의 장사는 현재 성황을 이루고 있다 Fortunately their business is prosperous [flourishing, thriving] at present.
▶그 하기 강습회는 대단한 성황이었다 The summer workshop was a great success. ⇌ There were [was] a large number of participants in the summer institute.
▶모임은 성황리에 끝났다 The meeting ended successfully.

성황당 城隍堂 the shrine for a tutelary deity ⇨ 서낭(~당)

성히 safely; safe and sound

섶[1] 〈옷의〉 a gusset; a gore

섶[2] 〈꼬챙이〉 a prop; a stay; a support; 〈누에의〉 cocoon holders ♦섶으로 나무를 받치다 support a plant with a stick

섶(나무) brushwood; firewood

세 〈셋〉 three ♦세 번 three times; thrice / 세 사람 three men

세 稅 a tax; a duty 《on goods》; an imposition; dues; 〈지방세 등〉 rates
♦세의 부담 a tax burden [load] / 세를 포함한 가격 the price with taxes included / 세를 포함한 급여 one's salary before taxes 《are deducted》 / 세를 공제한 급여 take-home pay; one's pay after taxes / 세를 부과하다 impose a tax 《on》
▶자동차에는 여러 종류의 세가 붙는다 A car is subject to several kinds of taxes.
■개인[법인] 소득— an individual [a corporate] income tax 고정자산— a fixed property tax 국[시]— a national [municipal] tax 도로 통행— a toll tax 상속— a death [succession, an inheritance] tax 소비— a consumption tax 영업[물품]— a business [commodity] tax 유흥— an amusement tax 입항[운항통행]— harbor [canal] dues 주민— a resident tax 증여—

a gift tax 지방— (美) a local tax; (英) the rates 직접[간접]— a direct [an indirect] tax

세 貰 rent (부동산의); hire (탈 것의); 〈임대·임차〉 lease (부동산의)
♦ 집[방]세 a house [room] rent / 세가 비싼[싼] 집 a high-[low-]rent(ed) house / 세가 오르다[내리다] the rent rises [falls]/ 세를 놓다 ⇨ 세놓다 세를 내다 ⇨ 세내다 / 세를 올리다[내리다] raise [lower] the rent / 세를 물다 pay the rent (on the house); pay for (the house)
▶ 이 방은 세가 한 달에 20만원이다 This room goes for 200,000 won a month. ⇌ The rent for this room is two hundred thousand won a month.

세 勢 influence ⇨ 세력(勢力)

-세 let us; let's; let (me, him)
▶ 가세 Let's go.
▶ 어디 보세 Let me see.
▶ 그의 말도 좀 들어보세 Let him have his say.
▶ 내일 또 만나세 See you again tomorrow.

-세 -世 1 〈대(代)〉 a generation; an age
♦ 헨리 3세 Henry III [the Third]
2 〔地質〕 an epoch ♦ 홍적세 the diluvial epoch

세간 household goods [furniture, furnishings, stuff, things, utensils, effects]
♦ 부엌 세간 kitchen utensils [appliances]; kitchenware / 세간이 별로 없는 방 a scantily furnished room / 세간이 많다 be well furnished

세간나다 establish [set up] a branch [separate] family; create a new family; establish *oneself* in a new family
▶ 그는 장가 들어 세간났다 He got married and made a new home.

세간내다 set up a separate home (for)
♦ 아들을 세간내다 set up a separate home for *one's* son

세게 〈강하게〉 strongly; stoutly; powerfully; firmly; intensely; 〈격렬하게〉 hard; severely; violently; 〈강조하여〉 with emphasis
♦ 세게 나오다 show a bold [unyielding] front; go strong; take the high hand with *sb* / 세게 때리다 hit [strike] hard [vigorously]
▶ 나는 머리를 세게 얻어맞았다 I was struck hard on the head. ⇌ I received a hard blow on the head.

세계 世界 1 〈온세상〉 the world; 〈지구〉 the earth; the globe
♦ 세계의 international; world / 세계에서 in the world; on earth / 세계의 끝까지 to the end of the world / 세계 각지로부터 from all over the world; from all parts [the four corners] of the world / 세계를 일주하다 go [trip] (a) round the world; travel (all over) the world / 내일의 세계를 건설하다 build [make] tomorrow's world
▶ 세계의 이목이 서울에 집중되어 있다 The eyes of the world are centered on Seoul.
▶ 세계는 하나다 The world is one.
▶ 교통의 발달로 세계는 작아졌다 The world [earth] has become smaller with the development of transportation.
▶ 그는 1년 동안 세계를 두루 여행했다 He traveled all over the world for a year.
▶ 금강산은 세계에서 가장 아름다운 산 가운데 하나다 Kŭmgangsan is one of the most beautiful mountain in the world.
2 〈우주〉 the universe; the cosmos; 〈그 일부〉 a world
♦ 달[별] 세계 the lunar [stellar] world
▶ 신은 세계를 창조하였다 God created the universe.
3 〈특수한 사회〉 a world; a society; circles; 〈영역〉 a realm
♦ 공상의 세계 the realm of fancy / 꿈의 세계 the realm of dreams; dreamland / 상상[음악]의 세계 the world of imagination [music]/ 이상의 세계 an ideal world
▶ 그들 무리는 새로운 세계를 찾아 이주했다 Their group emigrated in search of a new world.
▶ 아이들의 세계에는 어른들로서는 이해할 수 없는 것들이 있다 In the world of children there are things that are beyond the comprehension of grown-up people.
▶ 그들은 우리와는 전혀 다른 세계에서 살고 있다 They live in a world quite different from ours.
■ —경제 world [international] economy —관 an outlook on the world; a view of the world; a world view [outlook] —국가 the World State —기상기구 the World Meteorological Organization (略 WMO) —박람회 an international exposition; a world's fair —보건기구 the World Health Organization (略 WHO) —사(史) world history; the history of the world —사조 the current thoughts of the world —상(像) a picture of the world; a world picture —선수권 a world [an international] championship —시민 a citizen of the world —어 a world [a universal, an international] language —은행 the World Bank; the International Bank for Reconstruction and Development (略 IBRD) —인 a cosmopolitan —인권선언 the Universal Declaration of Human Rights —전쟁 a world [global] war —정부 the world government —정세 the situation of the world —정신 the world spirit [soul] —정책 a world [global] policy —제패 domination of the world; world hegemony —평화 world [global] peace; the peace of the world : 세계 평화의 꿈 the dream of global peace

세계기록 世界記錄 a world record
♦ 세계기록을 세우다 establish [make, set (up)] a world record (in)
■ —보유자 a world-record holder

세계대전 世界大戰 the World War
■ —제1[2]차— the First [Second] World War; World War I [II]

세계연방 世界聯邦 the World Federation of Nations ■ —주의 World Federalism —주의자 a World Federalist

세계일주 世界一周 a tour round the world; a round-the-world trip; 〈배로 하는〉 circumnavigation of the earth ♦ 세계일주 비행 a round-

the-world flight
▶ 그는 세계일주 여행을 하고 있는 중이다 He is making a journey round the world.

세계적 世界的 world; world-wide; international; global; universal
◆ 세계적 불황 a world-wide economic depression / 세계적 인물 a world figure; a person of world-wide fame / 세계적으로 유명한 가수 a world-famous singer
▶ 그는 세계적으로 유명한 식물학자다 He is a world-famous botanist.
▶ 그녀의 이름은 세계적으로 알려져 있다 Her name is known all over the world.

세계제일 世界第一 the greatest [best] in the world
◆ 세계제일의 정치가 a No. 1 statesman in the world / 세계제일을 자랑하다 beat [lead] the world 《in》 / …으로는 세계제일이다 be the best [greatest]…in the world
▶ 세계제일의 갑부는 누구냐? Who is the richest man in the world?
▶ 미국은 세계제일의 강대국이다 America is the greatest power on earth.

세계주의 世界主義 cosmopolitanism; internationalism ■—자 a cosmopolitan; a citizen of the world; an internationalist

세공 細工 work; workmanship; craftsmanship
◆ 정교한[공들인] 세공 delicate [elaborate] workmanship / 세공 솜씨가 좋다[어설프다] be of good [bad] workmanship
▶ 이 인형은 세공이 참 잘 되어 있다 This doll is of exquisite workmanship [craftsmanship].
—세공하다 work 《in, on》
◆ 보석에 세공하다 work on precious stone / 은으로 세공하다 work in silver
▶ 이 조가비에 세공할 수 있습니까? Can you work on this shell?
▶ 그 벽은 아주 정교하게 세공되었다 The wall was most cunningly wrought.
■그물— netting; network 금속— metalwork 조가비— shellwork ■—인 a worker; a craftsman; an artisan —품 a (piece of) work; handiwork; ware : 미술 세공품 an art object

세관 稅關 a custom(s)house; the customs
◆ 세관을 통과하다 pass [get through, go through] (the) customs / 세관에서 소지품을 신고하다 declare one's things / 세관에서 관세를 지급하다 clear goods
▶ 세관을 통과하는데 30분 이상이 걸렸다 It took more than thirty minutes to get through the customs.
▶ 세관에서 짐 검사를 받았다 I got my baggage inspected at the customs.
▶ 우리는 부산 세관에서 위험물을 가지고 있지 않은지 조사를 받았다 We were inspected at the Pusan customhouse whether or not we carried dangerous weapons.
■—감시선 a customs inspection boat; a revenue cutter —법규 customs regulations —보세창고 a customs warehouse —송장(送狀) a customs invoice —수수료 an entry fee; a customs fee —신고서 a customs declaration —압수품 customhouse seizures —원 a customhouse officer; a customs officer [inspector]; a customs agent —장(長) the superintendent [commissioner, director, controller] of a customhouse; a custom director —절차 customs formalities —창고 a customs shed

세광 洗鑛 ore washing —세광하다 wash 《ore》; scrub 《ore》 ■—반(盤) a frame —부(夫) an ore washer [scrubber] —조(槽) 〔鑛〕 a buddle; a hutch

세궁민 細窮民 the poor (and needy); the indigent; paupers

세균 細菌 a bacterium 《pl. -ria》; a bacillus 《pl. -li》; a microbe; a germ
◆ 세균의 bacterial; bacillar; bacillary / 세균을 죽이다 destroy germs
▶ 상처에 세균이 들어갔다 The wound has become infected.
▶ 상처는 세균에 감염되기 쉽다 Wounds are apt to become infected.
■—검사 a bacteriological examination; bacilloscopy : 세균검사를 실시하다 examine bacteriologically —배양 bacilliculture; bacterial culture; germiculture —병기 a bacteriological weapon —설〔醫〕 the germ theory —성 질병 a germ disease —전 bacteriological [germ] warfare —탄 a germ [microbe] bomb

세균학 細菌學 bacteriology; microbiology
■—자 a bacteriologist; a microbiologist

세금 稅金 a tax; 〈지방세〉《英》the rates; 〈관세〉 a duty 《on》; 〈통행세〉 a toll; 〈수수료〉 dues
〈세금이〉 세금이 붙다 be dutiable; be taxable; be subject to duty [taxation] / 세금이 붙지 않다 be exempted from taxation [a tax]; be free of duty; be duty-[tax-]free
▶ 여권을 제시하면 카메라를 사는데 세금이 붙지 않는다 If you present your passport, you can buy a camera free of tax [duty].
〈세금을〉 세금을 부과하다 impose a duty 《on an article》; levy a tax 《on sb》; charge a tax 《on an income》; assess a tax 《on land》 / 세금을 납부하다 pay a tax [duty] 《on》 / 세금을 징수하다 collect taxes 《from》; draw a tax 《from》 / 세금을 경감하다 lighten taxes / 세금을 물납하다 pay a tax in kind / 세금을 속이다 defraud a tax / 세금을 체납하다 let taxes fall in arrears; fail to pay a tax on the due date / 세금을 포탈하다 evade a tax
▶ 세금을 내고 나면 얼마 남지 않는다 We have little (money) left after taxes.
▶ 그는 세금을 면제받고 있다 He is exempt from taxation.
■—부담 a tax burden [load] —징수[납부] the collection [payment] of a tax —체납 tax delinquency —포털 tax evasion —혜택 a tax favor : 세금 혜택을 주다 give a tax favor 《to》

세금공제 稅金控除 the personal tax deduction —가격 the price after (deduction of) tax —급료 take-home pay; pay after (deduction of) tax; pay minus tax [with tax excluded]

세금포함 稅金包含 ■—가격 the price before (deduction of) tax —급료 pay [a salary] with tax; pay plus tax [with tax included]; a salary including [inclusive of] tax

세기 世紀 a century
♦ 21세기 the twentyfirst [21st] century / 세기의 대사건 the salient event of the century / 세기의 영웅 the hero of the century / 기원전 3세기에 in the third century B.C./ 금세기에 in our own century / 18세기 초[중, 말]엽에 in the early [mid, late] eighteenth century / 수 세기에 걸쳐 through [over] many centuries; for centuries
▶ 컴퓨터는 세기의 대발명이다 Computers are the great invention of the century.
▶ 21세기의 막이 올랐다 The 21st century opened.

세기말 世紀末 the end of the century; (프) fin de siècle
♦ 세기말적인 fin-de-siècle; decadent

세끼 three (regular) meals (a day); daily meals

세나다¹ 〈덧나다〉 《a burn, a rash or swelling》 get worse; grow

세나다² 〈잘 팔리다〉 sell [be selling] well; enjoy a good demand; command a large [good] sale; be a good seller; be much sought after ♦ 세나는 물건 a good [quick] sell(er)
▶ 이 물건은 세납니다 This article sells like fun [wildfire, hot cakes].
▶ 요즈음 달걀이 세난다 Eggs are selling well these days.

세내다 貰— lease; rent; hire; pay to use
♦ 건물을 세내다 take a lease of a building / 배를 세내다 hire a boat;〈용선 계약으로〉 charter a vessel / 자동차를 세내다 rent [hire, pay to use] a car / 집을 세내다 rent a house

세네갈 〈나라이름〉 Senegal;〈공식명〉 the Republic of Senegal ♦ 세네갈의 Senegalese
—말 Senegalese —사람 a Senegalese

세놓다 貰— hire out; let out on hire; rent (to); lease (out)
♦ 자동차를 세놓다 hire out a car; rent a car / 자전거를 세놓다 let bicycles out on hire / 집을 세놓다 rent a house 《to sb》

세뇌 洗腦 brainwashing; brainwash ♦ 전쟁포로의 세뇌 the brainwash of war prisoners —세뇌하다 brainwash; wash sb's brain
▶ 그는 세뇌되어 비밀을 누설하고 말았다 He was brainwashed into revealing the secret.

세다¹ 〈머리털이〉 turn gray [white]; become grizzled [grizzly];〈얼굴이〉 turn pale [white] 《with fear》
♦ 센 머리 gray [white, hoary] hair / 머리가 세다 one's hair turns gray; get gray-haired
▶ 그녀는 걱정으로 머리가 하얗게 세었다 Anxiety has turned her hair all gray.

세다² 〈수를〉 count; reckon; calculate; number; numerate; take count of
♦ 셀 수 없이 많은 too many 《stars》 to count / 열을 세다 count ten / 1에서 100까지 세다 count from one to one hundred / 10에서 1까지 거꾸로 세다 count back from ten to one / 대충 세어 …이 되다 be roughly estimated at…
▶ 열까지 세고 눈을 뜨십시오 Count ten, and open your eyes.
▶ 세어 보니 교실에 32명의 학생이 있었다 There were, by count, 32 students in the classroom.
▶ 요즈음 진짜 정직한 사람은 손가락으로 셀 정도다 Nowadays, the really honest people can be counted on your fingers.
▶ 잘못 센 것 같군요. 다시 한번 세어 주십시오 You seem to have counted wrong [have miscalculated, have miscounted]. Please count once again.
▶ 틀린 데가 셀 수 없을 정도로 많았다 There were countless errors.

세다³ **1**〈힘이〉 strong; powerful; tough; mighty;〈기운이〉 vigorous;〈근력이〉 muscular

> [解說] **strong**은 가장 일반적인 말로 육체적인 힘을 비롯해 체력·구조·조직·정신·효력·색·빛·감정 등에 쓰인다. **powerful**은 다른 것들보다 눈에 띄게 힘을 발휘하고 있음을 가리키며 보통 그 영향력을 암시하고 있다. **tough**는 사람이나 물건이 단단하고 강한 것을 말하며 쉽사리 굽히지 않음을 강조한다.

♦ 힘이 센 사람 a man of muscle; a powerful [strong] man / 완력이 센 남자 (美俗) a tough guy / 세 보이는 strong-looking / 기운이 무척 세다 be as strong as a horse; be of Herculean strength / 힘이 세지다 become [grow] powerful [strong]
▶ 이 세상에서는 힘이 센 자가 이기게 마련이다 In this world the strong are sure to win.
2〈마음이 강하다〉 firm; stubborn
♦ 고집이 세다 be stubborn [obstinate]/ 배짱이 세다 have pluck [mettle]; have iron nerves
3〈세차다·강렬하다〉 violent; strong; hard; severe; fierce; intense; heavy; rough
♦ 센 물살 a swift [strong] current; rapids / 센 바람 a strong [violent] wind / 센 빛 a strong [an intense] light / 화력이 세다 have strong caloric force
▶ 바람이 세다 It is blowing hard. ⇒ The wind blows hard.
▶ 파도가 세다 The waves are high. ⇒ The sea is rough.
▶ 빛이 너무 세다 The light is too strong.
▶ 강의 중류는 물살이 세다 The current is swift in the middle of the river.
▶ 바람이 세졌다 It began to blow hard.
4〈잘하다〉 good 《at》; strong 《in》
▶ 그는 영어가 세다 He is strong in English.
▶ 그녀는 수학이 세다 She is good at mathematics.
▶ 그는 바둑이 세다 He is a good *paduk* player. ⇒ He is good at *paduk*.
5〈주량이〉 drink heavily
▶ 그는 술이 세다 He is a heavy drinker. ⇒ He drinks quite a lot. ⇒ He can hold his liquor.
▶ 자네 술이 꽤나 세구먼 You are a fairly good drinker, aren't you?
6〈팔자 등이〉 unlucky; ill-fated; evil-[ill-]starred ♦ 팔자가 세다 be ill-fated; have a hard fate [lot]/ 터가 세다 a site is ill-omened;〈집이 주어〉 have an unlucky aspect
7〈물이〉 hard;〈풀기가〉 stiff ♦ 센 물 hard water / 풀기가 너무 세다 be starched too stiff

세단 〈자동차〉 a sedan (car); 《英》 a saloon

(car)

세단뛰기 〖競〗 hop, step [skip] and jump; the triple jump

세대 世代 a generation
♦세대 차[단절] a generation gap / 젊은 세대 the younger [rising] generation / 새로운 세대 the new generation / 다음[지난] 세대 the next [past] generation / 여러 세대에 걸쳐 for generations / 세대 교체를 부르짖다 call for a shift in generation
▶ 그것은 세대가 다르기 때문이다 That's because we belong to the different generation.
▶ 정계도 이제는 세대 교체가 필요하다 A change of generation is needed in political circles now.
▶ 여러분은 다음 세대를 이끌어가지 않으면 안됩니다 You are destined to lead the next generation.
■ 무성(無性)— 〖生〗 the asexual generation 유성— 〖生〗 the sexual generation ■—교번 〖生〗 alternation of generations

세대 世帶 a household; a family; a home
▶ 이 아파트에는 몇 세대가 살고 있습니까? How many households [families] live in this apartment house?

세도 勢道 power; authority; influence; (holding) the reigns of government
♦ 세도(를) 부리다 exercise [exert, wield] one's authority [power] (over); lord it over —세도하다 have one's own way about state affairs; seize political power; assume the reigns of the government
■ —가[꾼] a man of power [influence]; a person in power; an influential person

세도막형식 —形式 〖樂〗 ternary form

세레나데 〖樂〗 a serenade

세력 勢力 1 〈지배력〉 influence; power; might; sway; strength
♦ 세력이 있는 influential; powerful / 세력이 없는 uninfluential; powerless / 세력을 떨치다 wield influence [power] (over); exercise authority (over); 꺾다 break sb's power / 세력을 잃다 forfeit one's influence; lose one's power / 세력을 만회하다 regain [win back] one's power [strength] / 세력을 얻다 acquire [obtain, gain] influence; become influential [powerful] / 세력을 확대하다 extend one's power [influence]
▶ 신문은 사회에서 하나의 세력이다 The press is a power in society.
▶ 그 파벌은 세력이 기울고 있다 The influence of the faction is declining.
▶ 그의 세력은 늘어간다 His influence [power] is increasing [on the rise].
▶ 그는 원내에 큰 세력을 가지고 있다 He has a great influence with the House.
2 〈물리적인 힘〉 force; energy
♦ 세력을 더하다 〈바람 등이〉 gather strength
■ 안정— a stabilizing force [factor] ■—가 a man of influence [weight]; an influential person —균형 the balance of power; the power balance ■—다툼 a struggle [contest, grab, scramble] for power; a power grab

세력권 勢力圈 a sphere [scope] of influence; one's territory
♦ 세력권 내에 있다 be within one's territory [orbit, sphere of influence] / 세력권을 넓히다 widen [enlarge, expand] one's sphere of influence; extend one's territory / 깽패들이 세력권을 다투다 fight for sphere of influence between gangsters / 세력권을 침범하다 intrude [break] into sb's domain; trespass on sb's territory

세력범위 勢力範圍 a sphere of influence ⇨ 세력권

세련 洗練·洗煉 refinement; polishing; finish

세련되다 洗練— be polished; be refined [finished]; be sophisticated; be elegant
♦ 세련된 말 (use) refined language; cultivated speech / 세련된 문체 a polished style / 세련된 신사 a polished [refined] gentleman / 세련된 어법 elegant phraseology / 말을 세련되게 하다 refine (on [upon]) one's language
▶ 그녀의 세련된 매너에 모든 사람이 매료되었다 All people were charmed with her refined [elegant] manners.
▶ 그는 말씨가 세련되었다 He is refined in speaking.
▶ 그녀는 요즈음 세련되어 졌다 She has become refined lately.

세례 洗禮 baptism; palingenesis; christening
♦ 세례를 베풀다 baptize; administer baptism (to) / 세례를 받다 accept [receive] baptism; be baptized; be christened / 포화 세례를 받다 receive [undergo] one's baptism of fire; be under fire; be exposed to fire / 주먹 세례를 퍼붓다 hail blows upon sb
▶ 나는 갓난 아이 때에 세례를 받았다 I was baptized when I was a baby.
▶ 그녀는 세례를 받고 기독교도가 되었다 She was baptized into the Christian faith.
▶ 일본은 세계에서 원폭 세례를 받은 유일한 나라다 Japan is the only country in the world that has a real experience of the atomic bomb.
■ 침수[관수]— baptism by immersion [effusion] ■—명 a baptismal [Christian] name —식 baptism; a baptismal ceremony [service] —요한 John the Baptist —자 a baptist

세로 〈명사적〉 length; 〈부사적〉 vertically; perpendicularly; longitudinally; lengthwise; endwise

> 解說 우리말의 「세로」는 상하, 「가로」는 좌우의 방향으로 각각의 위치 관계가 명확히 정해져 있지만, 영어의 경우는 길이의 대소를 보아 긴 쪽이 **length**, 짧은 쪽이 width가 된다. 따라서 우리말의 「세로」가 영어로는 length가 아니라 width가 되는 수도 있으므로 번역시에 주의할 필요가 있다.

♦ 세로 3 피트 가로 2 피트 three feet by two; three feet long and two feet wide [broad]/ 세로로 쓰다 write vertically / 세로로 자르다 cut lengthwise; sliver
▶ 그 판자는 세로가 3 미터다 The board is three meters long. ⇌ The board measures

three meters in length.
▶ 나는 카드를 세로로 늘어놓았다 I lined the cards up lengthwise.
▶ 한글은 세로로도 쓸 수 있고 가로로도 쓸 수 있다 The Korean alphabet can be written both vertically and horizontally.
▶ 이 그림은 세로 60센티미터 가로 80센티미터 다 This picture measures 60 centimeters wide [in width] and 80 centimeters long [in length].
■─무늬 vertical stripes ─선[줄] a perpendicular [vertical] line; a (longitudinal) stripe; 〈장기판 등의〉 a file; [樂] a bar; ─세로선을 긋다 draw a vertical line ─쓰기 vertical writing ─축 a vertical [longitudinal] axis; [數] the axis of ordinates

세루 serge ⇨ 서지

세류 細流 a little [small] stream; a streamlet; a brooklet

세륨 [化] cerium ♦세륨을 함유하는 ceric

세르반테스 〈스페인의 소설가〉 Cervantes, Miguel de (1547-1616)

세리 稅吏 a tax collector; a revenue officer

세립 細粒 a granule; a small grain

세마치 a large (3-man) blacksmith's hammer

세말 歲末 the end of the year ⇨ 세모(歲暮)

세면 洗面 washing one's face
─세면하다 wash one's face; have a wash
■─기 (美) a washbowl; (英) a washbasin ─대 a washstand; a washing stand; (英) a washhand stand ─소 a washroom; a lavatory; a toilet room

세모 triangularity; 〈삼각형〉 a triangle
♦ 세모난 모자 a three-cornered [tricornered] hat / 세모지다[나다] have three corners; be three-cornered; be triangular
■─기둥 a triangular prism ─꼴 a triangle ─끌 a triangular file ─송곳 a triangular drill

세모 歲暮 the end [close] of the year; the year-end ♦ 세모의 거리 풍경 a year-end scene of the street / 세모 선물을 보내다 send sb a year-end present

세모래 細─ fine sand

세모시 細─ ramie cloth of fine texture

세목 細目 details; particulars; items; specifications ♦ 세목에 이르다 enter [go] into details [particulars] / 세목으로 나누다 itemize; specify
■─교수─ a detailed plan for instruction; a syllabus

세목 稅目 tax items; items of taxation

세무 稅務 taxation business
■─공무원 a revenue officer [official]; a tax collector ─사 a licensed tax accountant ─사찰[조사] a tax investigation [surveillance]; a tax probe ─상담소 a tax information office ─행정 tax administration ─회계 accounting for taxation

세무서 稅務署 a tax [taxation] office; a revenue office ■─원 a tax-office clerk; a tax collector [man] ─장 the superintendent of a revenue office

세물 貰物 an object for hire [rent] ■─전(廛) a renter's store: 세물전 영감이다 be well-informed

세미나 a seminar ♦ 환경문제 세미나 a seminar on environmental problems

세미다큐멘터리(영화) ─(映畫) a semidocumentary (film)

세미콜론 a semicolon ♦ 세미콜론을 찍다 put a semicolon 《to》

세미파이널 〈준결승〉 semifinals

세미프로(페셔널) a semiprofessional; (口) a semipro

세밀 細密 minuteness; elaborateness ─세밀하다 minute; detailed; fine; close; elaborate
♦ 세밀한 검사 close [minute] examination / 세밀한 관찰 close observation / 세밀한 서술 detailed description / 세밀한 주의 close attention; meticulous care / 세밀한 지시 detailed instructions
■─화(畫) a miniature

세밀히 細密─ minutely; in detail; closely
♦ 세밀히 조사하다 inquire minutely into 《a matter》; examine closely [minutely] / 실험 결과를 세밀히 분석하다 analyze the results of an experiment closely [minutely]; make a close [minute] analysis of the results of an experiment

세밑 歲─ the year-end; the end [close] of the year ⇨ 세말, 세모, 연말

세발 〈三각(脚)〉 tripod ─받침 a tripod ─솥 a tripod (kettle) ─자전거 a tricycle ─의자 a tripod (chair) ─테이블 a tripod (table)

세발 洗髮 (a) shampoo; hair wash(ing)
─세발하다 wash the hair
■─제(劑) a hair wash; a shampoo

세배 歲拜 a New Year's bow; a New Year's call [visit]
─세배하다 make a New Year's bow
♦ 세배하러 가다 pay one's respects 《to sb》 at the New Year; pay a New Year's call [visit] 《to sb》/ 세배하러 다니다 make (a round of) New Year's calls [visits]
■─꾼 a New Year's caller [visitor] 세뱃돈 a New Year's gift money; money given as a gift at the New Year: 아이에게 세뱃돈으로 만원을 주다 give a child 10,000 won as a New Year's gift

세법 稅法 the tax law

세별 細別 subdivision ⇨ 세분(細分)

세부 細部 details; particulars
♦ 세부에 걸쳐 조사하다 go into details [particulars]
▶ 우리는 그 계획을 세부적으로 재검토하였다 We reconsidered the plan in detail.

세부득이 勢不得已 by an unavoidable circumstance; by force of circumstances
─세부득이하다 unavoidable

세분 細分 subdivision; fraction(iz)ation; a breakdown
─세분하다 subdivide; fractionize; break into parts; itemize
♦ 20종으로 세분하다 subdivide into twenty (sets); itemize 《things》 into twenty; break down to twenty items
▶ 각 장은 5개 단락으로 세분되어 있다 Each chapter is subdivided into five sections.

세비 歲費 〈연간 경비〉 yearly pay; an annual allowance [salary]; 〈지출〉 annual expenditure

세살 three years of age ▶ 세살 먹은 어린아이도 안다 A mere child knows it.

세살부채 細— a fine-ribbed fan

세살적 버릇이 여든까지 간다 《속담》 As a boy, so the man. ⇒ What is learned in the cradle [A man's hobby] is carried to the grave.

세살창 細—窓 a slender-ribbed window

세상 世上 **1** 〈세계〉 the world; 〈사회〉 (a) society; 〈인생〉 life; *one's* lifetime

〈세상의〉 세상의 주목을 받게 되다 come in the limelight / 세상의 쓴맛 단맛을 다 보다 taste the sweets and bitters of life / 세상의 화제가 되다 become the talk of the town

〈세상이[은]〉 세상이 싫어지다 be [become] weary of life [the world]; get tired of life
▶ 그건 세상이 다 아는 사실이다 All the [The whole] world knows it. ⇒ It is a matter of common [universal] knowledge.
▶ 세상은 넓고도 좁다 The world is not as [so] wide as it appears.

〈세상을〉 세상을 떠나다 die; pass away; depart this life; leave [go out of] the world; end [close] *one's* days / 세상을 버리다 forsake [renounce] the world; hide *oneself* from the world / 세상을 살아가다 live; get along in the world / 정직하게 세상을 살아가다 live an honest life; pursue an honest career / 세상을 알다 know the world; have seen much of life / 세상을 모르다 be ignorant of the world; have seen (but) little of the world / 세상을 시끄럽게 하다 create a sensation; make a noise in the world
▶ 전직 대통령의 수뢰 사건이 세상을 떠들썩하게 했다 The bribery case of the former president caused a world sensation.
▶ 너는 세상을 도무지 모르는구나 You know nothing of the world.

〈세상에(서)〉 (자식 등을) 세상에 내보내다 send out to the world; place out in life / 세상에 나오다 〈태어나다〉 be born into the world; 〈사회로 나오다〉 go out into the world [in life]; start (in) life / 세상에 알려져 있다 be known to the world; be famous in the world / (소문 등이) 세상에 알려지다 get abroad; come to light; become public / 세상에서 잊혀지다 be buried in oblivion; be forgotten by the world
▶ 그 사람만한 학자도 세상에 드물다 A scholar like him is rarely to be met with.
▶ 그런 짓을 하면 곧 세상에 알려진다 If you do such a thing, it will soon get abroad.

2 〈시대〉 the age [era, period]; the times
◆세상에 뒤지다 fall [lag, get] behind the times; get out of the touch with the world / 세상에 뒤떨어지지 않게 하다 keep up with the times; keep abreast of [with] the times
▶ 지금은 정보화 세상이다 This is an information age.
▶ 세상은 변했다 Times have changed.

3 〈독무대〉 ◆…의 세상이다 be *one's* own master [boss]; have *one's* own way
▶ 그가 없어졌으니 이제 우리 세상이다 Now that he is gone we are our own masters.
▶ 여기는 내 세상이다 Here I am absolutely my own boss [master].

세상맛 世上— the sweets and bitters of life
◆세상맛을 다 본 사람 a man of the world; a worldly-wise man / 세상맛을 알다 know what the world is

세상물정 世上物情 things [ways] of the world; (the condition of) the world; worldly matters
◆세상 물정에 밝은 사람 a man of the world; a sensible man / 세상 물정을 알게 되다 get used to the ways of the world; become worldly-wise
▶ 그는 세상 물정을 모른다 He knows nothing of the world. ⇒ He has seen but little of the world.
▶ 그는 낙천적인 사람이며 세상 물정에 관심이 없었다 He was an optimist and didn't care about the worldly matters.

세상사 世上事 worldly affairs; mundane matters; the ways of life
◆세상사에 밝은 사람 a worldly-wise man; a man of the world / 세상사에 밝다 be worldly-wise; have seen much of life; know the world / 세상사에 어둡다 know little of (the ways of) the world; be ignorant of the world; be wanting in worldly wisdom / 세상사에 익숙해지다 get used to the world; grow accustomed to the world
▶ 그는 은퇴 후 세상사에 아주 어두워졌다 He became quite ignorant of the world after he went into retirement.

세상살이 世上— living; (the mode [way] of) life —**세상살이하다** lead a life; live; go through the world; go on in the world

세상없어도 世上— (not) for (all) the world; by all means; under [in] any circumstances; not...on any account; on no account; for the life of *one*; by hook or by crook; whatever may happen
▶ 세상없어도 찾아뵙겠습니다 I will come by all means.
▶ 난 세상없어도 목적을 달성해 보이겠다 I will move heaven and earth to attain my end.
▶ 세상없어도 말 못하겠다 Come what may, I can't tell you.

세상에 世上— 《how, what, who, where, why》 on earth [in the world, in God's name]
▶ 세상에 어디 갔다 왔니? Where on earth have you been?

세세하다 細細— detailed, minute
◆세세하게 in detail; minutely; in particular / 세세하게 설명하다 explain in particular

세속 世俗 〈세상의 풍속〉 common [popular, vulgar] customs; 〈세상〉 the (mundane, secular) world
◆세속의 취향에 영합하다 play down to the popular taste / 세속을 초월하다 stand aloof from [rise above] the trivialities of life; be free from the trammels of ordinary life; be unworldly

■**—주의** secularism **—화(化)** secularization

세속적 世俗的 worldly; earthly; mundane; popular; social; secular
♦세속적 명성[욕망] a worldly fame [desire] / 세속적 지위 one's social standing
▶ 그녀는 세속적인 생활에 싫증이 났다 She was bored by the mundane life she led.

세수 洗手 washing one's face
♦세수 수건 a washcloth; a towel
─세수하다 wash up; wash one's face; have a wash; wash oneself
■세숫대야 (美) a washbowl; (英) a washbasin; a washhand basin 세숫물 wash(ing) water; water for face-washing; 〈씻고 난〉 washings 세숫비누 toilet soap

세수 稅收 the yield of taxes; tax revenues
♦세수의 증대 the increase of tax revenues

세슘 (化) cesium; caesium (기호 Cs) ■─시계 a cesium clock

세습 世襲 heredity; (法) descent; inheritance
♦세습의[적인] hereditary; patrimonial
─세습하다 transmit from generation to generation
■─권 a hereditary right (to) ─재산 hereditary property [estate]; (a) hereditament; heritage; patrimony ─제도 hereditary system

세시 歲時 1 〈새해〉 the New Year; the beginning of the year
2 〈일년 중의 때때〉 times and seasons
─기(記) a book of seasonal events

세심 細心 carefulness; circumspection; prudence
─세심하다 careful; close; scrupulous; elaborate; attentive; prudent; circumspect
♦세심한 주의 scrupulous care; careful attention / 세심한 주의를 기울이다 pay close attention (to)
▶ 이 수화물 취급에는 세심한 주의가 필요하다 This baggage needs to be handled with careful attention.

세쌍둥이 ─雙─ triplets; 〈그 하나〉 a triplet
♦세쌍둥이를 낳다 have three at a birth

세안 洗眼 eyewashing ─세안하다 wash one's eyes ─약 an eye lotion; a collyrium (pl. ~s, -ria); an eyewash

세액 稅額 the amount of (a) tax; the tax amount; an assessment ♦세액을 정하다 assess ■결정─ the settled tax amount ─산정(算定) the assessment of a tax ─조정 settlement of a tax

세우다 1 〈서게 하다〉 make (a thing) stand; erect; raise; set up; put up (a notice board); set (a book) on edge [end]; stand (a long thing) on end; plant (a pillar); prick (up) (one's ears)
♦기념비를 세우다 set up a monument / 외투깃을 세우다 turn up the lapels of one's overcoat / 기둥을 세우다 set up a post / 사람을 일렬로 세우다 form people in a line; place [stand] people in a row / 사람을 두 줄로 세우다 draw up people in two lines / 상자를 세워 놓다 place a box on end
▶ 우리는「출입 금지」팻말을 세웠다 We put [set] up a notice "Keep off".
2 〈멈추게 하다〉 stop; put a stop to; bring to a stop [standstill]; hold up [on]
♦차를 세우다 bring a car to a halt / 택시를 세우다 〈손을 들어〉 stop [hold up, (美) flag (down)] a cab
▶ 그는 차를 현관 앞에 세웠다 He pulled the car up at the porch.
3 〈짓다·만들다〉 build; construct; erect (a statue, a monument); set [put] up
▶ 이 텔레비전 방송국은 5년 전에 세워졌다 This TV station was built five years ago.
4 〈설립·조직하다〉 establish (a school, a firm); found (a country); create; set up; organize
5 〈제도 등을〉 institute (a system); lay down (rules); establish (regulations); enact (a law)
6 〈계획을〉 form [make, lay] (a plan); shape; lay (down) (one's course); map out (a program)
▶ 계획을 잘 세웠습니까? Did you set your plan carefully?
7 〈예산을〉 ♦예산을 세우다 make a budget [an estimate]; budget for (the coming year)
8 〈이론·학설 등을〉 advance; set up; frame; set forth; put forward (an argument); lay down (a proposition); develop; formulate
♦새로운 이론을 세우다 set up [propose, advance] a new theory
9 〈뜻을〉 have (an object) in view; set (an object before one); be determined to (do); have (a fixed purpose) (in life); make up one's mind
▶ 한 번 뜻을 세웠으면 끝까지 노력해라 Once you have made up your mind to do something, keep up your efforts toward it to the very end.
10 〈성취하다〉 achieve; render; perform
11 〈사람을 어떤 자리에〉 put up; appoint; nominate (sb for mayor)
♦보증인을 세우다 find [give] surety [security] for; 〈신원 보증인을〉 give a reference / 후보자를 세우다 put up a candidate; have sb stand for (the House)
12 〈날을〉 put [forge] an edge (on); give an edge (to); edge; sharpen (a knife)
♦칼날을 날카롭게 세우다 put a sharp edge on a knife / 톱날을 세우다 set (the teeth of) a saw
13 〈체면을〉 keep up; save
♦체면을 세우다 save [keep up] appearances; save one's face [honor]
14 〈기대 놓다〉 put [rest, place, stand, lean] sth against
♦우산[사다리]을 벽에 세우다 stand an umbrella [a ladder] against the wall
15 〈생계를〉 support [maintain] oneself; earn one's living

세워총 ─銃 ♦세워총을 하다 order arms
▶ 세워총 (口令) Order arms!

세원 稅源 a source of taxation [tax revenue]; 〈과세 대상〉 an object of taxation

세월 歲月 1 〈시간〉 time (and tide); years (and months); days (and months)
♦긴[짧은] 세월 a long [short] period [space] of time / 세월이 감[흐름]에 따라 with the pas-

sage [lapse] of time [years]; as time passes on; as days [the years] go [roll] by / 오랜 세월이 지난 후 after long years; after (a lapse of) many years / 세월을 허송하다 pass time idly; idle [dawdle] *one's* time away
▶ 다리가 완성되기까지는 많은 세월이 걸렸다 It took a long time [years] to complete the bridge.
▶ 한국에 와서 10년의 세월이 흘렀다 Ten years have passed since I came to Korea.
▶ 세월이 약이다 (속담) Time is healer.
▶ 세월은 유수와 같다 (속담) Time flies like an arrow. ⇒ Time is fleeting.
▶ 세월은 사람을 기다리지 않는다 (속담) Time and tide wait for no man.
2 〈형편〉 the times; things; 〈시황〉 business; the market
▶ 세월이 어떻습니까? How is your business? ⇒ 〈생활 전반〉 How are you getting along? ⇒ How goes it (with you)?
▶ 세월이 좋다[없다] The times are good [bad, hard]. ⇒ Business [The market] is brisk [dull, quiet].
▶ 이 계절에는 세월이 없다 Business is slack at this season.

세율 稅率 the rate of taxation; tax rates; 〈관세의〉 a tariff
♦ 국정 세율 a statutory tariff / 세율 변경 the modification of the tax rates / 세율을 올리다 [내리다] raise [lower] the tax rates [the tariff] / 세율을 정하다 tariff 《goods》
■ ─표 a table of tax rates; a tariff

세이레 〈삼칠일〉 the twenty-first day after a baby's birth

세이셸 〈나라 이름〉 Seychelles; 〈공식명〉 the Republic of Seychelles

세이프 〔野〕 safe ♦ 세이프를 선언하다 declare safe

세인 世人 people; the world; the public
♦ 세인의 이목을 피하다 avert people's eyes; avoid public notice
▶ 그 사건은 세인을 놀라게 했다 The incident surprised the world.

세인트버나드 a Saint Bernard

세일 〈염가 판매〉 a sale
♦ 여름[겨울, 연말] 세일 a summer [winter, year-end] sale / 재고 정리 세일 a clearance sale
▶ 이 옷은 내가 몇해 전 여름 세일 때 샀다 I bought this dress at a summer sale some years ago.

세일러복 ─服 a sailor suit; 〈상의〉 a middy blouse

세일즈맨 〈남자 점원〉 a salesman

> 解說 *salesman*은 외판원뿐만 아니라 점원도 가리킨다. 일상적으로는 전자를 sales representative, 후자를 (美) salesclerk, (英) shop assistant라고 불러 구별한다. 여점원은 saleswoman, saleslady, salesgirl이라고 한다. 남녀 모두 복수형은 salespeople이다.

세일즈 엔지니어 〈판매 전문 기술자〉 a sales engineer

세입 稅入 tax revenues [yields]
♦ 세입의 증가[감소] an increase [a drop] in revenue

세입 歲入 〈국가의〉 an annual revenue; 〈개인의〉 an annual income
■ ─관세 revenue duties ─세출 revenue and expenditure ─예산 명세서 a detailed statement of estimated revenue ─예산안 a revenue bill ─예산액 an estimated amount of revenue; estimated revenues ─위원회 〈영·미국 하원의〉 the Committee on [(英) of] Ways and Means

세자 世子 the Crown Prince ⇨ 왕세자

세자 細字 small characters [letters]; small type [print]; fine print

세잔 〈프랑스의 화가〉 Cézanne, Paul (1839-1906)

세전 世傳 handing down from generation to generation ■ ─지물 heirlooms; things handed down from generation to generation

세전 歲前 ♦ 세전에 before the New Year

세정 世情 〈형편〉 the ways of the world; world; 〈인정〉 human nature; humanity
♦ 세정에 밝은 사람 a man of the world / 세정에 어둡다 know little of the world

세정 稅政 tax administration

세제 洗劑 a cleanser; cleaning material; a detergent ■ 중성[합성]─ a neutral [synthetic] detergent

세제 稅制 the taxation system [scheme]
■ ─개혁 a tax reform [revision]

세제곱 〔數〕 cube
▶ 3의 세제곱은 27이다 The cube of 3 is 27.
─세제곱하다 cube; raise 《a number》 to the third power
■ ─근(根) 〔數〕 a cubic root ─미터 a cubic meter ─비(比) 〔數〕 a triple [triplicate] ratio

세주다 貰 ─ 〈가옥·토지 등을〉 rent 《a house to sb》; rent out 《a mansion》; (英) hire [let] out 《a house》; lease; let out 《land》 on lease; grant a lease
♦ 방을 세주다 take in lodgers [roomers]; (美) rent a room; (英) let a room

세차 洗車 car washing; car wash ─세차하다 wash a car [an automobile] ■ ─장 a car wash

세차 歲差 〔天〕 precession ■ 분점─ precession of the equinoxes

세차다 violent; strong; vehement
♦ 세찬 바람 a strong [severe, violent, sharp] wind
▶ 바람이 세차게 분다 It blows furiously [smartly].
▶ 세찬 바람 때문에 파도가 더욱 거세졌다 Due to the strong wind, the sea waves got more and more furious.
▶ 비가 세차게 내렸다 It rained hard [heavily].

세차운동 歲差運動 〔天〕 precessional motion; precession ─세차운동하다 precess

세찬 歲饌 〈음식〉 food for serving New Year's guests

세책 貰册 a book for lending ⇨ 대본(貸本)

세척 洗滌 washing; cleansing; cleaning; rinsing; lavation; 〔醫〕 irrigation; 〈위·장 등의〉

세출

lavage; 〈수술 후의〉 toilet
—세척하다 wash; rinse (a bottle); rinse out (impurities); deterge; 〖醫〗 irrigate
♦ 위를 세척하다 carry out a gastric lavage
—기 a washer; a washing machine [apparatus]; a syringe —제 a wash; a detergent; an abstergent; an abluent

세출 歲出 annual expenditure(s)
■ 세입— revenue and expenditure ■ —예산액 estimated expenditures —외 자금 a non-appropriated fund —위원회 〈미국 하원의〉 the House Appropriation Committee

세칙 細則 detailed rules [regulations]; 〈부칙·준칙〉 bylaws ■ 시행— detailed rules for operation; detailed regulations relative to the application of the law

세칭 世稱 what is called [known as]; what people call; as they say; the so-called
♦ 세칭 일류 대학 a so-called prestige [leading] university

세컨드 1 〖野〗 〈2루〉 second base; 〈2루수〉 the second baseman 2 〖拳〗 〈보조자〉 a second 3 〈초(秒)〉 a second 4 〈첩〉 one's secondary wife

세쿼이아 〖植〗 a sequoia; a redwood

세탁 洗濯 a wash; washing; laundering; cleaning
♦ 물 세탁이 가능하다 be washable; stand washing
—세탁하다 wash; launder; clean; scour
♦ 세탁하러 보내다 send (one's clothes) to the wash [laundry]; send on [out] (one's clothes) for laundry
▶ 이것은 세탁하면 오그라든다 This shrinks in washing [in the wash].
▶ 그녀는 열심히 세탁하고 있었다 She was laboring over her wash.
▶ 나는 셔츠를 세탁하러 보냈다 I sent my shirts to the laundry.
■ —비 laundry charges —비누 laundry [washing] soap —소 a laundry; a cleaner's —업자 a laundryman; a washerman; a (dry) cleaner

세탁기 洗濯機 a washing machine; a washer
♦ 동전 투입식 자동 세탁기 launderette; (商標) Laundromat —전기— an electric washing machine; an automatic washer

세탁물 洗濯物 clothes to be washed [laundered]; washing; laundry
♦ 세탁물이 많다 have a lot of washing to do / 세탁물을 널다 hang out (the) washing to dry

세태 世態 an aspect of life; a sign of the times; the prevailing state of society; 〈사회정세〉 social conditions; the order [condition, current] of the world
▶ 대중 가요는 세태를 반영한다 Popular songs reflect the social conditions of the day.
▶ 이 소설은 당시의 세태를 사실적으로 묘사하고 있다 This novel is a perfect picture of people's life in the contemporary world.

세터 1 〈사냥개〉 a setter 2 〈배구에서〉 the person who sets up the ball

세톱 細— a fine-tooth saw

세트 1 〈한 벌〉 a set (of tableware)
♦ 응접 세트 a drawing-room suite / 커피 세트 a coffee (serving) set; a coffee service
2 〈무대 장치〉 a setting; 〈영화의〉 a set; a studio set
▶ 전쟁 장면을 세트로 촬영했다 They filmed the war scene on the set.
3 〈구기에서〉 a set
♦ 세트 포인트 a set point
4 〈수신기〉 a receiving set ♦ 텔레비전 세트 a television [TV] set
5 〈퍼머넌트 웨이브의〉 a (wave) set
■ —신 a set scene

세트포지션 〖野〗 the (pitcher's) set position

세파 世波 the rough-and-tumble of life
♦ 세파에 시달리다 be buffeted about in the world; be tossed about in the storms of life; taste the sweets and bitters of life
▶ 그는 세파에 시달렸다 He got [went] through the storms of life.

세퍼레이츠 〖服〗 separates

세평 世評 〈여론〉 public opinion; common talk of the town; 〈평판〉 reputation; 〈소문〉 rumor; hearsay
♦ 세평에 따르면 People [They] say...; It is said [reported] that... / 세평에 오르다 be the talk of the town; be talked about
▶ 그는 세평에는 관심이 없다 He does not care what people say about him.

세포 細胞 1 〖生〗 a cell
♦ 세포의 cellular; cell / 다세포의 multicellular / 단세포의 unicellular
2 〈조직의 작은 단위〉 a cell
♦ 공산당 세포 a communist cell [fraction] / 세포를 조직하다 organize a cell
■ 생식— 〖生〗 a gamete; a reproductive cell —막 〖生〗 the cell membrane —발 생 cytogenesis —분열 〖生〗 cell division —유전학 cytogenetics —융합 〖生〗 cell fusion —조직 cellular tissue —질(質) 〖生〗 cytoplasm —체 a cell body —학 cytology : 세포학의 cytological —학자 a cytologist —핵 〖生〗 a cell nucleus (pl. -clei, ~es)

섹셔널리즘 sectionalism ⇨ 섹트(~주의)

섹션 〈구획〉 a section ■ —페이퍼 〈모눈 종이〉 section paper

섹스 sex
■ —심벌 a sex symbol —어필 sex appeal; sexual attractiveness

섹시하다 sexy; sexually attractive [appealing] / 섹시한 여자 a sexy girl; (俗) a sexpot
▶ 그녀는 얼굴이며 목소리가 제법 섹시하다 Her face and voice are rather sexy.

섹트 〈분파〉 a sect ■ —주의 sectionalism; sectarianism

센 〈파리의 강〉 the Seine

센말 〖言〗 an intensive [emphatic] variant of a word

센머리 〈백발〉 gray [white, hoary] hair

센서스 〈국세·인구 조사〉 a census

센세이션 sensation ♦ 센세이션을 일으키다 create [cause] a sensation (in)

센스 a sense ♦ 센스가 있다[없다] have good [no] sense

센터 1 〈중심지·시설〉 a center

|解說| 「…센터」는 medical center, recreation center, sports center, leisure center, shopping center 등과 같이 *...center* 라고 하면 된다. trade center (무역 센터), commercial center (상업 중심지) 등에서는 center가 「종합적인 시설·건물」과 「…의 중심지」라는 두 가지 뜻을 갖고 있으므로, 후자의 뜻인 경우는 a center of trade, a center of commerce와 같이 써서 전자와 구별하기도 한다.

2 〔野〕 center field; 〈선수〉 a center fielder ■ 쇼핑— a shopping center ■ —백 〈배구 등의〉 a center back —포워드 〔蹴〕 a center forward

센터링 〔建〕 〈공가(拱架)〉 centering; 〔蹴〕 centering

센터플라이 〔野〕 a fly ball to center; a center fly ball ♦ 센터 플라이를 날리다 make [hit] a fly ball to center

센트 〈화폐단위〉 a cent (略 c.)
♦ 25센트 twenty-five cents; a quarter; (美俗) two bits (▶1 bit = 12.5 cents)/5[10, 25, 50]센트화 a nickel [dime, quarter (dollar), half dollar]

센트럴히팅 central heating

센티- 〈100분의 1〉 centi-
■ —그램 a centigram (略 cg.) —리터 a centiliter (略 cl.) —미터 a centimeter (略 cm)

센티멘털리즘 sentimentalism

센티멘털하다 sentimental

셀러리 〔植〕 celery

셀렌 〔化〕 selenium

셀로판 cellophane ■ —지(紙) cellophane (paper) —테이프 cellophane adhesive tape; (商標) Scotch tape

셀룰로오스 〔化〕 〈섬유소〉 cellulose

셀룰로이드 celluloid

셀링 포인트 〈판매시의 강조점〉 a selling point

셀프서비스 self-service ♦ 셀프서비스 식 상점 a self-service store / 셀프서비스 식 식당 a self-service restaurant; a cafeteria

셀프타이머 〔寫〕 〈자동셔터〉 a self-timer ♦ 카메라의 셀프타이머 a self-timer on a camera

셈 **1** 〈계산〉 calculation; account; counting; figures; reckoning; computation
♦ 셈이 빠르다[느리다] be quick [slow] at figures [accounts]/셈이 틀리다 make a mistake in calculation; miscalculate; calculate wrongly / 셈에 넣다 take 《a thing》 into account [consideration]/셈에 넣지 않다 leave 《a thing》 out of account
—셈하다 count; reckon; calculate; compute
♦ 돈을 셈하다 count money
2 〈지불〉 settlement of accounts; payment of bills
♦ 셈을 미루다 postpone *one's* payment
▶ 셈이 전부 얼마요? How much does the whole account come to?
▶ 셈은 따로따로 해주시오 Separate checks [bills], please!
▶ 나는 셈을 전부 치렀다 I've paid all my bills.
—셈하다 pay a bill; settle *one's* accounts; settle [square] accounts 《with *sb*》
3 〈작정·속셈〉 an intention; a design; a purpose
♦ …할 셈으로 with the intention [object, aim, idea] of doing; with a view to do
▶ 나는 그럴 셈이다 I have a mind to [mean to] do so. ⇌ I have the intention of [think of] doing so.
▶ 너는 언제 돌아올 셈이냐? When are you supposed to come back?
▶ 그들은 어쩔 셈일까? What are they going to do? ⇌ What do they intend to do?
4 〈셈판〉 the situation; circumstances; the matter; the case; reason; cause
▶ 어찌 된 셈이냐? Tell me why. ⇌ What's the story?
▶ 혹 떼러 갔다가 혹 붙인 셈이었다 It was an instance of the biter bit.
▶ 이번 생일이면 너도 스무 살이 되는 셈이구나 You'll be twenty years old next birthday.
5 〈분별〉 discretion; prudence; good sense; judg(e)ment

셈속 **1** 〈속 내용〉 the real state of affairs [things]
2 〈속마음〉 the mind; *one's* inmost thoughts [true motive]; *one's* heart of heart; the back of *one's* mind
♦ 셈속을 알 수 없는 사람 an inscrutable person; a person of very profound character
▶ 난 네 셈속을 알 수가 없다 I cannot read your inmost thoughts.

셈치다 **1** 〈계산하다〉 count; calculate; reckon
2 〈…한 것으로 생각하다〉 suppose; assume; grant
▶ 나는 영화 본 셈치고 저금하기로 했다 I have decided to save the money, not allowing myself to spend it for a movie.
▶ 그것은 잃어버린 셈치자 Let us suppose that we lost it.
▶ 나는 그 돈을 없어진 셈치고 있다 I regard the money as gone.
▶ 죽을 셈치고 해보자 Let us do or die.
▶ 나는 죽을 셈치고 휴전선을 넘어왔다 I came over the armistice line at the risk of my life.

셈판 〈형편〉 the situation; circumstances; 〈까닭〉 cause; ground; reason
▶ 나는 무슨 셈판인지 모르겠다 I don't know how the matter stands.
▶ 나보다 네가 먼저 알고 있으니 어찌 된 셈판이냐? How comes it that you know it before me?
▶ 그가 오지 않으니 무슨 셈판일까? What's the matter with him that he doesn't come?

셋 three; 〈로마 숫자〉 Ⅲ

셋돈 貰— rent (money) ♦ 셋돈을 내다 pay *one's* rent

셋방 貰房 (美) a room for rent; (英) a room [an apartment] to let; 〈세든 방〉 a rented room
♦ 셋방에 든 사람 a lodger; a tenant; (美) a roomer / 셋방살이하다 live in a rented room
▶ 셋방 있음 (게시) (美) Rooms for rent. ⇌ (英) Rooms to let.

셋잇단음표 —音標 〔樂〕 a triplet

셋집 貰— (美) a house for rent; (英) a house to

let; 〈세든 집〉 a rental [rented] house
♦셋집 주인 the owner of a house; a house owner; 〈남자〉 a landlord; 〈여자〉 a landlady / 셋집에 세든 사람 a tenant / 셋집에 살다 live [make *one's* home] in a rented house
▶그는 오늘 셋집을 구하러 나갔다 He went house-hunting today.
▶셋집 있음 (게시) (美) For rent. ⇌ (英) To let.
셋째 the third
셔링 〈주름〉 shirring
셔벗 〈빙과〉 sherbet; sorbet
셔츠 shirts

解説 우리말에서는 내의를 가리키는 경우가 많은데 내의는 undershirt이다. (英)에서는 vest 또는 singlet이라고 한다. 「와이셔츠」는 white shirt가 잘못 전해진 것인데 영어로는 그저 *shirt* 또는 dress shirt라고 한다.

─────── 셔츠 ───────

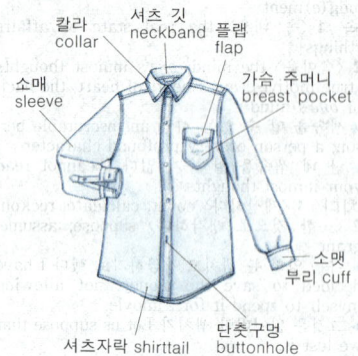

셔터 1 〈사진기의〉 a shutter
♦셔터를 누르다 press [release, snap, click] the shutter
2 〈덧문〉 a shutter
♦셔터를 내리다 pull down a shutter
▶가게는 이미 셔터가 내려져 있다 The store has already put up the shutters.
셧아웃 1 〈내쫓음〉 shutting out ─**셧아웃하다** shut out 2 〈野〉 a shutout (game) ─**셧아웃하다** shut out (the opposing team) ♦셧아웃당하다 get a shutout
셰르파 〈티베트 고산족〉 a Sherpa 《*pl.* ~ (s)》
셰리 〈술〉 sherry
셰이드 〈차양〉 a shade; 〈전등 갓〉 a (lamp) shade
셰이빙크림 〈면도용〉 shaving cream
셰익스피어 〈영국의 시인·극작가〉 Shakespeare, William (1564-1616)
♦셰익스피어 전집 the Complete Works of Shakespeare / 셰익스피어 작품 a (work of) Shakespeare / 셰익스피어의 Shakespearian; Shakespearean
셰퍼드 〈개〉 an Alsatian; a German shepherd (dog)
셸리 〈영국의 시인〉 Shelley, Percy Bysshe (1792-1822)
소¹ [動] 〈암소〉 a cow; 〈수소〉 a bull; (총칭) cattle; 〈거세한〉 an ox (*pl.* oxen); a bullock; 〈송아지〉 a heifer; a calf (*pl.* calves)

解説 소의 총칭은 ***cattle*** (집합명사로 복수취급)이지만 개별적으로는 ***bull*** (수소), ***cow*** (암소), ***calf*** (송아지), ***ox*** (노역용·식용의 거세한 수소)라고 한다. cow는 암소지만 흔히 일반어로 쓴다. 다만 동물학적으로는 ox로 쓴다. 소의 울음소리를 나타내는 말은 moo가 일반적이며 bellow는 특히 수소가 큰소리로 울 때 쓴다.
수사를 앞에 붙여 몇 「마리」라고 할 때는 head에 s를 붙이지 않는다.

♦식용용 소 beef cattle / 소 열 마리 ten cows / 소걸음으로 걷다 walk at a snail's [turtle's] pace / 덴 소 날뛰듯 하다 go on a wild rampage; rage [rave] in all (its) fury / (무게를 늘리려고) 소에게 물을 먹이다 force water down an ox / 소를 기르다 keep [raise] cattle / 짐나르는 마소처럼 부려먹다 use *sb* like a beast of burden
▶내 연구는 진척이 소걸음 같다 Progress on my research is proceeding at a snail's pace.
■─도둑 a cattle thief; (美口) a rustler ─떼 a herd of cattle

─────── 소 ───────

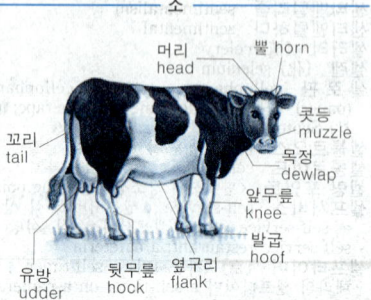

소² 〈만두·떡 등의〉 stuffing; a filling; dressing
♦소를 넣은 stuffed / 만두에 소를 넣다 stuff a dumpling
소 小 smallness ▶소를 죽이고 대를 살린다 Sacrifice a few to save the many.
소 沼 a swamp; a marsh; a pond; a bog
♦소가 많은 swampy; marshy; boggy
소- 小- small; little; minor; lesser; miniature
♦소극장 a little theater / 소위원회 a subcommittee / 소자본 a small capital
소가족 小家族 a small family
─제도 the small-family system
소각 燒却 incineration; cremation
─**소각하다** burn up [down]; incinerate; cremate; commit (a thing) to the flames
■─로[기] an incinerator; a trash burner ─장 a burning place

소간 所幹 〈용무〉 business; affairs; 〈일〉 work; an engagement ♦ 소간이 있다 have *sth* to do; be engaged

소간사 所幹事 business ⇨ 소간(所幹)

소갈머리 a disposition; (a) nature; (a) temper; (a) temperament ♦ 소갈머리가 좋은 narrow-minded; intolerate; thoughtless

소감 所感 one's feeling [thoughts, impressions, opinions] ♦ 소감을 말하다 express one's impressions 《of》
▶ 이 공연에 대해서 소감을 한 말씀 드리겠습니다 Let me say a few words about this performance.

소강 小康 a (temporary) lull; a (brief) respite; a letup; an easing; a breathing space [spell, time] (of peace [calmness, ease])
♦ 소강 상태가 되다 come to a (state of) lull; achieve [be allowed] a breathing space

소개 紹介 1〈서로 알도록 함〉 (an) introduction ♦ …의 소개로 through the introduction of…; with an introduction from…
ㅡ소개하다 introduce; present (a program)
♦ 모든 사람에게 소개하다 introduce *sb* all round / 정식으로 소개하다 introduce *sb* formally to *sb*
▶ 이 영화는 최근의 동남아시아 상황을 소개한다 This film presents the recent state of affairs in Southeast Asia.
▶ 제 친구 송 군을 소개합니다 Allow me to [Let me] introduce to you my friend, Mr. Song.
▶ 방금 사장님께서 소개한 김상수입니다 I am Kim Sang-su who has had the honor of being introduced to you by the president.
2〈어떤 사실・내용을〉ㅡ소개하다 ♦ 한국을 호의적으로 소개하는 기사 an article presenting Korea favorably
▶ 그는 두어 권의 신간 서적을 잡지에 소개했다 He reviewed a few new books in the magazine.
▶ 그 사건은 신문에 소개되었다 The incident was reported in the papers.
3〈추천・알선〉 good [kind] offices; a service; recommendation
♦ …의 소개로 through the good offices of…; at the recommendation of…
ㅡ소개하다 use [exercise] one's good offices; do *sb* a service
▶ 편집 고문을 한 사람 소개해 주십시오 Could you find [get] me an advisory editor?
■ 자기ㅡ (a) self-introduction : …이라고 자기 소개를 하다 introduce oneself as… ㅡ료 a commission; brokerage ㅡ소 ⇨ 직업 소개소 ㅡ업 brokerage; commission agency; go-between business ㅡ자 an introducer; 〈주선인〉 a go-between; 〈추천인〉 a recommender

소개 疏開 〈분산〉 (an) evacuation; 〈산개〉 dispersal; deployment
ㅡ소개하다 disperse; evacuate; remove
■ 강제ㅡ forced [compulsory] removal [evacuation] ■ ㅡ자 an evacuee ㅡ지 one's place of refuge; dispersal area

소개장 紹介狀 a letter of introduction
♦ 소개장을 받다 get a letter of introduction 《to》 / 소개장을 써 주다 write a letter of introduction 《for *sb*》

소거 消去 1〈말소〉 erasure ㅡ소거하다 erase 2 〖數〗 elimination ㅡ소거하다 eliminate

소견 所見 one's view [opinion]; 〈느낌〉 one's impressions
♦ 소견을 말하다 give [set forth] one's view [opinion] 《on》; express [voice] one's impressions 《of》
▶ 그는 소견이 좁다 He is narrow-minded.
■ 진단ㅡ a diagnostic view ■ ㅡ표 a school report; a report on a student's record

소결절 小結節 〖病理〗 a nodule

소경 1〈맹인〉 a blind [sightless] person; (총칭) the blind ♦ 소경이 되다 go [become] blind; lose one's sight / 소경으로 태어나다 be born blind
2〈문맹〉 an unlettered person; an illiterate (person); an ignoramus
▶ 그것을 모르다니 눈뜬 소경이로구나 You are a bat-blind person unable to recognize it.

소경 매질 하듯 (속담) at random; recklessly

소경 문고리 잡듯 (속담) A blind man may sometimes catch the hare.

소경 잠자나 마나 (속담) That's quite an inconspicuous deed.

소계 小計 a subtotal ♦ 소계를 내다 subtotal; do a partial sum ▶ 소계 2만원이다 It subtotals twenty thousand won.

소고 小鼓 〈농악기〉 a small hand drum

소곡 小曲 a short piece (of music); a sketch

소곤거리다 whisper; talk in a whisper; talk in a subdued tone ♦ 소곤거리는 소리 a whispering [suppressed] voice; a whisper / 소곤거리며 in a whisper; in whispers

소곤소곤 1〈작은 소리로〉 below [under] one's breath; in a suppressed [low] voice; in an undertone; in whispers
♦ 소곤소곤 이야기하다 talk in whispers; speak under one's breath
2〈은밀히〉 secretly; in secret; in confidence

소곳이 with one's head drooped

소관 所管 jurisdiction; competency; control
♦ 소관이다 fall under [be subject to] the jurisdiction 《of》; be under the control 《of》 / 소관 밖이다 be beyond the jurisdiction 《of》
▶ 그 문제는 우리 소관 밖의 일이다 The matter doesn't come within our jurisdiction.
■ ㅡ관청 the competent [proper] authorities; the authorities concerned ㅡ사항 matters within one's jurisdiction : 내무부 소관 사항 matters under the jurisdiction of the Ministry of Home Affairs

소관 所關 what is concerned
■ ㅡ사(事) one's business; one's concern; matters concerned : 그것은 네 소관사가 아니다 It is no affair [concern] of yours. ≒ It is none of your business.

소국 小國 a small country; a lesser [minor] power

소굴 巢窟 a den; a haunt; a nest; a hotbed
♦ 갱단의 소굴 a hangout for gangsters / 도둑의 소굴 a den [haunt] of robbers / 범죄의 소굴 a hotbed of crime

소개의 표현

사람을 소개할 때 동성(同性)인 경우에는 연소자를 연장자에게, 특히 여성끼리인 경우에는 미혼자를 기혼자에게, 이성인 경우에는 연령에 관계없이 남성을 여성에게 소개하는 것이 일반적인데 성명을 명료하게 천천히 말하는 것이 중요하다.
특히 한국 사람의 이름은 외국인들이 기억하기 힘들고 발음도 어렵다는 점에 유의해야 한다. 소개를 받았을 때는 Hi, John.이라든가 Nice to meet you, Su-ji.라는 식으로 상대의 이름을 부르며 인사하면 된다.

1. 친구 등의 소개
⟨**Dialog**⟩ (1) (인호가 Tom을 반 친구 수만에게 소개한다)
인호: 톰, 우리 반 친구 수만이야. 수만아, 이 애는 톰인데 캐나다에서 온 교환 학생이야 Tom, this is Su-man, a classmate of mine. Su-man, this is Tom. He is an exchange student from Canada.
톰 : 안녕, 수만. 만나서 반가워 Hello, Su-man, (I'm) glad to meet you.
수만: 안녕, 톰. 한국 생활이 재미있니? Hi, Tom. Are you enjoying your stay in Korea?
톰 : 응, 아주 좋아. 여름에는 좀 덥지만 말이야 Yes, very much. It's a little too hot in summer, though.
(2) (수만이 톰을 박선생님께 소개한다)
수만 : 박선생님, 톰을 소개합니다. 이 애가 톰 브라운입니다 Mr. Park, I'd like to introduce Tom to you. This is Tom Brown.
톰 : 처음 뵙겠습니다, 박선생님 How do you do, Mr. Park?
박선생: 잘 왔네, 톰군. 수만이한테서 자네 이야기는 많이 듣고 있었네. 이 학교가 마음에 들기 바라네 How do you do, Tom? Su-man has told me a lot about you. I hope you'll like our school.
톰 : 감사합니다 Thank you.

2. 격식 차린 자리에서의 소개
⟨**Dialog**⟩ (1) (대학생 미숙이가 친구 김인자를 스미스 교수에게 소개한다)
미숙: 스미스 교수님, 김양을 소개하겠습니다 Professor Smith, may I introduce Miss Kim?
교수: 아, 언젠가 말한 언어학에 관심이 있다는 아가씨로군. 맞지요 Oh, your friend who's interested in linguistics. Certainly.
(2) 미숙: 이쪽은 김인자 양입니다. 인자야, 스미스 교수님이셔 This is Miss Kim In-ja. In-ja, this is Professor Smith.
인자: 뵙게 돼서 영광입니다, 스미스 교수님. 진작부터 뵙고 싶었습니다 This is a great pleasure, Professor Smith. I have been looking forward to meeting you.
교수: 나도 만나게 돼서 반갑네 It's my pleasure. ⇌ The pleasure is mine.

3. 자기 소개
▶ 처음 뵙겠습니다. 저는 이수길입니다 May I introduce myself? My name is Lee Su-gil.
▶ 자기 소개를 하겠습니다 Please let me introduce myself. ⇌ Allow [Permit] me to introduce myself.
⟨**Dialog**⟩ (미국에서 한국으로 오는 비행기 안에서 수길과 보브가 같이 앉아 있다)
수길: 안녕, 너도 한국에 가니? Hi, are you going to Korea, too?
보브: 응, 대구에 사시는 아저씨를 방문해 Yes, I'm going to visit my uncle in Taegu.
수길: 뭐? 나 거기 사는데 Really? That's where I live.
보브: 그거 참 우연이로구나. 아 참, 나는 보브 그린이야 What a coincidence! Oh, my name is Bob Green.
수길: 나는 이수길이야 My name is Lee Su-gil.
보브: 그러니, 수길. 즐거운 여행이 되겠는데 All right, Su-gil. I think this is going to be an enjoyable flight.

▶ 이 주변에는 밀수단의 소굴이 있다 A smuggling ring has its base around here.
소권 訴權 〔法〕 the right to bring an action in a court 《against *sb* for a matter》
소규모 小規模 a small scale
 ◆소규모의 small-scale / 소규모로 on a small scale; in a small way
소극 消極 the negative; the cathode
 ■―론 a cautious approach ―주의 negativism ―책 passive measures
소극 笑劇 a farce
소극성 消極性 passivity; passiveness
소극장 小劇場 a little theater
소극적 消極的 passive; negative
 ◆소극적 저항 (a) passive resistance / 소극적 전법 passive tactics / 소극적 정책 a negative policy / 소극적으로 negatively; passively / 소극적 태도를 취하다 assume a negative attitude; act passively / 소극적으로 일하다 do things on negative lines

소금 salt
 ◆세상의 소금 〔聖〕 the salt of the earth / 식탁용 소금 table salt / 소금 한 스푼 a spoonful of salt / 소금을 뿌리다 scatter (a pinch of) salt / 소금을 치다 sprinkle salt on 《fish》; sprinkle 《fish》 with salt / 소금을 쳐서 〔젂어〕 먹다 eat with salt / 소금에 절이다 preserve in salt; ⟨야채를⟩ pickle with [in] salt
 ▶ 소금을 좀 건네 주십시오 ⟨식탁에서⟩ Will [Could] you pass (me) the salt?
 ▶ 소금을 좀 더 치면 맛있겠다 If you add a little bit more salt, it may taste better.
 ▶ 우리는 소금으로 간을 한다 We season with salt.
 ■―버캐 salt incrustation ―엣밥 a poor meal; plain fare [food]
소금구이 ◆도미 소금구이 a sea bream grilled with salt / 생선을 소금구이하다 broil [grill] fish with salt
소금기 ―氣 a salty [briny] taste; saltiness

소금물 salt water; brine
◆소금물에 담그다 soak [steep] in brine / 소금물로 입안을 가시다 gargle with salt water

소금쟁이 〔昆〕 a pond skater; a water strider [skipper]

소급 遡及 retroactivity; retroaction
—소급 지불되는 급료 retroactive [back] pay —소급하다 retroact 《to》; be retroactive 《to》
◆소급하여 retroactively; retrospectively / 소급해서 지불받다 get 《a sum of money》 in back pay
▶이 법률은 1월 1일자로 소급하여 적용된다 This law is effective retroactive(ly) to January 1.
■—력 retroactive [retrospective] power; retroactivity —법 〔法〕 a retroactive [retrospective] law

소기 所期 expectation; anticipation ◆소기의 expected; hoped-for; anticipated / 소기의 성과를 거두다 achieve the expected results
▶우리는 소기의 성과를 거둘 수가 없었다 We were unable to obtain the desired [expected] results. ⇌ The results fell short of our expectations.
▶인내없이 소기의 목적을 달성할 수는 없다 Without perseverance one cannot attain the desired end.

소기 笑氣 〔化〕 nitrous oxide; laughing gas

소꿉 toy flatware [kitchenware]; toy goods used in playing house ■—놀이 ⇨ 소꿉질

소꿉동무 a childhood friend; a friend [playmate] of one's childhood; a friend from one's childhood
▶그와 나는 소꿉동무였다 He and I were childhood friends.

소꿉질 playing house; playing at housekeeping —소꿉질하다 play (at) house; play at housekeeping
▶저 젊은 부부는 마치 아이들이 소꿉질하는 것 같다 That young couple are like children playing house.

소나기 a (sudden) shower; a sudden brief downpour; 〈열대의〉 a squall
▶소나기가 올 것 같다 It looks like we are going to have a shower.
▶오늘 소나기가 한 차례 있겠다 There will be a shower today.
▶소나기가 그쳤다 The shower has passed [is over].
▶나는 집에 돌아오는 길에 소나기를 만났다 On my way home I was caught in a shower.
■—구름 ⇨ 쎈비구름 —밥 sudden overeating —술 sudden overdrinking

소나무 〔植〕 a pine tree; a pine

소나타 〔樂〕 a sonata ■베토벤의 피아노 소나타 a piano sonata by Beethoven; a Beethoven piano sonata / 소나타 형식으로 in sonata form; in the form of a sonata

소낭 嗉囊 〈모이주머니〉 a crop; a craw

소네트 a sonnet ■—시인 a sonneteer

소녀 少女 a girl; a young [little] girl; a lass 《↔ lad》; a maiden

解說 *girl*은 5세 정도에서 20세 정도까지의 여자를 가리키는 말로 little girl은 생후 얼마 안 되는 여자아이부터 8세 정도까지의 여자아이를 말하고, young girl은 12세 정도에서부터 22세 정도까지의 여자, 특히 막연히 틴에 이저를 가리킨다.

◆10대 소녀 a teenage(d) girl; a girl in her teens / 소녀다운 girlish; maidenly; maidenlike
▶그녀는 소녀 때 매우 귀여웠다[예뻤다] She was very pretty [cute] when she was a girl.
■—가장 a girl head of a family —시절 young girlhood —취미 girlish tastes

소녀단 少女團 《美》 the Girl Scouts; 《英》 the Girl Guides ■—원 《美》 a girl scout; 《英》 a girl guide

소년 少年 a boy; a lad 《↔lass》

解說 *boy*는 5세 정도에서 19세 정도까지의 남자를 가리키는 말로 little boy는 생후 얼마 안 되는 사내아이부터 8세 정도까지의 남자아이를 가리킨다.

◆소년의 juvenile; children's / 소년의 꿈 a boy's [boyish] dream / 소년다운 boyish; juvenile
▶소년들이여 야망을 품어라 Boys, be ambitious.
■불량[비행]— a juvenile delinquent —기 ⇨ 소년시절 —노동 child labor —문학 juvenile literature —법 〔法〕 the Juvenile Act —보호 juvenile protection —소녀 (young) boys and girls; 《총칭》 young people —원 a reformatory; a juvenile detention home; 《英》 a community home —잡지 a children's magazine; a juvenile journal

소년단 少年團 the Boy Scouts ■—원 a boy scout

소년범죄 少年犯罪 juvenile delinquency
■—자 a juvenile delinquent [offender]

소년시절 少年時節 one's boyhood
◆소년 시절부터의 친구 a childhood friend / 소년 시절에 in one's boyhood [childhood]; when one was a boy
▶나는 소년 시절에 시골에서 행복하게 지냈다 I spent happy days in the country when I was a boy [in my boyhood]. ⇌ I had a happy boyhood in the country.

소농 小農 a small [petty] farmer; a peasant; 《총칭》 peasantry —가 a petty farmer; a peasant; a tenant farmer —계급 the peasant-proprietor class

소뇌 小腦 〔解〕 the cerebellum 《*pl.* ~s, -la》
◆소뇌의 cerebellar

소닉붐 〔物〕 〈음속 돌파음〉 a sonic boom

소다 〔化〕 soda ■가성— caustic soda 탄산— carbonate of soda; sodium carbonate ■—공업 the alkali industry —수 〈탄산수〉 soda water —유리 soda glass —크래커 a soda cracker —회(灰) soda ash

소달구지 an oxcart

소 닭 보듯 닭 소 보듯 하다 《속담》 look absent-mindedly 《about》; moon 《over》

소담스럽다 〈먹음직하다〉 appetizing; delicious-

looking; 〈탐스럽다〉 look nice and ripe
소담하다 appetizing; tempting; delicious-looking
♦소담한 꽃송이 a full-petaled flower / 소담하게 차린 식탁 a table with appetizing dishes
소대 小隊 a platoon ■―장 a platoon leader [commander] ―훈련 close-order drill
소댕 〈솥뚜껑〉 a kettle lid [cover]; the cap of an iron pot ■―꼭지 the handle of a kettle cover
소도 小刀 a small [short] knife
소도 小島 a small island; an islet
소도둑놈 〈도둑〉 a cattle thief [stealer]; 《美니》 a rustler; 〈욕심쟁이〉 an avaricious man; a grabber
소도시 小都市 a small city [town]
소독 消毒 disinfection; sterilization; 〈우유의〉 pasteurization; 〈훈증〉 fumigation; 〈정화〉 decontamination
―소독하다 disinfect; sterilize; pasteurize; fumigate; decontaminate
♦소독된 컵 a sterilized glass / 끓는 물로 소독하다 disinfect a thing by boiling / 상처를 소독약으로 소독하다 sterilize [disinfect] the wound by applying some antiseptic (to it) / 증기로 소독하다 sterilize by steam / 일광으로 소독하다 disinfect by the sun's rays
▶ 도시의 수돗물은 염소로 소독된다 City water is disinfected with chlorine.
―유황[증기]― sulfur [steam] disinfection ■―기 a sterilizer; disinfector ―력 the disinfective [sterilizing] power ―실 a disinfecting [sterilizing] room ―액 an antiseptic solution ―약[제] a disinfectant; an antiseptic ―의[복] a disinfected overgarment ―저 sanitary [sterilized] chopsticks
소동 騷動 〈사건〉 an affair; 〈법석〉 (a) disturbance; (an) uproar; an upheaval; a trouble 〈옥신각신〉 a strife; a dispute; 〈혼란〉 confusion; disorder; a row; 〈다툼〉 a quarrel; a brawl
♦큰 소동 a serious riot; a great disturbance / 소동을 일으키다[벌이다] raise [cause, create] a disturbance; stir up a riot / 소동을 가라앉히다 quiet [suppress] a disturbance; quell [put down] a riot
▶ 그것 때문에 소동이 벌어졌다 It raised a disturbance.
▶ 그의 발언이 소동을 일으켰다 His remarks caused wild confusion.
소두 小斗 〈닷 되들이 말〉 five-*doe* measure; a smaller [half] *mal* measure
소듐 〔化〕 sodium ⇨ 나트륨
소득 所得 〈수입〉 income; 〈수익〉 gain; earnings; profits
♦소득 범위 내에서 생활하다 live within *one's* income
▶ 그는 월 2백만원의 소득이 있다 He has a monthly income of two million won.
▶ 그는 소득이 아주 많다[적다] He has a very large [a very small] income.
■―개인[법인]― individual [corporate] income 국민― national income 근로[불로]― earned [unearned] income 명목― nominal income 순[총]― net [gross] income 실질―

real income 연간― annual income; yearly income 현물― income in kind ■―공제 tax reductions and allowances ―수준 an income level ―자 an income earner: 고액[저액] 소득자 people in the upper [lower] brackets of income ―정책 an incomes policy ―증대 increase of the income
소득세 所得稅 an income tax
♦소득세 신고 an income tax return
■―종합[개인, 법인]― the composite [individual, corporate] income tax 초과― an excess income tax ■―법 〔法〕 the Income Tax Law ―액 the amount of *one's* income tax
소득액 所得額 (the amount of) *one's* income
♦소득액의 사정 assessment of *sb's* income
▶ 그의 연간 소득액은 1억 이상이다 His annual [yearly] income is over one hundred million won. ≒ He earns one hundred million won or more a year.
소등 消燈 ♦소등 나팔을 불다 sound taps
▶ 소등시간은 열시입니다 Lights out is at 10.
―소등하다 put out [turn out] the lights
소라 1 〔貝〕 a top shell; a turbo
2 〈악기〉 a trumpet shell; a conch horn
♦소라를 불다 blow a trumpet shell
■―딱지 the shell of a turbo ―젓 salted turbos
소라게 〔動〕 soldier crab
소라고둥 〔貝〕 a trumpet shell; a conch
소란 騷亂 1 〈소동〉 a clamor; (a) noise; an uproar; a row
▶ 소란 떨지 마라 Don't make such a noise. ≒ Don't be so noisy.
―소란하다 noisy; loud; uproarious; clamorous; tumultuous 《crowd》
♦소란한 교실 a noisy classroom
▶ 소란해서 우리는 그의 목소리를 듣지 못했다 We could not hear him because of the noise. ≒ His voice was drowned out by the noise.
2 〈소요〉 (a) disturbance; (an) agitation; troubles; a commotion; a riot
♦소란을 일으키다 make a row; 〈어떤 일이〉 create [raise] a commotion [disturbance]; cause a riot
▶ 기동대가 소란을 진압했다 The riot squad suppressed the disturbance [put down the riot].
■―죄 the crime of rioting: 그들은 소란죄로 체포되었다 They were arrested on a [the] charge of raising a riot.
소란반자 小欄― 〔建〕 a compartment ceiling; coffering
소량 少量 a small quantity [amount, portion, dose]; a little
♦소량 거래 transactions in small lots / 소량 주문 a petty order / 소량의 버터 a little butter; a small amount [quantity] of butter
소령 少領 〈육군〉 a major; 〈해군〉 a lieutenant commander; 〈공군〉 《美》 a major; 《英》 a squadron leader
소로 小路 a (narrow) path; a lane; an alley; a trail
소론 所論 *one's* view [opinion]; the view *one* holds; *one's* argument

▶ 그는 그 문제에 대한 소론을 당당히 내놨다 He gave his opinion on the issue squarely.

소르르 1 〈잘 풀어지는 모양〉 easily; smoothly; readily ♦ 소르르 풀리다 unravel easily
2 〈바람이 부는 모양〉 softly; gently
♦ 소르르 부는 실바람 a gentle [light] breeze; a soft breath of air
3 〈졸음이 오는 모양〉 drowsily
♦ 잠이 소르르 오다 sleep steals upon *one*
▶ 날씨가 따뜻해서 그녀는 소르르 잠이 왔다 The warm weather made her sleepy [drowy].

소름 gooseflesh; goose pimples
♦ 소름이 끼치다 get (the) gooseflesh; feel a chill creep over *one* / 소름이 끼치게 하다 give *sb* gooseflesh; make *one's* blood run cold; horrify / 소름끼치는 이야기 a hair-raising [bloodcurdling] story
▶ 그 일은 생각만 해도 소름이 끼친다 The mere thought of it makes me shudder.
▶ 나는 그 광경을 보고 소름이 끼쳤다 I shuddered [was horrified] at the scene.

소리 1 〈음〉 (a) sound; 〈소음〉 (a) noise
♦ 높은[낮은] 소리 a high [low] sound / 큰[작은] 소리 a loud [soft] sound / 나팔 소리 notes of a bugle / 대포 소리 the cannon's roar; 〈멀리서 들리는〉 the booming of the gun / 벌레 소리 chirps of insects / 시계 소리 the ticking of a clock / 종소리 the sound [toll] of a bell / 파도 치는 소리 the splash of waves / 소리 없이 noiselessly; silently; quietly / 소리가 듣기 좋다 [나쁘다] sound sweet [harsh] / 소리를 작게 하다 lower the volume 《of a stereo》; tone down 《a transistor》
▶ 무슨 소리지? What's that noise?
▶ 밖에서 이상한 소리가 났다 I heard [There was] a strange noise outside.
▶ 소리는 공기중에서 매초 약 340미터의 속도로 전달된다 Sound travels at about 340 meters per second in (the) air.
▶ 차가 끽끽 소리를 내며 섰다 A car screeched to a stop.
▶ 문이 쾅 소리를 내며 닫혔다 The door shut with a bang.
▶ 새가 지저귀는 소리에 잠이 깼다 I woke to the call [chirp, song, twitter] of birds.
▶ 라디오 소리를 작게[크게] 해 주세요 Please turn the radio down [up].
2 〈목소리〉 a voice; a tone (of voice); 〈외침소리〉 a cry; an outcry
♦ 소리 없는 국민의 목소리 a soundless voice of people / 살려 달라는 소리 a cry for help / 속삭이는[목쉰] 소리 a whispering [hoarse, husky] voice / 성난 소리 an angry voice / 아름다운[날카로운, 부드러운] 소리 a beautiful [sharp, soft] voice / 소리를 내어 울다[읽다] weep [read] aloud / 국민의 소리를 무시하다 ignore the voice [opinion] of the people / 소리를 지르다 ⇨ 소리지르다 / 작은[큰] 소리로 말하다 talk in a low [loud, big] voice
▶ 소리가 안 들려요 〈전화에서〉 I can't hear you.
▶ 옆방에서 그들의 소리가 들렸다 I heard their voices in the next room. ⇌ I heard them talking in the next room.
▶ 더 큰 소리로 말해라 Speak up!
▶ 불이야 하는 소리를 듣고 그녀는 급히 피했다 She rushed for safety at the cry [alarm] of fire.
▶ 그 문장을 큰 소리로 읽어라 Read the sentence aloud.
3 〈말〉 a talk; a word; a remark
♦ 이상한 소리 같지만 It may sound strange, but… / 듣기 좋은 소리를 하다 say a pleasant thing
▶ 상사에게 감히 그런 소리를 하다니 How dare you say such a thing to your boss!
▶ 무슨 소리를 하고 있는 거야? What are you talking about? ⇌ What do you mean by that?
▶ 그의 논리적 논법에 모두 아무 소리도 못했다 His logic [logical argument] left everyone in silence.
4 〈노래〉 a song; a ballad; a folk song
♦ 소리를 잘하다 sing well
5 〈소식〉 news; a rumor
▶ 사장이 사임했다는 소리를 들었다 I've heard a rumor that the president resigned.

소리 小利 a small profit; a little gain; scanty earnings

소리개 〔鳥〕 a kite ⇨ 솔개

소리글자 〔言〕 a phonetic symbol; a phonogram

소리소리 in [with] a loud voice ♦ 소리소리 지르다 cry (out); shriek; scream; shout
▶ 한 여자가 소리소리 지르고 있었다 A woman was crying at the top of her voice.

소리 없는 고양이 쥐잡듯 《속담》 Silence catches a mouse.

소리지르다 1 〈크게 소리내다〉 shout; yell; scream; exclaim; cry (in a loud voice); speak loudly; bawl
♦ 괴로워서 소리지르다 cry out in [yell with] pain / 사람 살려달라고 소리지르다 cry [shout] for help / 목이 쉬게 소리지르다 shout *oneself* hoarse
▶ 그렇게 소리지르지 않아도 되네. 잘 들리니까 You needn't bawl; I can hear quite well.
2 〈큰 소리로 부르다〉 call out; hail

소리치다 shout; cry; yell; bawl ⇨ 소리지르다
▶ 누군가 「경찰이 왔다」고 소리쳤다 Someone cried, "A policeman is here!"
▶ 어떤 여자가 소리치는 것이 우리 귀에 들렸다 We heard a woman [woman's] scream.

소립자 素粒子 〔物〕 an elementary particle ■ ―론 the theory of elementary particles ―물리학 elementary particle physics

소말리아 〈나라 이름〉 Somalia; 〈공식명〉 the Somali Democratic Republic ♦ 소말리아의 Somalian ■ ―사람 a Somali; a Somalian

소망 所望 (a) desire; a wish; a hope
♦ 간절한 소망 an ardent desire; an earnest wish / 오랜 소망 a long-cherished desire / 소망을 들어 주다 grant *sb's* wish [desire]; fulfil *sb's* wish / 소망을 이루다 attain [accomplish, fulfill] *one's* desire; fulfill [gain, obtain] *one's* wish
▶ 네 소망이라면 함께 가겠다 If you wish, I will come with you.

소망(所望)의 표현

1. …이었으면(하고 생각)한다; …이라면 좋을텐데 (현재·미래의 소망)
wish + 주어 + 과거형
▶ 차가 있으면 좋겠다 I wish I had a car.
▶ 내가 슈퍼맨이었으면 좋을텐데 I wish I were [was] a superman.
▶ 그녀는 그가 부자라면하고 생각한다 She wishes he were [was] rich.
▶ 그는 영어를 잘했으면 한다 He wishes he spoke English well.
▶ 당신은 운전할 줄 알았으면하지 않습니까? Don't you wish you could drive a car?
▶ 그의 주소를 알면 좋을텐데 I wish I knew his address.
▶ 날씨가 좋아지면 좋을텐데 I wish the weather would improve.
[어법]
① wish 뒤에는 that을 쓰지 않는 것이 일반적.
② 1인칭, 3인칭에 was를 쓰는 것은 구어적 표현이다.

2. …이면 좋을텐데(하고 생각)했다; …이었으면(하고 생각)했다 (과거의 대화시의 소망)
wished + 주어 + 과거형
▶ 우리는 우리 집이 있으면 좋을텐데하고 생각했다 We wished we had a house of our own.
▶ 나는 그녀가 여기 있으면 좋을텐데하고 생각했다 I wished she was [were] here.
▶ 나는 영어가 이렇게 어렵지 않으면 좋겠다고 생각했다 I wished English were [was] not so difficult.
▶ 그는 영어를 알면 좋을텐데하고 생각했다 He wished he knew English well.

3. …이었으면 좋았을텐데(하고 생각)한다 (과거의 소망)
wish + 주어 + 과거완료
▶ 내가 그 일을 어제 알았다라면 좋았을텐데 I wish I had known about it yesterday.
▶ 그녀는 그와 결혼하지 않았다라면 좋았을 데하고 생각한다 She wishes she had not married him.
▶ 자네는 학생 시절에 좀더 열심히 공부했더라면 좋았을걸하고 생각하지 않는가? Don't you wish you had studied harder when you were in school?

4. …이었다면 좋았을텐데(하고 생각)했다 (과거의 대화시에서 본 과거의 소망)
wished + 주어 + 과거완료
▶ 나는 그의 충고를 들었더라면 좋았을걸하고 생각했다 I wished I had taken his advice.
▶ 그녀는 컴퓨터 사용법을 알았더라면 좋았을 텐데하고 생각했다 She wished she had known how to use the computer.
▶ 그는 대학 시절에 영어 회화 공부를 해 두었더라면 좋았을 것을하고 생각했다 He wished he had studied English conversation when he was in college.
[어법]
1, 2, 3, 4 전체의 구문에 걸쳐서「실제로는 그렇지 않다[않았다]」는 뜻이 숨어 있어서 유감의 뜻을 나타낸다. 보기 I wish I had a car. ⇌ I'm sorry I don't have a car. / He wished he knew English well. ⇌ He was sorry he didn't know English well. / I wished I had taken his advice. ⇌ I was sorry I hadn't taken his advice.

▶ 내 오랜 소망이 이루어졌다 My long-cherished dream has come true [has been realized].
— 소망하다 desire; wish for; hope (for)
▶ 우리는 행복을 소망한다 We want [hope for, wish (for)] happiness.
소매 a sleeve; 〈양복의〉 an arm
♦ 긴[넓은] 소매 a long [wide] sleeve / 소매 없는 드레스 a sleeveless dress; dress without sleeves / 소매가 긴[짧은] 셔츠 a long-sleeved [short-sleeved] shirt / 소매를 걷어붙이다 turn [roll, tuck] up one's sleeves; bare one's arms / 소매를 붙잡다 hold sb by the sleeve / 소매를 잡아당기다 pull sb by the sleeve / 눈물로 소매를 적시다 wet one's sleeves with tears; shed copious tears
 ■ —길이 the sleeve length —통 the sleeve width 소맷단 sleeve hem
소매 小賣 retail
♦ 소매로 by [at] retail(ing); retail sale
▶ 우리는 도매상이므로 소매는 하지 않습니다 We're wholesalers, so we don't sell retail.
▶ 이 공은 소매로 한 다스에 3만원입니다 These balls retail at [for] thirty thousand won a dozen.
— 소매하다 retail; sell retail; (美) sell at retail; (英) sell by retail
 ■ —가격 a retail price: 소매 가격은 도매보다 20퍼센트 비싸다 The retail price is 20 percent higher than the wholesale price. —물가지수 a retail price index —상품 retail goods —시장 a retail market —업 retail trade
소매상 小賣商 〈장사〉 retail trade; 〈상인〉 a retail dealer; a retailer
♦ 소매상을 하다 carry on a retail trade; run a retail business; be a retailer
▶ 내 동생은 스포츠용품 소매상을 하고 있습니다 My brother is a sporting goods retailer. ⇌ My brother retails sporting goods.
 ■ —인 a retail dealer; a retailer
소매점 小賣店 a retail store [shop] ♦ 소매점 주인 a storekeeper; (英) a shopkeeper / 소매점을 하다 run a retail store [shop]
소매치기 〈사람〉 a pickpocket; (美俗) a dip(per); 〈행위〉 pocket-picking; (美俗) dipping
▶ 소매치기 조심 (게시) Beware of [Watch out for] pickpockets. ⇌ Pickpockets operate here.
▶ 나는 열차에서 소매치기를 당했다 I have my purse stolen [my pocket picked] on [in] the train.
— 소매치기하다 pick sb's pocket; (美俗) dip

■一패 a gang of pickpockets
소맥 小麥 〈밀〉wheat; (英) corn ■一분 flour
소맷부리 〈옷의〉the edge [lower part] of a sleeve; 〈셔츠의〉a cuff ◆소맷부리를 뿌리치고 가다 tear *oneself* away 《from》
소맷자락 a sleeve; the bag of a sleeve
◆소맷자락을 눈물로 적시다 wet *one's* sleeves with tears / 소맷자락에 매달리다 cling to *sb's* sleeve; hold *sb* by the sleeve
소면 素麵 vermicelli; fine noodles; very thin white noodles
소면 梳綿 cotton carding; carded cotton ■一기(機) a carding machine; a card
소멸 消滅 〈없어짐〉extinction; disappearance; 〈실효〉extinguishment; nullification; extinction; lapse ◆권리의 소멸 extinguishment [lapse] of *one's* rights
一소멸하다 become extinct; disappear; vanish; 〈실효하다〉become null and void; be nullified; be extinguished; terminate; lapse
◆자연 소멸하다 cease to exist as a matter of course [in the course of time] / 소멸시키다 extinguish; nullify; 〈죄를〉expiate
▶ 이 협정은 4월 30일에 소멸된다 This agreement will terminate [cease to exist] on the 30th of April.
▶ 그 종(種)은 소멸되었다 That species has died out.
◆공유권— extinguishment of common property ■一시효 extinctive prescription
소명 召命 〈왕의 부름〉a royal summons; 〈종교상의〉calling ◆소명을 내리다 call; summon
소명사 小名辭 〔論〕a minor term
소모 消耗 〈써서 없어짐〉consumption; exhaustion; wear and tear; 〈체력의〉emaciation
一소모하다 consume; exhaust; use up
◆전력[연료]을 소모하다 consume electric power [fuel]
▶ 그 일로 나는 체력을 소모했다 I was worn out [exhausted] by the work. ⇌ The work wore me out.
▶ 하찮은 일로 정력을 소모해서는 안 된다 You shouldn't waste your energy on unimportant things.
■一비 wear and tear expenses 一병 a wasting disease 一열 hectic fever 一전(戰) a war of attrition
소모 梳毛 combed [carded] wool; 〈작업〉combing [carding] wool ■一기(機) a carding engine; combing machine; a comber; a card 一사(絲) worsted [wústid] yarn
소모품 消耗品 articles of consumption; expendable supplies; expendables ◆사무용 소모품 office supplies
소목장이 小木匠— a joiner; a cabinetmaker
소몰이 〈사람〉a cattle drover; a cowboy; 〈일〉cattle droving
소묘 素描 〈데생〉a dessin
소문 所聞 a rumor; hearsay; gossip; talk; a report ◆소문난 famous; well-known; renowned; 〈악명 높은〉notorious
▶ 그것은 뜬소문이다 It's an idle [a groundless, an unfounded] rumor.
▶ 그가 죽었다는 것은 헛소문이었다 The rumor [report] that he had died proved (to be) false.
▶ 그것은 소문일 뿐이다 It's a mere rumor. ⇌ It's just gossip. ⇌ It's only hearsay.
〈소문이〉소문이 나다 be talked [gossiped] about; become the talk 《of》; be in everybody's mouth; be in the air
▶ 요즘 그에 대한 소문이 많다 He is much talked about lately.
▶ 그가 사직했다는 소문이 있다 There is a rumor [Rumor has it, It is rumored] that he resigned. ⇌ He is rumored to have resigned. ⇌ I hear(d) [People say, They say, It is said, The story goes] that he resigned.
▶ 함께 있지 말자, 소문이 나니까 We'd better not to be seen together. People might talk.
〈소문을〉소문을 내다 start [circulate] a rumor; set a rumor afloat / 소문을 퍼뜨리다 spread scandal; tell tales
▶ 그에 대한 좋지 않은 소문을 들었다 I heard unpleasant stories about him.
▶ 그가 학교를 그만둔다는 소문을 들었다 I've heard a rumor that he will leave school [a rumor about his leaving school].
〈소문에[으로]〉소문으로 듣다 hear of; know by hearsay; (口) hear tell [say] of 《it》
▶ 소문으로 알고 있을 뿐이다 I know it only from [by] hearsay.
〈소문대로〉그녀는 소문대로 미인이다 She is as beautiful as she is reputed to be.
▶ 그는 소문대로 억센 사람이다 His sturdiness is true to his reputation.
소문난 잔치에 먹을 것 없다 (속담) Great boast and small roast.
소문만복래 笑門萬福來 (속담) Laugh and grow it. ⇌ Fortune favors cheerful homes.
소문자 小文字 a small letter; 〔印〕a lowercase letter
소박 素朴 simplicity; naivety; naiveté
一소박하다 simple (and honest); unsophisticated; unaffected; artless; naive
◆소박한 아름다움 simple beauty / 시골에서 소박한 생활을 하다 lead a simple life in the country
소박 疏薄 abuse; maltreatment; mistreatment; desertion (of *one's* wife)
一소박하다 abuse; maltreat (*one's* wife); desert; abandon
◆소박맞다 be abused [mistreated]; get deserted [divorced]
■一데기 an abused [a divorced, a deserted, an abandoned] wife
소박이 〈오이의〉cucumber *kimchi*; 〈음식〉stuffed food
소반 小盤 〈밥상〉a small (dining) table
소방 消防 fire fighting 一소방하다 put out and prevent fires; fight a fire
■一관 a fire officer; a fireman; a fighter 一대[단] a fire brigade; (美) a fire company; 〈공장・군대 등의〉a fire-fighting team [unit] 一대장 a fire marshal [chief]; the head of a fire-fighting group 一모 a smoke helmet; a fire hat 一비상선 a fire line 一사다리 a fire ladder; 〈신축식〉an extension ladder 一서 a

fire station; (美) a firehouse ―선(船) a fireboat ―연습 a fire drill; fire fighting practice ―용구 fire fighting apparatus ―용 도끼 a fireman's axe ―용 수전[호스] a fire cock [hose] ―조직[제도] the fire defense [fighting] organization [system] ―차 a fire engine [truck] ―펌프 a fire pump

소백반 燒白礬 〖化〗 burnt alum

소변 小便 urine; (俗) piss; (口) a pee
♦소변을 검사하다 examine [test] urine / 소변을 보다[누다] urinate; pass [discharge] urine; make [pass] water; piss; pee; have a pee; answer a call of nature / 길에서 소변을 보나 urinate [relieve *oneself*] in the street / 소변을 참다 hold *one's* water; contain *one's* urine
▶ 여기는 소변 냄새가 난다 This place smells [stinks] of (stale) urine.
▶ 소변이 마렵다 Nature calls (me).
▶ 소변 금지 (게시) No Urination
■―검사 urine analysis; urinalysis; uranalysis; urinoscopy [uroscopy] ―소 a urinal; (변소) a lavatory

소복 素服 〈흰옷〉 white clothes; 〈상복〉 (white) mourning clothes [garments]
▶ 그녀는 소복을 입고 있었다 She was dressed in white. ⇌ She was wearing [wore] mourning clothes.
―소복하다 wear white [mourning] clothes; wear white

소비 消費 spending; consumption
♦휘발유의 소비 consumption of gasoline
―소비하다 spend; consume; 〈시간·노력을〉 expend
♦시간의 대부분을 소비하다 expend [consume] most of *one's* time 《on the task》
▶ 쓸데없는 정력[시간]을 소비하지 마라 Don't waste your energy [time] on unnecessary things.
■―개인― personal consumption 자가― 〔經〕 self-consumption ■―감퇴 decrease of consumption; underconsumption ―경제 consumer economy; economy of consumption ―도시 a consuming [consumer] city ―물자 ⇨ 소비재(消費財) ―생활 *one's* daily life as a consumer ―성향 the propensity to consume; spending habits ―액 the amount of consumption ―인구 consumption population ―절약 economy in consumption ―제한 restriction on consumption ―혁명 the consumer revolution

소비세 消費稅 consumption tax; (美) sales tax
■―국내― an excise tax

소비자 消費者 a consumer
♦일반 소비자 the consuming public
■―최종― an ultimate consumer; an end-user ―가격 a consumer('s) price ―단체 a consumer organization ―물가지수 〔經〕 the consumer price index (略 CPI, c.p.i.) ―보호운동 a consumer movement

소비재 消費財 consumers' goods
■―산업 the consumption industry

소비자 협동조합 消費者 協同組合 a (consumers') cooperative society; (口) a co-op
■―매점 a cooperative store; (口) a co-op

소사 小史 a short [brief] history; a historical sketch

소사 小辭 〖論〗 a minor term

소사 燒死 death by fire
―소사하다 be burnt to death
▶ 그 화재로 여섯 명이 소사했다 Six people died [lost their lives] in the fire.
■―자 a person burnt to death; (총칭) the dead in fire ―체 a charred body

소사 掃射 machine-gunning; machine-gun [automatic weapons] fire; 〈공중에서〉 strafe
▶ 적기가 급강하하여 건물에 기총 소사를 퍼부었다 An enemy plane swooped down and raked the building with machine-gun fire.
―소사하다 sweep [rake] with fire; machine-gun; strafe

소산 所産 a product; 〈결과〉 an outcome; a result; 〈성과〉 fruits ♦노력의 소산 the fruits [product] of *one's* efforts [labors]

소산하다 消散― dissipate; disperse; vanish; evaporate ♦고약한 냄새를 소산시키다 get rid of a bad smell

소살 燒殺 killing by fire ―소살하다 burn sb to death; burn sb (alive)

소상 小祥 〈한 돌 제사〉 the first anniversary of *sb's* death

소상 塑像 a plastic [plaster] image; a clay figure [statue]

소상인 小商人 a small businessman [tradesman, trader]; a small-scale merchant

소상하다 昭詳― detailed; minute; full
♦소상히 in detail; at length; minutely / 소상히 설명하다 explain 《a matter》 in detail [to the minutest detail]; give a detailed [full] explanation
▶ 그는 그 문제를 소상히 설명했다 He stated the problem in detail.

소생 所生 〈자녀〉 *one's* children [offspring]
♦소생이 많다 have many children / 소생이 없다 be childless; have no children

소생 蘇生 revival; resuscitation
―소생하다 come to life [*oneself*]; revive; be resuscitated; be restored [recalled, brought back] to life
♦소생시키다 bring sb back to life; restore sb to consciousness; resuscitate; revive
▶ 오래 기다렸던 비가 오자 초목이 소생했다 The trees and plants came alive after the long awaited rain.
▶ 그 소녀는 죽은 것 같았는데 구조원이 소생시켰다 The girl seemed dead, but the lifeguard revived her.
▶ 그는 빈사지경이었으나 인공호흡으로 소생했다 He was nearly dead but they resuscitated [revived] him with artificial respiration.

소생 小生 〈자신을 낮추어〉 I; me; myself

-소서 I pray; please do; I beg you to do...
▶ 용소하소서 Please forgive me.
▶ 그를 불쌍히 여기소서 I pray you God, to take pity on him!
▶ 고이 잠드소서 〈묘비명에〉 Rest [May he rest] in peace.
▶ 주여 우리에게 자비를 베푸소서 May God have mercy on us!

소석고 燒石膏 plaster of Paris; calcined gypsum

소석회 消石灰 calcium hydroxide ⇨ 수산화(~칼슘)

소선거구 小選擧區 a small electoral [electorate] district [constituency]
■ —제 the small electoral [electorate] system; the minor constituency system; 〈1구 1인제〉 the single-member district system

소설 小雪 〈절기〉 20th of the 24 seasonal divisions according to the lunar calendar (about on November 22nd)

소설 小說 a novel; a story; a romance; (총칭) fiction
♦ 소설을 각색하다 dramatize a novel for the stage / 소설을 쓰다 write a novel / 소설화하다 make a novel [story] out of an affair; fictionalize; fictionize; novelize
▶ 이것은 업다이크의 소설이다 This is a novel by Updike. ⇌ This novel was written by Updike.
♦ 사실은 소설보다도 기이하다 (속담) Fact [Truth] is stranger than fiction.
■ 공상 과학— science fiction (略 SF) 단편— a short story; a storiette 대하— a saga 모험— a story of adventure 문제— a problem novel 신문— a serial story in a newspaper 심리— a psychological novel 역사— a historical novel 연애— a love story 연재— a story published serially (in a magazine); a serial 장편— a (full-length) novel 정치— a political novel 중편— a short novel; a novelette; a long-short story 추리— a detective [mystery] story; (美口) a whodun(n)it 통속— a light [popular, low-brow] story 현상— a prize novel [story] 현상 당선— a prize-winning story ■ —문학 novel literature —책 a storybook; a novel; a book of fiction

소설가 小說家 a novelist; a story [fiction] writer ♦ 인기 소설가 a popular novelist

소성 小成 a small success; small achievements ♦ 소성에 만족하다 be contented with one's small success

소성 塑性 〔工〕 plasticity ♦ 소성이 있다 be plastic

소성단 小星團 stardust

소소리바람 〈이른 봄의 찬바람〉 a bleak wind (in the early spring); a chilly spring wind; 〈회오리 바람〉 a whirlwind

소소하다 小小— little; small; trivial; trifling; insignificant ♦ 소소한 일에 신경을 쓰다 worry about little [trivial] things

소속 所屬 one's position [post, place]
♦ 민주당 소속 의원 an Assembly member of [belonging to] the Democratic Party / 소속 미정의 unassigned; unattached
▶ 그는 판매부 소속이다 He works [is] in the sales department. ⇌ He belongs to the sales department.
— 소속하다 belong (to); be attached (to); be under the command [control] 《of》
♦ 소속시키다 attach 《to》; assign 《to》
▶ 그녀는 그 위원회에 소속되어 있다 She is a member of the committee.
▶ 그는 그 부대에 소속되어 있다 He is attached [is assigned] to the unit.
■ —부대 one's unit

소송 訴訟 a suit; a lawsuit; litigation; 〈행위・절차〉 an action (at law); 〈사건〉 a case
♦ 소송을 일으키다[제기하다] institute [start, raise] a (law)suit 《against》; institute legal proceedings [action] 《against》; go to court 《against sb》 / 소송을 취하다 drop [withdraw] one's suit / 소송을 각하하다 dismiss an action [a case] / 소송에 이기다[지다] win [lose] a case / 소송 중이다 be at law; be on trial; be pending
▶ 나는 그들을 상대로 소송을 걸었다 I brought an action [a suit] against them.
— 소송하다 sue; accuse; litigate; bring an action [a suit]; go to suit; go to law
♦ 회사에 손해 배상 소송하다 bring [file, start] a suit for damages against the company; sue the company for damages; bring an action for damages against the company
▶ 그 사건을 소송하지 않고 해결하는 길은 없을까? Is there no way to settle the matter out of court?
■ 민사[형사]— a civil [criminal] suit: 민사[형사]— 소송법 the code of civil [criminal] procedure 손해배상— the action for damages 이혼— a suit [an action] for divorce: 이혼 소송을 내다 sue for divorce; file a divorce suit 행정— administrative litigation —각하 dismissal of a case —관계인 a litigant; (총칭) the litigants —기록 the records of a lawsuit —능력 litigation capacity —당사자 the parties (in [to] a lawsuit); the litigant parties; the litigants (in a lawsuit) —대리인 a counsel; an attorney —물 the object of a lawsuit —법 the code [law] of legal procedure —비용 the costs of a lawsuit; litigation costs [expenses] —위임장 a warrant of attorney —의뢰인 a client; (총칭) clientele —인 〈원고〉 litigator; a suitor; a plaintiff (↔ a defendant); 〈당사자〉 a (party) litigant; (총칭) the parties litigant —행위 an act of litigating; litigation

소송사건 訴訟事件 a legal [law] case; a lawsuit; a case in litigation
♦ (변호사가) 소송 사건을 맡다 take a brief
▶ 우리는 그 소송사건의 변호를 그에게 부탁했다 We asked him to defend us in the suit.

소송절차 訴訟節次 legal procedure; legal [judicial] proceedings ♦ 소송 절차를 밟다 take [institute] legal [judicial] action 《against sb, for one's right》

소수 小數 〔數〕 a decimal
♦ 대(帶)— a mixed decimal 유한[무한]— a finite [an infinite] decimal

소수 少數 a small number; a minority
♦ 소수 정예주의 elitism; the principle of the able minority / 소수의 사람들 a small number of people; a few persons
▶ 회의 참석자는 소수였다 A small number of people [Only a few (people)] were present at the meeting. ⇌ There was a small attendance at the meeting.
■ —민족 a minority race —의견 the opinion

of the minority; a minority opinion ―투표 the minor vote ―파[당] a minority group [party]; the minority : 그들은 소수파였다 They were in the minority [a minority group].
소수 素數 〔數〕 a prime number
소숫점 小數點 〔數〕 a decimal point
▶ 소숫점 이하 세 자리까지 계산하라 Calculate down to three decimals [the third decimal place].
▶ 소숫점 이하는 버려라 Discard decimals. ⇒ Discard [Omit] the numbers below the decimal point.
소스 sauce ♦고기에 소스를 치다 put [pour] sauce on [over] the meat ■화이트[브라운]— white [brown] sauce ■―그릇 (배 모양의) a sauceboat ―병 a sauce pot
소스라치다 be frightened; be taken aback; be startled; be stunned [shocked]
♦비명 소리에 소스라치다 be startled [frightened] at a scream
▶ 나는 소스라치게 놀라 말문이 막혔다 I was so astonished [flabbergasted] I couldn't say a word.
소슬하다 蕭瑟― dreary; chilly; lonely and desolate ♦소슬한 가을 바람 a bleak autumnal wind [blast] ▶ 바람이 소슬하게 불고 있다 The wind is blowing dolefully.
소승 小乘 Hinayana; the Lesser Vehicle ♦소승적 견해 a narrow (point of) view ■―불교 Hinayana Buddhism
소시민 小市民 a petit bourgeois; a member of the lower middle class
소시적 少時― (the time of) one's youth
♦소시적에 in one's youth; when young
▶ 그는 소시적에 제주도에 있었다 He was in Cheju Island when (he was) young [in his young days]. ⇒ He spent his youth in Cheju Island.
소시지 (a) sausage ♦소시지용 고기 sausage meat
■비엔나― Vienna sausage; (a) wiener 프랑크푸르트― frankfurter
소식 小食 light eating
―소식하다 do not eat much; have a small appetite; eat lightly
■―가 a small [light] eater
소식 素食 a meatless meal; plain fare
소식 消息 1 〈보도〉 news; tidings; word; 〈정보〉 information; intelligence; 〈서신 왕래〉 communication; correspondence; a letter; 〈통지〉 notice; a message
♦미국 소식 news from America
▶ 〔會話〕「김군 소식 좀 있니?」「몇년째 감감 무소식이야」 "Do you have any news of Mr. Kim?""We haven't heard from him for ages."
(▶hear from은 본인에게서 직접 편지나 전화로 안 것, hear of는 간접적인 소문 등으로 안 것을 뜻함)
〈소식이〉 소식이 있다 hear from; get a letter from; receive news [tidings] from / 소식이 없다 hear nothing [have no news] from
▶ 그는 통 소식이 없다 I have heard nothing [have no news, haven't heard] from him.
▶ 그건에 관해 무슨 소식이 있었습니까? Have you received any information on [about] the matter?
〈소식을〉 소식을 듣다 hear of; have [receive] news of / 소식을 보내다 write (a letter) to / 피난민의 소식을 전하다 bring the news of the refugees / 오랫동안 소식을 전하지 않다 keep silent for a long time
▶ 그의 사망 소식을 듣지 못했다 We were not notified of his death.
▶ 오랫동안 소식을 전해 드리지 못했습니다 I have been very remiss in writing to you.
▶ 그는 울산에서의 새생활 소식을 전해 왔다 He sent me word of his new life in Ulsan.
▶ 종종 소식을 주십시오 Please write (to) me once in a while. ⇒ Please let me hear from you from time to time.
2 〈동정(動靜)〉 movements
▶ 그는 이 방면의 소식에 밝다 He is in the know (about it). ⇒ He has some inside knowledge of it.
▶ 그는 중동 소식에 정통하다 He is well informed about the Middle East.
소식자 消息子 〔醫〕 a (surgical) probe; a sound
소식통 消息通 (well-)informed sources [quarters]; a source; 〈사람〉 a well-informed person; an insider; a man in the know
♦믿을 만한 소식통에 의하면 according to reliable sources of information / 정부 소식통에 의하면 …이다 According to official quarters…; Government circles say that…
소신 所信 〈믿는 바〉 one's belief [conviction]; 〈의견〉 one's opinion [view]
♦소신을 굽히지 않다 stick to one's views [beliefs] / 소신을 말하다[피력하다] give one's opinions; express one's beliefs / 소신을 바꾸다 reverse one's opinion / 소신대로 행동하다 act according to one's beliefs [convictions]
▶ 그녀는 소신을 굽히지 않는다 She is firm in her conviction.
소실 小室 〈첩〉 a mistress; a concubine
♦소실을 두다 keep a mistress
■―자식 a child by a concubine
소실 消失 disappearance; loss; vanishing; vanishment
♦권리의 소실 the lapse of a right ―소실하다 disappear; vanish
소실 燒失 destruction [loss] by fire ♦소실을 면하다 escape [be spared in] the fire
―소실하다 be destroyed by fire; be burnt down; burn down; lose by fire
♦가재 도구를 몽땅 소실하다 lose all one's household goods in the fire
■―가옥 burnt houses; houses destroyed by fire
소심 小心 1 〈겁많음〉 timidity; cowardice; 〈도량이 좁음〉 narrow-[small-]mindedness
―소심하다 〈겁많다〉 timid; cowardly; fainthearted; chicken-hearted; weak-willed; 〈도량이 좁다〉 narrow-minded
♦소심한 사람 a timid person; a coward
▶ 사슴은 소심한 동물이다 Deer are timid animals.

2 〈주의 깊음〉 prudence; scrupulousness; circumspection
—소심하다 prudent; cautious; scrupulous
소아 小我 one's smaller self; 〔哲〕 the ego
소아 小兒 a small [little] child; a baby; an infant ◆ 소아적인 생각 infantile [childish] ideas
소아과 小兒科 pediatrics; pediatry
■ —병원 a children's hospital —의사 a children's doctor; a pediatrician; a pediatrist
소아마비 小兒痲痺 infantile paralysis; poliomyelitis; polio
■ —예방주사 a preventive injection against poliomyelitis; a polio shot
소아병 小兒病 children's [infantile] diseases; (비유) infantilism
◆ 소아병적(인) infantilistic
소아시아 小— Asia Minor
소액 少額 a small [petty] sum
◆ 소액의 기부 a small contribution / 소액의 돈 a small sum of money
■ —금융 a small loan —대출금 a petty loan —보험 petty-sum insurance —예금 a petty deposit —지폐 a note [bill] of small [low] denomination —화폐 a fractional coin —환(換) a postal order 《for 30,000 won》 (略 P.O., p.o.); (美) a postal note
소야곡 小夜曲 〈세레나데〉 a serenade
소양 素養 〈교양〉 culture; 〈기초〉 a grounding; 〈지식〉 knowledge; 〈조예〉 acquirements; 〈수련〉 training
◆ 소양이 있다 have a grounding (in); be grounded (in); have knowledge of / 소양이 없다 have no knowledge; be poorly grounded / 중국 고전에 소양이 있다 have considerable knowledge of the Chinese classics
▶ 그녀는 프랑스어에 소양이 있다 She has some knowledge of French. ⇌ She knows some French.
▶ 그는 음악적 소양이 풍부하다 He is well grounded in music. ⇌ He has learned a good deal of music.
소양 搔痒 〈가려움〉 an itch; itching
—증 〔醫〕 pruritus; itching
소어 小魚 〈잔고기〉 (a) small fish
소연하다 騷然— noisy; clamorous; 〈소란하다〉 tumultuous; uproarious; confused
▶ 장내가 소연해졌다 The hall got confused. ⇌ The hall was thrown into a confusion [an uproar, a commotion].
소염제 消炎劑 an antiphlogistic (agent); an anti-inflammatory
소엽 小葉 1 〔解〕 a lobule; a lobelet **2** 〈작은 잎〉〔植〕 a foliole; a leaflet
소옥 小屋 a small house; a hut; a cottage; a shack
소외 疏外 estrangement; alienation
—소외하다 estrange; alienate; neglect; leave out; keep sb at a distance
◆ 소외당하다 be shunned [neglected]; be out of favor 《with》
▶ 그는 모든 사람으로부터 소외당하는 느낌이 들었다 He felt that he was left out of the group [neglected by all].
■ —감 a sense of alienation : 소외감을 느끼다 feel alienated; feel left out in the cold
소요 所要 what is needed [required]; requirement ■ —시간 the time required; the necessary time : 소요 시간은 두 시간이다 It takes two hours.
소요 逍遙 〈산책〉 a ramble; a stroll
—소요하다 walk leisurely; stroll [ramble, saunter] about; take a stroll
◆ 숲속을 소요하다 ramble in the wood
■ —학파 〔哲〕 the Peripatetic school
소요 騷擾 a disturbance; an agitation; a commotion; 〈폭동〉 an uprising; a riot
◆ 거리에서 소요를 일으키다 cause [make, raise] a disturbance in the street
■ —죄 a crime of sedition; a charge of rioting
소용 所用 〈쓰임〉 use; service; 〈유용성〉 usefulness; 〈필요〉 need; necessity; necessaries; 〈경비〉 expenses
◆ 어떤 일에 소용되는 기능 the skills necessary for a job; the necessary skills for a job / 소용 있다 be useful; be of use [service] / 소용에 닿다 serve the purpose; be useful [serviceable]/ 소용되다 be in need [want] of; be necessary; be needed; be required; be essential
▶ 이것은 네게 소용이 될 것이다 This will be good for you.
▶ 지금 이것을 배워두면 장차 소용이 될 것이다 Studying this now will prove of use someday.
▶ 이야기한들 무슨 소용이 있겠니? What is the use of talking?
소용돌이 a swirl; a whirlpool; a whirl; a vortex; a convolution; 〈작은〉 an eddy; 〈큰〉 a maelstrom; 〈나선〉 a spiral; 〈고동 등의〉 a gyration
◆ 전란의 소용돌이 속에 in the vortex of war / 소용돌이에 휘말리다 be drawn into a whirlpool [vortex]; (비유) be involved [entangled] in
▶ 그는 그 사건의 소용돌이에 휘말렸다 He got dragged into [involved in] the case.
소용돌이치다 whirl (around); flow in whirls; eddy; swirl; 〈연기가〉 curl ◆ 소용돌이치는 물 [급류] swirling waters [torrents]
▶ 그녀의 마음 속에 갖가지 생각이 소용돌이쳤다 Diverse thoughts were whirling around her mind.
소용없다 所用— useless; no good; of no use [avail]; fruitless
▶ 그것을 의논해 봤자 소용없다 It is useless [fruitless] (for us) to discuss it. ⇌ It is useless [no good, no use] discussing it. ⇌ There is no use [no good, no point, no sense] (in) discussing it.
▶ 그에게 충고해 봤자 소용없다 Your advice falls flat on him.
▶ 이제 그런 소리 해 봤자 아무 소용없다 It is no use to say such a thing now.
▶ 나는 이제 이 책이 소용없다 I have no (further) use for this book. ⇌ I don't want this book any more [any longer].
▶ 이제 와서 후회해 봐야 소용없다 It is no use crying over spilt milk.
소우주 小宇宙 a microcosm(os)

소웅좌 小熊座 〖天〗 the Little Bear ⇨ 작은곰자리

소원 所願 〈바람〉 a desire; a wish; (a) hope ♦이루지 못한 소원 an unfulfilled desire / 제발 소원이니 for God's sake; for mercy's sake / 소원을 이루다[성취하다] have [get] one's wish; have one's wish realized [fulfilled] / 소원을 들어 주다 fulfill [meet] sb's wishes / 소원을 품다 cherish [harbor, entertain] a desire
▶ 마침내 그녀의 오랜 소원이 이루어졌다 Her long cherished hope finally came true.
▶ 그녀의 소원은 미국에 가는 것이다 Her wish [dream] is to go to America.
▶ 소원대로 되었니? Did you get [have] your wish? ⇒ Did your wish come true?
▶ 하느님이 내 소원을 꼭 들어주실 것이다 I am sure God will grant my request.
▶ 그는 그녀의 소원을 들어주지 않았다 He turned a deaf ear to her entreaties.
▶ 모든 것이 내 소원대로 되었다 Everything turned out as I had hoped [wished, desired]. ⇒ Everything happened according to my expectations.

소원 疎遠 estrangement; alienation
—소원하다 estranged; alienated; distant
▶ 두 사람은 사이가 소원해졌다 The two became estranged from each other.

소원 訴願 a petition; an appeal —소원하다 petition; appeal ♦당국에 세금 면제를 소원하다 petition [appeal to] the authorities for exemption from taxation

소위 少尉 〈육군〉 a second lieutenant; 〈해군〉 〈美〉 an ensign; 〈英〉 a second sublieutenant; 〈공군〉 〈美〉 a second lieutenant; 〈英〉 a pilot officer

소위 所爲 〈행위〉 an act; a deed; one's doing [work]; behavior

소위 所謂 〈이른바〉 what is called; what they [we, you] call; as it is called; the so-called ♦소위 지식인 a so-called intellectual
▶ 그들이 소위 폭주족[과격파 학생]이다 They are what is called [what we call] hot rodders [radical students].
▶ 이것이 소위 '일석이조'라는 것이다 This is what you might call "Killing two birds with one stone."

소위원회 小委員會 a subcommittee

소유 所有 possession; ownership ♦김 선생 소유의 물건 articles owned by [belonging to] Mr. Kim
▶ 그 집은 부친 작고 후 내 소유가 되었다 The house came into my possession [fell into my hands] after my father's death.
▶ 그 물건은 지금 그녀의 소유로 되어 있다 The article is now in her possession.
—소유하다 have; own; possess; hold; be in possession of; be possessed of
▶ 이 차는 누가 소유하고 있습니까? Who owns this car? ⇒ Who is the owner of this car?
▶ 그 집은 그가 소유하고 있다 The house is owned by him. ⇒ The house belongs to him.
■개인[공동]— individual [joint] ownership

소유격 所有格 〖文法〗 the possessive [genitive] case

소유권 所有權 ownership; proprietorship; a right [title] 《to sth》; 〈토지의〉 dominium; dominion ♦소유권을 갖고 있다 have [hold] the ownership (of) / 집의 소유권을 A에게서 B에게로 이전하다 transfer the ownership of a house from A to B
▶ 그는 그 토지에 대한 소유권을 주장했다 He claimed title to the land.
■지적— intellectual property rights ■—이전 (a) transfer of ownership ─자 an owner ─침해 (an) infringement of sb's ownership

소유물 所有物 one's possession [property]; one's belongings [goods]
▶ 이 건물은 그 회사의 소유물이었다 This building was in the possession of the company. ⇒ The company was in possession of this building.

소유욕 所有慾 a desire to possess ♦본능적 소유욕 the possessive instinct / 소유욕이 강한 possessive; acquisitive; covetous

소유자 所有者 an owner; a proprietor ♦소유자가 없는 ownerless / 소유자가 바뀌다 〈사물이 주어〉 change hands; pass into the possession of another person; shift [change] its owner [proprietor]
▶ 이 집의 소유자는 누굽니까? Whose house is this? ⇒ Who(m) does this house belong to?
■공동— joint [common] owners; co-owners 단독— a sole owner

소유지 所有地 the land owned by [belonging to] one; one's (own) land; one's estate

소음 騷音 (a) noise; (a) din ♦거리의 소음 street noise / 귀가 멍해지는 소음 a deafening [earsplitting] noise / 소음을 내다 make a noise [din]
■—계 a noise [sound-level] meter ─공해 noise pollution ─방지 prevention of noise

소음기 消音器 a sound arrester; 〈차의〉 a muffler; 〈총의〉 a silencer; 〈피아노의〉 a damper pedal

소이 所以 〈까닭〉 a reason; (the reason) why…; grounds; a cause
▶ 이것이 그 이름이 생긴 소이다 Hence (comes) its name. ⇒ This is why it is so named.

소이탄 燒夷彈 an incendiary (bomb [shell]); a fire bomb

소인 小人 〈어린이〉 a child; 〈口〉 a little one; 〈난쟁이〉 a little man; a pigmy; a dwarf; 〈소인배〉 a small-minded person; a mean [small] fellow; 〈口〉 a nobody; a lightweight; 〈겸칭〉 I; me; myself
■—국(國) a land of pigmies; 〈걸리버 여행기의〉 Lilliput ─배(輩) 〈口〉 small fry : 그는 소인배의 농간에 말려들었다 He fell into the snare laid by the villains.

소인 素人 an amateur; a dilettante; a non-professional (⇨ 아마추어) ■—극 amateur theatricals; an amateur dramatic performance

소인 素因 a basic factor [reason]; a primary cause; 〖醫〗 a (pre)disposition; a diathesis

소인 消印 〈일부인〉 a postmark; a (postal) canceling [cancellation] mark

♦7월 14일자 소인이 찍힌 봉투 an envelope postmarked July 14 / 뉴욕의 소인이 찍힌 편지 a letter postmarked from New York [bearing a New York postmark] / 편지에 소인을 찍다 imprint a postmark on a letter; postmark a letter
▶ 엽서는 8월 31일자 소인이 찍힌 것까지 유효함 Cards should be postmarked not later than August 31.
—소인하다 postmark
소인수 素因數 〔數〕 a prime factor
소일 消日 killing [whiling away] time —소일하다 pass *one's* time; kill [while away] time; waste *one's* time
♦독서로 소일하다 spend *one's* time (in) reading / 텔레비전을 보며 소일하다 kill time by watching TV
▶그들은 며칠간을 할 일 없이 소일했다 They idled a few days away.
■—거리 a time killer; a pastime
소 잃고 외양간 고친다 (속담) It is too late to lock the stable when the house is stolen.
소임 所任 〈책임〉 a duty; responsibility; a charge; 〈임무〉 a task; a mission
♦소임을 다하다 fulfill [discharge, perform] *one's* duty; carry out *one's* task [mission] / 소임을 맡다 take a duty [job] on *oneself*; set about *one's* task
▶그는 어려운 소임을 훌륭히 해냈다 He successfully carried out [performed] the difficult duties left to him.
소자 小子 〈부모에게〉 I; me; myself
소자 素子 〔電子〕 an element; 〈TV·FM 안테나의〉 a circuit element
소자 消磁 〔電〕 demagnetization ■—기(器) a demagnetizer
소자본 小資本 (a) small capital; limited funds ▶그는 소자본으로 장사를 시작했다 He started his business with (a) small capital.
소작 小作 (farm) tenancy; tenant farming; (美) sharecropping —소작하다 tenant (a farm); (美) sharecrop
■—권 a tenant right —료 rent paid by a tenant farmer —인 a tenant (farmer); (총칭) tenantry; (美) a sharecropper —쟁의 a dispute between landlords and tenant farmers; a tenancy dispute [trouble] —제도 the tenant(-farming) system —지 tenanted land; (美) sharecropped land
소작 燒灼 〔醫〕 cauterization; cautery —소작하다 cauterize
■—제(劑) a cauterant; a caustic
소장 小腸 〔解〕 the small intestine ■—염 enteritis
소장 少壯 the young; vigorous youth
♦전도가 유망한 소장 실업가 a promising young businessman / 소장의 young and vigorous; youthful
■—파 the young group [faction] —학파 the young school
소장 少將 〈육군〉 a major general; 〈해군〉 a rear admiral; 〈공군〉 (美) a major general; (英) an air vice-marshal
소장 所長 a head [chief, manager] 《of an office, a factory》
소장 所藏 *one's* possession
♦김선생 소장의 서화 Mr. Kim's collection of writings and paintings; writings and paintings owned by [in the possession of] Mr. Kim / 소장 골동품 *one's* collection of curios; curios in *one's* possession
—소장하다 possess; own; collect
소장 訴狀 a (written) complaint; a petition
♦소장을 당국에 제출하다 present [submit] a petition to the authorities; file a complaint with the authorities
소재 所在 〈사람의〉 *one's* whereabouts; the place where sb is; 〈사물의〉 the place where 《a thing》 is (kept); 〈건물 등의〉 the site; 〈위치〉 the location; the position
♦소재를 찾아[알아]내다 discover [find out] *sb's* whereabouts; locate 《the enemy's camp》 / 책임 소재를 분명히 하다 clarify where the responsibility lies
▶서류의 소재를 알 수가 없다 The papers are missing.
▶나는 그의 소재를 모른다 I don't know his whereabouts [where he is]. ⇒ His whereabouts are [is] unknown.
▶그녀는 소재를 감추어 버렸다 She concealed her whereabouts. ⇒ She hid herself. ⇒ She disappeared.
■—지 a location; a site; a seat : 도청소재지 the seat of a provincial office / 그 호텔의 소재지를 알려 주세요 Can you tell me where the hotel is?
소재 素材 material; 〈소설 등의〉 a subject matter; a theme
♦소재를 모으다 gather [collect] material [data] / 소재를 살리다 make good use [take advantage] of *one's* material / (너무 많이 써서) 쓸 소재가 없다 write *oneself* out
■—신— a new material
소저 小姐 a young lady
소전 小傳 a biographical sketch; a short biography; a brief account of *sb's* life
소전제 小前提 〔論〕 a minor premise [premiss]
소절 小節 〔樂〕 a bar; a measure
♦제2 소절 the second measure; measure Ⅱ
소정 所定 ♦소정의 양 the stated amount / 소정의 용지 a prescribed form / 소정의 사항 designated items / 소정의 fixed; prescribed; designated; appointed / 소정의 시간과 장소에서 at the appointed time and place / 소정의 절차를 밟다 go through the regular course [the prescribed] formalities
▶소정의 학점을 취득한 자는 졸업할 수 있다 A person can graduate when he has received required credits.
소조 小潮 〈조금〉《at》 the neap (tide)
소조 塑造 modeling; molding ■—예술 plastic arts
소주 燒酒 *soju*; distilled spirits; a clear distilled liquor
소중하다 所重— important; weighty; significant; valuable; valued; precious; dear
♦소중한 물건 a valuable [treasured] article; a treasure / 소중히 carefully; with (much)

care; with caution / 소중히 하다 〈존중하다〉 value; treasure (up); prize; make much of; 〈애지중지하다〉 take (good) care of; cherish
▶ 평화보다 소중한 것은 없다 There's nothing more precious than peace.
▶ 그는 소중한 친구를 잃었다 He lost a valuable [his dearest] friend.
▶ 물은 사막에서 매우 소중하다 Water is very valuable in a desert.
▶ 그녀는 오래된 그 사진들을 소중히 간직하고 있다 She cherishes the old photographs.

소지 沼地 marshland ⇨ 소택지(~地)

소지 所持 possession
―**소지하다** 〈소유하다〉 possess; own; 〈휴대하다〉 have 《money》 about [with, on] one; bear; carry
▶ 그는 평소에 단검을 소지하고 다닌다 He usually carries a dagger.
■ ―금 money [cash] in hand ―인[자] a holder; a possessor; a bearer

소지 素地 〈소질〉 the makings; an aptitude (for, to); 〈바탕〉 groundwork; foundation
▶ 그는 음악가가 될 소지가 있다 He has the makings of a musician.
▶ 그는 훌륭한 배우가 될 소지가 있다 He has the makings of an excellent actor.
▶ 그들은 악습에 물들 소지가 있다 They have an aptitude to vices.

소지 燒紙 〔民俗〕 (the burning of) prayer paper ♦ 소지 올리다 burn prayer paper; burn paper for the dead

소지품 所持品 one's things [belongings]; one's personal effects; 〈수화물〉 (美) baggage; (英) luggage
♦ 소지품을 맡기다 check one's personal effects / 소지품을 조사하다 examine [check up on] sb's things
▶ 소지품을 챙기세요 Get your things ready.
▶ 소지품에서 사체의 신원을 알아냈다 The body was identified by his personal effects.
▶ 소지품 주의 《게시》 We are not responsible for loss of valuables.

소진 消盡 vanishing completely; total disappearance; exhaustion
―**소진하다** be exhausted; vanish completely
▶ 정상에 이르자 그는 기력이 소진했다 At the end of the climb, his strength was exhausted.

소진 燒盡 reduction to ashes; total destruction by fire
―**소진하다** 〈건물이〉 be burnt down; be destroyed [consumed] by fire; be reduced to ashes; 〈연료가〉 be burnt out; be exhausted
▶ 그 전쟁 중 화재로 많은 문화재가 소진했다 A lot of cultural properties were reduced to ashes by fires during the war.

소질 素質 〈자질〉 an aptitude 《for, to》; the makings; talent; temperament; character; nature; fiber; 〈체질〉 constitution; make-up; 〈경향〉 turn; a tendency
♦ 유전적 범죄 소질 inherited criminal tendencies / 문학적 소질이 있는 사람 a person of a literary turn (of mind) / 소질이 있다 have genius (for); have (in one) the makings 《of a scientist》 / 어학에 소질이 있다 have linguistic genius [talent]
▶ 그는 정치가[예술가]의 소질이 있다 He has (in him) the makings of a politician [an artist].

소집 召集 a call; a summons; 〈군대 등의〉 a muster; a levy; a call-up; 〈회의의〉 convocation ♦ 국회의 소집 the convocation of the National Assembly / 소집에 응하다 respond to the call
―**소집하다** 〈회의를〉 call; convene; convoke; summon; 〈군대를〉 levy; muster; call up [out]; mobilize 《동원하다》; 〈군대에〉 call sb into the army; (美) draft sb (for service)
♦ 임시국회를 소집하다 convene [summon] a special session of the National Assembly
▶ 데모 진압을 위해 군대가 소집되었다 Troops were mobilized to quell the demonstration.
▶ 임시국회가 내일 소집된다 A special session of the National Assembly will be convened tomorrow.
■ ―나팔 a bugle call ―령 (issue) a draft call ―영장 a call-up paper; a draft notice; a summons to the colors

소차 小差 a small [slight] difference; a narrow [slim] margin; a small majority; a short lead

소찬 素饌 〈나물 반찬〉 a plain [homely] dish; a plain dinner; a vegetarian dish

소채 蔬菜 greens ⇨ 채소

소책자 小冊子 a booklet; a pamphlet; a brochure; a tract

소철 蘇鐵 〔植〕 a cycad; a sago [fern] palm

소청 所請 a request ♦ 소청을 들어주다 grant [comply with] a request
▶ 나는 그의 소청을 거절하였다 I declined his request.

소총 小銃 a rifle; 〈총칭〉 small arms
■ 엠십육― an M-16 (rifle) 카빈― a carbine ―탄 a bullet; a rifleshot

소추 訴追 〈형사상의〉 prosecution; indictment; accusation ―**소추하다** prosecute [indict] 《sb for a crime》; accuse 《sb of a crime》; charge 《sb with》
▶ 그는 문서 위조로 소추되었다 He was charged with forgery.

소출 所出 〈수확〉 the yield; the crop ♦ 밀의 소출 wheat yields; a crop of wheat / 소출이 많은 heavily [highly] productive 《farm》
▶ 금년엔 밀의 소출이 좋다 We have a good crop of wheat this year.

소치 所致 what is brought [caused] by; the result ♦ 젊은 소치로 on account of one's youthful ardor; due to youthfulness
▶ 이것은 그의 근면의 소치다 This is due to his industry.
▶ 실패는 전적으로 내 불찰의 소치였다 The failure was caused entirely by my carelessness.

소켓 a socket ♦ 소켓에 끼우다 fit [screw] 《a light bulb》 into the socket; socket ■ 쌍[세가닥]― a two-[three-]way socket

소쿠리 a bamboo basket

소크라테스 〈고대 아테네의 철학자〉 Socrates (470?-399 B.C.)

소크백신 〈소아마비 예방용〉〔醫〕the Salk vaccine

소 탈 疎脫 informality; unceremoniousness; lack of ceremony
―**소탈하다** informal; free and easy; openhearted; frank; uncauremonious; unconstrained; bohemian; freely-thinking and freely-acting
▶ 그는 어딘지 소탈한 데가 있다 He has something free and easy about him.
▶ 그녀는 성품이 소탈하다 Her personality is openhearted.

소탐대실 小貪大失 incurring a great loss by pursuing a small gain [profit] ―**소탐대실하다** suffer a big loss in going after a small gain

소 탕 掃蕩 sweeping; clearing; a sweep; mopping up; a mop-up; a cleanup
―**소탕하다** sweep; clear; scour; stamp [wipe] out; get rid of; 〈잔적 등을〉 mop up; clean up; clear out
♦ 바다에서 적을 소탕하다 clear [sweep, rid] the sea of the enemy / 잔적을 소탕하다 mop up the remnants of the enemy
▶ 경찰은 거리의 부랑자를 소탕했다 The police cleared away the vagrants in the streets.
■―(작)전 a mopping-up operation [campaign]

소 택 沼澤 〈늪과 못〉 a marsh; a swamp; a bog
■―지 marshy ground; marshland; swampland; bogland; 《英》fenland

소 통 疏通 〈의사의〉 (good) understanding; 〈물 등의〉 drainage
♦ 의사 소통이 되지 않다 lack understanding; be at odds 《with》
―**소통하다** communicate; come to understand each other; come to a mutual (good) understanding; 〈물 등이〉 drain off
♦ 의사 소통하고 있다 have [keep] a good understanding 《with》

소 파 搔爬 〔醫〕curettage; curettement
♦ 소파 수술을 받다 undergo curettage
―**소파하다** curet(te); remove [scrape] with a curette

소 파 a sofa

소 편 小片 a small piece; a bit; a fragment; 〈도자기의〉 a shard

소 포 小包 a parcel; a package; a packet; a pack

소포우편 小包郵便 〈제도〉 parcel(s) post; a (postal) package; 〈우편물〉 a (postal) parcel
♦ 소포우편으로 보내다 send *sth* by parcel post; 《美》 mail *sth*《to》
▶ 이 책을 소포우편으로 보내려고 합니다 I want to send this book by parcel post.
■―료 parcel post postage [charge, rates]

소포클레스 〈고대 그리스의 시인〉 Sophocles (496?-406 B.C.)

소 폭 小幅 〈폭〉 single breadth; 〈범위〉 narrow range; narrow limits
♦ 소폭 등락 〈주식 등의〉 fluctuations of a narrow range / 소폭의 변동을 보이다 move within narrow limits
▶ 후장(後場)은 (주가가) 소폭 변동이나마 활발하였다 The afternoon market was brisk within a narrow range (of stock prices).

소 품 小品 〈문학의〉 short piece [work]; a (literary) sketch; 〈회화의〉 a small work of art; a small painting; 〈조각의〉 a small sculpture; 〔劇〕 (stage) properties; props
■―곡 a short piece of music; a musical sketch ―담당자 a property [(口) prop] man [master] ―실 a property room

소 풍 逍風 a picnic; an excursion; a holiday expedition; a walking tour; a hike; a tramp; an outing
♦ 학교의 소풍 a school picnic / 소풍을 가다 go on a picnic [an excursion] / 소풍에 데려가다 take 《children》 on an excursion
―**소풍하다** go on an excursion [a picnic, an outing, a hike]; take a long walk; take the air; get some fresh air
■―객 an excursionist; a holidaymaker

소프라노 〔樂〕 soprano; 〈가수〉 a soprano《*pl.* ~s, -ni》; a soprano singer ♦ 소프라노로 노래하다 sing in soprano

소프트볼 〈놀이〉《play》 softball; 〈공〉 a softball

소프트웨어 〔電算〕 software

소 피 所避 urination
♦ 소피보다 do *one's* needs; ease [relieve] nature; pay a call of nature; pass [make] water; urinate
▶ 소피보고 싶다 Nature calls [is calling] me.

소피아 〈불가리아의 수도〉 Sofia

소하어 遡河魚 an anadromous fish

소 할 所轄 jurisdiction ⇨ 관할(管轄)

소 항 遡航 sailing upstream ―**소항하다** sail upstream; go [sail] up the river

소 해 掃海 〈수뢰 등의 제거〉 sea clearing; mine sweeping [dragging]
―**소해하다** sweep up mines; sweep [drag] the sea for mines; clear the sea
■―작업 mine-sweeping [sea-clearing] operations; mine sweeping [dragging] ―정(艇) a mine sweeper

소 행 所行 an act; a deed; *one's* doing [work]
♦ 악마의 소행 the work of the Devil
▶ 이건 그의 소행임에 틀림없다 It must be his doing.
▶ 도대체 어느 놈의 소행이냐? Who the devil did it?

소 행 素行 〈품행〉 conduct; behavior; *one's* natural character
♦ 소행이 나쁜 사람 a man of bad [loose] conduct / 소행이 나쁘다 lead a fast [dissolute] life; be a loose fish

소행성 小行星 〔天〕 a minor [small] planet; an asteroid

소 형 小型 a small size; a pocket size
♦ 소형의 small-sized; small; midget; pocket-size(d); miniature
■―권총 a pocket pistol ―램프 a midget lamp ―미사일 a bantam missile ―비행기 a light plane; (총칭) light aircraft ―승용차 a compact [small] car; a minicar ―카메라 a miniature camera; a midget camera; a minicam ―트럭 a light (delivery) truck; a

pickup (truck) —판(判) a miniature [pocket] edition

소형화 小型化 miniaturization —**소형화하다** miniaturize

소홀 疏忽 〈태만〉 negligence; 〈부주의〉 carelessness; 〈무관심〉 indifference
—**소홀하다** negligent; neglectful; remiss; careless; indifferent
♦ 소홀함이 없이 〈근면하게〉 diligently; 〈충실히〉 faithfully / 소홀히 하다 neglect; disregard; be negligent [neglectful] (of); make light [little] of; pay no attention (to) / 공부를 소홀히 하다 neglect one's studies / 부모를 소홀히 하다 neglect [be unkind to] one's parents / 일[근무]을 소홀히 하다 neglect [scant, scamp] one's work [duties] / 일언반구도 소홀히 하지 않다 carefully weigh every word and phrase
▶ 그는 직무를 소홀히 했다 He was neglectful of his duties. ⇒ He neglected his duties.

소화 消化 1 〈음식의〉 digestion
♦ 소화가 잘 안되는 음식물[것] indigestible [heavy] food [substance] / 소화를 돕다 promote [help, aid] digestion
▶ 이 약은 소화에 도움이 된다 This medicine helps digestion.
▶ 이 생선은 소화가 잘 된다 This fish digests well [is easy to digest].
▶ 이것은 소화가 잘 된다[안된다] This digests well [ill].
—**소화하다** digest
♦ 소화하기 쉬운[힘든] digestible [indigestible]; (be) easy [hard] of digestion [to digest]
2 〈이해〉 digestion; assimilation ♦ 제대로 소화를 못한 외국 문화 ill-digested foreign culture —**소화하다** digest; assimilate; understand; take in
♦ 첫번째로 소화해야 할 문제 the first problem to be digested
3 〈소비〉 consumption
—**소화하다** consume
▶ 국내 시장만으로는 이들 제품을 도저히 소화시킬 수 없다 The home [domestic] market alone cannot consume all these goods.
■—**관(管)** 〔解〕 an alimentary [a digestive] canal [tract, duct] —**력** digestive power —**샘** 〔解〕 a digestive gland —**선** ⇨ 소화샘 —**액** digestive fluid [juice] —**작용** a digestive process —**제** a digestive; a digester; a peptic —**효소** digestive enzymes

소화 消火 fire extinguishing; fire fighting
♦ 소화용의[으로] for fire-extinguishing [fire-fighting] purposes / 소화에 힘쓰다 fight a fire
▶ 그들은 초기 소화에 실패했다 They failed to bring the fire under control in its early stages.
—**소화하다** put out [extinguish] a fire
■—**용수(用水)** water (available) for fire-fighting —**전(栓)** a (fire) hydrant; a fireplug —**호스[펌프]** a fire hose [pump]

소화 笑話 a funny [humorous] story; a joke

소화기 消化器 〔解〕 a digestive organ
■—**장애** (a) digestive trouble

소화기 消火器 a fire extinguisher

소화기

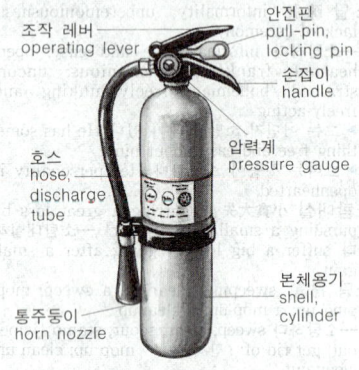

조작 레버 operating lever
안전핀 pull-pin, locking pin
손잡이 handle
호스 hose, discharge tube
압력계 pressure gauge
본체용기 shell, cylinder
통노즐이 horn nozzle

소화물 小貨物 a parcel; a packet; (美) a package ♦ 소화물로 보내다 consign [send] sth as a parcel
■—**차** a parcels [luggage] van —**취급소** a parcels office

소화불량 消化不良 dyspepsia; indigestion; bad [defective] digestion; digestive disorder
♦ 소화불량이 되다 suffer from indigestion; lose digestion
■—**환자** a dyspeptic

소환 召喚 a call; a summons; (a) monition; 〔法〕 (a) citation; a subp(o)ena
♦ 소환을 받다 receive a summons; be served with a subp(o)ena / 소환에 응하다 answer [obey] a summons
—**소환하다** summon; call; cite
▶ 법정에 소환되다 be summoned to (appear before) the court / 증인으로 소환되다 be summoned as a witness
■—**장** a (writ of) summons [subp(o)ena]; 〔法〕 a citation: 소환장을 발부하다 issue a summons (against sb)

소환 召還 (a) recall
—**소환하다** recall; call back
♦ 본국으로 소환되다 be summoned [recalled, ordered] home
▶ 주미 대사가 소환되었다 The ambassador to the U.S. was recalled.
■—**장** a letter of recall —**제도** the recall system

소회 所懷 one's impression

속 1 〈안〉 the inside; the interior; the inner part; 〈깊숙한〉 the innermost [inmost] recess; the heart
♦ 산 속 the heart of a mountain / 서랍[봉투] 속 the inside of a drawer [an envelope] / 그림 속의 꽃 the flowers in the picture / 숲 속 깊이 deep in the recesses of the forest / 물 속 깊이 deep in the water; at the bottom of the sea / 어둠 속에 in the dark / 모래 속에 파묻히다 be buried in the sand
▶ 그는 가난 속에서 죽었다 He died in poverty.

▶그 일행은 밀림 속에서 길을 잃었다 The party lost their way in the jungle.
▶이 병 속에는 무엇이 들어 있습니까? What is in this bottle?
▶이 상자 속에는 든 것이 없다 There is no substance in this box.
▶알맹이는 껍질 속에 있다 The nut is inside the shell.
2 〈마음・이면〉 the depth; the bottom; the heart
♦속이 들여다 보이는 짓을 하다 resort to shallow tricks / (마음) 속으로는 in the innermost [inmost, secret] recesses [depths] of one's heart [nature]; in one's heart of hearts; at heart / 속으로 웃다 laugh [smile] in [up] one's sleeve / 속을 알 수 없는 인물 a mysterious person; a sphinx; an enigma / 부모의 속을 몹시 썩이는 사람 the plague of one's parents / 속을 썩이다 worry oneself about / 서로 속을 떠보다 try to fathom the unexpressed intentions of others
▶그는 무언가 속에 간직하고 있는 것 같다 He seems to have something on his mind.
3 〈내용물〉 content(s); 〈실질〉 substance; 〈박제품・요리 등의〉 stuffing; a filling; 〈의자 등의〉 pad; padding; 〈이불 등의〉 wad; wadding; a filler
♦매트리스에 속을 넣다 stuff the mattress / 박속을 파내다 hollow out [excavate] a gourd
4 〈뱃속〉 insides; stomach
♦빈 속 empty stomach / 속이 비다 get hungry; feel empty / 속이 쓰리다 have a burning feeling in the stomach / 속이 좋지 않다 have something wrong with one's inside(s)
5 〈중심・핵〉 the center; the heart; 〈과일의〉 the core; 〈초목의〉 a pith; 〈뼛속〉 the marrow
♦사과의 속을 도려내다 core an apple
▶그는 뼛속까지 썩었다 He is rotten to the core.
▶이 재목은 속까지 썩었다 This timber is rotten throughout.
속 屬 〔生〕 a genus (pl. genera, ~es)
속 束 〈묶음〉 a bundle 《of fag(g)ot》
속 續 〈속편〉 a second series; a sequel
♦「속 미국 이야기」 The Story of America, Continued
속가 俗歌 a popular [folk] song; a ditty; a ballad
속가죽 the inside skin; an inner layer of skin
속간 續刊 continuation of publication
─속간하다 continue the publication 《of》
속감침 inside hemming
속개 續開 resumption; continuation
─속개하다 resume; continue ▶예산위원회는 내일 속개된다 The budget committee will resume its session tomorrow.
속겨 inner bran
속격 屬格 〔文法〕 the genitive (case)
속결 速決 a prompt [quick] decision
속계 俗界 the [this] world; earthly [secular] life
속고갱이 the (very) heart [core] ♦배추의 속고갱이 the heart of a cabbage
속곡 俗曲 a folk song; a popular song; a ballad
속곳 a slip; a petticoat; women's underwear
♦속곳 바람으로 with nothing on but a slip
속공 速攻 a swift attack ─속공하다 launch a swift attack against
속구 速球 〔野〕 a speed ball; a fastball
■─투수 a fast baller; a fastball pitcher; (美俗) a speed baller
속국 屬國 a dependency; a subject [vassal] state [country]; a tributary (state)
♦중국의 속국이 되다 come [pass] under the sway [rule, yoke] of China; become (a) tributary to China; be subject to China
속궁리 ─窮理 a contrivance; rumination
─속궁리하다 contrive; consider; deliberate; ponder 《over》; ruminate 《on》; reflect 《on》; (口) mull 《over》
속기 速記 **1** 〈속필〉 rapid [fast] writing
─속기하다 write [note down] fast [rapidly]; take rapid notes 《of》
2 〈속기술〉 shorthand 《writing》; stenography
♦속기를 배우다 learn shorthand; take lessons in stenography [shorthand]
─속기하다 write [take] down in shorthand; take stenographic notes 《of》; stenograph
▶그녀는 강의를 속기하였다 She wrote [took] down the lecture in shorthand.
■─록 a stenographic record; shorthand [stenographic] notes [records] ─문자 a stenographic character ─법 stenography ─사[자] a shorthand writer; a stenographer; a stenographist ─술 shorthand; stenography ─학교 a shorthand school
속꺼풀 the inner skin [covering]; an inner layer
속껍데기 an inner shell; an inner layer of skin; the derma
속껍질 an inner skin [coat]
속내 the internal conditions; the inside
♦속내를 들여다 보다 see behind the scenes / 속내를 알고 있다 have an inside know ledge 《of》; be in the know
속내평 the internal conditions ⇨ 속내
속념 俗念 worldly ideas; earthly desires; worldliness; worldly-mindedness ♦속념을 버리다 free oneself from earthly desires
속눈썹 eyelashes; lashes; (口) winkers ♦긴 속눈썹 long eyelashes ■─인조 false eyelashes
속다 be [get] deceived [cheated, deluded, hoaxed, defrauded, fooled]; be imposed on [upon]; be taken in; be caught in a trap
♦잘 속는 사람 a dupe; a gull; a pushover; a sucker; (口) an easy [a soft, a good] mark / 잘 속을 것 같은 모습 something green in sb's eyes / 잘 속는 be credulous; green / 감쪽같이 속다 be fairly taken in / 속아서 돈을 빼앗기다 be cheated [fooled] out of one's money; be stung 《for》 / 물건을 속아 사다 get gypped in buying an article / 가짜 물건을 속아 사다 be fobbed [palmed] off with a counterfeit
▶그는 쉽게 속았다 He was easily taken in.
▶그녀는 속아서 그 남자와 결혼하였다 She was tricked into marrying that man.
▶그들에게 속지 않도록 해라 Be on your guard

in dealing with them.
▶ 내가 만만히 속을 줄 아니? Do you see any green in my eyes?

속닥거리다 talk in whispers ⇨ 쑥덕거리다

속단 速斷 1 〈성급한 단정〉 a hasty conclusion ―**속단하다** make [draw] a hasty conclusion; decide hastily; jump [rush] to conclusions
▶ 그가 우리에게 한 말이 거짓말이라고 속단해서는 안된다 You must not jump to the conclusion that what he told us is a lie.
▶ 그는 내가 그것을 했다고 속단하였다 He ran away with the idea that I had done it.
2 〈빠른 판단〉 an immediate judgment; a prompt decision ―**속단하다** pass [form] an immediate judgment ((up)on); be prompt in deciding 《that…》

속달 速達 express [special] delivery
♦ 편지를 속달로 보내다 send a letter by express [by special delivery] / 소포를 속달로 보내다 express a parcel
▶ 이것을 속달로 보내면 얼마입니까? How much does it cost if I send this by express?
■ ―료 an express [a special] delivery charge; a special-delivery fee / ―우편 〈제도〉 express- [special-]delivery postal service; 〈우편물〉 (美) special delivery; (英) express delivery ―편지 a special-delivery letter

속달다 〈몸달다〉 jitter; be anxious [eager] (for, to do); be impatient (for, to do); be nervous (about); fret (oneself) (about)
♦ 나는 결과를 알지 못해 속달았다 I was anxious to know the result.
▶ 그는 기차가 연착해서 속달았다 He was impatient at the delay of the train.
▶ 그렇게 속달아할 것 없네 Don't jitter [fret yourself] like that.

속달뱅이 a small scale
♦ 속달뱅이로 on small scale

속담 俗談 a proverb; a (common) [an old] saying; an adage; a maxim (▶이 사전에서 우리말 속담은 찾아보기 쉽도록 독립 표제어로 하였다. 속담은 국어사전에서처럼 어순대로 찾으면 된다. 영어 속담은 해당 표제어에 풀이해 두었다)
♦ 속담에도 있듯이 as the proverb says [goes, runs]
▶ 속담에도 있듯이 시간은 금이다 As the proverb goes [says], time is money.

속답 速答 an immediate answer; a prompt reply

속대¹ 〈푸성귀의〉 the heart (of greenstuff)
속대² 〈댓개비의〉 bamboo pith

속도 速度 〔物〕 (a) velocity; (a) speed; a pace; (a) rate; 〔樂〕 (a) tempo
〈속도가〉 빠른[느리다] be fast [slow] in speed / 속도가 늘다 gain [increase] in speed; gather speed / 속도가 줄다 lose [decrease] in speed
〈속도를〉 속도를 늘이다 increase [accelerate] speed; speed up / 속도를 줄이다 [늦추다] decrease speed; slow down
▶ 속도를 줄이세요 (게시) Slow (down). ⇌ Reduce speed.
▶ 열차는 속도를 늦추었다 The train slowed down.
▶ 이 스포츠카는 어느 정도로 속도를 낼 수 있습니까? How fast does this sports car go?
▶ 우리 앞차가 갑자기 속도를 늦추었다 The car ahead of us suddenly slowed down.
〈속도로〉 빠른[느린] 속도로 at high [low] speed / 무서운 속도로 at terrible speed / 매초 15미터의 속도로 at the rate [at a speed] of fifteen meters a second
▶ 그는 매시 40마일의 속도로 차를 몰았다 He drove at a speed [rate] of 40 miles per hour.
▶ 태풍은 매시 300킬로미터의 속도로 북상하고 있었다 The typhoon was advancing northward at the rate of 300 kilometers per hour.
■ ―규정― the regulation speed 제한― (at) regulation speed; 《within》 the speed limit 최고― the maximum speed ■ ―계 a speedometer; a speed indicator; a tachymeter ―선택기 a velocity selector ―유량계 a velocity flow meter ―제어 장치 a speed control device ―조절기 a velocity governor; a speed regulator

속도위반 速度違反 speeding; violation of the speed regulations ♦ 속도위반으로 벌금을 물다 be fined for speeding ■ ―자 a violator of the speed regulations; a speeder

속도제한 速度制限 speed regulation; a speed limit ♦ 속도제한을 하다 set [place] a speed limit 《on》 ―속도제한 시속 40마일 (게시) Speed limit : 40 mph.
■ ―표지 a speed-limit sign

속독 速讀 rapid [speed, quick, fast] reading ―**속독하다** read fast [rapidly] ■ ―법 speed reading

속돌 〔鑛〕 (a) pumice (stone); a floatstone

속되다 俗― 〈세속적이다〉 secular; earthly; worldly; mundane; 〈통속적이다〉 common; popular; 〈천하다〉 vulgar; low; coarse
♦ 속된 사람 a vulgar fellow; a worldly people / 속된 욕망 worldly desires [ambitions] / 속된 욕망을 가지다 have [entertain] worldly ambitions
▶ 그는 아주 속된 사람이다 He is quite a vulgar fellow.

속등 續騰 a continued advance [rise] (in prices); a further rise [appreciation] ―**속등하다** continue to advance [rise] ▶ 물가가 속등하고 있다 The prices continue to rise.

속락 續落 a continued fall [drop]; a further decline; sagging; sliding ―**속락하다** continue to fall [drop]; keep declining [sagging, sliding]; fall persistently

속력 速力 (a) speed; (a) velocity; (a) rate
♦ 전속력으로 at full [top] speed; (口) (at) full lick / 매시 60마일의 속력으로 at a [the] speed [rate] of sixty miles per [an] hour
▶ 그 배는 점차 속력이 떨어졌다 The ship lost speed gradually.
▶ 그는 전속력으로 달렸다 He ran at full speed.
▶ 그 배는 평균 30 노트의 속력을 낸다 The ship makes an average speed of 30 knots.
▶ 이 자동차는 최대 시속 150마일까지 속력을 낼 수 있다 This motorcar develops a maximum

speed of 150 miles an hour
■ 경제— an economic speed ■ =시험 a speed test

속령 屬領 〈영토〉 a territory; a possession;〈속국〉 a dependency; a dependent domain [territory]; a subject province; a vassel state; a dominion; a colony

속론 俗論 a vulgar opinion [view]; a conventional view ◆ 그 문제에 관한 속론 the vulgar view of the matter / 속론에 반대하다 be against conventional views

속료 屬僚 a subordinate; (총칭) the staff

속리 俗吏 a petty official; (英) a bumble; a jack-in-office ■ —근성(根性) bumbledom

속립 粟粒 〈조의 낟알〉a German millet seed ■ —결핵 miliary tuberculosis —종(腫)〔醫〕a milium (*pl.* milia)

속마음 one's inmost heart [thought(s)]; one's real intention; the bottom of one's heart
◆ 속마음으로는 at (the) bottom; at heart / 속마음을 알 수 없는 인물 a person of very profound character; an inscrutable person; (口) a deep one
▶ 우리는 속마음을 잘 아는 사이다 We are close friends [well used to each other's ways].
▶ 그녀는 김선생에게 속마음으로 감사하고 있다 She thanks Mr. Kim from the bottom of her heart.
▶ 말은 그렇게 해도 속마음은 울고 있다 Though he says so, he is weeping at heart.

속말 a confidential [private] talk; a confidence ◆ 속말을 하다 have a private [confidential] talk 《with》; speak out of one's heart; make confidences 《to》

속명 俗名 〈통명〉a popular [familiar] name;〈속칭〉a common [vernacular] name;〔佛敎〕a secular name

속명 屬名 〔生〕a generic name [term]; a genus name

속무 俗務 worldly matters [cares]; secular work

속문학 俗文學 vulgar [low] literature; popular literature

속물 俗物 a worldly(-minded) person; a worldling; a snob; a person of low [vulgar] taste; (口) a snooty fellow ■ —근성 philistinism; snobbery; vulgarity

속바지 underpants; drawers; briefs

속박 束縛 (a) restraint; (a) restriction; shackles; fetters; trammels; a yoke
◆ 속박을 받다 be placed under restraint; be fettered 《by》 / 속박을 벗어나다 free *oneself* from restraint
▶ 그들은 당시 외국의 속박을 받고 있었다 At that time they were under the yoke of a foreign power.
—속박하다 restrain; restrict; trammel; shackle; enchain; fetter; tie; bind; lay [place] under restraint
◆ 아무의 자유를 속박하다 restrain *sb* of his liberty; restrict *sb's* freedom / 언론의 자유를 속박하다 place a gag upon freedom of speech / 행동을 속박당하다 be restricted in

one's movements

속박된 전자 束縛—電子 〔物〕a bound electron

속발 續發 successive [frequent] occurrence; a succession [series] 《of events》
—속발하다 happen [occur] in succession; come out [crop up] one after another
▶ 어제는 산불이 속발하였다 Forest fires broke out successively yesterday.

속방 屬邦 a dependency ⇨ 속국

속병 —病 〈위장병〉a gastroenteric disorder [trouble]; a digestive complaint that lingers;〈지병〉a chronic internal disease; a lingering constitutional malady
▶ 그는 오랜 속병 끝에 죽었다 He died after a chronic gastroenteric disease.

속보 速步 a quick pace; quicksteps;〔軍〕a quick march;〔馬〕a trot (▶ a walk와 a gallop의 중간속도); trotting ◆ 속보로 at a quick pace; at a trot

속보 速報 a bulletin; a prompt [quick] report [announcement]; a (news) flash
▶ 개표결과 속보가 있었다 There was a news flash of the results of the ballot counting.
▶ 오늘 아침 뉴스 속보로 그 열차 사고를 알았다 On a news flash this morning I learned about the train accident.
—속보하다 report promptly; announce quickly; make a quick report 《on》
■ 선거— prompt [hour-by-hour] reports of the election returns ■ —판 a bulletin board; (英) a newsboard

속보 續報 a continued [follow-up] report; a follow-up; further news; additional [further] particulars

속보이다 be transparent; be easily seen through; be conjecturable [inferable, surmisable]
◆ 속보이는 행동 a mean [shameful, despicable; contemptible] act / 속보이는 짓을 하다 resort to a shallow trick

속사 俗事 worldly [earthly, mundane] affairs; daily routine; common business; secular affairs ◆ 속사에 쫓기다 be busy with routine work; be engrossed in daily affairs

속사 速射 quick firing [fire]; firing in rapid succession; a snap shot —속사하다 fire quickly [in rapid succession]

속사 速寫 〈복사〉quick copying;〔寫〕snap-shooting; snapshot —속사하다 copy quickly [rapidly]; snapshoot; take a snapshot 《of》
■ —사진 a snap; a snapshot —카메라 a snapshot camera; 〈소형의〉a candid camera

속사정 —事情 the inside story; the unrevealed circumstances; the real state of affairs

속사포 速射砲 a quick-firing [quick-fire] gun; a rapid-firng gun; a quick-firer
◆ 속사포처럼 질문을 퍼붓다 fire off questions one after another in rapid succession

속삭거리다 whisper ⇨ 속삭이다
▶ 시험중에 속삭거리면 안됩니다 Don't whisper during the examination.

속삭속삭 in a suppressed [low] voice; under one's breath; in whispers —속삭속삭하다 ⇨ 속삭이다

속삭이다 whisper; murmur; talk in whispers; speak below [under] *one's* breath
♦서로 속삭이다 whisper to each other; exchange whispers / 귀에 대고 속삭이다 whisper in 《another's》 ear / 남의 귀에다 한두 마디 속삭이다 whisper a word or two into another's ear
▶ 그는 그녀의 귀에다 몇 마디 속삭였다 He whispered a few words in her ear.
▶ 그는 사랑의 말을 속삭였다 He murmured his words of love.

속삭임 a whisper; a murmur ♦사랑의 속삭임 sweet whispers of love; soft nothings / 시냇물의 속삭임 murmurs of a brook

속산 速算 a rapid calculation ━**속산하다** do [make] a rapid calculation; calculate rapidly

속살 1 〈옷 속의〉 the part of the body usually covered by clothing
♦속살이 내비치는 블라우스 a see-through blouse / 속살이 희다 have a fair skin
▶ 그는 말라 보여도 속살은 포동포동하다 He is apparently thin, but his body is substantially plump.
2 〈옹골찬 살〉 the inside flesh; the inner meat 《of a lobster》
3 〈쇠고기의〉 the meat from the inside of a cow's mouth

속살찌다 1 〈살찌다〉 be plumper than 《he》 looks; be solidly fleshy
2 〈실속있다〉 be substantial; be solid; be rich

속상하다 〈마음이 불편하고 괴롭다〉 feel sore 《about》; feel depressed [distressed]; be troubled; 〈분하다〉 be [feel] vexed 《at *one's* failure》; be annoyed; be exasperated 《at》; 〈사물이 주어〉 be troublesome; be distressing
♦속상하게 하다 hurt *sb's* feeling; cause *sb* distress / 속상해 하다 feel sore 《about》
▶ 아이 속상해 How vexing [disappointing]!
▶ 무엇이 그리 속상하니? What are you sore [mad] at?
▶ 기차를 놓쳐서 속상하다 I am mad at missing the train.
▶ 그는 실패를 해서[펜을 잃어버려서] 속상했다 He was [felt] chagrined at his failure [at losing his pen].
▶ 아들의 성적이 좋지 않아 아버지는 몹시 속상했다 The boy's low grades caused his father great distress.

속새 〔植〕 a horsetail; a scouring rush

속새질 scouring 《with a scouring rush》 ━**속새질하다** scour with a scouring rush

속생각 rumination ━**속생각하다** ruminate

속설 俗說 a common [popular] saying; a popular version 《of》; a conventional remark; 〈전설〉 folklore; 《a》 tradition; a legend

속성 俗姓 *one's* secular surname

속성 速成 quick mastery; rapid completion; 〈단기 양성〉 an intensive training 《in》
♦3개월의 영어 속성 강습 a three-month intensive course in English / 속성으로 영어 회화를 배우다 learn English conversation by cramming
■━과 a short [an intensive] course 《in French》 ━법 a shortcut [royal road] 《to》; a quick-mastery method ━재배 forcing [intensive] culture

속성 屬性 〔論〕 an attribute; a property; 〔生〕 a generic character

속성작용 續成作用 〔地〕 the diagenesis

속세 俗世 this [the] world; earthly existence; mundane life
♦속세를 등지다 turn *one's* back upon the world / 속세를 버리다 renounce [retire from] the world; go to live in seclusion
▶ 나는 속세를 떠나 선계에서 노닐고 있는 기분이었다 I felt as if I had left the everyday world and were enjoying life in a fairyland.

속세간 俗世間 this world ⇨ 속세

속셈 1 〈심산〉 an intention; inner thought(s) [calculation]; an ulterior motive [purpose]
♦속셈을 드러내다 reveal *one's* secret intention / …할 속셈으로 with the secret intention of…
▶ 그들은 속셈이 있어 나를 초대했다 They had some ulterior motive in inviting me.
▶ 그가 무슨 속셈으로 그렇게 말했을까? What did he really mean by that? ⇌ With what intention did he say that?
▶ 나는 그의 속셈을 모르겠다 I don't understand what he has in mind.
▶ 나는 그의 속셈을 뻔히 알 수 있다 I can see through his intentions.
▶ 그의 속셈은 우리를 갈라놓는 것이다 His design is to separate [drive a wedge between] us.
▶ 그가 나를 위해 일하는 것은 아마도 어떤 속셈이 있어서일 것이다 Probably he works for me with some secret intention.
2 〈암산〉 mental arithmetic [calculation, computation]

속셔츠 an underwear shirt; an undershirt; next-to-skin wear ♦속셔츠 바람으로 있다 have nothing on but an undershirt / 속셔츠 바람으로 일하다 work in *one's* undershirt

속속 續續 successively; in succession; one after another
▶ 사람들이 속속 달려왔다 A lot of people came running one after another.
▶ 세계 각지에서 편지가 속속 날아들었다 Letters poured in from various parts of the world.
▶ 주문이 속속 쇄도한다 Orders pour in. ⇌ We are flooded with orders.
▶ 새 집들이 속속 들어선다 New houses spring up like mushrooms.

속속들이 thoroughly; to the core; inside out
♦속속들이 썩다 be rotten to the core / 속속들이 알다 know *sth* through and through; have a thorough [full] knowledge 《of》; be quite at home 《on, in》 / 속속들이 젖다 be drenched [wet] to the skin / 비밀을 속속들이 캐내다 root out a secret / 정계를 속속들이 알고 있다 know the political world inside out
▶ 그렇게 속속들이 캐묻지 마라 Don't be so inquisitive.
▶ 이 근처는 그가 속속들이 안다 He knows every inch of this neighborhood.
▶ 그 장사는 내가 속속들이 알고 있다 I know

속손톱 the half-moon of [on] a fingernail; 〔解〕 the lunula 《*pl.* -lae》
속수무책 束手無策 resourcelessness; helplessness; being at *one's* wits' [wit's] end
◆속수무책이다 be at *one's* wits' [wit's] end; be at the end of *one's* resources; be quite at a loss (what to do)
▶나로서는 속수무책이다 It's all up with me. ⇌ There's nothing more I can do.
속썩다 feel sick at heart; be vexed [worried, troubled]; worry [trouble] *oneself* 《about》
속씨식물 —植物 an angiosperm
속아넘어가다 be deceived ⇨ 속다
속악 俗惡 vulgarity; inelegance; coarseness
—속악하다 vulgar; gross; unrefined; coarse; low; lowbrow; inelegant
◆속악한 취미 vulgar [low, philistine] taste
속어 俗語 a slang word; (총칭) slang
◆속어로는 in common speech / 속어를 쓰다 use vulgar speech
▶bread는 money의 속어 중의 하나다 'Bread' is one of the slang words for 'money.'
속어림 *one's* guess; *one's* conjecture / 속어림으로는 in *one's* estimation [estimate]; by guess [guesswork]; in *one's* thought
속없다 〈줏대가 없다〉 spineless; spiritless; backboneless; poor-spirited; (be) without settled convictions; 〈악의가 없다〉 innocent, harmless
◆속없는 말 an idle talk / 속없는 사람 a man without settled convictions; a spineless person
▶내가 속없이 한 말이다 I meant no harm.
속여먹다 deceive ⇨ 속이다
속연 續演 the continuation of a show
—속연하다 continue to perform [stage, put on] 《a play》; run 《a show》 consecutively
속영 續映 a continual run (of a film)
—속영하다 continue to show 《a film》; run 《a movie》 consecutively
▶그 영화는 3개월 이상 속영되고 있다 The movie has been running for more than three months.
속옷 underwear; underclothing; underclothes; an undergarment; underlinen; 〈여성용〉 lingerie [lɑ̀ːndʒəréi, læ̀n-, -ríː]; (口) undies
◆속옷을 갈아입다 change *one's* underlinen
속요 俗謠 a popular [folk] song; a ballad; a ditty ⇨ 속가(俗歌)
속음 俗音 a popular pronunciation [reading] of a Chinese character
속이다 deceive; cheat; trick; swindle; hoax; fool; falsify; take in; impose [play] upon
▶나이를 속이다 misrepresent [lie about] *one's* age / 이름을 속이다 give [assume] a false name / 적을 속이다 mislead an enemy / 자신을 속이다 deceive *oneself* / 장부를 속이다 falsify books [accounts]; cook [manipulate, juggle] accounts / 저울을 속이다 give short measure [weight] / 숫자를 속이다 juggle with figures / 계산서를 속이다 cook up a bill / 아무의 눈을 속이다 hoodwink *sb*; pull [draw] the wool over *sb's* eyes / 이름을 속이고 under [assuming] a false name / 아프다고 속이다 feign illness; pretend to be ill / 대학생이라 속이다 feign [pretend to be] a university student / 아무를 속여 돈을 빼앗다 cheat *sb* out of his money; swindle *sb* out of money; swindle money out of *sb* / 물건을 속여 팔다 sell a thing fraudulently / …시키다 cheat [deceive, trick] *sb* into doing *sth*
▶자신을 속이지 마라 Don't deceive yourself. ⇌ Be honest to yourself.
▶그는 경력을 속였다 He misrepresented the facts of his career. ⇌ He gave a false account of [lied about] his career.
▶나는 그의 말에 속았다 I was taken in by his talk.
▶그는 나를 속이려고 했다 He tried to play a trick on me.
▶그는 손가락이 아프다고 속이고 결석했다 He used his sore finger as a pretext for his absence.
▶그는 줄곧 나를 속이고 있었다 He has been fooling me all the time.
속인 俗人 〈세속적인 사람〉 a worldly person; 〈범인〉 an ordinary person; 〈무식자〉 an uneducated man; 〈평신도〉 a layman; (총칭) the laity
▶속인들이 생각하는 바는 비슷비슷하다 What worldly persons think differ little [are more or less the same].
▶그런 속인이기 때문에 그런 야한 장식에 만족하고 있을 것이다 He is satisfied with those gaudy decorations because he has such vulgar taste.
속인주의 屬人主義 〔法〕 the personal [nationality] principle; the principle of personal (privilege for) jurisdiction
속임수 (a) deception; a trick; a fake; trickery; camouflage; swindle; imposture
◆속임수를 쓰다 resort to tricks; play a trick on *sb*; serve *sb* a trick; practice deception on *sb*; cheat *sb* / 카드놀이에서 속임수를 쓰다 cheat at cards / 속임수에 걸리다[넘어가다] be cheated; be imposed upon; be taken in; become a victim of a deception
▶그의 친절은 속임수에 지나지 않는다 His kindness is nothing but a sham.
▶네 속임수에는 넘어가지 않는다 None of your tricks with me.
▶그에게는 속임수가 통하지 않는다 Deception won't work on him. ⇌ You can't put anything over on him.
속잎 inner leaves (of a vegetable)
속자 俗字 the popular [simplified] form of a Chinese character
속잠방이 short underpants
속장 〈책의〉 the inside pages
속장 屬長 〈감리교의〉 the leader of a sectional prayer meeting
속적삼 an undershirt; underwear
속전 贖錢 〈속금〉 (a) ransom
속전속결 速戰速決 an intensive [all-out] surprise offensive [attack]; (獨) a blitzkrieg
■—전법 blitz tactics

속절없다 hopeless; futile; vain; unavailing
♦속절없는 세상 the vain [futile] world / 속절없이 붙잡히다 be arrested [held] with no way out / 속절없이 굶다 starve helplessly
▶숙박할 곳이 없어 나는 속절없이 노숙해야 했다 Finding no lodging, I resigned myself to passing the night under the stars.

속죄 贖罪 atonement for [expiation of] one's sin(s); redemption; [神學] satisfaction
♦그리스도의 속죄 the (Vicarious) Atonement; the Redemption / 속죄의 기도 purgatorial prayers
─속죄하다 expiate [atone for] one's sin; make amends for one's offenses [crime]
♦과거를 속죄하다 make amends for the past / 죽음으로써 속죄하다 expiate a crime with death
▶그는 자기가 저지른 죄에 대해 이미 충분히 속죄했다 He has made atonement in full for the wrong he did.
─론 the doctrine of atonement

속주다 open one's heart (to sb); take sb into one's confidence; let sb know one's mind

속지 屬地 a possession; a dependency; a territory; a dominion

속지주의 屬地主義 [法] the territorial principle; the principle of territorial privilege for jurisdiction

속진 俗塵 the world; earthly [mundane] affairs ♦속진을 피하다[멀리하다] keep aloof from the earthly things [madding crowd]; live secluded from the world

속짐작 one's (personal) estimation; a guess; a conjecture; a surmise

속출 續出 successive [frequent] occurrence
─속출하다 appear [occur] in succession [one after another]; crop up
▶요즘 교통사고가 속출하고 있다 Traffic accidents have been occurring one after another recently.

속치마 an underskirt; a petticoat

속칭 俗稱 a popular [familiar] name; 〈학명에 대해〉 a common [vernacular] name
▶그 꽃은 속칭「아이리스」로 알려져 있다 The flower is commonly known as an iris.
▶속칭 그를 백두라고 했다 He was commonly called the white head.
─속칭하다 call [name] sth popularly [commonly]; be popularly [better] known as

속타다 be worried 《about, that》; be troubled [fretted] 《about》; feel impatient [anxious] 《about》; (口) be in [get into] a stew
♦속타는 마음 an aching [a troubled] heart / 속타는 일 the source [matter] of worry; worries; troubles; cares

속탈 ─頉 a stomach trouble [disorder, upset]
♦속탈이 나다 get one's bowels out of order; have stomach trouble

속태우다 1 〈자신을〉 worry [bother] (oneself) 《about》; trouble oneself 《with》; be anxious [nervous] 《about》; fret (oneself) 《about》; stew over; stew oneself 《into》; be stewed up 《with》
♦몹시 속태우다 fret oneself to death / 하찮은 일로 속태우다 worry over trifles / 속태우다 병이 나다 worry oneself ill [into illness]; fret oneself ill
▶네가 늦게 와서 그는 몹시 속태웠다 He was vexed at your delay.
▶그런 일로 속태우지 마라 Don't worry yourself about such a thing. ⇒ Don't let that worry you.
▶속태운다고 무슨 소용이 있나? What's the good of worrying?
2 〈남의 속을〉 worry; bother; trouble
▶아이가 어머니를 속태운다 The child worries the mother.

속편 續編・續篇 a sequel (of, to); a continuation (of); a follow-up; a supplementary [second] volume [film]

속표지 ─表紙 the front page; a title page; the title leaf

속필 速筆 quick writing; writing with a facile pen; a fast hand 《with pen》 ▶그는 속필이다 He writes fast.

속하다 屬─ belong (to); appertain (to); 〈사람・회사가〉 be affiliated (to, with); 〈문제가〉 come under (a head); fall within [under]
▶사자는 고양이과에 속한다 The lion belongs to the cat family.
▶인간은「포유 동물」이라는 큰 동물 집단에 속한다 Man belongs to the great group of animals called 'mammals.'
▶그는 민주당에 속해 있다 He is affiliated with the Democratic Party.
▶이 섬은 대한민국에 속한다 This island is annexed to Korea.
▶이것은 교향곡의 범주에 속한다 This comes under [belongs to] the category of symphonies.
▶주권은 국민에게 속한다 The sovereignty rests with the people.
▶거부권은 대통령의 권한에 속한다 The veto power is invested in the president.
▶이 그림은 그의 최고 걸작에 속한다 This painting counts among the best of his works.

속하다 續─ 〈계속하다〉 continue; 〈계승하다〉 succeed (to)

속하다 贖─ 〈대갚음하다〉 atone (for); redeem

속하다 速─ fast; quick; swift; rapid; speedy

속행 速行 〈빨리 감〉 going [walking] fast; 〈빨리 행함〉 prompt action ─속행하다 go [walk] fast [quickly]; take prompt [quick] action; carry out speedily

속행 續行 continuation; continuance
─속행하다 continue (to do, doing); go on 《with》; proceed 《with》
♦토의를 속행하다 continue [proceed with] debates / 교섭을 속행하다 continue negotiations 《with》
▶우리는 비가 그친 후 시합을 속행했다 We continued the game after the rain (had) stopped.

속화 俗化 popularization; vulgarization; secularization
─속화하다 popularize; vulgarize; secularize; 〈속화되다〉 be popularized [secularized, vul-

속환이 俗還— a person who has returned to secular life; an ex-monk; an ex-nun

속회 續會 resumption of a meeting —**속회하다** resume a meeting

속효 速效 (a) quick effect; an immediate effect; instant results
♦ 속효가 있다 have an immediate effect 《on》; cure...quickly; show [have] (a) quick effect; bring immediate results 《on》

속히 速— rapidly; quickly; fast; swiftly; hastily; promptly
♦ 속히 대답하다 answer promptly; make a prompt reply; give *sb* a prompt answer
▶ 속히 해 (Be) Quick! ⇌ Hurry up! ⇌ (口) Make it snappy!

솎다 thin out; cull 《plants》
▶ 농부는 부실한 무를 솎아낸다 The farmer thins out weaker radishes.
▶ 나는 토마토 모종을 솎아 이식했다 I thinned out tomato seedlings and transplanted them.

솎음(질) thinning out —**솎음(질)하다** thin out

손[1] **1**【수족】 the hand; 〈팔〉 the arm; 〈고양이 등의〉 the paw
〈**손이**〉 손이 곱다 fingers are numb with cold / 손이 닿는 곳에 있다 be within one's reach [grasp]; be within (the reach of) one's hands / 손이 닿지 않는 곳에 있다 be beyond one's reach; be out of one's grasp
▶ 왼손이 아프다 I have a pain in my left hand [arm]. ⇌ My left hand [arm] hurts.
▶ 선반까지 손이 닿지 않는다 I cannot reach to the shelf.
▶ 그는 천장에 손이 닿을 정도로 키가 크다 He is so tall (that) he can touch the ceiling.
▶ 이 상자는 늘 환자의 손이 닿는 [닿지 않는] 곳에 두십시오 Please place this case always within [out of] reach of the sick person.
▶ 손이 곱아 펜을 쥘 수 없다 My fingers are so numbed by cold that I cannot hold a pen.
〈**손을**〉 손을 내밀다 hold [stretch] out one's hands; offer one's hand 《to》 / 손을 놓다 loose [let go] one's hold 《on, of》; release one's hold 《of》 / 손을 대다 touch / 손을 들다 raise [hold up] one's hand ⇨ 손들다 / 손을 깍지 끼다 fold [clasp] one's hands / 손을 잡다 join hands; cooperate
▶ 나는 그의 손을 잡았다 I grasped [took hold of] his hand.
▶ 학생들은 손을 들었다 The pupils raised their hands.
▶ 나는 톰에게 잘 가라고 손을 흔들었다 I waved good-bye to Tom.
▶ 그는 호주머니에 손을 집어넣고 서 있었다 He was standing with his hands in his pockets.
▶ 그는 손을 뻗쳐서 잡지를 집어 들었다 He reached for the magazine and picked it up.
▶ 그는 손을 모아 기도했다 He prayed with his hands pressed together.
〈**손에**〉 손에 잡다[들다] take *sth* in one's hands / 손에 손을 잡고 걷다 walk hand in hand
▶ 그는 손에 펜을 들고 있다 He has a pen in his hand.
▶ 그녀가 손에 갖고 있는 것은 금메달이다 What she has in her hand is a gold medal.
〈**손으로**〉 손으로 만들다 make by hand / 손으로 만지다 feel *sth* with one's hand / 손으로 입을 가리다 cup one's hand to one's mouth
▶ 나는 모든 일을 손으로 더듬어서 해야만 했다 I had to do everything by feel [feeling].

2【일손】 a hand; a man; an agency; 〈도움〉 help; a helping hand
♦ 한 사람의 손으로 그린 두 장의 그림 two pictures by the same hand / 여러 사람의 손으로 된 번역 a translation by various hands / 손이 달리다[모자라다] be shorthanded; be short of hands; be undermanned / 손이 비다 〈할 일이 없다〉 have no work on hand; be disengaged; be free; be at leisure / 손을 빌다 ask for help; call in the aid of / 손을 빌리다 give [lend] a (helping) hand / 많은 사람의 손을 거치다 pass through many hands / 손에 익히다 get into practice; go into training; get one's hand in / 일이 손에 잡히지 않다 cannot go about [settle to] one's work; be in no mood for work
▶ 이 일은 여러 사람의 손이 필요하다 This work requires [calls for] many hands.
▶ 손이 많으면 일도 쉽다 Many hands make light work.
▶ 추수 때는 집안 식구만으로는 손이 모자란다 At harvest time only family members are not enough.
▶ 손이 비면 잔디 좀 깎아 주세요 Please mow the lawn if you are free.

3〈수중〉 the hands 《of》; possession
♦ 손에 넣다 get; obtain; secure; win; take [get, gain] possession of / 손에 들어오다 come into one's possession; come to [fall into] one's hands / 손에서 손으로 건너가다 pass from hand to hand / 남의 손에 넘어가다 fall into another's hands; pass into another's possession / 남의 손에 넘기다 hand over *sth* into another's hands
▶ 이 보석은 여러 명의 손을 거쳐 내 것이 됐다 This jewel came into my possession after going through the hands of many people.
▶ 그의 운명은 내 손에 달렸다 His fate lies in my hands. ⇌ His life is at my disposal.
▶ 그 편지가 그들의 손에 들어갔다 The letter fell into their hands.
▶ 손 안의 새 한 마리는 숲 속의 새 두 마리보다 더 낫다 《속담》 A bird in the hand is worth two in the bush.
▶ 이 고문서는 우연히 내 손에 들어왔다 These old documents came into my hands by chance. ⇌ I got these old documents quite unexpectedly.

4〈수고〉 trouble; 〈돌봄〉 care; charge
♦ 손이 많이 가다 take much trouble; require a lot of trouble [care]; be laborious; be troublesome / 손을 덜다 save trouble
▶ 그러면 크게 손을 덜 수 있다 That saves much trouble.
▶ 그 일에는 손이 많이 갔다 The work cost me much labor.

► 이것을 완성하려면 더 많은 손이 필요하다 It needs a lot more work to get this completed.
5 〈관계·교제〉 connection; meddling
♦손을 끊다 break with / 손을 대다 take up; touch / 손을 뻗치다 concern *oneself* with [in] *sth*
► 그는 새로운 프로젝트에서 손을 뗐다 He washed his hands of the new project.
► 그 연구에는 아직 아무도 손을 대지 않았다 Nobody has set his hand to that research work.
► 그 회사는 유럽 방면으로 손을 뻗치려 하고 있다 The firm is going to extend its relations in Europe.
6 〈물건에 대한 아량〉 generosity; liberality
♦손이 크다 freehanded
7 〈수단·방법〉 a means; a way; a device
♦손을 쓰다 take measures
► 그와 테니스를 하면 넌 손도 못 써 보고 질 걸 He'll easily defeat you in tennis.
► 나는 백방으로 손을 썼지만 아버지는 결국 돌아가셨다 Though I did everything I could, my father eventually died.
8 〈수완·간계〉 a trick; an artifice; a trap; a snare; an art
♦아무의 손에 걸리다 fall into *sb's* hand; fall into a trap [snare] of / 아무의 손에 걸려 죽다 die [fall] by *sb's* hand(s); meet *one's* death at the hands of...
► 그는 옛 원수의 손에 걸려 죽었다 He was killed by an old enemy. ⇌ He lost his life at the hand of an old enemy.
9 〈기타〉 ♦손에 땀을 쥐고 with suppressed excitement; in breathless suspense; with breathless interest / 손이 거칠다 thievish / 손이 맞다 be in [and] glove 《with》; (美俗) be in cahoot(s) 《with》
► 관객은 그 축구 시합을 손에 땀을 쥐고 보았다 The spectators were on the edge of their seats at that football game.
► 그 녀석은 언제나 손만 벌리니 귀찮아 죽겠다 I am plagued (to death) by his everlasting begging.

― 손 ―

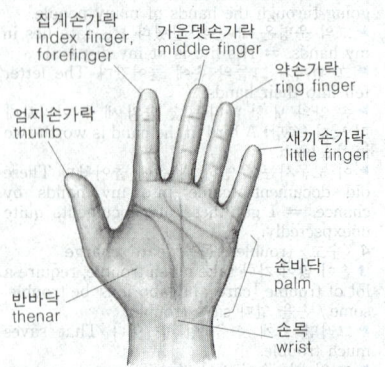

집게손가락 index finger, forefinger
가운뎃손가락 middle finger
약손가락 ring finger
엄지손가락 thumb
새끼손가락 little finger
손바닥 palm
반바닥 thenar
손목 wrist

손² 〈손님〉 a guest; a visitor; a customer; 〈길손〉 a traveller
손³ 〔民俗〕〈귀신〉 a wandering evil spirit
손⁴ 〈가정·양보〉 ♦농담이다손 치더라도 even in joke / 그것이 사실이다손 치더라도 granting it to be true [that it is true]; granted it is true
► 실패한다손 치더라도 해볼 만한 가치는 있다 It is worth attempting even though we fail.
손 孫 descendants ⇨ 후손
손 損 (a) loss; damage ⇨ 손해
손가락 a finger

> 解說 *finger*는 보통 엄지손가락(the thumb) 이외의 손가락을 말한다. 그러므로 집게손가락을 the first finger라 하며 the second finger(가운뎃손가락), the third finger(약손가락), the fourth finger(새끼손가락) 등으로 부른다. 그 밖에 집게손가락을 the index finger 또는 the forefinger라고도 하며, 가운뎃손가락을 the middle finger, 약손가락을 (주로 왼손가락의) the ring finger, 그리고 새끼손가락을 the little finger 또는 (美口)에서 pinkie 라고도 한다.

♦다섯 손가락 the five fingers; the thumb and fingers / 손가락 마디 a finger joint; knuckle / 손가락 하나 까딱않다 do not lift a finger; be laziness itself / 손가락을 입에 물다 take [put] a finger in *one's* mouth / 손가락 마디를 꺾다 crack *one's* fingers / 손가락으로 집어 먹다 eat with the fingers / 손가락에 끼다 place [put] 《a ring》 on a finger / 손가락으로 꼽다 count *sb* on *one's* fingers
► 합격자는 다섯 손가락으로 셀 정도밖에 되지 않았다 The successful candidates could be counted on the fingers of one hand.
► 그녀한테 손가락 하나라도 댔다간 혼날 줄 알아라 If you lay [put] a [your] finger on her, you shall smart for it.
► 당대 제일의 음악가라면 누구나 그를 첫 손가락에 꼽는다 Everybody points to [counts] him as the greatest musician of the day.
■—무늬 〈지문〉 a fingerprint; 〈엄지손가락〉 a thumbprint —자국 a 《dirty》 finger mark; 〈엄지손가락〉 a thumbmark

― 손가락 ―

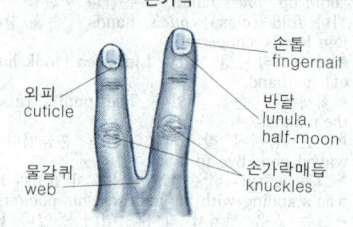

손톱 fingernail
외피 cuticle
반달 lunula, half-moon
물갈퀴 web
손가락매듭 knuckles

손가락질 1 〈가리킴〉 pointing 《at, to》
—**손가락질하다** point 《at, to》; point 《with》 the finger 《at, to》; indicate 《the door》
► 남을 손가락질하는 것은 실례다 It is rude to point at another.
► 그는 지도를 손가락질하며 설명했다 He ex-

plained it pointing to the map.
2 〈비난〉 pointing at; scorning; treating with contempt
♦ 손가락질(을) 받다 be pointed at [talked about] with scorn; be talked of in contempt; be an object of social contempt
▶ 남의 손가락질 받을 일은 절대로 하지 않겠다 I will never do anything which will bring contempt upon me.
―손가락질하다 point at *sb*; talk about *sb* with scorn [in contempt]
손가방 a briefcase; a portfolio; (美) a valise; 〈여성용의〉 a handbag
손거스러미 an agnail; a hangnail ♦ 손거스러미가 생기다 have a hangnail
손거울 a hand glass [mirror]
손거칠다 light-fingered; light of fingers; (美俗) sticky-fingered; thievish; 〈서술적〉 have light [sticky] fingers ♦ 손거친 사람 a kleptomaniac; a thievish person
손겪다 entertain a guest; play host 《to》
손결 the texture of the skin of the hand
▶ 그녀는 손결이 곱다 She has soft hands.
손곱다 《*one's* fingers [hands] are》 numb [stiff, benumbed] with cold; 〈서술적〉 have numb hands [fingers]
손금 the lines of the palm
▶ 그는 손금이 좋다[나쁘다] He has lucky [unlucky, ominous] lines in his hand.
▶ 그녀는 손금을 볼 줄 안다 She can read (in) a person's hand [palm]. ⇒ She can tell fortunes by the lines of the palm [hand].
■ ―쟁이 a palmist; a palm reader
손금 損金 a loss of money; pecuniary loss
손길 〈원조〉 a (helping) hand; 〈내민 손〉 an outstretched hand
♦ 손길(을) 잡다 link [join] hands with each other / 따뜻한 구호의 손길을 뻗다 extend a warm helping hand 《to *sb*》
손꼽다 count 《the days》 on *one's* fingers
▶ 그는 당시에는 손꼽는 화가였다 He was one of the world's foremost painters of his day.
▶ 그는 세계에서 손꼽는 명지휘자다 He is one of the leading [prominent] conductors in the world.
▶ 그런 사람은 손꼽을 정도밖에 없다 Such people can be counted on your fingers.
▶ 그들은 그의 귀국을 손꼽아 기다리고 있다 They are eagerly waiting for his return home.
▶ 나는 귀국할 날을 손꼽아 기다리고 있다 I am eagerly awaiting the day I go home.
손꼽아치다 rank 《among, with》; count for much; count 《among》 ▶ 그는 한국에서 손꼽아 치는 작가다 He ranks with the best Korean authors.
손끊다 break with; break away from; cut *oneself* free of; sever *one's* connections with; cease to deal with; wash *one's* hands
▶ 그는 그 여자와 손끊었다 He cut (off) all ties with that woman.
▶ 나는 그 일에서 아주 손끊었다 I washed my hands clean of that affair.
손끝 **1** 〈손가락의 끝〉 the tip of a finger; a fingertip
♦ 손끝이 닳도록 일하다 work *oneself* [*one's* fingers] to the bone; toil away; toil and moil / 손끝을 다치다 be injured in the fingertip; have *one's* fingertip wounded / 손끝(을) 맺다 remain idle; look on with folded arms [with *one's* hands in *one's* pockets] / 손끝으로 만지작거리다 finger; fumble 《with》
▶ 지금은 손끝 맺고 있을 때가 아니다 This is no time for us to remain idle.
2 〈일솜씨〉 manual dexterity
♦ 그녀는 손끝이 여물다 She is good [clever, dexterous, skillful] with her hands [fingers].
▶ 그는 손끝이 무디다 He is clumsy [awkward] with his hands. ⇒ His fingers are all thumbs.
3 〈모진 결과〉 an evil hand
♦ 손끝(이) 맵다 have an evil hand; have a contaminating touch; foul up 《everything》 *one* touches
손녀 孫女 a granddaughter
손놀림 a way of using *one's* hand
♦ 어색한[서투른] 손놀림으로 with clumsy hands; clumsily; awkwardly / 손놀림이 재다 have nimble fingers; be skillful [smart] with *one's* hand
손놓다 release [let go] *one's* hold 《of》; leave (off) [lay off] *one's* work
▶ 그 사건에서 손놓았다 I washed my hands of that affair.
손님 **1** 【내객】 〈방문객〉 a visitor; 〈호출인〉 a caller; 〈초대객〉 a guest; (口) company 《▶ 한 사람에도, 두 사람 이상에도 쓰이는데 항상 단수형이고 관사가 붙지 않음》
♦ 뜻밖의 손님 an unexpected caller / 손님을 맞다 receive [see] a caller [visitor]; receive company / 손님을 초대[접대]하다 invite [entertain] a guest / 다과회에 손님을 초대하다 invite company to tea / 시골에서 손님이 와 있다 have a country visitor
▶ 오늘 밤엔 집에 손님이 많다 We receive much company tonight.
2 【고객】〈구매자·단골〉 a customer; a patron; a buyer; (총칭) custom; 〈투숙객〉 a guest; 〈의뢰인〉 a client; (총칭) clientele; 〈관광객〉 a visitor
♦ 처음 온 손님 a first-time buyer / 손님의 질이 좋다 have good customers; have customers from the upper classes (of society); be patronized by wealthy [well-to-do] people / 손님을 끌다 attract customers; draw custom; 〈호객하다〉 tout; solicit 《customers》 / 손님에게 시중들다 wait on a customer
▶ 저 레스토랑은 손님이 많다[적다] That restaurant is well [poorly] patronized.
▶ 그 가게에는 언제나 손님이 들끓는다 The store is always full of [crowded with] customers.
▶ 이 호텔은 여름엔 숙박 손님이 많다 This hotel has a lot of guests [visitors] in summer.
▶ 한국을 찾는 외국 손님 가운데는 경주 관광을 희망하는 손님이 많다 Many foreign visitors to Korea want to see the sights of Kyŏngju.
▶ 그 변호사의 단골 손님 가운데는 유명 인사가

많다 The lawyer has many well-known clients. ⇒ The lawyer has many clients who are well-known individuals.
3 〈승객〉 a passenger; a fare
♦ (운전 기사가) 손님을 모시고 드라이브 a drive a fare
4 〈관객〉 audience; spectators
♦ 입장 손님이 많다[적다] have a large [poor] house
■—마마 〖醫〗 (the) smallpox

손대기 〈잔심부름꾼〉 an errand boy; a houseboy; a houseman

손대다 **1** 〈건드리다〉 touch; lay one's hands on
♦ 남의 돈에 손대다 make free with [dip into] another's money / 손대지 않고 그대로 두다 leave sth untouched [alone] / 손대지 못하게 하다 keep sth inviolate [intact]
▶ 진열품에 손대지 마시오 (게시) Don't touch the exhibits.
▶ 내 서류에 손대지 마라 Let my papers alone. ⇒ Don't touch my papers.
▶ 학생들이 그 문제에는 손댈 엄두도 못냈다 None of the students had tried to solve the problem.
▶ 손대지 말 것 (게시) Hands off. ⇒ Please don't touch.
2 〈관여하다〉 concern oneself with; have a finger in the pie; have one's hand in; meddle with; 〈착수하다〉 turn [put, set] one's hand to 《a task》 set about; take up; 〈관계하다〉 be on intimate terms with 《a girl》 have carnal connection with
♦ 투기에 손대다 dabble in [take to] speculation / 위험한 일에 손대다 dally with danger
▶ 무엇부터 손댈까요? Which shall I begin with?
▶ 그는 새로운 저술에 손대고 있다 He has a new work in hand.
▶ 슈퍼마켓 경영이 아버지가 처음 손댄 사업이다 Running a supermarket is my father's first business.
▶ 사업에서 성공한 뒤에 정치에 손대는 사람이 많다 There are many who dabble in politics after they have succeeded in business.
3 〈때리다〉 strike; hit; give sb a blow; take a fist (to)
▶ 누가 먼저 손댔느냐? Who started the fight? ⇒ Who struck the first blow?
▶ 어떤 일이 있어도 아이들에게 손대서는 안된다 You must not strike [raise your hand against] your children in any circumstances.

손대야 〈美〉 a (small) washbowl; 〈英〉 a washbasin; a handbasin

손대중 measuring [weighing] by hand; hefting ♦ 손대중으로 by hand measure / 손대중으로 재다 measure by hand; heft sth
▶ 그의 손대중은 상당히 정확하다 He measures by hand fairly accurately.

손도끼 a small ax(e); a hand ax(e); a hatchet; an adz(e)

손도장 —圖章 a thumbprint ♦ 문서에 손도장을 찍다 seal a document with one's thumb

손독 —毒 a hand-borne infection; hand poisoning
♦ 손독(이) 오르다 be sore [inflamed] by scratching; 《a sore》 become worse
▶ 상처를 건드리지 마라, 손독 오른다 Don't touch the wound, or it will be infected.

손들다 **1** 〈손을 올리다〉 raise [hold up] one's hand; 〈때리다〉 lift one's hand against [to]
▶ 손들어 Hold up!
2 〈지다〉 be defeated [beaten]; 〈항복하다〉 yield 《to》 surrender; give in; throw up one's hand
▶ 졌다, 손들었다 I'm beaten [done for]. ⇒ You win.
▶ 두번째 문제에는 손들었다 The second problem beat me. ⇒ I was stumped by the second problem.
▶ 더위에는 손들었다 I can't stand the heat.
▶ 저 바보한테는 손들었다 I don't know what to do with that fool.
▶ 일이 너무 힘들어 하루만에 손들고 말았다 It was such tough work that I was done up in a day.
▶ 그 문제는 워낙 어려워 그도 결국 손들고 말았다 The problem was so difficult (that) he gave in at last.
▶ 그 아이한테는 선생님도 손들고 말았다 The child was the despair of his teacher.

손등 the back of one's hand ▶ 그녀는 손등으로 입을 닦았다 She wiped her mouth with the back of her hand.

손때 〈만져서 묻은〉 finger marks; dirty marks; dirt from the handling
♦ 손때 묻은 책 a finger-marked book; a book soiled by the hand / 손때(를) 묻히다 soil sth with the hand
▶ 그 사진에는 몹시 손때가 묻어 있었다 The picture was badly thumbed.

손떼다 **1** 〈관계를 끊다〉 finish with; wash one's hands of; sever one's connections with; withdraw oneself 《from》
♦ 정치에서 손떼다 withdraw oneself from politics; put an end to one's political life
▶ 이제 와서 손뗄 수는 없다 It is too late now to get out of it.
▶ 그가 그것을 할 마음이 없다면 나도 손떼겠다 If he is not willing to do it, I will withdraw my hands (from it), too.
▶ 그녀는 갑자기 그 사업에서 손(을) 뗐다 She suddenly withdrew her hands from the enterprise.
2 〈끝내다〉 finish; bring to a close [an end]; get [be] through 《with》

손료 損料 hire; (a) rent ♦ 손료를 물다 pay for the hire 《of》

손모 損耗 wear (and tear); wastage; (a) loss
▶ 기계에 기름을 치는 것은 손모를 방지하기 위해서다 We lubricate the machine to protect it against wear.
—**손모하다** be worn out; wear out

손목 a wrist; 〖解〗 a carpus 《pl. -pi》 ♦ 손목이 가늘다 be slim-wristed / 손목을 잡다 take [grasp, grip] sb by the wrist; catch sb's wrist
■—시계 a watch; a wristwatch

손바느질 sewing by hand; needlework
—**손바느질하다** do needlework; sew by hand

손바닥 the palm [flat, hollow] of the hand;

the palm
♦손바닥만한 땅 a (small) strip [patch] of land / 손바닥을 뒤집듯이 〈쉽게〉 without the least trouble / 손바닥뒤집듯하다 change *one's* attitude [opinion] quite abruptly / 손바닥을 뒤집듯이 태도를 바꾸다 assume a completely changed attitude / 손바닥으로 찰싹 때리다 slap; give sb a slap; strike sb with the open hand; spank (a baby)
▶ 그녀는 꽃잎 하나를 손바닥에 올려놓았다 She laid a petal on the palm of her hand.
▶ 그는 이 도시를 자기 손바닥 들여다보듯 훤히 안다 He knows this town like the palm of his hand.
▶ 그의 배신은 손바닥을 보듯 뻔하다 His betrayal is as clear as day.

손바람 the swish [swing] of a hand
♦일에 손바람이 나다 get into the swing of *one's* work; warm to *one's* work

손발 hands and feet; hand and foot; the limbs; arms and legs
♦손발이 큰 big-limbed / 손발이 큰 사람 a person large of limbs / 손발이 맞다 be in hand [and] glove (with); (美俗) be in cahoot(s) (with) / 손발을 묶다 bind sb hand and foot / 손발을 못쓰게 되다 lose the use of *one's* limbs
▶ 나는 도둑에게 손발이 묶였다 I was bound hand and foot by the robber.
▶ 파업자들은 손발이 맞지 않았다 There was lack of unity among the strikers.
▶ 그녀는 아버지의 손발이 되어 일했다 She served her father as if she were his tool.
▶ 그는 사장의 손발이 되어 일했다 He waited on his boss hand and foot. (▶ hand and foot 는 「매우 충실히」라는 뜻의 부사구)

손버릇 any habitual action of the hands; 〈도벽〉a habit of stealing ▶ 그는 손버릇이 나쁘다 He is light-fingered [sticky-fingered]. ⇌ He has light fingers [thievish habits].

손보다¹ 〈손님을 만나다〉 see a visitor [guest]; receive company

손보다² 〈보살피다〉 see to it that there are no defects; care for; take care of; 〈수리하다〉 repair (a house); service (a car); mend; 〈수정하다〉 correct; touch up
▶ 집을 좀 손봐야겠다 My house wants [needs] repairing.

손봐주다 help; give [lend] a (helping) hand

손부끄럽다 be embarrassed ▶ 그가 돈을 꿔주지 않아 손부끄러웠다 I was embarrassed by his refusal of my request for a loan.

손빌리다 get [receive] help; get [obtain, receive] the aid (of) ♦손빌리지 않고 without another's help; unaided; single-handed

손뼉 the flat of *one's* hand
♦손뼉(을) 치다 clap *one's* hands
▶ 그가 손뼉을 치자 하녀가 나타났다 The maid appeared when he clapped his hands.
▶ 나는 손뼉을 쳐 웨이터를 불렀다 I clapped my hands for a waiter.
▶ 아이들은 손뼉을 치며 기뻐했다 The children clapped their hands with joy.
▶ 손뼉도 마주 쳐야 소리가 난다 (속담) It takes two to make a quarrel.

손상 損傷 damage; (an) injury; impairment
▶ 그의 차는 충돌 사고로 큰 손상을 입었다 His car sustained considerable damage in the accident. ⇌ His car was considerably damaged in the wreck.
—**손상하다** damage; injure; impair; mar; 〈法〉 damnify; (비유-) hurt
♦미관을 손상하다 mar [injure] the beauty (of) / 명예를 손상시키다 hurt [impair, injure] sb's honor; dishonor sb
▶ 그러한 행위는 그룹의 융화 정신을 손상한다 Such conduct will mar the spirit of harmony of the group.
▶ 그 교회는 제2차 세계대전 중에 폭격으로 손상되었다 The church was damaged by bombing during World War II.

손샅 the space between fingers

손색 遜色 inferiority
♦손색이 있다 be inferior (to); suffer by comparison (with) / 손색이 없다 be by no means inferior (to); suffer nothing by comparison (with); compare favorably (with)
▶ 그녀는 어떤 점에서는 그에 비해 손색이 있다 She is inferior to him in some respects.
▶ 이것은 외래품에 비해 조금도 손색이 없다 This compares quite well with foreign-made articles.
▶ 요즈음은 국산차가 외제차에 비해 손색이 없다 The home-manufactured cars these days are by no means inferior to foreign cars.
▶ 이것은 전문가의 작품으로써 손색이 없다 This work would do credit to a professional.

손서투르다 clumsy; bungling; unskillful; 〈서툴게〉 be a poor hand (at); be clumsy with *one's* hands; be all thumbs
▶ 하는 짓이 손서투르다 His fingers are all thumbs. ⇌ He has two left hands.

손수 〈제 손으로〉 with *one's* own hands; 〈몸소〉 in person; personally; 〈제 스스로〉 (do it) oneself
♦손수 만든 of *one's* own making; homemade / 어머니가 손수 만든 요리 food prepared by *one's* mother / 손수 가르치다 teach (a boy) oneself
▶ 이것은 손수 만드신 겁니까? Is this your own make?
▶ 식이 끝난 뒤 대통령이 손수 묘목을 심었다 After the ceremony the President planted young trees himself [in person, personally].

손수건 —手巾 a handkerchief
▶ 그녀는 배가 보이지 않을 때까지 손수건을 흔들었다 She kept waving her handkerchief until the ship was out of sight.

손수레 a handcart; a hand truck

손쉽다 easy; simple; light
♦손쉬운 일 an easy [a light] task [thing]; a soft job / 손쉬운 방법 the easy way / 손쉽게 easily; with ease [facility]; without difficulty [effort] / 돈을 손쉽게 벌다 make an easy gain
▶ 그것은 아주 손쉬운 일이다 That's nothing. ⇌ Nothing is easier. ⇌ (美俗) That's a cinch.
▶ 그는 그 일을 손쉽게 해냈다 He finished the task with ease.
▶ 그가 있는 곳을 손쉽게 알아냈다 I found out

his whereabouts easily. ⇒ I had no difficulty in discovering where he was.

손시늉 hand gestures [mimicry]; a hand signal

손실 損失 (a) loss
♦인명과 재산의 손실 a loss of life and property / 손실을 입다 suffer [sustain] a loss / 손실을 초래하다 incur a loss; bring a loss on oneself / 손실을 입히다 inflict [entail] a loss (on); cause a loss (to)
▶ 그의 죽음은 국가적 손실이다 His death is a national loss [a loss to the country].
▶ 이러한 홍수는 인명의 손실과 무서운 재난을 가져온다 These floods bring loss of life and terrible suffering.
▶ 우리는 큰 손실을 입었다 We suffered a great [big, heavy, serious] loss.
▶ 그는 손실을 만회하기 위해 열심히 일했다 He worked hard to retrieve [recover] his loss.

손싸다 quick-handed; nimble-fingered; deft; dexterous

손쓰다 〈조치를 취하다〉 take [adopt] measures; take a course; take action
♦교묘히 손쓰다 make a clever action / 미리 손쓰다 take preventive measures (against) / 달리 손쓰다 try some other means / 여러 모로 손쓰다 try every possible means / 어떻게 손쓰 볼 도리가 없다 be in a deadlock; be at one's wit's [wits'] end
▶ 위험을 피하려면 무언가 손쓰지 않으면 안된다 We must do something to avert the danger.
▶ 소방대원도 그 사나운 불길에는 손쓸 재간이 없었다 The firemen could do nothing with the raging flames.

손아귀 the space between the thumb and the fingers; 〈쥐는 힘〉 the (power of one's) grip; 〈수중〉 (in) the hands
♦손아귀에 넣다 take [gain] possession of; have sb under one's thumb [control]; have sb well in hand / 권력을 손아귀에 쥐다 hold the authority in the hollow of one's hand
▶ 그는 부하 대부분을 완전히 손아귀에 쥐고 있다 He manages most of his men completely.

손아래 juniority
♦손아래의 younger; junior; subordinate
▶ 그는 나보다 세 살 손아래다 He is my junior by three years. ⇒ He is three years my junior [younger than I].

손아랫사람 one's junior [inferior]; one's subordinate ▶ 손아랫사람한테 친절히 대하라 Be kind to your juniors.

손어림 measuring roughly with one's hands
—손어림하다 measure [weigh] roughly by (the) hand; use one's hands to make a rough estimate (of); heft

손위 seniority ♦손위의 older; elder; senior; superior
▶ 그는 나보다 다섯 살 손위다 He is my senior by five years. ⇒ He is five years my senior [older than I].

손윗사람 one's elder; one's senior; one's superiors

손익 損益 loss and gain; profit and loss; advantage(s) and disadvantage(s)
♦손익 없음 The losses and gains are on a par. ⇒ Neither lost nor gained.
■—계산서 a profit and loss statement; income statement —계정 the profit and loss account —분기점 a break-even point (略 BEP)

손익다 be skilled 《in》; be [get] accustomed 《to》 ♦손익은 일 accustomed work

손일 manual labor [work]; handwork; handicrafts

손자 孫子 a grandchild; a grandson
▶ 그 이야기는 손자의 대까지 전해질 것이다 The story will be handed down to future generations [to posterity].

손자귀 a small adz(e)

손잡다 1 〈손과 손을 마주 잡다〉 take sb by the hand; grasp another's hand; join hands 《with》
♦손잡고 울다 take each other's hands and weep
▶ 두 사람은 손잡고 기뻐했다 The two took [clasped] each other's hands in joy.
▶ 그는 그녀와 손잡고 걷고 있었다 He was walking hand in hand with her.
2 〈화해하다〉 make peace 《with》; 〈제휴·협력하다〉 clasp hands 《with》; cooperate 《with》; join hands 《in》; tie up 《with》; go hand in hand 《with》; 〈동맹하다〉 combine 《with》; join forces 《with》
♦…와 손잡고 일하다 work in concert [conjunction, cooperation] with / 손잡고 (협력하여) 일을 하다 do a job hand in hand
▶ 두 나라는 서로 손잡았다 The two countries made peace with each other.
▶ 그는 사전을 편찬하는 일에 동료와 손잡았다 He cooperated with his colleagues in compiling the dictionary.

손잡이 〈도구의〉 a handle; a grip; 〈문·서랍 등의〉 a doorknob; a knob; 〈칼 등의〉 a hilt; a haft; 〈창·도끼 등의〉 a shaft
♦손잡이를 달다 knob; furnish a knob; fix a handle / 손잡이를 돌리다 turn the handle [doorknob]
▶ 손잡이가 헐거워진다 The handle is coming loose.
▶ 손잡이를 당기면 물이 나옵니다 Pull the handle and water comes out.
▶ 손잡이가 떨어져 있다 The handle [knob] is off.

손잡이끈 〈버스 등의〉 a (hand)strap
♦손잡이끈을 잡다 hold on to a strap; hang from [on to] a strap; (口) straphang

손장난 fumbling; fidgeting; fiddling; trifling; toying with one's hands
—손장난하다 finger 《a button》; fumble [fiddle, fidget] with 《a coin》; 〈가지고 놀다〉 play [toy] with 《one's rings》; trifle with 《a pen》 / 시계[모자]를 가지고 손장난하다 fidget [fiddle] with one's watch [cap]

손장단 —長短 beating time with the hand
♦손장단을 치다 beat time with the hand; keep time by clapping 《one's hands》
▶ 우리는 손장단을 치면서 노래를 불렀다 We sang beating time with our hands.

손재간 —才幹 hand skill ⇨ 손재주

손재수 損財數 the doom to come off a loser; the forthcoming fate to lose *one's* possessions

손재주 —才— hand skill; dexterity [deftness] of hand; manual dexterity [adroitness]
♦손재주가 있는 사람 a handy [clever-fingered] man / 손재주가 없는 사람 a bungler; a botcher / 손재주가 있는 직공 a deft mechanic / 손재주가 있다 be dexterous; be deft; be deft-handed; be clever [skillful] with *one's* fingers; be good with *one's* hands / 목수일에 손재주가 있다 be deft at carpentry / 손재주가 없다 have heavy hands; be clumsy [not good] with *one's* hands; have two left hands; *one's* fingers are all thumbs

손전등 —電燈 (英) an electric torch; (美) a flashlight ♦손전등을 켜다[비추다] turn on [shine] a flashlight

손질 1〈수리〉repair(s); 〈주로 의류〉mending; remodeling
♦손질이 잘 안된 집 a house in bad repair / 손질중이다 be under repairs / 손질이 잘 되어 있다 be in a good state of repair; be (kept) in good repair
▶이 집은 많은 손질이 필요하다 This house needs a lot of repairs.
—손질하다 repair (a house); make repairs; mend (shoes); remodel
▶그들은 집을 손질하지 않고 내버려 두었다 They left the house unrepaired.
▶옛 성은 잘 손질되어 있었다 The old castle was (kept) in good condition.
2〈매만짐·보살핌〉care; trimming
♦손질이 잘 안 된 ill-kept; 〈나무 등〉unpruned; untrimmed
▶정원은 손질이 잘 되어 있다 The garden is well kept.
▶네 머리는 손질이 잘 되어 있구나 Your hair is well taken care of [is well trimmed].
—손질하다 care for; take care of; tend; trim (a tree); groom (a horse)
▶아버지는 지금 정원에 나가 국화를 손질하고 계신다 My father is out in the garden taking care of [trimming] the chrysanthemums.
3〈정정〉correction; retouch
—손질하다 correct; touch up; improve
▶나는 그 번역을 몇 번이나 손질했다 I reworked that translation a number of times.
▶내가 쓴 글을 손질하는 데 종일 걸렸다 I spent a whole day trying to improve what I had written.
▶이 문장을 좀 손질해 주세요 Please polish [brush] up this composition.

손짓 a gesture; signs; a hand signal; dumb show; gesticulation
♦손짓으로 이야기하다 talk in signs [sign language] / 손짓으로 아무를 가라고 하다 motion *sb* away / 손짓으로 아무를 부르다 motion toward *one*; beckon to *sb*
▶그는 손짓으로 외국인과 이야기했다 He made himself understood by (using) gestures with foreigners. ⇌ He used gestures to communicate with foreigners.
—손짓하다 gesture; make [use] gestures [signs]; motion 《for *sb* to do》; give a hand signal
♦아무더러 앉으라고 손짓하다 motion *sb* to sit down [take a seat]
▶나는 그에게 더 가까이 오라고[안으로 들어오라고] 손짓했다 I beckoned [motioned (to)] him to come nearer [come in].
▶그는 우리들에게 조용히 하라고 손짓했다 He motioned [signed] (to) us to keep quiet.

손찌검 〈구타〉a blow; beating; striking; hitting
—손찌검하다 beat; strike; knock; hit; slap; give [deal, deliver] *sb* a blow
♦아무를 손찌검하여 기절시키다 knock [beat] *sb* unconscious / 아무의 얼굴을 손찌검하다 slap *sb* on [in, across] the face
▶그 소년은 멍들 정도로 손찌검당했다 The boy was beaten (until he was) black and blue.

손치다¹ 〈여관 등에서〉take in lodgers; put up *sb*

손치다² 1〈매만져 바로잡다〉smooth; put in order (with *one's* hand); put *one's* hand to 《smoothing, ordering》
2〈어지르다〉get out of order; get mussed up [messed up]; get scattered

손치르다 〈손님을 대접하다〉entertain *one's* guests; give a party; play host (to)

손크다 1〈활수(滑手)하다〉freehanded; openhanded; generous; liberal; unsparing
♦손큰 사람 an openhanded [a generous] man; a liberal [bountiful, generous] giver
▶그는 어려운 사람에게 손크게 물건을 준다 He is generous to [toward] people in need.
▶그녀는 손크게 돈을 쓴다 She is generous [lavish, liberal] with her money.
2〈수단이 많다〉resourceful

손톱 a fingernail; a nail
♦손톱으로 할퀴다 scratch with *one's* nails
▶저 남자에게는 동정이라고는 손톱만큼도 없다 He doesn't have an atom [a scrap] of sympathy with others.
♦손톱을 기르다 have *one's* nails grow (long) / 손톱을 다듬다 do *one's* nails / 손톱을 치장하다 polish *one's* fingernails; manicure *one's* hands / 손톱을 깎다 pare [trim, clip, cut] *one's* nails / 손톱을 바싹 깎다 pare a nail to the quick / 손톱을 깨물다 bite [gnaw] *one's* nails / 손톱을 붉게 물들이다 red-polish *one's* nails; tint *one's* nails with red polish
▶네 손톱을 깎아야 되겠군 Your fingernails need cutting.
■엄지— a thumbnail ■—깎이 a nail clipper [nipper]; 〈가위〉nail-scissors —눈 the quick; the flesh around the fingernail —자국[상처] a nail mark [scratch, scar] —줄 a nail file; an emery board

손틀 〈기계〉a hand-operated [hand-worked] machine; 〈재봉틀〉a hand sewing machine

손티 〈마맛자국〉slight pockmarks; blemished skin ▶그녀는 손티가 있다 She is slightly pockmarked.

손표 —標 〔印〕〈손가락표〉an index; a fist (☞)

손풀무 a hand bellows

손풍금 —風琴 an accordion; a concertina; a

melodeon

손해 損害 〈물건의 패손〉 damage; (an) injury, harm (→damage는 무생물에, injury는 생물에 대하여 쓰일 때가 많음); 〈손실〉 a loss

♦ 200만원의 손해 damage [a loss] to the extent of [amounting to] two million won / 막대한 손해 dire [serious, heavy] damage / 경미한 손해 slight [trifling] damage / 사업상의 손해 a loss in business

〈손해가[는]〉 약 1억원의 손해가 나다 cause damage to the extent of [amounting to] some one hundred million won

▶홍수[화재]에 의한 손해가[는] 2천만원에 이른다[으로 추정되고 있다] The damage caused by the flood [fire] amounts to [is estimated at] twenty million won.

▶그 손해는 내가 부담하겠다 I'll stand the damage.

▶어제는 지진이 있었으나 실제로는 아무런 손해가 없었다 Yesterday we had an earthquake, but there was no real damage done.

〈손해를〉 손해를 주다[입히다] damage; injure; do harm (to); cause [do] damage (to); inflict [entail] a loss [an injury] on / 사업으로 큰 손해를 입다[보다] suffer heavy losses in the business / 손해를 보고 팔다 sell sth at a loss [sacrifice] / 손해를 메우다 make up for the loss; cover the loss; make good (for) the loss / 손해를 회복하다 retrieve one's loss

▶회사는 모든 손해를 배상했다 The company paid [compensated for] the total damage.

▶태풍으로 농작물은 큰 손해를 입었다 The crops suffered great damage by the storm. ⇌ The crops were greatly damaged by the storm. ⇌ The storm did [caused] great damage to the crops. ⇌ The storm damaged the crops greatly.

■물적— property damage ■—보험 insurance against damage [loss]; indemnity [nonlife] insurance —액 damages; the amount [extent] of damage

손해배상 損害賠償 (a) compensation for damage [the loss]; reparation for injury; indemnity (for damage done)

♦손해 배상 소송을 내다 go to law (against sb) for damages; sue sb for (one million won) in damages / 손해 배상을 청구하다 demand reparation for injury; claim [demand] damages

▶그는 부당한 해고에 대하여 회사에 1천만원의 손해 배상을 요구했다 He claimed ten million won (in) damages against the company for unfair dismissal.

▶자동차에 치인 남자는 5천만원의 손해 배상을 요구했다 The man who was run over by a car asked for fifty million won damages.

—손해배상하다 compensate sb for damages; indemnify sb for the loss; make reparation for damages [injury]; pay damages (to)

■—금 damages; a claim for compensation; a compensation claim; a claim for damage [loss]

손회목 the most slender part of a wrist

솔¹ (松) a pine (tree) ⇨ 소나무

솔² 〈브러쉬〉 a brush ♦옷솔[구둣솔] a clothes [shoe] brush / 머리솔 a hair brush / 솔로 털다[a hat]; brush away [off] / 네 상의는 솔로 털어야 되겠다 Your coat needs [wants] brushing.

♦ a seam ⇨ 솔기

솔⁴ (樂) sol; so; G솔 ♦솔 장조[단조] G major [minor] / 올림[내림]솔 G sharp [flat]

솔⁵ 〈표적〉 an archery target

솔⁶ (醫) skin pustules

솔가리 1 fallen pine needles **2** ⇨ 솔가지

솔가지 pine twigs for fuel

솔개 (鳥) a (black) kite

솔권 率眷 taking [leading] away one's family —솔권하다 take [lead] one's family away

솔기 〈옷의〉 a seam; a stitch

♦솔기를 풀다 undo [rip up] a seam / 터진 솔기를 꿰매다 stitch up the torn seam

▶내 드레스의 솔기가 터졌어 The seam of my dress has come apart [has come undone]. ⇌ My dress has torn along the seam.

솔깃하다 〈관심이 있다〉 be interested (in); be enthusiastic (about)

▶남의 이야기를 귀가 솔깃하여 듣다 listen to sb with interest [enthusiasm]; listen to sb with strained ears

▶그녀는 내 제안에 대해 아주 솔깃해했다 She showed great enthusiasm for my proposal.

▶그 말을 들으니 귀가 솔깃해지는군 〈제안을 받고〉 That's a tempting offer. ⇌ That sounds inviting.

솔나방 (蟲) an eggar ⇨ 송충나방

솔다¹ 1 〈폭이 좁다〉 narrow; 〈넓이가 좁다〉 small; close; cramp; cramped; 〈옷 등이〉 죄다; tight; skimpy

▶이 상의는 품이 솔다 This coat is skimpy.
2 〈아프고 가렵다〉 itchy and sore; irritating

솔다² **1** 〈귀가 아프게 되다〉 get [be] sick of hearing; hear more than enough of; have sore ears

▶그 이야기는 내 귀가 솔만큼 들었다 I am sick and tired of (hearing) the story. ⇌ I have heard enough of the story.

2 〈굳다〉 dry up; tighten up [contract] with dryness

▶찰흙이 솔 때까지 손을 대지 마라 Don't touch the clay until it gets hard [hardened].

3 〈푸솔다〉 〈a vegetable〉 decay from the damp; molder

4 〈소쿠라지다〉 foam; surge

솔대 1 (建) 〈솔대목〉 a lath; a thin slat **2** 〈활 쏠 때의〉 the prop for an archery target

솔따비 a weeder-plow used to dig out pine roots

솔딱새 (鳥) a Siberian flycatcher

솔래솔래 ♦솔래솔래 빠져나가다 steal [slip] out of (a room) inch by inch

솔로 (樂) a solo (pl. ~s, soli)

♦솔로로 노래하다 sing (a) solo; give a vocal solo / 솔로로 연주하다 play a solo; play alone
■피아노— a piano solo ■—악기 a solo instrument

솔로몬 제도 〈나라 이름〉 the Solomons Islands

솔리스트 〈독창[독주]자〉 a soloist

솔뮤직 〈흑인 음악〉 soul music
솔바탕 an archery field; a shooting range
솔발 鉾鈸 a small brass handbell ♦솔발(을) 놓다 ring a handbell; (비유) spread a rumor
솔방울 a pinecone; a cone
솔밭 a pine grove; a pinery
솔보굿 〈솔껍질〉 pine bark
솔봉이 a countryish-looking [boorish] young person; a young rustic clodhopper
솔부엉이 〔鳥〕 a brown hawkowl
솔불 a pine torch
솔뿌리 a pine root
솔선 率先 ─솔선하다 take the lead [initiative]; take up the running
♦솔선하여 …하다 be the first to 《do》; take the lead [initiative] in 《doing》; 〈솔선수범하다〉 set an example to others; act as a pioneer in 《doing》
▶그는 솔선하여 그 교착 상태를 타개했다 He took the initiative in breaking the deadlock.
▶그는 솔선하여 구조대에 가담했다 He was the first to join the rescue party.
솔 솔 1 〈거침없이〉 soft-flowing; smoothly; swimmingly; 〈막힘없이〉 fluently; facilely.
▶콩가루가 자루에서 솔솔 샌다 A tiny stream of soybean flour leaks out of the bag.
2 〈가볍게〉 lightly; gently; softly
▶이슬비가 솔솔 내린다 It drizzles lightly.
3 〈쉽게〉 easily; readily; with ease; effortlessly
▶얽힌 실이 솔솔 풀렸다 The tangled thread straightened out nicely.
4 〈유창하게〉 fluently; smoothly; glibly
▶그녀는 중국어를 솔솔 말한다 She speaks Chinese fluently. ⇌ She is a fluent speaker of Chinese.
5 〈부드럽고 가볍게〉 gently; lightly; softly
▶바람이 솔솔 불고 있었다 The wind was blowing gently [softly, lightly].
솔송나무 〔植〕 a Japanese hemlock
솔수펑이 a pinewood ⇨ 솔숲
솔숲 pinewood; pine forest; a pinery
솔 심어 정자라 〈속담〉 Count *one's* chicken before they are hatched.
솔이끼 〔植〕 hair [haircap] moss
솔잎 pine needle
솔잎상투 a topknot braided out of short hair
솔잣새 〔鳥〕 a crossbill
솔 직 率直 plainness; straightforwardness; frankness; candidness; openheartedness
─솔직하다 frank; candid; outspoken; straightforward; honest; plain; straight; openhearted; open-minded

解說 *frank*는 가장 일반적인 말로 자기가 생각하고 있는 것들을 숨김없이 말하는 것. *candid*는 자신에게 곤란한 점이 있더라도 감추지 않고 딱 잘라 말하는 것. *outspoken*은 감추는 편이 나을 듯한 것이라도 거침없이 말하는 것. *straightforward*는 정직하게 단도직입적으로 말하는 것.

▶그는 솔직한 사람이다 He is a straightforward [an openhearted, a candid, an outspoken] man.

▶그는 내게 솔직한 대답을 했다 He gave me a straightforward [frank] answer.
▶이 건에 대하여 자네의 솔직한 의견을 듣고 싶네 I'd like to hear your frank [candid, honest] opinion about this matter.
솔직히 率直─ straightforwardly; frankly; candidly; plainly; honestly; openheartedly
♦솔직히 말하면 frankly (speaking); in plain words [terms]; to be frank with you / 솔직히 말하다 speak [talk] plainly [frankly] / 솔직히 인정하다 admit candidly / 솔직히 고백하다 confess frankly / 솔직히 대답하다 give a straightforward answer
▶솔직히 말해서 네 계획은 실패하고 말거야 Frankly (speaking) [To be frank (with you), To be quite honest (with you)], your plan will fail.(▶상대방에게 난처하거나 불쾌한 것을 말할 때 표현을 부드럽게 하는 말씨로 speaking, with you는 흔히 생략됨)
▶그녀는 그에게 사랑하지 않는다고 솔직히 말했다 She told him straight out that she didn't love him.
▶나한테는 솔직히 이야기해라 Speak to me frankly. ⇌ Be frank [open] with me.
▶〔會話〕「그건 좋아하지 않니?」「솔직히 말하면 그래」 "Don't you like it?" "I don't, frankly."
솔질 brushing ─솔질하다 brush; give a brush 《to a coat》 ♦옷을 솔질하다 give *one's* clothes a brushing
▶네 상의는 솔질해야 되겠다 Your coat needs [wants] a brushing.
솔트 〈전략 무기 제한 협정〉 SALT [〈the *Strategic Arms Limitation Talks*〕
솔페주 〔樂〕〈계이름 부르기〉 solfège
솔페지오 〔樂〕〈도레미파 연습〉 solfeggio 《*pl.* -feggi, ~s》
솔포기, 솔폭 a small pine tree with thick branches
솜 cotton (wool)
♦솜같은 구름 fleecy [wooly] clouds / 이불 [옷]에 두는 솜 cotton wool; batting; wadding; padding / 탄 솜 whipped cotton (wool) / 귀를 솜으로 틀어막다 stop *one's* ears with cotton; plug *one's* ears with wads of cotton / 솜을 타다 whip [willow] cotton / 방석에 솜을 두다 stuff cotton into a cushion; stuff a cushion / 이불에 솜을 두다 pad bedclothes with cotton
▶겨울이 되면 사람들은 솜을 많이 둔 옷을 입는다 In winter people wear clothes stuffed with much cotton.
─덩이 a ball of cotton ─먼지 bits of cotton ─뭉치 a wad of cotton ─지스러기 waste cotton; flue; bits of down
솜대 〔植〕 a black bamboo
솜돗 a willowing mat (for cotton)
솜두루마기 〈한복〉 a padded outer coat
솜몽둥이 a cotton-tipped stick (used as a dauber)
솜바지 〈한복 등〉 padded trousers
솜반 〈반반한 솜조각〉 a thin layer of cotton
솜버선 cotton-padded socks; wadded socks
솜붙이 〈솜옷〉 (cotton-)padded clothes; wadded [padded] garments
솜사탕 ─砂糖 spun sugar; candy fluff [floss];

cotton candy

솜솜하다 〈마맛자국이 얕게 얽은〉 pockmarked
솜씨 〈손놀림〉 a way of moving [using] one's hands; 〈처리하는〉 performance; execution; 〈교묘함〉 skill; dexterity; deftness; knack; 〈세공의〉 workmanship; handicraft; make; hand; 〈수완·요령〉 ability; capacity; tact
♦ 뛰어난 솜씨 a masterly hand; matured skill / 솜씨있게 skillfully; neatly; expertly; finely /《do it》 fine; cleverly; tactfully / 솜씨있게 해치우다 settle tactfully; make a neat job of it
〈솜씨가[는]〉 솜씨가 좋다[서툴다] be skillful [awkward] 《in doing sth》; be clever [clumsy] 《at sth》; do a good [poor] job 《of sth》 / 솜씨가 늘다 get [become] skilled
▶ 그녀는 바느질 솜씨가 좋다 She is a good hand at sewing. ⇌ She is a good sewer.
▶ 이 청자를 만든 솜씨는 비상하다 This celadon is of excellent workmanship.
▶ 그녀의 솜씨는 정말 놀랄만한 것이었다 The way she handled it [used her hands] was just marvelous.
〈솜씨를〉 솜씨를 보이다 exhibit [display] one's skill / 솜씨를 겨루다 try one's skill with sb / 솜씨를 자랑하다 plume oneself on one's skill 《at》
▶ 이제 자네의 훌륭한 솜씨를 보여주기 바라네 I do hope that you will show your masterful skill now.
〈솜씨로〉 멋진 솜씨로 with great adroitness; with a deft hand / 서투른 솜씨로 젓가락을 쥐다 hold chopsticks awkwardly
▶ 그녀는 서투른 솜씨로 아기를 안아올렸다 She picked the baby up clumsily.
▶ 그녀는 능숙한 솜씨로 꽃꽂이를 했다 She arranged the flowers with dexterous hands [skillfully].
▶ 그는 익숙한 솜씨로 아기를 얼렸다 He played with a baby with practiced hands.
솜옷 wadded [padded, quilted] clothes; a wadded gown [garment, coat]
솜저고리 〈한복 등〉 a wadded jacket
솜채 a cotton-beating stick; a willowing stick
솜털 downy [fine soft] hair 《on a boy's face》; 〈새의〉 plumule [plúːmjuːl]; 〈복숭아 등의〉 down; pile; fluff; 〈식물의〉 tomentum
♦ 솜털이 난[로 덮인] downy; fluffy
▶ 저기 솜털이 많은 복숭아가 보이죠 You can see downy [fluffy] peaches there.
솜틀 a willow(er); a willowing machine; a cotton gin
솜화약 —火藥 guncotton; cotton powder
솟고라지다 〈끓어 오르다〉 boil up; 〈솟구쳐 오르다〉 leap up
솟구다 raise; make rise ♦ 몸을 솟구다 spring [leap, jump] up
솟구치다 raise quickly; make a quick rise; 〈불길이〉 blaze up; burn [go] up in a flame
솟다 1 〈높이〉 rise; tower; soar
♦ 하늘 높이 솟다 rise high into the sky / 구름 위로 솟다 rise [tower] above the clouds
▶ 마천루는 다른 건물 위로 우뚝 솟아 있다 The skyscraper towers above the other buildings.
▶ 뾰족탑이 하나 그 도시에 높이 솟아 있다 A spire towered [rose] high over the town.
2 〈샘 등이〉 gush out [forth]; spring
▶ 상처에서 피가 솟았다 Blood gushed [spurted] out of the wound.
3 〈불길이〉 flame up; blaze up; burst into flames
▶ 갑자기 불길이 솟았다 Suddenly the fire burst into flames [flamed up].
솟아나다 gush [spring] out [forth]; spout; spurt
▶ 나의 가슴에 희망이 솟아났다 Hope has begun to spring up in my heart.
▶ 그녀의 눈에 눈물이 솟아났다 Tears welled up in her eyes.
▶ 연기가 솟아났다 Smoke jetted out.
▶ 땀이 그의 이마에 솟아났다 The perspiration broke out on his forehead.
솟아오르다 tower; soar; rise high
▶ 해가 수평선에 솟아오른다 The sun is rising above the horizon.
▶ 여러 높은 봉우리가 하늘 높이 솟아올라 있다 Several mountains are towering [soaring] high into the sky.
▶ 굴뚝에서 연기가 솟아오르는 것이 보인다 Smoke is seen rising from the chimney.
솟을대문 —大門 a tall [lofty] gate; a house gate taller than the *haengrang* on either side
솟을무늬 embossed pattern on a cloth
송 宋 Sung; the Sung dynasty
〈남[북]송 Southern [Northern] Sung
송 頌 a eulogy ⇨ 송덕
송가 頌歌 an anthem; a hymn of praise
송골매 松鶻— 〔鳥〕 a peregrine falcon; a duck hawk
송골송골 〈땀·소름 등이〉《sweat, goose pimples appearing》 in profuse beads
송곳 〈도래 송곳〉 a gimlet; 〈가죽용의〉 an awl; 〈금속·돌 등을 뚫는〉 a drill; 〈목공용의〉 an auger; 〈종이용의〉 an eyeleteer
♦ 송곳 자루 a drill stock / 송곳의 끝 a drill bit / 송곳으로 구멍을 뚫다 bore a hole 《in sth》 with a gimlet [an awl]; drill a hole
▶ 송곳으로 이 나뭇조각에 구멍을 뚫어주세요 Please bore a hole in this piece of wood with a gimlet.
송곳니 a dogtooth; a canine (tooth); 〈특히 위의〉 an eyetooth; 〔解〕 a cuspid
송곳칼 a combination knife-drill
송과선 松果腺 〔醫〕 a pineal gland
송구 送球 1 〈공을 던져 보냄〉 passing a ball
▶ 송구가 늦었다 The throw was late.
▶ 2루에 송구가 늦었군요 The throw-down to second (base) is not in time!
—송구하다 throw [toss] a ball 《to》
2 ⇨ 핸드볼
송구스럽다 悚懼— 〈죄송하다〉 be sorry; be filled with awe; be overwhelmed with shame [gratitude]; be [feel] grateful 《of》; be sorry to trouble [for troubling] sb; 〈부끄럽다〉 feel [be] ashamed [embarrassed] 《of》; feel small
▶ 그는 자기의 무례함을 송구스러워하고 있다 He is ashamed of his bad manners. ⇌ His bad manners make him feel small.

▶ 치하를 하시니 도리어 송구스럽습니다 I am unworthy of your thanks [gratitude].
▶ 기다리게 해서 송구스럽습니다 I'm sorry to have kept you waiting.
▶ 그렇게 말씀하시니 정말 송구스럽습니다 I feel very much flattered by your compliments.

송구영신 送舊迎新 —**송구영신하다** see the old year out and the new year in; ring out the old and ring in the new; speed the old and welcome the new
♦송구영신 예배 a midnight service on New Year's Eve

송금 送金 (a) remittance; 〈생활비·용돈 등의〉 (an) allowance
—**송금하다** remit [send] money ((to)); send [make] (a) remittance ((to))
♦지불을 온라인으로 송금하다 remit [send] payment on the on-line system / 학비를 송금하다 supply sb with (his) school expenses / 매달 30만원씩 송금하다 allow sb three hundred thousand won a month
▶ 나는 가끔씩 아들에게 약간의 송금을 해준다 I sometimes send a small remittance to my son [send my son a small remittance].
■—수수료 a remittance charge; a charge for remittance —수표[어음] a remittance check [draft] —액 the amount of remittance —인 the remitter —처 〈수취인〉 the remittee

송기 松肌 pine endodermis ■—떡 a cake flavored with pine endodermis

송나라 宋— Sung ⇨ 송(宋)

송낙 a nun's hat (made of wisteria)

송낙뿔 an oxhorn whose ends bend outward

송년 送年 bidding the old year out ■—회 a year-end party

송달 送達 conveyance; delivery; dispatch
—**송달하다** convey; send; deliver; dispatch; forward ♦영장을 송달하다 serve a writ on sb; serve sb with a writ
■—부 a chitbook; a delivery book

송당송당 with hasty [random] whacks; letting the knife [needle] fall where it may
♦무를 송당송당 썰다 chop a radish; cut a radish into small pieces / 송당송당 바느질하다 sew hastily; jab away with the needle

송덕 頌德 eulogy —**송덕하다** eulogize; honor
■—문 a eulogy; an encomium; a panegyric —비 a monument (erected) in honor of sb

송독 誦讀 〈소리 내어 읽음〉 recitation; 〈외어 읽음〉 recitation from memory
—**송독하다** recite; recite from memory

송두리째 〈몽땅〉 root and branch; all; completely; thoroughly; whole; altogether; entirely
♦사과를 송두리째 먹다 eat an apple, rind and all / 노름으로 재산을 송두리째 날리다 gamble away all one's property
▶ 많은 집들이 홍수로 송두리째 떠내려 갔다 A lot of houses were completely washed away by the flood.
▶ 간 밤에 돈을 송두리째 도둑맞았다 All my money was stolen last night.
▶ 모든 악은 송두리째 근절시켜야 한다 All evil must be rooted out [rooted up; eradicated].

송로 松露 1 〈솔잎에 맺힌 이슬〉 dew on pine needles 2 [植] 〈송로과의 버섯〉 a truffle

송료 送料 〈화물의〉 carriage; freight (▶영국에서는 수상·항공 운송에만 씀); 〈우편의〉 postage
♦소화물의 송료 the carriage on a parcel / 송료 포함 2만원 20,000 won postage [carriage] included / 〈철도·트럭 등〉 송료 선불 carriage prepaid
▶ 송료 무료 (표시) Postage free.
▶ 미국까지 소포 송료는 얼마입니까? What is the postage for [on] a parcel to America?
▶ 이 책의 송료는 3천원입니다 The charge for the delivery of this book is 3,000 won.

송림 松林 pinewood ⇨ 솔숲

송백 松柏 the pine (tree) and the nut pine (tree)

송별 送別 a farewell; a send-off
—**송별하다** bid sb farewell; give sb a send-off
■—사 a farewell speech; a parting address: 그가 대표로 송별사를 했다 He made a farewell speech [address] on behalf of the groups. —연 a farewell dinner [party] given for sb before (his) departure —회 a farewell [send-off, good-bye] party: 우리는 김선생의 송별회를 베풀었다 We gave a farewell party [dinner] in honor of Mr. Kim.

송부 送付 sending; forwarding; 〈송금〉 remittance
—**송부하다** send; forward; 〈송금하다〉 remit
▶ 대금을 즉시 송부해주시오 Remit me the money at once.
■—처 〈수신인〉 the addressee

송사 訟事 a lawsuit; a suit; legal proceedings [steps]; litigation
♦송사를 취하하다 drop one's suit
▶ 그녀는 그를 상대로 손해 배상의 송사를 제기했다 She brought [filed, started] a suit [a lawsuit, an action] for damages against him.
—**송사하다** sue; file suit; take legal proceedings [actions] ((against))

송사 頌辭 a laudatory address; a eulogy; a memorial

송사리 1 [魚] a cyprinodont; top minnow; killifish (pl. -fish, ~es)
2 〈총칭〉 〈하찮은 사람〉 the small fry
▶ 거물급은 가만두고 송사리만 못 살게 구는 이유가 무엇이지? Why are they hitting the small fry while letting the big ones go free?

송송 1 〈잘게〉 (chop) into small pieces; finely
♦파를 송송 썰다 chop scallion into small pieces
2 〈구멍이〉 full of small holes; perforated
♦종이에 송송 구멍을 뚫다 perforate paper
3 〈땀방울·소름 등이〉 ▶ 그의 이마에는 땀방울이 송송 나 있었다 Beads of sweat [perspiration] stood (out) on his forehead. = There were beads of sweat [perspiration] on his forehead.

송수 送水 water supply; water conveyance
—**송수하다** supply water ((to)); supply ((a town)) with water; convey water ((to)) ♦어느 지역에 송수하다 supply a district with water
■—관 a water pipe —본관 a water [service]

송수신기 送受信機 〔通信〕 a transmitter-receiver
송수화기 送受話器 a handset
송시 頌詩 a poem of praise
송신 送信 transmission ―송신하다 transmit [dispatch] a message (to) ■―국[탑]― a transmitting station [tower] ―자 the sender; the transmitter
송신기 送信機 a transmitter; a transmitting set ―무전― a wireless [radio] transmitter
송아리 a small bunch [cluster] (of flowers)
송아지 a calf 《*pl.* calves》 ♦ 수― a male calf; a bullcalf ―가죽 calfskin; calf (leather) ―고기 veal
송악 〔植〕 a kind of ivy
송알송알 1 〈괴어 거품이 이는 모양〉 fermenting; bubbling ♦ 송알송알 괴다 ferment; undergo fermentation 2 〈땀·물방울이 엉긴 모양〉 in profuse drops ♦ 송알송알 땀이 나다 perspire profusely
송액 松液 〈송진〉 rosin; pine resin
송어 松魚 〔魚〕 a trout (▶단수·복수동형)
송연하다 竦然·悚然― fearful; timorous ♦ 송연하게 하다 terrify; horrify; strike *sb's* with terror; make *sb's* flesh creep / 송연해지다 be horror-struck; be terrified [horrified] (at)
▶ 괴담(怪談)을 듣고 우리는 모골이 송연해졌다 The eerie stories made our flesh creep.
송영 送迎 welcome and send-off; greeting and farewell; seeing off and welcoming back ―송영하다 welcome and send off
▶ 공항은 친구들을 송영하는 사람들로 붐볐다 The airport was crowded [alive] with people who had come to meet or see off their friends.
송영 誦詠 recitation (of a poem) ―송영하다 recite (a poem)
송유 送油 oil supply; sending oil ―송유하다 supply oil; send oil ■―관 an oil pipeline
송이 1 〈꽃의〉 a flower; a blossom; 〈과일의〉 a bunch; a cluster
♦ 한 송이 꽂이 꽃병 a single-flower vase / 포도 한 송이 a bunch [cluster] of grapes / 바나나 한 송이 a bunch of bananas / 송이로 피다 bloom in clusters
▶ (꽃이) 한 송이 두 송이 피기 시작한다 Flowers come out one by one.
2 〈눈의〉 a flake (of snow)
♦ 눈송이 a snowflake
3 〈종자 방울〉 a seed cone
♦ 잣 송이 a pine cone
송이 松栮 〈버섯〉 a songi mushroom
▶ 일요일에 우리는 송이를 따러 갔습니다 We went mushroom gathering [mushrooming] on Sunday. ♦ 양― a mushroom; a champignon
송이송이 in clusters; in bunches; in flakes
송장 a dead body ⇨ 시체(屍體) ♦ 산 송장 a living corpse ♦ 송장에 매질을 해서는 안 된다 You should not speak ill of the dead.
송장 送狀 an invoice
♦ 송장을 작성하다 invoice 《a shipment of goods》; make out an invoice / 송장을 보내다 send an invoice
■―본선도[선적도]― an F.O.B.[F.A.S.] invoice 세관[영사]― a customs [consular] invoice 수출[수입]― an export [import] invoice 운임 [보험료]포함― a C.& F.[C.I.F.] invoice
송장개구리 a ranid
송장벌레 〔昆〕 a burying beetle; a gravedigger
송장헤엄 the backstroke ⇨ 배영(背泳)
♦ 송장헤엄을 치다 do the backstroke; swim backstroke
송전 送電 transmission of electricity; power [electric] transmission; electric (power) supply
▶ 어젯밤 갑자기 송전이 중단되었다 Last night, the power supply was suddenly cut off.
―송전하다 transmit electricity (from...to...); supply (electric) power (to)
▶ 이 변전소에서 김포공항으로 송전하고 있다 Electricity is transmitted to Kimp'o Airport through this substation.
―력[용량] (power-)carrying [transmission] capacity ―선 a power-transmission line [wire]; 〈고압선〉 a power cable ―시설 power (transmission) facilities ―탑[소] a (power-)transmission tower [site]
송죽 松竹 pine and bamboo
송진 松津 pine resin; pitch; turpentine
송채 送綵 〔民俗〕 sending red and blue silk from the bridegroom's family to the bride's (after setting the date for the wedding)
송청 送廳 committal for trial ―송청하다 commit (a culprit) for trial; 〈서류를〉 send (the papers pertaining to a case) to the prosecutor's office
송축 頌祝 blessing; commendation and benediction; a eulogy ―송축하다 bless; eulogize
송충나방 松蟲― 〔昆〕 an eggar; an egger
송충이 松蟲― a pine caterpillar ♦ 송충이를 대하듯 싫어하다 hate *sb* like a serpent [viper]
송충이가 갈잎을 먹으면 떨어진다 〈속담〉 The cobbler should stick to his last.
송치 an unborn calf
송치 送致 sending; forwarding; transmittance; commitment ―송치하다 send; forward; transmit; commit
▶ 마약 밀매자는 검찰청으로 송치되었다 The drug peddler was sent to the Public Prosecutor's Office.
송판 松板 a pine board; a deal
송편 松― songp'yŏn; a half-moon-shaped rice cake
송풍 送風 ventilation ―송풍하다 send air (to); ventilate (a room) ♦ 지하실로 송풍하다 let some fresh air into a basement
■―갱 a ventilating shaft ―관 a blast pipe ―기 a blower; a ventilator; a fan
송화 松花 the flowers of the pine; pine pollen
송화 送話 transmission ―송화하다 transmit ―구 a mouthpiece ―기 a transmitter ―선 a transmitting line
송환 送還 sending back [home]; 〈포로 등〉 repatriation; 〈국외 도망 범인 인도〉 extradition; 〈불법 입국자의 국외 추방〉 deportation ―송환하다 send back; 〈본국으로〉 send home;

repatriate
▶밀항자는 송환되었다 The stowaway was sent back home.
▶포로들은 본국으로 송환되었다 The prisoners were repatriated.
=자 a deportee; a returnee; a repatriate

솥 a pot; a kettle; a ca(u)ldron
◆솥을 걸다 install a pot (in a furnace [fireplace])/한 솥 밥을 먹다 eat at the same mess; be a messmate (with)
▶그와 나는 한 솥 밥을 먹은 사이다 We have shared many things.
=밥= a rice-cooker; an iron pot 전기~ an electric rice-cooker 증기~ 〈요리용〉 a steam cooker ■=뚜껑 a kettle cover; a pot lid

솥땜장이 a tinker; a mender of old pots
솥발 the tripod base of a kettle; kettle legs
솥솔 a pot [kettle] brush; a scouring brush
솥전 廛 〈가게〉 a kitchen hardware shop

쇄 〈비바람 소리〉 with a sough; with a rushing [gushing] sound; with a cool gust; briskly
▶비가 쇄 쏟아졌다 The rain came lashing down.
▶바람이 나무 사이로 쇄 불고 있었다 The wind is soughing in the branches.

쇄쇄 with a great flow; (flow) freely [forcibly]; in torrents; briskly ▶시냇물이 쇄쇄 흐른다 A stream rushes past.

쇄골 鎖骨 (解) the collarbone; the clavicle
=쇄골의 clavicular

쇄광 碎鑛 crushing ore ■=기 an ore crusher; a stamp mill

쇄국 鎖國 national isolation; seclusion
=쇄국하다 close the country; close the door [one's doors] (to foreigners); exclude foreigners from the country
■=주의[정책] a national isolation policy; a policy of seclusion; seclusionism

쇄도 殺到 a rush; a stampede ◆주문[신청]의 쇄도 a rush of orders [applications]
=쇄도하다 come with a rush; rush [pour] in; 〈밀어닥치다〉 rush to (a place); storm (a place); swoop down on (the enemy)
◆신청이 쇄도하다 〈사람·단체에 주어〉 be flooded [deluged] with applications [offers]
▶아주 많은 손님이 특매장에 쇄도했다 A great number of customers rushed to the bargain floor.
▶주문이 쇄도했다 We've had a rush of orders.
▶군중이 출구로 쇄도했다 The crowd rushed to the exit.
▶문이 열리자 학생들이 실내로 쇄도했다 The students rushed in as soon as the door was opened.
▶전국에서 불평의 편지가 쇄도했다 Letters of complaint poured [flooded] in from all over the country.

쇄빙 碎氷 〈깨기〉 breaking the ice; 〈깬 얼음〉 rubble ice; fragmentary ice =쇄빙하다 break ice; smash [crush] ice ■=선 an icebreaker; an iceboat

쇄석 碎石 rubble; broken stones; debris; 〈土〉 〈토로포장용〉 macadam ◆쇄석 포장한 도로 a macadamized road
=쇄석하다 break stone; smash [crush] rock

쇄신 刷新 (a) reform; (a) renovation; (an) innovation; 〈숙청〉 a cleanup ◆생활 양식의 쇄신 a reform of the mode of living
▶우리는 현 입시제도의 일대 쇄신을 단행해야 한다 We should carry out a drastic renovation of the present entrance examination system.
▶그 정당은 조직의 대쇄신을 단행했다 The political party carried out a radical reform of its organization.
=쇄신하다 reform; introduce [make] a reform; renovate; innovate; clean up
◆인사를 쇄신하다 carry out a personnel reshuffle [shake-up]

쇄항하다 鎖港 close the ports; exclude foreigners from the ports

쇠 1 〈철〉 iron; 〈쇠붙이〉 metal ◆쇠로 만든 iron; (made) of iron 2 〈자물쇠·열쇠〉 a lock; a key 3 〈지남철〉 a compass 4 〈돈〉 money; (돈) chink; blunt; juice

쇠-¹ 〈작은 종류〉 a small one
=쇠고래 a small whale; a gray whale

쇠-² 〈소의〉 of cattle; ox-; cow-
쇠가죽 oxhide; cowhide
쇠갈고리 an iron hook
쇠고기 beef; 〈송아지 고기〉 veal
▶쇠고기를 두껍게 썬 것을 두 토막 주세요 Can I have two thick cuts of beef?
쇠고랑 handcuffs ⇨ 수갑(手匣) ◆쇠고랑을 차다 be arrested (for); be in irons
쇠고리 a metal hoop; an iron ring; a metal band; a clasp; a quoit ◆쇠고리 던지기 quoits
쇠골 cow's brains; 〈식용의〉 ox-brain
쇠공이 an iron pestle [pounder]
쇠귀 〈소의 귀〉 a cow's ears; ears of a cow
쇠귀나물 〈植〉 an arrowhead
쇠귀에 경읽기 〈속담〉 Talk to the wind.
▶나의 충고도 그에게는 쇠귀에 경읽기일 것이다 All my advice will fall flat on him. ≡ He will be deaf to my advice. ≡ He won't listen to my advice.

쇠기름 (beef) tallow
쇠꼬리 〈소의〉 a cow's tail; (an) oxtail
쇠꼬챙이 an iron skewer; a steel spit
쇠뇌 a catapult
쇠다 1 〈채소가〉 become tough (and stringy)
▶시금치가 쇠었다 Spinach has lost its tenderness and become tough.
2 〈병이〉 get [grow] worse; grow chronic
▶그의 고질병이 쇠었다 His chronic disease got worse.

쇠다² 〈명절 등을〉 observe; keep (one's birthday); celebrate
▶그는 설을 이국땅에서 쇠었다 He kept the New Year's Day in a foreign land.
▶그녀는 명절을 고향에서 쇠었다 She served [celebrated] a festival day in her old home.

쇠다리 a cow's leg; 〈고기〉 the shank of beef
쇠달구 an iron (ground) rammer
쇠도리깨 an iron flail; a flail
쇠똥¹ 〈쇠부스러기〉 iron slag; dross; scoria
쇠똥² 〈소의 똥〉 cattle dung

쇠뜨기 〔植〕 a field horsetail
쇠막대기 an iron bar; a metal rod; 〈곤봉〉 an iron club
쇠망 衰亡 a decline; decay; ruin; a fall; a downfall ―**쇠망하다** 〈멸망하다〉 go to ruin; be ruined; fall; go down; 〈쇠퇴하다〉 decline; decay; fall into decay
▶ 몇 세기에 걸쳐 번영했던 그 도시는 완전히 쇠망했다 The city, which had flourished for many centuries, was completely ruined.
쇠망치 an iron hammer
쇠머리 a cow's head; 〈고기〉 ox-head (meat)
쇠먹이 cattle feed; fodder
쇠못 an iron nail; a nail ▶ 그녀는 쇠못에 소매가 걸렸다 The iron nail caught her sleeve.
쇠몽둥이 an iron club [bar]
쇠문 —門 an iron gate [door]
쇠물닭 〔鳥〕 a moorhen; a water hen
쇠뭉치 a mass of iron; a pig
쇠백장 a butcher
쇠버짐 ringworm of the scalp
쇠붙이 〈살림용 기물〉 iron [metal] goods; metal [things]; ironware; hardware; 〈쇠장식〉 metal fittings
쇠비름 〔植〕 a purslane
쇠뼈 cow [bullock] bones; ox-bone
쇠뿔 a bull's [cow's] horn ▶ 그 투우사는 쇠뿔에 받혀 죽었다 The bullfighter was gored to death by a bull.
쇠뿔도 단김에 빼라 (속담) Strike while the iron is hot.
쇠뿔 잡다가 소 죽인다 (속담) ruin the whole by trying to correct a small fault
쇠사슬 a (metal) chain; an iron chain
♦ 쇠사슬에 묶인 포로 a war prisoner (shackled) in chains / 쇠사슬로 매다 enchain; chain up; put (men) in chains
▶ 그녀는 쇠사슬을 풀어 그를 달아나게 해주었다 She undid the chain and let him go.
쇠스랑 a scraper; a rake ♦ 쇠스랑으로 낙엽을 긁어 모으다 rake up fallen leaves
쇠시리 〔建〕 a molding; (英) a scotia
쇠약 衰弱 weakness; weakening; debility; infirmity; 〔醫〕 asthenia
♦ 건강의 쇠약 the decline of health
―**쇠약하다** weak; enfeebled; infirm; emaciated
♦ 쇠약해지다 weaken; grow weak; become feeble [low]; sink; be worn out / 건강이 쇠약해지다 decline in health; fall in one's health / 병으로 쇠약해지다 grow weak from illness
▶ 그녀는 오랜 병으로 쇠약해졌다 She has become weak from a long illness.
■ 신경— (a) nervous breakdown; neurasthenia 전신— general weakening
쇠운 衰運 declining fortune
♦ 쇠운에 접어들다 begin to decline [wane]; be going downhill; be on the wane [decline] / 쇠운을 만회하다 rebuild one's fortunes; regain one's former prosperity
▶ 사원들은 회사의 쇠운을 만회하려고 단결하였다 The workers united to retrieve the declining fortunes of their company.
쇠자루 a metal [an iron] handle [grip]

쇠잔 衰殘 decline ―**쇠잔하다** decline; fail; decay; wear off [out]
♦ 쇠잔한 몸 a wreck of one's former self
▶ 오랜 병 때문에 그의 몸이 많이 쇠잔해졌다 Because of a long illness, his health conditions are remarkably declined.
쇠죽 cattle feed boiled with grains and grass
■ —가마 a caldron to cook cattle-feed —통 a large tub [bucket] to contain cattle-feed
쇠줄 (iron) wire; a cable; a chain
쇠지레 a crow(bar); a jimmy
쇠진 衰盡 decay; exhaustion ―**쇠진하다** decay; be exhausted
쇠창살 —窓— an iron window bar; a grating; a grate; a grill(e)
쇠코뚜레 a cow's [bull's] nose ring; a cattle leader
쇠테 an iron frame; a metal [steel] rim
쇠톱 a hacksaw
쇠퇴 衰退 decline; decay
♦ 쇠퇴 일로에 있다 go [keep] on declining; decline gradually
―**쇠퇴하다** decline; decay; fall off [away]; fail; go downhill; ebb (away)
♦ 운이 쇠퇴하다 be down on one's luck / 쇠퇴해 가고 있다 be on the decline [wane]; be on the downgrade
▶ 늙어서 그녀는 기억력이 쇠퇴하였다 Old age has undermined her memory.
▶ 내 시력이 쇠퇴하기 시작했다 My eyesight has started to go.
쇠파리 〔昆〕 a warble fly; a gadfly
쇠푼 a small [petty] sum of money; some money
쇠하다 衰— 〈쇠약해지다〉 become weak; lose vigor; be weakened; waste away; be run down; 〈쇠퇴하다〉 fall off [away]; fail; ebb (away); decline; decay; go [fall] into decay; 〈기운 등이〉 sink; wane; collapse; slacken
♦ 건강이 쇠하다 decline in health; fall in one's health / 운이 쇠하다 be down on one's luck
▶ 그의 건강은 이미 쇠하기 시작했다 His health was already declining.
쇠혀 a cow's tongue; 〈식용의〉 (an) oxtongue
쇤네 I; me; your humble servant
쇳내 a metallic taste; a taste of iron ♦ 쇳내가 나다 taste iron [metallic]; smell metallic ▶ 이 물에서는 쇳내가 난다 This water has a metallic taste.
쇳덩이 a lump of metal [iron]
쇳독 —毒 metallic poison(ing)
쇳물 〈녹물〉 iron mold; a rust stain ▶ 내 셔츠에 쇳물이 묻었다 I have a rust stain on my shirt.
쇳소리 a metallic sound [clang]; 〈목소리〉 a piercing [shrill] voice ♦ 쇳소리가 나다 sound like something metallic
쇳조각 a steel scrap; scrap iron; a piece [scrap] of iron; bits of iron
쇼[1] 〈영국의 극작가〉 Shaw, George Bernard (1856-1950)
쇼[2] 〈구경거리〉 a show ▶ 우리는 쇼를 보러 갔다 We went to see a show. ■ 패션— a fashion show ■ —걸 a show girl —룸 a showroom

―보트 a showboat ―케이스 a showcase
쇼맨 a showman ■―십[기질] showmanship
쇼스타코비치 〈러시아의 작곡가〉 Shostakovich, Dimitri Dimitrievich (1906-75)
쇼윈도 a show window; a shopwindow
♦쇼윈도에 진열되어 있다 be on display in a show window / (물건을 사지는 않고) 쇼윈도를 들여다보고 다니다 window-shop; go window-shopping
쇼크 a shock ♦쇼크를 주다 give *sb* a shock; shock / 쇼크를 받다 be shocked 《at》; receive a shock
▶그의 갑작스러운 죽음에 나는 쇼크를 받았다 I was shocked at his sudden death.
▶그 뉴스는 나에게 큰 쇼크를 주었다 The news gave me a great shock. ⇌ The news was a great shock to me.
쇼크사 ―死 death from shock ♦페니실린 주사에 의한 쇼크사 shock death from penicillin injection
쇼크요법 ―療法 shock therapy [treatment]
쇼킹하다 shocking ♦쇼킹한 사고[사건] a shocking accident [event]
쇼트[1] 〈野〉〈유격수〉 a short; a shortstop ▶그는 쇼트를 맡아 봤다 He played shortstop.
쇼트[2] 〈電〉〈단락〉 a short circuit ―쇼트하다 short-circuit; short ▶전선이 쇼트되었다 The wire was shorted. ⇌ The wire had a short circuit.
쇼팽 〈폴란드의 작곡가〉 Chopin, Frédéric François (1810-49)
쇼펜하우어 〈독일의 철학자〉 Schopenhauer, Arthur (1788-1860)
쇼핑 shopping ♦쇼핑가다 go shopping 《to Myŏng-dong》
▶그녀는 쇼핑 갔습니다 She has gone shopping. ⇌ She is out shopping.
―쇼핑하다 shop; do *one's* [the] shopping
■―백 a shopping bag ―센터 a shopping center [district]
솔 a shawl ♦솔을 걸치다 shawl; wear a shawl
숄더백 a shoulder bag
솔로호프 〈구 소련의 소설가〉 Sholokhov, Mikhail Aleksandrovich (1905-84)
수[1] 〈생물의 남성〉 a male; a he ♦수꽃 a male flower / 숫염소 a billy goat; a he-goat / 수참새 a cock sparrow / 수캐 a male dog, a he-dog / 수탉 a cock; (美) a rooster
▶이 놈은 수고양이입니까? Is this cat a he?
수[2] **1**〈도리·수단〉 a way; a means; a measure; a resource; help; 〈착상〉 an idea; 〈비결〉 a key 《to》
♦무슨 수를 써서라도 by all means; at any cost; at all risks [costs] / 하는 수 없이 helplessly; unavoidably; inevitably; 〈마지못해서〉 reluctantly; against *one's* will / 갖은 수를 다 쓰다 use [try] all conceivable means
▶우리는 다른 수를 써 보겠다 We'll try in some other way.
▶어떻게 할 수가 없다 It cannot be helped. ⇌ There is no help for it.
▶무슨 수가 나겠지요 Something may be done for it.
▶〔會話〕「무슨 좋은 수가 없을까?」「나도 별 수가 없어」 "Do you have any good idea?" "No, I don't think I have."
2〈가능성·능력〉 possibility; likelihood; ability; capability ♦할 수 있는 데까지 as much [far] as *one* can; as much [far] as possible / 할 수만 있다면 if possible; if *one* can
3〈장기·바둑 등의〉 a move; an artifice; a trick; an idea ♦좋은 수 a clever move / 한 수 쓰다 make a move
▶네가 수 쏠 차례다 It's your move.
▶그는 바둑의 모든 수를 알고 있었다 He knew all the moves in playing *paduk*.
▶그는 실력이 너보다 한 수 위다 He is a cut above you.
수 秀 〈학업 성적의〉 Excellent; (美) A
▶그는 전과목 수를 받았다 He got straight A's.
▶그는 수학에서 수를 받았다 He got an Excellent [A] in mathematics.
수 首 **1**〈시나 노래의〉 a poem; a piece 《of poetry》 ♦시 한 수 짓다 compose a poem / 시 한 수 읊다 recite a poem **2**〈마리〉 ♦닭 50 수 fifty chickens
수 隋 〈중국의 왕조〉 Sui
수 壽 〈연령〉 age; 〈타고난 수명〉 *one's* life span; 〈천수〉 *one's* natural life; 〈장수〉 a long life; (a) longevity ♦수를 다하다 die a natural death
▶그는 백세 수를 누렸다 He lived to be a hundred (years old). ⇌ He was blessed with a longevity of a hundred years.
―수하다 live long; live to be a great age; enjoy longevity
수 數 **1**〈수효〉 a number; 〈자릿수〉 a figure

> [解說] 수학상의 수의 종류는 다음과 같다. 정수 (整數) a whole number; integer, 분수 fraction, 유[무]리수 (有[無]理數) a rational [an irrational] number, 양[음]수 (陽[陰]數) a positive [negative] number, 플러스 [minus] number, 실[허]수 a real [an imaginary] number, 홀[짝]수 an odd [even] number

♦큰[작은] 수 a high [low] number / 수적 우세 numerical superiority 《over》 / 두[세]자릿수 double [three] figures; a two [three] digit number / 수에 있어서는 in number / 수에 있어서 우세하다 be numerically superior 《to》; exceed *sth* in number; outnumber *sth*
〈수가[는]〉 수가 많아서 세는 데 시간이 걸린다 Since there are so many, it takes a long time to count.
▶자가용 차 수가 최근 증가했다 The number of private cars has increased recently.
▶불경기로 말미암아 실업자의 수가 늘고 있다 The number of people out of work is growing on account of business depression.
▶그 회의의 출석자 수는 적었다 There was a small attendance at the meeting.
〈수를〉 수를 세다 count; take count of / 수를 늘리다 increase [swell] the numbers 《of》 / 수를 채우다 make up the number
▶출석자 수를 세어 주시겠습니까? Will you

쇼핑에 관한 표현

1. 가게의 종류

▶ 소매점 a retail shop / 대형 소매점 a emporium / 백화점 a department store / 잡화점 a general store / 잡화 백화점 a dime store; a five-and-dime store (▶10센트 동전(dime) 한 개나 5센트 짜리로 살 수 있는 물건을 판다는데서 붙여진 이름. 근래에는 a variety store 또는 a discount shop 등으로 많이 부르고 있음. 여기서 발전하여 커다란 체인점이 된 것이 미국의 Woolworth's) / 드러그스토어 a drugstore (▶의약품을 중심으로 일용 잡화를 파는 가게) / 슈퍼마켓 a supermarket (▶식료품을 중심으로 가정용품 등을 파는 셀프 서비스 (self-service) 식의 가게로 미국의 Safeway가 유명) / 편의점 a convenience store (▶연중 무휴로 일용잡화나 식료품을 팖. 7-Eleven Food Stores가 대(大)체인점으로서 유명)

▶ 상점가 a shopping street [area, district] / 산책 쇼핑가 a shopping mall / 지하 상가 an underground center [market] / 아케이드 a shopping arcade / 쇼핑센터 a shopping center (▶교외 등에 주차장을 갖춘 상업시설의 종합체) / 시장 a market (place) (▶「장이 서는 날」은 market day); a baza(a)r (▶특히 중동의 시장을 가리키며 그밖에 『자선시』(바자)라는 뜻도 있음) / 어시장 a fish market / 야채시장 a vegetable market / 벼룩시장 a flea market [fair]

◆미국에서는 중고품이나 쓰지 않는 물건을 처분하는데 흔히 자기집 차고(garage)나 뜰안(yard)을 매장으로 하여 개라지 세일(garage sale), 야드 세일(yard sale)을 벌인다. 또 이 웃사람들이 공동으로 행하는 블록 세일(block sale), 자기가 만든 물품이나 쓰지 않는 물품을 교환하는 교환회(swap meet)도 볼 수 있다.

2. 판매·상품

▶ 손님 a customer; (shopping 하는 사람) a shopper / 소비자 a consumer / 상점 주인 (美) a storekeeper; (英) a shopkeeper / 점원 salesclerk; (英) a shop assistant; (여점원) a salesgirl / 매장 주임 a floor manager

▶ 가격 a price / 정가 a (list) price / 공정 가격 a fixed price / 가격표 a price list / 소매가격 a retail price / 공정가격 the official price / 할인가격 a reduced [discount] price / 덤핑가격 a bargain price / 도매가격 a wholesale price / 정가표 (정찰) a price tag

▶ 현금판매 a cash sale / 신용판매 (외상판매) a credit sale; selling on credit / 할부판매 the installment plan; the easy payment plan / 통신판매 catalog shopping; a mail order (▶미국의 Sears Roebuck 회사가 유명) / 방문판매 door-to-door selling; home selling / 텔레비전 쇼핑 television shopping; teleshopping

▶ 특매 (염가 판매) a bargain [discount, special] sale / 특매일 a special bargain day / 특매장 a bargain counter; a bargain basement (▶백화점 등에는 특매장이 보통 지하에 있다 때문에) / 재고처리 대매출 a clearance sale / 개점 대매출 a (grand) opening sale / 개점기념 대매출 an anniversary sale / 점포정리 대매출 (폐점 대매출) (美) a closeout; a closeout sale / 잡품 떨이 세일 (美) a rummage sale / 신학기용품 매출 a back-to-school sale / 바겐세일만 찾아다니는 사람 a bargain hunter

▶ 상품 an article; an item; 〈집합적〉 goods; merchandise / 운송게 (싼값에) 입수한 물건 a (lucky) find; a good buy / 싸게 산 물건 a bargain / 손님을 끌기 위한 상품 (美俗) a come-on; a loss leader (▶「손해를 보면서 사람을 끌어오는 것」이란 뜻에서) / 특선품 choice goods / 수입품 imported goods / 비매품 (an article) not for sale

▶ 영업 시간 business hours / 영업중 be open; (게시) Open. / 금일 휴업 (게시) Closed today.

▶ 상품권 a gift certificate; (英) a gift token / 쿠폰권 (상품 할인권) a coupon / 경품 스탬프 (美) a trading stamp

▶ 애프터 서비스 after-sales services; after-sale servicing / 환불 refundment; a refund

▶ 물품세 sales [commodity] tax (▶미국에서는 주(州)에 따라 세율이 다르지만 보통 5~8%의 물품세를 상품에 부과한다. 100달러의 정찰이 붙은 물건을 사더라도 세율이 5%면 합쳐 105달러를 지불해야 한다. 전혀 세금이 붙지 않는 주도 있음)

〈표현 예〉

▶ 會話 『어서 오십시오. 무엇을 드릴까요?』 『아니요, 잠깐 구경만 하고 싶습니다』 "Good morning [Good afternoon], sir. May I help you?" "(여성 손님에겐 ma'am을 씀) "Oh, no thank you. I'm just looking."

▶ 會話 『치약 팝니까?』『죄송합니다, 지금 없습니다』"Do you carry dental cream?" " I'm sorry, we don't have that in stock now."

▶ 그것은 적당한 가격입니다 It's a fair [reasonable] price.

▶ 會話 『모두 해서 얼마 입니까?』『합계 2만원 입니다』 "How much is it altogether?" "The total comes to 20,000 won."

▶ 會話 『10퍼센트 할인해주면 이것을 사겠습니다』『현금이라면 10퍼센트 할인해 드리겠습니다』 "If you give me a 10 percent discount, I'll buy this." "I'll knock 10 percent off if you pay in cash."

▶ 이 구두는 정말 싸게 샀다 These shoes were a real bargain.

▶ 이 워드프로세서는 매달 20만원씩 10개월 월부로 샀다 I bought this word processor in 10 monthly installments of 200,000 won each.

▶ 공항에서 한국인 관광객들이 면세품을 마구 사고 있었다 A group of Korean tourists were buying duty-free articles right and left at the airport.

▶ 그는 중고품 벤츠를 3,000만원에 구입했다 He bought a used Mercedes-Benz for 30 million won.

수와 양의 표현

1. 막연한 수·양의 표현
(1) 많다
▶많은 학생이 영어에 흥미를 가지고 있다 Many students are interested in English.
▶식당에는 많은 학생들이 있었다 There were a lot [lots] of students in the cafeteria.
▶한국에서는 제법 많은 고교생이 대학에 진학한다 In Korea, quite a few (high school) students go on to university.
▶대학 교육은 꼭 필요하다고 생각하는 사람이 적지 않다 Not a few people consider a university education essential.
▶한국은 중동에서 다량의 석유를 수입하고 있다 Korea imports a great [good] deal of petroleum from the Middle East. (▶of 뒤에는 보통 불가산 명사가 이어진다)
▶그 지진으로 엄청난 수의 사람이 죽었다 Great numbers of people were killed in the earthquake.

(2) 조금, 거의 …하지 않다
▶나는 선생님들을 몇 분 압니다 I can recognize a few of the teachers.
▶교실에 교과서를 갖고 있지 않은 학생이 몇 명 있었다 Some students in the class did not have their textbooks.
▶그 시험관 속에 염화나트륨은 거의 남아 있지 않다 There's little sodium chloride left in the test tube.
▶그 강연회에는 조금밖에 사람이 오지 않았다 Only a few people came to the lecture.

2. 수를 묻는 표현
▶형제[자매]가 몇 분이십니까? How many brothers [sisters] do you have?
▶그 방에는 몇 점의 가구가 있습니까? How many pieces of furniture are there in the room?
▶크리스마스까지 앞으로 며칠 남았습니까? How many more days are there till Christmas?
▶얼마나 자주 머리를 감습니까? How often do you wash your hair? (▶「1주일에 몇 번 …합니까?」는 "How often [How many times] do you…(in) a week?")
▶세계에서 두번째로 깊은 호수는 어디입니까? Which [What] lake is the second deepest in the world?
▶고교를 마치고 취직하는 학생의 비율은 어느 정도입니까? What is the percentage of students who get jobs when they graduate from high school?

3. 수에 관한 표현
▶내 왼쪽 눈의 시력은 1.0입니다 The eyesight in my left eye is 20/20. (▶twenty-twenty라고 읽는다. 「20피트 떨어진 곳에서 지표 20의 글자를 읽을 수 있음」이란 뜻으로 우리나라의 1.0에 해당)
▶내 봉급은 매년 10퍼센트씩 올랐다 My salary kept increasing by ten percent every year.
▶밑에서 세번째 줄을 번역할 수가 없습니다 I cannot translate the third line from the bottom.
▶그녀는 6개 국어나 말할 수 있다 She can speak as many as six languages. ⇌ She can speak no fewer than six languages.
▶그 섬까지는 배로 고작 20분 걸릴 것이다 It'll take at most twenty minutes by ship to the island.
▶이 항아리는 적어도 100만원은 한다 This vase is worth at least a million won.
▶그가 가지고 있는 돈은 겨우 500원이었다 He had no more than [only] five hundred won.

〈불특정 수의 표현예〉
▶그는 지금까지 수십번 학교에 지각했다 He has been late for school dozens of times.
▶그 전투에서는 몇 백 [몇 천, 몇 만] 이나 되는 병사들이 부상당했다 Hundreds [Thousands, Tens of thousands] of soldiers were wounded in the battle.
▶그 나라에서는 몇 백만이나 되는 사람들이 굶주리고 있다 Millions of people are starving in that country.
▶약 5천명의 고교생이 그 대학을 지원했다 Some 5,000 high school students applied for entrance to that university.
▶그의 나이는 아마도 30대 전반[후반]이다 He is probably in his early [late] thirties. (▶1990년대 전반[후반]에 in the early [late] 1990's)
▶그 책은 2, 3주일 전에 도서관에 반납했습니다 I returned the book to the library a couple of weeks ago.
▶그녀는 과반수의 득표로 회장에 선출되었다 She was elected chairperson by a majority.

---

count the people?
2 ⇨ 운수(運數)
수 繡 embroidery ⇨ 자수(刺繡)
♦금실로 꽃과 새가 수 놓인 치마 a skirt embroidered with birds and flowers in gold thread / 수(를)놓다 embroider; do [lay, make] embroidery 《on》
──실 embroidery thread ──틀 an embroidery frame; a tabo(u)ret
수- 數- a few; several; some ♦수주 several weeks / 수일 several [a few] days
▶그것은 수주 전에 일어났다 It happened some weeks ago.
-수- 囚 ♦미결수 an unconvicted prisoner / 사형수 a condemned criminal
수간 樹幹 〔植〕 a (tree) trunk; a shaft
수간 獸姦 bestiality
수간호사 首看護師 a head [chief] nurse
수감 收監 confinement; imprisonment; commitment
──**수감하다** confine [put] *sb* in prison [jail, gaol]; imprison ♦수감되어 있다 be (held [confined]) in prison [jail]
▶그는 현재 서울 근처 모 교도소에 수감되어 있

다 He is now (confined) in a certain prison near Seoul.
■—자 a prisoner; a prison inmate

수갑 手匣 handcuffs; (口) cuffs; manacles
♦수갑을 차고 in handcuffs / 수갑을 채우다 handcuff; manacle; slip [place, put] handcuffs [manacles] on *sb* / 수갑을 채워 호송하다 escort *sb* in handcuffs
▶그는 수갑을 차고 있었다 He was in handcuffs.

수강 受講 taking lectures ─수강하다 take lectures; attend a lecture (class)
♦하기(夏期) 강습을 수강히다 attend summer school [a summer course]
■—생 a trainee; a person present at a lecture class

수개 數個 a few pieces; several 《items》
♦수개월 several months

수갱 竪坑 〖鑛〗 a shaft; a pit ♦수갱을 파다 sink [put down] a shaft

수건 手巾 a (hand) towel; a washcloth
♦수건으로 닦다 wipe [rub] *sth* with a towel; dry 《one's hand》 on a towel
▶이 수건으로 손을 닦으세요 Dry [Wipe] your hands with this towel.
■세수— a face towel 손— a handkerchief
■—걸이 a towel rack [horse, hanger]

수검 受檢 having [undergoing] an examination [inspection]; being inspected ─수검하다 undergo [go through] an examination; be inspected ■—자 an examinee

수결 手決 〈사인〉 a signature; a handwritten monogram; a written seal ♦수결(을) 두다 sign; put [affix] one's signature to

수 경 水耕 〈물 재배〉 hydroponics; water [hydroponic, soilless] culture; aquiculture; tank farming ■—농장 a hydroponic farm —법 water culture —법식 농업 경영자 a hydroponist

수경성 水硬性 (化) hydraulicity ♦수경성의 hydraulic

수경시멘트 水硬— hydraulic cement

수계 水系 a water system

수계 水界 the hydrosphere

수고 trouble; labor; hardship(s); suffering(s); toil; pains; (an) exertion; service(s)

[解說]「수고」라는 단어를 쓰는 인사말은 상황에 따라 적당히 구별해서 번역할 필요가 있다. 회사 등에서 퇴근할 때 말하는「수고하셨습니다」는 Good-bye. 또는 See you tomorrow. 이다. 상대에게 수고를 끼쳤을 경우의「수고하셨습니다」는 Thank you very much.(다소 무관한 사이의 표현은 Thanks a lot.) 또는 Thank you for your trouble. 을 쓰는 것이 좋다. 또 회사에서 돌아온 남편에게 말하는「수고하셨어요」는 How was work today? 나 How was your day today? 정도가 적당하다. 그 밖에 만나면서「수고하십니다」는 How are you? 또는 Hi. 헤어지면서「그럼 수고하십시오」는 Good-bye. 또는 See you again. 미국식 표현으로는 Don't work too hard! 또는 Take it easy! 등을 상황에 맞게 쓴다.

♦헛수고 vain efforts / 수고를 끼치다 give *sb* trouble; trouble *sb*; put *sb* to [into] trouble/ 수고를 덜어주다 save *sb* trouble / 수고를 아끼다 be sparing of *oneself*; spare *oneself* trouble / 수고를 아끼지 않다 spare no efforts [pains, trouble] 《to do》; do not mind work
▶사전 찾는 수고를 아껴서는 안된다 You must always be ready to consult a dictionary.
▶너무 수고를 끼쳐 죄송합니다 I am sorry to have put you to so much trouble.
─수고하다 take pains [trouble] 《about》; take the trouble 《to do》; make efforts; have a hard time (of it); suffer [undergo, go through] hardships; labor (hard)
▶이 집을 짓는데 내가 얼마나 수고했는지 너는 모른다 You don't know what I had to go through to build this house.
▶수고한 보람이 있었다 My pains have been rewarded. ⇌ It was worth the trouble (I took).
▶ [話] 「그 사건을 조사하느라 여러 가지 수고하신 데 대해 감사합니다」「원, 별말씀을」"Thank you for all the trouble you took to investigate the matter." "Don't mention it."

수고스럽다 troublesome; toilsome; laborious; bothersome; painstaking
♦수고스러운 일 laborious [painstaking] work
▶젊은 사람들은 수고스러운 일을 회피하는 경향이 있다 Young people tend to evade laborious jobs.
▶수고스럽지만 이 편지 좀 부쳐 줘요 May I trouble you to post this letter?

수공 手工 manual arts [work]; handicraft; handwork; handiwork ■—품 a piece of handiwork; a product of one's fingers; (총칭) handicraft

수공업 手工業 manual industry; handicraft manufacturing; handicraft
■—자 a handicraftsman 《pl. -men》

수공예 手工藝 handicraft ■—품 a handicraft

수관 水管 a water pipe [tube, line]; 〖動〗 a siphon

수괴 首魁 the ringleader; the leader

수교 手交 handing ─수교하다 hand over *sth* into another's hands; hand *sth* to *sb*; deliver by hand ♦각서를 수교하다 hand a memorandum; deliver a note

수교 修交 amity; friendship; friendly relations ─수 교 하 다 form [establish] a friendly relationship 《with》
■—조약 a treaty of amity : 수교조약을 체결하다 conclude [sign] a treaty of amity [friendship] —훈장 the Distinguished Order of Diplomatic Service

수구 水球 water polo

수구 守舊 〈보수〉 conservatism; adherence to traditional customs ♦수구적인 conservative ─수구하다 adhere to traditional customs
■—정권 a conservative government —파 the conservatives; the old-liners

수국 水菊 〖植〗 a hydrangea

수군 水軍 the naval forces

수군거리다 talk [speak, say] in whispers ⇨

소곤거리다
수권 水圈 the hydrosphere
수권 授權 authorization; delegation of legal power ―**수권하다** give authority 《to sb》; authorize [empower] sb ■―**대리인** an authorized agent ―**자본** authorized capital
수그러지다 1〈머리가〉 hang down; become low; lower; sink; droop; drop
▶ 머리가 수그러진 채 서 있는 메리의 사진이 한 일간지에 소개되었다 Mary's standing picture, with her head drooping, was introduced in a daily newspaper.
▶ 그의 용기에는 머리가 수그러진다 I take off my hat to his courage.
2〈기세 등이〉 soften; become mild; be appeased; flag; 〈병세가〉 be relieved; be suppressed; be subdued; 〈바람 등이〉 go [die, calm] down; subside; sink; abate
▶ 바람이 수그러졌다 The wind has fallen.
▶ 더위가 수그러졌다 The heat diminished.
수그리다 hang down ⇨ 숙이다
수금 收金 collection of money; bill collecting ―**수금하다** collect money [bills] ♦ 수금하러 돌아다니다 make a round of calls to collect bills
▶ 그 가게 주인은 수금하느라 바쁘다 The proprietor of the store is busy collecting bills.
■―**원** a money [bill] collector
수금 竪琴 a harp; 〈고대 그리스의〉 a lyre
수금 水禽 a waterfowl ■ 물새
수급 首級 a severed head 《of the enemy》
수급 需給 supply and demand; demand and supply ■ 수요공급(需要供給)
♦ 수급을 조정하다 adjust supply and demand / 수급의 균형을 유지하다 keep supply and demand in balance
■―**계획** a supply and demand program ―**관계** supply-demand relation; relations between supply and demand ―**조정** adjustment of demand and supply
수급 受給 〈공급 받음〉 receipt
♦ 연금 수급 receipt of a pension
■―**자** a recipient: 노령 연금 수급자가 최근 증가하고 있다 The numbers of recipients of the old-age pension has increased recently. ―**자격** the right to receive; qualifications for receiving
수긍 首肯 assent; consent; a nod
♦ 수긍이 가게 하다 win sb's consent; bring the truth to sb's heart; convince [persuade] sb 《of》
▶ 네 설명은 충분히 수긍이 간다 Your explanation is sufficiently convincing.
―**수긍하다** assent 《to》; nod one's assent 《to》; consent 《to》; 〈납득하다〉 be convinced 《of, that》 ♦ 수긍할 수 있는[없는] convincing [unconvincing]
▶ 그는 형의 충고를 일일이 수긍하면서 들었다 He listened to his brother's advice nodding each time.
수기 手記 a note; a memorandum 《pl. -da, ~s》; (口) a memo 《pl. ~s》; 〈회상록〉 memoirs
▶ 그는 병원생활의 수기를 남겼다 He wrote a note about his stay in the hospital.

▶ 그의 수기는 사후 출판되었다 His notes [memoirs] were published after his death.
수기 手旗 a flag; 〈신호용〉 a signal flag
♦ 수기로 신호하다 signal with flags ■―**신호** semaphore; flag signaling
수꽃 〔植〕 a male [sterile, staminate] flower
수꽃술 〔植〕 a stamen; an androecium 《pl. -cia》
수꿩 〔鳥〕 a male pheasant; a cock-pheasant
수나다 數― have a stroke of luck; have sudden luck; (俗) hit the jackpot
수나사 a male [an external] screw
수난 水難 a disaster by water; 〈익사〉 drowning; 〈해난〉 a disaster at sea; a shipwreck; 〈수해〉 a flood (disaster) ♦ 수난을 당하다 suffer from a flood
수난 受難 ordeals; sufferings; severe trial
♦ 십자가의 수난 crucifixion / 예수의 수난 the sufferings of Christ (on the cross); the (Savior's) Passion
―**수난하다** suffer; undergo hardships [trials]
■―**곡** Passion music; the Passion ―**극** a Passion play ―**일** 〔基〕 Good Friday ―**절** Passiontide ―**주** the Passion Week
수납 收納 〈금전의〉 receipt ―**수납하다** receive ―**계** a receiver; 〈은행의〉 a receiving teller ―**액** the amount received ―**장** an account book ―**전표** a receipt (voucher); a receiving slip
수납 受納 receipt; acceptance ―**수납하다** accept; receive ■―**자** a recipient
수냉 水冷 ♦ 수냉식의 water-cooled / 수냉식 엔진 a water-cooled engine ―**수냉하다** water-cool
수녀 修女 a nun; a sister
♦ 수녀가 되다 enter a nunnery [convent]; go into a convent; take the vows of a nun
■―**원** a nunnery; a convent
수년 數年 several [some, a few] years
♦ 수년간 for [over] (several) years
▶ 나는 수년 전에 미국을 방문했다 I visited America some years ago.
▶ 땅 값은 지난 수년간 계속 상승해 왔다 The price of the land has been rising for the past few years.
▶ 지난 수년 동안에 시내의 면모가 완전히 바뀌었다 The town has completely changed in the last few years.
▶ 우리가 만난 지도 수년 됐구나 It is several years since we met.
수노루 a male roe deer; a roebuck
수놈 a male ⇨ 수컷
수놓다 繡― embroider; do embroidery ♦ 비단에 꽃을 수놓다 embroider flowers on silk
수뇌 首腦 a head; a chief; a leader; a top
♦ 정부 수뇌 the heads of the government / 수뇌가 되다 head 《a group》; lead; play the leading part 《in》
■―**부** the (top) management of a company ―**회담** summit [top-level] conference [meeting]; summit talks 《between》: 7개국 수뇌회담 the seven power summit conference
수뇌 髓腦 〔解〕 the myelencephalon
수뇨관 輸尿管 〔解〕 the ureter ⇨ 요관(尿管)

수니파 —派 〈이슬람교의 종파〉 Sunni
♦ 수니파 교의(教義) Sunnism / 수니파 교도 a Sunnite

수다 〈말이 많음〉 talkativeness; chattering; prattle; futile [empty] talk; (美口) a talkfest
♦ 수다 떨다 talk; chat; have a chat 《with》; prattle; chatter; gossip 《about》
▶ 수다 떨지 마라 Shut your big mouth!
▶ 우리는 수다를 떨며 3시간을 보냈다 We spent three hours just chattering.
▶ 우리는 전화로 30분 동안이나 수다를 떨었다 We kept on talking for half an hour on the phone.
—**수다스럽다** talkative; prattling; chattering; glib-tongued; garrulous; gossipy; wordy
♦ 수다스러운 아가씨들 magpie girls
▶ 그녀는 수다스러워 탈이다 Her tongue wags too freely.
■—**쟁이** a talkative [chatty] person; (口) a chatterbox: 그녀는 수다쟁이다 She is a great talker [chatterbox].

수다 數多 〈다수〉 a great number —**수다하다** numerous; many ♦ 수다한 학생 many students

수단 〈나라 이름〉 the Sudan; 〈공식명〉 the Republic of Sudan ■—**사람** a Sudanese

수단 手段 a means (▶단수·복수 동형); 〈방책〉 a measure; a way; 〈단계적 처치〉 a step; 〈편법〉 a shift; a resource
♦ 생계 수단 a means of livelihood / 안전한 수단 a safe [sure] card / 과감한 수단 a drastic step [measure] / 부정 수단 a foul means; a unjust step
▶ 교육은 목적을 달성하기 위한 수단일 뿐이다 Education is only a means to an end.
〈수단이〉 수단이 대단한 사람 a man of unlimited resource
▶ 그는 수단이 좋다 He is resourceful.
〈수단을〉 모든 수단을 다 쓰다 try every possible means; leave no means untried; leave no stone unturned; use every means / 비상 수단을 쓰다 take drastic measures / 수단(방법)을 가리지 않다 be indiscreet in employing means 《to》/ 수단을 강구하다 devise [find] a means 《to》/ 다른 수단을 쓰다 resort to other means; try some other means; play another trick upon
▶ 그는 목적을 위해서는 수단을 가리지 않는다 He makes no scruples of doing anything to attain his object. ⇒ He tries [takes] every possible means to achieve his purpose. ⇒ He goes all lengths to attain his goal.
▶ 그는 입국 비자를 얻기 위해 불법 수단을 썼다 He used illegal means to get an entry visa.
▶ 손실을 최소화하기 위해 효과적인 수단을 취하지 않으면 안된다 We must take effective measures [steps] to minimize the losses.
▶ 그는 온갖 돈벌이 수단을 알고 있다 He knows all the tricks of moneymaking.
〈수단으로〉 최후의 수단으로 as a [in the] last resort
▶ 그는 부정한 수단으로 원하는 것을 손에 넣었다 He got what he wanted by unfair [foul] means.
▶ 그는 최후 수단으로 차를 팔았다 He sold the car as a last resort.

수단추 a ball (of a snap fastener); a stud; a male snap [fastener]

수달 水獺 〔動〕 an otter —**피**(皮) an otter skin [fur]

수답 水畓 a paddy field

수당 手當 〈봉급 외에 지급되는 돈〉 extra benefits; an allowance; (美) a compensation; a stipend; 〈상여금〉 a bonus; 〈보험·연금 등〉 a benefit; a pension; 〈하사금〉 a bounty
♦ 수당을 주다 give an allowance; recompense sb for
▶ 내 동생은 월 10만원의 수당을 받는다 My brother is allowed a hundred thousand won a month.
—**가족**— a family allowance 근무지— a regional allowance 부양— a dependent [family] allowance: 나는 월 20만원의 부양(扶養) 수당을 받는다 I get a monthly allowance of two hundred thousand won for dependents. 시간외[초과근무]— an overtime allowance: 초과 근무 수당이 나옵니까? Will I get extra pay for overtime? 연말— a year-end allowance [bonus] 월— a monthly allowance 전시— a war allowance; 〔軍〕 a field allowance 제(諸)— sundry allowance 퇴직— a retiring [retirement] allowance; severance [separation] pay 특별— a special [an extra] allowance: 열심히 일하는 사람에게는 특별 수당을 주겠다 A bonus will be given to hardworkers.

수더분하다 good-natured; good-tempered; tenderhearted; not fussy; kindhearted ♦ 수더분한 사람 a good-natured person; a regular guy

수도 水道 **1** 〈급수설비〉 waterworks (▶단수·복수 취급); 〈상수도〉 water supply [service]; 〈수돗물〉 tap [running] water
♦ 수도를 놓다 lay a water pipe; have water pipes laid; have water supplied; lay on water / 수도를 틀다[잠그다] turn on [off] a faucet / 수도를 끊다 [단수하다] shut off the water
▶ 이 마을에는 수도가 없다 We have [There is] no water supply [service] in this village.
▶ 우리집 수도는 잘 나오지 않는다 The tap water in my house doesn't run well. ⇒ The water pressure at my house isn't good.
2 〈수로〉 a water course; a waterway; 〈해협〉 a channel; a gut
♦ 한려수도(閑麗水道) the Hallyōsudo
—**공사** waterworks —**관** a water [service] pipe; 〈본관〉 a water main —**국** 〈시의〉 the Waterworks Bureau; the bureau of waterworks —**료**[요금] water rates [charges] —**사업소** a waterworks office —**전**(栓)[꼭지] a faucet; (英) a tap

수도 水稻 paddy rice

수도 受渡 receipt and delivery; (a) delivery; transfer; payment
▶ 물품의 수도는 모두 끝났다 The goods have all been delivered.
—**수도하다** deliver 《goods》; transfer 《property》; hand over

수도 首都 the capital (city); a metropolis

▶ 서울은 한국의 수도다 Seoul is the capital of Korea. ■ —권 the metropolitan area

수도 修道 religious austerities; spiritual exercise; asceticism; 〔宗〕 discipline
—**수도하다** lead an ascetic life; practice asceticism [religious austerities]
■ —생활 an ascetic life; monasticism; a monastic life —승 a Buddhist monk —자 an ascetic; 〔가톨릭〕 a religious —회 a religious [monastic] order; an order

수도원 修道院 a religious house; 〈큰 것〉 an abbey; a cloister; 〈남자〉 a monastery; 〈여자〉 a convent; a nunnery
—**장** 〈남자〉 an abbot; the Father Superior; 〈여자〉 an abbess; the Mother [Lady] Superior

수돗물 水道— city [tap, piped] water; running water
▶ 공사 때문에 내일 아침 다섯시부터 일곱시까지 수돗물이 나오지 않습니다 Due to construction work, the water supply will be cut off from five o'clock until seven tomorrow morning.

수동 手動 manual [hand] operation
♦ 수동의 manual; worked by hand; hand-operated; manually operated
▶ 이 타이프라이터는 수동식이다 This typewriter is operated manually. ⇌ This is a manual typewriter.
■ —브레이크 a hand brake —제어장치 a manual control —펌프 a hand pump

수동 受動 passivity; passiveness
♦ 수동의[수동적인] passive / 수동적으로 passively / 수동적인 태도를 취하다 take a passive attitude 《toward》
■ —태[형] 〔文法〕 the passive voice [form]

수두 水痘 〔醫〕 varicella; chicken pox

수두룩하다 plentiful; abundant; numerous; a good deal of; (a) lot [wealth] of; plenty [lots] of
▶ 우리는 할 일이 수두룩하다 We have a plenty of works to do.
▶ 그런 사람들이 수두룩하다 There are lots [plenty] of people like that.

수때우다 數— forestall predicted bad luck; ward off evil with a prior, lesser ordeal

수땜 數— warding off bad luck with a prior, lesser ordeal ♦ 수땜으로 여기고 체념하다 resign *oneself* to hardship —**수땜하다** ward off evil with a prior, lesser hardship

수라 水剌 〈임금의 식사〉 the king's meal [food] —**간**(間) the royal kitchen —**상** the king's dinner table

수라장 修羅場 a scene of carnage; a shambles; a pandemonium; a scene of violence; a scene of utter confusion
♦ 수라장이 되다 become a scene of carnage; be turned into a (veritable) shambles
▶ 회장은 수라장이 되었다 The meeting hall was thrown into great confusion.

수락 受諾 acceptance; agreement
—**수락하다** accept 《an offer》; consent [agree] to; comply with
♦ 수락할 수 없는 unacceptable; disputable / 선뜻 수락하다 give ready consent 《to》 / 취임을 수락하다 accept the post 《of chairman》 / 아무의 요구를 수락하다 comply with *sb's* request
▶ 그들은 우리의 요구를 수락했다 They complied with our request.
▶ 그 제안은 만장일치로 수락되었다 The proposal was accepted with unanimity.
▶ 그런 조건은 수락할 수가 없다 I cannot accept such terms.
▶ 제의하신 건 기꺼이 수락하는 바입니다 In reference to your suggestion, we are very happy to be able to accept your request.
■ 서면[구두]— written [oral] acceptance 정식— formal acceptance

수란 水卵 a poached egg ♦ 수란을 뜨다 poach an egg —**짜** an egg poacher; a poacher

수란관 輸卵管 〔解〕 the oviduct; the Fallopian tube

수량 水量 the volume of water
▶ 강의 수량이 불었다 The river is swollen [in flood].
▶ 그 강은 수량이 풍부하다 The river has a great volume of water.
■ —계 a water gauge [meter]

수량 數量 quantity; volume
♦ 수량이 늘다[줄다] increase [decrease] in quantity
▶ 그들은 수량에서는 우월했다 They exceeded in quantity.
▶ 수량이 많을 경우에는 특별 할인해 드리겠습니다 We are prepared to allow special discounts for a large quantity [amount].

수렁 a slough; a quagmire; a mire; a morass; a bog
♦ 수렁에 빠지다 fall in the mire; sink in a bog; 《비유》 be bogged [mired] down; mire *oneself* 《in》 / 수렁에서 빠져나오다 pull *oneself* out of the mire; find a way out of the swamp
■ —논 a swampy paddy field —배미 a strip of swampy paddy field

수레 a wagon; a cart; 〈손수레〉 a handcart; 〈마차〉 a carriage
♦ 수레를 끌다 draw [pull] a cart / 수레에 싣다 load a cart [wagon] 《with goods》 / 수레로 운반하다 carry 《goods》 in a cart
■ —바퀴 a (wagon) wheel

수려하다 秀麗— graceful; beautiful; handsome; fine ♦ 이목구비가 수려한 청년 a very handsome young man

수력 水力 waterpower; hydraulic power
♦ 수력을 이용하다 make use of hydraulic power; 〈동력원으로서〉 harness waterpower
■ —공학 hydraulic engineering —기계 a hydraulic machinery —자원 waterpower resources —전기 hydroelectricity —터빈 a waterpower turbine —학 hydraulics; hydrodynamics

수력발전 水力發電 waterpower [hydroelectric power] generation ■ —소 a hydroelectric power [waterpower, hydropower] plant [station]

수련 修鍊 〈훈련〉 training; practice; drilling; discipline
♦ 여러해 동안 수련을 쌓다 go through many

years' [a long period of] training; undergo many years' of training (to become)
▶ 그는 학생들에게 자기 생각을 영어로 분명히 말하는 수련을 쌓도록 했다 He practiced his students in expressing themselves clearly in English.
—수련하다 train; discipline; drill
—의(醫) an intern(e); an apprentice doctor

수련 睡蓮 〔植〕 a water [pond] lily

수렴 收斂 1〈세금 등의〉 extortion [exaction] of taxes; levying and collecting of heavy taxes —수렴하다 extort [exact] heavy taxes《from》; tax heavily; collect strictly
2〈수축〉〔醫〕 astriction;〈物·數〉 convergence; convergency —수렴하다 be astringent; be astrictive; converge ▶ 혈관이 수렴한다 The blood vein is astringent.
3〈여론 등을〉 collecting; (a) reflection —수렴하다 collect
▶ 우리는 각계의 폭넓은 의견을 수렴했다 We took opinions from various strata of society into consideration.
■—급수 a convergent series (of numbers) —렌즈 a converging [convergent] lens —성 astringency —작용 astriction —제(劑) an astringent; an astrictive

수렴청정 垂簾聽政 regency by the queen mother from behind the veil

수렵 狩獵 〈사냥〉 a hunt; hunting; shooting
♦수렵하러 가다 go hunting [shooting]
▶ 그는 산으로 수렵하러 갔다 He went hunting [went on a hunt] in the mountains.
■—가 a hunter;〈여자〉 a huntress;〈英〉 a huntsman; a sportsman; a sportswoman —금지기 the closed 〔(英) close〕 season —기 the hunting [open] season —면허증 a shooting [hunting] license —모 a hunting cap —민족 a hunting people —법〔法〕 the game law —복 shooting clothes; a hunting suit —여행 hunting [shooting] trip —조 a game fowl —지 a hunting ground —해금일 the opening day of the hunting

수령 守令 〔古制〕 a chief magistrate [administrator]; a local governor

수령 受領 receipt; acceptance
—수령하다 receive; accept; be (the) recipient of ♦연금을 수령하다 receive a pension
▶ 정히 수령함 Received with thanks.
■—대장 a receipt book —자 a receiver; a recipient;〈어음 등의〉 a payee: 나는 아내를 보험금의 수령자로 했다 I made my wife the beneficiary of my insurance. —자격 qualification to be [as] a recipient —증 a receipt

수령 首領 a leader; a head; a chief; a boss; a chieftain ♦수령이 되다 become a leader; lead (others in sth)

수령 樹齡 the age of a tree ▶ 저 나무는 수령이 천년이 넘는다 That tree is over one thousand years old.

수로 水路 a waterway;〈관개용의〉 a watercourse;〈항해로〉 a lane;〈항구의〉 a fairway; a (water) channel;〈땅을 파서 만든〉 a canal; a ditch
♦수로로 가다 go by ship [water, sea]
■—관개— an irrigation canal [ditch] ■—관측소 a hydrographic observatory —도 a hydrographic map —측량(술) a hydrographical survey —표지 a beacon; a channel mark —학 hydrography —학자 a hydrographer

수로안내 水路案內 〈행위〉 piloting; pilotage;〈사람〉 a pilot ■—료 pilotage (dues) —선 a pilot boat

수록 收錄 gathering; collection;〈녹음·녹화〉 (video) tape recording; (video) taping
—수록하다 〈모으다〉 gather; collect;〈기록·녹음하다〉 record; tape; write down; mention; contain
▶ 이 사전에는 일상 생활에 필요한 표현이 모두 수록되어 있다 All necessary expressions used in daily life are found [included] in this dictionary.
▶ 우리는 그들이 수업하는 모습을 비디오 테이프에 수록했다 We videotaped their classroom work.
▶ 나는 이 회합에 모인 사람들의 의견을 테이프에 수록했다 I taped the opinions of those who attended the meeting.

수뢰 水雷 〈어뢰〉 a torpedo (pl. ~es);〈기뢰〉 a mine
♦수뢰를 발사하다 fire a torpedo (at) / 수뢰를 부설하다 lay a mine / 수뢰에 맞다 take a torpedo hit / 수뢰로 공격하다 torpedo《a vessel》
■부유(浮遊)— a floating [surface] mine 촉발— a contact mine ■—방어망 a torpedo net;〈총칭〉 torpedo netting —부설구역 the minefield —부설함 a minelayer —정 a torpedo boat

수뢰 受賂 bribery; accepting a bribe
♦수뢰 혐의로 on the charge of taking a bribe
▶ 그는 5억원의 수뢰죄로 고발당했다 He was charged with having accepted five hundred million won in bribes.
—수뢰하다 take [accept, receive] a bribe [payoff] from sb; graft
■—물 graft;〈美俗〉 boodle —사건 a bribery case; a graft [bribery] scandal —자 a bribee; a bribetaker; a grafter;〈美俗〉 a boodler

수료 修了 completion (of a course)
—수료하다 complete; finish
♦3학년 과정을 수료하다 finish the third-year course
▶ 나는 고등학교 전과정을 수료했다 I completed the whole course of study at a high school.
■—증서 a certificate

수류 水流 a (water) current; a stream (of water); a flow

수류탄 手榴彈 a hand grenade [bomb]; a grenade;〈軍俗〉 a pineapple ♦수류탄을 던지다 throw a hand grenade (at)

수륙 水陸 land and water
♦수륙 양용의 amphibian; amphibious
■—공동 작전 amphibious operations —양용(비행)기[전차] an amphibious plane [tank]; an amphibian —양용자동차 an amphibious car [vehicle]

수리 〔鳥〕 an eagle ♦수리의 aquiline ■—둥지 an eagle's nest; an aerie —새끼 an eaglet

수리 水利 〈물의 이용〉 utilization of water; 〈수운〉 water transport; 〈급수〉 water supply; 〈농경용의〉 irrigation
■―권 water (irrigation) rights ―사업 irrigation works [projects] ―시설 irrigation facilities ―조합 an irrigation association

수리 受理 acceptance; reception
―수리하다 accept 《a report》; receive; take up
♦ 청원서를 수리하다 receive a petition / 고소를 수리하다 take up a charge
▶ 그의 사표는 수리되었다 His resignation was accepted.

수리 修理 repair(s); mending
♦ 트럭의 수리 서비스 truck repair service / 수리중이다 be under repair
▶ 이 전기 면도기는 수리가 필요하다 This electric razor needs repairing. ⇌ (口) I have to repair this electric razor.
▶ 내부 수리중 임시 휴업 《게시》 Closed temporarily for remodeling [redecoration].
―수리하다 repair; mend; (美) fix (up)

> **解說** *repair*와 *mend*는 같은 뜻으로 쓰이지만 repair는 자동차·기계류 등 비교적 크거나 복잡하여 숙련을 요하는 경우에, mend는 비교적 단순한 것을 고치는 경우에 쓴다. (美)에서 mend는 보통 의류를 수리하는 경우에 쓴다. *fix*는 구어적인 말로 repair, mend 대신 쓴다.

♦ 구멍난 타이어를 수리하다 repair [patch] a flat tire / 수리할 필요가 있다 be in want of repair; need repairs [repairing] / 차를 수리하러 보내다 send *one's* car for repair(s)
▶ 이 차는 수리할 수 없다 This car can't be repaired. ⇌ This car is beyond [past] repair.
▶ 나는 시계를 수리했다 I had my watch repaired [mended, fixed].
▶ 우리는 하수구를 수리하기 위해 배관공을 불렀다 We called in the plumber to fix the drain.
■―공 a repairer; a repairman 《pl. -men》: 시계 수리공 a watch repairer ―공장 a repair shop; a garage : 자동차 수리공장 a car repair shop ―비 repairing charges; the cost of repairing ―점 〈라디오·전기기구의〉 a service station

수리 數理 〈수학 이론〉 a mathematical principle; 〈계산〉 mathematics
♦ 수리적(인) mathematical / 수리적으로 mathematically / 수리적 두뇌가 있다 have a head for mathematics; be clever at mathematics
▶ 그는 수리에 밝다 He is good at [strong in] mathematics.
■―경제학[통계학, 물리학, 철학] mathematical economics [statistics, physics, philosophy]

수리남 〈나라 이름〉 Suriname; 〈공식명〉 the Republic of Suriname

수리부엉이 〔鳥〕 an eagle owl

수림 樹林 a forest; a wood; a grove

수립 樹立 establishment; founding; setting-up
♦ 새 정당의 수립 the establishment of a new political party
―수립하다 establish; found; set up; plant
♦ 계획을 수립하다 devise [work out, formulate] a plan / 외교[우호] 관계를 수립하다 establish diplomatic [friendly] relations / 새 정부를 수립하다 establish [set up] a new government
▶ 그는 또 세계 신기록을 수립했다 He made [established, set] another new world record.

수마 水魔 〈수해〉 a disastrous flood ♦ 수마가 덮치다 be struck by a disastrous flood

수마 睡魔 〈졸음〉 somnolence; sleepiness; drowsiness; 〈전설·동화 등의〉 the sandman; the dustman; 〔神〕 Morpheus
♦ 수마가 덮치다 get sleepy; become drowsy / 수마와 싸우다 fight off sleep; try not to fall asleep

수마트라 〈인도네시아의 섬〉 Sumatra; (총칭) the Sumatrans ♦ 수마트라의 Sumatran
■―사람 a Sumatran ―어 Sumatran

수만 數萬 tens [scores] of thousands 《of》
♦ 수만의 청중 scores of thousands audiences
▶ 수만의 사람이 그 전쟁에서 죽었다 Tens of thousands of people were killed in the war.

수많다 數― a lot of; a great [great] many; numerous; numbers of; a (great) number of
♦ 수많은 사람들 a great number of [a great many] people; numbers [scores, crowds] of people / 수많은 인파에 시달리다 be jostled among the crowd
▶ 수많은 사람들이 광장에 모였다 Many [A large number of] people were assembled in the square.
▶ 전쟁은 수많은 인명을 앗아갔다 The war took the lives of innumerable [countless] people.
▶ 수많은 난관에도 불구하고 그는 마침내 그 사업에 성공했다 In spite of a great many difficulties, he finally succeeded in the business.

수말 a (male) horse; a stallion

수매 收買 (a) purchase; buying; 〈정부의〉 procurement ♦ 정부의 쌀 수매 가격 the government's buying [purchasing] price of rice
―수매하다 buy (out); purchase

수맥 水脈 1 〈뱃길〉 a water route; a channel; 〈항로〉 a sea route; a seaway
2 〈땅속에 흐르는 물줄기〉 a water vein
♦ 수맥을 찾아내다 strike (a vein of) water
▶ 애쓰고 있지만 아직도 수맥을 찾아내지 못했다 We've been trying, but haven't struck water yet.

수면 水面 the surface of the water
♦ 수면에서 3,4미터 위[아래] several meters above [below] the water / 수면에 떠오르다 come up [rise] to the surface of the water
▶ 나뭇잎 몇 개가 수면에 떠다니고 있다 Some leaves are floating on the water.

수면 睡眠 (a) sleep; (a) slumber
♦ 수면을 취하다 sleep; slumber; have a sleep / 수면을 방해하다 disturb [interrupt] *sb's* sleep [slumber]
▶ 수면을 방해하지 말아주세요 Please don't disturb my sleep.
▶ 아이들은 하루 열 시간 쯤의 수면이 필요하다

Children need about ten hours' sleep every day [night].
▶ 충분히 수면을 취했습니까? Did you have a good sleep?
▶ 그녀는 지금 수면중인데요 She is sleeping [asleep] now.
—수면하다 sleep; slumber; have a sleep [slumber]
■—병 sleeping [(英) sleepy] sickness —시간 hours of sleep; sleeping hours: 수면시간을 줄이다 curtail [cut down] sleep; rob *oneself* of sleep —제 a sleeping drug [medicine, pill, tablet]; sleeping powder [draught]; a sleep-inducing drug; a soporific (drug); 〈마취약〉 a narcotic; an anesthetic

수면부족 睡眠不足 lack [want] of sleep; insufficient sleep
▶ 수면부족은 몸에 나쁘다 Want [Lack] of sleep injures our health.
▶ 수면부족으로 현기증이 난다 I feel giddy from want of sleep.
▶ 나는 수면부족이다 I am short of sleep.

수명 壽命 1〈명의 길이〉the span of life; a life span; 〈생명〉 (a) life (*pl.* -ves); 〈일생〉 a lifetime
◆ 인간의 평균 수명 the average span [longevity] of human life [human beings]; 〈保險〉 the average life expectancy / 내각의 수명 the Cabinet's tenure of office
▶ 그의 선수 수명도 끝나가고 있다 His playing life [His life as a player] is nearly over.
〈수명이[은]〉 수명이 길다 be long-lived; have [enjoy] a long life / 수명이 짧다 be short-lived; have a short life / 수명이 길어지다[연장되다] take (on) [win] a new [fresh] lease of life / 수명이 길어져 가고 있다 be living longer
▶ 그녀는 수명이 길었다[짧았다] She was long- [short-]lived. ⇒ She had a long [short] life.
▶ 한국인의 평균 수명이 길어졌다 The average life span of the Korean has been extended [prolonged].
▶ 그 사고를 당했을 때 마치 수명이 단축되는 것처럼 여겨졌다 I felt as if my life were shortened when I met the accident.
▶ 두루미는 수명이 길다 Cranes live to a great age.
▶ 그의 수명은 얼마 남지 않았다 His days are numbered.
▶ 노인은 이미 자신의 수명이 다하고 있음을 알아챘다 The old man realized that the end of his life was in sight [drawing near].
〈수명을〉 수명을 늘이다[줄이다] lengthen [shorten] *one's* (span of) life / 수명을 다하고 죽다 die a natural death; die from a natural cause
▶ 그 일이 그의 수명을 연장했다[단축했다] It prolonged [shortened] his life.
▶ 그는 충분히 휴식을 취하지 않았기 때문에 수명을 단축했다 He shortened his life because he did not get enough rest.
2〈내구 기간〉 a life
◆ 자동차[건전지]의 수명 the life of a car [battery]; the expected life span of (motor) car [battery]

▶ 그 건전지는 수명이 다 됐을 거다 I wonder if the battery has run down.
▶ 이 책은 수명이 긴 베스트셀러다 This is a long-standing bestseller.
▶ 그 잡지의 수명은 불과 1년 남짓됐다 The magazine lived only for a year or so.

수모 受侮 scorn; contempt; disdain; slight
◆ 수모를 당하다 be held in contempt; suffer an insult; be insulted [despised] / 수모를 참다 bear an affront; pocket [swallow (down)] an insult; (美口) eat crow [dirt]; eat humble pie
▶ 나는 온갖 수모를 다 견뎌야 했다 I have to pocket not a few insults.

수목 樹木 trees; arbors ◆ 수목이 울창한 woody; wooded 《mountain》; arboreous / 수목이 없는 woodless; naked; bare (of trees)
■—숭배 tree worship; dendrolatry —원(園) a tree garden; an arboretum 《*pl.* ~s, -ta》 —재배 arboriculture —학 dendrology —한계선 timberline

수몰지역 水沒地域 submerged districts; an area (to be) under water

수몰하다 水沒— be submerged [submersed] (in); be flooded [inundated] (with water); be under water
▶ 홍수로 마을이 수몰되었다 The flood submerged the village. ⇒ The flood covered the village with water.

수묵 水墨 India(n) ink ◆ 수묵(이) 지다 get smudged with India ink ■—화 a painting [drawing] in black and white [Indian ink]

수문 水門 a water gate; 〈댐·저수지 등의〉 a sluice (gate); 〈운하·수로의〉 a floodgate; a penstock; 〈운하의〉 a lock gate
◆ 수문을 열다[닫다] open [shut] a water gate [sluice] / (배가) 수문을 통과하다 pass through a lock
■—감시장 a lockmaster —지기[관리인] a lockkeeper; a lockman —통행세 lockage; a lock fee

수문 守門 keeping [guarding] a gate
■—군(軍) guards; sentries —장 the chief of gatekeepers; the commander of guards

수미 愁眉 knitted brows; a worried look
◆ 수미를 펴다 feel relieved

수밀 水密 ◆ 수밀의 watertight ■—시험 a watertight test

수밀도 水蜜桃 a peach

수바 〈피지의 수도〉 Suva

수박 a watermelon ◆ 씨 없는 수박 a seedless watermelon

수박겉핥기 superficiality; shallowness
◆ 수박겉핥기 지식 a smattering; a superficial [half, shallow] knowledge / …을 수박겉핥기 식으로 알고 있다 have a smattering of
▶ 그는 수박겉핥기식 지식을 과시한다 He shows off his smattering of knowledge.
▶ 그의 영어는 수박겉핥기에 지나지 않는다 He has only got a smattering of English.

수반 首班 the head ◆ 내각의 수반 the head of a Cabinet / 김 수반 내각 the Cabinet with Mr. Kim at its head; the Kim-headed Cabinet
▶ 김씨가 내각 수반으로 지명되었다 Mr. Kim

was appointed [named] to the premiership.

수반 隨伴 accompaniment; concomitant ―수반하다 follow; attend; be attendant on [upon]; be concomitant with ♦위험이 수반하는 직업 a hazardous job
▶ 그 수술에는 다소의 위험이 수반된다 The operation is not without risk. ⇌ There is some risk in the operation.

수반 水盤 a basin; a flower tray

수방 水防 flood control; prevention of floods; defense against floods
♦수방 공사 anti-flood construction / 수방 대책 an anti-flood measure; a flood control measure; a measure to prevent floods

수배 手配 **1** 〈갈라 맡아서 하게 함〉 arrangements; preparations ♦수배가 잘 되어 있다[있지 않다] be well [badly] arranged (for) ―수배하다 arrange for; prepare for; make arrangements [preparations] for
▶ 차량은 수배되어있습니까? Have you arranged for a car?
▶ 여행사가 호텔 예약과 비행기표를 수배해 줬다 A travel agency has arranged for my hotel reservations and plane tickets.
2 〈수사망을 폄〉 (a) search ―수배하다 〈수사망을 펴다〉 institute [begin] a search for; cast a dragnet for; 〈배치하다〉 dispose 〈men〉; make dispositions
♦요소요소에 수배하다 make dispositions at important points
▶ 그는 강도 살인 혐의로 경찰이 수배하고 있다 He is wanted by the police for burglary and murder.
▪지명― arrangements for the search of an identified criminal ▪―자 a person wanted by the police; a wanted criminal ―자 사진 a photograph of a wanted criminal; (美俗) an art

수배 數倍 several times ♦수배로 늘어나다 increase several times
▶ 그는 자네의 수배의 책을 가지고 있네 He has several times as many books as you have.

수백 數百 hundreds (of) ♦수백 명 hundreds of people ▶ 광장에는 수백 명의 사람이 있었다 There were several hundred people [hundreds of people] in the plaza.

수백만 數百萬 millions ♦수백만 명 several million men; millions of people

수범 垂範 setting an example ―수범하다 set [give] an example to 〈others〉; exemplify *oneself* ♦〈남에게〉 솔선 수범하다 take the initiative and set an example (to others)

수법 手法 **1** 〈수단·방법〉 a method; a way; 〈속임수〉 a trick
♦범죄 수법 a method employed in a crime / 그 수법으로 in that way / 똑같은 수법 the same old trick / 새로운 수법의 사기 a swindle of a new type
▶ 이 수법은 용의자의 것과는 조금 다르다 This style of work is a little different from that of the suspect.
▶ 나는 그의 수법을 잘 알고 있다 I know his regular way [old trick].
▶ 그는 낡은 수법으로 나를 속이려 했다 He tried the old trick on me.
▶ 그건 전형적인 사기 수법이야 That is a classic swindling gambit, you know.
2 〈작품 제작 방법〉 a technique; a style
▶ 그는 한국화에 서양의 수법을 도입하고 있다 He is introducing a western technique into Korean drawing.

수병 水兵 a seaman 〈*pl.* -men〉; a sailor; a bluejacket; a Jack tar
▪―모 a sailor hat ―복 a seaman's uniform

수복 收復 recovery; reclamation ―수복하다 recover; reclaim; win back ▪―민 repatriated people ―지구 a reclaimed area

수복 修復 restoration (to the original state) ⇨ 복원(復元) ―수복하다 restore *sth* to the original state

수복 壽福 longevity and happiness
♦수복 강녕하다 be blessed with longevity, good health and happiness

수부 水夫 a sailor; a seaman 〈*pl.* -men〉; a mariner ♦수부가 되다 become a sailor; go to sea

수북수북 in heaps ―수북수북하다 〈서술적〉 be heaped up 〈with〉 ▶ 밥은 사발에 수북수북하게 담아드리세요 Serve the rice heaped up in bowls.

수북이 full(y); in a heap
♦사발에 수북이 담은 밥 a heaped-up [heaping] bowl of rice / 수북이 쌓이다 be piled up high; lie in a heap / 쟁반에 밤을 수북이 담다 heap a tray with chestnuts

수북하다 heaped up; heaping ♦수북하게 쌓인 쓰레기 a pile of garbage ▶ 접시에 과자가 수북하다 Cakes are heaped up on the plate.

수분 水分 water; moisture; humidity; 〈액즙〉 juice; 〈수액(樹液)〉 sap
♦수분이 많은 watery; moist; humid; succulent 〈plant〉; juicy 〈fruit〉 / 수분을 공급하다 restore moisture 〈to〉; rehydrate / 수분을 없애다 〈빼다〉 remove water [moisture] 〈from〉; 〈특히 식품을 가공할 때〉 dehydrate; 〈건조시키다〉 dry (up) / 수분을 흡수하다 absorb [suck up] water 〈from〉
▶ 이 사과는 수분이 많다 This apple is juicy.

수분 受粉 [植] pollination; fertilization ―수분하다 be pollinated ♦수분시키다 pollinate ▪인공― artificial pollination [fertilization] ▪―작용(作用) pollination

수불 受拂 receipts and payments; collection and disbursement
▶ 고객 예금의 수불은 은행의 주요 업무다 The receipts and payments of customers' deposits are important work of banks.
―수불하다 take in and pay out; collect and disburse
▪―금 incomes and outgoes; receipts and disbursements

수비 守備 **1** 〈방어〉 (a) defense; (英) (a) defence; defending; garrisoning; guard ♦수비를 강화하다 strengthen the defense ―수비하다 defend; guard; garrison
2 [野] fielding ♦깨끗한[서투른, 철통 같은] 수비 clean [poor, airtight] fielding / 수비를 보다 take the field / 수비가 좋다[허술하다] be

수비대 守備隊 a garrison; guards ◆국경— the border guards; a frontier garrison

수사 手寫 〈손으로 베낌〉 copying [transcription] by hand —수사하다 copy [transcribe] by hand ■—본(本) a book copied by hand

수사 修士 a monk; 〈탁발의〉 a friar

수사 修辭 a figure of speech; rhetoric ◆수사적인[상의] rhetorical / 수사 의문 a rhetorical question
▶그의 소설은 수사적 표현이 많다 His novels are heavy with rhetorical expressions.

수사 搜査 an investigation; (a) criminal investigation; 〈수색〉 a search; 〈美〉〈범인의〉 a manhunt
◆국립 과학 수사 연구소 the National Scientific Criminal Investigation Laboratory / 합동 수사반 the joint investigation team / 수사 선상에 나타나다[떠오르다] appear on the network of police search / 수사를 개시하다 start [institute] a search / 수사를 중단하다 give up [abandon] the search
—수사하다 investigate (a case); conduct [make] an investigation (into, of); 〈수색하다〉 search (for); make a search (for)
▶경찰은 그 범죄 사건의 원인을 수사하고 있다 The police are investigating the cause of the crime.
■ 과학(적)— scientific crime detection; criminalistics 범죄— criminal investigation : 범죄수사관 a criminal investigator; a police detective ■—과 the criminal investigation section [department] —반 a crime [criminal investigation] squad —본부 the investigation headquarters —주임 the chief investigator —카드 a 'wanted' card

수사 數詞 〔文法〕 a numeral —기(基)— a cardinal numeral 서(序)— an ordinal numeral

수사납다 數— unlucky; unfortunate; luckless ◆수사납게(도) by ill fortune; unluckily; unfortunately; as ill luck would have it
▶어제는 나에게 수사나운 날이었다 It was unlucky on me yesterday.

수사망 搜査網 the police dragnet ◆수사망에 걸리다 be caught in the police dragnet / 수사망을 펴다 spread [drop] a dragnet
▶온 시내에 수사망이 펼쳐져 있다 The dragnet is spread throughout the city.

수사슴 a stag; a buck; 〈5세 이상의〉 a hart

수사학 修辭學 rhetoric ◆수사학적인[상의] rhetorical / 수사학적으로[상으로] rhetorically ■—자 a rhetorician

수산 水産 marine [aquatic] products ■—가공품 processed marine products —대학[학교] a fisheries college [school] —물 marine [aquatic] products —시험장 a marine laboratory; a fisheries experiment station —식(료)품 seafood —업 fisheries —업협동조합 a fisheries cooperative —청 the Fisheries Administration; the Office of Fishery —학 the science of fisheries

수산 蓚酸 〔化〕 oxalic acid ⇨ 옥살산

수산화 水酸化 〔化〕 hydration ■—나트륨 sodium hydroxide —물 hydroxide —철 hydrated iron —칼륨 potassium hydroxide —칼슘[마그네슘, 아연] calcium [magnesium, zinc] hydroxide

수삼 水蔘 undried ginseng

수삼차 數三次 〈여러 차례〉 a couple of times; several times

수상 水上 ◆수상의 aquatic; water-surface / 수상(에)(서) on (the surface of) the water
▶축제는 수상에서 벌어졌다 The festival was held on the water.
■—가옥 a house built on stilts over the water —경찰 the water [harbor, marine] police —교통 water-borne traffic —(비행)기 a water plane; a hydroplane; a seaplane —운송 transportation by water; water transportation

수상 手相 the lines of the palm ⇨ 손금

수상 受像 〔物〕 receiving television pictures —수상하다 receive televisional [television] pictures; televise
■—관 a picture [an image-receiving] tube —기 a television receiver [set]; a TV set —면 the television screen; the telescreen

수상 受賞 receiving a prize [reward] —수상하다 receive a prize [reward]; win [be awarded] a prize
▶그는 작년에 동인 문학상을 수상했다 He got the Dong-In Literary Prize last year.
▶그 전람회에서 그는 처음으로 수상했다 For the first time he won a prize at the exhibition.
—자 a prize winner; an awardee : 노벨상 수상자 a Nobel-prize winner; a Nobel prizer; a Nobelist; a Nobel laureate / 수상자 명부 a (prize) winners' list —작품 a prize winner; an awarded work

수상 首相 the prime minister; the premier; 〈독일의〉 the chancellor ◆수상이 되다 hold (the) premiership; head a Cabinet ■—직 prime ministership; premiership; prime ministry

수상 殊常 suspiciousness —수상하다[쩍다, 스럽다] suspicious; suspicious-looking; questionable; dubious; shady; 〈口〉 fishy; queer
◆수상한 사람 a suspicious-looking man [fellow] / 수상한 장사 a shady business / 수상한 행동을 하다 act suspiciously
▶그는 나를 수상한듯이 바라보았다 He looked at me suspiciously.
▶사람들은 그의 행동을 수상히 여겼다 His behavior gave rise to suspicion.
▶저 사나이가 수상하다 He looks very suspicious. ⇌ I suspect him.
▶그는 수상쩍은 인물이다 He is a suspicious [dubious] character.

수상 授賞 awarding a prize; prize giving —수상하다 award [give] a prize ■—식 a prize-giving [an award-giving] ceremony

수상 隨想 occasional [random, desultory] thoughts ■—록 stray notes; jottings; (occasional) essays; memoirs

수상경기 水上競技 aquatic [water] sports; aquatics
■—대회 an aquatic competition

수상생활 水上生活 aquatic life; life on the water ■—자 a man who makes a living on the water

수상스키 水上— water skiing; 〈도구〉 water skis ◆수상스키를 하다 water-ski / 수상스키를 하러가다 go water-skiing / 수상스키를 하는 사람 a water-skier

수색 搜索 (a) quest; a search; (美)〈범인 수색〉 a manhunt; 〈수사〉(an) investigation
◆수색원을 내다 ask the police to search (for one's son); apply to the police for sb's search / 수색의 방향을 바꾸다 start a search in a new direction
▶ 눈보라 때문에 그들은 수색을 중단하지 않을 수 없었다 Because of the snowstorm, they had no choice but to give up the search.
—**수색하다** search [look, hunt] (for); make a search (for); rummage (a house for sth); drag (a river for a dead body)
◆철저히 수색하다 search thoroughly (for); comb (a region for sb) / 몸을 수색하다 frisk sb; rub down sb
■ 가택— a domiciliary search; house searching ■—대[기(機), 정(艇)] a search(ing) party [plane, boat] —영장 a search warrant

수색 愁色 a sad countenance; a worried [sorrowful, an anxious] look; a melancholy [gloomy] air; the traces of sorrow (in one's face) ◆(얼굴에) 수색을 띠다 wear a worried look; look sad [gloomy]

수생 水生 ◆수생의 living [growing] in the water; aquatic
■—동물 an aquatic animal —생물 (총칭) aquatic (life); water creatures: 여러 형태의 수생생물 many forms of aquatic life —식물 an aquatic [a water] plant; a hydrophyte

수서 水棲 ◆수서의 aquatic; living in the water ■—동물 an aquatic (animal)

수석 首席 〈석차·지위〉the top seat [place]; 〈수석자〉the head; the chief
◆외교단의 수석 the head of the diplomatic corps / 수석으로 졸업하다 graduate first (on the list) / 수석으로 합격하다 top the list at the examination
▶ 그는 반에서 수석이다 He is at the top of the class.
■—대표 the chief delegate; the head of the delegation —판사 the chief judge —학생 top [head] student

수선 noise; fuss; ado; bustle
◆수선피우다 make [raise] a fuss
■—쟁이 a bustling fellow; (口) a fussbudget; a fusspot; a rattler; a chatterbox

수선 垂線 〔數〕a perpendicular (line)
◆수선을 긋다 draw a perpendicular / 삼각형의 밑변에 수선을 내리다 drop a perpendicular line toward the base of a triangle

수선 修繕 fixing; repair(s); mending ◆수선중이다 be under repair; be undergoing repairs —**수선하다** repair; 〈구두를〉cobble; make repairs (on); mend; fix (up)
◆시계를 수선시키다 have a watch repaired [fixed] / 수선하러 보내다 send sth to (a shop) for repair(s) / 수선할 수 있다 be repairable / 수선할 수 없다 be beyond [past] repair
▶ 이 우산은 수선해야겠다 This umbrella needs fixing [repair].
▶ 이 구두는 수선해야겠다 These shoes need cobbling.
■ 응급— urgent [emergency] repairs ■—공 a repairer; a repairman (pl. -men); a mender —비 repairing expenses; the cost of repairs

수선거리다 be in commotion; create a commotion; make a noise; raise [make] a fuss; make a stir; buzz
▶ 그가 등단하니까 청중들이 수선거렸다 When he appeared on the platform, a stir ran through the audience.
▶ 교실 안이 수선거렸다 The class was in commotion.

수선떨다 fuss (about); make [raise] a fuss; bustle (about)
◆하찮은 일로 수선떨다 make a (great) fuss about trifles; make much ado about nothing
▶ 이것은 네가 수선떨 문제가 아니다 This is not a question you'll fuss about.

수선스럽다 boisterous; noisy; clamorous; vociferous; bustling ▶ 도대체 왜 이렇게 수선스러운 거냐? What on earth are you making such a noise for?

수선화 水仙花 〔植〕a narcissus (pl. ~es, -cissi) ■ 나팔— a daffodil; (口) a daffy 노랑— a jonquil

수성 水性 ◆수성의 aqueous ■—가스[도료] water gas [paint]

수성 水星 〔天〕Mercury ◆수성의 Mercurian

수성 獸性 animality; beastliness; bestiality; brutality; the brute [beast] (in man); (man's) brutal [animal] nature; brutishness

수성암 水成岩 〔地質〕an aqueous rock; a neptunian rock

수세 水洗 flushing; washing (by water); rinsing ■—식 화장실 a flush toilet; a water closet (略 W.C.)

수세 水勢 the force of water [a current]

수세 守勢 a defensive attitude [position]; the defensive ◆수세의 defensive; passive / 수세를 취하다 assume [take] the defensive; stand [be, act] on the defensive
▶ 우리는 그때 수세에 처해 있었다 We were on the defensive at that time.

수세 受洗 〔基〕receiving [taking] baptism —**수세하다** be baptized

수세공 手細工〈일 또는 수제품〉handiwork; handwork ▶ 많은 사람들이 그녀의 수세공을 칭찬하였다 Many people admired her handwork.

수세다 手— be good at; be a strong player (at); be a skilled hand (at)

수세미 a vegetable sponge; a pot cleaner; a scrub(bing) brush

수세미외 〔植〕a dishcloth [towel] gourd; a sponge cucumber [gourd]; a luffa; a loofah

수소 a bull; 〈거세한〉an ox (pl. oxen); a steer

수소 水素 〔化〕hydrogen

◆수소의 hydrogenous; hydric / 수소와 화합시키다 combine with hydrogen; hydrogenate; hydrogenize / 수소를 제거하다 remove hydrogen 《from》; dehydrogenize; dehydrogenate ━중— heavy hydrogen; deuterium: 3중수소 tritium ━가스 hydrogen gas ━산 hydracid ━이온 a hydrogen ion ━폭탄 a hydrogen [fusion, thermonuclear] bomb; an H-bomb ━화물(化物) a hydride

수소문 搜所聞 asking around ━수소문하다 ask around; inquire here and there
▶많은 곳을 수소문한 끝에 그 가게를 찾았다 I found the store after a great deal of asking around.

수속 手續 (a) procedure; formalities; steps (⇨ 절차) ▶입학 수속은 이미 마쳤습니까? Have you finished the entrance procedure yet?

수송 輸送 transport; transportation; transit; conveyance; traffic; deportation; carriage
◆수송중이다 be in transit [under shipment]
◆상품이 수송중에 파손되었다 The goods were damaged in transit.
━수송하다 convey; transport; deport; carry ━공중— aerial transport; an airlift 육상[해상, 철도, 항공]— transport [carriage] by land [sea, rail, air]; land [marine, railway, air] transport ━━계획 a schedule of transport ━기 a transport (plane) ━난 the difficulty of transportation; 〈난점〉 transportation difficulties ━대(隊) a transportation unit ━량 transport volume; (the volume of) traffic; 〈화물의〉 carloadings ━력 transport [transportation, carrying] capacity; carrying [transit] power ━로 a transport [transportation] route ━비 the cost of transportation; transporting expenses ━선(船) a transport (ship) ━선(線) a line of transportation; a transportation line ━시설 transportation facilities ━열차 a transport train

수수 〔植〕 an African [Indian] millet; 〈고량〉 a kaoliang ■━깡 a millet stalk

수수 收受 receipt ━수수하다 receive

수수 授受 giving and receiving; delivery and receipt [acceptance]; transfer 《of property》
▶두 사람 사이에 금전 수수는 없었다 There was no monetary transfer between the two.
━수수하다 give and receive; deliver; transfer

수수께끼 a riddle; a conundrum; a puzzle; an enigma; a mystery
◆풀기 어려운 수수께끼 a hopeless puzzle / 우주의 수수께끼 the riddle of the universe / 수수께끼같은 puzzling; mysterious; riddling; enigmatic
▶그것은 우리에게는 지금도 풀 수 없는 수수께끼다 It is still a riddle [sealed book] to us.
▶그는 정계의 수수께끼같은 인물이다 He is an enigmatic person in political circles.
〈수수께끼를〉 수수께끼를 내다 give *sb* a puzzle to guess [make out]; ask [set] *sb* a riddle to guess [make out]; put [propose] a riddle to *sb* / 수수께끼를 풀다[알아맞히다] solve [interpret, guess, undo, find out] a riddle; unriddle; answer [solve, work out, make out] a puzzle; solve [untangle] a mystery
〈수수께끼에〉 수수께끼에 싸여 있다 be wrapped up in (a) mystery
▶그 여객기의 폭발은 지금도 수수께끼에 싸여 있다 Mystery still cloaks the explosion of the airliner.
〈수수께끼로〉 수수께끼로 남다 remain an unsolved mystery

수수료 手數料 〈구전〉 a commission; a percentage; brokerage; 〈요금〉 a charge (for trouble); a fee
◆판매 수수료 a selling commission / 수수료를 내다 allow [give] a commission 《of 10% on sales》 / 수수료를 (천원) 받다 charge *sb* a (1000 won) commission
▶이것은 수수료가 없습니다 This is free of charge.
▶은행 송금에는 1000원의 수수료가 붙습니다 It costs one thousand won to make a bank transfer.
▶나는 그것에 대해 비싼 수수료를 물었다 I was charged heavily for it.

수수방관 袖手傍觀 looking on with folded arms ━수수방관하다 look on with folded arms; be [remain] an idle onlooker; stand by idly; take no part in 《a matter》; sit back and watch
▶지금은 수수방관할 때가 아니다 This is no time to stand by idly.

수수하다 mediocre; quiet; 〈빛깔 등이〉 sober; sedate; 〈검소하다〉 plain; simple; modest; 〈점잖다〉 unpretentious; undemonstrative
◆수수한 빛깔 a sober [sedate, quiet, soft] color; a subdued color / 인물이 수수한 여자 a woman of average beauty; a woman passable in appearance / 수수한 무늬 a plain pattern; a pattern of quiet elegance / 수수한 옷차림을 하고 있다 be soberly [quietly] dressed [attired] / 수수하게 살다 lead a plain living
▶그녀의 수수한 태도는 동료들에게 좋은 인상을 주었다 Her modest attitude impressed her co-workers favorably.

수순 手順 〈장기·바둑의〉 a schemed order of the move; an envisaged move order

수술 〔植〕 a stamen 《*pl.* ～s, stamina》; an androecium 《*pl.* -cia》

수술 手術 a surgical operation; an operation
◆간단한[어려운] 수술 a simple [difficult] operation / 수술을 받다 undergo [have, go through] an operation 《for gastric ulcer》; be operated (up)on 《for appendicitis》; go [be] under the knife
▶그 수술은 성공적이었다 The operation was a success.
▶그의 수술은 약 30분 걸렸다 He was in the operation room for about half an hour.
▶최근엔 내시경 수술이 높이 평가되고 있다 Recently endoscopic operations are highly evaluated.
━수술하다 operate 《on a patient for gastric cancer》; perform [conduct] an operation 《on *sb* for》
◆수술할 수 있는[없는] operable [inoperable] / 축농증으로 코를 수술하다 have *one's*

nose operated upon for ozena; undergo an operation on *one's* nose for ozena
■ 대[소]— a major [minor] operation 복부— an operation on the abdomen ■ 대[복] an operating table [gown] —비 charges for operation; operation charges —실 an operating room [[美] theater]; a surgery —자 an operator; an operating surgeon

수습 收拾 control ♦ 사태 수습에 힘쓰다 make an effort to put the situation under control ▶ 사태는 수습 불능이 되었다 The situation became uncontrollable. ⇌ The situation got out of control [hand].
—수습하다 get under control; control; disentangle; manipulate; manage; sort ((a problem)) out; settle; save
♦ 원만히 수습하다 reach a peaceful settlement; come to a perfect understanding / 혼란을 수습하다 disentangle the chaos
▶ 이 난국을 수습할 사람은 없다 Nobody can save the difficult situation.

수습 修習 training; apprenticeship; probation
▶ 그녀는 미용사 수습이 아직 끝나지 않았다 She is still in training to be a beautician.
—수습하다 learn ((the business routine of an office)); receive training ((in)); practice *oneself* ((in a trade))
■ 一간호사 a student nurse; [英] a probationer nurse —공 an apprentice —기간 a period of apprenticeship [probation]; a probationary [probation] period; a term of trial —기자 a cub reporter; a junior reporter —생 an apprentice student; a trainee; a probationer —선원 a landsman

수시로 隨時— 〈언제나〉 (at) any time; at all times; 〈필요에 따라〉 on [upon] occasion; as [whenever] occasion calls [demands, arises]; 〈때때로〉 from time to time
▶ 이 학원은 수시로 학생을 받는다 Students are admitted at any time into this institute.

수식 水蝕 erosion (by the action of water)
수식 修飾 〈장식〉 (a) decoration; ornamentation; embroidery; (an) adornment; (an) embellishment; [樂] (a) figuration; 〈문장 등의〉 [文法] modification; qualification; a rhetorical flourish
—수식하다 decorate; adorn; [文法] modify; qualify; ornament; [樂] figure; 〈윤색하다〉 embellish; embroider; garnish
♦ 명사를 수식하다 qualify [modify] a noun
■ 一어 a modifier; a qualifier
수식 數式 a numerical formula [expression]
수신 水神 the god of water; the water god
수신 受信 the receipt of a message; reception
—수신하다 pick up; receive a message [letter]; receive
▶ 그 방송은 보통 수신기로 수신됩니다 That broadcast can be received on an ordinary (receiving) set.
■ 一라디오— radio reception ■ 一국[소] a receiving station —기 a receiver; a receiving apparatus; a telegraph [radio] receiver; 〈라디오의〉 a receiving [wireless] set —료 a (radio, TV) receiving fee —부(簿) a letter and telegram register —안테나 a receiving antenna —장치 a receiving apparatus [set]

수신 修身 moral culture [training]
—수신하다 cultivate *oneself*; practice moral culture; order *one's* life
수신인 受信人 an addressee; a recipient
♦ 수신인 불명의 편지 a blind letter / 〈편지가〉 수신인 불명으로 돌아오다 be sent back labeled "blind" ["addressee unknown"]
■ 一지불 전보[통화] a collect telegram [call]
수신제가 修身齊家 moral culture and home management ♦ 유학자들은 수신제가를 강조했다 Confucianists emphasized the cultivation of moral culture and good home management. —수신제가하다 cultivate *one's* moral culture and manage [regulate] *one's* family
수심 水深 the depth of water ♦ 수심을 재다 sound [measure] the depth of water; take soundings
▶ 그들은 그곳의 수심을 쟀다 They sounded the depth of water there.
■ 一측량 sounding; plumbing —측량기 a depth-sounding apparatus
수심 垂心 [數] an orthocenter
수심 愁心 〈격정·근심〉 anxiety; gloom; pathos; worry; sadness; sorrow; grief; melancholy
♦ 수심에 잠기다 be sorrow-stricken; be oppressed with sorrow; be sunk [plunged] in grief / 수심을 띠다 wear a worried look; look concerned [anxious, gloomy, worried, sad] / 수심을 풀다 dissipate *one's* anxiety; distract *one's* mind from worry
▶ 그녀는 수심에 잠겨 있다 She is all anxiety.
수심 獸心 a brutal heart
수십 數十 (several) tens (of); scores [dozens] ((of))
♦ 수십대의 자동차 tens of motorcars / 수십만명 hundreds of thousands of people / 수십년간 for several decades / 수십명씩 (떼지어) 오다 people come in [by] scores
▶ 그곳에 수십번 가 보았다 I've been there dozens of times.
♦ 수십만명의 시위대들이 거리를 행진하였다 Hundreds of thousands of demonstrators marched the streets.
수압 水壓 hydraulic [water] pressure ▶ 수압이 약하다 The pressure of the water is low.
■ 一계(計) a water [hydraulic] pressure gauge —관 a hydraulic pipe; a penstock —기관 a hydromotor —력 hydraulic power —리프트 a hydraulic lift —시험 a hydraulic test
수액 樹液 sap; milk ♦ 수액이 많은 sapful; sappy / 수액을 채취하다 sap; tap a tree
수양 收養 adoption; fostering —수양하다 foster; adopt ■ 一부모 foster parents —아들[딸] a foster son [daughter] —아버지[어머니] a foster father [mother] —자식 a foster child; a fosterling
수양 修養 moral [mental] culture; cultivation of the mind; (mental) training; character-building
♦ 수양이 있는[없는] 사람 a cultured [an uncultured] mind [person] / 수양을 쌓다 train

[improve] one's mind [mental] culture; cultivate one's mind; build up one's character
▶ 너는 아직 수양이 모자란다 You are still in need of moral training [culture].
—수양하다 cultivate one's mind; improve oneself
■정신— moral [spiritual] culture ■—법 a method of moral training [culture]; how to cultivate one's mind
수양버들 垂楊— 〔植〕 a weeping willow
수업 修業 pursuit of knowledge; study
—수업하다 pursue knowledge; study
◆응용[이론]물리학을 수업하다 study applied [theoretical] physics
■—연한 the years required for graduation from a school; the years required for completing a course of study : 본교의 수업 연한은 3년입니다 The course of study in our school covers three years. ⇒ Our school requires three years of study. —증서 a certificate of study; a diploma
수업 授業 lesson; class; teaching; instruction; school(work); classwork; classroom work

> 解説 **lesson**은 개인 수업이나 학급의 집단적 수업을 말하고, **class**는 집단적 수업에만 쓰이며 (美에서는 lesson보다 널리 쓰인다. 둘 다 하나하나의 수업을 말할 때에는 가산명사 (countable noun)로 쓰인다. **teaching**은 가르친다는 사실 자체에 중점을 두며, **instruction**은 「조직적 방법으로 행해지는 모든 교육」을 가리킨다. **school**은 수업이 이루어지는 장소로서의 학교를 기능적인 면에서 본 말로서 관사 없이 쓴다.

▶ 김선생님은 지금 수업중입니다 Mr. Kim is teaching (his class) now.
〈수업은[이]〉 영어 수업은 1주일에 몇시간 있습니까? How many English classes [lessons] do you have a week?
▶ 〔會話〕「오늘밤 수업은 몇시부터 하니?」「7시입니다」"What time is class tonight?" "It's at 7:00."
▶ 수업은 8시 반에 시작한다 School begins at 8:30. (▶at 대신 from을 쓸 수 없음)
▶ 오늘 수업은 이것으로 끝 That's all for today. ⇒ I think that will be all for today. (▶교사의 말로 나중 문장이 정중함)
▶ 내일은 오전중 수업이 없습니다 We have no school [class(es), lesson(s)] tomorrow morning.
〈수업을〉 (선생이) 반의 수업을 마치다 dismiss a class / (학교가) 수업을 끝내다 dismiss school / 수업을 빼먹다 dodge [skip, cut] a lesson; play truant (from school)
▶ 그들은 한국사 수업을 받았다 They were taught the lesson on Korean history.
〈수업에〉 수업에 들어가다 〈선생이〉 go to one's class; teach (a school [class]); 〈학생이〉 attend school 〔(Miss N's) lesson〕
▶ 나는 A 선생의 수업에 들어갔다 I attended Mr. A's class.
〈수업중에〉 수업중에 during school hours; in class; at school / 수업중에 졸다 have a doze [nap] during a lesson
—수업하다 teach; instruct; give lessons; give classes ◆ 외국어로 수업하다 conduct a lesson in a foreign language
■ 과외— a special class; an extra lesson
■—료 school [schooling] fee; tuition (fee)
■—시간 school [lesson] hours; hours of teaching; 〈출석한〉 hours of attendance; (lesson) periods ■—일수 the number of school days
수없이 數— innumerably; countlessly; without [out of] number; beyond [out of] count
◆ 수없이 많은 전쟁 희생자 war victims [victims of war] without number; too many war victims [victims of war] to count / 같은 소리를 수없이 되뇌다 repeat the same thing a hundred times / 예를 수없이 들다 give no end of examples
수에즈 운하 —運河 the Suez Canal
수여 授與 〈증서 등의〉 conferment; presentation; 〈상품의〉 awarding ◆ 명예 학위의 수여 the conferment of an honorary degree
—수여하다 give; grant; confer (a degree on sb); award (a medal to a winner); present (sth to sb, sb with sth); 〈훈장을〉 decorate (sb with an order)
▶ 왕은 그에게 훈장을 수여했다 The King decorated him with [awarded him] the order.
수여리 〔昆〕 a female honeybee; a queen bee
수여식 授與式 a conferment ceremony
◆ 군기 수여식 presentation of the colors / 상품 수여식 distribution [awarding] of prizes / 졸업 증서 수여식 a graduation ceremony; (美) commencement exercises
수역 水域 (in) the water area (of, around); (in Korean) waters; 〈강의〉 river basin
■ 경제— an economic zone (off the coast) 공동 규제— a jointly controlled waters [fishing zone] 방위— a military zone 어로— a fishery zone 위험— 〈강의〉 a dangerous area of the river 전관— an exclusive zone : 어업 전관 수역 the exclusive fishing zone [waters] 중립— neutral waters
수연 水鉛 molybdenum ⇨ 몰리브덴
수연 水煙 〈물보라〉 water spray [mist]
수연 壽宴 a birthday feast for an old man (to celebrate his long life)
수열 數列 〔數〕 a series; (a) (numerical) progression; a sequence (of numbers)
■ 등비— a geometrical progression 등차— an arithmetical progression
수염 鬚髥 1 〔사람의〕 〈콧수염〉 a mustache; (英) a moustache; 〈턱수염〉 a beard; 〈구레나룻〉 whiskers
◆ 수염이 덥수룩한 얼굴 a bushy-bearded face / 수염이 있는 mustached; bearded; whiskered / 수염이 없는 beardless; 〈면도하여〉 clean-[smooth-]shaven / 수염을 기르다 grow [raise, cultivate] a mustache [beard]; 〈기르고 있다〉 wear [have] a mustache [beard] / 수염을 깎다 〈자기가〉 shave (oneself); (▶oneself는 생략하는 것이 일반적); 〈이발관에서〉 have [get, take] a shave; get shaved
▶ 수염을 깎아 주시오 I want [need] a shave.
▶ 매일 아침 수염을 깎습니까? Do you shave

every morning?
▶ 그는 보름 동안이나 수염을 깎지 않았다 He has a half month's beard on his chin.
2 【동식물의】 〈호랑이 등의〉 whiskers; 〈염소의〉 a (chin) tuft; 〈물고기의〉 a barbel; 〈보리의〉 barley beard; 〈옥수수의〉 corn silk [tassel]
■ 가짜— 《wear, remove》 a false mustache [beard] 염소— a goatee 황제— an imperial

수염

구레나룻
whiskers

콧수염
mustache

턱수염
beard

수염수리 鬚鷲— 〔鳥〕 a bearded vulture; a lammergeier
수염이 대 자라도 먹어야 양반이다 《속담》 Food comes first even in the maintenance of dignity. ⇌ Sharp stomachs make short graces.
수영 〔植〕 a (sour) sorrel
수영 水泳 swimming; bathing; a swim; 《英》 a bathe ◆수영의 명수 an expert swimmer / 수영을 배우다 learn how to swim; take lessons in swimming
▶ 그는 수영을 잘한다[못한다] He is a good [poor] swimmer. ⇌ He is good [poor] at swimming.
▶ 나는 수영을 전혀 못한다 I can't swim a stroke.
—수영하다 swim; bathe; have a swim
◆수영하러 가다 go for a swim [bathe]; go swimming [bathing]
▶ 우리는 한겨울에 수영하러 갔다 We went midwinter swimming.
■ —경기 (the sport of) swimming; a swimming race —대회 a swimming meet —모 a swimming [bathing] cap —복 a swimming suit; 〈여성용 원피스형〉 a swimsuit; a bathing suit [dress, costume] —선수 a swimmer; 《美》〈여자〉 a mermaid —장 a swimming [bathing] place; a swimming pool —팬츠 bathing drawers; (a pair of) swimming trunks
수예 手藝 handicraft; manual arts; 〈자수〉 fancywork ■ —전 an exhibition of handicraft(s) —품 a fancywork; a handicraft article; (총칭) handiwork; handicrafts
수온 水溫 the temperature of the water; water temperature
수완 手腕 ability; capability; capacity; 〈기량〉 skill; 《美口》 faculty ◆외교 수완 diplomatic ability
〈수완이[은]〉 수완이 있는[없는] 사람 a man of [of no] ability / 수완이 있는 able; capable; competent; talented / 수완이 없는 incapable; incompetent; inefficient
▶ 그의 경영[행정] 수완은 정말로 대단하다 His managerial [administrative] skill is truly amazing.
〈수완〉 정치적 수완을 발휘하다 show [exercise] one's political ability [skill] / 놀라운 수완을 보이다 show [display] remarkable [striking] ability 《in》
▶ 나는 수완을 충분히 발휘할 수 있는 직장을 찾았다 I have found a position where I can show [display] my ability [skill] to the full.
■ —가 a man of ability; an able [a capable] man; (口) a go-getter
수요 需要 demand; request
◆꾸준한 수요 steady demand 《for a commodity》 / 수요가 있다 be in demand / 수요가 크다 〈사물이 주어〉 be much in demand [request]; be in great demand; be greatly wanted / 수요를 충족시키다 supply [meet] the demand
▶ 여름에는 맥주의 수요가 많다 There is a great demand for beer in summer. ⇌ Beer is in great demand in summer.
▶ 공급이 수요를 따르지 못한다 The supply cannot meet the demand.
▶ 사과의 수요는 공급을 상회하고 있다 Demand for apples exceeds [is greater than] supply.
▶ 가격은 수요에 따라 변한다 The price varies with demand.
▶ 수요가 대폭 줄었다 The demand has considerably abated.
■ —곡선 a demand curve —독점 monopsony —예측 demand forecast —자 a consumer: 수요자 금융 the customer's finance system
수요공급 需要供給 supply and demand (▶우리말 어순과 반대) ◆수요공급의 법칙 the law of supply and demand
수요일 水曜日 Wednesday 《略 Wed.》
수욕 水浴 bathing; a bathe —수욕하다 bathe in water; have [take] a bathe
수욕 受辱 suffering insult; humiliation —수욕하다 suffer insult; be insulted; get humiliated; be disgraced
수욕 獸慾 animal [carnal] desires [passion(s)]; bestiality; lust ◆수욕적 bestial; lustful / 수욕에 불타는 lust-mad; (口) sex-crazy / 수욕을 채우다 satisfy [gratify] one's carnal desires
수용 收用 expropriation —수용하다 expropriate 《sb's estate, sb from 《his》 land》 ■ 토지— land expropriation: 토지 수용권 (right of) eminent domain
수용 收容 accommodation; reception; admission; seating; housing; 〈난파 선원 등의〉 picking up; a picking
—수용하다 accommodate 《travelers》; admit 《students to a school》; seat 《so many persons》; receive [take in] 《a patient》; intern [impound] 《prisoners》; house 《sufferers》; 〈구조하다〉 pick up 《shipwrecked sailors》
▶ 이 극장은 300명을 수용할 수 있다 This theater has a (seating) capacity of [has seats for, seats, holds, admits] 300 people.
▶ 그들은 부상자를 병원에 수용했다 They took [carried] the injured to the hospital.
■ —능력 〈극장 등의〉 a seating capacity 《of》; 〈호텔 등의〉 sleeping accommodation(s) 《for

200 persons》 —시설 accommodations —인원 the number of persons to be accommodated [admitted] —자 〈양로원 등의〉 inmates; 〈병원의〉 inpatients; 〈교도소의〉 prisoners

수용 受容 reception; acceptance ♦수용적 receptive; recipient —수용하다 receive; accept ■—력[성] receptive capacity; receptiveness; recipiency; receptivity; recipience

수용 需用 consumption —수용하다 consume ■—자 a consumer; a user; a customer: 전력 수용자 a consumer [user] of electricity —전력 (the amount of) electricity consumed

수용성 水溶性 ♦수용성의 water-soluble ■—비료 water-soluble manure

수용소 收容所 a home; an asylum; a concentration [an internment] camp ■포로— a prisoner of war camp (略 a POW camp)

수용액 水溶液 an aqueous [a water] solution

수용태세 受容態勢 preparedness [readiness, preparations] to receive 《new personnel》; a reception setup 《for immigrants》
♦수용 태세를 갖추다 prepare for (receiving); get ready to (receiving)

수운 水運 water transportation; transportation by water
♦수운의 편의가 좋다 have [enjoy] good water transportation facilities; have good facilities for water transport [transportation] (►transport는 주로 화물의, transportation은 주로 사람의 운송임)

수원 水原 the head [source] 《of a stream》; a riverhead; a fountainhead; a headspring; 〈상수도의 수원지〉 the source of water supply; 〈저수지〉 a reservoir ♦강의 수원을 탐색하다 trace (up) a river to its source
▶이 강의 수원은 히말라야 산중에 있다 This river has its source in [flows from] the Himalayas.

수원 受援 receipt of (foreign) assistance ■—국 a recipient country —태세 arrangements necessary for receipt of foreign assistance

수월 數月 a few months ⇨ 수개월

수월래놀이 〔民俗〕 singing and dancing the *Kanggangsuwŏllae*

수월찮다 〈일이〉 not easy; hard; difficult; 〈수·양이〉 not a few [little]; no small; many; much; considerable
♦수월찮은 큰 수입 a handsome [good, tidy] income / 수월찮이 돈이 들다 cost fairly much of money
▶해결책을 찾아내기란 수월찮은 일이다 It's no simple matter to find a solution.
▶그 책은 읽기가 수월찮다 You can't read the book easily. ⇌ The book is not easy to read.

수월하다 〈쉽다〉 easy; simple
♦수월한 일 an easy [a light] task / 풀기 수월한 문제 a simple [an easy] problem to solve; a problem easy [simple] to solve / 수월히 easily; readily; without difficulty; with ease [facility] / 수월하게 받아들이다 accept (it) readily / 하기가 수월하다 be easy [no trouble] to do; have no difficulty in doing
▶그의 글씨는 읽기가 수월하다 His writing is easy to read.
▶그는 수월하게 문제를 풀었다 He had no difficulty (in) solving the problem. ⇌ He solved the problem with ease.
▶그런 녀석을 이기는 것쯤은 수월하다 I can beat him hands down [easily].
▶이 펜은 저 펜보다 쓰기가 수월하다 This pen writes better than that one.
▶말하기는 수월해도 행하기는 어렵다 It's easier said than done.

수위 水位 a water level
♦수위가 높다[낮다] The water level is high [low].
▶댐의 수위가 1미터 내려갔다 The water level in the dam dropped [fell] by one meter.
■위험— the dangerous water level —계 a water gauge; a hydrograph —표 a watermark

수위 守衞 〈지키는 일〉 guard; 〈경비원〉 a (security) guard; 〈문지기〉 a doorkeeper; a doorman; (英) a porter; a janitor —수위하다 guard ■—실 a gatehouse; a guard office; a porter's lodge —장(長) the chief guard

수위 首位 the premier [first, top] place; the leading [foremost] position
♦수위 다툼 a struggle for primacy / 수위를 차지하다 occupy [win] (the) first place; rank [stand] first (in); head [top] the list (of) / 클래스에서 수위가 되다 be (at) the top of the class; be the best in the class (►be 대신에 become을 쓰면 잘못임)
▶그 팀은 센트럴리그 수위를 탈환했다 The team regained the lead in the Central League.
■—타자 (野) the leading hitter

수유 授乳 〈젖 먹이기〉 nursing; breast-feeding; suckling; lactation
—수유하다 nurse; feed; suckle 《a baby》; give suck [the breast] to 《a child》; lactate
■—기(期) a period of lactation; the lactation period

수육 〈삶은 쇠고기〉 boiled [cooked] beef

수육 獸肉 flesh of animals; 〈식용의〉 meat
♦갓 잡은 수육 green meat

수은 水銀 mercury; quicksilver; hydrargyrum
♦유기— organic mercury ■—광(鑛) mercurial ore —기압계[압력계, 온도계] a mercury barometer [manometer, thermometer] —농약 an agricultural chemical containing mercury —등 a mercury(-vapor) lamp —연고 mercurial [blue] ointment —오염 mercury contamination —전지 a mercury battery —제(劑) a preparation of mercury; a mercurial (preparation) —주 a column of mercury; a mercurial column: 수은주가 30도까지 올라갔다 The mercury went up to thirty degrees. —중독(증) mercurialism; mercurial [mercury] poisoning; hydrargyrism: 수은 중독에 걸리다 suffer from mercury poisoning

수음 手淫 masturbation

수의 壽衣·襚衣 a shroud; cerements; graveclothes; a winding-sheet

수의 隨意 voluntariness; option
♦수의의 voluntary; optional; free / 수의로 freely; voluntarily; at will; as *one* pleases; at *one's* pleasure [option]

—계약 a private [free] contract; a contract ad libitum —근(筋) [解] a voluntary muscle —선택 free choice —운동 voluntary movement

수의 獸醫 a veterinarian ; (英) a veterinary surgeon; (口) a vet
■—과 대학 a veterinary college —업 veterinary (surgeon's) business —학 veterinary science [medicine] —학과 the department of veterinary science

수의사 獸醫師 a veterinarian ⇨ 수의(獸醫)
■—법 the Veterinary License Law

수익 收益 earnings; 〈이익〉 gainings; gains; 〈매상고〉 proceeds; 〈자본에 대한〉 returns; a profit; 〈소득·수입〉 income
♦ 수익이 있는[없는] 거래 a profitable [an unprofitable] transaction / 수익이 있는 장사 a profitable [lucrative] job [business] / 수익을 올리다 realize [make, turn out] a profit; make [fetch] (a million won)
▶ 우리 회사의 수익은 매년 순조롭게 신장하고 있다 Our company's profits have climbed steadily every year.
▶ 음악회 수익은 전부 고아원에 기부됩니다 All the proceeds from the concert will be donated to the orphanage.
▶ 그 회사는 충분한 수익을 올렸다 The company made a satisfactory profit [sufficient profits].
─평균[순, 총, 예정]— average [net, gross, estimated] earnings ■—금 earnings; gains; proceeds —력 earning power —률 an earning rate; 〈주가(株價)의〉 price-earnings ratio —세 profit tax —자산 live assets

수익 受益 earnings (⇨ 수익(收益)) —수익하다 benefit (by an investment); receive benefits (from a project) ■—증권 a beneficiary certificate

수익다 手— 〈익숙해지다〉 get used to (the ways of doing *sth*); get familiar (with)
▶ 그녀는 수익은 솜씨로 양파를 얇게 썬다 She slices an onion with a practiced hand.

수익자 受益者 [經] a beneficiary; a person who stands to benefit (▶ a beneficiary 는 주로 유산·배당금 등을 받는 사람)
♦ 신탁업의 수익자 a beneficiary of a trust business / 수익자 부담의 원칙 the principle that beneficiaries should pay for part of (a project); the benefit principle
▶ 도로의 건설은 수익자 부담으로 한다 Those who will benefit have to bear the cost of road construction [works].

수인 囚人 a prisoner ⇨ 죄수
수인 數人 several persons; a few people
수인성전염병 水因性傳染病 waterborne contagious diseases
수일 數日 (for) a few [several] days
♦ 수일내에 in several [a few] days
▶ 나는 수일 전에 새 차를 샀다 I bought a new car a few days ago.
▶ 수일 후에 그는 나를 만나러 올 것이다 He'll call on me after [in] several days.

수임 受任 acceptance of an appointment [a nomination] —수임하다 be nominated; accept an appointment [office]; take office
■—자 a nominee; an appointee; [法] a mandatory; a mandatary

수입 收入 〈소득〉 an income; earnings; 〈세입〉 a revenue; 〈입금〉 receipts; 〈매상〉 proceeds; takings
♦ 수입과 지출 incomings and outgoings; receipts and expenses; 〈국가의〉 revenue and expenditure / 얼마 안 되는 수입 a scanty [meager, small, limited] income / 수입의 길이 막히다 lose the source of income
〈수입은[이]〉 수입이 좋은 직업 a gainful [profitable] occupation [profession]
▶ 이번 달은 뜻하지 않은 수입이 있었다 I got some unexpected money.
▶ 그는 수입이 많다 His income is large. ⇌ He has [earns, enjoys] a large income.
▶ 그녀는 월 80만원의 수입이 있다 She has an income of eight hundred thousand won a month. ⇌ Her monthly income is [Her monthly earnings are] eight hundred thousand won.
▶ 나의 수입은 5년 전의 2배가 되었다 My income is twice as large as it was five years ago. ⇌ I earn double what I did five years ago.
〈수입을〉 수입을 얻다 earn [gain, obtain] an income (of); derive [draw] *one's* income (from) / 수입을 늘리다 increase [augment] *one's* income
▶ 나는 바자의 수입을 자선 사업에 기부했다 I gave the proceeds from [of] a bazaar to charity.
〈수입으로〉 현재의 수입으로 살아갈 수 있다 I can get along on my present [current] income.
—고정— a periodical [regular, fixed] income 국가— national revenues 세— tax revenue; revenue from tax 실— a net income; net earnings 잡— miscellaneous earnings; sundry receipts 총— a total [gross] income; gross earnings ■—계정 revenue account —인지 a revenue [fiscal] stamp

수입 輸入 import; importation; 〈제도·문물의〉 introduction
♦ 수입의 자유화 the liberalization of imports / 해외로부터의 물자 수입 the imports of goods from abroad / 수입량의 통제 quantitative import controls / 수입을 금지하다 ban [prohibit] the import (of); place a ban on (oil) import / 수입을 제한하다 limit [restrict] the import (of)
▶ 수입(액)이 수출(액)을 웃돌고 있다 Imports exceed [are greater than] exports (in value).
▶ 한국은 외국으로부터의 자동차 수입을 장려 [규제]해 왔다 Korea has promoted [restricted] the import of cars from abroad.
—수입하다 import; introduce
♦ 수입할 수 있는 importable (goods)
▶ 한국은 중동으로부터 많은 원유를 수입하고 있다 Korea imports a lot of crude oil from the Middle East.
■밀— smuggling 자유— free import 직— direct import [importation] ■—가격 an import

수입품

price: 원유의 수입 가격이 올랐다 Import prices of crude oil have increased [gone up]. ―검사 import inspection ―계약 an import contract ―과징금 an import surcharge ―국 an importer; an importing country ―규제 control of imports ―금융 import finance ―금지 an import prohibition ―담보율 the import deposit [mortgage] rate ―대리점 an import agent [―무역 import [incoming] trade ―상[업자] an importer; an import trader [merchant] ―상사 an import firm [house, company] ―성향 the propensity of import ―세 an import duty [tariff] ―송장 an import invoice ―수속 the process of import; importation formalities ―승인서 import license ―신고서 an import declaration ―신용장 an import (letter of) credit ―신청서 〈세관에서의〉 an import entry ―액 the amount of imports ―어음 an import bill ―억제[금지]품목 an import-restricted[-banned] item ―원가 the imported cost; the import price ―의존도 the rate of dependence on imports ―장려금 an import bounty ―제한 import restrictions [controls] ―제한품목표 a negative list ―초과 an excess of imports (over exports); an unfavorable [adverse] balance of trade [trade balance]; a trade deficit; the deficit in the balance of trade; the balance of trade against a country ―할당 an import (allotment) quota ―할당제 the import quota system ―항 an import port; a port of entry ―허가제 the import license system ―허가증 an import license [permit] ―환 an import bill

수입품 輸入品 (overseas) imports; imports from abroad; imported articles [goods, commodities]; import goods; an import item; (총칭) the importation ▪밀― smuggled goods

수자리 〈국경 수비〉 guarding the frontier; 〈민병〉 border [frontier] guards; border posts [patrols] ―수자리하다 guard the frontier

수자원 水資源 water resources
♦수자원의 적극적인 개발 active development [exploitation] of water resources / 한국 수자원 개발공사 the Korea Water Resources Development Corporation / 수자원이 풍부하다 be rich in water resources

수작 秀作 an excellent [outstanding] work 〈of art〉

수작 授爵 〈작위를 줌〉 ennoblement; elevation to the peerage ―수작하다 create *sb* a peer; ennoble; raise [elevate] *sb* to the peerage

수작 酬酌 1 〈술잔을 주고 받음〉 an exchange of cups of wine; an exchange of wineglasses ―수작하다 exchange wineglasses [cups of wine]
2 〈말을 주고 받음〉 an exchange of words; exchanging words; 〈그 말〉 words exchanged; a talk
♦허튼 수작을 하다 talk nonsense; say silly things / (이성에게) 수작을 걸다 court; woo; pay court [*one's* addresses] (to); (口) make a pass [passes] at
―수작하다 exchange remarks [words]; talk back and forth

수잠 〈깊이 들지 않은 잠〉 a doze; 〈특히 낮잠〉 a nap; (口) a catnap ♦수잠을 자다 take [have] a doze [nap]; doze [drop, nod] off

수장 水葬 water burial; burial at sea [in the sea] ―수장하다 bury *sb's* body at sea [in the sea] ▶그의 유체는 수장되었다 His body was burried at sea. ▪―권 burial right at sea

수장 收藏 〈거두어 간직함〉 garnering; storage ―수장하다 garner (up); store up; keep [put] *sth* in storage
♦가구를 창고에 수장하다 put *one's* furniture in storage / 겨울에 대비하여 채소를 수장하다 store (up [away]) vegetables for winter use

수장 袖章 a sleeve badge; sleeve stripes; 〈갈매기표의〉 a chevron

수재 水災 〈범람〉 a flood (disaster); 〈침수〉 an inundation
▶태풍은 각지에 수재를 야기시켰다 The typhoon caused floods in many places [widespread flood disaster].
▪―민 flood sufferers [victims]; sufferers from a flood : 수재민 의연품 relief goods to flood victims

수재 秀才 〈재주〉 great ability [talent]; genius; 〈사람〉 a genius; a prodigy; a talented [bright, brilliant, a highly intelligent] person
♦대단한 수재 a great genius
▶그는 우리학교에서 제일가는 수재였다 He was the brightest [best] student in our school.

수저 spoon and chopsticks; 〈숟가락〉 a spoon
♦은수저 한 벌 a set of silver spoon and chopsticks ▪―통 a spoon stand

수적 數的 numerical
♦수적 우세 numerical superiority (over) / 수적 열세 numerical inferiority / 수적으로 우세하다 be numerically superior (to); exceed 《the enemy》 in number; outnumber 《the enemy》

수전 水田 a paddy field ⇨ 논

수전 水電 〈수력 전기〉 hydroelectricity

수전 水戰 〈해전〉 a battle on the water; water warfare

수전노 守錢奴 a stingy man; a miser; a niggard; a skinflint; a screw; (美俗) a tightwad; (口) a penny pincher ▶저 녀석은 수전노다 He is stingy [miserly, closefisted].

수전증 手顫症 〔韓醫〕 tremor of the hand

수절하다 守節 〈절의를〉 keep [remain faithful to] *one's* principles; hold [stick, live up] to *one's* principles; 〈정절을〉 defend *one's* chastity; retain *one's* virtue; 〈과부가〉 remain unmarried after the death of *one's* husband; remain a widow

수정 水晶 rock crystal; crystallized quartz
♦수정 목걸이 a necklace of crystals; a crystal necklace / 수정처럼 투명한 crystalline; (as) clear as crystal
▶이 호수는 수정처럼 맑다 This lake is crystal-clear.
▪―연(煙)― smoky quartz 자(紫)― amethyst ▪―궁 the Crystal Palace ―세공 crystal ware ―시계 a crystal [quartz] clock [chronometer] ―체 〈눈의〉 the crystalline lens

수정 受精 [生] fertilization; fecundation; [植]〈꽃가루받이〉pollination **―수정하다** be fertilized [fecundated]; be pollinated
■ 인공― artificial insemination: 인공 수정을 시키다 artificially fertilize (eggs) 접촉― fecundation by contact 체내― internal fertilization 체외― external fertilization; 〈인간의〉 in vitro fertilization ―능력 fertility; fertilizing power ―란 a fertilized egg: 미수정란 an unfertilized egg

수정 修正 〈법안·조문 등의〉 (an) amendment; 〈문서 등의〉 (a) revision; 〈계획·의견 등의〉 (a) modification; (an) alteration; 〈잘못의〉 (a) correction; (a) rectification
♦ 논문의 몇 군데에 수정을 가하다 make some modifications to one's thesis
―수정하다 revise; modify; correct; amend; rectify
▶ 위원회는 그 법안을 수정하기로 결정했다 The committee decided to amend the bill.
▶ 자구(字句)를 조금 수정하는 것이 좋겠다 You'd better make some changes [alterations] in the wording.
■ ―예산 a revised budget

수정 修整 〈고쳐 정돈함〉 adjustment; regulation; [寫] retouching; **―수정하다** adjust; regulate; [寫] retouch (a negative)

수정과 水正果 cinnamon flavored ginger punch

수정관 輸精管 [解] the deferent duct
♦ 수정관 절제 (수술) vasectomy

수정안 修正案 〈초안〉 a draft amendment; a proposed revision; 〈수정된 의안〉 an amended [a revised] bill; an amendment
♦ 수정안을 제출하다 propose [put forward] an amendment (to a bill)

수정주의 修正主義 revisionism ♦ 수정주의적인 revisionistic ■ ―자 a revisionist

수정 手製 ♦ 수제의 handmade; handwrought; made by hand
▶ 이것은 수제 스웨터입니다 This is a handmade sweater. ⇌ This sweater is handmade.
▶ 이 테이블은 수제입니다 This is a handmade table. ■ ―인형[폭탄] a handmade doll [bomb] ―품 a handmade article

수제비 soup with dough flakes ♦ 수제비를 뜨다 put flakes of dough into clear soup

수제자 首弟子 one's best [ablest] pupils (of); one's most distinguished disciples (of); one's leading disciple

수조 水槽 a cistern; a water tank ♦ 수조차 a tank car [truck]

수족 手足 hands and feet; the limbs ⇨ 손발
♦ 남의 수족처럼 일하다 serve sb like a tool; move [act] at sb's beck and call
▶ 조부께서는 뇌일혈로 수족을 못쓰게 되셨다 My grandfather came to lose the use of his limbs because of an apoplectic stroke.
▶ 나는 사장의 수족처럼 일했다 I served the president as if I were his tool.

수족 水族 sea creatures; aquatic animals; the finny race [tribe]; water life ■ ―관 an aquarium 《pl. ~s, -ia》: 해양 수족관 an oceanarium

수종 水腫 [醫] dropsy; 〈부종〉 (an) edema

―다리 ⇨ 수중다리

수종 隨從 1 ⇨ 시중 **2** 〈하인〉 an attendant; a servant

수주 受注 acceptance [receiving] an order; booking
▶ 수주가 줄고 있다 Orders are falling off. ⇌ The number of orders received is decreasing.
―수주하다 receive [accept] an order
■ ―액[고] the amount orders received

수준 水準 a level; a standard
♦ 수준 이상[이하]이다 be above [below] standard / …과 같은 수준이다 be on the same [at a] level with…; be on a par with… / 세계적 수준을 유지하다 maintain the world level / 지적 수준을 높이다 raise [improve] the intellectual level [standard] / 수준에 이르다 reach [attain] the level; come up to the standard
▶ 그의 최신작은 수준 이하다 His latest work is below par.
▶ 그녀의 작품은 예술가 수준이다 Her work is on the level of artists.
■ 문화― a cultural level 생활― a standard of living; a living standard: 생활수준을 높이다 [낮추다] raise [lower] the standard of living 세계― a world standard 최고― the highest level; the high-water mark ■ ―기 a level; a water level: 수준기로 측정하다 level; take a level ―선[면] a level line [surface] ―의(儀) a leveling instrument; a surveyor's level ―측량 leveling

수줍다 shy; bashful; timid; diffident; coy
♦ 수줍은 소녀 a modest [shy, bashful] girl / 수줍은 얼굴[미소] bashful looks [smile] / 수줍어 말도 못하다 be coy of speech
▶ 그 소년은 수줍어서 말을 하지[쳐다보지] 못했다 The boy was too shy to speak [look up].

수줍어하다 be [feel] shy; be abashed; be bashful; be embarrassed
▶ 그녀는 칭찬을 듣고 수줍어했다 She looked abashed at the praise she got.
▶ 수줍어하지 말고 네 의견을 말해라 Don't be shy about giving your opinion.

수줍음 bashfulness; shyness; self-consciousness; timidity ♦ 그녀는 수줍음을 잘 탄다 She is very shy [bashful]. ⇌ She is a very shy [bashful] girl.

수중 水中 underwater ♦ 수중의 underwater; subaqueous; aquatic / 수중에 in the water; under water / 수중에 가라앉다 sink under water; be submerged / 수중에서 작업하다 work under water / 수중으로 뛰어들다 jump [plunge] into the water; 〈배에서〉 leap overboard
■ ―발레 water ballet; synchronized swimming ―발사관 a submerged tube ―속력 〈잠수함의〉 an underwater [a submerged] speed ―식물 aquatic plant; hydrophyte ―안경 a hydroscope; a water glass; diving [swimming] goggles ―전파탐지기 a sonar; an asdic ―청음기 a hydrophone; an underwater sound detector ―촬영 underwater photography ―카메라 an underwater camera ―폭뢰 a depth charge [bomb] ―폭발 an underwater explosion [detonation] ―호흡기 a aqualung; a scuba

수중 手中 ♦수중의 돈 ready cash; the money in [on] hand / 수중의 in one's hands; within one's grip [grasp]/ 수중에 넣다 secure; capture; take [gain] possession of; get sth in one's pocket / 수중에 들어오다 come into one's possession; fall into one's hands / …의 수중에 있다 be in the possession [hands] of…; be at the mercy [disposal] of…
▶ 그 도시는 마침내 적의 수중에 들어갔다 The town fell into the enemy's [enemy] hands after all.
▶ 그는 그 회사를 완전히 수중에 넣는 데 성공했다 He succeeded in gaining [taking] full control of the company.

수중다리 a dropsical [dropsied] leg

수중익 水中翼 a hydrofoil ■—선 a hydrofoil (boat)

수증기 水蒸氣 〈자연의〉 (water) vapor; 〈가열한〉 steam ♦대기속의 수증기 the water vapor of the air [in the atmosphere]

수지 收支 income and expenditure; earnings and expenses; revenue and expenditure; balance
〈수지가[는]〉 수지가 맞다 have a balanced income and outgo; 〈장사가〉 pay well; pay off; be on a paying basis; be in the black; 〈직업 등이〉 be remunerative; be paying; 〈거래 등이〉 be profitable; 〈자리 등이〉 be advantageous / 수지가 맞지 않다 〈수지균형이〉 income does not cover [meet] the expenses; 〈장사가〉 do not pay; do not pay off
▶ 이 사업은 수지가 맞는다 This business pays.
▶ 한국의 국제 수지는 적자[흑자]다 Korea's international balance of payments is in the red [black].
〈수지를〉 수지를 맞추다 make (both [two]) ends meet; make 〈it〉
▶ 수지를 맞추느라 진땀을 빼고 있다 I have great difficulty making (both) ends meet.
■ —결산 settlement of accounts : 수지 결산을 하다 settle accounts (with); strike a balance —균형 the equilibrium between incomings and outgoings —일람표 a statement of income and expenditure; a balance sheet

수지 樹脂 〈진득진득한〉 resin; 〈고체의〉 rosin
♦수지의[가 많은] resinous / 수지 상태의 resinoid
■ 고무— gum resin 고형— galipot 천연— (a) natural resin 합성— synthetic resin —가공 plasticization : 수지 가공하다 resinate; resin; treat with resin —광택 resinous luster —비누 resin soup —성 물질 resinoid

수지 獸脂 〈짐승의 기름〉 grease; animal fat; tallow

수지 계산 收支計算 calculation; reckoning; accounts; balancing
♦수지계산을 맞추다 settle the accounts / 수지계산을 밝히다 account for income and expenditure / 수지계산만 따지다 〈타산적이다〉 be given to calculaton; be bent on gain; be calculative

수직 手織 handweaving ♦수직의 handwoven; homespun ■—기 a handloom —물 handwoven fabrics; domestics

수직 垂直 perpendicularity; verticality
♦수직으로 교차하는 두 직선 two lines crossing [meeting] vertically [at right angles]/ 수직의 perpendicular; vertical / 수직으로 perpendicularly; vertically / 제시된 선에 수직으로 선을 긋다 draw a line perpendicular [at right angles] to a given line
▶ 두 선이 수직으로 교차한다[만난다] Two lines cross [meet] at right angles.
▶ 기둥이 바닥과 수직이 아니다 The pole is not perpendicular to the floor.
▶ 헬리콥터는 수직으로 이륙할 수 있다 A helicopter can take off vertically.
■—강하 〔空〕 a vertical descent; a nose dive —경사 〔鑛〕 underlay (of ore) —단층 vertical fault —분포 vertical distribution —사회 vertical society —선[면] a perpendicular [vertical] line [plane] —운동 a vertical movement —이착륙기 a vertical take-off and landing (略 VTOL)

수질 水質 water quality; the quality of water
♦음료로서 적합한 수질 water (of a quality) fit to drink
■—검사 (an) examination of water; 〈분석〉 water analysis : 수질검사를 하다 examine [analyze] the water —관리 water-purity control —오염 water pollution —오염방지 water pollution control —오염방지법 the Water Pollution Prevention Law [Act]

수집 收集 collection; gathering —수집하다 collect; gather
▶ 재활용품의 수집일은 매주 수요일이다 Recyclable goods are picked up every Wednesday.

수집 蒐集 (a) collection; gathering; (an) accumulation
—수집하다 collect; accumulate; make a collection of
▶ 그는 외국 우표를 수집하고 있다 He collects foreign stamps.
▶ 그녀는 자기 책의 자료를 수집하러 한국에 왔다 She came to [visited] Korea to collect materials [data] for her book.
■ 우표— stamp collecting; philately ■—벽 (癖) a mania for collecting things; a collecting mania

수집가 蒐集家 a collector ■ 골동품— a curio collector 미술품— an art collector 우표— a stamp collector; a philatelist

수쪽 〈어음의〉 the right half of a transaction paper; the right half of an IOU [a check]

수차 水車 〈물레방아〉 a water mill; a water wheel; 〈양수기〉 a water meter [gauge]

수차 收差 〔物〕 aberration ♦렌즈의 수차 aberration of a lens ■—구면— spherical aberration

수차 數次 several times
▶ 그들은 수차 조사했다 They investigated several times.
▶ 수차의 시험 끝에 그 제품은 실용화되었다 After a series of tests the products were put into practical use.

수창 首唱 advocacy; originating —수창하다 advocate; promote; be first to 〈do〉 ■—자 an advocate; a pioneer

수채 a drain; a sink; a sewer; 〈설비〉 drainage
♦ 수채를 놓다 lay out a drain / 수채를 쳐내다 clean [scour] a drain [sewer]
▶ 수채가 막혀 있다 The drain is clogged up [blocked].
▶ 수채가 넘친다 The sewage has overflowed.
■—통 a drain pipe **수챗구멍** an outfall; a sinkhole

수채화 水彩畵 a watercolor (painting); a picture [painting] in watercolors
♦ 수채화를 그리다 paint with watercolors
■—가 a watercolor painter; a watercolorist —물감 water colors (▶주로 복수형) —법 water colors; an aquarelle

수척 瘦瘠 〈여윔〉 emaciation; gauntness; leanness; haggardness
—수척하다 thin and worn-out; skinny; emaciated; gaunt; haggard
♦ 수척한 얼굴[모습] a haggard [worn] face [figure] / 수척해지다 get [become] thin [haggard] / 근심걱정으로 수척해지다 be careworn
▶ 어머니께서는 오랜 병환으로 수척해지셨다 My mother has wasted away [has grown thin and worn out, has lost a lot of weight] because of her long illness.

수천 數千 several thousand; thousands
♦ 수천명 several thousand people; thousands of people / 수천만 tens of millions; countless numbers
▶ 그는 수천만원에 이르는 이익을 남겼다 He made a profit of tens of millions of won.

수첩 手帖 a notebook; a memorandum book; (英) a pocketbook
♦ 수첩에 주소를 적다 write [take, jot, put] down the addresses in one's pocketbook

수청 守廳 attendance on a high government official ♦ 수청들다 attend on a high official; 〈기생이〉 (a kisaeng) give sb bed service

수초 水草 〔植〕 a water [an aquatic] plant; a waterweed

수축 收縮 shrinking; shrinkage; contraction; constriction
—수축하다 shrink; contract; be constricted; be shortened; 〈부피가〉 deflate
▶ 이 셔츠는 빨아도 수축하지 않는다 This shirt won't shrink in the wash [in washing].
■—계수 a coefficient of contraction —근 〔解〕 contractile muscles —기 contraction period —력 contractile force [power] —성 contractibility; contractility —한계 shrinkage limit

수축 修築 repair —수축하다 repair; mend ♦ 집을 수축하다 repair a house; make repairs on a house

수출 輸出 export; exportation
♦ 녹다운 수출 〈현지 조립 수출〉 knockdown export / 수출을 늘리다 raise exports; increase the amount of export 《of》 / 농산물의 수출을 금지[허가]하다 prohibit [permit] the export of agricultural products
▶ 자동차의 수출은 금년에도 늘어났다 The export of automobiles [cars] has increased again this year.
▶ 수출은 한국에 있어서 매우 중요한 것이다 The export is essential to Korea.
—수출하다 export; ship abroad
▶ 호주는 한국에 양모를 수출하고 있다 Australia exports wool to Korea.
▶ 당신네 나라에서는 주로 무엇을 수출하고 있습니까? What are the chief exports of your country?
■기아— hunger export 무역외— invisible export 설비[플랜트]— plant export 재— re-export ■—가격 an export price —가득률 the rate of net exchange earning from exports —검사 export inspection —견본 an export sample —경기 an export boom —경쟁력 competitiveness in exports —공업단지 the export industrial complex [park, (英) estate] —국 an exporting country; an exporter (country) —금융 export financing —면장 an export permit —무역 export trade —보험 export insurance —산업 an export industry —상 an exporter; an export trader —상사 an export [a trading] company —세 an export duty —송장 an export invoice —승인서 〈통상산업부의〉 an export license —시장 an export markets: 수출시장의 다변화 diversification of export markets —신고 an export declaration —신용장 an export letter of credit —어음 an export bill —자율규제 voluntary export restriction; self-imposed export restraints —장려 encouragement of export —장려금 an export bounty; a bounty on exports —절차 export procedure [formalities] —제한 restriction of exports; export restriction —진흥정책 export promotion policy —초과 an excess of exports (over imports); a favorable balance of trade [trade balance] —통관수속 customs clearing procedure for exports —항 an export port; an outport —허가 an export permit —환 export exchange [bill]

수출금지 輸出禁止 an (export) embargo 《pl. ~es》; an export ban
♦ 금[무기] 수출금지 an embargo on the export of gold [arms]; a gold [an arms] embargo / 수출금지품 items on the embargo list; items subject to embargo / 수출금지를 해제하다 lift [remove] the embargo 《on》
—수출금지하다 put [place] an embargo 《on》; forbid [prohibit, ban] the export 《of》

수출목표 輸出目標 an export target [goal]
♦ 수출목표액을 50% 초과달성하다 surpass [exceed] the target amount of exports by 50 percent

수출실적 輸出實績 the actual exports; the actual amount exported
▶ 반도체의 수출실적이 근년에 늘어나고 있다 Semiconductor exports have grown in recent years.

수출액 輸出額 the amount of export; exports
▶ 작년은 수출액이 수입액을 밑돌았다 Last year's exports were less [lower] than imports (in value).
■총— the total export

수출업 輸出業 export trade; export business
■—자 an exporter; an export trader

수출입 輸出入 import and export
♦수출입의 차이 an import-export gap; the balance of trade / 수출입의 불균형 an imbalance between imports and exports; a trade imbalance
■—금지품 contraband (goods); contraband imports and exports —은행 an export-import bank; 〈미국의〉 Export-Import Bank (of the United States); Ex-Im Bank —품 the exports and imports

수출품 輸出品 an export (▶혼히 복수형); export [exported] goods [commodities]; articles of export (trade)
▶그들은 새 수출품을 개발중이다 They are developing new products for export.
▶전자기기[자동차]는 한국의 중요 수출품이다 Electronic machines [Automobiles] are the important [major] export of Korea.
■—전람회 an exports exhibition

수출할당 輸出割當 an export quota ■—제 the system of export allotment quotas; the export quota system

수취 受取 receiving; receipt
—수취하다 receive; accept
—어음 bills receivable (略 b.r., B.R., B/R) —인 a recipient; a receiver; 〈화물의〉 a consignee; 〈어음의〉 a payee; a remittee; 〈보험의〉 a beneficiary; 〈편지의〉 an addressee : 그 선적 화물의 수취인은 회사의 무역부다 The consignee of the shipment is the trade department of the company.

수치 羞恥 shame; disgrace; dishonor; humiliation
〈수치가〉 가난은 수치가 아니다 Being poor is no disgrace. ⇌ There is no shame in being poor.
▶그녀의 추문이 가족의 수치가 되었다 Her scandal brought shame [disgrace] on [to] her family.
〈수치를〉 수치를 느끼다 feel shame / 수치를 알다 be sensible to shame; have a sense of shame / 수치를 참다 bear up under one's shame / 수치를 당하다 be put to shame
▶나는 대중 앞에서 수치를 당했다 I was put to shame in public. ⇌ I was humiliated in public.
▶그녀는 수치를 모른다 She is shameless. ⇌ She has no sense of shame.
♦수치를 알아라 For shame! ⇌ Shame (on you)!

수치 數值 〔數〕 numerical value; 〈계산해 얻은 값〉 the result ♦수치를 구하다 evaluate / 대기 오염도를 수치로 설명하다 explain the state of air pollution in numbers
■—검사 numeric check —연산 numerical operation —제어 numerical control

수치스럽다 羞恥— 〈부끄럽다〉 shameful; disgraceful; dishonorable
♦수치스러운 일 a shameful thing; a shame / 수치러운 행실[행위] disgraceful [shameful] behavior [conduct]
▶수치스럽지만 나는 시험에 불합격했습니다 I am shamed to say [admit] it, but I have failed [flunked] the examination.

수치심 羞恥心 a sense of shame
♦수치심이 없는 여자 a shameless woman / 수치심이 없다 have no sense of shame; be lost to (all sense of) shame / 수치심으로 얼굴을 붉히다 blush for [with] shame; blush shyly

수치질 痔疾 〔醫〕 external hemorrhoids; blind piles

수카르노 〈인도네시아의 정치가・대통령〉 Sukarno, Achmed (1901-70)

수캉아지 a male pup; a he-puppy

수캐 a he-dog; a male dog

수컷 a male; 〈새의〉 a cock; 〈코끼리・고래・물소 등 큰 동물의〉 a bull; 〈토끼 등 작은 동물의〉 a buck; a he
◀염소의 수컷 a he-goat
▶그것이 수컷인지 암컷인지 알 수가 없다 I can't tell its sex.
▶이 개는 수컷입니까, 암컷입니까? Is this dog male or female [a he or a she]?

수키와 a convex (roofing) tile ♦수키와와 암키와 convex and concave (roofing) tiles

수탁 受託 trust
—수탁하다 be given in trust; be entrusted with sth; take charge of sth
—금 money given [placed] in trust [charge]; trust money —료 a depository —물 a thing put under [in] one's custody —법원 a court of requisition —자 a trustee; 〈판매의〉 a consignee; 〈권리 등의〉 an assignee —판사 a commissioned judge

수탈 收奪 plundering; exploitation —수탈하다 plunder; exploit; dispossess; deprive

수탉 a cock; 〈美〉 rooster

수태 受胎 〔임신〕 conception; 〔生〕 fecundation; fertilization
—수태하다 become [be] pregnant; conceive
♦수태시키다 have sb pregnant; fecundate; impregnate; fertilize
■—인공 artificial conception [fertilization] ■—고지(告知) 〔가톨릭〕 the Annunciation —(능)력 fertility —조절 conception [birth] control —현상 〔生〕 fertilization; fecundation; impregnation

수통 水桶 a water pail ⇨ 물통

수통 水筒 〈휴대용〉 a canteen; a (drinking) flask; 〈英〉 a water bottle ♦수통의 물을 냄비에 비우다 empty the water out of a canteen into a pan

수통 水筩 〈수관(水管)〉 a water pipe [tube]; a conduit; 〈수도전(栓)〉 a hydrant; a tap

수퇘지 a male pig; a boar

수틀 繡— a wooden embroidery frame; a tambour ♦천을 수틀에 끼우다 stretch a piece of cloth over a tambour

수판 數板 an abacus; a counting board; (a set of) counting beads
♦수판을 잘 놓다 be clever with one's abacus / 수판으로 계산하다 count [calculate] on the abacus / 수판으로 셈하다 use [work] an abacus; count [figure] on the abacus
■—알 a bead (on an abacus)

수평 水平 level; horizontality
♦수평의 level; even; 〈수직에 대해〉 horizontal / 수평으로 horizontally / 수평이 되게 하다

make 《a surface》 level / ···와 수평이다 be level with... / 가로대를 지면과 수평으로 하다 make [keep] a bar level [even] with the ground
▶ 그녀는 기운 액자를 수평으로 했다 She leveled the tilted frame.
■ ―각[거리] a horizontal angle [distance] ―갱도 horizontal gallery [tunnel] ―단층 horizontal fault ―동(動) a horizontal motion [movement, shock] ―력 horizontal force ―면 a horizontal plane; a level (surface) ―분포 horizontal distribution ―비행 (a) level flight: 비행기는 1만 미터 상공에서 수평비행으로 이동했다 The plane leveled off at ten thousand meters. ―(식)사고 lateral thinking ―이동 horizontal migration [mobility]

수평선 水平線 the horizon; 〈수평한 선〉 a horizontal line
♦ 수평선위로 뜨다[나타나다] rise [appear] above the horizon / 수평선 아래로 지다[사라지다] sink [disappear] below the horizon
▶ 수평선상에 지는 태양은 장엄하였다 The setting sun on the horizon was magnificent.

수평운동 水平運動 a social equality movement; a leveling movement ■ ―가 a (social) leveler

수포 水泡 〈물거품〉 foam; a bubble; 〈헛된 결과〉 naught; nothing
▶ 그의 모든 노력은 수포로 돌아갔다 All his efforts have come to nothing [have gone down the drain, have gone up in smoke].

수포 水疱 〔醫〕〈물집〉 a (water) blister; a vesicle (작은); a bulla (큰)
■ ―진(疹) 〔醫〕 vesicular exanthema

수폭 水爆 a hydrogen bomb ⇨ 수소(~폭탄)
■ ―실험 an H-bomb [a thermonuclear] test ―탄두 a hydrogen [thermonuclear] warhead

수표 手票 (美) a check; (英) a cheque
♦ 100 만원권 수표 a check for one million won / 박 선생 앞으로 발행한 수표 a check in favor of Mr. Park / 수표로 지급하다 pay by check; check out / 수표를 발행하다[끊다, 떼다] issue [write out, make out, draw] a check / 수표를 현찰로 바꾸다 cash a check / 수표에 배서하다 endorse a check
▶ 수표가 부도났다 The check is dishonored. ⇌ The check bounces.
■ 개인― a personal check 보증― a certified check; (美) a (bank) treasurer's check 부도― a dishonored check 분실[위조]― a lost [forged] check 여행자― a traveler's check 자기앞― a cashier's check 횡선― a crossed check ―발행인 the issuer of a check, a check drawer ―책[장] (美) a checkbook; (英) a chequebook

수표 數表 a numeration table; mathematical tables

수풀 〈숲〉 a forest; a wood; a grove; 〈덤불〉 a thicket; a bush; a (grass) tussock ♦ 수풀이 우거진 산허리 a thickly wooded hillside

수프 soup
♦ 진한[묽은] 수프 a thick [thin] soup / 수프를 먹다 have [take, eat] soup;〈그릇에 입을 대고〉 drink soup
▶ 수프를 먹을 때는 소리를 내지 마라 Don't make noise when you eat soup.
▶ 나는 저녁 식사에는 꼭 수프를 먹는다 I always have soup at dinner [supper].
■ 야채― vegetable soup ―접시 a soup plate [bowl];〈깊고 뚜껑이 있는〉 a (soup) tureen

수피 樹皮 (the coat of) bark; cortex ♦ 수피를 벗기다 strip the bark from a tree; bark a tree

수피 獸皮 a hide; an animal skin; a fell;〈모피〉 a fur

수필 隨筆 an essay; an occasional essay; random notes; miscellaneous [occasional] writings; a miscellany
♦ 수필을 쓰다 write an essay 《on, about》
▶ ―가 an essayist; a miscellanist ―란 a miscellany column; a column for literary jotting ―문학 essay literature ―집 (collected) essays; a collection of *one*'s essays

수하 手下 1〈손아래〉*one*'s junior
▶ 그는 나의 세살 수하일세 He is three years younger than me.
2〈부하〉a follower; a subordinate; an underling; (총칭) *one*'s men; a following
▶ 그는 많은 수하를 거느리고 있다 He has a lot of men under him. ⇌ He has a lot of followers.

수하 誰何 1〈누구〉who; anyone; anybody
♦ 수하를 막론하고 regardless [irrespective of] persons; whoever; anyone
2〈검문〉a challenge ♦ 보초에게 수하를 받다 be challenged by a sentry
―수하하다 challenge 《an unknown person》

수하다 壽― 〈장수하다〉live a long life; live to a ripe old age
▶ 그는 대대로 수하는 집안 출신이다 He comes from [of] a long-lived family.

수하물 手荷物 (personal) luggage ⇨ 수화물

수학 修學 study; learning; pursuit of knowledge
―수학하다 study; learn; pursue knowledge; get an education
▶ 우리는 홍교수 밑에서 경제학을 수학했다 We studied economics under Prof. Hong.

수학 數學 mathematics (▶ 단수취급); (美口) math; (英口) maths
♦ 수학적으로 mathematically / 수학적 재능이 있다 have a head for mathematics; be clever at mathematics
■ 고등[응용]― higher [applied] mathematics ―가[자] a mathematician ―문제 a mathematical problem; a problem in mathematics ―시간 a mathematics lesson [class]

수학능력시험 修學能力試驗 proficiency test for college education

수학여행 修學旅行 a school excursion [trip]; a study tour; a field trip

> [解說] 영국이나 미국에서는 우리나라에서처럼 학년 전체가 가는「수학여행」은 없으며 교과별로 특정한 시설이나 장소를 찾아가서 학습하는 ***field trip***(견학 여행)이 있다.

♦ 수학여행 가다 make [go on] a school

수해 水害 flood damage; damage by [from] a flood; a flood disaster
♦수해를 입다 suffer from floods; be damaged by flood
■―구제 flood relief ―대책 〈방지의〉 flood-control measures; 〈구제의〉 relief measure for flood victims ―방지 prevention of floods; flood control ―이재민 sufferers from a flood; flood victims ―지 a flooded [flood-stricken] district

수해 樹海 〈광대한 숲〉a sea of trees; a broad expanse of dense woodland

수행 修行 〈수련〉 training; 〈종교적〉ascetic practices; religious austerities
♦절에서 수행을 쌓다 practice religious austerities at a temple / 수행이 모자라다 be not sufficiently trained《in》
―수행하다 train *oneself*《in》; practice asceticism; lead an ascetic life
■―자 a trainee; an ascetic

수행 遂行 accomplishment; achievement; execution; performance; discharge
―수행하다 accomplish; perform; fulfill; carry out [through]; carry [put] into execution; achieve 《*one's* end》
♦임무를 수행하다 perform [carry out, execute] *one's* duties / 임무를 수행하는 중 순직하다 be killed in the pursuit of *one's* duties ▶나는 어떤 일이 있어도 이 일을 수행할 작정이다 I am determined to go through with the undertaking.

수행 隨行 attendance《on a journey》
―수행하다 accompany; follow; attend *sb* on a journey
▶그는 장관을 수행하여 호주에 갔다 He visited Australia as a member of the minister's party.
▶그녀는 무역사절단을 수행하여 싱가포르에 갔다 She accompanied the trade mission to Singapore.

수행원 隨行員 an attendant; a member of *sb's* party; 〈일단〉a party; a suite; a retinue; an entourage
♦장관 및 그 수행원 the minister and his party / 수행원을 거느리다 be accompanied by attendants; go with attendants

수향 水鄕 a riverside [lakeside] district

수험 受驗 undergoing [going through] an examination
♦수험을 준비하다 prepare《*oneself*》for an examination / 수험 준비를 지도하다 coach [tutor]《a student》for an examination
▶그는 수험 공부를 하고 있다 He is studying [cramming] for the examination.
―수험하다 take a test; take [sit for] an examination
■―과목 subjects of examination ―료 an examination fee ―번호 an examinee's (seat) number ―생[자] a student preparing himself for an examination; a testee; an examinee; a candidate for an examination ―자격 qualification for an examination : 수험 자격이 있다 be qualified for an examination ―지옥 the examination ordeal ―참고서 a reference book [manual] for entrance examinations; (口) a crammer ―표 an applicant's identification card; an admission ticket for an examination

수혈 竪穴 a pit; a shaft ■―주거 a pit-style site of an ancient dwelling

수혈 輸血 (a) blood transfusion; transfusion ▶수혈로 그의 목숨을 건졌다 A blood transfusion saved his life.
▶그는 수혈을 받았다 He had [was given] a blood transfusion.
―수혈하다 give a blood transfusion to *sb*; transfuse *sb's* blood《into another》; transfuse《a patient》
■―간염 transfusion hepatitis ―반응 a blood transfusion reaction ―자 a (blood) donor

수형 受刑 being under sentence
▶그는 수형중이다 He is serving [doing] his sentence [time]. ―수형하다 do [serve] time
■―자 a convict; a prisoner under sentence

수호 守護 protection; safeguard; defense
♦신의 수호로 through [by, as the result of] divine protection
―수호하다 protect; guard; keep guard《over, around》; defend
■―성인 a tutelary; 〔가톨릭〕a patron saint ―신 a guardian [tutelar(y)] deity [spirit] ―자 a protector; a guardian ―천사 a guardian angel

수호 修好 friendly relations; amity
♦수호조약을 맺다 conclude a treaty of amity [friendship]《with》

수화 水和 〔化〕hydration ―수화하다 hydrate
■―석회 ⇨ 수산화(~칼슘)

수화 手話 sign language
―수화하다 use [talk in] sign language
■―법 dactylology

수화기 受話器 a (telephone) receiver; an earpiece; 〈헤드폰의〉a handset; a headpiece; 〈무전의〉radio earphones; a receiving set
♦수화기를 들다 lift [take up, pick up] the receiver / 수화기를 내려 놓다 hang up [put back, replace] the receiver / 수화기를 귀에 대다 put [apply] the receiver to *one's* ear / 수화기를 제대로 놓지 않다 leave the phone [receiver] off the rest [cradle]
▶수화기가 제대로 놓여 있지 않다 The receiver [phone] is off the hook.

수화물 水化物 〔化〕a hydrate
수화물 手貨物 (personal) luggage; (美) (hand) baggage
♦수화물 3개 three pieces of baggage / 많은 수화물 much [a lot of] baggage / 수화물을 맡기다 have *one's* baggage checked
▶수화물은 60킬로그램까지 무료입니다 There is no charge for baggage under 60kg.
▶해외여행에는 수화물은 될 수 있는 대로 적게 가져가는 것이 좋다 You had better take as little baggage as possible when you travel abroad.
■―담당자 a luggage clerk; (美) a baggage clerk ―보관소 (美) a baggage room; a left-luggage office ―차 a luggage van; (美) a

baggage car —취급소 a luggage office —표 a luggage [baggage] claim ticket

수확 收穫 〈일〉harvesting; 〈수확물〉a crop; a harvest; a yield; (비유) the fruit (of labor)

> [解說] ***crop***은 가장 일반적인 말로 곡물·야채·과일 등의 수확을 말하며 ***harvest***는 주로 곡물의 수확을 말한다.

♦올해의 밀[쌀]수확 the yield of wheat [rice] this year
▶올해는 쌀의 수확이 좋다[나쁘다] We have a good [poor] crop of rice this year.
▶척박한 땅에서는 수확이 적다 Poor soil produces a small crop.
▶올해의 쌀 수확은 평년작을 밑돌 것으로 보인다 This year's rice crop is estimated to be below the average.
▶나는 그와 오래 이야기했지만 이렇다 할 수확이 없었다 I had a long talk with him, but it yielded nothing particular.
—수확하다 harvest; crop; gather (in) a harvest; reap; gather [take] in
▶바나나는 1년에 두 번 수확한다 Bananas bear two crops a year.
■—기(期) the harvesting season; the harvest time —기(機) a reaping machine; a reaper; a harvester —연도 a crop year —예상 a crop [harvest] estimate —체감 diminishing return

수확고 收穫高 the yield; the crop
♦쌀의 수확고 the rice crop; the yield of rice
♦예상— a crop [harvest] estimate

수회 收賄 acceptance of a bribe; corruption; (美) graft —수회하다 commit bribery; take [accept] a bribe; take graft
■—사건 a bribery case; (美) a graft scandal —자 a bribee; a bribetaker —죄 bribery

수회 數回 a number of times; several times; a few times ♦수회에 걸쳐 several times; on several occasions

수효 數爻 a number; an amount
♦주택의 수효 the number of houses
〈수효가〉수효가 많다[적다] be many [few]; be large [small] in number / 수효가 늘다 grow [increase] in number
▶이 회사는 여성의 수효가 남자보다 많다 In this company there are more women than men [women exceed men] in number.
▶그들은 우리보다 수효가 많았다 We were outnumbered by them. ⇌ We were inferior in number.
〈수효를〉수효를 늘리다[줄이다] increase [decrease] the number of / 수효를 세다 count; count (the) number; take count of

수훈 垂訓 teachings《of Christ》; instruction; a precept —수훈하다 teach; instruct (in)
■산상— (聖) the Sermon on the Mount

수훈 殊勳 distinguished [conspicuous] services; meritorious deeds
♦최고 수훈 선수 〈野〉the most valuable player (略 MVP) / 수훈을 세우다 render distinguished services; distinguish *oneself*《in a battle》
■—상 the outstanding performance award

—타 〈野〉a big [scoring] hit

숙고 熟考 careful consideration; deliberation; mature reflection
—숙고하다 consider *sth* carefully; ponder on [over]; deliberate
♦숙고한 끝에 after long [careful, mature] consideration; after deliberation
▶일을 착수하기 전에 숙고해야 한다 One must think twice before one undertakes anything.

숙군 肅軍 a purge in the army —숙군하다 purge disloyal [corrupt] elements from the army

숙녀 淑女 a lady ♦숙녀다운 ladylike; becoming (to) a lady

숙달 熟達 skill; proficiency; mastery
♦영어 숙달법 how to master English
—숙달하다 master; attain proficiency; become proficient [skillful, skilled]; be adept in [at]
♦숙달한 proficient; skilled; expert; adept / 심장 수술에 숙달한 외과의사 a surgeon skilled in heart surgery
▶1년 남짓으로 영어에 숙달할 수는 없다 You cannot master English in only a year or so. ⇌ It is impossible to attain proficiency in English in just a couple of years.
▶그녀는 프랑스어에 숙달해 있다 She has good command of French.
▶그는 대형화물차 운전에 숙달해 있다 He is an expert at driving large trucks.

숙당하다 肅黨 purge disloyal [corrupt] elements from the party

숙덕 淑德 feminine virtue ♦숙덕이 있는 부인 a virtuous lady; a woman of virtue

숙독 熟讀 careful reading; perusal
—숙독하다 read thoroughly [carefully, attentively, through and through]; peruse
♦서류를 숙독하다 read [examine] documents with great care

숙려 熟慮 careful thinking; deliberation ⇨ 숙고(熟考)

숙련 熟練 skill; mastery; dexterity
♦숙련을 요하는 일 a skilled [delicate] job; a job which requires a lot of skill
▶그것은 상당한 숙련을 요한다 It requires great skill.
—숙련하다 become skillful [dexterous]; get skilled
♦숙련된 파일럿 an expert [a skilled, a skillful] pilot / 숙련된 skilled; skillful; trained; practiced; experienced
▶그들은 연장 다루는 데 숙련되어 있다 They are skillful with [skilled in] tools.
■—자[가] a man of experience; an expert; a practiced [skilled] worker

숙련공 熟練工 a skilled worker [hand, laborer, craftsman]; a master mechanic; (총칭) skilled [trained] labor ■ 미— an unskilled laborer; (총칭) unskilled labor

숙맥 菽麥 1 〈콩과 보리〉beans and barley **2** 〈바보〉a fool; a foolish [stupid] person; a blockhead

숙면 熟眠 a sound [profound, heavy] sleep
—숙면하다 sleep well [soundly]; have a good

숙명

sleep; fall [sink] into a deep sleep
▶ 그는 숙면하고 있다 He is fast [sound, dead] asleep.
▶ 숙면했더니 기분이 상쾌하다 I had a good night's sleep and feel great.

숙명 宿命 fate; destiny; karma
♦ 숙명적(인) fatal / 숙명적으로 fatally
▶ 산에서 죽는 것이 그의 숙명이었다 It was his fate to die in the mountains. ⇌ He was destined to die in the mountains.
▶ 그녀는 유명해질 숙명이었다 It was her destiny to become famous.

숙명론 宿命論 fatalism ♦ 숙명론적(인) fatalistic ■ ―자 a fatalist

숙모 叔母 an aunt; the wife of *one's* father's younger brother

숙박 宿泊 (a) lodging; a stay; 〈군대의〉 billeting; quartering
―숙박하다 stay 《at, with》; lodge 《in, at》; put up 《at》; take up *one's* lodgings; be registered 《at a hotel》; 《美》 check in 《at a hotel》; 〈군대가〉 be billeted; be quartered
♦ 하룻밤 숙박하다 stop for the night; stay overnight / 친구 집에서 숙박하다 stay with a friend; stop at a friend's house / 피난민을 집에 숙박시키다 give the refugees lodging in *one's* home
▶ 그는 그랜드 호텔에 숙박하고 있다 He is registered at the Grand Hotel.
▶ 나는 그곳에서 이틀밤 숙박합니다 I am staying (for) [spending] two nights there.
■ ―계〈屆〉 ⇨ 숙박신고 ―설비 accommodations; hotel facilities ―인 a hotel guest; a lodger; 〈하숙인〉 a boarder

숙박료 宿泊料 hotel charges [expenses]; a hotel bill; accommodation [lodging] charges
♦ 숙박료를 치르다 pay a hotel bill [hotel charges]
▶ 하룻밤 숙박료는 얼마지요? What is the charge for a night?

숙박부 宿泊簿 a hotel register [book]; a visitors' book of a hotel [an inn]; a rooming list
♦ 숙박부에 적다 enter [register] *one's* name (and address) in a hotel register

숙박소 宿泊所 *one's* lodgings [quarters]; 〈여관〉 an inn; a hostel ■ 간이― a cheap lodging house; 《美口》 a flophouse 무료― a free lodging house

숙부 叔父 an uncle; *one's* father's younger brother

숙부드럽다 gentle; meek; modest; quiet

숙사 宿舍 a place to stay; a lodging house; lodgings; quarters; 〈군대의〉 a billet

숙성 夙成 precocity ⇨ 조숙(早熟)
―숙성하다 precocious; 〈서술적〉 be ahead of *one's* years; be big for *one's* age
♦ 숙성한 아이 a precocious child
▶ 그 아이는 나이에 비해 숙성하다 He is too grown-up [smart] for his age.

숙성 熟成 ripening; maturation; 〔電·化〕 aging
―숙성하다 ripen; mature; get mellow
■ ―온도 the ripening temperature

숙소 宿所 〈숙박소〉 *one's* lodgings [quarters]; *one's* (place of) abode; 〈여관〉 an inn; a hotel

♦ 숙소의 배정 assignment [allotment] of lodgings / 숙소를 잡다 take up *one's* lodgings [quarters] / 숙소를 옮기다 change *one's* hotel [lodgings]
▶ 오늘밤은 어디에 숙소를 정할까? Where shall we stay [put up] for the night?

숙수 熟手 a fancy [master] cook; a caterer

숙식 宿食 bed and board; room and board; board and lodging; lodging and boarding
―숙식하다 board and lodge
■ ―비 the charge for room and board : 한 달에 숙박비는 얼마입니까? What [How much] do you charge a month for room and board?

숙어 熟語 〈한자의〉 a Chinese compound word; 〈성구〉 a (set) phrase; an idiomatic phrase; an idiom ■ ―집 a phrase book; a dictionary of phrases

숙어지다 **1** 〈수그러지다〉 hang (down); fall; droop; sag; be bent [inclined]
▶ 나뭇가지들이 열매 무게로 숙어져 있다 The branches are drooping under the weight of the fruit.
2 〈기운이 줄다〉 become less energetic; decline

숙연하다 肅然― 〈조용한〉 silent; quiet; hushed; 〈엄숙한〉 solemn; austere; 〈경건한〉 reverent; reverential ▶ 우리는 모두 숙연하게 앉아 있었다 We all sat in silent awe.

숙영 宿營 billeting; quartering; 〈막사〉 military quarters; billets; a camp ―숙영하다 set up camp; camp; be billeted; be quartered 《in》
■ ―지(地) a billeting area [place]

숙원 宿怨 an old [a deep-seated] grudge; a long-harbored resentment [enmity]; 〈불화〉 an old [a long-standing] feud ♦ 숙원을 품다 have [harbor] an old grudge [resentment]

숙원 宿願 a long-cherished[-fostered] desire [dream]; *one's* heart's desire
▶ 런던에 가는 것은 나의 숙원이었다 I had always wanted to go to London.
▶ 마침내 숙원이 이루어졌다 My dream was finally fulfilled [realized]. ⇌ My dream finally came true.

숙의 熟議 deliberation; careful consultation; exhaustive discussion ―숙의하다 deliberate on; discuss fully; talk over
▶ 시간을 두고 모든 가능성을 숙의하시오 Take your time and talk over all the possibilities.

숙이다 hang down; bend *oneself* (forward); stoop
♦ 머리를 숙이다 bow *one's* head far down; lower *one's* head / 부끄러워 고개를 숙이다 hang [drop] *one's* head in shame / 고개를 수그리고 서다 stand with *one's* head hanging [drooping]
▶ 총소리를 듣자 우리는 모두 몸을 숙였다 We all ducked when we heard the shots.

숙적 宿敵 an old enemy [foe]; a sworn enemy

숙정 肅正 〈단속〉 regulation; enforcement; 〈정화〉 purification
―숙정하다 regulate; enforce; discipline
♦ 공무원의 기강을 숙정하다 enforce discipline among government officials
■ 관기― enforcement of official discipline

숙제 宿題 1 〈학교의〉 homework; a home task; 〈(his)〉 an assignment
♦숙제가 많다 have lots of homework to do / 숙제를 하다 do *one's* homework / 숙제를 도와주다 help sb with (his) homework
▶그 선생님은 언제나 많은 숙제를 낸다 That teacher always gives his students lots of homework [assignments].
2 〈미결 문제〉 a pending [an open] question
♦숙제를 해결하다 settle a pending question / 숙제로 남겨두다 leave sth for future solution
▶그 문제는 2년동안이나 숙제로 남아 있다 The matter has been pending for two years.
■ 방학— a holiday task ■ —장(帳) a homework notebook

숙주 宿主 〔生〕 a host
■ 중간— an intermediate host

숙주(나물) green bean sprouts

숙지 熟知 full knowledge; familiarity
—숙지하다 know well [fully, thoroughly]; be well aware [informed] of; be [become] familiar [well acquainted] with
▶그것은 여러분이 숙지하고 계신 사실입니다 It is a fact (that is) familiar to you all.

숙직 宿直 night duty; (a) night watch —숙직하다 be on night duty; keep night watch
▶누가 오늘 숙직하지요? Who is on duty tonight?
■ —실 a night watchman's room ■ —원 a person on night duty

숙질 叔姪 an uncle and his nephew [niece]
▶그분과는 숙질간입니다 He is my uncle.

숙청 肅淸 purging; a purge; liquidation
▶혁명후 일련의 숙청이 이어졌다 A series of (political) purges followed the revolution.
—숙청하다 purge; liquidate

숙체 宿滯 〔韓醫〕〈만성 소화 불량〉 chronic indigestion [dyspepsia]

숙취 宿醉 the aftereffects of excessive drinking; discomfort after heavy drinking; (美) a hangover; (口) a morning after
—숙취하다 suffer from a hangover; have a bad morning after

숙친하다 熟親— well-acquainted; familiar
▶우리는 숙친한 사이다 We [He and I] are close friends.

숙환 宿患 a long illness; a chronic disease; an inveterate disease; a deep-rooted disease
▶그는 숙환으로 앓고 있다 He is suffering from a protracted illness. ≒ He has been ill in bed for a long time.

순 旬 1 〈열흘 동안〉 (a period of) ten days
♦상[중, 하]순 the first [middle, last] ten days (of a month)
2 〈십년〉 a decade; ten years ▶그는 칠순이 넘었다 He is over seventy years old.

순 筍 a sprout; a shoot; a bud
♦대순 a bamboo shoot [sprout] / 순이 나다 bud; sprout (out); put forth buds / 순을 치다 trim off sprouts; cut [nip] off extra sprouts

순 順 〈순서〉 order; 〈차례〉 a turn
♦번호순 numerical order / 연대순으로 in chronologic(al) order / 연령순으로 by priority of age; according to seniority / 키순으로 서다 stand in order of height / ABC순으로 배열하다 arrange in alphabetical order
▶신청은 선착순으로 접수됩니다 Applications will be accepted in the order of arrival.

순 純 〈순수한〉 pure; genuine; 〈순전한〉 sheer; utter; absolute; 〈금·은 등의〉 pure; fine; sterling; 〈도금 등에 대하여〉 solid; 〈이익 등의〉 net
♦순 거짓말 a downright lie / 순 자산 net worth / 순 중량 net weight / 순 한국식 가옥 an traditional Korean-style house

순간 旬刊 ♦순간지 a magazine published [issued] every ten days

순간 瞬間 a moment; an instant; a second
♦순간의[적인] momentary; brief; instantaneous / 순간적으로 instantaneously; in a moment; in an instant; in a flash (of lightning)
▶우리는 결정적 순간을 기다렸다 We awaited the critical [decisive] moment.
▶한눈 파는 순간 차가 나무에 부딪혔다 My car ran into a tree the instant I took my eyes off the road.
▶모든 것은 순간적으로 일어났다 All that happened in a moment [an instant].
■ —온수기 an instaneous water heater —접착제 (a tube of) instant glue —최대풍속 the maximum instantaneous wind velocity

순견 純絹 pure silk ♦순견의 pure-silk; all-silk
♦ —양말 pure-silk [all-silk] stockings

순결 純潔 〈결백〉 purity; integrity; 〈티없음〉 innocence; immaculacy; 〈동정〉 chastity; virginal purity ♦순결을 잃다 lose *one's* chastity [innocence] / 순결을 빼앗기다 be deprived of *one's* virginity
—순결하다 pure; clean; immaculate; taintless; chaste
♦순결한 사랑 Platonic [pure] love / 마음이 순결한 사람 a purehearted person / 순결한 처녀 a chaste maiden; a virgin
■ —교육 education in sexual morality

순계 純系 〔遺〕 a pure line ■ —분리 a pure line separation ■ —설 a pure line theory

순교 殉敎 martyrdom —순교하다 die a martyr; be martyred; die for *one's* belief [faith]
■ —사(史) a martyrology —자 a martyr; 〈여자〉 a martyress

순국 殉國 dying for *one's* country
—순국하다 die (a martyr) for *one's* country; sacrifice *one's* life for *one's* country
■ —선열 a (patriotic) martyr —정신 the spirit of patriotic martyrdom; patriotism

순금 純金 pure [solid] gold
♦순금 반지 a solid-gold ring / 순금의 solid-gold; all-gold; pure-gold

순 대 (a) Korean-style sausage ♦ 순 대 국 Korean-style sausage soup

순도 純度 purity ♦금의 순도 gold purity / 순도가 높은[낮은] 금 gold of a high [low] degree of purity

순두부 —豆腐 watery [uncurdled] bean curd

순량 純量 net weight

순량하다 順良— good and obedient; gentle; meek; submissive ♦순량한 백성 (a) law-abiding people / 순량한 여자 a docile woman

순례 巡禮 a pilgrimage ―**순례하다** make [go on] a pilgrimage ■―**자** a pilgrim; a palmer ―**지** a place [destination, goal] of pilgrimage; a pilgrimage resort

순록 馴鹿 〔動〕 a reindeer 《*pl.* ~, ~s》; **(총칭)** reindeer

순리 順理 reasonableness; rationality; submission to reason
◆**순리적** reasonable; rational; right / **순리적으로** reasonably; rationally; properly
▶어머니가 자식을 사랑하는 것은 당연한 순리다 It is only natural [stands to reason] that a mother should love her children.

순리 純理 pure reason [logic] ◆**순리적인** rational; logical

순리론 純理論 〔哲〕 rationalism ◆**순리론적** rational; rationalistic ■―**자** a rationalist

순막 瞬膜 〔動〕 a nictating membrane

순면 純綿 pure cotton ◆**순면의** all-cotton ■―**직물[제품]** all-cotton stuff [fabrics]

순모 純毛 pure wool ◆**순모의** all-wool ■―**제품** all-[pure-]wool goods [fabrics]

순무 〔植〕 a turnip

순문학 純文學 pure [serious] literature; **(프)** belles lettres ◆**순문학파의 작가** a literary artist; a serious writer / **순문학의** belletristic ■―**소설** a purely literary novel

순물질 純物質 〔化〕 a pure substance

순박 淳朴·醇朴 (rustic) simplicity; homeliness
―**순박하다** 〈성질이〉 simple and honest; unsophisticated; naive; 〈풍속이〉 homely; simple-mannered
◆**순박한 시골 사람** an unaffected and honest [good-natured] countryman

순방 巡訪 a round of calls [visits] ―**순방하다** make a round of calls; visit one after another
◆**동남아 제국을 순방하다** visit [make a tour of] various Southeast Asian countries

순배 巡杯 ◆**한 순배** one round of drinks / **술잔이 한 순배 돌다** a winecup goes the round of the party / **모두에게 맥주를 한 순배 돌리다** serve out a round of beer to all
―**순배하다** pass 《a winecup》 round

순백 純白 snow white; pure [immaculate] whiteness ◆**순백의 식탁보** a pure-white [snow-white] tablecloth / **순백의** pure-white; white as snow

순번 順番 〈순서〉 order; 〈차례〉 one's turn
▶마침내 내 순번이 되었다 At last my turn came (around).

순보 旬報 a report [bulletin] issued every ten days

순분 純分 fineness ■―**도** 〈금·은의〉 fineness; a degree of purity; 〈금의〉 the number of carats

순사 殉死 suicide committed for one's country; killing oneself on the death of one's lord [master]
―**순사하다** 〈나라를 위하여〉 die for one's country; 〈왕·남편을 뒤따라〉 follow one's master to the grave

순산 順產 an easy delivery [childbirth]
―**순산하다** give an easy birth to; have an easy delivery
▶그녀는 아기를 순산했다 She gave an easy birth [delivery] to a baby. ⇒ The birth of a baby was performed without complications.

순색 純色 pure color; 〈원색〉 the original color; true color; unmixed shade

순서 順序 〈차례〉 (sequent) order; sequence; 〈절차〉 procedure; course; 〈방법〉 a system; a method
◆**식의 순서** the program [order] of the ceremony / **순서대로 말하다** speak in an orderly fashion / **순서가 엉망이다** be out of order [turn] / **순서가 틀리다** be in wrong order / **순서를 바로잡다** correct [adjust] the order / **순서를 뒤바꾸다** reverse [invert] the order / **순서를 어기다** follow the wrong order; upset [confuse] the order / **순서를 밟다** go through due formalities [the proper procedure]
▶순서 부동임 〈무순〉 No set [particular] order is observed. ⇒ In random order.
▶식은 순서대로 진행되었다 The ceremony went as was arranged.
▶상사에게 먼저 말하는 것이 마땅한 순서다 The proper procedure is to speak to the boss first.

순소득 純所得 net income ◆**월 50만원의 순소득** a monthly net income of 500,000 won

순손 純損 a net [dead] loss

순수 巡狩 a royal tour (of inspection) ◆**진흥왕 순수비** the monument commemorating King Chinhŭng's tour ―**순수하다** make a royal tour

순수 純粹 purity; pureness; genuineness
◆**한국어의 순수성을 보존하다** preserve the pure well of Korean undefiled
▶나는 그의 순수에 깊은 감명을 받았다 I was deeply impressed with his purity.
―**순수하다** pure; genuine; true; incorrupt; 〈잡물이 없는〉 unmixed; unadulterated; undiluted
◆**순수한 마음** a pure heart / **순수한 사랑** a genuine love / **음악에 대한 순수한 정열** genuine enthusiasm for music
▶나는 순수한 동기에서 그렇게 했다 I did it from unmixed motives.
▶그는 순수한 이탈리아인이다 He is an Italian born and bred in Italy.
■―**과학** pure science ―**논리학[수학]** pure logic [mathematics] ―**배양** pure culture: **순수배양하다** grow a pure culture ―**이성비판** 〈칸트의〉 *the Critique of Pure Reason* ―**주의** 〔美術〕 purism ―**주의자** a purist

순수입 純收入 net income [earnings, proceeds, receipts]

순순하다 順順― obedient; docile; submissive
◆**순순히** obediently; submissively; quietly; tamely / **순순히 자백하다** confess without concealment; own up / **순순히 물러서다** withdraw without making a fuss
▶그는 그녀의 충고를 순순히 따랐다 He followed her advice obediently. ⇒ He obeyed her advice.
▶그들은 이런 수모를 순순히 당하고 있을 사람들이 아니다 I bet they will not take this humiliation lying down.

순순하다 諄諄— kind and gentle 《in admonishing》 ◆ 순순히 gently; kindly; earnestly / 순순히 타이르다 admonish gently; reason [advise] patiently

순시 巡視 a tour [round] of inspection; an inspection; a round of visits
—순시하다 make a tour [go a round] of inspection; inspect; 〈담당 구역을〉 patrol; walk on one's beat
◆ 공장을 순시하다 inspect [go over] a factory / 학교를 순시하다 patrol the school ground
■ 연두— the new year inspection tour ■—선 a patrol boat —인[자] a patrolman; 〈백화점 매장의〉 a floorwalker

순시 瞬時 a moment; an instant
◆ 순시에 in a moment; in an instant / 순시도 《not》 even for a moment
▶ 나는 어머님 말씀을 순시도 잊을 수 없었다 I couldn't forget my mother's words even for a moment.

순식간 瞬息間 an instant; a moment; a second
◆ 순식간에 in a moment; in an instant; in [like] a flash; suddenly; instantly; in almost no time / 순식간에 먹어치우다 eat [devour] in an instant
▶ 그 소식은 순식간에 사내에 퍼졌다 The news got around fast in the office.
▶ 그것은 순식간에 일어났다 It happened in a moment [in the blink of an eye].

순양 巡洋 a cruise; cruising —순양하다 cruise; sail about

순양전함 巡洋戰艦 a battle cruiser

순양함 巡洋艦 a cruiser ■—경— a light cruiser 보조— an auxiliary [a converted] cruiser 중— a heavy cruiser

순연 順延 postponement; deferment
—순연하다 put off; postpone; defer
▶ 우천시에는 순연합니다 In the event [In case] of rain, it will be put off [postponed] till the next [first] fine day.

순열 順列 〔數〕 (a) permutation ◆ 순열과 조합 permutations and combinations

순위 順位 order; 〈서열〉 ranking; standing; precedence
◆ 순위가 위[아래]다 rank high [low]; be at the top [bottom] of the list / 순위를 다투다 contend for precedence / 순위를 결정하다 decide ranking
■—결정전 〈동점자끼리의〉 a play-off; 〈장애물 경주의〉 a jump-off; 〈사격의〉 a shoot-off; 〈펜싱의〉 a fence-off

순위표 順位表 a ranking [graded] list ◆ 순위표를 만들다 make a graded list 《of》

순은 純銀 pure [solid] silver ◆ 순은 숟가락 a solid-sliver spoon; a spoon of sterling silver / 순은으로 된 pure [solid] silver; all-silver

순음 脣音 〔音聲〕 a labial = 입술(~소리)

순응 順應 adaptation; accommodation; adjustment; sympathy
—순응하다 adapt [adjust, accommodate, (美) acclimate] oneself 《to new circumstances》
◆ 환경에 순응하다 adapt [adjust] oneself to the environment / 사회의 풍습에 순응하다 conform to social manners and customs / 대세에 순응하다 follow the general trend of the times
▶ 그는 시류에 순응하는 사람이다 He goes [swims] with the current of the times.
▶ 그녀는 쉽게 외국 생활에 순응했다 She easily adapted [adjusted] herself to life in a foreign country.
■—성 adaptability; flexibility

순이익 純利益 (a) net profit [gain]; net proceeds [earnings]
◆ 그 거래에서 백만원의 순이익을 올리다 net [make a net profit of] one million won on [from] the deal

순익(금) 純益(金) a net profit ⇨ 순이익

순일 純一 purity; genuineness; homogeneity
—순일하다 pure (and simple); genuine; sheer; uniform; unmixed; homogeneous
■—발생 〔生〕 homogenesis

순장 殉葬 burial of the living with the dead (as an attendant on the death of his lord)
—순장하다 bury sb alive together with 《his》 lord's [master's] body

순전하다 純全— pure; genuine; whole; real; absolute; perfect; downright; complete; out-and-out; thorough
◆ 순전한 바보 an absolute [a complete] fool / 순전한 개인 문제 a purely personal matter / 순전히 purely; wholly; completely / 순전히 돈 때문에 solely for money
▶ 그는 순전한 시인이다 He is a poet every inch of him.
▶ 그는 순전히 호기심에서 했을 뿐이다 He did it simply out of curiosity.
▶ 그녀는 순전히 혼자 힘으로 그 어려운 일을 해냈다 She carried out the difficult work all alone [by herself].

순정 純情 a pure heart [mind]; pure-minded feeling; naivety
◆ 순정적인 unsophisticated; naive; pure in heart / 순정을 바치다 love sb with one's pure and whole heart; love faithfully [sincerely]
■—소설 a love story; a boy-meets-girl story; (口) a puppy [calf] love story

순조 順調 a favorable [normal] condition; favorableness; 〈일의 진전〉 smooth progress

순 조 롭 다 順調— favorable; satisfactory; smooth; normal; 〈서술적〉 be in good condition; be in working order (기계 작동 등이)
◆ 순조로운 날씨 seasonable [favorable] weather / 순조롭게[순조로이] favorably; satisfactorily; smoothly; normally; without trouble; without a hitch / 순조롭게 진행되다 progress satisfactorily; proceed favorably; go smoothly [well]
▶ 엔진은 아주 순조롭다 The engine is in good top condition.
▶ 그는 모든 것이 순조로웠다 Everything went well [ran smoothly] with him.
▶ 그 도로공사는 순조로웠다 The road construction went smoothly [without a hitch].
▶ 환자의 수술 경과가 순조롭다 The patient has been making satisfactory progress since the operation.

순종

▶이 일은 순조롭게 진행되면 내달에 완성된다 This work will be finished next month if everything goes well [everything is O.K.].

순종 純種 a purebred
◆순종의 말 a thoroughbred; a pedigreed horse / 순종의 thoroughbred; purebred; of unmixed [genuine] breed [stock]
■―교배 purebred breeding

순종 順從 obedience; submission
―순종하다 follow obediently; obey meekly; submit to sb willingly
▶그녀는 일평생 남편에게 순종했다 She served her husband obediently [submissively] all her life.

순직 純直 naivety and honesty; simplicity and uprightness ―순직하다 naive and honest; simple and upright; unsophisticated

순직 殉職 death at one's post (of duty)
◆순직 경찰관 a policeman who died (while) on duty
―순직하다 die [be killed] in the line of duty; die at one's post (of duty); be killed at work [in the performance of one's duties]
■―자 a victim to one's duty

순진 純眞 naivety; purity; innocence
―순진하다 naive; innocent; pure; sincere
◆순진한 처녀 an innocent girl / 순진한 어린이들 innocent and naive children / 순진한 마음 a pure heart; a heart of gold / 순진한 사랑 pure [Platonic] love / 순진한 생각 a simple [an unsophisticated] idea
▶그에게는 아직도 순진한 데가 있다 There's still something innocent about him.
▶그 노부인은 소녀처럼 순진했다 The old woman retained her childlike innocence.

순차 order; turn
◆순차로[순차적으로] in (serial [consecutive]) order; successively; one after another; in turn
▶우리는 순차적으로 교장실로 불려갔다 We were summoned to the principal's office one by one.

순찰 巡察 a round of inspection; patrol
▶감시원은 3시간마다 순찰을 돌아야 한다 The watchman has to make his rounds every three hours.
▶그 경찰관은 지금 순찰중이다 The policeman is now on patrol (duty) [on his beat].
―순찰하다 make [go] a round of inspection; patrol; go [walk] the [one's] round(s)
■―구역 a beat; rounds ―대 a patrol party ―대원 a patrolman; a patrol officer ―차 a (police) patrol car; a squad car

순치음 脣齒音 〔音聲〕a labiodental [dentilabial] sound

순탄하다 順坦― 〈평탄하다〉even; level; smooth; 〈순조롭다〉favorable; peaceful; uneventful
◆순탄한 길 a smooth [level] road / 순탄한 생활 an uneventful life / 순탄하게 자라다 be bred in favorable circumstances

순풍 順風 a fair [favorable, tail] wind
▶요트는 순풍을 타고 달렸다 The yacht sailed before [with] the wind.
▶그의 사업은 순풍에 돛단듯 진행됐다 All's going well with his business.
▶인생은 순풍에 돛단듯이 되지는 않는다 Life is by no means smooth [plain] sailing.

순풍미속 淳風美俗 good manners and customs

순하다 順― 1 〈온순하다〉gentle; mild; meek; 〈고분고분하다〉obedient; submissive; docile
◆순한 성질 a gentle nature; a meek disposition / 순한 아이 a docile [an obedient] child
2 〈맛이 부드럽다〉mild; light
◆순한 담배 mild cigarettes
3 〈일이 잘 되다〉smooth; easy; trouble-free; uneventful

순항 巡航 cruising
▶그 유람선은 남태평양을 순항중이다 The pleasure boat is cruising in the South Pacific.
―순항하다 cruise; make a cruise
■―권(圈) a cruising circle ―선 a cruiser; a cruise boat ―속도 cruising speed

순행(운동) 順行(運動) 〔天〕direct motion

순혈 純血 pure blood ⇨ 순종(純種)

순화 純化 purification ―순화하다 purify; refine

순화 醇化 refinement; sublimation
―순화하다 refine; purify; sublimate
◆국어를 순화하다 refine [purify] the Korean language / 비행 소년을 순화하다 guide a delinquent boy upright

순환 循環 circulation; rotation; circle; cycle
◆계절의 순환 the cycle [round] of the seasons / 혈액의 순환 the circulation of blood
▶나는 혈액 순환이 잘 된다[되지 않는다] I have a good [bad] blood circulation.
▶목욕은 혈액 순환에 좋다 Taking a bath is good for the blood circulation.
―순환하다 circulate 《through》; rotate; cycle; recur; repeat; move in a cycle; go in cycles ; go in circles
▶계절은 순환한다 The seasons rotate [revolve].
▶호황과 불경기는 순환한다 Prosperity and depression move in a cycle.
▶혈액은 우리의 체내를 순환한다 Blood circulates in our body.
■―경기― a business [〔英〕trade] cycle: 경기순환설 the cycle theory 악― a vicious circle: 빈곤의 악순환 the vicious circle of poverty ―계통 the circulatory system: 순환계통의 병 a circulatory disease ―곡선 a recurring curve ―급수 〔數〕a recurring series ―기(期) circulation period ―기(器) a circulatory organ ―논법[논증] 〔論〕a circular argument [reasoning]; a vicious circle ―도로 a loop [circular] road: 남산 순환 도로 the Namsan Circular Road ―론 ⇨ 순환(~논법) ―버스 a loop-line [circular] bus ―선(線) a belt [loop] line; 〈철도의〉a circular railway ―소수 〔數〕recurring decimals

순회 巡廻 a round; a patrol; a tour
◆〈극단 등이〉순회중이다 be on tour; 〔美〕be on the road
―순회하다 go [walk] round; go the round(s); go [make] one's rounds; make the round (of); patrol; itinerate; make [go on] a tour (of)

♦담당 구역을 순회하다 make the round of one's assigned block [beat] / 명승지를 순회하다 make a tour of noted places
▶야간 경비원이 건물 안을 순회하고 있다 The night watchman is going around [making his rounds] in the building.
■지방— a provincial tour 《of a theatrical company》 ■—강연 a lecture [lecturing] tour —강연자 an itinerant lecturer; a circuit rider —극단 a touring company [theater, troupe] —대사 a roving ambassador —도서관[문고] an itinerant [itinerating] library; a traveling library; 〈차량〉 a library on wheels; 《美》 a bookmobile —진료소 a traveling clinic
순회공연 巡廻公演 a local [provincial] performance; a show on tour; a road show
♦순회공연 중인 배우들 actors on tour / 순회공연을 하다 take a company on tour
■—단 a theatrical company on the road; 《美》 a road company
순회재판 巡廻裁判 the assizes ■—구 a judicial circuit —소 a circuit court —소판사 a circuit judge
순후하다 淳厚— pure and honest; warmhearted
숟가락 a spoon
♦밥 한 숟가락 a spoonful of rice / 설탕 두 숟가락 two spoonfuls of sugar / 우유 세 숟가락 three spoonfuls of milk / 숟가락으로 뜨다 spoon out [up] / 숟가락으로 젓다 stir with a spoon
■—총 the handle of a spoon
술¹ 〈주류〉 liquor; alcoholic drinks; an intoxicant; wine; spirits; 《俗》 booze

|解說| 「알코올 음료」란 뜻으로는 *alcoholic drinks*나 *alcohol*이 일반적이다. *liquor*는 《英》에서는 널리 술을 의미하는 딱딱한 말인데 《美》에서는 *spirits*처럼 위스키나 브랜디 등 특히 독한 술을 가리킨다.

♦독한[약한] 술 a strong [weak] wine; a hard [light] liquor / 오래 묵은 술 old [aged] wine; old vintage / 술생각이 나다 get thirsty for drink / 술상대를 하다 keep company in drinking
〈술이〉 술이 세다 be a heavy drinker / 술이 약하다 get easily drunk; be easily overcome by drink; be a small [poor] drinker / 술이 늘다 gain in one's alcoholic capacity
▶그는 술이 들어가면 전혀 딴사람이 된다 He looks quite another man when the wine is in.
▶그 사람은 이내 술이 깼다 The man soon sobered up [off].
▶그 놀라운 소식에 그들은 모두 술이 깼다 The alarming news sobered all of them.
〈술을〉 술을 마시다 drink; take liquor; have a drink / 술을 빚다[담그다] brew rice wine / 술을 권하다 offer liquor; ask sb to have some liquor / 술을 대접하다 offer 《a guest》 a drink / 술을 데우다 warm up wine in a bottle; heat wine / 술을 따르다 serve sb with wine; pour out wine 《for sb》; fill sb's cup; fill 《a glass》 with liquor / 술을 삼가다 refrain [abstain] from drinking / 술을 끊다 quit [give up] drinking; cut out wine
▶그는 술을 곱게 마신다 He is merry in his cups. ⇌ He is a good drunk.
▶그는 술을 한 잔도 마시지 못한다 He is a teetotaler by nature.
▶그는 술을 한 잔만 해도 얼굴이 벌개진다 He is easily flushed with a single glass of wine.
▶그는 술을 마셔도 끄떡없다 He carries his liquor well.
▶손님에게 술을 억지로 권하지 마라 You must not press wine on your guest.
〈술에〉 술에 물을 타다 water wine / 술에 빠지다 indulge in wine; give oneself up to drinking; be addicted to drinking / 술에 젖다 be steeped in liquor; be soaked in drink; keep oneself saturated with wine / 술에 취하다 get drunk; become intoxicated
▶그는 술에 취했다 He is drunk.
▶술을 마시는 것은 좋지만 술에 먹히면 안된다 You may drink if you want to, but you must not get drowned in your liquor.
〈술로〉 술로 슬픔을 달래다 drown one's grief in drink / 술로 재산을 들어먹다 drink [guzzle] away one's fortune [property]
▶그는 그날 밤을 술로 지새웠다 They drank the night away.
▶그는 술로 인해 죽었다[병이 났다] He drank himself to death [into illness].
술² 〈쟁기의〉 a share beam
술³ 〈술대〉 a (bamboo) plectrum 《pl. ~s, -tra》; a pick
술⁴ 〈장식용의〉 a tassel; a tuft; a fringe
♦술이 달린 tassel(l)ed; tufted; fringed / 술을 달다 tassel
▶그것은 술이 달린 고급 커튼이었다 It was a fine, fringed curtain.
술⁵ 〈종이·피륙의 부피〉 the bulk 《of a paper》
술⁶ 〈분량〉 a spoonful; a small quantity
♦밥 한 술 a spoonful of rice
술값 〈술먹은 대금〉 (a) drink charge; 〈술 마실 돈〉 money for drink(ing); drink(ing) money; 《英口》 beer money
▶그는 술값을 안 내고 달아나는 버릇이 있다 He has a habit of running away without paying for his drink.
▶급료가 거의 술값으로 나가기도 한다 Sometimes nearly all my salary goes for drink.
술고래 a heavy drinker; a drunkard; a boozer; a tippler; a toper; a soaker
술과 안주를 보면 맹세도 잊는다 《속담》 When wine is in, the wit is out.
술기 —氣 intoxication ⇨ 술기운
술기운 intoxication; tipsiness
♦술기운이 돌다 grow [become, get] tipsy [drunk]; feel the effect of drink
▶그는 술기운이 돌기 시작했다 The liquor has started to affect him.
술김 the influence of liquor
♦술김에 하는 싸움 a drunken brawl / 술김에 부리는 객기 Dutch courage / 술김에 under the influence of liquor [alcohol]; emboldened by liquor / 술김에 싸우다 quarrel [brawl] under the influence of liquor

술꾼 a (heavy) drinker; a tippler; a sot; 〈애주가〉 a thirsty soul
술내 the smell [odor] of liquor; an alcoholic smell
♦술내가 나다 smell of liquor; reek of wine; have an alcoholic breath
술대 〈樂〉〈채〉 a (bamboo) plectrum; a pick
술도가 —都家 a brewery; a brew house; a distillery
술독 〈항아리〉 a liquor jug; 〈술고래〉 a sot; a tippler
술독 —毒 alcohol poisoning ⇨ 주독(酒毒)
술래 a tagger; it ■네가 술래다 You're it.
술래잡기 tag; tig; touch-last; (a game of) hide-and-seek; hy-spy; I-spy ━술래잡기하다 play tag [tig]; play hide-and-seek
술렁거리다 be disturbed [perturbed]; be uneasy [upset]; be unsettled; be in (a) commotion; stir
▶ 그녀의 발언에 순간 장내가 술렁거렸다 Her utterance caused a momentary stir among the audience.
▶ 그 소식으로 온 동네가 술렁거렸다 The whole village was astir with the news.
술맛 the taste [flavor] of wine ♦술맛을 보다 taste wine
술먹은개 a drunkard; a drunken person
술버릇 ♦술버릇이 나쁘다 be quarrelsome in one's cups; be a bad drunk; be a problem [quarrelsome] drinker / 술버릇이 좋다 be a good drunk
술법 術法 〈복술〉 divination; fortunetelling; 〈요술〉 magical tricks; conjury; magic; mysteries; sorcery
♦술법을 쓰다 use magic; practice sorcery [divination]; lay a spell
술병 —瓶 a liquor bottle
술병 —病 sickness caused by drinking; an alcoholic disorder [disease] ♦술병이 나다 drink oneself sick [ill]; be sick from drink
술부 述部 〈文法〉 the predicate
술살 ♦술살이 오르다 grow fat through (habitual) drinking
술상 —床 a drinking table ♦술상을 차리다 prepare dishes for drink; set a drinking table
술수 術數 1 ⇨ 술법(術法)
2 〈술책〉 an artifice; a trick; tactics; strategy; wiles; trickery
♦술수를 쓰다 use tactics [diplomacy]; resort to wiles [trickery, machination]
▶ 어떤 술수도 나한테는 안 통한다 None of your tricks will work on me.
술술 1 〈새어나오는 모양〉in a steady stream
▶ 주전자에서 술이 술술 샌다 Wine is leaking from the kettle in a steady stream.
2 〈비·바람이〉 gently; softly; lightly
▶ 봄바람이 술술 분다 The spring wind is blowing gently [softly].
▶ 비가 술술 내린다 It is raining softly [gently]. ≒ It is drizzling.
3 〈막힘없이〉 fluently; glibly; smoothly; 〈거침없이〉 swimmingly; without a hitch; 〈쉽사리〉 easily; with ease; readily; 〈솔직히〉 frankly; unreservedly

♦술술 말하다 speak fluently [off the reel, without hesitation] / 술술 자백하다 confess frankly [with a good grace] / 어려운 문제를 술술 풀다 solve a hard question easily [without (any) effort] / 목으로 술술 넘어가다 go smoothly down the throat
▶ 이 펜은 술술 써진다 I can write easily with this pen.
▶ 그의 입에서 말이 술술 자연스럽게 흘러나왔다 Words flowed easily and naturally from his lips.
▶ 그는 술이 들어가자 말이 술술 나왔다 Wine loosened his tongue.
▶ 그는 그 질문에 술술 대답했다 He gave a ready answer to the question.
▶ 그는 말을 술술 이어갔다 He went on talking with a flow of eloquence.
▶ 그는 영어를 술술 잘 한다 He speaks fluent English.
▶ 얽힌 실이 술술 풀렸다 The tangled thread straightened out nicely.
▶ 문제가 술술 풀렸다 The problem was solved smoothly.
술시중 serving [waiting] at table ♦술시중을 들다 serve wine; serve sb with liquor
술어 述語 〈文法〉 a predicate ♦술어로 쓰이다 be used as a predicate ■—동사 a predicate verb
술어 術語 a technical term; (총칭) technics; terminology ♦의학상의 술어 a medical term
술은 괼 때 걸러야 한다 (속담) Make hay while the sun shines.
술은 백약의 장 (속담) Wine is the best of all medicines. ⇌ Good wine makes good blood.
술자리 a drinking party ⇨ 주석(酒席)
술잔 —盞 a winecup; a wineglass; a goblet
♦이별의 술잔 a parting cup / 술잔을 돌리다 pass the winecup round; circulate the winecup / 술잔을 부딪치다 touch (their) cups / 술잔을 비우다 drain [drink off] the cup; drink the cup dry / 술잔을 주고받다 exchange cups of wine (with); help one another to wine / 술잔을 채우다 fill a cup / 술잔을 나누며 이야기하다 have a chat (with another) over winecups
술잔치 a drinking party [bout]; a carousal; a revel
♦술잔치를 벌이다 have [go on] a drinking bout; have a carousal
술장사 liquor(-selling) business [trade]
술장수 a liquor [wine] dealer; a wine seller
술집 a drinking house; a bar; a barroom; (美) a saloon; a tavern; (英) a public house; (英口) a pub
♦술집을 돌며 마시다 barhop; go barhopping; (英) do a pub crawl
■—주인 a barkeeper; a saloon keeper; (英) a publican
술찌끼 liquor lees ⇨ 재강
술책 術策 an artifice; a trick; a trap; wiles; resources; a stratagem; a policy
♦술책에 능한 사람 an artful [a resourceful] man; a man of resources; a tactician / 술책을 부리다 resort to tricks

▶ 우리는 적의 술책에 빠졌다 We have fallen into our enemy's trap. ⇌ We were entrapped [taken in] by our enemy. ⇌ We played into the hands of our enemy.

술추렴 pooling the expenses [collecting money] for a drinking bout [party]
―**술추렴하다** pool the expenses for a drinking bout [party]; have everyone chip in for a drinking bout; 《everyone》 give a drinking party by turns

술친구 ―親舊 a boon companion; a drinking companion

술타령 ―打令 indulgence in wine; asking for nothing but liquor
▶ 그는 술타령만 한다 He has nothing but drinking on his mind.
―**술타령하다** indulge in wine; ask for [suggest] nothing but liquor; think only of liquor; be always thirsty

술탈 ―頉 an accident [upset] due to drinking
술통 ―桶 a wine cask [barrel, keg]
술파제 ―劑 a sulfa [sulpha] drug; sulfa
술판 a drinking bout [party]
♦ 술판을 벌이다 hold [give, have] a drinking bout [party]

술회 述懷 〈생각을 말함〉 an effusion of one's thoughts (and feelings); 〈그 말〉 recollections; reminiscences
―**술회하다** relate one's thoughts [recollections]; speak reminiscently [reflectively]; reminisce
♦ 지난날을 술회하다 speak about [give reminiscences of] one's old days; relate the past
▶ 노인은 젊은 시절의 즐거웠던 일을 술회했다 The old man gave pleasant reminiscences of his younger days.

숨 1 〈호흡〉 a breath; breathing; respiration 〈숨이〉 숨이 가쁘다 breathe hard / 숨이 끊어지다 die; gasp one's life away; breathe one's last (breath) / 숨이 답답하다 be choky [stuffy] / 숨이 막히다 be choked / 숨이 아직 붙어 있다 be still breathing; be still alive; show signs of life
▶ 그녀는 숨이 가빠서 말을 잇지 못했다 She stopped talking for lack of breath.
▶ 더워서 숨이 막힐 지경이었다 We were stifled by the heat.
〈숨을〉 숨을 죽이고 with bated breath; in breathless suspense; with breathless interest [attention] / 숨을 들이쉬다 breathe in; take in breath; inhale / 숨을 내쉬다 breathe out [forth]; give out breath; exhale / 숨을 헐떡이다 gasp; pant (for breath); get out [short] of breath / 숨을 죽이다 hold [catch, bate] one's breath; stay with bated breath / 숨을 죽이고 듣다[지켜보다] listen [watch] with breathless attention / 숨을 거두다 die; breathe [gasp] one's last
▶ 구경꾼들은 숨을 죽였다 A hush fell on the onlookers.
▶ 그는 청중 앞에서 잠시 숨을 돌린 후 말문을 열었다 He began to talk to the audience after a little pause.
2 〈채소 등의〉 freshness; crispness 《of fresh vegetables》
▶ 배추가 숨이 죽었다 The cabbage has lost its crispness.

숨가쁘다 〈서술적〉 breathe hard; be out [short] of breath; be panting [puffing, gasping] for breath ♦ 숨가쁘게 out of breath; breathlessly; gaspingly

숨결 breathing; respiration ♦ 봄의 숨결 a breath of spring / 청춘의 숨결 the vigor of youth; youthful energy / 숨결이 거칠다 breathe hard [short, heavily]; be gasping

숨구멍 1 〈숨통〉 the windpipe 2 〔昆〕 a stigma 《pl. ~s, -mata》 3 ⇨ 숫구멍

숨기 ―氣 signs of breathing; a breath
♦ 숨기가 있다[없다] show signs [no sign] of life / 숨기가 약하다 breathe faintly / 아직도 숨기가 있다 be still breathing

숨기다 hide; conceal; bury; veil
♦ 몸을 숨기다 hide [shelter] oneself 《behind, under, in》 / 나이를 숨기다 conceal [make a secret of] one's age / 본색을 숨기다 wear [put on] a mask; disguise oneself / 사실을 숨기다 cover up [wrap up, disguise] a fact / 신원을 숨기다 conceal one's identity / 복병을 숲속에 숨기다 lay an ambush in a thick wood / 범행을 숨기기 위해 방화하다 set a fire to cover up the crime / 범인을 숨겨 주다 harbor a criminal; give shelter to a fugitive
▶ 그는 나무 뒤로 몸을 숨겼다 He hid himself behind the tree.
▶ 그는 차 열쇠를 좌석 밑에 숨겼다 He concealed the car keys under the seat.
▶ 그는 품속에 단도를 숨기고 있었다 He had a knife concealed under his shirt.
▶ 편지는 서류 밑에 숨겨져 있었다 The letter was buried under the papers.
▶ 이것은 숨길 수 없는 사실이다 The fact is not to be disguised. ⇌ This is a patent [an undeniable] fact.
▶ 그는 왼손으로 써서 필적을 숨겼다 He disguised his handwriting by writing with his left hand.
▶ 나는 그가 내게 뭔가 숨기고 있다는 것을 알았다 I knew he was keeping something back from me.
▶ 숨기지 말고 말해 Speak it out. ⇌ 《俗》 Spit it out.
▶ 대부분의 가정에는 남에게 숨기고 싶은 일이 있게 마련이다 Most families have a skeleton in the cupboard [closet].
▶ 그들은 한동안 이혼 사실을 숨기고 있었다 They kept their divorce secret for a time.

숨기척 a breath ⇨ 숨기

숨김 keeping sth secret; concealment; secrecy
♦ 숨김없는 사실 an obvious [a patent] fact / 숨김없는 frank; open (and aboveboard); honest
▶ 하나도 숨김이 없습니다 I am not holding anything back from you. ⇌ I have told you all I know.

숨김없이 without reserve [concealment]; frankly; openly; unreservedly
♦ 숨김없이 말하자면 to be frank with you; frankly speaking / 숨김없이 말하다 speak

(straight) out; be open [frank, straightforward] with sb; make a clean breast of 《a fact》
▶ 자네 생각을 숨김없이 말해 보게 Give me your honest opinion. ⇌ Tell me straight (out) what you think.
▶ 그는 진상을 숨김없이 내게 털어놓았다 He told me the whole truth. ⇌ He made a clean breast of it to me.

숨넘어가다 breathe *one's* last; gasp *one's* life away [out]; expire; die

숨다 **1** 〈몸을 숨기다〉 hide; hide [conceal] *oneself*; take cover; go into hiding; 〈피난하나〉 take [seek] refuge [shelter] 《in, under, behind, with》; 〈사라지다〉 disappear
♦ 숨어서 out of sight; in secret / 나무 뒤에 숨다 hide [cover] *oneself* behind a tree; go [disappear] behind a tree; conceal *oneself* among trees / 벽장 속에 숨다 hide *oneself* in a closet / 숨어 있다 be in hiding; keep out of sight
▶ 그는 나를 보자 재빨리 숨었다 He quickly disappeared when he saw me.
▶ 그 아이는 테이블 밑에 숨었다 The child concealed [hid] himself under the table.
▶ 여우는 바위 뒤에 숨어 있다 A fox is lurking behind the rock.
▶ 그는 틀림없이 이 근방 어딘가에 숨어 있다 He must be hiding somewhere about here.
▶ 나는 아무데도 숨을 곳이 없었다 I found no place to hide myself in.
▶ 달이 구름 뒤로 숨었다 The moon went behind the clouds.
2 〈은둔하다〉 live in seclusion; retire from the world
▶ 그는 속세를 떠나 산중에 숨어 살고 있다 He lives in the mountains, keeping his seclusion from the world.
3 〈알려져 있지 않다〉 be unknown; be anonymous
♦ 숨은 뜻 a latent [hidden] meaning / 숨은 자선가 an unknown [anonymous] philanthropist / 숨은 천재 a hidden genius / 숨은 인재를 찾다 look for an unknown man of talent
▶ 너에게 그런 숨은 재주가 있는 줄 몰랐다 I didn't know you had such a hidden talent.

숨돌리다 recover *one's* breath; take [gather] breath; take [have] a breather; pause for breath
♦ 숨돌릴 틈도 주지 않고 giving *sb* not a moment's respite
▶ 2, 3일 숨돌릴 겨를이 있었으면 좋겠다 I wish I could have a few days' breathing space.
♦ 숨돌릴 겨를도 없을 만큼 바쁘다 I'm too busy to find time for breath. ⇌ I'm so busy that I have hardly any breathing spell.

숨막히다 be choked; be suffocated; be stifled
♦ 숨막히는 더위 a suffocating heat / 숨막히는 접전 a breathtaking close game / 숨막힐 듯한 침묵[긴장] an oppressive silence [tension] / 숨막힐 듯한 쓰레기 냄새 choking odor of garbage / 숨막힐 듯한 속력으로 at a breathless speed
▶ 숨막힐 것 같은 회의 분위기에 진력이 났다 I was tired of the stuffy atmosphere of the meeting.

숨바꼭질 hide-and-seek; I spy; hy spy ─**숨바꼭질하다** play (at) hide-and-seek

숨소리 the sound of breathing ♦ 숨소리를 죽이다 hold [bate] *one's* breath

숨숨하다 slightly pockmarked [pitted]

숨쉬다 breathe; respire; draw (*one's*) breath; take breath
▶ 나는 숨쉴 사이도 없다 I have scarcely time to breathe. ⇌ I have hardly a breathing spell.
▶ 그는 숨쉴 때마다 그르렁거렸다 His throat made a wheezing sound at each breath.

숨어들다 get in by stealth; pass in secretly; steal in [into]
▶ 강도가 방안에 숨어들었다 The burglar stole [sneaked] into a room.
▶ 전쟁 중에 그들은 지하로 숨어들어 정치 활동을 계속했다 During the war they went underground in order to continue their political activities.

숨지다 breathe *one's* last; gasp *one's* life away [out]; expire; die ♦ 교통 사고로 숨지다 die [be killed] in a traffic accident

숨차다 be out [short] of breath [wind]; be breathless; be short-winded[-breathed]
▶ 먼 길을 달려왔더니 숨차다 I am out of breath after running such a long way.
▶ 완만한 비탈을 오르는 데도 숨차다 I pant for breath even when going up a gentle slope.

숨통 ─筒 the windpipe; the trachea 《*pl.* ~s, -cheae》

숫- pure; virgin; spotless; immaculate; undefiled; innocent ♦ 숫백성 the simple and honest people

숫구멍 〈갓난아이의〉 the fontanel(le)

숫기 ─氣 manly openness; boldness
♦ 숫기(가) 없다 be shy [bashful, diffident] / 숫기(가) 좋다 be unabashed [bold, confident, outgoing] / 숫기좋게 말하다 speak out unabashed [unreservedly] / 숫기가 없어 말도 못하다 be coy of speech; be too shy to speak

숫돌 a whetstone; a rubstone; a hone
▶ 소년은 칼을 숫돌에 갈고 있었다 The boy was sharpening [whetting] his knife on the whetstone.

숫되다 naive; artless; unsophisticated; unspoiled; unaffected ♦ 숫된 처녀 an innocent girl

숫보기 〈숫된 사람〉 an innocent [a simple] person; a dove; 〈숫총각〉 an innocent bachelor; 〈숫처녀〉 an innocent girl [virgin]

숫색시 an immaculate virgin ⇨ 숫처녀

숫실 繡─ embroidery thread

숫자 數字 a figure; a number; a numeral
♦ 정확한 숫자 exact [precise] figures / 숫자상의 잘못 a numerical error / 숫자상으로 numerically; in figures / 숫자를 들다 give [cite] figures / 숫자로 나타내다 state [express] in figures / 막대한 숫자에 달하다 reach [attain, amount to, mount up to] big figures
▶ 실업자 수가 기록적인 숫자에 달했다 The number of jobless people has reached record figures.

▶그는 숫자에 밝다[어둡다] He has a good [poor] head for figures.
■로마[아라비아]— Roman [Arabic] numerals 세자리— three figures 유효— significant figures 천문학적— astronomical figures

숫제 1 〈차라리〉 rather 《than》; better 《than》; sooner 《than》; 〈전적으로〉 (not) at all; from the first [beginning]
▶앓느니 숫제 죽지 I would rather [sooner] die than suffer from illness.
▶넌 숫제 포기하는 게 낫겠다 You had better give up.
▶이건 숫제 모르겠다 I can't make head or tail of this.
▶장사가 숫제 안됩니다 My business is no good at all.
▶그가 오리라고는 숫제 기대하지도 않았다 I did not at all expect that he would come.
▶나는 그 책을 숫제 펴보지도 않았다 I never even opened the book.
2 〈진실하게〉 sincerely; heartily; wholeheartedly

숫지다 〈순박하다〉 simple; simplehearted; innocent; homely; naive; 〈인정이 후하다〉 humane; kind

숫처녀 —處女 an immaculate [undefiled, innocent] virgin

숫총각 —總角 an innocent bachelor

숭고 崇高 sublimity; loftiness —숭고하다 lofty; sublime; noble; grand ♦숭고한 이상 a lofty ideal
▶그는 숭고한 정신의 소유자다 He is high-minded [noble-minded].

숭굴숭굴하다 1 〈성질이〉 affable; amiable; pleasant; pleasing; smooth; well-rounded; good-natured; good-humored; easy to get along with
♦숭굴숭굴한 사람 an amiable [a good-natured] person / 숭굴숭굴한 태도 a smooth [bland] manner
▶그는 사람이 숭굴숭굴해졌다 His character has been rounded off.
2 〈생김새가〉 chubby; plump (and buxom); good-looking
♦숭굴숭굴하게 생긴 아이 a chubby child; a plump and well-looking child

숭늉 scorched-rice water; water boiled with burned rice

숭배 崇拜 worship; adoration; admiration; cult; veneration
♦숭배의 대상 an object of veneration / 맹목적인 숭배 blind devotion
—숭배하다 worship; venerate; adore; admire; make an idol of
▶그들은 그를 살아 있는 신으로 숭배한다 They adore him as a living god.
▶그녀는 어느 누구보다도 남편을 숭배했다 She worshiped her husband more than anybody else.
▶그는 칸트를 열렬히 숭배하고 있다 He is an ardent admirer of Kant. ⇌ He has a sincere admiration for Kant.
■개인— the cult of personality; personality cult 영웅— hero worship 우상— idol worship; idolatry 조상— ancestor worship ■—자 a worship(p)er; an adorer; an admirer

숭상 崇尙 respect; veneration —숭상하다 respect; revere; esteem ♦무(武)를 숭상하다 pursue the policy of militarism

숭숭 《chop》 into small pieces ⇨ 송송

숭어 〔魚〕 a gray mullet

숯 charcoal
♦숯이 되다 become charcoal; be charred / 숯을 굽다 burn [make] charcoal
■—가루 charcoal powder [dust] —감 charcoal material —검정 charcoal soot —덩이 a lump of charcoal —등걸 charcoal cinders; half-burned charcoal —섬 a charcoal sack —장수 a charcoal dealer; 〈얼굴이 검은 사람〉 a black-[dark-]faced person

숯가마 a charcoal kiln
♦숯가마에 숯을 굽다 burn [make] charcoal in a charcoal kiln

숯내 the fumes of charcoal; smell of burning charcoal; charcoal smoke ♦숯내(가) 나다 smell charcoal burning / 숯내를 맡다 get poisoned by the fumes of charcoal

숯머리 a headache from inhaling charcoal fumes
♦숯머리를 앓다 be poisoned by the fumes of charcoal

숯불 charcoal fire ♦숯불에 구운 생선 fish grilled over a charcoal fire / 숯불을 피우다 make [build] fire with charcoal

숯이 검정 나무란다 《속담》 The pot calls the kettle black.

숱 thickness; density; richness; quantity
♦숱이 많은 머리 thick [abundant] hair / 머리 숱이 많다 have thick [heavy] hair; have a profusion [wealth] of hair / 머리 숱이 적다 have thin [spare] hair / 머리 숱을 치다 thin *one's* hair out

숱하다 plentiful; abundant; copious; rich; very many; bulky; much; numerous
♦숱한 잘못[불평, 결점] numerous errors [complaints, defects] / 숱하게 많다 be abundant 《in》; be plentiful
▶집에 쥐가 숱하게 많다 The house abounds in [with] rats.
▶그는 돈을 숱하게 쓴다 He spends a great deal of money.
▶숱하게 많은 사람이 그 역사적 유적을 찾는다 A large number of people visit the historic site.

숲 〈큰 숲〉 a forest; 〈작은 숲〉 a wood; woods; a grove
♦소나무 숲 a pine grove / 빌딩 숲 a forest of buildings / 깊은 숲 deep woods / 숲에 사는 사람[동물] a forest dweller [animal]; a forester / 숲으로 도망치다 take to the woods / 숲 속을 걷다[헤매다] walk [wander about] in the woods
▶너는 나무는 보고 숲은 보지 못하는구나 You cannot see the wood [forest] for the trees.
▶연못은 숲 한가운데 있다 The pond is in the middle of a wood.
▶우리는 숲으로 산책을 갔다 We went for a walk in the woods.

▶ 그 울창한 숲 속은 낮에도 어둡다 It is dark in the dense forest even during the daytime.
▶ 그 소나무 숲을 지나면 해안이 나온다 If you cross the pine groves [go through the pine woods], you will come out on the seashore.
■ ―길 a forest [woodland] path

쉬(이) Shoo! ▶ 그녀는 닭을 쉬(이) 하고 쫓았다 She shooed the rooster away.

쉬[1] 〈파리의 알〉 eggs of a fly; flyblows ♦ 파리가 쉬를 슬다 a fly lays eggs (upon food); a fly blows (food) ▶ 과일에 쉬를 스는 파리도 있다 Some flies blow fruit.

쉬[2] easily ⇨ 쉬이

쉬[3] 〈제지하는 소리〉 Hush!; Sh!; Mum! ▶ 쉬, 조용히 해라 Hush! ⇌ Be quiet! ⇌ Silence!

쉬[4] (兒) Pee!; Piddle!; Wee-wee!; (卑) Piss! ―쉬하다 pee; piddle; piss ♦ 바지에 쉬하다 wet one's pants

쉬다[1] 〈음식이〉 go bad; turn sour; stale; spoil ♦ 쉰 내 a sourish [stale] smell / 쉰 밥 spoiled rice / 쉰 음식 spoiled food
▶ 우유가 쉬었다 The milk has turned sour.
▶ 쉰 내가 난다 It smells as if it has gone bad.

쉬다[2] 〈목소리가〉 get [become, go, grow] hoarse [husky]; hoarsen ♦ 목이 쉬도록 소리지르다[응원하다] shout [cheer] oneself hoarse / 쉰 목소리로 이야기하다 talk in a husky [hoarse] voice
▶ 그는 너무 소리를 질러서 목이 쉬었다 He raved [shouted] himself hoarse.
▶ 나는 감기 때문에 목소리가 쉬었다 My voice is hoarse from a cold. ⇌ I have a hoarse voice from a cold.
▶ 나는 노래를 너무 많이 불러서 목이 쉬었다 I lost my voice by singing too much.
▶ 오늘은 목소리가 쉬어 노래를 못하겠다 My voice is husky today and I can't sing.

쉬다[3] 1 〈휴식하다〉 rest; take [have] a rest; take a break; relax ♦ 쉬는 시간 a break; a recess; an intermission / 쉬게 하다 give 《sb, a horse》 a rest; rest 《one's men》 / 쉬고 있다 be at rest; be resting / 쉴 사이도 없다 have no time to rest
▶ 좀 쉬자 Let's take [have] a rest for a while.
▶ 일은 좀 놓고 쉬지 그래 Why don't you leave work and take a rest?
▶ 두어 시간 쉬면 나아질 거야 A few hours' rest will set [put] you all right.
▶ 푹 쉬어서 몸이 가뿐하다 I feel thoroughly rested.
▶ 열중 쉬어 (口令) Parade rest!
▶ 편히 쉬어 (口令) At ease! ⇌ Stand at ease!
2 〈일·활동을〉 stop [drop, knock off] 《work》; take a rest from 《one's work》; give oneself rest; 〈중단하다〉 suspend; pause; discontinue; 〈결근·결석하다〉 be absent 《from》; stay [keep] away 《from》; do not attend 《school》; 〈휴가를 내다〉 take a holiday; have 《a day》 off; be off ♦ 일을 쉬다 take a rest from work / 하루 쉬다 take [have] a day off / 이삼일 쉬다 take a few days' holiday
▶ 감기때문에 어제 쉬었다 I took yesterday off on account of a cold.
▶ 그는 오늘 하루 쉬고 있다 He has a day off today.
▶ 당신은 한 달간 쉬어야 합니다 You need a month off.
▶ 휴일에는 모든 일을 쉰다 All work is laid aside on holidays.
▶ 오늘은 학교가 쉰다 We have no school today.
▶ 은행은 일요일엔 쉰다 Banks are closed on Sundays.
▶ 그 기계는 현재 쉬고 있다 The machine is now standing idle.
▶ 여름에는 장사를 쉽니다 We do not keep on this business in summer.
▶ 우리 공장은 일을 쉬고 있다 Work is suspended at our factory. ⇌ Our factory has suspended operation.
▶ 나는 어제 직장을 쉬었다 I was absent from the office yesterday.
3 〈머무르다〉 stop; put up 《at an inn》; stay 《with sb》
▶ 오늘밤은 저희 집에서 쉬시죠 Why don't you stay with us tonight?
4 〈자다〉 sleep; go to sleep [rest]
▶ 편히 쉬세요 Good night.
▶ 간밤엔 잘 쉬었습니다 I slept well last night.
▶ 그녀는 잘 쉬고 있다 She is fast asleep.

쉬다[4] 〈숨을〉 breathe; respire; take [draw] breath ♦ 깊이[길게] 한숨을 쉬며 with a deep [long] sigh / 한숨을 쉬다 sigh; heave [draw] a sigh / 깊이 숨을 쉬다 draw a deep breath / 안도의 숨을 쉬다 heave [give, breathe] a sigh of relief

쉬르리얼리즘 surrealism; superrealism ♦ 쉬르리얼리즘의 surrealistic

쉬쉬하다 hush [cover, smother] up 《a scandal》; (俗) hush-hush ♦ 쉬쉬하며 말하다 talk hush-hush

쉬엄쉬엄 with frequent rests; by easy [short] stages; off and on; on and off; in an off-and-on way; intermittently
▶ 우리는 쉬엄쉬엄 산에 올라갔다 We climbed the mountain resting at several intervals [with frequent stops to rest].
▶ 나는 쉬엄쉬엄 계단을 올라갔다 I went up the stairs taking a rest occasionally.

쉬이 1 〈쉽게〉 easily; readily; with ease; without difficulty ♦ 쉬이 풀 수 있는 문제 a problem easy to solve
▶ 그 문제는 쉬이 풀릴 것 같지 않다 The problem is not likely to be solved with ease.
▶ 그런 제의는 쉬이 받아들일 수 없다 I can't accept such an offer so readily.
2 〈곧〉 soon; before long; presently; shortly; by and by
▶ 나이를 먹으면 쉬이 피로해진다 One tires quickly with age. ⇌ You tire easily when you get old.
▶ 쉬이 또 찾아뵙겠습니다 I will call again one of these days.
▶ 쉬이 더워지는 방이 쉬이 식는다 (속담) Soon hot, soon cold.

쉬지근하다 somewhat stale-smelling; smell-

ing sourish
쉬척지근하다 quite stale-smelling; smelling very sour
쉰 fifty ♦쉰 살 fifty years of age / 나이 쉰을 바라보다 be close upon fifty; be getting on for [to] fifty
쉴새없이 incessantly; continuously; continually; unceasingly; ceaselessly; without a letup; without a break
♦쉴새없이 일하다 work without rest [stopping]/ 쉴새없이 지껄이다 talk without ceasing [a pause]; chatter ceaselessly; have no end of talk
▶쉴새없이 전화가 걸려왔다 I had calls one after another.
쉼표 ―標 〚樂〛 a rest; a pause ━**4분**― a quarter [英] crotchet] rest 온[2분]― a whole [half] rest 8분― an eighth rest
쉽다 1〈용이하다〉easy; simple; light;〈평이하다〉plain
♦쉬운 문제 a simple [an easy] question / 쉽게 readily; simply; plainly; with ease [facility]; without difficulty / 쉽게 말하면 plainly speaking; in plain speech / 쉽게 문제를 해결하다 solve a problem easily / 읽기 쉽다 be easy to read; be easily read / 쉬운 글로 쓰다 write in plain language
▶이 일이라면 쉽게 해낼 수 있다 I can finish this work without difficulty.
▶이렇게 쉬운 일도 없다 Nothing can be simpler [easier] than this.
▶쉽게 번 돈은 쉽게 나가는 법 (속담) Easy come, easy go.
▶말하기는 쉬우나 행하기는 어렵다 It's easier said than done.
▶얻기 쉬운 것은 잃기도 쉽다 (속담) Light come, light go. ⇌ Soon gotten, soon gone.
▶외국어를 마스터하기란 쉬운 일이 아니다 It is no easy job [not easy] to master a foreign language.
▶그 책은 쉬운 영어로 쓰여 있다 The book is written in simple [easy, plain] English.
2〈경향〉(be) apt [prone, liable, ready] ((to do))
♦감기에 걸리기 쉽다 be susceptible [sensitive, subject] to a cold; be apt to take a cold; be liable to catch (a) cold / 부서지기 쉽다 be easy to break; break easily
▶사람은 이기적이기 쉽다 People are liable [apt] to be selfish.
▶우리는 남을 나쁘게 생각하기 쉽다 We are apt to think ill of others.
▶젊은이들은 게을러지기 쉽다 The young men are inclined to be lazy.
쉽사리 easily; readily; with ease; without trouble [difficulty, effort]; with no effort; hands down
♦쉽사리 이기다 win easily; win an easy victory ((over)); beat *sb* hands down / 쉽사리 돈을 벌다 make easy money [gain]/ 쉽사리 접근할 수 없다 be difficult of access
▶그는 그 문제를 쉽사리 풀 수 있었다 He found no difficulty in solving the problem.
▶이 문은 쉽사리 열리지 않는다 This door will not open.
▶그의 병은 쉽사리 낫지 않았다 It was long before he got well.
▶그가 쉽사리 승낙할 것 같지 않다 I am afraid he will not consent readily.
슈미즈 a slip; a chemise
슈크림 a cream puff; (프) chou à la crème
슈트〈의복〉a suit ━케이스 a suitcase
슈퍼마켓 a supermarket
슈퍼맨 a superman
스가랴〚聖〛(The Book of) Zechariah (略 Zech.)
스내치〚力道〛the snatch ⇨ 인상(引上) 2
스낵《have, eat》a snack

[解說] *snack*은 샌드위치나 케이크 등의 「경식(輕食)」을 말하며 경식과 soft drink를 파는 가게를 snack bar라 한다. snack bar에서는 보통 술은 팔지 않는다.

━바 a snack bar [counter, stand]
스냅 1〚野〛a snap
▶투수는 스냅을 주어 볼을 던졌다 The pitcher threw a ball with a snap.
2 ⇨ 스냅사진
스냅사진 ―寫眞 a snapshot; a snap ♦스냅사진을 찍다 take a snapshot ((of)); snap(shot)
▶스냅사진을 두어 장 찍어 주시겠습니까? Would you take a few snapshots of me?
스님 1〈사승(師僧)〉one's teacher [master] in Buddhist faith;〈호칭〉(the) Reverend (略 Rev.) 2〈중〉a Buddhist priest [monk]; a bonze
스라소니〚動〛a lynx (*pl.* ~ (es))
스르르 gently; softly;〈저절로〉of itself
♦눈이 스르르 감기다 one's eyes close softly / 입에서 스르르 녹다 melt away in the mouth
▶매듭이 스르르 풀렸다 The knot came untied of itself.
-스름하다 1〈빛깔〉tinged with...; somewhat; -ish
2〈형상〉somewhat; -ish
스리랑카 Sri Lanka;〈공식명〉the Democratic Socialist Republic of Sri Lanka ♦스리랑카의 Sri Lankan
━사람 a Sri Lankan
스릴〈전율〉a thrill ♦스릴 있는 이야기 a thrilling story / 스릴을 느끼다 have a kick [thrill] ((from)); be thrilled ((by))
▶그 영화는 스릴 만점이었다 The film was full of thrills.
스릴러〈공포영화·소설〉a thriller
스마트하다 smart; stylish; spruce; chic
스매시〈탁구 등의〉a smash ━**스매시하다** smash (a ball)
스멀거리다 itch; feel itchy [creepy, crawly]; be creepy-crawly
▶등이 스멀거린다 I feel itchy in my back. ⇌ My back itches.
스멀스멀하다 itch
스모그 smog
♦스모그가 심한 smoggy
▶그 도시 상공에는 스모그가 짙게 깔렸다 A heavy smog hung over the city.

스무 twenty ⇨ 스물
♦ 스무살의 청년 a young man twenty years old; a young man of twenty / 공 스무개 twenty balls; a score of balls
■—날 the 20th day; twenty days —번째 the twentieth

스무드하다 smooth ▶ 만사가 스무드하게 진행되었다 Everything went smoothly. ≒ Everything went off without a hitch.

스물 twenty; a score; 〈스무살〉 twenty years of age; one's twentieth year
▶ 그는 아직 스물 안짝이다 He is still in his teens.
▶ 그 여자는 스물 한두 살쯤 되어 보인다 She is apparently in early twenties.

스미다 1 〈액체·기체 등이〉 soak through [into]; sink in [into]; infiltrate (into, through); permeate; penetrate; pierce
▶ 비가 천장으로 스며들다 The rain has soaked through the ceiling.
▶ 물은 천천히 땅속으로 스며들었다 The water slowly sank into the ground.
▶ 한기가 뼛속까지 스며들었다 I have been chilled to the bone. ≒ It has been bitingly cold.
▶ 상처에서 피가 스며나왔다 The wound oozed blood.
2 〈감정·사상 등이〉 sink into; be impressed (on one's mind); filter into [through]; be imbued
▶ 그의 마음속에 불안이 스며들었다 Anxiety crept into his mind.
▶ 그의 충고가 가슴에 스며들었다 His advice was well imprinted on our minds.
▶ 이런 새로운 사상이 그들의 마음에 스며들고 있었다 These new ideas were filtering into their minds.

스바냐 〔聖〕 (The Book of) Zephaniah (略 Zeph.)

스스럼없다 unreserved; unconstrained; free (from constraint)
♦ 스스럼없는 사이 (on) frank [intimate] terms (with) / 스스럼없는 대화 a frank [an unreserved] talk / 스스럼없는 태도 an unconstrained manner / 스스럼없이 unreservedly; freely; without reserve (ceremony, restraint] / 스스럼없이 이야기하다 talk in a familiar way; speak without reserve [restraint]
▶ 그사람하고는 스스럼없이 지내고 있다 I am on familiar terms with him.
▶ 그는 누구를 만나건 스스럼없이 사귄다 He makes friends with everyone he meets.

스스럽다 reserved; constrained; diffident; shy; coy
♦ 스스러워하다 feel constraint (in sb's presence); feel diffident; be reserved / 스스러워서 말을 못하다 be coy of speech; be too shy to speak up
▶ 필요한 것은 스스러워 마시고 말씀하십시오 Don't scruple to ask for anything you want.
▶ 그의 태도에는 조금도 스스러운 데가 없었다 His manner was altogether free from constraint.

스스로 1 〈저절로〉 of itself; of its own accord; naturally; spontaneously; automatically
▶ 상처는 스스로 나았다 The wound healed of itself.
▶ 문이 스스로 열렸다 The door opened all by itself.
2 〈자진하여〉 of one's own accord [free will]; voluntarily
▶ 그는 스스로 학교를 그만두었다 He left school voluntarily [of his own accord].
▶ 스스로 그 일을 완성하고 싶다 We'd like to complete the work (by) ourselves.
▶ 그것은 그가 스스로 한 짓이었다 He did it of his own accord.
▶ 그녀는 우리에게 스스로 자기의 과거를 이야기했다 She told us about her past life without being asked.
3 〈혼자서〉 for oneself; by oneself
♦ 스스로 결정하다 decide sth for oneself
4 〈명사적〉 oneself
♦ 스스로를 돌이켜 보다 reflect on oneself [one's own conduct]

스승 a teacher; a master; an instructor; a mentor; a preceptor
♦ 스승과 제자 master and disciple; teacher and pupil / 스승의 은혜 the favors [kindnesses] of one's teacher / 스승으로 섬기다 look up to sb as one's mentor [preceptor]

스웨덴 Sweden; 〈공식명〉 the Kingdom of Sweden ♦ 스웨덴의 Swedish ■—말 Swedish ■—사람 a Swede

스웨이드 〈가죽〉 suede

스웨터 a sweater; a sweat shirt; a jersey; a pullover
♦ 스웨터 차림의 소녀 a sweatered girl / 스웨터를 뜨다 knit a sweater

스위스 Switzerland; 〈공식명〉 the Swiss Confederation ♦ 스위스의 Swiss
■—사람 a Swiss

스위치 a switch ♦ 전등 스위치 a light switch / 라디오 스위치를 켜다 switch [turn] on the radio / 텔레비전 스위치를 끄다 turn [switch] off the TV
■—히터 〔野〕 a switch-hitter

스위트피 〔植〕 a sweet pea

스윙 1 〔樂〕 swing (music); jive
2 〔競〕 a swing ―스윙하다 swing (a bat)

스쳐보다 〈곁눈질로 보다〉 look askance (at); look with a sidelong glance (at); cast a sidelong glance [look] (at); squint [leer] (at); 〈대충 보다〉 run one's eyes through (a book); skim [run] through (a book)

스치다 graze; barely touch; brush (past, against, by); go past by sb; rub [scrape] (against, past); 〈수면 등을〉 skim along; scud; 〈생각 등이〉 flit
▶ 어둠 속에서 무엇인가가 내 손을 살짝 스쳤다 Something brushed my hand in the darkness.
▶ 총알이 내 어깨를 스쳐 갔다 The bullet grazed my shoulder.
▶ 그녀는 내 옆을 스쳐 지나갔다 She went past by me.
▶ 제비 한 마리가 호수의 수면을 스치며 날아갔다 A swallow went skimming the lake.

▶ 피부가 스쳐서 벗겨졌다 I've rubbed the skin off.
▶ 기발한 생각이 언뜻 뇌리를 스쳤다 A fanciful idea flitted through my mind.

스카우트 a scout
▶ 팀마다 신인 스카우트에 혈안이 되어 있다 Every team is searching frantically for new talent.
—**스카우트하다** scout (for) 《young talent》
▶ 그는 유망한 선수를 스카우트하러 다녔다 He scouted around for a promising player.

스카이 the sky
■ —**블루** sky blue

스카이다이빙 skydiving —**스카이다이빙하다** skydive

스카이라인 a skyline ◆ 스카이라인 위로 on the skyline

스카치위스키 Scotch whisky

스카치테이프 (商標) Scotch tape

스카프 a scarf 《pl. ~s, scarves》

스칸듐 〔化〕 scandium

스칸디나비아 Scandinavia ◆ 스칸디나비아의 Scandinavian
■ —**반도** the Scandinavian Peninsula —**사람** a Scandinavian

스캔들 a scandal ◆ 세상이 떠들썩한 스캔들 a sensational scandal / 스캔들에 말려들다 get involved in a scandal

스커드미사일 a Scud missile

스커트 a skirt
◆ 스커트 주름 a pleat [gather] on a skirt / 스커트를 길게[짧게] make the skirt longer [shorter] / 스커트를 입다[벗다] put on [take off, step out of] one's skirt
■ —**롱[쇼트]—** a long [short] skirt **미니—** a miniskirt **타이트—** a tight skirt **플레어[개더]—** a flared [gathered] skirt

스컬 〈경주용 보트〉 a scull

스컹크 〔動〕 a skunk

스케이트 〈기구〉 (a pair of) skates
◆ 스케이트를 타다 skate 《on the ice》; do skating / 스케이트를 타러 가다 go skating / 스케이트를 잘[못]타다 be a good [poor] skater
■ **롤러—** roller skates ■ —**장** a skating [an ice] rink —**화** skates

———— 스케이트화 ————

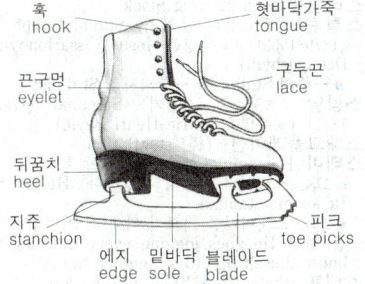

혹 hook
헛바닥가죽 tongue
끈구멍 eyelet
구두끈 lace
뒤꿈치 heel
지주 stanchion
피크 toe picks
에지 edge
밑바닥 sole
블레이드 blade

스케이팅 〈얼음 지치기〉 skating

■ **피겨[스피드]—** figure [speed] skating

스케일 〈규모〉 a scale; 〈인물의 도량〉 caliber

〔解說〕 **scale**은 「규모, 눈금, 척도」 등을 뜻하며 사람에 대해서는 쓰지 않는다. 사람에 대해서는 **caliber**를 사용한다.

◆ 스케일이 큰 사업 a large-scale undertaking / 스케일이 큰 사람 a man of large [high, remarkable] caliber / 스케일이 큰[작은] large-[small-]scale / 세계적인 스케일로 on a world [global] scale
▶ 그 사업은 공전의 스케일로 운영되고 있다 The business is conducted on an unexampled scale.

스케줄 a schedule; a program
◆ 일의 스케줄 a work schedule / 꽉 찬 스케줄 a crowded [crammed] schedule / 스케줄에 없는 unscheduled 《flight》 / 스케줄대로 as scheduled; on schedule; according to schedule / 스케줄을 짜다 make [map, lay] out a schedule 《of, for》; draw up a program 《of》 / 스케줄을 새로 짜다 reschedule
▶ 서울 시장으로서의 그의 스케줄은 꽉 짜여 있다 His schedule as the Mayor of Seoul is very tight.
▶ 파티는 스케줄대로 끝났다 The party finished on schedule.

스케치 〈사생〉 sketching; 〈사생화〉 a sketch —**스케치하다** sketch; make a sketch of sth
◆ 스케치하는 사람 a sketcher / 스케치하러 가다 go sketching / 꽃을 스케치하다 sketch a flower; make a sketch of a flower
■ —**북** a sketchbook

스코어 〈경기의〉 a score; 〈모음 악보〉 a (musical) score
◆ 스코어를 기록하다 keep the score 《of》
▶ 우리 팀이 3대 2 스코어로 이겼다 Our team won by a score of 3 to 2.
▶ 스코어는 9회에 3대 3 동점이 되었다 The score was tied at 3 to 3 in the ninth inning.
■ —**보드** a scoreboard —**북** a scorebook

스코치테리어 〈개〉 a Scotch [Scottish] terrier

스코틀랜드 Scotland ◆ 스코틀랜드의 Scotch; Scottish —**사람** a Scotchman; a Scot; 〈총칭〉 the Scotch [Scottish]; the Scots

스콜 〈열대의 소나기〉 a squall

스콜라철학 —**哲學** Scholasticism ■ —**자** a Scholastic

스콧 〈영국의 소설가·시인〉 Scott, Sir Walter (1771-1832)

스쿠너 〈범선〉 a schooner

스쿠터 a (motor) scooter ◆ 스쿠터를 타다 ride on a scooter; have [take] a ride on a motor scooter / 스쿠터로 달리다 go on a (motor) scooter

스쿠프 〈특종〉 a scoop; (美) a beat —**스쿠프하다** scoop 《news》; get a scoop 《on rival papers》; pull a scoop
▶ 그들은 그 독직 사건을 스쿠프하여 다른 신문들을 앞질렀다 They scooped [beat] all the other papers with the corruption scandal.

스쿨 a school

■―버스 a school bus

스퀘어댄스 a square dance ◆스퀘어댄스를 추다 dance [perform, take part in] a square dance

스퀴즈번트 〔野〕 a squeeze bunt ▶그는 절묘한 스퀴즈번트로 3루 주자를 불러들였다 He squeezed in a runner on third base with a perfect bunt.

스퀴즈플레이 〔野〕 a squeeze play

스크랩 (a) scrap ―스크랩하다 scrap ■―북 a scrapbook

스크럼 〔럭비〕 a scrum; a scrummage; scrimmage
◆스크럼을 짜다 form [line up for] a scrummage; scrimmage; (비유) join forces [hands] (to do) / 스크럼을 풀다 break up a scrummage
▶학생들은 스크럼을 짜고 거리를 행진하고 있었다 The students were marching along the street arm in arm.

스크루 〈나사〉 a screw; 〈배의 추진기〉 a screw (propeller) ■―드라이버 a screwdriver ―볼 〔野〕 a screwball

스크린 〈영사막〉 a screen; 〈영화계〉 the screen
◆스크린에 나오다 appear on the screen; play for the screen

스크립트 a (TV) script ■―걸 a script [continuity] girl

스키 〈경기〉 (snow) skiing; 〈기구〉 (a pair of) skis
◆스키를 타다 ski / 스키를 신다 put on skis / 스키를 배우다 learn to ski / 스키를 타러 가다 go skiing / 스키를 잘 타다 be good at skiing; be a good skier
▶겨울은 스키의 계절이다 Winter is the season for skiing.
▶매년 겨울이면 용평으로 스키 타러 간다 I go to Yongp'yŏng to ski every winter. ≒ I go skiing at Yongp'yŏng every winter.
■―대회 a ski meet ―복 a ski suit; a skiwear ―부대 a ski-borne troop ―장 a skiing ground [area] ―점프 a ski jump ―화 ski boots

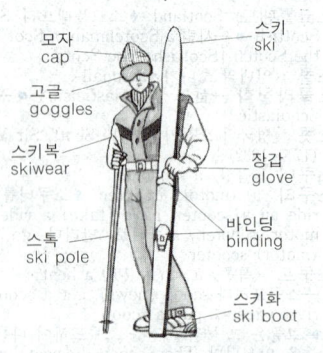
― 스키 ―
모자 cap
고글 goggles
스키복 skiwear
스톡 ski pole
스키 ski
장갑 glove
바인딩 binding
스키화 ski boot

스킨다이빙 skin diving

―스킨다이빙하다 skin-dive

스타 a star ◆스타가 되다 become a star ■―영화― a movie [film] star ■―시스템 the star system

스타덤 stardom ◆스타덤에 오르다 enter [achieve, rise to] stardom

스타디움 a stadium (*pl.* ~s, -dia) ■―올림픽― the Olympic Stadium

스타인벡 〈미국의 소설가〉 Steinbeck, John Ernest (1902-68)

스타일 a style; 〈몸매〉 one's form; one's figure

> **解說** ***style***은 「(건축·문예 등의) 양식」「(복장 등의) 형」「문체」 등을 가리킨다. 따라서 「(사람이) 스타일이 좋다」라고 표현할 때는 ***figure***를 써야 한다.

◆최신 유행 스타일 the latest style / 스타일 구기다 get out of shape; be put out of countenance
▶그녀는 스타일이 좋다[나쁘다] She has a good [poor] figure.
■―북 a stylebook

스타일리스트 〈문장의〉 a stylist; 〈복장의〉 a dandy

스타카토 〔樂〕 staccato

스타킹 (a pair of) stockings ◆스타킹을 신다 [벗다] pull stockings on [off]

스타터 〈출발 신호인〉 a starter; 〈시동장치〉 a (self-)starter

스타트 〈출발〉 a start; 〈경마·자동차의〉 (口) a getaway; 〈출발점〉 point of departure
◆스타트 신호를 하다 give a starting signal; give a signal to start / 스타트를 끊다 start; make a start; get off the mark / 스타트가 좋다[나쁘다] start well [poorly]; start quick [slow]; make a good [bad] start
▶그들은 일제히 스타트를 끊었다 They started all in one body.
▶「땅」하고 스타트 신호가 났다 "Bang!" went the starting signal.
▶그는 백화점 점원으로 인생의 스타트를 끊었다 He got his start in life as a clerk in a department store.
―스타트하다 start; make a start
■―라인 a starting line; a balkline : 스타트라인에 서다 toe the line

스타팅블록 a starting block

스탈린 〈구소련의 정치가〉 Stalin, Joseph V. (1879-1953) (▶본명은 Iosif Vissarionovich Dzhugashvili)
■―주의 Stalinism ―주의자 a Stalinist

스탕달 〈프랑스의 소설가〉 Stendhal (1783-1842) (▶본명은 Marie Henri Beyle)

스태그플레이션 〔經〕 stagflation

스태미나 stamina; staying power
▶그는 스태미나가 없다[왕성하다] He has no [a lot of] stamina.
▶그는 스태미나를 기르기 위해 매일 아침 조깅을 한다 He goes jogging every morning to build himself up [to strengthen himself].

스태프 the staff ◆스태프 일동을 대표하여 on behalf of all the members of the staff / 스태프의 일원이다 be on the staff; be a member

스탠더드 standard ■—넘버 [樂] a standard number
스탠드 1 〈관람석〉 the stands; 〈매점·노점〉 a (coffee) stand; a booth
▶ 스탠드는 만원이었다 The stands were full.
▶ 스탠드에서 우레와 같은 박수갈채가 터져나왔다 A storm of applause rose from the stands.
2 〈램프〉 a desk lamp; 〈마루에 놓는〉 a floor lamp
3 〈진열대〉 a stand
스탠드플레이 〈과잉 연기〉 a grandstand play
◆ 스탠드플레이를 하다 play to the grandstands [to the gallery]; (口) grandstand
스탠리 〈영국의 탐험가〉 Stanley, Sir Henry Morton (1841-1904)
스탠스 [野·골프] a stance ▶ 그는 스탠스가 좀 넓다 His stance is a little too wide.
■ 오픈— an open stance
스탬프 〈우표〉 a stamp; 〈도장〉 a datemark; 〈소인(消印)〉 a postmark
◆ 카드에 스탬프를 찍다 stamp a card; affix a stamp on a card
■ 기념— a commemorative stamp
스턴트맨 〈영화의 대역〉 a stunt man
스테레오 〈음향 장치〉 a stereo (*pl.* ~s); stereotype; 〈입체 음향 재생 방식〉 the stereophonic sound reproduction system
◆ 스테레오로 방송하다 broadcast in stereo / 교향곡 음반을 스테레오로 듣다 listen to a recording of a symphony on stereo / 스테레오로 녹음하다 make a stereo(phonic) recording of 《Chaikovski's sixth symphony》; record 《music》 in stereo
■ —녹음 stereophonic [stereo] recording —레코드 a stereo [stereophonic] record [disc] —음향 stereophony; stereo sounds —전축 a stereophonic [stereo] phonograph —테이프 a stereo tape
스테레오판 —版 [印] stereotype; stereo
스테아린 [化] stearin(e)
스테이션 a (railway) station ▶ 우주— a space station; an interplanetary station
■ —왜건 a station [beach] wagon; (英) an estate car [wagon]
스테이지 a stage ◆ 스테이지를 밟다[떠나다] go on [off] the stage ■ —댄스 a stage dance
스테이크 a (grilled) steak; a beefsteak
스테이터스심볼 a status symbol
스테이플 a staple ◆ 스테이플을 찍다 staple 《sheets of paper》 together
스테이플파이버 staple fiber; rayon staple
스테인드글라스 stained glass
스테인리스강 —鋼 stainless steel
스테인리스스틸 stainless steel=스테인리스강
스텐실 a stencil ■—페이퍼 stencil paper
스텝 a step ◆ 스텝을 밟다 dance; step
스토브 a stove; a heater

解說 우리말에서 「스토브」는 난방기구를 가리키는데 영어의 *stove*에도 그런 뜻이 없는 것은 아니지만 그 경우에는 potbelly [potbellied] stove (가운데가 볼록한 스토브) 같은 구식 난방기구를 가리키는 경우가 많다. 일반적으로 stove는 cooking stove 또는 cookstove (두가지 모두 요리용 레인지)로 쓰인다. 난방기구를 가리키는 가장 일반적인 말은 *heater*다.

◆ 스토브를 피우다 light a heater [stove]; make a fire in a potbelly stove / 스토브를 끄다[켜다] turn off [on] the heater [gas stove] / 스토브로 몸을 따뜻하게 하다 warm *oneself* by a heater
▶ 방에는 스토브가 잘 타고 있었다 The heater [stove] was going well in the room.
■ 가스[석유, 전기]— a gas [an oil, an electric] heater ■ —리그 (美俗) a stove league
스토아 —主의[哲學] Stoicism —철학자 Stoic
스토어 〈상점〉 a store ■ 드러그— a drugstore 체인— a chain store
스토코프스키 〈영국 태생의 미국 지휘자〉 Stokowski, Leopold (1882-1977)
스톡 1 ⇨ 재고품
2 〈스키의 지팡이〉 (a pair of) a ski sticks [poles]
스톡홀름 〈스웨덴의 수도〉 Stockholm
스톱 a stop —스톱하다 ⇨ 멈추다
스톱워치 a stopwatch ◆ 스톱워치로 시간을 재다 stopwatch
스튜 (a) stew ▶ 스튜 더 드시겠습니까? Would you care for some more stew?
■ 비프— beef stew; stewed beef ■—냄비 a saucepan; (英) a stewpan
스튜던트파워 student power
스튜디오 a studio (*pl.* ~s) ■ 영화— a film studio; (美) a movie lot
스튜어디스 a stewardess; an air hostess

解說 한때는 *air hostess*가 많이 쓰였지만 최근에는 잘 쓰이지 않는다. 요즈음에는 *stewardess*, air hostess처럼 성별을 구분하는 말을 피해서 flight attendant를 쓰는 항공사도 있다. 또 stewardess, purser 등의 승무원을 합쳐서 aircrew 또는 cabin crew라고 한다. 기내에서 stewardess에게 말을 걸 때에는 "Excuse me, stewardess."라고 하면 된다.

스튜어트 왕가 —王家 the Stuarts
스트라빈스키 〈러시아 태생의 미국 작곡가〉 Stravinsky, Igor Fédorovich (1882-1971)
스트라이크 1 〈파업〉 a strike; a walkout
◆ 스트라이크 중이다 be on (a) strike / 스트라이크를 하다[에 들어가다] go [come out] on (a) strike; walk out / 스트라이크를 중지하다 halt [call off] a strike
2 [野] a strike ◆ 스트라이크가 되다 score a strike
▶ 카운트는 투 스트라이크 스리 볼이다 The count is two strikes and three balls.
3 〈볼링〉 a strike
■ —존 [野] the strike zone
스트라이크아웃 [野] a strikeout ◆ 스트라이크아웃시키다 strike 《a batter》 out / 스트라이크 아웃 당하다 be [get] struck out
스트레스 stress
◆ 스트레스가 쌓이다 stress builds up / 스트레

스를 받고 있다 be under stress / 스트레스를 해소하다 get rid of stress (by engaging in sports); dispel a stress
▶ 스트레스를 해소하기 위해 골프를 치자 Let's play golf to get rid of stress.
▶ 나는 스트레스를 몹시 받아왔다 I've been under so much stress.
▶ 는 스트레스가 쌓이면 화를 잘 낸다 He becomes irritable when stress builds up.
■ ―학설 the theory of stress

스트레이트 **1** 〖拳〗 a straight punch (on); 〖野〗 a straight ball **2** 〈연속으로〉 ◆ 스트레이트로 이기다 win a straight victory / 스트레이트로 지다 suffer a straight defeat
▶ 우리 팀은 스트레이트로 이겼다 Our team won a straight victory. ⇌ We won in straight sets.
3 〈물을 타지 않은〉 (美) straight; (英) neat
◆ 스트레이트로 마시다 drink straight
▶ 그는 위스키를 보통 스트레이트로 마신다 He usually drinks whisky straight.

스트레치 〈직선 코스〉 the stretch
스트렙토마이신 〖藥〗 streptomycin
스트로 a (drinking) straw ◆ 스트로로 빨다 suck through a straw ■ ―해트 a straw hat
스트로보 〖寫〗 a stroboscope; a strobe
■ ―사진(술) stroboscopic photography ―전구 a strobe (light); a stroboscopic lamp
스트로크 a stroke ◆ 한 스트로크 차이로 이기다[지다] win [lose] by a stroke
스트론튬 〖化〗 strontium ■ ―석 strontianite
스트리크닌 〖藥〗 strychnine
스트리퍼 a stripper; a stripteaser
스트린드베리 〈스웨덴의 극작가〉 Strindberg, Johan August (1849-1912)
스트립쇼 a striptease; a strip show
스티렌 〖化〗 styrene ◆ 발포(發泡) 스티렌 styrene foam; styrofoam
스티븐슨 **1** 〈영국 소설가〉 Stevenson, Robert Louis Balfour (1850-94) **2** 〈영국의 증기기관차 발명자〉 Stephenson, George (1781-1848)
스티커 a sticker; an adhesive label
스틸[1] 〈강철〉 steel ■ ―기타 a steel guitar
스틸[2] 〈도루〉 〖野〗 a steal ◆ 더블― a double steal 홈― a home steal
스틸[3] 〈사진〉 a still (picture)
스팀 〈증기〉 steam ◆ 스팀 난방 steam heating; 〈장치〉 a steam heater / 스팀으로 방을 덥게 하다 heat a room by steam / 스팀이 들어오다 be steam-heated; be heated by steam
■ ―다리미 a steam iron ―엔진 a steam engine
스파게티 〈이탈리아식 국수〉 spaghetti
스파르타 Sparta ◆ 스파르타(식)의 Spartan
■ ―사람 a Spartan ―식 교육[훈련] Spartan education [training]
스파링 〖拳〗 sparring ■ ―파트너 one's sparring partner
스파이 a spy; a secret agent; 〈간첩 행위〉 espionage; 〈군사 정찰〉 (a) reconnaissance
◆ 스파이를 보내다 send a spy (into) / 스파이가 딸리다 set a spy on sb / 스파이 노릇을 하다 spy; act as spy
■ ―산업 industrial espionage; an industrial spy 이중― a double (secret) agent ■ ―망 a spy network ―비행 a spy [an espionage] flight ―영화[소설] an espionage movie [novel]; a spy film [story] ―위성 a reconnaissance satellite ―활동 espionage activites
스파이크 〈구두의〉 a spike; 〈배구의〉 spiking; a spike ―스파이크하다 〈배구에서〉 spike (the ball) ■ ―화[슈즈] a pair of spikes [spiked shoes, track shoes] ―힐 〈여성 구두의 높은 뒷굽〉 a spike heel
스파크 〈전기 불꽃〉 a spark
스패너 (美) a wrench; (英) a spanner
■ 멍키[자재]― a monkey wrench [spanner]
스퍼트 〈경주에서의 역주〉 a spurt; ◆ 마지막 스퍼트 the finishing [last] spurt ―스퍼트하다 spurt; make [put on] a spurt
스펀지 〈해면〉 a sponge; 〈인공 해면 물질〉 sponge ◆ 스펀지로 더러움을 닦아내다 sponge off the dirt
■ ―고무 sponge rubber ―볼 a sponge ball ―케이크 (a) sponge cake
스페셜리스트 〈전문가〉 a specialist
스페어 a spare ■ ―타이어 a spare tire
스페이드 〈트럼프의〉 a spade ◆ 스페이드의 여왕 the Queen of spades
스페이스 **1** 〈공간〉 (a) space; room ▶ 주차할 스페이스가 없다 There is no space to park a car. **2** 〈행간·간격〉 ◆ 더블 스페이스로 타자하다 type double-spaced **3** 〈우주〉 space ■ ―셔틀 〈우주 왕복선〉 a space shuttle
스페인 Spain; 〈공식명〉 the Kingdom of Spain
◆ 스페인의 Spanish ■ ―말 Spanish ―사람 a Spaniard; 〈총칭〉 the Spanish (people); the Spaniards
스펙터클 〈장관(壯觀)〉 a spectacle
■ ―영화 a spectacular film
스펙트럼 a spectrum 《pl. -tra, ~s》
■ ―분석 spectrum [spectroscopic] analysis ―사진 a spectrogram ―선 a spectral line
스펜서 **1** 〈영국 철학자〉 Spencer, Herbert (1820-1903) **2** 〈영국 시인〉 Spenser, Edmund (1552 ? -99)
스펠링 spelling ⇨ 철자(綴字)
■ 미스― misspelling
스포츠 a sport; 〈총칭〉 sports

[解說] 주로 승패를 가리는 운동을 「스포츠」라고 하지만 영어의 **sport**는 「사냥」 「낚시」 「경마」 등을 포함하는 보다 범위가 넓은 말이다. 따라서 sportsman 은 「사냥꾼」 「낚시꾼」을 포함한다.

◆ 스포츠를 좋아하는 sports-minded / 스포츠를 하다 take part in [participate in, practice, go in for] a sport
▶ 그는 스포츠를 관람하기보다 실제 참가하기를 좋아한다 He is a lover of participant sports, not of spectator sports.
■ ―계 sports circles; the sporting world; (美) sportsdom ―기자 a sportswriter; a sports reporter ―뉴스 sports news ―란 a sports section ―방송 sportscasting; a sportscast; a sportcast: 스포츠 방송을 하다 broadcast a sports event ―센터 a sports center ―신문 a

스포츠 용어

1. 스포츠 종목의 명칭

(1) 구기 ball games
▶ 야구 baseball / 소프트볼 softball / 축구 soccer; 〈英〉 association football / 배구 volleyball / 농구 basketball / 미식축구 football; 〈英〉 American football / 럭비 rugby / 핸드볼 handball / 필드하키 field hockey / 아이스하키 ice hockey
▶ 테니스 tennis; 〈연식〉 softball tennis; 〈남자 단식〉 men's singles; 〈혼합 복식〉 mixed doubles / 배드민턴 badminton (▶깃털공 a shuttlecock; a shuttle)
▶ 골프 golf / 크리켓 cricket / 볼링 bowling

(2) 육상 경기 track and field events
▶ 트랙 경기 track events / 단거리 sprinting; a sprint (race) / 중거리 a middle-distance race / 장거리 a long-distance race / 허들 hurdles; a hurdle race / 100미터 경주 a 100-meter dash / 400 미터 계주 a 400-meter relay
▶ 필드 경기 field events / 높이뛰기 the high jump (▶배면(背面)뛰기 Fosbury flop) / 멀리뛰기 the long [broad] jump / 세단뛰기 the triple jump; the hop, step and jump / 장대 높이뛰기 the pole vault / 창던지기 the javelin throw / 포환던지기 the shot put / 원반던지기 the discus throw / 해머던지기 the hammer throw
▶ 마라톤 a marathon / 경보 a walking race

(3) 체조 gymnastics
▶ 맨손 체조 free exercise / 마루 운동 floor exercise / 기구 체조 apparatus exercise / 기계체조 gymnastics (▶뜀틀 long horse; vaulting horse / 평행봉 parallel bars / 이단 평행봉 uneven parallel bars / 링 rings / 안마 pommel horse / 철봉 horizontal bar / 평균대 balance beam) / 턱걸이 hang / 도약 vault / 물구나무서기 handstand / 공중제비 somersault

(4) 수영 swimming
▶ 개인경영(競泳) an individual race / 자유형 free style (▶영법은 crawl) / 평영 breaststroke / 접영 butterfly (stroke) / 배영 backstroke / 개인 혼영 an individual medley / 단체 경기 종목 a team race / 자유형 계영 a freestyle relay / 혼계영 a medley relay
▶ 다이빙 diving
▶ 싱크로나이즈드 스위밍 synchronized swimming / 수구 water polo

(5) 격투기 combat sports
▶ 권투 boxing (▶플라이급 flyweight / 밴텀급 bantamweight / 웰터급 welterweight / 헤비급 heavyweight) / 레슬링 wrestling (▶자유형 freestyle wrestling / 그레코로망형 Greco-Roman wrestling)
▶ 펜싱 fencing / 유도 judo / 검도 swordplay; swordsmanship / 태권도 t'aekwŏndo

(6) 스키, 기타 skiing and others
▶ 알파인 종목 Alpine events (▶회전 slalom / 활강 downhill racing / 대회전 giant slalom / 노르딕 종목 Nordic events (▶점프 ski jumping / 크로스컨트리 crosscountry) / 수상스키 water ski
▶ 스피드 스케이팅 speed skating / 피겨 스케이팅 figure skating / 스케이트보드 skateboarding / 롤러 스케이팅 roller skating
▶ 사격 shooting / 클레이 사격 clay pigeon shooting
▶ 양궁 archery
▶ 마술 경기 an equestrian event / 장애물 경마 steeplechase
▶ 역도 weightlifting
▶ 자전거 경주 cycle racing
▶ 조정 경기 rowing and canoeing
▶ 근대 5종 경기 the modern pentathlon
▶ 서핑 surfing / 서프 보드 a surfboard / 스킨 다이빙 skin diving / 스쿠버 다이빙 scuba diving / 윈드서핑 windsurfing

2. 선수·임원·경기
▶ 아마추어 amateur / 프로 professional / 선수[경기자] an athlete; a player / 경기 참가자 a participant / 자기편 짝 a partner / 대전 상대 an opponent / 경쟁자 a contender / 팀 전체 a team / 시드 선수 a seeded player (▶선수는 각 종목에 ~er 또는 player를 붙인다. 그러나 때로는 ~ist로 쓰기도 한다: 골프 선수 a golfer / 수영 선수 a swimmer / 축구 선수 a football player / 테니스 선수 a tennis player)
▶ 감독 a manager / 코치 a coach / 트레이너 a trainer / 세컨드 a second / 경기 임원 an official (▶심판 포함) / 심판 an umpire; a referee / 선심 a linesman / 득점 기록원 a scorer (▶스코어 보드 a scoreboard) / 계시원 a timekeeper / 기록원 a record keeper
▶ 경기 a game / 시합 competition / 대항 시합 a match / 토너먼트 a tournament / 권투나 펜싱 등의 승부 a bout / 한 세트 a set / 스피드 경주 a race / 공식 경기 a formal game / 연습 경기 an informal game; a practice game / 교내 경기 an interclass tournament / 대학 대항 경기 intercollegiate tournament / 친선경기 를 하다 have a friendly match

3. 스포츠 시설
▶ 경기장 a stadium / 그라운드 ground / 필드 a field / 코트 a court / 수영장 a swimming pool / 링크 a skating rink / 링 a ring / 골프 코스 golf links; a golf course / 체육관 a gymnasium

4. 주요 스포츠 규칙, 용어
▶ 공격 offense / 수비 defense / 반칙 a foul / 벌칙 penalty / 페널티 박스[에어리어] a penalty box [area]
▶ 미식축구 태클(하다) tackle / 펌블 fumble / 킥오프 a kickoff / 터치다운 a touchdown / 엔드 존 end zone / 골포스트 goalpost
▶ 농구 슛하다 shoot / 골인하다 make a basket / 리바운드 볼 a rebound / 드리블 a dribble / 아웃 오브 바운드 out of bounds / 맨투맨 a-man-to-man defense

▶ 배구 서브(를 넣다) serve / 토스(하다) set up / 스파이크(하다) spike / 오버타임 overtime / 네트터치 a net touch / 블록 a block ▶ 테니스 서브 a service; a serve / 서브 득점 a service ace / 그라운드 스트로크 a ground stroke / 포핸드 스트로크 a forehand storke / 백핸드 스트로크 a backhand stroke / 스매시 a smash / 로브 a lob / 톱[백]스핀 a top[back] spin / 세트[브레이크, 매치] 포인트 a set [break, match] point / 어드밴티지 an advantage / 듀스 a deuce

5. 스포츠를「하다」
(1) play를 쓰는 것 — 대부분의 구기 종목
play tennis [table tennis, golf, baseball, basketball, football, volleyball, soccer, rugby, handball, badminton]
(2) 동사로 쓰는 것
ski, ice-skate, bowl, swim, skin-dive, surf, wrestle, box, climb, ride on a horse, fence
(3) go + ~ing「~하러 가다」
go skiing [swimming, shooting, riding, yachting, fishing, hiking, bowling]
(4) **practice**를 쓰는 것
practice *t'aekwŏndo* [judo, archery, gymnastics]

6. 올림픽 the Olympic Games; the Olympics ▶ 하계[동계] 올림픽 대회 the Olympic Summer [Winter] Games / 국제 올림픽 위원회 the International Olympic Committee (略 IOC) / 한국 올림픽 위원회 the Korea Olympic Committee (略 KOC) / 올림픽 선수촌 the Olympic Village / 성화(聖火) 〈주자가 갖고 있는〉 the Olympic Torch; 〈대회장에 있는〉 the Olympic Flame / 성화 릴레이 the sacred torch relay / 개회식 the opening ceremony / 폐회식 the closing ceremony / 개최국 the host country / 올림픽 헌장 the Olympic Charter / 금[은, 동] 메달 a gold [silver, bronze] medal

〈표현예〉
▶ 어떤 종목에 출전하십니까? What event do you participate in?
▶ 어떤 운동을 하고 있습니까? Do you do any exercise?
▶ 그는 100미터 경주의 2차 예선을 통과했다 He made it through the second heat in the 100-meter dash.
▶ 그는 예선에서 떨어지고 말았다 He was eliminated in the preliminaries.
▶ 그의 세계 기록은 5년간 깨지지 않고 있다 His world record has not been broken for 5 years.
▶ 조깅은 참여하는 스포츠지만 야구는 보는 스포츠라고 생각한다 I think jogging is a participation sport, whereas baseball is a spectator sport.

---

sporting newspaper [journal] —용어 sporting terms; sports jargon —용품 sports equipment; sporting goods —용품점 a sports shop —잡지 a sports magazine —카 a sports [sport] car —평론가 a sports commentator —하이라이트 sports highlights

스포츠맨 a sportsman (*pl.* -men); an athlete ◆ 스포츠맨다운 sportsmanlike / 스포츠맨답게 경기하다 play sportsmanlike ■ —십[정신] sportsmanship

스포크 〈바퀴살〉 a spoke; a radius

스포크스맨 〈대변자〉 a spokesman; a mouthpiece ◆ 정부의 스포크스맨 a spokesman of the Government

스포트라이트 〔劇〕 a spotlight ◆ 스포트라이트를 비추다 spotlight; direct a spotlight upon / 스포트라이트를 받고 있다 be in the spotlight

스폰서 〈후원자〉 a sponsor
◆ 스폰서[공동스폰서]가 되다 sponsor [co-sponsor] 《a TV program》 / 아무에게 스폰서가 되어 달라고 청하다 ask *sb* to sponsor
▶ 이 프로그램의 스폰서는 에이비사다 This program is sponsored by AB Company.

스폿 〈짧은 삽입 방송〉 a spot ■ —광고 spot advertising —뉴스 spot news

스푼 a spoon
◆ 설탕 두 스푼 two spoonfuls of sugar / 수프를 스푼으로 뜨다 spoon up [out] soup ■ —레이스 an egg-and-spoon race

스프레이 〈분무기〉 a spray

스프롤현상 —現象 〈대도시 교외의〉 urban sprawl

스프린터 〈단거리 경주자〉 a sprinter

스프링 1 〈용수철〉 a spring
◆ 스프링 침대 a spring bed; an inner-spring bed
2 〈봄〉 spring
■ —보드 〔泳〕 a springboard; a diving board —코트 a topcoat; a light overcoat

스프링클러 a sprinkler
■ —장치 a sprinkler system

스피노자 〈네덜란드 철학자〉 Spinoza, Baruch [Benedict] (1632-77)

스피드 〈속도·속력〉 speed
◆ 전 스피드로 at full speed / 보통 스피드로 at an ordinary speed / 무시무시한 스피드로 at a terrific [furious, breakneck] speed / 스피드를 내다 speed up; gather [get up, put on] speed; (口) step on it [the gas] / 시속 80킬로미터의 스피드를 내다 get [develop] a speed of 80 kilometers an hour / 스피드를 낮추다 reduce [decrease, slacken] speed; slow down [up] / 스피드를 위반하다 break [violate] the speed laws
▶ 그의 차는 시속 100킬로미터 이상의 스피드로 달렸다 His car was running at a speed of more than 100 kilometers an hour.
▶ 지금 스피드가 어느 정도인가? What speed are we doing now?

스푼

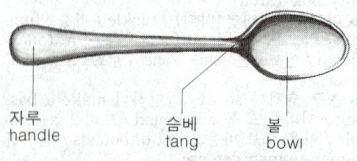

자루 handle / 슴베 tang / 볼 bowl

—광 a speed maniac [fiend, demon] **—레이스** a speed race **—볼** 〔野〕 a speedball **—시대** the age of speed **—위반** violation of the speed limit; speeding : 스피드 위반으로 나는 5만원의 벌칙금을 물었다 I was fined 50,000 won for speeding. **—위반자** a speeder; a speedster **—제한** speed regulation; a speed limit

스피드업 〈가속·능률 향상〉 speeding up; a speedup **—스피드업하다** speed up
▶ 모든 것이 스피드업되고 있다 Everything is getting speeded up.

스피로헤타 〔菌〕 a spiroch(a)ete
■ **—병** spiroch(a)etosis

스피츠 a spitz (dog)

스피치 a speech ♦스피치를 하다 make [deliver] a speech

스피커 〈확성기〉 a loudspeaker; 〈라디오의〉 a radio speaker ♦고음용[저음용] 스피커 a tweeter [woofer] / 스피커로 공표하다 announce through a loudspeaker

스핑크스 〈수수께끼의 인물〉 a sphinx 《pl. ~es, sphinges》; 〔그神〕 the Sphinx

슬개골 膝蓋骨 〔解〕 the kneepan; the kneecap; the patella 《pl. -lae》

슬관절 膝關節 〔解〕 the knee joint

슬그머니 1 〈남몰래〉 stealthily; by stealth; in secret; covertly; on the sly; 〈조용히〉 softly; quietly ♦슬그머니 알려주다 tell sb secretly / 슬그머니 들어오다[나가다] steal [slip] into [out of] 《a room》 / 슬그머니 보다 steal a glance at; look furtively at / 슬그머니 자리를 뜨다 leave one's seat quietly / 슬그머니 돈을 쥐어 주다 slip money (to sb, into sb's hand)
▶ 그는 슬그머니 교실을 빠져 나가다가 잡혔다 He was caught sneaking out of the classroom.
▶ 유령은 슬그머니 사라졌다 The ghost vanished silently.
▶ 나는 슬그머니 무서워졌다 Fear stole into my heart.
2 〈넌지시〉 indirectly; in a casual manner; in a roundabout way
♦슬그머니 경고하다 give a veiled warning

슬금슬금 stealthily; sneakingly; furtively; covertly; quietly
♦슬금슬금 다가서다 steal one's way (to) / 슬금슬금 훔쳐보다 cast covert glances at sb / 슬금슬금 달아나다 slip away; sneak [slink] off [away]; run away stealthily

슬기 wisdom; sense; sagacity; intellect; intelligence ♦슬기가 있다 be wise; have (good) sense; be intelligent

슬기롭다 intelligent; wise; sagacious; sensible; prudent ♦슬기로운 사람 a wise man; a man of wisdom [intelligence] / 슬기롭게 처신하다 conduct oneself intelligently; act wisely [sensibly] / 슬기롭지 못하다 be unintelligent; be injudicious; be dull

슬다¹ 1 〈채소 등이 시들다〉 wither; wilt; droop
▶ 꽃병의 꽃이 슬기 시작했다 The flowers in the vase were beginning to wilt.
2 〈사라지다〉 disappear; vanish; wither

슬다² 1 〈녹이〉 rust; get [become] rusty; 〈곰팡이가〉 become [get] musty [moldy, fusty]
♦버려두어 녹이 슬다 rust from disuse

2 〈알을 낳다〉 lay 《eggs》; 〈파리가〉 blow; 〈물고기가〉 spawn
♦파리가 쉬를 슬다 a fly blows eggs
▶ 연어는 알을 슬기 위해 바다에서 강으로 거슬러 올라간다 Salmon swim up a river from the sea to spawn.

슬라브 Slav ■ **—말** Slavic : 슬라브 말의 Slavic **—사람** a Slav; a Slavonian **—족** the Slavs : 슬라브 족의 Slavic **—주의** Slavism

슬라이더 〔野〕 a slider

슬라이드 〈환등〉 a (lantern) slide; 〈현미경의〉 a slide; 〈계산자〉 a slide rule ♦슬라이드를 스크린에 영사하다 project slides on the screen
■ **컬러—** a color slide **—영사기** a slide projector

슬라이드제 **—制** 〔經〕 a sliding scale
▶ 우리 급료는 물가 슬라이드제로 지불된다 We are paid on a sliding scale.

슬라이딩 〔野〕 sliding **—슬라이딩하다** slide into ▶ 그는 2루에 슬라이딩해서 가까스로 세이프되었다 He slide into second base just in time.

슬랄롬 〔스키〕 slalom

슬랙스 《a pair of》 slacks ♦슬랙스를 입은 여자 a woman in slacks

슬랭 〈속어〉 a slang word [expression, term]; a word of slang; 〈총칭〉 slang

슬러거 〔野〕 a slugger; a strong hitter

슬럼 a slum ♦슬럼화(化)하다 turn into slums
■ **—가** a slum district; slum quarters [areas]; the slums

슬럼프 a slump ♦슬럼프에 빠지다 hit [be in] a slump / 슬럼프에서 헤어나다 get [come] out of a slump
▶ 그는 요즘 슬럼프에 빠져 있는 것 같다 He seems to be in a slump these days.

슬레이트 〈석판〉 a slate; 〈총칭〉 slating
♦슬레이트로 덮은 지붕 a slated roof / 슬레이트 지붕의 집 a slate-roofed house / 지붕을 슬레이트로 이다 slate a roof; roof a house with slates

슬로건 a slogan ♦…라는 슬로건을 내걸고 under the slogan of… / 슬로건을 내세우다 publish a slogan
▶ "빈곤 추방"은 그 정당의 유일한 슬로건이었다 "Down with Poverty" was the sole slogan of the party.

슬로모션 slow motion ■ **—영화** a slow-motion picture [film]

슬로볼 〔野〕 a slow ball ♦슬로볼을 던지다 throw a slow ball

슬로프 〈경사면〉 a slope ♦완만한 슬로프 a gentle slope / 슬로프를 미끄러져 내리다 slide down a slope

슬리퍼 《a pair of》 slippers; 〈뒤축없는〉 backless slippers; mules; scuffs

> 解說 영어의 *slippers*는 우리나라에서 신는 「슬리퍼」와는 달리 보통 뒤축이 있는 가벼운 실내화를 가리킨다. 일반적으로 우리나라에서 뒤축 없이 걸쳐 신는 것을 *mules* 또는 *scuffs* 라고 하는데 이런 종류는 영국이나 미국에서는 별로 신지 않는다.

슬리퍼를 신다 have *one's* slippers on / 슬리퍼로 갈아 신다 change *one's* shoes for slippers

슬립 〈여자의 속옷〉 a slip; an underslip
▶ 네 슬립이 보인다 Your slip is showing.

슬며시 stealthily ⇨ 슬그머니

슬슬 1 〈천천히〉 slowly; leisurely
♦ 슬슬 걷다 walk slowly [leisurely]
▶ 시간이 있으니 슬슬 하시오 Don't hurry; there's plenty of time.
▶ 그들은 슬슬 걷고 있었다 They were walking slowly.
2 〈부드럽게〉 gently; softly; lightly ♦ 슬슬 문지르다 rub lightly; give *sth* a light rub
3 〈부지중에〉 unconsciously; imperceptibly
▶ 날씨가 따뜻해지자 눈은 슬슬 녹아버렸다 The snow unconsciously melted away when the warm weather came.
4 〈꾀거나 달래는 모양〉 ♦ 감언이설로 소녀를 슬슬 꾀다 entice [allure] a girl with fair words / 슬슬 달래서 하게 하다 coax *sb* to do [into doing]
5 〈점차〉 bit by bit; gradually; little by little; by degrees
▶ 날씨가 슬슬 더워지고 있다 It's getting warmer and warmer.

슬쩍 secretly (⇨ 살짝) ♦ 슬쩍 가지고 나가다 sneak *sth* out of / 옆 사람의 답안을 슬쩍 보다 peep stealthily at *one's* neighbor's paper / 옆구리를 슬쩍 찌르다 nudge *sb* in the ribs / 주먹을 슬쩍 피하다 parry a blow
▶ 나는 슬쩍 왼쪽으로 피했다 I swiftly dodged to the left side.
▶ 한 여자가 백화점에서 보석을 슬쩍 가지고 나갔다 A woman sneaked the jewels out of the department store.

슬퍼하다 bewail; grieve 《at, over》; feel sad 《about》; have a heavy [broken] heart; 〈한탄하다〉 deplore; lament; mourn 《over, for》; be distressed 《over》; regret
♦ 남의 불행을 슬퍼하다 feel sorry for another's misfortune / 남의 죽음을 슬퍼하다 mourn [lament] another's death; grieve [wail] over another's death
▶ 그는 때때로 자기의 기구한 팔자를 슬퍼한다 He sometimes bewails his hard fate.
▶ 지금은 슬퍼만 하고 있을 때가 아니다 This is no time to give way simply to sorrow.
▶ 아무리 슬퍼해도 죽은 사람은 돌아오지 않는다 No amount of grief will bring back the dead.

슬프다 1 〈마음이〉 sad; sorrowful; doleful; unhappy ♦ 슬픈 목소리로 in a sad voice / 슬픈 나머지 in (the excess of) *one's* sorrow [grief] / 슬픈 표정을 짓다 have a sad look on *one's* face / 슬픈 생각이 들다 feel sad [sorrowful]; be saddened; feel miserable [unhappy]
▶ 나는 아버지께서 돌아가셔서 슬프다 I am sad because my father has passed away.
▶ 그가 그렇게 젊은 나이에 죽다니 너무 슬프다 What a sad thing it is [What a pity] that he should have died so young.
▶ 너를 다시 못 본다고 생각하니 슬프다 I am so sad to think that I cannot see you again.
▶ 슬픈 노래는 듣고 싶지 않다 I don't like to hear sad [mournful] songs.
2 〈일이〉 sad; sorrowful; pathetic; plaintive; lamentable; grievous
♦ 슬픈 사정 a plaintive [doleful] case / 기쁠 때나 슬플 때나 in joy and in sorrow
▶ 우리의 미래에는 여러 가지 슬픈 일이 도사리고 있을지도 모른다 The future may hold many sorrows (in store) for us.

슬픔 sadness; sorrow; woe; 〈비애〉 grief; distress; 〈비탄〉 lamentation; mourning
♦ 슬픔에 찬 얼굴 a sad [sorrow-stricken] face; a sorrowful face / 슬픔에 잠기다 be overwhelmed with grief; be overcome with sorrow; cannot control *one's* grief / 슬픔에 잠기다 be grief-stricken 《at》; be in deep grief; be buried in grief; be plunged into grief / 슬픔을 참다 master *one's* sorrow / 슬픔 속에 살다 live in sorrow / 기쁨과 슬픔이 엇갈리다 have a mingled feeling of joy and sorrow
▶ 인생은 슬픔과 비탄으로 가득차 있다 Life is full of grief and sorrow.
▶ 때가 지나면 슬픔도 가라앉는다 Time blunts the edge of sorrow.
▶ 그녀에게는 자식은 슬픔의 씨앗이었다 Her son has been a sorrow to her.
▶ 그렇게 훌륭한 분을 잃다니 슬픔을 금할 수가 없다 The sadness of losing such a fine person is overwhelming.

슬피 sadly; sorrowfully; mournfully; dolefully; plaintively ♦ 슬피 울다 cry sorrowfully [in a mournful manner]

슬하 膝下 《under》 *one's* paternal roof [care]; the care of *one's* parents
♦ 부모 슬하에서 자라다 grow up under *one's* parental roof [care] / 부모 슬하에 있다 live with *one's* parents; live under *one's* parental roof / 부모 슬하를 떠나다 leave *one's* home
▶ 슬하에 자녀가 몇입니까? How many sons and daughters do you have (under your care)?

슴베 〈호미·칼 등의〉 the tang; the fang

습격 襲擊 an attack; an assault; a raid; a storm; a charge; an onset; an onslaught
─습격하다 attack; assault; raid; break into 《a house》; charge; make an attack [assault] on; make a raid on
♦ 불시에 습격하다 make a surprise attack 《on》; take 《the enemy》 by surprise; surprise
▶ 게릴라는 밤중에 경찰을 습격했다 The guerrillas attacked the police at midnight.
■ **─대** an attacking force; a storming party; an assault troop ■ **─자** a raider

습곡 褶曲 〔地〕 a fold ■ **─산맥** fold [folded] mountains

습관 習慣 〈관습·풍습〉 (a) custom; 〈버릇〉 a habit; a way; 〈관용(慣用)〉 a usage; 〈상습〉 a practice; a convention
♦ 평소의 습관 *one's* habitual ways / 예로부터의 습관 an old custom / 일찍 일어나는 습관 the habit of early rising / 담배 피우는 습관 the habit of smoking / 습관적인 habitual; customary; usual / 습관적으로 habitually; from [out of] habit / 습관이 붙다 acquire [con-

tract, form, pick up, take on] a habit; a habit grows upon *one* / …하는 습관이 있다 have [be in] the habit of (doing) / 습관을 들이다[붙이다] form (cultivate, build up) a habit / 습관을 버리다 abandon [discard, give up, throw aside] a habit; break (off [up]) [shake off] a habit / 나쁜 습관을 고치다 get rid of [get over] a bad habit; cure *oneself* of a bad habit / 남의 나쁜 습관을 버리게 하다 wean *sb* from a bad habit; break [cure] *sb* of a bad habit

▶ 그 습관은 지금은 없어졌다 The custom has died out.

▶ 일단 이 습관은 붙기만 하면 매우 고치기가 어렵다 Once you get into this habit, you will find it hard to get rid of it.

▶ 조반 전에 신문을 보는 것이 그의 습관이다 It is his daily routine to read the newspaper before breakfast.

▶ 습관은 제2의 천성이다 (속담) Habit [Custom] is (a) second nature.

습관성 習慣性 tendency ◆ 습관성이 있는 habit-forming / 습관성 의약품의 판매를 금지하다 ban sales of habit-forming medicines

▶ 이 약은 습관성이 있다 This medicine is habit-forming [addictive].

습기 濕氣 moisture; humidity; damp(ness) wet(ness)

◆ 습기가 찬 공기 humid air; air heavy with moisture / 습기가 많은[찬] damp; humid; moist / 습기가 없는 free from moisture; dry / 습기가 차다 be [get] damp; be moist; be humid; be wet; wet / 습기를 없애다 remove moisture ⦅from⦆

▶ 모피는 습기에 약하다 Furs are easily damaged by moisture [damp]

▶ 습기 차지 않도록 이것을 깡통 속에 넣어라 Keep this in a can so that it won't get damp.

▶ 이 약을 습기 없는 곳에 두어라 Keep this drug in a dry place.

습도 濕度 humidity ◆ 높은[낮은] 습도 high [low] humidity / 습도를 재다 measure the humidity ⦅of the atmosphere⦆ ▶ 습도는 80 퍼센트다 The humidity is 80 percent.

■—계 a hygrometer

습득 拾得 picking up

—습득하다 pick up; find

▶ 오늘 길에서 지갑을 습득하여 경찰에 신고했다 I found a purse on the road and reported it to the police today.

■—물 a find; a found article; a thing found [picked up] —자 the finder

습득 習得 learning; acquirement ◆ 기술의 습득 acquirement of technics

—습득하다 learn; master; acquire ⦅a foreign language⦆ / 완전히 습득하다 achieve a complete mastery ⦅of⦆

▶ 영어를 그렇게 단시일에 습득하기는 불가능하다 It is impossible to learn English in such a short time.

습성 習性 a habit; behaviour; *one's* way(s); a peculiarity; a habitude ⇨ 버릇

▶ 그는 개들의 습성을 조사했다 He investigated dogs' behaviour.

습성 濕性 wet; wetness ◆ 습성의 wet; moist; humid ■—늑막염 wet [moist] pleurisy; pleurisy with effusion —천식 humid asthma

습자 習字 ⟨펜의⟩ penmanship; ⟨붓의⟩ calligraphy ◆ 습자 연습을 하다 do practice in calligraphy [penmanship] / 습자를 배우다 take lessons in calligraphy / 습자를 잘하다[못하다] be a good [bad] hand

—습자하다 practice penmanship [calligraphy]

■영어— English penmanship ■—책 a writing book; a copybook

습작 習作 a study; ⟨프⟩ an étude

—습작하다 study

습전지 濕電池 a wet cell

습종 濕腫 ⟨韓醫⟩ ulcers on the legs

습증 濕症 diseases caused by dampness

습지 濕地 damp [marshy] ground [land]; ⟨美⟩ a moor, ⟨英⟩ a bog; a swamp

습진 濕疹 ⟨醫⟩ eczema; humid [moist] tetter

습포 濕布 a wet compress [pack, pad cloth]; ⟨약을 바른⟩ a poultice; a cataplasm

—습포하다 apply a poultice ⦅to⦆; put a wet compress ⦅on⦆

■냉— a cold compress [pad]; 간호사는 내 발에 냉습포를 했다 The nurse put a cold compress on my leg. 온— a stupe; a hot compress —제 (劑) poultice (medicine)

습하다 濕— damp; moist; wet; dampish; humid; ⟨축축하다⟩ soppy; soggy

◆ 습한 기후 a humid climate / 습한 날씨 soft weather; a damp [wet, muggy] day / 습한 공기 damp [dampish, humid] air

승¹ 乘 ⟨數⟩ multiplication ⇨ 곱셈

승² 乘 ◆ 500인승의 에어버스 a 500-seat [-passenger] airbus / 3인승의 우주선 a three-man spaceship / 2인승의 자전거 a bicycle (built) for two; a tandem (bicycle)

▶ 그의 스포츠카는 4인승입니다 His sportscar is a four-seater [carries four people].

승 勝 a victory; a win

▶ 우리 팀은 4승 3패 1무승부였다 Our team had four wins [victories], three losses [defeats] and one draw.

승강 昇降 ⟨오르내림⟩ going up and down; ascent and descent; ⟨파도가⟩ rise and fall; ⟨성쇠⟩ fluctuations

—승강하다 go [come] up and down; ascend and descend; rise and fall; fluctuate

■—구 (口) an entrance; ⟨배의⟩ a hatch(way) —기 an elevator; ⟨英⟩ a lift —타 (舵) ⟨空⟩ an elevator

승강이 昇降— a petty quarrel; wrangling; altercation ◆ 서로 승강이를 벌이다 wrangle against each other

▶ 옥신각신 승강이를 한 끝에 강경 수단이 취해졌다 After their repeated wrangles, drastic measures were taken.

—승강이하다 quarrel ⦅with⦆; wrangle ⦅with⦆; altercate ⦅with⦆

승객 乘客 a passenger; ⟨택시 등의⟩ (a) fare

◆ 승객을 태우다 ⟨기차·전차가⟩ take in passengers; ⟨배가⟩ take passengers on board

▶ 그 버스에는 승객이 별로 없었다 There were

승격

few passengers on that bus.
▶ 승객 이백 명과 승무원 다섯 명이 탑승한 여객기가 하와이로 운항중에 실종 되었다 A plane carrying two hundred passengers and a crew of five was lost on its way to Hawaii.
■ —명부 a register [list] of passengers; a passenger list; a waybill —안내소 an inquiry [information] office for passengers

승격 昇格 promotion in status; the raising [elevation] of status
—승격되다 be promoted [raised] to a higher status; be elevated to
♦ 부(部)로 승격하다 be raised to the status of a ministry / 시로 승격하다 be elevated to a city
▶ 그는 교수로 승격했다 He has been promoted to (the rank of) professor.
▶ 그 영사관은 대사관으로 승격되었다 The consulate was raised to the status of an embassy.

승계 承繼 succession ⇨ 계승(繼承)

승급 昇級 promotion to a higher grade; advancement; preferment
♦ 연공 서열에 의한 승급 promotion by seniority / 승급이 빠르다 win [get] speedy [rapid, quick] promotion
▶ 이 회사에서는 승급의 가망이 없다 There are no chance of promotion in this firm.
—승급하다 be promoted [advanced] ((to a higher grade)); obtain [get, win] promotion; rise in rank
♦ 승급시키다 promote; advance / 공로와 능력으로 승급하다 be promoted [win (a) promotion, rise in rank] by merit and abilities
▶ 그는 교장으로 승급했다 He was promoted to (the position of) principal.

승급 昇給 an increase [a rise] in pay [salary]; a payraise; (口) a wage [pay] hike
▶ 노조는 10퍼센트의 승급을 요구하고 있다 The union has asked for a ten percent increase in salary.
—승급하다 get a rise [raise] in one's salary [pay]; have one's salary raised
♦ 승급시키다 raise [increase] sb's salary; give sb a rise in pay
▶ 나는 올해 4퍼센트 승급했다 This year I got a four percent raise in (my) pay. ⇌ This year I had my pay four percent raised.
■ 정기— a periodic [a regular] pay raise: 연 1회의 승급 a set annual pay raise ■—률 the rate of pay raise

승기 勝機 a chance of victory; a chance to win / 승기를 놓치다 miss a chance to win; let a chance to win slip through one's fingers / 승기를 잡다 seize a chance of victory

승낙 承諾 assent; consent; agreement; acceptance; compliance
♦ 승낙을 얻어[승낙 없이] with [without] sb's consent / 승낙을 구하다 ask sb's consent ((to)) / 승낙을 얻다 obtain [win] sb's consent [assent]
▶ 그는 아버지의 승낙 없이는 아무것도 할 수 없다고 말했다 He said that he would not do anything, unless his father consented.
▶ 나는 그에게서 자동차 사용 승낙을 받았다 I got his consent [permission] to use his car.
—승낙하다 consent [agree, assent, accede] ((to)); comply ((with)); give one's consent [assent] ((to)); say yes ((to)); accept
♦ 제의를 승낙하다 accept a proposal / 쾌히[마지못해] 승낙하다 give a willing [a reluctant, an unwilling] consent ((to)) / 결혼을 승낙하다 give one's hand ((to)) / 설득하여 승낙하게 하다 talk [reason] sb into compliance / 위협하여 승낙하게 하다 intimidate sb into compliance
▶ 그는 그 요청을 즉석에서 승낙했다 He gave his ready consent to the request.
▶ 그는 수술을 승낙했다 The man consented to the operation.
■ 구두[서면]— a verbal [written] acceptance 사전— a previous consent 사후— ex post facto consent [approval] 조건부— a qualified consent ■—서 a written consent [acceptance]

승냥이 (動) a Korean wolf; a coyote

승단 昇段 〈태권도 등의〉 promotion
—승단하다 be promoted to a higher rank
▶ 그는 태권도 3단으로 승단했다 He was raised to the rank of the third grade of T'aekwondo.

승도(복숭아) 僧桃(—) 〔植〕 a nectarine

승려 僧侶 a (Buddhist) priest; bonze ⇨ 중
♦ 승려가 되다 become a bonze; enter the priesthood

승률 勝率 the percentage of victories (to the total number of matches [games])

승리 勝利 (a) victory; (a) triumph; (a) conquest; (a) success; 〈경기의〉 a win
♦ 승리를 거두다[차지하다] win (out) (over); carry [win] the day; come out on top
▶ 그 전투에서 아군은 대승리를 거두었다 Our troops won [had, gained] a great victory at the battle. ⇌ The battle ended in a great victory for our troops.
▶ 승리는 우리에게로 돌아왔다 The victory is ours. ⇌ We have triumphed.
—승리하다 win [gain] a victory; score a triumph; come out [emerge] victorious; come off victorious
■ 대— a great [signal, landslide] victory ■—자 a victor; a conqueror; 〈경기의〉 a winner —투수 〔野〕 the winning pitcher

승마 乘馬 horseback riding; riding; 〔競〕 equestrian
♦ 승마를 잘하다[못하다] ride [mount] a horse well [poorly]; be a good [poor] rider
▶ 나는 승마를 좋아한다 I like riding a horse.
▶ 내 취미는 승마입니다 My hobby is (horseback) riding.
—승마하다 ride a horse; mount [get on] a horse; ride horseback; take horse
♦ 승마하러 가다 go for a ride; go horse-riding
—교관 a riding master —바지 riding breeches —복 a riding clothes; a riding suit; 〈여성용〉 a riding habit —술 horsemanship —연습 riding exercise: 승마연습을 하다 take riding lessons; learn (how) to ride (a horse) —클럽 a (horse) riding club —학교[훈련소] a

riding school [academy]; a manege **—화 riding** [top] boots
승무 僧舞 a Buddhist dance; a dance in Buddhist attire
승무원 乘務員 a crewman; a member of the crew; (총칭) the crew
♦ 배에 승무원을 배치하다 man a boat [ship]
▶ 승무원은 전원 무사했다 All the crew were found safe.
▶ 그 배의 승무원은 몇 명입니까? What is the size of ship's crew?
▶ 그 배의 승무원은 여덟명입니다 The ship has a crew of eight men.
■ 여자— 〈여객기의〉 a stewardess; an air hostess ■ —명부 a crew list —실 the driver's [engineer's] cab [cabin]
승문 僧門 Buddhism; the Buddhist priesthood
♦ 승문에 들어가다 〈중이 되다〉 become a bonze; enter the priesthood
승방 僧房 a Buddhist nunnery; nuns' living quarters
승병 僧兵 a monk soldier; a fighting monk
승보 勝報 news of victory
승복 承服 1 〈동의〉 consent; 〈수락〉 acceptance; 〈굴복〉 submission; obedience
—승복하다 〈동의하다〉 consent [assent] (to); 〈수락하다〉 accept; 〈굴복하다〉 submit to (authority); yield to (power); obey (an order)
▶ 당신의 제안에는 승복할 수 없소 I can't consent to your proposal.
▶ 그의 이론은 남을 승복시키기에 충분하나 His theory is quite persuasive [convincing].
2 〈자백〉 confession [admission] of *one's* crime —승복하다 confess [acknowledge] *one's* guilt
승복 僧服 a clerical [priestly] robe; a monk's habit
승부 勝負 〈승패〉 victory or defeat; the issue; the outcome; 〈시합〉 a match; a game; a contest; a bout
♦ 무승부 a drawn game; a draw; 〈경주에서〉 a dead heat / 승부를 내다 [짓다] try conclusions (with); fight to the finish; fight it out; 〈동점 시합에서〉 play off / 승부를 다투다 contend for victory; compete; vie (in, with)
▶ 너하고는 승부가 안된다 〈상대가 우세하여〉 I am no match for you. ⇌ 〈상대가 열세하여〉 You stand no chance (whatever) against me.
▶ 좀처럼 승부가 나지 않았다 It was a close game [contest].
▶ 자포자기하여 승부를 포기하지 마라 Don't lose heart and give up the game.
승산 勝算 a chance of success [winning]; prospects of victory; odds
♦ 승산 없는 전쟁 a hopeless war; a lost cause / 승산이 있다 have [stand] a good [fair] chance of winning; have all the odds in *one's* favor
▶ 그에게는 승산이 없다 [충분히 있다] He has no [a good] chance of winning. ⇌ The odds are against him [strongly in his favor].
▶ 우리 팀의 승산은 반반이다 Our team has a fifty-fifty [an even] chance of winning.

승선 乘船 embarkation; boarding
—승선하다 embark (on [in] a ship); go [get] on board [aboard] (a ship); take (a) ship [boat]
▶ 그는 인천에서 승선하여 하와이로 향했다 He boarded a ship at Inch'ŏn bound for Hawaii.
▶ 우리는 저녁 5시까지 승선해야 한다 We have to be [go, get] on board by five (o'clock) in the evening.
■ —권 a passage ticket —료 passage money [fare]
승소 勝訴 winning a suit
—승소하다 〈사람이 주어〉 win [gain] the case [*one's* suit]; 〈사건이 주어〉 the case is decided in favor of *one*
▶ 그 재판은 피고가 승소했다 The defendant won the suit. ⇌ The case resulted [was decided] in favor of the defendant.
승수 乘數 〔數〕 a multiplier; multiplicator
■ 피(被)— a multiplicand
승승장구하다 乘勝長驅— make a long drive taking advantage of victory; press hard on the heels of the enemy; follow up *one's* victory
승압 昇壓 〔電〕 —승압하다 boost [raise] the voltage (of) —기 a booster —변압기 a step-up transformer
승용 乘用 ♦ 승용의 for riding / 말을 승용으로 쓰다 use a horse in riding
■ —마(馬) a riding horse; a saddle horse; a mount; a saddler —(자동)차 a motorcar [an automobile] for riding; a passenger car : 네 승용차에 태워주지 않겠니? Will you give me a ride [a lift] (in your car)?
승원 僧院 〈절〉 a temple; 〈수도원〉 a monastery; a cloister
승인 承認 1 〈인가〉 approval; (美口) an O.K. [OK, okay]
♦ 승인을 얻어 with *sb's* approval / 승인을 얻다 obtain [gain] *sb's* approval / 위원회의 승인을 요청하다 ask for the approval of the committee
▶ 그는 사장에게서 그 계약을 해도 좋다는 승인을 받았다 He received the president's approval to sign the contract.
—승인하다 approve; (美口) O.K. [OK, okay]
▶ 위원회는 그 계획을 승인했다 The committe approved the plan.
2 〈동의〉 consent; agreement; assent
♦ 저자의 사전승인 없이 without the author's prior consent
—승인하다 consent [assent] (to); agree (to)
3 〈인정〉 admission; recognition; acknowledgment ♦ 사실상의 승인 a de facto recognition
—승인하다 admit; recognize; acknowledge
▶ 그는 뇌물을 받았다는 것을 승인했다 He admitted taking [having taken] bribes.
▶ 미국은 즉시 이스라엘을 국가로서 승인했다 The United States promptly recognized Israel.
■ —서 a written acknowledgment —장 a letter of approval [assent]
승인 勝因 the cause of the victory
승자 勝者 a winner; a victor

승적 僧籍 the priesthood; the holy orders
▶ 그는 승적에 들었다 He became a priest. ⇌ He entered the priesthood.

승전 勝戰 a successful battle [war]; a victory; a triumph ―승전하다 win a war [battle]; gain [win] a victory
■―고(鼓) the drum of victory : 승전고를 울리다 beat victory on the drum

승제 乘除 〔數〕 multiplication and division
■가감― ⇨ 가감(～승제)

승직 僧職 priesthood; the clerical profession

승진 昇進 promotion; advancement; a rise in rank ◆승진이 빠르다 win speedy [rapid, quick] promotion; be quick in promotion / 승진이 늦다 be slow in promotion
―승진하다 obtain [win, get] promotion; be promoted [advanced] ((to)); rise (in rank); move up (to)
◆승진할 기회가 있다[없다] have a [no] chance of advancement [promotion]/ 승진시키다 promote; raise; advance
▶ 그는 최근 판매부장으로 승진했다 He was recently promoted to sales manager.
▶ 그 사원은 관리직으로 승진했다 The clerk was advanced to a managerial position.
▶ 그는 과장에서 부장으로 승진했다 He was promoted from section head to department manager.

승차 乘車 taking a train [car]; getting on a taxi; entrainment
◆승차를 거부하다 refuse (to accept) passengers; decline to pick up (prospective) fares
▶ 그 택시 운전 기사는 승차를 거부했다 The taxi driver rejected [refused to pick up] the passengers.
―승차하다 take a train [car, taxi]; get on a train; (美) board a train; get in [on] (a car); 〈군대 등이〉 entrain
▶ 여러분, 승차하시기 바랍니다 All aboard!
■―거부 refusal to pick up a passenger ―구 the entrance to the platform; (게시) Way In. ―규정 rules for passengers ―역 the [one's] entraining point [station]

승차권 乘車券 a (railway, subway) ticket; a passenger ticket
■―급행― an express ticket 무임― a free pass 우대― a complimentary pass 정기― ⇨ 정기승차권 할인― a cheap ticket ■―매표소 (美) a ticket office; (英) a booking office ―예매 the advanced sale of tickets for passengers

승천 昇天 〈그리스도의〉 the Ascension; 〈성모 마리아의〉 the Assumption; 〈죽음〉 death
―승천하다 ascend to [into] heaven; 〈죽다〉 go to heaven [glory]; die; pass away
■―일 〈그리스도의〉 Ascension Day; 〈성모 마리아의〉 the Assumption

승패 勝敗 victory or [and] defeat; the issue [outcome] (of a battle) ◆승패가 날 때까지 싸우다 fight to the finish [last]; fight it out
▶ 승패는 병가상사다 Victory and defeat are but ordinary events in a soldier's career.
▶ 승패를 떠나 최선을 다하라 Win or lose, do your best.

승홍 昇汞 〔化〕 〈속칭〉 corrosive sublimate ⇨ 염화(～제이 수은)

승화 昇華 〔化·心〕 sublimation ―승화하다 sublime; sublimate; be sublimated ◆승화시키다 sublime; sublimate ■―열〔化〕 the heat of sublimation

시¹ 〈감탄사〉 bah!; fie!; bowwow!; pshaw!; huh!; damn!

시² 〔樂〕 si; ti

시 市 1 〈도시〉 a city; a town; 〈행정구역〉 a municipality
◆온양시 Onyang City / 시 당국 the municipal authorities / 시의 municipal; urban / 시로 승격하다 be elevated to a city
▶ 이 읍은 내년에 시가 된다 This town will get city status [be municipalized] next year.
2 〈시장〉 a market; a fair
◆견본시 a sample fair / 야시 a night fair

시 時 〈시간〉 an hour; 〈시각〉 o'clock; time
◆아홉시 nine o'clock / 세시 반에 at half past three / 여덟시 반 기차로 by [(美) on] the 8:30 [eight thirty] train / 오전[오후] 다섯시에 at five (o'clock) in the morning [afternoon]; at 5 a.m. [p.m.]
▶ 넌 몇 시에 자니? What time do you go to bed?
▶ 그 프로그램은 8시 정각에 시작합니다 The program begins at eight o'clock sharp.

시 詩 (총칭) poetry; 〈한 편〉 a poem; lines; 〈운문〉 verse; 〈압운시〉 (a) rhyme [rime]
◆무운시(無韻詩) a blank verse / 산문시 a prose poem / 시를 감상하다 appreciate a poem / 시를 짓다 compose [write] a poem; write poetry
▶ 그녀는 감동을 시로 표현하고 싶었다 She wanted to make her impression into a poem.

시- 〈몹시〉 deep; very; intense; vivid
◆시꺼먼 very black; deep-black; jet-[coal-]black

시- 媤- (a brother) of the husband; (an aunt) on the husband's side

시가 市街 〈거리〉 the street; 〈시〉 a city; a town / 서울 시가 the street of Seoul / 시가를 행진하다 march [parade] along [down] the street
▶ 시가를 걸어가다가 선생님을 만났다 I met my teacher as I was going along the street.
■―신[구]― a new [the old] section of a city ■―전(戰) street fighting [battling, warfare]; street-to-street fighting ―전차 (美) a street car; (英) a tram(car) ―지 an urban district [area]; a town area ―지도 a city map ―행진 a demonstration; 시가 행진을 하다 stage a demonstration (parade); demonstrate

시가 市價 the market price [value]; the market quotations ◆상품을 시가로 팔다 sell goods at the market price
▶ 달러의 시가는 국제시장의 수요에 따라 변동한다 The market price of the dollar fluctuates according to the demands of the international marketplace.
■―기준 the market level ―변동 market movements [fluctuations]

시가 時價 the current price ◆시가로 쳐서 in current prices

▶이 다이아몬드는 시가로 쳐서 100만원 나간다 This diamond is valued at a million won today. ⇒ This diamond is [worth a million won in current prices.
■—위탁〔商〕the consignment with out limit
시가 媤家 one's husband's family [home]
시가 詩歌 songs and poems; poetry
■—선집 an anthology
시가 a cigar ▶그는 시가를 입에 물고 신문을 읽고 있었다 He was reading a newspaper with a cigar in his mouth.
시각 時刻 time; hour ⇨ 때, 시간
▶이 시각에 무얼 하고 있는거야? What (on earth) are you doing at this time of day?
▶열차는 제 시각에 도착했다 The train arrived punctually [on time].
■—약속— the appointed time [hour] ■—측정 (법) chronometry
시각 視角 **1**〔物〕the visual angle; an angle of vision [view]; the optic angle **2**〈시점〉a point of view; a viewpoint; an angle
시각 視覺 (the sense of) sight; visual sensation; vision; eyesight ◆시각적인 visual / 시각적으로 visually / 시각을 상실하다 lose one's eyesight [sight]; 〈일시적 상실〉〔空〕black out / 시각에 호소하다 appeal visually 《to》
■—교육 visual education —교재 visual aids —기관 an organ of sight [vision]; a visual [an optic] organ —중추 the visual center
시간 時間 an hour; time;〈수 업 시 간〉an hour; a period; a lesson; a class;〈여가〉leisure [spare] time
◆시간과 공간 time and space / 정확한 시간 the correct time / 장시간의 중노동 long hours of hard work / 근무 시간중에 during working hours
▶그것은 시간 문제에 지나지 않는다 It is only a question [matter] of time.
▶이제 잘 시간이다 It's time you were in bed. ⇒ It's time (for you) to go to bed. ⇒ It's bedtime [time for bed].
▶〔會話〕「여기서 서울까지 몇 시간 걸립니까?」「자동차로 2시간 반입니다」"How many hours [How long] does it take (to go) from here to Seoul?" "It takes two hours and a half to drive there." ⇒ "It is two and a half hours' drive there."
▶근무중 면회 사절 (게시) No interviews are allowed during office hours.
〈시간이[은]〉시간이 지남에 따라 as time goes by; with the lapse of time; in the course of time / 시간이 걸리다 take (a lot of) time / 시간이 걸리지 않다 don't take much time / 시간이 없다 have no time / 시간이 지나다 time passes [goes by] / 시간이 모자라다 have not enough time 《for, to do》
▶안양까지 가는데 그렇게 시간이 걸릴 리가 없다 It can't take you that long to get to Anyang.
▶아직 시간이 제법 있다 We still have plenty of time.
▶이제 시간이 다 됐다 Time is up.
▶운명을 결정짓는 시간이 시시각각 다가오고 있다 The fatal hour is approaching every moment.
▶무엇 때문에 그렇게 시간이 걸렸느냐? What kept [took] you so long?
▶시간은 돈이다 Time is money.
▶그 사고가 일어난 시간은 오후 6시 반이었다 The time of the accident was six thirty p.m. ⇒ It was at 6:30 [six thirty] p.m. that the accident occured.
〈시간을〉시간을 엄수하다 be punctual to the minute /〈시계의〉시간을 맞추다 set one's watch (aright) 《by》/ 시간을 내다 arrange hours; manage to find time / 시간을 낭비[절약]하다 waste [save] time / 충분한 시간을 들이다 give ample [much] time to / 시간을 보내다〈세월을〉pass away [while away] time;〈무료하게〉kill time / 빈둥거리며 시간을 보내다 idle one's time away
▶〔會話〕「잠깐 시간 좀 내 주시겠습니까?」「예, 좋습니다」"Can you spare me a few minutes [a minute]?" "Yes, sure."
▶시간을 내 주셔서 고맙습니다 Thank you very much for your time.
▶그는 여러 가지 구실을 삼아 시간을 끌려고 다 He tried to buy [play for, stall for] time by giving a lot of excuses.
▶천천히 생각할 시간을 주세요 Please give [allow] me sufficient time to think over it thoroughly.
▶그의 도착 시간을 가르쳐 주세요 Please let me know the time of his arrival [what time he is arriving].
▶그녀는 시간을 잘못 알고 음악회에 나갔다 She went out to concert at the wrong time.
▶나는 텔레비전의 시보에 시간을 맞추었다 I set my watch by the time-signal on television.
〈시간에〉일정한 시간에 at a certain [given] hour of the day / 제 시간에 punctually; on time / 역사 시간에 during a history lesson [the history hour] / 약속한 시간에 (오다) at the appointed [promised] time / 시간에 쫓기다 be pressed for time / 시간에 얽매이다 be restricted by time / (5시 30분의 기차) 시간에 대다 be in time (for the 5:30 train) / 시간에 늦다 be [come] late; be behind time
▶나는 시간에 쫓기고 있다 I am pressed for time.
▶기차는 제 시간에 도착했다 The train arrived on schedule [as scheduled, on time].
▶이런 시간에 그가 집에 있을 턱이 없다 He can't be at home at a time like this.
▶오늘 둘째 시간에 영어 시험이 있다 We have an English test in the second period today.
■배당— time assigned 《for a work》소요— the time required 수업— school hours 식사— meal time 점심— lunchtime 제한— limited time 집무[영업]— office [business] hours 취침— the time of [for] going to bed; bedtime 통금— curfew hours 표준[현지]— standard [local] time 휴식— a break; a recess ■—강사 a part-time lecturer —기록기 a time clock; a time recorder [register] —대(帶)〈동일 표준 시의〉a time zone; a period of time; a time period —문제 a question [matter] of time —엄수 punctuality —예술 arts based on

시각과 시간

1. 지금 …시입니다
- ▶ 지금 11시 정각입니다 It's just eleven (o'clock).
- ▶ 오전[오후] 11시입니다 It's eleven (o'clock) in the morning [evening]. ⇌ It's 11:00 a.m. [p.m.] (▶정오가 지나서 저녁 5시 경까지의「오후」는 in the afternoon이라고 한다)
- ▶ 11시 5분입니다 It's 11:05.(▶eleven O [ŏu] five로 읽는다) ⇌ It's five (minutes) past [때때로 (美) after] eleven.
- ▶ 11시 15분입니다 It's 11:15.(▶eleven fifteen 으로 읽는다) ⇌ It's a quarter past eleven.
- ▶ 11시 30분입니다 It's 11:30. ⇌ It's half past eleven.
- ▶ 11시 45분입니다 It's 11:45. ⇌ It's (a) quarter to twelve.(▶(美)에서는 to 대신 before나 of를 쓰기도 한다)

2. 지금 몇 시입니까?
- ▶ 지금 몇 시입니까? What time is it now? ⇌ What's the time? ⇌ 〈친한 사람끼리〉 What time do you have? ⇌ What time have you got?
- ▶〈공손하게 묻는 법〉 Could you tell me the time? ⇌ May I ask you the time?
- ▶ [會話]「당신 시계로 지금 몇 시입니까?」「내 시계로는 정각 4시입니다」 "What time is it by your watch?" "It's exactly four (o'clock) by my watch."
- ▶ [會話]「정확한 시간을 가르쳐 주십시오」「이제 30초 지나면 정오가 됩니다」 "Do you have the correct time?" "It'll be noon in thirty seconds."

3. …시에 ~하다
- ▶ [會話]「당신은 몇시에 학교에 갑니까?」「7시에 갑니다」 "What time do you leave for school?" "At seven."
- ▶ 오늘은 8시 30분쯤에 학교에 도착했습니다 I arrived at school (at) about eight thirty. (▶~쯤은 (美)에서는 around도 쓴다)
- ▶ 5시 정각에 그 열차는 출발했다 The train left at five sharp [on the dot].
- ▶ [會話]「순자야, 몇시에 전화하면 되겠니?」「글쎄. 오늘밤 10시까지 해줘」 "What time shall I call you, Sun-cha?" "Let me see. Call me by ten tonight, will you?"
- ▶ [會話]「하나야, 일어날 시간이다」「아직 6시 반밖에 안됐잖아」 "It's time to wake up, Hana." "It's only six thirty."

4. 시계에 관한 표현
- ▶ 내 시계는 3분 빠르다[늦다] My watch is three minutes fast [slow].
- ▶ 이 시계는 하루에 2분 더[덜] 간다 This clock gains [loses] two minutes a day.
- ▶ 나는 시계를 늘 5분 빠르게[늦게] 맞춘다 I always set my watch five minutes ahead [back].
- ▶ 이 시계는 아주 정밀해서 연차가 1초 이내야 This is a really precision watch, accurate to within of a second a year.
- ▶ [會話]「네 시계 정말 좋구나. 전자시계니?」「아니, 태엽을 감아줘야 해」 "Your watch is very nice. Is it a quartz watch?" "No, I have to wind it (up)."

5. 시간에 관한 표현
- ▶ 그 일은 너무 힘들어서 한 시간마다 10분씩 휴식을 취한다 The work is so hard that we take a ten minutes break every hour.
- ▶ [會話]「나, 저 레스토랑에서 아르바이트를 하고 있어」「그래? 시간당 얼만데?」 "I work part-time at that restaurant." "Do you? How much do you get an hour?"
- ▶ [會話]「3시 30분까진 시간이 얼마나 남았니?」「리포트 제출 마감 시간 말이구나. 이제 15분밖에 안남았어」 "How much time is there till three thirty?" "You're talking about the deadline for the report, aren't you? We've got only fifteen minutes."
- ▶ [會話]「그 사람 조금 전까지도 기분이 좋았는데」「걱정마. 두서너 시간만 지나면 나아질 거야」 "He was cheerful a little while ago." "Don't worry. He'll be in a better mood in a few hours."

tempo —절약 economy [economization] of time —제한 a time limit
시간급 時間給 payment by the hour; time wages ♦시간급의 일 timework / 시간급으로 일하다 work for hourly pay; be paid by the hour; be paid on an hourly basis
- ▶ 그의 시간급은 7천원이다 He is paid seven thousand won by the hour.
- ▶ 그는 시간급으로 고용돼 있다 He is engaged and paid on an hourly basis.
- ■—제 the hourly-wage system
시간급수 時間給水 an hour-restricted supply of water ♦상수도 시간 급수제 an hour-restricted water supply system; water rationing
시간외 時間外 ■—근무 working overtime; overtime work : 시간외 근무를 하다 work overtime [extra hours, after usual hours] —근무 수당 overtime allowance [pay]
시간제 時間制 ♦시간제의 일[노동] timework ♦시간제로 일하다 work by the hours
- ■—임금제 the pay-by-the-hour fare system
시간차 時間差 a time lag
- ■—공격 〈배구의〉 delayed spiking
시간표 時間表 a timetable; (美) a schedule ♦시간표대로 on schedule
- ■기차— a train timetable; (美) a railroad schedule 학교— a teaching schedule
시거에 〈우선〉 first of all; for the moment; hastily; 〈곧〉 at once; immediately
시건방지다 saucy ⇨ 건방지다
시게 grain [(英) corn] sold in the marketplace ■—전 market stalls that deal in grain 시겟금 the market price of grain [corn] 시겟바리 a

horseload of grain
시경 市警 ⟨수도의⟩ the Metropolitan Police ■―국장 the Metropolitan Police Director; the Chief Commissioner of the Metropolitan Police
시경 詩經 the Book of Odes [Poetry]
시계 時計 a timepiece; a timekeeper; ⟨벽시계⟩ a clock; ⟨회중・손목시계⟩ a watch; a wrist watch; ⟨자명종⟩ an alarm clock
♦ 정확한[부정확한] 시계 a good [bad, poor] timekeeper / 시계처럼 like a clock; like clockwork
⟨시계가[는]⟩ 시계가 서다 a watch stops
▶ 자네 시계는 몇 시인가? What time is it by your watch? ⇒ What time do you make it? ⇒ (美) What time do you have?
▶ 그 시계는 정확하다 The clock is correct [right]. ⇒ The clock keeps (good [right]) time.
▶ 이 시계는 3분 빠르다 [느리다] This watch is three minutes fast [slow].
▶ 내 시계는 하루에 2분 더[덜] 간다 My watch gains [loses] two minutes a day.
▶ 시계가 2시를 쳤다 The clock struck two (o'clock).
▶ 내 시계가 섰다 My watch has stopped [run down].
⟨시계를⟩ 시계를 차다 put on a watch / 시계를 맞추다 put one's watch right / 시계를 보다 look at [consult, refer to] one's watch / 시계를 고치다 repair a watch; put a watch [clock] in order / 시계를 앞으로 돌리다 put a clock [watch] on [forward, ahead]/ 시계를 늦추다 put a clock [watch] back / 시계를 라디오의 시보에 맞추다 set one's watch by the radio (time signal) [the time signal on the radio]
▶ 그는 시계를 10분 뒤로 늦추었다[앞으로 돌렸다] He put [set] his watch ten minutes back [ahead].
▶ 그는 시계를 9시에 맞췄다 He put the clock to nine. ⇒ He set his watch at nine.
▶ 그는 디지털 시계를 차고 있다 He is wearing a digital watch.
■ 뻐꾹― a cuckoo clock 야광― a glow [luminous] watch 전기―an electric clock 전자―an electronic watch 진자[추]― a pendulum clock 탁상― a table clock ―바늘 the hands of a clock [watch] ―소리 ⟨똑딱똑딱・재깍재깍⟩ ticking of a clock; ticktack ―수리공[제조자] a watchmaker ―장치 clockwork ―줄 a watch chain [guard] ―탑 a clock tower ―포(鋪) (美) a watch shop; a jeweler's; a jewelry store; (英) a watchmaker's
시계 視界 a field of vision ⇨ 시야 (視野)
▶ 시계 제로[양호] Zero [Good] visibility.
시계방향 時計方向 ♦ 시계 방향의 right-handed; clockwise / 시계 방향과 반대의 counterclockwise; anticlockwise
시고 詩稿 a draft poem; a draft of a poem
시고모 媤姑母 a husband's (paternal) aunt; an aunt (who is a sister of one's husband's father) ■―부(夫) the husband of an aunt on one's husband's side
시골 the country; ⟨전원⟩ a rural district

[area]; a countryside; the backcountry; (美口) the sticks; ⟨지방⟩ the provinces; ⟨고향⟩ one's home (country); one's hometown; one's birthplace
♦ 시골의 country; rural / 시골 태생의 country-born; born in the country / 시골 출신의 from the country / 시골에서 자란 countrybred / 시골에서 갓 올라온 fresh from the country / 시골에 가다 go into [down to] the country / 시골에서 자라다 be brought up in the country
▶ 시골의 환경은 건강에 좋다 A country enviornment is healthy.
▶ 시골 사람은 의리와 인정을 잘 간직하고 있다 Countryfolk know [understand] very well what duty and humanity are.
▶ 그는 도시보다 시골을 좋아한다 He prefers the country to the town.
▶ 그는 시골에서 살고 있다 He lives in the country [in a rural area].
▶ 노모께서는 지금도 시골에 혼자 살고 계십니다 My old mother still lives alone in our hometown.
▶ 올 여름 휴가에는 시골로 내려가려고 생각하고 있다 I'm planning to go back to my hometown during this summer vacation.
■ ―구석 a remote village; a secluded place ―길 a country lane [road] ―내기[사람] a rustic; (총칭) country folk ―뜨기 a countryman; a rustic; a bumpkin; a clodhopper ―말투 provincial accent ―사투리 a rustic [provincial, local] dialect; a provincialism ―생활 country [provincial, rural] life : 한가로운 시골 생활을 즐기고 있다 I'm enjoying an easy life in the country. ―집 a country house; a rustic dwelling ―풍경 rural scenery ―풍습 the manners and customs of the country
시골식 ―式 rustic manners; provincialism; localism; country style [fashion]
♦ 시골식의 countrylike; rustic
시골티 the rural [rustic, country] air
♦ 시골티 나는 rusticated; countrified; rustic
시공 施工 execution; operation; carrying out
―시공하다 execute; operate; carry out
▶ 우리는 그 건축 공사를 시공한다 We are executing the construction work.
■ ―도(圖) a contract drawing; a working [an execution] drawing [diagram] ―자 a (main) contractor; a builder; an operator
시공 時空 (物) space-time
♦ 시공 연속체 (數) a space-time continuum (pl. -tinua) / 시공의 spatial-temporal
시구 市區 a municipal district; streets ■―개편 town [city] replanning; street improvement
시구 始球 opening of a ball game
▶ 서울 시장의 시구로 경기는 시작되었다 The game was opened [started] with the first ball thrown by the Mayor of Seoul.
―시구하다 throw [pitch] the first ball
―식 opening ceremony of a ball game
시구 詩句 ⟨시의 한 행⟩ a line of a poem; ⟨시의 절⟩ a verse; a stanza; a stave
시국 時局 the situation; the (current) state of affairs [things]

시국 ♦어려운 시국을 수습하다 settle [sort out; straighten out] a difficult situation / 시국을 논하다 discuss the present [existing, current] situation / 시국에 대처하다 meet [deal with, cope with] the situation
▶이 심각한 시국을 타개할 길은 이것 밖에 없다 This is the only means we have to tide us over this grave situation [crisis].
■비상─ an emergency; 〈위기〉a crisis 《pl. -ses》; 〈전시〉wartime

시굴 試掘 trial boring [digging]; prospecting ─시굴하다 make a trial digging [boring]; prospect 《a mine》
♦유정을 시굴하다 drill an experimental oil well; bore for oil; (美) wildcat
■─권 a prospecting right ─자 a prospector; (美) a wildcatter

시궁 〈시궁창물〉sewage; waste in sewers or drains; 〈하수구〉a sewer; a cesspool; 〈도랑〉a ditch; a gutter ⇨ 시궁창
♦시궁을 치다 clear a sewer [gutter]
■─구멍 the opening of a cesspool

시궁쥐 a brown rat; a sewer [water] rat

시궁창 〈도랑〉a ditch; 〈하수구〉a gutter; a drain; a gully; a sewer; 〈괸 곳〉a cesspool
♦시궁창에 빠지다 fall into a ditch / 시궁창을 치다 clear (out) a ditch
▶시궁창이 흙으로 메워졌다 The drain [gutter] is clogged with mud.
■─물 ditch water; sewage

시그널 〈신호〉a signal ▶교통 시그널이 빨강으로 바뀌었다 The traffic signal [sign] turned red.

시그러지다 lose one's vigor [strength, energy]; become depressed [despondent]

시극 詩劇 a verse [poetic] drama; a drama in verse

시근거리다¹ 〈숨을〉breathe hard [roughly]; be short of breath; gasp; pant
♦시근거리며 panting(ly); out of breath / 시근거리며 말하다 pant [puff] out / 화가 나서 시근거리다 be in a huff; be really fuming

시근거리다² 〈관절이〉feel an arthritic [a neuralgic] pain ♦발목이 시근거리다 have a nagging pain in the ankle

시근시근¹ 〈숨을〉panting(ly); out [short] of breath; wheezing(ly)

시근시근² 〈관절이〉with an arthritic [a neuralgic] pain

시근하다 have a nagging [a neuralgic] pain

시글시글 in a swarm [crowd] ─시글시글하다 swarming ▶물고기가 못에 시글시글하다 Fish are swimming in schools in the pond.

시금 試金 assaying; 〈한번의〉an assay ─시금하다 assay; make an assay of
■─술 the art of assaying ─천칭 an assay balance

시금떨떨하다 sourish and astringent

시금석 試金石 1 〈돌〉a touchstone; a Lydian stone
2 〈시험〉a test; a test case
▶이 일이 나의 재능과 운명의 시금석이 될 것입니다 This work will be [will serve as] a test of my ability and fortune.

시금씁쓸하다 sour and bitter [astringent]

시금치 〔植〕spinach

시금하다 sourish; somewhat sour; tart

시급하다 時急─ urgent; pressing; immediate; imminent
♦시급한 문제 a pressing question; a problem of great urgency / 시급히 urgently; at once; without delay; in no time
▶시급히 착수해 주시오 Get to work at once [right away].

시기 時期 〈때〉time; a period; 〈계절・제절〉a season; the time of (the) year
♦이 중대한 시기에 at this crucial period / 적당한 시기에 at the appropriate season [time] / 시기가 좋다[나쁘다] be favorable [adverse] time for [to] / 시기가 너무 이르다[늦다] be too early [late] (to)
▶공부[수영]하기에는 지금이 좋은 시기다 Now is a good season for study [swimming].
▶아직은 그에게 말할 시기가 아니다 It is not yet the time to tell him.

시기 時機 〈기회〉an opportunity; a chance; 〈경우〉an occasion
♦시기에 알맞은[적절한] timely; appropriate; well-timed; opportune / 시기에 맞지 않는 inopportune; inappropriate; untimely; out of season / 시기를 기다리다 wait for a favorable time [a ripe opportunity]; bide one's time / 시기를 잡다[포착하다] seize [take] the opportunity / 시기를 놓치다 miss [pass up] an opportunity; let an opportunity slip by; lose one's chance
▶시기를 놓치지 마라 Don't miss a chance. ⇌ Strike while the iron is hot.
▶그녀의 발언은 여러 면에서 시기에 알맞다 Her remark is timely in more ways than one.
▶매사에는 다 시기가 있는 법이다 There is a time for everything.
▶지금이야말로 절호의 시기다 This is the time of all times.

시기 猜忌 jealousy; (green) envy
♦아무의 명성에 대한 강한 시기 fierce jealousy for sb's fame
─시기하다 be jealous [envious] (of); envy; feel envy; show jealousy (of)
▶그는 성적이 좋아서 반친구들이 시기하고 있다 He is envied by his classmates for his good record.
■─심 jealousy; envy : 시기심이 강한 envious; jealous / 그녀는 시기심에서 범죄를 저질렀다 She committed a crime out of jealousy.

시기상조 時機尚早 prematurity
▶결정하기에는 시기상조다 It is too early yet to decide.
▶지금 출발하기에는 시기상조다 The time is not yet ripe for starting.
▶그 계획을 실행하기에는 시기상조다 The time is not quite ripe [mature] for taking action on the plan.

시끄럽다 1 〈떠들썩하다〉noisy; loud; boisterous; uproarious; clamorous; tumultuous; (美俗) rip-roaring
♦시끄러운 소리 a noisy sound; a noise; 〈떠드는 소리〉a clamor / 시끄러운 텔레비전 광고 a

시끄러운 TV commercial / 시끄러운 음악 loud music / 시끄럽게 noisily; clamorously; boisterously; uproariously / 시끄럽게 떠들다 make a noise; clamor; shout
▶ 옆집 아이들은 항상 시끄럽다 My neighbor's kids are always making a noise.
▶ 이 가게는 시끄럽다 It is noisy in this shop. ⇒ This shop is full of noise.
▶ 그는 시끄럽게 기타를 쳤다 He played his guitar loudly [(口) loud].
▶ 그렇게 시끄럽게 굴면 야단 맞는다 You'll be scolded if you make so much noise.
▶ 시끄러워! 〈입닥쳐!〉 Shut up! ⇒ Shut your mouth! ⇒ Be quiet! ⇒ Don't be noisy. ⇒ Don't make a noise. ⇒ 〈말시키지 마!〉 Stop nagging (at me)!
2 〈여론 등이〉 controversial; much-talked-of; much-discussed; burning
▶ 공해 문제로 여론이 시끄럽다 The public is raising a clamor against environmental pollution.
▶ 세상이 시끄러워졌다 Times are [The world is] getting unsettled.
▶ 그 문제로 세상이 시끄러워졌다 The case caused [was] a sensation.

시끈가오리 〔魚〕 an electric ray

시나리오 a scenario (*pl.* ~s); a screenplay
♦ 텔레비전 드라마의 시나리오를 쓰다 write a scenario for a TV drama
■ —라이터 [작가] a scenario writer; a scenarist; a screenwriter

시나몬 〈향신료〉 cinnamon

시나브로 〈서서히〉 by imperceptible degrees; little by little; bit by bit; gradually; slowly
▶ 땅에 쌓인 눈이 시나브로 녹아 없어졌다 The snow on the ground has disappeared [melted] little by little.

시내 a small stream; a brook; a brooklet; a rivulet; a streamlet; (美) a creek
■ 시냇가 the bank of a stream: 시냇가를 걷다 walk along a stream

시내 市內 the town
♦ 시내에(서) in the city; within the city limits
▶ 제가 시내를 안내하겠습니다 I'll show you around [over] the city.
▶ 시내 배달은 무료입니다 Delivery within the city (limits) is free.
■ —거주자 a city resident —구경 sightseeing in the city —버스 a city bus —전차 a streetcar; (英) a tramcar —통화 a local call

시냇물 brook water; a stream; a small stream
♦ 시냇물 소리 the murmuring of a stream

시네라리아 〔植〕 a cineraria

시네라마 (商標) (映) Cinerama

시네마 (총칭) the movies; (英) the cinema; 〈영화 한 편〉 a movie; (英) a film

시네마스코프 (商標) (映) CinemaScope

시녀 侍女 a waiting woman [maid]; 〈여관〉 a lady's maid; a lady-in-waiting; a lady attendant

시누렇다 brightly [vividly] yellow ⇨ 싯누렇다

시누이 媤— *one's* husband's sister; a woman's sister-in-law

시늉 〈흉내〉 mimicry; imitation; aping; 〈몸짓〉 gesture; 〈체하기〉 (false) show; (a) pretense; make-believe; simulation
♦ 앓는 시늉을 하다 feign *oneself* to be sick / 귀먹은 시늉을 하다 assume to be deaf / 우는 시늉을 하다 pretend to be weeping; shed false tears / 죽은 시늉을 하다 feign death; pretend to be dead; play dead / 절망한 시늉을 하다 make a gesture of despair
▶ 그는 그녀에게 의자에 앉으라는 시늉을 했다 He motioned her to take a seat.
▶ 거미는 위급하면 죽은 시늉을 한다 A spider often plays dead when in danger.
▶ 그 소년은 선생님의 목소리 시늉을 하며 우리를 웃겼다 The boy made us laugh by mimicking the teacher's voice.
—시늉하다 〈흉내내다〉 imitate; mimic; gesture; make motion; 〈체하다〉 pretend; make believe; assume; (口) put on; feign; affect

시니시즘 cynicism

시니어 senior; 〈윗사람〉 *one's* senior

시니컬 —시니컬하다 cynical; cynic

시다¹ **1** 〈맛이〉 sour; acid; tart; 〈식초같은〉 vinegary
▶ 이 사과는 맛이 시다 This apple tastes sour.
2 〈시어지다〉 turn sour; get [become] sour
▶ 우유가 조금 시었다 The milk has gone a bit sour.

시다² **1** 〈뼈마디가〉 stinging; (inflammatorily) painful
▶ 무릎이 시고 아프다 I feel a dull pain in my knees.
2 〈비위에 거슬리다〉 detestable; offensive; disgusting; repulsive; offensively flattering
♦ 눈꼴이 신 아첨 fulsome compliments [flattery]
3 〈눈이 부시다〉 dazzling; glaring; blinding
▶ 밖에서 들어오는 빛에 눈이 시어서 한동안 볼 수가 없었다 I was blinded for a moment by the dazzling light from outside.

시단 詩壇 the world of poetry; poetical [poetic] circles

시달 示達 〈문서에 의한〉 written instructions [directions]; a directive; 〈공문에 의한〉 a public notification [notice]; an official notice; 〈명령〉 an order
♦ 시달대로 행하다 act according to directions; follow instructions
—시달하다 instruct; direct; give instructions [directions]; notify

시달리다 〈고생하다〉 be troubled ((with)); be worried ((with)); be annoyed ((by, with, at)); be harassed; be vexed; 〈병으로〉 suffer ((from))
♦ 가난에 시달리다 be distressed by poverty / 빚쟁이에게 시달리다 be hounded [persecuted] by *one's* creditors / 생활고에 시달리다 be in distress for *one's* livelihood / 악몽에 시달리다 have a (fit of) nightmare
▶ 어젯 밤에는 모기에 시달렸다 We were bothered [disturbed] by mosquitoes last night.
▶ 그는 신경통에 시달리고 있다 He is suffering from [tormented by] neuralgia.
▶ 그의 중상에 몹시 시달렸다 His backbiting caused me a great deal of trouble.

▶ 하루종일 아이들을 돌보느라 시달렸겠다 You must be all in, taking care of the children all day.
▶ 주정뱅이 남편 때문에 많이 시달렸다 My drunk of a husband caused me great distress [so much trouble].

시담 示談 〈사사로운 해결〉 settlement out of court; a private settlement [arrangement]; a mutual concession
▶ 회사는 그 건을 500만원의 시담(금)으로 해결했다 The company settled the case out of court [without going to law] for five million won.

시대 時代 1 〈시기〉 a period; an epoch; 〈연대〉 an age; an era
♦ 나폴레옹 시대 the era of Napoleon / 문예부흥 시대 the period [age, time] of the Renaissance / 우주 여행의 시대 the era [epoch] of space travel / 혁명 시대 the period [epoch, era, age] of the revolution / 청춘 시대 one's youth; one's youthful days / 다음 시대 사람 the next generation
▶ 전시품 가운데는 여러 시대의 것이 있었다 Among the exhibits were articles from different periods.
▶ 인공위성이 통신에 새 시대를 열었다 The artificial satellite marked a new epoch in communications.
▶ 이것은 시대를 초월한 예술 작품이다 This is the very work of art that transcends time.
2 〈세상〉 (the) times; time; day(s)
♦ 시대의 총아 the most popular figure of the times / 지금 시대에 (in) these days; nowadays / 시대에 앞서다 be ahead of the times; go before the times / 시대의 요청을 따르다 meet the demands of the times / 시대를 반영하다 reflect the times / 시대에 뒤지다 fall behind the times [the age, the day]; be old-fashioned [out-of-date]
▶ 시대가 바뀌었다 Times have changed.
▶ 너희 시대가 온다 Your time will come.
▶ 그는 시대에 뒤떨어지지 않으려고 열심히 공부하고 있다 He is studying hard to keep abreast of [pace with, up with] the time.
■기계― the machine age 봉건― the feudal age 빙하― the glacial period [age] 삼국― the era of the Three Kingdoms 석기[청동기, 철기]― the Stone [Bronze, Iron] Age 암흑― 〈중세의〉 the Dark Ages 우주― the space age 원자력― the atomic age 자동차― the motor age [era]; the age of motorcars ―감각 sensitivity to the spirit of the time(s) ―극 a historical play [drama]; a period piece ―사상 current thoughts [ideas, sentiments] ―사조 the trend [current] of the times ―상(相) the phases [indications] of the times [age] ―정신 the spirit of the times [age]; 〈독〉 Zeitgeist ―착오 anachronism : 시대 착오의 anachronistic; anachronic; out-of-date

시댁 媤宅 one's husband's family [home]; the family into which a woman has married

시도 示度 〈눈금 숫자〉 a reading; the recorded [registered] degrees; indication

시도 試圖 a try; a trial; (口) a tryout; 〈기도〉 an attempt; a venture; an experiment
♦ 새로운 시도 a new trial [attempt]; 〈사업 등의〉 a new venture
▶ 그건 좋은 시도였다 It was a good try.
―시도하다 try; try out; attempt (to do); make an attempt (at)
▶ 그는 불가능한 것을 시도하여 성공했다 He attempted the impossible and succeeded.

시도 視度 visibility ♦ 수평[사(斜)]방향 시도 the horizontal [slant] visibility

시도 市道 a city [municipal] road

시동 始動 〔機〕 starting
♦ 기계의 시동을 걸다 start a machine
▶ 엔진의 시동이 잘 걸리지 않는다 The engine does not start well.
―시동하다 start
■―기 a starter; a starting engine ―장치 a starting device [gear, system]

시동 侍童 a page; a boy attending a nobleman

시동생 媤同生 one's husband's younger brother; a woman's brother-in-law

시드 〔競〕 seeding ―시드하다 seed ■―선수 a seeded player; (口) a seed

시드니 〈호주의 도시〉 Sydney

시드머니 〈신규사업 착수금〉 seed money

시들다 1 〈초목이〉 wither; wilt; fade (away); droop; shrivel
♦ 시든 야채 withered vegetables
▶ 이 더위로 꽃이 시들어버렸다 The flowers have shriveled [dried] up in this heat.
▶ 자른 꽃은 쉽게 시든다 Cut flowers soon wither [fade].
2 〈기운이〉 weaken; lose strength; wane; 〈매력·청춘이〉 wither; wane
♦ 기력이 시들다 lose one's vigor [energy]/ 인기가 시들다 lose [fall in] popularity

시들부들, 시들시들 ―시들부들하다, 시들시들하다 slightly withered [wilted]
▶ 장미는 피었으나 며칠 후에 시들시들 져버렸다 The roses bloomed and withered away a few days later.

시들하다 〈불만이다〉 unsatisfactory; dissatisfied; 〈건성이다〉 halfhearted; unwilling; uninterested; unattractive; uninteresting; 〈하찮다〉 trivial; of no account [value]
♦ 시들한 이야기 a dull [an uninteresting] story / 삶이 시들해지다 lose interest in life; grow weary [get sick] of life / 시들하게 대답하다 answer in a halfhearted manner
▶ 나는 때로 일이 시들해질 때가 있다 I sometimes get tired of my job.
▶ 회의의 후반은 시들했다 The latter half of the meeting was dull.
▶ 그의 인기가 시들해지고 있다 He is losing popularity. ⇌ His popularity is waning.

시디 CD [〈compact *d*isc〕

시래기 dried radish leaves

시러큐스 〈미국의 도시〉 Syracuse

시럽 sirup; syrup ♦ 과일 시럽 fruit syrup / 팬케이크에 바른 메이플 시럽 maple syrup on pancakes

시렁 a (wall) shelf; a rack
♦ 시렁을 달다 put up a shelf / 시렁에 얹다 put

[place] *sth* on a shelf; shelve
시력 視力 sight; eyesight; vision; visual power [acuity]

> [해설] 영·미에서는 시력의 측정법을 **20 / 20 vision**으로 나타내어 **twenty-twenty vision**으로 읽는다. 이는「시력 정상」임을 나타낸다. 또 1.0의 2배 크기의 글자 밖에 읽지 못하는 시력은 **twenty-forty (20/40)**라고 한다.

〈시력이〉 시력이 약하다 have poor [bad, weak] sight; be weak-sighted; be weak in sight / 시력이 약해지다 *one's* eyesight fails
▶ 나는 오른쪽 눈의 시력이 1.0이다 My eyesight in my right eye is 1.0 ⇌ (美) I have 20/20 vision in my right eye. (▶20피트 거리에서 표시 20의 글씨가 보이는 것이 우리의 1.0에 해당함)
▶ 시력이 약하거나 떨어진 분에게는 큰 활자의 책이 있습니다 Books with large points are available for those with weak or failing eyesight.
〈시력을〉 시력을 잃다 lose *one's* eyesight; be deprived of *one's* eyesight / 시력을 회복하다 recover *one's* sight / 시력을 검사하다 test *sb's* eyesight
■─감퇴 amblyopia ─검사 an eye examination; an eyesight [a vision] test; optometry : 시력 검사용 안경 trial glasses / 나는 시력검사를 받았다 I had my eyesight tested. ─검사표 an eye examination chart; an eyesight [a vision] test chart; an eye chart ─계〈측정장치〉 an optometer

시련 試鍊·試練 a trial; a test; an ordeal; 〔神學〕 a probation
◆인생의 시련 the trials of life / 신의 시련 [시험] a divine test; 〈벌〉 an infliction from God / 모진 시련 a severe [bitter] trial; a trying [severe] ordeal / 시련을 받다 be tried 《by》; be tested 《by》; undergo [go through] an ordeal
▶ 그는 그 시련을 견디지 못했다 He could not endure [get over] the trial [ordeal].

시론 時論 〈시사론〉 comments upon current events; 〈일반적 의견〉 a current view; a contemporary opinion
◆시론을 무시하다 ignore the public opinion of the day

시론 詩論 an essay on poetry; a criticism of poems; a theory on [of] poetry; poetics

시론 試論 an essay 《in, on》 ◆문학적 시론 a literary essay

시료 施療 free medical treatment
◆시료를 받다 be treated free of charge
─시료하다 give *sb* free medical treatment; treat *sb* free of charge
■─병원 a charity hospital ─환자 a charity [free] patient

시료 試料 〈실험용의〉 materials for experiment; a sample ■─시험 a test on sample

시루 〈떡 찌는〉 a rice steaming pot; an earthenware pot for steaming rice ■─떡 steamed rice cake 시룻방석 a straw mat cover for a rice steaming pot

시루에 물 퍼붓기 (속담) It's like pouring water into a sieve. ⇌ It's waste of labor.

시류 時流 〈당시의 풍조〉 the current of the times; the trend (of the world); 〈유행〉 the fashion (of the day)
◆시류를 따르다[좇다] follow [pursue] the fashion of the day; swim [go] with the tide [current]/ 시류를 거스르다[역행하다] go [swim] against the stream [tide, current]; run counter to the times / 시류를 초월하다 stand aloof from the crowd; be independent of the trends of the times
▶ 그는 시류에 영합하여 명성을 얻었다 He won popularity by conforming to the current of the times (of puplic opinion).

시름 anxiety; uneasiness; worry; care; trouble; grief; sorrow
◆시름 많은 얼굴 a sorrowful look / 시름을 놓다[덜다] be relieved of *one's* anxiety; feel relieved; unload *one's* mind
▶ 그는 술로 시름을 달랬다 He drowned his cares [sorrows, grief] in drink.
▶ 나는 시름이 많다 I am full of cares [worries, troubles]. ⇌ I am care-laden.

시름시름 ◆시름시름 앓다 suffer from a lingering disease / 시름시름 앓다가 죽다 die after a lingering illness

시름없다 1〈근심·걱정으로 맥이 없다〉 worried; concerned; careworn; depressed; dispirited; disheartened; care-laden
2〈멍하다〉 absentminded; vacant

시름없이 1〈맥없이〉 worriedly; depressedly; dispiritedly; languidly; plaintively
2〈멍하니〉 absentmindedly; vacantly
◆시름없이 하늘을 쳐다보다 gaze up at the sky absentmindedly

시리다 〈손발 등이〉 (achingly, painfully) cold; chilled; chilly; 〈서술적〉 feel [have] a chill
▶ 발이 시리다 My feet feel cold.
▶ 병자는 흔히 손발이 시린다 The patient is apt to be cold at the extremities.

시리아 〈나라 이름〉 Syria; 〈공식명〉 the Syrian Arab Republic ◆시리아(사람)의 Syrian
■─사람 a Syrian

시리즈 a series; a serial

> [해설] 출판물이나 방송 프로그램의「연속물」에는 **a series, a serial** 양쪽 다 쓰인다. a series는 매회 완결되는 형태의 것, a serial은 전체로서 연속되는 것을 가리킨다.

◆영문학시리즈 the English Literature Series
▶ 출판사는 그의 소설을 시리즈로 냈다 The publisher published his novels in a serial form.
■─물 a serial

시립 市立 ◆시립의 municipal
▶ 이 도서관은 시립이다 The library is maintained at municipal expense.
▶ 이 유아원은 시립이다 This nursery is run by the city.
■─도서관 a city library ─병원 a municipal hospital

시말 始末 〈시종〉 the beginning and the end;

시맥 翅脈 〔昆〕 a vein (in an insect's wing); a nerve; nervure

시멘트 cement ◆벽에 시멘트를 바르다 cover [coat] a wall with cement; cement a wall ■—공사 cement work —공장 a cement factory [plant] —기와 a cement tile —믹서 a cement mixer

시목 市木 the official tree of a city

시무 始務 —시무하다 start work; 〈신년에〉 resume [reopen] office business after the New Year recess ■—식 the opening ceremony of official business (for the year)

시무룩하다 sulky; sullen; peevish; glum; grumpy; moody and taciturn
◆시무룩한 얼굴을 하다 pull a long face; wear a sullen look
▶그녀는 하루종일 시무룩했다 She was in [had] the sulks all day long.

시문 時文 contemporary writing
■—체 current [newspaper] style of writing

시문 詩文 prose and poetry; literature; 〈문학작품〉 literary works ■—선집 an anthology

시문 試問 a question; a test; an examination —시문하다 question sb; put a question to sb

시뮬레이터 a simulator

시민 市民 〈개인〉 a resident of a city; a citizen (▶원래 투표권이 있는 사람으로서의 국민·공민의 뜻이 더 강함); 〈총칭〉 the townsmen; the townspeople; the townsfolk; the citizens; the citizenry
◆수원 시민 the people [citizens] of Suwon; the residents of Suwon / 미국 시민 an American citizen / 온 시민 all the citizens; the whole city / 명예 시민 an honorary citizen
▶시민의 과반수가 현시장에게 투표했다 The majority of the citizens voted for the present mayor.
■—계급 (프) bourgeoisie —대회 a citizens' rally [mass meeting] —사회 civil society —생활 the civic life —세(稅) a municipal tax —운동 a citizens' campaign; a grass-roots movement —혁명 a people's [popular] revolution —회관 a civic hall

시민권 市民權 citizenship; civic [civil] rights
◆미국 시민권을 얻다 acquire [be granted] U.S. citizenship; become a U.S. citizen

시반 a death spot

시발 始發 the first departure (of a train [car]); 〈차〉 the first train
◆서울역 시발의 열차 a train starting from Seoul Station
▶시발은 오전 5시 5분이다 The first train [car] starts at 5:05 a.m.
—시발하다 start; leave; depart (a terminal)
■—역 a terminal; a starting station; the station of origin —점 a starting point

시방 時方 now ⇨ 지금

시방서 示方書 specifications ◆건축 설계 시방서 building specifications

시범 示範 showing an example; a model for others ◆시범적으로 by way of showing an example; as a model
—시범하다 show [set, give] an example
■—경기 an exhibition game [match] —농장 [학교] a model farm [school]

시베리아 Siberia ◆시베리아의 Siberian
▶그는 시베리아 경유로 유럽에 갔다 He went to Europe via [by way of] Siberia.
■—사람 a Siberian —철도 the (Trans-)Siberian Railway [Railroad]

시벨리우스 〈핀란드의 작곡가〉 Sibelius, Jean Julius Christian (1865 1957)

시보 時報 1〈보도〉 (current) news; a report; a gazette; a bulletin; 〈평론〉 a review
2〈방송의〉 a time signal; 〈라디오 등의〉 an announcement of (the) time; (美俗) a timecast ◆시계를 시보에 맞추다 set a watch by the radio time signal

시복 諡福 〔가톨릭〕 beatification —시복하다 beatify ■—식 a beatification

시부렁거리다 chatter; prattle; gossip; talk idly; talk nonsense ▶그녀는 한 시간이나 시부렁거렸다 She chattered (continuously) for an hour.

시부모 媤父母 the parents of one's husband; a woman's parents-in-law

시비 市費 municipal [city] expense; 〈경비〉 municipal [city] expenditure ◆시비로 at municipal expense; at the city's expense; at the expense of the city

시비 侍婢 a waiting woman; a maid

시비 施肥 fertilizing; manuring
—시비하다 fertilize; manure; spread fertilizer (on)

시비 是非 1〈잘잘못〉 right and [or] wrong; 〈적부〉 the propriety (of)
◆시비의 판단 discrimination of right and wrong / 시비를 가리다 discuss the rights and wrongs [merits and demerits]
▶네 나이쯤 되면 시비를 가릴 줄 알아야지 At your age, you ought to be able to tell right from wrong [good from bad].
2〈싸움〉 a dispute; a quarrel; an argument
◆시비를 걸다 pick a quarrel with sb; provoke sb to a fight
▶그들 사이에는 시비가 그치지 않는 것 같다 There seems to be no end to their quarrels.
—시비하다 quarrel (with); dispute [argue] (with); have a quarrel [dispute] (with)
▶사소한 일로 시비하다가 치고 받기에 이르렀다 A dispute over a trifle developed into an exchange of blows.

시비 詩碑 a monument inscribed [engraved] with a poem ◆박목월의 시비 the monument inscribed with Park Mok-wol's poem

시비곡직 是非曲直 right and [or] wrong; the rights and wrongs; good and evil [bad]
◆시비곡직을 따지다 inquire into the rights and wrongs; demand justice / 시비곡직을 가리다 discriminate the good from the bad; distinguish right from wrong

시비조 是非調 a quarreling attitude; a defiant manner; an aggressive attitude

♦시비조로 나오다 assume [take] a defiant attitude; provoke *sb* to a quarrel; pick a fight with *sb*

시뻘겋다 very red; deep red; crimson
♦시뻘겋게 단 쇠 red-hot iron / 시뻘겋게 핀 숯불 live [red-hot] charcoal
▶ 서쪽 하늘은 시뻘겋게 불타고 있었다 The western sky glowed with crimson.

시쁘다 〈불만이다〉dissatisfied ⇨ 시들하다

시사 示唆 〈암시〉(a) suggestion; a hint
—**시사하다** suggest; hint
♦시사적인 suggestive
♦시사하는 바가 많은 강의 a (very) suggestive [thought-provoking] lecture; a lecture full of suggestions
▶ 그 제안은 시사하는 바가 크다 The proposal is full of interesting suggestions.

시사 時事 current [present] events [affairs]; the events [news] of the day
♦시사를 논하다 discuss current events [the events of the day] / 시사에 밝다 be well-informed of current events [affairs] / 시사에 어둡다 be out of touch with the times
■ —영어 current English —평론 a contemporary review; a review of current topics —평론가 a news commentator

시사 試射 〈시험 발사〉(a) test [trial] firing —**시사하다** test-fire ■ —장 a (test-)firing range : 로켓 시사장 a rocket range —탄 a trial shot

시사 試寫 a preview; a private showing; a premiere show(ing)
—**시사하다** give [hold] a preview (of a film); preview (a film)
■ —회 a preview; 〈영화관계자만의〉 a trade premiere

시사문제 時事問題 issues of the day; questions of the day [times]; current topics
♦시사문제에 관한 기사 articles on current events / 시사문제를 논하다 discuss the events of the day [current events]

시사해설 時事解說 news commentary; comments on current topics —자 a commentator on current events; a news commentator; a TV [radio] commentator

시산 試算 a trial [test] calculation —**시산하다** calculate roughly [approximately]; make a trial balance
■ —표〔簿〕a trial balance (sheet)

시삼촌 媤三寸 *one's* husband's uncle
■ —댁 the wife of *one's* husband's uncle

시상 施賞 awarding (a prize)
—**시상하다** award [give] a prize
▶ 그는 시상되었다 He received [won] a prize.
■ —대 an honor platform —식 a ceremony of awarding prizes

시상 視床 〔解〕 a thalamus (*pl.* -mi); an optic thalamus

시상 詩想 the thought [sentiment] expressed in a poem; 〈시적 감정〉 poetic sentiment; 〈시적 착상〉 a poetical imagination [idea]; an inspiration
▶ 시상이 떠올랐다 Poetic sentiment [A poetic urge] has begun to stir in me.

시새 fine sand =모새

시새(우)다 be [feel] jealous [envious] 《of》; envy
♦몹시 시새우다 be green with jealousy; feel intense jealousy 《toward》
▶ 난 그의 성공을 시새우지 않는다 I feel no envy of [at] his success. ⇌ I don't envy his success at all.

시새움, 시샘 jealousy; envy
▶ 그녀는 시샘이 많은 사람이다 She is a very jealous woman.
▶ 그녀는 미모로 인해 반친구들의 시샘을 샀다 Her beauty made her classmates envious [jealous]. ⇌ Her beauty was envy of her classmates.

시생대 始生代 〔地質〕the Arch(a)eozoic (era)

시선 視線 *one's* eyes; *one's* gaze; a stare; a glance
♦시선을 딴데로 돌리다 turn *one's* eyes away (from); look away; glance away / 시선을 피하다 avoid *sb's* eye [gaze]
▶ 우리는 시선이 마주쳤다 Our eyes met.
▶ 모든 손님의 시선이 그녀에게로 쏠렸다 The eyes of all the guests were focused on her.
▶ 나는 누군가의 시선을 느꼈다 I felt someone looking [staring] at me.

시선 詩仙 a great poet; a poetic genius
♦시선 이백 the immortal poet, Li Po

시선 詩選 an anthology; selected poems; a selection of poems
♦현대영시선 Selection from [An Anthology of] Modern British [English] Poetry
■ 당(唐)— the Selection of Poems of the Tang Dynasty

시설 施設 〈설비〉 equipment; facilities; 〈공공기관〉 an institution; 〈공공건물〉 an establishment
♦시설이 좋은[나쁜] well-[poorly-]equipped; well-[poorly-]furnished
▶ 우리 시는 오락[위락] 시설이 부족하다 Our city needs more facilities for recreation.
▶ 이 도시에는 고아를 위한 시설이 있다 There is an institution [a home] for orphans in this town.
▶ 이 호텔은 시설이 나쁘다 This hotel is poorly-equipped.
—**시설하다** equip [provide, furnish] 《with》; install; establish
♦공공— 〈수도·전화 등〉 a public service; 〈학교 등〉 a public institution 교육— an educational institution [establishment]; educational facilities 군사— military installation [establishments] 복지— welfare facilities 산업— industrial facilities 오락— recreation(al) [amusement] facilities 항만— port [harbor] facilities 호텔— hotel facilities [accommodations] ■ —공사 installation work —비 installation expense; the cost of equipment

시성 詩聖 a great [master] poet; a poetic genius ♦시성 두보 the saint of poetry, Du Fu

시성 諡聖 〔가톨릭〕 canonization —**시성하다** canonize *sb*

시성식 示性式 〔化〕 a rational formula

시세 市稅 municipal [city] taxes

시세 市勢 1 〈상태〉 the demographic, social and economic conditions of a city; the status [condition] of a city
2 〈經〉 market conditions; the market ♦한산한 시세 a quiet [dull] market ■—조사 municipal census-taking; a municipal [city] census

시세 時世 the times ⇨ 시대 2

시세 時勢 1 〈시대의 형편〉 the tendency [trend] of the times; the signs of the times; the conditions of life; 〈시대〉 the times; the day
▶시세가 달라졌다 The times [Times] have changed.
2 〈시가〉 the current price; the market (price); a quotation 《on, for》; 〈경기〉 market conditions; the market
♦달러 시세 the exchange rate of the dollar; the dollar exchange rate / 소매[도매] 시세 the retail [wholesale] price / 쌀 시세 the price of rice; the market quotation on rice / 증권 시세 stock quotations [prices] / 최고 시세 the ceiling price / 최저 시세 the bottom price / 시세의 변동 fluctuations in the market price / 시세가 내리다 fall [go down] in price; quotations [prices] decline [fall] / 시세가 내릴 대로 내리다 prices reach the bottom / 시세가 오르다 rise [go up] in price; quotations [prices] advance [rise]
▶이 다이아몬드는 시세가 천만원입니다 This diamond is worth ten million won in today's money.
▶요즈음 증권 시세가 오르고 있다 Stocks have been rising [going up] of late.
▶시세가 없다 The market [business] is dull [quiet].
3 〈평가〉 estimate; (public) estimation; popularity
▶그 사건을 해결해서 그의 시세가 올라갔다 Since he solved that case his stock has risen.
▶대학 졸업자의 시세도 옛날같지 않다 University men are not so highly rated as they used to be.

시세폭 時勢幅 a price range; price changes [fluctuations] ♦큰[작은] 시세폭 a wide [narrow] range of price fluctuations

시소 a seesaw; a teeter(-totter) ▶아이들이 시소를 타고 놀고 있다 The kids are playing on a seesaw. ■—게임 a seesaw game [match]

시속 時俗 the manners and customs of the age [times]

시속 時速 speed per hour
♦시속 100킬로미터로 at 100 kilometers per [an] hour; at 100 k.p.h.
▶차는 시속 70킬로미터로 속도를 올렸다[내렸다] The car speeded up [slowed down, reduced] to 70 k.p.h.

시숙 媤叔 one's husband's brother; a woman's brother-in-law

시술 施術 (administration of) medical treatment; 〈외과수술〉 an operation; a surgical operation —시술하다 treat; operate; give medical treatment to a patient

시스템 a system ■—공학 systems engineering —화 systematization: 시스템화하다 systemize

시승 試乘 a trial ride —시승하다 test-drive; make [take] a test ride; test a car ▶그들은 지난 일요일에 새 차를 시승했다 They had a trial ride in a new car last Sunday.
■—차 a demonstrator; a demonstration model

시시 cc; c.c. [〈cubic centimeter]

시시각각 時時刻刻 every hour [moment, minute]; hourly; momently; momentarily; from one minute to the next ♦시시각각 변하는 날씨 ever-changing weather
▶형세는 시시각각으로 변하고 있다 The situation is changing every hour [moment].
▶주가는 시시각각 변한다 The stock prices change every moment [minute by minute].

시시덕거리다 chat and giggle; jest; talk nonsense; chatter; flirt (each other)
▶여자애들은 남자 친구에 대해 계속 시시덕거렸다 The girls chattered [prattled] on and on about their boyfriends.

시시로 時時— from time to time ⇨ 때때로

시시부지 1 〈아무렇게나〉 carelessly; half-heartedly; perfunctorily
—시시부지하다 careless; not thorough; sloppy; indifferent; halfhearted
♦일을 시시부지하게 하다 do one's work carelessly [roughly]; work in a slovenly way
2 ⇨ 흐지부지

시시비비 是是非非 1 〈잘잘못〉 right and [or] wrong ♦시시비비를 따지다[가리다] argue rights and wrongs [tell right from wrong]
2 〈싸움〉 ⇨ 시비 (是非)
■—주의 the principle of being fair and just [fairness and justice]

시시콜콜 inquisitively
♦시시콜콜 캐묻다 inquire of sb about every detail of 《a matter》
▶시시콜콜 따지지 마라 Don't nitpick. ⇌ Stop complaining about nothing [minor details].

시시티브이 CCTV [〈closed-circuit television]

시시하다 〈사소하다〉 trifling; trivial; insignificant; inconsiderable; petty; of little importance; of no account; of no consequence; 〈무가치하다〉 worthless; valueless; unworthy; trashy; 〈쓸모 없다〉 useless; of no use; 〈어리석다〉 stupid; foolish; silly; 〈재미없다〉 uninteresting; dull; 〈평범하다〉 common; prosaic; flat; 〈지리하다〉 boring
♦시시한 것 a matter of no importance [weight, consequence]; a trifling [trashy] thing [matter, affair]; rubbish / 시시한 강연 a poor [dull, boring] lecture / 시시한 녀석 a worthless [an insignificant, a good-for-nothing] fellow; a nobody; a person of no importance / 시시한 소리를 하다 talk nonsense; say silly things; talk rot / 시시한 일로 법석을 떨다 make a fuss about trifles
▶그의 시는 시시하다 His poems are poor stuff.
▶이 잡지는 정말 시시하다 This magazine is absolute rubbish [absolutely worthless].
▶그 파티는 시시했다 That was a dull party.
▶시시한 소리 작작해! Don't talk nonsense.

⇒ Nonsense! ⇒ Rot!
▶ 내가 대학을 다니지 않았다고 해서 날 시시하게 생각하는구나 Just because I didn't go to college, you think I'm nothing.
시식 試食 sampling; foretaste —시식하다 sample; taste; try; have a foretaste
▶ 그 냉동식품을 시식했는데 생각보다 맛이 있었다 I sampled the frozen food. It was more tasty than I expected.
■—회 a tasting [sampling] party
시신경 視神經 〔解〕 the optic [ophthalmic, visual] nerve ■—염(炎) optic neuritis
시실리 Sicily ♦ 시실리(섬 사람)의 Sicilian ■—(섬)사람 a Sicilian
시심 詩心 poetic sentiment [disposition; feeling, spirit]; a poetic turn of mind
시아버지 媤— a woman's father-in-law; one's husband's father
시아이시 CIC [〈Counter Intelligence Corps〕
시아이에이 CIA; C.I.A. [〈Central Intelligence Agency〕
시아파 —派 〈교파〉 Shi'a; Shia; Shiah; 〈신자〉 the Shi'ite; the Shiite
시안 試案 a tentative plan [draft, proposal]; a draft (plan) ♦ 행정 개혁의 시안을 작성하다 draw up [make out] a tentative plan for administrative reform
시안 〔化〕 cyanogen ♦ 시안의 cyanic / 시안화하다 cyanize ■—화물(化物) a cyanide —화법 cyaniding; cyanide process —화 칼륨 potassium cyanide
시암 Siam; Thailand ♦ 시암의 Siamese ■—어 Siamese —사람 a Siamese (▶단수·복수 동형); (총칭) the Siamese —쌍둥이 Siamese twins
시앗 〈첩〉 a mistress [concubine] of one's husband ♦ (남편이) 시앗을 보다 (one's husband) keep a mistress
시애틀 〈미국 북서부의 항구도시〉 Seattle
시야 視野 〈시력의 범위〉 a field [range] of vision [view]; a visual field; one's view; sight; 〈식견·사려의 범위〉 one's mental [intellectual] horizon; outlook
♦ 문학계 전체에 대한 넓은 시야 a range of knowledge that extends over the entire field of literature / 시야가 넓은[좁은] 사람 a man with a wide [narrow] outlook / 시야에 들어오다 come within the range [sweep]; come in sight; come into view / 넓은 시야로 사물을 보다 take a broad view of things / 시야 속[밖]에 있다 be within [beyond] one's (field of) vision / 시야를 벗어나다[에서 사라지다] go [get] out of sight; vanish from sight
▶ 짙은 구름으로 시야가 가려졌다 Our view was blocked by thick clouds.
▶ 위로 올라감에 따라 시야가 넓어졌다 As we climbed up, our field of vision [our view] broadened.
▶ 안개 때문에 시야가 나쁘다 Visibility is poor because of the fog.
▶ 호수가 시야에 들어왔다 The lake came into view.
시약 施藥 〈무료로 약을 지어줌〉 free dispensing of medicine; 〈무료 약〉 medicine dispensed free —시약하다 dispense [administer] medicine free
시약 試藥 〔化〕 a (chemical) reagent
■—병 a reagent bottle
시어 詩語 a poetic word; (총칭) poetic language [diction]
시어머니 媤— a woman's mother-in-law; one's husband's mother
시업 始業 opening; commencement of work; inauguration —시업하다 open; commence [begin, start] work ■—식 the opening ceremony; an inauguration (ceremony)
시에라리온 〈나라 이름〉 Sierra Leone; 〈공식명〉 the Republic of Sierra Leone ♦ 시에라리온의 Sierra Leonean ■—사람 a Sierra Leonean
시에프시 CFC [〈chlorofluorocarbon〕
시역 市域 the municipal area; the city limits
시역 弑逆 the murder of one's lord [parent]; 〈국왕의〉 regicide; 〈부모의〉 parricide
—시역하다 murder one's lord [parent]; assassinate; commit regicide [parricide]
시연 試演 a demonstration; a trial performance 《of a play》; a rehearsal —시연하다 give a trial performance [production] 《of an opera [a play]》; rehearse
시영 市營 municipal management [operation, ownership, enterprise, undertaking]
♦ 시영의 municipal; municipally operated [run, managed]; under municipal control / 시영화하다 municipalize
■—버스 a municipal [city] bus —사업 a municipal enterprise [undertaking] —주택 a municipal dwelling house
시오니즘 Zionism
시외 市外 the outskirts of a city; outside the city limits; 〈한 구획〉 a suburb; (총칭) the suburbs
♦ 시외의 out-of-town; suburban / 시외에 살다 live in a suburb [in the suburbs]
▶ 시외 부탁합니다 〈전화에서〉 (美) I want a toll call. ⇒ (英) Give me trunks.
▶ 학교는 인천 시외에 있다 The school is situated on the outskirts of (the city of) Inch'ŏn.
■—거주자 an out-of-towner —버스 a cross-country bus
시외전화 市外電話 a long-distance [an out-of-town, a toll] call; 〈회선〉 a toll line; (英) a trunk line ♦ 시외전화를 걸다 make an out-of-town [a long-distance] call
■—교환대 a toll (switch) board —국번 an area code
시용 試用 (a) trial ♦ 새 약의 시용 trying out a new medicine —시용하다 try; give sth a trial ♦ 기계를 시용해 보다 make a trial of a machine
▶ 사기 전에 시용해 보는 것이 좋다 You'd better give it a trial before you buy it.
시운 時運 the tide of the times
▶ 시운이 우리에게 불리하다 The times are against us.
▶ 그는 시운을 거스를 수가 없었다 He could not resist the current of the times.
시운동 視運動 apparent motion

시운전 試運轉 a trial [test] run [trip]; 〈기계의〉 a test; test working ♦엔진의 시운전 a test run of an engine
—**시운전하다** make a trial run; run a trial ▶그는 새차를 시운전해 보았다 He tried out the new car. ⇒ He gave the new car a trial.

시원섭섭하다 feel both relief and sorrow; feel relieved but sorry ▶딸을 시집보내고 나니 시원섭섭하다 I feel somewhat relieved but sad at marrying off my daughter.

시원스럽다 〈성격이〉 frank; unreserved; openhearted; not fussy; 〈동작이〉 brisk; active; spirited; prompt; quick
♦시원스러운 눈 bright, clear eyes; large, bright eyes / 시원스럽게 말하다 speak frankly [without reserve]; be outspoken; make a bright [brisk] statement
▶나는 그 문제를 시원스럽게 풀 수 있었다 I was able to solve the question quite easily [without any difficulty].

시원시원하다 frank ⇨ 시원스럽다
♦일하는 것이 시원시원하다 work briskly [energetically]; be efficient at *one's* work; be an efficient worker / 시원시원하게 대답하다 give a frank [candid] answer

시원찮다 〈좋지 않다〉 not good; poor; humble; 〈만족스럽지 않다〉 unsatisfactory; unsatisfying; boring; 〈시시하다〉 of little importance [value]; worthless
♦시원찮은 대답 an unsatisfactory answer / 시원찮은 음식 poor food / 시원찮은 책 a boring [an uninteresting] book / 성적이 시원찮은 학생 an undistinguished [a dull] boy
▶결과가 별로 시원찮다 The result is not much to our expectation [not satisfactory].
▶병세가 시원찮다 The patient is not making satisfactory progress. ⇒ There has been no improvement in the patient's condition.
▶요즈음은 사업이 시원찮다 These days my business has not been going well.

시원하다 1 〈서늘하다〉 cool ♦시원한 나무 그늘에서 in the cool shade of a tree / 시원한 곳에 두다 keep *sth* in a cool place
2 〈상쾌하다〉 refreshing; reviving; bracing; 〈산뜻하다〉 clean; clear; 〈개운하다〉 feel refreshed [relieved]; 〈가뿐하다〉 feel good; 〈만족스럽다〉 satisfactory
♦시원한 산 공기 the refreshing [crisp] mountain air / 시원한 바람 a refreshing breeze; a bracing wind
▶찬 물을 한 잔 마시니 시원해졌다 A glass of cold water refreshed me [was refreshing to me].
▶목욕하고 나면 시원해질 거다 You will feel refreshed after a bath. ⇒ A bath will freshen you up.
▶빚을 갚고 나니 속이 시원하다 Now that I have paid off my debt(s), I feel quite relieved.
▶불만을 털어 놓을 수 있어서 속이 시원하다 I feel better now that I have been able to air my grievance.
▶그 녀석이 없어지니 속이 시원하다 It is a great relief to get rid of him.
3 〈성격·동작이〉 ⇨ 시원스럽다

시월 十月 October (略 Oct.)

시위 示威 demonstration; show of force; (口) demo ♦시위적(인) demonstrative; threatening / 반정부 시위에 참가하다 take part in an antigovernment demonstration
—**시위하다** demonstrate 《against》; hold a demonstration
■**—가두** a street demonstration 전쟁반대— an antiwar demonstration ■**—대** (a group of) demonstrators **—행진** a demonstration parade

시위운동 示威運動 a demonstration; a parade ♦가두 시위 운동 a street demonstration / 집단 시위 운동 a mass demonstration / 시위 운동을 하다 carry out [have, stage, hold] a demonstration
■**—자** a demonstrator; a demonstrant

시유 市有 municipal [city] ownership ♦시유의 municipal; city-owned
▶공장 이전 후 당국은 부지를 시유화했다 After the move of the factory, the authorities municipalized the site.
■**—림** a municipal [city-owned] forest **—재산** municipal property **—지** city land

시음 試飮 sampling [tasting] 《wine》 —**시음하다** sample; taste;try ♦포도주를 시음하다 sample wine

시읍면 市邑面 cities, towns and villages; 〈자치 단체로서의〉 municipalities

시의 侍醫 a court physician; a medical attendant [physician] (to the king)

시의 時宜 opportuneness; timeliness; circumstances
♦시의에 맞다[맞지 않다] be opportune [inopportune]; be timely [untimely] / 시의에 맞는 조치를 하다 take timely [suitable] action / 시의에 따라 according to circumstances
▶그는 언제나 시의에 맞는 말을 한다 He always says the right thing at the right moment [time].

시의 猜疑 〈시기〉 jealousy; 〈의심〉 suspicion —**시의하다** be suspicious [jealous] of *sb*
■**—심** suspicious mind; suspicion; jealousy: 그녀는 시의심이 대단하다 She is extremely suspicious [jealous]. ⇒ She has a very suspicious [jealous] nature.

시의회 市議會 a municipal [city] assembly [council] ■**—의사당** a municipal assembly [council] hall **—의장** the president of a municipal assembly [city council]

시의회의원 市議會議員 a municipal assemblyman; a member of the municipal assembly
■**—선거** a municipal election

시인 是認 approval; acknowledgement; admission —**시인하다** approve of; acknowledge; admit
♦자기의 잘못을 시인하다 admit [acknowledge] *one's* mistake / 패배를 시인하다 admit *oneself* beaten ▶피고는 죄를 시인했다 The accused man admitted his guilt.

시인 詩人 a poet ♦여류 시인 a woman poet; a poetess / 엉터리 시인 a petty poet; a poetaster
▶그는 시인 기질이다 He is something of a

poet.

시일 時日 1 〈날짜〉 the date; the day ♦회의의 시일을 정하다 fix [set] a date for the meeting **2** 〈기간〉 time; days
♦시일의 경과 the passage [lapse, progress] of time / 시일이 경과함에 따라서 as time passes [goes by]; as the days go by; with the passing of time
▶이런 일은 많은 시일이 걸린다 This kind of work takes [requires] much time.
▶시일이 촉박하다 Time presses. ⇌ We are pressed for time. ⇌ We're running out of time.
▶시일이 지나면 누가 옳은지 알게 될 것이다 Time will show [tell] which of them is right.

시작 始作 the beginning; the start; the opening; the commencement; 〈발단〉 the outset; 〈기원〉 the origin; 〈초기〉 the early stage
♦시작이 좋으면 끝이 좋다 A good beginning makes a good ending.
▶무슨 일이나 시작이 어렵다 Everything is hard at the beginning.
▶그의 제안을 시작으로 열띤 토의가 벌어졌다 His proposal was the start of an enthusiastic discussion.
▶그것을 시작으로 그는 많은 것을 발명했다 With that as a beginning [starter], he invented many things.
▶그건 시작에 지나지 않는다 That's just [only, mere] the beginning.
▶더위는 이제 시작에 불과하다 This is only the beginning of the hot weather.
—**시작하다** begin; start; open; be opened; commence; make a start [beginning]; initiate; set about; take up; 〈계절〉 set in
♦3월 1일부터 시작하는 한 주일 동안의 스케줄 one's schedule for the week from March 1st / 새로 시작하다 begin afresh; make a new start; renew / 처음부터 다시 시작하다 begin again / 1페이지부터 시작하다 begin at page one / 읽기 시작하다 begin to read; begin reading / 식당을 시작하다 open a restaurant / 수영[음악]을 시작하다 take up swimming [music] / 조사를 시작하다 enter into investigation
▶우리 학교는 8시 반에 시작한다 Our school begins at eight-thirty.
▶사무실은 오전 9시에 시작한다 The office opens [Work begins] at 9 a.m.
▶회계 연도는 3월 1일에 시작한다 The fiscal year begins [starts] on March 1st.
▶어린애는 몇살 무렵부터 말을 하기 시작하나요? At about what age do babies begin to talk [use words]?
▶곧 갈테니까 먼저 시작하세요 I'll come right away, so please go on ahead.
▶오늘은 10페이지부터 시작합시다 Let's begin at page ten today.
▶비가 내리기 시작했다 It began [started] to rain [raining].
▶꽃이 피기 시작했다 The blossoms have started blooming.
▶그는 새 사업을 시작했다 He started a new business.
▶그는 빵집을 시작했다 He opened a bakery.
▶나는 20 살부터 담배를 피우기 시작했다 I began to smoke at the age of twenty.
▶아직 오지 않은 사람이 있지만 시간이 없으므로 시작하겠습니다 There are still some people who haven't come, but there's not much time, so we'll begin.
▶어디서부터 시작하면 좋을까요? Where should I begin?
▶그녀는 틈틈이 뜨개질을 시작했다 She has taken up knitting in her spare time.
▶우리가 음악당에 도착했을 때 연주회는 벌써 시작되었다 When we got to the hall, the concert had already begun.
▶아침 예배는 찬송가로 시작되었다 The morning service began [started, opened] with a hymn.
▶장마가 시작되었다 The rainy season has set in.
▶문예부흥은 이탈리아에서 시작되었다 The Renaissance started [originated] in Italy.
▶그 계획은 이미 시작되고 있다 The project is under way already.
▶그의 음주벽은 지금 시작된 것이 아니다 His drinking habit is an old one.

시작 詩作 composition of poems —**시작하다** write [compose] poems

시작 試作 1 〈시험 제작〉 trial manufacture —**시작하다** manufacture [produce] sth by way of trial [experiment]
♦설상차(雪上車)를 시작하다 make [produce] a snowmobile experimentally
2 〈시문의〉 a study; 〈프〉 an étude —**시작하다** write [compose] as an experiment
3 〈식물 등의〉 trial growing [rearing]
■ —공장 a pilot plant

시작이 반이다 (속담) Well begun is half done. ⇌ A good beginning [start] is half the battle. ⇌ A good beginning is always important [makes a good ending].

시장 hunger
—**시장하다** (be, go) hungry; (feel) empty; (口) starving; famished
▶몹시 시장하다 be very hungry; be savagely hungry; have a wolf in one's stomach
▶시장해서 죽겠다 I am dying with hunger. ⇌ I'm simply starving.

시장 市長 a mayor ♦런던 시장 the Lord Mayor (of London) / 서울 시장 the Mayor of Seoul / 조 시장 Mayor Cho
■ —부인 a mayoress —선거 a mayoral election —직[임기] mayoralty : 그는 5년째 시장직을 맡고 있다 He has been mayor of this city for five years.

시장 市場 a market (place); a mart
〈시장이[은]〉 시장이 부진하다[불황이다] The market is dull [depressed].
▶토요일에 시장이 선다 A fair is held on Saturday.
▶올 시장은 순조롭다 This year the market is fair.
〈시장을〉 시장을 개척하다 cultivate [open up] a market (for) / 시장을 확장하다 extend [develop] the market / 시장을 독점하다 engross [swipe] the market

시장개발

▶이 회사는 세계 곡물 시장을 장악하고 있다 This company controls the grain market of the world.
▶그들은 새 시장을 개척했다 They opened up [cultivated] a new market.
〈시장에〉시장에 가다 go to market / 시장에 내다 put [place] on the market; bring [take] to market; market 《a product》
▶4월에 신형 자동차가 시장에 출하될 것이다 In April new model cars will be (put) on the market.
▶새 제품은 곧 한국 시장에 판로를 열 것이다 The new products will soon find their way into the Korean market.
▶최신 봄 상품이 시장에 선뵈기 시작했다 The latest spring goods have appeared [made their appearance] on the market.
■고물[벼룩]— a flea market 공개— an open market 공설— a public [municipal] market 과점[독점]— an oligopolistic [a monopolistic] market 구매자— a buyer's market 국내— a home [domestic] market 금융— the money [financial] market; the investment market 노동[자본]— the labor [capital] market 노천— an open-air market 도매[소매]— a wholesale [retailing, retail] market 선물(先物)— a future's market 암— a black market 어— a fish market 외국[해외]— an oversea(s) [a foreign] market 주식— a stock exchange [market]: 주식 시장은 오늘 활황[부진]이었다 The stock market was active [dull, slack] today. 중앙— the central market 증권— a stock [stock-exchange] market 지방— a local market 청과(물)— a vegetable and fruit market 투기[투자]— the speculative [investment] market 판매자— a seller's market ■—가격 a market price [rate] / 금의 시장가격 the market value [price] of gold —가치 market value —경제 the market economy —분석 a market analysis —세분화 market segmentation —시세 a market price; quotations —점유율 a (market) share: 시장 점유율을 높이다 build up a market share; increase *one's* share of the market —조사 a market research; a marketing research —조작 market operations [manipulation]

시장개발 市場開發 market development; opening up new markets [the market]

시장개방 市場開放 opening 《Korea's》 markets 《to the world》
◆쌀 시장 개방 반대 캠페인 a campaign against rice market opening
▶외국으로부터의 시장 개방 요구가 거세지고 있다 There are growing foreign demands that we open our markets.

시장기 hungriness; hunger ◆시장기를 느끼다 feel hungry [empty] / 시장기를 달래다[덜다] appease [alleviate, allay] *one's* hunger 《with a slice of bread》

시장성 市場性 marketability ◆시장성이 있는 [없는] 물건 marketable [unmarketable] goods

시장이 반찬 (속담) Hunger is the best sauce. ⇌ Hunger makes hard beans sweet.

시재 詩才 poetic talent [genius] ▶그에게는 시재가 있다 He has a genius for poetry. ⇌ He is endowed with poetic genius.

시재 詩材 a subject for a poem; material for poetry

시저 〈로마의 장군·정치가〉 Caesar, (Gaius) Julius (100–44 B.C.)

시적 詩的 poetic; poetical
◆시적 생활 a poetical life / 시적 용어 poetic diction / 시적인 아름다움 poetic beauty / 시적 감흥이 일다 have a poetic inspiration
▶그의 문장은 시적 표현으로 가득하다 His composition is full of poetic expression.

시적거리다 《마지못해 하다》 do [speak] reluctantly [unwillingly, grudgingly]; do [speak] slowly [tardily, sluggishly, listlessly]

시절 時節 1〈계절〉 the season; the time of (the) year
◆꽃피는 시절 the flower season / 시절에 맞는 seasonable / 시절에 맞지 않는 out of season; unseasonable
▶해마다 이 시절에는 바람이 세차다 It generally blows hard at this time of (the) year.
2〈때·시기〉 the time(s); days; an occasion
◆청년 시절 the time of *one's* youth / 살기 힘든 시절 hard times / 소년 시절에 in *one's* boyhood [childhood]; when *one* was a boy / 그 시절에(는) in those days; at that times
▶어려운 시절이다 These are hard times.
▶저 사람도 좋은 시절이 있었다 That man has seen better days.
▶시절은 아직 그에게 불리했다 The time was still against him.

시점 時點 a point of [in] time
◆이 시점에 at this point of time [moment] / 오늘의 시점에서 as of today / 그가 결혼한 시점에서는 at the time [moment] of his marriage; when he got married / 이 시점까지 up to the present
▶그 시점에서 그녀는 유언을 바꾸기로 결심했다 She made up her mind at that moment to change her will.

시점 視點 〔生〕〈주시점〉 a visual point; 〈관점〉 point of view; a viewpoint

시접 a margin to sew up [to seam]; a tuck

시정 市井 1〈시가〉 a town; a street; streets
◆시정의 일 an event on [in] the street
▶그는 시정인으로 일생을 보냈다 He passed his life as an ordinary citizen.
2〈사람〉 a market tradesman

시정 市政 municipal [city] government [administration]
◆시정의 civic; municipal / 시정을 쇄신[개혁]하다 make a civic [municipal] reform / 시정에 참여하다 participate in municipal government

시정 是正 correction; rectification
—시정하다 correct; rectify; set *sth* to rights; put *sth* right ◆세계 무역의 불균형을 시정하다 rectify the unbalanced world trade / 폐습을 시정하다 redress abuses
▶잘못은 즉시 시정해야 한다 A mistake corrected promptly.
▶시정할 점이 몇 가지 있다 There are some

시정 施政 administration; government —**시정하다** administer; govern
■—방침 an administrative policy; 〈정당의〉 a party line : 시정 방침을 정하다 decide upon one's administrative policies
▶ 이런 폐습은 시정되어야 한다 It is necessary to straighten out these abuses.

시정 詩情 poetic(al) sentiment [feeling]; a poetic state of mind ◆ 시정이 풍부하다 be full of poetical interest
▶ 그는 시정이 풍부한 사람이다 He is a person full of poetical sentiment.
▶ 그의 수필엔 시정이 없다 His essay has no [little] poetry in it. ≒ His essay is prosaic.
▶ 이 시골은 내 시정을 일깨우는 곳의 하나다 This country is one of the places which awaken my lyre.

시정연설 施政演說 a policy speech; an administrative policy speech; a speech on one's administrative policy
▶ 대통령은 국회에서 시정 연설을 했다 The President set forth in the National Assembly the administrative policy of the government.

시제 市制 municipal system [organization] ◆ 시제를 실시하다 incorporate 《a town》 as a city; reorganize 《a town》 as a municipality; municipalize

시제 時制 〔文法〕 a tense ◆ 시제의 일치 sequence (of tenses) ■ 현재[과거, 미래]— the present [past, future] tense

시제 詩題 a poetic theme; a subject [theme] for a poem

시조 始祖 the founder; the originator; the progenitor; the father
◆ 인류의 시조 the progenitor of the human race / 조선 왕조의 시조 the founder of Chosŏn Dynasty / 무선 공학의 시조 the father of radio engineering

시조 時調 a *shijo*; a three-verse [three-stanza] Korean ode [poem] ◆ 시조를 짓다 compose [write] a *shijo* / 시조를 읊다 recite a *shijo*

시조새 始祖— 〔古生〕 an archaeopteryx 《pl. ~es》; an archaeornis

시종 始終 〈명사적〉 the beginning and the end; 〈부사적〉 from start [beginning] to finish [end]; from first to last; all the time [while]; throughout
◆ 시종일관하게 consistently / 시종여일하다 be consistent
▶ 그는 시종 묵묵히 그들의 토론을 듣고 있었다 He remained silent from first to last listening to their discussion.
▶ 그는 시종 냉정했다 He kept his calm all the time [throughout].
▶ 그는 시종일관 전쟁에 반대했다 He has consistently been against the war.

시종 侍從 a chamberlain; a gentleman in waiting; a lord-in-waiting
■ —무관 a military [naval] aide-de-camp [ADC] to His [Her] Majesty; an aide to His [Her] Majesty; an officer in attendance on the King [Queen] —장(長) the Grand Chamberlain

시주 施主 〔佛敎〕〈행위〉 donation; offering; 〈사람〉 a donator; an offerer; a benefactor —**시주하다** offer; make an offering 《to a temple》; donate

시준 視準 〔物〕 collimation —**시준하다** collimate 《a telescope》 ■ —기[의(儀)] a collimator —선 a collimation line —오차 a collimation error

시중 attendance; attending; serving; waiting on; 〈식탁에서의〉 service 《at table》
◆ 부모님의 시중을 들다 take care of one's parents / 식사 시중을 들다 wait on sb at table; wait (on) table
▶ 그녀는 수족처럼 남편의 시중을 들고 있다 She waits on [upon] her husband hand and foot.
—**시중하다** attend (on); wait on [upon]; serve sb; do sb a service; 〈돌보다〉 take care of

시중 市中 1 〈시내〉 the city; the town; the streets ◆ 시중에(서) in the city; on [in] the streets 2 〔金融〕 〈시장〉 the open market
■ —금리 the open market (interest) rate —시세 the open market quotation —은행 a city bank

시즌 a season ◆ 스키 시즌 the season for skiing / 야구 시즌 the baseball season / 시즌이 지난 off-season; out of season
▶ 호텔은 시즌 중에는 붐빈다 Hotels are crowded in season.

시지에스단위계 —單位系 cgs [c.g.s., C.G.S., CGS] system [<*centimeter-gram-second*>]

시집 媤— one's husband's family [home]

시집 詩集 a collection of poems; collected poems; 〈명시선〉 an anthology ◆ 엘리엇 시집 〈저서명〉 The Poetic Works [The Collected Poems] of Eliot

시집가다 媤— marry 《a man, into a family》; get [be] married 《to a man》; take a husband
◆ 시집간 여자 a married woman / 좋은 데로 시집가다 marry [get married] well; make a good marriage / 시집갈 나이가 지나다 be past the marriageable age / 시집갈 준비를 하다 prepare for marriage
▶ 그녀는 이씨 집안으로 시집갔다 She married into the Lee family.
▶ 우리 딸은 작년에 시집갔다 My daughter got married last year.
▶ 우리 딸은 드디어 시집갔다 My daughter finally got married.
▶ 그녀는 어떤 사업가에게 시집갔다 She married a businessman.
▶ 그녀도 이제 시집갈 나이다[나이가 됐다] She is old enough to be [get] married. ⇌ She has reached a marriageable age.

시집보내다 媤— marry 《one's daughter to a man》; give 《one's daughter》 (away) in marriage; marry 《one's daughter》 off
▶ 그들은 딸을 의사에게 시집보냈다 They married their daughter to a doctor.
▶ 부모는 딸을 시집보내기가 몹시 서운했다 The parents felt very sad to have their daughter married.

▶ 우리는 시집보낼 딸이 하나 있다 We have a daughter of marriageable age.
시집살이 媤— living with *one's* husband's parents; a woman's married life
시차 時差 〈지방시의 차〉 difference in time; time difference; 〔天〕 the equation of time
▶ 서울과 방콕은 시차가 2시간이다 There is a two hours' difference between Seoul and Bangkok time.
▶ 서울과 파리는 시차가 얼마나 납니까? What is the time difference between Seoul and Paris?
■ —을 equation of time —제 staggering work-hour system: 시차제 출근 《adopt》 staggered office [working] hours; differentiation of office attendance hours
시차 視差 〔天〕 (a) parallax ◆ 태양[두 눈]의 시차 solar [binocular] parallax
시찰 視察 (an) inspection; observation —시찰하다 inspect; make an inspection 《of》; visit ◆ 현장을 시찰하다 take a view of the scene / 현지를 시찰하다 make an on-site inspection 《of》
▶ 국회의원들이 공장을 시찰했다 Members of the National Assembly inspected the factory.
▶ 시장은 수해 현장을 시찰했다 The mayor made an on-the-spot inspection of the flooded district.
■ —단 a group of inspectors; an inspection team [party] —단원 a member of an inspection team —여행 an inspection [observation] tour; a tour of inspection; a study tour
시채 市債 a municipal [city] loan [debt]; 〈채권〉 a municipal bond ◆ 시채를 모집[발행]하다 raise [issue] a municipal loan
시책 施策 〈정책〉 a measure; a policy; 〈시행〉 enforcement of a policy
◆ 국가의 시책 state measures / 시책을 강구하다 take measure to meet; consider how to cope with 《the situation》 / 시책을 잘못하다 take a wrong measure [step]
▶ 정부는 폭동을 진압하기 위한 시책을 강구했다 The Government has taken measures [steps] to put down the riot.
—시책하다 enforce [execute] a policy.
시청 市廳 a municipal [city] office; 〈청사〉 a city hall ◆ 시청 직원 a city [municipal] official ▶ 그는 시청에 근무한다 He works at City Hall.
시청 視聽 looking and listening ◆ 텔레비전 시청료 a TV subscription fee; a viewer's fee —시청하다 look and listen; watch ◆ 텔레비전을 시청하다 watch television
시청 試聽 an audition —시청하다 audition; give an audition 《to *sth*》 ■ —실 an audition room
시청각 視聽覺 (the senses of) sight and hearing; the visual and auditory senses
■ —교실 a language laboratory; an audiovisual classroom —교육 audiovisual education [instruction] —교재[기기] audiovisual aids [materials]; audiovisuals
시청률 視聽率 〔TV〕 a program [an audience] rating; a rating

◆ 시청률이 높은[좋은] 프로그램 a television program with a high [good] rating / 시청률을 높이다 improve the audience ratings
▶ 그의 프로그램은 시청률이 가장 높다 His program is (the) highest in the ratings [is at the top of the ratings].
▶ 그가 그 프로그램에 나오게 되자 시청률이 10퍼센트 올랐다 After he (had) joined the program, the rating went up [improved, rose] (by) ten percent. ⇒ The program went up [improved, rose] in the ratings by ten percent after he (had) joined it.
■ —조사 《make》 an audience rating survey
시청자 視聽者 〔TV〕 a (television) viewer; a televiewer; 《총칭》 the television audience; the viewing public
■ —상담실 viewers' consultation room —여론조사 the audience response rating —참가 프로그램 an audience participation show [program]; 《美》 〈전화로 하는〉 a call-in; 《英》 a phone-in
시체 屍體 a (dead) body; 〈사람의〉 a corpse; *one's* remains; 〈해부용의〉 a cadaver; 《俗》 a stiff; 〈동물의〉 a carcass
◆ 시체의[와 같은] cadaverous / 신원 불명의 시체 an unidentified body [corpse] / 시체를 발견하다 find [recover] a body / 시체를 안치하다 lay the remains in state / 시체를 인도하다 hand *sb's* body over 《to》
▶ 현장에는 시체가 무더기로 쌓여 있었다 The bodies lay in heaps at the scene.
▶ 어머니는 아들의 시체를 확인하였다 The mother identified the body of her son.
▶ 어제 경찰은 시체를 발굴해냈다 Police carried out the exhumation of the body yesterday.
▶ 그는 시체로 발견되었다 He was found dead.
■ —타살— the body of a murdered person —검안 a postmortem (examination); an autopsy —안치소 a mortuary; a lich-house; a deadhouse; a morgue —유기[발굴] abandonment (exhumation) of a dead body: 그는 시체 유기 혐의로 체포되었다 He was arrested for abandoning a body. —해부 dissection of a dead body; necrotomy; 〈검시를 위한〉 an autopsy; a postmortem (examination)
시초 始初 the beginning; the inception; the start; the outset; 〈기원〉 the origin; the source; the genesis; 〈원인〉 the cause
◆ 만물의 시초 the genesis of things / 싸움의 시초 the original cause [ground] of the quarrel / 시초부터 from the beginning [start]
시추 試錐 drilling; boring —시추하다 drill; bore —석유— oil(-well) drilling —기(機) a drill; a drilling machine
시취 屍臭 the smell of a dead body; a putrid smell
시취 詩趣 poetical sentiment [interest] ◆ 시취가 있다 be poetic / 시취가 풍부하다 be full of poetry; be very poetic
시치다 tack; baste ◆ 주름을 시치다 tack down a fold
시치미 feigned [assumed] ignorance [innocence]; dissimulation; false pretenses

♦시치미를 떼고 with an air of innocence; affecting innocence [ignorance]; pretending not to know / 시치미를 떼다 feign [affect] ignorance; play the innocent
▶그는 모른다고 시치미를 뗐다 He pretended ignorance. ≒ He pretended not to know it.
▶나는 시치미를 떼고 물어 보았다 I asked him about it as if I did not know.
▶그는 시치미를 떼고 나를 방문했다 He called on me as if nothing had happened.
시침[1] feigned ignorance ⇨ 시치미
시침[2] tacking ⇨ 시침질
시침 時針 the hour [short] hand
시침질 tacking; basting
시카고 〈미국의 도시〉 Chicago ■—시민 a Chicagoan
시커멓다 deep-black; jet-black; coal-black; inky(-black) ♦마음보가 시커멓다 be black-hearted [evil-minded, wicked] / 시커멓게 타다 be scorched black
시큰둥하다 impertinent; saucy; pert ♦시큰둥한 대답 a pert answer; a saucy reply / 시큰둥한 소리를 하다 say saucy things
▶시큰둥한 소리 집어치워 Don't be saucy! ≒ None of your impudence [cheek, lip]!
시클라멘 〔植〕 a cyclamen
시큼하다 sourish ⇨ 시금하다
시키다 〈강제〉 make 《sb do》; cause 《sb to do》; force [compel] 《sb to do》; 〈허락·방임〉 let 《sb do》; allow 《sb to do》; 〈부탁·의뢰〉 get 《sb to do》; have 《sb do》; 〈주문하여〉 order 《sth from sb to do》
♦노래를 시키다 have sb sing a song; ask sb to sing / 대학 공부를 시키다 give sb a university education; let sb go to college / 서울 구경을 시키다 show sb round [over] Seoul / 영화 구경을 시키다 treat sb to a movie / 유학을 시키다 arrange for 《a student》 to study abroad / 일을 시키다 make sb work; put sb to work / 시키는 대로 하다 do as one is told 《to do》
▶나는 그들에게 그 방 청소를 시켰다 I made [had] them clean the room. ≒ I got them to clean the room. ≒ I had [got] the room cleaned by them.
▶나는 음식점에서 불고기를 시켰다 I ordered pulgogi at the restaurant.
▶그에게 그 일을 시키십시오 Make [Let] him do the work.
▶저 녀석이 시키는 대로 행동하지 마라 Don't let him make you dance to his tune.
▶한 번 더 시켜주십시오 Let me have another try!
-시키다 ♦사직시키다 force sb to resign; dismiss sb / 구두를 수선시키다 have [get] one's shoes mended / 연구시키다 make sb study [research]
▶그의 충고가 내 생각을 변화시켰다 His advice caused me to change my mind.
▶그를 만족시키기는 어렵다 It's hard to please him. ≒ He's hard to please.
▶그를 자백시켜야 한다 He must be made to confess.
시킴 〈인도의 주〉 Sikkim ■—사람 a Sikkimese

시토 SEATO [〈the Southeast Asia Treaty Organization]
시트 〈자리〉 a seat; 〈우표의〉 a sheet; 〈침대의〉 a (bed) sheet ♦시트를 깔다[갈다] spread [change] a sheet
시트론 〔植〕 a citron ■—수 citron water
시튼 〈영국 태생인 미국의 박물학자〉 Seton, Ernest Thompson(1860-1946)
시판 市販 marketing; sale at a market —시판하다 market; put [place] on the market; place on sale; sell at a market
♦시판되다 come into the market
▶이 약은 시판되고 있지 않다 This medicine isn't (put) on the market. ≒ This medicine hasn't come onto the market.
■ 공동— joint marketing ■—가능성 marketability —품 goods on the market
시판 試販 〈상품의〉 an adventure ■—품 goods on trial sale
시퍼렇다 1 〈빛깔이〉 deep blue; 〈안색이〉 deadly [ghastly] pale; pallid
♦시퍼런 바다 the deep blue sea / 시퍼렇게 멍든 눈 a black eye / 안색이 시퍼렇게 되다 turn (deadly) pale [go white, lose color] 《at the scene》
2 〈위풍·권세가〉 powerful; influential; stately ♦권세가 시퍼렇다 be very powerful [influential]
▶그는 서슬이 시퍼렇게 되어 나한테 덤벼들었다 He turned on me with an angry look.
3 〈날이〉 very sharp; sharp-edged ♦시퍼런 칼날 a well-sharpened [sharply honed] blade
시편 詩篇 1 〈책 속의 시 부분〉 the poetry section (of a book) 2 〈시를 편찬한 책〉 a book of poems; a volume of poetry 3 〔聖〕 (the Book of) Psalms (略 Ps., Psa.)
시평 時評 comments [criticism] on current events [topics]; 〈신문의〉 leaderettes; 《美》 editorial comments [notes] ♦문예 시평 a literary review
시풍 詩風 a style of poetry; a poetical style
시필 試筆 writing for trial —시필하다 write for trial; try one's hand at writing
시하 時下 〈부사적〉 nowadays; now; at present; at this time of (the) year ♦시하 추랭지절(秋冷之節)에 in this chilly autumn weather
시하 侍下 a person supporting his parents [grandparents]
시학 詩學 study of poetry; 〈시론〉 poetics; 〈운율학〉 prosody
시한 時限 the time limit; a limit of time; a deadline; 〈폐문 시간〉 closing time
■ 법적— the legal deadline ■—부 파업 a strike for a limited number of hours —폭탄 a time bomb; a delayed action bomb
시할머니 媤— one's husband's grandmother
시할아버지 媤— one's husband's grandfather
시합 試合 a match; a game; a contest; 〈권투 등의 한 승부〉 a bout; a fight; 《美俗》 an encounter; 〈일련의〉 a tournament; a series; 〈시합하기〉 play; playing ⇨ 경기
♦권투[레슬링] 시합 a boxing [wrestling] match / 야구[농구]시합 a baseball [basketball] game / 야간 시합 a night game / 연습 시

시행

합 a practice game / 시합 일정 the schedule of the matches / 일방적인 시합이 되다 end in a one-sided game
▶ 테니스[골프] 시합 결과는 어떻게 되었나? What was the outcome of the tennis [golf] match?
〈시합을〉 시합을 승낙하다 accept a challenge to a game 《from》 / 시합을 제의하다 challenge (a team) to a match; send *sb* a challenge to a game 《of tennis》
▶ 우리는 어제 중국 팀과 배구 시합을 했다 We played the Chinese team at [in] volleyball yesterday. ⇌ We played volleyball against the Chinese team yesterday.
▶ 그의 홈런이 시합을 결정지었다 《美口》 His homer put the game on ice.
▶ 양 팀 모두 멋진 시합을 벌이고 있었다 Both teams were playing well.
〈시합에〉 시합에 나가다 participate [take part] in a game / 시합에 이기다[지다] win [lose] a match [game, bout, tournament]
▶ 그는 팔 뼈가 부러졌어. 그래서 시합에 나갈 수 없었던 거야 He broke his arm. So he couldn't play.
—**시합하다** play [have] a match [game] 《with》; play with [against] 《*sb*》; have a tournament; have a bout; tilt; 〔野〕 cross bats 《with》

시행 施行 operation; enforcement
—**시행하다** carry out; conduct; 〈법률을〉 enforce; put in force; put into operation; give effect 《to》; carry [put] into effect; execute
♦ 시행되다 be enforced; be put in force; come into force [operation]; become operative [effective]; take [go into] effect; 《美》 become effective / 시행되고 있다 be in force [operation]
▶ 그 법률은 1998년 1월 1일부터 시행된다 The law will take effect [go into operation] on and after January 1 [《英》 1 January], 1998.
■ —규칙 enforcement regulations; regulations relative to the application [enforcement] of a law —기간 a period of effectiveness —기일 a date of enforcement —령 an Enforcement Ordinance —세칙 detailed enforcement regulations; detailed regulations for the application [enforcement] of a law

시행착오 試行錯誤 trial and error ▶ 그는 시행착오를 통해 석유에서 새 물질을 만들어냈다 Through trial and error he succeeded in making a new material out of oil.
■ —법 the method [rule] of trial and error

시허옇다 pure white; snow(y)-white; (as) white as snow
▶ 일어나보니 지면이 시허옇게 눈이 쌓여 있었다 I woke up to find the ground completely white with snow.

시험 試驗 **1** 〈지식 등의〉 an examination; 《口》 a test; an exam; 《美》 a quiz 《*pl.* quizzes》

解説 ***examination***은 학생·지원자의 지식·자격 등을 조사하는 일반적인 시험을 말하며 주로 문어체로 쓰이고, 회화에서는 ***exam***이 보통 쓰인다. ***test***는 학습의 이해도를 알아보는 단순한 시험 또는 객관적인 테스트를 말하며, 수업중에 행하는 간단한 테스트에는 ***quiz***를 쓴다.

♦ 수학 시험 a mathematics exam [examination, test]; an exam [a test] in mathematics / 3과(課) 〔불규칙 동사〕의 시험 an examination [a test] on Lesson three [irregular verbs] / 취직 시험 an employment examination; an examination for employment / 시험 성적의 통지 a report of *one's* score on a test / 시험 답 안지 an exam(ination) paper; 《美》 a test paper / 무시험으로 without examination
▶ 시험 결과는 언제 알 수 있습니까? When can I expect [get] the exam results?
▶ 시험 범위는 몇 과(課)나 됩니까? How many lessons is the examination going to cover? ⇌ How many lessons will we be tested on?
〈시험이〉 [會話] 「난 오늘 시험이 끝났어」 「좋겠다. 난 아직 두 번 더 있어」 "I've finished my exams today.""Great, I have two more (exams) to go."
▶ 내일 영어 시험이 있다 We have an English examination tomorrow.
〈시험을〉 시험을 치다[치르다, 보다] go [come] up for an examination; sit for an examination; take [undergo] an examination; go in for an exam (ination) / 시험을 감독하다 proctor an examination; 《英》 invigilate
▶ 선생님은 우리가 숙제를 해왔는지 확인하기 위해 시험을 쳤다 The teacher gave us a test [tested us] to see if we had done our homework.
▶ 다음 주에 수학 시험을 보겠습니다 I'm going to give you an examination in mathematics next week.
▶ 그는 의과 대학의 입학시험을 쳤다 He took [《英》 sat for] the entrance examination of a medical college.
▶ 이 학교에 입학하려면 시험을 치러야 한다 Entrance to this school is through examination.
▶ 시험을 잘 쳤니? How have you fared in your exam?
〈시험에〉 〔문제가〕 시험에 나오다 be asked [given] in an examination / 시험에 떨어지다 fail in an examination [a test]; fail an examination; 《美口》 flunk a quiz
▶ 이 문제는 시험에 꼭 나온다 This question is sure to be asked [given] in the examination.
▶ 그는 시험에 붙었다 He passed [succeeded in] the examination.
▶ 그는 시험에 대비하여 부지런히 공부하는 중이다 He is grinding for the exam.
—**시험하다** conduct [hold, give, set] an examination; give [make] a test; test; examine 《students》 in 《English》

2 〈실험〉 an experiment; a test; a trial; a try
▶ 부품 하나하나가 엄격한 시험을 받았다 Each of the parts was subjected to very severe tests.
▶ 마이크 시험중입니다 Testing, testing, testing. One, two, three —testing.

▶ 시험 결과는 우수하였다 It proved excellent on trial.
▶ 시험필 (게시) Tried.
—시험하다 experiment 《a substance》; make an experiment 《on, with, in》; test; put [give] *sth* to trial [the test]; try (out); have a try at; make a trial 《with, of》; 〈시식・시음하다〉 try; taste; sample
♦ 시험한 후에 on [upon] trial / 기계를 시험하다 test a machine; give a machine a trial [test, try]; put a machine through a trial
▶ 채용 전에 그의 인물됨을 시험할 필요가 있다 We need to put his character to the test before we employ him.
■ 강도[내구성]— a strength [durability] test 경쟁[검정, 구두]— a competitive [a license, an oral] examination 국가— a state examination 기말— a term examination 모의— a sham [trial] examination 본[예비]— a final [preliminary] examination 성능[능률]— an efficiency test 입학— ⇨ 입학시험 자격(검정)— a qualifying examination 중간— a midterm examination; the midterm 채용[선발]— an examination for service [selection] 최종[졸업]— the final examination; (口) the finals 필기— a written examination; an examination on paper 학과— examinations on academic subjects 학기[학년, 임시]— a term [an annual, a special] examination 학력— an achievement test ■—감독 proctoring of an examination; (英) an invigilation; 〈사람〉 a proctor; (英) an invigilator —결혼 a tentative [a trial, an experimental] marriage —공장 a pilot plant —과목 a subject for examination —관(官) an examiner; an examinant —기(器・機) a tester; a testing machine —기간 a testing [trial] period —기일 the date of an examination —단계 the testing stage —방법 the method of examination; (化) a test method —생산 pilot production —위원 an examination committee; the examination board; an examiner —제도 an examination system —지 an exam(ination) paper [sheet]; (化) a test [litmus] paper —지역 〈미사일 등의〉 a testing area —지옥 an ordeal of (entrance) examinations

시험공부 試驗工夫 cramming [preparation] for an examination —시험공부하다 prepare [cram] for an exam; slog [grind] (away) at examination subjects

시험관 試驗管 a test tube ■—배양 a (test-)tube culture —아기 a test-tube baby; a tubebaby

시험문제 試驗問題 questions for an examination; examination [exam] questions; test problems

시험발사 試驗發射 a test fire; testfiring —시험발사하다 test-fire 《a rocket》

시험비행 試驗飛行 a test [a trial, an experimental] flight; a flying test —시험비행하다 test-fly 《an airplane》 ■—사 a test pilot

시험삼아 試驗— by way of experiment [trial]; experimentally; on [for] trial; tentatively; as a test [a trial, an experiment]

♦ 시험삼아 해보다 try; have a try 《at》; make an attempt; do *sth* on [as a] trial / 시험삼아 1개월간 고용하다 employ *sb* for a month on a trial basis; engage *sb* on trial [probation]; give *sb* a month's trial / 시험삼아 먹어[마셔]보다 try; test; sample
▶ 그는 시험삼아 신형 워드 프로세서를 써보았다 He tried using a new-model word processor.

시험장 試驗場 1 〈학교의〉 an examination hall [room] 2 〈실험실・연구실 등의〉 a laboratory; an experimental station
■ 농사— an agricultural experiment station 위생— a hygienic laboratory

시험적 試驗的 experimental; tentative
▶ 나는 그 새로운 약을 시험적으로 사용하고 있다 I'm using the new medicine on an experimental basis.
▶ 그를 시험적으로 써보시오 Give him a trial. ⇌ Take him on trial.

시험준비 試驗準備 preparation for an examination ♦ 시험준비를 하다 prepare [cram] for an examination; study for a test

시험채용 試驗採用 (a) probation ■—기간 a probationary [trial] period; a probation

시현 示現 revelation; manifestation
—시현하다 reveal; manifest

시형 詩形 a form of verse; a verse [poetic] form —학 prosody

시호 諡號 a posthumous [pástʃəməs] name [title]

시화 視話 lip reading; lip language
■—법 visible speech

시화 詩畫 an illustrated [a pictorial] poem; 〈시와 그림〉 a poem and a picture ■—전 an exhibition of illustrated poems

시황 市況 the market; market conditions; the tone [condition, position, state, movements] of the market
♦ 침체한 시황 a depressed [flat, stagnant] market / 활발한 시황 an active [a brisk, a spirited] market / 시황의 전망 the market outlook [prospect]
▶ 시황이 부진[한산, 활발]하다 The market is inactive [quiet, brisk].
▶ 시황은 강세로 시작하여 약세로 끝났다 The market opened strong and closed weak [soft].
■ 증권— the stock market; stock exchange quotations ■—보고 a market report

시회 詩會 a poetry club

시효 時效 〔法〕 prescription
♦ 시효에 걸리다 be barred [extinguished] by prescription; prescribe; lapse / 시효에 걸리지 않다 be unprescribed / 시효에 의하여 권리를 주장하다 prescribe 《for, to》
■ 법정— legal prescription 취득[소멸]— acquisitive [extinctive] prescription; positive [negative] prescription ■—중단[정지] interruption [suspension] of prescription

시후 時候 〈계절〉 the season; the time of (the) year; 〈기후〉 climate; weather
▶ 시후가 바뀌는 때이니 몸조심하세요 Take good care of yourself at the change of season.

▶ 시후에 안 맞는 더위[추위]다 It is unseasonably hot [cold].
■—문안 the compliments of the season; the season's greetings

시흥 詩興 poetical inspiration ◆시흥이 나다 be inspired to verse [to compose a poem]

식 式 1〈의식〉a ceremony; rituals; rites; a (ceremonial) function; a celebration; an observance; (美) (inauguration) exercises
◆개회[폐회]식 an opening [a closing] exercise [ceremony] / 표창식 an awarding ceremony / 증정[수여]식 a presentation [conferment] ceremony / (대통령의) 취임식 (美) inauguration exercises / 식의 사회를 보다 preside at a ceremony / 식을 거행하다 hold [have, perform] a ceremony; celebrate 《a wedding》 / 식에 참석하다 attend a ceremony
▶ 식의 날짜는 정했습니까? Have you fixed the date for the ceremony?
▶ 졸업식[입학식]이 엄숙히 거행되었다 The graduation [entrance] ceremony was solemnly held.
▶ 우리는 지난 봄에 식을 올렸다 We were [got] married last spring.
▶ 장례식은 어디서 있습니까? Where are the funeral rites going to be?
2〈방식〉a method; 〔論〕a system; 〈양식〉a style; a form; a type; a fashion; a mode; a way; a manner; 〔建〕an order
◆고딕식 건축 Gothic architecture / 그레그식 속기법 the Gregg system of shorthand / 95년식 M [Model] 1995 / 한국식 사고방식 a Korean mode [way] of thinking / 하는 식을 터득하다 get the hang 《of》; catch [acquire] the knack 《of》
▶ 어떤 식의 집을 원합니까? What style of house do you want?
3〈수리의〉an expression; 〈공식〉a formula (pl. ~s, -lae); 〈방정식〉an equation
◆구조식 a structural [constitutional] formula / 대수식 an algebraic expression / 물의 분자식 a molecular formula for water / 2항식 a binominal expression [formula]; a binominal / 화학식 a chemical formula / 식으로 나타내다 formularize; formulate
▶ 내 이론을 식으로 하면 이렇게 된다 My theory can be formulated like this.

식 蝕 〔天〕an eclipse ◆식의 상(相) a phase of an eclipse

식간 食間 ◆식간에 (eat) between meals
▶ 이 약은 식간에 복용해야 한다 This medicine is to be taken between meals.

식객 食客 a hanger-on (pl. hangers-on); a dependent; a parasite; a sponger
◆식객 생활 parasitism / 식객 노릇을 하다 be a dependent on sb; feed [live, sponge] on sb
▶ 그는 식객 같은 사람이다 He is something of a hanger-on [parasite].

식견 識見〈판단력〉knowledge; judgment; insight; discernment; vision; intelligence;〈견해〉one's view; opinions; ideas
◆식견이 높은 사람 a man of exalted ideas; a man of great insight
▶ 저 사람은 식견이 높다 He is a man of keen perception [discernment].

식곤증 食困症 languor [languidness, drowsiness] after a meal

식구 食口 mouths to feed; one's dependents; members of a family; one's family; (美) (one's) folk
◆식구수 the number of mouths to feed; the number of dependents; the size of a family / 부양할[돌볼] 식구가 많다[적다] have many [few] mouths to feed; have a large [small] family to support [to take care of] / 식구를 부양하다 support one's family
▶ 우리는 네 식구다 Ours is a family of four. ⇒ My family members are four.
▶ 그에게는 식구가 없다 He has no dependents. ⇒〈독신이다〉He is single.
▶ 그와는 한 식구처럼 지낸다 We treat him just like a member of the family.

식권 食券 a meal [food] ticket [coupon]

> 解說 (美)의 *a meal ticket* 은 음식점이 주는 식사 할인권을 말함, (英)에서는 점심 식권으로 종업원에 지급되는 것을 *a luncheon voucher*라고 함

식균작용 食菌作用〈백혈구 등의〉phagocytosis

식기 食器 tableware; a table service;〈정찬용의〉a dinner set [service]; (美) flatware; (英)《a piece of》plate;〈주발〉a bowl ◆식기를 씻다 (美) do the dishes; (英) do the washing-up
■—실 a pantry —장 a cupboard; a sideboard

식나무 〔植〕a Japan(ese) laurel

식다 1〈차지다〉get cold; cool (down [off])
◆식은 땀 a cold sweat [perspiration] / 식은 죽[밥] cold gruel [rice] / 식지 않도록 해두다 keep sth hot
▶ 빨리 와서 드세요. 수프가 식어요 Come to the table quickly. Your soup is getting [going] cold.
▶ 수프는 아직 식지 않았다 The soup has not cooled down yet.
▶ 목욕물이 식기 전에 들어가세요 Take a bath while it is warm enough.
2〈열이〉abate; subside; lapse back [away];〈열성 등이〉flag; be dampened; cool down [off] ◆열의가 식다 lose interest 《in》; grow less enthusiastic
▶ 열이 식었다〈내렸다〉The fever has broken [dropped].
▶ 그의 영어열도 곧 식어버렸다 His enthusiasm for English died down soon.
▶ 쉬 덥는 방이 쉬 식는다 (속담) Soon hot, soon cold.
▶ 그의 야구열이 아무래도 식은 것 같다 He seems to have lost interest in baseball.

식단(표) 食單(表) a menu; a (menu) card; a bill of fare ◆식단표를 보다 cousult [study] a menu / 식단을 작성하다 make out a menu
▶ 오늘 저녁 식단은 무엇입니까? What are we having for dinner? ⇒ What's for dinner tonight?

식당 食堂 a dining room [hall];〈군대·공장 등의〉a mess hall;〈선박 내의〉a messroom;〈역·열차 내의〉a buffet; a refreshment room;

〈대학·교회 등의〉 a refectory; 〈음식점〉 an eating house; a restaurant ■ 간이— a lunchroom; (美) a lunch counter; (美) a snack bar; 〈셀프 서비스의〉 a cafeteria —차 (美) a dining car; (英) a dining coach; (英) a restaurant car; a diner; a buffet car: 그 열차에는 식당차가 딸려 있었다 The train had a dining car attached to it.

식대 食代 〈식당의〉 the charge for food; 〈식비〉 food expenses ⇨ 식비(食費)

식도 食道 [解] the gullet; the alimentary canal; the esophagus (*pl.* ~es, -gi) ■ —경 an esophagoscope —암 cancer of the esophagus —염 esophagitis —절개 esophagotomy

식도락 食道樂 epicurism; epicureanism; gourmandism ♦ 식도락의 epicurean ■—가 〈미식가〉 an epicure; a gourmet; a gourmand; a gastronome

식량 食糧 food; foodstuffs; provisions; 〈군대·탐험대 등의〉 ration
♦ (군인 등이 휴대하는) 1일분의 식량 a day's ration / 식량을 비축하다 lay [store] up provisions / 식량을 공급하다 provide [supply] sb with food; provide food 《for sb》; provision 《a district》
▶ 우리에 대한 식량 보급이 감소되었다 Our food supplies have diminished [run short].
▶ 우리의 식량은 1주일 밖에 가지 못했다 Our provisions lasted us only a week.
▶ 그 나라는 가뭄으로 인해 큰 식량 부족을 겪고 있다 That country is suffering from a shortage of food as a result of the drought.
▶ 식량이 떨어졌다 The provisions have run out. ⇌ We have run out of provisions.
▶ 우선 식량을 확보해야만 했다 To begin with, we had to secure foodstuffs.
▶ 우리는 탐험에 나서기 위해 식량을 사들였다 We lay in provisions to go on an expedition.
■ 비상— emergency rations 예비— a reserve of provisions ■ —관리[통제] food control —난 the difficulty of obtaining food —농업기구〈UN의〉 the Food and Agriculture Organization (略 FAO, F.A.O.) —대책 a food policy; food measures —문제 a food problem —배급 (food) rationing —부 족 a shortage of provisions; a food shortage —위기 a food crisis —정책 a food policy —혁명 the green revolution

식량사정 食糧事情 the food situation ♦ 식량사정의 악화 aggravation of the food situation
▶ 북한은 식량사정이 나빠졌다 The food situation in North Korea has taken an unfavorable turn.
▶ 인구의 급증과 거듭되는 흉작으로 그 나라의 식량사정은 심각하다 The food situation in that country is very serious because of a sharp increase in population and repeated crop failures.

식료 食料 food; foodstuffs; fare; victuals
식료품 食料品 an article of food; a foodstuff; (총칭) foodstuffs; provisions; groceries; eatables; victuals
▶ 식료품 값이 급속히 오르고 있다 Food prices are going up rapidly.
■ —상 a dealer in provisions; a grocer; a groceryman —점 a food store; (美) a grocery (store); (英) a grocer's (shop): 그는 식료품점을 하고 있다 He is in the grocery business. ⇌ He runs a grocery store.

식림 植林 forestation; afforestation; tree planting
—식림하다 afforest 《a mountain》; plant trees
▶ 그들은 그 지역에 식림했다 They planted the area with trees. ⇌ They forested the area.
—계획[사업] a tree-planting [an afforestation] project —정책 an afforestation policy —지 a plantation

식모 食母 a kitchen maid; a maidservant; a housemaid; a (home) help; (美) a domestic help ♦ 식모를 두다 keep a kitchen help
▶ 식모 구함 (광고) Domestic servant [kitchenmaid] wanted. ⇌ Wanted a maid. ⇌ Domestic help needed.
■ —살이 domestic service: 식모살이하다 be in domestic service

식모 植毛 a hair transplant
식목 植木 tree planting; forestation
—식목하다 plant trees; do planting
■ —운동 a tree planting campaign [drive] —일 (美) Arbor Day; a tree-planting day —주간 Arbor Week

식물 植物 a plant; a vegetable; plant life; (총칭) vegetation; a flora (*pl.* ~s, -rae); the botany 《of Korea》
♦ 다년생[1년생] 식물 a perennial [an annual] (plant) / 식물의 분포 a geographical distribution of plants / 한국의 식물을 연구하다 study the botany of Korea / 식물을 채집하다 collect plants; botanize; herborize
▶ 그의 정원에는 100종 이상의 식물이 있다 His garden contains more than a hundred (different) kinds of plants.
▶ 저 산에 식물이라곤 아무것도 나 있지 않다 That mountain is bare of vegetation.
■ 고산[열대]— an alpine [a tropical] plant 기생— a parasitic plant 양지[음지]— a sun [shade] plant 현화(顯花)[은화(隱花)]— a flowering [flowerless] plant; a phanerogam [cryptogam] ■—계 the vegetable [botanical, plant] kingdom —구계(區系) a flora —대 a floral [vegetation] zone; a zone of vegetation —병리학 plant pathology; phytopathology —분류학 systematic botany; plant taxonomy —상(相) a flora —생리학 plant physiology; physiological botany —생태학[조직학] plant ecology [histology] —세포 a vegetable cell —원 a botanical garden —인간 a human vegetable —지(誌) a flora; a herbal —지리학 geographical botany; plant geography —질 vegetable matter —표본 a botanical specimen; (총칭) a herbarium (*pl.* ~s, -ria) —플랑크톤 phytoplankton —해부학 phytotomy; plant anatomy —형태학 plant morphology; morphological botany —화학 plant chemistry; phytochemistry

식물성 植物性 vegetability; vegetable property

[nature] ◆ 식물성 기름[버터] vegetable oil [butter] / 식물성 단백질 vegetable albumin; phytalbumin / 식물성 섬유 a vegetable fiber

식물채집 植物採集 plant collecting; botanization; herborization
◆ 식물채집하러 가다 go botanizing [herborizing, plant collecting] 《in, at》
■ —가 a herborist; a herbalist; a plant collector —통 a vasculum 《pl. ~s, -la》

식물학 植物學 botany; phytology
◆ 식물학상 botanically; from the botanical point of view
■ —자 a botanist

식민 植民 colonization; settlement; 〈사람〉 a colonist; a settler
◆ 식민하다 colonize 《in》《a land》; settle 《in》《a region》; plant 《a country》 with colonists / 브라질에 식민하다 colonize Brazil; plant settlers in Brazil
■ —사업 colonization —정책 a colonial policy

식민지 植民地 a colony; a settlement; 〔史〕 a plantation ◆ 식민지의 colonial / 식민지를 건설하다 found [establish, settle] a colony; plant a settlement [colony]
■ 해외— an overseas colony ■ —정책 a colonial policy —주의 colonialism —총독 a proconsul; a viceroy

식민지화 植民地化 colonialization
—식민지화하다 colonialize

식별 識別 discrimination; discernment ◆ 색깔의 식별 color vision
—식별하다 discriminate 《A from B, between A and B》; distinguish; discern; tell [separate] 《A from B》
◆ 식별할 수 있는[없는] distinguishable [undistinguishable] / 어둠 속에서 사람들의 얼굴을 식별하다 distinguish people's faces in the darkness
▶ 산토끼와 집토끼는 쉽게 식별할 수 있다 We can easily differentiate a rabbit and a hare. ⇌ We can easily tell [know] a rabbit from a hare. ⇌ A rabbit and a hare are easily distinguishable.
■ —력 discriminating power; the power of discernment; discrimination

식복 食福 one's luck [blessing, bliss] of having things to eat ◆ 식복이 있다 be blessed with things to eat

식부 植付 planting
—식부하다 plant 《a section with corn》; do the planting
■ —면적 the acreage [area] under crop; the planted area [acreage]

식분 蝕分 〔天〕 a phase of an eclipse

식비 食費 food expenses; 〈하숙의〉 (the charge for) board; 〈가정의〉 table expenses
◆ 15만원의 식비를 내다 pay 150,000 won for one's board / 식비를 절약하다[줄이다] cut down on one's food expenses
▶ 식비가 늘어서 모두 곤란해 하고 있다 Everybody is suffering from increasing food cost.
▶ 우리는 월 12만원의 식비가 든다 Our food expenses come to 120,000 won a month.
▶ 나는 봉급의 3분의 1을 식비로 지출한다 I spend one-third of my salary to pay my food expenses.

식빵 食— 《a loaf [slice] of》 bread

식사 式辭 an address; 〈축사〉 a ceremonial [congratulatory] address; a speech
◆ 식사를 하다 give [make] an address

식사 食事 a meal; 〈정찬〉 dinner; 〈규정식〉 a diet; 〈하숙의〉 board

> 解說 *meal*은 한끼 식사란 말로 아침 (breakfast), 점심 (lunch), 저녁 (supper)을 총칭하는 말이다. 각각의 식사 이름이 뚜렷할 때는 meal을 쓰지 않는다 : 오늘 아침에는 늦은 식사를 했다 We had a late breakfast this morning. *dinner*는 하루 중에서 가장 주요한 식사다. meal에 관사가 붙는 것과 달리 breakfast, lunch, dinner에는 보통 관사가 붙지 않는다. 다만 위에서와 같이 형용사가가 붙는 경우에는 a를 붙이고 특정한 식사를 강조할 때는 the를 붙인다: 그 다음날 조반은 검소한 것이었다 The breakfast we were served the next morning was a simple [a frugal] one. *diet*는 병 치료나 체중 조절을 위해 규정된 식사를 가리킨다.

◆ 간단한[검소한] 식사 a simple [frugal] meal / 푸짐한 식사 a good [substantial, square] meal / 호사스런 식사 sumptuous dinner / 식사 준비를 하다 〈요리의〉 prepare [〈美〉 fix] a meal; 〈식탁의〉 set the table; lay the cloth; get a meal ready / 식사 대접을 하다 treat sb to a meal; serve sb with a meal; dine sb / 식사에 초대받다 be asked [invited] to dinner
〈식사를〉 식사를 제한하다 〈환자의〉 put 《a patient》 on a (restricted) diet; diet sb; 〈스스로〉 go on a (reducing) diet / 식사를 함께 하다 dine [have a meal] with sb / 가벼운 식사를 하다 have a light meal; 《口》 have a bite (to eat)
—식사하다 have [take, eat, get] a meal; dine
◆ 급히[일찍] 식사하다 eat a hurried [have an early] meal / 충분히 식사하다 have a good [hearty] meal / 밖에서 식사하다 have one's meal [dinner] out; dine [eat] out / 제때에 식사하다 have regular mealtimes
▶ 會話 「나하고 함께 식사하고 가세요」「고맙습니다, 기꺼이」 "Would you like to eat [have dinner] with me?" "Thank you. I'd love to."
■ —시간 a mealtime —예법 table manners

식산 殖産 〈증산〉 increase of production; higher productivity; 〈재산을 늘림〉 enhancement of one's fortune
◆ 식산을 도모하다 try to enhance [increase] one's fortune

식상 食傷 〈배탈〉 a stomach trouble [disorder, upset]; indigestion; 〈물림〉 surfeit; glut
—식상하다 have a stomach trouble; suffer from indigestion; 〈물리다〉 be surfeited [cloyed, sated, satiated] 《with》; be fed up 《with》; glut *oneself* 《with》; have enough 《of》
▶ 우리는 자기 자랑뿐인 그의 이야기에 식상했다 We are quite fed up with his boastful talk.
▶ 이제 그런 경기에는 식상했다 I've had more than enough of that sort of game.

식사와 요리

아침밥은 breakfast, **점심**은 lunch, 아침 늦게 점심을 겸해서 하는 식사는 brunch (breakfast+lunch)라고 한다. 간단히 하는 **저녁식사**를 supper, **정찬**을 dinner라고 한다. dinner는 「저녁 식사」뿐만 아니라 하루 중에서 낮에 주요한 식사를 하면 그것이 dinner이고 저녁식사는 supper가 된다. 각 식사의 중간에는 **차 마시는 시간**((美) a coffee break; (英) a tea break)이 있다. 영국에서는 이 tea break를 오전과 오후에 두 번 하는 것이 보통인데, 오전의 차를 a morning tea 또는 (口)로 elevenses라고 하고 오후의 차를 an afternoon tea라고 한다. 또 사람에 따라서는 high tea를 드는 수도 있는데, 이것은 저녁에 tea와 함께 하는 가벼운 저녁식사에 해당한다. 간식은 a snack; between-meals refreshments고, 야식은 a midnight snack이라고 한다.

1. 아침밥

(英)과 (美)는 큰 차이 없이 빵이나 곡물식(cereal)에다 마실것으로 커피나 홍차를 곁들여 아침 식사로 한다. 유럽에서 영국의 아침 식사는 English breakfast라 하여 ham, bacon, sausage, 달걀요리 등이 한 가지 이상이 더 나와, 빵과 커피나 홍차뿐인 유럽 대륙의 아침식사(Continental breakfast)보다 푸짐한 것으로 알려져 있다. 달걀 요리로는 영국에서는 베이컨 에그 (bacon and eggs), 미국에서는 햄 에그 (ham and eggs)가 많이 나온다.

(1) 빵과 곡물식(cereal)

식빵은 bread, 토스트(toast), 달걀과 우유에 담갔다가 구운 프렌치 토스트(French toast), 롤 빵(a roll), 과자빵 대니시(Danish pastry), 크루아상(a croissant), 소형의 둥근 빵 머핀(a muffin) 등의 빵 이외에 와플(waffle), 팬케이크(a pancake), 도넛(a doughnut)도 일반적이다. 토스트, 머핀, 와플, 팬케이크에는 버터(butter), 젤리(jelly), 마멀레이드(marmalade), 딸기잼(strawberry jam)이나 래즈베리 잼(raspberry jam) 등 각종 잼, 또는 꿀(honey), 단풍 당밀(maple syrup) 등을 발라서 먹는다. 토스트는 잘 구운 것을 dark, 살짝 구운 것을 medium brown이라고 한다. 한국에서는 흰 빵(white bread)이 많으나 영국이나 미국에서는 밀기울(bran)이 섞인 밀가루(whole-wheat flour)의 누런 빵(brown bread; whole-wheat bread) 쪽이 많이 쓰인다. 곡물식(cereal)에는 오트밀(oatmeal)처럼 따뜻하게 해서 먹는 것(hot cereal)과 그대로 먹는 것(dry cereal)이 있는데 모두 우유와 설탕을 타서 먹는다. 영국에서는 겨울에 오트밀을 우유로 죽을 쑤어서 버터와 흑설탕(brown sugar)을 쳐서 먹는 포리지(porridge; oatmeal)가 식탁에 많이 오른다.

(2) 달걀

달걀은 달걀프라이 (sunny-side up), 스크램블드 에그 (scrambled eggs), 달걀볶음 (parched eggs), 오믈렛(an omelet), 삶은 달걀(a boiled egg) 등으로 만들어 먹는다. 삶는데는 완숙(hard boiled)과 반숙(soft boiled)이 있다. 한국식 달걀부침은 a plain omelet로 표현하는 것이 가장 근사하다. 영미인은 날달걀(a raw egg)은 먹지 않는다. 「달걀을 어떻게 요리할까요?」는 "How do you like your eggs?"라고 하며 「달걀부침을 만들어 주세요」는 "I'd like mine scrambled."라고 한다.

(3) 음료

영국에서는 커피(coffee)보다 홍차(tea)를 많이 마시는데 거의가 밀크 티(milk tea; white tea)를 좋아하며 레몬 티(lemon tea)는 그다지 마시지 않는다. 커피를 마시는 식에는 설탕·크림을 넣지 않는 블랙(black coffee), 카페인을 줄인 커피(decaffeinated coffee), 대략 같은 양의 밀크를 넣는 카페오레(café au lait) 등이 있다. 「커피를 어떻게 탈까요?」 "How do you like your coffee?"라고 물으면 「밀크를 넣어 주세요」 "With milk please."라든가 「블랙으로 해주세요」 "Black please." 등으로 대답한다. 「진하게[약하게] 해주세요」는 "I'd like my coffee strong [weak]."이다.

주스(juice)는 100 퍼센트 과즙인 것만을 가리킨다. 프루트 주스는 fruits가 아니고 fruit로 단수를 써서 fruit juice라고 한다. 오렌지 주스(orange juice), 파인 주스(pineapple juice), 그레이프프루트 주스(grapefruit juice) 등이 있다. 야채 주스(vegetable juice)로는 토마토 주스(tomato juice)를 가장 많이 마신다.

2. 점심

영국이나 미국이나 점심은 가볍게 때우는 사람이 많다. 다만 영국에서는 지역에 따라 일요일에 점심을 잘 차려먹는 사람들도 있어서 그것을 dinner라고 한다. 일반적으로 영국이나 미국에서는 샌드위치(a sandwich), 햄버거(a hamburger), 핫도그(a hot dog)에다 커피, 홍차, 우유, 수프 등을 곁들인다. 그 밖에 영국에서는 피시 앤드 칩스(fish and chips)도 인기가 있다. 이것은 대구의 일종인 haddock을 토막내서 튀긴 것에다 감자를 채썰어 튀긴 것을 곁들인 요리다.

(1) 햄버거

치즈버거(a cheeseburger), 생선의 흰살을 튀긴 피시버거(a fishburger), 새우로 만든 슈림프버거(a shrimpburger), 칠면조의 터키버거(a turkeyburger) 등 여러 가지가 있다.

(2) 샌드위치

베이컨·양상추·토마토로 속을 채운 BLT (▶bacon, lettuce, tomato의 첫글자를 따온 이름), 토스트 세 쪽에 고기·양상추·토마토를 끼워 넣은 클럽 샌드위치(a club sandwich), 세 쪽의 빵 사이에 두 겹으로 쇠고기를 넣은 더블데커(a double-decker), 호밀빵에 콘 비프를 얹은 콘비프샌드위치(a corned beef sandwich), 달걀프라이와 햄으로 만든 햄 앤드 에거(a ham'n egger), 피넛 버터 잼 샌드위치(PB and J—peanut butter and jelly), 오이 샌드위치(a cucumber sandwich), 큰 프랑스 빵에 야채·햄·로스트 비프 등을 끼운 서브머린(a submarine; a sub—모양이 잠수함과 비슷하다고 해서) 등 많은 종류가 있다.

(3) 핫도그(a hot dog)

—세로로 쪼갠 롤빵에

다 프랑크푸르트 소시지(frankfurter)를 끼워 넣은 것으로 칠리 소스에 담가서 삶아내어 저민 고기를 넣은 칠리도그(a chili dog) 등이 있다. 소스로는 사우어크라우트(sauerkraut)도 인기가 있다.

3. 저녁 식사

풀코스의 순서는 다음과 같다.

식전 술(appetizer), 전채(hors d'oeuvre), 수프(soup), 생선요리(fish), 고기요리(entree), 로스트(roast), 샐러드(salad), 디저트(dessert), 커피나 홍차

(1) 수프— 양파 수프(onion soup), 콩소메(consommé), 치킨 수프(chicken soup), 치킨누들 수프(chicken noodle soup), 빈 수프(bean soup), 포타즈(potage), 고기·야채·마카로니를 넣은 차우더(chowder; clam chowder)

(2) 생선요리—대하(a lobster), 새우(a shrimp), 굴(an oyster), 연어(a salmon), 허넙치(a sole), 대구(a codfish), 무지개송어(a rainbow trout), 대합(a clam), 송어(a trout) 등 어개류(魚介類)를 주재료로 하며, 다음과 같은 종류가 있다.

어개류의 모듬요리— Captain's Plate (▶「무엇이 들어갑니까?」는 "What comes with the Captain's Plate?"라고 한다), 생선·고기·야채 등을 조가비에 담아서 오븐에다 굽는 에스캘럽(escal(l)oped; scalloped), 어개류·야채를 토마토 소스에 푹 끓여서 밥에 얹어 먹는 크레올(creole), 어개류를 소스로 무쳐서 조가비에 넣어 굽는 코키유(coquille), 생선살 경단 튀김(a fish cake; a fish ball), 생선에 밀가루를 입혀서 튀기는 프리터(fritters), 생선에 밀가루를 입혀서 버터구이하는 뫼니에르(meunière), 연어 토막의 스테이크(steak) 등이 있다.

(3) 고기요리—스테이크(steak)는 고기나 생선의 두꺼운 토막 또는 그것을 구운 것을 말하지만, 보통 스테이크라고 하면 비프스테이크(beefsteak), 새끼 양고기의 램스테이크(lamb steak)도 있다.

스테이크는 쇠고기의 부위에 따라서 다음과 같은 호칭이 있다. 설로인 스테이크(sirloin steak, 허리 상부의 고기), 샤토브리앙(châteaubriand, 필렛살의 가장 두꺼운 부분), 텐더로인 스테이크(tenderloin steak, 허리 부분과 늑골 중간부의 연한 고기), 필레 미뇽(filet mignon, 필렛살), 포터하우스 스테이크(porterhouse steak, 허리 상부와 갈비살 중간부), 립 스테이크(rib steak)

스테이크의 굽는 법은 설익힘(rare), 반익힘(medium), 잘익힘(well-done)의 3종류.「어떻게 구워 드릴까요?」는 "How would you like your meat?"라고 하고「잘 익혀 주십시오」는 "I'd like it well-done."이다.

고기 요리에 따라 나오는 야채로는 구운 감자(baked potato), 시금치 소테(spinach sauté), 버섯(mushroom), 삶은 당근(boiled carrot) 등. 스테이크의 조미료로는 서양 고추냉이(horseradish)를 많이 쓴다.

주요 샐러드— 각 레스토랑마다 특유의 주방장 샐러드(chief's salad), 치킨 샐러드(chicken salad), 모듬 샐러드(combination salad), 양상추만의 그린 샐러드(green salad), 양배추 채썬 것을 마요네즈드레싱·사우어 크림으로 무친 콜슬로(coleslaw), 양파·양상추·토마토 등에 드레싱을 친 토스 샐러드(tossed salad), 야채에 날달걀·치즈를 가미한 시저 샐러드(Caesar salad) 등

샐러드 드레싱—프렌치 드레싱(French dressing), 이탈리언 드레싱(Italian dressing), 사우전드 아일랜드 드레싱(Thousand Island dressing), 식초와 식용유의 드레싱(Oil and vinegar dressing), 블루 치즈 드레싱(Blue cheese dressing) 등 외에 레스토랑에서는 특제 드레싱(House dressing)을 준비해 두기도 한다.

4. 식사 시설

레스토랑 a restaurant / 식당 a dining room / (주로 일품 요리를 하는) 그릴 a grillroom / 해물 요리 전문 레스토랑 a sea food restaurant / (햄버거 등의) 패스트 푸드 레스토랑 a fastfood restaurant / (차 안에 앉아서 먹는) 드라이브 인 레스토랑 a drive-in restaurant / 커피숍 (간이 식당) a coffee shop / 수상 레스토랑 a floating restaurant

식생활 食生活 food [dietary] life; eating habits
♦ 한국인의 식생활 the eating habits of the Korean / 식생활이 빈약하다 eat poor food / 식생활을 개선하다 improve *one's* diet [eating habits]; eat more nourishing food [better food]

식성 食性 preference; taste; likes and dislikes in food
♦ 식성에 맞는[안 맞는] 음식 an agreeable [a disagreeable] food / 식성이 까다롭다 be particular [fastidious] about *one's* food; have a delicate taste / 식성에 맞다 suit *one's* taste [palate]; be to *one's* taste

식수 drinking water; water (fit) to drink; potable water

식수 植樹 tree planting ⇨ 식목

식순 式順 the program [order] of a ceremony

식언 食言 eating *one's* words
—식언하다 eat *one's* words; break [take back] *one's* promise; go back on *one's* word
▶ 군자는 식언하지 않는다 A virtuous man neither takes back his words nor breaks his promise.

식역 識閾〔心〕(below) the threshold of consciousness; the limen ((pl. ~s, limina))
♦ 식역의 liminal / 식역하의 subliminal / 식역상의 supraliminal

식염 食鹽 (table) salt ■—수 a solution of salt; a saline [salt] solution —주사 (a) salt [saline] injection

식욕 食慾 appetite (for food); desire to eat ⟨식욕이⟩ 식욕이 나다 *one's* appetite improves [increases]; feel an appetite / 식욕이 없다 have no [little] appetite; have a poor [weak] appetite; lack appetite (for food) / 식욕이 없어지다 *one's* appetite fails; ⟨사람이 주어⟩ lose *one's* appetite / 식욕이 왕성하다 have a keen

[sharp, strong, hearty] appetite / 식욕이 있다 have a good appetite
▶ 조금 운동하면 식욕이 난다 A little exercise will give you a good appetite.
▶ 그 소식을 듣고 식욕이 뚝 떨어졌다 I lost my appetite when I heard the news. ⇌ The news spoiled my appetite.
〈식욕을〉 식욕을 돋우다 stimulate [excite, tempt, quicken, arouse, sharpen, work up] *one's* appetite / 식욕을 감퇴[증진]시키다 diminish [increase] *one's* appetite / 식욕을 잃다 lose *one's* appetite / 식욕을 만족시키다 [채우다] satisfy [gratify, appease] *one's* appetite
▶ 향신료는 식욕을 자극한다 Spice stimulates our appetite.
■ ―억제제 an appetite suppressant ―제어중추 the appetite-controlling center (of the brain)

식용 食用 edibility
♦ 식용의 edible; eatable; used for food / 식용에 적합하다 be good [suitable] to eat; be edible; be esculent; be fit for food / 식용으로 쓰이다 be used for food; be eaten as food
▶ 이 식물은 식용으로 적합하지 않다 This plant is not good to eat.
―식용하다 use *sth* for food
■ ―개구리 an edible frog; a bullfrog ―근(根) edible roots ―버섯 edible mushrooms ―색소 food coloring ―식물 esculent plants; plants for food ―유 edible [cooking, food] oil ―품 ⇨ 식료품

식육 食肉 〈고기〉 meat; 〈먹기〉 eating flesh
♦ 식육용 소 (총칭) beef cattle ―식육하다 eat meat
■ ―가공업자 a meat processor ―류 carnivorous [predatory] animals; carnivores

식은땀 a cold sweat ♦ 식은땀을 흘리다[흘리고 있다] break into [be in] a cold sweat
▶ 그녀는 당황하여 식은땀을 흘렸다 She perspired with embarrassment.
▶ 그것은 지금 생각해도 식은땀이 날 지경이다 Even now I break into a cold sweat when I remember it.

식은죽 ―粥 cold gruel [porridge]
▶ 그런 일은 식은죽 먹기다 That's quite an easy task. ⇌ Nothing can be easier. ⇌ That's (as) easy as pie. ⇌ (美俗) That's a cinch.
▶ 저런 상대는 식은죽 먹기다 I can beat him hands down.

식음 食飲 eating and drinking ♦ 식음을 전폐하다 give up eating and drinking; fast
―식음하다 eat and drink

식이 食餌 a diet; food

식이요법 食餌療法 alimentotherapy; a diet [dietary] cure; a dietetic treatment ♦ 식이요법을 하다 be [go] on a (restricted) diet
▶ 그녀는 체중을 줄이기 위해 식이요법을 하고 있다 She is on a diet to reduce her weight.
▶ 의사는 환자에게 식이요법을 시켰다 The doctor put the patient on a diet.

식인 食人 man-eating; cannibalism
■ ―귀 a cannibal demon ―자 a man-eater; a cannibal ―종 a cannibalistic tribe; a cannibal race; cannibals

식자 植字 typesetting; composing; composition ―식자하다 compose [set (up)] type
■ ―공 a compositor; a typesetter; a typo 《*pl.* ~s》 (자동)―기 a typesetting [composing] machine; a typesetter ―대[가] a composing stand [frame] ―판 a galley

식자 識者 〈지식인〉 intelligent [informed, learned, intellectual] people; men of intelligence; the wise; thinking people; persons of good sense; the intellectuals; the intelligentzia
♦ 당대의 식자들 the intellects of the age / 식자의 의견 the opinions of the intelligent

식자우환 識字憂患 Where ignorance is bliss, 'tis folly to be wise.

식장 式場 the hall [place] of ceremony; a stateroom; a ceremonial hall
▶ 식장은 어딥니까? Where is the ceremony (going) to be held?

식전 式典 a ceremony ⇨ 식(式) 1

식전 食前 1 〈식사 전〉 ♦ 식전에 before a meal; before eating
▶ 그들은 언제나 식전 기도를 한다 They always say grace [offer a short prayer] before a meal.
▶ 식전 30분에 복용 〈약의 복용 지시〉 To be taken 30 minutes before meals [each meal].
2 〈이른 아침〉 the time before breakfast; early morning
♦ 식전 바람에 before breakfast; early in the morning

식중독 食中毒 food poisoning
♦ 식중독에 걸리다 be poisoned by food; be stricken by food poisoning; come down with food poisoning / 식중독을 일으키다 〈음식이 주어〉 disagree with *sb*

식체 食滯 indigestion; dyspepsia
▶ 피자를 먹으면 난 꼭 식체가 된다 Pizza always gives me indigestion. ⇌ Pizza always sits heavily on my stomach.

식초 食醋 vinegar ♦ 야채에 식초를 치다 pickle vegetables in vinegar; vinegar vegetables

식충 食蟲 1 〈행위〉 insect-eating; 〈생물〉 an insect-eater; an insectivore
2 ⇨ 식충이
■ ―동물[식물] an insectivore; an insectivorous animal [plant] ―류 Insectivora

식충이 食蟲― 〈탐식자〉 a glutton; a gourmand; a gorger; a belly-slave; 〈밥벌레〉 an idler; a good-for-nothing; a ne'er-do-well
▶ 저 남자는 식충이야 He is good for nothing.

식칼 食― a kitchen knife; 〈식탁용 고기 써는 칼〉 a carving knife; 〈푸주용〉 a cleaver; a butcher('s) knife

식탁 食卓 a (dining) table; a board; a dinner table; 〈함선의〉 a mess table
♦ 식탁 예절 table manners / 식탁용의[으로] for table use / 식탁을 치우다 clear the table; remove [take away] the cloth / 식탁에서 일어서다 get up from [leave] the table
▶ 식탁을 차리세요 Set the table.
▶ 7시에 식탁에 앉아 주세요 Please sit at

식탐

[down to] (the) table at seven.
▶ 산해진미가 식탁에 차려져 있었다 All sorts of delicacies were served on the table.
■ —보 a tablecloth —용 소금 table salt —용품 tableware

식탐 食貪 gluttony —**식탐하다** be greedy; be gluttonous; be voracious

식품 食品 (a) food; foodstuff(s)
■ 건강[냉동]— health [frozen] foods 불량— inferior [unwholesome, unsanitary] foodstuff; substandard [illegal] food 인스턴트— precooked food; convenience [jiffy cooking] food; (俗) instant 주요— staple foods; staples ■ —공업 the food industry —공학 food engineering —영양학과 the department of food and nutrition —의약국 (美) the Food and Drug Administration (略 FDA, F.D.A.) —의약품 안전본부 National Food and Drug Safety Headquarters —점 a grocer's shop; (美) a grocery (store) —첨가물 a food additive —학 sitology —회사 a food company

식품가공 食品加工 food processing
■ —업 the food processing industry —업자 a food processor

식품관리 食品管理 food control
■ —법 (法) the Staple Food Control Act —제도 the food control system

식품위생 食品衛生 food sanitation [hygiene]
■ —법 (法) the Food Sanitation Act

식피 植皮 (外科) skin grafting; dermatoplasty; dermoplasty
■ —술 a skin grafting operation

식혜 食醯 a sweet rice drink

식후 食後 ♦ 식후의 after-dinner (speech); (period) after a meal / 식후에 after dinner [a meal]
▶ 식후 30분에 복용 〈약의 복용 지시〉 To be taken 30 minutes after meals [each meal].

식히다 〈차게 하다〉 cool; let *sth* cool
♦ 더운 물을 식히다 cool hot water / 머리를 식히다 cool *one's* head; make *one's* head clear
▶ 열이 높아서 머리를 얼음으로 식혔다 I put ice on my head because I had a high fever.
▶ 그 약은 열을 식힌다 The medicine reduces [brings down] the fever.
▶ 머리를 식히고 잘 생각해 봐 Calm down and think carefully.

신¹ 〈신발〉 shoes; footwear; footgear
♦ 갖신 Korean leather shoes / 고무신 rubber shoes / 나막신 wooden clogs / 짚신 straw sandals / 신 한 켤레 a pair of shoes
▶ 이 신은 내 발에 꼭 끼인다 These shoes pinch [are too tight for] my feet.
〈신을〉 신을 신다 put on *one's* shoes; wear shoes / 신을 신고 있다 be in *one's* shoes / 신을 신기다 put shoes on *sb*; have *sb* put on (his) shoes / 신을 신고 with *one's* shoes on; in *one's* shoes / 신을 벗다 take off *one's* shoes / 신을 닦다 polish [black, clean, (美) shine] *one's* shoes
▶ 신을 신은 채로 계셔도 좋습니다 Keep your shoes on, if you please.
▶ 신을 벗고 들어가시오 〈게시〉 Do not enter with shoes on.

신² 〈신명〉 spirits; dash; elation; enthusiasm; excitement; warmth; fervor
♦ 신(이) 나다 be spirited; cheer up; be animated; be elated 《by, with》; warm (up) (to); become enthusiastic; get excited 《at, by》 / 신이 나서 말하다 speak with great fervor; talk enthusiastically / 혼자 신이 나서 지껄이다 give veins to *one's* tongue
▶ 그는 정치 이야기를 할 때면 신이 난다 He gets excited [spirited] when talking politics.

신 神 〈일신교의〉 God; 〈전능자〉 the Almighty; Providence; the Supreme Being; 〈주(主)〉 the Lord; 〈창조주〉 the Creator; 〈하나님 아버지〉 God the Father; the Divinity; 〈이슬람교의〉 Allah; 〈다신교의〉 a god; 〈여신〉 a goddess; a deity; a divinity; 〈신령〉 a spirit; 〈악신〉 a demon
♦ 신의 가호 divine protection; the protection of God / 신의 축복[은총] the blessing [grace] of God; divine blessing [grace] / 신의 자비 God's mercy / 신의 심판 the justice of Heaven; divine judgment / 신의 조화 God's engineering; divine work; work of God / 신에게 맹세하다 swear to God / 신을 경외하다 revere God / 신을 믿다 believe in God / 신에게 기도하다 pray to God
▶ 그것은 신의 뜻이다 It is the will of God.
▶ 신을 믿지 않는 사람들도 있다 There are people who don't believe in God.

신 腎 1 〈신장〉 the kidney **2** 〈음경〉 the penis

신 〈장면〉 a scene ♦ 라스트 신 the last scene / 러브 신 a love scene

신- 新- 〈새〉 new; novel; fresh; neo-; 〈현대적〉 modern; 〈신식〉 latest; up-to-date
♦ 신내각 a new cabinet / 신무기 a modern weapon / 신발명 a new invention / 신유행 the latest fashion

신간 新刊 〈신간 활동〉 new publication; 〈서적〉 a new publication [book, title]
■ —광고 an advance copy —광고 a book notice —목록 a list of new publications —서 a new book [publication] —소개 a book review —예고 a notice [an advertisement] of forthcoming books [publications]

신개척지 新開拓地 (a) newly-opened land; a newly-developed land

신격 神格 godhood; divinity

신격화 神格化 deification; apotheosis —**신격화하다** deify; apotheosize; make *sb* divine
▶ 과거에 어떤 나라 국민은 왕이나 지도자를 신격화하곤 하였다 In the past in some countries, people used to make their kings or leaders divine. ⇌ In the past in some countries, people used to deify their kings or leaders.

신경 信經 (基) a creed ■ 사도— The Apostles' Creed 아타나시오스[니케아]— The Athanasian [Nicene] Creed

신경 神經 1 〈기관〉 (解) a nerve
♦ 신경의 nerval; neural; nervine / 신경성의 nervous / 신경성 두통 a nervous headache **2** 〈감각〉 sensitivity; 〈감수성〉 sensibility
〈신경이〉 신경이 날카로워지다[곤두서다] *one's* nerves become edgy; 〈사람이 주어〉 become

excited [jittery, touchy]; **(英)** be nervy / 신경이 피로해지다 be mentally fatigued / 신경이 굵다 be daring; be bold; **(美)** have a lot of nerve
▶ 그는 신경이 민감하다 He is very sensitive.
▶ 그는 신경이 몹시 날카로워져 있다 He is all nerves. ⇒ His nerves are edgy [on edge].
▶ 그는 신경이 몹시 지쳐 있었다 His sensitivity was quite fatigued [frazzled].
⟨신경을⟩ 신경을 피로케 하다 exhaust *one's* nerves / 신경을 건드리다 irritate [jar on] *one's* nerves; set [put] *one's* nerves on edge; make *sb* jittery / 신경을 가라앉히다[안정시키다] soothe [quiet, tranquilize] *one's* nerves
▶ 그의 말투가 나의 신경을 건드렸다 His way of speaking irritated me.
⟨신경에⟩ 신경에 거슬리다 jar [get, grate, work] on *one's* nerves; irritate *one's* nerves / 신경에 부담을 주다 be a (great) strain on *one's* nerves; be trying to *one's* nerves
▶ 저 소리는 내 신경에 거슬린다 That noise gets on my nerves.
3 ⟨관심⟩ care; concern; consideration
◆ 신경이 쓰이다 strain *one's* nerves / 신경을 쓰다 care ⟨about⟩; concern *oneself* ⟨about, cerned⟩ ⟨about⟩; have a regard for *sb's* feelings / 신경을 쓰지 않다 do not care [mind]; care nothing for; be indifferent to; pay [have] no regard ⟨to⟩
▶ 네 일에는 네가 신경을 쓰거라 Look after your own things.
▶ 그녀는 외모에는 신경을 쓰지 않는다 She has no regard for her appearance. ⇌ She is quite indifferent to her appearance.
■—가스 〔軍〕 nerve gas —과 ⟨병원의⟩ the department of neurology —과⟨전문⟩의사 a neurologist —분포 innervation —섬유 nerve fiber —세포 a nerve cell; a neuron —안정제 [진정제] a nervous sedative; a nervine —외과 (학) neurosurgery —외과의사 a neurosurgeon —장애 neuropathy —전(戰) a war of nerves; a nerve war; psychological warfare; **(美)** a psywar —절(節) a (nerve) ganglion ⟨*pl*. ~s, -glia⟩ —절제 neurotomy —정신병 neuropsychosis —정신의학 neuropsychiatry —증 ⇨ 신경병 —학 neurology

신경계 神經系 〔解·動〕 a nervous system
■중추[자율, 말초]— the central [autonomic, peripheral] nervous system

신경과민 神經過敏 oversensitiveness; morbid sensitiveness
◆ 신경과민의 oversensitive; morbidly sensitive; high-strung; overstrung; jumpy; touchy; **(英口)** nervy / 신경과민이 되다 become hypersensitive; get nervous; suffer from nerves
▶ 그는 신경과민이다 He is all nerves.

신경단위 神經單位 〔解〕 a neuron ◆ 신경단위의 neuronic; neuronal

신경병 神經病 a nervous disease [disorder]; neurosis; neuropathy ■—전문가 a neuropathist; a nerve specialist —학 neurology —환자 a neuropath; a neurotic

신경병리학 神經病理學 neuropathology
■—자 a neuropathologist

신경쇠약 神經衰弱 〔醫〕 a nervous breakdown; neurasthenia; nervous prostration; nervous depression [exhaustion]
◆ 신경쇠약의 neurasthenic / 신경쇠약에 걸리다 suffer from nervous prostration [a nervous breakdown]; have a nervous breakdown
■—자 a neurasthenic

신경염 神經炎 〔醫〕 neuritis
■다발성(多發性)— multiple neuritis

신경조직 神經組織 nerve [nervous] tissue
■—학 neurohistology

신경중추 神經中樞 a nerve center ◆ 신경중추의 nerve-centric(al)

신경지 新境地 a new phase [field, vista]
◆ 신경지를 개척하다 open up a new phase ⟨in the art⟩; open a new field ⟨of art⟩

신경질 神經質 a nervous temperament [constitution]; nervousness; nervosity
◆ 신경질의 nervous; high-strung; **(英口)** nervy; jumpy / 신경질이 나게 하다 make *sb* nervous; get on *sb's* nerves / 신경질을 부리다 show nervousness / 신경질을 내다 get nervous [fretful, peevish]
▶ 그는 너무 신경질적이다 He is too nervous [all nerves].

신경통 神經痛 neuralgia ◆ 신경통을 앓다 suffer from neuralgia ■—약 an antineuralgic

신경해부학 神經解剖學 neuroanatomy
■—자 a neuroanatomist

신경향 新傾向 a new tendency [trend]

신고 申告 ⟨보고⟩ a report; a notification; ⟨소득세의⟩ a return; ⟨주장⟩ a statement; ⟨세관에서의⟩ a declaration; a notice; filing
—신고하다 report; declare; state; file ⟨a return⟩; register
◆ 소득세를 신고하다 file *one's* income tax return / 당국[관청]에 신고하다 report to the authorities [competent office] / 경찰에 신고하다 report to the police; notify the police / 세관에 신고하다 make a declaration at the customs house
▶ 〔會話〕 ⟨세관에서⟩ 「신고할 것이 있습니까?」 「아무것도 없습니다」 "Do you have anything to declare?" "(No, I have) nothing (to declare)."
■녹색— a greenpaper report ⟨on business income⟩ 사망— a notice of death 세관— a customs declaration 소득세— an income tax return 전입— a moving-in notification 출생— a register [notification] of birth 출항— a notice of clearance 확정— a final return [declaration] ■—가격 a reported price —마감일 the final day for filing the return —용지 a return form; ⟨세금의⟩ a tax form —자 a reporter; a filer; a declarer —제 the return system

신고 辛苦 ⟨고난⟩ hardship(s); ⟨시련⟩ trials; ⟨노고⟩ labor; pains; trouble ◆ 신고를 겪다 suffer [go through] hardships

신고납세 申告納稅 tax payment by self-assessment ■—자 a self-assessed taxpayer

신고서 申告書 a report; a notice; a declaration; a statement; ⟨세금의⟩ a (tax) return

■ 소득세— an income tax return 수출[수입] — an export [import] declaration

신고안 新考案 a new device; a novel contrivance; a new gadget

신곡 神曲 〈단테의〉 *The Divine Comedy*; (이) *Divina Commedia*

신곡 新曲 a new musical composition; a new tune [piece]

신골 a shoetree; a shoemaker's last; 〈장화용〉 a boot tree

신관 信管 a fuse ♦신관을 제거하다 remove the fuse; defuse / 신관을 장치하다 set a fuse ■시한[격발, 근접]— a time [percussion, proximity] fuse

신관 新官 a newly-appointed official; a new appointee ♦신관 지사 the newly-appointed governor

신관 新館 a new building; 〈증축 건물·별관〉 an annex; (美) an extension ▶ 그 호텔에 신관이 증축되었다 An annex has been built to the hotel.

신교 信敎 religion; a religious belief; a creed; faith
♦신교의 자유 freedom of religion / 신교의 자유를 보장하다 guarantee freedom of religion / 신교를 가지다 have a religious belief; believe [have faith] in a religion
▶ 신교의 자유는 헌법으로 보장되어 있다 Freedom of religion is guaranteed by the constitution.

신교 新敎 Protestantism; the Reformed Faith ♦신교의 선교사 a Protestant missionary ■—도 a Protestant

신구 新舊 the old and the new
♦신구 사장 the incoming and outgoing presidents / 신구 사상의 충돌 a collision between old and new ideas
▶ 신구 회장이 각각 5분간의 연설을 했다 The outgoing and incoming presidents each made an address of five minutes.
■—약 (聖) the Old and New Testaments

신국면 新局面 a new aspect [phase]
♦신국면을 전개하다 take on a new aspect

신권 神權 the divine right ■—정치 theocracy

신규 新規 a new one [type]
♦신규의 new; fresh / 신규로 anew; afresh; newly / 신규로 사람을 채용하다 employ a new hand
▶ 나는 은행에 신규계좌를 개설했다 I opened a new account at the bank.
■—사업 a new enterprise [business, project]; ▶ 우리는 신규 사업을 기획하고 있다 We are undertaking a new business project. —예금 [계좌] a new deposit [account]

신극 新劇 a new drama ■—여배우 a new-drama actress —운동 a theatrical reform movement; a new-drama movement

신근 伸筋 〔解〕 a protractor; an extensor (muscle)

신기 神技 superhuman [divine] skill; a miracle ♦신기를 갖고 있다 have divine skill

신기 神奇 a marvel; marvelousness; a miracle; miraculousness
—신기하다 wonderful; marvelous; wondrous; mysterious; miraculous; magic(al)
♦신기한 일[것, 사람] a marvel; a wonder / 신기하게 marvelously; mysteriously; wonderfully; like magic / 신기하게 여기다 marvel; wonder
▶ 그가 도피했다니 신기하기도 하다 His escape is miraculous.

신기 新奇 novelty; originality
—신기하다 novel; original; new
♦신기한 고안 a novel [an original] device / 신기한 듯이 curiously; with curiosity; with curious eyes / 신기한 것을 좋아하다 be fond of novelty / 신기하게 여기다 regard *sth* as a novelty [curiosity]
▶ 보고 듣는 모든 것이 그에게는 신기했다 Everything he saw or heard interested [was quite new to] him.
▶ 당시엔 그것이 아주 신기했다 It was then a great novelty.
▶ 그것은 이젠 신기하지 않다 It has lost [outgrown] its novelty.
▶ 외국인을 그렇게 신기하게 바라보지 마라 Don't look at foreigners so curiously.

신기다 〈신을〉 put (shoes) on *sb*; get *sb* to put on (shoes)

신기록 新記錄 a new record [mark]; (美口) a new high
♦한국 신기록 a new Korean record / 신기록을 세우다 make [establish, create] a new record; (美口) reach [hit] a new [an all-time] high
▶ 금년 크리스마스 이브 매상은 신기록을 냈다 Christmas Eve's sales this year have hit an all-time high.
▶ 이 달 들어 교통사고 건 수가 신기록을 세웠다 The number of traffic accidents has reached a new high this month.
■세계— a new world record

신기료장수 a cobbler; a vamper; a shoemaker ▶ 신기료 장수 마누라 신발보다 더 험한 신발이 또 있을까? Who is worse shod than the shoemaker's wife?

신기루 蜃氣樓 a mirage ▶ 신기루가 나타났다 A mirage appeared.

신기원 新紀元 a new epoch [era, stage]
♦신기원을 이루는 사건 an epoch-making [epochal] event / 신기원을 이루다 mark a new epoch [era]

신기축 新機軸 a new departure [device]; a novel contrivance ♦신기축을 이루다 make [mark] a new departure; set up a new milestone
▶ 그 회사는 정보산업에서 신기축을 이루었다 The company made a new departure in the information industry.

신나다 be very exhilarated [pleased, happy, rejoiced]; be elated; be on the top of the world; 〈사물이 주어〉 be very exhilarating [interesting, entertaining]; be highly amusing [exciting]
♦신나는 이야기 a highly amusing story; a very interesting [entertaining] talk
▶ 요트를 타고 가면 신날 거야 It will be jolly [fine, capital] fun if we go by yacht.

신나무 〔植〕 an Amur maple
신내리다 神— be possessed by a spirit; 《a shaman》 go [fall] into a trance
♦신내린 사람 a person (who is) possessed by a spirit
▶ 신내린 사람은 신내린 상태에서 그 신과 의사소통을 한다고 한다 It is said that a person possessed by a spirit can commune with the spirit in entrancement.
신년 新年 the New Year; a new year
♦신년초에 at the beginning of the New Year; early in the New Year / 신년을 맞이하다 see the new year in; greet the New Year / 신년을 축하하다 celebrate the New Year / 묵은 해를 보내고 신년을 맞다 see the old year out and the new year in / 제야의 종소리와 함께 신년을 맞다 ring out the old (year) and ring in the new
▶ 신년을 축하합니다 〈새해 복 많이 받으세요〉 Happy New Year! ⇌ I wish you a happy New Year.
■근하— (A) Happy New Year!; 〈연하장에서〉 I wish you a Happy New Year. ■—회 a New Year's party
신념 信念 belief; 〈신앙 등에 대한〉 (a) faith; one's faith; 〈확신〉 confidence, (a) conviction
♦굳은 신념 a firm faith [belief] / 확고부동한 신념 an unshaken [unshakable] faith / 신념이 강한[약한] 사람 a man of strong [weak] faith / 신념이 없다 lack faith (in) / 신념을 관철하다 carry through [stick to] one's convictions / 신념을 가지다 have [hold] faith (in) / 신념을 잃다 lose one's faith [belief] (in)
▶ 그는 자기의 신념을 발표하고 그 신념에 따라 행동하는 용기가 있었다 He had the courage of expressing his conviction and acted on it.
▶ 그녀는 사랑이 모든 것을 극복한다는 신념을 갖고 있다 It is her belief that love conquers all.
신다 put on; 〈신고 있다〉 wear (shoes); have (shoes) on
♦신을 신고 in one's shoes / 신을 신지 않고 barefoot(ed) / 구두를 신다 put on one's shoes / 양말을 신다 pull on one's stockings; put on one's socks / 신어 보다 try (shoes) on
▶ 그녀는 나일론 양말을 신고 있다 She has nylon stockings on.
▶ 그녀는 부츠를 신고 왔다 She came in boots.
신당 新黨 a new political party
신대륙 新大陸 a new continent; 〈아메리카 대륙〉 the New World [Continent]
신도 信徒 a believer; a devotee; a follower; (총칭) the faithful; 〈그리스도교의〉 the flock
■기독교— a Christian 불교— a Buddhist 회교— a Muslim (pl. ~, ~s); a Moslem
신도시 新都市 a new town
신동 神童 an infant genius; a (child) prodigy; a wonder child; a boy wonder; (독) a wunderkind (pl. -kinder, ~s)
▶ 그 아이는 신동이다 The child is an infant genius.
신뒤축 a (shoe) heel
♦신뒤축이 높다[낮다] have high [low] heels; be high-[low-]heeled

▶ 내 신뒤축이 닳았다 My shoes are down at heels [(the) heel]. ⇌ The heels of my shoes are worn out.
▶ 그는 신뒤축이 닳은 신을 신고 있었다 He was down at (the) heels. (▶초라한 차림의 뜻으로도 씀)
신드롬 〔醫〕 〈병리적 증후군〉 a syndrome
♦다운(씨) 신드롬 Down('s) syndrome
신들림 神— 1 〈신 명〉 getting enthusiastic; being entranced ♦신들린 inspired; fanatical
▶ 그는 신들린 듯한 연주를 했다 He gave an inspired performance.
2 ⇨ 신내리다
신디케이트 a syndicate
♦〈기사·사진 등이〉 신디케이트로 공급되다 be syndicated / 신디케이트를[로] 조직하다 form a syndicate; syndicate
▶ 그의 기고는 전세계에 신디케이트로 공급되었다 His column was syndicated throughout the world.
■—단원[회원] a member of a syndicate
신라 新羅 Silla ■—금관 a gold crown of the Silla era
신랄하다 辛辣— sharp; bitter; acrid; biting; cutting; harsh; poignant; acrimonious; pungent; incisive; severe
♦신랄하게 poignantly; scathingly; severely; incisively; acrimoniously
▶ 그는 신랄한 비평을 하였다 He made a sharp criticism.
신랑 新郎 a bridegroom; a groom; a newlywed husband
■—감 a prospective bridegroom ■—들러리 a groomsman; a best man ■—신부 the bride and bridegroom [groom]; a bridal pair; the newlyweds
신력 新曆 the new calendar; 〈태양력〉 the solar [Gregorian] calendar; 〈서양력〉 the Western calendar ♦신력으로 according to the solar calendar
신령 神靈 〈신〉 a god; a deity; a spirit; 〈망령〉 a soul ♦신령의 가호 divine protection
■산— the spirit of a mountain; the mountain spirit
신록 新綠 fresh green [verdure]; tender [spring] green; new foliage
♦신록의 계절 the season of fresh green [verdure]
▶ 5월은 신록의 달이다 May is a month of fresh green leaves.
▶ 산 전체가 신록으로 덮여 있다 All the mountains are covered with fresh green.
신뢰 信賴 confidence (in); 〈의지〉 reliance (on); dependence (on); 〈신임〉 trust (in)
♦신뢰에 보답하다 prove worthy of sb's trust; live up to sb's expectation
▶ 그는 양친의 신뢰를 어겼다 He betrayed his parents' trust [confidence] in him.
▶ 그는 나에게 신뢰를 가지고 있다 He has confidence in me. ⇌ He places his confidence in me.
■—하다 rely on; depend upon; trust (in); confide in; put confidence in; place reliance on

신망 ◆신뢰할 만한[신뢰할 수 있는] trustworthy; reliable; authoritative; dependable; worthy of *one's* trust / 신뢰할 수 없는 unreliable; untrustworthy
▶ 나는 네 말을 신뢰한다 I trust what you say.
▶ 그는 상사에게 신뢰받고 있다 He has [enjoys] the confidence of his boss.
▶ 그 뉴스는 신뢰할 만한 출처에서 나왔다 The news came from authoritative sources.

신망 信望 〈신용〉 confidence; 〈인망〉 popularity; prestige
◆신망있는 사람 a man of popularity / 신망이 있다 enjoy [possess] the confidence 《of》; be popular 《with》; have credit 《with》/ 신망을 잃다 lose the confidence 《of》
▶ 그는 세인의 신망을 얻으려고 노력하였다 He made an effort to win [gain, obtain] public confidence.

신명 身命 *one's* life ◆신명을 걸고 at the risk of *one's* life
▶ 그들은 조국을 위해 신명을 바쳤다 They laid down their life for their motherland.

신명 神明 a god [goddess]; a deity; a divinity ⇨ 천지신명

신명기 申命記 〔聖〕 The Book of Deuteronomy; Deuteronomy(略 Deut.)

신명나다 get [become] lighthearted [cheerful, gay(-spirited), enthusiastic]; be exhilarated; get excited
◆신명나는 enthusiastic; exhilarative; exciting / 신명 나게 enthusiastically; exhilaratingly; excitingly
▶ 한 농악팀이 사물놀이를 신명나게 선보였다 A farm music team presented enthusiastic performances of four farm music instruments.

신명지다 〈신나고 멋있다〉 merry; joyous; thrilled; cheerful

신묘 辛卯 〔民俗〕 the 28th binary term of the sexagenary cycle; the Year of the Hare

신묘하다 神妙― mysterious; marvelous; wondrous

신문 訊問 a query; a questioning; (cross-)examination 《of a witness》; an inquiry; an interrogation
―신문하다 question; (cross-)examine; interrogate
◆신문받다 be examined; be questioned
■반대― a cross-examination 유도― a leading question ■―자 an examiner ―(조)서 〔法〕 an interrogatory

신문 新聞 a newspaper; a paper; a journal; 〈총칭〉 the press
〈신문은〉 이 신문은 발행 부수가 많다 This paper has a large circulation.
▶ 신문은 세상에서 일어나는 일을 알려 준다 The newspapers tell us what is happening [going on] in the world.
〈신문을〉 신문을 구독하다 subscribe to a paper; take (in) a paper / 신문을 발행하다 publish [issue] a newspaper / 신문을 편집하다 edit a newspaper / 신문을 펴다[접다] spread [fold up] a newspaper / 신문을 발송[배달]하다 distribute [deliver] a newspaper
▶ 어떤 신문을 보십니까? What paper do you get [take, read]? ⇌ What paper do you buy [receive] regularly?
〈신문에〉 신문에 의하면 according to the newspapers / 신문에 싣다[내다] have 《an article》 printed [carried] in a paper / 신문에 광고를 내다 put [place] an advertisement in the newspaper / 신문에 나다[실리다] appear in a paper; get into a paper [the press]/ 신문에 투고하다 contribute an article to a newspaper / 신문에 논설을 쓰다 write an article [a leader] for a newspaper / 신문에 …이라고 나 있다 the paper says that…; it is reported in the paper that…; it says in the paper that…/ 자신의 이름이 신문에 나다 get *one's* name in the paper
▶ 그것은 신문에 날거야 It will appear [be reported] in papers.
〈신문에서〉 신문에서 보다 see [read] *sth* in the papers / 신문에서 호평을 받다 be favorably noticed by the press / 신문에서 가볍게 취급하다 relegate to inside pages; give little space / 신문에서 공격하다 open a newspaper campaign 《against》/ 신문에서 언어맞다 be attacked [pounded] in the press
▶ 그것을 신문에서 읽었다 I read it in the newspaper.
■영자― an English-language paper 일간[주간]― a daily [weekly] (paper); 〈총칭〉 the daily [weekly] press 전국― a national paper; a paper with national circulation 조간[석간]― a morning [an evening, an afternoon] paper 지방― a local (news)paper ■―값[요금] 〈신문구독료〉 the subscription ―광고 a newspaper advertisement; 〈항목별로 된 광고란의〉 (口) a classified ad ―구독자 a (newspaper) reader; a newspaper subscriber ―기사 a newspaper article [story, item, report]; press news: 신문기삿거리 a newspaper topic; data [materials] for a news item ―논조 press comments ―매점 a newsstand; (英) a newsstall ―발표 a press [news] release; a (press) handout ―발행인 (美) a newspaper publisher; (英) a newspaper proprietor ―보도 a press report ―소설 a serial story 《in a newspaper》 ―스크랩 a newspaper clipping; a newspaper [press] cutting ―업 newspapering; journalism; the newspaper industry ―열람실 a newspaper room ―용지 newsprint ―윤리 강령 the Canons of Journalism; the Press (Moral) Code ―인 a newspaperman ―철 a newspaper file; newspapers on file ―팔이 a newsboy; a newspaper boy; a news vendor ―편집국 an editorial office [board, bureau, (美) section]; a news office ―학과 〈대학의〉 a journalism course

신문계 新聞界 the newspaper world; the press; the newspaperdom ◆신문계에 투신하다 enter (the field of) journalism

신문구독료 新聞購讀料 the subscription (of [for] a paper) ◆일 개월치의 신문구독료 the monthly charge for the newspaper

신문기자 新聞記者 a newsman; a newspaperman; a journalist; (英) a pressman; a (newspaper) reporter
■―단 the press corps ―석 the press gallery

[box, section] —클럽 a press club —회견 a press interview [conference]

신문배달 新聞配達 〈사람〉 a newsboy; a newspaperboy; a paper boy; a [paper] carrier; 〈일〉 delivery of newspapers ◆ 신문배달을 하다 deliver newspapers; take a paper route

신문보급소 新聞普及所 (美) a newsdealer's shop; (英) a newsagent's shop; a newspaper agency —장 (美) a newsdealer; (英) a newsagent

신문사 新聞社 a newspaper publishing company; a newspaper office ◆ 신문사에 근무하다 be on (the staff of) a newspaper

신문지 新聞紙 a newspaper; the newspaper itself ◆ 헌 신문지 an old newspaper

신물 water brash ◆ 신물(이) 나다 have (a fit of) water brash; 〈불쾌하게 느끼다〉 be disgusted 《with》; loathe; get sick and tired 《of》

신민 臣民 a subject

신바닥 the sole [tread] of a shoe; a boot sole ⇨ 신창

신바람 high [exulted] spirits; elation ⇨ 신² ◆ 신바람 나서 cheerfully; delightedly; in high spirits; with great joy
▶ 소년들은 신바람 나서 집을 떠났다 The boys left home with great joy.

신발 footwear; (총칭) footgear; shoes ⇨ 신¹ ■ —가게 a footwear store [(英) shop] —장수 a footwear dealer

신발견 新發見 a new [fresh, recent] discovery [find]; a discovery ◆ 신발견을 하다 make a new discovery

신발닦개 a doormat; 〈철제 신발 닦개〉 a doorscraper; a (mud) scraper

신발명 新發明 a new [recent] invention ◆ 신발명을 하다 make a new invention

신방 申方 [民俗] the west-southwest

신방 辛方 [民俗] the north-northwest

신방 新房 a bride-chamber; a bridal room ◆ 신방에 들다 get into the bridal bed; consummate a marriage

신벌 神罰 divine punishment [retribution] ⇨ 천벌

신법 新法 〈법률〉 a new law; new regulations; 〈방법〉 a new method

신변 身邊 one's person; oneself ◆ 신변의 위험을 무릅쓰고 at the risk of one's personal safety / 신변이 위태롭다 be in personal danger
▶ 우리는 그의 신변이 염려된다 We are anxious about his personal safety.
▶ 그는 수술을 받기 전에 신변을 정리했다 He put his affairs in order before he had the operation.
■ —소설 a personal novel; a novel depicting the author's private life

신병 身病 (bodily) illness; (美) sickness ◆ 신병으로 because of [on account of, owing to] illness / 신병으로 드러눕다 be laid up with illness; take to one's bed / 신병으로 사직하다 resign on account of ill health

신병 新兵 〈징집병〉 a recruit; a (new) conscript; a newly-enlisted soldier; (口) a rookie; (美口) a conscriptee ■ —훈련 recruit [boot] training —훈련소 a recruit training center

신볼 the width of a shoe ▶ 내 신은 신볼이 좀 좁다 My shoes are a little tight across the instep.

신봉 信奉 belief; faith —신봉하다 believe [have faith] in; follow ◆ 불교를 신봉하는 사람들 those who profess [believe in] Buddhism ■ —자 a believer (in); a devotee (of)

신부 神父 〔가톨릭〕 a father; a priest ◆ 스미스 신부 father Smith ▶ 그는 신부가 되었다 He became a Catholic priest.

신부 新婦 a bride; a newlywed wife ◆ 신부감을 고르다 look for a bride; search for a wife —들러리 a bridesmaid; a maid-of-honor; (美) 〈신부를 돌보는 기혼부인〉 a matron of honor —의상 a bridal costume [dress]; a bride's outfit —학교 a finishing school; a school for domestic training

신분 身分 〈지위〉 one's social position [standing, station]; one's station in life; 〈신원〉 one's status; one's identity
◆ 신분이 높은 사람 a man of position; a person of high standing / 신분이 낮은 사람 a lowly person; a person of humble condition [low social standing] / 신분이 높다는 be high in social standing / 신분이 다르다 differ in social standing / 신분을 밝히다[숨기다] disclose [conceal] one's identity / 신분을 증명하다 identify oneself
▶ 그는 신분을 감추고 여행을 했다 He traveled incognito.
▶ 신분을 증명할 만한 것을 가지고 있습니까? Do you have anything to prove your identity?
▶ 여기서는 당신의 신분을 보장합니다 We guarantee your status here.
▶ 그는 대학교수로서의 신분을 버리고 작가로서 살기로 결심했다 He decided to give up his position as a college professor and live as a writer.
▶ 학생의 신분으로 벤츠는 지나친 사치다 A Benz is too luxurious for a student like you.
▶ 사람의 가치를 신분으로 판단해서는 안된다 You should not judge a man's worth by his social standing [status].

신분증명서 身分證明書 an identification [I.D., identity] card ◆ 신분증명서를 보이다 show identification 《to》

신불 神佛 gods and Buddha ▶ 그는 신불의 가호를 빌었다 He prayed for divine protection.

신비 神祕 (a) mystery
◆ 삶[우주]의 신비 the mysteries of life [the universe] / 신비에 싸인 사건 incidents wrapped in mystery
▶ 그것은 신비의 베일에 싸이고 말았다 That has been shrouded [wrapped] in mystery.
—**신비하다, 신비롭다** mysterious; mystic(al)
◆ 모나리자의 신비로운 미소 a mysterious smile of Mona Liza
▶ 그녀에게는 어떤 신비한 데가 있었다 There was something mysterious about her.
▶ 그녀는 신비로운 미소를 띠고 있었다 She had a mysterious smile on her face.

신빙성 信憑性 reliability; authenticity; credibility ♦ 신빙성이 있다 [없다] be reliable [unreliable]

신사 紳士 a gentleman; a man of honor
♦ 신사다운 gentlemanly; gentlemanlike / 신사용의 men's; for gentlemen's use / 신사인 체하다 play the gentleman; pose as [set up for] a gentleman / 신사적인 gentlemanly; gentlemanlike / 신사적으로 like a gentleman, in a gentlemanly manner / 비신사적인 ungentlemanly
▶ 그는 전형적인 신사다 He is a typical gentleman.
▶ 그는 신사답게 처신했다 He behaved himself like a gentleman.
▶ 그것은 신사로서의 체면 문제다 That would be beneath your dignity as a gentleman.
▶ 영국의 신사 계급은 귀족 다음 간다 The English gentry are next below the nobility.
■ —도(道) the code [ideals] of a gentleman —록 a Who's Who; (美) a social register —복 men's suit; (美)〈약의〉 a sack [business] suit; (英) a lounge suit —협정 a gentleman's [gentlemen's] agreement —화(靴) men's shoes

신산 辛酸 1〈맵고 쓴〉 bitter and sour 2〈고난〉 hardships; privations ♦ 온갖 신산을 맛보다 go through many hardships; suffer [undergo] many privations; taste the bitters of life

신산 神算 an ingenious stratagem; a very clever plan

신상 身上 1〈몸〉 one's person; one's body
▶ 나는 그녀의 신상을 염려했다 I felt concerned about her welfare [safety].
2〈처지〉 one's lot [condition, circumstances, situation]
▶ 그것을 멀리 하는 게 신상에 좋을게다 You'd better stay away from it for your own sake.

신상 神像 (an image [idol] of) a god; an idol

신상문제 身上問題 one's personal affairs
▶ 그 여자는 자주 그에게 자기 신상문제를 상담한다 She often consults him about her personal affairs.

신상상담 身上相談 consultation about one's personal affairs ■ —란〈신문 등의〉 a personal advice column; a home council column; an agony column

신상필벌하다 信賞必罰— reward good conduct [well-doing] and punish evil conduct [evildoing]
▶ 그는 항상 신상필벌하는 원칙을 지켰다 He always rewarded good conduct and punished evil conduct. ⇌ He never failed to reward a merit nor to let a fault go unpunished.

신생 新生 a new birth ■ —국 a newly emerging nation —대〔地質〕 the Cenozoic Era —아(兒) a newborn (baby); a neonate

신생활 新生活 a new life ■ —운동 a new-life movement

신서 信書 a letter ⇨ 편지

♦ 신서의 비밀을 지키다[침해하다] protect [violate] the privacy of (personal) correspondence

신서 新書 a new book [publication]; a newly-published book

신석기시대 新石器時代〔考古〕 the Neolithic Era [Age]; the New Stone Age

신선 神仙 a hermit; an unworldly man; a ascetic ■ —경(境) a fairyland —도 a picture of hermit's life

신선도 新鮮度 (the degree of) freshness
♦ 신선도가 높은[좋은] very fresh; lively / 신선도가 떨어지다 lose (some of) (its) freshness

신선로 神仙爐 a cooking brazier

신선미 新鮮味 freshness ▶ 그의 작품에서는 아무런 신선미를 느낄 수 없었다 I found nothing fresh in his work.

신선하다 新鮮— fresh; new
♦ 신선한 야채 fresh vegetables / 신선한 과일 fresh fruits / 신선한 공기 the fresh air / 아침의 신선함 the freshness of the morning / 신선하게 하다 make fresh; freshen; refresh
▶ 그 그림은 나에게 아주 신선한 느낌을 주었다 The picture made quite a new impression on me.

신설 新設 (new) establishment; organization; founding
♦ 신설의 new; newly-established; newly-organized
—신설하다 establish; organize; found
▶ 우리는 대학을 신설했다 We established [founded] a new university.
▶ 역 근처에 파출소가 신설되었다 A new police box has been set up near the station.
■ —회사 a new company; a newly-established [newly-organized] company

신설 新說〈학설〉 a new theory [doctrine];〈견해〉 a new light [view];〈해석〉 a new interpretation ♦ 신설을 제기하다 propound [advance] a new theory

신성 神性 divine nature; divinity; godhead; godhood

신성 神聖 sacredness; sanctity; holiness
♦ 신성 불가침의 sacred and inviolable; (비유) sacrosanct / 신성을 더럽히다[모독하다] violate [defile] the sanctity (of); desecrate; profane / 신성하게 하다 make holy; consecrate; sanctify; hallow / 신성시하다 regard [hold] sth as sacred
—신성하다 sacred; holy; sanctified; hallowed; consecrated; divine
♦ 신성한 직업 a divine occupation / 신성한 가르침 holy teachings
▶ 인도에서는 소가 신성한 동물이다 The cow is a sacred animal in India.
▶ 이곳은 신성한 장소다 This is a sacred [holy] place.
■ —동맹〔史〕 the Holy Alliance —로마제국〔史〕 the Holy Roman Empire —화(化) consecration : 신성화하다 make holy; consecrate; hallow

신성 新星 1〔天〕 a nova (pl. ~s, -vae) 2〈연예계 등의〉 a new face; a new (film) star

신세 (moral) indebtedness; a debt of gratitude; an obligation; 〈의지〉 dependence; 〈폐〉 (a) trouble

♦아무의 신세를 지다 be indebted [obliged] to *sb*; owe *sb* a debt of gratitude; be under indebtedness [obligation] to *sb*; 〈도움을 받다〉 depend on; be under the care of; 〈짐이 되다〉 be a burden to *sb*; live at *sb's* expense / 경찰의 신세를 지다 get in trouble with the police / 약의 신세를 지다 take to the help of medicine / 신세를 갚다 repay *sb* for 《his》 kindness; return [repay] *sb's* favor

▶ 아직도 부모의 신세를 지고 있니? Are you still dependent on your parents?
▶ 이런 일로 신세를 지고 싶지 않습니다 I don't want to trouble you about a thing like this.
▶ 여러가지로 신세(를) 많이 졌습니다 Thank you very much for all you have done for me.
▶ 어려울 때 난 그녀의 신세를 많이 졌다 She helped me a lot when I was in trouble.
▶ 2년 동안 삼촌 댁에서 신세를 졌다 I lived with my uncle for two years.
▶ 여관에 묵지 않고 친구 신세를 지고 있다 I'm not staying at a hotel, I'm staying with friends.

신세 身世 *one's* lot [condition, circumstances]; *one's* personal affairs

♦가련한 신세 pitiful circumstances; a sad lot / 딱한 신세 adverse circumstances / 거지 신세가 되다 be reduced to beggary
▶ 그는 술로 신세를 망쳤다 Alcohol was his ruin. ⇒ He ruined himself by drinking.

신세계 新世界 a new world; 〈신대륙〉 the New World

신세대 新世代 the new generation

신세타령 身世打令 a story of *one's* miserable life —신세타령하다 bewail *one's* ill fortune; grieve about *one's* hard [ill] luck

신소리[1] 〈말〉 nonsense; (俗) lip
▶ 신소리 작작해 Less [None] of your lip!

신소리[2] 〈신발소리〉 footsteps; the shuffling [scuff] of feet; the sound of *sb's* shoes make 《on the road》 ♦ 신소리가 들리다 hear *sb's* footsteps; hear *sb* walking in 《his》 shoes

신속 迅速 quickness; rapidity; swiftness; promptitude; expedition; speediness; dispatch —신속하다 quick; rapid; fast; swift; prompt; expeditious; immediate; speedy

♦신속한 움직임 rapid movement / 신속한 반응 a quick response / 신속한 행동 prompt action / 신속한 해결 speedy solution / 신속히 quickly; fast; rapidly; swiftly; expeditiously; promptly; with speed [promptitude, dispatch]; without delay; (口) like fury / 보도가 신속하다 be very quick in reporting
▶ 그의 반응이 신속한 게 놀랍다 The swiftness [speed] of his reactions is amazing.
▶ 그 문제의 신속한 해결이 요망된다 A prompt solution of the problem is expected.
▶ 그는 일을 신속하게 처리한다 He promptly [quickly] carries out his business. ⇒ He dispatches business with speed.

신수 身手 〈안색〉 (a) complexion; a countenance; 〈용모·풍채〉 looks; *one's* personal appearance

♦신수가 훤하다 have a fine appearance [presence]; have a good figure

신수 身數 *one's* fortune; *one's* luck; *one's* future

♦신수가 피다 be in luck's way; *one's* fortune changes for the better; fortune turns in *one's* favor / 아무의 신수를 봐주다 tell [read] *sb's* fortune / 신수를 보다 have *one's* fortune told; consult a fortune-teller
▶ 금년은 당신의 신수가 좋습니다[나쁩니다] This is a lucky [an unlucky] year for you.

신승하다 辛勝— win a game by a narrow [small] margin; (美俗) nose [edge] *sb* out
▶ 접전 끝에 우리가 신승했다 We won by a narrow margin after a close game.

신시 新詩 〈새로 지은〉 a new poem; 〈신체시〉 a new-style poem

신시대 新時代 a new age [epoch, era]

신식 新式 a new style [type]
♦신식의 new-style; new-type; new; 〈현대적인〉 up-to-date; new-fashioned; modern
▶ 이것은 아주 신식 어학 교수법이다 This is quite a new method of language teaching.

신신당부 申申當付 (an) entreaty; solicitation; supplication; imploration; an earnest [a repeated] request
—신신당부하다 ask [request] repeatedly [earnestly]; entreat; solicit; supplicate; implore

신실하다 信實— steady and honest; sincere; faithful
♦신실한 말 sincere words / 신실한 사람 an honest and trustworthy man; a steady [solid] character

신심 信心 〈믿음〉 faith; belief; devotion; piety
♦ 신심이 두텁다[깊다] be (deeply) religious; be devout; be pious

신안 新案 a new idea [design, device]
■실용— a utility model ■—제품 a newly-devised product

신안특허 新案特許 a new design patent; a patent on a new device
♦특허청에 신안특허를 출원하다 apply to the Patent Office for a patent on a new design / 신안특허를 따다 get [obtain] a new design patent 《on *one's* invention》

신앙 信仰 faith; belief; religion
♦신앙의 자유 religious liberty; freedom of religion [worship] / 신앙을 지키다 keep the faith / 신앙을 굳히다 strengthen [confirm] *one's* faith / 신앙을 버리다 abandon [give up, discard] *one's* faith
▶ 그것을 계기로 기독교에 대한 그의 신앙은 더욱 깊어졌다 That made him deepen his faith in Christianity.
—신앙하다 believe [have faith] in 《God》
■—개조(個條) the articles of faith; a creed
■—고백 a confession of faith; profession ■—요법 faith cure [healing]; divine healing ■—인 a believer; a devotee

신앙생활 信仰生活 a life of faith; a religious [pious] life
♦ 신앙생활을 하다 lead [live] a pious [religious] life; walk by faith / 신앙생활에 들어가다 begin [enter into] a religious life

신앙심

신앙심 信仰心 faith ◆신신앙심이 없는 impious; unbelieving ▶그녀는 신앙심이 두텁다 She is very religious [pious, devout]. ▶그의 신앙심은 흔들렸다 His faith was shaken.
신약 新藥 a new medicine [drug]
신약성경 新約聖經 the New Testament
신약성경 전서 新約聖經 全書 the Complete New Testament
신어 新語 a new [(newly-)coined] word; a new coinage; a neologism ◆신어를 만들다 coin a new word; neologize
신여성 新女性 a modern woman [girl]; the new woman
신역 新譯 a new translation [version]
—**신역하다** translate anew; make a new translation
신열 身熱 (a) fever; fever heat; a temperature
◆신열이 나다 become feverish; run [develop] a fever / 신열이 높다 have a high fever [temperature]/ 신열이 내리다 one's fever breaks [subsides, abates]; one's temperature falls [goes down]
▶신열이 좀 있나 보군요 You have a slight fever, don't you? ⇒ You seem to be a little feverish.
▶이 약을 드시면 신열이 금방 가라앉을 겁니다 This medicine will soon bring down your fever [temperature].
▶아이는 신열에 들떠 헛소리를 했다 The fever had made the child delirious. ⇒ The child was talking in delirium because of a fever.
신염 腎炎 〔醫〕 nephritis ⇨ 신장(~염)
신예 新銳 ◆신예의 new and powerful 《weapons》 ■—기 a newly produced airplane —병기 a new (powerful) weapon
신용 信用 confidence; trust; reliance; faith; credence; dependence; 〈상업상의〉 credit; 〈평판〉 reputation
〈신용이〉 신용이 있는 사람[가게] a person [store] of good credit [established reputation]; a reliable person [store]/ 신용이 있다 have [enjoy] the confidence 《of》; be trusted 《by》; have credit with sb / 신용이 없다 have no confidence 《of》; have no [enjoy little] credit with sb; lack sb's trust
▶그의 신용이 문제되고 있다 His sincerity is in question.
▶장사꾼에게는 신용이 무엇보다도 중요하다 Credit is everything [all in all] to a merchant.
▶이번 사건으로 그 회사의 신용이 땅에 떨어졌다 The present case has discredited the firm hopelessly with the public.
〈신용을〉 신용을 얻다 win [gain] the confidence 《of》/ 신용을 유지하다 maintain one's reputation / 신용을 손상하다 injure [impair] one's credit; sully one's reputation; stain one's good name / 신용을 잃다 lose one's credit 《with》; lose the confidence 《of》/ 신용을 회복하다 regain the confidence 《of》; retrieve [redeem] one's credit
▶그는 전적으로 주인의 신용을 얻고 있다 He has [enjoys] the fullest confidence of his master.
▶장사에서는 고객의 신용을 얻는 것이 제일이다 The first consideration in business is to gain the confidence [trust] of the customers.
▶한번 신용을 잃으면 회복하기가 쉽지 않다 It is by no means easy to regain confidence once lost.
〈신용에〉 신용에 관계되다 affect one's credit
▶그것은 우리 가게의 신용에 관계되는 문제다 It affects the reputation of our store.
—**신용하다** trust; put [have, place, repose] trust in; have faith in; place [have, put, show, repose] confidence in; place [feel, have, put] reliance on [in]; give credence to; rely on; give credit to
◆신용할 수 있는 trustworthy; reliable / 신용할 수 없는 untrustworthy; unreliable / 전적으로 신용하다 give full credit to 《a promise》/ 절대적으로 신용하다 repose absolute confidence in
▶그녀라면 신용할 수 있다 We can put trust in her.
▶그의 말을 어디까지 신용해도 좋은 건지 모르겠다 I don't know how far I can believe what he says.
▶그런 일을 계속한다면 아무도 그를 신용하지 않게 될 것이다 If he goes on doing such things, everyone will lose faith in him.
■—기관 an organ of credit —보증기금 〔經〕 the credit guarantee funds —보험 〈대손(貸損)에 대한〉 credit insurance; 〈고용인 등에 대한〉 fidelity insurance —사기 〈英〉 a confidence trick; 〈美〉 a confidence game; 〈口〉 a con game 〈英口〉 trick —조합 a credit association [union] —조회 a credit [confidential] inquiry —증권 an instrument of credit; a credit instrument
신용거래 信用去來 credit transactions; sales on credit ◆신용거래를 하다 deal [sell, buy] on credit; do [carry on] credit transactions 《with》 ■—처 a credit [charge] customer
신용대출 信用貸出 a credit loan; a loan on credit ◆신용대출로 on credit —**신용대출하다** give [extend] a credit 《for three million won to sb》
—장기[단기]— a long [short] credit
신용상태 信用狀態 a [one's] credit standing; one's financial status [standing] ◆회사의 신용상태를 조사하다 investigate [inquire into] the credit [financial] standing of a firm
신용장 信用狀 a letter of credit (略 L/C); a bill of credit; a credit
◆신용장의 발행[양도, 분할, 갱신] issuance [transfer, division, renewal] of a credit / 신용장을 개설하다 open [establish] a letter of credit 《with a bank, by cable, for a sum, against an order》/ 신용장을 발행[확인]하다 issue [confirm] a letter of credit
■—수출[수입]— an export [import] letter of credit 정액— a fixed letter of credit ■—개설[발행, 확인] 은행 a letter of credit opening [issuing, confirming] bank
신용조사 信用調査 a credit check; an inquiry [investigation] into [concerning] the finan-

cial status [credit standing] 《of》; 〈조회〉 a credit inquiry
━보고 credit information ━원 a credit man

신용카드 信用━ a credit card ▶ 신용카드 받습니다 《게시》 Credit cards (are) accepted here.

신우 腎盂 〔解〕 the pelvis (of the kidney); 〔生〕 the renal pelvis
━염 pyelitis

신울 the outer rim of shoes

신원 身元 〈정체〉 one's identity; 〈태생〉 one's birth and parentage; 〈경력〉 one's antecedents
♦ 신원 불명의 unidentified / 신원 불명의 피해자 an unidentified victim
▶ 신원 불명의 여자 사체가 발견되었다 The body of an unidentified woman has been discovered.
〈신원이〉 신원이 확실한 사람 a person with good references; a person who comes well recommended / 신원이 확실하지 않은 여자 a woman of shady antecedents / 신원이 확인되다 be identified 《as》
▶ 그는 신원이 밝혀졌다 He has been identified. ⇌ His identity has been established.
▶ 사체는 의복으로 신원이 판명되었다 The corpse was identified by the clothing.
〈신원을〉 ♦ 신원을 밝히다 reveal [disclose] one's identity; identify oneself 《as》 / 신원을 조사하다[캐다] inquire [look] into sb's antecedents [birth and parentage]; look into sb's family (and social) background; check up sb's record; 〈고용주 등이〉 inquire into sb's reliability / 신원을 조회하다 refer to 《a former employer》 for sb's character / 신원을 증명하다 prove one's identity / 사체의 신원을 확인하다 identify a corpse
▶ 경찰이 그의 신원을 조사하고 있다 The police are looking into his background.

신원보증 身元保證 (personal) reference; a certificate of good character
━금 security for good conduct; 《英》 caution money ━서 a reference; a character ━인 a guarantor; a surety; a reference : 신원보증인을 세우다 furnish [give] a security

신원하다 伸寃━ redress a grievance; vindicate oneself; exonerate [exculpate] oneself from a charge of guilt

신위 神位 an ancestral tablet

신음 呻吟 a moan; a groan
♦ 고통의 신음 소리 a moan of pain / 신음 소리를 내며 쓰러지다 fall with a groan
▶ 그는 부상병들의 신음 소리를 들었다 He heard the groans of the wounded soldiers.
▶ 나는 나도 모르게 신음 소리를 냈다 I uttered a moan of pain in spite of myself.
━신음하다 moan; groan; give [utter, heave] a groan
♦ 고통으로 신음하다 moan in distress; groan with pain
▶ 그는 병상에서 신음하고 있다 He is confined to bed suffering severely.
▶ 백성은 폭군 밑에서 신음하고 있었다 People groaned under the tyrant.

신의 信義 faith; fidelity; truthfulness; loyalty
♦ 신의 있는 faithful; true; loyal / 신의가 없는 perfidious; truthless; unfaithful; faithless / 신의를 지키다[저버리다] keep [break] faith 《with sb》; be loyal [disloyal] 《to》
▶ 그것은 신의에 어긋나는 짓이다 That is an act running counter to good faith.
▶ 그것은 회사의 신의에 관계되는 일이다 That affects the honor [reputation] of the company.

신의 神意 the divine will; God's will; Providence

신의 神醫 a wonderful physician; a great doctor

신인 神人 1 〈신과 사람〉 god and man
▶ 그 남자는 신인 공노할 죄를 지었다 He has sinned against God and man.
2 〈신같은 사람〉 a man of god; a man-god

신인 新人 a new figure [man]; 〈예능계의〉 a new face [star]; 〈스포츠의〉 a rookie
♦ 문단(文壇)의 신인 a new figure in literary circles / 정계의 신인 a new political figure; a novice in politics
━가수 a new singer ━왕 〈프로 선수의〉 the best rookie player of the year; the rookie king

신임 信任 trust; confidence; credence
♦ 신임을 얻다[받다] win [gain, obtain] the confidence 《of》; find credence 《with》 / 신임을 얻고 있다 enjoy the confidence 《of》; have sb's confidence; be trusted 《by》 / 신임을 잃다 lose the confidence 《of》 / 국민에게 신임을 묻다 make an appeal to the confidence of the whole nation
▶ 그는 사장에게서 신임을 받고 있다 He enjoys his boss's confidence.
▶ 그는 사장의 신임이 두텁다 He enjoys the full confidence of the president. ⇌ He is trusted by the president.
━신임하다 trust; confide 《in》; have [put, place] confidence 《in》; take sb into one's confidence

신임 新任 a new appointment
▶ 교장은 신임 인사를 했다 The principal made an inaugural address.
━신임하다 newly appoint to office
━교사[교장] a new teacher [principal] ━대사 the new [newly-accredited] ambassador; 〈취임 전의〉 the incoming ambassador; the ambassador designate ━자 a new appointee; an incomer ━지 a new post of duty

신임장 信任狀 credentials; a letter of credence; a credential letter
♦ 신임장을 제출하다 present one's credentials 《to》

신임투표 信任投票 a vote of confidence; a confidence vote
♦ 신임투표에 승리하다[패배하다] win [lose] the vote of confidence

신입 新入 ♦ 신입의 new; incoming; entering
━사원 a new employee; a new member of the staff; a new staff member ━생 a new pupil; a new student; 〈대학・고교의〉 《美》 a freshman; 《英》 a fresher ━자 a newcomer; a

신자 new face; 〈교도소의〉 a new bird
신자 信者 a believer; an adherent; a devotee; (총칭) the faithful
♦ 불교 신자 a believer in Buddhism / 기독교 신자가 되다 become a Christian; turn Christian; 〈개종하여〉 be converted to Christianity
▶ 그는 불교[기독교] 신자다 He is a Buddhist [Christian]. ⇌ He believes in Buddhism [Christianity]. ⇌ He is a believer in Buddhism [Christianity].
신작 新作 a new work [production, composition]
♦ 신작을 발표하다 publish a new (piece of) work; 〈음악 등을〉 perform a new work; give the first public performance of a new piece (of music)
신작로 新作路 a newly-constructed road; a new highway
신장 ─欌 a shoe chest; a boot cupboard
신장 身長 height; stature
♦ 신장이 작은 short of stature / 신장순으로 in order of height / 신장이 6피트다 stand six feet (high); be six feet tall [in stature, in height]
▶ 이 반의 남자 평균 신장은 165센티미터다 The average height of the boys of this class is 165 centimeters.
▶ 간호사는 환자의 신장을 쟀다 The nurse measured [took] the patient's height.
▶ 신장순으로 서주십시오 Stand in order of height, please.
신장 伸張 extension; elongation; expansion; stretch
♦ 국력의 신장 continued buildup of national strength / 사업의 신장 the expansion of a business
─신장하다 extend; expand; elongate
♦ 세력을 신장하다 extend one's influence / 수출을 신장하다 expand [increase] exports / 국위를 해외에 신장하다 extend the national prestige overseas
─계 ﹝機﹞ an extensometer; an extensimeter
─성 an expansibility; stretch property
신장 神將 1 〈장수〉 a divine general 2 〈귀신〉 a commanding [most powerful] spirit
신장 腎臟 ﹝解﹞ the kidney ♦ 신장의 renal / 신장이 나쁘다 have a kidney trouble
■ ─결석 a renal calculus (pl. -li); a kidney stone ─병 kidney [renal] trouble [disease]; 〈만성의〉 nephrism ─염 ﹝醫﹞ nephritis; inflammation of a kidney
신장 新裝 1 〈새로 장치함〉 refurbishment; redecoration; refurnishing
▶ 10월 10일 신장 개업 (게시) Closed for remodeling. Open Oct. 10.
─신장하다 give a new look (to); refurbish; redecorate; 〈개조하다〉 remodel
♦ 신장한 강당 the refurbished auditorium
2 〈새옷〉 new dress
3 〈장정〉 a new binding; rebinding
신저 新著 a new work [publication]
신전 神前 ♦ 신전에(서) before God [gods]; before the altar
신전 神殿 a shrine; a sanctuary; a tabernacle; a temple

신접 新接 〈새 살림〉 setting up a new home; 〈이사하여 삶〉 taking up one's abode (in a new place) ■ ─살이 a life in a new home
신정 新正 〈새해의 첫머리〉 the (solar) New Year; 〈양력 설〉 (美) New Year's; New Year's Day; the first [opening] day of the New Year
신제 新制 a new system
신제품 新製品 a new product; an article newly manufactured [produced] (by)
신조 信條 〈신념〉 a principle; a belief; 〈교조 (敎條)〉 a creed; a credo (pl. ~s); an article of faith
▶ 그들은 신조를 잘 지킨다 They are true to their creed.
▶ 그것은 나의 신조에 반한다 That is against my principles.
▶ 그는 성실을 신조로 삼는다 He makes it his principle to be sincere.
■ 생활─ one's principles in life; one's philosophy of life
신조 神助 the help of Heaven [God]; divine aid [grace, intervention] ♦ 신조로[에 의하여] by the grace of God [Heaven]
신조 新造 new construction [building]
▶ 신조중이다 It is being built.
─신조하다 construct [build] (anew); 〈말 등을〉 mint; coin
♦ 신조한 new; newly-built; newly-made; 〈말이 신조된〉 newly-coined
■ ─선(船) a new [newly-built] ship ─어 〈신어〉 a newly-coined word; a neologism
신종 新種 〈종자〉 a new species; 〈변종〉 a new variety; 〈형(型)〉 a new type
▶ 이것은 진귀한 신종 튤립이다 This is a rare new variety of tulip.
■ ─사기 a new type of swindling
신주 神主 an ancestral tablet ▶ 돈을 신주 모시듯 해야 한다 You should try to make the most of your money.
신주 新株 (美) new stocks [(英) shares] ♦ 신주를 공모하다 offer new stocks for public subscription ■ ─락(落) ﹝證﹞ ex-new ─인수권 preemptive rights
신중 愼重 care; caution; prudence; discretion; circumspection; deliberation
▶ 신중은 용기의 태반이다 (속담) Discretion is the better part of valor.
▶ 그 문제의 취급은 신중을 요한다 The treatment of the matter requires circumspection.
▶ 장관의 발언은 신중을 기하지 않았다 The minister was careless [imprudent] in making that remark.
▶ 계획을 실시하는 데는 신중을 기하지 않으면 안된다 You must show proper discretion in carrying out the plan.
─신중하다 careful; cautious; circumspect; discreet; prudent
♦ 신중한 대답 a careful answer / 신중한 태도 a cautious [prudent] attitude / 신중하게 행동 [처신]하다 act with discretion [prudence]; move with circumspection [caution and care]
▶ 그는 친구를 선택하는 데 신중하다 He is discreet in choosing his friends.

▶그 문제는 신중히 고려중이다 The matter is under careful consideration.
▶좀더 신중히 행동해 주기를 바란다 I wish you'd act more prudently [discreetly].
▶그들은 신중히 계획을 세웠다 They worked out their plan very carefully [with careful deliberation].

신지식 新知識 ⟨acquire⟩ new [up-to-date] knowledge [information]; advanced ideas
♦ 신지식의 소유자 a man with up-to-date knowledge

신지피다 神— be inspired by the spirit
▶그녀는 신지핀 사람처럼 말한다 She talks like one possessed [in a religious frenzy].

신진 新進 ♦신진의 rising; promising; new; up-and-coming ▶그는 신진기예의 학자다 He is a young and promising scholar.
■—작가 a rising writer [novelist]; a coming author

신진대사 新陳代謝 ⟨생리작용⟩ metabolism; metastasis; ⟨신·구 교체⟩ renewal; replacement of the old with the new; regeneration
♦신진대사가 되다 be renewed; be replaced; be regenerated / 신진대사가 활발하다[저조하다] have a high [low] metabolism
▶젊은 사람은 신진대사가 왕성하다 Young people have a high rate of metabolism.
▶인체는 항상 신진대사를 한다 The human body is subject to constant metabolism.
▶저 회사는 사원의 신진대사가 필요하다 That company needs some new blood. ⇒ The staff of that company needs an infusion of fresh blood [needs to be rejuvenated].
▶생물체 내에서는 끊임없이 신진대사가 이루어지고 있다 Metabolism is taking place continuously in living things.

신짝 a shoe; an odd shoe (of a pair) ♦헌 신짝처럼 버리다 reject sth as worthless; cast sth away like dirt

신착 新着 ⟨도착⟩ new arrival; ⟨물건⟩ a new arrival; newly-arrived goods ♦신착 양서(洋書) newly-imported foreign books

신찬 新撰 new compilation —신찬하다 newly compile [edit]

신참 新參 **1** ⟨고참에 대해⟩ a newcomer; ⟨美⟩ a freshman; ⟨처음 사람⟩ a new [green] hand; (口) a greenhorn; a novice
▶이 일에 저는 아직 신참입니다 I am new at this job.
2 ⟨공무원 등의⟩ a newly appointed official's first visit to his office

신창 a (shoe) sole ♦신창을 갈다 resole shoes
신천옹 信天翁 ⟨鳥⟩ an albatross
신천지 新天地 a new world ♦신천지를 개척하다 open up a new field [sphere] of activity; break new [fresh] ground

신청 申請 **1** ⟨출원⟩ (an) application; ⟨청원⟩ (a) petition; ⟨예약의⟩ subscription; ⟨法⟩ (a) motion
♦신청이 쇄도하다 be flooded [deluged] with applications [offers] / 신청을 마감하다 close the invitation to applications / 신청을 접수하다 receive [accept] applications [subscriptions] / 이의 신청을 하다 make [raise] an objection / 신청에 응하다 accept an offer [a challenge]; accept [agree to] a proposal; comply with a request / 변호인의 신청을 기각하다 reject a lawyer's motion
▶신청은 서면에 한함 Applications in writing only.
▶신청이 쏟아져 들어왔다 Applications came pouring in. ⇒ We were flooded with applications.
▶그 마라톤 경주에 1,000명의 참가 신청이 있었다 There were a thousand entries for the marathon race.
▶그 잡지의 구독 신청을 취소했다 I canceled my subscription for the magazine.
▶신청을 하면 팸플릿을 보내 드립니다 We will send you a pamphlet on request.
—신청하다 apply (for); make an application; petition ⟨for⟩; [法] move ⟨for⟩
♦신청하는대로 on application / 입회를 신청하다 apply for membership ⟨in⟩ / 법원에 신청하다 move the court ⟨for sth⟩
▶건축 허가를 신청하였습니까? Have you applied for a construction permit?
▶직접 신청해도 되고 편지로 신청해도 됩니다 You may apply in person or by letter.
▶그는 영사관에 비자 발급을 신청했다 He applied to the consulate for a visa.
▶그들은 마라톤 참가를 신청했다 They entered themselves for the marathon.
▶나는 그 잡지의 구독을 신청했다 I have subscribed to that magazine.
▶변호인이 증인 소환을 신청했다 The lawyer moved that the witnesses be summoned.
▶원고는 재심을 신청했다 The plaintiff moved for a rehearing.
2 ⟨제의⟩ a proposal; an offer (of marriage); an overture (of peace); ⟨요구⟩ a request (for an interview); ⟨도전⟩ a challenge (to a duel)
♦신청을 거절하다 decline an offer [a proposal]; refuse [reject, turn down] a request
▶그 가옥은 채권자의 신청에 따라 압류되었다 The house was attached at the instance of creditors.
—신청하다 propose ⟨marriage to sb⟩; make a proposal (of marriage); offer; make an offer; raise (an objection); overture; make overtures (to); request [ask for] ⟨an interview⟩; challenge ⟨another team to a baseball game⟩
■—기한 a time limit for application —료 application [subscription] money —인[자] an applicant; a petitioner; an offerer —접수처 a place for application; a place where (the) applications are accepted

신청서 申請書 a written application; an application (in writing); ⟨용지⟩ an application form [blank]
♦당국에 신청서를 제출하다 file an application with the authorities

신청순 申請順 the order of applications received; the subscription order
♦신청순으로 in the order of application

신체 身體 the body
♦신체의 bodily; physical; corporal / 신체의 결함 a physical defect / 신체의 자유 personal

liberty / 신체의 발달을 촉진하다 promote physical development / 신체가 건전하다 be sound in body / 신체를 단련시키다 build up *one's* health
▶ 건전한 신체에 건전한 정신이 깃든다 A sound mind in a sound body
▶ 어머니와 아기의 관계는 밀접한 신체 접촉으로 강화된다 The relationship between mother and baby is strengthened by close physical contact.
▶ 당신은 신체적으로 아무 이상이 없읍니다 You are physically all right.
■ ─발부 our body and all its members ─조직 (a) bodily tissue

신체검사 身體檢査 〈건강진단〉 a physical [medical] examination; a physical checkup; a physical; 〈소지품 검사〉 a body search; a security check; a frisk
♦ 신체검사를 하다 hold a physical examination [checkup]; 〈소지품의〉 search [frisk] 《*sb* for concealed weapons》/ 신체검사를 받다 undergo a physical examination; 〈소지품 조사〉 have *one's* person searched; be frisked / 신체검사에 합격하다 pass the physical (examination)

신체시 新體詩 a new-style poem; (총칭) the new-style poetry

신체장애자 身體障碍者 a (physically) handicapped person; a disabled person; (총칭) the physically handicapped
▶ 그는 교통사고로 신체장애자가 되었다 He became disabled [He lost the use of his limbs] in a traffic accident.
■ ─복지법 the Disabled Persons Welfare Law ─시설 facilities for the (physically) handicapped

신체제 新體制 a new system [structure, set-up, order, organization]

신추 新秋 〈초가을〉 early autumn

신축 伸縮 expansion and contraction
─신축하다 expand and contract; be elastic; be flexible
■ ─관세 (美) a flexible tariff ─사닥다리 an extension ladder

신축 新築 new construction
▶ 우리 집은 신축중이다 My house is being built [under construction].
─신축하다 build; construct
♦ 신축한 집 a new [newly-built] house
▶ 그들은 병원을 신축했다 They built [constructed] a new hospital.
■ ─건물 a new building ─계획 a building program

신축성 伸縮性 elasticity; flexibility
♦ 신축성이 없다 lack elasticity [flexibility] / 신축성을 주다 give elasticity to *sth* / 신축성을 잃다 lose (its) elasticity

신축자재 伸縮自在 elasticity ♦ 신축자재의 elastic; flexible; capable of expansion and contraction

신춘 新春 〈새봄〉 early spring; 〈새해〉 the New Year ▶ 나는 런던에서 신춘을 맞았다 I welcomed the New Year in London.

신춘문예 新春文藝 a literary contest in spring

♦ 신춘문예 소설 부문 당선작[입선작] a prize-winning entry in the department of novels of a spring literary contest

신춘휘호 新春揮毫 the first writing of the year; the New Year's writing

신출귀몰 神出鬼沒 elusiveness; preternatural swiftness
─신출귀몰하다 appear in unexpected places and at unexpected moments; suddenly appear and suddenly disappear; be elusive; be mysterious
♦ 신출귀몰한 강도 an elusive robber; a protean burglar; a Proteus / 행동이 신출귀몰하다 be elusive in *one's* movements

신출내기 新出─ a novice; a beginner; a greenhorn; a fledgling; (美) a tenderfoot; (口) a rookie
▶ 그 녀석 신출내기가 건방지다 He is saucy as a novice.
▶ 그 실수로 그는 아직 신출내기임이 밝혀졌다 The mistake proved that he was still green at his job.
■ ─기자 a cub reporter; (口) a cub ─음악가 a fledgling musician

신탁 信託 trust
♦ 신탁을 받다 hold *sth* in trust
─신탁하다 trust *sb* with *sth*; leave *sth* in trust with *sb*
▶ 그에게 재산을 신탁했다 I left my property in trust with him. ⇒ I trusted [entrusted] my property to him.
■ ─공익─ a charitable trust 금전[대출]─ a money [loan] trust 명목─ a nominal trust 법인[개인]─ a corporate [personal] trust 수익─ a beneficial trust 유한─ a limited trust 투자─ investment trust
─계정[계약] a trust account [agreement]
─관리인 a trust executor [administrator]
─기금 a trust fund : 신탁기금을 설정하다 establish [create, set up] a trust fund ─료 a trust fee ─물 a trust ─부〈은행의〉 a trust department ─수익자 a beneficiary ─업 trust business : 신탁업법 the Trust Business Law ─업무 trust [fiduciary] work ─자 a truster : 피신탁자 a trustee; a fiduciary ─재산 property [an estate] in trust; trust property; a trust estate ─증권 a trust instrument ─증서 a trust certificate [deed] ─투자 trust investment ─회사[은행] a trust company [bank]

신탁 神託 an oracle; a divine message [revelation] ♦ 꿈에 신탁을 받다 receive a divine revelation in a dream

신탁통치 信託統治 trusteeship
♦ 국제연합의 신탁통치 하에 두다 put [place] (a territory) under a UN trusteeship
■ ─령 a trust territory ─이사회 the Trusteeship Council

신토불이 身土不二 Homegrown farm produces are most wholesome.

신통 神通 supernaturalness; wonder; miraculousness

신통력 神通力 an occult power; a divine [supernatural] power; magic powers
▶ 요즘엔 그의 신통력도 시들기 시작했다 His

occult power has begun to wane recently.
신통치않다 神通— 〈좋지 않다〉 not good; poor; 〈불만스럽다〉 unsatisfactory; discouraging; 〈재미없다〉 uninteresting; unattractive; 〈활발치 못하다〉 dull; heavy; stagnant
♦신통치 않은 용모 a plain [homely] feature / 신통치 않게 여기다 think poorly of
▶실험 결과는 신통치 않았다 The results of the experiment were not encouraging [satisfactory].

신통하다 神通— wonderful; miraculous; marvelous; divine; admirable; extraordinary
♦신통한 아이 a wonder child; an extraordinary child / 신통하게 듣는 약 a medicine of marvelous efficacy; a drug of great virtue
▶그가 그런 일을 해냈다니 신통하군 It is marvelous that he should have done such a thing. ⇌ I marvel that he managed it.

신트림 the eructation of an acid fluid; acid eructation —**신트림하다** belch [eruct(ate)] an acid fluid

신파 新派 〈유파〉 a new school; 〈연극〉 a new-school drama ♦신파조로 in the spirit of the drama ■—배우 an actor of the new school; a new-school actor

신파극 新派劇 ⇨ 신파연극

신파연극 新派演劇 a new-school drama [play]

신판 新版 〈간행〉 a new publication; 〈개정판〉 a new [revised] edition ♦신판의 newly-edited; newly-published

신품 新品 a new article ▶그 구두는 신품이나 다름없었다 Those shoes looked brand-new. ⇌ Those shoes were as good as new.

신풍 新風 〈풍조나 풍속〉 a new phase ♦정계에 신풍을 불어넣다 breathe new life [introduce a fresh current] into political circles

신하 臣下 a subject; 〈가신〉 a retainer; 〈봉신·가신〉 a vassal

신학 神學 theology; divinity
■목회(牧會)— pastoral theology 사변— speculative theology ■—교 a theological [divinity] school; a seminary —박사 a Doctor of Divinity (略 D.D.) —생 a theological [theology, divinity] student —자 a theologian; a theologist; a divine

신학기 新學期 a new school term

신학문 新學問 the new learning; modern sciences

신형 新型 a new [the latest] style [model, fashion, design] ♦최신형 컴퓨터 an electronic computer of the latest model ■—차 a new-model car

신호 信號 a sign; a signal; signaling
♦호각 소리를 신호로 at the [a] whistle / 신호를 보내다 make [give] a signal [sign] / 신호를 올리다 raise [hoist, put up, display] a signal / 신호를 내리다 strike [haul down] a signal / (길에서) 신호를 기다리다 wait for a signal [(traffic) light] / 신호를 무시하다 disregard [ignore] a signal / 신호를 무시하고 건너다 (口) jaywalk / 발차 신호를 하다 give a starting signal / 신호를 잘못 보내다 make a wrong signal / 신호를 잘못 보다[읽다] mistake [misread] a signal / 신호에 주의하다 look to [look out for] a signal / 신호에 답하다 return a signal / 신호로 알리다 signal; semaphore / 신호로 구조를 청하다 signal for rescue; call for assistance [help] by signal
▶파란 신호로 바뀐 뒤에 건너시오 Cross the street after the light has turned to green. ⇌ Cross the street on the green light.
▶신호는 빨강이었다 The signal was red.
▶한 노파가 정지 신호를 무시하고 길을 건너려고 했다 An old woman was about to cross the street against a red traffic light.
▶빨간 등은 일반적으로 위험을 알리는 신호다 A red light is usually a signal for [of] danger.
—**신호하다** signal; make [give] a signal [sign]; sign [motion] 《*sb* to do》
▶그는 출발 준비가 되었다고 신호했다 He signed that he was ready to start.
▶그는 웨이터에게 차림표를 가져오라고 신호했다 He signaled (to) the waiter to bring the menu.
▶선원들은 낮에는 수기로 밤에는 등불로 신호한다 Sailors signal with flags by day and with lights at night.
▶순찰 경찰관은 그들에게 정지하라고 신호했다 The patrolman signed (for) them to halt there.
▶그는 출발하라고 손을 들어 신호했다 He raised his hand as a signal for starting.
■경계— a caution [warning] signal 교통— a traffic signal 기상— a weather signal 무선— a wireless signal 비상— an alarm (signal) 수기(手旗)— a flag signal; 〈군대의〉 a semaphore 위험— a red [danger] signal 음향— an acoustic [an audible, a phonic] signal 자동— an automatic signal 정지— a signal of "Stop"; a stoplight; a red light 조난— a distress signal; a signal of distress 주의— a precaution signal; a signal of "Caution" 철도— a railroad signal [semaphore] 출발— a signal for starting; a starting signal 통화— a busy signal; an engaged signal 호출— a call signal [sign] ■—기(旗) a signal flag; 〈선박의〉 a code flag —기(機) a signal; 〈철도의〉 a semaphore —등 a signal lamp [light]; 〈깜박이등〉 a blinker —방식 signaling system —법 signal code : 국제신호법 an international code of signals —소 (美) a signal tower; (英) a signal box —수 a flagman; a signalman; a signaler; (俗) 〔軍〕 a buzzer —전파 〔空〕 a beam : 신호 전파를 벗어나[타고] off [on] the beam —책 a signal (code) book; a code of signals —탑 a signal tower —통신 signal communication

신혼 新婚 a new marriage [wedding]
■—부부 a newly married [newly wed] couple; newlyweds —생활 newly married life

신혼여행 新婚旅行 a honeymoon; a wedding trip [tour, journey]; a bridal journey
♦신혼여행을 하다 honeymoon (in, at); make a wedding trip / 신혼여행을 떠나다 go (off) on a honeymoon; go on a bridal tour
▶신혼여행은 어디로 갑니까? Where are you going away for the [your] honeymoon?

▶신혼여행은 하와이로 갑니다 We are going to Hawaii for our honeymoon.
■—자 honeymooners
신화 神化 〈신격화〉 deification; apotheosis
—**신화하다** deify; apotheosize
신화 神話 a myth; 〈총칭〉 mythology
♦신화적 영웅들 mythical heroes / 신화의[적인] mythical; mythologic; mythological; fabulous / 신화와 전설로 유명하다 be famous in myth and legend
—건국— the birth myth of a nation 그리스— Greek mythology ■—극 a mythological play —학자 a mythologist
신효 神效 wonderful efficacy
—**신효하다** wonderfully efficacious
신흥 新興 ♦신흥의 newly-rising; rising; burgeoning; new / 신흥 공업국 newly industrializing country (略 NIC)
■—계급 a newly emerging [awakened] class; a newly-rising class —국(가) an emerging [a rising] nation; a newly emerging nation; an emergent [a developing] country —도시 a boom [new] town —부유계급 the new-rich (class) —산업 a rising industry —세력 the growing power; the new emerging forces —종교 a new (religious) cult
싣다 1〈수송수단에〉 load; freight (a ship with wheat); carry (goods); put [take] on board; take in [on]
♦석탄을 실은 배 a ship freighted with coal / 싣다 남은 짐 left-off goods / 야채를 실은 수레 a wagon loaded with vegetables / 이삿짐 트럭에 가재도구를 싣다 load household effects on to a moving van; load a moving van with household effects
▶트럭은 건축자재를 잔뜩 싣고 있었다 The truck was loaded with building materials.
▶이 위에 아무것도 싣지 마십시오 Don't put anything on this.
▶그들은 말에 짐을 싣고 있었다 They were packing the horse.
▶배는 500명의 승객을 싣고 있었다 The ship had five hundred passengers on board. ⇌ On board the ship were 500 passengers.
▶배는 그 항구에서 광석을 실었다 The ship took on [in] (a cargo of) ore at the port.
2〈출판물에〉 record; publish; put; carry (a story)
♦지난호에 실은 기사 an article we reported [carried] in the previous issue / 신문에 소설을 싣다 publish a novel in a newspaper / 잡지에 광고를 싣다 put an advertisement in a magazine
▶오늘 신문은 시험관 아기의 기사를 싣고 있다 Today's paper carries an account of a test-tube baby.
▶당신의 그 기사를 우리 잡지에 싣겠습니다 I will put that article of yours in our periodical.
▶그 축구 시합 기사라면 이 잡지에 실어도 재미 있을 것이다 The story of the soccer game would be interesting enough to run in the magazine.
3〈물에〉 impound [store] (water in a paddy [reservoir])
실 〈재봉용〉 thread; 〈직물・편물용〉 yarn
♦실을 꿴 바늘 a needle and thread / 실처럼 가는 as thin as a thread / 실을 감다 reel thread; wind the thread (on *sth*) / 실을 잣다 spin yarn; spin thread out of cotton / 바늘에 실을 꿰다 thread a needle / 고치에서 실을 뽑다 reel silk off cocoons / 엉킨 실을 풀다 unravel [unloose] tangled thread / 구슬에 실을 꿰다 thread beads on a string
▶실이 끊어졌다[엉켰다] The thread broke [tangled].
▶실과 바늘 좀 빌릴까요? Can I borrow a needle and (some) thread?
▶도무지 이 바늘에 실을 꿸 수가 없다 I just can't thread this needle.
■—뭉치 a ball of thread
실 實 〈진실〉 the truth; the reality; 〈실체〉 substance; essence ♦실은 really
-실 -室 〈방〉 a room
♦119호실 room number 119 / 기차의 1등실 the first-class compartment
실가 實價 〈진가〉 intrinsic [true] value; sterling worth; 〈실제 가격〉 the actual [real] price; 〈원가〉 the cost price
실각 失脚 1〈발을 헛디딤〉 a slip of the foot; losing *one's* footing
2〈요직을 잃음〉 loss of position [post]; a downfall; a fall
▶그 외교 정책의 실패가 대통령의 실각을 초래했다 The blunder in the foreign policy brought about the downfall of the President.
—**실각하다** lose *one's* position; fall (from power); be overthrown
♦실각한 정치가 a knocked-out [an ousted] politician / 대통령을 실각시키다 overthrow the President
▶그 추문으로 그는 실각했다 He lost his post [position] because of the scandal. ⇌ The scandal led to his downfall.
실감 實感 actual feeling [sensation]; solid sense; 〈체득〉 realization
♦실감나는 realistic (stage effect); true to nature; lifelike / 실감나게 노래하다 sing with feeling and expression
▶이 그림은 실감이 안난다 This picture is not realistic [not true to nature].
▶나는 아직 대학생이라는 실감이 나지 않는다 I don't yet really feel that I am a college student.
▶당시 우리는 전쟁에 패했다는 것이 충분히 실감나지 않았다 In those days we did not realize fully that we had lost the war.
—**실감하다** feel actually; realize; experience personally
—**온도** effective temperature
실감개 a spool; a bobbin; a reel ♦실감개에 감다 spool; reel; wind (thread) on a spool [bobbin]
실개천 a streamlet; a small stream; a brooklet; a rivulet; a rill
실격 失格 disqualification; elimination
▶그는 색맹이라서 그 직무에서 실격이 되었다 His color blindness disqualified him for the

job.
▶그녀는 어머니로서는 실격이다 She is far from what a mother should be. ⇒ She has no right to be called a mother.
―실격하다 be disqualified; be eliminated 《from, out of》; be put out of the race
▶그는 예선전에서 실격했다 He was rejected in the elimination match.
▶그는 주로를 벗어나 실격했다 He strayed from the course and was put out of the race.
■―선 수 a nonqualifier; a suspended player ―자 a disqualified person
실경 實景 the actual view [scene]
실고추 shredded red pepper
실과 實果 fruit ⇨ 과일
실과 實科 a practical course; a practicum
실국수 thin [threadlike] noodles
실권 失權 loss [forfeiture] of *one's* right(s); disfranchisement; 《권력의》 loss of power
―실권하다 lose *one's* right(s); forfeit *one's* power; be disfranchised
실권 實權 real [actual] power ♦실권이 없는 사장 a president in name only / 실권을 쥐다 [잡다] hold real power 《over》; hold the reins of 《government》
▶실권은 그들 수중에 있었다 Real power was in their hands.
▶그가 회사의 실권을 쥐고 있다 He has controlling interest in the company. ⇒ He exercises controlling influences on the company.
실그러뜨리다 misshape; distort; tilt
실그러지다 get out of shape; be distorted [tilted]
실금 〈가는 금〉 a fine crack; a thread-like fissure ▶찻잔에 실금이 갔다 The tea cup got a fine crack in it.
실금 失禁 〔醫〕 incontinence
실긋거리다 shift from side to side; be tilted up and down; wobble; be unsteady [shaky]
♦실긋거리는 탁자 a wobbly [shaky] table
실긋실긋 shiftingly from side to side; wobblingly
실긋하다 tilted; tipsy; unsteady; distorted
실기 失期 missing an appointed time
―실기하다 be [get] too late; be a day after the fair; lose the last possible chance
실기 失機 missing a chance [an opportunity]
―실기하다 miss [lose, fail to catch] a chance [an opportunity]; let slip [go] a chance
실 기 實技 practical technique [technics]; actual [practical] skill [talent]; 〈체육의〉 practical [physical] training
실기시험 實技試驗 practical (talent) examination; skill test ♦운전 실기시험 driving test / 미술 실기시험 fine arts talent test
▶나는 교통법규 시험에는 합격했지만 운전 실기시험에서 떨어졌다 I passed the test of traffic laws, but failed in the driving test.
실꾸리 a ball [skein] of thread [yarn]
실낱 a strand; a ply; a single thread
♦실낱 같은 목숨 a life hanging by a thread / 실낱 같은 희망을 갖고 with faint hope / 실낱 같은 목소리로 in [with] a feeble voice

실내 室內 the (interior of a) room
♦실내의 indoor / 실내를 장식하다 decorate a room 《with pictures》; 〈커튼·가구 등으로〉 upholster a room / 실내에 틀어박히다 stay [keep] indoors / 실내에서 놀다 play indoors [in the room]
▶실내공기가 너무 건조하다 The air in the room is too dry.
▶그는 실내를 둘러보았다 He looked around the room.
▶우리는 비가 와서 하루 종일 실내에 갇혀 있었다 We were kept indoors all day by the rain.
▶이 놀이는 실내에서도 할 수 있습니다 You can play this game indoors [in the room], too.
■―게임 an indoor [a parlor] game ―디자인 interior design ―복 a housedress; a dressing gown [robe] ―수영장 an indoor swimming pool ―악 chamber music ―악단 a chamber orchestra ―안테나 an indoor antenna ―운동 indoor exercise ―음악 chamber music ―전화 an interphone ―조명〔배관, 배선〕 interior illumination [piping, wiring] ―체육관 a gymnasium 《pl. ~s, -sia》 ―화 house shoes; slippers; scuffs
실내장식 室內裝飾 interior [house] decoration; interior design; upholstery
♦실내장식을 하다 upholster a room
■―가 an interior decorator; an upholsterer
실농하다 失農― miss the season for farming
실눈 narrow eyes
♦실눈을 뜨고 with *one's* eyes half-closed [slightly open]; through *one's* eyelashes / 실눈을 뜨다 open *one's* eyes a little / 실눈을 하다 narrow *one's* eyes
▶그는 실눈을 한 채 나를 보고 있었다 He was looking at me with his eyes half-closed.
실답다 實― dependable; trustworthy; faithful
♦실다운 청년 a trustworthy young man
실답지 않다 實― unreliable; untrustworthy; insincere
실덕 失德 losing *one's* reputation; loss of virtue ―실덕하다 lose *one's* virtue [reputation]
실뜨기 〈놀이〉 cat's cradle
♦실뜨기를 하다 play cat's cradle
실랑이(질) pestering [bothering] 《sb》
―실랑이질하다 bother [pester] 《sb》
실러 〈독일의 시인·극작가〉 Schiller, Johann Christoph Friedrich von (1759-1805)
실러블 a syllable ⇨ 음절
실력 實力 1 〈실제의 역량〉 real ability; capability; merit; efficiency; competency; competence
♦어학 실력 *one's* linguistic attainments [ability] / 실력이 있는 사람 a person of ability; a competent [an able] person / 실력 있는 의사 a competent doctor / 실력에 따라 according to *one's* ability [merits]; according to individual worth / 수학 실력을 기르다 improve *oneself* in mathematics / 영어 실력을 기르다 make *oneself* proficient in English / 충분히 실력을 발휘하다 show *one's* ability to the full; do *oneself* full justice in a contest
▶너는 영어 실력이 있다 You are good at

English. ⇌ You have a good knowledge of English. ⇌ You are proficient in English.
▶ 그는 수학 실력이 늘었다 He has improved himself in mathematics.
▶ 요즈음은 실력이 말하는 시대다 Nowadays abilities talk [count] in the long run.
▶ 골프 실력이 느셨군요 Your golf has improved, hasn't it?
▶ 그녀는 영어 실력이 대단하다 She has indeed a good command of English. ⇌ Her proficiency in [Her command of] English is marvelous.
▶ 나는 간판보다 실력을 중시한다 I value real ability more than titles.
▶ 남의 실력을 판정하기는 어렵다 It is difficult to judge a person's real ability.
▶ 그는 시험에서 충분히 실력을 발휘했다 He did himself justice in the examination.
▶ 각자 실력에 따라 최선을 다해 주기 바란다 Everyone is expected to do his best according to his ability.
▶ 그는 실력으로 출세했다 He rose (in the world) through ability.
▶ 그녀는 실력으로 사장이 되었다 She became the president through ability.
2 〈무력〉 arms; 〈완력〉 force
♦ 실력을 행사하다 use [employ] force; appeal to arms / 실력으로 탈환하다 recover *sth* by force
■ 一제도[주의] the merit system 一테스트 a proficiency test 《in English》 一파 a competent group 一행사 use of force; appeal [recourse] to arms; 〈파업〉 a strike

실력자 實力者 an influential person; a man of influence; a strong man 《in the government》
♦ 숨은 실력자 a behind-the-scenes strong man / 정계의 실력자 a strong man in politics
▶ 아저씨는 재계에서 숨은 실력자다 My uncle is a latent power in the financial world.

실례 失禮 rudeness; impoliteness; discourtesy; bad manners [form]; a breach of etiquette
♦ 실례의 말을 하다 say rude things; make a rude remark; use rude language / 실례를 무릅쓰고 …하다 take the liberty of 《doing》; make bold to 《do》 / 말씀중에 실례입니다만… Sorry to interrupt you, but…; I'm sorry to interrupt you while you are talking, but…
▶ 손님에게 실례가 되지 않도록 주의하시오 Take care not to be impolite to the customers.
▶ 실례지만 민선생 아니십니까? Excuse me, but are you not Mr. Min?
▶ 실례지만 무슨 일로 오셨습니까? May I ask what your business is?
▶ 실례지만 성함이 어떻게 되시는지요? Might I ask your name?
▶ 실례지만 우체국 가는 길 좀 가르쳐 주십시오 Excuse me, but won't you tell me how to get to the post office?
▶ 실례지만 회의에 참석하지 못하겠습니다 I should like to excuse myself from attending the meeting.
▶ 실례지만 오늘 찾아가 뵈어도 괜찮습니까? May I take the liberty of calling on you today?
▶ 여러 사람 앞에서 하품하는 것은 실례다 It is bad manners to yawn in company.
▶ 식사중에 담배 피우는 것은 실례다 It is against etiquette to smoke at table.
▶ 호주머니에 손을 넣은 채로 이야기하는 것은 실례다 It is rude to speak with your hands in your pockets.
一실례하다 be rude 《to》; act rudely 《toward》; behave discourteously 《to》; commit a breach of etiquette
▶ 실례합니다 (1)〈자리를 뜰 때〉 Excuse me (for) a moment (2)〈남의 앞을 지나칠 때〉 Excuse me (for passing before you). (3)〈남의 집에 찾아가서〉 May I come in?
▶ 먼저 실례합니다 Please excuse me my leaving earlier.
▶ 이만 실례하겠습니다 Well, I must be going now. ⇌ (I am afraid) I must say good-by(e).
▶ 실례했습니다 I am sorry to have bothered you. ⇌ I beg your pardon. ⇌ Pardon me.
▶ 오랫동안 기다리시게 하여 실례했습니다 I am sorry to have kept you waiting so long.

실례 實例 an example; an instance; a concrete case; a case in point; an illustration
♦ 단어의 뜻을 나타내는 실례 an illustration of the meaning of a word / 실례를 들다 cite [give] an instance; give [set] a concrete example [illustration] / 실례를 들어 요점을 설명하다 explain the point by giving examples; illustrate the point
▶ 실례는 교훈보다 낫다 Example is better than precept.
▶ 아직까지 그런 실례가 없다 There is no precedent for it.
▶ 실례를 하나 들겠습니다 Let me give an example.
▶ 이것은 많은 실례 중의 하나에 지나지 않는다 This is only one instance out of many.

실로 實— indeed; really; truly; in truth
▶ 실로 절경이로다 How beautiful the scenery is!
▶ 그는 실로 비범한 사람이다 He is indeed a remarkable man.
▶ 이것은 실로 인생의 비극이다 This is in truth one of life's tragedies.

실로폰 a xylophone

실록 實錄 an authentic [a true, a faithful] record [account] ■ 이조— a true record of the Yi Dynasty ■ 一물 a historical novel

실론 〈스리랑카를 이루는 섬〉 Ceylon ♦ 실론의 Ceylonese ■ 一사람 a Ceylonese 一차 Ceylon tea

실루엣 a silhouette ♦ 실루엣의 옆모습 a profile in silhouette

실룩거리다 twitch; work; jerk
▶ 그녀의 얼굴이 감동으로 실룩거렸다 Her face worked with emotion.
▶ 그의 입술이 심한 분노로 실룩거렸다 His lips twitched in exasperation.
▶ 소들이 파리를 쫓으려고 옆구리를 실룩거리고 있었다 The cows were twitching their flanks to drive off the flies.

실룩실룩 with twitches [jerks]; twitchingly

—실룩실룩하다 twitch ⇨ 실룩거리다
♦눈꺼풀[얼굴]을 실룩실룩하다 twitch *one's* eyelids [face]

실리 實利 utility; (an actual) profit; material gain [interests]; benefit
♦실리적(인) utilitarian; practical

실리다 1 〈기재·기록되다〉 be reported; be recorded [mentioned]; be published [printed]; be given 《in a program》; be carried; 〈적재되다〉 be loaded 《up》; be put on board
♦신문에 실린 논설 an article carried in a newspaper / 신문에 실리다 appear [be printed, be reported] in a newspaper; be carried [published] in a daily / 실려 가다 be carried [taken] away; **(口)** be carted away / 바람에 실려 오다 be wafted on the wind
▶그의 단편이 잡지에 실렸다 One of his short stories has been printed in a magazine.
▶어느 신문이나 그 사건의 기사가 1면에 실렸다 All the papers carried accounts of the affair on the first page.
▶이 사전에는 용례가 많이 실려 있다 This dictionary gives a lot of examples showing the actual use of words.
▶배에는 기름이 실려 있었다 The ship was loaded with oil.
▶부상병들은 그 병원으로 실려 왔다 The wounded soldiers were carried into the hospital.
2 〈싣게 하다〉 get 《goods》 loaded; have *sb* load 《up》《a car, goods》; load
♦기록에 실리다 put 《a matter》 on record / 신문에 광고를 실리다 put [insert] an advertisement in a paper / 신문[잡지]에 소설을 실리다 publish a novel in a newspaper [magazine] / 쌀을 짐차에 실리다 load a wagon with rice

실리주의 實利主義 utilitarianism
■—자 a utilitarian

실리카 〔化〕 silica
실리콘 〔化〕〈규소 수지〉 silicone
실린더 〔機〕 a cylinder
실링 a shilling (略 s.)

실마리 1 〈실의 첫머리〉 the end of a thread
2 〈발단〉 the beginning; a start; an inception
♦출세의 실마리가 되다 lead to success in life; become the first step to *one's* success in life
3 〈단서〉 a clue 《to do》; a key 《for doing》; a lead ♦이것을 실마리로 하여 with this clue to go upon / 실마리를 잡다 find a clue; make a beginning [start]; hit upon a clue 《to》
▶그것이 실마리가 되어 사건은 해결되었다 It served as the clue that led to the solution of the case.
▶그 비밀은 탐색할 실마리가 없다 The mystery has no clue to it.
▶그는 그 문제를 풀 실마리를 찾지 못했다 He could find no clue to the solution of the problem.

실망 失望 (a) disappointment; discouragement; 〈절망〉 despair; loss of hope; **(口)** (a) letdown
▶어머니는 그 소식을 듣고 실망의 빛을 감추지 못했다 My mother couldn't hide her disappointment at the news.
▶그의 실패는 내게는 큰 실망이었다 His failure was a great disappointment to me.
—실망하다 be disappointed 《in, of, with, at》; be discouraged; feel letdown; despair 《of》; lose *one's* hope(s)

> 〔解說〕 (1) *disappointed* 와 *disappointing*이 다른 점에 주의. 「그는 실망했다」는 He was disappointed. 라고 반드시 수동형으로 쓴다. He was disappointing.이라고 하면 「그는 남을 실망시키는 사람이었다」는 뜻이 된다. *discouraged* 와 *discouraging* 도 또한 마찬가지다.
> (2) disappointed 는 discouraged 보다 형용사적 성격이 강하다. (very) much 외에 very 단독으로도 수식할 수 있다.

♦실망하여 disappointedly; in disappointment; in despair / 실망한 듯이 with a disappointed look; disappointedly / 실망시키다 disappoint; let down; dash [crush] *sb's* hope / 실망한 기색을 보이다 look disappointed; show *one's* dejection 《at》
▶나는 그에게 크게 실망했다 I was much disappointed in him.
▶나는 그의 작품에 실망했다 I was disappointed at his work.
▶그의 대답에 나는 실망했다 His answer was a disappointment to me.
▶그녀는 그에게 실망하고 있었다 She was disappointed in him.
▶실망하지 마라 Don't be disappointed [discouraged]. ⇌ Don't lose heart.
▶그 결과는 나를 실망케 했다 The result disappointed me.
▶그녀는 너를 실망시키지는 않을 것이다 She will never let you down.
▶그녀는 실망한 나머지 자살을 꾀했다 She attempted suicide out of despair.
▶실망스럽게도 그 경기는 중지되었다 To our disappointment the game was called off.

실명 失明 the loss of eyesight [sight]
—실명하다 lose *one's* eyesight [sight]; become sightless; become [go] blind
▶그는 그 사고로 실명했다 He lost his sight because of the accident.
■—자 a blind [sightless] person; 《총칭》 the blind

실명 實名 *one's* real name
실명거래 實名去來 real-name financial transaction
실명계좌 實名計座 a real-name account
실명제 實名制 (the) real-name financial transaction system
실무 實務 (practical) business [affairs]; administrative work; business practice
♦실무에 재간이 있는 사람 a person of business talent / 실무적 practical; businesslike / 실무 경험이 충분히 있다 have enough business experience / 실무를 배우다[익히다] receive a training [train *oneself*] in practical business; study the practice of business / 실무에 종사하다 go into [engage in] business / 실무에 어둡다 be not familiar with office routine; be out

of touch with the world
▶그는 실무 능력이 있다 He has practical business ability.
▶나는 이 학교를 나오면 실무에 종사하게 될 것이다 I'll have to go into business when I graduate from this school.
■—가 a man of business; a businessman: 뛰어난 실무가 a good businessman —강습(회) a training class —연수(研修) in-service training —자 a clerk [a person, an official] in charge (of) —자(급)회담 a working conference; a working-level meeting

실물 失物 loss of goods [things]
—실물하다 lose one's goods [things]

실물 實物 1〈실제 물건〉the (real) thing; the (actual) object; 〈진짜〉 a genuine article [thing]; the original; 〈그림에 대하여〉 life
♦실물 크기의 사진 a life-size(d) photograph; a photograph as large as life / 실물보다 잘 그려진 초상화 a flattering likeness / 실물의 real; genuine
▶실물을 보지 않고는 말할 수 없다 I can't tell unless I see the thing itself.
▶실물을 보고 사든지 말든지 결정하겠다 After I actually see it, I'll decide whether to buy it.
▶그 박물관에 전시돼 있는 실물을 본 적이 있다 I've seen the original hung in the museum.
▶이 동상은 실물 그대로다 This bronze statue is quite lifelike [is true to life, looks just like a real person].
▶이 조화는 실물 그대로다 This artificial flower looks just like a real [natural] one. ≒ This artificial flower is true to nature.
▶이 초상화는 꼭 실물같다 This portrait is so lifelike [exact to the life].
▶너는 실물보다 사진이 낫다 You look better in the picture.
2 ⇨ 현물(現物)
■—거래 a spot transaction —경제 object economy —경제시대 the age of object economy —광고 object advertisement —교수(give) an object lesson; object teaching —묘사 model drawing

실물대 實物大〈실물 크기〉actual size; the size of the original
♦실물대의 초상화 a life-size portrait / 실물대로 확대한 사진 a life-size enlargement of a photograph / 실물대의 as large as life; life-[full-]size(d); of natural [actual] size
▶이 사진은 실물대다 This picture shows the actual size.

실바람 a slight air; a light breeze
실밥 1〈솔기의〉a seam; a stitch
♦실밥이 풀리다 a seam starts / 실밥을 뽑다 undo a seam; cut a seam open
2〈보무라지〉waste (pieces of) thread [yarn]; drawn thread; ravelings
실버들 a slender weeping willow
실보무라지 waste (pieces of) thread [yarn]; ravel(l)ings; odd ends of thread
실비 實費〈실제 비용〉actual expense(s); 〈원가〉 the cost price; the prime cost
♦물건을 실비로 제공하다 offer an article at cost / 실비로 팔다 sell sth at actual cost
▶이 물품을 실비로 드리겠습니다 I'll sell this article at cost.
■—생산 the cost [expense] of production —제공 a cost sale

실사 實寫 a photograph [picture] taken from life [taken on the spot] —실사하다 take a photograph [picture] on the spot

실사회 實社會 the (real) world; the actual world; a practical life
♦실사회에 나가다 go [get] out into the world; get a start in life; start in life

실상 實狀〈실제 상황〉actual circumstances; the actual [real] state of affairs; the actual condition [situation] ♦실상은 as things [matters] stand; the fact is 《that…》
▶그는 사태가 호전되리라고 말했지만, 실상은 오히려 악화돼 가고 있다 He said things would go better, but actually [as it is] they are getting worse.

실상 實相〈실제의 모습〉the real aspect [state]; 〔佛敎〕 reality
♦사회의 실상 a true picture of life / 사물을 실상대로 표현하다 present sth in its true aspect
▶그 조직의 실상은 외부인으로서는 알 수가 없었다 The true nature of the organization was impenetrable to outsiders.

실상 實像〔光〕a real image
실색 失色 losing one's color; changing color 《as from anger》; changing countenance
—실색하다 change [lose] color; turn pale
▶그는 그 소식을 듣자 실색했다 Color left his face when he heard the news.

실생활 實生活 real life; actual life; (the realities of) life; life in the real [workaday] world ♦실생활에서 취재한 이야기 a tale taken from real life
▶실생활에서는 그런 일이 있을 수 없다 I don't believe in it in real life.

실선 實線 a solid line; a real line
실성 失性 mental derangement; distraction; insanity; madness —실성하다 become mentally deranged [unbalanced]; go mad; become insane; go out of one's mind
♦실성한 사람 a madman; an insane person / 실성한 사람처럼 frantically; madly
▶그는 실연하여 실성했다 Disappointed in love, he has lost his head.

실소 失笑 sudden uncontrollable laughter; irrepressible laughter ♦실소를 금치 못하다 cannot help laughing 《at sth》; cannot repress [swallow] a laugh
—실소하다 laugh in spite of oneself

실속 實— substance; matter; 〈내용〉 contents
♦실속있는 장사 a solid business / 실속 없는 겉치레 a mere show without reality / 별로 실속 없는 강의 a lecture of little substance; a thin lecture / 실속 있는 substantial; solid; meaty; voluminous / 실속 없는 unsubstantial; empty 《talk》 / 허울을 버리고 실속을 차리다 discard the shadow for the substance

실속 失速〔空〕stall —실속하다 stall
▶제트기는 실속하여 추락했다 The jet plane crashed because of an engine stall [because the engine stalled].

실수 失手 〈잘못〉 a mistake; an error; a fault; a slip; 〈실책〉 a blunder; a bungle; a mess; (口) a mess-up
♦ 큰 실수 a great [serious] mistake; a gross error / 부주의로 저지른 실수 a careless mistake [error] / 실수로 by mistake; through mistake; in error / 실수 없이 without any mistake; successfully
▶ 실수로 꽃병을 깨뜨렸다 I broke a vase by accident.
▶ 그는 또 큰 실수를 저질렀다 He has blundered again.
▶ 그는 계산에서 큰 실수를 했다 He made serious errors [mistake] in calculation.
▶ 그가 하는 말을 정말이라고 생각하면 큰 실수다 It is a great mistake to think what he says is true.
―실수하다 make a mistake [slip]; commit an error [a fault]; err; blunder; bungle; make [commit] a blunder; botch; goof
▶ 그런 사람을 믿다니 내가 실수했다 I made a mistake in trusting such a man.
▶ 그건 내가 실수한 거다 I am to blame for it. ⇌ It is my fault.
▶ 그는 무대에서 대사를 실수했다 He bungled [faltered, blundered] in his words on the stage.
▶ 실수하지 않도록 조심해라 Be careful not to fail. ⇌ See that there is no failure [mismanagement].
▶ 누구든지 실수할 수 있는 법이다 Who can be entirely innocent of error? ⇌ To err is human.

실수 實收 〈실수입〉 a real [net] income; actual receipts; 〈급료의〉 one's take-home pay [wages, earnings]; 〈수확〉 actual [real] yield
▶ 금년의 실수는 예상보다 많다 The actual receipts for this year are greater than I expected.
▶ 내 월급은 세금을 제하고 실수 100만원이다 My monthly salary is 1,000,000 won after taxes.

실수 實數 1 〈실제의 수〉 the real [actual] number 2 〖數〗 a real (number)

실수요 實需要 actual demand ■ ―자 an end user

실습 實習 practice; (practical) exercise; drill; training; probation **―실습하다** practice; have (practical) training ♦ 요리를 실습하다 practice cooking
▶ 우리는 학교에서 배운 것을 병원에서 실습했다 We put into practice at a hospital what we had learned at school.
■ ―교육― teaching practice ■ ―기간 probation ―생 a trainee; a student apprentice; an apprentice ―시간 practice hours

실시 實施 enforcement; operation; execution; implementation; 〖法〗 effectuation
♦ 실시를 명하다 order (a program) into effect
―실시하다 enforce [give effect to] (a law); carry (a law) into effect; execute
♦ 계획을 실시하다 carry out a plan / 규칙을 실시하다 put rules into practice / 실시되다 be enforced; come [go] into effect [force, operation]; be put in force [into operation]; take effect
▶ 그 조사는 다음달에 실시된다 The investigation will be carried out [be conducted] next month.
▶ 새 법률은 언제부터 실시됩니까? When does the new law come into effect [become effective]?
▶ 여름철 요금 할인은 6월 1일부터 실시됩니다 Reduced summer fares will be effective on and after June 1.
▶ 새 규칙은 4월 1일부터 실시된다 The new regulations will come into operation on April 1 〔英〕 1 April〕.

실신 失神 a faint; a swoon; a fainting fit
―실신하다 faint; swoon; fall into a swoon; fall unconscious; 〈의식을 잃다〉 lose consciousness [one's senses] ♦ 실신해 있다[넘어지다] be [fall down] in a faint
▶ 그녀는 그 소식을 듣고 실신했다 She fainted at the news.
▶ 그는 그녀를 때려 실신시켰다 He knocked her senseless.

실실 with a silly snicker ♦ 실실 웃다 snicker; giggle

실어증 失語症 〖醫〗 aphasia
■ ―환자 an aphasi(a)c

실언 失言 a slip of the tongue; an improper remark; a verbal lapse; an impropriety in speech
▶ 그는 실언을 사과했다 He apologized for his slip of the tongue.
―실언하다 make a slip of the tongue; use improper language [words]; make an improper remark; one's tongue slips (in one's statement); (口) put [stick] one's foot in the [one's] mouth

실업 失業 unemployment; loss of employment; joblessness
▶ 불황으로 인하여 젊은이들의 실업이 늘고 있다 Youth unemployment is rising because of the recession.
▶ 현재 많은 사람이 실업중이다 A lot of people are out of work now.
―실업하다 lose one's employment [work, job]; fall [be thrown] out of employment [work]
■ ―계절적[주기적]― seasonal [cyclical] unemployment 잠재― potential [latent] unemployment ―대책 an unemployment policy; a countermeasure against unemployment; a relief measure for the unemployed ―대책사업 relief work for the unemployed ―률 an unemployment rate; a jobless rate ―문제 an unemployment problem : 실업문제가 심각해졌다 The unemployment problem has come to assume a grave aspect. ―보상 unemployment compensation ―보험 unemployment [jobless] insurance ―상태 the state of being out of work; joblessness ―조사 an unemployment census

실업 實業 〈산업〉industry; 〈상업·실무〉business ♦ 실업에 종사하다 be (engaged) in busi-

■—가 a businessman; a man of business; 〈산업가〉 an industrialist —계(界) the industrial [business] world; business circles: 실업계에 투신하다 enter the business world; enter business life; go into business —교육 industrial education; vocational training —단체 a business corporation —야구팀 a business baseball team —학교 a vocational [technical, business] school; a trade school

실업수당 失業手當 an unemployment allowance; 〈英口〉 the dole
♦ 실업수당을 지급하다 grant sb an unemployment allowance; put sb on the dole / 실업수당을 받다 go on [draw] the dole

실업자 失業者 an unemployed person; a person out of employment [work]; a jobless person; (총칭) the unemployed [jobless]
♦ 실업자의 구제 relief of the unemployed
▶ 이 나라는 실업자가 거의 없다 There is little unemployment in this country.
▶ 그 때문에 수백 명의 실업자가 생겼다 It created unemployment for hundreds of workers.
▶ 거리에는 실업자가 득실거린다 Unemployed workers fill the streets. ⇌ Workers are out of work all over the town.
■ 잠재[완전]— the potentially [completely] unemployed

실없다 實— 〈성실성 없다〉 insincere; faithless; unreliable; 〈무의미하다〉 nonsensical; silly; foolish; absurd
♦ 실없는 사람 an untrustworthy person; a senseless [silly] person / 실없는 소리 absurd remarks; silly talk; nonsense / 실없는 소리를 지껄이다 chatter idly; talk nonsense; say useless [irrelevant] things / 실없이 nonsensically; senselessly; frivolously; idly; uselessly; flippantly
▶ 실없는 소리하지 마 Don't talk nonsense!

실연 失戀 broken heart; disappointed [lost] love; disappointment in love
—실연하다 be disappointed in love
♦ 실연한 남자 a brokenhearted man
▶ 그녀는 실연하여 자살을 꾀했다 She attempted suicide out of disappointment in love.
▶ 전혀 사랑해보지 않은 것보다는 사랑하고 실연해본 것이 낫다 It's better to have loved and lost rather than never to have loved at all.

실연 實演 1 〈실제 해보임〉 a demonstration; an exhibition ♦ 댄스의 실연 a dancing demonstration
2 〈상연〉 a performance; (a) stage demonstration [performance] —실연하다 give a stage performance; act on the stage

실오리 a piece of thread [string]
♦ 실오리같은 희망 a shadow [ray, flash] of hope; the sole remaining hope
▶ 그녀는 몸에 실오리 하나 걸치지 않고 있었다 She was without a stitch of clothing on her.

실온 室溫 the temperature of a room; room temperature

실외 室外 the outdoors; the open air ♦ 실외의 outdoor; outside / 실외에(서) outdoors; out of doors

실용 實用 practical use; utility
♦ 실용 본위의 가구 utility furniture
—실용하다 put sth to practical use
■ —단위 (物) a practical unit —성 practicality; utility: 실용성이 있는[없는] of [of no] practical use —신안 a utility model; a new design for practical use; a design of practical utility —신안권 utility model right —영어 practical English —위성 applications satellite; a working satellite —품 a utility [useful] article; 〈일용품〉 daily necessities; utility goods; an article of utility [practical use]; 〈필수품〉 necessities

실용적 實用的 practical; useful; (intended) for practical [actual] use ♦ 실용적인 코트 a utility coat
▶ 책상은 실용적으로 만들어졌다 The desk is made [designed] for practical use.
▶ 그 옷은 품위가 있다기보다는 실용적이다 The clothes are more practical than elegant.
▶ 이 책은 논리적이기보다 실용적이다 This book is practical rather than theoretical.

실용주의 實用主義 utilitarianism; 〔哲〕 pragmatism ♦ 실용주의의 practical; 〔哲〕 pragmatic; pragmatistic ■ —(철학)자 a pragmatist

실용화하다 實用化— put sth to practical use; put sth in [into] practice
▶ 그의 발명이 실용화되었다 His invention has been put to practical use.

실은 實— in reality [fact]; in point of fact; as a matter of fact; to tell (you) the truth; really; actually
▶ 실은 정반대다 In point of fact, the reverse is the case.
▶ 실은 나도 잘 모르겠어 I must confess I am hardly better informed.
▶ 실은 그는 큰 빚을 지고 있어 To tell the truth he is in heavy debt.
▶ 실은 자네에게 한 가지 부탁이 있어 Actually, I have a favor to ask of you.
▶ 실은 그 여자가 무척 싫어 To be frank with you, I hate her.
▶ 그는 숙제를 자기가 했다고 하지만, 실은 그의 누이가 해준 거야 He says he did his homework by himself, but in fact [really, actually] his sister did it.

실의 失意 disappointment; despair; dejection
♦ 실의에 빠진 시절 one's period of adversity; one's dark days / 실의에 빠져 있다 be in the depths of despair
▶ 우리는 실의의 늪에 빠져 있었다 We were at the nadir of our hopes.

실익 實益 〈실수익〉 an actual [a net] profit; 〈실리〉 practical use; material gain; benefit; utility
♦ 실익이 없는 계획 an impractical scheme / 실익이 있다 be profitable; be lucrative; be useful
▶ 실익이 없는 거래는 하지 마라 Don't make an unprofitable deal.
▶ 이 일은 재미도 있고 실익도 있다 This work is profitable as well as interesting. ⇌ This

work gives me profit and pleasure at the same time.
▶낚시는 취미와 실익을 겸하고 있다 Fishing combines utility with hobby.

실잠자리 〔昆〕 a damselfly

실장 室長 the head of an office; the head of a laboratory; a section chief; a senior roommate

실재 實在 real [actual] existence; actual being; actuality; 〔哲〕 essence; entity
◆실재의 인물 a real person / 신의 실재를 믿다 believe in (the existence of) God
▶햄릿은 실재의 인물이었을까? Was Hamlet a real person?
━실재하다 exist (really); be (in existence); have a real existence
◆실재하는 real; actual; existent; substantive / 실재하지 않는 unreal; nonexistent; imaginary
■━론 〔哲〕 realism : 관념적 실재론 ideal realism ━론자 a realist

실적 實績 actual results; *one's* achievements
◆학문상의 실적 academic achievements [accomplishments] / 과거의 실적에 입각하여 based on previous results; on the strength of past achievements [performance] / 실적을 올리다[거두다] give [attain] actual [satisfactory] results; 〈성과를 올리다〉 bear fruit; bring results
▶일의 실적이 오르지 않았다 The work did not give actual results. ⇌ We did not have actual results with the work.
▶아무런 실적도 거두지 못했다 Nothing has come out of it.
■━수출━ actual exports; the actual export record 영업━ the (past) business showings; the results of business ■━제(美) the merit system

실전 實戰 actual fighting [battle, warfare]; a battle; an action
◆실전 경험이 있다 have experience in actual fighting / 실전에 임하다 serve in a campaign; see action; be in action [the field] / 실전에 참가하다 take part [engage] in actual fighting; be in action
▶우리는 실전을 경험했다 We experienced action at the front.
▶연습은 실전을 상정한 것이었다 The exercise simulated actual battle conditions.

실점 失點 points [runs] *one* allows *one's* opponent (in a game); points given up; 〈야구의〉 runs given up; 〈테니스의〉 points lost
━실점하다 lose a point; be beaten; be defeated

실정 失政 misgovernment; maladministration; misrule
▶거듭되는 실정으로 내각은 부득이 총사퇴했다 Cabinet was forced to resign in a body owing to a series of maladministration cases.
━실정하다 misgovern; misrule

실정 實情 actual circumstances; the actual [real] state of affairs; the real [actual] condition; the facts 《of a case》; the real situation; (口) the lowdown
◆실정을 알다 know the actual circumstances; know how the matter (really) stands / 실정을 털어놓다 take *sb* into *one's* confidence / 실정을 잘 모르다 be out of touch with things as they are / 실정을 그대로 말하다 state just how things stand; represent things as they are / 실정에 밝다 be in the swim / 실정에 어둡다 be out of the swim; be out of touch with things as they are
▶실정을 알아보겠습니다 I will find out how things stand.
▶그녀는 실정을 전연 모르고 있었다 She did not know at all how things stood [the actual circumstances].

실정법 實定法 〔法〕 the positive law

실제 實際 〈사실〉 a fact; 〈진실〉 the truth; 〈실지〉 practice; 〈현실〉 reality; actuality; 〈실정〉 the actual conditions
◆상상과 실제 imagination and reality / 이론과 실제 theory and practice
〈실제의〉 real; true; actual; 〈구체적인〉 concrete; 〈실지의〉 practical; 〈사실상의〉 effective; virtual
◆실제의 가치 real [actual] value / 실제의 비용 actual cost / 실제의 문제 a practical problem
▶그러나 실제의 생활은 결코 이처럼 논리적이지 않다 But actual life is never so logical as this.
▶우리는 약속만이 아니라 실제의 도움이 필요하다 We need actual help, not just promises.
〈실제는〉 in fact; as a matter of fact; 〈현실은〉 actually; really; in reality; 〈사실상〉 virtually
▶그는 의사라고 말했지만 실제는 그렇지 않았다 He said he was a doctor, but in fact [actually] he was not.
▶실제는 그가 회사의 사장이다 He is virtually [practically] the president of the company.
▶그가 젊게 보일지는 모르지만 실제는 50대다 He may look young but he is in his fifties.
▶그는 돈을 어디선가 잃어버렸다고 말하지만 실제는 써버린 거다 He says he has lost the money somewhere, but the fact is he has spent it.
▶실제는 내가 혼자 했다 As a matter of fact, I did it for [by] myself.
▶상상했던 것과 실제는 딴판이었다 I found the reality quite different from what I had imagined.
〈실제에〉 실제에 어두운 사람 an unpractical person / 실제에 응용하다 apply 《a rule》 to practice
〈기타〉 그가 한 말은 실제와는 아주 딴판이다 What he said was quite different from the facts.
▶사진에서는 실제보다 크게 보인다 It looks larger than life in the picture.
■━경험 practical [actual] experience; practical knowledge ━문제 a practical question ━소득수준 a real income level ━원가 a actual cost ━판매가격 a truth selling price

실제로 實際━ actually; really; as a matter of fact; in fact; practically
◆실제로 있었던 일 an actual occurrence; a real event

▶ 나는 그것을 실제로 내 눈으로 보았다 I saw it with my own eyes. ⇌ I actually saw it.
▶ 그 증거로는 실제로 이런 일이 있었다 As proof, this kind of thing actually happened.
▶ 실제로는 그는 그 일을 할 능력이 없어 As a matter of fact, he is not equal to the task.
▶ 다음 이야기는 실제로 있었던 거야 The following story is what actually happened.
▶ 무엇이든지 실제로 부딪쳐 보지 않으면 알 수가 없다 We cannot learn anything without having practical experience of it.
▶ 실제로 지금 이순간 전쟁으로 죽어가고 있는 사람이 있다 Some people are being killed in battle at this very moment.

실제적 實際的 practical; matter-of-fact; businesslike
♦ 실제적인 사람 a practical person / 실제적인 의견 a practical view / 영어의 실제적인 지식 a practical [working] knowledge of English / 실제적으로 in a practical manner; matter-of-factly / 실제적인 견지에서 from the practical point of view
▶ 실제적인 면에서 필요와 욕구를 구별하기란 쉽지 않다 In practice it is not easy to distinguish between needs and wants.

실족 失足 〈잘못 디딤〉 a false step; a misstep; 〈행동을 잘못함〉 a misdeed; a failure
—**실족하다** miss one's foot [step]; lose one's footing; make [take] a false step; slip; 〈행동에서〉 do an unwise act; fail in sth
♦ 계단에서 실족하다 miss one's footing on the stairs / 실족하여 추락사하다 lose one's footing and fall to death
▶ 실족하면 자칫 목숨을 잃을 판이었다 One misstep meant certain death.
▶ 사람은 한 번 실족하면 다시 돌이키기 어렵다 Once we make a false step, we can hardly recover our credit.

실존 實存 existence ♦ 실존의 existent —**실존하다** exist ■—**주의** 〔哲〕 existentialism —**주의자** an existentialist —**철학** existential philosophy

실종 失踪 disappearance; missing; abscondence
—**실종하다** disappear; run away; abscond; be [go] missing
▶ 그는 전투 중에 실종되었다 He was missing in action.
▶ 그가 실종된 지 사흘째다 He's been missing for three days.
■—**선고[신고]** adjudication [a report] of sb's disappearance —**자** a missing person; 〈도망자〉 a runaway

실주 實株 〔證〕 a real stock; a spot share
실증 實證 positive [actual] proof; corroborative evidence
♦ 실증적 positive / 실증적으로 positively / 실증을 잡고 있다 hold the actual proof (of)
▶ 아직 실증을 얻지 못했다 The proof has not yet been obtained.
—**실증하다** prove; corroborate (a proof); establish (a fact); prove; demonstrate; bear out; verify [justify] (one's reputation)
▶ 그는 내 진술을 실증했다 He substantiated my statement.
▶ 그가 명석하다는 것이 실증되었다 It has been proved that he is bright.
■—**론** positivism —**신학** positive theology

실증주의 實證主義 〔哲〕 positivism ■—**자** a positivist

실증철학 實證哲學 positive philosophy; positivism; 〈Comte의〉 Comtism ■—**자** a positivist; a Comtist

실지 失地 a lost territory ♦ 실지를 회복하다 recover the lost territory ■—**회복** recovery of the lost territory

실지 實地 practice; actuality; reality
♦ 실지의 practical; actual; real; personal / 실지로 practically; personally; in practice / 이론을 실지로 응용하다 put 《a theory》 into practice; make a practical application of the theory
▶ 실지는 이론처럼 쉽지 않다 It is not so easy in practice as in theory.
▶ 이 법칙은 간단한 것 같으나 실지로 응용하게 되면 그렇지도 않다 This rule may appear simple, but it is far from simple to put into effect.
■—**검증** on-the-spot inspection —**관찰** actual observation —**시험** a practical [field] test; a trail practice; 〈자동차의〉 a driving test —**연습** practice; practical exercise —**응용** practical application (of a theory) —**조사** an actual [on-the-spot] survey; the firsthand investigation —**지도** practical guidance —**훈련** on-the-job training

실지경험 實地經驗 practical [actual] experience; practical knowledge
♦ 실지경험이 있는 사람 a man of 《journalistic, teaching》 experience / 실지경험을 하다 have practical experience (in)
▶ 그는 장사의 실지경험이 부족하다 He lacks practical experience in business.

실지렁이 〔動〕 a tubifex 《pl. ~, -es》
실직 失職 unemployment; loss of employment
—**실직하다** lose one's job; be out of work
♦ 실직한 unemployed; jobless / 실직한 상태다 be unemployed; be out of job; have no job; 《英口》 be on the dole
■—**자** ⇨ 실업자

실질 實質 〈본질〉 substance; essence; 〈소질〉 quality; 〈재료〉 matter; material; 〈내용〉 contents
♦ 실질의 substantial; tangible / 비실질적인 논의 unsubstantial [impalpable, hollow, empty] argument
▶ 실질이 형식보다 중요하다 Substance is more important than form.
▶ 겉보기보다 실질을 택하라 Prefer substance to appearance [shadow].
■—**소득** a real income —**임금** real wages; a takehome pay

실질적 實質的 substantial; essential; material; solid ♦ 실질적 원조 substantial aid / 실질적 진보 substantial progress / 실질적으로 substantially; materially; practically
▶ 그런 사람들은 실질적으로는 로봇이다 Such people are practically [virtually] robots.

실책 失策 a blunder; a slip; a bungle; an error; a mistake; a misstep
♦대실책 a gross [huge] blunder [error]/ 사소한 실책 a small slip [mistake]/ 실책을 저지르다 commit a blunder [an error]; make a slip [mistake]; do *sth* amiss
▶1루수의 실책으로 그는 살았다 He reached the home plate on the first baseman's error.
▶저런 남자를 믿은 것이 실책이었다 I made a mistake in trusting such a man.

실천 實踐 practice
♦실천적인 practical / 실천적으로 practically —실천하다 practice; put (a theory) in [into] practice [action]; execute
♦자기가 가르치는 바를 실천하다 practice what *one* preaches.
▶그는 자신의 주장을 실천했다 He practiced what he had advocated.
■—가 a man of deeds [action]; a person of practical mind —도덕[윤리, 철학] practical morality [ethics, philosophy] —자 an executor; a performer —주의 activism

실천력 實踐力 power of execution; executive faculty [ability]; action ♦실천력이 있는 사람 a person [man] of action

실체 實體 〔哲〕 substance; matter; subject; entity; essence; the true nature (of)
♦실체적인 substantial; material; essential / 비실체적인 이론 an unsubstantial [incorporeal, inessential] theory / 실체를 알지 못하다 do not know what *sth* really is / …의 실체를 파악하다 grasp the facts of (a case) / 실체화하다 substantialize; substantiate
■—론 〔哲〕 substantialism; noumenalism —론자 a noumenalist —법 the substantive law; the law substantive —성 substantiality

실추 失墜 loss; fall
♦위신[면목]의 실추 loss of prestige
—실추하다 〈신용 등을〉 lose (*one's*) credit); forfeit; 〈신용 등이〉 fall; sink
▶유엔 총회에서 이 제안이 부결되어 미국은 크게 위신을 실추했다 When this proposal by the United States was rejected in the General Assembly of the United Nations, her prestige suffered a severe setback.

실측 實測 (actual) survey [measurement]; observation
—실측하다 survey; make a survey of (a forest); measure
■—도 a surveyed map: 2만분의 1 실측도 a 20,000 scale [1/20,000th] map

실컷 *one's* fill; to *one's* heart's content; to *one's* satisfaction; heartily; without reserve; unreservedly
♦실컷 울다 cry [weep] *one's* fill; have *one's* cry out; have a good cry; cry *oneself* out / 실컷 웃다 laugh heartily; have a good hearty laugh / 실컷 먹다 have [eat] *one's* fill (of); eat heartily / 실컷 마시다 drink *one's* fill
▶나는 지난 밤에 친구와 실컷 술을 마셨다 I drank heartily with my friend last night.
♦실컷 야단을 맞았다 I got a good scolding.

실크 silk ■—로드 the Silk Road —햇트 a silk hat; a top hat

실큼하다 be somewhat disliked (to do); be rather unpleasant [unpleasing]

실탄 實彈 〈소총의〉 a ball [live, loaded] cartridge; a solid (bullet); live ammunition; 〈대포의〉 a loaded [live] shell
♦실탄을 발사하다 fire ball cartridges
■—사격 〈소총의〉 ball firing; firing [target] practice with live shells [bullets]; 〈대포의〉 live-shell shooting [firing]

실태 失態 〈실수〉 a fault; an error; a blunder; 〈면목을 잃음〉 disgrace; ignominy
♦실태를 부리다 commit a blunder [an error]; disgrace *oneself*; expose *oneself* to ridicule

실태 實態 the actual condition [state]; the realities
♦소년 범죄의 실태를 조사하다 investigate the actual conditions of juvenile delinquency
▶그 종교 단체의 실태는 분명하지 않다 Not much is known with any certainty about the religious body.
■—조사 research on [an investigation into] the actual condition; a fact-finding survey

실터 the narrow empty area between one house and the next

실토 實吐 a true confession; telling the whole truth; speaking with sincerity
—실토하다 confess [own] (to); reveal *one's* real motive; disclose *one's* real intention
♦모조리 실토하다 make a clean breast of (the secrets); own up
▶그는 자기의 잘못을 서슴없이 실토했다 He confessed his faults readily enough.

실톱 〔機〕 a fret saw; 〈美〉 a jigsaw; 〈전동식의〉 a saber saw

실투 失投 〔野〕 a careless pitch [throw]; the careless delivery of a ball (by a pitcher) —실투하다 make a careless pitch

실파 a small green onion

실팍지다 solid ⇨ 실팍하다

실팍하다 solid; firm; strong; substantial; stout; strongly [sturdily] built
♦실팍한 토대 a strong [firm] foundation / 실팍한 사나이 a man of solid [sturdy] build
▶이 집은 실팍하게 지어졌다 This is a strongly built house. ⇌ The house is strongly built.

실패 〈실감개〉 a spool; a reel; a bobbin; a beam ♦실패에 감다 spool; reel; quill; wind (thread) on a spool [bobbin]

실패 失敗 (a) failure; unsuccess; miscarriage; ill success; 〈口〉 a flop; 〈俗〉 a washout
♦대실패 a glaring [a complete, an utter] failure; a fiasco (*pl.* ~es, ~s) / 실패로 돌아가다[끝나다] end [result] in (a) failure; prove [turn out] a failure; meet with failure; come to naught [a sorry end]
▶실험은 모두 실패로 끝났다 All the experiments failed [ended in failure].
▶내게는 실패가 도리어 약이 되었다 I learned a dear lesson by my failure.
▶같은 실패를 되풀이하지 말자 Let's try not to make the same mistake again.
▶그 작품은 완전한 실패작이다 The work is a complete failure [〈口〉 flop].
▶실패는 성공의 어머니 〈속담〉 Every failure is

a stepping stone to success. ⇌ Failure teaches success.
―실패하다 〈사람이 주어〉 fail; be unsuccessful (in); fall through; 〈영락하다〉 sink [come down]; 〈사물이 주어〉 fail; prove [turn out] a failure; end [result] in (a) failure; go wrong [amiss]
▶ 그는 시험에 실패했다 He failed [flunked] the examination.
▶ 그는 사업에 실패했다 He had a business reversal. ⇌ He failed in his business.
▶ 그들의 시도는 죄다 실패했다 Their attempts all met with failure.
▶ 우리의 계획은 실패했다 Our plans failed [fell through]. ⇌ Our plans went wrong [came to naught].
▶ 또 다시 실패하지 않도록 조심해라 See that you do not repeat your failure.
―자 a failure; 〈낙오자〉 a social failure
실하다 實― 1 〈튼튼하다〉 strong; solid; stout; firm; substantial; sturdy; strongly built
♦ 실한 몸 a strong [sturdy, stout] body / 실한 서가 a strongly built bookshelf
▶ 이 배는 실하게 만들어져 있다 This ship is solidly built.
2 〈재산이 넉넉하다〉 well-to-do; wealthy; solid; sound
♦ 장사 밑천이 실하다 have enough [sufficient] business funds
3 〈믿을 수 있다〉 reliable 《man》; trustworthy 《bank》; solid; substantial
▶ 그는 실한 사람입니까? Is he trustworthy [reliable, dependable]?
4 〈속이 옹골지다〉 full; substantial; solid; rich in content
♦ 내용이 실한 저작 a substantial work
▶ 이것은 내용이 실한 책입니다 This book is full of useful information.
실학 實學 practical science; realism ■―주의자 a realist ―파 a realistic [positive] school
실행 實行 〈실천〉 practice; action; deed; 〈명령·계획 등의〉 execution; performance; 〈이행〉 fulfilment; 〈법규의〉 enforcement; 〈실현〉 realization
♦ 실행 가능한 계획 a practicable project / 실행상 practically; in practice / 실행상의 practical; executive / 실행에 옮기다 translate 《it》 into action [reality, practice]; put 《it》 in action [practice]; set 《a plan》 going / 이론을 실행으로 옮기다 descend from theory to practice
▶ 그는 말뿐이지 실행이 따르지 않는다 He is a man of words, and not of deeds. ⇌ He is all talk and no action.
▶ 그 계획은 실행이 불가능하다 The plan [scheme] is not workable[impracticable]. ⇌ The plan is impossible (for us) to carry out.
―실행하다 practice; put *sth* in [into] practice; execute; implement; carry out 《a plan》; carry 《a plan》 into execution [effect]; enforce
♦ 실행할 수 있는 practicable; feasible; workable / 실행하기 어려운 impracticable; infeasible; unworkable / 계약을 실행하다 act up to an agreement
▶ 말한 것은 실행하라 Practice what you preach.
▶ 그런 계획을 실행하는 것은 식은 죽 먹기다 It's a cinch to carry out such a plan.
▶ 아무리 규칙이 좋아도 실행되지 않으면 소용이 없다 However good the rules may be, they are of no avail unless carried into effect.
―가 a man of action ―가능성 조사 a feasibility study ―력 ⇨ 실천력 ―예산 the operating [working] budget ―위원(회) the executive committee [commission]
실험 實驗 1 〈과학의〉 experimentation; 〈실험실에서의〉 laboratory work; 〈1회 마다의〉 an experiment; a test (▶experiment는 새 발견이나 이론의 실증, test는 기준에 적합한지의 검사가 목적임)
♦ 실험적(인) experimental; empirical / 실험적으로 experimentally; empirically; by way of [as an] experiment / 전기 실험을 하다 make an experiment in [on] electricity / 실험을 통해서 가르치다 demonstrate; teach by the help of experiments
▶ 그는 실험을 해서 성공했다 He carried out his experiment with success.
▶ 그 계획은 실험 중에 있다 The plan is still in the experimental stage. ⇌ The plan is under experiment.
―실험하다 experiment 《on, in》; make [conduct] an experiment [a test] 《on, in, with》; put *sth* to the test [proof]; experimentalize
2 〈경험〉 (practical) experience; one's personal experience
■ 동물― experiments with [using] animals; an experiment on animals 핵― a nuclear experiment [test]: 핵실험의 금지 a ban on nuclear tests 화학― a chemical experiment; an experiment in chemistry: 화학 실험을 하다 experiment in chemistry; make [carry out] a chemical experiment ―값 an experimental value ―과학 an experimental science ―극장 an experimental [a laboratory] theater; 〈라디오의〉 a radio workshop ―농장 an experimental [a pilot] farm ―단계 《be in》 an experimental stage ―도시 an experimental city ―동물 experimental animals ―론 [哲] positivism ―물리학 experimental physics ―소설 an experimental romance ―식 [化] an empiric(al) formula ―심리학 experimental psychology ―자 a tester; an experimentalist; an experimenter ―자료 an experimental data; 〈美〉 a guinea pig; a laboratory rabbit ―장 a proving [test] ground; a test center ―조수 a laboratory [(口) lab] assistant ―주택 a pilot house ―철학 empirical [positive] philosophy
실험대 實驗臺 a testing bench; an experiment stand; a laboratory table; 〈실험 대상〉 an experimental object
▶ 그들은 각종 신무기의 실험대가 되었을 뿐이었다 They were apparently just used as guinea pigs to test new weapons on.
실험실 實驗室 a laboratory; (口) a lab
■ (시청각)어학― a language lab 화학[물

리]— a chemical [physics] laboratory

실험주의 實驗主義 〈哲〉 experimentalism
■—자 an experimentalist

실현 實現 realization; attainment; actualization; materialization; fruition
♦ 꿈[희망]의 실현 the realization of *one's* dreams [hopes] / 실현 가능한 계획 a feasible plan
▶그 계획은 실현 단계에 이르렀다 The plan has reached the stage of realization.
―**실현하다** put 《a plan》 into practice; turn 《the dream of flight》 into reality; make 《a dream》 come true; bring 《an idea》 to fruition; 〈계획했던 일이〉 come off; materialize; realize; actualize; materialize; 〈예언 등이〉 come true
▶우주 여행은 머지않아 실현될 것이다 Manned space navigation will soon become an accomplished fact.
▶마침내 그의 소년 시절의 꿈이 실현되었다 His boyhood dream finally materialized [came true, became 《a》 reality].
▶나는 여름에 유럽으로 갈 예정이었으나 실현되지 않았다 I had planned to go to Europe for the summer, but it did not come off.
▶그의 예언은 아직 실현되지 않고 있다 His prediction remains unfulfilled.
▶그의 이상은 실현될 것 같지 않다 His ideal is unlikely to be realized [to be translated into reality].

실형 實兄 〈친형〉 *one's* own elder brother

실형 實刑 imprisonment; a prison [jail] sentence
▶그는 징역 3년의 실형을 선고 받았다 He was sentenced to three years in prison [three years' imprisonment] without a stay of execution. ⇌ They gave him a sentence of three years' penal servitude without a stay of execution.
■—판결 an actual prison sentence

실화 失火 an accidental fire
▶그 불은 실화가 아니고 방화였다 The fire was not accidental, but incendiary.
▶그 화재는 실화였다 The fire broke out through [was caused by] carelessness.
―**실화하다** have a fire started 《in a house》 by accident; start a fire through carelessness

실화 實話 a true story; a real-life story; an authentic account
♦ 실화를 토대로 한 영화 a film (that [which] is) based on a true story
▶이 짤막한 신상 이야기는 실화입니다 This brief history is a true story.
■—범죄— a factual account of crime ■—기사 fact articles 《of a magazine》

실황 實況 the real [actual] situation [condition]; the actual [real] state of things; the actual scene; 〈실지 상황〉 actual operation
♦ 실황을 시찰하다 inspect the real condition

실황방송 實況放送 〈텔레비전의〉 live broadcast; an on-the-spot telecast; 〈라디오의〉 minute-to-minute [on-the-spot] broadcasting; a running commentary; 〈스포츠의〉 play-by-play broadcasting; outside broadcasting
♦ 실황방송을 하다 broadcast live / 야구 경기를 실황방송하다 do a running [a play-by-play] commentary of a baseball game; broadcast a baseball game on the spot
■—자[아나운서] a play-by-play announcer; an on-the-scene commentator

실효 失效 a lapse; abatement; invalidation; becoming null and void ―**실효하다** lapse; lose effect; become null and void; be invalidated
♦ 실효된 lapsed

실효 實效 〈효과〉 practical [actual] effect; efficacy; practical results; 〈능률〉 efficiency
♦ 실효가 있다 be effective; be efficacious / 실효를 거두다 give satisfactory results; do good work; work
■—가격 an effective price 《of a commodity》 ―값[치] 〔電〕 an effective value ―성 effectiveness

싫건좋건 whether *one* will [likes it] or not; whether willing or not; willy-nilly
▶싫건좋건 난 혼자 그곳에 가야 한다 Whether I like it or not, I have to go there alone.

싫다 〈불쾌하다〉 disagreeable; unpleasant; distasteful; disgusting; offensive; (口) nasty; 〈달갑지 않다〉 undesirable; unwelcome; 〈지긋지긋하다〉 hateful; loathsome; abominable; 〈서술적〉 be unwilling [reluctant] 《to do》; do not like; dislike; hate; loathe; be loath 《to do》; abhor
♦ 싫은 것 what *one* does not like; *sth* offensive / 싫은 녀석 a disgusting [a disagreeable, an unpleasant, an odious] fellow; (俗) a stinker / 싫은 소리 words offensive [objectionable, unpleasant] to the ear / 싫은 일 an irksome [ungrateful] business; an ugly job; drudgery / 싫은 얼굴을 하다 make a wry face; make a grimaces; look offended [displeased]; frown
▶나는 그에게 듣기 싫은 소리를 해 주었다 I gave him a flea in his ear.
▶〔會話〕「월급날까지 만 원만 빌려줘」「싫어」 "Can you let me have ten thousand won till payday?" "No."
▶거저 줘도 싫다 I would not have it (even) as a gift.
▶남의 앞에 나서기 싫다 I don't want to be seen in company.
▶나는 그날은 누구도 만나기 싫었다 I was in no mood to see any caller that day.
▶〔會話〕「네 일이 마음에 드니?」「어떤 때는 싫습니다」 "Do you like your job?" "Sometimes I hate it."

싫어지다 come to dislike *sth*; become disgusted with; lose taste for; 〈물리다〉 become sick [tired, weary] of; lose interest in; 〈식상하다〉 be fed up with
♦ 사랑하던 여자가 싫어지다 fall out of love with *one's* girl
▶난 싫어진다 I am disgusted with myself.
▶너는 벌써 내가 싫어졌구나 You have lost interest in me, I suppose.

싫어하다 dislike; have a dislike to [for]; be unwilling [reluctant] 《to do》
♦ 싫어하는 abominable; detestable; loath-

싫증

some / 남들이 싫어하는 사람 a pest; an abominable [odious] person / 몹시 싫어하다 hate; loathe; detest; have a distaste for; abhor; be averse to / 돈을 내놓기를 싫어하다 grudge money / 폭력을 싫어하다 abhor violence
▶ 그녀는 접시 닦기를 몹시 싫어한다 She hates [detests, loathes] washing dishes.
▶ 이웃 사람들은 모두 그를 싫어한다 He is a nuisance to all the neighborhood.
▶ 그들은 결혼하기 싫어하는 딸을 시집보냈다 They married off their daughter against her will.

싫증 一症 aversion; repugnance; dislike; disgust; weariness
♦…에 싫증이 나다 be [get, grow] tired of…; get sick of…; be [become] disgusted with…; become weary of; lose interest in
▶ 나는 고전 음악에 싫증이 났다 I have lost interest in classical music.
▶ 그녀는 그의 촌스러운 태도에 싫증이 났다 She was repelled by his rustic manners.
▶ 그는 아무 것에나 곧 싫증을 낸다 He cannot stick to anything.
▶ 넌 매일 만화만 보면서 싫증나지도 않니 How can you read comics every day and not get tired of them?

심 心 1〈옷 등에 넣는 헝겊〉 interlining; a padding ♦심을 넣다 pad; interline 《a coat》
2〈양초심지〉 a wick
♦양초심지를 자르다 snuff a candle
3〈연필심〉 lead
4〈중심부〉 the center; 〈과실의 핵〉 the core; 〈고갱이〉 the heart; 〈뿌리〉 a string
♦심까지 썩다 be rotten to the core
5〈새알심〉 a dumpling

-심 心 a heart; a mind; a spirit; a sense
♦도덕심 a sense of public morality / 애국심 patriotism / 허영심 vanity

심각하다 深刻— serious; grave; keen; acute; poignant
♦심각한 인구문제 a serious population problem / 심각해지다 become intensified [aggravated]; assume an acute phase [a serious aspect]; become more acute [critical, urgent, strained]
▶ 얼굴이 심각한 데 무슨 일이냐? You look serious [grave]. What's the matter with you?
▶ 아프리카는 심각한 식량부족으로 고통 받고 있다 Africa is suffering from a serious food shortage.
▶ 그 일을 너무 심각하게 생각하지 마라 Don't be so serious about that matter.
▶ 금융 사정은 더욱더 심각해지고 있다 The financial condition is getting worse.

심경 心境 one's feelings; one's mood; a frame [state] of mind; a mental attitude [state]
♦심경의 변화 a change of mind / 평온한 심경 a tranquil [serene] mind / 현재의 심경 one's present state of mind / 심경을 털어놓고 express one's feelings; speak one's mind; open one's heart (to); talk about one's opinions (of)
▶ 심경의 변화로 그 계획을 단념했습니다 I changed my mind and abandoned the plan.

▶ 지금도 나의 심경에는 변함이 없다 My point of view has not changed since then.

심근 心筋 〔解〕 the myocardium 《pl. -dia》; a cardiac [heart] muscle ■—경색 myocardial [cardiac] infraction —경화증 cardiosclerosis —염 myocarditis —운동도 a myocardiogram

심금 心琴 heartstrings
▶ 그 소설은 독자의 심금을 울렸다 The novel struck a chord in the hearts of the readers.
▶ 그의 노래는 수많은 사람들의 심금을 울렸다 His song touched the heartstrings of many people.

심기 心氣 (a) humor; a temper; a mood; feelings
♦심기가 좋다 be in a good humor [mood]; be cheerful / 심기가 좋지 않다 be in an ill [a bad] mood [humor]; be out of humor [temper]; be displeased / 심기가 상쾌하다 feel refreshed

심기 心機 mental activity; the mind
♦심기 일전하다 one's mind takes a new turn; 〈사람이 주어〉 change one's mind; turn over a new leaf; become a new man
▶ 그는 심기 일전하여 사업에 전념했다 He changed his mind [turned over a new leaf] and put his soul into the business.

심기다 〈심게 하다〉 make [have] sb plant; 〈심어지다〉 get [be] planted

심난하다 甚難— extremely [very] difficult

심낭 心囊 〔動·解〕 a pericardium 《pl. -dia》; a heart sac

심내막 心內膜 〔解〕 an endocardium 《pl. -dia》 ■—염 endocarditis

심다 1〈식물을〉 plant; set (out); 〈옮겨 심다〉 transplant; 〈재배하다〉 grow; raise
▶ 그녀는 정원에 올리브나무를 심었다 She planted fragrant olives in the garden. ⇌ She planted the garden with fragrant olives.
▶ 우리는 감자를 심었다 We dibbled in potatoes.
▶ 밭에는 밀이 심어져 있다 The fields are planted with wheat.
▶ 우리는 뜰에 잔디를 심었다 We sodded our yard.
2〈사상 등을〉 implant; plant; fix; imbue
♦어린이의 마음에 건전한 신조를 심다 implant sound principles in a child's mind / 명확한 목적의식이 심어져 있다 be imbued with a sense of purpose
▶ 그 날 그의 행동은 그녀의 마음에 강한 불신감을 심어 놓았다 His conduct that day planted a strong distrust in her heart.

심대하다 甚大— very great; immense; enormous; tremendous; serious; heavy ♦심대한 손해[피해] a heavy [great] loss [damage] / 심대한 영향 a profound influence

심덕 心德 virtue; uprightness of heart

심도 深度 depth; fathom ♦심도를 재다 measure [plumb] the depth (of a lake); sound 《the sea》; take soundings (in)
■위험[안전, 잠험]— a critical [safe, submersible] depth ■—계 a depth gauge —측정 measurement of depth

심돋우개 心— a wick-raiser; a wick control

심드렁하다 1 〈탐탁지 않다〉 rather unwilling 《to》; uninterested 《in》; indisposed 《to do》 2 〈병이 오래 끌다〉 lingering; dragging ▶그는 병세가 심드렁하여 퇴원할 수 없었다 He was not released from (the) hospital because of his lingering illness.

심란하다 心亂— disturbed [confused] in mind; upset; agitated ▶편지를 읽고 그녀는 심란해졌다 The letter disturbed her.

심려 心慮 worry; anxiety; uneasiness of heart; concern; apprehensions ◆아무에게 심려를 끼치다 cause *sb* to feel anxiety; give *sb* trouble; trouble [worry] *sb* ▶많은 심려를 끼쳐 죄송합니다 I am sorry to have occasioned you (so) much anxiety. **—심려하다** worry about [over]; worry *oneself* about; be anxious [concerned] 《about》; apprehend

심령 心靈 spirit **—술**〈강신술〉spiritualism **—연구** psychical research; psychicism **—학** psychics **—학자** a psychicist **—현상** a spiritual [psychic] phenomenon

심로 心勞〈걱정〉cares; anxiety; worries;〈마음의 피로〉mental fatigue; worry; boredom **—심로하다** suffer from nervous strain; be mentally fatigued

심록 深綠 deep [dark] green

심리 心理 a state of mind; a mental state; psychology; mentality; the mind

> [解說] *a state of mind*는 일시적인 마음상태나 기분이고, *psychology*는 심리적인 상태나 기분, *mentality*는 정신능력을 강조한다.

◆미묘한 심리 delicate shades of psychology / 범죄자의 심리 the psychology of criminals / 보통 한국인의 심리 the mentality of an average Korean ▶넌 그녀의 심리를 이해하니? Do you understand her state of mind [psychology]? ▶나는 그의 심리를 통 알 수가 없다 I have no idea of his real state of mind. ▶이것은 보통 일본인의 심리를 잘 나타낸다 This speaks eloquently of the mentality of an average Japanese. ■**군중—** mass [mob] psychology ■**—묘사** (a) psychological description **—상태** a state of mind; a mental state; psychology **—사회학** psychosociology **—소설** a psychological novel **—언어학** psycholinguistics **—요법** psychotherapy **—작용** a mental process **—작전** psychological tactics **—전(쟁)** psychological warfare; 《口》a psywar **—주의**〔哲〕 psychologism **—테스트** a psycological test

심리 審理 (a) trial; (an) examination; (an) inquiry; (a) hearing ▶그 사건은 현재 심리중이다 The case is now under [on] trial. ▶심리중인 사항이므로 아무런 논평을 할 수 없습니다 It's sub judice, so I can make no comment on it. **—심리하다** try 《a case》; inquire 《into》; examine

심리적 心理的 mental; psychological ◆심리적으로 psychologically; mentally ▶이혼은 아이들에게 나쁜 심리적 영향을 준다 A divorce has bad psychological effects on children.

심리학 心理學 psychology; the science of mind; mental philosophy ◆심리학상(으로) psychologically ■**교육[민족, 사회, 아동]—** educational [folk, social, child] psychology **범죄[심층, 이상]—** criminal [depth, abnormal] psychology **산업—** industrial psychology **실험[임상]—** experimental [clinical] psychology **형태[위상 (位相), 행동주의]—** Gestalt [topological, behavioristic] psychology **—자** a psychologist

심마니 a (mountain) ginseng-digger ■**—말** ginseng-digger's jargon

심문 審問 a trial; a hearing; an inquiry; an examination; a formal interrogation ◆심문을 받다 be given a hearing; be tried; be examined ▶심문은 1주일 연기되었다 Hearing was postponed for a week. **—심문하다** try; hear 《a case》; give a hearing 《to a case》; put *sb* to trial; examine [inquire into] 《a case》; interrogate 《a witness》; question 《a witness》 ■**증인—** examination of a witness : 내일 증인 심문을 할 것이다 The examination of the witness will be made tomorrow.

심미 審美 esthetic appreciation; appreciation of the beautiful ◆심미적 esthetic(al) ■**—가** an esthete **—안** an eye for the beautiful; an esthetic sense; a sense of the esthetic : 그의 심미안은 뛰어나다 He has a good eye for the beautiful. **—주의** estheticism **—파** an esthetic school **—학** esthetics

심방 心房〔解〕an atrium 《*pl.* -ria》; an auricle

심방 尋訪 a visit ⇨ 방문

심벌 a symbol; an emblem ▶올리브 가지는 평화의 심벌이다 The olive branch stands for peace.

심벌리즘〈상징주의〉symbolism

심벌즈〈악기〉cymbals ■**—주자** a cymbalist

심병 心病〈근심〉anxiety; anguish; sickness at heart; worry;〈졸도〉a fainting fit

심보 心— nature ⇨ 마음보

심복 心服 admiration and devotion; honest [hearty] submission [obedience] **—심복하다** be devoted 《to》; serve *sb* faithfully;〈존경하다〉hold *sb* in high esteem

심복 心腹 1〈가슴과 배〉the heart and the stomach 2〈긴요한 것〉the indispensable; necessaries 3〈사람〉one's confidant [confident]; one's right-hand man ▶K의 심복이던 T가 암살당했다 T, who was K's confident, was assassinated. ■**—부하** a devoted [trusted, right-hand] subordinate

심부 深部 a deep part; a depth; the bottom ■**—감각**〔生〕deep sensation

심부름 an errand; a mission; a message; run-

심부전

ning errands
♦아이를 (우체국까지) 심부름 보내다 send a child (to the post office) on an errand / 심부름 가다 go [run] on an errand [a mission]; do [run] an errand
━심부름하다 do [run] an errand; run errands
▶유실물을 가져갈 누구 심부름할 사람 좀 사무실로 보내주시겠어요? Will you send someone to the office for what you've left here?
■━값[삯] a tip for [to] a messenger; an errand charge ━꾼 an errand boy; 〈사무실의〉 a messenger; an office boy

심부전 心不全 〔醫〕 cardiac insufficiency

심사 心事 the thoughts of the heart; cares; concerns

심사 心思 ill will; malicious intention; malice, malevolence
♦심사를 부리다 do *sb* something mean; 〈말로〉 say something spiteful; thwart; disturb; get in the way / 심사가 나쁘다[사납다] be malicious; be ill-natured; be evil-minded; be spiteful; be malevolent / 심사가 나다 get cross [sour]; bear malice
▶그녀에게 그토록 심사 부리지 마라 Don't be so mean [unkind] to her.

심사 深思 meditation; contemplation; deep thought; profound reflection; pensiveness
━심사하다 meditate 《on》; contemplate; ponder 《on, over》; muse 《on, upon》; be pensive; reflect profoundly; deliberate 《over》

심사 深謝 〈감사〉 hearty [sincere] thanks; deep [heartfelt] gratitude; 〈사과〉 a sincere apology
━심사하다 〈감사하다〉 thank *sb* heartily; express [extend] one's hearty [cordial] thanks; express *one's* sincere gratitude; 〈사과하다〉 make [offer] a sincere apology
▶베풀어주신 온정에 심사드립니다 〈편지투〉 I am deeply grateful to you for your kindness.

심사 審査 〈검사〉 (an) examination; (an) inspection; 〈조사〉 (an) investigation; 〈판정〉 judgment; 〈선발〉 screening
♦최종 심사 final screening / 심사에 합격하다 pass the examination; be accepted; be found eligible
▶정밀 심사 결과 그것이 허위임이 밝혀졌다 On closer inspection it proved to be false.
▶그의 그림은 국전 심사에 통과했다 His picture was accepted for the National Art Exhibition.
━심사하다 examine; inspect; investigate 《into》; judge; 〈美〉 screen
■━관[원, 위원] a judge; an examiner; a juror; 〈총칭〉 a panel of judges; a board of examiners; a judging [screening] committee; a jury ━위원장 〈시상식 등의〉 the president of the board of examiners; the chairman of the screening [awarding] committee

심사숙고 深思熟考 meditation; mature [due] consideration; deliberation; deep thought
♦심사숙고 끝에 after due [mature] consideration; after much [serious] thought
━심사숙고하다 meditate 《on》; contemplate; muse 《on, upon》; consider 《a matter》 well;

give deep thought; be lost in meditation; be sunk in deep thought
▶그는 그 돈을 어떻게 하면 좋을까 하고 심사숙고했다 He deliberated on what to do with the money.

심산 心算 an intention; a design; an idea; a purpose; a motive; calculation ⇨ 속셈 ①
♦…할 심산으로 with the intention [object, aim, idea] of…; with a view to 《doing》; in the hope of…; expecting that…/ …할 심산이다 intend to 《do》; will 《do》; have a mind to 《do》; mean to 《do》; think of 《doing》; be going to 《do》
▶무슨 심산인지 모르겠다 I cannot quite see [understand] his motive [idea].
▶그녀에게 무언가 심산이 있는 듯하다 She seems to have some secret idea.

심산 深山 a deep [remote] mountain; the depths of mountains; the heart of a mountain
■━유곡 steep mountains and deep valleys : 심산유곡에 깊이 deep in the mountains

심살내리다 have something to worry about all the time; be harassed by troubles

심상 心像 an image; a mental picture [image]

심상하다 尋常━ ordinary; common; usual; average; 〈평범하다〉 commonplace; 〈범상하다〉 mediocre; 〈표준이다〉 normal
♦심상치 않은 사태 a grave [critical, serious] situation / 심상치 않은 unusual; extraordinary; uncommon; serious; alarming; important / 〈일이〉 심상치 않게 되다 become [grow] serious [grave]; 〈affairs〉 take a serious turn
▶심상한 수단으로는 도저히 그를 이길 수 없다 Ordinary methods will not do to defeat him.
▶그는 심상치 않은 소리를 들었다 He heard an alarming sound.
▶일이 심상치가 않다 It is no common case [trivial matter].

심성 心性 〈마음씨〉 mind; mentality; 〈타고난 성질〉 nature; disposition; temperament
♦심성이 정직한 사람 a man of honest disposition / 심성이 곧은 사람 a man of firm character / 심성이 비뚤어진 ill-natured

심성암 深成岩 〔地質〕 plutonic [abyssal, hypogene] rocks

심술 心術 cross temper; ill nature; perverseness; crabbedness
♦심술굿은 perverse; cross; ill-natured; evil-minded; crabbed; wicked; malicious / 심술내다[부리다] give vent to *one's* cross [bad] temper; get [become, grow] cross [perverse]; do *sb* something mean; act surly [cross]
▶그는 심술궂은 말을 했다 He said spiteful things.
▶심술궂은 짓은 하지 마라 Don't be so nasty [mean].
▶그녀는 심술궂다 She is an ill-natured person [woman]. ⇌ She is mean.
▶그는 내가 늦게 왔다고 심술을 부렸다 He was cross with me for being late.
■━꾸러기[쟁이, 퉁이] an ill-natured person; a cross-grained[-tempered] person; a perverse [crabbed] person; a dog in the manger; a crosspatch ━패기 a contrary [perverse,

cursed, cross] child
심신 心身 mind and body; body and mind [soul] ♦ 심신을 단련하다 cultivate [train] *one's* body and mind / 심신이 상쾌해지다 feel refreshed in mind and body
▶ 그는 심신이 모두 건전하다 He is sound both in mind and body [mentally and physically].
▶ 그는 심신의 피로로 쓰러졌다 He collapsed from mental and physical exhaustion.
심신 心神 mind ♦ 심신이 혼란하다 be deranged; be unhinged in mind ■ —박약자 a weak-minded person —상실 〔法〕 lunacy
심실 心室 〔解〕 the ventricle of the heart; the cardiac ventricle ■ 우〔좌〕— the right [left] ventricle (of the heart)
심심소일 —消日 killing time ⇨ 심심풀이
심심풀이 killing time; a pastime; 〈기분 전환〉 (a) diversion
♦ 심심풀이가 되는 일〔것〕 a kill-time; a time-killer / 심심풀이로 by way of killing time; to kill (*one's*) time; to beguile an idle hour; to pass the tedious hours; as a pastime / 심심풀이로 장기를 두다 play chess to kill time [by way of killing time]/ 심심풀이로 텔레비전을 보다 watch TV as a pastime
▶ 나는 심심풀이로 거리를 어슬렁거렸다 I strolled along the streets as a diversion.
▶ 나는 심심풀이로 종종 추리소설을 읽는다 I often read detective stories to kill time. ≒ I often kill time (by) reading detective stories.
—**심심풀이하다** kill *one's* time; pass the time (away)
심심하다[1] 〈서술적〉 be bored; feel ennui; have a dull time
♦ 심심해 보이다 look bored; wear a bored look / 심심해서 독서를 하다 relieve *oneself* from ennui by reading
▶ 종일 비가 오는 바람에 심심한 일요일이었다 It turned out a boring Sunday because it rained all day.
▶ 난 심심해 죽겠다 I'm bored to death. ≒ I'm suffering from ennui. ≒ I've time on my hands.
심심하다[2] 〈조금 싱겁다〉 lightly salted; 〈서술적〉 be not salty enough; be [taste] slightly flat
심심하다 深甚— deep and profound
♦ 심심한 감사 profound gratitude; cordial [heartfelt] thanks / 심심한 사의를 표하다 express *one's* deepest gratitude [thanks] (to) / 심심한 경의를 표하다 express deep respect (for)
심안 心眼 *one's* mind's eye; inward eyes; mental vision ♦ 심안으로 보다 see with the eyes of the spirit; see with *one's* mind's eye / 심안을 뜨다 open *one's* eyes of the spirit
심야 深夜 the dead of night; midnight
♦ 심야까지 till late at night; until midnight / 심야에 at [in the] dead of night; at midnight
▶ 이 심야에 문을 두드리는 사람이 누굴까? Who is knocking on the door at this time of (the) night?
▶ 그는 심야까지 라디오를 듣고 있었다 He was listening to the radio far into the night [till late at night].
■ —방송 midnight broadcasting; a midnight [nightcap] broadcast [(radio [TV]) program] —영업 late-night operation : 심야 영업을 하고 있다 be open late at night —영화 a midnight movie —요금 a late-night charge —작업 midnight labor
심약 心弱 timidness; weak-mindedness; feeblemindedness; fainteartedness —심약하다 weak-minded; feebleminded; fainthearted
▶ 그는 심약한 남자다 He is a timid [fainthearted] man.
▶ 그렇게 심약한 소리 하지 말게 Don't get discouraged so easily.
심연 深淵 (out of) the depths; an abyss; a gulf; an abysmal chasm ♦ 마음의 심연을 들여다 보다 spy [look] into the depths of *sb's* heart [mind]
심오 深奧 profundity; deepness —심오하다 deep; profound ♦ 심오한 뜻 a deep [profound] meaning
심원 深遠 profundity; depth —심원하다 profound (theory); deep (meaning); abstruse (ideas); unfathomable (metaphors); esoteric
심원 心願 *one's* heart's desire; *one's* heartfelt wish; *one's* dearest wish
심원 深怨 deep grudge [resentment] ♦ 심원을 품다 bear *sb* a deep grudge; bear [have, (美)hold] a grudge against *sb*
심음 心音 heart [cardiac] sound ■ —기록계 a phonocardiograph —기록도 a phonocardiogram
심의 審議 deliberation; consideration; careful discussion; review; (美口) 〈철저한〉 a going-over
♦ 심의를 거듭한 끝에 after much deliberation; after due consideration / 심의중이다 be under consideration [discussion, deliberation]/ 심의에 부치다 refer 《a matter》 to discussion; bring 《a matter》 upon the tapis / 심의에 부쳐지다 be taken into deliberation / 심의를 종결하다 discontinue [cut short, leave off] deliberations
▶ 그 문제는 위원회의 심의에 부쳐졌다 The matter was referred [submitted] to the committee.
▶ 그 심의는 뒤로 돌리자 Let's table it for further deliberation.
▶ 그 법안의 계속 심의를 제안합니다 We propose that we should table the deliberations until the next session.
—**심의하다** deliberate (on) 《a subject》; consider; discuss; go through
♦ 축조 심의하다 discuss 《a bill》 article by article; review 《a document》 clause by clause
▶ 그 문제는 충분히 심의할 필요가 있다 We need to discuss the matter thoroughly.
■ —권 the right to deliberate —기관 an organ of consultation —미결사항 an unfinished matter [business] —미결의안 a pending bill; a bill shelved [(美) tabled] —회 a (deliberative) council; an inquiry commission : 교육〔경제〕심의회 an educational [economic] council
심이 心耳 1 〈마음과 귀〉 the mind and the ears

심인 心因 a psychological [mental] cause
♦심인성의 psychogenic 《symptoms》
■—성반응 (a) psychogenic reaction

심장 心臟 **1** 〔解〕 the heart
♦심장의 고동 the beating [throbbing] of the heart; a heartbeat / 심장의 기능 the function of the heart / 심장의 cardiac / 심장이 튼튼하다 have a strong [stout] heart / 심장이 약하다 [나쁘다] have heart trouble; have [suffer from] a weak heart
▶그는 심장 발작을 일으켰다 He had a heart attack.
▶그 소식에 나는 심장이 뛰었다 My heart beat fast at the news.
▶나는 심장이 멎는 것 같았다 My heart stood still. ⇌ I had my heart in my mouth.
▶나는 과로 때문에 심장이 약해졌다 My heart was weakened by overwork.
▶내 심장이 몹시 뛴다 My heart is beating violently [fast].
▶그의 심장의 고동이 멈추었다 His heart stopped beating.
2 〈배짱〉 nerve; cheek
♦심장이 약한 사람 a nerveless fellow / 심장이 약하다 be shy [timid] / 심장이 강하다 [강심장이다] be bold; be cheeky; be brazen-faced; have much nerve
▶넌 심장이 너무 약해 You want more nerve.
▶심장이 강하기도 하지 How cheeky he is! ⇌ What nerve he's got!
■—비대(증) hypertrophy of the heart; cardiac hypertrophy; cardiomegaly —수축 contraction of the heart; systole —염 inflammation of the heart; carditis —외과 heart [cardiac] surgery —이식(수술) a heart transplant [graft] (operation) —이완[팽창] dilatation of the heart; diastole —절개(수)술 cardiotomy —파열 rupture of the heart; cardioclasis

심장 深長 profundity —심장하다 profound; deep; abstruse
▶표현은 간략하되 의미는 심장하다 Simple in expression, deep in meaning. ⇌ The words are simple, but of profound significance.

심장마비 心臟痲痺 heart failure; paralysis of the heart; cardiac paralysis; a heart attack
▶그녀의 사인은 심장마비였다 She died of heart failure.
▶그는 심장마비를 일으켰다 He had a heart attack.

심장병 心臟病 a disease of the heart; a heart disease; heart trouble; cardiopathy
■—약 a heart medicine —환자 a patient with heart disease; a heart patient; a cardiac (patient)

심장부 心臟部 〔解〕 the region of the heart; 〈비유〉 the heart
♦서울의 심장부 the heart [center] of Seoul

심장판막 心臟瓣膜 a valve of the heart; a cardiac valve ■—증 〔醫〕 a valvular disease of the heart

심장학 心臟學 cardiology ■—자 a cardiologist

심재 心材 heartwood; duramen

심적 心的 mental; psychological
■—상태 a mental state; a state of mind; mentality —작용[결함] a mental action [defect] —태도 a mental attitude —포화 mental saturation —현상 a mental phenomenon

심전계 心電計 〔醫〕 an electrocardiograph

심전도 心電圖 〔醫〕 an electrocardiogram (略 ECG)

심정 心情 one's feelings; one's heart; one's sentiment ♦심정을 살피다 enter into sb's feelings [sentiment]; 〈동성하나〉 feel for sb; sympathize with sb
▶울고 싶은 심정이다 I feel like crying.
▶당신의 심정을 잘 알겠습니다 Of course I understand your feelings. ⇌ I can enter into your feelings.
▶그의 심정을 생각하니 나는 아무 말도 할 수가 없었다 I felt so sorry for him that I could say nothing.

심줄 a tendon ⇨ 힘줄

심중 心中 the heart; the mind; one's real intention; one's true motive
♦심중에 품다 keep 《a secret》 in one's bosom; cherish 《a hope》 in one's heart / 심중을 헤아리다 enter into [share] sb's feelings; sympathize with sb; feel for sb / 심중을 꿰뚫어 보다 see through sb's heart (to the core); penetrate sb's mind / 심중을 털어놓다 tell one's inmost thoughts (to); lay bare one's heart (to); take [admit] sb into one's confidence; unburden [unbosom] oneself (to sb)
▶그녀는 나에게 심중을 털어놓았다 She revealed [disclosed] what she felt to me.
▶나는 그녀의 심중을 헤아렸다 I deeply sympathized with her.

심증 心證 **1** 〔法〕 〈법관의 확신〉 a strong belief; a conviction
▶검사는 그 용의자가 진범이 아니라는 심증을 얻었다 The prosecutor had a firm belief [was convinced] that the accused was not the real culprit.
▶나는 그가 유죄라는 심증을 굳혔다 I was confirmed in my belief that he was guilty.
2 〈인상〉 an impression
♦심증을 나쁘게[좋게] 하다 give sb an unfavorable [a favorable] impression

심지 心— a (lamp) wick
♦양초의 심지를 자르다 snuff a candle / 램프의 심지를 자르다 crick [trim] a wick [lamp] / 램프의 심지를 올리다[줄이다] turn up [down] the wick; screw up [down] a lamp

심지 心地 nature; temper; disposition
♦심지가 고운 사람 a good-hearted person; a person with [who has] a heart of gold
▶그녀는 심지가 곱다 She is tender-hearted by nature. ⇌ She is good-natured.
▶그는 심지가 사나운 녀석이다 He has a crooked disposition. ⇌ He is warped by nature.

심지 心志 〈의지〉 (a) will (to do); 〈의도〉 (an) intention (to do); 〈목표〉 an aim

심지어 甚至於 even (as far as); to crown all;

the extreme case is...
▶그는 심지어 자기 이름도 쓸 줄 모른다 He cannot even write his own name.

심축 心祝 hearty congratulations; good wishes [blessings]
―**심축하다** congratulate *sb* heartily 《on》; offer *one's* hearty congratulations 《on》; bless *sb* inwardly; wish [pray] for *sb's* happiness from *one's* heart

심취 心醉 admiration; adoration; idolization; 〈몰두〉 devotion
―**심취하다** be fascinated [charmed] by; be devoted 《to》; adore; idolize
▶그는 김소월에 심취해 있다 He adores Kim So-wol.
■―**자** an ardent admirer [worshipper]; an enthusiastic devotee; an adorer

심층 深層 the depths 《of *one's* consciousness》
♦심층의 in-depth / 의식의 심층을 헤아리다 fathom the depths of *one's* consciousness
■―**구조** 〔言〕 deep structure ―**심리학** depth psychology

심통 心― bad disposition

심통 心痛 worry; anguish; mental agony; agony of mind; heartache
―**심통하다** worried; grievous
▶그녀는 심통한 나머지 자리에 누워버렸다 She has taken to her bed with worry.

심판 審判 〈재판 등의 판결〉 judgment; adjudgment; decision; 〈배심원의 판결〉 verdict; 〈경기의〉 refereeing; umpireship; umpirage; 〈사람〉 a referee; an umpire; 〈신의〉 judgment; trial
♦최후의 심판 the (Last) Judgment / 최후 심판의 날 the doomsday; the Judgment Day; the Day of Judgment / 공평[불공평]한 심판 a fair [an unfair] judgment / 심판을 받다 be judged; be tried; face *one's* trial
▶심판의 결정에 항의해 봤자 아무 소용이 없다 It's no use objecting [kicking at] an umpire's decision.
▶오늘 이 사건의 최종 심판이 내려집니다 The final judgment on this affair will be given today.
▶나는 오는 일요일에 열리는 야구[축구]의 심판을 부탁받았다 I've been asked to umpire the baseball game [referee the soccer match] next Sunday.
―**심판하다** referee 《a game》; umpire; act as (an) umpire; judge
■―**원**[관] a judge; an umpire; a referee; (口) a ref

심포니 a symphony ♦베토벤의 제9 심포니 Beethoven's Ninth Symphony ■―**오케스트라** a symphony orchestra

심포지엄 a symposium 《*pl.* ~s, -sia》 ♦대기오염에 관한 심포지엄을 열다 hold a symposium on air pollution

심하게 甚― 〈대단히〉 extremely; exceedingly; terribly; dreadfully; awfully; 〈격렬하게〉 violently; intensely; heavily; badly; 〈난폭하게〉 outrageously
♦심하게 굴다 behave [act] cruelly [harshly] / 심하게 다루다 treat *sb* severely [harshly, roughly]; be hard 《on, upon》 / 심하게 다투다 argue [quarrel] heatedly / 심하게 야단치다 scold severely; give *sb* a good scolding / 심하게 머리가 아프다 have a bad [an awful] headache
▶비가 심하게 오기 시작했다 It began to rain heavily [hard].
▶그 아이는 심하게 울기 시작했다 The baby began to cry horribly.
▶그는 그 자동차 사고로 심하게 부상당했다 He was badly [severely, seriously] injured in the car accident.

심하다 甚― 1 〈대단하다〉 extreme; excessive; terrible; 〈격렬하다〉 strong; severe; violent; intense; hard
♦심한 감기 a bad [nasty] cold / 심한 경쟁 (a) keen [hot, fierce, cutthroat] competition / 심한 노동 hard labor / 심한 바람 a violent [strong] wind / 심한 비 a heavy rain / 심한 손해 a heavy [stupendous] loss / 심한 통증 an acute [a severe, a violent] pain / 심한 기침을 하다 have a bad cough / 심한 상처를 입다 be badly [seriously] injured; hurt *oneself* badly [seriously]
▶그 거리는 교통 정체가 심하다 That street is heavily congested with traffic. ⇒ There is terrible traffic congestion in that street.
▶그의 병세는 더 심해졌다 His illness has taken a serious turn.
▶그녀는 심한 근시다 She is strongly [very] nearsighted.
2 〈잔인하다〉 cruel; bitter; harsh; rough; merciless; relentless; heartless; 〈난폭하다〉 outrageous; atrocious; 〈부당하다〉 unfair; unjust; unreasonable
♦심한 대우 (a) cruel treatment / 심한 말을 하다 say cruel [awful] things 《about》
▶그는 남에게 심한 짓을 한다 He treats others cruelly. ⇒ He is cruel to others.
▶그런 짓을 하다니 그녀도 참 심하구나 It is heartless [inconsiderate] of her to do such a thing.

심해 深海 the deep sea; the depths of the sea
■―**수심측량** bathymetry; deep-sea sounding ―**어** a deep-sea fish ―**어업** deep-sea fishing [fishery]

심혈 心血 the heart's blood; (비유) heart and soul; *one's* whole energy ♦심혈을 기울인 작품 *one's* most laborious work / 심혈을 기울여 heart and soul; with *one's* heart's blood
▶그는 그 작품에 심혈을 기울였다 He devoted himself to the work. ⇒ He put his heart and soul into the work. ⇒ He applied all his energies to the work.

심호흡 深呼吸 deep breathing [respiration]; a deep breath
―**심호흡하다** breathe deeply; do deep breathing; draw [take] a deep [full, long] breath; take deep breathing exercises; breathe in [inhale] deeply and then breathe out [exhale]

심혼 心魂 *one's* heart [soul] ♦심혼을 기울이다 put *one's* heart and soul into 《*one's* research》

심홍 深紅 〈빛깔〉 deep red; crimson

심화 心火 indignation; infuriation; (a) rage; heartburning; grief; fire of anger [jealousy]
♦ 심화가 끓어오르다 be infuriated [enraged]; be worried [distressed]; burn with wrath [jealousy]
▶ 자기 아들의 비행에 그녀는 심화를 끓였다 Her son's misconduct was the source of her distress [grief].

심화 深化 deepening —**심화하다** deepen

심황 −黃 〔植〕 a turmeric

심히 甚− very; quite; really; indeed ♦ 심히 유감스럽다 be really [quite] deplorable [shameful, regrettable]

십 十 ten; 〈로마숫자〉 X
♦ 제 십[10] the tenth / 수십번 scores [dozens] of times / 수십명의 사람 dozens of people / 10주년 기념일 a tenth anniversary; (美) a decennial / 10일 동안 for ten days

십각류 十脚類 〔動〕 decapod

십각형 十角形 〔幾〕 a decagon

십계명 十誡命 〔聖〕 the Ten Commandments; the Decalog(ue)

십구 十九 nineteen; 〈로마숫자〉 XIX
♦ 제 십구[19] the nineteenth / 19분의 1 a nineteenth; one-nineteenth / 19세기 the nineteenth century

십년 十年 ten years; a decade
♦ 10년간(間) for (the space [period] of) ten years / 10년전 a decade ago / 수십년 동안 for several decades / 10년마다 every ten years; once in ten years; once in a decade; decennially / 10년을 하루같이 without any change [a break] / 오랜 기간 / 십년 감수하다 have one's life shortened by ten years; 〈혼나다〉 have a narrow escape; have a hard [rough] time (of it)
▶ 한 번 실수로 십년 공부 나무아미타불 An hour may destroy what took an age to build. ⇌ A small miscalculation can ruin [wreck] one's hardwork.
▶ 십년이면 강산도 변한다 Ten years is an epoch.
—**지기**(知己) an old friend; a friend of long standing

십대 十代 〈연령의〉 one's teens

〔解說〕 영어에서는 13세에서 19세까지 즉, 연령을 나타내는 숫자에 **-teen**이 붙은 사람들을 **teen·ager**라고 부른다.

♦ 십대의 소년[소녀] a teen-ager; a teen-age boy [girl] / 십대의 teenage(d); of teen age; in one's teens / 십대 초반[후반]이다 be in one's early [late] teens
▶ 그녀는 10대에 결혼했다 She married in her teens.

십리 十里 10 *ri*

십만 十萬 a hundred thousand

〔解說〕 영어에는 「만」이란 단어는 없고 「1,000의 10배」로 생각해서 ten thousand라고 한다. 따라서 「10만」은 **a [one] hundred thousand**가 된다.

♦ 수십만의 사람들[희생자] hundreds of thousands of people [victims]

십배 十倍 ten times
♦ 6의 십배 ten times six / 십배의 ten times; tenfold / 십배로 하다 multiply ten ((the number)) times [by ten] /…보다 십배나 크다 be ten times as large as…

십분 十分 1 〈시간〉 ten minutes
2 〈십등분〉 division in ten ♦ 10분의 1 one-tenth; a tenth (part) / 10분의 6 six-tenths —**십분하다** divide *sth* into ten
3 〈충분히〉 enough; sufficiently; fully; in full; to the full; amply; plentifully; in plenty; satisfactorily
♦ 십분 이용하다 make full use of; make the best use of / 실력을 십분 발휘하다 show one's ability to the full

십사 十四 fourteen; 〈로마숫자〉 XIV
♦ 제 십사[14] the fourteenth / 14분의 1 a fourteenth; one-fourteenth
—**처**(處) 〔가톨릭〕 the stations of the cross
—**행시** fourteen-line verse; a sonnet

십삼 十三 thirteen; 〈로마숫자〉 XIII
♦ 제 십삼[13] the thirteenth / 13분의 1 a thirteenth; one-thirteenth / 13일의 금요일 Friday the thirteenth; Black Friday

십상 〈안성맞춤〉 the right thing (for); just the thing (for); 〈부사적〉 just (well); right; best; perfectly
♦ 십상인 ideal; suitable 《for》; fit 《for》; the very; right; best
▶ 여기는 책을 읽기에 십상인 장소다 This is a suitable [fit, good] place for reading.
▶ 하이킹하기에는 십상 좋은 날씨다 It is an ideal weather for hiking.
▶ 이 옷은 네게 십상 잘 어울린다 This dress fits you perfectly.

십시일반 十匙一飯 〔속담〕 All hands to the pump(s). ⇌ Every little helps.

십억 十億 (美) a billion; (英) a milliard; a thousand million(s) ♦ 수십억 달러 billions of dollars

십오 十五 fifteen; 〈로마숫자〉 XV
♦ 제 십오[15] the fifteenth / 15분의 1 a fifteenth; one-fifteenth / 1시간 15분 an hour and a quarter / 15주년 기념일 the fifteenth anniversary; a quindecennial / 10시 15분에 at (a) quarter past [after] ten

십오야 十五夜 a full moon night ⇨ 삼오야(三五夜)

십육 十六 sixteen; 〈로마숫자〉 XVI
♦ 제 십육[16] the sixteenth / 16분의 1 a sixteenth; one-sixteenth / 16 밀리미터 필름 a 16 mm (movie) film; a 16-millimeter film / 16분 음표 〔樂〕 a sixteenth note; a semiquaver

십이 十二 twelve; a dozen; 〈로마숫자〉 XII
♦ 제 십이[12] the twelfth / 12분의 1 a twelfth; one-twelfth
—**각형** 〔幾〕 a dodecagon —**사도**(使徒) the (Twelve) Apostles —**진법** 〔數〕 duodecimals; the duodecimal system

십이궁 十二宮 the twelve mundane houses; the (twelve) signs of the zodiac ■—**도** a diagram [figure] representing the zodiac; the

horoscope
십이면체 十二面體 〚幾〛 a dodecahedron
십이월 十二月 December (略 Dec.)
십이지장 十二指腸 〚解〛 the duodenum (*pl.* ~s, -na) ♦십이지장의 duodenal ■—궤양 a duodenal ulcer —염 〚醫〛 duodenitis
십이지장충 十二指腸蟲 〚動〛a hookworm; an ancylostome. —병 hookworm disease; ancylostomiasis; uncinariasis
십인십색 十人十色 So many men, so many minds. ▶사람의 취미는 십인십색이다 There's no accounting for tastes.
십일 十日 〈열흘〉 ten days; 〈열흘 날〉 the tenth ♦11월 10일에 on the tenth of November; on November 10
십일 十一 eleven; 〈로마숫자〉 XI ♦제 11 the eleventh / 11분의 1 an eleventh; one-eleventh
■—각형 an undecagon; a hendecagon —면 관세음보살 the eleven-faced Buddhist Goddess of Mercy
십일월 十一月 November (略 Nov.)
십일조 十一租 a tithe; 〈英〉 tithes ♦십일조를 내다[부과하다] tithe
십자 十字 a cross ♦십자로 crosswise / 십자(형)의 cross-shaped; cross; cruciform / 〈가슴에〉 십자를 긋다 cross *oneself*; make the sign of the cross on *one's* breast
■—낱말풀이 a crossword puzzle
십자가 十字架 a cross; 〚基〛 the (Holy) Cross ♦십자가에서의 죽음 the Crucifixion / 십자가 모양의 cruciform / 십자가를 지다 bear *one's* cross / 십자가에 못박다 crucify; put *sb* on the cross ■—성— the holy [real, true] cross
십자고상 十字苦像 〚가톨릭〛 a crucifix
십자군 十字軍 〚史〛 Crusade ■—전사(戰士) a crusader; a soldier [warrior] of the Cross
십자로 十字路 a crossroads (〈보통 단수 취급〉; crossing [intersecting] streets
♦십자로에 서다 stand at a crossroads
▶십자로를 오른쪽으로 도시오 Turn to the right at the crossroads.
십자매 十姉妹 〚鳥〛 a society finch
십자수 十字繡 a cross-stitch ♦십자수를 놓다 cross-stitch
십자포화 十字砲火 (a) cross fire ♦십자포화를 적에게 퍼붓다 pour fire on the enemy from different angles; pour a cross fire on the enemy
십장 什長 a foreman (of a group of workers); an overman; a gangmaster; 〈英〉 a gaffer; a boss
십종경기 十種競技 decathlon; an athletic contest in ten track and field events
■—참가자[선수] a decathlon contestant; a decathlonist
십주희 十柱戱 tenpins ⇨ 볼링
십중팔구 十中八九 〈부사적〉 in nine cases out of ten; ten to one; most likely; in all probability
▶이 병에 걸리면 십중팔구 죽는다 This disease proves fatal in most cases.
▶그녀는 십중팔구 온다 You can count on her coming.

▶십중팔구 그는 성공할 것이다 Ten to one he'll succeed.
십진 十進 progressing by tens ⇨ 십진법
♦십진의 decimal; denary
■—분류법 〈도서의〉 decimal classification; the Dewey [decimal] system
십진법 十進法 the decimal system [scale]; the denary scale [notation] ♦십진법으로 decimally; on the decimal system / 십진법으로 하다 decimalize
십철 十哲 ten sages ♦공자 문하(門下)의 십철 the ten leading disciples of Confucius
십칠 十七 seventeen; 〈로마숫자〉 XVII ♦제 17 the seventeenth / 17분의 1 a seventeenth / 방년 17세의 처녀 (a girl of) sweet sixteen (▶영어로는 16세)
십팔 十八 eighteen; 〈로마숫자〉 XVIII ♦제18 the eighteenth / 18분의 1 an eighteenth
■—금 18-carat gold; gold 18-carat fine
십팔기 十八技 18 martial arts
싯- deep; pure; intense
싯누렇다 bright [vivid] yellow
♦문을 싯누렇게 칠하다 paint the door vivid yellow
싱가포르 〈나라 이름〉 Singapore; 〈공식명〉 the Republic of Singapore
♦싱가포르의 Singaporean
■—사람 a Singaporean
싱겁다 1 〈짜지 않다〉 not salty enough; not well salted; slightly salted; 〈별맛이 없다〉 flat; tasteless; 〈술·담배 등이〉 weak; mild; watery [light, thin] 《liquor》
♦맛이 싱겁다 taste flat; be flat to the taste; be insipid / 싱겁게 먹다 cut down on the salt / 싱겁게 요리하다 salt food only slightly; use only a little salt in the seasoning
▶이 국은 싱겁다[약간 싱겁다] This soup needs more [a touch of] salt.
▶그 커피는 싱거웠다 The coffee was too weak.
2 〈언행이〉 dull; tedious; boring; wearisome; flat
♦싱거운 사람 a boring person; a bore; a wishy-washy person / 싱거운 소설 a dull novel
▶싱겁게 이겨서 감동이 없었다 It was such an easy victory that we weren't impressed.
싱그레 with a gentle [sweet] smile
♦싱그레 웃다 smile sweetly (at); smile a sweet smile; grin (with delight)
싱글 1 〚테니스〛 (a match of) singles ♦여자 싱글 결승전 a women's singles final match / 싱글 경기를 하다 play singles 《of tennis》
2 ⇨ 싱글 히트
3 〈미혼자〉 a single [an unmarried] person
4 〈양복〉 a single-breasted 《coat》
5 〈침대〉 a single bed
■—코트 〚테니스〛 a single court
싱글거리다 smile gently [sweetly]; beam with a gentle smile
싱글벙글 with a broad smile; with a smiling face; smilingly; beamingly
—**싱글벙글하다** smile happily [radiantly]; be all smiles; look happy

싱글히트 〔野〕 a single (hit); a one-base hit; a one-bagger ♦싱글히트를 치다 make a base hit
♦싱글벙글하는 얼굴 a smiling [beaming] face; a radiant [happy] look
▶그녀는 만족하여 싱글벙글했다 She beamed with satisfaction.

싱숭생숭하다 feel restless [fidgety, nervous, uneasy]; be ill at ease
▶나는 온종일 싱숭생숭했다 I spent the whole day in a state of nervous excitement.
▶그 생각만 해도 나는 싱숭생숭해진다 The thought of it makes me restless.

싱싱하다 fresh; young and fresh; fresh as paint; lively; 〈팔팔한〉 green
♦싱싱한 생선 a fresh fish; a fish fresh from the water / 싱싱한 야채[과일] fresh vegetables [fruits]
▶꽃은 물을 주면 싱싱해진다 Flowers revive in water.

싱어 〈가수〉 a singer ■재즈— a jazz singer

싱커 〔野〕 a sinker; a sinker ball

싱크 〈개수대〉 a sink; a water basin in a kitchen

싱크로나이즈드스위밍 〔泳〕〈수중 발레〉 synchronized swimming

싱크로트론 〔物〕 a synchrotron

싱크로플래시 〔寫〕 a synchroflash

싱크탱크 〈두뇌집단〉(口) a think tank

싱클레어 〈미국의 소설가〉 Sinclair, Upton Beall (1878-1968)

싶다 1 〈바라다〉 want 《to do》; hope 《to do》; wish 《to do》; like 《to do》; long 《to do》; be anxious; be [feel] inclined to 《do》; feel like 《doing》
♦꼭[몹시] …하고 싶다 be anxious [eager, impatient, dying] to 《do》 / …하고 싶지 않다 hate 《doing, to do》; be unwilling [reluctant, loath] 《to do》
▶나는 의사가 되고 싶다 I want [wish, hope] to be a doctor.
▶이번 여름에는 유럽에 가고 싶다 I want [would like] to go to Europe this summer.
▶꼭 해외유학을 하고 싶다 I am very anxious [eager, longing] to go abroad for study.
▶〔會話〕「영화보러 가려는데, 같이 갈래?」「가고 싶지만, 공부해야 해」 "I'm going to the movies. Do you want to come with me?" "I'd like [love (주로 여성)] to, but I have to study."
▶감기 때문에 아무것도 하고 싶지 않다 Because of my cold, I don't feel like doing anything at all.
▶네 생일 파티에 가고 싶었어 I wished [wanted, would like] to have come to your birthday party.
▶갖고 싶은 것은 무엇이든 사줄게 I will get you anything you want.
▶지금도 낚시하러 가고 싶은 생각이 없지는 않다 I have a half wish to go fishing even now.
▶그녀는 무엇이든 자기 하고 싶은 대로 했다 She did everything (as) she pleased [liked]. ⇒ She had her own way in everything.
▶십년만 더 젊었으면 싶다 I wish I were [(口) was] ten years younger.
▶그가 이번에는 합격했으면 싶다 I wish he would pass this time.
▶그 소식이 사실이 아니었으면 싶다 I hope [pray] the news will not prove true.
▶이 회사를 그만두고 싶다 I mean [intend] to quit this company.
2 〈추측되다〉 look; seem; appear; be likely 《to do》
▶눈이 올듯 싶다 It looks like snow. ⇒ It is likely to snow.
▶그는 아픈가 싶다 He seems to be sick. ⇒ I feel (that) he is sick.
▶그가 올성 싶지 않다 It is not likely that he will come. ⇒ He is not likely to come.
▶그녀는 성실하지 않은듯 싶다 I feel doubtful of her sincerity.
▶이 구두는 내 발에 맞지 않을 듯 싶다 I'm afraid these shoes will not fit me [my feet];

싶어하다 want to; wish to; desire; be eager to; be anxious to; long to; long for
♦무엇이든 알고 싶어하는 사람 an inquisitive person / 몹시 …하고 싶어하다 be eager [anxious, impatient] to 《do》
▶그는 배우가 되고 싶어한다 He wants to be an actor.
▶아버지는 내가 오랫동안 갖고 싶어한 자전거를 사주셨다 My father bought me the bicycle I had wanted for a long time.
▶그녀는 고향에 돌아가고 싶어한다 She longs to go back to her hometown.
▶그는 고향 소식을 듣고 싶어했다 He was anxious for [to hear] the news from home.
▶어머니는 어린시절에 대해 말하고 싶어하지 않으셨다 My mother was reluctant to talk of her childhood.
▶누구나 평온 무사한 생활을 하고 싶어한다 Everybody wishes to lead [wishes for] a peaceful and quiet life.

싸개 a wrapper; wrapping paper [cloth]; a covering; cover material; a (slip) cover
■책— a book jacket; a dustcover
—장이 an upholsterer —질 upholstering

싸개통 〈말다툼〉 a verbal quarrel; a squabble; a row; 〈욕먹기〉 a kangaroo court; trial by one's comrades

싸고돌다 1 〈에워싸다〉 crowd round; cluster [throng] around; turn around; rotate; 〈추종하다〉 form a small clique [an intimate circle, an inside group] around sb
▶그들이 사장을 싸고도는 자들이다 They are the president's followers [hangers-on].
2 〈두둔하다〉 protect; cover; favor; take sb under one's wings; shield [screen] 《sb from》
▶그녀는 막내만 싸고돈다 She is partial to [favors] her youngest child only.

싸구려 a cheap [low-priced] article; cheap goods
♦싸구려 구두 shoes of low price and poor quality / 싸구려 여인숙 a cheap inn
▶싸구려는 한눈에 알 수 있다 I can tell cheap articles at a glance.
▶이 시계는 싸구려지만 시간은 정확하다 This watch is cheap, but it keeps good time.

▶ 싸구려도 괜찮다 Something inexpensive will be fine.

싸느랗다 cool; chilly ♦ 싸느란 방 a chilly room

싸늘하다 1 〈차다〉 cold; chill(y); cool; icy; freezing
♦ 싸늘한 바람 a chilly [cold] wind / 싸늘해지다 become [get] cold [chilled, chilly]
▶ 난방이 안돼서 방이 싸늘했다 There was no heating and the room was chilly.
2 〈냉담하다〉 cold; distant; icy; indifferent; cold-hearted; cold-blooded
♦ 싸늘한 웃음 a cold smile / 싸늘한 태도 a cool [cold] attitude; a distant air
▶ 그들의 사이가 싸늘해졌다 Their relationship had gone [turned] cold.

싸다¹ 1 〈포장하다〉 wrap (in); pack (up) 《goods》; bundle 《clothes》
♦ 손수건[보자기]에 싸다 tie [do, wrap] up *sth* in a handkerchief [cloth wrapper] / 꾸러미를 싸다 make up a bundle [package] / 여행가방에 옷을 싸다 pack clothes in a suitcase / 도시락을 싸다 (美) fix a lunch; pack a lunch basket [box] / 단단히 싸다 pack well [securely]; wrap up tightly [fast] / 담요로 몸을 싸다 wrap *oneself* in a blanket
▶ 오늘밤에 짐을 싸는 편이 좋겠어 We had better pack our things tonight.
▶ 책을 모두 한데 싸주시오 Make one parcel of those books. ⇒ Put those books into one parcel.
▶ 선물용으로 싸주세요 Please gift-wrap it.
▶ 싸 드릴까요? Shall I wrap it up?
2 〈덮다〉 cover 《with》; veil 《in》
♦ 얼굴을 복면으로 싸다 veil *one's* face; cover *one's* face with a veil

싸다² 〈대·소변을〉 excrete 《urine, feces》; void; discharge; 〈사정하다〉 ejaculate
♦ 똥을 싸다 have a bowel movement; (卑) shit; defecate; (비유) have a hard time of it; get the worst of it; (俗) get a real raw deal / 오줌을 싸다 urinate; pass [discharge] urine; (俗) pee; (卑) piss / 이불에 오줌을 싸다 wet *one's* bed / 길에서 오줌을 싸다 urinate [relieve *oneself*] in the street

싸다³ 1 〈입이 가볍다〉 talkative; prattling; gossipy; glib(-tongued)
♦ 입이 싼 사람 a blabber (mouth); a tattler; a chatterbox
2 〈동작이 빠르다〉 swift; fast; nimble; quick
♦ 걸음이 싸다 be quick [swift] of foot; have a quick step / 싸게 걷다 walk with light steps
▶ 무엇이든 싸게 해치워라! Be quick in doing everything!
3 〈불길이 세다〉 intense; burning fast
▶ 불길이 싸서 머리카락을 그슬렸다 The heat of the fire was so great that my hair got singed.

싸다⁴ 1 〈값이〉 cheap; inexpensive; economical; low(-priced); of low price

解説 *cheap*에는 「싸구려의, 조악한」의 뜻이 있으므로 보통 *inexpensive*가 흔히 쓰인다. 이러한 경향은 (英)보다는 (美)에서 뚜렷하다.

「싼 값」은 *a low price,* 「값이 싸다」는 The price is low. 가 원칙이지만 격식을 차리지 않는 표현에서는 a cheap price, The price is cheap. 이라고도 한다.

♦ 싸게 치이다 cost little; come cheap / 싸게 사다 buy [get] cheap / 싸게 팔다 sell cheap; sell at low prices [a small profit] / 아주 싸게 팔다 sell dog-cheap [(口) dirt-cheap]; sell at the lowest possible price
▶ 요새는 사과가 싸다 Apples are cheap [low in price] now. ⇌ Apples are selling cheap now.
▶ 생활용품은 대개 싸다 Daily necessities are generally inexpensive.
▶ 싼 요금으로 차를 빌렸다 I rented a car at low rates.
▶ 싼 급료로는 지내기가 어렵다 I have a hard time getting by on my low salary.
▶ 그 값이면 싸다 It's cheap [a good bargain] at that price.
▶ 그는 차를 싸게 팔았다 He sold the car cheap [cheaply].
▶ 나는 시계를 싸게 샀다 I bought a watch cheap [at a low price]. (▶ sell, buy, get과 같이 쓰일 때는 cheaply보다 cheap이 보통)
▶ 좀더 싸게 해 주실 수 없어요? Can't you make it a little cheaper? ⇌ Can't you come down [reduce] the price a little more?
▶ 생각보다 싸게 샀다 I bought it cheaper than I (had) expected.
▶ 단체 해외 여행이 싸게 먹힌다 Going abroad on a package tour is economical.
2 〈마땅하다〉 be due; be well deserved
▶ 그런 인간은 벌을 받아 싸다 Such a person well deserves the punishment.
▶ 그래 싸다 It serve(s) you [him, her] right! ⇌ (美) You had it coming!

싸다니다 go [gad, wander] about; loiter; roam ▶ 하루종일 싸다니다 gad about all day long ▶ 밤중에 혼자 싸다니는 것은 위험하다 It is dangerous to go out alone at night.

싸데려가다 〈신랑이〉 《the groom》 give a dowry

싸라기 1 〈쌀의〉 broken rice; crushed [waste] rice 2 ⇨ 싸라기눈

싸라기눈 graupel; snow pellets; soft hail

싸락눈 snow pellets ⇨ 싸라기눈

싸리(나무) 〔植〕 a bush clover

싸매다 wrap *sb* up and tie; tie [bind] up
♦ 수건으로 머리를 싸매다 with a towel worn [tied] round *one's* head / 머리를 싸매고 공부하다 study as hard as *one* can / 머리를 싸매고 누워 있다 be [lie] in bed with a towel worn [tied]

싸우다 1 〈다투다〉 quarrel [have a quarrel] 《with *sb* over a matter》; exchange (angry) words; have a row 《with》; wrangle; brawl; 〈논쟁하다〉 dispute; argue; have a dispute [an argument]; engage in a controversy; 〈사이가 틀어지다〉 disagree 《with》; fall out 《with》; 〈치고 받고 하다〉 fight; scuffle; come to blows
♦ 자리를 차지하려고 싸우다 struggle [scramble] for a seat / 유산을 놓고 싸우다 quarrel

싸움

[argue] over the inheritance / 법정에서 싸우다 go to law 《with, against》; contend at law / 사소한 일로 싸우다 quarrel with *sb* about [over] trifles / 싸우게 하다 make *sb* fight with [against] 《another》; set *sb* to fight with 《another》
▶ 그는 언제나 살림살이를 놓고 아내와 싸운다 He always disputes with his wife about the housekeeping.
▶ 옆방에서 싸우는 소리가 들렸다 I heard the voices of people quarreling in the next room.
▶ 나는 대법원까지 가더라도 싸울 것이다 I won't drop the suit even if I have to take it all the way to the Supreme Court.
2 〈전쟁하다〉 make war 《on》; wage war 《against, with》; go to war; fight 《with, against》; fight a battle; engage in battle; battle; 〈1대 1로〉 combat 《with》; 〈소규모로〉 scuffle; 〈우연히 적과 마주쳐서〉 encounter
♦ 우세한 대군[적군]과 싸우다 fight against overwhelming odds [with an enemy] / 마지막 한 사람까지 싸우다 fight to the last man
▶ 영국은 프랑스와 함께 독일에 대항하여 싸웠다 Great Britain fought with France against Germany.
▶ 그들은 필사적으로 싸웠다 They fought in desperation.
▶ 그들은 새벽까지 적과 치열하게 싸웠다 They fought fiercely [a fierce battle] against their enemies until dawn.
3 〈경기하다〉 engage in contest; play games 《with》
♦ 정정당당하게 싸우다 play a fair game / 우승[선수권]을 걸고 싸우다 fight for championship; play for the title
▶ 정정당당하게 싸우자 Let's play fair.
4 〈곤란 등과〉 struggle 《against》; grapple 《with》; strive 《with》; contend 《with》
♦ 가난[고난]과 싸우다 struggle against [with] poverty [difficulties] / 더위와 싸우다 endure [bear, put up with, stand against] the heat / 운명과 싸우다 fight [struggle] against fate / 유혹과 싸우다 resist temptation / 졸음과 싸우다 fight off sleep; withstand sleepiness / 나라를 위하여 싸우다 fight for *one's* country / 자유를 위하여 싸우다 fight [struggle] for freedom / 평화를 위하여 싸우다 strive for peace / 최후[끝]까지 싸우다 fight to the end [to the death]; fight to a [the] finish; fight it out; see a war through
▶ 의사들은 암과 싸우고 있다 Doctors are carrying on a war against cancer.

싸움 1 〈말다툼〉 a quarrel; a wrangle; a brawl; a squabble; a row; 〈논쟁〉 a dispute 《on, over》; an argument; a controversy; 〈불화〉 feud; a conflict; disagreement; a discord; strife; 〈격투〉 a fight; a scuffle
♦ 큰[대판] 싸움 a big row; a big quarrel / 시시한 싸움 a petty quarrel / 학문상의 싸움 an academic controversy / 땅 소유권에 관한 이웃과의 싸움 a dispute with *one's* neighbors over the ownership of the land / 물을 둘러싼 부족간의 싸움 strife between the tribes over water / 싸움의 불씨[원인] the cause of a quarrel; a bone of contention; 〖그神〗 the apple of discord / 싸움을 벌이다 〈말다툼을〉 quarrel 《with》; have a quarrel; 〈주먹다짐을〉 come to blows; fall to (blows) / 싸움을 붙이다 make *sb* quarrel / 싸움을 말리다 [그만두게 하다] put down a fight; make people stop fighting / 싸움을 그치다 stop fighting; put down a fight / 싸움을 걸다 pick [seek, provoke] a quarrel with *sb*; provoke *sb* to a quarrel / 파벌 사이의 싸움에 말려들다 be dragged into [be involved in] factional conflicts [strifes, disputes]
▶ 두 집안 사이에는 싸움이 끊이지 않았다 The two families were constantly at feud with each other.
▶ 그가 싸움을 걸어와 맞붙어 싸웠다 He tried to pick a fight with me, so I accepted the challenge.
▶ 저 부부는 언제나 싸움을 한다 That couple is [are] always having a row.
2 〈전쟁〉 (a) war; warfare; 〈전투〉 a fight; a battle; 〈1대 1의〉 a combat; 〈소규모의〉 a scuffle; a skirmish
♦ 목숨을 건 싸움 a battle for life / 싸움에 대비하다 prepare for war / 싸움에 이기다 gain [win] a victory; gain [win, carry] the day; come out victorious (in a battle) / 싸움에 지다 lose the day [a battle]; be defeated (in a battle); be beaten in battle
▶ 두 나라간에 싸움이 터졌다 A war broke out [started] between the two countries.
▶ 두 나라는 싸움에 돌입했다 The two nations entered into [upon] a state of war.
▶ 그 사건은 두 나라간의 싸움으로 번졌다 The incident developed into war between the two countries.
3 〈경쟁·경기〉 a game; a contest; a contention; a competition
♦ 싸움을 걸다 challenge *sb* to a game [fight] / 싸움에 이기다[지다] win [lose] a game
4 〈투쟁〉 a struggle; a conflict
♦ 노사(勞使)간의 싸움 a struggle [trouble, dispute] between labor and management / 시간과의 싸움 *one's* fight against time / 암과의 싸움 a war against [on] cancer / 자유를 위한 싸움 a struggle [a fight] for freedom / 이성과 욕망간의 싸움 a conflict [struggle] between reason and desire
■ 눈— a snowball fight 부부— a matrimonial quarrel; a domestic skirmish 집안— a family quarrel [dispute, feud]; family [domestic] trouble(s) ■—꾼 a quarrelsome [contentious] person; a fire-eater; 《美俗》 a scrapper —닭 a fighting cock; a game cock —패 (a gang of) hooligans; hoodlums; rowdies; roughs; roughnecks

싸움터 a battlefield; a battlefront; a battleground; a war theater; the front
♦ 싸움터로 나가다 go to the front; take the field; go (off) to war
▶ 그 도시는 싸움터가 되어버렸다 The city turned into a battlefield [a scene of battle].

싸움판 a scene of a quarrel [fight]; a fight; a

brawl; a row; a scuffle
▶ 싸움판이 벌어졌다 A fight took place. ⇌ A dispute arose. ⇌ A quarrel broke out.
▶ 고성이 오가더니 싸움판이 벌어졌다 Harsh words for harsh words have led to a fight between them.
싸움하다 fight ⇨ 싸우다
싸이다 get [be] wrapped [covered] ⇨ 싸다¹
◆ 수수께끼에 싸이다 be wrapped up in (a) mystery / 화염에 싸이다 be enveloped in flames
▶ 선물은 예쁜 종이로 싸여 있었다 The present was wrapped up in beautiful paper.
▶ 그 도시는 스모그에 싸여 있다 The town is veiled [shrouded] in smog.
싸잡다 lump things together; round up
◆ 싸잡아서 altogether; in a lump; at wholesale / 싸잡아 비난하다 denounce indiscriminately [wholesale]; make a sweeping denunciation
싸전 —廛 〈곡물 가게〉 a rice store [shop]
■ —쟁이 a rice dealer
싸하다 〈박하맛처럼〉 minty; pepperminty; cool; 〈아리듯이〉 piquant; pungent; spicy; tongue-biting; sharp; 〈샴페인처럼〉 fizzy
▶ 연기로 눈이 싸하다 The smoke makes my eyes smart.
▶ 카레라이스가 싸했다 The curry and rice tasted hot [had a burning taste].
싹¹ 1 〈가지의〉 a sprout; a shoot; 〈어린 싹〉 a germ; 〈꽃눈〉 a bud; 〈감자의〉 an eye
◆ 싹이 트다[돋다] put forth [shoot out] buds; bud; sprout
▶ 감자는 싹이 나기 전에 먹어야 한다 You should eat potatoes before they start sprouting.
▶ 실수로 새싹을 꺾었다 I carelessly broke off a sprout.
2 ⇨ 싹수
싹² 1 〈완전히〉 entirely; completely; thoroughly; 〈갑자기〉 suddenly
◆ 싹 변하다 make a sudden change
▶ 과거는 싹 잊어버리시오 Forget all about the past.
▶ 그는 접시 위의 빵을 싹 먹어치웠다 He ate up the bread on the plate to the last crumb.
2 〈베는 소리·모양〉 with a swishing sound [motion]; with one clean stroke
◆ 종이를 싹 베다 cut paper with a snip / 천을 싹 찢다 rip [tear] a piece of cloth
싹독싹독 ◆ 싹독싹독 자르다 snip; clip / 무를 싹독싹독 썰다 chop up a radish into small pieces
싹둑 ◆ 싹둑 자르다 chop [nip, snip] off; cut with a snip / 가위로 가지를 싹둑 잘라내다 chop [lop] off a branch with scissors
싹둑거리다 cut up; slice; hash; mince; chop; snip
싹수 a good omen; hope(s); future; promise; prospects; a likelihood
◆ 싹수가 있다 be promising; be hopeful; show promise of success / 싹수가 없다 show no promise of success
▶ 싹수가 노랗다[틀렸다] (口) There is not a dog's [cat's] chance. ⇌ The matter [situation] is hopeless.
▶ 그가 시험에 통과할 싹수는 노랗다 There's little hope that he will pass the examination.
▶ 마침내 그의 일에 싹수가 보인다 His work is showing signs of success at last.
싹싹¹ 〈비는 모양〉 imploringly; entreatingly; humbly; earnestly
◆ 용서를 싹싹 빌다 beg [ask] one's pardon / 살려달라고 싹싹 빌다 beg [plead] for one's life
▶ 그녀는 어머니에게 잘못을 용서해 달라고 싹싹 빌었다 She asked humbly her mother to forgive her for her mistake.
싹싹² 〈완전히〉 completely; clean(ly); 〈힘들여〉 roughly
◆ 싹싹 씻다 wash roughly [vigorously] / 싹싹 쓸어내다 sweep out thoroughly / 타월로 몸을 싹싹 문지르다 scrub oneself with a towel / 통을 싹싹 문지르다 rub a tub hard; give a tub a good scrub
싹싹하다 friendly; pleasant; sociable; affable; amiable; good-humored
◆ 성품이 싹싹하다 have a sociable [friendly] nature
싹트다 bud; sprout; put forth buds [shoots]; shoot out buds
◆ 싹트는 꽃눈 sprouting flower buds
▶ 비가 와서 밀이 싹텄다 The rain has sprouted the wheat.
▶ 두 사람 사이에 사랑이 싹트기 시작했다 Love has begun to grow between the two.
▶ 젊은이들 사이에 새로운 사고 방식이 싹트고 있다 A new way of thinking is appearing among young people.
싼값 a low [cheap] price
◆ (…보다) 싼 값을 부르다 put a low price; underquote [underbid] / 싼 값에 사다 buy sth cheap; make a good bargain / (남보다) 싼 값으로 팔다 undersell (one's competitors)
▶ 나는 이 양복을 형편없이 싼값으로 샀다 I bought this suit at an unbelievably low price.
싼거리 a cheap [an inexpensive] article [item]; cheap goods; (口) a cheapie; a (good) bargain
싼 것이 비지떡 (속담) A cheap thing will cost you dear. ⇌ Buy cheap and waste your money.
쌀 (raw [uncooked]) rice (▶ 영어의 rice는 「벼·쌀·밥」을 포함하는 것이 보통)
◆ 쌀을 씻다[일다] wash rice / 쌀을 안치다 prepare rice for boiling
▶ 우리 한국인은 쌀이 주식이다 We Korean people live on rice.
▶ 한국의 농가에서는 쌀을 주로 논에다 재배한다 Korean farmers grow [raise, cultivate] most of their rice in paddies.
■ —가게 a rice store [shop] —가루 rice flour —가마니 a straw rice bag; a bag of rice —값 the price of rice : 쌀값을 올리다[내리다] raise [lower] the price of rice —겨 rice bran —광 a storeroom [barn] for rice; a rice granary —눈 an embryo bud (of rice) —생산지 a rice-producing district [region] —장사 dealing in

쌀농사 ―農事 〈재배〉 rice growing [farming]; rice cultivation; 〈수확〉 the rice crop [harvest]; the crop [harvest] of rice
▶ 올해의 쌀농사는 풍작[흉작]일 것 같다 This year's rice crop looks good [poor]. ⇌ The rice crop looks excellent [bad] this year.

쌀뜨물 water from washing rice; rice water
쌀밥 boiled [cooked] rice
쌀벌레 a rice weevil
쌀보리 〔植〕 rye
쌀쌀 ◆ 쌀쌀 쏘다니다 go [wander, gad] about; kick around on the loose

쌀쌀맞다 〈매정스럽다〉 cold; icy; 〈퉁명스럽다〉 blunt; curt; brusque; indifferent ⇨ 쌀쌀하다 2
◆ 쌀쌀맞는 대답 a curt answer; a brusque reply / 쌀쌀맞게 coldly; distantly; bluntly; curtly; brusquely / 쌀쌀맞게 대하다 treat *sb* coldly; give *sb* cold treatment

쌀쌀하다 1 〈날씨가〉 chilly; slightly cold; cool
◆ 쌀쌀한 공기 sharp air
▶ 오늘 아침은 쌀쌀하군요 It's rather chilly this morning.
2 〈사람이〉 cold; icy; cool; cold-hearted; curt; brusque; blunt; indifferent
◆ 쌀쌀하게 굴다 put on a distant [cool] air / 쌀쌀하게 대하다 give [show, turn] the cold shoulder to *sb*; keep [hold] *sb* at a distance; treat *sb* coldly; give a cold [frosty] reception (to) / 쌀쌀하게 거절하다 give a curt [flat] refusal; refuse flatly
▶ 우리가 처음 만났을 때 그녀는 쌀쌀했다 She was very cold to me [treated me very coldly] when we first met.

쌀알 〈한 톨〉 a grain of rice
쌀장수 a rice dealer
쌈[1] 〈음식〉 cooked [boiled] rice wrapped in lettuce [laver] ■ 상추— lettuce-wrapped rice
쌈[2] 1 〈바늘〉 a pack (of 24 needles) 2 〈금 백 냥중〉 100 taels of gold 3 〈피륙 뭉치〉 a bundle [package] (of cloth)
쌈지 a pouch ■ 담배— a tobacco pouch 부시— a purse for small flints
쌉쌀하다 slightly bitter; (taste) bitterish
◆ 쌉쌀한 맥주맛 dry [the slightly bitter taste of] beer
쌍 雙 〈짝〉 a pair; 〈암수〉 a couple; a breeding pair; a brace (▶ 단수·복수 동형)
◆ 꿩[오리] 한 쌍 a brace of pheasants [ducks] / 두 쌍의 백조 two pairs [couples] of swans / 한 쌍의 젊은 부부 a young (married) couple / 쌍을 이루다 make [form] a pair
쌍가마 雙— a pair of hair whirls on the head
쌍각류 雙殼類 a bivalve
쌍갈래 雙— a fork; a branch; bifurcation
■ 쌍갈랫길 a forked road
쌍 갈리다 divide [fork] into two; fork [branch] off in two
▶ 별장에 가는 길이 여기서 쌍갈지고 있다 The road to the villa branches off here.
쌍견 雙肩 *one's* shoulders
▶ 국가의 장래는 청년들의 쌍견에 달려 있다 The future of the country rests on the shoulders of the young.
▶ 회사의 운명이 그의 쌍견에 달렸다 The destiny of the firm depended on him.
쌍곡선 雙曲線 〔數〕 a hyperbola (*pl.* ~s, -lae); a hyperbolic curve ◆ 쌍곡선의 hyperbolic / 쌍곡선을 그리다 describe a hyperbolic curve
쌍곡선면 雙曲線面 〔數〕 a hyperboloid ◆ 쌍곡선면의 hyperboloidal
쌍구균 雙球菌 a diplococcus (*pl.* -cocci)
쌍극자 雙極子 〔物〕 a dipole
■ —모멘트 a dipole moment
쌍꺼풀 雙— a double(-edged) eyelid; an eyelid with a fold ◆ 쌍꺼풀지다 have a double eyelid / 쌍꺼풀지게 수술하다 give *sb's* eyelids a fold
쌍날 雙— a double blade [edge]
■ —칼 a double-edged [two-edged] sword
쌍녀궁 雙女宮 the Virgin ⇨ 처녀(—자리)
쌍두 雙頭 two head(s) (of cattle); a pair (of horses) ◆ 쌍두의 double-headed
■ —마차 a carriage and pair —정치 a dyarchy [diarchy]
쌍둥이 雙— twins; 〈그 한 사람〉 a twin
◆ 남녀 (의) 쌍둥이 mixed twins; a pigeon pair; twin boy and girl / 남자[여자] 쌍둥이 boy [girl] twins; twin brothers [sisters] / 그의 쌍둥이 형[아우] his twin brother / 쌍둥이를 낳다 give birth to twins / 쌍둥이로 태어나다 be born twins; be twinborn
▶ 그들은 쌍둥이다 They are twins.
▶ 그는 쌍둥이 중 한쪽이다 He is one of a pair of twins.
■ 네— quadruplets; (口) quads 세— triplets; 〈세 쌍둥이 중 한사람〉 a triplet ■ —자리 〔天〕 the Twins; Gemini
쌍떡잎 雙— 〔植〕 a dual cotyledon [seed leaf]
■ —식물 a dicotyledon; dicot; dicotyl : 쌍떡잎 식물의 dicotyledonous
쌍무 雙務 ◆ 쌍무적인 bilateral; reciprocal
■ —계약 a bilateral [reciprocal] contract —조약 a bilateral treaty —주의 bilateralism —협정 a bilateral [two-way, reciprocal] agreement
쌍무지개 雙— a double rainbow
쌍발 雙發 (having) twin engines [motors]
◆ 쌍발의 〔空〕 bimotor(ed); twin-engine(d) [-motor(ed)]; 〈총·포 등의〉 double-barreled [-chambered]
■ —기 a twin-motor(ed) [-engine(d)] plane; a bimotored airplane —총 a double-barreled gun; a double-chambered rifle
쌍방 雙方 both parties [sides]
◆ 쌍방의 이익 mutual benefit / 노사 쌍방의 주장 the claims of both labor and capital / 쌍방의 양보 mutual concessions / 쌍방의 의무 mutual obligation / 쌍방의 both; mutual; bilateral / 쌍방을 위하여 for mutual interests; for the benefit of both parties / 쌍방의 합의에 따라 by mutual consent [agreement]
▶ 나는 쌍방의 말을 듣지 않고는 판단을 내릴 수가 없다 I must hear the claims of both sides before I judge.
쌍벌 雙罰 punishing both sides; dual punishment ■ —규정 provisions of dual punishment —죄 a crime of dual punishment —주의 the

쌍벽 雙璧 the two greatest authorities; the matchless twin stars ▶그들 둘은 한국 연극계의 쌍벽이다 The two are the matchless twin stars of Korean theatrical troupe.

쌍봉낙타 雙峰駱駝 〔動〕 a Bactrian [two-humped] camel

쌍생아 雙生兒 twins ⇨ 쌍둥이
♦1란성 쌍생아 identical [one-egg, monozygotic, single ovum] twins / 2란성 쌍생아 fraternal [double ovum, two-egg, non-identical] twins

쌍수 雙手 both hands
♦쌍수를 들어 찬성하다 agree with sb wholeheartedly; second [support] sb with all one's heart; give one's hearty support 《to》 / 쌍수를 들어 환영하다 receive sb with open arms; extend open arms of welcome 《to》
▶나는 네 의견에 쌍수를 들어 찬성한다 I agree with you wholeheartedly.

쌍시류 雙翅類 〔昆〕 diptera 《*sing.* dipteron》

쌍심지 雙心― a double wick
♦눈에 쌍심지를 켜고 with hot angry [glaring] eyes / 쌍심지(가) 나다[서다] burn [be furious] with anger; have eyes glaring with anger; flare up
▶그는 눈에 쌍심지를 켜고 나를 노려보았다 He glared at me with hot angry eyes.

쌍쌍이 雙雙― two and [by] two; in pairs; in couples; by twos ▶그들은 쌍쌍이 걸었다 They walked in pairs.

쌍안 雙眼 both [two] eyes; a pair of eyes
■―리플렉스 카메라 a twin reflex camera ―망원경 a binocular (telescope) ―현미경 a binocular microscope

쌍안경 雙眼鏡 (a pair of) binoculars; 〈야외용〉 field glasses; 〈해상용〉 marine glasses; 〈오페라용〉 opera glasses ♦쌍안경으로 보다 look through field glasses

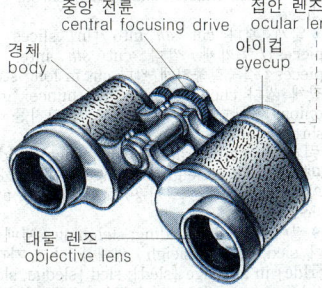
쌍안경
중앙 전륜 central focusing drive
접안 렌즈 ocular lens
경체 body
아이컵 eyecup
대물 렌즈 objective lens

쌍자엽 雙子葉 a dual cotyledon ⇨ 쌍떡잎
쌍지팡이 雙― (a pair of) crutches; two crutches [sticks]
▶외다리가 쌍지팡이보다 낫다 One leg is better than two crutches.
▶그는 남의 일에 쌍지팡이 짚고 나서기를 잘한다 He is always nosing into what doesn't concern him.

쌍칼잡이 雙― a two-sword fencer
쌍태 雙胎 twin embryos [fetuses, foetuses]
쌍화탕 雙和湯 〔韓醫〕 *ssanghwatang*, a kind of herb tonic tea

쌓다 1 〈포개어 올리다〉 pile (up); heap (up); stack; lay; make a pile; pile one above [on] another

|解說| ***pile*** (***up***)은 하나하나 착실하게, ***heap*** (***up***)은 어지럽게, ***stack*** (***up***)은 건초나 볏짚 등을 둥글거나 네모지게 정연히 쌓는 것을 말한다.

♦벽돌을 쌓다 lay bricks / 책상 위에 책을 쌓다 pile books on the desk / 쌓아올리다 pile [heap] up; pile in heaps / 산더미처럼 쌓아올리다 heap up (mountain-)high
2 〈구축하다〉 build; erect; raise; construct
♦돌담을 쌓다 build a stone wall / 강에 둑을 쌓다 embank a river; build an embankment along the river / 탑을 쌓다 erect a tower
3 〈축적하다〉 accumulate; acquire; store up; amass
♦경험을 쌓다 acquire [gain] experience; become experienced / 덕을 쌓다 cultivate virtue [moral character] / 학식[지식]을 쌓다 accumulate [store up] knowledge; stock *one's* mind with knowledge
▶지식은 젊을 때 쌓는 것이 좋다 You'd better store your mind with knowledge in your younger days.
▶그는 맨주먹으로 막대한 재산을 쌓았다 He built up a fabulous fortune from nothing.

쌓이다 1 〈퇴적되다〉 be piled up; lie 《on》
♦높이 쌓이다 be piled up high / 산더미 같이 쌓이다 be piled up mountain-high; lie in a heap [in heaps]
▶책상 위에 먼지가 잔뜩 쌓여 있었다 Thick dust lays on the desk.
2 〈일이 밀리다〉 stagnate; be stagnant; be left undone
▶일이 잔뜩 쌓여 있다 There is a good deal of work undone.
3 〈원한 등이〉 be pent up; be congested; 〈빚 등이〉 accumulate; get accumulated
♦쌓이고 쌓인 원한 pent-up hatred
▶그는 그녀에 대해 쌓인 원한을 나에게 말했다 He told me of a number of grudges he bore against her.

쌔비다 〈훔치다〉 pilfer; filch; steal; (口) sneak; (俗) pinch
쌘비구름 a cumulonimbus
쌨다 〈흔하다〉 plentiful; abundant; available as many [much] as 《you wish》
▶그 지역은 석탄이 쌨다 Coal abounds in the region.
▶그 만찬 파티에는 언제나 고기와 술이 쌨다 The dinner party is always with beef and ale galore.
▶이런 물건이야 어느 가게에나 쌔고 쌨다 Such a thing is available as many as you wish at any store.

쌩 〈바람소리〉 howling; whistling; whizzing; ping; zing; zip
♦ 쌩하는 소리 a whistling sound; a whiz; a zing / 쌩하고 날다 whiz(z); zing; zip; go zipping
▶ 겨울에는 바람이 쌩쌩 분다 The wind howls in winter.
▶ 온종일 바람이 쌩쌩 불었다 The wind was whistling all day long.

써내다 write and submit [hand in, turn in, give in]; write

써넣다 write in; fill in; enter; make an entry; inscribe (in); make [take, write] notes; 〈행간에〉 interline
▶ 그 용지에 써넣으십시오 Please fill in the form.
▶ 그 교수가 강의하는 동안 톰은 교과서에 메모를 많이 써넣었다 During the professor's lecture, Tom wrote a lot of notes in his textbook.

써다 〈조수가 빠지다〉 ebb; flow back; recede; 〈물이 줄다〉 subside; sink; go down
▶ 이곳 조수(潮水)는 저녁에 들어왔다가 아침에 썬다 The tide here inflows in the evening and ebbs in the morning.

써레 〔農〕 a harrow; a rake ♦ 써레질하다 harrow (the field); rake (the ground) ▪ 써렛발 the prongs [pegs, spikes, teeth] of a harrow

써리다 〔農〕 harrow (a field); rake (the soil smooth)

써먹다 〈사용하다〉 use; make use of; utilize
♦ 써먹을 만하다 be useful [usable]; be of use / 써먹을 데가 없다 be useless [of no use, unusable]; be good for nothing

썩 1 〈대단히〉 very; very much; exceedingly; greatly; so
▶ 이것은 썩 좋은 책이다 This is a very good book.
▶ 그녀는 노래를 썩 잘 부른다 She sings very well. ⇒ She is a very good singer.
2 〈즉시〉 at once; immediately; (美口) right away [off]
▶ 썩 나가 Get out of here right now!

썩다 1 〈부패하다〉 go bad [rotten]; rot; decompose; decay; spoil; corrupt; 〈달걀이〉 addle; 〈우유 등이〉 turn sour; 〈고기 등이〉 putrefy; 〈생선이〉 become stale; 〈물이〉 become foul; 〈금속이〉 corrode

[解說] *go bad*는「음식이 썩다」의 뜻을 가진 가장 구어적인 표현이다. *rot*은 특히 야채·고기 등이 세균이나 곰팡이 등으로 인해 썩는 것이며, *decay*는 보통 물질이 서서히 변질해서 썩는 것으로 rot보다는 전문적인 용어이다. *spoil*은 음식의 질이 손상된다는 뜻의 일상용어이다.

♦ 썩은 이 a decayed tooth / 썩은 〈버터·튀김이〉 rancid; rotten; bad; corrupt; decomposed; spoilt [spoiled]; putrid; 〈생선이〉 stale; 〈달걀이〉 addled / 썩기 쉬운 perishable / 썩지 않다 keep good
▶ 이 생선은 내일 아침이면 썩을거다 This fish will not keep (good) overnight.

2 〈활용되지 않다〉 gather rust; become [get] rusty; lie in the dust; be wasted
♦ 썩고 있는 재능 talents left to rust
3 〈은둔 생활을 하다〉 remain [live] in obscurity; be buried in oblivion; be kept away from the public eye
♦ 시골에서 썩다 bury *oneself* [be buried] in the country; live an obscure life in the country

썩둑 with a slash ⇨ 싹둑
썩둑썩둑 with a snip-snap ⇨ 싹둑싹둑
썩썩 imploringly; completely ⇨ 싹싹[1,2]

썩어도 준치 (俗談) A withered rose is still a rose. ⇌ An old eagle is better than a young crow.

썩어빠지다 rot [decay, go bad] completely; rot away; be utterly rotten
♦ 썩어빠진 사람 a morally bankrupt man

썩이다 1 〈부패시키다〉 rot; putrefy; corrupt; render putrid; spoil; let *sth* decay [rot]; 〈금속을〉 corrode; 〈달걀을〉 addle
♦ 사과를 썩이다 let an apple spoil
2 〈안쓰다〉 keep *sth* idle; let *sth* go to waste; leave *sth* to rust [unemployed, unused]
♦ 돈을 썩이다 keep *one's* money idle; let *one's* money stay unemployed / 책을 썩이다 let *one's* books gather [covered with] dust
3 〈마음을〉 worry (*oneself*); be worried (about, over); be depressed [discouraged, bother (*oneself*)] (about); feel [be] sick at heart; feel downhearted; eat [tear] *one's* heart out (with); lose heart over; make *one's* heart break
♦ 남의 속을 썩이다 give *sb* anxiety; worry another's heart
▶ 아이들은 곧잘 부모의 속을 썩인다 The children often bother their parents.
▶ 이런 사소한 일로 마음 썩어서는 안된다 You shouldn't be discouraged by such trifles.
▶ 그는 취직을 못해 속을 썩였다 His failure to find a job made him (feel) sick at heart.

썰다 cut (fine); chop (up); hack (to pieces); mince; hash (meat); slice; slash; shred; 〈얇게〉 shave
♦ 얇게 썰다 cut *sth* into [in] slices [thin pieces] / 두껍게 썰다 cut *sth* into thick pieces / 길쭉길쭉하게 썰다 cut in long strips / 잘게 썰다 chop (onion) fine; mince (garlic, onions) / 샐러드를 만들려고 캐비지를 썰다 shred cabbage for a salad

썰렁하다 chilly; rather [somewhat] cold

썰매 a sled; a sleigh; a sledge; 〈미국·캐나다의〉 a toboggan; 〈경기용〉 a bobsleigh; a bobsled
♦ 썰매 타기 sleighriding; sleighing / 썰매를 타다 sled; sledge; sleigh / 썰매를 타고 가다 go [ride] in a sledge [sled]; sled [sledge, sleigh] (along); travel by sleigh / 썰매를 타러 가다 go sleighriding

썰물 the ebb [ebbing, falling] tide; low tide [water] ▶ 내일은 아침 다섯시에 썰물이 된다 Ebb tide tomorrow is at five in the morning.

썸벅 1 〈쉽게 결단되는 모양〉 (cut) easily; with a light stroke

♦썸벅 썰다 cut *sth* lightly [nimbly] / 무릎 썸벅 썰다 slice a radish nimbly
2 〈절단되는 소리〉 sound of nimble cutting
♦썸벅썸벅 썰다 cut *sth* lightly and nimbly

쏘가리 〔魚〕 a mandarin fish

쏘다 **1** 〈화살·총 등을〉 fire; shoot 《an arrow, a bird》
♦한방 쏘다 fire a shot / 인공위성을 쏘다 launch [blast off, put up] an artificial satellite; put [get, fire] an artificial satellite into the sky / 쏘아 죽이다 shoot *sb* dead [to death]; kill by a shot
▶그 사냥꾼은 단 한방으로 곰을 쏘아 잡았다 The hunter killed the bear with single shot.
2 〈벌이〉 sting
▶벌이 쏜 데가 부었다 The sting of a bee has swollen up.
3 〈맛·냄새가〉 bite; sting
♦맛이 톡 쏘는 것 같은 biting to the taste
▶후추는 혀를 쏜다 Pepper bites [stings] the tongue.
4 〈말로〉 make cutting remarks; make a sharp [cutting] retort; say spiteful things; deliver *sb* pinpricks

쏘다니다 gad [wander] about; run [bustle] about; loiter; 《美俗》 bum around
♦잘 쏘다니는 사람 a regular gadabout / 쏘다니며 on the gad / 쏘다니며 시간을 보내다 spent time on the gad

쏘삭거리다 rummage ⇨ 쑤석거리다

쏘시개 a (fire) lighter ⇨ 불쏘시개

쏘아보다 glare [stare] at; scowl at; look fiercely [menacingly] 《at》; look sharply in the face; look daggers at
♦서로 쏘아보다 glare at each other

쏘아붙이다 speak daggers to; blame harshly
▶그들은 대통령의 수뢰사건을 폭로하면서 쏘아붙였다 They spoke daggers to the president disclosing his bribery case.

쏘아올리다 〈높이〉 shoot up; send up; 〈불꽃을〉 set [let] off; 〈인공위성을〉 launch
▶그들은 불꽃을 쏘아올렸다 They set off fireworks.
▶한국은 1995년 인공위성을 쏘아올렸다 Korea launched an artificial satellite in 1995.

쏘이다 be stung ♦벌에 쏘이다 get stung by a bee

쏙독새 〔鳥〕 a (Korean) goatsucker; a nighthawk; a nightjar

쏙쏙 rapidly ⇨ 쑥쑥

쏜살 a shot arrow [dart]
♦쏜살같다 be as swift as an arrow / 쏜살같이 as swift as an arrow; like an arrow [a dart, a shot] / 쏜살같이 달아나다 run away like an arrow
▶그 개는 쏜살같이 그 토끼를 쫓았다 The dog ran after the rabbit like a (shot) dart.
▶자동차가 우리 옆을 쏜살같이 지나갔다 A car shot by us.

쏟다 **1** 〈붓다〉 dash 《over》; pour 《in, into, out》; spill; empty
♦잉크를 쏟다 spill ink / 물을 양동이에 쏟다 pour water into a bucket / 물을 땅에 쏟다 dash water over the ground
▶나는 책상 위에 커피를 쏟았다 I spilled some coffee on the desk.
2 〈집중하다〉 concentrate 《one's efforts on *sth*》; pay [direct] 《one's attention to》; give 《one's mind to *sth*》; devote 《to》
♦아무에게 애정을 쏟다 devote [fix] one's affection on *sb*; be strongly attached to *sb* / 전력을 쏟다 focus [concentrate] one's efforts 《on》 / 연구에 전력을 쏟다 pour [put, throw] (all) one's energies [efforts] into one's research
▶그는 그 새로운 계획에 전력을 쏟았다 He concentrated his energies on the new project.
3 〈심중을〉 pour out; give vent 《to one's anger》
♦불평을 쏟다 complain 《about, of》; grumble 《at, over, about》 / 울분을 쏟다 vent [work off] one's (pent-up) anger 《on》

쏟뜨리다 dash 《⇨ 쏟다》 ♦책상 위에 잉크를 쏟뜨리다 spill ink on the desk

쏟아넣다 **1** ⇨ 쏟다 1 ♦자루에 보리를 쏟아넣다 pour barley in a sack
2 〈돈 등을〉 be spent on [went for]; put 《money》 into; invest 《capital》 in; sink 《money》 in
♦사업에 전재산을 쏟아넣다 put all one's fortune in an enterprise
▶그는 남은 돈을 모두 책에 쏟아넣었다 All his spare money went for [was spent on] books.

쏟아지다 pour on [cut, down]; 〈물 등이〉 gush out [forth]; spout; spurt; get [be] spilt
▶비가 쏟아진다 It rains hard on [pours on].
▶눈물이 한없이 쏟아졌다 Tears poured [streamed] ceaselessly down my cheeks.
▶많은 축하가 쏟아져 들어왔다 Congratulations came snowing in.
▶그들은 떼지어 쏟아져 나왔다 They poured out in crowds.

쏠다 gnaw; nibble
♦반자를 쏠아 구멍을 내다 gnaw a hole through a ceiling
▶쥐가 뒤주를 쏠아 구멍을 냈다 The rat gnawed a hole into the wooden rice box.

쏠리다 **1** 〈기울다〉 lean 《to, toward》; tilt; slant; lurch; incline 《to》
♦〈배가〉 좌현[우현]으로 쏠리다 《the boat》 list [heel] to port [starboard] / 한쪽으로 쏠리다 lean to one side / 걸을 때 몸이 앞으로 쏠리다 lean forward in walking
2 〈경향을 띠다〉 incline 《to》; tend 《to》; lean [trend] 《toward》
♦자연주의로 쏠리다 lean to naturalism
3 〈시선이〉 focus 《on, at》; center 《on, in, at》
▶모든 사람들의 시선이 그에게로 쏠렸다 All eyes were centered on him.

쏠쏠하다 passable ⇨ 쑬쑬하다

쏨뱅이 〔魚〕 a scorpion fish

쐐기[1] a wedge; 〈바퀴·원통을 괴는〉 a chock; 〈차바퀴 핀〉 a linchpin
♦쐐기꼴[모양]의 wedge-shaped; wedgewise / 쐐기꼴로 in (a) wedge / 쐐기를 박다 wedge; drive in a wedge
▶통나무를 쪼개기 위해 쐐기를 박았다 A wedge was driven into the log.

▶바퀴 밑을 쐐기로 괴었다 I set a chock under the wheels.
▶그가 약속을 지키도록 쐐기를 박아둘 필요가 있다 We must take steps to make sure that he will keep his promise.
쐐기² 〔昆〕 a caterpillar
쐐기풀 〔植〕 a nettle
쐬다 〈바람·연기 등을 받다〉 expose 《to the wind》; be exposed to
◆바람쐬다 〈물건을〉 expose sth to the air; 〈사람이〉 expose oneself to the wind; 〈바깥 공기를〉 air oneself; take a walk 《the air》/ 옷을 바람에 쐬다 air clothes; give clothes airing / 저녁 바람을 쐬다 air oneself in the evening; enjoy the cool of the evening
쑤다 make gruel [porridge]; make paste
◆밀가루로 풀을 쑤다 make gruel by boiling flour in water / 쌀로 죽을 쑤다 make gruel by boiling rice in water
쑤석거리다 〈뒤적거리다〉 ransack; rummage (in); stir up; poke [stir] about 《with a stick》; rake [poke up] 《the fire》
◆서랍속을 쑤석거리다 ransack [rummage (in)] a drawer 《for sth》/ 난로의 불을 쑤석거리다 poke up a fire in the stove
쑤셔넣다 push [squeeze] sth into; thrust in [into]; stuff into; poke [strike] into; ram [bump, jam] into ◆쓰레기를 부대에 쑤셔넣다 push litter in a bag
쑤시개 a pick; a poke ■이— a toothpick
쑤시다¹ 1 〈틈을〉 pick; poke
◆이를 쑤시다 pick one's teeth / 청소기로 파이프를 쑤시다 poke the pipe with pipe cleaners / 흙벽을 쑤시어 구멍을 내다 poke a hole in a mud wall
2 〈불을〉 stir 《the fire》; poke up; give 《the fire》 a stir
쑤시다² 〈아프다〉 ache; 〈배가〉 gripe; 〈손가락이〉 smart; tingle; 〈종기가〉 throb with pain; jump; fester; 〈염증이 나서〉 rankle; be sore; twinge; prick; prickle
◆귀가 쑤시다 have a sore ear / 이가 쑤시다 have a toothache / 머리가 쑤시다 have a splitting headache / 온 몸이 쑤시다 feel sharp pains all over one's body / 복통이 나 쑤시다 have a griping pain in one's stomach
쑥¹ 〔植〕 a mugwort; a wormwood
쑥² 〈못난이〉 a fool; a dupe; an ass; a donkey; a simpleton
◆어이구 이 쑥아 What a fool you are!
쑥³ 1 〈나오거나 들어간 상태〉 (protruded) way out; (sunken) way in
◆쑥 나온 턱 a prominent jaw / 쑥 들어간 눈 deep-set [sunken] eyes / 바다로 쑥 나온 갑 (岬) a cape that shoots out into the sea
2 〈밀어넣거나 뽑는 모양〉 with a jerk; with a vigorous pull
◆말뚝을 (땅에서) 쑥 뽑다 jerk a stake out of the ground / 칼을 쑥 뽑다 draw one's sword in a flash; whip out one's sword / 혀를 쑥 내밀다 stick one's tongue out
▶반지가 그녀의 손가락에서 쑥 빠졌다 A ring slipped off her finger.
▶문 손잡이를 잡아당겼더니 그대로 쑥 빠져버렸다 When I pulled on the doorknob, it came right off in my hand.
3 〈갑자기〉 suddenly; abruptly; all at once; unexpectedly
◆쑥 앞지르다 〈경주에서〉 shoot ahead / 팔을 쑥 내밀다 shoot out one's arm
쑥갓 〔植〕 a crown daisy
쑥대 a mugwort [wormwood] stalk; a stem of mugwort
쑥대밭 1 〈쑥밭〉 a mugwort field; an area overgrown with mugwort
2 〈황무지〉 wasteland; a wilderness; 〈폐허〉 the ruins
◆쑥대밭이 되다 be ruined [devastated]; be reduced [go] to complete ruin; fall into ruins; run waste / 쑥대밭을 만들다 lay waste; devastate 《land》; ruin; turn 《a place》 into ruins
쑥덕거리다 talk in whispers; exchange subdued remarks; talk in a subdued tone
◆아무개를 두고 쑥덕거리다 pick sb for the topic of their whispers
▶그들은 누군가를 두고 쑥덕거리고 있었다 They were whispering about somebody.
쑥덕공론 —公論 secret talks; a secret conference; a talk in whispers
◆머리를 맞대고 쑥덕공론을 하다 lay heads together in secret consultation / 쑥덕공론으로 계획을 세우다 plan 《a thing》 through secret talks
—**쑥덕공론하다** hold a secret conference [discussion]; discuss 《things》 under one's breath; exchange subdued remarks
쑥덕쑥덕 in undertones; in whispers; under one's breath ◆쑥덕쑥덕 이야기하다 talk in whispers; speak under one's breath
쑥떡 a mugwort rice cake; a rice-flour cake mixed with mugwort
쑥밭 a mugwort field ⇨ 쑥대밭 1
쑥부쟁이 〔植〕 an aster; a starwort
쑥스럽다 1 〈겸연쩍다〉 awkward
◆쑥스러워하다 feel awkward [shy, nervous] 《before an audience》; feel small [cheap, embarrassed] 《in company》; be [feel] abashed; be self-conscious
▶나는 어떤 사람에게 아는 사람인줄 알고 잘못 말을 걸었다가 아주 쑥스러웠다 I was very embarrassed when I mistakenly spoke to a person I thought I knew.
▶그의 아들은 손님에게 쑥스러워 하며 인사했다 His son greeted the guest awkwardly.
2 〈격에 맞지 않다〉 unbecoming; improper; unseemly; indecent
◆쑥스럽게 굴다 behave unseemly; cut a ridiculous figure
쑥쑥 1 〈들어가거나 나온 모양〉 all (protruded) way out; all (sunken) way in ◆쑥쑥 내밀다 protrude all way out / 쑥쑥 들어가다 sink all way in
2 〈솟는 모양〉 quickly; rapidly; very fast
◆쑥쑥 자라다 grow rapidly; be shooting up
▶그 사내아이는 쑥쑥 자라고 있다 The boy is growing rapidly [shooting up].
3 〈쑤시듯 아픈 모양〉 《hurt》 sharply from time to time

♦ 쑥쑥 쑤시다 shoot; prick; tingle; prickle
▶ 이가 쑥쑥 쑤신다 My tooth stings.
▶ 팔이 쑥쑥 쑤셨다 I had a twinge in my arm.
4 〈뽑아 내는 모양〉 pulling [jerking] out repeatedly ♦ 무를 쑥쑥 뽑다 uproot radishes

쑬쑬하다 passable; fairly good; so-so
♦ 쑬쑬히 (ㅁ) so-so; passably; tolerably / 생김 생김이 쑬쑬하다 be fairly good-looking

쓰개 headgear; 〈여자의〉 a headdress ■—**치마** an old-fashioned woman shawl used to cover the head and upper body when going out

쓰다¹ 〈글씨를〉 write (in ink [English]); 〈글을〉 compose (an essay, a poem); write (a story); pen (an article); 〈적다〉 put (down) (*one's* opinion) in writing; put [lay, write] down; 〈기술하다〉 describe
♦ 편지(를) 쓰는 법 how to write letters; letter-writing / 갈겨 쓰다 scrawl; scribble / 똑똑하게[크게, 작게] 쓰다 write plain [large, small] / 연필로 쓰다 write with a pencil [in pencil] / 영수증을 쓰다 write [make] out a receipt / 글씨를 잘[못] 쓰다 write a good [poor] hand / 문학작품을 쓰다 produce literary works / 틀리게 쓰다 make a mistake in writing; write amiss [wrong]; miswrite / 편지를 쓰다 write a letter / 잡지에 쓰다 write for a magazine / 술술 써내려가다 write [dash] off; write without much thinking
▶ 펜으로 써라 Write with a pen.
▶ 여기에다 이름을 쓰세요 Put your name down here.
▶ 잉크로 썼니? Did you write in ink?
▶ 이 연필은 쓰기 편하다 This pencil is easy to write with.
▶ 이 만년필은 잘 써진다 This fountain pen writes smoothly [runs smoothly on paper].
▶ 성함은 어떻게 쓰시죠? How do you spell your name?
▶ 나는 일기를 쓴다 I keep a diary.
▶ 이 책은 누가 썼지? Who wrote this book?
⇒ Who is the author of this book?
▶ 그는 새 소설을 쓰고 있다 He is working [at work] on a new novel.
▶ 그녀는 박사 논문을 쓰고 있다 She is working on a doctoral dissertation.
▶ 이것은 내가 쓴 수필입니다 This is the essay I wrote.
▶ 그 사건에 관해서는 더 이상 쓸 것이 없다 There is nothing more left to write about the incident.
▶ 아버지는 언제나 내게 편지를 받아 쓰게 하신다 Father is always dictating letters to me.
▶ 그의 편지에는 그가 내주 일요일에 서울에 온다고 쓰여 있다 His letter says he is coming up to Seoul next Sunday.
▶ 벽보에는 다음과 같이 쓰여 있다 The notice runs [reads] as follows.

쓰다² **1** 〈물건을〉 use; make use of; put to use; employ; 〈다루다〉 work [operate] (a machine); handle a tool; manipulate (an instrument)
♦ 유용[유효]하게 쓰다 make good use (of) / 남의 물건을 마음대로[자유로이] 쓰다 make free use of another's things; be at liberty to make use of (another's library); help *oneself* freely to (another's things) / 널리[일상] 쓰고 있다 be in general [daily] use / 쓸 수 있다 be usable [serviceable]; be fit for use [service] / 오래 쓸 수 있다 stand long use; give a long service / 쓰지 않게 되다 pass from use; fall into disuse; be [get, go, fall] out of use / 쓸 수 없다 be unusable; be unfit for use [service]; be useless
▶ 이것은 어디에 쓰는 겁니까? What is this (used [intended]) for?
▶ 이 방은 요즘 내 서재로 쓰고 있다 This room now serves as my study.
▶ 우리는 종이를 자르는데 가위를 쓴다 We use scissors to cut paper.
▶ 쇠 주전자는 쓸수록 광택이 난다 An iron kettle's luster improves with use.
▶ 그 원고는 쓸 만합니까? Is the manuscript (of) any good?
▶ 그런 책을 읽어서 무엇에 쓸 것인가? What's the good [use] of reading such a book?
▶ 알코올은 소독하는데 쓰인다 Alcohol is used for sterilization.
▶ 그 용어는 식물에는 좀처럼 쓰이지 않는다 The term is rarely applied to plants.
2 〈돈을〉 spend; 〈소모품을〉 use; consume
♦ 돈을 물 쓰듯이 쓰다 squander money; spend money like water / 책 사는 데 돈을 쓰다 spend money on books / 돈을 다 써버리다 use up; spend all *one's* money; go [run] through money; run [give] out of; consume; exhaust; squander
▶ 나는 예습하는데 세시간을 썼다 I spent three hours in preparing my lesson.
▶ 그녀는 옷[하찮은 일]에 많은 돈을 썼다 She spent a lot of money on clothes [the trifles].
▶ 한 달에 설탕을 얼마나 씁니까? How much sugar do you use [consume] a month?
▶ 돈을 많이 쓰시게 해서 미안합니다 I am sorry to have put you to a lot of expense.
▶ 그 돈은 마음대로 써도 됩니다 The money is at your disposal.
3 〈고용하다〉 employ; engage; hire; take *sb* into *one's* service; keep [have] *sb* in *one's* employ [service, pay]; keep (a servant); 〈잘 다루다〉 handle; manage
♦ 시험삼아 써보다 take *sb* on trial; give *sb* a trial
▶ 그 공장은 3백명의 근로자를 쓰고 있다 The plant gives employment to three hundred hands.
▶ 윗자리에 있는 사람은 인력을 가장 효율적으로 쓰는 방법을 잘 생각해야 한다 Leaders should think more about how best to use labor.
▶ 그는 나이는 젊지만 그 일에는 쓸 만하다 He is young, but quite useful at the job.
4 〈채택하다〉 adopt; 〈적용하다〉 apply
♦ 계략을 쓰다 adopt [use] a stratagem / 긴축정책을 쓰다 adopt a retrenchment policy / 별별 수단을 다 쓰다 use [try] every conceivable means / 최후의 수단을 쓰다 resort to the last measure
▶ 그는 멋진 꾀를 써서 이겼다 He won by

5 〈말하다〉 speak
♦고운 말을 쓰다 use corteous words / 거만한 말씨를 쓰다 use haughty language / 문자를 쓰다 talk like a book
▶이스라엘에서는 어떤 말을 씁니까? What language is spoken [do they speak] in Israel?
▶내 수업에서 한국어는 쓰지 마시오 You are not allowed to speak Korean in my class.

6 〈능력 등을〉 use; exercise; give play [scope] to; exert; call [bring] into play
♦머리를 쓰다 use one's head [brains]; exercise [use] one's wits; 〈머리를 짜내다〉 rack [cudgel] one's brains / 애를[힘을] 쓰다 take pains; exert oneself; make [bend one's] efforts; use one's strength [energy]; endeavor / 꾀를 쓰다 set one's wits to work; exercise one's brains [wits]/ 폭력을 쓰다 use [employ] violence [force] on sb
▶이 일은 머리를 많이 써야 한다 This work requires a lot of thinking.
▶그 일에 대해서는 신경을 쓰지 마라 Do not exercise yourself over the affair.

7 〈술법 등을〉 practice; play; do; resort to
♦최면술을 쓰다 practice mesmerism / 계략을 쓰다 resort to tricks / 요술을 쓰다 juggle; do conjuring tricks

8 〈유통하다〉 circulate; pass; utter
♦위조 화폐를 쓰다 pass a counterfeit coin

9 〈약을〉 administer 《a medicine》; dose 《a patient》; use; apply 《an ointment to》
♦하제를 쓰다 take a laxative

10 〈색을〉 색을 쓰다 copulate; (口) have sex

11 〈빚을〉 ♦빚을 쓰다 borrow money; raise a loan of money

12 〈대접하다〉 ♦한턱 쓰다 stand treat for 《one's friend》; give sb a treat; (口) stand 《sb dinner》

13 〈장기 등에서〉 ♦말을 쓰다 move a piece; make a move

14 〈합당하다〉 be suitable [proper, fit]; be all right
▶그에게 그런 말을 하면 쓰나 You ought not to say such a thing to him.

쓰다³ **1** 〈착용하다〉 put on; wear; have on

解説 *put on*은 「쓰다」라는 동작을, *wear*, *have on*은 「쓰고 있다」는 상태를 나타낸다. wear, have on은 put on과는 달리 Wear your hat during the day. (낮에는 모자를 쓰고 있어라)와 같이 기간을 표시하는 부사구[절]이 있는 경우 외에는 명령문에 쓰지 않는다.

♦가면을 쓰다 wear a mask; mask one's face; 〈감정 등을 숨기다〉 dissemble; 〈변장하다〉 disguise oneself 《as》; 〈위선적으로〉 play the hypocrite / 모자를 쓰다 put on a hat / 안경을 쓰다 put [have, hook] on one's glasses [spectacles]
▶그는 언제나 안경을 쓴다 He always wears [has on] glasses.
▶그는 모자를 쓰고 있었다 He wore a hat. ⇌ He had a cap on.
▶나는 모자를 쓰지 않고 한 시간 동안 햇볕에 서 있었다 I was standing bareheaded [uncovered] in the sun for an hour.

2 〈뒤집어쓰다〉 pour 《water》 on 《oneself》; be covered with 《dust》; pull [draw] 《the bedspread》 over 《one's head》
♦머리에 수건을 쓰다 cover one's head with a towel / 담요를 쓰고 자다 sleep with the blanket pulled over one's head

3 〈우산을〉 raise [put up] 《an umbrella》 over one's head
♦우산을 쓰고 under an umbrella

4 〈누명을〉 be falsely charged 《with murder》; be unjustly accused 《of stealing》

쓰다⁴ 〈뫼를〉 ♦뫼를 쓰다 bury in [at]/ 선산에 뫼를 쓰다 bury 《sb's remains》 in the family graveyard

쓰다⁵ 〈맛이〉 bitter; 〈쓰라리다〉 hard; trying
♦쓴 맛 a bitter taste / 쓴 약 a bitter medicine / 쓴다 달다 말 없이 without saying yes or no [this or that]; without response / 쓴맛 단맛 다 보다 taste the sweets and bitters of life / 입맛이 쓰다 〈미각〉 taste bitter; 〈기분〉 feel unpleasant; be disgusted 《with, at》
▶이 주스는 맛이 쓰다 This juice tastes bitter.
▶나는 쓴 경험을 했다 I had a bitter [hard] experience.

쓰다듬다 **1** 〈손으로 쓸어주다〉 stroke; pass one's hand over [across] 《one's face》; smooth; caress
♦대머리를 쓰다듬다 pass one's hand over one's bald head / 머리를 쓰다듬다 stroke sb's head / 머리카락을 smooth (down) one's hair / 새끼 고양이를 쓰다듬다 pat a kitten / 수염을 쓰다듬다 stroke one's beard/ 어린아이를 쓰다듬다 pat a child
▶그는 가끔 턱을 쓰다듬는다 He sometimes strokes his chin.
▶서늘한 바람이 그녀의 달아오른 볼을 쓰다듬고 지나갔다 The cool breeze fanned her hot cheeks.

2 〈달래다〉 soothe; allay; pacify; calm (down); stroke; caress ♦우는 아이를 쓰다듬다 soothe [still] a crying child

쓰디쓰다 very [extremely] bitter; bitter as bitter can be ♦쓰디쓴 웃음 《smile》 a bitter [grim] smile

쓰라리다 **1** 〈상처가〉 smart; sore; tingling; burning ♦가슴이 쓰라리다 have heartburn
▶긁힌 상처가 아직도 쓰라리다 The scratch still smarts.

2 〈괴롭다〉 painful; sore; bitter; trying; hard (to bear)
♦쓰라린 고생 a sore affliction / 쓰라린 생활 [세상] a hard life [world]/ 쓰라린 운명 / 쓰라린 경험을 하다 taste [go through] a hard [trying] experience
▶나는 쓰라린 경험을 했다 I had a bitter experience.

쓰라림 〈상처의〉 soreness; smartness; 〈괴로움〉 pain; bitterness; sorrow
♦가난의 쓰라림 the bitterness of want
▶만남의 즐거움은 조만간 이별의 쓰라림이 된다 The pleasure of meeting will bring the sorrow [wrench] of parting sooner or later.

▶ 그는 가난의 쓰라림을 모른다 He doesn't know what it means to be poor.
쓰러뜨리다 1 〈서 있는 것을〉 bring [throw] down; level 《a house to the ground》; 〈바람이〉 blow down; lodge; 〈농작물을〉 lay; 〈베어 넘기다〉 fell; 〈사람을〉 throw *sb* to the ground; floor *sb*; knock down; 〈발을 걸어〉 trip up; topple [bring down] *sb*
♦ 나무를 베어 쓰러뜨리다 fell a tree; cut a tree down / 집을 쓰러뜨리다 〈지진 등이〉 demolish [destroy] a house; 〈헐다〉 pull down a house
▶ 간밤의 폭풍이 많은 나무들을 쓰러뜨렸다 Last night's storm blew many trees.
2 〈멸망시키다〉 overthrow; ruin; 〈죽이다〉 kill
▶ 반란군은 그 왕가를 쓰러뜨렸다 The rebels overthrew [toppled] the dynasty.
3 〈경기에서〉 beat; defeat; topple
♦ 상대방을 쓰러뜨리다 topple [beat] *one's* opponent
▶ 신인 권투 선수가 챔피언을 쓰러뜨렸다 The new boxer outboxed the champion.
쓰러지다 1 〈서 있는 것이〉 fall; come [go] down; topple; collapse; 〈사람·동물이〉 fall; fall over [down]; drop; go [roll] over; be off *one's* feet; sink to the ground
♦ 쓰러져 가는 집 a tottering [tumbledown] house; a house ready to run down [collapse] / 앞으로[뒤로] 쓰러지다 fall forward [backward] / 쓰러져 가고 있다 be on the point of falling
▶ 트럭이 옆으로 쓰러졌다 The truck fell on its side.
▶ 바람에 가로수들이 쓰러졌다 The wind blew those roadside trees down.
▶ 태풍으로 많은 가옥이 쓰러졌다 A number of houses were leveled to the ground by the typhoon.
▶ 그 집은 다 쓰러져 간다 The house is rather rickety.
2 〈과로 등으로〉 break down 《from》; be down 《with a cold》; crack up; succumb [give way] to 《a disease》; 〈졸도하다〉 fall senseless; fall in a faint
♦ 일사병으로 쓰러지다 have a heatstroke; be laid low by sunstroke / 기진맥진하여 쓰러지다 break [sink] down from exhaustion / 허기가 져 쓰러질 듯하다 be faint with hunger
▶ 그녀는 과도한 긴장으로 쓰러졌다 She broke down [collapsed] from overstrain.
▶ 그는 정신을 잃고 길에 쓰러져 있었다 He was found lying unconscious on the road.
▶ 그는 너무 무리해서 쓰러졌다 He has taken ill from pushing himself too hard.
3 〈죽다〉 die; fall down dead; fall a victim [prey] to; succumb to 《the wound》
♦ 암으로 쓰러지다 die of [be carried off by] cancer / 아무의 손에 쓰러지다 fall [meet *one's* end] at the hand of *sb* / 쓰러질 때까지 싸우다 fight to the death; die fighting
▶ 많은 병사들이 기아로 쓰러졌다 Many soldiers died of hunger.
▶ 나는 자유를 위해 쓰러질 때까지 싸우겠다 I'll fight for freedom to the last.

4 〈망하다〉 go to ruin; be ruined; 〈도산하다〉 go [become] bankrupt; 《美口》 go broke; 〈와해·붕괴하다〉 collapse; fall; be overthrown
♦ 쓰러져가는 은행 a bank on the verge [brink, eve] of bankruptcy / 쓰러져 가다 be on the point of falling
▶ 수많은 중소기업이 불황으로 쓰러졌다 A number of minor enterprises went under because of the recession.
▶ 그 독재 정권은 혁명중에 쓰러졌다 The dictatorship fell during the revolution.
▶ 쿠데타로 정부가 쓰러졌다 The government was overthrown by the coup d'état.
쓰레기 garbage; trash; refuse; rubbish; litter; waste

> 解說 *garbage*는 주로 부엌에서 나오는 음식 찌꺼기이고 *trash*, *rubbish*는 휴지, 나무쪽, 넝마조각 등 조그맣고 물기 없는 쓰레기다. 그리고 *refuse*는 그보다 큰 폐기물을 말한다. *litter*는 도로 같은 데 흩어져 있는 휴지 조각. 빈 병, 빈 깡통 등이다.

♦ 쓰레기 버리는 곳 a garbage dump [pit]; a dump yard; a dumping ground; a dust shoot; 《英》 a dust hole / 쓰레기 처리 waste [rubbish] disposal / 쓰레기를 버리다 dump; throw out the garbage [trash] / 바닥의 쓰레기를 청소하다 sweep the dust off the floor
▶ 쓰레기를 버리지 말 것 《게시》 No dumping.
▶ 그는 쓰레기 같은 인간이다 He is a good-for-nothing.
▶ 이곳에 쓰레기를 버리지 마시오 Don't heap [pile] up rubbish here.
■ **부엌**— kitchen refuse; garbage **인간**— the dregs of mankind; the scum of society **—매립지** a sanitary landfill **—분리수거** collection of garbage by type **—소각로** a garbage furnace; an incinerator **—장** a dumping place [ground]; 《美》 a garbage dump **—종량제** the volume-rate [volume-base] garbage collection system **—종량제 봉투** a standard plastic garbage bag **—차** a garbage cart [truck]; 《英》 a dust cart; 《美》 a dumpcart; a dumper
쓰레기통 **—桶** a trash can; a refuse bin; a wastebasket; 〈부엌의〉 a garbage can [box]; 《英》 a dust bin; an ash bin [《美》 can]; 〈역·공원 등의〉 a trash basket [box]; 《英》 a litter bin
♦ 쓰레기통에 버리다 put 《refuse》 into a wastebasket
▶ 쓰레기를 모두 주워서 쓰레기통에 버려 주세요 Please pick up all the trash and put it into the trash can.
▶ 쓰레기는 쓰레기통에 버리시오 《게시》 Deposit litter in basket.
쓰레받기 a dustpan ♦ 쓰레받기에 쓸어담다 sweep into a dustpan
쓰레질 sweeping (and cleaning) **—쓰레질하다** sweep (and clean)
쓰르라미 [昆] a clear-toned [green-colored] cicada 《*pl*. ~s, -dae》
쓰르람쓰르람 chirr; chirp
쓰리다 1 〈아프다〉 sore; smart; tingling; burning

쓰리다¹
♦속이 쓰리다 have a burning feeling in *one's* stomach; have a sour stomach
2 〈마음이〉 sore; bitter; heartrending; heartaching

쓰이다¹ **1** 〈써지다〉 be written 《with》; write
♦글씨가 잘 쓰이는 종이 a paper on which a pen writes well / 편지에 이렇게 쓰여 있다 The letter says [reads] that...
▶ 이 볼펜은 글씨가 잘 쓰인다 This ballpoint pen writes well.
2 〈쓰게 하다〉 get *sb* to write 《a letter》; have 《a letter》 written
♦불러주어 쓰이다 dictate 《a letter》 to 《*one's* clerk》
▶ 그녀는 아들에게 편지를 쓰였다 She had her son write a letter.

쓰이다² **1** 〈사용되다〉 be used; be made use of; be utilized [employed]; be employed; serve
♦일상 생활에 쓰이는 물건 articles in daily [everyday] use / 항상 쓰이는 말 a word in general use / 쓰이고 있다 be in use / 널리[일반적으로] 쓰이다 be widely [generally] used / 쓰이게 되다 come into use; come to be used / 쓰이지 않게 되다 get [go, fall] out of use
▶ 맥주 만드는 데 홉이 쓰인다 Hops are used in brewing beer.
▶ 망치는 못을 박는 데 쓰인다 The hammer is used for driving in nails.
▶ 그 단어는 현재 쓰이지 않는다 The word is out of use [is obsolete].
▶ 이것은 무엇에 쓰이지? What is this (used [intended]) for?
▶ 그것은 식탁으로 쓰인다 It does the duty of [serves as] a table.
▶ 이 방은 지금 내 서재로 쓰인다 This room now serves as my study.
2 〈소비되다〉 be spent; be consumed; be used
▶ 겨울철에는 가스가 많이 쓰인다 A great deal of gas is consumed during the winter.

쓰적거리다 1 〈비벼지다〉 rub [chafe] against; be rubbed 《against》 **2** 〈대강 쓸다〉 sweep [broom] hastily [roughly]

쓱 〈슬쩍·가만히〉 quietly; stealthily; 〈가볍게〉 (wipe, rub) lightly; 〈빨리〉 quickly; hastily
♦방문을 쓱 열다 open the door quietly / 방에서 쓱 나가다 slip [steal] out of the room / 서류를 쓱 훑어보다 take a glance at [read hastily through] the document
▶ 그는 방을 쓱 둘러보았다 His glance swept about the room.
▶ 그는 이마의 땀을 손수건으로 쓱 닦았다 He mopped his brow with his handkerchief.

쓱싹거리다 make a sawing sound; emit a rasping sound

쓱싹쓱싹 with a (continuous) sawing sound

쓱싹하다 1 〈착복하다〉 pocket; embezzle; take *sth* to *oneself*; divert (public money) into *one's* own pocket ♦아무의 돈을 쓱싹하다 embezzle money from *sb*
2 〈비밀히 처리하다〉 settle 《a matter》 secretly; cover [hush] up
3 〈셈을 맞비기다〉 balance [square] the accounts; offset each other
▶ 나는 며칠 일해주고 빚을 쓱싹해 달라고 했다 I asked to square the debt by working a few days.

쓱쓱 〈비비는 모양〉 rubbing; scrubbing; 〈일 등을〉 easily; with ease; without (any) trouble [difficulty] ♦두 손을 쓱쓱 비비다 rub *one's* hands (together) / 머리를 쓱쓱 쓰다듬다 smooth (down) *sb's* hair / 일을 쓱쓱 해치우다 do a work with ease

쓴맛 a bitter taste; bitterness ♦쓴맛이 나다 taste bitter; be bitter

쓴맛단맛 the bitters and the sweets 《of life》; sorrows and joys; prosperity and adversity
▶ 나는 인생의 쓴맛 단맛을 다 맛보았다 I have tasted the sweets and bitters of life.

쓴웃음 a bitter [grim, sour, vinegary] smile; a strained [forced] laugh
♦쓴웃음을 짓다 smile a sour [wry] smile; give a forced [strained] laugh; force a smile
▶ 나는 그녀의 무례한 질문에 나도 모르게 쓴웃음을 지었다 I smiled bitterly [wryly] at her rude question in spite of myself.

쓸개 〖解〗 the gallbladder; the gall ♦쓸개 빠진 사람 a spiritless [pluckless] man; a weak-kneed person ■—즙 bile; gall

쓸다¹ 〈비로〉 sweep 《with a broom》
♦마루를 쓸다 sweep the floor / 쓸어내다 sweep (the dirt) out [away]; sweep out [up]
▶ 그녀는 방[오물]을 쓸어냈다 She swept out the room [dirt].
▶ 나는 정원의 쓰레기를 쓸어 모았다 I swept the litter in the garden into a heap.
2 〈유행병이〉 spread; sweep; prevail; be prevalent [widespread]; 〈홍수 등이〉 sweep; 〈황폐시키다〉 devastate
▶ 전염병이 마을을 쓸었다 An infectious disease prevailed throughout the town. ≠ An epidemic swept the town.
3 〈판돈을〉 sweep the (gambling) board; 〈경기에서〉 make a clear sweep [score]
♦판돈을 쓸다 win all the money

쓸다² 〈줄로〉 file; rasp (off, away) ♦줄로 쓸어서 반드럽게 하다 file 《a thing》 smooth; file away roughness

쓸데 (a) use; service; usefulness; 〈필요〉 necessity; need ♦쓸데가 많다 be of wide [extensive] use

쓸데없다 〈필요없다〉 needless; unnecessary; 〈쓸모·가치없다〉 useless; unserviceable; of no use [avail, good]; worthless; 〈군더더기의〉 superfluous; redundant; 〈달갑지 않은〉 uncalled-for; unwanted; uninvited
♦쓸데없는 녀석 a useless [good-for-nothing] fellow / 쓸데없는 말참견 an uncalled-for remark; uninvited advice / 쓸데없는 소리 empty [idle] talk; nonsense; 《美俗》 bunk / 쓸데없는 책 a book of no value; a worthless book / 쓸데없는 걱정을 하다 feel [give *oneself*] unnecessary [needless] anxiety; worry too much / 쓸데없는 말을 하다 say unnecessary things; make an uncalled-for remark
▶ 쓸데없는 소리 작작해 Don't talk nonsense [rubbish]!
▶ 쓸데없는 참견마라 Mind your own business.

⇌ It's none of your business. ⇌ Don't poke your nose into my affairs.

쓸데없이 useless; unnecessarily; futilely; idly; without avail; to no [little] avail [purpose]; wastefully
♦쓸데없이 걱정하다 worry (*oneself*) unnecessarily [needlessly] / 쓸데없이 돈을 쓰다 waste money; spend money wasted / 쓸데없이 시간을 허비하다 squander *one's* time / 쓸데없이 허세부리다 be vainly pretentious
▶ 쓸데없이 애만 썼다 I have labored in vain.

쓸리다 1 〈기울다〉 lean; incline; totter; tile
▶ 높은 탑이 한쪽으로 쓸리더니 넘어갔다 The tall tower tottered and fell.
2 〈문질러지다〉 rub [scrape] 《against》; be rubbed; 〈살갗이〉 be chafed; be grazed
▶ 오른발 뒤꿈치가 구두에 쓸려 까졌다 I've got a shoe sore on my right heel.

쓸모 usefulness; utility; use; service(ableness); worth; help; value
♦쓸모있는 사람 a useful [valuable, serviceable] man; *sb* of ability [worth, use] / 쓸모 있는 것 a useful thing; utilities; 〈편리한 것〉 a convenience / 쓸모없는 사람 a good-for-nothing (fellow); a useless person / 쓸모없는 것 a useless thing; trash; a piece of nothing / 쓸모있다 be useful [serviceable] 《to, for》; be helpful 《to, in doing》; be of use 《service, help》 《to, for》 / 쓸모없다 be useless; be unusable [unserviceable]; be unworthy; be of no [little] use [service]; be good-for-nothing / 쓸모가 많다 be of wide [extensive] use
▶ 미국에 있는 동안 내 영어도 꽤 쓸모가 있었다 My English served me well during my stay in America.
▶ 그는 아무 쓸모 없는 녀석이다 He is a good-for-nothing (fellow).
▶ 이 모터[그런 낡은 차]는 쓸모없다 This motor [Such an old car] is (quite) useless [of no use].

쓸쓸하다 1 〈적적하다〉 lonely; lonesome; 〈외롭다〉 solitary; 〈황량하다〉 desolate; deserted

> **解說** *lonely*는 외톨이기 때문에 쓸쓸하다는 것을 강조하는 일반적인 말이고, *lonesome*은 lonely보다 감정적인 말로서 특히 가까운 사람과 헤어져서 쓸쓸할 때에 쓴다.

♦쓸쓸한 거리 a lonely [deserted] street / 쓸쓸한 경치 a desolate [dreary] scene / 쓸쓸한 곳 a lonely place / 쓸쓸한 느낌 a feeling of loneliness / 쓸쓸한 웃음 a wan [melancholy, sad] smile / 타국에서 쓸쓸히 죽다 go to die forlorn in a foreign land / 쓸쓸하게 지내다[살다] lead [live] a lonely life
▶ 말 동무가 없어서 쓸쓸하다 I feel lonely having no one to talk to.
▶ 그녀는 쓸쓸하게 웃었다 She smiled a sad [melancholy] smile.
▶ 나는 혼자 남아 쓸쓸했다 Left by myself, I felt lonely.
▶ 그는 고향 마을에서 쓸쓸한 생활을 하고 있다 He lives a lonely life in his native village.
▶ 나의 형은 쓸쓸한 하숙생활을 하고 있다 My brother leads a solitary life in a boarding-house.
2 〈날씨가〉 gloomy; dreary; melancholy
▶ 날씨가 쓸쓸하다 The weather is gloomy.

쓸어들이다 sweep in; rake in ♦돈을 쓸어들이다 shovel up [in] money

쓿다 refine; polish 《grain》
♦쌀을 쓿다 polish rice

씀바귀 〈植〉 a lettuce

씀씀이 expense; expenditure
♦씀씀이가 헤픈 사람 an extravagant person; a spendthrift; a big [lavish] spender; a scattergood; (美俗) a high roller / 씀씀이가 헤프다 be too free [generous] with *one's* money; be wasteful of money; be a spendthrift; spend money lavishly; (口) spend money like water
▶ 그녀는 씀씀이가 너무 헤프다 She is too much of a spendthrift. ⇌ She throws away her money.

씁쓰레하다 slightly [somewhat] bitter; be [taste] rather bitter

씁쓸하다 somewhat bitter; bitterish

씌다 be possessed 《by [with] a spirit》; be obsessed 《by》 ♦무엇에 씐 사람처럼 행동하다 act like a man possessed
▶ 그는 마치 귀신이 씐 사람 같다 He seems to be possessed by [with] an evil spirit.

씌우다 1 〈머리에〉 put 《a hat》 on; 〈덮다〉 cover *sth* with 《a cloth》; 〈도금하다〉 plate *sth* with 《gold》
♦ 냄비에 뚜껑을 씌우다 put the lid on a pan / 아이에게 모자를 씌우다 put a cap on a child / 이에 금을 씌우다 crown a tooth with gold; put a gold crown on a tooth
2 〈죄 등을〉 charge; fix; fasten [pin] 《a crime on *sb*》; put 《the murder upon others》; 〈전가하다〉 shift [shuffle off] 《a responsibility》 on 《to another's shoulders》; 〈오명을〉 fasten 《a stigma upon *sb*》
♦아무에게 죄를 씌우다 lay the guilt upon *sb*; impute a crime to *sb* / 오명을 씌우다 cast a slur on *sb's* good name
▶ 그는 자기가 저지른 잘못을 나에게 씌웠다 He laid the blame upon me for what he had done.
▶ 남에게 책임을 씌우려 들지 마라 Don't try to shuffle off your responsibility on another's shoulder.

씨¹ 〈言〉 a part of speech ⇨ 품사

씨² 〈피륙의〉 the woof; the weft; the width-wide threads ♦씨와 날 woof and warp

씨³ **1** 〈종자〉 a seed 《*pl*. ~(s)》; 〈과실의 핵〉 a stone; 〈사과·배 등의〉 a pip
♦배추 씨 cabbage seeds / 씨가 많은 seedy / 씨가 없는 seedless 《watermelon》 / 씨가 생기다 seed; go [run] to seed / 씨를 받다 gather the seeds / 포도에서 씨를 빼내다 remove the seeds from grapes / 씨를 뿌리다 seed 《a garden》; sow 《the field》; plant 《the》 seed(s)
▶ 나는 어제 밭에 밀 씨를 뿌렸다 I sowed the fields with wheat yesterday.
2 〈동물의〉 a breed; a strain; a stock
♦씨 좋은 말 a horse of a fine [good] breed

[stock]; a thoroughbred / 씨가 좋다 be of [bred from] a good [fine] stock; be of a fine breed / 씨를 받다 breed from a stock / 씨를 받으려고 기르다 keep for breeding (purposes)
3 〈사람의 혈통〉 paternal blood
♦ 불륜의 씨 a child born in sin; a child born out of wedlock / 씨 다른 형제[자매] a half brother [sister] / 아무의 씨를 배다 be (big) with child by *sb*; conceive a child of *sb*
4 〈근원〉 a cause; a source
♦ 눈물의 씨 a cause of sorrow / 불화의 씨 an apple [the seeds] of discord / 불화의 씨를 뿌리다 sow (the seeds of) trouble [discord]; sow dissension / 악의 씨를 없애다 nip an evil in the bud
▶ 자기가 뿌린 씨는 자기가 거두어야 한다 You must reap what you have sown.
씨 氏 **1** 〈남자의 경칭〉 Mr. (*pl.* Messrs.); (英) Esq. (▶Esquire의 약어); 〈미혼 여성〉 Miss (*pl.* Misses); 〈부인〉 Mrs. (*pl.* Mmes.); Ms. (▶Ms.는 기혼·미혼의 구별을 하지 않는 여성의 경칭) / 민씨 Mr. Min / 제임스 베이커씨 James Baker, Esq. / 김, 조 양씨 Messrs. Kim and Cho / 김씨 내외 Mr. and Mrs. Kim / 모씨 Mr. So-and-so
2 〈씨족〉 a family; a clan
♦ 강씨(네) the Kang family [clan]; the Kangs / 김해 김씨 the Kims of Kimhae / 안동 김씨 남자 an Andong Kim male
3 〈특정인〉 the gentleman; he
♦ 씨에 의하면 according to him; in his opinion; He says that...
▶ 씨의 타계는 참으로 애석한 일이다 His passing away is really lamentable.
씨감자 a seed potato
씨닭 a breeding cock; a chicken raised for breeding
씨도둑은 못한다 (속담) Of evil grain no good seed.
씨돼지 a breeding pig; 〈수컷〉 a boar; 〈암컷〉 a breed [brood] sow
씨름 1 〈운동〉 wrestling; a wrestling match
♦ 씨름 대회를 열다 hold public wrestling matches / 씨름을 한판 하다 have a wrestling bout [match] 《with》 / 씨름에 이기다[지다] win [lose] a wrestling bout
—**씨름하다** wrestle 《with》
2 〈노력〉 a (hard) struggle; strenuous effort(s)
—**씨름하다** exert *oneself*; make a strenuous efforts; come to grips 《with》
♦ 문제와 씨름하다 wrestle with [tackle] a problem; face a problem squarely / 영어와 씨름하다 wrestle with English
▶ 나는 사전과 씨름하며 영문 소설을 읽었다 I went through an English novel by thumbing a dictionary. ⇌ I read an English novel by referring constantly to a dictionary.
▶ 그는 산더미 같은 숙제와 씨름하고 있다 He is grappling with a heap of assignments.
■ 발— ankle [shin, leg] wrestling 팔— arm [Indian] wrestling —꾼 a wrestler —판 〈경기〉 a wrestling match [bout]; 〈장소〉 the (wrestling) ring [arena]
씨말 a studhorse; a breeding horse; a (breed-ing) stallion; a sire; 〈암말〉 a broodmare
씨방 —房 〔植〕 an ovary
씨소 a (seed) bull=종우(種牛)
씨실 the woof; the weft
씨아 a (cotton) gin; a (cotton) ginning machine / 씨아로 목화씨를 빼다 gin cotton
씨알 〈종란〉 a hatching egg; 〈종자〉 a seed grain; 〈광물의 잔 알갱이〉 a grain [particle] of mineral
씨알머리 ♦ 씨알머리 없는 놈 an ill-bred fellow; a churl; a hangdog / 씨알머리 없다 be ill-bred; be nasty
씨암닭 a brood hen; a breeder
■ —걸음 mincing steps; waddling
씨앗 seeds (of grain [vegetables])
♦ 씨앗을 뿌리다 seed 《a garden》; sow [plant] seed(s); sow [plant] 《the field》
■ —가게 a seed(s) store —장수 a seed(s)-man
씨억씨억하다 of firm and lively [active, brisk] disposition
씨젖 〔植〕 an albumen ⇨ 배젖
씨족 氏族 a family; a clan; 〈고대 로마의〉 a gens (*pl.* gentes) ■ —사회 a clan society —제도 the family [clan] system
씨주머니 〔植〕 an ascus ⇨ 자낭(子囊)
씨줄 1 〈피륙의 씨〉 the woof; the weft
2 〈위선(緯線)〉 〔地〕 a parallel (of latitude)
씩[1] 씩 웃다 give a quick smile; grin
씩[2] 〈조금씩〉 little by little; bit by bit; inch by inch; 〈서서히〉 gradually; by degrees / 하나[한사람]씩 one by one; one after another / 둘[두 사람]씩 two by two; two at a time; by twos / 세 사람에 하나씩 one to every three persons / 하나에 오십원씩 fifty won apiece / 3일에 한 번씩 once in every three days / 1주에 두번씩 twice a week / 하루에 세번씩 three times a day / 아이들에게 천원씩 주다 give the children one thousand won each
▶ 이 시계는 하루에 3분씩 늦는다 This watch loses three minutes a day.
▶ 앞 줄에 있는 책은 한 권에 5천원씩입니다 The books in the front rank are five thousand won a copy.
▶ 이것들은 얼마씩입니까? How much are these apiece?
▶ 응모자들은 두세 사람씩 왔다 The applicants came by twos and threes.
▶ 그들은 셋씩 짝지어 거리를 순시했다 They patrolled the streets in threes.
▶ 책은 학생 두명에 한 권씩 뿐이었다 There was only one copy to [for] every two students.
씩둑거리다 tattle; prattle; chatter; talk idly [nonsense]
씩씩거리다 gasp (for breath); pant; breathe heavily [hard] ⇌ 화가 나서 씩씩거리다 huff and puff; fume with rage / 씩씩거리며 말하다 gasp [pant, puff] out
씩씩하다 〈원기 넘치다〉 lively; spirited; gallant; vivacious; manly; 〈용감하다〉 brave; valiant; courageous
♦ 씩씩한 기상 a dashing [brave, valiant] spirit / 씩씩한 남자 [젊은이] a dashing fellow

[youth]/ 씩씩하게 걷다 step lively; walk briskly / 씩씩하게 싸우다 fight bravely [gamely, gallantly]; fight a valiant battle
▶ 이윽고 한국 축구 선수들이 씩씩한 모습으로 나타났다 Before long the smart figures of Korean soccer players appeared.
▶ 그의 군복 입은 모습이 씩씩해 보인다 He looks dashing in army uniform.
▶ 그는 씩씩하게 위험에 맞섰다[싸움터에 나갔다] He confronted the danger heroically [went out to war gallantly].

씹 **1** 〈음문〉 the vulva; (卑) a cunt; (卑) a pussy
2 〈성교〉 (卑) fuck; (卑) screw
—**씹하다** fuck; screw

씹다 chew; masticate
♦ 씹는 담배 a plug; chewing tobacco / 껌을 씹다 chew gum / 잘 씹다 chew 《food》 well / 씹어 뱉듯이 말하다 speak disgustedly [snappishly, curtly]; snap [rap] out
▶ 음식을 잘 씹어 먹는 것은 건강에 좋다 It's good for the health to chew your food well.
▶ 그것을 꼭꼭 씹으면 단맛이 난다 Chew it well, and it will taste sweet.

씹히다 〈씹어지다〉 be chewed; be masticated; 〈씹게 하다〉 let *sb* chew [masticate] 《on》
♦ 잘 씹히다 be chewed well [easily] / 잘 씹히지 않다 be hard to masticate [chew]; 〈질겨서〉 be tough / 밥에 돌이 씹히다 bite on a grit in boiled rice

씻가시다 wash out; rinse 《out》 ♦ 병을 씻가시다 rinse [wash] out a bottle

씻개 ♦ 밑씻개 toilet paper

씻기다 **1** 〈수동〉 be washed [wiped]
♦ 잘 씻기다 be washed easily [well]/ 씻겨 내려가다 be washed [carried] away 《by a flood》; wash away
▶ 비에 길이 깨끗이 씻겼다 The road was washed clean with rain.
▶ 해변은 파도에 씻기고 있었다 The beach was awash in the waves.
▶ 밥그릇이 잘 씻기지 않는다 This rice bowl does not wash well.
2 〈사역〉 let [have] *sb* wash 《a thing》
♦ 때를 씻기다 have [let] *sb* wash [scrape, rub] off the dirt / 남편에게 그릇을 씻기다 have *one's* husband wash dishes

씻다 **1** 〈물 등으로〉 wash 《*one's* face》; have a wash; 〈상처를〉 cleanse 《a wound》; rinse 《a bottle》; bathe 《*one's* eyes in warm water》; 〈닦아내다〉 wipe away [off]; mop
♦ 몸을 씻다 wash *oneself* / 북북 씻다 wash roughly; 〈문지르다〉 give a good scrub / 쌀을 씻다 wash rice / 야채를 물에 씻다 wash vegetables in water / 잘 씻다 wash *sth* well; give *sth* a good wash / 씻어내다[버리다] wash away [off, out]; clean away / 샴푸를 씻어내다 rinse off the shampoo / 씻어내리다 flush 《a toilet [streets]》; wash away [down]; 〈벽 등을〉 clean down
▶ 손을 잘 씻어라 Wash your hands well.
▶ 이 때는 씻으면 없어질까요? Will the dirt come out in the wash?
2 〈오명·죄 등을〉 clean [clear] *oneself* 《of the stain》; wipe; mop 《up》
♦ 씻을 수 없는 치욕 an indelible disgrace; an ineffaceable [inerasable] humiliation / 누명을 씻다 clear *oneself* of a false charge / 오명을 씻다 wipe away *one's* dishonor; clear *oneself* of his disgrace / 죄를 씻다 wash away *one's* guilt
▶ 그는 그 행동으로 지난 번의 모든 불명예를 씻었다 By that act he blotted out all his previous [former] disgraces.

씻은듯이 clean(ly); completely; thoroughly; entirely
♦ 씻은듯이 잊다 forget all 《about it》; forget *sth* 《clear and》 clean
▶ 종기가 씻은듯이 나았다 The boil was all healed up.
▶ 하늘이 씻은듯이 맑다 The sky is as clear as can be.
▶ 약을 먹었더니 치통이 씻은듯이 가셨다 The toothache has clean gone by virtue of the remedy.

씽 with a whistle [whiz]; whistling; whizzing
♦ 씽하는 소리 a whistling sound; a whistle; 〈화살·총알 등의〉 a whizz
▶ 모터사이클이 씽하고 지나갔다 A motorcycle whizzed past.

씽씽 〈바람이〉 a sough
▶ 바람이 씽씽 불고 있었다 The wind was whistling [hissing, piping].
▶ 겨울에는 북풍이 씽씽 분다 The north wind howls in winter.

ㅇ

아 1 〈감탄·놀람 등〉 Ah!; Oh!; O!; O dear!; Why!; Well, well!
▶아, 깜짝이야 Oh, what a surprise!
▶아, 프랑스에 가고 싶다 Oh, I do wish I could go to France! (▶do는 wish의 뜻을 강조함)
▶아, 아름답다 Oh, beautiful!
▶아, 정말 기쁘다 Oh, how glad I am!
▶아, 큰일났네 Ah! That's the trouble.
2 〈슬픔·실망 등〉 Ah!; Alas!
▶아, 슬프다 Alas! ⇒ Woe is me!
▶아, 가엾어라 Ah, poor thing! ⇒ Ah, you poor fellow.
3 〈일깨움·맞장구〉 Oh; O; O yes; Ah; Well; Indeed
▶|會話|「이 버튼을 누르면 됩니다」「아, 그렇군요」 "Push the button here." "Oh, I see."
▶|會話|「브라운 씨를 알아요」「아, 그래요?」 "I know Mr. Brown." "Oh, do you?"
▶아, 왔다 왔다 Oh [Ah], here they come.
▶|會話|「민수야, 도와주겠니?」「아, 물론」 "Will you lend a hand, Min-su?" "Why, certainly."
▶|會話|「너 피곤하니?」「아, 그래」 "Are you tired?" "Yes, I am."
▶|會話|「상관 없지?」「아, 전혀」 "You don't mind, do you?" "No, not at all."
4 〈말을 걸 때〉 Oh; O; Well; I say; (美) Say; Listen; Look here
▶아, 여보세요 Hello! ⇒ I say!
▶아, 웨이터, 계산해 주세요 Oh, waiter! Check, please.

아- 亞- 〈다음 가는〉 sub-; second; near-
♦아류 an epigone; an (inferior) imitator / 아열대의 subtropical

아가 雅歌 〈聖〉 The Song of Solomon (略 Song of Sol.)

아가리 1 ⇨ 입
▶아가리 닥쳐 Shut up! ⇒ Stop [Hold] your jaw! ⇒ Hold your tongue!
2 〈그릇 등의〉 a mouth
♦병 아가리 the mouth of a bottle / 병 아가리를 열다[막다] take the lid off [put the lid back on] a bottle; open [close] a bottle
■—질〈말질〉a wrangle; a dispute; a quarrel; abuse; 〈악다구니〉 a brawl

아가미 the gill(s) 《of a fish》; the branchiae (sing. -chia) ♦아가미가 있는 gilled; branchiate
■—호흡 branchial respiration

아가씨 a young lady; (口) a missy; 〈부를 때〉 young lady; miss; (프) mademoiselle
♦시골 아가씨 a country girl [lass] / 어여쁜 아가씨 a lovely [sweet, (美口) cute] girl
▶저 아가씨는 누구죠? Who is the young lady?
▶아가씨, 이쪽입니다 This way, Miss.

아가위 the fruit of the hawthorn; a haw
■—나무 ⇨ 산사나무

아고산대 亞高山帶 〔地〕 a subalpine zone

아교 阿膠 glue ⇨ 갖풀

아구창 牙口瘡 〔韓醫〕 thrush; aphtha

아군 我軍 our forces [troops, army]; 〈우군〉 a friendly troop 〔army〕

아궁이 a fuel [fire] hole; the (fire) door 《of a furnace》; the burner door

아귀¹ **1** 〈갈라진 곳〉 a fork; a crotch ♦손아귀 the space between the thumb and the fingers
2 〈옷의 터놓은 데〉 side slits 《on an overcoat》; a placket 《in a skirt》 ♦두루마기에 아귀를 트다 provide a Korean overcoat with side slits
3 〈싹 나오는 곳〉 that part of a seed through which it sprouts ♦씨가 아귀 트다 a seed sprouts open
4 〈활의〉 the curved-in part of an archer's bow

아귀² 〔魚〕 an angler(fish)

아귀 餓鬼 **1** 〔佛敎〕 a starving [hungry] ghost; a famished devil [demon] **2** 〈식탐하는 사람〉 a greedy person; a person of voracious appetite ♦아귀 같은 greedy; gluttonous

아귀다툼 a quarrel ⇨ 말다툼

아귀맞추다 round out the number; bring it up to the proper amount; make it come out even

아귀세다 **1** 〈고집세다〉 obstinate; unyielding; stubborn ♦아귀센 사람 a stubborn [stiff-necked] fellow **2** 〈서술적〉 have a strong grip [grasping power]

아귀아귀 greedily; ravenously; gluttonously; voraciously ♦아귀아귀 먹다 eat greedily [voraciously]; devour; gobble away; wolf down

아그레망 approval; acceptance; (프) an agrément ♦아그레망을 요청하다 ask for an agrément / 아그레망을 주다 give an agrément

아그배나무 〔植〕 a toringo crab apple

아굿하다 **1** 〈겨우 미치다〉 barely come [measure] up to 《one's expectation》 **2** 〈틈이 조금 벌어져 있다〉 a bit open [apart]; a little ajar; do not quite fit; be not quite together

아기 **1** 〈갓난아이〉 an infant; a baby; a little child; (詩) a babe
▶아기는 사내애입니까, 계집애입니까? Is it [your baby] a boy or a girl?
2 〈딸·며느리〉 one's dear [darling]

아기똥거리다 **1** 〈걸음이〉 waddle; totter; walk with a waddling gait **2** 〈말·짓이〉 speak [behave] in an affected way

아기똥하다 〈교만하다〉 haughty; arrogant

아기서다 〈임신하다〉 conceive 《a baby》; get [become] pregnant; get with child

아기자기하다 1 〈잘 어울려 예쁘다〉 harmonious in appearance; visually charming; picturesque ◆아기자기하게 꾸민 방 a charmingly decorated room
▶그는 정원을 아기자기하게 꾸몄다 He made a garden tastefully [elaborately] laid out [designed].
2 〈잔재미가 있다〉 juicy; interesting; amusing; 〈분위기 등이〉 harmonious
◆아기자기한 이야기 a juicy story; an interesting [entertaining] talk
▶모임은 아기자기한 분위기 속에 끝이 났다 The meeting broke up in a very friendly atmosphere.
▶둘 사이가 아주 아기자기하다 〈친구끼리〉 The two are on very friendly terms. ⇌ 〈부부 사이〉 There is completely conjugal harmony between them.
아기작거리다 toddle; walk with a toddling gait
아기집 the womb ⇨ 자궁(子宮)
아까 〈조금 전〉 time ago; a little while ago; a short time ago ◆아까부터 for some time; since a little while ago
▶그는 아까 돌아왔습니다 He came back just a little while ago.
▶저 부인이 아까부터 기다리고 계십니다 That woman has been waiting for you some time.
▶아까 이야기는 비밀로 해주세요 Please keep secret what I told you a short time ago.
▶아까부터 그를 불렀는데 대답이 없었다 I have been calling him for a little while, but (have) got no answer.
아깝다 1 〈서운하다〉 regrettable; pitiful
◆아깝게도 regrettably; lamentably; sad to say / 아깝게도 절호의 기회를 놓치다 miss a golden opportunity
▶아깝게도 그는 요절했다 It's too bad that he died young.
▶1점차로 시합에 진 것이 아깝다 It's a shame [a pity, too bad] (that) we lost the game by one point.
2 〈소중하다〉 precious; valuable; worthy; dear
◆아까운 목숨 one's precious life / 아까워하다 set [put] much value on [upon]; make much of
▶정말 아까운 사람을 잃었다 His death is a great [true] loss to us.
▶시간이 아까우니 택시로 가자 We can't waste time; let's go by taxi.
▶목숨이 아까우면 꼼짝 마라 Stay where you are, if you want to stay alive.
3 〈애석·분하다〉 wasteful; too good (for); (be) unworthy (of)
◆아까운듯이 grudgingly; with an air of reluctance; reluctantly; unwillingly
▶버리기는 아깝다 It would be a waste to throw it away. ⇌ It's too good to be thrown away.
▶여배우가 될 수만 있다면 어떤 희생을 치러도 아깝지 않다 I would give anything in the world to be an actress.
아끼는 것이 찌로 간다 (속담) Penny wise, (and) pound foolish.

아끼다 1 〈절약하다〉 spare; economize; be frugal ((of)); 〈내놓기를 꺼리다〉 grudge; be stingy; be tightfisted; be a miser
◆돈을 아끼다 be frugal [chary] of one's money; begrudge [grudge] money / 물을 아끼다 economize water; use water sparingly / 돈을 아껴 쓰다 use one's money sparingly
▶그는 돈을 아끼지 않고 쓴다 He lavishes money. ⇌ He is liberal with his purse.
▶나는 노력을 아끼지 않겠다 I will not spare myself [my efforts].
2 〈소중히 하다〉 prize; value; esteem (highly); think [make] much of; hold sth dear; 〈알뜰히 하다〉 favor; treat tenderly [kindly]
▶그는 너무 바쁘기 때문에 일각이라도 아낀다 Because he is very busy, he values time.
▶그는 목숨보다 명예를 아꼈다 He valued honor above life.
아낌없는 unsparing; free; willing
▶지휘자는 아낌없는 박수 속에서 퇴장했다 The conductor left the stage amid thunderous [great, loud] applause.
▶그의 소설은 아낌없는 찬사를 받았다 His novel won [received] high praise. ⇌ He won [received] high praise for his novel.
아낌없이 unsparingly; ungrudgingly; without stint [reluctance, regret]; 〈후하게〉 freely; liberally; generously; lavishly
◆아낌없이 주다 give away freely; be generous ((with)) / 아낌없이 돈을 쓰다 be lavish with [of] one's money; spend money lavishly ((on))
▶저 사람은 자선사업에 많은 돈을 아낌없이 내놓았다 That man gave a lot of money freely to charities.
아나 1 〈여봐라·옜다〉 Hey!; Look!
▶아나, 네가 찾고 있던 책이다 Here's the book(s) you have been looking for.
2 〈고양이 부르는 소리〉 Here puss!; Kitty-kitty!
아나나스 〚植〛 an ananas
아나운서 an announcer ◆여자 아나운서 a woman [lady] announcer / 라디오[텔레비전] 아나운서 a radio [television] announcer
아나크로니즘 〈시대착오〉 anachronism
아나키스트 〈무정부주의자〉 an anarchist
아나키즘 〈무정부주의〉 anarchism
아낙 1 〈내간〉 a lady's private sitting room; the ladies' quarters; a boudoir
2 ⇨ 아낙네
아낙군수 —郡守 a person who stays at home all the time; a stay-at-home; (口) a homebody
아낙네 a woman; a wife ◆아낙네들 the womenfolk; women
아날로그 〚電〛 an analog(ue)
■—시계 an analog(ue) watch —컴퓨터 an analog(ue) computer
아내 〈처〉 a wife (pl. wives); (俗) one's better half; 〈배우자〉 〚法〛 a spouse
◆헌신적인 아내 a devoted wife / 훌륭한 아내 a good wife / 아내의 의무를 다하다 do one's wifely duties / 아내를 얻다 marry (a woman); take ((to oneself)) a wife; get married to a woman / 아내에게 충실하다 be faithful [true]

to *one's* wife / 아내로 맞다[삼다] make 《a woman》 *one's* wife; take 《a woman》 to wife [in marriage]
▶ 그녀는 그의 훌륭한 아내가 되었다 She made him a good wife. ⇒ She made a good wife for him.
▶ 2년 전에 그는 아내를 잃었다 He lost his wife two years ago. ⇒ His wife died two years ago.
▶ 그는 세 살 연상의 여자를 아내로 맞았다 He married a woman three years older.

아네모네 〔植〕 an anemone; a windflower; a snowdrop

아녀자 兒女子 〈어린이와 여자〉 children and women; 〈여자〉 a woman; a girl; 《俗》 a skirt

아노락 〈두건 달린 방한복〉 an anorak; a parka

아놀드 〈영국의 시인·비평가〉 Arnold, Matthew (1822-88)

아늑하다 snug; cosy; cozy ◆아늑한 장소 a cubbyhole / 작고 아늑한 집 a snug [cosy] little house

아니¹ 〈부정·반대〉 not; never; no
◆아니 가다[오다] do not go [come]
▶ 會話「내일 그녀 올까?」「아니 올걸」"Is she coming tomorrow?" "I don't think so." ⇒ "I think not."

아니² 1 〈대답이 부정일 때〉 no; nay; 〈대답이 긍정일 때〉 yes; 〈주저하여〉 well
◆아니라고 대답하다 say no; answer [reply] in the negative
▶ 會話「담배 한 대 어때?」「아니, 고마워, 내게도 있어」"How about a cigarette?" "No, thank you, I have my own."
▶ 그것은 1,000원, 아니, 100원의 값어치도 없다 It is worth 1,000 won, no, not even 100 won.
▶ 會話「어젯밤에 거기 없었니?」「아니, 있었어」"Weren't you there last night?" "Yes, I was."
▶ 會話「맥주는 안 좋아하니?」「아니, 좋아해」"Don't you like beer?" "Yes, I do."
2 〈놀람·의아〉 dear me; why; what; good heavens; well
▶ 아니 어떡하면 좋지? Well, what should I do?
▶ 아니 그런 놀라운 일이 있나 Why, it is a big surprise to me.
▶ 아니 어디서 그것을 구했니? Why, where did you find it?

아니꼽다 1 〈메스껍다〉 sick; nauseated; 〈서술적〉 be sick at the stomach; feel sick [nausea, queasy]
▶ 보기만 해도 속이 아니꼽다 The mere sight of it makes me sick [turns my stomach].
2 〈불쾌하다〉 sickening; revolting; offensive; repulsive; disgusting; detestable
▶ 그의 태도는 아니꼬웠다 His attitude disgusted [offended] me. ⇒ I was disgusted [was offended] at [by] his attitude. ⇒ His attitude was disgusting [very offensive] to me.
▶ 그는 아니꼬울 만큼 침착하다 He is provokingly cool.

아니나다를까 as *one* expected; as (was) expected; as feared; sure enough
▶ 아니나다를까 그녀는 결석이었다 As I had feared [expected], she was absent. ⇒ Sure enough, she did not show up.
▶ 아니나다를까 그는 거기 있었다 Sure enough, I found him there.
▶ 아니나다를까 급행은 붐볐고 좌석이 없었다 Just as I (had) feared, the express train was very crowded and I couldn't get a seat.

아니다 (be) not; no
◆~도 아니고 …도 아니다 neither ~ nor …
▶ 그는 말만 잘하는 것이 아니고 유능하기도 하다 He is as ready to work as to talk. ⇒ He is not only eloquent but also efficient.
▶ 會話「이거 네 거니?」「아니야」"Is this yours?" "No."
▶ 바보가 아닌 이상 그런 짓은 하지 않을거다 None but a fool would do such a thing.

아니 땐 굴뚝에 연기 날까 《속담》 There is no smoke [No smoke] without fire.

아니라고 (say) that it is not; saying that it is not ▶ 그는 암이 반드시 불치병은 아니라고 말한다 He says that cancer is not always a fatal disease.

아니라도 even if [though] (it is) not
▶ 설사 자기 것이 아니라도 낭비하는 것은 나쁘다 It is bad for anyone to waste things even if they are not his own.

아니면 〈택일〉 either … or; 〈그렇지 않으면〉 or; (or) else
▶ 네가 가든가, 아니면 그녀가 가야 한다 Either you are to go or she is. ⇒ Either you or she is to go.
▶ 더 주의해서 운전하든가, 아니면 운전을 해서는 안된다 Either you ought to be more careful, or (else) you shouldn't drive at all.
▶ 자유가 아니면 죽음을 달라 Give me liberty, or give me death!

아니스 〔植〕 anise

아니오 〈대답이 부정일 때〉 no; 〈대답이 긍정일 때〉 yes
▶ 會話「생선은 좋아하지 않습니까?」「아니오, 좋아합니다」"Don't you like fish?" "Yes, I do."

아니참 Well!; Oh!; Uh!; That reminds me.; I just happen to recall it.

아니하다 do not ⇨ 않다

아닌게아니라 just as *one* thought; as (was, may be, had been) expected; sure enough; indeed; truly; certainly
▶ 이것은 아닌게아니라 지금까지 내가 본 영화 중 최고다 This is certainly [surely] the best movie I've ever seen.
▶ 아닌게아니라 그렇다 Certainly it is.
▶ 아닌게아니라 네 말이 옳다 To be sure, what you say is right.
▶ 아닌게아니라 이것은 배신행위다 This is a clear breach of faith.

아닌밤중 —中 ◆아닌밤중에 at midnight; at dead of night; in the dead [depth] of the night / 아닌밤중에 홍두깨처럼 abruptly; all of a sudden; unexpectedly; like a thunderbolt from a clear sky
▶ 그가 아닌밤중에 홍두깨처럼 나타나는 바람에

놀랐다 I was surprised at his sudden appearance.
아닐린 〔化〕 aniline ■ —**염료[색소]** aniline dyes [colors]
아다지오 (이)〔樂〕adagio
아담 〔聖〕 Adam ♦**아담과 이브**〔하와〕 Adam and Eve
아담하다 雅淡— elegant; graceful; refined; 〈조촐하다〉 nice; neat; trim; tidy; 〈아늑하다〉 snug; cozy
♦**아담하니 지내기 좋은 방** a cozy [snug] room; a compact little apartment / **아담한 집** a trim [snug] house
아대륙 亞大陸 a subcontinent ♦**인도 아대륙** the Indian Subcontinent
아데나워 〈통일전 서독의 정치가·수상〉 Adenauer, Konrad (1876-1967)
아데노이드 〔醫〕 adenoids ♦**아데노이드 절제술** adenoidectomy / **아데노이드 증상이 있는 아이** an adenoidal child
아덴 〈예멘의 도시〉 Aden
아동 兒童 a child; a juvenile; 〈학동〉 a pupil; (총칭) children; boys and girls
♦**초등 학교 아동** a schoolchild; elementary [primary] school children / **취학 전의 아동** a preschool child / **아동의** juvenile / **아동용의** juvenile; (books) for children
■ —**교육** juvenile education; the education of children —**극**(劇) a juvenile drama; a play for children —**기**(期) (one's) childhood —**도서** children's books —**문학** juvenile literature; literature for children —**문학가** a writer of juvenile stories —**상담소** a child consultation center —**심리학** juvenile [child] psychology —**연구** the study of children —**연구소** a child research institute —**교** pedology
아동복지 兒童福祉 child welfare
■ —**법**(法) the Child Welfare Law —**시설** a child welfare institution
아둔패기 a dull fellow; (口) a blockhead
▶ **그걸 믿다니 자네도 아둔패기로군** How stupid of you to believe that!
아둔하다 stupid; dull; dull-witted; slow; 〈서술적〉 be thick [fat] in head
▶ **그는 아둔해서 완곡한 표현으로는 알아듣지 못한다** He is so thick-skinned that gentle hints are lost [wasted] on him.
▶ **그는 아둔해서 잘 속는다** He is so stupid that he is easily taken in.
아드님 your [his] esteemed son
아드득 1 〈이 가는 소리〉 with a grinding sound —**아드득하다** grate [gnash, grind] one's teeth 2 〈깨무는 소리〉 with a crunching sound —**아드득하다** ▶ **사자가 뼈를 아드득하고 깨물었다** The lion crunched the bone.
아드득아드득 with a crunching sound
아드레날린 〔生化〕 adrenaline
아드리아해 —海 the Adriatic Sea
아득하다 1 〈거리가〉 far; faraway; far-off; far distant; remote; 〈서술적〉 be a long way off ♦**아득히 먼 나라** a faraway [far distant, remote, far-off] country / **가도가도 아득한 천릿길** a long, long way to go
▶ **우리는 갈 길이 아득하다** We have a long way to go.
▶ **한라산 정상이 아득히 바라보인다** The top of Hallasan is seen a long way off [far away].
▶ **어딘가 멀리서 절의 종소리가 아득하게 들려왔다** Somewhere far-off, the peals of a temple bell sounded faintly.
2 〈시간이〉 remote; far-off ♦**아득한 옛날을 생각하다** think of the days long past; think of far-off times
▶ **아득한 옛날에 인간은 불을 사용하기 시작했다** Far in the past man began using fire.
3 〈정신이〉 vague; dim; hazy; obscure; indistinct; fuzzy
♦**아득한 기억을 더듬다** trace back a vague memory
▶ **그녀는 아득하게나마 그 사건을 알고 있다** She has only a vague idea of the incident.
아들 a son; a boy
♦**착한[못된] 아들을 두다** be blessed with a good son [cursed with a bad son]
▶ **저 노인은 아들 내외와 함께 살고 있다** That old man is living with his son and daughter-in-law.
—**딸** son(s) and daughter(s)
아들자 〈보조(補助)자〉 〔數〕 a vernier
아디스아바바 〈에티오피아의 수도〉 Addis Ababa
아디외 〈안녕〉 (프) an adieu (pl. ~s, ~x); good-by(e); so long
아딧줄 a brace
아따 (美俗) Gee!; Heavens!; Damn it!
▶ **아따, 이 양반 급하기도 하셔** Oh! Why are you in such a hurry?
▶ **아따, 그 여자 키도 크네** Gee [Jesus], what a tall woman she is!
▶ **아따, 걱정도 팔자야** Dammit, don't worry so much.
아뜩하다 〈아찔하다〉 suddenly dizzy; giddy; dazed; stunned ♦**아뜩한 높이에서** at a giddy [dizzy] height
▶ **나는 그 나쁜 소식을 듣고 정신이 아뜩했다** I was stunned at the bad news.
▶ **요 삼일 동안 아무것도 안 먹었더니 좀 아뜩하다** I feel slightly dizzy because I haven't had anything to eat these three days.
아라공 〈프랑스의 시인〉 Aragon, Louis (1897-1982)
아라모드 〈최신 유행〉 (프) à la mode
아라베스크 〔발레〕 an arabesque
아라비아 Arabia
♦**아라비아의** Arabian
■ —**고무** gum arabic —**낙타** an Arabian camel; a dromedary —**말** an Arabian horse; an Arab —**문자** Arabic script —**문화** Arabic culture —**반도** the Arabian Peninsula —**사람** an Arabian; an Arab∶**아라비아 사람의** Arabian; Arabic —**사막** the Arabian Desert —**숫자** Arabic figures [numerals] —**어**(語) Arabic∶ **아라비아어의** Arabic —**해** the Arabian Sea
아라비안나이트 〈천일 야화〉 The Arabian Nights' Entertainments (▶The Thousand and One Nights; The Arabian Nights라고도

아라한 阿羅漢 〔佛敎〕 an arhat; a Buddhist monk who attained Nirvana

아랄해 ―海 the Aral Sea

아람 〈밤·상수리 등의〉 fully ripened nuts

아람치 〈자기 차지〉 one's share; one's own

아랍 Arab
■ 범아랍주의 Pan-Arabism
■ ―게릴라 an Arab guerilla ―국가 an Arab state ―민족주의 Arab nationalism ―세계 the Arab world; Arabdom ―연맹 the Arab League

아랍에미리트 〈나라 이름〉 the United Arab Emirates

아랑곳 〈개의〉 concern; interest; 〈유의〉 heed; attention; notice; regard; 〈간섭〉 meddling; interference
◆ 아랑곳하다 be concerned about; concern oneself about; take (an) interest in; give heed [attention] to; take notice of; interfere in [with]; meddle in [with]; 〈상대하다〉 have to do with / 아랑곳하지 않다 do not care [mind]; be indifferent 《to》; neglect 《one's family》; be heedless of 《others》; care nothing 《about》
▶ 그는 남에게 폐가 되는 것은 아랑곳하지 않고 그것을 했다 He did it without regard to others' troubles.
▶ 그는 남의 기분은 아랑곳하지 않고 하고 싶은 대로 한다 He does what he likes regardless of other people's feelings.

아랑곳없다 〈서술적〉 have no concern with; have nothing to do with; have no interest in; be no concern of
◆ …에도 아랑곳없이 in the teeth of…; in defiance [spite] of…
▶ 그들은 경비 같은 것은 아랑곳없이 계획을 세웠다 They made a plan without thinking over [regardless of, without regard to] the expenses.
▶ 그가 뭐라고 하든 난 아랑곳없다 I am not concerned about what he may say.
▶ 그것은 나에게는 아랑곳없는 일이다 It's no concern of mine.

아래 1 〈하부·아래쪽〉 the lower part; the bottom; the foot; the base
◆ 아래의 under; lower / 아래에 under; beneath; below; 〈바로 아래〉 underneath / 아래(쪽으)로 down; downward(s) / 나무 아래서 under a tree
▶ 그녀는 아랫 서랍을 열었다 She unlocked the bottom drawer.
▶ 그 교회는 언덕 아래에 있었다 The church stood under [at the foot of] a hill.
▶ 그는 계단 아래서 기다리고 있었다 He was waiting at the foot of the stairs.
▶ 아래서 세번째 줄을 읽으시오 Read the third line from the bottom.
▶ 무릎 아래가 차가워진다 I feel chilly below the knees.
▶ 다리 아래에 소년이 있었다 There was a boy under [beneath] the bridge.
▶ 눈 아래에는 푸른 들판이 펼쳐져 있었다 A green field stretched below our eyes.
▶ 이야기를 할 때는 아래를 보지 마라 Don't look down, while talking.
▶ 한 쌍의 교각이 아래서 그 다리를 지탱하고 있다 A pair of piers support the bridge from below.
▶ 저녁 식사하러 아래로 내려오세요 Come down (stairs) for supper.
2 〈다음〉 below
▶ 아래와 같다 be as follows
▶ 아래 통계표를 보라 See the statistics in the chart(s) below.
3 〈하위·연하〉 ◆ 평균보다 아래 below the average / 아래에서 둘째 아이 the second youngest of one's children / 아래의 lower; subordinate; below; under / …의 아래서 일하다 work under…
▶ 그는 아래 학년입니다 He is in a lower class.
▶ 과장은 부장 아래다 The section chief is beneath the department head.
▶ 위로는 장관에서부터 아래로는 거지에 이르기까지 그것을 보러 왔다 All people, from ministers down to beggars, came to see it.
▶ 그녀는 오빠보다 다섯 살 아래다 She is five years younger than her brother. ⇒ She is younger than her brother by five years.
▶ 만원 아래로는 팔 수 없습니다 I can't sell it under [at less than] 10,000 won.
4 〈받음〉 ◆ …의 지휘[지도, 감독] 아래 under the command [direction, supervision] of… / …의 지원 아래 with the support [help] of…; through the sponsorship of… / …이라는 조건 아래 under the condition of [that]…; on condition of [that]…
▶ 시민 문화제가 시의 후원 아래 개최되었다 The citizens' cultural festival was held under the sponsorship of the city.
5 〈하체〉 the lower part of the body; 〈음부〉 the genitalia; one's private parts

아래옷 lower garment; bottom piece; trousers; breeches

아래위 the lower and upper parts; up and bottom; above and below
◆ 아래위로 《move》 up and down; upward and downward; above and below; high and low / 아무의 아래위를 훑어보다 survey sb from head to foot; measure sb with one's eyes
▶ 지진 때문에 집이 아래위로 흔들리는 것을 느꼈다 I felt the house shake up and down in the earthquake.
▶ 배가 아래위로 흔들렸다 Our ship pitched.

아래윗막이 〈양 마구리〉 end pieces; top and bottom pieces

아래윗벌 〈옷의〉 a suit 《of clothes》; upper and lower garment

아래짝 the lower one 《of a pair set》; the bottom member

아래쪽 1 〈아래 방향〉 down; lower direction
◆ 아래쪽으로 downward(s); down / 아래쪽으로 내려가다 go down [downward] / 아래쪽을 보다 look down 2 〈앞대〉 the southern part 《of a province》

아래채 an outhouse [outbuilding] (near the gate)

아래층 ―層 the lower floor [story]; the downstairs 《▶단수취급》 ◆ 아래층의 방 a

downstairs room / 아래층에〈서〉 downstairs; below stairs / 아래층으로 내려가다 go downstairs
▶ 그는 저녁 식사하러 아래층으로 내려갔다 He went downstairs to dinner.

아래턱 the lower jaw; the underjaw ♦ 아래턱을 쓰다듬다 stroke *one's* chin

아래통 the girth of the lower part 〈of *sth*〉

아랫것 〈하인〉 servants; employees; 〈손아랫사람〉 *one's* inferiors

아랫길 1〈길〉 the lower road; the way below 2〈품질〉 lower grade; inferior quality

아랫녘 1〈남부 지방〉 the southern part of Korea 2〈앞대〉 the southern part 〈of a province〉

아랫눈썹 the lower eyelashes

아랫니 the lower [under] teeth

아랫도리 1〈하체〉 the lower part [half] of the body
▶ 그는 아랫도리가 마비되었다 The lower part of his body is paralyzed. ⇌ He is paralyzed below the waist [from the waist down].
2〈하층 계급〉 the lower class; the grass roots
3〈아래옷〉 lower garment(s)

아랫동아리 1〈물건의〉 the lower 〈of a thing〉 2 ☞ 아랫도리

아랫막이 〈아래쪽 마구리〉 bottom piece

아랫머리 the bottom end; the bottom 〈of a thing having the similar top〉

아랫목 the warmer [lower] part of an *ondol* floor

아랫물 the water of the lower stream 〈of a river〉

아랫반 ―班 a lower [low] class [grade]; 〈英〉 a lower form ▶ 그는 아랫반 학생이다 He is in a lower class.

아랫방 ―房 a detached room

아랫배 the abdomen; the underbelly
♦ 아랫배의 abdominal / 아랫배가 아프다 have [feel] a pain in the abdomen / 아랫배에 힘을 주다 strain the abdomen; put *one's* whole strength in the abdomen

아랫벌 〈아래옷〉 lower garment

아랫볼 the lower cheeks

아랫사람 〈손아랫사람〉 *one's* junior; 〈부하〉 a subordinate; an underling; a follower
♦ 아랫사람이 되어 일하다 work under *sb*
▶ 아랫사람에게는 친절히 해라 Be kind to your junior.
▶ 그는 아랫사람들의 미움을 샀다 He was hated by his subordinates.

아랫사랑 ―舍廊 a guest room in the outer wing of a house

아랫수염 ―鬚髥 〈턱수염〉 a beard

아랫입술 the lower [under] lip ♦ 아랫입술을 깨물다 bit *one's* lower lip

아랫잇몸 the lower gum(s)

아랫자리 1〈낮은 곳의〉 a seat on a lower place; the seats below; 〈하위〉 a lower seat; a subordinate position; 〈아랫사람 자리〉 seats for *one's* juniors [subordinates] 2 〈數〉 one place down; the next decimal place

아랫집 the house just below [just down the way]

아량 雅量 tolerance; generosity; liberality; broad-mindedness; large-mindedness
♦ 아량이 있는 generous 〈to〉; broad-minded; tolerant / 아량이 없는 intolerant; narrow-minded / 아량을 보이다 show *oneself* to be generous

아련하다 dim; faint; vague
♦ 아련히 dimly; faintly; vaguely / 아련하게 보이다 be seen dimly
▶ 이제 그것은 아련한 기억으로 남아 있을 뿐이다 I have only a vague memory of it now.
▶ 멀리 탑의 윤곽이 아련하게 보였다 The vague outline of the tower was seen in the distance.

아령 啞鈴 a 〈pair of〉 dumbbell ■ ―體操 dumbbell exercise

아로새기다 engrave [carve] delicately; make an elaborate bas-relief
♦ 용을 아로새긴 기둥 a pillar of a subtly carved dragon / 나무에 이름을 아로새기다 cut *one's* name on a tree / 마음에 아로새기다 bear [keep] *sth* in mind
▶ 이 말들은 내 마음속에 깊이 아로새겨져 있다 These words are engraved on my mind. ⇌ These words are kept deep in my memory.

아롱다롱하다 unevenly striped; spotted; mottled; dappled; speckled; motley
♦ 무늬가 아롱다롱한 옷감 cloth with a spotted pattern

아롱지다 spotted; mottled; dappled; speckled; motley; variegated

아류 亞流 a follower; an 〈inferior〉 imitator; an adherent; a 〈bad〉 second; an epigone
▶ 그는 디킨즈의 아류다 He imitates Dickens. ⇌ He is a follower of Dickens.

아르 〈면적의 단위〉 an are

아르곤 〔化〕 argon

아르마딜로 〔動〕 an armadillo 〈*pl.* ~s〉

아르메니아 〈나라 이름〉 Armenia; 〈공식명〉 the Republic of Armenia ♦ 아르메니아의 Armenian
■ ―말 Armenian ―사람 an Armenian

아르바이트 a part-time job; work [a job] on the side

> 解說 독일어의 Arbeit (일, 연구)에서 온 말인데 영어 표현은 이와 다르다. 영어로는 ***part-time job*** 또는 ***job on the side*** 등으로 쓴다. 본업이 있으면서 부업으로, 특히 야간에 아르바이트하는 것을 moonlight라 하고, 그런 사람은 moonlighter라 한다.

♦ 아르바이트를 하고 있다 have a job on the side / 아르바이트로 학비를 벌다 work for *one's* school expenses
▶ 그는 아르바이트를 하여 대학을 나왔다 He worked his way through college.
▶ 나는 아르바이트로 여고생의 수학 가정교사를 했다 I tutored a high school girl in math for my school expenses.
―**아르바이트하다** work at a part-time job; 〈본업 이외에〉 go into other work
■ ―학생 a working student; a student worker

아르에이치 Rh
  ■**—마이너스**[음성] Rh negative (略 Rh⁻)
  —식 혈액형 (blood types of) Rh groups **—인자**〔醫〕an Rh [a Rhesus] factor; Rh antigen
  —플러스[양성] Rh positive (略 Rh⁺)
아르키메데스 〈그리스의 수학자·물리학자〉Archimedes (287?-212 B.C.)
  ■**—의 원리** the Archimedean [Archimedes'] principle
아르헨티나 Argentina; 〈공식명〉the Argentine Republic ♦**아르헨티나의** Argentine; Argentinean; Argentinian
  ■**—사람** an Argentine; an Argentinean; an Argentinian
아른거리다 flicker; shimmer ⇨ 어른거리다
아름 an armful; an armload
  ♦**한 아름의 책**[장작] an armful [armload] of books [firewood] / 한 아름이 넘는 기둥 a pillar so big (that) one cannot put one's arms around it / 몇 아름이나 되는 큰 나무 a big tree that takes several persons to circle it with outstretched arms; a big tree measuring several arms' stretches around
아름다움 beauty
  ♦자연의 아름다움을 감상하다 appreciate the beauties of nature / 경치의 아름다움에 넋을 잃다 be overpowered with the beauty of the scene
아름답다 pretty; beautiful; lovely; handsome; good-looking; fair; charming; comely; fine; picturesque; sweet
  ♦아름다운 경치 beautiful scenery; a picturesque [lovely, charming] scene / 아름다운 목소리 a sweet voice / 아름다운 여인 a beautiful lady; a beauty / 아름다운 이야기 a beautiful story / 아름답게 beautifully; prettily; charmingly; sweetly / 아름답게 하다 beautify; make sth beautiful [pretty] / 아름답게 차려 입다 dress oneself beautifully; dress up
  ▶그 꽃 참 아름답다 What a pretty flower it is!
  ▶그 소녀는 아름다운 마음씨를 가졌다 The girl was pure in [of] heart. ⇒ The girl had a pure heart.
  ▶그녀는 한복을 입으면 훨씬 더 아름답다 She looks even more lovely in Korean clothes.
  ▶그 홀은 꽃으로 아름답게 장식되어 있었다 The hall was decorated beautifully with flowers.
아름드리나무 a tree measuring more than one stretch [span] of one's arms
아리다 1〈맛이〉hot; pungent; acrid; biting; burning; 〈서술적〉taste hot; have a biting [burning] taste; bite
  ▶너무 매워서 혀가 아리다 It's so hot that my tongue is burning.
  2〈상처 등이〉smart; tingling; burning; biting; 〈수족이〉numb; asleep; benumbed
  ▶벤 데가 아직도 아리다 The cut still smarts.
  ▶연기 때문에 눈이 아리다 Smoke makes my eyes smart.
  ▶상처 입은 자리가 아려서 그는 잠을 이루지 못했다 The smart of the hurt kept him awake.
  ▶추위서 손가락이 아리다 My fingers are asleep with cold.
아리땁다 beautiful; charming; lovely; fascinating
아리송하다 vague; ambiguous; equivocal; indistinct; evasive
  ♦아리송한 답변[설명] an equivocal [evasive] answer [explanation] / 아리송하게 대답하다 give an equivocal [a vague] answer; give a noncommittal answer
아리스토텔레스 〈그리스의 철학자〉Aristotle (384-322 B.C.) ♦**아리스토텔레스 학파의 사람** an Aristotelian
아리아 〔樂〕an aria
  ♦오페라의 아리아 an operatic aria
아리안 〈인종〉the Aryan races; the Aryans
아리안어족 —語族 〈인도 유럽 어족〉the Indo-European (languages)
아릿하다 acrid; (bitterly) pungent; 〈서술적〉taste acrid; sting [bite] the tongue; be biting to the taste ♦아릿한 맛이 나다 taste acrid; be biting to the tongue
아마 perhaps; maybe; probably; likely; possibly; It is probable that...; in all likelihood [probability]; 〈걱정되어〉I am afraid; I fear; 〈의심할 때〉I suspect

> 解說 확률이 반반인 경우에는 **perhaps**나 **maybe**(미국 구어에서 즐겨 씀)를, 그 이상인 경우에는 **probably**를 쓴다. probably보다 다소 확률이 떨어지는 경우는 **likely**를, 가능성은 있으나 확실성이 적을 때는 **possibly**를 쓴다. probably는 문장 안에서, perhaps와 maybe는 문장의 첫머리에 쓰이다. likely는 문장의 첫머리나 중간의 어느 위치에서도 쓰이며 미래형의 경우는 very, most 등을 같이 쓴다.

  ▶아마 그것은 사실일 거야 Perhaps that's true. ⇒ It may well be true.
  ▶아마 오늘 밤엔 비가 올 거야 It will probably rain this evening. ⇒ Perhaps it will rain this evening.
  ▶아마 날씨가 좋아질 것이다 I hope it will be fine.
  ▶내일은 아마 제가 파티에 참석하지 못할 겁니다 I am afraid I shall not be able to join the party tomorrow.
  ▶했더라면 아마 그는 성공했을 것이다 If he had tried, he would probably have succeeded. ⇒ If he had tried his hand at it, he would have been successful.
아마 亞麻 〔植〕flax ♦아마(제)의 flaxen
  ■**—포**(布) linen
아마도 probably; in all probability; perhaps; maybe; likely ⇨ 아마
아마릴리스 〔植〕an amaryllis
아마인 亞麻仁 linseed; flaxseed ■**—유**(油) linseed oil
아마존 1〔그神〕an Amazon ♦아마존 같은 Amazonian 《woman》
  2〈강이름〉the Amazon ♦아마존(유역)의 Amazonian
아마추어 an amateur; a nonprofessional
  ♦아마추어의 nonprofessional / 아마추어다운 amateurish / 아마추어의 수준을 넘어서다〈일

이〉 be free from amateurishness; be far from amateurish; be as good as professional; 〈사람이〉 have more than amateur's skill
■—규정 requirements for amateurship —무선국 an amateur radio station —무선사 an amateur radio operator; a (radio) ham —정신 amateurism

아말감 〔化〕 amalgam
  금[주석]— gold [tin] amalgam ■—법(法) the amalgamation process

아메리카 America ▶**남북—** North and South America; the Americas **라틴—** Latin America **중앙—** Central America **—주[대륙]** the American Continent

아메리칸 American ▶**—인디언** American Indians; the Red Indians

아메리칸리그 the American League

아메리칸풋볼 American football

아메바 an amoeba 《*pl.* ~s, -bae》 ■**—성 이질** amoebic dysentery

아멘 Amen!; So be it!

아명 兒名 one's milk name; a childish name

아모스 〔聖〕 (The Book of) Amos

아무¹ 1 〈누구〉 anyone; anybody; any person; 〈부정〉 no one; nobody; none
  ▶아무도 못 만났다 I haven't seen anybody.
  ▶전쟁을 원하는 사람은 아무도 없다 Nobody wants war.
  ▶그가 누군지 아무도 모른다 Nobody [No one] knows who he is.
  ▶아무라도 좋으니 누가 좀 도와 주시오 I need some of you to help me. Anyone will do.
  ▶아무도 그 뜻을 알 수 없었으리라고 생각한다 I don't think anyone could understand the meaning.
  ▶그런 문제는 아무나 풀 수 있다 Anyone could solve such a problem.
  ▶아무나 좋아하는 사람을 고르시오 Choose who(m)ever [anyone] you like.
  2 ⇨ 아무개

아무² 〈어떠한·아무런〉 any; 〈부정〉 no; not at all
  ♦아무 까닭 없이 for nothing; without any reason / 아무 생각 없이 with no definite idea; unintentionally; unconcernedly / 아무 상관이 없다 have no relation [connection] whatever 《with》 / 아무 말 없이 결근하다 absent *oneself* from office without notice
  ▶아무 이상 없습니다 Nothing is wrong [the matter]. ⇌ 《美》 Everything's O.K.
  ▶뼈에는 아무 이상이 없다 The bone is not affected at all. ⇌ The bone is all right.
  ▶나는 그 일과는 아무 관련이 없다 I have no connection whatever [have nothing to do] with the matter.
  ▶그에겐 충고해봤자 아무 소용이 없다 Advice is no use to him.
  ▶교섭은 아무 탈 없이 잘 진행되었다 There was no hitch in the negotiations. ⇌ The negotiations went well [all right].

아무개 a certain person; Mr. X; Mr. [Mrs., Miss] So-and-so; such and such a person ♦이아무개 a certain (Mr.) Lee; a man called Lee; a [one] Mr. Lee / 아무개 박사 Dr. So-and-so
  ▶아무개가 그렇게 말했다 Mr. So-and-so said so.

아무것 anything; something; 〈부정〉 nothing; 〈사람〉 none
  ♦아무것이나 좋아하는 것 anything *one* likes / 아무것도 아닌 일 〈쉬운 일〉 an easy thing [task]; 〈사소한 일〉 a small [trifling] matter; a (mere) trifle / 아무것도 않고 without doing anything
  ▶나는 할 일이 아무것도 없다 I have nothing [no work] to do.
  ▶그 책에는 재미있는 것이 아무것도 없었다 I found nothing interesting in the book.
  ▶그는 학자도 아무것도 아니다 He is nothing of a scholar.
  ▶그에 비하면 나는 정말 아무것도 아니다 I am a mere nothing compared to him.
  ▶〔會話〕「무슨 일이 있었니?」「아무것도 아냐」 "What's wrong with you?" "Nothing serious."

아무데 any place; anywhere; 〈부정〉 nowhere
  ▶당신이 가는 곳이라면 아무데건 따라가겠소 I will follow you wherever you go.
  ▶나는 아무데도 안 간다 I am not going anywhere. ⇌ I am going nowhere.
  ▶그는 수년 동안 아무데도 가지 않았다 He has gone nowhere for years.
  ▶그 책은 아무데서도 구할 수가 없다 The book is nowhere to be had.

아무때 (at) any moment [time]; anytime; any (old) day; always; all the time; whenever
  ▶아무때나 좋다 Any time will do.
  ▶아무때든 오십시오 Come at any time you please.
  ▶아무때든 그가 좋을 때 만나겠다 I'll see him whenever he likes to come.
  ▶우리는 아무때고 출발할 수 있다 We are ready to start at a moment's notice.

아무래도 1 〈어찌되든·무관심〉 in any way; anyhow
  ♦아무래도 좋은 일 a matter of no consequence [of indifference]; a trivial matter; a trifle / 아무래도 좋다는 태도를 취하다 take an indifferent attitude 《toward》; be devil-may-care 《about》
  ▶결과는 아무래도 좋다 The result does not matter.
  ▶아무래도 좋으니 네 맘대로 해라 It doesn't matter, you may do as you please. ⇌ Have it your own way.
  2 〈아무리 하여도·결코·좀처럼·도저히〉 by any means; on any account; possibly; by any possibility; at all; for anything; for all the world
  ▶아무래도 가망이 없다 There is no hope at all [in the world].
  ▶그는 아무래도 회복될 것 같지 않다 His recovery is beyond hope.
  ▶아무래도 그의 이름이 생각나지 않는다 I just can't remember his name. ⇌ I can't, for the life of me, remember his name.
  ▶너한테는 아무래도 못 당하겠다 I am no match for you. ⇌ I cannot come near you.
  ▶이 문은 아무래도 열리지 않는다 This door

will not open.

3 〈아무리 보아도·불가피하게·틀림없이〉 any way you look at it; to all appearance(s); in every respect; in all respects; surely; inevitably
▶ 그는 아무래도 60은 넘었다 He must be over sixty.
▶ 아무래도 길을 잘못 든 것 같다 It looks as though we have taken the wrong road.
▶ 아무래도 비가 올 것 같다 It sure looks like rain. ⇒ I am afraid it is going to rain.
▶ 아무래도 그렇게 될 것 같다 There is every likelihood that it will come to that.
▶ 아무래도 10만원은 있어야겠다 I must have one hundred thousand won.
▶ 그 계획은 아무래도 실패다 The enterprise is doomed to failure.

4 〈싫건 좋건〉 whether willing or not; willingly or unwillingly; 〈결국〉 in the end; in the long run; after all; eventually; 〈필연적으로〉 inevitably; must (needs); infallibly
▶ 아무래도 가야겠다 I have no choice but to go. ⇒ I have to go whether I like it or not.
▶ 아무래도 실력이 이긴다 Real ability will win in the end.

아무러면 whatever it is; no matter what [how] it is; whatever anybody may do; whoever says it
▶ 옷이야 아무러면 어떠냐 It doesn't matter how your clothes look like. ⇒ Don't mind what you wear. ⇒ Don't bother to dress up.
▶ 사람들이 아무러면 어떠냐 Don't mind what people say.

아무런 any sort of; no
♦ 아무런 생각 없이 unconsciously; unintentionally; unwittingly / 아무런 예고도 없이 with no notice whatever
▶ 그것은 아무런 소용도 없다 It is of no value whatever.
▶ 아무런 의심의 여지도 없다 There is no doubt whatever.

아무런들 whatever it is ⇨ 아무러면
아무렇거나 anyhow; anyway; in any case; at any rate
▶ 아무렇거나 출발하세 Let's start anyway.
▶ 아무렇거나 꼭 오겠소 I will come at any rate.
▶ 아무렇거나 시험은 쳐보겠소 I'm going to take the examination whether I'll succeed in it or not.

아무렇게 in whatever way; however
아무렇게나 〈되는대로〉 at random; at [by] haphazard; haphazardly; casually; 〈건성으로〉 carelessly; indifferently; halfheartedly; in a slovenly way
♦ 아무렇게나 하는 말 a random [casual] remark / 아무렇게나 다루다 handle roughly [carelessly]; treat sb with neglect / 아무렇게나 말하다 talk at random; say irresponsible things / 아무렇게나 쏘다 shoot without aim; fire blindly / 일을 아무렇게나 하다 scamp [huddle over] one's work [duty]; do a slap-dash job / 재킷을 어깨에 아무렇게나 걸치다 throw one's jacket carelessly over one's shoulder
▶ 아무렇게나 좋을대로 생각하게 Take it any way you like.
▶ 대답을 아무렇게나 하지 마라 Don't give irresponsible answers.
▶ 그는 무슨 일이든 아무렇게나 해치운다 He leaves everything half-done.
▶ 그는 아무렇게나 나오는 대로 말해 버리는 버릇이 있다 He has the habit of saying whatever comes into his head.

아무렇게도 《not》 in any way (whatever); 〈조금도〉 nothing; not a bit; not at all
♦ 아무렇게도 생각 안하다 do not care a bit [feather, straw] 《about》; make little [nothing] 《of》
▶ 그 문제에 대해서는 아무렇게도 말할 수 없다 I cannot say anything definite on the matter.

아무렇든지 no matter what; at any rate; in any case [event]; at all events; anyway; anyhow ▶ 아무렇든지 출발 전에 알려 주겠다 In any event, I will let you know before I start.

아무렇지(도) 않다 〈태연하다·무관심하다〉 indifferent; unconcerned; nonchalant; 〈무사하다〉 safe; sound; all right
♦ 아무렇지도 않은 듯이 with an unconcerned air; in an indifferent [a lighthearted] manner [way]; lightly; casually / 아무렇지 않게 말하다 speak lightly 《of》 / 아무렇지도 않은 체하다 assume a nonchalant air [an air of indifference]
▶ 그는 약속 어기는 걸 아무렇지도 않게 여긴다 He doesn't give [care] a damn about breaking his promise.
▶ 나는 욕 얻어 먹는 것 쯤은 아무렇지도 않다 I am quite indifferent to abuse.

아무러니 〈설마〉 Impossible!; You don't say so!
▶ 아무러니 그럴 수가 있을까? I can't believe it. ⇒ It can't be so.
▶ 아무러니 그가 그런 짓을 했을라구 He is the last man to do such a thing.
▶ 아무러니 내가 문을 닫지 않았을라구 (You) Don't tell me I forgot to shut the door.

아무려면 Of course!; Certainly!; Naturally!; 《美口》 Sure!
▶ 가느냐구? 아무려면 가고 말고 Will I go, you say? Sure, I will.

아무렴 Of course! ⇨ 아무려면
아무르 〈강이름〉 the Amur
아무리 however; no matter how
▶ 아무리 늦어도 월요일까지는 돌아온다 I shall be back by Monday at the latest.
▶ 아무리 돈이 많아도 무위도식하면 안된다 No matter how rich you are, you ought not to lead an idle life.
▶ 아무리 기다려도 답장은 안 올 걸세 However long you (may) wait, no answer will come.
▶ 그 편지는 아무리 보아도 원래의 것과는 달랐다 The letter was, to all appearance(s), different from the original one.
▶ 우리의 일이 아무리 어려울지라도 우리는 포기할 수 없다 We cannot give up our work, however hard it may be.
▶ 아무리 그래도 그것은 너무하다 That's going

아무말 any word; ⟨한마디⟩ a (single) word; one word
▶ 아무말도 없었다 Not a word was said.
▶ 아무말도 할 것이 없다 I have nothing to say.
▶ 그는 아무말도 없이 나갔다 He went out without saying anything [a word].

아무아무 certain persons; such-and-such persons

아무일 something; anything; ⟨부정⟩ nothing
♦ 아무일 없이 without any accident [mishap]; without a hitch; quietly; peacefully; smoothly; uneventfully
▶ 종일 아무일도 없었다 Nothing happened all day. ⇌ The day passed quietly.

아무짝 any use
♦ 아무짝에도 못 쓸 인간 a good-for-nothing (fellow); a worthless fellow; **(美)** a no-good; **(英俗)** a rotter / 아무짝에도 못 쓰다 be good for nothing; be utterly useless

아무쪼록 as much [far] as *one* can; as much [far] as possible [practicable]; to the best of *one's* ability; by all means
▶ 아무쪼록 몸조심 하십시오 I hope you will take good care of yourself.
▶ 아무쪼록 결과를 알려 주십시오 Please let me know about the result.
▶ 아무쪼록 그이가 무사히 돌아왔으면 May he return in safety!

아무튼 anyway; anyhow ⇨ 어쨌든

아문센 ⟨노르웨이의 탐험가⟩ Amundsen, Roald (1872-1928)

아물거리다 1 ⟨어른거리다⟩ glimmer; shimmer; ⟨깜박이다⟩ flicker; ⟨희미하다⟩ be dim; be hazy; ⟨눈앞이⟩ be dizzy
♦ 아물거리는 기억 a dim memory / 아물거리는 등불 a flickering [glimmering] light / 먼데서 아물거리다 come in and out of sight in the distance
▶ 등불이 아물거린다 The lamp flickers.
2 ⇨ 어물거리다

아물다 ⟨낫다⟩ heal [close] up; be healed
▶ 상처가 아물었다 The wound has closed [healed up].

아물리다 1 ⟨상처를⟩ heal; make [help] (a wound) heal; treat (a wound)
♦ 상처를 고약으로 아물리다 help heal a wound with ointment
2 ⟨일을⟩ finish up; complete; conclude; bring (a matter) to an end [a close]; wind up
♦ 일을 아물리다 finish up *one's* work; bring *one's* work to a conclusion

아물아물 glimmeringly; shimmeringly; flickeringly; dimly; vaguely; dazzlingly
♦ 아물아물 보이다 come in and out of sight
—**아물아물하다** ⇨ 아물거리다

아미 蛾眉 the eyebrows of a beauty; fine [delicate] eyebrows

아미노산 一酸 〔化〕 an amino acid
■ 필수— the (eight) essential amino acids

아미타불 阿彌陀佛 〔佛敎〕 Amitabha; Amida (Buddha)

아방가르드 [⟨(프) avant-garde] the vanguard

아방튀르 [⟨(프) aventure] an amorous adventure; a love affair

아버님 a father ⇨ 아버지

아버지 a father; ⟨아빠⟩ papa; daddy; ⟨하나님⟩ Father
♦ 아버지의 사랑 fatherly [paternal] affection / 아버지 쪽의 친척 a relative on the father's [paternal] side / 아버지 없는 아이 a fatherless child / 아버지답게 fatherly; fatherlike / 아버지답지 않은 unfatherly / 아버지처럼 돌보다 father (a child); act as a father (to a child) / 아버지를 여의다 lose *one's* father; be left fatherless
▶ 아버지는 출판사에 다니십니다 My father works for a publishing company.
▶ 그 아버지에 그 자식 (속담) Like father, like son.

아범 ⟨비칭⟩ father; ⟨며느리가⟩ my husband; ⟨윗사람이⟩ your [his] father; ⟨하인⟩ an elderly manservant

아베마리아 Ave Maria

아베크 [⟨(프) avec] a couple [lovers] on a date; a pair of sweethearts; a rendezvousing couple; ⟨밀회⟩ a rendezvous; a date
▶ 이 공원은 젊은 남녀들이 아베크 장소로 애용하는 곳이다 This park is a favorite rendezvous for young men and women.
—**아베크하다** have a date with; go on a date with; rendezvous

아보가드로 ⟨이탈리아의 화학자·물리학자⟩ Avogadro, Amedeo (1776-1856)
■ —수 Avogadro's number; Avogadro constant ─의 법칙 the Avogadro's law

아부 阿附 flattery; adulation; sycophancy; toadyism
▶ 저 친구는 아부로 출세했다 That fellow got his present position by flattery [apple-polishing].
▶ 그에게는 아부가 통하지 않는다 He is proof against flattery.
—**아부하다** flatter; adulate; butter *sb* upon; court *sb's* favor; curry favor with
♦ 상사에게 아부하다 curry favor with *one's* boss; play up to [toady to] the boss
■ —꾼 a flatterer; a sycophant; a toadeater; a groveler

아비규환 阿鼻叫喚 (비유) agonizing cries; pandemonium
♦ 아비규환의 참상 an agonizing [a heart-rending] scene; a babel; a scene of dire confusion
▶ 가스 폭발로 현장은 아비규환의 도가니로 변했다 The gas explosion turned the scene into an inferno.
▶ 사고 현장은 그야말로 아비규환이었다 The scene of the accident was simply hell.

아비산 亞砒酸 arsenious acid
■ —염 (鹽) arsenite

아빠 papa; pa; (口) dad; daddy

아뿔싸 Gosh!; Oh dear!; Dear me!; Darn it!; Damn it!; Confound it!

아사

▶ 아뿔싸, 우산을 잊고 왔구나 Gosh! I forgot to bring my umbrella with me.
▶ 아뿔싸, 이 일을 어쩐담 O my! What shall I do?
아사 餓死 death from hunger; (death by) starvation
♦ 아사지경에 있다 be on the verge of starvation; be nearly dying from hunger
—**아사하다** starve [be starved] to death; die of hunger; perish [with] famine
▶ 많은 사람이 아사한 것으로 밝혀졌다 Many people were found dead from starvation.
아삭 with a crunch
♦ 사과를 아삭 베어 물다 bite at an apple with a crunching sound
—**아삭하다** crunch; be crunchy [crisp]
아삭거리다 be crunchy [crisp]; crunch; eat crisp
▶ 그녀는 사과를 아삭거리며 먹었다 She ate the apple with a crunching sound. ⇒ She crunched the apple.
아서라 No!; Oh no!; Oh, don't!; No, I say!; Stop!; Quit!; Ugh!; Gee!; Gosh!; Come come [now]!; Now now!
▶ 아서라, 싸우다니 Now now! Quit [Stop] your quarreling.
▶ 아서라, 그래봤자 별 수 있나 Oh, don't! It won't do any good.
아성 牙城 the inner citadel; the keep; the stronghold; the bastion; an impenetrable fortress
▶ 우리는 보수주의의 아성을 무너뜨리지 못했다 We couldn't pull down the stronghold of conservatism.
아성 亞聖 a sage of second order; 〈맹자〉 Mencius
아성층권 亞成層圈 the substratosphere
■—비행[비행기] a substratospheric flight [plane]
아세안 ASEAN [〈the *A*ssociation of *S*outh*e*ast *A*sian *N*ations]
아세테이트 〈인조 견사〉 acetate
아세톤 〔化〕 acetone
♦ 아세톤의 acetonic
아세트산 — 酸 〔化〕 acetic acid
■—무수물 acetic anhydride
아세틸 〔化〕 acetyl
아세틸렌 〔化〕 acetylene ■—가스 acetylene gas —램프 an acetylene torch —용접장치 acetylene welding equipment
아수라 阿修羅 〈산〉 Asura ■—왕 the King of the Asuras
아순시온 〈파라과이의 수도〉 Asunción
아쉬워하다 〈없어서〉 miss; feel the lack [want, loss] of; 〈서운해서〉 be unwilling [reluctant]; be loath
♦ 이별을 아쉬워하다 be unwilling [loath] to part (from *one's* friend); be reluctant to leave (*sb*, a place)
▶ 그가 떠나면 친구들이 매우 아쉬워할 것이다 He will be sorely missed by a circle of personal friends.
▶ 그녀는 모두가 아쉬워하는 가운데 학교를 떠났다 She left the school to the deep regret of all.
아쉰대로 though it is not enough [satisfactory]; inconvenient though it is; as a makeshift; as a temporary measure
▶ 아쉰대로 당분간은 이만큼 있으면 된다 We can do with this amount for the time being.
▶ 아쉰대로 이걸 쓰시오 Use this as a makeshift.
아쉽다 〈서술적〉 want for; miss; feel inconvenienced by the lack of
♦ 아쉰 소리를 하다 make a request (of *sb*); ask a favor of *sb* / 아쉬운 것 없이 지내다 live in plenty [comfort]; be comfortably off; be above want / 아쉬운 감이 들다 feel *sth* wanting [lacking]; feel a sense of loss
▶ 나는 돈이 아쉽다 I want for money.
▶ 그 기회를 놓친 것이 아쉽다 It is a pity that I failed to grasp that opportunity.
▶ 전체적으로 통일성이 결여된 점이 아쉽다 It's too bad that it lacks unity as a whole.
아스라이 〈아득히〉 far; far off [away]; in the distance; a long way off; 〈희미하게〉 faintly; dimly; vaguely
♦ 아스라이 들리는 소리 a faint sound / 아스라이 보이다 be seen dimly [at a dim distance]
▶ 아스라이 비행기가 날고 있는 것이 보였다 I saw an airplane flying in the distance.
아스라하다 〈아득하다〉 faraway; far-off; 〈희미하다〉 dim; faint; vague
아스러뜨리다 crush
아스러지다 1 〈덩어리가〉 crumble 2 〈살이〉 be grazed; be abraded; be chafed
아스타틴 〔化〕 astatine
아스트라한 〈모피〉 astrakhan
아스트린젠트 〈화장수〉 an astringent
아스파라거스 〔植〕 asparagus
아스팍 ASPAC ⇒ 아시아(~태평양 이사회)
아스팔트 asphalt ♦ 도로를 아스팔트로 포장하다 pave [lay] a road with asphalt; asphalt a road
■—길 an asphalt(ed) road
아스피린 〔藥〕 aspirin
아슬아슬하다 〈위태롭다〉 dangerous; risky; critical; perilous; 〈신나다〉 thrilling; exciting; 〈차이가 근소하다〉 close; narrow; hairbreadth
♦ 아슬아슬한 시합[플레이] a close game [play] / 마지막 아슬아슬한 고비에서 at the last moment; at the eleventh hour / 아슬아슬하게 도망치다[피하다] escape narrowly [by a hair'sbreadth]; have a narrow [hairbreadth] escape / 아슬아슬하게 세이프되다 be narrowly safe / 아슬아슬하게 이기다 win by a narrow margin; 〈경마에서〉 win by a neck
▶ 이 영화에는 아슬아슬한 장면이 많다 There are a lot of thrilling scenes in this film.
▶ 시합은 아슬아슬한 장면의 연속이었다 There were a series of exciting [thrilling] scenes in the game.
아시아 Asia ♦ 아시아의 Asian; Asiatic (▶인종을 말할 경우에 Asiatic은 경멸의 뜻을 내포하고 있어서 Asian이 더 많이 쓰임)
■ 동남— Southeast Asia 동북— Northeast Asia 소— Asia Minor 중앙— Central Asia ■—개발은행 the Asian Development Bank

(略 ADB) —경제협력기구 the Organization for Asian Economic Cooperation (略 OAEC) —극동경제위원회 the Economic Commission for Asia and the Far East (略 ECAFE) —대륙 the Asiatic Continent; the Continent of Asia —민족 an Asian nation —사람 an Asian; an Asiatic —생산성기구 the Asian Productivity Organization —영화제 the Asian Film Festival —인종 the Asian races —태평양이사회 the Asian and Pacific Council (略 ASPAC)

아시아아프리카 the Asian-African ♦아시아아프리카의 Asian-African; Afro-Asian
■—그룹 the Afro-Asian [African-Asian, Asian-African] Group; the A.A. Group —블록 the Afro-Asian [African-Asian] bloc —회의 the Asian-African Conference

아시안게임 the Asian Games

아식축구 —式蹴球 association football; soccer ⇨ 축구

아씨 〈경칭〉 madam; 〈호칭〉 your (good) lady; Mrs...; your ladyship; 〈하인이 부르는 소리〉 mistress; madam; ma'am

아악 雅樂 (classical) court music
♦아악을 연주하다 give performances of court music

아야 Ouch!
▶아야, 아파 Ouch, how it hurts!

아양 coquetry; flirtation
♦아양 떠는 여자 a coquette; a coquettish woman / 아양 떠는 목소리로 in a wheedling [an insinuating] voice / 아양(을) 떨다[부리다] purr at 《one's lover》; coquet(te); play the coquette 《with a man》; flirt 《with a man》

아양스럽다 be [look] coquettish

아어 雅語 an elegant word; a polite expression; a classical word; a refined diction

아역 兒役 〈역〉 a child's part [role] 《in a play》; a juvenile part; the role of a child; 〈사람〉 a child [juvenile] actor [actress]; an actor [actress] playing a child's part

아연 亞鉛 zinc
♦아연의 zincic; zincoid; zincous / 아연을 입힌 coated with zinc; galvanized / 아연을 입히다 zinc; zincify; coat with zinc
■—광 zinc ore —도금 zinc galvanizing; galvanization; zincification —블록판 anastatic printing; photozincography; 〈원판〉 an anastatic plate —철 galvanized iron —판(板) a zinc plate [sheet] —판(版) 〈제판용〉 zincography; 〈인쇄물〉 a zincograph; a zincotype

아연 俄然 〈부사적〉 suddenly; all at once; (all) of a sudden; abruptly
♦아연 긴장하다 be strained all of a sudden / 아연 활기를 띠다 suddenly begin to show signs of activity
—아연하다 sudden; abrupt

아연 啞然 ♦아연 실색하다 turn pale with surprise [fright]
—아연하다 (be) stunned; (be) dumbfounded; (be) tongue-tied; (be) struck dumb [speechless]
♦아연하여 agape 《with wonder》; aghast; startled; in mute [utter] amazement

그는 아연하여 말문이 막혔다 He was struck dumb with amazement.
▶그는 아연하여 그 광경을 보고 있었다 He stood aghast at the sight.
▶그들은 그 뜻밖의 재난에 아연할 뿐이었다 They stood aghast at the unforeseen disaster.
▶그 소식을 듣고 나는 한동안 아연했다 I was struck dumb by the news for a while.

아연화 亞鉛華 zinc flowers; flowers of zinc; zinc oxide
■—반창고 zinc adhesive plaster —연고 zinc (oxide) ointment

아열대 亞熱帶 the subtropical zones [regions]; the subtropics
♦아열대의 subtropic(al); near-tropical
■—기후 a subtropical climate —림 a subtropical forest —식물[동물] a subtropical plant [animal]

아예 〈애초부터〉 from the (very) first [start, beginning]; 〈절대로〉 (not) by any means; altogether; never; at all
▶선생 노릇 할 생각은 아예 말게 Never intend to be a teacher.
▶그럴 생각은 아예 없었다 I never intended to do so.
▶그것은 아예 문제가 되지 않는다 It is altogether out of the question.

아옹 with a meow; with a miaow —아옹하다¹ mew; meow; miaow

아옹다옹하다 quarrel; altercate; bicker; wrangle; bandy words 《with》

아옹하다² 1 〈오목하다〉 hollow; sunken; depressed
2 〈속좁은 사람이〉 sulky; disgruntled; complaining [griping] to *oneself*

아우 1 〈동생〉 a man's younger brother; a woman's younger [little] sister 2 〈동료간의〉 a junior 《in age》; a junior colleague

아우보다 have [get] a younger brother [sister]

아우성 shouting; an outcry; a clamor; a hubbub
♦아우성치다 clamor; bawl (out); raise a hubbub; bawl and squall; set up a shout [clamor]; 〈못마땅하여〉 let out a squawk
▶웬 아우성이냐? What are you bawling at?

아우타다 suffer a younger sibling; get thin from premature weaning (as a result of the mother's new pregnancy)

아우타르키 〈자급자족주의〉 autarchy; autarky

아우트라인 〈윤곽〉 an outline

아욱 〈植〉 a mallow

아울러 〈함께〉 (joining) together; 〈곁들여서〉 in addition; besides; at the same time
♦아울러 가지다 possess together 《with》; possess *sth* in addition 《to》; have both 《A》 and 《B》
▶사람은 누구나 선악 양면을 아울러 갖고 있다 There is a good and bad side to everyone.
▶인사차 찾아 뵙고 아울러 한 가지 부탁 드리려고 합니다 I intend to pay a visit and beg a favor of you in person.

아웃 1 〈野〉 an out; a put-out (略 po.)
♦아웃이 되다 be put out / 쳐서 아웃이 되다

아음속

hit into an out / 주자를 아웃시키다 pick a runner off (base); throw a runner out; retire a runner / 타자를 아웃시키다 put a batter out; 〈삼진으로〉 have a batter struck out ▶ 투 아웃 만루였다 The bases were loaded with two men out. ▶ 심판은 타자[주자]에게 아웃을 선언했다 The umpire called the batter [runner] out. ▶ 그는 레프트 플라이로 아웃이 되었다 He was out on a fly to left. ▶ 주자는 3루로 슬라이딩했지만 아웃이 되었다 The runner slid into third base but was out. **2** 〔골프〕 the outgoing course ■ ―드롭 〔野〕 an outdrop ―사이더 〈국외자〉 an outsider ―사이드 outside ―커브 〔野〕 an outcurve ―코너 〔野〕 the outside corner (of the plate): 공은 아웃코너를 벗어났다 The pitch missed the outside corner of the plate. ―파이팅 〔拳〕 outfighting ―풋〔電算〕 (the) output

아음속 亞音速 (at) subsonic speed ♦ 아음속의 subsonic (airplanes) / 아음속으로 at subsonic speed

아이 a child (*pl*. children); 〈젖먹이〉 a baby; 〈유아〉 an infant; 〈俗〉 a kid; 〈남아〉 a boy; 〈여아〉 a girl; 〈아들〉 a son; 〈딸〉 a daughter; 〈자손〉 〔法〕 issue; offspring

解說 *child*는 가장 흔히 쓰는 말로 보통 이유기 이후 14세 무렵까지를 가리킨다. 다만 아들, 딸의 뜻으로는 연령에 관계 없이 쓰인다. 또 "my child"라고 하여 아이를 부를 때도 쓴다. *baby*는 주로 말을 할 수 있을 때까지의 어린 애를 가리키는데 남녀를 구별할 때는 a baby boy, a baby girl 등으로 말하고, a boy baby, a girl baby 등으로는 하지 않는다. *infant*는 baby의 약간 딱딱한 말로, 〈英〉에서는 학령기 전의 아동한테도 쓰며 〔法〕에서는 미성년자를 가리킨다. child, baby, infant는 성의 구별 없이 it으로 받기도 한다.

♦ 우리집 아이 my son / 계집 아이 〈아기〉 a baby girl / 사내 아이 a boy-child; 〈아기〉 a baby boy / 어린아이 a (preschool) child; a baby / 큰 아이 a big boy / 뱃속의 아이 an expected [a coming] child / 아이 때부터 from one's childhood; from a child / 아이 취급하다 treat sb as a child; baby sb / 아이가 많다 have many children (to feed and clothe); have a large family (to provide for) / 아이가 없다 be childless; have no child [issue]; be without issue / 아이를 낳다 give birth to a child; bear a child; have a child / 아이를 배다 get [be] with child; conceive a child / 아이를 보다 tend a baby; 〈美〉 baby-sit / 아이 같이 굴다 behave childishly ▶ 아이를 울리지 마라 Don't make [let] the child cry. ▶ 그들에게 아이가 생겼다 A baby [child] was born to them. ▶ 그녀는 그와 살면서 예쁜 아이를 둘 낳았다 She gave him two beautiful children. ■ ―방 a nursery ―아버지 the father of (the) children; 〈남편〉 one's husband ―어머니 the mother of (the) children; 〈그녀〉 you; she

아이고(머니) **1** 〈반갑거나 좋을 때〉 Ah!; Oh! ▶ 아이고 고마워라 Thank you very much. ▶ 아이고 좋아라 What a delight! ⇌ Oh, how glad I am! ⇌ Hallelujah! **2** 〈놀라거나 기막힐 때〉 Oh!; O dear!; Dear me! (▶여성 용어); Gee whiz!; Good(ness) gracious!; Good Heaven(s)!; Good Lord!; God bless me!; My eye!; Why!; 〈아프거나 힘들 때〉 Ouch! ▶ 아이고머니나 Dear me! ▶ 아이고 나 죽네 Oh, I am dying. ▶ 아이고 내가 망쳐 놓았구나 Oh, no, I've made a mess of it! ▶ 아이고 너였구나 Why, was it you? ⇌ Oh, it was (only) you. ▶ 아이고 귀찮아 Good Lord, how annoying! ▶ 아이고 더워 How hot (it is)! ▶ 아이고 불쌍해라 What a pity! ⇌ Poor thing! ▶ 아이고머니 내 지갑이 없어졌네 Heavens! I have lost my purse somewhere. **3** 〈뒤늦게 깨달았을 때〉 Well!; Well now! ▶ 아이고머니 이 일을 어쩌나 Well, what am I to do now!

아이누 〈사람〉 an Ainu (*pl*. ~ (s)); an Aino (*pl*. ~s); 〈종족〉 the Ainus; the Ainos ■ ―말 Ainu; Aino

아이다호 〈미국의 주〉 Idaho (略 Id., Ida.); 〈속칭〉 Gem State ♦ 아이다호의 Idahoan ■ ―사람 an Idahoan

아이디어 an idea ▶ 기발한 아이디어가 떠올랐다 A good idea occurred [came] to me. ▶ 그는 아이디어가 풍부하다 He is full of new ideas. ■ ―맨 an idea man; an ideamonger; a man of ideas

아이러니 (an) irony

아이모 〈소형 촬영기〉 **(**商標**)** an Eyemo

아이보리 ivory ■ ―블랙 ivory black

아이보리코스트 〈코트디부아르의 영어명〉 the Ivory Coast

아이비엠 〈펀치카드 방식〉 IBM [〈*I*nternational *B*usiness *M*achines]; 〈기계〉 an IBM machine [computer]

아이섀도 eye shadow ♦ 아이섀도를 하다 apply [put on] eye shadow

아이소토프 〔物〕 an isotope ■ ―요법 isotope therapy

아이스 ice ■ ―댄싱 ice dancing ―링크 an ice rink ―박스 an icebox; an ice chest ―쇼 an ice show ―캔디 〈美〉 a popsicle; 〈英〉 an ice lolly ―커피 iced coffee ―크림 (an) ice cream; 〈英〉 an ice: 아이스크림 제조기 an ice-cream freezer ―하키 ice hockey : 아이스하키 선수 an ice hockey player; a puckster

아이슬란드 Iceland; 〈공식명〉 the Republic of Iceland ♦ 아이슬란드의 Icelandic ■ ―말 Icelandic ―사람 an Icelander

아이시 an IC [〈*i*ntegrated *c*ircuit〕

아이시비엠 〈대륙간 탄도탄〉 ICBM [《Inter-continental Ballistic Missile》]
아이아르 〈정보 검색〉 IR [《information retrieval》]
아이아르비엠 〈중거리 탄도탄〉 IRBM [《Intermediate Range Ballistic Missile》]
아이아르에이 〈아일랜드 공화국군〉 IRA [《Irish Republican Army》]
아이언 〈다리미〉 an iron; a smoothing iron; a flatiron; 〈모발용〉 a curling [waving] iron ◆아이언으로 다리다 iron (out) 《a shirt》; press 《the trousers》 ■전기[증기]— an electric [a steam] iron ■—대[틀] an iron board [stand]
아이언클럽 〔골프〕 an iron (club) ◆9번의 아이언클럽 a nine-iron
아이에스비엔 〈국제표준도서번호〉 ISBN [《International Standard Book Number》]
아이엔에스 〈고도 정보 통신시스템〉 INS [《Information Network System》]
아이엘오 〈국제 노동 기구〉 ILO [《International Labor Organization》]
아이엠에프 〈국제 통화 기금〉 IMF [《International Monetary Fund》] ◆아이엠에프 8조국 an IMF Article 8 nation
아이오시 〈국제 올림픽 위원회〉 IOC [《International Olympic Committee》]
아이오와 〈미국의 주〉 Iowa (略 Ia.); 〈속칭〉 Hawkeye State ◆아이오와의 Iowan ■—사람 an Iowan
아이오유 〔經〕〈차용증〉 I.O.U. [《I owe you》]
아이유 〈국제 단위〉 IU [《international unit》]
아이이에이 〈국제 에너지 기관〉 IEA [《International Energy Agency》]
아 이 젠 [《독》 Steigeisen》] climbing irons; crampo(o)ns
아이지다 have a stillbirth; have a baby born dead
아이지와이 〈국제 지구 물리 관측년〉 IGY [《International Geophysical Year》]
아이쿠 Oops!; Whew!; Gee whiz!; Wow!
아이큐 IQ [I.Q.] [《intelligence quotient》] ▶그는 아이큐가 120이다 He has an IQ of 120.
아이티 〈나라 이름〉 Haiti 〈공식명〉 the Republic of Haiti ◆아이티의 Haitian ■—사람 a Haitian
아인슈타인 〈독일 태생의 미국 물리학자〉 Einstein, Albert (1879-1955) ◆아인슈타인의 상대성 이론 Einstein's theory of relativity ■—항등식 the Einstein equation
아일랜드 〈나라 이름〉 Ireland; 〈공식명〉 the Republic of Ireland ◆아일랜드의 Irish ■—말 Irish; the Irish language ■—사람 an Irishman; 〈여성〉 an Irishwoman; (총칭) the Irish
아잇적 one's childhood ◆아잇적에 in one's childhood [infancy]; when [as] a child
아작아작 with a munching sound ◆아작아작 먹다 crunch; munch 《carrots》
아장거리다 1〈어린아이가〉 toddle; totter ◆아장거리는 어린아이 a toddler 2〈일없이 거닐다〉 ⇨ 어정거리다
아장아장 toddlingly; with toddling steps ◆아장아장 걷는 어린아이 a toddler; a toddling child / 아장아장 걷다 toddle along [about]; totter

아재 〈아저씨〉 one's uncle; 〈아주버니〉 one's husband's brother; a brother-in-law
아저씨 1〈삼촌〉 an uncle 2〈어른〉 a man; 〈호칭〉 Mister; Sir; Pop; Uncle ◆낯선 아저씨 a strange gentleman
아전 衙前 an official clerk
아전인수 我田引水 drawing water to one's own mill; turning sth to one's own advantage; seeking [promoting] one's own interests; arguing from a self-centered angle ◆아전인수의 self-seeking; self-centered / 아전인수 격 a selfish view ▶아전인수도 유분수지 Don't be so self-seeking. ▶그녀가 하는 말은 무엇이건 아전인수에 지나지 않는다 She's just turning every argument in her own favor [to her own advantage]. ▶아전인수로 들릴지 모르지만 그 계획은 모두에게 유익하다고 생각합니다 It may sound self-seeking, but I think the plan will be useful to everyone.
아제 〈자매의 남편〉 (a woman's [girl's]) sister's husband; (俗) 〈아저씨〉 one's uncle
아종 亞種 〔生〕 a subspecies (▶단수·복수 동형) ◆아종의 subspecific
아주¹ 1〈매우〉 very (much); greatly; exceedingly; excessively; extremely; remarkably ▶이 일은 아주 쉽다 This work is very easy. ▶그는 아주 좋은 친구다 He is quite a nice fellow. ▶여기는 아주 시끄럽다 It is so noisy here. ▶아주 피곤하다 I am tired to death. ▶그것은 5월의 아주 맑은 날이었다 It was an extremely fine day in May. ▶시골길을 걸으면 기분이 아주 좋다 It's quite pleasant walking along a country road. ▶나는 그것이 아주 즐거웠다 I have enjoyed it immensely. ▶아이는 그 장난감이 아주 마음에 들었다 The child was very much pleased with the toy. 2〈전혀·완전히〉 quite; utterly; entirely; completely; perfectly; altogether; 〈영영〉 for good (and all); forever ◆관계를 아주 끊다 break off entirely 《with》; sever one's connections 《with》; (美) be entirely through 《with》 ▶그들은 한국을 아주 떠났다 They left Korea for good. ▶그는 아주 바보는 아니다 He is not altogether a fool. ▶그는 아주 딴 사람이 되었다 He is quite another man now. ▶내가 들은 바와는 아주 달랐다 It was entirely different from what I had heard.
아주² 〈감탄사〉 Oh really! ▶아주, 너에게 질까봐 Damn it! See who is the stronger! ▶아주, 모르는 체하긴 As if you didn't know!
아주 阿洲 the Continent of Africa
아주 亞洲 the Continent of Asia
아주까리 〔植〕 a castor-oil plant ■—기름 castor oil; ricinus oil ■—씨 a castor bean
아주머니 〈숙모〉 an aunt; 〈부인〉 a lady ◆처음 보는 아주머니 a strange lady

아주버니 one's husband's brother; a brother-in-law

아지랑이 heat haze; waves of heat; heat waves; (a veil of) heat shimmer; shimmering of heated air
▶ 아지랑이가 일고 있다 The air is waving [shimmering] with heat. ⇌ The heat is waving the air.
■ ―현상 〔物〕 schlieren

아지작거리다 crunch; munch; champ
◆ 송과를 아지작거리다 munch a pine nut

아지작아지작 crunching; munching; champing ◆ 사탕을 아지작아지작 깨물다 munch candies

아지트 an agitating point; (美俗) a hideout

아직 〈여전히〉 (not) yet; still; as yet; so far; 〈계속해서〉 still more; 〈고작〉 only
▶ 일은 아직 끝나지 않았다 The work is not yet finished.
▶ 아직 할 일이 남아 있다 There is work yet to be done.
▶ 사건은 아직 해결되지 않았다 The matter remains unsettled. ⇌ The matter has not been settled yet.
▶ 너는 사랑을 하기에는 아직 어리다 You are too young to be in love.
▶ 정상까지는 아직 멀다 It is still a long way to the summit.
▶ 아직 3시밖에 안됐다 It's only three o'clock.
▶ 그의 기술은 전문가로서는 아직 멀었다 His skill is still far from that of an expert.
▶ 그 사실은 아직 증명되지 않았다 That statement remains to be proved.

아직까지 until [up to] now [the present]; so far; hitherto
▶ 아직까지 아무런 보고도 받지 못했다 No report has been received so far.
▶ 그것은 아직까지 발견된 것 중 최상이다 It's the best yet found.
▶ 나는 그런 사람은 아직까지 만나본 적이 없다 I have never met such a man before [in my life].

아직도 still; yet
▶ 아직도 비가 내리고 있다 It is still raining.
▶ 그것은 우리의 기억에 아직도 새롭다 It is still fresh in our memory.
▶ 그녀는 아들의 죽음이 아직도 믿어지지 않았다 She cannot yet accept her son's death.
▶ 그들은 아직도 진상을 모른다 They still do not know the truth.
▶ 아직도 할 일이 많이 남아 있다 Much yet remains to be done.

아질산 亞窒酸 〔化〕 nitrous acid
■ ―염 nitrite

아집 我執 egoistic attachment; self-indulgence; tenacity; obstinacy ◆ 아집을 버리다 overcome [get rid of] one's self-centeredness
▶ 그는 아집이 강한 사람이다 He is an egocentric man.

아찔하다 dizzy; giddy; faint
▶ 그는 보기에도 아찔한 절벽을 기어올랐다 He climbed a dizzying [giddy] cliff.
▶ 내 새 집의 호화스러움에 아찔했다 I was dazzled by the richness of my new home.
▶ 나는 정신이 아찔해졌다 I began to feel faint [woozy].

아차 Heavens!; By Jove!; Hang it!; Damn it!; Confound it!; Deuce take it!; Gosh!; Shucks!
▶ 아차 또 속았구나 Oh my! I have been fooled again!
▶ 아차 책을 잊고 왔구나 Shucks, I left my book behind.
▶ 그것은 아차 하는 순간에 일어난 일이었다 All this happened in an instant.

아첨 阿諂 flattery; adulation; sycophancy; toadyism ⇨ 아부
◆ 아첨의 말 a compliment; sugary [sweet] words / 아첨을 잘하다 have a well-oiled tongue / 아첨에 넘어가다 be taken in by flattery; swallow flattery
▶ 그는 사장한테 아첨을 일삼고 있다 He is always making [playing] up to the president.
▶ 나는 아첨을 할 줄 모른다 I am not in the way of making compliments.
■ ―아첨하다 flatter; apple-polish; toady 《to》; curry favor 《with one's superior》; fawn 《on, upon》; butter up 《to》
▶ 그에게 아첨해 봐야 소용없다 He is proof against flattery. ⇌ He is above flattery.
▶ 그 사내는 권력자에게 아첨하지 않는다 That man doesn't fawn on the powerful.
■ ―꾼[쟁이] a flatterer; a toady; a toadeater; a sycophant; an apple-polisher

아취 雅趣 elegance; tastefulness; artistry
◆ 아취가 있는 tasteful; elegant; graceful; refined / 아취가 없는 tasteless; inelegant; ungraceful; unrefined

-아치 〈종사하는 사람〉 ◆ 동냥아치 a beggar / 벼슬아치 a government official

아치 雅致 good taste; elegance; grace; artistic effect; gusto ◆ 아치있는 elegant; tasteful; artistic; (a)esthetic
▶ 그 정원은 자못 아치있게 꾸며져 있다 The garden is very tastefully laid out.

아치 an arch ◆ 아치형의 archwise; arched; arciform

아침¹ 〈때〉 morning; (詩) morn
◆ 아침마다 every morning / 아침 내내 all (the) morning / 아침 일찍 early in the morning / 아침부터 밤까지 from morning till night; all day (long) / 아침까지 until morning / 아침까지는 by (tomorrow) morning; before morning / 아침에 in the morning / 오늘[내일, 어제] 아침(에) this [tomorrow, yesterday] morning / 3일날 아침에 on the morning of the 3rd / 일요일 아침에 on Sunday morning / 어느 여름날 아침에 one summer morning / 아침 일찍[늦게] 일어나다 rise early [late] / 아침, 점심, 저녁 세끼 식사를 하다 have three meals a day, at morning, noon and evening
▶ 아침이 된다 Morning breaks [dawns].
▶ 아침이 되면서 비가 내리기 시작했다 It began to rain toward morning.
▶ 아침부터 비가 오락가락 하고 있다 It's been raining on and off since morning.
▶ 맑은 5월의 아침에 산책하는 것은 즐겁다 It is pleasant to take a walk on a fine May morning.

▶ 인생은 아침 이슬과 같다 Men's life vanishes like the dew. ⇒ Life is but a span.
2 〈조반〉 breakfast; the morning meal ♦ 아침 겸 점심 a late breakfast; (美口) brunch / 아침을 마치다 finish *one's* breakfast / 아침을 먹다 eat [take] (*one's*) breakfast; breakfast
■ —거리 breakfast makings; foodstuff for breakfast —결 the forenoon —기도 a morning prayer; 〈교회의〉 Mat(t)ins —나절 the forenoon; the first half of the day between breakfast and lunch —놀 the morning glow; the glow of sunrise in the sky —밥 ⇨ 아침 2 —상 a breakfast table [tray] —안개 a morning mist [haze, fog]; the pride of the morning —이슬 the morning dew —잠 a morning sleep —참 a breakfast break (in work)

아침저녁 morning and evening
▶ 아침저녁으로 서늘하다 We have cooler mornings and evenings now. ⇌ It is quite chilly in the mornings and evenings.

아침해 the morning sun; the rising sun
▶ 아침해가 뜬다 The sun rises.
▶ 아침해를 받아 이슬 방울들이 반짝반짝 빛났다 The dewdrops glittered brilliantly in the morning sun.

아카데미 an academy

아카데미상 —賞 〈映〉 the Academy Award; the Oscar ▶ 이 영화는 7개 부문에서 아카데미상을 수상했다 This film has won seven Oscars.
■ —수상배우 an Oscar actor [actress]

아카데미즘 academism; academicism

아카시아 〔植〕 an acacia

아카펠라 (이)〔樂〕〈무반주 합창곡〉 a cappella

아칸소 〈미국의 주〉 Arkansas(略 Ark.); 〈속칭〉 Land of Opportunity; Bear [Bowie] State
■ —사람 an Arkansan

아케이드 an arcade; an archway
♦ 아케이드가 있는 거리 an arcaded street

아코디언 〈손풍금〉 an accordion ■ —연주자 an accordionist; an accordion player

아코디언도어 an accordion door

아퀴 〔끝매듭〕 the final touches; finishing; settlement ♦ 일의 아퀴를 짓다 finish [wind up] *one's* work; bring a matter to a conclusion; give the final touches to the job

아크 〔電〕 an (electric) arc ■ —등 an arc lamp [light] —방전 arc discharge

아크라 〈가나의 수도〉 Accra

아크로메걸리 〔醫〕〈선단 비대증〉the acromegaly

아크로바트 〈곡예사〉 an acrobat

아크릴 〔化〕 acryloyl; acrylyl; acryl ■ —섬유 acrylic fiber —수지 acrylic (acid) resin

아킬레스건 —腱 〔解〕 the Achilles' tendon; (비유) *one's* Achilles' heel; a vulnerable point

아탄 亞炭 lignite; brown coal; soft coal
■ —가스 lignite gas

아테네 〈그리스의 수도〉 Athens
♦ 아테네의 Athenian ■ —사람 an Athenian

아토니 〔醫〕 atony ■ 위(胃)— gastric atony

아톰 〈원자〉 an atom

아트지 —紙 (美) coated paper; (英) art paper

아틀라스 **1** 〔그神〕 Atlas **2** 〈미국이 개발한 유도탄〉 an Atlas

아틀리에 〈작업장〉 (프) an atelier; a studio (*pl*. -dios); a workshop

아티스트 〈예술가〉 an artist

아파르트헤이트 〈인종 차별정책〉 apartheid

아파치(족) —(族) the Apache ♦ 아파치족의 Apachean

아파트 〈한 세대분의 방〉 (美) an apartment; (英) a flat; 〈건물 전체〉 an apartment building [house]; (英) a block (of flats)
♦ 아파트에서 살다 (美) live in an apartment; (英) live in a flat
▶ 아파트를 찾고 있어요[빌리고 싶어요] I am looking for [I would like to rent] an apartment [a flat].
▶ 그는 학교에서 가까운 아파트의 2층에 살고 있어 He lives on the second floor of an apartment building [house] near the school.
■ 고층— a high-rise apartment building 서민— an apartment building for the low incomers [income bracket] 임대[분양]— a rental [lot-sold] apartment 호화— a luxury apartment —군(群) an apartment block

아파하다 express [show] pain; complain of a pain ♦ 아파하는 pained 《look》 / 아파하고 있다 be in pain

아페리티프 〈식전 술〉 (프) an apéritif

아펜니노산맥 —山脈 〈이탈리아의〉 the Apennino Mountains; the Apennines

아편 阿片 opium ♦ 아편을 피우다 smoke [eat] opium; hit the pipe
■ —굴 an opium den [joint] —매매 traffic —분말 powdered opium —연 opium tobacco —쟁이 an opium eater: 그는 아편쟁이다 He is addicted to opium. —제(劑) an opiate; an opium product; a narcotic drug

아편전쟁 阿片戰爭 〔史〕 the Opium War

아편중독 阿片中毒 opiumism; opium habit
■ —자 an opium addict [eater, smoker]; a hophead; a dope

아포스테리오리 〔哲〕 (라) a posteriori

아포스트로피 an apostrophe

아폴로 〔그神〕 Apollo
■ —계획 the Apollo Project; Project Apollo

아폴리네르 〈프랑스의 시인〉 Apollinaire, Guillaume (1880-1918)

아프가니스탄 〈나라 이름〉 Afghanistan; 〈공식명〉 the Democratic Republic of Afghanistan
♦ 아프가니스탄의 Afghan
■ —말 Afghan —사람 an Afghan

아프다 **1** 〈신체·상처 등이〉 painful; sore; 〈서술적〉 hurt; pain 《him》

> 解說 ***painful***은 「아프다」의 가장 일반적인 말로서 정신적·육체적인 모든 아픔을 가리킨다. ***sore***는 표피의 상처·염증·근육통 등의 아픔을 가리킨다.

♦ 아픈 상처 a sore [painful] wound / 아픈 이 an aching tooth / 머리[배]가 아프다 have a headache [stomachache]; have [feel] a pain in the head [stomach]; *one's* head [stomach] aches / 먼지로 목이 아프다 have sore throat from dust / 얼얼하게 아프다 have a burning pain; smart / 따끔따끔 아프다 tingle; prickle;

feel prickly / 갑자기 쑤시듯이 아프다 feel a sudden griping pain / 아파서 울다 cry with pain; cry in one's pain / 아파서 몸부림치다 writhe with pain
▶그는 아파서 울고 있다 He is crying with pain.
▶아프니? Do you have [feel] any pain? ⇒ Are you in pain? ⇒ Does it hurt?
▶「아이고 아파, 거기야」하고 그는 외쳤다 "Ouch! That's where the pain is [where it hurts]," he cried.
▶〖會話〗「다리가 아파 견딜 수가 없어」「잠간 쉬어 가자」 "My feet are killing me. ⇒ My feet are all aching (from walking)." "Let's stop and rest for a while."
▶충치가 아프다 My cavity hurts me.
▶가끔 등이 아픕니다 Sometimes my back aches.
▶오른팔은 아직도 아파요 My right arm still hurts.
▶왼팔의 관절이 아프다 My left arm joint aches.
▶머리가 쪼개지는 것처럼 아프다 I have a splitting [throbbing] headache. ⇒ My head aches terribly.
▶등의 아픈 곳에 연고를 발랐다 I applied a plaster to a sore place on my back.
2 〖비유〗 ♦골치아픈 일 a headache; a cause of anxiety; a source of trouble; a worry / 배가 아파서 from jealousy; out of envy / 골치가 아프다 be in pain [distress, trouble]/(아무의) 아픈 곳을 건드리다[찌르다] touch sb on a sore place [the raw] / 사촌이 땅을 사면 배가 아프다 〖속담〗 envy sb (his) success
▶그 슬픈 소식에 가슴[마음]이 아팠다 I grieved at the sad news.
▶부모를 잃은 아이의 일을 생각하니 가슴이 아프다 It wrings my heart to think of the child who has lost his parents.
▶내 마음의 아픈데를 건드리지 말아줘 Don't touch upon my sore spots in my mind.
▶그녀는 그의 약한 데를 찔렀다 She took advantage of his weak point. ⇒ She touched him on the raw.
▶그것은 골치 아픈 문제다 That's a vexing question. ⇒ That problem gives me a headache.

아프레게르 〖프〗〈전후파〉 après-guerre; postwar
아프리오리 〖라〗〖哲〗 a priori
아프리카 Africa ♦아프리카의 African ■—대륙[주] ⇨ 아주(阿洲) —사람 an African —통일기구 the Organization of African Unity (略 OAU)
아프트식 —式 the Abt system
■—철도 an Abt-system railway
아플리케 〈오려대기〉 appliqué
♦아플리케(를 한) 에이프런 an appliqué apron
아픔 〈통증〉 a pain; an ache; a sore; 〈자통·격통〉 a sting [stinging pain]; 〈심통(心痛)〉 pain; a grief
♦가슴의 아픔 a pain in the breast / 상처의 아픔 the smart of a wound / 이별의 아픔 the pain of parting / 심한 아픔 a severe [a sharp, an acute] pain / 정신적[육체적] 아픔 mental [physical] pain / 아픔을 견디다 stand [bear, endure] the pain / 아픔을 느끼다[느끼지 않다] feel a [no] pain / 아픔을 없애다 remove [banish, kill] (the) pain / 아픔을 진정시키다 allay the pain; make the pain easier
▶주사로 아픔이 멈췄다 The injection stopped the pain.
▶아픔은 거의 가셨다 The pain has almost gone
▶나는 갑자기 위에 심한 아픔을 느꼈다 Suddenly I felt an awful pain in the stomach.

아하 Aha!; Ah!; Oh!; Dear me!; Well!; My goodness! ▶이하, 이제 알만헤 Oh! I understand it now.
아하하 ha, ha, ha ♦아하하 웃다 laugh aloud [loudly]
아한대 亞寒帶 〈북반구의〉 the subarctic zone; 〈남반구의〉 the subantarctic zone
■—식물 the subarctic [subantarctic] plant
아호 雅號 a pen [literary] name; a pseudonym; 〖프〗 a nom de plume
아홉 nine ♦아홉째(의) the ninth / 아홉째로 ninthly ■—수 numbers ending in 9 [19, 29, etc.]; years of age ending in 9, considered climacteric
아황산 亞黃酸 〖化〗 sulfurous acid
■—가스 sulfurous acid gas; 〈이산화황〉 sulfur dioxide —나트륨 sodium sulfite —소다 sodium sulfite; sulfite of soda —염 sulfite; sulphite
아흐레 〈아흡날〉 nine days **2** ⇨ 아흐렛날
아흐렛날 〈아홉째 날〉 the ninth day; 〈초아흐렛날〉 the ninth day (of a month)
아흔 ninety ♦아흔째 the ninetieth / 아흔째의 ninetieth
악¹ 〈모질게 쓰는 기운〉 desperation; desperate effort; franticness ♦악에 바치 in the fury of one's passion / 악을 쓰다 shout / 악에 바치다 become desperate
악² 〈남을 놀라게 할 때〉 Bo!; Boh!; Boo!;〈놀랐을 때〉 Ugh!; Oh!; Wow!; Ooh!
악 惡 badness; evil; wickedness; vice; wrong ♦악의 소굴 criminal quarters; the underworld / 악의 온상 a hotbed of vice / 악에 물든 생활 a life of vice / 악의 길로 유혹하다 tempt one into evil [wrong]/ 악을 선으로 갚다 return good for evil [evil with good]/ 악을 악으로 갚다 revenge wrong with wrong / 악에 물들다 be steeped in vice; sink into vice
▶그는 악의 화신이었다 He was the incarnation of wickedness.
▶악에 강한 자는 선에도 강하다 Extremes in wickedness make for extremes in goodness.
▶불량배들은 그를 유혹해서 악의 길로 들어서게 했다 The ruffians tempted him into vice.
▶그는 악에 물들고 말았다 He has taken on bad ways. ⇒ He has gone wrong.
■사회[필요]— a social [necessary] evil
악감정 惡感情 ill feeling; an ill will; animosity; an unfavorable impression
♦악감정을 품다 have bad [hard] feeling (toward); bear [harbor] ill feeling (toward, against); be ill disposed (toward) / 악감정을 사다 offend; make an unfavorable impression

(on another's mind); impress *sb* unfavorably
▶ 그들 사이에는 악감정이 있었다 There was bad blood between them.
▶ 남에게 악감정을 사지 않도록 주의하거라 Be careful not to impress others unfavorably.
▶ 그들은 우리에게 악감정을 품고 있다 They are ill-disposed toward us.
▶ 이 제안은 시민의 악감정을 야기할지도 모른다 This proposal might invite ill feeling [will] among the citizens.

악계 樂界 the musical world ⇨ 악단(樂壇)
악곡 樂曲 a tune; a piece of music; a musical piece [composition]
악골 顎骨 [解] a jawbone; a maxillary bone; the maxilla 《*pl.* ~s, -lae》
■ 상[하]— the upper [lower] jawbone
악공 樂工 a court musician
악구 樂句 a (musical) phrase
악귀 惡鬼 a devil; a demon; an evil spirit
악극 樂劇 a music drama ■-단 a musical troupe
악기 樂器 a musical instrument; an instrument
♦ 음악을 악기에 맞도록 편곡하다 arrange music for instruments; instrument
▶ 넌 악기를 연주할 수 있니? Can you play an instrument?
■ 관[현, 타]— a wind [string, percussion] instrument ■ -반주 instrumental accompaniments ■ -점 a musical instruments' shop [store]
악기류 惡氣流 a treacherous [dangerous] air current
악녀 惡女 〈독부〉 a wicked woman; 〈추녀〉 an ugly woman; a fright
악다구니 a name-calling quarrel; (exchange of) high [sharp] words; a brawl; an altercation ─악다구니하다 have high words [a row] 《with》; brawl; altercate
악단 樂團 an orchestra; a (musical) band
■ 교향— a symphony orchestra ■ -연주 band concert ─원 a bandsman; a member of an orchestra
악단 樂壇 the musical world; musical circles
♦ 악단에 데뷔하다 make *one*'s debut in the musical world
악담 惡談 **1** 〈저주의 말〉 a curse; a malediction; 〈욕〉 abusive [bad] language; abuse
♦ 악담을 퍼붓다 abuse *sb* soundly; heap abuses on *sb* / 갖은 악담을 늘어놓다 let out a stream of curses
▶ 그는 악담을 했다 He used bad language. ⇌ He swore.
─악담하다 swear at; curse; abuse; revile; call *sb* (bad) names
2 〈비방〉 backbiting; slander ─악담하다 backbite *sb*; speak ill of *sb*; bad-mouth
악당 惡黨 a blackguard; a rascal; a villain; a wrongdoer; 〈깡패〉 a hooligan; 《美口》 a hoodlum
악대 樂隊 a (musical) band; 〈취주악대〉 a brass band; 〈관현악대〉 an orchestra
♦ 악대의 연주회 a band concert
▶ 우리는 악대를 선두로 하여 행진했다 We marched on with the band at the head.

■ 육군[해군, 공군]— a military [a naval, an air force] band ■-원 a bandsman ─음악 band music ─장 a bandmaster
악덕 惡德 (a) vice; 〈타락〉 corruption; 〈부도덕〉 immorality ♦ 악덕을 쌓다 commit a series of vicious acts ─악덕하다 vicious; corrupt; vice-ridden; immoral
■ -기업주 a vicious entrepreneur ─변호사 《美口》 a shyster; 《美俗》 a fixer ─상인[업자] wicked [dishonest] dealers [traders] ─의사 a crooked doctor
악도리 a roughneck; a tough guy; a ruffian; a brawler; an ugly customer
악독 惡毒 infernality; atrocity; perversity; brutality; villainy ─악독하다 most wicked; infernal; atrocious; brutal; devilish; villainous
♦ 악독한 짓 an atrocious [infernal] act; an atrocity
악동 惡童 a bad [naughty] boy; a mischievous [roguish] boy; 〈도회지의〉 a street Arab
악랄 惡辣 viciousness; spitefulness; knavishness ─악랄하다 vicious; spiteful; crafty; knavish; villainous; wily; sharp; poisonous
♦ 악랄한 수단 knavish tricks; villainous measures; foul play / 악랄한 짓을 하다 play a wily trick; 〈상습적으로〉 be given to sharp practices; resort to knavish tricks
▶ 그는 그녀에게 악랄한 짓을 했다 He played her a dirty trick.
▶ 그들은 악랄한 수법으로 돈을 벌었다 They made money by hook or by crook.
악력 握力 grasping power; grip
▶ 나는 악력이 세다[약하다] I have a strong [weak] grip.
▶ 나는 악력이 약해졌다 My grip weakened.
▶ 그의 오른손 악력은 약 70킬로그램이다 He is able to exert a right-handed squeeze of 70 kg. or so.
■ -계(計) a hand [squeeze] dynamometer; 〈오락장의〉 a try-your-grip machine
악령 惡靈 an evil [a malevolent] spirit
♦ 악령을 쫓아내다 ward off evil spirits; drive out demons / 악령이 씌다 [들리다] be possessed by an evil spirit
악례 惡例 a bad example; an evil precedent
♦ 악례를 남기다 [만들다] set [establish, create] a bad precedent; set [leave] a bad [poor] example 《for》
악리 樂理 music theory; the theory of music
악마 惡魔 an evil spirit; a devil; a demon; a fiend; 〈기독교의〉 Satan [séitn]; the Devil; Old Serpent
♦ 악마의, 악마적인 satanic [Satanic] (influence); demonic 《power》 / 악마 같은 devilish; fiendish; demoniac(al) / 악마를 쫓아내다 drive out [drive away, exorcise] evil spirits 《from *sb*》
▶ 그녀는 악마같은 남편에게 한평생 시달렸다 She was suffered all her life because of her fiendish husband.
▶ 그는 악마가 씌었다 There is a demon inside him.
■ -주의[숭배] Satanism; diabolism ─파 the diabolists; the Satanic school

악명 惡名 a bad reputation [name]; ill repute [fame]; infamy; notoriety
♦악명 높은 사건 an infamous incident / 악명 높은 notorious (for his goings-on) / 악명이 높다 be notorious (for); be infamous / 악명이 자자해지다 become notorious; gain notoriety; be given a bad name; acquire a bad reputation ⟨as a miser⟩
▶그는 악명 높은 고리 대금업자다 He is a notorious loan shark.

악몽 惡夢 a nightmare; a bad [an unpleasant, a terrible] dream; a hideous dream; ⟨흉몽⟩ an ominous dream
♦악몽같은 경험 a nightmarish experience / 악몽을 꾸다 have (a) nightmare / 악몽에 시달리다 suffer from a nightmare; be troubled by a nightmare; be oppressed by a nightmare
▶나는 악몽을 꾸었다 I had a bad dream.
▶그는 악몽에서 깨어났다 ⟨제정신이 들었다⟩ He awoke from a nightmare. ⇒ He came to his senses.

악문 惡文 a bad style; poor writing
♦악문을 쓰다 write in a bad style

악물다 clench [set] ⟨one's teeth⟩
♦이를 악물고 견디다 bear (it) with clenched teeth / 이를 악물고 싸우다 fight bitterly [fiercely] / 이를 악물고 일하다 clench one's teeth and dig into the job; work with firm determination / 이를 악물고 고통을 참다 endure the pain by clenching one's teeth
▶이를 악물고 하면 안 되는 일이 없다 Nothing is impossible to a determined mind.

악바리 ⟨영악한 사람⟩ a hard shrewd person; ⟨모진 사람⟩ a (harsh) tough [ferocious] person

악법 惡法 a bad law; an evil law
▶아무리 악법이라도 법은 법이다 A law is a law, however undesirable it may be.

악벽 惡癖 a bad [vicious] habit; a vice

악보 樂譜 a musical note; ⟨총보⟩ a (musical) score; ⟨책⟩ a music book
♦악보를 읽다 read music / 악보를 보지 않고 연주[노래]하다 play [sing] by ear [without music, from memory] / 악보를 읽을 수 있다 be able to read music
▶나는 악보가 없으면 노래를 못 한다 I cannot sing by ear [without music].
▶그는 악보만 보고도 노래할 수 있다 He can sing at sight.
━관현— a full [an orchestral] score 단행(單行)— a sheet music 피아노— a piano score ━대 a music stand [rack] ━집 a music book

악사 惡事 ⟨악행⟩ an evil [a wicked] deed; a vice; ⟨나쁜 일⟩ a misfortune; an unfortunate incident ♦악사를 꾀하다 plot evil

악사 樂士 a bandsman; a musician ♦거리의 악사 a street musician; (俗) a busker

악사천리 惡事千里 Ill news runs apace [never comes too late]. ⇌ Bad news travels fast.

악상 樂想 ⟨樂⟩ a theme; a motif; a melodic subject ▶그는 갑자기 악상이 떠올랐다 A musical motif suddenly came into his mind.

악서 惡書 a bad [vicious] book; an [a morally] offensive book
♦악서를 추방하다 drive harmful books out of circulation; get rid of undesirable books

악선전 惡宣傳 vile [harmful] propaganda; pernicious propaganda; ⟨악의적인⟩ malicious propaganda; a sinister rumor
▶사람들은 악선전에 넘어갔다 People were misled by pernicious propaganda.
━악선전하다 make pernicious propaganda ⟨about⟩; spread a bad rumor ⟨about⟩; launch false propaganda ⟨about⟩

악성 惡性 malignancy; malignity; viciousness
♦악성의 malignant ⟨influenza⟩; virulent ⟨disease⟩; vicious
■━감기 a nasty [bad] cold: 형은 악성 감기에 걸렸다 My brother has a bad [nasty] cold. ━빈혈 pernicious anemia ━인플레이션 vicious [spiraling] inflation ━종양 a malignant tumor

악성 惡聲 ⟨소리⟩ a bad voice; an evil sound; ⟨악평⟩ a bad reputation

악성 樂聖 a celebrated [master] musician
♦악성 베토벤 Beethoven, the great master of music

악센트 an accent; ⟨강세⟩ a stress; ⟨억양⟩ a tone; accentuation
♦악센트가 있는 accented; accentuated; stressed / 악센트가 없는 unaccented; unaccentuated; unstressed; stressless / 첫 음절에 악센트가 있는 ⟨a word⟩ stressed on the first syllable / 악센트를 붙이다 accent ⟨a word on the second syllable⟩; accentuate ⟨a word⟩; stress ⟨the first syllable⟩; place an accent [lay stress] on ⟨a syllable⟩
▶이 단어는 첫째 음절에 악센트가 있다 This word is stressed on the first syllable.
▶그의 말씨에는 북부 악센트가 있다 He speaks with a Northern accent.

악송구 惡送球 【野】 ⟨make⟩ a bad throw ⟨to second base⟩

악수 握手 shaking hands; a handshake; shaking; ⟨화해⟩ reconciliation; ⟨제휴⟩ a union
♦굳은 악수 a firm handclasp / 악수를 나누다 exchange a handshake ⟨with⟩; shake hands with each other; shake each other by the hand / 아무에게 악수를 청하다 offer sb (his) hand; ⟨화해를 구하다⟩ ask sb for a reconciliation / 아무를 악수로 맞이하다 greet sb with a handshake
▶그들은 굳은 악수를 나누고 헤어졌다 They parted after exchanging a firm handshake.
▶그녀는 내게 악수를 청했다 She offered me her hand.
━악수하다 shake hands ⟨with⟩; shake sb by the hand; press [pump] sb's hand; handshake
▶과거는 잊어버리고 악수해라 You should forget the past and be friends.

악수 惡手 ⟨make⟩ a bad move ⟨at chess⟩; a wrong move

악순환 惡循環 【經·醫】 ⟨be in⟩ a vicious circle [cycle]
♦임금과 물가의 악순환 a vicious cycle [spiral] of prices and wages; a wage-price spiral
▶우리는 군비 경쟁의 악순환을 단절해야 한다 We should break the vicious circle of the

armaments race.
▶임금 인상과 물가 상승이 악순환을 이룬다 Wage raises and price hikes form a vicious circle.

악습 惡習 〈나쁜 버릇〉 a bad habit; a vicious [pernicious] habit; evil ways; 〈악폐〉 an evil practice; an abuse; a vice; 〈악풍〉 a bad custom
♦음주의 악습 the vice of intemperance / 악습이 붙다 contract a bad habit / 악습을 버리다 get rid [break *oneself*] of a bad habit / (사회의) 악습을 근절하다 extirpate evil practices
▶그것은 선거에 따른 악습의 하나다 It is an election abuse.
▶그는 과음하는 악습이 붙었다 He fell into the bad habit of overdrinking.
▶나는 이 악습을 고쳐야겠다 I'll break off [overcome, get rid of] this bad habit.

악식 惡食 〈음식〉 plain [gross] food; coarse [poor] food; 〈먹기〉 gross feeding
♦악식이 몸에 배다 become accustomed [get used] to coarse [plain] fare
—악식하다 eat poor food; be a gross feeder; live on coarse fare

악식 樂式 【樂】 musical form

악심 惡心 an evil intention; a malicious intent; an evil thought [impulse]; a sinister motive
♦악심이 있는 evil-minded; evil-disposed; malignant; malicious / 악심을 품다 become evilly inclined

악쓰다 1 〈소리지르다〉 shout [bawl] out; bawl and squall; yell (in anger, in protest)
♦남편에게 악쓰다 bawl at *one's* husband / 악쓰며 덤벼들다 bawl at *sb* furiously / 악써서 목이 쉬다 roar *oneself* hoarse
2 〈기를 쓰다〉 try hard; struggle; (美口) go all out
♦악쓰고 덤비다 grapple with *sb* desperately; tackle with all *one's* strength

악어 鰐魚 〈아프리카산〉 a crocodile; 〈북미산〉 an alligator; 〈중남미산〉 a caiman; 〈인도산〉 a gavial
■—가죽 crocodile skin [hide]; alligator skin [leather] : 악어 가죽 핸드백 an alligator handbag ■—류 the crocodilians

악언 惡言 bad language; evil speech; abuse
—악언하다 abuse; call names; speak ill of

악업 惡業 【佛敎】 (산) karma

악역 惡役 a villain's [ruffian's] part [role]; the part [role] of the (heavy) villain; (口) the heavy
♦악역을 맡다 play [act] the villain (in a film); play the part of a villain
■—배우 a villain [ruffian] actor; the (heavy) villain

악역 惡疫 a plague; an epidemic; a pestilence
♦악역이 유행하는 지역 a plague spot; a pestilence-stricken district

악연 愕然 ♦악연 실색하다 turn pale with consternation —악연하다 be amazed; be shocked (to find *sth*); be [stand] aghast at; be appalled at
♦악연히 in amazement; in [with] consternation / 악연케 하다 strike *sb* with terror; frighten

악연 惡緣 〈악업이 되는 인연〉 evil connection; a bad [an unfortunate] relation; 〈남녀의 인연〉 an undesirable yet unseverable relationship; fatal bonds

악영향 惡影響 a bad [harmful] influence; an adverse [a baleful, an ill] effect
♦악영향을 끼치다 have [exert] a bad [baneful] influence (upon) / 악영향을 받다 receive a bad influence (from); be adversely affected (by)
▶이런 잡지들은 청소년의 심성에 악영향을 끼친다 These magazines have a demoralizing influence upon the minds of young people.

악용 惡用 abuse; misuse; an improper use
—악용하다 abuse; make bad [wrong] use (of); use *sth* for a wrong [an evil] purpose; put [turn] *sth* to evil ends
♦금력을 악용하다 make an ill use of *one's* wealth / 남의 이름을 악용하다 use another's name evilly [for evil purposes]; make an illicit use of another's name / 지위를 악용하다 abuse *one's* position
▶그는 내 인내심을 악용한다 He presumes upon [takes advantage of] my patience.
▶그는 특권[권력]을 악용했다 He abused his privilege [power].

악우 惡友 a bad friend [companion]; (총칭) bad company
♦악우가 생기다 get [fall] into bad company / 악우를 사귀다 keep bad company / 악우 때문에 나쁜 길로 빠지다 be led astray by a bad friend

악운 惡運 〈나쁜 운수〉 bad [adverse] fortune; ill luck; ill fate; 〈악인이 잘되는 운수〉 the devil's (own) luck
♦악운이 세다 have the devil's luck; thrive in spite of *one's* evil courses / 악운이 다하다 come to the end of *one's* devil's luck
▶가엾게도 그녀에게는 항상 악운이 따라 다닌다 The poor woman is always pursued by bad fortune.

악음 樂音 a musical sound [tone]

악의 惡意 〈악심〉 ill will; malice; spite; 〈나쁜 의도〉 an evil intention; a malicious [wrongful] intent; a sinister motive; 〈적의〉 hostility
♦악의에 찬 비평 a vicious criticism / 악의적인 evil-minded; ill-disposed; malicious; hostile; ill-intentioned / 악의 없는 innocent; harmless; with no harm / 악의 없이 without malice [evil intentions] / 악의에 찬 spiteful; malicious / 악의에서[로] out of malice; from [out of] spite; maliciously; with malicious [evil] intent; in bad faith / 악의를 품다 bear [harbor] malice (to, toward); bear *sb* spite [ill will, malice]; mean ill (toward) / 악의로 해석하다 take *sth* amiss [ill]; take (another's word) in bad [evil, ill] part
▶그는 내게 악의를 품고 있다 He is hostile toward you. ⇌ (口) He has it in for you.
▶우리 아주머니는 악의가 없는 분이다 My aunt is a good-natured woman [a woman with malice toward none].

▶ 그녀는 언제나 악의에 찬 헛소문을 퍼뜨린다 She is always spreading malicious gossip.
▶ 그가 악의에서 그런 것은 아니다 He didn't do it out of [through] malice.
악의악식 惡衣惡食 poor [coarse] clothing and meager [poor] food ◆ 악의악식에 만족하다 be content with a simple life
—**악의악식하다** be poorly clad and eat meager food; be ill-clad and poorly fed
악인 惡人 a bad [wicked] man; a villain; an evildoer; 〈악당〉 a rogue; a scoundrel
▶ 악인에게는 평안이 없다 There is no peace for the wicked.
악인 惡因 a cause of evil
악인악과 惡因惡果 An evil cause produces an evil effect. ⇒ Sow evil and reap evil.
악장 樂長 a bandmaster; a music master; a conductor of a band; a musical director; an orchestra leader
악장 樂章 〔樂〕 a movement
◆ 제1악장 the first movement 《of the Pastoral Symphony》
악장치다 〈악을 쓰며 싸우다〉 brawl; quarrel with each other clamorously [noisily, wildly]
악 재(료) 惡材(料) 〔經〕 unfavorable [adverse] factors; depressing indications
악전 惡錢 〈부정한 돈〉 ill-gotten [dirty] money; 〈악화〉 a bad coin; crooked money
악전 樂典 〔樂〕 musical grammer
악전고투 惡戰苦鬪 hard fighting; a hard [desperate] fight; 〈경기의〉 a hard game; 〈경쟁의〉 a stiff contest
▶ 우리는 악전 고투 끝에 시합에 이겼다 We finally won the game after a tough fight.
—**악전고투하다** fight desperately [against heavy odds]; fight with one's back to the wall
▶ 그는 지사 선거에서 악전 고투했다 He had a close contest in a gubernatorial election.
악절 樂節 〔樂〕 a passage
악정 惡政 misgovernment; misrule; 〈실정〉 maladministration
◆ 악정을 펴다 misgovern a country
▶ 국민은 악정에 시달렸다 The people suffered from misgovernment.
악조건 惡條件 unfavorable [bad] conditions; a handicap
◆ 악조건을 극복하다 get over [surmount] a handicap / 악조건에서 뛰어난 성과를 거두다 achieve excellent results under unfavorable conditions
▶ 심한 악조건속에서도 사업은 잘 되었다 The business succeeded against a severe handicap.
▶ 그들은 악조건 아래에서 일할 수밖에 없었다 They could not help working under unfavorable conditions.
악종 惡種 〈나쁜 종류〉 a bad seed; 〈성질이 흉악한 사람〉 a bad egg; a bad [a wicked, an evil] fellow
악주 惡酒 a bad liquor; 〈밀주〉 bad hooch
악증 惡症 **1** 〈병〉 a bad disease
2 〈나쁜 짓〉 evildoing; a wicked act; a misdeed
악질 惡疾 a bad [malignant, foul, virulent] disease ◆ 악질에 걸리다 be seized with a malignant disease
악질 惡質 **1** 〈나쁜 성질〉 evil [vicious] nature; malignancy; wickedness; 〈모질고 나쁜 사람〉 a wicked fellow
◆ 악질적인 wicked; malignant; vicious; of a vicious nature; pernicious; vile; bad / 악질적인 계약[선거법] 위반 a vicious [flagrant] violation of the contract [Election Law]/ 악질적인 사기 a vicious fraud
2 〈못된 바탕〉 evil [ill] nature
■ —범죄 a flagrant offense —분자 bad [undesirable] elements; undesirables —선전 pernicious propaganda —업자 a wicked trader; a malicious businessman
악착 齷齪 toughness ⇨ 억척 ◆ 악착같이 〈끈덕지게〉 perseveringly; persistently; 〈악을 쓰고〉 desperately; (口) like hell / 악착같이 일하다 toil and moil; grub along; hack; persevere with one's work / 성공하기 위해 악착같이 노력하다 struggle hard to succeed (in)
▶ 그는 악착같이 절약하지 않으면 안될 형편이다 He is forced to pinch and scrape.
악처 惡妻 a bad wife; a Xanthippe
▶ 악처는 평생 골치다 A bad wife is the shipwreck [ruin] of her husband.
악천후 惡天候 bad [unfavorable, nasty] weather; 〈사나운 날씨〉 rough [stormy, inclement] weather
◆ 악천후를 무릅쓰고 in spite of bad weather; braving [facing] stormy weather / 악천후로 인하여 because of bad weather
▶ 서울은 여러 날 동안 악천후가 계속되고 있다 Seoul is having bad weather for many days.
▶ 우리는 악천후를 무릅쓰고 출발했다 We set out in spite of bad weather.
▶ 우리는 악천후때문에 그 일행의 구조 현장에 좀더 일찍 도착하지 못했다 The inclemency of the weather [Stormy weather] prevented us from arriving earlier at the place to rescue the party.
악취 惡臭 a bad [foul, nasty] smell; an offensive odor [smell]; a malodor; stink
◆ 지독한 악취 powerful stink / 악취가 나는 stenchy; stinking; fetid; bad-smelling; evil-smelling / 악취를 제거하다[없애다] remove a bad smell; drown [destroy] an offensive odor; deodorize / 악취를 풍기다 emit [give out] an offensive odor [a bad smell]; smell bad; stink
▶ 죽은 물고기의 악취는 견딜 수가 없다 I can't bear the nasty smell of dead fish.
▶ 음식 쓰레기가 악취를 풍겼다 The garbage stank [gave out a foul smell].
▶ 악취로 숨이 막힌다 The bad odor stifles me.
악취미 惡趣味 vulgar [bad] taste; 〈복장 등의〉 loud taste
악 티늄 〔化〕 actinium ■ —계 열 actinium series
악패듯 〈몹시 심하게〉 violently; furiously; severely; wildly
악편 萼片 〔植〕 a sepal; a calyx ⇨ 꽃받침
악평 惡評 〈나쁜 평판〉 a bad [an evil] reputation; ill fame [repute]; notoriety; 〈나쁜 비평〉 an unfavorable [adverse] criticism; an abu-

악평이 나 있는 사람 a person of ill repute [fame]; a person with a bad reputation / **악평을 받다** be criticized unfavorably; get a bad press / **악평을 퍼뜨리다** circulate scandal 《about sb》; speak ill of sb
▶ 그는 악평을 받고 있다 He is spoken ill of.
──**악평하다** speak ill of; make malicious remarks 《about》; 〈신문 등에서〉 criticize unfavorably [severely]; cut [cry, write] down
▶ 그녀[그의 책]를 너무 악평하지 마라 Don't criticize her [his book] too severely.

악폐 惡弊 a vice; an abuse; an evil [a corrupt] practice
◆ **악폐를 근절하다** uproot [extirpate] an evil practice; stamp [wipe] out evils / **악폐를 바로 잡다** remedy [correct] evils
▶ 그들은 사회적 악폐를 일소하려고 노력했다 They tried to sweep away social abuses.

악풍 惡風 〈악습〉 a bad custom; a vicious practice; a vice
◆ **악풍을 타파하다** break down [do away with] evil customs / **악풍에 물들다** be infected [be led astray] with the vices (practiced in the world around one)
▶ 이 지방에는 아직도 악풍이 좀 남아 있다 Some bad customs still exist in this district.
▶ 소년들은 사회의 악풍에 물들기 쉽다 Boys are easily infected with the corruption of the world.

악필 惡筆 bad [poor] handwriting; a poor [bad] hand
▶ 그는 악필이다 He is [writes] a poor [bad] hand. ⇌ He has bad handwriting.
──**가** a bad penman

악하다 惡── bad; evil; ill; sinful; wicked; malicious; villainous
◆ **악한 사람** a wicked man; a rascal / **악한 짓을 하다** do wrong [evil]; commit a sin [crime] / **성질이 악하다** be ill-natured
▶ 그들은 악한 수단으로 돈을 벌었다 They made money in a crooked [vicious] way.

악한 惡漢 a villain; a rascal; a scoundrel; a knave; a rogue

악행 惡行 evildoing; a wicked [bad] act; a misdeed; bad conduct; a sinful deed
▶ 보르지아가의 악행은 세계적으로 유명하다 The misdeeds of the Borgia are world-famous.
▶ 그는 악행에 악행을 거듭했다 He committed one crime after another.

악형 惡刑 a cruel [severe] punishment; torture ◆ **악형을 가하다** punish cruelly [severely]; inflict a severe punishment 《on》

악화 惡化 〈형세・상태의〉 a change for the worse; deterioration; getting worse [more serious]; 〔醫〕 ingravescence; 〈풍속 등의〉 degeneration; corruption
◆ **인플레이션의 악화** the aggravation of inflation
▶ 북한의 경제 상태는 악화 일로를 걷고 있다 The economic situation in North Korea is getting increasingly worse. ⇌ North Korean economic situation is going from bad to worse.
──**악화하다** worsen; become [grow] worse; go from bad to worse; deteriorate; 〈병세가〉 take a bad [serious] turn; take a turn for the worse; 〈사태가〉 grow more serious
◆ **악화시키다** make worse; worsen; aggravate; deteriorate; corrupt
▶ 아버지의 병세가 급격히 악화되었다 Father's condition took a sudden turn for the worse [suddenly grew serious].
▶ 날씨 때문에 사태가 악화되었다 The weather made it worse.

악화 惡貨 a bad coin; bad money ▶ **악화가 양화(良貨)를 구축한다** Bad money drives out good money.

안¹ 1 〈내부〉 the interior; the inside (↔ the outside)
◆ **안에** in; within; inside; inward / **집안에** within [in] the house; indoors / **안으로부터** from within; from the inside / **상자 안에 넣다** put sth into a box / **집안에 들어박히다** keep indoors [within doors]; stay at home / **안에서 열리다** open from within / **안에서 자물쇠를 잠그다** lock 《a door》 on the inside / **상점 안에서 기다리다** wait inside the store / **집 안에서 나오다** come from within the house / **안으로 들어가다** enter 《a house》; step [come, go] into 《a room》; go [come] inside 《the house》; get inside 《a church》 / **안으로 모시다** show sb in
▶ 집 안은 온통 어질러져 있었다 All was confusion within the house.
▶ 우리는 집 안을 들여다 보았다 We looked inside the house.
▶ 그의 장래는 내 손 안에 있다 I have his future in my hands [clutches].
▶ 안에는 아무것도 없었다 There was nothing inside.
▶ 문이 안에서 잠겼다 The door is locked from the inside.
▶ 방 안에서 무슨 일이 일어나고 있는 건가 I wonder what is happening inside the room.
▶ 아이들은 안에서 놀고 있었다 The children were playing inside.
▶ 할 말이 있으니 안으로 들어와라 Come inside, I've something to talk to you about.
▶ 손님을 안으로 모셔라 Show the guest in [into the parlor].

2 〈시간〉 ◆ **…안에** 〈이내에〉 within; 〈…중에〉 in (the course of); 〈…까지에〉 before; not later than / **그 날 안에** in the course of the day / **기한 안에** within the time limit / **며칠 안에** in a few days / **한 달 안에** within 〔美口〕 inside of] a month; in less than a month
▶ 너는 리포트를 마감 전까지 제출할 수 있다고 생각하니? Do you think you can submit the report before the deadline?
▶ 2, 3일 안에 찾아 뵙겠습니다 I'll visit you in two or three days.

3 〈범위〉 ▶ 교통비는 예산 안에 포함되어 있지 않다 Transportation costs are excluded from the budget.

안² 〈의복의〉 the lining; 〈뒤쪽〉 the back [reverse, other] side; the wrong side
◆ **안을 댄** lined; with a lining; backed

(cloth) / 안을 대지 않은 unlined / (옷이) 등에 안을 대지 않은 unlined at the back; openbacked / 안에 털을 댄 lined with fur; fur-lined (coat) / 안이 나와 있다 be wrong side out / 안을 대다 line 《a coat with fur》; back / 안을 뒤집다 turn 《a suit》
► 이 점퍼는 안으로 뒤집어 입어도 된다 This jumper is reversible.
► 그 코트는 안이 비단[털가죽]이다 The coat has a silk [fur] lining.

안³ 〈내실〉 the women's quarters of the house; the main (living) room; a boudoir
► 어머니는 안에 계십니다 Mother is in the main room.
2 〈아내〉 one's wife

안⁴ not ⇨ 아니¹

안 案 1 〈제안〉 a proposal; a proposition; 〈시사〉 a suggestion; 〈초안〉 a draft
♦ 안을 내다 present [submit] a plan; make a suggestion / 안을 짜다 prepare [frame] a draft / 안을 철회하다 withdraw a proposal
► 평화조약 안이 마련되었다 A draft of a peace treaty has been prepared [made out].
► 그 사업안은 실행 불가능하다 하여 거부되었다 The business proposition was rejected as impractical.
2 〈계획〉 a plan; a scheme; 〈고안〉 an idea; a device; a design
♦ 명안 a good idea / 안을 다듬다 elaborate a plan / 안을 세우다 make [draft] a plan; map out [devise] a plan; work out a program; plan [for]
► 그것은 훌륭한 안이다 That is an excellent idea.
3 〈의안〉 a bill
♦ …법 개정안 a bill for amending the... Act / 예산안 a budget bill / 정부안 a Government bill / 안을 제출하다 present [submit] a bill / 안을 통과시키다 pass a bill

안- 〈여자의〉 women's; female; feminine; woman; lady
♦ 안손님 a lady visitor [guest] / 안주인 〈주부〉 a mistress

안간힘 ♦ 안간힘을 쓰다 strain 《to》; struggle; make great [strenuous] efforts / 사업에 성공하려고 안간힘을 쓰다 struggle to succeed in business / 이기려고 안간힘을 쓰다 strain to win / 분노를 가라앉히려고 안간힘을 쓰다 try hard to restrain one's indignation
► 그녀는 터져 나오는 울음을 참으려고 안간힘을 썼다 She resisted an impulse to cry out.

안감 lining 《cloth》; cloth [material] for lining; 〈안찝〉 the lining of a garment
► 그 드레스는 안감을 대지 않았다 The dress is not lined [is unlined].

안강 安康 peace and good health; the best of health —안강하다 healthy; safe and sound; 〈노인이〉 hale and hearty

안강 鮟鱇 〔魚〕 an angler (fish) =아귀²

안개 (a) fog; (a) mist; (a) haze
♦ 바다[육지] 안개 (a) sea [ground] fog / 봄안개 spring haze / 옅은 안개 a thin [light, gauzy] fog; mist; haze / 짙은 안개 a heavy [thick] mist; fog / 안개낀 misty 《morning》; foggy; hazy / 안개가 짙은 foggy 《day, night, weather, street》 / 안개에 싸인 산들 hills veiled in mist / 안개에 싸이다 be wrapped in a fog; be shrouded by fog / 안갯속 〈미궁〉 mystery; a maze; a labyrinth : 《사건이》 안갯속에 싸이다 《a case》 be shrouded [wrapped] in mystery
► 안개가 낀다 The mist is settling [setting in]. ⇌ It is getting foggy.
► 안개가 걷혔다 The mist cleared [lifted, disappeared, broke away].
► 오늘 아침은 안개가 너무 짙어 차들이 빨리 달릴 수가 없다 It's so foggy this morning (that) cars can't go fast.
► 안개가 옅어졌다[짙어졌다] The fog [mist] thinned [thickened].
► 안개가 흩어졌다 The fog [mist] dispersed.
► 공항은 안개가 끼어 항공편이 재개될 때까지 두 시간을 기다려야 했다 The airport was fogbound, so we had to wait two hours for flights to restart.
► 산꼭대기는 짙은 안개에 싸여 있었다 The mountaintop was shrouded [wrapped] in fog.
■ 상자 안개 〔物〕 a cloud chamber

안건 案件 a matter; an item; a case; 〈의안〉 a bill ♦ 중요 안건 an important item; a matter of importance [significance]
► 이것은 회의의 중요 안건이다 This is an important item on the agenda for the conference.

안경 眼鏡 glasses; 《a pair of》 spectacles; 《口》 specs; 〈방진·방풍용의〉 goggles
♦ 근시[원시]용 안경 glasses for a nearsighted [farsighted] person / 도수가 높은 안경 powerful spectacles; strong glasses; 〈근시의〉 thick glasses [spectacles]; glasses with heavy lenses; thick-lensed spectacles / 도수가 낮은 안경 weak glasses / 도수가 없는 안경 plain glasses; plain-glass spectacles / 테 없는 안경 rimless spectacles / 안경 너머로 over [from above] one's spectacles / 안경을 닦다 polish [wipe] one's glasses / 안경을 벗다 take off one's glasses [spectacles] / 안경을 쓰다 put [hook] on one's glasses [spectacles] / 안경을 쓰고 있다 wear [be in] 《dark》 spectacles
► 저 안경 쓴 여자를 아세요? Do you know the woman with glasses on?
► 교수는 안경 너머로 그 학생의 얼굴을 바라보았다 The professor looked at the student's face over his spectacles.
► 나는 안경 없이는 책을 읽을 수 없다 I cannot read (books) without glasses.
► 안경이 뿌옇게 흐려졌다 My glasses have fogged over.
■ 〔會話〕 「네 안경은 도수가 얼마냐?」「7도야」 "How strong are your glasses?" "It is 7 (degrees)."
► 그는 도수가 높은 안경을 쓰고 있다 He wears strong(-lensed) glasses.
■ 검은 ─ dark glasses 금테 ─ gold-rimmed glasses 색 ─ colored glasses; 〈햇빛 가림용의〉 sunglasses : 그는 그 여자를 색안경을 쓰고 보았다 He viewed her with prejudice [bias]. ⇌ He took a jaundiced view of her. 외알 ─ a

monocle; an eyeglass 코―(프) a pince-nez [pǽns nèi] ―다리 (美) the bows [temples] of a pair of spectacles; (英) the sides of a pair of spectacles ―상(商) an optician ―알 a spectacle lens ―자국 imprints (on the skin) from wearing glasses ―쟁이 a bespectacled person; a glasses-wearer; (俗) a four-eyes ―집[케이스] a spectacle case ―테 the rim [frame] of a pair of spectacles

―――――― 안경 ――――――

프레임 frame / 더블 브리지 double bridge / 다리 temple / 코받침 nose pad / 테 rim / 브리지 bridge / 렌즈 lens

안계 眼界 the range [field] of vision; sight; the visual field; prospect; the sweep [reach] of the eye
♦안계가 넓다[좁다] have a wide [narrow] field of view; have a wide [narrow] mental horizon / 안계에 들어오다 come in (one's) sight; break [burst] upon one's view; 〈경치가〉 spread before one
▶숲을 나서자 안계가 탁 트였다 A wide prospect opened [revealed itself] as I came out of the forest.
▶작은 섬이 안계에 들어왔다 A little island was within [came in] sight.
▶폭격기 편대가 안계에서 사라졌다 The formation of bombers has vanished from [gone out of] sight.

안공 眼孔 an eyehole; an eye socket; the orbit of an eye

안과 眼科 [醫] 〈학문〉 ophthalmology; 〈병원의〉 the department of ophthalmology
■―병원 an ophthalmic hospital ―의사 an oculist; ophthalmiater; an ophthalmologist; 〈통속적으로〉 an eye doctor [specialist]

안광 眼光 〈눈의 정기〉 the glitter of one's eyes; 〈통찰력〉 penetration; discernment; insight
♦안광을 빛내며 with one's eyes glaring / 안광이 날카롭다 be sharp-eyed; have piercing [keen, penetrating] eyes

안구 眼球 [解] an eyeball; ophthalmus [oculous]
■―건조증 xerophthalmia; ophthalmoxerosis ―결막 ocular conjunctiva ―돌출(증) exophthalmos; exophthalmus ―염 ophthalmitis; ophthamia ―은행 an eye bank ―적출(술) (an) ophthalmectomy

안구 鞍具 saddle gear; saddlery; tack; harness; horse gear

안기다¹ 〈품속에 들다〉 be embraced; nestle in sb's arms; go [move] into sb's arms
♦엄마 품에 안겨 있는 아기 an infant nestling in its mother's bosom / 자연의 품에 안기다 be (nestled) in the bosom of nature / 아무의 품에 안겨 잠자다 sleep in sb's arms [bosom]
▶아기는 엄마의 팔에 안겨 (조용히 자고) 있었다 The baby was (sleeping quietly) in its mother's arms.

안기다² 1 〈안게 하다〉 make sb hold [take, carry] 《someone》 in his arms; make sb embrace [hug]
♦엄마에게 아기를 안기다 put the baby in its mother's breast [bosom]
2 〈책임을 지게 하다〉 charge 《sb with responsibility》; fix 《responsibility》 upon sb; lay 《the blame on sb》; put 《the responsibility for sth》 on sb; entrust 《sb with a task》
♦아무에게 비용을 안기다 charge the expenses to sb; make sb bear the expenses; make sb foot the bill / 아무에게 빚을 안기다 saddle sb with debts; hold sb liable for the debt / 친구에게 책임을 안기다 give a friend the responsibility
3 〈물건을 떠맡기다〉 force [press] sb to buy 《the wares》; force 《a sale》 on; intrude on; tout; 〈가짜를〉 palm off 《sth upon sb》; foist 《sth (off) on sb》
♦가짜를 진짜라고 안기다 pass a false article for a genuine one / 아무에게 나쁜 물건을 안기다 palm [impose] a bad article upon sb / 아무에게 선물을 안기다 press gifts on sb
▶상인은 그에게 가짜 물건을 안겼다 The merchant palmed off the bad article on him.
4 〈때리다〉 give [deal] sb a blow; strike sb a blow
♦아무의 머리에 한 대 안기다 give sb a punch [clout] on the head
▶나는 그의 미간에 한 대 안겼다 I dealt him a blow between the eyes.
5 〈알을 품게 하다〉 make 《a hen》 sit on 《eggs》; set 《a hen》 on 《eggs》
6 〈기타〉 ♦아무에게 물벼락을 안기다 pour [throw] water upon [over] sb

안나푸르나 〈히말라야 산맥의 산〉 Annapurna

안남 安南 〈옛왕국〉 Annam ♦안남의 Annamese ―말 Annamese ―미 Annam rice ―사람 an Annamese

안내 案內 1 〈인도〉 guidance; conduct; lead; 〈초대〉 invitation
♦뉴욕 안내 a guide to New York / 안내가 있는[없는] 여행 a conducted [an unconducted] tour / …의 안내로 under sb's guidance [conduct, lead]
▶나는 안내를 받고 거실로 들어가 그들과 이야기를 나누었다 I was shown into the parlor and had a talk with them.
▶그는 이름을 밝히고 안내를 부탁했다 He said his name and asked to be shown in.
▶내가 그 사람의 안내를 맡았다 I acted as his guide.
▶안내 말씀 드립니다 〈공항 등에서〉 Attention, please.
―안내하다 guide; lead; conduct; show sb over; act as a guide 《for sb》; show [ask] into 《a room》; usher sb in
♦길을 안내하다 show sb the way; 〈앞에서〉 lead the way 《to》 / 방안[좌석]으로 안내하다

show [usher] *sb* into the room [to *one's* seat]
▶ 원주민들이 탐험대를 산으로 안내했다 The natives guided the explorers into the mountain.
▶ 그녀는 손님을 거실로 안내했다 She ushered the visitor into the drawing room.
▶ 내가 수원까지 가니까 도중까지 안내해 드리지요 I am going as far as Suwon, so I will go part of the way with you.
▶ 좌석으로 안내해 드릴까요? May I show you to your seat?
2 〈통지〉 information; (a) notice; 〔商〕 advices
◆개점 안내 an announcement of the opening of a store
▶ 은행으로부터 지점 개설 안내가 있었다 I was informed by the bank that a new branch office had been opened.
─**안내하다** notify 《*sb* of, that...》; 〔商〕 advise 《*sb* of the dispatch of 《his》 order》
3 〈안내자〉 a guide
■길─ a guide 연예[극장]─〈신문 등의〉 an entertainment [a theater] guide ─도(圖) 〈소재지의〉 an information map, a guide map; 〈관광용의〉 a sight-seeing map ─별 a guide star ─서 a guide 《to Kyŏngju》; a guidebook 《to the National Museum》; a roadbook; a handbook : 수학 여행 안내서 a guide to the school excursion ─소 an information bureau [center]; an inquiry office: 여행 안내소 a tourist bureau ─양 an usherette; a conductress ─원 a guide; 〈호텔 등의〉 a clerk at the information desk; a desk clerk; 〈극장 등의〉 an usher 《남자》; an usherette 《여자》; a theater attendant [guide] ─자(인) a guide; an attendant; 〈명승 고적의〉 a cicerone ─장(狀) a letter [note] of invitation; an invitation 《card, note》; 〔商〕 an advice; an advice note ─판 〈역 구내 등의〉 a direction board

안녕 安寧 1 〈탈 없음〉 (public) peace [security]; tranquility; 〈복지〉 well-being; welfare
◆사회의 안녕 질서를 유지하다[어지럽히다] maintain the (public) peace and order [disturb the tranquility] of a society
▶ 정부는 안녕 질서의 회복을 위해 전력했다 The government tried hard to restore peace and order.
2 〈평안〉 peace; calm(ness); quiet(ness); tranquility; 〈건강〉 good health
─**안녕하다** 〈평안하다〉 peaceful; calm; uneventful; 〈건강하다〉 healthy; in good health; 〈노인 등이〉 hale and hearty; 〈서술적〉 be (quite) well
▶ 〔會話〕「아버님은 안녕하시냐?」「예, 안녕하십니다」 "How is your father?" "Thank you, he is fine."
▶ 안녕하십니까? How are you (getting on [along])? ⇒ 〈초대면〉 How do you do? ⇒ 〈아침 인사〉 Good morning! ⇒ 〈낮 인사〉 Good day! ⇒ 〈오후 인사〉 Good afternoon! ⇒ 〈저녁·밤 인사〉 Good evening! ⇒ 〈가볍게〉 Hello! ⇒ Hi!

〔解說〕 *Hello!* 나 *Hi!* 는 친한 사이에 특별히 이름과 함께 쓰이며 하루 중 밤낮을 가리지 않고 쓰인다. *Hi, Tom!* 또 *Good morning!* 은 오후 1시 무렵까지, *Good afternoon!* 은 그 이후 일몰 때까지 쓰는 데 조금 더 격식을 차린 표현이다. *Good day!* 는 지금은 잘 쓰지 않는 격식을 차린 표현이다.

▶ 안녕하셨습니까? How have you been?
▶ 안녕히 가십시오[계십시오] Good-by(e)! ⇒ Adieu! ⇒ So long! ⇒ 〈멀리 갈 때〉 Farewell!
3 〔인사말〕 〈작별할 때〉 Good-by(e)!; 〈口〉 So long!; Bye-bye!; 〈여행할 때〉 I wish you a pleasant journey!; 〈프〉 Bon voyage!; 〈오전의〉 Good morning!; 〈낮의〉 Good day!; 〈오후의〉 Good afternoon!; 〈밤의〉 Good night!; 〈편지의〉 With my love!

〔解說〕 작별 인사의 「안녕」에는 *Good-by(e)!* 그 밖에 《*I'll*》 *see you later!* / *See you tomorrow!* / *So long!* / *Take care* 《*of yourself*》 *!* / *Have a nice day!* 등이 있다. 친한 사이에는 *Bye!* / *Bye-bye!* 《▶ 본래는 유아어》 / *Bye* 《*for*》 *now!* 등도 쓰인다. 영국에서는 *Good morning!* / *Good afternoon!* / *Good evening!* 을 끝을 낮추어 말해서 「안녕」의 뜻으로 쓰기도 한다. 또 *Cheerio!* 는 영국의 독특한 친지간의 작별 인사다.

─**안녕하다** say good-by(e) to *sb*; wish [say] *sb* good-by(e); bid *sb* farewell
안노인 ─**老人** the old mistress [lady] of a household [family]
안다 1 〈팔·품에〉 hold [take] *sb* in *one's* arms; embrace; hug; give *sb* a hug; cuddle
◆끌어안다 draw *sb* closer to *one's* breast; clasp [hold] *sb* in *one's* arms / 아이를 품에 안다 embrace a baby; hug a child / 안아 일으키다 help *sb* up; get to *sb's* feet; raise *sb* in *one's* arms; 〈누워 있는 사람을〉 help *sb* sit up in bed
▶ 어머니는 내 여동생을 안고 급히 병원으로 달려갔다 Mother hurried to the doctor's carrying my sister in her arms.
▶ 그녀는 아기를 안아 올렸다 She took up [lifted] her baby in her arms.
▶ 아기가 참 예쁘군요. 좀 안아 봐도 되겠어요? What a cute baby! May I hold her a minute?
▶ 그녀는 아기를 품에 안고 잤다 She slept with her baby in her arms.
2 ⇨ 품다
3 〈떠맡다〉 undertake 《another's responsibility》; bear [assume, shoulder] 《the responsibility for [of]》; answer for
◆빚을 안다 hold *oneself* liable for a debt; 〈남의 빚을〉 shoulder another's debt
▶ 우리 젊은이들은 무거운 책무를 안고 있다 A great responsibility rests upon us young men.
4 〈맞받다〉 meet; confront
◆〈돛이〉 바람을 가득 안다 be filled [swollen] with wind / 바람을 안고 달리다 run against [in the teeth of] the wind
▶ 우리는 바람을 안고 항해했다 We sailed against the wind.
5 〈입다〉 suffer; incur; sustain; receive

◆손해를 안다 suffer [receive] damage; suffer [sustain] a loss / 마음에 상처를 안고 살아가다 live in agonies of a broken heart

안단테 (이) 〖樂〗 andante

안달 fret; fuss; impatience; (口) stew
◆안달이 나서 in a chafe [stew]; impatiently
▶ 그는 참지 못하고 안달이었다 He was fretting with impatience.
▶ 그녀는 그것이 보고 싶어 안달이 났다 She can hardly wait to see it.
▶ 그녀는 안달이 나서 돌아다니고 있었다 She was fussing about.
—**안달하다** fuss; be [grow] impatient 《to do, for》; be overanxious; be nettled; fret 《about》; be in the fidgets [a fidget]; (美口) stew 《over, about》; be in a stew 《about》
◆가고 싶어 안달하다 be anxious to go / 하찮은 일로 안달하다 fuss over [fret about] trifles / 안달하여 병이 나다 fret [worry] *oneself* ill
▶ 그는 고향에 가지 못해 안달했다 He was dying to go home.
▶ 무엇 때문에 안달하니? What are you fretting over?
▶ 그렇게 안달하지 마라 Don't fret yourself like that.
■—(뱅)이 a fretful person; (口) a worrywart

안대 眼帶 a patch; a eyepatch; an eye bandage ◆안대를 하다 have *one's* eye in bandage; have a bandage [patch] over *one's* eye

안데르센 〈덴마크의 동화 작가〉 Andersen, Hans Christian (1805-75)

안데스(산맥) —(山脈) the Andes
◆안데스 지방 사람 an Andean

안도 安堵 relief; reassurance
◆안도의 한숨을 내쉬다 heave [give] a sigh of relief; feel greatly relieved [reassured]
▶ 그 소식을 듣고 그녀는 안도의 한숨을 내쉬었다 At the news she gave a sigh of relief. ⇒ The news put her mind at ease.
—**안도하다** feel relieved [reassured]; feel at ease; set *one's* mind at rest
▶ 남편이 무사히 도착했다는 소식을 듣고 그녀는 안도했다 She was relieved to hear that her husband had arrived safely.

안도라 〈나라 이름〉 Andorra ◆안도라의 Andorran —**사람** an Andorran

안되다 1 〈유감이다〉 be [feel] sorry 《for, at, (to hear) that...》; feel bad 《about》; be a pity 《that...》; have [take] pity 《on》; feel pity 《for》; sympathize 《with》
◆이야기하기 안됐지만 to my regret; I regret to say that... / 보기에 안되다 be pitiful to see
▶ 그녀가 안됐다 I am sorry for her.
▶ 안됐습니다 I am sorry (for you). ⇒ It is a pity.
▶ 민 선생이 죽었다니 안됐다 We regret to hear the news of the death of Mr. Min.
▶ 그 여자가 불행을 당해서 참 안됐다 I feel so sorry for her misfortune.
2 〈금지〉 must [should] not 《do》; ought not to 《do》; be not allowed
▶ 안 돼 Oh, don't!
▶ 이 방에서 담배 피우면 안됩니다 You are not supposed [allowed] to smoke in this room. ⇒ You are forbidden to smoke [prohibited from smoking] in this room.
▶ 밖에 나가면 안 됩니까? May I not [Can't I] go out?
▶ 그런 곳에 가면 안된다 You must not go to a place like that.
▶ 그런 일을 그녀에게 말하면 안된다 You ought not to say such a thing to her.
3 〈필요·의무〉 must 《do》; have (got) to 《do》; need to 《do》; It is necessary 《to do》...
▶ 그녀는 누군가 도와주지 않으면 안된다 She is in need of help.
▶ 그 집은 수리하지 않으면 안된다 The house must be repaired. ⇒ The house needs [wants] repairing.
▶ 늦어도 8시 30분까지는 학교에 도착하지 않으면 안된다 I have (got) to be in school by 8:30 at the latest.
▶ 오늘은 병원에 가지 않으면 안된다 I have to go to the doctor's today.
▶ 우리는 싫든 좋든 규칙을 지키지 않으면 안된다 We ought to [should] observe the rule whether we like it or not.
4 〈도리〉 should 《do》; ought to 《do》; shall 《do》
▶ 부모에게 순종하지 않으면 안된다 One should be obedient to *one's* parents.
▶ 부모로서는 당연히 자녀를 교육시키지 않으면 안된다 It is in nature of things that parents should put children to school.
5 〈쓸모 없다〉 be useless; be of no use; won't do [work]
▶ 그 사람은 교사는 안된다 He is useless as a teacher. ⇒ As a teacher, he is a failure.
▶ 그 정도 돈으론 안된다 That amount of money will not do.
▶ 〖話〗 「연필도 됩니까?」 「안됩니다」 "Will the pencil do?" "No, it won't."
6 〈미달·실패〉 be a failure; be unsuccessful; fail ◆되든 안되든 간에 whether successful or not
▶ 이것으로는 교통비[커피 한 잔 값]도 안된다 This will not cover even the transportation expenses [is not enough for even a cup of coffee].
▶ 이 기계는 작동이 안된다 This machine does not work.
▶ 그는 서른 살이 채 안되었다 He is on this side of thirty.
▶ 금년에는 벼농사가 잘 안되었다 The rice crops have turned out ill [badly] this year.
▶ 되고 안되고는 전적으로 너에게 달렸다 Its success or failure solely depends upon you.
7 〈조심〉 ◆…하면 안되니까 for fear...may [should]; so as not to...; so that *one* may not 《be, do》; lest...should
▶ 늦으면 안되니까 서두르자 Let's hurry up, so that we may not be late.
▶ 잃어버리면 안되니까 이 돈은 내가 맡아 두겠다 I shall keep this money, lest you should lose it.

안드로겐 〖生化〗 an androgen

안드로메다 〖그神〗 Andromeda; 〖天〗 Andromeda ◆안드로메다 은하 the Andromeda Galaxy / 안드로메다 자리 Andromeda

안뜰 a courtyard; an inner court [garden]

안락 安樂 ease; comfort
—**안락하다** comfortable; easy; cozy
◆안락한 생활 an easy [a carefree] life; a comfortable living / 안락하게 살다 live comfortably [in (ease and) comfort]; live in easy circumstances; make a comfortable living; live on a bed of roses
▶ 그 남자와 결혼하면 너는 평생 안락하게 살 수 있을 것이다 If you marry him, you will be able to live in comfort [comfortably] all your life.
■—의자 an easy chair; an armchair; a club chair

안락사 安樂死 (artificial) euthanasia; mercy killing; an easy death
▶ 안락사는 의사들에게 중대한 윤리적인 문제를 제기하고 있다 Euthanasia poses a serious ethical problem for physicians.

안력 眼力 〈관찰력〉 insight; power of observation; 〈시력〉 eyesight ◆안력이 있는 discerning; penetrating
▶ 범인은 형사의 예리한 안력에 놀랐다 The detective's keen insight astonished the criminal.

안료 顔料 1 〈화장품〉 cosmetics; a face paint 2 〈도료〉 a paint; 〈색소〉 a pigment

안마 按摩 massage ◆안마를 받다 have [get] a massage; have *oneself* massaged
▶ 피곤할 때 안마를 잘 받으면 기분이 좋아진다 A thorough massage feels good when we are tired.
—**안마하다** massage; give a massage (to)
▶ 안마해 드릴까요? Shall I give you a massage?
■—사 a massager; 〈남자〉 a masseur; 〈여자〉 a masseuse; a rubber —치료 a massage treatment

안마 鞍馬 〔體操〕 〈기구〉 a pommel [side] horse; 〈종목〉 the pommel [side] horse

안면 安眠 a sound [good, restful] sleep; a comfortable sleep
◆안면을 못하다 have a troubled sleep; pass a bad night; cannot get a good [quiet] night's sleep / 안면을 방해하다 disturb *sb's* (quiet) sleep
▶ 개가 밤새도록 짖어대어 내 안면을 방해했다 Barking all night the dog kept me awake [disturbed my sleep].
▶ 이 약을 드시면 안면을 취할 수 있을 겁니다 This medicine is going to give you a quiet [peaceful] sleep.
—**안면하다** sleep well [soundly]; have a quiet [good] sleep; sleep in peace
■—방해 disturbance of sleep; nuisance at night : 라디오 좀 꺼라. 안면 방해다 Turn off the radio. I can't sleep for it.

안면 顔面 1 〈얼굴〉 the face ◆안면의 facial / 안면에 부상을 입다 get injured in the face
2 〈친분〉 acquaintance
◆안면이 있는 사람 an acquaintance / 안면이 넓다 have a wide acquaintance; have a large [wide] circle of acquaintances / 안면이 있다 be (personally) acquainted 《with》; know *sb* by sight / 안면이 없다 have no personal acquaintance 《with》; do not know *sb* by sight; be a stranger / 안면 박대하다 slight an acquaintance
▶ 그 사람과는 안면이 전혀 없다 He is quite a stranger to me.
▶ 나는 그 계통에 안면이 별로 없다 I have few acquaintances in that circle.
▶ 나는 그와 안면은 없으나 이름은 들어서 알고 있다 I don't know him by sight, but I know him by name.
■—각〔지수〕 〔人類〕 the facial angle [index] —경련 facial tics [spasm] —신경〔동맥, 근〕 the facial nerve [artery, muscle] —신경 마비 〔醫〕 facial paralysis —신경통 〔醫〕 facial neuralgia; face-ache

안면부지 顔面不知 ◆안면 부지의 인물 an utter [a total, a perfect] stranger; a man whom *one* has never met / 안면 부지이다 have no personal acquaintance with *sb* at all; be a total [an utter] stranger 《to me》
▶ 그 사람과는 안면 부지다 He is a complete stranger to me. = I have never met him.

안목 inside [interior] measure [dimensions, measurements] ◆안목으로 (재어) in the clear
▶ 안목이 열자다 It measures ten *cha* in the clear [on the inside].

안목 眼目 1 〈안식〉 an appreciative eye; discernment; a discerning [critical] eye; (a sense of) discrimination
◆전문가의 안목 an expert's(s) eye; a professional eye / 안목이 있는 사람 a discerning person; a man of judgment / 안목이 있다 have an eye [a discerning eye] 《for curios》 / 사물을 보는 안목이 있다 have the seeing eye / 예술에 대한 안목을 기르다 train [develop] artistic judgment [discrimination]/ 안목에 틀림이 없다 have an unerring critical eye / 긴 안목으로 보다 take a long(-range) view 《of》
▶ 그 여자는 도기에 대한 안목이 있다 She has an eye for pottery.
2 〈요점〉 the (main) point; the purport [gist]; 〈주안〉 the primary [main] object

안무 按舞 the arrangement of a dance; dance composition; 〈발레의〉 choreography
—**안무하다** design the (dance) postures; arrange a dance; choreograph; compose the choreography
■—가 a choreographer; a dance composer

안문 —門 an inner door [gate]; an inner window

안방 —房 the main living room; a boudoir; 〈주부가 거처하는〉 the women's quarters

안방샌님 —房— a stay-at-home; (美口) a homebody ▶ 그 사람은 안방 샌님이다 He is a family man.

안배 按排·按配 〈배치〉 arrangement; disposition; 〈배분〉 distribution; assignment
—**안배하다** arrange; distribute; assign 《work》
◆역할을 안배하다 assign duties

안벽 —壁 the inside of a wall; the inner wall

안벽 岸壁 〈항만·운하의〉 a quay (wall); 〈물가

의 벼랑〉 a bluff; palisades
♦배를 안벽에 대다 bring [moor] a ship alongside the pier / 안벽에 정박하다 come [be brought] alongside the quay

안보 安保 security ⇨ 안전보장
♦국가의 안보 문제 national security problems / 물샐 틈 없는 안보 태세 the watertight security posture / 한미 안보 조약 the Korea-U.S. Security Treaty / 한미 연례 안보 회의 the Annual Korea-U.S. Security Consultative Meeting
■ 집단[총력]— collective [all-out] security
■—외교 diplomacy for national security —의식 sense of national security : 국민의 안보 의식 the public perception of security

안부 安否 〈무사 여부〉 safety; 〈지내는 형편〉 sb's welfare; 〈문안〉 an inquiry; 〈문안 인사〉 regards; wishes
♦안부를 묻다 inquire [ask] after sb [sb's health] / 안부를 알리다 let sb know how one is / 안부를 염려하다 worry [be concerned] about sb's safety
▶ 그분께 안부 전해 주세요 Please give him my best regards.
▶ 댁내 여러분께 안부 전해 주십시오 Please remember me to all your family. ⇌ 〈편지의 끝맺는 말〉 With kind regards to all.
▶ 나는 고향의 부모님께 안부 편지를 드렸다 I wrote to my parents at home asking how they were getting on [along].
▶ 그들의 안부는 아직 모른다 Their safety is not known yet.
▶ 우리 동네에서 불이 나자 그는 즉시 안부를 물으러 왔다 He immediately came to inquire after us when a fire broke out in our neighborhood.
—**안부하다** inquire after sb's welfare; pay one's respects to

안부 鞍部 〈산의〉 a col; a saddle

안부인 —夫人 your [his] esteemed wife; madam; Mrs....

안분 按分 proportional division —**안분하다** divide [distribute] proportionally 《among》
▶ 우리는 그 돈을 청구자들에게 안분했다 We distributed the money pro rata [prorated the money] among all the claimants.
■—비례 proportional distribution : 안분 비례로 proportionally; in proportion; pro rata

안사돈 —查頓 a son's [daughter's] mother-in-law; a son-in-law's [daughter-in-law's] mother

안사람 (my) wife
안산 安產 an easy delivery ⇨ 순산
안산암 安山岩 〔鑛〕 andesite
안살림 household [home] management; housekeeping

안색 顔色 1 〈얼굴빛〉 (a) complexion; color
♦안색이 좋은[나쁜] 사람 a person with a healthy [bad] complexion / 안색이 변하다 change color / 안색이 좋다[나쁘다] look fine [bad, ill]; look well [unwell, pale, sick] / 안색이 좋아지다[나빠지다] look better [worse]; regain [lose] color / 안색이 희다[검다] have a fair [dark] complexion

▶ 그는 화가 나면 안색이 변한다 When he gets angry, his face changes color.
▶ 오늘은 안색이 훨씬 좋구나 You look much better today.
▶ 그는 안색이 창백해졌다 He turned pale.
2 〈표정·기색〉 a look; a countenance; an expression
♦안색을 살피다 try to gauge [judge] sb's feelings [state of mind] (from his expression); read sb's expression [face, countenance] / 안색에 나타나다 betray 《one's emotions》; show
▶ 그는 항상 내 안색을 살핀다 He always studies [reads] my face [expression].
▶ 그녀는 기분이 안색에 나타난다 Her feelings show in her expression [on her face].

안성맞춤 安城— the very thing wanted; the most suitable thing ; just the thing
♦안성맞춤의 (the most) suitable 《for》; fit 《for》; ideal; just / 안성맞춤의 날씨 ideal weather 《for》 / 안성맞춤의 일 the work sb is best fitted to undertake / 야영하기에 안성맞춤인 장소 an ideal place for camping
▶ 그 사람이야말로 그 일에 안성맞춤이다 He is just the man for the job.
▶ 이것이야말로 안성맞춤이다 This is just what we want. ⇌ This will fill the bill perfectly.
▶ 그 시간은 내게 안성맞춤이다 The time is convenient for me.

안손님 a woman caller; a lady visitor

안수 按手 〔基〕 the imposition; the laying on of hands —**안수하다** impose; lay hands on sb; confirm sb
■—례 〈신도의〉 the imposition of hands; the rite of confirmation; 〈성직의〉 the ordination

안슬프다 sorry and uneasy ⇨ 안쓰럽다

안식 安息 rest; repose —**안식하다** rest; repose
■—교 the Seventh-Day Adventist Church
—년 (年) a sabbatical year

안식 眼識 discernment; insight; a critical [discerning] eye; discrimination
♦안식이 있는 사람 a discerning person; a man of insight / 안식이 있다 have an eye 《for works of art》; be a connoisseur 《of old furniture》
▶ 그는 미에 대한 안식이 있다 He has an eye for beauty.

안식구 —食口 〈여자 식구〉 the female members of a family; 〈아내〉 one's wife

안식일 安息日 the Sabbath (day) ♦안식일을 지키다[어기다] observe [break] the Sabbath

안식처 安息處 a (safe) haven; a place to rest; a resting place; a refuge ♦종교에서 안식처를 구하다 seek refuge [solace, peace] in religion; find relief in religion

안식향 安息香 〔化〕 benzoin; gum benjamin [benzoin]

안심 安心 〈마음의 평안〉 peace of mind; freedom from care [anxiety]; 〈안도〉 (a sense of) relief; 〈안전〉 (a sense of) security; safety; reassurance
♦안심이 되다 feel relief; be reassured / 안심이 안 되다 feel uneasy 《about》; be anxious

《about》; fear
▶열이 내렸으니 이제 안심이다 The fever has gone down, and now I feel at ease [have no cause to worry].
▶그 사람이 그렇게 말하니 안심이 된다 I am reassured by his saying so.
▶그 소식을 들어도 안심이 안 된다 The news does not put my mind at ease.
—안심하다 feel easy 《about》; feel at ease [rest]; 〈마음을 놓다〉 feel [be] relieved; have [feel] no anxiety 《about》; relax; 〈안전하다고 여기다〉 feel reassured; be [rest] assured; be confident 《of》
♦안심할 수 없는 병세 a serious [dangerous, critical] condition / 안심할 수 있는 사람 a reliable [trustworthy] man / 안심할 수 없는 사람 an unreliable [a dangerous] man / 안심하고 〈근심없이〉 at 《one's》 ease; without anxiety; free from fear [care, anxiety]; 〈안도하여〉 with a sense of relief; 〈안전하다고 여기고〉 with a sense of security / 안심하고 죽다 die in peace / 안심시키다 set *sb* at ease; ease *sb's* mind; relieve *sb* of 《his》 anxiety
▶그 소식을 듣고 안심했다 I was [felt] greatly relieved at the news.
▶사건이 해결되어 모두 크게 안심했다 The matter has been settled to the great relief of everybody.
▶그 점은 안심하십시오 Put [Set] your mind at rest [ease] about that [on that score].
▶꼭 그리 갈테니 안심하세요 You may rest assured that I'll be there.
▶그에게는 안심하고 그 일을 맡길 수 있다 I can entrust him with the task.
▶그만큼 열심히 공부했으니 안심하고 시험을 봐라 Since you have worked so hard, you should take your examinations with confidence.
▶내가 그 일을 맡았으니 안심하고 일임하세요 Now that I've taken on the job, you can rest easy and leave it all to me.

안심찮다 安心— 1〈안심이 안 되다〉uneasy; anxious; uncertain; ill at ease
♦안심찮은 마음 a heart full of misgiving(s) / 안심찮게 여기다 feel uneasy; be anxious 《about》; be uncertain 《over》; have misgivings 《about》; be in suspense
▶그녀는 안심찮은 기색이다 She looks anxious.
▶나는 안심찮은 일이 많다 Many things weigh on my mind. ⇒ I am worried about many things.
2 〈미안하다〉 sorry
▶자네한테 폐를 끼쳐 안심찮네 I am sorry I have put you to so much trouble. ⇒ I am sorry for all the trouble I am causing you.

안쓰럽다 (feel) sorry and uneasy (for troubling [being helped by] *one's* inferior)

안아맡다 〈남의 일·책임을 떠맡다〉 undertake [shoulder] 《another's responsibility [debt]》; assume 《responsibility》

안아일으키다 raise [lift] *sb* in *one's* arms; help *sb* get to 《his》 feet; pick *sb* up; 〈누운 사람을〉 help *sb* sit up in bed

안압 眼壓 〔醫〕 intraocular pressure
안약 眼藥 eyewash; medicine for the eyes; eye drops; eyewater
♦안약을 넣다 apply eye drops [eyewash]; drop some eye lotion into *one's* eyes
▶나는 좀처럼 안약을 넣지 않는다 I seldom use eye drops. ⇒ I rarely put eye drops into my eyes.
안염 眼炎 〔醫〕 ophthalmia; inflammation of the eyes
안온 安穩 peace; quiet; tranquility; calmness
—안온하다 peaceful; quiet; tranquil; calm
♦안온한 생활 a placid life / 안온하게 peacefully; in peace; quietly; tranquilly / 안온하게 살다 live in peace
▶내가 지금 원하는 것은 시골에서 안온하게 살아가는 것 뿐이다 All (that) I want now is a peaceful life in the country.
안와 眼窩 〔解〕 an eye socket; an eyepit; an eyehole; an orbit
안위 安危 safety and danger; security; fate; destiny; welfare
♦국가의 안위 a national crisis
▶그는 자신의 안위를 돌보지 않고 물에 빠진 소년을 건져 주었다 Disregarding his own safety, he rescued a drowning boy.
▶이것은 국가의 안위에 관한 중대 문제다 This is a matter of vital importance to the destiny of the nation.
안이하다 安易— easy; easygoing
♦안이한 생각[사고 방식] an easygoing [a happy-go-lucky] way of thinking / 안이하게 easily; 〈태평하게〉 at ease; at *one's* ease / 안이한 생활을 하다 lead an easy life / 안이하게 생각하다 take things easy / 안이하게 타협하다 make an easy compromise
▶그는 생각이 너무 안이하다 He is too easygoing. ⇒ His view seems to be too optimistic.
▶그것은 안이한 영어 학습법이다 It is an easy approach to the study of English.
▶그것은 너무 안이한 생각[사고방식]이다 It is too easygoing a way of thinking.
▶세상 일을 너무 안이하게 생각하지 마라 Do not take things too lightly.
안일 housework; women's work; household affairs
안일 安逸 idleness; (idle) ease ♦무사 안일주의 a peace-at-any-price principle
▶안일에 빠지지 마라 Do not idle away your time [days]. ⇒ Do not lead an idle life
—안일하다 idle; indolent
▶그는 안일한 생활을 했다 He lived a life of ease. ⇒ He lived in idleness. ⇒ He led an idle life.
안장 安葬 burial; interment —안장하다 bury; entomb; inter; lay 《*sb's* body》to rest; commit to the earth [ground, grave] ▶그 분은 이곳에 안장되었다 He was laid to rest here.
—ㅈ a burial [burying] ground
안장 鞍裝 a saddle
♦안장을 얹다[내리다] saddle (up) [unsaddle] 《a horse》; put a saddle on [take a saddle off] 《a horse》/ 말에 안장을 얹지 않고 타다 ride bareback / 안장에 올라타다 take [get into]

the saddle; get onto *one's* horse ■—방석 a saddle blanket; a saddlecloth; a pad —코 a saddle nose; 〈사람〉a saddle-nosed person

안저 眼底 the eyeground; 〔解〕 the fundus oculi ■—검사〔醫〕funduscopy —출혈 〔醫〕 cerebral hemorrhage in *one's* eyes; hemorrhage in the eyeground

안전 安全 safety; security; freedom from danger

♦생명과 재산의 안전 security of life and property / 작업상의 안전 safety in work operations / 안전을 위해 for safety's sake / 교통의 안전을 위협하다 endanger safe traffic / 일신의 안전을 도모하다 look to *one's* own safety / 안전을 위협하다 threaten the security 《of》; imperil the safety 《of》

▶ 당신의 안전은 절대 보증합니다 You are assured of the complete security of your life.
▶ 그는 일신의 안전을 위해 해외로 도피했다 He fled abroad for his own safety.
▶ 길을 건너기 전에 안전을 확인해라 Make sure that it's free from danger before you cross the road.
▶ 안전 제일 (게시) Safety First.

—**안전하다** safe; secure; free from danger
♦안전한 장소 a place [zone] of safety / 안전한 투자 a sound investment / 안전하게 safely; in safety; securely

▶ 여기는 홍수 때도 안전합니다 This place is quite safe even during floods.
▶ 이 집은 어떠한 지진에도 안전합니다 This house is secure in any earthquakes.
■—계수 a factor of safety; a safety factor —계획 a safety program —관리 safety supervision —교육 safety education —규칙 safety regulations;〈교통의〉road safety rules —기 (器)〈기계·총 등의〉a safety bolt [catch, guard];〈전기의〉a (safety) cutout; a cutout switch; a circuit breaker; a safety fuse —등 (燈) a safety lamp —띠[벨트] a safety belt; a safety band;〈좌석의〉a seat belt —면도(날) a safety razor (blade) —모(帽) a safety helmet —밸브 a safety [relief] valve; an escape [a pop-off] valve —성 원자력의 안전성을 연구하다 study nuclear safety —시설 safety facilities —운동 safety campaign —율 safety rate [factor]; a factor of safety —점검 safety checks; safety inspection —제일주의 the safety first principle : 안전 제일주의로 행동하다 act on the principle [basis] of safety-first —조업 safety operation —주간 a safety week : 지금은 교통 안전 주간이다 Traffic Safety Week is being observed. —지대 a safety zone;〈도로의〉a safety [traffic] island

안전 眼前 ♦안전에서 before *sb's* eyes

안전권 安全圈 a safety zone ♦안전권에 들다 〈경기 등에서〉get [have, secure] a safety lead
▶ 그 후보는 안전권에 들었다 The candidate is now sure of election [safe to win the seat]. ⇌ The candidate is home free.

안전기준 安全基準 safety standards
▶ 방사능이 원자력 위원회가 정한 안전기준을 상회했다 The radioactivity rose above the safety levels established by the Atomic Energy Commission.

안전보장 安全保障 security
♦국가 안전 보장법 〈미국의〉 the National Security Act / 국가 안전 보장 회의 〈미국의〉 the National Security Council
■ 집단— collective security ■—이사회 the Security Council —조약 a security treaty [pact]

안전운전 安全運轉 safe [careful] driving
♦안전 운전을 하다 drive safely [carefully]

안전장치 安全裝置 a safety device [appliance]; a safety gear [system];〈총포의〉a safety bolt [catch, lock, lever]; a safety
♦안전 장치가 있는 총 a gun with the safety catch on / 안전 장치를 걸다 put 《a gun》 at [on] safety; put 《a rifle》 on safety /〈총의〉안전장치를 풀다 slip [push off] the safety catch

안전책 安全策 a safe plan [measure]
♦안전책을 강구하다 take a safe measure

안전핀 安全— a safety pin
♦안전핀을 꽂다 fasten 《a crape to *one's* sleeve》 with a safety pin / 안전핀을 뽑다 unfasten a safety pin

안절부절못하다 be [grow] restless; be fidgety; be impatient; get [have] the fidgets; jitter; be on pins and needles
♦안절부절 못하는 사람 a restless person; a fidgety man; a fidget / 안절부절 못하여 uneasily; restlessly; nervously; in a restless manner; in a fidget / 안절부절 못하게 하다 give *sb* the fidgets; make *sb* nervous; give *sb* the jitters
▶ 그 소식이 올 때까지 그녀는 안절부절 못했다 Until she heard the news, she was all on edge [in a fidget].

안정 安定 stability; stabilization; steadiness; 〈균형〉equilibrium; balance;〈침착〉settlement; composure
♦경제 [물가, 통화]의 안정 economic [price, currency] stabilization / 사회의 안정 social stability / 생활의 안정 the stabilization [stability] of livelihood; security of living / 안정을 결하다 lack stability; be unstable; be unsettled / 안정을 유지하다[잃다] keep [lose] equilibrium [balance, stability] / 생활의 안정을 얻다 secure *one's* livelihood; find a sure means of living
▶ 저 소녀는 정서의 안정이 결여되어 쉽게 흥분한다 The girl is emotionally unstable [lacks emotional stability] and is easily excited.
▶ 정부는 경제의 안정을 위해 노력하고 있다 The government is making efforts to stabilize the economy.

—**안정하다** be stabilized [settled]; become stable; balance; settle
♦안정되어 있다 be stable; be steady; be in equilibrium; be settled; be at rest / 안정시키다 stabilize; equilibrate; balance / 민심을 안정시키다 put the people's mind at rest
▶ 물가가 안정될 조짐은 아직 전혀 없다 There are no signs of prices stabilizing.
▶ 주식 시장은 안정되어 있었다 The stock market held firm.

안정

▶시세가 안정됐다 The market has settled [steadied].
■一고용 stable [safe, secure] employment —공황 a stabilization crisis —성장(률) a stable growth (rate) —세력 a stabilizing force [power]; a steadying influence —의(儀) a ship stabilizer —자금 a stabilization fund —장치 a stabilizing apparatus; a stabilizer —통화[화폐] a stabilized [stable] currency

안정 安靜 rest; quiet; repose
♦안정을 요하다 〈병·환자가 주어〉 require rest in bed
—안정하다 quiet; peaceful; at ease
♦안정하고 있다 lie quietly; keep quiet; stay in [keep to one's] bed / 안정시키다 set at ease; quiet / 식후 1시간 안정하다 have [take] an hour's rest after a meal; lie quietly for an hour after a meal
■절대— absolute [thorough] rest [quiet]; a complete rest: 의사는 그에게 절대 안정을 명했다 The doctor advised [prescribed] a complete [an absolute] rest for him. ■一요법 a rest cure [therapy]

안정 眼睛 the pupil of the eye ⇨ 눈동자
—피로 (疲勞) eyestrain; fatigue of the eyes; 【醫】asthenopia

안정감 安定感 a sense of security [stability]
♦안정감이 있는 stable; secure; well-balanced

안정도 安定度 stability ■一시험 a stability test

안정판 安定板 〈비행기의〉 a stabilizer
≠수직— a (vertical) fin; a vertical stabilizer 수평— a horizontal stabilizer

안존하다 安存— 1〈잘 있다〉 be at peace 2〈성질이〉 be quiet and gentle; be at ease

안주 安住 peaceful living; living in peace; a serene life; a comfortable life
♦종교에서 안주를 얻다 find peace in religion —안주하다 live in peace; lead a comfortable life [peaceful living]
♦안주할 자리를 찾다 seek a place where one can live in peace / 현재의 지위에 안주하고 있다 be content with one's present position
▶그는 서울에서 안주할 곳을 찾고 있다 He is seeking a place for peaceful living in Seoul.

안주 按酒 〈술의〉 a relish [tidbit] (taken with alcoholic drinks); a (side) dish; appetizers [(프)] hors d'oeuvres served with drinks; an accompaniment of wine; a dish eaten with wine ♦술과 안주 wine and some eatables / 안주로 as a side dish for wine
▶두부는 좋은 술안주가 된다 Bean curd is a good accompaniment of wine.
▶안주는 무엇이 있습니까? What eatables do you have with your wine? ⇒ What is the appetizer?
▶이것은 안주로 꼭 알맞다 This goes very well with wine.

안주머니 an inside pocket (of the coat); an inner pocket ♦안주머니에 넣어두다 keep sth in one of one's inside pockets

안주인 —主人 〈주부〉 the lady of the house; a wife; a mistress; 〈여관·하숙의〉 a landlady; a hostess

안중 眼中 1〈눈 속〉 inside of the eye; in the eye 2〈관심의 범위내〉 mind; heart; notice; attention
♦안중에 있는 in one's eyes / 안중에 없다 leave 《sb, sth》 out of account [consideration]; take no account [notice] (of); think nothing (of); be of no concern; ignore / 자기 이외에는 안중에 없다 think of none but oneself
▶나 같은 것은 그의 안중에도 없는 것 같았다 He apparently took no notice of me.
▶그녀에게 나 같은 것은 아예 안중에도 없었다 My presence was utterly ignored by her.
▶그런 녀석은 안중에 없다 I don't take notice of people like him. ⇒ He is a nobody. ⇒ He is beneath our notice.

안중문 —中門 a mid-gate (leading to the inner court)

안지름 the inside diameter

안질 眼疾 〈눈병〉 an eye disease [trouble, complaint, disorder]; sore eyes; an ophthalmic ailment [case]
♦안질을 앓다 suffer from an eye trouble; be afflicted with an eye disease

안집 〈안채〉 an inner building [wing]; the main building (of a house)

안짝 〈미만〉 inside a limit; within; less [not more] than; not exceeding
▶그의 월수입은 100만원 안짝이다 His monthly income is less than [under] one million won.
▶학교는 역에서 걸어서 30분 안짝에 있다 The school is within half an hour's walk of the station. (▶of 대신에 from은 잘못임) ⇒ The school is not more [less] than half an hour's walk from the station.
▶1시간 안짝에 돌아오겠다 I'll be back in less than [within] an hour.
▶리포트는 2천 단어 안짝으로 써 주세요 Write your report within [in less than] two thousand words.
▶여행 비용은 10만원 안짝으로 들어야 한다 The expense for the trip should not exceed [be within] one hundred thousand won.
▶【會話】「그녀는 언제 퇴원하니?」「의사는 10일 안짝으로 생각하나봐」"When will she be out of the hospital?" "The doctor thinks in ten days' time."

안짱다리 〈다리〉 varus; 〈사람〉 a knock-kneed [pigeon-toed] person
♦안짱다리의 knock-kneed; pigeon-toed / 안짱다리로 걷다 walk intoed [pigeon-toed]; walk with one's toes turned in [inward]

안쪽 the inside; the interior; the inner part
♦안쪽의 inside; inner; interior / 안쪽에 (on the) inside; within; inward / 안쪽에서 from within; on the inside / 안쪽에서 열다 open 《a door》 from within / 안쪽에서 잠그다 lock [fasten] 《a door》 from [on] the inside; lock 《a door》 from within
▶상자의 안쪽은 붉은 색으로, 바깥쪽은 흰색으로 칠해져 있다 The inside of the box is painted red, the outside white.
▶한 남자가 문 바로 안쪽에 서 있었다 A man was standing just inside the gate.

▶ 문은 방 안쪽으로 열렸다 The door opened inward into the room.
안쪽잡다 1 〈마음 속에〉 keep [bear] in mind 2 〈걸가량으로 헤아리다〉 grasp; take in; get the general idea; roughly understand
안찝 1 〈옷의 안감〉 the lining of a garment; (cloth for) lining 2 〈소·돼지 내장〉 the viscera 《*sing.* viscus》; the entrails 《of a pig or a cattle》; the guts 3 〈관(棺)〉 a coffin; (美) a casket
안차다 〈겁이 없고 깜찍하다〉 bold; fearless; daring; dauntless
▶ 저렇게 험한 산을 오르다니 너도 꽤 안차구나 It's a very bold [daring, fearless] of you to climb that steep mountain.
안착 安着 safe arrival; 〈물품의〉 safe receipt
◆ 안착을 알리다 inform *sb* of *one's* safe arrival
— **안착하다** 〈사람이〉 arrive safe [safely, in safety]; reach 《a place》 safe and sound; 〈물건이〉 duly reach; reach in good condition
▶ 우리는 가구가 안착되었다는 통지를 받았다 We received an acknowledgment of the safe receipt of the furniture.
안창 a shoe liner; an inner sole
◆ 구두에 안창을 깔다 put liners in shoes
안채 the main building of a house
안채 眼彩 the glitter of the eyes ⇨ 안광
안총 眼聰 sight; visual power ⇨ 시력
안출 案出 contrivance; invention
— **안출하다** contrive 《a plan》; devise; 〈창작하다〉 originate; 〈발명하다〉 invent; think [work, strike] out; study out
▶ 그 교사는 새로운 교수법을 안출했다 The schoolteacher has devised a new method of teaching.
■ —**자** a contriver; 〈창시자〉 an originator; 〈발명자〉 an inventor
안치 安置 1 〈잘 둠〉 installation; enshrinement
— **안치하다** install; enshrine; lay in state
▶ 그 절에는 작은 불상이 안치되어 있었다 There was a little Buddhist image enshrined in the temple.
▶ 그 장군의 유해는 2일간 홀에 안치되었다 For a couple of days the dead general lay in state in the hall.
2 〈귀양간 죄인을〉 — **안치하다** enclose [confine] 《a banished offender》 in
안치다¹ 〈어려운 일이 닥치다〉 press upon *one*; threaten; 〈절박하다〉 be imminent; impend; lie ahead
안치다² 〈솥에〉 get 《rice》 ready to cook; prepare 《rice》 for cooking ◆ 저녁을 안쳐 두다 leave the supper to cook 《on the stove》
안치수 —**數** 〈안쪽으로 잰 치수〉 inside [interior] measure [dimensions, measurement]; interior width ◆ 안치수로 재면 in the clear / 안치수가 10센티미터다 ten centimeters across [wide] on the inside
안타 安打 〔野〕 a hit; a safety; a base [safe] hit; (美) a crash
◆ 멋진[깨끗한] 안타 a clean hit / 3루를 빠지는 안타 a hit through third / 투수의 머리 위로 빠지는 안타 a hit over the pitcher's head / 5안타

를 치다 make five hits /(투수가) 타자에게 안타를 허용하다 allow a hit to the batter / 3타수 2안타를 치다 have two hits in three times at bat; go two for three at bat
▶ 그는 2루 강습의 안타를 쳐서 1타점을 올렸다 He sent a hard-hit ball to second for a run.
▶ 그 투수는 상대 팀을 무안타로 봉쇄했다 The pitcher kept [held] the opposing team hitless. ⇌ He pitched a no-hitter.
■ **내야** — an infield hit 산발— scattered hits 우전[좌전, 중전]— a hit to right [left, center]: 좌전안타를 치다 hit to the front of (the) left field 적시— a timely hit 집중— bunched hits; fireworks; a swat parade [streak]
안타까워하다 1 〈애태우다〉 be [feel] impatient; fret [be in a fret] 《about, at, over》; be fretful; be [feel] irritated; be tantalized [vexed] at; be nervous [agitated] about; 〈개탄하다〉 deplore 《a fact》; regret
◆ 몹시 안타까워하다 fret *oneself* to death / 결과를 알고 싶어 안타까워하다 be anxious to know about the results / 정치의 부패를 안타까워하다 deplore the corruption of politics
▶ 영어가 통하지 않았기 때문에 안타까웠다 I couldn't make myself understood in English and it was irritating [I was irritated].
2 〈딱하게 여기다〉 feel pity 《for》; pity *sb*
◆ 남의 불행을 안타까워하다 feel sorry for another's misfortune
▶ 나는 그 고아의 처지를 안타까워했다 I pitied [felt pity for, had pity on] the orphan.
안타깝다 1 〈사람이〉 impatient; irritated; nervous; vexed; sad; 〈사물이〉 irritating; tantalizing; vexatious; 〈개탄스럽다〉 deplorable, regretable; lamentable
▶ 그것은 정말 안타까운 일이다 It is really a matter for regret.
▶ 안타까워 죽겠다 How vexing [provoking]! ⇌ You try my patience.
▶ 네가 낙제했다니 참 안타까운 일이구나 It is sad that you failed (in) your examination.
▶ 보기만 하고 만지지는 못하다니 안타까운 일이야 It is tantalizing to see it but not to touch it.
◆ 안타깝게도 나에겐 돈이 없다 The trouble is [It is a pity] that I have no money.
2 〈딱하다〉 poor; pitiable; pitiful 《sight》; pathetic; touching
◆ 안타까운 처지 a miserable [pitiable] condition; a sad plight / 안타깝게 여기다 feel pity for *sb*; pity *sb*
▶ 안타깝게도 우리 아들은 6·25전쟁에서 전사했다 My poor son died in the Korean War.
안타깨이 an impatient person; a fidget; a fidgetter; a nervous [jumpy] person
안타깨비 a coarse silk woven from broken threads
안타다 ride in front of *sb* 《on a horse or a sedan chair》
안태 安泰 peace; 〈안전〉 security
안태우다 have [make] *sb* ride in front of *one* [in *one's* arms]
안택 安宅 〔民俗〕 calming the household god for the peace of the household — **안택하다** bring peace to the home by offering sacrifice

to the household god
안테나 (美) an antenna 《pl. ~s》; (英) an aerial (wire)
♦안테나를 세우다 set [put] up an antenna
■수신— a receiving antenna 실내— indoor antenna 쌍극— a dipole aerial 자동차용— an auto antenna 접지— an earthed antenna 지향[송신, 수직]— an antenna [sending, vertical] antenna ■—반사기[개폐기, 지주, 지향성도] an antenna reflector [switch, support, pattern] —축전기[전류, 애자] an antenna condenser [current, insulator] —회로 an antenna circuit
안 틀다 be less [lower] than 《a certain quantity or price》; be [fall] below 《the price》; cost less than
♦만원에 안튼 값 a price under ten thousand won
안티모니 〔化〕 antimony ⇨ 안티몬
안티몬 〔化〕 antimony; stibium ■—산(酸) antimonic acid —산화물 an antimony oxide
안 티 테 제 〔(독) Antithese〕 〈반정립〉 an antithesis 《pl. -theses》
안티피린 〔藥〕 antipyrin(e)
안팎 1〈안과 밖〉the interior and exterior; the inside and outside;〈안쪽과 겉쪽〉obverse and reverse; the ins and outs
♦나라 안팎의 정세 the internal and external state of affairs / 안팎의 internal and external / 안팎에 [으로] within and without; inside and outside 《the house》; in and out / 집 안팎에 both inside and outside the house; in and out of the house / 공항의 안팎을 순시하다 patrol in and around [inside and outside] the airport / 옷의 안팎을 뒤집다 turn a dress inside out
▶올해는 나라 안팎으로 다사한 해였다 This has been an eventful year (both) at home and abroad.
▶그 작가는 나라 안팎으로 유명하다 The writer is famous both at home and abroad [overseas].
2〈표리〉duplicity; the right and wrong sides
♦안팎이 다른 double-dealing; double-faced / 안팎이 없는 single-hearted[-minded]; faithful / 안팎이 다른 행동을 하다 play on [with] both hands
3〈대략〉some; about; or so; (美) around; approximately
♦1주일 안팎 a week or thereabouts
▶비용은 10달러 안팎이 들 것이다 It will cost about [around] ten dollars. ⇒ It will cost ten dollars or so.
▶그들의 나이는 20세 안팎이었다 They were in the neighborhood [vicinity] of twenty.
4〈아내와 남편〉man and wife
안팎곱사등이 a person with a humpback and a protruding chest
안팎노자 —路資 the round-trip fare
▶서울까지 안팎노자가 얼마입니까? How much is it round-trip to Seoul?
안팎벽 —壁 inner and outer walls
안팎심부름 inside and outside chores
안팎일 inside and outside work

안팎채 inner and outer buildings
안편지 —便紙 〈내간(內簡)〉a letter from a woman to a woman
안표 眼標 a sign; a mark; an earmark
—안표하다 make [leave, put] a mark 《on》
안피지 雁皮紙 unsized silk paper; tissue paper
안하 眼下 ♦안하에 below the eye / 안하에 under one's eyes; right [just] beneath one's eyes / 아무를 안하에 내려다보다 〈얕보다〉 look down upon sb; despise [slight] sb; put a slight upon sb
안하다 do not ⇨ 않다
안하무인 眼下無人 overbearance; arrogance
♦안하 무인의 high-handed; haughty; overbearing; domineering; arrogant; defiant; outrageous; insolent; audacious / 안하무인으로 haughtily; audaciously; insolently; high-handedly; overbearingly / 안하무인으로 굴다 [behave] high-handedly [overbearingly]
▶그는 안하무인이다 He disdains everybody.
안한 安閑 leisure; idleness
—안한하다 idle;〈서술적〉 be at leisure
♦안한한 생활 an idle life / 안한하게 idly; in idleness; lazily
안항 雁行 〈남의 형제의 경칭〉(your [his]) esteemed brothers
안해 〈바로 전해〉the previous year; the year before; last year
안형제 —兄弟 〈여자 형제〉a girl's sister
안호주머니 an inside (breast) pocket; an inner pocket ▶그는 돈을 오른쪽 안호주머니에 간수하고 있었다 He had the money stowed away in his right-hand inner pocket.
앉다 1〈자리에〉sit down; take [have] a seat; seat oneself;〈앉아 있다〉sit; be seated
♦단정하게 앉다 sit straight; sit up / 무릎을 꿇고 앉다 sit with one's legs under one; sit on one's knees / 피아노 앞에 앉다 sit down to the piano / 식탁에 앉다 sit at table / 의자에 앉다 sit in [on] a chair / 편히 앉다 sit at one's ease; make oneself comfortable [at home] / 잠자리에서 일어나 앉다 sit up in one's bed / 책상 앞에 앉다 sit at the desk / 털썩 앉다 plump [plunk] oneself down
▶〔會話〕「이 자리에 앉아도 됩니까?」「그럼요」 "May I take this seat?" "Certainly."
▶앉으십시오 Please sit down. ⇒ Please take [have] a seat. ⇒ Please be seated. (▶뒤로 갈수록 정중한 표현임)
▶그대로 앉아 계십시오 Keep your seat, please.
▶이 소파에는 3명이 넉넉히 앉을 수 있다 This sofa can seat three people easily.
2〈새 등이〉perch [alight, light, sit, settle] on;〈홰에〉roost
▶참새가 나뭇가지에 앉았다[앉아 있었다] The sparrow perched [sat, was sitting] on the branch.
▶파리가 천장에 앉아 있다 There is a fly on the ceiling.
3〈건물 등이〉be located [situated] 《in, on》; face 《on》
▶너의 집은 잘 앉았다 Your house is nicely situated [located].

4 〈지위에〉 take *one's* post; take [assume, come into] office 《as》
♦권력의 자리에 앉아 있는 사람들 men in the saddle; those in (position of) power / 경찰서장 자리에 앉다 take *one's* place as the chief of police / 높은 자리에 앉아 있다 hold a high rank 《among》; stand high 《among》
▶그는 회장 자리에 앉았다 He took office as president.
5 〈먼지 등이〉 lie 《on》; collect; gather; accumulate
♦책상 위에 먼지가 앉았다 Dust collected [gathered, accumulated] on the desk.
앉은걸음 ♦앉은걸음으로 가다 crawl on *one's* knees up (to); sidle [edge] up (to)
앉은검정 〈솥 밑에 붙은〉 the soot on the bottom of a kettle; kettle black
앉은뱅이 a cripple; a wheel-chair case ■─저울 a platform scale
앉은부채 〔植〕a skunk cabbage
앉은일 sedentary [seated, bench] work; a sedentary job ♦앉은일을 하는 사람 a sedentary / 앉은일을 하다 engage in sedentary work
앉은자리 **1** 〈좌석〉 *one's* seat; *one's* place
♦앉은자리에서 일어서다 stand up [rise] from *one's* seat [place]
2 〈즉석〉 ♦앉은자리에서 immediately; at once; on the spot; impromptu; offhandedly; 《美口》 off the cuff / 앉은자리에서 시를 짓다 improvise a poem / 앉은자리에서 만들다 make *sth* on the spot
▶수상은 앉은자리에서 기자 회견을 했다 The premier gave an impromptu press conference.
▶그는 앉은자리에서 돈을 지불했다 He was prompt in paying his bills.
앉은장사 sedentary business [trade, commerce] ♦앉은장사를 하다 keep a shop; run a store
앉은차례 ─次例 the order of seats [places]; the seating (order)
앉은키 *one's* sitting height
♦앉은키가 작은 short-bodied[-trunked] / 앉은키를 재다 measure *one's* sitting height
앉을깨 **1** 〈베틀의〉 the seat of a loom **2** 〈걸터앉는〉 a straddle seat
앉을자리 a place to sit; 〈물건의〉 a place to put *sth* on; 〈건물의〉 a site; an emplacement
앉음새 a sitting posture ⇨ 앉음앉음
앉음앉음 a sitting posture [position]; *one's* seated posture ♦앉음앉음을 바로잡다 sit up straight; sit upright; straighten *oneself*
앉히다 **1** 〈좌석에〉 seat [sit] *sb*; have *sb* sit down ♦상좌에 앉히다 seat a guest at the head of the table / 안락의자에 앉히다 seat [have] *sb* in an armchair
▶나는 아이를 의자에 앉혔다 I sat my child on a chair.
2 〈지위에〉 place [install] 《*sb* in a position》
♦아무를 그 학교의 교장에 앉히다 appoint *sb* [place *sb* as] principal of the school / 아무를 왕위에 앉히다 set *sb* on the throne; make *sb* king / 아무를 회장 자리에 앉히다 establish *sb* as president
않다 〈아니하다〉 be not; do not; have not

♦가지[먹지] 않다 do not go [eat] / 예쁘지[쉽지] 않다 be not pretty [easy] / 조금도 …않다 not…at all; not…in the least
▶그는 그 아가씨와 결혼하고 싶어하지 않는다 He doesn't want to get married to the girl.
▶성공할 가망이 없지도 않다 There is some hope of success.
▶그것을 알지도 못하거니와 또한 알고 싶지도 않다 I neither know nor care to know it.
않을수없다 cannot help 《doing》; cannot but 《do》; be compelled [forced, obliged] to 《do》
♦복종하지 않을 수 없다 be obliged to obey / 웃지 않을 수 없다 cannot help laughing
♦나는 계획을 포기하지 않을 수 없었다 I was compelled [forced] to give up my plan. ⇌ I had to [had no (other) choice but to] give up my plan.
▶그녀를 사랑하지 않을 수 없다 I cannot but love her.
▶그의 익살에 웃지 않을 수 없었다 I couldn't help laughing 《주로 美口》 couldn't help but laugh, could not but laugh] at his joke.
▶그는 최후 수단을 쓰지 않을 수 없었다 He was driven to extreme measure.
알¹ **1** 〈새·닭의〉 an egg; 〈물고기·패류의〉 spawn
♦알의 흰자[노른자] the white [yolk] of an egg / 갓 낳은 알 a new-laid [newly laid] egg / 신선한 알 a fresh egg / 한 배에 품은 알 a laying; a clutch of eggs / 알을 깨다 break [open] an egg / 알을 까다 hatch an egg / 알을 낳다 lay an egg; 〈물고기·패류가〉 spawn; shoot spawn / 알을 품다 sit on eggs; brood / 닭이 알을 품게 하다 set a hen on eggs
▶ 會話「알을 어떻게 드시겠습니까?」「반숙[완숙]으로 해주세요」 "How would you like your egg?" "I'd like mine soft-boiled [hard-boiled]."
2 〈작고 둥근 것〉 a ball; a bulb; a bead
♦안경 알 a (spectacle) lens; an eyepiece / 유리 알 a glass bead / 총알 a ball / 〈소총의〉 a bullet; 〈산탄의〉 a shot / 알이 고른 달걀 even-sized eggs; eggs of even size
3 〈작은 낟알·열매〉 a nut; a berry; a grain
♦한 알의 보리[쌀] a grain of barley [rice] / 알이 작은 오렌지 a small-sized orange / 알이 들다 go [run] to seed
▶이 오렌지는 알이 고르다 These oranges are all of a size [all the same size].
4 〈배추·양배추 등의〉 a bulb; a head
♦알이 잘 밴 양배추 a cabbage with a good head
알² the lower part ⇨ 아래
♦알로 내려가다 go [come] down
알- naked; bare; undressed; unclothed; unclad; uncovered; stripped; 〈알짜의〉 net; core; real; important; essential; thorough
♦알몸 a naked body / 알부피 net bulk / 알깍쟁이 a real tightwad
알갱이 〈낟알〉 a grain (of rice); a kernel; 〈미립자〉 a granule ♦한 알갱이의 보리 a grain of barley / 알갱이의 granular / 한 알갱이씩 grain by grain
알거지 a penniless person; a beggar; a person

알겨먹다 with no property but his own body

알겨먹다 swindle [wheedle, cozen, trick] *sb* out of *sth*; trick a weaker person out of some small thing

알결다 〈암탉이〉 cluck for a rooster (to mate with)

알곡 —穀 〈알곡식〉 pure grain with no grit in it; clean grain; 〈깍지 벗긴〉 husked grain

알과녁 〈과녁의 복판〉 the bull's-eye

알구지 〈지게 작대기의 아귀진 곳〉 the crotch of the supporting stick of an A-frame

알궁둥이 the naked buttocks; the bare bottom

알껍데기 an eggshell

알다 1 〈일반적으로〉 know; be aware 《of》; find out; learn; be acquainted 《with》
♦ 내가 아는 바로는 so [as] far as I know; for all I know / 아시다시피 as you know; as you are aware / 잘 알다 know well; be well aware 《of》; be well acquainted 《with》; be familiar 《with》; have a good knowledge 《of》; be well informed 《about》; be (well) versed 《in》; be (quite) at home 《in, at》 / 알고 싶어하다 be curious to know; be curious 《about》 / 이름[얼굴]을 알고 있다 know *sb* by name [sight] / 아는 체하다 have a knowing look; pretend to know; talk knowingly / 알지 못하다 do not know; be ignorant 《of》
▶ 그는 한국의 역사를 잘 알고 있다 He knows Korean history well. ⇒ He has a good knowledge of Korean history. ⇒ He is familiar with Korean history.
▶ 나는 체스를 둘 줄 안다 I know how to play chess.
▶ 나는 그녀의 이름만은 알고 있다 I know her by name.
▶ 그는 무엇이든지 아는 체한다 He pretends to know everything.
▶ 나는 지난 주에 그것을 알았다 I learned (of) [heard of, was informed of] it last week.
▶ 그는 그 일에 대해서 잘 알고 있었다 He was well informed with the matter.
▶ 그녀는 그 일에 대해서는 아무것도 알지 못했다 She knew nothing about the matter.
▶ 몹시 취해 있었기 때문에 엊저녁 일은 아무것도 알지 못했다 I was terribly drunk and remembered nothing of last night.
▶ 내가 아는 바로는 그녀는 유능한 교사다 As [So] far as I know she is an able teacher.
▶ 그가 어떻게 될 것인가는 아무도 알 수 없다 There is no knowing [No one can tell] what will become of him.
▶ 그 병은 의학 전문가들은 알고 있었으나 일반인은 알지 못했다 The disease was known by specialists in medicine but not to the public. (▶수동형에서는 to가 보통임. 다만 by는 동작자가 알고자해서 알게 된 결과로서의 상태를, to는 절로 알게 된다는 뜻을 내포함)

2 〈이해하다〉 understand; appreciate; know; see; comprehend; make sense 《of》; make out
▶ 저 아이는 빨리 알아 듣는다 That child is very quick to understand.
▶ 병이 들어서야 비로서 건강의 고마움을 알게 된다 We don't appreciate the blessing of (good) health till we lose it.
▶ 나를 알아주는 사람은 그녀뿐이다 She is the only one who understands me.

3 〈안면이 있다〉 be acquainted 《with》; know (▶전자는 단순히 「면식이 있다」는 뜻이지만, know는 보통 「잘 알고 있다」는 뜻을 내포하고 있음)
♦ 아는 사람 an acquaintance / 내가 아는 미국인 an American of my acquaintance / 우연히 알게 된 사람 a chance [casual] acquaintance / 알게 되다 become acquainted 《with》; make *sb's* acquaintance / 아는 사람이 많다 have a large [wide] circle of acquaintances
▶ [會話] 「김 선생을 아십니까?」 「잘 알고 있습니다」 "Do you know who Mr. Kim?" "Yes, I know him well."
▶ 나는 그를 소문을 들어서 알고 있지만 개인적으로는 모른다 I know of him, but I don't know him personally. (▶know him은 실제로 알고 있다, know of him은 간접적으로 알고 있다는 뜻임)
▶ 그와는 여러해 전부터 알고 있는 사이입니다 I have known him for years. ⇒ He and I have been acquainted with each other for years. (▶I and he는 잘못임)

4 〈인지·인식하다〉 recognize; realize; be aware 《of》; be convinced 《of》
♦ 자기의 잘못을 알다 be convinced of *one's* (own) error / 정직한 사람으로 알다 give *sb* credit for being an honest man / 중요성을 알다 recognize the importance of
▶ 그는 그녀를 믿을 수 없다는 것을 알았다 He found that she could not be trusted.
▶ 나를 무얼로 알고 있나? What do you take me for?

5 〈깨닫다〉 find; see; notice; perceive; realize; sense
♦ 자기의 결점을 알다 be sensible of *one's* (own) shortcomings / 낌새를 알다 have an inkling 《of》; get a scent 《of》
▶ 그 책을 읽고 평화의 소중함을 알았다 I learned [realized] the importance of peace when I read the book.
▶ 그가 진정한 친구라는 것을 알았다 I found that he was a true friend. ⇒ I found him (to be) a true friend. ⇒ I found a true friend in him.

6 〈느끼다〉 feel; be conscious 《of》; be sensible 《of, to》; be alive 《to》
♦ 부끄러움을 알다 have [be alive to] a sense of honor; be sensible to shame / 은혜를 알다 feel (*oneself*) indebted [obliged] 《to *sb* for doing》; have a sense of gratitude; be grateful
▶ 그는 몸이 들어올려지는 것을 알았다 He felt himself lifted up.
▶ 새들이 위험을 알고 일제히 날아가 버렸다 The birds sensed the danger and flew off all together.

7 〈기억하고 있다〉 remember; have [bear, keep] in mind
♦ 내가 알기로는 as far as I remember / 똑똑히 알고 있다 have a clear recollection 《of》; remember clearly / 어렴풋이 알고 있다 have a dim remembrance [recollection] 《of》;

remember vaguely
▶ 내가 알기로는 그는 60세에 죽었다 As I remember [As far as I recollect], he died at the age of 60.
▶ 내가 누군지 알겠습니까? Do you remember me?
8 〈식별하다〉 recognize
♦ 옳고 그른 것을 알다 know the difference between right and wrong; know right from wrong
▶ 목소리로 자네라는 것을 알았네 I've recognized you by your voice.
▶ 저 발소리가 누구의 것인지 알겠니? Can you recognize the footsteps?
▶ 사람은 그가 사귀는 친구로 알 수 있다 A man is known by the company he keeps.
9 〈미루어 헤아리다〉 infer; guess; gather ((from sb's talk))
♦ 눈을 보고 남의 마음을 알다 read sb's thought in ((his)) eyes
▶ 그녀가 어떤 의도를 갖고 있는지 알 수 없다 I can't guess [conjecture] what purpose she has in her head.
▶ 그 나머지는 미루어 알 수 있다 The rest may easily be inferred [imagined].
▶ 그의 말씨로 그가 배운 사람임을 알 수 있다 His speech suggests that he is a man of education.
10 〈아랑곳하다〉 be concerned with; have to do with
▶ 그것은 내가 알 바가 아니다 It's no concern of mine. ⇒ It's none of my business. ⇒ I have nothing to do with it. ⇒ It has nothing to do with me.
11 〈소양이 있다〉 have accomplishments; have some knowledge ((of)); 〈감상 능력이 있다〉 appreciate ♦ 문학을 잘 알다 have literary accomplishments / 서양 예절을 잘 알다 be well versed in [have a good knowledge of] Western etiquette
▶ 프랑스어를 잘 알지 못하면 이 일을 감당해 내지 못한다 You cannot tackle this job without some knowledge of French.
12 〈경험이 있다〉 have experience ((of)); taste (the fear of poverty)
♦ 남자를 알다 have carnal knowledge of man
▶ 그는 세상을 알고 있다 He has seen a lot of the world.
▶ 나는 가난이 어떤 것인지 알고 있다 I have known poverty. ⇒ I know what it is like to be poor. ⇒ I am no stranger to poverty.
13 〈동의·승낙하다〉 consent to; agree to
▶ 알았다 All right. ⇒ (美) O.K. ⇒ Sure! 〔通信〕 Roger!
▶ 알았어, 곧 간다고 전하게 All right. Tell him I will come at once.
14 〈…으로 보다〉 take ((for)); look upon ((as)); regard ((as))
♦ 잘못 알다 mistake [take] ((A for B))
▶ 처음에 나는 그가 독일인인 줄 알았다 At first I took [mistook] him for a German.
알데히드 〔化〕 an aldehyde
알돌 a round stone; a cobble(stone)
알땅 naked [unprotected, unvegetated] land

알뚝배기 a small unglazed pottery bowl
알뜯이 a crab with spawn removed
알들살뜰 thriftily
알뜰하다 **1** 〈아끼다〉 prudent; thrifty; frugal; saving; provident ((of))
♦ 알뜰한 주부 a thrifty housewife / 알뜰히 frugally; economically; with frugality / 알뜰히 하다 be frugal [economical]; use [practice] economy / 알뜰히 살다[지내다] live frugally; live [lead] a frugal life; live in a small way
▶ 그들은 도시의 외딴 곳에서 알뜰히 살고 있다 They are living in a small [frugal] way in an obscure part of the city.
▶ 그는 알뜰하게 해서 부자가 되었다 He has enriched himself by being provident with his money.
2 〈정성스럽다〉 careful and earnest; conscientious
♦ 알뜰히 carefully; wholeheartedly; earnestly / 알뜰하게 만들다 make with patient [the utmost] care
▶ 그는 알뜰한 장사꾼이다 He is a shrewd businessman.
알라 〈이슬람교의〉 Allah
알랑거리다 flatter; curry favor with sb; fawn upon sb; (口) soft-soap; butter sb up
♦ 알랑거리며 비위맞추다 tickle [titilate] sb by flattery; make insincere compliments / 상사에게 알랑거리다 cringe [suck up] to the boss
▶ 그는 정치가에게 알랑거리며 돈을 모았다 He made money by buttering up politicians.
알랑쇠 a flatterer; (美口) an apple-polisher; a yes-man; a toady
알랑수 a bit [piece] of flattery ♦ 알랑수에 넘어가지 않다 be above being flattered; be insusceptible [impervious] to flattery
알랑알랑 flatteringly; in a flattering manner
♦ 알랑알랑 여자를 꾀다 seduce a girl with flattery
알래스카 〈미국의 주〉 Alaska (略 Alas.) ♦ 알래스카의 Alaskan ■—공로(公路) Alaska [Alcan] Highway —사람 an Alaskan
알량하다 〈보잘 것 없다〉 trifling; trivial; 〈무가치하다〉 unimportant; trashy; rubbishy ♦ 알량한 녀석 a useless [good-for-nothing] fellow
▶ 그녀석 참 알량한 소리 하네 There is nothing important in what he says. ⇒ What he says is all rubbish.
알레그레토 (이) 〔樂〕 allegretto
알레그로 (이) 〔樂〕 allegro
♦ 알레그로 모데라토 allegro moderato
알레르기 allergy ♦ 알레르기성의 allergic / 우유에 알레르기를 일으키다 develop an allergy to milk ■—반응 (an) allergic reaction —성 질환 an allergic disease
알렉산더대왕 —大王 Alexander the Great (356-323 B.C.)
알렉산드리아 〈이집트의 항구도시〉 Alexandria
알려지다 **1** 〈남이 알게 되다〉 become known ((to)); come to sb's knowledge
♦ 잘 알려진대로 as everyone knows; as gener-

ally [well] known / 세상에 널리 알려지다 become generally known; be known to everybody; become public knowledge; 〈소문나다〉 get abroad; spread widely / 알려지지 않도록 하다 keep *sth* (secret) from *sb*; keep *sb* in the dark

▶ 감추어도 언젠가는 알려지게 되는거야 Even if you keep it secret, it will come out some day.

▶ 그에 관한 추문이 온통 알려지게 되었다 The scandal involving him became generally [widely] known.

2 〈판명되다〉 be found; be revealed [disclosed]; be identified

▶ 그의 사인(死因)은 아직 알려지지 않고 있다 The cause of his death still remains a mystery [unknown].

▶ 피해자는 김선생으로 알려졌다 The victim was found to be [was identified as] Mr. Kim.

3 〈유명해지다〉 become famous; earn [win] fame; come [rise] to fame

♦ 잘 알려진 famous; popular; renowned; well-known / 알려지지 않은 unknown; obscure; nameless

▶ 그는 국제적으로 알려져 있다 He is famous [well known] to the world.

알력 軋轢 friction; discord; dissension; disagreement; (a) strife

♦ 알력이 있다 be in discord [conflict]; be at strife [feud] / 알력을 야기하다[초래하다] produce [lead to] friction / 알력을 피하다 avoid friction

▶ 이 문제로 그들 사이에 알력이 생겼다 Friction developed between them over this matter. ⇌ They clashed over the matter.

▶ 두 나라 간에는 오랜 알력이 있어 왔다 The two countries have long been at odds.

알로까다 very shrewd [sharp]; very clever [smart] ♦ 알로깐 놈 a shrewd [smart] fellow

알로하셔츠 an aloha shirt; a short-sleeved sport(s) shirt

알루미이트 (商標) Alumite ■—주전자[냄비] an Alumite kettle [pot, pan]

알루미늄 aluminum; (英) aluminium ■—박(箔) an aluminum foil ―새시 an aluminum sash ―선 an aluminum wire ―제품[합금] aluminum ware [alloy]

알류샨열도―列島 the Aleutian Islands; the Aleutians

알리다 let *sb* know; tell 《*sb* about *sth*》; inform [advise, notify] 《*sb* of *sth*》; give notice of [that]; report (to); make *sth* known (to *sb*); 〈예고하다〉 give *sb* notice 《that...》

♦ 알리지 않다 keep *sth* secret from *sb*; keep *sth* to *oneself*; leave *sb* uninformed / 넌지시 알리다 hint (at); drop a hint; suggest / 미리 알리다 give *sb* previous notice / (시계가) 시각을 알리다 tell the time / 소식을 알리다 tell [bring] the news (to) / 전화로 알리다 let *sb* know by [through the] telephone; telephone 《*sb* that...》 / 화재를 알리다 give an alarm of fire

▶ 그 여자는 이름을 알리지 않고 갔다 The woman went away without giving [telling] her name.

▶ 그것은 편지로 알려 드리겠습니다 We'll let you know about it [make it known to you] by letter. ⇌ I'll write (to) you about it.

▶ 여러분께 알립니다 (광고) May I have your attention please!

▶ 바로 경찰에 알리시오 Report it to the police right away.

▶ 그가 네가 병으로 누워 있다고 나에게 알려 주었다 He told me (that) you are sick in bed.

▶ 그 소식을 아무에게도 알리지 마시오 Please don't tell the news to anybody.

▶ 퇴직하려면 1개월 전에 고용주에게 알려야 한다 If you want to quit your job, you must give one [a] month's notice to your employer.

▶ 될 수 있는대로 빨리 알려 드리겠소 I will let you know as soon as possible.

▶ 나의 의도는 이미 그에게 알려 놓았다 I have already informed him of my intentions.

알리바이 〈현장 부재 증명〉 an alibi

♦ 알리바이가 있다[없다] have an [no] alibi / 알리바이를 꾸미다[조작하다] frame [fake] an alibi / 알리바이를 깨뜨리다 break an alibi / 알리바이를 세우다 make [fix] an alibi

▶ 그에게는 움직일 수 없는 알리바이가 있다 He has an all-tight [ironclad] alibi.

▶ 그의 알리바이는 깨졌다 His alibi was broken down. ⇌ His alibi didn't hold up.

알맞다 suitable; suited; proper; fit; fitting; adequate; appropriate; 〈어울리다〉 becoming; matching; seemly

♦ 알맞은 운동과 수면 a proper amount of exercise and sleep / 그 가족에 알맞은 집 a house adequate for the family / 그 자리에 알맞은 사람 a person fit for the position [post] / 철에 알맞은 선물 a seasonable gift / 아이들에게 알맞은 책 a book right [fit] for children / 알맞은 조언을 하다 give good [timely, relevant] advice / 알맞은 처처를 하다 take proper measures / 알맞은 값으로 팔다 sell at a reasonable price / (책이) 초보자에게 알맞다 be good [suitable] for beginners / 먹기에 알맞다 be just right for eating / 알맞게 suitably; properly; adequately; appropriately / 알맞게 먹다[마시다] be moderate [temperate] in eating [drinking] / 알맞게 운동하다 do [have, get] moderate exercise; exercise in moderation

▶ 그 자리에는 그가 가장 알맞다 He is the best [very] person for the post. ⇌ He is perfect for the post.

▶ 그의 연설은 그 경우에 알맞은 것이 아니었다 His speech wasn't suitable [good, fit, appropriate, proper] for the occasion.

▶ 생선이[고기가] 알맞게 익었군 The fish [meat] is done beautifully.

▶ 술은 알맞게 마시면 최고의 영약이다 When taken in moderation wine is the best of all medicines.

알맹이 〈과실 속〉 a kernel; 〈실질〉 substance; 〈내용〉 contents; filling

♦ 호두 알맹이 the kernel of a walnut / 알맹이 있는 substantial; solid / 알맹이 없는 unsubstantial; empty / 알맹이가 있는[없는] 이야기 a speech of much [little] substance / 알맹이 없는 책 a book poor in contents [substance]

알몸 1 〈나체〉 a naked [nude] body; 〈나체상태〉 nakedness; nudity
♦ 알몸의 naked; nude / 알몸으로 with nothing on; stark-naked; in *one's* bare skin; in the nude / 알몸이 되다 become [strip *oneself*] naked; take off all *one's* clothes; strip *oneself* bare [stark-naked] / 알몸으로 만들다 strip *sb* of all 《his》 clothes; strip *sb* (down) naked / 알몸으로 헤엄치다 swim in the nude [(口) in the raw]
▶ 그들은 알몸이 되어 강으로 뛰어들었다 They took off their clothes and jumped into the river.
2 〈무일푼〉 pennilessness
♦ 알몸으로 성공한 사람 a self-made man / 알몸이 되다 be reduced to *one's* naked personal merit; be stripped of all *one's* possessions; go (clean) broke / 알몸으로 재산을 이루다 make a fortune from nothing / 딸을 알몸으로 시집보내다 marry off *one's* daughter with no dowry provided

알바니아 〈나라 이름〉 Albania; 〈공식명〉 the Republic of Albania
■ ─말 Albanian; the Albanian language ─사람 an Albanian: 알바니아 사람의 Albanian

알밤 a (shelled) chestnut

알배기 a (full-)roed fish ♦ 알배기 새우[게] a lobster [crab] in berry / 알배기 연어 a roed salmon

알부랑자 ─浮浪者 a real tramp; a regular rogue [villain]

알부민 〔生化〕 albumin; albumen

알부자 ─富者 a really rich [wealthy] man

알부피 net bulk [volume, capacity]

알사탕 ─砂糖 a (piece of) candy; (美) a sweet
♦ 알사탕을 빨다 suck on a piece of candy

알선 斡旋 〈주선〉 good offices; kind help; 〈조정〉 mediation; conciliation
♦ 화해의 알선 mediation for a settlement / 한선생의 알선으로 by [through] the good offices of Mr. Han / 알선을 부탁하다 ask for *sb's* good offices
▶ 그에게 취직 알선을 부탁했다 I asked him to find a job for me.
▶ 나는 김교수의 알선으로 그 자리를 얻었다 I got the position through [by] the kind [good] offices of prof. Kim.
▶ 파업은 정부의 알선으로 중지되었다 The strike was called off as a result of the conciliation of the Government.
─**알선하다** use [exercise, lend, offer] *one's* good offices (in settling a matter); do [render] a service; mediate 《between》; conciliate; go between (two parties)
♦ 일자리를 알선해 주다 help *sb* (to) find employment
▶ 내가 둘 사이를 알선해서 그 문제를 해결하겠소 I'll go [mediate] between the persons and settle the problem.
■ ─자 a mediator; an intermediary; a conciliator; a go-between

알슬다 〈물고기가〉 spawn; 〈파리가〉 blow; 〈곤충이〉 oviposit; lay [deposit] eggs ⇨ 슬다² 2

알심 〈동정〉 hidden sympathy [compassion]; 〈힘〉 hidden strength; 〈고갱이〉 the pith; the core

알싸하다 acrid; pungent; piquant; smart; smoky; biting ▶ 연기 때문에 코가[눈이] 알싸했다 The smoke irritated my nostrils [made my eyes smart].

알쏭달쏭하다 1 〈알록달록하다〉 variegated; motley; jumbled; intricate; complicated
2 〈애매하다〉 ambiguous; vague; obscure; equivocal; evasive; elusive; noncommittal; uncertain
♦ 알쏭달쏭한 말을 하다 equivocate; talk ambiguously / 알쏭달쏭한 태도를 취하다 take an uncertain attitude 《toward》/ 알쏭달쏭하게 대답하다 give an equivocal [a vague] answer
▶ 이 글은 뜻이 알쏭달쏭하다 The meaning of this sentence is ambiguous [uncertain].
▶ 뭐가 뭔지 알쏭달쏭하다 I can make neither head nor tail of it.

알아내다 〈찾아내다〉 find out; discover; dig out [up]; detect; 〈깨닫다〉 make out; understand
♦ 그의 소재를 알아내다 locate his whereabouts / 남의 비밀을 알아내다 dig *sb's* secret out; smell out *sb's* secret / 물어서 알아내다 elicit information by inquiring / 병원체를 알아내다 identify the virus
▶ 마침내 그 소문의 출처를 알아냈다 Finally we ran down the source of the rumor.

알아듣다 〈판별하다〉 hear out; recognize; tell (the difference) by hearing; 〈이해하다〉 understand; comprehend; catch [get] 《the meaning》; 〈납득하다〉 come to [listen to] reason
♦ 알아들을 수 없다 be inaudible; cannot catch / 알아듣도록 설명하다 explain convincingly [understandably] / 농담을 바로 알아듣다 see a joke quickly / 말뜻을 알아듣다 understand [get the gist of] what *sb* says
▶ 전화가 멀어서 알아듣기 힘들었다 The voice on the phone was faint and difficult to hear [catch].
▶ 그녀의 말은 거의 알아듣지 못하겠다 I could hardly hear her 《words》. ⇌ Her words were scarcely audible.
▶ 네 말은 너무 빨라서 알아들을 수가 없다 You speak so fast (that) I cannot catch you.

알아맞히다 guess right; make a good guess
♦ 수수께끼를 알아맞히다 guess a riddle right; find out a riddle; solve [answer] a riddle / 알아맞히지 못하다 miss *one's* guess; make a wrong guess; guess wrong / 용케 알아맞히다 make a good [happy] guess; guess right; hit it (to a tee)
▶ 내 나이를 용케 알아맞혔어요 You guessed (at) my age correctly. ⇌ You made a correct guess at my age.
▶ 누구인지 알아맞혀봐 Make a guess. ⇌ Guess who!

알아보다 1 〈문의하다〉 ask; inquire; make

알아주다

inquiries; 〈조사하다〉 investigate; examine; study; look into [over]; check (up on); 〈살피다〉 look [search] for; feel out
♦ 경력을 알아보다 probe into *sb's* past; trace *sb's* career / 사실을 알아보다 investigate [look into] the facts / 사실 여부를 알아보다 ascertain whether [if] it is true / 의향을 알아보다 sound *sb's* inclination / 사건의 원인을 알아보다 investigate the cause of the incident; find out what caused the incident / 장소를 지도에서 알아보다 look up a place on a map / 보도의 진위를 알아보다 check (up on) the truth of a news report
▶ 그는 셋집을 알아보고 있다 He is looking for a house for rent.
▶ 그녀는 날마다 직장을 알아보러 다닌다 She goes out every day to hunt for a job.
▶ 그것은 그에게 알아보면 된다 He will [can] tell you about it.
▶ 알아보니 그 소문은 거짓이었다 Upon inquiry the rumor turned out to be false.
2 〈식별하다〉 recognize; 〈판단하다〉 judge (of); 〈이해하다〉 understand
♦ 알아볼 수 없을 만큼 beyond [out of] recognition / 알아보기 힘든 글씨를 쓰다 write an illegible [a crabbed] hand
▶ 알아뵙지 못해 죄송합니다 Pardon me for not recognizing. ⇒ I'm very sorry, but I could not recognize you.
▶ 나는 도자기는 제대로 못 알아본다 I am no judge of ceramics.

알아주다 1 〈인정하다〉 recognize; admit; accept; appreciate; acknowledge; approve of
♦ 남의 진가를 알아주다 recognize *sb's* real worth
▶ 우리는 누구나 그의 능력을 알아주고 있다 All of us recognize his ability.
▶ 그의 알아줄 점은 알아주어야 한다 You must pay him the respect which is due to him.
2 〈이해하다〉 understand; sympathize (with); feel for [with]
♦ 남의 심중을 알아주다 enter into *sb's* feelings; sympathize with *sb*
▶ 저희가 처한 어려운 형편을 알아주십시오 I would like you to understand that we are in a difficult situation.

알아차리다 〈깨닫다〉 realize; understand; sense; find; notice; become aware of
▶ 그는 남의 마음을 잘 알아차린다 He is a good mind reader. ⇒ He is good at guessing what the other people are thinking.
▶ 그가 누구보다도 먼저 그들의 음모를 알아차렸다 He was the first to become aware of their plot.
▶ 그녀는 뒤에서 누군가가 따라온다는 것을 알아차렸다 She noticed [became aware] that someone was following her.
▶ 그녀는 자기 위험을 알아차리지 못했다 She was unaware of her danger.
▶ 그의 태도를 보아 나는 남아 있지 않아도 된다고 알아차렸다 I gathered from his attitude that I did not have to stay.

알아채다 〈낌새채다〉 notice; become aware [conscious] of; realize; sense; get scent [wind] of; suspect; be suspicious of
♦ 한눈에 상황을 알아채다 take in the situation at a glance
▶ 그의 표정으로 그가 불만인 것을 알아챌 수 있었다 I could see from his expression that he wasn't satisfied.
▶ 그는 뒤돌아보지 않고도 배후에서 벌어지고 있는 일을 알아챘다 He took in what was going on behind him without turning his head.

알아하다 do of *one's* own accord [choice, free will]; act at *one's* discretion [option]
♦ 알아하도록 하다 let *sb* have (his) way; let *sb* do as *one* pleases; put [place] *sth* at *sb's* disposal
▶ 그 일은 그가 알아하도록 맡기겠다 I will leave the matter entirely to his discretion.
▶ 가건 말건 알아해라 It's up to you to go out or not.

알알이 grain by grain; berry after berry; egg by egg ▶ 이 오렌지 주스에는 알맹이가 알알이 들어 있다 This orange juice has bits of orange pulp in it.

알알하다 1 〈맵다〉 pungent; piquant; 〈서술적〉 taste hot; have a burning taste ▶ 이 요리는 맛이 알알하다 This dish tastes hot [has a burning taste, is pungent].
2 〈아리다〉 smart (with pain)
▶ 상처가 아직도 알알하다 The wound still smarts.

알약 —藥 a tablet; a tabloid; 〈환약〉 a pill
♦ 비타민 알약 a vitamin pill [tablet]

알은체 1 〈남의 일에〉 interference; meddling —알은체하다 meddle; interfere
▶ 네가 알은체할 일이 아니다 You have no right to interfere in the matter.
▶ 나는 그것을 알은체하지 않았다 I feigned ignorance about it. ⇒ I pretended to know nothing about it.
2 〈사람에게〉 (a show [gesture] of) recognition —알은체하다 recognize; notice
▶ 그는 나를 보고 알은체했다 He nodded at me in recognition.
▶ 길에서 만났을 때 그녀는 나를 알은체하지 않았다 She cut me dead [pretended not to recognize me] when we met on the street.

알음 〈서로 앎〉 acquaintance(ship); 〈아는 것〉 knowledge
♦ 알음이 많다 have a profound [deep] knowledge of; be well informed in / 알음이 있다 have acquaintance (with)
▶ 그와는 아무 알음도 없다 I have no (personal) acquaintance with him.

알음알음 ♦ 알음알음으로 through some acquaintance(s) / 알음알음으로 취직하다 get a job through pull

알음알이 1 〈아는 사람〉 an acquaintance
♦ 알음알이가 많다 have a wide acquaintance; have a wide circle of acquaintance; (美) have many contacts; know a lot of people
2 〈자라나는 재주〉 the developing knowledge [talent] (of a child)
3 〈꾀바른 수단〉 a clever method

알음장하다 give [drop] a hint; clue; cursively allude to

알자리 a nest for laying eggs; a brooding place
알젓 (fish) roe [spawn] pickled in salt; pickled roe; salted spawn
알제리 〈나라이름〉 Algeria; 〈공식명〉 the Democratic and Pouplar Republic of Algeria
♦ 알제리의 Algerian ■―사람 an Algerian
알주머니 an ovisac; an egg case; an egg-containing capsule; 〈상어 등의〉 a sea purse
알짜 the best; the essence; the quintessence; the pick; the choice
♦ …의 알짜 부분 the pith and marrow of… / 알짜 서울 토박이 a true Seoulite; a Seoulite born and bred / 알짜만 뽑아내다 get the cream 《of》; extract the essence
알짝지근하다 〈조금 맵다〉 rather spicy [hot, peppery]; a bit pungent [piquant]; 〈알얼하다〉 feel a superficial stinging pain; somewhat smart; 〈술기운이 도는 듯하다〉 be slightly drunk
알짱거리다 〈알랑대다〉 flatter; curry favor; coax [cajole] 《sb to do》; 〈돌아다니다〉 hang around [about]; loaf around idly
알칼로이드 〖生化〗 an alkaloid
♦ 알칼로이드의 alkaloidal
알칼리 〖化〗 alkali ―금속 alkaline metals ―액 lye ―전지 an alkaline cell ―증(症) 〖醫〗 alkalosis ―화 alkalization
알칼리성 ―性 alkalinity ♦ 알칼리성의 alkaline; alkali
▶ 이 물은 알칼리성이다 This water is alkaline.
■―반응 alkaline reaction ―식품 alkaline food ―염료 alkaline dyes ―토양 alkaline soil
알코올 alcohol; liquor; spirits
♦ 알코올(성)의 alcoholic / 알코올에 담근 표본 a specimen (preserved) in alcohol / 알코올에 담그다 preserve in alcohol; alcoholize / 알코올류를 전혀 입에 대지 않다 abstain from all alcoholic drinks; do not touch any alcoholic drinks
■공업용― industrial alcohol 무수(無水)― absolute alcohol ―램프 an alcohol [a spirit] lamp ―분(分) (an) alcoholic content ―온도계 an alcohol thermometer ―음료 alcoholic drinks [beverages]
알코올중독 ―中毒 〖醫〗 alcoholism; alcoholic poisoning
♦ 급성 알코올중독 acute alcoholic poisoning / 알코올중독에 걸리다 suffer from alcoholism
■―방지협회 Alcoholics Anonymous (略 A.A., AA) ―자 an alcoholic
알타이 ♦ 알타이의 Altaic ■―산맥 the Altai Mountains; the Altais ―어족 the Altaic (family of) languages
알토 〖樂〗 alto ■―가수 an alto (singer) ―독창 an alto solo ―색소폰 an alto saxophone
알통 a knot of muscles; 〈팔의〉 the flexed biceps ♦ 팔을 굽혀 알통을 만들다 bend [flex] one's arm and make the biceps stand out
알파 alpha; α ♦ 알파와 오메가 alpha and omega / 플러스 알파 something; and a little extra [more] / 10만원 플러스 알파의 추가 지불로 합의하다 agree on a raise of 100,000 won plus a little extra

■―선 α-rays; alpha rays ―입자 an α [alpha] particle
알파벳 the alphabet
♦ 알파벳의 alphabetical(al) / 영어의 알파벳 the English alphabet / 알파벳순으로 하다 arrange alphabetically [in alphabetical order]
▶ 그녀는 경제학의 알파벳조차 모른다 She doesn't even know the fundamentals [ABC's] of economics.
알파인 ♦ 알파인의 Alpine ■―경기[종목] the Alpine events ―스키 Alpine skiing
알펜호른 an alpenhorn; an alphorn
알파카 〖動〗 an alpaca ♦ 알파카 코트 an alpaca coat
알프스 〈산맥〉 the Alps
알피니스트 〈알프스 등산가〉 an Alpinist; 〈등산가〉 an alpinist; a mountaineer
알현 謁見 an audience 《with the king》
―알현하다 be received in audience 《by His Majesty》; have [be granted] an audience 《with》; be presented 《to》
▶ 그 사절은 왕을 알현했다 The messenger had an audience with the king.
■―실 an audience [a presence] chamber
앎 knowledge; learning; information
♦ 앎은 힘이다 Knowledge is power.
앓는소리 a groan; a moan; a whimper; (비유) a complaint
♦ 앓는소리를 내다[하다] groan; give [heave] a groan; moan; 〈불평하다〉 make complaints
▶ 부상자의 앓는 소리가 들렸다 We heard the injured people groan. ⇌ We heard the groans of the injured people.
앓다 1 〈병을〉 be sick [ill, afflicted] 《with》; suffer from
♦ 독감을 앓다 suffer from flu / 앓아 누워 있다 be laid up with illness; be ill [sick] in bed
▶ 그는 신경통을 앓고 있다 He is suffering from [afflicted with] neuralgia.
▶ 나는 여섯 살 때 큰 병을 앓았다 I had a serious illness when I was six years old.
▶ 그녀는 어렸을 때 자주 병을 앓았다 She was frequently sick [ill] when she was a child. ⇌ She was a sickly child.
▶ 나는 좀처럼 병을 앓지 않는다 I rarely [seldom] get sick [fall ill]. ⇌ I am rarely taken ill.
2 (비유) be worried 《about》; be troubled [distressed, afflicted]
♦ 골치를 앓다 bother one's head 《about》; rack one's brains over; worry 《oneself》 《about》; suffer mental anguish
▶ 나는 앓던 이가 빠진 것 같았다 I felt quite relieved.
▶ 그런 일에 골치를 앓을 것 없다 Don't worry too much [be so nervous] about such a thing.
―앓이 ache ♦ 귀앓이 an earache / 배앓이 a stomachache / 이앓이 a toothache
암[1] 〈접두어적〉 female; she- ♦ 암캐 a bitch / 암염소 a she-goat; a nanny goat / 암코양이 a female cat; a she-cat; a tabby / 암탉 a hen / 암범 a tigress / 암비둘기 a she-dove; a she-pigeon
암[2] of course; certainly; (口) sure; surely;

no doubt
▶ 會話 「정말 그러니?」 「암, 그렇고 말고」 "Are you quite sure?" "Yes, I am."
▶ 會話 「내일 파티에 가실 거에요?」 「암, 가고 말고」 "Are you going to the party tomorrow?" "Of course, I will go."
▶ 會話 「그를 아십니까?」 「암, 알고말고」 "Do you know him?" "Indeed, I do."

암 癌 1 〈악성 종양〉 [醫] cancer
♦위암 stomach cancer / 방광암 cancer of the bladder / 암이 cancerous / 암이 생기다 develop [get] a cancer 《on》 / 암으로 죽다 die of cancer
▶ 그녀는 유방암이다 She has breast cancer [cancer of the breast].
▶ 그의 암이 간장으로 전위했다 The cancer spread to his liver.
2 〈폐단〉 a cancer
♦민주정치의 암 a curse [fatal impediments] to democracy / 사회적 암 persistent social evils; a cancer of [in, on] the society
■ —검진 an examination [a test] for cancer —세포 a cancerous cell —조직 cancer tissue —환자 a cancer patient

암갈색 暗褐色 dark brown (color); umber; dun ♦암갈색의 dark-brown; umber; dun

암거 暗渠 an underdrain; a culvert; a covered conduit; [建] a duct ■ —배수 drainage by a culvert; underdraining

암거래 暗去來 black market [under-the-table] dealings; underhand [undercover] transactions
♦암거래의 black market; illegal; shady; under-the-table / 암거래를 단속하다 crack down on the black market
▶ 이것은 암거래에서는 두 배 싸다 It is twice as less expensive in the black market.
—암거래하다 black-marketeer; black-market; sell [buy] (goods) in the black market
■ —물자[품] black market goods; 〈밀수입품〉 smuggled [illegally imported] goods

암구다 〈흘레붙이다〉 mate; pair (animals) for breeding

암굴 岩窟 a rock cave; a cavern; a grotto

암기 暗記 learning by heart; memorizing; memory work ♦영어단어 암기법 how to memorize English words
▶ 암기는 영어 학습에서 아주 중요하다 Memorizing is very helpful for the study of English.
—암기하다 learn by heart; memorize
♦암기하고 있다 know by heart; have by heart
▶ 나는 중요한 지명과 인명을 모두 암기했다 I've memorized all the important geographical and biographical names

암기력 暗記力 (one's powers of) memory; retentive power ♦암기력이 좋다 [나쁘다] have a good [bad, poor] memory
▶ 나이가 들면 암기력이 떨어진다 Our memory gets poorer as we get older.

암꽃 [植] a female [pistillate] flower
암꽃술 [植] a pistil
암나사 —螺絲 a female screw
암내 1 〈발정기의〉 the odor of a female animal in heat ♦암내(를) 내다 go in heat; get [come] on heat; be in [on] rut [heat]
2 〈겨드랑이의〉 axillary odor; body odor; 《美俗》 B.O. ♦암내가 심하게 나다 have a strong body odor; 《口》 have B.O.

암단추 a socket [female part] of a snap fastener [press stud]

암달러 暗— black-market dollar; illegally exchanged dollar ■ —거래 black-market dollar transactions —상 an illegal currency [dollar] dealer

암담하다 暗澹— dark; gloomy; dismal
♦암담한 전망 gloomy [dark] prospects
▶ 전도가 암담하다 The future looks gloomy.
▶ 기분이 암담하다 I am most depressed.

암띠다 〈비밀스럽다〉 secretive; reserved; not frank; 〈수줍다〉 shy; coy; timid; 《口》 sissy

암록 暗綠 dark green (color); bottle green

암루 暗淚 secret [silent] tears
♦암루를 흘리다 weep in silence; shed silent tears

암류 暗流 an undercurrent; an underflow

암만 〈수·양〉 a certain amount [sum]
▶ 소년들은 암만씩의 돈을 받았다 Each of the boys received a certain amount of money.

암만해도 no matter how [what]; however ⇨ 아무래도

암말 a mare; a female horse

암매매 暗賣買 black-marketing; illegal trade ⇨ 암거래(暗去來)

암매상 暗賣商 a black marketeer; a black-market trader [operator]; 〈특히 주류 밀매업자〉 《美俗》 a bootlegger

암매장 暗埋葬 secret burial ⇨ 암장(暗葬)

암모나이트 [古生] an ammonite
암모늄 [化] ammonium
암모니아 ammonia
■ 액체— liquid ammonia ■ —가스 ammonia gas —수 ammonia (water); aqueous ammonia; an ammonia solution

암묵 暗默 ♦암묵의 tacit; implicit / 암묵의 양해 a tacit [an implicit] understanding; an unspoken agreement / 암묵리에 tacitly; by a tacit consent [understanding]

암반 岩盤 base rock; a rock bed
암벽 岩壁 a rockwall; a rock face; a rock cliff
♦암벽을 오르다 climb a cliff
■ —등반(술) rock-climbing

암사슴 a doe ♦암사슴의 가죽 a doeskin
암사자 —獅子 a lioness
암산 岩山 a rocky [craggy] mountain
암산 暗算 mental arithmetic; mental calculation ♦암산으로 in mental arithmetic / 암산으로 답을 내다 work out an answer in one's head [in mental arithmetic]
▶ 그는 네 자리 암산을 할 수 있다 He can do four-digit mental calculation.
—암산하다 calculate mentally; do a sum in one's head; work mental sums

암살 暗殺 (an) assassination
♦암살을 꾀하다 plan to assassinate sb; make an attempt on sb's life; attempt sb's life
—암살하다 assassinate ♦암살당하다 be assassinated; fall a victim to an assassin
▶ 케네디 대통령은 1963년에 암살당했다

President Kennedy was assassinated in 1963. ■ —계획 an assassination plot against *sb* —미수 (an) attempted assassination —자 an assassin

암상 jealousy; (green) envy ♦ 암상 떨다 ⇨ 암상부리다 —암상하다[스럽다] jealous; resentful in rivalry —꾸러기 a jealous person

암상 岩床 a rock floor; a deposit [layer] of rock; 〔地〕 a sheet

암상부리다 show jealousy; burn with jealousy; feel envy toward; be green with envy

암새 a hen bird

암석 岩石 (a) rock; a crag; stones and rocks ♦ 암석이 많은 rocky; craggy 〈hill, coast〉 —층 a rock layer [stratum] —학 petrology —현미경 a petrographic microscope

암선 暗線 〈흡수선〉〔物〕 a dark line

암소 a cow; 〈어린 암소〉 a heifer

암송 暗誦 recitation; recital
♦ 시의 암송 a recitation of a poem —암송하다 recite; repeat from memory; say by heart [rote] ♦ 시를 암송하다 recite a poem

암쇠 〈자물쇠의〉 a keyhole plate; 〈돌쩌귀의〉 a gudgeon; 〈맷돌의〉 the rind [rynd] (of a millstone)

암수 male and female; both sexes; sex
♦ 색깔이나 크기로 암수를 구별하다 distinguish [tell] the male from the female by color or size

암수 暗數 〈속임수〉 a trick; trickery; a swindle; swindling ♦ 암수를 쓰다 practice fraud; swindle / 암수에 걸리다 fall into a trick

암술 〔植〕 a pistil

암술대 〔植〕 a style

암스테르담 〈네덜란드의 수도〉 Amsterdam

암시 暗示 a hint; a suggestion; an allusion; an implication
♦ 폭풍을 암시하는 선율 (a) melody suggestive of a storm / 암시적인 suggestive; revealing / 암시를 주다 hint; give [drop] a hint / 암시에 걸리다 be subjected to (hypnotical) suggestion / 암시에 걸리기 쉽다 be easily influenced by suggestion
▶ 그의 말에 암시를 얻어 문제를 풀었다 His words gave me the hint [clue] for solving the problem.
—암시하다 hint; give [drop] a hint; suggest; allude (to); imply
▶ 자기— an autosuggestion ■ —요법 suggestive therapy [cure]

암시세 暗時勢 a black-market price; off-the-books quotations ▶ 그것은 암시세로는 두 배다 It is twice as expensive on the black market.

암시장 暗市場 th black market
♦ 암시장에서 통제품을 팔다 sell controlled goods on the black market; black-market controlled goods

암실 暗室 a (photo) darkroom
♦ 암실용 램프 a darkroom lamp

암암리 暗暗裡 ♦ 암암리에 tacitly; implicitly; secretly; covertly / 암암리에 승낙하다 give tacit consent
▶ 그는 암암리에 돈을 요구했다 He made an indirect demand [indirectly asked] for money.
▶ 그들은 한밤중 암암리에 실험을 계속했다 They continued their experiments secretly in the middle of the night.

암야 暗夜 a dark [moonless] night
♦ 암야를 틈타서 under (the) cover of night [darkness]

암약 暗躍 secret maneuvers
▶ 그의 정치적인 암약으로 그런 결정이 내려졌다고 했다 He is said to have engaged in political maneuvers for the decision.
—암약하다 maneuver secretly; be active behind the scenes; engage in secret maneuvers; pull the strings

암양 —羊 a ewe; a female sheep

암염 岩鹽 rock salt; halite ♦ 암염을 캐내다 mine (rock) salt ■ —갱 a salt mine —채굴 saltmining

암영 暗影 a dark shadow; 〈불안〉 a gloom
♦ 암영이 감돌다 a gloom hangs 《over the school》 / …의 앞날에 암영을 던지다 cast a gloom [pall, cloud] over the future of...
▶ 전쟁은 국가에 암영을 던졌다 War cast a gloom over the country.

암운 暗雲 dark [murky, sullen] clouds
▶ 암운이 감돌고 있다 Dark clouds are hanging low.
▶ 정계에 암운이 감돌고 있다 Dark clouds are gathering over the political world.

암유 暗喩 〔修〕 (a) metaphor ⇨ 은유

암자 庵子 a small (Buddhist) temple; 〈승암〉 a hermitage; a (hermit's) cell [cottage]
♦ 암자를 짓다 build a hermitage / 암자에서 은둔하다 live seclude *oneself* in a hermitage

암자색 dark purple

암장 暗漿 〔地質〕 rock magma

암장 暗葬 〈암매장〉 secret burial —암장하다 bury (a body) secretly

암적색 暗赤色 dark red
♦ 암적색의 dark-red; garnet

암전 暗轉 〔劇〕 a dark change —암전하다 change scenes in the dark (without dropping the curtain)

암종 癌腫 〔醫〕 a carcinoma 《*pl.* ~s, -mata》; cancer ♦ 암종의 carcinomatous ■ —증 a carcinomatosis 《*pl.* -ses》

암죽 —粥 thin gruel (for a baby)

암중모색하다 暗中摸索— grope 《for, after》 in the dark; 〈무턱대고〉 search blindly 《for》; be at sea
♦ 보다 좋은 방법을 암중모색하다 grope for a better way in the dark
▶ 그 사건에 대해 경찰은 지금 암중모색하고만 있다 When it comes to that case, the police are just groping in the dark right now.
▶ 경찰은 그 살인사건의 단서를 잡으려고 암중모색하고 있었다 The police were groping for a clue to the murder case.

암중비약하다 暗中飛躍— be active behind the scenes; engage in secret maneuvers

암초 暗礁 a submerged [sunken] rock; an unknown reef; 〈비유〉 a deadlock; a rock
♦ 암초에 얹히다 be stranded on a reef; strike a rock; go [run, founder] on a rock; 〈계획·

암치질 〖醫〗 internal hemorrhoids
암캉아지 a she-puppy[-pup]
암캐 a she-dog; a bitch
암컷 a female (animal); a she 《*pl.* ~s》; 〈사슴·토끼·양 등의〉 a doe; 〈암새〉 a hen
▶우리 고양이는 암컷이다 Our cat is a female [she].
▶그것은 암컷이냐 수컷이냐? Is it a she [female] or a he [male]? ⇒ What is its sex?
암키와 〖建〗 a concave [upturned] tile
암탉 a hen; a pullet ◆암탉이 우는 집안 (비유) a house where the husband is henpecked by his wife; a house where the wife wears the pants / 암탉이 울다 (비유) henpeck
암탉이 울면 집안이 망한다 (속담) It is a sad house where the hen crows louder than the cock.
암탕나귀 a jenny (ass); a jennet
암톨쩌귀 the knuckle (joint) 《of a hinge》; a gudgeon; a pan
암퇘지 a female hog; a sow
암투 暗鬪 a secret feuding; a secret [smoldering] strife [feud]; veiled enmity
▶당원 간에 암투가 끊이지 않는다 There is a secret feud among the members of the party.
―**암투하다** be at a secret feud 《with》; feud silently 《with》
암팡스럽다 short but aggressive [plucky, spunky, tough] ◆암팡스럽게 말대꾸하다 answer back aggressively / 암팡스럽게 싸우다 fight dauntlessly [ferociously]
암팡지다 short but aggressive ⇨ 암팡스럽다
암페어 〖電·物〗 an ampere ■―계 amperemeter; an ammeter ―수 amperage ―시 an ampere-hour
암평아리 a pullet; a she-chick[-chicken]
암표 暗票 a scalper's [an illegal] ticket
◆암표를 팔다 scalp ■―상 〈행위〉 ticket-scalping; 〈사람〉 a (ticket) scalper; an illegal ticket-broker
암행 暗行 traveling incognito ―**암행하다** travel incognito [in secret, in disguise] ■―어사 〈조선시대의〉 a secret royal [regius] inspector
암호 暗號 a cryptograph; a cryptogram; 〈전신의〉 a cipher; a (secret) code; a secret language; 〈군호〉 a password; a watchword
◆암호를 풀다[해독하다] decode [decipher] / 암호로 적다 write in cipher [code]; cipher / 암호로 전보를 치다 send a telegram in code [cipher] / 암호화하다 code; encode
▶나는 암호로 전보를 쳐 보냈다 I wrote a telegram in code and sent it.
■―문자 a letter code 숫자― a figure code 전신― a telegraphic code ―명 code designation; a code name ―문 a cryptogram; a cryptograph ―법 cryptography ―전보 a code [cipher] telegram ―통신 a signal; cryptography ―해독 code-breaking; cryptanalysis ―해독관 a cipher officer

암흑 暗黑 darkness; blackness
◆사회[인생]의 암흑면 the dark [gloomy] side of society [life] / 암흑의 dark; black; gloomy; seamy
■―가 the underworld; a gangland ―계 the underworld ―대륙 〈과거의 아프리카〉 the Dark Continent ―시대 a dark age; 〈중세 유럽의〉 the Dark Ages
압각 壓覺 〖心〗 a pressure sensation
압권 壓卷 〈뛰어난 것〉 the best (part) 《of a book》; the highlight 《of the day》
▶이 그림은 현대 회화의 압권이다 This is a masterpiece of modern painting.
압도적 壓倒的 overwhelming
◆압도적으로 overwhelmingly / 압도적인 승리를 거두다 win an overwhelming [a sweeping] victory 《over》; 〈美〉〈선거에서〉 score a landslide (victory) / 압도적 다수로 당선하다 be elected by an overwhelming majority
▶그는 압도적인 다수로 국회의장에 재선되었다 He was reelected speaker of the National Assembly by an overwhelming majority.
압도하다 壓倒― overwhelm; overpower; overcome; crush; weigh down; 〈능가하다〉 surpass; excel; exceed; outrival
◆상대를 압도하다 overwhelm [exceed] an opponent; (口) snow under an opponent
압력 壓力 〖物〗 pressure; stress
◆대기의 압력 atmospheric pressure / 압력을 가하다[넣다] apply pressure to; put pressure upon; exert pressure on / 정치적 압력을 가하다 exercise political influence / 압력에 굴하다 bow [bend] to pressure
▶그는 사장의 압력으로 생각을 바꾸었다 He changed his mind under pressure from the company president.
■―계기― 〖物〗 gauge pressure 총[최대, 절대]― total [maximum, absolute] pressure ■―계 a manometer; a pressure gauge ―단체 a pressure group ―솥 a pressure cooker ―시험 a pressure test
압록강 鴨綠江 Amnokkang; the Yalu
압류 押留 〖法〗 attachment; seizure; 〈동산의〉 distraint; distress
◆압류를 해제하다 relieve sb's property from attachment / 압류 딱지를 붙이다 paste distraint paper 《on goods》
―**압류하다** attach; seize; distrain; place 《sb's property》 under distraint
◆물품을 압류하다 seize [distrain] sb's goods / 재산을 압류하다 attach sb's property / 압류당하다 have *one's* property attached [placed under distraint]
▶그는 재산을 압류당했다 His property was placed under distraint.
■―가 provisional attachment [seizure] 동산― personal (property) distress 부동산― real (property) attachment ―영장 a warrant [writ] of attachment ―인 a distrainer; a seizor : 피압류인 a distrainee ―재산 property under distraint; attached [seized] property ―집행 service [execution] of attachment ―품 seized [attached] goods ―품 경매 a distress sale; an auction to sell seized goods

압박 壓迫 pressure; oppression; coercion
♦생활의 압박 the stress [pressure] of life / 여론의 압박 the pressure of public opinion / 정신적 압박 moral pressure / 압박을 가하다 put [exert] pressure on; put the screw(s) on [to]; put under the screw; apply the screw to / 압박을 받다 be pressed [pressured]; be subjected to [come under] pressure
―**압박하다** press; oppress; suppress; 〈부담을 주다〉 strain; clamp down on
♦언론의 자유를 압박하다 suppress the freedom of speech
▶물가 상승은 가계를 압박했다 The rise in prices strained our family budget.
■―**감** a sense of oppression; an oppressive sensation ―**자** an oppressor

압복 壓服 overpoweringness
―**압복하다** overpower

압사 壓死 death from pressure
―**압사하다** be crushed [pressed] to death
▶그는 낙석(落石)에 깔려 압사했다 He was crushed to death under falling rocks. ⇌ Falling rocks crushed him to death.

압살 壓殺 crushing [squeezing] to death
―**압살하다** crush [squeeze] to death; suppress; snuff out
♦국민의 언론의 자유를 압살하다 suppress [snuff out] the people's freedom of speech; gag the people
▶그들의 희망은 압살되었다 Their hopes were crushed.

압생트 〈쓴 쑥맛이 나는 술〉 absinth(e)

압송 押送 〔法〕 sending 《a criminal》 in custody
―**압송하다** send 《a criminal》 under escort; transfer 《a convict》 in custody

압수 押收 〔法〕 (a) confiscation; (a) seizure
―**압수하다** attach; confiscate; impound; seize
♦밀수품을 압수하다 confiscate smuggled goods / 서류를 압수하다 capture [retain] papers / 재산을 압수당하다 have one's property confiscated
▶채권자는 그의 재산을 압수했다 The creditor seized his property.
▶당국은 밀수된 향수를 압수했다 The authorities confiscated the smuggled perfume.
■―**물** a seized article; seized property ―**영장** a warrant for seizure

압승 壓勝 an overwhelming [a landslide] victory
―**압승하다** win an overwhelming [a landslide] victory 《over》; defeat overwhelmingly
▶그 당은 총선거에서 압승했다 The party won a landslide victory in the general election.

압연 壓延 rolling ―**압연하다** roll ■**냉간[열간]**― cold [hot] rolling ―**강** rolled steel ―**공장** a rolling mill ―**기** a roller; a rolling machine

압운 押韻 〈시의 운을 맞춤〉 rhyme; rhyming
―**압운하다** rhyme; (美) rime
♦압운이 뚜렷한 시 heavily rhymed verse / 압운된[한] rhymed / 훌륭히 압운되다 be superbly rhymed
▶long은 song과 압운한다 'Long' rhymes with 'song'.
■―**시** rhymed verses ―**형식** a rhyme scheme

압인 壓印 〈날인〉 sealing ―**압인하다** seal; affix a seal 《to》 ■―**기** a stamping [sealing] machine; a stamper [sealer]

압정 壓釘 (美) a pushpin; a thumbtack; (英) a drawing pin ♦압정으로 고정시키다 tack down [up, together]; tack; thumbtack
▶이 포스터를 벽에 압정으로 붙여라 Tack this poster up on the wall.

압정 壓政 despotism ⇨ 압제

압제 壓制 〈압박〉 oppression; 〈학정〉 tyranny; 〈전제〉 despotism
♦압제적 oppressive; repressive; despotic / 압제에서 벗어나다 be freed from oppression [tyranny] / 압제로 신음하다 groan [crouch] under tyranny
▶국민들은 군사정권의 압제에서 벗어났다 The people were freed from the oppression of the military regime.
―**압제하다** oppress; tyrannize 《over》; rule with an iron hand
■―**자** an oppressor; a despot; a tyrant ―**정치** despotism

압지 押紙·壓紙 blotting paper; a blotter

압착 壓搾 pressure; compression; pressing
―**압착하다** press; compress
―**가스[공기]** compressed gas [air] ―**기** a compressor; a press ―**여과기** a filter press ―**펌프** a compression pump; a compressor

압축 壓縮 compression; constriction; condensation ―**압축하다** compress; compact; constrict; condense
♦압축할 수 있는 compressible; condensable ―**공기** compressed air ―**기[펌프]** a compressor ―**비 (比)** 〔機〕 compression ratio ―**언어** compressed speech ―**파 (波)** 〔物〕 compression waves

압출 壓出 pressure ―**압출하다** press out; extrude 《plastics》
■―**기** an extruder; an extruding machine; an extrusion press

앗 〈뜻밖이거나 놀랐을 때〉 Oh!; O dear!; Dear me!; Good(ness) gracious!; (Good) heavens!; By Jove!; God bless me!; Look!; Why!; Wow!; 〈아프거나 뜨거울 때〉 Ouch!
▶앗, 내 지갑이 없어졌다 Oh! My purse is gone!
▶앗, 기차가 온다 Look! There comes the train over there.
▶앗, 뜨거워 Wow! It's hot.

앗기다 be robbed of sth ⇨ 빼앗기다

앗다 **1** ⇨ 빼앗다
2 〈씨를 빼다〉 remove the seeds ▶목화의 씨는 씨아로 앗는다 Cotton seeds are removed by a cotton gin.
3 〈품을〉 get labor by paying in kind
♦품을 앗다 exchange labors
▶노동력 부족을 해결하기 위해 농부들은 관습적으로 서로 품을 앗는다 To solve the labor shortage, farmers customarily exchange labors.

앗아가다 take [snatch] sth away 《from sb》
♦강도에게서 권총을 앗아가다 snatch a pistol

앗아라 away from a robber
앗아라 No! ⇨ 아서라
앙 1 〈어린아이의 울음소리〉 ◆ 앙 하고 울다 cry loudly; burst out crying; mewl 2 〈남을 놀랠 때 지르는 소리〉 Bo!; Boh!; Boo!
앙가발이 1 〈다리가 짧고 굽은 사람〉 a short and bent-legged [bowlegged] person 2 〈찰거머리〉 a persistently sticky person; a leech
앙가슴 the middle of the chest
앙각 仰角 〔數〕 (an angle of) elevation ⇨ 올려본각
앙감질 〈한 발로만 뛰어가기〉 hopping (on one leg) ―앙감질하다 hop (on one leg)
앙갚음 〈복수〉 revenge; tit for tat; an eye for an eye; retaliation; 〈주로 국가간의〉 reprisal ◆ 앙갚음으로 in revenge [retaliation] 《for》; by way of retaliation
▶ 난 이 앙갚음은 꼭 할테다 I will pay you out for this.
▶ 테러리스트는 그 공격의 앙갚음으로 병원을 폭파했다 The terrorist blew up a hospital in retaliation for the attack.
―앙갚음하다 give [pay] tit for tat; revenge 《one's》 wrongs; revenge oneself 《on sb for sth》; pay off old scores; retaliate on sb; pay back
◆ 아무와 같은 식으로 앙갚음하다 pay sb in 《his》 own coin; serve sb with the same sauce
앙고라 〈고양이[토끼]〉 an Angora (cat [rabbit]) ―직물 angora
앙골라 〈나라 이름〉 Angola; 〈공식명〉 the Republic of Angola
◆ 앙골라의 Angolan ■―사람 an Angolan
앙괭이 〔民俗〕〈귀신〉 a witch who is supposed to visit houses on New Year's night in search of children's shoes to fit her feet
앙괭이그리다 blacken one's face; daub black on one's face
앙구다 1 〈밥그릇 등을 묻어두다〉 keep (food) warm 2 〈곁들이다〉 put (several kinds of food) on the same dish [plate] 3 〈동행케 하다〉 accompany [see] sb on 《his》 way
앙그러지다 1 〈먹음직하다〉 delicious-looking; appetizing; tempting ◆ 앙그러진 요리 an appetizing meal
2 〈모양이 보기 좋다〉 nice; smart; stylish
3 〈하는 짓이 어울리다〉 smart
앙글방글 1 《a child smiles》 beamingly; with a smile; smilingly 2 〈선웃음〉 with a smirk; with an insincere [a deceptive] smile
앙금 〈침전물〉 sediment; settlings; 〈술 등의〉 dregs; lees; 〈커피 등의〉 grounds
◆ 술의 앙금 the sediment of wine / 앙금이 앉다 the dregs settle / 앙금을 앉히다 settle dregs
앙금앙금 〈아기가〉 crawlingly; creepingly; sprawlingly ◆ 앙금앙금 기다 creep [crawl] about; creep on one's stomach; go on all fours
앙달머리 〈야심스레 구는 짓〉 high-flown behavior; 〈사람〉 a person swollen [puffed up] with inordinate ambition
◆ 앙달머리스럽다 inordinate; ambitious
앙등 昂騰 〈급등〉 a sudden [steep] rise (in prices); a jump (in prices)
◆ 물가의 앙등 a rise in prices / 생활비의 앙등 the rising [soaring] cost of living
▶ 땅값의 앙등으로 내 집을 갖겠다는 꿈이 깨졌다 The soaring [skyrocketing] land prices have ended our dream of having our own house.
―앙등하다 jump; soar; rise suddenly
▶ 최근 물가가 앙등했다 Prices have soared recently.
앙망 仰望 〈우러러 바람〉 looking up to with hope; 〈우러러 봄〉 looking up to sb
―앙망하다 〈바라다〉 wish; hope 《for》; be solicitous for; look forward to; 〈부탁하다〉 beg; ask 《for》; solicit; entreat
▶ 다음 일요일 식전에 참석해 주시기를 앙망합니다 You are cordially invited at the ceremony next Sunday.
▶ 조속한 회신을 앙망합니다 I am looking forward to your early reply [hearing from you soon].
앙모하다 仰慕― look up to; respect; adore; admire ◆ 스승으로 앙모하다 look up to sb as one's teacher / 대학자로서 앙모받다 be looked up to as a great scholar
앙바틈하다 〈짤막하고 딱 바라지다〉 thickset; short and thick; fat and short; stocky
앙버티다 〈고집하다〉 hold [stand, stick] it out; stand out stoutly; resist to the (bitter) end
앙살하다, 앙살부리다 oppose with feigned dismay [pain, hardship]; fuss [grumble] in opposition
앙상굳다 (very) gaunt [rugged, haggard]
앙상블 (프) an ensemble
앙상하다 thin; spare; 〈사람이 말라서〉 lean; haggard; scraggy; skinny
◆ 앙상한 사람 a skinny [lean] person; a (living) skeleton / 말라서 뼈만 앙상하다 be reduced [wasted away] to a mere skeleton [to skin and bones]
▶ 잎이 다 져서 나무들이 앙상해 보인다 The trees look thin with their leaves all gone off.
앙세다 〈약해 보이지만 다부지다〉 be weak-looking but have hidden strength
앙숙 怏宿 〈아무와〉 앙숙이다 be at enmity 《with》; lead a cat-and-dog life; be on bad terms 《with》
▶ 그들은 서로 앙숙이다 They are cat and dog. ⇌ They are at daggers drawn with each other.
앙심 怏心 spite; grudge; ill will; rancor
◆ 앙심을 품다 have [bear, harbor] a grudge against sb ▶ 그녀는 아직 그 일로 내게 앙심을 품고 있다 She still bears me ill will over that matter.
앙앙하다 怏怏 〈마음에 만족하지 않다〉 displeased; dissatisfied; discontented; dispirited; dejected; disheartened
앙양 昂揚 exaltation; enhancement; elevation; 《spiritual》 uplift ◆ 애국심의 앙양 an upsurge of patriotic sentiment
―앙양하다 exalt; enhance; uplift; raise; uphold ◆ 국위를 앙양하다 heighten [enhance, raise] national prestige / 사회도의를 앙양하다 promote social morality

▶ 첫 시합의 승리로 선수들의 사기가 앙양했다 The victory in the first match raised the morale of the team.
앙얼 殃孽 divine wrath ⇨ 앙화(殃禍)
앙증스럽다 disproportionately [extraodinarily] small [little]; tiny; miniature 《tube》
♦ 앙증스러운 인형 a little pretty doll
앙짜 1 〈점잔 뺌〉 putting on [giving *oneself*] airs; acting prim ▶ 애, 앙짜 그만 빼라 Stop acting so prim, son.
2 〈암상스러운 사람〉 a tenacious and jealous person
앙천대소하다 仰天大笑— have [laugh] a hearty laugh; burst out laughing; roar with laughter
▶ 우리 모두는 그 일로 앙천대소했다 We all had a good laugh about it.
앙카라 〈터키의 수도〉 Ankara
앙칼지다 1 〈악을 쓰고 덤비다〉 unyielding; furious; fierce; sharp; keen; aggressive
♦ 앙칼진 여자 an aggressive woman; a woman of violent temper / 앙칼지게 공격하다 make a fierce [furious] attack 《on》/ 앙칼지게 쏘아붙이다 snap *sb*; retort with a sharp remark
2 〈앙큼하다〉 overambitious; inwardly audacious; preposterous
앙케트 [〈(프) enquête] an inquiry; a questionnaire; an opinion poll

> 解説 (1) 프랑스말의 *enquête*에서 온 것으로 「조사」「설문」의 뜻이며 영어의 *inquiry*와 같은 계통의 말이다.
> (2) 「앙케트」에 해당하는 영어는 *questionnaire*이며 설문만이 아니라 설문용지도 가리킨다. 「여론조사」의 뜻으로는 *opinion poll*이라고 해도 좋다.

♦ 앙케트에 대한 회답 replies submitted to a questionnaire / 앙케트를 내다 send out a questionnaire / 전화로 앙케트를 조사하다 address a telephone questionnaire 《to *sb* on a matter》/ 앙케트에 기입하다[대답하다] fill out [reply to] a questionnaire
▶ 앙케트를 부탁합니다 (거리에서) May I ask you a few questions?
▶ 앙케트 조사는 주민 1,000명을 대상으로 행해졌다 The questionnairing was conducted on one thousand local residents.
■—용지 a questionnaire
앙코르 an encore

> 解説 「앙케트」처럼, 프랑스말의 *encore* (다시 한번)에서 왔다. 그러나 앙케트와는 달리 프랑스말을 그대로 영어에 쓴다. 「앙코르 곡목」도 encore로 나타낼 수 있다.

♦ 앙코르를 청하다 demand [call for] an encore
▶ 청중은 가수에게 앙코르를 청했다 The audience encored the singer.
▶ 피아니스트는 앙코르에 응하여 세 곡을 연주했다 The pianist played three encores.

앙큼상큼 with short steps; toddlingly ♦ 앙큼상큼 걷다 take short steps
앙큼하다 overambitious; audacious; presumptuous
앙탈 scheming to disobey; grumbling; 〈핑계대어 피함〉 trying to avoid what is right
▶ 네가 하는 말은 아무래도 앙탈인 것 같다 What you say seems to me very much like evasion.
▶ 무엇 때문에 그 앙탈이냐? What are the grounds of your complaint?
—앙탈하다[부리다] try to disobey; try to evade [shirk]; do against; whine
♦ 버릇없는 아이처럼 앙탈하다 whine like a spoiled child
▶ 그녀는 눈이 오는데도 바깥에 나가겠다고 앙탈부린다 In spite of the snow she is insistent on going out.
앙투카 〈경기장의 인조흙〉 (프) en-tout-cas
♦ 앙투카 테니스 코트 an en-tout-cas tennis court / 앙투카의 〈인조흙을 깐 전천후용의〉 en-tout-cas 《tracks》
앙티로망 (프) anti-roman; an antinovel
앙혼 仰婚 marriage with *sb* of higher status; a morganatic marriage **—앙혼하다** marry above *oneself*; marry into a higher status
앙화 殃禍 〈죄의 앙갚음으로 받는 재앙〉《incur》 divine wrath [punishment, retribution]; misfortune; calamities; woe ▶ 그에게 앙화가 닥쳤다 Misfortune [Evil] fell on him.
앞[1] 1 〈앞면〉 the front; the fore(part); 〈전방〉 ahead; beyond; away; off
♦ 앞바퀴 a front wheel / 앞자리[줄] a front seat [row] / 앞집 the opposite house
〈앞의〉 앞의 front; fore / 앞의 좌석에 앉다 take a front seat; sit in the front
▶ 앞의 단추를 채우시오 Do up [Put] the buttons in (the) [down the] front. (▶front 뒤에 of 구(句)가 이어지지 않을 때는 in 다음의 the는 생략할 수 있다)
▶ 역 앞의 책방은 대단히 크다 The bookstore across (the street) from the station is very large. 〈길을 건너서 역 앞에 있는 경우〉⇔ The bookstore in front of the station is very large. (▶역 바로 앞에 있는 경우)
〈앞이[은]〉 앞에 막혀 있다 It is blocked ahead.
▶ 그 마을은 뒤에는 산을 업고 앞은 바다를 면하고 있다 The village fronts [abuts] on the sea with hill at the back.
〈앞을〉 앞을 보다 look before / 건물 앞을 통과하다 pass the front of [in front of] the building
▶ 그는 앞을 못본다 He is blind. ⇔ He is a blind person.
▶ 그는 내 앞을 달리고 있다 He is running ahead of me.
▶ 앞을 보라 Look forward [ahead]. ⇔ Look to the front. ⇔ Look in front of you.
▶ 會話 「아이구, 미안합니다」 「앞을 좀 보고 다니세요?」 "Oh, sorry." "Why don't you look where you are going?"
〈앞에〉 …의 앞에 in [at] the front of… (▶특정한 공간내에서 앞부분을 말함. at은 위치를 강조하는 경우에 쓰임) / 바로 앞에 just [right] in

front 《of》; right before [opposite] *sb* / 집 앞에 before [in front of] a house
▶ 현관 앞에 줄서 주세요 Please line up in front of the entrance.
〈앞에서〉 우리는 둘 째줄에 앉았다 We sat in the second row from the front.
〈앞으로〉 앞으로 ahead; before / 앞으로 나아가다 go [move, step] forward / 곧장 앞으로 가다 go straight ahead / 한 걸음 앞으로 나아가다 take a step forward / 앞으로 나아가 악수하다 come forward [forth] and shake hands
▶ 나는 그를 좀더 잘 보려고 몇 줄 앞으로 나아갔다 I moved up several rows to see him better. (▶up은 문제가 되는 위치로 접근함을 나타냄)
▶ 앞으로 나란히 《口令》 Forward dress!
2 〈순서의〉 the head; the foremost; the first
♦ 행렬의 앞 the head of a procession / 〈열차의〉 제일 앞차 the headmost car / 제일 앞 부대 the foremost troop of an army / 앞 페이지에 on the preceding [previous] page / 앞을 다투어 …하다 strive to be first [for, in doing]; scramble for 《seats》 / 앞에 서서 가다 walk [go] ahead of 《others》; lead the way
▶ 내 이름이 제일 앞에 나와 있다 My name heads [leads] the list.
3 〈면전〉 presence
♦ 남의 앞도 아랑곳없이 in spite of the presence of others / 남 앞에서 in *sb's* presence [face, sight]; in the presence of a person / 사람들 앞에 나서기를 꺼리다 shun company [the public] / 주인 앞에 불려가다 be called before *one's* master / 청중 앞에서 연설하다 speak in front of [before] the audience
▶ 나는 남 앞에서 모욕을 당했다 I was insulted in front of other people [〈공공연히〉 in public].
▶ 그 사람[어머니] 앞에서는 그 일을 얘기하지 마세요 Don't talk about it in his presence [in the presence of my mother]. ⇒ 《口》 Don't talk about it when he [my mother] is there.
▶ 그는 위험 앞에서조차 냉정했다 He remained calm even in the presence of [in the face of] danger.
▶ 법 앞에서는 만인이 평등하다 All men are equal before [in the eye of] the law.
4 〈미래〉 the future
♦ 앞으로의 전망 the prospects; the outlook / …을 1주일 앞(에) 두고 with…one weeks ahead [off] / 10년을 내다보다 look (ten years) ahead; look into the future / 앞을 내다볼 줄 알다 have foresight; be farsighted / 앞으로 in (the) future; from now on / 앞으로 5일간 for the next five days; for five days ahead / 앞으로 몇 개월동안[오랫동안] for months [a long time] to come / 앞으로의 계획을 세우다 make plans for the future
▶ 會話 「잠깐 쉬는게 어때?」「아니야, 앞길을 서두르자」"Why don't we take a rest?" "No, let's be on our way."
▶ 앞으로 너는 어떻게 할 작정이냐? What is your plan for the future?
▶ 앞으로 어떤 일이 일어날지 모른다 We don't know what is in store for us.
▶ 그 일은 앞으로 전망이 있다[없다] The work has a bright [gloomy] outlook.
5 〈몫〉 a share; *one's* lot [portion, allotment, quota]
♦ 한 사람 앞에 사과를 3개씩 주다 give three apples each [per head]
▶ 그 유산은 대부분 장남 앞으로 갔다 Most of the legacy went to the eldest son.
▶ 겨우 이만큼이 내 앞으로 떨어졌다 This much has fallen to my lot.
▶ 그 계산은 내 앞으로 달아 놓으시오 Charge it [Put it down] to my account.
6 〈먼저 부분〉 the preceding part
♦ 앞에서 말한 바와 같이 as previously stated
▶ 그 문제는 앞에서 대충 언급한 바 있다 The subject has been referred to cursorily above.

앞² **1** 〈편지 등의〉 addressed to *sb*
♦ A씨 앞 편지 a letter for [addressed to] Mr. A / B씨 앞 소포 a parcel directed to Mr. B / 파리 지국 …앞으로 편지를 쓰다 write *sb* at the office in Paris
▶ 이 편지는 누구 앞으로 온 것인가요? Who is this letter for? ⇒ Who is this letter addressed [directed] to?
▶ 會話 「한국에 계신 어머니 앞으로 보내는 편지는 며칠 걸릴까?」「적어도 1주일은 잡아야 될 거야」"How long are letters to my mother in Korea taking?" "You ought to allow a week at least."
2 〈어음 등의〉 drawn in *one's* favor
♦ C씨 앞으로 우편환을 끊다 draw a postal money order for [in favor of] Mr. C
▶ 나는 H씨 앞으로 5백만원짜리 수표를 끊었다 I have issued a check for five million won in favor of Mr. H.

앞가림하다 have just enough education to get by ▶ 그 아이가 제 앞가림할지 모르겠다 I am afraid he is not old enough to look after himself.

앞가슴 the breast; the chest 《of the body, of a garment》

앞갈이 〔農〕 **1** 〈애벌갈이〉 the first plowing [《英》 ploughing] 《of a rice field》 **2** 〈첫농사〉 the first of the annual crops

앞길 **1** 〈갈길〉 the road ahead; *one's* way to go
♦ 앞길이 멀다 have a long [far] way to go / 앞길을 가로막다 block [close, stand in] *one's* way / 횃불로 앞길을 비추다 light *one's* way with a torch
▶ 우리의 앞길은 매우 험난하다 The road ahead of us is very rough.
2 〈전도〉 *one's* future; prospects
♦ 앞길이 유망한 청년 a promising youth; a young man (full) of promise / 앞길을 그르치다 〈사물이 주어〉 ruin [wreck] *one's* career [future] / 앞길을 비관하다 despair of *one's* future
▶ 그는 앞길이 양양하다 He has a bright [promising] future before him. ⇒ He has bright [excellent] prospects.
▶ 우리의 앞길은 다난하다 Many difficulties lie ahead of us [in our way].

앞날 the days ahead [to come]; *one's* future; 〈여생〉 the remaining years [days] 《of *one's*

life)
♦ 밝은 앞날 a bright [rosy] future / 어두운 앞날 a dark future; gloomy prospects
〈앞날의〉 앞날의 즐거움 the pleasure to come / 앞날의 계획을 세우다 form [lay] a plan for the future
〈앞날이〉 앞날이 촉망되는 젊은이 a young man of promise; a promising youth
▶ 그 남자의 앞날이 멀지 않다 His days are numbered [drawing to their close].
▶ 그는 앞날이 유망한 학자다 He is a (very) promising scholar. ⇌ He is a scholar with great promise [with good prospects].
〈앞날을〉 앞날을 바라보다 look ahead into the future / 앞날을 생각하다 think of the future 《of》; take thought for the future 《of》 / 앞날을 염려하다 be anxious about *one's* future / 앞날을 위해 저축하다 save money for the future
▶ 너는 네 자신의 앞날을 더 진지하게 생각해야 된다 You should think about your future more seriously.
▶ 그 결정은 신중한 그리고 앞날을 잘 내다본 것이었다 The decision was discreet and far-sighted

앞니 a foretooth; a front tooth; an incisor
▶ 나는 앞니가 두 개 빠졌다 I have two front teeth missing.
▶ 아기는 앞니가 하나 났다 The baby has cut a front tooth.

앞다리 1 〈네 발 짐승의〉 a foreleg; a front leg; a forelimb; 〈발톱 있는 짐승의〉 a paw
2 〈이사할 집〉 one's new house [residence] (to move into)
♦ 앞다리를 정해 놓고 집을 팔다 sell *one's* house after *one* has procured a new one
3 〈앞잡이〉 co-worker standing right in front
4 〈베틀 앞기둥〉 the beam stand of a hand loom

앞다투다 ♦ 앞다투어 기차를 타다 crush [push *one's* way] onto a train
▶ 사내애들은 앞다투어 자리를 잡으려고 했다 The boys scrambled for seats [to take the seat].

앞달이 〈구두의 앞부분〉 a vamp; a toe cap

앞당기다 advance; move [carry] up
♦ 사흘 앞당기다 advance 《the date》 by three days / 둘째 시간의 영어 수업을 첫째 시간으로 앞당기다 move up the English lesson from the second hour to the first / 회의를 앞당겨 열다 hold a meeting ahead of schedule
▶ 출발을 토요일에서 금요일로[1주일] 앞당겼다 We brought forward our departure from Saturday to Friday [by one week].

앞대 〈남쪽지방〉 the southern part 《of a country, a province》; the south; the southern district; the southland

앞대문 ─大門 the front gate

앞두다 have 《a period, a distance》 ahead; have 《an examination》 near [close] at hand
♦ 시험을 목전에 앞두고 with the examination just before on [near at hand] / 열흘을 앞두다 have ten days to go [run] / 10마일을 앞두다 have ten miles ahead (to cover)
▶ 우리는 새해를 앞두고 몹시 바쁘다 We are very busy with the New Year close at hand [just before us].
▶ 그는 미국으로의 출발을 이틀 앞두고 있다 He is waiting to start for America in two days. ⇌ 출발까지 앞으로 이틀 남았다 He has two days (left) until he starts for America.

앞뒤 1 〈위치〉 front and rear
♦ 앞뒤의[에] before and behind / 앞뒤로 backward(s) and forward(s); 〈앞뒤로 움직여〉 back and forth; in front and in (the) rear; 《口》 front and rear / 앞뒤를 둘러보다 look before and behind; look around [about] / 앞뒤로 적의 공격을 받다 be attacked both in front and in rear
▶ 앞뒤를 잘 봐요 Look carefully before and behind [to the front and the rear].
▶ 차를 후진시켜 차고에 넣을 때는 앞뒤를 잘 살피세요 Look around [about] (you) carefully when you back your car into the garage.
▶ 그들은 그 성을 앞뒤에서 공격했다 They attacked the castle in front and in the rear [front and rear].
▶ 그들은 음악에 맞춰 몸을 앞뒤로 흔들었다 They were swaying back and forth [to and fro] to the music.
2 〈순서〉 order
▶ 앞뒤가 전도되어 있다 The order is reversed.
3 〈전후 사정〉 circumstances; consequences
♦ 앞뒤 생각없이 indiscreetly; thoughtlessly; blindly; regardless [reckless] of the consequences / 앞뒤를 잘 가리다[재다] reflect on [think of] the consequences; be provident; be prudent
▶ 앞뒤 생각없이 경솔히 행동하지 마라 Don't behave imprudently regardless of [without reflecting on] the consequences.
4 〈일관성〉 coherence; consistency; 〈조리〉 logical sequence
♦ 앞뒤가 닿지 않는 변명[의논] a lame excuse [argument] / 앞뒤가 맞다[닿다] be coherent [consistent]; hang together / 앞뒤가 맞지[닿지] 않다 be (self-)contradictory; lack consistence [coherence] / 앞뒤가 맞지 않게 말하다 talk incoherently; say incoherent things; contradict *oneself*
▶ 그녀의 주장은 앞뒤가 맞지 않는다 Her argument is not coherent [incoherent].
▶ 그는 술에 취해[흥분하여] 앞뒤가 맞지 않는 말을 했다 He was incoherent with drunkenness [in agitation].
▶ 네 말은 앞뒤가 안 맞아 There is no logic [neither rhyme nor reason] in your remark.
5 〈문맥〉 the context
▶ 앞뒤 관계에서 낱말의 뜻을 추측할 수 있다 We can guess the meaning of a word from its context.
▶ 그의 말은 앞뒤 관계없이 인용되어 오해받았다 His words were quoted out of context and were misunderstood.

앞뒷집 two neighbor houses; two houses, one in front and the other in (the) rear
♦ 앞뒷집에 살다 live in the vicinity; be [live] next door to each other [neighbors]
▶ 그들은 내 앞뒷집에 살고 있다 They live in

the houses next to mine. ⇌ They live next door to me. (▸me 대신 my house는 잘못임) ⇌ They are my next-door neighbors.

앞뜰 a front yard [court, courtyard, garden]

앞마구리 〈걸채의 앞쪽에 가로댄 나무〉 the front end-board of a saddle-rack

앞머리 1〈정수리 앞쪽의 머리〉 the forehead; 〔解〕 the sinciput; 〈머리칼〉 a forelock; 〈단발머리의〉 a bang
  ♦앞머리를 단발머리로 하다 wear *one's* hair banged
  2〈물건의 앞쪽〉 the front end; the head
  3〈선두〉 the forefront; the head; the van; the vanguard
  ♦행렬의 앞머리 the van of a procession / …의 앞머리에서 in the van of…

앞못보다 1〈소경이〉 be blind; can't see what is going on 2〈무식하다〉 be illiterate; be ignorant

앞문—門 the front gate; the front door; the front entrance ♦앞문으로 들어가다 enter at [by] the front door

앞바다 the offing; coastal and off-shore areas
  ♦앞바다에 in the offing; offshore; off the shore [coast] / 속초 앞바다에서 off (the coast of) Sokch'o

앞바닥 the fore part of a sole

앞바람 1〈마파람〉 the south wind 2 ⇨ 역풍

앞바퀴 a front [fore] wheel

앞발 〈네발짐승·곤충 등의〉 a forefoot (*pl.* -feet); 〈개·고양이 등의〉 a paw; 〈굽이 있는 짐승의〉 a front hoof (*pl.* -hooves)
  —질 kicking with the forefeet; pawing

앞볼 〈버선 앞쪽에 덧대는 헝겊〉 a toe patch for Korean socks

앞산—山 a mountain [hill] (standing) in front (of a house)

앞서 1〈지난번〉 previously; earlier; before
  ♦앞서 말한 바와 같이 as previously stated / 앞서 편지로 말한 대로 as I have stated in my previous letter / 앞서 그를 만났을 때 when I saw him last
  ▶그것은 앞서 말한 대로입니다 It is just as I stated previously [above]. (▸above는 가로쓰기의 문장에서「위에」「앞에」의 뜻)
  2〈먼저〉 before; earlier (than); 〈…에 앞서〉 prior to; 〈앞장서서〉 ahead (of); in advance (of)
  ♦회의에 앞서 previous to the conference / 앞서 가다 go ahead (of another); go before; precede /예정 시간보다 앞서 떠나다 start [leave] earlier than the fixed [scheduled] time
  ▶그녀는 나보다 앞서 역에 도착했다 She got to the station before me [〈보다 빨리〉 earlier than I did, 〔口〕 earlier than me].
  ▶나는 편지하기에 앞서 전화를 걸었다 I had rung him before to writing.
  ▶회의에 앞서 환영회가 열렸다 The meeting was preceded by a reception.

앞서거니뒤서거니 neck and neck ♦앞서거니 뒤서거니하다 alternate for [in] the lead; run neck and neck; be nip and tuck
  ▶그들은 앞서거니 뒤서거니하며 결승선에 육박하고 있었다 They were coming toward the finish line neck and neck.

앞서다 go ahead (of another); go before; go in advance of; precede; head; lead (others); take precedence [the lead]
  ♦경주에서 앞서다 get the lead in a race / 시대에 앞서다 go ahead of the times [*one's* age]
  ▶그는 영어 과목이 다른 학생보다 앞서 있다 He is ahead of the other students in English.
  ▶이 분야에서 그의 솜씨는 어떤 동료보다도 다소 앞선다 He does a little better job than any of his colleagues in this field.
  ▶어떤 일이든지 돈이 가장 앞선다 Money is the first consideration [requisite].

앞세우다 1〈앞에 서게 하다〉 make *sb* go ahead; let lead [precede]
  ♦국기를 앞세우고 with the national flag at the head (of a procession) / 악대를 앞세우고 led [spearheaded] by a band
  ▶우리는 경제문제보다 도덕교육을 앞세워야 한다 We must give priority to moral education over economic problems.
  2〈먼저 여의다〉 survive [outlive] (*one's* son)
  ▶나는 딸을 앞세웠다 I survived [outlived] my daughter.

앞수표—手票 〈실제 발행일자보다 그 이후의 날짜를 기재한 수표〉 a postdated check [bill]

앞앞이 〈저마다의 앞에〉 before [in front of] each person; 〈몫몫이〉 to [for] each person; each; respectively
  ♦앞앞이 하나씩 one for each person; one piece each
  ▶그들은 사과를 앞앞이 세 개씩 집었다 They took three apples each.

앞어금니 〈소구치〉 a premolar; a bicuspid

앞에총—銃 ♦앞에총 자세 the port / 앞에총을 하다 port ♦앞에총 (口令) Port arms!

앞이마 〈사람의〉 the forehead; 〈동물의〉 the frontlet

앞일 things to come; the future
  ♦앞일을 걱정하다 worry about *one's* future / 앞일을 생각하다 think of [take thought for] the future (of) / 앞일을 예상하다[예측하다] predict [forecast] the future (of) / 앞일에 대비하다 provide [prepare] for the future
  ▶난 앞일이 걱정이다 I am anxious [feel gloomy] about my future.
  ▶앞일은 알 수 없다 You cannot tell the future. ⇌ There is no knowing what the future may bring forth.

앞자락 the front hem [skirt] (of a garment)

앞잡이 1〈인도하는 사람〉 a guide; a leader
  ▶앞잡이의 인도로 우리는 산에 올랐다 We climbed the mountain under the leadership of [following] the guide.
  2〈끄나풀〉 a cat's-paw; a tool; an instrument; 〈비유〉 a pawn
  ♦…의 앞잡이가 되다 be made a cat's-paw of [by]
  ▶그는 두목의 앞잡이에 불과하다 He is a mere tool of the boss.
  ▶그는 나를 앞잡이로 부렸다 He used me as a pawn [tool]. ⇌ He made a pawn [cat's-paw] of me.

▶ 그는 경찰의 앞잡이다 He is a pawn [tool] (in the hands) of the police.
앞장 the head; the lead; a leader; a pioneer; the forefront; the van; the vanguard
♦ 앞장 서다 be at the head (of); be in the van [forefront] 《of a parade》; take the lead [van] 《in》 / 유행에 앞장 서다 lead the fashion / 행렬에서 앞장 서다 head [lead] a procession / 앞장 서서 걷다 walk at the head (of) / 앞장 서서 …하다 take the lead in 《doing》; take the initiative in...
▶ 관악대가 행렬의 앞장을 섰다 The brass band led (the way for) the parade.
▶ 그는 앞장 서서 교육개혁을 실행했다 He took the lead [〈솔선하여〉 the initiative] in carrying out the educational reform.
앞정강이 the (fore-)shin; the shank
앞줄 the front row [rank] (▶the front rank는 주로 군대·택시의 줄을 말함)
♦ 앞줄 왼쪽에서 세번째 학생 the third student from the left in the front row / 앞줄에 앉다 [자리를 잡다] sit [take a seat] in the front row
앞지르다 〈추월하다〉 outrun; pass 《another in the race》; outstrip; outpace; pass 《another car》 ahead; 〈배가〉 outsail; get ahead of 《another》; 〈능가하다〉 outdo; 〈앞서다〉 overtake; 〈낫다〉 surpass
♦ 훨씬 앞지르다 get far ahead of 《another》; outdistance / 남의 이야기를 앞지르다 get ahead of [anticipate] *sb* telling a story / 다른 차를 앞지르다 pass another car ahead / 공업 생산에서 다른 모든 나라를 앞지르다 overtake [outstrip] all other nations in industrial production / 앞지름을 당하다 〈어떤 분야에서〉 be outdone by another; 〈경주에서〉 lose the lead to 《one's opponent》
▶ 좌측[커브]에서 앞질러서는 안된다 Don't pass on the left [on a curve].
▶ 내가 탄 택시가 버스를 앞질렀다 My taxi overtook [passed, got ahead of] a bus.
▶ 그는 수학에서 형을 앞질렀다 He got ahead of his brother in mathematics.
▶ 사장은 파업에 앞질러 그 책임자를 해고했다 The president forestalled the walkout by firing those responsible for it.
앞집 〈앞으로 이웃한〉 the house in front; 〈길 건너의〉 the opposite house
앞쪽 the front; 〈앞부분〉 the fore(part)
♦ 대열의 앞쪽으로 forward ranks / 앞쪽에 in front (of); ahead; forward; frontward / 멀리 앞쪽에 far ahead / 열차의 맨 앞쪽 차량에서 좌석을 찾다 find a seat in the foremost car [in the car at the front] of a train
앞차 —車 〈앞서 떠난 차〉 the last bus [train]; 〈앞에 가는 차〉 a preceding vehicle; the car (that goes) ahead
♦ 앞차와의 안전거리를 유지하시오 Keep a safe distance from the car that goes ahead.
앞차다 〈든든하다〉 strong and dependable; 〈믿음성이 있다〉 reliable
앞참 —站 〈다음에 머무를 곳〉 the next stage [stop]; the next post town
앞창 a half sole ♦ 앞창을 대다 half-sole; 〈수리 시키다〉 have *one's* shoes resoled
앞창 —窓 the front window
앞채 1 〈집의〉 the front wing of a house 2 〈가마·상여 등의 앞에서 메는 채〉 the front poles
앞치마 an apron ♦ 앞치마를 두르다 put on [wear] an apron

애¹ 1 〈근심·걱정〉 anxiety; worry; trouble
♦ 애가 타다 be anxious [nervous, worried] 《about》
▶ 그녀가 잠자코 있자 그는 애가 타서 그녀를 바라보았다 He looked at her irritatingly [impatiently] as she kept silent.
▶ 그는 부모에게 애만 먹인다 He is a constant source of anxiety to his parents.
2 〈수고〉 ⇨ 애먹다, 애쓰다
▶ 타이어가 구멍나서 애를 먹고 있다 I'm in a fix because I have a flat tire.
애² a child ⇨ 아이
애— 〈맨처음〉 the very first; 〈어린〉 infant; very young; fresh; 〈앳된〉 childish; boyish; green
♦ 애벌 the first time [round] / 애송이 a novice; (口) a greenhorn / 애순 a fresh sprot / 애호박 a young pumpkin
애가 哀歌 a song of sorrow; 〈만가〉 an elegy; a dirge ♦ 예레미야애가 [聖] the Lamentations (of Jeremiah)
애간장 —肝腸 the bowels (as the seat of the feelings)
♦ 애간장을 저미다 rend [wring] *one's* heart
애개 〈아뿔싸〉 My!; O dear!; Why!; Gosh!; Golly!; 〈작은 것을 업신여기는 소리〉 How puny [skimpy, little, paltry]!
▶ 애개 저 조그만 강아지 좀 봐 Look, what a tiny puppy it is!
애걸 哀乞 begging; imploring; pleading —**애걸하다** beg [plead] for; implore; cry *sb* mercy; ask for mercy
♦ 애걸복걸하다 beg earnestly; implore *sb* on *one's* knees; beg 《*sb* forgiveness》 on bended knees / 눈물을 흘리며 애걸하다 implore with tears in *one's* eyes
▶ 그녀는 왕에게 용서해 달라고 애걸했다 She implored the king to have mercy.
애견 愛犬 *one's* pet dog ♦ 애견을 품평회에 내다 enter *one's* pet dog in a dog show
▶ 아지는 내 애견의 이름이다 Aji is the name of my pet dog.
■ —가 a dog lover; a lover of dogs
애고 愛顧 patronage; favor; custom
♦ 애고를 바라다 solicit *sb's* patronage [custom] / 애고를 입다 be patronized 《by *sb*》; receive favors 《from》 / 애고에 보답하다 be worthy of [thankful for] *sb's* patronage
▶ 애고를 바라마지 않습니다 〈상용문 등에서〉 We solicit your (continued) patronage.
▶ 변함없는 애고를 바랍니다 Your usual patronage will be much appreciated.
—**애고하다** patronize; favor
애고대고 crying and wailing —**애고대고하다** cry and wail
애곡 哀哭 mourning; lamentation; grief; wailing —**애곡하다** mourn 《for, over》; lament 《for》; grieve 《at, over》; wail
▶ 그는 아버지의 죽음을 애곡했다 He mourned

over the death of his father.

애교 愛嬌 charm; amiability; attractiveness; courtesy
◆ 애교있는 웃음[소녀] a charming [a winning, an attractive] smile [girl] / 애교있는 charming; attractive / 애교없는 unattractive; blunt; curt / 애교가 넘쳐흐르다 be overflowing with smiles / 애교를 떨다 turn on the [*one's*] charm / 애교를 떨며 알랑거리다 court *sb's* favor; ⟨여자가⟩ traffic in *one's* charms / 애교있는 눈을 하고 있다 have charming [cute] eyes
▶ 그녀는 애교있고 머리도 좋다 She is smart as well as charming.
▶ 저 아기는 눈매에 애교가 있다 That baby has charming eyes.
▶ 그녀는 애교가 없다 She is curt.
▶ 그녀는 언제나 애교없는 대답을 한다 She always gives a blunt [curt] answer.
▶ 그녀는 애교가 넘쳐흐른다 She overflows with smiles.

애교심 愛校心 love of [for] *one's* school; attachment to *one's* alma mater [old school]
▶ 그는 애교심에 불타고 있다 He dearly [deeply] loves his school.

애구 Oh!; Oh, my goodness!; Oh, my God!

애국 愛國 patriotism; love of [for] *one's* country
◆ 애국적(인) patriotic / 비애국적인 unpatriotic
▶ 그는 애국의 정열에 불타고 있다 He loves his country passionately [deeply]. ≒ He is very patriotic.
━선열 deceased [previous] patriots ━운동 a patriotic movement ━자[지사] a patriot; ⟨광신적인⟩ a chauvinist ━정신 patriotism

애국가 愛國歌 the Korean national anthem
▶ 우리는 힘차게 애국가를 불렀다 We sang powerfully the Korean national anthem.

애국심 愛國心 patriotism; nationalism; patriotic spirit [sentiment, feeling]
◆ 애국심이 강한 청년 a patriotic young man / 애국심에 불타는 마음 *one's* heart burning [glowing] with patriotism / 애국심이 있다 be patriotic; have a love for *one's* country
▶ 그는 애국심이 강하다 He is very patriotic. ≒ He loves his (own) country very much.
▶ 그는 청년들에게 애국심을 고취했다 He inspired young men with the spirit of patriotism.

애기 愛機 ⟨비행기⟩ *one's* (own) airplane; an airplane for *one's* personal use

애기잠 ⟨누에의 첫잠⟩ the first dormant period of the silkworm

애꾸 1 ⇨ 애꾸눈 **2** ⇨ 애꾸눈이

애꾸눈 blindness of [in] one eye
◆ 애꾸눈이 되다 lose one eye; become blind in one eye; lose the sight of one eye

애꾸눈이 a one-eyed person

애꿎다 innocent; blameless; guiltless; undeserved ◆ 애꿎은 사람 an innocent [a blameless] person

애끊다 feel *one's* heart torn [rent] to pieces; feel as if *one's* heart were breaking
◆ 애끊는 슬픔 heartrending [breaking] sorrow
▶ 그 슬픈 소식을 듣고 내 마음은 애끊는 듯했다 My heart broke when I heard the sad news. ≒ My heart bled to hear the sad news.

애끓다 be worried (about); fret (about); worry (*oneself*) (about); ⟨口⟩ be in a fidget [stew] (about) ▶ 그는 무엇 때문에 애끓고 있느냐? What's worrying him?

애늙은이 a stuffy youngster; a person who looks [acts] older than his years

애니메이션 ⟨동화(動畫)⟩ (an) animation

애니미즘 ⟨정령숭배⟩ animism

애달다 be anxious (to, about); be impatient (at); worry; fret (about, over)
▶ 나를 애달게 하지 말고 어서 보여 주렴 Don't keep me in suspense, but show it to me.
▶ 그는 성적이 나빠 애달아한다 He is worrying over his low marks.

애달프다 heartbreaking; heartrending; anguishing; sorrowful; painful
▶ 그가 죽다니 정말 애달픈 노릇이다 It is really heartbreaking to hear of his death.

애당심 愛黨心 party loyalty; party [partisan] spirit

애당초 ━當初 the beginning ⇨ 애초

애도 哀悼 sorrow; regret; condolence; sympathy; mourning; grief; lamentation
◆ 애도의 뜻을 표하는 편지 a letter of condolence [sympathy] / 애도의 뜻을 표하다 express *one's* regret (over); ⟨유족에게⟩ offer *one's* condolence ⟨to sb on his bereavement⟩; express *one's* sympathy ⟨for sb on the death of his father⟩
▶ 애도의 뜻을 표합니다 I sympathize with your grief.
▶ 진심으로 애도의 말씀을 드립니다 Please accept my deep sympathy. ≒ Allow me to offer my sincere condolences.
▶ 나는 부친을 잃은 친구에게 애도의 말을 했다 I expressed my condolences to my friend on the death of his father.
━애도하다 mourn (for, over); lament (for); grieve (at, on, for); regret
━가(歌) a lamentation; an elegy ━사 a funeral oration : 애도사를 하다 make a condolatory address ━자 a condoler; a mourner

애독 愛讀 reading for pleasure; love of reading
━애독하다 enjoy reading; like reading; read (a book) with pleasure; be fond of reading (a book); ⟨신문·잡지를 정기 구독하다⟩ read (a paper, a magazine) regularly; subscribe to [for]
▶ 나는 「전쟁과 평화」를 애독하고 있다 I am a lover of *War and Peace*.
▶ 그 책은 교양있는 여성에게 애독되고 있다 The book is very popular [a great favorite] among cultured women.
━서 *one's* favorite book

애독자 愛讀者 an avid reader ⟨of Hamlet⟩; an admirer ⟨of Keats⟩; ⟨정기 구독자⟩ a regular reader ⟨of⟩; a subscriber ⟨for [to] The Times⟩
▶ 그 잡지는 애독자가 많다 The magazine has

a lot of readers.
▶ 그의 소설은 애독자가 많다 His novels have a large circle of readers.
▶ 나는 그 신문의 애독자다 I am a regular reader of that newspaper.

애드 (口) 〈광고〉 an ad(vertisement); advertising ■—**맨** (口) an adman

애드리브 〈즉흥적인 대사[연주]〉 an ad lib
♦애드리브로 개그를 집어넣다 ad-lib some jokes; throw in some jokes that are not in the script

애드벌룬 an advertising balloon
♦애드벌룬을 띄우다[내리다] float [pull down] advertising balloon

애디슨병 —病 〈만성부신 기능장애〉 Addison's disease

애락 哀樂 grief and joy; sadness and pleasure

애련 哀憐 pity; compassion ♦애련의 정을 금치 못하다 be overwhelmed with pity 《for》 —**애련하다** piteous; pitiable; pitiful; poor; touching
♦애련한 노래 a plaintive song

애로 隘路 **1** 〈좁고 험한 길〉 a narrow path; 〈산속의〉 a defile **2** 〈장애〉 a bottleneck
♦애로가 되다 cause a bottleneck / 애로를 타개하다 break (through) [resolve] a bottleneck; push through an impasse
▶ 농촌에서는 엄청난 일손 부족이 애로가 되어 있다 In rural districts an extraordinary shortage of farmhands has created a bottleneck.
▶ 우리는 생산에서의 애로를 타개하도록 노력하지 않으면 안된다 We must try to break the bottleneck in production.

애리조나 〈미국의 주〉 Arizona (略 Ariz., Az.) ■—**사람** an Arizonan; an Arizonian

애림 愛林 loving the forests; cherishing [protecting] the forests; conservation [care, protection] of forests; forestry conservation —**애림하다** take care of trees [forests]
■—**녹화** 〈게시〉 Keep the Trees Green; Save the Trees —**사상** interest in forest conservation

애마 愛馬 one's favorite horse; one's pet horse; a horse one keeps with tender care; one's cherished mount

애매 曖昧 vagueness; ambiguity; obscurity —**애매하다** 〈의미가 막연하다〉 vague (expression); 〈두가지 이상의 뜻이 있는〉 ambiguous 《wording》; 〈분분명한〉 unclear; uncertain; 〈모호한〉 obscure 《vowels》; 〈언질을 주지 않는〉 noncommittal; 〈회피적인〉 evasive
♦애매한 기사 news of doubtful authority / 애매한 태도 an ambiguous attitude / 애매한 대답 a vague answer; an evasive answer; a noncommittal answer / 애매하게 vaguely; ambiguously / 애매한 대답을 하다 make an ambiguous answer; give a vague [an indefinite] answer / 애매한 말을 하다 equivocate; prevaricate; talk ambiguously / 애매한 진술을 하다 quibble; make an ambiguous statement / 애매한 태도를 취하다 take an uncertain [a noncommittal] attitude 《toward》; do not commit oneself
▶ 그의 대답은 애매하다 His answer is uncertain.
▶ 그는 내게 애매한 대답을 했다 He gave me a noncommittal [an equivocal, an evasive, an ambiguous, an obscure, a vague] answer.
▶ 이 규칙에는 애매한 점이 많다 These regulations are full of ambiguities.
▶ 그는 이 일에 대해 애매한 태도를 취하고 있다 He is taking an uncertain attitude on this matter.

애매하다 falsely charged 《with》; unjustly [falsely, wrongly] accused 《of》
♦애매한 사람을 들볶다 pester an innocent person / 애매한 사람을 감옥에 가두다 cast [put] an innocent person into jail / 애매한 사람을 죽이다 kill an innocent person / 애매하게 꾸중을 듣다 get an unwarranted scolding / 애매하게 의심받다 be unjustly suspected of a guilt

애먹다 have a hard time of it; have trouble; be greatly embarrassed; be in a bad [pretty] fix; be stumped 《by》; suffer [go through] hardships; be hard put to it
♦설득에 애먹다 have a great tug to persuade
▶ 그 사건을 수사 하는 데 무척 애먹었다 We had a hard time solving the case.
▶ 입시문제가 어려워서 나는 몹시 애먹었다 The entrance examination questions were difficult and I had a lot of trouble.
▶ 그는 그 일에 무척 애먹었다 He had much trouble with the business.
▶ 나는 수학문제를 푸는 데 애먹었다 I tried hard to solve a mathematical problem.

애먹이다 annoy; plague; give sb much trouble; put sb in a fix; put sb out

애면글면 struggling with all one's might; doing one's feeble best —**애면글면하다** do one's feeble best

애모 愛慕 attachment; affection
▶ 그녀는 선생님에게 깊은 애모를 품게 되었다 She formed a profound attachment for her teacher.
▶ 그들은 서로에게 깊은 애모의 정으로 결합돼 있다 They are deeply attached to each other. —**애모하다** be attached to; love; long [yearn] 《for》

애무 愛撫 caress; caressing; endearment; (口) petting
—**애무하다** caress; 〈동물을 어르다〉 pet (▶ (口)로는 이성간의 애무를 나타냄); 〈포옹·키스 등으로〉 fondle; dandle
▶ 그녀는 고양이 새끼를 애무했다 She petted the kitten.
▶ 그의 손이 그녀의 얼굴을 다정하게 애무했다 His hands caressed her face lovingly.

애물 **1** 〈어려서 죽은 자식〉 one's child who died young **2** 〈애태우는 것〉 a cause of worry [anxiety]

애바르다 be alive to one's interests; be keen [sharp] in moneymaking; be shrewd in business

애바리 〈애바른 사람〉 a shrewd man of business [in moneymaking]

애버딘 〈스코틀랜드의 도시〉 Aberdeen

애벌 the first [preliminary] stage (in the

procession of work)
♦애벌 손질을 하다 make rough preparations ((for)) / 애벌 찌다 steam ((food)) for the first time
■—갈이 〔農〕 a first [primary] plowing —김 〔農〕 primary rough weeding —빨래 a rough washing —일 spadework; preliminary work —칠 (a) rough coating; an undercoat; the first [ground] coat; 〔建〕 a primary coat : 애벌칠을 하다 give (the wall) a first coat

애벌레 〔昆〕 a larva ((*pl*. -vae)); a green caterpillar; a grub

애별리고 愛別離苦 〔佛敎〕 the anguish of parting from *one's* loved person

애사 哀史 a sad [tragic, pathetic] story [history]

애사 愛社 —**애사하다** be loyal to *one's* company; love *one's* company
■—심[정신] loyalty [devotion] to *one's* company; company loyalty : 그는 애사심이 강하다 He devotes himself to his company.

애살스럽다 mean and stingy; penny-pinching

애서 愛書 love of books; bibliophilism ■—가 a book lover; a bibliophile; a lover of books

애서다 〈임신하다〉 get with child; become pregnant [impregnated]; conceive

애석 哀惜 〈슬픔〉 lamentation; grief; sorrow; 〈유감스러운 일〉 pity; 〈서운함〉 regret
—**애석하다** 〈슬프다〉 sad; sorrowful; mourn over [lament] ((*sb's* death)); doleful; plaintive; 〈유감스럽다〉 pitiful; 〈서운하다〉 regrettable
♦애석한 일 a matter of sadness [to be regretted]; a grief / 애석한 표정으로 with a sad look; with a regretful glance / 애석하게도 regretfully; to *one's* regret / 애석해 하다 〈슬퍼하다〉 grieve [sorrow] ((over *sb's* death)); 〈서운해 하다〉 regret
▶그건 애석한 일이다 It's too bad. ⇒ It's a pity.
▶그녀는 애석하게도 낙선했다 To our regret, she was defeated in the election.
▶그 평화주의자의 비보를 접하며 애석한 마음을 누를 길이 없다 The news of the pacifist's death filled me with grief.

애소 哀訴 〈슬픈 호소〉 an appeal ((to *sb*)); an entreaty; a petition
—**애소하다** appeal((*to sb*)); entreat ((*sb* to do)); make an appeal ((to)); implore; petition

애송 愛誦 love of reading a poem ; reciting with pleasure
—**애송하다** love to read [recite] a poem; read [recite] with pleasure
▶그녀는 워즈워스의 시를 애송한다 She loves to recite [read] Wordsworth's poems.
■—시 *one's* favorite poem —시집 a collection [an anthology] of *one's* favorite poems

애송이 a very young [a new] person; a green [raw] youth; (口) 〈미숙련자〉 a greenhorn; a novice ■—기자 a cub reporter

애수 哀愁 sadness; sorrow; grief
♦애수에 찬 얼굴 a sorrowful face / 애수를 느끼다 feel sad [sorrow] / 애수를 자아내다 make *sb* feel sad; induce sadness in *sb* / 애수에 잠기다 be merged in a sentiment of sadness
▶우리는 가을에는 곧잘 애수를 느낀다 We often feel sad in autumn.
▶바이올린의 높은 가락이 애수를 자아냈다 The high-pitched tune of the violin made us feel sad.

애순 —筍 young buds; fresh [tender] shoots; sprouts

애써 with effort; laboriously; hard; as much [far] as possible
♦애써 번 돈 hard-earned money / 애써 일찍 자다 go to bed as early as possible
▶나는 애써 평정을 가장했다 I tried to look calm.
▶나는 애써 냉정하려고 했다 I made an effort [strove] to compose myself.
▶그는 병약해서 애써 일하지 않도록 하고 있다 He doesn't work more than he can help, as he is weak.
▶아내는 양친을 모시느라 애써 노력했다 My wife attended to my parents as much as she could.

애쓰다 try ((to do)); make an effort [efforts] ((to do)); exert *oneself* ((to do)); endeavor; strive; take pains [trouble] ((to do)); 〈돕다〉 render assistance [service] ((to)); 〈마음 쓰다〉 take care to ((do)); be careful to ((do))
♦애쓰지 않고 without trouble [effort]; easily / 애쓴 보람이 없다 labor in vain [for nothing]; make vain [fruitless] efforts / 나라를 위해 애쓰다 render services to the state / 문제를 풀려고 애쓰다 set *oneself* to solve a problem
▶내게는 애쓴 보람이 있었다 My pains have been rewarded.
▶애쓴 보람이 없었다 My labors were fruitless [unavailing].
▶나는 웃지 않으려고 애썼다 I tried not to laugh.
▶그가 애써준 덕택에 나는 파산을 면했다 Thanks to his efforts, I was saved from bankruptcy.
▶그녀는 남편을 금연케 하려고 애썼다 She tried to make her husband give up [quit, abstain from] smoking. ⇒ She tried to cure [break] her husband of the habit of smoking.

애연가 愛煙家 a habitual [regular] smoker; a heavy smoker ▶그는 애연가다 He is a heavy [habitual] smoker. ⇒ He is addicted to smoking.

애오라지 〈부족하나마 겨우〉 in some degree; to some extent; more or less; somewhat; 〈오로지〉 solely; exclusively

애옥살이 〈고생스런 살림〉 a poor household; hard [poor] living
—**애옥살이하다** make a poor living; live in sad [pinching] poverty

애옥하다 〈살림이 구차하다〉 poor; poverty-stricken; indigent

애완 愛玩 ♦애완견 a pet dog
—**애완하다** pet ((a dog)); fondle; make a pet of; prize; value; treasure
▶그녀는 앵무새를 애완하고 있다 She keeps a parrot as a pet.
▶그는 고려 자기를 애완한다 He treasures

Koryŏ porcelain.
■—가 a lover; 〈동식물의〉 a fancier —동물 a pet (animal) —물 a cherished [prized] article

애욕 愛慾 love (and lust); (sexual) passion; sexual desire; lust
♦ 애욕이 원인이 된 범죄 a crime of passion / 애욕에 빠지다 give *oneself* up to passion
▶ 그 여자는 애욕의 노예가 되었다 She has become a slave to passion [fallen a prey to passion].

애용 愛用 *one's* favorite use; habitual use
—애용하다 use *sth* habitually [regularly]; make habitual use of; patronize
♦ 애용하는 카메라 a camera for 《*one's*》 personal use; *one's* favorite camera / 애용하는 *one's* favorite 《fountain pen》; *one's* beloved 《pipe》 / 국산품을 애용하다 use [buy] home-made articles
▶ 이것은 내가 애용하는 사전이다 This is my favorite dictionary. ⇌ I use this dictionary constantly.
▶ 수입품을 애용하는 젊은이가 많다 A lot of young people prefer imported goods.
▶ 좀더 국산품을 애용해야 한다 We should buy more domestic products.
■—자[가] a habitual [regular] user; a patron: 수면제 애용자 a chronic user of sleeping pills

애원 哀願 (an) entreaty; a plea; an appeal; supplication
—애원하다 implore [entreat] 《*sb* to do》; make a (humble) petition 《to *sb*》; appeal 《to *sb* for mercy》; beg 《for》; supplicate 《to *sb*, for *sth*》
♦ 애원하는 눈으로 보다 give *sb* a pleading [an appealing] look / 도와달라고 애원하다 appeal [implore] *sb* to help 《*one*》
▶ 그는 아버지에게 재정적 원조를 애원했다 He appealed to his father financial help.
▶ 그녀는 우리에게 그를 처벌하지 말아 달라고 애원했다 She begged us not to punish him.
■—자 an implorer; a supplicant

애육하다 愛育— bring up [nurse, foster] with tender care; coddle up
▶ 그들은 외아들을 애육했다 They brought up their only son with tender care and affection

애음 愛飲 drink habitually ⇨ 애주
■—가(家) ⇨ 애주(~가)

애인 愛人 〈남자〉 a lover; a boyfriend 〈여자〉 a love; 〈口〉 *one's* (best) girl; 〈남녀공용〉 a sweetheart; 《美》 *one's* steady
♦ 그의 애인 his love / 한 쌍의 애인 a pair of lovers / 애인이 있다 have a lover [ladylove] / 애인이 생기다 get a girlfriend
▶ 그녀가 그의 애인이니? Is she his love [girlfriend]?
▶ 한 쌍의 젊은 애인들이 손에 손을 잡고 걸어갔다 A pair of young lovers walked hand in hand.

애자 哀子 I, the chief mourner
애자 愛子 *one's* dear [beloved] son [child]
애자 碍子·礙子 〔電〕 an insulator
애잔하다 1 〈아주 약하다〉 weak; delicate; feeble; fragile; frail
2 〈애처롭다〉 touching; pathetic; plaintive

애장 愛藏 —애장하다 treasure; cherish
♦ 애장하는 고미술 *one's* treasured antique
■—본 *one's* cherished book

애저 —豬 a piglet; a pigling
■—구이 roast of suckling pig; grilled piglet

애절하다 哀切— pathetic; plaintive; mournful; sorrowful; sad
♦ 애절한 장면 a pathetic scene / 애절하기 그지없는 이야기 a most pathetic story

애정 哀情 pity; sadness; grief
♦ 애정을 느끼다 feel sad / 애정을 자아내다 excite *one's* pity [sympathy]

애정 愛情 (a) love 《for, of》; 〈지속적인 사랑〉 (an) affection 《for》; 〈애착〉 an attachment 《to, for》; devotion; 〈동정심〉 pity; compassion; sympathy
♦ 애정생활 *one's* love life / 애정없는 결혼 a loveless marriage / 애정이 깊은 사람 a person of deep affections / 따뜻한[열렬한] 애정 warm [strong] affection / 애정어린 말 affectionate words / 애정있는 affectionate; loving; warmhearted / 애정이 없는 loveless; cold-hearted; unfeeling / 애정에 굶주린 love-starved 《children》 / 애정을 품다[갖다] be fond 《of》; have [cherish] affection 《for》; feel affection 《toward》 / 애정을 쏟다 give *sb* great affection
▶ 한국 사람은 자연에 대해 깊은 애정을 가지고 있다 The Korean have a deep love for [of] nature.
▶ 그는 애인에게 열렬한 애정을 품고 있었다 He had a burning love for his girlfriend. ⇌ He loved his girlfriend passionately.
▶ 그녀는 그의 애정어린 편지[말]에 마음이 움직였다 She was moved by his affectionate letter [words].
▶ 그녀는 애정없는 결혼을 청산했다 She dissolved her loveless marriage.
▶ 많은 어머니들은 자기 자식들에게 깊은 애정을 품고 있다 Most mothers feel deep affection for [toward] their children.

애제자 愛弟子 *one's* favorite pupil; *one's* beloved student

애조 哀調 〈슬픈 가락〉 plaintive strains [notes]; sad [sorrowful] tone; a sad melody
♦ 애조띤 노래 a sad song [piece]; a plaintive melody; an elegy / 애조띤 doleful; mournful; plaintive; wailful; elegiac

애조 愛鳥 *one's* pet bird ■—가(家) a bird fancier [lover]

애족 愛族 love of *one's* people [nation]
—애족하다 love *one's* people
■ 애국— love of *one's* country and people

애주 愛酒 habitual drinking; love of wine [liquor] —애주하다 drink liquor habitually; be fond of drinking
■—가 a habitual [regular] drinker

애증 愛憎 love and hatred [hate]
♦ 애증이 뒤얽힌 관계 a love-hate relations / 애증의 감정이 강하다 have a strong partiality; be too passionate

애지중지 愛之重之 valuing *sth* highly; dotingness

—애지중지하다 treasure; prize; cherish; set great value on; think [make] much of; 〈귀여워하다〉 coddle 《a child》; lavish love 《on》; fondle
♦ 애지중지하는 골동품 one's prized curio / 애지중지하는 딸 one's loving [favorite] daughter / 애지중지하는 것 a treasure / 보석을 애지중지하다 treasure jewels / 손자를 애지중지하다 love one's grandchild as the apple of the eye

애착 愛着 attachment; affection; love; devotion
♦ 자녀에 대한 애착 attachment to one's children / 애착을 느[갖]다 become attached 《to》; form an attachment to [for]
▶ 나는 그 여자에게 애착을 느끼게 되었다 I become attached to her.
▶ 그는 고향산천에 애착을 느끼고 있다 He is attached to the rivers and mountains of his hometown.
—애착하다 attach oneself 《to》

애창 愛唱 —애창하다 love to sing 《a song》
■ —가(歌) one's favorite song : 그는 민요를 애창한다 He loves to sing folk songs.

애창곡집 愛唱曲集 a collection of popular songs; a songbook

애채 a newly sprouted branch of a tree; a shoot; a sprout ♦ 애채가 나다 《a tree》 put out new shoots

애처 愛妻 one's (beloved [dear]) wife
■ —가 a devoted [an uxorious] husband : 그는 애처가다 He is a devoted husband.

애처롭다 pitiful; touching; pathetic; sad; plaintive; dolorous
♦ 애처로운 이야기 a pathetic [touching] story / 애처로운 처지 a pitiable situation / 애처롭게 여기다 pity sb; feel pity for sb
♦ 아이들은 애처로울 정도로 야위었다 The children are pitiably [miserably] thin.

애첩 愛妾 one's (favorite) concubine; one's mistress

애초 the beginning; the very first; the outset [start]
♦ 애초 예산 the original budget / 애초의 계획 the original plan / 애초의 목적 the primary object / 애초의 first; primary / 〈원래의〉 original / 애초에 in [at] the beginning; at the (very) outset / 애초에는 at first; 〈본래의〉 originally / 애초부터 from [at, on] scratch; from the first [beginning, start]
▶ 우리는 애초의 목표를 달성할 수가 없었다 We could not achieve our original goal.

애칭 愛稱 a term of endearment; a pet [an affectionate] name
♦ 애칭으로 부르다 call sb by 《his》 pet name
▶ 베시는 엘리자베스의 애칭이다 Bessie is a nickname for Elizabeth.
▶ 톰은 토머스의 애칭이다 Tom is a term of endearment for Thomas.

애타 愛他 〈이타〉 altruism ♦ 애타적인 altruistic ■ —심 altruism; an altruistic spirit —주의 altruism —주의자 an altruist

애타다 be anxious [worried] 《about, for》; be nervous 《about》; be in suspense

♦ 애타는 모습 worried looks / 애타게 그리다 burn with love 《for》; long for / 아기의 병이 낫지 않아서 애타다 be in anguish on account of one's child's protracted sickness
▶ 누이의 귀가 시간이 늦자 어머니는 애타셨다 My sister was late coming home and my mother was worried about her.
▶ 그는 일이 뜻대로 되지 않아 애탔다 He was all hot and bothered that things didn't turn out the way he wanted.

애태우다 〈남을〉 bother; worry; fidget; fret sb's heart; cause sb anxiety; 〈자기에 대해〉 worry oneself 《about》; be anxious 《about》; bother oneself 《about》; fidget [jitter] 《about》
♦ 부모를 애태우다 come one's parents anxiety; bother one's parents / 아무가 돌아오기를 애태우며 기다리다 wait in anxious suspense for sb's arrival
▶ 동수의 병은 그의 양친을 애태웠다 Dong-soo's illness caused his parents great anxiety.

애통 哀痛 〈슬픔〉 grief; sorrow; sadness; 〈비탄〉 lament; lamentation
♦ 애통터지다 be quite worried; be very anxious 《about》
—애통하다 grieve 《at, over》; be [feel] sad 《at》; be [feel] sorrowful; deplore; lament; mourn 《for, over》
♦ 애통한 나머지 in the excess of one's grief
▶ 숙희는 어머니의 죽음을 애통해 하고 있다 Suk-hi mourns for her dead mother.
▶ 애통하게도 그의 아버지는 고기잡이를 나간 후 돌아오지 않았다 Sad to say his father went fishing never to return.

애틋하다 1 〈애가 타는 듯하다〉 anxious; worried; nervous; troubled
♦ 애틋한 사랑을 고백하다 confess one's affectionate love
2 〈애석하다〉 regrettable; pitiful; deplorable
▶ 우리 모교가 폐교되었다니 참으로 애틋하다 It is greatly regrettable that our old school was closed.
3 〈정을 끄는 맛이 있다〉 lovable; affectionate; dear
♦ 애틋한 정 tender [deep] affection

애티 childishness
♦ 애티 나는 childlike; juvenile / 애티가 흐르다 be childlike; look childish / 애티를 벗다 leave childhood behind; grow up
▶ 그 소년은 애티를 벗었다 The boy in him has died.

애틀랜타 〈미국 조지아 주의 도시〉 Atlanta (▶1996년 올림픽 대회 개최지)

애팔래치아산맥 —山脈 〈미국 동부에 있는 산맥〉 Appalachian Mountains

애프터서비스 after-sales (service)

애플파이 an apple pie

애해 Well!; Ha(h)!; Eh!; Pshaw!; Oh yeah!

애햄 ahem; hem —애햄하다 hem; clear one's throat

애향 愛鄕 loving one's hometown [birthplace]
—애향하다 love one's native place [hometown] ■ —심 love of one's native place [hometown]

애호 愛好 love 《for, of》; a liking 《for》; fondness 《for》
  ♦ 평화애호국민 a peace-loving nation
  ―애호하다 love; be fond of; like; have a fancy [liking] for; be devoted of
  ♦ 애호받다 be beloved 《by》
  ▶ 그는 음악[낚시]을 애호한다 He is fond [a lover] of music [fishing]. ⇌ He is devoted to music [fishing].
애호 愛護 〈보호〉 protection; preservation; conservation; 〈돌보기〉 kind(ly) treatment; tender care
  ♦ 동물 애호 정신 kindness to animals / 동물애호협회 the Society for the Prevention of Cruelty to Animals (略 S.P.C.A.)
  ―애호하다 protect; preserve; conserve; treat 《an animal》 kindly; be kind to 《an animal》; cherish; love and protect; take care of
애호가 愛好家 a lover 《of literature》; 〈동식물 등의〉 a fancier 〈예술 등의〉 a devotee; a dilettante 《pl. ~s, -ti》; 〈열광자〉 an enthusiast; a fan; a maniac
  ■ 야구[영화]― a baseball [movie] fan 연극― a theatergoer; a playgoer 음악― a lover of music
애호박 a young pumpkin
애화 哀話 〈슬픈 이야기〉 a sad [pathetic] story [episode]; a tragic tale
애환 哀歡 joys and sorrows
  ♦ 인생의 애환 the joys and sorrows of life
애휼 愛恤 pity; charity; beneficence
  ―애휼하다 pity and help; give to charity
액 厄 〈사나운 운수〉 evil fortune; an evil; ill [bad] luck; a misfortune; a disaster
  ♦ 액을 막다 ward off evil fortune; protect *sb* from [against] evils / 액을 면하다 escape the disaster / 액을 쫓아내다 exorcise; drive out an evil
  ▶ 그들은 액을 면하기 위해 이런 일을 한다 They do such things to avoid bad luck.
액 液 〈액체〉 liquid; 〈유동체〉 fluid; 〈액즙〉 juice; 〈수액〉 sap; 〈분비액〉 secretion; 〈용액〉 a solution
-액 額 〈분량〉 a quantity; a volume; 〈금액〉 an amount; a sum
  ♦ 소액 지폐 a note of a small denomination / 생산액 the amount of production; the volume of manufacture / 거액에 달하다 reach a colossal amount
  ▶ 손해액은 5천만원이다 The damage amounts to fifty million won.
액년 厄年 an unlucky [a bad, an evil] year; 〈나이의〉 a climacteric [critical] age
액달 厄― an unlucky [a bad, an evil, a critical] month
액땜 厄― an escape from a worse calamity
  ♦ 액땜으로 여기고 참다 bear [a misfortune] as the price for the escape from worse evils
  ―액땜하다 forestall a disaster with a lesser sacrifice
액량 液量 liquid quantity [measure]
액막이 厄― driving off evils; exorcism; warding off evil; preventing misfortune ―액막이하다 exorcise; ward off [prevent] evil [misfortune]
  ▶ 이 부적을 지니고 있으면 액막이가 된다 This charm will protect you from evil.
  ■ ―굿 an exorcism (usually held in the beginning of the year) ―부적 an amulet [a charm] against evil
액면 額面 1 〈증권·공채 등의 권면(卷面)〉 face value; (nominal) par; a denomination
  ♦ 액면 이상으로[이하로] above [below] par; at a premium [discount] / 액면에 달하다 reach par
  2 〈외양〉 a mere outlook
  ♦ 소문을 액면대로 받아들이다 take [accept] a rumor at face value
  ▶ 그는 그녀의 말을 액면대로 받아들였다 He took her at her word.
  ▶ 그의 말은 액면대로 받아들일 수 없다 You'd better discount his story.
  ■ ―가격 face value; par value : 액면가격으로 at par ―상환 redemption at par value
액모 腋毛 〈겨드랑이 털〉 hairs of the armpit
액사 縊死 〈목매어 죽음〉 death [suicide] by hanging *oneself*
액상 液狀 a liquid state
  ♦ 액상의 liquid; in liquid form
액세서리 accessories; accessaries; 〈보석류의 장신구〉 jewelry

> 解說 (1) 우리는 장신구를「액세서리」라고 말하지만 영어의 ***accessory***는 모자, 핸드백, 장갑, 스카프, 손수건 등을 가리키며 그 범위가 우리말의 「액세서리」와는 다르다.
> (2) 영어에서 귀고리, 목걸이 등 보석류의 장신구는 ***jewelry***라고 한다.

  ♦ 액세서리를 달다 wear accessories
  ▶ 그녀는 액세서리를 하고 있다 She is wearing accessories.
액셀러레이터 〈가속 페달〉 an accelerator (pedal)
  ♦ 액셀러레이터를 밟다 step [press] on the accelerator; press [tread] on the gas / 액셀러레이터를 떼다 release the accelerator
액션 action ■ ―드라마[영화] an action drama [film] ―페인팅 action painting (▶추상화의 일종)
액수 額數 〈금액〉 a sum; an amount 《of money》
  ♦ 많은[적은] 액수 a large [small] amount 《of money》 / 막대한 액수에 달하다 amount [come up] to enormous figures
  ▶ 피해액수는 20억원에 달한다 The damage amounts to two billion won.
액운 厄運 〈불운〉 (a) misfortune; adverse [bad] fortune; a bad luck; a hapless fate; an evil [untoward, adverse] fate
  ♦ 액운을 물리치다 drive out an evil fate
액월 厄月 an unlucky month ⇨ 액달
액일 厄日 〈운수 사나운 날〉 an evil [unlucky] day; a day when one might encounter with an evil spirit
  ▶ 어제는 나의 액일이었다 I had a very unlucky day yesterday. ⇌ Yesterday was an unlucky day for me.

액자 額子 a (picture) frame
♦액자에 끼우다 set [put] (a picture) in frame; frame (a picture)
액자 額字 letters written on a tablet
액정 液晶 〔化〕 a liquid crystal
■ ―폴리머 liquid crystalline polymer ―표시 liquid crystal display (略 LCD): 액정 표시 텔레비전 LCD television
액체 液體 liquid (body); fluid
■ ―공기[암모니아] liquid air [ammonia] ―동력학 ⇨ 유체(~역학) ―비중계 a hydrometer; an areometer; a spindle ―비중 측정법 hydrometry; areometry ―산소[수소, 질소] liquid oxygen [hydrogen, nitrogen] ―압력 hydraulic pressure ―연료 liquid fuel ―열량계 [온도계] a liquid calorimeter [thermometer] ―정역학(靜力學) hydrostatics ―탄산 liquid carbon dioxide
액화 液化 liquefaction
―액화하다 be liquefied; liquefy; 〈조해(潮解)하다〉〔化〕 deliquesce
♦액화되다 be liquefied
♦석탄― liquefaction of coal ■ ―가스 liquefied [liquid] gas ―기 a liquefier ―산소 liquefied oxygen ―석유가스 liquefied petroleum gas (略 LPG) ―온도 the temperature of liquefaction ―제(劑) liquefacient ―천연가스 liquefied natural gas (略 LNG)
앤더슨 〈미국의 소설가〉 Anderson, Sherwood (1876-1941)
앤저스조약 ―條約 ANZUS [〈Australia, New Zealand and the United States Pact〉]
앤티노크제 ―劑 〈내폭제(耐爆劑)〉 antiknock (agent)
■ ―가솔린 antiknock gasoline ―제(劑) an antiknock (agent)
앨라배마 〈미국의 주〉 Alabama (略 Ala., AL)
♦앨라배마의 Alabaman; Alabamian
■ ―사람 an Alabaman; an Alabamian
앨범 an album

〔解說〕 album이란 말에는 사진첩 뿐만 아니라 우표, 서명, 신문 스크랩, 한 사람의 작품이나 레코드, 졸업기념책, 방명록 등도 포함된다.

♦레코드 앨범 an album / 〈미국의 대학, 고교의〉 졸업 앨범 a yearbook / 앨범에 붙이다[끼우다] paste [slip] (a picture) in an album
▶ 그녀의 포크송 앨범은 다음 달에 판매된다 Her album of folk songs will be out next month.
▶ 이 노래는 「한국의 사계절」이라는 그의 앨범중의 한 곡이다 This is one of the songs on his album titled "The four seasons in Korea."
■사진[우표]― a photo (graphic) [stamp] album
앰풀 〈주사약 1회 분량의 용기〉 an ampul(e); an ampoule
앰플리파이어 〈증폭기〉 an amplifier
♦앰플리파이어 내장 레코드 플레이어 a record player with a built-in amplifier
앳되다 young; childish; boyish; green; innocent; puerile
♦나이보다 앳돼 보이다 look young for [younger than] one's age
▶ 너는 갓난아기처럼 앳되다 You're as innocent as a newborn babe.
앵¹ 〈날벌레가 나는 소리〉 humming buzzing; with a hum [buzz] ⇨ 왱 ―앵하다 buzz; bum; make a bumming sound
▶ 벌 한 마리가 내 귓가에서 앵하고 있다 A bee is buzzing around my ears.
앵² 〈불쾌할 때〉 Tut!; Shucks!; Phew!; Pshaw!; Fie!; Hang it all!
앵글 1 〈각·각도〉 an angle ♦45도 앵글 an angle of 45°
2 〈관점〉 ▶우리는 이 문제를 여러 앵글에서 고려해야 한다 We must consider this matter from various angles.
■카메라― a camera angle
앵글로색슨 an Anglo-Saxon
■ ―어[인(人)] Anglo-Saxon ―족 the Anglo-Saxons
앵돌아지다 become [get] sulky [cross, peevish]; sulk; pout; take the pet
♦앵돌아진 sullen; sulky; sour / 앵돌아져서 in a pet; be in the sulks
▶ 그 애는 제뜻대로 안된다고 앵돌아져 있다 The child has the sulks because things aren't going just as he expects.
앵두 a cherry ♦앵두같은 입술 cherry [rosy, red] lips / 앵두빛 pink; cerise ■ 〔植〕 a cherry (tree)
앵무 鸚鵡 〔鳥〕 a parrot ⇨ 앵무새 ―병 parrot fever; 〔醫〕 psittacosis
앵무새 鸚鵡― 〔鳥〕 a parrot; a cockatoo (pl. ~s) ♦앵무새처럼 남의 말을 흉내내다 repeat sb's words like a parrot; repeat [echo, mimic] another's words (mechanically); parrot sb's words
앵무조개 鸚鵡― a nautilus (pl. ~es, -tili)
앵앵 buzzing; humming; droning; with a buzzing [humming] sound; with a whiz [zoom] ―앵앵거리다[대다] buzz; hum; drone; make a humming sound
♦앵앵 거리고 있다 be buzzing [humming]
▶ 벌 한 마리가 내 귓가에서 앵앵거리고 있다 A bee is buzzing around my ears.
▶ 파리떼가 앵앵댄다 The flies are buzzing around [their wings).
앵초 櫻草 〔植〕a primrose
앵커 1 〈닻〉 an anchor
2 〈이어 달리기의 최종 주자〉 the anchor; the anchor (man) (on a relay race team)
3 〈뉴스 해설자〉 ♦앵커맨[우먼] 〔放〕 an anchor man [woman]
앵커리지 〈미국 알래스카 주의 도시〉 Anchorage
앵하다 chagrined; resentful; (feel) bitter
♦앵하게 느끼다 be [feel] chagrined at
야¹ 1 〈한정·강조〉 ▶너야 반대하지 않겠지 You won't object to it, will you?
▶ 결과야 어찌 되건 내가 알 바 아니다 I don't care for what may come of it.
▶ 건강을 잃고서야 건강의 고마움을 안다 You cannot appreciate the blessing of health until you lose it.
2 〈호칭〉 ▶ 애야 Buster!; My boy!

▶창수야 My dear Chang-soo!
야² 1〈놀람〉Oh!; Ah!; Oh my!; Dear me!; Wow!; Good gracious!; Good heavens!; Gosh!; (美俗) Gee!; Boy!
▶야, 이건 너무했다 By heavens! This is really too much!
▶야, 이거 재미있다 Why, this is quite interesting.
2〈호칭〉Hullo; Hello; Halloo; Hey (there); (美) Hi; I say
야 野〈들〉a field; 〈야당〉a party out of power; the Opposition (party); 〈민간〉being outside the government
♦야로 물러나다〈개인이〉go out of public office; retire into private life; 〈정당이〉go out of power
야간 夜間 night; nighttime
♦야간의 night; nocturnal / 야간에(는) at night; during the night; in the nighttime; 〈주간에 대해〉by night
▶미성년자는 야간에 그런 장소에서 일할 수 없다 A minor is not allowed to work in such a place at night.
■ㅡ근무 ➪ 야근 ㅡ당직 a night watch [duty] ㅡ비행 a night flight; night flying ㅡ시합[경기] a night game [match] ㅡ연습 a night practice [exercise] ㅡ열차 a night train ㅡ작업(자) a night shift ㅡ촬영 photographing at night; night photography ㅡ통행금지 (impose) a curfew ㅡ폭격 night bombing ㅡ학교 a night school
야간부 夜間部 the evening session of a school
ㅡ학생 a night-school student; a student in the evening session of a college
야경 夜景 a night view [scene]
▶홍콩의 야경은 장관이다 The night view of Hong Kong is wonderful.
야경 夜警 night watch; 〈사람〉a night watchman
♦야경(을) 돌다 make the round 《of a district》 at night; go on *one's* rounds at night / 야경(을) 서다 keep watch at night; stand [be] on night watch
■ㅡ꾼 a night watchman [watch]; a night watcher
야고보서 ㅡ書 〔聖〕(The General Epistle of St.) James (略 Jam.)
야곡 夜曲 〔樂〕a serenade＝소야곡
야광 夜光 noctilucence
♦야광의 noctilucent; noctilucous
■ㅡ도료 a luminous paint ㅡ시계 a luminous [glow] watch; a watch with a luminous [an illuminated] dial ㅡ주(珠) a gem that emits light at night ㅡ충(蟲) a noctiluca 《*pl*. ～s, -cae》
야구 野球 baseball; (口) ball
♦야구계의 스타 a star player in the baseball world / 야구 사상 최고의 유격수 the best shortstop in the history of baseball / 야구를 하다 play baseball / …과 야구 시합을 하다 play a baseball game with... / 야구 시합을 시청하다 enjoy a baseball game on television
■ㅡ어린이ㅡ〈빈터에서 하는〉sandlot baseball ㅡ프로ㅡ professional baseball ■ㅡ광〔팬〕a baseball fan ㅡ모(帽) a baseball cap ㅡ부 a baseball club ㅡ부 the president of a baseball club ㅡ선수 a baseball player; a baseballer ㅡ연맹 a baseball league ㅡ열 baseball fever; a mania for baseball ㅡ장 a baseball ground [field]; a ballpark ㅡ팀 a baseball [ball] team
야근 夜勤 night duty; night work; a night shift
▶한 달에 여러 번 야근을 한다 I take night duty [night shift] several times a month.
▶그는 오늘 야근이다 He is on duty tonight.
ㅡ야근하다 be on night work [shift]; take night duty
ㅡ수당 night-work allowance ㅡ시간 night shift; night-work hours ㅡ자 a night worker; (총칭) night shift
야금 冶金 metallurgy ■ㅡ학[술] metallurgy ㅡ학자 a metallurgist
야금 野禽 a wild fowl; a game bird
야금거리다 eat by bites
야금야금 little by little; bit by bit; by nips
♦야금야금 먹다 eat (a cake) bit by bit [little by little] / 야금야금 먹어 들어가다 encroach upon [make an inroad into] gradually
야긋야긋하다 notched; jagged; indented; have teeth
야기 夜氣 night air; the cool of the night
▶차가운 야기가 방으로 들어왔다 The cool of the night crept into the room.
▶야기는 몸에 좋지 않다 The night air isn't good for you.
야기부리다 complain aloud; make a noise [fuss] with dissatisfaction; give vent to *one's* dissatisfaction
▶그는 골이 나면 누구에게나 야기부린다 He works off his anger [bad temper] on everybody around him.
야기하다 惹起 cause; bring about [on]; give rise [birth, occasion] to (a trouble); lead to 《confusion》
▶그의 발언이 큰 논쟁을 야기했다 His words gave rise to a big controversy.
▶그 사건이 전쟁을 야기했다 The incident caused [brought about] the war.
▶전쟁은 재정 위기를 야기했다 The war brought about [on] a financial crisis.
야뇨증 夜尿症 〔醫〕 nocturnal enuresis; bed-wetting
야다하면 if there is no help for it; if compelled [forced]
야단 惹端 1〈소란·소동〉a clamor; an uproar; a row; a commotion; a tumult; a racket; a stir
♦야단이 나다 a commotion breaks out; a stir is created; be uproarious; be clamorous; be in commotion / 입장시키라고 야단이다 clamor for admission / 임금을 올리라고 야단이다 clamor for a higher wage; cry for a boost in pay / 시시한 일로 야단이다 make a great fuss about trifles; raise the wind over trifles
▶웬일로 이 야단이냐? What's all this noise?
▶왜 야단들이냐? What's the racket?
2〈질책〉(a) scolding; a chiding; a rebuke; a lecture; a nagging

♦야단 치다 scold; chide / 호되게 야단 치다 scold severely; give *sb* a good [sharp] scolding [sound rating] / 야단 맞다 be scolded [rebuked] 《by》; (美口) catch [get] it hot 《from》; catch [get] hell 《from》
▶ 그는 아들을 호되게 야단 쳤다 He heaped reproaches on his son.
▶ 지각하여 선생님께 야단 맞았다 The teacher gave me a sharp scolding for being late for school.
―야단하다 scold; chide; rebuke; give *sb* a scolding; have [call] *sb* on the carpet
3 〈곤란〉 a trouble; a difficulty, 〈곤경〉 a predicament; a quandary; a plight; a fix
♦야단나다 come to [reach] a nice [pretty] pass; get into trouble; get [be] in a fix
▶ 비가 쉬 오지 않으면 야단인데 If it doesn't rain soon, we'll be in a hell of a fix.
▶ 참, 야단났다 All the fat is in the fire. ⇒ Well, what a fine fix this is! ⇒ Things have come to a pretty pass! ⇒ Here's a pretty go!

야단법석 野壇法席 a boisterous merrymaking; an uproaring festivity; a great stir; a bustle; a racket; a spree; a fuss; a row
♦야단법석을 떨다 make a bustle; make a great stir [fuss]; kick up a row / 술 마시고 야단법석이다 have a hilarious time; hold high jinks; go on a spree
▶ 아무것도 아닌 일로 왜 이리 야단법석이냐? Why do you make such a fuss about [over, of] nothing? ⇒ What a lot of excitement over nothing!

야단스럽다 惹端— uproarious; noisy; clamorous; tumultuous 《crowd》; vociferous

야담 野談 an unofficial version of a historical tale ―가 a (professional) historical-story teller ―책 a historical-story book; a book of historical romances

야당 野黨 the opposition (party); a party out of power; a nongovernment party; the outs
♦야당의 공세 an offensive (move) taken by the outs against the government / (정당이) 야당으로 있다 be in opposition
■제1― the leading opposition; the second largest party ―기관지 the opposition organ ―당수 an opposition leader; the leader of the opposition ―연합 a combination of parties out of power; coalition between nongovernment parties ―의석 the opposition benches ―의 원 a member of the opposition ―통합 merger of the opposition parties

야독 夜讀 reading at night; night study
―야독하다 read in the night; study till late at night

야드 a yard (略 yd.) ―자 a yard measure; a yardstick ―파운드법 the yard-pound system

야들야들하다 smooth [soft] and shiny; tender; velvet(y); silky
♦야들야들한 가죽 supple leather / 야들야들한 살결 a silky smooth skin / 야들야들한 손 soft and delicate hands / 감촉이 야들야들하다 feel soft; be soft to the touch

야료 惹鬧 disturbing; interruption; heckling; catcalling; hooting; booing; jeering
▶ 그의 연설은 청중의 야료를 받았다 His speech was disturbed by the greet of boos and hisses from the audience.
▶ 그는 연설을 하려고 일어섰다가 청중의 야료로 물러났다 He stood up to speak but his audience cried [hissed] him down.
―야료하다 disturb; interrupt; obstruct; heckle; make sport [fun] of *sb*; hoot; catcall; jeer; boo

야릇하다 odd; queer; strange; peculiar; curious; mysterious
♦야릇한 꿈 a strange dream / 야릇한 친구 a queer fish [duck, guy] / 야릇한 운명의 장난으로 by the curious irony of fate / 야릇하게 굴다 behave oddly; be particular / 야릇한 경험을 하다 have an odd experience / 야릇한 기분이 들다 feel 《it》 strange; have a strange sensation
▶ 운명이란 참 야릇하다 Fate plays strange tricks.

야만 野蠻 savagery; savageness; barbarism; barbarity ▶ 전쟁은 야만 그 자체다 War is barbarism itself.
■―국 an uncivilized country; a savage country ―시대 the barbaric times [age]; barbarous days ―인 a barbarian; a savage; an uncivilized man; savage people

야만적 野蠻的 barbarous; savage; uncivilized
♦야만적 풍습 uncivilized manners; a barbaric custom / 야만적 행위 a barbarous act; (acts of) barbarity
▶ 그들은 아직도 야만적 생활을 하고 있다 They are still living in barbarism.
▶ 이런 야만적 풍습은 당장 없애야 한다 We must abolish such barbarism [a barbarous practice] at once.

야말로 the very; just; indeed; precisely; exactly; really
▶ 그야말로 적임자다 He's the right man (for it).
▶ 사자야말로 백수의 왕이다 The lion is indeed (the) king of beasts.
▶ 이거야말로 우리가 찾던 책이다 This is the very book that we have been looking for.
▶ 저야말로 용서를 빌어야겠습니다 It is I who must apologize.
▶ 지금이야말로 우리가 궐기할 때다 Now is the time for us to rouse ourselves to action.

야망 野望 (an) ambition; (an) aspiration
♦야망이 있는 ambitious; aspiring / 야망을 이루다 realize *one's* ambition / 야망을 품다 have [cherish, harbor] an ambition; aim high; aspire after greatness
▶ 그는 대정치가가 될 야망을 품었다 He had the high ambition to be a great statesman.
▶ 천하를 평정하겠다는 그의 야망은 실현[좌절]되었다 His ambition to conquer the whole country was realized [frustrated].

야맹증 夜盲症 night blindness; 〔醫〕 nyctalopia

야멸스럽다 cold; cold-hearted; hardhearted; heartless; inhuman; inhumane; inconsiderate; harsh; pitiless; merciless
♦야멸스런 행동 an inconsiderate action / 야멸스런 짓을 하다 behave callously [in a heartless manner] / 야멸스럽게 말하다 speak cru-

elly; say a harsh [mean] thing / 야멸스럽게 거절하다 give a point-blank refusal
▶ 넌 정말 야멸스럽구나 How inconsiderate you are! ⇒ How unkind of you!

야멸치다 cold-hearted
♦ 야멸치게 뿌리치다 reject [refuse] flatly

야무지다 hard; strong; tough; firm; solid
♦ 야무진 사람 a man of firm [strong] character / 야무진 성품 a stout-minded [hardheaded] man; a staunch character / 야무지게 묶다 tie tightly [fast]; fasten tight / 솜씨가 야무지다 be clever with *one's* hands; be dexterous; be defthanded
▶ 그는 체격이 야무지다 He has a well-built physique.
▶ 그는 야무진 데가 없다 He lacks firmness of character. ⇒ He has no backbone.

야물다 1 〈씨가익다〉 get [become, grow] ripe; ripen; mature ♦ 야문 씨앗 ripe seeds
2 ⇨ 야무지다

야바위 〈사기〉 trickery; swindle; imposture; fraud; deception; a hoax
♦ 야바위치다 cheat; deceive; swindle; take [let] *sb* in; bilk; play off a fraud《upon》; play a trick《upon》; practice an imposture《on》/ 야바위에 걸리다 be imposed upon; be cheated; be taken in; become a victim of a deception
▶ 그는 친구에게 30만원을 야바위당했다 He was swindled out of three hundred thousand won by his friend.
■—꾼 an impostor; a swindler; a cheat; a trickster

야박하다 野薄— unfeeling; heartless; coldhearted; stonehearted; pitiless
♦ 야박한 세상 a hard world (to live in); hard times / 야박한 말 unkind words; heartless speech;《say》harsh things
▶ 그녀는 친구에게 야박하게 굴었다 She acted cruelly toward(s) her friend. ⇒ She treated her friend cruelly.
▶ 그녀의 말은 야박하게 들렸다 Her words sounded unkind [cruel].

야반 夜半 midnight ⇨ 한밤중

야반도주 夜半逃走 run away under cover of night; flight by night;《英口》moonlight flit(ting)
▶ 그의 출국은 야반도주나 다름없었다 His departure from the country was the same as running away under cover of darkness [night].
—**야반도주하다** do a moonlight (flit); flee by night
▶ 그들은 집세도 물지 않고 야반도주했다 They did a midnight disappearing act [did a moonlight flit], leaving the rent unpaid.
—**자**《美口》a fly-by-night(er)

야밤중 夜—中 midnight ⇨ 한밤중

야번 夜番 〈일〉night watch; duty at night; 〈사람〉a night watchman; a night watcher ♦ 야번을 서다 keep night watch; be on duty at night

야비하다 野卑— vulgar; coarse; base; mean; low; unrefined; boorish; ill-mannered; gross
♦ 야비한 사람 a vulgar [coarse, low] person; a person without manners; 〈본데없는〉 an ill-bred person; 〈교양이 없는〉 an uncultured person / 야비한 말《use》vulgar [coarse, gross] language / 야비한 취미 unrefined [boorish, vulgar] taste / 야비한 태도 a boorish [low, coarse] manner
▶ 그는 말하는 것이 야비하다 He uses vulgar language. ⇒ His language is vulgar.

야사 野史 an unofficial [unauthorized] history [chronicle]

야산 野山 a hillock; a hill (on a plain)

야살 perverseness; peevishness; crabbedness; impertinence; impudence
♦ 야살 떨다[부리다] behave perversely; act cross; behave in a saucy manner
■—쟁이[이] a peevish [cross] fellow; a crab; a saucebox

야살스럽다 perverse; peevish; cross-grained; crabbed; impertinent; impudent; saucy ♦ 야살스런 여자 a brash and impertinent woman

야생 野生 wildness
♦ 야생의 wild; feral; savage; undomesticated; uncultivated / 야생마를 길들이다 tame a wild horse
—**야생하다** 〈식물이〉grow wild; 〈동물이〉live in the wild state
▶ 벼는 야생하지 않는다 Rice does not grow wild.
■—**동물** a wild [feral] animal;《총칭》wildlife
—**식물** a wild plant; a wilding

야선 野選 〔野〕 a fielder's choice ⇨ 야수(野手)〔~선택〕

야성 野性 wild nature
♦ 야성적인 wild; savage; rude; rough / 야성으로 돌아가다 revert to a wild state / 야성을 발휘하다 〈동물이〉run wild; 〈사람이〉give vent to *one's* savage instinct; commit barbarity
▶ 우리에 갇힌 늑대는 야성을 잃었다 The caged wolf has lost its wild nature.
▶ 그 남자에게는 야성적인 데가 있다 There is something rough [rude] about that man.
■—**미** unpolished beauty

야속하다 野俗— unkind; unfeeling; heartless; coldhearted; inhospitable; unsympathetic; pitiless
♦ 야속하게 굴다 be hard on *sb*; behave coldly [heartlessly]《towards》/ 야속하게 여기다 feel bitter《against *sb*》
▶ 그는 야속하게도 내 청을 들어주지 않았다 He was so unkind as to refuse my request.

야수 野手 〔野〕 a fielder ■—내— an infielder 외— an outfielder ■—선택 (be safe on) a fielder's choice

야수 野獸 a wild beast [animal]; beasts of the field
♦ 야수적 본능 a brutal instinct / 야수와 같은 사람 a brutal person; a brute of a man / 야수적인[같은] brutal; beastly; beastlike; bestial
■—**성** brutality; beastliness; brutal [bestial] nature : 야수성을 나타내다 show *one's* brutality —**파** 〔美術〕〈사람〉a fauvist, 〈주의〉fauvisme

야숙 野宿 camping(-out) ⇨ 노숙(露宿)

야스락거리다 talk glibly [eloquently, smooth-

야스퍼스 〈독일의 철학자〉 Jaspers, Karl (1883-1969)

야습 夜襲 a night attack [raid, assault]; a nocturnal assault; a surprise [sudden] attack by night
▶우리는 적에게 야습을 감행했다 We made a night attack on the enemy. ⇒ We made an attack on the enemy under cover of night.
―야습하다 make [attempt] a night attack 《on the enemy》; attack 《the enemy》 at night

야시(장) 夜市(場) a night market; a night fair

야식 夜食 a midnight meal [snack]; a late snack ◆야식을 먹다 take a midnight snack [meal] / 야식으로 라면을 먹다 have instant noodles for a midnight snack
―야식하다 take [have] a midnight snack [meal]

야심 夜深 being late at night
―야심하다 late at night ◆야심하도록 책을 읽다 read a book till midnight [far into the night]; burn [consume] the midnight oil / 야심할 때까지 일하다 work far into the night; work till late at night

야심 野心 1 〈야망〉 (an) ambition
◆야심이 있는 ambitious; designing; treacherous / 야심이 없는 unambitious; disinterested
▶그는 정치적 야심은 전연 없다 He has no political ambitions whatsoever.
▶그는 신진작가로서 야심만만하다 He is a rising [promising] novelist who is full of ambition.
▶그는 회장이 될 야심을 품고 있었다 He had designs on the president. ⇌ The presidency was his ambition.
▶그는 이 대륙을 걸어서 횡단한다는 야심적인 계획을 가지고 있다 He has an ambitious plan to walk across this continent.
2 〈몰래 품은 소망〉 an ill [a sinister] design; an intrigue
◆엉뚱한 야심 an inordinate ambition / 영토적 야심 a territorial ambition; territorial designs
▶그가 내 누이한테 친절한 것은 어떤 야심이 있어서가 아닐까 I am afraid he has some hidden purpose [ulterior motive] in being kind to my sister.
■―가 a man of ambition; an ambitious person; a highflier ―작 an ambitious work

야업 夜業 a night shift ⇨ 야간(~작업)

야영 野營 camping; camp-out; encampment; bivouac; 〈야영소〉 a camp
―야영하다 camp (out); make [pitch, go into] camp; encamp; bivouac ▶그들은 골짜기에서 야영했다 They encamped in the valley.
―지[장] a camp, a campground; a campsite; a camping ground [site]; a bivouac

야옹 mewing; meowing ◆야옹 하고 울다 mew; meow; miaow

야외 野外 〈들〉 the field; 〈옥외〉 the open air; 〈교외〉 the outskirts 《of a town》; the suburbs 《of a city》
◆야외의 field; open-air; outdoor / 야외로 나가다 go out into the field 《to observe wild animals》 / 야외에서 점심을 먹다 have lunch out of doors [in the open air]; have lunch outdoors [outside]
▶아이들은 야외에서 놀기를 좋아한다 Children like to play in the open (air).
▶선생님은 선사시대의 마을을 발굴하느라 야외에서 여름을 보냈다 The teacher spent his summer in the field, excavating the prehistoric village.
■―강연 a field [an open-air] lecture ―경기 field games ―극 an outdoor play; a pageant ―극장 an open-air [outdoor] theater ―사생 outdoor sketching ―연설 an outdoor speech ―연습 field exercises; field work ―연주회 an open-air concert ―운동 outdoor sports ―작업 field work; field study ―촬영 location: 야외촬영 중이다 be on location

야운데 〈카메룬의 수도〉 Yaoundé

야위다 become thin; be worn out; lose (one's) weight ◆야윈 얼굴 a haggard face / 고통으로 야위다 be careworn / 병으로 야위다 become worn out from illness

야유 野遊 a picnic; an outing ■―회 a picnic party [group]

야유 揶揄 banter; raillery; 〈극장 등에서의〉 catcalling; 〈의회에서의〉 heckling
▶그의 말에 야유가 터져 나왔다 His remark was greeted by boos and hisses.
▶그들은 연사에게 야유를 보냈다 They heckled [jeered at] the speaker.
▶야유가 심해서 그의 연설은 아무도 듣지 못했다 There was so much hooting and jeering that no one could hear his speech.
―야유하다 make sport [fun] of; tease; banter; ridicule; heckle; hoot [catcall, boo] 《at》 ◆세상을 야유하는 경구 an epigram that makes fun of society / 야유하여 강단에서 물러나게 하다 boo sb out of the platform

야음 夜陰 darkness of the night
◆야음을 틈타 under cover of darkness [night]; under the screen [cloak] of night; taking advantage [availing oneself] of darkness

야인 野人 1 〈시골 사람〉 a rustic; a boor; a countryman
2 〈예절없는 사람〉 an uncouth person
3 〈재야의 사람〉 a private citizen
◆야인으로 있다 be in private life; remain out of public office; be out of office [power]
▶그는 정계에서 은퇴한 후에는 일개 야인으로 지냈다 After he retired from politics, he lived as a private citizen.

야자 椰子 1 ⇨ 야자나무 2 〈열매〉 a coconut ■―유(油) palm [coconut] oil
야자나무 椰子― 〈植〉 a palm (tree); a palmetto (pl. ~s, -es)

야적 野積 open-air storage (of freight [goods]) ―야적하다 pile up 《coal》 out in the open ■―장(場) an open-air yard

야전 夜戰 night operations [battles] ―야전하다 engage in night operations

야전 野戰 field operations [battles]; open [field] warfare; an open battle
―야전하다 engage in field warfare

야군 ━軍 a field army ━병원 a field hospital; a clearing hospital; an ambulance ━우체국 a field post office ━우편[전화, 통신] the field post [telephone, telegraph] ━잠바 a field jacket ━장비 field equipment ━포병중대 a field battery

야조 野鳥 a wild bird; 《총칭》 wild fowl

야죽거리다 make provocative ⇨ 이기죽거리다

야차 夜叉 《산》 a yaksa; a (female) demon; a (she-)devil ▶ 보살같은 얼굴에 야차같은 마음 An angel without, a devil within.

야찬 夜餐 〈밤참〉 a midnight [late-night] snack [meal] ⇨ 야식

야채 野菜 (green) vegetables; greens; greenstuff; 〈시판용의〉 《美》 garden truck
♦ 야채를 가꾸다[재배하다] grow [raise] vegetables; grow garden truck
━가게 a greengrocery ━밭 〈가정의〉 a kitchen [vegetable] garden; 〈대규모의〉 《美》 a truck farm; 《英》 a market garden ━샐러드 [수프] vegetable salad [soup] ━요리 a vegetable [vegetarian] dish ━장수 a greengrocer; 〈행상〉 a vegetable peddler

야청 ━靑 a dark blue colo(u)r

야초 野草 wild grass

야취 野趣 rural [rustic] beauty; a rural air; rusticity ♦ 야취를 띤 rural; rustic; pastoral

야크 〔動〕 a yak 《pl. ~s, ~》

야트막하다 very shallow

야틈하다 somewhat [rather] shallow; shallowish ♦ 야틈한 개울[접시] a shallowish stream [dish]

야포 野砲 a field gun; 《총칭》 field artillery
━대 a field artillery corps; a field battery 《중대》

야하다 野━ showy; gaudy; loud 《color》; noisy 《color, necktie》; flashy
♦ 야한 장식품 gaudy decorations / 화장이 야한 여자 a woman wearing heavy makeup / 야한 농담을 하다 make an excessive joke / 야하게 차려 입다 be gaudily [loudly, flashily] dressed
▶ 이 색깔은 야하다 This color is gaudy [loud].
▶ 그녀는 화장이 너무 야하다 She uses too much makeup.

야학 夜學 an evening [a night] class 《of a night school》 ♦ 야학에 다니다 attend [go to] an evening [a night] school [class]
━교 an evening [a night] school ━생 an evening [a night] school student

야합 野合 1 〈남녀간의 사통〉 an illicit union [connection]; 〈공모〉 collusion; conspiracy
━야합하다 contract an illicit intimacy 《with》; misconduct *oneself* 《with》; 〈공모하다〉 plot together; conspire 《with》
♦ 야합한 부부 a common-law couple / 야합하여 in collusion [conspiracy, league] 《with》 / 야합하여 부부가 되다 marry [jump] over the broomstick
2 〈몰래 관계를 맺음〉 ▶ 두 당은 야합한 게 틀림없다 There must be some collusive agreement between the two parties.

야행 夜行 night [nocturnal] traveling; traveling by night ━야행하다 travel [go] by night

야행성 夜行性 〔動〕 the nocturnal habits 《of an animal》 ♦ 야행성의 nocturnal
━동물 a nocturnal animal

야화 夜話 an evening story

야화 野火 a field [bush] fire; a prairie fire

야화 野花 a wild [field] flower

야화 野話 a folk tale [story]

야회 夜會 an evening party; a soiree; 〈무도회〉 a ball ━복 〈남녀의〉 (an) evening dress; (a) party dress; 〈남자의〉 a dress coat [suit]; 〈여자의〉 an evening gown; a dress suit

약 葯 〔植〕 an anther=꽃밥

약 藥 1 〈의약〉 (a) medicine; a remedy; a drug; 《口》 a physic; 〈약제〉 a medical substance; a pharmaceutical; a medicament

┌─────────────────────────────┐
│ **解說** **drug**는 최근에는 「마약」의 뜻으로 쓰이 │
│ 는 일이 많다. 약의 형태에 따라서 tablet (정 │
│ 제), pill (알약), capsule (교갑), powdered │
│ medicine (가루약), liquid medicine (물약) │
│ 등으로 부른다. │
└─────────────────────────────┘

♦ 내복 약 an internal medicine / 바르는 약 an ointment / 배 아픈 데 먹는 약 a medicine for stomachache / 덴 데 바르는 약 a remedy for burns / 약(의) 성분 medicinal properties / 약의 효능 the virtue(s) of a medicine [remedy] / 약을 먹이다 administer [give] a medicine 《to a patient》 / 약을 바르다 apply an ointment 《to》 / 약을 복용하다 take medicine [a drug]
▶ 이틀치 약을 드리겠습니다 I will give you medicine for two days.
▶ 이 약을 한 첩 드시면 아픈 것이 금방 가실 겁니다 A dose of this medicine will soon cure your sickness.
▶ 이 약은 두통에 잘 듣는다 This medicine is effective for headache.
▶ 이 약은 너무 써서 못 먹겠다 This medicine is too bitter for me to take.
▶ 이 약은 전혀 효과가 없다 This medicine does not work at all.
▶ 식사 30분 전에 이 약을 드십시오 Take this medicine 30 minutes before meals.
▶ 나는 이 약 저 약 다 먹어 보았다 I tried all sorts of drugs.
2 〈화학 약품〉 chemicals; chemical preparations; pharmaceuticals
♦ 광내는 약 polishing wax [material]; polish
▶ 이 전지는 약이 다 됐다 This battery is dead.
3 〈유익한 것〉 benefit; good; remedy
▶ 모르는 게 약이다 《속담》 Ignorance is bliss.
▶ 불면증에는 운동이 약이다 Exercise is good for insomnia.
▶ 건강에는 신선한 공기와 햇빛이 가장 좋은 약이다 Fresh air and sunshine are the best things for your health.
4 〈뇌물〉 a bribe; 《俗》 palm oil
♦ …에게 약을 쓰다 grease the palm [hand, fist] of...
5 〈기타〉 ▶ 그는 친절이라고는 약에 쓰려 해도 없는 녀석이다 He has not a spark of kindness

in him.
▶ 그에게 양심이라곤 약에 쓰려 해도 없다 He doesn't have an ounce of conscience in him.
▶ 그에게 지성이라곤 약에 쓰려 해도 없다 He doesn't have an ounce of brains.
■ ―기운 the effect [power] of a medicine ―상자 a medicine chest [cabinet, case] ―장 a medical locker ―장수 a traveling patent-medicine salesman; a medicine peddler

약 約 about; some; approximately; roughly; round; nearly; (美口) around; or so

> [해설] 「약」이라는 뜻으로는 *about*가 가장 일반적이며 *around*는 구어적인 표현. *some*은 이들로서도 막연한 수를 가리키는데 쓴다. *or so*는 「…일까 그 쯤」의 뜻. *approximately*는 조금 딱딱한 표현이지만 문어체·구어체의 양쪽에서 흔히 쓰인다.

◆ 약 1마일 about a mile / 약 100권의 책 some hundred books / 약 한 시간 an hour or so
▶ 그 보석은 약 1만 달러로 평가된다 The jewel is estimated roughly at ten thousand dollars.
▶ 현장에는 약 오백명이 모였다 Approximately five hundred people gathered at the site.

-약 -弱 a little less than; a little short of; a little under ◆1 마일 약 a little less than a mile; a short mile

약가심 藥― chasing the aftertaste of the medicine
◆ 약가심으로 캔디 한 개를 먹다 eat a piece of candy to chase the bitter taste of the medicine
―약가심하다 chase [kill, take off] the aftertaste of the medicine

약간 若干 a few; a little; some; somewhat; more or less; to some extent [degree]
▶ 그 모임에는 여자도 약간 있었다 There were a few women at the meeting, too.
▶ 그것은 사실과 약간 다르다 It is some way from the truth.
▶ 오늘은 약간 춥다 It is rather cold today.
▶ 꽃은 바람에 약간 흔들렸다 The flower slightly swayed in the wind.
▶ 그에게는 약간 시인다운 데가 있다 He is a bit of a poet.

약값 藥― the price of medicine; the charge for a medicine; a medical fee [charge]
◆ 약값을 치르다 pay (the charge) for medicine; pay a pharmacist's bill

약골 弱骨 〈사람〉 a weakling; a weak [feeble] fellow; 〈골격〉 a weak [feeble, delicate] constitution

약과 藥果 1〈과줄〉 a fried cake made of wheat flour, honey and oil
2〈쉬운 일〉 an easy task [job]; (口) a piece of cake
▶ 그까짓것 약과다 That's nothing. ⇌ Nothing is easier. ⇌ (美口) That's (as) easy as pie. ⇌ (美口) That's a cinch.

약관 約款 a stipulation; a provision; an article; a clause

약관 弱冠 1〈남자 나이 스무살〉 twenty years of age; a youth of twenty
▶ 그는 약관으로 등과했다 He passed the higher civil service at the early age of twenty.
2〈약년(弱年)〉 youth; an early age
▶ 그는 약관 열 여덟 살에 세계적으로 유명한 음악 콩쿠르에 입상했다 He won a prize at the world-famous music contest at the early age of 18.

약국 藥局 (美) a drugstore; (英) a chemist's (shop); a pharmacy; 〈병원의〉 a pharmacist's office; a dispensary; a (doctor's) medicine room

약기 略記 a brief [short] sketch; an outline
―약기하다 give a rough sketch 《of》; give an outline 《of》; make a short sketch 《of》

약다 clever; shrewd; smart; cunning; keen; wide-awake; 〈영리하다〉 tactful
◆ 약은 녀석 a smart guy; a shrewd fellow; an old fox / 약은 수법 a shrewd way 《of handling business》 / 약게 굴다 act smartly [cleverly]; be tactful
▶ 그는 약아서 자기가 다칠 일은 하지 않는다 He is too clever [smart] to do anything that might hurt him.

약대 (動) a camel ⇨ 낙타

약대 藥大 a college of pharmacy

약도 略圖 a rough sketch 《of》; 〈지도〉 an outline map; a route [sketch] map 《of》; 〈설계〉 a rough plan 《of》
◆ …의 약도를 그리다 take a rough sketch of; draw a route map 《from… to…》
▶ 공원에서 그녀의 집까지 가는 약도를 그려 주시오 Please sketch a map showing the way to her house from the park.

약동 躍動 a lively motion; a throb; a stir; a palpitation
▶ 나는 자연에서 생명의 약동을 느낀다 I can feel the throbbing pulse of life in nature.
―약동하다 move lively; be quick with life; stir; throb
▶ 봄에는 만물이 약동한다 Everything moves lively in spring.

약력 略歷 a sketch of *one's* life; a brief personal record [history]; a brief outline of *one's* career
▶ 나의 약력은 다음과 같습니다 My brief personal history is as follows. ⇌ The following is a brief outline of my career.

약령(시) 藥令(市) a drug [medicinal stuff] market / 약령 보다 shop for drugs at the drug market / 약령 서다 hold a drug market

약리 藥理 ■―유전학 pharmacogenetics ―작용 a pharmacological action ―학 pharmacology ―학자 a pharmacologist

약막대기 藥― a medicine strainer stick

약물 藥― 〈약수〉 medicinal [mineral] water; 〈약을 우린 물〉 an infusion; 〈약을 다린 물〉 a (medical) decoction; 〈약을 탄 물〉 a solution of a drug; 〈약을 달일 물〉 water for decoction
■―꾼 a spa visitor ―터 a mineral spring; a spa

약물 藥物 medicines; drugs; medicinal substances; medicament
■―검사 examination by medicine ―요법

pharmacotherapy; medicament therapy ―중독 medicinal poisoning ―학 pharmacology; materia medica
약밥 藥― a sweet rice dish
약방 藥房 〈약국〉 a pharmacy ⇨ 약국
약방문 藥方文 a (medical) prescription ⇨ 처방(～전)
약방에 감초 〈속담〉 a man who is in on everything; a person active in all sorts of affairs
약변화 弱變化 〔文法〕〈동사의〉 weak conjugation
약병 藥瓶 a medicine bottle; a prescription bottle; a phial; (美) a vial
약봉지 藥封紙 a (paper) packet of medicine
약분 約分 〔數〕 reduction of fraction; abbreviation; cancellation
―**약분하다** reduce; abbreviate; cancel
◆약분할 수 있는 reducible / 약분할 수 없는 irreducible / 3/9를 1/3로 약분하다 reduce 3/9 to 1/3
약빠르다 shrewd; sharp; smart; quick-witted
◆약빠른 사람 a shrewd [quick-witted] man; a smart fellow / 약빠르게 굴다 move smartly; act shrewdly
▶ 약빠른 그는 그 기회를 놓치지 않았다 It was very smart of him not to miss the chance.
약사 略史 an abbreviated [outline] history; a shortened history; a historical sketch 〈of〉
◆한국의 약사 an outline [a shortened] history of Korea
약사 藥師 a pharmaceutist; a pharmacist; a dispenser; (美) a druggist; (英) a (pharmaceutical [dispensing]) chemist
약사발 藥沙鉢 1 〈약 그릇〉 a medicine bowl **2** 〈독약 사발〉 a bowl of poison
◆약사발을 내리다 bestow poison (for an official to kill *himself* with) / 약사발을 받다 be bestowed poison
약사법 藥事法 〔法〕 the Drugs, Cosmetics and Medical Instruments Law
약삭빠르다 shrewd ⇨ 약빠르다
약산 弱酸 〔化〕 a weak acid = 약한 산
약석 藥石 medicine and acupuncture
◆약석의 효험도 없이 in spite of all the medical treatment; all remedies having proved unavailing [inefficacious]
약설 略說 a brief explanation; summarization
―**약설하다** summarize; abridge; sum up; give an outline of; outline
약세 弱勢 〔證〕 a bearish trend [sentiment]; a slack ◆약세의 weak; bear; bearish; easy / 약세가 되다 slacken ■―시장 a weak [bear] market
약소 弱小 the weak and small; the weak; the minor; the lesser; 〈약하고 작음〉 puniness
―**약소하다** small and weak; puny
■―국(가) a lesser [minor] power; a small and weak nation ―민족 the people of a small and weak power
약소하다 略少― 〈적다〉 few; little; scanty; 〈보잘것없다〉 trifling; slight; trivial; meager
◆약소한 돈 a petty sum of money
약속 約束 a promise; 〈회합 등의〉 an engagement; an appointment; 〈남녀간의〉 (美口) a

date; 〈협정〉 an agreement; 〈매매의〉 a bargain; 〈관례〉 a convention
◆구두 약속 a verbal promise / 거짓 약속 a false [an empty, a hollow] promise / 무대상의 약속 stage conventions / 약속 장소 the appointed place; the place agreed upon / 약속의 땅 [聖] the Land of Promise; the Promised Land / 약속 시간에 at the hour named; at the appointed time; at the time agreed upon; true to *one's* time / 약속대로 as promised; true [according] to *one's* word [promise] / 약속을 지키다 keep *one's* word [promise]; be true to *one's* word [promise]; abide by an agreement
▶ 그는 약속 시간에 오지 않았다 He did not come at the appointed time.
▶ 오늘 저녁 약속이 있습니까? Do you have any appointment this evening? ⇌ Are you busy this evening?
▶ 일곱시에 김교수와 만날 약속이 있습니다 I have a seven o'clock engagement with Prof. Kim. ⇌ I have an engagement [appointment] to see Prof. Kim at seven o'clock.
▶ 약속은 어떻게 되었니? You gave us your word, didn't you?
▶ 약속은 어기지 않을테니 안심하십시오 You may rest assured that we shall honor [observe] our commitment.
▶ 약속을 했으면 지켜야 한다 Once you have made a promise, you should keep it.
▶ 우리 모임에는 지켜야 할 약속이 있다 Our association has some rules which must be observed.
▶ 그는 여덟시에 오기로 한 약속을 어겼다 He broke his promise to come here at eight.
▶ 그는 나에게 약속의 이행을 요구했다 He claimed my promise.
▶ 나는 그런 약속은 하지 않았다 I didn't bargain for that.
▶ 그것은 전생의 약속이다 It is decreed by predestination.
▶ 모두 약속이나 한듯이 침묵했다 All fell dumb as if with one accord.
―**약속하다** promise; give [pass] *one's* word [promise]; make an appointment [engagement]
▶ 그는 나를 도와 주겠다고 약속했다 He promised me his help.
▶ 그녀는 절대 늦지 않겠다고 약속했다 She promised (me) never to be late.
▶ 그에게는 중역 자리가 약속되어 있다 He is a certainty for a directorship. ⇌ He is expected to be [become] a director.
▶ 그녀의 미래에는 행복이 약속되어 있다 Her future happiness is guaranteed.
▶ 그 계획은 멋진 미래를 약속할 듯이 보였다 The plan seemed to augur [bode] well for the future.
약속어음 約束― a promissory note ◆약속어음을 발행하다 issue [write] a promissory note ■―발행인 a promisor; a marker
약손 藥― 1 〈약손가락〉 the third finger **2** 〈만지면 낫는 손〉 a soothing touch of the hand; a medicinal hand
약손가락 藥― the third finger; 〈왼손의〉 the

ring finger

약솜 藥— surgical [sanitary] cotton; 〈탈지면〉(美) absorbent cotton; (英) cotton wool

약수 約數 〔數〕 a measure; a divisor
♦공약수 a common measure [divisor] / 최대 공약수 the greatest common measure

약수 藥水 mineral [medicine] water ■—터 a mineral spring; a spa

약술 略述 an outline; a summary —**약술하다** summarize; give an outline of; sum up

약술 藥— a medicinal wine [liquor]

약시 弱視 〔醫〕 weak [poor] eyesight; weakness of sight; amblyopia
♦약시의 weak-sighted[-eyed]; amblyopic
▶ 요즈음에는 약시인 아이들이 많다 We have more weak-sighted children these days.

약식 略式 informality
♦약식의 informal; summary / 약식으로 informally; in an informal way; without formality [circumstance]
■—기소 a summary indictment; information —명령 a summary order —복장 ordinary [informal, everyday] clothes [dress] : 약식 복장으로 해주십시오 Please come in informal clothes. —재판 summary proceedings; a summary trial —절차 summary procedure —처분 summary disposition

약식 藥食 a sweet rice dish ⇨ 약밥

약실 藥室 1 〈약제실〉 a pharmacist's office; a pharmacy 2 〈탄약을 재는 부분〉 a powder [cartridge] chamber

약어 略語 an abbreviation; an abbreviated word ⇨ 준말
▶ R.O.K.는 무엇의 약어입니까? What does R.O.K. stand for?
▶ Oct.는 October의 약어다 Oct. is an abbreviation of [abbreviated from] October.

약언 略言 a brief statement; a summary; an epitome; an outline —**약언하다** summarize; state briefly; sum up; epitomize; outline

약연 藥碾 a druggist's [(英) chemist's] mortar

약오르다 藥— 1 〈성나다〉 get angry; chafe; be [feel] sore (at, about); feel irritated [injured]; feel vexed [annoyed] (with sb, at sth); be chagrined (at); be nettled
♦약오르는 말 a provoking remark / 약올라 있다 be in a bad temper; be out of temper
2 〈고추 등이 익다〉 ripen to its full flavor

약올리다 藥— chafe; provoke; irritate; vex; grate on sb's nerves; sting [cut] sb to the quick; try sb's patience

약용 藥用 medicinal use
♦약용의 medical; medicinal; for medicine —**약용하다** use sth for medicinal purposes
■—비누 medicated soap —식물 a medicinal plant [herb] —크림 medicated cream —포도주 medical wine

약육강식 弱肉強食 the survival of the fittest; the law of the jungle; the right of the strongest —**약육강식하다** the stronger [strong] prey upon the weaker [weak]; the weak become the victim of the strong

약음기 弱音器 〔樂〕 a mute; a sordino; a damper; a sordine ♦현에 약음기를 달고 with muted strings

약자 弱者 a weak person; a person of feeble strength; (총칭) the weak
♦약자편을 들다 stand by [side with] the weak (underdog] / 강자에 대항하여 약자를 돕다 champion the weak against the strong
▶ 그는 언제나 약자를 못살게 군다 He is always bullying.
▶ 약자를 못살게 굴지 마라 Don't bully the weak.
▶ 오늘날 우리 사회는 약자를 보호할 대책을 좀더 강구해야 한다 We should take more measures today to protect the weak in our society.

약자 略字 〈한자의〉 a simplified form (of a Chinese character); an abbreviated form

약장 略章 a miniature medal [decoration]; a service ribbon ♦약장을 달다 wear a (service) ribbon

약장 略裝 〈약식 복장〉 informal [ordinary] dress

약재 藥材 medicinal stuffs; medicines; drugs

약전 弱電 〈약한 전류〉 a weak electric current
■—기기 (器機) a light electrical appliance —메이커 light electrical appliance manufacturers

약전 略傳 a biographical sketch

약전 藥典 a pharmacop(o)eia
♦약전에 따른 처방전 an official prescription —대한(大韓) — the Korean Pharmacop(o)eia; Pharmacop(o)eia Koreana

약점 弱點 a weak point; a weakness; a soft spot; a foible; a drawback; a defect; 〈결점〉 shortcomings; 〈불리한 점〉 a disadvantage; 〈아픈 곳〉 a sore spot [place]
♦약점을 가지고 있다 have a weakness; have a weak point [spot] / 약점을 드러내다 betray one's weak point; show the white feather / 약점을 이용하다 take advantage of 《another's》 weak point; avail oneself of 《another's》 disadvantage / 아무의 약점을 건드리다 touch sb on the raw / 아무에게 약점을 잡히다 give a handle to sb / 약점을 찔리다 be struck at one's most vulnerable point
▶ 거기가 그의 이론의 약점이다 That is a weak point [drawback] of his theory.
▶ 그는 약점을 극복하려고 애썼다 He tried to overcome his weaknesses [short comings].
▶ 자기의 약점은 보이지 않는 것이 좋다 You'd better not expose [reveal] your own shortcomings.
▶ 그는 남의 약점을 이용한다 He takes advantage of another's weak points.
▶ 누구든지 약점은 있게 마련이다 Everyone has his own weaknesses.
▶ 그 장사꾼은 언제나 사람의 약점을 이용한다 The merchant will always take advantage of the helpless condition of others.

약정 約定 〈약속〉 a promise; an engagement; 〈계약〉 a contract; a compact; 〈매매〉 a bargain; 〈협정〉 an agreement; an understanding; an arrangement; a convention; 〈계약·협정 조항〉 a stipulation
♦약정의 promissory; contracted; agreed / 약정에 따라 by agreement; by arrangement

—약정하다 promise; agree; engage; contract; bargain for *sth*; stipulate for *sth*; make a contract
■—구두— a verbal promise; a spoken agreement /—기한 the stipulated time —서 a (written) contract; a deed of contract; an agreement; a bond; a pact: 가약정서 a provisional contract [agreement] —이자(利子) the rate of interest agreed upon; the agreed rate of interest

약제 藥劑 (a) medicine; drugs; a remedy
—사 약사(藥師) a pharmacy; a drugstore; a pharmacist's office

약조 約條 〈언약〉 a promise; a pledge; 〈규정〉 rule; an agreement; a condition ♦ 약조를 지키다 keep *one's* pledge [engagement]; keep faith with *sb*
—약조하다 promise; pledge ♦ 약조한 바에 따라 according to the agreement
■—금 a contract deposit

약졸 弱卒 a cowardly [weak] soldier; a poltroon ▶ 용장 밑에 약졸없다 Brave soldiers under a brave general.

약종 藥種 medicines ⇨ 약재 ■—상 a seller of materia medica; an apothecary; (美) a druggist; (英) a chemist

약주 藥酒 1〈약술〉a medicinal wine 2〈청주〉refined rice wine

약지 藥指 the third finger ⇨ 약손가락

약진 弱震 a weak shock (of an earthquake); a minor tremor; a slight earthquake tremor ▶ 오늘 아침 약진이 있었다 A slight earthquake tremor was felt this morning.

약진 躍進 a rush; a dash; a charge; an onrush; an onslaught; rapid progress [advance]
♦ 한국 경제의 약진 the rapid [remarkable] progress of the Korean economy / 약진에 약진을 거듭하다 advance by leaps and bounds
▶ 우리 회사는 작년에 대약진을 했다 Our company made a great advance [rapid strides] last year.
—약진하다 advance rapidly [remarkably]; make rapid [remarkable] progress; 〈돌진하다〉 rush 《for, at》; dash 《for, at》; make a rush [dash] 《for, at》; make an onslaught; take [make] great [rapid] strides
▶ 저 팀은 3위에서 1위로 약진했다 That team jumped from the third place to the top.
▶ 그 회사는 급속히 성장하여 일류 기업으로 약진했다 The company grew by leaps and bounds into a first-rate enterprise.

약질 弱質 a weak [feeble] fellow; *sb* of feeble strength; a weakling

약체 弱體 〈약한 몸〉 a weak body; 〈조직체〉 a weak system ♦ 약체의 weak; effete / 약체화하다 weaken; become weak [effete]
▶ 그들의 집행부는 약체다 They have a weak executive.
▶ 개선(改選)으로 보수당은 약체화되었다 The conservative party was weakened by the election.
■—내각 an effete [a weak] Cabinet —보험 substandard (life) insurance —정부[회사] a weak government [concern]

약초 藥草 a (medical) herb ■—상 a herbalist —원 a herb garden; a herbary —채집가 a herbalist —학 medical botany —학자 a herbalist; a medical botanist

약칭 略稱 an abbreviation (of)
▶ MVP는 최우수 선수의 약칭이다 MVP is short for "most valuable player."

약탈 掠奪 plunder; pillage; loot; spoilage; spoliation; despoilation; despoilment
▶ 약탈이 행해지고 있을 때 군인들이 왔다 During the plunder the soldiers came.
—약탈하다 plunder; pillage; despoil; loot; sack; strip 《*sb* of *sth*》; ravage 《a land》
▶ 군인들이 그 도시를 약탈했다 The soldiers plundered [sacked] the city.
▶ 도적들은 그 집에서 값비싼 물건들을 모두 약탈했다 Thieves stripped the house of everything valuable.
▶ 해적들은 마을을 약탈하기 시작했다 The pirates began to plunder the town.
■—농법 plunder farming; a slash-and-burn method of agriculture —자 a despoiler; a plunderer; a marauder; a looter; a sacker —자산 a looted property —주의 a policy of spoliation —품 spoils; loot; plunder; booty

약탕관 藥湯罐 a clay pot in which medicines are prepared; a pipkin for preparing decoctions

약포 藥包 1〈약을 싸는 종이〉 a chartula 《*pl.* -lae》 2〈발사용 화약〉 a cartridge

약포 藥圃 〈약초밭〉 a herb garden; a garden for medical herbs [plants]

약품 藥品 medicines; drugs; medical supplies
■불량— illegal [fraudulent] drugs; a quack medicine 화학— chemicals ■—명 the name of a medicine [drug]

약하다 略— abridge ⇨ 생략(~하다)

약하다 弱— weak; feeble; 〈부서지기 쉽다〉 frail; fragile; 〈허약하다〉 weakly; infirm; 〈섬약하다〉 delicate; 〈술 등에〉 light; mild; 〈소리·빛 등이〉 faint; 〈서투른〉 poor
♦ 약한 사람 a weak person; (총칭) the weak / 약한 빛 a feeble light / 약한 술 weak wine / 약한 팀 a weak team / 마음이 약한 fainthearted; timid / 약한 소리로 in a weak [feeble, faint] voice / 의지가 약하다 have a weak will / 심장이 약하다 have a weak heart; be weak in the heart; (비유) be shy; be timid / 시력이 약하다 have weak [poor] eyes [eyesight] / 바둑이 약하다 be a poor hand at *paduk* / 술에 약하다 get drunk easily; cannot drink much; be a poor drinker; have a low tolerance for liquor / 열에 약하다 be weak against heat / 감기에 약하다 catch cold easily; 〈저항력이 없다〉 have little resistance to colds
▶ 그는 몸이 약하다 〈건강상〉 He is delicate [poor, frail] in health. ⇌ He is in delicate [poor] health. ⇌ 〈체질상〉 He has a weak [delicate] constitution.
▶ 이 팀은 외야가 약하다 This team is weak in fielding.
▶ 놀라게 하지 마라. 나는 심장이 약하다 Don't scare me. I have a weak heart.
▶ 그녀는 위가 약하다 She has poor digestion.

▶ 비닐은 열에 약하다고 한다 Vinyl is said to melt easily.
▶ 나는 수학에 약하다 I am weak in [at] mathematics.
▶ 나는 술에 약하다 I get drunk easily.
▶ 그의 맥박은 아주 약했다 His pulse was very feeble [faint].
▶ 나는 더위에 약해서 여름에는 거의 공부하지 못한다 I am so sensitive to heat (that) I can hardly study in summer.
▶ 약한 자여, 그대 이름은 여자니라 Frailty, thy name is woman.

약학 藥學 pharmacy; 〈약리학〉 pharmacology; 〈조제학〉 pharmaceutics
♦ 약학의 pharmaceutical
■ —과 the pharmaceutical department —대학 a pharmaceutical college; a college of pharmacy —사[박사] a Bachelor [Doctor] of Pharmacy (略 Phar. B. [D.]) —자 a pharmacologist

약한산 弱—酸 《化》 a weak acid

약해 藥害 harmful effects of a medicine; 〈농약의〉 damage from (agricultural) chemicals
▶ 보시는 바와 같이 작물은 심한 약해를 당했습니다 As you see, the crop is badly damaged by agricultural chemicals.

약해지다 弱— weaken; grow weak [feeble]; be enfeebled; fall in health; 〈바람 등이〉 abate; 〈빛·힘·명성 등이〉 wane
♦ 과로로 약해지다 run down from overwork / 몸이 약해지다 decline [go down] in health
▶ 그의 시력은 40대에 약해졌다 His eyes weakened in his forties.
▶ 불길이 약해졌다 The flames have sunk.
▶ 그의 맥박이 갑자기 약해졌다 His pulse has suddenly become feeble.
▶ 그녀는 앓고 난 뒤에 몸이 약해졌다 She became weak after the illness.

약협 藥莢 a cartridge (case)

약호 略號 《電信》 a code [cable] address
■ 전신— a telegraphic address (略 T.A.); a cable address

약혼 約婚 an engagement; a betrothal
♦ A양과 B군의 약혼 the engagement of Miss A to Mr. B / 약혼중인 두 사람 an engaged couple; the betrothed pair / 약혼을 발표하다 announce the engagement (of one's daughter to a man) / 약혼을 파기하다 break (off) one's engagement (with)
■ —약혼하다 make an engagement; engage oneself (to sb, to marry sb); betroth oneself (to sb); be engaged [betrothed] (to)
▶ 존은 앨리스와 약혼했다 John got engaged to Alice. ⇌ John and Alice got engaged.
▶ 그들은 3월에 약혼하고 9월에 결혼했다 They got engaged in March and married in September.
■ —기간 the term of engagement; the engagement period —반지 an engagement ring —선물 a betrothal present [gift] —식 an engagement ceremony —자 〈남자〉 a fiancé; 〈여자〉 a fiancée —피로연 a betrothal party; a feast of betrothal

약화 弱化 weakening; enfeeblement
♦ 지도력의 약화 the decline in one's leadership ability
■ —약화하다 weaken; become weak [weaker]
♦ 약화시키다 make weak [weaker]; weaken; enfeeble; debilitate
▶ 겨울 동안 운동 부족으로 내 몸이 약화되었다 My muscles have gotten soft through lack of exercise in winter.
▶ 과로로 체력이 약화되었다 Overwork weakened my health.

약화 略畵 《draw》 a sketch ♦ 약화를 그리다 sketch; make a rough sketch (of); draw a (line) sketch (of)

약화학 藥化學 pharmaceutical chemistry

약효 藥效 the effect [virtue, efficacy] of a medicine ♦ 약효가 나타나다 tell on; take effect ▶ 서서히 약효가 나타났다 The medicine took effect gradually.

얄궂다 〈성질이 괴상하다〉 odd; queer; eccentric; 〈얄망궂다〉 erratic; 〈이상하고 짓궂다〉 curious; ironical
♦ 얄궂은 사람 an eccentric person; a queer [a strange, an odd] fish / 얄궂은 운명 a curious [strange] irony of fate / 얄궂게도 mysteriously; strangely enough; by a strange irony of fate
▶ 암의 명의가 암으로 죽다니 얄궂은 운명이다 It is an irony (of fate) that a great cancer doctor should die of cancer himself.

얄궂거리다 quiver; be rickety [shaky]; be reckety ▶ 책상 다리가 좀 얄궂거린다 The legs of the table are a bit shaky.

얄기죽거리다 swing [sway] one's hips

얄라차 Oops!; Gosh!; Oh!

얄망궂다 erratic; imprudent; frivolous

얄망스럽다 erratic ⇨ 얄망궂다

얄밉다 hateful; detestable; disgusting; spiteful
♦ 얄미운 아이 a horrid [hateful] boy / 얄미운 짓 hateful behavior / 얄밉게 hatefully; detestably; provokingly / 얄밉게 굴다 behave detestably [provokingly]
▶ 그는 그녀가 얄미워졌다 She was becoming repugnant [odious] to him.
▶ 그는 종종 얄미운 소리를 한다 He often uses aggressively provoking language.

얄타 〈우크라이나 공화국 남부의 항구〉 Yalta
■ —협정 the Yalta Pact —회담 the Yalta Conference

얄팍하다 〈아주 얇다〉 rather thin; small 《volume》; sleazy 《blanket》; 〈천박하다〉 shallow 《argument》; shallow-minded; superficial 《knowledge》 ♦ 얄팍한 교양 a thin veneer of education [culture] / 얄팍한 생각 a shallow [superficial] thinking

얇다 thin
♦ 얇은 종이 thin paper / 얇은 옷 a flimsy [thin] dress / 얇게 thinly / 얇게 하다 thin / 얇게 썰다 cut into thin slices; slice 《ham》 / 입술이 얇다 have thin lips; be thin-lipped / 얇아지다 thin; become thin
▶ 사전에는 보통 얇은 종이를 사용한다 Thin paper is usually used for a dictionary.
▶ 빵을 좀더 얇게 썰어 주세요 Please slice the bread thinner.

얌냠 yum-yum ⇨ 냠냠
얌생이 ◆얌생이 몰다 sneak; pilfer; steal ■—꾼 a sneak; a pilferer; a filcher
얌심 jealousy ◆얌심스럽다 jealous; envious / 얌심부리다 show [display] jealousy ■—데기 a jealous person
얌전떨다 be prudish; behave nicely
얌전하다 1〈유순·침착하다〉gentle; mild; meek; quiet; dovelike;〈착하다〉good;〈고분고분하다〉obedient; submissive; docile;〈정숙하다〉modest;〈행실이 좋다〉well-behaved;〈어린아이가〉as good as gold; well-[mild-]mannered
◆얌전한 소녀 a lamb of a girl / 얌전한 태도 a humble attitude / 얌전히 gently; meekly; obediently; quietly / 얌전히 듣다 listen to *sb* patiently
▶이 아기 참 얌전도 하다 How quiet [meek] this child is!
▶장난치지 말고 얌전히 굴어라 Don't be naughty. Behave yourself.
▶너는 오늘 참 얌전하다 You have been good all day.
▶그 여자는 아주 얌전한 여성이다 She is a very modest woman.
▶그 여자는 얌전해 보여도 성미가 무척 급하다 She looks meek but she has a very quick temper.
▶그 애는 선생님 앞에선 아주 얌전하다 The boy is very quiet [meek] in front of his teacher.
2〈일·솜씨 등이〉nice; neat; good
◆얌전한 솜씨 good workmanship / 일을 얌전하게 하다 do a nice job
얌체 a selfish person; a shameless fellow; a person of no sense of shame
얏 ◆얏하고 외치며 with a cry [yell] / 얏하고 던지다 throw 《*one's* opponent》 with a yell [with all *one's* might]
양 1〈가장〉◆학자인 양하다 set up for a scholar / 시인인 양하다 pose as a poet
2〈작정〉◆…할 양으로 with the idea [intention, aim] of 《doing》; for the purpose of 《doing》
양 羊 a sheep (▶단수·복수 동형);〈숫양〉a ram [tup];〈암양〉a ewe [juː];〈거세한〉a wether
◆새끼 양 a lamb / 양떼 a flock of sheep / 양가죽〈제본용〉sheepskin; roan / 양고기 mutton; (美) lamb / 양털 [모] wool / 양우리 a sheepfold; sheepcot / 양 지키는 개 a sheep dog / 양치는 사람 a shepherd / 양가죽을 쓴 늑대 a wolf in sheep's clothing / 양의 울음소리 a bleat / 양처럼 순하다 be as gentle as a lamb
양 胖〈소의〉ox-stomach; the cud pouch;〈처녑〉tripe
양 陽 1 the positive;〔哲〕Yang
◆양과 음 the positive and the negative; the male and the female / 양의 positive; plus
2〈겉으로 드러내어〉▶그녀는 음으로 양으로 나를 돕고 있다 She helps me both in private and in public.
3〔數〕positive; plus
양 量 1〈분량〉(a) quantity; (an) amount; volume; magnitude
◆양의 증가 an increase in quantity / 많은[적은] 양 a large [small] quantity 《of》 / 양이 늘다[줄다] gain [diminish] in quantity [volume] / 양이 많다[적다] be large [small] in quantity
▶양보다 질이다 Quality before [rather than] quantity.
▶일의 양이 꾸준히 늘고 있다 The amount of work [The number of jobs] is steadily increasing.
▶우리는 그 세 배[두 배]의 양이 필요합니다 We need three times [double, twice] the amount [quantity].
▶막대한[상당한, 어느 정도의, 일정한] 양의 휘발유가 이들 탱크에 저장되어 있다 There is a huge [a considerable, some, a fixed] amount of gasoline stored in these tanks.
▶올해는 비의 양이 많았다[적었다] We had a lot of [a little] rain this year. ⇌ We had a large [a small] amount [quantity] of rain this year.
▶ IC 생산은 양적으로도 질적으로도 많이 늘었다 The production of ICs has grown a great deal in terms of both quantity and quality [both quantitatively and qualitatively].
▶밥 양이 너무 많아요, 좀 덜어주세요 This is too much rice. Please take away a little.
▶시간은 많이 걸리는데 일한 양은 너무 적다 You work for a long time but accomplish very little.
▶저 사람의 독서의 양은 대단하다 He reads so many books!
▶이 일에는 양보다 질이 중요하다 Quality matters more than quantity in this work.
2〈먹는 분량〉◆양이 큰[작은] 사람 a great [small] eater / 양이 크다[작다] be a great [small] eater / 양에 차지 않다 have not eaten enough; have *one's* appetite still unsatisfied / 양껏 먹다 eat *one's* fill; feast *oneself* to repletion
양 兩 〈둘〉a pair; both; a couple; two
◆양다리 both feet / 양쪽에 on either side [both sides] / 양국 both countries / 양끝 both ends
양 洋 Western; European; foreign
◆양장 Western dress / 양담배 foreign cigarettes; imported tobacco / 양요리 Western food [dishes]
양 養 〈수양〉foster; adopted ◆양아들 a foster [an adopted] son / 양어머니 a foster mother
-양 孃 Miss ◆김 양 Miss Kim / 이 양 자매 the Miss Lees
양가 良家 a good [respectable] family
◆양가의 자녀 sons and daughters of good families / 양가에서 (곱게) 자라다 be brought up (with tender care) in a good family
▶그는 양가 출신이다 He is [comes] of a good family. ⇌ He is a man of (good) family.
▶이들 학교는 양가 자녀를 대상으로 하고 있다 These schools are for sons and daughters from good families [parentage].
양가 兩家 two houses; both families

양가 ▶자, 여러분, 이선생과 김선생 양가의 번영을 빌며 건배를 합시다 Now, ladies and gentlemen, may I ask you all to join me in drinking a toast to the prosperity of both Lee and Kim families?

양가 養家 *one's* adoptive family ▶이 사진에 있는 사람들은 그의 양가 부모들이다 These persons in this picture are his adoptive parents.

양각 陽刻 relief; engraving in relief; relievo ―**양각하다** emboss; carve [sculpture] in relief ―**세공** relief (work); embossed work; embossment

양갈보 洋― a foreigners' whore [prostitute]

양감 量感 〈그림에서의〉 massiveness; volume ◆양감이 있는 석조 건물 a massive stone building / 양감이 있는 voluminous / 양감이 있다 be massive

양갱 羊羹 〈단팥묵〉 sweet beans jelly; a fine sweet paste

양견 兩肩 (both) soulders; the two shoulders

양계 養鷄 poultry farming [keeping]; chicken raising ▶그는 양계로 생계를 유지한다 He makes his livelihood by poultry farming [raising poultry]. ―**양계하다** raise poultry [chickens] ■―**업** poultry farming; poultry [egg] industry ―**업자** a poultryman; a poulterer; poultry farmer [breeder]; a chicken raiser ―**장** a poultry farm [yard]

양곡 洋曲 Western [European] music

양곡 糧穀 grains; corns; cereals ◆정부 양곡의 방출가격 the selling prices of staple grains held by the government / 양곡을 운반하다 haul grain; (英) carry corn ■―**거래소** the grain exchange center ―**관리법** the grain management law ―**도입** imports [importation] of corn ―**수급계획** a plan for demand and supply of cereals ―**수매자금** the cereal purchase fund ―**정책** a cereals policy ―**창고** a granary; a (grain) elevator

양과자 洋菓子 a cake; (총칭) Western confectionery

양관 洋館 1 〈서양식 집〉 a house built in Western style; a Western-[European-]style house 2 〈서양 각국의 공관〉 legation [missions] of the Western Powers in Korea

양광 陽光 〈태양빛〉 sunlight; sunshine; sunbeam

양국 兩國 the both [two] countries [nations] ◆양국간의 유대 (friendly) ties between the two countries

양군 兩軍 both [two] armies; 〈양 팀〉 both [two] teams

양궁 洋弓 〈활〉 a Western-style bow; 〈궁술〉 archery ◆양궁 선수권 대회 the Archery Championships

양귀비 楊貴妃 1 〈사람〉 Yang Kuei-fei 2 〈植〉 a poppy ◆양귀비씨 a poppy seed

양극 兩極 〈양끝〉 both extremities; 〈남북 양극〉 the two [north and south] poles; 〈양극과 음극〉 the positive and negative poles ◆양극의 bipolar ■―**지방** the polar circles [areas]

양극 陽極 〔電〕 the anode; the positive pole [electrode]; 〈전지의〉 the zincode ■―**단자** the positive terminal ―**선(線)** anode ray; positive ray; canal ray ―**전류** plate current ―**판(板)** a positive plate ―**회로** plate circuit

양극단 兩極端 both extremes ▶양극단은 일치한다 Two extremes meet. ▶그는 행불행의 양극단을 경험했다 He experienced the extremes of fortune. ▶그들은 의견이 양극단으로 갈라져 있었다 They were poles apart in their opinions.

양근 陽根 〔化〕 a positive radical

양금 洋琴 a kind of zither ◆양금채 같은 목소리 a sweet voice / 양금채 같다 〈생김새가〉 be fine and delicate; 〈목소리가〉 be sweet

양기 陽氣 1 〈햇볕의 기운〉 sunshine; sunlight 2 〈남자의 기운〉 vitality; vital power; vigor; energy; virility ◆양기 좋은 사람 a man of energy; an energetic man

양끝 兩― both ends; either end ◆막대기의 양끝을 자르다 cut a stick at both ends

양난 兩難 a dilemma ―**양난하다** be in a dilemma [fix]; be on the horns of a dilemma

양날 兩― 〈양날의〉 double-edged ■―**톱** a double-edged saw

양녀 洋女 a Western [European, an American] woman

양녀 養女 an adopted [a foster] daughter ◆아무의 양녀가 되다 be adopted as daughter by *sb* / 양녀로 기르다 foster 《a girl》 as *one's* daughter

양념 〈향신료〉 spice(s); condiment(s); (총칭) spicery; 〈조미료〉 a seasoning; a flavoring ◆양념을 많이 한 highly spiced [seasoned] / 요리에 양념을 하다 spice a dish / 고기를 양념에 무치다 season meat with spices / 수프에 양념을 넣다 put spices into soup ―**양념하다** season; flavor; spice; give flavor to ■―**그릇**〔병〕 a cruet; a castor

양다리 兩― ◆양다리 걸치는 사람 a double-dealer; a timeserver; an opportunist; a fence sitter / 양다리(를) 걸치다 have [play] it both ways; play double; sit on [stand on, straddle, walk] the fence ▶그 계획은 양다리를 걸치려다 실패하고 말 것이다 The attempt will fall between two stools.

양단 兩端 both ends; both extremes; either end

양단 兩斷 cutting in two; bisection ―**양단하다** bisect; break [split] in two; cut *sth* in two ◆양단되다 get split in two; be bisected / 일도 양단하다 cut in two at a single stroke of the sword; (비유) take a drastic measure

양단 洋緞 〈비단의 일종〉 brocade; foreign satin

양단간 兩端間 〈둘 가운데〉 between the two; one or the other; this or that; 〈좌우간〉 at any rate; in any case [event]; anyhow ◆양단간에 단안을 내리다 decide between two choices

▶양단간에 내가 해야 한다 I must do it anyhow. ⇌ It must be done somehow or other.
양달 陽― a sunny place [spot] ♦양달쪽 the sunny side / 양달에 내놓다 keep *sth* in the sun / 양달에 말리다 dry in the sun
양담배 洋― imported tobacco; a foreign [an American] cigarette; American tobacco
양당 兩黨 ♦양당의 bipartisan; bipartizan; two-party
■―외교 (美) a bipartisan diplomacy ―정치 [제도] the two-party politics [system]
양도 兩刀 two swords ■―논법 [論] dilemma
양도 糧道 supply of provisions ♦적의 양도를 끊다 cut off the enemy's supplies [supply of provisions]
양도 讓渡 transfer; alienation; 〈어음의〉 negotiation; assignment; 〈권리의〉 cession
―양도하다 transfer; alienate (land to *sb*); negotiate (secutities); (法) assign; convey *sth* to *sb* by deed
♦양도할 수 있는 transferable; alienable; 〈어음〉 negotiable / 재산을 양도하다 transfer property to *sb* / 소유권을 양도하다 transfer [yield] ownership (of *sth* to *sb*)
■재산― alienation of property ■―가격 a transfer price ―성 예금증서 a negotiable certificate of deposit ―소득 income from transfer; capital gains ―소득세 a transfer income tax ―약관 assignment clause ―인 a transferer; a releasor; an assignor ―자산 transfer property; property (to be) transferred ―증서 a transfer; a conveyance; an assignment
양도체 良導體 [物] a good conductor (of heat)
양돈 養豚 pig farming; pig [hog, swine] raising ―가 a pig breeder; (美) a hog raiser ―업 the hog raising industry ―업자 a pig breeder [farmer]; (美) a hog raiser ―장 a swinery; a pig farm; a hog yard
양동이 洋― a (metal) pail; a bucket
♦양동이로 물을 긷다 draw water with a pail
양동작전 陽動作戰 a feint operation; diversionary activities ♦양동작전을 펴다 make a feint; feint
양돼지 洋― a hog of Western breed; a Western hog [pig]
양두 兩頭 two heads ♦양두의 double-headed; dicephalous ■―사(蛇) an amphisbaena
양두구육 羊頭狗肉 advertising [crying] wine, and selling vinegar
양두정치 兩頭政治 dyarchy; diarchy ♦양두정치의 dyarchical; diarchic
양딸기 ― [植] a strawberry
양떼구름 洋― an altocumulus ⇨ 고적운(高積雲)
양력 揚力 [物] lift force
■―계수 a lift coefficient
양력 陽曆 the solar [Julian] calendar ♦양력 10월 10일 October 10 by the solar calendar
양로 養老 provision for old age; taking good care of the aged
■―보험 old-age insurance; endowment insurance; (英) endowment assurance: 양로보험에 들다 be insured against old age ―시설 an institution for the aged ―연금 an old-age pension; an endowment annuity: 양로연금을 받다 draw an old-age pension ―원 an asylum [a home] for the aged; an old people's home: 유료 양로원 a paid home for old folks ―자금 an endowment
양론 兩論 both arguments; both sides of the argument
양륙 揚陸 landing; unloading; disembarkation ―양륙하다 unload goods; disembark; discharge
■―비(費) landing charges ―선 a lighter; a barge ―인부 a dockhand; a stevedore; a longshoreman (*pl.* -men) ―장(場) a landing place; a wharf ―절차 landing formalities ―지(地) a designated landing place ―항 a port of discharge; an unloading port
양립 兩立 coexistence; compatibility
―양립하다 coexist (with); be compatible [consistent] (with); stand together
♦양립할 수 없다 be incompatible (with); cannot exist together
▶태만과 성공은 양립하지 않는다 Idleness is not compatible [incompatible] with success.
▶일과 취미는 양립하기 어렵다 It is rather difficult to combine one's work and hobby.
양막 羊膜 [解] the amnion (*pl.* ~s, -nia)
■―강(腔) an amniotic cavity ―염 amnionitis
양말 洋襪 〈짧은〉 socks; 〈긴〉 stockings; (a pair of) hose
♦양말 한 켤레 a pair of socks [stockings] / 양말을 신고[신은 채] with *one's* socks [stockings] on / 양말을 신다[벗다] put on [take off] *one's* socks [stockings]
▶당신 양말은 올이 풀려 있어요 Your stocking has a run (in it).
양말 糧秣 provisions and fodder
양면 兩面 both [two] faces
♦양면 접착 테이프 (a piece of) tape that is sticky on both sides / 인생의 명암 양면 both bright and seamy sides of life / 양면의 double-faced; both-sided / 사물의 양면을 보다 look both sides of things
▶모든 문제에는 양면이 있다 There are two sides to every question.
▶나는 유리창의 양면을 닦았다 I cleaned both sides of the windowpane.
■―작전 double-sided operations ―정책 a two-pronged policy
양명 揚名 fame; distinction; renown
―양명하다 make a [*one's*] name; win [make] a name for *oneself*; win [get] *oneself* a name; rise to fame; achieve fame
양명학 陽明學 the doctrines [teachings] of Wang Yang-ming
양모 羊毛 wool ♦양모의 wool; woolen (cloth)/ 양모로 만든 woolen
―공업 the woolen and worsted industry ―상 a wool merchant; a woolman ―제품 woolen goods ―지(脂) wool fat [grease]; lanolin(e); yolk ―직 woolen fabric [textiles]
양모 養母 a foster [an adoptive] mother

양모제 養毛劑 a hair tonic
양미 兩眉 two eyebrows ♦양미간을 찌푸리다 knit [gather, bend] *one's* brows; frown 《at, on》
양미 糧米 rice; provisions
양민 良民 law-abiding [good] citizens [people]; (총칭) good citizenry ■—학살 massacre of innocent people
양반 兩班 1 [古制] (the) *yangban*; the nobility; the aristocratic class
2 〈점잖은 사람〉 a gentleman; a man; a nobleman
♦우리집 양반 my old man; my husband / 주인양반 the master 《of a house》
양방 兩方 both; both parties [sides]; the two
양배추 洋— (a) cabbage
양변 兩邊 both sides [directions]
양병 養兵 building up an army —양병하다 bulid up [maintain, support] an army
양병 養病 1 〈병조리〉 curing a disease; nursing *one's* health
—양병하다 seek a cure for an illness; give attention to the recovery of *one's* health
2 〈병의 악화〉 —양병하다 aggravate [worsen] *one's* disease
양보 讓步 concession ♦서로의[상호의] 양보로 by mutual concession
▶우리는 그들의 요구에 굴욕적인 양보를 했다 We made a humiliating concession to their demand.
—양보하다 concede 《to》; make a concession; yield place to *sb*; give way to *sb*
♦아무에게 자리를 양보하다 make room for *sb*; offer *one's* seat *sb* / 서로 양보하다 make mutual concessions; meet each other halfway / 마지못해 양보하다 reluctantly grant [make] a concession
▶우리는 서로 양보해 합의했다 We reached an agreement through concession.
▶서로 양보하여 삼십만원으로 매듭을 지읍시다 Let us split the difference and do business at three hundred thousand won.
▶나는 기차에서 노부인에게 자리를 양보했다 I gave [offered] my seat to an old lady in the train.
▶그들은 후진에게 길을 양보해야 한다 They should make way for younger people.
▶나는 좌회전하는 차에 길을 양보하였다 I gave way [yielded] to the car turning (to the) left.
▶그는 한발자국도 양보하지 않았다 He would not budge an inch.
■—절 [文法] a concessive clause
양복 洋服 a suit; a dress; 〈한복에 대하여〉 Western [European] clothes
♦양복을 입다[벗다] put on [take off] *one's* clothes / 양복을 한 벌 맞추다 have [get] a suit of clothes made
▶양복은 활동하기에 편하다 Western clothes are easier to work in.
▶너는 한복보다 양복쪽이 더 잘 어울린다 Western clothes suit you better than traditional Korean ones.
▶양복을 입으세요[벗으세요] Put on [Take off] your clothes.
—걸이 a coat hanger —장 a wardrobe; a clothespress —장이 〈양복을 만드는 사람〉 a tailor —쟁이 〈입은 사람〉 a man in Western clothes —점 a tailor's (shop); a tailor —지 [감] suiting; cloth; stuff —짜리 (부) a man in foreign [Western] clothes
양봉 養蜂 beekeeping; bee culture; apiculture
♦양봉에 종사하다 engage in apiculture; keep bees
—양봉하다 keep [culture] bees
■—가 a beekeeper; an apiarist —상자 a wooden beehive; a movable comb [hive] —업 bee-farming —장 a bee yard; an apiary
양부 良否 〈좋음과 나쁨〉 whether 《a thing》 is good or bad
♦양부를 알아내다 ascertain the quality 《of a thing》 / 물건의 양부를 조사하다 examine the quality of an article; examine an article to see whether it is good or bad
양부 養父 a foster [an adoptive] father
양부모 養父母 adoptive parents
양분 兩分 bisection —양분하다 cut in two; bisect; divide *sth* into two parts; halve
양분 養分 nourishment; nutrient
♦양분이 있다 be nourishing [nutritious]; contain nourishment / 양분을 주다 nourish / 양분을 섭취하다 take nourishment 《from》
▶식물은 뿌리에서 양분을 섭취한다 A plant takes nourishment from its roots.
■—비(比) nutrient ratio —표 a nutrient table —흡수 nutrient absorption
양비 兩非 wrong of both sides
■—론 theory that both sides are wrong —론자 a theorist who thinks both sides are wrong [to blame]
양비둘기 洋— [鳥] a rock dove [pigeon]
양산 洋傘 an umbrella
♦양산의 살 〈한개〉 a rib; 〈전체〉 a frame / 양산을 펴다 unfold [spread, open] an umbrella / 양산을 접다 close [fold, shut] an umbrella / 양산을 쓰다 put up [raise] an (open) umbrella
양산 陽傘 a sunshade; a parasol
♦양산을 받다[펴다, 접다] put up [open, close] a parasol
양산 量產 mass production
—양산하다 mass-produce 《bicycles》
▶지금은 마이크로컴퓨터까지 양산되고 있다 Even microcomputers are being mass-produced now.
■—계획 a plan for the mass production 《of》
양상 樣相 an aspect; a phase
♦양상을 일변시키다 change the whole situation [climate]
▶사태는 심상치 않은 양상을 띠고 있다 Things are taking on [assuming] a serious aspect.
▶철도가 놓이자 마을의 양상이 새로워졌다 The village entered upon a new phase because a railway was constructed.
양생 養生 〈몸의〉 care of health; recuperation; curing
♦양생을 위해 for *one's* health
—양생하다 take care of *oneself*; improve

양보의 표현

1. **…하지만 (그러나) ~ …, but ~**
▶ 그는 차가 있지만 버스를 자주 이용한다 He has a car, but he often uses buses.
▶ 그는 늠름하지는 않지만, 여성들은 그에게 끌린다 He is not a handsome man, but women find him attractive.

2. **…하기는 하지만 ; …인데도 불구하고**
(1) Although [Though]…, ~
▶ 그는 차가 있기는 하지만 버스를 자주 이용한다 Although [Though] he has a car, he often uses buses.
▶ 그는 늠름하지는 않지만 여성들은 그에게 끌린다 Although [Though] he is not a handsome man, women find him attractive.
(2) ~ though [although]…
▶ 그는 차가 있기는 하지만 버스를 자주 이용한다 He often uses buses though [although] he has a car.
▶ 그는 늠름하지는 않지만 여성들은 그에게 끌린다 Women find him attractive though [although] he is not a handsome man.
(3) in spite of…; in spite of the fact + that clause
▶ 폭우에도 불구하고 그녀는 쇼핑을 갔다 In spite of the heavy rain(,) she went to the store. ⇌ She went to the store in spite of the heavy rain.
▶ 그는 화가 났음에도 불구하고 내게 말을 걸었다 In spite of his anger [In spite of being angry] he spoke to me.
▶ 그는 차가 있는데도 불구하고 버스를 자주 이용한다 In spite of the fact that he has a car, he often uses buses.
[어법]
① though와 although 사이에 의미상의 구별은 없다.
② 이 형식은 첫머리나 끝머리에 모두 쓸 수 있으나 첫머리에는 although, 끝머리에는 though를 쓰는 것이 좋다는 견해도 있다.
③ 끝머리에 although를 쓸 때에는 거기에 이어지는 clause를 강조한다.
④ although나 though에 이어지는 clause가 주절보다 앞에 올 때는 보통 콤마가 필요하고 주절 다음에 이어질 때는 콤마가 필요치 않다.

3. **어떻게 …하더라도 ; 아무리 …하더라도**
(1) however…, ~
▶ 여러분이 어떻게 하더라도 저 사람은 마음에 들지 않을 것입니다 However you do it, he won't like it.
▶ 어떻게 가더라도 3시간 걸립니다 However you travel, it'll take you three hours.
(2) however [no matter how] + 형용사[부사] + 주어 + 동사
▶ 아무리 바쁘더라도 그 책은 꼭 읽어야 한다고 생각합니다 However [No matter how] busy you are, I think you should read the book.
▶ 아무리 시간이 걸리더라도 나는 영어를 공부할 생각입니다 However [No matter how] long it takes me, I'm going to study English.
(3) however [no matter how] + 형용사 + 명사 + 주어 + 동사
▶ 주시는 돈이 아무리 적더라도 우리들에게는 도움이 됩니다 However [No matter how] little money you can give, it will help us.
▶ 당신이 아무리 많은 돈을 가지고 있더라도 나는 당신과 결혼할 생각이 없습니다 However [No matter how] much money you have, I still don't want to marry you.
[어법]
① however clause는 주절 다음에 오는 경우도 있다.
② however clause에 「may + 동사의 원형」을 쓸 수도 있다.
  [보기] However much he may like her, he is not likely to marry her. (그가 아무리 그녀를 좋아했다 하더라도 그는 그녀와 결혼할 것 같지는 않다)

4. **무엇이[무엇을]…라 하더라도 ; 어떠한 …라도**
(1) whatever…
▶ 무슨 일이 일어나더라도 네 마음이 변해서는 안된다 Don't change your mind, whatever happens.
▶ 네가 뭐라고 하든, 나는 네 말을 믿지 않아 Whatever you say, I won't believe you.
▶ 무슨 실수를 하더라도 걱정하지 마라 Whatever mistakes you make, don't worry about them.
(2) no matter what + 주어 + 동사, ~
▶ 무슨 일이 일어나더라도 마음이 변해서는 안된다 No matter what happens, don't change your mind.
▶ 네가 뭐라고 하든, 나는 네 말을 믿지 않아 No matter what you say, I won't believe you.
[어법]
① whatever…, no matter what…의 clause는 첫머리나 끝머리에 모두 쓸 수 있다.
② 다음과 같은 말도 같은 구문으로 쓸 수 있다 Don't open the door, whoever it is. ⇌ Don't open the door, no matter who it is. (누구든간에 문을 열지 마라)
  Whichever road you take, drive your car carefully. (어떤 길을 가더라도 조심해서 운전해라)
  Wherever I go, he follows me. (내가 어디를 가든 그는 따라온다)

5. **설령 …라 하더라도**
▶ 설령 비가 오더라도 갈 겁니다 I'll go even if it rains. (▶even if…의 clause가 주절 다음에 이어질 때는 콤마는 필요 없음)
▶ 설령 돈을 주더라도 나는 그것을 하지 않을 것입니다 Even if you pay me, I won't do it.
▶ 설령 5년이 걸리더라도 나는 영어를 공부하기로 결심했습니다 Even if it takes me five years, I've made up my mind to study English.

양서 [promote] one's health; 〈병후에〉 recuperate oneself
  ■ —법 rules for healthy living; hygiene
양서 良書 a good book; a valuable work ◆ 양서를 구하다[고르다] seek [choose] good books
양서 洋書 a foreign [Western] book
양서 兩棲 ◆양서의 amphibious ■—동물 an amphibious animal; an amphibian —류 Amphibia
양성 良性 benignancy ◆양성의 〔醫〕 benign [benignant] 《disease》
양성 兩性 both [the two] sexes ◆양성의 bisexual
  ■—관계 sex relations —구유(具有) hermaphroditism; androgyny —구유자 a hermaphrodite; an androgyne —생식 amphigony; gamogenesis; bisexual reproduction —체 〔動·植〕 a bisexual —화 〔植〕 a bisexual flower; a hermaphrodite
양성 陽性 1 〔醫〕 positivity
  ◆양성으로 전화(轉化)하다 turn positive
  ▶ 내 투베르쿨린 반응은 양성으로 바뀌었다 My tuberculin reaction has changed to positive.
  2 〈적극적인 성질〉 a positive [an active, an extrovert, a sunny] disposition
  ◆성격이 양성인 사람 a man of positive [sunny] disposition
  ■—반응 (a) positive reaction —전환 change to positive
양성 養成 〈훈련〉 training; education; cultivation
  —양성하다 〈기술자 등을〉 train; educate; 〈재능·품성 등을〉 cultivate; develop
  ◆간호사를 양성하다 train nurses / 전문적 지식을 양성하다 cultivate [develop] a technical knowledge / 인내력을 양성하다 cultivate one's patience
  ▶ 그 학교에서는 기술자를 양성하고 있다 They train technicians at that school.
  ■—기간 a training period; the period of apprenticeship
양성소 養成所 a training school [center, institute] ■ 교원[간호사]— a training school for teachers [nurses]
양소매책상 兩—册床 a kneehole desk
양속 良俗 a good [fine] custom
  ■ 미풍— good morals and manners
양손 兩— both [two] hands ⇨ 양수(兩手)
양손녀 養孫女 an adopted [a foster] granddaughter; an adopted daughter of one's son
양손(자) 養孫(子) an adopted [a foster] grandson; an adopted son of one's son
양송이 洋松栮 a mushroom; a champignon
  ■ —재배 mushroom cultivation
양수 羊水 amniotic fluid
  ▶ 양수가 터졌다 The waters broke.
양수 兩手 〈양손〉 both [two] hands
  ■—걸이 〈일 등의〉 playing (a) double (game); 〈장기 등의〉 scoring a double point with a single move —겸장(兼將) 《announce》 a double check; 〈서양 장기의〉 a fork —잡이 〈사람〉 an ambidexter; 〈장기 등의〉 scoring a double point with a single move

양수 揚水 —양수하다 pump (up) water
  ■ —기 a water pump
양수 陽數 〔數〕 a positive number
양수 讓受 (acquisition by) transfer; inheritance —양수하다 obtain sth by transfer; take over; inherit
  ■ —인 a grantee; an assignee; a transferee —증 (a certificate of) receipt; a receipt form
양수기 量水器 a water meter
양순 良順 gentleness; meekness; docility
  —양순하다 good; gentle; meek; docile
  ◆양순한 아이 a docile [meek] child / 양순한 백성 law-abiding [obedient] people / 양순하게 말을 듣다 do as told without objection
양식 良識 good sense; common sense; sound judgment
  ◆양식이 있는 사람 a man of good sense; a sensible man / 양식이 없다 lack [be lacking in] good sense / 양식이 있는[없는] 행동을 하다 act sensibly [foolishly]
  ▶ 그런 짓을 하지 않을 만큼의 양식은 있다 I have enough good sense not to do that.
  ▶ 나는 그의 양식을 의심했다 I doubted his good sense [sound judgment].
양식 洋式 foreign [European, Western, Occidental] style [manner]
  ◆양식 방 a room furnished in Western style
양식 洋食 Western [European, foreign] food [dishes] ■ 양식 먹는 법 Western table manners —요리(법) Western cooking —집 a restaurant (serving foreign dishes)
양식 樣式 a form; a mode; 〔建〕 (a) style; an order
  ◆일정한 양식 a (fixed) form
  ▶ 당신은 어떤 양식의 집을 지을 겁니까? What style of house are you planning to build?
  ■ —건축— a style of building 생활— a style [mode] of living; a way of life: 과학의 발전이 우리의 생활양식을 바꿨다 The progress of science has changed our mode of living.
양식 養殖 raising; farming; culture
  —양식하다 rear; raise; breed; cultivate
  ◆물고기를 양식하다 raise [cultivate, farm] fish
  ■ —진주— culture of pearl; pearl culture:이 지역은 진주 양식으로 유명하다 This area is famous for its pearl culture. ■ —업 cultivating [breeding] industry —장 a nursery; a farm —진주 a culture(d) [cultivated] pearl
양식 糧食 food; provisions; supplies
  ◆생명의 양식 〔聖〕 the bread of life / 마음의 양식 mental food / 양식이 떨어지다 provisions give out; run out of provisions / 양식이 넉넉하다 have an ample supply of food / 양식을 대다 provision; provide with food
양실 洋室 a Western-style room; a European-style room
양심 良心 (a) conscience
  ◆양심의 가책 the pangs of conscience; a sting of conscience / 양심상 for conscience sake; for the sake of one's conscience
  ▶ 그것은 양심의 문제다 That's a matter of conscience.

▶ 나는 그와의 약속을 어긴 데 대해 양심의 가책을 느꼈다 I felt guilty [prick of conscience] about having broken my promise to him. 〈양심이〉 양심이 있는 conscientious / 양심이 없는 conscienceless / 양심이 명하는대로 따르다 follow [obey] the dictate of *one's* conscience; do what conscience dictates
▶ 양심이 허락지 않아서 거짓말을 하지 못했다 My conscience did not allow me to tell a lie.
▶ 그에게는 양심이 없다 He has no conscience.
▶ 도둑질은 그의 양심이 절대로 용납지 않았다 His conscience would not let him [allow him to] steal.
〈양심에〉 양심에 따르다[따라 행동하다] follow [act according to] *one's* (own) conscience / 양심에 거리낌 없다[떳떳하다] have a clear [good] conscience / 양심에 걸리다 have sth on *one's* conscience; lie heavy on *one's* conscience / 양심에 거리끼다[부끄럽다] have a guilty [bad] conscience / 양심에 호소하다 address [appeal] to *sb's* conscience / 양심에 맡기다 leave *sb* to (his) conscience
▶ 양심에 반하는 명령에는 따르지 않겠다 I shall [will] never obey orders that go against my conscience.
▶ 나는 양심에 부끄러운 점이 없다 I have a clear conscience. ⇌ My conscience is clear.
▶ 그렇게 하는 것이 좋은지 나쁜지 너의 양심에 물어봐라 Your conscience will tell you whether you should do so or not.

양심적 良心的 ◆ 양심적인 상인 an honest merchant / 양심적인 conscientious / 양심적으로 conscientiously
▶ 그는 양심적으로 일을 하는 사람이다 He is a conscientious worker. ⇌ He is conscientious about his work. ⇌ He works concientiously.
▶ 저 가게는 무척 양심적이다 They're very honest [conscientious] at that store.

양아들 養— an adopted [a foster] son ⇨ 양자(養子)
양아버지 養— an adoptive father ⇨ 양부
양아치 〈넝마주이〉 a ragpicker; a ragman
양악 洋樂 Western [European] music; foreign music ■—가 a musician [player] of Western music
양안 兩岸 (both) banks; either bank
◆ 양안에 on either bank; on both banks
양안 兩眼 〈두 눈〉 both eyes ◆ 양안이 다 멀다 be blind in both eyes ■—실명 total blindness in both eyes
양약 良藥 a good [an efficacious] medicine
▶ 양약은 입에 쓰다 (속담) Good medicine is bitter in the mouth. ⇌ Bitter pills may have wholesome effects. ⇌ Good advice sounds harsh to the ear.
양약 洋藥 Western [European] medicine(s); a foreign drug ■—국 (美) drugstore; (英) chemist's (shop) ■—재(材) imported pharmaceuticals
양양하다 洋洋— 〈바다가〉 wide; vast; boundless; broad; 〈장래가〉 bright; promising; rosy
◆ 양양한 바다 the boundless ocean; the vast [boundless, broad] expanse of the ocean / 양양한 앞길 a bright [rosy] future; rosy prospects
▶ 그는 앞길이 양양한 젊은이다 He is a young man with a bright [rosy, great] future (ahead).
양양하다 揚揚— elated; exultant; triumphant
양어 養魚 fish farming [breeding]; pisciculture ■—양어하다 breed [raise] fish
■—가 a fish farmer [breeder, culturist]; a pisciculturist ■—못[지] a fishpond; a fish pool; a breeding pond ■—장 a fish farm; a breeding ground [place] ■—조(槽) a rearing tank
양어깨 兩— both [*one's*] shoulders
양어머니 養— an adoptive mother
양어버이 養— adoptive parents=양부모
양언하다 揚言— say [speak] publicly; assert (in public); declare; proclaim; announce
양여 讓與 concession; 〈양도〉 transfer; assignment; 〈영토의〉 cession
■—양여하다 concede (a privilege to *sb*); yield possession of *sth*; transfer; assign
◆ 소유권을 양여하다 yield [transfer] ownership (of *sth* to *sb*)
양옥 洋屋 a Western-[European-]style house; a house in Western-[European-]style
▶ 그는 양옥에서 살고 있다 He is living in a house of foreign style.
양요 洋擾 〔史〕 an invasion of Korea by a Western power
양요리 洋料理 Western food [dishes]; 〈요리법〉 Western cooking [cookery]
양용 兩用 (for) double use ◆ 수륙양용전차[비행기] an amphibious tank [plane]
양우리 羊— a sheepfold; a sheepcot(e); (英) a sheep-pen
양원 兩院 both [the two] Houses
◆ 양원일치의 의결 a concurrent vote of both Houses / 양원을 통과하다 pass both Houses ■—상하— the Lower House and the Upper House; the House and the Senate; (英) the House of Paliament ■—제(도) the bicameral [two-chamber] system ■—협의회 a joint conference of the two Houses
양위 讓位 abdication of the throne; demise of the crown ■—양위하다 abdicate (from) the crown [throne]; demise the throne
양육 羊肉 mutton; 〈새끼의〉 lamb
양육 養育 bringing-up; rearing; upbringing; breeding; care; fostering ■—양육하다 bring up; raise; rear; nurse; foster
■—법 the method [way] of bringing-up children; the care and feeding of children ■—비 the expense [cost] of bringing-up a child; fostering expenses ■—원 a workhouse; a poorhouse; 〈고아의〉 a home for orphans; an orphanage; 〈버려진 아이의〉 a foundling home ■—자 a fosterer; a rearer; a breeder
양은 洋銀 albata; nickel [German] silver ■—그릇 nickel silver ware
양의 良醫 a good [skilled] physician [doctor]
양의 兩義 a double meaning; two meanings
양의 洋醫 a Western physician; a Western (medical) doctor
양이 攘夷 the exclusion [expulsion] of foreigners ■—론 〔史〕 anti-alienism; exclu-

양이온 陽— 〔物〕 a positive ion; a cation
양익 兩翼 two wings; 〈대형의〉 both flanks
양인 兩人 two persons ⇨ 양자(兩者)
양인 洋人 a Westerner; a foreigner
양일 兩日 two days; a couple of days
♦ 양일간 during [for] two days / 양일간에 in [within] two days
양자 兩者 two persons; both; both sides [parties]; a couple; a pair ♦ 양자 합의 하에 by mutual consent [agreement]
양자 陽子 〈양성자〉〔物〕 a proton
양자 量子 〔物〕 a quantum (略 q)
 ■—론 the quantum theory —물리학 quantum physics —수 quantum number —역학 quantum mechanics
양자 養子 an adopted son; one's son by adoption
 ♦ 양자로 삼다 adopt sb as one's son; make an adopted child of / 양자로 가다[들다] be adopted (into a family); become sb's adopted child / 양자 보내다 give one's child to sb as (his) heir
 ▶ 그들은 그 아이를 상속자로서 양자를 삼았다 They adopted the child as their heir.
양자택일 兩者擇一 selecting one alternative
 —양자택일하다 select one alternative; choose between the two
양잠 養蠶 sericulture; silkworm culture; silk culture [raising]
 —양잠하다 rear [raise, breed] silkworms
 ■—가 a sericulturist; a silk grower [raiser] —농가 a silk-raising farmer —업 the sericultural [silk-raising] industry
양장 羊腸 1 〈창자〉 sheep's intestines
 2 〈길〉 a winding [tortuous] path; a narrow meandering road
양장 洋裝 1 〈복장〉 foreign [Western] style of dress
 —양장하다 be dressed in foreign [European] style; wear Western(-style) clothes
 ♦ 양장한 숙녀 a lady in Western clothes
 2 〈제본〉 binding a book in Western style
 —양장하다 bind (a book) in foreign [Western] style
 ■—점 a dressmaking shop
양재 良材 1 〈재목〉 good material; good timber 2 〈인재〉 a man of ability [fine caliber]
양재 洋裁 foreign-style dressmaking
 ♦ 양재를 배우다 learn [take lessons in] dressmaking
 ▶ 그녀는 올봄부터 양재를 배우고 있다 She has been taking lessons in dressmaking since this spring.
 ■—사 a dressmaker —학교 a dressmaking school
양재기 洋— enamelware; an enameled iron bowl [pot]
양잿물 洋— 〈수산화나트륨〉 caustic soda; lye; alkaline solution
양적 量的 ♦ 양적인 quantitative / 양적으로 quantitatively; in (terms of) quantity
 ■—증가 an increase in quantity

양전기 陽電氣 〔物〕 positive [plus] electricity
양전자 陽電子 〔物〕 positron; positive dectron
양전하 陽電荷 〔物〕 positive electric charge
양정 糧政 〈행정〉 food administration; 〈정책〉 a food policy
양젖 羊— sheep('s) milk; goat('s) milk
양조 釀造 〈맥주의〉 brewing; brewage; 〈위스키의〉 distillation
 —양조하다 brew (beer); distill (whisky)
 ▶ 맥주는 보리를 양조해 만든다 Beer is brewed from barley.
 ■—법 the method of brewing; brewage —업 the brewing industry; the brewery business —자[인] a brewer; a distiller —장 a brewery; a brewhouse
양종 洋種 a foreign breed; Western kinds [seeds]
양주 洋酒 foreign wine [liquors]
양지 洋紙 machine-made paper; Western paper
양지 陽地 a sunny place [spot]; a sunshine
 ■—식물 a sun plant; a heliophyte
양지 諒知 understanding; appreciation
 —양지하다 understand; apperciate; know
 ♦ 양지하시는 바와 같이 as you know [see, are well aware]
 ▶ 모쪼록 양지해서 들어 주세요 I beg you to be very attentive.
양지가 음지되고 음지가 양지된다 〈속담〉 Life is full of ups and downs [vicissitudes].
양지 바르다 陽地— sunny; full of sunshine; 〈서술적〉 admit ample sunshine
 ♦ 양지바른 방 a sunny room / 양지바른 집 a house with a sunny aspect
양지쪽 陽地— the sunny side; a sunny spot
 ♦ 양지쪽에 in the sun
양진영 兩陣營 both camps; the two opposing blocs ♦ 동서 양진영 the camps of East and West
양질 良質 good quality ♦ 양질의 옷감 high quality texture
양쪽 兩— both; both sides [parties]; either side; 〈부정〉 neither (of them)
 ♦ 양쪽 다 both; the two / 길 양쪽에 on either side [both sides] of the street
 ▶ 그녀는 양쪽 손에 사과를 가지고 있었다 She had apples in both (her) hands.
 ▶ 당신은 양쪽의 이유를 다 들어야 합니다 You should listen to the cause of either party.
 ▶ 사고의 책임은 너희들 양쪽에 다 있다 Both of you are responsible for the accident.
 ▶ 그 답은 양쪽 다 맞는다 Both (of) those answers [Both (the) answers] are correct. ⇌ Those answers are both correct.
 ▶ 양쪽 다 서로 상대방을 잘 알고 있다 Each knows the other well.
양쯔강 揚子江 the Yanzi (Jiang); the Yangtze (Kiang); the Chang Jiang
양차 兩次 two times; twice
양찰 諒察 sympathetic understanding [consideration] —양찰하다 consider; take into consideration [account]; sympathize with; enter into sb's feelings
 ▶ 저의 입장을 양찰해 주십시오 Please consider my position.

양책 良策 a good plan [scheme]; a good [wise] policy

양처 良妻 a good wife ♦양처가 되다 make a good wife ■현모— a good [faithful] wife and wise mother

양철 兩凸 double-convex ■—렌즈 a biconvex [convexo-convex, double-convex] lens

양철 洋鐵 〈아연을 입힌〉 galvanized iron (sheet); 〈주석을 입힌〉 tinned (sheet) iron; a tin plate
■—가위 〈작은 것〉 (a pair of) snips; 〈큰 것〉 tinman's shears —공 a tinman; a tinner; a tinsmith —제품 tinware —지붕 a tin roof —집 a tin-roofed house —통 a tin pail; a metal bucket —판 galvanized sheet iron; a tin plate

양초 洋— a candle; a taper
♦양초를 켜다[끄다] light [put out, blow out] a candle
▶양초가 타고 있다[꺼져 간다] A candle is burning [burning low].
■—심지 a candlewick; the wick (of a candle) 양촛대 a candlestick; a candleholder; a flambeau (*pl.* -beaux, ~s)

양춘 陽春 〈봄〉 spring; the springtime; 〈음력 정월〉 the first lunar month
—가절 the pleasant springtime

양측 兩側 both; both parties [sides]

양치 養齒 brushing *one's* teeth ⇨ 양치질

양치기 羊— 〈일〉 sheep raising; 〈사람〉 a shepherd

양치류 羊齒類 〔植〕 the ferns

양치질 養齒— 〈이 닦기〉 brushing *one's* teeth; 〈입안을 가심〉 rinsing *one's* mouth; gargling —양치질하다 brush [clean] *one's* teeth (with a toothbrush); rinse (out) *one's* mouth; gargle
♦소금물로 양치질하다 rinse *one's* mouth with salt and water
■—그릇 a gargling bowl —물 gargling water —소금 salt for cleaning teeth; dentifrice salt

양친 兩親 (*one's*) parents ⇨ 부모

양코 洋— a Westerner's nose; a large protruding nose ■—배기 a Westerner; 〈미국 사람〉 a Yankee

양키 a Yankee; a Yank ■—기질 Yankeeism

양탄자 洋— a rug; a (felt) carpet
♦두꺼운 양탄자가 깔린 마루 a thick-carpeted floor / 양탄자를 깔다 spread [lay] a rug; lay (a room) with a carpet

양털 羊— wool ⇨ 양모(羊毛)

양토 養兎 rabbit rearing [raising]
—양토하다 raise [breed] rabbits
■—장 a rabbitry; a (rabbit) warren

양파 洋— an onion ♦양파껍질 the coats of an onion

양팔 兩— both [two] arms ♦양팔을 펴다 hold out both arms / 양팔로 끌어안다 embrace

양편 兩便 both; both sides [parties]

양푼 a (large) brass bowl [basin]

양품 洋品 Western-style apparel and accessories; fancy goods; haberdashery
■—상 〈남자용〉 a haberdasher; (英) a hosier —점 a haberdasher's (store); a haberdashery

양풍 良風 a good [laudable] custom ⇨ 미풍 (~양속)

양풍 洋風 foreign [European, Western] style [manner]

양피 羊皮 sheepskin; 〈제본용〉 a roan
■—구두 sheepskin shoes

양피지 羊皮紙 parchment; sheepskin

양학 洋學 Western [European] learning
■—자 a scholar of Western learning

양항 良港 a good [fine] harbor

양해 諒解 〈이해〉 (an) understanding 《on, about》; 〈용납함〉 agreement 《on, about》; consent
♦무언의 양해 tacit agreement [understanding] / 양해를 얻어서 with *sb's* consent / 양해 하에에 on the understanding 《that…》 / 양해 가 이루어지다 come to [arrive at] an understanding [agreement] 《with》 / 양해를 얻다[구 하다] get [ask for] *sb's* consent [(口) O.K.]
▶두 사람 사이에는 무언의 양해가 있었다 There was a tacit understanding between them.
▶그는 병 때문에 귀국이 늦어진다는 데 대하여 정부의 양해를 구했다 He sought the government's consent to delay his return home on account of illness.
—양해하다 understand; consent 《to》; agree 《to, with, in, upon》
▶회사는 내가 야간학교에 다니는 것을 양해해 주었다 The management consented to my going to night school.
■—사항 items of understanding; an agreed item

양행 洋行 1 〈외국으로 감〉 going [traveling] abroad —양행하다 go [travel] abroad; go on a foreign travel [tour]
2 〈상점〉 a firm; 〈중국의〉 a hong

양형 量刑 assessment of a case; weighing of offense [(英) offence] ▶재판관의 양형은 타당 [부당]했다 The judge handed down a reasonable [an excellent] sentence.

양호 良好 good —양호하다 good; fine; excellent; favorable; satisfactory ♦아주 양호한 성 적 an excellent result ♦수술 후 환자의 상태는 양호하다 The patient is getting better [recovering satisfactorily, making good progress] after the operation.

양호 養護 nursing; protection
▶그들은 국가의 양호가 필요하다 They need the protection of the state.
—양호하다 protect; nurse; give protective care
■—교사 a nurse-teacher —시설 a protective institution —실 a dispensary

양홍 洋紅 carmine; crimson ♦양홍색의 carmine; crimson

양화 良貨 good money ▶악화는 양화를 구축한 다 Bad money drives out good money.

양화 洋畵 1 ⇨ 서양화
2 〈영화〉 a foreign film

양화 洋靴 shoes 〈구두〉 ■—점 (美) a shoe store; a shoemaker's: 양화점 주인 a shoemaker; a shoe dealer

양화 陽畵 〔寫〕 a positive (picture)

양회 洋灰 cement ⇨ 시멘트

얕다 1 〈깊지 않다〉 shallow
♦얕은 못 a shallow pond / 얕은 물에서 헤엄치다 swim in shallow water / 얕은 상처 a slight injury
▶물이 얕은 곳에서 수영하라 Swim where the water is shallow.
▶강물이 가장 얕은 곳으로 건너라 Cross the stream where it is shallowest.
▶물은 얕은 곳으로 흐른다 Water finds its level.
▶얕은 내도 깊게 건너라 One cannot use too much caution. ⇌ You should make it doubly [double] sure.
2 〈경험·지식이 적다〉 shallow; superficial
♦얕은 생각 a superficial way of thinking [view]; a shallow [foolish] idea / 생각이 얕은 사람 a shallow-brained[-minded] person; a shallow thinker
▶나는 컴퓨터에 대한 지식이 아직 얕다 My knowledge of computers is still limited.
▶네 역사관은 얕다 Your view of history is superficial.
▶그는 아직 경험이 얕다 He lacks experience. ⇌ He is still green.
3 〈정도가〉 slight
♦얕은 잠 (a) light sleep

얕보다 〈얕잡아보다〉 make light [little] of; slight; belittle; depreciate; underestimate; undervalve; underrate; 〈멸시하다〉 look down upon; despise; disdain *sb*
♦얕보는 웃음 a contemptuous laugh / 얕보는 태도로 with superior airs
▶나를 얕보지 마라 Don't underestimate me [my power].
▶상대를 절대로 얕보아서는 안된다 Never underrate your opponent.
▶우리는 그들이 얕볼 수 없는 적임을 알았다 We found in them no despicable foes.

얕잡다 look down upon; think lightly [meanly] of; hold *sb* cheap; underrate; belittle ⇨ 얕보다
▶이건 여간 어려운 일이 아니야, 얕잡지 마라 This is quite a job, don't make light of it.
▶그들은 그를 어리다고 얕잡았다 They made light of him as only a boy.

애 1 〈자식을 부를 때〉 Sonny; My boy; 〈남을 부를 때〉 Hi!; Hellow; You; Hey; Here; There
▶애, 너 이리 오너라 Hey you, come here!
▶애, 그만 둬 Come on, stop it!
2 〈이 애〉 this child [boy, girl]
▶애가 왜 이래？ What's the matter [What's wrong] with this boy [girl]？
▶ 會話「애, 저 사람 누구니？」「세일즈맨이야」 "Say, [I say], who's that?" "He's a salesman."

어 〈놀라움〉 Oh!; Dear!; Why!; Well!; 〈대답〉 Yes; Yea
▶어, 내 펜이 어디 갔지？ Where is my pen, I wonder? ⇌ 〈여성적 표현〉 Oh, my! Can't find my pen.
▶어！ 인수가 오네 Oh! [Why!] Here comes In-su!
▶ 會話「어, 10시가 다 됐네」「빨리해」 "Why! [(My) goodness!] It's nearly ten o'clock." "You'd better hurry up."

-어 -語 〈단어〉 a word; 〈전문어〉 a (technical) term; 〈국어〉 a language
♦모국어 one's mother tongue / 비어 a vulgar word; a vulgarism / 200어 이내로 in less than two hundred words

어가 御駕 a royal carriage

어간 〈넓은 사이〉 a space (in a house); 〈시공〉 (a) distance; an interval
♦어간 대청 a floored hall between the rooms

어간 語幹 the stem of a word; a stem

어감 語感 〈말소리〉 sensitivity to words; a keen sense of language; 〈말투〉 a nuance; connotation; word feeling
♦어감이 나쁘다 sound jarring [cacophony]; lack euphony / 어감이 좋다 sound well; be euphonic
▶그녀는 어감이 예민하다[무디다] She can [cannot] distinguish delicate [fine] shades of meaning.

어개 魚介 fish and shellfish; (총칭) fishery products

어거하다 馭車— 〈소·말을 몰다〉 drive [handle] 《a horse, a carriage》; 〈제어하다〉 manage; control; handle

어구 語句 words; words and phrases ♦어구의 용법 wording ▶어구의 용법 하나로 문장에 생기가 난다 Good wording gives life to a composition.

어구 漁具 fishing implements; (총칭) fishing gear [tackle]

어구 漁區 a fishing ground [area]; a fishery

어군 魚群 a school [shoal] of fish
■—탐지기 a fishfinder; a fish detector

어군 語群 〈文法〉 a word group

어귀 an entrance; an entryway
♦강 어귀 the mouth of a river; an estuary / 마을 어귀 the edge of a village; an approach to a village / 절 어귀 a gateway to a temple / 터널 어귀 the beginning of a tunnel

어귀어귀 greedily; voraciously; devouringly ⇨ 아귀아귀 ▶먹어치우다 devour; munch; eat up greedily

어귀차다 〈매우 세다〉 strong; firm; tough; unyielding ♦어귀차게 쥐다 grip; clasp; clutch; hold tightly

어그러지다 1 〈모양이 틀어지다〉 be out of joint [order]; be dislocated
▶내 구두 모양이 어그러졌다 My shoes have lost their shapes.
2 〈어긋나다〉 be against [contrary to]; go bad [against]; depart; deviate
♦신뢰에 어그러지다 betray [prove false to] *sb's* trust / 기대에 어그러지지 않다 comply with [satisfy, obey] *sb's* wishes / 사람의 도리에 어그러지다 be out of line with humanitarian principles
▶내 기대가 어그러졌다 Things did not turn out the way I expected [wanted them to]. ⇌ It fell short of [didn't come up to] my expectation.
▶내 계획은 완전히 어그러졌다 My scheme was completely failed.

▶ 그것은 규정에 어그러진다 That is against the rules.
▶ 그의 행동은 예의에 어그러진 것이다 His behavior is a violation [breach] of etiquette.
▶ 그녀의 연기는 우리의 기대에 어그러졌다 Her performance didn't meet [come up to] our expectations.
3 〈사이가 나빠지다〉 become estranged [alienated] (from); get into discord 《with》
▶ 둘 사이가 점점 어그러졌다 The relationship between the two grew estranged.

어근 語根 the root of a word; 〖文法〗 a radix (*pl.* ~es, radices)

어근버근하다 〈사개가 맞지 않다〉 loose; loosely fitted 〈화합하지 않다〉 discord 《with》; be discordant 《with》; be on bad terms 《with》; do not get along well with each other

어금니 a molar (tooth); a back tooth; a grinding tooth; a grinder ♦ 어금니를 악물다 clench *one's* teeth

어금막히다 lie crisscross [crosswise]; be placed across [obliquely, at an oblique angle]

어금버금하다, 어금지금하다 nearly [much] alike; much the same; (口) much of a muchness
▶ 둘다 어금지금하다 There is little difference between the two.

어긋나다 1 〈교차하다〉 cross each other; 〈벗어나다〉 be [come] off; be out of joint
▶ 무릎뼈가 어긋났다 My knee came out of joint.
▶ 그녀의 발목이 어긋났다 She has sprained her ankle.
2 〈엇갈리다〉 go crisscross 《with》; run [go, act] counter (to); be contrary (to); go against; go amiss [awry]; clash 《with》
♦ 길이 어긋나다 cross [pass] each other (on the way) / 의견이 서로 어긋나다 differ [vary] in opinion / 도의에 어긋나는 행동을 하다 act contrary to morality
▶ 모든 것이 어긋났다 Everything went against me.
▶ 생각이 서로 어긋나서 우리는 아무 결정도 못했다 We didn't decide anything because we couldn't agree.
▶ 그녀의 말은 사실과 어긋난다 What she has said is contrary to the fact.
▶ 기대에 어긋나지 않도록 최선을 다하겠습니다 I'll do my best to meet your expectations.
▶ 그것은 인도에 어긋나는 행위다 Such conduct is against humanity. ⇒ It's an inhuman act.

어긋놓다 put [place, set, lay] *sth* crisscross

어긋맞다 be [meet] crisscross; be at odd angles from each other
♦ 잎이 줄기에서 어긋맞게 나다 leaves grow at alternating intervals on either side of a stem

어긋매끼다 stack [insert] in alternation; arrange (in positions) alternately on either side; cross [intersect] each other

어긋물리다 dovetail; engage [join] crisscross; mesh together crisscross ▶ 윗니와 아랫니가 어긋물리고 있다 The upper teeth and the other meet crisscross.

어긋버긋하다 be out of joint (with each other); coarse; uneven

어긋하다 a bit out of joint; slightly opened

어기 漁期 a fishing season ▶ 연어의 어기가 시작되었다 The salmon (fishing) season has opened [begun].

어기다 1 〈지키지 않다〉 break; violate; disobey; disregard; go [act] against; be contrary to; run [go, act] counter (to)
♦ 관례를 어기다 violate [break] the custom [traditional practice] / 명령을 어기고 행동하다 act in defiance of orders / 약속을 어기다 break *one's* word [promise] / 시간을 1분도 어기지 않다 be punctual to the minute
▶ 그는 절대로 약속을 어기지 않는다 He always keeps his promises. ⇒ He is true to his word. ⇒ He never breaks his word.
▶ 그는 나의 경고를 어기고 혼자 등산갔다 He went climbing alone in spite of [despite] my warning.
▶ 그는 부모의 뜻을 어기고 대학을 중퇴했다 He dropped out of college against his parents' wishes.
2 〈위반하다〉 violate 《a law》; break 《the regulations》; transgress [trespass] against; offend against
♦ 교통 법규를 어기다 violate [break] the traffic rules
▶ 너는 교칙을 어긴 것이다 You have acted against [violated] the school regulations.
▶ 법을 어기면 처벌을 받는다 If you break [violate] the law, you will be punished.

어기대다 〈반항하다〉 disobey; defy ▶ 그는 상사에게 어기대다가 해고되었다 He defied his boss and was fired [dismissed, sacked].

어기뚱거리다, 어기뚱대다 shuffle along; waddle

어기뚱하다 〈교만스럽다〉 (slightly) impudent [saucy, arrogant]; 〈틈이 생겨 있다〉 partially opened; slightly opened; cracked

어기적거리다, 어기적대다 waddle 《along》; walk heavily and clumsily; walk in an awkward way

어기중하다 於其中— be in the middle; be middle; be medium; be moderate
▶ 그의 학업성적은 어기중하다 His grades are mediocre [neither good nor bad]. ⇒ He is about average in grades.

어기차다 determined; obstinate; willful; firm
♦ 어기찬 아이 a headstrong child / 성질이 어기차다 have an unyielding spirit [nature]

어김 a breach; (a) violation; a failure

어김없다 unerring; infallible

어김없이 without fail; surely
▶ 내일 어김없이 와 주시오 Be sure [Don't fail] to come tomorrow. ⇒ Please come tomorrow without fail.
▶ 그는 어김없이 올 것이다 He will surely [certainly] come. ⇒ I'm sure [certain] that he will come. ⇒ He won't fail to come.
▶ 그녀는 시내에 가면 어김없이 책방에 들른다 She never goes to town without stopping at the bookstore.

어깨 1 〈인체의〉 the shoulder

♦처진[벌어진] 어깨 sloping [square] shoulders / 어깨 너머로 보다 look at sb over one's shoulder
〈어깨가〉 어깨가 좁다[넓다] be narrow-[broad-]shouldered / 어깨가 뻐근하다 feel stiff in one's shoulder(s)
〈어깨를〉 어깨를 드러내다 bare one's shoulders / 어깨를 으쓱거리다 raise [draw up] one's shoulders / 어깨를 축 늘어뜨리다 droop one's shoulders / 어깨를 나란히 하고 걷다 walk shoulder to shoulder [side by side] (with)
▶ 누군가가 내 어깨를 툭툭 쳤다 Someone tapped [patted] me on the shoulder.
〈어깨에〉 짐을 어깨에 메다 carry a package on one's shoulder
▶ 그는 총을 어깨에 메고 걸어나갔다 He walked out with a rifle on his shoulder.
▶ 우리의 승리는 그의 어깨에 걸려 있다 Our victory rests on his shoulders.
2 〈의복의〉 a shoulder
▶ 블라우스의 어깨가 뜯어졌다 My blouse is ripped at the shoulders.
3 〈俗〉〈불량배〉 a rowdy; a roughneck; a thug; a rogue; a ruffian
♦어깨와 어울리다 keep bad [rough] company; join a gang of hoodlums [hooligans]
4 〈책임·사명〉 (a) responsibility; duty ♦어깨가 무겁다 be a burden to sb; be too much [hard, heavy] for sb; feel loaded with one's duties [responsibilities]
▶ 가게의 운영으로 그는 어깨가 무겁다 Running the store is a burden to him.
▶ 아들이 대학을 나와서 어깨가 가벼워졌다 My son's graduation from the university took a load off my shoulders.
▶ 빚을 모조리 갚고 나니 어깨가 가벼워졌다 When I repaid loan in full, I finally relieved myself of a heavy burden.
5 〈대등한 위치〉 an equal; a match; a rival
♦어깨를 겨루다 rival; vie with; compete with
▶ 이론물리학에서 그와 어깨를 겨룰 자는 없다 He has no equal [match, rival] in (the field of) theoretical physics.

어깨걸이 a shawl; a wrap ♦어깨걸이를 걸치다 put on a shawl; wear a shawl around one's shoulders

어깨결림 the stiffness of shoulders; a stiff shoulder ♦어깨결림으로 고생하다 suffer from a stiff shoulder; have stiff shoulders

어깨너멋글 picked-up knowledge ♦어깨너멋글로 배우다 acquire [pick up] knowledge by overhearing others; learn by watching other people

어깨동무 a childhood friend; an old playmate —어깨동무하다 hook each other's shoulders ♦어깨동무하고 걷다 walk shoulder to shoulder [side by side, abreast]

어깨받이 a shoulder pad ♦어깨받이를 넣다 pad the shoulders / 어깨받이를 넣은 상의 a jacket with padded shoulders

어깨뼈 a shoulder blade [bone]; a bladebone; (라) a scapula (pl. -lae, ~s)
♦어깨뼈가 부러지다 get one's bladebone broken

어깨총 —銃 (口令) Shoulder arms!; Slope [Carry] arms!
▶ 우로 [좌로] 어깨총 Right [Left] shoulder arms!
—어깨총하다 〔軍〕 come to the shoulder

어깨춤 ♦어깨춤을 추다 dance with one's shoulders moving up and down; 〈기뻐서〉 dance for [with] joy
▶ 그녀는 그 소식을 듣고 어깨춤을 추면서 좋아했다 She danced for [with] joy at [to hear] the news.

어깨통 the breadth of one's shoulders; the shoulder width

어깻바대 a reinforcement strip inside the shoulder of a jacket

어깻바람 〈어깻짓〉 swinging [swaying] one's shoulders with delight [exultation]; 〈뽐냄〉 swaggering
♦어깻바람이 나서 in high [jolly] spirits / 어깻바람을 내며 걷다 walk with a swagger; swagger [strut] about; strut along
▶ 그는 경주에서 이겨 어깻바람이 나 있다 Having won the race he has got quite elated lately. ⇒ He is boasting [bragging] of having won the race.

어깻숨 ♦어깻숨을 쉬다 gasp for breath; breathe hard; breathe rapidly in short gasps; pant

어깻죽지 the shoulder joint ▶ 그말을 듣자 그는 어깻죽지를 축 늘어뜨렸다 His shoulders dropped when he heard it.

어깻짓 swinging [moving] one's shoulders ♦어깻짓으로 사람들을 비집고 나가다 shoulder one's way through the crowd.

어꾸수하다 rather tasty; amusing; plausible=엇구수하다

어눌하다 語訥— be slow of speech; speak [talk] falteringly [hesitantly]; stammer; stutter ♦어눌하게 설명하다 [변명하다] falter [stammer] out an explanation [excuse]

어느 **1** 〈의문〉 which; what...
▶ 어느 가방이 네 것이냐? Which is your bag? ⇒ Which bag is yours?
▶ 어느 색을 좋아합니까? What color do you like?
▶ 어느 계절을 제일 좋아하니? Which [What] season do you like best?
▶ 어느 TV 프로그램을 보고 싶은 거야? Which [What] TV program do you want to watch?
▶ 나는 어느 쪽이 옳은지 모르겠다 I don't know which is right [the right one].
2 〈한〉 a; one; 〈어떤〉 (a) certain; some
♦어느날 아침 [저녁] one morning [evening]/ 어느 경우에는 on some occasion; in some cases / 어느 의미에서는 in a (certain) sense / 어느 정도(까지) to some [a certain] extent [degree]
▶ 어느 사내아이가 도망치고 있다 Some boy is running away.
▶ 어느 책엔가 그렇게 쓰여 있었다 It was written in a certain book.
3 〈그 중의 어느〉 whichever; any
♦어느 …도 whichever; any; every; 〈부정〉

none; neither / 어느 사람이나 anyone; anybody; 〈모두〉 everybody; 〈부정〉 no one; nobody; none / 어느모로 보나 in every respect [all respects]; from every point of view; every inch《a soldier》/ 어느라도[든지] (at) any time; at any hour you like
▶어느 쪽의 이야기도 진실이 아니다 Neither story is true.
▶어느 열차나 만원이었다 Every train was [All the trains were] full.
▶어느 학생이든 각자 개성을 가지고 있다 Each [Every] student has his [(口) their] own personality. ⇌ All students have their own personality.
▶이 책은 어느 서점에서든지 판다 This book is to be had at any bookseller's.
▶어느 책을 읽어도 된다 You can read any book.
▶어느 누구에게도 너의 비밀을 말하지 않겠다 I will not tell your secret to anyone whatever.
▶어느 길로 가도 미술관에 갈 수 있습니다 Whichever road you take, you will come to the art gallery. ⇌ Any of the roads will lead you to the art gallery.
▶어느 것을 고르셔도 상관없습니다 No matter which [Whichever] (one) you choose, it doesn't matter to me.

어느것 which one; which
◆어느것이라도 any; all; every / 어느것도 any and every; all and singular / 어느것이든 any; any one; whichever; 〈둘중의〉 either
▶어느것이 맞는지 모르겠다 I don't know which is right [the right one].
▶〔會話〕「어느것이 좋으니?」「어느것도 싫어」 "Which do you like better [prefer, (口) like best]?" "Neither. ⇌ I like neither (of them). ⇌ I don't like either of them."
▶〔會話〕「커피나 차, 어느것으로 할까요?」「커피를 주세요」 "Which would you like, coffee or tea?" "Coffee, please."
▶나는 어느것이 어느것인지 모르겠다 I cannot tell which is which.
▶이 중에서 어느것이든 맘대로 가지시오 Take whichever you like of these.

어느겨를에 when with so little time to spare
▶어느겨를에 해외 여행을 하겠는가? How can I spare [find] enough time to go on an overseas trip?
▶지금 몹시 바빠요. 어느겨를에 아이를 본 단 말이오 I have so many things to do now, I cannot find the time for babysitting.

어느누구 anybody; anyone; somebody; someone; Mr. [Miss, Mrs.] So-and-so; who; whoever ⇨ 누구, 아무.¹
▶어느 누구도 완전하지 않다 No one is perfect. ⇌ Everyone has his faults.

어느덧 before *one* knows [realizes]; before *one* is aware (of it); without *one's* knowledge [knowing it]; unnoticed
▶어느덧 밤이 깊어갔다 The night was far advanced unnoticed [without our noticing of it].
▶그때부터 어느덧 10년이 지났다 Ten years elapsed [slipped] past [by, away] since then.
▶봄방학도 어느덧 지나가고 말았다 The spring vacation has passed all too soon.
▶어느덧 가을이 왔다 Autumn has stolen on [over] us.

어느때 when; (at) what time
◆어느때든지, 어느때나, 어느때고 (at) any time; always; whenever; no matter when; (at) some time [day] or other / 일년 중 어느때나 at any season of the year
▶어느때나 출발할 수 있습니다 I'm ready to leave anytime.
▶어느때고 좋을 때 오너라 Come whenever [(at) any time] you like.
▶신분증을 어느때든 가지고 다니시오 Carry your identification card with you at all times.

어느분 who; anybody; somebody ⇨ 누구
▶어느분이든 좀 도와주십시오 Would someone please help me?
▶어느분이시지요? 〈전화에서〉 May I have your name, please? ⇌ Who is calling please?

어느새 before *one* knows; so [all too] soon
▶어느새 그녀가 없어졌다 She was gone before we knew it. ⇌ We were unaware that she had gone.
▶어느새 파티는 끝나 있었다 The party was over all too soon.

어느세월에 —歲月— 〈어느 천년에〉 when on earth…; by what time; when
▶어느 세월에 이 다리가 완공될 건가 I wonder when this bridge will be completed.

어느정도 —程度 in a [some] measure; in some degree; to some [a certain] degree [extent]; somewhat; more or less; partly; 〈의문〉 how far; to what extent
▶그것은 어느 정도 정말이다 It's true to some [a certain] extent. ⇌ There is some truth in it.
▶어느 정도의 손해는 피할 수 없다 Some losses cannot be helped.
▶이 탑은 높이가 어느 정도입니까? How high [tall] is this tower? ⇌ What is the height of this tower?
▶그를 어느 정도(까지) 믿어야 하는지 알 수가 없다 How far can I trust him, I wonder?

어느쪽 1〈어느편〉 which (side); which person [thing, one]
◆어느쪽인가[이든] either; whichever / 어느쪽 이든 간에 in either case; either way; anyhow; anyway / 어느쪽인가 하면 rather; rather than; otherwise; as likely as not
▶어느쪽이 이겼지요? Which side [Who] won?
▶미국과 캐나다는 어느쪽이 더 크지? Which is bigger, the United States or Canada?
▶어느쪽이든 더 맘에 드는 것을 골라라 Choose whichever you like better.
▶어느쪽이 어느쪽인지 분간할 수 없다 I can't tell which is which.
2〈방향〉 which way [direction]; what side
▶그는 어느쪽으로 갔지요? Which way did he go?

어느틈에 when with so little time; before *one* knows

어는점 —點 〔化〕a freezing point ■ —내림 a

freezing point depression

-어도 **1** 〈양보·가정〉 but; however; though; (even) if; no matter 《who, what, etc.》
♦늦어도 at (the) latest / 적어도 at least / 어떤 일이 있어도 whatever [no matter what] may happen [come]; come what may [will]
▶파티에 가고 싶어도 못갑니다 I'd like to go to the party, but I can't.
▶그에게 아무리 전화를 걸어도 받지 않더라 I tried to call him many times, but he didn't answer.
2 〈승낙·양해〉 ▶ 口話 「창문을 열어도 괜찮나요?」「그래, 괜찮아」 "May I [Is it all right to] open the window?" "Yes, you may [it is]."

어두 語頭 the beginning of a word ♦어두의 음 the sound at the beginning of a word

어두워지다 **1** 〈날이〉 (it) become [get] dark [dim]; darken
♦어두워진 뒤에 after dark / 어두워지기 전에 before (it gets) dark
▶요즈음은 일찍 어두워진다 Night falls [The light fails] earlier now.
▶날이 어두워지자 별들이 보였다 As it got dark, stars were seen.
2 〈눈·귀가〉 귀가 어두워지다 become hard of hearing; become weak in hearing / 눈이 어두워지다 become weak in sight / 돈에 눈이 어두워지다 be blinded by the lure of money
▶그녀는 요 몇달 사이에 눈이 점점 어두워졌다 Her eyesight has been weakening [failing] for the last several months.

어두커니 at the peep of dawn [day, the morning]; in the gray of the morning; in the dim light of daybreak

어두컴컴하다 dark; dusky ♦어두컴컴한 밤 a dark night; a pitch-black[-dark] night ▶굴은 어두컴컴했다 The cave was very dark.

어둑새벽 (at) the dusk of dawn; the early dawn ▶아버지는 어둑새벽에 일어나신다 My father gets up while it is still dark.

어둑어둑하다 dusky; gloomy; dim ♦어둑어둑한 새벽에 떠나다 start in the dusk of dawn [before daybreak] ▶밖이 어둑어둑해졌다 It is getting dark outside.

어둑하다 〈조금 어둡다〉 gloomy; dusky; dim ♦어둑하게 하다 《美》 dim out ▶무대의 조명이 차차 어둑해졌다 The stage lights slowly darkened.

어둔하다 語鈍— tongue-tied; slow of speech; clumsy in speaking; speak haltingly
♦어둔한 사람 a poor speaker

어둠 darkness; the dark
♦밤의 어둠 the shadows of night / 어둠 속에서 in the dark; in darkness / 어둠 속으로 사라지다 disappear [be swallowed up] in the darkness / 어둠속에서 길을 잃다 lose one's way in the darkness / 어둠속에서 2층까지 더듬어 올라가다 grope one's way upstairs in the dark

어둠상자 —箱子 〖物〗 a black box

어둠침침하다 gloomy; somber; dusky; dim
♦이 방은 어둠침침하다 This room is poorly lighted.
▶전등이 어둠침침하다 The electric light is dim.

어둡다 **1** 〈빛이〉 dim; faint; 〈색깔이〉 dark
♦어두운 방 an ill-lit [a dimly lighted] room / 어두운 빨강[파랑] dark red [blue]/ 등불을 어둡게 하다 turn down a lamp / 전등을 어둡게 하다 dim the light
▶등불이 어둡다 The lamp is dim [not bright enough].
▶어두운 데서 독서하는 것은 눈에 나쁘다 Reading in dim [poor] light is bad for the eyes.
2 〈잘 모르다〉 be not familiar 《with》; be ignorant 《of》; be ill informed 《of》; be a stranger 《to》
♦물정에 어둡다 know [have seen] very little of the world
▶나는 사정에 어둡기 때문에 아무 말도 하지 않았다 I said nothing because I didn't know what was going on.
▶나는 이 근처의 지리에 어둡다 I am a stranger here. ⇒ I am new to this part of the town.
3 〈비유〉 ♦어두운 얼굴 a clouded face; a gloomy look / 어두운 과거가 있는 여자 a woman with a shady past
▶그는 성격이 어둡다 He has a gloomy character.
▶우리의 전망은 어둡다 Our prospects are gloomy. ⇒ We face a black [bleak] future.
4 〈눈·귀가〉 weak 《in sight, in hearing》 ♦눈이 어둡다 be weak-sighted; have bad [weak] sight
▶그는 귀가 어둡다 He is hard of hearing. ⇒ His hearing is poor.
▶그녀는 밤눈이 어둡다 She has a night blindness.
▶그녀의 얼굴에 어두운 그림자가 비쳤다 A cloud passed over her face.

어디¹ **1** 〈의문〉 where; what place; 〈어디쯤〉 whereabout(s); 〈어떤 곳〉 somewhere; 〈의문문에서〉 anywhere
♦어디(에서)든지 anywhere; 《美口》 anyplace; 〈도처에〉 everywhere / 어딘가에 somewhere; 《美口》 someplace / 어디(에)서 from where; whence
▶여기는 서울의 어디입니까? Where in Seoul am I?
▶시청은 어디입니까? Where's the city hall?
▶스위스의 수도는 어디입니까? What is the capital of Switzerland?
▶가장 가까운 지하철 역은 어디일까? Which is the nearest subway station?
▶제일 씨뿌리기 좋은데가 어디일까? Where's the best place to plant seeds?
▶그들은 어디 있지? Where are they now?
▶어디까지 가십니까? How far are you going (to go)?
▶그것을 어디서 찾았니? Where did you find it?
▶어디서 전화하는 거니? Where are you calling from?
▶어디 가니? Where are you going?
▶너는 어디 출신이냐? Where are you from? ⇒ Where were you born?

▶ 會話 「야, 멋있다, 거기가 어디지?」「영국이야」「영국의 어디지?」"Oh, that's nice. Where's that?" "It's England." "Where abouts in [What part of] England?"
▶ 어디를 가나 친절한 사람이 있다 Wherever [No matter where] you go, you'll find kind people.
▶ 그것은 이방의 어디에 두어도 된다 You can put it anywhere in this room.
▶ 어디를 보나 물뿐이었다 All was water as far as the eye could reach [see].
▶ 여기는 추우니 어디 따뜻한 데로 가자 It's cold here. Let's go somewhere warm.
▶ 그는 이 근처 어디엔가 살고 있다 He lives somewhere about here [in this neighborhood].
2 〈어떤 점〉 in some respects; in some ways
▶ 그녀는 어딘지 내 어머니 같다 She looks like my mother in some ways. ⇌ She has [bears] some resemblance to my mother.
▶ 그에게는 어딘지 사람을 끄는[이상한] 데가 있다 There's something attractive [strange] about him.
▶ 그 사람의 어디가 좋으냐? What (good) do you see in him?
어디² 〈강조〉 well; now; well now; let me see
▶ 어디 두고 보자 You will have to [You'll] pay for this. ⇌ I won't let you get away with this.
▶ 어디 이야기 좀 들어봅시다 Well [Now], let me hear the story.
▶ 어디, 좀 쉬자 Well, let's take a break.
▶ 그게 어디 말이나 되니? This is absurd [ridiculous]. ⇌ It is quite out of the question.
어디까지 how far; to what extent
▶ 어디까지 가십니까? How far are you going?
▶ 어디까지 가야 호텔이 있습니까? How far do we have to go to find a hotel?
▶ (교실에서) 요전에 어디까지 배웠던가요? How far did we go last time?
▶ 그녀를 어디까지 믿어야 할지 모르겠다 I don't know how far [to what extent] she can be trusted [I can trust her].
어디까지나 1 〈어디에든지〉 anywhere; to the end of the world [earth]; endlessly
♦어디까지나 이어지는 사막 an endless desert
▶ 옥수수밭이 어디까지나 계속되고 있었다 The corn fields extended endlessly.
▶ 너하고 함께라면 어디까지나 가겠다 I would go to the world's end with you.
2 〈최후까지〉 to the end; 〈어떤 일이 있어도〉 through thick and thin
▶ 난 어디까지나 네 편이다 I'm with you all the way.
▶ 나는 그 계획에는 어디까지나 반대다 I am against the plan from beginning to end.
3 〈어느 모로 보나〉 in all respects; in every point; after all
▶ 사내아이는 어디까지나 사내아이다 (속담) Boys will be boys.
어디여 〈소를 모는 소리〉 gee!; gee-ho!; gee-up!
어딘가, 어딘지 somehow; in some ways; without knowing why ⇨ 어디 2, 어쩐지 ▶ 어딘지 이상하다 Somehow [For no special reason], it seems strange.
어따 〈였다〉 Here! ▶ 어따 이것 가져라 [먹어라] Here, take [eat] this. ⇌ Here you are!
어때 How; How [what] about
▶ 오늘 아침은 기분이 어때? How are you feeling this morning?
▶ 장사는 어때? How about your business?
▶ 이렇게 하면 어때? How [What] about doing this?
▶ 어때, 마음에 드니? Well, do you like it?
어떠하다 be how ⇨ 어떻다
어떠한 a certain ⇨ 어떻다
어떤 1 〈무슨〉 what 《book》; what kind [sort] of 《book》; like what
♦어떤 이유로 why; for what reason / 어떤 식으로 how; in what manner [way]
▶ 그는 어떤 사람이냐? What sort of (a) man is he? ⇌ What is he like?
▶ 어떤 영화를 보고 싶니? What [Which] movie do you want to see?
▶ 네가 말하는 사랑이란 어떤 뜻이니? What do you mean by the word "love"?
2 〈여하한〉 ♦어떤 일이든 anything; everything; 〈부정〉 nothing / 어떤 짓을 해서라도 at all costs; at any cost; by any means / 어떤 일이 일어나도 whatever may happen; under [in] any circumstances; (not) for all the world
▶ 어떤 말을 해도 그는 들으려 하지 않는다 He won't listen to me, no matter what I say.
▶ 어떤 일이 있어도 생각을 바꾸지 마라 Don't change your mind, no matter what [whatever] happens.
3 〈어느〉 a certain; some; one; a
♦어떤 것 something / 어떤 날 one (fine) day / 어떤 사람 a certain person; someone; a Mr. So-and-so
▶ 찬 어떤 것을 마시고 싶다 I want something cold to drink.
▶ 4월의 어떤 날[밤, 일요일] 그녀는 여행을 떠났다 She set out on a trip one day [one evening, on a Sunday] in April.
▶ 어떤 남자 아이가 네가 없는 동안에 찾아왔더라 Some [A, One] boy came to see you while you were out.
▶ 어떤 의미에서 그것도 옳다 That is correct in a (certain) sense.
어떻게 1 〈어찌〉 how; in what way [manner]; by what means
▶ 어머님은 어떻게 지내십니까? How is your mother?
▶ 요즘 어떻게 지내십니까? How are you getting along these days?
▶ 어떻게 그렇게 했는지 모른다 I have no idea how it was done.
▶ 그 사람과 어떻게 알게 됐나? How did you come to know him?
▶ 어떻게 해야 좋을지 모르겠다 I am at a loss what to do.
▶ 넌 그를 어떻게 생각하느냐? What do you think of him?
2 〈몹시〉 how (much); so; what
▶ 너를 만나 어떻게 기쁜지 모르겠어 I'm so glad to see you.

어떻게 되다

▶어떻게나 더운지 모두가 물을 잔뜩 마셨다 It was so hot that everybody was drinking a lot of water.
▶이 상자는 어떻게 무거운지 꿈적도 하지 않는다 The box is so heavy (that) I can't lift it.
3 〈어떻게든〉 anyway; anyhow; somehow; some way or other
▶어떻게 좀 할 수 없어? Couldn't you do something?
▶8시까지 어떻게 거기에 가 볼게요 I'll be there by eight somehow or other. ⇌ I'll manage to be there by eight.
▶그것은 내가 어떻게 해볼게요 I'll see to the matter.

어떻게 되다 1 〈사람·일이〉 how it turns out
▶그가 오지 않으면 어떻게 되지? What if he doesn't come?
▶ 會話 「결과는 어떻게 되었지?」「잘 되었지요」 "How did it turn out? ⇌ What was the result?" "It turned out (to be) fine. ⇌ It was good [Ok]."
▶이게 어떻게 된 거야? What's all this?
▶그래 그 개는 어떻게 되었지? And what became of the dog?
▶어떻게 되든 내버려 둬 Let it take care of itself.
2 〈그럭저럭〉 turn out somehow (or other); 〈마련되다〉 be managed one way or another
▶어떻게 되겠지 Somehow it will come out all right.
▶십만원 필요한데 어떻게 안 될까? I need one hundred thousand won. Can you manage the money for me?

어떻게든 anyway; anyhow; somehow (or other); by some means (or other); by any means; one way or another
▶내가 어떻게든 해 보겠소 I'll see to it.
▶그녀는 어떻게든 생계를 꾸려갈 것이다 She will manage to earn her (own) living.

어떻게 하다 do [manage] by some means or other; do [manage] somehow; manage; see to...
♦어떻게 해서든 at any cost; at all costs [risks]; by all means
▶나는 어떻게 해서든 목적을 달성합니다 I'll achieve my goal at all costs.
▶어떻게 해서든 그것을 갖고 싶다 I want to get it somehow or other [one way or another].
▶그 건에 대해서 어떻게 좀 해주실 수 없을까요? Couldn't you do something about it?
▶어떻게 하면 그를 만날 수 있을까? What should I do in order to meet him?
▶낙방하면 어떻게 하지? What (would you do) if you should fail?
▶ 會話 「내가 도와줄까?」「괜찮아, 어떻게 해서든 내가 해볼게」 "Do you want me to help?" "No thanks, I can manage (it)."
▶그것은 인간의 힘으로는 어떻게 할 수 없다 It's beyond human control. ⇌ There is no help for it.
▶그의 병은 어떻게 할 수가 없다 There's no way to cure his illness. ⇌ Nothing can be done about his illness.

어떻다 be how; be like what
♦어떻게 how; in what manner [way]; by what means
▶ 會話 「오늘은 좀 어떻습니까?」「덕분에 많이 좋아졌습니다」 "How do you feel today?" "I feel much better, thank you."
▶가족 분들은 어떠신지요? How is your family?
▶요즈음 어떻습니까? How are you (getting on [along]) these days?
▶어떻습니까, 마음에 드십니까? Well, do you like it?
▶학교생활은 어떠냐? How do you like your school?
▶커피 맛이 어떻습니까? How do you find the coffee?
▶당신 의견은 어떻습니까? What is your opinion?
▶이것을 한번 써 보시면 어떻겠습니까? What do you say to trying this one? ⇌ How about trying this one? ⇌ Why don't you try this one?

어떻든지 anyway; anyhow; in any way; in any case; at any rate; either way; one way or the other; at all events
♦그것은 어떻든지 no matter what it may be; however it may be
▶어떻든지 내가 그 모임에 출석해야 한다 In any [either] case you have to go to the meeting.
▶어떻든지 마찬가지입니다 It makes no difference either way.

어뜩 for an instant; quickly; at a glance; by chance
▶호수가 어뜩 보였다 The lake appeared for an instant. ⇌ We had [caught] a glance of the lake.
▶불안이 어뜩 마음속에 스쳐갔다 A feeling of uneasiness flashed across my mind.

어뜩하다 〈서술적〉 be [feel] dizzy; get [feel] giddy [faint]
▶정신이 어뜩하더니 쓰러졌다 I felt faint and fell down.

-어라 1 〈명령〉 Do!
▶좀 숙녀답게 굴어라 Why don't you behave [act] a little more like a lady?
▶담배를 끊어라 Do give up smoking.
2 〈감탄〉 how...!; what...!
▶아이고 가엾어라 What a pity!

어란 魚卵 spawn; (hard) roe; fish eggs; 〈젓〉 salted roe

어람 御覽 〈왕이 봄〉 a royal inspection

어량 魚梁 〈어살〉 a weir

어런더런 hustling and bustling; boisterously going and coming ♦어런더런한 시장 골목 a bustling [crowded] market alley

어럽쇼 Look!; Listen!; Oh, my!; Oh, dear!
▶어럽쇼, 벌써 10시야 Why! [(My) Goodness!] It is ten.
▶어럽쇼, 벌써 돌아가야 할 시간이야 Why! It's time to go home already.
▶어럽쇼, 우산을 두고 올뻔했네 Oh dear [Dear]! I've nearly [almost] left my umbrella behind.

어레미 a coarse sieve; a riddle ◆ 어레미질하다 riddle; sift

어려움 〈곤란〉 (a) hardship; (a) difficulty; 〈곤경〉 distress; adversity; 〈수고〉 trouble; 〈고뇌〉 affliction; suffering(s); 〈시련〉 a disaster; a trial; an ordeal
◆ 어려움을 겪다 be in difficulties [trouble, distress]; have trouble; have a hard [rough] time of it / 어려움을 견디내다 endure *one's* hardships [sufferings] / 어려움에 빠지다 get into difficulties / 재정적 어려움에 처해 있다 be in financial difficulties [trouble]
▶ 그는 나를 어려움에서 구해 주었다 He rescued me from the trouble I was in.
▶ 어떤 어려움이 닥치더라도 너는 그것을 성취해야 한다 Whatever difficulty you may find [meet], you must accomplish it.

어려워하다 be [feel] anxious (about); feel constraint; have a regard for; hold back; hold *sb* in fear
◆ 어려워하는 기색 a constrained manner [air]; an air of constraint / 어려워하지 않고 without reserve [scruple] / 어려워하지 않다 make *oneself* free and easy
▶ 어려워할 것 없네 You needn't trouble yourself about me.
▶ 원하는 것이 있으면 어려워하지 말고 말하세요. Don't hesitate to ask if you want anything.
▶ 저 두 사람은 서로 어려워하고 있다 Those two are very reserved with each other.

어련무던하다 〈괜찮다〉 not so bad; fair; pretty good [well]; so-so; 〈성질이〉 moderate; gentle; mild ▶ 그는 어련무던한 사람이다 He is a mild-mannered person.

어련하다 〈의문형으로 만〉 certain; natural; infallible; reliable; trustworthy
▶ 그의 말이니 어련하겠나 We have every reason to believe in his words.
▶ 그 분 생각이 어련하겠소 He is a man of discretion [good sense]. ⇌ We can rely on his idea.

어련히 naturally; surely; certainly; undoubtedly; as a matter of course; infallibly
▶ 염려마, 어련히 그가 돌아올라구 Don't worry about him, he will surely be back.
▶ 그에게 모두 맡게. 어련히 알아서 할까 Leave everything to him. He'll show his skill [efficiency].

어렴성 〈어려워 하는 기색〉 constraint; regardfulness for *sb's* feelings; discretion
◆ 어렴성 없는 indiscreet; unreserved [unconstrained]; free from constraint / 어렴성 없이 without constraint; at (*one's*) ease; freely / 어렴성 없이 말하다 talk without reserve; speak bluntly
▶ 그는 어렴성이 없다 He is indiscreet. ⇌ He has bad manners.
▶ 그 소녀는 어렴성도 없이 대통령과 악수했다 The little girl boldly shook hands with the President.

어렴풋이 dimly; faintly; vaguely; slightly
◆ 어렴풋이 기억하고 있다 have a dim memory (of); remember dimly
▶ 산이 멀리 어렴풋이 보였다 The mountain was dimly visible in the distance.
▶ 나는 그녀를 어렴풋이 기억할 뿐이다 I have only dim [vague, indistinct] memories of her.
▶ 그의 말은 어렴풋이 이해될 뿐이다 I have only a vague idea of what he said.

어렴풋하다 faint; vague; dim; indistinct; obscure
◆ 어렴풋한 소리 a faint sound / 어렴풋한 기억을 더듬다 trace back a vague [faint] memory / 멀리 어렴풋한 빛이 보였다 I saw a faint [dim] light in the distance.
▶ 그 시절에 대한 기억은 어렴풋하게 남아있을 뿐이다 I have but dim remembrance of those days.

어렵 漁獵 fishing and hunting; 〈어업〉 fishery

어렵다 1 〈힘들다〉 hard; difficult
◆ 어려운 문제 a hard [tough] question / 어려운 일 a hard task; a rough job / 직업을 구하기가 어렵다 have difficulty in finding a job
▶ 시험은 아주 어려웠다 The examination was [I found the examination] very hard [extremely difficult].
▶ 그녀가 그 문제를 풀기는 어렵다 It is difficult for her to solve the problem. ⇌ The problem is difficult for her to solve. ⇌ She has difficulty (in) solving the problem.
▶ 그를 설득하기는 어렵다 It is hard to convince him. ⇌ He is hard to convince.
▶ PC 조작법을 배우는 것이 내게는 아주 어렵다 It's extremely difficult for me to learn how to operate a personal computer.
▶ 말하기는 쉽고 행하기는 어렵다 Easier said than done.

2 〈까다롭다〉 troublesome; 〈미묘하다〉 delicate; 〈거북하다〉 awkward
◆ 어려운 수술 a delicate operation / 다루기 어려운 기계 a machine hard to handle / 대답하기 어려운 질문 an awkward question
▶ 거기가 어려운 대목이다 That is a trickish [delicate] point.

3 〈조심스럽다〉 ◆ 말씀드리기 어렵습니다만 Excuse me but...; I hardly venture to say that... / 어려워서 말을 못하다 be silent out of deference
▶ 선배들이 어려워서 그녀는 의장직을 사양했다 Out of deference to her superiors she refused to accept the post of chairperson.

4 〈가난하다〉 poor; needy; poverty-stricken; destitute
◆ 어려운 사람을 돕다 help a person out of a (financial) difficulty / 살아가기가 어렵다 find it difficult to make a living
▶ 어려울 때 돕는 친구야말로 참된 친구다 A friend in need is a friend indeed.
▶ 그들은 어렵게 살고 있다 They are needy [in poverty].
▶ 이웃에는 어려운 사람들이 아직도 많다 There are still many needy people in this neighborhood.

어령칙하다 〈기억이〉 have a dim [vague] memory of it ▶ 돌아가신 아버님의 기억이 어령칙하다 I dimly [vaguely] remember my dead father.

어로 漁撈 fishing; fishery ■ ―금지구역 a re-

어록 語錄 quotations; analects; sayings
■ 모택동— the sayings of Mao Zedong 윈스턴 처칠— Quotations from Winston Churchill

어롱 魚籠 a fish basket; a creel

어뢰 魚雷 a torpedo (*pl.* ~es)
♦ 어뢰를 맞다 take a torpedo hit / 어뢰를 발사하다 launch [fire] a torpedo
■ —발사관 a torpedo tube; a launching tube —방어망 a torpedo net —정 a torpedo speedboat; a PT boat

어룡 魚龍 〔古生〕 an ichthyosaur

어루다 wheedle; coax; (口) sweet-talk; lure [tempt, seduce] by flattery; cheat
▶ 그는 그녀를 어루꾀어 주식을 사게 했다 He talked her into buying stock.

어루더듬다 grope for...; feel about [around] for... ♦ 어두운 방에서 전화기를 어루더듬다 grope (about) for the telephone in the dark room

어루러기 〔醫〕 pityriasis [tinea] versicolor; chromophytosis

어루만지다 1 〈쓰다듬다〉 stroke; pat; pass *one's* hand over [across]; smooth down; 〈애무하다〉 caress
♦ 고양이를 어루만지다 stroke a cat / 대머리를 어루만지다 pass *one's* hand over *one's* bald head / 머리털을 어루만지다 smooth *one's* hair down / 수염[턱]을 어루만지다 stroke *one's* beard [chin] / 아기의 볼을 어루만지다 pat a child on the cheek
▶ 그녀는 머리를 어루만지고 있었다 She was stroking her hair.
▶ 개는 배를 어루만지면 좋아한다 Dogs like to be rubbed [stroked] on the stomach.
2 〈달래다〉 soothe; ease; calm (down); pacify; appease

어룽거리다 be dappled [mottled, spotted, varicolored]; be variegated

어룽이 mottles; spots; 〈점·무늬〉 patches; 〈동물〉 a mottled [spotted] animal

어룽지다 mottled; varicolored; variegated; be with spots or streaks of different shades ⇨ 아롱지다

어류 魚類 fish; fishes; the finny tribe; (총칭) the Pisces ♦ 어류의 piscine; ichthyic / 어류, 수류(獸類) 및 조류 fin, fur, and feathers
■ —학 ichthyology —학자 an ichthyologist

어르다 fondle; dandle; play with (a baby); lull; pacify; please (a baby)
♦ 어르고 빨래는 사람 a Job's comforter / 아이를 어르고 달래서 약을 먹게 하다 coax a child to take a medicine
▶ 그는 아이를 무릎에서 얼렀다 He bounced the baby up and down [dandled the baby] on his knee.
▶ 어머니가 아이를 얼러서 잠들게 했다 The mother lulled her baby to sleep.
▶ 그녀는 우는 아이를 장난감을 주어 얼렀다 She calmed [humored] the crying child by giving him a toy.
▶ 고양이가 쥐를 어르고 있다 The cat is toying with a mouse.

어르신네 〈남의 아버지〉 your [his] father; 〈노인·연장자〉 elders; seniors; older people than *one* ♦ 어르신네를 공경하다 be respectful to *one's* elders [seniors]
▶ 어르신네께서는 안녕하신가? How is your father?

어른 1 〈성인〉 a man; a woman; a grown-up (person); an adult
♦ 어른의 세계 the adult [grown-up] world / 어른이 되다 grow up (to be a man [woman]); become a man [woman]; grow into a man [woman]; come of age / 어른처럼 굴다 act [behave] like a grown up / 어른티를 내다 assume a grown-up person's air
▶ 어른이 되면 뭐가 되고 싶니? What do you want to be when you grow up?
▶ 입장료는 어른 한 명에 3천원이다 The admission fee is 3,000 won per adult [for adults].
2 〈윗사람·노인〉 an elder; a senior; an older [elderly] person (than *one*)
♦ 마을의 어른들 village seniors [elders]; elders of the village / 집안의 어른 the head of a family
▶ 어른을 공경하라 Respect your elders.
▶ 어른 앞에서 담배를 피워서는 안된다 You shouldn't smoke in the presence of your elders.

어른거리다 〈눈앞·마음에〉 flicker; glimmer; shimmer; quiver; 〈빛이〉 blink
▶ 빛이 나뭇잎 사이로 어른거리는 것이 보였다 We saw light on and off through the leaves of the trees.
▶ 아버지의 성난 얼굴이 눈앞에 어른거렸다 The angry face of my father flashed before my eyes.
▶ 그녀의 모습이 마음속에서 어른거린다 Her image keeps [coming back to haunt me] flickering around my mind.
▶ 물위의 그림자가 어른거렸다 The reflection on the water flickered and danced.
▶ 촛불이 어른거리다가 꺼졌다 The candle flickered and soon went out.

어른스럽다 be [look] like a grown-up (person); 〈조숙한〉 precocious
♦ 어른스럽게 굴다 act [behave] like a grown-up / 어른스럽게 말하다 talk like a grown-up
▶ 그 애는 나이에 비해 어른스럽다 The boy looks quite mature for his age.
▶ 요즈음 그녀는 갑자기 어른스러워졌다 Recently she's suddenly become more grown up.

어른어른 glimmering(ly); shimmering(ly); flickering(ly)
♦ 물위에서 어른어른하는 햇빛 sunlight playing on the water
▶ 촛불이 바람에 어른어른한다 The candle is flickering in the breeze.

어름 〈맞닿는 자리〉 a junction; 〈한가운데〉 the very middle

어름거리다 〈언행을〉 act [talk] ambiguously; equivocate; 〈일을〉 shuffle along [through]
♦ 대답을 어름거리다 equivocate in replying; evade a question; give a vague answer / 말을 어름거리다 speak ambiguously

어름어름 1 〈불분명하게〉 ambiguously; vague-

ly; equivocally
♦ 어름어름 말하다 talk ambiguously; talk nonsense / 어름어름 변명하다 falter (out) an excuse
▶ 웃으며 어름어름 하지 마라 You can't laugh it off [smile it away].
2 〈엉터리로〉 carelessly; in a slovenly way
♦ 어름어름 일하다 scamp *one's* work; be careless [sloppy] about *one's* work

어릉 御陵 a royal tomb [mausoleum]
어리 〈병아리의〉 a coop
어리광 a child's winning ways; palying the baby
♦ 어리광 피우는 아이 a pampered child / 어리광 부리다 [피우다, 떨다] play the baby; behave like a spoilt child; (口) make up to
▶ 어리광 떨지 마라 Don't act like a baby.
▶ 아이들은 계모에게 어리광을 부리지 않았다 The children never made up to the stepmother.

어리굴젓 salted and spiced oysters
어리다¹ **1** 〈눈물이〉 (tears) come to [gather in] *one's* eyes
♦ 눈물 어린 눈 moist [tearful] eyes / 눈물 어린 눈으로 with tears in *one's* eyes / 눈에 눈물이 어리다 tears stand [well up] in *one's* eyes
▶ 그녀의 눈에 눈물이 어려 있었다 There were tears in her eyes. ⇌ She had tears in her eyes.
2 〈깃들다〉 be filled (with)
♦ 진심어린 감사의 말 heartfelt words of gratitude / 애정어린 편지 an affectionate letter
▶ 그의 말에는 진심이 어려 있었다 He spoke from the heart.
▶ 그녀의 노래에는 애수가 어려 있다 There is a pathetic note in her songs. ⇌ A melancholy mood runs through her songs.

어리다² **1** 〈나이가 적다〉 infant; (very) young; juvenile; of tender age [years]
♦ 어린 가지 a shoot / 어린 나무 a young plant [tree] / 〈묘목〉 a sapling / 어린 마음 a childish [juvenile] mind / 어린 아이 〈보통 2~6세〉 a little boy [girl]; a very young boy [girl] / 어린 양 a lamb; 〈하나님의〉 the Lamb of God / 〈어릴 때〉 어릴 때의 기억 *one's* childhood [early] memory / 어릴 때의 동무 a childhood friend; a friend [playmate] of *one's* childhood / 어릴 때에 in *one's* infancy [childhood, early life]; when (*one* was) a child / 어릴 때부터 from *one's* childhood
▶ 그는 나보다 세살 어리다 He is three years younger than I [me]. ⇌ He is my junior by three years.
▶ 어린 마음에 그는 무척 슬펐다 Child that he was, he felt very sad.
▶ 그의 아이들은 아직도 어렸었다 His children were still very young.
▶ 그는 나이는 어리지만 분별이 있다 He has an old head on young shoulders.
▶ 나는 어린 마음에도 슬퍼서 눈물이 나왔다 Mere child that [as] I was, I felt sad and shed tears.
2 〈유치하다〉 childish; immature; green; inexperienced
♦ 생각하는 것이 어리다 have a childish [an infantile] idea; *one's* way of thinking is childish [immature]
▶ 그는 큰 소리치지만 아직 어리다 He talks big but he is still a greenhorn

어리대다 hang [linger] about [around]; ramble; wander; idle
어리둥절하다 puzzled; confused; stupefied; stunned; dumbfounded; bewildered
♦ 어리둥절하여 어찌 할 바를 모르다 be quite at a loss what to do / 어리둥절하게 하다 amaze; perplex; puzzle
▶ 나는 어려운 질문을 받고 어리둥절했다 I was thrown off balance by the difficult question.
▶ 그녀가 갑자기 키스를 해서 그는 어리둥절했다 He was embarrassed when she suddenly kissed him.

어리마리 drowsily —**어리마리하다** half-asleep; drowsy; sleepy-headed
▶ 어리마리하는 동안에 강의가 끝났다 While I was dozing, the lecture came to an end.

어리벙벙하다 dumbfounded; bewildered; dazed; absentminded; disconcerted
▶ 어리벙벙해서 나는 어찌할 바를 몰랐다 I was at a loss [at my wit's end] what to do.
▶ 나는 그 소식을 듣고 한동안 어리벙벙했다 The news struck me speechless [dumb] for a while.
▶ 그녀가 너무 몰라서 나는 잠시 어리벙벙했다 I was dumbfounded for a moment by her crass ignorance.

어리보기 a half-wit; a dim-wit; a dullard; a simpleton
어리석다 foolish; silly; stupid
♦ 어리석은 생각 a foolish [stupid, ridiculous] notion [idea] / 어리석도록 고지식한 사람 a person who is honest to a fault / 어리석은 짓을 하다 do a foolish [stupid, silly] thing; act foolishly; play the fool; commit a folly
▶ 어리석은 소리 작작해 Don't say silly things!
▶ 그런 말을 했다니, 너는 참 어리석다 What a fool [How foolish] you were to say such a thing!
▶ 그의 어리석음은 조처가 사태를 악화시켰다 His stupidity made the matter [situation] worse.
▶ 그녀는 그것을 그대로 믿을 정도로 어리석지는 않다 She is not so naive as to believe that.

어리숭하다 1 〈희미하다〉 dim; hazy; indistinct; vague; obscure
♦ 기억이 어리숭하다 have a dim memory; remember dimly
2 〈어리석은 듯하다〉 look foolish; naive
▶ 그는 어리숭하지만 바보가 아니다 He looks foolish but he is no fool [he is not a fool].
▶ 나는 쓸데없는 것에 돈을 쓸만큼 어리숭하지는 않다 I am not so foolish as to waste my money on trifles.

어리어리하다 〈희미하다〉 dim; hazy; vague; indistinct; 〈잡다하다〉 variegated; mottled
어리치다 〈정신이 흐릿해지다〉 lose consciousness; get fuzzy; faint (away); swoon
어리칙칙하다 〈어리석은 체하다〉 pretend to be stupid [foolish]; put on an air of ignorance
어린것 a little one [child]; *one's* child [kid]
어린녀석 a little chap; a mischievous young-

어린아이 　ster; a brat; an urchin

어린아이　a child (*pl.* children); a youngster; a little one; (俗) a kid; a kiddy; 〈남아〉 a boy; 〈여아〉 a girl; 〈젖먹이〉 a baby; 〈유아〉 an infant; (총칭) little ones [fellows]
♦ 어린아이다운 childlike; infantile / 어린아이 같은 〈유치한〉 childish / 어린아이같은 말을 하다 talk like a child; say childish things / 어린아이를 좋아하다 be fond of children
▶ 너도 이제는 어린아이가 아니다 You are no longer a child.
▶ 그녀는 아직 어린아이가 없다 She has no children as yet ⇒ She is still childless.
▶ 어머니는 나를 언제나 어린아이 취급하신다 My mother always treats me like a child [(口) as if I was a little child].
▶ 그런 것은 세 살 먹은 어린아이라도 알고 있다 A mere child knows it.
▶ 어린아이 같이 굴지 마라 Don't be so childish [such a child].

어린이　a child ⇨ 어린아이
♦ 어린이의 juvenile / 어린이를 위한 juvenile; of a child
▶ 우리는 어린이가 셋입니다 We have three children.
▶ 그녀는 어린이처럼 남편을 믿고 따랐다 She followed her husband with children's trust.
■ —날 Children's Day　—대공원 Children's Grand Park　—방 a child's room; a children's room　—시간 〈라디오·TV의〉 the children's hour　—신문 a children's newspaper　—영화 a film for children　—옷 children's clothing [garments, wears]; 〈유아의〉 smallclothes; shortclothes　—요금 children's fare　—헌장 the Children's Charter; the Charter for Juveniles; the Young People's Charter

어림　a rough [gross] estimate [estimation; calculation]; an approximation; 〈짐작〉 a (rough) guess
♦ 어림으로 at a rough estimate; roughly; by guesswork
▶ 우리는 100만원이 넘게 손해본 것으로 어림잡았다 We estimated roughly that our damage was over one million won.
—**어림하다**　estimate [calculate] roughly; make a rough estimate (of); guess
♦ 건축비용을 어림하다 estimate the building cost
▶ 열차 승객의 수는 어림해서 500명 정도다 The number of train passengers is roughly estimated at 500.
■ —셈 a rough estimate [computation, calculation]　—수 round numbers [figures]; approximate figures

어림없다　wide of the mark; off the point; far (from); 〈당치않다〉 absurd; ridiculous; nonsensical; unreasonable; out of the question; impossible
▶ 그를 이기려들다니 어림없는 이야기다 It is utterly impossible to beat him.
▶ 그 일을 혼자하다니 어림없는 노릇이다 The job is too much for one person.
▶ 그 일은 천만원 가지고는 어림없다 Ten million won is far from sufficient for the pur-pose.
▶ 이 일은 내 힘으로는 어림없다 This work is far beyond my capacity.
▶ 그에게 도움을 청해? 어림없는 이야기야! Ask him for help? Impossible!

어림짐작　a rough [random, wild] guess; guesswork
♦ 어림짐작으로 대답하다 answer with a guess / 어림짐작으로 알아맞히다 guess right
—**어림짐작하다**　guess (at); make a guess (at); make a (random [wild]) guess; try a shot in the dark

어릿거리다, 어릿대다　be dull [slow]; be unlively; move sluggishly
▶ 어릿거리지 마라 Make it snappy!

어릿광대　a clown; a jester; a comedian

어마　Oh, well; 〈주로 여성어〉 Oh my!; Dear me!; Oh dear!; Good gracious [heavens]
▶ 어마, 귀여워라 How cute [nice, lovely]!
▶ 어마, 꽃이 예쁘기도 해라 O my, what a beautiful flower!

어마어마하다　〈엄청나다〉 tremendous; enormous; colossal; 〈많다〉 innumerous; stupendous; countless; 〈당당한〉 grand; majestic; showy
♦ 어마어마한 돈 a vast [an huge; an immense] sum of money / 어마어마한 부자 a man of great [colossal] wealth / 어마어마한 빚 staggering debts / 어마어마한 우주비행 계획 a colossal space flight project / 어마어마한 인파 a tremendous turnout of people; a mammoth crowd / 어마어마한 직함 a grandiose [an ostentatious, a high-sounding] title
▶ 우리는 주식매매에서 어마어마한 손해를 봤다 We suffered heavy losses on the stock market.
▶ 그는 어마어마한 재산을 상속했다 He inherited an enormous fortune.

어망 漁網　a fishing net　♦ 어망을 치다 pitch [lay, stretch] a fishing net

어머나　Oh!; My!; O my!; Oh, my goodness!; Heavens!; Good gracious!; 〈주로 여성어〉 Dear me!; Oh dear!
▶ 어머나, 그래요? Oh, really?
▶ 어머나, 그래서요? Well, then?
▶ 어머나, 가엾어라 Dear, dear! I'm sorry to hear that.

어머니　**1** 〈모친〉 a mother; (兒) mom; mamma, mama
♦ 어머니의, 어머니 같은[다운] motherly; maternal / 어머니같은 여성 a motherly woman / 어머니를 여의다 lose *one's* mother; be left motherless
▶ 그녀는 곧 어머니가 된다 She is going to have a baby. ⇒ She is expecting.
▶ 그 여자는 좋은 어머니가 될 것이다 She will make a kind [loving] mother.
2 〈사물의 근원〉 origin; source; cause; the mother (of)
▶ 필요는 발명의 어머니 (속담) Necessity is the mother of invention.
■ —회 〈조직〉 a mother's association; 〈모임〉 a mother's meeting

어멈　〈하녀〉 a (married) housemaid; a maid;

a woman servant; an amah; 〈어머니의 낮춤말〉 a [one's] mother

어명 御命 a king's [royal] command [mandate] ♦어명을 내리다[받다] issue [receive] a royal mandate

어묵 魚— boiled fish paste

어물 魚物 fishes; 〈말린 것〉 dried fishes; stockfish ■—상〈사람〉 a fish dealer; (英) a fishmonger —전〈가게〉 a fish shop; a dried-fish store

어물거리다 〈주저하다〉 waver; hesitate; be hesitant; be irresolute; 〈모호하게 하다〉 talk [act] ambiguously; be ambiguous; be non-committal
♦ 대답을 어물거리다 give a vague answer / 결단을 못 내리고 어물거리다 waver in one's determination
▶ 어물거릴 시간이 없다 There's no time to lose. ⇒ We mustn't dillydally.

어물다 immature; undeveloped

어물어물 〈주저하며〉 hesitantly; hesitatingly; waveringly; 〈모호하게〉 indefinitely; vaguely; evasively; ambiguously; noncommittally
♦문제점을 어물어물 넘기다 hedge upon a point
—어물어물하다 waver ⇨ 어물거리다
♦ 일을 어물어물하다 do a slapdash job / 어물어물하다가 기회를 놓치다 dally away one's opportunity
▶ 그는 식사를 다하고도 어물어물하고 있었다 He lingered at the table after the meal.

어물쩍 equivocally; quibblingly; evasively
♦어물쩍 대답하다 give an evasive [a vague] reply / 질문을 어물쩍 넘기다 evade [dodge] a question
—어물쩍하다 equivocate; prevaricate; quibble

어물쩍거리다 speak ambiguously; pussyfoot around; equivocate; prevaricate; quibble

어미 〈어머니의 낮춤말〉 a mother; 〈동물의〉 a female parent; a dam; a mother animal
♦어미개 [고양이, 새] a mother dog [cat, bird]

어미 語尾 〖文法〗 the ending (of a word)
♦어미가 -sh로 끝나는 말 words ending in -sh ■—변화 inflection; 〈명사・형용사의〉 declension

어민 漁民 fishermen; fisherfolk

어버이 parents
♦친어버이 one's real [true] parents / 어버이의 사랑 parental love [affection] / 어버이 없는 아이 a child with no parents; an orphan; an parentless child / 어버이의 parental / 어버이다운 parentlike; parental / 어버이를 부양하다 support one's parents / 어버이를 잃다 lose one's parents; be deprived of one's parents / 어버이를 따르다 obey [be obedient to] one's parents / 어버이에게 효도하다 serve one's parents devotedly; be dutiful toward one's parents

어벌쩡하다 quibbling; deceitful; tricky; cajoling; wheedling ♦어벌쩡하여 남의 것을 빼앗다 cajole sb out of sth
▶ 외판원은 나를 어벌쩡하여 그 차를 사게 했다 The salesman wheedled me into buying the car.

어법 語法 (a mode of) expression; usage (of language); wording; phraseology; 〈문법〉 grammar; diction
♦현대 미국 영어의 어법 modern American usage; (a) modern Americanism / 어법에 어긋나다 be solecistic
■—위반 a solecism; a breach of syntax

어변성룡 魚變成龍 rising from poverty to wealth and honor

어별 魚鼈 1 〈물고기와 자라〉 fish and snapping turtles **2** 〈해산 동물〉 (총칭) sea creatures

어보 魚譜 an atlas of fish

어복 魚腹 belly of fish ♦어복을 채우다 〈익사하다〉 become food for fishes; find a watery grave

어부 漁夫 a fisherman; a fisher
▶ 어부지리를 얻다 (속담) A third party makes off with the profits. ⇒ Someone horns in on the profits. ⇒ Two dogs fight for a bone and the third runs away with it.
▶ 그는 적끼리 싸우게 해놓고 감쪽같이 어부지리를 얻었다 He succeeded by playing his enemies off against each other.

어부슴 魚— 〖民俗〗 a fish-feeding exorcism (on the 15th of lunar January)

어분 魚粉 fish meal

어불성설 語不成說 lack of logic; illogicality; unreasonable talk ♦어불성설이다 be illogical [unreasonable]; be contrary to logic; do not hold any water; lack logic

어비 魚肥 fish fertilizer [manure]

어빙 〈미국의 작가〉 Irving, Washington (1783-1859)

어사 御史 a royal censor [inspector]

어사 御使 a king's messenger

어사리 漁— fishing with a net; netting
—어사리하다 fish with a net; net

어살 魚— a weir; a kiddle; a fishpound

어상 —商 a cattle dealer

어상 魚商 a fish dealer

어상반하다 於相半— much the same; nearly alike; almost equal
♦ 생계비의 상승에 어상반한 급료 pay proportionate to increased living cost / 나이가 어상반하다 be about the same age
▶ 수입에 어상반한 생활을 하세요 You should live according to [within] your means [income].

어새 御璽 the royal seal

어색하다 語塞— 1 〈말이 막히다〉 be at a loss for a word; be stuck for words; stumble at one's words; falter
▶ 어색하여 말이 나오지 않았다 Words stuck in my throat. ⇒ I was choked up for words.
2 〈열적다・거북하다・부자연스럽다〉 feel awkward [embarrassed, (con)strained, nervous]; feel [be] ill at ease; feel diffident; find it hard to
♦ 어색한 미소를 짓다 smile an artificial [a forced] smile / 어른과 같이 있기가 어색하다 feel ill at ease in the presence of elders
▶ 그는 어색한 태도로 내게 인사했다 He greet-

ed me in an awkward manner.
▶ 그의 거동이 어색했다 His movements were awkward. ⇌ He was awkward in his movements.
▶ 여기 있기가 좀 어색하다 I feel out of place here.
3 〈서투르다〉 awkward; clumsy; stiff; 〈딱딱하다〉 crude; unrefined
♦ 어색한 문장 an awkward [a stiff] style
▶ 그의 문장은 어색하다 He writes in a crude style.
▶ 외국인들은 어색한 손놀림으로 젓가락질을 하고 있었다 The foreigners were using chopsticks clumsily [with clumsy hands].

어서 1 〈빨리〉 quick(ly); promptly; fast; without delay [hesitation]
▶ 어서 가거라 Go right away [at once, immediately].
▶ 어서 해라 Be quick! ⇌ Hurry (up).
▶ 어서 오너라 Come quick.
▶ 어서 대답해라 Answer promptly. ⇌ Give me a prompt answer.
2 〈부디〉 please; kindly
▶ 어서 들어오십시오 Come right in, please.
▶ 어서 오십시오 Welcome! ⇌ 〈점포에서〉 Good morning [afternoon, evening], sir [madam]. What can I do for you [I show you]? ⇌ 〈호객시에〉 Walk up! Walk up!

-어서 (and) so; and then; to; for; from; as; so as to; so... that...; because (of); on account of
▶ 이것이 너무 적어서 나누기가 어렵다 This is too little to divide.
▶ 너무 늦어서 미안합니다 I'm sorry to be so late.

-어서가 not that... (but that...)
▶ 일이 싫어서가 아니라 시간이 없기 때문입니다 Not that I dislike the work, but that I have no time.

-어서도 too; also; either; as well
▶ 품질은 물론 크기에 있어서도 이것이 제일이다 This comes the first in (point of) size as well as quality [to say nothing of quality].

-어서야 (only) if; when; not until
▶ 밤이 늦어서야 그는 돌아왔다 It was not until late at night that he returned home.
▶ 이렇게 늦어서야 어떻게 떠나겠니 How can we start when it's so late now?

어석거리다 crunch; crush with one's teeth; chew with a crushing [crunching] sound
어석소 a grown calf=어스럭송아지
어석송아지 a grown calf=어스럭송아지
어선 漁船 a fishing boat [vessel, craft]; a fisherboat; 〈활어조를 갖춘〉 (美) a smack
—단 a fishing fleet

어설프다 〈조밀하지 않다〉 coarse; rough; loose; 〈탐탁찮다〉 poor; awkward; clumsy; careless; 〈걸핥기로 알다〉 imperfect; incomplete; smattering; superficial
♦ 어설픈 변명 a clumsy apology / 어설픈 지식 a smattering, a superficial [half] knowledge / 어설픈 표현 a clumsy expression
▶ 그는 솜씨가 어설프다 He is clumsy with his hands.
▶ 그는 물리학을 어설프게 알고 있다 He has a smattering of physics.
어설피 〈조밀하지 않게〉 coarsely; roughly; loosely; 〈탐탁찮게〉 poorly; clumsily; imperfectly; in a clumsy [slovenly, sloppy] way
♦ 어설피 지은 집 a poorly built house
어세 語勢 a tone (of voice); emphasis; stress
♦ 어세를 높이다 emphasize; lay stress [emphasis] on [upon] (a word) / 어세를 높이어 말하다 speak emphatically [with emphasis]
어수룩하다 unsophisticated; naive; simple; simple-minded; 〈어리석다〉 half-witted; somewhat stupid
♦ 어수룩한 사람 a simple soul; a simple-minded person / 어수룩한 생각 a simple [an unsophisticated] idea / 사물을 어수룩하게 보다 take things simple and easy
▶ 그런 이야기에 속아 넘어가다니 너도 참 어수룩하군 It's pretty naive of you to be taken in by such a story.
▶ 그를 믿다니 너도 어수룩하군 How stupid you are to believe him!
▶ 그는 좀 어수룩하다 He is somewhat weak in the head.
▶ 내가 그것을 믿을 만큼 어수룩해 보입니까 Do you think I am so naive as to believe it?
어수선하다 1 〈사물이〉 be in disorder [disarray, confusion]; be out of order; be in a mess [muddle]
♦ 어수선한 머리 unkempt [disheveled] hair
▶ 바닥에 책이 어수선하게 쌓여 있다 Books are heaped in disorder [in a mess] on the floor.
▶ 그의 방은 언제나 어수선하다 His room is usually in a mess.
2 〈세상이〉 (be) troublous [tumultuous]
♦ 어수선한 세상 troublous [troubled, unsettled] times; wild [stormy] times
▶ 세상이 어수선해지고 있다 Times are [The world is] getting unsettled.
3 〈마음이〉 (be) agitated [confused]; flurried; distracted; upset
♦ 어수선한 감정 a feeling of unrest / 어수선한 마음을 가라앉히다 collect [gather] one's scattered wits
▶ 나쁜 소식으로 그의 마음이 온통 어수선해졌다 The bad news completely upset his mind.
어순 語順 〖文法〗 word order
♦ 어순을 틀리다 make an error in the arrangement of words
어숭그러하다 1 〈일이〉 turn out pretty well [good, favo(u)rable, satisfactory, smooth]
♦ 어숭그러하게 진행되다 progress pretty satisfactorily; go pretty well
2 〈사람이〉 (be) easy to get along with
어스 〖電〗 (美) (a) ground; (英) (an) earth
♦ 어스선 a ground [an earth] wire
어스러기 a fray; a frayed end
어스러지다 1 〈말·풍채가〉 become abnormal [eccentric, erratic]; go off the rails [track]; go contrary (to)
▶ 그의 행동은 아주 어스러져 있다 His conduct is very eccentric [abnormal].
▶ 어스러진 행동은 일절 없도록 해라 You must avoid all deviations from the normal (course of action).

2 〈솔기가〉《the seam》turn; become unstraight

어스럭송아지 〈중송〉 a grown calf

어스레하다 〈어둑하다〉 dusky; gloomy; dim
♦ 어스레한 빛 dim [feeble, faint] light / 어스레해지다 become rather dark / 아침 어스레할 동안에 출발하다 start in the morning twilight
▶ 해가 져서 주변이 어스레해졌다 The sun set and it became dark around there.
▶ 첫 지하철을 타기 위해 아침 어스레할 즈음에 집을 나섰다 I left home in the morning twilight in order to catch the first subway train.

어스름 dusk; 〈어스레한 빛〉 dim [feeble, faint] light ♦ 어스름달 a clouded [dim, hazy] moon / 어스름 달밤 a misty moonlight night; a night with a hazy [misty] moon

어슬렁거리다 stroll about; ramble about; saunter [loiter] along; gad about; prowl; 〈배회하다〉 hang [linger] about [around] 《a place》
♦ 거리를 어슬렁거리다 stroll around the streets / 공원을 어슬렁거리다 saunter about a park / 바닷가를 어슬렁거리다 take a stroll on the beach / 숲속을 어슬렁거리다 ramble [stroll] (around) in the woods
▶ 둘이서 이른 오후에 공원을 어슬렁거렸다 The two rambled about in the park early in the afternoon.

어슬렁어슬렁 ♦ 어슬렁어슬렁 걷다 stroll [ramble] about; saunter [lounge] along; walk at a leisurely pace
▶ 삼삼오오로 숲속을 어슬렁어슬렁 걷고 있다 People are walking leisurely by twos and threes in the woods.
▶ 곰은 어슬렁어슬렁 가버렸다 The bear lumbered away.

어슴새벽 early [murky] dawn; daybreak
♦ 6일 어슴새벽에 before dawn [daybreak] on the morning of the 6th / 어슴새벽부터 일하다 work from early dawn
▶ 그 배는 15일 어슴새벽에 부산에서 샌프란시스코를 향해 출항했다 The ship sailed [set sail] from Pusan for San Francisco before dawn [daybreak] on the 15th.

어슴푸레 dimly; faintly; hazily
♦ 어슴푸레 밝아오는 하늘 the dawning sky
♦ 어릴때의 일을 어슴푸레 기억하고 있다 I vaguely remember my childhood.
▶ 나는 할머님의 일을 어슴푸레 기억하고 있다 I have a dim memory of my grandmother.
―어슴푸레하다 dim; faint; misty; vague
▶ 어둠속에 어슴푸레한 빛이 보였다 We saw a dim [faint] light in the darkness.

어슷거리다 drag one's feet listlessly

어슷비슷하다 〈서술적〉 be much [nearly] the same; be much of a muchness; be six of one and half a dozen of the other; be about and about
▶ 자네와 그의 영어실력은 어슷비슷하네 Your English ability is just about the same as his.
▶ 두 사람의 처지는 어슷비슷하다 There is little [not much] to choose between the two persons in their circumstances.

어슷하다 〈비뚤어져 있다〉 slant; oblique; diagonal ♦ 어슷하게 aslant; obliquely; diagonally / 어슷해지다 slant; incline / 모자를 어슷하게 쓰다 wear one's hat on the side of one's head

어시장 魚市場 a fish market

어슷하다 chivalrous; generous

어안렌즈 魚眼― a fisheye lens

어안이벙벙하다 be struck dumb; be dum(b)-founded; be dazed [astonished] ♦ 어안이 벙벙하여 dum(b)founded; in blank [mute] amazement; in openmouthed astonishment
▶ 우리는 어안이 벙벙하여 할 말을 잊었다 We were so amazed [astonished] (that) we couldn't speak. ⇒ We were struck dumb with amazement.
▶ 모두 어안이 벙벙하여 그녀의 얼굴을 보았다 Everybody looked at her with blank disbelief [in amazement].

-어야 1 〈당연・의무・필요・유감〉 should [ought to] 《do, have done》; must [have to] 《do》
▶ 그 일은 벌써 해두었어야 했다 The work ought to have been done long ago.
▶ 너는 그와 의논했어야 했다 You ought to have consulted him.
▶ 제가 미리 말씀 드렸어야 했는데요 I probably should have told you beforehand.
▶ 돈이 있어야 미국에 갈 수 있다 It takes money to go to America.
2 〈암만 …해도〉 however... one may [might] 《do》; to whatever extent
▶ 그가 암만 핑계를 대어야 우리는 그의 말을 안 믿는다 Whatever excuses he may make, we do not believe him.
▶ 그는 아무리 늦어야 10시까진 올 것이다 He will be here by 10 at the latest.

-어야지 1 〈가벼운 의지〉 would; be going to
▶ 내일 그녀와 점심을 먹어야지 Tomorrow, I am going to have lunch with her.
▶ 그녀에게 이 책을 사주어야지 I am going to get this book for her.
2 〈아쉬움・실망〉
▶ 피서를 가고 싶은데 돈이 있어야지 I want to go to a summer resort, but I have no money with me.

어어 〈의외의 일을 당했을 때〉 Oh-oh!; Good Gracious!; (My) God!; Why!

어언간 於焉間 〈어느새〉 before one knows (it) [realizes, is aware (of it)]; without one's knowing [realizing] it; (all) too soon
▶ 어언간 가을도 지나갔다 Autumn has gone all too soon.
▶ 어언간 한 해가 지나갔다 A year sped on.
▶ 어언간 여름방학도 지나가 버렸다 The summer vacation has passed all too soon [simply flown by].

어업 漁業 fishery; the fishing industry
■ 근해― coast [offshore] fishery 연안― inshore [coastal] fishery 원양― pelagic [deep-sea, ocean] fishery ―권 a fishery [fishing] right: 공동 어업권 common of fishery ―법 Fisheries Law [Act] ―전관수역 exclusive fishing waters [fishery zone] ―조합 a fishermen's union [association] ―허가증 a fishing license ―협동조합 a fishermen's cooperative

association —협정 a fisheries agreement

어여머리 〈예장용 큰머리〉 a woman's wig 《in a ceremonial occasion》

어여차 yo-ho; yo-heave-ho
▶ 그는 어여차 어여차 하며 바위를 옮기고 있었다 He was yo-hoing again and again while (he was) moving the rock.

어엿하다 respectable; decent; good; honorable; stately; imposing; unblamable ◆ 어엿한 변호사 a full-fledged barrister / 어엿한 신분의 집안 a decent family / 어엿한 신사 a decent [an honorable] gentleman / 어엿한 풍채 a stately [an imposing] air [appearance] / 어엿한 행동 respectable behavior
▶ 그녀는 어엿한 여성이 되었다 She became a full-fledged woman.
▶ 나도 이제 어엿한 가장이다 Now I am a respectable master of my own house.

어용 御用 king's [royal] use; government use [service]
■ —기자 a journalist in government pay —신문 a kept press; 〈기관지〉 a government organ; a mouthpiece organ; a state-controlled press [newspaper] —의원 a government-controlled Assemblyman —조합 a company [kept] union —학자 a government patronized scholar; an unprincipled scholar

어우러지다 〈조화되다〉 get joined [be put] together (in good harmony); be well-matched (with); be harmonized [united]
▶ 식물원에는 온갖 꽃이 어우러져 피어 있다 A variety of flowers are in their glory [have bloomed fully] all over the botanical garden.

어우르다 〈한 덩어리가 되게 하다〉 put [join] together; unite; combine; 〈협력하다〉 go hand in hand (with)
◆ 공동 정신에 의해 어우른 사람들의 집단 bodies of men united by a common spirit / 힘을 어우르다 unite their strength; join efforts; cooperate

어울리다 1 〈어우르게 되다〉 associate (with); join (with); mix [mingle] (with); keep company (with)
◆ 좋은[나쁜] 친구와 어울리다 keep good [bad] company / 아이들과 어울려 놀다 join in the children's play
▶ 그녀는 다른 사람들과 잘 어울린다 She mixes well [easily] with others.
▶ 저런 녀석과 어울리지 마라 Don't go around [associate] with that man. ⇒ You should stay away from a person like that man. ⇒ You should not keep company with that man.
▶ 그녀는 누구와도 잘 어울린다 She gets on well with anybody.
2 〈조화되다〉 suit; become; match; befit; go (well) (with); be becoming (to); harmonize (with); be suitable (to, for)
◆ 어울리는 부부 a well-matched[-mated] couple / 어울리지 않는 부부 an ill-matched [-mated] couple / 어울리지 않다 do not suit [match, go well with]; be unbecoming (to, in); be unsuitable (for) / 신분에 어울리지 않는 생활을 하다 live above *oneself*; live beyond *one's* social standing
▶ 그 감색 드레스는 네게 아주 잘 어울린다 That dark blue dress becomes [suits] you very well. ⇒ That dark blue dress looks very good [nice] on you. ⇒ You look very well [good, nice] in that dark blue dress.
▶ 그 넥타이는 네 옷에 잘 어울린다 The tie suits your coat well. ⇒ The tie goes well with your coat.
▶ 그녀에게는 긴 머리가 제일 어울린다 She looks best with long hair. ⇒ Long hair suits her best.

어웅하다 sunken; hollow

어원 語源 the derivation [origin] of a word; etymology
◆ 어원상의 etymological / 어원을 조사하다 trace a word to its origin; study the etymology of a word / 단어들을 어원적으로 연구하다 make an etymological study of words
▶ 이 말의 어원은 무엇이냐? What is the etymology of this word?
▶ 그 단어의 어원은 독일어다 The word is derived [comes] from German. ⇒ This is a word of German origin.
▶ 이 말들은 어원이 같다 These words have the same pedigree [origin].
▶ 이 낱말의 어원은 분명하지 않다 The etymology of this word is doubtful. ⇒ The origin of this word is unknown.
■ —학 etymology —학자 an etymologist

어유 魚油 fish oil

어육 魚肉 〈생선〉 fish (meat); 〈생선과 고기〉 fish and meat

어음 語音 〈말의 음조〉 the sound of a word; the pronunciation

어음 a bill; a draft; a note ◆ 백만원짜리 어음 a draft [bill] for 1,000,000 won
〈어음이[은]〉 어음이 만기가 되었다 The bill falls due.
▶ 이 어음은 30일간 유효하다 This bill has thirty days to run.
▶ 이 어음은 지금 기한이 지났다 This bill is overdue.
〈어음을〉 어음을 발행하다 draw a bill [credit] (on *sb* for); 〈약속 어음을〉 give a promissory note / 어음을 부도(를) 내다 dishonor a bill / 어음을 인수하다 accept a bill / 어음을 할인하다 discount a bill / 어음을 개서(改書) 하다 renew a bill
▶ 다음주 지급의 어음을 받았다 I received a draft payable [that matures] next week.
▶ 그는 백만원짜리 어음을 발행했다 He drew a bill for 1,000,000 won.
〈어음으로〉 어음으로 지불하다 pay by draft (▶지급 수단을 나타내는 by 뒤에는 관사가 없음)
■ 개인— a private bill 기일경과[만기]— an overdue [a matured] bill 기한부— a term bill; usance (bill) 단기[장기]— a short[long] (-dated) bill 단독— a sole bill 부도— a dishonored [bad] bill [draft] 사고— a foul bill 상업— a commercial [mercantile] paper [bill] 약속— a promissory note; a note of hand 요구불— a note on demand; (英) a cash order (환어음) 유통— a negotiable bill 융통—

an accommodation bill 일람불— a note at sight; a sight [presentation] bill; a demand draft 지급— a bill payable 지참인[지시인]불 — a note payable to (the) bearer [to order] 할인— a discount bill 환— a bill of exchange (略 B/E); a draft ■—담당 a note-teller; a bill clerk —소지인 a bill holder —수취인 the payee of a bill —유통기간 the currency of a bill —재할인 rediscounting of a bill —지급 payment by a bill

어음교환 —交換 bill clearing; clearing (of bills); (bill) clearance
■—소 a clearing house —액 bank clearings

어음발행 —發行 drawing a bill
■—인 the drawer [maker] of a bill [draft]

어음인수 —引受 acceptance of a bill
■—인 an accepter of a bill

어음할인 —割引 discounting a bill
—율 a discount rate

어의 御醫 a royal physician

어의 語義 the meaning of a word ◆어의를 명확히 하다 define [clarify the meaning of] a word

어이¹ 〈어찌〉 how; why
▶그렇게 적은 수입으로 어이 살았는가? How have you been getting along on such a small income?
▶어이해서 그는 자살을 했을까? Why did he kill himself?

어이² 〈평교 이하의 사람에게〉 hullo; halloa; hello; hey; say; (英) I say; (look) here; there
▶어이, 여보게 Hey, you.
▶어이, 창문을 열어주게 Say, open the window.
▶어이, 그만둬 Come on, stop it.
▶어이, 잠깐 기다려 Hey, just a minute!

어이구 O!; Oh!; Ah!; Ouch!

어이어이 〈곡소리〉 wailing of mourners; a funeral lament; Alas!; Woe!
◆어이어이 울다 cry [wail] bitterly

어이없다 〈기가 막히다〉 amazing; shocking; absurd; ridiculous; 〈서술적〉 be amazed (at); be dum(b)founded; be stunned (by); be [stand] aghast (at)
◆어이없는 가격 a fabulous price; an exorbitant [extravagant, absurd] price
▶그건 어이없는 거짓말이다 That's a damned [whopping] lie [a whopper].
▶그의 수치스러운 행동에 어이없어 말도 못했다 I was dumbfounded by his shameful conduct.

어이없이 shockingly; helplessly; easily; all too soon [easily] ◆어이없이 지다 be easily beaten; be beaten too easily / 어이없이 죽다 die a sudden death; drop dead

어이쿠 Oh!; Ouch! ⇨ 어이구

어장 漁場 a fishing ground [place]; fishing banks; a fishery
◆연어 어장 a salmon fishery / 근해[원양]어장 an inshore [offshore] fishery

어저귀 〈植〉 an Indian mallow

어저께 yesterday ⇨ 어제

어적거리다 munch; eat with a munching sound; champ ◆과자[사과]를 어적거리며 먹다 munch a cake [an apple]

어적어적 with a munching [crunching]

어전 御前 (in) the presence of the king; (in) the king's [royal] presence
◆…의 어전에 부름을 받다 be summoned into the presence of… / 어전에 나가다[에서 물러나다] come into [leave, withdraw from] the king's presence
■—회의 a council in the royal [king's] presence

어정 1 〈실속없음〉 having form but no content; all show and no substance
2 〈건성으로 대강함〉 doing sth half-heartedly (and poorly); sloppiness; negligence
▶그녀는 일을 어정으로 한다 She does her work carelessly. ⇌ She works in a slovenly way.

어정거리다 hang [loiter, hover, linger] about [around] (a place)
◆공원을 어정거리다 saunter about a park / 늦게까지 어정거리다 loiter late
▶부랑자가 집 주변에서 어정거리는 것을 보았다 I saw a tramp hanging about the house.

어정뜨다 careless; negligent; slovenly; slipshod; sloppy ▶그녀는 일을 어정뜨게 한다 She does her work carelessly. ⇌ She works in a slovenly way.

어정뱅이 1 〈벼락부자〉 an upstart; a parvenu
2 〈어정대는 사람〉 a negligent [sloppy] person

어정버정 loiteringly; loungingly
—어정버정하다 loiter; lounge [stroll, saunter] about; hover (about, in); wander (about)
▶너무 어정버정하면 남한테 의심받는다 If you loiter too much, people will get suspicious.

어정쩡하다 1 〈꺼림하다〉 (feel) uneasy [ill at ease] (about); (be) uncertain (over); (be) in suspense; dubious
◆아무를 어정쩡하게 하다 keep sb in suspense / 어쩐지 좀 어정쩡하다 feel [have] some misgivings (about)
▶어떻게 하면 좋을지 어정쩡하다 I feel dubious (about [as to]) what to do.
2 〈어중간하다〉 noncommittal; ambiguous; equivocal
◆어정쩡한 대답 a noncommittal [a vague, an equivocal] answer / 어정쩡한 태도를 취하다 take a noncommittal attitude; do not commit oneself
3 〈기억이 흐릿하다〉 vague; dim; faint; misty; indistinct ◆어정쩡한 추억 a misty recollection / 어정쩡한 기억 indistinct memories
4 〈난처하다〉 perplexed; awkward; (be) at a loss ◆어정쩡한 상황 an awkward situation / 어정쩡한 표정으로 with a perplexed expression

어제 yesterday ◆어제 신문 yesterday's paper / 어제 아침[오후] yesterday morning [afternoon] / 어젯밤 last night [evening]
▶우리가 함께 테니스를 치던 일이 어제 같다 It seems like yesterday that we used to play tennis together.
▶그녀는 「어제 공원에서 그와 마주쳤어」라고 말했다 She said, "I ran into him in the park

yesterday." ⇒ She said that she had run into him in the park the day before [the previous day].
▶ 그것은 어제의 적이 오늘의 친구인 에다 It's a case of yesterday's enemy, today's ally [friend].

어조 語調 a tone; an accent; a note; a strain
♦ 놀란 어조 frightened tones / 부드러운[흥분한] 어조로 in gentle [excited] tones / 어조가 좋다 sound good [agreeable, rhythmical]; be euphonious / 어조가 나쁘다 do not sound well [pleasant]; lack euphony; be unpleasant to the ear / 어조를 낮추다 lower the pitch / 어조를 부드럽게 하다 tone down; soften one's voice / 신랄한 어조로 말하다 speak in acid tones
▶ 그녀는 슬픈 어조로 말했다 She spoke in a sad tone.
▶ 이 단어 쪽이 어조가 좋다[나쁘다] This word sounds much better [lacks euphony].

어조사 語助辭 〔言〕 a particle (in classical Chinese)

어족 魚族 fishes; the finny tribe; the Pisces

어족 語族 〔言〕 a family of languages; a linguistic family 우랄알타이[인도유럽]— the Ural-Altaic [Indo-European] languages

어좌 御座 〈옥좌〉 the king's chair; 〈왕위〉 the (royal) throne

어줍다 1 〈언행이〉 awkward; stiff; constrained; dull; slow ♦ 어줍은 대답 a noncommittal reply / 어줍은 사람 a dull person; an irresolute person / 어줍은 태도 a constrained attitude
2 〈솜씨가〉 unskilled; clumsy; awkward; unhandy; poor ♦ 바느질 솜씨가 어줍다 be clumsy with one's sewing

어중간하다 於中間— 〈거의 중간이다〉 (be) about halfway [midway]; 〈엉거주춤하다〉 noncommittal; fence-riding
♦ 어중간한 지식 half [shallow, smattering] knowledge; a smattering (of) / 어중간한 태도를 취하다 take a noncommittal attitude; sit on the fence
▶ 그는 무슨 일이든 어중간하게는 안 한다 He does nothing by halves.

어중되다 於中— (be) either too small [little, short] or too big [much, long]; (be) unsuitable [insufficient] either way; (be) not perfectly fit
♦ 어중되어 쓸모가 없다 be good for neither one thing nor the other
▶ 지금 나서면 시간이 어중됩니다 If we start now, we shall arrive there at an awkward time.

어중이떠중이 all the world and his wife; (every) Tom, Dick and Harry; every man; (anybody and) everybody; the rabble; the ruck; the ragtag and bobtail; all sorts and conditions of men
♦ 정계의 어중이떠중이들 political mongers; the rank and file of political circles / 어중이떠중이를 상대로 일장 연설을 하다 make a speech for the masses

어지간하다 〈상당하다〉 fair; tolerable; passable; considerable
♦ 어지간한 금액 a good sum of money; a sizable amount of money / 어지간한 미인 a rather good-looking woman / 어지간한 수입 a handsome [good, tidy] income
▶ 그는 주식 시장에서 어지간한 돈을 벌었다 He made a considerable sum of money on [in] the stock market.
▶ 화재로 어지간한 손해를 입었다 We suffered considerable loss from the fire.

어지간히 fairly; pretty; tolerably; passably; considerably
♦ 이지간히 가파른 비탈 a rather [pretty] steep slope / 책을 어지간히 갖고 있다 have a good many books / 영어를 어지간히 말할 줄 알다 speak English fairly [tolerably] well
▶ 그녀는 작년보다 어지간히 수척해졌다 She is considerably thinner than (she was) last year.
▶ 오늘은 어지간히 덥다 It is pretty [rather, fairly] hot today. (▶rather는 불쾌함을, fairly는 알맞음을 내포함)
▶ 여기도 비가 어지간히 왔다 A fair amount of rain has fallen here.

어지러뜨리다 scatter (things) (about); put [throw] (a room) into disorder [confusion]; disarrange; disarray
♦ 방을 어지러뜨리다 leave a room untidy [in disorder, out of order]
▶ 책상 위에 책이나 잡지가 어지러뜨려져 있다 The desk was littered with books and magazines.

어지러이 dizzily; dazedly; giddily
♦ 총을 어지러이 쏘다 fire a gun at random

어지럼 giddiness; dizziness; the whirl of the brain; 〔醫〕 (a) vertigo (pl. ~es, ~s)
♦ 어지럼을 느낄만큼의 높이 a dizzy [giddy] height / 어지럼을 타다 (be liable to) feel dizzy [giddy]; be subject to dizziness

어지럽다 1 〈눈·정신이〉 dizzy; giddy; dazing; 〈서술적〉 feel dizzy [giddy]; have [get] a dizzy spell ♦ 종종 어지럽다 have frequent dizzy spells / 어지러울 정도의 속도로 at a dizzy speed / 마음이 어지러워지다 lose one's composure / 마음의 평화를 어지럽히다 disturb the peace of mind
▶ 〔會話〕 「어디 탈이라도 났습니까?」 「예, 조금 어지러워요.」 "Is anything wrong with you?" "Yes, I feel a little dizzy [woozy]."
2 〈어수선하다〉 confused; disorderly; untidy; disturbed; agitated; troubled; chaotic
♦ 어지러운 방 a disorderly room / 어지럽게 돌아가는 세상 the bustling world; the dizzy [dazing] bustle of life
▶ 신문에 의하면 중동 정세는 어지럽게 변하고 있다 The newspapers tell us that the situation in the Middle East is rapidly changing.
▶ 이 방은 어지럽기 짝이 없구나 This room is in a terrible mess [clutter].

어지르다 scatter (about); (口) mess up; put in [throw into] disorder [confusion]; disarrange; clutter (up); 〈잡동사니를〉 litter (up) (one's room)
♦ 장난감을 온 방에 어지르다 scatter toys

around [all over] the room / 주방을 어질러 놓다 leave the kitchen untidy [in a mess, in disorder] / 어질러진 방을 치우다 tidy (up) a disordered [cluttered] room
▶ 방을 어지르지 마라 Don't mess up the room. ⇒ Don't leave your room in a mess [disorder].
▶ 어질러 놓아서 미안합니다 I'm sorry everything is all over the place.
▶ 운동장에 종잇조각을 어지르지 않도록 주의합시다 Be careful not to leave scraps of paper scattered around the playground.

어지빠르다 〈정도가 넘고 처지다〉 miss being right; be too big or little to be right; be not what is wanted; unsuitable

-어지이다 〈기원〉 ◆어머니의 건강이 속히 회복되어지이다 I wish my mother a speedy recovery to health. ▶ 그의 영혼이 편안히 쉬어지이다 May he rest in peace!

어지자지 [醫] a hermaphrodite

어진 御眞 King's portrait; His [Her] Majesty's portrait

어질다 〈너그럽다〉 gentle; good-natured 〈kind-hearted〉; 〈인자하다〉 benign; benevolent; merciful; humane; gracious; 〈덕이 있다〉 virtuous
◆어진 남편 an affectionate [a fond, a loving] husband / 어진 마음 a gentle heart; a compassionate heart / 어진 사람 a good-natured person; 〈덕있는〉 a man of virtue / 어진 임금 a benignant sovereign / 어진 통치 a benign rule

어질더분하다 〈지저분하다〉 be all messed up

어질어질 dizzily; giddily; in a whirl
─어질어질하다 (feel) dizzy [giddy]; faint
▶ 머리가 어질어질하다 My head reels [swims, spins]. ⇒ I feel dizzy.
▶ 오늘 아침에 일어나니 머리가 어질어질했다 My head swam [I felt dizzy] when I got up this morning.

어째서 why; for what reason; (口) what... for; (俗) how come; 〈근거〉 on what ground
◆어째서 그러냐 하면 because; for; The reason is...
▶ 會話 「그녀는 프랑스에 있는 줄 알았어」「어째서 그렇게 생각했니?」 "I thought she was in France." "Where did you get that idea from?" ⇒ "What made you think so?"
▶ 어째서 그가 그런 짓을 했을까? What made him do such a thing, I wonder?
▶ 오늘은 어째서 늦었니? Why are you late today? ⇒ What kept you [made you late] today?
▶ 그는 어째서 그 모양이냐? How can he be like that?

어쨌든 at any rate; in any case [event]; anyway; anyhow; somehow or other; 〈…은 차치하고〉 setting aside [apart]; aside [apart] from; not to mention; 〈…이건 말건〉 whether...or not; whatever; however
◆그것은 어쨌든 be that as it may; be the matter as [what] it may / 비용 문제는 어쨌든 setting aside [apart from] the question of expense / 평소에는 어쨌든 whatever may be the case at normal times
▶ 어쨌든 우리 계획을 추진하자 Anyway [At any rate], let's go ahead with our plans.
▶ 비가 올지도 모르지만, 어쨌든 난 가겠다 It may rain, but I will go anyway [anyhow, in any case]. (▶ at any rate은 쓸 수 없음; 이 문장에서 쓰인 anyway, anyhow는 「비록 그렇더라도」의 뜻임)
▶ 會話 「어쨌든 그는 사과했어」「당연하지」 "At least he apologized." "So I should think."
▶ 이기고 지는 일이야 어쨌든 정정당당하게 싸워야 한다 Whether you win or not [win or lose], you must play fair.

어쩌다(가) **1** 〈가끔〉 occasionally; at times; now and then; once in a (long) while; on rare occasions
◆어쩌다 있는 일[사례] a rare occurrence [instance]; a thing of infrequent occurrence / 어쩌다 찾아오다 show up in a long while
▶ 어쩌다가 그의 소식을 듣는다 I occasionally hear from him. ⇒ I get an occasional letter from him.
▶ 會話 「그가 서울에 오는 일이 있나요?」「아주 어쩌다가요」 "Does he ever come to Seoul?" "Only very occasionally."
▶ 어쩌다가 외식도 하자 Let's go out to a restaurant for a change.
2 〈뜻밖에·우연히〉 accidentally; casually; unexpectedly; by (some) chance; by accident
◆어쩌다 알게 된 사람 a casual [chance] acquaintance / 나에게 어쩌다 무슨 일이 생기면 if anything should happen to me (▶ 「어쩌다가 죽으면」의 완곡한 표현) / 어쩌다 온 방문객 a casual visitor
▶ 두 사람은 어쩌다가 같은 기차를 탔다 As it happened [chanced], they took the same train.

어쩌면 **1** 〈도대체 어떻게 해서〉 what; how
▶ 어쩌면 저렇게 사람이 많을까 What a lot of people! ⇒ (口) What crowds of people! (▶ 「어쩌면 저렇게 많은…」은 How many [much]... 대신에 보통 What a lot of...를 씀)
▶ 어쩌면 그림이 이렇게 아름다울까 What a fine picture!
▶ 어쩌면 사람이 저럴지? How can he be like that?
▶ 어쩌면 이렇게 추울까 How cold it is!
2 〈아마〉 possibly; probably; maybe; perhaps; It may be that...
▶ 어쩌면 오늘은 그녀가 오지 않을지도 모른다 It may be that she will not come today.
▶ 어쩌면 그는 입시에 실패할지도 모른다 He may possibly fail in the entrance examination.

어쩐지 **1** 〈어찌된 까닭인지〉 somehow; without knowing why; in some ways; for some (vague) reason or other; vaguely
◆어쩐지 불안하다 feel uneasy without knowing why
▶ 오늘 아침은 어쩐지 즐거운 기분이 들었다 I had a vague feeling of joy this morning.
▶ 그와 함께 있으면 어쩐지 난 두렵다 I have an unaccountable [a vague] fear when I am with him.
▶ 나는 어쩐지 그녀가 참 좋다 I like her very much for some reason or other [somehow].

▶어머니가 없는 가정은 어쩐지 쓸쓸하다 A family without a mother is somehow sad.
2 〈그런 연유로〉 so that is why; (it is) no wonder
▶창문이 열려 있었구나 — 어쩐지 춥더라 The window was left open — so that's why I've felt cold.

어쩔수없다 1 〈불가피하다〉 inevitable; beyond one's control; unavoidable; 〈긴급하다〉 urgent; pressing
◆어쩔 수 없이 unavoidably; inevitably; 〈강요로〉 under compulsion; 〈마지못해〉 reluctantly; against one's will / 이쩔 수 없이 …하다 be obliged [forced] to 《do》
▶그는 어쩔 수 없이 거짓말을 했다 He was compelled to tell a lie under the pressure of necessity.
▶약간의 사소한 실수는 어쩔 수 없다 Some small mistakes are unavoidable [cannot be helped].
▶어쩔 수 없는 사정으로 결석했습니다 Inevitably I was absent. ⇒ My absence was inevitable.
▶그때는 어쩔 수 없었다 I had no other choice then.
2 〈논의의 여지가 가다〉 incontestable; indisputable; undeniable
◆어쩔 수 없는 사실 an undeniable [indisputable] fact; a fact beyond dispute
▶혈통은 어쩔수 없다 Blood will out.

어쭙지않다 saucy; pert; forward; conceited; cheeky; 〈비웃을 만하다〉 laughable; ridiculous
◆어쭙지않은 말을 하다 say pert things; be cheeky
▶부친에게 거역하다니 넌 어쭙지않은 짓을 했다 It was saucy of you to contradict your father.
◆어쭙지않게 내게 충고를 하겠다고? You to offer advice to me? How ridiculous!

어찌 1 〈어떠한 이유로〉 why; how;for what reason; (口) what... for; (俗) how come
▶오늘은 어찌 늦었느냐? Why are you late today? ⇒ What kept you [made you late] today?
▶그는 어찌 자살했을까? Why did he kill himself?
▶너는 사람이 어찌 그러냐? How can you be like that?
▶(會話)「어찌 안색이 좋지 않소」「아무렇지도 않은데요」 "You look pale." "Nothing (is the matter with me)."
2 〈어떤 방법으로〉 how; in what way [manner]; by what means; 〈감탄사적〉 how; why; what
◆어찌할 바를 모르다 do not know what to do; be at a loss; be all at sea; be at one's wit's [wits'] end; be unable to make up one's mind
▶그는 기뻐서 어찌할 바를 몰랐다 He danced for joy. ⇒ He was beside himself with joy.
▶나는 어찌할 도리가 없었다 I couldn't do anything about it. ⇒ I was quite powerless [helpless].
3 ⇒ 어찌나

어찌나 how; what; 〈너무도〉 too; too much; excessively; very; quite
◆어찌나 기쁜지 in a rapture of delight; in the excess of one's joy / 어찌나 슬픈지 in a passion of grief; in one's grief
▶어찌나 좋은지 믿기 어렵다 It's too good to be true.
▶그녀는 어찌나 기뻤던지 눈물이 글썽해졌다 She was so happy that she brought tears to her eyes.
▶그녀는 어찌나 친절한지 모두가 좋아하고 있다 She is so kind [such a kind girl, so kinda girl] (that) everybody likes her.

어쩔어쩔 dizzily ⇒ 어질어질
어차피 於此彼 〈어떻게 하든지〉 anyway; anyhow; at all events; at any rate; in any case; 〈결국〉 after all
▶그는 어차피 실패할 것이다 I'm sure (that) he will fail. ⇒ He will finally fail [fail in the end].
▶나는 어차피 그걸 해야 한다 I must do it sooner or later.

어채 魚菜 boiled fish sticks and vegetables
어처구니없다 〈어이없다〉 absurd; ridiculous; nonsensical; outrageous
◆어처구니 없는 생각 a fabulous idea / 어처구니 없는 값 an exorbitant price / 어처구니 없는 요구 a preposterous demand / 어처구니 없는 잘못 a gross (fatal, grievous) mistake; an astounding mistake
▶네가 그와 우승을 다투다니 어처구니없다 It is utterly ridiculous [absurd] that you should contend with him for the championship.
▶어처구니없는 일이군 Nothing can be more absurd!
▶(會話)「그녀의 의상은 꽤 별났어, 안 그래?」「어처구니없더라」 "Her costume was rather odd, wasn't it?" "It was incredible."
▶정말 어처구니없어서 말도 안 나온다 It is too absurd [ridiculous] to be taken seriously.

어초 漁礁 《build》 a fish-breeding ground [reef]; a breeding ground [reef] for fish
어촌 漁村 a fishing village [hamlet]; a sea village
어치 〔鳥〕 a jay (bird)
-어치 worth ◆과자 천원어치 one thousand won('s) worth of sweets ▶그건 한 푼의 값어치도 없다 It's not worth a penny [a straw]. ⇒ It's worth nothing.
어치렁거리다 〈힘없이 어슬렁거리다〉 trudge along ◆어치렁어치렁 trudgingly; totteringly
어치브먼트테스트 〔敎〕 an achievement test ◆어치브먼트 테스트를 받다 take an achievement test
어칠거리다 trudge along ⇒ 어치렁거리다
어칠비칠 staggeringly; totteringly; unsteadily ▶그는 술에 취해 어칠비칠 걸었다 He got drunk and walked unsteadily.
―어칠비칠하다 stagger
어탁 魚拓 a fish print;《make》an ink rubbing of a fish; a print made of a fish
어택 〈공격〉 an attack; 〈노래 할 때 명료한 소리를 내는 방법〉 an attack; 〈도전〉 an attack; 〈배

구·펜싱에서〉 an attack;〈하키에서 맨 앞줄에 있는 다섯 선수〉 an attack
어투 語套 one's manner of speaking ⇨ 말투
어퍼컷〔拳〕 an uppercut
▶ 도전자는 챔피언의 턱에 어퍼컷을 먹였다 The challenger landed [dealt, delivered] an uppercut on the chin of the champion.
어폐 語弊 defects in expression; a faulty [misleading] expression
♦ 어폐가 있다 be misleading; be liable to be misunderstood / 이렇게 말하면 어폐가 있을지 모르지만… I doubt the propriety of the word [expression], but…; I'm afraid this expression may be misleading, but…; This may be the wrong word, but…
▶ 그 말은 어폐가 있다 It is not the proper word. ⇌ The word is misleading. ⇌ The word has a bad connotation.
어포 魚脯 dried slices of fish seasoned with spices
어프로치〈접근〉 approach;〈연구대상의 포착·방법〉 an approach /영문학의 어프로치 an approach to English literature
■一샷〈그린에 공을 올려놓기 위한 타구〉 an approach (shot)
어필 御筆 His Majesty's autograph; the writing of a king
어필 an appeal ━어필하다 appeal 《to》; have an appeal 《to》 ▶ 우리는 여론에 어필해야 한다 We should appeal [make an appeal] to public opinion.
어학 語學 language study; linguistics
♦ 어학 지식[실력] linguistic knowledge [ability, attainments] / 어학의 천재 a born linguist; a genius in language [for languages] / 어학의 재능이 있다[없다] have considerable [no] linguistic talent; have an [no] aptitude for languages / 어학에 강하다 be good at [proficient in] languages; be a good [clever] linguist
▶ 그는 어학에 강하다[약하다] He is strong [weak] in languages. ⇌ He is a good [bad] linguist.
▶ 그는 학창 시절에 어학을 잘했다 He did very well in languages at school.
■一교육 linguistic education; language instruction ━자 a linguist
어항 魚缸 a gold fish basin;〈유리로 만든〉 a gold fish bowl;〈둥근〉 a gold fish globe;〈큰〉 an aquarium
어항 漁港 a fishing port; a fishery harbor
어허〈문득 깨달음〉 Why!; Oh!; Heavens!; Dear me!
▶ 어허, 이거 야단났군 Oh! I have made a mess of it.
▶ 어허, 벌써 열 한시네 Why! It is eleven.
어험〈기침 소리〉 Hem!; Ahem!;〈거드름 부릴 때〉 Hum hum!
♦ 어험하고 기침을 하다 hem; clear one's throat
▶ 어험, 내가 우리 반에서 1등을 했단 말야 Look at me! I am at the head [top] of the class.
어혈 瘀血〔韓醫〕 extravasated blood

어형 語形 a word form; a form of a word; a form ■一론〔文法〕accidence;〔言〕morphology ━변화〔文法〕an inflection;〈동사의〉conjugation ━변화표〔文法〕a paradigm
어화 漁火〈어선의 등불·횃불〉a fishing fire; a fish-attracting torch; a fisherman's fire (to lure fishes)
어회 魚膾 slices of raw fish ⇨ 생선(~회)
어획 漁獲 fishing
♦ 어획이 많다 get [make] a good catch; the catches are large
━고[량] a haul [catch] (of fish); a fishery; taking : 한국 근해에서는 어획고가 많다 The catches are large in the sea near Korea. ━기 fishing season ━할당량 《salmon》 fishing [catch] quota
어휘 語彙 a vocabulary; a glossary
♦ 풍부한 어휘 an abundant [an extensive, a copious] vocabulary / 빈약한 어휘 a meager [small, poor] vocabulary / 어휘를 풍부하게 하다[늘리다] enrich [increase, enlarge] one's vocabulary
▶ 이 사전은 어휘가 풍부[빈약]하다 This dictionary contains a rich [meager] vocabulary.
▶ 그는 어휘력이 풍부하다[부족하다] He has a large [small, limited] vocabulary. (▶ He has many [(a) few] vocabularies. 라고는 쓰지 않음)
■━집 a wordbook; a vocabulary
억 億 a [one] hundred million
♦ 1억2천만 one hundred and twenty million / 10억 (美) a billion; (英) a thousand million / 수 억년 several hundred millions of years
억누르다 press [hold, keep] down; force down;〈진압하다·억압하다〉suppress; put down; subdue; repress; get under; control; bring [keep] under control; oppress;〈억제하다〉restrain; control; master; suppress; repress; contain; keep down
♦ 억누를 수 없는 uncontrollable; irrepressible; irresistible / 분노를 억누르다 contain [swallow] one's anger; repress [keep down] one's anger; master one's wrath / 감정을 억누르다 restrain one's feelings; stifle one's emotions / 반란을 억누르다 get under [put down, suppress] a revolt; stifle a rebellion / 언론의 자유를 억누르다 suppress the freedom of speech / 웃음을 억누르다 stifle a laugh; repress a smile
▶ 나는 하품을 억누르고 그의 연설을 들었다 I suppressed [stifled] a yawn and listened to his speech.
억눌리다 get pressed down
억단 臆斷〈억측 판단〉a conjecture; a hypothesis 《pl. -ses》; a guess; a guesswork; a surmise
▶ 그것은 아무 근거 없는 억단에 지나지 않는다 That's (a) mere conjecture having no authority [without foundation].
━억단하다 guess; presume; conjecture; surmise
▶ 우리는 우리 팀이 승리한다고 억단했다 We conjectured that our team would win the victory.

억류 抑留 〈억지로 머물게 함〉 detention; detainment; internment; 〈붙잡아 둠〉 seizure
▶ 많은 사람이 억류중에 있다 Many people are under detention.
━하다 detain; intern; hold in custody; 〈붙잡다〉 seize; arrest
▶ 그는 종전될 때까지 억류되어 있었다 He was interned until the end of the war.
■ ━국 a detaining country ━선 an interned ship ━소 a detention [a concentration, an internment] camp ━자 a detainee; an internee; a detained person

억만 億萬 billions ■ ━년 countless years ━장자 a billionaire; a multimillionaire

억매흥정 抑賣━ 〈억지 흥정〉 forced merchandising
◆ 물건을 억매 흥정으로 팔다 be forced to sell a thing

억병 〈한 없이 술을 마심〉 a large drinking capacity
◆ 억병으로 마시다 drink heavily / 억병으로 취해 있다 be [get] dead [beastly] drunk; be as drunk as a lord
▶ 그는 억병으로 취해 집에 돌아왔다 He came home dead drunk.

억보 〈억지 센 사람〉 a headstrong [stubborn] person; a bigot / 그녀는 억보다 She is a stubborn [an obstinate] woman.

억새 〔植〕 a eulalia ■ ━반지기 〈억새가 많이 섞인 풋잠[땔나무]〉 a firewood mixture largely consisting of eulalia

억설 臆說 〈억측의 말〉 a hypothesis; one's private ideas; a notion without foundation; a conjecture; a surmise; speculation; an assumption; a supposition
◆ 억설을 내세우다 make a conjecture

억세다 1 〈뻣뻣하고 세다〉 tough; hard; stiff
◆ 억센 머리털 a wiry [bristly] hair / 억센 수염 a tough beard
2 〈몸이〉 stout; sturdy; strong; hefty; 〈뜻이〉 strong; tough; resolute; tenacious; unyielding
◆ 억센 의지 a strong [an iron] will; tenacity of purpose / 억센 젊은이 a powerfully-built young man; a sturdy youth; a strongly-built lad; (口) a husky boy / 억센 정신 a mind of steel; a stout heart / 억센 팔 muscular [brawny, sinewy] arms / 체격이 억세다 have a strong frame; be of stout build / 힘이 억세다 have great physical strength

억수 a pouring [driving, heavy] rain; a pelting rain [shower]; a downpour (of rain); a torrential rain
▶ 비가 억수로 쏟아졌다 It rained heavily [in torrents]. ⇒ It rained (in) buckets. ⇒ It rained cats and dogs.
▶ 비가 오기만 하면 억수로 쏟아진다 It never rains but it pours. ⇒ (美) When it rains, it pours.

억압 抑壓 a check; (a) restraint; (an) oppression; (a) suppression; (a) repression
━하다 oppress; repress; check; suppress; restrain; keep [hold, put] down ⇨ 억누르다
◆ 언론의 자유를 억압하다 repress freedom of speech
▶ 왕은 재위중에 백성을 억압했다 The king oppressed his people during his reign.

억양 抑揚 〔言〕 intonation; accent; swell; modulation; inflection
◆ 억양이 있는 modulated; intoned / 억양이 없는 toneless; monotonous; singsong; unaccentuated (voice) / 억양을 붙여 with a certain intonation / 억양을 붙이다 intone; intonate
▶ 의문문은 맨 끝에 억양이 온다 Questions end on a rising intonation.
■ ━부호 the circumflex (accent)

억울하다 抑鬱━ mortified; (feel) chagrined
◆ 억울한 벌 an undeserved punishment / 억울한 대우[조처] unfair [unjust] treatment / 억울한 누명 a false [an unjust] charge [accusation]; groundless [unfounded] suspicion / 억울한 누명을 쓰다 be falsely [unjustly, wrongly] accused (of stealing); be falsely charged (with murder) / 억울한 누명을 씌우다 accuse (sb of theft) unjustly; charge sb unjustly (with bribery) / 억울한 책망을 듣다 get an undeserved scolding / 억울해서 눈물을 흘리다 shed tears in one's mortification [chagrin]
▶ 억울하게도 그 제안은 거부되었다 To my disappointment [chagrin], the proposal was turned down.
▶ 억울합니다 You do me wrong [an injustice]. ⇒ I am innocent of the charge.

억제 抑制 control; restraint; suppression; repression; holdback; constraint; check; curb; 〔心〕 inhibition
━하다 control; repress; suppress; restrain; inhibit (one's desire); check; hold [keep] in check; hold back; curb [put a curb upon] (one's passions); bring [keep] (it) under control
◆ 억제할 수 없는 unrestrainable; uncontrollable; irrepressible; irresistible / 감정을 억제하다 control [restrain, repress] one's emotion / 자기의 감정을 억제하다 control oneself / 충동을 억제하다 inhibit [resist] an impulse (to do) / 인플레이션을 억제하다 check [control] inflation / 성장을 억제하다 arrest [stunt] the growth [development] (of)
▶ 그녀는 격한 감정을 억제할 수 없었다 She could not control her strong emotion.
▶ 정부는 휘발유 가격을 억제했다 The government held down gasoline prices.
■ ━인플레이션 an inflation curb ■ ━력 restraint; control ━작용 inhibitory [inhibitive] action ━재배 late raising (of plants)

억조 億兆 1 〈억과 조〉 a hundred million and a trillion (英) a billion 2 〈썩 많은 수〉 billions; myriads; numberless
■ ━창생 myriads of people; the (common) people; the multitude; the masses; the million(s)

억지 willfulness; headstrongness; stubbornness; obstinacy; unreasonableness; perversity
◆ 억지 해석 a farfetched [strained] interpretation / 억지가 세다 be stubborn [obstinate, headstrong] / 억지 부리다[쓰다] insist on having one's own way; persist (in) [insist (on)]

unduly; act [behave] willfully [perversely]; 〈강요하다〉 make unreasonable demand 《of sb》;〈궤변을 부리다〉 quibble; sophisticate
▶ 억지 부리지 마라 Don't be obstinate, you know.

억지 抑止 〈제지〉 determent; check; restraint; suppression
―억지하다 deter; check; hold back
■―력 the deterrent potential [force] 《of a weapon》;〈물체〉a deterrent : 핵무기가 억지력으로 작용한다고 믿는 사람은 아직도 많다 A lot of people still believe that the nuclear weapons act as a deterrent.

억지로 1 〈강제로〉 by force; forcibly; compulsorily; under compulsion
♦싫어하는 것을 against sb's will / 어린애에게 억지로 약을 먹이다 make the child take the pill; force [compel] the child to take the pill (▶두 용례 모두 the child 대신에 oneself를 쓰면「자기가 억지로 마시다」의 뜻이 됨. force, make는「싫어하는 것을 하게 하다」라는 강한 강제력을 뜻함. compel은 force보다 강제력이 약함) / 억지로 웃다 force a smile; give a forced smile / 억지로 갖다붙이다 sophisticate / 억지로 눈물을 짜내다 force tears from the eyes / 억지로 승낙시키다 force [coerce] sb into consent; force sb to agree to 《the terms》
▶ 나는 가고 싶지 않았는데 그가 억지로 나를 가게 했다 I didn't want to go, but he forced me (to) [made me (go)].
2 〈간신히〉 with difficulty [much effort]
♦억지로 (돈을) 마련하다 scrape together a sum of money
▶ 그는 억지로 생계를 유지하고 있다 He is eking out a scanty livelihood. ⇌ He is making a bare [scanty] living.
▶ 그녀는 시험에 억지로 붙었다 She passed the examination with difficulty. ⇌ She scraped through the examination.

억지스럽다 〈억지가 세다〉 willful; obstinate; stubborn; headstrong; 〈불합리하다〉 unreasonable; 〈부당하다〉 unjustifiable; 〈부자연스럽다〉 unnatural; 〈강제적이다〉 compulsory; forcible
▶ 그렇게 억지스럽게 굴지 마라 Don't be so obstinate.
▶ 그는 그것의 인수를 억지스레 거부했다 He obstinately [stubbornly] refused to accept it.
▶ 그는 자기의 의견을 억지스레 주장했다 He persisted in his opinion.
▶ 할아버지는 너무 억지스러워 결정하신 일은 바꾸는 법이 없으셨다 My grandfather was so stubborn that he wouldn't change his decision.

억지웃음 a forced [strained] laugh; a feigned smile
♦억지웃음을 짓다 laugh a forced smile; put on a feigned smile; force a smile [a laugh]; give a forced smile [laugh] 《at》
▶ 그녀는 억지웃음을 지었다 She forced a smile. ⇌ She forced herself to smile.

억지춘향이 ―春香― doing against one's will; coercion; compelling; compulsion; forcing; something narrowly done by force
♦억지춘향이로 by force; unnaturally; against one's will; under compulsion

억척 〈끈질기고 억셈〉 being unyielding [unwieldy]; toughness; stiffness; stubbornness
♦억척같은 여자 a tough [strong-minded] woman / 억척같다[스럽다] unyielding; unrelenting; tough; strong-minded; dogged; spirited]/ 억척을 떨다[부리다] act [behave] unyieldingly [toughly, persistently]; show toughness [stubbornness]
■―꾸러기[보두] a tough [hard-headed] person; an unrelenting [indefatigable, dauntless] person ―빼기 a tough [stubborn] child; an unruly child

억측 臆測 a guess; a conjecture; speculation; a surmise; a supposition; an inference
♦당치 않은 억측 a wild [wrong] guess / 억측으로 by [at a] guess; by guesswork; as a shot / 다분히 억측의 범위를 벗어나지 않다 be little better than guesswork [a guess]; be largely conjectural
▶ 그는 억측을 하고 있을 뿐이다 He is only guessing [speculating].
▶ 그 문제에 대해서는 갖가지 억측이 있다 There are various conjectures about the matter.
―억측하다 guess 《at, about》; suppose; surmise; conjecture; speculate 《about, on》; give [make] a guess; make a conjecture
♦멋대로 억측하다 indulge in speculation; give flight to one's fancy

억판 〈몹시 가난한 처지〉 extremely needy circumstances; abject [acute, dire] poverty
♦사는 것이 억판이다 live in the most abject [dire] poverty
▶ 그는 억판의 상태에서 죽었다 He died very poor.
▶ 그는 사는 것이 억판이다 He lives in extreme poverty. ⇌ He is as poor as a church mouse.

억패듯 harshly; relentlessly; violently; without mercy
♦억패듯 벌주다 punish sb without pity [mercy]; punish sb pitilessly [mercilessly]
▶ 그는 그녀를 억패듯 빗속으로 내쫓았다 Without a shred of compassion, he thrust her out into the rain.

억하심정 抑何心情 ♦무슨 억하심정으로 …할까 It is hard to understand why…; I wonder why…; Why [How] on earth [in the world]…?

언감생심 焉敢生心 ♦언감생심 …하느냐 How dare you …?
▶ 언감생심 내앞에서 그런 말을 하느냐? How dare you say such a thing in spite of my presence?

언감히 焉敢― 〈어찌 감히〉 how dare
▶ 나한테 네가 언감히 그따위 말을 하느냐? How dare you speak to me like that?

언거번거하다 〈말이 많다〉 talkative; garrulous; long-tongued; long-winded

언걸 〈남 때문에 당하는 해〉 undeserved affliction [loss, blame, responsibility] incurred on another's account; involvement; embroilment; a by-blow

◆언걸 입다[먹다] get involved [mixed up] ⟨in⟩
▶나는 그들의 싸움 때문에 언걸을 입었다 I was [got] involved in their quarrel.

언구럭 ⟨감언이설로 남을 농락하는 태도⟩ a slick manner in wheedling
◆언구럭 부리다 act slick; wheedle

언급 言及 reference; mention; comment; allusion
—**언급하다** refer [allude] to; mention; make reference [allusion] to; make mention of; touch upon (▶make mention of는 보통 부정문에서 쓰임)
◆앞서 언급한 above-mentioned; above alluded to; as stated above
▶너는 그 문제점에 대해서는 언급하지 않고 있다 What you say doesn't touch the point at issue.
▶그것은 두 서너 가지 예를 언급하는 것으로 충분할 것이다 It will be sufficient to refer to a few examples.
▶특별히 언급할 만한 말은 없다 There is nothing worth special mention.

언니 an elder [older] sister; ⟨형⟩ an elder [older] brother

언더그라운드 ⟨지하운동·그 조직⟩ the underground ◆제2차 세계대전 중 프랑스의 언더그라운드 the underground of France in World War II

언더라인 an underline ◆언더라인을 긋다 underline ⟨a word⟩; underscore ⟨a phrase⟩

언더셔츠 (美) an undershirt; (英) a undervest

언더스로 〔野〕 an underhand [underarm] throw [delivery]; underhand [underarm] pitching ◆언더스로로 던지다 throw ⟨the ball⟩ underhand [underarm]

언더웨어 ⟨속옷⟩ underwear; underclothes

언덕 1 ⟨나지막한 산⟩ a hill; ⟨작은⟩ a hillock; a height; a rise; ⟨둥근⟩ a knoll
◆언덕 꼭대기 the top of a hill / 언덕을 오르다 [내려가다] go up [down] a hill
▶그 성은 언덕 위[중턱]에 서 있다 The castle stands on ⟨the top of⟩ a hill [on the side of a hill, on a hillside].
2 ⟨비탈진 곳⟩ a slope; an incline
◆가파른 언덕 a steep slope [ascent, acclivity]/ 완만한 언덕을 내려가다 go down [descend] a gentle [gradual] slope
■—길 a slope; a sloping [slanting] road : 샌프란시스코에는 언덕길이 많다 There are a lot of hills in San Francisco. —**밥** rice boiled partly soft and partly hard (by putting the raw rice slopingly in the pot) —**배기** ⟨경사가 심한 곳⟩ a steep [sharp] hillside; ⟨꼭대기⟩ a hilltop; the top of a hill

언덕지다 sloping; slant; slanting; inclined

언도 言渡 a sentence ⇨ 선고(宣告)

언동 言動 ⟨말과 행동⟩ speech and behavior [conduct] ⇨ 언어행동 (言語行動)

언두부 —豆腐 ⟨얼려 말린 두부⟩ dried bean curd

언뜻 ⟨잠깐⟩ in an instant; in a flash; quickly; suddenly; ⟨무심결에⟩ by chance [accident]
◆언뜻 듣다 ⟨사람이 주어⟩ happen to ⟨over⟩hear ⟪that⟫/ 언뜻 보다 take a quick glance [look] at ⟪a thing⟫
▶언뜻 보니 그녀는 아주 매력적이다 She looks very charming at first sight [glance].
▶그 생각이 언뜻 떠올랐다 The idea crossed [flashed across] my mind.
▶그는 언뜻 바다가 보고 싶어졌다 He was suddenly taken by the idea of seeing the sea.

언론 言論 speech; discussion; views
◆언론의 자유 freedom of speech [opinion]; the right of free discussion; ⟨출판의⟩ freedom of the press / 언론의 단압 pressure on discussion [public opinion]; a gag upon freedom of speech [the press] / 언론의 힘 power of speech / 언론의 자유를 침해하다 infringe on the freedom of discussion / 언론을 통제하다 control speech
■—**계** the press (▶일반적으로 신문·잡지를 가리키지만 종종 텔레비전·라디오도 포함시킴) —**기관** an organ of expression [public opinion] (▶종종 organs of...의 형태로 쓰임); the mass media (▶보통 복수 취급) —**전** wordy warfare; a verbal battle; a war of words

언막이 堰— ⟨둑⟩ a dam; a barrage; a weir

언명 言明 declaration; statement; affirmation; assertion
◆언명을 피하다 make no comment ⟪on⟫
▶나는 그 문제에 대해 명확한 언명을 피했다 I avoided making any definite statement on the subject.
—**언명하다** declare; affirm; assert; make an assertion [a statement]; proclaim; voice
◆대통령이 언명한 바에 의하면 according to the president's declaration / 사직을 언명하다 make a statement of *one's* resignation; pledge *oneself* to resign

언문 諺文 the Korean alphabet ⇨ 한글

언문 言文 the colloquial and the literary
■—**일치** unification of the written and spoken language; unity of speech and writing : 언문일치체로 쓰다 write in a colloquial style [the spoken language]

언밸런스 ⟨불균형⟩ unbalance; imbalance

언변 言辯 oratorical talent [skill]; ⟨능변⟩ eloquence
◆언변이 좋은 사람 an eloquent speaker; a good conversationalist; a gifted speaker; a person who has the gift of ⟨the⟩ gab (▶the의 생략은 (美)) / 언변이 없다 be awkward in speaking; be a poor speaker / 언변이 좋다 be gifted with eloquence; have an oratorical talent; have a fluent [ready] tongue

언비천리 言飛千里 ⟨소문이 빠르고도 멀리 퍼짐⟩ A word [rumor] flies [spreads, travels] far and fast.

언사 言辭 ⟨말씨⟩ words; speech; language; an expression
◆외교적 언사 diplomatic language / 무분별한 언사 imprudent words
▶무례한 언사는 삼가라 Don't use improper language. ⇌ Be prudent in speech.

언설 言說 ⟨설명⟩ a statement; ⟨논평⟩ remark; a comment

언성 言聲 a voice; a tone ⟨of voice⟩

♦언성을 높여 loudly; aloud; roughly; in a rough [hard] voice; in a harsh tone; in an angry voice / 화가 나서 언성을 높이다 raise 《one's》 voice in anger

언약 言約 *one's* word; a verbal promise [contract]; a pledge; a vow
♦언약을 지키다[어기다] keep [break] *one's* word [promise]
―언약하다 make a verbal promise [agreement]; give *one's* word 《to do》; promise by word of mouth
◈굳게 언약하다 make a solemn promise; give *one's* word of honor
▶그에게서 단순한 언약만이 아니라 반드시 서면 약속을 받아두시오 Be sure to get not a mere verbal promise but a written one from him.

언어 言語 language; speech; words (▶일반적으로「언어」를 가리킬 때는 language이지만, 어느 한 나라의「언어」를 말할 때는 a [the] language가 됨)
♦언어에 의한 묘사 a verbal picture 《of a scene》 / 언어의 verbal; wordy; linguistic; lingual / 언어가 통하다 a language is used [understood]; make *oneself* understood
▶태풍의 피해는 언어로 표현할 수 없었다 The extent of damage from the typhoon was beyond description.
▶프랑스에서는 언어가 통하지 않아 고생했다 Because of trouble with the language I had a hard time in France.
■―감각 a linguistic sense ―교정 speech clinic ―능력 language [linguistic] ability [abilities, competence]; (the faculty of) speech ―불통 language difficulty ―사회학 sociolinguistics ―심리학 linguistic psychology; psycholinguistics ―연대학 glottochronology ―예술 language arts ―장애 aphasia; speech impediment [defect]; an impediment in *one's* speech ―중추 the speech center; the speech-control centers of the brain ―지리학 linguistic geography; geographical linguistics ―지역 a speech area ―철학 philosophy of language ―형태학 morphology; accidence ―활동 speech function

언어도단 言語道斷 ♦언어도단의 나쁜 품행 abominable [shocking] dissipation / 언어도단의 요구 a preposterous [an absurd] demand / 언어도단의 unspeakable; unutterable; 〈용납할 수 없는〉 outrageous; abominable; 〈어이 없는〉 absurd; preposterous
▶그는 언어도단의 요구를 했다 He made a preposterous [an absurd] demand.
▶그들의 집단 범죄는 정말 언어도단이다 The group crime they committed is simply unpardonable.

언어학 言語學 linguistics; philology
♦언어학적 연구 a philological study / 언어학적 [상의] philological; linguistic(al) / 언어학상 philologically; linguistically
■―구조[비교]― structural [comparative] linguistics 민족― ethnolinguistics ■―과 the philological department ―자 a philologist; a linguist ―회 a linguistic society

언어행동 言語行動 words and actions; speech and behavior; *one's* words and deeds
♦언어행동을 조심하다[삼가다] be careful in speech and behavior; mind *one's* P's and Q's
▶그의 언어행동은 일치하지 않는다 His words do not agree with his deeds. ⇌ He says one thing and does another. ⇌ He is a man of words and not of deeds. (▶man of his words 는 「언행이 일치하는 사람」의 뜻임)

언외 言外 ♦언외의 unspoken; implied; unexpressed / 언외의 뜻을 간파하다 catch the implied meaning 《of》; read between the lines
▶그녀는 언외로 이혼을 암시했다 She hinted at her divorce.
♦영시를 감상할 때는 언외의 의미를 간파하지 않으면 안된다 In appreciating English poetry you have to try to read between the lines.

언쟁 言爭 a quarrel; a bickering; a (verbal) dispute; an argument
―언쟁하다 quarrel 《with *sb* about [for, over]》; dispute; altercate; wrangle; have [bandy] words 《with》
▶김선생은 친구와 언쟁했다 Mr. Kim bandied words with his friend.

언저리 the edge; the rim; bounds
♦입 언저리 parts around the mouth / 접시 언저리 the brim of a dish / 목 언저리가 서늘하다 feel cold around *one's* neck

언제 1〈어느 때〉 when; (at) what time; how soon

> 解說 ***when***은 현재완료형과 같이 쓰이지 않는다 When did you finish [(×) have you finished] it? (언제 그것을 끝마쳤습니까?) 다만 since when …? 의 경우, 경험을 나타내는 경우, 수사(修辭)의문의 경우에는 가능하다 When have you been to London? (언제 런던에 간 적이 있었습니까?) / When have I said such a thing? (도대체 언제 내가 그런 말을 했어?)

▶會話「당신의 생일은 언제입니까?」「9월 9일이에요」"When is your birthday?" "(It's on) September 9." ⇌ "What day is your birthday?" "(It's) September 9." (▶9는 (the) ninth로 읽는다. 또 9th로 쓰기도 함)
▶언제 떠날까? When shall we start?
▶서울에는 언제 왔니? When did you come to Seoul?
▶언제가 좋을까요? What time [day] will be convenient for you?
▶언제 어디서 그를 만났습니까? When and where did you meet him? ⇌ When did you meet him, and where? (▶앞의 말보다 강조적)
▶시합은 언제 시작합니까? When [(At) what time] will the game start? (▶will 대신 does 도 가능함. will은 막연한 미래를 나타내지만 does 는 거의 확실하여 변경될 수 없는 예정을 나타내며「언제 시작하기로 되어 있습니까?」의 뜻임)
▶그가 언제 나타날지는 아무도 모른다 Nobody knows when he will appear.
▶언제 가면 좋을지 말씀해 주십시오 Please tell me when to go [I should go].

▶ 시계 수리는 언제 될까요? How soon will you fix the watch? ⇒ How long will it take you to fix the watch?
2 〈일간에〉 some time (or other); some day; someday ◆ 언제 또 some other time [day]; another time
▶ 언제 한번 놀러 와라 Come and see me one of these days.
3 〈항상〉 always; (美) anytime; (英) (at) any time; all the time; 〈언제나〉 every time; whenever
▶ 바다는 언제 보아도 좋다 I never get tired of looking out over the sea.

언제고 〈미래의〉 some time (or other); some day; someday; 〈때가 오면〉 in (due course of) time ◆ 언제고 형편 좋은 때에 at some convenient time / 내주 중 언제고 sometime next week
▶ 언제고 그것을 후회할 때가 있을 것이다 The time will come when you will repent it.
▶ 언제고 그 일이 생각날 것이다 Some day you will remember it.

언제까지 how long; till when; by what time [day]; how soon
▶ 언제까지 귀가해야 합니까? By what time must I come back home?
▶ 자네 일은 언제까지나 잊지 못할거야 I'll never forget you (as long as I live).
▶ 나는 언제까지 학생이고 싶다 I wish I could remain a student forever.
▶ 언제까지 그것을 하면 됩니까? How soon do you want it to be done?
▶ 언제까지라는 기한은 없어요 There's no time limit.
▶ 이 은혜는 언제까지나 잊지 않겠습니다 I will not forget your kindness as long as I live.
▶ 네가 언제까지나 젊음을 간직할 수 있는 것은 아니다 You cannot stay young forever.

언제나 〈항상〉 always; all the time; 〈평소〉 usually; 〈습관적으로〉 habitually; 〈변함없이〉 invariably; 〈끊임없이〉 constantly; 〈…할 때마다〉 every time; whenever
▶ 그는 언제나 부모에게 근심만 끼친다 He is a constant source of anxiety to his parents.
▶ 그들은 언제나 만나면 다툰다 They never meet without quarrelling. ⇒ They quarrel every time [whenever] they meet.
▶ 우리는 토요일 밤에 언제나 외출한다 We usually go out on Saturday nights.
▶ 저놈은 언제나 불평을 투덜댄다 That fellow is grumbling all the time [always grumbling].
▶ 당신은 언제나 아름답습니다 You are as beautiful as ever.
▶ 나는 언제나처럼 아침 식사 전에 산책했다 I took a walk before breakfast as usual.
▶ 그는 언제나 자기 자리에 앉아 있었다 He was sitting in his customary [habitual] seat.
▶ 그는 언제나 그렇게 말했다 He used to say so.

언제든지 〈어느 때라도〉 (at) any time; anytime; 〈항상〉 always; (美) all the time; whenever ◆ 날씨만 좋으면 언제든지 Whenever the weather permits, ….
▶ 언제든지 떠날 준비는 되어 있다 We are ready to start at a moment's notice.

언젠가 **1** 〈과거의〉 the other day; some time ago; once; on one occasion; at one time
▶ 언젠가 내가 말한 내 누이를 만나 주십시오 I want you to meet my sister I spoke of other day.
▶ 언젠가 기차 안에서 그를 만난 적이 있다 I have seen him once on [(美) in] the train.
▶ 언젠가 당신을 만난 적이 있는 것 같습니다 I think I have met you once.
2 〈미래의〉 some time (or other); some day; someday; one day; one of these days; before long ◆ 언젠가는 some time or other; 〈조만간〉 sooner or later
▶ 지금 열심히 공부해 두지 않으면 언젠가 후회하게 될거다 Unless you study hard now, the time will surely come when you regret that you have not done so.
▶ 언젠가 휴가가 되면 오시지요 Please come and see us sometime during the vacation.
▶ 나머지 일은 언젠가 또 하겠습니다 I'll do the rest of the work another time.
▶ 그 여자는 언젠가는 결혼하겠지 She will probably marry one day.
▶ 그 새로운 연구는 언젠가는 완성될 것이다 Someday the new research work will be completed.

언중유골 言中有骨 the implied meaning in a remark; implications in a remark [statement] ▶ 그가 하는 말은 언중유골이다 He speaks up with implied bitterness.

언질 言質 a pledge; a promise; a commitment ◆ 언질을 주다 give a pledge; give *one's* word (to do, that…); make a promise; commit *oneself* (on a matter, to do) / 언질(을) 잡다 take [get, seize] *sb* pledge / 언질이 잡히지 않도록 말하다 avoid [speak without] committing *oneself*; make a noncommittal statement / 확실한 언질을 주지 않다 make no (firm) commitment (for)
▶ 나는 그것에 대해 언질을 주었기 때문에 이제 와서 물러설 수가 없다 I've committed myself to it and I can't draw back now.

언짢다 **1** 〈불쾌하다〉 unpleasant; disagreeable; offensive; ill-humored; (feel) bad
◆ 언짢은 기분 an unpleasant mood / 언짢은 얼굴 a displeased [an offended] look / 남의 기분을 언짢게 하다 put *sb* in(to) a bad humor
▶ 나는 기분이 언짢다 I feel out of sort. ⇒ I feel depressed.
2 〈불길하다〉 ill; ill-omened; bad; unlucky; sinister; 〈꺼림칙하다〉 hateful; loathsome; abominable; 〈마뜩찮다〉 undesirable; unwelcome; repulsive
◆ 언짢은 꿈 a bad [an ominous] dream / 언짢은 소식 sad [ill, unwelcome] news / 언짢은 징조 a bad [an ill] omen / 남을 언짢게 말하다 speak ill [evil] of *sb*; talk against *sb*
▶ 나를 언짢게 생각지 마세요 Don't think ill [hard] of me. ⇒ No hard feelings!
3 〈몸이 불편하다〉 sick; ill; bad; indisposed; (feel) unwell
◆ 몸이 언짢다 feel unwell [out of sorts]; (美)

feel mean / 뱃속이 언짢다 have a complaint in *one's* stomach
▶나는 그런 음식은 보기만 해도 속이 언짢아진다 My stomach revolts at (the sight of) such food.

언책 言責 1〈책임〉responsibility for a statement [for *one's* words]
♦언책을 지다 be responsible for a statement
2〈책망〉a verbal reprimand; verbal reproof

언청이 (a person with) a harelip, a split lip
♦언청이의 harelipped / 언청이다 be harelipped; have a split lip / 언청이 아니면 일색 have only one fault, but what a fault it is

언턱 a raised part; a hump; a ridge
♦언턱지다 be bumpy [uneven]
■문— a doorsill; a threshold

언턱거리 the cause (of a dispute; of a quarrel); excuse; pretext

언필칭 言必稱〈말할 때마다 꼭〉as *one* always [habitually, invariably] says; never fail to 〈say〉; in *one's* favorite phrase [saying]
▶그는 언필칭 자식 자랑이다 He never opens his mouth without boasting of his son.
▶젊은이들은 언필칭 남녀 동등권을 외친다 The youngmen talk of nothing but the equality of the sexes.

언하 言下 ♦언하에 promptly; readily; flatly
▶나는 그의 제안을 언하에 거절했다 I flatly [decidedly] rejected his proposal.

언해 諺解 Korean annotation [translation] of Chinese classics —언해하다 annotate 《a Chinese classic》 in Korean

언행 言行 *one's* words and deeds [action]; *one's* saying and doings; speech and behavior
♦언행이 일치하다 live up to what *one* says; *one's* words correspond with *one's* actions / 언행을 일치시키다 mate *one's* words with deeds; substantiate *one's* statements with *one's* conduct
▶그는 언행이 일치하는 사람이다 He is a man of his words.
▶그는 언행이 일치하지 않는다 He says one thing and does another. ⇌ His deeds do not agree with his words.
▶언행을 삼가라 Be careful in your speech and behavior [words and deeds].
■—록 a memoir; a chronicle of *sb's* sayings and doings

얹다 put on; place [lay, set] *sth* on 《a shelf》
♦어깨에 손을 얹다 set [lay] *one's* hand on *sb's* shoulder / 난로[불] 위에 주전자를 얹다 put a kettle on the stove [fire] / 지붕에 기와를 얹다 tile a roof

얹어주다 〈덤으로 주다〉give an extra; throw *sth* in (for good measure) ♦돈을 조금 얹어주다 pay a little extra 《to *sb*》

얹혀살다 be a dependent on *sb*; depend upon *sb* for support; feed [live, sponge] on *sb*; live at the expense of 《*one's* friend》
♦얹혀사는 사람 a dependent [dependant]; a hanger-on 《*pl.* hangers-on》; a sponge
▶그는 아직도 부모에게 얹혀산다 He still sponges [lives] on his parents.
▶그는 아저씨에게 얹혀 살아가려고 했다 He tried to sponge on his uncle for a living.

얹히다 1〈놓이다〉be placed [put] on 《a table》
▶모자가 선반 위에 얹혀 있다 The hat is put on the shelf.
2 ⇨ 얹혀살다
3〈체하다〉lie [sit] heavy on the stomach; remain undigested in the stomach
♦음식이 속에 얹히다 food lies heavy on the stomach
▶이 음식은 잘 얹힌다 This food sits [lies] heavy on the stomach. ⇌ This is not easily digested.
4〈좌초하다〉strand; be stranded; run [go] ashore; run aground;〈일부러〉beach
♦암초에 얹히다 run on a sunken rock; go [be] ashore on a reef
5〈얹게 하다〉make *sb* put [place, lie] 《*sth* on》

얻다 1〈손에 넣다〉get; have;〈노력·계획하여〉obtain; acquire;〈애써서〉secure; procure; derive 《from》;〈일하여〉earn;〈경쟁하여〉win;〈받다〉receive; be given;〈채취하다〉produce《gas from coal》;〈추출하다〉extract
♦명성을 얻다 make a name; win fame / 승리를 얻다 win [achieve, score] a victory 《over》/ 신용을 얻다 win *sb's* confidence; gain [enjoy] credit 《with *sb*》/ 이익을 얻다 make [realize] profits / 1주일간의 휴가를 얻다 take a week's vacation [holiday] / 자격증을 얻다 obtain [take] a certificate / 지위를 얻다 get [attain] a position / 책에서 지식을 얻다 acquire [gain] knowledge through books / 크게 얻는 바가 있다 gain [get] much 《from, by》; get [derive] much benefit 《from》; learn a great deal 《from》
▶나는 책을 읽고 많은 것을 얻었다 I got [learned] a lot out of the book I read [out of reading the book]. ⇌ I learned [gained] a lot of things by reading the book.
▶그는 열심히 일해서가 아니라 도박으로 그 돈을 얻었다 He didn't earn the money by working hard but won it by gamble.
▶좋은 친구를 얻기는 어렵다 It is not easy to find good friends.
▶노력한 결과 그는 부와 지위를 얻었다 As a result of his efforts he required wealth and position.
▶그녀는 그 시로 명성을 얻었다 She became famous because of her poetry. ⇌ Her poetry brought her fame.
▶지식은 주로 책에서 얻어진다 Knowledge is acquired chiefly through books.
▶그는 어떤 일에서도 얻는 바가 있다 He turns everything to good account. ⇌ He takes advantage of every situation.
▶언제 약을 얻으러 올까요? When shall I call for the medicine?
▶잃은 것은 많고 얻은 것은 적다 The gain is outweighed by the loss.
2〈아내를 맞다〉marry 《a woman》; take 《a woman》in marriage; take 《a woman》to wife; take a wife
♦과부를 얻다 marry a widow

얼어걸리다

3 〈줍다〉 pick up; find 《a book》 ◆ 길에서 지갑을 얻다 pick up a wallet on the road
4 〈앓게 되다〉 catch 《flu》; contract 《a disease》; get 《cancer》; be attacked [affected] by 《a disease》

얻어걸리다 find; get; come by
◆ 밥이 얻어걸리다 be treated 《to a dinner》/ 일이 얻어걸리다 find employment [a job]; (口) land a job

얻어듣다 hear of; be informed [told] of [about]; hear [learn] from others; learn [know] by hearsay; happen to hear 《of, about》
◆ 얻어들은 영어 English that one has picked / 얻어들은 지식 knowledge acquired along the way; picked-up knowledge; a smattering of knowledge / 얻어들은 바로는 according to what I (have) / 이웃으로부터 얻어듣다 get (it) out of a neighbor

얻어맞다 1〈매를 맞다〉 get [receive] a blow; be beaten [knocked, struck, hit, thrashed, punched]; be licked ◆ 머리를 얻어맞다 be struck [hit] on the head / 몽둥이로 얻어맞다 be drubbed; be clubbed
▶ 또 얻어맞고 싶으냐? Do you want another thrashing?
▶ 그런 짓을 하면 얻어맞는다 If you do such a thing, you will got licked.
2 〈공격받다〉 be criticized; take a beating; get a rap ◆ 신문에서 얻어맞다 be attacked [by] the newspaper / 여론에 얻어맞다 be flayed by public opinion

얻어먹다 1 〈음식 등을〉 beg one's bread; 〈빌어먹다〉 beg food; 〈대접받다〉 get treated to; rely [depend] on sb for one's food; live off sb ◆ 밥을 얻어먹다 beg one's food
▶ 우리는 다과를 얻어먹었다 We were entertained with refreshments.
2 〈욕 등을〉 get called (names); suffer (harsh words); be abused; be slandered
◆ 욕을 얻어먹다 get called names; be spoken ill of

얼 〈정신〉 spirit; mind; 〈혼〉 soul
◆ 애국의 얼 patriotic spirit; patriotism / 한국의 얼 the spirit of Korea

얼간 salting slightly [lightly]
◆ 얼간 고등어 lightly-salted mackerel / 얼간 생선구이 salted and broiled fish
▶ 나는 얼간 생선구이를 좋아한다 I like light-[slightly-]salted roast fish.

얼간이 a simpleton; a stupid [dull] fellow; a fool; a half-wit; a fathead
▶ 저 아이는 얼간이야 He is stupid [dumb]. ⇒ He is half-[slow-]witted.

얼갈이 1 [農] 〈대충 갈아엎는 일〉 winter plowing **2** 〈겨울에 푸성귀를 심는 일〉 growing vegetables in the wintertime; 〈그 푸성귀〉 winter-grown vegetables; winter-sown greens
■—김치 kimch'i made with winter-grown cabbage

얼결 the confusion of the moment ⇨ 얼떨결

얼굴 1〈낯〉 a face; a visage; 〈이목구비〉 features; 〈안색〉 a complexion
◆ 희고 갸름한 얼굴 a fair and oval face / 예쁜 [못생긴] 얼굴 a beautiful [an ugly] face / 수척한[여읜] 얼굴 a haggard [pinched] face / 모난[둥근, 통통한, 깡마른, 홀쭉한, 혈색이 나쁜] 얼굴 a square [round, plump, bony, lean, sallow] face / 납작한 얼굴 a flat face / 윤곽이 뚜렷한 얼굴 face clear-cut features [person] / 주름진 얼굴 a wrinkled face

〈얼굴이[은]〉 얼굴이 잘 생긴 사람 a good-looking person
▶ 나는 부끄러워 얼굴이 빨개졌다 I blushed for [with] shame.
▶ 그녀는 어머니와 얼굴이 닮았나 She has mother's looks.
▶ 내 얼굴이 기억나니? Do you recognize [remember] me?

〈얼굴을〉 얼굴을 들다 lift one's face [head]; look up 《from the paper》 / 얼굴을 맞대고 앉다 sit face to face 《with》; sit tête-à-tête 《with》 / 아무의 얼굴을 똑바로 보다 look sb in the face / 두 손에 얼굴을 묻다 drop one's face on one's hands / 얼굴을 마주보다 look at each other; exchange glances [looks] / 얼굴을 씻다 wash oneself; have a wash / 얼굴을 붉히다 become red in the face; color up
▶ 그는 창밖으로 얼굴을 내밀었다 He put [stuck] his head out of the window.
▶ 그녀가 내쪽으로 얼굴을 돌렸을 때 나는 그녀에게 손을 흔들었다 When she turned her face to me, I waved to her.
▶ 그들은 얼굴을 마주보았다 They looked at each other [each other's faces].
▶ 나는 부끄러워서 그의 얼굴을 정면으로 바라볼 수가 없었다 I am so ashamed that I can't look him (straight) in the face [eye].
▶ 나는 그의 얼굴을 보는 것도 싫다 I hate to see him. ⇒ I hate [I'm sick of] the sight of him.
▶ 나는 그녀의 얼굴을 응시했다 I stared her in the face.
▶ 나는 그 여자의 얼굴을 알고 있다 I know her by sight.
▶ 선생님은 학생들이 시끄러워 얼굴을 찡그리셨다 The teacher frowned at the noisy pupils.

2 〈표정〉 a face; a look; a countenance; (an) expression
◆ 즐거운[슬픈] 얼굴 a happy [sad] face [look, countenance] / 웃는 얼굴 smiling faces / 실망한 얼굴로 나를 보다 give me a disappointed look; look at me with an expression of disappointment

〈얼굴이〉 얼굴이 험상궂은 너석 an ill-looking fellow
▶ 그 소식을 듣자 그 여자의 얼굴이 갑자기 밝아졌다 When she heard the news, she suddenly looked happy [her face suddenly brightened up].

〈얼굴을〉 불안한 얼굴을 하다 look uneasy; have a concerned look / 행복한[슬픈, 실망한] 얼굴을 하다 look happy [sad, disappointed] / 험악한 얼굴을 하다 bear an evil look
▶ 그녀는 걱정스런 얼굴을 했다 She looked troubled.
▶ 그는 불만스런 얼굴을 했다[하고 있었다] He made [wore] a long face.

▶그는 화난 얼굴을 하고 나왔다 He came out with an angry look.
▶왜 그렇게 비참한 얼굴을 하고 있니? Why are you looking to miserable?
▶그는 그 일에 아무것도 모르는 듯한 얼굴을 하고 있다 He looks [acts] as if he knew nothing about that.
▶가족들은 그의 머리맡에서 걱정스런 얼굴을 했다 The family looked worried at his beside.
▶어머니는 그 소식을 듣고 놀란 얼굴을 했다 Mother looked surprised to hear the news.
▶나도 파티에 참석했지만 그녀는 나를 모른다는 얼굴을 했다 I was also attending the party, but she ignored me [(口) out me dead].
▶우리 딸은 도와달라고 하면 언제든지 싫은 얼굴을 한다 My daughter always scowls [frowns] when I ask her to help.
▶그는 뭔가 미심쩍은 얼굴을 하고 있었다 He put on [wore] a questioning look.
〈얼굴에[로]〉 분노를 얼굴에 나타내지 마라 Don't show (your) anger.
▶성실한 사람이라는 것이 그의 얼굴에 드러나 있었다 Sincerity was written on his face. ⇌ It showed on his face that he was sincere.
▶그녀는 비웃는 얼굴로 나를 보았다 She threw a look of contempt at me.
3 〈체면〉 honor; prestige
♦얼굴이 깎이다 be put out of countenance; lose *one's* honor; lose face / 얼굴이 서다 save *one's* face / 얼굴에 똥칠[먹칠]을 하다 cause *sb* to lose face; disgrace [shame] *sb*
▶네 얼굴을 봐서 한잔 더 마시겠다 I'll drink just one beer on your account.
▶넌 내 얼굴에 먹칠[똥칠]을 했어 You made me lose face.
얼굴빛 complexion; color; countenance
♦얼굴빛이 좋아지다 gain color / 얼굴빛이 희다[검다] have fair [dark] complexion / 남의 얼굴빛을 살피다 read *sb's* face; hang on *sb's* smiles
▶그는 얼굴빛이 안좋다 He looks pale.
▶그는 아들이 죽었다는 소식을 듣는 순간 얼굴빛이 흙빛으로 변했다 The moment he heard the news of his son's death, he turned pale.
▶어떻게 너는 얼굴빛도 변하지 않고 그런 것을 말할 수 있었니? How could you tell such a thing with a straight face?
얼근하다 **1** 〈맛이〉 rather hot; somewhat peppery [pungent] ♦얼근하게 양념하다 season (food) somewhat hot
2 〈술이〉 mellow; tipsy
♦얼근하게 취한 half-drunk [-drunk] / 얼근히 취하다 get half drunk / 얼근히 취해 있다 be tipsy; (俗) be half-seas over
얼기설기 《be heaped》 in a disorderly way; confusedly; complicatedly; in a disorderly heap ♦얼기설기 얽힌 사정 a complicated state of things / 얼기설기 얽히다 be tangled confusedly
▶일이 얼기설기 얽혔다 The matter has become quite complicated.
얼김에 〈다른 일이 되는 바람에〉 on the spur [impulse] of the moment; under the impulse (of); in spite of *oneself*

♦얼김에 말해버리다 say on the spur of the moment; let slip
얼다 **1** 〈결빙하다〉 freeze; be frozen; 〈응결하다〉 congeal
♦꽁꽁 얼다 be frozen up / 몸이 꽁꽁 얼다 be benumbed with cold / 딱딱하게 얼다 freeze (up) solid / 온통 얼어붙다 《a pond》 freeze [be frozen] all over / 얼어 죽다 be frozen [freeze] to death; die of cold
▶물은 영도에서 언다 Water freezes at 0℃.
▶나는 추위로 몸이 얼었다 I am almost frozen with cold.
▶연못은 전체가 3인치 정도 얼어 있다 The pond is frozen over about three inches thick.
▶오늘밤은 몸이 얼만큼 춥다 It is freezing tonight.
▶뼛속까지 얼만큼 춥다 It is so cold (that) I feel chilled to the bone.
▶손이 얼지 않도록 장갑을 끼고 나가거라 Go out with gloves on, so that your hands will not become benumbed.
▶난 얼어 죽을 것 같다 I am freezing to death.
2 〈기가 죽다〉 be cowed [intimidated]; be scared stiff; feel timid [small]; 〈긴장하여〉 get nervous
▶무대에서 얼다 have [get] a stage fright; suffer from stage fright / 시험에서 얼다 get nervous at an examination
얼떨결 the confusion of the moment; a moment of bewilderment
♦얼떨결에 in the confusion of the moment; in a moment of bewilderment
▶그건 얼떨결에 말한 거야 That was just a slip of the tongue.
▶그는 얼떨결에 그렇게 말해 버렸다 He said so in his bewilderment.
얼떨떨하다 〈정신을 못 차리다〉 confused; flurried; perturbed; bewildered; perplexed; puzzled; upset
♦얼떨떨한 표정[기색] a puzzled look [expression] / 얼떨떨하여 in a flurried; in a puzzle; in a perplexity; in a flurry / 얼떨떨하게 하다 flurry; perplex; puzzle
▶느닷없는 질문에 나는 잠시 얼떨떨했다 I felt dazed for a moment at the sudden question.
얼떨하다 1 ⇨ 얼떨떨하다
2 〈머리가 울리고 아프다〉 dizzy; giddy; stupefied; groggy ♦얼떨해 하다 fluster *oneself*; be all in a flurry / 고단해서 정신이 얼떨하다 be faint with fatigue
▶나는 머리가 얼떨하다 My brain reels. ⇌ My head swims [spins]. ⇌ I feel dizzy.
얼뜨기 a half-wit; a dimwit; a ninny; a dunce; a blockhead
▶그는 얼뜨기다 He is a regular stick.
▶이 얼뜨기야! You idiot! ⇌ (俗) What an ass you are!
얼뜨다 〈어리석다〉 slow-witted; dim-witted; stupid; foolish; silly; 〈얼 빠지다〉 absent-minded; abstracted; 〈겁이 많다〉 cowardly; chicken-hearted
♦얼뜬 사람 a half-wit ⇨ 얼뜨기 / 얼뜬 짓을 하다 do a stupid thing; make a fool of *oneself*
▶그는 좀 얼뜨다 He is a bit soft (in the

얼러맞추다 humor 《*one's* husband》; please *sb's* humor [whim]; play up to; fawn upon; flatter; curry favor with *sb*
♦ 얼러맞추기 힘들다 be hard to please

얼러먹다 eat together; eat at the same table

얼러붙다 grapple with *sb*; wrestle with
♦ 얼러붙어 싸우다 fight hand to hand; fight a close fight

얼러치다 1 〈때리다〉 strike [hit, knock] at one time 2 〈함께 값을 셈하다〉 lump [put] together; sum up ♦ 얼러쳐서 all put together; in total; (all) in all; in the lump
▶ 얼러쳐서 모두 얼마요? How much (is it) all together?

얼럭 〈반점〉 spots; stains ⇨ 얼룩

얼럭덜럭하다 spotted ⇨ 얼룩덜룩하다

얼렁뚱땅하다 1 〈엉터리로 남을 속이다〉 play a trick on; hoodwink; 〈말을〉 palter (with a person); prevaricate
♦ 얼렁뚱땅하여 돈을 빼앗다 juggle *sb* out of his money
▶ 얼렁뚱땅하지 말고 똑똑히 대답해 Don't shuffle, give a clear answer.
2 〈적당히〉 일을 얼렁뚱땅 해치우다 scamp [muddle with] *one's* work; do a slapdash work / 대학을 얼렁뚱땅 졸업하다 muddle through college

얼렁장사 〈여럿이 어울러서 하는 장사〉 cooperative business; joint management

얼레 a reel; a spool ♦ 얼레에 실을 감다 spool; reel; wind thread on a reel / 얼레에서 실을 풀다 unwind thread from a reel

얼레빗 a coarse-tooth comb

얼레살풀다 start to dissipate *one's* fortune

얼레지 〔植〕 a dogtooth violet
■ 얼레짓가루 dogtooth violet starch; starch

얼룩 1 ⇨ 반점(斑點)
♦ 희고 검은 얼룩이 있는 개 a white and black dog / 얼룩이 있는 spotted; mottled; dapple(d); 〈작은 반점의〉 speckled; varicolored; motley; 〈새·짐승 등의〉 pied; spotted; 〈호랑이 무늬의〉 brindle(d)
▶ 나는 얼룩이 있는 개를 기르고 있다 I have a spotted dog.
2 〈자국〉 stain; a blot; a spot; a blob; a smut; a smear; a smudge; a blotch
♦ 비가 샌 얼룩 a patch of damp / 잉크 얼룩 an ink stain [spot] / 지위지지 않는 얼룩 an indelible stain / 얼룩이 있는 stained; smeared; blotted; spotted / 얼룩이 없는 stainless; spotless; clean / 얼룩이 생기다 a stain appears [comes out] / 옷에 얼룩이 지다[가다, 생기다] *one's* clothes get spotted / 얼룩을 묻히다 stain; blot / 얼룩을 빼다 take [get] out a stain [blot]; remove stains [blotches] 《from》 / 빨아서[닦아서] 얼룩을 없애다 wash [wipe] out a stain
▶ 나는 비를 맞아 흰 겉옷에 얼룩이 졌다 I got spots on my white coat from the rain.
▶ 그 얼룩은 아무리해도[빨아도] 지워지지 않는다 The stain will not come [wash] out.
■ ─고양이 a tabby (cat) ─말 a zebra; a piebald horse ─소 a brindled ox [cow]

얼룩덜룩하다 spotted; mottled; dapple(d); 〈잔무늬〉 speckled; variegated; varicolored; parti-colored; motley; 〈새·짐승 등의〉 pied; 〈호랑이 무늬처럼〉 brindle(d)
♦ 얼룩덜룩한 남방셔츠 a dappled aloha shirt / 얼룩덜룩한 옷감 varicolored cloth / 얼룩덜룩한 옷을 입은 wearing pied clothing

얼룩이 1 ⇨ 얼룩 1
2 〈동물〉 a spotted [dappled, dotted] animal; a piebald; 〈고양이〉 a tabby

얼룩지다 become stained [smudged]; stain; take a stain
♦ 얼룩진 stained; spotted; blotted; smeared / 얼룩지게 하다 stain; blot; smear; smudge
▶ 그 부인은 옷이 얼룩지지 않도록 조심했다 The woman was very careful so as not to get her clothes stained.
▶ 소녀는 얼굴이 눈물로 얼룩져 있었다 The girl's face was smudged with tears.

얼룽덜룽하다 spotted; dappled; mottled; motley; 〈짐승이〉 brindled; 〈흑백으로〉 piebald

얼른 〈빨리〉 quickly; speedily; rapidly; swiftly; fast; in a hurry; hastily; 〈즉시〉 at once; immediately; promptly; in a moment; (美口) right [straight] away
▶ 얼른 가거라 Go right away. ⇌ Go quickly.
▶ 얼른 해라 (Be) quick! ⇌ Hurry up!
▶ 얼른 대답해라 Answer promptly.
▶ 나는 얼른 대답할 수 없었다 I was at a loss for a ready answer.
▶ 그의 이름이 얼른 떠오르지 않았다 I couldn't think of his name offhand [instantly].

얼른거리다 flicker ⇨ 어른거리다

얼리다¹ join with ⇨ 어울리다, 어우르다

얼리다² 〈얼게 하다〉 freeze; congeal; refrigerate ♦ 물을 얼리다 freeze water; turn water into ice / 생선을 얼리다 refrigerate [freeze] fish / 얼음을 얼리다 make ice; make ice form

얼마 1 〈값〉 how much; what price; some [a certain] price; 〈금액〉 what sum [amount] 《of money》; some amount
▶ 값이 얼마요? What is the price? ⇌ How much is it? ⇌ How much are you asking? ⇌ What do you charge? ⇌ How much do you charge?
▶ 이 사과는 얼마죠? How do you sell these apples? ⇌ How much do you sell your apples for?
▶ 이 책은 얼마죠? How much is this book? ⇌ What is the price of this book?
▶ 차비는 얼마에요? What is the car fare?
▶ 그 쇠고기는 1파운드에 얼마입니까? How much is this meat a pound [per pound]?
▶ 저 모자는 얼마입니까? How much is that hat?
▶ 얼마에 팔겠습니까? What do you ask for it?
▶ 얼마에 샀습니까? What did you pay [give] for it? ⇌ How much did it cost you?
▶ 비용은 얼마 되지 않았다 The expenses were small.
▶ 서울까지의 요금은 얼마입니까? What [How much] is the fare to Seoul?
2 〈기간〉 a while; some length of time

♦얼마 전 some time ago / 얼마 안되어 soon; presently; shortly; before (very) long; in a short time; in no time / 얼마 있으면 some time after; after a (little) while; later on
▶ 학교가 설립된지는 얼마 안된다 It is not (very) long [It is only a short time] since our school was founded.
▶ 그에게서 얼마 동안 소식이 없었다 I haven't heard from him for a while.
3 〈수〉 how many; 〈양〉 how much; what number [amount]; a certain number [amount, quantity] 《of》; some; so much 《water》; 〈정도〉 some degree 《of》
♦얼마 안되는 수입 a meager [slim] income
▶ 내게 돈이 얼마 있다 I have some money with me.
▶ 너는 돈이 얼마 있니? How much money do you have?
4 〈무게·높이·거리 등〉 what weight [measure]; some weight [measure]; 〈거리〉 what distance; some distance
▶ 이 수박은 무게가 얼마입니까? How much does this watermelon weigh? ⇌ What is the weight of this watermelon?
▶ 그는 키가 얼마입니까? How tall is he?
▶ 여기서 런던까지의 거리는 얼마입니까? How far is it from here to London?
5 〈비율〉 ♦ 한 시간당[1인당] 얼마로 at so much an hour [a head]/ 한 다스에 얼마로 팔다 sell (things) by the dozen
6 〈일부분〉 (a) part 《of》; a portion 《of》; some 《of》; something
♦수입에서 얼마를 저축하다 save *sth* from *one's* income
7 〈끝수·우수리〉 odd
▶ 會話 「어느 정도 있나?」「백 얼마 있습니다」 "How many are there?" "There are a hundred and odd."

얼마간 ─間 **1** 〈다소〉 some; somewhat; a little; to some extent; in some degree; more or less; 〈일부분〉 partly; in part
♦얼마간의 돈 some money; a certain sum of money
▶ 나는 이 사업에 얼마간의 자본을 투자했다 I have invested some capital in the business.
▶ 그는 내 생각을 얼마간 이해하고 있다 He understands my thinking to some extent.
2 〈얼마동안〉 for some time (to come); some time; for a while [time]
▶ 그는 친구집에서 얼마간 묵을 생각을 하고 찾아갔다 He visited his friend for some stay.

얼마나 **1** 〈값〉 how much; what; 〈수량〉 how many [much]
▶ 그 책값은 얼마나 주었습니까? How much [What] did the book cost you? ⇌ What did you give for your book?
▶ 댁은 장서를 얼마나 가지고 있습니까? How many books do you have? ⇌ How large is your library?
▶ 새 집을 짓는 데 비용이 얼마나 듭니까? How much did it cost you to build the new house?
▶ 너는 돈이 얼마나 필요하니? How much money do you need [want]?
▶ 커피에 설탕을 얼마나 넣나요? How much sugar would you like in your coffee?
2 〈정도〉 how 《large, deep, high, wide, thick, far, long, old, etc》; how much
▶ 당신은 회사에서 하루에 얼마나 근무[일]합니까? How much a day do you work for the company?
▶ 그 호수의 깊이는 얼마나 됩니까? How deep is the lake?
▶ 그 나무의 높이는 얼마나 됩니까? How tall is the tree?
▶ 이 상자에는 사과가 얼마나 있습니까? How many apples are there in this box?
▶ 오늘 책은 얼마나 팔렸습니까? How many books were sold today?
▶ 그것을 고치는 데 (시간이) 얼마나 걸리요? How soon can you fix it?
▶ 당신의 체중은 얼마나 됩니까? How much do you weigh? ⇌ What is your weight?
▶ 그는 당신보다 얼마나 나이가 많습니까? How much older is he than you?
▶ 여기서 얼마나 멉니까? How far is it [What is the distance] from here?
▶ 집에서 학교까지는 거리가 얼마나 됩니까? How long [many hours] does it take from your house to the school?
▶ 여기서 역까지는 걸어서 얼마나 걸릴까요? How long will it take to walk from here to the station?
▶ 여기서 얼마나 머물게 됩니까? How long are you staying here?
▶ 당신 차는 얼마나 손상을 입었습니까? How badly damaged is your car?
▶ 그녀는 얼마나 피아노를 칠줄[영어를 할줄] 압니까? How well can she play the piano [speak English]?
▶ 그가 얼마나 열심히 공부했는지 너 아니? Do you know how hard he studied?

얼마든지 〈원하는 만큼〉 as many [much] as *one* likes; any number [amount] of; 〈한없이〉 without limit; ever so many [much]; 〈금액〉 any sum; any price
♦얼마든지 있다 be available as many [much] as *one* wishes
▶ 그는 돈은 얼마든지 있다 He has no end of money.
▶ 나는 시간은 얼마든지 있다 I have tons of time.
▶ 교통사고로 죽은 사람은 얼마든지 있다 Many a man has been killed in traffic accidents.
▶ 값은 얼마든지 좋으니 꼭 구해 주십시오 Get it for me, whatever it costs.

얼마만큼 **1** 〈어느 정도〉 to some [a certain] degree [extent]; up to a certain point; partly; (in) part; how; to what extent [amount]
♦얼마만큼 참말이 섞인 거짓말 a lie that is part truth
▶ 나도 그 일에는 얼마만큼 책임이 있다 I am partly responsible for the problem.
2 ⇨ 얼마나

얼멍덜멍하다 〈덩어리지다〉 lumpy; fuel of lumps

얼밋얼밋하다 **1** 〈미루다〉 defer gradually; hesitate; put off [postpone] from day to day;

얼바람둥이 a crackpot; a senseless fellow; an absurd person

얼바람맞다 behave absurdly; act silly

얼버무리다 1 speak ambiguously; equivocate; prevaricate; shuffle; quibble; palter; do not commit *oneself*
♦농담으로 얼버무리다 turn (a matter) off with a joke / 대답을 얼버무리다 equivocate in replying; give a vague [a noncommittal, an evasive] answer / 요점을 얼버무리다 evade the point
▶그는 자신의 과실을 얼버무렸다 He glossed over his errors.
▶그는 웃음으로 얼버무리기를 잘한다 He often smiles things away [laughs things off].
▶얼버무리지 말고 분명히 대답해라 Don't shuffle. Give me a definite answer.
2 〈음식을〉 swallow 《one's food》; bolt
3 〈버무리다〉 roughly mix

얼보다 can't see straight [clearly]; have a vague view of

얼보이다 〈바로 보이지 않다〉 be seen distortedly; be blurred; 〈흐릿하게 보이다〉 be seen vaguely [indistinctly]
▶글씨가 얼보여서 읽기 어렵다 The writing is blurred and difficult to read.
▶거울에 나의 투영(投影)이 얼보인다 My reflection in the mirror is distorted.

얼부풀다 expand from freezing

얼빠지다 be abstracted [stupefied] 《with fear》; be dazed [stunned] 《by the news》; be absent-minded; look blank
♦얼빠진 짓 a foolish act; foolery / 얼빠진 사람 a dunce; a lackwit; a bonehead; a stupid person; 《美俗》 a softhead / 얼빠진 얼굴 a vacant look; 《美俗》 a moony face / 얼빠진 abstracted; stupid; silly; foolish / 얼빠진 듯이 바라보다 look with an abstracted gaze
▶그런 짓을 하다니 나도 얼 빠졌다! How stupid of me to do such a thing!

얼빼다 daze; stun; stupefy; drive *sb* out of 《his》 mind; make *sb* senseless; bewilder; infatuate; 〈매혹시키다〉 fascinate
♦소란을 피워 얼빼다 stupefy *sb* with a clamor

얼싸 〈흥겨워 내는 소리〉 Yippee!; Whoopee!; Goody-goody; Oh boy! ♦얼싸 좋다! Yippee-hurry!

얼싸안다 embrace; hug; give *sb* a hug; hold [take] *sb* in *one's* arms; clasp to *one's* bosom
♦목을 얼싸안다 throw [lock, fold] *one's* arms around [about] another's neck / 서로 얼싸안다 embrace [hug] each other; go into in each other's arms
▶어머니는 기뻐서 그를 얼싸안았다 His mother hugged him for joy.
▶그 두 사람은 기뻐서 얼싸안고 춤을 추었다 The couple danced with joy in each other's arms.

얼쑹덜쑹하다 1〈줄·점이〉 intricate; confusing; mixed-up; 〈빛깔이〉 varicolored; variegated; dapple(d); motley; mottled; piebald
♦얼쑹덜쑹한 무늬 a bewildering [mixed, jumbled] pattern
2 ⇨ 알쏭달쏭하다

얼씨구 Whoopee!; Yippee!; Hurrah!; Hurray!; Oh boy!; Goody-goody
▶얼씨구 좋다! What a delight!
▶얼씨구 잘한다! Well done!; Capital!; Good for you!

얼씬거리다 make frequent appearances; frequent; haunt; hang [hover] around
▶이 근처에 얼씬거리지도 마라 I don't want to see you around.

얼씬못하다 dare not come round [show up]; cannot appear before *sb's* eyes at all
♦아무도 집에 얼씬 못 하게 하다 forbid *sb's* access to the house; turn *sb* from *one's* doors
▶그는 다시는 감히 내 집에 얼씬 못 할거다 He will never dare to enter my house again.

얼씬하다 appear briefly; make [put in] an appearance; show *oneself*; show [turn] up
♦얼씬하지 않다 do not appear at all
▶그는 요새 얼씬하지도 않는다 I have seen nothing of him lately.

얼어붙다 freeze (on) 《to》; be frozen fast [hard] 《to》
♦얼어붙은 도로 a frozen [an icy] road / 얼어붙을 것같이 추운 freezing cold
▶창문이 얼어붙었다 The window have iced up [over].
▶길은 꽁꽁 얼어붙어 있었다 The road was frozen hard [like ice].

얼얼하다 1〈매워서〉 piquant; hot; burning; pungent; biting; stinging
▶혀가 얼얼하다 *one's* tongue smarts [stings, burns]
2〈살갗이 다쳐서〉 smart; tingling; prickly
▶추위로 얼얼한 귀 ears tingling with the cold
▶햇볕에 타서 등이 얼얼하다 My sunburnt back smarts [tingles].

얼음 ice ♦얼음 넣은 위스키 whisky with ice; whisky on the rocks / 얼음에 채운 수박 iced watermelon; a watermelon in ice / 얼음의[같은] ice; icy; icelike; glacial / 얼음이 얼다 freeze; be frozen (over) / 얼음을 깨다 crush ice; break [crack] ice / 얼음을 지치다 skate (on the ice); do skating / 얼음에 채우다 ice; put *sth* on (the) ice; cool *sth* with ice / 얼음에 갇히다 be locked by ice; be icebound / 얼음으로 뒤덮이다 be covered with ice; be iced [frozen] over
▶화씨 32도면 얼음이 언다 Ice forms [It freezes] at a temperature of 32°F.
▶어젯밤에 얼음이 꽁꽁 얼었다 It froze hard last night.
▶얼음이 갈라진다 The ice breaks [cracks, gives way].
▶호수의 얼음은 스케이트를 탈 수 있을 만큼 두꺼웠다 The ice on the lake was thick enough for skating.
▶연못의 얼음이 녹기 시작했다 The ice on the pond began to melt.

▶ 나는 여름에 얼음으로 차게 한 맥주를 좋아한다 I like beer cooled with ice in summer.
▶ 계곡물은 얼음같이 찼다 The water of the mountain stream was icy.
■—가게 an ice shop —과자 ices ⇨ 빙과(氷菓) —덩이 an ice lump; a block [lump] of ice; a cake of ice: 잘게 깬 얼음덩이 cracked [chipped] ice; chips of ice —물[냉수] iced water; ice water —베개 an ice pillow —사탕 rock [sugar] candy —장수 (美) an iceman; an ice dealer —점 ice point —주머니 an ice bag [pack] —집 an igloo —집게 an ice claw; ice tongs —찜 applying an ice bag [pack] —창고 an icehouse

얼음박이다 〈사람이 주어〉 be [get] frostbitten; get [have] chilblains (on *one's* hand); 〈국부가 주어〉 be affected with chilblains; become frostbitten
♦ 얼음박인 발가락 frostbitten toes / 귀가 얼음박이다 get *one's* ears frostbitten

얼음장 a layer [coat, sheet] of ice; a flat piece of ice ▶ 방바닥이 얼음장같다 The floor is as cold as (a sheet of) ice.

얼음판 an icy ground; the ice ♦ 얼음판에서 미끄러지다 slip and fall on the ice / 얼음판에서 썰매를 타다 slide on the ice in a sled

얼쩍지근하다 1 〈맵다〉 somewhat hot [pungent, biting, stinging]; a bit spicy
2 〈아프다〉 smart; prickly; tingling 《pain》
3 〈술이 거나하다〉 tipsy, slightly drunk

얼쩡거리다 flatter ⇨ 알짱거리다

얼쭝거리다 flatter; butter *sb* up; curry favor with *sb*; curry *sb's* favor; court *sb's* favor; fawn on *sb*
▶ 나는 그녀가 그럴듯하게 얼쭝거리는 바람에 넘어갔다 I was imposed upon by her plausible flattery.

얼쭝얼쭝 flatteringly; by honeyed words; with fair words

얼씀얼쑴 hesitatingly; irresolutely; vacillatingly —얼씀얼쑴하다 hesitate; waver; falter; pause; hang back; vacillate
▶ 그 위험이 너무 컸기 때문에 나는 얼씀얼쑴했다 The danger was so great that I hesitated.
▶ 그는 두 의견 사이에서 얼씀얼쑴하였다 He vacillated between the two views.

얼찐거리다 flatter ⇨ 얼쭝거리다

얼추 nearly; almost; practically; well-nigh
▶ 일이 얼추 끝났다 The work is almost [practically] finished.
▶ 그는 나이가 나와 얼추 같다 He is about my age.

얼추잡다 estimate roughly; make a rough estimate (of); make a draft; lay an outline
♦ 비용을 얼추잡다 make a rough estimate of the expense 《for》
▶ 비용은 얼추잡아 50만원이다 The costs are roughly estimated at 500,000 won.

얼치기 an in-between thing; something half-and-half
♦ 얼치기 기술자 a half-trained mechanic
▶ 그는 일을 얼치기로 하지 않는다 He does not do things by halves.
▶ 일을 얼치기로 하지 마라 Don't do things by halves. ⇌ Don't leave things unfinished.
▶ 얼치기로 아느니 아예 모르는게 낫다 One may as well know nothing than know things by halves.

얼크러지다 tangle; get [become] entangled [complicated] ♦ 얼크러진 머리 tangled hair

얼큰하다 rather hot ⇨ 얼근하다

얼토당토않다 〈당치 않다〉 exorbitant; incongruous; unreasonable; absurd; preposterous; nonsensical; irrelevant; wide of the mark; 〈관련 없다〉 have nothing to do with
♦ 얼토당토 않은 사람 a wrong man / 얼토당토 않은 요구 an unreasonable [a preposterous] demand / 얼토당토 않은 질문 questions irrelative to the subject / 얼토당토 않게 exorbitantly; stupendously; unreasonably / 얼토당토 않은 말을 하다 say extraordinary [absurd] things; talk wild / 얼토당토 않은 짓을 하다 bark up the wrong tree; bring [drive] *one's* pigs to a fine [a pretty, the wrong] market
▶ 이곳 식품 가격은 얼토당토 않게 비싸다 The price of food here is exorbitantly expensive.
▶ 너의 비방은 얼토당토 않다 You lay the blame at the wrong door.
▶ 너의 추측은 얼토당토 않다 Your guess is wide of the mark.

얽다¹ 1 〈얼굴이〉 be [get] pockmarked; be pitted [pocked] 《with the smallpox》
♦ 얽은 얼굴 a pockmarked [pitted] face / 얽은 자국 pockmarks; pocks
▶ 얽은 얼굴에 복이 있다 (속담) Luck resides in a pitted face.
2 〈물건의 표면이〉 be uneven [rugged, jagged, ragged]

얽다² 1 〈묶다〉 bind; tie [fasten] up ♦ 새끼로 얽다 bind *sth* with a rope / 짐을 얽다 tie up goods; fasten up a parcel 2 〈날조하다〉 fabricate; fake; forge; concoct; frame [make] up

얽동이다 bind up; tie up; truss up
♦ 단단히 얽동이다 tie hard [fast] / 포대를 새끼로 얽동이다 rope a bale

얽둑얽둑 ♦ 얽둑얽둑 얽은 사람 a person with a pocky face ▶ 그는 얼굴이 얽둑얽둑 얽었다 His face is covered with pockmarks.
—얽둑얽둑하다 pocky; pockmarked; pitted

얽매다 bind ⇨ 얽어매다
♦ 단단히 얽매다 tie fast [hard] / 규칙으로 얽매다 restrict *sb* by rule

얽매이다 be bound; be restricted [restrained]; be tied down; be chained (to)
♦ 시간에 얽매이다 be restricted by time / 일에 얽매이다 be chained to *one's* business [work]; be tied up in *one's* business / 인습에 얽매이다 be fettered [enslaved] by convention [tradition] / 의리에 얽매이다 be fettered by the bonds of obligations / 규칙에 얽매여 있다 be screwed down to a rule
▶ 그녀는 규정에 얽매여 융통성이 없다 She adheres to regulations and is not flexible.
▶ 나는 무슨 일에나 얽매이기 싫다 I am impatient of any restraint.

얽빼기 a pockmarked [pitted] person
얽어매다 tie up; bind; fasten; truss
♦ 새끼로 얽어매다 bind *sth* with a rope / 아무

의 손발을 얽매다 bind *sb* hand and foot
얽이 〈얽어매기〉 tying [trussing, binding] *sth* up securely; 〈윤곽〉 an outline [a sketch] (of a plan); a rough idea (of a matter); 〈짜임새〉 structure
▶너의 소설은 얽이가 치밀하지 않다 Your novel lacks in elaborate structures.
얽적얽적하다 lightly pockmarked [pitted]
얽히다 1 〈줄에〉 be tied; 〈감기다〉 twine [coil] round; get coiled round; get entangled 〈in〉; be tangled 《with》
♦복잡하게 얽힌 문제 the tangle of problems / 일이 복잡하게 얽히다 be at sixes and sevens / 얽히게 하다 intertwine; interlace; entangle; entwine; interlock 《with》
▶실이 얽혀 있다 The thread is in a tangle.
▶그 문제에는 여러 가지 사정이 얽혀 있다 Various circumstances are entangled in the matter.
▶낚싯줄이 해초에 얽혔다 My fishing line got entangled in some seaweed.
2 〈연루되다〉 be [get] involved in; 〈관련되다〉 be related 《to》
♦그 나무에 얽힌 전설 the legend that is related to the tree / 얽히고 설킨 이야기 an involved story / 삼각 관계로 얽히다 get involved in a love triangle
엄격 嚴格 austerity; strictness; sternness; severity; rigo(u)r
─**엄격하다** strict; stern; rigorous; severe
♦엄격한 가정 a sternly moral family / 엄격한 검사 a rigid inspection / 엄격한 구별 a sharp distinction / 엄격한 사람 a stern [straitlaced] man / 엄격한 생활 an austere [a hard] life / 엄격한 아버지 a stern [strict] father / 엄격한 훈육[규율] stern [rigorous] discipline / 엄격히 strictly; sternly; rigorously / 엄격히 말하자면 strictly speaking / 엄격히 기르다 bring up (a child) rigorously [sternly]
▶차내 흡연은 엄격히 금지되어 있다 Smoking in the car is strictly prohibited.
▶그 선생은 학생들에게 엄격하다 The teacher is severe with his students.
▶어머니는 아이들을 엄격히 양육하였다 The mother strictly brought up her children.
▶우리는 공사의 구별이 엄격해야 한다 We must make a sharp distinction between public and private affairs.
엄금 嚴禁 strict prohibition; a ban
▶화기 엄금 〈게시〉 Caution : Flammables. ⇌ No Fire. ⇌ Inflammable.
─**엄금하다** prohibit [forbid] *sth* strictly; interdict; place *sth* under a ban; taboo
♦외출을 엄금하다 strictly [rigidly] forbid *sb* to go out
엄니 〈멧돼지 등의〉 a tusk; 〈개 등의〉 a fang
♦엄니를 드러내다 show its fangs; 〈으르렁거리다〉 snarl 《at》; growl 《at》
엄동 嚴冬 a rigorous [hard, severe] winter; the cold of winter
■─**설한** 〈인〉 a hard [severe] snowy winter
엄두 the very thought (of doing *sth*); daring
♦엄두를 못내다 never dream of; be unimaginable; cannot even conceive the idea 《of doing》
▶나는 그녀와의 결혼은 엄두도 못냈다 I never dreamed of myself marrying her.
▶그는 올 엄두도 못냈다 He did not dare to come.
▶그에게 물어볼 엄두가 안났다 I have never dared (to) ask him.
엄마 mam(m)a; mammy; mummy; (美) mom; (口) ma
엄매 〈송아지가〉 엄매 울다 bleat; moo
엄명 嚴命 a strict order [command]; a rigid instruction [injunction]
♦사령관의 엄명 orders from the commander / 엄명으로 under [by] a strict order (of) / 엄명을 내리다 issue [give] rigorous instructions
─**엄명하다** give a strict order 《that...》; strictly order 《to do》
엄밀 嚴密 〈엄중·세밀〉 strictness; closeness; rigidity; exactness; preciseness; 〈비밀〉 strict secrecy
─**엄밀하다** strict; precise; close; rigid; strictly confidential
♦엄밀한 검사 a close [rigid] examination / 엄밀한 과학적 정의 a rigorously scientific definition / 엄밀한 의미에서 in the strict sense of the word / 엄밀히 strictly; exactly; closely; rigidly; in strict secrecy / 엄밀히 말하면 strictly speaking; to be exact / 엄밀히 조사하다 investigate (a case) closely
엄벌 嚴罰 a severe [heavy] punishment
♦엄벌에 처하다 punish *sb* severely; inflict a severe punishment on *sb* ─**엄벌하다** punish *sb* severely ■─**주의** a severe punishment policy
엄벙덤벙 halfheartedly; at random; slovenly; sloppily; loosely ─**엄벙덤벙하다** act thoughtlessly; go at it halfheartedly [carelessly]
엄벙하다 1 〈떠벌리다〉 inflated; 〈애매하다〉 ambiguous; evasive ♦엄벙하게 말하다 speak ambiguously [evasively]; quibble
2 〈착실하지 못하다〉 insincere; sloppy; slipshod; slack 《in *one's* work》 ♦일을 엄벙하게 하다 do a doubtful job of it
엄부 嚴父 a stern [strict] father
엄살 exaggeration [pretension] of pain [hardship]; much ado [a great fuss] about nothing
─**엄살하다** exaggerate pain
■─**꾸러기** a fussy person; a crybaby; a fusser; a fussbudget; a fusspot
엄살부리다 exaggerate [pretend] pain [hardship]; make a (great) fuss (about trifles)
▶그만한 상처로 엄살부리다니 What a fuss about such a scratch!
엄선 嚴選 careful selection ─**엄선하다** select [screen] carefully; make a careful choice
♦엄선된 rigidly selected / 엄선한 것 a choice
엄수 嚴守 〈시간의〉 punctuality; 〈규칙 등의〉 strict observance; rigid adherence 《to rules》
─**엄수하다** observe [keep] strictly; rigidly adhere to ♦명령을 엄수하다 obey *sb's* orders rigidly / 비밀[약속]을 엄수하다 keep a secret [promise] strictly / 시간을 엄수하다 be very punctual
엄수 嚴修 〈의식의〉 conducting 《a service》

solemnly
—엄수하다 conduct [hold] 《a service》 with solemnly
▶장례식은 엄수되었다 The funeral was conducted with great solemnly.

엄숙 嚴肅 solemnly; dignity; gravity; seriousness; 〈엄정〉 rigor
—엄숙하다 solemn; dignified; grave; serious
♦엄숙한 현실 the stern realities of life / 엄숙한 의식 a solemn ceremony / 엄숙한 얼굴로 with a grave [dignifed] countenance / 엄숙히 solemnly; with solemnity; gravely; seriously / 엄숙하게 말하다 speak gravely / 인생을 엄숙하게 보다 take a solemn view of life; take life seriously

엄습 掩襲 a surprise [sudden] attack
—엄습하다 make a surprise [sudden] attack 《on the enemy》; surprise 《the fort》; take by surprise; 〈감정이 사람을〉 come over; 〈재난 등이〉 visit; strike (down); sweep; hit
♦공포감이 엄습하다 be seized with fear / 엄습당하다 be attacked unawares; be taken by surprise; be visited [hit] 《by》 / 폭풍우에 엄습당하다 be visited by [caught in] a storm
▶태풍이 어디를 엄습할지 예측할 수 없다 It is impossible to predict where the typhoon will hit.
▶심한 피로감이 그를 엄습했다 An intense weariness took him.

엄연하다 儼然— grave; solemn; stern; majestic ♦엄연한 사실 a grim [solid, hard] fact; an undeniable fact; a stern [grim] reality / 엄연히 solemnly; solidly; gravely; with dignity [authority]
▶이 벌칙은 지금도 엄연히 존재한다 This penal regulation is still in full force.

엄전하다 decent; decorous; majestic; dignified

엄정 嚴正 exactness; strictness; severity; rigidness; rigor; strict fairness
—엄정하다 exact; strict; rigorous; (strictly) fair; impartial
♦엄정한 비판 an impartial criticism / 엄정한 재판관 an impartial judge / 엄정한 심사 결과 after careful consideration / 엄정하게 strictly; rigorously; fairly; impartially / 엄정하게 다루다 deal with 《an affair》 in strict fairness
▶모든 작품은 엄정하게 심사되었다 Each work has been fairly judged.
—중립 《observe》 strict neutrality

엄존 儼存 real existence —엄존하다 〈사실이〉 (really) exist; 〈법률이〉 be in full force

엄중 嚴重 severity; strictness; rigor; closeness
—엄중하다 strict; stringent; severe; stern; rigorous; rigid; close
♦엄중한 검사 a severe [close] inspection / 엄중한 경계 (a) strict [close] watch / 엄중한 규칙 a strict [rigorous] rule / 경찰의 엄중한 단속 strict police supervision / 엄중한 조사[심문] a close examination / 엄중히 strictly; severely; sternly; rigorously; rigidly; closely / 엄중히 처벌하다 punish sb severely / 엄중히 금하다 prohibit strictly / 엄중히 단속하다 exercise strict control 《on, over》
▶그는 엄중한 조사를 받았다 He received a close examination.
▶공항은 경비가 엄중하였다 The airport was strongly guarded.

엄지 the thumb; the first digit
■—발가락 the big [great] toe —발톱 the big toenail —손가락 the thumb; the big finger —손톱 the thumbnail

엄지머리 총각 —總角 a lifelong bachelor

엄지벌레 an imago 《pl. ~(e)s, imagines》

엄징 嚴懲 severe punishment ⇨ 엄벌

엄책 嚴責 a severe [stern] reprimand [rebuke] —엄책하다 reprimand [rebuke] severely [harshly]; give a severe rebuke

엄처시하 嚴妻侍下 being under *one's* wife's thumb ▶그는 엄처시하다 He is tied to his wife's apron strings. ⇌ He is a henpecked husband.

엄청나다 exorbitant; extraordinary; extravagant; excessive; absurd; preposterous
♦엄청난 값 an exorbitant [a prohibitive] price / 엄청난 소리를 하다 speak extravagant [preposterous] things / 엄청난 돈을 치르다 pay through the nose / 엄청나게 exorbitantly; extraordinarily / 엄청나게 큰 awfully big; huge; gigantic; colossal; whopping / 엄청나게 싸다 be ridiculously cheap; be dog-cheap / 엄청나게 비싸다 be absurdly [exorbitantly] expensive

엄친 嚴親 a father; my father

엄탐 嚴探 a strict [close] search
▶범인은 지금 엄탐중이다 A strict search is being made for the offender.
—엄탐하다 search strictly [closely] 《for》; be on a sharp lookout 《for》

엄파이어 〈심판원〉 an umpire

엄평소니 〈속임수〉 a trap; a trick; trickery

엄평스럽다 deceitful; dishonest; fraudulent; swindling ♦엄펑스러운 술책 a fraudulent scheme

엄폐 掩蔽 cover; obscuration —엄폐하다 cover up; mask; screen; conceal
■—물 a cover; a shelter —호 a covered trench; an entrenchment; a dugout; a bunker

엄포 empty menaces [threats]; bluff; bluster; intimidation
♦엄포 놓다 utter empty threats 《against》; use empty menaces [threats] 《to》; bluster 《out, forth》
▶그는 엄포만 놓을 뿐이다 He blusters but does nothing.

엄하다 嚴— grim; severe; strict; stern; rigid; rigorous; austere; stringent; 〈가혹하다〉 hard; harsh
♦엄한 감독 strict [rigorous] control / 엄한 규칙[검사] strict regulations [inspection]/ 엄한 벌 a severe punishment / 엄한 분부 a strict order; severe instructions / 엄한 심문 a searching [rigorous] examination / 엄한 아버지 a stern [strict] father / 엄한 표정 a stern [grave] look / 지나치게 엄하다 be too strict [severe]; err on the side of severity / 아이들에게 엄하다 be strict with [stern to] *one's* children / 엄하게 strictly; rigidly; with rigor; closely / 엄하게 꾸짖다 scold severely / 엄하게

명하다 direct [command, order] strictly / 버릇을 엄하게 가르치다 be strict in discipline
엄한 嚴寒 the intense [severe] cold; the rigor of winter
엄형 嚴刑 a severe punishment ⇨ 엄벌 (嚴罰)
엄호 掩護 cover(ing); protection
―엄호하다 cover; protect; shelter; screen
◆ 퇴로를[측면을] 엄호하다 cover the retreat [flank] / 해병대의 상륙을 엄호하다 cover the marine's landing
■ ―대 a covering force [party] ―사격 covering [curtain] fire ―진지 a covering position ―포화 a wall [cover] of fire; a barrage
엄혹하다 嚴酷― severe; harsh ⇨ 엄하다
업 〔民俗〕 a luck animal [person]
업 業 1 〈직업〉 an occupation; a calling; a profession; a vocation; work; a business; a trade
◆ 문필을 업으로 삼다 adopt [take up] writing as a profession / 의술을 업으로 삼다 practice medicine; be a physician by profession / 아버지의 업을 잇다 succeed one's father in his occupation
2 〈산〉〔佛敎〕 karma
업계 業界 the business world [community]; business circles; the industry; manufacturers; the trade
◆ 택시업계의 사람들 people in the taxi trade
▶ 그는 업계의 거물이다 He is a big shot in the business world.
▶ 업계의 재개편이 불가피하다 It is necessary to reorganize the industry.
■ ―지(紙) a trade paper ―지(誌) a trade magazine
업다 1 〈등에〉 carry sth on one's back
◆ 아기를 (등에) 업다 carry a baby on one's back; have a baby strapped to one's back
▶ 나는 갓난아기를 업고 있는 여자에게 자리를 양보했다 I offered my seat to a woman with a baby on her back.
2 〈끌고 들어가다〉 implicate; involve in
▶ 그는 죄를 혼자 지지 않고 친구들을 업고 들어갔다 Refusing to take the guilt upon himself alone, he dragged his friends into it too.
업무 業務 business; work; service; duty; operation; affairs
◆ 업무용의 for business use [purposes] / 업무를 게을리하다 neglect one's business / 업무를 방해하다 impede [interfere with] sb's business / 업무를 확장하다 expand (its) operations / 업무에 힘쓰다 apply oneself to one's work; attend to one's business with diligence
▶ 이 엘리베이터는 업무용이다 This elevator is for business use.
▶ 업무상의 비밀을 남에게 알리면 안된다 You must not let out our trade secrets to anybody.
■ ―관리 business control [management] ―방해 interference with sb's duty ―보고 a report on operation(s); a business report ―부 the Operation [Business, Sales] Department ―상과실치사 manslaughter through professional negligence ―상횡령 embezzlement of corporate funds ―시간 office [business] hours ―일지 a business log ―집행의 관리[conduct] of business; the execution of one's duty : 업무 집행 방해 interference in the execution of one's duty

업보 業報 〔佛敎〕 karma effects; effects of karma
업숭이 a stupid [dull] fellow; a dunce
업신여기다 despise; slight; make light of; look down on [upon]; hold sb in contempt
◆ 부모를 업신여기다 slight one's parents
▶ 그는 사람을 업신여기는 버릇이 있다 He has a habit of looking down upon people.
▶ 약하게 보인다고 그를 업신여기면 안된다 You mustn't despise him because he seems weak.
▶ 결국 그를 업신여긴 것이 실패의 원인이었다 It was because I despised him that I failed at last.
업신여김 contempt; disdain; slighting; disregard
◆ 업신여김을 받다[당하다] be held in contempt; be slighted; be held cheap
업어치기 〔柔道〕 a back [shoulder] throw
업자 業者 a trader; a dealer; a tradesman; (총칭) the trade
◆ 업자간의 거래 trade sales / 업자를 모으다 call in traders concerned
▶ 업자간의 경쟁이 치열하다 There is keen competition among the traders concerned.
■ ―관계― traders [dealers, businessmen] concerned 악덕― a crooked dealer
업적 業績 〈scholarly〉 achievements; 〈sales〉 results; contributions
◆ 훌륭한 업적을 올리다 [쌓다] get [achieve] good 〈business〉 results; produce brilliant 〈scientific〉 achievements
▶ 그는 자연과학 분야에서 큰 업적을 이뤘다 He produced remarkable results in the area of natural science.
▶ 건축계에서의 위대한 업적으로 그에게 상이 수여됐다 A prize was given to him for his great achievements in the world of architecture.
■ ―보고 a business report
업종 業種 a type of industry; a category of business [trade]
업종별 業種別 industrial classification; classification by industry
◆ 업종별로 나누다 classify by industry
■ ―임금 prevailing wages by industry ―전화번호부 a telephone directory classified by (type of) industry
업체 業體 a business enterprise; an enterprise
■ 민간[개인]― a private enterprise 부실― an insolvent enterprise 생산[수출]― a production [an export] enterprise
업태 業態 business conditions [status]
■ ―조사 an inquiry into the business status; a business conditions survey
업화 業火 〔佛敎〕 hellfire; the fire of retribution
업히다 be carried on sb's back; ride [get] on sb's shoulder [back]; pickaback [piggyback] 〈on sb〉
◆ 엄마 등에 업히다 be on one's mother's

back; get on *one's* mother's back

없다 1 〈존재하지 않다〉 there is [are] no...; do not exist
▶ 그런 것은 없다 There is no such thing.
▶ 양동이에는 물이 없다 There is no water in the bucket.
▶ 이 도시에는 교회가 없다 There is no church in this town.
▶ 유령 따위는 없다 There are no such beings as ghosts. ⇌ Ghosts do not exist.
▶ 그것을 모르는 사람은 없다 There is no one who doesn't know it.
▶ 이 자동차는 낡았지만 없는 것보다는 낫다 This car is old, but it's better than nothing.
▶ 개량의 여지는 거의 없다 There is little room for improvement.
▶ 나는 책이 없어도 살 수 있다 I can live without books. ⇌ I can live even if there are no books in the world.
▶ 그녀는 우리에게 없어서는 안될 사람이다 We cannot do without her.
▶ 태양이 없으면 생물이 살 수가 없다 Without [If it were not for] the sun, no creatures could live.
▶ 네 도움이 없었더라면 나는 실패했을 것이다 Without [If it had not been for] your help, I would have failed.
▶ 그런 약속은 없었던 것으로 해달라 Forget that there was any such agreement.

2 〈가지고 있지 않다〉 have no...; be without; 〈보이지 않다〉 be missing; cannot be found
▶ 난 돈이 없다 I have no money. ⇌ I haven't got any money.
▶ 그에게는 자식이 없다 He has no children.
▶ 이 방에는 창이 없다 This room has no windows.
▶ 지금은 아무것도 할 일이 없다 I have nothing to do now.
▶ 그는 스포츠에 흥미가 없다 He is not interested in sports. ⇌ He takes no interest in sports.
▶ 내 이름이 명단에 없다 My name is missing from the list.
▶ 이 과일은 한국에는 없다 This fruit is not found in Korea.
▶ 방금 책상 위에 두었던 책이 없다 I cannot find the book that I just put on the table.

3 〈갖추고 있지 않다〉 want; lack; be wanting [lacking]
♦ 버릇이 없다 be wanting in politeness / 재미가 없다 be devoid of interest; be uninteresting / 재수가 없다 be unlucky / 용기가 없다 lack [be wanting in] courage / 의리가 없다 have no sense of honor; be ungrateful
▶ 그는 상식이 없다 He lacks [is lacking in] common sense.
▶ 그 전집은 제2권이 없다 The second volume is missing in the complete works.
▶ 이 백화점에는 없는 것이 없다 This department store carries everything.
▶ 이 문장은 문법에는 맞지만 의미가 없다 This sentence is grammatical but meaningless.
▶ 이 자료는 나의 연구에 없어서는 안되는 것이다 These data are indispensable for my study.
▶ 그에게는 자기의 계획을 실행할 힘이 없다 He lacks [wants] the power to carry out his ideas.

4 〈다 없어지다〉 run out 《of》; be out 《of》; run short 《of》
▶ 이젠 술이 없다 The wine is all gone.
▶ 우물에 물이 없다 The well has run dry.
▶ 가솔린이 없다 We have run out of gas.

5 〈생겨나지 않다〉 be free [clear] from [of]
♦ 불순물이 없는 물 water free of impurities / 잘못[결점]이 없다 be free from mistakes [faults] / 혐의가 없다 be clear from suspicion / 통로에는 장애물이 없다 The passage is clear [free] from obstacles.

6 〈죽고 없다〉 be deceased [defunct]
▶ 부모 없는 아이 an orphan
▶ 그는 아버지가 없다 His father is deceased. ⇌ He has no father.
▶ 그는 이제 가고 없다 Alas! He is no more!

7 〈가난하다〉 poor; needy
♦ 없는 사람들 the poor (and needy); poor people / 있는 사람과 없는 사람 the haves and the have-nots / 없는 집에 태어나다 be born poor [in a poor family]

8 〈기타〉 ▶ 어찌할 수 없다 I can't help it.
▶ 그로부터는 아직도 전화가 없다 I haven't had a (telephone) call from him yet.
▶ 나는 웃을 수밖에 없었다 I could not help laughing.
▶ 나는 없는 돈이나마 가진 걸 몽땅 주었다 I gave him what (little) money I had.

없애다 1 〈제거하다〉 take away; take off; remove; eliminate; clear; exterminate; get rid of; leave out; 〈폐지하다〉 abolish; do away with
♦ 화근을 없애다 remove [eliminate] the root of an evil / 잡념을 없애다 put idle thoughts out of *one's* mind / 장애물을 없애다 remove obstacles; clear the way of obstacles / 해충을 없애다 exterminate harmful insects / 허례를 없애다 do away with formalities / 밭의 잡초를 없애다 clear the field of the weeds / 집에서 쥐를 없애다 rid a house of rats / 불순물을 완전히 없애다 remove all the impurities
▶ 나쁜 버릇을 없애기는 쉽지가 않다 It is not easy to get rid of your bad habits.
▶ 주민의 불안을 없애는 일이 가장 중요하다 The most important thing is to remove [dispel] the anxiety of the inhabitants.

2 〈잃다〉 lose; 〈낭비하다〉 waste; spend; throw away
♦ 시간을 없애다 waste [spend] time / 쓸데없는 것들에 돈을 없애다 waste *one's* money on useless things
▶ 나는 돈을 다 없앴다 I spent all my money.
▶ 그는 1년도 안되어 물려받은 재산을 몽땅 없앴다 He lost [ran through] his entire inheritance in less than a year.

3 〈죽이다〉 kill; murder; 〈숙청하다〉 liquidate; (美俗) blot (out); erase; make [do] away with
▶ 없애버려라 Down with him! ⇌ Finish him!

없어지다 1 〈잃게 되다〉 be [get] lost; be missing; be gone
♦ 없어진 책 a lost [missing] book / 없어진 셈

치고 단념하다 give up for lost
▶지갑이 없어졌다 I have lost my purse [wallet]. ⇒ My purse [wallet] is missing.
▶금고 속의 서류가 없어졌다 The papers that were in the safe are gone.
2 〈다 쓰게 되다〉 run short [out] (of); be gone; be out; be used up; be exhausted
▶돈이란 금방 없어지는 것이다 Money soon goes.
▶그의 재산은 거의 다 없어졌다 His property shrank almost to nothing.
3 〈사라지다〉 disappear; vanish; be gone
▶입맛이 없어졌다 I have lost my appetite. ⇒ My appetite has failed.
▶시합에 이길 가망은 완전히 없어졌다 All hope of winning the game vanished. ⇒ There is no hope of our winning the game.
▶버릇은 한번 들면 좀처럼 없어지지 않는다 A habit is very difficult to get rid of [shake off] once it is formed.

없이 without
♦예외 없이 without exceptions / 휴일도 없이 without holidays / 없이 살다 live in poverty [want] / 없이 지내다 do without; dispense with / 돈 없이 여행하다 go on a trip without money / 한 푼 없이 되다 become penniless
▶그는 지도없이 여행을 떠났다 He went on a journey without a map [maps].
▶미국에서는 차 없이는 못 산다 You can't do without a car in America.
▶공기 없이는 하루도 살아갈 수 없다 Without [Were it not for] air, we could not live even a single day.
▶오늘은 점심 시간도 없이 일을 해야 될 것 같다 My work is likely to carry over into the lunch break today.

없이하다 remove; get rid of ⇨ 없애다
엇가다 go astray ⇨ 엇나가다 2
엇각 —角 〖數〗 alternate interior angles
엇갈리다 cross paths; pass [cross] (each other); miss each other on the way
▶우리는 도중에서 길이 엇갈린것 같다 We seem to have missed each other on the way.
▶그들은 의견이 서로 엇갈려 있다 They have different [conflicting] opinions. ⇒ There is a discrepancy in their opinions.
▶나는 희비가 엇갈렸다 I have mixed feelings about it. ⇒ Joy and grief alternated in my heart.

엇걸다 cross (each other); join (things) crosswise ♦국기를 엇걸다 cross national flags / 총을 엇걸다 stack [pile] rifles
엇걸리다 be crossed; lie across; cut [cross] each other; be intersected; intersect
엇결 〈나뭇결〉 cross-grain
엇구수하다 〈맛이 구수하다〉 rather tasty; 〈이야기가 그럴 듯하다〉 plausible; amusing
엇나가다 **1** 〈줄 등이〉 stray (from); deviate (from a course); 〈일이〉 go awry [wrong]
2 〈언동이〉 deviate [go away] from the right path; go contrary to reason; go astray [wild]
엇대다 **1** 〈어긋나게 대다〉 put [fix, join] askew [cockeyed]; apply obliquely
♦옷에 형겊을 엇대다 put a patch on one's clothes cockeyed
2 〈빗대다〉 make an insinuating remark (at); make an oblique [a sly] hint (at)
엇되다 〈건방지다〉 somewhat pert; uppish; saucy; perky ♦엇된 놈 a saucy fellow
엇뜨기 a squinter ⇨ 사팔뜨기
엇뜨다 squint (at)
엇먹다 **1** 〈비꼬다〉 have a sly dig (at); insinuate; satirize **2** 〈톱이 비뚜로 켜들어가다〉 〈a blade〉 cut at an angle; cut crooked
엇메다 sling (a bag, a rifle) over the shoulder and across the breast ♦가방을 엇메다 sling a satchel from the shoulder across one's chest
엇바꾸다 exchange (books) with each other; interchange
엇베다 cut (off) aslant [obliquely]; cut diagonally [at an angle]; make an oblique cut
♦천을 엇베다 cut cloth (on the) bias
엇비슷하다 similar; like; 〈서술적〉 be nearly the same; be (about) alike
▶그들은 성격이 엇비슷하다 They are alike in character.
▶엇비슷하게 알아맞혔다 That isn't far off the mark.
엇서다 〈거세게 맞서다〉 oppose; go [act] against; act contrary to
엇섞다 mix in alternation
엇셈 an offset; settlement [balancing] of accounts; cross liquidation; striking a balance
—**엇셈하다** offset; settle [balance] accounts; strike a balance
엇송아지 a young ox; a calf
-었겠다 〈추측〉 I should think; I suppose (it) would be ▶그녀는 서른 살은 넘었겠다 She is over thirty, I should think.
-었느냐 〈의문〉 (why, what, where, etc.) did you [he, she]? ▶어디서 그런 이야기를 들었느냐? Where did you get that story?
-었는지 〈불확실〉 whether (it) was [did]
▶어디를 읽고 있었는지 잊어버렸다 I forgot where we were reading.
-었으나 처음에는 꽤 문제가 되었으나 이제는 순조로이 진행된다 At first it was quite a problem, but now it's going smoothly.
엉거능측하다 〈능청스럽다〉 crafty; wily; snaky; 〈서술적〉 be full of sly ways
엉거시 〖植〗 a cotton [Scotch] thistle
엉거주춤하다 **1** 〈앉지도 서지도 않다〉 be in half-rising [half-sitting] posture
▶엉거주춤하지 말고 서든지 앉든지 해라 Either stand up or sit down.
▶그런 엉거주춤한 자세로 치면 공이 멀리 날아가지 않아 The ball won't fly far if you hit it with your rear stuck out like that.
2 〈망설이다〉 hesitate (to do); waver; hover ▶엉거주춤하지 말고 결정하시오 Get off the fence and make up your mind.
▶시장은 엉거주춤하게 답변했다 The mayor answered irresolutely [without confidence].
엉겁 the condition of being covered with goo ▶손에 엿이 엉겁을 했다 The hands were all sticky with taffy.
엉겁결에 in a moment of bewilderment; in

the confusion of the moment
▶ 엉겁결에 나는 거짓말을 했다 I involuntarily [unintentionally] told a lie.
▶ 엉겁결에 그런 말이 나왔다 The words just escaped my lips.

엉겅퀴 〔植〕 a thistle

엉구다 〈마련하다〉 make [get] 《a plan》 ready; form 《a plan》 out; work out; 〈성사시키다〉 effect; materialize; bring out

엉그름 a mud crack

엉글벙글 smilingly; beamingly; with a sweet smile ━**엉글벙글하다** smile radiantly 《at》; smile a sweet smile; beam 《upon》

엉금엉금 on all fours ♦ 엉금엉금 기다 crawl; creep / 엉금엉금 기어가다 go on all fours; creep [crawl] to [toward]

엉기다 1 〈뭉치어 굳어지다〉 coagulate; congeal; clot; curdle
♦ 엉긴 피 a clot of blood; clotted blood / 구두에 엉겨붙은 진흙 mud caked on the shoes
▶ 우유가 엉긴다 Milk curdles.
2 〈일이 뒤얽히다〉 be all tangled up
3 〈허둥거리다〉 busy *oneself* ineffectively
4 〈간신히 기어가다〉 crawl with effort; creep

엉기정기 in disorder; pell-mell; in (utter) confusion

엉너리 tricksy [deceitful] ingratiation; bamboozlements to ingratiate *oneself* ♦ 엉너리치다 ingratiate *oneself* 《with *sb*》 tricksily; try all sorts of tricks to win favor

엉너릿손 the skill of tricksy ingratiation

엉덩방아 a fall on *one's* behind [backside, buttocks]; (美口) a pratfall
♦ 엉덩방아를 찧다 fall on *one's* behind [backside, buttocks]; land on *one's* rear; (美口) take [have] a pratfall
▶ 의자에 앉다가 잘못되어 엉덩방아를 찧었다 I missed the chair and sat right down on the floor.

엉덩이 the buttocks; the hips; (口) the behind; the bottom; the rear
♦ 엉덩이가 가볍다 do not stay long 《in a place》 / 엉덩이가 무겁다 be slow to act; be slow in starting work; be sluggish / 엉덩이를 붙이다 stay too long; outstay *one's* welcome / 엉덩이를 흔들다 swing [wag] *one's* hips [behind]
▶ 그녀는 엉덩이가 크다 She is big in the hips. ⇒ She is broad-hipped. ⇒ She has broad hips.

엉덩잇바람 swaying *one's* hips (as *one* walks)

엉덩잇짓 swinging *one's* hips; hip-swinging ━**엉덩잇짓하다** swing *one's* hips

엉덩춤 hip dancing; a hip dance; a hula

엉덩판 the hips ⇨ 엉덩이 ♦ 엉덩판이 큰 여자 a woman broad in the beam

엉두덜거리다 〈투덜거리다〉 grumble; complain; mutter; (口) grouch

엉뚱하다 extraordinary; extravagant; eccentric; preposterous; inconsistent; irrelevant; absurd; unexpected; wild; wrong
♦ 엉뚱한 사람 a different person; a person not related 《to the affair》; 〈무모한 사람〉 an extravagant [a venturesome] fellow / 엉뚱한 생각 a wild [an inordinate] idea / 엉뚱한 말을 하다 say something quite beside the point; utter some incoherent remarks / 엉뚱한 질문을 하다 ask [《口》 pop] an unexpected question / 엉뚱한 데로 가다 go in the wrong direction
▶ 그는 엉뚱한 짓을 잘 한다 He is always doing wild things.
▶ 우리는 그녀의 엉뚱한 제안에 당황했다 We were puzzled at her absurd suggestion.
▶ 그런 엉뚱한 요구는 받아들일 수 없다 We cannot accept such a preposterous demand.
▶ 그는 엉뚱한 대답을 했다 His answer was far off the mark.

엉망 mess; wreck; ruin; (in) bad shape; disorder; higgledy-piggledy; topsy-turvy; confusion
♦ 엉망이 되다 get out of shape; be spoiled; go to wreck / 엉망을 만들다 make a mess of; mess; wreck; mess up 《matters》
▶ 큰 비가 와서 길이 엉망이다 The road is very bad after a heavy rain.
▶ 그의 갑작스런 죽음으로 모든 것이 엉망이 되었다 His sudden death threw everything into confusion.
▶ 기차가 늦게 도착하는 바람에 우리의 모든 계획이 엉망이 되었다 The late arrival of the train messed up all our plans.
▶ 방안이 엉망이다 The room is topsy-turvy [in wild disorder].

엉망진창 higgledy-piggledy; topsy-turvy ⇨ 엉망

엉성하다 1 〈짜임새가 없다〉 loose; careless; 〈성기다〉 sparse; coarse
♦ 엉성한 그물 a net of large meshes / 엉성한 문장 a loose piece of writing / 엉성하게 자란 나뭇가지 loosely grown twigs / 엉성하게 뜨개질하다 knit with large stitches
▶ 이 잡지는 편집이 엉성하다 This magazine is carelessly edited.
2 〈마르다〉 lean; haggard; gaunt
♦ 가지만 엉성한 나무 a bare [leafless] tree
3 〈탐탁하지 않다〉 unsatisfactory; 〈조잡하다〉 slipshod; slovenly
♦ 엉성한 세공품 a slipshod piece of work / 일 솜씨가 엉성하다 be of bad [slovenly] workmanship

엉엉 ♦ 엉엉 울다 weep noisily; cry loudly [bitterly]; cry *one's* heart out; boohoo

엉엉거리다 1 ⇨ 엉엉
2 〈하소연하다〉 complain of [about] *one's* poverty; deplore *one's* misfortune [hard life]

엉정벙정 with useless things scattered about; in a clutter ━**엉정벙정하다** be all cluttered up

엉클다 tangle; entangle ⇨ 헝클다

엉클어지다 tangle; get tangled; be [get] entangled

엉큼대왕 ━大王 a man of wild [grandiose] ambition; a deep one

엉큼성큼 with long [big] strides ♦ 엉큼성큼 걷다 stride 《along》; stalk

엉큼하다 overambitious; preposterous; inwardly bold [audacious]; wily; deep; sly
♦ 엉큼한 사람 a man swollen with suppressed

엉키다

ambition / 엉큼한 생각 a wild ambition; a wily scheme; an inordinate desire / 엉큼한 질문 a sly question / 엉큼한 처사 underhand dealings

엉키다 be entangled ⇨ 엉클어지다
▶호트러진 실은 쉽게 엉킨다 Loose string is easily entangled.

엉터리 1 〈미덥지 못한 사람〉 a fake; a quack; a sham; a gyp; 〈허울만 좋은 것〉 a gimcrack; a gewgaw
♦엉터리 시인 a poetaster; a rhymester / 엉터리 약 a quack medicine / 엉터리 의사 a quack / 엉터리 회사 (美) a bogus concern
▶이 라디오는 엉터리다 This radio is not so good as it looks.
▶그는 일을 엉터리로 한다 He does his work anyhow. ⇌ He does a slapdash job.
2 〈윤곽〉 an outline; a sketch; framework
♦일의 엉터리를 잡다 grasp the general idea [outline] of a job
3 〈터무니〉 a ground; a foundation
♦엉터리없는 보도 news from an unreliable source / 엉터리없는 소문 a groundless rumor / 엉터리없는 이야기 a made-up [trumped-up] story; a (pure) fabrication / 엉터리없는 짓을 하다 do a foolish [stupid] thing

엊그저께 a few days ago; the day before yesterday

엊저녁 last night; yesterday [last] evening
♦엊저녁에 가족을 데리고 외식을 했다 Last night I took my family out to eat.

엎다 turn over; turn [lay] upside down; turn face down; overthrow; undermine; subvert
♦잔을 엎다 set a glass bottom up [upside down] / 상자를 엎다 overturn a box

엎드러지다 fall on *one's* breast [nose]; fall down
♦돌에 걸려 엎드러지다 fall [tumble] over a stone / 엎드러지면 코 닿을 데에 있다 be close at hand; be only a little away (from); be within [at] a stone's throw (of, from)

엎드리다 lie on *one's* face; lie (with *one's*) face down [downward]; lie [be] prone; throw *oneself* flat; prostrate *oneself*
♦왕의 발 아래 엎드리다 prostrate *oneself* before the king / 땅[마룻바닥]에 납작 엎드리다 lie flat down on the ground [floor] / 엎드려 자다 sleep on *one's* face / 엎드려 기어가다 creep [move] on *one's* stomach / 엎드려 용서를 빌다 beg *sb's* pardon prostrating *oneself* on the ground
▶엎드려 (口令) Lie down!
▶그 슬픈 소식을 듣고 그녀는 소파에 엎드려 울었다 At the sad news, she lay on her face on the sofa and cried.

엎어놓다 put 〈a thing〉 face [top] down [upside down]

엎어지다 1 〈넘어지다〉 fall on *one's* breast [nose, face]; fall down; 〈뒤집히다〉 be turned over
▶그는 발을 헛디뎌 엎어졌다 He lost his footing and fell on his face.
▶은행은 우리 집에서 엎어지면 코 닿을 거리에 있다 The bank is very close to my house.

2 〈망쳐지다〉 be spoilt; be ruined; be overthrown

엎지르다 spill; slop
▶바닥에 잉크를 엎지르지 않도록 조심해라 Take care not to spill the ink on the floor.
▶테이블을 흔들지 마라, 커피가 엎질러진다 Don't shake the table, or the coffee will spill (on it).

엎지른 물을 도로 담을까 (속담) It is no use crying over spilt milk. ⇌ Let bygones be bygones.

엎치다 turn over ⇨ 엎다

엎치락뒤치락 up-and-down; turning over and over ─엎치락뒤치락하다 toss about; turn over and over
♦엎치락뒤치락하는 경기 a seesaw [dingdong] game [match]
▶그는 잠이 오지않아서 엎치락뒤치락했다 He tossed about in bed unable to get to sleep.

엎친데덮치다 make things worse; add to *one's* troubles; have one misfortune after another
♦엎친 데 덮친다 (속담) Misfortunes never come singly. ⇌ One misfortune rides upon another's back.
▶엎친 데 덮치기로 비까지 왔다 To make matters worse, it started to rain.
▶엎친 데 덮치기로 그는 직장까지 잃었다 To complete the sum of his miseries, he lost his job.

에¹ 1 〈장소·위치〉 at; in; on
♦방에 in the room / 대문(곁)에 at [by] the gate / 책상 위에 on the desk / 양쪽에 on both sides / 강가에 살다 live on the banks of a river / 강물 위에 뜨다 float on the river / 벽에 기대다 lean against the wall / 목적지에 닿다 arrive at *one's* destination / 입에 담뱃대를 물다 have a pipe in *one's* mouth
▶그녀는 지금 파리에 살고 있다 She lives [is] in Paris now.
▶나는 내일 집에 있을 예정이다 I will be (at) home tomorrow.
▶그 의자에 앉으세요. Please sit on the chair.
2 〈방향〉 to; in; into; for; on; toward
♦학교에 가다 go to school / 집에 들어가다 enter [go into] the house / 싸움터에 나가다 go to the front; go (off) to war / 땅에 떨어지다 fall to the ground / 상자(속)에 넣다 put *sth* in [into] a box
3 〈원인〉 at; with; of; from; owing to; because of; for
♦더위에 시달리다 suffer from heat / 추위에 떨다 shiver with [from] cold / 술에 취하다 get drunk / 그렇기 (때문)에 such being the case
▶서두르는 바람에 책을 가져가는 것을 잊어버렸다 In my hurry I forgot to bring the book.
▶그녀는 수치심 때문에 얼굴이 붉어졌다 She blushed for shame.
4 〈시간〉 at; on; in
♦3시에 at three (o'clock) / 7시 10분에 at 10 past [after] 7 / 정오[새벽]에 at noon [dusk] / 아침[오후, 저녁]에 in the morning [afternoon, evening] / 겨울에 in (the) winter / 3일

에 on the 3rd / 일요일 저녁에 on Sunday evening / 해마다 이 시기에 every year / 여행이 끝날 무렵에 toward the end of *one's* journey
▶ 기차는 3시에 도착할 예정이다 The train is due (to arrive) at three.
▶ 막 떠나려던 차에 그녀가 왔다 She came just as I was leaving.
5 〈나이〉 at; in
♦ 나이 서른에 죽다 die at (the age of) thirty / 십대에 결혼하다 marry in *one's* teens
6 〈비율·단위〉 at; in; for; per; by
♦ 하루에 세 끼의 식사 three meals a day / 한 달에 40만원의 용돈 a monthly allowance of 400,000 won / 10년에 한 번 once in ten years; once every ten years / 한 사람에 열 발의 탄약 10 rounds of ammunition per man / 양복 한 벌을 20만원에 팔다 sell a suit at [for] two hundred thousand won / 1년에 얼마로 집을 빌리다 rent a house by the year
▶ 그녀는 한 달에 두 번씩 상경한다 She comes (up) to Seoul at least twice a [every] month.
▶ 이 잡지는 1년에 네 번 발간된다 This magazine is issued four times a [per] year.
7 〈관련〉 for; to; in; with; of; on
♦ 그 사람에 관해서 concerning that person / 건강에 좋다 be good for health / 질문에 대답하다 answer [reply to] a question / 어떤 일에 관계하다 relate to [be connected with] a certain matter
8 〈수단〉 on; in; to; 〈작인(作因)〉 by; with
♦ (현관) 매트에 신발흙을 털어내다 wipe *one's* shoes on the doormat / 완력에 호소하다 resort to force [violence] / 손잡이에 매달리다 hang on [by] the strap / 바늘에 찔리다 be pricked with a needle / 눈에 파묻히다 be buried under [in] snow / 총(알)에 맞다 be hit by a bullet
▶ 가지가 바람에 흔들린다 Branches sway in the wind.
9 〈표준〉 by; to; at; 〈기준〉 on
♦ 크기에 따라서 according to size / 시계를 시보에 맞추다 set a watch by the timecast / 기본 원칙에 입각하여 행동하다 act on the basis of fundamental rules
10 〈열거〉 and; in addition to; and the like
▶ 술에 고기에 잘 먹었다 I have had enough drinks, meat and the like.
11 〈대비〉 on; against; and; in contrast 《with》
♦ 청색 바탕에 금빛 글자 gold characters on a blue ground
▶ 그녀는 노랑 저고리에 다홍 치마를 입었다 She wore a yellow coat and a pink skirt.
12 〈소속·종사〉 in
♦ 군대에 가 있다 be on the army
에² **1** 〈못마땅할 때〉 oh; fie
▶ 에, 속상해 How vexing!
▶ 에, 보기 싫어 Fie, for shame!
2 〈말하는 도중에〉 well; let me see; er; hum
에게 **1** 〈행동이 미치는 대상〉 to; at; for; of
♦ 아들에게 책을 사주다 buy a book for *one's* son / 아이에게 밥을 먹이다 feed a child / 어머니에게 편지를 쓰다 write a letter to *one's* mother / 죄인에게 돌을 던지다 throw [pelt] stones at an evildoer
▶ 그에게 덤벼들어라 At him!
▶ 그것은 나에게 큰 도움이 된다 It is of great help to me. ⇌ It is very helpful [useful] to me.
2 〈행동을 일으키는 대상〉 by; from
▶ 나는 그에게 속았다 I was fooled by him.
▶ 그것을 누구에게 들었느냐? From whom did you hear that? ⇌ Who told you about it?
에게도 also; too; as well; even to
♦ 아무에게도 뒤지지 않다 be second to none; have no equal / 낯선 사람에게도 친절하다 be kind even to strangers
▶ 너에게도 그걸 주마 I'll give it to you too.
에게로 to; toward; at
▶ 허물이 누구에게로 돌아갈까? Who(m) does that mistake go back to?
▶ 책임을 그에게로 돌리지 마라 Don't lay the fault to his charge.
에게서 from; of
♦ 아버님에게서 온 편지 a letter from *one's* father / 친구에게서 돈을 조금 빌리다 borrow some money of a friend
▶ 이 돈은 누구에게서 나왔느냐? Who(m) did this money come from?
에게해 —**海** 〈지중해 동부 해역〉 the Aegean Sea
에고 the ego; self
■ —**이스트** a selfish [self-centered] person; an egoist —**이즘** 〈이기주의〉 selfishness; egoism —**티즘** 〈자아주의〉 egotism
에구구 Oh! oh!; O dear! ▶ 에구구, 가엾기도 해라 O dear, what a pity!
에그 oh my! ⇨ 에끼¹
에그머니 Ah! ⇨ 아이고
에그프라이 fried eggs
에끼¹ Oh my!
에끼² 〈못마땅해 하는 소리〉 Ugh!; Fie!; Phew!; Pshaw! ▶ 에끼, 이 고얀 놈 Ugh! You rascal [scoundrel]!
에나멜 enamel ♦ 에나멜을 입히다 enamel
■ —**구두** enameled shoes; patent (leather) shoes —**선** an enamel wire —**질(質)** enamel —**페인트** enamel paint
에너지 〔物〕 energy
♦ 에너지를 비축하다 conserve energy
▶ 태양은 우리의 가장 귀중한 에너지원이다 The sun is our most precious energy source.
■ **결합**— binding energy **열**— thermal energy; heat energy **운동**— kinetic **위치**— potential energy **잠재**— latent [potential] energy **정지**— rest energy **태양[핵]**— solar [nuclear] energy ■ —**량** energy content 《of cosmic rays》—**론** energetics —**보존 법칙** the law of energy conservation —**위기** the energy crisis —**혁명** energy revolution —**효율** an energy efficiency
에누리 **1** 〈더 얹어 부르는 값〉 an overcharge
▶ 에누리 없이 얼마니까? What is your lowest price?
—**에누리하다** ask a fancy price [two prices]; overcharge
♦ 에누리하지 않다 do not overcharge; ask only one price
2 〈할인〉 (a) reduction in price; (a) discount
▶ 그 드레스는 너무 비싸요. 에누리는 안 되나

요? The dress is too expensive. Can you lower [bring down] the price?
▶ 에누리는 일절 없습니다 We never make a reduction. ⇒ We never ask two prices. ⇒ 〈게시〉 No reduction allowed.
—에누리하다 bring [beat, knock] down the price; reduce [abate, lower] the price; make a reduction [discount]; discount
♦ 천원으로 에누리하다 beat down the price to 1,000 won / 1할을 에누리하다 cut 10% off the price
▶ 그렇게 에누리하지 마십시오 Don't bid so low.
▶ 조금 에누리해 드리지요 We will make it a little cheaper.
3 〈과장〉 (an) exaggeration; (an) overstatement
♦ 에누리 없이 말하다 state the fact as it is; give *one's* honest opinion; speak without exaggeration
—에누리하다 exaggerate; overstate
♦ 좀 에누리해서 말하면 if I may be allowed a little exaggeration

에는 as for; for; to; at; on; in
♦ 필요할 경우에는 in case of need / 내 생각에는 in my opinion / 눈에는 눈 an eye for an eye
▶ 올 여름에는 어디로 갑니까? Where do you go for this summer?
▶ 이번에는 꼭 이기겠다 I will win this time for sure.
▶ 그는 낮에는 농사를 짓고 밤에는 책을 읽는다 He works on a farm by day and reads books by night.

에다[1] 〈예리한 것으로 도려내다〉 cut [scoop, scrape] out; gouge (out)
♦ 에는 듯한 아픔 poignant [lancinating] pain / 살을 에는 듯한 북풍 a cutting [biting, piercing] north wind
▶ 바람은 살을 에는 듯이 차가왔다 The wind was cutting [biting] cold.

에다[2] to; and ⇨ 에다가

에다가 to; in; on; at; for; and
♦ 벽에다가 연필로 낙서를 해놓았다 There are pencil scribblings on the wall.
▶ 3에다가 7을 더하면 10이 된다 Three and seven make [are] ten. ⇒ Three plus seven is ten.

에덴 Eden ■—동산 the Garden of Eden
에델바이스 〔植〕 an edelweiss
에도 also; too; as well; even
♦ 몽매간에도 even while asleep; awake or asleep / 낮에도 어둡다 be dark even in the daytime / 밤에도 자지 않다 do not sleep even at night; do not sleep at night either / 마음에도 없는 소리를 하다 say what *one* does not mean; say what is not in *one's* mind
♦ 알래스카에 갈 수 있으리라고는 꿈에도 생각지 못했다 I never dreamed that I would be able to go to Alaska.
▶ 그곳은 한여름에도 서늘하다 It is cool there at [in] the height of summer.
▶ 흰여우는 한국에도 일본에도 없다 The silver fox is found neither in Korea nor in Japan.

에돌다 hover around shy; hang around [about] hesitantly; linger over (*one's* work)
♦ 선뜻 일하지 않고 에돌다 loaf on the job; (口) lie down on the job

에두르다 **1** 〈둘러 막다〉 encircle; enclose (with, in); surround (with, by)
♦ 집을 울타리로 에두르다 enclose the house with a fence
2 〈둘러서 말하다〉 make a roundabout statement; suggest; hint; euphemize
▶ 그는 에둘러 말하는 버릇이 있다 He has a tendency to talk in a roundabout way [to beat around the bush].

에든버러 〈영국 스코틀랜드의 중심 도시〉 Edinburgh
에디슨 〈미국의 발명가〉 Edison, Thomas Alva (1847-1931) ■—축전지 an Edison cell
에디터 an editor ⇨ 편집(~자)
에디푸스콤플렉스 〔心〕 Oedipus complex
에라 **1** 〈체념〉 Oh well; All right; Oh my!; Gee!; Gosh!
▶ 에라 그만 두자 All right, let's give it up. ⇒ Well, let's quit.
2 〈주위 환기〉 Hey there!; You there!
▶ 에라 비켜라 Move [Step] aside!; Get out of the way!
3 〈금지〉 Don't!; Stop!
4 ⇨ 에루화

에라스무스 〈네덜란드의 인문학자〉 Erasmus, Desiderius (1466?-1536)
에러 〈야구 등의〉 an error
♦ 야수의 에러 a fielder's error / 투수[포수]의 에러를 a battery error / 에러를 범하다 make an error / 유격수의 에러로 3루에서 세이프되다 be safe on third base on an error by the shortstop
▶ 저 유격수는 에러를 잘 범한다 That shortstop often makes errors.

에로 〈에로티시즘〉 eroticism; 〈형용사적〉 erotic; sexy; sensual; obscene
■—문학 pornography —영화 a sex film; (美俗) a purple film

에로스 〔그神〕 Eros
에로티시즘 〈성애〉 eroticism
에로틱하다 erotic; sexy; lewd; sensual
에루화 Oh, what fun!; Delightful!
에르그 〔物〕 〈에너지의 단위〉 an erg
에르븀 〔化〕 erbium
에만 **1** 〈장소〉 only to [in, at, on]
♦ 집에만 틀어박혀 있는 사람 a stay-at-home; (美俗) a homebody / 술집에만 드나들다 do nothing but frequent drinking houses
▶ 그는 왼손에만 장갑을 끼고 있었다 He had a glove only on the left hand.
2 〈사물〉 only; simply; …alone
▶ 그는 한 가지 일에만 열중하고 있다 He is absorbed in only one thing.

에머슨 〈미국의 시인·사상가〉 Emerson, Ralph Waldo (1803-82)
에메랄드 〔鑛〕 emerald
에멜무지로 **1** 〈헛일 겸 시험삼아〉 on [for] trial; by way of experiment ♦ 에멜무지로 한번 써보다 give *sth* a trial; employ *sb* on trial
2 〈느슨하게 묶어서〉 loosely; poorly; badly
에베소서 —書 〔聖〕 The Epistle of St. Paul

(the Apostle) to the Ephesians; 〈약칭〉 the Ephesians (略 Eph.)

에보나이트 ebonite; vulcanite; hard rubber

에볼라바이러스 〔醫〕 the Ebola virus

에비 Boo! ▶에비, 만지지 마라 Boo! Don't touch it!

에서 1 〈장소〉 in; at; on
▶ 나는 플랫폼에서 그녀를 만났다 I saw her on the platform.
▶ 어느 역에서 갈아타야 합니까? At what station should I change trains?
▶ 이 열차를 타고 수원에서 내리시오 Take this train and get off at Suwon.
▶ 이 방에서 잠시 기다려요 Wait in this room for a while.
▶ 그는 2층에서 공부하고 있다 He is studying upstairs.
2 〈출발점〉 from; out of; off; through; down; over; 〈기산점(起算點)〉 from
◆ 시골에서 갓 올라온 처녀 a maiden fresh [green] from the country / 일곱살에서 열두살까지의 아이들 children (ranging) from seven to twelve / 1시에서 3시 사이에 between one and three o'clock / 기차에서 내리다 get off a train; alight [get out] from a train / 방에서 나오다 come out of the room / 사다리에서 떨어지다 fall off [from] a ladder / 벼랑에서 떨어지다 fall over a precipice / 30쪽에서 시작하다 begin at page 30 / 5에서 3을 빼다 subtract 3 from 5 / 봉급에서 공제하다 deduct 《a sum》 from one's salary
▶ 해는 동쪽에서 뜬다 The sun rises in the east.
▶ 바다에서 불어오는 바람은 시원하다 The wind from the sea is cool.
▶ 그는 찬장에서 위스키를 꺼내어 마시기 시작했다 He took the whisky out of the cupboard and began to drink it.
▶ 가격은 오백원에서 천원까지 여러 가지입니다 The prices range from 500 won (up) to 1,000.
3 〈주격 조사〉 ◆ 국가에서 정한 (법정) 공휴일 a national holiday / 법에서 정한 바에 따라 as provided by law
▶ 이 비용은 회사에서 부담한다 The firm bears the whole expense of this.
4 〈동기・원인〉 from; out of; in; through
◆ 원한에서 out of spite / 책임감에서 from a sense of duty / 호기심에서 out of curiosity
▶ 이것은 모두 질투에서 빚어진 일이다 All this was done through envy.
▶ 그것은 자책감에서 나온 말이다 He said that out of self-accusation.
5 〈근거・관점〉 by; from; on; according to
◆ 교육적 견지에서 (보면) from the [an] educational point of view / 다른 각도에서 보다 view (life) from a different angle
▶ 교사도 학생의 입장에서 생각해 주었으면 한다 We hope that the teacher will try to think, putting himself in the student's place.
6 〈비교〉 than
▶ 이에서 더한 불행[사랑]은 없다 There can be no greater misfortune [love] than this.

에서는 in; at; to; as to; as for; in the case of; in point [respect] of; concerning
▶ 광주에서는 삼촌 집에서 묵었다 In Kwangju I stayed at my uncle's. ⇒ I stayed with my uncle in Kwangju.
▶ 그 점에서는 당신과 완전히 동감입니다 In that respect, I agree with you completely.

에서도 even in [at, from]; also at [in, from]
▶ 어떤 상황에서도 사람을 죽여서는 안된다 You must not kill human beings under any circumstances.
▶ 이 문제를 놓고 해외에서 뿐마나라 국내에서도 열띤 논쟁이 있었다 This question has been heatedly discussed at home as well as abroad.

에서만 only [just] in [at, from] ◆ 서울에서만 팔리다 sell only in Seoul / 흙에서만 검출되다 be detected only from the soil

에세이 an essay

에센스 essence

에스 1 〈알파벳 자모〉 the letter "S" 2 〈치수〉 S; small (size) 3 〈동성애자〉 (口) one's sister [sis]; one's pet

에스겔 〔聖〕 (The Book of) Ezekiel (略 Ezek.)

에스더 〔聖〕 (The Book of) Esther (略 Esth.)

에스라 〔聖〕 (The Book of) Ezra

에스에프 SF [《science fiction》]

에스 엘 비 엠 SLBM [《submarine-launched ballistic missile》]

에스오에스 〈조난 신호〉 an SOS; a signal of distress ◆ 에스오에스를 보내다 flash [send out] an SOS / 에스오에스를 수신하다 pick up an SOS

에스컬레이션 (an) escalation

에스컬레이터 an escalator; a moving staircase

에스코트 〈행위〉 escort; 〈사람〉 an escort
▶ 그가 파티에서 나를 에스코트해 주었다 He was my escort at the party.

에스키모 an Eskimo (pl. ~(s)) ; an Esquimau (pl. -maux, ~) ◆ 에스키모의 Eskimo ■ ─개 an Eskimo dog; a husky ─말 Eskimo; Esquimau

에스테르 〔化〕 an ester

에스토니아 〈나라 이름〉 Estonia; 〈공식명〉 the Republic of Estonia ◆ 에스토니아의 Estonian ■ ─말 Estonian; the Estonian language ─사람 an Estonian

에스파냐 España ⇨ 스페인

에스페란토 〈국제어〉 Esperanto

에스프리 〈정신・기지〉 spirit; (프) esprit

에야디야 Yo-ho!; Yo-heave-ho!

에어 〈공기〉 air
■ ─라인 〈항공로〉 an air line [route]; 〈항공회사〉 an airlines ─메일 airmail ─백 an air bag ─버스 an airbus ─컨디셔너 an air conditioner ─터미널 an air terminal ─포켓 〔空〕 an air pocket [hole] ─포트 an airport

에어로빅스 〈운동법〉 aerobics

에우다 1 〈둘러싸다〉 encircle; surround 2 〈지우다〉 cross [strike] out [off]; blot out; erase 3 〈딴 길로 돌리다〉 go round

에움길 a roundabout way [route]; a detour
◆ 에움길로 가다 go a roundabout way

에워가다 1 〈둘러가다〉 go round; go by a roundabout way; take [make] a detour; take

에워싸다 a circuitous route
2 〈지워 나가다〉 strike [cross] out one by one
에워싸다 enclose; surround; encircle; 〈군대가〉 besiege; lay siege to (a town)
♦집을 담으로 에워싸다 enclose a house with a wall / 요새를 에워싸다 lay siege to a fortress / 적을 겹겹이 에워싸다 surround the enemy thick and fast / 삼면이 산으로 에워싸이다 be surrounded by hills on three sides
▶그들은 우르르 그를 에워쌌다 They thronged around him.
▶그는 손자들에게 에워싸인채 미소를 짓고 있었다 He was smiling, encircled [ringed around] by his grandchildren.
에의 to; at; in ♦성공에의 지름길 a shortcut to success
에이비시 〈알파벳〉 the alphabet; 〈초보〉 the ABC's; the elements; the fundamentals; the first step
▶그는 영문법의 에이비시도 모른다 He does not know even the ABC's of English grammar.
▶이름은 에이비시 순입니다 The names are arranged alphabetically [in alphabetical order].
에이스 〈카드놀이〉 the ace; 〈최고 선수〉 a leading player; 〔野〕 the top [first-line, outstanding] pitcher (on a team)
에 이 엠 AM 〈*a*mplitude *m*odulation〉 ■—방송 AM broadcasting
에이전시 〈대리점〉 an agency
에이전트 〈대리인·대리점〉 an agent
에이즈 〔醫〕 AIDS [〈*a*cquired *i*mmune *d*eficiency *s*yndrome〉]
에이커 an acre ▶부지는 10에이커다 The grounds contain ten acres.
에이트 〈보트경주〉 an 《Oxford》 eight
에이티시 ATC [〈*a*utomatic *t*rain *c*ontrol〉]
에이티에스 ATS [〈*a*utomatic *t*rain *s*top〉]
에이프런 〈앞치마〉 an apron
♦흰 에이프런을 두른 김여사 white-aproned Mrs. Kim / 에이프런을 두르다 wear an apron; be in an apron / 에이프런에 손을 닦다 wipe *one's* hands on *one's* apron
▶그녀는 에이프런을 두르고 있다 She is wearing an apron.
▶어머니는 에이프런을 두른 채 손님을 맞았다 Mother in her apron met a stranger.
■—스테이지 〔劇〕 an apron stage; a forestage; the apron of a stage
에이피 AP [〈the *A*ssociated *P*ress〉]
에인절피시 〔魚〕 an angelfish
에잇 〈놀람·분노 등〉 Eh!; Oh!; 〈혐오·경멸 등〉 Pshaw!; 〈기합〉 Come on! ▶에잇, 빌어먹을 Damn it! ⇒ Hang it!
에지 〔스키·스케이트〕 an edge
에참 Phew!; Hang it all!; Shucks!; Tut!
▶에참, 또 내가 가야해 Shucks! Again, have I to go?
에칭 〈기법〉 etching; 〈작품〉 an etching
에카페 ECAFE [〈the *E*conomic *C*ommission for *A*sia and the *F*ar *E*ast〉]
에코 〈메아리〉 an echo
에콰도르 Ecuador; 〈공식명〉 the Republic of Ecuador ♦에콰도르의 Ecuadorian ■—사람 an Ecuadorian
에크 Oh my! ⇨ 에크나
에크나 〈놀람〉 Dear me!; Oh (my)!; Heavens!; Gosh! ▶에크나, 큰일났네 Gee! What have I done!
에탄 〔化〕 ethane
에탄올 〔化〕 ethanol
에테르 〔化〕 ether; aether ♦에테르의 ethereal / 에테르로 마취시키다 etherize
에토스 〔哲〕 ethos
에튀드 〔樂〕 a study; (프) an étude
에트랑세 a stranger; (프) an étranger
에티오피아 Ethiopia; 〈공식명〉 the Federal Democratic Republic of Ethiopia ♦에티오피아의 Ethiopian ■—사람 an Ethiopian
에티켓 etiquette; good manners
♦에티켓을 알고 있다[지키다] know [observe] the rules of etiquette / …은 에티켓에 어긋난다 It is not good to do...; It is a break of etiquette to do...
▶그의 행동은 에티켓에 어긋난다 His behavior is against (the rules of) etiquette.
에틸 〔化〕 ethyl ■—알코올 ethanol; ethyl [grain] alcohol
에틸렌 〔化〕 ethylene ■—글리콜 ethylene glycol
에페 (프) 〔펜싱〕 an épée
에펠탑 —塔 the Eiffel Tower
에폭시수지 —樹脂 〔化〕 epoxy resins
에프비아이 FBI [〈the *F*ederal *B*ureau of *I*nvestigation〉]
에프에이오 FAO [〈the *F*ood and *A*griculture *O*rganization〉]
에프엠 FM [〈*f*requency *m*odulation〉]
▶이 라디오는 에프엠 채널이 들립니까? Does this radio have an FM channel?
▶이 라디오로 그 에프엠 프로그램을 들을 수 있나요? Can you get that FM program at this radio?
■—방송 FM broadcasting ■—방송국[라디오] an FM station [radio]
에프티시 FTC [〈the *F*ederal *T*rade *C*ommission〉]
에피소드 〈삽화〉 an episode; 〈일화〉 an anecdote
에피쿠로스 〈고대 그리스의 철학자〉 Epicurus (341-270 B.C.)
에필로그 〈종결부〉 an epilogue (↔ prologue)
에헴 hem; ahem ♦에헴하고 소리내다 hem; clear *one's* throat ▶그는 내 주의를 끌기 위해 「에헴」 소리를 냈다 He made a sound of "Hem!" to call my attention.
엑스 1 〈미지수〉 an x; an unknown quantity
2 ⇨ 가위표
엑스선 —線 X rays; Roentgen rays
♦엑스선으로 보다 watch through X rays
■—검사 an X-ray examination; X-ray inspection : 나는 엑스선 검사를 받으러 병원에 갔다 I went to a hospital for an X-ray examination.
—사진 an X-ray [a Roentgen] photograph; a roentgenogram; roentgenograph : 엑스선 사진을 찍다 take an X-ray photograph (of); X-ray
—요법 X-ray therapy

엑스터시 〈황홀 상태〉ecstasy
엑스트라 〈임시고용 배우〉an extra (hand); a supernumerary; (口) a super ◆엑스트라 노릇을 하다 play an extra part (in a movie)
▶그 한 장면을 찍기 위해 수천명의 엑스트라가 고용되었다 Thousands of extras were hired for that one scene.
엑스퍼트 〈전문가〉an expert (at, in)
엔간하다 〈적당하다〉moderate; reasonable; proper; suitable; 〈보통이다〉average; ordinary; common
▶엔간히 마셔라 Don't drink too much.
▶허풍을 떨어도 엔간히 떨어야지 There is a limit to bragging.
엔도르핀 〔生化〕endorphin
엔들 〈반어적〉even; also; too ▶필요하다면 어디엔들 못가랴 I would go any place if (it is) necessary.
엔지 〔映〕N.G.; no good ◆엔지를 내다 spoil [ruin] a sequence
엔지니어 an engineer
엔진 an engine ◆엔진을 걸다 start an engine; set an engine going [at work] / 엔진을 멈추다 stop an engine / 엔진을 덥게 하다 warm up the engine
▶엔진이 걸려 있다 The engine is running.
▶엔진이 꺼졌다 The engine stopped [ran down].
▶엔진이 고장났다 The engine stalled.
■가솔린— a petrol [gasoline] engine 디젤— a diesel (oil) engine 선박용— a marine engine 항공— an aeroengine ■—고장 stalling of a motor [an engine]; an engine failure [trouble]; 〈제트 엔진의〉a flameout
엔트로피 〔物〕entropy
엔트리 an entry
엘그레코 〈스페인의 화가〉El Greco (1541-1614)
엘레지 〈비가〉an elegy
엘렉트라콤플렉스 〔心〕the Electra complex
엘리베이터 (美) an elevator; (英) a lift
◆엘리베이터의 단추 the signal; the up [down] button / 엘리베이터가 있는 아파트 an elevator apartment; an apartment with an elevator / 엘리베이터가 없는 건물 (美) a walk-up (building) / 엘리베이터를 운전하다 run [operate] an elevator / 엘리베이터를 타다 take an elevator ((to the fifth floor)) / 엘리베이터를 타고 올라가다[내려가다] go up [down] in an elevator
▶이 엘리베이터는 올라갑니까, 내려갑니까 ? Is this elevator going up or down?
▶이 엘리베이터는 층마다 섭니다 This elevator stops at every floor.
▶엘리베이터를 타고 5층에 갑시다 Let's take the elevator to the fifth floor.
■—운전자 an elevator operator [boy, girl]
엘리엇 1〈영국의 여류작가〉Eliot, George (1819-80) (▶본명은 Mary Ann Evans) 2〈영국의 시인・비평가〉Eliot, Thomas Stearns (1888-1965)
엘리트 (총칭) the elite (of society); the chosen (few)
◆엘리트 코스를 밟다 be on course for membership of the elite; be destined for high [higher] things
▶그는 엘리트다 He is an elitist.
■—사원 an elite employee —의식 elitism : 그는 엘리트 의식이 강하다 He assumes himself to be rather elite. —주의 elitism : 엘리트주의자 an elitist —파워 the power elite ((inside the government))
엘살바도르 El Salvador; 〈공식명〉the Republic of El Salvador ◆엘살바도르의 Salvadoran; Salvadorian
■—사람 a Salvadoran
엘에스디 LSD [〈lysergic acid diethylamide]; (美俗) acid
엘에스아이 LSI [〈large scale integration]
엘에스티 LST [〈landing ship, tank]
엘엔지 LNG [〈liquefied natural gas]
엘피지 LPG [〈liquefied petroleum gas]
엘피판 —板 an LP record [〈a long-playing record]
엠브이피 MVP [〈the most valuable player]
엥 〈짜증・뉘우침〉Shucks!; Pshaw!; Gee!
엥겔 〈독일의 통계학자〉Engel, Ernst (1821-96)
■—계수 Engel's coefficient —법칙 Engel's law
엥겔스 〈독일의 사회주의자〉Engels, Friedrich (1820-95)
-여 -餘 〈…을 넘는〉above; over; more ((than)); beyond; 〈이상〉...and over [more]
◆10여년간 for ten odd years; for over ten years / 2천여명 two thousand (and) odd men / 70여년 three score and ten-odd years
여가 餘暇 leisure; leisure hours [time]; spare time [moments]; free time
◆업무의 여가에 in spare moments from one's business; in the intervals of business / 여가가 있다 be free; have time; be not busy; be at leisure / 여가가 없다 have no leisure [time to spare]; be busy [occupied] ((with one's work)) / 여가를 이용하다 make use of one's spare moments
▶오후에는 여가가 좀 있습니다 I have some free time in the afternoon.
▶나는 언제나 여가가 없다 I am always busy. ⇒ I never have any time to spare.
▶그녀는 여가만 나면 피아노를 친다 All her spare time is spent (in) playing the piano. ⇒ She plays the piano whenever she has the time.
▶그는 독서하며 여가를 보냈다 He spent his leisure [spare time] (in) reading.
여가수 女歌手 a female [woman] singer
여각 餘角 〔幾〕the complementary angle; the complement
여간 如干 ordinarily; commonly; normally
◆여간 기뻐하지 않다 be greatly [highly] delighted / 여간 놀라지 않다 be not a little surprised / 여간 어렵지 않다 be awfully [exceedingly, very] difficult
▶오늘은 10월 치고 여간 추운 날씨가 아니다 The cold today is unusual [not normal] for October. ⇒ Today it is unusually [exceptionally] cold for October.
▶그녀는 커피를 여간 좋아하는게 아닌 모양이다 She seems to be very fond of coffee.

여간내기 如干— an ordinary [a common] person
▶ 그는 여간내기가 아니다 He is no common [ordinary] man.

여간아니다 如干— uncommon; unusual; extraordinary
♦ 여간아닌 미인 a rare beauty / 여간아닌 사람 a remarkable man; a man of unusual ability / 더위가 여간아니다 be very [terribly] hot / 재주가 여간아니다 have an unusual talent; have rare ability
▶ 오늘 추위는 여간아니다 It is terribly cold today.
▶ 이 일을 마치느라고 고생이 여간아니었다 It was a hard strain for me to finish the work.

여간하다 如干— ordinary; normal; common
▶ 이건 여간한 일이 아니다 〈쉽지 않다〉 It is no easy thing to do. ⇒ 〈큰일이다〉 It is a matter of no small magnitude.
▶ 이 문제는 여간해서 풀리지 않는다 This problem is not easily solved.

여객 旅客 〈승객〉 a traveler; a passenger; 〈관광객〉 a tourist
■ —기 a passenger plane; an airliner: 초음속 여객기 a supersonic transport (略 SST) —명단 a list of passengers —선 a passenger ship [boat]; a (passenger) liner —수화물 (美) traveler's baggage; (英) traveller's luggage —안내소 a travel bureau; (英) an inquiry office —열차 a passenger train —운송 passenger transport —운임 passengers' fares —전무 a train master; a passenger guard

여건 與件 a given condition; [論] a datum (*pl.* data) ♦ 여건이 허락하면 if the circumstances permit

여걸 女傑 a heroine; a great woman; (비유) an amazon

여겨듣다 listen carefully [intently, attentively] 〈to〉; listen with all *one's* mind

여겨보다 watch carefully; see closely; have a good look 《at》

여격 與格 〔文法〕 the dative

여경 女警 a policewoman (*pl.* -women); (口) a woman cop

여계 女系 the female line; the maternal side (of a family); the mother's side of the family; the distaff side (of a house)
■ —친(親) a relative in the female line [on the mother's side]

여고 女高 a girls' high school ⇨ 여자고등학교

여공 女工 a factory girl; a woman worker; a workwoman; a female operative [mill hand]

여과 濾過 filtering; filtration; percolation
—여과하다 filter; filtrate; pass (a liquid) through a filter; percolate
♦ 커피를 여과하다 percolate coffee / 모래로 물을 여과하다 filter water through the sand / 불순물을 여과해내다 filter off impurities / 물의 더러운 것들을 모두 여과해 내다 filter out [off] all the dirt of water
■ —법(作用) filtration —성 filterability —성병원체 〔醫〕 a filterable virus —액(液) filtrate —장치 a filter —지(池) a filter bed [basin] —지(紙) ⇨ 거름종이 —층 a filter layer —통 a filter box

여과기 濾過器 a filter; a percolater; a strainer
♦ 여과기로 물을 정화하다 purify water by a filter

여관 旅館 a hotel; an inn
♦ 여관의 손님 a hotel guest; a guest (staying) at a hotel / 여관 주인 a landlord; an innkeeper; 〈여자〉 a landlady / 여관을 경영하다 run [keep, operate] a hotel / 여관에 들다 put up [register] at a hotel [an inn]; (美) check in / 여관에 묵다 stay [stop] at a hotel / 여관에서 나가다 (美) check out
▶ 어젯밤에는 시내 여관에서 묵었다 I stayed [put up] at a hotel in the city last night.
▶ 이 사람이 여관 주인입니다 This is the owner of the hotel.
■ —방 a hotel room —비 hotel charges [expenses]; a hotel bill —업 the hotel business: 아버지는 여관업을 하신다 My father owns [runs] a hotel. —업자 a hotelman

여광 餘光 1 an afterglow; remaining [lingering] light
2 ⇨ 여덕(餘德)

여광기 濾光器 〔寫·光·電〕 a light filter; a color screen

여교사 女敎師 a schoolmistress; a woman [female, lady] teacher

여군 女軍 〈병사〉 a woman soldier; 〈군대〉 Women's Army Corps

여권 女權 women's [woman's] rights; the rights of women; 〈참정권〉 woman suffrage
—신장[확장] the extension [expansion] of women's rights —(신장)론 feminism —(신장)론자 a feminist; a woman suffragist; 〈여자〉 a suffragette —신장운동[주의] feminism; women's liberation

여권 旅券 a passport
♦ 여권을 교부하다 issue a passport 〈to〉; furnish *sb* with a passport / 여권을 발급받다 have a passport issued; get a passport / 여권을 사증에 받다 have [get] *one's* passport visaed / 여권을 신청하다 apply for a passport
■ 관용— an official passport 외교관— a diplomat's passport ■ —사증 a passport visa

여급 女給 〈접대부〉 a waitress; a waiting maid; 〈바의〉 a barmaid; a hostess

여기 here; this place [point]
♦ 여기 사람들 the people here / 여기쯤 hereabouts; about [around] here; in this neighborhood
▶ 여기는 인천보다 따뜻하다 It's warmer here [in this place] than in Inch'ŏn.
▶ 〔會話〕 「여기는 어딥니까?」「동대문입니다」 "Where are we [am I] now?" "We are [You are] at Tongdaemun."
▶ 여기가 우리 집이야 This is my house.
▶ 여기가 중요한 대목이니까 잘 들어라 This is the important point. Listen attentively!
▶ 네 시계는 여기 있다 Your watch is here.
▶ 〔會話〕 「연필이 어디 있더라?」「여기 있어」 "Where is the pencil?" "Here it is." ⇌ "Right here." ⇌ "Here you are."
▶ 그는 조금 아까 여기 있었다 He was (right) here a moment ago.

▶ 아니, 여기 있네. 별데를 다 찾아다녔잖아 Oh, here you are. I've been looking everywhere for you.
▶ 나는 여기서 태어나 여기서 자랐다 I was born and brought up here.
▶ 여기서 역까지는 걸어서 5분 걸린다 It is a five-minute walk from here to the railroad station.
▶ 여기에 오신 지 몇 해나 되셨습니까? How long have you been here?
▶ 여기서는 담배를 삼가 주십시오 Please refrain from smoking in here.
▶ 어제 여기서 그를 만났다 I saw him here [at this place] yesterday.
▶ 여기서 나갑시다 Let's get out of here [this place].
▶ 여기까지는 잘 해왔다 We have done well so far.
▶ 오늘은 여기까지 합시다 〈교실에서〉 So much for today. ⇌ We shall [Let us] leave off here.

여기 餘技 a hobby; an avocation
♦여기로 그림을 그리다 paint as a hobby; take up painting as a hobby

여기다 think; consider (as); deem; regard (as); treat (as); hold; wonder (if, whether)
♦귀엽게 여기다 hold sb dear / 대수롭지 않게 여기다 think little [nothing] of; have a low opinion of / 좋게 여기다 think well of sb / 바보로 여기다 consider sb (to be) a fool; look upon sb as a fool / 불쌍하게 여기다 feel pity (for); have a pity (on) / 돈을 하찮게 여기다 treat money cheap
▶ 저 사람은 우리가 베푸는 친절을 고맙게 여기지 않는다 That man doesn't feel grateful for the kindness we show him.
▶ 그녀는 그의 위협을 농담으로 여겼다 She treated his threat as a joke.
▶ 그가 실패했다고 이상하게 여길 것은 없다 What wonder if he failed?

여기자 女記者 a woman [lady, female] reporter; a newspaperwoman; a newswoman; (美) a newshen

여기저기 here and there; from place to place; in (several [various]) places; 〈산재하여〉 sporadically; 〈모든 곳〉 everywhere
♦여기저기 여행하다 travel from place to place / 여기저기 벗어져 있다 be off in places / 여기저기를 보다 look this way or that (way) / 여기저기를 찾다 look for sth here and there; search everywhere / 여기저기서 모이다 come from all over the place
▶ 우리는 한 시간쯤 여기저기 걸어다녔다 We walked up and down for about an hour.
▶ 나라의 여기저기에 국립공원이 있다 There are national parks scattered throughout the country.
▶ 공원 여기저기에 아름다운 꽃이 피어 있다 Beautiful flowers are in bloom here and there in the park.
▶ 사람들이 여기저기서 모여들었다 The people flocked from far and near.
▶ 산비탈에는 아직도 여기저기 눈이 남아 있다 On the slopes of the mountain snow still remains here and there.
▶ 그녀에 관한 일은 여기저기서 듣고 있다 I hear things now and again about her.
▶ 잉크가 여기저기로 튀었다 The ink splashed in all directions.

여난 女難 trouble with women ▶ 그는 여난을 겪을 상이다 He seems to be destined to have trouble with women.

여남은 some ten odd; more than [somewhat over] ten ♦여남은 사람 a dozen men; a little over ten men / 연필 여남은 자루 a dozen pencils / 여남은 해 ten-odd years

여념 餘念 distraction; divided attention
♦여념이 없다 be intent (on); be absorbed (in); give undivided attention (to); be devoted (to) / 노는 데 여념이 없다 be absorbed [deep] in play
▶ 그는 연구에 여념이 없다 He studies with his whole heart. ⇌ He devotes himself to his studies.
▶ 그는 일에 여념이 없었다 He was intent on his job.

여느 〈보통의〉 ordinary; usual; common; 〈그 밖의 다른〉 other
♦여느 날 a usual day / 여느 때 ordinary times / 여느 사람 an ordinary man; an average mortal; (총칭) the common run of people / 여느 때의 〈평소의〉 usual; ordinary; 〈매일의〉 everyday; 〈습관적〉 habitual / 여느 때처럼 as usual; in one's usual way / 여느 때보다 일찍 earlier than usual / 여느 때와는 달리 unusually; contrary to one's habit / 여느 때와 다름없이 in an ordinary way
▶ 그에게는 어딘가 여느 사람과는 다른 데가 있다 There is something extraordinary about him.
▶ 나는 여느 때보다 일찍 교회에 도착했다 I arrived at the church earlier than usual.
▶ 그는 여느 때와는 달리 그날 밤은 퍽 늦게 돌아왔다 That night he came home much later than usual.

여단 旅團 〔軍〕 a brigade ♦여단으로 편성하다 form into a brigade; brigade
■ 보병─ an infantry brigade 혼성─ a mixed [composite] brigade ■ ─장 a brigade commander; a brigadier

여닫다 open and shut [close] ♦문을 여닫다 open and close [shut] the door

여닫이 1 〈열고 닫음〉 opening and shutting [closing] ▶ 그 문은 여닫이가 좋지 않다 The door doesn't work well [fits badly].
2 〈미닫이〉 a sliding door; a hinged door; 〈내리닫이〉 a sash window

여담 餘談 a digression; a by-talk
♦여담이지만 if you'll allow a slight digression; by the way; Incidentally [In passing] I may say that...; Let me say in passing that... / 여담은 그만하고 to return to the (main) subject; to cut short the digression / 여담으로 흐르다 digress from the subject things; go aside from the main issue; make a digression
▶ 그의 얘기는 여담이 많았다 There were a lot of digressions in his speech.
▶ 여담은 이 정도로 해두자 So much for the

여당 興黨 the Administration party; the party in office [power]; the government [ruling, ministerial] party ◆여당(측)의 ministerial ■ 준(準)— a quasi-government party —의 원 a member of the government party

여대 女大 a women's college [university] ■ —생 a college woman; a student at a women's college; 〈남녀공학의〉(美口) a co-ed

여덕 餘德 the influence of great virtues ◆조상의 여덕 the influence of one's ancestors

여덟 eight ◆여덟번 eight times / 여덟번째 the eighth

여덟팔자걸음 —八字— a splayfooted walk

여독 旅毒 sickness from the fatigue of travel ◆여독을 풀다 banish the fatigue of travel; take a rest after the fatigue of one's journey

여독 餘毒 the remaining effect of poison; the aftereffect of a sickness

여드레 〈8일〉 eight days; 〈초여드레〉 the eighth day (of a month) ◆8월 여드렛날 August 8(th); the eighth of August

여드름 a pimple; an acne; a comedo (pl. ~s, ~nes); 〈표면이 검은〉 a blackhead ◆여드름 자국 an acne spot [pit] / 여드름이 난 얼굴 a pimpled [pimply] face; (英口) a spotty face / 얼굴에 여드름이 난 소녀 a pimple-faced girl / 여드름이 나다 pimples break [come] out (on [in] one's face) / 여드름을 짜다 squeeze a blackhead / 얼굴에 여드름 투성이다 have pimples [acne] all over one's face

여든 eighty ◆여든살 노인 an old man [woman] of eighty; an eighty-year-old man [woman] / 여든번째 the eightieth / 여든이 넘다 be over eighty

여러 several; many; various; diverse ◆여러 번 several times; many times / 여러 날 동안 for (many) days; for many a day; for a number of days / 여러 달 several [many] months / 여러 사람 several [many] people / 세계 여러 곳에서 in various parts of the world / 그 문제를 여러 각도에서 살피다 investigate the matter from different angles
▶나는 여러 번 시도해 보았지만 성공하지 못했다 I tried again and again, but couldn't succeed.

여러가지 a (great) variety (of); different kinds [sorts]; all sorts (of); various kinds (of) ◆여러가지 의견 diverse views; various opinions / 여러가지의 various (kinds of); many; different; varied; diverse; of different kinds [sorts] / 여러 가지 이유로 for various reasons / 여러가지로 variously; in many [various, different] ways / 여러가지로 애쓰다 try to do in various ways [in every way]; try every means (possible)
▶그는 여러가지 책을 읽고 있다 He reads several [many] different (kinds of) books.
▶그들에게는 여러가지 동기가 있었다 They had various [a variety of] motives.
▶여러가지 차가 홀에 전시되어 있다 A variety of cars are displayed in the hall.
▶여러가지를 고려하여 사직하기로 결심했습니다 Taking various considerations into account [Taking everything into consideration], I decided to resign.
▶여러가지로 실험해 보았으나 실패했다 I experimented in many ways, but my efforts did not bear fruit.
▶그는 그녀를 여러가지로 환대했다 He entertained her in various ways.
▶여러가지로 고마웠습니다 Thank you very much for everything.

여러모로 in various [many] ways; in more ways than one; one way or another
▶그것은 여러모로 쓸모가 있다 It is useful for one thing or another.

여러분 all of you; everybody; ladies and gentlemen ◆신사 숙녀 여러분 Ladies and gentlemen! / 여러분, 안녕하십니까 Good morning, everybody.

여러해살이 〔植〕 perennation ■ —식물 a perennial (plant)

여럿 〈많은 수〉 a large number; 〈많은 사람〉 many; many people

여력 餘力 remaining power [strength]; surplus strength [energy]; 〈여유〉 a reserve (of energy); 〈돈의〉 money to spare
▶그에게는 아직 더 뛸 여력이 남아 있었다 He still had the energy left to keep on running.
▶그는 시험에 대비하여 여력을 축적하고 있다 He has saved his energy for the examination.
▶그에게는 만원을 기부할 여력이 없었다 He didn't have enough money to make a contribution of 10,000 won.

여로 旅路 a journey ◆먼 여로 a long journey / 여로의 끝 (at) one's journey's end / 여로에 오르다 start on a journey
▶그럼, 즐거운 여로가 되시길 (빕니다) A pleasant journey to you! ⇒ I wish you a good [happy] journey.

여론 輿論 public opinion; the popular voice; public [general] sentiment ◆세계의 여론 world opinion / 여론의 동향 the trend of public opinion / 여론을 무시하다 defy public opinion / 여론을 조작하다 manipulate public opinion / 여론을 불러일으키다 arouse [stir up] public opinion / 여론에 귀를 기울이다 pay careful attention to public opinion / 여론에 호소하다 appeal to public opinion / 여론에 따르다 obey the dictates of public opinion; act in accordance with public opinion
▶여론은 그 계획을 강력하게 지지했다 Public opinion was strongly in favor of the project.
▶증세에 반대하는 여론이 비등하고 있다 The public is clamoring against the tax increase.
▶그것에 관해 여론이 나뉘고 있다 Public opinion is divided on it. ⇒ There is a polarity of public opinion on it.
▶그 기사는 그 문제에 관한 여론의 일치를 나타내고 있었다 The article expressed the consensus of public opinion about the problem.
▶그의 발언은 여론을 자극했다 His remarks gave an impetus to public sentiment.
▶위정자는 여론에 귀를 기울여야 한다 Statesmen should give careful attention to the trends of public opinion [(美) keep their ears

여론 international opinion ■—비판 the forum [tribunal] of public opinion —연구소 an institute of public opinion

여론조사 輿論調査 a survey of public opinion; a public-opinion census [poll]; 〈지상(紙上)의〉 a straw poll
♦여론조사를 하다 take a public-opinion poll; conduct a poll
■—원 a polltaker; a pollster

여류 女流 the fair sex; womankind
■—문학가 a lady of letters; a literary woman —비행사 a woman [lady] aviator; an aviatrix 《*pl.* ~es, -trices》 —시인 a poetess —작가 a woman [lady] writer [novelist] —화가 a woman [lady] painter

여름 summer; summertime
♦여름 용품 summer goods; articles for summer use / 올 여름 this summer / 무더운 여름 a hot summer / 여름용의 suitable for summer; for summer use [wear] / 여름에는 in (the) summer / 초여름에 early in summer; in (the) early summer / 한여름에 in the height [middle] of (the) summer; in midsummer / 여름을 나다 pass [spend] the summer《at a place》/ 여름을 타다 suffer from the summer heat; lose weight in summer
▶여름에 이 곳은 무척 덥다 It is very hot here in (the) summer [summertime].
▶우리는 프랑스 남부에서 여름을 났다 We summered in the south of France.
■—감기 a summer cold —날 a summer day —모자 a summer hat —옷 summer wear [clothes]; a summer suit —철 summertime; the summer season —학교 a summer school

여름방학 —放學 the summer vacation [《英》holiday(s)]
♦여름방학 숙제 *one's* homework for (the) summer vacation / 두달 동안의 여름방학 a two-month vacation for the summer
▶우리 학교는 내일부터 여름방학에 들어갑니다 Our school begins its summer vacation tomorrow.
▶여름방학은 어떻게 지낼 거니? How are you going to spend your summer vacation?
▶나는 올 여름방학에 홍도에 갈 예정이다 I am going to make a trip to Hongdo during this coming summer vacation.
■—책 a summer exercise book; 《美》a workbook for the summer vacation

여리꾼 a shill 《for a shop》; a tout; a barker; a decoy

여리다 1 〈연하다〉 soft; tender; delicate; 〈약하다〉 weak; fragile ♦여린 피부 a tender skin / 감정이 여리다 be tender-hearted; be easily moved
2 〈모자라다〉 short; insufficient; lacking; 〈서술적〉 be not enough

여망 餘望 the remaining hope

여망 輿望 〈신망〉 popularity; reputation; 〈신뢰〉 credit; trust
♦국민의 여망 the trust [confidence] of the whole nation

여명 黎明 dawn; daybreak
♦여명기의 문학 literature at the dawn of a new age / 여명부터 일몰까지 from dawn till dark
▶우리는 7월 3일 여명에 산정에 도착했다 We reached the summit at (the break of) dawn on July 3.
▶우리는 지금 우주시대의 여명기에 있는 것이다 We now stand at the dawning of the space age.

여명 餘命 *one's* remaining days; the remainder [rest, remnant] of *one's* life
▶그는 여명이 얼마 남지 않았다 He is not long for this world. ⇌ He has but a few years [days] to live. ⇌ His days are numbered.

여물¹ 〈마소의 먹이〉 chaff; fodder; forage; feed
♦소에게 여물을 주다 feed a cow with fodder; give a cow fodder
■—죽 boiled cattle feed

여물² 〈우물물〉 brackish well water

여물다 1 〈익다〉 grow [get, become] ripe; ripen; mature
▶벼가 여물다 rice corns
2 〈살림이 헤프지 않다〉 firm; tight; steady
▶그녀는 여문 주부다 She manages her household frugally. ⇌ She is of an economical turn of mind.

여미다 adjust; arrange; fix ♦옷깃을 여미다 adjust *one's* dress; adjust [straighten] *oneself*

여반장 如反掌 〈쉬운〉 being very easy; 《口》a piece of cake
▶그것쯤은 여반장이다 That's nothing. ⇌ That's as simple as turning one's hand. ⇌《口》 That's 《as》 easy as pie.

여배우 女俳優 an actress ♦최우수 여배우상 the Best Actress award
■—주연 the principal actress ■—지망자 a would-be [prospective] actress

여백 餘白 〈공백〉a space; a blank; 〈난외의〉a margin ♦여백을 메우다[채우다] fill in [up] the blank / 여백을 남기다 leave a space
▶그는 책의 여백에 써 넣었다 He wrote down in the margin of the book.
▶이 페이지의 여백을 채울 만한 것이 필요하다 Something is needed to fill up the space in this page.

여 벌 餘— remainings; remnants; surplus; spare ♦여벌 바지 spare trousers [pants]; an extra pair of trousers [pants] / 여벌의 spare; reserved

여병 餘病 a complication; a secondary disease ⇨ 합병증

여보 1 〈남에게〉 ⇨ 여보세요 2 〈부부 사이에〉 (my) darling; (my) dear; (my) honey; sweetheart

여보게 Hey!; Hi!; Hey there!; Look here!
▶여보게, 창수 Hi [Hey], Chang-su!

여보세요 Excuse me!; Hello!; Hey!; I say!; Look here!; Please!; 《美》 Say!
▶여보세요, 누구십니까? 〔電話〕 Hello, who is speaking?
▶여보세요, 지금 몇시지요? Excuse me, but could you tell me the time?

여복 女服 a (female) dress; a lady's costume; women's clothing

여봐란듯이 for show; out of display; to show off; demonstratively; ostentatiously; showily
▶ 그녀는 여봐란듯이 다이아몬드 반지를 낀 왼손을 흔들었다 She waved her left hand about to show off her diamond ring.

여부 與否 yes or no; whether or not; if
▶ 사실 여부를 모르겠다 I don't know whether it is true or not.
▶ 우리의 성공 여부는 여러분의 노력에 달려 있습니다 Our success depends on your efforts.
▶ 우리는 그 제안의 수락 여부를 논의했다 We discussed whether or not we should accept the offer.

여부없다 與否— sure; certain; unquestionable; beyond call; no question; out of question
▶ 회화 「그가 네 계획에 찬성할까?」「여부없지」 "Will he agree to your plan?" "No doubt about it!"

여북 how (much); very much; greatly
▶ 여북 창피할까 I imagine how shamed he is. ⇌ His shame must be beyond imagination.
▶ 여북 슬펐을까 How sad she must have been!
▶ 그가 이 소식을 들으면 여북 마음이 놓일까 How relieved he must be to hear the news!

여분 餘分 an extra; an excess; a surplus
♦여분의 extra; spare; too much / 여분의 표가 한 장 있다 have one extra ticket
▶ 내게는 여분의 시간이 없다 I have no time to spare [no spare time].
▶ 여분의 돈은 가져오지 마십시오 Please don't bring too much money.

여비 旅費 traveling expenses
▶ 부산까지의 여비는 왕복 얼마입니까? How much does it cost to go to Pusan and back?
▶ 여비는 각자 부담입니다 You must pay your own traveling expenses.
▶ 여비는 회사에 청구할 수 있다 Traveling expenses are chargeable to the company.
▶ 싸구려 여인숙에서 숙박해서 여비를 절약했다 I saved the traveling expenses by staying at a cheap inn.

여사 女史 Mrs.; Miss; Madame
♦S 여사 Miss [Mrs.] S; Madame S

여사감 女舍監 a housemother; a matron

여사무원 女事務員 an office woman [lady]; a female clerk

여색 女色 〈미색〉 a woman's beauty [charms]; feminine charms; 〈미인〉 a beautiful woman; 〈색욕〉 lust; sensuality; carnal pleasure [desire]
♦여색을 멀리하다 eschew women; keep away from women / 여색을 좋아하다 be licentious; be a womanizer / 여색에 홀리다 be fascinated by a woman; fall into a woman's charms / 여색에 빠지다 be infatuated with women; be engrossed in fleshly love

여생 餘生 the rest [remainder] of one's life [days]; one's remaining years
♦여생을 교육에 바치다 devote the rest of one's life to education / 여생을 편안히 보내다 spend one's remaining years in comfort
▶ 그는 고향에서 여생을 보냈다 He spent his remaining years in his native place. ⇌ He lived in his hometown for the rest of his life.

여섯 six ♦여섯째 the sixth

여성 女性 1 〈여자다움〉 womanhood; femininity; 〈여자〉 a woman (pl. women); a female; (총칭) womankind; the female sex
♦여성의 권리 women's rights / 여성다운 상냥함 womanly [feminine] tenderness / 여성적인 남자 a womanish [an effeminate] fellow; (美口·英俗) a sissy / 여성의 female
▶ 회화 「저 사람은 여성입니까, 남성입니까?」 「여성입니다」 "Is that person male or female [a man or a woman]?" "It's a woman."
▶ 그는 여성적인 남자다 He is a womanish [an effeminate] man.
▶ 이 디자인은 여성 취향인 편이지요 This design rather suits the taste of ladies.
2 〔文法〕 the feminine gender
■—관 one's view of womanhood —란 the women's [ladies'] section [column] —명사[어미] a feminine noun [ending] —문제 a women's problem —미 womanly [female, feminine] beauty —상위사회 a female-dominated society —어 female language —지 a women's magazine —해방운동 women's liberation (movement); (口) women's lib —호르몬 the female hormone —화 feminization: 여성화하다 feminize

여성 女聲 a woman's [female] voice
—합창 a female [women's] chorus

여세 餘勢 surplus power [energy]; reserve energy; momentum (pl. ~s, -ta); impetus
▶ 우리는 여세를 몰아 적을 맹공했다 Following up the victory, we made another attack on the enemy. ⇌ Encouraged by the success, we delivered a further attack against the enemy.
▶ 그는 대성공의 여세를 몰아 다른 사업을 시작했다 Encouraged by his great success, he started on another enterprise.

여송연 呂宋煙 a cigar ⇨ 엽궐련

여수 女囚 a female prisoner

여수 旅愁 loneliness on a journey; a traveler's melancholy; sadness felt while on a journey
♦여수를 달래다 relieve one's loneliness [lighten one's melancholy] on one's journey / 여수를 느끼다 feel lonely on one's journey

여승 女僧 a Buddhist nun [priestess]

여식 女息 a [one's] daughter

여신 女神 a goddess; a female deity
♦자유의 여신 the Goddess of Liberty
▶ 마침내 운명의 여신이 그에게 미소를 지었다 Destiny finally smiled (up)on him.

여신 與信 loan; credit
■—업무 a loan business —한도(액) a line of credit

여신 餘燼 〈타고 남은 불기운〉 embers; cinders

여실 如實 reality; vividness
—여실하다 real; realistic; vivid
♦여실히 vividly; realistically; exactly; true to life; as they are; as it is / 사건을 여실히 묘사하다 describe an event just as it happened
▶ 한장의 사진이 그 피해의 막심함을 여실히 보여주고 있다 One picture gives a vivid [graphic] account of the heavy damage.

여심 女心 a woman's heart
여아 女兒 〈여자아이〉 a little [baby] girl; a female child; 〈딸〉 a daughter
여야 與野 the Government [Ruling] party and the Opposition party; the ins and the outs; the in party and the out party
여열 餘熱 remaining heat ◆엔진의 여열 the residual heat in the engine
여염집 閭閻— an ordinary home; a respectable home [family] ■—여자 an honest [a respectable] woman
여왕 女王 1 a queen; 〈군주〉 a queen regnant ◆영국 여왕 빅토리아 Victoria, Queen of England / 여왕 엘리자베스 2세 Queen Elizabeth Ⅱ / 여왕같은 queenly; queenlike
▶여왕 폐하가 그 식에 참석하신다 Her Majesty the Queen will be present at the ceremony.
2 (비유) a belle; a queen; a mistress ◆사교계의 여왕 a queen [mistress] of society; a society queen
▶그녀는 무도회의 여왕이었다 She was the belle of the ball.
■—개미 a queen ant —국 a queendom —벌 a queen bee
여우 a fox; 〈암컷〉 (俗) a vixen
◆여우같이 교활한 늙은이 an old fox [bird]; a foxy fellow; a sly [cunning] man / 여우같은 foxy; vulpine / 여우에 홀리다 be bewitched by a fox
▶여우가 울고 있다 A fox is barking [yelping].
▶그는 여우에 홀린 것 같은 얼굴이었다 He had a puzzled expression on his face.
■—가죽 a fox fur; a fox skin —굴 a fox burrow —꼬리 a foxtail; a fox brush —목도리 a fox-fur muffler —비 a shower in the sunshine; a sun shower —사냥 fox hunting —새끼 a cub
여우 女優 an actress ⇨ 여배우
여우별 a short [brief] spell of sunshine on a rainy day; intermittent sunshine
◆여우볕이 나다 the sun comes out for a while on a rainy day
여우원숭이 〔動〕 a lemur
여우자리 〔天〕 Vulpecula
여운 餘韻 〈악기 등의〉 a lingering [trailing] tone; resonance; 〈종 등의〉 reverberations; echoes; 〈영향〉 an aftertaste; an aftereffect; 〈글 등의〉 suggestiveness
◆여운이 있는 reverberative; suggestive / 여운이 많은 full of suggestion
▶우리는 그 시의 여운을 감상했다 We appreciated the lingering imagery [subtle overtones] of the poem.
여울 shallows; rapids; a shoal; a ford ◆여울을 건너다 cross a ford; ford a rapid; wade across a ford
■—목 the neck of rapids
여위다 lose weight [flesh]; become [get] thin [lean]; grow gaunt; pine away
◆여윈 말 a thin [lean] horse / 몹시 여윈 사람 a living skeleton; a bag of bones / 여윈 얼굴 a thin [haggard, meager] face / 여위어 피골이

상접하다 be reduced to a mere skeleton [skin and bones]; be worn to a shadow
▶그녀는 앓고 나서 많이 여위었다 She has lost a lot of weight since her illness. ⇌ She got a lot thinner after her illness.
여유 餘裕 1 〈여지〉 room; 〈시간적〉 time (to spare); 〈잉여〉 a surplus; a margin

解說 빡빡하지 않고 남음이 있는 것을 「여유」라고 하며 공간 뿐만 아니라 시간이나 기분에 대해서도 쓰는데 이에 해당하는 한 단어로 된 영어는 없다. 따라서 공간적인 것은 *room* 등으로, 시간적인 것은 *time* 등으로 나타낸다.

◆여유가 없는 스케줄 a tight schedule
▶차 안은 한 사람분의 여유가 더 있다 We have enough room for one more in the car.
▶나는 돈에 여유가 없다 I have no money to spare. ⇌ I am pressed for money.
▶생각할 시간적 여유를 주세요 Give me time to think.
▶그들은 여유있는 생활을 하고 있다 They live in comfort [comfortably]. ⇌ They are well-off.
▶버스가 출발하기까지는 20분의 여유가 있다 We have twenty minutes left before the bus leaves.
2 〈침착성〉 composure; calmness
◆여유가 있는 태도 an easy and graceful attitude / 여유를 잃다 lose composure; lose *one's* presence of mind / 여유만만하다 calm and confident; easy and relaxed
▶그녀는 마음의 여유가 없어서 안절부절 못했다 She was irritated from lack of confidence.
여유작작하다 餘裕綽綽— calm and composed
▶그는 아주 차분한 것이 시험 전날에도 여유작작해 보였다 He was very calm and looked as if he had plenty of confidence even on the day before his examination.
여의다 1 〈사별하다〉 have *sb* die; lose; be bereaved [deprived] of ◆남편을 여의다 lose *one's* husband; be widowed / 자식을 여의다 survive [lose] *one's* child
▶나는 어려서 아버지를 여의었다 I lost my father when I was a child.
2 〈멀리 보내다〉 send *sb* far away
3 〈시집보내다〉 marry off *one's* daughter 《to *sb*》
여의사 女醫師 a woman [female] doctor
여의주 如意珠 a magic stone that bestows omnipotence on *sb* who acquires it
여의찮다 如意— 〈서술적〉 go contrary to *one's* wishes; go wrong [amiss]
▶만사가 여의찮다 Nothing goes as I wish. ⇌ Everything goes wrong with me.
여인 女人 a woman 《*pl.* women》
▶여인 금제(禁制) (게시) Off limits [No admittance] to women.
■—천하 petticoat government
여인숙 旅人宿 an inn; a lodging house ◆싸구려 여인숙 a cheap inn; (美俗) a flophouse; (英俗) a doss house / 여인숙에 들다 stay up [put up] at an inn
여일 如一 〈한결같음〉 constancy; consistency

—여일하다 constant; consistent; unvarying; 〈서술적〉 be just the same; be unchanged
♦시종여일하게 constantly; consistently; without any change; invariably from first [beginning] to last [end]
▶그의 행동은 시종여일했다 He was consistent in his actions.

여자 女子 a woman, a female; a lady; a girl; (총칭) the fair [female, gentle] sex; womankind; 〈정부〉 a mistress
♦여자용 시계 a ladies' watch; a watch for ladies [women] / 여자 같은 사내 a womanish [an effeminate] fellow; (美口·英俗) a sissy / 여자다운 여자 a womanly woman / 여자만의 모임 (口) a hen party / 여자용의 ladies'; women's; for ladies' use / 여자 꽁무니를 따라다니다 dangle after [hang about] a girl; run after a woman
▶대개 여자 목소리는 남자보다 높다 The female voice is generally higher than the male voice.
▶그녀는 여자다운 데가 없다 There is little of the woman in her.
〈여자가[는]〉 대개 여자가 남자보다 수명이 길다 Women live generally longer than men.
▶그는 여자가 있는 것 같다 It looks as if he's got a woman [he is having an affair with a woman].
〈여자를〉 여자를 농락하다 make a toy [plaything] of a woman / 여자를 싫어하다 have an aversion for women; be a woman hater
▶저 회사에서는 아직도 여자를 차별한다 That company still discriminates against women.
▶그는 아직 여자를 모른다 He still hasn't had a woman. ⇌ He's still a virgin.
▶그는 여자를 잘 다룬다 He has a way with women.
〈여자에게〉 당신은 여자들에게 약하군요 You are too nice to women.
■—감독 〈노동자의〉 a forewoman; 〈영화의〉 a female director —교육 the education of girls [women]; female education —기숙사 a women's [girls'] dormitory —역 a female role [part] —차장 a conductress; a female [woman] conductor —친구 a girl friend; a woman friend (pl. women friends)

여자고등학교 女子高等學校 a girls' (senior) high school; a girls' upper secondary school
■—학생 a high-school girl

여자중학교 女子中學校 a girls' junior high school; a girls' middle school
■—학생 a middle-school girl

여장 女裝 dressing in female attire; disguising as a woman
—여장하다 dress up like a woman; disguise oneself as a woman; put on a female dress
♦여장한 남자 a man in a woman's dress
▶그 살인범은 여장하고 도망쳤다 The murderer made his escape disguised as a woman.

여장 旅裝 a traveling outfit [kit] ♦여장을 꾸리다 make preparations [prepare] for a journey [trip] / 여장을 풀다 take a rest after a journey
▶그들은 여장을 꾸려 출발했다 They prepared [equipped] themselves for a journey and started.
▶여장을 풀고 나니 안심이 되었다 It was a relief to rest after our journey.

여장부 女丈夫 a brave [great] woman; (비유) an amazon

여재 餘財 one's remaining fortune

여전하다 如前— 〈서술적〉 remain unchanged; be as before [ever]; be as usual; be just as it was
♦여전히 as ever; as (it was) before; as always; as (it) used to be; as usual; still / 여전히 게으르다[가난하다] be as idle [poor] as ever / 여전히 행방불명이다 be still missing
▶ 會話「상수는 어땠어?」「여전했어」 "How was Sang-su looking?" "Just the same as he always was."
▶ 會話「장사는 어때?」「여전해」 "How's your business going?" "Only, so-so."
▶그 노인은 기력이 아직도 여전하다 The old man is still going strong as usual.
▶파도는 여전히 높다 The waves are as high as ever.
▶그들은 그 계획에 여전히 반대다 They are still against the plan.
▶그녀는 여전히 젊어 보인다 She looks as young as ever [before]. ⇌ She still looks young.
▶어머니는 휴일인데도 여전히 바쁘시다 Even though it's a holiday, my mother is (as) busy as usual.

여점원 女店員 a saleswoman; a salesgirl; a shopgirl; (美) a female sales-clerk

여접 餘接 (數) a cotangent ⇨ 코탄젠트

여정 旅情 traveler's sentiment
▶그 아름다운 경치는 나그네의 여정을 자아내기에 부족함이 없었다 The beautiful scene appealed to the travelers' sentiments.

여정 旅程 〈거리〉 the distance to be covered; 〈일정〉 the plan [schedule] of a journey [trip]; an itinerary
▶그들은 하루 30킬로미터의 여정을 갔다 They covered (a distance of) 30 kilometers a day.
▶그들은 상세한 여정을 짰다 They made up the exact plan of their journey.

여제 女帝 an empress; a queen

여존남비 女尊男卑 putting [placing] women above men; respect for woman at the expense of man

여종 女— a female slave [servant]

여죄 餘罪 〈그 죄 외의 다른 죄〉 other [further] crimes [offenses]
♦여죄를 심문하다 question about other crimes

여주 〔植〕 a balsam pear

여주인공 女主人公 a heroine

여중 女中 a girls' middle school ⇨ 여자중학교

여지 荔枝 〔植〕 a litchi; a lichee

여지 餘地 room; a margin; a place; a space; 〈여백〉 a blank
♦개량[발전]의 여지 room for improvement [development] / 타협의 여지가 있다[없다] admit of compromise [no compromise]; leave room [no room] for compromise / 여지없이

패하다 meet with complete defeat; suffer a crushing defeat
▶ 그의 성공은 의문의 여지가 없다 There is no doubt about his success. ⇒ He will no doubt succeed.
▶ 회장은 만원으로 입추의 여지도 없었다 The hall was so full that there was no standing room [no room for anyone to step in].

여진 餘震 an aftershock; an after tremor [earthquake] ▶ 합계 여덟의 여진이 있었다 There were eight aftershocks altogether.

여질 女姪 〈조카 딸〉 a niece

여짓거리다, 여짓대다 keep hesitating to speak; falter in *one's* speech

여쭈다 1 〈아뢰다〉 tell; inform; say ♦ 인사를 여쭈다 greet (a superior) 2 〈문의하다〉 ask; inquire ▶ 좀 여쭈어 봐도 될까요? May I ask you a question?

여차여차하다 如此如此— such and such
♦ 여차여차한 사람 such and such a man / 여차여차한 사정[까닭]으로 for such and such reasons; such being the case; in [under] these circumstances / 여차여차한 경우에 on such occasions
▶ 사정이 여차여차하다고 그는 내게 설명했다 He explained the circumstances to me.

여차하다 如此— such; like this; of this kind; of the sort [kind] ♦ 여차한 사람 such a man; a person like this ♦ 이유는 여차하다 The reason is such and such.

여차하면 in case [time] of need [emergency]; in an emergency; if need be
▶ 여차하면 내가 도맡겠소 I'll take it when I have to [if (it is) necessary].
▶ 여차하면 사직할 테다 If it comes to the crunch, I'm ready to quit my job.

여체 女體 a woman's body; the body of (a) woman

여축 餘蓄 〈모아둠〉 savings; (a) stock; storage; reserve; supplies
♦ 다소 여축이 있다 have some savings; have some money saved
▶ 나는 한푼의 여축도 없다 I have no savings [no money saved].
▶ 식량의 여축이 줄어들고 있다 Our stock of food is running short.

여치 〔昆〕 a (long-horned) grasshopper; (美) a katydid

여탕 女湯 the women's section of a public bath (house)

여태 till now ⇨ 여태까지

여태까지 till [until, up to] now [the present]; so [thus] far; by [by, all] this time; yet; still
♦ 여태까지 없었던 사건 an unprecedented event / 여태까지 알려져 있지 않은 사실 a fact hitherto unknown
▶ 그는 여태까지 오지 않고 있다 He has not come yet. ⇒ He hasn't showed up yet.
▶ 그 집은 여태까지 비어 있다 The house is still vacant [is vacant even now].
▶ 여태까지 이렇게 재미있는 책을 읽어 본 적이 없다 I have never read such an interesting book as this. ⇒ This is the most interesting book I have ever read.

▶ 그는 여태까지 고용주에 대해 원망을 품고 있다 He still bears a grudge against his employer.

여파 餘波 〈풍파 뒤의〉 a trail; 〈영향〉 an aftereffect (▶보통 복수로 씀); an aftermath; a consequence
♦ 석유파동의 여파 the aftereffects of oil shock / 전쟁의 여파 the aftermath of the war / …의 여파를 받다 be affected by (the sequel of)
▶ 미국의 경기 후퇴의 여파가 우리나라에도 미치기 시작했다 The effects of the recession in America began to be felt in our country.

여편네 1 〈기혼녀〉 a married woman 2 〈아내〉 *one's* wife

여폐 餘弊 the surviving evil [vice, abuses]
♦ 봉건시대의 여폐 a holdover from the feudal age

여필종부 女必從夫 wives should be submissive
▶ 여필종부가 가정의 행복의 최고 덕목이라는 말은 커다란 시대착오다 The saying that the best way to maintain domestic happiness is for the wife to follow the husband's lead [to be obedient to the husband] is a pure anachronism.

여하 如何 how; what
♦ 여하한 how; what
▶ 성공은 너의 노력 여하에 달려 있다 Success depends [rests] on your efforts. ⇒ Whether you succeed or not depends on your efforts.
▶ 그것은 너의 결정 여하에 달려 있다 The decision rests with you. ⇒ It is up to [rests with] you to decide.

여하간 如何間 ♦ 여하간(에) 〈여하튼〉 anyway; anyhow; in any case [event]; at any rate; 〈별도로 치고〉 apart from; to say nothing of; 〈우선〉 above all things
▶ 여하간 계획을 추진하자 Anyway [At any rate], let's go ahead with our plans.
▶ 여하간 나는 끝까지 버틸 것이오 Anyhow, I am going to stick it (out).

여하튼 如何— anyway ⇨ 여하간

여학교 女學校 a girls' (high) school

여학생 女學生 a schoolgirl; a girl [female] student; (口) 〈대학의〉 a co(-)ed

여한 餘恨 a smoldering [lingering] regret; ill will; enmity
▶ 이제 나는 죽어도 여한이 없다 Now I can die happy [without regrets].

여한 餘寒 the lingering cold (of early spring); the cold of late winter
▶ 초봄에는 아직 여한이 심하다 The lingering cold is still severe in early spring.

여행 旅行 travel; 〈짧은〉 a trip; 〈역방(歷訪)〉 a tour; 〈긴 여행〉 a journey; 〈유람〉 an excursion; 〈바다의〉 a voyage

> [解說] 가장 일반적인 말은 ***travel***이지만 이 말은 명사보다는 동사로 사용되는 경우가 많다. ***trip***은 주로 단기간의 여행, ***tour***는 주유하는 여행을 가리킨다. 또 ***journey***는 볼일·유람에 관계없이 보통 육상의 오랜 여행을 말하며 인생을 여행에 비유할 때에도 이 말을 쓴다.

여행의 계절 a tourist season / **긴[짧은] 여행** a long [short] trip [journey] / **하루의 여행** a day's journey; a day trip / **여행중에** during one's journey; while (one is) traveling; on a journey / **여행을 떠나다** start [set out, go] on a [one's] journey / **세계 여행을 하다** travel around the world; make a world tour
▶ 제주도 여행은 어땠습니까? How was your trip to Cheju-do?
▶ 미국인은 여행을 좋아한다 Americans like to travel.
▶ 우리 어머니는 12일간의 유럽관광 여행을 하고 계신다 My mother is on a 12-day tour of Europe.
▶ 소년들은 다음주에 캠프여행을 떠난다 The boys are going on a camping trip next week.
▶ 즐거운 여행을 하시기를 Have a nice trip! = Bon voyage!
▶ 그는 지금 여행중입니다 He is away on a trip. = He is on a trip now.
—여행하다 travel; journey; make [take, go on, undertake] a journey [trip, tour]; make a voyage; make an excursion
♦ **자동차[버스]로 여행하다** travel by car [bus] / **두루 여행하다** travel widely (extensively, far and wide) / **육지와 바다로 여행하다** travel on land and sea / **미국을 여행하다** make a tour of America; travel in America
▶ 가벼운 차림으로 여행하세요 I advise you to travel light.
■ **강연—** a lecture tour **관광—** a sight-seeing tour **기차—** railway traveling; (美) a train journey [trip] **달—** a voyage [a trip] to the moon **도보—** a walking tour; a journey on foot **무전—** a penniless journey **세계일주—** a round-the-world trip **수학—** a school excursion [trip] **시골—** a journey into the country **시찰—** an inspection tour **신혼—** a honeymoon; a wedding trip **우주—** a space travel **주말—** a weekend trip **항공—** an air trip; travel by plane [air] **해외—** a trip abroad; an oversea trip; foreign travel ■ **—자** a traveler; 〈유람객〉 a tourist **—가방** a traveling [traveler's] bag; a suitcase; 〈단기용〉 an overnight bag **—담** an account of one's travels; a travelog(ue) **—사** a travel agency; a tourist [travel] bureau **—(상해)보험** travel (accident) insurance

여행 勵行 careful [faithful] observance **—여행하다** observe strictly; enforce rigidly
여행기 旅行記 a book of travel; a travel book; a record [an account] of one's travels; travels
♦ **걸리버여행기** Gulliver's Travels / **미국 여행기** a record of one's travels in America
여행안내 旅行案內 guidance to travelers; 〈책〉 a guidebook
■ **—서** guidebook; a traveler's handbook; a traveler's guide; 〈간단한〉 a travel brochure [pamphlet] **—소** a travel [tourist] agency; a tourist [travel] (information) bureau **—인** a tourist guide; a tour conductor
여행일정 旅行日程 a plan [schedule] of one's journey; one's travel schedule; an itinerary

♦ **여행일정을 짜다** make plans for a trip; make travel plans
▶ 우리는 하루의 여행일정을 마치고 여관[호텔]에 들었다 We settled down at an inn [a hotel] after a day's journey.
여행자 旅行者 a traveler; a tourist
■ **—수표** a traveler's check (略 T.C.)
여행지 旅行地 〈목적지〉 one's destination in travel; 〈체재지〉 the place where one is staying ♦ **여행지에서 병이 나다** be taken ill while traveling
여현 餘弦 〔數〕〈코사인〉 a cosine (略 cos)
여호수아 〔聖〕 (The Book of) Joshua (略 Josh.)
여호와 〔聖〕 Jehovah ♦ **여호와의 증인** 〈기독교의 일파〉 Jehovah's Witnesses
여화 餘話 gossip ♦ **정계 여화** choice bits of political gossip
여흥 餘興 〈아직 남은 흥〉 unexhausted merriment [fun]; 〈연예나 오락〉 (an) entertainment; a sideshow
♦ **여흥으로** by way of entertainment; for an amusement / **여흥을 보여주다** put on an entertainment
▶ 그가 여흥으로 피아노를 쳤다 He entertained us by playing the piano.
여히 如— as like ♦ **하기와 여히** as follows; as in the following / **상술한 바와 여히** as stated [mentioned] above
역 逆 the opposite; the contrary; contrariness; (the) reverse; the inverse; 〔論·數〕 converse
♦ **역으로** contrary; reverse; opposite / **역으로** conversely; in the opposite direction; contrariwise; on the contrary
▶ 역 또한 진(眞)이다 The converse is also true.
▶ 역은 반드시 진이 아니다 The opposite [reverse] is not always true.
▶ 역의 경우도 많다 There are many cases to the contrary.
역 閾 〔心〕 a threshold
♦ **식역(識閾)** the threshold of consciousness
역 驛 a station; (美) a railroad [(英) a railway] station; a train station; (美) a depot; 〈지하철〉(美) a subway [(英) an underground] station
♦ **서울역** Seoul Station / **역전 광장** a station plaza [square]
▶ 저는 다음 역에서 내립니다 I'll get off at the next station.
역 役 〈연극·영화의〉 a role; a part
♦ **알맞은 역** a part well-suited to sb / **호평을 받은 역** a successful role [part] / **…의 역을 맡아하다** play [take, act, perform, enact] the part [role] of; play; do; personate / **역을 맡기다** cast a part [role] to sb; cast sb for a part / **형사역으로 등장하다** make one's debut in the role of a detective
▶ 그는 그 극에서 무슨 역을 합니까? What role [part] will he play in the drama?
■ **아—** a juvenile part [role]
역譯 (a) translation ⇨ 번역
▶ 이 책의 한국어역은 읽기 어렵다 The Korean version of this book is hard to read.

역가 力價 〔化〕 titer
역겹다 逆— sick; disgusting; sickening; nauseating; nauseous; detestable
♦역겨운 냄새 a sickening smell / 역겨운 광경 a nauseating sight
▶그것은 보기만 해도 역겨웠다 The mere sight of it made me sick.
역경 易經 the I Ching; the Book of Changes
역경 逆境 adversity; adverse situation; adverse [unfavorable] circumstances; misfortune
♦역경을 극복하다 tide over a difficult situation / 역경에 빠지다 fall into adversity / 역경에 처하다 be in [under] adversity; be in time of adversity
▶그는 일생을 역경과 싸웠다 All his life he struggled against [with] adversity.
▶그녀는 역경에서도 최선을 다했다 She has done her best under [in] adversity.
▶그는 역경에서도 희망을 잃지 않았다 Though things seemed [went] against him, he did not give up hope.
역광선 逆光線 backlight; counterlight; 〈조명법〉 backlighting ♦역광선에서 사진을 찍다 take a picture against [into] the light
■사진 a backlighted shot; a shadowgraph
역군 役軍 a laborer; (英) a navvy; a hard worker; 〈유능한 일꾼〉 an able worker
♦사회의 역군 the driving force of society
역기 力技 〔스포츠〕 weight lifting ⇒ 역도(力道)
역기 力器 〔스포츠〕 a barbell; the weight ♦역기를 들다 lift a barbell
역내 域內 ♦역내에서 within the area ―무역 intratrading
역년 曆年 〈책력의 일년〉 a calendar [civil] year; 〈연월〉 time
■―년령 chronological age
역단층 逆斷層 〔地質〕 a reverse fault
역담보 逆擔保 (a) counter-security
역대 歷代 successive generations
♦역대(의) 대통령 all the past presidents
▶그는 역대 총리 중에서 가장 젊다 He is the youngest prime minister (that) Korea has ever had.
■―기(記) 상[하] 〔聖〕 The First [Second] Book of Chronicles; 〈약칭〉 I [II] Chronicles ―내각 successive cabinets ―왕 successive kings
역도 力道 〔스포츠〕 weight lifting
♦역도를 하다 lift weights; do weight lifting / 역도로 몸을 단련하다 fortify one's body by lifting [hoisting] weights
■―선수 a weight lifter
역도 逆徒 traitors
역독 譯讀 reading and translating; oral translation ―역독하다 read and translate
역두 驛頭 the front of a station ⇒ 역전
역랑 逆浪 ♦역랑이 이는 바다 a choppy sea
역량 力量 ability; capability; capacity; talent
♦역량이 있는 사람 a man of ability [talent]; an able [a talented] man / 역량이 있는 able; capable; competent / 역량을 보이다 display [show] one's ability / 역량을 시험하다 test [try] sb's ability; put sb through (his) paces / 자기의 역량을 알다 know one's limitations / 그 일을 할 만한 역량이 있다 be equal to [be competent for] the work; have the ability to do the work
▶그 일에는 내 역량이 미치지 못한다 I'm not equal to [not capable of] the task. ⇌ The task is beyond me [my power].
▶그는 그런 일에 역량을 충분히 발휘하지 못한다 At a job like that, he cannot bring his ability into full play.
역력하다 歷歷— obvious; evident; vivid; clear; plain; manifest; unmistakable
♦역력한 사실 an obvious [a glaring] truth / 역력한 증거 manifest [self-evident] evidence / 역력히 clearly; plainly; obviously; manifestly; evidently; vividly; unmistakably
▶격전의 흔적이 역력하게 남아 있었다 There remained the unmistakable traces of a fierce battles.
▶그녀가 거짓말하고 있는 것이 역력하다 It is evident [clear, obvious] that she is lying.
역류 逆流 〈거슬러 흐름〉 a back current; 〈거슬러 흐름・역수〉 a return flow; 〈조수의〉 an adverse tide [current]; 〈거슬러 올라감〉 flowing backward; 〈체액・음식의〉 reflux; regurgitation
♦역류를 저어가다 row against the stream [current] ―역류하다 flow backward [upstream]; surge back
역리 疫痢 〔醫〕 children's dysentery; infant diarrhea
역리 逆理 irrationality; absurdity; unreasonableness
역링크제 逆―制 〔經〕 a counter link system
역마 驛馬 〔古制〕 a post horse ⇒ 역말
역마을 驛― a post town [village]
역마차 驛馬車 a stagecoach; a stage
역말 驛― 1 〈역참의 말〉 (古) a post horse; a relay horse ♦역말을 갈아타다 take another relay
2 a post town ⇒ 역마을
역모 逆謀 a treasonable conspiracy; a plot of treason
▶역모는 사전에 발각되었다 The treason was detected before it was carried out.
―역모하다 plot treason (against); conspire (to rise against)
역무 役務 (a) labor; (a) service
♦역무배상 reparation in services
역문 譯文 a translated sentence [passage]; a translation ♦자연스런[부자연한] 역문 a natural [an unnatural, an awkward] translation
역반응 逆反應 〔化〕 a reverse reaction
역법 曆法 the calendar; the method of establishing the calendar ♦역법의 개정 a reform of the calendar
역병 疫病 〈유행병〉 an epidemic (disease); 〈악성유행병〉 a pestilence; a plague ♦역병 유행지 a plague spot; a plague-stricken[-infected] district
역본 譯本 a translation
♦안네 프랑크의 일기를 영어 역본으로 읽다 read the Diary of Anne Frank in an English translation; read the English translation [ver-

sion] of *the Diary of Anne Frank*
역부족 力不足 being beyond one's power [capacity]
▶나로서는 그 일에 역부족이다 The work is beyond [too much for] me.
역분사 逆噴射 reverse thrust; 〈로켓의〉 retrofiring (of a rocket)
역불급하다 力不及— beyond one's power; not competent enough; not equal to
역비 逆比 〔數〕 inverse [reciprocal] ratio
역비례 逆比例 〔數〕〈반비례〉 inverse [reciprocal]proportion ◆역비례하다 be in inverse proportion (to)
역빠르다 shrewd ⇨ 약빠르다
역사 力士 a strong man ⇨ 장사(壯士)
역사 役事 construction work; public [engineering] works ◆간척과 매립의 대역사를 벌이다 initiate [undertake] an ambitious reclamation and inning project
―**역사하다** do construction [engineering] work
역사 歷史 1 〈변천의 자취〉 history; 〈사서(史書)〉 a history; annals; a chronicle
◆고대의 역사 an ancient history / 세계의 역사 world history / 한국의 역사 Korean history; the history of Korea / 의학의 역사 the history of medicine / 역사 이전의 prehistoric / 역사 이전에 in prehistoric times; before the dawn of history
〈역사의〉 역사의 선생(님) a history teacher
〈역사는[가]〉 역사는 되풀이한다 History repeats itself.
▶냉전은 이제 과거의 역사가 되었다 The Cold War has already passed into history.
▶역사는 밤에 이루어진다 History is made at night.
〈역사를〉 역사를 거슬러 올라가다 go back in history / 역사를 더듬다 trace the history (of) / 역사를 전공하다 (美) major in [(英) read] history
▶그 사건은 세계 역사를 바꾸어 놓았다 The event changed the history of the world.
〈역사에〉 역사에 남다 go down in history; find a place in history / 역사에 길이 남다 remain long [live] in history / 역사에 이름을 남기다 leave one's mark on history / 세계 역사에 영향을 미치다 affect world history [the history of the world] / 세계 역사에 유례가 없다 be unparalleled in the annals of the world history
▶그 사건은 역사에 실려 있지 않다 The event is not mentioned in history. ⇌ History is silent about [on] it.
2 〈유래〉 history; 〈전통〉 tradition
◆역사 있는 학교 a school with a long history; a historied school; an old [ancient] school
▶우리 은행은 80년의 역사를 간직하고 있다 Our bank has a history of eighty years.
■―**가** a historian; 〈연구가〉 a history student, a student of history ―**관** a historical view ―**극** a historical play ―**소설** a historical novel ―**연표**(年表) a history chart ―**이야기** a historical story ―**철학** historical philosophy; the philosophy of history ―**학** ⇨ 사학(史學) ―**학파** the historical school ―**화** a history picture ―**화가** a history painter
역사 轢死 being killed by a vehicle [a train, an automobile]
―**역사하다** be (run over and) killed by a vehicle [an automobile, a train]
▶그는 선로를 건다가 역사했다 While walking on the tracks, he was run over and killed by a train.
■―**자** a person run over and killed
역사 驛舍 a station building [house]
역사상 歷史上 historically; from the historical point of view
◆역사상의 인물 a historical figure [personage] / 역사상 유명한 곳 a historic spot [scene]; a place of historic interest / 역사상의 historical; historic
▶이 건물은 역사상 중요하다 This building is of historical importance.
역사적 歷史的 historical; historic
◆역사적 건물 a historic building / 역사적 발명 a historic invention / 역사적 사건 a historic event / 역사적 사실[인물] a historical fact [person] / 역사적으로 (보아) historically; from a historical point of view
▶우리는 몇몇 역사적으로 유명한 곳을 찾아보았다 We visited some historic sites.
역산 逆産 1 〔醫〕 cross birth; footpresentation; an agrippa 2 〈반역자의 재산〉 the property [possessions] of a traitor
역산 逆算 inverse [reverse] operation ―**역산하다** count [reckon] backward; calculate back (to)
역살하다 轢殺— run over and kill; kill by running over ▶그 차가 고양이를 역살했다 The car ran over a cat and killed it.
역서 曆書 〈책력〉 an almanac; a calendar
역서 譯書 a translation [version]
▶토인비의 「역사의 연구」를 우리말 역서로 읽다 read Toynbee's "*A Study of History*" in a Korean translation
역선 力線 〔物〕 line of force
역선전 逆宣傳 counterpropaganda ―**역선전하다** carry on [out] counterpropaganda
역설 力說 emphasis; stress
―**역설하다** emphasize; lay [put] emphasis [stress] on; stress; insist upon; urge (on *sb*)
▶그는 타인에 대한 배려의 중요성을 역설했다 He emphasized [stressed] the importance of consideration for others.
▶그녀는 공해방지책의 필요성을 역설했다 She urged the need for antipollution measures.
역설 逆說 〔論〕 a paradox
◆역설적(인) paradoxical
▶역설적으로 말하면 그의 말도 일리가 있다 Paradoxically speaking there is some truth in what he says. ■―**가** a paradoxist
역성 favoritism; (undue) partiality; nepotism
―**역성하다[들다]** be partial to; favor; show partiality [favoritism] to; take part [sides] with; take up for
▶그녀는 막내아이를 역성든다 She favors her youngest child.
▶교사는 어느 학생에게 역성들면 안된다 A

역성 逆成 〔言〕 back-formation
▶타자 치다(typewrite)는 타자기(typewriter)에서 역성된 말이다 Typewrite is a back-formation from typewriter.
■—어 a back-formation

역성비누 逆性— invert soap

역수 逆數 〔數〕 a reciprocal (number); an inverse number ▶x의 역수는 1/x이다 The reciprocal of x is 1/x.

역수입 逆輸入 reimportation; reimport
—역수입하다 reimport
▶국산 수출품 중 어떤 것은 외국 상표를 붙여 역수입된다 Some of Korean-made exported products are reimported with foreign trademarks.

역수출 逆輸出 reexportation; reexport
—역수출하다 reexport
▶수입 외제품 중 어떤 것은 외국 시장에서의 원자재값 상승으로 역수출된다 Some imported foreign goods are reexported due to the price increases of raw materials in the foreign markets.

역습 逆襲 a counterattack; counteroffensive; 〈말로써의〉 a retort
—역습하다 counterattack; make [deliver] a counterattack 《on, against》; 〈말로써〉 retort 《on, against *sb*》; give a retort 《on, against *sb*》; turn the tables 《on *sb*》
◆역습당하다 meet with a reverse; have the tables turned upon 《*one*》

역시 譯詩 a translated poem; a poem in translation

역시 亦是 1 〈또한·마찬가지로〉 too; also; (not) either; as well; likewise
▶그는 교육 전문가며 당신도 역시 그렇습니다 He is an educator, you are another [so are you].
▶우리도 역시 그렇다 That is also the case with us.
▶그도 역시 우리와 마찬가지다 He is like the rest of us. ⇒ He is no exception.
2 〈여전히〉 still; all [just] the same
▶역시 서울에 사십니까? Are you still living in Seoul?
▶아무리 따뜻하여도 역시 겨울은 겨울이다 Warm as it is, winter is still winter.
3 〈결국〉 after all
▶그는 역시 사기꾼이었다 He turned out to be a swindler after all.
4 〈그래도〉 but then; notwithstanding; nevertheless; though; however; in spite of; with all; none the less; for all
▶그는 많은 재산이 있지만 역시 행복하지는 않다 He is none the happier with all his wealth.
5 〈생각했던 대로〉 as (was) expected; true to *one's* expectations; as *one* expected
▶역시 그는 실패했다 He failed as I feared.

역신 疫神 〔民俗〕 the spirit of smallpox; 〈병〉 smallpox

역신 逆臣 〈역적〉 a rebellious subject; a rebel; a traitor

역암 礫岩 〔地質〕 conglomerate; pudding stone

역어 譯語 a translated word; words [terms] used in a translation
◆같은 뜻의 영어 역어 an English equivalent / 역어를 고르다 choose apt [appropriate] terms for translation
▶「세계화」는 영어의 "globalization"의 역어다 "Segyehwa" is the Korean (equivalent) for the English "globalization."
▶이 한국어에 맞는 영어 역어를 나는 발견할 수 없다 I can't find the proper English equivalent for this Korean word.

역연 歷然 〈뚜렷함〉 distinctness
—역연하다 clear; glaring; manifest; obvious; evident; plain; unmistakable
◆역연한 사실 a glaring [an obvious, an undeniable] fact

역영하다 力泳— swim with powerful strokes; swim with might and main
▶골[목표지점]에 접근하자 그는 더욱 역영하였다 He swam with might and main as he approached the goal.

역외 域外 ◆역외에서의 자동차 부품제조 an offshore manufacture of car parts / 병기 탄약을 역외에서 구입하다 purchase arms and ammunitions offshore
■—구매 an offshore purchase —어업 offshore fisheries —조달 offshore procurement

역용 逆用 a reverse use —역용하다 make a reverse use 《of》; turn *sth* to *one's* own advantage
▶그는 그녀의 친절을 역용했다 He turned her kindness to his own advantage.

역원 驛員 a station employee [attendant, worker]; (총칭) station personnel [staff]

역임 歷任 successive [consecutive] service in various posts
—역임하다 successively fill [hold] various posts
◆여러 관직을 역임하다 fill various government posts
▶그는 여러 요직을 역임했다 He has consecutively [successively] occupied a number of important posts.

역자 譯者 a translator

역작 力作 a labored [great] work; a major work; a masterpiece; a work requiring tremendous labor
▶이것은 그의 근래의 역작이다 This is one of his latest works which cost him painstaking efforts.
▶그가 최근 개인전에 소개한 미술품들은 한결같이 역작들이다 The art works at his recent exhibition are all equal masterpieces.
—역작하다 make [produce] a masterpiece; work laboriously [strenuously] 《on》

역작용 逆作用 an adverse effect; a reaction

역장 力場 field of force; force field

역장 驛長 〈큰 역의〉 a stationmaster (at Seoul); (美) 〈작은 역의〉 a station agent
■—실 the stationmaster's [station agent's] office

역저 力著 a literary effort; a fine literary work

역적 逆賊 a rebel; a traitor; an insurgent; 〈반

역행위〉 (a) revolt; (a) rebellion ◆역적 모의하다 conspire to rise in revolt 《against》 ■―질 rebellion; (an act of) treason

역전 力戰 hard fighting; a hard [good, desperate] fight ―**역전하다** fight hard [well, desperately]; put up a good fight ▶ 그는 역전했으나 그 시합에 패했다 He lost the game though he fought hard.

역전 逆轉 a reversal; a reversion; a turnabout; a turnaround; 〔空〕 a loop; 〔氣〕〈기온의〉 an inversion ―**역전하다** reverse 《*itself*》; go into reverse; be reversed; invert; 〈비행기가〉 loop the loop; 〔海〕〈항로가〉 work aback ▶ 형세가 역전했다 The situation has reversed (itself).

역전 歷戰 〈많은 싸움을 겪음〉 long record of active service ◆역전의 용사 a (combat) veteran; a veteran soldier; a hero of many battles; a seasoned soldier

역전 驛前 the front of a (railroad) station; the station front ◆역전에서 at [in front of] a station ―**광장** the station plaza [square] ―**파출소** a police booth near the station

역전경주 驛傳競走 a long-distance relay road race

역전승 逆轉勝 a come-from-behind victory ―**역전승하다** win a come-from-behind victory 《over》

역전패 逆轉敗 suffering a come-from-behind defeat ―**역전패하다** suffer a come-from-behind defeat 《to》

역점 力點 1〈중점〉 emphasis; stress ◆역점을 두다 emphasize; lay [put] emphasis [stress] on 《a matter》; accent(uate) ▶ 이 회사는 인화(人和)에 경영의 역점을 두고 있다 In this company we emphasize harmonious personal relations as a managing principle.
2〔物〕 the point (of a lever) where the force is applied

역점 易占 divination

역정 逆情 anger ⇨ 성 ◆역정이 나다 become [get, grow] angry / 역정을 내다 be angered by [at] ▶ 너는 역정이 날 만도 하다 You have good reason to be angry. ▶ 그 남자는 사소한 일로 역정을 냈다 He was angered at trifles.

역조 力漕〈보트 등을 힘껏 저음〉 a spurt of row; a row with all *one's* might ―**역조하다** row with all *one's* might; row powerfully [with powerful strokes]

역조 逆潮〈풍향과 반대의〉 weather tide; a counter tide; a head tide; 〈배의 진로와 반대의〉 an adverse current

역조 逆調 an adverse [unfavorable] condition ―**무역―** an adverse balance of trade; an unfavorable balance of trade

역종 役種〈병역의 종류〉 the classification of (military) service status

역주 力走 a spurt running with all *one's* might; running as fast [hard] as *one* can; 〈단거리에서〉 sprinting ―**역주하다** run as fast [hard] as *one* can; 〈경주에서〉 make a spurt; spurt

역주 譯註 translation and annotation; translation with notes ―**역주하다** translate and annotate; translate with notes ◆김교수가 역주한 「리어왕」 "Kings Lear" translated and annotated by professor Kim ―**서(書)** a copy of translation with notes

역진 力盡 exhaustion (of strength) ―**역진하다** *one's* strength is gone [ebbs]; 〈사람이 주어〉 be exhausted [spent up]

역청 瀝靑〔鑛〕 (mineral) pitch; bitumen ◆역청질의 bituminous ―**암[석]** pitchstone ―**탄** bituminous [pitch, soft] coal

역추진로켓 逆推進― a retro-rocket ◆역추진로켓에 점화하다 retrofire ―**엔진** a retro-rocket engine

역코스 逆― the reverse course ◆역코스를 가다 take the reverse [opposite] course

역탐지 逆探知〈전화 발신자 추적〉 tracing the phoner ―**역탐지하다** trace (the phoner) ▶ 경찰은 그의 전화를 역탐지했다 The police traced his (phone) call. ―**장치** a tracer; a tracing system

역투 力投〔野〕 a hard pitch; pitching hard [with all one's might]; all-out pitching ―**역투하다** pitch [hurl] with might and main; pitch hard ▶ 그는 게임 끝까지 역투했다 He pitched hard throughout the game.

역투 力鬪 a hard fight ―**역투하다** fight hard [gamely]; fight with might and main

역풍 逆風 an adverse [a contrary, a foul, an unfavorable] wind; a head wind ◆역풍을 향하여[무릅쓰고] in the teeth of foul wind ▶ 주자는 역풍을 안고 뛰었다 The runner ran against an unfavorable [a head] wind

역하다 逆― sickening; nauseating; repulsive; repellent; revolting; disgusting; offensive ◆역한 냄새 a repulsive smell; a disgusting odor

역학 力學 dynamics; mechanics ◆역학적(인) dynamic(al) / 역학상[적으로] dynamically ―**공기[항공]―** aerodynamics **동(動)―** kinetics **생체(生體)―** biodynamics : 생체 정력학 **biostatics 양자―** quantum dynamics **열―** thermodynamics **응용―** applied mechanics **정(靜)―** statics

역학 易學 the science of divination

역할 役割 a role; a part; 〈임무〉 duty; function; service ◆역할을 다하다 discharge [perform, fulfill] *one's* duty / 역할을 정하다 allot roles; assign a part / 중요한 역할을 하다 play an important part [role] 《in a matter》 / 형용사 역할을 하다 serve for [as] an adjective; function as an adjective ▶ 그는 자기의 역할을 훌륭히 해냈다 He performed his part most effectively.

역행 力行 endeavor; strenuous efforts; exertion —역행하다 make strenuous efforts; endeavor; exert *oneself*; exert *one's* powers

역행 逆行 retrogression; retrogradation; reverse [backward] movement; countermarch; 〔天〕 retrograde motion
♦역행적인 retrogressive
—역행하다 go back; move [go] backward; retrogress; retrograde; run counter 《to》; be contrary 《to》
♦민주주의에 역행하다 run counter to democracy / 시대에 역행하다 go against the times; put back the clock
▶그의 생활방식은 시대에 역행한다 His life style goes against the times.

역행운동 逆行運動 〔天〕 retrogradation; the retrograde motion 《of a planet》

역회전 逆回轉 spinning the opposite way; 〔테니스·탁구〕 backspin; 〔스케이트〕 a counter

역효과 逆效果 a counter effect [result]; a contrary [reverse] effect; a backfire; an adverse effect [reaction]
♦역효과를 가져오다[초래하다] backfire; have a reverse [an adverse] effect 《on》; produce a contrary result; bring about a contrary effect
▶우리의 경고는 그에게 역효과를 초래했을 뿐이었다 Our warning only produced a reverse effect on him.

엮다 1 〈뜨다〉 weave; plait; entwine
♦대바구니를 엮다 weave a bamboo basket / 화환을 엮다 weave flowers into a wreath; weave a garland of flowers
2 〈꾸미다〉 weave 《in, into》; 〈편찬하다〉 compile; edit
♦역사를 엮다 compile [edit] a history / 이야기를 엮다 weave a tale [story]
▶〈책에 대해서〉 김선생 엮음 Compiled by Mr. Kim.

연 年 a year
♦연 1[2]회 once[twice] a year / 연 1회의 yearly; annual / 연 2회의 half-yearly; biannual; semiannual —수입 an annual [a yearly] income —평균 the yearly mean

연 鉛 lead ⇨ 납

연 鳶 a kite
♦연을 날리다 fly a kite / 연을 내리다 draw [reel] in a kite / 바람에 연을 올리다 let up a kite with the wind
—날리기 kite-flying —실 a kite string; a string [twine] for a kite —싸움 a kite fighting (contest)

연 蓮 〔植〕 〈an Indian〉 lotus ■—꽃 a lotus flower [bloom]

연 緣 preordained tie ⇨ 연분

연 延 the total; the aggregate
♦연인원[연일수] the total number of (working) days; the total man-days / 연톤수 total tonnage / 연면적 the total floor area

연- 連- 〈연속〉 consecutive(ly); in succession; successive(ly); continuous(ly); continual(ly); without a break
♦역사흘 《for》 three consecutive days
▶연이틀 비가 오고 있다 It has been raining for two consecutive days.

연가 戀歌 a love song [poem]; an amatory poem

연간 年刊 〈책〉 a yearly ♦연간의 published once a year; yearly 〈annual〉 《magazine》

연간 年間 (for) a year
■—계획 a program for the year —매상고 a yearly [an annual] turnover —생산고 a yearly [an annual] output —수입(收入) an annual income

연감 年鑑 a yearbook; an almanac
■—경제— an economic yearbook 통계— a statistical yearbook

연감 軟— a ripe and soft persimmon

연갑 年甲 a contemporary; a person (of) about the same age
♦우리 연갑들 our contemporaries

연강 軟鋼 mild [soft] steel

연거푸 連— successively; in (quick) succession; consecutively; one after another; again and again; repeatedly; on end
♦연거푸 때리다 strike; give repeated blows / 연거푸 세번 이기다 win three consecutive [straight] victories / 연거푸 우유를 석 잔 마시다 drink three glasses of milk in quick succession / 연거푸 질문하다 fire questions in rapid succession
▶그는 연거푸 술을 마셨다 He drank glasses of wine in quick succession [one after another].
▶그는 내 멱살을 잡고 연거푸 때렸다 He seized me by the collar and hit me again [struck me repeatedly].

연건평 延建坪 the total floor space

연결 連結 connection; coupling; joining; linking
—연결하다 connect; couple; attach; interconnect; join; interlink; link
♦급행 열차에 연결한 식당차 a dining car coupled on to an express / 객차 10량(輛)이 연결된 열차 a ten-car[-carriage] train / 기관차를 열차에 연결하다 couple [attach] a locomotive to a train
▶이 도로는 서울과 인천을 연결한다 This road connects [links] Seoul and Inch'ŏn.
▶이 다리는 그 섬과 본토를 연결한다 This bridge joins [links] the island to the mainland.
▶전화가 연결되었다 The call was put through. ⇌ The connection was made.
■—기(器) a coupler; a connector; a connecter —장치 a coupling device

연계 連繫 connection; linking; liaison; contact; touch ♦…와 긴밀한 연계가 있다 be closely connected with…
■—동작 a conjoint action; a combination —자금 a stopgap fund —플레이 a combination play

연고 軟膏 (an) ointment; (an) unguent; salve; inunction
♦연고를 바르다 apply ointment 《to》
▶상처에 연고를 발라라 Put some ointment on the cut.
■—수은[붕산]— mercurial [boric] ointment

연고 緣故 〈관계·연분〉 relation; connection; affinity; a tie-in; (口) (a) pull
♦ 이순신 장군의 연고지 a place noted [remembered] in connection with General Yi Sun-shin / 연고권을 인정하다 give *sb* preemptive right
▶ 두 사람 사이에는 아무런 연고도 없다 There is no connection between the two.
■ —자 a relative; a relation —지 a place one has relation with —채용 hiring *sb* through personal connection

연고로 緣故— therefore; accordingly; because of that

연골 軟骨 1 〔解〕〈여린 뼈〉 cartilage; gristle **2** 〈어린 사람〉 a young person; a man of tender age
■ 갑상(甲狀)— the thyroid cartilage ■ —막 a perichondrium (*pl.* -ria) —세포 a cartilage cell; a chondrocyte —어류 a cartilaginous fish —조직 cartilaginous tissue —한(漢) a weak-willed man; a weak character

연공 年功 〈오래 근속한 공로〉 long [continued] service; 〈경험〉 long experience
♦ 연공을 쌓은 사람 an old timer; a veteran / 연공을 쌓다 serve long (in a firm); have long [a lot of] experience (in) / 연공으로 승급시키다 raise *sb* salary as a reward for long service
▶ 승진은 연공에 따라 한다 Promotion goes by seniority.
▶ 이 회사에서는 연공이 아니라 공적에 따라 승진한다 Promotions in this company are based on merit rather than seniority.
■ —가봉(加俸) a long service allowance; a good service pension; an additional salary for long service; [美軍] longevity pay —서열제도 the seniority system [rule]

연공 年貢 an annual [a yearly] tribute (to)
♦ 연공을 징수하다[바치다] collect [pay] the land tax

연관 鉛管 a lead pipe; a lead tube; (총칭) plumbing ■ —공 a plumber —공사 plumbing (work)

연관 聯關 1 ⇨ 관련 **2** 〔遺〕 linkage

연광 鉛鑛 1 〈납을 캐는 광산〉 a lead mine; lead deposits **2** 〈광석〉 a lead ore

연구 研究 (a) study (*pl.* -dies) (of, on, in); research(es) 《on, in》; investigation

> 解說 *study*는 지식을 얻기 위한 연구나 공부를 이르는 말로서, *one's* studies라 하여 흔히 개인 연구활동을 가리키기도 한다. *research*는 새로운 사실 등을 발견하고자 하는 study보다 학술적인 연구·조사를 가리킨다. 불가산(不可算)명사이므로 a나 수사 등을 붙이지 않으나 복수형으로 쓸 때가 있다.

♦ 문학의 연구 the study of literature / 칸트의 연구 *Studies on Kant* (▶학문영역에서는 on대신 in을 씀: Studies in Philosophy); 〈논문명〉 A Study of Kant / 물리학 분야에서의 최근의 뛰어난 연구 an excellent piece of recent research in the field of physics / 연구중인 문제 the subject under investigation / 〈출판물로〉 연구를 발표하다 publish the results of *one's* research work (in a bulletin); 〈구두로〉 read *one's* paper / 연구를 계속하다 continue *one's* study / 연구를 끝내다 complete [conclude] *one's* study / 연구를 지도하다 direct *sb's* study [research] / 연구에 종사하다 be engaged in research (work); pursue [follow, carry on] *one's* studies; conduct researches (in)
▶ 나는 (학교를) 졸업하더라도 연구를 계속할 작정이다 I will continue my studies even after graduation.
▶ 그는 이론 물리학 연구에 열의를 보이고 있다 He's attending to his studies of theoretical physics.
▶ 그는 연구에 열심이다 He is eager in his studies.

—연구하다 study; make [do, conduct] a study (of); research (in, into, on)
♦ 깊이 연구하다 go deep into the study (of); devote deep study (to) / 전문적으로 연구하다 make a special study (of); make a specialty (of); specialize (in)
▶ 그는 손 교수 밑에서 철학을 연구했다 He studied philosophy under Professor Son.
▶ 그는 문학을 연구하고 있다 He is studying literature.
▶ 그들은 방사능을 연구하고 있다 They are doing research(es) on [into] radioactivity. ≠ They are engaged in radioactivity research.
▶ 이 문제는 깊이 연구하고 나서 내게 답변해 주세요 Give the matter careful consideration before you give me a reply.
■ 문법— a study in [of] grammar 문학— literary researches; study of literature 위탁— researches commissioned ■ —가 a student; a scholar; an investigator —과 a postgraduate course; a seminar —기관 a research institution —논문 a research paper; 〈전공논문〉 a treatise (on); a monograph; 〈학위논문〉 a dissertation —단체 a research organization —반[팀] a research team —발표회 a meeting for reading research papers —방법 a method of study [research] —보고 a report of research; 〈보고서〉 a research paper —보조금 a research-aid fund —비 research funds [expenses] —생[원] a (research) student [worker, scientist]; a specialty student; a laboratory man; (口) a labman (*pl.* -men) —수당 research allowances —시설 a research installation —심 the spirit of study; the love of study; an inquiring mind —자 a research worker [scholar]; a student; a researcher —자료[재료] the materials [data] for *one's* study; research materials [data] —제목 a subject for study [inquiry]; a laboratory subject —활동 research activities

연구 聯句 a linked verse; a couplet

연구개 軟口蓋 〔解〕 the soft palate; the velum (*pl.* -la) ♦ 연구개의 velar ■ —음 〔音聲〕 a velar (sound) —자음 a velar consonant

연구소 研究所 a research institute; a (research) laboratory; (口) a lab ■ 화학— a chemical laboratory

연구실 研究室 a study room; 〈대학의 세미나 용의〉 a seminar room; 〈화학 등의〉 a laboratory; (口) a lab
 ♦ (교수의) 개인 연구실 a professor's office / 연구실 비치 도서 a laboratory collection of books

연구회 研究會 〈단체〉 a society for the research [study] 《of》; 〈일시적인 모임〉 a study meeting
 ♦ 경제문제연구회 a society for the study of economic problems

연극 演劇 1 〈극〉 a play; 〈희곡〉 a drama; 〈무대의〉 a theatrical [dramatic] performance
 ♦ 연극적 dramatic(al); theatrical / 연극을 상연하다 stage a play / 연극을 전공하다 major in theater [drama] / 연극을 보러 가다 go to the theater; go to (see) plays / 연극에 미치다 be stagestruck
 ▶ 그는 그 연극에 출연했다 He played a part in that play. ⇌ He was [acted, appeared] in the play.
 ▶ 그 연극은 지금 S극장에서 상연중이다[상연하고 있다] The play is now on [showing] at the S theater.
 ▶ 학교 축제에서 그들은 셰익스피어의 연극을 상연했다 They gave a Shakespearian play at their school [campus] festival.
 2 〈거짓 꾸미기〉 acting; playacting; a fake
 ♦ 연극을 하다 playact; pretend; use [play] trick; put on an act; put up a false show
 ▶ 그녀는 연극을 하고 있다 She is just putting on an act. ⇌ She is only acting a part.
 ■ ―계 the dramatic [theatrical] world [circles] ―과(科) a course of dramatics ―구경 theatergoing; playgoing ―박물관 a theater museum ―비평가 a dramatic critic ―애호가 a playgoer; a play enthusiast [fan] ―운동 a dramatic movement ―인 a man of the theater; theatrical people ―학교 a dramatic school

연근 蓮根 〔植〕 a lotus root [rhizome]

연금 年金 an annuity; a pension
 ♦ 연금을 주다[받다] grant [receive, draw] an annuity *sb* / 연금을 받고 퇴직하다 retire on an annuity / 연금을 주어 퇴직시키다 pension *sb* off / 연금으로 살다 live on a pension [on *one's* annuity]
 ▶ 그는 연금으로 생활하고 있다 He lives on a [his] pension.
 ■ 양로― an old-age pension (略 O.A.P.) 종신― a life annuity 질병― an invalidity pension 퇴직― a retirement pension ■ ―생활자 a pensioner ―수령자 an annuitant; a pensioner ―제도 the pension system ―증서 an annuity bond [certificate]

연금 軟禁 informal confinement; house arrest
 ―연금하다 confine *sb* informally 《in room》; place [put] *sb* under house arrest
 ▶ 그는 자택에 연금되어 있다 He is confined informally in his own house. ⇌ He is [placed] under house arrest.

연금술 鍊金術 alchemy [ǽlkəmi] ■ ―사(師) an alchemist

연급 年給 an annual salary ⇨ 연봉(年俸)

연기 年期 a term; a period; a limited period of time

연기 延期 delay; (a) postponement; deferment; 〈회의 등의〉 adjournment; extension
 ♦ 2주간의 연기를 허락하다 allow two week's postponement
 ▶ 심판은 게임의 연기를 선언했다 The umpire declared a delay in the game.
 ―연기하다 put off; postpone; defer; delay; adjourn

 解説 *put off*나 *postpone*은 정해진 시기까지 일이나 행위를 연기하는 것이나 put off가 더 구어적이다. *defer*는 의도적으로 연기하는 것으로 격식을 차린 표현이며 *delay*는 사람이 우물쭈물하거나 사고 또는 나쁜 일기 등으로 지연되는 것을 말한다. *adjourn*은 회의 등을 다음번까지 중단시키는 것을 말한다.

 ♦ 2, 3일 연기하다 put off for a few days / 기한을 연기하다 extend [prolong] the term / 출발을 월요일까지[일주일] 연기하다 put off [postpone, delay] *one's* departure till monday [for a week]; put off [postpone, delay] leaving till monday [for a week] / 청구서의 지급을 연기하다 defer payment of [paying] *one's* bills
 ▶ 파티는 일주일 연기되었다 The party was postponed [put off] for a week.
 ▶ 시합은 비 때문에 연기되었다 The game was put off [was postponed] because of (the) rain.
 ▶ 전람회는 꼭 1주일간 연기되었다 The exhibition was extended for just a week.
 ▶ 그 로켓 발사는 다음 수요일까지 연기되었다 The launching of the rocket was postponed [put off] until next Wednesday.

연기 連記 listing; writing down together
 ―연기하다 list 《the names》; make a list
 ♦ (투표에서) 2명을 연기하다 write down two names on a ballot

연기 煙氣 smoke; fumes; a smother
 ♦ 담배 연기 cigarette smoke; tobacco fumes / 한 줄기의 연기 a column [streak] of smoke / 뭉게뭉게 피어 오르는 연기 a cloud [volumes] of smoke / 굴뚝에서 뿜어대는 연기 smoke shot up from a chimney / 연기가 나다 smoke; smolder / 연기를 내뿜다 emit [give out] smoke; 〈기관차 등이〉 puff out [off] smoke / 연기에 질식해 죽다 be suffocated to death by smoke / 연기처럼 사라지다 vanish into thin air; 〈계획 등이〉 end [go up] in smoke
 ▶ 공장의 굴뚝에서 검은 연기가 뿜어 나오고 있다 Black smoke is coming out of the factory chimney.
 ▶ 나는 연기에 숨이 막혀 피로웠다 I was suffering from the choking smoke. ⇌ I was choking from the smoke.
 ▶ 아이들은 연기에 질식해 죽었다 The children were choked [stifled, suffocated, smothered] to death by smoke.
 ▶ 연기에 눈이 매웠다 The smoke irritated my eyes.

연기 演技 a performance; acting
 ▶ 그녀는 연기가 훌륭했다 Her performance

was excellent. ⇌ She gave an excellent [〈감동적인〉a moving] performance. ⇌ 〈감명을 받았다〉 I was very impressed with her performance.
▶ 그의 연기는 일류였다 His acting was first-rate.
▶ 그것은 다만 연기에 지나지 않았다 That was only a gesture [a fake, (口) an act].
—연기하다 perform; act; play
▶ 당신은 우리의 동정을 사기 위해 연기하고 있을 뿐이다 You are only acting to get our sympathy.
■—자 a performer

연내 年內 ◆연내에 before the end of the year; within the year; before the year is out

연년 年年 〈해마다·매년〉 every year; yearly; annually ■—세세(歲歲) every year; year in and year out

연년 連年 consecutive [successive] years; year after year; every year

연년생 連年生 a child born within a year of another; children born in consecutive years
▶ 나와 형은 연년생이다 I am only one year younger than my brother.
▶ 그 형제는 연년생이다 They are brothers born within a year of each other.

연년익수 延年益壽 prolonging one's life; longevity —연년익수하다 live long; prolong one's life

연놈 (卑) the man and woman; a chap and a bitch

연단 演壇 a (speaker's) platform; a rostrum (pl. ~s, -tra)
◆연단에 서다 stand on [take, appear on] a platform; take the rostrum

연달 練達 skill; dexterity —연달하다 be skilled; become skillful [dexterous]; get skilled
◆연달한 expert (in); skilled (in)

연달다 連— continue; keep on; occur in succession; follow one after another
◆연달은 3승 three consecutive [straight] victories / 불행한 일이 연달다 have a run of ill luck; misfortune comes one after another
▶ 나는 연달아 기침이 나왔다 I had a fit of coughing.
▶ 모든 그의 계획은 연달아 실패했다 All his plans have failed one after another.

연대 年代 〈세대〉 an age; an epoch; a period; 〈연원〉 years
◆1990년대 전반에 in the early 1990's
▶ 그것은 1980년대에 일어났다 It happened in the nineteen-eighties [1980's].

연대 連帶
◆연대의 joint and several / 연대로 돈을 빌리다 borrow money under joint signature
■—감[의식] the feeling of togetherness

연대 聯隊 〔軍〕 a regiment ◆연대(소속)의 regimental
■보병[기병]— a foot [cavalry] regiment
■—기 the regimental colors [standard] —병력 a regimental force [strength] —본부 regimental headquarters —장 a regimental commander; the colonel of the regiment

연대기 年代記 a chronicle; annals

연대보증 連帶保證 joint and several liability on guarantee ◆연대보증을 서다 stand [go] joint and several surety (for) ■—인 a surety liable jointly and severally

연대순 年代順 chronological order; order of date ◆연대순의 chronological / 연대순으로 chronologically; in chronological order

연대채무 連帶債務 joint and several obligation [debt] —자 a joint and several debtor —증서 a joint and several bond

연대책임 連帶責任 joint and several liability; 〈내각의〉 collective responsibility
◆연대책임으로 on joint and several [collective] liability [responsibility] / 연대책임을 지다 assume joint [collective] responsibility (for); 〔法〕 be jointly liable (for)

연대학 年代學 chronology
■—자 a chronologist; a chronologer

연도 年度 the year; 〈회계연도〉 a fiscal year
◆1996 회계연도 1996 fiscal year; fiscal 1996 / 1997회계연도 예산 the budget for the 1997 fiscal year / 1997년도의 S대 졸업생 a graduate of the S University in the class of 1997 / 학년도말 the end of the school year / 연도별의 《a financial report》 by year / 내년도로 이월하다 carry over 《an account》 to the next fiscal year
■본— the current year 사업— a business year —보고 an annual report —초[말] (at) the beginning [end] of the fiscal year

연도 沿道 the roadside; the wayside; a route
◆연도의[에] along the route [road]; by the roadside
▶ 그 퍼레이드를 보기 위해 군중들은 연도에 줄지어 섰다 Crowds of people lined the route to see the parade.

연도 煉禱 〔가톨릭〕〈위령 기도〉 a litany

연독 鉛毒 〔醫〕 lead poisoning ⇨ 납(~중독)
◆연독에 걸리다 suffer from lead poisoning

연돌 煙突 a chimney ⇨ 굴뚝

연동 聯動·連動 interlock; 〔機〕 gears; gearing; linkage
■—기 a clutch —장치 an interlocker; interlocking device —전환장치 a gearshift

연동 蠕動 1 〈벌레가 꾸물꾸물 움직임〉 vermiculation
—연동하다 move in a wormlike manner
2 ⇨ 연동운동

연동운동 蠕動運動 〔生理〕 peristalsis; a peristaltic motion [movement] ◆연동운동을 하다 move peristaltically

연두 年頭 the beginning of the year; 〈새해〉 the New Year('s) Day
■—교서 the State of the National Message; 〈미국 대통령의〉 the (President's annual) State of the Union Message (to Congress)

연두색 軟豆色 yellow green; yellowish (light) green ◆연두색의 yellow-green

연락 宴樂 merrymaking; festivities; revelry; conviviality

연락 連絡 〈관계〉 (a) connection; 〈접촉〉 (a) contact; touch; 〈통신〉 communication; 〈연계〉 liaison

♦긴밀한 연락 a close contact
〈연락이〉 연락이 끊기다 lose contact 《with》/ 연락이 닿(고 있)다 be in touch [liaison] 《with》/ …와 연락이 있다 have connection with…; be connected [linked] with…
▶나는 옛친구와 연락이 끊어지고 말았다 I have lost contact [touch] with my old friends.
▶여러번 전화한 끝에 겨우 그와 연락이 되었다 I finally made contact with [could reach, could get] him after calling several times.
▶홍수로 전화연락이 끊어졌다 Telephone communication was cut off by the flood.
▶요트는 태평양 한가운데서 연락이 끊어졌다 The cruiser lost [went out of] communication in the midst of the Pacific Ocean.
▶숙부한테서 오지 못한다는 연락이 왔다 Word came that my uncle couldn't come.
▶그에게서 곧 연락이 갈 것으로 생각한다 You'll hear from him soon.
〈연락을〉 연락을 취하다 get in touch 《with》; effect liaison 《with》 / 연락을 강화하다 strengthen the contact 《with the police》 / 무전으로 연락을 유지하다 keep in radio touch 《with》; maintain radio contact 《with》
▶나는 그와 연락을 취하고 있다 I am [keep] in touch [contact, communication] with him.
▶어머니는 전화로 의사와 연락을 취했다 Mother contacted the doctor by telephone.
—연락하다 contact; make contact 《with》; connect [be connected] 《with》; get in touch; communicate with
♦경찰과 연락하다 contact the police
▶그 섬은 기선으로 본토와 연락하고 있다 The island is connected with the mainland by a steamer.
▶될 수 있는대로 속히 연락해 주게 Let me know it as soon as you can.
■—선(線) a connecting line —소 a liaison office —역 〈갈아 타는 역〉 a junction —장교 a liaison officer
연락선 連絡船 a ferryboat; a ferry steamer
연래 年來 (for) some [a number of] years; these [recent] years
♦연래의 현안 long-pending question [problem] / 20년래의 친구 a friend of twenty years' standing / 연래의 of long standing; long-cherished 《desire》
▶10년래의 대설이다 This is the heaviest snowfall for [(美) in] ten years. ⇌ This is the heaviest snowfall (that) we have had for the past [last] ten years.
▶연래의 숙원이 이루어졌다 My long-cherished desire was fulfilled.
▶올해의 쌀 수확량은 10년래의 풍작[흉작]이다 The rice crop this year is the best [worst] in the last [past] ten years.
▶그는 20년래의 친구다 He has been my close friend for twenty years.
연령 年齡 age ⇨ 나이
♦연령의 차 disparity [discrepancy] of age / 선박의 연령 the age of a vessel / 모든 연령의 of all ages / 연령별로 by age / 연령에 비해서는 for one's age
▶이곳은 모든 연령의 사람이 방문한다 People of all ages visit this place.
▶그녀는 연령보다 훨씬 젊어 보인다 She looks much younger than [very young for] her age.
▶어떤 연령의 아이도 만화를 좋아한다 Children of all ages like comics.
▶연령·성별에 관계없이 그 일에 응모할 수 있다 Anyone, regardless of age or sex, can apply for the job.
■결혼— the marriage [marriageable] age 정신— one's mental age 평균— the average age (of) ■—제한 (set) the age limit —층 (an) age group [bracket]
연례 年例 yearly custom ♦연례의 yearly; annual ■—보고 an annual report —총회 an annual general meeting —행사 an annual function [event]
연로 年老 agedness; oldness —연로하다 aged; old ▶그는 연로한 부모를 모시고 있다 He has old parents to support.
연료 燃料 fuel
♦연료를 공급하다 provide 《a country》 with fuel / 석유[석탄]를 연료로 사용하다 use oil [coal] as [for] fuel
▶연료가 떨어져 가고 있다 We are running out of fuel.
▶연료가 몹시 부족하다 Fuel is badly needed [in very short supply].
▶비행기는 연료가 떨어져 불시착했다 The airplane was out of fuel and made an emergency landing.
▶비행기는 런던에 머물러 연료를 보급했다 The plane stopped over at London and (was) refueled.
▶그 배는 연료를 보급받기 위해 입항했다 The ship put into port to fuel.
▶고장은 연료계통이다 The trouble is in the fuel line.
▶석탄이나 나무는 값싼 연료다 Coal and wood are cheap fuels.
■액체[기체, 고체]— liquid [gaseous, solid] fuel ■—보급 refueling —보급소 a fueling station —부족 lack [dearth] of fuel —비 cost of fuel; fuel expenses [charge] —유[가스, 탄] fuel oil [gas, coal] —탱크 a fuel tank
연루 連累 implication; involvement; complicity —연루하다 be implicated in 《a crime》; be involved in 《an affair》
▶그는 그 수뢰 사건에 연루되어 있다 He is implicated in the bribery case.
▶이 사건에 그가 연루되어 있는 것 같다 He seems to be involved in this case.
■범죄— complicity with another in a crime ■—자 an accomplice; a confederate; a person concerned [involved]
연륜 年輪 〈나이테〉 an annual ring 《of a tree》
연리 年利 annual interest
♦연리 13퍼센트로 은행에서 500만원을 빌리다 borrow five million won from the bank at an annual interest of 13 percent [at 13 percent interest a year]
▶연리 13퍼센트로 은행에서 돈을 빌렸다 I got a loan from the bank at an annual interest rate of 13 percent.
연립 聯立 alliance; coalition; union

—연립하다 ally *oneself* 《with》; be allied; coalesce 《with》; unite 《with》
■—내각 a coalition cabinet —방정식 〔數〕 simultaneous equations —정부 a coalition government —주택 《live in》 a tenement house; row houses

연마 研磨·練磨 **1** 〔機〕 grinding; abrasion; polishing
—연마하다 grind 《a knife, lens》; polish 《up》; whet
2 〈연구·단련〉 training; practice; drilling
◆다년간의 연마 덕택에 by virtue of many year's training
—연마하다 study hard; apply *oneself* to the study 《of》; polish up
◆잘 연마된 기술 consummate skill / 기술을 연마하다 improve *one's* skill; practice an art / 신체를 연마하다 improve *one's* physical fitness / 정신을 연마하다 cultivate [school, train] *one's* mind
■—기 a grinder; a polishing [an abrasive] machine; 〈렌즈 등의〉 a polisher —분 polishing powder —제 an abradant; an abrasive —지 abrasive paper; polishing [emery] paper

연막 煙幕 a smoke screen
◆연막을 치다 lay a smoke screen
▶그는 본심을 간파당하지 않으려고 여러 가지로 연막을 쳤다 He tried one thing after another by way of a smoke screen so as not to have his real intentions seen through.
■—전술 smoke-screen tactics —탄 a smoke shell

연만하다 年滿— old (enough); far [well] advanced in years; senile ◆연만한 사람들 old men; people far advanced in life

연말 年末 (at) the end [close] of the year; (at) the year-end
◆연말에 in the last days of the year; at the end of the year
■—대매출 a year-end (bargain) sale —상여금 a year-end bonus —정산 〈세금의〉 year-end (tax) adjustment

연맥 燕麥 〔植〕 oats ⇨ 귀리

연맹 聯盟 a league; a union; a federation; a confederation
◆…과 연맹으로 in league with…/ 연맹을 조직하다 form a league [federation] / 연맹을 탈퇴하다 resign [secede] from a league / 연맹에 가입하다 join a league
—국제— the League of Nations 육상경기— the Federation of Athletic Associations
■—국 allied countries

연면하다 連綿— consecutive; continuous; uninterrupted
◆연면한 가계 an old, uninterrupted family tree / 연면한 혈통 a long, uninterrupted lineage / 연면히 continuously; consecutively; uninterruptedly / 연면히 이어져 온 전통 an old tradition handed down from generation to generation

연명 延命 〈겨우 살아감〉 maintenance of a scanty existence; 〈수명 연장〉 the prolongation of (human) life
◆내각의 연명을 도모하다 try to prolong the life of the cabinet / 연명책을 강구하다 make plans for prolonging *one's* life
▶당신의 경우는 운동이 유일한 연명책입니다 In your case exercise is the only way of prolonging your life.
—연명하다 prolong *sb's* life; eke out a scanty existence [livelihood]; keep body and soul together
◆박봉으로 겨우 연명하다 eke out a livelihood on *one's* meager pay

연명 連名 a joint signature
◆연명의 joint / 연명으로 (send an invitation) under joint signature
▶우리는 연명으로 그 회사에 공개 질의서를 보냈다 We jointly sent a written public inquiry to the company.
—연명하다 sign jointly; join *one's* name 《to a circular》
■—진정서 a joint petition

연모 〈도구〉 an instrument; a tool; 〈재료〉 material

연모 戀慕 love (and yearning); attachment; the tender emotions
—연모하다 love; fall in love with; become attached to; long for; yearn for
◆애타게 연모하다 be desperately in love 《with》; burn with passion 《for》 / 연모받다 be loved; be yearned for
▶그는 친구의 여동생을 연모했다 He loved his friend's sister.
▶그녀는 남몰래 그를 연모했다 She secretly pined for his affection.

연모 軟毛 soft [downy] hairs; down

연목 軟木 softwood; soft timber

연목구어 緣木求魚 attempting the impossible; seeking a fish in a tree

연못 蓮— a lotus pond; a pond

연무 煙霧·烟霧 smoke and fog; (a) mist; (a) fog; (a) haze ▶연무 때문에 시계가 좋지 않다 Visibility is poor because of the mist.

연무 演武 military exercises; practice of martial [military] arts —연무하다 practice military arts; engage in military exercises

연무 鍊武 a military drill; training in the military arts —연무하다 practice a military drill; have a drill

연문 戀文 〈연애편지〉 a love letter

연문학 軟文學 light [erotic, amatory] literature

연미복 燕尾服 a swallow-tailed coat; a dress coat; a swallowtail; a tailcoat

연민 憐憫 pity; compassion; mercy
◆연민의 정을 느끼다 feel compassion [pity] 《for, toward》; be touched with compassion 《for》 / 연민의 정을 일으키다 excite [arouse] compassion [pity] 《for》
▶기아에 허덕이고 있는 어린이들에게 연민의 정을 느끼지 않는 사람은 아무도 없을 것이다 There mustn't be anyone who doesn't feel pity for the children suffering from starvation.

연발 延發 delayed departure —연발하다 start late ▶기차가 30분 연발했다 The train started thirty minutes late [behind schedule].

연발 連發 running fire; a volley
♦ 사고의 연발 a series of accidents / 질문의 연발 a running fire [volley] of questions / 연발로 사격하다 fire many shots in rapid [quick] succession
―**연발하다** fire in rapid succession [in volleys]
♦ 질문을 연발하다 ask one question after another; put questions 《to *sb*》 in rapid succession; fire questions at *sb* in rapid succession
▶ 사고가 연발했다 Accidents occurred one after another.
■ ―**총** a magazine rifle [gun]; a revolver: 6연발 권총 a six-shooter; a six-shot [six chambered] revolver; (美口) six-gun

연방 continuously; ceaselessly; without a break [interruption]
♦ 연방 전화가 걸려오다 have telephone calls almost without a break / 연방 지껄이다 chatter incessantly
▶ 차들이 연방 길을 지나간다 There is a constant stream of motorcars along the street.

연방 聯邦 a federal union; a federation; a confederation; a commonwealth; a federal state
♦ 연방의 federal; confederate
■ **영국―** the British Commonwealth of Nations ■ ―**수사국** (美) the Federal Bureau of Investigation (略 FBI) ―**재판소** a federal court ―**정부** a federal government ―**제도** a federal system; federalism ―**준비 은행** (美) the Federal Reserve Bank ―**최고 재판소** the Supreme Court (of the United States) ―**회의** a confederate [federal] council

연배 年輩 〈나이〉 similar age; 〈사람〉 a person of one's age; 《one's》 contemporary; a coeval
♦ 동년배의 of [about] the same age
▶ 그들은 모두 같은 연배다 They are all the same age.
▶ 그는 나와 연배가 비슷합니다 He is about my age.

연백 鉛白 (化) white lead; lead foil
연백분 煉白粉 paste powder
연변 沿邊 the area [country] along 《a road, a river, a railway, a border》
♦ 도로 연변의 찻집 a teahouse by [along] the roadside [wayside] / 철도연변의 집들 houses along a railway (line)

연병 練兵 a military drill; troop training
―**연병하다** drill; have a drill; drill troops ―**장** a drill ground [field]; a parade ground

연보 年報 an annual report [bulletin]; annual returns
연보 年譜 a chronological (personal) history; a chronological record 《of *sb's* career》
연보 捐補 contribution 《to help other》; 〈교회의〉 offering ―**연보하다** contribute 《money》 to 《a fund》; donate; subscribe
■ ―**함** an offertory box **연봇돈** an offering; offertory money

연보라 light purple; lilac; lavender; orchid
연봉 年俸 an annual [a yearly] salary; a yearly stipend
♦ 연봉 10만 달러로 at (a salary of) $100,000 a year
▶ 그는 연봉이 3천만원이다 His salary is [He draws a salary of] thirty million won a year.
▶ 그는 급료를 연봉으로 받는다 He is paid by the year.
■ ―**제** annual [yearly] pay system

연봉 連峯 a mountain range; a range [chain] of mountains ♦ 히말라야[알프스]의 연봉 the peaks of the Himalayas [Alps]

연부 年賦 a yearly [an annual] installment
♦ 3년 연부로 in installments covering [over] a period of three years / 연부로 사다 buy *sth* by [in] yearly installments / 연부로 지급하다 pay 《for a thing》 by yearly installments 《of 200,000 won》
■ ―**금** a yearly installment ―**상환** redemption by [in] yearly installments

연분 緣分 preordained tie; karma relation; predestination; 〈부부의〉 fate to have conjugal relation
♦ 연분이 있으면 if fate so ordains / 희한한 연분으로 by a happy chance / 연분이 없다고 단념하다 give it up as an impossible union / 연분을 맺다 form a connection 《with》 / 부부의 연분을 맺다 tie the nuptial [marriage] knot / 부부의 연분을 끊다 break off conjugal relations
▶ 그 부부는 천생 연분이다 They are made for man and wife. ⇌ They are a well-matched couple.
▶ 연분이 있어서 그 둘은 부부가 되었다 Fate made the two man and wife.

연분홍 軟粉紅 light [soft] pink
연불 延拂 deferred payment ♦ 연불방식으로 on a deferred payment basis ―**수출** deferred-payment export; export on easy-payment term

연비 連比 〔數〕 a continued ratio
연비례 連比例 〔數〕 a continued proportion
연뿌리 蓮― a lotus root
연사 演士 a (public) speaker; an orator; a lecturer ■ **초청―** a guest speaker
연사 撚絲 〈꼬은 실〉 twisted thread [yarn]; twine ―**견**(絹)― twisted silk yarn; thrown silk ■ ―**공** a twister; a throwster ―**기** a twisting machine
연삭 硏削 grinding ■ ―**기** a grinder ―**반** a grinder; a grinding machine ―**숫돌** a grinding stone
연산 年産 a yearly [an annual] production [output] ♦ 자동차의 연산 대수 the annual output of automobiles
▶ 이 공장의 카메라 생산량은 연산 100만대다 This plant produces 1,000,000 cameras a year.
■ ―**능력** annual capacity of production
연산 連山 a range [chain] of mountains; mountain ranges ♦ 남북으로 뻗은 연산 a range of mountains running north and south
연산 演算 〔數〕 operation ♦ 연산을 하다 carry out an operation ―**역―** an inverse operation
■ ―**자** 〔數〕 an operator ―**제어장치** 〔電算〕 an arithmetic and control unit
연상 年上 seniority (in age) ♦ 연상의 아내 a wife older than her husband

▶그는 나보다 세살 연상이다 He is my senior by three years. ⇌ He is three years older than I.
▶누가 연상이냐? Which is older?

연상 聯想 association of ideas
◆연상으로 by association
▶그것을 보자 여러가지 연상이 떠올랐다 An association of ideas welled up [It reminded me of many things] when I saw it.
—**연상하다** remind *sb* of; be reminded of; associate 《A with B》
◆…을 연상시키다 remind *sb* of …; suggest *sth* to *sb's* mind; produce [give *one*] an impression of …; bring up the image of …
▶외국인들은 한국하면 태권도를 연상한다 Foreigners associate [connect] Korea with Taekwondo.
▶이 교향곡은 「랩소디 인 블루」를 연상시킨다 This symphony suggests [is suggestive of] "Rhapsody in Blue".
▶이것을 보면 무엇이 연상되니? What does this remind you of?
■—관념 an associate —검사 a word association test

연서 連署 〈공동 서명〉 a joint signature
◆연서로써 under the joint signature
▶이 서류에는 본인과 보증인의 연서가 필요하다 These papers require the joint signature of a person himself and a guarantor.
—**연서하다** sign jointly; countersign
—인 a cosignatory; a joint signer

연석 宴席 a feast; a banquet
◆연석을 베풀다 hold a banquet; give a dinner party / 연석에 참석하다 attend a banquet / 연석에서 연설하다 speak at a banquet

연석 連席 sitting together; 〈참석〉 attendance; presence
◆…의 연석하에 with…in attendance
—**연석하다** sit [be seated] in a row; attend; be present at ◆회의에 연석하다 sit as a member at a meeting
■—자 attendants; 〈총칭〉 attendance —회의 a joint meeting: 정부·여당 연석회의 a government-ruling party joint conference

연선 沿線 the area along the (railroad) line
◆연선의 along a railway line / 연선의 주민들 the people living along the railroad line / 철도 연선에 있다 be on a railway
▶철도 연선에 시가지가 형성되었다 Towns were built along the railroad line.

연설 演說 a speech; 〈공식적인〉 an address; 〈식사〉 an oration; 〈강연〉 a lecture
◆5분 연설 a five-minute speech / 준비된 연설 a prepared speech / 연설 원고 작성자 a speech writer / 연설조로 말하다 speak in a declamatory [an oratorical] tone / 일장 연설을 하다 make a speech / 연설을 속기하다 take down a speech in shorthand / 연설을 시작하다 open a speech / 아무의 연설을 방해하다 interrupt *sb* in his speech / 연설을 중지시키다 cut short the speaker
▶나는 연설 부탁을 받았다 I was called upon to make a speech.
▶그런 형편없는 연설은 아직 들어본 적이 없다 That was the worst (-delivered) speech I have ever heard.
▶그는 연설을 잘한다[못한다] He is a good [bad] speaker.
—**연설하다** give [make, deliver] a speech; address 《an audience》; speak (in public)
◆대중 앞에서 연설하다 speak at a large gathering [audience] / 라디오와 텔레비전을 통해 국민에게 연설하다 address the nation over radio and television / 원고를 보면서 연설하다 make a speech from [referring to] notes / 즉석 연설하다 improvise a speech; give an impromptu speech
▶국무총리가 개회식에서 연설했다 The prime minister delivered a speech at the opening ceremony.
▶그는 역 앞에서 대중에게 연설했다 He addressed the public in front of the station.
■기조— a keynote address [speech] 선거— a campaign speech 시정— an administrative policy speech 영어— an English speech; a speech in English ■—가 a (public) speaker; an orator —법 elocution; oratory; oration —회 an oratorical [a speech] meeting —회장 a meeting hall

연성 延性 〔物〕 ductility ◆연성의 ductile
연성 軟性 softness; mildness
■—세제 a soft detergent —하감 〔醫〕 a soft chancre; chancroid

연세 年歲 (years of) age ⇨ 나이
◆연세가 높다 be advanced [well up] in years [age]; be old
▶할머니는 연세가 80이시다 My grandmother is eighty years old.

연소 年少 〈어림〉 youth; juvenility
—**연소하다** young; juvenile
◆연소한 독자 a juvenile reader / 연소하다는 이유로 on account of [in consideration of] *one's* minority
▶그는 그 동아리에서 최연소자다 He is the youngest in the group.
■—노동자 a minor worker; a child laborer

연소 延燒 the spread of a fire
◆연소를 막다 check the spread of a fire
▶우리집만 연소를 면했다 Only my house escaped the fire next door.
—**연소하다** spread; burn down by the spreading fire
◆집이 연소되다 have *one's* house burnt by a spreading fire
▶애석하게도 그의 집이 어젯밤에 연소되었다 It's a pity that he had his house burnt by a spreading fire last evening.
▶불은 바람부는 쪽으로 연소했다 The fire spread leeward.
■—가옥 a house burnt by a spreading fire

연소 燃燒 combustion; burning; ignition
▶산소가 없으면 연소는 불가능하다 Nothing can burn without oxygen.
—**연소하다** burn; ignite
■불완전[완전]— imperfect [perfect] combustion: 완전연소장치 a smoke-consumer 자연— spontaneous combustion ■—기 (器) a (gas) burner —물 combustibles; inflammable

articles —성 combustibility; inflammability: 연소성의 combustive; inflammable —시간 burning time —실 a combustor; a combustion chamber; 〈제트엔진의〉 a burner —열 heat of combustion

연소자 年少者 a youth; young people; juniors; 〈미성년자〉 a minor
♦동아리[반]에서 최연소자 the youngest in the group [class]
▶ 연소자 입장 금지 (게시) No admittance to children. ⇌ No minors. ⇌ Adults only.
■—범죄 juvenile delinquency

연속 連續 continuity; succession; continuation; continuance; sequence; a series; a chain
♦실패의 연속 a succession of failures / 연속적인 사건 a chain [series] of events / 연속적인 continuous; successive; consecutive / 24시간 연속의 around-the-clock; round-the-clock / 연속적으로 continuously; continually; consecutively; successively / 2주동안 연속 공연하다 run a show for a fortnight
▶ 그는 두 게임 연속 투구했다 He pitched in two consecutive games.
▶ 그 팀은 2년 연속 우승했다 The team won the championship for two years running.
—연속하다 continue; be continuous
♦연속해서 in succession; one after another
▶ 그 영화는 6개월간 연속해서 상영되었다 The movie had a run of six months [a six-months' run].
■—강연 a series of lectures: 4회 연속 강연 a series of four lectures —경기 〈美〉 doubleheader —극 a serial drama: 일일[주간] 연속극 a daily [weekly] serial drama / 텔레비전 연속극 a television serial —만화 a comic (strip); the funnies —물 a serial: 4회 연속물 a serial in four installments —방송극 a serial radio [television] drama —상영 consecutive [continuative] showing of a film —성 continuity —안타 a barrage of (three) singles —홈런 (two) consecutive homers

연쇄 連鎖 a chain; a link; a series; a connection; 〈유전자의〉 linkage
■—도산 chain reaction bankruptcies —반응 (a) chain reaction: 연쇄 반응을 일으키다 cause [touch off, set off, trigger] a chain reaction —살인 사건 a chain [series] of murder cases —충돌 a chain collision: 어제 고속버스 4대의 연쇄 충돌로 2명이 죽고 20명이 부상을 입었다 Two persons were killed and 20 others injured yesterday in a chain collision of four express buses.

연쇄구균 連鎖球菌 〔植〕 a streptococcus (pl. -cocci)

연쇄점 連鎖店 〈美〉 a chain store; 〈英〉 a multiple shop

연수 年收 an annual [a yearly] income
▶ 그는 연수 2,200만원이다 He draws an annual income of 22,000,000 won.
▶ 그는 연수 3천만원이 못된다 His annual income is less than thirty million won.

연수 年數 (the number of) years; many years
♦그 다리를 완공하는 데 필요한 연수 the number of years to complete the bridge / 연수가 지나다 pass a number of years

연수 延髓 〔라〕〔解〕 the medulla oblongata; bulb (of the spinal cord)
♦연수의 bulbar

연수 軟水 soft water ♦〈경수를〉 연수로 만들다 soften water ■—제 water softener

연수 研修 research study; train; study and training; 〈사원 등의〉 an induction course; in-service training
▶ 사원들에게 월 1회 판매 연수가 실시된다 Training in salesmanship is given to the company staff once a month.
—연수하다 study; master; pursue the study (of)
■—생 a trainee —원 a [an in-service] training institute: 사법 연수원 Judicial Training Institute —제도 the in-service training system

연수정 煙水晶 smoky quartz; cairngorm (stone); morion

연수표 延手票 a postdated check

연숙 鍊熟 dexterity; adroitness; expertness; mastery —연숙하다 trained; skilled; skillful; practiced; expert

연습 演習 1 〈연습(練習)〉 practice; drill; an exercise
▶ 자네에게 필요한 것은 보다 많은 연습일세 What you need is more practice.
—연습하다 practice; carry out exercises
2 〈모의전〉 simulation; a sham fight [〈美〉 battle]; mimic warfare; 〈기동 연습〉 maneuvers
—연습하다 hold [carry out] maneuvers
3 〈대학의〉 a seminar ♦미국 문학 연습 a seminar in American literature
■—방공— an antiair raid drill; air defense maneuvers 사격— rifle [target] practice 영작문— exercises in English composition 예행— a rehearsal; a preliminary exercise : 내일 연극 예행 연습이 있다 We'll have a rehearsal of the play tomorrow. ■—림 an experimental plantation —실 a seminar room

연습 練習 practice; training; a drill; an exercise; 〈경기 전의〉 a warm-up; 〈연극 등의〉 (a) rehearsal
♦연습을 시작하다 go into training / 연습을 쉬다 break training / 연습을 시키다 give sb training / 속셈 연습을 시키다 drill 《students》 in mental arithmetic / 듣기 연습을 하다 train one's ears; practice hearing / 경주에 대비하여 맹연습을 하다 go into hard training for the race; start training hard for the race
▶ 연극 연습은 강당에서 한다 Reheasal of the play will take place in the auditorium.
▶ 너는 연습이 부족하다 You need more practice.
▶ 나는 연습 부족으로 실패하였다 I failed because I didn't practice enough.
▶ 서두르자, 축구 연습에 늦겠다 Let's hurry, or we'll be late for the soccer practice.
▶ 그들은 연극 연습에 바쁘다 They are busy rehearsing for the play.
—연습하다 practice; train; drill; exercise

(*oneself*) 《in》; rehearse
▶바이올린을 연습하다 practice (on [at]) the violin / 학생들에게 영어 발음을 연습시키다 drill students in the pronunciation of English / 수영을 연습하다 exercise *oneself* in swimming
▶선수들은 체육관에서 연습하고 있었다 The players were working out at the gym.
▶연습하면 무엇이나 잘하게 된다 Practice makes perfect.
▶그 팀은 6시간 동안 호되게 연습했다 The team did [had] six hours of grueling practice.
▶그는 조금 연습한 후 발음이 좋아졌다 He improved his pronunciation after a few drills.
■무대— a stage rehearsal 총— a run-through —곡 (樂) an étude, a study —경기 a practice game [match] —기 a trainer; a training plane —량 the amount of practice (*one can put in*) —문제 (do) exercises —비행 a practice (training) flight —생 a student; a trainee —선 a school ship —시합 a practice game —장 an exercise book; a workbook; a drill book —항해 a training [practice] cruise

연승 連勝 straight [successive, consecutive] victories; a series of victories
▶우리 팀은 지금 7연승 행진을 벌이고 있다 Our team is having a seven-game winning streak.
—연승하다 gain [win] consecutive [successive] victories; win victory after victory
◆3연승하다 win three consecutive [successive] victories 《over》 / 연전 연승하다 win every battle [game]
▶다저스 팀은 양키스 팀에게 2연승했다 The Dodgers defeated the Yankees two games in a row.
—단식〈경마의〉perfecta; exacta —복식〈경마의〉quiniela

연시 年始 〈연초〉the beginning of the year; 〈설날〉New Year's Day

연시간 延時間 the total number of hours; the total man-hours ◆연시간 3백 시간 300 man-hours

연식 軟式 nonrigid [soft] type

연실 鳶 a kite string ◆연실을 감다[풀다] reel in [pay out] the kite string

연실 蓮實 〈연의 열매〉a lotus pip

연안 沿岸 the coast; the shore
◆연안의[에] on [along] the coast; coastal / 지중해 연안 지방 the districts along the shore of the Mediterranean / 황해 연안 the coast of the Yellow Sea
▶그 도시는 태평양 연안에 있다 The city is on the Pacific coast.
▶허리케인이 플로리다 연안을 덮쳤다 The hurricane struck the coasts of Florida.
▶내 고향은 강원도의 동해 연안에 있습니다 My hometown lies on the coast of the East Sea in Kan·gwon·do.
■—경비대 the coast guard —무역 coasting trade —선 a coastline —어업 coastal fishery; inshore fishing —지방[평야] a coastal region [plain] —항로 coastal [coastwise] route; coasting service [line] —항해 coastal [coastwise] navigation —항해선 a coasting vessel; a coaster

연애 戀愛 love; amour; affection; a love affair
◆순결한[정신적인] 연애 pure [platonic, spiritual] love / 연애하고 있다 be in love with each other; have an affair 《with》
▶연애는 신성하다 Love is sacred.
▶그녀의 첫 연애는 실패했다 Her first love affair was a failure.
▶그는 그 소녀와 연애중이다 He is in love with the girl.
—연애하다 fall [be] in love 《with》
▶나는 그녀와 연애한 지 2년 되었다 I have been in love with her for two years.
■ 동성— homosexual [unisexual] love; homosexuality; 〈남자의〉 sodomy; 〈여자의〉 lesbian love; lesbianism 삼각— a triangular love affair; a love triangle 자유— free love —결혼 a love marriage: 그는 그녀와 연애 결혼했다 He married her for love. —관 a view [theory, philosophy] of love —대장 a Don Juan; a great lover —사건 a love affair; an amour; a romance —소설 a love story —시 (詩) a love poem —지상주의 love for love's sake —편지 a love letter

연액 年額 an annual sum; a yearly amount
◆연액 2천만원의 이익 an annual profit of [amounting to] twenty million won
▶회비는 연액 12만원이다 The membership fee is 120,000 won a year.
■—보장임금제 the guaranteed annual wage system

연야 連夜 night after night; every night
◆연야의 nightly / 3일동안 연야로 작업하다 work for three consecutive nights

연약 軟弱 weakness; effeminacy; tenderness
—연약하다 tender; mild; 〈지반 등이〉 soft weak; feeble; weak-kneed; delicate; frail
◆연약한 여자의 힘으로 with the weak hands of a woman / 연약해지다 weaken; be enfeebled
▶연약한 여성에게는 그 일이 힘든 일이다 The work is too heavy for a tender woman.
■—외교 weak-kneed diplomacy

연어 鰱魚 〔魚〕 a salmon ◆소금에 절인[훈제] 연어 a salted [smoked] salmon

연역 演繹 deduction (↔ induction); deductive reasoning —연역하다 deduce; evolve
▶그는 이미 알고 있는 원리에서 모르는 진리를 연역한다 He deduces unknown truths from principles already known.
■—법 the deductive method [logic]; deduction

연역적 演繹的 deductive ◆연역적으로 deductively
■—추론 deductive inference [reasoning]

연연 戀戀 attachment 《to, for》; affection
—연연하다 cling to (*one's* position); be ardently [fondly] attached to 《a girl》
◆연연 불망하다 be strongly attached to; pine [long, yearn] 《for》
▶그는 아직도 떠난 여자에게 연연하고 있다 He is still attached to the girl who left him.
▶그는 자기 지위에 연연하는 사람이 아니다 He

is not a man who is reluctant to give up his position [clings to his position].
연예 演藝 a performance; 《dramatic, musical》 entertainments ▶ 만찬 후 연예 공연이 있었다 After dinner there was entertainment.
■ —기자 an entertainments reporter —란 the entertainments column [section]
연예계 演藝界 (men in) the entertainment world [business]; (the world of) show business [(口) biz] ▶ 그녀는 연예계에 뛰어들었다 She entered show business.
연예인 演藝人 a public entertainer; an artiste; a performer; a person in show business; (총칭) showfolk ♦ 인기 연예인 a star [principal] performer [artiste]; (美口) a headliner
연옥 軟玉 〔鑛〕 kidney stone ■ —색 light bluish green
연옥 煉獄 〔가톨릭〕 the purgatory
♦ 연옥의, 연옥에 빠진 purgatorial 《sufferings》/ 연옥의 영혼 souls in purgatory / 연옥의 고통을 겪다 go through the purgatory
연와 煉瓦 〔벽돌〕 (a piece of) brick ♦ 연와조 건물 a brick building; a building in brick
연운 年運 the luck [fortune] of the year
연원 淵源 an origin; a source; a fountainhead ♦ …의 연원을 찾다 trace the origin of...; trace *sth* to its source
▶ 이러한 사회 불안은 실업의 증가에 그 연원이 있다 This social unrest has its origin in [can be traced to] increasing unemployment.
연월일 年月日 a date
♦ 연월일 순으로 (file documents) in order of date; in chronological order / 연월일 없는 undated (letters) / 연월일을 기입하다 date; put the date to (a paper)
연유 煉乳 condensed milk
연유 緣由 〈유래〉 the origin; the root; the source; the derivation;〈사유〉(a) reason; (a) cause; ground(s)
▶ 이런 관습이 생긴 연유를 아십니까？ Do you know how this custom came about?
— **연유하다** originate (in); be derived (from); date back (to); be caused (by)
연음 延音 a prolonged [held] sound
연 의 演 義 〈부연〉 expansion; expatiation; amplification;〈개작〉 a popular version; an adaptation (for popular reading)
— **연의하다** expatiate (on); amplify (on); 〈개작하다〉 adapt (a story) for popular reading
■ **삼국지** — a popular version of the novel *Samgukchi*
연이나 然— however; but; still; and yet; nevertheless; while
연이율 年利率 an annual rate of interest ⇨ 연리
연익 年益 an annual [a yearly] profit; the profit per annum
연인 連印 a joint signature ⇨ 연서
연인 戀人 〈남자〉 a lover;〈여자〉 a love; a sweetheart; (口) a sweetie
♦ 한쌍의 연인 a pair of lovers
▶ 그녀는 내 연인이다 She is my girl.
▶ 그들은 연인 사이다 They love [are in love with] each other.

연인원 延人員 the total number of persons [workers]; the total man-days
♦ 그것은 연인원 10만명이 넘는 대공사였다 It was a huge construction project requiring over 100,000 man-days.
연일 連日 every day; day after [by] day; day in, day out; several days in succession
▶ 연일 내린 비로 둑이 무너졌다 The banks gave way because of the rain day after day.
▶ 우리는 연일 연야 그 문제를 논의했다 We discussed the problem day and night.
연일수 延日數 the total number of days; the total man-days
연임 連任 reappointment;〈재선〉 reelection
— **연임하다** be reappointed; be reelected; resume the office
▶ 은행장에는 민 행장이 연임되었다 Mr. Min has been reappointed president of the bank.
연잇다 連—〈연속하다〉 continue; follow one after another;〈연결하다〉 join together; piece [put] together
♦ 연이어 continuously; successively; in succession / 연이은 불행 a train [series, succession] of misfortunes; the consecutive misfortune / 종이 몇 장을 연잇다 join some pieces of paper together / 연이어 손해를 보다 suffer series of losses; suffer loss upon loss
▶ 우리 야구팀은 연이어 세 경기에서 이겼다 Our baseball team won three successive games.
▶ 8일간 연이어 비가 왔다 It rained for eight successive days.
▶ 집에 손님이 연이었다 We had relays [a constant stream] of visitors [callers].
연잎 蓮— a lotus leaf
연자매 研子— a millstone worked by a horse or an ox ■ **연자맷간** a beastworked mill
연자방아 研子— a millstone worked by a horse or an ox
연작 連作 1 〈작물의〉 repeated cultivation; continuous cropping
— **연작하다** plant (a field) with the same crop over and over [every year]
2 〈작품의〉 a work [novel] written by several writers in collaboration
— **연작하다** produce a work [novel] in collaboration
연작 燕雀 〈제비와 참새〉 swallows and sparrows;〈소인〉 a small-minded [narrow-minded] person
♦ 연작류의 새 a passerine (bird)
▶ 연작이 어찌 홍곡의 뜻을 알랴 Only a hero can understand heroism [a hero].
연장 a tool; an instrument; an implement; a utensil
♦ 농사용 연장 a farm tool; an agricultural tool [implement] / 목수의 연장 a carpenter's kit / 연장 한 벌 a kit; an outfit
■ —궤[통] a toolbox —주머니[자루] a toolbag
연장 年長 seniority ♦ 연장의 older; elder; senior
▶ 그는 나보다 네 살 연장자다 He is four years older than I. ⇌ He is four years my senior. ⇌ He is my senior by four years.

연장

■ —자 a senior; an elder: 집안[일행 중]의 최고 연장자 the oldest man in a family [the party]/ 연장자는 공경해야 한다 Age should be respected.

연장 延長 extension; prolongation; elongation; 〈기한의〉 put-off; postponement
♦ 버스 노선의 연장 the extension of the bus service (into a city)
▶ 이 강은 연장 1천 킬로미터에 이른다 This river extends for 1,000 kilometers.
▶ 대학은 단순히 고등학교의 연장이 아니다 A university is not a mere continuation [extension] of a high school.
—**연장하다** extend; prolong; draw out; lengthen; elongate
♦ 3미터 연장하다 make (a thing) three meter longer; prolong by three meters / 영업시간을 연장하다 extend *one's* business hours / 체류를 일주일간 연장하다 prolong *one's* stay a week
▶ 절찬리에 공연을 일주일간 연장합니다 The performance will be continued another week because it has been so well received.
▶ 나는 그 잡지의 예약 구독을 연장했다 I renewed my subscription to the magazine.
▶ 의약품의 발달은 수명을 연장시켜 주었다 The development of drugs extended the life expectancy.
▶ 지하철이 이 근처까지 연장됩니다 The subway line is going to be extended out this way.
▶ 국회 회기가 이달 말까지 연장되었다 The current National Assembly session was extended until the end of this month.
■ —선 an extension (line); a prolongation; 〈敷〉 a production

연장전 延長戰 an extended game; 〔野〕 an extrainning game ▶ 시합은 연장전으로 들어갔다 The game went [ran] into an extra inning.

연재 連載 serial publication; serialization
♦ 신문에 연재중인 소설 a novel which is now appearing serially in the newspaper
—**연재하다** publish (a novel) serially; give in serial form; serialize
♦ 소설을 연재하다 publish a novel serially [in installments]/ 잡지에 연재되다 be published [appear] serially in a magazine; be serialized in a magazine
▶ 그는 신문에 문예 평론을 연재하고 있다 He is writing a series of articles on literary criticism for a newspaper.
▶ 그 소설은 월간지에 연재되었다 The novel appeared in a series in a monthly magazine.
■ —만화 a serial comic strip; (口) serial comics —소설 a serial novel

연재물 連載物 a serial (story)
♦ 신문[잡지]의 연재물 a serial story in a newspaper [magazine]; a newspaper [magazine] serial / 연재물로서 in serial form; in serials / 연재물을 쓰다 write a serial story

연적 硯滴 a water dropper for preparing ink; a container for (Chinese) ink slab water

연적 戀敵 a rival [corrival] in love; a rival suitor

연전 年前 the other year ♦연전에 some [a few] years ago; a few years back [before]

연전 連戰 a series of battles; successive battles; battle after battle; 〔野〕 consecutive games ♦ 자이언츠와 타이거즈의 3연전 three consecutive games between the Giants and the Tigers
▶ 우리 팀은 먼저 인천에서 3연전을 치른다 First, our team will play three consecutive games in Inchŏn.
—**연전하다** fight a series of battles

연전연승 連戰連勝 a succession [series] of victories
▶ 우리 육군과 해군은 연전연승을 거두었다 There was an unbroken series of victories for our army and navy.
—**연전연승하다** win battle after battle; win [gain] consecutive victories; win every battle *one* fights
▶ 우리편은 연전연승했다 Our side won battle after battle.

연전연패 連戰連敗 a succession [series] of defeats —**연전연패하다** lose [be defeated in] every battle; lose one battle after another; lose battle after battle; lose every battle

연접 連接 connection; junction; combination
—**연접하다** connect; combine; interlock
■ —봉 〔機〕 a connecting rod; (美) a pitman (*pl.* ~s) —부 〔─〕 synapse [sínæps]

연정 戀情 (a feeling of) love; tender passion [feeling] (for, to); attachment
♦ 불타는 연정 a burning passion; an ardent love / 연정을 고백하다 confess *one's* love (to) / 연정을 느끼다 feel attached to (a girl) / 연정을 품다 cherish [have] attachment (for); have a tender passion (to) / 연정에 불타다 burn with love (for)
▶ 연정은 이성과 합치하지 않는다 Love and reason do not go together.

연제 演題 the subject of an address [a speech, a lecture]; the theme
▶ 그는 「언어와 정신」이라는 연제로 연설[강연]했다 He spoke [lectured] on the subject of "Language and Mind".

연좌 連坐 〈앉음〉 sitting down in a row; 〈연루〉 implication; involvement; complicity
—**연좌하다** be implicated [involved] in (the bribery case); sit down in a row
■ —데모 (go) a sit-in [sit-down] demonstration —스트라이크 a sit-down strike —전술 (resort to) sit-down tactics —제도 the guilty-by-association system; the involvement system

연주 演奏 a (musical) performance; rendering; rendition; 〈독주〉 a recital
▶ 내일 그 악단의 연주가 있다 The band will give a concert tomorrow.
▶ 연주 중에는 입장하면 안된다 You may not go inside during the performance.
—**연주하다** play (the piano); perform; give a performance [recital]
♦ 바이올린을 연주하다 play the violin / 피아노로 쇼팽을 연주하다 play Chopin on the piano
▶ 오케스트라는 교향곡 제5번을 연주했다 The

orchestra played [performed] the Fifth Symphony.
■ —곡목 a (musical) program; a repertoire —기술 technical skill; technique —법 execution; interpretation —여행 a recital [concert] tour —자 a player; a performer: 그는 유명한 하프[기타] 연주자다 He is a famous harp player [guitarist].
연주창 連珠瘡 〔韓醫〕 scrofula; the king's evil
연주회 演奏會 a concert; 〈독주〉 a recital
♦ 피아노 연주회 piano recital / 연주회에 가다 go to [attend] a concert
▶ 우리는 올 봄에 연주회를 연다 We are going to give a concert this spring.
연줄 鳶— a kite string ⇨ 연실
연줄 緣— connections; a relation; (口) (a) pull; influence
♦ 좋은 연줄이 있다 have good connections; have a good [strong] pull / 경찰에 연줄이 있다 have a pull with the police
▶ 그 회사에 연줄이 있니? Do you have any pull in that company?
▶ 그가 취직을 한 것은 자기 아버지가 그 회사에 연줄이 있었기 때문이다 He got his job because his father had some influence in that company.
연줄연줄 緣—緣— through one's connections; through one connection after another
▶ 친구의 거처를 연줄연줄 알아보았다 I located [inquired into] my friend's whereabouts through my acquaintances.
연중 年中 the whole year; all times of the year; (all) the year round
♦ 연중 내내 throughout the year; in all seasons (of the year); at any season
▶ 연중 무휴 (게시) Open throughout the year.
▶ 농가는 연중 바쁘다 Farmers are busy all the year round.
♦ 영화관은 연중 무휴다 Movie theaters are open throughout the year.
연중행사 年中行事 (regular) annual events [affairs, functions]; the year's celebrations
▶ 추수 감사절은 미국 사람들의 연중 행사의 하나다 Thanksgiving is one of the year's celebrations [annual events] of American life.
연지 臙脂 rouge; lipstick ♦ 입술에 연지를 바르다 put on lipstick; rouge one's lips
▶ 그녀는 볼에 엷게[진하게] 연지를 발랐다 She slightly [thickly] rouged [put rouge on] her cheeks.
■ —볼 (cheek) rouge ■ —분 rouge and powder; cosmetics —색 red; crimson
연직 鉛直 〈수직〉 perpendicularity; plumb
♦ 연직의 perpendicular; vertical
♦ —면 a vertical plane; a perpendicular —선 a vertical [plumb] line
연진 煙塵 dirt and soot
연차 年次 ♦ 연차의 annual; yearly / 연차적으로 chronologically
■ —계획 a yearly program —보고 an annual report —총회 an annual general meeting —휴가 an annual (paid) holiday
연착 延着 delayed [late] arrival; delay in arrival —연착하다 arrive late; be delayed; be overdue
▶ 그 열차는 폭설로 2시간 연착했다 The train was delayed two hours by a heavy snowfall.
▶ 그 배는 두 시간 연착해서 인천에 도착했다 The ship arrived at Inchŏn two hours late [behind time].
연착륙 軟着陸 a soft landing —연착륙하다 make a soft landing 《on the moon》; soft-land 《on》
연창 —窓 an outer window; a storm window; a shutter
연천하다 年淺— short in age [years, time]; young; not long ▶ 그 회사는 연륜이 아직 연천하다 It is only a short time since the company was founded.
연철 軟鐵 〔冶〕 soft iron
연철 鍊鐵 〔冶〕 wrought iron ■ —로(爐) a puddling furnace; a puddler —법 puddling
연체 延滯 〈지연〉 delay; procrastination; 〈체납〉 arrear —연체하다 be delayed; 〈지불 등이〉 be in arrear(s)
▶ 집세가 두 달 분 연체되어 있다 The rent is two months overdue.
▶ 나는 가스 요금 지불이 연체되었다 I'm behind [late] in paying of my gas bill.
■ —금 (money in) arrears; arrearage; 〈벌금〉 arrearage charge —대출금 outstanding loan [debt]; a loan in arrear —이자 overdue interest; interest for delay —일 days in arrears —자 a person who is in arrears; a delinquent
연체동물 軟體動物 a mollusk; 〈총칭〉 Mollusca
연초 年初 the beginning of the year
♦ 연초에 at the beginning [in the fresh] of the year; early in the next year
연초 煙草 tobacco ⇨ 담배
연출 演出 〈美〉 direction; 〈英〉 production
♦ 연출 김기문 directed [produced] by Mr. Kim Ki-mun —연출하다 direct; produce; stage; represent; present
▶ 이 연극은 유명한 극작가가 연출했다 This play was produced by a famous playwright.
■ —가 a director; 〈英〉 a producer —대본 an acting copy [script] —법 the manner of performance; execution; dramatics; dramaturgy —효과 stage effect
연충 蠕蟲 〔動〕 a worm; 〈기생충〉 a helminth
연타 連打 a barrage of blows
—연타하다 strike [beat, knock] repeatedly; deliver a barrage of blows 《at, against》; rain [shower] blows 《on》; 〈종 등을〉 ring [clang] 《a bell》 repeatedly
연탄 連彈 〔樂〕 a four-hand playing (on the piano) ■ —곡(曲) a piece for four hands
연탄 煙炭 a briquet(te) ♦ 연탄을 갈다 change a briquet
■ —가스(중독) briquet gas (poisoning): 연탄 가스 중독으로 죽다 die from briquet gas poisoning —공장 a briquette manufactory [factory] —난로 a briquet stove —불 briquet fire —재 a used briquet
연통 煙筒 a chimney; 〈난로의〉 a stovepipe; 〈공장의〉 a smokestack; 〈기관차·기선의〉 a funnel ♦ 연통의 갓 a chimney cap
▶ 연통이 막혔다 The stovepipe is choked up.

연투 連投 〔野〕 pitching in successive games
—**연투하다** pitch 《two》 successive games; go on [take] the (pitcher's) mound in 《three》 consecutive games

연파 軟派 1 〈온건파〉 the moderate party; the moderates ♦ 연파 의원 a moderate member **2** 〈문예상의〉 ♦ 연파 작가 a writer of erotic novels **3** 〈신문·잡지의〉 ♦ 연파 기자 a social affairs journalist; a society writer

연파 連破 successive [consecutive] victories
—**연파하다** gain [win, get] 《three》 successive [straight] victories 《over *one's* opponent》
▶ 자이언츠는 다이거스를 연파했다 The Giants won successive victories over the Tigers.

연판 連判 a joint signature [seal]
♦ 연판으로 under joint signature
■ —자 a cosignatory —장 a compact [covenant] under joint signature

연판 鉛版 a stereotype; a stereo 《*pl*. ~s》
♦ 연판을 뜨다 stereotype; make a stereotype of / 연판으로 인쇄하다 stereotype
■ —공(工) a stereotyper —인쇄 stereotypography —인쇄공 a stereotypographer

연패 連敗 successive [consecutive] defeats; a series [succession] of reverses
▶ 우리는 연전 연패의 쓰라린 경험을 했다 We had a bitter experience of losing one game after another.
—**연패하다** suffer [meet with] successive [straight] defeats
♦ 3연패하다 lose three games straight [in a row, in succession]; lose three consecutive games [battles]; be defeated three times in succession

연패 連覇 winning the championship for 《three》 consecutive years
♦ 프로야구 한국 시리즈의 3연패를 달성하다 win three successive Korean pro-baseball championships
—**연패하다** win first place for 《three》 years in a row [for 《three》 straight years]

연평수 延坪數 the total [gross] floor space 《of a building》
▶ 이 집은 연평수가 72평이다 The total floor space of this house is 72 *pyong*.

연표 年表 a chronological table; a chronology
♦ 세계사 연표 a chronological table of world history

연풍 軟風 a gentle [light, soft] breeze [wind]; 〈詩〉 a zephyr

연필 鉛筆 a (lead) pencil
♦ 끝이 뾰족한 연필 a pencil with a sharp point / 끝이 뭉툭한 연필 a pencil with a dull point; a blunt pencil / 연필을 깎다 sharpen a pencil / 연필로 그리다 draw with a pencil / 연필로 쓰다 write in [with a] pencil; pencil (down) / 연필로 선을 긋다 draw a pencil line
▶ 사생에는 무른 연필이 좋다 Soft leads are better for sketching.
▶ 나는 그의 말을 연필로 받아 썼다 I wrote [took] down his words.
■ 몽당— a stubby pencil; a stub 색— a color(ed) pencil: 빨간[파란] 색연필 a red[blue] colored pencil 제도— a drawing pencil ■ —깎

이 a pencil sharpener —끝 a pencil point —뚜껑 a (pencil) point protector —심 the lead of a pencil; (a) pencil lead —토막 a (pencil) stump; a stub —통 a pencil case —화 a picture in pencil; a pencil picture [sketch]; 〈화법〉 pencil drawing

연하 年下 juniority; a junior ♦ 연하의 younger; junior ▶ 그녀는 나보다 2년 연하다 She is two years younger than I (am). ≒ She is my junior by two years.

연하 年賀 the New Year's greetings [wishes]; 〈연하장에서〉 (A) Happy New Year (to you)

|解說| 설날 또는 정초에 신년 인사를 하는 것은 우리 나라의 풍습이며 영·미에서는 크리스마스를 성대히 축하하고, 그때 I wish you a Merry Christmas and a Happy New Year. 라든가 Greetings and sincere good wishes for Christmas and the New Year. 같은 신년을 축하하는 인사장을 친척·친구 등에게 보낸다.

■ —객 a New Year's caller [visitor] —우편 New Year's mail

연하 嚥下 〈꿀꺽 삼킴〉 (the act of) swallowing; deglutition —**연하하다** swallow; gulp down; gorge ■ —물 things swallowed

연하다 連— 〈잇닿다〉 adjoin; be connected (to); range; 〈계속하다〉 continue
▶ 산들이 남북으로 연해 있다 The mountains range north and south.
▶ 한국과 만주는 서로 연해 있다 Korea and Manchuria adjoin each other.
▶ 송림이 눈길 닿는 데까지 길게 연해있다 There is a long stretch of pine groves as far as the eye can reach.

연하다 軟— 1 〈질기지 않다〉 soft; tender
♦ 연한 고기 tender meat / 연해지다 become soft [tender]; soften; go soft / 연하게 하다 soften; make soft [tender]; 〈식육 등을〉 tenderize
2 〈빛깔이〉 light 《color》; mild 《shade》; mellow 《light》
♦ 연한 빛 a light color; a soft [subdued] light / 연한 청색 light [pale] blue (▶pale이 더 연한 의미임)/ 빛깔이 연하다 be light in color / 그림에 연한 색을 칠하다 paint a picture in pale colors / 빛깔을 연하게 하다 lighten the color

-**연하다 然—** 〈체하다〉 pretend to be; act as if 《*one* were...》; pose as
♦ 학자연하는 사람 a pedantic scholar / 대가연하다 put on the airs of an authority

연하장 年賀狀 a New Year's card
♦ 연하장을 보내다 send *sb* a New Year's card [the New Year's greetings]

연한 年限 a period; a term ▶ 연한이 끝났다 The term (of service) has expired [is up].
■ 복무[수업]— a term of service [study] 의무— an obligatory [a compulsory] term of service

연합 聯合 combination; union; confederacy; concert; incorporation; league; 〈정당의〉 coalition; 〈기업의〉 a combine; 〈동맹〉 an alliance;

〔心〕 association
—연합하다 combine 《with》; unite 《with》; merge 《with》; confederate 《with》; league 《with》; ally *oneself* 《with a power》; coalesce 《with a party》
▶ 24개 조합이 새 조직을 결성하기 위해 연합했다 The twenty-four associations united to form a new organization.
▶ 여러 나라가 연합하여 국제연합을 만들었다 Many countries combined to form the United Nations.
▶ 야당이 연합하여 여당을 공격했다 The opposition parties combined together and attacked the government. ⇌ The opposition parties attacked the government in concert.
■ **국제—** the United Nations (略 UN) **—고사** a unified entrance examination **—군** the allied forces; the Allies; the combined forces **—단체** a federation **—작전** combined operations **—전선** a united front : 연합전선을 펴다 present a united front **—함대** a combined fleet

연합국 聯合國 〈1, 2차 대전 때의〉 the Allied Powers [Nations]; the Allies;〈1차 대전 때의〉 the Allied and Associated Powers
■ **—점령군** the Allied Occupation Forces **—총사령부** the General Headquarters of the Allied Powers

연해 沿海 〈육지에 인접한 바다〉 the inshore; the sea along the coast; the coastal waters; 〈바다에 임한 육지〉 the coast
♦ 연해의 coastal; inshore; longshore; littoral
■ **—도시** coast cities [towns] **—무역** coastal [coasting] trade **—선(船)** a coasting vessel; a coastal trader **—어업** inshore [coastal] fishery; longshore fishing

연해 煙害 injury from smoke; smoke damage [pollution]

연해 連— continuously; uninterruptedly; successively; without intermission

연해안 沿海岸 the coast; the shore
■ **—지대** the littoral zone; the coastland **—지방** the districts along the shore

연해주 沿海州 〈시베리아의〉 the Maritime [Littoral] Province of Siberia

연행 連行 taking 《*sb* to the police station》
—연행하다 take [lead, walk, haul, drag] 《a suspect to the police station》
♦ 경찰서로 연행되다 be taken to the police station
▶ 경찰은 용의자를 경찰서로 연행했다 The policeman took the suspect to the police station.

연혁 沿革 the history 《of》;〈변천〉 changes
♦ 방문객에게 학교의 연혁을 설명하다 brief visitors on the school history

연호 年號 the name of an era
▶ 그 해에 연호가 바뀌었다 A new era began that year.
▶ 연호가 태평으로 바뀌었다 The new era was named Tai-Pyung.

연화 軟化 softening; mollification
♦ 골 연화증 softening of the bones
—연화 하 다 become soft; soften; tone down; 〈사람이〉 be mollified; become conciliatory
▶ 과격파의 태도가 크게 연화되었다 The radicals have considerably softened their attitude.

연화 軟貨 soft money; paper money

연화 蓮花·蓮華 a lotus flower
■ **—대** a lotus pedestal 《of a Buddha's image》 **—좌(座)** a lotus position [posture]

연회 宴會 a party; a feast; a banquet; a social dinner; a convivial meeting
♦ 연회를 베풀다 hold a banquet; give a dinner; give [have] a (dinner) party / 연회에 참석하다 attend [join] a party; attend a banquet / 연회석상에서 연설하다 make a speech at a banquet
■ **—장** a banquet hall

연후 然後 ♦ 연후에 after that; afterwards; (and) then

연휴 連休 consecutive holidays; holidays in a row ♦ 징검다리 연휴 a series of holidays with working days in between / 연휴를 즐기다 enjoy straight holidays
▶ 이달에는 4일 연휴가 있다 We have four straight holidays this month.

열 ten; half a score
♦ 열번째 the tenth / 열 사람 ten persons [people, men]/ 열 시 ten o'clock / 열 살 쯤 되는 소년 a boy about ten years old / 하나를 보고 열을 안다 judge the whole by a part; be very clever
▶ 총명한 사람은 하나를 들으면 열을 안다 A word to the wise is enough.
▶ 그 수는 열을 넘지 않는다 They might be counted on the fingers.
▶ 그는 하나에서 열까지 자기 뜻대로 하지 않고는 못 배기는 사람이다 He must have his own way in every particular [all without exception].
▶ 이 영화는 열 번 이상 보았다 I've seen this movie ten times or more.

열 列 〈줄〉 a row; a line;〈층으로 된〉 a tier; 〈세로의〉 a file; a column;〈가로의〉 a rank; 〈행렬〉 a procession;〈차례를 기다리는〉 a queue
♦ 전[후]열 the front [rear] rank [row]/ 2열 횡대[종대] a double line [file]/ 제1[제2]열의 좌석 a seat in the front [second] row / 3열로 in three columns [rows]/ 열을 가로지르다 cross a line; break through a line 《of》 / 열을 지어 서다 stand in line / 2열로 나아가다 advance two abreast [in a double line]/ 일렬로 서다 line up / 열을 정돈하다 dress to ranks / 열에 끼어들다 break into a line [queue] of people 《waiting for a train》
▶ 많은 사람이 극장 앞에 열을 지어 서 있었다 Many people queued up [formed a queue] in front of the theater.
▶ 일열로 서서 기다려라 Wait in (a) row.
▶ 집 네 채가 일열로 서 있었다 Four houses stood in a row.
▶ 군인들이 열을 지어 행진했다 The soldiers marched in ranks [files].
▶ 사내 아이 몇이 열을 이탈했다 A few boys left [dropped out of] the lines.

열 熱 1 〈열기〉 heat; warmth
◆열의 전달 heat transfer [transmission]/ 열의 thermic; thermal / 열을 가하다 apply heat (to); heat / 열을 발산[복사]하다 give off [radiate] heat / 열을 발생하다 generate [produce] heat
▶ 철은 열을 잘 전달한다 Iron transmits heat well.
▶ 검은 천은 흰색 천보다 열을 잘 흡수한다 Black cloth absorbs more heat than white cloth.
2 〈몸의〉 (a) temperature; 〈신열〉 (a) fever; fever heat
◆좀처럼 내리지 않는 열 a lingering fever / 열이 나다 become feverish; develop a fever; come to have fever / 열이 높다 have a high fever [temperature] / 열을 내리게 하다 lower [send down] the temperature; allay [diminish, reduce, bring down] the fever
▶ 열이 올랐다 My fever [temperature] rose.
▶ 열이 좀 있군요 You have a slight fever. ⇌ You are slightly [a little] feverish.
▶ 나는 열이 38도[37도 8분]입니다 My temperature is thirty-eight degrees [thirty-seven point eight].
▶ (열을) 재보니까 열이 있었다 I took my temperature and found that I had a fever [temperature].
▶ 오후만 되면 열이 납니다 I have fever every afternoon.
▶ 환자는 열이 정상으로 내렸다 The patient's temperature has fallen to normal.
▶ 열이 어느 정도 되시죠？ What is your temperature?
▶ 아침에는 열이 없어집니다 The fever leaves me in the morning.
▶ 그녀는 열에 들떠 있다 She is delirious with fever. ⇌ Fever has made her delirious.
3 〈열광·흥분·유행〉 a mania; a craze; a rage; fever; enthusiasm
◆문학열 a craze [mania] for literature / 스포츠열 enthusiasm for sports / 야구열 enthusiasm for baseball; baseball fever / 우표 수집열 a stamp-collecting craze; a rage for stamp collecting / 부동산 투기열 speculation fever on real estate / 열을 올리다 become enthusiatic (about, over, for); (美口) enthuse (about, over); be mad [crazy] (after, over); have a crush (on a girl); lose one's head (over a woman) / 열을 식히다 dampen [chill, cool down] sb's enthusiasm (for)
▶ 게임은 열이 오르기 시작했다 The game heated up.
▶ 그는 점점 이야기에 열을 올리기 시작했다 He was gradually warmed up to his subject.
4 〈정열·열의〉 zeal; ardor; passion; enthusiasm; vehemence
◆열이 없는 연설 a speech lacking [that lacks] fire / 열이 없다 have no enthusiasm (for); show [manifest] no zeal (for); be indifferent (to) / 공부에 열을 안 내다 take little interest in one's school work
▶ 오늘은 어쩐 일인지 일에 열이 나지 않는다 Somehow I don't feel like working today.

▶「그 소설은 정말 재미있어요」라고 그녀는 열을 올려 말했다 "That novel is wonderful", she announced with tremendous enthusiasm.
5 〈기염〉 animation ◆열을 올려 떠들어대다 give rein to one's tongue; tell (a story) in an excited tone (of voice)
6 〈화〉 anger; offense; rage; wrath; passion
◆열이 나다 be offended [provoked] (by); become indignant (at an insult, with sb); get into a passion / 열이 나서 in a fit of anger; in the heat of passion; spurred by anger
열각 劣角 〔數〕 a minor angle
열강 列強 the Great Powers (of the world); the World Powers
열거 列舉 enumeration
—열거하다 enumerate; list (the names) (in a long line); specify; go [run] through the list [catalogue] (of virtues)
▶ 그는 내게 철도 여행의 장점을 일일이 열거했다 He enumerated to me the advantages of traveling by train.
▶ 그런 사건은 일일이 열거할 수도 없다 Such cases are too numerous to mention.
열관리 熱管理 control of heat; heat control
—사 a heat controller
열광 熱狂 wild enthusiasm; frenzy; fanaticism; mania; furor; excitement
—열광하다 be wildly excited (at, over, by); go [get] wild [mad] with excitement (over); be enthusiastic (over)
◆열광한 excited; frantic; mad / 열광하여 with wild [feverish] excitement; madly; wildly; with great enthusiasm / 열광시키다 thrill; excite; enrapture; arouse [excite, stir up] sb's enthusiasm
▶ 열광한 관중들은 일제히 갈채를 보냈다 Excited spectators burst into applause.
▶ 그의 묘기는 팬들을 열광시켰다 His fine play enraptured the fans.
열광적 熱狂的 enthusiastic; wild; mad; frantic
◆열광적인 박수 rapturous [enthusiastic] applause / 열광적인 팬 an ardent fan
▶ 대통령은 열광적인 환영을 받았다 The president was given an enthusiastic welcome.
열국 列國 the powers; the countries [nations] of the world; all countries [nations]
◆유럽 열국 the European powers
열기 列記 enumeration ⇨ 열거(列擧)
열기 熱氣 1 〈더운 공기〉 heat; hot air; 〈열광적인 기분〉 fevered air; a heated atmosphere
◆열기띤 논쟁[토론] heated controversy [discussion] / 열기가 식다 cool down / 열기를 띠다 get [become] heated; become excited
▶ 토론은 열기를 띠었다 The discussion got [grew] heated.
▶ 홀은 열기로 가득했다 The hall was filled with excitement.
2 〈신열〉 feverishness ◆열기가 있다 be a little feverish; have a slight fever
열기관 熱機關 a heat engine; a thermomotor
열 길 물 속은 알아도 한 길 사람의 속은 모른다 (속담) It is hard to fathom the real minds and intentions of men. ⇌ Human nature is unfathomable.

열김 熱— **1** 〈열의 운김〉 fervor; ardor; passion; enthusiasm ◆ 열김에 under the impulse of (strong) passion; in the excess of passion; driven by *one's* emotion ▶ 토론 중 열김에 그렇게 말했다 I spoke like that in the heat of discussion. **2** 〈홧김〉 (a fit of) anger; fume; indignation ▶ 그는 열김에 자리에서 벌떡 일어났다 He started from his seat in indignation.

열나다 熱— **1** 〈몸에〉 become feverish; run a temperature [fever]; come to have fever **2** 〈열중하다〉 become enthusiastic 《about, over, for》; be mad [crazy] 《about, over》 ◆ 돈 벌기에 열나다 be intent on making money **3** 〈화나다〉 get [become, grow] angry ▶ 그녀는 나를 열나게 하는 짓만 한다 She always rubs me (up) the wrong way.

열넷 fourteen ◆ 열네째 the fourteenth

열녀 烈女 a virtuous [chaste, constant] woman; a faithful wife ▶ 열녀는 불사 이부 A woman of virtue marries but once.

열다[1] 〈열매가 맺다〉 〈나무가 주어〉 bear (fruit); produce [bring forth] fruit; fruit; 〈열매가 주어〉 grow 《on a tree》 ◆ 열매가 잘 여는 나무 a fruitful tree; a good bearer / 열매가 열지 않게 된 나무 a tree past bearing / 많이 열다 bear much [abundant] fruit; bear well / 주렁주렁 열다 grow in clusters ▶ 이 나무는 열매가 잘 연다 This tree bears well [a lot of fruit]. ▶ 나무에는 사과가 잔뜩 열려 있었다 The trees were heavily laden with apples. ◆ 돈이 여는 나무는 내게 없다 I've got no bush money grows on.

열다[2] **1** 〈닫힌 것을〉 open; unlock; uncover; 〈뚜껑을〉 lift ◆ 창문을 열다 open a window / 문을 당겨서 [밀어서] 열다 pull [push] a door open / 뚜껑을 열다 lift [take off, undo] the lid [cover] / 문을 홱 열다 swing [fling] a door open / 문을 발로 차서 열다 kick the door open / 문을 억지로 열다 open a door by force; force [burst] a door open / 지레로 상자 뚜껑을 비집어 열다 pry [prize] up the lid of a box; prize a box open; pry the top off a box / 창문을 조금 열어 두다 keep [leave] the window ajar [slightly open] **2** 〈개최하다〉 hold 《a meeting》; give [(美) throw] 《a party》; open 《a conference》 ◆ 만찬회를 열다 give a dinner 《party》 / 무도회를 열다 give a ball [dance] / 운동회를 열다 hold an athletic meeting / 동양화 전시회를 열다 hold [open] an exhibit of oriental pictures ▶ 저 미술관에서는 피카소전이 열리고 있다 That art museum is holding [having] a Picasso exhibition. **3** 〈개시하다〉 open 《a shop》; start [set up] 《a store》; commence ◆ 식당을[사무소를] 열다 open a restaurant [an office] ▶ 그는 강남에 점포를 열었다 He opened a store in Kangnam. ▶ 은행은 9시까지는 열지 않는다 Banks don't open [are closed] till nine. ▶ 그 가게는 7시에 연다 The shop opens at seven. **4** 〈길·계기를〉 clear 《the way for》; open (up) 《a new way》; break 《a road》; make 《way for *sb*》 ◆ 길을 열다 open a road; cut a road 《through》 / 출세 길을 열어 주다 open a way for *sb's* promotion [advancement] / 후진을 위해 길을 열어 주다 give the young fellows [men] a chance; open the way for the promotion of *one's* juniors ▶ 그는 내게 길을 열어 주었다 He made way for me. ▶ 성경은 내게 새로운 세계를 열어 주었다 The Bible opened up a new world to me.

열다섯 fifteen ◆ 열다섯째 the fifteenth

열대 熱帶 the torrid zone; the tropics ◆ 열대의 과실 tropical fruit(s) / 열대의 뜨거운 공기 the hot air of the tropics / 열대의 tropic(al) ■—병 a tropical disease —성 저기압 a tropical depression —식물 a tropical plant; (총칭) tropical flora —야(夜) a sweltering night —어 a tropical fish —조 a tropic bird —지방 the tropics; the tropical regions: 열대 지방에 살다 live in the tropics

열댓 about fifteen; fifteen or so ◆ 열댓 사람 about [some] fifteen people / 열댓 살의 사내아이 a boy about fifteen years old

열도 列島 an archipelago 《*pl.* ~(e)s》; a chain [group] of islands ■ 알류산— the Aleutian Islands

열도 熱度 〈신열의 도수〉 degrees of heat; 〈열심의 정도〉 degree of enthusiasm

열두 가지 재주 가진 놈이 저녁 거리가 없다 (속담) Jack of all trades, and master of none.

열둘 twelve ◆ 열두째 the twelfth

열등 劣等 inferiority; a low grade [class] —열등하다 inferior; low(-grade); of poor [lower] quality ◆ 품질이 열등하다 be of inferior quality ▶ 어떤 면에서는 남자가 여자보다 열등하다 Man is inferior to woman in some respects. ■—생 a backward pupil; a poor student —아(兒) a feeble-headed [feeble-minded] child; a subnormal [an inferior] child —품 an article of inferior quality; low-grade goods

열등감 劣等感 inferiority complex; a sense of inferiority ◆ 열등감을 가지다 have a sense of inferiority; be possessed by inferiority complex ▶ 나는 한때 열등감에 시달리던 때가 있었다 I once suffered from an inferiority complex.

열띠다 熱— 〈서술적〉 get [grow] excited; become heated; (英) hot up ◆ 열띤 경기 hot fighting; a close game / 열띤 논쟁 heated controversy / 열띤 어조로 말하다 speak with fervor ▶ 우리는 그의 열띤 연설에 큰 감명을 받았다 We were very much impressed by his impassioned speech.

열락 悅樂 pleasure; joy; rapture; mirth

열람 閱覽 reading; perusal ▶ 열람 환영[사절] (게시) Inspection free [declined].

—**열람하다** read; look through; peruse
▶ 그 책을 도서관에서 열람할 수 있다 You can look over [through] that book at the library.
■ —권 a library admission ticket —료 a admission fee 《of a library》 —실 a reading room —자 a reader; a visitor —표 a call slip

열량 熱量 the amount of heat; heat [thermal] value; 〈칼로리〉 calorie; calory
♦ 열량이 많은 high-caloried / 열량이 많다[적다] be high [low] in calorie
▶ 그 음식은 1천 칼로리의 열량이 있다 The diet represents a heat value of 1,000 calories.
▶ 물질의 비열이란 그 물질의 온도를 1도 올리는 데 필요한 열량을 말한다 The specific heat of a substance is the amount of heat required to raise its temperature one degree.
■ —계(計) a calorimeter —측정(법) calorimetry

열렬하다 熱烈— ardent; passionate; vehement; fervent; enthusiastic
♦ 열렬한 구애 impassioned wooing / 열렬한 사랑 an ardent [a passionate] love / 열렬한 신앙 lively faith / 열렬한 애국자 an ardent patriot / 금주 운동의 열렬한 지지자 an ardent supporter of the temperance cause / 열렬히 ardently; fervently; vehemently / 열렬한 환영을 받다 be received with great enthusiasm
▶ 그는 타이거즈의 열렬한 팬이다 He is an enthusiastic fan of the Tigers.
▶ 그는 열렬한 음악 애호가다 He is a great fan of music. = He is an ardent lover of music. = He is passionately fond of music.
▶ 그녀는 그 운동을 열렬히 지지하고 있었다 She was an ardent supporter of the movement.
▶ 그녀는 그를 열렬히 사랑했다 She adored him.

열뢰 熱雷 〖氣〗 a heat thunderstorm
열루 熱淚 hot [burning, scalding] tears
열리다¹ 〈문 등이〉 open; be opened
♦ 열려 있는 문 an open door / (문이) 홱 열리다 fly open; be thrown [flung] open / 삐걱하고 열리다 creak open / (문이) 안에서 열리다 open from within / 안으로 열리다 open inward / 열려 있다 be open; 〈빠끔히〉 be (standing) ajar
▶ 문은 매일 아침 9시에 열린다 The gate opens at nine every morning.
▶ 당신 등 뒤의 지퍼가 열렸습니다 The zipper is open on your back. = Your back is unzipped.
▶ 그 대답에 나는 열린 입이 다물어지지 않았다 I was struck dumb by the answer.
▶ 아무리 해도 문이 열리지 않는다 The door will not open.
2 〈개최되다〉 be held; take place; 〈개시되다〉 open; begin; start; commence
♦ —의 주최로 열리다 《a seminar》 be held under the auspices of...
▶ 전시회는 월요일에 열린다 The exhibition opens on Monday.
▶ 김박사의 수상 축하연이 열렸다 A party [dinner] was held [given] to celebrate Dr. Kim's receiving the prize.

3 〈트이다〉 open; be open(ed)
♦ 승진 길이 열리다 the way [door] to promotion is opened; be given a chance to rise (in rank) / 출세 길이 열리다 be given a chance of success in life
▶ 글을 읽을 수 있게 되자 그에게 새로운 세계가 열렸다 The ability to read opened up a new world for him.

열리다² 〈나무가 주어〉 bear (fruit); fruit; be in fruit; 〈열매가 주어〉 grow 《on a tree》
♦ 열매가 잔뜩 열린 나무 a tree laden with [full of] fruit; a tree covered with fruit
▶ 감이 주렁주렁 열려 있었다 Persimmons were growing in clusters (on the tree).
▶ 올해는 복숭아가 많이 열렸으면 좋겠다 I hope the peach trees will bear well [a lot of fruit] this year.
▶ 이 지방에서는 귤이 열리지 않는다 Orange trees won't bear fruit in this area.

열망 熱望 an ardent wish [desire]; a fervent [an eager] hope [aspiration]
—**열망하다** desire earnestly [eagerly]; be eager [anxious] 《for sth》; have a great [an eager] desire 《for sth, to do》; 《俗》 be dying 《for sb, to do》
▶ 그는 명성을 열망했다 He had a fervent aspiration after fame.
▶ 사람들은 그의 복귀를 열망하고 있었다 People were eager [longing] for him to make a comeback.
▶ 전세계 사람들은 평화를 열망하고 있다 People all over the world are eager for peace.

열매 fruit; 〈견과〉 a nut; 〈장과(漿果)〉 a berry
♦ 열매가 잘 열리는 나무 a fruitful tree; a good bearer / 열매가 열리지 않는 fruitless; unfruitful; infructuous; barren / 열매를 열다 bear [produce] fruit / 열매가 잘 열다 fruit well / 열매가 열려 있다 be in bearing / 열매가 익다 [여물다] grow ripe; ripen / 열매를 맺다 bear [produce, bring forth] fruit; (비유) produce a result; come [be brought] to fruition; bear fruit
▶ 두 사람의 사랑이 열매를 맺었다 Their love matured into marriage.

열무 a young radish
■ —김치 young radish *kimchi*

열반 涅槃 1 〖佛敎〗〈해탈〉 Nirvana; salvation; supreme enlightenment ♦ 열반에 들다 enter [pass into] Nirvana; attain Buddhahood
2 〈입적〉 death of a Buddhist priest

열 번 찍어 아니 넘어가는 나무 없다 (속담) The repeated stroke will fell the oak.

열변 熱辯 a fervent [an impassioned, a vehement] speech; passionate [fiery] eloquence
▶ 그는 셰익스피어에 관해 열변을 했다 He delivered a fervent speech on Shakespeare.
▶ 그는 불을 토하는 듯한 열변을 토했다 He made a fiery speech.

열병 閱兵 inspection of troops; a military review; a parade —**열병하다** inspect troops; review (troops); pass troops in review; inspect soldiers at a parade
■ —식 (hold) a review (of troops); (hold) a military review —식장 a parade ground

열병 熱病 a fever; a febrile disease; pyrexia
♦열병에 걸리다 catch [suffer from] a fever
▶그녀는 열병을 앓고 있다 She is sick [ill] with a fever. ⇌ She is ill of fever.

열분해 熱分解 〔化〕 pyrolysis
—열분해하다 pyrolyze

열비 劣比 〔數〕 a minor ratio; a ratio of lesser inequality

열사 烈士 a man of fervid loyalty; a patriot; a hero ■순국— a martyr

열사병 熱射病 〔醫〕 heatstroke; heat prostration [exhaustion] ♦열사병에 걸리다 suffer from [be affected by] heatstroke

열상 裂傷 a laceration; a lacerated wound
▶나는 얼굴[등]에 열상을 입었다 I had my face [back] lacerated. ⇌ My face [back] was lacerated.

열생학 劣生學 〔生〕 dysgenics

열석 列席 attendance ⇨ 출석

열선 熱線 〔物〕 thermic [heat] rays; 〈적외선〉 infrared rays; 〈가열 도선(導線)〉 a hot wire
■—전류계 a hot-wire ammeter

열성 劣性 〈열등〉 inferiority; 〔遺〕 recessive
♦열성의 〔遺〕 recessive; 〔生〕 dysgenic ■—유전 a recessive heredity —형질 a recessive (character)

열성 列聖 〈대대의 임금〉 successive kings; 〈여러 성인〉 a number of saints ■—조(朝) successive reigns

열성 熱誠 earnestness; ardor; zeal; warmth; enthusiasm; fervor; 〈헌신〉 devotion; 〈성실〉 sincerity
♦열성적으로[을 다하여] with zeal [devotion, sincerity]; heart and soul; enthusiastically; devotedly / 열성이 넘치다 overflow with enthusiasm
▶나는 열성어린 환영을 받았다 I was accorded [given] a warm reception [hearty welcome].
▶그 배우는 자기 배역에 열성을 쏟고 있다 The actor throws himself into his roles with fervor.
▶너는 열성이 부족하다 You lack zeal. ⇌ You are lacking in zeal.
▶그는 열성적으로 나라에 이바지했다 He served his country with ardent zeal.
—**열성스럽다** enthusiastic; earnest; ardent; zealous; devoted; sincere
♦열성스러운 교육가 an earnest educationist
■—가 an enthusiast; a devotee; 〈열광자〉 a zealot —분자 earnest [enthusiastic, devoted] elements (of a party)

열세 劣勢 inferiority in strength [numbers]; numerical inferiority
♦열세를 만회하다 rally from an inferior position; regain one's strength / 열세에 있다 be inferior in numbers [strength]
—**열세하다** inferior in numbers [strength]

열셋 thirteen ♦열셋째 the thirteenth

열 손가락 깨물어 안 아픈 손가락 없다 (속담) Every child is dear to his parents.

열쇠 **1** 〈자물쇠를 여는〉 a key
♦여벌의 열쇠 a false [duplicate, skeleton] key; a master key / 현관문[금고] 열쇠 a key to the front door [safe] / 열쇠를 돌리다 turn the key (in a lock); give the key a turn / 열쇠를 자물쇠에 꽂다 fit a key to a lock; put [insert] a key in a lock / 열쇠를 채워두다 keep sth under lock and key
▶그가 천천히 열쇠를 돌리자 문이 삐걱 열렸다 He gave the key a slow turn and the door swung open.
▶열쇠로 열어라 Unlock [Open a lock] with a key.
2 〈단서〉 a key; 〈실마리〉 a clue
♦가로[세로]의 열쇠 〈십자낱말풀이의〉 the across [down] clues / 문제의 열쇠 a key to the question; 〈중요점〉 the clue of the problem / 사건 해결의 열쇠 (hold) the key to the solution of the case / 성공의 열쇠 a key to success
▶그가 이 사건의 열쇠를 쥐고 있다 He holds the key to this affair.
■—고리 a key ring —구멍 a keyhole : 열쇠 구멍으로 들여다 보다 look [peep, spy] through a keyhole —다발 a bunch of keys —제조업자 a keysmith

열심 熱心 enthusiasm; zeal; fervor; ardor; eagerness; earnestness
♦음악[스포츠]에 열심인 사람 a person full of zeal for music [sports]; an enthusiast for music [sports] / 열심이다 be eager (about, for, to do); be intent [keen] (on); be devoted (to); be enthusiastic (about, in)
▶그는 연구에 열심이다 He is intent on [devoted to] his studies. ⇌ He applies himself closely to his studies.
▶그는 스포츠[축구]에 열심이다 He is keen on sports [about soccer].
▶그는 무슨 일에나 열심이기 때문에 아마 크게 성공할 것이다 He is enthusiastic about everything, so he will probably become very successful.

열심히 熱心— eagerly; earnestly; enthusiastically; ardently; warmly; zealously; in (good) earnest; with zeal [ardor]; with (great) keenness
♦열심히 기도하는 사람 a fervent prayer / 열심히 공부하다 study hard; apply oneself closely to one's studies / 학생을 열심히 가르치다 teach student cordially
▶그는 언제나 열심히 일한다 He always works very hard.
▶나는 그의 강연을 열심히 들었다 I listened attentively [intently] to his lectures.
▶나는 열심히 기도를 드렸다 I prayed fervently [with my whole heart].
▶좀더 열심히 해라 Do it with more enthusiasm [zeal].

열십자 —十字 a cross ⇨ 십자(十字)
♦열십자형의 cross-shaped / 열십자로 crosswise / 열십자로 묶다 tie crosswise / 열십자를 긋다 cross oneself; cross one's heart [brow]

열씨 列氏 Reaumur; Réaumur (略 R) ♦열씨 70도 70° [seventy degrees] R ■—온도계 a Réaumur thermometer

열아홉 nineteen ♦열아홉째 the nineteenth

열악하다 劣惡— inferior; poor; coarse; of poor quality

▶열악한 노동 조건에도 불구하고 그는 불평 한 마디 없이 일했다 He worked without the slightest complaint in spite of the poor working conditions.

열애 熱愛 ardent [passionate] love; a strong attachment
―열애하다 love fervently [passionately, ardently]; be passionately in love 《with sb》 ▶그는 그녀를 열애했다 He loved her passionately. ⇒ He was madly in love with her.

열어젖뜨리다 swing [throw] open; open wide
♦문을 열어젖뜨리다 fling a door open

열없다 1 〈부끄럽다〉 awkward; shy; bashful; ill at ease
♦열없게 bashfully; awkwardly / 열없어 하다 be [feel] abashed [shy]; feel small (in company); feel awkward [nervous] 《before an audience》/ 열없이 웃다 grin sheepishly ▶그는 여자 앞에서는 열없어서 말을 못한다 He is shy to speak in front of girls.
2 〈겁이 많다〉 timid; fainthearted; chickenhearted; white-[lily-]livered
♦열없는 사람 a pudding heart; a faintheart; (口) a softy

열에너지 熱― 〔物〕 heat [therma] energy
열여덟 eighteen ♦열여덟째 the eighteenth
열여섯 sixteen ♦열여섯째 the sixteenth
열역학 熱力學 〔物〕 thermodynamics
열연 熱演 an enthusiastic [fervent, impassioned] performance
―열연하다 perform [play] enthusiastically [with fire]; give an impassioned [a spirited] performance
▶그녀는 무대에서 열연했다 She gave a performance with zest on the stage.

열왕기 列王記 〔聖〕 The (Books of) Kings
♦열왕기상[하] The First [Second] Book of the Kings

열용량 熱容量 〔物〕 thermal [heat] capacity
열원 熱源 heat source [reservoir]
열의 熱意 enthusiasm; zeal; ardor; eagerness
♦불타는 열의 fiery zeal / 열의가 있는 zealous; enthusiastic / 열의(가) 없는 unenthusiastic; halfhearted
▶그는 그 일에 대한 열의가 대단하다 He has a great deal of interest [enthusiasm] in the undertaking.
▶그는 그 계획에 큰 열의를 보였다 He showed great enthusiasm for the plan.
▶그들은 대단한 열의를 가지고 그 일을 시작했 다 They started the work with great eagerness.

열이온 熱― 〔物〕 a thermion
■―검파기 a thermionic detector ―관(管) a thermionic tube ―방사(放射) thermionic emission ―전류 a thermionic current

열일곱 seventeen ♦열일곱째 the seventeenth
열자기 熱磁氣 〔物〕 thermomagnetism
■―효과 a thermomagnetic effect

열적다 shy; timid ⇨ 열없다
열전 列傳 a series of biographies
♦위인 열전 the lives of the great men

열전 熱戰 a fierce [hard] fight; 〈경기〉 a hot contest; a close [tough] game; 〈냉전에 대해〉 a hot war
♦열전을 벌이다 put up a hard fight 《with》; run a neck-and-neck race 《with》
▶열전이 벌어지고 있다 A close [An exciting] game is going on.
▶나는 그와 우승컵을 놓고 열전을 벌였다 I had [put up] a hard fight with him for the cup.

열전기 熱電氣 〔物〕 thermoelectricity
♦열전기의 thermoelectric
■―온도계 a thermoelectric thermometer

열전도 熱傳導 heat [thermal] conduction
■―율 heat [thermal] conductivity

열전류 熱電流 a thermoelectric current, a thermocurrent

열전자 熱電子 a thermion; 〔物〕 a thermoelectron; a thermal electron ♦열전자의 thermionic; thermoelectronic
■―관 a thermionic tube ―전류 a thermionic current

열정 劣情 low [animal] passions; carnal desires; licentious impulses; lust
♦열정을 자극하는 소설 a suggestive [lascivious] novel / 열정을 도발하다 excite [inflame] the low passions

열정 熱情 1 〈열중하는 마음〉 passion; fervor; ardor
♦애국의 열정 patriotic ardor / 젊은이의 열정 《burn with》 youthful ardor / 열정적인 passionate
2 ⇨ 정열(情熱)

열중 熱中 absorption; enthusiasm; craze; zeal
―열중하다 become enthusiastic (in, about, over); have a mania [craze, rage] 《for》; have a zeal 《for》; be absorbed [engrossed] 《in》; 〈전념하다〉 devote *oneself* 《to》; give *oneself* up [over] 《to》
♦열중하는 성격의 enthusiastic; ardent; singleminded; concentrative / 공부[놀이]에 열중하 다 be absorbed in *one's* studies [in play] / 독 서에 열중하다 be absorbed [immersed] in reading; pore over a book / 여자에 열중하다 be infatuated with a woman / 음악에 열중하 다 enthuse about [over] music / 자기 일에 열 중하다 go heart and soul into *one's* job; be deep in *one's* work
▶그는 그 계획에 열중했다 He warmed to the plan.
▶그녀는 여성해방운동에 열중해 있다 She is full of enthusiasm for feminism.
▶그는 돈벌이에 열중한 나머지 다른 일은 돌보 지 않는다 He is too intent [bent] on money making to think anything else.
▶그는 무슨 일에나 열중하는 성미다 He goes heart and soul into anything he tries his hand at.

열증 熱症 〔醫〕 a fever (case)
열진 熱震 a violent earthquake
열차 列車 a train; a railroad [《英》 railway] train
♦오후 7시 도착 예정의 목포발 열차 a train from Mokp'o due (to arrive) at 7 p.m. / 오전 9시 출발 서울행 급행열차 the 9 a.m. express (train bound) for Seoul / 10량 편성 열차 a train ten cars long; a train (made up) of ten

cars [coaches] / 열차의 전복을 꾀하다 attempt to wreck a train / 열차를 편성하다 form a train / 열차를 운행하다 run [operate] a train / 열차에 타다 take a train; (美) board a train / 오후 3시 30분 열차로 출발하다 start by the 3:30 p.m. train
▶ 열차의 도착 예정 시간은 오후 8시 30분입니다 The train is due at 8:30 p.m.
▶ 열차가 도착한다[들어온다] The train is in.
▶ 열차가 탈선했다 The train ran off the track.
▶ 역이 가까워지자 열차가 속도를 늦췄다 The train slowed down as it approached the station.
▶ 나는 우연히 그가 열차에 타는[에서 내리는] 것을 보았다 I happened to see him get on [off] a train.
▶ 그는 열차를 잡아탔다[놓쳤다] He caught [missed] the train.
▶ 숙부님은 오후 5시 열차로 부산을 떠나셨다 My uncle left Pusan by the 5 p.m. train.
─급행─ an express [a fast] train 병원─ an ambulance [a hospital] train 보통─ an accommodation [a way, (英) a local] train 상행[하행]─ a train going toward [away from] (Seoul); an up [a down] train 야간─ a night train 여객─ a passenger train 임시[특별]─ a special train : 임시 열차를 편성하다 form [put on] a special train 직행─ a through train 특급─ a limited express (train): 초특급 열차 a super express (train); a bullet train; (俗) a cannonball train 화물─ (美) a freight (train); (英) a goods train ─도둑 a train thief ─도착홈 an arrival platform ─방해 railway obstruction [sabotage] ─사고 a train [railroad] accident ─시간표 a railroad schedule; a railway timetable ─운임표 a railway tariff ─운행 operation of trains; train service ─운행표 a schedule; a diagram : 열차 운행표대로 되지 않았다 The trains are not running on schedule. ─자동 정지 장치 an automatic train stop (略 ATS) ─자동 제어 장치 an automatic train control (略 ATC) ─전화 a train (tele)phone ─집중 제어 장치 a central train control (略 CTC) ─차장 a passenger conductor

열처리 熱處理 heat treatment
─열처리하다 treat with heat; heat-treat
■─공 a heat treatment worker ─장치 a heat treatment equipment

열탕 熱湯 boiling [hot] water
♦ 열탕 소독을 하다 scald (an instrument); disinfect (an instrument) in boiling water / 열탕에 데다 be scalded with boiling water; get a scald from boiling water

열통적다 〈거칠다〉 unmannerly; crude; 〈조심성이 없다〉 imprudent; rough; rude; 〈미련하다〉 dull
♦ 열통적은 말 coarse speech; rough words / 열통적은 사람 a boorish [rude] fellow; an imprudent person / 거동이 열통표다 be rude mannered

열파 熱波 〔氣・物〕 a hot [heat] wave
열패 劣敗 (a) defeat (through one's inferiority); (a) setback ─열패하다 be defeated (through one's inferiority); get bested

열팽창 熱膨脹 〔物・化〕 thermal expansion
■─률[계수] a coefficient of thermal expansion; thermal expansivity

열풍 烈風 a violent [strong, severe] wind; a gale

열풍 熱風 a hot wind [blast]; (a blast of) hot air; 〈사하라 사막의〉 a sirocco (pl. ~s); 〈북아프리카・아라비아 사막의〉 a simoom [simoon]; 〈용광로의〉 a hot blast ■─건조 hot-air drying ─로(爐) a hot stove; a hot blast

열하나 eleven

열하루 〈열한 날〉 eleven days; 〈제11일〉 the eleventh (day) ♦ 3월 열하루 the eleventh of March; March 11th

열학 熱學 〔物〕 thermotics; calorifics

열핵 熱核 thermonuclear
■─반응 thermonuclear reaction ─병기[미사일, 탄두] a thermonuclear weapon [missile, warhead] ─실험[전쟁] a thermonuclear test [war] ─융합[동력] thermonuclear fusion [power] ─폭발 a thermonuclear explosion

열혈 熱血 hot [warm] blood; 〈열정〉 fiery zeal [spirit] ■─남아[한(漢)] a hot-blooded man; a fervent soul

열호 劣弧 〔數〕 a minor [inferior] arc

열화 烈火 a blazing [raging] fire; furious flames ♦ 열화같이 노하다 fire [flare] up; flame [burn, be red] with anger; blaze [flush] with fury
▶ 그 점원의 오만한 태도에 그는 열화가 치밀었다 The arrogant attitude of the clerk made him burn [boil] with anger.

열화학 熱化學 thermochemistry
─자 a thermochemist

열확산 熱擴散 thermal diffusion; thermodiffusion ■─율 thermal diffusivity

열효율 熱效率 〔物〕 thermal efficiency

열흘 〈10일간〉 (for) ten days; 〈제10일〉 the tenth (day)
♦ 열흘도 못 되어 in less than ten days / 매월 열흘에 봉급을 타다 get paid on the tenth of every month
■─날 〈초열흘〉 the tenth day (of the month)

엷다 〈두께가〉 thin
♦ 엷은 종이[담요] thin paper [blanket] / 엷게 눈에 덮인 한라산 Hallasan lightly covered with snow / 엷게 thinly / 엷게 썰다 cut into thin slices; cut (meat) thin; slice (ham)
2 〈빛깔이〉 light (color); light-colored; pale; faint
♦ 엷은 황색 light [pale] yellow / 엷은 색깔로 (paint a picture) in pale colors / 엷게 lightly; faintly / 빛깔이 엷다 be light in color; be of a light color [shade]
3 〈인정이〉 shallow; superficial; shortwitted; shortsighted
♦ 속이 엷은 사람 a shallow [frivolous] fellow

염 殮 washing and clothing the dead ⇨ 염습
염 鹽 salt ⇨ 소금

염가 廉價 a moderate [low, cheap] price
♦ 염가의 low-priced; moderate-priced; cheap (↔dear) / 염가로 at low prices; at a bargain / 염가로 사다 buy (things) cheap [at a

bargain price] / 염가로 팔다 sell (things) cheap [at a moderate price]; 〈재고 정리로〉 clear off; 〈남보다 싸게〉 undersell
■ —판 a cheap [popular] edition (of a book) ■ popular-priced [low-priced] goods
염가판매 廉價販賣 a bargain sale; 〈투매〉 a sacrifice —**염가판매하다** sell cheap; sell at a reduced [low] price
▶ 고본[중고차] 염가판매함 (광고) Secondhand books [cars] sold cheap. ⇒ Bargain-priced used books [cars].
▶ 저 상점에서는 매일 한번씩 염가판매한다 They have a (bargain) sale at that store once a month.
염광 鹽鑛 a salt mine
염교 〔植〕 a scallion; a shallot
염기 鹽基 〔化〕 a base
♦ 염기성의 basic; positive
♦ 유기— an organic base ■—도(度) basicity —류 the bases; the basic group —성 반응 basic reaction —성 산화물 a basic oxide —성암(鑛) a basic rock —성염 a basic salt —성 염료 basic dyestuffs [dyes] —성 탄산염 ceruse —화 basification: 염기화하다 basify
염두 念頭 mind; thought; one's attention
♦ 염두에 두다 give one's mind [a thought] (to); bear [have, keep] sth in mind / 염두에 있다 be in one's thought [mind]; be on one's mind / 염두에 떠오르다 occur to one [one's mind]; come across one's mind; come to mind / 염두에서 떠나지 않다 〈사물이 주어〉 be stamped upon memory; occupy [haunt] one's mind; 〈사람이 주어〉 be unable to forget; cannot put (a matter) out of one's mind
▶ 어디 제품을 염두에 두고 계십니까? What make do you have in mind?
▶ 그런 것은 그의 염두에도 없었다 He gave no thought to it.
▶ 그 걱정이 내 염두에서 사라지지 않는다 The anxiety has been haunting me.
▶ 그런 것은 염두에 두지 마라 Don't think [care] about it. ⇒ Dismiss it from your thought [mind].
▶ 그녀는 가사 같은 것은 염두에도 없었다 She never cared about household affairs [housework].
염라 閻羅 〈염라대왕〉〔佛敎〕 Yama; 〔그神〕 Pluto; the King of Hell; (the Lord of) Hades ■—國 Hades; Hell; the Underworld; the Nether World
염려 念慮 anxiety; concern; fear; solicitude; uneasiness; worry
♦ 염려가 있다[되다] have some fear (for one's future); be apprehensive (of) / 염려가 없다 have no concern (for); have no apprehension [fear] (of) / 염려스럽다 be [feel] uneasy (about); be anxious (about)
▶ 염려 마세요, 다 잘 될 겁니다 Don't worry, everything will be all right.
▶ 지붕이 무너질 염려가 있다 The roof is in danger of collapsing.
▶ 이런 악천후에는 비행기가 연착할 염려가 다분히 있다 In this bad weather, there is a strong possibility of the plane arriving late.

▶ 염려를 끼쳐 드려 죄송합니다 I'm sorry to have caused you so much worry [anxiety].
—**염려하다** be anxious (about, at); feel anxiety [concern]; concern oneself (about); care; fear; apprehend (danger); be apprehensive (of, for); have [feel] misgivings (about)
♦ 건강을 염려하다 feel concern about one's health; fear for [be anxious about] sb's health / 장래를 염려하다 feel some misgivings about the future / 염려할 필요가 없다 there is no need of apprehension; be beyond apprehension
▶ 나는 그의 건강이 염려된다 I feel uneasy [am anxious] about his health.
▶ 우리는 네가 규칙을 위반하지나 않았나 염려된다 We are afraid you may have violated the regulations.
▶ 그 점에 대해서는 염려하지 마십시오 You may put your mind at rest on that point.
▶ 비용에 대해서는 염려하지 마세요 Never mind (about) the expenses.
염료 染料 dyestuffs; dyes; colors
▶ 염료가 좋다[나쁘다] The dye is fast [weak].
♦ 다색(천연)— polygenetic [natural] dyes 염기성[합성, 인조]— basic [synthetic, artificial] dyes 직접— a direct dye ■—工業 the dye industry —製造 dye making [manufacture]
염류 鹽類 salts ♦ 염류의 saline ■—泉(泉) a saline spring; a mineral salt spring
염마 閻魔 ⇨ 염라(閻羅)
염매 廉賣 a bargain [cheap] sale —**염매하다** sell cheap [at low prices]; sell at a bargain ■—價格 a bargain price —競爭 a price war [competition] —市場 a bargain [cheap] market; 〈지하의〉 a bargain basement —品 bargain-priced [low-priced] goods
염모 染毛 hairdyeing ■—劑 a hairdye
염문 艶文 a love letter ⇨ 염서(艶書)
염문 艶聞 (rumor of) a love affair; one's episode of love; a romance
♦ 염문이 있다 be associated with a love affair; have a romance / 염문이 나돌다 be talked about for one's love affair
▶ 그 여자는 염문이 끊이지 않는다 Her love affairs provide constant fuel for the gossip mills.
▶ 그는 염문이 자자하다 His love affair is in everybody's mouth.
염병 染病 typhoid fever ⇨ 장티푸스
염병할 染病— (卑) Go to hell!; Go to the devil!; Curse upon you!; Devil take you!
염분 鹽分 salt; salinity
♦ 염분이 있는 salty; saline / 염분을 다량으로 함유하다 contain much salt / (담수로 만들려고) 바닷물의 염분을 없애다 desalt [desalinate] the seawater
▶ 바닷물에는 염분이 많다 Seawater contains [holds] much salt.
염불 念佛 〔佛敎〕 a Buddhist invocation; a prayer to Amitabha [Amida Buddha]; repetition of the sacred name of Amitabha
—**염불하다** pray [offer prayers] to Amitabha;

chant [say] a prayer to Amitabha; tell [say] one's beads

염산 鹽酸 〔化〕 hydrochloric acid; 〈상품명〉 muriatic acid ■―가스 hydrochloric acid gas ―아닐린 aniline salt ―염 hydrochloride

염색 染色 dyeing ◆염색이 잘 되다[잘 되지 않다] dye well [badly]; be well [badly] dyed ▶그 염색은 바래지 않을겁니다 The dyeing will not go off [fade (out)].
―염색하다 dye
◆다시 염색하다 redye (the clothes); dye again / 빨갛게[여러가지 빛깔로] 염색하다 dye (cloth) red [in multicolor] / 바래지 않게 염색하다 dye fast
■머리― hair dyeing [coloring]: 머리염색약 a hairdye ―공[업자] a dyer ―공장[집] a dyeworks; a dyehouse ―기(機) a dyeing machine [range] ―력 covering [coloring, dyeing] power ―법 (a process of) dyeing; how to dye ―분체(分體) 〔生〕 a chromatid ―사(絲) 〔生〕 a chromonema (pl. -mata) ―통 a dyeing bathtub

염색질 染色質 〔生〕 chromatin; karyotin
■ 비(非)― achromatin 진정(眞正)― euchromatin ―소멸 chromatolysis

염색체 染色體 〔生・遺〕a chromosome
◆염색체의 구성 chromosomal composition (of male and female body cells) / 염색체의 chromosomal 《defect》
■성(性)― a sex chromosome ■―수 the chromosome number (of) ―이상 (a) chromosome aberration ―입자 a chromiole ―지도 a chromosome map

염서 炎暑 intense [extreme, scorching] heat (of summer days)
▶나는 한여름의 염서에는 견딜 수가 없다 I can't stand the hot summer weather. ⇒ The summer heat is unbearable.

염서 艶書 a love letter; 〈프〉 a billet-doux (pl. billets-doux)

염세 厭世 pessimism; world-weariness; weariness of life [the world]
◆염세적인 사상 a pessimistic idea / 염세적(인) pessimistic; world-weary; sick of life
▶그 소설가는 염세적이다 The novelist is pessimistic. ⇒ The novelist has a pessimistic temperament.
▶그는 염세적이 되었다 He got sick of life.
―가 a pessimist ―관 a pessimistic view of life; pessimism ―자살 a suicide from being sick of life: 그는 염세 자살했다 He got sick of life and killed himself. ⇒ He committed suicide from a disgust for existence. ―주의 pessimism ―철학 pessimistic philosophy

염소 a goat ◆염소치는 사람 a goatherd
▶언덕 위에서 염소 한 마리가 매하고 울고 있었다 A goat was bleating on the hill.
■새끼― a kid; a kidling; a goatling; a young goat 숫― he-goat; a billy goat 암― a shegoat; a nanny goat ■―가죽 goatskin; goat leather; 〈구두・장갑용〉 kid: 이것은 염소가죽 장갑입니다 These are kid gloves. ―수염 a goatee ―자리 〔天〕 the Goat; Capricornus

염소 鹽素 〔化〕 chlorine

◆염소의 chlorine; 〈염소를 함유한〉 chlorous / 염소로 소독[살균]하다 chlorinate 《the water》/ 염소와 화합하다[시키다] chlorinate; chloridize
■액체― liquid chlorine ■―가스 chlorine gas ―법 a chlorine method ―소독[살균] chlorination; chlorine disinfection ―수 chlorine water

염소산 鹽素酸 〔化〕 chloric acid
■―나트륨 sodium chlorate ―염 chlorate ―칼륨 potassium chlorate

염소화처리 鹽素化處理 chlorination
■―시설 a chlorination plant

염수 鹽水 brine; salt [saline] water
■―선(選) brine assortment

염습 殮襲 washing and clothing the dead
―염습하다 wash and shroud sb's dead body; prepare [dress] the body for burial

염열 炎熱 extreme [scorching, intense] heat (of summer days) ⇨ 염서(炎暑)

염오하다 厭惡― dislike; detest; abhor; loathe
■염오할 disgusting; loathsome

염원 念願 one's heart's [cherished] desire; one's dearest [heartiest] wish; one's prayer
▶파리에 가서 미술 공부를 하려는 그의 오랜 염원이 이루어졌다 His long-cherished desire to go to Paris for the study of painting was fulfilled.
―염원하다 desire; wish (for); pray (for)
▶그들은 세계평화가 영원히 계속되기를 간절히 염원했다 They prayed with all their hearts for everlasting world peace.

염장 鹽醬 salt and soy sauce; (a) seasoning; spices

염장하다 鹽藏― preserve with salt; salt (away) ◆생선[쇠고기, 돼지고기]을 염장하다 salt fish [beef, pork]
―물[식품] salted foods

염쟁이 殮― a corpse shrouder; 〈장의사〉 a mortician; an undertaker

염전 厭戰 war-weariness ◆염전적인 가요 war-weary mood songs ―염전하다 grow war-weary

염전 鹽田 a salt farm [field]; a salt pan; a saltern ■―화(化) salternization: 염전화하다 salternize

염접하다 trim the edges of cloth [paper]; even up the edges of 《cloth》 by folding

염좌 捻挫 a sprain; a wrench
―염좌하다 sprain (one's ankle); have a sprain (in one's wrist)

염주 念珠 〔佛教〕 a (Buddhist) rosary; (prayer) beads ◆염주를 굴리다[세다] finger [count] one's beads (of a rosary)
2 〔植〕 Job's-tears; tear grass
■―나무 a kind of linden ―알 〈한 개〉 a bead; 〈전체〉 a string of beads; the beads of a rosary: 염주알을 세며 기구하다 tell [say] the beads (of a rosary)

염증 炎症 〔醫〕 (an) inflammation
◆염증성의 질병 an inflammatory disease / 염증을 일으키다 inflame; cause inflammation; 〈환부가 주어〉 become [be] inflamed
▶상처에 염증이 생기지 않도록 조심해라 Be

염증 careful to keep the wound from getting inflamed [infected].
▶이런 상처는 염증을 일으키기 쉽다 Such a wound is apt to get inflamed.

염증 厭症 an aversion; a repugnance
♦염증이 나다 get sick (of); become disgusted (with); be tired (of doing the same things)

염직 染織 ―**염직하다** dye and weave
■―공장 a dyeworks

염천 炎天 1〈몹시 더운 날씨〉 hot [broiling] weather; 〈땡볕〉 the blazing [scorching] sun
♦염천 아래서 걷다 walk in [under] a burning [scorching] sun
▶그는 이 염천 아래 밭에서 일을 하고 있었다 He was working in the fields in this broiling sun [under the scorching sun].
2〈남쪽 하늘〉 the southern sky

염출하다 捻出― 1〈각출하다〉 contrive to raise; manage to make
♦자금을 염출하다 contrive to raise funds / 재원을 염출하다 hit on a new source of revenue
2〈안출하다〉 contrive; devise
♦새로운 채무 변제 방법을 염출하다 work out a new plan for financing one's obligations

염치 廉恥 (have) a sense of shame [honor]
♦염치가 있는 사람 a man of honor / 염치 없는 놈 a shameless fellow / 염치가 있다[없다] have a [no] sense of honor; be alive [lost] to shame / 염치를 알다 be sensible to shame; be (keenly) alive to the feeling of honor / 염치를 중히 여기다 hold honor high / 염치 불구하고 …하다 bear shame to (do); stoop to (do)
▶그 놈은 염치가 없다 He has no sense of shame.
▶그는 염치도 없이 더 달라고 했다 He had the nerve [cheek, impudence] to ask for more. ⇌ He impudently [shamelessly] asked for more.
▶그는 염치라고는 없다 He is dead to all sense of shame. ⇌ He is brazen-faced.

염탐 廉探 spying (upon); making secret observations
―**염탐하다** spy (up)on; spy into (a secret); make secret observations; fell (out); 〈동정을 살피다〉 pry about [into]
♦적정을 염탐하다 spy on [upon] the enemy's movements / 형세를 염탐하다 feel out the situation / 회사의 내부 사정을 염탐하다 investigate the inside affairs of a company
■―꾼 a spy; a secret agent; a scout

염통 the heart ⇨ 심장(心臟)

염하다 殮― wash and shroud sb's dead body ⇨ 염습(~하다)

염호 鹽湖 a salt [saline] lake ⇨ 함수(~호)

염화 鹽化 〔化〕 chloridation; salification
―**염화하다** chloridate; chloridize; salify
■―나트륨 sodium chloride ―물(物) a chloride ―비닐 vinyl chloride; chloroethylene ―수소 hydrogen chloride ―연[납] lead chloride ―은 silver [argentic] chloride ―제이수은 corrosive sublimate; mercuric bichloride; bichloride of mercury ―철 iron chloride ―칼륨 postassium chloride ―칼슘 calcium chloride

엽견 獵犬 a hound ⇨ 사냥개

엽관운동 獵官運動 office hunting [seeking]; place hunting ♦엽관운동을 하는 사람 a place hunter; an office seeker; a spoilsman / 엽관운동을 하다 run [hunt] for office; seek election to an office

엽궐련 葉― a cigar; 〈가늘고 작은 것〉 a cigarillo
♦엽궐련을 물고 with a cigar in one's mouth / 엽궐련을 피우다 smoke a cigar; puff at one's cigar

엽기 獵奇 bizarrerie hunting; grotesquerie hunting
♦엽기적인 살인 사건 a grotesque murder case / 엽기적인 bizarre; bizarrerie-seeking; curiosity-hunting
■―문학 bizarre literature ―소설 a bizarre story [novel] ―심 curiosity ―취미 a taste for [love of] the bizarre

엽기 獵期 the shooting [hunting, open] season ♦사슴은 지금이 엽기이다 Deer are now in season. ▶엽기가 되었다 The shooting season has opened.

엽록소 葉綠素 〔植〕 chlorophyl(l) ♦엽록소의 chlorophyllous

엽록체 葉綠體 〔植〕 chloroplast

엽맥 葉脈 〔植〕 a vein; a nerve ⇨ 잎맥

엽병 葉柄 a leafstalk ⇨ 잎자루

엽상 葉狀 〔植〕 ♦엽상의 leaflike; foliated; foliaceous; foliar; phylloid ■―식물 a thallophyte ―조직 phyllome ―체 a thallus (pl. ~es, -li); a frond; a phyllome

엽색 獵色 philandering; lewdness
■―꾼 a philanderer; a libertine: 그는 아주 엽색꾼이다 He is a real philanderer.

엽서 葉序 〔植〕 a phyllotaxis ⇨ 잎차례

엽서 葉書 〈관제〉 a postal card; (英) a postcard; (美口) a postal

> 解説 영・미에서는 그림엽서 외에는 거의 엽서를 쓰지 않는다. 따라서 **postcard**라고 하면 보통 그림엽서를 가리킨다. 간단한 사신(私信)도 보통 겉봉을 봉한 편지로 한다.

▶나는 그녀에게 엽서를 보냈다 I sent a postcard to her.
▶내가 그에게 엽서로 그 일을 알려 주어야겠다 I will inform him of it by postcard.
▶그녀는 엽서로 회답을 보내왔다 She answered by postcard.
■―그림― a picture [an illustrated] postal card [postcard] ―반신용― a reply (postal) card ―봉함― a letter card ―왕복― a return postal card [postcard]

엽전 葉錢 a Korean brass coin (with a square hole in the middle)

엽조 獵鳥 a game bird; (총칭) (winged) game

엽차 葉茶 coarse (green) tea

엽초 葉草 leaf tobacco =잎담배

엽총 獵銃 a hunting gun; a shotgun; 〈새잡이용〉 a fowling piece

엿¹ 〈식물〉 taffy; (英) toffee
♦엿을 빨다 suck taffy
■―가래 a stick of taffy [(英) toffee] ―물

엿² 〈여섯〉 six ◆엿 말 six *mal*

엿기름 dried barley sprouts; germ barley; (barley) ◆엿기름을 만들다 malt ■—가루 powdered malt —물 mash

엿듣다 eavesdrop 《on *sb* [*sth*]》; overhear; listen secretly 《to》
◆엿듣는 사람 an eavesdropper / 남의 이야기를 엿듣다 eavesdrop on the conversation; overhear another's talk / 문에 서서 엿듣다 eavesdrop at the door / 전화를 엿듣다 tap the wires; listen in on *sb's* telephone conversation
▶엿보거나 엿들어서는 안된다 You must not peep or eavesdrop.
▶나는 우연히 그들의 이야기를 엿들었다 I accidentally overheard their conversation [what they were saying].

엿보다 1 〈훔쳐보다〉 steal a glance at; look furtively at; watch *sb* with a furtive eye; 〈들여다보다〉 peep into [through]; 〈살피다〉 spy on
◆안색[눈치]을 엿보다 study *sb's* face furtively / 형세를 엿보다 wait and see how the wind blows [lies] / 틈새로 엿보다 peep through a crack [crevice]
2 〈때를 노리다〉 watch [wait] for 《a chance》
◆도망갈 기회를 엿보다 watch for an opportunity to run away
▶그는 반격할 기회를 엿보고 있었다 He was looking for a chance to counterattack.

엿새 six days; 〈엿샛날〉 the sixth (day) (of a month)

엿장수 a taffy seller [vendor] ◆엿장수 마음대로 at *one's* convenience; as *one* pleases; arbitrarily

엿치기 a taffy-breaking game —**엿치기하다** play a taffy-breaking game

영¹ (straw) thatch ⇨ 이엉

영² 〈밝은 기운〉 a clean bright atmosphere 《in a house [room]》 ◆영이 돌다 have a clean bright atmosphere about it

영 令 〈명령〉 an order; a command; 〈법령〉 an ordinance; a law
◆영을 내리다 order; command; dictate; issue a decree; promulgate a law / 영을 거역하다 disobey [protest against] *sb's* order
2 ⇨ 약령(藥令)

영 零 zero; naught; nought; nothing; a cipher
▶우리는 그 시합에서 2대 0으로 이겼다[졌다] We won [lost] the game by the score [at the score] of 2 to zero.
▶3에 영을 곱하면 영이다 Multiply three by nothing, and the result is nothing.

영 嶺 a (mountain) pass; a ridge; a high hill

영 靈 〈신령〉 a divine spirit; 〈영혼〉 the spirit; the soul ◆영의 생활 the spiritual life / 영과 육(肉) the spirit and the flesh / 죽은 사람의 영을 모시다 worship the soul of a dead person

영가 靈歌 a spiritual ■흑인— a Negro spiritual

영감 令監 1 〈존칭〉 lord; sir
2 〈늙은이〉 an old man; an elderly man
◆고집쟁이 영감 an old diehard
3 〈남편〉 *one's* husband ▶여보, 영감 Dear. ⇌ Darling. ⇌ My dear [darling].

영감 靈感 (an) inspiration; 〈시인·예언가의〉 afflatus; 〔心〕〈초감각적 지각〉 extrasensory perception (略 ESP)
▶그는 자연으로부터 영감을 받았다 He was inspired by nature. ⇌ He drew his inspiration from nature.
▶나는 산속에서 갑자기 영감이 떠올랐다 I had a sudden inspiration in the mountain. ⇌ An inspiration burst upon me in the mountain.

영걸 英傑 〈사람〉 a great man; a hero; a mastermind; 〈기상〉 heroic qualities [character]

영검 靈— divine response [answer] to *one's* prayer; a miracle; miraculous virtue
—**영검하다[스럽다]** wonder-working; all-powerful; magical [miraculous] in its effect; wonderfully efficacious
◆영검스러운 약 a medicine of marvelous efficacy [sovereign virtue]

영겁 永劫 eternity; perpetuity ⇨ 영원
◆영겁 불변의 eternal; everlasting; immutable ■—회귀(回歸) Eternal Recurrence

영결 永訣 the last [final] parting [farewell]; separation by death —**영결하다** part forever; bid *one's* farewell to the dead; pay *one's* last respects to the deceased
■—식 a funeral ceremony [service]; the ceremony of bidding farewell to the deceased

영계 —鷄 a spring chicken; 〔農〕 a broiler
■—백숙 a boiled chicken

영계 靈界 〈정신계〉 the spiritual [psychical] world [sphere]; 〈영혼의 세계〉 the world of the spirit [soul]
◆영계의 현상 a spiritual [psychic] phenomenon / 영계와 교신하다 communicate with the world of the spirit

영고(성쇠) 榮枯(盛衰) prosperity and decline; rise and fall; ups and downs of life; the vicissitudes of fortune
▶영고성쇠는 인간 상사다 A man's life has its ups and downs. ⇌ Human life has many vicissitudes [ups and downs]. ⇌ In all human things there is a rise and a fall.

영공 領空 〔地〕 territorial air; airspace
▶국적 불명기가 우리나라의 영공을 비행하고 있다 An unidentified plane is flying over our territory.
▶국적불명의 제트 전투기가 한국의 영공을 침범했다 A jet fighter of unknown nationality violated [invaded] Korea's territorial sky [airspace].
■—권 aerial domain —침범 the violation of the territorial sky; an intrusion of 《a country's》 airspace

영관 領官 〈육군〉〈총칭〉 a field officer; a major (소령); a lieutenant colonel (중령); a colonel (대령); 〈해군〉 a captain (대령); a commander (중령); a lieutenant commander (소령)
■—급 the field grade: 영관급 장교 a field grade officer

영관 榮冠 the crown (of glory); the garland; the laurels; the palm

영광

♦승리의 영관을 쓰다 be crowned with victory; win [gain] the laurels; gain [carry away] the garland

영광 榮光 a glory; an honor
♦신의 영광 the glory of God / 신의 영광을 찬미하다 glorify God / 분에 넘치는 영광을 얻다 receive undeserved honor / 승리의 영광으로 빛나다 win a great [glorious] victory / 영광으로 여기다 feel honored
▶ 영광입니다 I am honored. ⇌ You do me proud.
▶ 분에 넘치는 영광입니다 The honor is more than I deserve.
▶ 와주셔서 영광입니다 I take your visit as a great honor.
▶ 이 모임에서 여러분께 말씀드리게 된 것을 영광으로 생각합니다 I esteem it a great honor to address you at this meeting.
—**영광스럽다** glorious; honorable; honored
♦영광스러운 역사 a glorious history / 영광스럽게도 …하다 have the honor of doing…; have the pleasure [honor] to do…

영구 永久 permanence; perpetuity; eternity
♦ 영구적 lasting; permanent / 반영구적인 semipermanent 《equipment》 / 영구 불변의 everlasting / 영구 불변하다 remain unchanged forever
—**영구하다** permanent; perpetual; eternal; lasting; everlasting
♦영구히 eternally; permanently; perpetually; forever; for good (and all); (美俗) for keeps
■ 一성 permanency 一연금 a permanence annuity 一운동 〔物〕 a perpetual motion 一자석 a permanent magnet 一치〔齒〕 a permanent tooth; the second teeth

영구 靈柩 a coffin; (美) a casket ■ 一차 a (motor) hearse; a funeral car [coach]

영국 英國 〈나라 이름〉 England; Britain; Great Britain; 〈공식명〉 the United Kingdom of Great Britain and Northern Ireland (略 U.K.)

> 解說 *England*는 본래 대(大)브리튼 섬에서 Scotland와 Wales를 제외한 부분이지만, 영국 전체의 의미로도 쓰인다. England, Scotland, Wales를 총칭하여 *Great Britain*이라고 한다. 여기에 북아일랜드를 포함한 공식명이 *the United Kingdom of Great Britain and Northern Ireland*이며, 그 약칭이 *U.K.* 그 밖에 the Commonwealth (of Nations) (영연방), the British Empire (대영제국—영국 본토 및 자치령과 보호령을 포함하는 영연방의 옛이름), the British Isles (영국 제도) 등의 명칭이 있다.

♦영국의 English; British; Britannic; Anglican / 영국제의 English-made; of English make; made in England
■ 一공군 the Royal Air Force (略 R.A.F.) 一국교회 the Church of England; the Anglican Church 一국기 the Union Flag; the Union Jack 一국민 a British subject; a British national 一국왕[여왕] the King [Queen] of England 一군인 a British soldier; 〈별명〉 a Tommy; Tommy Atkins 一사람 ⇨ 영국인 一정부 the British Government; H.M.'s Government; Whitehall; Downing Street: 영국정부의 호평을 받다 find favor in Downing Street 一톤 a British ton; a gross [long] ton 一해협 the English Channel 一황태자 the Prince of Wales

영국인 英國人 an Englishman; 〈여자〉 an Englishwoman; 〈본국인〉 a Britisher; 〈대브리튼 사람〉 a Briton; 〈별명〉 John Bull; (총칭) the English; the British
■ 一기질 Anglo-Saxonism; John Bullism

영국풍 英國風 Anglicism; Britishism; (美) Briticism ♦영국풍으로 하다 Anglicize

영군 英軍 the British forces

영금 〈곤욕〉 (a) bitter humiliation
♦영금을 당하다 undergo bitter humiliation; be much humiliated; feel much insulted

영남 嶺南 the Yŏngnam district [area]; the Kyŏngsang-do provinces; the southeastern part [section] of Korea

영내 領內 ♦한국의 영내에 within Korean territory

영내 營內 〈병영의 안〉 inside barracks ♦영내 생활을 하다 live in barracks ■ 一거주 living in barracks 一근무 service in barracks 一생활 a barrack life

영년 永年 many years; a long time ♦영년에 걸쳐 for many years 一근속 continuous service for many years 一근속자 a longtime worker [employee] 一변화 〔地〕 long period change; secular change

영농 營農 agricultural [farm] management; farming ♦영농의 기계화 agricultural mechanization; mechanization of farming
一영농하다 farm; manage farmland
■ 一가 an agriculturalist; a farmer 一자금 a farming fund

영단 英斷 〈결단〉 a wise and prompt decision; a decisive judgment; 〈조치〉 a drastic measure [step]
▶ 대통령은 영단을 내렸다 The president took drastic steps [measures].
▶ 당신의 영단을 기대합니다 The decision rests with you. ⇌ It's up to you to decide.

영단 營團 a corporation; a management foundation ■ 一주택 the Housing Corporation

영달 榮達 distinction; advancement (in life)
▶ 그는 한평생 일신의 영달만을 꿈꾸었다 He only dreamed all his life of distinguishing himself.
▶ 지금 나는 일신의 영달 따위를 생각할 여유가 없다 I have no time to be concerned with my own personal advancement.

영대차지 永代借地 a perpetual leasehold; 〔英法〕 a fee farm ■ 一권 a perpetual lease; a lease in perpetuity 一인 a perpetual leasee; a life tenant

영도 零度 〈도수 기점〉 zero; the zero point; 〈어는점〉 the freezing point
♦영도 이하의 날씨 sub-zero weather / 영도 이하의 온도 a sub-zero temperature / 영도 이상이 되다 rise above zero / 영도 이하로 내려가다 fall below zero
■ 一절대— 〔物〕 the absolute zero degree [point]

영도 領導 leading; lead; guidance; direction
♦…의 영도하에 under the leadership [guidance, direction] of... / 영도적 역할을 하다 play the part of the leader; take the lead; play a leading part [role] 《in》
—영도하다 lead; take the lead; guide; direct
■—력 the capacity as a leader; leadership
—자 a leader; the mentor of a group

영동 嶺東 the Yŏngdong district [area]; the Kang-won-do provinces

영락 零落 ruin; downfall
▶나는 영락은 했지만 그래도 염치는 안다 I have fallen pretty low, but still I am a man of honor.
—영락하다 be ruined; get shabby; go downhill; go to ruin; sink [come] down in the world; sink in *one's* fortunes; be reduced to poverty
♦거지로 영락하다 be reduced to beggary / 영락한 생활을 하다 live a wretched life; live in poverty; be down and out; be down at heel

영락없다 零落— invariably right; infallible; unfailing; quite free from mistakes [errors]
♦영락없는 서울내기 Seoulite to the core / 영락없이 without fail; without any slip; infallibly; surely; for sure
▶너는 영락없는 거지 꼴이구나 You look like a beggar, every inch of you.

영령 英領 〈영국 영토〉 (a) British territory; 〈직할식민지〉a crown colony ▶지브롤터는 영령이다 Gibraltar is British territory.

영령 英靈 the spirit of the departed [deceased]《war heroes》▶영령이여, 고이 잠드소서 May your noble soul rest in peace!
■호국— the spirits of the fallen patriots

영롱하다 玲瓏— brilliant; clear and bright; translucent; lucid ♦영롱한 구슬 a bright gem / 영롱한 문체 a crystal-clear style / 영롱한 아침 이슬 a translucent morning dew

영리 營利 moneymaking; profit; gain
♦비영리적인 단체 a nonprofit organization / 영리적인 profit-making; money-making / 영리를 도모하지 않고 without any thought of gain [profit] / 영리에 급급하다 be bent solely upon profit
▶나는 영리만을 목적으로 사업을 하고 있는 것이 아니다 I am not in business only for commercial gain.
▶그는 영리를 전연 생각지 않는다 He has no thought of gain.
■—법인 a profit-making corporation; a juridical person established for profit —사업 a profit-making enterprise; an undertaking for profit; a commercial enterprise —자본 lucrative capital —주의 commercialism

영리하다 怜悧— bright; clever; intelligent; wise; brainy; sensible; smart
♦영리한 아이 a bright child / 영리한 체하는 사람 a knowing chap / 영리한 체하다 try to appear smart / 영리해 보이다 look brainy [intelligent, smart]; have an intelligent face
▶그는 영리하게 생겼다 He looks intelligent.
▶그는 영리한 사람이다 He has lots of brains. ⇒ He is a sensible man.
▶개는 영리한 동물이다 The dog is a clever [smart] animal.
▶그는 때로 너무 영리해서 탈이다 His cleverness often overshoots itself.

영림 營林 forest management [administration]; forestry; 〈식림〉 afforestation; reforestation ■—서 a local forestry office

영마루 嶺— the top of a (mountain) pass

영매 靈媒 a (spiritualistic) medium《pl. ~s, -dia》

영매하다 英邁— wise and great; brave and sagacious ♦영매한 군주 an illustrious sovereign [lord]

영면 永眠 eternal sleep [rest]; death
▶스위스가 그의 영면의 땅이 되었다 Switzerland was [became] his final resting place.
—영면하다 pass away; die; sleep *one's* final sleep; take *one's* last sleep

영명 令名 a fair name; good repute; (a) reputation; fame
▶그는 숙련된 외과의로서 영명이 높다 He has a high reputation as a skillful surgeon.
▶그는 지휘자로서 영명을 떨치고 있다 He is well-known [distinguished] as a conductor.

영명하다 英明— perspicacious; sagacious; clear-sighted; clearheaded; intelligent; wise

영묘 靈廟 a mausoleum《pl. ~s, -lea》; a tomb

영묘하다 靈妙— miraculous; mysterious; inexplicable; exquisite; ethereal
♦영묘한 아름다운 ethereal beauty / 영묘한 피리 소리 an exquisite [a heavenly] note from a flute
▶그 비행 물체는 영묘한 빛을 발산했다 The flying object sent out inexplicable light.

영문 〈까닭〉(a) reason; (a) cause; ground; the matter; the case; 〈형편〉circumstances; the situation; the state of things [affairs, matters]
♦영문 모를 살인 a wanton murder / 무슨 영문인지 모르지만 for some unknown reason; for no reason that could be discovered / 영문을 캐묻다 inquire into the circumstances
▶어떻게 된 일인지 영문을 모르겠다 There is neither rhyme nor reason about it.
▶나는 무슨 영문인지도 모르고 그를 따라갔다 I followed him, not knowing exactly why.
▶그는 필시 처음부터 영문을 알고 있었을 것이다 It is certain that he was in the secret from the beginning.

영문 英文 English (writing); an English sentence
♦영문을 잘 쓰다 write English well; be a good writer of English / 영문으로 읽다 read 《a story》in English / 영문으로 쓰다 write《a letter》in English
▶다음 영문을 번역하시오 Put [Translate] the following English sentences into Korean.
■—국역 (an) English-Korean translation; translation from English into Korean —기자 a writer of English on the editorial staff —소설 an English novel; a novel [story] in English —타이피스트 a typist in English —타자 English typewriting —편지 an English letter; a letter in English —해석 construing English

영문 營門 〈병영의 문〉 a barrack [camp] gate
영문법 英文法 English grammar ■—책 an English grammar book
영문학 英文學 English literature
  ◆영문학을 전공하다 specialize [(美) major] in English literature
  ■—과 〈전공과목〉 the English literature course; 〈학부〉 the department of English literature —사 a history of English literature —자 a scholar in [of] English literature
영물 靈物 a spiritual being; 〈영리한 짐승〉 a very intelligent animal ■—학 pneumatology
영미 英美 England and America; Britain and the United States ◆영미의 English [British] and American; Anglo-American
  ■—법 Anglo-American law —인 the British [English] and the Americans
영민하다 英敏— bright; intelligent; clear-headed; sagacious ◆영민한 두뇌 a clear head; a keen intellect / 머리가 영민한 사람 a nimble-witted person
영바람 high spirits; exhilaration; elation
  ◆영바람이 나서 in high spirits; in fine [good] feather; exultantly; triumphantly / 영바람이 나다 be exulted [elated, exhilarated]
영법 泳法 a style of swimming; a swimming style [form, stroke]
영법 英法 the English law
영별 the last parting [farewell]
  ◆영별을 고하다 bid one's last farewell (to) —영별하다 part forever; part never to meet again; be parted from sb forever
영봉 零封 〈완봉〉 a shutout —영봉하다 shut out
  ▶그 신인 투수는 자이언츠를 4대 0으로 영봉했다 The rookie pitched a 4–0 shutout win over the Giants.
영봉 靈峰 a sacred [hallowed] mountain
영부인 令夫人 〈남의 부인〉 your [his] wife
  ▶홍박사와 영부인이 그 식전에 참석했다 Dr. and Mrs. Hong attended the ceremony.
영불 英佛 England [Britain] and France
  ◆영불의 Anglo-French
영빈관 迎賓館 a reception hall; a guest house
영사 映寫 projection —영사하다 project [throw] 《a picture》 on a screen
  ▶8밀리미터 짜리 필름을 영사합시다 Let's project the 8 mm film on the screen.
  ■—기 a (movie) projector; a cineprojector; a cinematograph —기사 a projectionist; an operator —막 a screen —시간 the running time for a film: 이 뉴스 영화의 영사 시간은 20분이다 This newsreel runs for twenty minutes. —실 a projection room [booth]; the booth
영사 領事 a consul; a consular representative
  ◆봄베이 주재 한국 영사 the Korean consul at Bombay
  ■대리— an acting consul 명예— an honorary consul 부— a vice-consul 총— a consul general —관 a consulate —관원 a consular attaché; (총칭) the staff of a consulate —(증명)송장(送狀) 〔商〕 a consular invoice
영산 靈山 a holy mountain
영상 映像 〈TV 등의〉 a picture; an image; 〈수면·거울에 비치는〉 a reflection 《in the mirror》; 〈그림자〉 a shadow; a silhouette
  ◆흐린 영상 a blurred image; a picture out of focus / 레이더에 비치는 영상 a blip on the radar screen
  ▶텔레비전의 영상이 흐리다 The picture on the TV screen is blurred [out of focus].
  ■—디자인 silhouette design —주파수 a image frequency
영상 零上 above zero ◆영상 8도 eight degrees above zero
영생 永生 eternal life; immortality
  —영생하다 live eternally; enjoy immortality
영생이 〔植〕 peppermint ⇨ 박하
영서 英書 an English book
영선 營繕 building and repairs —영선하다 build and repair ■—과(科) a building and repairs section —비 building and repairing expenses
영성 靈性 divine nature; divinity; spirituality
영성체 領聖體 〔가톨릭〕 (Holy) Communion
  ■—송(頌) Communion; communion hymn
영세 永世 all ages; all generations; eternity; permanence ◆영세토록 forever; to all ages; through all eternity; eternally; permanently
  ■—중립국 the permanent neutral state
영세 領洗 〔가톨릭〕 baptism ⇨ 세례
영세 零細 being paltry [petty]
  —영세하다 trifling; small; paltry; petty
  ▶이 부근에는 영세한 공장이 많다 There are many small factories in this neighborhood.
  ▶우리는 자금이 영세해서 그들과 경쟁이 되지 않는다 Having only small funds we cannot compete with them.
  ■—기업 a small business —농[농가, 농민] a petty farmer —어민 a poorly-equipped fisherman —업자 a small-scale businessman
영세민 零細民 a needy [destitute] person; a poverty-stricken [poverty-ridden] person; (총칭) the destitute [indigent]; the poor [needy]
  ◆영세민을 돕다 relieve the poor [destitute]; give aid to the poor (and needy)
  ■도시— the low-income citizens
영세불망 永世不忘 everlasting remembrance; eternal gratitude —영세불망하다 remember [bear in mind] forever
영세중립 永世中立 permanent neutrality
  ■—국 a permanently neutral country [state]
영속 永續 permanency; perpetuity; perpetuation; long continuance [duration]
  ◆영속적인 lasting; everlasting; permanent; perpetual; continual
  —영속하다 last [endure] long; remain permanently; continue forever
  ▶양국의 우호관계는 영속하지 않았다 The friendly ties between the two nations were short-lived [did not last long].
영속성 永續性 perpetuity; permanence; permanency
  ◆영속성이 있는 lasting; permanent; of long standing / 영속성이 없는 not lasting; transient; of short duration
  ▶이 사업은 영속성이 없다 This business will not last [prosper] long.

영손 令孫 your [his, her] grandson [grandchild]

영솔 領率 〈거느림〉 commanding; leading; directing —**영솔하다** command; lead; direct
♦K장군이 영솔하는 군대 the army under the command of General K

영송 迎送 meeting and farewell —**영송하다** welcome [meet] and see [send] off

영수 領收・領受 receipt
▶영수필(畢)(표시) Received. ⇌ Paid.
—**영수하다** receive
▶일금 백만원을 정히 영수했습니다 I certainly received [acknowledge receipt of] (the sum of) one million won. ⇌ 〈증서에〉 Received (from [of] Mr. Kim) the sum of ₩1,000,000.
■—**인** a receiver; a recipient

영수 領袖 a leader; a chief; a boss
♦정당의 영수 a leader of a political party; a political [party] leader; a boss

영수증 領收證 a receipt (for); a voucher (for); an acknowledgment (for)
♦영수증을 받다 get a receipt (made out) / 영수증을 쓰다 write [issue] a receipt (for) / 영수증을 써주다 make sb out a receipt; give sb a receipt (for)

영습자 英習字 English penmanship

영시 英詩 an English poem; a poem in English; (총칭) English poetry [verse]

영시 零時 〈자정〉 twelve (o'clock) midnight; 〈정오〉 noon (▶군대에서는 24시간제의 경우 오전 영시는 0000로 써서 zero hours라고 읽음)
♦영시 30분에 at half past twelve; 〈밤의〉 at half past twelve at night
▶막차는 영시 출발입니다 The last train leaves just at twelve midnight.

영식 令息 〈남의 아들〉 your [his, her] son

영아 嬰兒 an infant; a baby; a newborn child; a nursling ■—**사망률** infant mortality; the death rate of infants —**살해** infanticide

영악 獰惡 〈모질고 악착스러움〉 fierceness; ferocity —**영악하다** fierce; ferocious; savage; cruel ♦영악한 짐승 a fierce animal

영악하다 bright; smart; shrewd; sharp; clever
♦영악한 아이 a smart [bright] boy; a clever child

영안실 靈安室 a mortuary (of a hospital)
♦영안실에 안치하다 place a dead body in a mortuary of a hospital

영애 令愛 〈남의 딸〉 your [his, her] daughter ⇨ 영양

영약 靈藥 a wonder drug; a miraculous medicine [remedy]; a royal elixir
♦불로장생의 영약 an elixir of life

영양 令孃 〈남의 딸〉 your [his, her] daughter; 〈미혼여성〉 a young lady

영양 羚羊 【動】 an antelope

영양 營養 nourishment; nutrition; alimentation; sustenance
♦영양이 많은 음식물 nutritious [nourishing] food; nutriment / 영양이 좋은 well-fed; well-nourished / 영양이 모자라다 be undernourished [underfed] / 영양을 섭취하다 take [get] nourishment (from)
▶계란에는 영양이 풍부하게 들어 있다 Eggs are very nutritious.
▶나는 항상 영양에 신경을 써서 조리한다 I am careful to have a balanced diet when I cook.
■—**과다** supernutrition; hypernutrition —**물** nutritious [nourishing] food; nutriments; aliment —**분[소]** nutritive substance [elements]; a nutriment; a nutrient —**불량** ⇨ 영양부족 —**사** a dietitian; a dietician; a nutrition technician; a nutritionist —**상태** nutritive conditions —**식** a nourishing meal —**연구소** a dietetic laboratory; a nutrition research institute —**요법** a dietary cure —**장애** nutrition lesion [disorder] —**제** a medicine for promoting nutrition; a nutrient; a tonic —**지수** an index of nutrition

영양가 營養價 nutritive [food] value; nutritive qualities ♦영양가가 높은 of high nutritive value; highly nutritious

영양부족 營養不足 undernourishment; undernutrition; insufficient nourishment [nutrition]; malnutrition
♦영양부족의 undernourished; ill-fed; poorly fed / 영양부족으로 through lack of nourishment; from insufficient nourishment

영양실조 營養失調 unbalanced nutrition; malnutrition; dystrophy; dystrophia
♦심한 영양실조에 걸린 아이들 children suffering from severe malnutrition / 영양실조의 underfed

영양학 營養學 the science of nutrition; dietetics ■—**자** a nutritionist; a dietitian; a dietician

영어 英語 English; the English language
♦산 영어 living English / 서툰 영어 broken [poor] English / 세련된 영어 polished [refined] English / 정확한 [어법에 맞는] 영어 correct [idiomatic] English / 영어가 늘다 improve [make progress] in one's English / 영어 실력을 기르다 improve one's ability in English / 영어를 유창하게 하다 speak English fluently; speak fluent English / 영어로 말하다 [쓰다] speak [write] in English / 영어로 옮기다 translate [put, render] into English
▶그는 영어가 서툴다 He is poor at English.
▶그녀는 영어로 의사 소통이 가능하다 She can make herself understood in English.
▶우리 영어 선생님은 아주 엄하시다 Our English teacher is very strict. (▶「영어 선생님」의 경우는 teacher보다 English에 강세를 둠. teacher를 강하게 발음하면 「영국인 선생님」으로 들릴 수 있음)
▶영어는 이제 세계어다 English is now a world [an international] language.
▶이 꽃은 영어로 뭐라고 합니까? What is this flower called in English? ⇌ What is the English (word) for this flower?
▶「사랑」은 영어로 뭐라고 합니까? What is the English for "sarang"?
■ **고대[중세, 근세]—** Old [Middle, Modern] English **구어—** colloquial English **미국[국]—** American [British] English **상업—** commercial [business] English **순수—** 〈영국〉 the Queen's [King's] English **시사—** current

English 실용— practical [living] English 일상— everyday English 표준— standard English 현대— current [present-day] English ■—교사 a teacher of English; an English teacher —교육 the teaching of English; English-language teaching —극 a theatrical performance given in English —(사용)국민 an English-speaking people —소설 an English novel; a novel in English —시험 an examination in English —연설 an English speech —책[잡지] an English book [magazine] —편지 a letter (written) in English —학 English philology [linguistics] —회화 English conversation

영업 營業 〈업무〉 business; 〈장사〉 trade; 〈판매〉 sales; 〈운영〉 operation
♦영업상의 비밀 a trade secret / 남의 영업을 방해하다 obstruct [interfere with] one's business / 영업을 쉬다 suspend business; close one's shop / 영업을 시작하다 open [commence] business / 영업을 허가하다 authorize sb to carry on the business / 영업 허가를 받다 secure a license to operate
▶ 영업중 (게시) Open.
▶ 영업이 잘 되고 있습니다 We're enjoying a successful business.
▶ 그는 어떤 영업을 하고 있습니까? What line of business is he in?
—**영업하다** do [conduct] business; engage in business; carry on [run, operate] business
▶ 은행은 영업하느냐? Are banks in operation?
▶ 일요일에도 영업합니까? Are they open on Sundays, too?
▶ 일요일에는 영업하지 않습니다 They are closed on Sundays.
▶ 일요일을 제외하고는 매일 영업합니다 Business goes on daily except on Sunday.
▶ 이 가게는 밤 열 한 시까지 영업합니다 This store stays open till eleven o'clock at night.
■—감찰 a business [trade] license —금지 prohibition of business —방침 a business policy; 회사의 영업방침을 정하다 set company policies —방해 obstruction of business —보고 a business [financial] report —부 the business department —부장[주임] the business manager —부진 a business slump; lack of business —비 working [operating, running, business] expenses; overhead charges —상태 business standing [status] —성적 the results of operations 《for 1997》 —세 business tax —소 a business office; a place of business —소득 operating income —수익 operating revenue —시간 business [office] hours : 영업 시간 오전 여덟시부터 오후 다섯시까지 (게시) Open from 9 a.m. to 5 p.m. ⇌ Business hours: 9 a.m. - 5 p.m. —실적 business results; business turnover —안내 a business guide; a catalog —연도 a business year —외수익 non-operating income [revenue] —자 a trader; a business manager —자본[자금] a working capital —장소 a business site; a place of business —정지 suspension [discontinuance] of business —종목 the description [kind, line] of business —주 a business proprietor —창고 a business warehouse

영업권 營業權 right of trade [business]; 〔商〕 goodwill ♦영업권을 팔다 sell out one's business; sell the goodwill / 가게의 영업권을 넘기다 transfer the goodwill of one's store

영업용 營業用 ♦영업용의 for business (purpose) ■—기물 office furniture —자동차 cars kept for business (purposes) —자산 operating assets

영역 英譯 translation into English; (an) English translation [version]
▶ 이것은 황순원의 소설 「소나기」의 영역이다 This is an English translation of "A Shower", a novel by Hwang Sun-won.
▶ 나는 톨스토이의 작품을 영역본으로 읽었다 I have read Tolstoy's works in English version [translation].
—**영역하다** translate [render, turn, put] into English
▶ 다음 문장을 영역하시오 Translate [Put] the following sentences into English.
■—국문— translating Korean into English; Korean-English translation

영역 領域 〈영토〉 a territory; a domain; 〈분야〉 a province; a sphere; an area; a field
♦과학의 영역 the domain [territory, sphere, realm] of science / 전문 영역이 아닌 out of one's realm [proper domain] / 영역을 정하다 fix the territory [domain] / 남의 영역을 침범하다 encroach [invade, trespass] on another's province
▶ 이 경계 너머는 캐나다의 영역이다 The land beyond this boundary is Canadian territory [belongs to Canada].
▶ 천문학은 나의 영역이 아니다 Astronomy is not in my line [sphere].
▶ 그것은 과학의 영역을 넘어서 있다 It is beyond the limits of science.
▶ 그 학문은 인간생활의 모든 영역에 걸쳐 있다 The discipline covers all areas of human life.

영역 靈域 sacred ground; a holy place; holy precincts

영영 永永 eternally; permanently; perpetually; to (all) eternity; forever; for good (and all); for all time
♦조국을 영영 떠나다 leave one's homeland permanently [for good, never to return]
▶ 그후 그로부터는 영영 소식이 없다 Nothing whatever has been heard of him ever since. ⇌ I have heard nothing from him ever since.

영예 榮譽 honor; glory ⇨ 명예
▶ 이보다 더한 영예가 어디 있겠는가 No greater glory could be gained (than this).
▶ 그 영예는 그에게로 돌아 가는 것이 마땅하다 The honor should go to him.
—**영예롭다** honorable; glorious ♦영예로운 죽음 an honorable death

영외 營外 outside barracks ♦영외 거주를 하다 live outside [out of] barracks; take one's lodgings outside barracks

영욕 榮辱 honor and disgrace

영웅 英雄 a hero 《pl. ~es》; a great man
♦일세의 영웅 the greatest hero of the age /

전쟁의 영웅 a war hero / 영웅적인 행위 a heroic deed; (an act of) heroism / 영웅답게 like a hero; heroically / 국민적 영웅이 되다 become a national hero / 영웅화하다 make a hero of sb
▶영웅호색 All great men are also great lovers [womanizers]. ⇌ Heroes enjoy the pleasures of flesh.
■—숭배 hero worship —주의 heroism

영원 永遠 eternity; perpetuity; permanence; 〈불멸〉 immortality
◆지상에서 영원으로 from here to eternity
—**영원하다** eternal; everlasting; perpetual; permanent; immortal; timeless
◆영원한 사랑 everlasting love / 영원한 생명 [진리] an eternal life [truth] / 영원한 평화 everlasting [permanent] peace / 인생의 영원한 수수께끼 the eternal riddle of life / 영원히 [영원토록] forever; eternally; perpetually; everlastingly; for ever and ever; from everlasting to everlasting; for good (and all); permanently; in eternity; through all ages / 영원히 잠들다 sleep the eternal [last] sleep; take *one's* last sleep; go to *one's* eternal rest / 이름을 영원히 남기다 immortalize *one's* fame [name]
▶그것은 영원한 수수께끼로 남을 것이다 It will remain a riddle forever.
▶우리는 그의 작품에서 위대한 예술의 영원한 아름다움을 본다 We see the timeless beauty of great art in his work.
■—성 eternal nature; eternity; perpetuity

영원 蠑蚖 〔動〕 a newt; 〈美〉 an eft

영위 營爲 management; operation; running
—**영위하다** manage; run; operate; carry on; conduct ◆정직한 삶을 영위하다 lead an honest life

영유 領有 possession
▶그 섬은 전승국의 영유가 되었다 That island was annexed to the victorious nation.
—**영유하다** possess; get [be in] possession of —**권** dominium —**지**[물] a possession

영육 靈肉 soul and body; body and spirit
▶그들은 영육 일치를 목표로 수행하고 있다 They are training themselves aiming at the unity of body and soul.

영의정 領議政 the prime [chief] minister; the premier

영인 影印 a facsimile 《of a manuscript》; a photographic reproduction; photostating
—**영인하다** photostat; facsimile
■—본 a photographic edition; a phototype

영일 寧日 〈좋은 날〉 a peaceful [quiet] day; rest ▶하루도 영일이 없다 Not a single day passes quietly.

영자 英字 an English letter ■—신문 an English (language) paper; a newspaper in English

영작(문) 英作(文) 〈학과목〉 English composition; 〈쓴 것〉 an English composition
■—자유— free (English) composition

영장 令狀 a warrant; a writ
◆영장에 의한[의하지 않은] 체포 an arrest with [without] a warrant / 영장을 발부하다 [청구하다] issue [request] a warrant 《for sb's arrest》 / 영장을 집행하다 execute a warrant; serve a writ on sb
■—소집— a call-up paper [card] 수색— a search warrant 체포[구속]— a warrant of arrest; an arrest warrant ■—송달자 〔法〕 a process server

영장 靈長 a supreme creature
▶인간은 만물의 영장이다 Man is the lord of (all) creation.
■—류(類)〔動〕 Primates

영재 英才 〈재주〉 talent; genius; brilliant parts; 〈사람〉 a brilliant [talented, gifted] person; a man of ability [talent, parts]; a genius
■—교육 specific education for the gifted

영적 靈的 spiritual; incorporeal ■—교류 spiritual sympathy —생활 the spiritual [inner] life

영전 榮轉 promotion; preferment; a promotional transfer; transference on promotion
▶그는 영전의 기회를 놓쳤다 He missed a chance of being promoted to a high post.
▶영전을 축하합니다 Congratulations on your promotion.
—**영전하다** be promoted [transferred] to a higher post
▶그는 본사 총무부장으로 영전했다 He was promoted to the general manager of the head office.

영전 靈前 ◆영전에 before the spirit of the departed [deceased] / 고인의 영전에 바치다 offer sth to the spirit of the departed
▶그는 영전에 화환을 바쳤다 He offered a wreath to the spirit of the departed.
▶그녀는 영전에 엎드려 빌었다 She bowed before the deceased and prayed.

영점 零點 1 〈무득점〉 (a) zero 《pl. ~s, ~es》; no points; no marks; a duck; a duck's egg
◆영점을 받다 get zero (in English); receive a zero marking [mark]; 〈경기에서〉 get a duck
2 〈무능·무성과〉 nothing; nought; a failure
▶그는 교사로서는 영점이다 As a teacher he is a failure [he is useless].

영접 迎接 reception; meeting ◆영접을 받다 be met [greeted, received] 《at the station》 —**영접하다** receive; greet; meet

영정 影幀 (a scroll of) the painted picture of sb; a portrait (scroll) ◆고(故) 민 선생의 영정 a picture of the late Mr. Min

영조 營造 building; construction —**영조하다** build; construct ■—물 an establishment; a building; a structure

영조 靈鳥 a sacred bird

영존 永存 permanence; perpetuity; permanent existence —**영존하다** exist [remain] forever [permanently]

영주 永住 permanent residence
—**영주하다** settle down (for good); reside permanently in 《Korea》; take up a permanent residence [abode]
▶그는 페루에 영주했다 He made Peru his permanent home.
▶나는 네팔에 영주하고 싶다 I want to reside [settle down] in Nepal permanently.

영주 —권 denizenship; permanent residentship: 영주권을 얻다 be denizened; obtain permanent residentship **—민[자]** a permanent resident; a settler; a denizen **—지** one's (permanent) home; a place of permanent residence; a permanent domicile

영주 英主 a wise ruler; an illustrious king

영주 領主 a (feudal) lord; the lord [proprietor] of a manor

영지 英智 wisdom; intelligence; sagacity

영지 領地 1 ⇨ 영토
2 〈봉토〉 a feud; a fief; feudal tenure [domain]

영지 靈地 a holy ground [land]; a sacred place

영차 yo-ho!; yo-heave-ho!; heave-ho! ⇨ 이영차

영창 詠唱 〈樂〉 an aria ⇨ 아리아

영창 營倉 〈건물〉 a guardhouse; a guardroom; a detention camp; 〈형(刑)〉 detention in the guardhouse ▶ 그는 영창에 갇혔다 He was confined in [to] the guardhouse.

영천 靈泉 a wonder-working [magical] fountain; 〈온천〉 a hot spring (with miraculous virtue); a spa

영치 領置 〔法〕 provisional holding; keeping in custody **—영치하다** detain; place in the custody 《of the prison officer》
—금 money in custody

영탄 詠嘆 〈읊음〉 recitation; 〈감탄〉 exclamation; admiration **—영탄하다** recite 《a poem》; exclaim; admire; express [give voice to] one's admiration 《for》

영토 領土 (a) territory; (a) dominion; (a) domain; territorial possessions
◆ 한국의 영토 Korean territory; the land belonging to Korea / 영토를 확장하다 extend one's territory / 영토를 획득하다 acquire a territory / 영토적 야심을 품다 harbor [have] territorial ambitions [designs]
▶ 독도는 한국의 영토다 Tokto belongs to Korea.
▶ 간도(間島)는 원래 한국의 영토였다 Kando used to be Korean territory.
—권 territorial rights **—문제** the territorial problems **—보전** territorial integrity **—분쟁** a territorial dispute **—주권** sovereignty upon land; territorial sovereignty **—침범** encroachment upon the territory 《of another country》 **—획득** acquisition of territory

영토확장 領土擴張 expansion of territory; territorial expansion [aggrandizement]
—론자 an expansionist **—정책** a policy of territorial expansion; expansionism

영특하다 英特— wise; sagacious; perspicacious; exceptional; outstanding

영판¹ 〈길흉을 맞힘〉 true [inspired] fortunetelling; 〈길흉을 잘 맞히는 사람〉 a wonderful diviner

영판² 〈아주〉 just; exactly; quite
◆ 영판 같다 be exactly alike; be the exact image [likeness] 《of》 / 영판 다르다 be quite different 《from》

영패 零敗 a whitewash; a shutout; 《美俗》 a skunk ◆ 겨우 영패를 면하다 barely miss being shut out
—영패하다 fail to score; be shut out; 《美俗》 be skunked ◆ 영패시키다 shut out; whitewash; 《美俗》 skunk
▶ 우리 팀은 요전 시합에서 영패했다 Our team was shut out [failed to score] in the last game.
▶ 그녀는 그 테니스 토너먼트에서 영패했다 She was defeated in a love game at the tennis tournament.

영하 零下 ◆ 영하의 기온 a sub-zero temperature / 영히 3도 three degrees below zero / (기온이) 영하 10도로 떨어지다 fall [drop] to 10 degrees below zero [below the freezing point]
▶ 바깥의 기온은 영하 20도다 The temperature in the open air is minus twenty degrees.

영한 英韓 English-Korean
—대역본 an English book with the Korean translation on opposite pages **—사전** an English-Korean dictionary

영합 迎合 flattery; adulation; ingratiation
—영합하다 flatter; curry favor with; fawn upon; ingratiate oneself with 《one's superior》; cater to
◆ 여론에 영합하다 accommodation oneself to public opinion / 권력에 영합하다 follow [wait on] the wishes of the powers / 남의 의견에 영합하다 echo [cater to] another's opinion / 시류에 영합하다 go with the current of the times; swim [go with] the tide
—주의 opportunism; timeserving

영해 領海 〔地〕 territorial seas; a closed sea
▶ 그들은 한국의 영해 안[밖]에서 조업하고 있다 They are engaged in fishing within [out of] the territorial waters of Korea.
—선(線) a territorial water line **—침범** violation of territorial waters

영행렬 零行列 〔數〕 a zero matrix

영향 影響 influence; effect; consequences; repercussions
◆ 불교의 영향 the influence of Buddhism / 원폭의 영향 the effects of the atomic bomb / 외국의 영향 a foreign influence / …의 영향으로 under the influence of...; owing to...; in consequence of... / 영향을 미치다[주다] influence; affect; have [exert, exercise] an influence on [upon, over, with] / …의 영향을 받다 be affected [influenced] by...; be subjected to the influence of...
▶ 내가 영어를 좋아하게 된 데는 누이의 영향이 크다 It is largely because of my sister that I have come to like English.
▶ 지난 전쟁의 영향이 아직도 생활의 여기저기에서 느껴진다 The influences [repercussions] of the last war are still felt in every aspects of our life.
▶ 물가 상승은 국민생활에 직접 영향을 끼친다 A rise in prices has [exert] a direct influence upon the livelihood of the people.
▶ 날씨는 농작물에 영향을 미친다 The weather affects [has effect on] the crops.
▶ 나이는 기억력에 영향을 준다 Age tells on

the memory.
▶이 만화는 아이들에게 나쁜 영향을 줄 것이다 This comic strip will be a bad influence on children.
▶정신적 압박이 그녀의 신체에 영향을 미치기 시작했다 The strain began to affect her physically.
▶나는 형의 영향을 받아 화학을 좋아하게 되었다 Influenced by my brother, I came to like chemistry.

영향력 影響力 influence; the influencing power; the power of influence ◆영향력이 있다 be influential; be powerful / 영향력을 행사하다 exercise *one's* influence 《over》

영험 靈驗 a miracle ⇨ 영검

영혼 靈魂 a soul; a spirit
◆육체를 떠난 영혼의 안식처 the abode of the departed souls / 영혼의 존재를 믿다 believe in spirits / (망자의) 영혼을 달래다 propitiate [appease] the souls [manes] of
▶그들은 영혼의 불멸성을 믿고 있다 They believe in the immortality of the soul.
■―불멸설 the doctrine of the immortality of the soul

영화 英貨 〈파운드〉 British [English] currency [money]; the pound; sterling
◆영화 5 파운드 five pounds sterling / 영화로 환산하여 100 파운드 one hundred pounds [£ 100] in English money / 영화로 환산하다 convert into British currency
▶이 책은 영화로 얼마가 됩니까? How much would this book be in English currency?

영화 映畫 a movie, a film; a picture; a moving [motion] picture; (총칭) the movies; the screen; (英) the cinema
◆영화를 제작하다 produce a film / 영화를 촬영하다 take a motion picture; shoot pictures; film / 영화를 개봉[상영]하다 release [show] a film / 영화를 보러 가다 go to a movie [the movies, the pictures, the cinema] / 영화에 나오다 appear on the screen; appear in a movie; be in the movies / 영화화하다 make a movie 《of》; (美) picturize; make into a movie; (英) cinematize
▶영화를 좋아하십니까? Are you interested in the movies?
▶여기서 재미있는 영화가 상영중 입니다 An interesting movie is showing here.
▶그 영화는 단성사에서 상영중입니다 The picture is now on (show) at the Tansŏngsa.
▶이 소설은 영화로 적합하다[적합하지 않다] This novel films well [ill].
■갱― a gangster film 교육― an educational film 기록― a documentary (film) 뉴스― a news film; a newsreel 단편[소형]― a short; a briefie 만화― an animation; a cartoon film 입체― a 3-D [stereoscopic] film 천연색― a techni(color) movie 흑백― a black and white movie ■―가(街) the cinema quarters ―각본 ⇨ 시나리오 ―감독 a (film) director; (英) a producer ―검열 film censorship ―극 a film [screen] play [drama]; a photoplay ―대본 a (dialogue) script; a continuity ―배급회사 a film distributing company; a movie distributing agency ―사업 the movie industry ―상영권 film rights ―스타 a cinema [film, screen] star; (美俗) a cinestar ―윤리위원회 the Motion Picture Ethics Commission ―인 a movieman ―제 a film festival: 아시아 영화제 the Asian Film Festival ―촬영소 a film [movie] studio ―팬 a movie [cinema, film] fan; a moviegoer ―편집자 a movie editor ―평 a film review; a movie criticism ―평론가 a film critic

영화 榮華 〈번영〉 prosperity; 〈호화〉 splendor; pomp; 〈영예〉 glory
◆속세의 영화의 pomps and glories of the world; vain glories / 잠시의 영화 a brief span of prosperity / 영화의 극치에 이르다 be at the height [zenith] of *one's* prosperity; live in splendor / 영화에 도취하다 revel in prosperity

영화계 映畫界 the world at movies; the filmland; the film [movie] world; (英) the cinema world ◆영화계에 들어가다 enter the movie world; go into the movies

영화관 映畫館 a movie theater; (英) a cinema; a picture hall ■―주인 a cinema house proprietor; a film exhibitor

영화배우 映畫俳優 a film [movie, screen] actor [actress]; a photoplayer
◆영화배우가 되다 appear on the screen
■―지망자 an aspirant to a screen career

영화제작 映畫製作 filmmaking
■―소 a movie [cinema] studio ―업 the film producing industry ―자 a movie [film] producer; a moviemaker ―회사 a film producing company

영화화 映畫化 filming; cinematization; (英) picturization
―영화화하다 cinematize; film; make a screen play of; screen; (英) picturize; filmize
◆소설을 영화화하다 make a film of a novel

옅다 1 〈깊지 않다〉 shallow ⇨ 얕다
2 〈색깔이 묽다〉 light 《color》; pale; faint
◆옅은 하늘색 light blue

옆 〈측면〉 the side; the flank; 〈근처〉 neighborhood; vicinity
◆길 옆의 집 a house by the road / 옆의 side; nearby; next to; neighboring; close to / 옆에 by; by the side of; beside sb; 〈가까이에〉 near in the neighborhood [vicinity] 《of》 / 바로 옆에 near [close] by; just beside one / 옆으로 aside; to *one's* side; sideways; sidelong / 옆에 놓다 put sth beside [by the side of] / 대문 옆에 서다 stand by the gate / 옆으로 가다 go to one side; 〈다가가다〉 draw to *sb's* side / 옆으로 걷다 walk sideways / 옆으로 비키다 step aside / 옆의 강으로 고기를 잡으러 가다 go fishing in a nearby river [a river nearby, a river in the neighborhood]
▶그들은 탁자를 옆으로 치웠다 They moved the table aside.
▶그들은 날 옆으로 밀어 붙였다 They pushed me away.
▶옆으로 눕힐 것 (표시) Keep flat. ⇌ Stow level.
▶옆으로 눕히지 말 것 (표시) Never lay flat. ⇌ Not to be laid flat.

▶ 해안 옆에 공원이 있다 There is a park by [near] the beach.
▶ 그는 내 옆에 앉았다 He sat beside [next to] me. ⇒ He sat by [at] my side.
▶ 화재가 났을 때 옆에 아무도 없었다 No one was by when the fire broke out.

옆구리 the side; the flank
♦ 오른쪽 옆구리 the right side; the right flank / 오른쪽 옆구리가 결리다 have a stitch in *one's* right side / 옆구리를 쿡 찌르다 give a poke in *sb's* ribs; dig [poke] *sb* in the ribs / 가방을 옆구리에 끼고 오다 come holding a bag under *one's* arm
▶ 갑자기 왼쪽 옆구리가 아팠다 I suddenly had a pain in my left side.

옆길 a byroad; a side-road; a side road
옆들다 help; aid 《in a fight》; take the side of
옆머리 the side of the head
옆모습 a profile; the side face ♦ 옆모습을 그리다 draw *sb's* profile; draw *sb* in profile
옆문 ―門 a side entrance 《of a house》; a side door ▶ 옆문을 이용하시오 《게시》 Side entrance. ⇒ Use next door.
옆바람 a side wind; 〔空〕 a crosswind
옆발치 the place at the feet of *sb* lying down
옆방 ―房 the next room; the side room
옆자리 the next seat; 〈버스 등의〉 a side seat
▶ 나는 그녀의 옆자리에 앉았다 I sat at her side [by her (side)].
옆줄 a side line; 〔魚〕 a lateral line
옆질 〈자동차·배의〉 rolling ―옆질하다 roll 《from side to side》; 《a boat》 rock
옆집 a neighboring [an adjoining] house; a neighbor's house; the next-door house; the house next door
♦ 옆집에 살다 live next-door to *one's* house / 한 집 건너 옆집에 살다 live next door but one down
■―사람 a next-door neighbor: 오른쪽 옆집 사람 *one's* neighbor on the right / 우리 옆집 사람은 새를 기른다 My next-door neighbor has some pet birds.
옆쪽 the side; the flank
옆폭 ―幅 a side board; the sidepiece
옆홀이(대패) a side grooving planer

예¹ 〈예전〉 old times; a long time ago; bygone days ♦ 예로부터의 관습 an old [a traditional] custom
▶ 예나 지금이나 다름이 없다 It is the same now as it was in the days gone by.

예² 1 〈대답〉 yes; certainly; all right; very well; 〈부정 의문일 때〉 no
▶ 예 알겠습니다 Yes, certainly. ⇒ All right, sir.
▶ 〔會話〕「헤엄칠 줄 모릅니까?」「예」 "Can't you swim?" "No, I can't."
2 〈호명시의 대답〉 yes, sir; here (sir); present
3 〈재우쳐 묻는 소리〉 eh?; what?
▶ 예? 그러세요? Is that so? ⇒ Really?

예 例 1 〈실례·유례〉 an example; an instance; 〈증명·설명을 위한〉 an illustration; 〈사례(事例)〉 a case
♦ 비슷한 예 a similar case; a parallel instance / 흔한 예 a familiar instance / 예를 들면 for example [instance] / 예를 들다 cite [give, show, point out] an instance / 예를 들어 설명하다 explain (it) by (giving) examples / 예로 들다 give... as an example; take... for instance
▶ 이것은 다만 한 가지 예에 지나지 않는다 That is only one example.
▶ 그는 자신의 유럽 생활을 예로 들었다 He took illustrations from his own life in Europe.
▶ 이것이 그 좋은 예다 This is a case in point.
2 〈개인적인 습관〉 a habit; 〈사회적 관습〉 a custom
♦ 예와 같이 as usual; as is usual with one
3 〈전례〉 a precedent
▶ 그러한 파업은 예가 없다 There is no precedent for such a strike. ⇒ Such a strike is unprecedented [quite without precedent].
⇒ There is no precedent for it.

예 禮 1 ⇨ 예의(禮儀)
♦ 예를 갖춘 인사 a polite greeting / 예를 다하여 손님을 대접하다 treat the guest with the utmost courtesy [most courteously] / 손윗사람에 대한 예를 차릴 줄 알다 know how to behave around [act with] *one's* seniors / 예를 잃으면 be impolite; be rude
2 〈경례〉 a salute; a salution; a bow
3 ⇨ 의식(儀式)

예각 銳角 〔數〕 an acute angle
■―삼각형 an acute(-angled) triangle

예감 豫感 a feeling; a hunch; 〈특히 나쁜〉 foreboding a presentiment; a premonition
♦ 불길한 예감 an ominous presentiment; a gloomy foreboding / 재앙이 있을 것 같은 예감이 들다 have a premonition of disaster
▶ 나는 그가 이길 것 같은 예감이 든다 I have a hunch that he will win.
―예감하다 have a hunch [foreboding]; feel a premonition; forebode 《disaster》
♦ 죽음을 예감하다 have a premonition of death

예견 豫見 foresight; foreknowledge ―예견하다 foreknow
▶ 이렇게 변화무쌍한 세상에서는 1년 앞의 일도 예견할 수 없다 We cannot foresee what will happen a year hence, as we are in such an ever-changing world.

예고 豫告 〈통지〉 an advance notice; a preliminary announcement; a (previous) notice; 〈영화·연극의〉 advance billing; 〈경고〉 (a) warning
♦ 예고 없이 방문하다 pay a visit without (previous) notice; pay a surprise visit 《to》 / 3개월 전의 예고로[예고 없이] 해고되다 be dismissed at three months' notice [without notice]
―예고하다 announce beforehand; notify beforehand; make a preliminary announcement (for); give notice; warn *sb* of *sth*
♦ 예고한 대로 as already [previously] announced / 책의 근간을 예고하다 announce a book as in preparation / 아무에게 1개월 전에 해고[퇴직]를 예고하다 give *sb* a month's notice; give a month's notice to *sb*

■신간— the announcement [notice] of new [forthcoming] books ■—편 〈영화의〉 a trailer; a preview
예과 豫科 a preparatory course [department]; 〈의과대학의〉 a premedical course ♦예과를 수료하다 complete the preparatory course ■—학생 a preparatory course student
예광탄 曳光彈 a tracer; a light tracer; a flame tracer; a tracer bullet [shell]
예규 例規 an established rule [regulation] ♦예규를 벗어나다 deviate from an established rule / 예규에 따라 처리하다 dispose of 《a matter》 in accordance with the established regulations
예금 預金 (a) deposit; money on deposit ♦예금을 찾다[인출하다] draw *one's* deposit 《from a bank》; 〈계좌에서〉 withdraw 《₩100,000》 from *one's* account / 은행에 예금계좌를 개설하다 open an account at a bank ▶예금 잔고를 가르쳐 주시겠습니까? Could you tell me my balance? ▶그의 예금이 늘었다 His bank account grew. —예금하다 deposit 《money in a bank》; bank ♦100,000원을 예금하다 deposit [make a deposit of] 100,000 won 《in a bank》 ▶나는 그 돈을 전부 예금했다 I put all the money in my account. = I deposited all the money. ▶그는 그 은행에 많은 돈을 예금하고 있다 He keeps [has] a large deposit in the bank. ▶그는 그 은행에 50만원을 예금해 두고 있다 He has a deposit of 500,000 won in the bank. ■당좌— 《美》 a checking [《英》 current] account 별단(別段)— a miscellaneous deposit 보통— an ordinary deposit 신탁— a trust deposit 은행— a bank deposit [account]; a deposit in a bank 저축— 《美》 a savings account; 《英》 deposit account 적립— an installment deposit 정기— a time deposit; 정기예금을 들다[해약하다] buy [cancel] a time deposit ■—계 the deposit department [section] 《of a bank》; 〈사람〉 a deposit teller —계좌 《美》 a bank account; 《英》 a deposit account —대출 a deposit loan —액 the deposited amount —이자 interest on [of] deposits —준비금 a reserve for deposit —증서 a certificate of deposit; a deposit certificate —통장 a bankbook; a deposit book
예기 銳氣 (animated) spirit; dash; vigor ♦예기있는 spirited; dashing; mettlesome / 예기 발랄하다 be in exuberant spirits / 예기를 꺾다 shake [break] *one's* spirits
예기 豫期 〈예상〉 expectations(s); (an) anticipation —예기하다 expect; anticipate ♦예기치 않은 결과 an unexpected [undesigned] effect / 예기한 대로 되다 meet [come up to] *one's* expectations ▶예기치 못한 일이 그곳에서 일어났다 Unexpected things happened there. ▶예기한 대로 좋은 회답이 왔다 A favorable answer came as I had expected.
예끼 〈나무라는 소리〉 Damn it!; Damn you! ♦예끼 나쁜 놈 You rascal!
예납 豫納 payment in advance; prepayment

—예납하다 pay in advance; prepay ♦회비를 예납하다 pay the membership fee in advance
예년 例年 〈평년〉 an ordinary year; a normal year; 〈매년〉 every year; annually ♦예년의 행사 an annual event / 예년에 없는 풍작 an exceptionally good harvest / 예년의 〈평년의〉 normal; usual; 〈매년의〉 annual / 예년에 비해서 compared with other year ▶금년 겨울은 예년에 없이 춥다 It is unusually cold [colder than usual] this year. ▶축제는 예년처럼 행해졌다 We had [held] the festival as in other years. ▶금년의 수확고는 예년 수준이다 The crops this year are about (up to) (the) average.
예능 藝能 public entertainments ■—계(界) the world of entertainment [show business]: 스무 살에 예능계에 들어가다 join [start in, enter] the world of entertainment at twenty —과 the art course —교육 art education —인 an entertainer
예니레 six or seven days
예닐곱 six or seven
예단 豫斷 (a) prediction ▶사건의 결과는 예단을 불허한다 There is no telling [It is impossible to tell] what the development of the affair will be like. —예단하다 presuppose; guess; predict ▶실제 무엇이 일어날지는 예단할 수 없다 We can't [Nobody can] tell what will actually happen. = There is no predicting [knowing] what will actually happen.
예답다 禮— polite; courteous; ceremonious
예대 禮待 (an) honorable treatment —예대하다 receive *sb* cordially; treat *sb* with respect
예도 藝道 (an) art; accomplishments ♦예도에 전념하다 devote *oneself* to the cultivation of *one's* art
예라 1 〈그만 둬라〉 Stop!; Cut it out!; Get away! ▶예라 저리 가라 Be off with you! = Stop! = Cut it out! ▶예라 그런 말 마라 Stop talking like that! 2 〈결단·체념〉 all right; good; well ▶예라 모르겠다 Well then, I'll have nothing more to do with it.
예레미야서 —書 〈聖〉 (The Book of) Jeremiah (略 Jer.)
예루살렘 Jerusalem ■—사람 a Jerusalemite
예리하다 銳利— 1 〈날카롭다〉 sharp; keen ♦예리한 무기 a sharp [trenchant] weapon / 예리한 칼[면도칼] a sharp knife [razor blade] ▶시체는 예리한 칼에 찔려 있었다 The body was stabbed with a sharp knife. 2 〈정확하다〉 acute; keen; sharp ♦예리한 눈 piercing eyes / 예리한 비판 pungent criticism ▶그녀는 예리한 두뇌의 소유자다 She has a keen mind [clear head].
예망 曳網 a seine; a dragnet; a draw net
예매 豫買 advance purchase; subscription —예매하다 buy [purchase] in advance; subscribe for [to]
예매 豫賣 booking; an advance sale; a sale in

예매 advance ◆예매 좌석이 매진되다 be booked up —예매하다 sell (it) in advance; book ▶그들은 지정석을 예매하고 있다 They are selling reserved seats in advance.
■—권[표] an advance ticket; a ticket sold in advance: 예매권은 여기서 팝니까? Can I get an advance ticket here?

예멘 〈나라이름〉 Yemen; 〈공식명〉 the Republic of Yemen ◆예멘의 Yemeni; Yemenite ■—사람 a Yemeni; a Yemenite

예명 藝名 a stage name; (프) a nom(s) de guerre (pl. noms de guerre); 〈영화 배우의〉 a screen name

예모 禮貌 courtesy; etiquette; (good) manners ◆예모가 없다 be wanting in politeness; be ill-mannered / 예모를 지키다 observe good manners

예문 例文 an example (sentence); an illustrative sentence; an illustration
◆예문을 들다 give an example sentence ▶영작문을 공부하는 데는 가능한 한 많은 예문을 외우는 것이 필요하다 It is necessary for you to learn as many model sentences as possible by heart in the study of English composition.

예물 禮物 1〈사례물〉 a gift; a present; an offering
2〈결혼의〉 a wedding present for the bride
3〈신랑 신부의〉 wedding gifts exchanged between the bridegroom and bride
◆예물을 주고 받다 exchange wedding presents [gifts]

예민하다 銳敏— 〈감각 등이〉 sharp; keen; acute; sensitive
◆예민한 감각 a keen [fine, quick] sense / 예민한 관찰자 an acute observer / 예민한 두뇌 a keen intelligence; a clear head / 귀가 예민하다 have sharp [keen] ears; be keen of hearing
▶개는 코가 예민하다 Dogs have an acute [sharp] sense of smell. ≒ Dogs have a keen nose.

예바르다 禮— courteous; polite; civil; refined ▶그는 예바른 사람이다 He has good manners [is well-mannered].

예방 豫防 〈방지〉 prevention ((of, against)); protection ((from, against)); 〈주의〉 (a) precaution; 〔醫〕 (a) prophylaxis
◆범죄 예방 the prevention of crime / 화재[병] 예방 the precaution of fire [disease] / 예방의 preventive; precautionary
▶예방이 치료보다 낫다 Prevention is better than cure.
—예방하다 prevent; protect ((from, against)); take preventive measures ((against)); take precautions ((against))
◆전염병을 예방하다 prevent an epidemic
■—법 a prophylactic measure —약 a preventive (medicine) ((of, against)) —위생 preventive hygiene [sanitation] —의학 preventive medicine —전쟁 a preventive war —접종〈병원균 등의〉 (a) prophylactic inoculation; 〈백신의〉 (a) vaccination: 장티푸스의 예방접종을 맞다 be inoculated typhobacterin

—주사 a preventive inoculation: 나는 유행성 감기의 예방주사를 맞았다 I had [got] an injection against influenza. —책 a precautionary measure

예방 禮防 a courtesy visit [call] —예방하다 pay a courtesy visit ((to)); make [pay] a courtesy call ((at, on))

예배 禮拜 worship; a worship service; a (church) service
◆예배드리다 worship; attend divine [church] service; attend chapel / 예배 중이다 be at church
▶이 교회에서는 주일날 세번 예배를 드린다 This church hold [has] three services every Sunday.
—예배하다 worship (God); adore
■가정— family worship 새벽— morning service 주일— a Sunday service ■—자 a worshiper

예법 禮法 etiquette; manners; courtesy; decorum(s)
◆예법을 모르다 be ill-mannered; have no manners / 예법을 지키다 observe the proprieties [decorums] / 예법에 어긋나다[맞다] go against [conform to] etiquette
▶우리 양친은 예법에 아주 까다롭다 My parents are very particular about manners.

예보 豫報 a forecast; 〈예측〉 (a) prediction
▶오늘 밤에는 비가 온다는 예보다 Rain is forecast for this evening.
▶요즘의 예보는 잘 맞지 않는다[맞는다] The recent forecasts often prove wrong [right].
—예보하다 forecast; predict
■일기— a weather forecast: 텔레비전[라디오]의 일기예보를 듣다 listen to the weather forecast on TV [the radio] 장기— a long-range forecast 지진— an earthquake prediction [forecast]

예복 禮服 full dress; ceremonial [formal] dress; a dress suit; 〈야회복〉 evening dress; 〈군인의〉 a dress uniform
◆예복을 입다 be in [wear] full dress
▶당일은 예복을 착용할 것 A dress coat to be worn on the occasion.
■결혼—〈남성의〉 a wedding suit; 〈여성의〉 a wedding dress 궁중— a court suit; a full court dress

예봉 銳鋒 a sharp [keen] point; 〈기세〉 the brunt ◆예봉을 꺾다 break the brunt of ((the enemy's attack)) / 공격의 예봉에 맞서다 bear the brunt of an attack

예불 禮佛 the worship of Buddha
—예불하다 hold worship in front of Buddha

예비 豫備 preparation; a reserve; a spare ◆예비의 〈여분의〉 reserve; spare; 〈사전의〉 preparatory
▶나는 예비로 돈을 좀 가지고 있었다 I had a little money in reserve.
—예비하다 prepare ((for)); provide ((for)); reserve; keep [have] sth in reserve
■—검사 preliminary examination —공작 spadework; preliminaries —교 a preparatory school; (口) a prep (school) —교섭 preliminary negotiations [talks] —병 a reser-

vist —부품 spare parts —사단〔軍〕 a reserved division —선거〔美〕 a preliminary [primary] election —선수 a reserve player —인원 reserve men —점검[검사] (a) preliminary inspection [examination] —조사 a preliminary examination [investigation] —지식 a preliminary [background] knowledge —타이어 a spare tire : 예비 타이어가 트렁크 안에 있다 The spare tire is in the trunk. —회담 a preliminary conference [talks]

예비군 豫備軍 (the) reserve forces
■ 직장[지역]— workplace [regional] reserve forces 향토— the homeland reserve forces: 향토예비군 소집일 a reserve forces muster day
■ —소대[중대] a reserve forces platoon [company] —훈련 reserve forces training

예비역 豫備役 service in the first reserve
◆ 예비역에 편입되다 go into the first reserve; be placed on the reserve list
■ —장교 a reserve officer

예쁘다 pretty; beautiful; lovely; good-looking
♦ 예쁜 꽃 a pretty [beautiful, lovely] flower / 예쁜 소녀 a beautiful [pretty, lovely, good-looking] girl / 예쁜 얼굴 a fair countenance [face] / 예쁜 목소리로 노래하다 sing in a sweet voice / 예쁘게 꾸미다 decorate; make (*sth*) beautiful
▶ 그녀는 늘 옷을 예쁘게 차려 입는다 She always dresses herself beautifully.
▶ 튤립이 예쁘게 피어 있다 Tulips are in beautiful bloom.
▶ 그녀는 글씨를 예쁘게 쓴다 She writes a clear [good] hand.

예사 例事 〈보통의 일〉 an ordinary affair; a commonplace event; a common practice; (a) usage; 〈일상사〉 an everyday occurrence [affair]
◆ 예사가 아닌 unusual; extraordinary; uncommon / 예사로 여기다 do not hesitate; make little of / 예사로 거짓말하다 make no [do not] scruple of lying
▶ 버스는 예사로 연착한다 Delayed arrival of buses on a regular route is a matter of almost daily occurrence.

예사롭다 例事— common; ordinary; commonplace
◆ 예사로운 일 a commonplace event; an everyday occurrence
▶ 나는 사태가 예사롭지 않다는 것을 알았다 I realized that the situation was serious.

예산 豫算 〈견적〉 an estimate; 〈예산안〉 a budget; an estimated cost
♦ 1997년도의 예산 the budget for the fiscal year 1997 / 3천만원의 예산으로 at an estimated cost of 30 million won
〈예산의〉 예산의 균형 budgetary balance / 예산의 삭감 reduction of appropriation; a curtailment in the budget / 예산의 집행 execution of the budget / 예산(의) 편성 compilation of the budget / 예산의 범위 내에서 within (the limit of) the budget
〈예산은[이]〉 그 예산은 얼마나 잡고 계십니까? About how much would you like to spend [pay]? ⇌ What price range do you have in mind?
▶ 해외 여행을 할 예산이 없다 I can't afford [allow] a trip abroad.
▶ 사회복지예산이 대폭 삭감되었다 The budget for social welfare was cut drastically.
〈예산을〉 예산을 삭감하다 cut (down) [reduce] a budget / 예산을 세우다[편성하다] make [write, compile] a budget; draw up and estimate; prepare a budget / 국회에서 예산을 통과시키다 pass the budget through the national assembly
〈예산에〉 교제비를 예산에 넣다 include social expenses in a budget; budget social expenses / 예산에 계상하다 budget funds for; set down in the budget
—예산하다 estimate; budget 《for》
▶ 건축비는 5천만원으로 예산한다 The cost of building is estimated at fifty million won.
■ 경비— an estimated appropriation 본— the principal [original] budget 수정— a revised budget 잠정— a provisional budget 총— the total budget 추가— the supplementary budget 평시[전시]— a peace [war, wartime] budget
■ —결손[부족] a budgetary deficit —관리 budget control —연도 a budget year —위원회 the budget committee —조치 《take》 a budgetary measure —초과 an excess over the estimates —할당 budgetary allocations

예산안 豫算案 a draft budget; 〈의안〉 a budget bill
◆ 예산안을 심의하다 discuss the budget bill / 예산안을 국회에 제출하다 open the budget; submit a budget to the national assembly
▶ 예산안은 부결[통과, 승인]되었다 The budget was rejected [passed, approved].
■ 추가— a supplementary budget bill ■ —심의 discussion on the budget bill

예산외 豫算外 〈예산비 지출명목 외 것〉 outside the budget; 〈예상 밖〉 unexpected; unforeseen
■ —수입 receipts outside of budget —지출 defrayment unprovided for in the budget; extraordinary disbursements

예상 豫想 〈예측〉 (a) prospect; a forecast; 〈추측〉 a guess; 〈예기〉 expectation(s); anticipation
◆ 예상대로(의) true to *one's* expectation; as (was) expected / 예상 밖에 beyond (*one's*) expectation(s); 〈예상과 반대로〉 against [contrary to] (*one's*) expectation(s)
〈예상이〉 그의 예상이 들어 맞았다[빗나갔다] He guessed right [wrong]. ⇌ His guess was right [wrong].
▶ 어떤 일이 일어날지 예상이 되지 않는다 It is impossible [isn't possible] to tell what will happen.
〈예상을〉 예상을 뒤엎다 go [be] against *one's* expectations / 예상을 웃돌다 exceed [surpass] 《*one's*》 expectations
〈예상으로〉 내 예상으로 그들은 다음달에 혼인할 것이다 My guess is [I guess] that they will get married next month.
—예상하다 expect; forecast; estimate
▶ 그들은 나라의 보조를 예상하고 그 질환의 연

예상사

구를 시작했다 They began their studies of the disease in anticipation of government aid.
▶ 그녀는 여비를 100만원으로 예상한다 She estimates the traveling expenses at a million won.
■ ─수확고 the estimated production [crop, yield]; a crop estimate ─액 an estimated amount; estimates ─이익 an estimated [anticipated] profit ─착오 a miscalculation

예상사 例常事 an ordinary affair ⇨ 예사(例事)

예상외 豫想外 ◆예상외의 unexpected; unlooked-for; unanticipated / 예상외로 beyond *one's* expectation(s); contrary to [against] (*one's*) expectation / 예상외로 돈이 들다 be more expensive than (*one*) expected
▶ 그 시험은 예상외로 어려웠다 The exam was more difficult than (I had) expected [(口) than I expected].
▶ 결과는 예상외였다 The result exceeded my expectations.
▶ 성적이 예상외로 좋다[나쁘다] The result is better [worse] than I expected.

예서 隸書 the square, ornamental style of Chinese writing

예선 曳船 〈끌기〉 towing; 〈배〉 a tugboat; tug; towboat

예선 豫選 〈달리기 등의〉 a (trial [preliminary]) heat; 〈경기 등의〉 a preliminary; a tryout; 〈축구 등의〉 a qualifying round [heat, game]; 〈선거의〉 a provisional election; a preelection; (美) a primary (election)
◆예선에서 탈락하다 be rejected in an elimination match; be eliminated [disqualified] ((from)) / 예선을 통과하다 get through a preliminary
─예선하다 hold a preliminary match [contest]; 〈선거하다〉 select [elect] provisionally; preelect
■ 제1차─ the first elimination round ■ ─통과자 a qualifier

예속 隸屬 subordination ─예속하다 subordinate *oneself* (to); be subordinate [subject] ((to)) ◆ A를 B에 예속시키다 subordinate A to B ■ ─국 a subject nation; a dependency

예수교 ─教 Christianity ■ ─도[인] a Christian

예수그리스도 Jesus Christ

예순 sixty; threescore ◆예순 살의 노인 an old person of sixty

예술 藝術 art; the arts
◆예술적인 artistic / 비예술적인 inartistic
▶ 그의 연주는 예술적이었다 His playing was artistic. ⇌ He gave artistic performance.
■ 현대─ modern art ■ ─가 an artist; a man of art ─원 the Art Academy ─작품 a work of art; (총칭) art; works of art

예스 yes ◆ ─맨 a yes man
▶ 예스냐 노냐 둘 중의 하나야 The only alternative is yes or no.
▶ 예스냐 노냐 분명히 대답해 Answer me with a plain yes or no.

예스럽다 old-fashioned; of old style; 〈보수적인〉 conservative; antique; antiquated; archaic ◆예스러운 말투 an archaic expression / 예스러운 건물 an old-fashioned [old-sytle] building / 예스럽게 in the old fashion

예스페르센 〈덴마크의 언어학자〉 Jespersen, (Jens) Otto (Harry) (1860-1943)

예습 豫習 preparation (of lessons)
◆예습과 복습 preparations and reviews of *one's* lessons
▶ 나는 내일 수업의 예습을 해야 한다 I must prepare (for) tomorrow's classes.
▶ 내일 예습 다 했니? Have you finished your preparation for tomorrow's lessons?
▶ 예습은 저녁 식사 후에 하겠다 I'll do my homework after dinner.
─예습하다 〈집에서 자습하다〉 do *one's* homework; 〈수업 준비를 하다〉 prepare *one's* lessons
▶ 그는 언제나 예습하지 않고 학교에 간다 He always goes to school without doing any preparation.

예시 例示 illustration; exemplification
─예시하다 illustrate; exemplify
▶ 이 도표는 내가 말하고자 하는 바를 예시한다 This diagram illustrates my point.

예시 豫示 indication; adumbration ─예시하다 indicate beforehand; show signs of

예식 例式 an established form

예식 禮式 a ceremony; a celebration; 〈결혼식〉 a wedding (ceremony) ■ ─장 a wedding [ceremony] hall

예심 豫審 〔法〕 a preliminary hearing [trial]; a pretrial hearing
◆예심중이다 be under preliminary hearings ■ ─법정 the preliminary court of inquiry ─조서 the protocol of preliminary hearings ─판사 an examining [a preliminary] judge

예약 豫約 1 〈호텔 방·탈것의 좌석 등의〉 (英) a booking; (美) a reservation
▶ 그 레스토랑은 예약이 필요하다 You need a reservation for the restaurant.
▶ 다음달까지 예약이 다 됐습니다 We're fully reserved [booked up] until next month.
▶ 주말에는 어느 호텔이나 예약이 다 되있습니다 All the hotels are fully reserved [booked] for the weekend.
▶ 9월 1일부터 예약을 받습니다 We take reservations beginning on September 1 [1 September].
▶ 예약을 취소하고 싶은데요 I'd like to cancel my reservation.
▶ 〔會話〕「예약은 되어 있는지요?」「예, 얼마전에 전화로 했습니다」 "Do you have a reservation sir?" "Yes, I made it by phone a while ago."
─예약하다 (美) reserve; make a reservation; (英) book
▶ 나는 그 비행기의 좌석을 둘 예약했다 I have reserved [booked] two seats on the plane.
▶ 표를 한 장 예약해 드릴까요? Shall I reserve [book] a ticket for you? ⇌ Shall I book you a ticket?
▶ 빨리 예약하십시오. 그렇지 않으면 콘서트 표를 못 사실 겁니다 Book now, or you won't get a ticket for the concert.

2 〈진료・면회 등의〉 an appointment
♦ 내일의 예약을 취소하다[변경하다] cancel [change] *one's* appointment for tomorrow
▶ 의사와 5시에 예약이 되어 있다 I have an appointment with the doctor at five.
—예약하다 make an appointment 《with》
▶ 치과에는 내일 오후 3시로 예약했다 I made an appointment with the dentist for 3 p.m. tomorrow.
3 〈신문・잡지의〉 subscription; 〈상품의〉 an advance order
▶ 귀하의 잡지 예약은 다음달에 끝납니다 Your subscription to the magazine runs out next month.
—예약하다 subscribe to [for]
▶ 타임지의 1년간 구독을 예약했다 I made a subscription [subscribed] to [for] Time magazine for a year.
■ —가격 a subscription price —금 a deposit —독자 a registered reader; a subscriber —모집 invitation for subscription —좌석 a reserved seat —주문 an advance order: 그들은 그 기계의 예약 주문을 받았다 They received an advance order for the machine. —판매[출판] sale [publication] by subscription

예언 豫言 (a) prophecy; (a) prediction
▶ 그 예언은 빗나갔다[적중했다] The prophecy failed [came true].
—예언하다 predict; prophecy; foretell
▶ 그는 그 도시에 대지진이 일어날 것을 예언했다 He predicted that a great earthquake would strike the city.
▶ 그것은 아무도 예언할 수 없다 That is impossible for anyone to foretell.
■ —자 a prophet; a prophetess (여자); a predictor

예외 例外 an exception
♦ 예외적(인) exceptional; unusual / 예외적으로 exceptionally; unusually; as an exception / 예외 없이 without exception / …는 예외로 하고 except(ing)…; with the exception of…
▶ 예외 없는 규칙은 없다 There is no rule without exceptions. ⇌ There is an exception to every rule.
▶ 우리는 예외를 인정치 않는다 We won't admit [allow] of no exception.
▶ 그녀의 자녀는 예외 없이 고명한 학자가 되었다 Without exception, all her children became prominent scholars.
▶ 예외가 있다는 것은 곧 규칙이 있다는 증거다 The exception proves the rule.

예우 禮遇 (an) honorable treatment; a courteous reception
—예우하다 receive *sb* with respect
♦ 외교상 최고로 예우하다 give the highest protocol treatment 《to》
▶ 우리는 그를 각별히 예우했다 We received him with marks of distinction.
▶ 그는 국빈으로 예우 받았다 He was accorded a courteous reception as a guest of the state.

예의 銳意 eagerly; zealously; vigorously; earnestly; ardently
♦ 예의 검토하다 inquire into *sth* assiduously; examine *sth* in earnest / 예의 주시하다 pay sharp attention to; watch
▶ 나는 민주주의를 위해서 예의 힘쓸 작정이다 I'm determined to devote myself to the cause of democracy.

예의 禮儀 courtesy; politeness; civility; etiquette; manners
♦ 예의바른 courteous ⇨ 예바르다 / 예의바르게 politely; courteously / 예의 없는 indecorous; impolite / 예의상 by courtesy; out of courtesy [politeness]; for courtesy's sake
▶ 저 녀석은 예의를 모른다 He has no manners. ⇌ He is rude [impolite, ill-mannered].
▶ 그런 짓은 예의에 어긋난다 It is bad manners to act like that. ⇌ Such behavior is against (the rules of) etiquette.
▶ 그는 아주 예의바른 사람이다 He is a very courteous [polite] person.
▶ 아무리 친한 사이라도 예의는 지켜야 한다 There should be courtesy even between close friends.
■ —범절 courtesy; etiquette; manners; decorum; proprieties: 예의범절을 가르치다 give *sb* lessons in manners [etiquette]

예이츠 〈아일랜드의 시인〉 Yeats, William Butler(1865-1939)

예인선 曳引船 a tug; a tugboat; a towing vessel

예장 禮狀 ♦ 예장을 보내다 send *sb* a letter of thanks

예장 禮裝 full dress ⇨ 예복 ♦ 예장을 하고 in full [ceremonial] dress —예장하다 wear ceremonial dress; be in full dress

예전 former days [times]
♦ 예전의 ancient; old; old-time; 〈이전의〉 former; past; bygone / 예전에는 〈옛날〉 in old times [days]; 〈지난날〉 in former times [days, years]; formerly / 예전부터 from old times
▶ 예전에는 여기에 성이 있었다 There used to be a castle here. ⇌ There was a castle here in old [ancient, olden] times.
▶ 그는 예전 그대로다 He is just as he always was. ⇌ He hasn't changed (one bit).
▶ 예전에 그를 만난 기억이 난다 I remember meeting him a long time ago.
▶ 모든 것이 예전과 달라졌다 Things are not what they used to be.
▶ 예전에는 참 좋았었다 Things were better in the old days.

예절 禮節 courtesy ⇨ 예의(禮儀)
♦ 예절을 모르다 have no sense of propriety; have no manners / 예절을 지키다[어기다] observe [offend, against] the proprieties
▶ 그들은 예절을 존중한다 They think much of propriety.
▶ 그는 예절을 어느 정도 안다 He has some sense of propriety.
▶ 의식이 족해야 예절을 차릴줄 안다 (속담) Well fed, well bred.

예정 豫定 〈계획〉 a plan; a program; a schedule; 〈준비〉 previous arrangement; 〈예상〉 expectation; anticipation; prearrangement
♦ 출발[도착] 예정 시간 the expected time of departure [arrival] / 출산 예정일 the expected date of confinement / 출항 예정일 the

scheduled date of sailing / 예정 시각에 at the appointed [set] time; on (scheduled) time / 예정대로 as prearranged [previously arranged]; according to plan [program, schedule]
▶ 공사가 예정대로 진행되고 있다 The construction is going as scheduled [according to schedule].
▶ 비행기는 예정대로 3시 15분에 떠난다 The plane will depart on schedule [as scheduled] at 3:15.
▶ 예정이 변경되었다 The schedule has been changed.
▶ 열차는 예정보다 2시간 연착했다 The train arrived two hours behind schedule [time].
▶ 그녀와 10시에 만날 예정이다 I'm going to meet her at ten.
▶ 저는 12월에 출산 예정입니다 I'm expecting a baby in December.
▶ 그는 내일 서울에 도착할 예정이다 He is expected (to be) in Seoul tomorrow.
▶ 기차는 6시 도착 예정이다 The train is due at six.
▶ 배는 5월 2일 출범 예정이다 The ship is scheduled [slated] to sail on May 2.
▶ 그는 금년 3월에 졸업할 예정이다 He is expected to graduate from his school in March this year.
—예정하다 plan; schedule; make a plan; 〈기대하다〉 expect
▶ 모임은 내일 2시로 예정되어 있다 The meeting is scheduled for 2 p.m. tomorrow.
■—액 the estimated amount —자 an expectant; 입후보 예정자 an expectant candidate —표 a schedule —행동 (개시) 시각 〔軍〕 the zero hour
예제 here and there; this place and that (place); (in) places
예제 例題 〈보기〉 an example; 〈연습 문제〉 an exercise ▶ 아래 예제에 따라 다음 두 물음에 답하시오 Answer these two questions according to the example given below.
예조 禮曹 〔古制〕 the Board of Rites
예증 例證 (an) illustration; an instance; an example ◆ 예증으로(서) by way of illustration; as an example / …의 예증이 되다 serve as an example of…; be illustrative of…
▶ 나는 다만 예증으로서 그 사실을 들었다 I only presented the fact as an example [instance].
▶ 그것은 이 사실의 뚜렷한 예증이 된다 It affords a striking illustration of the fact.
—예증하다 illustrate; give evidence; exemplify
예지 豫知 foreknowledge; foresight; prescience; 〈예언〉 foreboding; prediction —예지하다 foresee; foreknow; 〈예언하다〉 predict; foretell
예지 叡智 wisdom; sagacity; intelligence; 〔哲〕 intellect
예진 豫震 a foreshock; a preliminary tremor
예찬 禮讚 worship; praise; adoration; admiration; glorification
▶ 그의 용기는 전시민의 예찬을 받았다 His bravery was admired by the whole citizenry.
▶ 그의 연기는 대단한 예찬을 받았다 He won great praise for his performance.
—예찬하다 worship; praise; adore; idolize; glorify; sing the praises of
■—자 a worshiper; an adorer; an admirer
예측 豫測 prediction; an estimate; estimation; a forecast ◆ 예측이 틀리다 make a wrong estimate [forecast]
▶ 결과가 어떻게 될지 예측을 못하겠다 How the result may turn out is beyond imagination.
▶ 그의 예측대로 되었다 His prediction came true.
▶ 우리의 예측은 어긋났다 We made an incorrect estimate.
—예측하다 estimate; forecast; presuppose; guess beforehand
▶ 결과는 아무도 예측할 수 없다 How it may turn out is anybody's guess.
▶ 어느쪽이 이길지 예측하기 어렵다 It is difficult to predict which will win.
▶ 그는 종종 예측할 수 없는 언동을 한다 He is often unpredictable.
예치금 預置金 a deposit; money on deposit
예치물 預置物 an article left in charge; a charge; a deposit
예컨대 例— 〈예를 들면〉 for instance; for example; e.g.; 〈이를테면〉 such as; say
▶ 몸에 해로운 것, 예컨대 술이나 담배를 삼가는게 좋다 It is much better to abstain from things which harm the body, such as alcohol and tobacco.
예탁 預託 depositing; deposition —예탁하다 deposit ■—금 a deposit; deposit money —자 a depositor
예탐 豫探 previous inquiry; spying —예탐하다 inquire beforehand; spy on [upon]; sound [feel] out ■—꾼 a spy
예편하다 豫編— place sb on the reserve list; transfer sb to the first reserve ◆ 예편되다 go into the first reserve; be placed on the reserve list
예포 禮砲 a salute (gun) ◆ 예포를 쏘다 fire [give] a salute ▶ 그들은 세 발의 예포를 쏘았다 They fired a salute of three guns.
예품 藝風 one's [the] (distinctive [trademark]) style of acting [performance]
예항 曳航 towing —예항하다 take [have] 《a ship》 in tow; tow 《a ship》
예해 例解 an illustration; an example; an exemplification —예해하다 illustrate; exemplify; explain by examples
예행 豫行 rehearsal; (preliminary) run-through [tryout] —예행하다 rehearse; try out; perform preliminarily ◆ 졸업식을 예행하다 have [go through] a rehearsal of the graduation ceremony
예행 연습 豫行演習 a (dress) rehearsal; preliminary exercises ◆ 예행 연습을 하다 rehearse; run through 《a play》
예후 豫後 〈병후의 경과・회복〉 convalescence; 〔醫〕 〈병의 경과와 결과에 대한 전망〉 prognosis 《pl. -ses》 ▶ 그는 예후가 좋다[좋지 않다] He [is not] convalescing satisfactorily.

엣장 Oh dear!; Oh no!; Darn!; Damn!; Pshaw!; Goodness!; Gee whiz!

옐친 〈러시아의 정치가·연방 대통령〉 Yeltsin, Boris (1931-)

옛 old; ancient; olden; antique
▶이 지방에는 옛 풍습이 많이 남아 있다 Many old customs still exist in this area.

옛글 ancient writings; 〈고전〉 classics

옛날 〈오래 전〉 a long time ago; long ago; 〈한때〉 once; 〈전에〉 before; formerly; in former times [days]; 〈과거에〉 in the past; in old [ancient] times; 〈형용사적〉 old; ancient
▶옛날에는 여성에게 선거권이 부여되지 않았다 Formerly [In former times], the right to vote was not given to women.
▶옛날 옛날 한 마을에 한 노인이 살고 있었다 Once upon a time [Long long ago] there lived an old man in a village.
▶옛날엔 사람들이 동굴에서 살았다 Long ago, people lived in caves.
▶옛날에는 지구가 둥글다는 것을 사람들이 알지 못했다 In old(en) times people did not know that the earth is round.
▶그녀는 그의 옛날 여자 친구다 She is his former girl friend.
▶그는 옛날의 그가 아니다 He is not what he used to be.
▶우리는 같이 놀던 옛날을 회상했다 We remembered the old days when we played together.
▶이 지방에서는 옛날 그대로의 방식으로 농사를 짓고 있다 In this region, people still farm the same way as they did in ancient times.

옛말 1 〈고어(古語)〉 an archaism
2 〈옛사람의 말〉 an old saying [proverb]
3 〈지난 일〉 ▶그 마을의 번영도 이미 옛말이 되었다 The prosperity of the town is now a thing of the past.

옛모습 old familiar faces; traces; remains; vestiges
◆옛모습을 찾아볼 수 없다 〈사람의〉 be but the shadow of *one's* former self; 〈사물의〉 be a mere shadow of its former prosperity; 〈자취의〉 have gone (all) to pot
▶그는 옛모습 그대로다 He is just as he used to be. ⇒ He has not changed a bit since then.

옛사람 ancient people; men of old (times); (총칭) the ancients

옛사랑 a bygone romance; 〈애인〉 *one's* old flame

옛상처 一傷處 an old wound; a scar ◆옛상처를 들추다 rake up *sb's* past misdeeds [scandals]

옛식 一式 an old type; 〈구습〉 an old custom [rite] ◆옛식의 old-fashioned / 옛식을 따라 in accordance with the old custom

옛이야기 an old tale [story]; 〈전설〉 a legend; 〈회고담〉 *one's* past stories; stories of *one's* past [youth]; reminiscences
◆옛이야기를 하다 〈회고담〉 talk about [over] old times / 아이들에게 옛이야기를 들려주다 tell old tales to children
▶그들은 노인의 옛이야기에 귀를 기울였다 They listened to the old man's reminiscences.
▶지금은 그것도 옛이야기가 되었다 It is now an old story [a thing of the past].

옛일 〈과거사〉 a thing gone by; bygones; a thing of the past ◆옛일을 생각하다 think of *one's* past ▶그것도 이제는 옛일이 되고 말았다 It is now a thing of the past.

옛적 〈오래전〉 long ago ⇨ 옛날

옛정 一情 old friendship ⇨ 구정(舊情)

옛집 *one's* former residence; an old nest [haunt]; *one's* old home [house] ◆옛집이 그립다 have a longing for *one's* old haunt / 옛집으로 돌아가다 return to *one's* old haunt

옛추억 一追憶 the memory of *one's* early days; *one's* old memory ◆옛추억을 더듬다 think of *one's* good old days

옛친구 一親舊 an old friend

옜다 〈남이 찾던 물건을 건네 줄 때〉 Here it is!; 〈선물 등을 줄 때〉 This [It] is for you!
▶옜다, 이것 가져라 Here, take this.

오 1 〈아〉 Oh!; O; O dear!; Ah!
▶오 슬프도다 Alas! ⇌ Woe is [to] me.
▶오 주여, 우리를 악에서 구하옵소서 O Lord, deliver us from evil.
2 〈대답〉 Yes!; Oh; all right; very well
▶오, 알았어 Yah, I see [understand].

오 五 five ◆제 오 the fifth / 오 배(의) five times 《as large》; fivefold; quintuple / 오분의 일 one-fifth

오가다 come and go
◆오가는 사람들 passersby / 오가는 길에 on the [*one's*] way to and from
▶나는 걸어서 학교를 오간다 I walk to and from school.
▶회사를 오가는 길에 타는 버스는 언제나 복잡하다 The bus I take on my way to and from the office is always crowded.

오가리 〈호박고지〉 dried chips [slices] of pumpkin ◆오가리 들다 wither ⇨ 오갈들다

오각형 五角形 a pentagon
◆오각형의 five-angled; pentagonal

오갈들다 1 〈오글쪼글해지다〉 wither; wilt; shrivel; be shriveled up 2 〈겁먹다〉 be in a (blue) funk 《of *sth*》; (口) get [have] cold feet

오갈병 一病 〔植〕 wilt; wilt disease

오감 五感 the (five) senses

오감하다 〈만족하다〉 (quite) satisfactory; enough ▶그 정도면 나로서는 오감합니다 I can hope for nothing better than that.

오개년계획 五個年計劃 a five-year plan [program] ■경제개발— a five-year economic development plan

오경 五經 the Five Chinese Classics (of Confucianism)

오계 五戒 〔佛敎〕 the five commandments [precepts] (of Buddhism)

오곡 五穀 〈다섯 가지 곡식〉 the five grains; 〈곡식의 총칭〉 all kinds of cereals; (staple) grains ■—밥 boiled rice with four other staple cereals

오공 五共 the Fifth Republic Government of Korea

오관 五官 the five sensory organs; the five organs (of sense)

오그라들다 shrink; shrivel (up); contract;

curl; curl (oneself) up; be shortened
◆추워서 오그라들다 be pinched with cold
▶이 스웨터는 세탁하면 오그라든다 This sweater shrinks in the wash.
▶나일론 섬유는 세탁해도 오그라들지 않는다 Nylon fabrics will not shrink when (they are) washed.
▶마른 오징어는 구우면 오그라든다 A dried cuttlefish curls when grilled.

오그라지다 1 〈오므라지다〉 shrivel (up); curl; contract ◆나뭇잎이 오그라지다 leaves shrivel up (in the hot sun)
2 〈움푹해지다〉 dent ◆오그라진 냄비 a dented pan ◆양철은 잘 오그라진다 Tin dents easily.
3 〈우그러지다〉 warp; be contorted

오그랑이 〈물건〉 a shrunk object; a shriveled [curled] thing; 〈사람〉 a crooked [perverse] person ▶그는 구제불능의 오그랑이다 He is an impossible crooked person.

오그랑장사 a dwindling [diminishing, failing] business

오그랑하다 somewhat shriveled [curled]; slightly dented

오그르르 〈물 끓는 소리〉 hubble-bubble; 〈벌레가 많은 모양〉 in swarms
▶주전자에 물이 오그르르 끓는다 The water in a kettle is boiling with a hubble-bubble.
▶개미 떼가 쿠키 주위에 오그르르 모여 있다 Ants are swarming around a cookie.

오그리다 1 〈몸을〉 curl [roll] up (one's body); draw up [in] (one's legs)
◆다리를 오그리고 자다 sleep with one's legs drawn in / 몸을 오그리고 자다 sleep curled up
▶몸을 오그릴 만큼 춥다 It is cold enough to shrivel one up.
2 〈물건을〉 shrink; dent; indent; bend
◆양동이를 오그리다 indent a pail [bucket] / 철사를 오그려 고리를 만들다 bend a piece of wire into a ring

오글거리다 〈물이〉 simmer; boil with a hubble-bubble; 〈벌레가〉 swarm

오글보글 hubble-bubble —**오글보글하다** boil with a hubble-bubble [bubbling sound]

오글쪼글하다 crinkled; shriveled; wrinkled; crumpled; rumpled
◆오글쪼글한 노파 a crone; a withered old woman / 오글쪼글한 손 a withered hand; a hand full of wrinkles / 오글쪼글해진 사과 a shriveled apple / 오글쪼글해지다 be crumpled; crumple; be wrinkled

오금 the back [hollow] of the knee
◆오금(이) 뜨다 be always on the gad [move] / 오금이 저리다 (겁나서) feel one's legs tremble; 〈죄 때문에〉 be conscious of one's fault; feel guilty; have a guilty conscience / 오금을 못쓰다 be unable to use one's knees; (비유) 〈겁먹어〉 be transfixed (with fear); be under sb's control [thumb] / 오금(을) 박다 squelch [snub] sb's contradiction / 오금(을) 펴다 stretch one's knees
▶저 외나무 다리를 건널 때 나는 오금이 저리는 것을 느낀다 I feel my legs tremble when I cross the single-log bridge.
▶그는 아내 앞에서 오금을 못쓴다 He is under his wife's thumb.

오금탱이 an inner curve

오긋이 with a slight cave-in [curve, dent, indent] toward center; a little pressed in

오긋하다 〈서술적〉 have a slight cave-in toward center; be somewhat dented [indented]; be pressed in slightly
▶이 나무 쟁반은 가운데가 오긋하다 This wooden tray has a slight cave-in toward center.

오기 傲氣 〈지기 싫어하는〉 a competitive [an unyielding] spirit; haughtiness; 〈자존심〉 pride
◆오기로 in a spirit of rivalry / 오기를 부리다 be game enough to compete (another); refuse to yield (to) / 오기가 세다 be reluctant [unwilling] to admit defeat / 오기로 버티다 endure through pride; try to endure beyond one's power
▶그녀는 워낙 오기가 세서 남에게 지고는 못산다 She is never content to be (the) second best. ⇒ She is never content unless she is the best.

오기 誤記 an error in writing; a clerical error; a misentry; a slip of the pen
—**오기하다** write incorrectly; miswrite; make a slip of the pen; 〈철자를〉 misspell (a word)
◆주소를 오기하다 address (a letter) wrongly; write a wrong address

오나가나 〈늘〉 always; all the time
▶그는 오나가나 말썽이다 He is a constant troublemaker.
▶그것은 내가 오나가나 주장한 바다 That is what I have always insisted.
▶그는 오나가나 팔자를 탓한다 He always grumbles at his lot.

오나니즘 〈자위〉 onanism

오냐 〈그래〉 Yes; 〈동의〉 All right; O.K. ◆오냐 알았다 Yes, I understand [have got it]. ◆오냐 그렇게 해라 All right, you may do so.

오뇌 懊惱 (an) agony; anguish; worry; trouble —**오뇌하다** be in agony; be anguished [worried, troubled]

오누이 brother and sister

오뉴월 五六月 May and June ◆오뉴월 긴긴 해에 in May and June when days are long

오는 next; coming ◆오는 화요일(에) next Tuesday; on Tuesday next / 오는 총선거 the forthcoming general election

오는 말이 고와야 가는 말이 곱다 〈속담〉 Claw me, and I'll claw thee. ⇒ Scratch my back and I will scratch yours.

오늘 today; this day

> 解說 「지난 주의 오늘」에 해당하는 영어에는 (ⅰ) a week ago today (ⅱ) (美) today [this day] last week (ⅲ) (英) today [this day] week (ⅳ) (英) (a) week today 등이 있다. (ⅲ)과 (ⅳ)는 문맥에 따라서「다음주의 오늘」의 뜻으로 쓰이는데 그 구별은 동사의 시제로 판단된다. 「다음주의 오늘」로는 이 밖에도 a week from [now] today next week가 쓰인다.

♦ 내년[작년]의 오늘 today [this day] year; a year from [ago] today / 바로 오늘 this very day / 오늘 신문 today's newspapers / 오늘 오전[오후] this morning [afternoon] / 오늘부터 1주일 동안 for a week from today / 오늘까지 up to now; till [until] this day / 오늘 따라 today of all days / 오늘부터(는) from this day forth; from now on
▶ 오늘은 며칠이냐? What day of the month is this?
▶ 오늘은 1월 3일이다 This is the third of January.
▶ 오늘은 무슨 요일이냐? What day of week is this?
▶ 오늘은 월요일이다 Today is Monday.
▶ 오늘은 이만 This much for today. ⇌ Let's call it a day.
▶ 그는 오늘 내일 하는 중태다 He is so ill that it is feared he will be for this world only a day or two.
▶ 오늘의 한국은 10년 전의 한국이 아니다 Today's Korea isn't what it was ten years ago.
▶ 오늘 할 수 있는 일을 내일로 미루지 마라 Never [Don't] put off till tomorrow what may be done today.

오늘날 today; these days [times]; the present day
♦ 오늘날의 학생들 students of today / 오늘날의 한국 the Korea of today; Korea today / 오늘날에는 nowadays; today; these days; at present / 오늘날에 이르기까지 until [to] the present; to this day / 원자력 시대인 오늘날에 in this age of atomic energy / 생존경쟁이 격심한 오늘날에 in these days of severe struggle for existence
▶ 오늘날 젊은이들에게 가장 인기 있는 스포츠는 무엇입니까? What sport is (the) most popular among the young nowadays?

오늘밤 this evening; tonight
♦ 오늘밤 중에[안으로] in the course of the night; before the night is out
▶ 오늘밤 찾아뵈어도 되겠습니까? May [Can] I come and see you this evening?
▶ 오늘밤은 대단히 춥지요? It is very cold tonight, isn't it?

오늬 the nock [notch] 《of an arrow》
♦ 오늬를 붙이다 nock [notch] 《an arrow》

오닐 〈미국의 극작가〉 O'Neill, Eugene (Gladstone) (1888-1953)

오다 **1**〈일반적으로〉come ♦ 오는 길에 on one's way here / 가까이 오다 come nearer; draw closer [near] / 가지러 오다 come for sth / 데리러[모시러] 오다 come for sb
▶ 이리 오너라 Come here.
▶ 저기 버스가 온다 There comes a bus!
▶ 그는 약속하고서도 오지 않았다 He didn't come in spite of his promise.
▶ 이쪽으로 오시오 Come [Step] this way, please.
▶ 여기는 한 번 온 적이 있다 I have been here once.
2 〈닿다〉 reach; arrive 《at, in》
▶ 버스가 온다 Here comes our bus.
▶ 자, 다 왔다 Here we are.
▶ 엄마, 잘 다녀왔습니다 I'm home, Mom.
▶ 편지 온 게 있니? Any mail for me today?
▶ 전화 왔어요 You are wanted on the phone.
▶ 선생님은 아직 안 오셨다 The teacher hasn't showed up yet.
3 〈방문하다〉 call 《on sb, at a house》; come to see; visit
▶ 바쁠 때 사람이 오면 반갑지 않다 I don't like to have people come when I am busy.
▶ 내일 다시 오겠습니다 I will call again tomorrow.
▶ 김선생이 오셨습니다 Mr. Kim has been over here [wants to see you].
▶ 잘 오셨습니다 You are welcome.
4 〈눈·비 등이〉 fall; come down; rain; snow
▶ 비가 올 것 같다 It looks like rain.
5 〈잠·졸음이〉 ♦ 졸음이 오다 become [feel] sleepy [drowsy]
6 〈계절·시간이〉 come 《round [around]》
▶ 겨울이 오면 봄도 멀지 않겠지? If winter comes can spring be far behind?
▶ 이 지방에는 봄이 늦게 온다 Spring is late coming in this part of the country.
7 〈전기 등이〉 be lighted; come [go] on
▶ 전깃불이 올 때가 됐어 It is the time for the light to go on.
8 〈전래하다〉 come 《from》; be introduced 《into, from》; 〈유래하다〉 derive from
♦ 그리스어에서 온 말 a word derived from Greek; a word of Greek origin
▶ 그 사상은 인도에서 왔다 The ideas originated in India.
9 〈기인·결과〉 come of [from]; be due to; be caused by ▶ 그의 병은 과식에서 온 것이다 His illness comes of overeating.
10 gradually come 《in doing》; become; grow
▶ 떠날 날이 가까워 온다 The day is drawing near when we are to leave.

오다가다 〈이따금〉 occasionally; at times; now and then; once in a while; sometimes; 〈어쩌다가〉 casually
♦ 오다가다 만난 부부 a free-love couple; a couple of free union / 오다가다 들르는 뜨내기 손님 a casual visitor / 오다가다 만나다 meet by chance
▶ 제인으로부터 오다가다 소식이 있다 I hear from Jane once in a while.

오달지다 〈체격이〉 solid; sturdy; 〈성질이〉 hardheaded; sharp; shrewd; smart

오답 誤答 an incorrect [a wrong] answer
오대양 五大洋 the Five Oceans
오대주 五大洲 the Five Continents
오더 **1** 〈주문〉 an order **2** 〈순서〉 (an) order
▶ 오늘의 라이온즈 팀 배팅 오더는 다음과 같다 The batting order of the Lions today is as follows.

오도 悟道 〈佛敎〉〈깨달음〉 spiritual enlightenment; 〈길〉 the way of enlightenment ―**오도하다** attain (the) supreme wisdom; be spiritually enlightened

오도 誤導 misguidance ―**오도하다** mislead; misguide; misdirect; lead sb astray

오도깝스럽다 flippant ⇨ 호들갑스럽다

오도독 〈깨무는 소리〉 with a crunching sound ♦ 오도독 오도독 crunching; munching / 오도독 깨물다 champ; crunch
—**오도독하다[거리다]** crunch; munch; make a crunching sound
■ —뼈 cartilage; gristle

오도방정 flightiness; giddiness; frivolity; flippancy; slapdash ♦ 오도방정을 떨다 act frivolously; behave in a giddy [slaphappy] way

오도카니 absentmindedly and lonely; blankly ⇨ 우두커니
▶ 노승은 불단 앞에 오도카니 앉아 있었다 The old priest was sitting lonely and quietly before the altar.
▶ 연잎에 작은 개구리 한 마리가 오도카니 앉아 있다 A little frog is sitting on a lotus leaf quietly and lonely.

오독 誤讀 misreading; misinterpretation
—**오독하다** misread; misinterpret; read wrongly

오돌오돌하다 〈좀 단단하다〉 somewhat hard to chew; gristly; cartilaginous; 〈잘 삶아지지 않다〉 half-boiled
▶ 이 생선꼬치는 씹으니까 오돌오돌하다 This fish stick is gristly and somewhat hard to chew.

오동나무 梧桐— 〖植〗 a paulownia; an empress tree; a princess tree; a karritree

오동통하다 chubby; plump; short and fat; pudgy; thick and short ♦ 오동통한 소년 a chubby boy

오동포동하다 pudgy; plump(y); chubby ♦ 볼이 오동포동한 젖먹이 a baby with plump(y) cheeks

오두막(집) —幕(—) a hut; a shack; a shed; a hovel; a (humble) cottage; a shanty
♦ 오두막 집을 짓다 put up a shanty [hovel]
▶ 오두막집이라도 내 집이 제일이다 There's no place like home, however humble it may be.

오드콜로뉴 (프) eau de cologne; Eau de Cologne; cologne

오든 〈영국 태생의 미국 시인·극작가〉 Auden, Wystan Hugh (1907-73)

오들오들 trembling; shivering; shuddering
♦ 오들오들 떨다 quiver; tremble; shiver 《with cold》; 두려워서 오들오들 떨다 tremble [shudder] with fear; shudder at 《the sight》 / 오들오들 떨게 하다 strike terror into *sb's* heart; terrify

오디 〈뽕의〉 a mulberry
오디세우스 〖그神〗 Odysseus
오디션 〈연예인 채용 테스트〉 an audition
♦ 오디션을 받다 audition (for a part); have an audition / 오디션을 받게 하다[부과하다] audition; give an audition to
▶ 나는 그 배역을 맡기 위해 오디션을 받았다 I auditioned for the part.
▶ 신인 배우에게 오디션을 부과했다 We auditioned [gave an audition to] a new actor.

오디오 audio (equipment) ■ —비주얼 audiovisuals —애호가 an audiophile —테이프 audiotape

오뚝 high ⇨ 우뚝

오뚝이[1] 〈완구〉 a tumbler; a roly-poly; a self-righting toy

오뚝이[2] 〈오뚝하게〉 high; aloft
♦ 오뚝이 서다 overtop 《*sth*》
▶ 나는 연못의 연꽃이 연잎 위에 오뚝이 서 있는 것을 보았다 I saw a lotus flower that overtopped the lotus leaves in a pond.

오라 a rope for binding a criminal
♦ 오라를 지우다 bind *sb's* hands behind 《his》 back / 오라에 묶이다 be bound with a rope; be arrested / 죄인을 오라로 묶다 bind a criminal with a rope; arrest a culprit

오라기 a piece, a bit
♦ 실 오라기 a piece of thread [string] / 헝겊 오라기 a piece [strip] of cloth / 실 오라기 하나 걸치지 않고 stark-naked; with nothing on; without a stitch of clothing 《on》

오라버니, 오라범 a woman's [girl's] elder brother ■ —댁 the wife of a woman's elder brother

오라지다 have *one's* hands tied behind *one's* back ▶ 오라질 Damn [Blast, Dash, Hang] it! ⇌ The devil! ⇌ Confound (it [you])!

오라토리오 〖樂〗 an oratorio (*pl.* ~s)

오락 娛樂 〈즐거움〉 amusement(s); pleasure; entertainment; 〈기분전환〉 recreation; pastime; 〈취미〉 a hobby
♦ 오락으로 for pleasure; for *one's* recreation [amusement]; by way of pastime; as a recreation
▶ 당신은 오락으로 무엇을 하십니까? What do you do as a pastime?
▶ 하이킹은 건전한 야외 오락이다 Hiking is a good outdoor recreation.
■ 실내— indoor amusements [entertainment] —물 a plaything; 〈영화의〉 a film for amusement —비 recreation expenditure —서적 recreational readings —설비[시설, 기관] recreation(al) facilities; a means of public amusement; amusement facilities —실 an amusement hall; a recreation [rumpus, game] room; 〈군대의〉 a service club; 〈청소년의〉 a video game room —잡지 a magazine for amusement —장 a place of amusement [entertainment]; a recreation center —프로그램 an entertainment program

오락가락 〈왔다갔다·비나 눈이〉 coming and going; to and fro; back and forth; off and on
—**오락가락하다** fitful; come and go; move [go] back and forth
♦ 오락가락하는 바람 a fitful wind
▶ 비가 오락가락한다 It rains fitfully [off and on, by fits and starts].
▶ 그는 정신이 오락가락하는 모양이다 His mind seems to wander [stray].

오랑우탄 〖動〗 an orang(o)utan(g)
오랑캐 a barbarian
오랑캐꽃 〖植〗 a violet=제비꽃
오래 〈시간상으로 길게〉 long; for long; for a long time [while]

> 解說 *long, for (very) long*은 보통 부정문·의문문에 쓰인다. 다만 다음 경우에는 긍정문에서도 가능하다. (i) so, as, enough 등으로 수

식되든가 비교급으로 쓰이는 경우: The rain will last longer. (비는 좀더 오래 계속될 것이다) (ii) 「have long+신념·상정(想定)·태도 등을 나타내는 동사」의 꼴로 쓰이는 경우: I have long thought of doing that. (나는 오래 그것을 하려고 마음먹어 왔다) (▶I've been thinking of doing that for a long time. 은 구어적인 표현임).

◆오래전에 long ago [before] / 오래 걸리다 take long; take a long time; require a lot [plenty] of time / 오래 머물다 stay long; make a long stay / 오래 살다 live long; enjoy longevity
▶ 오래 살고 볼 일이다 **(속담)** Live and learn.
▶ 이 비는 오래 계속되지 않을 것이다 This rain will not last long.
▶ 버스가 오래 오지 않았다 The bus didn't come for a long time.
▶ 오래 기다리시게 해서 죄송합니다 I'm sorry to have kept you waiting so long.

오래다 (be) durable; (keep, last, stay) long
◆오래가는 우정 durable friendship / 바래지 않고 오래가는 색 a durable color / 오래가는 신발 a durable pair of shoes / 오래가지 않다 do not last long [a long time]; be not durable
▶ 이 좋은 날씨는 오래갈 것 같지 않다 I'm afraid this fine weather will not hold [last, stay] long.

오래간만 ◆오래간만에 after a long time [interval, silence, absence, separation]; for the first time in a long time
▶ 오래간만입니다 I haven't seen you for a long time. ⇌ It is ages since I saw you last. ⇌ It's been quite a time since we met. ⇌ Long time no see.
▶ 그녀에게서 오래간만에 전화가 왔다 I had a call from her for the first time in a long time.

오래다 long; of long standing; long continued; of many years; 〈서술적〉 be a long time (since)
◆오랜 전설 an old legend / 오랜 전통 a time-honored tradition / 오랜 세월 many years; a long time / 오랜 옛날 the remote ages; the far-off days; the far past; great antiquity / 오랜 친구 a longtime friend / 오래지 않아 before long; not long after
▶ 그를 본 지 오래다 I haven't seen him (for) a long time. ⇌ It is a long time since I saw him last.
▶ 그는 죽은 지 오래다 He has been long dead. ⇌ It has been a long time since he passed away.

오래도록 for long; for a long time; 〈늦게까지〉 till late
◆오래도록 기다리다 wait a long while
▶ 오래도록 그를 못만났다 I haven't seen him for a long time.
▶ 오래도록 소식 전하지 못해 미안합니다 I must apologize to you for my long silence.

오래되다 1 〈시간이〉 of long standing 2 〈낡다〉 old; aged; antiquated; time-honored; old-fashioned
◆오래된 풍습 an old custom / 아주 오래되다 be as old as the hills [world]

오래오래 for a long long time; very long; 〈영원히〉 forever; eternally; everlastingly
◆오래오래 살다 live long; live to a ripe old age
▶ 양친은 딸이 오래오래 행복하기를 염원한다 The parents hope their daughter will be happy for ever and ever.

오랫동안 〈긴 세월〉 long; **(for)** a long time; **(俗) (for)** dog's age; **(for)** donkey's years [ears]; 〈장시간〉 **(for)** a good while
▶ 우리는 그에게서 오랫동안 소식을 듣지 못했다 We haven't heard nothing from him for long.
▶ 오랫동안 소식 전하지 못해 죄송합니다 I'm sorry that I haven't contacted you for so long.

오레오마이신 (商標)〔藥〕Aureomycin
오렌지 an orange ◆오렌지색의 orange ■ㅡ주스 orange juice
오려내다 cut [clip] (out) ((from)); scissor out ((from)) ⇨ 오리다
◆오려낸 신문 기사 **(美)** newspaper clippings; **(英)** press cuttings
오로라 〈극광〉 an aurora **(**pl.**** ~s, -rae)
■남극— ⇨ 극광(남~) 북극— ⇨ 극광(북~)
오로지 only; wholly; entirely; exclusively; earnestly; very hard
▶ 그는 오로지 암세포 연구에만 전념했다 He devoted himself entirely [heart and soul] to his study on cancer cells.
▶ 그들은 오로지 평화를 기원했다 They earnestly prayed for peace.
오롯하다 〈완전하다〉 perfect; complete; 〈원만하다〉 faultless; harmonious
오류 誤謬 a mistake; an error; a fallacy
◆오류를 깨닫다 realize *one's* errors / 오류를 범하다 make a mistake [an error]; fall into the error (of) / 오류를 바로잡다 correct the errors; rectify a mistake
▶ 제 영어는 오류투성이죠? My English is full of mistakes, isn't it?
오륜 五倫 the five principal moral rules to govern the human relations; the five principles of morality
오륜 五輪 the Olympics ⇨ 올림픽
오르가슴 [〈프〉 orgasme] 〈성적 쾌감의 절정〉 (an) orgasm
오르간 an organ
◆오르간을 연주하다 play the organ
■리드— a reed organ; a cabinet organ; a harmonium 전자— an electric organ 파이프— a pipe organ 연주자— an organist
오르골 [〈네〉 orgel] a music box; **(英)** musical box
오르내리 ascent and descent; rise and fall; 〈시세의〉 ups and downs; fluctuations
오르내리다 1 〈높은 곳을〉 go [walk] up and down; ascend and descend
▶ 계단을 오르내릴 때 조심하시오 Be careful in going up and down the stairs.
2 〈물가·열 등이〉 fluctuate; rise and fall; go up and down
▶ 물가가 오르내린다 The prices fluctuate.

▶ 온도계가 섭씨 30도선에서 오르내렸다 The mercury hovered around 30℃.
3 〈입에〉 be talked [gossiped] about
▶ 그의 이상한 행동이 이웃 사람들 입에 오르내렸다 His strange behavior became the talk of the neighborhood.
4 〈음식이〉 do not settle 《in the stomach》
오르다 1 〈위로〉 rise; 〈높은 곳에〉 ascend; go [walk] up; climb; make an ascent of

解説 *go up*은「오르다, 올라가다」를 뜻하는 가장 일반적인 말이다. *rise*는 go up보다 문어적인 말인데 거의 같은 뜻으로 쓰인다. *climb*은 보통「손발을 움직여서 한발자국씩 높은 곳에 오르다」는 뜻이지만 그냥「오르다」의 뜻으로도 쓰인다. *ascend*는 격식 차린 말로 climb과는 달리 반드시 노력이나 곤란의 뜻을 포함하지 않고「서서히, 당당히」란 뜻이 있다.

♦ 계단을 오르다 go [walk] up the stairs / 나무에 오르다 climb a tree / 산에 오르다 climb [go up] a mountain / 지붕에 오르다 go up on the roof / 연단에 오르다 step on [mount] the platform
▶ 막이 올랐다 The curtain rose.
2 〈탈것 등에 올라타다〉 mount; get [step] on; ride; ride on; get in [on, into]
♦ 기차[비행기]에 오르다 board a train [an airplane] / 차에 오르다 ride on a car
3 〈값이〉 rise; advance; go [come, look] up 《to》
▶ 물가가 오른다 Prices go up [advance].
▶ 전기요금이 올랐다 The power rate is increased [raised, pushed up].
4 〈남의 이야깃거리가 되다〉 be gossiped about; become the talk of
♦ 물망에 오르다 be popularly [widely] expected
▶ 그가 회장에 선출될 거라는 얘기가 사람들 입에 오르고 있다 The talk is [There are rumors] that he will be elected chairman.
5 〈의제 등에〉 be placed before; be brought up; come up; 〈무대에〉 be presented [put] on; 〈식탁에〉 be served
♦ 회의 의제로 오르다 be brought up at the meeting for discussion
▶ 그가 쓴 각본이 무대에 오를 것이다 The play he wrote will be presented on the stage.
▶ 야채 요리가 매일 아침 식탁에 오른다 A vegetable dish is served on the table every morning.
6 〈승진·승급하다〉 rise 《to》; be promoted 《to》; be raised 《to》; 〈왕위에〉 ascend; accede 《to》
♦ 권좌에 오르다 rise to power / 왕위에 오르다 accede [come] to the throne; ascend the throne / 계급이 오르다 rise in rank / 지위가 오르다 rise in status / 지위가 높이 오르다 be promoted [rise] to a higher position / 월급이 오르다 have *one's* salary raised; get a raise [《英》 rise] in salary; get a salary raise
7 〈나아지다〉 progress; make progress [headway]; advance; improve
♦ 능률이 오르다 improve [increase] in efficiency / 수학 성적이 오르다 show better marks in mathematics
8 〈떠나다〉 start; set out; leave
♦ 귀로에 오르다 leave for home; start on a homeward journey
9 〈실리다〉 be recorded [registered] 《on, in》; be put [placed] 《in, on》; be entered [included]
♦ 명단에 오르다 be put [placed] on the list
10 〈살이 붙다〉 put on [gather, gain] 《flesh》
▶ 그녀의 볼에 살이 올랐다 Her cheeks filled out.
11 〈열·온도 등이〉 rise; go up; get higher
♦ 신열이 오르다 the fever gets higher / 온도가 오르다 the temperature rises
12 〈병독이〉 be infected 《with》; be affected 《by》
♦ 옻이 오르다 be poisoned with lacquer; get [have] poison ivy
13 〈연기·불길이〉 rise; coil up
▶ 헛간에서 갑자기 검은 연기가 올랐다 Black smoke rose all of a sudden in the barn.
14 〈기운 등이〉 rise; show; become high-spirited
♦ 사기가 오르다 become full of 《fighting》 spirit / 술이 오르다 be flushed [dazed] 《by liquor》; become [get] tipsy [intoxicated]; get into *one's* head
15 〈물이〉 rise
♦ 나무에 물이 오른다 The sap rises.
▶ 지금은 이른 봄, 버드나무에 물이 오르고 가지가 파릇파릇해지고 있다 Now is the early spring when the sap rises in the willows and the twigs are becoming green.
16 〈화가 나다〉 get angry; feel vexed 《with, at》; 〈고추 등의 약이〉 ripen to full flavor
17 〈때가 묻다〉 get dirty; become dirty [filthy]
18 〈악귀등이 몸에 덮치다〉 be possessed 《by a spirit》
▶ 무당에게 신이 올랐다 A spirit entered into the 《female》 shaman.
오르되브르 〈전채〉 《프》 an hors d'oeuvre 《*pl*. ~(s)》
오르락내리락 going up and down; rising and falling; 〈물가 등이〉 fluctuating
—**오르락내리락하다** go up and down
오르막 an ascent; an upward slope; a rising hill; an uprise ♦ 완만한[가파른] 오르막 a gradual [steep] ascent ▶ 여기서부터 길은 오르막이다 From here the road is running uphill.
오르막길 an uphill [a sloping] road [path]; an ascent
오르페우스 〔그神〕 Orpheus
오른 the right (side) ⇨ 오른쪽 ♦ 오른다리 [눈] the right leg [eye]
오른손 the right hand
■ —잡이 a right-handed person : 오른손잡이의 right-handed
오른쪽 the right; the right side
♦ 오른쪽에 있는 사람 a person on *one's* right / 오른쪽의 right-hand; right 《arm》/ 오른쪽에 on the right 《of》; on [at] 《its》 right / 오른쪽으로 to the right 《of》/ 오른쪽에 앉다 sit at

오른 the right (of) / 오른쪽으로 돌다 turn right; turn to the right

오른팔 〈팔〉 the right arm; 〈심복〉 one's right-hand man; one's right-hand
▶ 그는 내 오른팔이다 He is my right-hand man.

오른편 the right (side) ⇨ 오른쪽

오름세 —勢 〈물가의〉 an upward tendency 《of the market》; a rising trend; an advance; 〔證〕 a bull (market)

오름차 —次 〔數〕 an ascending power
♦ 오름차순으로 in ascending power

오리¹ 〈가는 조각〉 a strip 《of cloth, wood, etc.》 ■나무— a strip of wood 실— a piece of thread

오리² 〔鳥〕 a (wild) duck; a mallard; 〈수컷〉 a drake ■새끼— a duckling ■—떼 a flock of wild ducks —사냥 ducking; duck-shooting : 오리 사냥가다 go ducking [duck-shooting]

오리 五里 〈길이의 단위〉 five 里

오리 汚吏 a corrupt official

오리건 〈미국의 주〉 Oregon (略 Oreg., OR)

오리나무 〔植〕 an alder

오리너구리 〔動〕 a duckbill; a platypus

오리다 cut [clip] (out) 《from》
♦ 가위로 종이를 오리다 cut paper into strips with scissors / 신문에서 기사를 오리다 clip [cut] an article from a newspaper; scissor out a paragraph from a newspaper

오리목 —木 〔建〕 a scantling

오리무중 五里霧中 ♦ 오리무중이다 be in a fog; be (all) at sea; be in the dark; lose one's bearings ▶ 우리는 이 문제에 관해서 오리무중이다 We are all at sea on this subject.

오리발 1 〈물갈퀴〉 〔動〕 a web; 〈발〉 a webfoot 2 〈딴전·발뺌〉 ♦ 오리발을 내밀다 (비유) show false evidence to pretend ignorance [innocence]
▶ 오리발 내밀지 마라 Don't show false evidence [play innocent].

오리엔테이션 orientation ♦ 신입생 오리엔테이션 orientation for (incoming) freshmen

오리엔트 〈동방·동양〉 the Orient ■—학자 an Orientalist

오리엔티어링 〈야외 스포츠〉 orienteering ■—참가자 an orienteer

오리온자리 〔天〕 Orion

오리지널 an original ♦ 오리지널 작품 an original work 《of art》

오막살이 (life in) a grass hut [cottage]
—오막살이하다 lead a hut living; live in a grass hut; be a hut-dweller

오만 五萬 fifty thousand; 〈잡다한〉 various; of every sort and kind; all sorts of; 〈수많은〉 innumerable; countless; thousands; millions
♦ 오만가지 일 all sorts of things / 오만가지 물건을 팔다 sell various kinds of articles

오만 傲慢 arrogance; haughtiness
♦ 오만 불손하게도 …하다 be so insolent as to (do); be insolent enough to (do)
—오만하다 arrogant; haughty; conceited; insolent; overbearing; puffed-up; stuck-up
♦ 오만한 태도 a haughty [proud] attitude [demeanor, air]

오만 〈나라 이름〉 Oman ■—사람 an Omani 〈공식명〉 the Sultanate of Oman

오만상 五萬相 a distorted [frowning, wry] face; a grimace; a scowl
♦ 오만상을 찌푸리다[찡그리다] distort one's face; make a wry face; make grimaces

오매불망 寤寐不忘 〈자나깨나 잊지 못함〉 thinking of sb [sth] day and night
♦ 오매불망의 unforgettable; never-to-be-forgotten
▶ 나는 오매불망 그녀 생각뿐이다 I think of her day and night.
—오매불망하다 cannot forget waking or sleeping; bear in mind all the time; hold…in remembrance

오메가 〈그리스문자〉 omega (▶Ω, ω로 표시함); 〈사물의 최후〉 the last
♦ 알파에서 오메가까지 from alpha to omega; from the first to the last

오명 汚名 a stigma (pl. ~s, -mata); one's bad reputation; a taint; a stain on one's good name; 〈불명예〉 dishonor; disgrace; a spot on [to] one's honor
♦ 오명을 남기다 leave a bad name behind one / 오명을 씻다 clear one's name (of a stigma); remove the stigma [disgrace] that has (been) attached to one's name

오목 五目 omok ♦ 오목을 두다 play omok

오목거울 a concave mirror

오목렌즈 a concave lens

오목오목 with pits [indents, dents]; into small hollows —오목오목하다 dented all over; sunken here and there [in places]

오목조목 with dents ⇨ 오목오목

오목하다 dented; indented; sunken; hollow; concave
♦ 눈이 오목한 사람 a person with sunken [deep-set] eyes; a hollow-eyed person / 오목한 곳 a pit; a dent; a small depression
▶ 그 학교 운동장에는 몇 군데 오목한 곳이 있다 There are some hollow spots in the school ground.

오묘 奧妙 profundity; depth; abstruseness
—오묘하다 profound; abstruse; deep; recondite ♦ 오묘한 뜻 deep meaning / 오묘한 통찰력 profound insight

오물 汚物 〈분뇨·인분〉 night soil; 〈더러운 것〉 muck; filth; dirt; 〈하수의〉 sewage; 〈부엌의〉 garbage
■—수거인 〈분뇨의〉 a nightman; 〈쓰레기의〉 (美) a garbageman; (英) a dustman ■—차 a night-soil cart ■—처리시설 filth-treating equipment; sanitation facilities

오물거리다 1 〈벌레·물고기 등이〉 wriggle; swarm; squirm
▶ 수조에 모기 애벌레가 오물거리고 있다 The water tank teams with mosquito larvae.
▶ 그 연못에는 민물고기가 오물거리고 있었다 The pond was alive with freshwater fish.
2 〈음식을〉 mumble; munch
♦ 샌드위치를 오물거리며 먹다 mumble (on) sandwiches
3 〈말을〉 mumble 《words》
▶ 오물거리지 말고 하고 싶은 말을 똑똑히 해라

오물오물

Don't mumble and speak up what's on your mind.

오물오물 1 〈벌레·물고기 등이〉 with a wriggle; in swarms —오물오물하다 ⇨ 오물거리다 1
2 〈음식을〉 mumblingly —오물오물하다 ⇨ 오물거리다 2
3 〈말을〉 mumblingly —오물오물하다 ⇨ 오물거리다 3

오므라들다 〈틈 등이〉 become narrower; narrow; 〈입이〉 pucker; purse; 〈줄어들다〉 shrink; contract; draw
▶ 모직물은 뜨거운 물에 빨면 오므라든다 Wool shrinks when washed in hot water.
▶ 이 금속은 냉각시켜도 오므라들지 않는다 This metal won't contract in cooling.
▶ 상처가 오므라들고 있다 The wound is closing.

오므라이스 an omelet filled with fried rice, seasoned with ketchup

오므리다 make narrower; shut; close; 〈입을〉 pucker; purse
♦ 발을 오므리다 draw in one's legs / 입을 오므리다 pucker up one's mouth; purse (up) one's lips
▶ 나는 손바닥을 오므려서 빗방울을 받았다 I hollowed the palm of my hand and caught a few raindrops.

오믈렛 an omelet; 〈英〉 an omelette

오미 〈물이 괴이는 곳〉 a (land) sink

오미 五味 the five tastes (▶sour, bitter, pungent, sweet and salty)

오밀조밀하다 奧密稠密 1 〈솜씨가〉 elaborate; exquisite; delicate
♦ 오밀조밀한 디자인 an elaborate design / 오밀조밀한 세공품 an elaborate handiwork / 오밀조밀하게 꾸민 거실 a living room of tasteful layout
2 〈성질이〉 minute; scrupulous; sedulous

오발 誤發 accidental firing —오발하다 fire [shoot] 《a gun》 by accident [mistake]

오방 午方 〔民俗〕 the Direction of the Horse; the south

오배 五倍 quintuple; five times 《as many as》 —오배하다 multiply 《a number》 by five; quintuplicate

오버 1 〈초과〉 over; exceeding —오버하다 go over; exceed ▶비용은 예산액수를 오버했다 The expenses exceeded the estimate.
2 ⇨ 오버코트
3 〔通信〕 over

오버랩 〔映〕 an overlap
—오버랩하다 overlap 《into another scene》

오버런하다 overrun
▶ 그는 2루를 오버런하여 아웃이 되었다 He overran second base and was tagged out.

오버슈즈 〈방수용 덧신〉 《a pair of》 overshoes; 〈고무제의〉 〈美〉 gumshoes

오버스로 〔野〕 an overhand throw=오버핸드스로

오버코트 〈외투〉 an overcoat; a coat; 〈英〉 a greatcoat

오버타임 1 〈초과 근무〉 《work》 overtime
♦ 오버타임 수당 overtime pay [allowance]
2 〔排〕 overtime
▶ 그들은 오버타임 페널티를 받았다 They were penalized for keeping the ball too long [playing the ball too many times in succession].

오버핸드스로 〔野〕 an overhand throw

오버행 〔登山〕 an overhang

오버홀 〈분해 검사〉 an overhaul —오버홀하다 overhaul 《an engine》

오벨리스크 〈방첨탑〉 an obelisk

오변형 五邊形 〔數〕 a pentagon ⇨ 오각형

오보 誤報 an incorrect [an erroneous, a false] report; wrong information; misinformation
▶ 그것은 오보였다 The report proved false. ⇌ The report turned out (to be) incorrect. ⇌ The information was wrong.
▶ 그 신문에는 가끔 오보가 실린다 That paper often gives wrong information.
—오보하다 give a false report; misreport; misinform 《on》

오보에 an oboe ■—연주자 an oboist

오복 五福 the five blessings (▶longevity, wealth, health, virtue and peaceful death)

오불관언 吾不關焉 a detached [an unconcerned] air; an indifferent attitude
♦ 오불관언의 태도를 취하다 assume an attitude of indifference
▶ 그는 그 논의에는 오불관언하고 잠자코 있었다 He said nothing as if the argument was [were] none of his business. ⇌ He kept silent without showing interest in the argument.
▶ 그는 정치에는 오불관언이다 He is indifferent to politics.

오붓이 〈오붓하게〉 substantially

오붓하다 〈허실이 없다〉 substantial; sufficient; adequately enough; 〈살림이 포실하다〉 moderately wealthy
♦ 오붓한 살림 a comfortable living / 오붓하게 살다 live in peace and competence; live in ease [plenty]; be well [comfortably] off; be well-to-do

오븐 an oven ♦ 오븐에 케이크를 굽다 bake a cake in an oven

오블라토 〔<(포) oblato〕 a wafer (for wrapping a dose of powdered medicine)
▶ 이 약은 오블라토에 싸서 먹으면 좋다 You had better take this medicine wrapped in a wafer.

오비 1 〈졸업생〉 a graduate; an old boy; 〈美〉 〈남자〉 an alumnus 《pl. -ni》; 〈여자〉 an alumna 《pl. -nae》
♦ 연고대의 야구 오비전 a baseball game between the Yonsei and Korea old boys
2 〔골프〕 out of bounds

오비다 poke ⇨ 우비다

오비이락 烏飛梨落 the strange [casual] coincidence (arousing suspicion); misinformation
▶ 이 무슨 오비이락이람 What a strange coincidence!

오빠 a girl's older [elder] brother

오사리 五— the early catch of fish at high tide

오사리잡놈 五—雜 a debauchee; a reprobate

오산 誤算 〈잘못 셈함〉 miscalculation; miscomputation; wrong reckoning [estimate]; 〈잘못된 추정·판단〉 misjudgment
♦ 전략상의 오산 a strategical miscalculation
▶ 그의 득표 예상은 큰 오산이었다 He made a huge [gross] error in estimating the number of possible votes he would get.
—**오산하다** miscalculate; make a miscalculation; make a wrong estimate; misjudge

오상 五常 **1** ⇨ 오륜(五倫)
2 〈다섯가지 덕〉 the five cardinal virtues (▶ benevolence, justice, politeness, wisdom and fidelity)

오색 五色 the five (cardinal) colors; 〈여러 가지 빛깔〉 various colors
♦ 오색 구름 five-colored clouds; glowing [iridescent] clouds / 오색의 five-colored; multicolored ⟨tapes⟩; ⟨garments⟩ of many colors

오색딱따구리 五色— 〔鳥〕 a great spotted woodpecker

오색영롱 五色玲瓏 shining brilliantly in various colors —**오색영롱하다** 〈서술적〉 resplendent; very colorful; shine brilliantly in various colors

오색잡놈 五色雜— a reprobate; a rogue; a scamp

오선 五線 〔樂〕 the staffs; the stave
오선지 五線紙 〔樂〕 music paper; music sheet
오성 悟性 〔心〕 wisdom; 〔哲〕 understanding
■—론 〔哲〕 rationalism

오성장군 五星將軍 〈육군·공군〉 a five-star general; 〈해군〉 a five-star admiral

오세아니아 〈대양주〉 Oceania ♦ 오세아니아의 Oceanian; Oceanic

오소리 〔動〕 a badger; an old-world badger
오손 汚損 stain [soilage] and damage
—**오손하다** stain; soil; damage ♦ 오손되다 be stained [soiled] ▶ 이 천은 오손되어 있다 This cloth is spoiled.

오솔길 a (narrow) path; a (lonely) lane; a trail ♦ 숲속의 오솔길 a forest path
▶ 그녀는 오솔길을 걸어서 호숫가로 나왔다 She followed the lonely path [track] to the lake.

오수 午睡 〈낮잠〉 a nap
오수 汚水 dirty [foul] water; 〈하수〉 sewage; polluted water; 〈구정물〉 (kitchen) slop(s)

오순도순 chummily; intimately; in amity [harmony]; harmoniously
♦ 오순도순 의좋게 지내다 live harmoniously [happily, in harmony] / 오순도순 이야기하다 have a nice little tête-à-tête ⟨with⟩

오스뮴 〔化〕 osmium
오스카상 —賞 〔映〕 an Oscar ⇨ 아카데미상
오스트레일리아 Australia; 〈공식명〉 the Commonwealth of Australia
♦ 오스트레일리아의 Australian
■—사람 an Australian

오스트리아 Austria; 〈공식명〉 the Republic of Austria ♦ 오스트리아의 Austrian
■—사람 an Austrian

오슬로 〈노르웨이의 수도〉 Oslo
오슬오슬 shiveringly
♦ 오슬오슬 춥다 feel (a) chill; feel chilly
♦ 오늘 아침은 오슬오슬 춥다 It's shivering(ly) cold this morning.
▶ 밖에 나갔다가 추위에 오슬오슬 떨었다 I shivered with cold when I went outside.
—**오슬오슬하다** shivery; chill; chilly
♦ 열이 나서 오슬오슬하다 have chills [shakes] with the fever

오시 午時 〔民俗〕 〈십일시의〉 the 7th of the 12 hour periods (▶11:00 a.m.—1:00 p.m.); 〈이십사시의〉 the 13th of the 24 hour periods (▶11:30 a.m.—12:30 p.m.)

오식 誤植 〔印〕 〈인쇄상의 잘못〉 a typographic(al) error; a misprint; 〈인쇄공의 잘못〉 a printer's error; a slip of the press
♦ 오식이 없는 책 a book free from misprints / 오식투성이인 책 a book full of misprints / 오식이 많다 teem with [be full of] misprints / 오식을 정정하다 correct errors in proof [in printing]
—**오식하다** misprint
■—정정표 ⇨ 정오(~표)

오신 誤信 misbelief —**오신하다** misbelieve; believe erroneously

오실로그래프 〈진동 기록기〉 〔物〕 an oscillograph

오실로스코프 〈역전류 검출관〉 〔物〕 an oscilloscope

오심 惡心 〈토할 듯한 기분〉 〔韓醫〕 nausea; qualm; retch; a sickly feeling

오심 誤審 **1** 〔競〕 wrong refereeing [decision]
—**오심하다** referee wrongly
2 〔法〕 (a) miscarriage of justice; (a) misjudgment; mistrial
—**오심하다** misjudge; judge wrongly

오십 五十 fifty
♦ 제 오십 the fiftieth / 오십년 fifty years; half a century / 오십분의 일 a fiftieth part / 오십대에 in one's fifties
▶ 오십보 백보다 There is little difference [not much to choose] between the two.
▶ 나는 오십대의 신사를 소개받았다 I was introduced to a gentleman of about fifty.

오싹 with one's blood running cold; with (cold) chills running up and down one's spine

오싹오싹 shiveringly —**오싹오싹하다** 〈추위로〉 feel a chill; feel chilly; shiver with cold; 〈공포로〉 feel creepy

오싹하다 shiver [tremble, shudder] ⟨with cold, with fear⟩; feel a chill
♦ 오싹한 bloodcurdling; hair-raising; gruesome; grisly; eerie; eery; (美) morbid / 오싹하게 하다 〈사물이 주어〉 make one's blood run cold; send a thrill [chill] through one; give one the shivers; make one's flesh creep [crawl]; give one gooseflesh
▶ 온몸이 오싹했다 A shiver went through me.
▶ 그 사고를 보고 그녀는 등골이 오싹했다 The sight of the accident sent a shiver [shivers] down her back.

오아시스 an oasis ⟪pl. -ses⟫
오얏 a plum ⇨ 자두
오에이에스 OAS[⟨the Organization of American States⟩]
오에이유 OAU [⟨the Organization of African Unity⟩]

오에이펙 OAPEC [《the *O*rganization of *A*rab *P*etroleum *E*xporting *C*ountries]

오엑스 true-false ■ —문제 true-false questions —식 테스트 a true-false test

오역 誤譯 a mistranslation; an incorrect translation; a mistake [an error] in translation ◆ 오역이 없다 be free from errors of translation ▶ 이 책은 오역투성이다 There are a lot of errors in this translation. —오역하다 mistranslate; make an error [a mistake, a slip] in translation

오연 傲然 〈거만한 태도〉 arrogance; 《attitude of》 haughtiness —오연하다 arrogant; haughty; overbearing ◆ 오연히 arrogantly; haughtily; overbearingly ▶ 그는 우리를 오연히 내려다보았다 He looked down on all of us in [with] arrogant contempt.

오열 五列 the Fifth Column ⇨ 제오열(第五列)

오열 嗚咽 sob; weeping —오열하다 sob; weep; choke ▶ 그녀는 오열하면서 이야기했다 She talked between sobs.

오염 汚染 〈주로 화학물질에 의한〉 pollution; 〈주로 세균·독물에 의한〉 contamination —오염하다 pollute; taint; contaminate ▶ 도시의 공기는 자동차 배기 가스로 몹시 오염되어 있다 The air in cities has been heavily polluted by vehicle emissions. ▶ 그것은 오염된 물에 의해 일어나는 병이다 It is a disease caused by contaminated water. ■ 대기— air pollution : 대기오염은 대도시의 중대한 문제다 Air pollution is a serious problem in large cities. 방사능— radioactive contamination [pollution] 수질— water pollution 환경— environmental pollution ■ —계(計) a contamination meter —대책 antipollution measures —도 a pollution level —물질 a pollutant; a contaminant —방지 prevention of 《air, water》 pollution —원 a pollution source —제거 decontamination

오욕 汚辱 〈불명예〉 disgrace; dishonor; ignominy; 〈모욕〉 《an》 insult ▶ 오욕을 당하느니 차라리 죽음을 택하는 것이 낫다 I would rather choose death than dishonor. —오욕하다 disgrace; dishonor; bring disgrace upon *sb*

오용 誤用 〈부적절한 용법〉 misuse; 〈틀린 용법〉 wrong use; 〈적용의 잘못〉 misapplication —오용하다 misuse; misapply; use *sth* for a wrong purpose; put *sth* to an improper use

오월 五月 May ◆ 오월의 여왕 a May queen

오월 吳越 Wu and Yüeh (the two rival states in ancient China)

오월동주 吳越同舟 bitter [implacable] enemies (placed by fate) in the same boat

오유 烏有 〈아무것도 없이 됨〉 reverting to nothing; vanishing away ◆ 오유로 돌아가다 be reduced to ashes; be burnt down; revert [come] to nothing; be nullified

오의 奧義 secret principles; secrets; hidden [inner] mysteries; the mysteries 《of an art》; the heart 《of things》 ◆ 오의를 전수받다 be initiated into the secrets [mysteries] 《of》

오이 〔植〕 a cucumber ▶ 오이를 거꾸로 먹어도 제 멋 《속담》 There is no accounting for tastes. ⇌ Every man to his taste. ≒ Tastes differ. ■ —생채 sliced cucumbers seasoned with vinegar —소박이(김치) stuffed cucumber *kimchi* —지 cucumber pickle

오이시디 OECD [《the *O*rganization for *E*conomic *C*ooperation and *D*evelopment]

오이엠 OEM [《the *o*riginal *e*quipment *m*anufacturer]

오인 誤認 a mistake; misconception; misunderstanding; an erroneous assumption —오인하다 mistake [take] 《a thing》 for 《another》; misunderstand; misconceive ▶ 그들은 아군을 적으로 오인했다 They took [mistook] their allies for the enemy. ▶ 전차 운전사는 신호를 오인했다 The motorman misread the signal.

오인 吾人 〈나〉 I; 〈우리〉 we

오일 五日 five days; the fifth day (of the month)

오일 oil; petroleum; gasoline ■ —달러 oil dollar; petrodollar —버너 an oil burner —쇼크 the oil crisis —스토브 an oilstove —탱커 an oil tanker —펜스 oil fence

오일장 五日葬 《have》 a five-day funeral

오입 誤入 womanizing; wenching; whoring; philandering —오입하다 womanize; wench; whore; consort with a whore; philander ■ —쟁이 a womanizer; a woman chaser; a whoremonger; a philanderer

오자 誤字 a wrong [miswritten, misused] letter [character]; 〈인쇄의〉 an erratum; a misprint ◆ 오자투성이의 작문 a composition full of wrong letters; a badly misspelled composition / 오자투성이다 be full of [bristle with] wrong words

오장 五臟 〔韓醫〕 the five viscera (▶liver, lungs, heart, kidneys and spleen) ■ —육부(六腑) five viscera and six entrails; the bowels; the internal organs in general

오쟁이 〈짚으로 만든 작은 섬〉 a small straw bag

오쟁이지다 be made a cuckold of; wear the horns ◆ 오쟁이진 사내 a cuckold

오전 午前 the forenoon; the morning; a.m.; A. M.

〔解說〕 ***morning***은 새벽부터 정오까지 또는 자정부터 정오까지의 사이를 말한다. ***a.m.***, ***A. M.***은 자정부터 정오까지의 시각을 나타내는 숫자 뒤에 붙여서 쓴다. 시각표나 표제 이외에 주로 문어에서는 보통 소문자나 소형 대문자 《A.M.》을 쓴다. 《英》에서는 마침표는 보통 생략한다.

◆ 오전중에 in the morning / 일요일 오전중에 on Sunday morning / 9월 1일 오전중에 on the

morning of September 1 [英] 1 September] (➤단독으로 「오전중에」일 때는 in, 날짜·날씨 등을 나타내는 말과 같이 쓸 때는 on을 씀) / 오늘 [그날] 오전중에 this [that] morning / 내일 [어제] 오전중에 tomorrow [yesterday] morning (➤this, that, tomorrow, yesterday와 함께 써서 부사의 역할을 할 때는 전치사를 쓰지 않음)
▶ 어느 추운 날 오전중의 일이었다 It happened on one cold morning.
오전 誤傳 a false [an incorrect] report; an unfounded [a groundless] rumor; 〈틀린 정보〉 wrong information; misinformation
—**오전하다** misreport; misinform; give a false report
오점 汚點 a spot; 〈얼룩·불명예스러운 점〉 a blot; a stain; a taint; a smear; a bad mark; 〈흠〉 a flaw; 〈결점〉 a blemish
♦ 오점이 없는 stainless; spotless / 오점을 찍다 spot; flecksoil; stain; bring a blot (on); put a black mark 《on》/ 평생 씻을 수 없는 오점을 남기다 leave an indelible stain [blot] on *one's* name [character, reputation, honor]
▶ 그 수뢰 사건은 우리 나라 정치사에 큰 오점을 남겼다 The bribery case left a great blot [stain] on the political history of our nation.
오정 午正 noon ⇨ 정오(正午)
오조 〈일찍 익는 조〉 an early-ripening millet
오존 [化] ozone ♦ 오존의 ozonous; ozonic
—**발생기[장치]** an ozonizer; an ozonator; an ozone apparatus —**층[대(帶)]** an ozone layer: 오존층의 소멸 the depletion of the ozone layer / 오존층의 보호 the protection [preservation] of the ozone layer —홀 a hole in the ozone layer; an ozone hole
오종경기 五種競技 pentathlon
♦ 오종경기의 선수 a pentathlete / 근대 오종경기 the modern pentathlon
오종종하다 〈빽빽하다〉 dense; thick; compact; 〈얼굴이〉 meager (face); narrow-minded 《look》
오죽 how; how much; very; indeed
▶ 그가 성공했다는 소식을 듣고 그녀는 오죽 기뻐했겠느냐 How glad she must have been to hear the news of his success!
▶ 그의 슬픔은 오죽이나 할까 I can imagine just how sad he is.
오죽잖다 (be) not up to par; trivial; trifling; small; ungainly
▶ 그녀는 오죽잖은 일로 늘 걱정하고 있다 She is always worring over trifles.
▶ 그는 오죽잖은 인간이다 He is a mere nobody.
오줌 urine; (卑) piss, (卑) pee; (兒俗) water; 〈마소의〉 stale
♦ 오줌의 urinous; urinary; [化] uric / 오줌이 마렵다 have a desire [feel the urge] to urinate [pass water]; feel nature's call; want to piss / 오줌을 누다 urinate; pass [discharge] urine; make [pass] water; (卑) piss; 〈마소가〉 stale / 오줌을 참다 control *one's* need to urinate; hold back *one's* urine / 자다가 오줌을 싸다 wet the bed (at night)
▶ 그는 오줌이 잦다 He has a frequent need to urinate. ⇌ He needs to go to the bathroom frequently.

■—**똥** urine and feces; excreta —**버캐** urine incrustations —**소태** [醫] pollakiuria; micturition —**싸개** a bedwetter —**장군** a urine barrel —**통** [生] 〈방광〉 the bladder; 〈통〉 a urine pail; a urinary; 〈변기〉 a urinal
오중 五重 〈다섯 겹〉 five layers
♦ 오중의 fivefold; quintuple
—**주[창]** [樂] a quintet(te)
오지 glazed earthenware ⇨ 오지그릇
오지 五指 the five fingers (of the hand)
오지 奧地 the hinterland; the interior; the back region [country, land]
♦ 오지의 inland; up-country 《farms》/ 오지로 《go》 up-country, 《head》 for [toward, into] the interior / 아마존의 오지에서 in the upper reaches of the Amazon
오지그릇 glazed earthenware; pottery (with darkbrown glaze); potter's work [ware]
오지다 sturdy ⇨ 오달지다
오지랖 the lapels of an outer garment
♦ 오지랖(이) 넓다 〈아무 일에나 참견하다〉 interfere [meddle] (in); (口) nose (into); intrude; be forward; (口) be pushy
오직 merely; simply; solely; only; but; alone; entirely
♦ 오직 한 번 only [but] once / 오직 혼자서 (all) alone; solely; by *oneself*
▶ 그녀는 오직 울기만 하고 있다 She does nothing but cry. ⇌ She just [only] cries.
▶ 오직 의견이 맞지 않는다는 것만으로 그는 종업원을 해고했다 He dismissed his employees just [simply, only, merely] because they disagreed with him.
▶ 방법은 오직 하나다 There is but one way left.
▶ 너는 오직 그가 하는 말을 듣기만 하면 된다 You only have to listen to him. ⇌ All you have to do is listen to him.
오직 汚職 (official) corruption ⇨ 독직(瀆職)
오진 誤診 [醫] an erroneous [a wrong] diagnosis —**오진하다** make a wrong diagnosis; diagnose erroneously [wrongly]; make an error in diagnosis; misdiagnose
▶ 의사는 그녀의 폐렴을 감기로 오진했다 The doctor misdiagnosed her pneumonia as a cold.
▶ 어떤 명의라도 오진하는 수가 있다 The most experienced doctor sometimes makes a wrong [mistaken] diagnosis of a person's illness.
오짓물 glaze; glost ♦ 오짓물을 올리다 glaze
오징어 〈뼈가 있는〉 a cuttlefish; a cuttle; 〈뼈가 없는〉 a squid; an inkfish —**뼈** a cuttlebone; a pen —**잡이 어선** a squid boat [jigger] —**포** dried cuttlefish
오차 誤差 [數] an error
♦ 허용(되는) 오차의 폭 a tolerance; an (acceptable) error range / 오차 1밀리미터 미만이다 be in error by less than one millimeter; be correct [accurate] (to) within less than a millimeter
▶ 오차가 있다 There is an error.
■**개인**— a personal error [equation] **관측**— an observational error **우연**— an accidental

오찬 午餐 a luncheon; a lunch (▶luncheon은 lunch보다 형식적이며 공식적인 접대 등에 씀) ◆오찬에 초대하다 invite sb to a luncheon / 아무와 오찬을 나누다 (take) lunch with sb ■—회 a luncheon party: 오찬회를 베풀다 give a luncheon party

오채 五彩 〈다섯 가지 채색〉the five colo(u)rs (▶blue, yellow, red, white, black)

오체 五體 the whole body [frame] ▶ 그 갓난 아이는 오체에 결함이 없다 The baby has no physical defects.

오촌 五寸 〈종숙〉a male cousin of one's father; 〈종질〉a (first) cousin once removed

오층탑 五層塔 a five-storied pagoda

오칭 誤稱 a misnomer —오칭하다 call by a wrong name; call wrongly [erroneously]

오카리나 〈악기〉an ocarina

오케스트라 〈관현악단〉an orchestra ◆50인 편성의 오케스트라 a 50-piece [50-member] orchestra / 오케스트라의 반주로 to an orchestral accompaniment ▶ 오케스트라의 단원은 모두 귀가했다 The orchestra have all gone home. ■실내[심포니]— a chamber [symphony] orchestra

오케이 O.K.; OK; okay; all right; 〈승낙〉an O.K. (pl. O.K.'s); an okay; (an) approval ▶ 會話「내일 꼭 와」「오케이」"Be sure to come tomorrow." "O.K." ▶ 會話「무슨 문제가 있니?」「아냐, 만사 오케이야」"(Is there) anything wrong?" "No, everything is all right." ▶ 그 일에 대해서는 아버지한테서 오케이를 받아 놓았다 My father approved [OK'd] it.

오크라 〈植〉(an) okra

오클라호마 〈미국의 주〉Oklahoma (略 Okla.) ◆오클라호마 사람 an Oklahoman

오타와 〈캐나다의 수도〉Ottawa ■—시민 an Ottawan

오탁 汚濁 corruption —오탁하다 corrupt; foul; filthy and turbid ◆오탁한 공기[물] foul air [water]

오토레이스 〈모터사이클의〉a motorcycle race; 〈자동차의〉a motor [an auto] race ◆오토레이스 선수 〈모터사이클의〉a motorcycle rider; 〈자동차의〉a racing driver

오토매틱 automatic ▶ 이 기계는 오토매틱이다 This machine is automatic.

오토메이션 automation ◆완전히 [고도로] 오토메이션화한 공장 a fully [highly] automated factory / 오토메이션으로 (operate the equipment) by automation

오토바이 a motorcycle ⇨ 모터(~사이클)

오토자이로 〈空〉an autogiro; an autogyro

오톨도톨하다 rough ⇨ 우툴두툴하다

오트밀 oatmeal; 〈英〉porridge

오판 誤判 misjudgment; miscalculation; a mistrial; miscarriage of justice [law] ◆오판으로 국제간의 분쟁을 빚어내다 lead to international trouble by misjudgement ■—사례 a misjudgment case

오팔 〈鑛〉opal

오퍼 〈貿易〉an offer ◆오퍼를 내다 offer; make an offer (for goods); put forward [submit] an offer / 오퍼를 받다 receive an offer / 오퍼를 갱신[수정, 연기]하다 renew [modify, extend] an offer —오퍼하다 make an offer ▶ 이 상품은 표시 가격의 10%를 할인해 오퍼합니다 We offer you these goods at 10 percent off list price. ■구매— a buying [buyer's] offer; a bid 반대— a counter offer 원(原)— an original offer 판매— a selling offer; an offer 확정— a firm offer —기간 the offering period

오퍼레이터 an operator

오페라 an opera ⇨ 가극 ■그랜드— a grand opera; (이) an opera seria ■—가수 an opera singer —극장[하우스] an opera house —단 an opera company [troupe]

오페레타 〈經(輕)가극〉an operetta

오펙 OPEC [〈the Organization of Petroleum Exporting Countries〉]

오펜바흐 〈프랑스의 작곡가〉Offenbach, Jacques (1819-80)

오펜하이머 〈미국의 이론물리학자〉Oppenheimer, Julius Robert (1904-67)

오포 午砲 (fire) the midday [noon] gun

오프더레코드 off the record ▶ 장관은 오프 더 레코드 조건으로 이야기했다 The minister spoke off the record.

오프라인 〈電омп〉—시스템 an off-line system —처리 off-line process

오프리미츠 〈출입 금지〉〈美〉off limits; 〈英〉out of bounds

오프사이드 〈蹴〉offside ◆오프사이드가 되다 be offside / 오프사이드를 범하다 commit an offside penalty

오프셋인쇄 —印刷 offset printing [lithography]; offset ◆오프셋 인쇄를 하다 print offset; offset ■—기 an offset (printing) press

오프시즌 an off-season

오픈 ■—샌드위치 an open sandwich —숍 an open shop —전 (戰)[게임] a preseason [an off-season] exhibition game; an exhibition game —카 a convertible

오피스 an office ■—오토메이션 office automation —워커 a office worker

오하이오 〈미국의 주〉Ohio (略 OH) ◆오하이오 사람 an Ohioan

오한 惡寒 a chill; a cold [shivering] fit; 〔醫〕rigor; algor; ague ◆오한이 나다 feel [catch, take] a chill; have a shivering fit ▶ 갑자기 오한이 났다 Suddenly I caught a chill. = Suddenly a chill came over me.

오합지졸 烏合之卒 a (mere) rabble; a disorderly crowd; an undisciplined mob; the ruck ▶ 시위대는 오합지졸처럼 우르르 도망쳤다 The demonstrators stampeded like a herd of cattle.

오해 誤解 misunderstanding; misapprehension ◆오해를 받다 be misunderstood / 오해를 사다 cause [invite] misunderstanding; 〈사물이〉lead to 《serious》 misunderstanding / 오해를 풀다 remove the misunderstanding

▶그녀가 냉정하다고 생각한다면 자네 오해다 If you think she is cold-hearted, you are mistaken.
▶그것은 내 오해였다 That was a misunderstanding on my part.
▶그녀는 그 문제에 대해 오해를 가지고 있다 She has a misunderstanding on the matter.
▶네 행동은 오해를 사기 쉽다 Your actions are open to [liable to cause] misunderstanding.
▶그의 오해를 풀기 위해 그와 한번 더 얘기해 보는 것이 좋겠다 You had better talk to him once more to clear up his misunderstanding.
—오해하다 misunderstand; misinterpret; have a false idea (of); have misunderstanding (about); 〈어구를〉 put a wrong construction (on); misconstrue
♦오해받기 쉽다 〈사람이〉 be apt to be misunderstood; 〈일이〉 be liable to cause misunderstanding; 〈어구 등이〉 be misleading
▶그는 자유라는 것을 오해하고 있다 He has a false idea of liberty.
▶자네는 저 사람을 전적으로 오해하고 있네 You've got that man all wrong.
▶우리를 오해하지 말게. 자네를 비판하는 것은 아니니까 Please don't misunderstand us. We are not criticizing you.
오행 五行 the five elements (such as metal, wood, water, fire, and earth)
오헨리 〈미국의 작가〉 O. Henry (1862-1910) (▶본명은 William Sidney Porter)
오호 嗚呼 Alas!; (古) Alack!; (古) Wo(e)!
▶오호라 Alas!
▶오호 슬프다, 그녀는 이제 가고 없구나 Alas, she is dead and gone!
오호츠크해 —海 the Sea of Okhotsk
오후 午後 afternoon; p.m.; P.M.; PM (▶p.m.으로 쓰는 것이 보통임)
♦오늘[그날] 오후 this [that] afternoon / 내일[어제] 오후 tomorrow [yesterday] afternoon / 오후 수업 afternoon classes / 오후에 in the afternoon / 토요일 오후에 on Saturday afternoon / 어느날 오후에 one afternoon / 10일 오후에 on the afternoon of the 10th / 오후 5시에 at five (o'clock) in the afternoon; at 5 p.m. / 오후 늦게 in the late afternoon
▶오후가 되자 폭풍우가 심하게 몰아치기 시작했다 A storm began to rage here in the afternoon.
▶아버지는 오후 6시 30분 차로 도착하실 겁니다 Father is arriving on the 6:30 p.m. train.
▶그 일은 어느 추운 날 오후에 일어났다 It happened on a cold afternoon.
▶내일 오후 5시에 내게 오도록 하세요 Come and see me at five o'clock tomorrow afternoon.
오히려 1 〈반대로〉 on the contrary; instead
♦섣불리 아는 것은 오히려 위험하다 A little learning is rather dangerous.
▶술을 약간 마시는 것은 오히려 약이 된다 A little drink does you more good than harm.
▶자네는 잘못이 없네, 잘못한 것은 오히려 날세 You are not to blame; on the contrary it is I who am to blame.
▶그는 고마워하기는커녕 오히려 나를 비난했다 Far from thanking me, he blamed me, instead.
▶그의 호의가 오히려 해가 되었다 His kind intentions brought harm.
2 〈차라리〉 rather; 〈그만큼 더〉 all the more [better, worse]
▶그는 작가라기보다는 오히려 평론가다 He is not so much a writer as a critic.
▶무척 걱정했지만 사태는 오히려 호전되는 것 같다 We were rather anxious, but if anything, things seem to be improving.
옥 玉 〔鑛〕 jade; 〈보석〉 a precious stone; a gem; a jewel; (총칭) jewelry
♦옥을 굴리는 듯한 목소리로 in a silvery voice
■—가락지 a jade ring
옥 獄 a prison ⇨ 감옥
옥고 玉稿 your [his] (esteemed) manuscript
옥고 獄苦 the hardships of prison life
♦옥고를 견디다 endure the hardships of prison life / 옥고를 치르다 groan [languish] in prison; serve *one's* term of imprisonment
옥내 屋內 the interior [inside] of a house
♦옥내의 indoor; covered / 옥내에(서) indoors; within doors
■—경기〔스포츠〕 an indoor game [sport] —경기장 a gymnasium (pl. ~s, -sia); (口) a gym —배선 interior [house] wiring —선 〈전기의〉 a service wire; 〈전화의〉 a telephone drop; 〈라디오·TV의〉 a lead-in (wire); a (down-)lead —풀장 an indoor pool
옥니 an inturned tooth
■—박이 a person with inturned teeth
옥다 1 〈오그라져 있다〉 (be) turned [bent, curved] inward; bent out of shape
2 〈밑지다〉 lose (money) (by a business); suffer a loss; operate at a loss; sell (an article) below cost
옥답 沃畓 a rich [fertile] paddy field
옥당목 玉唐木 calico of inferior quality
옥도 沃度 〔化〕 iodine; iodin ⇨ 요오드 ■—정기 tincture of iodine; iodine tincture
옥돌 玉— a gem stone; jade
옥돔 玉— 〔魚〕 a tilefish
옥동자 玉童子 a precious son; a darling baby boy
옥리 獄吏 a jailer ⇨ 옥사쟁이
옥문 獄門 a prison gate
옥바라지하다 獄— send in private supplies for a prisoner; supply a prisoner with clothes and food from outside the prison
옥배 玉杯 a jade cup; a beautiful cup
옥사 獄死 death in prison
—옥사하다 die in prison; end up in jail
옥사 獄舍 a prison house; a jail; (英) a gaol; 〈감방〉 a cell
옥사 獄事 the handling [administration] of major crimes [criminal cases] (▶murder and high treason)
옥사쟁이 獄— a jailer; a prison guard; (美) a warden
옥살산 —酸 〔化〕 oxalic acid ■—암모늄 ammonium oxalate; oxalate of ammonium —염 an oxalate
옥살이 獄— prison life; life behind bars

옥상 屋上 the rooftop; the housetop; the roof
♦옥상에[에서] on [from] the roof
■—정원 a roof garden —주택 a penthouse

옥상가옥 屋上架屋 building on top of a building ▶그것은 옥상가옥이나 마찬가지다 That's like carrying coals to Newcastle. ⇌ That's like putting a fifth wheel on a coach.

옥새 玉璽 the Royal [Imperial] Seal; (英) the Privy Seal

옥색 玉色 jade green

옥석 玉石 〈옥돌〉 a gem [precious] stone; jade; 〈좋은 것과 궂은 것〉 wheat and tares

옥석구분 玉石俱焚 indiscriminate destruction of the good and bad alike

옥석혼효 玉石混淆 a jumble [medley] of wheat and tares [chaff and grain]; a mixture of wheat and chaff
♦옥석혼효 되어 있다 be a mixture [jumble] of good and bad; be a jumble of wheat and tares [chaff and grain]
▶이 반 학생들은 그야말로 옥석혼효다 The students of this class are of very uneven ability.

옥소 沃素 iodine ⇨ 요오드

옥쇄 玉碎 death for honor
♦옥쇄를 택하다 seek an honorable death rather than an ignoble surrender
—옥쇄하다 suffer [meet with] an honorable death; die in honor
▶연대는 전원 옥쇄했다 The whole regiment died an honorable death rather than surrender.
■—전법 suicide tactics

옥수 玉手 〈임금의〉 the king's hand; 〈미인의〉 white hands (of a beautiful woman); a 《woman's》 beautiful hand
♦섬섬옥수 a slender [delicate] hand

옥수 玉水 clear [crystal] water

옥수수 〔植〕 Indian corn; maize; (美) corn
♦옥수수 낟알 a kernel [an ear] of corn / 옥수수를 재배하다 grow corn
■—가루 corn flour —밭 (美) a cornfield; a field of corn —수염 corn floss [silk]; a tassel —재배 지대 (美) the Corn Belt 옥수숫대 (英) a cornstalk

옥스퍼드 〈영국의 도시〉 Oxford ■—대학 Oxford University; 〈정식 명칭〉 the University of Oxford: 옥스퍼드 대학 학생 an Oxonian

옥시던트 〔化〕 an oxidant

옥시풀 〔藥·化〕 oxygenated water; hydrogen peroxide solution; (hydrogen) peroxide; (商標) Oxyful

옥신각신 arguing; wrangling —옥신각신하다 argue [dispute, wrangle] 《with》; altercate 《with》; have a (petty) quarrel 《with》
♦서로 옥신각신하다 wrangle with each other; have [bandy] words with each other / 아무와 사소한 일로 옥신각신하다 fight [argue] with *sb* over trifles

옥안 玉顔 〈임금의 얼굴〉 the king's face; the royal visage [countenance]; 〈아름다운 얼굴〉 a beautiful (woman's) face

옥야 沃野 a fertile [rich] plain ♦옥야 천리 a vast stretch of fertile plain [land]

옥양목 玉洋木 (英) calico; (美) muslin

옥양사 玉洋紗 fine calico

옥에도 티가 있다 〈속담〉 Nothing is perfect in the world. ⇌ Everything has its drawback. ⇌ No silver [gold] without its dross. ⇌ There are spots even in the sun.

옥에티 玉— 〈속담〉 a fly in the ointment; a flaw in *one's* perfect character / a blot on *one's* record [reputation]
▶그 여자는 수다스러운 것이 옥에 티다 Her talkativeness is the fly in the ointment.
▶그는 완고한 것이 옥에 티다 The only trouble with him is (that) he is very stubborn. ⇌ Stubbornness is his only flaw [the only flaw in his character].

옥외 屋外 the open (air); the outdoor
♦옥외의 outdoor; open-air; out-of-door / 옥외에서 《exercise》 in the open air; outdoors; out of doors / 옥외로 나가다 go outside [outdoors, out of doors]
▶나는 한가할 때는 옥외에서 시간을 보냈다 I spent my spare time in the open (air).
■—경기 an outdoor game [contest] —광고판 《set up》 an outdoor billboard —노동자 an outdoor [open-air] laborer —배관[배선] outdoor piping [wiring] —스포츠[운동] outdoor [open-air] sports [exercise] —연설[집회] an open-air speech [meeting]

옥이다 bend *sth* in ⇨ 욱이다

옥장이 玉匠— a lapidary; a jade cutter

옥졸 獄卒 a jailer ⇨ 옥사쟁이

옥좌 玉座 the king's chair; the Royal seat; the throne ♦옥좌에 앉다 sit on the throne; take the Royal seat

옥죄이다 get tightened [cramped]; be too tight for *one*; be fitting too close
▶그의 두 손을 묶은 포승줄이 몹시 옥죄여 들었다 The rope with which his hands were tied cut into the flesh.

옥중 獄中 ♦옥중에(서) in prison [jail]; during prison life ■—기 a diary written in prison

옥체 玉體 〈임금의 몸〉 the person of the king; the Royal [His Majesty's] person; the King's body; 〈편지에서의 경칭〉 your health [body]; you

옥타브 〔樂〕 an octave
▶목소리를 한 옥타브 올려라[내려라] Raise [Drop] your voice an octave higher [lower].

옥탄 〔化〕 octane —가(價) an octane number [rating]: 옥탄가 높은 휘발유 high-octane gasoline; gasoline with a high octane rating

옥토 沃土 fertile land; rich [fat] soil ♦불모지를 옥토로 만들다 make barren soil fertile

옥토끼 玉— 〈전설상의〉 the rabbit (supposed to be) in the moon; 〈흰토끼〉 a white rabbit

옥편 玉篇 a Chinese-character wordbook; a wordbook of Chinese characters

옥호 屋號 the name [style] of a store; a shop name

옥화 沃化 〔化〕 iodation ⇨ 요오드화

옥황상제 玉皇上帝 the King of Heaven (of Taoism); Heaven

온 1 〈전부의〉 all; whole; entire; total; com-

plete
- 온 누리 the whole universe / 온 백성 the whole nation; all the people / 온 세상 all the world / 온 집안 the whole family; all the family / 온 몸에 all over the body; from head to foot / 온 얼굴에 all over the [*one's*] face / 온 힘을 다해 with all *one's* might
▶ 온 동네가 그를 환영했다 The whole village turned out to welcome him.
▶ 나는 온 몸이 아프다 I ache all over.
2 ⇨ 온갖

온각 溫覺 〔生理〕 thermesthesia
온감 溫感 the sense of heat [warmth]
온갖 all; every; each and every; every possible [single, last]
- 온갖 종류의 all sorts [kinds, manner] of; of all sorts; of every kind / 온갖 방법을 다하여 (in) every way / 온갖 수단을 다 써보다 try every means available; try every possible [imaginable] means [method] / 온갖 죄를 다 저지르다 go through the catalog of crimes; have a long list of criminal acts / 온갖 불평을 다 늘어놓다 make all sorts of complaints; grumble *one's* fill
▶ 나는 이번 일에 온갖 노력을 쏟고 있다 I am really putting forth great efforts for this job.
▶ 그는 온갖 고생을 다 했다 He went through all kinds of hardships imaginable.

온건 穩健 moderateness; moderation
—**온건하다** moderate; temperate; sound
- 온건한 수단 a mild measure / 온건한 의견 a moderate [sensible] view
▶ 그는 생각하는 것이 온건하다 He has moderate views.
■ —주의 moderatism —주의자 a moderatist —파 a moderate party [faction]

온고지신 溫故知新 taking a lesson from the past; reviewing the old and learning the new; understanding the new by exploring the old

온기 溫氣 warmth; warm air
- 온기가 있다[없다] be [be not] warm / 술을 마셔 몸에 온기가 돌다 get warmed [heated] with wine
▶ 물[방석]에는 아직도 온기가 남아 있다 The water [cushion] is still a little warm [warm from the body of someone else].

온난 溫暖 warmth —**온난하다** warm; genial; mild; temperate
- 온난한 기후 a mild climate / 온난한 지방에 살다 live in a temperate climate
▶ 그 지역의 기후는 온난하다 The climate of the region is mild.
■ —전선 〔氣〕 a warm front

온당하다 穩當— reasonable; proper; modest; just; right; appropriate; fitting
- 온당한 말 proper language / 온당한 요구 a reasonable claim / 온당한 조치 just and proper measures
▶ 그 해석은 온당하다 That is a sensible interpretation of the passage.
▶ 그의 요구는 온당하다[온당치 않다] His claim is reasonable [unreasonable].
▶ 그가 생각하는 방식은 온당치 않다 His way of thinking is not proper.

▶ 장례식에서 웃고 농담하는 것은 온당치 못하다 Laughing and joking are improper at a funeral service.

온대 溫帶 the Temperate [Variable] Zone
■ —식물[동물] the flora [fauna] of the temperate zone —(성) 저기압 an extratropical cyclone —지방 the temperate regions [latitudes]

온더록스 ◆ 위스키[버번]를 온더록스로 마시다 drink whisky [bourbon] on the rocks

온데간데없다 suddenly disappear [vanish]; vanish without leaving a trace; be completely out of sight
▶ 그 모습은 온데간데없이 사라져 버렸다 The figure suddenly vanished like a phantom [dissolved into the air].

온도 溫度 (a) temperature; heat
- 온도의 변화 a temperature change / 온도를 조절하다 adjust [control] the temperature / 온도를 측정하다 take [measure] the temperature (of)
▶ 온도가 높다[낮다] The temperature is high [low].
▶ 온도가 내려갔다 The temperature [mercury, thermometer] fell [went down].
▶ 어젯밤에는 온도가 영하 10도였다 The temperature was [The thermometer stood at] ten degrees below zero last night.
▶ 온도[수은주]가 올라갔기 때문에 나는 스위치를 껐다 I turned off the switch because the temperature [mercury] rose [went up].
■ 실내— room temperature; the indoor temperature : 실내온도를 높이세요 [낮추세요] Keep the room at a high [low] temperature. 절대[표준]— 〔物〕 the absolute [standard] temperature 체감— sensible temperature 평균— the (annual) mean temperature: 연간 평균 온도는 얼마나 됩니까? What is the annual mean temperature? ■ —조절 thermostatic control —조절장치 a thermostat; a thermoregulator —측정기 a thermometer; a thermoscope

온도계 溫度計 a thermometer
▶ 온도계는 그늘에서 섭씨 20도를 가리키고 있다 The thermometer registers [reads, indicates, stands at] 20℃ in the shade. (▶twenty degrees Centigrade라고 읽음)
■ 섭씨[화씨]— a Centigrade [Fahrenheit] thermometer 자기(自記)— a recording [self-registering] thermometer 최고[최저]— a maximum [minimum] thermometer

온돌 溫突 an *ondol*; a Korean underfloor heating system; a hypocaust
■ —방 a hot-floored room; an *ondol* room

온두라스 〈나라 이름〉 Honduras; 〈공식명〉 the Republic of Honduras
- 온두라스의 Honduran; Honduranian
■ —사람 a Honduran; a Honduranean

온라인 〔電算〕 ◆ 온라인의[으로] on-line
■ —방식 the on-line information processing system; 〈은행의〉 the on-line banking system

온랭 溫冷 warmth and coldness
온량 溫凉 warmth and coolness
온면 溫麪 noodles served in hot soup; warm

온몸 noodles

온몸 the whole body ♦온몸에 over *one's* whole body; all over *one's* body / 온몸이 멍투성이다 be black and blue all over / 온몸에 화상을 입다 get burns all over the body
▶넘어진 뒤부터 나는 온몸이 쑤셨다 After I fell, I ached all over.
▶독이 그의 온몸에 퍼졌다 The poison pervaded [passed into] his (whole) system.

온밤 all night; the whole night; all the night through ▶간밤엔 온밤을 뜬눈으로 새웠다 I stayed awake all night yesterday.

온상 溫床 a hotbed; a warm nursery; a breeding ground [place] ♦악[범죄]의 온상 a hotbed [nursery] of vice [crime] / 온상에서 묘목을 기르다 raise seedlings in a hotbed
▶빈민굴은 질병과 범죄의 온상이다 Slums are hotbeds of disease and vice.

온색 溫色 a warm color

온수 溫水 warm [hot] water ♦냉·온수 설비를 갖춘 아파트먼트 an apartment with hot and cold (running) water / 온수 설비를 하다 install hot water / 온수 꼭지를 틀다 turn on a hot tap
—공급 hot-water supply —기 a water heater: 순간 온수기 an instantaneous water heater —난방 hot-water heating —보일러 a hot-water boiler —시설 a hot-water supply system —탱크 a hot-water tank —풀 a heated (swimming) pool

온순하다 溫順— gentle; docile; obedient; meek ♦양처럼 온순하다 be as meek as a lamb
▶서커스 동물들은 대체로 온순하다 Most circus animals are tame.
▶그는 아주 온순한 친구다 He is just a mild-mannered guy.

온스 an ounce (略 oz.)

온실 溫室 a greenhouse; a hothouse; 〈촉성재배용〉 a forcing house; 〈英〉 a glasshouse
♦온실에서 재배하다 grow [cultivate] (plants) under glass / (비유) 온실에서 자라다 be brought up on a bed of roses; be brought up like a tender plant; never taste the bitter cup of life.
—멜론 a greenhouse melon —식물 a hothouse plant —재배[배양] glass culture —효과 the greenhouse effect

온열요법 溫熱療法 thermotherapy

온욕 溫浴 (take) a warm [hot] bath
—요법 a hot-water cure

온유하다 溫柔— gentle; mild; genial; docile ♦기질이 온유한 사람 a person with mild [gentle] disposition

온음 —音 〔樂〕 a whole tone [note]
—계 the diatonic scale —음계 the whole-note [whole-tone] scale —표 〈美〉 a whole note; 〈英〉 a semibreve

온장 —張 〈종이·피륙의〉 a whole sheet (of paper [cloth]); uncut paper [cloth]

온전하다 穩全— whole; sound; intact; flawless ♦온전하게 두다 keep [leave] *sth* intact
▶집안에 온전한 접시가 하나도 없다 There is not a plate left whole [unbroken] in the house.

온점 溫點 〈피부의 감각점〉 a hot point [spot]

온정 溫情 a warm heart; a kindly feeling; consideration
♦온정있는 kindly; warm-hearted
▶그는 다른 사람들의 온정으로 먹고 산다 He is living on other people's kindnesses.
—주의 paternalism

온존하다 溫存— keep; preserve; retain; set aside [apart] (for later use)
♦옛 전통을 온존하다 cherish old traditions / 훗날을 위해 힘을 온존하다 keep *one's* power in reserve

온종일 —終日 all day (long); the whole day ⇨ 종일(終日)
▶온종일 비가 온다 It rains all through the day.
▶그는 온종일 빈둥거리며 지냈다 He idled away the whole day.

온집안 〈가족〉 the whole family; all (members of) the family; 〈가옥 안〉 all over the house
♦온집안을 뒤지다 search all over the house
▶저희는 온집안이 무고합니다 My family are all well.
▶열쇠를 찾느라 온집안을 샅샅이 뒤졌다 I searched every nook and corner of the house for the key.

온천 溫泉 a hot spring; a hot well; 〈광천〉 a spa ♦온천욕을 하다 take a hot spring bath
▶아버지는 요양차 수안보 온천에 가셨다 My father went to Suanbo hot spring for his health.
—마을 a hot-spring town —마크 a hot-spring mark —물 the water of a spa —여관[호텔] an inn [a hotel] at a hot-spring resort; a hot-spring inn [hotel] —요법 a hot-spring cure —장 a hot-spring resort; a spa

온축 蘊蓄 a great [*one's* vast] stock of knowledge; profound [extensive] knowledge; erudition

온타리오 1 〈캐나다의 주〉 Ontario
2 〈5대호의 하나〉 Lake Ontario

온탕 溫湯 **1** 〈온천물〉 the hot water of a spa [hot spring] **2** 〈더운 물〉 warm (bath) water

온통 all; wholly; totally; entirely
♦온통 불바다가 되다 be entirely enveloped in flames / 온통 …투성이다 be covered [filled] with …; be full of…
▶소년은 벽에 온통 그 배우의 사진을 붙여놓았다 The boy pinned pictures of the actor all over the wall.

온폭 —幅 the full width [overall breadth] (of paper [cloth])

온풍 溫風 a warm breeze ♦(기계장치로) 온풍을 보내다 send a warm current of air 《to》
—기 a warm air circulator

온혈 溫血 warm blood
—동물 a warm-blooded animal

온화하다 溫和— 〈성질·거동이〉 mild; gentle; mild-tempered; genial; 〈기후·날씨가〉 mild; temperate; morderate; benign; clement
♦온화한 기후 a mild [genial] climate / 온화한 미소 a gentle smile / 온화한 봄날의 오후 a mild afternoon in spring / 온화한 사람 a gentle [genial] person / 온화한 성질 sweet [good] temper

▶이 섬은 기후가 온화하다 This island has a mild [temperate] climate.
▶오늘은 바람 한 점 없는 온화한 날씨다 It is a pleasant, windless day today.
▶그 사람은 성격이 온화해서 좀처럼 화를 내는 일이 없다 He is a very gentle soul and seldom gets angry.
▶나는 성질이 온화한 사람을 쓰고 싶다 I want (to employ) a man of gentle [mild] nature.

온후하다 溫厚— gentle; mild-mannered; suave; courteous
♦온후한 신사 a courteous gentleman
▶그는 온후한 사람이다 His personality is gentle and sincere.
▶나는 그의 온후한 성품이 무척 마음에 든다 His gentle character fascinates me.

올¹ this year ⇨ 올해
♦올여름 this summer / 올안에 before the end of this [the] year; before the year-end
▶그것은 올 예산에 들어 있다 It is included in the budget for the current fiscal year.
▶올에는 눈이 많이 왔다 We have had a lot of snow this year.

올² 〈가닥〉 a strand; a ply; 〈피륙의〉 warp
♦머리카락 한 올 a strand of hair / 스타킹의 풀린 올 a run [(英) ladder] in a stocking / 두 올 실 two-ply thread / 올이 풀리지 않는 스타킹 runproof stockings / 올이 밴[성긴] close [coarse]
▶이 스타킹은 올이 풀렸다 There is a run in this stocking. ⇌ This stocking has a run.

올- 〈조숙한〉 precocious; early-ripening
♦올밤 an early chestnut / 올벼 an early-ripening rice plant

올가미 a noose; a lasso; a loop; 〈함정〉 a snare; a trap; a cheat
♦올가미를 씌우다 〈동물에게〉 put a rope on [round]; 〈사람에게〉 trap *sb* / 올가미에 걸리다 be ensnared / 올가미로 야생마를 잡다 lasso a wild horse

올곧다 1 〈마음이〉 honest; upright; straightforward; right-minded
♦올곧은 사람 an upright person / 마음이 올곧다 be upright at heart / 올곧게 살다 lead an honest life; live straight
▶우리는 그의 올곧은 성품을 높이 사고 있다 We duly appreciate his sincere personality.
2 〈줄이〉 straight; direct

올내년 一來年 this and next year
올되다 1 〈피륙의 올 등이〉 be tight
2 〈조숙하다〉 mature young [early]; be precocious; be forward 《for *one's* age [years]》
♦올된 아이 a precocious [forward] child
▶그녀는 중학생 치고는 올되었다 She is too forward for a middle school girl.
3 〈농작물이〉 ripen early
♦올되는 품종 a variety of early ripening

올라가다 1 〈높은 데로〉 go [walk] up; mount; climb (up); rise; ascend
♦나무에 〔꼭대기까지〕 올라가다 climb [climb to the top of] a tree / 산에 올라가다 climb [go up] a mountain / 연단에 올라가다 step on [mount] the platform / 2층에 올라가다 go upstairs / 절벽을 올라가다 scale a cliff
▶이 계단을 올라가세요 Go up these stairs, please.
▶엘리베이터는 천천히 올라갔다 The elevator ascended slowly.
▶나는 지붕에 올라갔다 I went up on the roof.
2 〈배 등이 강을〉 sail [stream, go] up 《a river》; go upstream; 〈물고기가〉 run up 《a river》
▶강을 올라가자 곧 작은 절이 나타났다 I went up the river and soon found a small temple.
3 〈진보·진출하다〉 advance; progress; make progress [headway]; improve
♦결승에 올라가다 go into [move into] the finals; get [win *one's* way] into the finals / 성적이 올라가다 show a better school record
▶그 아이는 학교 성적이 많이 올라갔다 He has made good progress in his studies.
▶영업 실적이 올라가지를 않는다 Our business is not improving.
4 〈지위 등이〉 rise; be promoted [raised]; be advanced [elevated]
♦명성이 올라가다 rise in fame / 지위가 올라가다 rise in rank; be promoted to a higher position / 대학으로 올라가다 go on to college
▶우리 아들은 금년에 3학년으로 올라갑니다 My son will enter the third grade this year.
▶그는 한 계급 올라갔다 He was promoted one grade in rank.
▶그녀의 지위는 크게 올라갔다 Her position has been greatly raised.
▶그 일로 그의 명성이 올라갔다 That made him famous.
5 〈서울로〉 go up to Seoul; go up to the capital
▶아버지는 사업차 서울에 올라가셨습니다 My father went to Seoul on business.
6 〈물가·온도 등이〉 advance; go [look] up; rise; 〈급히〉 soar; shoot up; skyrocket
▶내일은 기온이 3도 정도 올라갈 것이다 The temperature will probably rise about 3 degrees tomorrow.
7 〈건축되다〉 be built [erected]; go up; rise
♦쑥쑥 올라가다 shoot up
8 〈없어지다〉 lose; 《money》 be lost; be spent uselessly
♦경마로 300만원이 올라가다 lose three million won on the turf

올라서다 1 〈높은 데로〉 get up on a higher place; mount [ascend] 《a platform》
▶그는 의자 위에 올라서서 천장의 먼지를 털었다 He stood on the stool to dust the ceiling.
2 〈지위가 높아지다〉 rise to higher level of rank; 〈출세하다〉 rise in the world
♦1위로 올라서다 move into the first place
▶그 배우는 단 2, 3년 사이에 일약 스타 자리에 올라섰다 The actor shot to stardom in a couple of years.

올라오다 rise; ascend; come up
♦서울로 올라오다 come up to Seoul / 2층에 올라오다 come upstairs
▶방금 육지에 올라와서 아직도 뱃멀미가 나는 것 같다 As I have just come ashore, I still feel a bit seasick.

올라타다

올라타다 1 〈탈것에〉 ◆뛰어 올라타다 jump on (a horse); jump in (a bus, a moving car)
▶ 버스가 오자 그는 뛰어 올라탔다 The bus came in and he swung into it.
▶ 그는 달리는 열차에 뛰어 올라탔다 He swung aboard a moving train.
2 〈고미하다〉 line; cover; tread

올랑출랑하다 slop; splash (in a tub); lap (against)
▶ 물결이 물가에 부딪쳐 올랑출랑한다 The waves are lapping [slapping] (against) the shore.
▶ 물통의 물이 올랑출랑한다 The water in the pail is slapping hither and thither.

올려놓다 put *sth* (up) on (a place, *sth*)
▶ 손을 탁자 위에 올려놓다 rest *one's* hands on a table / 책을 선반에 올려놓다 put a book (up) on a shelf

올려본각 —角 〔數〕 an angle of elevation

올리고세 —世 〈신생대 제 3기의 하나〉 〔地質〕 the Oligocene

올리다 1 〈위로〉 raise; lift (up); elevate; put [get] up; hold
◆닻을 올리다 heave up the anchor; weigh anchor / 깃발을 올리다 hoist [lift, 〈줄을 당겨〉 run up] a flag / 무대에 올리다 put (a play) on the stage; stage (a play) / 불꽃을 쏘아 올리다 set off [let off, shoot, display] fireworks
▶ 나 좀 올려 주시오. Help me up. ⇌ Let me up.
▶ 죄송하지만 이 가방 좀 선반에 올려 주세요 Would you please put this suitcase up on the rack?
2 〈등급·지위를〉 raise; promote; elevate
◆계급을 올리다 raise *sb's* rank; promote *sb* to a higher rank / 급수를 한 급 올리다 promote *sb* to a higher class
3 〈증가시키다〉 increase; 〈인상하다〉 raise; keep up; advance; (口) hike; boost
◆가격을 올리다 raise [put up] the price / 급료를 올리다 raise *sb's* salary (to); give *sb* a raise [(英) rise] / 세금[세율]을 올리다 raise the tax rates / 요금을 올리다 raise the charge [rate]
4 〈바치다〉 offer; give; present
◆공양을 올리다 make an offering / 기도를 올리다 pray; offer a prayer / 미사를 올리다 say [read] mass / 잔을 올리다 offer a cup (to *one's* senior)
▶ 나는 아버지께 진지를 올렸다 I served my father with dinner.
▶ 이것을 선생님께 올리겠습니다 Here is something for you, sir.
▶ 제가 써 올리지요 I will write it for you.
5 〈좋은 결과를〉 achieve (good results); advance
◆매상을 많이 올리다 have a good [great] sale; enjoy a brisk sale / 좋은 성과를 올리다 obtain [get, gain, attain, win] excellent results / 순익 200만원을 올리다 gain a net profit of two million won
▶ 우리 팀은 10득점을 올렸다 Our team scored 10 points.
▶ 어제는 100만원의 매상을 올렸다 The sales of yesterday totalled one million won.
6 〈차리다〉 serve; prepare
◆상에 올리다 serve [set] (dishes) on the table
7 〈식을〉 hold; observe; perform; solemnize
▶ 그들은 5월에 결혼식을 올릴 계획이다 They plan to hold [have] their wedding (ceremony) in May.
8 〈기록하다〉 enter (a name); put *sth* on record
◆기록에 올리다 place [put] (a matter) on record / 새 낱말을 사전에 올리다 enter a new word in a dictionary / 이름을 전화번호부에 올리다 enter *sb's* name in the telephone book [directory] / 장부에 올리다 enter (an item) in an account book / 호적에 이름을 올리다 have *sb's* name entered in the family register
9 〈상정·제출하다〉 bring up; present
◆의제에 올리다 place (a matter) on the agenda; bring up (a matter) for discussion
10 〈입히다〉 paint (with); coat; apply; 〈도금하다〉 plate; gild
◆구리에 은을 올리다 plate copper with silver
11 〈지붕에〉 roof / 지붕에 기와를 올리다 roof with tiles; tile a roof
12 〈소리를〉 raise; give
◆환성을 올리다 raise [give, let out, send up] a cheer; shout for joy
13 〈병균을 옮기다〉 infect (*sb* with a disease)
▶ 그는 내게 옴을 올렸다 He has given me his itch [scabies].
14 〈기타〉 ◆기세를 올리다 arouse *one's* spirits / 약을 올리다 grate on *sb's* nerves; try *sb's* patience; provoke

올리브 〔植〕 an olive ■—나무 an olive tree —색 olive color —유 olive oil

올림[1] 1 〈증정〉 presentation; proffering; with the compliments of
▶ 김 선생님께 지은이 올림 To Mr. Kim, With the Compliments of the Author.
2 〈편지에서〉 Yours very truly

올림[2] 〔樂〕 ■—표 sharp (▶#로 표시함): 2중 올림표 a double sharp / 올림표를 붙이다 sharp —활 a up-bow

올림픽 the Olympics; the Olympic Games; the Olympiad
◆국제 올림픽 위원회 the International Olympic Committee (略 IOC) / 한국 올림픽 위원회 the Korean Olympic Committee (略 KOC) / 한국 대표로 올림픽에 나가다 represent Korea in the Olympic Games
▶ 올림픽은 4년에 한 번씩 열린다 The Olympic Games are held every four years.
■국제기능— the International Vocational Training Competition 국제 장애자— the International Paraplegics Olympic Games 근대— the modern Olympics 동계— the Olympic Winter Games; the Winter Olympic Games; the Winter Olympics 프레— the Pre-Olympics; the Pre-Olympic Games ■—경기[대회] the Olympic Games; the Olympics; the Olympiad —경기장 the Olympic Stadium —기 the Olympic flag —기록 an Olympic record —선수 an Olympian —선수촌 an Olympic village

—성화 the Olympic Flame; 〈릴레이의〉 the Olympic Torch —조직위원회 the Olympic Organizing Committee (略 O.O.C.) —찬가 the Olympic anthem [hymn] —헌장 the Olympic Charter —회의 the Olympic Congress

올망졸망 in lots of small units [pieces, lumps]; in a lovely huddle; in abundance; in clusters
▶감이 올망졸망 달려 있다 There are a lot of small persimmons of about the same size.
—**올망졸망하다** 《be》 of various small sizes
◆올망졸망한 아이들 little children of about [roughly] the same size / 올망졸망한 집들 a cluster of small houses

올무 a snare; a noose ◆올무를 놓다 lay [set] a snare

올바로 〈곧게〉 straightly; straightforwardly; uprightly; 〈옳게〉 correctly; properly; 〈정당하게〉 right; rightfully; 〈정직하게〉 honestly; truthfully; frankly; 〈건전하게〉 soundly; morally
◆올바로 말하다 speak frankly; speak straight out / 올바로 살다 lead an honest life; pursue an honest career; live straight / 올바로 행동하다 behave properly [correctly]

올바르다 〈정당하다〉 right; reasonable; 〈정직하다〉 honest; upright; 〈정확하다〉 exact; correct; 〈적절하다〉 proper; 〈건전하다〉 sound; healthy; 〈합법적·도덕적이다〉 lawful; legitimate; moral

> 解說 *right*는 사실·기준·도리에 합당하며 사람의 판단력이나 의견이 올바른 것, 또 행위 등이 법률·도덕·사회 통념에 비추어 올바른 것 등과 특정 목적에 가장 적합하고 올바른 것을 가리킨다. *correct*는 결점이나 잘못이 없이 정확하고, 또 예의나 규칙에 어긋나지 않고 올바른 것. *proper*는 방법 등이 목적·상황·예의에 부합되게 올바른 것을 뜻하는 약간 딱딱한 말이다.

◆올바른 대답 the correct [right] answer 《to the question》 / 올바른 방법 the proper way; the correct method / 올바른 사람 a righteous [upright] man / 올바른 재판관 an upright judge / 올바른 행위 right conduct / 올바른 일을 하다 do a right thing; do right / 올바른 인식을 갖게 하다 make *sb* have correct understanding 《of》 / 올바르게 살다 live an honest life; live straight
▶나는 항상 올바른 일을 하려고 애쓰고 있다 I always try to do what is right.
▶그 표현은 문법적으로는 올바르지 않다 Grammatically the expression is not correct.
▶외국어를 올바르게 발음하기는 어렵다 It is hard to pronounce a foreign language correctly.

올밤 an early chestnut
올벼 an early-ripening (variety of) rice plant
올봄 this spring
올빼미 〔鳥〕 an owl ◆올빼미 새끼 an owlet
▶나는 올빼미가 우는 소리를 들었다 I heard an owl hooting.

올새 〈천의〉 texture; weave

◆올새가 성긴[촘촘한] 천 cloth of open [close] texture; cloth with a loose [close] weave / 올새가 거칠다 be rough [coarse]

올스타 ◆올스타전[게임] an all-star game / 올스타 캐스트 〔映〕 an all-star cast

올차다 〈사람이〉 energetic; solid; firm; tough; 〈곡식이〉 early-ripening ◆올찬 사람 a man of compact [substantial] build

올챙이 a tadpole; 《美方》 a polliwog
■—기자 a cub reporter —배 a potbelly —작가 a cub writer

올커트 〈미국의 여류 작가〉 Alcott, Louisa May (1832-88)

올케 the wife of a girl's brother; a girl's sister-in-law

올통볼통하다 uneven ⇨ 울퉁불퉁하다

올해 this year; the current [present] year
◆올해의 예산 the budget for the current year / 올해 안에 before the end of the year; within the year
▶올해는 풍년이다 This is a bumper year.
▶올해는 윤년이다 This is a leap year.
▶올해도 며칠 남지 않았다 We have only a few days left before the end of the year.

옭다 1 〈잡아매다〉 bind; fasten
◆단단히 옭다 tie firmly [tightly]; tie up 《a luggage》
2 〈올가미로〉 put the noose on; noose; 〈꾀로〉 ensnare; snare; entrap; rope in
◆밧줄로 목을 옭다 noose a rope round the neck 《of a dog》 / 염소를 옭다 put the noose on a goat
3 〈죄를 씌우다〉 entrap *sb*; fasten the crime on *sb*
◆남을 옭아 넣다 put *sb* under a false charge / 남을 옭아서 …하게 하다 entrap *sb* by a trick into 《doing》
▶그녀는 기회만 있으면 그를 옭아 넣으려고 했다 She never lost an opportunity to set a trap for him.

옭매다 tie 《a shoestring》 in a flat [reef] knot; reef-knot 《a shoestring》

옭매듭 a square knot; a flat [reef] knot

옭아내다 1 〈올가미로〉 put the noose on 《an animal》 and drag 《it》 out; noose 《an animal》 out 2 ⇨ 우려내다 1

옭아매다 1 〈올가미로〉 cast [put] a noose round 《the neck》 and tie to; tie up
◆개를 기둥에 옭아매다 put a noose on a dog and leash it to a post
2 〈없는 죄로〉 make a false charge 《of espionage》 against *sb*

옭히다 1 〈잡아매이다〉 be tied (up); be bound [fastened]; 〈올가미로〉 be noosed; get roped; be caught in a snare
▶사슴이 올가미에 옭혀 있었다 A deer was caught in a snare.
2 〈걸려들다〉 be ensnared; be entrapped; be entangled (in an affair); be [get] involved (in, with)
◆살인 사건에 옭혀 곤욕을 치르다 be mixed up in a murder case and get a rough going-over
3 〈얽히다〉 be tied in a knot; be entangled
▶실이 옭혀 풀리지 않는다 Thread is so tan-

옮겨붙다 〈불이〉 catch [take] fire; spread to ▶불은 옆집으로 옮겨붙었다 The fire spread to the next house.

옮겨심다 transplant; replant ▶그는 묘목들을 집 뒤에 옮겨 심었다 He reset the nursery trees behind the house.

옮기다 1 〈이전·이동하다〉 move [remove, shift, transfer] 《to, into》
♦가구를 옮기다 move furniture 《from one room to another》 / 짐을 한 손에서 다른 손으로 옮기다 shift a bundle from one hand to the other / 학교를 옮기다 transfer to another school / 다른 회사로 옮기다 change to another firm / 지금의 집에서 새 집으로 옮기다 move out of *one's* house into a new one / 다른 배로 옮겨 싣다 transship / 화차에서 트럭으로 짐을 옮겨 싣다 transfer goods from a freight car to a truck
▶난 수원으로 집을 옮겼다 I moved to Suwon.
▶그 회사는 본사를 뉴욕에서 시카고로 옮겼다 The company has transferred its main office from New York to Chicago.

2 〈말을〉 pass 《words》 on 《to another》; tell (at second hand)
▶이 말을 다른 사람에게 옮기지 마라 Don't tell this to anyone. ⇒ Keep this secret.

3 〈전염시키다〉 give; infect 《*sb* with a disease》
▶그녀가 아이에게 감기를 옮겼다 She has given the child her cold.
▶아기에게 감기를 옮기지 않도록 주의해라 Be careful not to infect the baby with your cold [pass your cold on to the baby].

4 〈용기에〉 transfuse; pour 《into》; empty
♦술을 통에서 병으로 옮기다 pour wine from the cask into a bottle
▶그녀는 주전자의 더운 물을 보온병에 옮겨담 았다 She emptied [poured] the hot water of the kettle into the vacuum bottle [flask].

5 〈실행·이송하다〉 transfer; carry
♦계획[결심]을 실천[실행]에 옮기다 carry a plan into practice [put *one's* decision into effect] / 사건을 대법원으로 옮기다 transfer [carry] a case to the Supreme Court
▶다음 문제로 옮깁시다 Let's get on to the next problem.

6 〈돌리다·향하다〉 divert; turn; direct 《to》
♦주의를 딴 데로 옮기다 turn [divert] *one's* attention from one thing to another / 집으로 발길을 옮기다 direct *one's* step toward home

7 〈번역하다〉 translate [render, put] 《into》
♦한국어를 영어로 옮기다 translate [put] Korean into English
▶다음 문장을 우리 말로 옮기시오 Put [Render, Translate] the following (sentences) into Korean.

옮다 1 〈이전하다〉 move *one's* residence; move [remove] 《to, into》
2 〈병·버릇·사상 등에 전염되다〉 be infected 《with》; catch; take; contract
♦옮기 쉬운 infectious 《disease》; contagious 《fever》; catching 《disease》
▶너한테 감기가 옮았다 You've given me a cold.
▶그녀는 남편한테서 병이 옮았다 She caught the disease of [from] her husband.
▶그녀는 미국식 사고방식이 크게 옮았다 She has been greatly influenced by the American way of thinking.
▶그는 아버지의 습관이 옮았다 He got [picked up] the habit from his father.
▶하품은 옮는다 Yawning is catching.

3 〈물이 들다〉 dye
▶포장지의 색깔이 상자에 옮았다 The color of the wrapping paper rubbed off on the box.

옮아가다 1 〈이전하다〉 move [remove] 《to, into》 ♦교외로 옮아가다 change *one's* abode [move] to the suburbs
2 〈퍼져가다〉 spread; circulate
▶소문은 금방 옮아간다 Rumors circulate rapidly.
▶독감이 이웃 마을로 옮아갔다 Influenza spread to a neighboring village.

옮아오다 1 〈전입하다〉 move in [into]; transfer 《to this place》
♦지점에서 본점으로 옮아오다 be transferred from a branch to the head office
2 〈퍼져오다〉 spread 《to this place》

옳다¹ 〈바르다〉 correct; exact; 〈정당하다〉 right; rightful; 〈정의롭다〉 righteous; just; 〈합법적〉 lawful; legitimate; legal
♦옳은 답 a correct [right] answer 《to a problem》 / 옳지 않은 wrong; unjust; dishonest; incorrect / 옳은 일을 하다 do a right thing; do right; do what is right / 옳다고 생각하다 consider [think] (it) right / 어느 쪽이 옳은지 조사하다 find out on which side the right lies
▶네 말이 옳다 You are right. ⇒ What you say is true.
▶두 사람 중 누가 옳은가? Which of the two men is in the right?
▶그는 옳은 것을 옳다고 하고 그른 것을 그르다 고 한다 He calls a spade a spade.
▶네가 옳게 맞혔어 You guessed right. ⇒ You hit it.

옳다² Right!; O.K.!; All right!; Good!; Capital!
♦옳다구나 하고 제의를 받아들이다 jump [snatch] at a proposal [an offer]
▶옳다, 됐다 Good! I've got it!
▶옳다, 알았다 Eureka!
▶옳다, 이제 알겠다 Oh, now I get it!

옳아 ▶옳아, 바로 네가 그랬구나 I see, you are the very one who did it.

옳은길 the path of righteousness; the right track ♦옳은 길을 걷다 tread the path of righteousness / 옳은 길로 이끌다 guide *sb* into the right path; set *sb* on the right track

옳은말 an honest speech; the truth; a reasonable remark ♦옳은 말만 하는 사람 a person who always makes reasonable remarks [tell what is right]

옴¹ 1 〖醫〗 the itch; scabies(▶단수취급); 〈말·개 등의〉 mange
♦옴이 오르다 catch [have] the itch; be infected with scabies
▶그는 옴이 옮았다 He has [suffers from]

scabies.
2 〈젖꼭지에 좁쌀처럼 돋은 것〉 a granular process on the teats of a nursing mother ■—딱지 scabies scabs

옴² 〈전기저항의 단위〉〈電〉an ohm ♦옴의 법칙 Ohm's law ■—계(計) an ohmmeter —저항 ohmic resistance

옴니버스 〈단편을 모은 것〉 an omnibus ■—영화 an omnibus film [movie]

옴니암니 sundry expenses; expenses for this and that

옴부즈맨 〈행정 감시위원〉an ombudsman; (英) a parliamentary commissioner for administration

옴살 bosom friendship; intimacy

옴실거리다 swarm; squirm [wriggle] (in swarm) ▶ 돌 밑에서 지렁이들이 옴실거리고 있다 A loaf of earthworms are wriggling under the stone.

옴쏙 ♦눈이 옴쏙 들어간 사람 a person with sunken [deep-set] eyes; a hollow-eyed person —옴쏙하다 hollow; sunken

옴질거리다 1 〈자꾸 움직이다〉 squirm; move slowly ♦벌레가 옴질거리다 a worm wriggles **2** 〈주저하다〉 hesitate; be slow (in doing); linger
♦일을 옴질거리다 linger over *one's* work
3 〈오물거리다〉 mumble; chew on 《something hard》

옴질옴질 1 〈옴실옴실〉 wrigglingly; squirmingly; crawlingly
2 〈오물오물〉 mumblingly
♦빵 껍질을 옴질옴질 먹다 mumble on a crust
3 〈머뭇머뭇〉 hesitatingly; hesitantly; irresolutely; lingeringly

옴쭉달싹 with a very slight move
♦옴쭉달싹 않다 do not budge [move] (an inch); stand as firm as rock / 옴쭉달싹 못하다 cannot move [stir, budge] an inch; be stuck; be in a (pretty [fine]) fix; bog down in; be helpless / 자금부족으로 옴쭉달싹 못하다 find *oneself* stuck for want of funds / 옴쭉달싹 못하게 되다 be [get] stuck 《with》; be in a fix [pinch]

옴찔하다 be taken by surprise ⇨ 움찔하다

옴츠러들다 〈공포로〉 shrink (up with fear); 〈움찔하다〉 flinch (from)
▶ 그는 두려움으로 옴츠러 들었다 He was huddled up with fear.

옴츠러뜨리다 1 〈옴츠리다〉 contract; curl up; draw [pull] in
♦다리를 옴츠러뜨리다 draw in *one's* legs
2 〈겁을 먹고〉 make *sb* shrink up; scare
♦고함을 질러 아무를 옴츠러뜨리다 scare *sb* with a loud shout

옴츠러지다 1 〈추워서〉 be curled [huddled] up; curl [huddle] (*oneself*) up
▶ 나는 추워서 몸이 옴츠러진다 I am huddled up with cold.
2 〈무서워서〉 cower; quail 《at, before》; shrink [flinch] 《at, before, from》; cringe 《at》; wince 《under》
▶ 나는 얻어 맞고도 옴츠러지지 않았다 I didn't wince under the blow.

옴츠리다 contract; shrink (up); huddle [curl] up; 〈쏙 들여보내다〉 draw [take, pull] in; withdraw; retract
♦목을 옴츠리다 duck *one's* head; pull in *one's* head / 몸을 옴츠리다 curl [huddle] *oneself* up; squeeze *oneself* (in); 〈용기를 잃고〉 shrink (up) (within *oneself*); cower; wince; flinch; quail / 다리를 옴츠리다 sleep with *one's* legs drawn in / 옴츠리게 하다 make *sb* shrink up; 〈질려서〉 scare *sb*
▶ 나는 추위로 몸을 옴츠렸다 I shrinked up with the cold.
▶ 나는 두려움으로 몸을 옴츠렸다 I was huddled up with fear.
▶ 그녀는 남편의 노기 띤 말에 몸을 옴츠렸다 She winced at her husband's angry words.
▶ 그 일에서는 나도 몸을 옴츠렸다 Even I shrank from the task.

옴큼 a handful [fistful] 《of earth》

옴파다 gouge out; hollow out; bore; excavate ♦나무판에 구멍을 옴파다 bore a hole in the board

옴팡눈 〈눈〉 sunken [deep-set] eyes; 〈사람〉 a sunken-eyed person ▶ 그녀는 옴팡눈이다 She has deep-set eyes.

옴패다 〈오목하게 파지다〉 be hollowed [scooped, gouged] out; get excavated; 〈오목해지다〉 become hollow [depressed]; get sunken; sink; pit

옴폭 ♦옴폭 패인 땅 a hollowed place
—옴폭하다 hollow; deep; sunken; dented; depressed ♦옴폭한 눈 sunken eyes

옵서버 〈참관인〉an observer
▶ 나는 그 회의에 옵서버로 참석했다 I attended the meeting as an observer.

옵션 〈선택 가능물〉an option

옵티미스트 〈낙천주의자〉an optimist (↔ a pessimist)

옷 clothes; a garment; 〈주로 여자·어린이용〉 a dress; (총칭) clothing
♦헌[낡은] 옷 used clothes / 속옷 underwear / 겉옷 outer garments / 잠옷 pajamas / 가벼운 여름옷 a light clothes for summer
▶ 그녀는 옷 입은 모습이 잘 어울린다 She is very attractive [looks very nice] in a dress.
▶ 나는 옷엔 관심이 없다 I don't care how I dress.
〈옷이[은]〉그녀는 옷이 많다[별로 없다] She has a large [small] wardrobe.
▶ 그 옷은 너한테는 잘 맞는다 The dress fits you perfectly.
▶ 나는 입고 갈 옷이 없었다 I had nothing to go in.
▶ 옷은 어머니가 입혀 주신다 My mother helps me on with my dress.
▶ 아이가 자라서 옷이 전부 맞지 않는다 The child has outgrown all his clothes.
〈옷을〉옷을 입다 put on *one's* clothes; get into *one's* clothes; dress (*oneself*) / 옷을 갈아 입다 change (*one's*) clothes / 옷을 급히 입다 rush into *one's* clothes; throw *one's* clothes on / 옷을 껴입다 wear *one's* garment over the other / 옷을 얇게 입다 dress lightly; be thinly dressed (in) / 좋은[허름한] 옷을 입고 있다 be

옷가슴 the breast (of a garment) ◆옷가슴이 넓다[좁다] be loose [tight] across the chest [breast] / 옷가슴을 여미다 tidy oneself

옷가지 several garments; pieces of clothing

옷 감 (plain) cloth; material; 〈직물〉 texture; 〈복지〉 suiting; 〈美〉 goods
◆두꺼운[얇은] 옷감 heavy [light] stuff; thick [thin] cloth / 부드러운 옷감 soft cloth / 여름 [겨울] 옷감 cloth for summer [winter] use; summer [winter] goods / 좋은[나쁜] 옷감 good [bad] stuff / 옷감의 견본 sample cloth; a swatch / 옷감을 마르다 cut (out) cloth / 옷감을 재다 measure a piece of cloth

옷걸이 a coat [dress] hanger; a dress rack

옷고름 a breast-tie (of a Korean coat); a coat string ◆옷고름을 매다[풀다] fasten [loosen] breast-ties; tie [untie] one's coat

옷기장 the length of one's dress; one's dress length

옷깃 〈양복의〉 a collar; 〈한복의〉 the neckband; a lapel; 〈셔츠 등의〉 a neck
◆옷깃이 없는 collarless (blouse) / 옷깃을 여미고 듣다 listen with respectful attention / 코트의 옷깃을 세우다 turn up the collar of one's overcoat / 옷깃을 여미다 adjust oneself [one's dress]; straighten oneself
▶추워서 코트의 옷깃을 세웠다 It was so cold (that) I turned my coat collar up.
▶옷깃을 바로하고 들어주십시오 Straighten up and listen to me. ⇌ Listen to me carefully.

옷농 —籠 a clothes chest ⇨ 옷장

옷단 a tuck; 〈옷의 가장자리를 감친 것〉 a hem
◆옷단을 감치다 hem; overcast; put in a tuck

옷단장 —丹粧 —옷단장하다 dress (oneself) up; deck (oneself) out; (口) doll (oneself) up

옷맵시 the appearance of one's clothes
◆옷맵시가 좋다[좋지 않다] wear one's clothes stylishly [poorly]; dress oneself in good [bad] shape; dress well [badly]

옷보 —褓 a cloth wrapper for clothes

옷본 —本 a pattern; a paper pattern

옷상자 —箱子 a box [chest] for clothes

옷셋집 —貰— a rental clothier's shop

옷이 날개다 (속담) Fine clothes make the man. ⇌ Fine feathers make fine birds. ⇌ The tailor makes the man.

옷자락 the lower end of clothes; the dress hem; 〈양복바지의〉 the bottom; 〈긴 치맛자락〉 the train
◆옷자락을 걷어올리다 tuck up one's skirt / 옷자락을 끌다 trail the skirt(s)

옷장 —欌 a clothes chest; a wardrobe

옷차림 (an) appearance; dress; attire; getup; outfit
◆옷차림이 훌륭하다[초라하다] be well [ill] dressed / 옷차림을 상관하지 않다 be careless about one's dress [appearance] / 초라한 옷차림을 하고 있다 be poorly [shabbily] dressed / 옷차림을 단정히 하다 tidy (oneself) up; get (oneself) up
▶옷차림으로 사람을 판단하지 마라 Don't judge people by their appearances.

옷치레 rich attire
◆옷치레를 좋아하는 사람 a lover of finery
—옷치레하다 wear [put on] fine clothes; dress (oneself) up

-옹 —翁 an old [aged] man; old Mr. ...
◆박 옹 (the) old Mr. Park

옹고집 壅固執 obstinacy; stubbornness; perversity; bigotry
◆옹고집의 obstinate; stubborn; bigoted; headstrong / 옹고집을 부리다 be obstinate; do not give in
▶그 소년은 대단한 옹고집이었다 The boy was as stubborn as a donkey.
■—쟁이 a stubborn person

옹골지다 〈알차다〉 substantial; solid; meaty; 〈단단하다〉 firm; well-knit; compact
◆옹골진 과일 hard fruits

옹골차다 strong and hard; substantial; solid
◆옹골찬 사람 a man of firm [solid] build [physique]; a man of well-knit frame

옹그리다 huddle [curl] (oneself) up; roll oneself up; crouch; squat; stoop
◆추워서 옹그리다 be huddled up [huddle oneself up] with the cold / 옹그리고 자다 sleep curled up; lie huddled up in bed
▶고양이는 방석 위에서 몸을 옹그렸다 The cat huddled itself up on the cushion.

옹기 甕器 pottery; crockery; earthenware
■—장수 a pottery [crockery] dealer —장이 a potter —전 a pottery shop

옹기종기 in a small close group; in crowds
◆옹기종기 텔레비전 앞에 모이다 form a little knot of togetherness around the television

옹달- small and hollow
◆옹달샘 a small fountain [spring] / 옹달솥 a small iron pot / 옹달우물 a small well

옹두리 a knot (on a tree); a knob; a gnarl; a node; a knurl; a knar
■—뼈 the leg bone (of cattle)

옹립 擁立 〈왕으로〉 enthroning; 〈지지〉 backing
—옹립하다 〈임금으로 세우다〉 help to the throne; 〈떠받들다〉 give backing to; back (up); support
▶그들은 어린 왕자를 옹립했다 They supported [backed up] the young prince to the throne.

옹벽 擁壁 a retaining wall

옹색하다 壅塞— 1 〈생활이 군색하다〉 needy; straitened
◆살림이 옹색하다 be in needy circumstances; be badly off; live in poverty / 돈에 옹색하다 be pinched [pressed] for money; be hard up for money
▶우리 집은 요즘 살림이 옹색해졌다 My fam-

ily has fallen on hard times.
2 〈비좁다〉 narrow and close; cramping; cramped
♦옹색한 방 a narrow (and close) room
옹생원 —生員 a narrow-minded person
옹송그리다 curl *one's* body up; huddle; crouch
▶ 할머니는 불가에 옹송그리고 앉아 계셨다 The old woman squatted down by the fire.
▶ 그는 방 한구석에 옹송그리고 앉아 있다 He huddles himself up in a corner of the room.
옹송옹송하다 confused; hazy; muzzy; muddled; dazed
옹스트롬 〔物〕 an angstrom (unit)
옹알거리다 murmur; mumble; mutter
▶ 우리 아기가 혼자 옹알거리고 있다 My baby is mumbling to himself.
옹이 a knar; a knot; a node; a gnarl; a knurl; a knob
▶ 이 나무는 옹이투성이다 This wood is full of knars.
▶ 나무 옹이에 머리를 부딪쳤다 I knocked my head against a knot of the tree.
옹자배기 a tiny earthenware bowl
옹졸하다 壅拙— narrow-minded; illiberal; intolerant; ungenerous; hidebound
♦옹졸한 사람 a narrow-minded person
옹주 翁主 a princess by a concubine
옹크리다 huddle (*oneself*) up ⇨ 옹그리다
옹호 擁護 〈지지〉 support; defense [(英) defence]; 〈보호〉 protection; 〈변호〉 vindication; 〈조력〉 assistance; help
—옹호하다 protect; defend; safeguard; vindicate; support; back up; help
♦인권을 옹호하다 defend [protect] human rights / 헌법을 옹호하다 safeguard the constitution / 그의 의견을 옹호하는 발언을 하다 speak in defense [support] of his opinion
▶ 그는 출판의 자유을 옹호하는 일에 몸을 바쳤다 He committed himself to the protection of a free press.
▶ 만일 당신이 스스로 권리를 옹호하지 않으면 아무도 그걸 가져다 주지 않습니다 If you don't stand up for your rights no one else will do it for you.
■—자 a defender; a supporter; a backer; a protector; a bulwark
옻 lacquer; japan; 〈중독〉 lacquer poisoning
♦옻을 lacquered
옻나무 〔植〕 a lacquer tree; a poison ivy
옻오르다, 옻올리다 be poisoned with lacquer; have poison ivy
▶ 나는 옻올랐다 I was poisoned with lacquer.
옻칠 —漆 lacquering; 〈옻〉 lacquer
—옻칠하다 lacquer; varnish with lacquer
♦옻칠한 lacquered
옻타다 be sensitive [allergic] to lacquer poison
와[1] 〈갑자기〉 suddenly; 〈일제히〉 all at once; 〈떠드는 모양〉 with a great roar; loudly
♦와 떠들다 make a great noise [roar]; clamor / 와 달아나다 run away in a panic / 와 밀어닥치다 advance on 《the enemy》 with a rush / 와 웃다 burst into laughter; burst out laughing; roar with laughter
▶ 소녀들 중 한 명이 와 울었다 One of the girls burst into tears.
▶ 관객은 그 광경을 보자 환성을 와 올렸다 The spectators sent up [raised, let out] cheers at the sight.
와[2] **1** 〈열거〉 and ♦너와 나 You and I
▶ 저희는 아버지와 어머니께 감사하다는 말씀을 드리고 싶습니다 We want to thank father and mother.
2 〈함께〉 with; along [together] with; in company with
▶ 그는 여자 친구와 영화를 보러갔다 He went to the movies with his girlfriend.
3 〈대상·대립〉 against; with
♦원수와 싸우다 fight against [with] an enemy
▶ 3년만에 그와 통화했다 I talked with [to] him on the phone for the first time in three years.
▶ 전에는 아우와 곧잘 싸우곤 했지요 I used to quarrel [argue] with my brother.
4 〈합치·협력〉 with
♦친구와 협력하다 cooperate with *one's* friend
5 〈접촉〉 with
▶ 그 군인은 본부와 연락을 취하면서 행동했다 The soldier acted in conjunction with the headquarters.
6 〈분리〉 with; from
♦친구와 헤어지다 part with [from] *one's* friend; 〈절교하다〉 break with [off from] *one's* friend
7 〈관계〉 with
▶ 나는 그와 거래가 있다 I have dealings with him.
8 〈비교·선택〉 with
▶ 우리 나라와 비교하면 한국이 더 따뜻합니다 Korea is warmer than my country. ⇌ Compared with my country, Korea is warmer.
▶ 차와 커피 중 어느 것을 좋아합니까? Which do you prefer, tea and coffee?
9 〈유사〉 as; like; (similar) to; 〈차이〉 (different) from
♦여느때와 같이 as (is) usual / 이와는 달리 different from this
10 〈혼합〉 with
♦우유와 물을 섞다 mix water with milk
와[3] 〈마소를 멈추는 소리〉 Whoa!; Wo!; Woa!; Halt there!
와가 瓦家 〈기와집〉 a house roofed with tiles; a tile-roofed house
와각거리다 clatter; rattle
와각와각 rattlingly; clatteringly; with a rattling noise
와글거리다 1 〈북적거리다〉 throng; crowd; swarm
▶ 나는 사람들이 와글거리는 곳은 좋아하지 않는다 I hate crowded places, you know.
2 〈떠들다〉 make a lot of noise; raise a clamor; be boisterous [clamorous]
♦와글거리는 사람들 a clamorous crowd of people
3 〈끓어오르다〉 be boiling [seething]

와글와글 1 〈북적북적〉 in swarms [crowds, throngs]; 〈시끄럽게〉 noisily; clamorously ▶ 옆방에서 와글와글 떠드는 소리가 들렸다 We heard noisy voices in the next room. ―와글와글하다 make a noise; make a hullabaloo; raise a clamor 2 boilingly; seethingly

와닥닥 with a hurl; with a thud; 〈갑자기〉 suddenly; 〈급히〉 hastily
◆ 방에서 와닥닥 나가다 rush [dash, fling] out of the room / 계단을 와닥닥 내려가다 hurry [tumble] down the stairs
▶ 학생들이 와닥닥 열차에 들이닥쳤다 A lot of students crowded hastily into our train.

와당탕 with a bang [crash]; thumpingly; with a bump; 〈요란하게〉 noisily
◆ 벽에 와당탕 부딪치다 bang into a wall
▶ 뒤차가 와당탕 내 차를 들이받았다 The car behind banged [crashed] into my car.
―와당탕하다 make a thumping [bumping] sound; make a noise

와들와들 tremblingly; shiveringly
◆ 무서워서[화가 나서] 와들와들 떨다 tremble with fear [anger] / 추워서 와들와들 떨다 shiver with cold; quiver from cold
▶ 손이 와들와들 떨려서 글씨를 잘 쓸 수가 없었다 My hands were shaking so badly that I could not write well.
▶ 나는 무릎이 와들와들 떨렸다 My knees shook together. ⇌ I felt wobbly about the knees.

와락 with a sudden jerk [tug]; with all *one's* might; at a breath; 〈갑자기〉 suddenly; all at once; abruptly
◆ 와락 잡아당기다 pull with a sudden jerk; pull suddenly / 와락 울음을 터뜨리다 burst out crying; burst into tears
▶ 어머니는 자기 아이를 와락 껴안았다 The mother hugged [embraced] her child tightly.

와룡 臥龍 a lying dragon; 〈인물〉 a great man in obscurity; a man of great promise [potentiality]

와류 渦流 eddy

와르르 1 〈무너지는 모양〉 in a confused heap; 〈소리〉 clatteringly; rattlingly; with a crash
◆ 와르르 무너지다 fall (down) [collapse] with a crash; fall down to pieces
▶ 짐더미가 와르르 무너졌다 The piles of cargo collapsed with a crash.
▶ 바위가 와르르 무너져 내렸다 The rock came hurtling down.
2 〈천둥소리〉 rollingly; rumblingly; thunderingly
▶ 천둥소리가 와르르 난다 The thunder is rumbling.
3 〈끓는 소리〉 hubble-bubble; seething; boiling
▶ 물이 와르르 끓고 있다 The water is boiling away [furiously].
▶ 냄비가 와르르 끓는다 The pot is boiling
4 〈몰려드는 모양〉 in crowds; with [in] a rush
◆ 사인을 받으려고 영화배우에게 와르르 몰려들다 crowd [swarm] around the movie star [asking] for autographs

와륵 瓦礫 〈기와 조각과 자갈〉 tiles and pebbles; debris; rubble (▶복수형 없음)

와병하다 臥病― be ill in bed; be laid up (with illness); (美) be sick in bed
▶ 그는 와병한지 1주일이다 He has been ill in bed for one week.

와삭 rustle-rustle; rustling(ly); with a rustle; with a rustling sound
▶ 낙엽이 와삭 굴러갔다 Fallen leaves rustled away.
―와삭하다[거리다] rustle; give a rustle
▶ 갈대가 바람에 와삭거렸다 The wind rustled the reeds.

와스스 with a rustling noise; rustling
◆ 와스스 무너지다 crumble down; fall with a swish
▶ 상자가 와스스 나갔다 The box went to pieces.
▶ 나뭇잎이 와스스 떨어졌다 The leaves fell off with a rustling sound.

와신상담 臥薪嘗膽 sustained endurance of hardship(s); determination and perseverance
▶ 그는 와신상담 4년 후에 사법 시험에 합격했다 After persevering for four years, he finally passed the bar examination.
―와신상담하다 go through hardships and privations; struggle against difficulties for the sake of vengeance

와우 蝸牛 〈달팽이〉 a snail
◆ 와우 각상(角上)의 싸움 petty strife
■ ―각(殼) the shell of a snail; 〔解〕 a cochlea (*pl.* ~s, -leae)

와이 〈영어 자모〉 Y
■ ―염색체〔生〕 a Y chromosome ―자형 Y shape: 와이자형 강(鋼) Y-beam steel ―축 the Y-axis

와이더블류시에이 Y.W.C.A. [《*Y*oung *W*omen's *C*hristian *A*ssociation》]

와이드스크린 a wide screen

와이드프로그램 a marathon (TV) program

와이셔츠 a shirt; a dress shirt
◆ 반소매 와이셔츠 a short-sleeved shirt / 와이셔츠 차림의 사무원 an office worker in *one's* shirtsleeves

와이어 wire; 〈기중기의〉 a crane cable
■ ―글라스 wire glass ―로프 a wire rope ―브러시 a wire brush

와이어리스 wireless ―마이크 a wireless microphone ―헤드폰 a wireless headphone

와이엠시에이 Y.M.C.A. [《*Y*oung *M*en's *C*hristian *A*ssociation》]

와이오밍 〈미국 북서부의 주〉 Wyoming (略 Wyo., Wy.)

와이트 〈영국의 섬〉 the Isle of Wight

와이퍼 a wiper; 〈자동차의〉 a windshield wiper; (英) a windscreen wiper ◆ 차의 와이퍼를 작동시키다 turn on the windshield wipers

와이프 a wife; *one's* wife

와인 wine ◆ 화이트[레드, 로즈] 와인 white [red, rose] wine ―글라스 a wineglass

와인드업 〔野〕 a windup ―와인드업하다 wind up

와일드 〈아일랜드의 시인·극작가·소설가〉 Wilde, Oscar (1854-1900)

와일드피치 〔野〕 a wild pitch

와전 瓦全 (living) a life of ease and inactivity; (living) a midiocre life
와전 訛傳 a false [misleading] report; distorted information; a canard
—**와전하다** misinform; give a false report
▶ 그 말은 와전된 것이었다 The report turned out false [incorrect].
와중 渦中 a vortex ◆와중에 휩쓸리다 be drawn into the maelstrom [vortex] of; be involved [entangled] in 《a dispute》
▶ 그는 그 사건의 와중에 말려들어갔다 He got [dragged] into [involved in] the incident.
와지끈 crashing; smash; crack
◆와지끈 뚝딱 with a crash [smash]; crashing; smashing / 와지끈 깨지다 break [be broken to pieces; be shattered [smashed] / 와지끈 부수다 smash [break] *sth* into fragment
와짝 〈힘껏〉 forcefully; (good and) hard; 〈갑자기〉 all of sudden; suddenly; briskly; rapidly; 〈많이〉 a great deal; in quantities
◆와짝 당기다 give 《it》 a vigorous [strong] pull
▶ 사람들이 와짝 현장에 몰려들었다 People rushed [thronged] to the spot.
와트 〔電〕 a watt; wattage ◆60와트의 전구 a 60 watt (light) bulb ■—계 a wattmeter —시 (時) 〔電〕 a watt-hour
와플 〈과자〉 a waffle
와해 瓦解 collapse; breakup; fall; downfall
◆정당의 와해 the collapse of a political party
—**와해하다** collapse; break up; fall down; be ruined
▶ 그 나라의 독재체제가 와해되었다 The dictatorship in that country collapsed [fell].
왁다그르르 rattlingly; with a rattle
—**왁다그르르하다** roll clattering
왁스 wax ◆가죽[마루]에 왁스를 칠하다 wax leather [a floor]
왁시글거리다 swarm with; cluster around; flock together; be crowded [thronged] (with)
왁자그르하다 be noisy; be boisterous [clamorous]; be uproarious
◆왁자그르하게 웃다 roar with laughter; burst into laughter
▶ 소녀들은 왁자그르하게 떠들어댔다 The girls gabbled and made a lot of noise.
왁자지껄하다 noisy ⇨ 왁자하다
왁자하다 〈떠들썩하다〉 noisy; loud; clamorous; uproarious; 〈소문나다〉 be much-talked of [about]; famous; sensational
◆왁자한 교실 an uproarious classroom
왁친 〔醫〕 vaccine = 백신
완강하다 頑強— stubborn; obstinate; dogged
◆완강한 우익주의자 a die-hard rightist / 완강히 stubbornly; doggedly; obstinately / 완강히 부인하다 deny persistently [obstinately] / 완강히 저항하다 resist stoutly [stubbornly]; put up (a) stubborn resistance
▶ 그는 그 보도를 완강히 부인했다 He obstinately denied the report.
완결 完結 completion; conclusion; termination; the end
◆완결편 the last [concluding] program [episode] of a series
—**완결하다** complete; conclude; finish; end
◆완결되다 be completed [concluded, finished]; come to a conclusion [to an end]/ 사건을 완결짓다 bring a matter to a conclusion
◆완결됨 Concluded.
▶ 다음회에 완결됩니다 To be concluded next time.
완고하다 頑固— obstinate; stubborn; headstrong; bigoted; 〈끈질기다〉 persistent; dogged; mulish
◆완고한 노인 an obstinate [a stiff-necked] old man / 완고하게 obstinately; stubbornly; persistently
▶ 그는 언제나 완고하게 자기 의견을 고집한다 He always persists in his opinion.
완곡 婉曲 —완곡하다 roundabout; indirect; euphemistic; circumlocutional
◆완곡한 표현 a periphrastic [roundabout] expression; a euphemism / 완곡하게 말하다 speak in a roundabout way; euphemize
▶ 그녀는 나의 제안을 완곡하게 거절했다 She refused my offer in a roundabout way.
■—**법** 〔修〕 euphemism; periphrasis
완골 腕骨 〔解〕 wrist bones; the carpus
완공 完工 completion ⇨ 준공 (竣工)
완구 玩具 a toy; a plaything ■—**상** 〈사람〉 a toy dealer; 〈가게〉 a toy shop —**함** a toy box
완급 緩急 fast and slow motion; high and low speed
◆문제를 완급에 따라 잘 처리하다 be discrete in dealing with the matter / 어떤 비상 사태에도 완급에 따라 응할 대책을 갖추다 make every arrangement to meet any emergency
■—**기호** 〔樂〕 musical notes showing tempo
완납 完納 full payment; 〈물건의〉 full delivery
—**완납하다** pay in full; pay the whole amount of; complete the delivery of
◆세금을 완납하다 pay (up) all *one's* taxes; pay *one's* taxes in full
완두 豌豆 〔植〕 a pea ◆완두 껍질을 까다 shell peas
완력 腕力 physical [muscular] strength; 〈폭력〉 (brutal) force; violence
◆완력이 세다 have strong arms; have great physical strength; be strong-muscled
◆완력을 쓰지 마라 Don't use force [violence].
▶ 그는 완력에서는 아무에게도 진적이 없다 He never met his match in physical strength.
완료 完了 finishing; completion; conclusion
—**완료하다** finish; complete; conclude
◆완료되다 be completed [concluded, finished]; be over
◆준비는 완료되었습니다 Our preparations are complete [all set]. ⇌ We're quite ready now.
■**현재[과거]—** 〔文法〕 the present [past] perfect ■—**시제** 〔文法〕 the perfect tense
완만하다 緩慢— 〈속도가〉 slow(-moving); slow(-going); sluggish; inactive; slack; dull; 〈경사가〉 gentle
◆완만한 흐름 a slow stream / 완만하게 slowly; gently / 동작이 완만하다 be slow in action; be slow-moving
▶ 차는 완만한 언덕을 천천히 올라갔다 The car went up the gentle slope slowly.

완목 腕木 〈받침대〉 a bracket; 〈전주 등의〉 a crosspiece

완미하다 玩味 ― 〈맛보다〉 taste; relish; savor; 〈진가를〉 appreciate ◆숙독 완미하다 read with appreciation

완미하다 頑迷 ― 〈완강하여 사리에 어둡다〉 bigoted; wrong-headed; pig-headed; bull-headed; (stupidly) obstinate; stubborn; obdurate

◆완미한 노인 an old fogy
▶그는 완미하게도 진찰받기를 거절했다 He refused to see a doctor out of sheer stubbornness.

완벽 完璧 perfection; completeness
◆완벽을 기하다 aim for perfection
―**완벽하다** perfect; flawless; faultless; impeccable
▶그녀의 알리바이는 완벽하다 Her alibi is perfect [flawless].
▶그녀의 연주는 거의 완벽했다 Her performance was virtually flawless.
▶그는 불어를 완벽하게 구사한다 He has a perfect command of French. ⇒ His French is perfect.

완본 完本 a complete book [volume]; an unabridged edition ◆셰익스피어의 완본 a complete [full] set of Shakespeare's works

완봉 完封 〔野〕 a shutout; (口) a whitewash
―**완봉하다** 〔野〕 shut out; pitch a shutout; whitewash

완비 完備 perfection; completion; full equipment ―**완비하다** perfect; complete; furnish [provide, equip] completely
◆가구가 완비된 방 a fully-furnished room / 완비되어 있다 be supplied well; 〈설비가〉 be fully equipped
▶이 학교는 급식 설비가 완비되어 있다 This school is completely equipped with catering facilities.
▶주차장이 완비되어 있다 A parking lot is available.

완상 玩賞 appreciation; enjoyment
―**완상하다** appreciate; enjoy; cherish
◆골동품을 완상하다 take delight in viewing antiques

완성 完成 completion; accomplishment
▶그 작품의 완성에 3년 걸렸다 The work took three years to complete.
―**완성하다** finish; complete; accomplish; achieve; bring to completion [perfection]
◆완성되다 be finished; be completed; be perfected [accomplished]; come [be brought] to perfection / 일을 완성하다 bring one's work to completion
▶새 교사가 완성되었다 The new school building has been completed.
▶도로는 6월에 완성될 예정이다 The road will [is to] be completed in June.
▶내주까지 완성해 주시오 I want to have it ready [finished] by next week.
■자기― perfection of self ■―품 a finished product

완수 完遂 accomplishment; completion
―**완수하다** accomplish; complete; carry through [out]
◆대사업을 완수하다 accomplish [complete] a great undertaking [work] / 목적을 완수하다 attain one's object; accomplish one's aim / 책임을 완수하다 fulfill one's responsibility

완숙 完熟 full ripeness [maturity] ―**완숙하다** fully ripe [ripened]; in full maturity
◆완숙한 토마토 a fully-ripened tomato
■―계란 a hard-boiled egg

완승 完勝 a complete [total] victory; a sweeping triumph
▶우리는 상대팀에 완승을 거두었다 We won a sweeping victory over the opposing team.
―**완승하다** win [score] a complete victory ⟨over⟩

완역 完譯 a complete translation
―**완역하다** make a complete translation; translate in full [the whole text]

완연하다 宛然― obvious; evident; clear; unmistakable ▶봄이 완연하다 Spring has already come.

완월하다 玩月― enjoy (viewing) the moonlight; admire the moon

완자 a fried meatball [dumpling]

완장 腕章 an armband; an arm strap; a brassard ◆완장을 두르다 put on an armband

완전 完全 perfection; completeness
◆완전에 가깝다 be nearly perfect
―**완전하다** perfect; complete; whole; entire
◆완전한 성공[실패] a complete success [failure] / 완전무결한 자유 absolute [perfect] liberty / 완전무결한 perfect and faultless; absolutely perfect / 완전하게 perfectly / 완전하게 하다 perfect; make sth perfect; bring sth to perfection
▶실험은 완전한 실패였다 The experience was a complete failure.
▶네 답안은 몇 개의 철자 잘못 이외에는 완전하다 Your examination paper is perfect except for a few spelling mistakes.
■―가동[조업] full operation ―고용 full [perfect] employment ―범죄 a perfect crime ―시합 a perfect game ―연소 complete [perfect] combustion ―주의 perfectionism

완전히 完全― perfectly; to perfection; completely; entirely; wholly; thoroughly; 〈전적으로〉 quite; all
◆완전히 달라지다 change completely / 완전히 잊어버리다 forget all about 《it》
▶그는 완전히 잊혀졌다 He was entirely [completely] forgotten.
▶나는 그를 완전히 믿는 것이 아니다 I don't fully trust him.
▶완전히 준비가 끝나 있었다 All the preparations had been made. ⇒ Everything was ready.

완제 完濟 full payment; liquidation ◆대부금의 완제 paying off [repayment of] a loan

완주하다 完走― run the whole distance; stay the course; complete [finish] the course [race]

완충 緩衝 shock-absorbing; buffing
―**완충하다** absorb shock; buff; buffer
■―국 a buffer state ―기(器) 〈철도 차량의〉 a

완치 完治 a complete cure
▶ 그는 완치 1주일을 요하는 상처를 입었다 He suffered an injury that would take [require] one week to heal completely.
—**완치하다** cure [heal] ⟪a person, a disease⟫ completely ◆ 완치되다 be completely cured; heal completely

완쾌 完快 complete recovery ⟪from *one's* illness, of *one's* health⟫
—**완쾌하다** recover completely ⟪from *one's* illness⟫; be completely restored to health
▶ 당신은 완쾌하는 데 1주일의 자택 요양이 필요합니다 You need a week's convalescence at home for complete recovery [to recover completely].
▶ 귀하께서 조속히 완쾌되시기를 빕니다 I hope you will get well soon. ⇒ I hope you will be soon restored to health.

완투 完投 —**완투하다** pitch the whole game; pitch the full nine innings; go the whole distance ■—투수 a thoroughgoing pitcher; a pitcher who goes the (entire) route

완패 完敗 a complete [crushing] defeat
—**완패하다** suffer a complete defeat; be completely [decisively] defeated [beaten]; (口) be beaten hollow

완하제 緩下劑 a (mild) laxative; an aperient
완행 緩行 going [running] slow —**완행하다** go slow ■—열차 a slow [local] train
완화 緩和 easing; relief; relaxation; mitigation; alleviation
◆ 국가간의 긴장 완화 détente; the easing of strained relations between nations
—**완화하다** ease; soften; relieve; mitigate; alleviate; relax
◆ 고통을 완화하다 mitigate [alleviate] pain / 교통난을 완화하다 relieve traffic congestion; ease a traffic jam / 규제를 완화하다 relax [ease] restrictions (on)
▶ 그의 부드러운 미소가 그녀의 긴장을 완화시켜 주었다 His gentle smile relieved [relaxed] her tension.
▶ 외국무역의 규제가 완화되었다 Restrictions on foreign trade have been eased [relaxed].
▶ 그것은 긴장된 상황을 완화시키는 힘이 있다 It has a moderating influence on the strained situation.
■—정책 an appeasement policy —제 〔醫〕 a lenitive; a mitigative; a demulcent —책 neutralizing [alleviating] measure

왈 曰 ⟨가로되⟩ say; ⟨소위⟩ so-called
◆ 공자 왈 Confucius [The Master] says.../ 왈 신세대 a so-called new generation

왈가닥 a spirited [spunky] woman; a pert [impudent] young girl; (口) a minx
▶ 저 여자는 왈가닥이야 She is a tomboy. ⇒ She is an aggressive woman.

왈가닥거리다 rattle; clatter; lutter; jerk
◆ 왈가닥거리는 짐차 a truck jerking along noisily / 왈가닥거리며 with a rattling sound

왈가왈부 曰可曰否 arguments for and against; the pros and cons
—**왈가왈부하다** argue for and against *sth*; discuss; the pros and cons of *sth*
▶ 우리는 이 행사에 참가여부를 놓고 왈가왈부 했다 We discussed whether or not we ought to take part in this event.
▶ 회의는 논쟁만 왈가왈부할 뿐 결론이 나지 않았다 The meeting was a seesaw battle of arguments for and against with no conclusion being reached.

왈왈하다 quick-tempered; hot-tempered; impatient; impetuous

왈츠 a waltz ◆ 왈츠를 추다 dance a waltz; waltz ■ 비엔나— a Vienna [Viennese] waltz

왈칵 suddenly (with force); all of a sudden; in a rush
◆ 왈칵 게우다 throw up [vomit] suddenly / 왈칵 뒤집히다 be overturned [upset] all of a sudden / 왈칵 성을 내다 burst into a furious rage / 왈칵 피를 토하다 vomit [spit] blood; cough up blood
▶ 그 소녀는 왈칵 울음을 터뜨렸다 The girl burst into tears [burst out crying].
▶ 참았던 말이 그녀의 입에서 왈칵 쏟아져 나왔다 The suppressed words gushed [poured] from her lips.

왈칵하다 quick-tempered; hot-tempered; impatient; rash; restless

왈패 曰牌 a rowdy fellow; a tomboy

왔다갔다하다 come and go; walk up and down; go [walk] back and forth
▶ 그녀는 진열장을 곁눈질하면서 왔다갔다 했다 She went back and forth looking sideways at the shopwindow.
▶ 그들은 서로 왔다갔다 하는 사이다 They are on visiting terms with each other.

왕 ⟨말·소를 멈출 때⟩ Whoa!; Wo!; Ho!
왕 王 ⟨임금⟩ a king; ⟨군주⟩ a monarch; ⟨지배자⟩ a ruler
◆ 영국왕 조지 6세 George VI, King of Great Britain / 왕중왕 the King of Kings / 석유[자동차] 왕 an oil [automobile] magnate / 왕의 [다운] kingly; royal / 왕을 옹립하다 enthrone a king / 왕을 폐하다 dethrone [depose] a king
▶ 사자는 백수의 왕이다 The lion is (the) king of beasts.

왕- 王- big; large; king-size(d) ◆ 왕개미 a carpenter ant / 왕거미 a garden spider

왕가 王家 a royal family [house] ▶ 그는 왕가 출신이다 He's from a royal family [house].
왕게 王— 〔動〕 a king crab
왕겨 王— chaff; rice husks [hulls]
왕고모 王姑母 a grandaunt; a grandfather's sister
왕골 〔植〕 a sedge ◆ 왕골 자리 a sedge mat
왕관 王冠 a (royal) crown; a diadem
◆ 왕관을 쓰다 put on [wear] a crown; ⟨왕위에⟩ 오르다 be crowned king
왕국 王國 a kingdom; ⟨군주국⟩ a monarchy
왕궁 王宮 a king's [royal] palace; a palace
왕권 王權 royal authority [power(s)]; sovereignty ◆ 왕권을 쥐다 hold regal sway

왕기

■—신수설 (the theory of) the divine right of kings

왕기 王旗 a royal standard; (英) the King's Color

왕녀 王女 a royal princess; a princess of the blood (royal)

왕년 往年 the years gone by; bygone years
♦왕년에 in the past [former times]
▶그는 왕년의 명투수다 He was a famous pitcher in the days gone by.
▶그에게서는 왕년의 모습을 찾아볼 수 없다 He is a mere shadow of the former self.

왕눈이 王— a person with big eyes; a large-eyed [goggle-eyed] person

왕당 王黨 the Royalists; monarchists
♦왕당파 the royalist faction

왕대비 王大妃 the Queen Dowager; the Queen Mother

왕도 王都 the (royal) capital; the seat of the royal government

왕도 王道 the rule of right [virtue]; righteous government
▶학문에는 왕도가 없다 (속담) There is no royal road to learning.

왕래 往來 1〈통행〉traffic; come-and-go; comings and goings
♦사람의 왕래 pedestrian traffic / 왕래가 잦은 길 a busy street [road]; a crowded [bustling] road / 왕래를 금지하다 block [close] traffic; be closed to traffic
▶도로에는 사람의 왕래가 끊어졌다 The streets were deserted.
▶왕래가 많다[적다] Traffic is heavy [light].
▶요즈음 차의 왕래가 늘어났다 Recently traffic has increased.
▶이 길은 왕래가 거의 없다 There is little traffic on this road.
—왕래하다 come and go
♦왕래하는 사람 a passerby (*pl.* passersby)
2〈서신의〉correspondence; communication
▶그와는 5년간이나 서신 왕래가 있었습니다 I have been corresponding [exchanging letters] with him for five years.
▶두 사람 사이에 편지 왕래는 없었다 No letters have passed between them.
—왕래하다 visit each other; communicate; exchange 《letters with》

왕릉 王陵 a royal tomb

왕림 枉臨 your coming [visit, presence, attendance]
▶왕림하여 주시기 바랍니다 Kindly favor [honor] us with your company. ⇌ Your presence will be highly appreciated.

왕립 王立 ♦왕립 공원[도서관] a royal park [library] / 왕립의 royal
■—미술관 (英) the Royal Academy of Arts

왕명 王命 an order of the king; a royal order
♦왕명에 의하여 by order of the king; in obedience to the king's order [command]

왕모래 王— coarse sand

왕밤 王— a large chestnut

왕방 往訪 a visit
—왕방하다 visit; pay a visit (to); come [go] to see; go and see

왕방울 王— a large bell ♦눈이 왕방울 같다 have big eyes; be big-eyed [goggle-eyed]
■—눈 a big eye; an ox eye

왕벌 王— a wasp ⇨ 말벌, 호박벌

왕복 往復 coming and going; going and returning; two ways; a round trip
♦왕복 버스 요금 a bus fare both ways [for a round trip]
▶거기까지 왕복 20마일이다 It's twenty miles there and back.
▶나는 왕복 길을 꼬박 서 다녔다 I had to stand both ways.
—왕복하나 go and return [come back]; go to and from; make a round trip; 〈다니다〉run; 〈배가〉ply 《between》
♦비행기로 왕복하다 go and back by plane
▶배가 강을 하루 5회 왕복한다 A boat goes up and down the river five times a day.
▶나는 주 1회 서울-부산 간을 왕복한다 I go back and forth [make a round trip] between Seoul and Pusan once a week.
▶이 버스는 공항과 호텔 사이를 (정기적으로) 왕복한다 This bus shuttles between the airport and the hotel.
▶런던까지 왕복하는데 몇 시간 걸립니까? How long will it take to and from London?
■—비행 a double-trip flight —승차권[차표] a round-trip ticket; (英) a return ticket (▶(美)에서는〈귀로의 차표〉)—여행 a double journey; (美) a round trip —엽서 a double postcard (with a replycard attached) —운동〔機〕reciprocation; an alternating motion —운임〔요금〕round-trip fare —운행 shuttle service

왕비 王妃 a queen; a queen consort ♦왕비의 queenly

왕생 往生 〔佛敎〕—왕생하다 go to Nirvana after death; go to heaven; die an easy and peaceful death
■—극락 ⇨ 극락(~왕생)

왕성 王城 〈성〉a royal castle; 〈왕도〉the royal capital

왕성하다 旺盛— flourishing; prosperous; thriving; active; excellent
♦왕성한 식욕 a strong [keen, sharp] appetite / 혈기 왕성한 젊은이 a hot-blooded young man / 혈기 왕성한 때에 in the prime of *one's* youth / 기운이 왕성하다 be in high [fine] spirits; be full of energy [vigor]; be energetic / 식욕이 왕성하다 have a good [an excellent] appetite
▶그는 지식욕이 왕성하다 He is very eager for knowledge. ⇌ He has a great thirst for knowledge.
▶그 팀의 사기는 매우 왕성하다 The morale of the team is very high [excellent].
▶그는 70세지만 기력이 왕성하다 He is 70 years old and still very active [energetic, vigorous].

왕세손 王世孫 the eldest son of the Crown Prince

왕세자 王世子 the Crown Prince; the Heir Apparent to the Throne
♦왕세자로 책봉되다 be proclaimed [designated] Crown Prince

■—비 the Crown Princess; the consort of the Crown Prince

왕손 王孫 a grandson of a king; a royal grandchild [descendant] ◆왕손이다 be of royal blood

왕수 王水 〔化〕 aqua regia

왕시 往時 ◆왕시에 in past days; in the past; formerly

왕신 〈사람〉 a choosy [picky, cantankerous] person; a person hard to get along with; a crank

왕신 往信 a letter sent; a message sent out to get a reply

왕실 王室 the royal family [house]; the royal household ◆왕실용품 공급상 a purveyor to the royal household

왕업 王業 royal rule [reign, sway]

왕오색나비 〔昆〕 a giant purple butterfly

왕왕 往往 〈이따금〉 now and then; once in a while; occasionally; at times; from time to time; 〈종종〉 often; frequently
▶ 그것은 왕왕 있는 일이다 It is a matter of no uncommon occurrence.
▶ 과도한 음주는 왕왕 간장 장애를 일으킨다 Excessive drinking tends to cause liver trouble.
▶ 왕왕 노력의 대가를 보상받지 못할 때도 있다 Our efforts are not always rewarded.

왕위 王位 the throne
◆왕위를 다투다[빼앗다] contend for [usurp] the throne / 왕위를 잃다 forfeit *one's* crown / 왕위를 잇다 succeed to the throne [crown] / 왕위에 오르다 come to [accede to] the throne / 왕위에 있다 be on the throne / 왕위에서 물러나다 step down from the throne
▶ 그 왕자는 10살때 왕위에 올랐다 The prince came to the throne [was crowned] at the age of ten.
■—계승 succession to the throne: 스페인의 왕위계승전쟁 the War of the Spanish Succession

왕자 王子 a Royal prince ◆에드워드 왕자 Prince Edward

왕자 王者 〈임금〉a king; a monarch; 〈통치자〉 a ruler; a sovereign; 〈제1인자〉 a champion
◆마라톤의 왕자 the marathon champion / 왕자의 권력 royal power / 왕자의 royal; kingly; regal

왕잠자리 〔昆〕 a large dragonfly

왕정 王政 〈정치〉royal rule [regime]; 〈정체〉 monarchy
■—복고 the restoration of royal rule; 〈영국왕 찰스 2세의〉 the Restoration

왕조 王朝 a dynasty ◆왕조의 dynastic

왕족 王族 the royal family; royalty; 〈개인〉 a (member of) royalty ▶ 그는 왕족 출신이다 He is of royal blood.

왕좌 王座 the throne; supremacy
◆테니스계의 왕좌를 다투는 열전 a heated match contesting supremacy in the tennis world / 왕좌에 오르다 come to [ascend] the throne; 〈제1인자가 되다〉 come to the top; win the championship
■—결정전 a championship contest [match]

왕지 王旨 a royal order [instruction] ◆왕지를 받들어 in obedience to the royal order

왕진 往診 a doctor's visit to a patient; a call on a patient; a house [home] call from a doctor
◆왕진 요청에 응하다 take a call
▶ 나는 의사의 왕진을 받았다 I had a (house [home]) call from the doctor. ⇌ I got the doctor to visit me.
—왕진하다 go and see [visit] a patient at his house [home]
▶ 저 의사는 오후에 왕진한다 That doctor makes a house call in the afternoon.
■ 야간— a night call **■—료** a doctor's fee for a visit **—시간** hours for visiting patients

왕청되다, 왕청스럽다 〈차이가 엄청나다〉 quite [widely, entirely] different 《from》; poles apart 《in》; 〈서술적〉 differ entirely [completely] 《from》

왕토 王土 the royal domain [territory]

왕통 王統 the royal lineage [legitimacy]

왕화 王化 the civilizing influence of the king; a king's rule of virtue

왕후 王后 〈왕비〉 a queen; a queen consort

왕후 王侯 〈제왕과 제후〉 the king and peers; crowned heads; royalty
◆왕후귀족 royalty and titled nobility / 왕후같은 생활을 하다 live like a prince [lord, king]

왜 1 〈이유〉why; for what reason; what…for; 〈근거〉 on what ground
▶ 왜 그럴까? What can be the reason?
▶ 왜 지각했는지 말해봐라 Tell me why you are late.
▶ 왜 그녀를 의심합니까? On what grounds do you suspect her?
▶ 왜 미국에 갑니까? What are you going to America for? ⇌ For what purpose are you going to America?
▶ 왜 여기 왔니? What brought you here?
▶ 왜 울었니[화를 냈니]? What made you cry [angry]?
2 〈감탄사로〉 Why?; What?
▶ 〔會話〕「이리와」"Come here." "Why?"
▶ 〔會話〕「왜, 그러니?」 "What's up?" ⇌ "What's the matter?"
▶ 〔會話〕「그가 내게 몹시 화를 내고 있어」「왜?」「모르지」 "He's very angry with me." "How come?" "I don't know."

왜 倭 Japan; 〈접두어적〉 Japanese

왜가리 〔鳥〕 a (gray) heron

왜간장 倭—醬 Japanese soysauce

왜곡 歪曲 distortion
—왜곡하다 distort; twist; contort; warp
◆왜곡된 견해 a distorted view / 뜻을 왜곡하다 distort [warp] the meaning / 사실을 왜곡하다 distort [twist, disrepresent] a fact
▶ 사실이 왜곡되어 보도되었다 The facts were falsely represented in the news. ⇌ The news report distorted [twisted] the facts.

왜건 a wagon

왜골 a rude giant; a big [large] rough; a clumsy [ill-mannered] person

왜구 倭寇 〔史〕Japanese pirates

왜그르르 ▶ 벽이 왜그르르 무너졌다 The wall

왜냐하면

fell in with a crash. —왜그르르하다 crumbly
♦ 밥이 왜그르르하다 rice is too flaky; rice is not sticky enough
왜냐하면 because; 〈문두에서〉 since; as; for; the reason is that
▶ 고래는 포유동물이다. 왜냐하면 고래는 태생이기 때문이다 The whale is a mammal because it is viviparous.
▶ 나는 오늘 버스로 출근했다. 왜냐하면 철도업이 있었기 때문이다 I went to the office by bus today, because there was a railroad strike. ⇌ Since [As] there was a railroad strike, I went to the office by bus.
▶ [회화]「왜 나는 가면 안됩니까?」「왜냐하면 너무 어리니까」"Why can't I go?" "Because you're still too young."
왜뚜리 〈큰 물건〉 a large [bulky] thing
왜뚤삐뚤 zigzag ⇨ 왜틀비틀
♦ 글을 왜뚤삐뚤 쓰다 scrawl; squiggle; write crooked letters; write a clumsy hand
왜림 矮林 a thicket [bush, grove] of shrubs
왜말 倭— Japanese; the Japanese language; 〈단어〉 a Japanese word
왜바람 a changeable [fitful, choppy] wind
왜색 倭色 Japanese ways [manners]; Japanese style [fashion]; things Japanese
♦ 왜색을 일소하다 make a clean sweep of Japanese manners; clear away [drive away, stamp out] the Japanese ways
왜성 矮星 〔天〕 a dwarf star
왜소 矮小 dwarfishness
—왜소하다 dwarfish; diminutive; undersized
♦ 왜소한 나무[짐승] a dwarf tree [animal]
왜옥 矮屋 a small flat house
왜인 倭人 a Japanese; (口) a Jap
왜인 矮人 〈난쟁이〉 a dwarf; a midget; a pygmy
왜자기다 〈떠들다〉 make (a) noise; be noisy
왜자하다 widespread; rife
▶ 소문이 왜자하게 퍼졌다 The rumor spread like wildfire [quickly].
왜정 倭政 the Japanese rule
—시대 the period of the Japanese rule in Korea (1910-45)
왜죽왜죽 with rapid strides ♦ 왜죽왜죽 걷다 walk with rapid strides
왜퉁스럽다 queer and silly; odd; rash and insensible
왜틀비틀 zigzag; in zigzag; falteringly
♦ 왜틀비틀 걷다 walk zigzag [in zigzags]; stagger [reel] along
▶ 그 노인은 왜틀비틀 걸어갔다 The old man walked along with tottering [unsteady, faltering] steps.
왜풍 倭風 Japanese customs [manners]; Japanese style [fashion]
왝왝 keck keck!; puke puke! ♦ 왝왝 게우다 throw up; (口) upchuck; (口) puke; (美俗) barf
—왝왝하다 keck; retch
왱 with a hum [buzz]
▶ 벌이 왱 날아갔다 A bee buzzed away.
▶ 소방차가 사이렌을 왱 울리면서 달려갔다 Fire engines sped away with sirens wailing.
—왱하다 hum; buzz; whiz(z)

왱그랑댕그랑 tinkle-tinkle; ting-a-ling; with a jangle [jingle]
▶ 풍경이 처마밑에서 왱그랑댕그랑 울리고 있다 The wind chime is tinkling under the eaves.
—왱그랑댕그랑하다 tinkle; clink; jingle-jangle
왱왱 1 〈날벌레가〉 buzz-buzz; humming; 〈돌팔매가〉 with a twang; 〈센바람이〉 whistling
▶ 모터가 왱왱 돌고 있다 The motor is purring.
—왱왱하다 hum; buzz; whiz(z); whine
▶ 모기가 귓전에서 왱왱거렸다 The mosquitoes buzzed around my ears.
▶ 바람이 전선에서 왱왱거리고 있다 The wind is whining in the electric wires.
2 〈아이들이 책읽는 소리〉 aloud; noisily
▶ 아이들이 책을 왱왱 읽고 있다 Children are reading books at the top of voices.
외 a cucumber ⇨ 오이
외— single; sole; only
♦ 외아들 an only son (▶ the only son은 「그 외아들」의 뜻, 뒤에 한정 어구가 따를 때에 한해서 사용됨) / 외딸 an only daughter / 외톨이 an only child
▶ 톰은 그의 외아들이다 Tom is the only son (that) he has.
외 外 1 〈밖〉 outside; outer; foreign
♦ 시외 outside the city
2 〈이외〉 except; with the exception of; outside of...; 〈...이상은〉 beyond; 〈게다가〉 besides; in addition to 〈this〉; apart [(文) aside] from
♦ 학생 외의 사람들 people other than students / 브라운씨 외에 세 명 Mr. Brown and three other; three (people) besides Mr. Brown / 권한 외의 행위를 하다 do an act in excess of one's authority
▶ 그 외에 아무도 그 질문에 대답하지 못했다 Nobody except [but] him was able to answer the question.
▶ 정규 회원 외에 한 사람 더 데려와 주십시오 Please bring one more person in addition to our regular member.
▶ 나는 낚시질 외에는 취미가 없다 I have no hobby except fishing.
▶ 주말에는 조깅 외에 보통 무엇을 합니까? What do you usually do on weekends besides go jogging? (▶do가 앞에 올 때는 besides 다음에는 to 없는 부정사가 따름)
▶ 나는 이것 외에는 아무것도 모른다 I know nothing beyond [more than] this.
외 根 〔建〕〈흙을 바르기 위해 벽에 엮는 가는 나뭇가지〉 laths; wattles
외가 外家 one's mother's old home; the mother's (side of the) family
♦ 외가의 on the mother's [maternal, distaff] side; maternal / 외가 쪽 친척 a relative on one's mother's side
▶ 어머니는 외가에 가 계십니다 My mother has been staying with her parents' home.
외가닥 a (single) strand [ply]
외각 外角 〔數〕 an exterior angle; 〔野〕 the outcorner; the outside
♦ 외각구 an outside ball / 외각 낮은 공 a ball low (and) on the outside
외각 外殼 a shell; a crust

외간 外艱 〈아버지의 상사〉 mourning for a father ♦외간을 당하다 meet with the death of *one's* father / 외간을 입다 go into [take to] mourning for a father

외갈래 a single fork
■—길 road with a single fork; a road without a branch; a straight road

외감 外感 1 [韓醫] 〈고뿔〉 a cold **2** [心] 〈외부 감각〉 sense; (external) sensation; feeling

외객 外客 〈딴 곳에서 온 사람〉 a guest; a visitor; 〈외국 손님〉 a foreign visitor [tourist]

외견 外見 external appearance ⇨ 외관

외겹 〈단 한겹〉 one [a single] layer 《of cloth》; one ply
♦외겹의 single; one-ply; onefold

외경 外徑 an external diameter ⇨ 바깥지름

외경 畏敬 awe

외계 外界 the external [outside] world; the outside; 〈지구 밖〉 the outer space
♦외계의 사물 outward things / 외계와 차단되다 be secluded [shut off] from the outer world / 외계와의 접촉을 피하다 avoid contact with the outside world
▶그 교도소는 외계로부터 완전히 차단되어 있었다 The prison was completely shut off from the outside world.

외고집—固執 (single-minded) stubbornness; obstinacy; perversity
♦외고집의 obstinate; stubborn; headstrong; perverse / 외고집을 부리다 get stiff-necked
▶그는 말리면 더 외고집이 된다 If you try to dissuade him, he will become only the more obdurate.
■—쟁이 a pigheaded person : 외고집쟁이 영감 a stiff-necked [an obstinate] old man / 저런 외고집쟁이는 만나보기 드물다 Such a pigheaded person is rarely met with.

외골목 a single alley

외곬 a single way [track]
♦외곬으로 생각하는 사람 a person with a single-[one-]track mind / 외곬으로 with a single-[one-]track mind; single-mindedly; with only one purpose (in mind) / 외곬으로 생각하다 see things from only one point of view
▶그는 오직 외곬으로만 연인을 생각하고 있다 He thinks only of his girlfriend. ⇌ He has a single-minded[-hearted] affection for his love.
▶그녀는 발레만을 위해 외곬으로 살아왔다 She has devoted herself entirely to the ballet.

외과 外科 surgery; 〈병원의〉 the department of surgery; the surgical department
■임상[성형]— clinical [plastic] surgery ■—과장 a chief surgeon ■—병동 a surgical ward 《of a hospital》 ■—수술 a surgical operation : 외과 수술을 받다 be operated on 《by》; undergo a surgical operation ■—수술실 an operating room (略 OR) ■—의사 a surgeon ■—적 치료 surgical treatment

외과피 外果皮 〔植〕 the epicarp; the exocarp

외곽 外廓 〈바깥 성〉 the outer wall; the outwall; 〈테두리〉 the outer block; the contour
■—단체 〈보조기관〉 an auxiliary organ; 〈정부기관 외의 단체〉 an extra-governmental [departmental] organization [body]

외관 外觀 external [outside] appearance; an outward show [aspect]; an exterior view (▶특히 「바깥 쪽」를 강조하고 싶을 때는 external [outward, outer] appearance로 함)
♦외관상(으로) externally; apparently; in appearace; to all appearance / 외관을 꾸미다 make outward show; put on a show
▶사람을 외관으로 판단해서는 안된다 You shouldn't judge a person by his appearance [looks].
▶외관은 훌륭하지만 내부는 대차지 않다 The interior is not so fine as its outer appearance would suggest.

외교 外交 1 〈외국과의 교섭〉 diplomacy; 〈정책〉 a foreign [diplomatic] policy; 〈국교〉 diplomatic intercourse
♦한국의 대미외교 Korea's policy toward America [the United States]; Korea's American policy / 외교상의 비밀 a diplomatic secret / 외교상(으로) diplomatically
▶군인이 정치나 외교에 간섭하는 것은 바람직하지 않다 It is not desirable for military men to interfere in politics or diplomatic relations.
2 〈섭외〉 outside duty [service]; canvassing; soliciting
▶그녀는 그 문제에 외교 수단을 이용했다 She used diplomacy [showed diplomatic skill] in dealing with the issue.
▶그는 외교술이 뛰어나서 누구와도 잘 지낼거야 He is so diplomatic [tactful, sociable] that he can get along with anybody. (▶diplomatic은 「사람을 능숙하게 다루는」, tactful은 「재치있는」, sociable은 「사교적인」의 뜻)
■강경[약체]— a strong [weak, weak-kneed] foreign policy **경제—** economic diplomacy (toward) **공개[비밀]—** open [secret] diplomacy **굴욕—** humiliating diplomacy **다각—** multilateral diplomacy **달러[무력]—** dollar [armed] diplomacy **초당파—** a supraparty [bipartizan] diplomacy ■—가 a diplomat; a diplomatist; a diplomatic person **—경로** diplomatic channels : 그들은 그 분쟁을 외교 경로를 통해서 해결했다 They settled the dispute through diplomatic channels. **—계** diplomatic circles **—교섭[협상]** diplomatic negotiations **—기관** diplomatic channels [machinery] **—단절** diplomatic cessation **—문서** diplomatic documents (▶단수 취급) **—문제** a diplomatic question [issue, problem, affair] : 그는 외교문제의 전문가다 He is an expert in foreign affairs [diplomatic problems]. **—백서[청서]** the White Paper [Blue Book] (published by the Foreign Office) **—사령**(辭令) diplomatic language **—사절단** a diplomatic mission : 주한 외교사절단 the Diplomatic Corps in Korea **—소식통** diplomatic sources **—수완** diplomacy; diplomatic talent [skill]; **(美)** 〈세일즈맨 등의〉 salesmanship : 외교수완을 발휘하다 give full play to *one's* diplomatic skill **—특권** diplomatic privileges (and immunities)

외교관 外交官 a diplomatic official; a diplo-

외교관계

matist; a diplomat; (총칭) the diplomatic service
♦ 외교관이 되다 enter the diplomatic service / 외교관이다 be in the diplomatic service; be a diplomat
▶ 그는 외교관이 되고 싶어한다 He wants to become a diplomat.
■직업— a career diplomat ■—면책 특권 diplomatic immunity —시험 the Diplomatic Service Examination

외교관계 外交關係 diplomatic [foreign] relations
♦ 외교관계가 있다 have a diplomatic relations (with) / 외교관계를 단절하다 sever [cut off, break off] diplomatic relations (with) / 외교관계를 수립하다 establish diplomatic relations (with) / 외교관계를 재개하다 reestablish diplomatic relations (with)
▶ 그들은 적국과의 외교관계를 단절했다 They broke off diplomatic relations with the enemy.

외교원 外交員 a canvasser ⇨ 외무원

외구 外寇 a foreign enemy ⇨ 외적

외구 畏懼 fear; dread; awe ♦ 외구심을 갖다 feel fear (of)
—외구하다 fear; dread; be struck with awe; stand in awe (of)

외국 外國 a foreign country [nation] (▶ nation이 더 격식을 차린 느낌)
♦ 외국의 foreign; alien (▶ foreign이 일반적임. alien은 보통 시민권이 없는 외국인에 대해 쓰며 배타적인 느낌이 있으므로 일반적으로 사용을 피함); 〈해외의〉 overseas / 외국으로 abroad; overseas (▶ 거의 같은 뜻이지만 overseas의 용도가 더 넓음) / 외국에서 온 유학생 a foreign student (▶ 다음의 표현이 정중함); an overseas student; a student from overseas (▶ a student overseas는 외국에서 공부하는 유학생) / 외국산의 foreign produced (fruit); of foreign production [growth, origin] / 외국제의 (cars) of foreign manufacture [make]; foreign-made / 외국 태생의 foreign-born / 외국으로 보낼 foreign-going; outbound; outgoing (mails) / 외국땅을 밟다 step [set foot] on foreign soil / 외국의 영향을 받지 않다 be untouched by alien influences / 외국의 침략을 받다 be invaded by a foreign country / 외국에서 돌아오다 return [come back] from abroad [overseas, a foreign country] / 외국으로 가다 go abroad [overseas]; go to foreign country

解說 go abroad와 go overseas는 같은 뜻이지만 우리나라처럼 반도국에서 해외로 가는 경우는 후자를 쓰는 것이 좋다. (美)에서는 go to England, go to America 처럼 행선지를 구체적으로 말하는 경우가 많다.

▶ 우리 형은 외국에서 살고 있다 My brother is living in a overseas [abroad].
▶ 나는 외국에 간 적이 없다 I have never been abroad [overseas].
■—무역 foreign [overseas] trade —사절[사신] a foreign envoy —상사 foreign firm [company] —생활 life overseas —시장 overseas [foreign firm] market —우편 foreign [international] mail —자본 foreign capital —전보 international telegram; cablegram (▶격식차린 말) —풍 foreign manners [ways]; exotic fashion; exoticism —항로 overseas route; a foreign (service) route: 외국 항로의 배 a vessel on a foreign route

외국 外局 an extra-ministerial bureau

외국어 外國語 a foreign language [tongue] (▶ tongue을 쓰는 것은 격식차린 말씨)
♦ 외국어를 읽을 수 있게 되다 acquire a reading knowledge of a foreign language / 외국어로[의] in a foreign language
▶ 그는 여러 외국어에 능숙하다 He's quite a linguist. ⇌ (수개 국어에 통달한 사람이다) He is a polyglot.
▶ 외국어로 자기 생각을 말하기란 아주 힘들다 It is very hard to express oneself in a language that is not one's own.
■제이— a second foreign language ■—학교 a foreign language school

외국인 外國人 a foreigner; 〈시민권이 없는 외국 거주인〉 an alien

解說 foreigner는 「이방인」이라는 느낌이 들어 person [people] from abroad [other countries]를 쓰는 것이 좋다.

■—관광객 a foreign tourist —노동자 foreign worker [laborer] —등록 alien registration —등록법 the Alien Registration Law

외국환 外國換 foreign exchange ⇨ 외환(外換)

외근 外勤 working away from [outside] the office; outside duty [service]; canvassing
♦ 외근의 on outdoor service; on outside duty; 〈취재 근무〉 on reportorial duty
▶ 넌 외근이냐 내근이냐? Do you work outside or inside?
—외근하다 work outside; do outside work
■—경찰 a patrol(man) —기자 a reporter; a legman —자 a person on outside duty; 〈외무원〉 a canvasser —직원 an outdoor service employee

외기 外氣 the (open) air; (the) fresh air; the air outside
♦ 외기를 쐬다 air oneself; take the air / 외기에 쐬다 air; expose sth to the air
▶ 방안이 무답다. 창문을 열어 외기로 통풍시키자 The air in the room is close. We'd better open the windows and let in some fresh air.
■—권 the exosphere

외길 〈한 군데로만 난 길〉 the only road; road with no forks
■—목 a junction of roads [paths]

외나무다리 a log bridge; a single-log bridge
♦ 외나무다리를 건너다 cross (a stream) by a log bridge / 외나무다리에서 원수를 만나다 meet bad luck one cannot escape from

외날 a single edge
♦ 외날 면도기 a single-edged blade

외눈박이 a one-eyed person ⇨ 애꾸눈이

외다¹ 〈외우다〉 recite; learn by heart

외다² 〈물건 쓰기가 불편하다〉 unhandy; un-

wieldy; inconvenient; 〈서술적〉 be out of place; be off to *one* side
♦손이 외다 be out of the way; be hard to reach; be unhandy
▶그 보따리는 들어나르기가 외다 The pack is unhandy [inconvenient] to carry about.

외대다[1] 〈반대로 일러주다〉 tell [inform] *sb* contrary to the facts; give *sb* a false report

외대다[2] **1** 〈소홀히 대접하다〉 treat [receive] *sb* coldly [unkindly]; give *sb* a cold reception; treat slightingly; give the cold shoulder to *sb*
2 〈배척하다〉 reject; keep away from; shun

외대머리 〈혼례전의 쪽머리〉 an unmarried woman who wears her hair as if married

외대박이 1 〈외돛단배〉 a single-sail[-masted] boat
2 a one-eyed person
3 〈무·배추의 한 포기로 한 단을 만든것〉 a bundle of one cabbage [radish]

외 덩굴에 가지 열릴까 〈속담〉 An onion will not produce a rose.

외도 外道 1 〈바르지 않은 길〉 a way of doing contrary to the truth; a wrong way ━외도하다 stray [deviate, swerve] from the right path
2 〈오입〉 womanizing

외돌다 〈남과 어울리지 않다〉 keep [remain, stand] aloof 《from》

외돌토리 〈홀몸〉 a single [solitary, lonely] person; being alone
♦외돌토리 노인 a solitary [lonely] old man
▶그는 외돌토리였다 He was (all) alone. ⇌ He was living in complete solitude.

외동딸 〈외딸〉 an [*one's*] only daughter
외동아들 〈외아들〉 an [*one's*] only son
외동이 *one's* beloved only son
외등 外燈 an outdoor lamp [light]
외따로 lonelily; solitarily; all alone; in isolation
♦외따로 살다 live in isolation (from other) / 외따로 앉아 있다 sit all alone
▶들판에 나무 한그루가 외따로 서 있다 A solitary tree stands in a field.

외딴 〈멀리 떨어진〉 isolated; out-of-the-way; solitary
♦외딴 섬 a solitary island / 외딴 시골 a secluded village / 외딴 집 a lonely house; a house remote from any village or town; an isolated house / 외딴 곳 an out-of-the-way [a secluded] place; a lonely spot
▶그는 인가에서 멀리 떨어진 외딴 집에 살고 있다 He lives in a solitary cottage far from human habitation.
▶그곳은 외딴 마을이었다 It was a remote [an out-of-the-way] village.

외딴치다 〈혼자 판을 치다〉 stand unrivaled [unchallenged]; play a one-man show

외딸 an only daughter (▶the only daughter는 「그 외딸」의 뜻이거나, 뒤에 한정 어구가 따를 때에 한해서 사용함. 외아들의 경우도 마찬가지임)
▶제인은 그녀의 외딸이다 Jane is the only daughter (that) she has.

외딸다 〈홀로 떨어져 있다〉 isolated; secluded; out-of-the-way; separated; lonely

외떡잎식물 ━植物 〔植〕 monocotyledon

외람 猥濫 〈분수·도리가 지나침〉 presumption; forwardness; foreign; alien
━외람하다 presumptuous; impertinent; impudent
♦외람된 말씀이오나 I dare [venture to] say...; Allow me to tell you that... / 외람된 말을 하다 say pert things
▶그는 외람되게도 우리의 제안을 거절했다 He had the presumption [audacity, (口) cheek] to refuse our offer.
▶외람되나 이 안을 위원회에 제의하겠습니다 Allow me to suggest this plan to the committee.

외래 外來 ♦외래의 (coming) from abroad; imported; foreign; alien
■━문화 foreign [imported] culture ━사상 an idea of foreign origin; foreign [alien, imported] ideas ━어 an adopted [a loan, a borrowed] word; a word of foreign origin ━인 a stranger; an alien; a visitor ━자 a visitor; a stranger : 〈게시〉 외래자 출입금지 Outsiders are requested to keep out. ━종 〈식물 등〉 an introduced species ━환자 an out-patient; a day-patient

외래품 外來品 foreign [imported] goods
━상점 a foreign goods store

외력 外力 〔物〕 external force

외로 1 〈왼쪽으로〉 on the [*one's*] left (-hand); left-side; to [toward] the [*one's*] left (side)
▶다음 모퉁이에서 외로 도세요 Turn (to the) left at the next corner.
▶외로 보이는 것이 서울역입니다 On your left you (can) see Seoul Station.
2 〈비뚤게〉 to the wrong direction [way, path]
♦외로 가다 go to the left; go astray; fall into evil ways / 외로 기울다 incline [lean] to the left (side)

외로움 solitude; loneliness
♦외로움을 느끼다 feel lonely

외로이 〈외롭게·혼자서〉 lonelily; alone; lonesomely; solitarily
♦외로이 지내다 live in loneliness [solitude]; live alone [a lonely life]; lead a solitary [lonely] life / 이국땅에서 외로이 죽다 die forlorn in a foreign land

외롭다 〈쓸쓸하다〉 lonely; lonesome; solitary; 〈의지할 곳이 없다〉 friendless; helpless; forlorn
♦외로운 사람 have no person to depend upon [on]; a solitary [lonely] person / 외로운 생활을 하다 lead a lonely [solitary] life
▶남편이 죽은 뒤 그녀는 외로운 생활을 하고 있다 Since her husband's death, she has been leading a lonely life.

외륜 外輪 〈바깥쪽 바퀴〉 an outer ring; the rim (of a wheel); a tire; 〈기선의〉 a paddle wheel
■━산 〔地質〕 a somma ━선 a paddle steamer; a side-wheeler

외마디 1 〈한 동강〉 a single section [piece]

외마디소리

《of a bamboo》 2 〈한 마디 소리〉 a short outcry
■―설대 a bamboo pipestem without a joint

외마디소리 a short outcry [scream]; a scream
♦외마디 소리를 지르다 scream; shriek 《with pain》; give [utter] a shriek; give a shrill cry
▶그 한적한 거리에서 외마디 소리가 들렸다 I heard a scream come [coming] from that quiet street.

외면 外面 〈겉면〉 the outside; the exterior; 〈바깥 모양〉 outward appearance
♦건물의 외면 the outside [exterior] of a building / 외면의 outside; outward; exterior; external / 외면은[으로는] outwardly
▶외면이 좋다고 해서 반드시 내부가 좋은 것은 아니다 What is good externally is not always good internally.
■―묘사 an external description

외면하다 外面― turn one's face away 《from》; look away 《from》; 〈무시하다〉 disregard
▶그가 말을 걸었을 때 나는 외면했다 I looked the other way [looked away, turned away] when he spoke to me.
▶그는 외면하며 지나갔다 He passed by, looking the other way.

외모 外貌 outward appearance; external features; looks
♦장사꾼같은 외모 merchantlike appearance / 외모(로)는 outwardly; in appearance; to all appearances / 사람을 외모로 판단하다 judge sb by 《his》 appearances [looks]

외목 1 ⇨ 외길(~목)
2 〈외목장사〉 (a) monopoly; a monopolistic business
■―장수 a monopolizer; a monopolist

외몽고 外蒙古 Outer Mongolia

외무 外務 1 〈외교 사무〉 foreign [external] affairs 2 ⇨ 외근
■―위원회 the Foreign Affairs Committee

외무부 外務部 the Ministry of Foreign Affairs
■―장관 the Minister of [for] Foreign Affairs; Foreign Minister ―재외공관 an overseas agency of the Ministry of Foreign Affairs ―차관 the Vice Minister of Foreign Affairs ―차관보 the Deputy Minister of Foreign Affairs

외무원 外務員 a canvasser; (美) a solicitor; a (traveling) salesman; 〈판매의〉 a commercial traveler ♦외무원을 하다 travel for 《a Seoul publisher》
■보험― an insurance salesman [canvasser]

외박 外泊 〈밖에서 잠〉 stopping [staying] out 《overnight》
♦외박을 허가하다 permit staying out
―외박하다 stay out [be away] overnight [for the night]; sleep away from home; 〈군인이〉 stop out of barracks
▶나는 2, 3일 외박할 예정이다 I'm going to stay out for a few nights.
▶그는 무단으로 외박했다 He stayed out overnight without notice.

외발제기 playing a shuttlecock with one foot

외방 外方 1 〈서울 밖의 지방〉 districts away from the capital [Seoul]; the country outside of Seoul; the provinces
♦외방의 provincial; local
2 〈바깥쪽〉 the outside
■―살이 an official life in the provinces

외배엽 外胚葉 〔生〕 the ectoderm; the ectoblast

외배젖 外胚― 〔生〕 a perisperm

외벌매듭 a single [simple] knot

외벽 外壁 〔建〕 an outer [external] wall

외보 外報 news from abroad; oversea(s) [foreign] news

외부 外部 the outside; the exterior; 〈외계〉 the outside world
♦외부의 outside; outer; external; exterior / 외부에서 보면 when seen from the outside / 외부에 나타나다 appear on the outside / 외부와 완전히 고립되다 be entirely isolated [cut off] from the outside world
▶이 정보가 외부로 새나가지 않도록 매우 조심해라 Be very careful not to let this information leak out.
▶도움은 외부로부터 왔다 Help came from the outside.
▶이것이 마을과 외부를 잇는 유일한 통로다 This is the only passage that connects the village with the outside world.
■―간섭 outside intervention [interference] ―기생 〔生〕 external parasitism ―사람 an outsider ―침략 external aggression

외분비 外分泌 〔醫〕 external secretion
■―선 an exocrine gland

외분하다 外分― ♦선분을 외분하다 divide a segment externally

외빈 外賓 〈외국 손님〉 a foreign guest [visitor]; 〈외부 손님〉 a guest [visitor]

외사 外史 1 〈외국 역사〉 foreign history; history of a foreign country
2 〈야사〉 unofficial [unauthorized] history

외사 外事 external [foreign] affairs
■―과 〈경찰의〉 the foreign affairs section

외사촌 外四寸 a cousin (on the mother's side); one's maternal cousin

외삼촌 外三寸 an uncle (on the mother's [maternal] side); one's maternal uncle
―댁 ⇨ 외숙(~모)

외상 credit; trust; (美) a check; charge account; (口) a tick; credit account
♦외상이 밀리다[늘다] run a credit; run up a score 《at a grocery store》 / 외상을 갚다 clear [pay] off one's credits [bills] / 외상으로 사다 buy 《sth》 on credit [(美) on the cuff]/ 외상으로 주다 give credit
▶내 앞으로 외상을 달아주세요 Put it on my bill [(口) tab]. ⇌ Charge it to my account [to me].
▶외상 사절 (게시) No credit given. ⇌ For cash only.
■―값 an account; a bill ―거래 credit transactions ―매입 credit purchase ―매출[판매] credit sale; sale on credit ―매출계정 charge [credit] account ―매출금 a credit account

—손님 a charge [credit] customer —수금원 a bill collector

외상 一床 〈독상〉 a table for *one*; an individual table ♦ 외상을 받다 be served food on an individual table

외상 外相 〈외무부 장관〉 the Foreign Minister ■ —회담 a foreign minister's conference

외상 外傷 an external wound [injury]; a trauma (*pl.* ~s -mata)
♦ 외상을 입히다 traumatize
▶ 그는 교통사고로 심한 외상을 입었다 He received [suffered] a heavy injury in the traffic accident.

외상 外商 〈외국 상인〉 a foreign merchant; 〈외국 상사〉 a foreign firm

외상말코지 〈돈을 먼저 주지 않으면 일을 빨리 안해줌〉 difficulty in getting things (done) without paying in advance

외생 外甥 〈사위의 자칭〉 I your humble son-in-law

외서 外書 a foreign book

외선 外線 〈전기의〉 outside wire [cable]; the outer line; 〈전화의〉 an outside line
▶ 외선은 영(번)을 돌리세요 Dial zero for [to get] an outside line.
▶ 이 전화로 외선을 걸 수 있습니까? Can I make an outside call [Can I call outside] by this phone? ⇌ Can I get outside on this phone?

외설 猥褻 obscenity [əbsénəti]; indecency
—외설하다 obscene; indecent; lascivious
♦ 외설한 그림 an obscene picture / 외설한 농담 a dirty [an indecent, a lewd] joke / 외설한 영화 an obscene [an indecent] movie / 외설한 행위 indecent behavior [act]; pornographic act / 외설한 이야기를 하다 tell a dirty story; talk dirty
▶ 그 영화는 외설한 부분을 자른 다음 상영이 허가되었다 The film was permitted to be shown after the obscene parts had been [were] cut [censored] (out).
■ —문학 obscene literature [writings]; pornography —사진 French postcard —서 an obscene [a pornographic] book —죄 public indecency

외세 外勢 〈바깥 형세〉 external conditions [situation]; 〈외국 세력〉 outside [foreign, alien] influence [power]
♦ 외세를 배척하다 denounce [reject] the foreign power / 외세에 의존하다 depend on the power [influence] of a foreign country

외손 〈한쪽 손〉 one hand ■ —뼉 single palm —잡이 a one-handed person

외손 外孫 *one's* grandson [grandchild]; a daughter's son ■ —녀 *one's* granddaughter; a daughter's daughter —자 *one's* grandson; a daughter's son

외손뼉이 울지 못한다 (속담) It takes two to make a quarrel.

외손지다 get deprived of the use of one hand

외수 外需 〈외국 수요〉 foreign demand

외수 外數 〈속임수〉 deceit; trick

외숙 外叔 a maternal uncle; a brother of *one's* mother ■ —모 an aunt; the wife of a maternal uncle

외시골 外— 〈먼 시골〉 a remote country place; outlying [remote] country districts

외식 外食 eating [dining, boarding] out
—외식하다 dine out; eat [take] *one's* meals ticket
▶ 매일 외식하는 사람들은 편식하기가 쉽다 Those who dine out every day are liable to have an unbalanced diet.
■ —권 a meal ticket —산업 fast food chains industry; the food service industry —자 a diner-out

외식 外飾 〈면치레·겉치레〉 a face-lifting; outward show

외신 外信 a foreign telegram [cable]; a report from overseas; foreign news
♦ 런던발 외신에 의하면… News from London says…; According to news from London…
▶ 파리에서 보내온 외신에 따르면 정상 회담이 2월 1일부터 열릴 예정이라고 한다 According to a dispatch from Paris, the summit conference is to be held on February 1 [(英) 1 February, the 1st of February].
■ —부 the foreign news department [section, desk] —부장 〈신문사 등의〉 a foreign news editor; editor of the foreign news department

외실 外室 a guest room for men ⇨ 사랑(舍廊)

외심 外心 〔數〕 a circumcenter; an outer center; 〈딴마음·두마음〉 duplicity; a double heart; two hearts

외 심은데 콩나랴 (속담) An eagle does not hatch a dove.

외씨버선 slender Korean socks

외아들 an only son

외야 外野 〔野〕 the outfield ▶ 그는 오늘 외야를 수비한다 He plays in the outfield today.
■ —석 the outfield stands; (美) 〈지붕없는〉 bleachers —수 an outfielder; a fielder

외양 外洋 the open sea; the ocean
♦ 외양 항로의 ocean-going ■ —선 〈정기선〉 an ocean liner; an ocean-going vessel [ship] —어업 deep-sea fishing [fishery]

외양 外樣 〈겉모양〉 outward appearance [show, look]; external appearance
♦ 외양이 그럴듯하다 have a good appearance / 외양을 꾸미다 make outward show; keep up appearances
▶ 그는 외양에 너무 신경을 쓴다 He cares too much about how he looks.
▶ 사람들은 사물을 외양으로 판단하려는 경향이 있다 People are apt to judge you by your appearance.
▶ 그의 슬픔[동정]은 외양뿐이다 His sorrow [sympathy] is mere show.

외양간 喂養間 〈말의〉 a stable; (美) a (horse) barn; 〈소의〉 a cowhouse; a cowshed
▶ 소 잃고 외양간 고친다 (속담) It is too late to lock the stable door after the horse is stolen.

외어서다 step [move] aside (from); get out of the way (of) ▶ 차가 오고 있어, 어서 외어서라 A car is coming. Get out of the way.

외연 外延 〔論〕 denotation; extension

외연기관 外燃機關 an external combustion

engine

외올 a single strand ■—뜨기 single-strand knitwork —베 hemp cloth woven in single-strand —실 single-strand thread

외욕질 〈욕지기〉 nausea; qualm; retch

외용 外用 external use [application] —외용하다 use [apply] externally
■—약 a medicine [lotion] for external use [application]; 〈약병 등의 글〉 "For external use only"

외우 外憂 1 〈외환(外患)〉 foreign troubles; the pressure [invasion] of a foreign enemy
2 ⇨ 외간(外艱)

외우 畏友 〈존경하는 벗〉 one's respected [esteemed] friend

외우다 1 〈암송하다〉 recite; say...by heart; repeat...from memory
♦ 시를 외우다 recite a poem / 염불을 외우다 repeat [chant] the name of Buddha / 주기도문을 외우다 chant the Lord's Prayer / 주문을 외우다 utter a magic formula
2 〈암기하다〉 learn by heart; 〈기억하다〉 memorize; commit (it) to memory; get (off) by heart
▶ 우리는 교과서의 인명과 지명을 외웠다 We memorized the geographical and biographical names in the textbook. ⇒ We learned the geographical and biographical names in the textbook by heart.

외원 外苑 the outer gardens (of the royal palace)

외원 外援 〈외부의 도움〉 external help; 〈외국원조〉 foreign aid [assistance]

외유 外遊 a foreign travel [tour, trip]; a trip abroad; an overseas trip; travel abroad (▶an abroad trip은 안됨)
♦ 외유길에 오르다 start on a tour abroad [a foreign tour]/ 외유에서 돌아오다 return home from one's foreign tour
▶ 송선생은 외유중입니다 Mr. Song is abroad now. ⇒ Mr. Song is traveling abroad.
▶ 나는 내년에 외유하려고 생각하고 있다 I'm planning to go abroad next year. ⇒ I'm planning (to take) a trip abroad [an overseas trip] next year.

외유내강 外柔內剛 being gentle in appearance, but sturdy in spirit; an iron hand in the velvet glove
▶ 그는 외유내강한 사람이다 He is gentle in appearance, but sturdy in spirit.

외음부 外陰部 the external genitals; the vulva

외의 外衣 an outer garment

외이 外耳 〔解〕 the external ear; the concha (pl. -chae); the auricle
■—염 〔醫〕 otitis externa

외이도 外耳道 〔解〕 an external auditory canal [meatus]

외인 外人 1 〈외국인〉 a foreigner; an alien
♦ 외인 관광객 a visitor from abroad [overseas]; a foreign visitor
2 〈국외자〉 an outsider; a stranger
▶ 이 일은 외인이 알아서는 안 된다 This is between ourselves.

▶ 외인 출입금지[사절] (게시) No admittance. —재류— foreign residents —부대 a foreign legion —상사 a foreign (business) firm —주택 foreign residents' houses

외자 外資 foreign capital [money, funds]
■—도입 the induction [introduction] of foreign capital [funds] —수용 태세 preparation for the receipt of foreign investments —유입 the inflow [influx] of foreign capital

외장 外裝 1 〈겉포장〉 wrapping(s); the outside packing
—외장하다 wrap; cover; pack
2 〈바깥 장식〉 (a) facing (material); the exterior (finish) (of a building); (a) cladding
■—검사 packing inspection —공사 exterior work —재(材) coverings; wrappings —케이블 an armored cable

외장골 外腸骨 〔解〕 the external iliac [flank] bone ■—동맥[정맥] the (external) iliac arteries [veins]

외적 外敵 a foreign enemy [invader]
♦ 외적의 침입 foreign invasion / 외적의 공격을 받다 suffer an attack from a foreign country; be attacked by a foreign enemy

외적 外的 external; outward; outside
♦ 외적 증거 external evidence / 외적인 조건 external conditions / 외적인 이유 ostensible reasons

외전 外電 a foreign telegram ⇨ 외신

외접 外接 〔數〕 circumscription —외접하다 circumscribe (a polygon); be circumscribed
■—원 a circumscribed circle; a circumcircle

외정 外征 a foreign expedition [campaign]
—외정하다 go on a foreign expedition; send an army abroad
■—군 an expeditionary army [force]

외정 外政 diplomatic [foreign] affairs; foreign policies

외제 外製 ♦ 외제의 of foreign manufacture [make]; foreign-made
■—차 a foreign [a foreign-made, an imported] car —품 foreign-made articles; imported articles [goods]; goods of foreign make

외조모 外祖母 a maternal grandmother; a grandmother on one's mother's side

외조부 外祖父 a maternal grandfather; a grandfather on one's mother's side

외족 外族 maternal relatives; a relative [relation] on [by] the mother's side

외종사촌 外從四寸 a cousin ⇨ 외사촌

외주 外注 an outside order
♦ (자사 제품의) 기계 부품을 외주를 내다 place an order with an outside supplier for parts of a machine (produced in one's plant)
▶ 이 부품은 외주를 낸다 We order these parts outside the company.
—외주하다 place an order (with) outside
♦ 부품을 모두 외주하다 contract out all the parts
■—지정공장 a factory designated for subcontract —품 outside product

외주 外周 the outer circumference

외주물집 〈보잘 것 없는 집〉 a shabby house that is open to the road; an open shack

외줄 a single line; 〈전깃줄 등의〉 solid wire
외줄기 a single stem [stalk]
외지 外地 **1** 〈다른 고장〉 another countryside; a place away from home; an outlying region ♦외지로 생활비를 벌러가다 go to an outlying region to earn *one's* living
2 〈외국〉 a foreign [an alien] land; an oversea(s) land
3 〈해외 영토〉 an external territory ■―근무[생활] overseas service [life] ―수당 an overseas allowance
외지 外紙 〈외국 신문〉 a foreign newspaper; 〈총칭〉 the foreign press ♦…이라고 외지는 보도하고 있다 It is reported in the foreign newspaper that...
외지다 out-of-the-way; remote; isolated; secluded; sequestered ♦외진 마을 a remote [an out-of-the-way] village / 외진 산길 a remote mountain trail [path]
▶ 그의 가족은 외진 산촌에 살고 있었다 His family lived in a remote mountain village.
외직 外職 a government post away from the capital; a local [provincial] government post
외진 外診 〔醫〕 an external examination
외짝 an odd one (of a pair)
♦외짝 구두[장갑] an odd shoe [glove]
▶ 아내 없이 와보니 파티에서는 나 혼자만 외짝 손님이 되었다 Coming without my wife, I found myself the odd guest at the party.
외쪽 1 〈한 쪽〉 one side; one way (▶다른 쪽의 the other side)
2 〈한 조각〉 a single piece
♦외쪽 눈이 안 보이다 be blind in one eye
▶ 이 장갑의 외쪽이 안 보여요 I can't find the mate to [of] this glove.
■―생각 one-sided thinking
외채 a single house ⇨ 외챗집
외채 外債 〔經〕〈차관〉 a foreign loan; 〈채권〉 a foreign bond; 〈부채〉 foreign debt
♦외채를 모집[발행]하다 raise [float] a foreign loan / 외채를 상환하다 redeem [refund] a foreign loan / 외채를 상환하지 못하다 default on foreign loans
▶ 정부는 8,000만 달러의 외채를 모집하기로 결정했다 The Government decided to raise an eighty million dollar foreign loan.
■―모집[상환] floatation [redemption] of a foreign loan
외챗집 a single [an independent] house
외척 外戚 a maternal relative [relation]; a relation on *one's* mother's side
외청도 外聽道 an external auditory canal ⇨ 외이도(外耳道)
외촌 外村 a village outside of a town; an outlying [outside] village
외축하다 畏縮― 〈두려워서 움츠리다〉 flinch; shrivel; shrink 《from》; cower [quail] 《before》; recoil 《from》
외출 外出 going out; an outing; an airing
♦외출을 좋아하는 사람 (口) a gadabout / 외출을 싫어하는 사람 a homebody / 외출허가를 받다 be allowed out / 〈군인의〉 외출을 금지 당하다 be confined to the barracks
▶ 아버지는 지금 외출중이십니다 Father is out now.
▶ 일요일에는 외출이 허용된다 They have their Sundays out.
―**외출하다** go out (of doors); take an airing
♦외출하지 않다 stay at home; keep [stay] indoors / 외출했다가 돌아오다 come home [back] from a visit
▶ 그들은 외출할 채비를 하고 있다 They dress themselves for the street [outdoors]. ⇌ They get ready to go out.
▶ 어제는 비 때문에[아파서] 외출할 수 없었다 Rain [Illness] kept [prevented] me indoors [from going out] yesterday.
■―금지 〈군인의〉 confinement (to the barracks) ―금지령 a curfew (order) ―복 street clothes ―시간 〈군인의〉 leave-time ―일 a leave day ―허가증 a leave slip
외출혈 外出血 〔醫〕 external hemorrhage (↔ internal hemorrhage)
외치 外治 **1** ⇨ 외교 **2** 〈외과적 치료〉 〔醫〕 external [surgical] treatment
―**외치하다** treat externally; apply external [surgical] treatment
외치다 cry; shout; yell; 〈새된 소리로〉 shriek; scream; 〈감탄하여〉 exclaim

┌──────────────────────────────────────┐
│ **解說** *cry*는 가장 넓게 사용되는 말로 반드시 │
│ 큰소리에 국한되지는 않는다. ***shout, yell***은 │
│ 소리를 질러 외치다, ***shriek***는 「새된 소리로 │
│ 외치다」를 말한다. │
└──────────────────────────────────────┘

♦개혁을 외치다 cry (loudly) for reform / 원폭 실험금지를 외치다 cry out for an atomic ban / 아파서 외치다 cry [shout, scream] with pain; give a cry [shout, scream] of pain / 성나서 외치다 roar with anger / 목이 쉬도록 외치다 shout *oneself* hoarse / 「도둑이야」라고 외치다 cry "Thief!" / 「불이야, 불」이라고 외치다 cry "Fire, fire!" / 「찬성」이라고 외치다 give a cry of approval
▶ 「이겼다」라고 그는 외쳤다 "I won!" he cried [shouted, exclaimed]. (▶he 대신 명사의 주어를 쓸 경우에는 "I won!" cried my brother. 처럼 「동사+주어」의 어순도 가능함)
▶ 그녀는 살려달라고 큰 소리로 외쳤으나 그에게는 들리지 않았다 She cried out [shouted out, yelled out, screamed] for help, but he couldn't hear her.
외침 a shout; a cry; an outcry; an exclamation; a yell; a clamor; a shriek; a scream
♦반전의 외침 a cry [clamor] for opposition to war
외탁하다 外― take after *one's* mother's side of the family
▶ 그는 용모가 외탁했다 He is very (much) like [really takes after, really resembles] his mother in appearance. ⇌ He really looks like his mother. ⇌ He and his mother look very (much) alike.
외톨이 a single ⇨ 외돌토리
외톨 1 〈한 톨만이 여문 알〉 a single ripened chestnut [garlic bulb]
2 ⇨ 외돌토리
■―밤이 〈밤〉 a chestnut-bur with a single

nut; 〈마늘〉 a garlic made up of a single bulb
외통 〈장기〉 checkmate ■ —**수** a checkmate move : 외통수로 몰리다 be checkmated —**장군** checkmate; mate
외투 外套 〈美〉 an overcoat; 〈英〉 a greatcoat; 〈망토〉 a cloak
♦ 남자용[여자용] 외투 a man's [woman's] overcoat
▶ 그는 외투를 입고 있다 He wears an overcoat. (▶wear는 몸에 걸치고 있는 상태를 나타내는 동사)
▶ 그는 외투를 입고 있었다 He had on [was wearing] an overcoat. ⇌ He had an overcoat on. (▶현재 입고 있는 것을 표현할 때는 have on이 쓰임)
▶ 그는 외투를 입었다 He put his overcoat on. (▶옷을 입는 1회의 동작을 나타내는 가장 일반적인 동사는 put on, 벗는 것은 take off임)
▶ 나는 그녀에게 외투를 입혀[벗겨] 주었다 I helped her on [off] with her overcoat.
■ —**감** overcoating —**걸이** an overcoat rack —**막** 〈연체동물의〉 a mantle
외판 外販 (a) traveling sale; canvassing
♦ 서적 외판을 하다 go from house to house selling [peddling] books
▶ 그는 보험 외판으로 생계를 꾸려가고 있다 He sells insurance for a living.
■ —**원** a salesman; a canvasser; a commercial traveler : 서적 외판원 a (door-to-door) salesman in books
외팔 〈한쪽 팔〉 one arm ■ —**이** a one-armed person
외포 畏怖 〈두려워함〉 awe; fear; dread; terror
▶ 전설 때문에 마을 사람들은 그 숲에 외포의 염(念)을 품고 있다 The legend had given the villagers the fear of the forest.
▶ 천재가 사람들에게 외포의 감(感)을 일으키게 했다 Disaster inspired the people with awe.
외풍 外風 1 〈새어드는 바람〉 〈美〉 a draft (of air); 〈英〉 a draught ♦ 외풍을 막다 cut off the drafts / 외풍이 있는 drafty (room)
▶ 이 집은 외풍이 들어온다 This house is drafty [〈英〉 draughty]. ⇌ There's a draft [a draught] in this house.
2 〈외국 풍습〉 exotic fashion; foreignism; Western [foreign] style [manners]
외피 外皮 〈살갗〉 a skin; 〔解 · 動〕 an integument; 〈과일씨 · 종자 등의〉 a husk; 〈곡물의〉 a hull; 〈패류 등의〉 a shell; 〈파이 · 빵 등의〉 a crust
외할머니 外— a maternal grandmother
외할아버지 外— a maternal grandfather
외항 外航 a foreign [an overseas] voyage
■ —**선** a ship for overseas service; an ocean-going ship; an ocean liner
외항 外港 an outer port; an outport
외항 外項 〔數〕 an outer [external] term; the extreme
외해 外海 〈만 · 항구 밖 해역〉 the open [main] sea; 〈공해〉 the high seas; 〈대양〉 the ocean
♦ 외해로 나가다 sail out to the open sea
외향성 外向性 〔心〕 extroversion
♦ 외향성인 extrovert(ed); extroversive / 외향성인 사람 an extrovert

외형 外形 1 〈겉형상〉 an external [outward] form [shape]; 〈겉모양〉 external [outward] appearance ♦ 외형의 external; outward 2 〔經〕 the gross sales [proceeds]; the turnover ■ **당기(당)월** the sales for this term
외화 外貨 1 〈화폐〉 foreign currency [money]
♦ 외화를 획득하다 obtain foreign currency
▶ 외화를 획득하기 위해 정부는 수출을 장려하고 있다 The government encourages exports to earn foreign currency.
2 〈화물〉 foreign goods
♦ 외화의 배척 the boycott of foreign goods
■ —**가 득액[률]** foreign-exchange earnings [earning rate] —**관리** management of foreign currency holdings —**보유고** foreign currency holdings; foreign exchange reserves —**어음** a foreign money bill —**유출** the diversion [outflow] of foreign currency —**자금** foreign currency funds —**절약** foreign currency saving —**준비금** foreign currency reserve —**획득** the acquisition of foreign currencies
외화 外畫 a foreign film [movie]
▶ 영화로 말하면, 방화(邦畵)와 외화 중 어느 쪽을 더 좋아하세요? Speaking of movies, which do you like better, Korean movies or foreign ones?
■ —**수입쿼터** the foreign film import quotas
외환 外患 fears of foreign [outside] invasion; foreign troubles; the invasion of a foreign enemy
외환 外換 〈외국환〉 foreign exchange
■ —**관리법** 〔法〕 the Foreign Exchange Control Law —**시장[시세]** a foreign exchange market [rate] —**은행** a foreign exchange bank
왼 left; left-hand(ed) ♦ 왼눈 one's left eye / 왼발[팔] the left foot [arm] / 왼쪽의 the left (side)
왼소리 〈부음〉 news of one's death ♦ 왼소리를 듣다 hear of sb's death
왼손 the left hand
♦ 왼손편에 on the left-hand side / 왼손으로 글을 쓰다 write with one's left hand
■ —**잡이** a left-handed person; a left-hander; a lefty : 너는 왼손잡이냐 오른손잡이냐? Are you right-handed or left-handed?
왼쪽 the left (side)
♦ 왼쪽 끝 the left-hand edge / 왼쪽에 on the left (hand); left / 길 왼쪽에 on the left(-hand) side of the road / 왼쪽에서 오른쪽으로 ((write)) from left to right / 왼쪽으로 돌다 turn to the left; turn left
▶ 이 길을 곧장 가시면 왼쪽에 은행이 있습니다 Go straight down this road, and you will come to a bank on the left-hand side.
왼편 —便 the left ▷ 왼쪽
♦ 강의 왼편 기슭 the left bank of a river
욀총 —聰 a good memory; a retentive mind
욋가지 根— 〔建〕 a lath; 〈총칭〉 lathing
요¹ 1 〈얕잡아 하는 말〉 this little (one)
♦ 요놈의 the fellow [guy]; you rascal / 요까짓… such a (little)…
2 〈시간 · 거리〉 this; these; 〈오는〉 next; coming; 〈지난〉 last; past

요새 these days; nowadays; recently; lately / 요 며칠 (동안) / 〈지금까지〉 these few days; for some days past; 〈금후〉 the next few days; for some days to come / 요 근처에 in this neighborhood
▶요 며칠 사이에 아주 시원해졌다 It has got very cool these past few days.
▶그 마을은 요 고개 너머에 있습니다 The village lies beyond the ridge.

요² 〈침대용〉 a sleeping pad; 〈한국식〉 a Korean mattress ◆요 깔다 lay a Korean mattress; make the bed / 요를 개다 put away a Korean mattress
■—이불 sleeping pads and quilts

요 要 〈요점〉 the main [essential] point; 〈정수〉 the essence; 〈목적〉 the aim ◆요는 what is essential [important] is...; the point is...; in a word; in short
▶요는 위험을 무릅쓰고 싶지 않다는거야 In short, I don't want you to run the risk.

요가 yoga ◆요가의 수행자 a yogi / 요가를 하다 do [practice] yoga

요각 凹刻 〈數〉 an intaglio; a reentering angle

요강 尿䀇 〈실내용의〉 a (close)stool; a chamber pot; a commode; 〈환자용의〉 a bedpan

요강 要綱 〈대요〉 the outline; the gist; a summary; 〈대체적 계획〉 the general plan; 〈취지서〉 a prospectus
■모집— guidebook for applicants; an application guidebook : 모집요강을 한 부 보내주십시오 Please send me a copy of the guidelines for applicants. 입학— a list of the entrance requirements 《for a college》 지시— the essential points for guidance

요건 要件 〈중요 용건〉 an important business [matter]; 〈필요 조건〉 a necessary [required] condition 《of》; 〈자격 등의〉 a requirement
◆요건을 구비하다 meet [satisfy] the necessary conditions [requirements] 《for》
▶근면은 성공의 요건이다 Diligence is the basic requisite for success.
▶입주자격 요건을 좀더 완화해 주시기 바랍니다 We hope necessary conditions for the tenant will be made easier.

요격 邀擊 an ambush; intercept; interception —요격하다 lie in wait [ambush] 《for》; ambush; waylay; intercept 《raiding bombers》
▶그들은 적의 폭격기를 요격하기 위해 날아올랐다 They took off in order to intercept enemy bombers.
■—기 an interceptor (plane) —미사일 an interceptor missile; an ABM; an antiballistic missile; an antimissile

요결 要訣 **1** 〈비결〉 a key; a secret; an essential principle
▶건강의 요결은 일찍 일어나는 것이다 Early rising in the morning is a key to good health.
2 〈긴요한 뜻〉 an essential meaning

요골 腰骨 the hipbone; the hucklebone
요골 橈骨 〔解〕 a radius 《pl. ~es, -dii》
요관 尿管 a ureter
요괴 妖怪 a specter; a demon; a ghost; an apparition; 〈괴물〉 a goblin —요괴스럽다 (be) wicked and mysterious; weird; uncanny; eerie; monstrous

요구 要求 a demand; 〈청구〉 a request; 〈권리에 의한〉 a claim; 〈필요〉 requirement
◆시대의 요구 the needs [requirements] of the times / 정당한 요구 a reasonable claim / 부당한[터무니없는] 요구 an unreasonable [inordinate] demand / 요구에 따라 on [upon] demand; at *one's* request / 요구에 따르다 accede to [meet] *sb's* demand; admit [accept] *sb's* claim 《for compensation》 / 요구를 거절하다 reject *sb's* claim [demand] / 요구를 충족시키다 meet [satisfy] the requirement; 《口》 fill the bill
▶우리의 요구가 받아들여져 매주 토요일과 일요일이 휴무가 됐다 Our demands being accepted, we shall have holidays on Saturday and Sunday every week.
▶너의 기본적인 요구는 뭐냐? What are your basic need?
▶이 법안은 시대적 요구에 부합하는 것이다 This bill meets the needs of the times.
▶자네의 요구는 들어줄 수가 없네 I cannot comply with your request.
▶그는 우리의 요구를 받아들였다[거절했다] He accepted [turned down] our demand.
—요구하다 demand; claim 《damages》; require; request; call 《for》; call upon 《*sb* to do》; ask [make a demand] for 《money》

<blockquote>解說 ***demand***와 ***claim***은 「당연한 권리로서 요구하다」인데 보다 강하고 명령적으로 요구하는 것이 demand이다. ***require***는 규칙·의무상 당연하고 필요한 것을 요구하다, ***ask***는 위에서 말한 것보다 부드러운 「바라다」「원하다」의 뜻이다.</blockquote>

◆설명을 요구하다 demand an explanation 《from [of] him》 / (사장에게) 승급을 요구하다 ask (the boss) for a pay raise/ …에게 지불을 요구하다 demand payment from [of] *sb* / 손해배상을 요구하다 put in a claim for the damage; claim 《a million won》 for damages
▶나는 빌린 돈을 갚으라고 그에게 편지로 강력하게 요구했다 I wrote a strong letter demanding that he return the loan.
▶학교는 학생들에게 제복을 입도록 요구했다 The school required the students to wear uniform. ⇌ The school required that the students (《美》 should) wear uniforms.
▶우리의 몸은 언제나 물을 요구한다 Our body always needs waters.
▶그녀는 그 보험회사에 지불을 요구했다 She filed a claim with insurance company.
▶그는 내게 아무것도 요구하지 않았다 He never asked me for anything.
▶그들은 총리에게 사임할 것을 요구했다 They called upon the prime minister to resign.
▶그는 우리에게 곧 떠나라고 요구했다 He demanded that we (should) leave at once.
▶그 배우는 계약 조건으로 주역을 요구했다 The actor stipulated that he should take the lead.

요구르트 yog(h)urt
요구불 要求拂 ■—어음 a note [bill] on

요귀 妖鬼 a demon ⇨ 요괴

요금 料金 a charge; a fee; a rate; 〈탈것의〉 fare; 〈유료도로 등의〉 a toll
♦요금을 내다 pay a charge [rate] / 요금을 받다 charge; make a charge 《for admission》 / 요금을 받지 않다 make no charge 《for》 / 요금을 올리다[내리다] raise [lower] the charge [rate] / 요금을 징수하다 collect fees [rates, charges]
▶배달에는 약간의 요금이 붙습니다 There is a nominal charge for the delivery.
▶이것은 사용하는 것만으로는 요금은 없습니다 Mere use of this is free of charge.
▶도시가스와 수도 요금이 많아서 걱정입니다 We suffer from the high cost of city gas and water.
▶학생은 특별히 싼 요금으로 영화를 볼 수가 있습니다 Students can see movies at a special low fee.
▶지하철의 최저요금은 400원입니다 The minimum subway fare is four hundred won.
■가스[전기, 전화]— the gas [power, telephone] rate 우편— postal charges [rates] 입장— an admission fee 택시[버스]— a taxi [bus] fare 특별— an extra charge ■—별납 charges paid separately : 요금 별납으로 100통의 편지를 부쳤다 I mailed a hundred letters postpaid. —인상[인하] a raise [reduction] of the charge [rate]; 《美》 a charge hike [cut] —징수소 a tollgate; a tollhouse; a tollbooth —표 a tariff; a list [table] of charges; a price list

요기 妖氣 a weird [ghostly] air
▶이 방에는 요기가 서려 있었다 There was something ghostly in the room.

요기하다 療飢— satisfy one's appetite 《on potatoes》; appease [alleviate, allay] one's hunger; stay [stave off] hunger
▶우리는 사과로 요기했다 We allayed our hunger with some apples.

요긴 要緊 essential importance
—요긴하다 essentially important; of vital importance; vital; indispensable 《to》
♦요긴한 때에 when badly needed; at a critical moment
▶이것이 가장 요긴한 점이다 This is the key [most important] point.
▶돈을 빌려주셔서 정말 요긴하게 썼습니다 Thank you for the money you lent me — it was a great help to me.
■—목 〈길목의〉 a critical position [place, point]

요나서 —書 〔聖〕 (The Book of) Jonah

요녀 妖女 an enchantress; a temptress ⇨ 요부 (妖婦)

요다음 next; next time; another time ♦요다음 토요일에 next Saturday; on Saturday next
▶요다음에 가기로 하자 Let's go there some other time.

요담 要談 an important talk [conference]
♦요담중이다 be in an important discussion [talk]
▶사장님은 지금 요담중이십니다 The president is now having an important business meeting.
—요담하다 have an important talk 《with sb on sth》
▶두 나라 외상이 모종의 외교문제로 요담했다 The Foreign Ministers had important talks on some diplomatic question pending between the two countries.

요도 尿道 〔解〕 the urethra [ju(ə)riːθrə] 《pl. ~s, -thrae》
■—검사 urethroscopy —경 a urethroscope —관 the urethral canal —염 〔醫〕 urethritis; inflammation of the urethra —협착 stricture of the urethra

요독증 尿毒症 〔醫〕 uremia; urine [uremic] poisoning

요동 搖動 shaking;〈배의 전후의〉pitching;〈좌우의〉rolling;〈수레의〉jolting
▶배의 요동이 그치지 않았다 The boat kept pitching [rolling].
—요동하다 tremble; shake; quake; wobble; 〈수레가〉jolt;〈배가〉pitch and roll; rock
▶배는 전후좌우로 심하게 요동했다 Our ship rolled and pitched heavily.

요들 〈알프스 지방의 민요〉 a yodel ♦요들을 부르다 yodel a song ■—가수 a yodeler

요란 搖亂·擾亂 uproar; clamor; a tumult; a commotion; disorders; disturbance
—요란하다 noisy; loud; boisterous; uproarious; clamorous; tumultuous
♦요란한 반대의 소리 an uproar [a loud clamor] against 《the measure》; 《arouse》 stormy opposition 《to》/ 요란하게; noisily clamorously / 요란하게 떠들다 clamor; make much noise
▶국민은 정부에 요란하게 항의했다 The public protested loudly against the government.
▶아이들은 요란하게 떠들며 전차에 올라탔다 The children got on the train making a noise [noisy].
▶구급차가 요란하게 사이렌을 울리며 거리를 달려갔다 An ambulance ran through the street with the siren wailing furiously.

요람 要覽 a survey;〈안내서〉an outline; a handbook ■회사— a general survey of a company

요람 搖籃 a cradle; a swinging cot
♦요람을 흔들다 rock 《a child》 in a cradle
▶애기를 요람에 재워주세요 Please put the baby in the cradle.
▶복지국가에서는 요람에서 무덤까지 생활이 보장된다 In a welfare state the people are guaranteed security from (the) cradle to (the) grave.
■—기[시대] the cradle; the infancy —지 the cradle; the place of origin; the birthplace : 문명의 요람지 the cradle of civilization

요략 要略 a summary ⇨ 요약

요량 料量 〈생각하여 헤아림〉 an idea; a thought; a plan; an intention; 〈판단〉 judgment; discretion
♦요량없는 말[짓] an absurd remark [act] / 요량없다 lack common sense; be absurd [crazy] / 삼촌을 만날 요량으로 with the intention of seeing one's uncle

▶ 모든 것이 그 사람의 요량에 맡겨져 있었다 Everything was left to his own discretion.
▶ 그 일의 해결은 그의 요량으로 가능하다 It is within his discretion to settle the matter.
—요량하다 plan out; use *one's* discretion; consider carefully

요령 要領 1 〈요점〉 the point; the gist; the sum and substance; 〈개요〉 an outline; 〈요지〉 the purport; the import
♦ 요령있는 강의 a pointed lecture / 요령있게 말하다 speak to the point
▶ 그의 설명은 간결하고도 요령이 있었다 His explanation was brief and to the point.
▶ 그의 대답은 요령이 없다 His answer is off the point.
▶ 그가 하는 말은 요령이 없다 His speech is pointless. ⇒ His remark do not come to the point.
▶ 그 사건에 관해 요령있게 얘기해라 Tell me the gist of the case.
2 〈비결·기교〉 a knack; the trick; tack; (口) the hang; (美) know-how
♦ 사람을 다루는 요령 the art of handling people / 요령이 필요하다 require tact [skill] / 요령을 알다 have a knack 《at, for》 / 요령을 터득하다 get the hang [knack] 《of》
▶ 조사 요령은 그가 설명해 줄 것입니다 He will brief us on how to investigation.
▶ 곧 그 기계의 조작요령을 알게 될거다 You'll get the knack [hang] of operating the machine soon.
▶ 그는 그 일을 요령있게 했다 He did the job efficiently. ⇒ He was efficient in doing the job.
▶ 그녀는 어떤 일을 하든 요령이 없다 She is clumsy in everything.
▶ 그는 요령이 좋은[없는] 놈이다 He is a smooth [clumsy] fellow.

요령 搖鈴 a handbell

요령부득 要領不得 pointless; impertinency
▶ 그의 말은 언제나 요령부득이다 What he says is always not to the point. ⇒ His statement is always ambiguous.
—요령부득하다 pointless; vague; ambiguous; impertinent; noncommittal
♦ 요령부득한 말을 하다 speak beside the purpose; say nothing to the purpose [point]
▶ 그는 언제나 요령부득한 대답만 한다 He always gives evasive [noncommittal] answers.

요로 尿路 the urinary tract

요로 要路 1 〈길〉 the principal road; an important road; a main artery 《of traffic》
♦ 교통의 요로에 있다 be in the main traffic artery / 국내 교통의 요로다 be an important road in the internal communication
2 〈지위〉 an important post [position]; an influential post; high office; 〈당국〉 the authorities
♦ 요로의 고관 a high-ranking official / 요로의 사람들 those in (high) authority / 요로에 있다 occupy [hold] an important position; be in authority

요르단 Jordan; 〈공식명〉 the Hashemit Kingdom of Jordan ♦ 요르단의 Jordanian

■—강 the (River) Jordan —사람 a Jordanian

요리 料理 1 〈음식 만들기〉 cooking; 〈요리법〉 cookery; 〈나라·지방 특유의〉 cuisine; 〈음식〉 food; a dish 《*pl.* ~es》
♦ 가벼운 요리 a light meal; a snack / 쇠고기와 야채의 요리 a dish of beef and vegetables / 맛있는 요리 a nice [delicious] dish / 정성들여 만든 요리 an elaborate dish / 야외요리 cook out / 1인분의 요리 a plate / 서양 요리를 먹다 eat Western food [dishes] / 요리를 준비하다 prepare a dish / 요리를 내놓다 serve dishes / 한국 요리를 먹다 have a Korean meal
▶ 그녀는 요리 솜씨가 뛰어나다[나쁘다] She is a good [poor, bad] cook. ⇒ She is good [poor, bad] at cooking.
▶ 이것이 내가 좋아하는 요리다 This is my favorite dishes.
▶ 어머니가 요리의 비결을 가르쳐 주셨다 My mother taught me the secrets of cooking [how to cook].
▶ 이 요리는 맛이 없다 The cooking is bad.
▶ 그 호텔의 요리는 뛰어나다 The cuisine of that hotel is good.
▶ 그 요리는 품절입니다 That dish is off.
▶ 요리가 다 되었다 The dishes are ready. ⇒ Dinner is ready.
▶ 이 종류의 생선은 요리가 어렵다 It's hard to cook this kind of fish. ⇒ This kind of fish doesn't cook well.
▶ 저 음식점은 맛있는 요리를 내놓는다 They serve good food at that restaurant.
▶ 그는 스스로 요리를 한다 He cooks his own meals.
▶ 젊은 여자는 프랑스 요리를 좋아한다 Young girls like [are fond of] French food [dishes, cuisine].
—요리하다 cook; do the cooking; prepare; (美 口) fix; dress

해설 (1) **cook**은 열을 가해 조리하는 것이므로 cook salad라는 표현은 안된다. 그러나 **prepare**, **fix**는 가열하는 요리나 가열하지 않는 요리에 다 쓰이며, **dress**는 내장을 빼내고 토막을 내어 요리하는 것을 말한다.
(2) cook에 따르는 요리법에는 다음과 같은 것이 있다: boil (찌다, 삶다, 데치다), fry (프라이팬을 사용해 기름으로 볶다, 튀기다), deep-fry (기름을 많이 넣고 튀기다), bake (빵, 케이크 같은 것을 오븐 등에 굽다), toast (이미 만들어져 있는 빵 등을 가볍게 굽다), grill (고기 등을 석쇠, 철판 위에서 굽다), roast (오븐 또는 불에 굽다).

♦ 생선을 요리하다 cook fish; dress fish / 구워 [석쇠에 올려놓고, 오븐으로] 요리하다 cook by broiling [on a gridiron, in an oven]
2 〈처리〉 handling; management
—요리하다 handle; manage; conduct; defeat
♦ 일을 요리하다 manage the work / 국정을 요리하다 manage [conduct] state affairs; administer the affairs of state
▶ 그는 상대를 간단히 요리했다 He defeated his opponent easily [hands down].
▶ 이 일은 나 혼자서는 도저히 요리할 수 없다 I

요리조리 cannot manage the work alone.
- 고급— haute cuisine 고기[생선, 야채]— a meat [fish, vegetable] dish 서울식— Seoul fare [dishes] 일품— one-course dinner —대 a dressing table; a dresser —도구 a cooker; kitchen [cooking] utensils —법 cookery; cooking; the culinary art; a recipe —사 a cook; (프) a chef —책 a cookbook —학 gastrology —학원 a cooking school

요리조리 this way and that way; here and there
♦ 자동차의 홍수를 요리조리 피해가다 dodge (one's way) through a mass of vehicles / 요리조리 핑계를 대다 make one excuse [pretext] or another; resort to all kinds of excuses / 책임을 요리조리 피하다 be cunning in dodging one's responsibility

요릿집 料理— a restaurant; a cookshop
- 고급— a fashionable restaurant 중국— a Chinese restaurant

요마 妖魔 a specter; a demon ⇨ 요괴(妖怪)

요만큼 this (little) bit; to this small extent
▶ 나는 요만큼밖에 모른다 I know only this much.
▶ 저 사람은 양심이라고는 요만큼도 없다 He hasn't a particle [an ounce] of conscience in him.

요망 妖妄 wickedness; frivolity —요망하다[스럽다] frivolous; capricious; fickle; flippant —요망떨다[부리다] act [behave] frivolously [capriciously]

요망 要望 a cry; a demand (for); 〈소망〉 a desire; a request; 〈희원〉 a wish
♦ 요망에 따라 in compliance with the wishes (of) / 시대의 요망에 따르다 meet the demand of the age / 요망을 들어주다 comply with one's wishes; satisfy what one wants
—요망하다 demand; request; cry for; desire
▶ 국가는 그와 같은 인물을 요망하고 있다 The nation demands men of such type.

요면 凹面 concave; a concave surface; 〈요상(凹狀)〉 concavity ♦ 요면의 concave / 요면이다 be concavely curved
- 경(鏡) a concave mirror

요목 要目 principal [important] items; essential points; 〈적요〉 an epitome; 〈교수의〉 a syllabus (pl. -bi, -buses)
- 교수— a syllabus (of lectures) - 색인 an index of principal items

요물 妖物 〈요사스런 물건〉 an uncanny thing; 〈간악한 사람〉 a wicked [crafty and malicious] person
▶ 여우는 요물이라고 한다 The fox is regarded as a mysterious animal.

요민 饒民 the people of ample means; the well-off [well-to-do] people

요밀하다 要密 〈빈틈없다〉 meticulous; circumspect; 〈세밀하다〉 minute; close; detailed

요번 — this time ⇨ 이번

요법 療法 a remedy; a (method of) treatment; a cure; therapy
- 가정[정신]— home [psychic] treatment : 그는 정신요법을 받고 있다 He is undergoing mental treatment. 민간— a folk remedy 전기— electrotherapy 지압— finger-pressure therapy

요변 妖變 〈괴이쩍은 사건〉 a mystery; a mysterious event; 〈요사스런 행동〉 strange [mysterious, uncanny] behavior
—요변스럽다 strange; suspicious; queer; treacherous; erratic; fishy
—요변떨다[부리다] act [behave, work] suspiciously [strangely]

요부 妖婦 a vamp; an enchantress; a siren; a vampire; 〈탕녀〉 a jilt ♦ 요부형의 여자 a vamp type woman

요부 要部 the principal [important, essential] part ♦ 요부를 이루다 form an important part (of a thing)

요부 腰部 the waist; the hips; the loins; the lumbar region

요사 夭死 an early death ⇨ 요절(夭折)

요사 妖邪 capriciousness; fickleness
—요사하다[스럽다] capricious; fickle; treacherous; weird; uncanny; wicked; evil; vicious; crafty; cunning
—요사떨다[부리다] behave in a capricious [treacherous, wicked] way; act capriciously [treacherously, weirdly]

요사 寮舍 1 a dormitory (for Buddhist monks) 2 〈기숙사〉 a hostel; a dormitory

요사이 now ⇨ 요새

요산 尿酸 〔化〕 uric acid - 염 a urate

요새 〈최근〉 now; nowadays; (in) these days; 〈요즈음〉 recently; lately; of late; a few days ago; 〈요전부터〉 for some days [time] past; these few days
♦ 요새의 경향 recent tendency [trend] / 요새 기온 the current temperature / 요새 청년 the young men of today; today's youth / 요새 학생 기질 the way of thinking of the students of these days / 요새 일어난 일 a recent event
▶ 요새 흔히 볼 수 있는 것들이다 Lots of things are to be met with nowadays.
▶ 요새 어떻게 지내십니까? How are you these days?
▶ 나는 요새 아주 바쁘다 I'm very busy at present [at the moment].
▶ 요새 학생들은 많은 책을 읽지 않는다 The students of today [students today, today's students] don't read many books.
▶ 요새 이곳은 비가 오고 있다 It's raining here now.
▶ 요새 학생들은 상당히 현실적이다 Students of today [nowadays] are considerably materialistic.

요새 要塞 a fortress; a stronghold; fortifications ♦ 하늘의 요새 a flying fortress / 난공불락의 요새 an impregnable fortress / 요새화하다 fortify
▶ 그들은 적의 공격에 대비해 요새를 구축했다 They constructed a fortress to defend themselves from the attack of the enemy.
▶ 두 병사가 요새 입구를 지키고 있었다 Two soldiers guarded the entrance of the fort.
- 사령관 the commander of a fortress - 지(대) a fortified [strategic] zone

요석 尿石 〔醫〕 a urolith; a urinary calculus

요설 饒舌 talkativeness; garrulity —요설하다 become [get] talkative; be garrulous ♦ 요설한 garrulous; loquacious; talkative; chatty ■—가 a talkative person; a chatterbox
요섭 [聖] Joseph
요소 尿素 [化] urea ■—계(計) ureameter —수지(樹脂) urea resins
요소 要所 an important point; [軍] a strategic point ♦ 요소요소에 at important places; at every strategic point / 요소의 방비를 강화하다 fortify strategic positions
▶시의 요소에는 경찰관이 배치되어 있었다 Policemen were posted at key places in the city.
요소 要素 an element; a factor; a requisite ♦ 요소를 이루다 be essential to *sth*; form an important factor [an essential part] of
▶건강은 행복의 요소다 Health is essential to happiness.
▶관용도 사회생활의 한 요소다 Tolerance is another factor in public life.
▶희극에도 비극의 요소는 있다 Even a comic contains some tragic elements.
■—구성— a constituent element; a component (element)
요술 妖術 1 〈마술〉 magic; black art; witchcraft; sorcery
♦ 요술을 걸다 cast [lay, put, set] a spell 《on [upon, over] *sb*》; bind *sb* by a spell / 요술을 부리다 practice sorcery; use magic
2 〈기술(奇術)〉 a juggler's trick; a conjuring trick; jugglery
♦ 요술을 부리다 juggle; play [perform] conjuring tricks / 요술을 잘하다 be good at sleight of hand / 요술로 모자에서 토끼를 꺼내다 conjure a rabbit out of a hat; produce a rabbit from a hat by magic
▶그는 여흥으로 몇가지 요술을 부렸다 He did some juggling for an entertainment.
■—방망이 the Aladin's lamp; a mallet of luck —쟁이 〈마술사〉 a magician; a wizard(남자); a witch(여자); 〈기술사〉 a juggler; a conjurer
요승 妖僧 an evil-working Buddhist priest
요시찰인 要視察人 a person under (close) surveillance; people on a surveillance list [blacklist]
■—명부 a black [surveillance] list
요식 要式 (the necessary) formalities
■—계약[행위] a formal contract [act]
요식업 料食業 restaurant business ■—자 a restaurant owner
요신 妖神 an evil spirit; a demon
요약 要約 a summary (of); condensation; summing up; 〈문학작품 등의〉 an outline; a digest; a résumé
—요약하다 summarize; epitomize; digest; condense; sum up; abridge; (美) brief
♦ 요약하면 to sum up; to make a long story short; in short [brief]; in a word / 요약해 말하다 tell briefly; give the outline (of); sketch / 그 문제를 간결하게 요약하다 sum up the matter briefly
▶그 이론을 요약하면 이렇다 This is a summary of the theory.
▶이 논평을 200자로 요약하십시오 Summarize [Give a summary of] this commentary in two hundred words.
—판 an abridged edition; an abridgment
요양 療養 〈치료〉 (a) medical treatment; 〈병후의〉 recuperation; recruitment
♦ 현재 요양중이다 be now under medical treatment; be now recuperating
▶그는 전지 요양을 갔다 He went away for a change of air.
—요양하다 receive medical treatment; recuperate (*oneself*, *one's* health)
▶의사는 내게 1개월 가량 병원에서 요양하라고 말했다 The doctor told me to receive medical treatment in the hospital for a month or so.
■—병후— convalescence 자택— home treatment; recuperation at home : 그녀는 지금 자택 요양중이다 She is now recuperating at home.
■—비 medical expenses —소 a sanatorium 《*pl.* ~s, -ria》; (美) a sanitarium 《*pl.* ~s, -ria》 —지 a health resort
요언 要言 summarizing the essential points; a summing-up
요업 窯業 the ceramic industry; ceramics
■—가 a ceramist —소 a pottery
요엘서 —書 [聖] (The Book of) Joel
요연하다 瞭然— clear; evident; plain; easy to see
요염 妖艶 voluptuous beauty; sensual charm
—요염하다 fascinating; bewitching; voluptuous; enchanting; charming
♦ 요염한 미소 a bewitching smile / 요염한 미인 a voluptuous beauty / 요염한 여자 a charmer; an alluring woman / 요염한 자태 a charming [bewitching] figure / 요염한 눈길을 보내다 cast a coquettish [voluptuous] glance (at) / 요염하게 보이다 look charming 《in that dress》
▶그녀는 그 요염한 아름다움으로 파티에 있던 사람들의 눈길을 끌었다 Her bewitching beauty held the eye of the people present at the party.
요오드 [化] iodin(e) ■—제 an iodine preparation —팅크 tincture of iodine; iodine tincture —포름 iodoform
요오드화 —化 iodatium —요오드화하다 iodize ■—나트륨 sodium iodide —물 an iodide —아연 zinc iodide —은 silver iodide —칼륨 potassium iodide
요우 僚友 a colleague; a comrade; a fellow worker
요원 要員 workers required; personnel necessary [required] 《for》; (총칭) needed personal
▶기상(機上)에는 일곱 사람의 요원이 있었다 There were seven airline personnel aboard.
■—기간— a skeleton staff; 〈배의〉 a skeleton crew 보안— security personnel : 보안요원은 몇명 필요합니까? How many workers do you require for security?
요원 燎原 〈불이 난 초원〉 a prairie on fire
♦ 요원의 불 a prairie fire; wildfire
▶그 소문은 요원의 불길처럼 퍼졌다 The rumor spread [ran] like a wildfire.

요원하다 遙遠— very far away; (far) distant; remote; far off [away] ◆전도 요원하다 〈사람이 주어〉 have a long way to go; 〈사물이 주어〉 be far [a long way] off
▶우리가 목표에 이르려면 아직 요원하다 We are yet far from our object [goal].

요의 尿意 ◆요의를 느끼다 have a desire to urinate [pass water]

요인 要人 a very important person; a V.I.P. [VIP] 《*pl.* VIPs》 ◆산업계의 요인 a leading [figure] of the industrial world / 재계의 요인 a VIP in the financial world / 정부 요인 key figures in the government

요인 要因 a main [chief] cause; a primary factor [element]; a cause
▶싸움의 요인은 무엇이었습니까? What was the cause of the trouble?
▶성실함이 그가 성공한 최대의 요인이었다 Honesty was the most important factor in his success.

요일 曜日 a day of the week
▶오늘은 무슨 요일입니까? What day (of the week) is it today?
▶오늘은 토요일입니다 It's Saturday today. ⇒ Today is Saturday.
▶요일에 상관없이 놀러오세요 Please come to see me any day of the week.

요전 —前 〈며칠 전〉 the other day; some [a few] time ago; not long ago; 〈최근〉 recently; lately; 〈지난〉 last; before; last time
◆요전의 last; previous; former / 요전 모임 the recent [last] meeting / 요전 편지 *one's* last [previous] letter / 요전부터 for some days [time] past / 바로 요전에 only the other day; quite recently / 요전 일요일 last Sunday; on Sunday last / 요전에 말한 것처럼[바대로] as I told you last time
▶요전에는 실례가 많았습니다 I am sorry I caused you much trouble the other day.
▶요전 일요일에 낚시하러 갔다 I went fishing last Sunday [on Sunday last].
▶요전에 어디서 일했니? Where did you work last?
▶요전에 그를 만났을 때 의기소침해 보였다 When I saw him last [The last time I saw him], he looked depressed.
▶바로 요전에 그의 편지를 받았습니다 I had a letter from him only the other day [only a few days ago].

요절 夭折 an early [a premature, an untimely] death —**요절하다** die young; die at an early age; die prematurely
▶형은 사고 때문에 요절했다 My brother died young because of an accident.

요절나다 1 〈물건이 못쓰게 되다〉 be broken; be wrecked; go [fall] to ruin; be ruined [spoilt]; be damaged; be destroyed
▶내 모자가 요절났다 My hat are worn out.
▶그의 차는 트럭과 충돌해 요절났다 His car has collided with a truck and broken down.
2 〈일이 실패하게 되다〉 be spoiled; be ruined; fall through; go to pot
▶그 계획은 인력부족으로 요절났다 The plan fell through due to the shortage of manpower.
▶지난번의 폭풍으로 모든 계획이 요절났다 The recent storm upset the whole plans.

요절내다 spoil; ruin; upset; mar; destroy; demolish

요절하다 腰絶— hold [shake, split] *one's* sides with laughter; have a sidesplitting laugh; laugh *oneself* into convulsions
▶참, 요절할 노릇이다 It is really sidesplitting. ⇒ How ridiculously amusing!

요점 要點 the gist; the main [essential, vital, principal, crucial] point; the essentials; the pith; the crux
◆문제의 요점 the point of a subject; the essence of a matter / 요점을 말하다 give the gist of 《an account》 / 요점을 벗어나다 wander from [be beside] the point / 요점을 찌르다 hit the (right) nail on the head / 요점을 파악하다 grasp [catch] the point 《of a subject》 / 요점만 간단히 말하다 summarize; recapitulate
▶요점만 말씀해 주십시오 To the point, please.
▶그것은 요점이 없는 얘기다 That is a pointless story.
▶나는 그가 말하는 요점을 모르겠다 I cannot understand [see] what he is talking about.
▶그의 강의는 요점을 파악하기가 어려웠다 It was very difficult to get the point of his lecture.

요정 了定 〈완관〉 (a) decision; (a) settlement; 〈끝마침〉 completion; finish
—**요정나다** 〈끝나다〉 end; be concluded; come to an end; 〈결정되다〉 be decided 《upon》
—**요정짓다** 〈끝내다〉 end; finish; complete; conclude; put an end to; 〈결정짓다〉 decide 《on》

요정 妖精 a fairy; a sprite; an elf 《*pl.* elves》; a spirit; a nymph
◆요정의 fairy; elfin / 물의 요정 a naiad; a (water) nymph / 바다의 요정 an ocean [a sea] nymph / 숲의 요정 a (tree) dryad / 꽃의 요정 sprite of a flower / 요정의 나라 a fairyland; an elfland

요정 料亭 a (Korean style) restaurant; a *kisaeng* house

요주의 要注意 ▶김 선생은 요주의 인물이다 Mr. Kim requires special attention. ⇒ Mr. Kim is black-listed.

요즈음 〈오늘날〉 now; these days; nowadays; 〈최근〉 recently; lately
◆요즈음의 of today; today's; current / 요즈음의 젊은이 the young people of today; young people today [these days]; today's youth / 요즈음의 학생 present-day students; students these days / 요즈음의 교육의 경향 present-day tendencies in education / 요즈음에 일어난 사건 a recent event
▶요즈음엔 물가가 비싸다 Prices are high these days [nowadays].
▶요즈음의 아이들은 안심하고 길에서 놀 수 없다 The children of today [Children today, Present-day children] can't play safely on the street.

▶ 나는 요즈음 그녀와 만나지 못했다 I haven't seen her lately.
▶ 요즈음 세상에 그렇게 욕심없는 사람은 드물다 These days we seldom meet with such an unselfish person. ⇌ Such an unselfish man is rarely to be met with nowadays.
▶ 요즈음 나는 몸이 좋지 않다 Recently I have not been well.

요지 要旨 〈요점〉 the point; the gist; the essentials; the major points; the substance; the amount; 〈취지〉 the purport; the keynote; 〈서적 등의〉 the argument; 〈적요〉 a summary
▶ 이야기의 요지를 알겠습니까? Have you got the gist of the speech?
▶ 그의 연설의 요지는 기독교적 사랑이었다 The keynote of his speech was Christian love.
▶ 나는 질문의 요지를 노트에 적었다 I wrote down the essential points of the questions in my notebook.

요지 要地 an important place; a critical location; a strategic point ◆ 상업상의 요지 a place of great commercial importance

요지경 瑤池鏡 a (device for) peep show [raree-show]; a magic glass
▶ 세상은 요지경속이다 Life is kaleidoscopic.

요지부동 搖之不動 steadfastness
—요지부동이다 stand as firm as rock; be unshakable [steadfast, unyielding]

요직 要職 an important post [office]; a responsible [key] position
▶ 그는 회사의 요직에 임명되었다 He was appointed to an important position in the company.
▶ 그는 중앙정부의 요직에 있다 He holds a responsible post [office] in the central government.

요철 凹凸 unevenness; ruggedness; irregularity ◆ 요철이 있는 rugged; uneven; irregular

요청 要請 a request; a demand; a requirement
▶ 사장의 요청으로 중국에 가게 되었다 I am going to China at the request of the president.
▶ 나는 연설을 해달라는 요청을 받았다 I was called upon to make a speech.
▶ 여기서는 요청을 할 때만 버스가 선다 Buses stop here only by request.
▶ 부부의 맞벌이도 시대의 요청이다 The times demand working in double harness.
▶ 그 법률은 시대의 요청에 부응한다 The law meets the needs of the times.
—요청하다 request; demand; ask [call on] sb for [aid]
▶ 그들은 사장과의 면담을 요청했다 They requested an interview with the president.
▶ 그에게 시장에 출마할 것을 요청했다 We requested [asked] him to run for mayor.

요체 要諦 the secret; the cardinal point
요추 腰椎 〔解〕 the lumbar (vertebra)
요충 要衝 a key point ⇨ 요충지
요충 蟯蟲 〔動〕 a threadworm; a pinworm
요충지 要衝地 a key point; an important position; a place of strategic importance ◆ 변방의 요충지 an outlying post of strategic importance

요컨대 要— in short; in brief; in a word; after all; to sum up; to make a long story short
▶ 요컨대 그에게는 시간이 없다 In short [In a word], he has no time.
▶ 요컨대 이런 것이다 To make a long story short, it's like this.
▶ 요컨대 그는 우리의 적이다 After all [To sum up], he is our enemy.

요탓조탓 with this excuse and that; on some pretext or other

요통 腰痛 〔醫〕 lumbago (pl. ~s)
▶ 나이가 들면 요통을 호소하는 사람이 많다 Many aged people complain of lumbago.

요트 a yacht ◆ 요트를 타다 yacht; cruise in a yacht / 요트를 타러 가다 go yachting ■경주용— a racing yacht / ■—경주 a yachting race; yachting —조종자 a yachtsman

요판 凹版 〈오목판〉 an intaglio (pl. ~s)
■—인쇄 intaglio printing

요포대기 a baby quilt

요하다 要— require; need; want; demand; take; call for
▶ 그 집은 수리를 요한다 The house needs [wants] repairing.
▶ 그것은 세심한 주의를 요하는 문제다 The matter demands [calls for] close attention.

요한복음 —福音 The Gospel according to St. John

요함 僚艦 a consort; a comrade vessel
요항 要港 a strategic port; an important harbor ▶ 그곳은 그 나라 북부의 유일한 요항이다 It is the only strategic port in the northern part of the country.

요항 要項 the essential points; the essentials; 〈개요〉 the gist; an outline
▶ 노트에 요항을 적어 두시오 Write down the points in your notebook.
■지시— the essential points for guidance

요해(처) 要害(處) a key point ⇨ 요충(지)
◆ 지중해의 요해 지브롤터 Gibraltar, the key to the Mediterranean

요행 僥倖 (good) luck; good fortune; a lucky chance; a fluke; a godsend; a windfall
◆ 요행히[으로] by (a stroke of good) luck; luckily; by good fortune / 요행을 바라고 on the off [outside] chance / 요행을 바라다 rely on chance; lean on a false hope
▶ 그는 요행으로 합격했다 He passed the examinations by a lucky fluke [by a freak of chance].
▶ 물론 요행으로 맞은 거다 Of course, it is only a hit by chance [a chance hit]. ⇌ It is nothing but a fluke, no doubt.

요행수 僥倖數 a lucky stroke; a chance hit; a fluke ◆ 요행수로 이기다 win by a fluke

요혈 尿血 〔醫〕 bloody urine; hematuria

욕 辱 1 〈욕설〉 abuse; abusive [foul] language; curses; a swearword
▶ 그는 우리에게 욕을 마구 퍼부었다 He hurled a storm of curses at us. ⇌ He heaped all sorts of abuse upon us.
▶ 그런 욕을 한다고 기죽지 마라 Don't be discouraged with such abuse.
—욕하다 speak ill [evil] of; call sb names;

욕

abuse; swear 《at》; use abusive language 《against》
▶ 뒤에서 남을 욕하는 것은 좋지 않다 It's no good to speak ill of others behind their backs.
2 〈치욕〉 shame; disgrace; humiliation; insult; 〈능욕〉 rape
♦욕을 달게 받다 eat humble pie / 욕을 보이다 put *sb* to shame
3 〈수고〉 trouble(s); hardship(s); pains
♦욕을 보다 have a hard time

욕慾·欲 a desire; a thirst; an appetite
♦권세욕 the will to power / 금전욕 love of money / 명예욕 a desire for fame / 소유욕 a desire to possess / 지식욕 a thirst [an appetite] for knowledge

욕가마리 辱— a person deserving of abuse
욕감태기 辱— a butt of abuse
욕객 浴客 〈대중탕의〉 a bather; 〈온천장의〉 a visitor at a spa
욕계 欲界 [佛敎] the world of desires
욕구 欲求 want(s); (a) desire [wish] 《for》; craving 《for》; an urge 《to do》
♦생의 욕구 the will to live / 성적 욕구 sexual desire / 생리적 욕구를 채우다 satisfy one's natural urge
▶ 그녀는 지적 욕구가 강하다 She has a strong desire to learn.
▶ 나는 뭔가 나의 욕구를 충족시켜 줄 만한 것을 찾고 있다 I'm looking for something that satisfies my wants.
■—불만 [心] frustration; unsatisfied desires

욕기 慾氣 greediness; covetousness
♦욕기 부리다 covet; be covetous [avaricious]; be greedy 《for》
▶ 웬 욕기가 그리 많나 How covetous you are!
▶ 너무 욕기 부리지 마라 You must not be so grasping [avaricious].

욕념 欲念 (a) desire; wish(es); passions
욕되다 辱— be a disgrace [dishonor, shame] 《to》; bring disgrace [shame] upon *oneself*
▶ 욕되게 사느니 죽는 편이 낫다 I would rather die than be disgraced. ⇌ I don't want to live in disgrace.
▶ 그것은 네 가문을 욕되게 하는 짓이 된다 You will disgrace [shame] your family if you do anything like that.

욕망 欲望 a desire; an appetite; a craving; an ambition; [經] wants
♦「욕망이라는 이름의 전차」 *A Streetcar Named Desire* / 마음속에 있는 사악한 욕망 an evil desire in one's heart / 욕망을 채우다[억제하다] satisfy [suppress] one's desire / 욕망을 품다 harbor an ambition
▶ 그의 욕망을 다 채워줄 수는 없다 It is impossible to fully gratify [satisfy] his desires.

욕먹다 辱— **1** 〈욕설을 듣다〉 be abused; be reviled; be called (bad [rough]) names
2 〈악평을 받다〉 have one's name scandalized; be stigmatized; be spoken ill of; 〈신문 등에서〉 be criticized unfavorably; be attacked
▶ 그는 욕먹을 짓을 했다 His conduct deserves criticism.

욕보다 辱— **1** 〈고생하다〉 have trouble; have a hard time (of it); undergo [suffer] hardships; take pains
▶ 범인을 잡느라고 욕봤다 I had a hard time hunting up the culprit.
▶ 그동안 욕봤네 Many thanks for your trouble. ⇌ I thank you for your kind labor. ⇌ You have done a fine job!
2 〈치욕을 당하다〉 be put to shame; disgrace *oneself*; be humiliated [disgraced, dishonored, insulted]
▶ 그는 욕보느니 차라리 죽음을 택했다 He preferred death to dishonor.
3 〈능욕당하다〉 be raped; be violated; be outraged

욕보이다 辱— **1** 〈치욕을 주다〉 disgrace; dishonor; humiliate; insult; put *sb* to shame
♦가문을 욕보이다 bring disgrace upon (the name of) one's family
2 〈능욕하다〉 violate; outrage; rape
3 〈폐를 끼치다〉 put *sb* to trouble; give *sb* trouble

욕설 辱說 abuse; abusive language; slander; curses; swearwords
▶ 모두가 그녀에게 욕설을 퍼부었다 All the people gave her much abuse. ⇌ All the people heaped abuse upon her.
—**욕설하다** abuse; swear 《at》; revile; use abusive language 《to, against》
♦서로 욕설하다 call each other names

욕실 浴室 〈목욕실〉 a bathroom; a bath; (美) a toilet (room) ♦욕실이 있다 be furnished with a bathroom

욕심 慾心 greed; avarice; cupidity; desire
♦욕심이 나서 from selfish motives; out of greed; guided by self-interest / 욕심을 부려 avariciously; covetously / 욕심(이) 많다[사납다] be avaricious; be grasping; be selfish / 욕심이 없다 be unselfish; be disinterested; be simple / 욕심에 눈이 멀다 be blinded by love of gain; be ruled by avarice
▶ 욕심이 지나치면 다 잃는다 Grasp all, lose all.
▶ 그는 욕심 덩어리다 He is the incarnation of avarice. ⇌ He is greed(iness) itself.
▶ 남의 것에 욕심 내지 마라 Do not covet things which belong to others.
▶ 아버지는 욕심이 없는 분이셨다 My father was a man of few wants. ⇌ My father was far from selfish.
▶ 수전노는 돈에 악착같이 욕심 낸다 A miser lusts after [for] gold.
▶ 욕심 같아서는 그의 키가 조금 더 컸으면 싶다 I wish he were a little taller.
■—**쟁이[꾸러기]** an avaricious person; a grasping person; a grabber; (美) a grab-all

욕의 浴衣 a bathrobe; a bath gown
욕쟁이 辱— a foul-mouthed[-tongued] person; a slanderer; (美俗) a knocker
욕정 欲情 passion; sexual desire
욕조 浴槽 a bathtub; a bath ♦욕조에 몸을 담그다 have [take] a bath; bathe *oneself* in the bathtub

욕지거리 辱— abuse; abusive language (⇨ 욕설) —**욕지거리하다** curse
욕지기 nausea; qualm; queasiness; retch; a

sickly feeling; sickness at the stomach
♦욕지기 나는 냄새 a nauseous [sickening] smell / 욕지기가 날 정도로 to a sickening degree; revoltingly / 욕지기(가) 나다 feel nausea; feel sick [sickish]; (美) feel queasy / 욕지기 나게 하다 make *sb* sick at the stomach; provoke [cause] nausea
▶ 조개를 날로 먹는다고 생각하니 욕지기가 난다 The idea of eating raw shellfish nauseates me.
▶ 보기만 해도 욕지기가 난다 The mere sight of it makes me sick [turns my stomach].

욕창 褥瘡 a bedsore
욕탕 浴湯 a bath ⇨ 목욕탕
욕화 浴化 the influence of virtue; moral influence ―욕화하다 be influenced [reformed] by virtuous examples
욕화 欲火 〔佛敎〕 burning [ardent] desire; a flame of desire
욥기 —記 〔聖〕 (The Book of) Job
옷속 batting [wadding] for a mattress
옷잇 a sheet-covering (for a mattress)
용 茸 an antler ⇨ 녹용
용 龍 a dragon ♦용이 구름을 얻은 듯하다 be in *one's* element
▶ 개천에서 용 난다 (속담) A great person may rise from humble family.
▶ 미꾸라지 용 됐다 (속담) He has come a long way from rags to riches [from a small fly to a big shot].

-용 -用 for (the use of)
♦가정용 비누 soap for home use / 수출용 도자기 chinaware for export / 여자[남자]용 장갑 gloves for ladies [gentlemen]; ladies' [gentlemen's] gloves / 어린이용 건전 영화 a wholesome moving picture for children
▶ 이 수건은 손님용이다 These towels are for the guests.
▶ 이것은 중학생용 사전이다 This is a dictionary for the use of junior high school students.

용감 勇敢 bravery; valor; gallantry ―용감하다 brave; gallant; valiant; courageous
▶ 그는 조국을 위해 용감하게 싸웠다 He fought bravely for his country.
▶ 그의 용감한 행위는 모든 사람의 칭찬을 받았다 His gallant [brave, heroic] deed was applauded by everybody.

용건 用件 business; a matter (of business)
▶ 용건을 말씀하십시오 Come to the point, please.
▶ 아버지는 급한 용건으로 출타하셨습니다 My father went out on urgent business.

용골 龍骨 〈화석〉 mastodon bones; 〈선골(船骨)〉 the keel
용공 容共 pro-communist ■―사상 pro-communist thought ―정책 ((take up)) a pro-communist policy
용광로 鎔鑛爐 a smelting [blast] furnace
용구 用具 a tool; an instrument; an implement
▶ 이 용구는 작은 구멍을 뚫는 데 적합하다 This tool is suitable for making a small hole.
■ 교육― teaching aids 운동― sporting goods
용궁 龍宮 the Dragon King's Palace

용기 用器 an instrument; a tool ■―화(畵) instrumental [mechanical] drawing
용기 勇氣 courage; valor; bravery
♦용기 있는 사람 a courageous [brave, plucky] man; a man of courage / 용기 없는 사람 a coward / 용기가 꺾이다 be discouraged; lose courage / 용기가 나다 be encouraged (at, by); take heart / 용기를 꺾다 discourage; dispirit; unnerve / 용기를 내다 screw [pluck, muster] up *one's* courage; take [collect] courage [heart]
▶ 그는 용기를 잃었다 His heart [courage] failed him.
▶ 용기있는 사람만이 미인을 얻을 자격이 있다 (속담) None but the brave deserve the fair.
▶ 다시 해볼 용기가 안 난다 I am discouraged from trying again.
▶ 나에게는 그의 잘못을 지적할 용기가 없다 I don't have the courage [heart] to point out his mistake.
▶ 한번 실패했다고 용기를 잃으면 안된다 You mustn't lose heart [be discouraged] just because you failed once.
▶ 용기를 내서 최후까지 싸우시오 Muster up your courage and fight to the last.
▶ 그의 말에 우리는 용기 백배했다 His words inspired us with redoubled courage.

용기 容器 a vessel; a receptacle; a container
용기병 龍騎兵 a dragoon
용꿈 龍― a lucky dream; a dream about a dragon ♦용꿈(을) 꾸다 dream [have] a lucky dream; dream [have a dream] about a dragon
용납 容納 toleration; permission; admission; allowance; approval; 〈용서〉 pardon; forgiveness ―용납하다 permit; admit; tolerate; allow; approve; pardon; forgive
♦용납할 수 없는 unpardonable; intolerable / 지연을 용납하지 않다 admit of no delay
▶ 그 누구도 내 앞에서 그를 비난하는 것을 용납하지 않겠다 No one is going to criticize him in my presence.

용녀 傭女 〈하녀〉 a maidservant
용녀 龍女 〈용왕의 딸〉 the Princess of the Dragon King
용뇌 龍腦 〔藥〕 camphol; borneol
용단 勇斷 a decisive [resolute, drastic] measure; a courageous decision
♦용단을 내리다 take a resolute [decisive] step; make a (manly) resolution; decide courageously
▶ 관계 당국의 용단이 기대된다 The authorities concerned are expected to take drastic measures.
▶ 사장의 용단으로 그는 해고를 면했다 He escaped being fired thanks to the president's decision.

용달 用達 delivery; delivery [messenger] service ―용달하다 deliver ((goods, messages))
■―사 a delivery agency ―업 the delivery business ―차 a delivery van
용담 龍膽 〔植〕 a gentian; an autumn bellflower
용도 用度 supplies; expenditure

용도 用途 a use; service
▶ 석유는 용도가 다양하다 Oil has various uses. ⇌ Oil is used for many purposes. ⇌ Oil is useful in various ways.
▶ 이 빈 상자의 용도를 알아 보시오 Find a use for this empty box.
▶ 용도를 알아야 돈을 주든지 말든지 하지 Whether I'll give you money or not depends on what it is for.

용돈 用— pocket money; spending money; an allowance; 〈아내·딸 등에게 주는〉 pin money ◆용돈을 벌기 위해 일하다 do an odd job to earn some money for *one's* own petty expenses / 자식에게 용돈을 주다 allow *one's* child pocket money
▶ 나는 매달 십 만원씩 용돈을 받고 있다 I receive a monthly allowance of 100,000 won. ⇌ I get a hundred thousand won a month for pocket money. ⇌ My monthly allowance is a hundred thousand won.
▶ 그는 용돈을 벌기 위해 아르바이트를 한다 He works part time for spending money.
▶ 그는 용돈으로 아내에게 줄 선물을 샀다 He bought a present for his wife out of his own pocket.

용두 龍頭 〈시계의〉 a (winding) crown; a stem ◆용두로 감는 시계 a stem-winding watch; a stem-winder; 〈英〉 a keyless watch

용두사미 龍頭蛇尾 bright beginning and dull finish; an anticlimax; much cry and little wool; a tame ending
▶ 그의 연설은 용두사미로 끝났다 His speech started well and ended in a fiasco. ⇌ His speech failed miserably after a good start.
▶ 그 영화는 용두사미로 끝났다 The film's last scene was an anticlimax.

용두질 masturbation

용략 勇略 courage and strategy; bravery and artifice

용량 用量 〈약의〉 dosage; 〈1회의〉 a dose

용량 容量 capacity; content; volume
◆용량 2 리터들이 병 a bottle with the capacity of two liters /…의 용량을 재다 gauge (a cask); measure the capacity (of)
■ 열[전기]— thermal [electric] capacity
■ —분석 〈부피 분석〉〔化〕 volumetric analysis (*pl.* -ses)

용력 勇力 manly strength; undaunted power; fearless [dauntless] vigor; valor and strength ◆용력이 대단하다 be very powerful and strong

용렬하다 庸劣— mediocre; commonplace; foolish; stupid ◆용렬한 사람 a foolish fellow / 용렬한 짓을 하다 do a very stupid thing; act foolishly

용례 用例 an example; an illustration
▶ 이 동사가 어떻게 쓰이는지 용례를 하나 들어 주시오 Give me an example of how this verb is used.

용립 聳立 rising aloft; soaring; towering
—용립하다 rise aloft; tower (up); soar

용마 龍馬 a swift horse; a fleet steed

용마루 the ridge (of a roof)

용마름 ridge thatch; straw thatch for the ridge

용매 溶媒 〔化〕 a solvent; a dissolvent

용맹 勇猛 bravery; intrepidity; dauntlessness; valor; pluck
—용맹하다 intrepid; undaunted; dauntless; plucky; valiant; lionhearted

용맹스럽다 勇猛— intrepid

용맹심 勇猛心 a dauntless spirit; intrepid courage ◆용맹심을 불러 일으키다 be inspired with courage

용명 勇名 fame for *one's* bravery ◆용명을 떨치다 be famous for *one's* bravery; win fame as a brave man

용명 溶明 〔映·TV〕 a fade-in ◆용명이 되다 fade in

용모 容貌 looks; features; the face; (personal) appearance; (a) countenance
◆용모가 아름다운 여자 a beauty; a good-looking woman / 용모에 자신이 있는 여자 a girl proud of her (own) good looks [personal beauty] / 용모가 추한 사람 an ugly [ill-favored] person / 용모가 괴이한 사람 a man of imposing appearance; a man with an impressive face
▶ 그의 용모가 마음에 안 든다 I don't like the look of him.
▶ 용모보다 마음씨 (속담) Handsome is as [that] handsome does.

용무 用務 business (to attend to); a thing to do ◆급한 용무로 on urgent business
▶ 무슨 용무로 오셨습니까? What is your business here? ⇌ What business have you here?
▶ 급한 용무가 있어서 늦었다 I was late on account of urgent business.
▶ 회사 용무로 부산에 갔다 I went to Pusan on the business of the firm.
▶ 그는 중요한 용무로 출발했다 He started on some important business.

용법 用法 (the) use 《of》; how to use; (a) usage; the directions (for use)
◆전치사의 용법 uses of prepositions / 용법을 그르치다 misuse; make a wrong use 《of》 / 용법을 모르다 do not know how to use / 용법을 잘 알고 있다 be familiar with the use 《of》 / 정해진 용법을 지키다 follow the directions
▶ 그는 전치사의 용법을 정확하게 가르쳐 주었다 He taught us how to use prepositions correctly.

용변 用便 ◆용변 후 after stool / 용변(을) 보다 go to stool; go to the lavatory [bathroom, restroom]; relieve *oneself*; ease nature; wash *one's* hands

용병 用兵 tactics; manipulation of troops
◆용병에 능하다 be well versed in tactics
—용병하다 manipulate [maneuver] the troops ■ —술 tactics; the science of war

용병 傭兵 a mercenary (soldier); a hired soldier

용부 勇夫 a brave [courageous] man

용부 庸夫 a mediocrity; a mediocre [an inferior] man

용불용설 用不用說 〔生〕 the theory of use and disuse; Lamarckism

용비 冗費 unnecessary [wasteful, useless]

expenses

용사 勇士 a brave man [soldier]; a man of courage; a hero (*pl.* ~es); (총칭) the brave ◆ 역전의 용사 an experienced soldier / 용사중의 용사 the bravest of the brave / 하늘의 용사 an air ace; an intrepid flyer [flier]

용상 龍床 the king's seat; the (royal) throne

용색 用色 sexual intercourse; performance of a sexual act —용색하다 have sexual intercourse; (口) have sex

용색 容色 features; (good) looks; personal appearance
▶ 그녀의 용색도 언젠가는 쇠한다 Her personal beauty [charming features] will fade sooner or later.
▶ 그녀의 용색이 예전만 못하다 She is not so beautiful as before.

용서 容恕 pardon; forgiveness; mercy; allowance ◆ 용서 없는 merciless; unsparing / 용서 없이 without mercy; mercilessly / 용서를 받다 find pardon / 용서를 빌다 ask for pardon; beg *one's* pardon
—용서하다 pardon; forgive; excuse; have mercy on *sb*; 〈눈감아주다〉 overlook; pass over ◆ 용서하지 못할 말 an unforgivable remark
▶ 너의 행위는 용서할 수 없다 What you have done is unpardonable.
▶ 아무쪼록 용서해 주십시오 I humbly beg your pardon.
▶ 대접이 소홀했던 점을 용서하십시오 I hope you will pardon us for our poor service.
▶ 이번만은 너의 무례를 용서해 주마 This time I will excuse your bad manners.
▶ 서로 용서하고 우리가 한 일을 잊어 버리자 Let's forgive each other and forget what we have done.

용선 傭船 chartering; 〈배〉 a chartered ship [vessel] —용선하다 charter [let, hire] a ship ■—계약 charter; chartering —계약서 a charter (party) —료 charterage; charter money —자 a charterer

용설란 龍舌蘭 〈植〉 an agave; a pita

용소 龍沼 the basin [bottom] of a waterfall

용속하다 庸俗— mediocre; banal; commonplace; vulgar

용솟음 湧— 〈끓어 오름〉 boiling; seething; bubbling up; 〈분출〉 gush; leaping; gushing out —용솟음하다 ⇨ 용솟음치다

용솟음치다 湧— boil; seethe; bubble up; gush out ◆ 피가 용솟음치는 것을 느끼다 feel the bounding blood in *one's* veins / 피가 용솟음치게 하다 cause the blood to tingle; inflame the blood (of); stir *one's* blood
▶ 그 바위 틈에서 수정같이 맑은 물이 용솟음치고 있다 Crystal-clear water is welling from a crevice of the rock.

용수 a rice-wine [soy-sauce] strainer ◆ 용수 지르다 put a strainer into fermented rice wine [soy sauce] ■—뒤 the last of the wine; wine dregs

용수 用水 1 〈상수도〉 service water; city water; 〈관개용의〉 water for irrigation; 〈허드렛물〉 water for sundry [miscellaneous] uses 2 〈물을 씀〉 the use of water ■ 공업[농업]— water for industrial [agricultural] use; industrial [agricultural] water ■—로 〈관개용의〉 an irrigation canal [channel]; 〈발전용·목재를 띄워 보내는〉 a flume

용수철 龍鬚鐵 a spring
▶ 이 인형은 용수철로 움직인다 This doll moves if you wind it up.
▶ 그는 용수철로 움직이는 장난감을 가지고 놀았다 He played with a toy worked by a spring.
■—저울 a spring balance

용신 容身 1 〈몸을 놀림〉 moving (around) —용신하다 move *one's* body; stir
▶ 방이 좁아서 용신할 수도 없다 The room is so narrow that I can't even move.
2 〈겨우 살아감〉 a scanty livelihood —용신하다 eke out *one's* living

용신 龍神 the Dragon God ⇨ 용왕 ■—제 the Dragon God festival

용심 〈심술〉 ill will; malice; spite ◆ 용심 부리다 be cross with *sb*; wreak *one's* spite [jealousy] ■—꾸러기[쟁이] a malicious [spiteful] person

용심 用心 concentration of the mind; care; attention; precaution —용심하다 take care 《of》; be cautious 《of》; devote [pay] *one's* attention 《to》 ◆ 화재에 대해 용심하다 exercise the reasonable care against fires

용쓰다 1 〈힘쓰다〉 put forth *one's* energy at a time; exert *one's* utmost strength; strain [exert] *oneself*; concentrate *one's* energy 2 〈참다〉 force *oneself* to bear up under stress

용안 龍眼 〈植〉 a longan ■—육(肉) longan

용안 龍顏 the king's [royal] countenance ◆ 용안을 배알하다 be received in audience by His Majesty [the king, the emperor]

용암 溶暗 〈映·TV〉 a fade-out ◆ 용암이 되다 fade out

용암 熔岩 lava
▶ 저 화산에서는 때때로 용암이 흘러나온다 Sometimes lava flows out from that volcano. ■—대지 a lava plateau —류 a stream of lava; a lava flow —층 a lava bed

용액 溶液 a solution
◆ 묽은 용액 a weak [dilute] solution / 진한 용액 a strong [concentrated] solution

용약 勇躍 high spirits; elation; exultation
◆ 용약 장도에 오르다 go on an expedition in high spirits / 용약 진격을 시작하다 launch a spirited attack —용약하다 be spirited; be in high spirits; be encouraged 《by》

용어 用語 〈술어〉 terminology; a term; 〈말씨〉 wording; diction; phraseology; language; 〈어휘〉 (a) vocabulary
▶ 자네는 용어에 좀 더 신경을 써야겠어 You should be more careful about your wording [diction].
▶ 우리 선생님은 용어에 까다로우시다 Our teacher is particular about his choice of words.
▶ 이것을 의학 용어로 뭐라고 합니까? What is the medical term for this?
■ 관청— official language 법률— legal terms

전문[학술]— technical [scientific] terms

용언 用言 〚文法〛 a declinable word

용역 用役 service ■ —단 service corps : 민간 용역단 civilian service corps —수출 service export

용왕 龍王 the Dragon King [God]

용왕매진 勇往邁進 advance in a dashing spirit; a vigorous forward dash
♦ 용왕매진의 기상 a dashing [daring] spirit —용왕매진하다 dash [push] on [forward]; make a dash [push]; advance bravely

용융 熔融 〚化〛 fusion; melting —용융하다 melt; smelt; fuse —섬 〈녹는섬〉 the melting [fusing] point

용의 用意 1〈주의〉 care; mindfulness; precautions; prudence
▶ 그는 만사에 용의주도하다 He is very careful and prudent in everything.
▶ 그는 용의주도한 계획을 세웠다 He made a very careful plan.
2〈준비〉 preparedness; readiness
▶ 그는 목숨을 걸 용의가 되어 있다 He is ready to risk his life.

용의 容疑 (a) suspicion

용의자 容疑者 a suspect; a suspected person; a person under suspicion
♦ 살인 (사건의) 용의자 a suspected murderer; a suspect in a murder; a murder suspect / 유력한 용의자 a key suspect

용이 容易 easiness; ease; simpleness; facility —용이하다 easy; simple; facile
▶ 비행기로 인해 여행이 용이해졌다 Airplanes have made travel easier.
▶ 영어에 숙달한다는 것이 용이한 일은 아니다 It is not easy [no easy matter] to master English.

용익권 用益權 〚法〛 a usufruct; a usufructuary right ■ —자 a usufructuary

용인 容認 admission; approval; acceptance; toleration
—용인하다 admit; approve of; accept; tolerate
▶ 당신의 조치는 용인하기 어렵다 I cannot agree with the measures you took.
▶ 그것은 많은 사람에 의해 용인된 사실이다 It is a fact accepted by many people.

용자 勇者 a hero (*pl.* ~es); a brave [courageous] man; a man of valor [courage]; (총칭) the brave

용자 容姿 the face and figure; figure; *one's* appearance
▶ 그녀는 용자가 아름답다 She has a graceful figure [beautiful style]. ⇌ She looks good from head to toe.

용자리 龍— 〚天〛 the Dragon; Draco

용장 冗長 wordiness; prolixity; diffuseness; verbosity —용장하다 wordy; prolix; diffuse (style); redundant (passage); verbose

용장 勇壯 bravery —용장하다 brave; heroic; gallant; valiant

용장 勇將 a brave general ▶ 용장 밑에 약졸 없다 No cowardly soldiers under a brave general. ⇌ 〈속담〉 Like master, like man.

용재 用材 〈재료〉 material; 〈재목〉 timber; (美) lumber ■ 건축— building materials

용재 庸才 a mediocre talent; inferior intelligence

용적 容積 〈용량〉 capacity; 〈부피〉 cubic volume [content(s)]; volume
♦ 용적 1.8 리터들이 병 a bottle with a capacity of 1.8 liters / 용적이 큰 capacious; bulky
▶ 이 통의 용적은 40 리터입니다 This barrel has a capacity [volume] of forty liters.
■ —량 the measure of capacity —톤 a measurement ton

용전 勇戰 a brave fighting ♦ 용전 분투하다 fight a battle courageously —용전하다 fight bravely [desperately]; fight a brave fight

용전여수 用錢如水 spending money like water; lavish use of money
—용전여수하다 spend money like water; be extravagant; be too lavish [free] with money; lavish [squander] *one's* money 《on》

용점 熔點 〚化〛 the melting point ⇨ 녹는점

용접 鎔接 welding
▶ 용접이 보다 잘 되는 금속이 있다 Some metals weld better than others.
—용접하다 weld 《to, together》 ♦ 부러진 쇠막대를 용접하다 weld a broken rod
▶ 이 합금들은 제각기 다른 온도에서 용접된다 These alloys weld at different heats.
■ 가스[전기]— gas [electric] welding —공 a welder —기[공장] a welding machine [shop] —봉 a welding rod —제 a welding agent

용제 溶劑 〚化〛 a solvent
▶ 알코올은 수지성 물질의 용제다 Alcohol is a solvent for [of] resinous substances.

용졸 庸拙 mediocrity —용졸하다 mediocre; shabby; inferior

용지 用地 a lot; a site ♦ 용지를 선정하다 choose a site (for a new school) / 철도 용지를 매수하다 buy railroad land
■ 건축— a building lot [site]; a vacant lot 농업— farmland

용지 用紙 a (blank) form; a blank; stationery
♦ 소정의 용지 the printed form
■ 시험— an examination paper 신청[원서]— an application blank [form] 전보— a telegraph form [blank] 주문— an order blank 투표— a ballot (paper)

용진 勇進 a brave advance; dashing forward
—용진하다 advance [march] bravely; dash forward bravely; make a dash

용질 溶質 〚化〛 a solute

용출 湧出 eruption; gush ♦ 북해 유전의 연간 원유 용출량 the annual yield of crude oil in the North Sea oil fields —용출하다 gush out [forth]; erupt; well up

용춤 ♦ 용춤 추다 yield to flattery / 용춤 추이다 cajole [wheedle] *sb* into 《doing》

용태 容態 condition; state
▶ 환자의 용태가 악화되었다 The patient took a sudden turn for the worse.
▶ 〚회화〛 「그의 용태는 어떻습니까?」 「별로 좋지 않습니다」 "How is he?" "He isn't in very good condition."

용퇴 勇退 voluntary retirement [resignation]
—용퇴하다 retire voluntarily; resign *one's*

post with good grace
▶그는 정계에서 용퇴했다 He retired voluntarily from the political world.
▶그는 정년을 앞두고 용퇴했다 He retired [resigned his post] voluntarily just before reaching the age limit.
▶그는 후진에게 길을 열어 주기 위해 용퇴했다 He retired (from his post) (in order) to give a chance to a younger person.

용트림 a big burp [belch] made on purpose —**용트림하다** force out a loud belch on purpose; let out a big burp

용품 用品 an article; supplies ■가정— household utensils [articles, appliances] 부엌— kitchen utensils; kitchenware 사무— office supplies 스포츠— sports equipment 캠핑— a camping outfit 학— school supplies [things]

용필 用筆 the use of a brush; 〈운필〉 one's command of the brush; 〈필치〉a stroke of the brush
—**용필하다** use [handle] a brush

용하다 1 〈재주가 뛰어나다〉skillful; deft; dexterous; adroit; ingenious; (be) good 《at》
♦용한 의사 an excellent [a skilled] physician / 그림에 용하다 draw deftly well / 용하게 (알아) 맞히다 hit the (right) nail on the head / 병을 용하게 고치다 be a noted physician / 무엇에나 용하다 be a good hand at all things; be skillful in everything
▶저 점쟁이는 꽤나 용하다 That fortune-teller often makes good hits.
2 〈기특하다〉admirable; laudable; wonderful; great
▶혼자서 그런 큰일을 했다니 참으로 용하다 It is admirable that you did such a great work by yourself.

용해 溶解 melting; solution; dissolution; liquefaction
—**용해하다** melt; dissolve; liquefy
▶일반적으로 금속은 물에 용해되지 않는다 Generally speaking, metals cannot be dissolved in water.
▶얼음은 물에 용해된다 Ice melts [dissolves] into water.
▶설탕은 뜨거운 물에 금방 용해한다 Sugar is readily soluble in hot water.
■—도 solubility —력 solvency —성 solubility : 용해성의 soluble; liquefactive —점 the melting point

용해 鎔解 〈금속의〉melting; smelting; fusion
—**용해하다** melt; smelt; fuse
♦불에 용해하다 smelt [melt] in the fire; be fused by the fire
■—로 a melting furnace —성 fusibility : 용해성의 fusible / 불용해성의 infusible —점 the smelting point

용호 龍虎 〈용과 범〉the dragon and the tiger; 〈두 영웅〉the two rival heroes

용호상박 龍虎相搏 a well-matched contest; a Titanic struggle; diamond cut diamond
♦용호상박의 결전 a decisive battle fought between two mighty rivals

용화 熔化 melting; fusion —**용화하다** melt; fuse ▶구리와 아연은 용화되어 놋쇠가 된다 Copper and zinc are fused to make brass.

용훼 容喙 interference; meddling —**용훼하다** put in a word; interfere [meddle] 《in》 ♦남의 일에 용훼하다 meddle in another's affairs; poke one's nose into another's business

우 〈일시에 몰리는 모양〉all at once; with a rush; in a crowd [body]
♦우 몰려 나오다 come out with a rush; rush out / 우 달아나다 run away in a panic / 방으로 우 몰려 들어오다 pour [throng, crowd] into the room
▶소녀들은 배우의 사인을 받으려고 우 몰려들었다 The girls stormed the actor for autographs.
▶사람들이 현장으로 우 몰려갔다 A crowd of people rushed to the scene.

우 右 the right
▶우로 나란히 (口令) Right, dress!
▶우로 봐 (口令) Eyes right!
▶우향우 (口令) Right, turn [face]!

우각 牛角 a cow's horn ⇨ 쇠뿔
—**호** 〔地質〕an oxbow lake

우간다 Uganda; 〈공식명〉 the Republic of Uganda ♦우간다의 Ugandan
■—사람 an Ugandan

우거 寓居 1 〈임시로 삶〉a temporary abode [residence] —**우거하다** reside [live] temporarily; take up one's (temporary) quarters
♦산중에 우거하다 live temporarily in the mountains
2 〈자기 집〉my humble cottage

우거지 1 〈야채의〉outer leaves (of a cabbage, etc.) 2 〈새우젓 등의〉the (tasteless) top layer of a crock of salted shrimps [pickles]

우거지다 grow thick [luxuriant]; luxuriate; be luxuriant [thick]; grow (thick and) rank
♦나무가 우거진 산 a thickly-wooded mountain
▶뜰에는 잡초가 우거져 있다 The garden is overgrown with rank weeds.
▶그 산에는 수목이 우거져 있다 The mountain is thickly wooded [covered with trees].

우거지상 —相 a sour [wry] face; distorted features; a grimace ▶그는 우거지상을 했다 He made a sour face. ⇒ He frowned.

우걱뿔 an inflexed horn ■—이 an ox with inflexed horns

우겨대다 stubbornly insist 《that...》; maintain persistently 《that...》; keep saying; persist 《in》
▶그는 끝까지 모른다고 우겨댔다 He persisted in denying his knowledge of it.

우격다짐 〈억지〉compulsion; coercion; high-handedness
▶그건 우격다짐이다 That's forcing things.
▶그는 부하들을 우격다짐으로 다룬다 He domineers over his men.
—**우격다짐하다** force [compel] sb to 《do》; coerce sb into 《doing》; resort to high-handed measures

우격으로 by (main) force; perforce; by brute strength; 《美》by a strong-arm method
♦우격으로 밀고 나가다 force [bulldoze] through / 우격으로 승낙하게 하다 force sb

우견

into consent
▶ 그는 우격으로 딸을 집으로 데려왔다 He took his daughter home by force.
♦ 싫다는데도 그는 우격으로 나에게 술을 먹였다 He made me drink against my will.

우견 愚見 1 〈어리석은 소견〉 a foolish view; a silly opinion 2 〈자기 의견〉 my opinion [view] ♦ 우견으로는 from my point of view; in my (humble) opinion; to express my opinion

우경 右傾 leaning [tending, turning] to the right
▶ 그는 우경화 되고 있다 He is becoming more right-wing.

우계 雨季 the rainy season ⇨ 우기(雨期)
우골 牛骨 cow [bullock] bones
우국 憂國 patriotism; love of *one's* country
■ 一지사 a patriot; a public-spirited man 一지심 a public spirit; a patriotic spirit 一충정 *one's* intense patriotism; 〈열정〉 a fire of patriotism: 우국 충정에서 우러나오다 be motivated by *one's* ardent patriotic sentiment

우군 友軍 friendly troops [forces]; 〈동맹군〉 an allied army
우그러지다 dent ⇨ 오그라지다
우그리다 indent; dent ⇨ 오그리다
우글거리다 swarm; be crowded; be overflowing; teem (with)
▶ 거리에 거지가 우글거린다 The streets swarm with beggars.
▶ 설탕에 개미가 우글거린다 The sugar is alive with ants.
▶ 연못에 물고기가 우글거린다 The pond teems with fish.
▶ 그 나라에는 실업자가 우글거렸다 There were an enormous number of unemployed people in that country.

우글부글 simmeringly; with a bubble
一우글부글하다 simmer; bubble (up); seethe
우글우글 in swarms
一우글우글하다 ⇨ 우글거리다 ♦ 사람들이 우글우글하다 be crowded [thronged] with people
▶ 쓰레기통에는 구더기가 우글우글했다 The garbage can was crawling [alive] with maggots.

우글쭈글하다 crumpled; rumpled; wrinkled; creasy
♦ 우글쭈글한 노파 an old withered woman; a crone / 우글쭈글한 손 a hand full of wrinkles / 우글쭈글해지다 be crumpled [wrinkled, rumpled]; crumple; become creased; cockle
▶ 사과가 시들어 우글쭈글해졌다 The apple is all shriveled up.
♦ 종이는 바르면 우글쭈글해질 때가 있다 Paper sometimes cockles when you paste it.

우기 雨氣 signs of rain ♦ 우기를 띤 하늘 a watery sky
우기 雨期 the rainy [wet] season ▶ 우기로 접어들었다 The wet [rainy] season has set in [begun].
우기다 insist 《on, that...》; persist 《in》; assert 《*oneself*》

♦ 결백하다고 우기다 insist that *one* is innocent / 자기 의견이 옳다고 우기다 stick to *one's* own opinion / 억척스레 우기다 insist stubbornly; stickle
▶ 그는 여전히 모른다고 우긴다 He keeps saying that he does not know.
▶ 그는 혼자 그곳에 가겠다고 우겼다 He insisted in going there alone.
▶ 그는 자기만 옳다고 우겼다 He insisted he was the only one who was right.

우김성 一性 obstinate character; obstinacy
♦ 우김성이 많다 be headstrong; be self-opinionated / 우김성이 있다 have [be a person of] obstinate character
▶ 그 아이는 우김성이 강하다 The boy asserts himself strongly.

우는소리 a complaint; a whimper; slush
▶ 그는 불경기가 어쩌고 하며 늘 우는소리만 한다 He is always complaining about the hard times.
一우는소리하다 complain 《about, of》; grumble 《about》; whine 《about》
▶ 나한테 우는소리해봐야 소용없다 It's no use whining about it to me.

우는 아이 젖 준다 〈속담〉 No song, no supper.
⇌ A squeaky wheel gets the grease.
우단 羽緞 velvet ♦ 검은 우단 옷을 입다 be dressed in black velvet / 우단처럼 부드럽다 be as smooth as velvet
우당 友黨 an allied [a friendly] (political) party
우당탕 with a thumping [bumping] noise
♦ 우당탕 뛰어나가다 stamp out of
▶ 그는 우당탕 층계를 내려갔다 He went bump down the stairs.
▶ 빈 드럼통이 길아래로 우당탕 소리를 내며 굴러 갔다 An empty drum was banging along down the road.
一우당탕하다 thump; stamp [stomp] 《about, along》

우대 優待 favorable [preferential] treatment
一우대하다 give preferential treatment to *sb*; treat *sb* favorably; discriminate in favor of *sb*; 〈급료 등을〉 pay a good salary (to)
♦ 우대받다 be treated well [favorably]; 〈급료 등을〉 be paid well; be shown hospitality
▶ 유경험자는 우대합니다 An experienced man will be paid a good salary [be well-paid].
一권 a complimentary ticket; 〈할인권〉 a discount coupon 一금리 prime rate

우두 牛痘 〔醫〕 cowpox; vaccinia
♦ 우두를 놓다 vaccinate; inoculate *sb* for [against] smallpox / 우두를 맞다 take [undergo] vaccination; be vaccinated for [against] smallpox
♦ 우둣자국 a vaccination scar
우두둑 1 ⇨ 오도독 2 〈부러지는 소리〉 with a snapping sound
우두망찰하다 be bewildered [flustered, disconcerted, flurried]; be upset; be at a loss
▶ 그의 죽음으로 식구가 모두 우두망찰하고 있다 His death has bewildered the whole family.
우두머리 〈사람〉 the chief; the head; the boss;

우두커니 absent-mindedly; vacantly; blankly; 〈하는 일 없이〉 idly
♦우두커니 바라보다 look vacantly 《at》 / 우두커니 앉아 있다 sit idle / 우두커니 보고만 있다 remain an idle spectator / 우두커니 생각에 잠겨 있다 be in a brown study
▶그는 우두커니 창밖을 내다보고 있었다 He stood gazing vacantly out the window.
▶그는 대문간에 우두커니 서 있었다 He was standing stolidly in the doorway.

우둔하다 愚鈍— stupid (as an owl); dull; obtuse; thick-headed
▶그 녀석은 참 우둔하다 He is real dummy [blockhead].

우듬지 the top of a tree; a treetop

우등 優等 excellence; honors ♦영어에 우등이 되다 take honors in English
▶그는 전과목 우등으로 상을 받았다 He won the prize for excellence in all subjects.
▶그는 우등으로 고등학교를 졸업했다 He graduated from a high school with honors [(라) cum laude].
■—상 an honor [a special] prize: 우등상을 받다 be awarded an honor prize —생 an honor student

우뚝 high; aloft
▶눈 덮인 산이 하늘로 우뚝 솟아 있다 The snowy mountain soars high into [stands out against] the sky.
—**우뚝하다** high; towering; soaring; 〈뛰어나다〉 conspicuous ♦우뚝한 코 a high nose / 키가 우뚝하다 be tall in stature

우라늄 〔化〕 uranium ♦초우라늄 원소 a transuranic element
■농축— enriched [concentrated] uranium 천연— natural uranium ■—광 uranium ore

우락부락하다 coarse-grained; rough; tough; rowdy
♦우락부락한 사내 a rough (fellow) / 우락부락한 행동 rowdy behavior / 우락부락하게 굴다 behave rudely
▶그 사람 우락부락하게 생겼지만 마음씨는 곱다 He looks wild but he has a tender mind.

우랄산맥 —山脈 the Urals
우랄알타이어족 —語族 the Ural-Altaic
우람지다 〈서술적〉 be [appear] imposing [stately, grand]
우람하다 stately; imposing; grand; magnificent; majestic ♦체격이 우람한 남자 a big brawny [muscular] man
우량 雨量 (a) rainfall ⇨ 강우량
♦서울의 연평균 우량 the average annual rainfall in Seoul / 우량을 재다 gauge [measure] the rainfall
■—계 a rain gauge; a pluviometer
우량 優良 superiority; excellence —우량하다 superior; excellent ♦우량한 성적 an excellent result
—기업 a blue-chip company —도서 best [excellent] books —아(兒) a prize-winning child in a health contest; a superior child; a physically perfect child; 우량아 선발 대회 a baby contest [show] —종(種) a good breed —주(株) blue chips; blue-chip stocks —품 excellent goods; articles of superior quality

우러나다 soak out; come off; 〈차 등이〉 draw; infuse ♦차를 우러나게 하다 draw tea / (물 등에 담가) 냅킨의 얼룩이 우러나게 하다 soak a stain out of a napkin
▶이 차는 잘 우러난다 This tea draws well.

우러나오다 spring up; well up
♦진심에서 우러나오는 감사 thanks from the bottom of one's heart
▶나는 그녀에게 마음에서 우러나오는 축하를 보냈다 I sent her my heartfelt congratulations.

우러러보다 1〈위를 쳐다보다〉 look up 《at》; turn one's face upward (to)
▶그는 하늘의 별들을 우러러보았다 He looked up at the stars in the heavens.
2〈앙모하다〉 respect; look up to; revere
▶그들은 그를 스승으로 우러러보고 있다 They look up to him as their teacher.

우러르다 1〈쳐들다〉 raise [lift] one's head; look up ▶하늘을 우러러 한점 부끄러움이 없다 I am not morally ashamed of myself before God.
2〈공경하다〉 respect; revere; look up to
♦신으로 우러러 받들다 deify

우럭우럭 〈불이〉 flaringly; furiously; 〈술기운이〉 with a flush
♦술기운이 얼굴에 우럭우럭 오르다 one's face grows flushed with drunkenness
▶불이 우럭우럭 일고 있다 The fire is burning furiously.

우렁쉥이 〔動〕 an ascidian; a sea squirt
우렁우렁 thunderingly; with a rumble
♦우렁우렁 울리다 rumble; roll
우렁이 〔動〕 a mud snail; a pond snail
우렁잇속 inscrutability; mystery
♦우렁잇속 같다 be inscrutable [impenetrable]
▶그는 마음이 우렁잇속 같다 What he has in his mind is a mystery to me.

우렁차다 rotund; rich and full; sonorous
♦우렁찬 목소리 a rotund voice
▶그들은 우렁차게 국가를 불렀다 They sang the national anthem with a sonorous voice.

우레 thunder ⇨ 천둥
♦우레같은 박수갈채 a storm [thunder] of applause; thunderous applause / 우레 같은 환호 thundering cheers
▶우레같은 박수가 터졌다 There was a thunderous clapping of hands.
▶그녀는 우레같은 박수를 받으며 홀을 떠났다 She left the hall amid a storm of applause.

우레탄 〔化〕 urethane
우렛소리 a peal [clap, roll] of thunder; a thunderclap
▶멀리서 우렛소리가 연속해서 들려왔다 A succession of rolling sounds of thunder was heard in the distance.

우려 憂慮 anxiety; concern; apprehension(s); solicitude ♦실패할 우려가 있다 run a chance of failure
▶홍수로 다리가 떠내려갈 우려가 있다 It is feared that the bridge will be washed away in the flood.
—**우려하다** fear; worry 《over》; apprehend; be concerned 《about》; be apprehensive 《of》
♦우려할 만한 결과 a grave consequence / 우려할 만한 사태 a serious [grave] situation
▶그들은 사태를 크게 우려하고 있다 They are deeply worried over the situation.

우려내다 1 〈신액 등을〉 infuse; steep 《in a liquid》
♦약초를 우려내다 infuse herbs in water
2 〈빼앗다〉 screw 《money》 from [out of] *sb*; extort [squeeze] 《money》 from *sb*; 《口》 bleed [milk] *sb*
♦국민들로부터 세금을 우려내다 wring taxes from the people

우려먹다 infuse; screw 《money》 from *sb* ⇨ 우려내다
▶그 고리대금업자는 불쌍한 농민들로부터 돈을 우려먹었다 The loan shark squeezed money out of the poor farmers.

우련하다 dim; vague; obscure; misty
♦우련하게 보이다 be seen dimly [at a dim distance] / 우련하게 나타나다 loom 《in sight》; appear indistinctly
▶배가 안개 속에 우련하게 나타났다 The ship loomed through the mist.

우로 雨露 rain and dew
♦우로를 맞다 be exposed to the elements; be weather-beaten / 우로를 피하다 shelter *oneself* from the weather
▶그들은 겨우 우로나 피하며 살았다 They barely made a living.
■—**一**지택(之澤) universal kindness [benevolence] 《of a sovereign》

우론 愚論 a foolish opinion; an absurd view; 〈자기 의견〉 my opinion [view]

우롱 愚弄 mockery; derision; ridicule
—**우롱하다** mock; deride; fool; make fun [a fool] 《of》; ridicule
♦우롱하는 derisive; derisory; mocking
▶사람을 우롱해도 유분수지 You shouldn't make too much fun of me.
▶그것은 독자를 우롱하는 짓 밖에 안된다 That's just making a fool of readers.

우루과이 Uruguay; 〈공식명〉 the Oriental Republic of Uruguay
♦우루과이의 Uruguayan
■—**一**사람 an Uruguayan

우루과이라운드 the Uruguay Round

우르르 1 〈몰려가는 모양〉 in crowds [droves]; with a throng; with a stampede
♦우르르 따라가다 follow in a troop at the heels of *sb* / 우르르 달아나다 run away in a panic; stampede
▶사내아이들이 체육관으로 우르르 몰려들었다 Boys came crowding into the gym.
▶학생들은 선생님 주위로 우르르 몰려들었다 The students gathered around the teacher noisily.

2 〈무너지는 모양〉 in a confused heap; together; with a rumble
♦우르르 무너지다 fall down all of a heap
▶사과가 자루에서 우르르 쏟아졌다 Apples tumbled out of a sack all over.
3 〈끓어오름〉 ▶물이 우르르 끓고 있다 The water is boiling [bubbling] up.
4 〈천둥소리〉 with a rumble; thunderingly
♦우르르 울리다 rumble; boom; thunder
▶멀리서 우르르 천둥이 울린다 Thunder grumbles [growls] in the distance.

우리¹ 〈맹수의〉 a cage; 〈가축의〉 a pen; 〈corral [cote〉; 〈삭은 동물의〉 a hutch; 〈돼지의〉 a pigsty; 〈양의〉 a fold
♦우리에 갇힌 호랑이 a caged tiger / 우리에서 태어난 《animals》 born behind bars; 《chimpanzees》 born in captivity / 사자를 우리에 가두다 cage a lion / 우리에 넣다 cage in; coop; impound

우리² 〈우리들〉 we; 〈나〉 I
♦우리의 것 ours / 우리들 일동 all of us; we all / 우리 아버지 my father / 우리 아이 my son [daughter] / 우리 자신 ourselves / 우리 집 my house [home] / 우리 집사람 my wife / 우리 한국인 we Koreans / 우리의 our / 우리를[에게] us / 우리끼리 이야기지만 between ourselves [you and me]
▶우리 한국인은 축구를 매우 좋아합니다 We Koreans like soccer very much.
▶우리는 서로 사랑합니다 We love each other.
▶그렇게 되면 승리는 우리 것이다 It means that victory [success] is ours.
▶우리에게 자유를 다오 Give us liberty.
■—**나라** our country; this country 《of ours》: 우리 나라의 인구가 꾸준히 늘고 있다 The population of our country is increasing steadily.
—**말** our language; our mother tongue; Korean

우리다¹ 〈햇볕이〉 stream [shine] in

우리다² 1 〈우러나게 하다〉 steep [soak] out; infuse ♦도라지를 우리다 soak the bitterness out of broad bellflower roots / 물에 우리다 bleach [steep] 《herbs》 in water; soak 《the color out of *sth*》
2 〈때리다〉 slap hard ♦빰을 우리다 slap *sb* on the cheek
3 〈우려내다〉 wring

우마 牛馬 oxen and horses; (horses and) cattle ♦우마처럼 혹사시키다 work *sb* like a beast of burden; drive *sb* hard (like a horse)

우매 愚昧 stupidity; asininity; ignorance
—**우매하다** stupid; ignorant; unenlightened
♦우매한 백성 ignorant [unenlightened] people / 우매한 짓 a [an act of] folly; a foolish move [act]

우먼리브 〈여성 해방 운동〉 women's lib; women's liberation (movement)

> 解說 ***women's lib***는 ***women's liberation (movement)***의 약칭이다.

우먼파워 womanpower; female power
우멍하다 hollow; sunken
우모 羽毛 a feather; a plume; (총칭) plumage

우모가 있는 feathered
우무 agar(-agar) ⇨ 한천(寒天)
우묵하다 hollow ⇨ 오목하다
우문 愚問 a stupid [silly] question
  ■―우답 a silly dialogue ―현답 a wise answer to a silly question
우물 a well ◆깊이 판 우물 a deep-drilled well / 우물을 치다 clean a well / 우물을 파다 sink [dig, bore] a well / 우물에서 물을 긷다 draw water from a well
  ▶ 우리 집 우물이 말라버렸다 Our well has dried up.
  ■―물 well water: 이 우물물은 마셔도 됩니까? Is the water from this well good [fit] to drink?
우물가 the well side ■―공론 housewives' (well-side) gossip
우물거리다[1] 〈벌레 등이〉 squirm [wriggle about] in swarm; 〈장소가〉 swarm [be crowded] 《with》
  ▶ 땅에 벌레가 우물거리고 있었다 The ground was simply crawling with worms.
우물거리다[2] 〈우물우물 씹다〉 mumble; chew ineffectively; 〈중얼거리다〉 mumble; mump
  ◆대답을 우물거리다 mumble *one's* answer / 빵 껍질을 우물거리다 mumble on a crust
  ▶ 그녀는 무슨 말을 하려다 말고 우물거렸다 She started to say something but faltered.
우물귀신 ―鬼神 the spirit of a person drowned in a well ◆우물귀신이 되다 drown *oneself* in a well
우물 안 개구리 〈속담〉 a man of narrow outlook; a person of limited scope
우물에 가 숭늉 찾겠다 〈속담〉 He seeks wool on an ass.
우물우물 mumblingly
  ◆우물우물 말하다 mumble 《*one's* words》/ 우물우물 씹다 mumble
  ▶ 그는 우물우물 말꼬리를 흐렸다 He mumbled the end of his words [sentence].
  ▶ 저 노파가 우물우물 뭐라고 하는데 무슨 소린지 모르겠다 That old lady is mumbling something, but I cannot understand her.
우물을 파도 한 우물을 파라 〈속담〉 Every man must walk [labor] in his own calling [trade]. ⇌ Success comes to him who can stick to his pursuit.
우물지다 1 〈보조개가 생기다〉 dimple
  ▶ 그녀는 웃으면 한쪽 볼이 우물진다 She has a dimple when she smiles.
  2 〈우묵해지다〉 become hollow; form a hollow [dimple]
  ▶ 비가 와서 땅이 우물졌다 There came out hollows in the ground after the rain.
우물쭈물 hesitantly; irresolutely; indecisively; vaguely ◆우물쭈물 말하다 speak hesitantly; talk ambiguously / 우물쭈물 일하다 work sluggishly; do a slow job
  ―우물쭈물하다 be irresolute [indecisive]; be hesitant; hesitate
  ▶ 우물쭈물하지 마라 No hanging back.
  ▶ 우물쭈물하고 있을 때가 아니다 There is no time to lose. ⇌ There is not a moment to be lost.

우뭇가사리 〔植〕 an agar-agar
우미하다 優美― graceful; elegant 《design》
  ◆고아 우미한 자태 a refined and elegant figure
우민 愚民 ignorant [untaught] people
  ◆우민을 선동하다 instigate [agitate] the mob / 국민을 우민 취급하다 regard the people as foolish [ignorant]
  ■―(화) 정책 an obscurantist policy
우박 雨雹 hail; 〈한 알〉 a hailstone
  ◆우박에 의한 농작물의 피해 the damage done to the farm crops by a hailstorm
  ▶ 우박이 온다 It hails.
  ▶ 우박이 쏟아져 밭 채소가 피해를 입었다 Vegetables in the field suffered damage from a hailstorm.
우발 偶發 accidental [incidental] occurrence
  ◆우발적인 accidental; incidental; adventitious / 우발적으로 accidentally; incidentally
  ―우발하다 happen; occur [come about] by chance
  ■―사고 an (unforeseen) accident; an incident; a contingency ―성 contingency ―전쟁 accidental warfare; war through accident: 우발 전쟁의 위험을 방지하다 preclude the danger of accidental warfare
우방 友邦 a friendly nation [country]
우범 虞犯 liability to crime ■―자 a person liable to committing a crime ―지대[지역] a crime-ridden district; a crime-prone area
우변 右邊 the right side ◆우변의[에] on the right
우부 愚夫 a foolish man
우분 牛糞 cattle dung=쇠똥[2]
우비 雨備 a rain outfit; (총칭) rainwear ◆우비를 입다 put on a raincoat
  ▶ 우비는 준비했습니까? Are you prepared for rain?
우비다 scrape [scoop] out; bore; poke; 〈긁어내다〉 pick
  ◆귀를 우비다 clean *one's* ears / 담뱃대를 우비다 poke a pipe / 콧구멍을 우비다 pick *one's* nose / 귀에 솜을 우비어넣다 stuff *one's* ears with cotton
우비어파다 1 〈깊이 파다〉 scrape [scoop] out; gouge ◆벽에 구멍을 우비어파다 bore a hole in the wall
  ▶ 나는 칼로 사과 속을 우비어팠다 I dug out the apple core with a knife.
  2 〈내막을 캐다〉 pry 《into》; ferret out; poke 《at》 ◆남의 일을 우비어파다 pry into other people's affairs
우비적거리다 keep poking [scraping out, picking]; scoop repeatedly ◆콧구멍을 우비적거리다 keep picking *one's* nose
우빙 雨氷 silver thaw; sleet; (美) glaze; (英) glazed frost
우사 牛舍 a stable ⇨ 외양간
우산 雨傘 an umbrella
  ◆우산을 받다[쓰다] put up [raise, hold] an umbrella / 우산을 받고 가다 go [walk] under an umbrella / 우산을 접다 close [fold, shut] an umbrella / 우산을 펴다 open [spread, unfold, unfurl] an umbrella

▶ 그녀는 내게 우산을 받쳐 주었다 She held her umbrella over my head.
▶ 우산을 가져가요 Take [Carry] an [your] umbrella with you.
▶ 우산 좀 같이 쓰고 가십시다 Will you let me walk under [May I share] your umbrella? (▶ May I share~로 쓰는 것이 일반적임)
▶ 바람이 사나워서 우산이 뒤집혔다 The strong blast of wind blew [turned] my umbrella inside [wrong side] out.
■ ―꽂이 an umbrella stand ―살〈한 개〉a rib; a stretcher; 〈전체〉a frame ―손잡이 a handle ot an umbrella; the umbrella handle

우산이끼 雨傘― 〔植〕a (common) liverwort; a hepatica

우상 羽狀 ◆우상의 〔植〕pinnate ■―엽〔植〕a pinnate leaf

우상 偶像 an idol; an icon
◆우상을 숭배하다 worship idols / 젊은이의 우상이 되다 be an idol of the young people
■―숭배 idol worship; idolatry [aidálətri] ―숭배자 an idol worshiper; an idolater ―파괴 iconoclasm ―파괴자 an iconoclast ―화 idolization : 우상화하다 idolize; make an idol (oɪ)

우색 憂色 〈근심하는 표정〉a worried [an anxious] look; a melancholy [gloomy] air
◆우색을 띠고 with a look of anxiety on one's face / 우색을 띠다 wear a worried look; look concerned [anxious, sad]
▶ 그녀의 얼굴은 우색을 띠고 있었다 She wore [had] a worried look.

우생학 優生學 eugenics
◆우생학상으로 eugenically (speaking)
■―자 a eugenicist; a eugenist

우선 優先 〈선택 등의〉preference; 〈순서・시간 등의〉priority; 〈순서・중요성 등의〉precedence ―우선하다 be prior (to); have priority (to, over); have preference (to); take precedence (over)
▶ 공공 복지는 개인의 행복에 우선한다 Public welfare comes before private happiness.
▶ 헌법은 다른 모든 법률에 우선한다 The Constitution takes priority [precedence] over all laws.
■ 공익― precedence of public interest ■―배당 preference [preferred] dividends ―사항 a priority item [matter] ―순위 the order of priority : 이 계획에 대해 우선 순위를 결정하기는 어렵다 It is hard to decide the order of priority for these plans. ―주(株) (美) preferred stocks [shares]

우선 于先 **1**〈먼저〉first; first of all; before [above] everything; to begin with; in the first place
▶ 우선 119에 전화부터 걸어라 The first thing for you to do is to dial 119.
▶ 우선 서면으로 문안 드립니다 I take this first opportunity to inquire after you by letter.
▶ 우선 자금을 조달하지 않으면 안된다 First of all [To begin with], we have to raise the funds.
▶ 아침에 우선 이 약부터 먹어라 Take this medicine (the) first thing in the morning.
2〈아쉬운대로〉for the moment; for the present; for the time being
▶ 적당한 아파트를 구할 때까지 우선 나한테 있어라 You can stay with me for the moment until you can find a good apartment.
▶ 우선 이 10만원으로 견디어 보세요 Please tide yourself over for the present with this one hundred thousand won.

우선권 優先權 (the right of) priority [preference]; a preferential [prior] right; 〈통행상의 우선권〉right-of-way
◆우선권이 있다 have priority (rights) (to, over); have preference (to) / 우선권을 얻다 [주다] acquire [give] a priority
▶ 이 건에서는 나보다 당신에게 우선권이 있습니다 You have priority over me in this matter.
▶ 이 계약에서는 너보다 내가 우선권이 있다 I have priority over you in this contract.
▶ 곧 해결을 요하는 문제는 회의에서 우선권이 주어질 것이다 The problems requiring immediate solution will be given priority at the meeting.

우선적 優先的 preferential
◆우선적으로 preferentially / 최우선적으로 with first [top] priority / 우선적으로 다루다 give priority [precedence] to
▶ 그 일은 최우선적으로 다루어졌다 The job was given top [the highest] priority.

우성 優性 〔遺〕dominance ◆우성의 법칙 a law of dominance / 우성 유전 dominant heredity / 우성의 dominant ■―인자 a dominant gene ―형질 a dominant trait [character]

우세 〈남에게서 받는 비웃음〉derision; ridicule; shame; humiliation ―우세하다 be put to shame; be humiliated ◆우세스럽다 be shameful [scandalous, humiliating]

우세 優勢 〈힘・수 등의 우위〉(pre)dominance; preponderance; superior power; 〈우월〉superiority; 〈우세해짐〉the lead; ascendancy
◆우세를 유지하다 maintain a superior position / 간신히 우세를 유지하다 hold a slight lead / 우세를 차지하다 have the preponderance; get [gain] the better (of)
―우세하다 superior (in force, in number); leading; ascendant; predominant; dominant
▶ 우리는 수적으로 우세한 적과 교전했다 We encountered an enemy superior in number.
▶ 우리의 의견이 그 회의에서 우세해졌다 Our opinion was predominant at the conference.
▶ 그 후보자가 처음부터 우세했다 The candidate led from the first.

우송 郵送 (美) mailing; (英) posting; sending by mail [post]
―우송하다 (美) mail; (英) post; send [forward] sth by post [mail]; send sth through the post
◆우송되다 go by post
▶ 미국에 있는 친구에게 어제 소포를 우송했다 I mailed a package to my friend in America yesterday. ⇒ I sent a package to my friend in America by mail yesterday.
■ 무료― postage free : 무료 우송의 post-free; postage-free ■―료[비] postage (on): 이 소포의 우송료는 얼마입니까? What is the postage

on this package?

우수 1 〈덤〉 something thrown in; a giveaway; 《美口》 a freebie; 〈추가〉 an addition; 〈상품・경품 등〉 a premium; an extra; a bonus
2 ⇨ 우수리

우수 右手 the right hand

우수 雨水 1 〈빗물〉 rainwater 2 〈절기〉 the first rainfall of the year, the second of the 24 seasonal divisions 《about February 18》

우수 偶數 an even number = 짝수

우수 憂愁 〈근심〉 melancholy; 〈우울〉 gloom
♦우수의 melancholy; gloomy; anxious; worried / 우수의 빛을 띤 미소를 짓다 wear a melancholic smile

우수 優秀 superiority; excellence
―**우수하다** superior; excellent; best; leading; admirable; crack; 〈탁월한〉 outstanding; fine
♦우수한 학생 an excellent student; a student of superior ability / 시험에서 우수한 성적을 거두다 get excellent [brilliant] results on [《英》 in] the exam; get high marks on [《英》 in] the exam
▶그는 우수한 성적으로 입학이 허가되었다 He was admitted to the school with excellent grades [high marks].
▶그는 우리 회사의 우수한 사원이다 He is an able [excellent] member in our company.
▶그는 나보다 화학이 우수하다 He is superior to me in chemistry.
■―**성** excellency; prowess ―**팀** a crack team

우수리 1 〈끝수〉 a fraction; 〈금액〉 an odd sum
♦우수리의 fractional; odd 《sum》 / 우수리를 떨다 omit [round off] fractions
▶우수리를 떨어버리면 딱 50이 된다 If you omit fractions, you get exactly fifty.
2 ⇨ 거스름돈

우수수 in great masses; in a multitude; 〈떨어져 흩어지는 모양〉 rustling down
♦우수수 떨어지다 fall in great masses; rustle down
▶바람에 나뭇잎이 우수수 떨어졌다 A gust of wind shook a multitude of leaves off the trees.

우스개 〈농담〉 a joke; a jest; 〈웃기는 짓・말〉 comicality; drollery; jocularity
♦우스개로 삼다 make fun [sport] of; turn *sth* into ridicule; make a jest of
▶그는 늘 동료들의 우스갯 거리가 된다 He is a standing jest of all his companions.

우스갯소리 〈농담〉 a joke; a jest; fun; 〈우스운 이야기〉 a humorous [funny] story
♦우스갯 소리를 하다 crack [make] a joke; joke; jest
▶걱정하지마라. 그저 우스갯 소리야 Don't be upset. I was only joking. ⇒ It was only a joke. ⇒ It was only in fun.
▶이건 우스갯 소리가 아니야 It's no matter for jest. ⇒ It's no joke. ⇒ I mean what I say.

우스갯짓 clownery; comicality; drollery; waggery
♦우스갯짓을 하다 jest; joke; play the fool; play droll tricks; make a spectacle of *oneself*
▶그는 선생님에 관한 우스갯짓을 잘한다 He is good at playing jokes on his teachers.

우스꽝스럽다 ridiculous; ludicrous; funny; comic(al); droll ♦우스꽝스러운 사람 a funny person; a figure of fun
▶그 모자를 쓰니 네 모양이 우스꽝스럽다 You look funny in the hat.

우스터 〈영국의 도시〉 Worcester
■―**소스** Worcester [Worcestershire] sauce

우습게보다 〈얕보다〉 make [think] light of; think [take] lightly [little] of; attach no importance to; 〈소홀히 하다〉 slight; despise; belittle; 〈업신여기다〉 disdain; look down (up)on *sb*; have contempt for *sb*
▶생명을 우습게 보아서는 안된다 You should not make light of your life.
▶그녀는 상대방을 우습게 보고 있다 She belittles [thinks nothing of] her opponent.
▶그녀는 선생님의 충고 같은 건 우습게 보았다 She paid no attention to [made light of] the teacher's advice.
▶그들은 그 계획에서 그의 역할을 우습게 보았다 They played down his part in the scheme.

우습다 1 〈재미있다〉 laughable; ridiculous; ludicrous; sidesplitting; funny; droll; comic(al); amusing
♦우스운 녀석 a funny fellow / 우스운 이야기 〈즐거운〉 an amusing story / 〈절로 웃음을 자아내는〉 a funny story / 우스운 실수를 하다 make a laughable mistake / 우스워 죽겠다 be tickled to death / 우스워하다 be amused 《at, by, with》; be tickled 《at, by》
▶그의 농담은 조금도 우습지 않다 His joke wasn't funny at all. ⇒ 〈웃기지 않았다〉 His joke didn't make us laugh at all.
▶무엇이 그렇게 우스운가? What makes you laugh so much? ⇒ What's so funny [amusing]?
▶헐렁헐렁한 바지를 입은 너의 모양이 우습다 In your baggy pants you look ridiculous [comic(al)].
2 〈하찮다〉 trifling; trivial; small; slight; insignificant
♦우스운 일로 말다툼하다 argue about pinpoints
▶두 사람은 우스운 일로 종종 싸운다 The two often quarrel over a trifle.
▶그녀는 우스운 일로 늘 걱정한다 She is always worrying over trifles.
▶그건 우습게 여길 일이 아니다 It is not a small matter. ⇒ It is not an easy job.
3 〈가소롭다〉 laughing; laughable; ridiculous; absurd
▶그 참 우습군 What a joke! ⇒ You make me laugh!
▶그녀를 설득하려고 하다니 참 우습다 How absurd to try to persuade her!
▶그녀가 사장 비서로 선임되다니 우습기 짝이 없다 How ridiculous [What nonsense] it is that she should be elected as a secretary to the president.

우승 優勝 〈승리〉 the victory; 〈선수권〉 championship
♦단체[개인종합] 우승 a team [an overall individual] championship
―**우승하다** win [capture] the victory [cham-

pionship]; come off [out] the victor [winner]; come off victorious; win the title
▶ 우리 팀이 우승하게 틀림없다 Our team will definitely win the championship [(美) pennant].
■—준— coming out second best ■—결정전 a deciding match [contest] in a competition for a cup [pennant] —다툼 a competition for victory —시합 a championship tournament; the finals; a cup event —팀 a championship [winning, victorious] team

우승기 優勝旗 a championship flag [banner]; a (winner's) pennant

우승배 優勝杯 a championship cup; a trophy; (英) a cup ♦우승배를 주다 honor 《a winner》 with a trophy

우승열패 優勝劣敗 the survival of the fittest
▶ 우승 열패는 흔한 세상의 이치다 The survival of the fittest is the way of the world.
—**우승열패하다** the weakest goes to the wall; the fittest survives

우승자 優勝者 the (first-prize, pennant) winner; the victor; a successful contestant; a champion; a titleholder; a titlist

우승후보 優勝候補 a hopeful; a favorite; a likely winner (of the championship)
♦올림픽의 우승후보 an Olympic hopeful / 제 1 우승후보 the top favorite [choice] for the championship; the best bet for the title

우시장 牛市場 a cattle fair [market]

우심방 右心房 〔解〕the right atrium (of the heart) 《pl. -ria》

우심실 右心室 〔解〕the right ventricle (of the heart)

우심하다 尤甚— extreme; more severe [intense, violent, harsh]; heavier ♦우심한 손해 heavier loss ▶ 올핸 추위가 우심했다 We've had a more severe cold winter this year.

우썩 vigorously; rapidly; noticeably; markedly; remarkably
♦우썩 늘다 〈학문·기술등〉 make steady [rapid] progress / 우썩 줄다 decrease rapidly ▶ 키가 우썩 자랐구나 You've really grown.

우아 〈기쁠 때〉 Hurrah!; Hurray!; Wow!
▶ 우아 예쁘다 Oh! How beautiful!
▶ 우아, 이겼다 Hurrah! We've won.
▶ 우아, 모두 맛있겠는걸 Boy [Wow], everything looks so good.

우아하다 優雅— 〈고상하고 품위 있는〉 elegant; 〈정숙하고 점잖은〉 graceful; 〈세련된〉 refined; urbane; dainty; exquisite
♦우아한 문체 an elegant style / 우아한 부인 a graceful lady / 우아하게 in a graceful manner; gracefully; gently; elegantly
▶ 그녀는 몸가짐이 우아하다 She has a graceful carriage.
▶ 그녀는 우아하게 춤추었다 She danced with grace [gracefully].

우악스럽다 愚惡— rough; rude; wild; violent; rowdy; disorderly; cruel; hard; brutal
♦우악스러운 사람 a wild fellow; a rowdy; a rough; (美俗) a rough neck / 말씨가 우악스럽다 use violent language; be rough-spoken / 우악스럽게 생기다 have a ferocious look / 아무를 우악스럽게 다루다 get rough with *sb*
▶ 그는 그녀에게 우악스럽게 대한다 He is rough on her.

우악하다 優渥— 〈은혜가〉 a gracious; benevolent

우안 右岸 (on) the right bank 《of》

우애 友愛 〈우정〉 friendship; fellowship; comradeship; 〈형제간의 사랑〉 fraternity; brotherliness; brotherly love
♦우애롭다 be friendly; be brotherly
■—결혼 (a) companionate marriage

우어 〈말·소를 멈추게 할 때 내는 소리〉 Whoa!; Wo-back!, Halt there!

우언 寓言 〈교훈적인〉 an apologue; an allegory; 〈종교적인〉 a parable; 〈동물을 의인화한〉 a fable

우엉 〔植〕 a burdock; a cocklebur(r)

우여 〈새 등을 쫓는 소리〉 Shoo!

우여곡절 迂餘曲折 〈뒤얽힌 사정〉 twistings; complications; vicissitudes 《of fortune》
♦인생의 우여곡절 the vicissitudes [ups and downs] of life / 많은 우여곡절을 거쳐 after much meandering; after many twists and turns
▶ 그 법안이 통과되기까지 우여곡절이 많았다 There was a lot of bargaining [give-and-take] before the bill was passed.
▶ 두 사람이 결혼하기까지는 우여곡절이 많았다 There were many problems before they got married.

우역 牛疫 〈소의 전염병〉 cattle plague; rinderpest

우연 偶然 〈운에 좌우되는 일〉chance; 〈우발적인 사건〉an accident; fortuity; 〈우연의 일치〉 coincidence
▶ 콜럼버스가 1492년 아메리카를 발견했지만, 그의 아메리카 발견은 정말〔단순한〕 우연이었다 Columbus discovered America in 1492. But his discovery of America was a sheer [mere] chance.
▶ [會話]「오늘밤 그 콘서트에 갈거야」「나도 갈건데, 그것 참 우연이구나」"I'm going to go to the concert tonight." "So am I [(口) Me, too). What a coincidence!"
—**우연하다** accidental; chance; casual; haphazard; fortuitous
♦우연한 만남 an accidental [a chance, a casual] meeting / 우연한 사건 an accident / 우연히 by chance [accident]; accidentally; unexpectedly; casually; incidentally; by haphazard
▶ 내가 찾던 바로 그 책을 우연히 발견했다 By accident I found the very book I wanted.
▶ 그들의 만남은 우연한 일이었다 Their meeting was accidental.(▶chance, casual은 불가)
▶ 나는 서울에서 우연히 그녀를 만났다 I met her in Seoul by chance. ⇒ I happened [chanced] to meet her in Seoul. ⇒ (口) I ran into her in Seoul.
▶ 그는 길거리에서 우연히 지갑을 발견했다 He found a wallet on the street. (▶ happened to find라고는 하지 않음. 우연성을 함축한 동사는 happen과 함께 쓰지 않음)
▶ 우연히 그녀와 같은 버스에 타게 되었다 I

happened to ride in the same bus with her.
■—론 accidentalism; casualism; fortuitism —성 contingency; possibility

우열 優劣 superiority or inferiority; merits and demerits; relative merits [superiority, excellence]
♦우열이 없는 equal; level; even / 우열을 겨루다 contend [vie] for superiority; struggle for mastery
▶우리는 이 두 작품의 우열을 논했다 We discussed the merits and demerits of these two works.
▶그들의 학교 성적은 우열을 가릴 수 없다 Their school records are just about equal.
▶그 둘은 전혀 우열을 가릴 수 없다 There is little difference between the two. ⇌ There is nothing to choose between the two.

우왕좌왕하다 右往左往— run [move] about in (utter) confusion; rush about to no purpose; go this way and that [in all directions]; go hither and thither; go right and left
▶출구를 찾아서 관객은 회관 안을 우왕좌왕했다 Looking for a way out, the spectators ran around in confusion in the hall.

우울 憂鬱 〈우울증〉 melancholy; dejection; gloom; 〈마음이 울적함〉 depression; low spirits; gloominess; the dumps; 《俗》 the blues
—우울하다 melancholy; cheerless; dejected; depressing; out of [in low] spirits; blue; gloomy; dispirited; 〈불안해서〉 uneasy
♦우울한 날씨 gloomy [depressing, miserable] weather; a gloomy [sullen] sky / 우울한 음악 melancholy [sad] music / 우울한 기분으로 with a heavy heart; in a depressed mood; in a melancholy frame of mind / 우울한 얼굴을 짓다 draw [pull] a long face; look sad [blue]; be long-faced / 우울하게 만들다 give sb a melancholy feeling; cast a gloom on sb; make sb melancholy [gloomy]
▶그는 우울해 보인다 He looks blue.
▶내일 시험을 생각하니 우울하다 I feel uneasy [cannot feel relaxed] when I think of tomorrow's exam.
▶비오는 날은 마음이 우울해진다 I feel depressed [melancholy, 《口》 blue] on rainy days. ⇌ Rainy days give me a feeling of depression [melancholy]. ⇌ Rainy days are depressing to me [depress me].

우울병 憂鬱病 melancholia; hypochondria
우울증 憂鬱症 〈우울한 현상〉 the blues; the dumps; mental depression
♦우울증에 걸려 있다 be in the blues [dumps]; suffer from [be afflicted with] depression

우월 優越 superiority; supremacy; predominance; preponderance
—우월하다 be superior (to); supreme; be predominant 《over》; preponderant; surpassing ♦남보다 우월하다 be better than [superior to] another [others]

우월감 優越感 a sense of superiority; 〔心〕 (a) superiority complex (▶원래는 정신 분석 용어였으나 지금은 구어적 표현에도 쓰임)
♦우월감을 갖다[품다] have a sense of *one's* own superiority to 《others》

우위 優位 predominance [superiority] 《over others》; a dominant [prominent] position; a position of advantage
♦우위를 차지하다 gain [get] an advantage 《over》; hold a dominant position; attain [establish, realize] superiority 《over》; gain [get] the upper hand of 《others》 / 우위에 서다[있다] be [stand] at advantage 《over》; have an advantage 《over》; have (the) precedence 《of, over》; hold priority 《to》
▶공업 기술에 있어서는 그들이 우리보다 우위에 있다 Their technology is superior to [on a higher level than] ours.

우유 牛乳 cow's milk
♦신 우유 sour milk / 아기를 우유로 기르다 feed [raise] a baby on cow's milk; bring up a baby on the bottle / 우유를 짜다 milk a cow / 우유를 끓여서 살균하다 boil and sterilize milk / 우유를 배달하다 deliver milk
▶누이동생은 우유로 자랐다 My little sister was raised on cow's milk.
■ 분말— milk powder; powder(ed) milk; dry [dried, desiccated] milk 살균— pasteurized milk 탈지— skim [skimmed] milk ■ —배달원 a milkman; a milk roundsman —배달차 a milk wagon [cart] —병 a milk bottle —팩 milk carton [container]

우유부단 優柔不斷 indecision; lack of decision; irresolution; indetermination; vacillation
—우유부단하다 irresolute; indecisive; undetermined; weak and vacillating; shilly-shally
▶그 사람처럼 우유부단한 남자는 본적이 없다 I have never seen such an indecisive [irresolute] man.
▶그는 참으로 우유부단한 사람이다 He is a very indecisive [irresolute] man. ⇌ He can never make up his mind.

우의 友誼 〈친구 사이의 정의〉 friendship; fellowship; friendly relations [ties]; fraternity; comradeship
♦우의를 돈독히 하다 promote friendship 《between》; form a fast [close] friendship 《with》
▶그는 우의가 두텁다 He is true [kind] to his friends.

우의 雨衣 a raincoat ⇨ 비옷
우의 寓意 〈교훈〉 a moral; 〈숨은 뜻〉 a hidden meaning; allegory; an implication
♦우의적인 allegorical

우이 牛耳 1 〈쇠귀〉 the ears of an ox
2 〈우두머리〉 the leader; the head
♦우이를 잡다 take command 《of》; head; lead; take the leadership

우이독경 牛耳讀經 〈쇠귀에 경읽기〉 ♦우이독경이다 It's like preaching to deaf ears [to the wind]. ⇌ It's like water off a duck's back.

우익 右翼 1 the right wing [flank, column]
♦적의 우익을 치다 attack the enemy's right wing
2 〈보수 당파〉 the right wing; the right faction; 〈사람〉 the right-wingers; the rightists
3 〔野〕 right field; 〔蹴〕 the right wing
♦우익으로 날린 3루타 a triple into right field
■ —단체 a right-wing organization —수 〔野〕

우인 a right fielder
우인 友人 〈벗〉 a friend ⇨ 벗
우자 愚者 〈어리석은 사람〉 a fool; a simpleton; an idiot; a stupid person; a dunce
우장 雨裝 〈우비를 차림〉 preparations against [for] rain; 〈우비〉 rain gear; rainwear; a rain outfit; a raincoat
▶ 우장이 없어서 우리는 흠뻑 젖었다 We got soaking wet because we had nothing to protect us from the rain.
우적우적 1 ⇨ 우썩
2 〈씹는 소리·모양〉 munching; with a munching sound
♦ 우적우적 씹어 먹다 munch; eat with a munching sound
3 〈무너지는 모양·소리〉 squeaking; creaking
▶ 벽이 우적우적 소리를 내며 무너졌다 The wall broke with a cracking sound [crack].
우접다 1 〈뛰어나게 되다〉 become outstanding [superior]
2 〈선배를 이겨내다〉 surpass one's superiors
우정 友情 friendship; fellowship; friendly feelings [spirit]; friendliness; comradeship
♦ 우정의 유대 the bonds of friendship / 참다운 우정 true friendship / 우정에서 out of friendship / 우정이 없는 unfriendly; cold to one's friends / 우정이 두텁다 be kind [warm] to one's friend(s); be cordial [tender] in friendship / 우정을 돈독히 하다[굳히] cultivate [break up] a friendship 《with》 / 변함없는 우정을 서로 맹세하다 pledge to maintain a permanent [an everlasting] friendship
▶ 그와 나 사이의 우정은 오래도록 지속되었다 The friendship between him and me lasted for a long time.
우정 郵政 postal services [administration]
우제 虞祭 〈삼우(三虞)의 총칭〉 a sacrificial rite at the conclusion of a burial
우족 右族 1 〈적자(嫡子)의 계통〉 the descendants of the legitimate son [the heir]
2 〈고귀한 집안〉 the nobles
우졸 愚拙 〈어리석고 못남〉 stupidity and clumsiness —우졸하다 stupid; clumsy
우주 宇宙 the universe; the cosmos; (outer) space

解說 모든 천체를 포함한 우주의 뜻으로는 the universe를 쓰며, 질서있는 통일된 우주는 the cosmos로 「혼돈」(chaos)에 대응하는 말이다. 다만 「우주의」 뜻으로는 이것의 형용사형인 cosmic을 쓰고 universal은 쓰지 않는다. 또한, 일반적인 과학용어로서 우주 공간은 space라고 하며, 특히 지구에서 생각하는 경우는 outer space라고도 한다.

♦ 아득한 우주의 공간 deep space / 우주의 cosmic / 인간을 우주로 보내다 launch [put] a man in space; send a man into space
▶ 우주로 발진하는 물체는 지구의 인력을 벗어나야만 한다 An object traveling into (outer) space must escape the earth's gravity.
■ 대— macrocosm; macrocosmos 소— microcosm; microcosmos ■ —계획 a space program [project] —공간 (outer) space —공학 space engineering —공항 a spaceport —관 a cosmic view —국제법 the international law of outer space —대폭발생성론 the big-bang theory —로켓 a space [cosmic] rocket —론 cosmic philosophy; cosmism; cosmology —모 (帽) a space helmet —병[멀미] space sickness —병기 a space weapon; outer-space arms —복 a space suit —비행 a space flight; space flying —비행사 a spaceman; a spacewoman; 〈미국의〉 an astronaut; a space pilot; 〈러시아의〉 a cosmonaut; a cosmonette (여자) —산업 the aerospace industry —생물학 exobiology; space biology —선 (線) cosmic rays —센터 a space center —소설 space fiction —속도 space (flight) velocity —시대 the space [cosmic] age [era] —식 (食) space food —실험실 a space lab; a Skylab —연구 space research —위성 a space satellite —유영 a spacewalk —의학 space medicine —인 a spaceman; a saucerman; a man from outer space —인력 〔物〕universal attraction [gravitation] —자기 〔物〕 cosmical magnetism —정거장 a space [satellite] station; a space platform —중계 (communications) satellite transmission: 우주 중계로 via (communication) satellite —진〔먼지〕 cosmic dust; 〈통속적으로〉 star dust —진화론 cosmogony —총 a space gun; a jet gun —캡슐 a space capsule —탐사 space [celestial] exploration —탐사기 a space probe —탐험 space exploration —통신 space communication —항공학 astronautics; cosmonautics —항법 space navigation; astronautics; astrogation —협정 a space agreement
우주개발 宇宙開發 space development
■ —경쟁 a space race —계획 a space development project [program]
우주과학 宇宙科學 space science
■ —자 a space scientist
우주선 宇宙船 a spaceship; a spacecraft; a space shuttle; a space vehicle

解說 로켓 추진의 우주선은 spaceship, 기타 우주 여행이나 우주 탐색을 위한 위성(satellite) 등을 포함하여 넓은 의미로는 spacecraft라고 하며 우주 왕복선은 space shuttle이라고 한다.

우주여행 宇宙旅行 a space travel [journey, trip]; a travel [journey] in (outer) space
■ —자 a space traveler
우주왕복선 宇宙往復船 a space shuttle
우주학 宇宙學 cosmology
■ —자 a cosmologist
우줄거리다 〈몸을〉 keep dancing [swaying]; 〈뽐내다〉 keep swaggering
우줄우줄 〈몸을〉 with a swinging motion; dancing [swaying] rhythmically; 〈걸음을〉 with a swagger [rolling gait]
♦ 우줄우줄 걷다 walk with a swagger; swagger; roll / 우줄우줄 춤추다 dance up and down
우줅거리다 〈어기적거리며〉 toddle; trudge
우줅우줅 toddling; trudging; waddling
—우줅우줅하다 toddle

우줅이다 〈말려도 듣지 않고〉 go ahead and do; persist in doing *one's* own way

우중 雨中 ◆우중에 in the rain / 우중에도 불구하고 in spite of the rain; ignoring the rain; though it is raining
▶그들은 우중에도 불구하고 게임을 속행했다 In spite of the rain they continued the game.

우중충하다 〈어둡고 침침하다〉 gloomy; dismal; somber; dark
◆우중충한 날씨 gloomy [dull] weather / 우중충한 방 a gloomy room / 우중충한 색 a dull [dark] color / 우중충한 하늘 a somber sky; a clouded sky; a dull [gloomy] sky; an overcast

우지 〈울보〉 a crybaby; a blubberer
우지 牛脂 〈쇠기름〉 (beef) tallow; suet
우지끈 with a crack [smash]
▶강풍으로 전봇대가 우지끈 부러졌다 The strong wind brought [blew] down a utility pole with a crack.

우지끈거리다 〈우지끈 소리가 자꾸 나다〉 make cracking noises ▶대들보가 우지끈거리며 내려 앉았다 The crossbeam collapsed [fell] with a crashing noise.

우지끈뚝딱 with a crack [crackle, thud, thump]

우지끈우지끈 with crackles [cracks, snaps]
—우지끈우지끈하다 make cracking noises ⇨ 우지끈거리다

우지직 1 〈타는 소리〉 cracking; crackling; sputtering ◆우지직 타는 도화선 a sputtering fuse / 우지직 타다 crackle; burn crackling
▶마른 잔가지가 우지직 소리를 내며 탔다 Dry twigs crackled as they burned.
2 〈부러지는 소리〉 with a snap [crack]
▶정원사는 소나무 가지를 우지직 꺾었다 The gardener broke a pine twig with a snap.

우직 愚直 simple honesty; tactless frankness
—우직하다 honest to a fault; stupidly honest
◆우직한 남자 a simple and honest man / 우직한 〈고지식한〉 simple and honest

우집다 1 〈남을 업신여기다〉 despise [look down on] people
2 ⇨ 우겁다

우짖다 1 〈지저귀다〉 sing; chirp; chirrup; twitter; warble ▶새가 우짖는 소리에 잠에서 깨었다 I was awakened by the chirping [twittering] of the birds.
2 ⇨ 울부짖다

우쭐하다 be proud (of); be pompous; be [get] puffed up (by, with); be [get] self-conceited; 《美口》 have [get] a swelled head; 《英口》 get a swollen head; be [feel] elated (with, by); be inflated (exultant) (over); exult (in, at, over); swell with pride (at)
◆우쭐하여 exultantly; proudly; elatedly / 우쭐해서 말하다 speak in an elated manner
▶그렇게 우쭐하지 마라 Don't flatter yourself so much.
▶머리가 좋다고 우쭐해서 공부하지 않으니까 점점 성적이 떨어지는 거야 Because you think yourself smart and don't study, your marks are getting worse and worse.
▶영어를 조금 말할 수 있다고 해서 우쭐해 하지 마라 You should not have a high [good] opinion of yourself just because you can speak English a little.

우차 牛車 an oxcart
우책 愚策 〈졸렬한 술책〉 a stupid plan
우천 雨天 〈비가 오는 날씨〉 rainy [wet] weather; 〈비가 오는 날〉 a rainy [wet] day
◆우천 때문에 owing to [on account of] the rain
▶오랫동안 우천이 계속되었다 We have had a long spell of rainy weather.
▶우천일 경우라도 수업은 한다 We have classes if it rains [in case of rain].
▶우천 순연(順延) 《게시》 To be postponed till the first [next] fine day in case of rain.

우체국 郵遞局 a post office
■군사— an army post office (略 A.P.O.)
■—장 a postmaster; a postmistress (여자)
—직원 a post-office clerk; 《美》 a mail [mailing] clerk; 《英》 a postal clerk

우체부 郵遞夫 a postman ⇨ 우편집배원
우체통 郵遞筒 《美》 a (roadside) mailbox; 《英》 a postbox; 〈기둥모양의〉 a pillar box; a letter box; a post
◆우체통에 편지를 넣다 mail a letter (at a mailbox); post a letter; put a letter into a mailbox
▶우체통에 편지 넣는 것을 잊었다 I forgot to mail [《英》 post] my letter.

우측 右側 the right; the right side; the right hand; 〈배·항공기의〉 the starboard
◆우측의 right-hand; on the right / 우측에 on [at] the right (of); at [on, to] *one's* right hand / 〈도로의〉 우측을 다니다 keep to *one's* right side of the road
▶우측으로 첫번째 방이 내 연구실이다 The first room on the right is my office.
▶우측통행 《게시》 Keep to the right.
▶한국에서는 사람은 좌측으로 차는 우측으로 다닌다 In Korea pedestrians keep to the left and cars to the right.

우쿨렐레 〈악기〉 a ukulele; 《口》 a uke
우크라이나 the Ukraine; 〈공식명〉 the Republic of Ukrainian ◆우크라이나의 Ukrainian
■—말 Ukrainian ■—사람 a Ukrainian

우툴두툴하다 〈평평하지 않은〉 uneven; 〈매끈하지 않은〉 rough 《surface》; 〈거칠거칠한〉 rugged 《features》; 〈길이〉 bumpy; ragged; 〈나무·가죽이〉 granulated 《wood, leather》
◆우툴두툴한 길 a rough road; a bumpy [bumping] road / 우툴두툴한 목재 a knotty timber
▶우리는 우툴두툴한 산길을 따라갔다 We followed a rough [rugged] path up the mountain.

우파 右派 the right wing ⇨ 우익
우파니샤드 〈옛 인도의 철학서〉 Upanishad
우퍼 〈저음 확성기〉 a woofer
우편 右便 the right side ◆우편에 on the right side (of); on *one's* right

우편 郵便 《美》 mail; 《英》 post; 〈제도〉 mail [postal] service; 〈우편물〉 mail; postal matter
◆우편을 배달하다 deliver mail / 우편을 부치다 post [mail] (a letter); put (a letter) in the post; mail (a letter) at a mailbox / 우편으로

알리다[보내다, 주문하다] inform [send, order] by post [mail]
▶내 앞으로 온 우편이 있나요? Is there any mail [post] for me?
■군사— army [military] post [mail] 등기— (by) registered mail [post] 선내(船內)— sea post [mail] 속달— special delivery; express mail [post]; 〈편지〉 a special delivery letter; (英) an express(-delivery) letter: 이 편지를 속달 우편으로 부탁합니다 I'd like to send this letter by special delivery [(英) express], please. 외국[국내]— foreign [domestic] post [mail] 항공— air mail ■—기(旗)(船) a mail flag —낭[가방] (美) a mailbag; 〈가죽〉 a mail pouch; (英) a postbag —료 ⇨ 우편요금 —소액환 a postal order —소인 (消印) a postmark; a post-office stamp —소포 a postal package; parcel —업무 mail [postal] service —연금 a post-office [postal] annuity; 〈제도〉 the mail pension system —엽서 ⇨ 엽서 —전신환 a postal telegraphic transfer —제도 the postal system —조례[규칙] the postal regulations —조약 a postal treaty [convention] —주문 a mail order —차 [열차] a mail train (▶a post train은 잘못된 표현임); 〈한칸〉 a mail car; a post van; 〈자동차〉 a mail truck; a mailcoach —투표 voting by mail —함 〈각 가정의〉 (美) a mailbox (pl. ~es); (英) a letter box (pl. ~es)

우편물 郵便物 postal matter; mail; (英) post ◆우편물을 분류하다 sort mail
■제3종— third-class mail —구분대 a mailing table —투입구 a letter drop

우편배달 郵便配達 mail delivery; delivery of mail
■—구역 a postal delivery zone [(英) district]; (美) the zone —부 ⇨ 우편집배원

우편번호 郵便番號 〈전체〉 (美) zip code; (英) postcode; 〈개개의〉 (美) a zip code [postal code] number; a (postal) zone number
■—제도 the postal zoning system; (美) the zip code system

우편사서함 郵便私書函 a post-office box (略 POB, P.O.B., P.O. Box) ◆우편사서함 광화문 300번 P.O. Box Kwanghwamun 300

우편선 郵便船 a mail steamer [boat]; a mailer; (英) a post boat
■정기— a regular mail liner

우편요금 郵便料金 postage 《on a letter》; postal charges
▶우편요금 선불 Postage prepaid.
▶우편요금 지불필 Postage paid.
▶이탈리아로 부치는 편지의 항공우편 요금은 얼마지요? What [How much] is the airmail postage for [on] a letter to Italy, please?

우편저금 郵便貯金 postal savings; postal deposit
▶이 돈을 우편 저금 하고 싶다 I want to deposit this money in the post office.

우편집배원 郵便集配員 (美) a mailman; (英) a postman; a postboy; (美) a mail carrier
▶우편 집배원은 편지를 하루에 두 번 배달한다 The mailman delivers letters twice a day [makes two deliveries per day].

우편환 郵便換 (美) (postal) money order (略 P.M.O.); (英) a postal order (略 P.O.); money order; 〈내국 우편환〉 inland money order; 〈외국 우편환〉 international money order
◆우편환으로 3만원을 보내다 send 30,000 won by money order (英) postal order] (▶a mail order는 「우편에 의한 주문」의 뜻) / 우편환을 발행하다[지불하다] draw [cash] a postal money order / 우편환을 현금화하다 have a postal money order cashed

우표 郵票 a (postage) stamp
◆400원짜리 우표 a four hundred won stamp / 우표를 붙이다 put a stamp on (the envelope); stamp (a letter)
▶이 편지에는 얼마짜리 우표를 붙입니까? What is the postage for this letter?
■—첩 a stamp album [book, booklet]

우표수집 郵票蒐集 stamp collecting; philately
■—가 a stamp collector; a philatelist —열 the stamp craze

우피 牛皮 oxhide ⇨ 쇠가죽

우향 右向 ◆우향 우 (口令) Right turn [face]!
◆우향 앞으로 가 (口令) Right wheel!

우현 右舷 (海) the starboard; the right side (of a ship)
◆우현에 배가 보이다 sight a ship to (the) starboard / 키를 우현으로 잡다 starboard the helm; put the helm starboard
▶배는 좌현에서 우현으로 침로를 바꾸었다 The ship changed its course from port to starboard.

우호 友好 friendship; amity
◆우호적인 분위기 a cordial atmosphere / 우호적인 태도 a friendly attitude / 우호적인 friendly; fraternal; amicable (▶friendly는 적극적인 「우정·우호」를 나타내고 amicable은 단순히 적의가 없음을 나타냄) / 우호적으로 in a friendly way
■—관계 (establish) friendly [cordial, amicable] relations: 올림픽의 목적은 세계 여러 민족의 우호관계를 증진하는 데 있다 The purpose of the Olympics is to foster friendly relations among the peoples of the world. —국 a friendly nation [state, power] —사절 a goodwill delegate —조약 treaty of friendship [amity]; friendship treaty —통상조약 a treaty of comity and commerce

우화 羽化 〈번데기의〉 emergence; eclosion; hatch —우화하다 emerge; eclose; hatch ◆갓 우화한 나비 a newly emerged butterfly

우화 雨靴 (a pair of) rain shoes; 〈고무덧신〉 galoshes; overshoes

우화 寓話 a fable; 〈교훈적인〉 an allegory; a parable ◆이솝 우화 Aesop's Fables
■동물— an animal fable —작가 a fable writer; a fabler

우환 憂患 1 〈걱정거리〉 trouble; care; worry; anxiety; 〈불행〉 a calamity; a misfortune
◆우환이 있다 have worries [anxieties]; be worried; be agonized / 우환이 끊이지 않다 suffer a series of misfortunes
2 〈질병〉 illness
◆집안의 우환 family illness

우황 牛黃 [韓醫] ox bezoar

우회 迂廻 〈멀리 돌아감〉 a roundabout way;

an indirect route; a circuit; 〈교통 장애에 의한〉 a detour
—우회하다 take a long way around; make [take] a circuit 《round》; make a detour; detour; take a roundabout [circuitous] way [route]
▶도로가 보수중이어서 우리는 우회했다 The road was under repair, so we made a detour [detoured, took an indirect route].
▶우리는 우회하여 산길을 따라갔다 We made a detour through the mountains.
▶[會話]「집에 데려다 주시는 건 고맙지만 저 때문에 우회하는 건 아닌지요?」「아닙니다. 그렇지 않습니다」 "It's kind of you to take me home, but won't it take you (far) out of your way?" "No, it won't."
■—로 a roundabout way [route]; a detour; a bypass —무역 commodity shunting —생산 circuitous production; a roundabout method of production —선 a roundabout route —작전 an outflanking action

우회전 右廻轉 a right turn
▶우회전 금지 (게시) No right-turn.
—우회전하다 turn right; turn to [toward] the right ♦〈기계가〉 우회전하는 dextrorotatory; right-handed 《propeller》

우후죽순 雨後竹筍 ♦우후죽순처럼 나타나다 spring [crop] up like (so many) mushrooms after rain; mushroom; increase rapidly (in number)
▶유사한 회사들이 우후죽순처럼 설립되었다 Many similar companies were established one after another.

욱기 —氣 〈욱하는 성질〉 an inflammable [impulsive] nature
♦욱기가 있는 excitable; hot-brained; hot-headed; hot-tempered; impulsive

욱다 1 〈우그러지다〉 dent; become dented [hollow, depressed] 2 〈기운이〉 lose vigor; be enfeebled [weakened, enervated]

욱시글거리다 swarm 《with》; be crowded [thronged] 《with》; teem 《with》

욱신거리다 1 ⇨ 북적거리다 2 〈쑤시다〉 shoot; sting; have a shooting pain 《in》; feel a smart pain 《in》; tingle [throb] (with pain)
♦욱신거리는 상처 a shooting wound / 욱신거리는 아픔 (a) throbbing pain
▶상처가 욱신거렸다 The wound throbbed with pain.
▶머리가 (두통으로) 욱신거린다 My head throbs.
▶이가 욱신거린다 My tooth stings.

욱이다 〈안쪽으로 욱게 하다〉 bend sth in [inward]; dent; make a dent in
▶새 주전자를 테이블 모서리에 부딪뜨려 욱였다 I hit the new kettle against the edge of the table and made a dent in it.

욱일 旭日 the rising [morning] sun
▶그는 욱일 승천의 기세다 His star is rising [in the ascendant].

욱적거리다 bustle ⇨ 북적거리다

욱죄이다 be fastened [bound] tight; 〈목을〉 be throttled [choked]; get cramped [tightened]

욱지르다 intimidate; browbeat; cow
▶그는 그녀를 욱질러 그 서류에 서명하게 했다 He frightened [intimidated] her into signing the paper.

욱하다 excite oneself; rouse up; burst forth; be stirred; flare up; get impetuous
♦사소한 일에 욱하다 flare up at the slightest thing / 욱하고 성을 내다 be roused to anger; flare up 《in anger》; burst into a sudden anger
▶그는 내 말을 듣고 욱했다 He lost his temper [got very angry, got furious, flew into a rage] at what I said.
▶그는 모욕을 당하고 욱했다 He was roused to anger by the insult.

운 運 〈천명〉 destiny; fate; (a) lot; 〈인생을 좌우하는〉 fortune; 〈그때뿐의〉 luck; 〈우연의〉 chance
♦운좋게 fortunately; luckily; as (good) luck would have it; by (a piece of) good luck / 운좋게…하다 be lucky enough to 《do》; have the (good) fortune to 《do》; have the luck to 《be》 / 운 나쁘게 unluckily; unfortunately; by ill luck; by a stroke of bad luck [misfortune]
▶그는 운 나쁘게 그 사고에 말려들었다 Unfortunately [Unluckily], he was involved in the accident.
▶나는 운좋게 1등상을 받았다 I had the (good) luck to win (the) first prize.
▶그의 운도 기울었다[내리막이다] His star has set. ⇌ His (good) luck has run [played] out.
〈운이〉 운이 기울다 be down on one's luck / 운이 나쁘다 be unlucky [unfortunate]; be out of luck; have no luck / 운이 좋다 be lucky [fortunate]; have [be blessed with] a good luck; be born under a lucky star / 운이 트다 be in luck's way; one's fortune changes for the better; fortune turns in one's favor / 운이 트지 않다 have constant ill [bad] luck; have no luck; luck goes [runs] against sb
▶운이 나빴군 Bad [Hard, Tough] luck!
▶운이 내게 트이고 있다 Luck is coming my way.
▶여기서 널 만나다니 정말 운이 좋군 How lucky [What a stroke of luck] to meet you here!
▶오늘은 운이 없다 I'm out of luck today. ⇌ My luck is out today.
〈운을〉 운을 하늘에 맡기다 trust to Providence [Heaven]; leave one's fate to Heaven / 운을 시험해 보다 try one's luck [fortune]
▶운을 하늘에 맡기자 Let's take a chance. (▶흥하든 망하든 해보자는 뜻)
▶이렇게 되면 운을 하늘에 맡기는 수밖에 없다 There is nothing to do but to leave our fate to Heaven.
〈운에〉 운에 맡기다 trust to chance [luck]; leave 《a matter》 to chance; take the risk / 운에 맡기고 해보다 take [try] one's chance
▶매사를 운에 맡기지 마라 Don't leave anything to luck [chance].

운 韻 a rhyme; 《美》 a rime
♦운이 맞다 rhyme [make a rhyme] with 《some words》 / 운을 내다 propose [provide]

the rhymes / 운을 맞추다 rhyme the lines
운각 雲刻 〈구름 모양의 새김〉 cloud-shaped carved decorations
운각 韻脚 〈시의〉 a (metrical) foot
운경 雲鏡 〔氣〕〈운속계〉 a nephoscope
운고 雲高 〈구름의 높이〉 the height of the cloud ceiling; the ceiling
운급 雲級 〔氣〕〈10종 기본 운형의 분류〉 ◆10종 운급 the classification of clouds into ten categories / 〈국제〉 운급도 an (international) atlas of clouds
운김 1 〈남은 기운〉 remaining warmth
▶그 방에는 아직도 운김이 있다 There is still a little warmth lingering in the room.
2 〈울력〉 an impetus; an impulse
▶나는 운김에 그 일을 마쳤다 I finished the work on the spur [impulse] of circumstances.
운니지차 雲泥之差 〈매우 심한 차이〉 a great [wide] difference; miles of difference (between)
▶A와 B는 운니지차가 있다 There is a great difference [a vast difference, all the difference in the world] between A and B.
운동 運動 1〈물리적 움직임〉 motion (▶이론적·추상적인 뜻에서의 움직임); movement (▶방향성을 갖는 구체적인 움직임)
◆운동의 원리[법칙] the principle [laws] of motion / 운동중인 물체 a body in motion
─운동하다 move; be in motion
2 〈신체적 움직임〉 exercise; 〈경기〉 (athletic) sports; athletics; games
◆가벼운[과격한] 운동 light [(a) violent, (a) hard] exercise / 매일 한 시간씩의 운동 an hour's daily exercise
▶수영은 체중 감량에 좋은 운동이다 Swimming is a good exercise to lose weight.
〈운동은[이]〉 적당한 운동은 건강에 좋다 A little [Some, Moderate] exercise is good for the health [will do you good].
▶나는 운동이 더 필요하다 I need more exercise.
〈운동을〉 그는 운동을 잘한다 He is good at sports.
▶그는 운동을 위해 늘 걸어서 학교에 간다 He always walks to school for exercise.
▶식후 바로 심한 운동을 하지 마세요 Try not to take hard exercise soon after meals.
〈운동에〉 적어도 하루에 두 시간은 운동에 투자해야 한다 Not less than two hours a day should be spend on exercise.
─운동하다 take (bodily) exercise; exercise
3 〈사회적·정치적 활동〉 a movement; canvassing; a campaign; a drive; a crusade; an agitation; 〈의회의〉 lobbying (operations)
▶그는 대학 시절에 학생 운동에 가담했다 He was a student political activist when he was in college.
〈운동의〉 운동의 조직자 a campaign organizer / 그 운동의 발기인 the initiators of the movement
〈운동은[이]〉 대통령선거 운동은 1주일 전에 시작되었다 The presidential campaign began a week ago.
▶마약 판매 금지 운동이 시작되었다 A movement was begun to stop selling drugs.
〈운동을〉 운동을 벌이다 start a movement [crusade]; start [initiate, drive] a campaign; launch a drive [campaign] / 모금 운동을 하다 drive a fund-raising / 의안 통과 운동을 하다 lobby a bill
▶그는 그 운동을 지지하여 기꺼이 돈을 냈다 He willingly gave money [opened his purse] to support the movement.
─운동하다 conduct [carry on] a campaign (for, against); canvass (for); campaign (for, against); agitate; lobby (a bill)
■금주─ a temperance [prohibition] movement; a temperance crusade 상하— an up-and-down motion 선거— an election campaign; electioneering 실내— an indoor sport [game] 옥외— an outdoor sport [game]; field sports 임금 인상— an agitation [a movement] for an increase of wages 정치[노동]— a political [labor] movement 종교— a religious movement ─가[선수] an athlete; a sportsman ─감각 the sensation of movement ─경기 athletic sports; athletics ─권 학생 activist students for the political struggle; the students in the sphere of activism ─기구 ⇨ 운동구 ─량 quantity of motion; 〔物〕 momentum; impetus ─마찰 〔物〕 kinetic friction ─모 a sports cap ─복 〈한벌〉 sports clothes; sportswear; 〈상의〉 a sports coat [jacket] ─부 〈학교의〉 an athletic club ─셔츠 a sports shirt ─시설 sports facilities ─열 a passion for sports; love of sports ─원 〈선거의〉 a canvasser; an electioneer; an electioneering [a canvassing] agent; 〈정치상의〉 an agitator; a campaigner ─자금 campaign funds ─장 a playground; an athletic ground [field]; a sports field; (美) a park; (英) a playing field; 〈학교의〉 a schoolyard; 〈경기장〉 a stadium ─장애 〔醫〕 motor disturbance ─정신 sportsmanship ─화 sports [gymnasium, gym] shoes; (美口) 〈고무창을 댄〉 sneakers
운동구 運動具 sporting [athletic] goods [apparatus]; gymnastic equipment; sport outfits ─점 a sports store [shop]
운동방정식 運動方程式 〔物〕 the equation of motion
운동법칙 運動法則 〔物〕 law of motion
운동부족 運動不足 lack [shortage, want] of exercise; underexercise ◆운동부족으로 through lack of exercise
▶그는 운동부족으로 입맛이 떨어졌다 He has little appetite for lack [want] of exercise.
운동신경 運動神經 〔解〕 motor nerves
▶나는 운동신경이 둔하다[발달해 있다] I have slow [good, fast] reflexes.
운동회 運動會 〈트랙과 필드의 육상경기를 중심으로 한〉 an athletic meeting [(美) meet]; a field (and track) meet; a sports meeting

> 解説 *athletic meeting* [(美) *meet*]에는 둘 이상의 학교나 회사 등이 서로 승부를 겨룬다는 느낌이 다분하다.

♦학교 운동회 the school sports
▶나는 운동회의 100미터 경주에서 이겼다 I won the 100 meter dash in the sports.
■—날 (美) a sports day; a field day

운두 the height of shoes [bowls]
♦운두가 높은[낮은] 신 a high-cut [low-cut] shoes

운명 運命 〈숙명〉(a) destiny;〈필연·결정적인 운〉fate;〈우연·맹목적인 운〉(a) lot;〈(미래의) 운수〉(good, ill) fortune;〈천명〉kismet;〈악운〉doom; the inevitable
〈운명의〉운명의 순간[결단] a fateful moment [decision] (▶fateful은 「운명을 결정하는」, fatal은 「치명적인」의 뜻) / 운명의 짓궂음[장난]으로 by the irony [a quirk, a twist] of fate / 실패를 운명의 탓으로 돌리다 blame one's failure on fate
▶운명의 여신은 용감한 자의 편이다 Fortune favors the brave.
▶운명의 여신이 그에게 미소를 보냈다[그의 편에 섰다] Fortune smiled on [favored] him.
〈운명이[은]〉어떤 운명이 기다리고 있는지 아무도 모른다 No one knows what fate [destiny] is in store for him. ⇌ No one can tell what fate [destiny] awaits him.
▶나는 의사가 되고 싶었으나 운명이 그것을 허락하지 않았다 I wanted to be a doctor, but fate had decided otherwise. (▶스스로 어떤 상황을 타개하지 못한 결과로 불행했던 경우이므로 destiny는 쓸 수 없음)
▶병사의 운명은 가혹했다 A soldier's lot (in life) is a hard one.
〈운명을〉운명을 결정하다 decide [(口) seal] sb's fate / 운명을 타개하다 work [carve] out one's destiny / 운명을 받아들이다 accept one's fate;〈내맡기다〉be resigned [resign oneself] to one's fate (▶이것은 자유의지가 아니므로 destiny는 부적당함) / 운명을 좌우하다 affect the fate [destiny] 《of》 / 운명을 함께 하다 share sb's fate; throw in one's lot 《with sb》
▶아무도 자신의 운명을 모른다 Nobody knows his own destiny [fate]. ⇌ Nobody knows what his destiny [fate] will be.
〈운명에〉운명에 맞서다 rebel against 《one's》 destiny (▶이와 같이 자유의지의 가능성이 있는 경우 fate는 부적당함) / 운명에 맡기다 abandon [leave] 《sb oneself, sth》 to fate
▶우리는 모두 같은 운명에 처해 있다 We are all in the same boat.
▶그는 요절할 운명이었다 He was fated [doomed, destined] to die young. ⇌ It was fated that he ((英)) should) die young. ⇌ It was his fate to die young. ⇌ He was doomed to an early death.
〈운명에서〉우리는 자신의 운명에서 벗어날 수 없다 We cannot escape our destiny [fate].
〈기타〉운명으로 돌리다 resign oneself to one's fate; accept the inevitable / 운명과 싸우다 struggle [strive] against one's destiny
■—론 fatalism —론자 a fatalist —선 〔手相〕 the line of Fate [Destiny, Saturn]

운명 殞命 〈숨을 거둠〉death —운명하다 die; pass away; breathe one's last ▶남편은 4년 전에 운명했다 My husband died [passed away] (on me) four years ago.

운모 雲母 〔鑛〕 mica; isinglass ■ 금— phlogopite 백— muscovite; talc 흑— biotite
■—지 mica paper —판 a mica plate —편암 mica schist [slate]

운무 雲霧 cloud and mist [fog] ♦운무에 싸이다 be shrouded in cloud and fog

운문 韻文 〈산문에 대하여〉verse;〈시〉a poem; poetry;〈총칭〉metrical composition
♦운문으로 쓰다 compose [write] in verse
—극 a verse drama; a play in verse

운반 運搬 conveyance; transfer; transport; transportation; carriage
—운반하다〈손·손수레 등으로〉carry;〈배·비행기·열차 등으로〉transport;〈연속적인 배송 수단으로〉convey; deliver
♦손수레로 운반하다 carry by the [on a] cart; cart
▶물건을 트럭으로 운반하는 데 하루 걸렸다 It took all day to transport the goods by truck.
■—기계 a conveyor; a transporter —비 carriage; haulage;〈인부의〉porterage;〈찻삯〉cartage —인 a porter; a carrier;〈광산의〉a putter; a headsman

운반작용 運搬作用 〔地〕 transportation

운반차 運搬車 a cart; a wagon;〈자동차의〉a (motor) lorry; (美) a (motor) truck;〈이삿짐차의〉a removal van
■이삿짐— a moving [furniture] van 환자[부상자]— an ambulance (car)

운산 運算 operation; calculation ⇨ 연산(演算)
—운산하다 operate; calculate; cipher; figure out; do [work] sums
▶그는 방정식을 운산하지 못했다 He couldn't work out the equation.

운산무소하다 雲散霧消— disperse like mist; go up in smoke; vanish like smoke [into thin air]
▶그 계획은 운산무소했다 The plan came to nothing. ⇌ The plan went up in smoke. ⇌ The plan vanished like (the) mist.

운석 隕石 a meteorite [míːtiərɑ̀it]; a meteorolite; a meteoric [falling] stone ■—학 astrolithology

운성 隕星 a shooting star ⇨ 유성(流星)

운송 運送 conveyance; shipping; (英) transport; (美) transportation; carriage; traffic; forwarding; (美) freight
▶그 금괴는 운송중에 없어졌다 The gold ingots disappeared in transit.
—운송하다〈보내다〉send;〈수송하다〉transport;〈운반하다〉convey; carry; forward; ship
♦철도[배]로 운송하다 transport 《goods》 by rail [ship]
▶물품은 트럭으로 운송합니다 We will send [(美) ship] the goods by truck. ⇌ (口) We will truck the goods.
■—트럭 trucking 해상[육상]— transportation [conveyance] by sea [land]; carriage by sea [land] 화물— 〔商〕 goods transport ■—계약 a contract of carriage —기능 transportation function —료 forwarding [shipping]

charges; freight (rates); carriage; 〈운반차 운임〉 cartage ━보험 transportation insurance ━비 cost of transport freight; carriage (of [on] goods); shipping expenses [charges] ━선 a transport (ship); a cargo vessel; a freighter ━시설 transportation facilities ━인 a carrier; a porter ━점 a forwarding [shipping] agency; 〈사람〉 a forwarding [shipping] agent; a carrier; (美) an expressman ━차〈운송회사의〉 an express cart [wagon] ━화물 freight; goods ━회사 a transport [a shipping, a freight, an express] company; 〈자동차로 운송하는〉 a trucking company; 〈특히 이삿짐 운송 등의〉 moving company; mover

운송업 運送業 transport [freight, shipping] industry; transportation [forwarding] business ■━자 a shipping [a freight, a forwarding, an express] agent; an expressman

운송주선업 運送周旋業 forwarding business

운수 運數 *one's* star; fortune; luck
♦운수가 좋다[나쁘다] be fortunate [unfortunate]; be lucky [unlucky, ill-starred] / 운수를 보아 주다 tell [read] *sb's* fortune / 점쟁이에게 운수를 물어보다 have *one's* fortune told by a fortuneteller
■━소관 a matter pertaining to luck [fortune]; a matter of chance

운수 運輸 traffic (service); 〈수송〉(美) transportation; (英) transport; 〈운송〉 conveyance
■여객[철도]━ passenger [railway] traffic 해상[육상, 내국]━ marine [overland, inland] transportation ■━국(局) the traffic department ━기관 means of conveyance [transportation] ━능력 carrying capacity ━량 traffic ━사업 the transportation business ━협정 a traffic agreement ━회사 a transportation company; an express company

운신 運身 (a) movement; a stir
━운신하다 move (*one's* self); stir
▶우리는 초만원인 기차 안에서 운신조차 할 수 없었다 We could not even move in the overcrowded train.

운영 運營 operation; management; administration; conduct
━운영하다 operate; manage; administer; 〈경영하다〉 run
▶그가 위원회를 운영했다 He chaired the committee.
▶그 학교는 다섯 명의 이사가 운영하고 있다 The school is managed by five directors.
▶그는 큰 사업을 운영하고 있다 He runs a big business.
■━비 working expenses ━위원회〈국민 등의〉 a steering committee; 〈미국 하원의〉 Committee of Rules ━자금 working [operating] funds

운용 運用 (practical) use; working; employment; operation; 〈적용〉 application; 〈투자〉 investment
♦법률의 운용 the applicaton of the law ━운용하다〈쓰다〉 use; make use of; employ 《capital》; 〈적용하다〉 apply (to); 〈실시하다〉 put into practice; enforce; 〈투자하다〉 invest (in); 〈운전하다〉 operate; work
▶그는 지식을 운용하는데 훌륭하다 He is good at putting his knowledge to practical use.
■━의무시간 compulsory operating hours ━자본 working capital; operational funds

운운 云云 so and so; and so forth; and so on; (라) et cetera (略 etc., &c.); and the like ━운운하다 say *sth* or other (of, about); 〈비판하다〉 criticize; comment (on); 〈언급하다〉 mention; refer to
♦운운하는 such and such; certain (reason)
▶당신이 한 일을 운운할 생각은 아니었다 I didn't mean to criticize [comment on] what you did.

운율 韻律 〈운문의〉(a) meter [(英) (a) metre]; 〈리듬〉 (a) rhythm; a measure
♦운율의[적인] rhythmical; metrical / 운율이 없는 rhythmless
▶영어의 운율은 강세가 있는 음절이 규칙적으로 나타나는 것이 특징이다 English rhythm is characterized by the regular recurrence of emphasized syllables.
■━학 metrics; prosody

운임 運賃 **1**〈여객의〉 a (passenger) fare; 〈요금〉 charge; tariff
♦운임을 올리다[내리다] raise [lower] the fares / 할증 운임을 받다[내다] charge [pay] an extra fare
▶버스 운임이 또 올랐다 Bus fares have increased [been raised] again.
▶서울에서 대전까지의 왕복운임은 얼마입니까? What is the double [(美) round-trip, (英) return] fare from Seoul to Taejŏn?
2〈운송료〉 freight; freightage; freight [goods] charges [rates]; carriage; portage; 〈적화료〉 cartage; 〈용선료〉 shipping expenses [charges]
♦운임 무료 (게시) Carriage free
■━국내[해양, 항공]━ inland [ocean, airway] freight 반액━ a half fare 편도[왕복]━ a single [double, return] fare 할인━ a reduced fare ■━보험료 포함 가격 C.I.F. (〈cost, *i*nsurance and *f*reight〉 ━선불 carriage [freight] forward ━지불필 carriage paid ━청구서 a freight bill (略 f.b., FB) ━포함 가격 cost and freight (略 C. & F.) ━표〈여객〉 a fare table; 〈화물〉 a freight list; a (railway) tariff ━협정 [경쟁] a tariff agreement [war]

운자 韻字 〈한시의 각운자〉 a rhyming [rhyme] character

운적토 運積土 (地) transported soils

운전 運轉 〈자동차 등의 조종〉 driving; 〈교통기관의 운행〉 a run; 〈기계의 조작〉 operation; 〈자금 등의 운용〉 working
♦기계의 운전 the operation of a machine / 운전중인 기계 a machine in operation / 운전 교습을 받다 take driving lessons; take a driving course
▶자동차 운전을 가르쳐 주세오 Please teach me how to drive a car.
━운전하다〈차를 몰다〉 drive; take the wheel; 〈교통 기관을 운행하다〉 run; 〈자금을 운용하다〉 work; 〈기계를 조작하다〉 operate
♦기계를 운전하다 run, operate a machine / 운전하기 쉽다[어렵다] be easy [hard] to drive

▶ 그녀가 운전 했다 She took the wheel.
▶ 그는 차를 잘못 운전하여 시궁창에 빠졌다 He lost control of the car and it ended up in the ditch. ■시(험)— a trial run [operation] 음주— drunken [(口) drunk] driving ■—면허(증) 《美》a driver's license; 《英》a driving license: 그녀는 운전면허를 따고 싶어 한다 She wants to take a driver's license. —면허시험《take》a driving test —자금[자본] working capital [funds]; operational funds: 우리는 운전 자금이 부족하다 We are short of working fund.

운전사 運轉士 〈전동차 등의〉 a motorman; a (streetcar) driver; 〈기차의〉 an engineer; a locomotive engineer; 《英》 an engine driver; 〈승용차의〉 a driver; 〈자가용차의〉 a chauffeur; 〈택시의〉 a cabdriver; a cabman; a taxi driver; 〈버스의〉 a bus driver; 《英》 a busman; 〈트럭의〉 a truck [《英》 lorry] driver; 〈기계의〉 an operator; a runner
■ 교대— a co-driver 모범— an exemplary driver

운제 雲梯 a turret; a high [scaling] ladder
운지법 運指法 〔樂〕 fingering
운 집 하 다 雲集— swarm; crowd; gather [assemble] in crowds; throng
운철 隕鐵 〔鑛〕 a meteoric iron; siderite
운치 韻致 refinement; elegance; grace; artistic effect; gusto; daintiness
♦예술적 운치가 있는 유명한 작품 works of noble gusto / 운치가 있는 elegant; graceful; refined; tasteful; artistic; (a)esthetic / 운치가 없는 bald 《prose style》

운크라 UNKRA 〔《*United Nations Korean Reconstruction Agency*》〕
운크타드 UNCTAD 〔《*United Nations Conference on Trade and Development*》〕
운필 運筆 〈서법〉 calligraphy; 〈필법〉 strokes of the brush [pen]; 〈운필법〉 the use of [manner of handling] the brush [pen]
운하 運河 a canal [kənǽl]; a waterway
♦운하를 파다[만들다] dig [build, construct, cut, excavate] a canal; canalize
■ 수평[수문]— a level [a lock] canal 파나마 [수에즈]— the Panama [Suez] Canal ■ —통과료 canal tolls
운항 運航 〈항공기의〉 flight; 〈배의〉 service
♦운항중인 배 a ship in service
▶ 태풍 때문에 모든 비행기의 운항이 중지되었다 All flights were canceled because of the typhoon. ⇒ Air transportation services were completely halted because of the typhoon.
—운항하다 operate; run; ply
♦포항과 울릉도간을 운항하는 배 a ship that runs [plies] between P'ohang and Ullŭngdo —자중 operating empty weight
운해 雲海 1 〈구름이 덮인 바다〉 a clouded [overcast] sea
2 〈널리 깔린 구름〉 a sea of clouds; 〈광대하게 이어진 구름〉 a vast stretch of cloud(s)
▶ 시야 아래로 운해가 널리 펴져 있었다 There was a sea [vast stretch] of cloud(s) down below.
운행 運行 1 〈천체의 공전〉 revolution; 〈운전하며 진행함〉 movement; motion; race
♦천체의 운행 the movement of heavenly bodies
—운행하다 revolve [go, move, orbit, travel] 《round the sun》
▶ 지구는 지축을 중심으로 돌면서 태양의 주위를 운행하고 있다 The earth revolves [goes, moves] around the sun, while rotating [turning] on its axis.
2 〈열차·버스 등의〉 running; operation; service
▶ 대설로 열차의 운행이 중단되었다 The trains [Trains, Rail services] were disrupted due to (the) heavy snow.
—운행하다 run; operate
▶ 버스는 10분마다 운행하고 있다 The buses [Buses] run every ten minutes. ⇒ There is a bus every ten minutes.
■ 임시 열차— extra train service ■ —기록계 tachograph —노선 a 《bus》 route [line]; an operation system 《of streetcars》 —노선 번호 a route number —정지 the suspension of operation 《for 3 days》 —표 〈철도의〉 a train schedule; a time table
운형 雲形 〔地〕 cloud form
운형자 雲形— 〔數〕 〈곡선자〉 a curved rule; a French [a draftsman's an irregular] curve
운휴 運休 〈운행 일시 중지〉 the suspension [stoppage] of bus [train] service; 〈운행편의 취소〉 the cancellation 《of a bus [train]》
—운휴하다 〈일시 중지하다〉 suspend; 〈취소하다〉 cancel
▶ 사고 때문에 7시 20분 발 열차가 운휴했다 The 7:20 train was canceled because of the accident.

울¹ 〈이 편의 힘이 될 겨레붙이〉 kinsmen; kin; relatives; *one's* people; folks
울² 1 〈울타리〉 a fence; a hedge; a railing; an enclosure
♦높은 울 a high hedge / 울이 있는 정원 a garden surrounded with [by] a hedge / 울 안에(서) within [inside] an enclosure; in the compound; on the premises / 울을 치다 enclose 《a house》 with a fence; fence round [about] 《a house》; fence up 《a field》
▶ 그 집 주위에는 울이 둘러져 있다 The house is fenced around [about].
2 〈신울〉 the rim 《of a shoe》
울³ 〈양모〉 wool
♦울 코트 a wool 《a woolen》 coat / 울 100%인 스웨터 a pure-wool [an all-wool] sweater
울가망하다 〈마음이 불편하다〉 feel distressed [worried, uneasy, anxious]
울거미 〈얽어맨 것의 거죽에 댄 테〉 an outer rim; a hoop for a wrapped bundle; 〈짚신의 총을 꿴 끈〉 a long rim cord sewing sidewings to sandals
울걱거리다 wash 《water》 around in *one's* mouth; gargle and swish 《water》 between *one's* teeth
♦소금물로 울걱거리다 gargle with salt water
울겅거리다 〈잘 씹히지 않고 미끌대다〉 chew on 《sinewy stuff》; mumble; be hard to chew; be tough

울근거리다 mumble; chew

울근불근하다 1 〈서로 으르대다〉 feud [be at feud] 《with》; be in discord; be at daggers drawn 《with》; be at odds; be at swords' point; (美) be at loggerheads 《with》; be at outs 《with》
▶ 그들은 항상 하찮은 일로 울근불근하고 있다 They are always at odds about some little thing.
2 〈야위어서 갈빗대가 드러나다〉 very lean; bony; scraggy; rawboned
♦ 뼈가 울근불근한 사람 a skinny person; a bag ot bones

울근울근 mumbling; chewing

울굿불굿 in various [divers] colors
―울굿불굿하다 of various [divers] colors; manycolored; colorful
♦ 울굿불굿한 옷 colorful clothes / 울굿불굿한 우산 umbrellas of various colors
▶ 우리집 뜰에는 울굿불굿한 장미꽃이 피어 있다 Roses of various colors are blooming in my garden.

울기 鬱氣 〈답답한 기분〉 depression; gloom; low spirit pentup feelings

울꺽 1 〈갑자기 토하려는 모양〉 kecking; retching ♦ 울꺽 토하다 vomit; throw [cast] up
2 〈분기가 치미는 모양〉 ♦ 화가 울꺽 치밀다 have a fit of anger; get into a rage

울다 1 〈소리내어 울다〉 cry; 〈눈물을 흘리다〉 weep; shed tears; 〈흐느끼다〉 sob; 〈울먹이다〉 blubber; 〈통곡하다〉 wail; lament

> [解說] 우리말에서는 「야옹야옹 울다」와 같이 「울다」에 의성어를 붙여서 우는 모양을 나타내지만 영어에서는 ***meow, bellow, crow*** 등 동사 하나만으로 그 모양을 모두 나타낸다.

♦ 울며 겨자 먹기로 with (a) bad [(an) ill] grace / 울면서 with tears in *one's* eyes; weeping; crying / 거짓으로 울다 shed sham [false] tears; pretend to weep / 기뻐서[슬퍼서] 울다 weep for joy [from sorrow] / 남몰래[소리없이] 울다 weep in silence; shed silent tears / 눈이 붓도록 울다 cry *one's* eyes out / 분해서 울다 cry for vexation; shed tears in *one's* chagrin / 슬피 울다 cry bitterly / 실컷 울다 weep *oneself* out; cry *one's* heart out / 아파서 울다 cry with pain / 엉엉 울다 cry loudly / 훌쩍훌쩍 울다 whimper / 울면서 말하다 speak with tears; say *sth* between sobs; sob out / 울며 애원하며 빌다 beg [implore] in tears / 울며 헤어지다 part in tears
▶ 그 아기는 젖을 달라고[우유를 달라고] 울고 있다 The baby is crying for milk.
▶ 아기가 울고 있어요 The baby is crying!
▶ 나는 울고 싶어졌다 I felt like crying.
▶ 그녀는 울지 않으려고 이를 악물었다 She clenched her teeth to hold back the sobs [tears].
▶ 그 아이는 의사 앞에서 마구 울어댔다 The child screamed [howled] in front of the doctor.
▶ 그 이야기를 듣고 울지 않을 사람은 없다 No one can listen to the story with dry eyes.

2 〈벌레·새가〉 sing; chirp; twitter; 〈명금(鳴禽)이〉 warble; 〈수탉이〉 crow; 〈암탉이〉 cluck; cackle; 〈병아리가〉 peep; pip; 〈칠면조 등이〉 gobble; 〈기러기가〉 honk; 〈까마귀가〉 caw; croak; 〈까치가〉 clatter; 〈귀뚜라미가〉 chirrup; 〈독수리가〉 scream; shriek; 〈두루미가〉 whoop; 〈비둘기가〉 coo; 〈앵무새가〉 screech; 〈오리가〉 quack; 〈올빼미가〉 hoot
♦ 풀숲에서 우는 벌레 소리 the singing of insects in a thicket
▶ 벌레가 울면 가을이 가까워진 것을 안다 The chirping of insects tells us that fall is near.
▶ 새들이 나무 사이에서 운다 Birds are singing [chirping, twittering] in the trees.
▶ 어디선가 뻐꾸기가 울고 있다 Somewhere a cuckoo was calling.
3 〈짐승이 소리내다〉 cry; 〈개·늑대 등이〉 짖다; howl; roar; bark; yelp; whine; 〈개구리가〉 croak; 〈고양이가〉 mew; meow; caterwaul; 〈귀가〉 bray; 〈말이〉 neigh; whinny; nicker; 〈소가〉 low; moo; bellow; 〈사슴이〉 bell; 〈염소·양이〉 baa; bleat; 〈쥐가〉 squeak; 〈코끼리가〉 trumpet
4 〈우글쭈글하여지다〉 become wrinkled [puckered]; gather into folds; wrinkle; crease; cockle; pucker
♦ 바느질하면서 천이 울게 하다 pucker cloth in sewing
5 〈저절로 소리나다〉 creak; squeak
▶ 이 문은 열 때마다 운다 This door creaks [grates, squeaks] whenever it is opened.
6 ⇨ 울리다 3
7 〈귀울다〉 sing; ring
▶ 내 귀가 운다 I have a buzzing in my ears. ⇌ My ears are ringing. ⇌ My ears sing.
8 〈어려운 체하다〉 complain 《about, of》; make complaints; grumble 《about》; gripe; whine 《about》
▶ 「난 그 일은 못해요」라고 그녀는 우는 소리를 했다 "I can't do the job", she whined [complained].
▶ 그는 더 이상 걷지 못하겠다고 우는 소리를 했다 He complained that he could not walk any farther!
▶ 우는 소리 작작해! Never say die! ⇌ Don't show any sign of weakness. ⇌ Stop whining.

울대 〈명관〉 the vocal organ of a bird; 〔動〕 the syrinx 《*pl.* syringes, ~es》

울퉁불퉁 1 〈불거진 모양〉 ―울퉁불퉁하다 rough; rugged; scraggy; bumpy; 〈나무 등이〉 knotty; knagged; gnarled; 〈근육이〉 (enormously) muscular
2 ⇨ 울뚝울뚝

울뚝울뚝 roughly; wildly; rashly; impatiently
―울뚝울뚝하다 rough; violent; wild; rash; impetuous
♦ 울뚝울뚝한 성미 a short [quick] temper

울란바토르 〈몽골의 수도〉 Ulan Bator

울렁거리다 1 〈두근거리다〉 go pit-a-pat; throb; pound; beat (fast); palpitate
♦ 가슴을 울렁거리며 with a leap of *one's* heart; with a throbbing heart / 울렁거리는 마음을 진정시키다 suppress *one's* agitation; collect *oneself*

2 〈출렁거리다〉 surge; roll; swell
3 〈메슥거리다〉 feel nausea; feel [be] sick (in the stomach); feel like vomiting

울렁울렁 〈두근두근〉 pit-a-pat; thumpingly; poundingly; 〈출렁출렁〉 surgingly; rollingly; tossingly; sickeningly; nauseatingly
—**울렁울렁하다** ⇨ 울렁거리다

울룩불룩하다 uneven; bumpy; rough; rugged
▶ 우리는 울룩불룩한 산길을 올라갔다 We followed a rough [rugged] path up the mountain.

울름대다 threaten with a suggestion of violence; intimidate with an overbearing [imperative] manner; browbeat

울리다 1 〈울게 하다〉 make *sb* cry; move [touch] *sb* to tears; 〈속상하게 하다〉 give *sb* trouble; worry
♦ 심금을 울리는 이야기 a touching [moving] story / 여자를 울리는 남자 a lady-killer
▶ 그 기록 영화가 나를 울렸다 The documentary film moved me to tears. ⇌ I was moved to tears by the documentary film.
2 〈종을〉 ring (a bell); 〈불어서〉 sound; 〈쳐서〉 chime; clang; 〈나팔을〉 blow; 〈북을〉 beat; 〈방울을〉 jingle
♦ (자동차의) 경적을 울리다 sound [honk, toot] the horn / 벨을 울리다 give the bell a ring; 〈초인종〉 ring the doorbell
3 〈소리가〉 sound; 〈벨・종을〉 ring; peal; 〈쾅하고〉 roar; 〈울려 퍼지다〉 thunder; rumble; 〈뇌성이〉 roll; 〈대포가〉 boom; 〈반향하다〉 resound; echo
♦ 귀가 울리다 *one's* ears sing [ring]; have a singing in *one's* ears
▶ 초인종이 울리고 있습니다 There goes the doorbell.
▶ 내 차는 경음기가 잘 울리지 않는다 My car horn doesn't sound well.
▶ 총 소리가 울렸다 We heard the report of a gun.
▶ 심한 바람으로 미닫이 문이 울렸다 The violent wind rattled the sliding doors.
▶ 전화벨이 복도에 울렸다 The telephone bell rang throughout the hall.
▶ 귀청이 떨어질 것 같은 굉음이 터널 안에 울렸다 A deafening roar echoed [resounded] in [through] the tunnel.
▶ 구급차가 사이렌을 울리면서 사고 현장으로 달려가고 있었다 An ambulance was racing to the scene of the accident with the siren wailing.
4 〈널리 퍼지다〉 wield; sway; dominate; 〈널리 알려지다〉 be widely [well] known; be famous [celebrated]
♦ 세도가 쩡쩡 울리다 wield influence [power]; hold sway
▶ 그의 명성이 온 나라에 울리고 있었다 His name echoed [His fame resounded] throughout the country.
5 〈진동하다〉 vibrate; move; shake; swing
▶ 트럭이 지나갈 때마다 이 집이 울린다 Every time a truck passes, this house shakes.

울림 〈음향〉 a sound; 〈소음〉 a noise; a roar; a rumble; 〈굉음〉 a peal; 〈공명〉 a boom; 〈반향· 여운〉 an echo (*pl.* echoes); (a) reverberation; 〈진동〉 a vibration
♦ 기계의 울림 the hum of a machine / 북의 울림 the sound of a drum / 멀리서 들려오는 뇌성의 울림 distant peal [rumble] of thunder / 파도의 울림 a roar of (the) waves

울먹이다 sob; whine; blubber
♦ 울먹이는 소리로 with a sob in *one's* voice / 울먹이며 주장하다 insist in a tearful voice

울병 鬱病 depression; melancholia; a depressive psychosis

울보 a crybaby; a blubberer

울부짖다 cry; scream; shriek; screech; wail; yell; howl; roar ♦ 살려달라고 울부짖다 cry [scream] for help / 아파서 울부짖다 cry [scream] with pain

울분 鬱憤 pent-up feelings; (pent-up) anger [fury, rage]; frustration; resentment; enmity; wrath
♦ 울분을 참다[억누르다] control [restrain] *one's* anger / 울분을 풀다[터뜨리다] let out [give vent to] *one's* (pent-up) anger [smothered grievance]; let [blow, work] off *one's* steam

울상 —相 a face ready to cry; a tearful [sad] face
♦ 울상을 짓다[이 되다] wear a tearful face; almost cry (in tears); be near [close] to cry; be nearly sobbing [crying]
▶ 그녀는 결코 남 앞에서 울상을 짓지 않는다 She never shows her tears to others.

울새 (鳥) a robin

울쑥불쑥하다 uneven; rugged; jagged
♦ 울쑥불쑥한 산 rugged mountains

울안 a yard; a court; a courtyard; a compound; an enclosure; premises; precincts

울울하다 鬱鬱— 〈답답하다〉 dejected; melancholy; gloomy; 〈무성하다〉 luxuriant; dense
♦ 울울한 숲 a thick [dense] forest/ 울울한 심사 a gloomy [depressed] feeling [mood]

울음 weeping; crying; a cry
♦ 울음을 그치다 stop crying [weeping]; cry *oneself* out / 울음을 참다 repress *one's* tears; gulp down *one's* tears / 울음을 터뜨리다 burst [break] into tears; burst out [fall to] crying; be moved [give way] to tears / 거짓 울음을 울다 shed feigned [crocodile] tears
▶ 그녀는 울음을 터뜨릴 뻔했다 She was on the verge of [close to] tears.

울음소리 a cry; 〈새의〉 a song of birds; chirping; 〈개의〉 a bark; 〈고양이의〉 a meow; 〈말의〉 a neigh; a whinny
♦ 까마귀의 울음소리 the cawing of a crow

울음주머니 vocal sac

울적 鬱寂 melancholy; gloom; mental depression; low spirits; heaviness of mind
—**울적하다** (feel) depressed; frustrated; gloomy; dejected; melancholy; out of [in low] spirits
♦ 울적한 기분으로 with a heavy heart; in a depressed mood; in a melancholy frame of mind
▶ 나는 하루 종일 울적했다 I felt gloomy [blue, out of sorts] all day.

울적 鬱積 〈울적함이 쌓임〉 smolder

―울적하다 pent-up
♦ 울적한 기분 pent-up feelings
▶ 그에게는 불만이 울적되어 있었다 His mind is fulled with smoldered discontent.
▶ 그는 울적된 노여움을 그들에게 터뜨렸다 He vented his pent-up fury them.

울짱 a fence; a palisade; a stockade

울창하다 鬱蒼 thick; dense; luxuriant
♦ 울창한 삼림 a dense [thick] forest / 울창하게 thickly; densely
▶ 골짜기는 나무가 울창하였다 Trees were [grew] thick in the valley.

울컥 1 〈급히 토하는 모양〉 suddenly; abruptly
♦ 먹은 것을 울컥 다 토하다 vomit [throw up] suddenly all one has eaten
2 〈꽉 치미는 모양〉 all of a sudden; with a burst; flaring [burning] up
♦ 울컥 화가 치밀다 have a fit of anger; get angry all of a sudden
▶ 참았던 말이 그녀의 입에서 울컥 튀어나왔다 The suppressed words gushed [poured] from her lips.

울타리 a fence; 〈산울타리〉 a hedge; a paling; a stockade; a palisade; 〈목책〉 railings
♦ 낮은 울타리 a low fence / 대나무[잡목] 울타리 a bamboo [brushwood] fence / 울타리가 없는 fenceless; unfenced / 울타리를 두르다 enclose with a fence; fence in [up]; rail in

울툭불툭하다 uneven; rough; rugged; jagged
♦ 울툭불툭한 면 an uneven [rough] surface

울퉁불퉁하다 uneven ⇨ 울툭불툭하다
♦ 울퉁불퉁한 길 a rough [bumpy] road; a washboard (road)
▶ 그 차는 산간의 울퉁불퉁한 길을 나아갔다 The car jolted along the rough [bumpy] road in the mountains.

울프 〈미국의 소설가〉 Wolfe, Thomas (1900-38); 〈영국의 여성작가〉 Woolf, Virginia (1882-1941)

울 혈 鬱血 〔醫〕 congestion; engorgement; hyperemia ♦ 울혈이 되다 be congested [engorged] with blood

울화 鬱火 resentment; pent-up anger [fury, rage]; frustration; feeling of bitterness; rancor; a grudge
♦ 울화가 치밀다 feel the surge of anger [frustration]; boil with rage / 울화가 터지다 burst into a fit of rage; lose *one's* temper
■―병 a disease caused by pent-up resentment

울화통 鬱火― resentment ⇨ 울화
♦ 울화통이 터지다 get very angry [furious]; burst into a fit of rage [temper]; explode with anger; (I) blow *one's* top [cap]
▶ 그는 그 말에 울화통이 터졌다 He flew into a rage at the word.

움[1] 〈싹〉 a bud; a sprout; a shoot; an offshoot
♦ 움이 트다 put forth buds; come into bud; sprout up

움[2] 〈움막〉 a dugout mud hut; 〈땅광〉 a cellar; a storehouse; a pit; earthen warehouse
♦ 움에 저장하다 keep *sth* in a cellar

움돋다 put forth buds ⇨ 움트다

움라우트 〔言〕 (an) umlaut ♦ 움라우트 기호 an umlaut

움막 ―幕 〈토막〉 a sheltered dugout; a shed; a storage cellar ■ ―살이 life in a mud hut

움실거리다 〈화분 밑에는 많은 지렁이가 움실거리고 있었다〉 squirm [wriggle about] in swarm; throng ▶ 화분 밑에는 많은 지렁이가 움실거리고 있었다 A lot of earthworms were wriggling under the flowerpots.

움쑥하다 hollow; sunken; dented; caved in

움씰하다 flinch; shrink (back); hold back; hang back; recoil ▶ 그녀는 그 엄청난 광경에 움씰했다 She shrank back from [recoiled at] the terrible sight.

움직거리다 〈자꾸 움직이다〉 keep on moving; go around [about]; move around; 〈움질거리다〉 wriggle; squirm

움직이다[1] **1** 〈이동·동작시키다〉 move; remove; shift
♦ 손발을 움직이다 move [exercise] *one's* arms and legs / 허리를 좌우로 움직이다 sway *one's* hips
▶ 팔을 아래위로 움직여 봐라 Move your arms up and down.
▶ 그 바위는 너무 커서 아무도 움직이지 못한다 The rock was so big that no one could move [remove; 〈조금〉 budge] it.
▶ 그는 조금도 움직이려 하지 않았다 He wouldn't budge an inch.
2 〈운전하다〉 operate; set [put] in motion; run; drive
♦ 기계를 움직이다 set [put] a machine in motion; set a machine going [runnig; working]; 〈다루다〉 work [run] a machine / 차를 움직이다 run [drive] a car; start a car
▶ 물이 물레방아를 움직인다 Water moves [drives, runs] the waterwheel.
3 〈동요시키다〉 move; touch; affect; impress; influence; have influence on
♦ 아무의 마음을 움직여 …하게 하다 move [incite] *sb* to do
▶ 그의 호소가 많은 사람의 마음을 움직였다 His appeal touched the hearts [worked on the minds] of many people.
▶ 사람을 움직이는 것은 정성이다 Sincerity is what moves [touches] people. ≒ Sincerity is what winds [stirs] people's heart.
4 〈동원하다〉 ♦ 군대를 움직이다 mobilize troops
5 〈부정하다〉 deny
♦ 움직일 수 없는 사실 an undeniable [indisputable, established] fact
▶ 움직일 수 없는 증거를 찾아내다 find positive [incontestable] evidence
6 〈변경하다〉 change; alter; 〈흔들다〉 shake
♦ 움직일 수 없는 결심 an unshakable [a firm, an immovable] resolution
▶ 그는 돈으로 움직이는 사람이다 He is [can be] influenced by money.

움직이다[2] **1** 〈동작하다〉 move; stir; budge; shift
♦ 움직이고 있다 be in motion; be moving [stirring]/ 움직이지 않다 do not move [stir]; remain still
▶ 나는 지쳐서 한 발짝도 움직이지 못한다 I'm exhausted and can't move another step.

▶차가 천천히 움직이기 시작했다 The car slowly began to move. ⇒ The car started slowly.
▶내가 돌아올 때까지 여기서 움직이지 마라 Stay right [Don't move, Keep still] here till I come back.
▶움직이면 쏜다 If you move [stir], I'll shoot.
▶정전으로 기차가 움직이지 않게 되었다 The train stopped [halted, came to a standstill] because of power failure.
▶우리 차는 눈 때문에 움직이지 못하게 되었다 My car stuck in the snow.
2 〈흔들리다〉 shake; swing; sway
♦(나뭇잎 등이) 바람에 움직이다 tremble in the breeze; sway to the wind
▶이 나사는 움직인다 This screw is loose.
3 〈운전되다〉 run; work, operate; go
▶모터는 전기로 움직인다 The motor works [runs, goes] on electricity. ⇒ The motor is run [powered] by electricity.
4 〈일하다〉 work; 〈행동하다〉 act; move
♦아무의 명령대로 움직이다 act on *sb's* order
▶부하가 제대로 움직여 주지 않는다 My men will not work as they should.
▶마침내 경찰이 움직이기 시작했다 Finally the police went into action.
5 〈좌우되다〉 be influenced; be swayed; 〈동요하다〉 waver; fluctuate; vacillate; be shaken
♦감정에 움직이다 be swayed by sentiment / 돈에 움직이다 be influenced by the power of money
▶그녀의 눈물[말]에 그는 마음이 움직였다 He was moved by her tears [words].
6 〈마음이〉 be moved; be touched; be affected
♦…에 마음이 움직이다 be moved [touched, influenced, affected]
▶허영심 많은 사람은 아첨에 잘 움직인다 Vain people are susceptible to flattery.
7 〈변하다〉 vary; change
♦A와 B 사이를 움직이다 range between A and B
▶세계 정세가 움직이고 있다 The world situation is changing.
8 〈전임되다〉 be transferred (to another position)
▶인사이동으로 많은 인원이 회사내에서 움직였다 There was a lot of shifting in our company because of the personnel changes.
움직임 〈이동〉 (a) movement; (a) motion; a move; 〈활동〉 activity; 〈동향〉 a trend; a drift [movement]; a development
♦물가의 움직임 changes in prices / 세계 경제의 움직임 trends in world economics / 여론의 움직임 the drift of public opinion
▶기계의 움직임을 보아라 See how the machine is moving.
▶세상의 움직임이 하도 빨라서 따라가기가 힘들 때가 있다 The world is changing so rapidly (that) I am sometimes unable to keep with it.
움질거리다 1〈움직이다〉 move about [around]; run around; 〈꿈틀거리다〉 squirm; wriggle **2** 〈주저하다〉 hesitate; shrink **3** 〈오물거리다〉 munch; mumble
움집 a dugout mud hut; a sheltered cellar; a shed; a storehouse; a pit dwelling
♦움집살이 하다 dwell in a shed
움찔하다 be taken by surprise; be startled; be shocked; feel a shock; flinch (from); shrink back (from)
♦소식을 듣고 움찔하다 be shocked at [by, to hear] the news
▶나는 검은 그림자를 보고[큰 소리에] 움찔했다 I started at the sight of a dark figure [at the loud noise].
움츠리다 contract ⇨ 움츠리다
움켜잡다 hold firmly; take [catch, grab] hold of; grasp; grip; grab (at); seize
♦멱살을 움켜잡다 seize *sb* by the collar / 밧줄을 양손으로 움켜잡다 grasp a rope with *one's* hands
움켜쥐다 hold tight in *one's* hand; clasp; grip; grasp tightly; clutch; clench; take fast [firm] hold 《of》
♦권력을 움켜쥐다 get [seize] power / (남의) 손을 움켜쥐다 squeeze *sb's* hand / 주먹을 움켜쥐다 clench *one's* fist
▶그 아이는 엄마 손을 움켜쥐고 놓지 않았다 The child took [caught] hold of his [her] mother's hand tightly and never let it go.
▶그녀는 무서워서 내 손을 움켜쥐었다 She gripped [clutched] my hand in fear.
움큼 ♦쌀 한 움큼 a handful of rice
▶그녀는 그들에게 땅콩을 한 움큼씩 주었다 She gave them a handful of peanuts each.
움키다 1〈잡다·쥐다〉 catch; grasp; grip; clutch; clasp; seize; take [catch] hold of
♦사탕을 한 움큼 움키다 grasp [grab] a handful of candy
2 〈움켜 채다〉 claw hold of; seize [hold] *sth* (with the claws)
♦(솔개 등이) 병아리를 움켜 채가다 pounce away with a chicken
움트다 put forth [shoot out] buds; sprout up; shoot; bud
▶그들 사이에 사랑이 움텄다 Love has begun to grow between them.
▶감자는 움트기 전에 먹어야 한다 You should eat potatoes before they start sprouting.
움파 a Welsh onion grown in a cellar [storehouse]
움펑눈 sunken [deep-set] eyes ⇨ 옴팡눈 ▶그는 움펑눈이다 His eyes are sunk deep in his head.
움푹 deeply; hollowly ♦움푹 들어가다 become hollow; sink —움푹하다 sunken; hollow; dented ♦눈이 움푹하다 have deep-set eyes
웃기다 make *sb* laugh; move *sb* to laughter; excite *one's* laughter; cause a laugh; provoke laughter [a smile]; 〈재미나게 하다〉 amuse *sb*
▶그는 농담으로 우리를 웃겼다 He made us laugh by telling jokes. ⇒ His joke set us laughing [amused us].
▶웃기지마! Don't be ridiculous. ⇒ You are talking nonsense.
▶이건 정말 웃기는 일이야 This is a matter for a good laugh.
▶그가 음악가라고? 정말 웃기네 He is a musician? Don't make me laugh!

웃다 1 〈기뻐서〉 laugh; smile
♦웃으면서 with a laugh [smile]; laughingly; smilingly / …을 보고[듣고] 웃다 laugh at…/ 껄껄 웃다 laugh loudly; cackle / 낄낄[킬킬] 웃다 chuckle (to *oneself*); giggle; snicker / 방긋[방글방글] 웃다 smile sweetly; beam 《upon》; smile radiantly 《at》/ 싱긋이 웃다 grin 《at》; give *sb* a broad grin / 와자그르 웃다 roar [howl] with laughter / 억지로 웃다 smile a forced smile; force a laugh / 너털웃음을 웃다 give a horselaugh; guffaw / 쓴 웃음을 웃다 smile a bitter [wry] smile / 웃으며 헤어지다 part good friends / 웃지 않을 수 없다 cannot help laughing; cannot but laugh
▶ 큰 소리로 웃는 것은 점잖지 못하다 It is not good manners to laugh loudly.
▶ 낯선 사람이 내게 웃으면서 다가와 이야기를 걸었다 A stranger came up to me with a smile and started talking.
▶ 그 여자는 그것 봐란듯이 웃었다 She smiled an I-told-you-so smile.
▶ 그는 억지로 웃어보였다 He smiled a forced smile.
▶ 웃어요〈사진 찍을 때〉 Say cheese!
▶ 그것은 웃을 일이 아니다 That's no laughing [joking] matter at all.
▶ 그녀는 웃으며 승락했다 She smiled her approval.
▶ 나는 눈물이 나도록 웃었다 I laughed (myself) to (the point of) tears.
▶ 웃는 집안에 복이 들어온다 《속담》 Fortune comes in [enters] by [through] a merry gate. ⇌ Laugh and be [grow] fat.
▶ 이것은 웃어 넘길 일이 아니다 This is no matter to be laughed away.
2 〈비웃다〉 laugh at; ridicule; deride; jeer [sneer, scoff] at; make fun of
▶ 그 문제를 못 풀면 남이 웃는다 You'll be laughed at if you can't solve the problem.
▶ 울지 마라, 남들이 웃는다 Don't cry and make yourself ridiculous.
웃는 낯에 침 뱉으랴 《속담》 Laugh and the world laughs with you. ⇌ Docility disarms anger. ⇌ A soft answer turns away wrath.
웃돈 〈할증금〉 an extra; a premium; surcharge; a bonus
♦약정한 금액에 10만원의 웃돈을 주다 add one hundred thousand won to the agreed amount; give an extra one hundred thousand won
▶ 그는 웃돈을 얹어 주고서야 그 집을 살 수 있었다 He had to pay a premium before he could buy the house.
웃돌다 be more [better] than; exceed; surpass
♦백 명을 웃도는 사람들 over [more than] a hundred people
▶ 수입이 수출을 천만 달러 웃돌았다 Imports exceeded export by ten million dollars.
웃어른 *one's* elders; *one's* seniors
웃옷 1 〈겉옷〉 an outer garment; outerwear
2 〈상의〉 a jacket; a coat; an upper garment
▶ 그는 웃옷을 벗고 일하고 있었다 He was working in his shirt-sleeves.
웃음 a laugh; laughing; 〈큰 웃음〉 laughter; 〈미소〉 a smile; 〈비웃음〉 a sneer

♦눈물 섞인 웃음 a tearful smile / 억지 웃음 a forced [strained] laugh; a feigned [forced] smile / 웃음 소리 (the sound of) laughter; a laughing voice / 웃음이 나오게 하다 move *sb* to laughter; provoke [excite] a laugh / 웃음을 띠다[짓다] wear a smile / 웃음을 사다 incur laughter; be laughed at; draw ridicule upon *oneself* / 웃음을 참다 suppress [swallow] *one's* laughter; keep from laughing / 웃음를 터뜨리다 burst out laughing; burst into (fits of) laughter / 웃음을 팔다 sell *oneself* for money; prostitute; walk the streets
▶ 옆방에서 웃음소리가 들렸다 I heard laughter from the next room.
▶ 그녀는 행복한 웃음을 짓고 있었다 She had [wore] a happy smile on her face.
▶ 웃음 속에 칼이 있다 Bees that have honey in their mouths have stings in their tails.
웃음거리 〈일〉 a laughingstock; a joking matter; a standing jest [joke]; 〈사람〉 a fool
♦웃음거리가 되다 make *oneself* a laughingstock; make a fool of *oneself* / 아무를 웃음거리로 만들다 make a fool of *sb*
▶ 나는 웃음거리가 되기 싫다 I hate being laughed at.
▶ 그는 모두의 웃음거리다 Everybody laughs at him. ⇌ He is ridiculed by everyone.
▶ 너는 남의 웃음거리가 되지 말아야 한다 You must not make yourself a laughingstock.
웃통 〈상체〉 the upper part of the body; the upper part; 〈상의〉 an upper garment; a coat; a jacket
♦웃통을 벗다 strip *oneself* to *one's* waist 《for an X-ray》
웅그리다 roll *oneself* up; crouch ⇨ 웅크리다, 움크리다
웅긋쭝긋하다 pointing up [upward]; sticking up ♦웅긋쭝긋한 첨탑들 steeples dotting up skyward
웅기중기 in crowds ⇨ 웅기종기
웅담 熊膽 a bear's gall [bladder]
웅대 雄大 grandeur; magnificence; sublimity; majesty; greatness
—**웅대하다** grand; magnificent; sublime; majestic; great
♦웅대한 구상 a grand conception [idea] / 알프스의 웅대한 경치 a magnificent [grand, majestic] view of the Alps / 나이아가라 폭포의 웅대함 the grandeur [magnificence] of the Niagara Falls
웅덩이 a (stagnant) pool; a puddle; a water hole
♦웅덩이가 진 puddled; sloppy / 도로의 웅덩이에 빠지다 slip [fall, take a false step] into a puddle in the road
웅도 雄途 a heroic departure
▶ 그들은 히말라야 등정의 웅도에 올랐다 They have started out on the brave undertaking of trying to conquer the Himalayas.
웅도 雄圖 an ambitious enterprise [plan]; a great undertaking
▶ 그의 웅도는 좌절되었다 His ambitious plan miscarried [failed, fell through].
웅변 雄辯 eloquence; fluency (of speech); (a

flood of) oratory
♦ 웅변을 토하다 speak with great eloquence ((on)); make an eloquent speech ((on)) / 웅변으로 말해주다 be eloquent [be an eloquent proof] ((of))
▶ 그의 웅변에는 당할 자가 없다 Nobody is a match for him in eloquence.
■―가 an eloquent [a fluent] speaker; an orator ―대회 an oratorical [a speech] contest: 대학의 교내 웅변대회 intramural oratorical contest of a university ―술 oratory; the art of public speaking

웅변은 은이요 침묵은 금이다 《속담》 Speech is silver [silvern], silence is gold [golden].

웅비 雄飛 a great leap [flight]; an ambitious flight
♦ 해외에서 웅비하고 있는 한국인들 the Korean people who are actively engaging in various enterprises abroad / 해외로 웅비하다 go abroad with a great ambition; leave for abroad full of ambition

웅성 雄性 maleness ■―배우자 male gamete ―식물 a male (plant) ―호르몬 male hormone

웅성거리다 be noisy; be in a commotion; buzz ♦ 웅성거리는 말소리 a buzz [hum] of conversation
▶ 그녀가 등장하자 장내는 일순간 웅성거렸다 When she appeared on the platform, there was a momentary stir in the audience.

웅숭깊다 1 〈도량이 크다〉 broad-[large-]minded; magnanimous
2 〈깊이가 있다〉 deep; profound; subtle
♦ 웅숭 깊은 생각 a profound [prudent] idea
3 〈드러나지 않다〉 quiet; inconspicuous

웅얼거리다 murmur; mutter; mumble; grumble ♦ 알 수 없는 말을 혼자 웅얼거리다 mutter [grumble] *sth* indistinct to *oneself*
▶ 그 노인은 뭔가를 웅얼거렸다 The old man mumbled (out) something.

웅예 雄蕊 〔植〕 a stamen ⇨ 수술

웅자 雄姿 a brave [a gallant, an imposing] figure ♦ 웅자를 드러내다 cut a gallant figure; make an imposing appearance
▶ 알프스의 웅자가 눈앞에 있었다 There was a magnificent [an imposing] view of the Alps before us.

웅장 雄壯 grandeur; magnificence; splendor ―웅장하다 grand; majestic; magnificent; splendid
♦ 웅장한 경치 a grand spectacle; a magnificent view / 웅장한 궁전 a magnificent [grand, splendid] palace / 웅장한 대저택 an imposing residence

웅지 雄志 〈큰 뜻〉 a noble aspiration; a great ambition ♦ 웅지를 이루다 attain [accomplish] *one's* great ambition [goal]

웅천 an unreliable person; a braggart

웅크리다 crouch; huddle [curl] *oneself* up; squat ♦ 웅크리고 in a crouch; in a crouching position / 웅크리고 앉다 sit crouching [hunched up]; squat *oneself*; squat down / 웅크리고 자다 sleep huddled [curled] up
▶ 그녀는 그 자리에 웅크리고 앉았다 She squatted down on the spot [right there].

웅편 雄篇 〈걸작〉 a great [monumental] work; a masterpiece; (라) a magnum opus

웅혼하다 雄渾― 〈웅대하여 막힘이 없다〉 grand; sublime; vigorous; daring ♦ 웅혼한 문장 a vigorous style / 웅혼한 필치 a grand [bold] hand

워 〈영국의 작가〉 Waugh, Evelyn (Arthur St. John) (1903-66)

워낙 1 〈본디부터〉 from the first [beginning]; by nature
▶ 그는 워낙 게으름뱅이다 He is inherently a lazy creature. ⇌ He was born idle.
▶ 그녀는 워낙 몸이 약하다 She is constitutionally weak. ⇌ She was born weak.
▶ 그는 워낙 호기심이 많다 He is by nature curious.
2 〈아주〉 very; too much; excessively; (美) overly; 〈부정〉 ((not)) very [quite, much]
▶ 이 책은 워낙 어려워서 읽을 수가 없다 This book is too difficult for me to read.
▶ 그녀는 워낙 피곤해서 더 걸을 수 없었다 She was so tired (that) she couldn't walk any further.
▶ 그는 워낙 부자니까 걱정할 것 없다 There is no need to worry, because he's a millionaire.

워드프로세서 a word processor
♦ 한글 워드프로세서 a word processor for Korean / 워드프로세서로 상용문을 타이핑하다 [쓰다] type [write] a business letter on a word processor

워리 〈개 부르는 소리〉 Doggy!; Here doggy!

워밍업 warming-up ♦ 워밍업을 하다 warm up; limber up
▶ 달리기 전에 워밍업을 충분히 해야한다 You need a good warm up before running.

워싱턴 1 〈미국의 주〉 Washington; 〈미국의 수도〉 Washington, D.C.(▶D.C.는 District of Columbia의 약칭임).
2 〈미국 초대 대통령〉 Washington, George (1732-99)
■―시민[주민] a Washingtonian

워워 〈말·소에게 멈추라는 외침〉 whoa

워크로드 〈작업 부담〉 work load

워크맨 (商標) a Walkman

워크북 a workbook ♦ 워크북의 문제를 공부하다 do exercise in a workbook

워크숍 〔敎〕 a workshop

워크스테이션 〔電算〕 a workstation

워크아웃 〈동맹 파업〉 a walkout

워키루키 〈휴대용 텔레비전 카메라〉 a walkie-lookie

워키토키 a walkie-talkie

워터게이지 〈수면계〉 a water gauge

워터마크 〈종이의 비침 무늬〉 a watermark
♦ 워터마크를 넣다 watermark

워터슈트 a water chute

원¹ 〈화폐 단위〉 a won
♦ 오천원짜리 지폐 a 5,000 won note

원² Well!; Oh, dear!; Indeed!; What!; How!
▶ 원, 별소리 다 듣겠네 Don't talk nonsense! ⇌ Rubbish!
▶ 원, 이렇게 돈이 들어서야 I cannot indeed afford such an expense.

► 원, 세상에 그럴 수가 What a surprise! ⇒ No, it cannot be true! ⇒ How ever did that happen?

원 元 〈중국의 왕조〉 Yüan; the Yüan dynasty; 〈중국의 화폐 단위〉 a yüan (▶단수·복수동형)

원 圓 a circle
◆ 원의 중심[반경, 직경] the center [radius, diameter] of a circle / 컴퍼스로 원을 그리다 draw [describe] a circle with a pair of compasses / 원을 그리며 날다 fly in a circle; circle / 원을 그리며 춤추다 dance in a circle [ring, round]
■ ―운동 circular motion [movement]

원

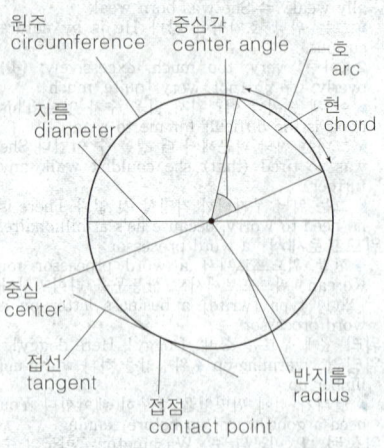

원주 circumference
중심각 center angle
호 arc
지름 diameter
현 chord
중심 center
접선 tangent
접점 contact point
반지름 radius

원 願 〈소원〉 a desire; a wish; a hope; 〈부탁〉 a request; an entreaty
◆ 원이 이루어지다 one's wish comes true / 원을 들어주다 grant a wish; comply with a request
► 원에 의하여 면직함 You are relieved of your post at your own request.

원- 元-·原- 〈이전의〉 former; previous; 〈원래의〉 original; 〈기본적〉 primary; fundamental; 〈원시의〉 primitive
◆ 원계획 the original plan / 원주인 the former owner / 원회원 the founding [original] member

-원 員 〈일의 관계자〉 a member; an employee
◆ 사무원 an office worker / 수금원 a bill collector / 편집원 a member of the editorial staff

-원 願 〈원서〉 an application ◆ 입학원 an application for admission

원가 原價 the cost price; the prime [initial] cost ◆ 원가로 팔다 sell at cost / 원가 이하로 팔다 sell with loss on cost; sell below cost
■ 공장― manufacturing cost 구입― purchasing cost 생산― cost of production; the production cost ―계산 cost accounting ―계산서 a cost statement ―고 high cost

원거리 遠距離 a long [great] distance; a long range ◆ 원거리의 long-distance; long-range / 원거리에 at a long distance
► 원거리 통근은 피곤하다 Commuting long distances is tiring.

원격 遠隔 ◆ 원격지 a remote [distant] place / 원격의 remote; far; faraway; far-off
■ ―제어 remote control ―조종기 a remote-control plane ―탐사 remote sensing

원경 遠景 a distant view; a perspective view
► 저 산은 원경이 아름답다 Seen from far away, that mountain is beautiful.

원고 原告 〈소송 제기자〉 [法] a plaintiff; an accuser; a complainant ―대리인 the plaintiff's representative ―측 the plaintiff; the prosecution ―측 변호인 the plaintiff's lawyer; (총칭) counsel for the plaintiff

원고 原稿 〈인쇄용의〉 a manuscript (略 MS.); a copy; 〈투고〉 a contribution; 〈초안〉 a draft
◆ 타이프로 친 원고 a typescript / 원고를 쓰다 write [prepare] a manuscript / 연설 원고를 쓰다 make out a draft of a speech / 원고 없이 말하다 speak without notes
► 원고는 월말까지 제출하시오 Turn in your manuscript no later than the end of the month.
► 나는 잡지에 원고를 쓰고 있다 I am writing an article for a magazine.
► 나는 그 작가의 자필 원고를 읽은 적이 있다 I have read the writer's hand-written manuscript.
■ ―료 pay (for the writing); a manuscript fee; payment for a manuscript ―(용)지 manuscript paper; a writing pad 낱장으로 떼어 쓰는: 200자 원고지 10장 ten sheets of manuscript paper with squares for two hundred characters

원광 圓光 〈후광〉 a halo; a nimbus

원교 遠郊 the outlying suburbs; the remote outskirts

원군 援軍 a reinforcement; reliefs
◆ 원군을 보내다 send reinforcement(s) (to)/ 5천명의 원군을 보내다 send five thousand more men / 원군을 기다리다 [청하다] wait [ask] for reinforcement(s)

원그래프 圓― a circular graph [chart]

원근 遠近 far and near; distance ◆ 원근을 불구하고 from far and near; irrespective [regardless] of distance
► 한쪽 눈을 감고 보면 원근의 구별이 잘 안된다 With one eye closed we cna't see things in the right perspective.
■ ―조절 〈눈의〉 accommodation

원근법 遠近法 perspective; perspective representation ◆ 원근법에 맞다 [맞지 않다] be in [out of] perspective

원금 元金 〈자본〉 capital; 〈이자에 대하여〉 the principal ◆ 원금과 이자 principal and interest / 원금 1000만원에 대한 이자 interest on the principal of ten million won

원급 原級 1 [文法] the positive degree 2 〈원래의 급〉 the original class

원기 元氣 vigor; energy; vitality; stamina; spirits; (口) go; pep

◆원기왕성하다 be in high [fine] spirits; be full of energy [vigor]; be very much alive / 원기를 돋우다 invigorate; strengthen / (口) pep up / 원기를 회복하다 recover one's spirits [strength]
▶그녀는 예순 살인데도 원기왕성하다 She's full of energy [vigor, vitality] at the age of sixty.
▶그는 원기 백배하여 다시 일을 시작했다 He came back to his work with increasing vigor.
원기둥 圓— 〔建〕 a column; 〔數〕 a circular cylinder; 〔幾〕 a cylinder
원내 院內 ■—교섭 단체 a group of national assemblymen having a legislative bargaining position in the national assembly —부총무 the deputy floor leader —총무 the leader of the house; (美) the floor leader; (英) the (party) whip —활동 (the) activities in the national assembly; (the) activities as a national assemblyman
원년 元年 the first year of a reign
◆광무 원년 the first year of Kwangmu / 세종 원년 the first year of King Sejong's reign
원념 怨念 grudge; hatred
원단 元旦 the morning of New Year's Day; the first day of the year
원대 原隊 one's (original) unit ◆원대 복귀하다 return to one's unit
원대하다 遠大 far-reaching; great; grand; long-range ◆원대한 계획 a farseeing program; a great [an ambitious] plan / 원대한 이상 a lofty idea / 원대한 포부 a great ambition; a lofty aspiration
원동기 原動機 a motor; a prime mover
원동력 原動力 motive power [force]; driving [moving] force; 〔동기〕 a motive ◆사회 발전의 원동력 the driving force in the development of society
▶애국심이 그 운동의 원동력이었다 Patriotism was the impelling power of [behind] the movement.
원두막 園頭幕 a lookout shed for a melon patch [field]
원둘레 圓— the circumference (of a circle)
◆원둘레가 2미터인 원 a circle two meters round [in circumference]
▶그 동전은 원둘레가 7센티미터다 The coin is about seven centimeters in circumference.
원래 元來·原來 〔본디〕 originally; primarily; 〔선천적으로〕 naturally; by nature; 〔본질적으로〕 essentially; in and for itself; 〔처음부터〕 from the first [start, beginning]; 〈첫째로〉 first; in the first place
▶「아름다움」이란 원래 주관적이다 "Beauty" is essentially [in itself] subjective.
▶이 계획은 원래 그가 생각해낸 것이다 This plan originated with him.
▶그는 원래 정직한[성급한] 사람이다 He is honest [quick-tempered] by nature.
▶그 많은 땅은 원래부터 내것이었다 The estate was mine from the start.
원래 遠來 ◆원래의 방문객 a visitor from a distant place [from afar]
원려 遠慮 forethought; foresight; prudence

원로 元老 〈정계의〉 an elder [a senior] statesman; 〈일반적으로〉 an elder; a senior (member); an old-timer; a veteran ◆재계의 원로 an elder [old-timer] in financial circles
▶그는 문단의 원로적 존재다 He is an influential senior member of literary circles.
■—원 〔史〕 the senate; the senate house —정치 government strongly influenced by elder statesmen
원로 遠路 a long way [distance]; a long journey ◆원로의 여행 a long [far] journey
▶그는 나를 만나러 원로를 왔다 He came all the way to see me.
원론 原論 a (general) theory; the principles 《of》 ■경제학[사회학]— the principles of economics [sociology]
원뢰 遠雷 distant thunder
원료 原料 raw [crude] materials ◆원료를 확보하다 secure [procure] raw materials
▶포도주는 포도를 원료로 한다 Wine is made from grapes.
▶나일론의 원료는 무엇입니까? What is nylon made from?
▶우리나라는 원료를 수입하고 제품을 수출한다 We import raw materials and export manufactured goods.
■—공업 the raw material industry; the primary product industry
원류 源流 〈수원〉 a headstream; headwaters; 〈기원〉 the origin [beginning] 《of》
원리 元利 principal and interest
◆대부금의 원리 합계액 the amount of a loan with interest added [included]
원리 原理 a principle; a theory; the fundamental truth
◆궁극적 원리 the ultimate principle / 아르키메데스의 원리 Archimedes' principle / 교육의 근본 원리 the fundamental principle of education / 지렛대의 원리를 응용하다 apply the principle of leverage 《to》/ …의 원리를 규명하다 go [inquire] into the principles [the ultimate truth] of...
▶다수결은 민주주의의 가장 중요한 원리의 하나다 Decision by the majority is one of the most important principles of democracy.
▶그것에 대해 이 원리를 적용할 수 있다 We can apply this theory to it.
원만 圓滿 〈완전〉 perfection; integrity; completeness; 〈만족〉 satisfaction; 〈원활〉 smoothness; 〈조화〉 harmony; 〈평온〉 peace
—원만하다 perfect; integral; happy; harmonious; peaceful; satisfactory; amicable
◆원만한 가정 a happy home / 원만한 부부 a harmonious couple / 원만한 성격 a peaceful character / 원만한 해결 a happy [satisfactory] compromise; an amicable settlement / 원만히 harmoniously; satisfactorily; smoothly; peacefully; amicably / 원만히 살다 live in harmony
▶그 쟁의는 원만히 해결되었다 The dispute has been settled amicably.
▶그들은 사이가 그다지 원만하지 못했다 They didn't get on [along] well together.
원망 怨望 a bitter [an ill] feeling; resentment;

원망

〈비난〉 a grievance; a reproach; a complaint
♦ 원망의 말을 하다 say spiteful [bitter] things (of *sb*) / 원망을 사다 incur *sb*'s grudge; make an enemy of *sb*
▶ 그는 많은 사람의 원망을 샀다 He incurred enmity from many people. ⇌ He invited the rancor of many people.
▶ 나는 원망을 억누르고 조정에 응했다 I suppressed my resentment [bitterness] and agreed to the mediation.
▶ 나는 남의 원망을 살 일은 한 기억이 없다 I don't remember having done anything to incur the resentment of others.
—원망하다 feel bitter about *sb*; feel [show] resentment at *sb*; resent; 〈비난하다〉 blame [reproach] (*sb* for *sth*)
♦ 자신을 원망하다 reproach *oneself* (for)
▶ 그는 나를 원망하고 있다 He is bitter [has resentment] against me.
▶ 그는 그 사고에 대해 나를 원망했다 He blamed me for the accident.
▶ 하늘의 뜻을 원망하지 마라 Do not quarrel with Providence.

원망 願望 〈원하고 바람〉 a desire; a wish; an aspiration —원망하다 desire; wish (for)

원망스럽다 怨望— reproachful; spiteful; 〈유감스럽다〉 regrettable
♦ 원망스러운 얼굴 a reproachful look / 원망스러운 듯이 resentfully; with a reproachful look; 〈어투가〉 in a reproachful tone
▶ 그는 비가 몹시 원망스러웠다 He was terribly disappointed by the rain.
▶ 나 자신의 부주의가 몹시 원망스러웠다 I bitterly regretted my own carelessness.

원맨 an autocrat; a dictatorial leader [chief] —쇼 a one-man show —정치 a one-man rule [government]

원면 原綿 raw cotton
원명 原名 the original name
원모 原毛 raw wool
원모 遠謀 a farsighted [long-sighted] plan [scheme] ♦ 원모를 짜내다 a farsighted plan
원목 原木 log; lumber; material; wood; 〈펄프 용재〉 pulpwood
원무 圓舞 a round dance; a waltz ■—곡 a waltz
원문 原文 〈본문〉 the text; 〈원서의 글〉 the original ♦ 원문의 잘못 a textual error / 원문대로 (라) sic 〈◆원문 인용 어구 뒤에 써 넣음〉 / 〈번역이〉 원문에 충실하다 closely follow the original
▶ 원문은 아래와 같이 되어 있다 The original text runs [reads] as follows [like this].
▶ 그는 셰익스피어의 작품을 원문에 충실하게 번역했다 He made a translation of Shakespeare's works faithful to the original.
▶ 나는 햄릿을 원문으로 읽었다 I read Hamlet in the original.

원반 圓盤 a disk; (英) a disc; 〈원반던지기 용의〉 a discus (*pl.* ~es, disci) ♦ 하늘을 나는 원반 a flying saucer
■—던지기 the discus throw
원반 原盤 the original record
원방 遠方 a remote [distant] place [area]; a distant district
♦ 원방의 distant; remote; faraway; far-off / 원방에 far away; in the distance / 원방에서 오다 come from far away [from a distant place]

원병 援兵 a reinforcement ⇨ 원군
원본 原本 the original (work); the original copy [text]; 〈copy에 대하여〉 〔法〕 the script
▶ 이것이 이 사본들의 원본이다 This is the original of these copies.
원부 怨婦 a spiteful woman; a woman with a grudge
원부 原簿 the original register (book)
원뿔 圓— a circular cone ■—곡선 a conic section —꼴 a cone: 원뿔꼴의 coneshaped; conic(al) —대(臺) a circular truncated cone —면(面) a circular conical surface

— 원뿔 —

꼭지점
vertex

모선
general line

높이
altitude

축
axis

밑면
base

원사이드게임 a one-sided game
원산 原産 ♦ 열대 원산의 originating in the tropics ▶ 키위는 중국 원산이다 The kiwi fruit came from China originally.
원산물 原産物 a primary product
원산지 原産地 the place [country] of origin; 〈동식물의〉 the home; the habitat; the native environment ♦ 감자의 원산지 the (original) home of the potato / 원산지 불명의 of doutful provenance
▶ 벚나무는 제주도가 원산지다 The cherry tree is native to Chejudo.
—증명서 〈수입품 등의〉 a certificate of origin (略 C.O.)
원상 原狀 the original state; the former condition [state]; 〔法〕 the status quo ante
♦ 원상 회복(복구)하다 return to the original [former] state / 원상으로 회복시키다 restore *sth* to its original state; 〔法〕 reestablish [restore matters to] the status quo ante
원색 原色 a primary color
♦ 원색으로 인쇄하다 print (a picture) in color ■삼— the three primary colors ■—사진 a color photograph —인쇄 color printing: 원색 인쇄 조류 도감 a book of birds illustrated in color [with color illustrations] —판(版) a heliotype
원색동물 原索動物 a protochordata
원생 原生 〔生〕 abiogenesis ■—대(代) the Proterozoic Era —동물류 a Protozoa —림 ⇨ 원시(~림) —생물 Protist —생물계 Protista kingdom —식물 a protophyte —암 primary rocks —액(液) primordial soup [broth]
원서 原書 the original (work) ⇨ 원전(原典)
▶ 헤밍웨이를 원서로 읽었다 I read Hem-

ingway in the original.
▶너는 켄터베리 이야기를 원서로 읽을 수 있니? Can you read *The Canterbury Tales* in the original?
—강독 reading original texts in class

원서 願書 an application
♦원서를 마감하다 stop receiving applications / 원서를 쓰다[에 기입하다] fill out [in] an application blank [form] / 원서를 접수하다 receive [accept] an application 《starting March 1》/ 원서를 제출하다 present [file] an application 《for》; send [hand] in an application 《to the office》
▶나는 그 대학[회사]에 원서를 냈다 I applied for the university [company].
■입학— an application for admission into a school

원석 原石 a raw ore; an ore ♦다이아몬드 원석 a rough [an uncut] diamond / 루비 원석 ruby in the rough

원성 怨聲 a complaint; a murmur (of grievances)

원소 元素 〔化〕 an element; a chemical element ♦몇 개의 원소로 분해하다 resolve into several elements
■동위— an isotope 불안정— an unstable element ■—기호 the symbol of element —분석 ultimate [elementary] analysis —주기율 the periodic law of the elements

원손 遠孫 a remote [distant] descendant

원수 元首 〈국가 원수〉 a sovereign; a ruler; the chief [head] of state

원수 元帥 〈육군〉(美) a general of the army; (英) a (field) marshal; 〈해군〉(美) a fleet admiral; (英) an admiral of the fleet; 〈공군〉(美) a general of the air force; (英) a marshal of the Royal Air Force
♦맥아더 원수 General of the Army Douglas MacArthur

원수 怨讐 〈사람〉 a foe; an enemy; 〈사물〉 the object of *one's* grudge [vengeance]
♦불구대천의 원수 a deadly enemy [foe; a [*one's*] mortal [sworn] enemy / 원수지간 mutual enemies / 원수지다 become an enemy 《of》; become enemies to each other / 원수를 갚다 revenge *oneself* on *sb*; take vengeance [avenge *oneself*] 《upon》
▶그들은 서로 원수지간이다 They are enemies to each other.
▶그는 돌아가신 아버지의 원수를 갚았다 He avenged his father's death.
▶그들은 주인이 암살당한 원수를 갚았다 They avenged the assassination of their master.
▶그녀는 은혜를 원수로 갚았다 She returned evil for good.

원수폭 原水爆 atomic and hydrogen bombs; A-and H-bombs
▶우리는 원수폭을 반대한다 We are against atomic and hydrogen bombs.
■—전쟁 atomic and hydrogen warfare

원숙 圓熟 maturity; ripeness; perfection; mellowness
♦원숙미를 더하다 get [become] mellower 《with age》/ 원숙기에 접어들다 come to the ripening period
▶그의 기예는 나이 서른 살에 원숙의 경지에 들었다 His art reached [attained] maturity at thirty.
—원숙하다 mature; ripe; fully developed; perfect ♦원숙한 문체 a mellowed style / 원숙한 사람 a man of mellow [rounded] character / 원숙해지다 mature; mellow; ripen; come to maturity
▶사람은 나이와 경험이 쌓임에 따라 원숙해진다 We mature by age and experience.

원숭이 a monkey; 〈꼬리가 없는〉 an ape
♦원숭이 같은 사람 a monkey of a man / 원숭이 상을 한 사람 a monkey-faced person
▶인간은 원숭이에서 진화했다 Man has evolved from the ape.

원숭이도 나무에서 떨어진다 (속담) Even Homer sometimes nods. ⇒ The best workman may miss.

원시 原始 the beginning; genesis; origin
♦원시적 본능 a primitive instinct / 원시적 상태 a primitive state / 원시적 생활 a primitive (form of) life; primeval life / 원시적(인) primitive; primeval / 원시적인 방법으로 in a primitive way
■—공동체 a primitive community —공산주의 primitive communism —기독교 primitive Christianity —대기(大氣) primitive atmosphere —동물 a protozoan —림(林) a virgin [primeval] forest —사회 primitive society —산업 the primary industry —생명체 a primitive organism —시대 the primitive ages; primitive times —언어 〔電算〕 source language —인 an early man; a primitive [dawn] man —종교 a primitive religion —프로그램 〔電算〕 source program

원시 遠視 long sight; farsightedness (↔ nearsightedness); (英) longsightedness; 〔醫〕 hyperopia; hypermetropia; 〈사람〉 a farsighted person
▶그 여자는 약간 원시다 She is a bit farsighted.
■—경 glasses for the farsighted —안 a longsighted eye

원심 怨心 a bitter [an ill] feeling; a grudge; a spite ♦원심을 품다 have a grudge against *sb*; harbor rancor toward *sb*

원심 原審 the original judgment [decision]
♦원심대로 as originally decided / 원심을 파기하다 reverse the original sentence [decision]; overrule the original judgment

원심 圓心 〔數〕 the center of a circle

원심 遠心 〈운동의 바깥쪽으로 작용하는 힘〉
■—력 〔物〕 centrifugal force: 물체의 원심력은 그 물체의 질량에 비례한다 The centrifugal force on a body is proportional to its mass. —분리기 a centrifugal separator [machine]; a centrifuge; a centrifugal filter —성신경 a centrifugal nerve —추 fly weight —탈수기 a hydroextractor; a spin drier —펌프 a centrifugal pump

원아 園兒 kindergarten children

원안 原案 the original bill [draft, plan]
♦원안을 수정하다 amend the original bill / 원

안을 작성하다 make [prepare] a draft [plan] 《of》/ 원안을 제출하다 produce a draft proposal / 원안에 찬성하다 support the original motion [proposal] / 원안대로 가결하다 pass 《a bill》 in 《its》 original form [without amendment]
▶ 그들은 원안을 서너 군데 수정했다 They amended the original bill in some points.
▶ 그 의안은 원안대로 통과되었다 The bill passed as drafted [in its original form].

원앙 鴛鴦 〔鳥〕 a mandarin duck
◆ 한쌍의 원앙 (비유) a couple of lovebirds; a happily married couple

원앙금 鴛鴦衾 a quilt embroidered with a pair of mandarin ducks; the marriage bed
◆ 원앙금을 나누다 share the marriage bed

원액 元額・原額 the original amount [sum]

원액 原液 an undiluted solution 《of》

원야 原野 wasteland; a wilderness; a plain; a field

원양 遠洋 an ocean; a deep sea ■ ─구역 deep-sea district ─어선 pelagic fishing boat ─어업 deep-sea [pelagic] fishery [fishing]

원양항로 遠洋航路 an ocean lane [route]
■ ─정기선 an oceangoing vessel; an ocean liner

원양항해 遠洋航海 ocean navigation; an ocean voyage; a long-distance cruise ◆ 원양항해 길에 오르다 set out on a long-distance cruise; set out on the ocean voyage

원어 原語 the original word [language]
▶ 그는 원어로 노래했다 He sang the song in the original [in its original language].

원언 怨言 〈원망하는 말〉 spiteful [grudging] remarks; a complaint; repining

원영 遠泳 a long-distance swim
◆ 원영을 하다 have a long-distance swim

원예 園藝 gardening; horticulture; 〈화초 재배〉 floriculture ◆ 원예를 잘하다 be a good gardener; (美) have a green thumb; (英) have green fingers
■ 가정─ home gardening ■ ─가[사] a gardener; a horticulturist; a horticultural expert ─과 the department of horticulture ─수 a garden plant ─술 the garden craft ─시험장 a horticultural experiment(al) station ─용구 gardening tools

원외 院外 ◆ 원외의 outside the House [Congress, parliamentary]; non-parliamentary; (美) non-Congressional
■ ─단 〈단체〉 the lobby; the lobbyists ─세력 an outside pressure group; outside influences ─운동[활동] (美) lobbying; lobbyism : 원외 운동을 벌이다 lobby ─투쟁 an out-of-the-national assembly struggle

원용하다 援用─ claim; 〈인용하다〉 quote 《an article》; 〈법률 조항 등〉 invoke
◆ 조항을 원용하다 invoke a clause
▶ 변호사는 언론 자유의 권리를 원용하여 피고의 무죄를 주장했다 The lawyer maintained that the defendant was innocent, quoting the right of free speech.

원유 原油 crude oil [petroleum]; crude
■ ─가격 crude oil price

원유회 園遊會 a garden [lawn] party ◆ 원유회를 열다 give [hold] a garden party

원음 原音 the original sound 《of a character》

원의 原意 **1** 〈의사〉 the original intention **2** ⇨ 원의(原義)

원의 原義 〈원래의 뜻〉 the primary [original] meaning 《of a word》

원의 院議 a parliamentary decision; a decision of the house [national assembly]
◆ 원의를 존중하여 in deference to the decision of the national assembly [house]

원인 原人 〔人類〕 a primitive man; a hominid; Early [Dawn] Man ■ 베이징[북경]─ Peking man; Sinanthropus 직립(直立)─ Homo erectus

원인 原因 a cause; 〈근원〉 the origin; 〈요인〉 a factor
◆ 분쟁의 원인 the cause of dispute [a quarrel] / 불평의 원인 the cause of complaint / 실패의 원인 the cause of one's failure / 화재의 원인 the origin of a fire / 원인과 결과 cause and effect / 원인 불명의 unaccountable; 《a fire》 of an unknown origin / …이 원인이다 be caused by…; start [arise] from…; be due to…; result from… / 원인을 규명하다 trace the origin 《of》; trace sth to its origin / 원인을 밝히다 clear up the cause / 오해의 원인을 없애다 remove the sources of misunderstanding / 실패의 원인을 …에 돌리다 attribute [ascribe] the failure to…
▶ 그녀의 병은 피로가 원인이다 Her sickness is the result of fatigue.
▶ 원인 없는 결과는 없다 There are no results without causes. ⇌ An effect presupposes a cause.
▶ 이 병의 원인은 아직 밝혀지지 않고 있다 The causes of this illness are not found yet.
▶ 그 사고의 원인은 운전자의 부주의였다 The accident was due to [caused by] the carelessness of the driver.
■ 간접[직접]─ an indirect [a direct] cause 근본─ the root cause 주요─ a major cause ─결과 cause and effect

원인 猿人 〔人類〕 an ape-man; a pithecanthrope ■ 자바─ the Java man; Pithecanthropus erectus

원인 遠因 a remote [distant] cause; an underlying cause
▶ 그가 파티에서 내 손수건을 주워 주었는데 그것이 우리 결혼의 원인이 되었다 He picked up my handkerchief at the party, which was the remote cause of our marriage.
▶ 그것이 전쟁의 원인을 이루고 있다 It is [forms] a remote cause of the war.

원일점 遠日點 〔天〕 the aphelion (↔ perihelion)

원자 原子 〔物〕 an atom; a corpuscle
◆ 원자의 atomic
▶ 모든 것은 원자로 구성되어 있다 All things are composed of atoms.
■ ─가 valence; valency ─구조 atomic structure ─기호 the atomic symbol ─량 atomic weight ─로(爐) an atomic pile; a nuclear re-

actor; power reactor; reactor; atomic furnace —론 atomic philosophy [theory]; atomistics —무기 atomic weapons [arms] —물리학 atomic physics —물리학자 an atomic physicist —번호 an atomic number: 우라늄의 원자 번호는 92다 The atomic number of uranium is 92. —병(환자) (a sufferer from) an atomic disease —시계 an atomic clock —식 an atomic formula —에너지 atomic [nuclear] energy —역학 atomic mechanics —열 atomic heat —운 an atomic cloud —질량(단위) atomic mass (unit) —탄두 an atomic warhead —포 an atomic gun —폭발 atomic explosion

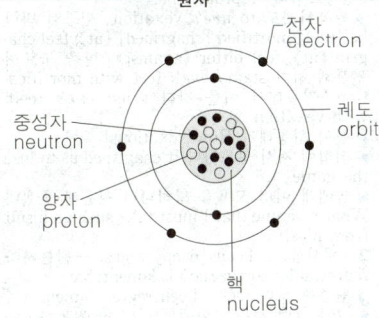
― 원자 ―
전자 electron
궤도 orbit
중성자 neutron
양자 proton
핵 nucleus

원자력 原子力 atomic [nuclear] energy; nuclear power
♦국제 원자력 기구 the International Atomic Energy Agency / 한국 원자력 연구소 Korea Atomic Energy Research Institute / 원자력의 평화적 이용 peaceful uses of atomic energy / 원자력 추진의 nuclear-propelled / 원자력으로 움직이는 atomic-powered; nuclear-powered
▶원자력은 평화적인 목적에 이용해야 한다 Atomic energy should be used for peaceful purposes.
■—관리 atomic energy control —발전 atomic power generation —발전기 an atomic power generator —발전소 an nuclear power plant; an atomic power plant —선 a nuclear power ship; an atomic-powered ship [liner] —시대 the atomic age —엔진 an atomic engine —연료 atomic [nuclear] fuel —위원회 the Atomic Energy Commission (略 AEC) —잠수함 an atomic-powered [a nuclear-powered] submarine —추진 atomic [nuclear] propulsion —항공모함 an atomic-powered [a nuclear-powered] carrier —협정 an atomic energy agreement
원자폭탄 原子爆彈 an atomic bomb; an A-bomb ♦원자폭탄으로 공격하다 atom-bomb
원자핵 原子核 an atomic nucleus ■—분열[융합] nuclear fission [fusion] —파괴장치 an atom smasher; an atom smashing machine
원작 原作 an original (work) ♦원작 황순원, 각색 김철수 written by Hwang Sun-won and adapted [dramatized] by Kim Chŭl-su

원장 元帳 a ledger (略 led.) ♦원장에 기장하다 enter 《an item》 in a ledger / 원장과 대조하다 check 《the account》 with the ledger
원장 院長 the director 《of a hospital》; the president 《of an academy》
원장 園長 the chief; the head; the director
♦동물원 원장 the zoo director / 유치원 원장 the head of a kindergarten
원저 原著 the original (work) ⇨ 원작
■—자 the author; the writer
원적 原籍 1〈원래의 본적〉an original domicile **2** ⇨ 본적
■—지 the place of *one's* domicile of origin; [法] the domicile of origin
원전 原典 the original (text); a source book
▶나는 원전을 찾아 보았다 I consulted the original text.
원점 原點 〈출발점〉the starting point; [數] the origin ♦원점으로 돌아가다 go back to the starting point
원정 遠征 〈정벌〉an expedition;〈운동 선수의〉 a playing tour
♦나폴레옹의 러시아 원정 Napoleon's expedition to Russia
▶그들은 시베리아 원정길에 올랐다 They started on an expedition (in)to Siberia.
—원정하다〈정벌하다〉go on [make] an expedition;〈운동 선수가〉make a playing tour 《of》; visit
▶그 하키 팀은 9월 12일부터 10월 9일까지 캐나다에 원정한다 The hockey team will visit Canada from September 12 to October 9.
■—군[대]〈군대〉an expedition; an expeditionary force [army];〈스포츠의〉a visiting [touring] team: 원정군을 파견하다 dispatch an expedition —시합 a road game
원정 遠程 a long road [way, distance]
원조 元祖〈시조〉the father; the first ancestor;〈창시자〉the originator; the founder;〈발명자〉the inventor;〈제조원〉the original maker
▶그는 우리 나라 서양 의학의 원조라고도 할 수 있는 사람이다 He is, so to speak, the father of Western medical science in our country.
원조 援助 assistance; aid; support; help
♦재정적 원조 financial help [aid] / 피원조국 an aid-receiving nation; an aid-recipient country; a recipient country / 원조의 손길을 뻗치다 stretch out [lend] a helping hand (to); extend assistance 《to》 / 원조를 바라다 ask for assistance / 원조를 얻다 receive [secure] assistance / 원조를 주다 give [afford] assistance [aid] to / 경제[군사] 원조를 제공하다 hand out (＄ 50 million) in economic [military] aid
▶그에게 원조를 청해서는 안된다 You must not ask for his help [assistance].
▶이 옛 건물은 우리의 원조로 복원되었다 This old building was reconstructed with our assistance.
▶그들은 우리 계획에 원조를 약속했다 They pledged support for our plan.
—원조하다 assist; help; support; aid; stand by
■—국[금] an aid country [fund] —물자 aid

goods —자 a supporter
원족 遠族 〈먼 일가〉 a distant relative [connection]
원죄 原罪 〔基〕 original sin
원죄 寃罪 a false charge; a false accusation
♦ 원죄를 쓰다 be falsely charged (with burglary); be falsely accused (of murder)
▶ 그는 자신의 결백을 증명하고 싶었으나 원죄를 벗는다는 것이 그에게 너무 어려운 일이었다 He wanted to prove his innocence, but it was very difficult for him to clear himself of false charge.
원주 圓周 the circumference (of a circle) ⇨ 원둘레 ♦ 원주의 circumferential
■ —각 angle of circumference —율 the ratio of the circumference of a circle to its diameter; pi
원주 原註 original notes
원주민 原住民 a native; the natives; an aborigine; the aborigines; (총칭) the native population ♦ —보호주의 nativism
원지 原紙 〈등사판의〉 stencil paper; a stencil; a master sheet ♦ 원지를 긁다 cut a stencil
원지점 遠地點 〔天〕〈달이나 인공 위성의〉 an apogee ♦ 원지점에 달하다 reach an apogee
원진 圓陣 a circle
♦ 원진을 치다 form a circle
▶ 선수들은 벤치에 원진을 치고 앉았다 The players sit in a circle in front of the bench.
원질 原質 a protyle ■ 유전— a gene
원창 圓窓 a round [circular] window
원천 源泉 the source; the fountainhead; an origin ♦ 지식의 원천 a source of knowledge [information]
■ —과세 taxation at the source; (英) pay-as-you-earn (略 P.A.Y.E.); (美) a withholding tax
원천징수 源泉徵收 withholding —원천징수하다 withhold (taxes at the source (of income))
■ —제도 a system of withholding taxes —표 a withholding slip; (美) a W-2 form
원체 元體 by nature ⇨ 워낙
원촌 原寸 an actual size
♦ 원촌 크기의 사진 a life-size photograph / 원촌 크기의 full-scale; life-size(d)
원촌 遠寸 〈먼 친척〉 distant kinship
♦ 원촌 사람 a distant relative
원추꽃차례 圓錐— 〔植〕 a panicle
원추리 〔植〕 a day lily
원칙 原則 a principle
♦ 기본 원칙을 세우다 establish a fundamental [an essential] principle
▶ 그것이 교육의 대원칙이다 That's the fundamental [essential] principle of education.
▶ 원칙적으로 나는 밤 10시에 잔다 I generally go to bed at ten at night.
▶ 원칙적으로는 당신에게 찬성합니다 In principle I agree with you.
▶ 원칙적으로 학기말 시험은 1년에 두 번 있다 As a general rule two term-end exams are given.
▶ 원칙적으로는 그 생각이 옳다고 생각한다 I think the idea is all right in principle.

▶ 나는 원칙적으로 남에게 책을 빌려 주지 않는다 I make it a rule not to lend books.
원컨대 願— I pray you; I hope...; I wish...; Would (to Heaven) that...
▶ 원컨대 남편이 어서 무사히 돌아오기를 I pray my husband will soon come back safely.
▶ 하느님, 원컨대, 그를 불쌍히 여기소서 I pray you, God, to take [have] pity on him. ⇒ May God take [have] pity on him.
원탁 圓卓 a round table ♦ 원탁의 기사들 the Knights of the Round Table [King Arthur]
■ —회의 a round-table conference
원통 寃痛 1 〈분〉 vexation; chagrin —원통하다 〈분하다〉 vexatious; vexing; mortifying; 〈원망스럽다〉 reproachable
♦ 원통하게도 to one's vexation / 원통해 하다 be [feel] mortified [chagrined] (at); feel chagrin (at); feel bitter (against) / 발을 구르며 원통해 하다 stamp one's feet with mortification / 원통해서 이를 갈다 grind one's teeth with vexation
▶ 아이 원통해라 How vexatious!
▶ 시합에 져서 원통했다 It chagrined us to lose the game.
▶ 놈에게 이런 모욕을 당하다니 원통해 죽겠네 What a shame that I must take such an insult from him!
2 〈애석함〉 a keen [deep] regret —원통하다 regrettable; sorry; rueful; lamentable
♦ 원통해 하다 feel a keen regret; lament
▶ 그가 그런 젊은 나이에 죽다니 참 원통하구나 What a pity that he should have died so young!
원통 圓筒 a cylinder ♦ 원통형 도장 a cylinder (seal) / 원통형의 cylindric(al)
원투 〔拳〕 a one-two (punch)
원판 the original state; 〈부사적〉 originally ⇨ 원래
원판 原板 〔寫〕 a negative (plate)
원판결 原判決 the original sentence ⇨ 원심 (原審)
원폭 原爆 an atom(ic) bomb; an A-bomb
■ —기지 an atomic base —실험 an atomic test; an A-test; a nuclear test —전 atomic warfare —증 an atomic bomb disease —투하 atomic bombing —희생자 an A-bomb victim
원피 原皮 raw hide; green hides [skins]
원피스 a one-piece dress; a one-piecer
원하다 願— 〈바라다〉 wish; desire; hope 《for》; want; 〈부탁하다〉 ask 《for》; 〈기원하다〉 pray

> 解說 *wish*는 기본적으로 실현이 불가능하거나 곤란한 일에 대한 바람을 나타낸다. *desire*는 딱딱한 말로서 wish보다 강도 높은 바람을 나타내는데, 그 바람을 실현시키려는 노력을 암시한다. *hope*는 성공을 바라는 기대를 나타내며 wish보다 실현 가능성이 높다. *want*는 hope와 마찬가지로 실현이 가능한 바람이지만 hope보다 의미가 강하여 부족한 것이나 필요한 것에 대하여 어떻게 해서든지 이를 충족시키려는 노력을 암시한다.

♦ 원하는 대로 〈부탁하는 대로〉 at one's re-

quest [desires]; 〈마음대로〉 at (one's) pleasure; 〈바라는 대로〉 to one's wish(es) / 원한다면 if one wishes [desires]; 〈상대방이〉 if you wish [want, please, like]
▶ 그는 의사가 되기를 원한다 He wishes to be a doctor.
▶ [會話] 「우리 부모님은 내가 결혼하기를 원하셔」「부모님들은 다 그러시지」 "My parents want me to marry." "I guess all parents do."
▶ 그것이 내가 원하는 거야 That is exactly what I want.

원한 怨恨 a grudge; resentment; a spite; ill will
♦ 원한이 뼈에 사무치다 have a deep-rooted rancor 《against》 / 원한을 풀다 pay off one's old scores; revenge oneself on sb / 아무에게 원한을 품다 have [harbor, bear] a spite [grudge] against sb; bear [owe] sb a spite [grudge]
▶ 그 범죄는 원한에 의한 것으로 판결되었다 The crime was judged as the result of a grudge.
▶ 우리는 그에게 아무런 원한도 없다 We have no rancor (at heart) against him.

원해 遠海 the open sea ━어 a pelagic fish
원행 遠行 〈먼 여행〉 a long journey ━원행하다 go a long way; take a long journey
원형 原形 the original form
▶ 그 집은 지진으로 원형을 알아볼 수 없을 정도로 망가졌다 The house was reduced to rubble by the earthquake. ■━질 [生] protoplasm
원형 原型 〈본보기〉 a pattern; a prototype; an archetype; a model; 〈治〉 a pattern
원형 圓形 a circle; a round shape [form]
♦ 원형의 건물 a circular building / 원형의 round(-shaped); circular
■━극장 an amphitheater
원호 援護 〈원조〉 support; 〈보호〉 protection; 〈구제〉 relief; help; 〈후원〉 backing
━원호하다 help; back (up); protect; lend [give] support to; give relief to
━기금[성금] a relief fund [donation] ━대상자 a relief recipient ━연금 a relief annuity
원호 圓弧 a circular arc; 〈원주의 일부〉 an arc of circle ♦ 원호를 그리다 draw an arc
원혼 寃魂 a malignant [vengeful] ghost
원화 原畵 an original picture [painting]
♦ 피카소의 원화 a Picasso original; the original picture by Picasso
원화 ━貨 the won (currency)
원활하다 圓滑━ smooth
♦ 원활하게 smoothly; 〈거침없이〉 without a hitch
▶ 만사가 원활하게 진행되었다 All went smoothly.
▶ 일은 원활하게 진척되었다 Things went (on) smoothly. ⇒ Things were carried without a hitch.
원훈 元勳 〈노신〉 a veteran statesman held first in merit; 〈훈공〉 the first order of merit
원흉 元兇 a ringleader; the chief instigator; the head [leader] 《of a riot》
월 月 〈문장론〉 a sentence
월 月 〈달〉 the moon; 〈한달〉 a month ⇨ 달

♦ 월 평균 on a monthly average / 월 1회의 once a month; monthly / 월 2회의 twice monthly; bimonthly
▶ 우리는 월 한번[두번] 모인다 We meet once [twice] a month.
▶ 내 월수입은 일정치 않다 My monthly income varies from month to month.
월간 月刊 monthly publication [issue]
♦ 월간의 monthly ■━잡지 a monthly (magazine [periodical])
월간 月間 ♦ 월간 목표 a monthly object / 월간 생산고 a monthly output / 월간의 monthly
월갈 〈문장론〉 syntax
월경 月經 menstruation; (the) menses; one's period; the monthlies; catamenia
━월경하다 menstruate; have the menses [monthlies]
▶ 그녀는 월경하는 중이다 She's having her period [menstruation].
■━곤란 difficult menstruation; dysmenorrhea ━과다 profuse menstruation ━기간 (the period of) menstruation; the menstrual period ━대 (帶) a hygienic band; a sanitary belt ━불순 irregular menstruation ━순조 regular menstruation ━이상 the disorder of menstruation ━주기 menstrual cycle ━통 menstrual pain ━폐쇄기 the climacteric; the menopause; the change of life
월경 越境 crossing the border; 〈불법의〉 border transgression; violation of the border
━월경하다 cross a [the] border; 〈불법으로〉 transgress the border; violate a frontier
▶ 그는 월경하여 도주했다 He escaped over [across] the border.
━사건 a border incident
월계 月計 a monthly account; monthly expenses ━월계하다 cast accounts monthly
■━표 [商] monthly trial balance
월계관 月桂冠 〈관〉 a laurel crown; a crown of laurel 〈honors〉
♦ 월계관을 쓰다 be crowned with laurels; win [gain, reap] laurels; bear [carry off] the palm
월계수 月桂樹 [植] a laurel
월계화 月季花 [植] a China [monthly] rose
월광 月光 〈달빛〉 moonlight; moonshine; 〈한 줄기의〉 a moonbeam
■━곡 〈곡명〉 the Moonlight Sonata
월권 越權 abuse of confidence; a stretch of authority; arrogation
▶ 그렇게 하는 것은 월권이다 It is beyond your right to do so.
━월권하다 overstep one's authority; go beyond [exceed] one's powers
■━행위 an act of arrogance: 그는 월권 행위를 했다 It has exceeded [(口) overstepped] his authority.
월급 月給 a (monthly) salary; (monthly) pay
♦ 많은 월급 a high [large] salary / 적은 월급 a low [small] salary / 세금을 포함한 월급 pay [salary] with tax / 세금 공제 월급 take-home pay / 월급이 오르다 [내리다] get a raise [cut] in one's salary / 적은 월급으로 살다 live on a small salary

▶ 그의 월급은 150만원이다 His monthly pay [(monthly) salary] is 1,500,000 won. ⇌ He gets a (monthly) salary of 1,500,000 won. ⇌ He gets 1,500,000 won a month.
▶ 會話 「네 월급은 얼마니?」「100만원이야」 "What [How much] is your monthly pay?" ⇌ "What [How much] salary do you get?" "It's 1,000,000 won." ⇌ "I get 1,000,000 won (a month)."
■ —날 a payday —봉투 a pay envelope [(英) packet] —일 a salaried man [worker]; a salaried employee

월남 越南 Vietnam ⇨ 베트남

월남하다 越南— 〈경계를 넘다〉 come south over the border; 〈북한에서〉 come from north Korea (over the 38th parallel)

월내 月內 ♦ 월내에 〈이 달 안에〉 before the end of this month; 〈한 달 안에〉 within a month

월년생초본 越年生草本 a biennial herb

월당 月當 a monthly sum ⇨ 월액

월동 越冬 passing the winter; wintering ♦ 월동 준비를 하다 prepare for the (coming of) winter
—하다 〈겨울을 나다〉 pass [spend] the winter 《at, in》; 〈피하하다〉 winter 《at, in》
▶ 그들은 남극에서 월동했다 They passed [spent] the winter in the Antarctic.
■ —자금 a winter allowance; a winter relief fund

월드시리즈 〔野〕 the World Series
월드컵 〔스포츠〕 the World Cup

월등하다 越等— 〈서술적〉 be by far the best; stand out conspicuous 《among》; be outstanding; be prominent
▶ 저 팀은 월등하다 That team is far and away the best.
▶ 그 가게에서는 카메라를 월등히 싸게 판다 That shop sells cameras at incredible low price.
▶ 동생이 나보다 월등히 영어를 잘한다 My brother is by far the better speaker of English.
▶ 그는 월등히 빨리 달렸다 He was an unusually [exceptionally, uncommonly] fast runner.

월령 月齡 the age of the moon
월례 月例 ♦ 월례의 monthly ■ —보고 a monthly report
월리 月利 monthly interest
월말 月末 《at, toward》 the end of the month ♦ 월말에 at [toward] the end of the month / 월말까지 by the end of the month
▶ 월말까지는 이 일이 끝납니다 I'll finish this work by the end of this month.
■ —지급[청산] month-end payment [settlement]
월면 月面 the surface of the moon; the moon's surface ♦ 월면을 밟다 walk on the moon's surface ■ —차 a moon buggy [car]; a lunar rover; a lunar roving vehicle —착륙 a lunar [moon] landing; a landing on the moon
월변 月邊 monthly interest
월별 月別 ♦ 월별(의) 판매 성적 sales records for each month / 월별(의) 생산고 monthly production
▶ 가스료와 전기 요금은 월별로 지급한다 I pay for the gas and electricity by the month.

월보 月報 a monthly report [bulletin]; monthly returns
월봉 月俸 one's monthly pay; a (monthly) salary
월부 月賦 a installment plan; an easy payment plan; a monthly installment [payment]
▶ 나는 냉장고를 월부로 샀다 I bought a refrigerator on a monthly installment plan [in monthly installments].
▶ 나는 매월 5만원씩 12개월 월부로 텔레비전을 샀다 I bought a television in twelve monthly installments [payments] of fifty thousand won each.
■ —불(拂) payment by [in] monthly installments —액 the amount allocated per month —판매제 (美) the (monthly) installment (paying) system [plan]; the easy payment plan; (英) the hire purchase (system)

월북하다 越北— 〈경계를 넘어가다〉 go north over the border; 〈북한으로 가다〉 go to north Korea

월비 月費 monthly expenses
월사금 月謝金 a monthly fee; a monthly tuition
월산 月産 a monthly production; a monthly output
월색 月色 moonlight; moonshine
월세 月貰 monthly rent ♦ 월세 20만원의 방 (live in) a 200,000 won-a-month room
▶ 이 방은 월세 80만원이다 This room rents for [at] 800,000 won a month.
월세계 月世界 〈달의〉 the lunar world; the moon
▶ 월세계 여행은 이제 꿈이 아니다 A journey to the moon [moon journey] is no longer a dream.
월수 月收 〈월수입〉 a monthly income
▶ 그의 월수는 200만원이다 His monthly income amounts to 2,000,000 won. ⇌ He has an income of 2,000,000 won a month.
월수당 月手當 a monthly allowance
월식 月蝕 〔天〕 an eclipse of the moon; a lunar eclipse ■ 부분[개기]— a partial [total, entire] eclipse of the moon
월액 月額 a monthly sum [amount, installment] ♦ 월액 30만원의 수당 a monthly allowance [pay] of 300,000 won
월여 月餘 〈한 달 남짓〉 more than a month ♦ 월여간이나 for more than a month / 월여전에 more than a month ago
월요일 月曜日 Monday (略 Mon.)
월일 月日 〈달과 해〉 the moon and the sun; 〈달과 날〉 months and days; 〈날짜〉 the date ♦ 생년 월일을 적다 write the date of one's birth
월전 月前 〈한 달 전에〉 a month ago
월정 月定 ♦ 월정의 monthly / 월정으로 구독하다 subscribe by the month
■ —구독자 a regular [monthly] subscriber
월진 月震 〈달의 지진〉 a moonquake

월차 月次 ♦월차의 monthly / 월차 보고 a monthly report
월초 月初 (at) the beginning of the month
월튼 〈영국의 수필가·전기 작가〉 Walton, Izaak (1593-1683)
월편 越便 (on) the opposite [other side]
월평 月評 a monthly review
월폴 〈영국의 소설가·수필가〉 Walpole, Horace (1717-97)
월표 月表 a monthly list [table]; monthly returns
웨딩 〈결혼식〉 wedding ■—드레스 a wedding dress ─마치 a wedding march ─케이크 a wedding [groom's] cake
웨스턴 〈서부극〉 a Western; 〈음악〉 Western music
웨스턴아일스 〈영국의 주〉 Western Isles
웨스트민스터 〈런던시 중앙의 한 구〉 Westminster
■—대성당 Westminster Cathedral ─사원 Westminster Abbey
웨스트버지니아 〈미국의 주〉 West Virginia (略 W. Va., WV)
웨스트서식스 〈영국의 주〉 West Sussex
웨이스트 〈허리〉 the waist 《of a dress》; one's waist
▶ 그녀의 웨이스트는 58센티미터다 Her waist measures 58 centimeters around. ⇒ She is 58 centimeters around the waist.
■—라인 the waistline
웨이터 a waiter
웨이트리스 a waitress
웨이퍼 〈과자〉 a wafer
웨일스 Wales ♦웨일스의 Welsh; Welch
■—사람 a Welshman 《pl. -men》; 〈여자〉 a Welshwoman; (총칭) the Welsh; the Welch
웩웩거리다 〈게우려고〉 keck; retch
웬 〈어떤, 한〉 a certain; one; some; unnamed
♦ 웬 사람 a certain person; someone
♦ 웬 사람이냐? Who is the man?
웬걸 〈의심·의외·부정을 나타낼 때〉 Oh!; Why!; Well!; on the contrary
▶ 會話 「수고하셨습니다」「웬걸요」 "I thank you for your kind labor!" "Not at all. ⇒ Don't mention it."
▶ 會話 「인제 끝났니?」「웬걸, 막 시작한 참이야」 "Have you finished?" "Why, I have only just begun."
웬만큼 〈다소, 어느 정도〉 to some degree [extent]; more or less; 〈어지간히, 꽤, 제법〉 pretty; fairly; tolerably; considerably; 〈알맞게〉 moderately
♦ 웬만큼 마시다 〈알맞게〉 drink temperately; be moderate in drinking / 웬만큼 살다 〈곧잘〉 make a decent living
▶ 그녀는 골프를 웬만큼 친다 She is not half bad at golf. ⇒ She is rather good at golf.
▶ 이것은 웬만큼 그린 그림이다 〈제법〉 This picture is done pretty well.
▶ 운동도 웬만큼 해야지 지나치면 오히려 해롭다 〈알맞게〉 An excessive amount of exercise will do you more harm than good.
웬만하다 〈꽤 좋다〉 good; fair; pretty [fairly] well; 〈어지간하, 상당하다〉 considerable; tolerable; passable; respectable; decent
♦ 수입이 웬만하다 〈꽤 된다〉 have a handsome income / 웬만하면 if you please [like]; if you don't mind
▶ 값이 웬만하면 사겠소 I will buy, if the price is reasonable.
웬일 what; whatever; what matter
♦ 웬일로 on what business / 웬일인지 for some unknown reason; without knowing why
▶ 웬일이냐? 〈어찌된 일이냐?〉 What is the matter (with you)?
▶ 웬일인지 모르겠다 I don't know why.
▶ 그는 웬일로 그런 짓을 했을까? I wonder why he did such a thing.
▶ 「왜, 안 왔었니?」「이유는 모르지만 웬일인지 오고 싶지 않았어」 "Why didn't you come?" "I don't know why, but I didn't want to."
▶ 미국엘 간다니 웬일이냐? For what purpose are you going to America? ⇒ What are you going to America for?
웰링턴¹ 〈뉴질랜드의 수도〉 Wellington
웰링턴² 〈영국의 장군·수상〉 Wellington, 1st Duke of Arthur Wellesley (1769-1852)
웰스 〈영국의 소설가〉 Wells, Herbert George (1866-1946)
웰터급 —級 the welterweight class
♦ 웰터급의 선수 a welterweight; a welter
웹스터 〈미국의 사전편찬가〉 Webster, Noah (1758-1843)
위 1 〈위쪽〉 the upper part; 〈표면〉 the surface; 〈테이블 등의〉 the top; 〈위층〉 the upstairs
♦ 위의 up; upward; upper
▶ 그 집의 위층은 아직 완성되지 않았다 The upstairs floor on the house haven't been completed yet.
▶ 산의 위쪽은 눈으로 덮여 있다 The upper part of the mountain is covered with snow.
▶ 비행기가 구름 위를 날고 있다 An airplane is flying over the clouds.
▶ 호수 위에 구름이 덮여 있다 Clouds hang over the lake.
▶ 위에서 보면 사람이 개미같이 작아 보인다 Seen from above, people looked as small as ants.
▶ 그는 내 방의 3층 위에 살고 있다 He lives three floors up from my room.
▶ 우리 사무실은 위층에 있다 Our office is upstairs. ⇒ We have an office upstairs [above].
▶ 그녀는 식탁 위에 식탁보를 씌웠다 She spread a tablecloth over the table.
▶ 이 책을 선반 위에 놓아라 Put this book on the shelf.
▶ 산 위로 달이 떠올랐다 The moon rose above the mountain.
▶ 좀더 위로 가면 아래 풍경을 잘 볼 수 있다 If we go up a little higher, we can see the scenery below very well.
▶ 좀더 위로 올라가자 Let's climb farther upward.

解說 ***on, above, over, on(to), up*** 의 용법
(1) ***on***: 표면에 접촉해 있는 경우를 가리킨다. 위쪽 면만 아니라 아래쪽, 옆면에 접촉해 있는

위

것도 나타내므로, 우리말의 「…의 위에」와 꼭 일치하지 않는다: 책상 위의 책 a book on the desk / 벽에 걸려 있는 지도 a map on the wall / 천장에 앉아 있는 파리 a fly on the ceiling
(2) *on*과 *upon*: *upon*은 딱딱한 느낌을 가지고 있어서 (口)에서는 보통 *on*이 쓰인다. 그러나 글의 리듬이나 관용상 upon을 사용하는 경우도 있다: 벽돌을 차곡차곡 쌓다 pile brick upon brick
(3) *on*과 *on top of*: *on top of* 「…의 꼭대기에」란 뜻으로 쓰인다: 내 머리 꼭대기에 on top of my head
(4) *above*와 *over*: (a) 「…에서 떨어져 위에」란 뜻이다: 벽난로 위에 걸린 그림 a picture above [over] the fireplace. 그러나 over는 바로 위 (directly above)를 암시하여 right over로도 쓰인다: 그의 방은 내 방 위[바로 위]에 있다 His room is above [(right) over] mine.
(b) over에 「…을 가리다」란 뜻이 있을 때가 있다: 두 손을 머리위에 올리다 hold *one's* hands above [over] *one's* head(▶above는 양손을 어깨위로 똑바로 올리는 것, over는 머리 위에서 손을 깍지끼어 머리를 가리는 자세임). 또 「…의 위로 뻗치다」의 뜻으로도 쓰인다: 발코니는 뜰 위로 튀어나와 있다 The balcony projects over the garden. 다만 상하관계만을 나타낼 때는 above를 쓴다: 구름 위로 보이는 봉우리 a peak seen above the clouds
(c) over에 「…을 넘어서」의 뜻이 더해지는 경우가 있다: 비행기가 머리 위를 날아갔다 A plane flew over my head [overhead]. (▶above를 쓰면 단순히 머리 위를 난 사실을 서술하는 것이다. my head를 생략하면 (3)의 용법이 됨)
(5) over: 물건을 덮는 경우: 마루 위에 깐 양탄자 a rug over [on] the floor (▶on은 단순히 마루와의 접촉을 나타내지만, over에는 마루를 덮는다는 느낌이 더 있음) / 강 위에 놓여 있는 다리 a bridge over the river. 또 「…의 위에 겹쳐서」란 뜻으로는 on top of도 사용된다: 그녀는 스웨터 위에 재킷을 끼어입었다 She wore a jacket over [on top of] her sweater.
(6) *on*과 *upon*과 *onto*: 「…의 위로[위에]」란 뜻으로 이동·운동을 나타내며, 강조하여 upon을 사용하는 수가 있다. (口)에서는 onto가 많이 쓰이며, (英)에서는 이따금 on to로 쓴다: 그는 말 위에 뛰어올랐다 He jumped on (to) [upon] the horse.
(7) *up*: 위쪽을 향한 동작·운동을 나타낸다: 소떼는 산 위로 이동하기 시작했다 Herds of cows began to move up the hill.

2 【꼭대기】 the top; a head
◆ 맨 위의 topmost; uppermost / 책상 왼쪽의 맨 위의 서랍 the left-hand top drawer of a desk / 페이지의 맨 위에 at the top [head] of the page / 위에서 다섯째 줄에 on the fifth line from the top
▶ 산 위는 몹시 춥다 It is very cold on the top of the mountain.
▶ 산 위에 오두막집이 하나 있다 A cottage

stands at the top of the mountain.
▶ 그는 나를 머리 위에서 발끝까지 훑어 봤다 He looked at me from top to toe.
▶ 언덕 위에서 바라본 경치는 장관이다 We can have a splendid view from the top of the hill.
▶ 그녀의 집은 언덕 위에 있다 Her house stands on the top of a hill.

3 【보다 나은 쪽】 superior ⟨to⟩; seniority
◆ 위의 better ⟨than⟩; above…; over…; advanced; upper; higher ⟨than⟩; more than; above / 위로부터의 명령 an order from *one's* superior [boss]
▶ 이것이 저것보다 품질이 위다 This is superior to that in quality.
▶ 그는 능력에서는 나보다 훨씬 위다 He is far superior to me in ability.
▶ 피아니스트로서는 그녀가 나보다 훨씬 위다 As a pianist, she is far above me.
▶ 그의 학교 성적은 평균보다 조금 위다 His schoolwork is a little above [better than] (the) average.
▶ 영어 회화 능력은 우리 반에서 네가 제일 위다 You're the best speaker of English in our class.
▶ 경험으로는 네가 나보다 위다 You have more experience than I do [(口) than me].

4 【연령이】 the elder [(美) older]
▶ 내 위의 누이는 초등학교 교사가 되었다 My older [elder] sister became an elementary school teacher.
▶ 그는 나보다 다섯 살 위다 He is five years older than I. ⇌ He is my senior by five years.
▶ 그녀는 나보다 1학년 위였다 She was a year ahead of me in school.
▶ 두 사람 가운데 내가 나이가 위다 I am the older [elder] of the two.

5 【전술·전기한】 the above
◆ 위에 말한 바와 같이 as we have said above; as stated [mentioned] above
▶ 위의 그림을 보라 See the picture above.
▶ 위와 같은 이유로 나는 그것에 반대한다 I am opposed to it for the above reasons.

위 位 1 ⟨등급⟩ a position; a post; a place; ⟨a⟩ rank; ⟨등수⟩ a class; a grade; ⟨지위⟩ a situation; a location
◆ 제4위의 the fourth-ranking ⟨Dodgers⟩/ 2위가 되다 take [win, gain] second place; be placed second; ⟨경주에서⟩ finish [come] second; come in second ⟨place⟩; finish ⟨a race⟩ in second place / 제 1[3] 위를 차지하다 win (the) first [third] place; rank first [third] / 제1위이다 be [stand, rank] first; head [top] the list / 제5위다 be fifth [in fifth position] / 3위로 떨어지다 drop to third place
▶ 그는 학급에서 10위로 떨어졌다 He has dropped to the tenth (place) in his class.
2 ⟨위패의 수⟩ ◆ 영령 5 위 five heroic souls

위 胃 [解] a stomach; ⟨동물·새·벌레의⟩ a craw
◆ 위의 gastric / 반추동물의 제1[2, 3, 4]위 the paunch [honeycomb, manyplies (▶단수·복수 동형), maw] / 위의 내용물을 검사하다 examine the contents of ⟨an animal's⟩ stomach
▶ 위가 아프다 I feel [have] a pain in the

stomach. ⇌ I have a stomachache.
▶ 나는 위가 약하다[튼튼하다] I have a weak [good] digestion. ⇌ I have a weak [strong] stomach.
▶ 아이스크림을 먹고 위가 탈이 났다 The ice cream has upset my stomach. ⇌ Ice cream has put my stomach out of order.
▶ 오늘 아침 먹은 햄이 위에 얹혀 거북하다 The ham I ate this morning still lies heavy on my stomach.
■ —간막(間膜) a mesogastrium (*pl.* -tria) —세척(洗滌) 〔醫〕 gastrolavage; gastric irrigation: 위 세척을 하다 wash out the stomach; carry out a gastric lavage —세척기 〔醫〕 a stomach pump —신경증 gastric neurosis —절개(술) gastrotomy —점막 the gastric mucous membrane —카메라 a gastrocamera —카타르 〔醫〕 catarrh of the stomach; gastric catarrh
위 緯 1 〈위도〉 latitude **2** 〈피륙의 씨〉 the woof; woof threads
위강 胃腔 gastral cavity
위경 危境 a critical situation [stage]; an emergency; a crisis (*pl.* ~es)
♦ 위경을 당하다 face a crisis / 위경에 처해 있다 be at a crisis; be in a critical condition / 위경에서 벗어나다 get [pass] through a crisis
위경 胃鏡 〔醫〕 a gastroscope —검사법 gastroscopy
위경련 胃痙攣 〔醫〕 stomach cramps; convulsion [a spasm] of the stomach ♦ 위경련을 일으키다 have a stomach cramp; get stomach cramps
위계 位階 grade of ranks; a (court) rank
♦ 위계가 높은 사람 a person high in rank
■ 성직(聖職)— order —제(制) a hierarchy
위계 僞計 〈거짓 꾀〉 a deceptive plan; a fraudulent stratagem ♦ 위계를 쓰다 use a deceptive scheme
위고 〈프랑스의 시인·소설가·극작가〉 Hugo, Victor Marie (1802-85)
위공 偉功 a meritorious service; a great deed [achievement] ♦ 위공을 세우다 render great services; achieve a great success
위관 尉官 〈육·공군의〉 officers below the rank of major; (美) a company officer; 〈해군의〉 an officer below lieutenant commander; a subaltern
위관 偉觀 a grand sight; a fine view [sight]
▶ 한라산이 위관을 드러내고 있다 Hallasan presents a magnificent view.
위광 威光 authority; power; influence
♦ 대통령의 위광 the authority of the president / 엄친의 위광으로 through the influence of *one's* father / 일족의 위광을 손상시키다 disgrace the dignity of the family
위구 危懼 fear; misgivings; apprehensions
♦ 위구심을 품다 feel [entertain] misgivings (about); be apprehensive (about, of)
위구르 ♦ 위구르어 Uighur / 위구르 사람 a Uighur; (총칭) the Uighur people
위국 危局 a critical situation; a crisis
위국하다 爲國— serve *one's* country; do much for [render service to] *one's* country
위궤양 胃潰瘍 〔醫〕 an ulcer of the stomach; a gastric [stomach] ulcer ▶ 그는 위궤양에 걸려 있었다 He had a stomach ulcer.
위급 危急 an emergency; a crisis (*pl.* crises); an exigency
♦ 위급한 때 an [a time of] emergency; a critical moment [hour] / 이렇게 위급한 때에 in this exigency / 위급을 구하다 save *sb* from imminent danger; help *sb* out of a crisis / 위급을 알리다 give the alarm
▶ 우리는 위급에 대비해야 한다 We must provide against emergencies.
▶ 우리는 위급에 처해 있다 We are in peril [imminent danger].
▶ 그들은 내 위급을 구해줬다 They helped me out of my distress [crisis].
▶ 우리는 돈을 빌려서 위급을 극복했다 We weathered the pinch by borrowing money.
—위급하다 critical; exigent; imminent; crucial
♦ 위급한 critical / 위급한 경우에(는) in case of emergency; in time of need [danger, crisis]; at a crisis; at a critical moment
▶ 우리는 위급한 경우에 대비해야만 한다 We must prepare for emergencies.
▶ 위급한 때는 그가 도와주겠지 He will stand by me in a pinch.
위기 危機 a crisis (*pl.* crises); an emergency; a critical [crucial] moment; a critical situation [stage]
♦ 정치적 위기 a political crisis / 위기에 처하여 at a crisis; in an emergency / 위기를 극복하다 get [pass, come] through a crisis; tide [get] over a crisis / 위기에 직면하다 face a crisis [an emergency] / 위기에 처하다 come to a crisis; be in danger condition
▶ 정치적 상황은 위기 국면이다 The political situation is critical [in a critical condition]. ⇌ We have a touch-and-go political situation.
▶ 금년 말에는 경제위기가 올 것이다 There will be an economic crisis at the end of this year.
▶ 그의 도움으로 우리는 재정적 위기를 극복했다 His help tided us over the financial crisis.
위기일발 危機一髮 the critical moment; the eleventh hour; hairbreadth; imminent danger
♦ 위기일발에서 at the critical moment; in the (very) nick of time / 위기일발에 처해 있다 be in imminent danger; be touch-and-go; hang by a thread [hair] / 위기일발에서 살아나다 escape (death) by a hairbreadth [by the skin of *one's* teeth]; have a narrow [hairbreadth] escape
▶ 나는 위기일발에서 벗어났다 I had a narrow escape.
위난 危難 (a) danger; (a) peril; (a) hazard; 〈조난〉 distress
♦ 국가의 위난을 구하다 save *one's* country / 위난을 당하다 meet with [encounter, face] a danger / 위난을 모면하다 escape from [get out of] danger / 위난에 빠지다 get into danger [a dangerous situation]
▶ 그는 위난이 닥쳐오는 것을 모르고 있었다 He was not aware of the approaching danger.
위남자 偉男子 a brave man; a man of higher character

위대 偉大 greatness; grandeur; mightiness
—**위대하다** great; 〈힘있는〉 mighty; 〈웅대한〉 grand
♦ 위대한 국민 a great nation / 위대한 업적 a great achievement [performance]
▶ 그는 한국이 낳은 위대한 학자다 He is a distinguished scholar Korea has ever produced.
▶ 어머니는 내게 열심히 공부해서 위대한 사람이 되라고 말씀하셨다 My mother used to tell me, "Study hard and become a great man."
▶ 그는 위대한 시인이다 He is a great poet.
▶ 그를 만나보면 그의 위대함을 알게 될 것이나 When you see him, you'll understand his greatness [how great he is].

위덕 威德 virtue and influence

위도 緯度 latitude (略 lat.)
♦ 위도의 latitudinal / 위도상(으로 보아) latitudinally / 위도를 달리하다 be in different latitudes (from) / 위도를 측정하다 determine the latitude
▶ 파리의 위도는 몇도지요? What is the latitude of Paris?
▶ 그 천문대의 위도는 북위 32도 15분이다 The latitude of that astronomical observatory is thirty-two degrees a quarter [fifteen] minutes north.
▶ 그 도시는 서울과 위도가 같다 The city is in [at] the same latitude as Seoul.
■ —선 a parallel

위독 危篤 a critical [serious] condition of illness
—**위독하다** 〈서술적〉 be dangerously [seriously] ill; be in a critical condition; 〈입원환자가〉 be on the danger [critical] list
♦ 위독해지다 〈사람이 주어〉 fall into a dangerous [critical] condition; 〈병이 주어〉 take a critical turn
▶ 그는 위독하다 He is dangerously [seriously] ill. ⇌ He is in a critical condition. ⇌ His condition is critical.
▶ 오늘 그는 조금 좋아졌지만 아직 위독한 상태를 벗어난 것은 아니다 He is slightly better today, but he is not out of danger yet [is still in danger].

위락시설 慰樂施設 recreation facilities

위략 偉略 an outstanding stratagem; an excellent tactics

위력 威力 power; might; 〈권력〉 authority; 〈세력〉 influence
♦ 돈의 위력 the power of money [wealth] / 위력 있는 powerful; influential / 위력을 떨치다 (口) throw [check] one's weight about [around]; exercise one's power (over) / 위력으로 굴복시키다 bring sb into submission by a show of one's power
▶ 돈의 위력으로 그는 그 지위를 얻었다 He used the power of (his) money [weath] to gain his position.
▶ 그 폭탄의 가공할 위력은 그 전쟁에서 증명되었다 The terrible power of the bomb was proved in the war.
▶ 바람이 위력을 더해가고 있다 The wind is gathering its force.
▶ 투수는 위력있는 공을 던져 타자 셋을 연달아 아웃시켰다 The pitcher fired the ball with such power that he retired three consecutive batters in one stretch.

위력 偉力 great power; mighty force

위령 威令 authority; authoritative order

위령 違令 〈명령을 거스름〉 violation of an order [a command]
—**위령하다** disobey [violate, break] an order; act contrary to sb's orders

위령 慰靈 —**위령하다** honor sb's memory; console the souls of a dead person
■ —제 a memorial service (in honor of [for]): 전몰자위령제 a memorial service for the war dead —탑 a memorial tower; a war memorial; the Cenotaph

위로 慰勞 1 〈수고를 치하함〉 appreciation of sb's efforts [services]; recognition of sb's services
—**위로하다** acknowledge [recognize] sb's services
♦ 장병들을 위로하다 provide troops with comforts
▶ 사장은 우리의 노고를 위로해 주었다 Our president showed his appreciation of our efforts.
2 〈위안〉 consolation; comfort
—**위로하다** console; comfort
♦ 남의 불행[슬픔]을 위로하다 console sb in (his) misfortune [sorrow] / 서로를 위로하다 comfort [console] each other / 심적으로 위로받다 be comforted internally
▶ 그녀는 외로우면 언제나 음악으로 마음을 위로했다 She always comforted herself with music when she was lonely.
▶ 많은 격려 편지가 내 슬픔을 위로해 주었다 Many letters of encouragement refreshed my sad heart.
▶ 슬픔에 잠겨 있는 그녀를 위로할 말이 없다 I don't have the proper words to comfort her in her deep sorrow.
▶ 세상이란 그런거라 생각하고 위로받으세요 Console yourself with the thought that such is the way of the world.
■ —금 (get) a bonus; a reward for one's services —연 a dinner party given in appreciation of one's services: 직원들에게 위로연을 열어 주다 give a party by way of rewarding one's employees for their services —휴가 a special holiday given in recognition of one's services

위막 胃膜 【解】 the coats of the stomach

위망 威望 〈위력과 명망〉 power and fame; authority and popularity

위망 僞妄 falsehood (and absurdity); falsity

위명 威名 fame; renown; prestige
♦ 위명을 떨치다 win (a) wide fame

위명 僞名 〈가명〉 a false [an assumed] name; 〈범죄자들이 사용하는〉 an alias
▶ 위명으로 under the false [an assumed] name (of) / 위명을 사용하다 use [give] a false name / 위명을 대다 give a false name / 위명으로 생활하다 live under an assumed name

위무 慰撫 pacification; appeasement
—**위무하다** pacify; soothe; appease; solace

위문 慰問 〈위로〉 consolation; sympathy; 〈문안〉 a call of sympathy; an inquiry after *sb's* health
♦ **위문을 가다** go and comfort *sb*; go to express *one's* sympathy; pay a sympathetic visit (to)
▶ 그의 극단은 양로원을 방문하여 위문 공연을 했다 His theater troupe gave a performance to cheer up the residents of the old people's home.
—**위문하다** 〈위로하다〉 console; 〈문안하다〉 inquire after *sb's* health; visit (a sick friend)
■—**대** (袋) a comfort bag [kit] —**방문** a call of inquiry —**편지** a consolatory letter; a letter of sympathy —**품** (little) comforts; a comfort article; a gift

위반 違反 a breach; (a) violation; contravention ((to [of] the law); infringement; transgression; infraction
▶ 그것은 법률 위반이다 That's against the law. ⇒ That's a violation of the law. ⇒ You are breaking the law.
▶ 그는 선거법 위반으로 기소되었다 He was prosecuted for a breach of the Election Law.
▶ 그의 경기는 규칙 위반이다 His play is against the rule.
—**위반하다** infringe; contravene; violate; break (a promise); disobey (orders); transgress against (rules); act [be] against (the law)
♦ **규칙을 위반하다** infringe [violate] a rule
▶ 규칙을 위반하면 벌을 받는다 There is a punishment for infringing the rules.
▶ 이 법률을 위반하는 자는 벌금에 처한다 Any violation of this law is to be punished with a fine.
■—**계약**— a breach of contract **교통**— a violation of traffic regulations; a traffic violation **법률**— an offense against [violation of] the law **주차**— a parking violation **헌법**— an anticonstitutional [unconstitutional] act ■—**자** an offender; a violator; a transgressor —**행위** an offense

위배 違背 a breach ⇨ 위반

위법 違法 illegality; unlawfulness; lawbreaking
♦ **위법의** illegal; unlawful; lawbreaking / **위법적으로** illegally; unlawfully; against the law
▶ 여기에 주차하는 것은 위법이다 It is illegal [against the law] to park here. ⇒ Parking here is against [is a violation of] the law.
▶ 폭발물을 차 안에 가지고 들어가는 것은 위법이다 It is illegal [against the law] to bring explosives in [to] the coach.
■—**성** illegality —**자** a lawbreaker; an offender —**행위** an illegal act; a violation of the law; illegality; 〔法〕 a delict; 〈관리 등의〉 a malfeasance: **위법 행위를 하다** commit an illegality [an illegal act]

위벽 胃壁 〔解〕 the walls of the stomach; the stomach walls

위병 胃病 a stomach trouble [disorder]; 〔醫〕 〈위약〉 dyspepsia ♦ **위병을 앓다** suffer from a stomach trouble ■—**학** gastrology —**환자** a dyspeptic

위병 衛兵 a guard; a sentinel; a sentry
♦ **위병을 서다** stand guard; serve as guard; be on guard / **위병을 세우다** post a guard
▶ 우리는 버킹엄 궁전의 위병 교대를 구경하러 갔다 We went to see the changing of the Guard at Buckingham Palace.
■—**근무** guard duty —**소** a guardhouse; a guardroom —**장교** an officer (in charge) of the guard

위복하다 威服— 〈복종케 하다〉 force [awe] *sb* into submission; 〈굴복하다〉 submit [obey] to power

위본 僞本 a spurious copy; a forgery; 〈해적판〉 a pirated edition

위부 委付 〔法〕 abandonment
—**위부하다** abandon

위산 胃散 〈위병에 쓰는 가루약〉 (medicinal) powder for the stomach

위산 胃酸 〔醫〕 gastric acid; acid in the stomach ♦ **위산과다의** hyperacid ■—**과다증** 〔醫〕 acid dyspepsia; gastric hyperacidity

위상 位相 〔電·物〕 a phase
■—**계** (計) a phase meter —**계수** phase coefficient —**공간** 〔數〕 topological space; 〔物〕 phase space —**기하학** topology —**변조** 〔電〕 phase modulation —**속도** 〔物〕 phase velocity —**수학** topology; analysis situs —**정수** (定數) 〔物〕 a phase constant —**조정** phase adjustment —**조정변압기** a phase compensating transformer —**차** (差) phase difference —**차 현미경** a phase-contrast [phase] microscope

위생 衛生 sanitation; hygiene; health
♦ **위생(상)의, 위생적인** sanitary; hygienic / **위생상** for reasons of sanitation; for sanitary reasons / **위생에 좋은** good for the health; healthy; wholesome / **위생에 주의하다** be careful of *one's* health; attend to sanitation / **위생에 해로운** insanitary; unwholesome; unhealthy
▶ 그들은 위생관념이 없다 They have no sense of hygiene [sanitation].
▶ 요리를 할 때에는 위생상 모자를 쓰십시오 When you cook, wear a hat for sanitary reasons.
▶ 이 방은 위생에 나쁘다 This room is bad for the health.
▶ 더러운 손으로 음식을 먹는 것은 비위생적이다 It's unhygienic [insanitary] to eat with dirty hands.
■—**공중**— public health **정신**— mental hygiene —**공학** sanitary engineering —**관리** health control [administration]; hygienics —**대** (帶) a sanitary belt; a hygienic band —**법** hygiene; hygienics —**병** a hospital orderly; (口) 〔an army〕 medic —**상태** sanitary conditions —**설비** health facilities —**시설** sanitary facilities —**시험장** a hygienic laboratory —**실** the medical room —**컵** 〈종이로 만든 컵〉 a sanitary cup —**학** hygienics; sanitary science

위서다 〈후행하다〉 accompany a bride [bridegroom] (to); 〈수행하다〉 attend [follow] an important person

위선 偽善 (a) hypocrisy

♦ 위선적(인) hypocritic(al); double-faced / 위선을 행하다 do hypocrisy; play the hypocrite; behave hypocritically; be a hypocrite

■ 一자 a hypocrite; a pharisee; a wolf in sheep's clothing

위선 緯線 〔地〕 a parallel (of latitude); a latitude line

위성 衛星 〔天〕 a satellite

▶ 달은 지구의 위성이다 The moon is a satellite of the earth.

■ 기상— a weather satellite 방송— a telecommunication satellite 인공— an artificial [a man-made] satellite 정찰— a reconnaissance satellite 통신— a communications satellite ■ 一국 a satellite country [state] 一도시 a satellite city [town] 一중계 satellite relay: 위성중계로 by [via] satellite relay / 위성중계하다 transmit (an event) via satellite

위세 威勢 power; might; influence; authority; 〈기세〉 (high) spirits

♦ 위세 당당한 high spirited; full of high spirits / 위세 당당하게 in high spirits; vigorously; gallantly; (口) full of go / 위세를 부리다 exercise [wield] one's authority over (others) / 위세에 굴복하다 bow to authority / 위세 좋게 돈을 쓰다 spend one's money freely [generously]; lavish one's money (on)

▶ 군인들은 위세를 보이려고 행군했다 The soldiers marched to show their strength.

위수 衛戌 〔軍〕 a garrison

■ 一령 Garrison Decree —병 garrison troops —사령관 the commandant of a garrison —임무 garrison duty —지 a garrison town

위스콘신 〈미국의 주〉 Wisconsin (略 Wis., Wisc., WI)

♦ 위스콘신주 사람 a Wisconsinite

위스키 whisky; whiskey

▶ 나는 위스키를 물에 타서[스트레이트로] 마셨다 I had a whisky and water [straight].

■ 一글라스 a whiskey glass —소다 (a) whiskey and soda; (a) highball

위시하다 爲始— begin; start; commence

♦ 위시하여 including...; ...and; as well as...

▶ 김선생을 위시하여 많은 명사가 그 회의에 참석했다 Many dignitaries, including Mr. Kim attended the meeting.

위신 威信 〈위엄〉 dignity; prestige; 〈권위〉 authority

♦ 위신을 되찾다[손상시키다] restore [injure] the prestige (of) / 위신을 잃다 lose prestige; lower [lose] one's dignity / 위신을 지키다 maintain one's dignity [prestige]

▶ 그녀에게 사정하는 것은 내 위신을 떨어뜨리는 일입니다 It is beneath my dignity to ask a favor of her.

▶ 그 교사의 위신은 땅에 떨어졌다 The teacher has lost his prestige. ⇒ The prestige of the teacher has gone.

위아래 ups and downs; 〈신분상의〉 high and low; the upper and lower

♦ 위아래가 뒤바뀌다 be upside-down; be topsy-turvy / 위아래로 움직이다 move up and down / 남을 위아래로 훑어보다 look sb up and down; survey sb from head to foot

위아토니 胃— 〔醫〕 gastric atony

위안 慰安 〈위로〉 (a) consolation; (a) solace; (a) comfort; easement; 〈오락〉 (a) recreation; (an) amusement

♦ 다소의 위안이 되다 some comfort can be drawn 《from》 / 위안을 받다 take comfort (in) / 위안을 주다 give comfort (to)

▶ 음악을 들으면 위안이 된다 I feel relieved when I listen to music.

▶ 그는 음악에서 위안을 찾았다 He sought consolation [solace, comfort] in music.

—위안하다 comfort, console; solace; amuse; entertain

♦ 스스로를 위안하다 comfort [divert, amuse] oneself

■ 一물 a comfort; a solace —부 a comfort girl [woman] —처 an oasis

위암 胃癌 〔醫〕 a stomach [gastric] cancer; (a) cancer of the stomach

위압 威壓 coercion; high-handedness; browbeating

♦ 위압적인 coercive; browbeating; high-handed / 위압적으로 coercively; overbearingly; with a high hand / 위압적으로 복종시키다 force [awe] sb into obedience

▶ 그는 위압적인 태도만 고치면 한결 괜찮은 사람이 될텐데 If he changed his high-handed [coercive] attitude, he would be a more likable person.

—위압하다 coerce; overawe; browbeat; daunt; treat with a high hand

♦ 위압당하다 be overawed (by); be cowed (before)

▶ 나는 그의 노려보는 눈초리에 위압되었다 I was intimidated by his stare.

위액 胃液 〔生〕 gastric [stomach] juice ♦ 위액의 분비 gastric secretions ■ —분비선 a gastric gland

위약 胃弱 〔醫〕 dyspepsia; indigestion; weak digestion —위약하다 dyspeptic; 〈서술적〉 have a weak stomach

위약 違約 a breach of a contract; 〈특히 혼약의〉 a breach of a promise; a default

—위약하다 infringe a contract; break [do not keep] one's word [a promise, a contract, an agreement]; default

▶ 그는 그 회사와 위약했다 He broke the contract with the company.

■ 一금 a penalty; a forfeit; an indemnity —자 a person breaking a contract; a defaulter

위엄 威嚴 dignity; majesty

♦ 위엄있는 사람 a man of dignity [dignified appearance] / 위엄있는 majestic(al); dignified; stately; commanding / 위엄 없는 undignified; unimpressive; cheap / 위엄을 보이다 show one's dignity / 위엄을 손상시키다 impair [damage, lower] one's dignity / 위엄을 유지하다[지키다] keep [maintain] one's dignity / 위엄을 잃다 lose one's dignity / 위엄을 차리다 get on one's dignity / 위엄에 눌리다 be overawed; be cowed (before)

▶ 재판관은 위엄있는 복장을 하고 있었다 The judge was clothed with dignity.

▶그의 연설에는 대통령다운 위엄이 없었다 His speech lacked the dignity worthy of a president.
위업 偉業 a great work [achievement, undertaking] ◆공전의 위업 an achievement of unprecedented magnitude
▶그는 위업을 달성했다 He achieved a great piece of work.
위없다 supreme; unsurpassed; matchless
위여 〈새떼를 쫓는 소리〉 Shoo!
위염 胃炎 〔醫〕 gastritis; inflammation of the stomach
위요하다 圍繞— surround ⇨ 둘러싸다
위용 威容 a dignified [majestic] appearance [air]; a dignified mien; dignity
◆위용을 갖추고 in a dignified attitude / 위용을 갖추다 assume a dignified attitude / 위용을 보이다 present a grand [magnificent] appearance
▶우리는 그랜드 캐니언의 위용에 감동했다 We were struck with the grandeur of the Grand Canyon.
▶사람들은 그의 위용에 압도되었다 People were overwhelmed by his dignified appearance.
위원 委員 a member of a committee; a committeeman; 〈정부의〉 a commissioner; (총칭) a committee
◆위원을 임명하다 appoint a member of a committee
▶그는 위원의 한 사람이다 He is [sits] on the committee.
▶그 위원회는 여섯 명의 위원으로 구성돼 있다 The committee consists of six members.
▶그는 7인 위원회 위원으로 선출되었다 He was elected (as) [chosen (to be)] a member of the seven-member committee.
▶나는 위원입니다 I am on the committee.
■국무— a cabinet member; a minister 논설— an editorial writer; an editorialist 상임— (총칭) a standing [permanent] committee 전문— an expert advisor; a technical expert 조사— a commission of inquiry 집행— (총칭) an executive committee 학급— a class secretary ■—장 a chairman [〈남녀〉 a chairperson] of a committee : 부위원장 a vice-chairman [cochairman, assistant chairman] of a committee / 위원장직을 맡다 chair a committee
위원회 委員會 a committee; a commission; a board; 〈회의〉 a meeting of a committee
◆4인 위원회 a four-member [four-man] committee / 위원회를 소집하다 call a meeting of the committee; call a committee into session; call a committee meeting / 위원회를 열다 hold a committee meeting / 위원회를 조직[설치]하다 form [set up] a committee / 위원회를 해산하다 discharge a committee meeting / 위원회에 제출[회부]하다 submit (a subject) to a committee / 위원회에 참석하다 sit [be] on a committee
▶위원회가 개회중이다 The committee is in session.
▶위원회는 그 문제를 심의하고 있다 The committee is in session on that question.

▶그 의안은 위원회를 통과했다 The bill got through [passed] the committee.
■교육— the 《Seoul》 Board of Education 군사정전— the Military Armistice Commission 분과— a subcommittee; 〈회의〉 a sectional committee meeting 상임— a standing committee 소— a small committee; a subcommittee 예산— a budget committee 운영— a steering committee 원자력— the Atomic Energy Commission 전문— an expert committee 전형— an examination body 조사— an investigation committee 준비— an arrangement committee 집행— an executive committee
위의 威儀 〈위엄〉 dignity (of demeanor); majesty; solemnity; 〈몸가짐〉 a dignified mien
◆위의 있는 dignified; solemn; stately / 위의를 갖추고 in a dignified [solemn] manner; in great state; solemnly / 위의를 갖추다 compose one's appearance
위의당당 威儀堂堂 a majestic air ⇨ 위풍
위인 偉人 a great man; a respectable person; a great [master] mind
◆과거의 위인들 the great names of past ages / 불세출의 위인 the greatest man that ever lived / 역사상의 위인들 the great names of history / 위인이 되다 attain greatness
■—전 the life of a great man
위인 爲人 〈됨됨이〉 one's personality [person, character]; 〈사람된〉 a person
▶그는 출세할[강도질할] 위인이 못된다 He is not the sort of man to succeed in life [commit robbery].
위임 委任 trust; commission; 〈권력·권한 등의〉 delegation; authorization; 〔法〕 mandate
◆권한의 위임 delegation of authority
—위임하다 entrust [charge] sb with (a matter); entrust [leave] (a matter) to sb; commit (a matter) to sb's care [management]; authorize [empower] sb to (do)
▶나의 부재시에는 모든 업무를 김 전무에게 위임하고 있습니다 All business is in the Managing Director Kim's charge during my absence.
▶나는 그에게 전권을 위임했다 I entrusted him with full powers.
■—권 power of attorney —권한 competency of mandate —대리 representation of mandate —대리인 an authorized agent —자 the mandator : 피위임자 a trustee —장 a letter [warrant] of attorney; (a letter of) proxy —제도 a mandate system —투표 proxy voting : 위임투표하다 vote by proxy
위임통치 委任統治 mandate; mandatory rule [administration]
◆유엔의 위임통치를 받다 be placed under the United Nations mandate / 위임통치를 하다 carry out a mandate
■—국 a mandatory (power); a mandatary —권 a mandate: 위임통치권을 행사하다 exercise a mandate —령(領) a mandatory [mandated] territory; territories under mandate
위자료 慰藉料 consolation money; a solatium 《pl. -tia》; (口) heart [love] balm; 〈별거 수당〉 an alimony
◆위자료를 청구하다 demand compensation

▶그녀는 그가 헤어지자고 하자 위자료를 내라고 요구했다 She demanded that he pay consolation money when he wanted to leave her.
위작 僞作 a forgery; a fake; 〈문학작품〉 an apocryphal work ▶저 그림은 밀레의 위작이다 That drawing is a forgery of a Millet. ⇒ That is a fake drawing of a Millet.
위장 胃腸 the stomach and intestines [bowels]
◆위장의 gastroenteric / 위장을 해치다 injure the stomach and bowels
▶나는 위장이 튼튼하다[약하다] I have a strong [poor] digestion.
▶나는 위장에 탈이 났있나 I had indigestion.
■—병[장애] a gastroenteric [gastrointestinal] disorder [trouble] —약 digestive medicine; a digestive —염 gastroenteritis
위장 僞裝 (a) camouflage; 〈변장〉 (a) disguise —위장하다 disguise; camouflage (a ship)
■—공작 operations to disguise the face —귀순 defection in disguise —망 a camouflage net —매매 〔證〕 a wash sale —실업 hidden unemployment —폭탄 a booby trap (bomb)
위장부 偉丈夫 a brave man ⇨ 위남자
위재 偉才 〈사람〉 a great man; a gifted person; 〈재주〉 a great talent
위적 偉績 a great deed; signal merits; glorious exploits; brilliant achievements; distinguished services
위정자 爲政者 〈정치가〉 a statesman; 〈행정가〉 an administrator; 〈통치자〉 a ruler
위조 僞造 〈문서의〉 forgery; fabrication; 〈화폐 등의〉 counterfeiting
▶그 그림은 위조됐다 The picture was a fake.
—위조하다 forge; counterfeit; fabricate
◆수표를 위조하다 forge a check
▶그는 문서를 위조했다 He fabricated a document.
■공문서— the forgery of official papers —단 a counterfeit ring —문서 false papers; a fake [forged] document —수표 a forged check —자 a forger; a faker; a counterfeiter —지폐 a counterfeit [forged] (bank) note: 1만원짜리 위조 지폐 a counterfeit ten-thousand-won bill / 위조 지폐를 사용하다 pass a counterfeit [forged] note —품 a forged [spurious] article; a forgery; a counterfeit [fake] —화폐 counterfeit [bogus, bad] money; 〈경화〉 a counterfeit [false] coin
위주 爲主 the chief [principal] aim; the first consideration
◆남성 위주의 사회 a male-oriented society / 성장 위주의 경제 정책 growth-oriented economic policy / 아동 위주의 교육 a child-centered education / 영리 위주의 학원 an (educational) institute run for profit / 자기 위주의 사고 방식 self centered thinking / 위주로 하다 put first (in importance); give the first consideration to 《do》
▶그 회사는 실력 위주로 사람을 쓴다 "Ability first" is their motto in employing men.
위중하다 危重— 〈서술적〉 be dangerously [critically] ill; be in a critical condition
▶그는 아버지가 위중하시다는 전보를 받았다 He got a wire announcing [telling him of] his father's critical [serious] condition.
위증 僞證 〔法〕 false evidence [testimony] —위증하다 give false evidence; bear false witness 《against》
■—자 a perjurer —죄 perjury: 위증죄를 범하다 commit perjury; perjure *oneself* / 위증죄로 구속하다 put *sb* into custody on charges of perjury
위지 危地 a dangerous position; a critical situation
◆위지를 벗어나다 get [find *one's* way] out of danger / 위지에 뛰어들다 get into danger; put *one's* head into a lion's mouth / 위지에 빠지다 get [run, fall] into danger / 위지에 빠뜨리다 endanger; put *sb* in danger
위 집하다 蝟集— swarm [throng] 《round, about》; throng 《a place》; gather in a swarm [flocks]; crowd together
위짝 the upper (one) (of a pair of things)
위쪽 〈방향〉 the upper direction; 〈부분〉 the upper part [side]; upside; the surface
◆위쪽의 upper / 위쪽에 up; above / 위쪽으로 above; upward(s) / 위쪽을 보다 look upward / 위쪽으로 뻗다 grow upward / 내를 위쪽으로 거슬러 올라가다 follow a stream upward; go up a stream
▶벽 위쪽에 틈새가 있다 There is a crack in the upper part of the wall.
위차 位次 order; the rank [order] of seats [precedence] ◆궁중(宮中) 위차 the order of precedence at the Court
위채 an upper house [building]; 〈큰채〉 the main house
위촉 委囑 〈위임〉 commission; entrusting; 〈의뢰〉 request; 〈임명〉 appointment
◆위촉으로[에 따라] by request; at *sb's* request
—위촉하다 ask [request] *sb* to 《do》; commission 《a painter to paint a mural》; give *sb* charge of 《a matter》
▶어째서 그렇게 중요한 일을 그에게 위촉했느냐? Why did you entrust him with such an important task?
위축 萎縮 withering; shriveling; contraction —위축하다 〈물체가〉 wither; shrivel; shrink [flinch] 《from》; 〈기관이〉 become atrophied; atrophy; 〈사람이〉 be daunted 《by failure》; be dispirited; cower 《before》
위층 —層 the upper floor [story]
◆위층 방 an upstairs room; the room above / 위층에(서) upstairs / 위층으로 올라가다 go upstairs
▶내 방은 위층에 있습니다 My room is upstairs [on the upper floor].
위치 位置 1 〈장소〉 a place; a position; a situation; a location; a site
◆침대의 위치 the position of a bed / 위치가 좋다[나쁘다] be in a good [bad] position; be well [ill] situated [located] / 위치를 바꾸다 shift [change] *one's* position / 위치를 잡다 take *one's* position [place]; go into [take up] position / 위치를 정하다[파악하다] locate / 유리한 위치를 차지하다 occupy a vantage ground; be on favorable ground / 〈배 등이〉

별을 보고 자기 위치를 알리다 take [get] a fix by the stars
▶ 그 호텔은 위치가 좋다 The hotel stands in a good position.
▶ (지도에서) 괌의 위치를 좀 알려주세요 Please locate Guam for me (on the map).
▶ 수원은 좋은 위치에 있는 도시다 Suwon is a favorably situated city.
―위치하다 be situated; be located; 〈나라 등이〉 lie; 〈산 등이〉 stand
◆ 시의 중앙에 위치하다 be situated in the center [heart] of a city
▶ 케이프타운은 아프리카 남단에 위치해 있다 Cape Town lies [is located] at the southern extremity of Africa.
2 〈입장〉 a place; a stand; 〈처지〉 a situation; 〈지위〉 a position; 〈신분〉 one's status; standing
▶ 그 여자는 회사에서 높은 위치에 있다 She holds a high position in her company.
■―선정 location; positioning ―에너지 potential energy

위친하다 爲親― be devoted to [do for] one's parents

위카메라 胃― 〔醫〕 a gastrocamera

위카타르 胃― 〔醫〕 the catarrh of the stomach; gastric catarrh

위클리 a weekly (magazine) ⇨ 주간(〜지)

위탁 委託 trust; commission; 〈판매의〉 consignment
◆ 위탁으로 상품을 발송하다 send [ship] goods on consignment; consign goods (to) / 위탁으로 책을 서점에 보내다 send out books to booksellers on sale or return
▶ 나는 물품을 위탁으로 송달받았다 I had the articles sent on consignment.
―위탁하다 entrust 《sb with a thing [a thing to sb]》; deposit 《documents with sb》; place sth in sb's charge; commission 《sb to do》; 〈상품을〉 consign 《goods for sale to a firm》
◆ 위탁받다 be entrusted; have sth to do on commission / 상품판매를 위탁하다 consign goods (for sale) to 《an agent》
▶ 그는 집을 (팔아 달라고) 중개업자에게 위탁했다 He consigned his house (for sale) to a house agent.
■―가공 processing of brought-in materials ―금 money in trust; trust money ―보증금 consignment guarantee money ―생 a scholarship student sponsored by government offices or business concerns ―수수료 a consignment fee; a commission ―인수인 a trustee; a consignee ―자 a truster; a consignor: 피위탁자 a trustee ―품 a trust; an article consigned; consignment goods

위 탁 판 매 委託販賣 commission [consignment] sale; sale on commission
◆ 위탁판매로 on consignment
―위탁하다 sell 《goods》 on commission
■―인 a commission merchant [agent]

위 태롭다, 위태하다 危殆― **1** 〈위험하다〉 dangerous; risky; precarious; perilous; 〈병세가〉 critical; grave; serious
◆ 위태로운 짓을 하다 make a risky attempt; 〈법이나 도덕적으로〉 sail near [close to] the wind / 위태로운 지경에서 구출되다 be rescued from danger / 위태로워지다 become dangerous; run [fall] into danger / 위태롭게 하다 endanger; imperil; compromise; jeopardize
▶ 이것은 위태로운 도박이다 It's a risky bet.
2 〈아슬아슬하다〉 narrow; close
◆ 위태로운 사업 a touch-and-go business

위태위태하다 危殆危殆― precarious ⇨ 위태롭다
▶ 그의 걸음걸이가 위태위태하다 He is unsteady on his feet.
▶ 그의 지위가 위태위태하다 His position is very precarious.

위턱 the upper jaw

위통 胃痛 a pain in the stomach; a stomach-ache

위트 wit ◆ 위트가 있는 witty 《man, speech》
▶ 그는 위트가 있는 사람이다 He is witty.

위트릴로 〈프랑스의 화가〉 Utrillo, Maurice (1883-1955)

위패 位牌 a mortuary [memorial] tablet
◆ 선조의 위패 an ancestral tablet

위폐 僞幣 〈위조 지폐〉 counterfeit [fake] money; 〈경화〉 a counterfeit [false] coin; 〈지폐〉 a false bank note; 《美》 bogus money
◆ 1백 달러 짜리 위폐 a counterfeit one-hundred-dollar bill / 위폐를 유통시키다 pass bogus money
■―범 a counterfeiter; a (bank-note) forger; a coiner ―사용자 a user [passer] of counterfeit money; 《俗》 a smasher

위품 位品 (court) rank; official rank

위풍 威風 dignity; an imposing [a majestic] air; a commanding presence ◆ 위풍에 압도되다 bend to sb's dignity; be overawed by sb's imposing air
▶ 그는 주위를 압도하는 위풍을 지니고 있었다 He had a commanding presence. ⇌ He had an awe-inspiring air about him.

위풍당당하다 威風堂堂― ◆ 위풍당당한 인물 a man of commanding presence / 위풍당당한 awe-inspiring; commanding; imposing; majestic / 위풍 당당하게 majestically; in a stately [dignified] manner; with an imposing air
▶ 그는 왕으로서 위풍당당하게 행동했다 He behaved with the dignity of a king.
▶ 이윽고 장군이 위풍당당하게 나타났다 Presently, the general made his majestic appearance.

위필 僞筆 forged [feigned, disguised] handwriting; a forgery ◆ 위필의 forged; imitated / 위필로 in a forged [disguised] hand
―위필하다 forge; counterfeit

위하다 爲― 〈이롭게 하다〉 do for the good [benefit] of; do in favor [behalf] of; 〈공경하다〉 serve; honor; respect; revere; worship; 〈사랑하다〉 care for; love; 〈소중히 하다〉 make [think] much of; value; esteem; have regard for; take good care of
◆ 남편을 위하는 아내 a devoted wife / 예술을 위한 예술 art for art's sake / 위하여 for; for the sake of; in the interests of; on behalf of; in the favor of / …하기 위하여 to; in order to;

so as to; so that; with a view to; for the purpose of / 건강을 위하여 for (the benefit of) one's health / 너를 위하여 for your own sake / 사회를 위하여 in the interests [service] of society / 조국을 위하여 for the sake of one's fatherland / 정의를 위하여 in the cause of justice / 남편을 위하다 attend to one's husband with devotion; be devoted to one's husband / 명예를 목숨보다 더 위하다 esteem honor above life / 몸을 위하다 take care of oneself / 부모를 위하다 take good care of one's parents; be devoted to one's parents; honor one's parents / 어린애를 위하다 be kind to children; love children / 자기를 위하다 seek one's own interests; look for one's interests / 공익을 위해서 일하다 work for the public good / 나라를 위해 죽다 die for one's country / 남을 위해 일하다 work for the good of others / 돈을 위해 일하다 work for money / 학교를 위하여 진력하다 exert oneself on behalf of the school / 학생들을 위해 책을 저술하다 write a book for the benefit of students / 조국을 위해 몸을 바치다 lay down one's life for the sake of one's fatherland / 회사를 위해 일하다 work in the interests of the company
▶ 황 선생을 위한 송별회가 열렸다 A farewell party was given in honor of Mr. Hwang.
▶ 그는 토론을 위한 토론을 좋아한다 He likes to argue just for argument's sake.
▶ 그는 학교를 위하는 마음에서 그렇게 했다 He did so out of concern for the school.
▶ 그렇게 날 위하는 체하는 소리는 난 이제 듣기 지겁다 I'm tired of hearing about how it'll be good for me [how it's all for my own good].
▶ 그는 대학 진학을 위해 열심히 공부하고 있다 He is studying hard so that he can enter a [the] university.
▶ 그는 친구를 마중하기 위해 공항에 갔다 He went to the airport (in order) to meet his friend.
▶ 나는 집을 짓기 위해 땅을 샀다 I have bought land with a view to building a house.
▶ 너는 화재 예방을 위해 각별히 주의해야 한다 You should take special precautions to prevent fire.
▶ 이것은 너를 위해서 하는 말이다 I say this for your (own) good.
▶ 만일을 위해서 당신께 묻고 싶은 것이 있습니다 I would like to ask you something just to make sure.
▶ 사람은 먹기 위해 사는 게 아니라 살기 위해 먹는다 Man does not live to eat, but eats to live.

위하수 胃下垂 〔醫〕 gastroptosis; gastric ptosis; downward displacement of the stomach

위해 危害 an injury; harm
♦ 위해를 가하다 do sb harm [an injury]; inflict an injury on sb; hurt; injure / 위해를 면하다 escape unhurt [unharmed]; escape with a whole skin / 위해를 입다 sustain [receive] an injury 《from》; be harmed [injured] 《by》
■—물 a dangerous [hazardous] article

위헌 違憲 unconstitutionality; (a) violation of the constitution
▶ 이 법률은 위헌의 소지가 많다 This law has serious doubts about its constitutionality.
▶ 그것은 위헌적인 처사다 That is an unconstitutional measure.
▶ 그것은 분명히 위헌이다 It is decidedly against the constitution.
■—성 unconstitutionality —입법 unconstitutional legislation

위험 危險 (a) danger; (a) peril; (a) risk; (a) hazard; jeopardy

〔解說〕 *danger*는 위험을 뜻하는 가장 일반적인 말이며 *peril*은 예측 불허의 절박하고 커다란 위험을 나타낸다. *risk*는 불이익·불행 등을 당할 위험성을 가리키는 말로 흔히 스스로 그것을 무릅쓴다는 뜻을 내포하며 *hazard*는 우연한 또는 피할 수 없는 위험을 말한다.

〈위험이〉 그 약을 매일 복용하면 중독될 위험이 있다 Daily use of the medicine may cause poisoning.
▶ 이런 유의 수술에는 다소의 위험이 따른다 Operations of this kind involve some risk.
▶ 등산에는 상당한 위험이 따른다 There is considerable danger in mountain climbing.
▶ 자연을 파괴할 위험이 있다 There is a danger of destroying nature.
▶ 인화 폭발의 위험이 있다 There is some fear of the inflammables blowing up.
〈위험을〉 그녀는 생명의 위험을 느꼈다 She felt a danger to her life.
▶ 위험을 무릅쓰지 않는 사람은 전진하지 못한다 A man who will not take a risk will never get ahead.
▶ 우리는 위험을 무릅쓰고 전진했다 We advanced in the face of danger.
▶ 그는 위험을 무릅쓰고 불 속으로 뛰어들었다 Braving the danger, he ran into the fire.
▶ 원자력 이용은 인류 파멸의 위험을 내포하고 있다 The use of nuclear power can possibly lead to the total destruction of mankind.
〈위험에〉 불이 나자 호텔의 투숙객은 위험에 빠졌다 Fire endangered the hotel's guests.
▶ 그의 생명은 끊임없는 위험에 처해 있었다 His life was always exposed to danger. ⇌ His life was in constant danger.
▶ 그 건물은 붕괴의 위험에 직면해 있다 The building is on the verge of collapse.
—**위험하다** dangerous; perilous; risky; hazardous; critical; breakneck 《speed》
♦ 위험한 놀이 a dangerous game / 위험한 투자 a risky investment of money / 위험한 처지에 놓이다 be exposed to danger; have a dangerous experience
▶ 그것은 위험한 내기다 It's a risky [hazardous] bet.
▶ 환자는 위험한 고비를 넘겼다 The patient has passed the crisis. ⇌ The patient is out of danger now.
▶ 불장난은 위험하다 It is dangerous to play with fire.
▶ 이 강에서 헤엄치는 것은 위험하다 It's dangerous to swim in this river.
■—부담 〔保險〕 risk bearing —분자 danger-

ous elements; risks ―사상 dangerous thoughts ―상태 a dangerous [critical] condition ―속도 critical speed [velocity] ―수당 danger money ―신호 a danger signal ―인물 a dangerous man [character]; 〈국가안보상의〉 a security risk ―지대[구역] a danger spot [zone, area] ―표지 a warning (sign) post

위험물 危險物 a dangerous article [thing] ▶위험물 반입 엄금 (게시) No Dangerous Objects. ⇒ Dangerous Articles Forbidden.

위험성 危險性 a possibility of danger; dangerousness; riskiness ♦위험성이 많은 risky; dangerous / 위험성이 없는 safe; sure; secure

위험시하다 危險視― regard sb [sth] as dangerous; regard 《an attempt》 as risky

위험천만하다 危險千萬― extremely dangerous ♦위험천만한 짓을 하다 perform a hazardous feat; sleep on a volcano; fly in the face of danger; risk one's neck

위협 威脅 (a) menace; intimidation; a threat ♦위협적인 menacing; threatening; intimidatory / 위협적으로 menacingly; threateningly / 위협적인 태도를 취하다 take [assume] a threatening attitude
▶우리는 끊임없이 전쟁의 위협을 받고 있다 We are constantly threatened by war. ⇒ We are always exposed to the menace of war [under (a) threat of war].
▶그의 말투는 위협적이었다 There was menace [a threat] in his tone.
▶그것은 세계평화에 대한 중대한 위협이다 It's a grave menace [threat] to world peace.
―**위협하다** menace; intimidate; threaten; scare
▶그는 총으로 위협했다 He menaced with a gun.
▶게릴라들은 우리를 죽이겠다고 위협했다 The guerrillas threatened to kill us.
▶경찰은 그를 위협하여 자백시켰다 The police frightened him into confessing.
▶우리 팀은 그들을 크게 위협할 것이다 Our team will pose them a real threat.
―**사격** an intimidating fire : 위협 사격을 하다 fire warning shots ―**자** an intimidator

위화감 違和感 a sense of incompatibility; a feeling that one does not belong (in a place)
▶그 방에서 나는 웬지 위화감을 느꼈다 I felt somehow out of place in that room.

위확장 胃擴張 〔醫〕 dilatation of the stomach; gastric dilatation

위효 偉效 a great [signal] effect

위훈 偉勳 a feat; a great achievement; a brilliant [glorious] exploit; a distinguished merit ♦위훈을 세우다 accomplish a great achievement; render distinguished services

윈도 a window ■―**쇼핑** window-shopping : 윈도쇼핑을 하다 go window-shopping; window-shop

윈드서핑 windsurfing

윈치 a winch; a hoist

윌리엄스 〈미국의 극작가〉 Williams, Tennessee (1911-83)

윌슨 〈미국의 28대 대통령〉. Wilson, Thomas Woodrow (1856-1924)

윔블던 〈영국의 도시〉 Wimbledon
―**선수권대회** the Wimbledon Open

윗- 〈위의〉 the upper; the above; the outer ♦윗눈꺼풀 the upper eyelid / 윗학교에 가다 attend a higher institution; go to the upper school

윗길 1 〈길〉 the upper road
2 〈등급〉 superior quality; better grade
▶이것이 그것보다 윗길이다 This is superior in quality than that.

윗니 the upper (set of) teeth

윗도리 〈상체〉 the upper body

윗동아리 the upper part 《of sth》

윗목 the upper part of an ondol floor; the part of a room farthest from the fireplace

윗물 the water of the upper stream [course] 《of a river》; the upper waters 《of a river》

윗물이 맑아야 아랫물이 맑다 (속담) Like master, like man. ⇒ As is the king, so is the people.

윗반 ―班 an upper class; a higher class

윗방 ―房 the upper room

윗배 the upper part of the belly

윗변 ―邊 〔數〕 the upper base

윗사람 〈연장자〉 one's elders; one's seniors; 〈상관〉 one's superior(s)
▶불평은 윗사람에게 하시오 Take your complaint to your boss [superior].

윗수염 ―鬚髥 a moustache

윗입술 the upper lip

윗잇몸 the upper gum(s)

윗자리 〈상좌〉 an upper [a higher] seat; the top seat; 〈주빈의 자리〉 the seat [place] of honor; 〈높은 지위〉 a high position [rank] ♦윗자리에 앉다 sit at the head 《of the table》; take the top seat; 〈높은 지위에〉 be highly placed; attain a high rank

윙 〔球〕 a wing

윙(윙) 〈벌레 소리〉 with a buzz; 〈기계 소리〉 with a whir; 〈바람 소리〉 with a whistle [whiz] ▶바람이 윙윙 불어댔다 The wind hissed and raged.

윙윙거리다 〈벌 등이〉 buzz; hum; make humming sounds; drone; 〈바람 소리가〉 whistle; 〈탄알이〉 whiz(z)
▶전선이 바람에 윙윙거리고 있다 The wire are whizzing in the wind.
▶벌이 윙윙거리며 날아왔다 A bee came buzzing its wings.

윙크 a wink ―**윙크하다** wink 《at》; give a wink 《to》

유 有 〈존재〉 existence; being ♦무에서 유를 창조하다 make sth out of nothing
▶무에서 유는 생기지 않는다 Out of nothing, nothing comes. ⇒ Nothing comes of [from] nothing.

유 類 1 〈종류〉 a sort; a kind; a class; a type; the like 《of it》 ⇨ -류(類)
▶난 이런 유의 음악은 싫다 I don't like music of this sort.
▶저런 유의 사람을 나는 다루기 어렵다 That sort of man is hard for me to deal with.
▶이 골동품들은 다른 것들과 유를 달리 한다 These antiques are a different type [different

유가 in kind] from the others.
2 〈무리〉 a group
3 ⇨ 유개념

유가 有價 1 〈값이 정해져 있음〉 having a fixed price; valuableness ◆유가의 valuable; negotiable
2 〈금전상의 가치〉 having value

유가 儒家 a Confucianist; a Confucian scholar

유가족 遺家族 a bereaved family
■군인— a war-bereaved family

유가증권 有價證券 (marketable) securities; a negotiable instrument

유감 遺憾 〈안된 마음〉 regret; a pity
◆유감의 뜻을 표하다 express *one's* regret / …은 유감 천만이다 it is really regrettable that…; it is much to be regretted that…; it is a thousand pities that…
▶ 그것은 유감이지만 사실이다 It is only too true.
▶ 매우 유감이지만 사절하겠습니다 I shall refuse it with many regrets [with much regret].
▶ 유감 천만이지만 그것을 사실로 인정하지 않을 수 없습니다 I cannot but admit, though with much regret, that it is a fact.

유감스럽다 遺憾— 1 〈섭섭하다〉 regrettable; deplorable; (be) sorry

解說 (1) ***sorry***가 가장 일반적인 말이다.「유감스러운」이란 뜻으로는 반드시 사람이 주어가 되고 서술적으로 쓰인다: I am sorry (that) I failed the test. (나는 시험에 떨어져서 유감이다)
(2) ***regrettable***과 ***regretful***: regrettable은 「유감스러운, 아쉬운, 애석한」이란 뜻으로 보통 사물에 관해서만 사용하지만, regretful은 사람이나 사물 양쪽에 다 쓰므로「사람이 아쉬워하고 있다」또는「(표정 등이) 아쉬움을 나타낸다」는 뜻이다: his regretful face (그의 아쉬운듯한 얼굴) / regrettable [disappointing] news (유감스러운 소식) / He is regretful about that.(그는 그 일을 애석하게 생각하고 있다)

▶ 사상자를 낸 것은 유감스러운 일이다 We regret [It is regrettable] that there were some casualties.
▶ 유감스럽게도 그 계획은 단념하지 않을 수 없었다 To my regret, the plan had to be given up.
2 〈불만족하다〉 unsatisfactory
◆유감스러운 점이 있다[많다] leave *sth* [much] to be desired

유감없다 遺憾— satisfactory; gratifying; 〈서술적〉 have nothing to regret; feel no regret
◆유감없이 (most) satisfactorily; to *one's* heart's content; 〈완전히〉 perfectly; 〈충분히〉 fully / 유감없이 재능을 발휘하다 give full [free] play to *one's* abilities
▶ 그는 그 시험에서 유감없이 실력을 발휘했다 He fully displayed his real ability in the examination.

유감지진 有感地震 a felt [sensible] earthquake

유개 有蓋 ◆유개의 covered; closed; lidded
■—마차[자동차] a covered carriage; (美)〈트럭의〉 a covered wagon —화차 (美) a boxcar; (英) a box [covered] waggon

유개념 類槪念 〔論〕 a genus

유객 幽客 a recluse; a hermit; an anchorite; an anchoret

유객 遊客 1 〈유람객〉 an excursionist; a tourist; a man on a pleasure trip **2** 〈건달〉 an idler; an idle man; 〈방탕아〉 a fast liver; (美口) a playboy

유거 幽居 〈주거〉 a sequestered retreat; a solitary [retired] residence; 〈생활〉 a secluded [retired] life —유거하다 live in seclusion; lead a retired life

유격 遊擊 〔軍〕 an attack by a mobile unit; a hit-and-run attack
■—대 a flying column [corps, army]; mobile forces; a corps of rangers; a commando unit —병 a ranger; a commando —수 〔野〕 a shortstop; a short —술 guerilla tactics; the hit-and-run tactics —전 guerilla warfare

유계 幽界 〈저승〉 the other world ⇨ 저승

유고 有故 〈사고〉 an accident; (a) trouble; a mishap; 〈사정〉 reason(s); circumstances
◆유고시에는 at the time of an accident
■—결석 absenting *oneself* from school owing to unavoidable circumstances

유고 諭告 1 〈타이름〉 advice; counsel; instruction; (an) admonition —유고하다 advise; counsel; admonish; give instructions
2 〈포고〉 official announcement; a decree; an ordinance; a proclamation —유고하다 proclaim; announce

유고 遺稿 posthumous works [manuscripts]; the writings left by the deceased
◆K씨의 유고를 정리하다 edit the unpublished writings [manuscripts] left by the late Mr. K

유고슬라비아 Yugoslavia; Jugoslavia; 〈공식명〉 the Federal Republic of Yugoslavia
◆유고슬라비아의 Yugoslav(ic); Yugoslavian; Jugoslav(ian)
■—사람 a Yugoslavian; a Jugoslav(ic)

유곡 幽谷 a deep valley [ravine]; a glen
■심산— steep mountains and deep valleys

유골 遺骨 the (skeletal) remains; ashes
◆유골을 줍다 gather *sb's* ashes
■—단지 a (cinerary, mortuary) urn

유공 有功 meritoriousness ◆유공의 meritorious —자 a person of merit —(훈)장 a merit medal; a medal for merit

유공충 有孔蟲 〔動〕 a foraminifer

유과 油菓 *yoogwa*; oil-and-honey pastry ⇨ 밀과

유곽 遊廓 licensed [gay] quarters; (美) a red-light district; 〈집〉 a bawdy house; a brothel
◆유곽에 드나들다 frequent houses of ill fame

유관 有關 being related [concerned]; having relation [concern] ■—업체 a concern interested; its associated company

유관 油管 an oil pipe

유관속 維管束 〔植〕 a vascular bundle
■—식물 a vascular plant

유광지 有光紙 glossy [glazed, coated,

유괴 誘拐 kidnap(p)ing; abduction
—유괴하다 kidnap 《a child》; abduct 《sb from sb's home》; carry off 《a boy》; lure away
▶ 그는 몸값을 노리고 그 아이를 유괴했다 He kidnapped [abducted] the child for ransom.
▶ 테러분자들은 그 정치가를 유괴하여 거액의 몸값을 요구했다 The terrorists kidnapped [abducted] the politician and demanded an enormous ransom.
▶ 그녀는 유괴된 것이 분명하다 She must have been abducted.
■ —사건 an abduction [《美》a snatch] case —자[범] an abductor; a kidnap(p)er —죄 abduction

유교 儒敎 Confucianism ◆유교의 (감화) Confucian (influence) ■ —사상 Confucian ideas

유구 琉球 Ryukyu; 〈열도〉 the Ryukyu [Loochoo] Islands; the Ryukyus
■ —사람 a Ryukyuan

유구무언 有口無言 ▶ 나는 유구무언이다 I have no word to say in excuse.

유구하다 悠久— eternal; everlasting; perpetual; permanent ◆유구한 역사 history from time immemorial / 유구한 역사의 흐름 the eternal flow of history / 유구한 옛날부터 from time immemorial

유군 幼君 a young [boy] king

유권자 有權者 the holder of a right; 〈선거의〉 an elector; a voter; (총칭) the electorate
▶ 그 시의 유권자는 20만명이다 The electoral roll of the city amounts to two hundred thousand.

유권해석 有權解釋 an authoritative interpretation ◆중앙 선거 관리 위원회의 유권해석 the ruling of the Central Election Management Committee

유근 幼根 〔植〕 a radicle; a rootlet

유금류 游禽類 〔鳥〕 natatorial [swimming] birds; the web-footed birds

유급 有給 ◆유급의 paid; salaried
■ —외판원 a salaried canvasser [salesman] —위원 a salaried [paid] committee man —직원 staff members on the payroll —휴가 a paid vacation [holiday]; paid leave: 나는 2주간의 유급휴가를 받았다 I had two weeks off with pay.

유급 留級 remaining in the same class
—유급하다 remain [stay two years] in the same class
▶ 그는 1년 유급하게 되었다 He is to stay in the same class for another year.
■ —생 a student remaining in the same class; a repeater

유기 有期 ◆유기의 terminable; limited; for a (definite) term
■ —공채 〔經〕 a terminable loan —연금 a terminable [limited] annuity —형 a sentence for imprisonment for a definite period [term]: 유기형을 받다 be sentenced to imprisonment for a definite term

유기 有機 ◆유기적 세계관 the organic view of the world / 유기적 통일체 an organic whole / 유기적(인) organic / 유기적으로 organically
■ —물 organic matter [substance]; an organism —비료 (an) organic fertilizer —염기 an organic base —질 an organic matter [substance]: 유기질 비료 an organic fertilizer —체 an organism; an organic body —화학 organic chemistry —화합물 an organic compound

유기 遺棄 abandonment; dereliction; desertion —유기하다 abandon; desert; leave behind [unattended]; leave
▶ 그들은 사체를 유기하고 달아났다 They ran away, leaving the body behind.
■ 직무— neglect of duty ■ —물 an abandoned thing; a left article; 〈해상의〉 a derelict —시체 an abandoned corpse —자 a deserter

유기 鍮器 〈놋그릇〉 brassware

유기음 有氣音 〔音聲〕 an aspirate; an aspirated sound

유난 〈보통이 아님〉 unusualness; uncommonness; 〈괴팍〉 fastidiousness; fussiness
◆유난을 떨다 behave fastidiously / 아무것도 아닌 일을 가지고 유난을 떨다 make much ado [a great fuss] about nothing; make a mountain (out) of a molehill
—유난하다[스럽다] unusual; uncommon; special; extraordinary; exceptional; fastidious; particular 《about》
◆유난히 눈에 띄다 outshine others / 옷차림이 유난한 여자 a fantastically dressed woman
▶ 올 겨울은 유난히[유난스럽게] 춥다 It is exceptionally [unusually] cold this winter. ⇌ This is an unusually cold winter.
▶ 그는 음식에 대해서 유난하다 He is very particular [fussy] about his food.
▶ 이 일에 대한 그의 흥미는 유난하다 His interest in this matter is extraordinary.

유네스코 UNESCO [〈the United Nations Educational, Scientific and Cultural Organization] —쿠폰 a Unesco coupon —헌장 the Constitution of UNESCO

유년 幼年 infancy; childhood ◆유년의 juvenile; puerile / 유년 시절을 외국에서 보내다 spend one's childhood in a foreign country

유년기 幼年期 infancy; childhood
◆유년기에[부터] in [from, since] one's childhood [infancy] / 유년기부터 성년기까지 from aprons to full beards
▶ 항공기 산업은 아직 유년기에 머물러 있다 Aviation was still in its infancy.

유념 留念 attention; consideration; regard; mindfulness —유념하다 bear [keep, have] sth in mind; be mindful of; take sth to heart

유뇨증 遺尿症 〔醫〕 enuresis

유능 有能 ability; competence; capability
—유능하다 able; capable; competent; talented
◆유능한 교사 a competent teacher / 유능한 사람 a man of ability [talent]; an able man
▶ 그는 아주 유능한 변호사로 알려져 있다 He is known as a very able [competent] lawyer.

유니버설 universal

유니버시아드 〈국제학생경기대회〉 the Universiade

유니버시티 a university

유니세프 〈국제연합아동기금〉 UNICEF [〈the

유니언숍 a union shop
유니언잭 〈영국국기〉 the Union Jack
유니테어리언 〈사람〉 a Unitarian
유니폼 a uniform ◆유니폼 차림의 (clad) in uniform; uniformed
유다 (聖) Jude; Judas ■—서 The General Epistle of St. Jude (略 Jude)
유다르다 類— uncommon; unusual; special; especial; exceptional; conspicuous
◆유다른 사람 a unique person; a rare man / 유나른 행동 peculiar behavior
유단자 有段者 a grade holder; a holder of a rank
유달리 類— uncommonly; unusually; extraordinarily; exceptionally; especially; particularly
▶오늘 밤은 유달리 춥다 It's particularly [especially] cold tonight.
▶올해는 유달리 비가 많이 내렸다 We have had an exceptional amount of rain this year.
▶그녀의 모자가 유달리 눈에 띄었다 Her hat stood out from the rest. ⇌ Her hat attracted the most attention.
유당 乳糖 〔化〕 milk sugar ⇨ 젖당
유대 紐帶 bonds; ties; 〈관계〉 relation; a relationship
◆사업상의 유대 business ties / 정신적 유대 spiritual bonds / 긴밀한 유대를 맺다 come [be brought] into close relation 《with》 / 정치적으로 강한 유대를 갖다 have strong ties 《with》 politically
▶무역협정으로 양국의 유대가 강화되었다 The trade agreement has strengthened the bonds between the two countries.
▶그 사건은 한미간의 유대를 공고히 하는 데 도움이 되었다 The event helped to place Seoul-Washington ties on a firm footing.
유대류 有袋類 〔動〕 the marsupials ◆유대류의 동물 a marsupial; a pouched animal
유덕 遺德 the influence [virtue] of the departed; posthumous influence ◆유덕을 기리다 speak highly of the virtue of the departed
유덕하다 有德— virtuous; good ◆유덕한 사람 a virtuous person; a man of virtue
유도 柔道 judo
◆유도를 하다 practice judo / 유도 시합을 하다 have a judo match 《with sb》
▶그는 유도 5단이다 He is a judo expert of the fifth tan.
■—복 a suit for judo practice —사범 an instructor of judo —유단자 a rank-holding judo man
유도 誘導 leading; guidance; incitement; inducement; 〈교도〉 instruction; 〔化·數〕 derivation; 〔電〕 induction; influence
▶비행기는 관제탑의 유도를 받아 착륙했다 The plane landed following the instructions of the control tower.
—유도하다 induce; incite; guide; lead; derive
▶선장은 난파선을 항구로 유도했다 The captain led the damaged ship to the port.
▶나는 그녀가 말을 하도록 유도해 보았다 I tried to lead her to talk.
■원격— teleguidance 자기(自己)— self-induction 전자기(電磁氣)— electromagnetic induction ■—기 기(機器) an induction machine —기 전력 induced electromotive force —력[성] inductivity —병기 a guided weapon —신호기 a calling signal —자(者) an inducer; a conductor —장치〈미사일 등의〉 a guidance system; guidance equipment [controls]; 〈관제탑의〉 a talking-down system —전기[자기] induced electricity [magnetism] —전동기 an induction motor —전류 an induced current —체 〔化〕 a derivative —코일 an induction coil —탄 ⇨ 미사일(유도~)
유도 儒道 Confucianism
유도신문 誘導訊問 a leading question
◆유도신문을 하다 lead 《a criminal suspect》 to the point in question / 유도신문에 걸려들다 be led 《against one's will》 to make a disadvantageous statement by deliberate questions
유독 有毒 noxiousness; venomousness
—유독하다 poisonous; venomous; noxious
■—가스 (a) poisonous gas —물질 a poisonous [toxic] substance —식물 a poisonous [noxious, virulent] plant
유독 惟獨 only; solely; singly; uniquely; alone
▶유독 너만이 그렇게 생각하고 있어 Nobody thinks so but [except] yourself.
▶유독 돈벌이만이 인생의 목적은 아니다 Moneymaking is not the sole end and aim of existence.
유동 流動 a flow; flowing; floating; 〈점성 물질의〉 flowage; 〔數〕 flux
▶사태는 유동적이다 The situation is fluid. ⇌ Things are still unstable.
■—물 fluid substance —상태 a state of flux; a fluid situation —성 liquidity; fluidity; 〔社〕 mobility —식 liquid food; a liquid diet —인구 a floating population —자본 floating [circulating, liquid] capital —자산[자금] floating [current] assets [fund] —체 a fluid; a liquid
유동활차 遊動滑車 a floating block; a loose [an idle] pulley
유두 乳頭 〔解〕 a nipple; a teat
—륜(輪) an areola (pl. ~s, -lae); a halo (pl. ~(e)s) —염 thelitis; acromastitis —종 (腫) a papilloma
유들유들 impudently; shamelessly; brazenfacedly
—유들유들하다 impudent; audacious; brazenfaced; barefaced; shameless; 《俗》 cheeky; brassy
▶그의 유들유들한 태도에는 구역질이 난다 His brazen-faced manner disgusts me.
유디티 〈수중 파괴반〉 U.D.T. [《underwater demolition team》]
유라시아 Eurasia; Europe and Asia
■—대륙 the Eurasian Continent
유라톰 〈유럽원자력 공동체〉 Euratom [《the European Atomic Energy Community》]
유락 遊樂 amusement; enjoyment; pleasure
◆유락에 빠지다 give oneself up to pleasure; be given to pleasure —유락하다 enjoy

[amuse] *oneself*; make merry

유람 遊覽 an excursion; a pleasure trip; sightseeing; a sightseeing tour
▶나의 외국 여행은 유람이 목적이 아니다 The object of my trip abroad is not to have fun [a good time].
▶그는 일과 유람을 겸해서 미국에 갔다 He went over to America on business and for pleasure.
―유람하다 go sightseeing 《to》; tour
▶그들은 지금 전국을 유람하고 있다 They are making [taking] a sightseeing trip throughout Korea.
■―객 a sightseer; a tourist; an excursionist; a holiday maker ―단체 a tourists' [an excursion, a sightseeing] party ―버스 a sightseeing bus ―선 an excursion steamer; a pleasure boat ―여행 a sightseeing tour; a pleasure trip; (美) touristing

유랑 流浪 wandering; roaming; roving; vagrancy; vagabondage
―유랑하다 wander [roam] about [from place to place]; rove
▶그들은 각지를 유랑한다 They roam [rove] from place to place.
■―민 a nomadic people; nomads ―생활 a wandering [nomadic] life ―자 a wanderer; a tramp; a vagabond

유래 由來 〈기원〉 the origin; 〈내력〉 the history; 〈출처〉 the source; the derivation
◆절의 유래 the history of the temple / 유래가 있는 집 a family with a history / 유래를 캐다 trace 《a custom》 to its source [origin]
▶이 단어의 유래를 아십니까? Do you know the origin of this word?
▶그 유래를 듣고 싶다 Tell me the whole story of it.
―유래하다 result 《from》; originate 《in》; be derived 《from》; date back 《to the time of...》
▶이 단어는 그리스어에서 유래한다 This word derives from Greek.

유량 流量 〔物〕 flow rate; flux ■―계 a flowmeter

유량계 油量計 an oil gauge

유럽 Europe
◆유럽의 European / 유럽을 여행하다 go over [make a trip] to Europe
■―경제공동체 the European Economic Community (略 EEC) ―경제협력기구 the Organization for European Economic Cooperation (略 OEEC) ―공동시장 the European Common Market (略 ECM); the Common Market ―공동체 the European Community (略 EC) ―대륙 the European Continent ―사람 a European

유려하다 流麗― flowing; elegant; refined; fluent ◆유려한 문장 a flowing and elegant style

유력 有力 being powerful
―유력하다 powerful; strong; influential; leading; weighty; convincing
◆유력한 경쟁 상대 a powerful rival / 유력한 단서 a promising [an important] clue / 유력한 신문 a leading newspaper / 유력한 실업가 an influential businessman / 유력한 용의자 a highly probable [most likely] offender / 유력한 후보자 a strong candidate / 가장 유력한 우승 후보 the likeliest winner 《of the championship》
▶그 문제에 관한 유력한 정보를 입수했다 We have received reliable information on the subject.
▶그의 무죄를 뒷받침할 유력한 증거가 있다 There is valid [strong] evidence that he is innocent.
▶차기 사장에는 그가 유력하다 He is likely to be the next president.

유력 遊歷 traveling; a tour; an itinerancy
―유력하다 travel [tour] about; make a tour; tour 《the district》; itinerate

유력자 有力者 an influential [a leading] person; a person of consequence [influence, weight] ◆지방의 유력자 a boss of the district; a magnate of the town

유령 幽靈 a ghost; a spirit; (口) a spook; an apparition; a specter; a phantom
◆유령이 나오는 집 a haunted house / 유령 같은 ghostly; ghostlike
▶그 성에는 유령이 나온다고 한다 That castle is said to be haunted by a ghost. ⇌ They say that castle is haunted by a ghost.
▶유령이라도 나타날 것같은 밤이었다 It was a ghostly night.
■―선 a phantom [ghost] ship; The Flying Dutchman ―이야기 a ghost story ―인구 a ghost [bogus] population ―회사 a bogus [phantom] company

유례 類例 a similar case [example, instance]
◆유례 없는 unparalleled; without parallel; unique; unprecedented / 역사상 유례가 없다 be unparalleled in history
▶이것은 유례가 없는 사건이다 This is a unique [an unparalleled] event.
▶그것은 범죄 역사상 유례가 없는 사건이었다 It was a case without parallel [unparalleld] in the history of crime.

유로달러 〔經〕 a Eurodollar

유로비전 Eurovision [〈the *Euro*pean *Television*]

유료 有料 a charge ◆유료의 charged; with charge [fee]／유료로 for pay
▶입장은 무료입니까, 유료입니까? Is the admission free or is there a charge?
▶입장은 유료입니다 There is a charge for admission. ⇌ There is an admission charge.
■―도로 a toll road ―변소 a pay toilet ―시사회 a charged preview ―입장 paid admission; admission by fee ―주차장 a toll parking place [lot]

유루 遺漏 〈빠짐〉 (an) omission; oversight; a slip; 〈새어 없어짐〉 leakage; a leak
◆가스의 유루 a gas leak／유루 없이 without omission; 〈철저하게〉 exhaustively; thoroughly／유루를 막다 stop a leak
▶만사 유루 없도록 하시오 See [Take care] that everything is done well. ⇌ Pay attention even to the smallest detail.
―유루하다 〈빠지다〉 be omitted[overlooked]; be passed over [by]; 〈새다〉 leak; escape

유류 油類 oil ■—파동 an oil crisis
유류분 遺留分 〔法〕 a legal portion of an heir; a reserve
유류품 遺留品 an article left (behind); a lost article; lost property
▶범행 현장에는 많은 유류품이 남아 있었다 There were many things left behind at the scene of the crime.
■—보관소 a lost property room
유리 有理 rationality ■—수〔함수〕 a rational number〔function〕 —식 a rational expression
유리 流離 wandering; roaming; roving
—유리하다 wander; roam; rove; (口) knock about —걸식 roving around begging
유리 琉璃 glass
◆한 장의 유리 a sheet of glass / 유리 자르는 칼 a glass cutter / 유리같은 glassy / 창에 유리를 끼우다 glaze a window; put a pane of glass in the window
▶유리는 잘 깨진다 Glass breaks easily.
▶유리는 광선과 열을 통과시킨다 Glass is pervious to light and heat.
■—색 stained [colored] glass 안전— safety glass 젖빛— opal [frosted] glass 창— a pane; a windowpane 판— plate glass ■—가게 a glass shop —공장 a glass factory; a glassworks —관 a glass tube —구슬 glass beads —그릇 glassware —문 a glass [glazed] door —병 a glass bottle;〈작은〉a vial —상자 a glassed case —섬유 glass fiber —세공 glasswork; glazing —솜[면(綿)] glass wool —장수 a glazier; a glassman —제조 glass manufacture —조각[파편] a broken piece of glass; a piece of broken glass; a glass splinter —직공 a glassworker; a glassblower —창 a glass window
유리 遊離〔化〕isolation; extrication;〈분리〉separation
—유리하다 isolate; separate; extricate
▶이 정책은 현실에서 유리된 것이다 This policy is unrealistic [far from realistic].
▶저 작가는 사회에서 유리되어 있다 That writer is alienated [isolated] from society.
■—상태 a free state —에너지 free energy
유리색 瑠璃色 lapis lazuli; bright blue; azure
유리하다 有利— profitable; gainful; lucrative; remunerative; paying;〈형편에 좋다〉advantageous; favorable
◆한국에 유리한 조건 terms advantageous [favorable] to Korea / 피고에게 유리한 증언 a witness favorable to the accused / 회사에 유리하다 be profitable to the firm / 유리해지다 turn (out) to one's advantage / 의심스러운 점을 피고에게 유리하게 해석하다〔法〕give the defendant the benefit of the doubt
▶당신은 유리한 입장에 있다 You are in an advantageous position.
▶그는 남보다 유리한 위치를 차지했다 He had the advantage [the upper hand] of the others.
▶그는 공격하는 데 유리한 위치에 있었다 He was in an advantageous position to attack.
▶유리한 조건을 살리면 너는 틀림없이 성공한다 If you make the most of the advantageous [profitable, favorable] conditions, you are sure to succeed.
▶국면은 우리에게 유리하게 전개되었다 The state of affairs turned to our advantage.
▶이 조건으로는 나보다 당신이 유리하다 This condition is more favorable to you than to me.
유린 蹂躪 trampling down; overrunning;〈침해〉violation; infringement; outrage
—유린하다 trample upon [on]; tread down; devastate; ravage; override; infringe upon (personal rights); violate (a woman); outrage
◆개인의 자유를 유린하다 trample on the right of personal liberty / 남의 권리를 유린하다 ride roughshod over the rights of others / 국토를 유린하다 override [overrun] a country; trample a country under foot
▶경찰은 우리의 인권을 유린했다 The police infringed upon our human rights.
▶우리의 조국은 침략군에게 유린되었다 Our country was overrun by the invading army.
유림 儒林 Confucianists; Confucian scholars
유막 油膜〔機〕an oil film
유망 有望 a bright prospect [future]; promise; hopefulness
—유망하다 promising; hopeful; favorable; full of promise
◆유망한 장래 a bright [rosy] future; rosy prospects; a promising career / 유망한 투자 분야 a promising field for investment / 유망하지 않다 give little [no] hope
▶그는 전도가 유망한 청년이다 He is a promising youth. ⇌ He is a young man (full) of promise.
▶우리 사업은 앞날이 유망하다 Our business has bright prospects. ⇌ Our business prospects are bright.
▶그녀는 가수로서 전도가 유망하다 She shows great promise as (a) singer.
■—주 (株)〈사람〉an up-and-coming (player);〈주식〉active stocks
유망 流網 a drift net ■—어업 drift-net fishing
유머 (美) humor; (英) humour;〈농담〉joke

> 〔解說〕 *humor*는 인간적이며 훈훈한 우스갯말을 가리킨다. 농담이나 익살은 *humor*보다는 *joke*에 가깝다.「유머러스」는 영어의 *humorous*지만 *funny*나 *amusing*으로 나타내는 것이 좋을 경우도 많다.

▶그는 유머가 있다 He has a (fine) sense of humor.
▶그의 소설에는 유머가 풍부하다 His novels are full of [rich in] humor.
▶그는 유머를 모르는 사람이다 He has no sense of humor.
■—감각 a sense of humor —소설 a humorous novel [story] —작가 a humorous writer [novelist]
유머러스하다 humorous
▶그는 매우 유머러스한 사람이다 He is a very funny [amusing, humorous] person.
▶그는 매우 유머러스하게 얘기했다 He spoke

with much humor.
유머리스트 a humorist
유명 幽明 〈저승과 이승〉 this and the other world; 〈어둠과 밝음〉 light and darkness
♦ 유명을 달리하다 die; pass away; depart (from) this life
유명 遺命 one's dying injunctions [wishes]; the last wishes 《of the king》 ♦ 선친의 유명에 따라 according to one's late father's will
유명계 幽冥界 〈황천〉the other world; Hades
유명무실하다 有名無實— (be) in name but not in deed [reality]; in name only; (merely) nominal; titular
▶ 그것은 유명무실한 위원회다 It is a nominal committee.
▶ 그 규정은 유명무실하다 Nobody follows that rule.
▶ 그 조약은 유명무실해졌다 The treaty has now become a mere scrap of paper.
유명세 有名稅 the price of fame; a penalty of greatness [popularity]; noblesse oblige
▶ 그것은 일종의 유명세다 That's an instance of noblesse oblige.
유명인 有名人 a well-known person; a man of distinction [fame]; a celebrity; a notable
유명하다 有名— famous; well-known; noted; celebrated; renowned; 〈악명높다〉 notorious
♦ 유명한 사기꾼 a notorious swindler / 유명한 역사가 a famous historian / 세계적으로 유명한 학자 a scholar of worldwide reputation / 유명해지다 become famous; acquire [earn] fame; gain renown; win a reputation; come to fame; 〈악명을 얻다〉 gain notoriety
▶ 그는 교육계에서는 유명한 인물이다 He is a big name in education.
▶ 이 지역은 범죄가 많기로 유명한 곳이다 This is an area notorious for crime.
▶ 한국의 노동자들은 근면하기로 유명하다 Workers of Korea are famous [well-known] for their diligence.
▶ 이 레스토랑은 프랑스 요리가 맛있기로 유명하다 This restaurant is noted [famous] for its good French food.
▶ 그 여자는 화가로 유명해졌다 She became famous [gained fame] as a painter.
유모 乳母 a nurse; a wet nurse; (英) a nanny
♦ 아기를 유모에게 맡기다 leave a baby with a nurse; place a baby under the care of a nurse
▶ 갓난아기는 유모에게 맡겨졌다 The baby is at nurse.
유모차 乳母車 (美) a baby carriage [buggy, stroller]; (英) a perambulator; a pram
▶ 그녀는 유모차를 밀고 쇼핑을 간다 She goes out for shopping, wheeling her baby carriage.
유목 流木 〈물 위를 흐르는 나무〉 driftwood; drifting wood [logs]; 〈강에 떠내려 보내는 나무〉 floating of timber down a river
유목 遊牧 nomadism ▶ 그들은 유목 생활을 했다 They lived a nomadic life. **—유목하다** lead [live] a nomadic life; nomadize ▶ **—민** nomads **—민족** a nomadic [nomad] tribe
유무 有無 existence and nonexistence; presence and absence ▶ 경험의 유무에 관계 없이 능력있는 사람을 채용합니다 We will employ an able person regardless of whether he has experience or not.
유무상통하다 有無相通— supply [minister to] each other's wants; fill each other's needs ▶ 두 사람은 서로 유무상통하는 것 같다 There seems to be a mutual understanding between them. ⇌ They seem to supplement each other's weak points.
유묵 遺墨 autographs of a departed person
유문 幽門 〔解〕 the pylorus 《pl. -ri》 ■ **—반사** the pyloric reflex **—절개술** pylorectomy **—협착** stricture of the pylorus
유문암 流紋岩 〔鑛〕 rhyolite
유물 遺物 relics; remains; vestiges
♦ 과거의 유물 relics of the past / 봉건시대의 유물 a holdover from the feudal times / 석기시대의 유물 remains [vestiges] of the Stone Age
▶ 그 박물관은 구석기시대의 유물이 많기로 유명하다 The museum is famous for its large collection of Paleolithic relics.
유물론 唯物論 〔哲〕 materialism ■ **변증법적 [사적(史的)]—** dialectical [historical] materialism ■ **—자** a materialist
유물변증법 唯物辨證法 〔哲〕 dialectical materialism=변증법(~적 유물론)
유물사관 唯物史觀 〔哲〕 historical materialism=사적(~유물론)
유물주의 唯物主義 〔哲〕 materialism ⇨ 유물론
유미 乳糜 〔生理〕 chyle ■ **—관** 〔解〕 a lacteal (vessel) **—즙** 〔生理〕 chyme
유미 柳眉 lovely [crescent] eyebrows
유미적 唯美的 aesthetic; esthetic
유미주의 唯美主義 (a)estheticism ■ **—자** an (a)esthete
유민 流民 drifting [wandering, roaming] people; displaced people
유민 遊民 idle people; idlers; nonworkers; the unemployed
유밀과 油蜜菓 oil-and-honey pastry
유발 乳鉢 〈막자 사발〉 a mortar
유발 誘發 induction
—유발하다 induce; cause 《one's anger》; bring about; give rise to; trigger; touch off
♦ 전쟁을 유발하다 give rise to a war; set [touch] off a war
▶ 지나친 흡연은 폐암을 유발시킬 수 있다 Too much smoking may cause [trigger] lung cancer.
▶ 낙반은 지진으로 유발되었다 The cave-in was caused [brought about] by the earthquake.
유방 乳房 the breast(s) ♦ 유방이 작은[큰] 여자 a small-[large-]breasted woman
유방암 乳房癌 〔醫〕 breast [mammary] cancer; cancer of the breast
유배 流配 banishment; exile; (英) transportation; deportation
—유배하다 send sb into exile; exile; deport
▶ 그는 붙잡혀 머나먼 섬으로 유배되었다 He was arrested and was banished [exiled] to a far-off island.
■ **—지** a place of exile

유백색 乳白色 ♦유백색의 milk-white; milky
유별 有別 (a) distinction; (a) discrimination ▶남녀 유별이다 There is a distinction between man and woman.
유별 類別 categorization; classification; assortment ―유별하다 a categorize; classify; grade; assort
유별나다 有別― uncommon; extraordinary; abnormal; particular
♦유별난 사람 a particular [peculiar] person / 유별나게 uncommonly; extraordinarily; particularly; peculiarly
▶그녀는 오늘 유별나게 신경질적이시 않니? She's unusually nervous today, isn't she?
유보 留保 reservation ―유보하다 reserve; withhold ♦결정을 유보하다 reserve *one's* decision ▶우리의 재산권은 유보되었다 Our right of property was reserved.
유복 有服 relatives for whom mourning is due =유복지친
유복 有福 being blessed ―유복하다 blessed; fortunate; lucky ♦유복한 사람 a blessed person
유복 裕福 affluence; prosperity; opulence ―유복하다 rich; wealthy; well-off; affluent; well-to-do
♦유복한 사람 a well-off [well-to-do] person / 유복하게 자라다 grow up lapped in luxury / 유복하게 살다 live well; be well off; be comfortably off; live in easy circumstances
▶그는 유복하다 He is well-off [well-to-do].
▶누구든지 유복하게 살고 싶어 한다 Everyone wants to live well [be well off].
▶그는 유복한 가정에 태어났다 He was born into a rich family.
유복자 遺腹子 a posthumous child
유복지친 有服之親 relatives for whom mourning is due
유봉 乳棒 a pestle
유부 油腐 (a piece of) fried bean curd
■―국수 noodles with fried bean curd ―초밥 fried bean curd with vinegared rice
유부남 有婦男 a married man
유부녀 有夫女 a married woman
유비 類比 〈비교함〉 comparison; 〔論〕〈유추〉 analogy
유비무환 有備無患 Fast bind, fast find. ⇒ Providing is preventing. ⇒ Keep something for the sore foot.
유빙 流氷 drift ice
유사 有史 the beginning of history
♦유사 이래의 대홍수 the greatest flood in history / 유사 이전 prehistoric times / 유사의 historic / 유사 이전의 prehistoric; of prehistoric times / 유사 이래 since the dawn of history; in history / 유사 이전에 in prehistoric times; before the dawn of history
▶유사 이래 그런 일이 일어난 적은 없었다 Such a thing had not taken place since the dawn of history.
유사 有事 emergency ♦유사시에 in time [case] of emergency; in an emergency / 유사시에 대비하다 provide for a rainy day
▶유사시에는 군대가 출동한다 The army will be mobilized in case of emergency.
유사 流砂 quicksand; drift sand
유사 類似 (a) resemblance; (a) similarity; (a) likeness; an analogy; an affinity
▶그 두 언어 사이에는 유사성이 있다 There is an affinity between the two languages.
―유사하다 similar (to); like; alike; 〈서술적〉 resemble
♦다소[아주] 유사하다 bear some [a striking] resemblance (to)
▶지금 네 상황은 내 경우와 유사하다 Your present situation is similar to mine.
▶인간의 심장은 펌프와 유사하다 There is an analogy between the human heart and a pump. ⇒ The human heart is analogous to a pump.
■―뇌염 a suspected encephalitis case ―어〔言〕an analogue; an analogous term ―종교 a pseudo-religion ―증 an analogous case of a disease ―환자 a suspected case
유사분열 有絲分裂 〔生〕 mitosis; mitotic cell division
유사점 類似點 a similarity; a similar point
▶양자 사이에는 유사점이 없다 There is no similarity [analogy] between the two.
▶이것과 저것과는 조금도 유사점이 없다 I see no likeness whatever between this and that. ⇒ This has nothing in common with that.
▶그의 입장과 네 입장에는 유사점이 전혀 없다 There's no analogy between his position and yours.
유사품 類似品 〈모조품〉 an imitation; 〈비슷한 물건〉 a similar article; similar goods
♦유사품에 주의(게시) Beware of Imitation.
유산 乳酸 〔化〕 lactic acid ⇨ 젖산
유산 流産 **1**〈태아의〉(an) abortion; (a) miscarriage ―유산하다 miscarry; abort; have a miscarriage ♦유산시키다 produce an abortion; procure abortion
▶그녀는 유산했다 She had a miscarriage.
▶그녀는 임신 3개월에 유산했다 She had a miscarriage in the twelfth week of pregnancy.
2 (비유) (a) failure
―유산하다 fail; miscarry; prove abortive
♦유산되다 〈모임 등이〉 be called off
▶그의 계획은 모두 유산되었다 All his plans have sadly miscarried.
■인공― an artificial abortion [miscarriage]
유산 遊山 a picnic; an excursion; an outing; a jaunt ―유산하다 picnic; go on a picnic; go on an outing; jaunt ―객 a picnicker
유산 遺産 〈상속재산〉 an inheritance; property [an estate] left (by a deceased person); 〈유언에 따른〉 a legacy; a bequest; 〈조상 전래의〉 a heritage
♦무형의 유산 incorporeal hereditament / 유산을 분배하다 divide *one's* property (among *one's* children) / 유산을 상속하다 come into a legacy [an inheritance] / 유산을 상속받다 inherit a fortune [property, an estate]
▶그녀는 할아버지로부터 많은 유산을 상속받았다 She received a large inheritance from her grandfather.

▶ 그는 아들에게 막대한 유산을 남겼다 He left a vast legacy to his son.
▶ 이 유서깊은 건물은 국가적 유산이다 This old building is a national heritage.
▶ 시골 집을 어머니로부터 유산으로 받았다 I received the country home by inheritance from my mother.
▶ 책은 위대한 천재들이 인류에게 남기는 유산이다 Books are the legacies that great geniuses leave to mankind.
■ 문화— cultural legacy [asset, heritage] —관리 administration —관리인 an administrator; 〈여자〉 an administratrix —분배 division [partition] of an estate —상속 inheritance; succession to property : 그의 재산은 유산상속에 의한 것이었다 His fortune came to him by inheritance. —상속세 succession duty; (美) an inheritance tax —상속인 an inheritor; 〈남자〉 an heir; 〈여자〉 an heiress —싸움 a quarrel over the inheritance

유산계급 有產階級 the propertied [moneyed, bourgeois] classes; the bourgeoisie ▶ 그는 유산계급 출신이다 He comes from a bourgeois family.

유산자 a bourgeois (▶단수·복수 동형); a man of property

유산탄 榴散彈 a shrapnel (shell)

유상 有償 compensation; consideration
♦ 유상의 onerous / 유상으로 취득하다 obtain *sth* for countervalue
■ —계약 an onerous contract —몰수 confiscation with compensation [for value] —원조 credit assistance —증자 issue of new shares to be purchased —취득 acquisition for value

유상 油狀 ♦ 유상의 oily 《matter》; like oil

유상무상 有象無象 1 〈만상〉 all things in nature; all nature; the whole creation; the universe
2 〈어중이떠중이〉 the rabble; the mob; (口) a bunch of average joes; the ragtag and bobtail; the ruck

유상액 乳狀液 (an) emulsion

유상화 乳狀化 emulsification

유색 有色 ♦ 유색의 colored ■ —인종 colored races; non-white people

유생 幼生 〔動〕 larva 《*pl.* -vae》 ■ —기관 a larval organ

유생 儒生 a Confucian (scholar); a student of Confucianism

유생물 有生物 the animate; life; living things

유서 由緒 a history
♦ 유서깊은 곳 a spot with its old associations; a place with a historic background / 유서깊은 historied; great-historied
▶ 이 유서깊은 건물이 허물어지기 시작하고 있다 This historic building is beginning to fall apart.
▶ 그녀는 유서있는 집안 출신이다 She is of noble birth. ⇌ She comes from a noble family.
▶ 이것은 유서있는 건물이다 This is a historic building.

유서 遺書 〈유언장〉 a (written) will; note left behind by a dead person [suicide]; 〈유언〉 a will; a testament; *one's* last will and testament
♦ 자살자의 유서 a suicide note; a testamentary letter / 유서를 남기다 leave a will
▶ 그는 재정적인 이유로 자살한다는 유서를 남겼다 He left a note saying he would kill himself because of financial problems.
▶ 자살자의 유서는 없었다 The suicide left no note behind.

유서 類書 books of the same kind; similar books
▶ 이 책에는 유서에서는 볼 수 없는 특징이 있다 This book has a characteristic which distinguishes it from other books of the same kind.

유선 有線 cable; closed-circuit ♦ 유선의 wire; wired
■ —방송 cable broadcasting [broadcasts] —식 the wire system —전신[전화] wire telegraph [telephone] —텔레비전 cable [closed-circuit] television; 〈공동안테나〉 community antenna television (略 CATV) —통신 communication by wire

유선 乳腺 〔解〕 the mammary [lacteal] gland ⇨ 젖샘
■ —염 〔醫〕 mastitis

유선 流線 〔物〕 a line of flow; a streamline

유선형 流線型 a streamline (form); a streamlined shape
♦ 유선형의 streamline(d) / 유선형으로 만들다 streamline
▶ 이것은 유선형 자동차다 This is a streamlined car.

유설 謬說 a fallacy; a wrong [an erroneous] remark; a false [wrong] view

유성 有性 ♦ 유성의 gamic; sexual ■ —생식 〔生〕 sexual reproduction —세대 〔生〕 the sexual generation

유성 油性 oiliness ♦ 유성의 oil; oily; greasy; 〈기름을 주성분으로 한〉 oil-based; oleaginous ■ —도료 an oil paint —페니실린 penicillin oil

유성 流星 a meteor; a shooting [falling] star ■ —군 a meteor swarm —우(雨) a meteor shower; a star shower

유성 遊星 a planet ⇨ 행성(行星)

유성 有聲 ♦ 유성의 voiced (↔ voiceless); vocal ■ —영화 a talking film [picture]; a talkie —음 voiced sounds; voice —음화 vocalization; voicing —자음 voiced consonants

유성기 留聲機 a phonograph ⇨ 축음기

유세 有稅 ♦ 유세의 taxable; dutiable
■ —지 dutiable land —품 dutiable goods

유세 有勢 being powerful ⇨ 유력(有力)

유 세 遊說 canvassing; electioneering; (美) stumping
—유세하다 canvass; (美) stump; take to [go on] the stumps; (美口) 〈지방을〉 barnstorm
♦ 유세하러 다니다 go on a stumping tour [(美) the stump]; go campaigning
▶ 그는 전국을 유세했다 He went about the country electioneering.
▶ 그는 지금 경기지방을 유세하고 있는 중이다 He is now stumping the Kyŏnggi districts.
▶ 후보자들은 선거 전에 선거구를 유세했다 The candidates stumped the district before

election.
▶ 대통령 후보자는 서해안을 유세하며 돌았다 The presidential candidate barnstormed (through) [stumped (around)] the west coast.
■—여행 a stumping tour; a canvassing trip; an electioneering tour —자 〈후보자〉 stumping candidate [politician]; a stumper; 〈운동원〉 a canvasser; 〈美〉 a stump speaker

유소 幼少 childhood; infancy ⇨ 유년(기)
◆유소의 infantile; young; juvenile
—유소하다 infant; young; juvenile
◆유소할 때부터 from one's infancy; from the cradle / 유소할 때 in early life; in one's infancy

유속 流速 the speed of a running [moving] fluid; 〈조류의〉 the drift of a current
■—계 a current meter; a tachometer —측정 tachometry

유속 遺俗 〈유풍〉 hereditary customs

유수 有數 ◆유수의 prominent; leading; foremost; eminent; distinguished
▶ 그는 한국 유수의 영문학자다 He is one of the best [most distinguished] scholars of English literature in Korea.
▶ 그는 한국 유수의 수학자다 He is one of the prominent [foremost] mathematicians in Korea.
▶ 독일은 세계 유수의 경제 대국이다 Germany is one of the world's leading economic powers.
—유수하다 prominent

유수 幽囚 imprisonment; confinement
◆바빌론 유수 〔聖〕 the Babylonian captivity

유수 流水 running water; a stream ▶ 세월은 유수와 같다 Time flies (like an arrow).

유수정책 誘水政策 a pump priming policy

유숙 留宿 (a) lodging —유숙하다 lodge 《at》; put up 《at》
▶ 지금 나는 할아버지댁에 유숙하고 있다 Now I'm staying with my grandfather.

유순 柔順 obedience; docility; submissiveness; meekness
—유순하다 obedient; submissive; 〈다루기 쉽다〉 docile; 〈얌전하다〉 gentle; meek
◆유순하게 obediently; submissively; gently; meekly / 유순하게 말을 잘 듣다 do as told without objection
▶ 그녀는 매우 유순하다 She is as meek as a lamb.

유스타키오관 —管 〔生〕 the Eustachian tube

유스호스텔 〈숙박시설〉 a youth hostel

유습 遺習 〈유풍〉 hereditary customs

유시 幼時 childhood; infancy ◆유시에 in one's infancy [childhood]; at an early age

유시 流矢 a stray arrow

유시 諭示 admonition; injunction; instruction; inculcation
◆대통령의 유시 a presidential instruction [message]
—유시하다 admonish; give admonition 《to》; instruct; inculcate

유시계비행 有視界飛行 visual flying; a visual flight

유식 有識 scholarship; learning
—유식하다 learned; educated; erudite
◆유식한 사람 an educated [a learned] person; a man of culture / 유식한 체하다 pretend to know much; assume an air of wisdom

유신 維新 〈혁신〉 renovation

유신론 有神論 theism (↔ atheism) ■—자 a theist; a deist

유실 流失 losing to the flood [waves]
—유실하다 lose to the flood; wash out
◆유실될 be washed [carried, swept] away
▶ 홍수로 가옥이 십여채 유실되었다 Ten-odd houses were washed away by the flood. ≒ A dozen or so houses were carried away by the flood.
■—가옥 houses washed [carried] away by the flood

유실 遺失 loss —유실하다 lose; leave behind ■—자 a loser; the owner of lost property

유실물 遺失物 a lost article; a missing thing; lost property ◆청구인이 없는 유실물 an unclaimed lost article / 유실물을 청구하다 reclaim a lost article
■—광고 a lost advertisement —신고 a report on lost property —취급소 a lost and found office; 《英》 a lost property office

유심 唯心 ◆유심적(인) spiritual; ideal; mentalistic ■—론 〔哲〕 idealism; spiritualism; mentalism —론자 a spiritualist; an idealist; a mentalist

유심하다 有心— attentive; careful; mindful; cautious
◆유심히 attentively; with attention [care, caution]; carefully; mindfully; cautiously / 유심히 듣다 hear attentively [mindfully]; listen attentively to / 유심히 보다 look hard [mindfully] at sb

유아 幼兒 a baby; an infant
◆유아의 infant; infantile; infantine
▶ 이것은 유아의 손이 닿지 않는 곳에 두어야 한다 It must be kept beyond the reach of a baby.
■—교육 preschool children's education —기 babyhood —보호소 a public nursery; a day nursery —사망률 infant mortality —세례 infant baptism —용품 infant's needs —원 a nursery

유아 幼芽 〔生〕 a germ; a young sprout

유아 乳兒 〈젖먹이〉 a suckling; a nursling; an infant; a baby ■—식 baby food

유아 遺兒 1 a child left after its father's [mother's] death; an orphan
▶ 빌은 스미스씨의 유아다 Bill is the son of the late Mr. Smith.
2 〈기아〉 an abandoned child

유아독존 唯我獨尊 〈독선〉 self-conceit; vainglory
▶ 천상천하 유아독존 I am my own Lord [Holy am I alone] throughout heaven and earth. ≒ I am not any man's man, but my own.

유아등 誘蛾燈 a light trap; a luring lamp

유아론 唯我論 〔哲〕 solipsism ■—자 a solipsist

유안 硫安 〔化〕 ammonium sulfate ⇨ 황산(~암모늄)
유암 乳癌 〔醫〕 breast [mammary] cancer; cancer of the breast=유방암
유압 油壓 oil pressure ■—계 an oil pressure gauge —브레이크[잭] a hydraulic brake [jack]
유액 乳液 1 〈식물의〉 latex (*pl.* ~es, latices); milky liquid (in plants)
2 〈화장용 크림〉 a milky lotion
유야무야 有耶無耶 ▶노사간의 대화는 유야무야 끝났다 The talk between labor and management yielded no definite results.
▶그들은 그 추문을 유야무야 덮어버리려 했다 They tried to hush up [hugger-mugger] the scandal.
—유야무야하다 mystifying; vague; indefinite; indecisive
♦유야무야한 대답을 하다 give a vague reply; do not commit *oneself* / 일을 유야무야해 버리다 leave a matter unsettled [undecided] (and do nothing definite about it)
▶우리는 그 일을 유야무야해선 안된다 We shouldn't leave the matter unsettled.
유약 柔弱 weakness; unmanliness
—유약하다 weak; fragile; unmanly; effeminate
♦유약한 태도 a weak-kneed attitude
▶저 남자는 유약한 사람이다 He is a weak character [weak-kneed man].
유약 釉藥 glaze; enamel; luster; glost; 〈마무리 하는〉 overglaze ♦유약을 칠하다 put glaze on (pottery); glaze; enamel (a brooch)
유어 類語 a synonym (↔ antonym); an associate [a kindred] word
▶idle은 lazy의 유어다 "Idle" is a synonym of "lazy." ⇌ "Idle" is synonymous with "lazy."
—사전 a thesaurus (*pl.* ~es, -ri)
유언 流言 a rumor; a false report
♦유언을 퍼뜨리다 set a false rumor afloat; spread a wild story
▶우리 가운데 유언에 혹된 사람은 아무도 없었다 None of us were misled by false rumors.
유언 遺言 a will; 〈구두의〉 one's last words; a verbal will; one's last injunctions [request]; one's deathbed wish; deathbed injunctions; 〈서면의〉 a testament
♦유언을 집행하다 administer [carry out] *sb's* will
▶그는 유언을 남기고[남기지 않고] 죽었다 He died testate [intestate].
▶그의 유언에 따라 그의 전재산을 대학에 기부했다 All his property was left to the university in accordance with [by] his will.
▶그는 아버지의 유언으로 이 농장을 상속받았다 He inherited this farm by the will of his father.
—유언하다 express *one's* dying wish; leave [make] a (verbal) will (that...); will (that...)
▶그는 전재산을 둘째아들에게 주라고 유언했다 He willed all his property to his second son. ⇌ He willed his second son all his property. ⇌ He left all his property to his second son in his will.
■—자 〈남자〉 a testator; 〈여자〉 a testatrix
—집행자 an executor
유언비어 流言蜚語 a groundless [wild] rumor; a canard
♦유언비어를 퍼뜨리다 spread [circulate] a false rumor; set a false rumor afloat [abroad] / 유언비어에 현혹되다 be misled by false rumors
▶유언비어를 퍼뜨려 민심을 어지럽게 하지 마라 Don't make people feel uneasy by circulating false reports.
유언장 遺言狀 a (written) will; a testament; *one's* last will and testament ♦자필 유언장 a holograph will / 유언장을 작성하다 make [draw up] a will
유업 乳業 the dairy industry [business]
유업 遺業 work left [unfinished] (by *sb*); an unfinished work ♦유업을 계승하다 take over *sb's* unfinished work
▶그는 아버지의 유업을 완성했다 He completed the work left unfinished by his father.
유에프오 〈비행 접시〉 a flying saucer; 〈미확인 비행물체〉 a UFO (*pl.* UFO's) [〈*u*nidentified *f*lying *o*bject〕
유엔 U.N. [〈the *U*nited *N*ations〕
■—경찰군 the U.N. Emergency Forces (略 UNEF) —기 the United Nations flag —대사 the Ambassador to the U.N. —데이 United Nations [U.N.] Day —본부 the U.N. Headquarters —사무총장 the Secretary-General of the U.N. —세계 인권 회의 World Conference on Human Rights —안전보장이사회 United Nations Security Council —인권위원회 Commission on Human Rights —총회 the U.N. General Assembly —평화유지군 the U.N. Peacekeeping Forces —헌장 the Charter of the United Nations; the U.N. Charter —회원국 a U.N. member (nation)
유엔군 —軍 the U.N. Forces [Army]; the United Nations Forces
■—사령관 the United Nations Forces Commander; the UNC Commander —총사령부 the United Nations Command; the U.N. Command (略 UNC)
-유여 -有餘 〈남짓〉 over; above; 〈이상〉 more than
♦1,000명 유여의 수험생 more than [over] one thousand candidates for examination; 1,000-odd candidates for examination / 10년 유여의 고생 *one's* hard work for over [more than] ten years
유역 流域 a basin; 〈큰 강의〉 a valley
♦한강 유역 the basin of the Han-gang / 양쯔강 유역 the Yangtze valley
▶낙동강 유역에는 농지가 풍부하다 The Naktonggang [The basin of the Naktonggang] has much good [rich] farm area.
유연 柔軟 softness; pliability; suppleness; flexibility
—유연하다 soft; pliant; supple; flexible; lithe
▶치타의 몸은 지극히 유연하다 A cheetah has a pliant body.
■—성 softness; suppleness; pliancy; pliableness; flexibility —체조 light gymnastics; 〈미

용체조〉 cal(l)isthenics

유연 悠然 an attitude of perfect composure —**유연하다** composed; self-possessed; calm; serene ◆유연하게 calmly; with an air [in an attitude] of perfect composure

유연탄 有煙炭 〔鑛〕 soft [bituminous] coal

유영 游泳 swimming; 〈처세〉 conduct of life; carrying *oneself*
■우주— a space walk ■—기관 〔動〕 a natatorial organ; the flipper —동물 〔動〕 nekton —술 the art of swimming; how to get along in the world: 그는 인생의 유영술에 밝다 He knows well how to get along in the world

유영 遺影 ◆김 선생의 유영 a picture of the late Mr. Kim

유예 猶豫 〈연기〉 (a) postponement; 〈기간의 연장〉 (an) extension; 〈지연〉 (a) delay; (a) deferment; 〈지급 등의〉 grace; 〈망설임〉 hesitation; 〔法〕 〈권리집행의〉 forbearance; 〈형의〉 a reprieve; a respite; 〔法〕 〈사형의〉 a stay (of execution); 〈법 적용의〉 dispensation
◆유예를 구하다 ask for a postponement (of three days)/유예를 얻다 gain time; get (an extension of) time
—**유예하다** 〈연기하다〉 put off; postpone; 〈지급을〉 allow [grant] delay [grace, respite]; give *sb's* grace; give time; 〈망설이다〉 hesitate; 〈형 집행을〉 reprieve (a condemned man)
▶그 대금의 지급을 5일 동안 유예해 드리겠습니다 I'll give you five days' grace to pay me the money.
▶그는 형 집행을 유예받았다 He was given [was granted] a reprieve.
▶일각도 유예할 처지가 아니다 There is no time to lose [be lost]. ⇒ We have not a minute to lose. ⇒ The situation requires no delay.
▶그는 형 집행을 1년간 유예받았다 He was reprieved for a year.
■지급— indulgence; postponement; grace of payment 집행— a stay of execution; a reprieve; suspension of a sentence; 〔法〕 probation: 그는 3년간의 집행유예를 받았다 He was placed [was put] on [under] three years' probation. 징병— temporary exemption from conscription ■—미결 postponement and suspension —일수 days of indulgence [allowance]; 〈어음지급의〉 days of grace

유예기간 猶豫期間 〈어음 지급・보험료 불입의〉 (美) a grace period; (英) days of grace
■법정— 〔法〕 〈채무 이행의〉 legal delay

유용 流用 diversion; (an) appropriation; 〈착복〉 (a) misappropriation
—**유용하다** apply [appropriate] (the money) to (some other purposes)
▶그는 공금을 유용했다 He appropriated public money for his own use.
▶그 돈은 다른 목적에 유용되었다 The fund was diverted to some other purposes.

유용 有用 —**유용하다** useful; of use; good; valuable (for students); available; helpful
◆유용한 것 a useful thing; utilities/유용한 사람 a valuable [useful] man/유용케 하다 turn *sth* to account/돈을 유용하게 쓰다 put money to a good use
▶소나 말은 유용한 동물이다 Cows and horses are useful animals.
▶이 사전은 영어 공부에 무척 유용하다 This dictionary is very useful for studying English.
■—가격 〔經〕 value in use —식물 a useful plant

유원지 遊園地 an amusement park; a recreation [pleasure] ground [area]; a pleasure resort; a public garden ◆어린이 유원지 an amusement park for children

유월 六月 June (略 Jun.)

유월절 逾越節・踰月節 〔유태教〕 the Passover

유위하다 有爲— 〈유능하다〉 capable; able; talented; competent; useful; 〈유망하다〉 promising

유유낙낙 唯唯諾諾 —**유유낙낙하다** do as told without objection; be obedient ◆유유낙낙하게 obediently; quite willingly; readily

유유상종 類類相從 affiliation among those of the same class —**유유상종하다** 〈속담〉 Birds of a feather flock together. ⇒ Every Jack has his Jill.

유유아 乳幼兒 an infant; a baby

유유자적하다 悠悠自適— live in easy [comfortable] retirement; live free from worldly cares
▶그는 그 사업에서 물러나 유유자적한 나날을 보냈다 He retired from the business and lived in great comfort.

유유하다 悠悠— 〈침착하다〉 calm; quiet; composed; 〈여유있다〉 leisurely; 〈썩 멀다〉 eternal; remote; far-off
◆유유히 〈침착하게〉 calmly; 〈여유있게〉 in a leisurely way [manner]; slowly; 〈편안히〉 at ease; in comfort/유유히 살다 live in comfort/유유히 여생을 보내다 spend the rest of *one's* life free from worldly cares
▶그는 유유히 맥주를 마시고 있었다 He was drinking a glass of beer in a leisurely manner.
▶그는 우산도 없이 빗속을 유유히 걸어갔다 He walked on calmly in the rain without an umbrella.

유의 留意 attention; heed; consideration; regard —**유의하다** regard; mind; care about; attend to; give heed [consideration] to; take care [account, notice] of; pay attention to; be mindful (of)
◆건강에 유의하다 take (good) care of *oneself* [*one's* health]/유의하여 듣다 listen attentively to; be all attention [ears]
▶우리는 그점에 유의하지 않으면 안된다 We must call attention to the point.
▶건강에 특히 유의하시기 바랍니다 Please pay special attention to your health.

유의어 類義語 a synonym

유의의 有意義 significance; meaningfulness —**유의의하다** significant; meaningful

유익하다 有益— beneficial; helpful; profitable; salutary; 〈교육적이다〉 instructive; edifying; 〈건전하다〉 wholesome; 〈유용하다〉 useful; serviceable

♦유익한 교훈[이야기] an instructive [edifying] lesson [story]/ 유익한 경험 a profitable experience / 유익한 정보 useful information / 유익한 조언 helpful advice / 유익한 읽을 거리 edifying reading / 유익하게 쓰다 put sth to a good use; use sth profitably; turn sth to advantage / 시간을 유익하게 쓰다 make good use of one's time
▶ 꿀벌은 인간에게 유익하다 Bees are useful [beneficial] to human beings.
▶ 그녀의 이야기는 유익했다 Her talk was instructive.
▶ 이 책은 아주 유익하다 This book is very rewarding.

유인 有人 ♦유인의 manned; piloted ■─기(쪽) a manned [piloted] airplane; (총칭) piloted aircraft ─우주비행 (a) manned space flight ─우주선[위성] a manned spaceship [satellite]

유인 誘引 enticement; attraction; allurement; seduction; inducement; incitement
─유인하다 entice [invite] 《sb to do sth》; beguile; induce; attract; allure; seduce
♦ 죄를 짓도록 유인하다 tempt sb to sin

유인 誘因 a cause; a motive; 〔心〕 an incentive 《to an action》; an inducement 《to》; an (immediate) occasion 《for》
♦ …의 유인이 되다 cause; induce; occasion; be the occasion [cause] of…; lead (up) to…; bring about…

유인물 油印物 printed matter
유인원 類人猿 〔動〕 an anthropoid (ape)

유일무이하다 唯一無二─ the one and only; 〈비길데 없다〉 peerless; unique ♦ 유일무이한 기회 a unique [golden] opportunity / 유일무이한 친구 the one and only friend one has

유일신 唯一神 (worship) the one and only God ■─교 ⇨ 일신교

유일하다 唯一─ the only; the sole; the one (and only); solitary; single; unique; exclusive
♦ 유일한 예[예외] a solitary [an isolated] instance [exception]/ 유일한 친구 one's only [sole] friend/ 남아 있는 유일한 방법 the only measure left
▶ 그는 그 일을 할 수 있는 유일한 사람이다 He is the only person that can accomplish the task.
▶ 독서가 그의 유일한 일이다 He has nothing to do but to read books.

유임 留任 remaining in office ♦ 유임을 권하다 advise sb to stay in office / 유임 운동을 벌이다 start a movement to have sb remain in office
─유임하다 remain [stay] in office; continue to serve as
▶ 그는 3월말까지는 은행장으로 유임할 것이다 He will continue to serve as (the) president of the bank until the end of March.

유입 流入 (an) inflow; (an) influx; incoming
─유입하다 flow [come, stream] in [into]
▶ 그 강은 호수로 유입한다 The river flows into a lake.
■ ─외자 an inflow [influx] of foreign capital

유자 柚子 〔植〕 a citron ■ ─나무 a citron

유자 遊資 unemployed capital ⇨ 유휴(~자본)

유자격자 有資格者 a (properly) qualified person 《for a post》; an eligible 《for》; (총칭) the [those] (properly) qualified ■ 교원[조종사] ─ a licensed [certified] teacher [pilot]

유자형 U字形 ♦ 유자형의 U; U-shaped 《conference table》
■ ─커브 a U curve [turn]; a U-shaped curve [turn]; a hairpin bend [curve, turn]

유작 遺作 posthumous works ▶ 그의 유작집이 곧 출판될 것이다 A collection of his posthumous works will be published soon.

유장 乳漿 whey; plasma

유장하다 悠長─ 1 〈오래 다〉 long; long-standing ♦ 유장한 세월 a long stretch of time 2 〈느긋하다〉 leisurely; slow; easy-going
♦ 유장한 태도[이야기] a leisurely manner [story]/ 유장하게 여행하다 travel leisurely

유저 遺著 posthumous works ⇨ 유작(遺作)

유적 遺跡 remains; ruins; vestiges; relics
♦ 고대 문명의 유적 the vestiges of ancient civilization / 선사시대의 유적 a prehistoric site / 역사적 유적 a place of historic interest; a historic site [relic]/ 태고의 유적 the relics [remains] of an ancient age / 로마의 유적을 찾다 visit the ruins of Rome

유전 油田 an oil [a petroleum] field [well]; oil land ♦ 유전을 발견하다 discover [find] an oil field; hit oil ■ ─개발[탐사] oil exploration ─지대 an oil (producing) region

유전 流轉 1 〈끊임없는 변천〉 flux; perpetual motion; constant mutation; vicissitudes
─유전하다 move perpetually; change [mutate] constantly
▶ 만물은 유전한다 All things are in a state of flux. ⇌ Impermanency is the nature of things.
2 〈유랑〉 vagrancy; wandering
─유전하다 wander [rove, roam] about
3 〈윤회〉 transmigration; metempsychosis
─유전하다 transmigrate

유전 遺傳 heredity; (hereditary) transmission; (genetic) inheritance; ancestral influence
♦ 유전의 법칙 the laws of heredity / 유전적인 결함 a genetic defect [fault, flaw]/ 유전적 영향 genetic effects / 방사능에 의한 유전적 장애 genetic damages caused by radioactivity / 유전의 hereditary; inherited / 유전성의[적인] genetic; of hereditary nature; hereditary; transmissible; transmittable; (in)heritable / 유전적으로 hereditarily
─유전하다 run in the family [blood]; be inherited; be transmitted 《from the parents》; be handed down
▶ 그 집안에는 정신병이 유전하고 있다 Insanity runs in that family.
■ ─론[설] hereditism ─론자 a hereditarian ─병 a hereditary [family, constitutional] disease ─암호 the genetic code ─인자 ⇨ 유전자 ─학 genetics ─학자 a geneticist

유전 誘電 〔電〕 ■ ─분극(分極) dielectric polarization ─율(率) dielectric constant; per-

mitivity —체(體) a dielectrics
유전스 usance ■—빌 a usance bill; a bill drawn at usance —제도 the usance bill system
유전자 遺轉子 a gene ♦ 유전자의 인위적 조작 genetic manipulation; manipulation of genes / 유전자에 의한 genetic; genic
■ 면역 반응 억제— an immune response inhibiting gene 성결정— a sex determining gene 열성[우성]— a recessive [dominant] gene 인간— a human gene 인공— an artificial gene 합성— a synthesized gene ■—공학 genetic engineering —군 a gene cluster —은행 a gene bank —장애 genetic defects —재조합 gene recombination —지도 a genetic [chromosome] map —치료 gene therapy —형 a genotype
유정 油井 an oil(-producing) well
유정 遺精 (have) involuntary emission of semen; 〔醫〕 spermatorrh(o)ea; nocturnal [night] pollution; a wet dream
유제 油劑 an oily medicine; a drug containing oil
유제 乳劑 〔化〕 an emulsion
유제 類題 similar questions
유제동물 有蹄動物 an ungulate (animal); a hoofed animal
유제류 有蹄類 〈각질(角質) 발굽이 있는 초식동물류〉 the ungulates
유제품 乳製品 dairy products
유조 油槽 an oil tank ■—선 a [an oil] tanker; an oiler —차 a tank car; an oil car
유족 裕足 abundance; affluence; opulence
—유족하다 affluent; opulent; rich; wealthy; well-to-do; well-off; comfortably off, (口) well-heeled
♦ 유족하게 살다 live well; be well off / 유족해지다 grow rich; spring into affluence
유족 遺族 a bereaved [surviving] family; the family of the deceased; the survivors
▶ 그의 유족으로는 부인과 두 딸이 있다 He left his wife and two daughters behind. = He was survived by his wife and two daughters.
■ 전사자— the war bereaved —부조금 an allowance to a bereaved [surviving] family [to the family of the deceased]; survivors' benefits —연금 〈개인 보험의〉 a survivor's annuity; 〈사회 보험의〉 a survivor's pension
유종 有終 having an end; consummation; finishing; perfection
♦ 유종의 미 a successful conclusion / 유종의 미를 거두다 round off 《one's career》; crown sth with perfection; carry sth to perfection; bring sth to a successful conclusion
▶ 그는 고별 시합에서 홈런을 쳐서 선수생활에 유종의 미를 거두었다 He rounded off his playing career with a home run in his farewell game.
유종 乳腫 〔醫〕 mastitis
유죄 有罪 guiltiness; guilt; culpableness; culpability; criminality
♦ 유죄로 판결되다 be found [adjudged] guilty 《of a crime》/ 유죄를 선고하다 convict sb of a crime; give sb the verdict of "guilty"; declare sb guilty
—유죄하다 guilty; culpable
■—인 a guilty person —판결 a judgment of "guilty"; 《get》 a conviction
유죄 流罪 transportation ⇨ 유형(流刑)
유증 遺贈 testation; 〈동산의〉 bequest; bequeathal; 〈부동산의〉 devise —유증하다 leave sth by will [testament]; bequeath; legate; devise
■—물 a bequest; a legacy —자 a legator; a devisor
유지 有志 **1** 〈뜻이 있음〉 having an interest ; having public spirit **2** 〈세상 일을 근심하는 사람〉 a volunteer; a supporter; a sympathizer; an interested person; those [people] interested 《in a matter》 **3** 〈유력가〉 an influential person; a man of influence [power]
▶ 그는 그 고장의 유지다 He is quite influential in the place.
■ 지방— those who work for the good of the locality; public-spirited men of the locality —일동 all the persons concerned
유지 乳脂 cream (in milk)
■—비누 curd soap
유지 油脂 oils and fats ■—공업 the oil and fat (manufacturing) industry
유지 油紙 oilpaper; oiled paper
유지 維持 maintenance; preservation; upkeep; support; conservation; sustenance
▶ 현상 유지도 어려울 것 같다 It seems certainly difficult even to maintain [preserve] the present state of things [status quo].
—유지하다 maintain; preserve; keep sth going; keep [hold] up; sustain 《an institution》; support 《life》
♦ 건강을 유지하다 maintain [keep, preserve] one's health / 질서를 유지하다 keep [maintain, preserve] order
▶ 그 협회는 어떻게 유지해 가고 있니 ? How is the society kept up?
▶ 나는 가게를 유지할 수가 없다 I am unable to maintain my store [to keep my store open].
▶ 언제까지나 젊음을 유지할 수는 없다 One cannot retain one's youth [stay young] forever.
■—비 upkeep [maintenance] expenses [cost]; (the cost of) maintenance: 유지비를 감당할 수 없다 I cannot pay for its upkeep. —책 a measure for maintenance
유지 諭旨 〈왕의 지시〉 an imperial message
유지 遺志 the desire [wish, intention, will] of a deceased person; one's dying wishes [will]
♦ 고인의 유지를 받들어 in obedience to the will of the deceased / 고인의 유지를 따르다 follow the intention of the deceased
▶ 그는 돌아가신 아버지의 유지를 따라 새 회사를 설립하였다 In accordance with the intention of his deceased father, he established a new company.
유지자 有職者 the employed; a person in employment
유질 流質 〔法〕 foreclosure (of the mortgage); a mortgage forfeit

유질하다 be foreclosed; be forfeited; run out ◆유질된 카메라 a foreclosed camera / 유질시키다 foreclose a mortgage; forfeit a pledge [pawn] ━공매 처분 a foreclosure sale ━물 an unredeemed pawn [pledge]; a forfeited article

유착 癒着 adhesion; union; conglutination; healing up ━유착하다 glue [knit] together; adhere 《to》; unite; conglutinate; heal [close] up ■━늑막━ 〔醫〕 pleural adhesion ■━불능〈골절의〉 nonunion

유창 流暢 fluency; facility ━유창하다 fluent 《in French》; flowing; smooth; facile ◆유창한 문장 a flowing [an easy] style / 유창한 연설 fluent speech / 유창하게 fluently; with fluency [facility]; smoothly / 유창하고 세련된 영어로 in fluent and polished English ▶나는 그가 독일어를 유창하게 하는 데 놀랐다 I was surprised at the fluency with which he spoke German.

유채 油菜 〔植〕 a rape; a cole ■━꽃 rape blossoms

유체 有體 ◆유체의 tangible; corporeal ■━동산 corporeal movables ━물 a materiality; 〔法〕 a corporeal thing ━자산 〔簿〕 tangible assets [property]; tangibles; 〔法〕 corporeal property

유체 流體 〔物〕 a fluid ◆유체의 fluid ■━공학 hydraulic engineering ━압력 fluid pressure ━역학 hydrodynamics; fluid dynamics [mechanics]

유체 遺體 〈송장〉 the (dead) body; the remains ◆유체를 안치하다 lay out the body [remains] ■━안치소 a mortuary

유추 類推 (an) analogy; analogism ◆유추적인 analogical ━유추하다 analogize; infer; know [reason] by analogy ◆일부로 전체를 유추하다 analogize the whole out of a part ■━해석 analogical interpretation

유출 流出 (an) effluence; (an) outflow; (an) efflux; an outward flow; exodus; 〈용암의〉 extrusion ◆금화[정화(正貨)]의 유출 the outflow [drain, exodus] of gold [specie] 《from a country》 ━유출하다 flow [run] out; issue; discharge; escape; drain out; debouch ▶금이 해외로 유출됐다 There was an outflow of gold from the country. ■━두뇌━ (口) the brain drain ■━구〈하천의〉 a debouchment ━률 the rate of flow

유충 幼蟲 a larva ⇨ 애벌레 ◆유충의 larval ■━기 the larval stage

유층 油層 reserves [a pool] of oil; an oil stratum 《pl. -ta》 ◆유층을 발견하다 strike oil

유치 幼稚 infancy; babyhood; crudeness ━유치하다 childish; infantile; babyish; puerile; immature; inexperienced; 〈미숙한〉 crude; raw; 〈원시적〉 primitive ◆유치한 생각[사상] a crude [a childish, an infantile] idea [thought] ▶이 나라의 농업은 아직 유치하다 Agriculture in this country is still primitive [in its infancy].

유치 乳齒 a milk [deciduous, baby, calf's] tooth

유치 留置 1〈억류〉 detention; custody; lock-up ━유치하다 detain; keep sb in custody; lock up; (美) hold ◆경찰에 유치하다 take sb into custody of the police; detain sb at a police station ▶그 사내는 절도 혐의로 경찰에 유치되었다 The man was detained at the police station on suspicion of theft. 2〈우편물의〉 being left till called for ━유치하다 leave until called for ■━권 a lien ━우편 poste restante; (美) general deliver : 편지를 유치우편으로 보내다 send a letter poste restante; (美) send a letter to general delivery ━전보 (프) télégraphe restante

유치 誘致 attraction; lure; enticement; induction ━유치하다 attract; lure; decoy; entice; induce; invite ◆공장을 유치하다 invite a factory / 외국인 관광객을 유치하다 try to attract foreign tourists / 외자를 유치하다 attract [draw, induce, invite] foreign capital

유치원 幼稚園 kindergarten; a nursery school; (美) a preschool; (英) a infant school ◆유치원에 보내다 send 《a child》 to kindergarten ■━보모[선생] a kindergartener; a kindergarten teacher ━원아[생] a kindergarten pupil; a kindergartener

유치장 留置場 a detention room; a house of custody; a police cell [pen]; a lockup ◆유치장에 갇히다 be detained in the police cell

유칼리나무 〔植〕 a eucalyptus 《pl. ~es, -lypti》; a eucalypt; a blue [red] gum

유쾌 愉快 pleasure; delight; fun; enjoyment ━유쾌하다 pleasant; enjoyable; delightful; joyful; amusing; cheerful; jolly ◆유쾌한 대화 a pleasant conversation / 유쾌한 사람 a jolly [cheerful, pleasant] fellow / 유쾌한 이야기 an amusing story / 유쾌하게 pleasantly; delightfully; cheerfully; merrily / 유쾌하게 웃다 smile cheerfully [happily] / 유쾌하게 시간을 보내다 enjoy *oneself*; have a good [pleasant, (口) heavenly] time 《of it》 ▶그는 무척 유쾌한 사람이다 He is a very cheerful [jolly] person. ⇌ He is good [great] fun. ▶김 선생은 유쾌한 사람이기 때문에 누구든지 좋아한다 Mr. Kim is a pleasant person and everyone likes him. ▶어제 하루는 유쾌하게 지냈다 I had a good [wonderful] time 《of it》 yesterday. ▶오늘은 일에 대해 잊어버리고 유쾌하게 놀자 Let's forget about work today and have some fun. ▶파티는 무척 유쾌했습니다 We had a very good time [enjoyed ourselves very much] at the party. ▶오늘 저녁은 참으로 유쾌했습니다 I have had a very good time this evening. ⇌ I have enjoyed myself very much this evening.

유클리드 〈그리스의 수학자〉 Euclid
■ ―기하학 Euclidean geometry

▶ 우리는 해안에서 무척 유쾌한 시간을 보냈다 We had a very enjoyable time at the (sea) shore.

유타 〈미국의 주〉 Utah (略 Ut., UT) ◆유타주의 Utahan ■ ―사람 a Utahan

유탄 流彈 a stray bullet [shot]; a random shot ◆유탄에 맞다 be struck [hit] by a stray bullet / 유탄에 맞아 죽다 be killed by a stray bullet

유탄 榴彈 a shell; a high-explosive projectile ■ ―발사기 a grenade launcher ―포 a howitzer

유태 猶太 Judaea [dʒuːdíːə]
◆유태의 Jewish; Judaic(al)
■ ―교 Judaism ―교도 a Jew; a Judaist ―교회 a synagogue ―력 the Jewish calendar ―민족 the Jews; the Hebrew people ―민족주의 Zionism ―인 a Jew; a Hebrew; (총칭) Jewry : 유태인의 Jewish; Judaic(al) / 유태인 거리 a ghetto (pl. ~s, ~es); the Jewish quarter

유택 幽宅 a grave; a tomb
유턴 〈U자형 선회〉 a U-turn
▶ 유턴 금지 (게시) No U-turn.
유토피아 (a) Utopia ◆유토피아의 Utopian
유통 流通 1 〈화폐의〉 circulation; currency; 〈어음의〉 negotiation; 〈상품의〉 distribution
―유통하다 circulate; pass current ◆유통시키다 circulate; put (it) in(to) circulation
▶ 백원권 지폐는 지금은 유통되지 않는다 100-won bills are not in [are out of] circulation now.
▶ 약 1,000장의 위조지폐가 유통되고 있는 것으로 추산된다 It is estimated that about one thousand forged notes are in circulation.
2 〈공기의〉 circulation; ventilation
◆공기의 유통을 잘 되게 하다 facilitate ventilation; facilitate the circulation of air
―유통하다 circulate; ventilate; flow
▶ 이 방은 공기가 잘 유통되고 있다[있지 않다] This room is well [poorly] ventilated. ≒ The circulation of air in this room is good [bad].
■ ―구조[기구, 경로, 망] a distribution structure [system, channel, network] ―량 the amount of circulation: 화폐의 유통량 the amount of current [circulating] money ―산업 the distribution industry ―시장 a circulation market ―어음 a negotiable bill ―자본 a circulating [floating] capital ―증권 a negotiable instrument [security, document] ―질서 distribution order: 유통질서의 확립 establishment of order in the circulation (of) ―혁명 a distribution revolution ―화폐 currency in circulation; circulating [current] money

유파 流派 a school ▶ 그는 한국 무용의 새로운 유파를 창시했다 He created [founded] a new school of Korean dancing.

유폐 幽閉 confinement; imprisonment; incarceration ―유폐하다 confine (sb in a house); imprison; shut [lock] up; incarcerate; constrain
▶ 왕은 오랫동안 동굴에 유폐되어 있었다 The king was confined [imprisoned] in the cave for a long time.

유포 流布 circulation; diffusion; spread
―유포하다 〈퍼지다〉 circulate; run current; be [put] in circulation; spread; get abroad [afloat]; 〈퍼뜨리다〉 circulate; spread; disseminate; diffuse; put in circulation
▶ 이 이야기는 널리 유포돼 있다 This story has obtained (a) wide circulation. ≒ This is a story spread far and wide.
▶ 여러가지 소문이 유포돼 있다 There are a lot of rumors going around [getting about].

유품 遺品 relics; an article left by the deceased, mementoes (of the dead)
◆셰익스피어의 유품 Shakespear's relics

유풍 遺風 a custom handed down from the preceding generations; hereditary customs; a remnant; tradition
◆봉건시대의 유풍 customs of the feudal age / 중세의 유풍 survivals of medieval customs

유프라테스강 ―江 〈아시아 서부의 강〉 the Euphrates [juːfréitiːz]

유피 柔皮 dressed skin; tanned leather ■ ―법 (the art of) tanning ―업 tannery ―업자 a tanner

유피아이 UPI [〈the United Press International〉]

유하다 留― 〈머무르다〉 stay; stop; lodge; put up 《at a hotel》 ◆하룻밤 유하다 stay overnight; take a lodging for the night

유하다 柔― 1 〈부드럽다〉 soft; mild; gentle; tender; kindly; affectionate; sweet
◆유한 사람 a genial person
2 〈걱정이 없다〉 carefree; easy(going)
◆유한 성질 an easygoing disposition

유학 留學 study [studying] abroad
▶ 나는 해외 유학의 경험이 없다 I am inexperienced in studying abroad.
―유학하다 study abroad; go abroad to study
◆해외로 유학하다 study abroad
▶ 그는 2년간 독일에 유학하고 있다 He has studied in Germany for two years.
▶ 나는 영문학을 공부하기 위해 내년에 영국에 유학할 예정이다 I'll go to England to study English literature next year.

유학 遊學 studying away from home ◆4년간의 서울 유학 four years' study in Seoul
―유학하다 study away from home

유학 儒學 Confucianism
■ ―자 a Confucianist; a Confucian scholar

유학생 留學生 a student studying abroad
◆영국에서 온 교환 유학생 an exchange student from Britain / 한국에 있는 외국인 유학생 a foreign student in Korea

유한 有限 limitedness; finiteness ―유한하다 limited; 〔數〕 finite ◆유한한 생명 a mortal life
■ ―급수 〔數〕 a finite series ―법화(法貨) limited legal tender ―수[소수] 〔數〕 a finite number [decimal] ―연금 a limited annuity ―직선 〔數〕 a finite straight line ―책임 limited liability: 유한 책임 사원 a partner with limited liability ―(책임)회사 (美) a corporation; (英) a limited liability company

유한 有閑 〈한가함〉 having leisure ■ ―계급

유한 遺恨 a grudge; (an) enmity; rancor; spite ♦유한을 품다 have [bear] a grudge ((against *sb*)); own *sb* a grudge / 유한을 풀다 pay off *one's* old scores; get *one's* revenge [revenge *oneself*] ((on *one's* father's murderer)); be revenged ((on *sb* for *sth*))
▶ 그들은 그에게 유한을 품고 있었다 They held a grudge against him.
▶ 나는 그에 대한 유한을 풀었다 I took revenge on him.

유합 癒合 〔醫〕 agglutination; conglutination; adhesion —유 합 하 다 agglutinate; conglutinate; knit; heal by intention

유해 有害 noxiousness; harmfulness; hurtfulness —유해하다 harmful; injurious; noxious; hurtful
♦ 유해한 곤충 noxious insects / 유해한 화학약품 harmful [noxious] chemicals / 건강에 유해한 detrimental [injurious] to (the) health; bad for (the) health / 작물에 유해한 harmful to the crops / 풍기상 유해한 prejudicial [destructive] to public morals
▶ 최근 청소년들에게 유해한 텔레비전 프로그램이나 주간지가 많다 These days there are many television programs and weekly magazines that are harmful to young people.
▶ 담배를 지나치게 피우는 것은 건강에 유해하다 Too much smoking is bad for [harmful to] our health.
▶ 수면부족은 건강에 유해하다 Lack of sleep is bad for health.
▶ 지나친 운동은 유해하다 Too much exercise will do one harm.
■ —물 a harmful object —식품 poisonous [harmful] food

유해 遺骸 a (dead) body; a corpse; *sb's* remains; 〈유골〉 ashes; bone
▶ 그의 유해는 흑석동의 국립묘지로 운구되었다 His corpse was carried to the national cemetery at Hŭksŏkdong.

유행 流行 1 〈의복 등의〉 (a) fashion; (a) vogue; 〈유행형(型)〉 a style; a mode; 〈일시적 대유행〉 a craze; a fad; 〈대중적 인기〉 popularity
▶ 이것이 올해의 유행이다 This is the fashion style this year.
▶ 당시의 여성들은 무릎까지 오는 가죽 부츠를 신는 것이 유행이었다 It was the fashion of the time for women to wear knee-length leather boots.
〈유행의〉 유행의 변천 changes of fashion / 유행의 첨단을 걷다 lead the fashion; set the fashion ((to the motoring world))
▶ 파리는 유행의 본고장이다 Paris is the wellspring of fashion.
▶ 이것이 최신 유행의 수영복이다 This is the latest fashion in swim suits.
▶ 그녀는 최신 유행의 머리 모양을 하고 있었다 She wore her hair in a modish [the latest] style.
〈유행이[은]〉 유행이 지나가다 go out of fashion [vogue]; become old-fashioned; lose popularity
▶ 유행은 변하기 쉬운 것이다 Fashion is changeable.
▶ 유행은 사라지는 법이다 A thing in fashion soon goes out of it.
▶ 여성복의 유행은 빨리 왔다 빨리 사라진다 Women's fashions [Fashions in women's clothings] come and go quickly.
▶ 여성복의 유행은 파리에서 시작된다고 한다 It is said that fashions in women's clothes begin in Paris.
▶ 컴퓨터 게임의 유행은 전국적으로 확대되었다 A craze [A vogue] for computer games spread all over the country.
〈유행을〉 유행을 창조하다 set the fashion / 유행을 좇다 follow [run after] the fashion; take up the latest fad [fashion]; follow the latest styles
▶ 그녀는 언제나 유행을 좇고 있다 She is always following (the) fashion. ⇌ (口) She is a trendy girl.
▶ 이 스타일의 슈트는 유행을 타지 않는다 A suit of this style is not subject to changes in fashion.
▶ 나는 유행을 따르는 것은 별로 좋아하지 않는다 I don't particularly like to follow the fashions.
〈유행에〉 유행에 뒤지다 be behind the fashion / 유행에 따르다 conform to (the) fashion / 유행에 뒤떨어지지 않도록 하다 keep up with (the) fashion
▶ 그는 유행에 민감하다 He is susceptible to changes in fashion.
▶ 그녀는 유행에 뒤떨어지지 않으려고 애썼다 She tried hard to keep up with the fashions.
▶ 그것은 단지 한때의 유행에 지나지 않는다 It is only a passion fad [fancy].
—유행하다 be in fashion; come into vogue; become popular
♦ 유행하기 시작하다 come into fashion [vogue]; become popular / 굉장히 유행하고 있다 be much in fashion [vogue]; be very popular; have a great vogue / 유행시키다 set the fashion; bring into fashion; popularize
▶ 롱 스커트가 유행한 것이 언제였지? When did long skirts come into fashion [become fashionable]?
▶ 올 봄에는 굽이 낮은 구두가 유행할 것 같다 Flat shoes are going to be in fashion [vogue] this spring.
▶ 이 노래는 학생들 사이에서 굉장히 유행하고 있다 This song is much in vogue [very popular] with the students.
2 〈병·폐단의〉 prevalence ♦ 콜레라의 유행 the prevalence of cholera
—유행하다 prevail; be widespread
▶ 지금 학생들 사이에 감기가 유행하고 있다 Colds are widespread now among the pupils.
▶ 열병이 온나라에 유행하고 있었다 The fever raged throughout the country.
▶ 뇌물이 널리 유행하고 있다 Bribery is widely prevalent.
■ —어 a word [phrase] in fashion; a popular [cant] word [phrase]; a cant; a catchword —형(型) a fashionable style [shape]; an up-

유행가 流行歌 a popular song ■—가수 a popular-song singer; a singer of popular songs

유행병 流行病 an epidemic ◆유행병을 없애다 stamp out an epidemic ▶유행병이 돌고 있다 An epidemic is raging [prevalent].

유행성 流行性 〔醫〕 epidemicity ◆유행성의 epidemic ■—뇌염 〔醫〕 epidemic encephalitis —안염 an epidemic ophthalmia

유행성감기 流行性感氣 (an epidemic of) influenza; grippe; (口) (the) flu ▶그는 유행성감기에 걸려 있다 He is suffering from influenza. ▶그녀는 심한 유행성감기로 며칠 째 누워 있다 She has been laid up with a bad cold for a few days.

유행지 流行地 an infected district [area] ◆콜레라의 유행지 a cholera-infected district

유향 乳香 olibanum; frankincense

유혈 流血 bloodshed ◆유혈 참사 a bloody [sanguinary] affair / 유혈의 참극을 빚다 create a scene of bloodshed / 유혈사태로 번지다 develop into an affair of bloodshed / 유혈이 낭자하다 be covered with blood / 유혈을 피하다 prevent bloodshed / 유혈로 끝나다 result in bloodshed ▶그 반정부 시위는 유혈 참사를 불러일으켰다 The anti-government demonstration developed into a bloody affair [led to bloodshed].

유형 有形 materiality; concreteness ◆유형의 material; concrete; physical; 〔法〕 tangible / 유형화하다 materialize; embody ■—무역 visible trade —문화재 tangible cultural properties —물 a material being; a concrete object —자본 a corporeal capital —재산 [자산] material [tangible] assets; material [corporeal] property; tangibles —체 a material body

유형 流刑 transportation; (a) banishment; exile ◆유형에 처하다 condemn sb to exile; banish; exile; transport; deport ▶나폴레옹은 프랑스로부터 종신 유형에 처해졌다 Napoleon was exiled from France for life. ■—수 an exile; a deported criminal; a deportee —지 a penal colony [settlement]; a place of exile

유형 類型 a type; a pattern; a group ◆유형적인 stereotype(d); typical ▶유형별로 분류하시오 Classify according to the types. ■—학 typology

유형무형 有形無形 ◆유형무형의 material and immaterial [spiritual]; visible and invisible; tangible and intangible ▶나는 그에게서 유형무형의 많은 도움을 받았다 I received great support, both material and moral, from him.

유혹 誘惑 (a) temptation; (a) lure; (詩) (an) allurement; (a) seduction ◆대도시의 유혹 the allurements [temptations] of a big city / 바다의 유혹 the lure [call] of the sea / 술의 유혹 the temptation of drink / 유혹에 견디다 resist [withstand] temptation / 유혹에 이기다 overcome a temptation / 유혹에 빠뜨리다 lead sb into temptation / 유혹에 빠지다 fall into temptation / 유혹과 싸우다 fight [struggle] against temptation / 술을 마시고 싶은 유혹에 넘어가다 give way to [yield] to the temptation to drink ▶서울은 유혹이 많다 Seoul is full of temptations [enticements]. ▶대도시에는 젊은이들을 파멸로 이끄는 유혹이 많다 There are in big cities various temptations which lead young people to ruin. ▶유혹에 넘어가면 안된다 Don't yield [give way] to the temptation. ▶나는 그 드레스를 사고 싶은 유혹을 뿌리칠 수 없었다 I could not resist the temptation to buy the dress. —유혹하다 tempt; lure; entice; seduce

---
解說 ***tempt***는 유혹하여 선악의 판단을 잃게 하는 것, ***lure***는 사람의 욕망·호기심을 불러일으켜 나쁜 일에 끌어들이는 것, ***entice***는 교묘한 설득 등으로 나쁜 일을 하도록 만드는 것이며, ***seduce***는 특히 젊은 여자를 유혹하는 것을 나타낸다.

▶뇌물로 나를 유혹하려고 해도 소용없다 It's no use trying to tempt me with a bribe. ▶그 남자는 소녀를 달콤한 말로 유혹했다 The man seduced the girl with honeyed words.

유화 乳化 emulsification —유화하다 emulsify ■—제 an emulsifier

유화 油畫 an oil painting; a picture in oils ▶그는 젊었을 때 종종 유화를 그렸다 He often painted in oils when young. ■—구(具) oil paints; oil colors; oils —전람회 an exhibition of oils —화가 an oil painter

유화 宥和 appeasement; propitiation —유화하다 appease; placate ■—론자 an appeaser —정책 an appeasement policy: 유화정책은 종속을 의미한다 Appeasement signifies subjection.

유화 類化 〈동화(同化)〉 assimilation —유화하다 〈동화하다〉 assimilate

유황 硫黃 〈황〉 sulfur; sulphur; brimstone ◆유황의 sulfurous; sulphurous; sulfuric; sulphuric / 유황분[질]을 빼다 desulfur(ize) ■—연고 sulfur ointment —천 a sulfur spring —화(華) flowers of sulfur; sublimed sulfur

유회 流會 the adjournment of a meeting —유회하다 adjourn a meeting —유회되다 be adjourned; be called off ▶총회는 참석자가 적어서[정원 미달로] 유회되었다 The general meeting was adjourned on account of scanty attendance.

유효 有效 〈법적인〉 validity; 〈표 등의〉 availability; 〈약의〉 effectiveness; effectuality; efficiency; efficacy —유효하다 valid; available; effective; effectual; efficacious; 〈서술적〉 hold [be, stand] good; 〔法〕 remain in force ◆유효한 계약 a valid contract / 4월 1일부터 유효한 규정 a rule effective from April 1st / 유효한 방법 an effectual measure / 유효하게 쓰다 put (*one's*) money [time]) to a good use; make good use of ((it))

▶ 이 계약[규정]은 1년 더 유효하다 This agreement [rule] holds [stands] good [remains in force] for another year.
▶ 이 표는 발행 당일에 한해 유효하다 This ticket is valid [good] on the day of issue only.
▶ 도서 대출 카드는 1년간 유효하며 갱신할 수도 있다 The library card is valid [good, available] for a year and renewable.
▶ 새 규정은 내달부터 유효하다 The new rules will go into effect [come into force] next month.
▶ 그 판결은 아직 유효하다 The decision still stands.
■ ―기간 〔法〕 the term of validity [availability]; the available period : 유효기간의 만료(일) the expiration (date) of the validity time / 유효기간은 3일이다 hold [be available] for three days ―사거리[사정] the effective [available] range 《of a gun》 ―수요 an effective [effectual] demand ―숫자 《數》 a significant digit [figure] ―열량 available heat ―전압 effective voltage ―증명 a certificate of validity ―타(打) a telling blow ―투표 a valid ballot ―표 an available ticket

유훈 遺訓 instructions [teachings] left by the departed; one's last [dying] injunctions
♦ 스승의 유훈을 소중히 여기다 cherish the teachings left by one's master

유휴 遊休 idleness; unemployment
■ ―공장 a nonoperating plant ―물자 idle goods ―생산[노동]력 idle production capacity [labor] ―시설 idle facilities; unused equipment ―자금 idle [uninvested] money; floating money; money lying idle ―자본 unemployed [idle] capital; idle [dormant, sleeping] funds ―자산 idle properties ―자재 idle materials; materials lying idle

유흥 遊興 (worldly) pleasures; merrymaking; amusements; diversion; 〈俗〉 a spree
▶ 그는 요즘 유흥에 빠져 있다 He indulges in pleasure these days.
―유흥하다 make merry; make pleasures; disport oneself; be [go] on the spree
■ ―가 ⇨ 환락(～가) ―비 entertainment costs; expenses for pleasures [a spree]; 《俗》 the price of a spree ―세 the amusement [entertainment] tax ―업소 a merrymaking place; a pleasure resort ―음식세 the tax on amusement, food and drink ―장[지] an amusement quarter; gay quarters; a pleasure resort

유희 遊戲 a play; 〈놀이〉 a game; 〈경기〉 sports; 〈오락〉 a pastime; amusements
♦ 유희를 즐기다 enjoy a game; amuse oneself at a game
▶ 그것은 말의 유희이다 It's a play on words.
―유희하다 play; play a game
■ ―본능 play [sportive] instinct ―실 a recreation [美口 rec] room; 〈어린이의〉 a playroom ―장 a playground; 〈오락장〉 an amusement center; a place of amusement; a recreation [美口 rec] hall

육 六 six
♦ 제 육[6] the sixth / 6분의 1 one-sixth / 6세

된 사내 아이 a boy of six / 6대 1 six of one / 6대 도시 the six biggest cities / 6자(字)를 쓰다 write a six

육 肉 (the) flesh
♦ 영과 육 flesh and spirit

육가 六價 〔化〕 ♦ 육가의 sexivalent ■ ―원소 a hexad ―크롬 hexavalent chromium

육각 六角 〈육모〉 six angles; a hexagon; a sexangle
♦ 육각의 hexagonal; sexangular ■ ―형 a hexagon; a sexangle

육감 六感 〈직감〉 the sixth sense; a hunch; (an) intuition; extrasensory perception
♦ 육감으로 《guided》 by the sixth sense
▶ 나는 항상 육감으로 행동해 왔다 I've always played my hunches.
▶ 나는 육감으로 그가 어떤 중대한 일을 우리에게 감추고 있다는 것을 알았다 I had a hunch that he was hiding something important from us.
▶ 나는 육감으로 그것을 알 수 있다 My sixth sense tells me that.

육감 肉感 〈육체적 느낌〉 the senses of the flesh; 〈성적인〉 sexual feeling; animal passion; carnal desire; sensual pleasure
♦ 육감적인 여자 a sexy woman / 육감적 미인 a voluptuous beauty / 육감적인 입술 sensual lips / 육감적(인) suggestive; sensual; voluptuous / 육감을 도발하다 excite one's lust [carnal desire]
■ ―주의 sensualism

육갑 六甲 〈육십 갑자〉 the sexagenary cycle of human life; 〈시시한 생각〉 a nonsense idea
♦ 육갑 떨다 speak [talk] sheer nonsense

육개장 肉― spicy stew like beef soup

육계 肉桂 〔藥〕 cinnamon; cassia (bark)

육공육호 六０六號 〈매독치료용(用)으로〉 〔藥〕 six-o-six("606") remedy; 〈商標〉 Salvarsan

육교 陸橋 an overbridge; (美) an overpass; 〈인도교〉 a footbridge; a girder bridge; a viaduct; 〈두 육지를 연결하는〉 〔地〕 a land bridge

육군 陸軍 the army; the military service
♦ 육군의 military; army
▶ 그는 육군에 들어가기를[입대하기를] 원한다 He wants to enter [enlist in] the army.
■ ―군악대 a military band ―대장 a general ―대학 the Military Staff College; the War College ―무관 〈대사관의〉 a military attaché ―본부 the Army Headquarters ―사관[장교] a military [an army] officer ―사관학교 the Military Academy ―사관학교 생도[사관 후보생] a military cadet ―참모총장 the Army Chief of Staff

육대주 六大洲 the Six Continents

육도 陸稻 〈밭벼〉 rice grown in a dry field; upland rice

육두구 肉豆筵 〔植〕 a nutmeg (tree)

육로 陸路 a land [an overland] route
♦ 육로로 by land; by an overland route; overland
▶ 그들은 북경에서 파리까지 육로로 여행했다 They traveled overland from Beijing to Paris.
■ ―수송 transport by land; overland trans-

육류 肉類 meat; flesh; flesh-meat

육면체 六面體 〔數〕 a hexahedron 《pl. ~s, -hedra》 ◆육면체의 hexahedral ■정— a regular hexahedron; a cube

육모 六— a hexagon; a sexangle ◆육모난 hexagonal; sexangular ■—방망이 a six-sided club [cudgel]

육미 六味 〈여섯가지 맛〉 the six flavors 《= bitter, sour, sweet, pungent, salty and flat》

육미 肉味 meat dishes ■—붙이 meat; meat dishes

육박 肉薄 —육박하다 press sb hard; close in upon sb; come to close quarters 《with》; 〈경쟁에서〉 tread close on sb's heels; run sb hard [close] ◆적진에 육박하다 carry the fighting to the enemy's camp
▶ 아군은 적진에 육박했다 Our troops pressed the enemy's positions [camp] hard.
■—전 bitter fighting at close quarters; a hand-to-hand fight; 〈경기〉 a close contest [game]; a hard-fought game

육발이 六— a person with six toes; a car with six wheels

육배 六倍 six times; sextuple

육법 六法 the six codes (of laws) ■—전서 a Compendium of Laws; the Statute Book; a complete book of the Six Major Laws

육봉 肉峰 〈낙타 등의 혹〉 a hump
▶ 단봉 낙타[아라비아 낙타]는 등에 육봉이 하나 있고 쌍봉 낙타는 육봉이 두 개 있다 The dromedary [Arabian camel] has one hump, and the Bactrian camel has two humps on the back.

육분의 六分儀 a sextant ■—자리 〔天〕 the Sextant; Sextans

육붕 陸棚 〔地〕 a continental shelf ⇨ 대륙붕

육붙이 肉— 〈고기 요리〉 meat dishes ⇨ 육미 (~붙이)

육삼삼제 六三三制 〔教〕 the 6·3·3 system of education; the 6·3·3 educational [schooling] system

육상 陸上 (the) land; (the) ground; 〈선상(船上)에 대하여〉 (the) shore ◆육상의[으로, 에서] on land [shore]; ashore
▶ 그들은 채소를 육상으로 수송하고 있다 They transport vegetable by land.
■—경기 field and track events; athletic sports —경기대회 a track and field meet —근무 〈선박에 대하여〉 shore duty [service]; service ashore; 〈항공에 대하여〉 ground duty [service] —부대 a land force —생활 life on land [shore] —운송 overland [ground] transport —운송비 overland freight

육서 陸棲 ◆육서의 〔動〕 terrestrial; living on land; land-dwelling; land-living ■—동물 terrestrial animals —생물 the terrestrial

육성 肉聲 a (natural) voice; a (human) voice ◆육성과 같은 음색을 내다 produce the correct sounds of the human voice
▶ 마이크 소리는 육성과는 다르다 Voices through a microphone differ from natural voices.

육성 育成 〈길러냄〉 raising 《children》; upbringing; rearing —육성하다 bring up; rear; raise; foster; nurture; train; educate; encourage

육성회 育成會 a parent-teacher association ■—비 〈학교의〉 school supporting fees

육속하다 陸續— 〈계속하여 끊이지 않다〉 be successive; be continuous; be consecutive
◆육속하여 successively; in succession; in a row; continuously; one after another

육손이 六— a person having six fingers

육송 陸送 land transportation; ground [overland] transport ■—화물 overland freight

육수 肉水 meat juice; meat [beef] stock; gravy; broth

육순 六旬 〈60일〉 sixty days; 〈60세〉 sixty years of age ◆육순의 sexagenarian ■—노인 a sexagenarian

육식 肉食 〈고기를 먹음〉 meat-eating 《사람》; flesh-eating 《동물》; 〈요리〉 a meat dish
◆육식의 carnivorous / 육식을 끊다 abstain from meat dishes [meat and fish]
▶ 나는 육식보다 채식을 좋아한다 I prefer a vegetable diet to meat dish.
—육식하다 〈사람이〉 eat meat; 〈동물이〉 eat flesh; live on flesh
■—가 a meat-eater —동물 a carnivore; a carnivorous [flesh-eating, predatory] animal; an animal of prey; (총칭) Carnivora —인종 a meat-eating race —조 a bird of prey; a predatory bird —충 a predacious [predatory] insect

육신 肉身 the flesh; the body; flesh and blood

육십 六十 sixty; threescore
◆제 육십[60] the sixtieth / 60주년 기념제 the sixtieth [diamond] anniversary / 60대의 사람 a sexagenarian; a sexagenary; a person in his sixties

육아 肉芽 〔醫〕 granulation ◆육아가 생기다 granulate ■—종(腫) a granuloma 《pl. ~s, -mata》

육아 育兒 baby care; childcare; infant rearing; nursing [upbringing] of infants [children] —육아하다 nurse [bring up] infants; rear children
■—법 a method of child-rearing; the art of rearing infants; how to rear [nurse] infants —비 childcare expenses —시간 nursing time —식(食) baby food —실 a nursery —원(園) a baby farm —원(院) 〈버린 아이의〉 a foundling hospital; 〈고아의〉 an orphanage; 〈일반의〉 a nursery home; (美) a nursery school —(전)서 a book on child-rearing [childcare] —휴가 a maternity leave

육안 肉眼 the naked [unaided] eye
◆육안으로 보이는 별 stars visible to ordinary sight / 육안으로 검사하다 examine with the naked [unaided] eye / 육안으로 보다 see with the naked eye / 육안으로 보이다 can be observed by the naked eye; be visible to the naked eye
▶ 그것은 육안으로 볼 수 없을 만큼 작다 It is too small to be visible to the naked eye.
■—검사 examination with the naked eye;

macrography

육연풍 陸軟風 〔地〕 a land breeze ＝육풍(陸風)

육영 育英 〈영재를 기름〉 education **—육영하다** educate
■**—사업** a scholarship program; educational work **—자금** a scholarship **—제도** a scholarship system **—회[재단]** a scholarship society [foundation]

육욕 肉慾 carnal desires [lust]; the appetites [lusts] of the flesh; animal passions; sensual appetite
♦육욕을 억제하다 restrain [control] *one's* passions; be continent / 육욕을 채우다 gratify *one's* lusts; satisfy *one's* sensual appetites
▶그는 도덕적으로 타락하여 육욕에 빠졌다 He was morally ruined and indulged in sensual pleasures.
■**—주의** sensualism; carnalism

육우 肉牛 beef cattle ▶그는 육우 100두를 기른다 He raises 100 head of beef cattle.

육운 陸運 〈육상운송〉 land carriage [transportation]; transportation by land; overland transportation ■**—회사** a land transportation company

육전 陸戰 a land combat [battle]; land warfare [fighting]; warfare on land **—육전하다** fight on land

육종 肉腫 〈종양〉 〔醫〕 a sarcoma (*pl.* ~s, -mata)

육종 育種 (selective) breeding of animals [plants]; developing new varieties of plants [breeds of animals] **—육종하다** breed
■**교배—** breeding by crossing **교잡—** breeding by hybridization ■**—가(家)** a breeder **—학** breeding science **—학자** a breeding scientist

육중주 六重奏 〔樂〕 a sextet(te) ■**—단** a sextet(te)

육중창 六重唱 〔樂〕 a sextet(te)

육중하다 肉重— 〈몸피가〉 bulky and heavy; 〈건물이〉 massive; massy; ponderous; 〈몸집이〉 heavily built; stout
♦육중한 걸음걸이 a heavy tread; a clamp [clump] / 육중한 구조물 a massive [ponderous] structure / 체격이 육중한 사람 a man of heavy frame

육즙 肉汁 meat juice; gravy; broth

육지 陸地 (the) land; 〈배에서 본〉 (the) shore
♦육지 동물 a land animal / 육지가 보이는 곳에서 within sight of land / 육지를 밟다 set foot on land / 육지에 살다 live on land / 육지에 오르다 go ashore [on shore]; get to land / (배가) 육지에 접근하다 stand in for the shore; approach land / 육지로 둘러싸이다 be landlocked
■**—측량** a land survey

육질 肉質 flesh; fleshy substance; 〈과육〉 pulpy substance; pulp ♦다(多)육질의 과실 fleshy fruit

육척 六尺 six feet
♦육척의 사나이 a six-footer; a 6-foot man

육체 肉滯 〈고기를 먹고 생긴 체증〉 indigestion due to eating meat

육체 肉體 the flesh; the body
♦육체와 정신 body and soul / 육체적 결함 a physical defect / 육체적 고통 bodily pain; physical suffering / 육체적 만족 sensual gratification; gratification of the flesh / 육체적 욕망 the appetites of the flesh / 육체적 충동 the body urge / 육체적 쾌락 sensual pleasures; the pleasures of the senses [the flesh] / 육체의 corporal; carnal; fleshly; bodily; physical; sensual
■**—관계** connection; sexual relations [intercourse] **—미** physical beauty; the beauty of the body **—미인** a woman of great physical beauty; a curvaceous woman **—파여인** 〈성적 매력이 있는〉 a glamorous girl; (口) a glamor girl

육체노동 肉體勞動 physical labor [work]; manual [muscular] labor ♦육체노동을 하다 do physical [manual] labor ■**—자** a (physical [muscular]) laborer; a manual worker

육촌 六寸 **1** 〈재종(再從)〉 a second [secondary] cousin; the sixth degree of consanguinity **2** 〈여섯 치〉 six inches

육친 六親 the six family relations (▶*one's* father, mother, older brother(s), younger brother(s), wife and children)

육친 肉親 〈관계〉 blood relationship; 〈혈족〉 blood relatives; *one's* (own) flesh and blood
♦육친에게 버림받다 be given up by *one's* own flesh and blood

육탄 肉彈 a human body (to be) used for suicide attack; a human bullet [bomb]
■**—공격** a suicide [sacrifice] attack **—전** a suicidal attack; a hand-to-hand battle [fighting]

육포 肉脯 a slice of dried meat [beef]; jerked meat; jerky

육품 陸風 〔地〕 〈육지에서 바다로 부는〉 a land breeze

육필 肉筆 *one's* own handwriting; an autograph (⇨ 친필) ♦육필 편지 a handwritten letter / 육필로 in *one's* own handwriting

육해공 陸海空 land, sea and air
♦육해공의 입체 공격 a coordinated attack of the army, navy and air forces
■**—군** the land, sea and air forces; the army, navy and air forces **—군 장병** officers and men of the armed forces **—합동 작전** joint [concerted] operations of the army, navy and air forces

육해군 陸海軍 the army and navy; military and naval forces; the land and sea forces
■**—인** soldiers and sailors

육혈포 六穴砲 a six-chambered revolver; a six-shooter; a pistol

육회 肉膾 a dish of minced [sliced] raw beef

윤 潤 gloss ⇨ 윤기
▶그녀의 머릿결은 윤이 난다 She has glossy hair. ⇌ Her hair has a fine gloss.

윤- 閏- 〈윤으로 든〉 embolism; intercalation
■**—초** a leap second

윤간 輪姦 multiple rape 《of a girl》; gang rape
—윤간하다 commit gang rape

윤곽 輪廓 **1** 〈겉모양〉 contour; outlines;

profile; 〈사진·책표지 등의 윤곽선〉 a fillet
♦ 얼굴의 윤곽 the contour of *one's* face
▶ 그녀의 얼굴은 윤곽이 뚜렷하다 She has very regular [well-chiseled] features.
▶ 그는 내 얼굴의 윤곽을 연필로 그렸다 He outlined my face with a pencil.
2 〈개략〉 an outline 《of a scheme》; a sketch
♦ 윤곽을 파악하다 grasp the general idea [outline] 《of》
▶ 검사는 사건의 윤곽을 말했다 The prosecutor gave an outline of the affair.

윤기 潤氣 gloss; brightness; luster; polish; shine; sheen

> 解說 *gloss*는 광택제를 바르거나, 갈고 닦거나 또는 특수한 끝손질을 해서 생기는 표면적인 광택, *luster*는 빛의 반사에 의하여 생기는 광택, *polish*, *shine*은 갈고 닦아서 낸 광택, *sheen*은 천·깃털·광물 등의 표면 광택이다.

♦ 윤기 있는 얼굴 a bright complexion / 윤기 있는 glossy; lustrous; bright; shiny / 윤기가 없다 have no gloss; be lusterless [dull, dry, muddy]; 〈얼굴에〉 look pale; have an unhealthy complexion / 윤기가 흐르다 have fine luster; have a good polish
▶ 그녀는 얼굴에 윤기가 돈다[없다] She has a ruddy [bad] complexion.
▶ 이 진주 목걸이는 윤기가 좋다 This pearl necklace has a fine luster.

윤나다 潤— be glossy [lustrous, bright, shiny, polished]; 〈얼굴이〉 be sleek [slick]

윤내다 潤— gloss; glaze; make (it) glossy; bring out the luster; brighten; put a polish [gloss] on; polish

윤년 閏年 a leap year; an intercalary [a bissextile] year ▶ 윤년은 4년마다 든다 A leap year occurs [comes] every four years.

윤달 閏— a leap month; an intercalary [a bissextile] month

윤독 輪讀 reading by rotation —**윤독하다** take turns in reading; read 《a book》 in turn [by turns]

윤락 淪落 ruin; fall; corruption
—**윤락하다** be ruined; ruin *oneself* 《by dissipation》; be corrupted; go to the bad
■ —가 a brothel —여성 a ruined [an abandoned, a fallen] woman; a delinquent girl

윤리 倫理 ethics; morals
♦ 윤리적 행위 a moral act / 윤리적 ethical; moral / 윤리적으로 ethically; morally
▶ 그는 윤리적 판단이 결여돼 있었다 He lacked [was lacking in] ethical judgments [moral sense].
■ 실천— practical ethics ■ —학 ethics; moral philosophy —학자 an ethicist; a moral philosopher

윤무 輪舞 a round dance ⇨ 원무(圓舞)
윤번 輪番 turn; rotation
♦ 윤번으로 in turn; by turns; alternately; by [in] rotation
▶ 경비원들은 윤번으로 경계를 섰다 The guards stood on watch in turn [by turns, alternately].

—**윤번하다** take turns 《at driving》 in rotation; rotate

윤번제 輪番制 a rotation system ▶ 그들은 윤번제로 의장이 되었다 They took the chairman in rotation. ▶ 우리는 윤번제로 당번을 선다 We are on duty by [in] rotation.

윤삭 閏朔 a leap month ⇨ 윤달
윤색 潤色 (an) embellishment; coloring
—**윤색하다** embellish; color 《a report》; adorn; ornament; give color to 《*one's* account》; dress 《the facts》 up ♦ 이야기를 윤색하다 embellish *one's* story

윤생 輪生 〔植〕 verticillation ⇨ 돌려나기
윤선 輪船 a steamship ⇨ 기선
윤월 閏月 a leap month ⇨ 윤달
윤음 綸音 〈임금의 말씀〉 the king's words; a royal message

윤일 閏日 a leap day; an intercalary day
윤작 輪作 〔農〕 crop rotation ⇨ 돌려짓기
윤전 輪轉 rotation —**윤전하다** rotate; revolve
■ —기 (印) a rotary press [machine] —등사기 a rotary mimeography

윤지 綸旨 the king's words ⇨ 윤음
윤창 輪唱 〔樂〕 a troll; a round ⇨ 돌림노래
—**윤창하다** troll ▶ 소녀들은 즐겁게 윤창했다 The girls trolled merrily.

윤택 潤澤 **1** 〈광택〉 (a) gloss; (a) luster; glaze
2 〈풍부〉 abundance; plenty
—**윤택하다** 〈풍부하다〉 abundant; ample; bountiful; bountiful; 〈살림이 넉넉하다〉 rich; wealthy; well-to-do; well-off
♦ 윤택한 살림 a comfortable circumstance; a well-off living / 윤택하게 abundantly; in abundance; plentifully; plenteously / 윤택하게 살다 live well; be well-off; be comfortably off; live in easy [comfortable] circumstances / 윤택해지다 grow rich; become prosperous; come to wealth

윤허 允許 royal permission [grant, approval, sanction] ♦ 윤허를 바라다 ask for [submit for] royal sanction —**윤허하다** grant (royal) sanction; be pleased to give sanction 《to》

윤형 輪形 〈바퀴같은 둥근 모양〉 a circle; a ring (shape) ♦ 윤형의 ring(-shaped); wheel-shaped; circular

윤화 輪禍 a traffic accident ♦ 윤화를 입다 meet with a traffic accident ▶ 그는 윤화로 죽었다 He was killed in a traffic accident.

윤활 潤滑 lubrication
—**윤활하다** lubricous; smooth
■ —유 lubricating oil; lubricant; (美) lube oil: 윤활유 역할을 하다 help (to) smooth —장치 a lubricating device —제 a lubricant

윤회 輪廻 **1** 〈차례로 돌아감〉 rotation; constant mutation —**윤회하다** rotate; mutate constantly
2 〔佛敎〕 metempsychosis; transmigration of souls; the cycles of life —**윤회하다** transmigrate
■ —설 transmigrationism

율 律 **1** 〈법규〉 a law; a rule; a regulation; a statute; 〈계율〉 (Buddhist) commandments; 〈기율〉 discipline; order
2 〈운율〉 a rhythm

율 率 〈비율〉 a rate; a ratio; a proportion; a percentage; 〔物〕 an index; 〔數〕 a constant ♦ 높은 출생[사망]률 the high birth [death] rate ■ 백분— (a) percentage 팽창률 a coefficient of expansion 평균— the average rate 할인— a discount rate

율동 律動 〈리듬〉 (a) rhythm; 〈주기적 운동〉 (a) rhythmic movement ♦ 율동적인 rhythmic; rhythmical
■ —감각 a rhythmical sense —미 rhythmical beauty —체조 rhythmic gymnastics

율령 律令 a statute; a law; an ordinance

율리우스력 —曆 the Julian calendar

율모기 〔動〕 a grass [ring] snake

율무 〔植〕 adlay; adlai

율법 律法 〈법률〉 (a) law; 〈규칙〉 a rule; 〈계율〉 commandments; 〈신이 내린〉 a divine law ♦ 율법을 따르다 obey the law / 율법을 지키다 keep the rule / 율법을 정하다 establish [lay down, make] a law [regulations]
▶ 그는 신의 율법을 배반했다 He violated [broke] a divine law.

율시 律詩 a stanza of eight lines (with rhymes, tones, and antitheses); a style of Chinese verse

융 絨 (cotton) flannel

융 〈스위스의 심리학자〉 Jung, Carl Gustav (1875-1961)

융기 隆起 a protuberance; bulging; rising; 〔地質〕 elevation; upheaval; upthrust
♦ 지표의 융기 upheavals on the earth
— 융기하다 rise; upheave; protrude; bulge
■ 화산성— a volcanic upheaval — 해안 an uplifted coast

융단 絨緞 a carpet
♦ 두꺼운 융단을 깐 마루 a thick-carpeted floor; a floor covered with a deep-pile carpet / 마루에 융단을 깔다 lay [put down] a carpet on the floor; carpet the floor
▶ 화단은 진홍색 융단을 깐 것 같았다 The flower bed was (like) a scarlet carpet.
▶ 들에는 들꽃이 만발하여 융단을 깔아놓은 것 같았다 The fields were carpeted with wild flowers in full glory.
■ 페르시아[터키]— a Persian [Turkish] carpet [rug] ■ —폭격 carpet [blanket, area] bombing

융모 絨毛 wool; 〔解〕 a villus 《pl. -li》
■ —조직 〔植〕 villosity

융비술 隆鼻術 〔醫〕 rhinoplasty; nasal plastic surgery; a rhinoplastic operation

융성 隆盛 prosperity
▶ 나라의 융성은 국민의 노력에 달렸다 National prosperity depends upon the efforts of the people.
— 융성하다 prosperous; flourishing; thriving
♦ 융성해지다 grow in prosperity; prosper; flourish
▶ 그 나라는 18세기 후반에 한창 융성했다 The nation reached the summit [zenith] of prosperity in the latter half of the eighteenth century.

융숭하다 隆崇— hospitable; cordial; heartwarming
♦ 융숭히 cordially; hospitably / 융숭한 대접을 받다 be received cordially; be entertained [treated] hospitably / 융숭히 대접하다 entertain *sb* hospitably
▶ 우리는 융숭한 대접을 받았다 We were hospitably received.

융자 融資 financing; 〈대부금〉 a loan; an advance
▶ 그는 집을 사기 위해 은행에 1천만원의 융자를 의뢰했다 He asked the bank for a loan of 10,000,000 won to purchase a house.
— 융자하다 finance 《an enterprise》; accommodate *sb* with a loan; loan *sb*; furnish funds 《to》
▶ 은행은 우리 회사에 융자해 줄 것이다 The bank will furnish our firm with funds.
▶ 은행이 신규사업에 융자하기는 쉽지 않다 It is not easy for the bank to finance a new business.
■ 구제— relief financing ; a relief loan 긴급— an emergency loan 단기— a short(-term) loan; 〈은행간 요구불의〉 a call loan ■ —금 a loan —신청 a request for a loan

융점 融點 the melting point ⇨ 융해(~점)

융통 融通 1 〈돌려씀〉 accommodation; finance; (a) loan; 〈유통〉 circulation
— 융통하다 〈유통하다〉 circulate; 〈빌려주다〉 lend; 《美》 loan (money); accommodate 《*sb* with a loan》
♦ 기업에 자금을 융통해주다 finance an enterprise / 아무에게 5백만원을 융통해 주다 lend *sb* 5,000,000 won
▶ 돈 좀 융통해 주시오 Please lend me a little money.
▶ 나는 은행에서 5백만원을 융통했다 The bank accommodated [supplied] me with a loan of 5,000,000 won.
▶ 그는 내게 2만원을 융통해 주었다 He accommodated me with twenty thousand won.
▶ 3만원을 융통해 줄 수 있겠니? Can you lend me thirty thousand won?
▶ 월말까지 200만원을 융통해 주시겠습니까? Will you lend me two million won until the end of the month?
2 ⇨ 융통성
■ —력 *one's* financing ability —어음 an accommodation bill; a negotiable paper —자본 a circulating capital —증권 a negotiable instrument

융통성 融通性 flexibility; elasticity; versatility; adaptability
♦ 융통성이 없는 사람 a straitlaced person / 융통성이 있는 elastic; versatile; adaptable; accommodating / 융통성이 없는 unadaptable; hidebound; inflexible; inelastic / 융통성 있게 처신하다 adapt *oneself* to (altered) conditions [to new circumstances]
▶ 그는 융통성이 있는 사내다 He is a versatile person.

융합 融合 fusion; union; 〈융화〉 harmony; unity ♦ 형식과 내용의 완전한 융합 a total fusion [harmony] of form and content
— 융합하다 fuse [blend] into one; unite; merge; become one [merged] 《with》; 〈융화하다〉 be in harmony 《with》

▶ 놋쇠는 구리와 아연을 융합해 만든다 They make brass by fusing copper and zinc.
■ 핵— 〔物〕 nuclear fusion
융해 融解 〔物〕 fusion; melting; dissolution
—융해하다 fuse; melt; dissolve; thaw
▶ 납은 다른 금속보다 낮은 온도에서 융해된다 Lead will fuse at a lower temperature than some other metals.
■ —열 the heat of fusion; the melting heat —점[온도] the melting point [temperature]
융화 融化 〔化〕 deliquescence
—융화하다 deliquesce; soften
융화 融和 〈조화〉 harmony (between, among); melting; 〈화해〉 reconciliation
▶ 다민족 국가에서는 인종의 융화가 큰 문제다 Multiracial nations usually have a big problem with racial integration.
—융화하다 harmonize [get along] with; 〈화목하다〉 be melted together; 〈화해하다〉 be reconciled (with)
▶ 그는 누구와도 쉽게 융화한다 He becomes friends with anyone easily.
융흥 隆興 prosperity; rise —융흥하다 prosper; flourish; thrive; rise
윷 1 〈놀이〉 (the game of) yut; a stick game 2 〈윷짝 네 개가 모두 젖혀진 것〉 4 points (made by a cast of yut sticks) 3 ⇨ 윷짝
윷놀이 playing yut; a game of yut
—윷놀이하다 play (a game of) yut
윷밭 checks on a yut board
윷짝 yut sticks; the sticks used in playing yut
♦ 윷짝 가르듯 (distinguish) sharply
윷판 〈말판〉 a yut board; 〈윷노는 자리〉 the scene of a yut game
으깨다 〈부수다〉 crush (up [down]); 〈짓이기다〉 mash; squash; squeeze (into pulp) ♦으깬 감자 mashed potatoes / 포도주를 만들려고 포도를 으깨다 crush grapes for wine
-으나 1 〈그러나〉 but; though
♦ 그는 나이는 젊으나 though he is young; young as he is
▶ 그녀는 돈은 많으나 불행하다 Though she is rich, she is unhappy.
▶ 그는 문제를 풀려고 했으나 헛수고였다 He tried to solve the problem in vain.
2 〈…건 간에〉 whether...or; or what not
♦ 크나 작으나 관계없이 regardless of it's size
▶ 싫으나 좋으나 너는 그 일을 해야 한다 You must do it whether you like it or not.
▶ 날씨가 좋으나 나쁘나 나는 가겠다 I shall go regardless of weather.
3 〈강조〉 very; quite; ever so (much)
♦ 넓으나 넓은[깊으나 깊은] 바다 a sea that is ever so wide [deep]
▶ 그녀는 젊으나 젊은 나이에 과부가 되었다 She became a widow when she is still quite young.
-으나마 though; but; however
▶ 보잘것 없으나마 제 차를 쓰시지요 You may use my car, such as it is.
▶ 적으나마 없는 것보다는 낫다 Half a loaf is better than no bread [none].
-으니 1 〈…하니까〉 since; as; now (that)
▶ 그 말을 들으니 무척 기쁘다 I am so glad to hear that.
▶ 소문을 들으니 자네 곧 미국에 간다더군 They say that you are going to America shortly.
2 〈… 했더니〉 as; when; (and) then
▶ 그에게 이름을 물으니 송인수라고 하더라 I asked his name, he said he was Song In-su.
3 〈설명의 계속〉 ▶ 그 해에 그가 대학 입시에 합격하였으니 그 나이 겨우 15세 때였다 He passed the college entrance exam in that year, when he was only fifteen years old.
-으니까 since ⇨ -으니 1
으드득 with a crump; with a crunching noise
♦ 으드득 깨물다 crump; crunch (a bone)
으드득거리다 〈깨물다〉 crunch; crump
으드득으드득 with a crump ⇨ 으드득
▶ 그는 밤을 으드득으드득 씹어 먹었다 He crunched chestnuts.
으뜸 1 〈첫째・최고〉 the first [best]; the first place; the top; (美口) number one
♦ 으뜸가는 first; best; foremost; leading; matchless; peerless; (口) top-notch; number one / 학급에서 으뜸가는 학생 the best student in the class; the head [top] boy in the class
▶ 그 남자는 당대에 으뜸가는 화가다 He is the greatest painter of our time.
▶ 돈 버는 데는 장사가 으뜸이다 The best (way) to make money is to go into business.
2 〈기본・근본〉 the root; the basis (pl. bases); the foundation
▶ 효도는 윤리의 으뜸이다 Filial piety [devotion] is at the root of moral principles.
으뜸음 —音 a tonic; a keynote
으뜸화음 —和音 tonic chord
-으라 〈기원〉 ▶ 이 나라에 평화가 있으라 Let there be peace in this country.
▶ 신의 은총이 있으라 May God bless you!
-으라고 ▶ 그에게 앉으라고[씻으라고] 해라 Tell him to sit down [get wash].
-으라는 〈…하라는〉 ▶ 그가 받은 명령은 그 자리에 머물러 있으라는 것이었다 The orders given to him were to stay where he was.
-으락 ▶ 그는 화가 나서 얼굴이 붉으락 푸르락했다 His face got red and blue with anger.
▶ 그녀의 이야기를 들으면서 그는 얼굴이 붉으락 푸르락 했다 His color came and went as he listened to her.
-으러 〈목적〉 ▶ 그는 점심 먹으러 나갔다 He went out for lunch.
으레 〈틀림없이〉 without fail; 〈늘〉 always; every time; whenever; 〈습관적으로〉 as a rule
▶ 내가 산책을 가려하면 으레 비가 온다 Whenever I get in the mood to take a walk, it rains.
▶ 그들은 만나기만 하면 으레 싸운다 They never meet without quarreling.
2 〈마땅히〉 naturally; (as a matter) of course; 〈말할 것도 없이〉 needless to say
▶ 그것은 으레 그래야 한다 That is the natural thing to be expected.
-으려고 with the intention of ⇨ -려고
▶ 나는 모임에 늦지 않으려고 급히 서둘렀다 I hurried so as [in order] not to be late for the meeting.
▶ 나는 3년 더 있으려고 한다 I intend to stay

another three years.
-으려도 ▶아무리 참으려도 웃음이 나왔다 I could not help laughing.
-으려면 ▶고기를 잡으려면 그물이 있어야 한다 A net is needed for catching fish.
▶런던에 닿으려면 한시간 정도 걸린다 It will take about an hour to reach London.
-으려마는 ▶비가 와 주었으면 좋으련마는 I wish it would rain. ▶갈 수만 있다면 좋으련마는 If I could go, I should be glad.
-으렴 ▶이 소설책을 읽고 싶으면 읽으렴 You may read this novel if you like.
▶마음에 드는 옷으로 입으렴 Wear what clothes you please.
으로 1〈수단·방법〉by; by means of; through; 〈도구〉with; on; in
♦열차[항공]편으로 by train [air] / 맨주먹으로 with bare hands / 돈으로 사다 buy sth with money / 붓으로 벌어 먹다 live by one's pen; depend upon the pen for bread / 서면으로 알리다 let sb know by letter / 펜으로 쓰다 write with a pen / 현미경으로 보다 look 《at sth》 through a microscope; see sth under a microscope
▶그는 순전히 실력으로 출세했다 He succeeded in life simply on the strength of ability.
2〈방향〉for; to; toward
♦수원으로 가는 차 the train for Suwon / 이쪽으로 this way / 부산으로 떠나다 leave for Pusan / 집안으로 들어가다 come into the house
▶그는 남쪽으로 갔다 He went toward the south.
▶이제 집으로 가 보자 Now we'd better head for home.
3〈원인·동기〉because of; owing to; with; from; for; as; due to; through
♦폭풍으로 in a storm / 병으로 누워 있다 lie in bed with illness / 직무태만으로 면직되다 lose one's position through neglect of duty
▶그는 암으로 죽었다 He died of cancer.
▶그는 병으로 학교를 결석했다 He absented himself from school on account of illness.
▶나는 수면 부족으로 기분이 좋지 않다 I feel unwell from lack of sleep.
▶그들은 굶주림으로 고생하고 있다 They are suffering from hunger.
4〈원료·재료〉from; of; out of; in
♦대리석으로 지은 집 a house made of marble / 플라스틱으로 여러 가지 용기를 만들다 make various containers from [out of] plastic / 진흙으로 말을 만들다 model a horse in clay
▶그는 헌 궤짝으로 책상을 만들었다 He made a table out of an old box.
5〈근거〉by; from; according to
♦안색으로 알다 know sth from one's looks / 행동으로 판단하다 judge (of) sb by his conduct
▶겉모습으로 사람을 판단하면 안 된다 You must not judge people by their appearances.
6〈척도·단위·액수〉by; for
♦만원권으로 in ten thousand-won notes / 월급으로 고용하다 hire sb by the month / 일당으로 일하다 work by the day / 하루 7천원으로 살다 live on seven thousand won a day
▶시간제 근무자는 시간으로 고용한다 Part-time workers [Part-timers] are hired by the hour.
7〈지위·신분〉as; for
♦개인 자격으로 in one's individual [private] capacity / 서민으로 자라나다 be born and bred among the common people / 외교관으로 미국에 가다 go to America as a diplomat
▶19살까지는 미성년으로 간주한다 Up to 19 you are counted [considered as] a minor.
8〈형식·형태〉in ♦서양식으로 in Western style / 물품으로 지급하다 pay in kind
9〈내용〉of; with ♦설탕으로 가득하다 be full of sugar / 우유와 빵으로 간단한 식사를 하다 have a simple meal of milk and bread
10〈구성〉of; in
♦3장으로 구성되다 consist of 3 Chapters
▶그 팀은 20명으로 구성되어 있다 The team has twenty members.
11〈변화·결과〉into; in; to
♦바다가 산으로 변하더라도 though seas turn to mountains / 헌것을 새것으로 바꾸다 change an old one for a new one
▶그 마을이 쑥대밭으로 변했다 The village has been reduced to a field of sagebrush.
12〈상태·정도〉with; in
♦가벼운 마음으로 with a light hart / 전속력으로 달리다 run at full speed
▶그는 한복 차림으로 파티에 갔다 He went to the party in Korean clothes.
13〈선택〉▶빵은 어떤 것으로 드릴까요? What shall I bring you in the way of bread?
▶우리 독일 빵으로 하자 Let's make it German bread.
14〈시간·경과〉by; at ♦밤낮으로 by day and (by) night; day and night
▶이제 아침 저녁으로 서늘해졌다 We have cooler mornings and evenings now.
15〈통과·경로〉through; by
♦문으로 드나들다 go in and out by the door
♦달빛이 창문으로 비쳐든다 The moon shines through the window.
으로나 ♦어느 면으로나 in all respects [every respect] / 양으로나 질로나 in quantity and [or] in quality / 힘으로나 스피드로나 in strength and [or] in speed
▶그 남자는 시인으로나 기자로나 실패했다 He was a failure both as a poet and as a news reporter.
으로는 ♦내 생각으로는 in my opinion
▶이것으로는 안 된다 This won't do.
▶내 힘으로는 그런 일은 할 수가 없다 Such things are beyond my powers.
으로도 ▶그는 장군으로도 이름이 있다 He is noted as a general also.
으로서 as ⇨ 로서 ♦사람으로서 as a human being / 여흥으로서 by way of entertainment
▶양심 있는 정치인으로서 어떻게 그런 말을 할 수 있는가? As a politician with a conscience, how can you say such a thing?
으로써 with ⇨ 로써 ♦유가증권으로써 보석금을 대신하다 substitute negotiable securities

for the bail money / 죽음으로써 속죄하다 atone for a crime with death

으르다 〈위협하다〉 threaten; menace; browbeat 《sb into doing》; frighten
♦ 으르고 달래고 하여 what with threats and (what with) entreaties / 죽인다고 으르다 threaten [menace] sb with death / 을러서 자백시키다 frighten [scare] sb into confession

으르렁 with a snarl [growl, roar]

으르렁거리다 1 〈짐승 등이〉 roar; snarl; growl
▶ 그 개는 나를 보고 으르렁거렸다 The dog snarled at me.
2 〈다투다〉 quarrel [dispute, wrangle] 《with》; be at daggers drawn 《with》; feud [be at feud] 《with》 ♦ 〈부부가〉 으르렁거리며 살다 lead a cat-and-dog life
▶ 그 부부는 늘 서로 으르렁거린다 The couple are always fighting [quarreling] with each other.

으름 〔植〕 an akebi fruit ■—덩굴 an akebi

으름장 a threat; intimidation; browbeating; blackmail
♦ 으름장을 놓다 threaten; make threats; menace; utter threats 《of violence》
▶ 지금은 아이들이 약아빠져서 으름장을 놓아도 먹히지 않는다 The children are too smart now for threats to work.

-으리까 ▶ 두 시까지 여기 있으리까? Shall I remain here till two o'clock?

-으리니 ▶ 조부님은 쉬 돌아가시지 않으리니 마음 놓게 Take it easy, since your grandfather will not die soon.

-으리라 may ⇨ -리라 ▶ 두번 다시 그런 장소에는 가지 않으리라 I won't go to such places again.

으리으리하다 〈훌륭하다〉 magnificent; 〈웅대하다〉 grand; 〈당당하다〉 imposing; stately
♦ 으리으리한 저택 a stately [a magnificent, an imposing] mansion
▶ 그 방은 장식이 으리으리했다 The room was gorgeously decorated.

-으며 1 〈동시에〉 and; while ▶ 어린애가 어머니를 찾으며 울었다 The child cried for his mother. **2** while ⇨ -으면서

-으면 if; when
♦ 이가 기회를 잘 잡으면 if he gets a fair chance / 네가 시간이 있으면 if [when] you have time / 그렇지 않으면 otherwise; or else; or / 네가 열심히 공부하지 않으면 unless you work hard / …하지 않으면 안 되다 ought to [should] do… / …했으면 한다 I wish [hope] that…
▶ 자동차가 있으면 좋으련만 I wish I had a car.
▶ 너무 많이 걸으면 피곤해진다 If you walk too much, you get tired.
▶ 아파서 1주일만 쉬었으면 I'd like to be excused to absent myself from the office for a week as I am sick [because of illness].

-으면서 while; at the same time (that)…; over; with
♦ 웃으면서 with a smile / 걸으면서 책을 읽다 read a book as *one* walks / 웃으면서 말하다 speak with a smile / 음악을 들으면서 신문을 읽다 read a newspaper while listening to the music
▶ 나는 라디오를 들으면서 그에게 편지를 썼다 Half listening to the radio, I wrote a letter to him.

-으면서도 while…yet; (al)though
▶ 그 이론은 올바른 것 같으면서도 납득이 안 간다 The logic seems sound, but it does not convince me.
▶ 그는 돈이 없으면서도 있는 체한다 He pretends as though he is rich [has much money].

-으므로 since; as; so; for
▶ 나한테 가진 돈이 없었으므로 그것을 살 수 없었다 Since I had no money with me I could not buy it.
▶ 날이 어두워졌으므로 우리는 곧 돌아왔다 As it was getting dark, we soon turned back.
▶ 개가 굶고 있었으므로 우리는 먹이를 주었다 The dog was hungry, (and) so we fed it.

-으소서 please (do); I pray [beg] you (that)
▶ 아무쪼록 주의해서 들으소서 I beg you to be very attentive.
▶ 제 말씀을 들으소서 Pray listen to me.

으스대다 be proud [overbearing]; swagger 《about》; lord (it) 《over》; give *oneself* [assume, put on] airs
♦ 으스대며 in a lordly manner; with an air / 재산 좀 있다고 으스대다 swagger about *one's* possessions / 으스대며 걷다 swagger; walk with an air / 으스대며 말하다 speak in a lordly [high and mighty] manner
▶ 나한테 으스대게 놓아두지 않겠다 I will not be lorded over.
▶ 그는 성공했다고 으스대다 He is puffed up with success.

으스름달 a hazy [dim] moon
■—밤 a misty [faint] moonlit night; a night with a hazy moon

으스름하다 hazy; misty; dim

으스스 ♦ 으스스 추워지다 take [catch] a chill; have [feel] a chill; be [feel] chilly
▶ 나는 으스스 추워서 잠이 깼다 I felt cold and shivery, so I awoke from my sleep.

으스스하다 1 〈춥다〉 chilly; rather cold; coldish
▶ 오늘 아침에는 으스스하더라 It was shivering this morning.
▶ 그 날은 꽤 으스스한 날씨였다 It was rather chilly that day.
2 〈무시무시하다〉 ghastly; spooky; weird; uncanny
♦ 으스스한 장소 a spooky place / 유령의 울음소리처럼 으스스한 weird [uncanny] as a wailing of a ghost
▶ 그 일은 생각만 해도 으스스해진다 It chills my blood to think of it.

으슥하다 retired and quiet; covert; lonely; deep
♦ 으슥한 곳 a secluded spot; an out-of-the-way place / 으슥한 구석 a covert nook / 으슥한 산길 a remote [lonely] mountain path [trail] / 으슥한 숲속에서 in the gloom [depths] of a forest

으슬으슬 ▶ 으슬으슬 춥다 I feel [am] chilly.
—**으슬으슬하다** chilly; somewhat cold

♦ 으슬으슬한 날씨 chilly weather
▶ 열이 나서 몸이 으슬으슬하다 I have chills [shakes] with the fever.
으슴푸레하다 hazy; misty; dim ♦ 으슴푸레한 달빛 아래서 in the misty moonlight
▶ 달빛이 으슴푸레하게 비친다 The moon shines dimly.
으쓱[1] 〈추위로〉 shrinkingly with cold; 〈무서워서〉 shrink into oneself with horror
―**으쓱하다** 〈춥다〉 cold; chilly; 〈무섭다〉 horrible; blood-curdling; hair-raising
으쓱[2] with a shrug (of one's shoulders); 〈우쭐해서〉 swaggeringly
―**으쓱하다** shrug; 〈우쭐하다〉 be elated [exultant] 《over, with》; be puffed up 《by, with》; puff oneself up 《with》
▶ 그는 어깨를 으쓱했다 He shrugged his shoulders.
▶ 그는 국회의원이 되어 어깨가 으쓱했다 He was highly elated at becoming a member of the National Assembly.
▶ 그 일이 성공하자 그는 으쓱했다 The success has turned his head.
으쓱거리다, 으쓱대다 raise [draw up] one's shoulders in pride; swagger; perk oneself up; (口) act big
으악 1 〈놀래줄 때〉 Boo; Bo; Boh; 〈놀랐을 때〉 Ugh; Wow; Gee ♦ 으악 소리를 지르다 shriek; scream 2 〈울컥〉 with a puke
으지적 ♦ 으지적 깨물다[씹다] crunch; munch
▶ 그 사내 아이는 사탕을 으지적 깨물어 먹었다 The boy munched on the hard candy.
윽박다 put down with threats ⇨ 윽박지르다
윽박지르다 put down with threats; treat with a high hand; bully 《sb into [out of]》
♦ 제안을 승낙하도록 윽박지르다 browbeat sb into accepting a proposal
▶ 그들은 그를 윽박질러서 침묵시켰다 They shouted him down.
-은 1 〈형용사 어간에〉 …that [which, who] is
♦ 낡은 모자 a hat which is old; an old hat / 맑은 공기 fresh air / 맑은 물 clear water / 작은 나무 a little tree
2 〈동사 어간에〉 …that [which, who] 《one》 did [has done]
♦ 내가 받은 선물 the present that I received / 상을 받은 사람 the man who won a prize / 내가 어제 읽은 책 the book that I read yesterday / 잘 닦은 구두 well-polished shoes
은 銀 silver; argentum
♦ 은색의 silver; silvery / 은 같은 silvery / 은으로 된 silver; made of silver / 은을 입힌 silver-plated / 은을 입히다 silver; plate sth with silver
■ 순― fine [pure, refined] silver ■ ―가락지 a silver ring ―가루 silver dust; powdered silver ―그릇 silverware; (총칭) 은―도금 silvering; silver-plating; silver gilt: 은도금한 수저와 젓가락 a silver-plated spoon and chopsticks ―메달 a silver medal ―본위(제) the silver standard (system) ―종이 tinfoil; silver paper
은거 隱居 living in retirement; retirement (from active life)
▶ 그는 편히 은거 생활을 하고 있다 He is living in easy retirement.
―**은거하다** live [dwell] in retirement; live a retired life; estrange from practical life
♦ 산 속에 은거하다 retire to hermitage in the mountain
▶ 아버님은 정계를 은퇴하고 고향에 은거하셨다 My father retired from politics to a secluded life in his hometown.
은고 恩顧 favors; patronage ♦ 은고를 입다 receive favors 《from sb》; be patronized 《by》
―**은고하다** favor; patronize
은공 恩功 a favor and (meritorious) service; merits ♦ 부모의 은공 paternal love / 스승의 은공 one's debts to one's teacher / 은공을 잊다 lose one's gratitude
은광 銀鑛 a silver mine
은괴 銀塊 a silver ingot; 〈막대 모양의〉 a silver bar; (총칭) silver bullion
은근 慇懃 1 〈정중함〉 politeness; courtesy; civility ―**은근하다** polite; courteous; civil
♦ 은근한 말씨 polite language / 은근한 태도 a polite [courteous] manner / 은근히 politely; courteously; with much courtesy
2 〈은밀함〉 quietness; inwardness; secrecy; implicitness; suggestiveness
―**은근하다** inward; implicit; suggestive; indirect; secret; private
♦ 은근한 미소 a quiet smile / 은근한 협박 a veiled [implicit] threat / 은근히 in one's heart; indirectly; secretly; privately; in confidence [private] / 은근히 걱정하다 feel anxious in one's heart [inwardly] / 은근히 꿇리다 cheat sb on the sly / 은근히 내비치다 hint 《at》; give [drop] a hint; suggest / (남의 마음을) 은근히 떠보다 beat about the bush; sound 《sb about》 / 은근히 바라다 have a secret desire to 《do》; have a sneaky urge to 《do》
▶ 나는 그를 은근히 비꼬아 주었다 I had a quiet dig at him.
▶ 나는 너를 은근히 기다렸다 I've been expecting you.
3 〈정이 깊음〉 intimacy; friendship
―**은근하다** intimate; friendly
♦ 은근한 사이다 be intimate 《with》; be on intimate terms 《with》
은근짜 〈밀매음녀〉 a woman of a certain description; an unlicensed prostitute; a whore; 〈의뭉스런 사람〉 a sly [crafty, cunning, foxy] person
은기 銀器 〈은그릇〉 silverware
은니 銀泥 silver paint
은닉 隱匿 concealment; secretion
♦ 장물 은닉죄 secretion of stolen goods / 중죄범 은닉죄 (法) misprision of felony
▶ 그 남자는 범인 은닉죄로 기소되었다 He was charged with sheltering [harboring] a criminal.
―**은닉하다** conceal; hide; secrete; 〈숨겨주다〉 shelter; harbor 《the culprit》
■ ―물 자 concealed goods [commodities] ―처 a hiding place: 범인에게 은닉처를 제공하다 provide shelters to criminals
은덕 恩德 a favor; a benefit
♦ 은덕을 베풀다 do sb a favor; (英) confer a

은덕 benefit ((upon)) / 조상의 은덕을 입다 receive the blessings of *one's* ancestors ▶ 나는 그 분이 베풀어 주신 은덕에 감사했다 I was grateful for the benefits I received from him.

은덕 隱德 a stealthy benefaction ⇨ 음덕

은둔 隱遁 retirement [seclusion] (from the world); withdrawal from ordinary life ―은둔하다 retire [sequester *oneself*] from the world; live in seclusion; seclude [isolate] *oneself* from society; renounce the world ▶ 그는 지금은 조용하고 경치 좋은 산촌에서 은둔해 있다 He has now kept his seclusion [secluded himself] from the world in a quiet, beautiful village among the hills. ■―생활 a retired [secluded, sequestered] life; a life in seclusion : 은둔 생활로 여생을 보내다 live the rest of *one's* life in seclusion ―자 a recluse; a hermit ―처 a place of seclusion; a hermitage; a retreat

은막 銀幕 〈영사막〉 the silver screen; 〈영화계〉 the (silver) screen ♦ 은막의 여왕 the movie queen; the queen of the (silver) screen; the heroine of the silver screen

은밀 隱密 privacy; secrecy ―은밀하다 covert; secret; private; confidential ♦ 은밀히 covertly; secretly; privately; confidentially; in confidence [private, secret] / 은밀히 처리하다 deal with (a matter) in secret [privately] / 은밀히 만나기를 요청하다 ask a private interview (with *sb*) / 은밀히 이야기하다 tell confidentially / 은밀히 조사하다 make confidential inquiries / 은밀히 해결하다 settle (a matter) privately [out of court] ▶ 그 남자는 그와 은밀한 이야기를 나누었다 The man had a private talk with him. ▶ 은밀히 드릴 말씀이 있습니다 I should like to speak to you confidentially [in private]. ▶ 이건 너에게만 은밀히 하는 이야기야 This is for your private ear.

은박 銀箔 〈얇은〉(a piece of) silver leaf; 〈두꺼운〉 silver foil ■―지 silver paper

은반 銀盤 〈쟁반〉 a silver plate; 〈달〉 the (silvery) moon; 〈스케이트장〉 a skating [an ice] rink ♦ 은반의 여왕 the queen on the ice

은발 銀髮 silver(y) [gray] hair ♦ 은발의 노인 an old man with silvery hair; a gray-haired old man ▶ 나이가 들어 그 부인의 머리는 은발이 되었다 Age had silvered her hair.

은방 銀房 a silversmith's; a silver shop

은방울꽃 銀― 〔植〕 a lily of the valley; a May lily

은배 銀杯 a silver cup ⇨ 은잔

은백(색) 銀白(色) silver gray ♦ 은백(색)의 silver-white; silver-gray; silvery; argentine

은붙이 銀― (총칭) silverware

은빛 銀― silver (color); silveriness ♦ 은빛의 silver-colored; silver(y)

은사 恩師 *one's* (former) teacher; *one's* respected [honored, beloved] teacher ▶ 나는 오래 뵙지 못한 고등학교 시절의 은사님을 만났다 I met my old high school teacher after a long separation.

은사 隱士 a retired [hermit] scholar; a recluse

은산 銀山 a silver mine

은색 銀色 silver color ⇨ 은빛

은세계 銀世界 a silver world; a vast snowy scene ▶ 들판이 온통 은세계다 The whole field is covered with [mantled with] snow.

은세공 銀細工 〈세공〉 silverwork; 〈세공품〉 an article of silver; (총칭) silverware ―은세공하다 work silver ■―인 a silversmith

은수 恩讐 love and hate; benefit and enmity

은수저 銀― (a set of) silver spoon and chopsticks

은신 隱身 hiding *oneself*; rendering *oneself* invisible ―은신하다 hide [conceal] *oneself*; 〈가려서〉 take cover; 〈피신하다〉 take [seek] refuge [shelter]

은신처 隱身處 a hiding place; a refuge; a hideaway; 〈도둑의〉 a den; 〈범인의〉 a hideout ▶ 경찰은 범인의 은신처를 찾아냈다 The police found the criminal's hideout.

은실 銀― silver thread; spun silver

은어 銀魚 〔魚〕 a sweetfish ♦ 산란하기 위해 강을 내려가는 은어 a sweetfish going downstream for spawning

은어 隱語 secret language; a jargon; 〈특정 계층·직업인의〉 a cant; 〈도둑 등의〉 an argot; an underworld slang ▶ 그들은 자기들끼리의 은어로 이야기했다 They talked in the jargon of their trade.

은연중 隱然中 tacitly; implicitly; indirectly; under cover; in a roundabout way ♦ …하기를 은연중 바라다 have a secret desire to (do) / 은연중 사의를 비치다 hint at *one's* resignation / 은연중에 친구를 돕다 help a friend on the quiet

은연하다 隱然― underlying; latent; secret; hidden ♦ 은연한 세력 hidden [covert] influence; a latent power / 은연한 실력자 a behind-the-scenes strong man

은유 隱喩 〔修〕 (a) metaphor ♦ 은유적인 metaphorical / 은유적으로 metaphorically

은은하다 殷殷― roaring; bellowing; booming; reverberating ▶ 은은한 포성이 잠잠해졌다 The roar of guns was hushed. ▶ 예포가 은은히 울렸다 Salute guns roared [boomed].

은은하다 隱隱― **1** 〈어렴풋하다〉 dim; vague; indistinct; misty ♦ 은은한 향기 a subtle perfume / 은은하게 보이다 be seen dimly; be made out faintly (in the distance) ▶ 난초 향기가 은은하게 풍겼다 There was a faint smell [fragrance] of an orchid. **2** 〈소리가〉 dim; faint; distant (to the ears) ▶ 종소리가 은은히 들려왔다 There came the dim sound of a bell to my ears.

은의 恩義·恩誼 a favor; an obligation; a debt of gratitude; indebtedness ♦ 은의에 보답하다 repay *sb* for (his) kindness

은익 銀翼 silver(y) wings; 〈비행기〉 an airplane

은인 恩人 a benefactor; 〈여자〉 a benefactress;

〈후원자〉a patron; 〈여자〉a patroness
▶ 당신은 내 생명의 은인입니다 I owe you my life. ⇌ I owe my life to you.
▶ 그는 나의 은인입니다 I am indebted to him.

은인 隱忍 patience; endurance
▶ 그는 은인 자중하여 때가 무르익기를 기다렸다 He waited patiently for the time to be ripe [opportunity to mature].
―**은인하다** be patient; endure; put up with; bear up

은자 隱者 a hermit; a recluse; a solitary
은잔 銀盞 a silver (wine)cup [goblet]
은장 銀匠 a silversmith; a jeweler
은장도 銀粧刀 a silver-decorated knife
은전 恩典 a favor; grace; a privilege
♦ 은전을 입다 receive [be granted] a favor
은전 銀錢 a silver; a silver coin
은정 恩情 benevolent [gracious] affection
은제 銀製 ♦ 은제의 made of silver ▶ 이 수저는 은제다 This spoon is made of silver. ■―품 silverware
은줄¹ 銀― 〔鑛〕 a vein of silver
은줄² 銀― 〈줄〉a silver cord [string]
은종이 銀― silver [silver-colored] paper; 〈과자·담배 등을 싸는〉 tin foil
은총 恩寵 grace; favor
♦ 신의 은총 (by) the grace of God / 신의 은총을 받다 receive [enjoy] the grace of God / 은총을 잃다 lose sb's favor; 〈신의〉 lose [fall out of] God's favor; fall from grace / 신의 은총을 빌다 pray for God's grace / 은총을 입고 있다 be in favor with sb; stand in sb's favor
은침 銀鍼 silver needle used for acupuncture
은테 銀― a silver rim ■―안경 silver-rimmed spectacles
은퇴 隱退 retirement (from active [public] life); 〈권투 선수의〉 retire from ring; 〈연예인 등의〉 retire from the stage
―**은퇴하다** retire (from active life); withdraw from public life; go into retirement; 〈사퇴하다〉 resign
♦ 은퇴한 정치가 a retired politician / 은막에서 은퇴하다 retire from the screen / 은퇴하여 넉넉하게 살다 retire with a handsome competence
▶ 그는 고령으로 2년전에 정계를 은퇴했다 He retired from political life two years ago because of his old age.
―■―경기[연주회] a farewell match [concert]
―**생활** a retired life: 은퇴 생활을 하다 live in retirement; live a retired life
은파 銀波 silvery [white] waves; whitecaps
은폐 隱蔽 concealment; hiding; cover-up
―**은폐하다** conceal; hide; cover (up); draw a veil (over); hush up (a scandal); sweep (a troublesome problem) under the rug
♦ 사실을 은폐하다 suppress [cover up] a fact; slur a fact over
▶ 그들은 추문을 은폐하려 하고 있다 They are trying to put a lid on the scandal.
▶ 우리는 그의 성명 가운데서 고의로 진실을 은폐한 것을 묵과해서는 안 된다 We must not overlook the deliberate concealment of truth in his statement.

은하 銀河 〔天〕 the Milky Way; the Galaxy
♦ 은하(계)의 galactic
■―**계** the Milky Way galaxy [system]; the Galaxy; the galactic system ―**군** group of galaxy ―**면** the galactic plane ―**수** =은하
―**좌표** galactic coordinates

은행 銀行 a bank
♦ 은행에 많은 예금이 있다 have much money (deposited) in a bank / 은행에서 돈을 빌리다 get a loan at a bank / 은행과 거래를 시작하다 [중단하다] open [close] an account with a bank / 은행에서 돈을 인출하다 draw [withdraw] money from the bank
▶ 이 중에서 10만원을 은행에 예금하겠다 I will put [deposit] 100,000 won out of the sum in the bank.
▶ 나는 은행에 예금이 2백만원 있다 I have [keep] 2,000,000 won in the bank.
▶ 그녀는 은행에서 10만원을 찾았다 She drew 100,000 won from the bank.
■―**국립**― a national bank 국제 부흥 개발― the International Bank of Reconstruction and Development (略 IBRD) 국책― a national [state] policy bank 발권― a bank of issue 보통― an ordinary commercial bank 상업― a commercial bank 세계― the World Bank 수출입― an export-import bank 시중― a city bank 신탁― a trust bank 안구― an eye bank 외환― a foreign exchange bank; 〈한국의〉 Korea Exchange Bank 저축― a savings bank 중앙― a central bank 지방― a local [provincial] bank 혈액― a blood bank ―**가** a banker ―**감독원** the Bank Inspection Board ―**강도** 〈사람〉 a bank burglar; 〈짓〉 bank robbery ―**계** banking circles ―**계정** a bank account ―**권** a bank note; (美) a bank bill ―**법** 〔法〕 the Banking Law ―**부기** bank bookkeeping ―**어음** a bank draft (略 B/D); a bank bill; a banker's bill; (총칭) bank paper ―**업** banking (business) ―**업무** banking (services) ―**영업 시간** banking hours ―**예금** bank deposits [savings] ―**원** 〈개인〉 a bank clerk [employe(e)]; (총칭) the staff of a bank ―**융자** bank accommodation; a bank loan ―**이자** bank interest; bank rate ―**장**[총재] the president of a bank ―**주**(株) bank stocks ―**지급 준비금** a bank reserve fund; bank reserves ―**통장** a bankbook; a passbook ―**할인** bank discount ―**환** a banker's draft; a bank bill

은행 銀杏 a ginkgo nut ■―**나무** a ginkgo [gingko] (tree)
은행거래 銀行去來 bank account; (英) banking account [transactions]
♦ 은행거래가 있다 be in [have an] account with a bank / 은행거래를 트다[끊다] open [close] an account with a bank
은현잉크 隱現― invisible [secret] ink
은혜 恩惠 1 〈은공〉 an obligation; a debt of gratitude; 〈친절〉 kindness; a favor; goodness

[解說] 타인 특히 윗사람으로부터 받은 온정·친절·호의를 「(언젠가는 갚아야 할) 은혜」로 해석하는 사고 방식은 유럽과 미국에서는 흔한

일이 아니므로 여기에 꼭 맞는 대응어가 영어에는 없다. 따라서 (**an**) ***obligation*** (도덕적 의무, 정신적 부채), (**a**) ***kindness*** (친절), (**a**) ***favor*** (호의) 등을 적절히 구분해서 써야 한다.

◆부모의 은혜 parental love / 스승의 은혜 one's debt to one's teacher; obligations [what] one owes to one's teacher / 은혜를 갚다 repay an obligation / 은혜를 모르다[잊다] be ungrateful; be thankless / 은혜를 베풀다 do sb a favor; do a favor for sb; bestow a favor on sb / 은혜를 알다 be grateful (to sb, for sb's kindness); have a sense of gratitude / 은혜를 입다 receive benefits [favors]; enjoy benevolent influence / 은혜에 보답하다 repay sb for his kindness
▶이 은혜는 결코 잊지 않겠습니다 I shall never forget your kindness [what you have done for me].
▶그 분의 은혜는 갚겠다 I'll repay [return] his kindness.
▶나는 그에게 큰 은혜를 입고 있습니다 I owe him a great debt of gratitude. ⇒ I am deeply [greatly] indebted to him.
▶자식을 가져 봐야 부모의 은혜를 안다 Without child, without true filial gratitude.
▶그는 은혜를 원수로 갚을 녀석이다 When you pat him, he snaps at you.
▶이 은혜를 어떻게 갚아야 할지 모르겠습니다 I don't see how I can ever repay your kindness.
2 〈신의〉 divine favor [grace]; (a) blessing
◆은혜를 입다[받다] receive divine favors / …에게 은혜를 베풀어 달라고 빌다 implore sb for mercy

은혼식 銀婚式 a silver wedding
◆은혼식을 거행하다 celebrate (their) silver wedding (anniversary)

은화 銀貨 〈개개의〉 a silver coin; (총칭) silver currency [coin, coinage]
■—본위제 the silver standard

은화식물 隱花植物 〈植〉a cryptogam
은회색 銀灰色 silver gray / ◆은회색의 silver-gray
은휘하다 隱諱— conceal; hide; cover up
읽을 〈타동사의 목적〉◆신문을 보다 read [look at] the newspaper / 컵에 물을 채우다 fill a glass with water
▶그 선생님은 우리에게 음악을 가르치신다 He teaches us music [teaches music to us].
▶그녀는 그들을 비웃었다 She laughed at them.
▶웬 낯선 사람이 내 얼굴을 빤히 쳐다 보았다 A stranger stared at me in the face.
▶그는 아들을 자랑스럽게 생각한다 He is proud of his son.
▶그 학생은 내년에 대학 입학을 목표로 열심히 공부하고 있다 The student is studying hard aiming at entering college next year.
2 〈수동태의 목적〉◆발목을 채다 get a kick [get kicked] on the ankle / 물건을 빼앗기다 be robbed of sth
3 〈위치〉◆강을 건너가다 cross a river / 산을 넘다 go over [cross] a mountain / 하늘을 날다 fly (in) the sky
4 〈동작의 기점〉◆관식을 물러나다 resign from one's official post / (열차가) 역을 떠나다 get clear of the station / 인천을 떠나다 leave Inchŏn
5 〈동작의 목적·방향〉◆세계 일주 여행을 떠나다 set out on a round-the-world trip / 영화 구경을 가다 go to see a movie
6 〈차례〉◆1등을 하다 go [rank] first
7 〈동안〉◆두 시간을 자다 sleep (for) two hours / 사흘을 굶다 starve for three days / 하루 8시간을 일하다 work for eight hours a day
8 〈관계〉◆병을 구실로 under the pretext of illness / 부산을 기점으로 with Pusan as the starting point
9 〈동족목적어〉◆꿈을 꾸다 dream a dream / 숨을 쉬다 breathe a breath / 잠을 자다 sleep a sleep / 춤을 추다 dance a dance
10 〈구어적〉◆마음을 먹다 make up one's mind / 앞장을 서다 stand at the head; be in the lead
11 〈생략〉▶하늘에는 영광을, 땅에는 평화를 Glory be in the heaven, and peace on earth!
12 〈강조〉▶자유가 아니면 죽음을 달라 Give me liberty, or give me death.

을 乙 〈제2〉 the second; B; 〈후자〉 the latter; 〈등급의〉 second grade [class]
을러대다 threaten; menace; browbeat; 《美》 bulldoze ◆을러메어 by threats [intimidation] / 죽인다고 을러메다 threaten [menace] sb with death
-을망정 although ⇨ ㄹ망정
◆늙었을망정 though he is old; old as he is / 남루한 의복을 입었을망정 though he is (clad) in rags (and tatters)
을씨년스럽다 **1** 〈쓸쓸해 보이다〉 (look) lonesome; (look) deserted; (look) shabby; 〈날씨·광경 등이〉 dreary; dismal; gloomy
◆을씨년스러운 곳 a lonely [dreary] place / 을씨년스러운 날씨 gloomy weather; a leaden sky
2 〈군색하다〉 poor; badly off; miserable
◆살림이 을씨년스럽다 lead a miserable [wretched] life; live poor [in poverty]
을종 乙種 grade [class] B; second grade
-을지언정 even if ⇨ -ㄹ지언정
▶죽을지언정 그런 짓은 안 한다 I would rather die than do it.
▶굶을지언정 그에게 청을 안 하겠다 Even though I were starving I would not ask a favor of him.
읊다 〈낭송하다〉 chant; sing; recite; 〈(시가)짓다〉 compose 《an ode》; write 《a poem》
◆시를 읊다 recite a poem
읊조리다 recite 《a poem》; chant 《a hymn》
음 音 〈소리〉 a sound; 〈음조〉 a note; a tone
◆높은[낮은] 음 a high [low] sound / 아름다운 음 a melodious [musical] sound / 음높이 pitch / 음을 내다 emit [produce] a sound
2 〈한자의〉 the pronunciation
◆한자(漢字)를 음으로 읽다 read Chinese characters phonetically
음 陰 **1** 〈哲〉 Yin; the negative [female] principle in nature

2 〔그늘〕 shade; 〔어둠〕 dark; secrecy
◆음으로 양으로 implicitly and explicitly; publicly and privately; in every possible way
3 〔數〕 negative number; minus quantity
◆음의 부호 a negative [minus] sign

음가 音價 〔音聲〕 a phonetic value; 〔樂〕 a note value

음각 陰刻 〔美術〕 intaglio; sunk relief; cavo-relievo; depressed engraving [carving] —**음각하다** intaglio; engrave [carve] in intaglio

음감 音感 a sense of sound ■—**교육** acoustic education; auditory education

음경 陰莖 〔解〕 the penis (*pl.* ~es, penes); the phallus (*pl.* ~es, -li); 〔卑〕 the cock —**숭배** phallicism

음계 音階 〔樂〕 the (musical) scale; the gamut
◆음계를 연주하다 play *one's* scales
▶그녀는 피아노로 음계를 연습했다 She practiced scales on the piano.
■단[장]— the minor [major] scale 반[온]— a chromatic [diatonic] scale

음곡 音曲 〔곡조〕 a tune; a melody; 〈음악〉 music —**금지** the prohibition of musical entertainments [performances]

음극 陰極 〔電〕 the negative pole [electrode]; the cathode ■—**관(管)** a cathode-ray tube(略 CRT) —**선** the cathode ray —**판** a negative plate

음기 陰氣 gloominess; dreariness; a chill; chilliness ◆음기가 서린 묘지 the dreary graveyard

음낭 陰囊 〔解〕 the scrotum (*pl.* ~s, -ta)

음녀 淫女 a lewd [wanton, dissolute] woman ⇨ 음부(淫婦)

음담 淫談 a filthy [an obscene, a foul, a dirty] talk; a dirty [sexual] story
◆음담을 하다 tell a dirty story; talk dirty [smut, filth] ■—**패설** a filthy talk

음덕 陰德 a stealthy benefaction; good done by stealth; a secret act of charity
◆음덕을 베풀다 do good secretly

음덕 蔭德 *one's* ancestor's virtue
▶그는 선조의 음덕을 입고 있다 He is indebted to his forefathers.

음독 音讀 〈소리내어 읽음〉 reading aloud; 〈한자의〉 straight reading
▶시를 이해하기 위해서는 우선 음독을 해야 한다 To understand a poem, you should first read it aloud.
—**음독하다** 〈소리내어〉 read aloud; 〈한문을〉 read 《a Chinese text》 phonetically [straight on]

음독 飮毒 taking poison
◆음독 자살하다 kill *oneself* [commit suicide] by taking poison; poison *oneself* to death
—**음독하다** take poison

음란 淫亂 incontinence; lewdness; lasciviousness; lechery; salacity
—**음란하다** licentious; lewd; incontinent; lustful; obscene; salacious; lascivious; indecent; wanton ◆음란한 여자[남자] a lewd [lustful] woman [man]

음란증 淫亂症 symptoms of lewdness

음량 音量 volume (of the radio music); sound volume ◆스테레오의 음량을 줄이다[높이다] turn down [up] the stereo / 라디오의 음량을 최고로 하다 turn a radio all the way up [on full blast]

음력 陰曆 the lunar calendar
◆음력을 쓰다 use [follow] the lunar calendar / 음력으로 세다 reckon according to the lunar calendar
▶오늘은 음력 4월 10일이다 Today is April 10 of the lunar month.
—**설** lunar New Year's Day

음료 飮料 a drink; a beverage; drinkables
◆알코올성 음료 an alcoholic drink / 알코올분이 없는 음료 a nonalcoholic drink [beverage]; 〔美〕 a soft drink / 음료로 쓰다 use for drinking purpose
▶무슨 음료를 드릴까요 What kind of drink [beverage] would you like?
■청량— a cooling drink 혼합— concoctions; cocktail; 〔美〕 highball ■—**수** drinking water; water to drink; potable water

음률 音律 (a) rhythm; a tune; pitch

음매 〈소 우는 소리〉 moo ◆음매(하고) 울다 moo; low

음모 陰毛 〔解〕 pubic hair; pubes

음모 陰謀 a plot; an intrigue; an underhand design; a machination; 〔美口〕 a frame-up
◆암살음모 designs against *sb's* life; a conspiracy to kill *sb* / 음모를 꾸미다 plot; lay [hatch, brew, frame, weave, concoct] a plot; form a conspiracy against 《*sb's* life》; intrigue against 《*sb*》 / 음모를 뒤엎다 thwart a conspiracy / 음모를 적발하다 expose [lay bare] a plot; unmask a conspiracy / 음모에 가담하다 be implicated [initiated] in a plot
▶그들은 대통령의 암살 음모를 꾸몄다 They plotted to murder the President. = They attempted to take the life of the President.
—**음모하다** plot; conspire ◆암살을 음모하다 plot against *sb's* life
▶그는 정부의 전복을 음모한 죄로 기소되었다 He was indicted for conspiring against the government.
■—**단** a band of conspirators; a cabal; a junto —**자** a plotter; a conspirator; an intriguer

음문 陰門 〔解〕 the vagina; the vulva

음미 吟味 **1** 〈감상〉 appreciation; savoring —**음미하다** appreciate; savor; relish
▶시를 음미하다 enjoy poems
2 〈검토〉 close examination [investigation]; inquiry; scrutiny; critical study
—**음미하다** examine closely; investigate (minutely); inquire [search] into; scrutinize; study (critically)

음반 音盤 a (phonograph) record; a disc

음보 音譜 a (musical) score ⇨ 악보(樂譜)

음부 音符 a (musical) note ⇨ 음표(音標)

음부 陰部 the pubic region; the private [secret] parts; genital organs; genitals ◆음부의 pubic —**외** — pudenda; external genital organs : 외음부의 pudendal

음부 淫婦 a lewd [wanton, bawdy] woman; a woman of easy virtue [of loose morals]; a vamp; a bitch

음산 陰散 dreariness; weirdness; gloominess
—**음산하다** dreary; dismal; weird; gloomy
♦ 음산한 날씨 dismal weather
▶ 시국이 자못 음산하다 The state of affairs is very gloomy.

음색 音色 a tone quality [color]; the quality of a tone [sound]; (프) timbre
♦ 음색이 좋다 sound beautiful; have a good timbre
▶ 이 거문고는 음색이 좋다 This *Keomunko* sounds beautiful.

음서 淫書 a foul [lascivious] book; (총칭) obscene literature; pornography ♦ 춘화(春花)가 많은 음서 obscene literature with many pornographies

음성 音聲 a voice; a sound
♦ 음성을 높이다[낮추다] raise [lower] *one's* voice / 음성이 변하다 *one's* voice breaks / 음성이 좋다 have a fine voice
■ —기관 the vocal organs —기호 a phonetic sign [symbol]; a phonetic notation —다중방송 multiplex broadcasting —테스트 audition

음성 陰性 1 〈소극성〉 passive character; passivity; passiveness; 〔電〕 negativity; 〈병의〉 dormancy
♦ 음성의[적인] negative; passive; minus; 〔電〕 electronegative; 〈병이〉 dormant; atonic; 〈성격이〉 gloomy; dismal
▶ 에이즈 검사 결과는 음성이었다 The result of the AIDS examination was negative.
2 〈떳떳하지 못한〉 shadiness; unfairness
♦ 음성적인 shady; unfair; illegal
■ —거래 shady [unlawful, illicit, under-the-table] transaction [deal] —수입[소득] ill-gotten [illicit] gains; 〈관리의〉 spoils; 《get》 a perquisite —콜레라 dormant cholera

음성학 音聲學 phonetics
♦ 음성학의 phonetic(al) ■ —자 a phonetician

음 소 音素 〔音聲〕 a phoneme ■ —론(論) phonemics; 음소론자 a phonemicist

음속 音速 sonic speed; the speed [velocity] of sound; acoustic velocity
♦ 음속의 벽 the sonic [sound] barrier / 음속의 벽을 돌파하다 break through the sonic barrier
▶ 마하 1은 음속, 마하 2는 음속의 2배를 말한다 Mach one is the speed of sound, and Mach two means twice the speed of sound.
▶ 이 미사일은 음속의 2배로 비행한다 This missile flies at Mach 2 [double the speed of sound].
■ 아(亞)— subsonic (speed) 초— supersonic [ultrasonic] (speed) : 이 비행기는 초음속으로 비행한다 This aircraft flies supersonic.

음수 陰數 〔數〕 a negative (number); a minus [negative] quantity; a minus

음순 陰脣 〔解〕 the labia (*sing.* -bium); the lips of the vulva
■ 대— the labia majora 소— the labia minora; the nymphae

음습 陰濕 shadiness and dampness
—**음습하다** shady and damp; unsunny and moist ♦ 음습한 곳 a shady and damp place
▶ 이 식물은 음습한 땅에서 자란다 This plant grows in damp, shady places.

음식 飮食 〈음식물〉 food and drink; food; foodstuffs; a meal; refreshments
♦ 가벼운[기름진] 음식 light [rich, heavy] food / 영양분이 많은 음식 nourishing [nutritious] food / 소화가 잘되는[안되는] 음식 digestible [indigestible] food / 음식을 들다 eat and drink; take food and drink; take some refreshments / 음식이 좋다[나쁘다] 〈기숙사 등에서〉 be well-[ill-, badly-]boarded / 음식을 조심하다 be careful about *one's* food [*one's* diet, what *one* eats]/ 음식을 절제하다 be temperate in food
▶ 그는 음식에 대해서 까다롭다 He is fastidious [particular, nice] about food.
▶ 그는 음식에 까다롭지 않다 He is not a fastidious eater.
▶ 여름에는 음식에 조심해라 Be careful about what you eat and drink in summer.
▶ 나는 음식을 스스로 요리해서 먹었다 I cooked and ate (the food) by myself.

음식물 飮食物 food and drink ⇨ 음식

음식점 飮食店 an eating house; a restaurant; a cookshop; (口) a chophouse; (口) an eatery

음신 音信 〈소식〉 correspondence; (a) communication; 〈편지〉 a letter

음심 淫心 a zest for lechery; an inclination toward lewdness [licentiousness]; lustful desire

음악 音樂 music
♦ 음악의 밤 a musical evening / 음악적 재능 musical talent / 음악적인 musical; rhythmical; melodious / 음악을 좋아하는 musical; philharmonic; music-loving / 음악을 모르다 be deaf to music; have no ear for music / 음악을 배우다 take lessons in music / 음악을 연주하다 play music / 음악에 맞추어서 노래하다 sing to music
▶ 그는 음악을 모르는 사람이다 He is a man who has no music in himself.
■ 고전— classical music 교회— church music 구체— concrete music; (프) musique concrète 레코드— recorded [transcribed] music 실내— chamber music 전자— electronic music 절대— absolute [abstract] music 표제— program music ■ —가 a musician; a man of music —감독 〈영화의〉 a music director —감상실 a music hall —계 the musical world [circle] —교육 musical education —당 a concert hall; 〈옥외 연주용〉 a bandstand —대학 the college [school] of music —사 the history of music —선생 a music teacher —성 musicianship —애호가 a music lover; a lover of music —영화 a musical (film) —이론 musical [music] theory —콩쿠르 a musical contest —평론가 a music critic —학 musicology —학교 a music school [academy]; a conservatory —효과 musical effects; the (background) music

음악대 音樂隊 a (musical) band
■ —장 the band master

음악회 音樂會 a concert; a recital ♦ 음악회를 개최하다 give a concert [recital] ■ 야외— an outdoor concert 자선— a charity [benefit] concert

음양 陰陽 Yin and Yang (▶the dual characters facing each other in the nature, corresponding to moon and sun, female and male, shade and light, negative and positive)
♦음양의 조화 the harmony of the male and female principles
■一家 a fortune-teller; a diviner —오행설 (五行說) the theory of the five natural elements of the Yin and Yang (composing the nature)
음역 音域 〔樂〕 compass; a pitch extent; a (singing) range; a register ♦음역이 넓은 목소리 a voice of great compass; a voice with a wide range
■고[저]— the upper [lower] register
음역 音譯 transliteration
—음역하다 transliterate
▶베이징은 중국 수도의 중국어 발음을 음역한 것이다 Beijing is the transliteration of Chinese pronunciation of the capital city of China.
음영 吟詠 singing; recital; chanting —음영하다 recite [chant] (a poem) ♦시를 음영하다 give a recital of a poem; recite a poem
음영 陰影 shadow; shade
음욕 淫慾 improper carnal desire [passion]; sensual [sexual] appetite; lust
♦음욕을 억제하다 restrain [control] one's passion; rule lust
음용 飮用 ♦음용도 for drinking; potable; 〈마실 수 있는〉 drinkable; fit to drink / 음용에 적합하다 be potable; be fit [good] to drink; be drinkable / 음용에 적합하지 않다 be not good to drink; be unfit to drink; be undrinkable
—음용하다 drink
■一水 potable water; drinking water; water to drink; (계시) Fit to drink
음운 音韻 the phonological structure of a word; the initial sound and final rhyme of a Chinese syllable
■—론[학] phonemics; phonology : 음운학자 a phonologist —법칙 phonological law —변화 phonetic change; phonological transition —조직 the sound system
음울 陰鬱 gloom; gloominess; dismalness
—음울하다 gloomy; cheerless; melancholy; moody 《temperament》; dismal
♦음울한 날씨 gloomy [miserable, dull] weather / 음울한 하늘 an overcast [a leaden, a cloudy] sky / 음울하게 gloomily; drearily; dismally
▶음울한 날씨가 계속되었다 We've had a spell of gloomy [dull] weather.
▶그는 음울해 보였다 He looked gloomy [depressed, glum].
음위 陰痿 〔醫〕 impotence ♦음위의 impotent
음유시인 吟遊詩人 a wandering [strolling] minstrel; 〈남 프랑스의〉 a troubadour
음으로 陰— implicitly; covertly; privately; indirectly ♦음으로 양으로 implicitly and explicitly; publicly and privately / 음으로 양으로 은혜를 입다 be favored directly and indirectly
▶나는 그녀를 음으로 양으로 도왔다 I helped her implicitly and explicitly.

음이름 音— 〔樂〕 a pitch name; the name of a (musical) note; (총칭) pitch notation
음이온 陰— 〔化〕 an anion; a negative ion
음자리표 音—標 〔樂〕 a clef
음전 音栓 〈오르간의〉〔樂〕 a stop (knob); 〈관악기의〉 a fipple
음전기 陰電氣 negative electricity
음전자 陰電子 a negative electron; a negatron
음절 音節 〔音聲〕 a syllable
♦단(單)음절의 낱말 a monosyllable; a monosyllabic word / 2 음절의 낱말 a dis(s)yllable; a dis(s)yllabic word / 3 음절의 낱말 a trisyllable; a trisyllabic word / 다(多)음절의 낱말 a polysyllable; a polysyllabic word / 음절의 syllabic / 음절로 나누다 syllabicate; syllabify; divide into syllables
■一文字 a syllabic (character [symbol]); a syllabary
음정 音程 〔樂〕 a distance between tunes [tones]; an [a musical] interval; a step
♦음정이 맞다[틀리다] be in [out of] tune; be on [off] key [pitch]
▶그녀의 노래는 음정이 맞다 She sings on key.
■단[장]— a minor [major] (interval) 반— a semitone; a half step 4분— a quarter tone 전— a tone; a whole step
음조 音調 〈곡조〉 a tune; 〈음색〉 a tone; 〈운율〉 (a) rhythm; 〈가락〉 (a) melody; 〈소리의 높낮이〉 a pitch ♦음조의 변화 modulation; inflection of voice / 음조가 좋은 euphonious; melodious / 음조를 바꾸다 modulate
▶그녀는 갑자기 음조를 바꾸었다 She suddenly changed her tone.
음주 飮酒 drinking
♦음주를 삼가다 abstain from drinking; keep oneself sober / 음주로 패가 망신하다 drink one's fortune away
▶그 교통사고 이후로 그는 음주를 삼갔다 After the traffic accident, he kept himself sober.
▶음주로 인하여 그는 직장을 잃었다 His drinking caused him to lose his job.
—음주하다 drink; take wine
■—家 a drinker —벽 inebriety; drinking habit —운전 drunk [drunken] driving
음지 陰地 a shaded lot [ground]
♦음지와 양지 light and shade
▶음지가 양지되고 양지가 음지된다 Joy and sorrow are next-door neighbors.
음질 音質 the quality of sound; tone quality; (프) timbre
음차 音叉 〔物〕 a tuning fork; a diapason
음치 音癡 tone deafness ♦음치의 tone-deaf
▶그녀는 음치다 She is tone-deaf. ⇒ She has no musical sense [ear for music].
음침하다 陰沈— gloomy; dismal; dreary; melancholy; tricky; sly; wily ♦음침한 방 a gloomy room / 음침한 하늘 gloomy skies
음탕 淫蕩 dissipation; profligacy; debauchery; lewdness —음탕하다 dissipated; dissolute; licentious; profligate; debauched; lewd
♦음탕한 눈으로 보다 give sb an amorous glance / 음탕한 말을 하다 say improper [indecent] things / …에게 음탕한 짓을 하다 do something dirty to…

음파 音波 〖物〗 a sound [a sonic] wave ■—측정기 a phonometer —측정(법) phonometry —탐지기 a sound navigation and ranging
음판 陰板 〖電·寫〗 a negative (plate)
음편 音便 〖言〗 a euphonic change ♦음편상 for the sake of euphony; euphonically
음표 音標 〖樂〗 a nota; a note; notation ♦음표를 읽다[그리다] read [write] notes [musical scores]
■겹점— a double dotted note 고— the treble (score) 4분— a quarter-note 32분— a thirty-second note; (英) a demisemiquaver 16분— a sixteenth-note; (英) a semiquaver 온[전]— a Taktnote; (英) a semibreve 64분— (美) a sixty-fourth note; (英) a hemidemisemiquaver 2분— Zweitelnote; a minim; a half note 저— the bass (score) 점— a dotted note 8분— an eighth note
음표문자 音標文字 a phonetic alphabet [symbol, sign]; a phonogram ■만국[국제]— the International Phonetic Alphabet (略 IPA)
음핵 陰核 〖解〗 the clitoris
음행 淫行 a lewd [an obscene, an immoral] act
음향 音響 (a) sound; 〈소음〉 a noise ♦음향을 막다 arrest sound / 음향을 흡수하다 absorb sound; be sound-absorbent ▶그 강당은 음향 상태가 좋다[좋지 않다] The acoustics of the auditorium are excellent [bad, faulty].
■—실〈악기의〉 a sound box —전파 sound propagation —조절 acoustic control —측심기 an echo sounder; an echo-sounding device —탐지기 a sound detector —효과 sound [acoustic] effects; acoustics
음향학 音響學 acoustics ■—자 an acoustician
음험하다 陰險— guileful; insidious; tricky; sly; wily; crafty; dark; snaky; treacherous; designing; double-dealing ♦음험한 사람 an insidious man; a deep one; a snake / 음험한 수단을 쓰다 use subtle tricks; play a deep game / 눈초리가 음험하다 have a nasty look in one's eye
음화 陰畫 〖寫〗 a negative (picture)
음흉 陰凶 wickedness; treacherousness ▶그는 음흉 주머니이다 He is a black-hearted [treacherous] person. ⇌ He is a snake in the grass.
—음흉하다 black-hearted; wicked; treacherous; crafty; viperous ♦음흉한 웃음 a wicked smile
읍 邑 eup; a town ♦읍에 가다 go up to town ■—민 inhabitants of a town; the townsfolk; the townspeople; townsmen —사무소 a town office —소재지 the seat of a town office —장 a town headman
읍 揖 a polite bow with one's hands in front —읍하다 make a polite [low] bow with one's hands in front of the chest
읍내 邑內 (in) a town ⇨ 읍(邑)
읍례 揖禮 a polite bow with one's hands in front of the chest ⇨ 읍(揖)
읍소하다 泣訴— implore [supplicate, appeal to] sb for mercy with tears in one's eyes
응 1 〈대답할 때〉 yeah; yes; well; h'm!; hum!; all right; OK
▶〖會話〗「커피 좀 들래?」「응, 부탁해」 "Would you like some coffee?" "Yes, please."
▶〖會話〗「안 올 거니?」「응, 안 가」 "Won't you come?" "No, I won't."
2 〈대답을 구할 때〉 OK?; huh?
▶야구하자, 응? Let's play ball, huh?
응결 凝結 〈엉김〉 coagulation; curdling; 〈시멘트의 응고〉 setting; 〈액체의 고체화〉 congelation; solidification; freezing; 〈기체의 액화〉 condensation
—응결하다 coagulate; congeal; solidify; freeze; curdle; set; condense
▶수증기는 응결하여 물이 된다 Steam condenses into water.
▶물은 응결하여 얼음이 된다 Water freezes into ice.
▶우유는 오래 두면 응결한다 Milk curdles when kept too long.
■—고도 the condensation level —열 the heat of condensation —핵 〖氣〗 a condensation nucleus —효소 〖化〗 a coagulating enzyme
응고 凝固 〈굳어짐〉 solidification; 〈엉김〉 coagulation; 〈curdling〉; congelation; setting; freezing
—응고하다 solidify; congeal; coagulate; set; freeze; fix
■급 냉—rapid solidification ■—약 a coagulant: 항(抗)응고약 an anticoagulant —열 heat of solidification —점 the solidifying [freezing, setting] point
응급 應急 ♦응급의 emergency; 〈임시〉 temporary; 〈임시방편〉 makeshift; stopgap
■—물자 emergency supplies —수단 an emergency measure ⇨ 응급조처 —실 a first-aid room; an emergency room —책 an expeditious measure ⇨ 응급조처 —처치 ⇨ 응급치료 —환자 a first-aid patient
응급조처 應急措處 an emergency [expeditious] measure; a makeshift [stopgap] measure; a temporary expedient
♦응급조처를 취하다 take a temporary expedient; employ a stopgap measure
응급치료 應急治療 first aid; first-aid treatment
♦화상의 응급치료(법) the first-aid treatment of burns / 응급치료를 하다 give [administer] first aid [first-aid treatment] (to); apply first-aid dressing ((to)) / 응급치료 훈련을 하다 train sb in first aid
■—소 a first-aid room [station]
응낙 應諾 consent; agreement; assent; acceptance 〈承諾〉
—응낙하다 agree with sb; agree to (a plan, a proposal, a request); give one's consent (to); accept
▶그녀는 고개를 끄덕여 응낙했다 She nodded her assent.
응달 the shade; the shady place [side]
♦응달의 shady; in the shade / 응달이 지다 be shaded ((by)) / 응달에서 말리다 dry sth out of

응답 應答 a response; an answer; a reply
▶무선전화의 호출에 금방 응답이 왔다 The radiophone calls were soon responded to.
▶그는 무슨 질문이든 응답에 막힘이 없다 He can give ready answers to any questions.
▶너의 기도는 하나님의 응답을 받을 것이다 Your prayers will be answered by God.
■질의— questions and answers; answers to queries ■—자 a respondent

응당 應當 for sure; to be sure; without fail; naturally; duly; necessarily; as a matter of course ♦응당 해야 할 일 a thing *one* ought to do [should do]

응대 應對 〈접대〉 a reception; 〈회견〉 a meeting ♦응대를 잘하는 사람 a man of good [pleasing, winning] address / 응대가 서투른 사람 a man of awkward address
—응대하다 receive (a guest); interview (with); 〈점원이〉 serve; wait on (a customer)
▶손님에게 정중히 응대하시오 Wait on customers politely.
▶나는 응접실에서 손님을 응대했다 I received my guest in the parlor.

응력 應力 〔機〕 stress

응모 應募 〈예약・기부의〉 (a) subscription; 〈입학・취직의〉 (an) application; 〈병역의〉 enlistment; 〈경기 등의〉 (an) entry
—응모하다 subscribe for; apply for; make an application for; enlist (as a volunteer) for; enter for (a race); come forward
▶그는 그 회사의 기술자 모집에 응모했다 He applied for a position as an engineer in the company.
▶신춘문예에 많은 사람이 응모했다 A lot of people applied for the literary contest in spring.
■—신청 an application for subscription —액 the amount subscribed; the subscription —요령 how to apply [enter] —용지 a written application; an application form [blank] —원고 manuscripts of contestants (for the prize)

응모자 應募者 an applicant (for a school); a subscriber (to); an entrant; a volunteer ■현상 논문— a prize essayist

응보 應報 retribution; retributive justice; 〈천벌〉 nemesis
▶그것은 네가 저지른 나쁜 짓에 대한 응보다 It's a punishment for the wrong you did. ⇒ That's what you get for doing wrong.
▶나쁜 짓을 하면 무서운 응보가 뒤따른다 An evil deed calls forth fearful retribution.

응분 應分 ♦응분의 appropriate; due; reasonable; suitable / 응분의 몫을 하다 do *one's* due share / 응분의 기부를 하다 contribute according to *one's* means; contribute what [as much as] *one* can afford / 응분의 대우를 받다 be given proper [due] treatment / 응분의 처우를 하다 give [render] *sb* his due

응사 應射 a return shot; firing back ♦응사를 받다 bring [draw] return fire (from the enemy)

응석 (a child's) playing on another's affection; playing the baby (to)
♦응석(을) 받다 be indulgent to (one's child); indulge (one's child); make much of; pamper; spoil / 응석(을) 부리다 play on (another's) affection; behave like a spoilt child; play the baby (to)
▶이 아이는 응석이 심하다 This is quite a spoilt child. ⇒ This boy is quite spoiled.
▶아이들은 지나치게 응석을 받아 주면 안된다 Children must not be indulged too much.
▶아저씨한테 응석 부리면 안돼요 Don't make up to your uncle like that.
■—꾸러기[둥이, 받이] a spoiled [spoilt] child; a pampered child; a brat

응소 應召 answering a call —응소하다 answer the call; get drafted; join the colors; obey the call-up ■—병 a conscript; an enlisted man; a draftee; 〔美〕 a selectee —율 draft quota

응소 應訴 acceptance of a legal suit; an answer —응소하다 accept [answer] a legal suit; meet sb's lawsuit [charges]

응송 應訟 an answer ⇨ 응소(應訴)

응수 應酬 〈대답〉 a reply; an answer; a response; 〈말대꾸〉 a retort; a repartee; 〈답례〉 a return; 〈교환〉 an exchange; give and take ♦비난의 응수 hurling accusation at each other
—응수하다 respond; reply; return; counter; give [make] a (sharp) retort

응수 應手 〈바둑・장기의〉 a countermove; a response —응수하다 countermove; make a countermove; answer a move

응시 凝視 a stare; a gaze
—응시하다 stare at; gaze at; fix [fasten] *one's* eyes on; look hard [steadily] at
▶그는 먼데를 응시하고 있었다 He was staring into the distance.
▶그녀는 별을 응시하고 서 있었다 She stood gazing at the stars.
▶그녀는 겁내지 않고 내 얼굴을 응시했다 She looked at me with a fearless gaze.

응시 應試 applying [〔英〕 sitting] for an examination
—응시하다 apply [sit] for an examination
▶내년에는 어느 대학에 응시할 생각이냐? Which university are you going to apply for next year?
■—자 a participant in an examination; an applicant (for)

응애응애 newling; whimpering ♦응애응애 울다 newl; pule; whimper

응어리 1 〈근육 등의〉 stiffness; a lump
▶어깨에 응어리가 생겼다 I feel stiff in the shoulder.
▶응어리가 없어도 유방암일 수 있다 Breast cancer can be present without a lump.
2 〈과실의 속〉 the core; a kernel; 〈사물의 핵심〉 the heart (of a matter)
♦사과의 응어리를 도려내다 core an apple
3 〈맺힌 감정〉 a bad feeling; an ill [unpleasant] feeling
▶그 사건은 두 사람 사이에 감정적 응어리를 남

겼다 The case left an antagonistic feeling [hard feelings] between the two.
▶ 우리 두 사람 사이의 응어리는 풀렸다 There is no more ill feeling between us.
▶ 두 사람 사이에는 아무런 응어리도 남지 않았다 There were no bad feelings left between them.

응용 應用 (practical) application
▶ 이 기술은 응용 범위가 넓을 것으로 기대된다 This technology is expected to have a wide range of application.
—응용하다 apply 《science to industry》; put 《knowledge》 to practical use; put 《theories》 into practice
▶ 이 과에서 배운 것을 응용하시오 Put to use what you have learned in this lesson.
▶ 과학을 실지에 응용하는 것이 필요하다 It is necessary to put science to practical use.
▶ 그는 영어교육에 언어학을 응용하려 하고 있다 He is trying to apply linguistics to English teaching.
▶ 그들은 유전공학을 신품종 개발에 응용하고 있다 They apply genetic engineering to the development of new breeds.
■ —경제학 [과학, 수학] applied economics [science, mathematics] —문제 an applied problem [question] —미술 applied fine arts

응원 應援 〈원조〉 aid; assistance; help; 〈지지〉 support; 〈경기의 성원〉 cheering; (美) rooting
♦ 응원을 요청하다 ask *sb* for aid [support]; call in *sb's* aid; send for an assistance
▶ 우리는 여학생들의 응원에 고무되었다 We were encouraged by the cheering of the girls.
▶ 하루 종일 야구 응원을 했더니 목이 쉬었다 I lost my voice because I was cheering at a baseball game all day.
—응원하다 aid; assist; help; give help [aid] (to); support; back (up); cheer; (美口) root (for)
▶ 관중은 모두 자기의 팀을 응원했다 All the crowd cheered [rooted for] his team.
▶ 그들은 모두 나를 응원해 주었다 They all cheered for me.
■ —가 a rooters' song —군 reinforcements —기 a rooters' pennant —석 a cheering section; (美口) the rooter's seat —자 a supporter; a backer; a cheering enthusiast [fan]; (美口) a rooter

응원단 應援團 a cheering [supporting] party [squad]; a cheering [rooting] group; a party of fans [enthusiasts, rooters]; (美口) rah-rah boys —장 a cheerleader; (美) a head rooter

응전 應戰 a response
♦ 도전과 응전 challenge and response
—응전하다 accept [take up] a challenge; accept battle; respond [reply] to 《a fire》; return fire; fight back
▶ 그들은 용감하게 응전했다 They fought back bravely.

응접 應接 〈응대〉 (a) reception; 〈접견〉 an interview ▶ 나는 손님 응접으로 바빴다 I was busy with visitors.
—응접하다 receive 《a visitor》; meet 《one's guests》; hold an interview with; see 《company》
■ —세트 drawing-room suite

응접실 應接室 a drawing [reception] room; (美) a parlor ♦ 손님을 응접실로 안내하다 show a visitor into a parlor

응집 凝集 〈엉겨 모임〉 cohesion; aggregation
—응집하다 cohere; aggregate ■ —력 cohesive force; cohesion-tension: 응집력이 있는 cohesive —반응 [醫] agglutination reaction —소 agglutinin —원 agglutinogen

응징 膺懲 〈징계〉 chastisement; punishment
—응징하다 chastise; punish ♦ 악을 응징하다 chastise vice; punish the wicked

응축 凝縮 〈엉기어 줄어듦〉 condensation —응축하다 condense ♦ 가스를 액체로 응축하다 condense a gas to a liquid ■ —기 condenser

응하다 應— 1 〈대답하다〉 answer; reply; respond; accept
▶ 내 이야기를 마친 뒤 질문에 응하겠습니다 I will answer your questions after I have finished my speech.
▶ 그 부름에 아무도 응하는 사람이 없었다 There was nobody who responded to the call.
2 〈승낙하다〉 accept 《an invitation》; comply with; consent to
▶ 기꺼이 상담에 응하겠습니다 I will be happy to give you advice, if necessary.
▶ 아무 때라도 도전하면 응해 주마 I am ready to accept your challenge any time.
▶ 이 초대에 응해야 되는 건가? I wonder if I have to accept this invitation or not.
3 〈모집에〉 apply for; make application for; enter
♦ 신입생 모집에 응하다 apply for admission to a school / 회원 모집에 응하다 apply for membership in a society
▶ 현상소설 모집에 응했지만 실패했다 I entered a prize-contest for stories, but I lost.
4 〈충족하다〉 meet; satisfy; fulfill; supply; answer
♦ 수요에 응하다 meet [supply] the demand / 새 시대의 필요와 요구에 응하다 meet the needs and demands of a new age
▶ 손해에 대한 일체의 배상 요구에는 응할 수 없습니다 We will never satisfy all claims for damage.

응혈 凝血 a clot; a coagulum; gore
—응혈하다 clot; coagulate

응회암 凝灰岩 (a) tuff

의 1 〈소유·소속〉 -'s; of; belonging to

[解說] (1) 생물의 경우에는 's를 붙이고 무생물에는 of를 써서 소유격을 만드는 것이 원칙이다. 그러나 무생물의 경우에도 시간·거리·중량·가격·지명 등을 나타내는 말에 대해서는 관용적으로 's를 붙여서 말하는 수가 있다: 오늘 신문 today's newspaper / 한국의 장래 Korea's future. 다만「오늘의 한국의 정세」라고 할 때는 today's Korea's situation과 같이 's를 이중으로 쓸 수는 없고 Korea's situation (of) today라고 쓴다.
(2) 일반적으로 of를 쓰는 편이 객관적이고 정확하며 딱딱한 말투가 되지만 정보의 초점이란 관점에서 's와 of를 구분해야 할 때가 있다.

the title of the novel과 the novel's title의 경우는 둘 다 쓸 수가 있지만, 전자는 novel에 초점을 두고 후자는 title에 초점을 둔 어법이라 할 수 있다.

♦나의 서재 my study / 형의 책 my brother's book / 너의 드레스 your dress / 집의 지붕 the roof of a house / 우리의 꿈 our dream / 클럽의 회원 a member of a club / 인간의 가치 a man's worth; the worth of a man / 돈의 가치 the value of money; monetary value / 한국의 경제 Korea's economy; the economy of Korea; Korean economy
▶이 책은 나의 것이다 This book belongs to me. ⇌ This book is mine.
▶부산에서는 숙부의 집에 머물렀다 In Pusan I stayed at my uncle's. ⇌ I stayed with my uncle in Pusan.
▶그는 아이의 머리를 때렸다 He struck the child on the head.
2 〈인적 관계〉 -'s; of; between; to
♦톰의 아버지 Tom's father / 나의 친구 a friend of mine; one of my friends / 송선생의 조카 a nephew of Mr. Song's; 《be》 nephew to Mr. Song / 사제지간의 관계 the relations between teacher and pupil
3 〈장소 관계〉 at; in; on; over; from
♦강변의 도시 a town on a river / 모스크바의 겨울 the winter in Moscow / 서울의 야경 the night view of Seoul / 고향의 부모 one's parents at home
4 〈시간 관계〉 of; in
♦오늘의 뉴스 today's news / 그 시대의 사람들 men of that time; men in those days / 젊은 시절의 꿈 the romantic vision of youth
5 〈작가〉 by; of; -'s
♦헤밍웨이의 소설 a novel (written) by Hemingway / 셰익스피어의 희곡 the plays of Shakespeare / 피카소의 그림 a painting by Picaso; a Picaso / 슈베르트의 미완성 교향곡 Schubert's *Unfinished Symphony*
6 〈구성·분량〉 of
♦가축의 떼 a herd of cattle / 다섯 마리의 새끼 고양이 five kittens / 40킬로그램의 쌀 forty kilograms of rice / 한 줌의 모래 a handful of sand
▶수십만 명의 사람이 직업을 잃었다 Hundreds of thousands of people have lost their jobs.
7 〈부분〉 of
♦학생의 반수 half (of) the students / 그 문제의 일부 part of the problem
8 〈산출〉 (coming) from; produced in; of
♦대구의 사과 apples from Taegu / 안성의 유기 brassware from Ansŏng / 제주도의 말 a Cheju-do horse
9 〈재료·수단〉 of; from; in
♦대리석의 상(像) a statue in marble
10 〈동격·정의(定義)〉 of; (such) as
♦백미터의 거리 a distance of 100 meters / 5년의 기한 a term of five years
11 〈동작의 주체〉 -'s; of; by
♦그의 양친의 동의 his parents' consent / 정부의 결정 the government's decision; the decision of [by] the government / 열차의 도착 the train's arrival; the arrival of the train
12 〈동작의 목적〉 -'s; for; of
♦가족의 부양 the family's support; the support of the family / 아이들의 교육 children's education; education for [of] children / 진리의 탐구 the quest of truth / 과세의 대상 property liable for taxation
13 〈동작의 대상〉 of; to
♦사장의 심부름 an errand for the president / 유산의 상속 succession to property / 성공의 열쇠 the key to success
14 〈…에 관한〉 about; on; of; in
♦경제학의 권위 an authority on economics / 세계사의 시험 an exam on [in] world history
15 〈기타〉 in; of
♦방년 열 여섯 살의 처녀 a girl of sixteen summers [of sweet sixteen] / 문제의 사나이 the man in question / 음악의 도시 비엔나 Vienna, the city of music / 최대의 겸손 the greatest humility / 반대의 의견 an opinion to the contrary

의 義 1 〈정의〉 justice; righteousness; 〈덕의〉 morality; 〈신의〉 faith; 〈충의〉 loyalty; 〈의기〉 chivalry
♦의를 중시하다 respect justice / 의를 위해 일어서다 stand for a good cause / 의를 위해 죽다 die in the cause of justice
▶의를 알고 행하지 않음은 용기가 없어서이다 To see what is right and not to do it shows want of courage. ⇌ Knowing what is right without practicing it betrays one's cowardice.
2 〈정리(情理)〉 relationship; relations; ties; bonds
♦친구의 의 the ties of friendship / 형제의 의를 맺다 swear to be brothers / (부모가) 자식과의 의를 끊다 cut off relationship with *one's* son
3 〈뜻〉 a sense; (a) meaning; signification
의 誼 〈사이〉 relations; relationship; terms; 〈정의〉 friendship; intimacy; good will; 〈화합〉 harmony; concord
♦의좋은 부부 a devoted [happy] couple / 의가 좋다[나쁘다] be on good [bad] terms 《with》 / 의가 상하다 break 《with》; quarrel [fall out] 《with》; be estranged 《from》 / 의좋게 지내다 chum up with
▶그는 이웃 사람과 의가 좋다 He lives in harmony with his neighbors.
▶그 부부는 의가 나빠졌다 The husband and wife are estranged [alienated] from each other.
의가 衣架 a coat hanger ⇨ 옷걸이
의거 義擧 a noble [worthy] undertaking [uprising]; a heroic [patriotic] deed; a movement in public interests
■ **4.19―** = 4.19혁명
의거하다 依據― 〈근거·입각하다〉 be based 《on, upon》; be founded 《on》; be grounded 《on, upon, in》; 〈준거하다〉 conform 《to》; accord 《with》
♦자료에 의거하여 on the basis [authority] of the data / 헌법에 의거하여 in conformity [accordance] with the constitution / …의 규정에 의거하여 under the provisions of… / …에

의거하여 행동하다 act on (the basis of)...
의걸이(장) 衣―(欌) a wardrobe chest
의견 意見 an opinion; a view; an idea; a suggestion
♦다른 의견 different [divergent] opinions / 다수[소수]의 의견 a majority [minority] opinion / 명확한[솔직한] 의견 a definite [frank] opinion / 상반되는 의견 a contrary opinion; an opposite view / 전문가의 의견 an expert opinion; expert advice; professional advice / 내 의견으로는 in my opinion / 남의 의견에 따르다 bow [yield] to *sb's* opinion / 다수의 의견에 따르다 agree to the views of the majority
〈의견의〉 의견의 교환 an exchange of opinions [views] / 의견의 일치 the consensus; unanimity of opinion; an agreement in views [opinions] / 의견의 불일치 a discord of opinion; disagreement in opinion / 의견의 대립 a split of opinion / 의견의 충돌 a conflict [collision, crash] of opinions / 온건한 [과격한] 의견의 소유자 a man of moderate [extreme] opinions
▶ 요컨대 그것은 의견의 차이다 In other words it is a difference of opinions.
▶ 두 사람은 끝까지 의견의 일치를 보지 못했다 No agreement was reached between the two until the end.
〈의견은[이]〉 그의 의견은 정반대였다 His opinion was quite to the contrary.
▶ 그의 의견은 네 의견과 정반대다 His opinion is directly opposite to yours.
▶ 나는 그들과 의견이 맞지 않는다 My opinion is different from theirs. ⇌ I disagree with them.
▶ 이 문제에 대해 의견이 분분하다 There are conflicting opinions on this matter.
▶[會話]「무슨 의견이 있으시면 말씀해 보시죠」「아뇨, 별로 말씀 드릴 것이 없습니다」"If you have anything to say, please go ahead." "No, I have nothing special to say."
▶ 이 점에서는 대체로 의견이 일치되어 있다 There is a general agreement on this point.
〈의견을〉 그것에 관해 당신의 의견을 듣고 싶습니다 I want to have your comment on it.
▶ 나는 각자의 의견을 물었다 I asked each person's opinion.
▶ 기탄없이 의견을 말씀해 주십시오 Will you please state your opinion without reserve? ⇌ Will you please let us hear your frank opinion?
▶ 내 의견을 말씀 드리겠습니다 I'm going to express my opinion.
▶ 우리는 각자 자기의 의견을 피력했다 Each of us expressed our opinion.
▶ 우리는 허심탄회하게 의견을 나누었다 We have exchanged our views very frankly.
▶ 그들은 서로 의견을 달리 했다 They disagreed with each other.
▶ 그는 그것에 관해 상당히 진보적인 의견을 가지고 있다 He has [holds, entertains] a rather liberal opinion about it.
▶ 그녀는 그 문제에 관해 확실한 의견을 밝히려고 하지 않았다 She would not commit herself about that issue.

의견서 意見書 *one's* written opinion ♦의견서를 제출하다 present a written opinion [a statement of *one's* views]
의결 議決 a decision; a resolution
♦…의 의결을 거쳐야 하다 be subject to the decision of...
―**의결하다** decide; resolve; 〈투표로〉 pass a vote 《of》; vote 《for, against》
▶ 위원회는 교육비의 지출을 의결했다 The board voted the money for education.
▶ 내각 불신임안이 의결되었다 A motion of nonconfidence in the cabinet was passed.
■―**권** a voting right; the right to vote [of voting] ―**기관** a legislative [deliberative] organ ―**사항** 〈결정해야 할〉 matters for decision [resolution, deliberation]; 〈기결된〉 matters settled [decided upon]
의고 擬古 imitation of ancient [archaic, classical] style ♦의고적인 pseudoarchaic; archaistic; classical
―**의고하다** write [constitute, compose] in (imitation of) classical style
■―**문** a pseudoclassical style ―**주의** classicism; classicalism; archaism ―**주의자** a classicist; an archaist
의곡 歪曲 distortion ⇨ 왜곡(歪曲)
의과 醫科 the medical department (of a university)
♦의과를 나오다 graduate from a university in medicine; graduate from a medical college
■―**대학** a medical college ―**대학생** a medical student
의관 衣冠 〈옷차림〉 dress and hat; clothing and headgear; attire ♦의관을 갖추다 be in full dress; be decently dressed / 의관을 정제하다 dress *oneself* properly; tidy oneself
의구 依舊 〈옛 모습과 다름 없음〉 being unchanged ―**의구하다** 《remain》 unchanged; 〈서술적〉 remain as it was; be as (it was) before
의구 疑懼 apprehension; suspicion; doubt; uneasiness ―**의구하다** apprehend; suspect; doubt; fear
의구심 疑懼心 misgivings; apprehensions; fear; doubts; suspicion
♦의구심을 품다 entertain [have] doubts 《about》; harbor suspicion; feel misgivings [apprehensions] 《about》
▶ 실험의 결과에 대해 약간의 의구심이 있었다 There were some misgivings [doubts] about the outcome of the experiment.
▶ 나의 의구심은 풀렸다 My suspicion has been cleared away. ⇌ My doubts have been dispelled.
의기 意氣 〈기운〉 spirit(s); heart; 《美》 grit; vigor; 〈사기〉 morale
♦의기가 왕성하다 be in high spirits; be elated; be in exaltation
▶ 좋지 않은 소식이 우리의 의기를 꺾었다 The bad news dampened our spirits.
의기 義氣 〈의협심〉 chivalrous spirit; chivalry; heroism; 〈공공심〉 public spirit
의기상투 意氣相投 mutual understanding ⇨ 의기투합
의기소침 意氣銷沈 depression [loss] of spirits;

의도의 표현

1. …할 생각이다; …하려고 생각하고 있다
(1) be going to do
▶ 자네는 대학을 졸업하면 무엇을 할 생각인가? What are you going to do when you leave college?
▶ 그녀는 커서 피아니스트가 되려고 생각하고 있다 She is going to be a pianist when she grown up.
▶ 나는 올 여름에는 자동차 운전을 배울 생각이야 I'm going to take driving lessons this summer.
▶ 이곳에는 1주일동안 머물 생각입니다 I'm going to stay here for a week.
▶ 우리는 그들과 그것을 논의할 생각은 없습니다 We're not going to discuss it with them.
[어법]
① be going to는「의도+계획」을 나타낸다.
② 때를 나타내는 어구가 없을 때에는「지금 곧」이란 뜻으로 아주 가까운 미래를 나타낸다.
[보기] I'm going to tell you an interesting story. (재미있는 이야기를 들려 주마)
③ I was going to call on you yesterday. (어제 당신을 방문할 생각이었다)와 같이 was [were] going to do는 실현되지 않은 의도를 표시한다.

(2) intend to do
▶ 저는 새 차를 살 생각입니다 I intend to buy a new car.
▶ 저는 의사가 될 생각입니다 I intend to become a doctor.
▶ 여러분들은 여름 휴가를 어디서 보낼 생각이십니까? Where do you intend to spend your summer vacation?
▶ 내일 날씨가 좋으면 드라이브를 할 생각입니다 If it is fine tomorrow, I intend to go for a drive.
▶ 나는 그에게 편지 쓸 생각은 없어요 I don't intend to write to him.

(3) 기타: plan to do; be thinking of doing

▶ 고등학교를 졸업하면 무엇을 할 생각이냐? What do you plan to do after finishing high school?
▶ 우리는 금년 여름에는 캠핑을 갈 생각이다 We plan [are planning] to go camping this summer.
▶ 당신은 정남씨와 결혼할 생각입니까? Are you thinking of marrying Mr. Chŏng-nam?
[어법]
plan의 본래의 뜻은「꾀하다, 계획하다」, be thinking of doing은「어떻게 할지 고려중이다」라는 뜻을 나타낸다.

2. …할 생각이었다 (그러나 실제로는 하지 않았다: 실현되지 않은 과거의 계획)
had intended to do; intend to have + 과거분사
▶ 나는 설악산으로 피서갈 생각이었다 I had intended to go to Mt. Sŏraksan for the summer. ⇌ I intended to have gone to Sŏraksan for the summer.
▶ 당신을 방문할 생각이었으나 비가 와서 가지 못했습니다 I had intended to call on you, but the rain prevented me from doing so. ⇌ I intended to have called on you, but the rain prevented me from doing so.

3. (아무)의 생각은 …하려는 것이다; …하려는 것이 (아무)의 생각이다
one's intention is to do; it is one's intention to do
▶ 그의 생각은 내년에 집을 지으려는 것이다 His intention is to build a house next year. ⇌ He intends to build a house next year.
▶ 내년에 집을 지으려는 것이 그의 생각이다 It is his intention to build a house next year.

4. …할 생각[의도]은 없다
have no intention of doing
▶ 그는 그곳에 갈 생각은 없다 He has no intention of going there.
▶ 그녀는 그와 결혼할 생각은 전혀 없다 She doesn't have the least intention of marrying him.

---

dejection; discouragement ―**의기소침하다** be dispirited [disheartened]; be depressed (in spirits); be in low spirits
▶ 그는 의기소침해 있다 He is depressed [in low spirits].
의기양양 意氣揚揚 elation; a triumphant air ―**의기양양하다** triumphant; exultant
♦ 의기양양한 표정 a triumphant [proud] look / 의기양양하게 exultingly; exultantly; elatedly; proudly; triumphantly; with a triumphant air [look]; in good [high] spirits
▶ 그는 의기양양한 모습이었다 He looked proud [triumphant]. ⇌ He put on a triumphant air.
▶ 그들은 의기양양하게 귀국했다 They went home in high spirits. ⇌ They left for home triumphantly.
의기저상 意氣沮喪 depression of spirits ⇨ 의기소침

의기충천하다 意氣衝天― one's spirits rise to the skies; be in royal [high, towering, roaring] spirits
의기투합 意氣投合 mutual understanding; affinity ―**의기투합하다** be of congenial temper; be of a [one] mind; find a kindred [congenial] spirit in sb
▶ 그들은 의기투합한다 They are like them minded. ⇌ There is a great affinity between.
의념 疑念 a (feeling of) doubt; suspicion; misgivings; distrust ♦ 의념을 품다 have doubts [misgivings]; suspect
의논 議論 consultation; (a) conference; a talk ♦ 의논 상대 an adviser; a counselor / 의논 끝에 after consultation; 〈합의하여〉 by common [mutual] consent / 의논중이다 be in council [consultation] / 의논 상대가 되다 give [offer]

의당 counsel [advice] to sb / 이마를 맞대고 의논하다 lay [put] their [our] heads together (about sth)
▶ 그에게는 의논 상대가 없다 He has no one to talk to [consult with, turn to for advice].
—**의논하다** consult 《sb, with sb about sth》; discuss 《sth with sb》; talk 《with sb over sth》; confer 《with》
▶ 어떻든 상대방과 의논해 봅시다 Anyway let's have a talk with the other side.
▶ 그들은 모처에서 장시간 의논했다 They conferred at a certain place for a long time.
▶ 그것은 가족들과 의논한 뒤 결정하고 싶다 I'd like to decide after discussing it with my family.
▶ 나는 그 계획에 관해 부모님과 의논했다 I talked with my parents about the plan. ⇌ I discussed the plan with my parents.
▶ 그들은 자기들끼리 의논해서 집을 팔았다 They sold their house by personal [private] negotiation.

의당 宜當 naturally; duly; justly; properly; deservedly; (as a matter) of course
▶ 너는 의당 알고 있을 줄 알았다 I took it for granted (that) you knew it.
▶ 그는 의당 출발을 연기했어야 했다 He should [ought to] have postponed his departure.
▶ 빚진 것은 의당 갚아야 한다 One ought to pay what one owes.
—**의당하다** proper; just; natural; deserved; due
▶ 나는 의당한 일을 했다 I did what was right and proper.
▶ 네가 그의 충고를 듣는 것이 의당한 일이다 It is natural that you (should) listen to his advice.

의대 衣帶 clothes and belts
의대 醫大 a medical college ⇨ 의과(~대학)
의도 意圖 〈의향〉 an intention; an intent; 〈목적〉 an aim; a purpose
♦ 의도적인 intentional; deliberate / 의도적으로 on purpose; intentionally
▶ 네 의도를 모르겠다 I don't understand your intentions [what you mean].
▶ 그는 그것을 훔칠 의도는 없었다 He had no intention of stealing it.
▶ 결과는 우리의 의도와는 반대가 되버렸다 The result was contrary to our purpose.
▶ 그녀는 의도적으로 나를 방해했다 She got in my way intentionally [on purpose].
—**의도하다** intend (to do); aim (at); drive (at)
▶ 이것은 내가 의도한 바가 아니다 This is not what I intended.

의례 依例 〈의전례〉 following precedent
—**의례하다** follow precedent; take example
의례 儀禮 etiquette; courtesy; 〈전례〉 formality; 〈의식〉 a ceremony
♦ 의례의, 의례적인 ceremonial; formal / 외교적인 의례 diplomatic etiquette / 가정의례준칙 (the) family rite rules / 의례적으로 out of courtesy; by courtesy / 의례적인 방문을 하다 pay a formal [courtesy] visit (to); make a courtesy call (at)

의례건 依例件 a matter of course; customary affairs; a common practice
의례히 依例— habitually; always ⇨ 으레
의론 議論 an argument; a discussion; a debate; a dispute; a controversy
▶ 그 문제로 의론이 분분했다 There was much heated [hot] discussion about the matter.
▶ 그것은 의론의 여지가 없다 It is beyond (all) dispute. ⇌ It admits of no dispute.
의롭다 義— righteous; rightful; right-minded; just
♦ 의로운 사람 a righteous man; (총칭) the righteous / 의로운 일을 하다 do a right thing; do right / 대의를 위해 의롭게 죽다 sacrifice oneself for the sake of justice
의롱 衣籠 〈옷농〉 a wardrobe
의뢰 依賴 **1** 〈의지〉 dependence; reliance
—**의뢰하다** depend [rely] upon; lean on; turn [look] to 《sb for》
2 〈부탁〉 a request; solicitation; 〈위탁〉 trust; commission
▶ 그는 우리의 거듭된 원조 의뢰를 거절했다 He declined [refused] our repeated requests for help.
▶ 그의 의뢰로 나는 그의 사무실로 전화했다 I telephoned his office at his request.
—**의뢰하다** request; make sb a request; ask 《sb to do》; entrust 《sb with a matter》; commission 《sb to do》; place 《a matter》 in sb's hands
♦ 변호사에게 의뢰하다 commit [leave] 《a matter》 to a lawyer
▶ 그는 사건을 변호사에게 의뢰했다 He left the case in the hands of the lawyer.
■ —서명 a letter of request; a written request —인 a client

의뢰심 依賴心 reliance; dependence ▶ 자네는 너무 의뢰심이 지나쳐 You rely too much upon others.
의료 衣料 clothing; articles of dress
의료 醫療 medical care; medical service
♦ 국립의료원 the National Medical Center
■ —기계 medical instruments [appliances] —기관 a medical institution —법인 a medical corporation —봉사 volunteer medical service —비 a medical fee; medical expenses; a doctor's bill —산업 the medical industry; the medical care industry —시설 medical facilities —실 a clinic room —요구 medical requirement —용품 a medical supply
의료보험 醫療保險 medical (care) insurance.
♦ 한국 의료보험 관리 공단 the Korea Medical Insurance Management Corporation
■ —비 medical insurance premiums —제도 the medical insurance [security] system —혜택 (expand) medical insurance benefits 《for》 —혜택자[수혜자] the beneficiaries of medical insurance
의료수가 醫療酬價 the charge for medical treatment; a medical fee ■ —규정[기준] the rules [standards] for medical fees
의류 衣類 clothing; clothes; garments; wear
♦ 남자용 의류 men's clothing / 여자용 의류

의뢰의 표현

1. …해 주십시오
Please…; …, please (명령문에 붙여서 씀)
▶ 문을 좀 열어주십시오. Please open the door. ⇌ Open the door, please.
▶ (식탁에서) 버터를 좀 건네주세요 Please pass the butter. ⇌ Pass the butter, please.
▶ 당신이 가주십시오. 나는 집에 있을테니까 You go, please, and I'll stay home. (▶명령·의뢰를 받는 상대를 나타낼 때가 있음)
▶ 커피를 두 잔 주십시오 Two coffees, please.
▶ 결혼 반지를 보여주십시오 Wedding rings, please. (▶동사를 생략할 때는 please를 끝에 씀. Please wedding rings.라고는 하지 않음)

2. …해 주겠습니까?
(1) Will you…?; Will you please…?; Will you…, please?
▶ 이 편지를 좀 부쳐주겠습니까? Will you mail this letter for me?
▶ 내 대신 전화 좀 받아주겠습니까? Will you answer the telephone for me?
▶ 좀 기다려 주겠습니까? Will you please wait a few minutes?
▶ 사고를 목격하신 분은 가까운 경찰서로 연락 좀 해 주겠습니까? Will anyone who saw the accident please communicate with the nearest police station?
▶ 창문 좀 열어주겠습니까? Will you please open the window? ⇌ Will you open the window, please?
▶ 여기에 서명 좀 해 주겠습니까? Will you sign your name here, please?
[어법]
① please는 문장 중간이나 끝 어디에나 써도 된다.
② please를 문장 끝에 쓸 때는 그 앞에 콤마를 찍는다.
③ 명령에 가까운 의뢰의 표현일 때는 물음표(?) 대신에 마침표(.)를 찍을 때도 있다. 이때의 억양은 문장의 끝이 내려간다.
④ Will you?를 문장 끝에 쓰는 경우는 친한 사이에서 쓰는 말투로서 그다지 정중한 어법은 아니다.
[보기] Pass the butter, will you? (버터를 좀 건네 줄래?) 이 경우 Will you pass the butter, please? 라고 하는 것이 정중한 말투다.

(2) Can you…?; Can you…, please?
▶ 시간을 좀 알려 주겠습니까? (지금 몇 시 입니까?) Can you tell me the time?
▶ 창문을 닫아주겠습니까? Can you close the window, please?

3. …해 주시겠습니까? (정중한 표현)
(1) Would you…?; Would you please…?; Would you…, please?
▶ 이 편지 좀 부쳐 주시겠습니까? Would you mail this letter for me?
▶ 우체국으로 가는 길을 좀 가르쳐 주시겠습니까? Would you tell me the way to the post office?
▶ 창문 좀 열어 주시겠습니까? Would you please open the window? ⇌ Would you open the door, please?
▶ 여기서 서명 좀 해 주시겠습니까? Would you sign your name here, please?
[어법]
① Would you…?는 과거의 형태지만 현재의 의뢰를 나타내며, Will you…? 보다 정중한 표현이다.
② Would you…?는 문장 끝에 쓸 수가 있다. 이 표현은 친한 사이에서 쓴다.
[보기] Pass the butter, would you? (버터 좀 건네 줄래?) 이 경우에는 Would you pass the butter, please?가 정중한 표현이다.

(2) Could you…?; Could you…, please?
▶ 여기서 잠깐 기다려 주시겠습니까? Could you wait here a minute, please?
▶ [會話] 「좀 더 천천히 말씀해 주시겠습니까?」 「네, 알았습니다」 "Could you speak a little more slowly, please?" "Yes, Certainly."
▶ 누가 저를 좀 도와 주시겠습니까? Could somebody help me? (▶이처럼 주어로 someone, somebody 등을 쓸 수도 있음)
[어법]
(2)는 Can you…? 보다 공손한 말투다.
Will you…?; Can you…? 보다는 Would you…?; Could you…?를 쓰는 편이 공손한 말투가 된다.

(3) Would [Do] you mind doing?
▶ 창문을 좀 열어주시겠습니까? Would you mind opening the window?
▶ 잠시 기다려 주시겠습니까? Would you mind waiting a few minutes, please? (▶이 와 같이 문장 끝에 please를 덧붙일 수가 있음)
▶ 이 짐 좀 들어 주시겠습니까? Do you mind helping me with this baggage? (▶Do you mind…? 보다는 Would you mind…? 라고 하는 것이 보통)

(4) Would you mind not doing? (「…하지 말아 주시지 않겠습니까」란 뜻)
▶ [會話] 「이 방에서는 담배를 삼가해 주시겠습니까?」 「예, 미안합니다」 "Would you mind not smoking in this room?" "Oh, I'm sorry me!"
▶ 그렇게 떠들지 말아 주시지 않겠습니까? Would you mind not making so much noise?

4. …해 주게 [주십시오]라고 말했다 (간접화법)
ask sb **to do**
▶ 그는 비서에게 이것을 타이핑해달라고 부탁했다 He asked his secretary to type it for him. (← He said to his secretary, "Will you type this for me?")
▶ 그는 나에게 거기에 서명해달라고 말했다 He asked me to sign my name there. (← He said to me, "Could you sign your name here, please?")

women's garments / 작업용 의류 working clothing / 의류 한 점 an article of clothing

의리 義理 〈도리〉 justice; (the principle of) righteousness; 〈의무〉 (a) (social) duty; (an) obligation; 〈신의〉 fidelity; faithfulness
♦ 친구간의 의리 the ties of friendship / 의리상 out of social obligation; out of a sense of duty / 의리가 있다 be faithful [dutiful, reliable]; keep faith 《with》; have a keen [strong] sense of honor [duty]; be alive [faithful] to duty / 의리가 없다 have no sense of duty; be a stranger to the sense of duty
▶ 그는 의리상 그렇게 했다 He was obliged to do so. ⇒ He did so from a mere sense of duty.
▶ 그는 의리를 아는 사람이다 He is a man of honor.
▶ 그는 친구에게 의리를 지켰다 He kept faith with his friend. ⇒ He was faithful to his friend.
▶ 이번에는 의리상으로라도 그를 만나 주지 않을 수 없다 I ought to see him this time even for mere decency's sake.

의모 義母 〈의붓 어미〉 a stepmother; 〈수양 어머니〉 a foster mother; 〈의로 맺은 어머니〉 a sworn mother

의무 義務 (a) duty; an obligation; liability 《for》; 〈책임〉 responsibility
♦ 납세의 의무 liability for tax payment [to pay taxes] / 병역의 의무 liability for military service / 법률상의 의무 a legal obligation / 의무적인 obligatory; compulsory
▶ 그것을 하는 것은 너의 의무다 It's your duty to do it. ⇒ You are bound to do it.
▶ 국민은 납세의 의무가 있다 A person has the duty to pay [of paying] taxes.
▶ 우리는 법을 준수해야 할 의무가 있다 We must obey the law.
▶ 부모는 자식을 돌볼 의무가 있다 Parents have an obligation to take care of their children.
▶ 국가에 대한 의무를 태만히 하지 마라 Do not neglect your duty to your country.
▶ 권리를 주장하려거든 먼저 의무를 다 해라 You must do [perform, fulfill] your duties before you assert your rights.
▶ 부모는 자녀를 양육할 의무를 지고 있다 Parents are responsible for bringing up their children.
▶ 그는 자식으로서의 의무를 다 해야 한다 He should perform his duty as a child.
▶ 그는 의무적으로 그 일을 했다 He did the work out of a mere sense of duty.
■ ─면제 excuse from duty ─병역 〈징병〉 compulsory (military) service ─연한 an obligatory [a compulsory] term of service ─이행 performance of a duty ─자 an obligator; a debtor; a responsible person; 〔法〕 an obligor

의무 醫務 medical affairs
─실 a doctor's [medical treatment] room

의무감 義務感 a sense of duty [obligation]
♦ 의무감에서 from a sense of duty [obligation]; at duty's call

의무교육 義務教育 compulsory education
♦ 의무교육을 받다 receive compulsory education
■ ─제도 a compulsory education system

의문 疑問 a doubt; a question

〔解說〕 ***doubt***는 막연하여 이유를 말할 수 없는 의문을 말하고 ***question***은 이유가 있는 의문을 뜻하므로 의문 쪽이 doubt의 정도가 강하다. question은 「질문」의 뜻일 때는 가산명사 (countable noun)로 취급한다.

♦ 의문의 죽음 a mysterious death / 의문의 doubtful; questionable; problematic(al) / 의문을 품다 doubt; be doubtful 《of, about》; have doubts 《about》
▶ 그가 성공할지는 의문이다 It is questionable [doubtful] if [whether] he will succeed. ⇒ I doubt if [whether] he will succeed.
▶ 그것은 의문의 여지가 없다 There's no question about it.
▶ 마침내 오랜 의문이 풀렸다 I could finally remove the doubts that had long been in my mind.
▶ 그는 나의 의견에 아직도 의문을 느끼고 있다 He still feels doubtful about my opinion.
■ ─대명사〔부사, 형용사〕 an interrogative pronoun [adverb, adjective] ─문 an interrogative sentence ─부 〈물음표〉 a question [an interrogation] mark ─사 an interrogative ─점 a doubtful point; a point in question

의뭉스럽다, 의뭉하다 sly; wily; dark; disingenuous; covertly guileful; 〈표리가 있는〉 double-dealing
♦ 의뭉스러운 웃음 a sly smile / 의뭉한 사람 a double-dealer

의미 意味 〈뜻〉 (a) meaning; (a) sense; 〈중요성〉 significance; 〈취지〉 the import; the purport
♦ 참된 의미의 민주주의 democracy in the true sense [the real meaning] of the term [word] / 의미있는 표정 a look full of meaning; a meaning [significant, suggestive] look / 어떤 의미로는 in a sense / 넓은[좁은] 의미로 in a broad [narrow] sense
▶ 그것은 무슨 의미입니까? What do you mean by that?
▶ 그가 「겁쟁이」라고 말한 것은 무슨 의미였을까? What did he mean by "coward"?
▶ 이 단어는 두 가지 의미로 쓰인다 This word is used in two senses.
▶ 이 구절은 그다지 의미가 없다 There isn't much meaning in the passage.
▶ 그 여자는 의미있는 미소를 지었다 She gave a meaningful smile.
▶ 그녀는 나에게 의미있는 시선을 던졌다 She gave me a significant glance. ⇒ She glanced at me meaningfully [with meaning].
▶ 그녀의 「예스」라는 대답은 나에게 특별한 의미를 준다 Her "Yes!" has a special significance for me.

의미론 意味論 〔言〕 semantics

의미심장하다 意味深長─ very meaningful; full of meaning; profound in meaning; 〈서술적〉 have a [be of] profound significance;

mean much [a great deal]
▶ 그녀는 의미심장한 눈빛으로 나를 보았다 She looked at me with eyes full of meaning [as if she knew something].
▶ 그는 의미심장한 말을 남기고 갔다 He said something very significant as he left.

의법 依法 (in) accordance [conformity] with law ♦의법 조치하다 decide (a case) according to law
■—처단 punishment [penalty] in accordance with [according to] law —처분 disposition [measures] according to law

의병 義兵 a loyal [patriotic] soldier; (총칭) a loyal [righteous] army
♦의병을 일으키다 raise an army in the cause of justice [loyalty]; raise a loyal army

의병 疑兵 (軍) dummy troops [soldiers]

의복 衣服 clothes; clothing; dress
♦의복을 벗다 undress *oneself*; take off *one's* clothes / 의복을 입다 dress *oneself*; put on *one's* clothes
■—비 a clothing allowance

의복이 날개라 (속담) Clothes make the man. ⇌ Fine feathers make fine birds.

의부 義父 〈의붓 아비〉 a stepfather; 〈수양아버지〉 an adoptive [a foster] father; 〈의로 맺은 아버지〉 a sworn father

의분 義憤 (righteous) indignation ♦의분을 느끼다 have (righteous) indignation (at, against, with) / 의분을 참다 repress *one's* (righteous) indignation

의붓딸 a stepdaughter
의붓아들 a stepson
의붓아비 a stepfather
의붓어미 a stepmother

의붓자식 —子息 a stepchild; 〈아들〉 a stepson; 〈딸〉 a stepdaughter

의사 義士 a righteous person; a martyr

의사 意思 〈의향〉 an intention; an intent; a purpose; a mind; 〈생각〉 an idea; (a) thought ♦의사를 묻다 ask *sb's* intention / 의사를 밝히다 speak *one's* mind; reveal [express] *one's* intention / 서로 의사가 통하다 understand each other
▶ 자네의 권리를 무시할 의사는 없네 I have no intention of ignoring your rights.
▶ 가든 안 가든 네 의사에 달렸다 You may go or stay at will.
▶ 편지로는 의사 전달이 어려울 때가 가끔 있다 It's sometimes difficult to get things across in a letter.
▶ 아직 영어로는 의사 전달이 충분히 안된다 I can't make myself fully understood in English yet.

의사 擬似 ■—콜레라 a suspected case of cholera; false cholera

의사 醫師 a (medical) doctor; 〈개업의〉 a medical practitioner; 〈내과의〉 a physician; 〈외과의〉 a surgeon

> 解說 *doctor*는 영국에서는 보통 *physician* (내과의)을 가리키고 미국에서는 *surgeon* (외과의), 치과의 (dentist) 등을 나타낸다.

♦의사를 부르다 call (in) a doctor / 의사를 부르러 사람을 보내다 send for a doctor / 의사에게 보이다, 의사의 진찰을 받다 consult [see] a doctor; seek medical advice [aid, assistance] / 의사의 치료를 받고 있다 be under medical treatment; be under a doctor's care / 의사로 개업하다 set up as a doctor; enter medical practice; become a medical practitioner
■단골— a family doctor; *one's* regular physician [doctor] 돌팔이— a quack (doctor); a charlatan ■—국가시험 (試驗) the national examination for medical practitioners —면허 a medical license —법 the Medical Law —회 a medical association [society]

의사 議事 〈토의〉 deliberation; conference; consultation; 〈심의사항〉 proceedings; business (of the day)
♦의사를 끝내다 close the proceedings / (회의 전에) 의사를 정리하다 arrange the proceedings (for a conference) / 의사에 들어가다 commence the proceedings
■—규칙 parliamentary rules —기관 a deliberative organ

의사능력 意思能力 mental capacity ♦의사능력이 없다 be devoid of mental capacity

의사당 議事堂 an assembly hall ♦국회 의사당 the National Assembly (Building); (美) the Capitol; (英) the Houses of Parliament; (일 등) the Diet Building

의사록 議事錄 a minute book; reports; minutes; proceedings; journals ♦의사록을 만들다 take minutes of (the proceedings) / 의사록에 올라 있다 be on the minutes

의사방해 議事妨害 (美) filibustering; filibuster
■—연설 (美) filibusterism —연설자 (美) a filibusterer —자 (美) a filibuster(er)

의사봉 議事棒 a gavel ♦의사봉을 두드리다 tap at (the table) with a gavel; bang the gavel

의사일정 議事日程 the agenda; the order of the day
♦의사일정에 넣다 include (an item) in the agenda / 의사일정에 오르다 be placed on the agenda; (美) go on the calendar
▶ 의사일정을 변경해야 한다 We have to make a change in the agenda.
▶ 그 항목은 의사일정에서 제외되었다 The item was excluded from the agenda.

의사진행 議事進行 progress of proceedings
▶ 그가 의사진행을 맡았다[방해했다] He expedited [obstructed] the proceedings.

의사표시 意思表示 declaration of intention; a gesture ♦별다른 의사표시가 없을 때에는 in the absence of any different declaration of intention / 의사표시를 하다 indicate *one's* intention; express *one's* will

의산 蟻酸 〈포름산〉 (化) formic acid

의상 衣裳 clothes; clothing; dress; garments; apparel; 〈무대용〉 costume
▶ 그녀는 의상이 꽤 많다 She has a lot of dresses. ⇌ She has a very large wardrobe.
▶ 그는 카우보이[인디언] 의상을 입고 나타났다

He appeared in a cowboy [an Indian] costume.
■무대— theatrical [stage] costume 신부— a trousseau; a bride's outfit ■ —담당자 〔劇〕 a dresser; a (theatrical) costumer —실 a (clothes) closet; a wardrobe; 〔劇〕 a property room;〈양장점〉 a dressmaker; a dressmaker's (shop)

의생 醫生 a herb doctor; a herbalist
의생활 衣生活 clothing habits
의서 醫書 a medical book; a book on medicine
의석 議席 a seat (in an assembly hall); a parliamentary seat; (총칭) the floor (국회의)
♦의석을 차지하다 win *one's* seat / 의석에 앉다 take *one's* seat / 의석을 잃다 lose *one's* seat
▶그는 처음으로 국회에 의석을 획득했다 He won a seat in the House for the first time.
▶신당은 선거에서 20석의 의석을 확보했다 The new party won twenty seats [places] in the election.

의성 擬聲 〔音聲〕 onomatopoeia
■—법 〈성유법〉 onomatopoeia —어(語) an onomatopoeic [echoic] word; an onomatopoeia; an onomatope

의수 義手 an artificial arm [hand]

의술 醫術 medicine; the medical [healing] art
♦의술을 업으로 하다 practice medicine; be a physician by profession
▶의술은 인술이다 Medicine is a benevolent art.

의식 衣食 food and clothing [clothes]
▶그에게는 의식 걱정을 안해도 될만큼 수입이 있다 He has an income enough to support himself.

의식 意識 consciousness; awareness; *one's* senses
♦의식의 흐름 the stream of consciousness / 의식이 있는 conscious / 의식이 없는 unconscious; impassive / 의식을 잃다 lose consciousness; lose *one's* senses; become unconscious / 의식을 회복하다 recover [regain] consciousness [*one's* senses]; come [be restored] to *one's* senses
▶그녀는 더위로 의식이 몽롱해졌다 She grew faint from the heat.
▶그는 머리를 맞고 의식을 잃었다 He lost his consciousness when he was struck on the head.
▶나는 머리를 맞고 나서도 몇 분 동안은 의식이 있었다 I remained conscious for a few minutes after being struck on the head.
▶그는 죽을 때까지 의식이 말짱했다 His mind remained clear to the last.
▶그는 곧 의식을 회복할 것이다 He will regain consciousness [come to himself] soon.
▶그녀는 노상에서 의식을 잃고 쓰러졌다 She fell senseless on the street.
▶호흡은 의식적인 노력을 요하지 않는다 Breathing does not require conscious effort.
▶의식적으로 노력하지 않고도 사람은 모두 숨을 쉰다 We all breathe without any conscious efforts.
▶그녀는 의식적으로 나를 피했다 She avoided me on purpose.
—의식하다 be conscious [sensible] (of); feel; be aware (of)
▶그는 그 위험을 의식하고 있었다 He was aware of the danger.
▶그는 누가 뒤를 밟고 있다는 것을 의식하게 되었다 He became conscious [aware] of being followed by somebody.
■계급 [민족]— the class [race] consciousness 미— a sense of beauty 사회— the social consciousness 위기— a sense of crisis 죄— consciousness of guilt : 그 소년에게는 죄의식이 없었다 The boy had no sense of guilt. ⇒ The boy was unconscious of his guilt. —구조 *one's* way of thinking; a line of thinking

의식 儀式 〈식전〉 a ceremony; a ceremonial (function); 〈예식〉 formality; 〈종교상의〉 a rite; a ritual; a service ♦의식의[적인] ceremonial; ritual(istic); formal / 의식을 거행하다 perform [administer] a ceremony
—주의 formalism

의식이 족해야 예절을 안다 (속담) Well fed, well bred. ⇒ It is hard for an empty sack to stand straight.

의식주 衣食住 food, clothing [clothes] and shelter [housing] ♦의식주를 제공하다 feed, lodge and clothe *sb*

의심 疑心 〈의혹〉 (a) doubt; 〈의문〉 a question; 〈불신〉 (a) distrust; (a) mistrust; 〈혐의〉 (a) suspicion
♦의심 많은 사람 a distrustful person; a man with a suspicious nature / 의심 없이 without doubt [question]; undoubtedly; doubtless(ly); unquestionably / 추호의 의심도 없이 without [beyond] a shadow of doubt / 의심이 없다 be beyond doubt [dispute]; be certain; there is no doubt (that, as to)
▶너는 매사에 의심이 너무 많다 You are too suspicious about everything.
▶그의 당황한 태도에 의심이 갔다 His flurried manner aroused my suspicion.
▶그녀는 너의 행동에 의심을 품고 있다 She has her suspicions about your behavior. ⇒ She is suspicious [doubtful] about your behavior.
▶남한테 의심을 받을 행동은 하면 안 된다 You should refrain from doing suspicious behavior.
▶그것은 의심 없는 사실이다 There is no denying the fact.
▶마침내 나의 의심이 풀렸다 At last I was cleared of suspicion.
▶그가 정직한 사람이라는 데는 의심의 여지가 없다 There is no room for doubt that he is an honest man.
—의심하다 doubt (of); be doubtful of; have [feel] a doubt (as to, about); distrust; mistrust; suspect; be suspicious of [about]
▶나는 내 눈을 의심했다 I couldn't believe my own eyes.
▶공연히 남을 의심해서는 안된다 Be on sure ground before you suspect anyone.
▶그것은 의심할 여지가 없다 It admits of no

doubt [dispute].
▶ 모두가 그를 살인범으로 의심하고 있다 Everybody suspects that he is [was] the murderer.

의심스럽다 疑心— doubtful; dubious; suspicious; questionable; uncertain; unreliable; incredulous

> 解說 *doubtful*은 확실성·정당성에 대해 불신을 품을 때, *dubious*는 의미·가치에 대해 신뢰를 갖지 못할 때, *suspicious*는 선악·진실성·가치에 대해 의문을 품을 때, *questionable*은 성실성·확실성에 문제가 있다고 볼 때 쓴다.

♦ 의심스러운 인물 a suspicious [doubtful, questionable] character / 의심스러운 듯이 doubtfully; incredulously; suspiciously; with suspicion
▶ 나는 그의 의도가 의심스럽다 I suspect his intentions.
▶ 이 약의 효능이 의심스럽다 The effect of the medicine is doubtful.
▶ 그 소문이 사실인지 의심스럽다 It is doubtful [questionable] whether the rumor is true.
▶ 그의 언행에는 의심스러운 데가 있다 There is something questionable in his speech and conduct.
▶ 단어의 뜻이 의심스러울 때는 사전을 찾아 봐라 When in doubt about the meaning of a word, consult your dictionary.

의아 疑訝 doubt; suspicion
—**의아하다** dubious; suspicious
▶ 그녀는 무슨 일이냐고 의아해서 물었다 She asked dubiously what was the matter.

의아스럽다 疑訝— dubious; suspicious
▶ 그는 의아스러운 표정을 지었다 He looked dubious [suspicious]. ≒ He gave a dubious look.

의안 義眼 an artificial [a false] eye; 〈유리로 만든〉 a glass eye

의안 議案 a bill; a measure
♦ 의안을 기초하다 draw up a bill / 의안을 국회에 제출하다 introduce [present] a bill to the National Assembly / 의안에 찬성[반대]하다 support [oppose] a bill / 의안을 가결[부결]하다 adopt [reject] a bill

의약 醫藥 〈의약품〉 medicine; physic; 〈의술과 시약〉 medical practice and dispensary
■—분업 separation of dispensary from medical practice

의약품 醫藥品 medical and pharmaceutical products; medical supplies
▶ 그 나라에는 의약품이 부족하다 They don't have enough medical supplies in the country.

의업 醫業 the medical profession; medical practice
♦ 의업에 종사하다 be in medical practice; practice medicine

의역 意譯 a free translation; a paraphrase
▶ 이것은 의역이 지나치다 This translation is too free.
▶ 우리는 원문의 숨은 뜻을 분명히 하기 위해 종종 의역을 한다 We often paraphrase [make a paraphrase] to reveal some hidden meaning in the original.
—**의역하다** translate freely; give a free [broad] translation; paraphrase; make a paraphrase

의연금 義捐金 a contribution; a subscription; a donation; alms
♦ 의연금을 모으다 raise [collect] contributions (for); invite [start a campaign for] subscriptions (to) / 의연금을 내다 contribute (to); donate (to); give alms (to)
■—수재— a relief fund for flood victims [sufferers]

의연하다 依然— 〈서술적〉 be as it used to be; be as (it was) before; be as of old
♦ 구태 의연하다 remain unchanged; be just as it was

의연하다 毅然— resolute; firm; dauntless
♦ 의연하다 태도를 취하다 take a resolute [firm, dauntless] attitude 《toward》 / 의연히 역경을 이겨 내다 heroically [stoically] endure adversity
▶ 그는 끝까지 의연함을 잃지 않았다 He never lost his fortitude.
▶ 그녀의 의연한 태도에 우리는 깊은 감명을 받았다 Her firm [resolute, dauntless] attitude impressed us deeply.

의열 義烈 nobility of soul; heroism
—**의열하다** noble; heroic; gallant ■—지사(之士) a man of heroic and noble mind

의예과 醫豫科 the premedical (course) 《of a medical college》; (口) premed(ic) ■—학생 a premedical student; (口) a premed(ic)

의옥 疑獄 a bribery case; a corruption scandal; (口) a graft case ♦ 정치적 의옥 사건 a political scandal / 의옥에 연루되다 be involved in a scandal

의외 意外 surprise; unexpectation; an unexpected [unforeseen] matter; an accident
♦ 의외의 unexpected; surprising / 의외로 contrary to *one's* expectation; beyond expectation; unexpectedly
▶ 그것은 전연 의외의 사건이었다 That was a totally unexpected event.
▶ 사건은 의외의 결말을 맞았다 The case came to a surprising conclusion.
▶ 그는 의외로 빨리 도착할지도 모른다 He may arrive earlier than is expected.
▶ 시험은 의외로 쉬웠다 The examination was easier than I had expected.

의욕 意慾 (a) will; (a) desire; volition
▶ 그녀는 학습 의욕이 없다 She lacks a will to study.
▶ 그들은 배우려는 의욕이 대단하다 They are keen on learning.
▶ 그는 신기술 개발에 의욕적이다 He is eager to develop a new technique.
▶ 그는 그 일에 의욕적으로 달라붙었다 He tackled the task with a will [with enthusiasm].

의용 義勇 〈충의와 용기〉 loyalty and courage; 〈의를 위한 용기〉 heroism; bravery for a righteous cause
■—군[병] a volunteer army [soldier]

의용 儀容 〈태도〉 a mien; bearing; presence; manners
♦ 의용을 갖추다 tidy *oneself*

의원 依願 〈in〉 accordance with *one's* request
■ —면직 dismissal [retirement] at *one's* own request

의원 醫員 a physician; a doctor; a member of the medical staff; (총칭) the medical staff [corps]

의원 醫院 〈美〉a doctor's [physician's] office; 〈英〉a (doctor's) surgery; 〈의사 2인 이상의〉a clinic
♦ 최 의원 Dr. Choi's Office ■ —장 the head physician [surgeon]

의원 議員 a member of an assembly; an assemblyman; 〈국회의원〉 a member of the National Assembly; an Assemblyman
♦ 의원의 임기 the term of membership / 서울 시의회 의원 a member of the Seoul Metropolitan Assembly / 민주당 소속 의원 an Assemblyman of the Democratic Party / 서울 출신 의원 P씨 Mr. P, a representative for [from] Seoul / 의원이 되다 obtain a seat (in Parliament) / 의원직을 사퇴하다 resign *one's* membership [seat] (in the National Assembly) / 의원으로 당선되다 be elected a member (of) / 의원이다 have a seat (in the House [National Assembly])
—평— an ordinary [average] member; 〈英〉a backbencher ■ —석 (총칭) the floor —입법 legislation by Assembly members —총회 a general meeting of the Assembly members —회관 Members' Office Building

의원 議院 the (National) Assembly chamber; the House; the Parliament
■ —내각제 the parliamentary government (system)

의의 意義 〈의미〉(a) meaning; (a) sense; 〈중요성〉 significance; import
♦ 인생의 의의 the meaning of life / 의의 있는 인생 a life worth living; a meaningful life / 의의(가) 깊은 of deep significance / 의의(가) 없는 meaningless; senseless; purposeless / 의의 없는 생활을 하다 live to no purpose
▶ 대학 생활의 의의를 생각해본 적이 있습니까? Have you ever thought of the significance of your college life?
▶ 곤경에 맞서는 데 인생의 의의가 있다 The meaning of life lies in challenging difficulties.
▶ 그는 의의 있는 생활을 했다 He led [lived] a meaningful life.
▶ 그 운동에 정치적 의의는 전혀 없다 The movement has no political significance.

의인 義人 a righteous man

의인 擬人 personification; impersonation
—의인하다 personify; impersonate
■ —법 personification

의인화 擬人化 personification —의인화하다 personify
▶ 고대인은 자연을 의인화했다 Ancient people personified nature.

의자 椅子 〈보통의〉 a chair; a stool; 〈긴〉 a bench; a sofa; a lounge; a couch; a divan (벽에 붙인); 〈직위〉 post

|解說| ***chair***는 의자의 총칭으로 쓰이지만 보통 등이 있는 1인용 의자를 가리키며 등이 없는 의자는 ***stool***이라 한다. 2인 이상이 앉을 수 있는 옆으로 긴 의자는 ***bench*** 또는 ***sofa***라고 한다.

♦ 의자를 권하다 offer *sb* a chair / 의자에 앉다 sit in [on] a chair; take a seat on a chair; take a chair / 의자를 당겨서 앉다 draw up a chair and sit down / 의자에서 일어서다 rise [get up] from the chair [seat]
▶ 방에는 앉을 의자가 없다 There is no chair to sit on [in] in the room.
▶ 그는 과장 의자에 눈독을 들이고 있었다 He had an eye on the post of section chief.
▶ 그가 죽은 후 계장 의자는 그대로 비어 있다 Since his death, the chief clerk's post has remained vacant.
■ 안락— an armchair 전기— an electric chair; (美俗) a hot chair 회전[흔들]— a swivel [rocking] chair —커버 a chair cover

의장 衣欌 a wardrobe; a chest of drawers
■ 단층[이층]— a single [double] chest of drawers

의장 意匠 a design; a decorative [an artistic] design
♦ 참신한 의장 a novel design; a creation / 등록된 의장 a registered design / 의장을 고안하다 think [work] out a design / 의장에 공을 들이다 elaborate [work hard on] a design
■ 공업— an industrial design ■ —가(家) a designer; an artistic designer —권 a design right; the copyright in registered designs —등록 registration of designs —료 a design fee

의장 艤裝 rig(ging); outfit; equipment (of a ship)
—의장하다 rig [equip] (a ship for sailing); fit out (a ship for sea)
♦ 원양 항해에 대비하여 배를 의장하다 fit out a ship for a long voyage
■ —가(家) a rigger —품 fittings

의장 議長 a president; a chairman (▶ 여성의 경우에도 쓸 수 있음); a chairperson; the Speaker; 〈호칭〉 Mr. Chairman! (남성); Madam Chairman! (여성); Mr. Speaker!
♦ 의장의 지위 presidency; chairmanship / 의장으로 취임하다 take over the presidency
▶ 그 회의의 의장은 누구였습니까? Who chaired the meeting?
▶ 그가 그 회의의 의장을 맡았다 He presided [took the chair] at the meeting.
▶ 그녀가 그 위원회의 의장으로 뽑혔다 She was elected chairman [chairperson] of the committee.
■ 공동— a cochairman; a joint chairman 국회— the Chairman of the National Assembly 부— a vice-chairman; a deputy chairman; 〈영국 하원의〉 the Deputy Speaker 임시— an acting chairman ■ —대리 a deputy chairman —직권 authority of the president

의장 議場 an assembly hall; a chamber; 〈의회〉 the House; the floor
▶ 의장은 난장판이었다 The House was in (an)

의치

uproar [in (a) turmoil].
▶그는 의장의 질서를 회복하려고 애썼다 He tried to restore order on the floor.
의장대 儀仗隊 a guard of honor; an honor guard
♦의장대를 사열하다 inspect [review] an honor guard
의적 義賊 a chivalrous [generous] robber; a benevolent picaroon
의전 儀典 a ceremony ⇨ 의식(儀式)
■―관 a master of ceremonies; a ceremonial officer ―비서 a protocol secretary ―실 the Office of Protocol
의절 義絶 severing of connection; dissolution of a tie; a break of relations; a breach (of friendship); 〈자녀와의〉 disowning; disinheritance
―의절하다 break off relations [friendship] 《with *sb*》; break with [off from] *sb*; cut [sever] *one's* connections 《with》; 〈자녀와〉 disown; disinherit; cut off relationship with 《*one's* son [daughter]》
▶그는 못된 아들과 의절했다 He disowned his wicked son.
의젓이 in a dignified manner; with dignity; imposingly; majestically
의젓잖다 undignified; unimposing; cheap; frivolous; flippant; lacking dignity
의젓하다 stately; dignified; grand; imposing; majestic(al); commanding
▶그는 아주 의젓한 청년으로 자랐다 He has grown into a very presentable young man.
▶그때 그의 태도는 의젓했다 The attitude he took then really commanded our admiration.
의정 議定 agreement (by conference)
―의정하다 confer and agree upon; confer and decide ■―서 a protocol
의정 議政 parliamentarism ⇨ 의회(~정치)
♦의정 단상에 서다 become [be elected] an assemblyman
의정 擬晶 [鑛] mimetic crystal
의제 義弟 a sworn [pledged] younger brother
의제 擬制 [法] a (legal) fiction
■―자본 watered [fictitious] capital
의제 議題 a subject [topic] for discussion; an agenda item; (총칭) an agenda
♦의제에 오르다 come [be brought] up for discussion; be placed on the agenda / 의제로 삼다 bring [take] up 《a matter》 for discussion; place 《a matter, a subject》 on the agenda
▶그 건은 오늘 의제에 올립니다 Today we are going to place the matter on the agenda. ⇌ The matter will be on the agenda today.
의족 義足 an artificial [a wooden] leg
♦의족을 한 사람 a wooden-legged person / 의족을 하고 있다 wear [be wearing] an artificial leg
의존 依存 dependence; reliance
―의존하다 depend [rely] 《on, upon》; be dependent 《upon》
▶이 나라는 원자재를 주로 외국에 의존한다 This country depends chiefly upon foreign countries for raw materials.

▶그는 실직중이라서 아내의 벌이에 의존하고 있다 He is out of a job and dependent upon his wife's earnings.
의중 意中 *one's* mind; *one's* heart
♦의중의 사람 the person *one* has in mind / 남의 의중을 떠보다 sound *sb's* views; feel *sb's* pulse / 의중을 밝히다 open *one's* heart; unbosom [explain] *oneself* 《to》; speak [lay bare] *one's* mind / 의중을 헤아리다 read *sb's* mind
의지 依支 1 〈몸을 기댐〉 leaning; 〈그 대상〉 a support
―의지하다 lean 《on》 a rest 《against》
♦지팡이에 몸을 의지하다 support *oneself* with a cane / 지팡이에 의지하여 걷다 walk leaning on [with the help of] *one's* stick
2 〈의존〉 reliance; dependence; help; 〈의지할 대상〉 a support; a prop
♦노후의 의지 the stay of *one's* old age; a prop for *one's* old age
―의지하다 rely [depend] 《on, upon》; trust 《on》; 〈도움을 바라다〉 look [turn] to *sb* for help [support, assistance]
♦금전적으로 아들에게 의지하다 depend [rely, be dependent] upon *one's* son for money
▶그녀에게는 의지할 친척이 한 사람도 없었다 She had no relative to depend upon [turn to for help].
▶남을 의지해서는 안 된다 You must not count upon another's help.
▶그는 남에게 의지하지 않는다 He is self-reliant.
▶신앙에 의지하지 않았다면 나는 그때 살아나가지 못했을 것이다 If I had not been supported by my faith, I would not have been able to go on living.
의지 意志 will; volition
♦굳은[약한] 의지 a strong [weak] will / 불굴의 의지 an indomitable [iron] will / 의지가 강한 사람 a person of strong [iron] will; a strong-willed [steadfast] man / 의지가 약한 사람 a feeble-minded [weak-willed] person / 의지의 힘으로 by the force of *one's* will
▶그는 자기 의지로 그것을 했다 He did it of his own (free) will. ⇌ He did it voluntarily.
▶그녀는 자기 의지에 반하여 거기 가야 했다 She had to go there against her will.
■―자유― free will ■―력 willpower: 의지력으로 이기다 win by willpower [the strength of will] ―박약 (a) lack of willpower
의지 義肢 an artificial leg [arm]; an artificial limb
의지가지없다 helpless; forlorn; alone; lonely
♦의지가지없는 고아 a helpless orphan ▶그녀는 의지가지없는 처지다 She has no one to depend on [turn to for help].
의처증 疑妻症 a morbid [pathological] suspicion about *one's* wife's chastity
의취 意趣 〈의향〉 an intention; 〈취향〉 wishes
의치 義齒 an artificial [a false] tooth;〈한 벌의〉 a denture ♦의치를 해박다 have a false tooth put in [inserted]
▶그의 이는 모두 의치다 He wears a full set of false teeth [dentures].

총[부분]— a full [partial] (set of) denture
—술 dental prosthesis; prosthetics

의탁 依託 〈맡김〉 trust; 〈의존〉 reliance
—의탁하다 entrust to sb's care; trust (to); rely [depend] (on)
♦ 몸을 의탁하다 entrust *oneself* to sb's care
▶ 나는 몸을 의탁할 곳이 없다 I have no one to entrust myself to [rely on].
▶ 그는 숙부집에 몸을 의탁했다 He went to live with his uncle. ⇒ He became dependent on his uncle.

의태 擬態 〔生〕 (biological) mimicry; mimesis, simulation; camouflage **—색** mimic coloration **—어** 〔言〕 a mimetic word; an imitative word; mimesis

의표 意表 a surprise ♦ 아무의 의표를 찌르다 take sb by surprise; baffle sb's expectations
▶ 그의 의표를 찌른 계책은 대성공이었다 His unexpected strategy really worked.

의하다 依— 1 〈의거하다〉 depend [turn, hang] on sth; 〈근거를 두다〉 be based [founded, grounded] on sth
♦ 소문에 의하면 as report has it [goes]
▶ 신문에 의하면 그는 사임할 것이라고 한다 Newspapers say that he is going to resign his post.
▶ 누전에 의한 화재에 조심하시오 Beware of fires caused by short circuits.
▶ 승진은 근속 연수에 의한다 Promotion goes by the length of service.
▶ 그의 의견은 경험에 의한 것이다 His opinion is based [founded, grounded] on his experience.
2 〈(수단에) 호소하다〉 do 《anything》 by (means of); appeal to; have recourse to
♦ …에 의하지 않고 without recourse to…; disregarding…
3 〈말미암다〉 ▶ 그 사고는 부주의에 의한 것이다 The accident was caused by [due to] carelessness.

의하여 依— 〈…에 따라서〉 according to; in accordance with [with]; 〈…에 응하여〉 in compliance with; 〈…에 근거하여〉 on the ground of; by [in] virtue of; 〈말미암아〉 because of; on account of; owing to; due to; 〈…의 수단으로〉 by means [dint] of; by; through
♦ 관례에 의하여 in conformity with [according to] custom / 부탁에 의하여 at *one's* request / 그의 원조에 의하여 by his help / 의사의 권고에 의하여 on the doctor's advice
▶ 아메리카 대륙은 콜럼버스에 의하여 발견되었다 America was discovered by Columbus.
▶ 음주운전은 법에 의하여 금지되어 있다 Driving under the influence of alcohol is prohibited by law.
▶ 그는 규정에 의하여 해고되었다 He was dismissed as the rules stipulated.
▶ 나는 그의 지시에 의하여 그것을 했다 I have done it according to [in accordance with] his instructions.
▶ 불가피한 사정에 의하여 갈 수 없었다 Unavoidable circumstances prevented me from going.
▶ 사상은 언어에 의하여 표현된다 Thoughts are expressed by means of language.

의학 醫學 medical science; medicine
♦ 의학적(으로) medical(ly) / 의학을 배우다 study medicine [medical science] / 의학 실습을 하다 act as an intern; intern
▶ 의학은 크게 진보하고 있다 Medical science is making great progress.
—계 the medical world; medical circles **—도[생]** a medical student **—박사** 〈사람〉 a doctor of medicine; 〈학위〉 Doctor of Medicine (略 M.D., D.M.) **—부** the medical department; (美) a medical school **—사** 〈사람〉 a bachelor of medicine; 〈학위〉 Bachelor of Medicine (略 B.M., M.B.) **—서** a medical book **—실습생** (美) an intern; (英) a houseman **—자** a medical man; a doctor

의향 意向 an intention; an inclination; *one's* mind [idea]; wishes; views
♦ …할 의향이 있다 be inclined [disposed] 《to do》; have a mind [an intention] 《to do》 / …할 의향이 없다 have no mind 《to do》; be in no mood 《to do, for》 / 남의 의향을 따르다 obey sb's wishes / 남의 의향을 떠보다 tap sb's views; sound sb on (his) intention [about (his) idea]
▶ 나는 그의 의향을 알고 싶다 I want to know his intention.
▶ 이 계획에 대한 당신 의향은 어떻습니까? What is your opinion about [on, of] this plan? ⇒ What do you think [How do you feel] about this plan?

의협 義俠 chivalry; gallantry; heroism
♦ 의협적인 chivalrous; gallant; knightly

의협심 義俠心 a chivalrous spirit; chivalry; gallantry ♦ 의협심이 있는 chivalrous; heroic
▶ 그는 의협심이 있는 사람이다 He is chivalrous [heroic]. ⇒ He has a chivalrous spirit.

의형 義兄 a sworn [pledged] (elder) brother [friend]

의형제 義兄弟 sworn [pledged] brothers
▶ 두 사람은 의형제를 맹세했다 The two men took a pledge of brotherhood. ⇒ The two men swore themselves brothers.

의혹 疑惑 suspicion; doubt; mystification
♦ 의혹의 눈으로 보다 look at sb suspiciously [with doubtful eyes]; eye [regard] sb with (an eye of) suspicion / 의혹을 일소하다 dispel all doubts [suspicions] / 의혹을 풀다 clear *oneself* of suspicion / 의혹을 품게[사게] 하다 excite [arouse, provoke] sb's suspicion / 의혹에 싸여 있다 be wrapped in a shroud of suspicion
▶ 나는 그의 설명에 의혹을 품고 있다 I am suspicious of his explanation. ⇒ I have doubts about his explanation.
▶ 의혹의 눈으로 보면 사물이 의심스럽게 보인다 When you regard things with suspicion, they begin to look suspicious.

의화학 醫化學 medical chemistry

의회 議會 an assembly; 〈한국의〉 the National Assembly; 〈영국, 프랑스, 이탈리아, 캐나다, 오스트레일리아의〉 Parliament; 〈미국의〉 Congress; 〈일본의〉 the Diet
♦ 의회의 지도자들 Congressional leaders / 의회를 소집하다 call the Assembly [Congress]

into session; convoke (a session of) the Assembly / 의회를 해산하다 dissolve the Assembly / 의안의 의회 통과를 추진하다 push a bill through the Assembly
▶ 의회는 어제 개회되었는데 1개월의 회기로 열린다 The Assembly was convened yesterday, and will be in session for a month.
▶ 의회가 산회했다 The Assembly was adjourned.
■—민주주의 parliamentary democracy —소집 convocation —정치 parliamentary politics [government] —제도 parliamentary institution [system] —주의 parliamentarism

이¹ 1 〈입안의〉 a tooth 《pl. teeth》; 〈총칭〉 dentition
♦ 썩은 이 a bad [decayed, ruined] tooth 〈이를〉 이가 고르다[고르지 않다] have a regular [an irregular] set of teeth / 이가 빠지다 a tooth comes [falls] off [out] / 이가 들뜨다 set one's teeth on edge; loose one's teeth / 이가 튼튼하다 [상하다] have good [bad] teeth
▶ 나는 이가 아프다 I have a toothache. ⇌ My tooth aches.
▶ 찬물을 먹으면[마시면] 이가 시리다 The tooth smarts when I drink chilled water.
▶ 너무 단것을 먹으면 이가 상한다 If you eat too many sweets, your teeth will decay.
▶ 이 아기는 이가 나고 있다 This child is teething [cutting a tooth].
〈이를〉 이를 닦다 clean [brush] one's teeth / 이를 빼다 pull out [extract] a tooth; 〈빼게 하다〉 have a tooth (pulled) out [extracted] / 이를 쑤시다 pick one's teeth / 이를 치료받다 have a tooth treated [fixed] / 이를 해박다 have a false tooth put in / 분해서 이를 갈다 grind [grate, gnash] one's teeth with vexation [chagrin]
▶ 그녀는 이를 악물고 모욕을 참았다 She clenched her teeth to bear the insult.
▶ 개가 으르렁거리며 이를 드러냈다 The dog bared [showed] its teeth in a rage.
2 〈기구·기계의〉 a cog; a tooth; a dent
♦ 톱니바퀴[톱]의 이 the teeth of a gear [saw]
3 〈사기그릇 등의〉 a chip; broken [jagged] edges [brim]
♦ 이(가) 빠진 칼 a sword with a nicked edge
▶ 이 접시는 이가 빠져 있다 The edge of this dish is chipped. ⇌ This dish has a chipped edge.

─────── 이 ───────

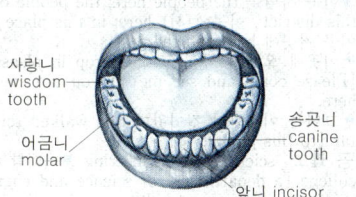

사랑니 wisdom tooth
어금니 molar
송곳니 canine tooth
앞니 incisor

이² 〖昆〗 a louse 《pl. lice》
♦ 이투성이의 lousy / 이가 끓다 become lousy; be infested with lice / 이를 잡다[없애다] rid of [get rid of] lice; delouse / 이 잡듯하다 search thoroughly
▶ 경찰은 범인을 잡으려고 집집마다 이 잡듯이 뒤졌다 The police made a from-door-to-door search for the criminal.

이³ 〈사람〉 a person; a man; someone; one
♦ 젊은이 a young person / 지은이 〈책의〉 the author; the writer; 〈작곡가〉 the composer
▶ 그는 절대로 그런 짓을 할 이가 아닙니다 He would be the last man [person] to do such a thing.

이⁴ 1 〈자기·현재로부터 가장 가까운 것〉 this; these; present; current
♦ 이 달 this month / 이 분 this man [gentleman] here
▶ 이 귀로 똑똑히 들었다 I heard it with my own ears.
▶ 이 바보야 You (damn) fool!
2 〈이것〉 this; it; things
♦ 이대로 as it is; as they are / 이밖에 besides; in addition to this / 이후에 after this; in the future
▶ 이를 잊어서는 안 된다 You must not forget this.
▶ 이는 그가 무식하기 때문에 일어난 사건이다 This is an accident that had been caused by his ignorance.
▶ 수표를 이에 동봉합니다 I enclose herewith a check.
▶ 그 물고기는 이만큼 컸다 The fish was this big.
▶ 이로써 제 말씀을 끝맺고자 합니다 Let me conclude my speech with this.

이⁵ 1 〈주격〉 ▶ 하늘이 아주 맑다 The sky is all clear.
2 〈대상〉 ▶ 나는 돈이 필요해 I need money.
▶ 나는 바다보다 산이 좋다 I like the mountains better than the sea.
▶ 그는 아들이 셋인데 모두 의사다 He has three sons and they are all doctors.
3 〈결과〉 ▶ 내 머리가 백발이 되어간다 My hair is turning [going] gray. ⇌ My hair is graying.
4 〈부정〉 ▶ 그것은 말이 아니고 노새다 It is not a horse but a mule.

이 利 1 〈나은 점〉 an advantage
♦ 지리적인 이 a geographic advantage / 지세의 이를 얻다 get the advantage(s) of (strategic) position
▶ 그건 내게 이가 된다 It is to my advantage.
2 〈이득〉 gain; profit; 〈이익〉 benefit; interests
♦ 이 많은 장사 a profitable [lucrative] business / 이가 남다 bring profits; yield a profit / 이를 보다 make [gain] a profit; profit / 이가 적다[박하다] give little profit; do not pay much / 너무 이만 따지다 think only of profit
▶ 그것은 이가 별로 없다 It won't yield much profit [pay at all].
▶ 그는 상당한 이를 보고 그것을 팔았다 He sold it at a considerable profit.
3 ⇨ 이자(利子)

이 理 1 〈불변의 법칙〉 principle; truth; nature ◆자연의 이를 따르다 follow the rules of nature
2 ⇨ 도리
이 哩 a mile
이 浬 〈해리〉 a nautical [sea] mile
이 釐・厘 one hundredth; one percent
이 二・貳 〈둘〉 two; 〈제2〉 the second
◆2 대(代) two generations / 제2대 the second generation
▶8에 2를 더하면 10이 된다 Tow added to eight makes ten.
이가 二價 〔化〕 bivalence; divalence
◆이가의 bivalent; divalent; diatomic
■—원소 〔化〕 a dyad
이간 離間 alienation; estrangement
◆이간을 붙이다 separate from
▶그는 양편의 이간을 꾀했다 He tried to estrange [drive a wedge between] the two parties.
—이간하다 alienate [estrange] ⟪sb from another⟫; separate [sever] from
■—쟁이 a mischief-maker —책(策) an alienating measure; a discord-producing intrigue; a scheme to provoke estrangement
이간질 離間— alienation ⇨ 이간
이감하다 移監— 〈수감자를〉 transfer a prisoner [detainee, internee] to another prison [cell]
이같은 such; like this; such...as this; this kind [sort] of; of this kind [sort]
◆이같은 일 a thing of this sort; such a thing (as this) / 이같은 날에 on a day like this; on such a day (as this) / 이같은 사정으로 such being the case; in [under] these circumstances
▶이같은 짓은 두 번 다시 하지 마라 Don't do such a thing [it] again.
▶이같은 말은 들어본 적이 없다 I have never heard such a story [a story like this]. ⇌ I have never heard a story of this kind [sort].
이같이 like this; thus; in this way [manner, fashion]; 〈정도〉 so; so much
◆이같이 많은 돈 such a big sum of money; so much money / 이같이 많이 so many [much]; (口) this many [much]
▶이같이 좋은 사람은 본 적이 없다 I've never met such a nice [so nice a] person.
▶이같이 하시오 Please do it like this [this way].
▶이같이 해서 그는 그 다이아몬드를 손에 넣었다 In this way [Thus] he acquired the diamond.
이거 〈놀람〉 O!; Oh!; Well!; Good Heavens!; Oh, my God! ◆이거 큰일났다 Good God! ⇌ What on earth should I do?
이것 1 〈사물〉 this (pl. these); this one
▶「이것이다」라고 그는 외쳤다 "That's it!" he cried. ⇌ "I've got it!" he cried.
▶이것 가져라 This is for you. ⇌ Here is something for you.
▶이것이면 되겠소? Will this do?
▶내가 아는 것은 이것 뿐이다 This is all I know about it.

2 〈얕잡아 부를 때〉 ▶이것봐 Look here! ⇌ Listen! ⇌ Say! ⇌ Hey!
▶이것봐 어디 가냐? Here [Say] where are you going?
이것저것 this and [or] that; this, that and the other (thing); one thing and [or] another
◆이것저것 모두 (anything and) everything; every and all / 이것저것 걱정하다 worry about this and that matter; be worried over one thing or another
▶이것저것 이견이 나와서 우리는 결론을 내리지 못했다 With various opinions presented, we couldn't reach a conclusion.
▶이것저것 망설이다가 그는 전직하기로 결정했다 After vacillating this way and that, he finally decided to change jobs.
이겨내다 conquer [triumph over]; defeat; overpower ⇨ 이기다
◆병을 이겨내다 get over a disease / 고난을 이겨내다 overcome all hardships [various difficulties]
▶그는 신체장애를 이겨내고 대학을 졸업했다 He overcame his physical handicap and graduated from college.
이견 異見 a different view; a dissenting opinion ◆이견을 내세우다 present a different view; 〈반대하다〉 raise an objection
이경 耳鏡 〔醫〕 an otoscope; an auriscope
이경 離京 departure from the capital
—이경하다 leave the capital
이고 1 〈한편〉 and; while; and also; or
▶그는 저명한 시인이고, 아들은 음악가다 He is a well-known poet, while [and] his son a musician.
2 〈…이건〉 any; -ever; whether it is...or...
◆무엇이고 anything; whatever
▶귤이고 사과이고 네가 좋아하는 대로 가져라 You can have whatever you like — an orange, an apple, or anything.
▶그는 무엇이고 해보고 싶어한다 He wants to try anything and everything.
▶당신 분부면 무엇이고 따르겠습니다 I shall obey whatever orders you give me.
이골 a fixed habit ◆이골(이) 나다 grow [become] accustomed ⟪to⟫; get used ⟪to⟫; be an expert
▶그는 철야하는 데 이골이 났다 He is accustomed to staying [sitting] up all night.
▶그녀는 그것에 워낙 이골이 나 있다 She is quite [very well] used to it.
이곳 this place; here
◆이곳 사람들 the people here; the people of this district / 이곳에(서) here; in this place / 이곳 저곳에 here and there
▶이곳에 오시면 꼭 들르세요 Drop in please [Please come and see me] if you are ever here.
▶그녀는 이곳까지 걸어왔다 She walked this far [to this point].
이공 理工 science and engineering ■—대학 a college [a department] of science and engineering —학부 the faculty of science and engineering
이공 耳孔 〔解〕 an ear hole; the auditory canal

이과 耳科 〔醫〕 otology ■ —전문의 〔醫〕 an ear specialist; an otologist
이과 理科 〈학문〉 science; natural science; 〈학과〉 the science department [course]
▶ 넌 대학을 이과로 진학하는 것이 좋다 You should take the science course in college.
■ —대학 a college of science
이관 耳管 〔解〕 an auditory tube
이관 移管 transfer of control [administration] —이관하다 transfer the control of
▶ 이 계획은 시에서 도로 이관되었다 This project was transferred from the municipal authorities to the control of the province.
■ 군원— transfer of the Military Assistance Program
이교 異敎 a foreign religion; 〈기독교에서 본〉 heathenism; paganism; a heresy
♦ 이교의 pagan; heathen; heretical
▶ 기독교는 한국인에게는 이교였다 To the Korean Christianity was a foreign religion.
▶ 부활절은 원래 이교의 축제였다 Easter was originally a pagan feast.
■ —국 a heathen country; (총칭) heathendom —도 a pagan; a heathen; a heretic
이구동성 異口同聲 a unanimous voice ♦ 이구동성으로 with one voice; unanimously; in chorus; in unison / 이구동성으로 찬성하다 agree unanimously
▶ 그들은 이구동성으로 「그렇다」고 했다 They all said "yes" with one voice [in unison, in chorus].
이구아나 〔動〕 an iguana
이국 異國 a foreign country [land]; a strange land ♦ 이국적(인) foreign; exotic / 이국에서 죽다 die in a foreign land
■ —인 a foreigner —정서 an exotic mood [atmosphere]; exoticism —풍 exoti(ci)sm; foreign customs
이군 二軍 〔野〕 a farm [scrub] team
▶ 감독은 그를 2군으로 돌렸다 The general manager farmed him out.
■ —선수 a farm hand; a scrub
이궁 離宮 1 〈세자궁〉 the Palace of the Crown Prince 2 〈별궁〉 a detached palace [villa]; a Royal villa
이권 利權 rights and interests; 〈개발의 특권〉 (a) concessions
♦ 아라비아에서의 미국의 석유 이권 the United States oil interests in Arabia / 외국인에게 광산개발의 이권을 주다 give foreigners mining concessions / 이권을 획득하다 acquire concessions [rights] / 이권을 포기하다 renounce one's interests
■ —양도 transfer of rights [concessions] —운동 graft(ing); hunting for a concession —운동자 a concession hunter; a profiteer —획득 acquisition of concessions; (美) graft
이극 二極 ♦ 이극의 bipolar; dipolar
■ —분화 bipolarization —성 bipolarity —(진공)관 a diode
이글 1 〈독수리〉 eagle 2 〈골프〉 eagle ♦ 이글을 치다 shot an eagle
이글거리다 blaze; glare
이글루 〈얼음집〉 an igloo; an iglu

이글이글 (burning) aglow; glowing lively
♦ 정욕으로 이글이글 불타는 눈 eyes burning with passion / 석양으로 이글이글 타는 하늘 the sky aglow with the setting sun / 숯불이 이글이글 피다 the charcoal burns lively
▶ 태양이 보도에 이글이글 내리쬐었다 The sun blazed [scorched] down on the pavement.
▶ 그의 두 눈은 분노로 이글이글 타올랐다 His eyes flashed with anger.
—이글이글하다 burning; blazing; glowing
이금 泥金 gold ink; gold paint
이급 二級 the second class ♦ 2급의 second-class; second-grade ■ —면허장 a second-class license
이기 二期 two terms [periods]
▶ 총장은 현재 2기째다 The president is in his [her] second term. ■ —작 a semiannual crop —제 a two-term system
이기 利己 self-interest; selfishness; egoism
♦ 이기적인 요구 a self-centered demand / 이기적인 selfish
■ —심 egoistic [selfish, self-centered] mind: 그는 이기심이 없어서 누구에게나 신뢰받는다 He is unselfish man and is relied upon by all
이기 利器 a convenience; a device
♦ 문명의 이기 a modern convenience; facilities of civilization
▶ 컴퓨터는 많은 현대 이기 중의 하나다 Computers are one of many modern conveniences.
이기다¹ 1 〈승리하다〉 win; gain [win] a victory (over); be [come off] victorious; be a winner; 〈정복하다〉 conquer; 〈패배시키다〉 defeat; overcome; beat
♦ 이기든 지든 win or lose / 경주[경기]에서 이기다 win a race [game] / 소송에 이기다 win a case; gain a lawsuit / 선거에서 이기다 win an election / 적에게 이기다 defeat [beat] the enemy; gain [win] a victory over the enemy / 투표에서 이기다 beat sb at the poll / 테니스[체스]에서 이기다 win at tennis [chess] / 2대 1[1점차]로 이기다 win by a score of 2 to 1; win the game 2 to 1 / 간신히 이기다 win a close victory (over) / 쉽게 이기다 win an easy victory; walk over / 크게 이기다 gain a great [sweeping] victory / 이길 가망이 있다 [없다] have a [no] chance of winning
▶ 어느 팀이 이기고 있습니까? Which team is winning [leading]?
▶ 신인 권투선수가 챔피언을 이겼다 The new boxer outboxed the champion.
▶ 누가 이기나 해보자 We will see which of us is master.
2 ⇨ 이겨내다
♦ 병을 이기다 triumph over disease / 유혹[시험]을 이기다 〔基〕 overcome the Temptation / 자기자신을 이기다 control oneself
이기다² 〈반죽하다〉 knead; temper
♦ 진흙을 이기다 work [knead] clay / 밀가루와 물을 섞어 이겨서 반죽을 만들다 mix flour and water, then knead into dough
이기적 利己的 selfish; egoistic; self-interested
♦ 이기적인 동기에서 from a selfish motive
▶ 그는 이기적이다 He is selfish [egoistic]. ⇌ He is a greedy [selfish] person.

이기주의 利己主義 egoism ■ —자 egoist
이기죽거리다 make provocative, insinuating remarks [jokes]; jeer; hoot (at); heckle
이까짓 so trifling [trivial, small, little]
♦이까짓 것[일] such a trifle; little [trivial] things / 이까짓 돈 such a small [trifling] sum of money; (口) chicken feed; (口) peanuts
▶이까짓 일로 소동을 피우지 마라 Don't make a fuss about such a little thing.
▶이까짓 일로 걱정하지 마라 You shouldn't let such a small thing worry you.
이깔나무 (植) a larch (tree)
이끌다 1 〈데리고 가다〉 take [have] along [with one]; 〈거느리다〉 lead; conduct; head; 〈지휘하다〉 command; 〈관심을〉 attract
♦장군이 이끄는 군대 an army under the command of [commanded by, led by] a general / 노구를 이끌고 in spite of *one's* old age / 군대를 이끌다 be in command of the army
▶그는 자기 자식들을 이끌고 동물원에 갔다 He took his children with him to the zoo.
▶김박사는 친선사절단을 이끌고 도미했다 Dr. Kim went to America, heading a good will mission.
▶도박이 그를 파멸로 이끌었다 Gambling led [brought] him to ruin.
▶그 그림이 나의 마음을 몹시 이끌었다 The painting appealed to me enormously.
2 〈인도하다〉 guide; lead; teach
♦젊은이들을 바른 길로 이끌다 guide [lead] the young men into the right path / 나라를 번영의 길로 이끌다 steer [guide] *one's* country to prosperity
▶그는 자기가 좋아하는 화제로 이야기를 이끌어 갔다 He led up to his favorite topic.
이끌리다 1 〈지휘받다〉 be led; be commanded; 〈인도되다〉 be led; be conducted; be guided
♦선생님에게 이끌린 아동들 a group of schoolchildren headed [led] by their teacher / 이끌리어 가다 be led away; be taken along
▶저런 유형의 남자는 나쁜 길로 이끌리기 쉽다 A man of that type is easily led [tempted] into evil ways.
2 〈정에〉 be drawn; be driven; be overcome [moved]; be touched
♦호기심에 이끌리어 out of curiosity; under the impulse of curiosity / 허영심에 이끌리다 be spurred on vanity
▶그는 그녀의 매력에 이끌리었다 He was attracted [fascinated, drawn to her] by her charm.
이끼[1] (植) moss; a lichen
♦이끼 낀 moss-grown[-covered]; mossy / 이끼 낀 해묵은 비석 a monument mossed by time / 이끼 낀 고목 the lichened trunk of an old tree; an old tree trunk covered with lichen
▶돌에 이끼가 끼었다 The stones have become moss-grown.
▶구르는 돌에는 이끼가 끼지 않는다 (속담) A rolling stone gathers no moss.
이끼[2] 〈놀란 소리〉 Oh!; Oh my goodness!
▶이끼, 이게 뭐야? What happened? ⇒ What a surprise! ⇒ 〈사람을 보고〉 Oh, you scared me!
이나 1 〈그러나〉 but; (and) yet; 〈한편〉 while; meanwhile; 〈…하기는 하나〉 however; in spite of this
▶그는 지독한 사람이나, 내 형이라네 He's an awful person [no good]—still [nevertheless], he is my brother.
2 〈정도〉 as many [much] as; no less [fewer] than; nearly; about
♦열 번이나 as often as ten times / 열 살이나 위다[아래다] be *sb's* senior [junior] by ten years; be older [younger] by ten years / 빚이 백만원이나 되다 be in debt to the extent of a million won / 3시간이나 기다리다 wait for good three hours
▶난 빗속을 두 시간이나 걸어야 했다 I had to walk as long as two hours in the rain.
▶이 물건은 100만원이나 했다 This article cost no less than [all of] one million won.
3 〈선택〉 any
▶박군이나 내가 가야만 한다 Either Mr. Park or I must go.
▶그는 1주일이나 2주일 후에 돌아온다 He will come back in a week or two.
▶그녀는 무엇이나 할 수 있는 사람이다 She can do [is good at] anything.
▶책이라면 무엇이나 좋다 Any book will do.
이나마 〈아쉬운 대로〉 although; though; even if; at least
▶조그만 선물이나마 받아 주십시오 Here's a small present for you I hope you like it.
▶성함이나마 가르쳐 주십시오 Can [Could] you let us know your name?
▶그가 전화 한통이나마 해주어야 할텐데 He might at least give me a call.
이날 〈오늘〉 today; this day; 〈바로 오늘〉 this very day; 〈당일〉 the day; that day
♦5년전의 이날 five years ago today; this day five years ago / 이날의 연사 the speaker of the day / 이날까지 till [until, up to, to] this day; until today; up to now
▶이날은 비가[눈이] 왔었다 It rained [snowed] on that day.
▶이날은 날씨가 좋았다 The occasion was favored by fine weather.
▶이날 면접하러 오지 않은 사람은 실격이 됩니다 Those who do not come for interviews on the day will be disqualified.
이날저날 from day to day; day after day
♦이날저날로 연기하다 put off from day to day ▶우리는 당신이 오기를 이날저날 하고 기다리고 있었다 We've been expecting you day after day.
이남 以南 south 《of》 ♦38선 이남 south of the 38th parallel / 한강 이남 지역 the area south of the Han-gang / 대전 이남은 비가 오고 있다 It is raining in Taejŏn and southward.
이남박 a rice-washing bowl; a rice washtub
이내[1] 〈흐릿한 기운〉 an evening haze; dusk
이내[2] 1 〈곧〉 soon; without delay; at once; promptly; immediately; (美) right away [off]
♦이내 팔리다 find quick buyers
▶이내 돌아오겠다 I'll be right back [in a moment, in a minute].

▶ 약 기운이 이내 나타났다 The medicine took immediate effect.
▶ 그녀의 열은 이내 내릴 것입니다 Her fever will soon go down.
2 〈그후 내처〉 ever since
▶ 이내 그들은 서로 사랑하게 되었다 From that time on [From then on], they came to love each other.

이내 以內 within; less than; not more than; 《美口》 inside of
♦ 5천원 이내의 금액 a sum less than [not exceeding] five thousand won / 10분 이내에 within [in less than] ten minutes
▶ 호텔은 역에서 차로 10분 이내에 있다 The hotel is within ten minutes' drive [ride] of the station.
▶ 100단어 이내로 답하시오 Answer in less than 100 words.

이냥 as it is; as it stands; (in) the same way as this ♦ 이냥 두다 〈현 상태로〉 leave *sth* as it is; leave *sth* intact
▶ 환자를 이냥 둘 수 없으니 의사를 부르시오 Call [Send for] a doctor, we can't leave the sick man like this.

이네(들) these people ▶ 이네들과는 일면식도 없다 These men are total strangers to me.

이년 this woman; 〈계집애〉 this chit
▶ 이년(아) You bitch!; You slut!

이년 二年 two years ♦ 2년 마다 every other year; every two years ■ーい생 a second-grade [-year] pupil [student]; 〈대학・고교의〉《美》a sophomore ーい생 식물 a biennial plant

이념 理念 an idea; a philosophy; an ideology; a doctrine
♦ 김박사의 교육 이념 Dr Kim's educational philosophy / 이념적 ideological / 이념적으로 ideologically / 이념 분쟁을 벌이다 have an ideological dispute 《with》

이노신산 ー酸《化》inosinic acid ■ ー나트륨 sodium inosinate

이놈 this man [fellow, guy, chap] ▶ 이놈(아) You villain [rascal, scoundrel, fool]!

이농 離農 rural exodus ーい농하다 give up [abandon] farming ■ーい가 a farmer who has given up farming

이뇨 利尿《醫》urination; diuresis ーい뇨하다 urinate; pass water
■ ー제 a diuretic; a hydragog(ue) : 수박에는 이뇨제 효능이 있다고 한다 Watermelon is said to have a diuretic effect.

이니 1〈열거〉 and; as well as; or
♦ 쌀이니 간장이니 된장이니 그밖의 여러 식품 rice, soy sauce, soybean paste, and various food stuffs
▶ 컵이니 칫솔이니 여러가지를 샀다 I bought a cup, a toothbrush and what not.
2〈의문〉▶ 이것은 무엇이니? What is this?
▶ 무슨 일이니? What happened?

이니(까) as; since; because; because of; so; owing to
▶ 우천이니까 외출하지 않았다 Because [Since, As] it was raining, I didn't go out.
▶ 가수가 병으니까 연주회는 연기되었다 The concert was postponed owing to [on account of] the singer's illness.
▶ 성탄절이니까 그는 귀향했다 He went home for Christmas as a matter of fact.
▶ 환자는 자는 중이니까 1시간 정도 기다려 주십겠습니까? As the patient is sleeping now, could you wait about an hour?

이니셜 *one's* initials ♦ 서류에 이니셜로 서명하다 sign documents with *one's* initials; initial documents

이닝〔野〕an inning; 《英》innings (▶ 단수 취급)

이다¹ 1〈머리에〉put [bear] on the head; carry on the head ♦ 물동이를 이다 carry a water jar [jug] on *one's* head
2〈지붕을〉cover; 〈짚으로〉thatch; 〈기와로〉tile over; 〈판자로〉shingle; 〈슬레이트로〉slate
▶ 그 농가는 짚으로 이어져 있다 The farmer's cottage is thatched.
▶ 우리집 지붕은 기와로 이은 것이다 The roof of my house is covered with tiles [is tiled].

이다² 1〈단정하는 말〉be
▶ 그는 학생이다 He is a student.
▶ 그녀의 머리는 갈색이다 She has brown hair.
▶ 전쟁이 끝난 것은 그 해이다 It is in that year that the war ended.
▶ 그녀의 태도는 우호적이다 Her attitude is friendly.
2〈…이 되다〉come; make; be
▶ 둘 더하기 셋은 다섯이다 Two and three make(s) five.
3〈수량이〉number; 〈도량이〉measure; 〈무게가〉weight; 〈면적이〉cover
▶ 그는 키가 6피트이다 He is six feet tall.
▶ 그는 체중이 60킬로그램이다 He weighs sixty kilograms.
▶ 그 다리는 길이가 150 미터이다 The bridge measures one hundred fifty meter in length.

이다지(도) this much; so (much); like this; to this degree [extent]; thus
♦ 이다지도 오래 so long (like this)
♦ 이다지도 좋은 기회는 절대로 없을 것이다 There will never be such a good chance like this.
▶ 비가 이다지도 많이 오는 것은 드물다 It is rare to have so much rain [such (a) heavy rainfall] here.
▶ 이다지도 좋은 시를 쓰는 사람은 극히 드물다 Few (people) can write poems so well [such fine poems].

이단 二段 ♦ 신문의 이단 광고 a two column advertisement / 이단 표제 a two-line [two-column] heading

이단 異端 heresy; 〈기독교 입장에서〉paganism; heterodoxy
♦ 이단의 heretic(al); pagan; heathen / 이단적 견해를 발표하다 express a heretical doctrine
▶ 그의 학설은 이단시되었다 His doctrine was considered heretical [regarded as unorthodox].
■ ー사설 (邪說) heresy and heterodoxy ーい자 a heretic; a heathen

이달 this month; the current [present] month
♦ 이달치 월급 *one's* salary for the month; this month's pay / 이달 호 잡지 the current number [issue] of the magazine / 이달 초에 at the

이대로 beginning of this month / 이달 10일에 on the tenth (of) this month / 이달 중에 in the course of this month; before the end of this month
▶ 이달은 비가 많이 왔다 We have had a lot of rain this month.
이대로 as it is [stands]; at they are; as *one* is; like this
♦ 이대로 내버려 두다 leave *sth* off as it is
▶ 이대로 하시오 〈똑같이〉 Please do it like this [in the same way].
▶ 이대로 가만 있을 수는 없다 Something must be done. ⇌ I can't overlook this.
▶ 경찰이 올 때까지 이 방은 이대로 놔 둬야 한다 We should leave this room intact [untouched, as it is] until the police arrives.
이대정당 二大政黨 two major political parties
■ 一제도 a two-party system
이데아 〔哲〕 an idea; 〈이상〉 an ideal
이데올로기 an ideology
♦ 이데올로기의 대립 an ideological conflict / 이데올로기의 ideological
▶ 그와 나는 이데올로기가 다르다 He and I have different ideologies.
이도 吏道 the duty of officials; officialdom
■ 一쇄신 renovation of officialdom
이도음정 二度音程 〔樂〕 a second
이동 以東 east (of)
♦ 서울 이동에[의] (to the) east of Seoul; at Seoul and eastward
▶ 경기 이동은 눈이 올 것입니다 It will snow in the regions east of Kyŏnggi province.
이동 異同 (a) difference; (a) dissimilarity
▶ 양자간에는 이동이 없다 There is no difference between the two. ■ 一식별 identification
이동 異動 change; shifting; reshuffle
♦ 공무원의 이동 changes among [of] public officials / 내각의 이동 a reshuffle of the Cabinet personnel
■ 대一 a wholesale [sweeping] change; (美) a shake-up: 회사 임원의 대이동이 있었다 Sweeping personnel changes have been made among the company officers. 인사— personnel changes: 이번 인사 이동에서 그는 울산으로 전근되었다 In the recent personnel changes he was transferred to the Ulsan office.
이동 移動 (a) move; (a) movement; (a) transfer; migration
♦ 게르만 민족의 대이동 〔史〕 the Germanic [Gothic] migration
—이동하다 move; remove; transfer; migrate
▶ 유목민은 목초를 찾아 항상 이동하고 있었다 The nomads were constantly on the move looking for grass.
■ 민족— a racial migration 인구— the movement [drift] of population ■ 一경찰 mobile police; railroad [highway] police 一극단 a traveling [an itinerant] theatrical troupe —노동자 a migratory laborer —도서관 a traveling library; (美) a bookmobile —외과병원 a mobile surgical hospital —전시회 a mobile [an itinerary] show —진료소 a traveling clinic
이동성 移動性 ♦ 이동성의 rambling; roving

■ 一고기압 〔氣〕 a migratory anticyclone
이두박근 二頭膊筋 〔解〕 the biceps of the arm
이드거니 in rather large quantity [amount]; at regular intervals; quite a bit of
▶ 우리는 이드거니 기다렸다 We waited for quite a long time.
▶ 오랜 가뭄 끝에 이드거니 비가 왔다 A great deal of rain has fallen after a long spell of drought.
이득 利得 profits; gains; returns
■ 부당— an undue [excessive] profit; profiteering: 부당이득세 the excess profits tax
이든(지) any; ·ever; whether...or; either...or; or
♦ 그것이 사실이든 아니든 간에 no matter whether it is true or not
▶ 무엇이든지 먹고 싶은 것을 먹어라 Eat anything [whatever] you like.
▶ 무슨 질문이든지 좋다 Any question will do [will do OK].
이듬 〈논밭의〉 the second weeding [hoeing]; the second plowing —이듬하다 give a second hoeing [plowing]
이듬— 〈다음의〉 next; following; succeeding; ensuing
이듬해 the next [following] year; the year after ▶ 그녀는 귀국한 이듬해 결혼했다 She got married the year after she returned home.
이등 二等 **1** 〈등급〉 the second class
♦ 2등의 second-class; second-rate; second-grade / 이등으로 여행하다 travel second class [〈배의〉 cabin]
2 〈순위〉 the second place number 2 [No. 2]
♦ 경주에서 2등이 되다 come in [finish] second in the race
▶ 그는 마라톤에서 2등 했다 He was second [runner-up] in the marathon.
▶ 그녀는 3학년생 중에서 2등이다 She is the second best [is second] of the third-year students. ⇌ She ranks second among the third graders.
■ 一국가 a second-rate power —상 a second prize [award] —차[선실, 승객, 차표] a second-class car [cabin, passenger, ticket] —품 second-grade articles [goods]
이등변삼각형 二等邊三角形 〔幾〕 an isosceles [equilateral] triangle
이등병 二等兵 〈육군·해병〉 a private second class; 〈해군〉 a seaman recruit; 〈공군〉 an airman ♦ 이등병으로 a private (2nd class)
이등분 二等分 bisection
—이등분하다 divide *sth* into two equal parts [portions]; cut in half
♦ 원을 이등분하다 bisect the circle
■ 一선 a bisector
이등친 二等親 a relation [relative] in the second degree ((to))
이디엄 (an) idiom ♦ 영어의 이디엄 English idioms
이따(가) (a little) later; after a while [short time] ▶ 이따가 전화하겠소 I'll call [phone, (英) ring] you later (on).
▶ 이따가 봅시다 I'll see [See] you later!
이따금 sometimes; once; in a while; occasion-

ally ♦이따금 편지를 받다 receive occasional letters from
▶전문가도 이따금 실수를 저지른다 Even experts sometimes mistake.
▶이따금 번개가 쳤다 Lightning flashed now and then.
▶이따금 텔레비전을 보지요. 그러나 보통은 너무 바빠요 I occasionally watch television, but usually I'm far too busy.

이따위 such a thing [a person] as this; like this; this kind [sort] of; of this sort [kind]
♦이따위 책 this kind [sort] of worthless book
▶이따위 것을 두려워해선 안된다 You should not fear such a little thing.
▶이따위 웃기는 얘기는 생전 처음 듣겠다 I've never heard anything so funny. ⇌ This is the funniest thing I've ever heard.
▶이따위를 믿을 정도로 그녀는 어리석지 않다 She is not so foolish as to believe something like this.

이때 ♦이때에 at this [that] time [moment, point] / 바로 이때(에) at this very moment [instant] / 이때까지 until [up to] now; till now / 이때까지 쭉 all this while
▶이때처럼 이렇게 훌륭한 경치를 본 적이 없다 I have never seen such a beautiful sight as this.
▶이때는 그가 아직 대학생이었다 He was still in college at that time [then].

이똥 a hard, yellowish deposit on the teeth; 〈치석〉 tartar

이라 ▶병이라 그는 결석했다 He was absent because of [on account of, owing to] illness.
▶교통체증이라 기차를 놓쳤다 I missed my train because of a traffic jam.

이라고 ▶김선생이라고 하는 분이 오셨습니다 A Mr. Kim [A man named [called] Kim] has come to see you.
▶그가 시인이라고? 설마? (口) Him a poet? What a joke?
▶뭣이라고? What is that you say?

이라는 that is (called) ♦존슨이라는 학생 a student named Johnson
▶「집」이라는 단어는 영어로 무엇이냐? What is the English word for "chip"?
▶그녀는 나를 도울 수 없을 것이라는 편지를 보내왔다 She sent me a letter to the effect [saying] that she could not help me.

-이라니 ⇨ -라니 ▶그런 사람이 장군이라니? 농담이겠지 Him a general? You're kidding.
▶책이라니, 어느 책 말이냐? Which book do you mean?
▶아니, 또 라면이라니? What instant noodles again?

이라도 ♦무엇이라도 anything, whatever / 우천이라도 even if it rains [should rain]
▶어느 것이라도 좋다 Either will do.
▶제1권이라도 인쇄했어야 하는데 We should have printed the first volume at least.
▶영웅이라도 두려움을 느낄 때가 있다 Heroes experience moments of fear, too.

-이라면 ⇨ -라면 ▶돈이라면 걱정할 것 없다 As far as money is concerned, you may put your mind at rest. ▶바둑이라면 그는 일류다 He is a first-rate player of [at] paduk.

이라크 Iraq; 〈공식명〉 the Republic of Iraq
♦이라크의 Iraqi ■—사람 an Iraqi

이락 利落 ex interest; ex int. ■—채권 an ex interest bond

이란¹ Iran; 〈공식명〉 the Islamic Republic of Iran ♦이란의 Iranian ■—사람 an Iranian

이란² that is (called) ⇨ 이라는
♦존슨이란 (이름의) 회사 a firm by the name of Johnson / 사슴이란 동물 an animal called the deer / 천만원이란 큰 돈 such a large sum as ten million won
▶창이란 창은 모두 깨졌다 Every window was broken.

이란성쌍둥이 二卵性雙— (one of) two-egg [biovular, fraternal] twins

-이람 ▶웬 이렇게 많은 사람이람! What a lot of [(口) What crowds of] people!
▶그 사람 웬 바보짓이람! How stupid (it is) of him to do that!
▶계집애가 엄마한테 그게 무슨 말버릇이람! For a girl to talk to her mother like that!

이랑¹ 〈두둑〉 a ridge in the ground; 〈고랑〉 a furrow; ridge and furrow
♦이랑이 진 furrowed; corrugated / 이랑을 일구다 plow into ridges; furrow

이랑² and ⇨ 랑 ▶어제 여동생이랑 쇼핑갔었다 I went shopping yesterday with my sister.
▶귤이랑 사과랑 과일을 많이 샀다 We bought a lot of fruit—oranges, apples and what not [so on].

이래 以來 since; from ♦그 이래 since then; from that time on; 〈줄곧〉 ever since / 천지개벽 이래 since the beginning of the world / 10년 이래 for the past [last] ten years; these ten years
▶그는 학교 창립 이래의 수재라고 한다 He is said to be the brightest by the school has had since it was founded.
▶이건 20년 이래의 대설이다 This is the heaviest snowfall (that) we have had for the past [(美) twenty years.

이래 〈…이라 하다〉 they say; I hear
▶그녀가 병이래 (I am not sure but) I hear she is sick [ill].

이래라저래라 ▶나로서는 그에게 이래라저래라 할 수가 없다 I am not in a position to tell him what to do.
▶당신이 이래라저래라 할것 없어요 You don't have the right to say anything about it. ⇌ It's none of your business.

이래봬도 you may not take 《me》 as such, but…; I don't know what you take 《me》 for, but…
▶이래봬도 나도 날리던 사람이야 You behold [see] in me one who has seen better days.
▶이래봬도 내가 젊었을 때는 한량이었다네 Though I may not look like it, I was considered a playboy when I was young.

이래저래 what with this and (what with) that; for one thing or another
▶나는 이래저래 바쁘다 I am busy with one thing and another.

이랬다저랬다

▶이래저래 그를 만날 기회를 놓쳐 버렸다 Something or other came up, and I missed my chance to see him.

이랬다저랬다 this way and that way
♦이랬다저랬다하다 〈마음이〉 be capricious [whimsical]; be temperamental; 〈행동이〉 play fast and loose
▶그녀는 이랬다저랬다 변덕이 심하다 She often changes her mind [is so whimsical].

이러 〈마소를 모는 소리〉 Giddap!; Giddup!; 〈빨리 몰 때〉 Gee-ho!; Gee-up!

이러구러 (in the) meantime; meanwhile
▶이러구러 10년이 지났다 Ten years have passed all too soon. ⇒ Meanwhile, ten years went by.

이러나저러나 anyway; at any rate; in any case [event]
▶이러나저러나 그것은 내게는 마찬가지다 It is all one [the same] to me.
▶이러나저러나 해보는 게 좋다 At all events you had better try.

이러니저러니 this and that ⇨ 이러쿵저러쿵
▶이러니저러니하지 말고 빨리 이거나 해 Do this quickly without argument [grumbling].
▶이러니저러니하지 말고 빨리 따라와 Just shut up and follow me.
▶지금 와서 이러니저러니해봐야 소용없다 It is too late now to raise any objections.

이러다 ▶서둘러라, 이러다 기차 놓치겠다 Hurry up, or we will miss the train.

이러루하다 like this (one); nearly the same as this; like [similar to] this

이러므로 for this reason; on this account

이러이러하다 so-and-so; such and such
♦이러이러한 이야기 such and such a story / 이러이러한 까닭으로 for such and such reasons; such being the case; under this circumstances
▶아버지께서 이러이러한 경우에는 이러저러하게 하라고 가르쳐주셨다 My father advised me to do so-and-so on such and such an occasion.

이러저러하다 so-and-so ⇨ 이러이러하다

이러쿵저러쿵 this and [or] that; one thing or another
♦이러쿵저러쿵 말할 것 없이 without saying this or that; without (useless) objections / 이러쿵저러쿵 말하다 say this and that (about); 〈반대하다〉 make objections to sb / 이러쿵저러쿵 말대답하다 answer back
▶이러쿵저러쿵 말하지 마라 Hold your tongue! ⇒ Shut up!
▶오늘날 젊은이들에 대해 이러쿵저러쿵 말하지 마라 Don't criticize young people today.
▶그는 이러쿵저러쿵 남의 일을 간섭하기 좋아한다 He is liable to put his nose into other people's business.
▶남의 일에 이러쿵저러쿵 참견하지 마라 Don't interfere [meddle] in other's affairs.
▶그녀의 복장을 이러쿵저러쿵 말하지 마라 Don't be so critical about what she wears.

이러하다 this; of this kind [sort]; like this ⇨ 이런¹
♦이러한 일 a thing [an affair] of this sort / 이러한 사람 such a one; a person like this / 이러한 사정 these circumstances
▶이야기인 즉 이러하다 I will tell you what [how, why].

이럭저럭 1 〈그냥저냥〉 somehow or other; one way or the other
♦이럭저럭 살아가다 manage to keep the pot boiling / 이럭저럭 해나가다 get along somehow
▶그는 이럭저럭 생계를 꾸려나갔다 He eked out a scanty livelihood.
▶이럭저럭 위기는 모면했다 We somehow managed to ride out the crisis.

2 〈어느덧〉 before one knows [is aware]; unnoticed
♦이럭저럭 하는 동안에 (in the) meantime; meanwhile
▶이럭저럭 날이 저물었다 In the meanwhile the sun went down.
▶이럭저럭 하는 사이에 일주일이 지나가 버렸다 A week has passed all too soon.

이런¹ 〈이러한〉 such; like this; 〈이〉 this; such... as this; 〈이 종류의〉 of this kind [sort]
♦이런 일 such a thing (as this) / 이런 기후에는 in this kind of weather / 이런 때에 at a time like this; at such a time / 이런 까닭에 for this reason; on this account
▶이런 훌륭한 사람을 만난 적은 없었다 I've never met such a nice [so nice a] person.
▶인생이란 이런 것이다 Such [This] is life.
▶이런 재미있는 책은 읽은 적이 없었다 I have never read such an interesting book.

이런² 〈놀라운 일이 있을 때〉 Oh!; Oh dear!; Dear me!; Gosh!; Good Gracious!
▶이런, 이게 뭐야? Why! What is this?
▶이런, 어처구니가 없군 Oh, how stupid!
▶이런, 벌써 10시잖아 My, is it already ten o'clock?
▶이런, 그 집 번지를 잊어버렸군 By Jove, I've forgotten the number of the house.

이런저런 this and that; one thing or [and] another; something or other
♦이런저런 생각 끝에 after fully considering the matter; after much thinking
▶이런저런 이유를 내세워 그는 그 제안에 동의하지 않았다 For one reason or another he did not give his consent to the proposal.
▶이런저런 일로 바쁘다 I am busy with one thing and another.
▶그 지도교사는 이런저런 일로 항상 바쁘다 The guidance teacher is always busy with one thing or another.

이렁저렁 somehow or other ⇨ 이럭저럭 1

이렇게 like this; in this way; so
♦이렇게 많은 〈수가〉 so many; 〈양이〉 so much / 이렇게 된 이상에는 now that things have come to this (pass) / 이렇게 아침 일찍 at this early hour of (the) morning / 이렇게 밤늦게 at this late hour of (the) night / 이렇게 비가 오는데도 for all this rain
▶이렇게 해라 Do it (in) this way [like this].
▶나는 이렇게 될 줄 알았다 I knew it would turn out like this.
▶이렇게 훌륭하게 되리라고는 예상하지 못했다 I did not expect it to be done so excellently.

▶이렇게 놀란 것은 생전 처음이다 I was never so frightened in all my life.
▶이렇게 좋은 기회는 다시 없을 것이다 There will never be such a good chance as this again.
▶나는 이렇게 생각한다 This is what I think [how I feel] about it.

이렇다 like this; this way; as follows ⇨ 이러하다
♦이렇다 할 재주가 없는 사람 a person with no particular skill / 이렇다 할 이유도 없이 without any particular reason / 이렇다 할 목적도 없이 without any definite object
▶그의 이야기는 대강 이렇다 His story runs somewhat like this.
▶우리 집에서는 만사가 이렇다 This is the way things go at home.
▶이렇다 할 어려움은 없다 There is no serious difficulty.
▶두 사람 사이의 의견에 이렇다 할 차이는 보이지 않는다 I see no substantial difference of opinion between them.
▶그는 아직 이렇다 할 작품을 내지 못했다 He has produced no works to speak of.
▶나는 이렇다 할 까닭도 없이 꾸지람을 들었다 I was scolded without any particular reason.

이렇다저렇다 this or that ⇨ 이러니저러니, 이러쿵저러쿵

이렇든저렇든 whether it is this or that; anyway; in any case; at any rate

이렇듯 like this (⇨ 이렇게) ▶그는 이렇듯 위대한 교사였다 As I have said, he was a great teacher.

이레 1 ⇨ 이렛날 **2** 〈일곱 날〉 seven days

이렛날 the seventh day (of a month)

이력 履歷 one's personal history [record]; 〈경력〉 one's career; 〈배경〉 one's background
♦이력이 나다 become experienced; get skill [used] / 이력이 좋다 [시원찮다] have an honorable [a poor] record of service
▶그는 이력이 좋다[나쁘다] He has a good [poor] record of service.
▶그녀의 이력은 훌륭하다 She is a woman of good background [antecedents].
▶그는 이 방면에 많은 이력을 쌓은 사람이다 He is rich in experience in this line.
▶우리는 그의 이력에 대해서 아는 것이 별로 없다 We know little of his career [what his career is].
■—서 a personal history; a curriculum vitae (略 c.v.); (美) a resume

이례 異例 an exception; an exceptional case
♦이례적인 exceptional; 〈전례없는〉 unprecedented
▶이런 장마는 8월에는 이례적이다 Such a long spell of rainy weather is exceptional for August.
▶이 결정은 이례적이다 This is an exceptional [unprecedented] decision.
▶그는 이례적인 승진으로 부러움을 샀다 Because of his exceptional promotion he was envied.

이로 理路 reasoning; argument ▶그는 그 회의에서 이로정연한 주장을 했다 He expressed logical [reasonable] opinions at the conference.

-이로되 it is but; though it is
▶밥은 밥이로되 선밥이다 It sure is boiled rice, but it is undercooked.
▶가장은 가장이로되 실권없는 가장이라 Though he is the head of a family, he has no power.

이로부터 1 〈금후〉 after this; from this time on; from now on; hence(forth); hereafter
♦이로부터 몇 달 동안 for a few months ahead / 이로부터 2년 뒤에 two years hence
2 〈이 때문에〉 for this reason; as a result of this; out of this
▶이로부터 희망봉이란 이름이 생겼다 Hence (comes) the name Cape of Good Hope.
▶이로부터 여러가지 문제가 발생했다 Out of this many troubles arose!

이로써 herewith; with this ♦이로써 판단하건대 judging from this ▶이로써 그는 끝장이다 This will be the end of him.

이론 異論 〈이견〉 different opinion; a divergent view; 〈이의〉 an objection; a protest; a dissent
♦이론을 제기하다 object (to); take exception (to); raise an objection (to, against)
▶이론이 있습니까? Do you have any objection (to it)?
▶나는 네가 그렇게 하는 것에 이론이 없다 I have no objection to your doing so.
▶그는 그 계획에 이론을 제기했다 He objected to the plan.

이론 理論 (a) theory
♦이론과 실천 theory and practice / 이론적인 theoretical / 이론을 세우다 theorize
▶그는 이 분야의 이론적 연구에 종사하고 있다 He is engaged in the theoretical study of the field.
▶그는 이론을 실천했다 He put his theory into practice.
▶그 실험은 이론상으로는 가능하다 The experiment is theoretically possible.
■상대성— the theory of relativity ■—가 a theorist; a theoretician ■경제학 theoretical economics ■물리학 theoretical physics ■투쟁 a theoretical dispute [controversy]

이롭다 利— 〈유리하다〉 advantageous; favorable; 〈이익이 있다〉 profitable; lucrative; remunerative; beneficial; salutary; 〈좋다〉 good 《for》
♦국민들에게 이로운 교훈 an instructive lesson to people / 이로운 사업 a profitable [paying] business / 이로운 조건 advantageous terms / 학생들에게 이로운 책 books good for students / 건강에 이롭다 be good for the health / 이롭게 하다 benefit oneself; promote one's benefit
▶그것은 이로우면 이롭지 해는 없다 It has everything to gain and nothing to lose.
▶그 경험은 내게 이로운 점이 많았다 That experience taught me a lot.
▶그 일이 그에게는 이롭지 않았다 He gained nothing from the work. ⇌ The work did him no good.

이루

▶ 모든 일이 내게 이롭게 전개되었다 Things turned out favorably for me.

이루 《cannot》 possibly
♦ 이루 말할 수 없는 unspeakable; beyond description; inexpressible; indescribable / 이루 헤아릴 수 없는 numberless; countless; innumerable / 이루 헤아릴 수 없다 be simply too many to count / 이루 형용할 수 없다 can hardly describe it
▶ 그 경치는 이루 말할 수 없이 아름답다 The wonderful scene is indescribably beautiful.
▶ 그들의 참상은 이루 다 말할 수 없었다 Their misery was beyond all expression.

이루 二壘 〔野〕 second base ▶ 주자는 2루로 진출했다 The runner got [advanced] to second. ■—수 a second baseman —타 a two-base hit; a two-bagger

이루 耳漏 〈귀에서 고름이 나오는 병〉 running ears; 〔醫〕 otorrhea

이루다 1 〈완성하다〉 finish; fulfill; complete; 〈성취하다〉 accomplish; achieve; attain; 〈실현하다〉 realize
♦ 못다 이룬 꿈 unfinished dream / 이룰 수 없는 소망 an unrealizable wish / 뜻을 이루다 have *one's* will; realize *one's* desire / 목적을 이루다 attain *one's* object; gain *one's* end
▶ 그 목표는 이루기 어렵다 The object is beyond attainment.
▶ 이룰 수 없는 사랑이라 단념해 버렸다 I gave it up as a hopeless love.
2 〈형성하다〉 form; make; constitute
♦ 원을 이루고 in a circle / 사회를 이루다 form a society
▶ 나는 결혼하여 새 가정을 이루었다 I got married and made a new home.
▶ 마침내 나는 바라던 바를 이루었다 I have fulfilled my wish at last.
▶ 그는 이미 일가를 이루었다고 말할 수 있다 We can safely say that he is an acknowledged authority.
▶ 저 산들이 이 성의 자연적인 성벽을 이룬다 Those mountains form natural walls for this castle.

이루어지다 1 〈성취되다〉 be accomplished; 《*one's* purpose》 be realized [fulfilled, attained, completed]; 〈소원·기도 등이〉 be answered [heard]; 〈실행되다〉 be carried out
▶ 내 기도가 이루어졌다 My prayer was heard.
▶ 내 오랜 숙원이 이루어졌다 My long-cherished desire has been realized.
2 〈구성·형성되다〉 be formed [composed] of; be made up of; 〈성립되다〉 be made [concluded, arranged, settled]
▶ 야구팀은 아홉명으로 이루어진다 A baseball team is made up of [consists of] nine players.
▶ 물은 산소와 수소로 이루어진다 Water consists [is composed] of oxygen and hydrogen.
▶ 포드사와 피아트사 간에 계약이 이루어졌다 The contract has been made between Ford (Motor Company) and Fiat. ⇒ Ford concluded a contract with Fiat.
▶ 이런 인플레이션하에서는 영업도 이루어지지 않는다 With this inflation we cannot manage [carry on] our business.

이룩하다 1 〈이루어내다〉 achieve; accomplish; complete; gain; win 《out, over》
▶ 과학은 괄목할 만한 발전을 이룩했다 Science has made remarkable advances.
▶ 소리보다 빨리 난다는 것은 사람의 힘으로는 이룩할 수 없는 일로 오랫동안 생각되었다 Flying faster than sound was long thought to be beyond human achievement.
2 〈세우다〉 found; establish; build ♦ 나라를 이룩하다 found [establish] a country / 회사를 이룩하다 establish a company

이류 二流 ♦ 이류의 second-class; middling; 〈시시한〉 inferior
▶ 그는 이류 음악가다 He's a minor musician.
■—시인 a minor poet —작가 a minor novelist [writer]: 그는 이류 작가다 He's a second-rate novelist. —호텔 a second-class [second-rate] hotel

이륙 離陸 a takeoff
—이륙하다 take off; leave the ground
▶ 비행기는 유럽을 향해 이륙했다 The airplane took [flew] off for Europe.
▶ 공항은 안개가 심했으나 비행기는 3시 정각에 순조롭게 이륙했다 The airport was foggy, but the plane took off smoothly [made a smooth takeoff] just at three.
■—거리 takeoff distance —시간 takeoff time —지점 a takeoff point —활주 a takeoff run

이륜차 二輪車 a two-wheeled vehicle; a two-wheeler; a bicycle ♦ 원동기를 단 이륜차 a motorized two-wheeled vehicle

이르다¹ 1 〈닿다〉 arrive 《at, in》; get to
▶ 그 길로 가면 국경에 이른다 The road leads to the border.
▶ 우리는 정오 무렵 목적지에 이르렀다 We arrived at our destination 《at》 about noon.
▶ 나는 2킬로미터 쯤 걸어서 산 오두막에 이르렀다 I walked some two kilometers and arrived at a mountain hut.
2 〈미치다〉 come to; extend to; get to; lead to; result [end] in
♦ 10월부터 12월에 이르는 3개월 동안 for three months 《extending》 from October to December / 극단적인 조치를 취하기에 이르다 go to extreme measures
▶ 그는 노름 때문에 자멸하기에 이르렀다 He ruined himself through gambling.
▶ 그 손해는 억대에 이르렀다 The damage ran into hundreds of million.
▶ 나는 그의 청렴함을 의심하기에 이르렀다 I came to doubt his integrity.
▶ 그 건물의 총공사비는 수백만 달러에 이르고 있다 The total cost of the building runs into millions of dollars.
▶ 어린아이에서 노인에 이르기까지 모두 그의 이름을 알고 있다 His name is known to everybody from children to elderly people.
▶ 이제 일이 여기에 이르렀으니 계획을 포기하는 수 밖에는 다른 도리가 없다 Now (that) things have come to this point, we have no choice but to give up the plan.
▶ 그의 기술은 아직 완벽한 경지에 이르지 못했다 His technique has not yet attained to perfection.

이르다² **1** 〈말하다〉 say ◆속담에 이르듯이 as the saying goes
▶너에게 이를 말이 있다 I have got something to say to you.
2 〈알리다〉 tell; make know; report
▶언제 서울로 떠날지 일러 주십시오 Tell me when you will depart for Seoul.
▶그는 자기의 결심을 내게 일러 주었다 He informed me of his decision.
3 〈알아듣게 말하다〉 explain; advise; teach; tell ◆…하는 방법을 일러주다 explain to *sb* how to 《do》
▶아버지는 아들에게 공부를 열심히 하라고 일렀다 The father advised his son to study hard.
▶형님은 내게 결혼을 너무 서두르지 말라고 일렀다 My brother advised me against marrying in haste.
4 〈고자질하다〉 tell on; tell tales 《about *sb*》; tattle
◆일러바치는 사람 a talebearer
▶누이 동생은 아버지한테 이르지 않겠다고 내게 약속했다 My sister promised not to tell father on me.

이르다³ 〈시기가〉 early; premature ◆이른 봄 early spring
▶아직 때가 이르다 It is yet too early for that.
▶네가 유학을 가기엔 아직 이르다 You are not old enough to go abroad for study.
▶금년엔 벼가 이르다 The rice crop is early this year.
▶우리는 이른 아침에 산책했다 We went out for a walk early in the morning.

이르집다 〈껍질을 뜯어내다〉 pull [strip] off; 〈지어내다〉 fabricate; make up
◆사건을 이르집다 frame up an affair; make up an incident

이른바 what is called; what we [people] call; so-called
◆이른바 지식인[신사] a so-called intellectual [gentleman]
▶그들은 이른바 과격파 학생이다 They are what is called [what we call] radical students. ⇌ They are so-called radical students.
▶그는 이른바 천재다 He is what you might call a genius.
▶때때로 우리는 이른바 친구라는 사람들에게 배신당하기도 한다 We are sometimes betrayed by our so-called best friends.
▶그들은 이른바 보호색으로 자신을 지킨다 They protect themselves by what is called protective coloring.

이를테면 so to say [speak]; such as; (let us) say; for example [instance]
◆채소, 이를테면 당근이나 오이 vegetables, for example, carrots and cucumbers; vegetables, such as [(口) like] carrots and cucumbers
▶어떤 도시, 이를테면 인천이나 부산은 항구로 유명하다 Some cities, such as Inch'ŏn and Pusan are famous for their ports.
▶누구든지, 이를테면 유치원 아이라도 그것은 안다 Anyone, say, a kindergarten kid knows it.

이름 **1** 〈성명〉 a name

[解說] 영・미에서 보통 *name*은 John Stuart Mill처럼 쓴다. 맨 앞의 John은 이름으로 first [Christian, (美) given] name, 가운데의 Stuart는 middle name, 맨끝의 Mill은 성으로 family [last] name, 또는 surname이라고 한다. 또한 앞의 둘은 J.S. Mill처럼 머리글자로 표시하기도 하는데 약자를 쓰지 않은 정식 이름을 full name이라고 한다. 성을 표시할 때는 Mill, J.S.나 Mill, John Stuart처럼 쓰기도 한다. Mr.를 붙일 때는 Mr. John Stuart Mill, Mr. Mill처럼 쓰며 Mr. John이라고는 안쓴다.

◆피터라는 이름의 남자 a man named Peter; a man by the name of Peter / 이름없는 갓난아기 a nameless baby / 이름 모르는 남자 an unidentified man / 이름을 대다 tell [mention, give] *one's* name / …의 이름을 따다 take the name of… / 이름을 밝히다 disclose *one's* name; reveal *one's* identity / 이름을 밝히지 않다 withhold *one's* name; be [remain] anonymous / 이름을 사칭하다 impersonate 《another》; assume *sb's* name / 이름을 속이다 assume a false name; give a wrong name / 저명인사의 이름을 (자랑삼아) 들먹이다 name-drop / 이름을 짓다 give a name; name; christen
▶[會話] 「미안하지만, 이름을 다시 한번 말해주세요」「페인이오, 존 페인」"Sorry, what's your name again?" "It's Paine, John Paine."
▶[會話] 「아기 이름을 뭐라고 지을 겁니까?」「줄리, 만일 여자애라면요」"What are you going to name [call] the baby?" "Julie, if it's a girl."
▶[會話] 「첫아이 이름을 뭐라고 지었습니까?」「아주머니 이름을 따서 케이트라고 지었어요」"What did you name your first child?" "We named her Kate after my aunt."
▶나는 그 사람 이름만 압니다 I know him only by name [by name only]. (▶「얼굴은 알지만 이름은 모른다」는 I know him by face, but not by name.)
▶나는 남의 이름을 잘 잊어버린다 I have a bad [poor] memory for names.
▶그는 「소월」이라는 이름으로 작품을 썼다 He wrote under the name of "Sowol."
2 〈명칭〉 a name; a title; 〈명의〉 a name
▶그는 이름뿐인 매니저다 He is the manager in name only.
▶그 책 이름은 「미래의 충격」이다 The book is titled "Future Shock."
▶저 나무 이름은 뭐라고 합니까? What is that tree called?
▶우리는 학교 이름으로 조의금을 냈다 We gave some condolence money in the name of the school.
3 〈명성〉 (a) reputation; fame
◆이름 있는 famous; noted; celebrated; well-known; renowned; reputed / 이름을 날리다 become famous; make *oneself* famous; gain [earn, obtain, win] distinction / 이름을 후세에 남기다 leave *one's* name behind / 세계적으로 이름을 떨치다 gain a worldwide reputation / 이름을 소중히 하다 respect honor / 이름을 팔다 trade on *one's* name [reputation]; take advantage of *one's* name

▶ 그는 그 작품으로 이름을 날렸다 He established distinction by the work.
▶ 그의 행위는 작가로서의 자기 이름을 더럽혔다 His behavior disgraced his reputation as an author.
▶ 아버지의 이름을 욕되지 않게 해라 Live up to your father's reputation.
▶ 사람은 죽어도 이름은 남는다 A man lives but for one generation; his name for many.
▶ 그 일로 그는 이름을 얻었다 That made him famous.
4 ⇨ 명분, 구실

이름나다 become famous [renowned] (for); make a name for *oneself*; gain [win] fame [renown] (for); win a reputation
♦ 문단에 이름난 사람 a celebrity in the literary world
▶ 진해는 벚꽃의 명승지로 이름났다 Chinhae has become a popular cherryviewing site.
▶ 그는 자선가로 이름났다 He has the name of philanthropist.
▶ 그녀는 피아니스트로서 이름났다 She made her name [became famous] as a pianist.
▶ 그는 영국에서는 이름난 작가다 He is a well-known [famous] writer in England.

이름씨 〔文法〕 a noun ⇨ 명사
이름자 —字 the characters of *one's* name
이름표 —標 a nameplate ⇨ 명찰 ♦ 어린이의 이름표 a child's identification tag
▶ 그는 옷깃에 이름표를 달고 있다 He has a name card on his lapel.

이리¹ 〔動〕 a wolf (*pl.* wolves)
♦ 이리떼 a pack of wolves
▶ 그는 사람의 탈을 쓴 이리다 He is a wolf of a man.

이리² 〈물고기의〉 milt; soft roe ■ —박이 a soft-roed fish

이리³ **1** 〈이러하게〉 in this way [manner]; like this; thus
▶ 왜 이리 서러울까? Why thus sad?
2 〈이곳[이쪽]으로〉 this way [direction]; here; hither
▶ 이리 오십시오 (Come) this way, please. ⇒ 〈멀리 있는 사람에게〉 Over here, please.
▶ 역은 그쪽이 아니고 이리 갑니다. The station is this way, not that way.
▶ 이리 앉아라 Sit here.

이리듐 〔化〕 iridium
이리이리 〈이러고 이러하게〉 thus and thus; (美) thus and so; such and such; so and so
♦ 아무에게 이리이리하라고 이르다 tell *sb* to do thus and thus

이리자리 〔天〕 the Wolf; Lupus
이리저리 **1** 〈이러하고 저러하게〉 like this way and that; thus and thus
♦ 이리저리 생각하다 turn 《it》 over in *one's* mind
▶ 이리저리 생각하다가 한숨도 못잤다 I could not sleep at all, thinking about this and that.
2 〈이쪽 저쪽으로〉 this way and that; from one place to another; here and there
♦ 이리저리 거닐다 wander [walk, roam, ramble] about 《the street》; go [walk] round / 방안을 이리저리 거닐다 pace up and down the room / 이리저리 찾다 search [look for] up and down / 이리저리 둘러보다 look about 《for》 / 이리저리 끌고 다녀 괴롭히다 lead *sb* a pretty dance / 이리저리 들고 다니다 carry *sth* about
▶ 그녀는 늘 이리저리 일자리를 바꾸고 있다 She is always changing from this job to that.

이리하다 〈이와 같이 하다〉 do like this; do in this way [manner]; do in such a manner
♦ 이리하여 thus; after this manner
▶ 이리 해주세요 Please do it like this [this way].
▶ 이리될 줄 예상하고 있었다 I expected that it would turn out this way [like this].
▶ 이리하면 어찌 된다는 것을 알고 있다 I know what is what [which is which].
▶ 이리하여 그는 그녀의 마음을 사로 잡았다 In this way [Thus] he won her heart. ⇒ That's how he won her heart.

이마 the forehead
♦ 주름진 이마 a furrowed forehead [brow]
▶ 그는 이마가 훤하다[좁다] He has a broad [narrow] forehead. ⇒ He is high-browed [low-browed].
▶ 사람은 이마에 땀 흘려 일해서 살아야 한다 Man must live by [in] the sweat of his brow.
▶ 선생님은 이마를 잔뜩 찌푸렸다 The teacher knitted [her] brows.
▶ 그들은 이마를 맞대고 의논했다 They put their heads together. (▶heads 대신에 forehead는 쓰지 않음)

이마적 〈요사이〉 these (few) days; recently; lately; nowadays

이만 〈이것만으로써〉 by this (much); this far; here; only to this extent; 〈명령형〉 Enough !; No more !; Stop!
▶ 오늘은 이만 합시다 That's all for today. ⇒ Let's call it a day. ⇒ Let's leave off here today.
▶ 이만 물러가겠습니다 I must say good-bye now.

이만저만 〈이만하고 저만하게〉 to this extent [point] or that; this much or that; so-so; tolerably
♦ 이만저만 아닌 not just so-so; extraordinary; great; prodigious 《amount》 / 이만저만 아니게 애쓰다 take much pains; make great efforts
▶ 나는 이만저만 놀라지 않았다 I was not a little surprised.
—이만저만하다 〈어지간하다〉 (be) this much or that; tolerable; ordinary
▶ 차를 굴린다는 것은 이만저만한 일이 아니다 It is no easy thing [task] to have a car.
▶ 그녀는 이만저만한 미인이 아니다 She is a girl of unsurpassed beauty.
▶ 그 일을 끝내기가 이만저만한 일이 아니었다 It was a hard strain to finish the work.

이만큼 〈분량〉 about this [so] much; 〈수〉 about so many; 〈크기〉 about so large; 〈길이〉 about so long; 〈폭〉 about this width; 〈정도〉 to this degree [extent]
♦ 이만큼 큰 about as large as this
▶ 이만큼 재미있는 이야기를 들은 적이 없다 I have never heard such an interesting story as

this.
▶작년에도 이만큼 여기에 모였다 About this many people gathered here last year.
▶아이라도 이만큼은 알고 있다 Even a child knows this much.
▶돈이 이만큼 있으면 당분간은 족할 것이다 This much money will do for the time being.

이만하다 〈서술적〉 be (about) this much [size]; be as much [many, large, long, wide] as this
▶그의 키는 이만합니다 He's about as tall as this. ⇒ (口) He's this tall.
▶이만하면 충분할 거야 This will [would] be enough.
▶이만한 폭풍에 놀라지마라 Don't be startled by a small storm like this [such a small storm as this].

이맘 〈이슬람교의 지도자〉 an imam

이맘때 about [around] this time; at this time of (the) day [night, year]
♦작년[내년] 이맘때 at this time last [next] year / 내일[어젯밤] 이맘때 about this time tomorrow [last night]
▶어제 이맘때는 소나기가 억수같이 쏟아졌다 We had a heavy shower about this time yesterday.
▶이맘때 진달래가 피다니 참 이상하다 It is strange that azaleas come out at this time of the year.
▶나는 다음 달 이맘때는 파리에 가 있을 거다 I'll have gone to Paris by this time next month.
▶작년 이맘때는 중국에 있었다 I was in China about this time last year.

이맛살 〈이마의 주름살〉 wrinkles in [on] the forehead ♦이맛살을 찌푸리다 wrinkle (up) one's forehead; knit one's brows; frown; produce wrinkles in the forehead

이맞다 〈이가 들어맞다〉 fit together; meet closely; 〈이빨이〉 occlude; 〈톱니가〉 gear (into, with); be in gear 《with》; mesh 《with》; engage 《with each other》

이며 and; or; and/or
♦낮이며 밤이며 night and day; day and night
▶그는 학자이며 시인이기도 하다 He is both a scholar and (a) poet.
▶책이며 연필이며 하는 것들을 샀다 I bought books, pencils and the like.

이면 二面 1〈두개의 면〉 two faces [sides] 2〈신문의 둘째 면〉 the second page
♦이면 기사 items on the second page
■—작전 double-sided operations

이면 裏面·裡面 1〈물건의 안쪽〉 the back; the reverse (side); the inside
♦표지의 이면 the inside of the cover / 동전의 이면 the reverse (side) of a coin
▶이면을 보시오 (표시) See overleaf [the back page].
▶이면에 계속 Please turn over. (略 P.T.O.) ⇒ Continued overleaf.
2〈겉으로 드러나지 않는 부분〉 the background; the inside; the reverse; the other side
♦인생[사회]의 이면 the dark [seamy] side of life [society] / 이면에 숨은 진상 the truth behind the facts / 이면에서 조종하다 pull the wires [strings] / 이면에서 활약하다 play in the background
▶누군가 이면에서 움직이고 있다 Someone is operating behind the scenes [in the background, in secret].
▶틀림없이 이면에 무엇인가 있다 I am sure something lies behind it. ⇒ Something is going on behind the scenes.
■—공작 behind-the-scene [backstage] maneuvering [maneuvers]; undercover work; wirepulling —사(史) an inside history

이면 if; in case that; provided [supposing] (that)
▶만일 내일 비가 오는날이면 안 가겠다 If [(美) In case] it rains tomorrow, I'll stay at home.
▶내가 당신이면 그런 일은 안해요 I would not do a thing like that if I were you.
▶이만한 양식이면 열흘은 가겠다 This much food will last ten days.

이명 耳鳴 a singing [ringing] in the ears
▶나는 이명이 있다 I have a ringing in my ears. ⇒ My ears are ringing.
■—증(醫) tinnitus

이명 異名 〈별명〉 another name; an alias; a nickname ▶그는 오랫동안 존 스미스라는 이명으로 통했다 He went by the alias of John Smith for many years.

이모 姨母 a maternal aunt; an aunt; one's mother's sister

이모부 姨母夫 an uncle; the husband of a maternal aunt

이모작 二毛作 double-cropping; two crops a year —**이모작하다** raise two crops a year; double-crop —**지대** a two-crop area

이모저모 every facet [side, aspect] 《of a matter》; this angle and that
♦이모저모로 바라보다 look at (it) from another angle [various angles] / 이모저모로 논하다 discuss (it) in all its aspects / 이모저모로 생각하다 view 《a matter》 from every angle

이목 耳目 〈귀와 눈〉 the eye and ear; 〈주목〉 one's attention [notice]
♦세상의 이목을 끌다 attract [arrest] public attention; catch the public eye / 세인의 이목을 놀라게 하다 startle the world; surprise the ears and eyes of the world; create a sensation / 세인의 이목을 피하다 avoid public notice
▶그의 대담한 모험은 세간의 이목을 끌었다 His bold adventure attracted public attention.

이목구비 耳目口鼻 〈얼굴 각부의 배열〉 (a set of) features; 〈용모〉 looks
▶그는 이목구비가 반듯하다 He has regular [fine] features.
▶그는 이목구비가 잘 생겼다 He is good-looking [handsome].
▶그녀는 이목구비가 그다지 잘 생긴 편은 아니다 She is rather plain [plain-looking, (美) homely]. ⇒ She has plain features.

이무기 [動] an anaconda; a boa (constrictor)

이문 利文 a profit margin; profit(s); gains; returns
♦이문을 많이[적게] 보다 make a big [small] (margin of) profit; yield much [little] profit
▶그는 적은 이문으로 만족하고 있다 He is satisfied with a small margin of profit [profit margin].
▶그들은 이문을 반분했다 They divided the profits [gains] equally among them.
▶상당한 이문이 있다 There is a fair margin of profit.

이문 異聞 a strange report [rumor]; curious information [news]

이물 〈배의 머리〉 the bow; the prow; the stem
♦이물에 fore / 이물에서 고물까지 from stem to stern / 해안으로 이물을 돌리다 head for the shore

이물 異物 an alien [a foreign] substance [matter]

-이므로 as; because; since ⇨ -므로

이미 1 〈벌써〉 already; yet (▶yet은 의문문에 씀); (not) any longer
♦이미 아시는 바와 같이 as you are already aware
▶내가 오늘 아침 일어났을 때 그는 이미 떠나고 없었다 He had already left when I got up this morning.
▶때는 이미 늦었다 It is too late.
▶그 다음 주에 가 보았더니 그는 이미 그곳에 살고 있지 않았다 The next week I found him no longer living there.
2 〈앞서〉 previously; before
♦이미 말한 바와 같이 as previously stated; as stated [mentioned] above
▶나는 이미 그곳에 간적이 있다 I have been there before [already].

이미지 an image
▶그의 이미지는 좋다 He has a good [positive] image.
▶그의 이미지는 좋지 않다 He has a bad [negative] image.
▶그녀는 자신의 이미지를 바꾸려고 한다 She is trying to change her image.
▶그의 성공은 회사의 이미지 향상에 큰 도움이 되었다 His success brought a higher reputation [better image] to his company. ⇌ His success went far toward improving his company's image.

이미테이션 (an) imitation
▶그녀의 진주 반지는 이미테이션이다 Her ring is an imitation [artificial] pearl.

이민 移民 〈외국으로의〉 emigration; 〈외국으로부터의〉 immigration; 〈입국자〉 an immigrant; 〈출국자〉 an emigrant
▶오스트레일리아는 유럽계 이민으로 정착되었다 Australia was settled by European immigrants.
—**이민하다** 〈출국하다〉 emigrate 《from, into, to》; 〈입국하다〉 immigrate 《from, into, to》
▶그는 가족을 데리고 브라질로 이민할까 생각중이다 He is thinking of emigrating to Brazil with his family.
■—국 immigration office —법 [法] an immigration law —알선자[회사] an emigration [emigrant] agent [company] —제한법 the Immigration Restriction Law

이바지하다 1 〈공헌하다〉 contribute to [toward] 《one's country》; make a contribution to 《the community》; render services to; conduce to 《sb's success》; help (toward)
♦사회복지에 이바지하다 contribute one's share to social welfare
▶그는 세계 평화에 크게 이바지했다 He contributed greatly to world peace. ⇌ He made a great contribution to world peace.
▶그녀는 한국 의학계에 크게 이바지했다 She rendered great services in the medical science world of Korea.
▶그는 양국의 유대에 크게 이바지했다 He contributed much towards establishing [made a great contribution to establish] ties between the two countries.
2 〈공급하다〉 provide; furnish; supply

이박자 二拍子 [樂] two-part time; duple time [measure]

이반 離反 〈인심이 떠나 배반함〉 (an) estrangement; alienation; desertion; defection 《from sb》; 〈탈퇴〉 (a) secession
—**이반하다** be estranged [alienated] 《from》; 〈탈퇴하다〉 secede 《from》; break away 《from》
♦민심이 이반하다 lose public support
▶민심은 이미 현정부에서 이반되어 있다 The public is already alienated from the present government.

이발 理髮 a haircut; hairdressing
♦이발을 해야겠다 I must have a haircut.
—**이발하다** have one's hair cut
▶나는 이발하러 갔다 I went to have hair cut. ⇌ I got [had] a haircut.
■—기 〈바리캉〉 hair-clippers; hairdressing implements —사 a barber; a hairdresser —소 a barbershop; (英) a barber's (shop) —업 barbering; hairdressing —요금 the charge for a haircut

이밥 〈쌀밥〉 plain boiled rice

이방인 異邦人 〈시민권이 없는 사람〉 an alien; 〈외국인〉 a foreigner; 〈낯선 사람〉 a stranger; 〈방관자〉 an outsider

이배 二倍 double; twice
▶이것은 저것의 2배 크기가 된다 This is twice as large as that.
▶땅값은 5년전의 2배가 되었다 The price of land is double what it was five years ago. ⇌ Land price has doubled in five years.
▶18은 9의 2배다 Eighteen is the double of nine.

이번 —番 1 〈이 차례〉 this time; 〈지금〉 now
♦이번만[뿐] just this time; for (this) once; once (and) for all / 이번 시험 the last [recent] examination
▶이번에는 같이 가 주지만 다시는 안돼 I'll go with you this time but never again.
▶이번에는 네가 이야기할 차례다 Now it is your turn to speak.
▶이번만은 내 좋은대로 하게 해줘요 Just for once [Just this once] let me do as I like.
2 〈다음 번〉 next time; some other time; another time

이번 시험 the coming [next, forthcoming] examination / **이번 일요일** next Sunday
▶ 이번에 올 때 그것을 가지고 오세요 Bring it to me (the) next time you come.
▶ 그녀는 이번에 미국에 가게 되었다더군 She is going to the United States shortly, I hear.

이번 二番 No. 2; number two; the second
▶ 어제 그는 2번 타자였다 He batted second in yesterday's line-up.
■ —타자 the second batter

이법 理法 a law ♦ **자연의 이법** the law [order] of nature; natural laws

이베리아 〈유럽의 반도〉 the Iberian Peninsula; Iberia

이변 異變 〈예상치 않은 사건〉 an accident; 〈불행한 사건〉 a mishap; an untoward [extraordinary] event; 〈재난〉 a disaster; a calamity; 〈이상한 사건〉 something unusual
♦ **기후의 이변** unusual [unseasonable] weather / **태양의 이변** an extraordinary phenomenon in the sun
▶ 그의 신변에 무슨 이변이 일어난 것 같다 I am afraid [I fear] something wrong has happened to him.

이별 離別 parting; separation; farewell; 〈이혼〉 divorce
♦ **이별의 눈물** tears at parting / **이별의 슬픔** the wrench [sorrow] of parting / **이별을 아쉬워하다** be [feel] loath to part; express regret at parting / **이별을 슬퍼하다** feel sorrow at parting; lament a separation / **이별의 눈물을 흘리다** shed parting tears
▶ 그는 그것이 그들의 마지막 이별일 줄은 꿈에도 몰랐다 Little did he know that it was to be their parting for life.
—**이별하다** part from *sb*; separate [be separated] from *sb*; 〈이혼하다〉 divorce *sb*
▶ 나는 2년 전에 아내와 이별했다 I divorced my wife two years ago.
■ —가[주] a farewell song [drink]

이병 罹病 〈병에 걸림〉 contraction《of a disease》; 〈감염〉 infection
—**이병하다** contract [catch] a disease; suffer from illness; 〈감염하다〉 be infected 《with》
■ —률 the attack rate; the (rate of) incidence《of influenza》 —자 a sufferer 《from cholera》; a case《of typhoid fever》; a victim : 에이즈의 **이병자** a sufferer from AIDS / **폐암의 이병자를 줄이다** decrease the incidence of lung cancer

이보다 《more, less, better, worse》than this
♦ **이보다 앞서** before this; previously
▶ 이보다 더한 기쁨이 없다 Nothing will please me more than this.
▶ 이보다 더 재미있는 소설을 읽은 적이 없다 I never read a more interesting novel than this.

이복 異腹 having a different mother
■ —형제[자매] a brother [sister] by a different mother; half brothers [sisters]

이본 異本 〈내용·글자가 다소 다른 책〉 a variant text; an alternative version; 〈진본〉 a rare book

이봐 〈부르는 말〉 Look here!; Hullo!; Hello!; Hey!; 《英》 I say; 《美》 Say; Listen!; 〈설득·도전 등을 나타내어〉 Come on!
▶ 이봐, 자네 Hey, you.
▶ 이봐, 창문 좀 열어 Say, open the window.
▶ 이봐, 그만 둬 Come on, stop it.
▶ 이봐, 왜 말한대로 못하는 거야 Look! Why can't you ever do as you're told?

이부 二部 〈두 부분〉 two parts; 〈제 2 부분〉 the second; part II; 〈학교의 야간부〉 night school; 〈책의〉 two copies [volumes]
▶ 이 연극은 2부로 나누어져 있다 This play is divided into two acts.
▶ 「햄릿」을 2부 샀다 I bought two copies of "Hamlet".
■ —수업 instruction in two shifts; the double-shift school system —작 work made up of two parts —합주[합창] ⇨ 이중(~창[주])

이부 異父 a different father ■ —형제 uterine [half] brothers; brothers by a different father

이부자리 〈침구〉 bedding; bedclothes; mattress and quilt
♦ **이부자리를 깔다[펴다]** make a bed; lay out the bedding / **이부자리를 개다** fold up the bedding

이부제 二部制 a two-shift (school) system
■ —학교 a school operated on the two-shift system

이북 以北 1 north《of》 ♦ **서울 이북** north of Seoul; at Seoul and northward / **38선 이북** north of the 38th parallel
2 〈북한〉 North Korea ▶ 그는 이북 사람이다 He comes from North Korea.

이분 二分 division into two parts
♦ **2분의 1** one [a] half / **2분의 2박자 (이)** 〔樂〕 alla breve / **2분의 1의 half**
—**이분하다** divide *sth* in two [into two parts]; halve
▶ 선생님은 학생을 A그룹과 B그룹으로 이분했다 The teacher divided the students into two groups, A and B.
■ —음표 〔樂〕 a half note; a minim —점[경선]《經線》〔天〕 the equinoctial point [colure]

이분자 異分子 〈이색 분자〉 a foreign [an alien] element; 〈외부에서 들어온 사람〉 an outsider

이불 〈침구 전체〉 bedding; bedclothes; 〈요〉 mattress; 〈솜이나 깃털 이불〉 a quilt; 《美》 a comforter [comfortable]
♦ **이불을 개다** fold up the bedding / **이불을 덮다** put on a quilt / **이불에 솜을 넣다** stuff a quilt with wadding
▶ 소년은 이불을 뒤집어쓰고 자고 있었다 The boy was sleeping with his bedclothes over his head.
■ —누비— a quilt ■ —속 fillings —잇 a quilt cover

이브 〔聖〕 Eve (▶「하와」의 영어명); 〈전야〉 an eve
♦ **크리스마스 이브에** on Christmas Eve

이브닝드레스 〈여성용 야회복〉 an evening dress [gown]

이비 耳鼻 the nose and ears
■ —과 otorhinology

이비인후 耳鼻咽喉 the nose, ear, and throat
■ —과(科) otorhinolaryngology —과전문의 a nose, ear, and throat specialist; an

이사 otorhinolaryngologist

이사 二死 〔野〕 two outs; two players out ▶이사만루 Two down, bases filled [loaded].

이사 理事 a director; 〈대학 등의〉 a trustee ◆이사가 되다 obtain a seat on [become a member of] the board of directors
■대표— a representative director 상무[상임]— a managing director 전무— an executive director —관 a grade-Ⅱ-A official —국 〈UN의〉 a member of the council of the United Nations —장 the director general; the chief director; the chairman of a board of directors [trustees] —회 〈기구〉 a board of directors [trustees]; a directorate; a council; 〈회의〉 a directors' meeting

이사 移徙 a move; house-moving; a removal ◆이사 가다[오다] move out [in] ▶이곳에 이사 온 지 벌써 10년이 되었다 It is now ten years since I moved here.
—**이사하다** (美) move (to, into); move house; change *one's* abode [residence] (to) ◆새집으로 이사하다 move into a new house ▶그 집은 부산으로 이사했다 The family moved to Pusan. ▶언제 이사합니까? When are you moving out [in]? ▶나는 그가 새 집으로 이사하는 것을 거들었다 I helped him move to [into] his new house.
■—비용 moving expenses; removal expenses 이삿짐 *one's* furniture [property] to be moved 이삿짐운반업자 (美) a mover; (英) a remover 이삿짐운반차 a removal van

이사야 〔聖〕(The Book of) Isaiah

이삭 〈곡물의〉 an ear; a head; a spike; 〈땅에 떨어진〉 gleanings ◆벼 이삭 an ear of rice / 이삭 줍는 사람 a gleaner / 이삭이 패다 come into ears; ear (up) / 이삭이 완전히 패어 있다 be in full ear / 이삭을 줍다 gather ears of grain after the reapers; glean (a field) ▶벼가 이삭이 되었다 The rice plants are in (the) ear. ▶보리 이삭이 다 팼다 The ears of barley are all out.
■—줍기 gleaning

이산 離散 separation; dispersion; scattering ▶그 일가는 이산의 쓰라림을 겪었다 The family met such hardship as to be broken up.
—**이산하다** scatter; disperse; be dispersed [scattered]
■—가족 dispersed [separated] families: 나는 이산 가족의 감동적인 재회를 텔레비전으로 지켜 보았다 I watched on television the emotional reunion of separated families. —가족 찾기 운동 a campaign for reunion of dispersed family members

이산화 二酸化 〔化〕 ■—규소 silicon dioxide —망간 manganese dioxide —물(物) a dioxide —탄소 carbon dioxide

이삼일 二三日 two or three days; a few [a couple of] days ▶이삼일만 기다려 주십시오 Please wait for a few days.

이상 以上 **1**〈수량〉not less than; or more; and over;〈그 수를 포함하지 않는〉over; above; more than ◆두 시간 이상 two hours or more; more than two hours / 60이상 60 and over; above sixty / 60이상 100까지 60 through 100; (from) 60 up to 100 ▶70점 이상 받은 지원자들만 합격했다 Only those applicants who got 70 or more passed the examination. ▶나는 한 시간에 4킬로미터 이상 걸을 수 있다 I can walk more than 4 kilometers in an hour. ▶그 제안은 3분의 2 이상의 다수로 채택되었다 The proposal was adopted by a majority of two-thirds. ▶그는 한 시간에 반 이상의 일을 했다 He did a good part of the work in an hour. **2**〈정도〉beyond; past; above; more than; further ◆기대[상상] 이상이다 be beyond *one's* expectation(s) [imagination] ▶그는 수입 이상의 생활을 한다 He lives beyond his means. ▶그 이상은 모른다 I know nothing beyond that. ▶그 이상은 할 말이 없소 I have nothing more [further] to say. ▶그의 작품은 우리의 기대 이상으로 잘 팔렸다 His works sold better than we had expected. **3**〈상기〉◆이상에 말한 the above(-mentioned); above-stated; the aforementioned; the aforesaid / 이상 말한 바와 같이 as mentioned [stated] above / 이상과 같은 이유로 for the reasons I have mentioned ▶제 이야기는 이상입니다 That's all that I have to say for now. ▶이상은 우리 신기획의 개요입니다 The above is the outline of our new project. ▶이상은 몇가지 예에 불과하다 The foregoings are only a few of the examples. **4**〈…한[하는] 바에는〉now that; since; once; seeing that;〈…하는 한〉so long as ◆살아 있는 이상 일을 해야 한다 So long as we live, we must work. ▶일이 이렇게 된 이상 나는 이 문제에서 손을 뗀다 Now things have come to this I wash my hands of the matter [I'll have no more to do with it]. ▶시작한 이상 끝을 내라 Now that [Once] you've started it, finish it. **5**〈끝〉the end;〔通信〕over [out];〈완결〉concluded ▶이상입니다 That is all.

이상 異狀 〈고장〉something wrong; an accident;〈변화〉(a) change;〈정신의〉derangement; disorder; abnormality;〈신체의〉(an) indisposition ◆이상이 있다〈맥박 등이〉be abnormal;〈기계 등이〉be out of order; something is wrong (with) / 정신에 이상이 있다 be mentally disturbed; be deranged / 이상이 없다 be all right; be normal; be in good order ▶엔진에 이상이 있다 Something is wrong with the engine. ⇌ The engine is out of order. ▶방에 이상은 없습니까 Is there [Do you find] any change in your room?

▶ 아무 이상 없습니다 Everything is all right.
▶ 그녀는 몸의 이상을 호소했다 She complained of indisposition.
▶ 여행 중에는 아무 이상도 없었다 We had no accident while traveling.
▶ 금고에는 이상이 없었다 The safe remained intact [untouched].
▶ 전원 이상 없음〈점호에서〉 All present and correct [accounted for].

이상 異常 strangeness; extraordinariness; uncommonness; abnormality
—**이상하다[스럽다]** 〈보통과 다르다〉 unusual; extraordinary; abnormal; singular; 〈기이하다〉 strange; odd; curious; 〈불가사의하다〉 mysterious; unaccountable
♦이상하게 unusually; abnormally; strangely; queerly / 이상하게 들리다 sound strange [queer] / …은 이상할 것이 없다 It's no wonder that... / 이상하게 보이다 look queer [strange] / 이상하게 여기다 wonder 《at》; think [feel] 《it》 strange; feel queer
▶ 그에게서 아무 소리가 없다니 이상하다 It is strange that he should remain silent.
▶ 이상하다, 내 책이 어디 갔지 That's odd, where has my book gone?
▶ 너 오늘 참 이상하구나 You are not quite yourself [usual self] today.
▶ 참 이상한 일도 다 있다 What a strange thing (this is)!
▶ 너 이상한 소리를 하는구나 What you say sounds funny [strange] (to me).
▶ 그에게는 조금도 이상한 데가 없다 There is nothing abnormal [out of the way] about him.
▶ 그의 눈이 이상하게 빛났다 A strange light shone in his eyes.
▶ 그것이 내게는 이상하게 생각되었다 It struck me as singular.
■—**건조** abnormal dryness —**건조주의보** a dry-weather alert —**기상** abnormal weather —**난동**(暖冬) an unusually warm winter —**반응** an allergy —**성격** abnormal character —**심리** abnormal mentality —**아(兒)** an abnormal child —**체질**〔醫〕 (a) diathesis

이상 理想 an ideal
♦이상을 실현하다 attain [realize] one's ideal / 이상을 쫓다 follow [pursue] an ideal / 이상에 맞다 meet [conform to] one's ideal
▶ 그는 이상의 여인과 결혼했다 He married the woman of his dreams.
▶ 그녀는 이상이 높다 She has lofty ideals. ≒ She aims high.
▶ 인간은 모름지기 이상을 품어야 한다 We should aspire after something noble.
■—**주의** idealism —**주의자** an idealist —**향** an ideal land; a Utopia —**형** an ideal type

이상론 理想論 ▶ 당신의 말은 이상론입니다 What you say is idealistic.

이상야릇하다 異常— queer; strange; odd; funny
▶ 나는 기분이 이상야릇하다 I feel queer.
▶ 나는 그 그림을 보고 이상야릇한 감동을 느꼈다 I experienced a singular sensation on seeing the picture.

이상적 理想的 ideal ♦이상적으로 ideally
▶ 이 땅은 우리 연구소를 세우는 데 이상적이다 This is an ideal site for building our laboratory.
▶ 화창하고 따뜻한 날씨는 소풍가기에 이상적이다 A fine warm day is ideal for a picnic.

이상화 理想化 idealization
—**이상화하다** idealize; sublimate
▶ 그녀는 어렸을 적에 돌아가신 아버지를 이상화했다 She idealized her father who had died when she was a child.

이색 二色 ♦이색(성)의 dichroic; dichromatic
■—**인쇄** two-color printing

이색 異色 〈다른 색〉 a different color; 〈색다름〉 novelty
♦이색적인 out of the ordinary; unique; novel
▶ 그는 이색적인 신인 선수다 He is a unique rookie.
▶ —**작품** a unique [novel, rare] work

이서 以西 west (of) ♦수원 이서에[의] (to the) west of Suwon; Suwon and westward
▶ 서울 이서는 따뜻한 날씨가 되겠다 Warm weather will prevail west of Seoul.

이서 裏書 (an) endorsement ⇨ 배서(背書)

이설 異說 a divergent view [opinion, theory]; a divergent opinion; conflicting views [opinions] ♦이설을 내세우다 evolve another theory; dissent from sb's view

이성 異性 〈다른 성〉 the other [opposite] sex; 〈다른 성질〉 different nature; 〔化〕 isomerism
♦이성관계 relations with opposite sex / 이성간의 intersexual / 이성을 알다 know a woman [man]
▶ 그는 이성교제가 넓다 He has a large acquaintance of the opposite sex.
▶ 그는 스무살에 이성을 처음 알았다 He was sexually initiated [had his first sexual experience] at the age of twenty.
■—**애** heterosexuality; sexual love —**체**(體)〔化〕 an isomer

이성 異姓 a different surname [family name]

이성 理性 reason; reasoning power
♦이성이 없는 reasonless; irrational / 이성적인 reasonable; rational / 이성과 경험에 비추어 in the light of reason and experience / 이성에 호소하다 appeal to [listen to] reason
▶ 인간은 이성적인 동물이다 Man is a rational being.
▶ 그녀는 정신적 충격으로 이성을 잃었다 She lost her ability to reason because of a shock.
▶ 그는 이성에 따라 행동했다 He acted with [according to] reason.
■—**순수[실천]—**〔心〕 pure [practical] reason
■—**론**〔哲〕 rationalism

이세 二世 1 〈현세와 내세〉 this and the next world; the present and the future existence
2 〈다음 세대〉 a second [next] generation; 〈제2대〉 the second; Junior; Jr.
♦2세 국민 the children of the next [coming] generation / 헨리 2세 Henry II / 존 D. 록펠러 2세 John D. Rockefeller, Junior
3 〈이민자의 자녀〉 ♦재미 한국인 2세 an American-born Korean; a second-generation Korean-American

이솝이야기 *Aesop's Fables*

이송 移送 transfer; removal ♦사건의 이송〔法〕removal [transfer] of a case
—이송하다 transport; transfer to; remove
♦용의자를 구치소로 이송하다 take a suspect to the prison
▶사건은 고등 법원으로 이송되었다 The case was sent [transferred] to an appellate court.

이수 利水 irrigation; water-utilization
—이수하다 utilize water 《for irrigation》
—공사 irrigation works

이수 里數 〈거리〉 mileage; 〈마을의 수〉 the number of villages

이수 履修 completion —이수하다 complete [finish] 《a college course》
♦전[정규] 과목을 이수하다 finish [complete] all the subject [the regular course]

이수하다 離水— 〈수상 비행기가〉 take [hop] off from the water; leave the water

이스라엘 Israel; 〈공식명〉 the State of Israel
♦이스라엘의 〈현대의〉 Israeli; 〈고대의〉 Israelite ■—사람 〈현대의〉 an Israeli; 〈고대의〉 an Israelite

이스탄불 〈터키의 도시〉 Istanbul
이스트 〈효모〉 yeast
이스트서시스 〈영국의 주〉 East Sussex
이슥하다 far advanced
♦이슥한 밤에 late at night; deep in the night / 밤이 이슥하도록 (till) late at night
▶밤이 이슥해졌다 The night was getting on [well advanced].

이슬 dew; 〈방울〉 a dewdrop
♦이슬같은 목숨 a life as evanescent as the dew / 이슬이 맺힌 dewy 《flowers》; bedewed / 이슬에 젖다 be wet [moist, damp] with dew / 전장의 이슬로 사라지다 fall [die] in battle
▶이슬이 내린다 It dews. ⇒ The dew [Dew] falls.
▶그녀의 눈에 이슬이 맺혀 있었다 Her eyes were bedewed with tears.
■밤[아침]— nightly [morning] dew

이슬라마바드 〈파키스탄의 수도〉 Islamabad
이슬람 Islam ♦이슬람 세계 the Islamic world / 이슬람의 Islamic ■—교 Islam —교국 Islam —교도 an Islamite; a Muslim —원리주의 Islamic fundamentalism

이슬받이 〈이슬 내릴 무렵〉 dewfall; 〈길〉 a footpath across dewy grassland; a dew-laden path; 〈도롱이〉 a dew-kilt; 〈사람〉 a dew-clearer

이슬비 a drizzle; a mizzle; a misty [fog] rain
▶이슬비가 오락가락했다 It drizzled on and off. ♦이슬비가 내리고 있다 It's drizzling.

이슬점 —點 〔物〕 the dew point
이승 〔佛敎〕 this life [world]; this existence
♦이승의 worldly; earthly; mundane / 이승에서 in this world / 이승을 떠나다 die; pass away / 이승에서의 이별을 고하다 bid *sb* a last farewell
▶이젠 미련[여한] 없이 이승을 떠날 수 있다 Now I can die happy [with no regrets].
▶그녀는 그것이 그와 이승에서의 마지막 작별이 되리라고는 생각하지 못했다 She didn't know it was to be the last time she would ever see him in this life.

이시 〈유럽 공동체〉 EC [〈*E*uropean *C*ommunity〕
이식 二食 《take》two meals a day
이식 利息 interest ⇨ 이자
■—계정 the interest account —법 the rule of interest —산 ⇨ 이자(~산) —조견표 a ready reckoner (of interest)
이식 利殖 〈재물을 불림〉 moneymaking
■—법 the secret of moneymaking
이식 移植 transplanting; transplantation; 〈다른 나라 동식물의〉 implantation; 〔醫〕〈피부·각막·뼈 등의〉 grafting; 〈장기 등의〉 a transplant
♦근육 이식법[수술] flesh (and muscle) transplantation [operation] / 심장 이식(수술) a heart transplant (operation) / 〈피부·장기 등의〉 피이식자 the (graft) recipient; the host / 신장 이식을 받다 receive a kidney transplant
—이식하다 〈식물을〉 transplant; replant; 〈외국산 식물을〉 implant; 〈피부·뼈 등을〉 graft; transplant ♦다른 화분에 이식하다 plant in another pot; repot

이신론 理神論 〔哲〕 deism ♦이신론의 deistic(-al) ■—자 a deist
이실직고하다 以實直告— report [tell] the truth; speak out honestly; state facts as they are
이심 二心 duplicity; 〈배반하는 마음〉 treachery ♦이심이 있는 사람 a double-dealer / 이심을 품은 double-hearted; double-faced; treacherous / 이심을 품다 have two faces
이심 二審 〔法〕〈제이심〉 the second instance
▶그는 2심에서 유죄판결을 받았다 He was found guilty at the second trial.
이심 異心 a treasonous intention [design]; treachery ♦이심을 품다 harbor treacherous intentions
이심 離心 ■—각〔數〕 an eccentric angle —궤도〔天〕 an eccentric orbit —률〔數〕 eccentricity
이심전심 以心傳心 telepathy; tacit understanding; immediate communication 《of truth》 from one mind to another; communion of mind with mind [heart with heart]
♦이심전심으로 by telepathy; telepathically; tacitly
▶우리는 이심전심으로 통하는 사이다 We are in tune with each other. ⇒ There is a sort of telepathy working between us. ⇒ We can understand each other without (the use of) language.
이십 二十 twenty; a score; 〈로마 숫자〉 XX
♦20번째 the twentieth / 20대의 여자[청년] a woman [a young man] in her [his] twenties / 20분의 1 a [one] twentieth / 20분의 5 five twentieths
▶나는 아직 20대 초반밖에 안됐습니다 I am still in my very early twenties.
■—세기 the twentieth century
이십사시간 二十四時間 twenty-four [24] hours
♦24시간 내내 《work》(a)round the clock; all day and night
▶나는 24시간 내내 바빴다 I was kept busy

around the clock [all day long].
■ —제 the 24-hour system; the around-the-clock system —조업[노동] a round-the-clock operation

이쑤시개 a toothpick

이아치다 1 〈손해를 끼치다〉 cause damage; lead to loss; spoil; ruin
2 〈방해가 되다〉 stand in *one's* way; 〈방해하다〉 obstruct; hinder

이악하다 mercenary; keen [greedy] for gain; wide-awake to *one's* own interest

이안 二眼 ■ —리플렉스 카메라 a twin-lens reflex camera

이알 a grain of (boiled) rice

이알이 곤두서다 〈속담〉 Don't be so cocky.

이앓이 (a) toothache ♦이앓이를 하다 have a toothache; suffer from a toothache

이앙 移秧 transplantation of rice seedlings; rice transplantation
—이앙하다 transplant rice (seedlings)
■ —기 the rice-planting machine

이야 〈강조〉 the very; just; indeed; 〈제한〉 only
♦ 말이야 바른 말이지 to be plain [frank, honest] (with you); plainly speaking
▶그 옷이야 내가 어디 입을 수 있니? How on earth could I wear that dress?
▶그는 뒷일이야 어찌되든 나 몰라라 하는 식이다 He does everything without any regard for the consequences.
▶풍경이야 한국이 제일이지 As for scenery, there is no country like Korea.

이야기 1 〈대화〉 a talk; (a) conversation; 〈한담〉 a chat; a gossip; 〈말〉 a remark; a statement; 〈화제〉 a topic
♦ 근거없는 이야기 a groundless talk / 뒷 이야기 an inside story / 쓸데없는 이야기 an idle talk / 사업 이야기 a business talk / 이야기 상대 a companion (to talk with) / 이야기를 잘 하는[못하는] 사람 a good [poor] talker / 다른 이야기지만 by the bye [way]; to change the subject / 우리 끼리 이야기지만 between ourselves [you and me] / 이야기가 이상하게 들릴지 모르지만 It may sound strange, but… / 이야기가 통하다 find each other's company enjoyable / 이야기 꽃을 피우다 engage in animated conversation / 이야기를 꺼내다 draw out conversation / 이야기를 계속하다 keep up the conversation / 이야기를 그치다 stop talking / 하던 이야기를 도중에서 그치다 break the threads of a talk [story] / 이야기를 독점하다 do all the talking; monopolize conversation / 이야기를 딴데로 돌리다 turn the conversation to other matters / 이야기로 밤을 새우다 talk all [through] the night; talk away the night 《with *sb*》 / 이야기에 열중하다 forget *oneself* in *one's* chat / 낚시 이야기를 하다 talk about fishing / 정치 이야기를 하다 talk politics / 자기 직업[전문] 이야기를 하다 talk shop
▶네게 할 이야기가 좀 있다 I have something to tell you.
▶이야기는 밤에 어느 항구 근처에서 시작된다 The story begins near a harbor at night.
▶차 한 잔 하면서 이야기나 나눕시다 Let's have a chat over a cup of tea.
▶그들은 전화로 30분이나 이야기를 계속 했다 They kept on talking for half an hour on the phone.
—이야기하다 talk; speak; chat 《over》; have a talk [chat] 《with》; 〈일러주다〉 tell; 〈진술하다〉 state; mention
♦ 아무를 붙들고 긴 이야기하다 buttonhole *sb* / 사실을 이야기하다 speak [tell] the truth / 영어로 이야기하다 speak in English
▶어머니는 자식에게 민족의 역사를 이야기해 주었다 The mother told her child about the history of their people.
▶나는 그에게 그 일을 대충 이야기해 주었다 I outlined [sketched] the matter to him.
▶이 건축은 고대인의 우수한 기술을 뚜렷이 이야기해 주고 있다 The architecture shows clearly that the people in ancient times had marvelous technique.
▶이것은 아무에게도 이야기하면 안된다 This is strictly between you and me.
▶이야기하자면 길다 It's a long story.
▶그는 이야기할 친구도 없이 혼자 살고 있다 He lives alone with no friend to talk to.
2 〈사실담〉 an account; a description; 〈설화〉 a tale; a story; a narrative; 〈전설〉 a legend; a romance; 〈우화〉 a fable; 〈삽화〉 an episode
♦ 신상 이야기 an account of *one's* life / 연애 이야기 a romance / 고생한 이야기 an account of *one's* sufferings / 꾸며낸 이야기 a story; a made-up story; a fiction / 허황한 이야기 a tale of a roasted horse / 이야기를 지어내다 fabricate [forge, invent] a story
▶아이들은 이야기 듣기를 좋아한다 Children love to listen to a story.
▶그거 마치 거짓말 같은 이야기로군 That sounds like (a) fiction. ⇌ 〈믿을 수 없는〉 It is an incredible story.
—이야기하다 tell a story [tale]; relate; narrate; give an account 《of》; (口) spin a yarn
3 〈소문〉 a rumor; a report; news
▶그 이야기는 곧 전국민에게 알려졌다 The news rapidly spread over the whole nation.
▶네 이야기는 자주 들었다 I have often heard about [of] you.
▶그렇게들 이야기를 하더라 So I understand. ⇌ So I am told.
4 〈상의〉 a consultation; 〈교섭〉 negotiations; an agreement; an understanding
♦ 이야기가 되다 come to [arrive at] an understanding 《with》; reach (an) agreement 《with》
▶나는 그 문제로 그들과 몇 차례 이야기를 나누었다 I had several talks with them about that matter.
—이야기하다 talk 《with》; discuss 《a matter with *sb*》; 〈교섭하다〉 negotiate 《with》; arrange 《with》
▶그들은 경영자 측과 노동 조건 개선에 대해 이야기했다 They negotiated with the management for the amendments of labor terms.
▶나는 결정할 수가 없으니 사장과 이야기하는 것이 나을 겁니다 I cannot make the decision, so you had better consult (with) the president.

이야기꾼

5 〈사정〉 the facts; reasons; 〈부탁〉 a request

이야기꾼 a storyteller; a raconteur

이야기책 —冊 a storybook ◆그림이 있는 이야기책 an illustrated storybook

이야깃거리 a topic of conversation; a subject of talk
▶ 그는 이야깃거리가 무궁무진하다 He has no end of things to talk about.
▶ 우리는 이야깃거리가 금방 떨어졌다 We soon ran out of topics of conversation.

이야말로[1] 〈이것이야말로〉 this very one [thing]; this...indeed [just]
▶ 이야말로 인성맞춤이다 This is the very thing for us [our purpose].
▶ 이야말로 내가 찾던 책이다 This is the very book (that) I have been looking for.
▶ 이야말로 일석이조다 This is a typical case of killing two birds with one stone.

이야말로[2] just; indeed; precisely; exactly; none other than
▶ 그 분이야말로 바로 국왕이었다 He was none other than the king himself.
▶ 그 말이야말로 내가 하고 싶은 말이다 That is just what I mean.

이양 移讓 transfer; relinquishment; handing over **—이양하다** transfer; turn [hand] over; relinquish ◆정권을 이양하다 hand over the reins of government
▶ 우리는 그에게 권한을 이양했다 We transferred our rights to him.

이어 俚語 a slang ⇨ 이언(俚諺)

이어받다 succeed to; inherit 《sth from sb》; take over 《a task》; be [fall] heir to
◆뜻을 이어받다 follow in the footsteps of 《another》
▶ 그는 아버지가 돌아가시자 가업을 이어받았다 He succeeded to [took over] the family business when his father died.
▶ 그녀는 어머니의 침착한 성격을 이어받았다 She inherited her mother's staid character.

이어서 〈그후에〉 soon after; after; then; 〈다음에〉 next; secondly; 〈연달아〉 continuously; successively; in succession; subsequently
◆연이어서 one after another; in succession
▶ 이어서 베토벤 교향곡 제9번이 연주되었다 Then [Next] the Ninth Symphony by Beethoven was performed.
▶ 송 선생에 이어서 김 선생이 교장이 되었다 Mr. Kim has succeeded Mr. Song as principal.

이어지다 be [get] connected; be joined [linked] together
▶ 길은 여기서부터 북쪽으로 이어진다 The road goes [runs] north from here.
▶ 그 두 도시는 다리로 이어져 있다 The two towns are connected by a bridge.

이어짓기 continuous cropping

이어폰 an earphone ◆이어폰을 끼다 put on an earphone / 이어폰으로 라디오를 듣다 listen to the radio through [with] an earphone

이언 二言 duplicity; double-dealing
—이언하다 break [go back on] one's word [promise]; be double-tongued

이언 俚言 〈속된 말〉 the language of the common people; a slang (word [expression])

이언 俚諺 a traditional [folk] saying; a proverb [maxim]

이언정 though ⇨ -ㄹ지언정

이엄이엄 uninterruptedly; continuously; without a break

이엉 (straw) thatch ◆이엉으로 지붕을 인 집 a thatch-roofed house / 이엉으로 지붕을 이다 thatch 《a house》 (with straw) ■—집 a straw-thatched house

이에 hereupon; on this; thereupon; therefore

이에서 than this ⇨ 이보다

이에짬 a joint; a juncture; a junction

이여 ▶ 서울이여 안녕 Adieu [Good-bye] to Seoul. / 신이여 우리를 불쌍히 여기소서 Oh, God! Have pity on us.

이여차 Yo-heave-ho! ⇨ 이영차

이역 二役 a double part [role] ⇨ 일인(一役)

이역 異域 〈이국〉 a foreign country [land]; an alien land; 〈먼곳〉 a remote place; a strange land
◆이역에서 살다 live far away from home; be a stranger in a strange land
▶ 아버지는 이역에 뼈를 묻으셨다 My father died in a foreign land.

이역시 —亦是 this too [also, again]
▶ 이 역시 미봉책에 불과하다 This again is a mere temporary measure.
▶ 이 역시 가짜다 This, too, is an imitation.

이연 離緣 〈양자의〉 the dissolution of adoption; 〈부부의〉 a divorce
—이연하다 cancel adoption; divorce

이연발 二連發 ◆2연발 총 a double-barreled gun; a double-chambered rifle

이열 二列 two rows; 〈횡렬〉 a double line; 〈종렬〉 a double file
◆2열로 in two rows [ranks]; in a double file; two abreast / 2열로 걷다 walk in two rows; walk two abreast / 2열로 서다 form two rows
■—종대 (縱隊) a double file: 2열 종대로 걷다 walk in a double file

이열치열 以熱治熱 〈속담〉 Like cures like. ⇒ The smell of garlic takes away the stink of dunghills. ⇒ Fight fire with fire.

이염 耳炎 〔醫〕 inflammation of the ear; otitis
■—중(내, 외)— otitis media [interna, externa]

이염화물 二鹽化物 〔化〕 a bichloride

이영차 Heave-ho!; Yo-heave-ho!; Yo-ho!
◆이영차 하고 짐을 나르다 carry a load with the cry of "heave-ho" / 이영차 하고 들어올리다 lift up sth with the cry of yo-ho

이오늄 〔化〕 ionium

이오니아 Ionia ◆이오니아의 Ionian; Ionic
■—식 the Ionic order: 이오니아식 건축 Ionic architecture

이온 〔化〕 an ion
■—수소— a hydrogen ion 양— a cation; a positive ion 음— an anion; a negative ion ■—교환수지 ion exchange resin —층[권] ionosphere —화 ionization: 이온화하다 ionize

이완 弛緩 laxity; slackness; 〔醫〕 atony
◆도덕의 이완 moral corruption [laxity]
—이완하다 slacken; relax; lax

이왕(에) 已往(—) already; now that; since

▶이왕(에) 가기로 했으면 가야지 Once you have decided to go, you had better go.
▶이왕(에) 할 바엔 큰 일을 해라 If you do anything at all, do something great.
▶이왕 왔으니 묵어 가도록 해라 Now you're already here, why not stay?

이왕이면 已往— if...must [should]; if...at all
▶이왕이면 일찍 떠나라 Start early if you want to go.
▶이왕이면 힘껏[철저히] 해라 If you do it at all, do it with all your might [thoroughly].
▶이왕이면 큰 것을 갖겠다 I will take the large one, if I must take either.

이왕지사 已往之事 the past; bygones
▶이왕지사는 어쩔 수 없다 What is done cannot be undone.
▶이왕지사는 묻지 말자 《속담》 Let bygones be bygones.

이외 以外 ◆…이외에 〈…을 제외하고〉 except (for); other than; excepting; but; save (for); 〈…밖에도〉 besides; in addition to
▶나는 영어 이외의 외국어는 하나도 모릅니다 Other than English I don't know any foreign languages.
▶여기는 학생 이외에는 들어갈 수 없습니다 People other than students are not allowed to enter.
▶우리 가게는 자전거 이외에 자동차 부품도 취급합니다 We deal in auto parts in addition to bicycles.
▶나는 그것 이외에도 하고 싶은 일이 많았다 I had many other things I wanted to do besides that.

이욕 利慾 greed; avarice; covetousness
◆이욕을 탐하다 be greedy for gain / 이욕에 눈이 멀다 be blinded by avarice
▶그는 이욕이 강하다 He is avaricious.
▶그는 이욕에 눈이 멀었다 Greed blinded him.

이용 利用 1 〈유리하게 씀〉 utilization; (good) use
▶원자력의 평화적 이용에 관한 토의가 있었다 A discussion was held on the peaceful use of atomic energy.
—이용하다 utilize; make (good) use of; take advantage of; employ profitably; turn *sth* to (good) account
◆시간을 잘 이용하다 make good use of *one's* time / 최대한도로 이용하다 make full [the best] use of; take full advantage of; utilize *sth* to the fullest / 돈[여가]을 잘 이용하다 make good use of *one's* money [leisure]/ 천연 자원을 이용하다 exploit natural resources
▶네 지식을 잘 이용해라 Turn your knowledge to good account.
▶나는 도서관을 자주 이용한다 I often use the library.
▶시간을 잘 이용하도록 해라 Try to make the most of your time.
▶여름 방학을 이용하여 경주를 여행했다 I took advantage of the summer vacation to travel to Kyŏngju.
▶태양에너지는 이미 난방에 이용되고 있다 Solar energy is already being utilized [used] to heat houses.

2 〈자신에게 편리하게 하는데 씀〉 **—이용하다** avail *oneself* of; take advantage of; trade [capitalize] on; 〈우려먹다〉 exploit; 〈수족처럼 부리다〉 make a cat's-paw of *sb*
◆이용할 수 있는[없는] available [unavailable] / 남의 무지[약점]를 이용하다 take advantage of [trade on] another's ignorance [weakness]
▶그들은 우정을 가장하여 우리를 이용했다 They exploited us under the guise of friendship.
▶그는 그 기회를 이용했다 He availed himself of the opportunity.
■폐품— the utilization of waste material
■—률 coefficient of utilization —법 utilization; a use; how [a way] to use: 이 기계의 이용법을 가르쳐 주시오 Tell me how to use [operate] this machine. —자 a user; 〈도서관의〉 a visitor; a reader

이용 理容 a haircut; hairdressing ⇨ 이발
이용가치 利用價値 usefulness; utility value
◆이용가치가 있다[없다] be of [be of no] utility value
▶이 데이터는 이용가치가 있다[없다] This data is worth [not worth] using.

이우다 help 《a woman》 (to) put 《loads》 on the head

이울다 1 〈시들다〉 wither; droop; wilt
▶꽃과 아름다움은 이우는 법이다 Flowers and beauty wither.
2 ⇨ 기울다 4
◆운세가 이울다 be down on *one's* luck
▶그의 가세가 이울어 가고 있다 He is in declining circumstances.

이웃 〈근처〉 the neighborhood [vicinity]; the next door; 〈사람〉 a neighbor
◆이웃 마을 the next town / 이웃 사람들 neighbors; people in the neighborhood / 이웃 아이들 neighbor children / 이웃의 next; neighboring; neighbor; adjacent / 이웃에 in the neighborhood 《of》/ (한 집 걸러) 이웃에 살다 live next door (but one) to *one's* house / 이웃과 사귀다 associate on the terms of neighbors; neighbor 《with》/ 이웃과 사이가 좋다[나쁘다] get along well [badly] with *one's* neighbors
▶브라운 씨는 내 친한 이웃입니다 Mr. Brown is a good neighbor of mine.
▶이웃의 정리상 나는 그렇게는 못하겠다 Our neighborly duty [feeling] won't let me do so.
▶네 이웃을 네 몸같이 사랑하라 You should love your neighbor as yourself.
▶나는 이웃과는 별로 교제가 없다 I don't have much to do with the neighbors.
▶김선생이 이웃으로 이사왔다 Mr. Kim has moved into the neighborhood.
—이웃하다 neighbor 《to》; adjoin (each other); be adjacent [next door] 《to》
▶그녀는 부모님과 이웃해서 살고 있다 She lives next door to her parents.
■—간 (be) next-door neighbors: 그 사람과 나는 이웃간이다 He and I are next door to each other. —나라 a neighboring [an adjacent] country: 한국과 중국은 이웃 나라다 Korea and China are neighbors (to each other). —돕

기웃동 a help-your-neighbor campaign —사랑 love of one's neighbors; good Samaritanism —집 a next-door [a neighboring, an adjacent] house: 그녀는 우리 이웃집에 산다 She lives next door to me.

이웃사촌 —四寸 (속담) A good neighbor is better than a brother far off.

이원 二元 duality ♦이원적인 dual; dualistic ■—론 [哲] dualism —론자 a dualist —방송 a simultaneous broadcast from two stations —방정식 [數] a dual equation —성(性) dualism; duality

이원권 以遠權 the beyond (traffic) rights

이원제 二院制 the bicameral system ⇨ 양원(~제)

이월 二月 February (略 Feb.)

이월 移越 a transfer; 〈차기로의〉a carry-over; carrying forward [over]; 〈전기로부터의〉 bringing forward [over]
—이월하다 transfer 《to, from》; 〈다음으로〉 carry forward 《to》; carry over 《to》; 〈앞에서〉 bring forward [over, down]
♦다음 연도로 이월하다 carry 《a sum》 forward to the next year / 차기로 이월하다 carry the balance to the next account
▶ 이달에는 3만원이 이월되었다 There was a thirty thousand won balance carried forward this month.
■—금〈전기로부터의〉the balance [amount of money] brought forward 《from the previous account》; 〈차기로의〉the amount of money carried forward 《to the next account》 —손익 losses and profits brought forward —잉여금〈차기로의〉a reserve carried forward; 〈전기로부터의〉a reserve brought forward

이위 二位 〈석차〉the second place [rank]; 〈사람〉a runner-up ♦2위가 되다 be [rank] second; be placed second
▶ 그는 경주에서 민수에 이어 근소한 차이로 2위를 했다 He made [finished] a close second to Min-su in the race.

이유 理由 1 〈까닭〉(a) reason; cause; 〈근거〉ground(s); occasion; account; why
♦그럴듯한 이유 a plausible reason / 정당한 이유 a justifiable reason; a just cause 《for war》 / 퇴직 이유 a reason for one's resignation / 이유 있는 reasonable; 〈정당한〉justifiable; well-grounded / 이유 없는 causeless; groundless; 〈부당한〉unjustifiable; unreasonable / 이유없이 without reason [cause]; 〈부당하게〉unreasonably / 이렇다 할 이유없이 for no particular reason / 이유 여하를 막론하고 on any account; irrespective of reason / 무슨 이유로 for what reason; on what ground [account]; why / …이라는 이유로 for the reason that…; by reason of [that…]; because of; on account [grounds] of; on the ground(s) of [that…] / 이유를 규명하다 inquire into the reason 《of》; investigate [study] the cause 《of》 / 이유를 대다 give a reason 《for》; state one's reasons / 이유를 묻다 ask sb for reason [explanation] 《of a case》 / 이유를 밝히다 clarify the reason / 지각한 이유를 설명하다 explain (the reason) why one is late
▶ 충분한 이유없이 아이를 꾸짖어서는 안 된다 You must not scold a child without good reason.
▶ 그가 온 이유가 분명치 않다 The reason why he came is not clear.
▶ 그의 말을 의심할 이유가 없다 There is no reason to doubt his word.
▶ 그가 그곳에 간 이유는 어머니를 기쁘게 해 드리고 싶어서였다 He went there simply because he wanted to please his mother.
▶ 그의 행동에 대해 불평할 이유는 없다 There is no ground for complaining of his behavior.
▶ 그가 나를 헐뜯는 이유를 모르겠다 I cannot understand why he speaks badly of me.
▶ 어떤 이유로 그것이 옳다고 말하는 겁니까? On what ground do you say that it is true?
2 〈구실〉a pretext; an excuse
▶ 이렇게 늦을 수 밖에 없었던 이유가 뭔가? What is your justification for being so late?
▶ 그런 이유는 통하지 않는다 Such an excuse won't do.
▶ 그는 (종종) 별의별 이유로 회사를 쉰다 He (often) stays away from the office for various unusual reasons.
3 〈고려〉consideration
♦어리다는 이유로 in consideration of one's youth; considering that one is under age
4 〈동기〉a motive
♦자살의 이유 a motive for a suicide
■존재— reason for being; (프) raison d'être —서 a statement of reasons; an explanatory statement

이유 離乳 weaning; ablactation; (라) ablactatio
▶ 그 아기는 아직 이유를 못했다 The baby is not yet weaned.
—이유하다 wean; be weaned
♦어린아이를 이유시키다 wean a baby from its mother
■—기 the weaning period —식 baby food

이윤 利潤 (a) profit; gain; returns
♦이윤이 높은 장사 a profitable [paying] business
▶ 이 가게는 월 300만원의 이윤을 올린다 This store makes a profit of three million won a month.
■정상[초과, 한계]— normal [excess, marginal] profits ■—율 a profit rate; a rate of profit —통제[추구] control [pursuit] of profits —폭 a profit margin

이율 利率 the rate of interest; the interest rate
♦이율 6%의 채권 a bond on a yield basis of 6% / 월 2%의 이율로 돈을 꾸어주다 lend money at the rate of 2% per month / 이율을 인상하다 raise [increase] the rate of interest
▶ 이 주식은 이율이 좋다[나쁘다] The stocks yield [bear] a good [bad] return.
▶ 그 은행은 지난달에 이율을 인상[인하]했다 The bank raised [lowered] the rate of interest last month.
■법정[협정]— the legal [conventional] rate of interest 은행[시장]— the bank [market] rate

이율배반 二律背反 〔哲〕 antinomy ♦이율배반의 antinomic
이윽고 in a (little) while; after a while; shortly (after); before long; by and by
▶이윽고 비가 그쳤다 By and by it stopped raining.
이음 異音 〔音聲〕 an allophone
이음매 a joint; a juncture; 〈솔기〉 a seam
♦이음매가 없는 jointless; one-piece / 이음매가 없는 레일 a welded rail / 이음매 없는 스타킹 seamless stockings
▶굴뚝의 이음매로 연기가 새어나오고 있다 Smoke is leaking through a joint in the chimney.
이음새 a joint ⇨ 이음매
이의 異義 〈다른 뜻〉 a different meaning; another meaning; 〈다른 주의〉 a different principle [doctrine]
♦동음 이의어 a homonym
이의 異議 〈반대〉 an objection; a complaint; 〈항의〉 a protest; 〈동의하지 않음〉 dissent; 〔法〕 a demurrer
♦이의없이 without dissent [any objection] / 이의가 있다[없다] have an [no] objection《to, against》/ 이의를 제기하다 raise [lodge] an objection《to》; voice a protest
▶이의 있소 Objection! ⇌ I object!
▶그 건에 대해서는 이의 없습니다 I have no objection on the matter.
▶위원회는 예산 삭감에 이의를 제기했다 The committee protested against the budget cut.
—신청 an exception; a formal objection: 이의 신청을 하다 take [make an] objection to / (재판장이) 이의 신청을 인정[기각]합니다 Objection sustained [overruled]. —신청서 a statement of protest —신청인 〔法〕 a demurrant
이이시 〈유럽경제공동체〉 EEC〔‹*European Economic Community*〕
이익 利益 1 〈이득〉 (a) profit; gain(s); returns
♦이익이 있는[없는] 거래 a profitable [an unprofitable] transaction / 이익을 보지 않고 without profit / 이익이 나나 yield a profit / 이익이 있다 be paying / 이익이 적다 bring little profit; do not pay much / 이익을 얻다[보다] make [earn, secure, obtain] a profit 《of 10,000 won》/ 이익 배분을 하다 give sb a profit participation
▶그는 이익을 위해서는 무슨 짓이라도 한다 He will do anything for the sake of profit.
▶이것은 이익이 있는[없는] 장사다 This is a profitable [unprofitable] transaction.
▶목전의 이익에만 급급해선 안된다 You must not think about your immediate profit only.
2 〈편익〉 benefit; profit; advantage; good; interests
♦이익이 있는[되는] beneficial; advantageous / 서로의 이익을 위하여 for mutual advantage [interests] / 이익을 얻다 profit [benefit] by 《reading》; get [receive] benefit from 《reading》/ 이익을 주다 benefit; do sb good / 자신의 이익을 도모하다 look out for [look after, pursue] one's own interests / 공동의 이익을 증진하다 promote 《our [their]》 common interests

▶이 책을 읽으면 꼭 이익이 있습니다 You are sure to get some benefit from this book.
▶그것은 아무 이익도 없다 No good will come (out) of it. ⇌ It will do no good.
■ 미 배당— undivided profit 순— a net [clear] profit ■—금 a profit; gains; 〈수익고〉 proceeds; returns —분배 ⇨ 이익배당 —준비금 an earned [a reserved] surplus
이익배당 利益配當 distribution of profits; profit sharing; 〈돈〉 a dividend ♦이익배당을 받다 participate [have a share] in the profit
이인 二人 two men; two persons
■ —삼각(三脚) 〈경주〉 a three-legged race —승 a two-seater; a double-seater —조 a duo (*pl.* duos, dui); a twosome: 2인조 강도가 그 집에 침입했다 A gang of two burglers broke into the house. —칭 〔文法〕 the second person —칭대명사 a personal pronoun for the second person
이인 異人 〈비범한 사람〉 an extraordinary man; a man of unusual ability; 〈다른 사람〉 a different person ■ 동명— a (different) person of the same name
이인종 異人種 an alien [a different] race
이임 離任— leave [quit] one's office [post]
이입 移入 introduction; import; shipping in
—이입하다 introduce; import; bring in; ship in
■ 감정— 〔心〕 empathy : 감정 이입하다 empathize 《with》
이자 〔解〕〈췌장〉 the pancreas
이자 利子 interest
♦비싼[싼] 이자로 at high [low] interest / 무이자로 free of interest; without interest; interest-free / 이자가 붙다 yield [bear] interest 《at 12%》/ 이자를 붙여서 갚다 pay back 《money》 with interest / 이자로 살다 live on the interest of one's money
▶그는 이자를 받고 돈을 빌려 주었다 He lent [put out] his money at interest.
▶정기 예금의 이자는 얼마입니까? What interest is allowed on fixed deposits?
■ 연체— accrued interest ■ —계산서 an interest note —산 calculation of interest —소득 the income from interests; interest income —평형세 the interest equalization tax
이자 —者 this man [fellow, guy]
이자락 利子落 〈이자・이익 배당 지급필〉 ex interest (*略* ex int.); interest off ■ —가격 ex interest value
이자부 利子附 ■—증권 an interest-bearing security —채권 an active [interest-bearing] bond
이자액 —液 〔生〕 pancreatic juice
이자지불 利子支拂 interest payment
—정지 suspension of interest payment
이장 里長 the head [man] of a village; a village headman [chief]
이장 移葬 reburial (to an other place)
—이장하다 rebury (to an other place); remove 《sb's body》 from one grave to another
이재 理財 financial management; finance; economy ♦이재에 밝다 be adept at money-

이재

making; be efficient at financial affairs
―이재하다 manage financial affairs
■―가(家) an economist; a financier ―학 political economy

이재 罹災 〈재해를 입음〉 suffering 《from an earthquake》; affliction
―이재하다 suffer 《from floods》; fall a victim 《to a disaster》; be hit [visited] 《by a typhoon》
■―구호 기금 a 《disaster》 relief fund ―율 〔保險〕 the frequency of loss ―지역 the afflicted [stricken, affected] district [area]

이재민 罹災民 the afflicted people; the sufferers; the victims 《of》
♦이재민을 구호하다 carry out the relief of victims of a disaster
■수해― sufferers from a flood; flood sufferers [victims] 전쟁― war victims ■―수용소 a refugee camp

이적 利敵 benefiting the enemy
■―행위 an act to serve the interest of the enemy; an act advantageous to the enemy: 그것은 이적행위다 It is profitable only to the enemy.

이적 異蹟 a miracle; a marvel ♦이적을 행하다 work [perform] miracles; do wonders

이적 移籍 transfer of the register
―이적하다 transfer *one's* registration 《from, to》; be transferred 《to》
▶그는 작년에 자이언츠로 이적했다 He was transferred [traded] to the Giants last year.
■―료 transfer fee (of a pro baseballer)

이적하다 離籍 have *one's* name removed from the family register

이전 以前 1 〈이제 보다 전〉 before
♦이보다 이전에 previous [prior] to this; before this time
▶김씨 이전에는 누가 지사였습니까 Who was the governor prior to Mr. Kim?
2 〈아주 전〉 former times [days]
♦이전에 formerly; in former times; of old; 〈한때〉 once / 이전에는 formerly; in old days / 이전의 동료 a former colleague
▶나는 그를 이전에 만난 적이 있다 I have seen him before.
▶그는 이전에는 대학 교수였다 He was formerly a professor at a university.
▶물가가 올라 생활이 이전처럼 쉽지 않다 As prices are going up, life isn't so easy as it used to be.

이전 利錢 〈이문〉 gain; profit; interest

이전 移轉 〈이사〉 (house) moving; a move; a removal; a change of address [residence]; 〈양도〉 transfer (권리 따위의); demise (재산의)
―이전하다 move; remove; change *one's* residence; 〈물건 등을〉 transfer
♦이전할 수 있는 권리 transferable rights / 가옥과 토지를 아내 명의로 이전하다 transfer *one's* house and estate to *his* wife
▶다음 주소로 이전하였습니다 We have moved to the following address.
■권리― a transfer of rights ―등기부 a transfer book ―신고 a report of removal; a report of change of address ―통지 a notice of change of address; a removal notice

이점 利點 an advantage
▶이 기계는 다루기가 쉽다는 이점이 있다 This machine has the advantage of easy handling.
▶근처에서 장을 볼 수 있는 것이 도시생활의 이점이다 Nearby shopping is an advantage of living in the city.

이정 里程 mileage; (a) distance
♦서울까지의 이정 the distance to Seoul
■―표(表) a table of distances ―표(標) a milestone; a milepost

이제 now ♦이제 막 just (now); a moment ago / 예나 이제나 in these days as in those; now as in ages past / 이제껏 내내 [죽] all this while
▶이제나 저제나 기다리고 있었습니다 I was expecting you to arrive at any moment.
▶이제 가을이다 It's fall now.
▶이제 그가 올 때가 되었다 It's (high) time he came.
▶그는 이제 어린애가 아니다 He is no longer a boy.
▶이제야말로 기회다 Now is the chance. ⇌ Now or never.
▶우리는 이제 끝장이다 It's all up with us now. ⇌ It's all over now.

이제까지 until now; hitherto; so [thus] far; up to this time [day]
♦이제까지처럼 as before; as ever (before)
▶이제까지는 그만하다 So far so good.
▶이것은 내가 이제까지 본 영화 중에서 가장 재미있다 This is the most interesting movie (that) I have ever seen.

이제부터 1 〈지금부터〉 from now on; from this time forth [forward]; after this; (美口) from here on in; hence
▶자, 이제부터 업무에 들어갑시다 From now on, let's get down to business.
▶이제부터는 더욱 조심해야 하네 Be more careful hereafter.
▶이제부터는 어떻게 살아가시렵니까? How will you get along in the future?
2 〈여기서부터〉 from here
▶이제부터 길은 숲속으로 들어선다 Here the road runs into woods.

이제와서 now; after so long a time; at this belated time [hour] ♦이제와서 생각하니 when I think of [look back to] it now; in hindsight
▶이제와서는 어쩔 수 없다 It can't be helped now.
▶그 제안은 당시는 비판을 많이 받았으나 이제 와서 생각하면 정치적으로는 의미가 있다 That proposal was much criticized at the time, but it makes political sense in hindsight.

이젤 〔美術〕 an easel

이조 吏曹 〔史〕 the Board of Civil Servants

이조 李朝 the Yi Dynasty ■―실록 the True Records of the Yi Dynasty

이족 異族 〈민족〉 a different race; 〈씨족〉 a different clan

이종 二種 two kinds; 〈제2종의〉 the second class ♦제2종 우편물 second-class mail (matter)

이종 姨從 a maternal cousin
이종 移種 〈모종 옮겨심기〉 transplanting (of a sapling)
—이종하다 transplant; plant out
이종 異種 a different kind [species]; a variety ■—개체군 interspecies population —교배〔動〕 hybridization; crossbreeding —번식〔生〕 cross breeding
이주 移住 migration; 〈외국으로의〉 emigration; 〈외국으로부터의〉 immigration; 〈이사〉 a move; a removal
—이주하다 migrate 《from, to》; settle 《in》; emigrate 《to》; immigrate 《into》; 〈이사하다〉 move; remove
▶ 그는 3년 전에 브라질로 이주했다 He emigrated to Bragil three year ago.
▶ 아메리카 인디언은 먼 옛날 아시아에서 이주해 왔다고 한다 American Indians are said to have come [migrated] from Asia to America in ancient times.
■—자[민] an emigrant; an immigrant; a migrant; a settler
이주일 二週日 two weeks; 《英》 a fortnight
♦이주일에 한 번씩 fortnightly; every two weeks / 이주일에 한 번 발간하는 간행물 a fortnightly; a biweekly
이죽거리다 make provocative remarks ⇨ 이기죽거리다
이중 二重 duplication; doubleness
♦이중의 double; duplex; dual; duplicate; twofold / 이중의 의미 a double meaning / 이중으로 doubly; twice; over again / 이중으로 하다 [되다] double; duplicate / 이중으로 기입하다 make an entry twice / 이중으로 지불하다 pay for sth twice (over)
▶ 이 창들은 이중으로 되어 있다 These windows are double ones.
▶ 이 표현에는 이중의 의미가 있다 This expression has a double meaning.
▶ 그렇게 하면 이중의 수고를 하게 된다 That would double the trouble.
■—간첩 a double agent —결합〔化〕 a double bond —곡가제 the dual grain price system; the dual [double] price system of grain [corn] —과세(課稅) double taxation —과세(過歲) celebrating both the solar New Year and the lunar New Year —구조 dual structure —노출 double exposure —뚜껑 double lid —모음〔音聲〕 a diphthong —문(門) double doors —방송 dual broadcasting —벽 a double (-framed) wall —부정〔文法〕 a double negative —성(性) duality; duplicity —외교 dual diplomacy —인화 double printing; superimposing —임금제 a two-tier wage system —장부 (have) a double accounting system —적분〔數〕 a double integral —조종 dual control —주머니 a double bag —창〔주〕〔樂〕 a duet; a duo; (이) a duetto 《pl. ~s, duetti》 —촬영 (a) superimposition; an overlap —판매 double sale —하이픈 a double hyphen
이중가격 二重價格 a dual price —제 a dual price system; a two-tier price system
이중결혼 二重結婚 bigamy ♦이중결혼의 bigamic ■—자 a bigamist

이중국적 二重國籍 dual nationality [citizenship] —자 a dual national
이중생활 二重生活 a double life; a dual existence ♦이중생활을 하다 maintain two households; lead a double life [dual existence]; live two lives
이중인격 二重人格 〔心〕 dual [double] personality ♦이중인격의 Jekyll-and-Hyde
■—자 a double-faced person; a Jekyll and Hyde
이중창 二重窓 a double window ♦이중창이 달린 방 a double-windowed room
이중턱 二重— a double chin
♦이중턱의 double-chinned
이즈베스티야 〈러시아의 신문〉 Izvestia
이즈음, 이즘¹ nowadays ⇨ 요즈음
이즘² 〈주의·학설〉 an ism ▶ 현대는 이즘의 시대다 This is the age of isms.
이지 理智 intellect; intelligence
♦이지의 번득임 flashes of intellect / 이지적인 사람[얼굴] an intellectual person [face]
▶ 나는 이지적인 여성을 좋아한다 I like intellectual women.
■—주의 intellectualism
이지러지다 1 〈한 귀퉁이가 떨어지다〉 chip (off); break (off); be broken ♦이지러진 잔 a chipped cup 2 〈한쪽이 차지 않다〉 wane
▶ 달이 이지러진다 The moon is on the wane.
이직 移職 〈직장을 옮김〉 a change of occupation ⇨ 전직(轉職)
이직 離職 〈직장을 떠남〉 separation 《from one's position [service]》 —이직하다 leave [quit] one's job
■—률〔勞〕 the separation rate —자 an unemployed person; 〈총칭〉 unemployed people; the jobless; the unemployed
이진법 二進法 〔數〕 the binary scale; the dyadic system ♦이진법의 binary
이진숫자 二進數字 〔電算〕 a bit; a binary digit
이질 姨姪 a nephew [niece] (who is the child of one's wife's sister)
이질 異質 heterogeneity ♦이질의 of a different nature; heterogeneous; 〈외래의〉 foreign; extraneous ■—문화 culture of a different nature; foreign culture
이질 痢疾 〔醫〕 dysentery ■ 세균성— a dysentery bacillus 아메바성— amoebic dysentery ■ —환자 a dysentery [dysenteric] patient
이질풀 痢疾— 〔植〕 a cranesbill
이집트 〈나라이름〉 Egypt; 〈공식명〉 the Arab Republic of Egypt ♦이집트의 Egyptian
■—사람 an Egyptian; 〈총칭〉 the Egyptians
이쪽 1 〈이편〉 this side; this way [direction]
♦이쪽 저쪽 this way and that / 이쪽 저쪽으로 hither and thither; to and fro
▶ 이쪽으로 오십시오 Please come [step, walk] this way. = This way, please.
▶ 학교는 강 이쪽입니까? Is the school (on) this side (of) the river?
2 〈우리 편〉 our part(y); we; us
♦이쪽과 저쪽 we and they
▶ 이쪽에서는 계약을 지켰습니다 The agreement was kept on our [my] part.
이차 二次 1 〈두번째〉 second; secondary; 〔數〕

이차적

quadratic; quadric
♦이차의 secondary; second; 〔數〕 quadratic; quadric / 제이차 세계대전 the Second World War; World War II
2 ⇨ 이차회(二次會) ▶ 자 이차로 가세 Let's go bar-hopping. ⇌ 〈英〉 Let's do a pub-crawl.
■—감염[공해] secondary infection [pollution] —방정식 〔數〕 a quadratic equation —산업 the second industry —성징 a secondary sex character(istic) —전자[전지] a secondary electron [battery] —제품 secondary products

이차적 二次的 secondary
▶ 그것은 이차적인 문제다 That is a matter of secondary importance. ⇌ That is a secondary consideration.

이차회 二次會 〈2차 술자리〉 an afterfeast; a second party [feast]; a party after a party
♦이차회를 하다 have another spree at another place; go bar-hopping; 〈英〉 do a pub-crawl

이착 二着 〈2위〉 the second place; 〈차점자〉 a runner-up

이착륙 離着陸 taking off and landing

이채 異彩 a conspicuous [prominent] color
♦이채로운 conspicuous; shining; brilliant; remarkable / 이채를 띠다 be conspicuous; cut a conspicuous [prominent, brilliant] figure; stand out from others

이처럼 like this; in this manner [way]; as you see ♦이처럼 많이 so many [much]; (口) this many [much]
▶ 나로서 이처럼 고마운 일은 없다 Nothing is more welcome to me than this.
▶ 그가 이처럼 바보일 줄은 몰랐다 I didn't know he was so silly.
▶ 이처럼 일찍 어딜 갔다 오세요 Where have you been at this hour of (the) morning?

이첩 移牒 notification to the authorities concerned; communication
—이첩하다 transmit (an order) to the office [official] concerned; pass (the information) on (to); notify (of, that); refer (to); communicate (to); give notice (to)
▶ 그 명령은 도 교육청으로 이첩되었다 The orders were transmitted to the provincial office of education.

이체 異體 a variant ■—동심(同心) being two in body but one in mind —동형(同形) 〔生〕 homomorphy

이초 離礁 〈좌초선이 다시 뜸〉 refloatation —이초하다 refloat; get off the rock [sunken reef] ♦이초시키다 refloat (a ship); get (a ship) off the rocks

이초점렌즈 二焦點— a bifocal lens
이초점안경 二焦點眼鏡 bifocals
이축하다 移築 dismantle (a historic building) and reconstruct (it) at a different place
▶ 이것은 경주의 민가를 이축한 것이다 This is an old house brought over from the Kyŏnju district and reassembled here.

이출 移出 shipment; export —이출하다 ship; export

이취 異臭 a nasty [a foul, an offensive] smell; (口) a stink; a stench ♦이취를 풍기다 give out a foul smell [stench]; stink

이층 二層 〈美〉 the second floor; 〈英〉 the first floor; (the) upstairs

> 解說 〈美〉에서는 일층이 *the first floor*이므로 이층은 *the second floor*가 되지만, 〈英〉에서는 일층을 the ground [street] floor로 나타내므로 이층은 the first floor가 된다. 또한 floor는 보통 건물 내부의 특정한 층을 나타내는 데 대해 story [〈英〉 storey] 는 건물 외부에서 본 층을 나타낸다.

♦이층의 방 an upstairs room; a room on the second [〈英〉 first] floor / 이층의 창 an upstairs window / 이층에서 내려오다 come downstairs / 이층으로 올라가다 go upstairs
▶ 그의 사무실은 이층에 있다 His office is on the second floor.
▶ 그의 집은 이층집이다 His house has two stories [is two stories high].
▶ 이층으로 통하는 통로는 이쪽이다 This is a passage leading upstairs.
■—버스 a double-decker —집 a two-storied [-story] house; a house of two stories

이치 理致 1 〈도리〉 reason; 〈논리〉 logic
♦당연한 이치 a matter of course / 이치에 맞는[맞지 않는] 말 a reasonable [an unreasonable] words / 이치에 따라서 in accordance with reason [what is reasonable]; in line with reason / 이치를 깨우치다 make sb see reason / 이치를 따지다 reason with sb / 이치에 맞다 be reasonable; stand to reason / 이치에 맞지 않다 be unreasonable; do not stand to reason / 이치에 어긋나다 be contrary to reason
▶ 그에게 이치를 따져도 소용없다 It is no use reasoning with him.
▶ 자네가 하는 말은 이치에 맞지 않는다 What you say is against reason [irrational].
▶ 남녀 관계는 이치만으론 설명할 수 없다 The relationship between man and woman is beyond reason or logic.

2 〈원리〉 a principle
♦자연의 이치 a natural law / 이치를 탐구하다 go [inquire] into the principles of
▶ 자식을 사랑하는 것은 자연스런 이치다 It is in the nature of things that parents should love their children.

이칭 異稱 another name [title]; a different title

이카오 〈국제 민간 항공 기구〉 the ICAO [《*International Civil Aviation Organization*》]

이퀄 equal ▶ 2 더하기 3 이퀄 5 Two and [plus] three equal [are, is] five.
▶ 5 빼기 1 이퀄 4 One from five [Five minus One] leaves [is] four.
▶ 2 곱하기 3 이퀄 6 Two times three is [are] six.
▶ 6 나누기 3 이퀄 2 Six divided by three is two.

이키(나) Oh!; Oh my (goodness)!; Dear me!; Gosh!; (美俗) Gee!

이타 利他 altruism ♦이타적인 altruistic

■―주의 altruism ―주의자 an altruist
이탄 泥炭 peat; furf ■―지 a peat bog [moor]; a turbary
이탈 離脫 (a) secession; a breakaway; (a) separation
―**이탈하다** break [drift] away from; leave 《a party》; secede from
♦직장을 이탈하다 desert *one's* post; quit *one's* job
▶ 그들은 연맹에서 이탈했다 They left [broke away from] the league.
▶ 그는 보수당에서 이탈하여 새 당을 만들었다 He left the conservative party and formed a new party.
■―국적― the renunciation of *one's* nationality
―**자** a seceder
이탈리아 〈나라이름〉 Italy; 〈공식명〉 the Italian Republic ♦이탈리아의 Italian
―**말** Italian ―**사람** an Italian
이탓저탓 with this excuse [complaint] and that; on one pretext or another; on some pretext or other
이태 two years ♦이태 동안 for a couple of years
이탤릭 〈활자〉 italics; italic type ♦이탤릭으로 [이탤릭체로] 하다 print in italics
▶ 예문은 이탤릭체로 인쇄되어 있다 The examples are printed in italics [italic type].
이테르븀 〔化〕 ytterbium
이토 泥土 mud; mire ■―층 〔地質〕 a dirt bed
이토록 so much; this much; like this
♦이토록 부탁하는데도 for all my request
▶ 영어를 가르치기가 이토록 힘들 줄은 몰랐다 I little dreamed that it was so hard work to teach English.
이트륨 〔化〕 yttrium
이통 耳痛 (an) earache ⇨ 귀앓이
이튿날 1 〈다음날〉 the next [following] day; the day after ♦이튿날 아침 the next morning
▶ 그녀는 그 이튿날 또 한번 왔다 She came again the next day.
▶ 대학을 졸업한 이튿날 그는 고향을 떠났다 He left home the day after he graduated from college.
2 〈둘째 날〉 the second day; 〈초이틀〉 the second (day of a month)
이틀¹ 〈2일간〉 two days; 〈둘째 날〉 the second (day)
♦구월 초이틀 the second of September; September 2(nd) / 이틀 밤 two nights / 이틀 후에 after two days; two days after [later, afterward] / 이틀마다 every two days; every other day / 하루 이틀에 in a day or two
▶ 그는 이틀 걸러 한번씩 병원으로 어머니 문병을 간다 He goes to the hospital to inquire after his sick mother every third day [three days].
▶ 파리에는 이틀밖에 있지 않았다 I was in Paris for only two days.
이틀² 1 〈치조 (齒槽)〉 the socket of a tooth; 〔解〕 an alveolus 《*pl.* -li》; an alveole
2 〈의치상 (床)〉 a denture; a dental [tooth] plate ♦이틀을 해박다 insert a dental plate; fix a denture

이틀거리 〔韓醫〕 a tertian fever [malaria]; vivax malaria ♦이틀거리에 걸리다 be taken with tertian fever
이판암 泥板岩 〔鑛〕 shale
이팔 二八 sixteen ■―청춘 sixteen years of age; the prime of youth; sweet sixteen; 〈사람〉 a maiden of sixteen
이페리트 〔化〕 yperite; mustard gas
이편 1 〈이쪽〉 this side [way]; 〈이것〉 this
▶ 우리 집은 길 이편에 있다 My house is on this side of the street.
▶ 저편보다 이편이 마음에 든다 I prefer this to that one.
2 〈자기〉 I; we ♦이편의 잘못 my [our] fault; a fault on my [our] part
▶ 이편으로서는 이의가 없습니다 For my part there is no objection.
이피반 ―盤 an EP [extended-play record]
이핑계저핑계 this excuse or that; (on) one excuse [pretext] or another; (on) some pretext or other
▶ 일꾼이 이핑계 저핑계 대며 일을 자꾸 미룬다 The worker keeps putting the matter off with one excuse after another.
―**이핑계저핑계하다** make one excuse or another
이하 以下 1 〈수량·정도〉 ...(and) downward; not exceeding; 〈미만〉 less than...; below

| 解説 | 우리말로「100 이하」라고 할 때는 100을 포함하지만, 영어의 ***less than*** 100에는 100을 포함하지 않는다. 따라서「100개 이하의 주문에는 할인되지 않습니다」는 There will be no discount on an order for 100 pieces or less 라고 해야 한다. |

♦0도 이하 below zero / 5세 이하의 어린이 children of five and under; children less than six years old / 10킬로미터 이하의 거리 a distance of under ten kilometers / 보통 이하 below the general level; below the average [mark, standard] / 중류 이하의 below the middle class / 천원 이하의[로] not exceeding 1,000 won; 1,000 won and less / 원가 이하로 팔다 sell below (the) cost
▶ 이곳은 겨울에 추워서 영도 이하로 내려가는 때가 있다 It's cold in the winter here and the temperature sometimes drops below zero.
▶ 이것은 1만원 이하로는 팔지 않습니다 I won't sell this for less than [under] 10,000 won.
▶ 총액은 예상 이하다 The sum total falls under what was expected.
▶ 올해의 쌀 수확고는 평년 이하였다 This year's rice crop was below the average.
▶ 그의 월소득은 150만원 이하다 His monthly income is less than [under] 1,500,000 won.
▶ 6세 이하는 입장 무료 《게시》 Admission free for children under six.
2 〈하기 (下記)〉 the following; the rest
♦이하 동문 same as above / 이하 20쪽에 계속됨 continued on page 20 / 이하 같음 and so forth [on]; etc
▶ 이하 다음 편[쪽]에 To be continued.
▶ 이하 생략 The rest is omitted.

▶이하 이에 준함 The same rule applies correspondingly to the following. ⇌ The same shall apply hereinafter.
▶결과는 이하와 같다 The result is as follow.
▶이하의 리스트를 참고하세요 Please refer to the following list.

이하선 耳下腺 〔解〕 the parotid (gland)
■(유행성)—염 〔醫〕 (epidemic) parotitis; parotiditis; mumps (virus) : 이하선염에 걸리다 catch [come down with] the lmumps

이학 理學 science ♦이학의 scientific
■—계 the scientific world —박사〈사람〉a doctor of scicncc;〈학위〉Doctor of Science (略 D. Sc.) —부 the department of science —사〈사람〉a bachelor of science;〈학위〉Bachelor of Science (略 B. Sc.) —자 a scientist

이한 離韓 one's departure from Korea —이한하다 leave [depart, go away from] Korea

이함 離艦 〔空軍〕 takeoff (of an aircraft) from a ship

이합집산 離合集散 meeting and parting ♦정당의 이합집산 changing of alignment of political parties

이항 二項 ♦이항의 〔數〕 binomial; binomial
■—방정식 a binomial equation —분포 〔統計〕 binomial distribution —식 a binomial expression [formula]; a binomial —정리〔定理〕the binomial theorem

이항 移項 〔數〕 (a) transposition
—이항하다 transpose (a term)

이해 this year; the current [present] year
♦이해 겨울에 this winter; in winter this year / 이해 안으로 by the end of this year

이해 利害 advantages and disadvantages; loss and gain; profit and loss; interests; concern
♦공동의 이해 common interests / 이해의 일치 identity of interests / 이해의 충돌 a clash [conflict] of interests / 이해를 초월한 사랑 disinterested love / 이해에 관계되다 affect one's interests / 이해 득실을 논하다 discuss the advantages and disadvantages (of)
▶그들의 우정은 이해의 대립으로 무너지고 말았다 Their friendship ended because of a dash [conflict] of interests.
▶이 문제에서는 그들의 이해가 일치한다 They have [share] common interests in this matter.
▶이 사건에서는 그들의 이해가 상반[충돌]하고 있다 Their interests conflict [clash] in this matter.
▶공통의 이해가 두 사람을 결합시키고 있다 Common interests bind [unite] the two.
▶이 문제는 너의 이해와 밀접한 관계가 있다 The question touches your interest closely.
■—상반 (相半) equalness of loss and gain; advantages and disadvantages in half: 이해 상반하다 break even —상반 (相反) a conflict [clash] of interests

이해 理解 understanding; comprehension;〈파악〉grasp; apprehension; appreciation
♦충분한 이해 a full understanding / 상호(간)의 이해 mutual understanding / 이해 있는 사람 an understanding person; a person of understanding / 이해가 빠르다 be quick of apprehension [understanding] / 이해가 부족하다 do not fully understand; want [lack] sympathy /…에 대하여 이해가 없다 have no understanding of...; lack sense [understanding] of... / 서로의 이해를 증진하다 promote [increase] mutual understanding
▶우리 아버지는 등산에 이해가 없다 My father is unsympathetic toward mountain climbing.
▶그는 예술에 이해가 있다 He knows how to appreciate art. ⇌ He appreciates art.
▶그의 말은 이해가 안 간다 What he says does not make sense.
—이해하다 understand; comprehend; apprehend; appreciate; grasp; (口) make out; see
♦이해할 수 있는 understandable; comprehensible / 올바로 이해하다 have a right [proper] understanding (of) / 서양문화를 바르게 이해하다 appreciate western culture
▶그가 왜 학교에 무단결석하는지 도저히 이해할 수 없다 I just can't understand why he cuts school. ⇌ I just can't understand his [(口) him] cutting school.
▶그는 이 문제를 분명히 이해하고 있다 He understands this matter clearly. ⇌ He has a clear understanding of this matter.
▶너는 이 점을 그에게 분명히 이해시키지 않으면 안된다 You must put [get] this point across to him clearly.
▶어린이는 선악을 이해하지 못한다 A child has no knowledge of good and evil.
▶이 책은 이해하기 쉽다[어렵다] This book is easy [difficult] to understand.
▶시장은 자신의 새로운 계획을 시의회에 이해시키지 못했다 The mayor was unable to make the city council understand his new project.
▶나는 그의 얘기를 들었지만 의미가 이해되지 않았다 I heard his speach but did not comprehend his meaning.
▶그가 하는 말을 이해할 수 없었다 I couldn't understand [make out, (美口) figure out, grasp] what he said.
▶그것은 이해할 수 없다 It is beyond my comprehension ⇌ It is incomprehensible to me.
▶부부 사이에는 서로 이해하는 것이 필요하다 Mutual understanding is necessary between husband and wife.
▶그의 작품은 당시에는 충분히 이해되지 않았다 His works were not fully appreciated at that time

이해관계 利害關係 interests
♦상충하는 이해관계의 조절 the adjustment of conflicting interests / 이해관계가 있다 have an interest [a concern] (in)
▶이 협회는 저 회사와 이해관계에 있다 This institution has an interest [a stake] in that firm.
■—자 those [the persons] concerned [interested]; the interested party

이해득실 利害得失 loss and gain; profit and loss; advantages and disadvantages; interest;〈장단〉merits and demerits
♦새 제도의 이해득실 the advantages and dis-

advantages [the pluses and minuses] of the new system / 이해득실을 논하다 discuss the advantages and disadvantages 《of》 / 이해득실을 따지다 calculate [reckon] the loss and gain 《of》; balance the profits and loss 《of》 / 이해득실을 재다 weigh losses against gains 《in doing *sth*》; weigh [compare] the advantages and disadvantages [merits and demerits] 《of》
▶ 모든 것은 각기 이해득실이 있다 Everything has its merits and demerits [faults].
▶ 이 방법의 이해득실을 설명해 주십시오 Would you explain the advantages and disadvantages [pros and cons] of this method?
▶ 그는 이해득실에 밝다 He knows where his interests lie.

이해력 理解力 the power to understand; the comprehensive faculty; understanding
♦ 이해력이 좋은 사람 a person quick to understand; a sensible person / 이해력이 모자라다 have a poor understanding / 이해력이 없다 lack understanding / 뛰어난 이해력이 있다 have an excellent understanding / 이해력을 기르다 cultivate the power of understanding
▶ 그는 고전에 대한 이해력이 모자란다 He lacks the ability to understand [appreciate] the classics.

이해심 理解心 understanding; consideration; sympathy ♦ 이해심이 있는 어머니 an understanding mother / 이해심이 없는 아내 an unsympathetic wife / 이해심이 부족하다 want [lack] sympathy [understanding] / 이해심이 있다 be considerate 《of other people's feeling》; be sympathetic 《about》 / 이해심이 없다 be inconsiderate 《of》
▶ 그녀는 남의 기분에 대한 이해심이 있다 She is considerate of other people's feelings.

이해타산 利害打算 〈계산〉 calculation [reckoning] of the loss and gain [the profits and losses]; 〈욕심〉 self-interest
♦ 이해타산을 떠나서 apart from the consideration of gain; unfettered by *one's* self-interest
▶ 그의 행위는 이해타산을 넘어선 것이었다 He did it from disinterested motives.

이행 移行 〈전환〉 changeover; 〈추이〉 a translation —**이행하다** change over [to]; move [proceed] 《to》; shift over 《to》 ♦ 평화산업으로 이행하다 switch over to peace industry
▶ 중국 경제는 급속하게 자본주의로 이행해 가고 있다 The economy of China is rapidly shifting over to capitalism.
■ ―기간 a transitional period ―조치 a transitional measure

이행 履行 performance; fulfillment
♦ 계약의 이행 fulfillment of a contract
—**이행하다** fulfill; carry out; perform; discharge; execute ♦ 약속을 이행하다 fulfill [carry out, keep] a promise / 채무를 이행하지 않다 default on debt payments
▶ 그는 자기의 직무를 이행하기 위해 사생활을 희생했다 He sacrificed his private life to perform his public duties.
▶ 그는 계약을 이행하려 하지 않았다 He didn't even try to carry out [fulfill] the contract.

■ ―자 a performer

이향 異鄕 a foreign country [land]; a strange land

이향 離鄕 leaving *one's* home town —**이향하다** depart [leave] *one's* native place; leave *one's* home town

이현령비현령 耳懸鈴鼻懸鈴 ▶ 그의 대답은 이현령비현령이었다 His answers were ones that could be interpreted in various ways. ⇌ He made equivocal answers.

이형배우자 異形配偶者 〔生〕 heterogamate

이형분열 異型分裂 〔生〕 heterotype division

이호 二號 〈둘째〉 No. 2; number two
▶ 그 잡지의 2호는 다음달 초에 발행된다 The second issue of the magazine will be published early next month.

이혼 離婚 《a》 divorce; divorcement
♦ 이혼을 요구하다 seek [claim] a divorce
▶ 이혼이 늘고 있다 Divorce is on the increase.
▶ 그들의 결혼생활은 결국 이혼으로 끝났다 Their marriage ended in divorce.
—**이혼하다** divorce 《*one's* husband》; get a divorce 《from》; be [get] divorced 《from》
▶ 그는 아내와 이혼하고 자신의 비서와 결혼했다 He divorced his wife and married his secretary.
▶ 양친이 이혼했을 때 나는 다섯 살이었다 When my parents divorced, I was five years old.
▶ 그는 최근에 아내와 이혼한 것 같다 He seems to have divorced his wife recently.
■ 법정— a judicial divorce 합의[협의]— a divorce by consent [agreement] ■ ―수당 an alimony ―수속 divorce procedure [formalities] ―율 a divorce rate ―자 a divorcee; a divorced person

이혼소송 離婚訴訟 a divorce suit; a suit for divorce; divorce proceedings ♦ 이혼소송을 제기하다 sue [bring a suit] for a divorce; file a suit [petition] for divorce 《against》; start divorce proceedings 《against》

이혼신고 離婚申告 a report [notice] of divorce ♦ 이혼신고를 하다[내다] notify *one's* divorce; register a divorce; send in a divorce notice

이화명충 二化螟蟲 a rice(-stem) borer; a grass webworm

이화수정 異花受精 〔植〕 cross-fertilization; allogamy —**이화수정하다** cross-fertilize
♦ 이화수정시키다 cross-fertilize

이화작용 異化作用 〔生・生理〕 dissimilation; catabolism

이화학 理化學 physics and chemistry; physicochemistry ♦ 이화학의 physicochemical
■ ―교실 a science room; 〈계단식〉 a science theater ―기기(機器) physical and chemical appliances [apparatus] ―연구소 an institute of physical and chemical research; a physicochemical research institute

이환 罹患 affection
■ ―율 〔醫〕 the morbidity rate; morbidity ―자 a sufferer 《from cholera》; a case 《of influenza》; a victim 《of a disease》

이회 二回 twice; two times
♦ 1일 2회 twice a day / 월 2회 twice a month;

이후 以後 after (this); from now on; hereafter; henceforth
◆그 이후의 사건 later [subsequent] events / 4월 8일 이후 on and after April 8; from April 8 on / 그 이후 오늘까지 from that time down to this day / 오후 11시 이후에는 집에 있다 stay at home after 11 p.m. [from 11 p.m. on] / 오늘 이후 술을 금하다 give up drinking from this day on
▶병은 치료됐지만 이후 좀더 조심해 주십시오 You recovered this time, but be more careful in the future [from now on].
▶그는 5월 3일 이후 소식이 없다 He has not been heard of since May 3.
▶이후 좀더 주의하겠습니다 I'll be more careful from now on.
▶그는 1990년 이후 내내 뉴욕에 살고 있다 He has lived in New York since 1990.
▶3월 동안은 바쁘니까 4월 이후에 만났으면 합니다 I'll be busy during March, so let's meet in April or later.

익곡 溺谷 〔地〕 a drowned valley; 〈리아스식〉 a ria

익년 翌年 the next [following, ensuing] year; the year after
▶그녀는 귀국한 익년에 결혼했다 She got married the year after she returned home.

익다¹ 1 〈열매·과일이〉 ripen; become [get] ripe (▶get은 구어적임); mellow; mature; come to maturity
◆익은 ripe; mature; mellow / 너무 익은 overripe / 익지 않은 unripe; green 《fruits》
▶토마토는 빨갛게 익을 때까지 따서는 안된다 Don't pick the tomatoes until they are red and ripe [〈아직 덜 익었을 때〉 while they are still green].
▶벼는 익을수록 고개를 숙인다 (속담) The more noble the more humble.
2 〈기운(機運)이〉 ripen; mature; be ripe for 《action》; 〈음모 등이〉 come to a head
▶바야흐로 개혁의 때가 익었다 The time is ripe for initiating (some) reforms.
▶시운이 익을 때까지 기다려라 Wait till the time is ripe.
▶기회가 익었다 The opportunity has matured [ripened].
3 〈날것이〉 boil; be boiled; be done; cook; be cooked
◆너무 익다 be overdone; be cooked too much / 잘 익은 well-done[-cooked]
▶그 고기는 잘 익어서 연하다 The meat is cooked well [nicely] and tender.
▶이 콩은 잘 익는다 These beans cook quickly.
▶잘 익었니? Is it cooked well? ⇒ Is it well done?
4 〈술·장 등이〉 ferment; mature; be [get] matured; become seasoned
◆익은 술 mature [ripe] wine
▶김치가 잘 익었다 The *kimchi* has pickled up flavor. ⇒ The *kimchi* has become seasoned.
5 〈살갗이〉 turn red; redden; color
◆〈열 등으로〉 발갛게 익은 얼굴 a glowing face 《with heat》

익다² 1 〈서투르지 않다〉 skilled; skillful; trained; experienced; practiced; expert
◆익지 않은 unskilled; inexperienced; green / 익은 솜씨로 with practiced [clever] hands; skillfully
▶난 이런 종류의 장사에는 익지 않다 I am not experienced [am inexperienced] in this kind of business. ⇒ 〈별로 경험이 없다〉 I don't have much experience in this kind of business.
▶그는 익은[익지 않은] 솜씨로 숟가락을 사용했다 He used spoon with a practiced hand [〈어색하게〉 awkwardly].
2 〈설지 않다〉 familiar; accustomed; 〈서술적〉 get [be] used 《to》; grow [become] accustomed to; grow familiar 《with》; become experienced in
◆귀에 익은[익지 않은] 목소리 a familiar [strange] voice / 익지 않은 new; unfamiliar; unaccustomed; strange / 고난에 익다 be inured to hardships / 눈[귀]에 익다 get used to seeing [hearing]; be accustomed to see [hear]
▶이런 광경은 어렸을 때부터 눈에 익어 있다 I have been used [been accustomed] to seeing such scenery since I was a child.
▶그의 강의는 귀에 익을 때까지는 이해하기 어렵다 His lectures are hard to understand before you get used to them.

익룡 翼龍 〔古生〕 a pterosaur

익명 匿名 〈본인을 숨김〉 anonymity; 〈가명〉 a pseudonym; a cryptonym; an anonym
◆익명의 기부인 a donor whose name was withheld / 익명의 독지가 an anonymous benefactor / 익명의 작가 an anonymous author [writer] / 익명의 투서[무고] an anonymous letter [contribution] / 익명의 anonymous; innominate; 《a prince》 incognito / 익명으로 anonymously; incognito
▶익명의 투서를 받았다 I received an anonymous [a nameless] letter.
▶그는 익명으로 어떤 기사를 썼다 He wrote an article anonymously. ⇒ 〈익명의 조건으로〉 He wrote article on condition of anonymity.
━━광고 a blind advertisement ━━비평 pseudonymous criticism ━━사원 a silent [dormant] partner; 《英》 a sleeping partner ━━자 〈남자〉 an incognito 《*pl.* ~s》; 〈여자〉 an incognita; an anonym ━━조합 a dormant partnership ━━투표 a secret ballot

익모초 益母草 〔植〕 a motherwort

익사 溺死 (death from [by]) drowning
◆익사 직전의 어린이를 구하다 save a child from drowning / 익사를 모면하다 escape a watery grave
━━하다 be [get] drowned (to death); drown; 〈스스로〉 drown *oneself*

〔解說〕 영어의 ***be drowned, drown*** 「익사하다」에는 확실히 「죽다」의 뜻이 있으므로 「그는 익사할 뻔했으나 다행히 살았다」고 할때 He drowned, but was happily saved.라고 할 수 없고, 살아난 경우에는 almost, nearly를

붙여야 한다. He nearly [almost] drowned, but... 또는 He was drowning, but...이라고 해야 한다.

▶그는 강에서 익사했다 He drowned [(英) was drowned] in the river. (▶drowned [was drowned] to death라고 하지는 않음)
▶그는 아이가 익사하는 것을 살렸다 He saved [rescued] the child from drowning.
▶나는 하마터면 강에서 익사할 뻔했다 I was nearly drowned in the river.
■—자 a drowned person [body]: 올 여름에는 익사자가 많다 There are a number of deaths from drowning this summer. —체 a drowned body; the body of a drowned person: 실종자는 해안에서 익사체로 발견되었다 The missing person was found drowned on the beach.

익살 comicality; drollery; waggery; clownery; jocularity; 〈농담〉 a joke; a jest; (a) pleasantry; humor; 〈기지〉 a witticism; 〈신소리〉 a pun
♦상스러운 익살 a vulgar joke; jesting; a buffoonery; tomfoolery; burlesque / 세련된 익살 a refined witticism / 익살을 이해하다[못하다] have a (fine) [no] sense of humor
▶그는 익살이 통하지 않는 사람이다 He can't take a joke.
—**익살스럽다[맞다]** comic(al); funny; humorous; waggish; jocular; jocose; jesting; clownish; antic; droll; 〈천하게〉 burlesque; 〈짓궂게〉 facetious
♦익살맞은 사람 a funny person; a figure of fun / 얼굴이 익살스러운 사람 a funny-looking man / 익살스러운 이야기 a funny story; a laughter-provoking story / 익살 떨다 play droll tricks
▶그는 익살맞은 말을 해 우리를 웃겼다 He kept us laughing with his funny remarks.
▶그의 말에는 익살스러운 데가 있다 His talk is tinged with humor.
■—꾼 a joker; a jester; a jokester; a buffoon; a clown; a harlequin; a comic; a comedian; a humorist; a droll; a wag; a funny man

익살부리다 〈일부러 익살스런 태도를 보이다〉 play the fool [clown]; play droll tricks; play antics [the joker]; clown; 〈말로〉 speak humorously; say funny things; crack [make] jokes; joke; jest
♦익살부린 연기 a clownish [funny] performance / 어설프게 익살부리다 tell [make, (口) crack] a cheap [bad, poor] joke (▶tell 대신 say를 쓰는 것은 잘못임); make a poor [bad] pun

익숙하다 1 〈친숙하다〉 familiar; accustomed; well acqnainted (with) experienced; 〈서술적〉 be at home in [on]; be well informed of (a fact)
♦익숙한 길 the familiar road [path, trail] / 익숙하지 않은 일 unaccustomed work / 익숙해지다 get used [accustomed] (to) (▶앞의 것이 구어적임); become accustomed (to); grow familiar (with); become inured (to hardships); become habituated (to dangers)
▶그는 곧 새로운 환경에 익숙해졌다 He soon got used to new surroundings. ⇌ He soon acquainted himself to new surroundings.
▶드디어 나는 이 타자기를 사용하는 데 익숙해졌다 I have at last got accustomed to using this typewriter.
▶나는 이런 일에는 익숙하지 못합니다 I am unaccustomed [strange, raw] to this kind of business.
▶나는 서울의 만원 버스에 익숙해질 수가 없다 I can't accustom myself to the crowded bus of Seoul.
▶나는 그 일[사정]에 대해서는 익숙해 있다 I am well informed about the matter [on the situation]
▶그녀는 영어로 말하는 데 익숙해 있다 She is quite experienced in speaking English.
2 〈능숙하다〉 skilled; skillful; trained; experienced; practiced; expert
♦익숙한 사람 a man of experience; an expert; a practiced [skilled] hand; an old hand (at); a (past) master / 익숙한 솜씨로 skillfully; with practiced [clever] hands / 익숙해지다 become skillful [dexterous, expert] (in [at] the trade); get skilled (in riding); acquire skill
▶초심자를 위한 익숙한 선생님을 원한다 We want an experieced teacher for the beginners.
▶그는 교정에 익숙하다 He is an old hand at [in] proofreading. ⇌ He is a veteran proofreader.
▶나는 차 운전에는 익숙하지 않다 I don't have much experience (at) driving.
▶우리는 오랫동안 익숙한 사이다 We've been close friends [(口) near pals] for years.

익숙히 with skill; skillfully; adroitly; expertly; with practiced [sure, clever] hands; like an old hand [a veteran]
♦프랑스어를 익숙히 구사하다 have a good command of French
▶그는 아주 익숙히 젓가락질을 한다 He uses chopsticks very skillfully. ⇌ He has great skill with chopsticks.

익애 溺愛 dotage; blind love
—**익애하다** show too much fondness to... (▶다소 설명적 표현); dote on [upon]; love sb passionately; lavish one's love upon (a child)
♦손자를 익애하다 dote on one's grandson; love one's grandson blindly

익월 翌月 the next [following] month
익일 翌日 the next [following] day; the day after
▶대학을 졸업한 익일 그는 고향을 떠났다 He left home the day after he graduated from college.

익조 益鳥 a useful [beneficial] bird
익충 益蟲 a useful [beneficial] insect
익히 with skill ⇨ 익숙히
♦익히 알다 know well; be well informed of (a fact); be familiar [well acquainted] with (a matter); be at home in [on] (things Chinese)
▶그 공원은 내가 익히 알고 있는 곳이다 The park is quite familiar to me. ⇌ I know the park very well. ⇌ I've often been to the park.
익히다[1] 1 〈열매 등을〉 make ripe; ripen; mel-

low; mature
▶ 햇볕이 과일을 익힌다 The sun ripens fruit.
2 〈날것을〉 boil; cook
▶ 고기를 잘 익힌다 get the meat well-done
▶ 어머니는 부엌에서 감자를 익히고 있다 Mom is boiling [cooking] potatoes in the kitchen.
3 〈술·장 등을〉 mature; ferment; brew; age
◆술을 익히다 brew (rice) wine / 김치를 익히다 get *kimchi* seasoned [flavored]
4 〈살갗을〉 redden; color
5 〈익숙해지다〉 make *oneself* familiar with; familiarize *oneself* with; habituate *oneself* to; inure *oneself* to; acclimate *oneself* to; accustom *oneself* to; acquaint *oneself* with; get *sb* accustomed to; accustom *sb* to; 〈숙련하다〉 develop [gain] skill in; 〈습득하다〉 learn; practice; acquire 《French》
◆고된 일(을 하는 데)에 몸을 익히다 habituate *oneself* to (doing) hard work / 열대의 기후를 익히다 get acclimatized to the tropical climate / 음악을 익히다 practice music; take [have] lessons in music; study music / 장사를 익히다 train *sb* to a trade / 자동차 운전을 익히다 learn how to drive a motorcar / 몸을 추위[생활]에 견딜 수 있도록 익히다 inure *oneself* to (bear) the cold [life] / 몸을 새로운 환경에 익히다 acclimate [acclimatize] *oneself* to the new environment / 노동을 익히다 accustom *sb* to labor; get *sb* accustomed [used] to labor
▶ 나는 미국 생활을 익히는 데 꼬박 1년이 걸렸다 It took me a whole year to adjust myself to the American life-style.
▶ 너는 영어 듣기를 더 익힐 필요가 있다 You need more practice (in) listening to English.
▶ 살아나가려면 기술을 익혀 두어야 한다 You ought to acquire some art [skill] useful in making a living.
인 仁 1 〈유교의〉 perfect virtue; 〈인애(仁愛)〉 benevolence; humanity; 〈박애〉 philanthropy; charity
◆자신을 희생하여 인도(人道)의 극치를 성취하다 sacrifice *oneself* for the good of others
2 〔植〕 〈씨〉 a stone; a kernel; 〈핵〉 a core; nucleolus
인 印 a seal ⇨ 도장
인 燐 〔化〕 phosphorus; phosphor
◆인의 phosphorous (3가의); phosphoric (5가의); (俗) phossy / 인과 화합한 phosphuret(t)ed / 인과 화합시키다[을 가하다] phosphorate
■ —중독 phosphorism
-인 -人 a man
◆한국인 a Korean / 체육인 an athlete / 경제인 a financier
인가 人家 house; a human habitation; a dwelling(-house)
◆인가가 드문 sparsely-populated 《area》; thinly-settled / 인가가 없는 deserted; desolate; uninhabited / 인가에서 동떨어져 far from human habitation / 인가가 많다 be crowded with houses; be thickly inhabited; be densely populated
▶ 이 주변은 인가가 밀집해 있다[드문드문하다] The area around here is crowded [dotted] with houses. ⇌ This area is densely [sparsely] populated.
인가 認可 approval; authorization; license; permission; (official) sanction
◆교육부 인가의 authorized by the Ministry of Education / 인가를 받고 under license / 인가를 받다 obtain [secure, get] sanction [authorization] 《from》; obtain a license [permit] 《from》; be authorized [sanctioned] 《by》 / 당국의 인가를 신청하다 apply for the approval of the authorities
▶ 이 도로는 경찰의 인가를 받은 차 외는 통행할 수 없다 No vehicle is [vehicles are] allowed on this road without police permission.
—인가하다 approve; authorize; permit; recognize; give permission [license, sanction] (to); sanction; (美) approbate
◆의사의 개업을 인가하다 license *sb* to practice as a doctor
▶ 시장이 빌딩 건축을 인가했다 The construction of the building was authorized by the mayor. ⇌ The mayor gave sanction to the construction of the building.
▶ 새 병원 건립을 보건복지부가 인가했다 The construction of the new hospital was authorized by the Ministry of Health and Welfare.
▶ 시는 그 주택계획을 인가했다 The city authorized the housing project.
■ —영업 a licensed business —증 a permit; a license; a certificate; a warrant; 〈법인 단체 설립의〉 a charter —학교 an authorized school; a school approved by the authorities
인가 隣家 〈이웃집〉 a neighbor's house; the house next door; 〈이웃집 사람〉 next-door neighbor
인각 印刻 engraving **—인각하다** engrave [cut] a seal
인간 人間 a human being; a human; (a) man (*pl*. men); a mortal; 〈인물〉 character; 〈인류〉 mankind

> 〔解說〕 (1) ***a human being, a human***은 동물 등과 대비해서 인간을 가리키나 a human being이 일반적이다. man은 성별에 관계없이 일반적으로 사람을 가리키며 보통 무관사다.
> (2) man은 또 mankind의 뜻으로 인류 전체를 말하며 보통 단수 취급하여 대명사는 it으로 받는다. 단, 남성 중심으로 되는 것을 피하여 man 대신에 ***human beings, people***을 mankind 대신에 ***the human race*** (단수취급)를 쓰기도 한다.

◆보통의 인간 an ordinary person; the common run of men [mortals] / 인간으로서의 약점 human weaknesses; a human weak point / 인간다운 manly; manlike / 인간다운 행동을 하다 behave like a human being / 인간다운 생활을 하다 live a decent life; lead a life worthy of man
▶ 그는 원만한 인간이다 He is a man of rounded [mellow] character.
▶ 나는 그런 일을 할 수 없는 인간이다 I am not born [given] that way.
〈인간의〉 인간의 존엄성 human [man's] dig-

nity / 인간의 탈을 쓴 악마 a demon in human shape [form] / 인간의 human; mortal
▶ 인간의 손으로는 이 이상 잘 할 수 없다 No man living could do better.
▶ 그렇게 하는 것이 인간의 의무다 It's a man's duty to do that. (▶부정관사에 주의)
〈인간은[이]〉그것은 인간이 할 수 있는 일이 아니다 It is humanly impossible. ⇌ It is beyond human power.
▶ 인간은 누구나 자유롭게 살 권리가 있다 All human beings have [All men have, Everyone has] a right to live free.
▶ 인간은 환경에 적응해 왔다 Mankind [The human race] has been adjusting itself to its surroundings.
▶ 인간은 만물의 영장이다 Man is the lord of creation.
▶ 인간은 죽음을 면치 못한다 **(속담)** Man is mortal.
■ —개조 reform in humanity —계 the world (of mortals); the terrestrial world —고(苦) (common) sufferings of men; human sufferings; bitterness of life —고락 the delights [joys] and sorrows of life; the sweets and bitters of life —공학 human engineering; ergonomics —관계 〈사회 등에서의〉 human relations (略 HR) —문화재 human cultural assets [properties] —사회 human society; the community of men —생태학 human ecology —자원 human resource —애 human love; 〈인정〉 humanity; 〈인류애〉 philanthropy —존중 respecting man's life and dignity —탐구 pursuit [the study] of man —폭탄[어뢰] a human bomb [torpedo] —형성 character building

인간미 人間味 (touches of) humanity; a human touch; humaneness
♦ 인간미가 있는 사람 a humane [a warm-hearted] person (▶humane은 「자비롭고 동정심이 있는」의 뜻) / 인간미가 넘치는[없는] 이야기 a story with a lot of [with no] heart / 인간미가 넘치는 책 a book full of human touches / 인간미가 있는 humane; 〈마음이 따뜻한〉 warm-hearted / 인간미가 없는 lack the touch of humanity; be cold-hearted

인간성 人間性 〈인간의 본성〉 human nature; 〈인간으로서의 덕성〉 humanity (▶「동물성」「신성(神性)」에 대비하여 씀.「인간성에 반하다」는 be against humanity)
♦ 인간성을 말살하다 dehumanize; divest sb of human qualities

인간혐오 人間嫌惡 misanthropy
■ —자 a misanthrope; a misanthropist; a man-hater: 그는 인간 혐오자다 He doesn't like people. ⇌ He is a misanthrope.

인감 印鑑 〈도장〉 one's seal [signet]; 〈인발〉 a seal impression (▶영미(英美)에서는 공문서 등 이외에는 보통 서명만 하며, 인감은 없음)
■ —도장 one's registered [legal] seal: 이 서류에는 인감 도장을 찍어야 합니다 You must stamp these papers with your registered seal.
—등록[신고] the registration of a seal impression —증명서 a certificate of seal impression: 나는 인감 증명서를 받았다 I had a certificate of my seal impression issued.

인건비 人件費 personnel expenses [expenditures]; labor costs (▶보통 복수형으로 제조업 등의 인건비를 나타내는 일반적인 표현)
♦ 높은 인건비 high personnel expenses
▶ 인건비가 높아지고 있다 Personnel expenses [expenditures] are going up.
▶ 이렇게 인건비가 올라서는 회사를 운영해 가는 것도 큰 일이다 It's difficult to get the company going with personnel expenses running as high as this.

인걸 人傑 a remarkable [great, prominent] man [character]; an extraordinary man; a hero

인격 人格 〈사람의 품격〉 character; 〈개성·인간성〉 personality (▶전자는 도덕적인 면에서의 개인의 성질, 후자는 대인관계에서의 개인의 내면적인 특성을 말함); individuality
♦ 인격적 감화 moral influence / 인격을 갖춘 사람 a man of character / 인격이 높다 have a great personality / 인격을 함양하다 build up one's character / 인격을 존중[무시]하다 respect [ignore] sb's personality
▶ 그의 인격은 환경에 의해 형성된 것이다 His character was formed by his environment.
▶ 그는 인격에 조금 문제가 있다 There are a few problems about his personality.
▶ 어린이의 인격을 무시해서는 안된다 We shouldn't disregard a child's personality [the personality of a child].
■ —교육 character building —권 personal rights —도야 formation [cultivation] of character; character building —문제 a question touching one's honor —소실[상실] 〔哲〕 depersonalization —주의 〔論·哲〕 personalism —형성 character shaping [molding]

인격자 人格者 a man [person] of character; 〔法〕 a person
♦ 훌륭한 인격자 a person of noble character
▶ 그는 상당한 인격자다 He is a man of very good character. (▶character 대신에 personality를 쓰는 것은 잘못임)

인격화 人格化 impersonation; personification
—인격화하다 impersonate; personify

인견 人絹 〈인조견〉 artificial [imitation] silk; rayon ■ —사 rayon yarn

인견 引見 an interview; an audience
▶ 여왕은 대사를 인견했다 The queen received the ambassador in audience. ⇌ The queen granted an interview [audience] to the ambassador.

인경 〈통행금지를 알려 주던 큰 종〉 a (large) curfew bell; a curfew ♦ 인경을 치다 toll the curfew bell

인경 隣境 〈인접한 땅의 경계〉 an adjacent region; a neighbo(u)ring land

인경 鱗莖 〔植〕〈비늘줄기〉 a scaly bulb

인계 引繼 〈직무 등의〉 take-over 《another's duties》; transfer of business one's successor; 〈계승〉 succession 《to》; handing [turning] over 《one's duties》
▶ 새 경영진은 지장없이 인계를 했다 The new management executed a smooth take-over
—인계하다 〈직무를〉 take over 《another's

duties); hand [turn] over (one's duties) to (another); transfer (one's business) to (another); 〈계승하다〉 succeed (to)
♦ (이어달리기에서) 배턴을 인계하다 pass [hand over] the baton to 《the next runner》 / 사무를 인계받다 take over business [the charge of an office] 《from another》
▶ 나는 그에게서 일을 인계받았다 I took over the business from him.
▶ 나는 재산을 인계받을 의사가 전혀 없다 I have no intention of succeeding the property at all.
▶ 내 일을 누구에게 인계해 줄까? To whom shall I hand over my business?

인공 人工 human work [labor]; 〈기교〉 art; human skill; artificiality
♦ 자연과 인공의 조화 the harmony between nature and art (▶between 대신에 of를 쓰는 것은 잘못임) / 인공의 artificial; man-made [-created]; unnatural / 인공을 가하다 work upon [apply work to] 《natural scenery》; touch up sth by human skill
▶ 그 호수는 자연적으로 만들어진 것이 아니고 인공으로 만들어진 것이다 The lake is made not by nature but by art.
▶ 자연계에는 인공으로 모방할 수 없는 것이 많다 There are many things in nature which defy human ingenuity to imitate them.

[解説] 「인공의」라는 형용사로는 *man-made*가 일반적이지만 man이 남성을 연상시키므로 최근엔 *artificial* (인위적인), *handmade* (손으로 만든), *mechanical* (기계로 움직이는), *machine-made* (기계로 만든), *manufactured* (대량 생산된) 등을 많이 쓴다.

■─감미료 an artificial sweetener ─강우〈비〉 artificial rainfall ─미 man-created beauty; the beauty of art ─배양 artificial culture ─부화(법) 〔動〕 artificial incubation ─수분 〔植〕 artificial pollination ─수태(법) 〔醫·動〕 artificial conception ─심장 mechanical heart ─심폐 artificial heart-lung ─어초 artificial reef ─언어 〔電算〕 artificial language ─임신중절 artificial termination of pregnancy ─잔디 artificial grass [turf] ─접종 〔獸醫〕 artificial infection ─지능 artificial intelligence ─진주 an artificial [imitation] pearl ─태양광선 artificial sunlight ─피부 artificial skin ─피임(법) artificial contraception ─항 an artificial harbor ─혜성 an artificial comet ─호 artificial lake ─호흡 artificial respiration

인공두뇌 人工頭腦 a mechanical [electronic] brain ■─학 cybernetics: 인공두뇌학의 cybernetic ─학자 a cyberneticist

인공수정 人工受精 〈동물의〉 artificial fertilization ■─아(兒) a test-tube baby

인공영양 人工營養 〈환자의〉 artificial nourishment; 〈유아의〉 artificial feeding; bottle-feeding; artificial alimentation ■─아 a bottle-fed baby

인공위성 人工衛星 an artificial [a man-made] satellite; an earth satellite
♦ 인공위성을 발사하다 launch [blast off, shoot up] an earth satellite
▶ 그들은 인공위성을 궤도에 올려놓는 데 성공했다 They succeeded in putting an artificial satellite in orbit.
■─기상관측─ a weather satellite

인공적 人工的 artificial; unnatural; man-made [-created]
♦ 인공적으로 artificially; by art
▶ 대부분의 공업용 다이아몬드는 인공적으로 만들어지고 있다 Most industrial diamonds are artificially made.

인공호흡 人工呼吸 artificial breathing [respiration]
♦ 인공호흡을 하다 practice [try, use] artificial respiration 《on sb》; give sb artificial respiration
■─기(器) an artificial respiratory machine [apparatus]; a pulmotor

인과 因果 cause and effect; 〔佛敎〕 karma; a retribution
♦ 피할 수 없는 인과 an inevitable retribution
▶ 그에게 인과로 설득하여 시도를 단념하게 했다 I persuaded him to give up his attempt, telling him to reconcile himself to his lot.
▶ 무슨 인과로 그런 일을 해야하는가? What irony of fate makes me do such a thing?
■─관계 the relation of [between] cause and effect; dependence of effect on cause; causal relation [dependence, chain]; causation; causality ─론[설] causationism ─율 the causality; the law of causality ─응보 a reward in accordance with a deed; the law of cause and effect; retribution; retributive justice in the universe

인광 燐光 〔物〕 a phosphorescence ♦ 인광을 발하다 phosphoresce; emit phosphorescence
▶ 그 심해어는 인광을 발하고 있다 The deep-sea fish emitted [gave out] phosphorescence.
■─안료 phosphorescent pigment ─체 a phosphorescent substance

인광 燐鑛 rock [mineral] phosphate

인구 人口 population (▶population은 총인구 수이며 보통 단수형, 두 지역 이상의 총인구의 누계인 경우만 복수형으로 함. 구체적으로 한 지역의 인구에서는 a population); the number of the inhabitants
〈인구의〉 인구의 도시 유입 the drift of population to cities; an influx of people into cities / 인구의 증가[감소] an increase [a decrease] in population
▶ 세계 인구의 절반 이상이 북반구에 살고 있다 More than half of the world's population live(s) in the Northern hemisphere.
〈인구가[는]〉 인구가 300만인 대도시 a big city of three million inhabitants [people] (▶이 경우 population을 쓰는 일은 잘못) / 인구가 조밀[희박]하다 be densely [sparsely] populated; be thickly [thinly] peopled / 인구가 늘다[줄다] increase [decrease] in population
▶ 그 도시는 인구가 많다[적다] The city has a large [a small] population. (▶many [a few] population이라고는 하지 않음)
▶ 한국의 인구는 얼마나 됩니까? What [How

large] is the population of Korea? (▶How many population이라고는 하지 않음)
▶ 농업 인구는 매년 줄고 있다 The farm(ing) population is decreasing(↔ increasing, growing) each year.
▶ 이 도시의 인구는 5만이다 This city has a population of 50,000.
■과잉— surplus [excess, overflowing] population; overpopulation 낚시[골프]— the angling [golf-playing] population《of Korea》유령— a "ghost" [bogus, spurious] population 총— the total population 최적(最適)— optimum population ■—계획 population planning —과밀 overpopulation —과소 underpopulation —과잉 overpopulation —동태[정태] 통계 dynamic [static] statistics of population —문제 a population problem —밀도 population density: 인구 밀도가 높은 도시 a densely [a thickly] populated city —분포 population distribution —이동 population migration —정책 a population policy —조사 a census: 인구 조사를 하다 take a census (of the population) —증가율 a rate of population increase —통계 vital [population] statistics —폭발 (a) population explosion —학 demography

인국 隣國 a neighboring [an adjacent] country [state]
▶ 한국과 중국은 서로 인국이다 China and Korea are neighbors (to each other).

인권 人權 human [people's] rights; personal rights; the rights of man; (美)〈시민권〉civil right
◆인권을 박탈하다 proscribe《a man》/ 인권을 유린하다 trample upon [infringe upon, commit an outrage on] personal [human] rights / 인권을 존중[옹호]하다 respect [uphold] human rights
▶ 그가 한 짓은 인권 유린[침해]이다 What he did is an outrage against [a violation of an infringement on] human rights.
■기본적— the fundamental human rights —문제 a question of personal rights —선언 the Declaration of Human Rights —유린[침해] a violation of human rights; civil rights violation —주간 Human Rights Week —헌장 the Civil Liberties Charter

인권옹호 人權擁護 the protection [defending] human rights [civil liberty]
■—운동 a human [civil] rights movement —위원 a Commissioner for the Protection of Fundamental Human Rights —협회 the Civil Liberty Association —활동 civil liberty activities

인근 隣近 the neighborhood; the vicinity
◆인근의 neighboring; nearby《hospital》/ 인근 주민들 neighbors / 이 인근에 in this neighborhood; about [around, near] here
▶ 이 사건은 인근에서 모르는 사람이 없다 Everybody in the neighborhood knows about this accident.
▶ 이 인근 사람들이 모두 그곳에 있었다 The whole neighborhood was there.

인금 人— one's personality

인기 人氣 popularity; popular favor; public interest
◆일시적[덧없는] 인기 a passing [an ephemeral] popularity / 폭발적 인기 tremendous popularity / 세계적인 인기 가수 a singer of international appeal / 흘러간 인기 가요 a once-popular song dear to the people's hearts / 인기를 얻다 become popular《among, with》; get into public favor; win [attain, gain] popularity / 인기가 있다[좋다] be popular《with, among》; enjoy popularity; be in (good) favor《with》; be a favorite《with》/ (흥행 등이) 인기를 끌다 be good box office; make a stir / 인기를 높이다[올리다] heighten [enhance] one's popularity / 대중의 인기를 누리다 command [win (its) way to] general popularity / 인기를 유지하다 maintain one's popularity / 인기를 잃다 fall [come] into disfavor《with, among》; lose one's popularity; become unpopular《with, among》
▶ 김교수는 학생에게 인기가 있다 Professor Kim is very popular with [among] his student. (▶with는 「…에게」, among은 「…(많은 사람) 중에서」라는 뜻. with가 구어적임)
▶ 이 쇼는 인기를 얻을 것이다 This will be a good box-office show.
▶ 그 책은 인기를 모았다 (口) The book took well.
▶ 그녀는 주연보다 더 인기를 끌었다 She stole the show.
▶ 그 전학생은 학급 여학생의 인기를 독차지했다 (주목의 대상이 되었다) The transfer student became the focus of attention of all the girl students in the class.
■—경쟁 a popularity contest —배우 a popular actor [actress]; a screen [stage] idol; a film [stage] favorite; a star —선수 a star [popular] player —순위표 a popularity list —연기자 a show stopper —연예인 some popular entertainers and singers —영화배우 a screen [film, movie] star —작가 a popular writer; a literary favorite [star, luminary] —주(株) an active share [(美) stock]; a market leader; 〈우량주〉blue chips —직업 an occupation largely dependent on public favor —품목 a popular item [article]; a drawing card —프로그램 a hit program

인기척 人— 《show》an indication [a sign] of sb being around
◆인기척이 없는 거리 a deserted [an empty] street / 인기척이 없다 show no signs of people being around; there is no sign of life
▶ 그 집에는 인기척이 없었다 There was [I could see] no sign of anyone at the house. ⇌ The house seemed to be deserted [〈사람이 살고 있지 않은〉uninhabited].
▶ 복도에 인기척이 났다 I felt [sensed] someone approaching along the hallway.

인기투표 人氣投票 a popularity vote [poll]
◆인기투표를 하다 take a poll《on the most popular actor》

인내 忍耐 〈적극적인 노력〉perseverance; 〈참을성〉patience; 〈감내〉forbearance; 〈특히 오래 참음〉endurance; long suffering; 〈불굴〉

인대

fortitude; 〈극기〉 stoicism

♦인내심이 강한 persevering; patient; stoical / 인내력이 없는 lacking in perseverance; impatient

▶ 나도 마침내 인내의 한계에 이르렀다 My patience is worn out at last.

▶ 그와의 교섭에는 많은 인내가 필요하다 It requires a considerable amount of perseverance to deal with him.

—**인내하다** persever (in); be patient (with); have patience (with); endure; bear; stand; put up with 《an insult》; forbear

인대 靱帶 〔解〕 a ligament; a cord ♦인대의 ligamental

인더스강 —江 〈인도 북부의 강〉 the Indus (River)

인더스문명 —文明 the Indus (valley) civilization

인덕 人德 〈타고난〉 *one's* natural [inborn] virtue; 〈인복〉 blessedness with friendly people

▶ 그것은 그의 인덕 덕분이다 That depends on his natural virtue [personal charm].

-인데 1 〈연결어미〉 and; so; but; however; whereas; when

▶ 고된 일인데 나는 즐겁게 하고 있다 It is hard work, but [(and) yet] I enjoy it.

▶ 무일푼인데 내가 어떻게 집을 삽니까? How can I buy the house when I have no money?
2 〈종결어미〉 ▶ 그 여자 정말 미인인데 She's good-looking [pretty], isn't she?

▶ 정말 절경인데 What a grand view [sight]!

인덱스 〈색인〉 an index (*pl*. ~es, indices); 〈지수〉 an index 《number》

▶ 책에 인덱스를 달았다 I indexed a book. ⇌ I provided a book with an index.

▶ 그녀는 ABC 순으로 인덱스를 만들었다 She compiled an alphabetical index.

■—**카드** 〈색인용·지수용 카드〉 an index card

인도 人道 1 〈인간으로서의 마땅한 도리〉 humanity; 〈도의〉 morality

♦인도를 무시하다 ignore humanity; disregard the laws of humanity / 인도에 어긋나다 be contrary to (the laws of) humanity; be inhumane; be against humanity

▶ 그들의 행위는 인도에 어긋나는 것이다 Their actions are against humanity.

2 〈보도〉 (英) a (side) pavement; a footway; 〈비포장의〉 a footpath; (美) a sidewalk; 〈포장한〉 a foot pavement

■—**교(橋)** a footbridge; a pedestrian bridge —**문제** a question touching [affecting] humanity

인도 引渡 〈물품의〉 delivery; 〈부동산 등의〉 transfer; handing [turning] over; 〈범죄자 등의〉 surrender; 〈해외 도피자의〉 extradition

▶ 그들은 물품의 인도를 거절했다 They refused delivery of goods.

▶ 경찰은 도주한 살인 용의자의 인도를 요구했다 The police demanded the handing over [transference] of the fleeting murder suspect.

—**인도하다** deliver; transfer; hand [turn, make] over; give away; 〈권리 등을〉 deliver up; resign; 〈포로·범인을〉 hand over; surrender; 〈경찰 등에〉 give 《a thief》 in charge; 〈국제간의 지명 수배자를〉 extradite

♦인도할 수 있는 deliverable / 화물을 인도하다 deliver goods; make [effect] delivery of goods 《to》/ 재산을 인도하다 transfer [make over] *one's* property / 시체를 가족에게 인도하다 hand over *sb's* body to (his) family

▶ 그 남자는 경찰에 인도되었다 The man was handed [turned] over to the police.

■**공장—** ex works [factory, mill] **대금 상환—** cash [collect] on delivery (略 C.O.D.) **도착항—** free port of destination **보세창고—** ex bond; delivery in bond **본선—** free on board (略 FOB, f.o.b.) **부두—** ex wharf [quay] **선측—** free alongside ship (略 F.A.S.) **수확—** harvest delivery **역—** ex station; delivered at station **즉시—** spot delivery **화차—** free on rail (略 F.O.R.); (美) free on board (略 FOB, f.o.b) ■—**가격** delivered cost —**부족** short delivery —**식** a handing-over ceremony —**인** a deliverer —**일**〔시기〕 the date [time] of delivery —**장소** a place of delivery —**지시서** delivery order (略 D/O) —**청구** a petition for eviction —**필** delivered

인도 引導 guidance; (a) lead; showing the way —**인도하다** guide; lead; show [usher] in; show the way

♦젊은이를 바른길로 인도하다 guide [lead] the young men to the right path

▶ 은행원이 강도를 인도했다 A bank clerk acted as guide for the burglar. ⇌ A bank clerk helped the burglar (to) break in.

▶ 손님은 여주인에게 서재로 인도되었다 The visitor was shown [ushered] into the study by the hostess.

인도 印度 India; 〈공식명〉 the Republic of India ♦인도의 Indian

■—**말** Indian; 〈공용어〉 Hindi —**사람** a Hindu; a Hindoo (*pl*. ~s); an Indian (▶ 현재는 보통 「아메리칸 인디언」을 뜻함) —**양** the Indian Ocean

인도네시아 Indonesia; 〈공식명〉 the Republic of Indonesia

♦인도네시아의 Indonesian

■—**말** Indonesian —**사람** an Indonesian

인도어 indoor ■—**게임** indoor games

인도유럽어족 —語族 Indo-European (languages)

인도적 人道的 humane; 〈인도주의적인〉 humanitarian

♦비인도적 inhumane / 인도적인 입장[견지]에서 from a humanitarian point of view / 가장 인도적인 방법으로 문제를 해결하다 solve the problem in the most humane way

▶ 그것은 인도적인 이유에서 용서할 수가 없다 That is unforgivable for humanitarian reasons.

▶ 인도적인 견지에서 포로를 석방했다 They set the prisoners (of war) free because of their humanitarian point of view.

인도주의 人道主義 humanitarianism; humanism

♦인도주의의 humanitarian; humanistic

■—**자** a humanitarian; a humanist —**작가** a humanistic writer

인도차이나 印度— Indochina
♦인도차이나 전쟁 the Indo-China War / 인도차이나의 Indo-Chinese
■—말 Indo-Chinese —반도 Indochina; the Indo-Chinese Peninsula

인동덩굴 忍冬— 〔植〕honeysuckle

인두 〈바느질의〉a (hot) iron; a flatiron; a smoothing iron;〈납땜용〉a soldering iron;〈의료용〉a searing iron; a cautery (iron);〈낙화(烙畫)용〉an iron for pyrography;〈이발용〉a curling iron; curling pins [tongs]
■—질 ironing; soldering: 인두질하다 iron; solder; sear

인두 咽頭 〔解〕the pharynx (*pl.* ~es, pharynges) ♦인두의 pharyngeal; pharyngal
■—염 pharyngitis [fæ̀rəndʒáitəs]

인두겁 人— 〈사람의 겉형상〉human shape [form]; a human face
▶그는 인두겁만 썼지 짐승이나 다름없다 He is man in face, (but) brute in mind.

인두세 人頭稅 a poll [head, per capita] tax; a capitation (tax)

인듐 〔化〕indium

인들 〈…이라고 할지라도 어찌…이라도〉even; even if [though] (it were so); admitting [granting] that (it is so); whatever; however
▶단돈 한 푼인들 줄 수 없다 I won't give a single penny. ⇌〈강조〉Not a single penny will I give.
▶영웅인들 별 수 있나 Even a hero cannot help it.

인듯하다 look (like) ⇨ 듯하다

인디고 〈물감〉indigo

인디아 India ⇨ 인도(印度) ■—페이퍼 India paper

인디애나주 —州 〈미국의〉Indiana (略 Ind.)
■—사람 an Indianan; an Indianian

인디애나폴리스 〈미국 인디애나주의 주도〉Indianapolis

인디언 1〈인도사람〉an Indian
2〈아메리카 원주민〉an American Indian
■아메리칸— an American [a Red] Indian; an Amerind

인력 人力 1〈사람의 힘〉man power; human power [strength]
2〈사람의 노력〉human efforts;〈인원수〉manpower
♦인력으로는 불가능하다 be beyond the power of man; be not within the control of human power
■—감사 manpower inspection —구조 manpower structure —난 manpower problems [shortage] —수출 manpower export

인력 引力 〔物〕〈물체간의〉attraction; attractive force;〈천체의〉gravitation
♦인력의 법칙 the law of gravitation; the (Newton's) law of gravitation / 인력이 있는 attractive
▶두 물체간의 인력은 그 질량에 정비례한다 The force of attraction between two objects is directly proportional to their masses.
▶조수의 간만은 달의 인력에 기인한다 The ebb and flow of the tide are due to the gravitation of the moon.
■모세관[분자]— capillary [molecular] attraction 반대— counterattraction 우주[만유]— universal gravitation 지구— terrestrial gravitation; the earth's gravitational force —권 the sphere of gravitation —설 the theory of gravitation

인력거 人力車 a ricksha; a rickshaw
♦인력거를 끌다[타다] pull [take, ride in] a ricksha / 인력거로 가다 go by rickhsa
■삼륜(三輪)— a trishaw ■—꾼 a rickshaman; a rickshawman; a ricksha-puller

인롱 印籠 1〈도장을 넣는 궤〉a seal case
2〈약을 넣는 궤〉a medicine case

인류 人類 mankind; the human (race); human beings; humanity; man; (라) Homo sapiens
♦인류의 행복 human happiness [welfare]
■—사 the history of man; human history —사회 human society —애 love for humanity [mankind] —화석 mankind fossil

인류학 人類學 anthropology
■문화[사회]— cultural [social] anthropology 자연— physical anthropology ■—자 an anthropoligist

인륜 人倫 1〈인도(人道)〉humanity; human duties
2〈오륜〉morality; moral principles; moral rules to govern the Five Human Relations
♦인륜에 위배되는 행위 an immoral behavior; an act contrary to morality
▶그는 인륜에 위배되는 생활을 해왔다 He has lived an immoral life.
3〈인간관계〉human relations
■—대사 important matter of life —도덕 ethics and morality

인망 人望 popularity; popular favor; public esteem; reputation
♦인망있는[없는] popular [unpopular] 《with》/ 인망이 높다 enjoy a high reputation; be very popular 《with, among》/ 인망을 잃다[얻다] lose [gain, win, acquire] *one's* popularity; forfeit [gain] public esteem; become unpopular [popular]
■—가(家) a popular person

인멸 湮滅 〈없어짐〉extinction;〈없앰〉destruction —인멸하다 be extinct;〈인위적으로〉destroy; annihilate
♦증거를 인멸하다 destroy [make away with] the proofs (of); destroy [stifle] evidence

인명 人名 a person's name
■—록 a directory; a Who's Who —부 a roll; a roster; a list of names; a name list; a directory —사전 a biographical dictionary

인명 人命 human life; life
♦인명을 희생하여 at the sacrifice [cost, expense] of life / 인명에 관계되다 affect people's lives; endanger life
▶그 사고에 인명의 손실은 없었다 No lives have been lost in the accident.
▶우리는 인명을 존중해야 한다 We should have respect for human life.
■—구조 saving a life; lifesaving —손실 a loss of lives; the toll of lives

인문 人文 1〈윤리·질서 등〉humanity
2〈문화〉civilization; culture

인문주의

♦인문의 발달 the advance of civilization; enlightenment
■—과학 cultural sciences —지리학 human geography; anthropogeography

인문주의 人文主義 humanism ♦인문주의의[적인] humanistic ■—자 a humanist

인물 人物 1〈사람〉 a person; 〈좀 유별난〉 a man; a character; 〈거물〉 a figure; a personage; 〈인격자〉 a man of character
♦세계적인 인물 a world figure; a person of worldwide fame / 작은 인물 a small [little] man; a man of small caliber / 훌륭한 인물 a worthy (man); a man of worth; a fine character / 자신을 상당한 인물로 생각하다 think oneself a somebody
▶그는 재간은 있으나 인물이 작다 He has talent enough, but lacks greatness.
▶그들은 상당한 인물로 보이려고 노력하였다 They tried to look like somebodies.
▶그는 어떤 인물이냐? What sort [style] of (a) man is he?
2〈인격·품성〉 character; personality; individuality; the quality of man
♦인물이 좋다 be of good character / 인물을 보증하다 answer for sb's character / 인물을 조사하다 make inquires into sb's character / 인물을 평가하다 read character; take sb's measure
▶인물을 보고 결혼해야 한다 You must marry for character.
3〈인재〉 an able man; a talented man; a man of ability [parts]; a talent
▶저 정당에는 인물이 많다 That party has many able men.
4〈용모〉 personal appearance; features; looks
♦인물이 잘 생긴 소녀 a good-looking girl / 인물이 못 생기다 be plain-looking [ill-favored, 《美》homely]; be ugly
5〈소설·극 중의〉 a character; a person; a personage; 〈그림의〉 a human figure; a figure subject
♦인물을 그리다 〈그림에서〉 paint a human figure; 〈소설에서〉 draw [delineate] a character; characterize sb
▶이 소설은 인물이 잘 묘사되어 있다 The characters are all well delineated in this novel.
▶그는 몇마디 적절한 말로 그녀의 인물을 묘사했다 He characterized her in a few well-chosen words.
■등장— characters ((in the drama [novel])); the cast 위험— a dangerous character 작중— the characters in the story [novel] 중요— an important figure; a leading spirit; (口) a very important person (略 VIP) ■—가 난 a shortage of talent —묘사 character painting [portrayal, portraiture] —보증서 a character reference

인물평 人物評 comments on (sb's) personality; personalities; a character [personality] sketch; characterization
♦인물평을 하다 comment on (sb's) personality; make a character sketch ((of))

인물화 人物畫 a figure painting [picture, piece]; a portrait; 〈화법〉 figure [portrait] painting
▶나는 인물화에 서투르다 I am a poor figure painter. ⇌ I am poor at figure painting.
■—가 a portrait painter

인민 人民 the citizens; the people; 〈민중〉 the public; the populace; 〈신민〉 the subjects
♦인민의 권리 the civil rights / 인민의 복지 the popular welfare / 인민의, 인민에 의한, 인민을 위한 정치 government of the people, by the people, for the people / 인민을 보호하다 protect the people
■—공화국 a people's republic —위원회 executive council of people's committee —재판 a people's court; 〈사형(私刑)〉 a kangaroo court: 인민 재판을 하다 subject sb to a kangaroo court —전선 the people's [popular] front —해방군 the People's Liberation Army

인박이다 be addicted ((to))
♦마약[아편]에 인박인 사람 a drug [an opium] addict
▶그는 담배[술]에 인박였다 He is addicted to smoking [alcohol].

인보이스 〔商〕〈송장〉 an invoice ♦인보이스를 보내다[받다] send [accept] an invoice

인복 人福 luck with good acquaintances

인본주의 人本主義 humanism
■—자 a humanist

인부 人夫 a laborer; a worker; a navvy; a coolie; 〈운반인〉 a porter; a carrier; 〈부두의〉 a longshoreman
■토목— a construction worker; a navvy ■—감독 a boss; a foreman ((pl. -men))

인분 人糞 human excrement; night soil
■—비료 human manure; night soil (for manure)

인비 人秘 secrecy of personnel affairs

인사 人士 a man of good breeding; a person; 〈명사〉 a society personage
♦거물급 인사 an important figure; a man of figure; (口) a VIP

인사 人事 1〈사교상의〉 a greeting; civilities; (a) salutation; recognition; 〈아침·저녁의〉 the time of day; 〈인사말〉 compliments; 〈식에서의〉 an address
♦(선채로) 수인사하다 pass the time of day ((with)) / 인사를 주고 받다 exchange civilities [greetings, salutations, the time of day] / 아침 인사를 하다 say good morning ((to)) / 저녁 인사를 하다 wish sb a good evening
▶그는 인사도 하지않고 떠나버렸다 He left without so much as saying goodbye.
—인사하다 greet; salute; present one's compliments; recognize; say hello; 〈식에서〉 give an address
♦인사하러 가다〈경의의 표시로〉 call on sb to pay one's respects / 인사시키다 introduce
2〈절〉 a bow; 〈여자의〉 a courtesy
—인사하다 bow ((to)); make a bow; bow [incline] one's head; make [drop, bob] a courtesy; make ((to)) one's manners
♦어른에게 인사하다 make a bow to one's elder / 서로 인사하다 exchange bows
3〈예의〉 (good) manners; courtesy; civility; decorum(s); etiquette; propriety

♦외교상의 인사 치렛말 idle words of diplomacy / 인사차 방문하다 pay a visit of courtesy 《to》
4 〈감사〉 thanks; gratitude; acknowledgement; appreciation
▶그에게 선물받은 인사를 무엇으로 할까? What shall I give him in return for his present?
─인사하다 thank [give thanks to] 《*sb* for *sth*》; express [extend] one's thanks [gratitude] 《to *sb* for *sth*》
5 〈사람이 해야할 일〉 human business
♦인사를 다하다 try every possible means / 인사를 다하고 천명을 기다리다 do one's best and leave the rest to Providence
6 〈개인에 관한 사항〉 personal affairs
7 〈의식〉 one's senses; consciousness
■작별─ a farewell greeting [address]; parting words; a valediction ─고과 performance appraisal ─관리[행정] personnel management [administration] ─국[부, 과] the bureau [division, section] of personnel; the personnel (affairs) bureau [division, section] ─권 the right of personnel management ─기록 a personnel record ─담당관 a personnel manager ─란 〈신문의〉 the personal column; (美) the personal ─말 greetings; compliments; 〈연설〉 an address ─비밀 secrecy of personnel affairs ─소송 personal suit ─위원회 a personnel committee ─이동 personnel changes; 〈대이동〉 a (sweeping) shake-up ─장 a letter of greeting; a greeting card

인사교류 人事交流 an interchange of personnel 《between》
♦부처간의 인사교류 interministerial personnel reshuffle
▶관계 당국에 의하면 4월에는 부처간의 인사교류가 있을 것이라고 한다 According to the authorities concerned, there will be interministerial personnel reshuffles in April.

인사불성 人事不省 〈기절〉 unconsciousness; loss of consciousness; insensibility
♦인사불성이 되다 lose consciousness; fall [become] unconscious [insensible, senseless]; lose one's senses; faint (away); fall into a swoon; lapse into unconsciousness; go into coma; (口) pass out
▶그녀는 인사불성이 되었다 She lost consciousness.

인사성 人事性 〈예의 바름〉 politeness; courteousness; sociability
♦인사성이 밝다[없다] have good [no] manners; be well-[ill-]mannered

인사이드 inside

인산 燐酸 〔化〕 phosphoric acid
■─마그네슘 magnesium phosphate ─비료 phosphatic manure [fertilizer]; phosphate ─석회 phosphate of lime ─염 phosphate ─칼륨 potassium phosphate ─칼슘 phosphate of calcium; calcium phosphate

인산인해 人山人海 a great [large] crowd (of people)
▶그 쇼는 인산인해를 이루었다 The show drew [attracted] a large crowd of spectators.
▶거리는 인산인해를 이루고 있었다 There were large crowds of people in the streets. ⇌ A great multitude gathered in the streets.

인삼 人蔘 a ginseng

인상 人相 looks; physiognomy; facial features; lineaments
♦고귀한 인상 a noble cast of countenance / 인상이 좋은[좋지 않은] 남자 a man of good [evil] physiognomy; a good- [ill-, evil-]looking man / 인상이 천한 vulgar looking
▶그 남자의 인상이 마음에 들지 않는다 I don't like the looks of the man.
■─학 physiognomy ─학자 a physiognomist

인상 引上 **1** 〈물가 등의〉 raising; a raise; (an) increase; boosting; pull-up
♦물가의 인상 an advance [a rise] in price; a price hike / 임금의 인상 a raise [a rise, an increase] in wages; a wage hike / 20퍼센트의 임금 인상 twenty percent increase [raise, boost] of wages / 임금 인상을 요구하다 demand a rise in (one's) wages; ask for higher wages
─인상하다 raise; increase; hike; (口) up; draw up; pull up; lift (up)
♦급료를 인상해주다 give *sb* a raise
▶나는 지난 주에 봉급이 인상되었다 My salary was stepped up [I got a raise] last week.
2 〔力道〕 the snatch ▶인상은 역도 종목의 하나다 The snatch is an item of the divisions of weight lifting.

인상 印象 an impression
♦나쁜 인상 a bad [an unfavorable] impression / 좋은 인상 a good [favorable] impression / 첫 인상 the first impression(s) / 지울 수 없는[지워지지 않는] 인상 an indeniable [ineffaceable] impression / 잊을 수 없는 인상 an unforgettable impression / 인상이 좋은 얼굴 affable looks; agreeable features / 인상 깊은 [에 남는] impressive; memorable / 좋은[나쁜] 인상을 주다 give *sb* a favorable [an unfavorable] impression / 나쁜 인상을 남기다 leave a bad impression behind [on] / 인상을 말하다 voice [give] one's impressions 《of》/ 인상을 받다 be impressed; receive [get, gain] an impression 《of, that》
▶런던의 인상은 어떠했습니까? How did London impress [strike] you? ⇌ What is your impression of London?
♦내가 받은 인상을 결코 잊을 수가 없다 I shall never forget the impression made upon me.
▶그녀의 인상은 내 마음 속에 깊이 새겨져 있다 Her image is deeply impressed on my mind.
▶그녀의 연설은 청중에게 깊은 인상을 주었다 Her speech produced a deep impression on the audience.

인상 鱗狀 〔動〕〈비늘 모양〉 scaliness
♦인상의 scalelike; scaly; squamous

인상서 人相書 the description of one's looks; a (personal) description ♦인상서와 들어맞다 answer [fit, meet] the description of *sb*

인상적 印象的 impressive; imposing
♦인상적인 풍경 a striking [an impressive] scene / 인상적으로 impressively

인상주의 印象主義 impressionism ♦인상주의

의 impressionistic ■신— neo-impressionism ■—자 an impressionist

인상파 印象派 the impressionist school; impressionism; the impressionists
♦인상파의 그림 an impressionist(ic) painting ■후기— the postimpressionists

인색 吝嗇 stinginess; miserliness; parsimony; screwing and scraping
—인색하다 stingy; mean; niggardly; tight; tight-fisted; miserly; parsimonious; pinchpenny; (俗) screwy

> [解說] **stingy**는 「인색한」의 가장 일반적인 말이며, **mean**은 돈을 내기 싫어하는 것이고, **tight(-fisted)**는 인색한 사람이어서 일단 돈이 들어오면 좀처럼 내놓지 않는 것을 말한다. **miserly**는 약간 격식을 갖춘 말로 돈 모으기를 좋아하여 어떤 일에도 돈 쓰기를 싫어하는 것을 말한다.

♦인색한 사람 a miser; a stingy fellow; a niggard; a skinflint; (英口) an screw / 돈에 인색하다 be niggardly of money; be close with *one's* money; stint *one's* money
▶ 그는 인색하게 살며 돈을 모으고 있다 He is saving (up) money by living close.
▶ 인색하게 굴지 마라 Don't be so stingy. ⇌ Be liberal.

인생 人生 human life; man's life; life
♦인생의 가시밭길 the thorny path of life / 인생의 덧없음 the frailty [transience] of human life / 인생의 목적[의미] the aim [meaning] of life / 인생의 부침(浮沈) ups and downs of fortune / 인생의 여로 life's journey / 인생의 즐거움 the pleasures of life / 인생의 종말 the end of *one's* life; *one's* journey's end / 인생의 human; life / 인생을 낙관하다 look on the bright side of life; take a cheerful [an optimistic] view of life / 인생을 비관하다 look on the dark side of life; take a gloomy [pessimistic] view of life / 인생을 꿈결 처럼 보내다 dream away *one's* life / 인생에 싫증이 나다 find life a bore
▶ 인생 겨우 50년 Life is (but) a span.
▶ 인생은 일장춘몽이다 Life is like a daydream. ⇌ Life is but an empty dream.
▶ 인생은 항해와 같다 Life is compared [likened] to a voyage.
▶ 인생 칠십 고래희(古來稀)란 옛말이 있다 We have an old saying "Men seldom [Few peolpe] live to be seventy."
▶ 이것이야말로 진짜 인생이다 This is the life.
■—기록 a human document —문제 the problem of life —예찬 a psalm of life —철학 the philosophy of life —행로 the tenor [path] of *one's* life; *one's* course of life; stages in a man's career

인생관 人生觀 *one's* view of life; *one's* theory [conception] of life; an outlook on [attitude toward] life; *one's* viewpoint on life
♦밝은[어두운] 인생관 a cheerful [gloomy] outlook on life; an optimistic [a pessimistic] view of life

인선 人選 the selection of men [the personnel]; the choice of a suitable person
♦각료의 인선 the selection of Cabinet members / 인선에 빠지다 find difficulty in choosing a suitable person (for a position)
—인선하다 choose a man; select a suitable person ((for a post)); make a choice from a list of names
▶ 우리는 인선하는 중이다 We are looking for a candidate suitable for the post.

인성 人性 〈본성〉 human nature; 〈본능〉 human instinct; humanity; humanism
■—론 *A Treatise on Human Nature* —주의자 a humanist

인세 印稅 a royalty ((on, for)); 〈인지세〉 the stamp duty
▶ 그는 소설의 인세로 5백만원을 받았다 He has received five million won in royalties [a royalty of five million won] on his novel.
▶ 출판업자는 저자에게 정가의 10%를 인세로 지급했다 The publisher paid the author a ten percent royalty on the published [retail] price of his book.

인솔 引率 leading; commanding
—인솔하다 lead [conduct] ((a party)); head
♦…을 인솔하여 leading a party of...; at the head of...
▶ 우리 선생님은 학생들을 인솔하고 설악산에 올라갔다 My teacher conducted his students up Sŏraksan.
▶ 나는 학생들을 인솔하고 박물관에 갔다 I led [took] a group of students to the museum.
■—자 a leader; a captain; a commander; 〈관광의〉 인솔자 a tour conductor [guide]

인쇄 印刷 printing
♦인쇄의 오식(誤植) a misprint / 책을 인쇄에 부치다 put a book to (the) press; put a book into print; send a book through the press
▶ 이 책은 인쇄가 잘[잘못] 되었다 This is well [poorly] printed.
▶ 그 책은 지금 인쇄중이다 The book is being printed [is in the hands of the printer] now. ⇌ The book is in [at] (the) press now.
▶ 이 사전의 초판 인쇄는 10만부였다 This dictionary had a first printing of one hundred thousand copies.
▶ 당신의 원고는 벌써 인쇄에 부쳤습니다 Your manuscript has already gone to (the) press [the printer].
—인쇄하다 print; put into print
♦대본을 인쇄하다 print a script; put a script into print / 팜플렛을 1,000부 인쇄하다 print (off) one thousand copies of the pamphlet
▶ 이 책은 5,000부 인쇄했다 This book had a printing of five thousand copies.
▶ 인쇄는 언제쯤 끝납니까? When will it be off the press?
▶ 그 뉴스는 급히 인쇄되었다 The news was rushed into print.
■4색— four-color printing 컬러— colored [color] printing ■—공 a printer; a pressman —공장 a printshop —기 a (printing) press; a printing machine —기술 a printing technique —기술자 a typographer —물 〈우편물로서의〉 printed matter; 〈배포용의〉 a handout —소 a

press; a printing house —술 (the art of) printing; typography —업 printing (business) : 인쇄업을 하다 engage in printing business —업자 a printer —용 (for) printing purpose —용지 printing paper —잉크 printing [printer's] ink —체 문자 a print letter; a disjoined [printing] hand —판 a printing plate; a press plate

인수 人數 the number of persons ⇨ 인원수(人員數)

인수 引受 1 〈물건·권리 의〉 taking over; undertaking; charge; assumption
▶ 업무의 인수 인계가 끝났다 Transfer of business has been completed.
—인수하다 take over 〈another's business〉; undertake; 〈임무 등을〉 assume; 〈시체·분실물을〉 claim; 〈책임지다〉 answer for; be responsible for; hold *oneself* responsible for
♦ 사건을 인수하다 take (up) an affair in hand / 정권을 인수하다 assume the reins of government
▶ 그는 그들의 사업을 인수했다 He took over [succeeded (to)] their business.
▶ 미안하지만 이 일은 인수하지 못하겠습니다 I'm sorry, but I can't take on this work.
2 〈공채 등의〉 underwriting; 〈주식의〉 subscription; 〈환어음의〉 acceptance; 〈보증〉 guarantee; guaranty; security
—인수하다 accept; honor; consent; comply with
▶ 내가 그 발행주를 인수하겠다 I'll agree to buy an issue of stocks.
■—거절 nonacceptance (of a bill); dishonor —어음 an accepted [acceptable] bill —은행 an accepting [underwriting] bank —필(畢) accepted

인수 因數 〔數〕 a factor ▶ 2와 3은 6의 인수다 Two and three are factors of six.
■ 소(素)[공통]— a prime [common] factor —분해 factorization; resolution into factors: 인수분해하다 factorize [factor] 《an expression》; resolve [break up] 《a quantity》 into factors / 다음의 식을 인수분해 하시오 Resolve the following expression into factors. ＝ Factorize the following expression.

인수인 引受人 〈환어음의〉 an acceptor; 〈공채 등의〉 an underwriter; 〈시체·분실물 등의〉 a claimant; 〈보증인〉 a surety; a guarantor ♦ 인수인이 없는 시체 an unclaimed body

인술 仁術 the healing art
▶ 의술은 인술이다 Medicine is a benevolent [caring, humanitarian] profession.

인슈트 〔野〕 an inshoot

인슐린 〔生化·藥〕 insulin ■—쇼크 an insulin shock

인스턴트 instant ■—식품 precooked [fast] food; convenience food —커피 instant coffee

인스피레이션 〈영감〉 (an) inspiration
♦ 인스피레이션을 얻다 receive [get] an idea [*one's* inspiration] 《from》; be inspired 《by》
▶ 그때 인스피레이션이 떠올랐다 Just then I had an inspiration [(美) a brainstorm, (英) a brain wave].

인습 因習 〈관습〉 a long-established custom [usage]; convention; conventionality; (a) tradition
♦ 인습적인 conventional / 인습을 타파하다 do away with conventionalities / 인습에 얽매이다 be a slave to convention; be bound by convention / 인습에서 벗어나다 depart from convention
▶ 나는 다만 인습을 따랐을 뿐이다 I just followed convention.
▶ 과거의 형식적인 인습을 타파할 용기를 가져라 Have the courage to break [abandon] the formal conventions of the past.
▶ 인습에 얽매여선 안된다 Don't be a slave of [to] convention. ＝ Don't be conventional.

인시류 鱗翅類 〈나비목〉 〔昆〕 Lepidoptera
♦ 인시류의 곤충 a lepidopteran 《*pl.* -tera》 / 인시류의 lepidopteran ■—연구가 a lepidopterist —학 lepidopterology

인식 認識 recognition; cognizance; perception; realization; 〈이해〉 understanding; 〈지식〉 knowledge; 〔心〕 noesis
♦ 우리의 인식을 깊게 하다 deepen [promote] our understanding 《of》 / 인식을 새로이 하다 see (it) in a new [fresh] light; be awakened to (its) new significance
▶ 그는 이 문제에 관해서는 인식이 부족하다 He has very little understanding [knowledge] of this matter.
▶ 웬일인지 이 문제에 관해서는 인식이 부족한 사람이 많다 I don't know why but there are many people who lack proper knowledge of this matter.
▶ 나는 여성해방 운동에 대한 인식을 새로이 했다 I saw the women's liberation movement in a new [fresh] light.
—인식하다 cognize; recognize; be cognizant of; perceive; realize; appreciate; 〈이해하다〉 understand
♦ 실태를 바르게 인식하다 understand the true situation correctly; have a correct understanding of the true situation 《of》; duly recognize 《a fact》
■—력 cognitive faculty [power] —비판 〔哲〕 critique of cognition —작용 〔哲·心〕 cognition —표 〔軍〕 an identification tag [disk]; (俗) a dog tag

인식론 認識論 〔哲〕 epistemology; the theory of knowledge ♦ 인식론(상)의[적인] epistemological
■—(학)자 an epistemologist

인식부족 認識不足 lack of understanding [knowledge]; ignorance
♦ 인식부족이다 be ignorant 《of》; be ill-informed 《about》
▶ 그것은 너의 인식부족이다 You don't know much about it. ＝ You've little understanding of it.

인신 人身 〈몸〉 the human body; 〈신상〉 *one's* person
■—보호령 〔英史〕 the Habeas Corpus Act

인신공격 人身攻擊 a personal abuse 《on》; personal remarks; character assassination
♦ 논쟁에서 인신공격을 하다 bring personalities into [(口) get personal in] an argu-

ment; become personal in a dispute
—**인식공격하다** indulge in [resort to] personalities; be personal
♦ 아무에 대해 인식공격하다 make a personal attack [personal remarks] on *sb*

인신매매 人身賣買 traffic in human beings; slave trade; human traffic ■—**자** a slave dealer [trader]

인심 人心 1 〈사람의 마음〉 a man's mind [heart]; 〈인정〉 human feeling; sympathy; the heart
♦ 인심이 좋다 be good-hearted; be generous; be genial / 인심을 쓰다 give with an open hand; grant *sb* a favor / 남의 것으로 인심 쓰다 be generous at another's expense
2 〈민심〉 people's mind [heart]; the public [popular] feeling(s)
♦ 인심을 무마하다 appease the people; pacify popular feeling
▶ 인심이 흉흉하다 The people are panic-stricken [are in alarm].
▶ 인심이 동요되었다 The people were agitated.
▶ 정부는 인심을 잃었다 The government lost the supports of the people.

인심 仁心 a benevolent heart; benevolence; humanity

인애 仁愛 humanity; benevolence; charity; humane affection ♦ 인애심이 있는 benevolent; humane
▶ 인애의 마음을 가지고 가난한 사람들을 대해야 한다 You should treat the poor with humanity.

인양 引揚 pulling [drawing] up; 〈침몰선의〉 refloatation; salvage; 〈시체 등의〉 recovery
—**인양하다** pull [draw] up; refloat; salvage; salve
▶ 그 침몰선은 해안으로 인양되었다 The sunken ship was raised to the shore of the sea.
■—**작업** refloatation [salvage] operations; salvage work

인어 人魚 1 〈상상의 동물〉 a mermaid (여자); a merman (남자)
2 〔動〕 a dugong; a sea pig

인연 因緣 1 〈연분〉 affinity; connection
♦ 부모 자식간의 인연 the ties that bind parent and child together / 인연이 깊다 be closely bound up together; be closely connected 《with》 / 인연을 끊다 cut [sever] *one's* connections 《with》; break [off] 《with》 / 인연을 맺다 form ties [a connection] 《with》
▶ 나는 그와 적지 않은 인연이 있다 I have a close tie [connection, relation] with him.
▶ 그는 우리와는 전혀 인연이 없는 사람이다 He is a perfect stranger to us.
▶ 이 회사와 이 지역 사회간에는 깊은 인연이 있다 There is a close connection between this company and the local community.
2 〈인과〉 cause and occasion; 〈운명〉 *one's* (the) fate; destiny; 〔佛敎〕 karma
▶ 이것도 인연이다 There is an act of providence in it.
▶ 우리가 여기서 만난 것도 어떤 인연이었으리라 We were possibly destined [predestined] to meet here.

인욕 忍辱 fortitude; endurance; forbearance; long-suffering

인용 引用 quotation; citation ♦ 성서에서의 인용 a quotation from the Bible
—**인용하다** quote [cite] from 《an auther》; adduce 《a quotation from》; borrow from ♦ 인용할 가치가 있는 quotable; quoteworthy
▶ 그는 셰익스피어의 한 구절을 인용했다 He quoted a passage from Shakespeare.
▶ 그는 롱펠로가 지은 다음의 시를 인용했다 He cited the following verses from Longfellow.
▶ 대통령은 링컨의 말을 인용하며 연설을 끝맺었다 The president finished his speech with a quotation from Lincoln.
■—**구[문]** a quotation; a quoted passage; (口) a quote : 인용구[인용문]의 출처를 밝히다 identify a quotation; trace a quotation to its original source —**부호** quotation marks; (口) quotes : 인용부호로 묶다 put in quotation marks [quotes] —**서** reference books; books referred to

인원 人員 〈사람수〉 the number of persons; 〈작업의〉 hands; 〈총칭〉 the staff; the personnel
♦ 인원을 늘리다[줄이다] increase [reduce, (口) cut down (on)] the staff [personnel] / 인원을 제한하다 limit the number of persons
▶ 회사는 인원이 너무 많다[부족하다] The company is overstaffed [understaffed].
▶ 필요한 인원을 확보하게 되면 이 일은 한 달 안에 끝낼 수 있다 If we can get the necessary number of persons, we'll finish this work within one month.
■—**가동** available hands ■—**구성** the personnel setup —**배치표** a personnel allotment table —**점검[점호]** a roll call; the muster : 인원점검을 하다 call the roll; hold a muster —**정리** a personnel reduction [slash, cut]: 인원정리를 하다 cut down the personnel

인원수 人員數 the number of persons [people]; numerical strength
♦ 인원수가 많다[적다] be large [small] in number / 인원수가 부족하다 be lacking in number / 인원수를 늘리다 increase the number 《of men》 / 인원수를 세다 count heads [noses] / 인원수를 제한하다 limit the number / 인원수를 채우다 fill up number; gather a number of people 《for event》; make up the numbers 《of》
▶ 인원수가 찼다 The number filled up.
▶ 지원자의 인원수가 늘었다[줄었다] The applicants increased [decreased] in number.
▶ 인원수는 얼마나 됩니까? What is the number? ⇌ How many are there?

인위 人爲 〈인공(人工)〉 human work; art; artificiality
♦ 인위적인 시세 artificial [manipulated] market prices / 인위적인 artificial; unnatural; factitious / 인위적으로 가격을 올리다 raise the price artificially
■—**법** an artificial law —**사회** 〔社〕 an artificial society —**선택** 〔生〕 artificial selection (↔ natural selection)

인육 人肉 human flesh ■—**시장** a house of

prostitution [ill fame]; a whorehouse; 〈백인의〉 a white slave market
인의 仁義 humanity [benevolence] and justice [righteousness]
■—**예지신** benevolence, righteousness, propriety, wisdom and sincerity
인자 人子 1 〈사람의 아들〉 a son 2 〈그리스도〉 the Son of Man
인자 仁者 〈어진 사람〉 a humane [benevolent, kindhearted] person; a man of virtue; a humanitarian
인자 仁慈 benignancy; benignity; benevolence; clemency —**인자하다** benign; benignant; merciful; kindly and gracious ♦인자한 아버지 a clement father
인자 因子 〈인수〉〖數〗 a factor; 〈유전자〉〖生〗 a gene
인자 印字 〈글자를 찍음〉 printing; typing; 〈그 글자〉 a printed letter; a typewritten letter —**인자하다** print; type (out)
인장 印章 a seal ♦인장을 새기다 engrave [cut] a seal / 인장을 위조하다 counterfeit [forge] a seal / 인장을 찍다 set [stamp, put] *one's* seal 《on》
■**위조—** a forged seal; a counterfeit [false] seal —**위조** forgery of a seal —**위조자** a forger of a seal
인재 人材 (a man of) talent; a capable man; a talented [competent] person; a man of ability [talent]; a capable [an able] person; **(총칭)** talent
♦인재를 구하다 look for talent / 인재를 등용하다 open the offices to talent / 인재를 모으다 gather capable [talented] people
▶ 저 회사에는 우수한 인재가 있다 That company has an excellent staff.
▶ 널리 인재를 모아 등용하는 과감한 방법을 취하지 않으면 안된다 We must take a bold step to call in the best brains and open the offices to them.
■—**등용** selection of fit persons for higher positions —**발굴** talent hunt —**은행** a talent bank
인재 人災 a man-made [man-caused] disaster [calamity]; a disaster caused by man ▶ 이것은 천재(天災)가 아니라 인재다 This is not a natural calamity, but a man-made one.
인적 人的 human ■—**담보** personal security —**손실** the loss of man power —**자원** human resources; manpower : 인적 자원의 부족 lack of human resources
인적 人跡 human traces [footsteps]
♦인적 미답의 땅 an untrodden [unexplored] region / 인적이 드문 산길 an unfrequented mountain path / 인적이 끊기다 be completely deserted
인절미 a square cake made from glutinous rice (coated with bean flour)
인접 隣接 adjacency; contiguity; proximity —**인접하다** adjoin; be adjacent (contiguous] to; be [stand, lie] close by; border [abut] on
♦인접한 도시들 nearby [neighboring] cities / 학교에 인접한 공원 a park next [adjacent] to the school
▶ 화재는 인접한 공장으로 번졌다 The fire spread to the adjacent [neighboring] factory.
▶ 그의 집은 교회에 인접해 있다 His house adjoins the church.
▶ 그 두 마을은 인접해 있다 The two villages adjoin [are adjacent to] (each other).
■—**가옥** adjacent houses —**국가** a neighbor nation; a neighboring country —**지** adjacent [adjoining] land
인정 人情 1 〈동정심〉 sympathy; compassion; humane feelings; 〈자비심〉 mercy; charity; benevolence; 〈친절〉 kindness; tenderness; 〈연민〉 pity
♦인정이 있는 사람 a man of heart; a kindhearted man / 인정머리 없이 without mercy [pity]; relentlessly / 인정에 끌리다 be touched with pity / 인정에 약하다 be easily moved; tenderhearted / 인정에 호소하다 appeal to *sb's* sympathy
▶ 그는 인정사정없이 그녀를 빗속으로 쫓아냈다 Without a shred of compassion he thrust her out into the rain.
▶ 나는 그를 인정상 해고할 수 없었다 I didn't have the heart to dismiss him.
▶ 그는 인정이 없다 He is cold-hearted. ⇒ He has an unfeeling heart.
▶ 너는 참 인정머리가 없다 You are really ruthless [merciless].
▶ 그에게도 약간의 인정은 있었다 He had a touch of sympathy.
2 〈인간적 감정〉 human feelings; 〈인간성〉 human nature; humanity; 〈마음〉 heart [mind] of people
▶ 그런 경우 그렇게 하는 것이 인정이다 It's quite natural to do on such an occasion.
▶ 누구나 출세하고자 하는 것이 인정이다 It's only natural for everyone to want to get ahead in the world.
■—**극** a human-nature play —**풍속** the customs and manners 《of a people》
인정 認定 〈승인〉 approval; 〈인식〉 recognition; acknowledgment; 〈법원의〉 finding; 〈동일하다는 것의〉 identification; 〈허가〉 permission; 〈인가〉 sanction
—**인정하다** approve of; admit; recognize; acknowledge; 〈자격을 주다〉 qualify
♦옛부터 인정되어 온 요법 an old and established remedy / 세상에서 인정받지 못한 작가 an obscure [unacknowledged] writer / 자기의 잘못을 인정하다 admit [allow, (美) concede] that *one* was wrong; admit [own] *oneself* (to have been) in the wrong / 필요성을 인정하다 recognize the necessity 《of》; recognize *sth* as necessary / 크게 인정받다 receive [meet with] much recognition / 자기의 주장을 사회적으로 인정받다 gain public acceptance for *one's* contention
▶ 나는 그의 노력을 인정한다 I think highly of his efforts.
▶ 그는 패배를 인정했다 He recognized that he was lost.
▶ 배심원은 그를 무죄로 인정했다 The jury found him innocent.
▶ 그는 자기 잘못을 인정했다 He admitted his

▶ 이 교과서는 교육부로부터 인정받았다 This textbook was authorized by the Ministry of Education.
▶ 그는 인정받는 작가다 He is a writer of established reputation.
■―과세 taxation with the standard of assessment fixed by the authorities ―서 a certificate; a written recognition 《of championship》

인정미 人情味 〈인간다운 맛〉a human touch; humanity; 〈따뜻함〉humane feelings
◆인정미의 발로 a touch of nature
▶ 그는 인정미가 있다 He has a human touch.
▶ 요즘 사람들은 예전 같은 인정미가 없다 These days people are not as warm-hearted as before.

인정신문 人定訊問 〔法〕 identity questioning; an identity interrogation ―인정신문하다 question the identity

인제 〈이제〉now; before long; 〈이제부터〉from now on; 〈곧〉soon ◆인제 와서 생각해 보니 when I think of it now
▶ 인제 생각이 난다 Now I remember.
▶ 인제 알게 될 거다 Time will tell. ⇌ You shall see.
▶ 인제라도 늦지 않다 It is not too late to do so.

인조 人造 artificiality; 〈모조〉imitation ◆인조의 artificial; man-made; 〈모조의〉imitation; 〈합성의〉synthetic
■―가죽 synthetic [American] leather ―견사 artificial silk; (美) rayon ―고무 synthetic rubber ―금 imitation gold ―대리석 artificial [imitation] marble ―버터 margarine ―보석 a paste gem; paste ―비료 artificial fertilizer; 〈화학비료〉chemical fertilizer [manure] ―상아[석(石)] imitation ivory [stone] ―석유 synthetic oil [petroleum] ―섬유 (a) synthetic fiber; staple [chemical] fiber ―육(肉) synthetic meat ―인간 a robot; a mechanical man ―진주 an artificial [a pasteboard, an imitation] pearl

인종 人種 a (human) race
◆인종적 편견 racial [race, color] prejudice; racialism / 인종적 평등 racial equality / 인종적 대립 race antagonism [rivalry]
▶ 그것은 인종적 편견에 깊이 뿌리박고 있다 It is deeply rooted in racial prejudice.
■―유색― colored races 황[백]― the yellow [white] race ■―문제 the race [a racial] problem [issue] ―분규 a racial conflict ―폭동 a race [color] riot ―학 ethnology; the science of races ―학자 an ethnologist

인종 忍從 submission; endurance; self-surrender; resignation ▶ 옛날에는 여성을 대부분이 인종의 생활을 했다 Most women suffered lives of submission in old times.

인종차별 人種差別 racial discrimination; 〈미국 흑인에 대한〉 segregation
◆인종차별을 하다 discriminate against non-white [colored] people; draw the color line; segregate 《Negroes》/ 인종차별을 당하다 be racially discriminated against; suffer from racial discrimination
■―정책 a racial discrimination policy ―주의 racism ―주의자 a racist ―폐지 abolition of racial discrimination; 〈미국의〉desegregation; integration

인주 印朱 cinnabar [vermilion] seal-ink; sealing ink

인즉 〈으로 말하면〉speaking of; to speak of; as for
◆사실인즉 in fact; to tell [speak] the truth; as a matter of fact
▶ 기회인즉 아주 좋소 As for the opportunity, it is a good one.

인증 引證 quotation; citation ―인증하다 quote 《a fact》; cite 《an instance》; adduce 《evidence》; exemplify

인증 認證 〔法〕 authentication; attestation; certification; validation ―인증하다 certify; attest; authenticate; confirm
■―서 a certificate of attestation; a note of authentication

인지 人智 human intelligence [knowledge, understanding]
◆인지가 미치지 못하는 beyond human knowledge [understanding]; beyond the wit of man
▶ 인지의 발달은 멈추는 법이 없다 The advance of human knowledge will never cease.

인지 印紙 a stamp
◆1,000원짜리 인지 a 1,000-won stamp / 인지를 붙이다 put [stick] a stamp 《on》; affix a stamp 《to》/ 영수증에 인지를 붙이다 put a stamp on a receipt / 인지로 지불[납입]하다 pay in stamps
▶ 이 증서에는 500원 짜리 인지를 붙여야 한다 We must put a 500-won stamp on [affix a 500-won stamp to] this document.
■ 수입― a revenue stamp : 구석에 1,000원 짜리 수입 인지를 붙이세요 Stick [Put, Affix] a 1,000-won revenue stamp in the corner.
■―세 (the) stamp duty ―세법 〔法〕 the Stamp Act ―판매소 a stamp-seller's office

인지 認知 1 〈인정하여 앎〉perception; recognition; acknowledgment; 〔心〕 cognition ―인지하다 perceive; recognize
2 〈친자로의〉〔法〕 filiation; (legal) acknowledgment
―인지하다 acknowledge [own, recognize] 《a child》 as one's own
▶ 그는 그 아이를 인지했다 He acknowledged the child as his own.
■ 사생아― 〔法〕 filiation; affiliation : 사생아 인지 사건 a paternity case ■―소송 a paternity suit ―심리학 cognitive psychology

-인지라 so; as; therefore; because
▶ 그는 게으름뱅이인지라 언제나 성적이 뒤떨어진다 He is lazy, so he is always behind others in his class.
▶ 그는 젊은 사람인지라 그 일을 감당하지 못했다 Young as he was, he was not equal to the task.

인지상정 人之常情 human nature; human feelings ▶ 그렇게 생각하는 것이 인지상정이다 It is human nature to think so.

인질 人質 a hostage
♦인질이 되다[로 잡히다] be taken [held] as a hostage / 아무를 인질로 잡다 take [hold] *sb* as a hostage
▶주인을 인질로 잡고 그들은 그 건물에서 농성했다 Taking the boss as hostage, they shut themselves up in the building.
━석방금[몸값] (a) ransom

인찰지 印札紙 ruled [lined] paper

인책하다 引責— assume the responsibility (for); take the responsibility on *oneself*; hold *oneself* responsible (for)
♦인책하여 사직하다 take the responsibility on *oneself* and resign
▶시장은 독직 사건으로 인책하여 사직할 수 밖에 없었다 The mayor had to resign from the office holding himself responsible for the corruption [bribery] case.

인척 姻戚 a relative [relation] by marriage; a matrimonial relation; 〈美口〉 an in-law ▶그는 결혼함으로써 김 선생과 인척관계가 된다 He is related to Mr. Kim by marriage.

인체 人體 a human body ♦인체에 유해하다 [무해하다] be harmful [harmless] to humans / 인체에 위해를 가하다 inflict an injury upon *sb*; inflict (a) bodily injury on *sb* ■━구조 the structure of the human body ━모형 an anatomical model (of the human body); a manikin ━실험 human experimentation; an experiment on a human body; a living-body test ━해부도 an anatomical chart ━해부(학) human anatomy

── 인체 ──

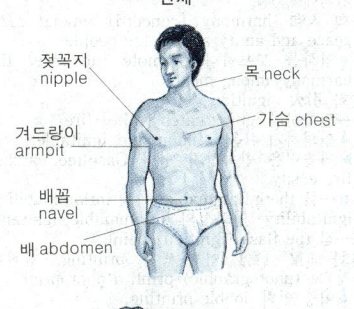

젖꼭지 nipple
목 neck
겨드랑이 armpit
가슴 chest
배꼽 navel
배 abdomen

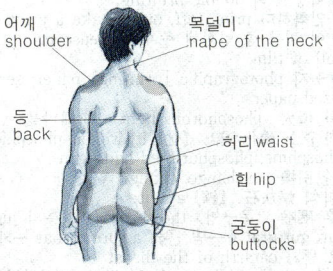

어깨 shoulder
목덜미 nape of the neck
등 back
허리 waist
힙 hip
궁둥이 buttocks

인축 人畜 men and [or] cattle [livestock]
▶인축에 무해 (표시) No harm to humans or animals.

인출 引出 〈예금 등의〉 (a) withdrawal; drawing out
━인출하다 draw out [from]; withdraw (from)
♦은행에서 돈을 인출하다 withdraw *one's* money from the bank
▶나는 매달 은행에서 50만원씩 인출해 쓴다 Every month I withdraw [draw out] five hundred thousand won from the bank and spend it.

인치 an inch (略 in.) ♦7피트 3인치 seven feet three inches; 7 ft. 3 in.; 7′ 3″
▶그는 키가 6피트 1인치다 He is six feet one inch tall. ⇒ He is [stands] six-foot-one.

인칭 人稱 〔文法〕 person ♦1[2, 3]인칭 the first [second, third] person ■━대명사 a personal pronoun

인커브 〔野〕 an incurve
♦인커브를 던지다 throw an inside breaking curve (ball)

인터내셔널 〈국제적〉 international; 〈국제 노동자 동맹〉 International
■제1[2, 3, 4]— the First [Second, Third, Fourth] International

인터넷 〔電算〕 Internet [<*Inter*national *Com*puter *Net*work]

인터벌 〈간격〉 an interval ♦인터벌을 두다 make an interval

인터뷰 an interview
♦기자와의 인터뷰 a press interview / 인터뷰를 하는 사람 an interviewer / 인터뷰를 받는 사람 an interviewee / 인터뷰를 청하다 ask *sb* for an interview / 인터뷰에 응하다 have an interview (with *sb*); give an interview (to *sb*)
━인터뷰하다 interview *sb*; have an interview (with *sb*)
♦단독— (have) an exclusive interview 전화— a telephone interview

인터셉트하다 〔球〕 intercept (a forward pass)

인터체인지 〈입체 교차로〉 an interchange
■클로버— a cloverleaf (interchange)

인터페론 〈바이러스 증식 억제물질〉 〔生化〕 interferon (▶interfere에서 유래함)

인터폰 an interphone; 〈口〉 the intercom [<*intercom*munication system]

인터폴 Interpol [<the *Inter*national Criminal *Pol*ice Organization]

인턴 〈수련의〉 〈美〉 an intern(e); 〈英〉 a houseman
▶그는 지금 적십자병원에서 인턴으로 근무하고 있다 He is now serving his internship [as an intern(e)] at the Red Cross Hospital. ⇒ He is now interning at the Red Cross Hospital.
■━제도 the internship system

인테리어 〈내부〉 the interior

解說 우리말에서 「인테리어」는 「실내장식」의 뜻으로 쓰는 경우가 많지만 영어에서 *interior*는 「실내(의), 내부(의)」라는 뜻밖에 없다. 따라서 「실내 장식」의 뜻을 제대로 나타내려면 interior decoration으로 해야 한다.

인텔리겐치아 〈지식인〉 an intellectual; an educated man; 《美口·蔑》 an egghead; 《美俗》 a double-dome; (총칭) the intelligentsia; the intellectuals

> [解説] 인텔리겐치아는 러시아어의 intelligentsiya에서 온 말이며 *the intelligentsia*는 총칭적으로 지식 계급을 가리킨다. 인텔리겐치아 개개인은 *an intellectual*이라고 하며 *an educated man*으로도 표현할 수 있다. 특히「경멸」의 뜻으로 쓰일 때는 *egghead* 등을 쓴다.

■—계급 the intellectual [educated] class —여성 an intellectual [educated] woman

인텔샛 Intelsat [〈the *Int*ernational *Tel*ecommunications *Sat*ellite Organization]

인토네이션 〈억양〉 intonation
♦상승— 〈 rising intonation 하강— (a) falling intonation 하강·상승— (a) falling-rising intonation

인트로덕션 〈서주부〉 〔樂〕 an introduction; (口) an intro 《pl. ~s》

인파 人波 a crowd; a surging crowd (of people); waves [a tide] of humanity
♦인파를 헤치고 나아가다 jostle through a crowd / 인파에 밀리다 be jostled in the crowd; be buffeted by the waves of humanity

인파이터 〈접근전에 능한 선수〉〔拳〕 an infighter

인파이트 〈접근전〉〔拳〕 infighting

인편 人便 ♦인편에 by someone / 인편에 보내다 send sth by someone / 인편에 말을 전하다 send words [a message] by someone

인편 鱗片 a scale; 〔動〕 a squama 《pl. -mae》; 〔植〕 a ramentum 《pl. -ta》

인품 人品 〈품격〉 character; personality
♦점잖은 인품 gentle personality / 인품이 좋다 have a fine personality
▶그는 인품이 강직하다 He is a man of strong character.

인풋 〈입력〉〔電算〕 input

인플레이션 inflation (of currency)
♦인플레이션을 억제하다 check [curb, counter, curtail] inflation / 인플레이션을 초래하다 cause [bring on] inflation
■악성— 〔經〕 an inflationary spiral; vicious [unsound, spiral] inflation 잠재적— latent inflation 잠행성— creeping inflation ■—경기 an inflation boom —경향 an inflationary trend —대책 an anti-inflation measure —정책 an inflationary policy

인플루엔자 influenza; (口) (the) flu
♦인플루엔자에 걸리다 contract [have, suffer from] influenza; catch [get] the flu
■악성— malignant influenza; fludemic

인피 靱皮 〈외피 안쪽의 세포 조직〉 〔植〕 bast
■—부 phloem; liber —섬유 bast fiber

인하 引下 (a) reduction; lowering; a cut
♦물가 인하 the reduction [lowering] of prices; 〈통제에 의한〉 a rollback / 임금 인하 (a) reduction in wages; a wage cut / 20% 가격 인하 markdown of 20%
—인하하다 lower; bring down; reduce; cut down
♦가격[임금]을 인하하다 reduce [lower, cut, put down] the price [wages]

인하다 因— 〈말미암다〉 be caused by; be due to; be owing to; result from; start [arise] from
♦기아로 인한 사망 die from hunger / 운전 부주의로 인한 사고 an accident due to [caused by] careless driving / …으로 인하여 because of…; by reason of…; on account of…; owing to…; due to…
▶나는 병으로 인하여 결석했다 I was absent from school on account of illness.
▶그는 사고로 인하여 죽었다 He died from an accident.

인해전술 人海戰術 human sea [wave] tactics
♦인해전술을 쓰다 send out more and more people

인허 認許 approval ⇨ 인가(認可)

인형 人形 a doll; 〈꼭두각시〉 a puppet; a marionette
♦인형의 집 a baby house; a dollhouse; a doll's house / 말하는 인형 a talking doll / 인형 같은 dollish / 인형을 가지고 놀다 play (with) dolls / 인형을 조작하다 manipulate a puppet [marionette]
■—극 a puppet play [show]; a marionette performance

인형 仁兄 〈친구에 대한 존칭〉 Dear Friend (▶편지에 씀)

인화 人和 harmony [concord] among men; peace and amity among the people
♦인화를 도모하다 promote [advance] the harmony among men

인화 引火 ignition
—인화하다 ignite; catch [take] fire
♦인화하기 쉬운 inflammable; ignitable
▶가솔린은 인화하기 쉽다 Gasoline catches fire easily.
■—물 the inflammables —성 inflammability; ignitability: 인화성의 inflammable; ignitable —점 the flash [ignition] point

인화 印畫 〔寫〕 printing; 〈인화된 것〉 a (photographic) print; a photoprint
♦이중 인화 double printing
—인화하다 print (off, out); make a print of
▶이 필름 좀 인화해 주세요 Please print this roll of film.
■—지 photographic [printing] paper; sensitized paper

인화 燐火 phosphorous light ⇨ 도깨비불

인화수소 燐化水素 〔化〕 hydrogen phosphide; phosphine; phosphuretted hydrogen

인환 引換 exchange; change ⇨ 상환

인회석 燐灰石 〔鑛〕 apatite

인후 咽喉 〈목구멍〉 the throat ♦인후의 jugular; guttural —염 〔醫〕 a sore throat —카타르 〔醫〕 catarrh of the throat

일 1 〈작업〉 a job; work; business; 〈할당된 과업〉 a task; 〈임무〉 a mission; *one's* duties; 〈직업〉 employment; an occupation

> [解説] **job**은 「(수입이 있는) 구체적인 일, 일자리」란 뜻이고 **work**는 「직업, 작업」이란 뜻의 추상 개념을 나타낸다.

♦힘든 일 a hard job; a difficult task / 하루 꼬박 걸리는 일 a good day's work / 일을 더 하는 사람 a slow worker [hand] / 일이 있다 have work to do; have a business to attend to / 일이 없다 have no work on hand; be out of work [employment, a job]; be jobless; be free / 일이 손에 잡히지 않다 be unable to get *oneself* [to make *oneself* settle down] to work; cannot concentrate on *one's* work / 일을 떠맡다 accept [take] a job; take a task upon *oneself* / 서둘러 일을 하다 rush *one's* work / 일을 맡기다 entrust *sb* with a task; give work to *sb* / 일을 마치다 bring *one's* work to a close; be through with *one's* work / 일을 마치고 집으로 돌아가다[돌아오다] go [come] home from work / 일을 계속하다 continue [carry on] *one's* work / 일을 그만두다 quit [leave off] work; 〈직장을 그만두다〉 throw up *one's* job / 일을 찾다 hunt [look (out) for] a job; seek [look for] work; seek for employment / 일을 싫어하다 be work-shy; be lazy / 일을 적당히 하다 do *one's* work in a rough-and-ready way; 〈날림으로〉 scamp [skimp] *one's* work / 일을 할당하다 assign a task to *sb* / 일을 중단하다 stop work; lay *one's* work aside / 일을 시작하다 begin to work; begin working; start work; set to work; get on the job / 일에 착수하다 fall to work; take up work; get (down) to business; set to work; go into harness
▶그것은 쉬운 일이 아니다 It is no easy work [task]. ⇌ It is quite a job. ⇌ It is no soft job.
▶내 일은 끝냈다 I have finished my work. ⇌ I am through with my work.
▶나는 힘든 일은 질색이다 I don't like hard work.
▶나는 할 일이 많다 I have a lot of work to do.
▶일은 잘 진척되고 있다 We are getting along very well with the work.
▶나는 일이 즐겁다 I enjoy my work.
▶그녀는 일에 쫓기고 있다 She is swamped with work.
▶그는 일을 잘한다 He is good in his job.
2 〈용무〉 business; an engagement; 〈심부름〉 an errand
♦일이 있어서 on business; 〈심부름으로〉 on an errand / 일을 보다 do *one's* business / 심부름 마치다 finish *one's* business / 아무에게 일이 있다 have business with *sb*
▶나에게 뭔가 (볼)일이 있습니까? What do you want with [of] me? ⇌ What do you want me for?
▶일이 있으면 부르십시오 Call me if I am wanted [if you want me].
▶한국에는 무슨 일로 오셨습니까? What have you come to Korea for? ⇌ What business has brought you to Korea?
▶이 일은 내가 맡으마 I'll take care of this matter [business].
3 〈경우·사물〉 a case; a thing; a matter; an affair; a business; (口) a concern; 〈문제〉 a question; 〈사실〉 a fact; 〈어떤 일〉 something
♦그런 일 such a thing; a thing like that / 나의 일 my concern [business] / 남의 일 other person's affairs / 난처한 일 an awkward affairs / 불쾌한 일 an unpleasant matter; something unpleasant / 금전상의 일 money [pecuniary] matters; a matter of money / 정신적인 일 things of the mind / 자기 일은 자기가 하다 mind [look after] *one's* own business; take care of *oneself*
▶제 일은 걱정하지 마십시오 Don't trouble yourself about me [on my account].
▶그는 남의 일에 참견을 잘한다 He often meddles [interferes] in other people's affairs.
▶그것은 이상한 일이다 It is a curious thing. ⇌ It is a strange [queer] business.
4 〈사정〉 circumstances; 〈사태〉 things
♦곤란한 일 a pretty [nice] kettle of fish / 무슨 일이 있어도 under [in] any circumstances; at any cost; in any case
▶일이 더 커지지는 않았다 It did not develop into serious situation.
▶그는 학교에 지각하는 일이 종종 있다 He is sometimes late for school.
5 〈사건〉 an incident; an event; a happening; an occurrence; 〈사고〉 an accident; 〈귀찮은〉 trouble
♦일을 저지르다 cause trouble / 무슨[위험한] 일이 있을 때는 in an emergency; in case of emergency
▶나는 일을 저지르고 싶지 않다 I don't want to cause trouble.
▶큰일이 벌어졌다 A terrible accident occurred.
▶그거 큰일났네 That's serious.
▶이제부터가 큰일이다 Now we have come to the most difficult part of the work.
6 〈계획〉 a plan; a program(me); a project; a scheme; 〈음모〉 a plot; 〈예정〉 a schedule
♦일을 꾀하다 make [form, lay] a plan; form [forge] a scheme; 〈음모를〉 hatch [brew] a plot / 일을 진행시키다 carry a program forward; carry forward a scheme
▶일이 순조롭게 되어간다 The plan is on a fair way to success.
▶일을 착착 진행시켜야 한다 We must carry out our plans steadily.
7 〈경험〉 an experience
♦…한 일이 있다[없다] have ever [never] done; once [never] did
▶당신은 러시아에 가 본 일이 있습니까? Have you ever been to Russia?
▶그녀에게서 한번 편지를 받은 일이 있다 I once got a letter from her.
8 〈업적〉 an achievement; merits; services
♦훌륭한 일을 하다 render distinguished services (to)
9 [物] work ▶증기기관은 열을 일로 바꾼다 A steam engine converts heat into work.

일 一 〈하나〉 one; 〈로마숫자〉 Ⅰ; 〈주사위 등의〉 an ace ♦5분의 일 one fifth; a fifth part

일 日 a day ◆2, 3일 a few days; a couple of days; two or three days / 7월 4일 ((on)) the Fourth of July; ((on)) July 4

일가 一家 1 〈가정〉 a family; a household; a home; 〈가족〉 one's family ◆민씨 일가 the Min family; the Mins / 일가가 단란하게 사는 in the bosom of one's family / 일가를 거느리다 keep house; manage one's household
2 〈일족〉 kin; a family; a clan; 〈친척〉 a relative; one's kinsfolk; one's folks
◆먼[가까운] 일가 a distant [near] relative [relation]
3 〈독자적 형식〉 a style; 〈유파〉 a school
◆일가를 이루다 develop a style of one's own; make a name; establish one's fame ((as a novelist))
■—문중 one's kinsfolk; one's clan —친척 one's relatives in blood and law [by blood and marriage]

일가 一價 〈化〉 monovalence; monovalency; univalence; univalency ◆일가의 〔化〕 monovalent; univalent —원소 〔化〕 a monad

일가견 一家見 an opinion peculiar to one; one's own opinion; a personal view

일가족 一家族 a family; a household; 〈전가족〉 the whole family; all the family

일각 一角 〈한 귀퉁이〉 a corner; a nook; 〈하나의 뿔〉 a horn
◆빙산의 일각 the tip of an iceberg / 정계의 일각 a section of political circles
▶이번 사건은 빙산의 일각에 불과하다 The present case is only the tip of the [an] iceberg.
■—수 (獸) a unicorn

일각 一刻 a minute; a moment
◆일각을 다투는 문제 a problem that needs a speedy solution; a burning question / 일각이라도 빨리 without a moment's delay; as soon as possible
▶일각을 다툰다 Not a moment is to be lost. ⇌ There is no time [not a moment] to lose.
▶일각이 삼추같다 Every minute seems like years [seems like a lifetime].
▶결승전은 각일각 다가오고 있었다 The run-off was coming closer every moment.

일간 日刊 daily publication [issue]
◆일간의 daily
■—신문[지] a daily newspaper; a daily; (총칭) the daily press: 이 신문은 일간지다 This paper is published daily [a daily].

일간 日間 〈부사적〉 one of these days; in the near future; at an early date
▶일간 다시 들르겠네 I'll call again one of these days.

일갈 一喝 a scolding —**일갈하다** scold in a voice of thunder; thunder (out); roar

일개 一介 ◆일개의 mere; only ▶나는 일개 미천한 서생에 지나지 않는다 I am only [no more than] a humble student.

일개 一箇 one; a piece ⇨ 한개

일개미 a worker ant ⇨ 개미(일~)

일개인 一個人 an individual ⇨ 개인(個人)

일거 一擧 one effort; one action; one coup
◆일거에 at a [one, a single] stroke; by [at] one effort; at a blow; at one coup [sweep, try]; at [in] one (fell) swoop / 적을 일거에 분쇄하다 beat [crush] the enemy at a blow

일거리 things to work with; a task; a piece of work; a job; business
◆일거리가 있다 have work to do; have a business to attend to / 일거리가 없다 be out of work; have nothing to do / 일거리를 주다 assign a task ((to sb)) / 일거리를 집에 가지고 오다 bring work home ((with one))

일거수일투족 一擧手一投足 one's every action ⇨ 일거일동

일거양득 一擧兩得 killing two birds with one stone ◆일거양득을 노리다 aim to kill two birds with one stone; try to make sth serve two purposes [ends]
▶그리하면 일거양득이다 It serves two ends.

일거일동 一擧一動 one's every action; every movement; everything one does
◆일거일동에 조심하다 be prudent in doing every little thing / 남의 일거일동을 주시하다 watch every movement [move] of others
▶이웃 사람들은 그녀의 일거일동을 지켜보고 있다 Her movements are being carefully watched by her neighbors.

일건 一件 an affair; a case

일격 一擊 a blow; a stroke; (口) a wallop
◆최후의 일격 a finishing stroke [blow] / 일격에 by (a single) blow; at a [one] blow [stroke]; with one stroke [blow] / 일격을 가하다 strike [give] sb a blow; strike [deal, launch] a blow ((at, on, against))
▶내가 그의 턱에 일격을 가했다 I gave him a blow on the jaw.

일견 一見 1 〈한번 봄·언뜻 봄〉 a look; a sight; a glance; a glimpse
—**일견하다** have [take, give] a look ((at)); glance; cast a glance ((at)); get [catch] a glimpse ((of))
◆일견하여 at a glance; at first sight / 일견할 가치가 있다 be worth seeing
▶나는 그것을 일견하고 진짜인 줄 알았다 I saw at a glance that it was genuine.
2 〈언뜻 보기에〉 apparently; seemingly
▶그는 일견 교사 같았다 He was apparently a teacher.

일계 日計 〈매일의 계산〉 a daily account; daily expenses ■—표 daily trial balance

일고 一考 consideration; a thought
◆이것은 일고를 요하는 문제다 This problem demands [calls for] our careful consideration.
—**일고하다** give a thought ((to)); bestow a thought ((on)); take ((a matter)) into consideration; bestow some consideration ((on))
◆일고한 뒤에 after consideration
▶그것은 일고해 볼 여지가 있다 It leaves room for consideration.

일고 一顧 a notice ▶그것은 일고의 가치도 없다 It does not deserve even the slightest notice.

일곱 seven ◆일곱개 한 벌 a heptad / 일곱살 먹은 아이 a child of seven years old; a seven-year-old (child) / 일곱째 (의) the seventh

일과 一過 ♦태풍 일과 후에 after the passage of typhoon ━일과하다 pass away
일과 日課 〈학과〉 a daily lesson; 〈일〉 a daily task; daily work; 〈매일의 습관〉 daily routine ♦일과를 게을리하다 neglect one's daily work ▶그는 아침 식사 전에 산책하는 것이 일과다 He makes a point of taking a walk before breakfast.
━━표 a daily schedule; a schedule 《of lessons》
일과성 一過性 ♦일과성의 temporary; fleeting; transient; transitory / 일과성 발열 a transient fever
일곽 一郭・一廓 a block; a quarter
일관 一貫 〈시종여일〉 consistency; coherence ▶정부의 교육 정책에는 일관성이 없다 The government lacks consistency in its educational policies.
━일관하다 be consistent; be coherent
♦일관하여 consistently; coherently; from first to last
▶그 당에는 일관된 정책이 없다 The party has no consistent policy.
▶그녀는 일관된 태도를 보였다 She kept the same attitude throughout [to the last]. ⇌ She was consistent in her attitude.
▶그는 시종 일관해서 암 연구에 전념했다 He was devoted to cancer research throughout his career.
━━작업 a thorough process; integrated work; 〈공정의〉 the conveyor system; assembly-line operation
일괄 一括 a bundle; a lump
▶그 법안들은 일괄 상정되었다 Those bills were brought up en bloc [in block, together] for discussion.
━일괄하다 make [tie up] into a bundle; lump together; sum up; summarize
▶취사 도구를 일괄해서 구입하고 싶다 I want to buy cooking utensils in one lot.
▶그것은 일괄해서 사는 것이 이득이다 It is economical to buy it in bulk.
━━계약 a blanket contract; a package deal ━━구입 a blanket purchase ━━사직 a wholesale resignation; a resignation en bloc [in a body] ━━소송 a wholesale suit; a package suit ━━제안 a package proposal ━━지급 a lump-sum payment ━━타결 a package [an overall] settlement ━━판매 (a) sale by bulk
일광 日光 sunlight; the sun; sunshine; sunbeams; the rays of the sun; the solar rays

> 解說 **sunlight**는 태양에서 오는 빛을 뜻하고 **sun, sunshine**은 태양에서 오는 빛과 열을 가리킨다. 이들은 모두 불가산명사다. **sunbeam**은 태양 광선을 나타내는 약간 문어적인 말인데 가산명사로서 복수형으로 쓰이는 일이 많다.

▶이 약은 일광이 들지 않는 곳에 두시오 Keep this medicine out of the sun.
━━직사 direct sunlight ━━반사기 〔物〕 a heliotrope ━━소독 sterilization by sunning; disinfection by sunlight; 일광소독을 하다 disinfect by sunlight ━━스펙트럼 a solar spectrum ━━시(時) the daylight hours; the span of daylight ━━요법 heliotherapy
일광욕 日光浴 a sunbath; a solar bath; sunbathing ━일광욕하다 bathe [bask] in the sun; sunbathe; take a sunbath
일교차 日較差 daily [diurnal] (temperature) range
일구다 1 〈개간하다〉 bring 《wasteland》 under cultivation; reclaim 《wasteland》; break up 《the soil》
▶그 땅은 채소밭을 만들려고 일구어 놓았다 The land has been dug up for a vegetable garden.
2 〈두더지가〉 《a mole》 raise a mound; burrow in
일구월심 日久月深 《with》 the lapse [passage] of time; 〈부사적〉 more intently [fervently] as time passes by
▶그녀는 일구월심 그 남자만을 생각했다 She conceived a single-minded affection for him.
일구이언 一口二言 being double-tongued; double-dealing; duplicity
━일구이언하다 be double-tongued; be double-dealing; talk out of both sides of the mouth; break [go back on] one's word; contradict oneself
일국 一國 〈한 나라〉 one country; one state; one nation; 〈나라 전체〉 the whole country
♦일국의 총리 a prime minister of a country / 일국을 뒤흔들어 놓은 사건 an event that shook [jolted] the whole country
일군 一軍 1 〈전군〉 the whole army [force] 《of a nation》
♦일군의 지휘관 a commander-in-chief / 일군을 거느리다 at the head of an army
2 〈제1군〉 the First Army
3 〔野〕 the first team
▶그는 아직 2군에서 1군으로 올라오지 못했다 He still hasn't made it (up) from the farm to the first team.
━━사령관 the Commander of the First Army
일군 一郡 〈한 군〉 one county; 〈군 전체〉 the whole county
일그러지다 be distorted; be contorted; be twisted
▶그녀는 고통으로 일그러진 얼굴을 하고 있었다 She had a face distorted [twisted] with pain.
▶나는 그의 일그러진 마음이 싫다 I don't like his crooked mind.
일금 一金 (the sum of) money ♦일금 십 만원 (the sum of) a hundred thousand won
일급 一級 1 〈최상급〉 the first class
▶그의 솜씨는 일급이다 His skill is excellent [first-class].
2 〈한 계급〉 one class; 〈등급〉 one grade
♦일급 승진하다 be promoted one grade
━━품 first-class goods; A 1 articles: 이 포도주는 일급품이다 This wine is (of) the best quality.
일급 日給 daily wages [pay]; a day's wage
♦일급으로 일하다 work by the day

일기 ▶내 일급은 5만원이다 I get [They pay me] fifty thousand won a day. ■ー노동자 a day laborer ―제 the day-rate plan

일기 一期 1〈일생〉one's span of life; one's whole life ▶그는 70세를 일기로 세상을 떠났다 He died at the age of seventy. 2〈한 기간〉a term ▶나는 소득세를 일기분에 5만원 낸다 I pay an income tax of 50,000 won for a term. ■ー배당금 a regular [quarterly] dividend

일기 一騎 a (single) horseman ◆일기 당천(一騎當千)의 용사 a match for a thousand; a matchless [mighty] warrior ▶병사들은 전원 일기 당천의 용사이었다 Each of the soldiers was a man of unsurpassed prowess.

일기 日記 a diary; a journal ▶나는 지금까지 10년 동안 계속 일기를 써왔다 I have kept my diary for ten years now. ▶자기 전에 일기 쓰는 일을 가끔 잊는다 I sometimes forget to write in my diary before going to bed. ■ー문학 diaries (as a branch of literature) ―장 a diary

일기 日氣 the weather ⇨ 날씨 ◆일기를 예보하다 make a weather forecast; forecast the weather ▶4월에는 일기가 고르지 못하다 The weather is changeable in April. ■ー개황 general weather conditions; a meteorological summary ―도 a weather map [chart] ―불순 unseasonableness [changeableness] of weather

일기예보 日氣豫報 a weather report ▶서울지역의 일기예보는 어떻습니까? - What's the weather report for the Seoul area? ▶일기예보에 의하면 오후에 소나기가 내리겠다고 합니다 The weather forecast says we'll have a shower in the afternoon. ▶오늘의 일기예보는 맞았다[틀렸다] The weather forecast was accurate [wrong] today. ■ー관 a weather forecaster; a weatherman

일기죽거리다 swing one's hips ⇨ 얄기죽거리다

일깨우다 1〈잠을 깨우다〉wake sb up early in the morning 2〈알게 하다〉make sb aware of; 〈깨닫게 하다〉awaken; open sb's eyes; 〈계몽하다〉enlighten ◆잘못을 일깨우다 convince sb of his errors / 몽매한 사람들을 일깨우다 enlighten the ignorant

일껏 with much trouble [effort]; at [with] great pains ▶일껏 재배한 채소가 홍수에 모두 유실되었다 All the vegetables I grew with great effort were washed away by the flood.

일꾼 1〈일하는 사람〉a worker; 〈품팔이〉a wage earner; a wageworker; 〈노동자〉a laborer; a workman ◆집안의 일꾼 the breadwinner 2〈유능한 사람〉an able person; a man of ability [capacity, resources] ▶그는 우리 회사에 없어서는 안될 일꾼이다 His work is indispensable to our firm. ▶그는 사회의 큰 일꾼이 될 것이다 He will become a pillar of society.

일끝 one end of a job [an event] ◆일끝을 맺다 finish the matter up; tie up the loose ends

일년 一年 a year; one year ◆일년에 한번 once a year; annually / 일년에 한번의 annual; yearly / 일년에 두번의 biannual; semiannual ▶일년은 365일이다 There are 365 days in a year. ⇌ A year has 365 days. ▶그 산의 정상은 일년 내내 눈으로 덮여 있다 The top of the mountain is covered with snow throughout the year [all the year round]. ■ー갈 ⇨ 토마토 ―생 a first-year [first-grade] student; a first grader; 〈대학·고교의〉a freshman; (口) a freshie ―생 식물 an annual [a yearly] plant

일념 一念 〈일심〉a single heart; a concentrated mind; a determined soul; 〈소원〉a wholehearted desire; an ardent wish ▶그녀는 그를 만나 보고 싶은 일념으로 상경했다 She has come to Seoul out of sheer desire [an ardent wish] to see him.

일다¹ 1〈생기다〉happen; rise ▶큰 바람이 일었다 A great wind arose. ▶이 비누는 거품이 잘 인다 This soap lathers well. 2〈성해지다〉grow violent [fierce]; rise [increase] in violence; 〈번창하다〉prosper; grow prosperous ◆살림이 일다 rise to fortune; come to wealth / 세력이 일다 increase in power; gain in influence ▶거리의 한 모퉁이에서 불길이 일었다 A fire broke out in one corner of the town. 3〈보풀 등이〉be nappy [fluffy] ◆보풀이 인 천 cloth with a rough nap

일다² 〈쌀 등을〉wash; clean by washing ◆사금을 일다 wash for gold; 〈냄비로〉pan gold / 쌀을 일다 wash rice to remove grit; clean rice

일단 一段 1〈단계〉a stage; the first stage ◆로켓의 제 일단 the first [bottom] stage of a rocket / 일단 기어 장치 a single gear 2〈층계의〉a stair [step] 《of a staircase》;〈사다리의〉a rung 3〈등급〉a grade; 〈초단〉the first grade ▶(바둑 등이) 일단인 사람 a first grader 4〈문장의〉a passage; a paragraph; 〈신문 등의〉a column

일단 一端 〈한쪽 끝〉one end; 〈일부〉a part; 〈대체〉an outline ▶나에게도 일단의 책임이 있다 I take partial responsibility for it. ▶그는 새로운 계획의 일단을 밝혔다 He revealed a part of the new project.

일단 一團 a group; a body; a party; a band; 〈악한의〉a gang ◆일단의 관광객 a party of tourists / 일단이 되어 in a body [group]

▶일단의 소년들이 버스 정류장에서 버스를 기다리고 있었다 A group [troop] of boys were waiting for the bus at the bus station.

일단 一旦 〈한 번〉 once; 〈우선〉 first; beforehand; in advance 《to》; 〈일시〉 for the time being; for the present; 〈만일〉 in the event of; in case of
◆일단 유사시에는 in case of [in an] emergency; should emergency arise
▶그는 일단 결심하면 꼭 실행한다 Once he makes up his mind, he will always follow through (on his decision).
▶일단 요령만 익히면 그 일은 결코 어렵지않다 Once you've got the knack of the work, it is not difficult at all.
▶내달에 일단 귀국하겠습니다 I'll go home temporarily next month.
▶이만 일단 끝냅시다 Let's stop here for the present.

일단락 一段落 a pause
▶그들은 교섭을 일단락지었다 They have finished [wound up, wrapped up] the first phase of the negotiations.
▶이것으로 이 일도 일단락되었다 The work has been brought to an end for the present [for the time being]. ⇌ We have completed the first stage of the work.

일당 一黨 1 〈한 패거리〉 fellow conspirators; a party 《to a plot》; a ring; a gang; a clique
▶은행은 강도 일당의 습격을 받았다 The bank was held up by a gang of robbers.
▶일당이 체포되었다 All the fellow conspirators were nabbed.
▶그는 강도의 일당으로 오인받았다 He was mistaken for one of the burglars.
2 〈한 정당〉 a party; a league
◆일당을 이끌다 lead a party / 일당 일파에 치우치다 be partial to a specific party
■一국회 a one-party legislature —독재 one-party rule [dictatorship]

일당 日當 a daily [per diem] allowance; a per diem; daily wages
◆일당으로 지급하다 pay by the day / 일당 5만 원을 지불하다 pay 50,000 won a day / 일당 4만 원을 받고 일하다 work for 40,000 won a day
▶그는 부산까지의 여비와 일당을 받았다 He was paid transportation to Pusan and a daily allowance.

일당백 一當百 ◆일당백의 용사 a match for a hundred; a very brave [strong] man

일대 一代 〈일세〉 a [one] generation; 〈일생〉 one's lifetime; 〈당대〉 the age; the day
▶나폴레옹은 일대의 영웅으로 추앙 받았다 Napoleon was respected as the greatest hero of his age [day].
■一기 a biography; a life history; a life

일대 一帶 the whole place [area, district]
▶중서부 일대에 큰 눈이 내렸다 There was a heavy snowfall all over the middle west region.
▶이 일대에는 병원이 없다 There is no hospital in the entire district.

일대 一隊 a company (of soldiers); a party (of mountaineers); a bevy (of school girls)

일대 一大 〈형용사적〉 one great [grand, large]; very important; of great importance
◆일대 발견 a discovery of great importance / 일대 성황을 이루다 be a great success; be well attended / 일대 용단을 내리다 take a decisive step [a drastic measure]

일대사 一大事 〈큰일〉 a matter of great importance [grave concern]; a serious [grave] affair; an emergency
◆국가의 일대사 an affair of vital importance to the State

일대일 一對一 one to one
◆일대일의 대응 a one-to-one correspondence / 일대일의 승부[대결] a single (-handed) combat [fight]; a man-to-man fight / 일대일로 싸우다 fight man to man

일더위 the early summer heat; the heat of early summer

일도 一度 a [one] degree

일도양단 一刀兩斷 ◆일도양단의 조치를 취하다 take a drastic [decisive] measure; solve a problem once for all; resort to a drastic measure; cut the Gordian knot
—일도양단하다 cut *sb* [*sth*] in two with a single stroke of the sword

일독 一讀 a perusal; a (single) reading
—일독하다 peruse; read through 《a book》 once; run one's eyes over 《a paper》
▶그 책은 일독할 가치가 있다 The book is worth reading.

일동 一同 all (of us [them]); all the persons concerned [present]; the whole 《staff》
◆가족 일동 all one's family / 사원 일동 the whole [entire] company / 일동을 대표하여 on behalf of 《us》 all
▶그는 일동을 대표하여 인사를 했다 He extended greetings on behalf of the company.

일되다 〈올되다〉 mature early; grow [ripen] early ▶올해는 벼가 일되었다 We have had an early crop of rice this year.

일등 一等 the first class [rank, grade, place]; A 1; 〈제1위〉 the first place
▶그녀가 일등으로 들어왔다 She came in first.
▶이것이 단연 일등이다 This is by far the best of all.
▶나는 웅변대회에서 일등을 했다 I got the first place in the speech contest.
▶그는 학급에서 영어 점수가 늘 일등이다 He is always at the top of the class in English.
■一국 a first-class power; 일등국이 되다 become a first-class power; rank among the greatest powers of the world —급 first degree —기관사 a first engineer —병 〈육군·해병〉 a private first class (略 PFC, Pfc.); 〈공군〉 (美) an airman second class; (英) a senior aircraftman —상 the first prize: 일등상을 타다 win (the) first prize; win first place —성(星) 〔天〕 a star of the first magnitude —승객 a first-class passenger —차 a first-class carriage [car] —친(親) 〔法〕 a relation of the first degree —품 a first-class article; the first on the market; the first stuff —항해사 the first officer; 〈상선의〉 the chief mate

일락 逸樂 idle pursuit of pleasure; ease; com-

일락서산 fort ♦일락에 빠지다 indulge in pleasure

일락서산 日落西山 the sunset on the western hills —일락서산하다 the sun sets on the western hills

일란성 一卵性 〔醫〕 ♦일란성의 monovular; monozygotic; monozygous —쌍생아 〈양쪽〉 identical twins; 〈한쪽〉 an identical twin

일람 一覽 〈일견〉 a look; a glance; an inspection; 〈개요〉 a summary; 〈안내서〉 a catalog(ue)
♦일람후 30일불(拂) payable at thirty days after sight
—일람하다 take [have] a look at; glance through; run one's eyes through; peruse; take a view of
▶샘플을 일람하신 후 주문해 주시기 바랍니다 Please look through [take a careful look at] the sample before you place an order.

일람불 一覽拂 ♦일람불의 payable at sight ■一어음 a bill [draft] (payable) at sight [on demand]; a sight bill (略 S/B); a demand draft (略 D/D); a sight draft

일람표 一覽表 a table; a list; a schedule; a catalog(ue) ♦시험 성적을 일람표로 만들다 make a list of the exam results

일러 두 기 explanatory notes; introductory remarks; 〈지도 등의〉 a legend

일러두다 tell; order; instruct; charge; request; bid; direct
♦…하라고 일러두다 tell [order, request] sb to 《do》/ 단단히 일러두다 give strict orders

일러바치다 inform 《one's superior against sb》; tell [squeal] on sb; tell [carry] tales 《about, against, upon sb》; (美俗) tick off
▶다시 한번 그런 짓을 하면 선생님께 일러바칠 거야 If you do it again, I'll tell on you to the teacher.

일러스트레이션 〈삽화〉 an illustration
일러스트레이터 〈삽화가〉 an illustrator
일러주다 〈알려주다〉 let sb know; tell 《sb about sth》; inform [advise, notify] 《sb of sth》; 〈가르쳐 주다〉 show; inform; teach; instruct; initiate 《in, into》
♦넌지시 일러주다 intimate; hint (at); drop a hint; suggest / 장사의 비결을 일러주다 initiate sb in [into] the tricks of the trade
▶언제 도착하는지 일러주십시오 Please tell me [let me know] when you will arrive.

일렁거리다 sway; waver; toss 《on the waves》; rock; 〈앞뒤로〉 pitch; 〈옆으로〉 roll
▶배가 일렁거려 속이 안좋다 The pitch and roll makes me sick.

일렁일렁 swayingly; in a wavering [swaying] manner

일렉트론 〔物〕 electron
일력 日曆 a daily pad [block] calendar
일련 一連 ♦일련의 a series of 《questions》; a chain [train] of 《events》
▶그 일련의 사건은 1995년에 시작되었다 The whole train [chain] of events began in 1995.

일련번호 一連番號 consecutive [running] numbers; serial numbers ♦일련번호를 매기다 number 《the cards》 serially [consecutively]

일련탁생 一蓮托生 〈극락왕생〉 rebirth together on lotus flower; 〈행동·운명의〉 casting one's lot with another; sharing the fate with others; rising or sinking together

일렬 一列 a line; a row; a queue; a file; a rank
▶학생들은 선생님 앞에 일렬로 섰다 The pupils stood in a single file in front of their teacher.
▶매표구 앞에 사람들이 일렬로 서 있다 People are making [forming] a line in front of the ticket window.
▶선수들은 일렬 종대로 행진했다 The players marched in a line [file].

일례 一例 an example; an instance; one instance from many; a case; an illustration
♦일례로 for example; for instance; by way of example [illustration]; as an example
▶이것은 일례에 지나지 않는다 This is only one instance [a case in point] among many.

일로 一路 a straight road; one road; 〈곧장〉 straight; directly
♦증가〔감소〕 일로에 있다 go [keep] on increasing [decreasing] / 악화 일로를 걷다 keep [go] on worsening; be steadily getting worse; grow worse and worse / 일로 매진하다 go [advance] straightly; 〈노력하다〉 strive only for 《a matter》/ 일로 샌프란시스코로 향하다 head [go] straight for San Francisco

일루 一縷 a single thread ♦일루의 희망 a ray [flush, shadow] of hope / 일루의 희망을 걸다 cling to one's last hope; entertain some faint hope 《that…》
▶아들이 죽자 그녀는 일루의 희망마저 없어졌다 Her son's death deprived her of her last hope.

일루 一壘 〔野〕 first base
♦1루를 맡다 play first base / 사구로 1루에 나가다 get [go] to first base on balls; walk
■—수 the first baseman —측 스탠드 the right stand —타 a base hit

일류 一流 the first class [rank]
▶이 부근에는 일류 호텔이 늘어서 있다 There stand first-class hotels around here.
▶그는 당대의 일류 경영자로 꼽힌다 He is one of the best [foremost] managers of today.
■—가수 a top class singer —극장 a first-class theater; 〈영화관〉 a first-run movie house [theater] —기술자 a top-notch [an A-1] engineer —선수 a ranking player —신사 a gentleman of the best standing —외교관 a diplomat of the first rank —작가 a first-rate writer; one of the best [leading] writers —학교 a prestige school —학자 a scholar of the first order [highest standing] —회사 a leading company [firm]

일루미네이션 〈조명〉 illumination ♦일류미네이션 장식을 하다 illuminate 《a building》

일륜 日輪 the orb of day; the sun
일률 一律 〈한결같음〉 uniformity; evenness; equality; 〈무차별〉 indiscrimination
♦일률적인 uniform; even; indiscriminate / 일률적으로 uniformly; evenly; indiscriminately; sweepingly / 일률적으로 논하다 make a sweeping statement
▶그들을 전부 일률적으로 논할 수는 없다 We

cannot apply the same rule to them all.
일리 一理 some reason; some truth
▶ 너의 말에도 일리가 있다 There is some [a grain of] truth in what you say. ⇒ One facet of what you say is true.
▶ 그것도 일리가 있다 There is something [some reason, some truth] in that.
일리노이 〈미국의 주〉 Illinois (略 Ill.)
일막 一幕 〈한 막〉 one act; 〈제1막〉 the first act ■一극 a one-act play; a one-acter
일말 一抹 a touch 《of melancholy》; a tinge 《of sadness》
◆일말의 불안을 느끼다 feel slightly uneasy; feel some [a certain] anxiety 《about》
▶ 그의 눈에 일말의 불안감이 비쳤다 There was a touch of uneasiness in his eyes.
▶ 너에게도 일말의 양심은 있을 거 아냐? You have a bit [particle] of conscience, don't you?
일망무제 一望無際 endlessness; boundlessness —**일망무제하다** endless; boundless
◆일망무제한 바다 an unlimited [a boundless] expanse of waters; a boundless ocean
일망타진 一網打盡 making a wholesale arrest; a roundup
—**일망타진하다** catch 《the whole herd》 with one throw; make a wholesale arrest 《of》; make a roundup; round up
▶ 경찰은 밀수꾼을 일망타진했다 The police made a wholesale arrest of all the smugglers.
일매지다 〈가지런하다〉 even; uniform; regular 《teeth》
일맥상통하다 一脈相通— have a thread of connection 《with》; have sth in common 《with》
▶ 양자간에는 일맥상통하는 점이 있다 There is a thread of connections between the two.
▶ 저 두 사람은 뭔가 일맥상통하는 것 같다 The two persons seem to have something in common.
일면 一面 1 〈한 면〉 a facet; one side; a phase
▶ 그것은 문제의 일면에 지나지 않는다 It means only one side [phase] of the issue.
▶ 나는 그 사건의 다른 일면을 알고 있다 I know another phase of the case.
2 〈한편〉 on the other hand; while on the other 《hand》
▶ 그녀는 무척 상냥하지만, 일면 엄격한 데도 있다 She is very gentle, but on the other hand there's something stern about her.
3 〈신문 등의〉 the first [front] page
▶ 그것에 관한 기사가 일면의 톱에 실렸다 An article about it appeared at the top of the front page.
일면식 一面識 a slight acquaintance; a bowing [nodding] acquaintance ◆일면식도 없는 사람 an utter [a total, a perfect] stranger / …과 일면식이 있다 be slightly acquainted with sb; be on bowing terms with sb
일명 一名 1 〈한 사람〉 one person
▶ 점원 일명 구함 《광고》 Wanted: a clerk.
2 〈별명〉 another name; a second name; an alias
▶ 미국의 경찰관은 일명 캅으로 불린다 A cop is another name for the policeman in the United States. ⇒ A policeman is sometimes called a cop in the United States.
일명 一命 a life ◆나라를 위해 일명을 바치다 offer [lay down] one's life for one's country
일모 日暮 〈일몰〉 nightfall; sunset; (美) sundown; 〈황혼〉 dusk; twilight
■一도궁 (途窮)[도원 (途遠)] 〈노쇠〉 loneliness and woe; senile decay
일모작 一毛作 raising a single-crop (of rice) a year; single-crop farming
▶ 이곳은 일모작 지역이다 This is a single-crop area. ■一답 a single-crop field
일목요연하다 一目瞭然— quite obvious; as plain as the day; as clear as day
▶ 그것은 일목요연하다 It is (as) clear as day [daylight]. ⇒ It is obvious at a glance.
일몰 日沒 sunset; (美) sundown
◆일몰후[전] after [before] sunset [sundown] / 일출부터 일몰까지 from sunrise till sunset; (美) from sunup to sundown
▶ 그는 일몰 전에는 돌아오지 않을 것이다 He won't be back before sunset.
▶ 일몰이 가까워지면서 바람이 가라앉았다 The wind died away toward(s) sunset.
일무 一無 nothing; not even one
■一소득 no profit [gain] at all ―소식 no tidings [news] at all; not a single word
일문 一門 1 〈일족〉 a family; a clan; 〈가족〉 one's kinsfolk; 〈종파〉 the whole sect
◆왕씨 일문 the Wang clan
2 〈대포 하나〉 a piece of gun; a cannon
일문일답 一問一答 a series of questions and answers; a question and an answer; a dialogue; Q & A
—**일문일답하다** give an (immediate) answer to each question; have a detailed dialogue 《about》; exchange questions and answers
일물 逸物 a superb article; an excellent specimen; a thing of the first rate; 〈걸작〉 a masterpiece
일미 一味 a superb [good] flavor; relish
▶ 이 요리는 정말 일미다 This dish is quite delicious.
일박 一泊 a night's lodging; an overnight stay
—**일박하다** stay overnight; stop for the night; pass [spend] a night (at, in)
▶ 그날 밤은 시내의 호텔에서 일박했다 I stayed [put up] at a hotel in the city for the night.
■一여행 (make) an overnight trip 《to》
일반 一般 〈일반의〉 the whole; 〈전반〉 the whole; 〈매한가지〉 the same 《as》 ◆일반 사람들 the general [common] run of people; 〈문외한〉 outsiders; 〈비전문가〉 laymen; men on [(英) in] the street / 일반의 예상 general expectations / 일반용의 for popular use / 일반에 공개하다 open …to the public / 일반에 알리다 make (it) generally known / 일반에 널리 알려지다 become public knowledge; become known to a wide public
▶ 나는 과학 일반에 관심이 있다 I'm interested in science in general.
▶ 이것은 일반에 잘 알려진 일이다 This is a matter of common knowledge.

일반적

▶사실은 일반 사람들이 믿고 있는 것과는 반대다 The fact is contrary to popular belief.
■—감각 (心) general sensation —감사 a general audit —개념 [論] a general concept [idea, notion] —교서 (美) the (President's) State of the Union Message (to Congress) —교양 general [liberal] culture —교양 과목 the subjects for general education —교양 과정 [教育] liberal education —규정 a general [universal] rule; general provisions —대중 the general public; the public at large; the masses: 그것이 일반 대중의 생각이다 It is how the masses think. —독자 general readership; common readers —론 general consideration —명사 (名辭) a general term —법 a general law [statute] —사면 a general pardon —석 〈극장 등의〉 a general admission seat —성 generality —식 (數) a general expression —원칙 broad [general] principles —의 (醫) a general practitioner —입찰 an open public tender [bid] —직 〈공무원의〉 regular government service —투자자 the investing public; a general investor —투표 a referendum (pl. ~s, -da); a popular [national] vote —화 generalization; popularization: 일반화하다 generalize; popularize —회계 the general account

일반적 一般的 〈전반적〉 general; universal; widespread; 〈보통의〉 common; ordinary; usual; average
◆일반적으로 알려진 일 a matter of common knowledge / 일반적으로 generally; universally; popularly; in general; at large; as a (general) rule
▶태양 숭배는 원시인들 사이에서는 일반적인 관습이었다 Worshipping the sun was a universal practice among primitive peoples.

일발 一發 a (single) shot; a round
▶그는 멧돼지를 향해 일발을 쏘았다 He fired a shot at the boar.
▶나는 밤의 어둠 속에서 일발의 총성을 들었다 I heard a shot [the report of a gun] in the darkness of the night.
▶사냥꾼은 일발로 곰 한 마리를 잡았다 The hunter killed a bear with a single shot.

일방 一方 〈한 쪽〉 one side [hand]; 〈다른 쪽〉 the other side [hand]; 〈편도〉 one-way
■—무역 one-way [lopsided] trade —통행 one-way traffic —통행로 a one-way street [road]

일방적 一方的 one-sided; lopsided
◆일방적인 경기 a one-sided game / 일방적으로 one-sidedly; unilaterally / 일방적인 승리를 거두다 win a runaway [an easy] victory / 조약을 일방적으로 파기하다 abrogate a treaty one-sidedly

일번 一番 the first (place); number one; No. 1
◆일번의 first; foremost; top; second to none
▶그의 야구 유니폼 번호는 일번이었다 His baseball uniform number was 1.
■—열차 the first train —타자 (野) a lead-off man [batter]

일벌 (昆) a worker bee; a worker
일벌백계 一罰百戒 an exemplary punishment
◆일벌백계로 다스리다 punish sb as a warning to all the others

일변 一變 a (complete) change ◆형세의 일변 a drastic [sweeping] change of the situation —일변하다 change completely [entirely, altogether]; undergo a (complete) change
◆태도를 일변하다 change [reverse] one's attitude; change front
▶사태는 일변했다 The situation has [Things have] completely changed. ⇒ The situation has taken a new turn.
▶그 일이 있은 후 그의 성격이 일변했다 After the incident he has become another man.

일변 日邊 daily interest; interest per diem
◆일변으로 빌린 돈 money loaned at daily interest

일변도 一邊倒 wholehearted [complete] devotion to one side
▶그들은 대미 일변도다 They are completely pro-America. ⇒ They are wholly devoted to American interests.
■—정책 a lean-to-one-side policy

일별 一瞥 a glance; a look; a glimpse
—일별하다 glance (at, on); cast a glance (at); shoot a look (at)
◆일별하여 at a glance / 일별할 가치도 없다 be beneath notice

일보 一步 a [one] step
◆일보 전진[후퇴]하다 take a step forward [backward] / 일보도 양보하지 않다 do not yield a step [an inch] / …의 일보 직전에 있다 be on the eve [brink, verge] of (ruin)
▶이것은 확실히 일보 전진이다 This is certainly a forward [positive] step. ⇒ This is a step in the right direction.
▶우리는 정밀 기구의 제조에서 그들보다 일보 앞섰다 We got one step ahead of them in the manufacture of precision instruments.
▶서로 솔직하게 이야기하는 것이 상호 이해의 제일보다 To talk frankly with each other is the first step toward a better mutual understanding.

일보 日報 a daily report [bulletin]; 〈신문〉 a daily (newspaper)
◆문화 일보 the Munhwa Daily News

일보다 carry on [attend to] one's business
▶사장 부재시에는 부사장이 대리로 일본다 In the absence of the president, the vice-president acts for him.

일본 日本 Japan
◆일본의 Japanese / 일본식으로 in Japanese style
■—뇌염 [醫] Japanese encephalitis [cerebritis] —사람 a Japanese; (총칭) the Japanese (people) —어 Japanese; the Japanese language —열도 the Japanese Islands [Isles, Archipelago] —요리 Japanese-style dish [cuisine] —제품 Japanese-made goods; a Japanese product

일부 一夫 〈한 사내〉 one man; 〈한 남편〉 one husband
◆일부 종사하다 serve but one husband / 일부 종신하다 have but one husband during [throughout] one's life
■—다처제 polygamy: 일부다처제의 polyga-

mous —다처주의자 a polygamist —일처제 monogamy: 일부일처제의 monogamous —일처주의자 a monogamist

일부 一部 **1** 〈한 부분〉 a part; a portion; a section
♦일부 사람들 some people / 일부의 partial; sectional / 일부는 in part; partly / 일부를 수정하다 amend partially [in part]; make a partial amendment 《of》 / …의 일부를 이루다 form (a) part of…
▶이 지도는 일부 수정이 필요하다 This map should be corrected in part.
▶그녀는 내 논문의 일부밖에 읽지 않았다 She read only part [a section] of my paper.
▶우리는 그 사업의 일부를 끝냈다 We have completed part of the project.
▶우리 집은 낡았지만 일부 수리하면 아직 살만 하다 Though my house is old, it is still livable if it is fixed up a little.
2 〈한 권〉 a copy 《of the book》
3 〈한 벌〉 a complete set 《of》
■—용선(傭船) a partcargo charter —주권국 a state having partial sovereignty; a semi-independent country

일부 日附 a date; dating
■—변경선 the (international) date line —인 a date stamp; 〈회전식의〉 a dater

일부 日賦 〈날짜〉 daily installment
♦일부로 갚다 pay by daily installments
■—금 daily installment payment —판매 sale on daily-installment terms

일부러 〈고의로〉 purposely; on purpose; intentionally; deliberately; 〈짐짓〉 knowingly; wittingly; 〈특별히〉 specially; especially; expressly
▶그것 때문에 일부러 왔다 I am here for that express purpose.
▶먼 데까지 일부러 와 주셔서 감사합니다 It is very kind of you to come all this way to see us.
▶당신을 일부러 피한 것은 아닙니다 I had no intention of avoiding you.

일부분 一部分 a part ⇨ 일부(一部) 1

일분 一分 **1** 〈백분의 일〉 (one) hundredth; one percent **2** 〈시간〉 a minute
♦일분 일초도 어김없이 as accurate as a chronometer; to the minute [very moment]; on the minute / 일분도 어기지 않다 be punctual to the minute

일사 一死 〔野〕 one (man) out ▶일사 만루가 되었다 The bases were loaded with one out.

일사 一事 one thing
■—부재리(不再理) 〔法〕 (the principle of) not subjecting sb to double jeopardy —부재의 (不再議) 〔法〕 (the principle of) not deliberating the same measure twice during the same session (of the National Assembly)

일사병 日射病 sunstroke; heatstroke; siriasis
♦일사병에 걸리다 have [suffer from] sunstroke; be affected by sunstroke; be sunstruck

일사분기 一四分期 the first quarter (of the year)

일사불란하다 一絲不亂— 《be》 in perfect [strict] order; thoroughly consistent; shipshape
♦일사불란한 논지 a thoroughly consistent argument / 일사불란한 팀워크 fine teamwork / 일사불란하게 in perfect [strict] order; shipshape; in a shipshape manner
▶그들은 일사불란하게 움직였다 They moved in perfect order.

일사천리 一瀉千里 dashing flow of torrents; rapid advance
♦일사천리로 일을 해치우다 finish off [get through with] one's work at a stretch; rush through one's work / 법안을 일사천리로 통과 시키다 rush a bill through
▶그는 일사천리로 리포트 하나를 썼다 He dashed off a report.

일삯 wages; pay

일산 日産 〈매일의 생산고〉 (a) daily output
▶이 공장은 일산 20톤의 강재를 생산한다 This factory produces [turns out] twenty tons of steel a day.

일산 一酸 〔化〕 ♦일산의 monoacid(ic)
■—염기 a monoacid base —화물 monoxide —화질소 nitrogen monoxide —화탄소 carbon monoxide: 일산화탄소 중독으로 죽다 die from [of] carbon monoxide

일삼다 〈일로 삼다〉 make it one's business to 《do sth》; 〈전념하다〉 devote oneself to; engage in; 〈탐닉하다〉 give oneself up to; do nothing but…; be given [addicted] to; indulge in; be absorbed in

일상 日常 every day; daily; usually; always
♦일상의 daily; everyday; usual; routine; ordinary
▶그녀는 일상 건강에 유의하고 있다 She always takes care of her health.
▶나는 일상 회화에 필요한 영어 단어를 배웠다 I learned several English words necessary for daily [everyday] conversation.
■—(다반)사 a daily event [occurrence, happening]; an everyday affair —복 everyday dress —생활 daily [everyday] life: 물은 우리의 일상생활에 불가결하다 Water is a necessity in [for, of] our daily [everyday] life. —업무 daily [ordinary] business [work]; routine work; (daily) routine : 그는 신체상 일상 업무에 지장이 없다 He is physically fit for ordinary work. —용어 everyday words —필수품 a thing of daily necessity

일색 一色 **1** 〈한 빛깔〉 one color ♦노랑 일색으로 칠하다 paint sth all in yellow
2 〈미인〉 a beautiful woman; a stunning beauty
3 (비유) ▶서울은 야당 일색이었다 Seoul was swept by the Opposition.
■—천하— a rare [an extraordinary] beauty; a woman of unmatched [matchless] beauty

일생 一生 one's (whole) life; one's lifetime
♦일생의 사업 one's lifework; a lifelong work / 일생의 소원[소망] one's lifelong desire; a desire cherished for life / 일생의 lifelong; for life
▶그 사전을 만들자면 당신 일생이 걸릴 것이오 It would take your (whole) lifetime to make the dictionary.
▶그녀의 일생은 소설 같다 Her life is just like

a novel.
▶사람의 일생은 짧다 The span of life is short.
▶조부는 80세로 일생을 마치셨다 My grandfather died at the age of eighty.
▶그는 암 연구에 일생을 바치기로 결심했다 He made up his mind to devote his whole life to the study of cancer.
▶그녀는 행복한 일생을 보냈다 She lived a happy life.
▶그런 일은 일생에 한번 밖에 일어나지 않는다 Something like that happens only once in a lifetime.
▶그녀는 일생을 독신으로 지냈다 She remained single all [throughout] her life.

일생일대 一生一代 ♦일생일대의 대사업 a once-in-a-lifetime venture / 일생일대의 once in a lifetime; of *one's* lifetime
▶이 소설은 그의 일생일대의 걸작이다 This is the best novel that has ever come out of his pen.

일석 一夕 one evening

일석이조 一石二鳥 killing two birds with one stone ▶그것은 일석이조다 It serves a double purpose.

일선 一線 1〈하나의 선〉a line ♦최후의 일선을 넘다 go beyond [exceed] the limit
▶A와 B 사이에 일선을 긋기는 어렵다 It is hard to draw a (demarcation [dividing]) line between A and B.
2〈최전선〉the first [foremost] line; 〈전선〉the fighting line; the front; 〈싸움터〉a battlefront; a battleground ♦일선에 서다 stand [be] in the forefront (of) / 일선에서 활약하다 be active at the forefront
■—근무 field [active] service

일설 一說 another report; 〈의견〉a view; an opinion
♦일설에 의하면 according to another account [report, view, version]; One theory holds that...; (口) Someone says that...

일성 一聲 ♦사장의 취임 제일성은 책임에 관한 것이었다 The first speech he made after becoming the president was on responsibility.

일세 一世 1〈일대〉a generation; an age; 〈일생〉a lifetime; 〈이민의〉a first-generation immigrant
2〈그 시대〉the time; the age
♦일세의 영웅 the hero of the age [day] / 일세를 풍미한 사상 the predominant thinking of the day / 일세를 풍미하다 command [rule] the world [age]
3〈왕조의 초대 군주〉the first ♦헨리 일세 Henry the First; Henry I

일세기 一世紀 a century; one hundred years

일소 一笑 a laugh ♦일소에 부치다 laugh *sth* off [away]; dismiss [carry off] *sth* with a laugh / 파안 일소하다 break into a big smile
▶의사가 암이 아닐까 하는 나의 우려를 일소에 부쳤다 The doctor laughingly dismissed my fears of cancer.

일소 一掃 a (clean) sweep; a cleanup
▶그는 주자 일소 2루타를 쳤다 〈야구에서〉He hit a double to clean the bases.
—일소하다 sweep away [off]; wipe out; clear out [away]; 〈근절하다〉stamp [root, sweep] out; eradicate ♦부정을 일소하다 eradicate [root out] injustice
▶시당국은 빈민가를 일소하는 계획을 입안했다 The municipal authority worked out a plan to clear away the slums.

일손 1〈사람〉a worker; a hand; 〈도움〉help; assistance
♦농가의 일손 a farm hand / 일손 부족 a shortage of help [hands] / 농촌의 일손 돕기 운동 a (nationwide) drive to help farmers《in their busiest harvest season》/ 일손이 모자라다 be [run] short of workforce; be shorthanded; suffer from a lack of man power / 일손을 빌다 get help [assistance] from another; ask for another's help / 심각한 일손부족에 직면하다 face an acute labor shortage
▶이 일에는 많은 일손이 필요하다 This work requires many hands.
▶일손이 아직도 세 사람 필요하다 We need [want] three more hands [helpers, workers].
2〈일〉work in hand
♦일손을 놓다 stop working; lay *one's* work aside / 일손을 쉬다 take a break / 일손이 몹시 바쁘다 be very busy and short-handed / 일손이 잡히다 get warmed up; be in top condition / 일손을 잡다 start work(ing); begin to work

일수 日數 1〈날의 수〉(the number of) days
♦남은 일수 the remaining days
▶그것은 일수가 얼마나 걸릴까? How long [How many days] will it take?
2〈그날의 운수〉*one's* luck for the day
♦일수가 좋다[나쁘다] have a lucky [an unlucky] day
▶오늘은 일수가 터졌어 This is my lucky day.

일수 日收〈하루 수입〉a daily (cash) income; 〈빚 등의〉daily installment [payment]; day-to-day loan
♦일수로 갚다 pay back by daily installments / 일수로 돈을 빌려 주다[빌다] lend [borrow] money on a daily installment basis
■—놀이 moneylending by [in] daily installments ■—쟁이 a moneylender who collects by daily installments **일숫돈** money payable by daily installments

일수불퇴 一手不退 ▶이 판은 일수불퇴다 〈장기에서〉Let's not have any withdrawals [retractions] or halts in this game.

일수판매 一手販賣 an exclusive sale ⇨ 총판

일숙박 一宿泊 a night's lodging; an overnight stay ⇨ 일박(一泊)

일순 一巡 a round; a tour; 〈경찰의〉a patrol —일순하다 make a round [tour] 《of》; tour
♦시내의 명소를 일순하다 tour [make a tour of] the sights of the town
▶우리는 그 구내를 일순했다 We walked around the premises.

일순간 一瞬間 an instant; a moment
♦일순간의 momentary / 일순간에 in an instant [a moment, a flash, a wink]
▶그녀는 일순간 주저했다 She hesitated a moment.
▶그것은 일순간에 일어난 일이었다 All that

일습 一襲 〈용기·용구의〉 a (complete) set 《of》; 〈옷의〉 a suit; 〈가구의〉 a suite ♦ 가구 일습 a suite of furniture / 동복 일습 a suit of winter clothes / 다기(茶器) 일습 a set of tea things / 등산 용구 일습 a complete outfit [a complete set of equipment] for mountain climbing

일승일패 一勝一敗 one win and [against] one defeat ♦ 일승일패의 경기 an even match; 〈무승부〉 a tie; a draw
▶ 지금까지 우리 팀은 일승일패를 거두었다 So far our team has won one game and lost one.

일시 一時 **1**〈동시〉 a [one] time
▶ 학생들이 일시 떠들기 시작했다 The students got noisy all at once.
▶ 모두가 일시 말했다 Everybody spoke at the same time [at once, together].
2〈한동안〉a short time [while]; a spell; 〈과거의 한때〉 once; one time; 〈부사적〉 at one time; for a while
♦ 일시의 temporary; momentary; casual / 종업원을 일시 해고하다 lay off the workers / 일시 실신하다 have a fainting spell
▶ 그 환자는 일시 위독했다 The patient was in a critical condition for a time [while].
▶ 그것은 일시의 유행일 따름이었다 It was only a passing fashion.
■ 一給(給) a lump-sum allowance

일시 日時 the time; the date; the date and hour ♦ 회의의 일시를 알리다 inform sb of the time and date of the meeting

일시동인 一視同仁 〈공평〉 impartiality; impartial treatment;〈동포애〉universal brotherhood [benevolence]

일시보관 一時保管 temporary custody
♦ 짐을 일시보관을 시키다 check one's baggage; leave one's baggage at a checkroom
■ 一所 a cloakroom; 《美》 a checkroom; a baggage checking office ■ 一證 a claim check

일시에 一時— 〈동시에〉 at the same time; at a time; at once;〈갑자기〉all at once
▶ 일시에 두가지 일을 할 수는 없다 No one can do two things at the same time [at a time].
▶ 모두가 일시에 웃었다 Everybody laughed all together.

일시적 一時的 temporary; passing; momentary; transient; causal
♦ 일시적 감정 transient emotion / 일시적 인기 ephemeral popularity / 일시적 쾌락 temporary pleasures / 일시적 현상 a passing phenomenon / 일시적 충동으로 on a momentary impulse; on the impulse [spur] of the moment / 일시적으로 〈임시로〉 temporarily; provisionally;〈잠시〉 for a time [while]; for the moment; for the time being

일시해고 一時解雇 a (temporary) layoff

일식 日蝕 〔天〕 a solar eclipse; an eclipse of the sun ▶ 지난 달에 일식이 있었다 A solar eclipse occurred last month. ⇒ There was an eclipse of the sun last month. ■ 개기[부분]— a total [partial] eclipse of the sun

일신 一身 oneself; one's self
♦ 일신의 이해관계를 생각지 않고 regardless of one's own interests / 일신의 안전을 도모하다 look to one's own safety / 일신의 이익만을 생각하다 think only of one's own interests

일신교 一神敎 monotheism
■ 一徒 a monotheist

일신상 一身上 ♦ 일신상의 중대사 a matter of great personal importance / 일신상의 personal / 일신상의 문제를 상의하다 consult sb about one's own affairs
▶ 그는 일신상의 사정으로 회사를 그만두었다 He left the company for (some) personal reasons.

일신하다 一新— 〈새롭게 하다〉 renew; renovate; reform; change sth completely; 〈새로워지다〉 be renewed [renovated, reformed]
♦ 면목을 일신하다 put on quite a new aspect; undergo a complete change / 생활을 일신하다 begin a new life

일심 一心 **1**〈한마음〉one mind
♦ 일심이 되다 become one in mind [spirit]; function as one mind
2〈전심〉 a single heart; wholeheartedness; 〈전심〉concentration of mind
♦ 일심으로 wholeheartedly; with one's [a] whole heart; intently / 일심으로 …하다 devote [bend] oneself to…; put one's heart and soul into…; be absorbed in…

일심 一審 the first instance [trial]
♦ 제일심 법정〔法〕a court of first instance / 일심에서 무죄[유죄]가 되다 be acquitted [be found guilty] at the first trial

일심동체 一心同體 being one in body and spirit
▶ 우승하려면 팀이 일심동체가 되어야 한다 In order to win the championship, a team must function as one mind and one body.
▶ 부부는 일심동체다 Man and wife are one in body and mind [are of one soul and flesh].

일심불란 一心不亂 one's whole heart
▶ 그녀는 일심 불란으로 그림을 그리고 있었다 She was completely absorbed in drawing the picture.
— **일심불란하다** be absorbed 《in》; be intent 《upon》; put one's whole soul 《into》
♦ 일심불란하게 absorbedly; with one's whole heart; (with) heart and soul / 일심불란하게 기도하다 pray to God fervently [wholeheartedly]

일심전력하다 一心專力— concentrate one's thoughts and energies 《on》; devote all one's energies 《to》
▶ 그는 그 번역에 일심전력했다 He devoted himself exclusively to that translation.

일쑤 〈명사적〉 a common [habitual] practice;〈부사적〉 frequently; often; usually
▶ 그는 학교에 지각하기가 일쑤다 He is often [habitually] late for school.
▶ 그것은 일쑤 있는 일이다 It's the kind of thing that happens everyday. ⇒ That's (fairly) common.

일안리플렉스(카메라) 一眼— 〔寫〕 a single-lens reflex (camera)

일약 一躍 at a bound; at [with] a jump [leap]; suddenly ♦ 일약 유명해지다 spring [leap] into fame / 일약 갑부가 되다 become a

일양일 一兩日 a day or two ◆일양일중에[간에] in [for] a day or two

일어나다 1 〈기상하다〉 get up; rise (from *one's* bed); 〈병상에서〉 leave *one's* bed
◆아침 일찍 일어나다 get up [rise] early (in the morning) / 벌떡 일어나다 jump [start] out of bed / 일어나 있다 be out of bed; have got up / 병이 나아 일어나게 되다 get well enough to leave *one's* bed [to get on *one's* feet]
▶빨리 일어나! Get up [Rise, Pick up yourself] quick(ly)!
▶내가 잠을 깼을 때 모두 일어나 있었다 When I woke up, everybody was up.
2 〈일어서다〉 stand up; get up; rise; regain *one's* feet; pick *oneself* up; recover *one's* legs
◆간신히 일어나다 scramble [stagger, struggle] to *one's* feet / 벌떡 일어나다 spring [leap, start] to *one's* feet
▶아기가 혼자 일어났다 The baby stood up on its own.
▶그 부상자는 한번 일어났으나 바로 쓰러졌다 The injured person got up once, but immediately collapsed again.
▶그 아이는 넘어졌으나 일어나서 다시 달리기 시작했다 The child fell, got up and then started to run again.
3 〈발생하다〉 happen; occur; take place; break out; develop; 〈원인 등이〉 arise from; result from
◆대중 사이에서 자연 발생적으로 일어난 운동 a movement which arose spontaneously from among the people / 일어날 듯하다 be likely to happen
▶어젯밤에 세 건의 화재가 일어났다 There were three fires last night.
▶그녀는 히스테리가 일어났다 She had a fit of hysteria.
▶제2차 대전은 1939년에 일어났다 World War II broke out in 1939.
▶끔찍한 사고가 일어났다 A terrible accident has occurred.
▶이 도시에 큰 변화가 일어났다 A great change has taken place in this city.
▶그 전쟁은 왜 일어났을까? What was the cause of the war? ⇒ What brought about the war?
▶이 실패는 과신에서 일어난 것이다 This failure resulted from [came of] overconfidence.
▶그 분쟁은 주민의 이기심에서 일어났다 The trouble originated in the self-centered attitude of the residents.
▶무슨 일이 일어나도 놀라지 마라 Don't be frightened no matter what happens [whatever may happen].
4 〈열·전기 등이〉 be generated; be produced
▶물체를 마찰하면 열과 전기가 일어난다 Friction generates heat and electricity.
▶합성섬유 내의는 정전기가 일어나기 쉽다 Underwear of synthetic fibers easily generate static electricity.
5 〈번성해지다〉 flourish; grow
▶그의 집안은 그의 대에 크게 일어났다 In his days, the family prospered.

일어서다 1 〈기립하다〉 stand up; get up (on *one's* feet); rise (to *one's* feet)
▶그녀는 자리에서 일어섰다 She stood up [rose] from her seat.
▶그는 일어서서 손님을 맞이했다 He stood up [got up, rose] to welcome the guest.
▶그는 노인에게 자리를 양보하려고 일어섰다 He stood up to give his seat to an old man.
▶그녀는 비틀비틀 일어섰다 She staggered to her feet.
2 〈분기하다〉 rise (up) 《against》; rouse *oneself* (to action)
▶그들은 독재에 대항하여 무기를 들고 일어섰다 They rose (up) in arms [took up arms] against dictatorship.
3 〈회복하다〉 recover; improve ◆충격에서 일어서다 recover from [get over] *one's* shock
▶우리 회사는 꽤 큰 손실을 보았으나 3개월만에 일어섰다 Our company suffered a rather heavy loss, but recovered from it in three months.

일언 一言 a (single) word; one word
▶그녀는 나의 요구를 일언지하에 거절했다 She flatly refused my request.
▶남아일언은 중천금이다 A man's word (of honor) is as good as a bond. ⇒ On my word as a gentleman, I really mean what I say.

일언거사 一言居士 a ready critic; a person who has something to say about anything and everything

일언반구 一言半句 a [one] word
◆일언반구도 하지 않다 say nothing; do not utter a word; keep absolute silence; hold *one's* tongue
▶그녀는 일언반구의 사과도 없이 가버렸다 She went away without (saying) a single word (of apology).

일언이폐지하다 一言以蔽之— boil down to one word; express in a single word
◆일언이폐지하면 in a [one] word; in short; to sum up

일없다 1 〈필요없다〉 unnecessary; needless; unwanted; 〈서슴〉 do not want; be done 《with *sb*》 ◆일없는 것을 버리다 throw away [get rid of] things which are no longer useful
▶나는 일없다는 말씀이군요 I see that I'm not wanted. ⇒ Do you mean to say that you are done with me [that you have nothing more to do with me]?
2 〈괜찮다〉 (be) all right
▶이 물은 마셔도 일없을까요? Is this water safe [good] to drink?

일엽편주 一葉片舟 a small [tiny] boat
일요 日曜 Sunday ⇨ 일요일
■ —예배 Sunday service —판[특집] 〈신문의〉 a Sunday edition [supplement] —화가 a Sunday [weekend] painter

일요일 日曜日 Sunday ◆일요일 아침에 on Sunday morning / 다음[지난] 일요일에 next [last] Sunday; on Sunday next [last]

▶우리는 일요일에는 교회에 간다 We go to church on Sunday.
▶나는 일요일에도 쉴 수 없을 정도로 너무 바쁘다 I am so busy I can't take even a Sunday rest.

일용 日用 daily [everyday] use ♦일용의 of daily necessity; for everyday use; everyday ■―잡화 miscellaneous goods for daily use ―품 daily necessities; articles for daily use

일우 一隅 〈한쪽 구석〉 a corner; a nook

일원 一元 ♦일원의[적인] unitary; unified; 〔哲〕 monistic ■―론 〔哲〕 monism ―발생설 〔生〕 monogenesis ―화 unification; centralization : 일원화하다 unify

일원 一員 a member ♦우리팀의 일원 a member of our team

일원 一圓 the whole place [district] ⇨ 일대 (一帶) ♦충청 지방 일원에 all over [throughout] the Ch'ungch'ŏng district

일원제 一院制 the single chamber [unicameral] system ■―의회 a unicameral legislature

일월 一月 January (略 Jan.)
♦일월 상순[하순]에 early [late] in January / 1998년 1월에 in January of 1998; in January(,) 1998 / 1998년 1월 15일에 on the 15th of January 1998; (美) on January 15, 1998; (英) on 15(th), January,(,) 1998

일월 日月 〈해 와 달〉 the sun and the moon; 〈세월〉 time; years ■―성신 the sun, the moon and the stars; the host(s) of heaven, the heavenly bodies [hosts] ―식 solar and lunar eclipse(s)

일위 一位 〈첫째 지위〉 the first place; the first rank [rate]
♦일위를 다투다[빼앗다] fight for [take over] the first place / 일위를 차지하다 stand [rank] first; head [top] the list
▶누가 너의 반에서 일위니? Who is first in your class? ≒ Who is at the top of your class?

일으키다 1 〈일으켜 세우다〉 raise up; set up; set upright; pick up
♦넘어진 사람을 일으키다 set [get] sb on 〈his〉 legs; help sb (back) up [get up, to 〈his〉 feet] / 쓰러진 기둥을 일으키다 put a fallen pole up again
▶그는 침대에서 몸을 일으켰다 He raised himself [sat up] in bed.
♦일어날 힘이 없어요, 날 좀 일으켜 주세요 Help me up, I'm too weak to pick myself up.
2 〈시작하다〉 commence; begin; start; launch
♦소송을 일으키다 start a lawsuit against
▶회사가 새 사업을 일으켰다 The company began a new project.
3 〈야기하다〉 cause; give rise to; bring about [on]; create
♦분쟁을 일으키다 cause [trigger] a dispute / 연쇄반응을 일으키다 cause [trigger] a chain reaction / 폭풍을 일으키다 raise a storm
♦음주운전은 사고를 일으킨다 Drunk(en) driving causes [leads to] accidents.
▶말썽을 일으키지 말고 천천히 운전해라 Don't run into trouble, drive slowly.

▶그의 저작이 큰 사회적 물의를 일으켰다 His writing has brought about [provoked] (a) public controversy.
4 〈발생시키다〉 produce
♦(정)전기를 일으키다 generate (static) electricity / 마찰로 열을 일으키다 generate [produce] heat by friction
5 〈발병하다〉 fall [get, be taken] ill with; be seized with; be attacked with; 〈원인이 주어〉 cause; set up / 기관지염을 일으키다 cause [bring on, set up] bronchitis
▶그는 너무 먹어 복통을 일으켰다 He ate too much and had a stomachache.
6 〈깨우다〉 wake (up); arouse 《sb from sleep》; 〈각성시키다〉 awake ♦지식에 대한 욕구를 일으키다 awake a desire for knowledge
7 〈설립하다〉 establish [start, set up] 《a school》; found
♦새 회사를 일으키다 set up a new firm
8 〈흥하게 하다〉 revive; restore; resuscitate
♦나라를 일으키다 cause a nation to prosper; make a nation prosper
▶그가 회사를 이 정도로 일으켰다 He has brought the company to its present level of prosperity.

일의대수 一衣帶水 ▶영국과 유럽은 일의대수를 끼고 있을 뿐이다 Only a narrow strip of water lies between Britain and Europe.

일이 一二 one or two; a few
♦일이년 one [a] year or two / 일이회 once or twice / 일이를 다투다 compete for first place
▶이 도시는 서해안에서 일이위를 다투는 어항이다 This town is one of the largest fishing ports in the west coast.

일익 一翼 a part [role] (to play)
♦일익을 담당하다 play its [one's] part 《in》; act [perform] a part [role] 《of》; contribute 《to》 / 개발도상국의 산업 발전에 일익을 담당하다 play a role [part] in the industrial development of the developing countries

일익 日益 〈날로 더욱〉 day by day; from day to day; every day; as day follows day
▶사태가 일익 악화되고 있다 The situation is getting more serious day by day.
▶귀사의 일익 번창하심을 기원합니다 We wish you every success in your business.

일인 一人 one person; one man
■―독재 one-man dictatorship ―이역 〈연극 등에서〉 a double role ―일기 a man, a skill [trade] ―일표 one man, one vote ―지배 one-man control

일인당 一人當 for each person; per capita [head, man]
▶입장료는 일인당 천원입니다 The entrance [admission] fee is one thousand won per capita.

일인분 一人分 a portion for one person; one helping [serving]
♦일인분에 5,000원 five thousand won for one person / 일인분 for one person; of one man
▶카레라이스 일인분 주세요 One order of curry and rice, please.
▶일인분을 추가할 수 있습니까? Can you

일인승 —人乘 ◆일인승의 single-seated
■—비행기[자동차] a single-seater
일인자 —人者 the leading person; the greatest [foremost] person
◆국제법의 일인자 a recognized authority on international law / 당대의 문예비평의 일인자 the leading [foremost] literary critic of the day
▶그는 기타 연주의 일인자다 He is an A 1[a No. 1] guitarist.
일인칭 —人稱 〔文法〕 the first person
■—단수[복수] the first person singular [plural] —소설 a first-person novel; an "I" story
일일 —日 〈하루〉 a [one] day; 〈초하루〉 the first day (of a month)
◆제 일일 the first day / 일일 2회 two times a day / 일일 역장[파출소장] 근무를 하다 act as stationmaster [police box chief] for a day / 일일 일선(一善)을 행하다 do some little good each day; do one good turn a day / 일일 여삼추로 애타게 기다리다 feel as if the days were three years long / 일일지장(之長)이 있다 be a little ahead of sb; be one's superior (in)
일일이 〈일마다〉 everything; every single thing; without omission
◆일일이 간섭하다 meddle in everything
▶그는 내가 하는 일을 일일이 트집잡는다 He finds fault with everything I do.
▶내가 시도한 것이 일일이 잘 되었다 Everything I attempted turned out well.
▶나에게 일일이 상의할 것 없다 You don't have to talk about everything with me.
▶그들의 제안은 일일이 거부되었다 All their proposals were rejected.
일일이 ——— 1 〈하나 하나〉 one by one; one after another; separately ◆제품을 일일이 점검하다 check the products one by one
▶그는 서류에 일일이 서명했다 He signed all the papers one by one.
2 〈상세히〉 in detail; in full; fully
▶미안합니다만 지금 일일이 설명할 수가 없습니다 I'm sorry I cannot go into details [particulars] now.
일임하다 —任— leave sth entirely to sb [to sb's discretion]; leave sb in full charge (of sth); entrust sb with the task (of)
▶그들은 그건을 나에게 일임했다 They left the matter to me [in my hands, to my discretion].
▶운전이라면[요리라면] 나에게 일임해라 Leave the driving [cooking] to me.
일자 —字 〈한 글자〉 one letter
▶그에게서는 일자 소식도 없다 So far I have received no word from him.
일자 日字 〈날짜〉 the date
◆6월 9일자의 편지 a letter dated June 9th
▶인사 이동은 3월 1일자로 발령되었다 The personnel reshuffle was announced as of [effective] the 1st of March.
일자리 〈직업〉 employment; work; a job; 〈직장〉 a position; a situation
◆일자리가 없는 unemployed; jobless / 일자리를 얻다 obtain [secure] employment; find [get] work; get a job / 일자리를 잃다 lose one's job [employment, position] / 일자리를 찾다 seek employment [work]; look [hunt] for a job [place]
▶나는 지금 일자리가 없다 I am out of work [a job] now.
▶귀사에 무슨 일자리 좀 없습니까? Don't you have any job opening [positions vacant]?
▶그는 내게 슈퍼마켓의 일자리를 얻어주었다 He found me employment [a job] in a supermarket.
일자무식 —字無識 illiteracy; ignorance
◆일자무식의 illiterate; ignorant
▶그녀는 경제에는 일자무식이다 She is quite ignorant of economics. ⇒ She knows nothing about economics.
■—꾼 an (utterly) illiterate person; an ignoramus
일장 —場 1 〈한바탕〉 ◆일장 연설을 하다 make [deliver] a speech [an address]
2 〈연극의〉 a scene; the first scene (제1장)
일장일단 —長—短 merits and demerits; advantages and disadvantages
▶어느 후보나 일장일단이 있다 All of the candidates have their merits and demerits [strong points and shortcomings].
일장춘몽 —場春夢 an empty dream
◆일장춘몽처럼 사라지다 vanish like a dream
▶인생은 일장춘몽이다 Life is but an empty dream. ⇒ How brief is the span of (human) life.
일전 —戰 〈전투〉 a battle; an engagement; 〈승부〉 a game; a contest; a bout
◆일전을 벌이다 fight [engage in] a battle (with); engage (an enemy); 〈승부를 가리다〉 have a game [bout]
▶그들이 우리 제의를 거절하면 일전도 불사할 것이다 If they reject our proposals, we shall not hesitate to fight.
일전 —轉 〈한 번 돎〉 a turn; 〈사태가 아주 변함〉 a complete change
▶무대 배경은 일전하여 봄의 강변 경치가 되었다 The scene changed to one of a riverside in spring.
▶형세가 일전하여 우리 팀이 유리해졌다 The situation reversed itself and our team gained the advantage.
일전 日前 the other day; some days [a few days] ago; recently; lately
▶그것에 대해서는 일전에 편지로 알려드렸습니다 I wrote about it in my last [latest] letter.
▶내가 일전에 말한 것처럼 금년에는 외국에 나가지 않는다 As I said before [mentioned previously], I won't go abroad this year.
일절 —切 ◆일절 …하지 않다 never…; not… at all
▶그 일은 일절 모릅니다 I know nothing at all about it.
▶외상은 일절 사절합니다 We never sell on credit. ⇒ (게시) Positively no credit.
일절 —節 〈문장의〉 a paragraph; a passage; 〈시의〉 a stanza; 〈말의〉 a syllable; 〈노래의〉 a verse
일점 —點 〈한 점〉 a point; a speck; a dot; 〈한

개〉 a particle; 〈한 품목〉 an article 《of clothing [furniture]》; an item
▶ 그는 나의 일점 혈육이다 He is the only son of my flesh and blood.
▶ 그녀는 우리 회사의 홍일점이다 She is the only woman in our company.
▶ 나는 양심에 일점의 가책도 없다 I have a clear [clean] conscience.

일정 日程 a day's schedule [program]; a daily routine; 〈의사(議事) 진행의〉 the order of the day; the agenda; 《美》 the calendar; 〈여행의〉 an itinerary; 〈경기의〉 a fixture
♦ 꽉 짜인 일정 a tight [crowded, crammed] schedule / 일정을 정하다 form a schedule; make a program; make out the schedule (for) / 시험 일정을 발표하다 announce the dates of the examination / 일정에 올라 있다 be on the day's agenda
▶ 그는 일정을 바꾸어 한 달 늦게 출발했다 He changed the schedule and left one month later.
▶ 오늘 무슨 일정이 있으십니까? Do you have any plans [anything scheduled] for today?
■ —표 a schedule; a program; 〈영국 하원의〉 an order paper [book]; 〈여행의〉 an itinerary

일정하다 一定— fixed; definite; established; regular; 〈한결같다〉 constant; uniform
♦ 일정한 규격의 부품 standardized parts / 일정한 금액 a specific [specified] sum [amount] (of money) / 일정한 서식 the prescribed form / 일정한 수입 a fixed income; a regular income / 일정하지 않은 irregular; variable; inconstant / 일정한 비율로 at a fixed rate / 일정한 시간 내에 within the set [given] time / 방의 온도를 일정하게 유지하다 keep the temperature of the room constant / 일정한 속도로 차를 몰다 drive at a uniform [constant] speed
▶ 카세트 테이프의 규격은 일정하다 Cassette tapes are standardized.
▶ 물품세는 주(州)에 따라 일정하지 않다 The sales tax varies according to the state.

일제 日帝 Japanese imperialism; imperialist Japan ♦ 일제의 압제에 고통받다 suffer under tyranny of the Japanese imperialism

일제검거 一齊檢擧 a wholesale [blanket] arrest; a roundup / 일제검거하다 round up; make a wholesale arrest of 《criminals》

일제사격 一齊射擊 a burst of shots; 〈대포의〉 a salvo; volley firing; a volley (fire)
—**일제사격하다** shoot simultaneously; fire a volley; deliver a volley of fire

일제히 一齊— 〈모두〉 all together; 〈동시에〉 all at once; simultaneously; 〈이구 동성으로〉 with one voice; unanimously; in unison; in chorus
▶ 벨이 울리자 그들은 일제히 일어났다 The moment the bell rang, they all stood up at once.
▶ 개표는 전국에서 일제히 시작될 것이다 Ballot counting will begin simultaneously [at the same time] throughout the country.

일조 一助 a help; an aid ♦ 일조가 되다 be a help 《to》; be of a help

일조 日照 sunshine ■ —계 a heliograph —권 the right to (enjoy) sunshine —시간 the duration of sunshine; daylight hours; hours of sunshine —율 the percentage of sunshine

일조 一條 1 〈한줄〉 a line; a stripe; a streak **2** 〈절·조항〉 a passage; an article
♦ 대한민국 헌법 제1조 Article one of the Constitution of the Republic of Korea

일조일석 一朝一夕 ♦ 일조일석에 in a (single) day; overnight; in a short [brief] time
▶ 이 분쟁은 일조일석에 해결될 문제가 아니라고 생각된다 I don't think this conflict will be settled [solved] in a short time.
▶ 로마는 일조일석에 이루어진 것이 아니다 《속담》 Rome was not built in a day.

일족 一族 〈일가족〉 one's (whole) family; one's people [folks]; 〈친족〉 kinsmen; relatives; 《총칭》 kin ♦ 일족을 거느리고 with one's whole clan [family]

일종 一種 a kind; a sort; a type; 〈변종〉 a variety ♦ 일종의 a kind [sort, species, variety] of / 일종의 차 tea of a kind [sort]; tea of sorts
▶ 그것은 물고기의 일종이다 That's a kind [sort] of fish.
▶ 늑대는 개의 일종인가? Is the wolf a kind [species] of dog?
▶ 그는 일종의 이상주의자다 He is a kind [sort] of (an) idealist.

일주 一周 〈한 바퀴 돎〉 one [a] round; 〈1회전〉 a revolution
♦ 세계일주여행 a round-the-world trip; a tour [trip] round the world; globe-trotting / 세계 일주 여행을 하다 make [take] a trip around [round] the world
—**일주하다** make a round 《of》; go [walk, run, travel] round; 〈회전하다〉 revolve; make a revolution
▶ 지구는 1년 걸려 태양을 일주한다 The earth goes [moves] around the sun once a year.
■ —기(期) 〔天〕 a period —여행 a round trip

일주 日周 〔天〕 ■ —권(圈) the diurnal circle —시차(視差) the diurnal parallax —운동 diurnal motion

일주기 一周忌 the first anniversary of sb's death

일주년 一周年 a full year —기념일 the first anniversary: 오늘은 우리의 결혼 일주년 기념일이다 Today is the first anniversary of our wedding.

일주야 一晝夜 a whole day and night
♦ 일주야 교대 근무 a 24-hour shift / 일주야 계속해서 (a)round the clock / 일주야 교대로 일하다 work all day and night

일주(일) 一週(日) a [one] week
♦ 일주일의 휴가 a week's holiday [leave, vacation] / 일주일 이내에 within a week / 일주일 단위로 지불하다 pay by the week
▶ 이 잡지는 일주 일회 발행된다 This magazine is published once a week. ⇒ This is a weekly (magazine).
■ —노동 시간 《美》 workweek —5일 노동 a five-day workweek

일지 日誌 a diary ⇨ 일기(日記)
■ 항해— a log; a logbook

일지도모르다 may [might] 《be, do》; maybe; perhaps
▶ 그것은 진실일지도 모른다 It may [might] be true. ⇌ Perhaps [Maybe] it is true.
▶ 네가 말하는 대로 일지도 모른다 I guess you are right.

일직 日直 day duty ▶ 오늘은 내가 일직이다 I am on duty today.
■ —장교 an officer of the day; 《英》 an orderly officer —하사관 a noncommissioned officer of the day

일직선 一直線 ◆일직선으로 in a straight line; in a beeline / 일직선으로 나아가다 go [keep] straight on; make a beeline 《for》; make straight 《for》
▶ 그들은 일직선으로 섰다 They stood in a straight line. ⇌ They lined up straight.

일진 一陣 1 〈군사의 진〉 a military camp; 〈선진(先陣)〉 the van 《of an army》; the vanguard; 〈선발대〉 an advanced party
2 〈바람 등이 한바탕 일어남〉 a gust [blast] 《of wind》; a puff [whiff] 《of breeze》; a gale 《of wind》 ▶ 일진 광풍이 남서에서 불어왔다 A violent gale came in from the southwest.

일진 日辰 1 〈날의 60갑자〉 the binary designation of the day according to the sexagenary cycle **2** 〈운수〉 the day's fortune
▶ 오늘은 일진이 좋다 Today is a lucky day.
▶ 오늘은 일진이 사납다 This just isn't my day. ⇌ This is not a lucky day for me.

일진월보 日進月步 rapid progress ⇨ 일취월장(日就月將)

일진일퇴 一進一退 advance and retreat; ebb and flow
◆일진일퇴의 now advancing and now retreating; 〈경기·시세 등이〉 fluctuating; seesaw
▶ 게임은 일진일퇴의 접전이었다 It was a close [seesaw] game.
—**일진일퇴하다** advance and retreat; ebb and flow; fluctuate

일찌감치 a little early; earlier (than usual); ahead of time
◆일찌감치 떠나다 make an early start
▶ 그는 일찌감치 미술에 대한 재능을 발휘했다 He displayed a talent for art at an early age.

일찍 early
◆아침 일찍 early in the morning; in the early morning / 일찍 일어나는 사람 an early riser / 30분 일찍 도착하다 arrive 《at a place》 thirty minutes ahead of time / 저녁을 일찍 들다 have an early supper
▶ 암은 일찍 치료하면 나을 수 있다 Cancer can be cured if treated in time.
▶ 일찍 자고 일찍 일어나는 것은 사람을 건강하고 유복하고 현명하게 만든다 Early to bed and early to rise makes a man healthy, wealthy and wise.
▶ 아침을 조금 일찍 준비했다 I prepared breakfast a little earlier than usual.
▶ 더 일찍 오지 그랬니 You should have come earlier.
▶ 일찍 자고 일찍 일어나는 것이 건강에 좋다 It's good for health to keep early hours.
▶ 일찍 일어나는 새가 벌레를 잡는다 (속담) The early bird will catch the worm.
▶ 그는 일찍 죽었다 He died at an early age. ⇌ He died young.

일찍이 〈전에 한번〉 once; (at) one time; before
◆일찍이 계획했던 여행 the trip *one* has been planning to make for some time / 일찍이 1392년에 as early as 1392
▶ 일찍이 그것에 대해 들어 알고 있습니다 I have heard [have been told] about it.
▶ 그는 일찍이 배우였던 적이 있다 He was at one time an actor.
▶ 이런 아름다운 경치는 일찍이 본 적이 없다 I have never seen such a beautiful sight (as this). ⇌ This is the most beautiful sight (that) I have ever seen.

일차 一次 〈한 번〉 one time; once; 〈첫번〉 the first
◆일차의 first; primary; 〔數〕 linear; of the first degree
■ —방정식 〔數〕 a linear [simple] equation; an equation of the first degree —변환 〔數〕 linear transformation —부등식 〔數〕 a linear inequality —산품(産品) primary products —시험 a primary examination; 〈예비시험〉 preliminary examination —식 a linear expression —전지 a primary battery [cell] —함수 〔數〕 a linear function —항 〔數〕 a linear term

일차원 一次元 〔數·物〕 one dimension ◆일차원의 of one dimemsion; unidimensional

일착 一着 〈경주 등의〉 the first arrival; the first 《in the race》; 〈바둑 등의〉 a 《good [bad]》 move
—**일착하다** finish [come in] first; be the first to come in; win the first place
▶ 100미터 경주에서 일착했다 I finished first [won (the) first place] in the 100-meter dash.

일책 一策 a plan; an idea ▶ 내게 일책이 있다 I've got a good idea. ▶ 그가 일책을 안출했다 He worked out [devised] a plan.

일처다부 一妻多夫 polyandry ◆일처다부의 polyandrous

일천 日淺 being a few days old
—**일천하다** short; not long (since...)
▶ 이 대학은 역사가 아직 일천하다 It's not been long [It's only a short time] since this college was founded. ⇌ This college was founded only a short time ago. ⇌ This college is quite a new [recent] foundation.

일체 一切 〈전부〉 all; everything; the whole; 〈부사적〉 wholly; entirely; absolutely
◆일체의 편의를 제공하다 offer [afford] every facility; afford every convenience 《to *sb*》
▶ 일체의 비용은 내가 부담한다 I will pay the whole [total] expenses.
▶ 노인은 화재로 일체의 재산을 잃었다 The old man lost all his [his whole, his entire] fortune in the fire.
▶ 그녀는 그와 일체의 관계를 끊었다 She has cut all relations with him.
▶ 일체가 명백해졌다 Everything has become clear. ⇌ Everything has been disclosed.
▶ 나한테 일체를 맡기시오 Leave everything to

me.
■—중생 〔佛敎〕 all living beings [things]; all creatures; all life; the whole mankind

일체 一體 〈한 몸〉 one body ♦일체가 되어 in one; in a [as one] body
▶ 부부는 일체다 Husband and wife are one flesh.
▶ 그들은 일체가 되어 행동했다 They acted in one [a] body.
▶ 작은 그룹이 결합하여 일체가 되었다 Small groups were united into one.
■—감 a sense of unity [togetherness] —화 unification; integration

일촉즉발 一觸卽發 ♦일촉즉발의 국제정세 an explosive international situation / 일촉즉발의 위기; a hair-trigger crisis / 일촉즉발의 touch-and-go; delicate
▶ 양국 관계는 일촉즉발의 상태에 있는 것으로 전해지고 있다 The relationship between the two countries is said to be in an explosive situation.

일축 一蹴 〈한번 참〉 a kick; 〈단호히 거절함〉 a flat rejection [refusal]; 〈단번에 물리침〉 beating easily
—**일축하다** reject [refuse] 《sb's demand》 flatly; spurn; turn down; brush off; beat [defeat] easily
▶ 그는 그 제의를 일축했다 He said no to the proposal. ⇒ He turned down the request. ⇒ He flatly rejected [refused] the proposal. ⇒ He gave a flat refusal to the proposal.

일출 日出 sunrise; 《美》 sunup
♦일출에서 일몰까지 from sunup to sundown; between sunup and sundown / 일출을 지켜보다 watch the sunrise [the rising sun] / 산꼭대기에서 일출을 보다 see the sunrise from a mountaintop
■—시각 the time of sunrise [sunup]

일취월장 日就月將 daily progress and monthly advance; steady advance; rapid progress
—**일취월장하다** make rapid progress [steady advance]
▶ 과학[공업 기술]이 일취월장하고 있다 Science [Industrial technology] is making steady advance [rapid progress].
▶ 전자공학은 일취월장하고 있다 Electronics is advancing by [in] leaps and bounds.

일층 一層 1 〈맨 아래층〉 《美》 the first floor [story]; 《英》 the ground floor; 〈공공건축물 등의〉 the street floor / 일층 앞좌석 《美》 〈극장의〉 the orchestra; the parquet
2 〈한층·한결 더〉 more; still [much] more; the more; all [only] the more ♦일층 열심히 일하다 work much [far, still, even] harder; work harder than ever
■—집 a one-storied house; a house of one story

일치 一致 〈합치〉 agreement; accord; 〈의견의 일치〉 consensus 《of opinion》; 〈부합〉 conformity; 〈상응〉 correspondence; 〈우연의〉 coincidence; 〈단합〉 unity; 〔文法〕 concord; agreement
♦언행의 일치 the correspondence of *one's* words with *one's* actions; consistency of speech and action / 여론의 일치 a unified public opinion / 우연의 일치 a casual [strange] coincidence 《of》 / 의견의 불일치 diversity of opinion / 전원 일치의 판정 an unanimous decision / 의견의 일치를 보다 reach a consensus 《on》; 〈합의에 이르다〉 reach [arrive at, come to] an agreement 《about, on》
▶ 참 우연의 일치구먼 What a coincidence! (▶ coincidence는「(시간·장소 등의) 우연한 일치」를 뜻함)
▶ 그는 전원 일치의 표결로 의장에 선출되었다 He was elected chairman by a unanimous vote.
—**일치하다** agree 《with》; (be in) accord 《with》; concur 《with》; conform 《to》; be congruous 《with》; coincide 《with》; correspond 《with》; tally 《with》; be identical 《with》; be of one accord
♦일치하여 in unison [union, concert]; unitedly; with one accord / 일치하지 않다 disagree [conflict] 《with》; be incongruous [inconsonant] 《with, to》; differ 《from》 / 의견이 일치하지 않다 differ [vary] in opinion; be divided in opinion
▶ 우리의 이해는 일치한다 Our interests coincide.
▶ 그와는 모든 점에서 의견이 일치한다 I am in agreement [accord] with him on all points.
▶ 당장 출발하는 것으로 의견이 일치했다 We agreed to start [on starting] at once. ⇒ We agreed that we should start at once.
▶ 네 이야기는 그의 이야기와 일치하지 않는다 Your story disagrees [does not agree] with what he says.
▶ 그는 언행이 일치하지 않는다 His saying and doing do not go together [are two different things]. ⇒ He says one thing and does another.
■—단결 〈단결〉 union; 〈결속〉 solidarity : 일치단결하다 unite; act together [in union] / 우리는 일치단결해서 일에 대처했다 We dealt with the affair as a unified group. ⇒ We united (together) to deal with the affair. —점 a point of concurrence : 상호간에 아무런 일치점도 없다 have no congruity with one another —협력 united [combined] efforts [strength]; union: 일치 협력하다 unite efforts; join forces 《with》; work together

일컫다 1 〈칭하다〉 call; name; term; designate
♦고산이라고 일컫는 사람 a man called [by the name of] Gosan / …이라 일컬어지다 be said [reputed, cracked up] to be...
▶ 그는 자신을 사서의 전문가라고 일컫고 있었다 He represented himself as an expert on dictionaries. (▶ 실제로는 그렇지 않다는 것을 함축하고 있음)
▶ 초서는 영시의 아버지라고 일컬어진다 Chaucer is called the father of English poetry.
▶ 하와이는 흔히 태평양의 낙원으로 일컬어진다 Hawaii is often referred to as the Paradise of the Pacific.
2 〈칭찬하다〉 praise; laud; admire; extol

일탈 逸脫 deviation; a breakaway 《from》

일터

▶ 그것은 규칙 일탈이다 It deviates from the rules.
―**일탈하다** deviate 《from》; break away 《from》; overstep 《the bounds》
♦ 일탈한 행동 〈규범을〉 deviant behavior
▶ 그의 행위는 상식을 일탈한 행동이다 His conduct goes against common sense.

일터 〈직장〉 one's place of work; one's job 〔site〕; 〈작업장〉 a workplace; a workshop; 〈회사〉 a company; 〈사무실〉 one's office

[解說] 영어에서는 「일터」의 종류에 따라서 「회사」 *company*, 「사무실」 *office*, 「공장」 *factory*, 「작업장」 *workplace*, *workshop* 등 구체적으로 쓰는 경우가 많다.

♦ 일터에서 돌아오다 come home from work / 일터로 가다 go to work; leave home for work
▶ 그는 2년후 일터에 복귀했다 Two years later he returned to work. (▸work는 명사)
▶ 내 일터는 도심에 있다 My place of work 〔office〕 is in the heart of the city.
▶ 내 일터에는 여성이 적다 There are few women in my office.

일파 ―派 〈유파〉 a school; 〈종파〉 a sect; 〈큰 종파〉 a denomination; 〈당파〉 a party; 〈파벌〉 a faction; 〈부문〉 a section; 〈집단〉 a group
▶ 감리교는 신교의 일파다 The Methodists are a Protestant denomination.

일패 ―敗 one defeat ♦ 9승 1패 nine wins and one defeat

일편 ―片 a piece; a bit; a fragment; a scrap

일편 ―篇 a piece 《of poetry》

일편단심 ―片丹心 passionate 〔single-hearted〕 devotion; a sincere heart
♦ 일편단심으로 single-mindedly; devotedly; with 《single-hearted》 devotion / 일편단심으로 섬기다 serve faithfully; devote *oneself* to

일평생 ―平生 a lifetime ⇨ 한평생

일폭 ―幅 〈한 폭〉 a scroll; a piece 《of picture》 ♦ 일폭의 동양화 a scroll of Oriental painting / 일폭의 그림같은 경치 a picturesque view

일품 逸品 〈품질이 뛰어난 물품〉 an excellent article 〔item〕; 〈진품(珍品)〉 a rare item; a rarity; 〈걸작〉 a masterpiece; a jewel in the crown
▶ 그 조각은 정말 일품이다 It is really a fine piece of sculpture.

일필 ―筆 〈한 번 쓰기〉 one stroke 《of a brush 〔pen〕》
▶ 그는 그 스케치에 마무리의 일필을 가했다 He added the finishing touches 〔strokes〕 to the sketch.
―**일필하다** make a stroke with a brush; write with a stroke of the brush

일하다 work; labo(u)r; do one's work 〔job, task〕; serve 《at》; be in the service 〔employ〕 《of》
♦ 일하고 있다 be working; be at work / 지나치게 일하다 work too hard 〔much〕; overwork / 아침부터 밤까지 〔종일, 밤낮으로〕 일하다 work from morning till night 〔all day 〔long〕, day and night〕 / 일하면서 대학을 나오다 work one's way through college / 열심히 일하다 work hard; be hard at work / 부지런히 일하다 work diligently; work 〔toil〕 away; toil and moil / 일하러 가다 〈출근하다〉 go to work 〔business〕
▶ 나는 주 5일 일한다 I work five days a week.
▶ 아버지는 공장에서 일하신다 My father works in〔at〕 a factory.
▶ 일하지 않는 자는 먹지 마라 No work, no pay 〔dinner〕. ⇒ The rule is that nonworkers shall not eat.

일할 ―割 ten percent 〔per cent〕; 10%
♦ 일할의 수수료 10 percent commission
▶ 일할 깎아 드리지요 I will make a discount of ten percent.
■―**할인** a ten percent discount; a reduction of 10%: 일할 할인으로 그것을 샀다 I got a ten percent discount when I bought it.

일행 ―行 1 〈일단〉 a party (▸특히 단기간에 공통의 목적으로 모인 사람들); 〈수행원〉 staff; suite; 〈총칭〉 entourage; a company; 〈배우·곡예사 등의 일단〉 a troupe
♦ 관광객 일행 a company of tourists; a touring company / 대사 일행 the ambassador and his staff / 김선생 일행 Mr. Kim and his party 〔suite〕 / 일행 5명 a party of five / 일행에 끼다 join a party
▶ 일행은 모두 10명이다 The party is ten in all 〔consists of ten members〕.
2 〈한 줄〉 a line
▶ 일행 걸러 써라 Write on every other line.

일혈 溢血 〔醫〕 extravasation; effusion of blood 《on the brain》

일호 ―號 No. 1; Number One ■―**홈런** 〔野〕 the virgin homer

일화 日貨 〈일본 화폐〉 Japanese currency 〔money〕; the yen; 〈일본 수입 상품〉 Japanese goods

일화 逸話 an anecdote; an episode
▶ 그 사람에게는 재미있는 일화가 많다 There are many interesting 〔amusing〕 anecdotes about him. ⇒ Many amusing anecdotes are told of him.
■―**집** an anecdotage

일확천금 ―攫千金 making a fortune at a stroke ♦ 일확천금의 〈美〉 get-rich-quick
▶ 그는 일확천금을 꿈꾸고 있다 He dreams of making a fortune overnight 〔striking it rich〕.
―**일확천금하다** make a fortune at a stroke

일환 ―環 〈고리 중의 하나〉 a link 《in a chain》; 〈밀접한 관계의 일부분〉 (a) part (▸a는 붙지 않는 것이 보통임)
♦ …의 일환으로서 as a part of… / 계획의 일환을 이루다 form a link in the chain of the program
▶ 이것은 우리나라 외교정책의 일환이다 This is 〔forms〕 (a) part of our foreign policy.

일회 ―回 〈한 번〉 once; a 〔one〕 time; 〈승부의〉 a round; a game; an event; 〔野〕 the first inning(s)
♦ 일회 말 the bottom of the first inning / 주〔월, 연〕 일회 once a week 〔month, year〕 / 일회에 at a time
▶ 정제를 일회에 3정씩 복용하시오 Take the

pills three at a time.
■ —분 〈약의〉 a dose; 〈총서·연재물의〉 an installment 《of a serial story》 —전 the first game; the first round: 우리 팀은 일회전에서 패했다 Our team lost [was defeated in] the first game.

일회용 —回用 ♦ 일회용 라이터 a disposable (cigarette) lighter / 일회용 컵 a disposable [throwaway] paper cup / 일회용의 disposable; throwaway
▶ 지금은「일회용 시대」다 We live in the "throwaway age."

일훈 日暈 the halo of the sun ⇨ 햇무리

일흔 seventy; 〈인간의 수명〉〔聖〕threescore (years) and ten

일희일비 —喜—悲 alternation of joy and sorrow —일희일비하다 be sometimes happy, sometimes sad; have joy and sorrow in quick alternation; be now glad, now sad; be glad and sad by turns

읽기 reading; 〈학과〉 a reading lesson
♦ 읽기, 쓰기, 셈 reading, writing and arithmetic; the three R's / 읽기를 연습하다 practice reading

읽다 1〈책 등을〉 read; peruse; 〈낭독하다〉 recite 《an ode》; 〈경을〉 chant 《a sutra》; 〈건너 뛰며〉 skip; 〈신문 등을 대충 훑어보다〉**(美口)** scan; 〈탐독하다〉 devour; 〈그래프·지도 등을〉 study 《a graph》 (▶ 문자 이외의 것을 주의깊게 보고 이해하는 경우)
♦ 되풀이해서 읽은 다음 after repeated reading / 다시 읽다 reread; read (over) again / (책을) 다 읽다 finish reading 《a book》; have done with 《a novel》; 〈통독하다〉 read 《a book》 through / 잘못 읽다 misread; read wrong / 소리내어 읽다 read aloud; read out / 큰 소리로 읽다 read loud [loudly] / 급히 읽다 read hurriedly; 〈대충 훑어보다〉 glance over [through] / 술술 읽다 read fluently; read on without pause / 따라 읽다 echo [follow] 《one's teacher》in reading / 군데군데 빼먹고 읽다 read skipping here and there; skim [skip] (over, through) / 요점만을 골라 읽다 pick up chief points
▶ 그는 그 책을 원서로 읽었다 He read the book in the original.
▶ 책을 읽고 있는데 갑자기 전화가 울렸다 The telephone rang suddenly while I was reading.
▶ 그가 자살한 것을 신문에서 읽었다 I read the paper that he committed suicide. ⇌ I read about [of] his suicide in the paper. (▶ that 절이나 of 구에서는「…을 읽어서 알고 있다」의 뜻으로 know에 상당함. about 구에서는「…에 대하여 자세히 읽다」의 뜻으로 수동형도 가능함)
▶ 아이에게 책을 읽어줘 재웠다 I read the child to sleep.
▶ 어머니는 내게 성경을 읽어주셨다 Mother read me the Bible. ⇌ Mother read the Bible to [for] me.
▶ 소년은 책을 읽다가 잠들었다 The boy read himself to sleep.
▶ 이 책은 읽을 만하다 This book is well worth reading.

2〈뜻을 알다〉see; 〈마음·안색을 읽다〉guess; figure
▶ 그의 다음 수를 잘못 읽었다 〈바둑 등에서〉 I failed to guess his next move.

읽을거리 reading; reading matter; literature
♦ 가벼운 읽을거리 light reading / 좋은 읽을거리 good reading / 어린이의 읽을거리 reading for children; children's books
▶ 이것은 어린이에게 좋은 읽을거리입니다 This is a good book for children.
▶ 그의 수필은 즐거운 읽을거리다 His essays make pleasant reading.

읽히다 1〈읽게 하다〉 get sb to read; set sb to reading; have 《a book》 read 《by sb》
2〈읽어지다〉 be read
▶ 이 책은 고교생 사이에서 많이 읽힌다 This book is widely read by high school students.
▶ 그 신문은 널리 읽히고 있다 The paper is widely read. ⇌ It's a widely-read paper. ⇌ The paper has a wide [large] circulation.
▶ 성경은 모든 책 중에서 가장 많이 읽힌다 The Bible is the most read of all books.

잃다 〈재산·소지품 등을〉 lose 《one's fortune》; 〈기회 등을〉 miss 《a chance》; 〈죽다〉 be deprived [bereaved] of 《one's father》
♦ 재산[인기, 명성, 기억]을 잃다 lose one's fortune [popularity, fame, memory] / 모든 희망을 잃다 lose [give up] all (one's) hope / 남편을 잃다 lose [survive] one's husband; be bereaved of one's husband / 길을 잃다 lose [miss] one's way; lose oneself; get [be] lost; stray / 신용을 잃다 lose one's credit; lose the confidence 《of》; fall [bring] into discredit 《with》
▶ 이번 사전으로 내가 잃은 것이 크다 I lost a great deal in this incident.
▶ 지각을 하면 일자리를 잃게 된다 Lateness will lose [cost] you your job. ⇌ You will lose your job because of being late.
▶ 그녀는 비행기 사고로 목숨을 잃었다 She died [was killed] in a plane crash.

잃어버리다 lose ⇨ 잃다
▶ 잃어버린 청춘은 두 번 다시 돌아오지 않는다 Lost youth never returns [will never come back again].

임 〈남자〉 a lover; 〈여자〉 a sweetheart
♦ 옛 임 one's old flame; an old flame of one's / 임을 그리워하다 miss one's love

임간 林間 the interior of a forest [wood]

임간학교 林間學校 an open-air [outdoor] school; camp(ing) school

임검 臨檢 〈현장 검사〉 an (official) inspection; a visit of inspection; 〈수색〉 a raid; a search; 〈배의〉 boarding
—임검하다 〈검사하다〉 visit and inspect; 〈수색하다〉 (raid and) search [make a raid on] 《a house》; raid into; 〈배를〉 (board and) search 《a ship》
▶ 경찰관은 범행 현장을 임검했다 The police made an inspection of [viewed] the scene of the crime.
▶ 세관원이 배를 임검했다 The customs officers inspected [boarded and searched] the ship.

■—반 a raiding party

임계 臨界 ♦임계의 [物] critical / 임계에 달하다 〈원자로가〉 go critical; reach the critical state
■—실험 a critical experiment —실험장치 [物] a critical assembly —압력 [각, 값, 고도, 상태, 온도, 점, 현상] the critical pressure [angle, value, altitude, state, temperature, point, phenomenon] —질량 [物] critical mass

임관 任官 (an) appointment to an office; 〈장교의〉 a commission
—임관하다 be appointed 《to an office》; 〈장교로〉 be commissioned
♦소위로 임관하다 be commissioned second lieutenant
—식 an inaugural ceremony —장교 a commissioned officer

임균 淋菌 a gonococcus
■—성 요도염 gonorrheal urethritis

임금 賃金 wages; pay; a salary (→wages는 보통 육체노동에 지불되는 임금, pay는 급료의 뜻, 월급이나 연봉은 a salary임)
♦임금을 올리다 increase [raise] wages / 임금을 내리다 lower [cut down] wages / 임금을 받다 get [receive] wages
▶ 우리는 생활에 필요한 임금을 요구할 권리가 있다 We have the right to a living wage.
▶ 남녀의 임금 격차가 크다 There is wide inequality [a big difference] in wages between men and women.
■ 기본— basic [standard] wages 기아— starvation wages 기준— the standard [basic] wages 능률— efficiency wages 명목— nominal wages 생활— living wages 시간제— time wages 실질— real wages; (美) take-home pay 작업량제— piece wages 저— low wages [pay] 전시특별— war wages 최고— maximum wages 최저— minimum wages (▶이 경우는 보통 단수) : 최저임금제 the legal [uniform] minimum wage system 할증— extra wages 현물— wages in kind ■—격차[차등] wage differential [disparity] —노동 wage labor; wageworking —노동자 a wage earner; (美) a wageworker —대장(臺帳) a wage ledger; a payroll; (英) a pay sheet —동결 a wage freeze; a freeze on wages —률 a wage [pay] rate —물가체계 the wageprice structure —생활자 a wage earner; a wageworker —수준 a pay level; a wage level [scale] —슬라이드제[연동제(連動制)] the sliding scale system of wages; the elevator system —인상 a wages raise [hike, increase]; a pay raise [boost] : 임금인상을 요구하다 demand a raise in 《one's》 wages; demand [ask for] higher wages —인하 a wage cut [decrease]; wage cutting —정책 a wage policy —제(도) a wage system —지급일 a payday —지수 a wage index —체계 a wage [payment] system —통제 wage control —투쟁 a wage struggle; a (labor) struggle for a wage hike

임기 a term [period] of office [service]; 《one's》 tenure (of office); 〈의원의〉 a term of membership
♦남은 임기 the remainder of one's term of office / 대통령으로서 (두 번째) 임기 중에 during his (second) term as President / 임기 만료 전에 before the term expires / 임기 만료와 동시에 at the expiration [completion] of one's term of office [membership tenure] / 임기가 만료되다 one's tenure [term of office] expires 《as, of》 / 임기를 연장하다 extend one's term / 임기를 마치다[채우다] wind up one's service; finish up one's tenure of office; serve out one's term
▶ 대통령의 임기는 5년이다 The President's term of office is five years. ⇌ The President holds office for five years.

임기응변 臨機應變 adaptation to circumstances
♦임기응변의 수완 the talent of accommodating [adapting] oneself to circumstances / 임기응변의 expedient / 임기응변으로 as occasion demands [arises, requires]; according to circumstances
▶ 그들은 임기응변의 조치를 취했다 They took emergency [proper] steps to meet the situation.
▶ 비상시에는 임기응변으로 행동해야 한다 In case of emergency we should act as the occasion demands [according to circumstances].
▶ 그것은 임기응변의 조치였다 They were the proper steps [measures] to meet the situation.
—임기응변하다 adapt oneself to circumstances; act according to the circumstances

임대 賃貸 〈부동산의〉 lease; hire; 〈물품 등의〉 hiring out; 〈배의〉 charter
♦5년간의 임대로 집을 빌리다 rent a house on a five-year lease; take a five-year lease on a house / 부동산 임대로 수입이 있다 have an income from property rentals
—임대하다 〈토지·가옥 등을〉 lease out; locate; rent [let out]; 〈물품 등을〉 hire out; 〈배를〉 charter
—가격 a rental value; a value of lease —계약 a lease contract —료 (a) rent 《for》; a rental; 〈자동차 등의〉 hire; 〈배의〉 charterage —업 leasing service —인 a lessor

임대차 賃貸借 lease; letting and hiring; 〈선박의〉 charter

임독 淋毒 〔醫〕 gonorrh(o)ea; (卑) the clap

임립하다 林立— stand close together; bristle 《with》

임면 任免 appointment and dismissal [removal]
—임면하다 appoint and dismiss [remove]
■—권 the power to appoint and to dismiss [remove]: 이 회사에서는 누가 임면권을 가지고 있습니까? Who has the right [power] to appoint and dismiss [hire and fire] (the) employees of [in] this company?

임명 任命 appointment; nomination; designation; assignment
—임명하다 appoint 《sb to an office》; nominate [name] 《sb to [for] a post》; ordain 《sb to [for] an office》; designate 《sb as, for》; assign 《sb to a post》
♦성직에 임명되다 be ordained priest [to the priesthood]

▶ 수상은 그를 자신의 후임자로 임명했다 The Prime Minister appointed [nominated, named] him (as [to be]) his successor. (▶ 보통 as, to be는 생략됨)
■ —권 the power to appoint; the appointive power(s) —권자 a person who has the appointive powers —자 an appointer

임무 任務 〈의무〉 duty; 〈직무〉 office; 〈부여된 일〉 a task; 〈파견된 자의 임무·사명〉 a mission
◆ 중대한 임무 an important duty; a great task [mission] / 특별한 [어떤] 임무를 띠고 on a special [certain] mission / 임무를 부여하다 place a duty upon 《sb》; assign 《sb》 to a task / 임무를 수행하다[다하다] discharge [do, perform, carry out] one's duty [duties]; accomplish one's task; fulfill one's mission / 임무를 게을리하다 neglect one's duties / 임무를 수행하지 못하다 fail in one's duty
▶ 나는 그 임무를 맡을 수 없습니다 I cannot take up [over] the task.
▶ 그들은 특별한 임무로 외국에 갔다 They went abroad on a special mission.
▶ 여러분의 임무는 등산 조난자를 구조하는 일입니다 Your mission is to rescue the climbers in distress.
▶ 나는 다만 임무를 수행했을 뿐이다 I have only done what it was my duty to do.

임박 臨迫 approaching; impending
—임박하다 draw near; approach; impend; be imminent; be close [near] at hand
◆ 임박한 전쟁 impending war
▶ 사태는 아주 임박해 있었다 The matter was quite urgent.
▶ 시간이 시시각각 임박하고 있다 Time is pressing every moment.
▶ 그는 죽음이 임박해 있다 He is dying. ⇒ He is on the verge [brink, point] of death.
▶ 시험이 임박했다 The examination is near [close] at hand. ⇒ The examination is just around the corner.

임부 妊婦 a pregnant woman; a woman in the family way; a woman in pregnancy [in a delicate condition]; an expectant mother

임산물 林産物 forest products (▶ 보통 복수형)

임산부 姙産婦 expectant and nursing mothers; pregnant women and nursing mothers

임상 林床 forest floor

임상 臨床 ◆ 임상적 연구 a clinical study 《of》/ 임상의 clinical; bedside / 임상적으로 clinically
■ —강의 a clinical lecture; a clinic —교수 clinical teaching —병리학 clinical pathology —신문 a clinical examination —실습 bedside and clinical training —실험 a clinical trials [tests]: 임상실험중이다 be in clinical trials 《on men》 —심리학 clinical psychology —의 (醫) a clinician; a therapist —의학 clinical medicine —일지 a physician's diary —진단 (a) clinical diagnosis —진찰 a clinical examination: 임상진찰을 하다 clinically examine; pursue a clinical examination

임석 臨席 〈출석〉 attendance; presence; 〈동석〉 company
◆ 아무의 임석하에 with sb in attendance; in the presence of sb
—임석하다 attend; be present 《at》
▶ 교육부장관이 그 모임에 임석했다 The Minister of Education attended [was present at, presented himself at] the meeting.
■ —경찰관 a policeman in attendance —자 a person present; (총칭) those present; the attendance: 그 모임의 임석자는 예상 외로 많았다[적었다] There was unexpectedly a large [small] attendance at the meeting.

임시 臨時 ◆ 임시의 〈일시적인〉 temporary; provisional; interim; 〈임시변통의〉 expedient; makeshift; stopgap; 〈급히 만든·즉흥적인〉 improvised 《seat》; 〈시험적인〉 tentative; 〈특별한 경우의〉 special; extra; extraordinary; emergent / 임시로 〈당분간〉 for the present; for the time being; temporarily; provisionally; 〈임시변통으로〉 as a makeshift; 〈특별히〉 specially; extraordinarily / 임시로 짓다 rig 《a building》
■ —결의 a provisional resolution —결정 a tentative decision —고용인 a temporary employee —공(工) a casual (laborer) —공사 provisional construction work —구호본부 a temporary rescue headquarters —국회 an extraordinary session of the National Assembly —규정 provisional [tentative] rules —내각 a stopgap cabinet —뉴스 a special newscast; news special —면허 a temporary [provisional] license —열차 a special train: 임시열차를 운행하다 run a special train —예산 a provisionary budget —의장 an acting president [chairman] —정류소 a temporary car [bus] stop —정부 a provisional government: 상해임시정부 Korean Provisional Government which was in Shanghai (during Japanese occupation of Korea); 〈미승인·사실상의 임시정부〉 de facto government —지출 extraordinary expenditure; a contingent outlay —직 a temporary post [position, office] —직원 a temporary employee; 〈견습 사원〉 a probationer —증간 an extra [a special] issue [edition] 《of a magazine》 —채용 appointment on trial [probation]: 임시 채용하다 take on trial; engage sb on probation —총회 an extraordinary general meeting —특례 a provisional exception —프로그램 a tentative program —협정 a provisional agreement —휴교 a temporary school closing; cancellation of classes —휴업 (게시) Closed today.; No business today. —휴일 an extra [a special] holiday

임시변통 臨時變通 a makeshift; a stopgap; a temporary expedient [measure]
◆ 임시변통의 대책 a makeshift [stopgap] measure [action] / 임시변통으로 만든 것 a makeshift; a make-do / 임시변통의 temporary; patch-up; makeshift / 임시변통으로 for a shift; by way of makeshift / 임시변통으로 맞추다 patch up
—임시변통하다 make shift 《with》; manage 《with》; temporize; make do with 《for the present》

임신 姙娠 pregnancy; conception; gestation; gravidity

임야

♦임신중인 딸 a daughter in the family way / 임신중에 during pregnancy / 임신중이다 be pregnant; be in a [the] family way; be (big) with child; be going to be a mother; be expecting a baby; 〈짐승이〉 be with young / 임신 8개월이 되다 be eight months pregnant; be in the eight month of pregnancy
—**임신하다** conceive; become pregnant [impregnated] ♦임신시키다 cause pregnancy; impregnate; get 《a woman》 with child
■상상— pseudopregnancy; false pregnancy; pseudocyesis 자궁외— extrauterine [ectopic] pregnancy; extrauterine gestation ■—가능기간 an impregnable period —가능연령 impregnable age —기간 a pregnancy period; the length of pregnancy —부 ⇨ 임부(姙婦) —조절 ⇨ 산아제한 —중독증 toxemia of pregnancy —중절 (an) artificial abortion; interrupted [interruption of] pregnancy —진단 pregnancy diagnosis

임야 林野 forests and fields; a forest land

임업 林業 forestry ■—경제 forestry economics —시험장 a forestry experiment station —연구원 the Forest Research Institute —지역 forestry region

임용 任用 appointment ♦공무원 임용령 the Official Appointment Regulations —임용하다 appoint 《an official, sb to a post》

임원 任員 〈단체의 간부〉 a leading member; 〈총칭〉 the board [staff]; 〈회사의 이사〉 a director; an executive
■조합— a union officer [official] ■—석 directors' seats —수당 an executive allowance —회 a directors' [executives'] meeting; the board of directors

임의 任意 voluntariness; option; discretion
♦임의의 장소 any place / 임의의 optional 《with》; voluntary; discretionary; free / 임의로 at one's option [discretion]; at 《one's》 pleasure; as one pleases [chooses]; at will; of one's own accord [free will]; voluntarily / 임의로 행동하다 act at one's discretion; do as one pleases / 시골을 임의로 돌아다니다 wander at will through the countryside
▶ 임의로 처분해도 좋다 You can do with it as you please. ⇒ It is within [in] your discretion to dispose of it.
▶ 학생들은 프랑스어나 독일어 중에서 임의로 선택할 수 있다 It is optional with the student to take either French or German.
■—보험 voluntary insurance —선택 option; free choice —성 voluntariness —자백 a voluntary confession —조정 voluntary arbitration —추출법〔統〕random sampling —출두 voluntary appearance [attendance]; 임의 출두를 요구하다 ask sb's voluntary appearance —표본 random sample

임자 1 〈소유주〉 the owner; the proprietor
♦임자없는 개 an ownerless dog / 임자없는 집 a vacant [deserted] house / 임자없는 ownerless; belonging to nobody / 임자가 바뀌다 change [shift] its owner [proprietor]
▶ 그는 자기가 그 차의 임자라고 주장했다 He claimed the ownership of the car.

▶ 이 모자의 임자는 누구입니까? Whose hat is this?
2 〈부부간〉 (my) dear; darling; honey
♦임자 있는 여자 a woman who has her husband; a married woman

임장감 臨場感 presence ⇨ 현장감

임전 臨戰 presence at a battle
—**임전하다** go into action
■—무퇴 no retreat at the battlefield —태세 preparations for action: 임전태세를 갖추다 be prepared for war

임정 臨政 a provisional government ⇨ 임시(〜정부)
—**요인** leading figures of the provisional government

임종 臨終 1 〈죽음에 임함〉 one's dying [last] moment ♦임종의 자리 one's deathbed
—**임종하다** be on one's deathbed; be at the moment of death; be dying
♦임종하는 날[때]까지 to [until] one's dying day; to one's last moment / 임종이 가깝다 be at death's door [near death]
2 〈부모의 사망 때 그 자리에 같이 있음〉 attendance [presence] at one's parent's deathbed
—**임종하다** be present at one's parent's death; attend [be at] one's parent's deathbed
♦임종하지 못하다 be unable to attend one's parent's deathbed

임종시 臨終時 one's last moments; the hour of death; the dying hour
♦임종시의 유언 one's dying injunctions / 임종시의 고백 a deathbed confession / 임종시에 at the moment of death; at a [on one's] deathbed; in one's last moments
▶ 이것이 그의 임종시의 말이었다 This was his dying words. ⇒ This was what he said in his last moments.

임지 任地 the place of one's appointment
♦임지로 떠나다 go to [leave for] one's (new) post

임지 林地 forestland

임진왜란 壬辰倭亂 〔史〕Japanese invasion of the Yi dynasty in 1592

임질 淋疾 〔醫〕gonorrhea; gonorrhoea; 〈俗〉 the clap ♦임질의 gonorrheal ■—환자 a gonorrheal patient [case]

임차 賃借 hire; hiring; lease; renting; rental
♦임차용 가옥 house for rent / 임차로 by [on] lease
—**임차하다** lease; take [hold] 《land, a house》 by [on] lease; rent 《a house》; hire 《a car》; charter 《a ship》
■—가격 the value of a lease —권 the right of lease; a lease —료 rent 《of a house》; hire 《of a car》 —부동산 leasehold estate —인 a hirer; a lessee; a leaseholder; 〈토지·가옥의〉 tenant —지 leased land

임팩트론 an impact loan

임피던스 〈전류 저항〉 impedance

임하다 任— 〈임명하다〉 appoint 《sb Mayor》; nominate 《sb to a post》; place; install [put] 《sb in an office》; institute; 〈장교로〉 commission 《sb as colonel》

임하다 臨— 1 〈면하다〉 look out on [upon]; face; look toward
♦ 바다에 임한 집 a house facing the sea
▶ 인천은 황해에 임해 있다 Inch'ŏn is situated on the Yellow Sea.
2 〈당면하다〉 meet; face; be confronted 《by》; 〈임박하다〉 be on the verge of 《a war》
♦ 죽음에 임하여 on *one's* deathbed; at the moment of death / 조용히 죽음에 임하다 meet *one's* death calmly
3 〈임석하다〉 attend 《a ceremony》; be present at 《a meeting》
♦ 졸업식에 임하다 be present at the graduation ceremony
4 〈대하다〉 deal with
♦ 부하에게 관대하게 임하다 deal with *one's* subordinates with generosity

임학 林學 forestry; dendrology
■ —자 a forestry expert; a dendrologist

임항 臨港 —선[철도] a harbor railway [railroad] —열차 a boat train

임해 臨海 seaside; coast
■ —공업지대 a coastal [seaside] industrial zone [region] —실험소 a marine (biological) laboratory —지역 a littoral district; a littoral —학교 a seaside school

입 1 〈사람·동물의〉 a mouth; 〈부리〉 a bill; 〈맹금의〉 a beak; 〈입술〉 lips
♦ 입속 the buccal [oral] cavity / 오므린 입 a puckered mouth; pursed lips / 꽉 다문 입 a firm(ly)-set mouth / 입의 oral; [解] buccal 〈입이〉 입이 작은[큰] smallmouthed [bigmouthed] / 입이 닳도록 말하다 tell over and over again / 입이 화근이다 out of the mouth comes the evil
▶ 입이 아프지도 않은가 보구나 You have a tireless jaw.
〈입을〉 입을 벌리고 with *one's* mouth open; agape / 입을 삐죽거리며 말하다 say poutingly / 입을 다물다 shut *one's* mouth; clamp *one's* lips together / 입을 오므리다 purse up *one's* lips; pucker up *one's* mouth / 입을 삐죽 내밀다 pout *one's* mouth [lips] / 입을 막다 stop *sb's* mouth
▶ 그는 입을 크게 벌리고 하품했다 He yawned wide.
▶ 마침내 그녀가 입을 열었다 At last she began to talk.
▶ 그는 입을 열기만 하면 경제를 논한다 Economy is always on his lips.
〈입에(서)〉 입에 가득한 mouthful / 입에 풀칠하다 earn *one's* living / 입에 거미줄 치다 can't afford to buy food; eat nothing; lose *one's* means of living; starve; go hungry / 입에 발린 말을 늘어놓다 speak claptrap / 입에서 입으로 전해지다 pass [be whispered] from mouth to mouth / 입에 물다 mouth / 입에서 냄새가 나다 have (a) foul [bad] breath / 입에 대지 않은 채 두다 leave untasted
▶ 그는 알코올성 음료는 전혀 입에 대지 않는다 He never touches alcoholic drinks.
〈입으로〉 ▶ 그는 자기 입으로 그런 말을 했다 He said so with his own lips.
2 〈말〉 tongue; speech; words; 〈소문〉 rumor; gossip
♦ 입만 아플 뿐이다 only waste *one's* breath [words] / 입 밖에 내다 disclose; betray; reveal divulge; 〈말하다〉 express; put into words; mention; mouth 《a word》; give mouth to / 입 밖에 내지 않다 keep 《a matter》 to *oneself*; keep mum 《about》; keep 《it》 a secret / 입이 아주 무겁다 be as close as an oyster / 남의 입에 오르내리다 be the talk of the town; be talked about by people; be on the tongues of people / 입을 조심하다 be careful of *one's* speech [language]; be cautious of *one's* tongue; restrain *one's* tongue / 입을 열다 tell; speak 〈it〉 out; disclose [reveal, betray] 《a secret》 / 입을 다물다 〈말하다가〉 cease to speak; 〈말하지 않다〉 keep *one's* mouth shout
▶ 그런 말은 입 밖에도 내지 마라 Don't show the slightest signs of it.
▶ 그 말은 입에 담기도 싫다 The language will not bear repeating.
3 〈맛〉 《*one's*》 taste; 《*one's*》 palate
♦ 입이 떡은 떡 just what *one* wants indeed / 입이 고급이다 be born with a dainty tooth; have a pampered taste / 입이 까다롭다 have a delicate taste; be particular about food / 입에 맞는 suit *one's* taste [palate]; be to *one's* taste
4 〈식구〉 a dependent; mouths
♦ 입이 많다 have a large family to support

입가 ♦ 입가에 about the mouth / 입가에 미소를 띠고 with a smile about *one's* lips [mouth]

입가심 a savo(u)ry; (口) chaser; (美口) wash
♦ 입가심으로 to kill the aftertaste
▶ 쓴 약이니까 입가심으로 과자를 먹어라 Eat cake to kill the bitter taste of the medicine.
—입가심하다 kill [take off] the aftertaste; (口) chase

입각 入閣 entry into the Cabinet [Ministry]
—입각하다 enter [join] the Cabinet [Ministry]; become a Cabinet member

입각 立脚 〈근거로 함〉 a footing; being based [grounded]
—입각하다 be based [grounded, founded] on
♦ …에 입각하여 based on…; on the basis of… / 기록에 입각하다 be based on records
▶ 현실에 입각하여 결정을 해야 한다 Your decision should be based on reality.

입감 入監 imprisonment ♦ 입감중이다 be in jail [prison]; be behind the bars
—입감하다 be sent to prison [jail]; be imprisoned

입갱 入坑 〈갱도로 들어감〉 entering an adit [a pit] —입갱하다 enter an adit; enter a pit

입거 入渠 docking; entering a dock
—입거하다 enter a dock; come [go, get] into 《a》 dock; dock ■ —료 dockage —시설 docking facilities; dockage

입건 立件 —입건하다 book 《*sb*》 on charge
♦ 아무를 기소하기 위해 입건하다 book to prosecute *sb* for a crime
▶ 경찰은 그를 절도 혐의로 입건했다 The police booked him on a charge of theft.

입경 入京 entering [arriving in] the capital city —입경하다 enter the capital; arrive in

입고 入庫 〈상품의〉 warehousing; 〈차량의〉 entering the (car) shed
―**입고하다** 〈상품을〉 stock [warehouse] (goods); put (goods) in a warehouse; 〈차량을〉 enter the (car) shed
▶ 신 제품이 많이 입고됐다 Great quantities of new products have been stocked.

입고병 立枯病 〔植〕 damping-off=모잘록병

입관 入棺 placing the corpse in the coffin
―**입관하다** place a corpse in a coffin

입교 入校 entrance into a school ⇨ 입학

입교 入敎 1 〈종교를 믿기 시작함〉 beginning to believe in religion
2 〈기독교인이 됨〉 becoming a Christian after being christened; conversion
―**입교하다** enter religion; 〈기독교인이 되다〉 become a Christian; be [get] converted

입구 入口 an entrance; a way in; an entry (to); the mouth 《of a cave》; the door (to); an approach [entrance] (to); the gate 《to》
◆ 극장의 입구 the entrance to a theater / 공원의 입구 a park gate / 고속도로 입구 the entrance ramp to an expressway / 입구에서 at the entrance; at the gate / 입구를 막다 block the entrance [entry]

입국 入國 entry [entrance] into a country; 〈이민의〉 immigration
◆ 입국을 허가하다 admit sb into a country / 입국하다 거절하다 deny [refuse] entry [admission] into a country
―**입국하다** enter a country; be admitted into a country; 〈이민이〉 immigrate into a country
■ 불법― illegal entry : 불법 입국자 an illegal entrant 재(再)― reentry; reentrance ■ ―금지 prohibition of entry ―사증 entry visa ―세 a landing tax; an entry tax ―수속[절차] entry formalities ―심사 inspection of an entry visa ―자 an immigrant ―허가서[증] a permit of entry; an entry permit

입국 立國 the founding [establishment] of a nation ―**입국하다** found a nation
■ ―산업 national foundation [prosperity] on the basis of industries

입궐 入闕 attendance at [entry into] the Royal Court ―**입궐하다** go [proceed] to the Royal Court; enter the palace

입금 入金 〈수령〉 receipt of money; 〈수납금〉 money received [paid in]; receipts; 〈수 납할 돈〉 money due; money coming in
―**입금하다** receive
■ 내― part payment : 내입금으로 50만원을 입금하다 make a part [partial] payment of five hundred thousand won 월별― receipts by month ■ ―전표 a deposit [paying-in] slip; receiving slip

입김 the steam of breath; puffs of one's breath
◆ 입김이 세다 breathe hard; (비유) be influential [powerful] (in); have influence 《over》 / 입김을 불다 breathe upon; blow on 《frozen hands》
▶ 사람의 입김 때문에 유리창이 흐려졌다 The windowpanes were steamed up with people's breaths.

입납 入納 addressed to 《Mr. Kim》; Please deliver to 《Mr. Kim》; To 《Mr. Kim》

입내[1] 〈말·소리의 흉내〉 mimicry
◆ 입내를 내다 mimic sb [sb's talk]; imitate sb's way of talking
▶ 그는 누나의 목소리를 입내낸다 He mimics his sister's voice.
■ ―쟁이 a mimic; a mimicker

입내[2] 〈입냄새〉 bad [foul] breath; 〔醫〕 halitosis

입노릇 〈먹는 일·군것질〉 eating (some refreshment); munching; having a bite
―**입노릇하다** eat some refreshments, munch, have a bite
▶ 이 사람들은 하루에 여러번 입노릇한다 These people eat many times a day.

입다 1 〈몸에〉 put [get] on; 〈걸치다〉 slip on; 〈입고 있다〉 wear; be dressed [clad] in
◆ 머리부터 입다 pull over / 맵시있게 입다 wear (a dress) stylishly / 옷을 입은 채로 자다 sleep in one's clothes / 새 옷을 입어보다 try on one's new clothes; try a new suit on
▶ 그는 일상복을 입고 있다 He is dressed in plain clothes.
▶ 그녀는 나들이옷을 입고 있다 She clothes herself in her best.
▶ 너는 이제 너무 커서 이 옷들을 입을 수 없다 You have outgrown these clothes.
▶ 그 바지는 아직 입을 수 있다 Those trousers [pants] are still good for wear.
2 〈도움 받다〉 be favored 《with》; get [receive] (a favor); enjoy; 〈피해를〉 suffer [incur] (a loss); sustain 《damage》
◆ 은혜를 입다 bask (in sb's favor); owe an obligation 《to》; be indebted 《to》; own sb a debt of gratitude / 문명의 혜택을 입다 bask in civilization's comfort / 부상을 입다 be [get] wounded [injured]; get hurt; suffer an injury 《to a knee》 / 손해를 입다 suffer [receive] damage; suffer a loss
▶ 우리는 이 태풍으로 막대한 피해를 입었다 We suffered great damage because of this typhoon.
3 〈상(喪)을〉 ◆ 상을 입다 mourn; go into [take to] mourning 《for sb》; observe mourning / 상을 입고 있다 be in mourning

입단 入團 joining [entering, enrolling in, entry into (an organization)]
―**입단하다** join [enter, enroll in] (an organization)
▶ 그는 보이스카우트에 입단했다 He joined the Boy Scouts.

입담 glibness; the gift of (the) gab; volubility
◆ 입담이 좋다 be good at talking; be glib-[smooth-, voluble-]tongued; be a glib talker

입당 入黨 joining a political party
―**입당하다** join a political party
■ ―자 an incoming member

입대 入隊 enlistment; enrollment; joining the army
―**입대하다** join [enter] the army; enroll [be enrolled] in a unit; 〈징병되어서〉 be conscripted [drafted] into the army
■ ―식 a parade [ceremony] of new recruits

입사

—자 a recruit

입덧 〔醫〕 morning sickness ◆입덧이 나다 suffer from [have] morning sickness / 입덧이 심하다 have bad morning sickness

입도 立稻 unharvested [standing] rice crop
―선매 selling rice before the harvest

입동 立冬 the first day [beginning] of winter (according to the solar calendar)

입력 入力 1〈전기의〉(power) input
2〈컴퓨터의〉input ―입력하다 input
◆컴퓨터에 정보를 입력하다 input information / 컴퓨터에 데이터를 입력하다 feed a computer with data
■―신호 an input [incoming] signal ―장치 an input unit ―전류 an input current

입론 立論 argument; argumentation
―입론하다 argue 《for, against》; make [put forward, set forth, build up] an argument

입막음하다 close [stop] sb's mouth; forbid sb to speak 《it》; hush up 《a matter》; muzzle sb; tie sb's tongue
◆입막음하는 돈 hush money; a bribe / 입막음하는 돈을 주다 put a gold muzzle
▶입막음하는 돈으로 그에게 50만원을 주었다 I bought his silence for 500,000 won.

입맛 appetite; one's taste; one's palate
◆입맛이 떨어지다〈주어 사람이〉lose one's appetite; (비유) lose one's interest in / 입맛이 당기다[없다] have a good [poor] appetite / 입맛 돋우다 stimulate [excite, arouse] one's appetite / 입맛을 잃다 lose one's appetite / 입맛에 맞다 be pleasant [mellow] to the taste; be palatable [tasty, savory, easy to take]; suit one's palate
▶운동을 좀 하면 입맛이 난다 A little exercise will give you a good appetite.
▶열이 나서 입맛이 없다 I have no appetite because I've got a fever.
▶이 포도주는 입맛에 맞는다 This wine tastes nice. ⇒ This wine is mellow.

입맛다시다 1〈먹고 싶어하다〉smack one's lips; lick one's lips [chops]
◆요리를 보고 입맛다시다 lick one's chops at the sight of dishes
2〈일이 난처하여〉click [clack] one's tongue; tut-tut
◆남이 하는 일이 못마땅해서 입맛다시다 click one's tongue at sb's behavior
3〈욕심내다〉have a desire; have an itch for
▶그녀는 보는 것마다 갖고 싶어 입맛다신다 She wants everything she sees.

입맛쓰다 be bitter [unpleasant, displeased, disgusting]
◆입맛 쓴 경험 a bitter experience / 입맛 쓴 듯이 with a perplexed air
▶그는 입맛 쓰다는 듯이 우리를 바라보았다 He looked at us with disgust.

입맞추다 kiss sb; press one's lips against
◆볼에 입맞추다 kiss sb on the cheek / 느닷없이 입맞추다 snatch a kiss

입멸 入滅 〔佛敎〕 entering Nirvana; death of a Buddhist saint ―입멸하다 enter Nirvana

입모습 the shape of one's mouth
◆입모습이 예쁘다 have a pretty mouth

▶그의 일모습은 어머니를 닮았다 His mouth looks like his mother's.

입목 立木 〈수목〉a standing [living, growing] tree; 〈목재〉standing timber

입문 入門 1〈첫걸음〉a guide; a primer
◆문학 입문 an introduction to the study of literature / 물리학 입문 the ABC of physics / 영작문 입문 a first manual of English composition
2〈문하생이 됨〉entrance into a private school
―입문하다 enter a (private) school; become a pupil [disciple] of sb
■―서 a primer; a guide; a manual; a handbook; an introduction

입바르다 plainspoken; outspoken; straightforward; unreserved
◆입바른 소리 plain speaking; a straight talk / 입바른 소리를 잘하는 사람 a plainspoken person; an outspoken person / 입바른 소리를 하다 speak plainly; speak in a straightforward manner; speak without reserve; call a spade a spade

입방 立方 〔數〕 cube ⇨ 세제곱

입방근 立方根 〔數〕 the cube root ＝ 세제곱(～근)

입방아찧다 prattle; chat; nag 《at》; gossip; (口) jaw

입방체 立方體 a cube; a regular hexahedron
◆입방체의 cubic(al)

입버릇 〈말버릇〉a habit of saying; 〈잘 쓰는 말〉one's favorite phrase; 〈되풀이하는 말〉a parrot-cry
◆입버릇처럼 말하다 always say; be in the habit of saying; keep saying; be never tired of saying
▶어머니는 '정신 차려라'하는 말씀을 입버릇처럼 하신다 My mother has a habit of saying [always says] "safety first."
▶'최선을 다해라'는 것이 그의 입버릇의 하나다 "Do your best" is one of his favorite phrases.

입법 立法 legislation; lawmaking
◆입법의 취지 the purpose of legislation / 입법상의 legislative; legislatorial / 입법 정신에 위배되다 be contrary to the spirit of legislation
―입법하다 legislate; make [enact] laws
■―권 (exercise) legislative power: 국회가 입법권을 가지고 있다 The National Assembly has legislative power. ―기관 a legislative [lawmaking] organ; the legislature ―부 the legislature ―자 a legislator; a lawmaker ―화 legalization

입병 ―病 a sore mouth; a mouth disease; a mouth infection

입사 入社 joining a company [firm]
―입사하다 join [get a job with] a company; enter a firm
▶나는 무역회사에 입사하고 싶다 I would like to join a trading company.
▶〘會話〙"당신은 언제 입사했습니까?"「지난 4월에요」"When did you join us?" "It was in April."

입사 入射 〔物〕 incidence ■ —각 an incidence angle; an angle of incidence —광선 incident rays

입사 立嗣 〈상속인을 세움〉 designating an heir —입사하다 designate *sb* as heir

입사시험 入社試驗 an entrance examination; an examination for service in a company
♦그 회사의 입사시험에 응모하다 apply for a job with the company / 큰 회사의 입사시험에 합격하다 succeed in the examination [test] for service in a big firm

입산 入山 —입산하다 1 enter a mountain area; go into a mountain 2 〈절에 들어가다〉〔佛敎〕 enter a monastery; enter the priesthood; become a monk
—금지구역 a restricted area

입상 入賞 winning a prize
—입상하다 win a prize
♦1등에 입상하다 win the first prize
▶그녀는 웅변대회에서 3등에 입상했다 She won third prize [was placed third] in the oratorical contest.
—자 a prize winner; a winning contestant

입상 立像 a statue; 〈소형의〉 a statuette; a standing image [figure] 《of》

입상 粒狀 ♦입상의 granular; granulous; granulated; graniform / 입상으로 만들다 granulate ■ —전분〔녹말〕 granular starch —조직 granular texture

입석 立席 〈극장 등의〉 the gallery; 〈美〉 standing room
▶입석도 만원이다 There's no room even for standing.
▶입석 이외 만원 (게시) Standing Room Only. (略 S.R.O.)
—손님 a standee

입선 入選 —입선하다 be accepted; be selected
▶내 작문이 콘테스트에 입선했다 My composition was accepted by [selected for] the contest.
▶그의 그림이 금년도 국전에 입선하였다 His painting was accepted [selected] for this year's National Art Exhibition.
■ —논문 a winning essay —자 a winner; a winning [successful] competitor [contestant] —작(品) a winning (piece of) work

입성 入城 a triumphal entry into a fortress [city] —입성하다 enter a castle

입 센 〈노르웨이의 극작가〉 Ibsen, Henrik (1828-1906)

입소 入所 1 〈훈련소・연구소 등에의〉 entrance 《into》; admission 《to》
—입소하다 enter [be admitted to] an institute 2 〈교도소의〉 imprisonment; 〈수용소의〉 internment; confinement
♦입소중이다 〈교도소에〉 be in prison [jail]; 〈수용소에〉 be in a camp
—입소하다 〈교도소에〉 be put into prison; be sent to jail; be imprisoned; 〈수용소에〉 be put into [sent to] a (concentration) camp; be interned
♦입소시키다 〈교도소에〉 put [cast] *sb* into prison; commit [send] *sb* to prison; 〈수용소에〉 intern; send *sb* to a camp

입속말 a murmur; a mumble; muttering
♦입속말로 중얼거리다 speak under *one's* breath —입속말하다 mutter; grumble 《at, over, about》; murmur 《at, against》
▶혼자서 입속말하다 mutter to *oneself*

입수 入手 acquisition; procurement; receipt
—입수하다 obtain; get; come by; receive; 〈사물이 주어〉 come to hand
♦입수할 수 있는 obtainable; available; accessible
▶넌 어디서 그 정보를 입수했니? Where did you pick up that information?
▶이런 종류의 그림은 입수하기 어렵다 This kind of picture is hard to obtain.
■ —경로 means of acquisition —난 difficulty of obtaining

입술 a lip
♦두툼한 입술 full [thick] lips / 터진 입술 chapped [cracked] lips / 얇은 입술 thin lips / 입술의 〔解・動〕 labial / 입술이 두툼한 full-lipped / 입술이 얇은 thin-lipped / 입술을 깨물다 bite *one's* lips; 〈아랫입술을〉 chew on *one's* lower lip / 입술을 삐죽 내밀다 pout *one's* lips / 입술을 오므리다 purse (up) *one's* lips / 입술을 핥다 lick *one's* own lips
▶그는 분해서 입술을 깨물었다 He bit his lips in (his) mortification.
■ —윗〔아랫〕— the upper [lower] lip ■ —성형수술 chiloplasty —소리 〔音聲〕 a labial

입술연지 —臙脂 〔립스틱〕 (a) lipstick; a lip pencil; 〈루주〉 rouge
♦입술연지를 바르다 paint *one's* lips; put lipstick on *one's* lips; rouge *one's* lips / 입술연지를 고치다 touch up *one's* lipstick

입시 入試 an admission examination (⇨ 입학시험) —지옥 the entrance examination evil; exam hell

입신 立身 success in life; a rise in the world —입신하다 rise in the world; succeed [advance, rise] in life
▶그는 중소기업가로서 입신했다 He established himself as a minor enterpriser.
■ —양명 rising in the world and winning [gaining] fame; achieving glory —욕 a desire of personal advancement —출세 success in life; a successful career —출세담 *one's* success story

입심 talkativeness; eloquence
♦입심이 좋은 사람 a glib talker; a man with a facile tongue / 입심이 사납다 have a bitter tongue / 입심이 좋다 be loquacious [talkative, glib]; have a facile tongue

입싸다 talkative; rash of speech; blabbing; glib-tongued; leaky
♦입싼 사람 a blabber(mouth); a leaky person / 입싸게 지껄이다 blab; babble; prattle
▶그는 입싼 사람이다 He has a loose tongue.

입쌀 unglutinous rice

입씨름 〈말다툼〉 a dispute; repeated argument; a bickering ♦공연한 입씨름을 벌이다 have a fruitless dispute
—입씨름하다 argue; bicker; dispute; altercate; wrangle; carry on a dispute; have an argument [altercation] 《with》; get into a shout-

입씨름 ing match 《with》
입씨기다 pay hush money; buy *sb's* silence
입씨이 1 〈입막음돈〉 hush money; a gold muzzle; a bribe 2 ⇨ 입가심
입아귀 the corner(s) of the mouth
입안 立案 〈안을 세움〉 drawing up a plan; 〈초안 작성〉 drafting; planning; design; scheme
　—**입안하다** make a plan; plan (out); devise; design; draft
　▶ 이것은 그 남자가 입안한 것이다 This idea originated with him.
　▶ 대통령은 새로운 외교정책을 입안했다 Mr. President designed a new foreign policy.
　▶ 이것은 누가 입안했습니까? Who planned this? ⇌ Who made [drew up] this plan?
　■ —**자** a designer; a drafter; a deviser; a planner: 도시계획의 입안자 a city planner
입양 入養 adoption
　—**입양하다** adopt 《a child》; receive 《a boy》 into *one's* family as a son; affiliate; be adopted into 《a family》; enter 《a family》 as an adopted son
　■ —**신고** a report of adoption of an heir —**아** an adopted child; a foster child
입어권 入漁權 an entrance right to a piscary; a right of entry into a fishing ground; the common of piscary
입어료 入漁料 charges for fishing in another's piscary
입영 入營 enlistment ⇨ 입대
　♦ **입영중이다** be in the army; be serving with the colors
　—**입영하다** 〈지원하다〉 enlist in the army; join [enter] army; 〈징병되다〉 be drafted [conscripted] into the army
　♦ **병졸[지원병]로 입영하다** enlist in the army as a private [volunteer]
입욕 入浴 a bath; bathing
　—**입욕하다** take [have] a bath; bathe; tub; (口) have [take] a tub
　▶ 환자를 입욕시키는 것은 무척 힘든 일이다 You will find it hard to give a patient a bath.
입원 入院 admission to a hospital; hospitalization
　▶ 그는 입원중이다 He is in (the) hospital.
　▶ 곧바로 입원을 신청하세요 Apply for treatment in [admission to] a hospital right away.
　▶ 그는 입원과 퇴원을 되풀이하고 있다 He has been in and out of the hospital.
　—**입원하다** go into [go to, enter] (the) hospital; be hospitalized; check into a hospital
　♦ **입원시키다** send [take] *sb* to hospital; put *sb* into hospital / 입원하여 치료를 받다 receive treatment in hospital
　▶ 우리는 그 여자를 곧 입원시켰다 We sent [took] her to the hospital at once.
　▶ 그는 오늘 아침 입원했다 He was hospitalized this morning.
　▶ 그는 한 달 동안 입원하고 있다 He has been in the hospital for a month.
　▶ 그녀를 곧 입원시키는 게 좋겠다 You had better send her to a [the] hospital at once.
　▶ 당신은 1주일 더 입원해야 합니다 You must stay in hospital for another week.
　■ —**가료[치료]** hospital treatment —**비[료]** hospital charges —**실** a (sick) ward —**절차** formalities connected with hospital treatment —**환자** an inpatient(▶ 외래환자(outpatient)에 대응하는 말로 보통은 patient라고 함); an inmate of a hospital

입자 粒子 〖物〗 a particle; a grain
　■ —**경(輕)—** a lepton 반(反)— an antiparticle
　—**량** particle weight
입장 入場 〈어떤 장소에 들어감〉 admission; 〈입장 허가〉 admission; admittance
　♦ **입장을 허가하다** admit *sb* into 《a place》; give *sb* admission 《to, into》 / 입장을 거절당하다 be denied [refused] admittance; be turned away
　▶ 그는 박물관 입장을 허가받았다 He was admitted [granted admission] into the museum.
　▶ 관계자외 입장 금지 《게시》 No Admittance Except on Business.
　▶ 입장 무료 《게시》 Admission (is) free.
　▶ 18세 미만의 중·고등학생은 입장불가 《게시》 No admission to middle and high school students under 18 years of age.
　▶ 미성년자 입장 사절 《게시》 Adults only.
　▶ 학생에 한하여 입장 무료 《게시》 Admittance free to students only.
　—**입장하다** enter; get in; 〈관객 등이〉 be admitted 《into》
　♦ **경기장에 입장하다** enter the stadium / 무료로 입장하다 have a free pass; be allowed in free / 무료로 입장시키다 free admission to 《children》
　▶ 나는 늦어서 입장할 수 없었다 As I was late, I was unable to gain admittance.
　▶ 전 선수가 경기장에 입장했다 All the players entered the stadium.
　▶ 표 없는 분은 입장할 수 없습니다 Admission to ticket holders only.
　■ —**무료—** free admission ■ —**권(權)** ingress; entree —**세** an admission [amusement] tax —**식** an entrance [opening] ceremony —**행진** an entrance march [procession]
입장 立場 1 〈처지·경우〉 a situation; a ground; a position; a footing; a stand
　♦ **정치적 입장** *one's* political stand / 남의 입장이 되어 보다 put *oneself* in [into] another's place [shoes] / 남의 입장을 존중하다 respect *sb's* position / 대등한 입장에 있다[서다] be [stand] on an equal footing 《with》 / 난처한 입장에 처해 있다 find *oneself* in a dilemma
　▶ 내 입장이 돼 봐라 Put yourself in my position [place].
　▶ 이 문제에 관한 당신의 입장은 어떤 것입니까? What is your stand on this matter?
　▶ 나는 그것에 대해서 확실한 말을 할 입장이 아니다 I am not in a position to tell you anything definite about it.
　▶ 미안하지만 당신을 도울 입장이 아닙니다 I'm afraid I'm not in a position to help you.
　▶ 내가 지금 어떤 입장에 있는지는 잘 알고 있을 것입니다 You know very well where I stand.
　▶ 입장에 따라 생각도 다르다 One's opinion varies according to one's position.
　▶ 그가 실패해서 나를 곤란한 입장에 빠뜨렸다

His failure put me in an awkward position.
▶ 네가 내 입장이라면 어떻게 하겠니? If you were in my place, what would you do?
▶ 만약에 내가 당신의 입장이었다면 그런 폭풍 우 치는 밤에는 나가지 않았을 것입니다 If I were in your place, I wouldn't go out on such a stormy night.
▶ 내 입장이 어렵다는 것을 네가 이해해 주기를 바란다 I hope you will understand the difficulties of my situation.
2 〈태도〉 an attitude
♦애매한 입장을 취하다 fence; take a noncommittal attitude
▶ 당신은 자신의 입장을 분명히 해야 합니다 You should make your standpoint [position] clear.
3 〈견지〉 a point of view; a viewpoint; an angle; 〈관점〉 a standpoint; 〈견해〉 a position; a stand
♦입장을 바꾸어 보다 look at (it) from a different standpoint [angle] / 입장을 밝히다 make *one's* position clear; define / 서로의 입장을 존중하다 define each other's position [point of views]
▶ 그는 그 문제에 대해 강경한[현실적인] 입장을 취했다 He took a strong [realistic] stand on the issue.

입장권 入場券 an admission ticket; 〈역 구내의〉 a platform ticket
♦입장권을 판매하다[발행하다] sell [issue] admission tickets
■ 무료— a complimentary ticket; an order; a free card [pass]; a pass 일반— a general admission ticket 특별— a complimentary ticket ■—매 표 소 (美) a ticket office [counter]; (英) a booking office —소지자 a ticket holder : 입장권 소지자에 한하여 입장을 허가함 (게시) Admission by ticket only.

입장료 入場料 an entrance [admission] fee (of 5,000 won); admission; 〈도박장 등의〉 a door fee; 〈골프장의〉 green(s) fee
♦입장료를 내다 pay admission; pay for an admission ticket / 입장료를 받다 charge admission
▶ 입장료가 있습니까? Is there an admission fee?
▶ (그 극장의) 입장료가 얼마지요? What is the admission (fee to the theater)?
▶ 입장료 5,000원 (게시) Admission ₩ 5,000.
■ —수 입[매 상 고] the total admission receipts; the proceeds from the box office

입장자 入場者 a visitor; a spectator; (총칭) an attendance
▶ 그녀의 연주회에는 입장자가 많았다 There was a large attendance at her recital.
■ 무료— a free visitor; 〈초대권을 가진〉(口) a deadhead 유료— a paid attendance; paying visitors [customers]

입적 入寂 〈죽음〉 [佛敎] entering Nirvana; death of a Buddhist saint —입적하다 enter [pass into] Nirvana

입적 入籍 〈호적에 올림〉 entry in the family register —입적하다 have *one's* name entered in the family register

입전 入電 a telegram received
▶ 워싱턴으로부터의 입전에 의하면 according to a telegram from Washington

입정 〈입버릇〉 a way of saying; 〈입노릇〉 a move of the mouth

입정 入廷 〈법정에 들어감〉 entrance into the courtroom —입정하다 enter [appear in] the courtroom

입정놀리다 keep *one's* mouth busy to eat

입정사납다 1 〈입버릇이 점잖지 못하다〉 foul-tongued; foul-mouthed; violent-tongued
♦입정사나운 사람 a foul-tongued [violent-tongued] person; an abuser
2 〈게걸스럽다〉 greedy; gluttonous; ravenous; 〈서술적〉 eat like a hungry dog

입주 入住 moving into (an apartment); living in (a house)
▶ 즉시 입주 가(可)(광고) Ready for immediate occupation.
—입주하다 move into (a flat); 〈가정교사 등이〉 live in (a house); live with (a family); 〈동거자가〉 become an inmate of (a house)
♦새 아파트에 입주하다 move into a new apartment
▶ 그녀는 가정교사로 아저씨 댁에 입주하고 있다 She lives in her uncle's (house) as a tutor.
■ —가정부 a resident maid —자 a tenant; an occupant; an inhabitant; a dweller —제(도) the living-in system

입증 立證 proof; establishment (of a fact); demonstration
—입증하다 give proof; prove; establish (*sb's* guilt); substantiate (*one's* statement); 〈일을〉 testify (a fact); attest to (a fact); bear out; bear *one's* testimony
♦유죄[무죄]를 입증하다 prove *sb* guilty [not guilty]
▶ 나는 그것을 입증할 수 있다 I can testify to that.
▶ 증인의 증언이 피고의 무죄를 입증했다 The testimony of witness vindicated the defendant.
▶ 그들은 날짜가 적힌 영수증을 보이며 자기들의 주장을 입증했다 They substantiated their claim by producing dated receipts.
■ —자료 supporting evidence

입지 立地 〈장소의 자연 환경〉 a location
■ —조건 locational condition; site condition: 저 공장은 입지조건이 좋다[나쁘다] That factory is conveniently [inconveniently] located.

입지 立志 〈뜻을 세움〉 determination to make a success in life —입지하다 determine to make a success in life; fix *one's* aim in life; decide *one's* purpose in life
■ —전 the biography of a self-made man; *one's* success story: 그는 입지전적 인물이다 He is a self-made man.

입질 〈낚시에서〉 a bite; a strike
▶ 입질이 있었다[많았다] I had a bite [a lot of bites].
—입질하다 〈물고기가〉 bite; take a bait; 〈사람이〉 have a bite

입짧다 have a little appetite; eat like a bird
♦입짧은 사람 a small [light, poor] eater

입찰 入札 (英) a tender; (美) a bid
◆ 상품을 입찰에 부치다 sell articles by (public) tender
▶ 그는 그 그림을 입찰에 부칠 작정이다 He is going to sell the picture by tender.
—**입찰하다** tender [bid] 《for》; offer [submit, put in] a tender [bid] 《for》
◆ 남보다 낮게[높게] 입찰하다 underbid [outbid] others
▶ 그는 그 피아노에 1,500달러로 입찰했다 He bid one thousand five hundred dollars for the piano.
■ **경쟁[일반]**— a public [an open] tender; sealed tender [bid]; competitive bids **지명**— a private tender; a tender of a specified contractor **최고[최저]**— the highest [lowest] tender [bid] ■ —**가격** the price tendered; a bid [bidding] price —**공고** a notice [an advertisement] of tender 《for》—**매매** tender sales and purchases —**보증금** security for a tender; bid bond —**일** the day of tender [bidding] —**제도** a bid system
입찰자 入札者 a tenderer; a bidder; a tendering party
■ **지명**— a specified [an approved] tenderer **최고[최저]**— the highest [lowest] tenderer [bidder]: 최고 입찰자에게 넘겨지다 be sold to the highest bidder
입천장 —天障 the palate ⇨ 구개
입체 立替 payment for another
—**입체하다** pay [defray] for another
▶ 그의 숙부가 입학금을 입체해 주었다 His uncle advanced him the (school) entrance fee.
▶ 그가 회비를 입체해 주었다 He paid the membership fee on my account.
입체 立體 a solid (body); stereo
◆ 입체의 solid; cubic / 입체적 three-dimensional / 입체적으로 in three dimensions [3-D]
▶ 우리는 그 문제를 입체적으로 조사했다 We investigated the matter from all angles.
■ —**각** 〔數〕 a solid angle —**감** cubic effect; three-dimensional effect: 그림에 입체감을 주다 give a painting a three-dimentional effect —**경** stereoscope —**기하학** solid geometry —**도형** solid figure —**묘사** cubic [solid] delineation —**미** solid beauty —**방송** a stereophonic broadcast [radio system] —**사진(술)** stereophotograph —**영화** a three-dimensional [3-D] film [movie] —**음향** a stereophonic sound —**전** three-dimensional warfare —**주차장** a multi-story parking garage —**화법** stereography

──────── **입체** ────────

구/공 원기둥 원뿔 입방체
sphere cylinder cone cube

입체교차 立體交叉 solid crossing; grade separation; a cloverleaf ■ —**로** a freeway; a flyover roadway; 〈육교〉 an overpass; 〈지하도〉 an underpass —**주차장** sky parking
입체파 立體派 〔美術〕〈화풍〉 cubisme; 〈단체〉 the cubists ■ —**그림** a cubist picture —**예술가** [화가, 조각가] a cubist
입초 入超 the excess of imports ⇨ 수입초과
입초 立哨 watch; standing guard; 〈경찰관 등의〉 point duty; 〈경비원〉 a guard; a watchman; 〈입초병〉 a sentinel; a sentry
◆ 입초 서다 stand guard [watch]; 〈경찰관이〉 stand [be] on point duty / 입초를 세우다 place [mount] a guard
▶ 나는 입구에서 입초섰다 I stood guard [kept watch] at the entrance.
입추 立秋 〈이십사 절기의 하나〉 the first day [beginning, onset] of fall [autumn]
입추 立錐 ◆ 입추의 여지도 없다 be closely packed; be packed full; be densely crowded; be filled to capacity
▶ 회장은 입추의 여지없이 청중으로 가득 찼다 The hall was filled with such a large audience that there wasn't even standing room.
입춘 立春 〈이십사 절기의 하나〉 the first day [beginning, onset] of spring
입출력 入出力 〔電算〕 input/output (略 I/O)
입출력관리 入出力管理 input/output management
입출력설계 入出力設計 input/output design
입출력처리기 入出力處理機 I/O processor
입태자 立太子 〈태자를 정함〉 the official investiture of the crown prince as heir apparent to the throne
입하 入荷 a fresh supply of goods; receipt [arrival] of goods
▶ 오늘 아침은 토마토의 입하가 없습니다 We don't have a fresh supply of tomatoes this morning.
—**입하하다** arrive; be received
▶ 그 책은 언제 입하됩니까? When will that book be available?
■ —**통지** an arrival notice
입하 立夏 〈이십사 절기의 하나〉 the first day [beginning, onset] of summer
입학 入學 entrance [admission] into a school; 〈대학에의〉 matriculation
◆ 입학을 지원하다 apply for admission to / 입학을 허가하다 admit 《a student》; grant admission (to); 〈대학에〉 matriculate 《a student》/ 무시험으로 입학을 허가하다 admit 《a student》 on certificate into a school
▶ 그는 옥스퍼드 대학의 입학이 허가되었다 He had [was granted] admission to Oxford.
—**입학하다** enter a school; be admitted to a school; be registered [enrolled] at a school; matriculate 《in a university》
▶ 그는 올 봄에 이 학교에 입학했다 He entered this school this spring.
▶ 이 대학에 입학하기 위해서는 어떤 자격이 필요합니까? What qualification(s) do I need to be admitted to this university?
■ **재**— reentrance [readmission] into a school ■ —**규칙** admission rules —**금** an

입학시험 entrance [admission] fee; a matriculation fee —난 the difficulty of entering 《a college》 —식 an entrance ceremony —자 new [incoming] students; matriculates; freshmen —자격 requirements [qualifications] for admission —절차 entrance formalities; registration 《for a school》 —지원자 a candidate [an applicant] for admission —허가 admission 《to a school》

입학시험 入學試驗 an admission [entrance] examination [《口》 exam] 《for, of, to》; an examination for entrance 《to》
▶ 그는 T대학의 입학시험을 봤다 [힘격했다, 불합격했다] He took [passed, failed] the entrance examination for T University.

입학원서 入學願書 application for admission [entrance]; application form
♦ 입학원서를 내다 send [hand] in an application for admission
▶ 입학원서는 우송할 것 The application 《form》 should be sent in by mail [《英》 post].
■—용지 an application blank [form]

입항 入港 arrival in 《a》 port; entry into port
♦ 입항중이다 be in port
—입항하다 《도착하다》 arrive at a port [in a harbor]; enter 《a》 port; 〈기항하다〉 call at 《a》 port
▶ 배는 내일 인천항에 입항한다 The ship is scheduled to arrive at [come into, enter, call at] Inch'ŏn port tomorrow.
■—선 an incoming [inbound] vessel —세 port [harbor] dues —수수료 an entrance fee —신고 an entrance notice —예정일 the expected time of arrival 《略 ETA》 —절차 clearance inwards

입향순속 入鄕循俗 〈속담〉 When in Rome, do as the Romans do.

입헌 立憲 establishment of a constitution; constitutionalization
■—국 a constitutional state —군주 a constitutional sovereign —군주국 a constitutional monarchy [country] —민주정체 constitutional democracy —정치 constitutionalism; constitutional government —주의 constitutionalism

입헌적 立憲的 constitutional ♦ 입헌적으로 constitutionally

입회 入會 〈허가〉 admission; 〈가입함〉 entrance
♦ 입회를 원하다 desire membership in a society / 입회를 허락하다 admit sb to membership [into a society]
▶ 테니스 클럽에 입회를 신청했다 I applied for admission [membership] to a tennis club.
—입회하다 〈회원이 되다〉 become a member 《of》; join [enter] a society; be admitted into an association
▶ 그는 작년에 영어 연구회에 입회했다 He joined [became a member of, was admitted to, entered] an English society last year.
▶ 누구든지 입회할 수 있다 The membership is open to all.
■—권 [法] (the right of) common —금 an entrance [admission, enrollment, initiation] fee: 입회금을 내다 pay 《for》 one's footing —식 an initiation —자 a new member: 입회자는 해마다 늘고 있다 The membership has been increasing with years.

입회 立會 〈참석〉 presence; 〈출석〉 attendance; witnessing; 〈증권 거래소의〉 a session
♦ 전장[후장]의 입회 the morning [afternoon] session / 증인[경찰] 입회하에 in the presence of a witness [policeman] / 입회를 요청하다 request [ask for] sb's presence 《at》
—입회하다 attend; be present at; 〈증인으로서〉 witness
▶ 몇 사람이 개표에 입회했다 Some people witnessed [were present as witness for] the vote count.
■—경찰관 a policeman in attendance —인 an observer; a witness; an attestant —증인 an attester; an attestor

입후보 立候補 《美》 candidacy; 《英》 candidature
♦ 입후보를 등록[취소]하다 file [withdraw] one's candidacy / 입후보를 사퇴하다 decline the nomination for candidacy / 입후보를 선언[단념]하다 announce [give up] one's candidacy 《for》
—입후보하다 《美》 run; 《英》 stand for
♦ 국회의원에 입후보하다 run for election to the national assembly / 서울에서 입후보하다 run as a candidate in Seoul
▶ 그는 하원의원에 입후보할 것이다 He will run [be a candidate] for the house of representatives.
▶ 그는 지사 선거에 입후보할 작정이다 He intends to run [stand] for governor.
▶ 올가을 대통령 선거에는 누가 입후보하지? Who is going to be a candidate for president in the election this fall?
▶ 그는 다음 선거에서 무소속으로 입후보할 것이다 He will run as an independent candidate in the next election.
■—자 a candidate: …의 입후보자가 되다 be a candidate for...

입히다 1 〈입게 하다〉 dress; clothe; put on
♦ 웃옷을 입혀 보다 try a coat on sb; 〈가봉하여〉 fit 《it》 on
▶ 그녀는 아이에게 나들이옷을 입혔다 She dressed her child in his [her] best clothes.
▶ 그녀는 딸을 거들어 한복을 입혀주었다 She helped her daughter on with her Korean clothes. ⇌ She helped her daughter to put on her Korean clothes.
▶ 이 옷을 딸에게 입히고 싶다 I want to get this dress for my daughter.
2 〈도금하다〉 plate; coat; gild; 〈덧붙이다〉 cover; veneer
♦ 금을 입힌 액자 a gilded frame / 은을 입힌 《watch chain》 of plated silver; silverplated 《handle》 / 설탕을 입힌 천 sugar cloth 《tablets》 / 고무를 입힌 rubber-coated / 주석을 입히다 coat 《copper》 with tin
3 〈당하게 하다〉 inflict 《injury upon》; cause 《damage to》; subject sb to
♦ 손해를 입히다 inflict losses upon sb / 화를 입히다 do sb an evil / 피해를 입히다 damage; do damage 《on》

잇 a cover [covering] 《for a mattress》
♦베갯잇 a (pillow) slip; a pillowcase

잇꽃 〔植〕 a safflower

잇다 1 〈맞대어 붙이다〉 connect; link; join; couple; joint; knot 《a broken string》
♦줄을 잇다 piece [tie] strings together / 2개의 밧줄을 잇다 tie together two pieces of rope / 이야기를 잇다 resume [take up] the thread of a story
▶이 도로는 서울과 수원을 잇고 있다 This road connects Seoul with [and] Suwon.
▶이 다리는 그 섬과 본토를 잇고 있다 This bridge joins [links] the island to the mainland.
2 〈계승하다〉 succeed 《to *one's* father's trade》; inherit
♦대를 잇다 carry on a family line / 가산을 잇다 inherit the estate / 가업을 잇다 succeed to *one's* family trade
▶그는 부친의 뒤를 이어 의사가 되었다 He followed in his father's footsteps and became a doctor.
▶그는 박선생의 뒤를 이어 회장이 되었다 He succeeded Mr. Park as president [to the presidency]. ⇌ He took over as president when Mr. Park retired.
3 〈유지하다〉 sustain [maintain, preserve] 《life》
♦겨우 목숨을 이어가다 keep body and soul together; barely keep alive

잇달다 1 〈연달다〉 continue; keep; occur in succession; succeed one another; follow (one after another)
♦잇달은 continued; successive / 잇달은 쾌청한 날씨 a long spell of fine weather / 잇달은 행운 a run of good luck
▶우리 집안에서는 오랫동안 불운한 일이 잇달았다 My family had a series of misfortunes for a long time.
2 〈잇대어 붙이다〉 join; put together; link; connect; attach
♦객차를 잇달다 join [couple] a passenger car with 《a train》

잇달아 successively; in (rapid) succession; consecutively; one after [following] another
♦네 번 잇달아 four consecutive times; four times running / 닷새 잇달아 for five consecutive [successive] days / 잇달아 손해보다 suffer a series of losses / 잇달아 일어나다 happen later; follow; ensue
▶사고가 잇달아 일어났다 Accidents occurred one after another [in succession].
▶질문이 잇달아 그에게 쏟아졌다 One question after another was fired at him.

잇닿다 be connected; adjoin; be adjacent to
▶그의 땅은 내 땅과 잇닿아 있다 His land borders (on) [adjoins] mine.

잇대다 1 〈서로 잇닿게 하다〉 join; link; connect; couple; attach; put together; piece up [together]; patch together
▶그는 밧줄의 두 끝을 잇대었다 He joined the two ends of a rope.
2 〈계속하다〉 continue; keep up; go on 《with》; carry on

♦잇대어 continuously; uninterruptedly; without intermission; without a break

잇따르다 continue ⇨ 잇달다

잇몸 the gum(s); the teethridge

잇바디 a row [set] of teeth ⇨ 치열(齒列)
♦고른 잇바디 even teeth

잇새 gaps in the [*one's*] teeth
♦잇새에 끼이다 get in between the teeth / 잇새에 끼인 음식 찌꺼기를 제거하다 remove bits of food lodged between the teeth
▶나는 잇새가 뜨다 My teeth are loose.

잇속 〈이의 생김새〉 the shape of a tooth [of *one's* teeth] ♦잇속이 좋다 [나쁘다] have a good [bad] set of teeth; have a regular [an irregular] set of teeth

잇속 利— 〈실속〉 substantial gain [profit]; 〈사리사욕〉 self-interest
♦잇속이 있는 장사[투자] a profitable [paying] business [investment] / 잇속만 차리는 사람 a selfish [greedy] person / 잇속이 있는 profitable; gainful; lucrative; paying / 잇속이 없는 unprofitable; gainless / 잇속을 차리다 profit; make a profit / 잇속에 밝다 have a quick eye for gain

잇자국 〈이빨 자국〉 an impression of the teeth; a tooth mark 《*pl.* teeth marks》
♦잇자국이 나 있다 have [show] a tooth mark

잇줄 利— a lucrative [profitable] connection; a road to gains

잇집 the socket of a tooth ⇨ 치조(齒槽)

있다 1 〈존재하다〉 there is [are]; be; exist; be in existence; be found
♦있으나마나 한 것 a chip in porridge [pottage] / 있을까 말까한 few [little] or no; few [little], if any
▶유령이 있다고 생각합니까? Do you believe (that) ghost exists? ⇌ Do you believe in ghost?
▶테이블 위에 사과가 있다 〈한 개〉 There is [(口) There's] an apple on the table. ⇌ 〈여러 개〉 There are some apples on the table.
2 〈위치하다〉 be; be situated; be sited; be located; 〈산 등이〉 stand; 〈도시·집·섬 등이〉 lie; 〈길·강이〉 run
▶그 열쇠는 테이블 위에 있었다 The key was on the table.
▶한국은 중국의 동쪽에 있다 Korea lies to the east of China.
▶우리 학교는 언덕 위에 있다 Our school is [stands] on the hill.
▶집 뒤에 시내가 있다 There runs a brook behind the house.
▶그 도시는 한강 서쪽에 있다 The city lies [is located, is situated] to the west of the Hangang.
▶자, 여기 있다 Here you are.
3 〈거주하다〉 live; dwell; reside; 〈머무르다〉 stay; remain; stop
▶더 있다 가거라 Stay a little longer.
▶나는 숙모댁에 있다 I live [am living, am staying] with my aunt [at my aunt's]. (▶진행형에는 일시적으로 살고 있다는 뜻이 내포됨)
▶미국에는 얼마나 있었습니까? How long have you been in America?

► 會話 「죽 여기에 있었나?」「가끔 떠나 있기도 했어」 "Have you been here all this time?" "Off and on."
4 〈서식하다〉 inhabit; live 《in》; be found
► 강원도에는 흑곰이 있습니까? Do black bears exist in Kangwondo?
► 이 물고기는 바다에 있다 These fishes inhabit the sea.
5 〈소유하다〉 have; possess; own; keep; 〈축복받다〉 be blessed with; 〈저주받다〉 be cursed with; 〈부여받다〉 be endowed [gifted] with
♦ 있는 나라와 없는 나라 haves and have-nots / 있는 집안에 태어나나 be born rich [to wealth] / 있는 힘을 다 내다 put forth all one's strength / 재산이 있다 be rich; be wealthy
► 그녀는 음악에 재능이 있다 She has a gift for music.
► 돈이 있으면 있을 수록 더 갖고 싶어한다 The more money we have, the more we want.
► 너한테 하고 싶은 이야기가 산더미처럼 있다 I have [I've got] a lot of things to tell you.
► 엽서와 우표가 있습니까? Do you have postcards and stamps?
► 그에겐 막대한 재산[풍부한 재능]이 있다 He has [possesses] great wealth [great talent]. (▶보통 진행형·명령형·수동형은 쓰지 않음)
► 하나 있기는 있지만 보잘 것 없다 I do have one, but it is worthless.
► 있을 때 아껴쓰지 않으면 아낄 것도 없다 It is too late to spare when the bottom is bare.
► 벌에는 침이 있다 The bee is armed with a sting.
► 나는 급한 볼 일이 있다 I have some urgent business to attend to.
6 〈부착되다〉 have sth attached to 《it》; 〈갖추다〉 be equipped [fitted, provided] with
► 그의 차에는 카 스테레오가 있다 His car has [is equipped with] a car stereo.
7 〈포함되다〉 be contained [included] 《in》
► 수험 과목 중에는 영어가 있다 English is included in the subjects of the examination.
► 레몬에는 비타민 C가 많이 있다 A lemon contains a lot of vitamin C. (▶contain 대신 includes는 쓸 수 없음)
► 이 책에는 재미있는 이야기가 많이 있다 This book contains many interesting stories.
8 〈입수되다〉 be got [had]; 〈찾아내다〉 be found
► 그 책은 자료실에 있다 The book can be got [be found] at data room. ⇌ You can get [find] the book at data room.
► 會話 「너희는 여기에 종종 오니?」「기회 있을 때마다 와」 "Do you come here often?" "Every chance I get."
9 〈경험하다〉 ► 그 사람과는 만난 일이 있다 I have seen him once. ⇌ I once saw him.
► 會話 「지금까지 미국에 가 본 적이 있나요?」「예, 있어요 [아니오, 없어요]」 "Have you (ever) been [《美》 Have you gone] to America?" "Yes, (I have) once [No, never]." ⇌ "Did you ever go to America?" "Yes, (I did) once [No, never]."
10 〈발생하다〉 there is [are]; happen; occur; arise; take place

♦ 사고가 있었던 곳 the scene of a disaster / 무슨 일이 있든지 whatever may come; no matter what may come
► 어젯밤 근처에서 화재가 있었다 A fire broke out [occured, started] in my neighborhood last night. ⇌ There was a fire last night in my neighborhood.
► 같은 일이 과거에도 있었다 The same thing happened in the past.
► 그것은 흔히 있는 일이다 It could happen to anyone. ⇌ It's the kind of thing that happens every day. ⇌ It's just one of those things. ⇌ It's an everyday occurrence.
► 그런 일이 있을 수 있을까? How can that be? ⇌ That's impossible.
► 이곳은 4월에도 매우 추울 때가 있다 It can be very cold here even in April.
11 〈거행·개최하다〉 be held; take place; come off; be open
► 음악회는 내일 있다 The concert will be held [take place] tomorrow.
► 오늘은 수업이 4시간 있다 I have four classes today.
12 〈실제로 있다〉 be
♦ 있을 법한 이야기 a likely [believable] story / 있을 수 있는 일 a possibility / 있을 수 없는 impossible / 있지도 않은 말을 퍼뜨리다 spread a false report / 사물을 있는 그대로 받아들이다 take things as they are
► 그런 것[일]이 있을까? Is there such a thing as that, I wonder?
► 그런 일은 있을 수 없다 It is impossible. ⇌ It is out of the bounds of possibility.
► 혹시 그런 일이 있었는지 모르겠다 It may have been.
13 〈놓여 있다〉 consist 《in》; lie 《in》; 〈달려 있다〉 depend 《on》
► 사람의 가치는 재산보다는 사람됨에 있다 A man's worth lies not so much in what he has as in what he is.
► 책임은 너한테 있다 It is you that [who] is to blame for it. ⇌ The blame rests with you.
► 이 시의 매력은 형용사의 용법에 있다 The charm of this poem consists in its use of adjectives.
14 〈품다·지니다〉 have; cherish; conceive
♦ 아기를 배고 있다 be (big) with child; be pregnant / 생리가 있다 have the menses [monthlies]
15 〈상태의 계속〉 go; 〈죽 …이다〉 keep; 〈여전히 …이다〉 remain; 〈동작의 계속〉 be (do)ing; 〈…인 채로 있다〉 stay
♦ 독신으로 있다 remain single / 먹지 않고 있다 go without food / 보고 있다 keep watching / 일을 하고 있다 be working; be at work
► 그의 부친은 그 회사에서 오랫동안 일하고 있었다 His father worked for the company for a long time.
► 문이 열려[닫혀] 있다 The door is open [is shut, is closed].
► 그는 죽 잠자코 있었다 He kept [remained, stayed] silent.
► 기차는 만원이어서 서 있어야 했다 I had to stand because the train was crowded.

▶그녀는 밤새도록 자지 않고 있었다 She was [stayed] awake all night.
16 〈관계하다〉 ◆…에 있어서 as for [to]…
▶크기에 있어서는 이것이 제일이다 This comes the first in (point of) size.
▶문제에 있어서는 더할 나위 없다 As for the style, it leaves nothing to be desired.

있다가 afterward(s); later (on); after a time [while]
◆닷새 있다가 five days later [after] / 오래 있다가 long afterwards
▶話「지금 지불해야 됩니까?」「있다가 주셔도 좋습니다」 "Should I pay you now?" "Later will be fine."
▶있다가 전화하겠습니다 I'll call you later (on) [afterward].

있음직하다 possible; probable; likely
◆있음직한 이야기 a likely [a believable] story / 있음직한 일 a possibility; a probability / 있음직하지도 않은 impossible
▶그건 있음직한 일이다 It is quite probable. ⇌ It is a likely story.
▶있음직하지도 않은 일은 말도 마라 Don't talk about things which are not likely to happen.

잉걸불 live charcoal; embers
잉굿 〔工〕 an ingot
잉글랜드 England ⇨ 영국
잉꼬 〔鳥〕 a parakeet; a macaw
잉부 孕婦 〈임신부〉 a pregnant woman
잉아 〔織〕 a heald ◆잉앗대 a heald bar
잉어 ─魚 〔魚〕 a carp 《*pl.* ～s, ～》
잉여 剩餘 a surplus; an overplus; 〈나머지〉 the remainder; 〔數〕 the remainder
　■─가치〔經〕 surplus value ─금〈수지의 차액〉 a surplus (fund); balance in hand ─노동력 surplus labor ─농산물 surplus farm produce [agricultural products] ─물자 surplus articles [goods, commodities] ─물자매각 surplus sales ─식량 surplus food ─재료 surplus materials
잉잉 a whimper; a blub; a blubber ◆잉잉 울다 whimper; blub; blubber; be in a blubber
잉카 Inca ◆잉카의 Inca ─문명 the Incan Civilization ─사람 an Inca(n) ─제국 the Inca Empire ─족 the Incas
잉크 ink ◆잉크로 쓰다 write in [with] ink / 잉크로 지우다 ink out
▶잉크 얼룩이 지워지지 않는다 Ink stains don't come off.
　■만년필용─ ink for the fountain pen ─롤러 ink roller ─병 an ink bottle; a bottle of ink ─스탠드 an inkstand ─장치 ink arrangement ─지우개 an ink eraser ─찍기 ink stamping ─통 an inkpot
잉태 孕胎 pregnancy ⇨ 임신(妊娠)

잊다 **1** 〈망각하다〉 forget; be forgetful [oblivious] 《of》; 〈일이 주어〉 slip *one's* mind; escape [slip] *one's* memory
◆잊을 수 없는 unforgettable; never to be forgotten 《event》 / 배웠던 라틴어를 잊다 lose *one's* Latin / 이름을 잊다 forget *sb's* name / 잊지 말고 [않고] without forgetting [fail] / 잊지 않도록 적어두다 take notes for future reference / 잊기를 잘하다 be forgetful [oblivious] 《of》 / 잠시도 잊지 않다 keep the matter in view; be ever present in *one's* mind
▶편지를 우체통에 넣는 것을 잊지마라 Don't forget to mail the letter.
▶나는 전등을 끄는 것을 잊었다 I forgot [have forgotten] to turn out the light.
▶나는 여기에서 당신을 만났던 것을 결코 잊지 않습니다 I'll never forget meeting you here. (▶과거에 있었던 일을 잊는다는 뜻에서는 이처럼 동명사와 함께 씀)
▶그 사람이 오늘 나를 만나러 온다는 것을 잊고 있었다 I forgot that he was coming to see me today.
▶그의 이름을 깜빡 잊었다 His name escapes me.
▶이 은혜는 평생 잊지 않겠습니다 I shall always remember your kindness to me.
2 〈단념하다〉 dismiss *sth* from *one's* mind; put [get] *sth* out of *one's* mind; think no more 《of》
◆어떤 일을 완전히 잊어버리다 banish *sth* from memory / 뜬 세상의 고뇌를 잠깐 동안 잊으려고 하다 try to snatch a moment's oblivion from the pain of life / 술로 슬픔을 잊다 drink down *one's* sorrow
▶지난 일은 잊어버리자 Let's forget (about) what happened. (▶「애써 잊다」의 뜻)
▶그 일은 이제 잊어버려라 Dismiss the matter from your mind.
▶잊을래야 잊을 수 없다 The memory always haunts me.
3 〈두고 기억해내지 못하다〉 mislay; misplace; leave *sth* behind; forget *sth*
▶자동차 열쇠를 깜빡 잊고 집에 두고 왔다 I have left my car key (behind) at home.
▶내가 장갑을 어디다 잊고 왔지? Where have I left my gloves?
▶나는 지갑을 깜빡 잊고 집에 두고 왔다 I left my purse at home.
▶나는 열쇠를 어디다 두었는지 잊었다 I mislaid [misplaced] the key somewhere.
▶기차에서 내리실 때는 잊으시는 물건이 없도록 주의하십시오 Don't forget anything when you leave the train.
잊어버리다 completely forget ⇨ 잊다
잊히다 be forgotten; pass out of mind [*one's* memory]; be buried in oblivion
◆잊히지 않는 unforgettable; never to be forgotten / 세상에서 잊히다 die from the memory of the public; fall [go, pass, sink] into oblivion

잎 〈잎사귀〉 a leaf 《*pl.* leaves》; 〈나뭇잎〉 (총칭) foliage; 〈침엽〉 a needle; 〈잎새〉 a blade
◆무성한 잎 thick foliage / 병든 잎 diseased [blighted] leaves / 잎의 겉면 [뒷면] the upper [under] surface of a leaf / 잎이 보기 좋은 나무 a tree with handsome foliage / 잎이 무성한 [없는] leafy [leafless, bare] / 잎이 질 무렵 the fall of the leaf / 잎이 무성하다 《美》 be leaved out / 잎이 돋아나다 come into leaf / 잎이 떨어지다 become leafless
▶나뭇잎이 다 떨어졌다 The leaves are all gone off the trees. ⇌ The trees are bare of leaves.

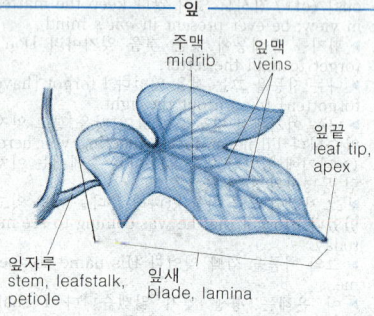

잎
- 주맥 midrib
- 잎맥 veins
- 잎끝 leaf tip, apex
- 잎자루 stem, leafstalk, petiole
- 잎새 blade, lamina

잎나무 〈잎이 달린 땔나무〉 brushwood
잎눈 a leaf [foliar] bud
잎담배 leaf tobacco
잎맥 —脈 〔植〕 a vein (of a leaf); a nervure; a rib; a nerve; a midrib
잎벌레 〔昆〕 a (green-)leaf insect
잎사귀 a leaf; a leaflet ▶ 나무 잎사귀는 가을이 되면 (황금) 빛깔로 변한다 Leaves change color [turn (yellow)] in (the) fall.
잎샘 〈봄에 잎이 나올 때의 추위〉 a cold spell in early spring (when the trees start leafing) —**잎샘하다** get cold in leafing time
잎자루 〔植〕 a petiole; a leafstalk; a stem; a stalk; a stipe
잎장식 —裝飾 〈무늬〉 foliage
잎차례 〔植〕 a phyllotaxis; a phyllotaxy
잎파랑이 〔植〕 chlorophyl(l) ⇨ 엽록소

자[1] **1** 〈길이를 재는〉 a measure; 〈자막대기〉 a rod; a ruler; a (measuring) rule; a square ◆직선자 a straightedge / 줄자 a tape measure / 3미터 줄자 a three-meter tape measure / 30센티미터 직선자 a thirty-centimeter straightedge / 1미터 막대자 a meter rod / 1미터 자 a meter rule / 자로 그은 선 a ruled line / 자로 재다 measure with a rule / 자로 잰듯이 to a T / 자를 대고 자르다 cut with a ruler **2** 〈길이의 단위〉 a *cha* ◆자로 재다 measure 《the length of》/ 한 자에 얼마로 팔다[사다] sell [buy] *sth* by the *cha*

― 자 ―

T 자형 자
T square

곧은자
ruler

삼각자
triangles

자[2] 〈재촉할 때〉 come now; come; now (then); well (now); 〈달래어〉 there; please
▶자, 가자 Come, let's go!
▶자, 자, 울지마 There, there! Don't cry.
▶자, 버스가 왔다 Here comes our bus.
▶자, 좋은 기회다 Now's our chance.
▶자, 여기 있다 Here you are.
▶자, 이것 좀 봐 Just look at this.
▶자, 드십시오 Now, help yourself, please.
▶자, 덤벼라 Come on!
▶자, 이걸 받아라 〈선물 등을 주면서〉 Now, this is for you.
▶자, 비켜라 비켜 Hey, get out of there [here]!
▶자, 이쪽을 봐요 Now, look this way, please.
▶자, 어디 해보자 Well, let's try.
▶자, 다 왔다 Here we are.
▶자, 이만하면 됐다 All right. This will do.

자 子 **1** 〈십이지(十二支)의 첫째〉 the Rat (as the first of the twelve zodiac [horary] signs of the Orient)
2 〈자식〉 a son; a child
3 〈공자(孔子)〉 Confucius
◆자왈(子曰) Confucius says...
■―년(年) the year of the Rat ―시(時) the hour of the Rat (▶from 11 p.m. to 1 a.m.)

자 字 **1** 〈글자〉 a character; a letter; 〈표의 문자〉 an ideograph; an ideogram

◆한자 Chinese character
2 〈낱말〉 a word
◆몇자 적다 jot down a line [a few words]
3 〈본이름 외의 이름〉 one's nickname; a pseudonym
▶한국의 유명한 학자 이황의 자는 경호, 호는 퇴계였다 The famous Korean scholar Lee Hwang's nickname was Kyŏng-ho, and his pen name, T'oe-gye.

자 者 〈사람〉 a person; a fellow; one
◆그 자 he; that man [fellow] / 어리석은 자 a fool
▶학식이 많은 자는 말수가 적다 《속담》 Who knows most says least.

자― 自― 〈부터〉 from ◆자오전 9시 지오후 5시 from 9 a.m. to 5 p.m.

자― 雌― 〈암컷〉 female; she

―자 1 〈권유〉 let 《us》; let's
▶한번 해보자 Let's try once.
▶좀 기다려 보자 Let's wait and see.
▶어디 가 보자 Let's go and see.
2 〈…하자 곧〉 as soon as; no sooner...than...; hardly [scarcely]...when...; the moment [instant]...; on ...ing
◆한국에 도착하자 on arriving in Korea / 대문을 나서자 as soon as *one* goes out of the gate
▶우리는 사고 소식을 듣자 곧 출발하였다 We started as soon as we heard about the accident.

자가 自家 〈자기 집〉 one's own house
◆자가 양조 포도주 homemade wine / 자가 재배의 homegrown; 《vegetables》 of one's own growing
■―발전장치 an independent (electric) power plant ―생식 〔植〕 autogamy ―소화 autolysis; autodigestion ―수분(受粉) 〔植〕 self-pollination ―수정(受精) 〔生〕 autogamy; self-fertilization

자가당착 自家撞着 self-contradiction
◆자가당착의 self-contradictory / 자가당착에 빠지다 contradict *oneself*

자가용 自家用 **1** 〈개인용〉 private [family] use **2** 〈자가용차〉 one's (own) car; an owner-driven car; an automobile for one's personal [private] use
■―족 owner-drivers

자가용차 自家用車 one's own car ⇨ 자가용 2
자가중독 自家中毒 〔醫〕 autotoxemia; autointoxication ◆자가중독을 일으키다 cause autointoxication

자가치료 自家治療 self-treatment; home treatment

자각 自覺 (self-)consciousness; awareness; awakening self-knowledge ―자각하다 be conscious [aware] of 《one's》 duty); realize; awake [be awakened] to

자기의 역량[결점]을 자각하다 realize one's own strength [deficiencies]/ **죄를 자각시키다** wake [awake] *sb* to a sense of sin
▶ 그는 자신의 역부족을 자각하지 못한다 He is not aware of his lack of ability.
■ **—증상[증세]** 〔醫〕 symptoms of which the patient is conscious; subjective symptoms

자간 子癇 〔醫〕 eclampsia

자갈 gravel; pebbles; 〈해안 등의〉 shingle; 〈궤도에 까는〉 ballast
♦ **자갈을 깔다** lay [cover] (a road) with gravel; gravel (a road); 〈철도·도로에〉 ballast (a railroad)
■ **—기초** gravel foundation **—길** a gravel road [walk]; a pebbly street **—밭** a gravelly [stony] place

자갈색 紫褐色 purplish brown

자강 自强 strenuous efforts
—자강하다 make strenuous efforts
■ **—불식** ceaseless efforts; keeping efforts for self-support **—술** the art of health building

자개 (a lamina of) mother-of-pearl [nacre]
♦ **자개빛이 나는** nacreous / **장에 자개를 박다** inlay a cabinet with mother-of-pearl [nacre]
■ **—단추** mother-of-pearl [nacre] buttons **—상[그릇]** a (lacquered) table [vessel] inlaid with mother-of-pearl **—세공** (inlaid) mother-of-pearl work; nacre work **—세공인** a shell-worker

자객 刺客 an assassin; an assassinator
♦ **자객의 손에 쓰러지다** fall a victim to an assassin; be assassinated

자격 資格 〈요건〉 qualification(s); requirement(s); 〈능력〉 competence; 〈신분〉 capacity
♦ **개인자격으로** in one's individual [private] capacity / **…의 자격으로** in the capacity of / **자격이 있다** have qualifications (for); be qualified [competent]; be eligible for (membership) / **자격을 부여하다** qualify (*sb* as a teacher); entitle (*sb* to do) / **자격을 얻다** obtain a qualification (for); qualify (to, for) / **자격을 빼앗다[박탈하다]** disqualify (*sb* from [for]) / **자격을 상실하다** be disqualified (from, for)
▶ 나는 고등학교 교사의 자격이 있다 I am qualified as a high school teacher.
▶ 그녀는 의사 자격증을 땄다 She has obtained a physician's [medical] licence.
▶ 회원 자격에 남녀의 제한은 없다 Membership is not limited by sex.
■ **선거—** qualifications for an elector **입학—** admission requirements **입회—** requirements for membership; eligibility ■ **—(검정)시험** a qualifying examination **—상실** disqualification **—심사** an examination of the applicants' qualification; a screening **—증(명서)** a certificate of qualifications

자격지심 自激之心 a guilty conscience; (a feeling of) self-reproach

자결 自決 〈자기 결정〉 self-determination; 〈자살〉 suicide **—자결하다** determine for [by] *oneself*; commit suicide; kill *oneself*

자계 自戒 self-discipline **—자계하다** caution *oneself* (against); admonish *oneself*

자계 磁界 〔物〕 a magnetic field ⇨ 자기장(磁氣場)

자고 鷓鴣 〔鳥〕 a francolin

자고깨면 whenever one awakes from one's sleep; whenever it dawns; every dawn; always
▶ 매일 새벽 자고깨면 밖엔 눈이 내려 있었다 It snowed every dawn. ⇌ Whenever we awoke from our sleep, there was snow outside.

자고로 自古— from ancient [old(en)] times; from of old; since early times; traditionally
▶ 자고로 한국 사람은 예의를 중히 여긴다 Koreans traditionally attach great importance to courtesy.

자고새면 when the day breaks; when another day dawns

자괴지심 自愧之心 a sense of shame

자구 字句 words and phrases; terms; 〈어투〉 expressions; wording
♦ **자구(상)의** verbal / **자구에 구애되다** be letter-bound; adhere to the letter / **자구를 수정하다** make verbal modifications
▶ 이 문장은 자구대로 해석[번역]해서는 안된다 You should not take [interpret] this sentence literally.

자구 磁區 〔物〕 a magnetic domain

자국 〈닳은 자리〉 a mark; a print; 〈더럼〉 a stain; 〈지나간 흔적〉 a trace; a track; a trail; 〈상처의〉 a scar
♦ **발자국** footprints; footmarks / **손가락자국** a finger mark / **신발 자국** the print of shoes / **핏자국** a bloodstain / **차가 지나간 자국** the trace [track] of a car / **종두 자국** a vaccination scar / **이빨 자국** tooth marks / **긁힌 자국** a scratch / **물린 자국** a bite
▶ 그녀의 등에는 수술의 자국이 있다 She has a scar from an operation on her back.

자국 自國 one's (own) country; 〈고국〉 one's native land; one's home(land)
♦ **자국의** native; home; 〈언어의〉 vernacular / **자국 제품의** homemade
■ **—민[인]** one's fellow countrymen

자국나다 get marked; form a scar; leave a trace [track]

자국어 自國語 one's mother [native] tongue; one's (native) language; the vernacular (language)
♦ **자국어 신문** newspapers of one's native language; vernacular dailies / **자국어의** of one's mother tongue; of one's native language; vernacular

자궁 子宮 the womb; 〔醫〕 the uterus (*pl.* -ri)
■ **—경** a hysteroscope **—병** a uterine disease **—암** uterine cancer **—외 임신** extrauterine pregnancy **—절개** hysterotomy **—절제(술)** hysterectomy **—탈** prolapse of uterus

자귀 an adz(e); a hatchet **—질** adzing: **자귀질하다** adz(e) **자귓밥** chips [splinters] produced in adzing

자그레브 〈크로아티아의 수도〉 Zagreb

자그마치 〈작게〉 in a smallish way; on a smallish scale; 〈적지 않게〉 not a little; as much [many] as
▶ 자그마치 3만의 관중이 야구장에 모였다 No less than 30,000 spectators were present at

the ball park.
▶술 좀 자그마치 마셔라 Don't drink too much.
▶이 작은 집에 자그마치 10명이 산다 This small house accommodates as many as ten people.

자그마하다 smallish; somewhat small [little]; small-sized; undersized
♦키가 자그마하는 사내 a man of small build [stature]; a small-statured man; a man short in stature; a short man
▶그녀는 키가 자그마하다 She is rather short in height [stature].

자극 刺戟 〈자극하기〉 stimulation; incitation; incitement; irritation; 〈격려〉 encouragement; 〈자극물〉 a stimulus (*pl.* -li); an impetus; an incentive
♦자극성 음식 pungent food / 자극성의 stimulative; pungent / 자극적인 stimulative; exciting; sensational / …에 자극 받아 under the stimulus of… / 자극이 되다 act as a stimulus 《to》; serve as an incentive 《to》 / 자극을 주다 give a stimulus [an impetus] 《to》 / 자극을 찾다 look for some excitement; seek a thrill 《in》 / 자극을 받다 be spurred 《by》 / 자극을 완화하다 〔醫〕 abirritate
▶그들은 자극적인 포스터를 내붙였다 They put up a sensational poster.
▶그 연기는 자극적인 냄새가 났다 The smoke had a pungent smell.
─**자극하다** stimulate; incite; stir (up); excite; irritate
♦신경을 자극하다 stimulate the nerves; get on *one's* nerves / 자극하여 …시키다 stimulate *sb* to 《some action》; sting *sb* into 《doing》
▶그 냄새는 내 식욕을 자극했다 The smell stimulated my appetite.
▶그 이야기는 소년의 상상력을 자극했다 The story stirred (up) the boy's imagination.
■─제 a stimulant; an excitant

자극 磁極 〔物〕 a magnetic pole
■─성 magnetic polarity

자금 資金 funds; a fund; (a) capital; money
♦자금이 있다[떨어지다] be in [out of] funds / 자금이 풍부하다 have ample funds / 자금이 부족하다 be short of funds / 자금을 대다 finance; raise funds 《for》 / 자금을 대다 furnish [provide] funds 《for》; finance / 자금을 회전시키다 turn money / 자금을 융통해주다 accommodate *sb* with money
▶그녀는 결혼자금을 마련하기 위해 일하고 있다 She is working for money to marry on.
▶자금이 부족하다[풍부하다] We are short of funds [have ample funds].
▶자금 조달에 애를 먹었다 We had difficulty in raising capital [funds].
■ 구제─ a relief fund 비(祕)─ secret funds 사업─ an enterprising fund 선거─ an election campaign fund 운동─ a campaign fund 운전─ working funds 장학─ a scholarship fund 정치─ money for political activities 준비─ reserve funds 회전─ revolving funds
■─난 financial difficulty; stringency of capital: 자금난으로 for lack of funds ─부족 insufficiency [shortage] of funds ─압박 the financial strains ─조달운동 a campaign for raising funds ─출처 《dig into》 the sources of operation funds

자금화 資金化 capitalization ─자금화하다 capitalize; convert 《goods》 into money

자급 自給 self-support; self-supply; self-sustenance
─**자급하다** support *oneself*; provide for *oneself*; be self-supporting
♦자급하는 self-supporting; self-supplying
─경제주의 autarky ─기(器) a self-feeder ─적 농업 subsistence farming [agriculture]

자급자족 自給自足 self-sufficiency
♦식량의 자급자족 foodstuff self-sufficiency / 자급자족의 self-sufficing; self-sufficient
─**자급자족하다** be self-sufficient
♦경제적으로 자급자족하다 achieve economic self-sufficiency
▶그는 자급자족하는 생활을 하고 있다 He provides for himself. ⇌ His life is self-sufficient.
■경제적─ economic self-sufficiency; autarky ■─경제 self-sufficient economy ─정책 a self-supporting and self-sufficient policy

자긍 自矜 self-conceit; pride; 〈자찬〉 self-praise

자기 自己 *one's* self; *oneself*; 〈자아〉 self
♦자기의 *one's* own; personal; private / 자기 멋대로 of *one's* own accord [own free will] / 자기의 생존을 위해서 일하다 work for *one's* life / 자기 이익을 도모하다 look to *one's* own interests / 자기 일만 생각하다 think of *oneself* only; be self-centered / 자기 생각대로 하다 act as *one* pleases [likes] / 자기 일을 자기가 하다 mind [look after] *one's* own business / 자기의 길을 가다 go *one's* 《own》 way / 자기를 돌아보다 reflect on *oneself* / 자기 자신을 알다 know *oneself*
▶그는 자기 입으로 그렇게 말했다 He himself said so. ⇌ He told me so himself.
▶그녀는 자기 말로는 스무살이라고 한다 She is twenty upon her own statement.
▶자기가 뿌린 씨는 자기가 거두게 마련이다 As you sow so shall you reap.
▶그에게는 자기 집이 있다 He has a house of his own.
▶그는 무엇이나 자기가 한다 He does everything for himself.
▶자기 일은 자기가 돌봐야 한다 We must mind our own business.
▶자기 일은 자기가 해라 Look after yourself.
■─유도 〔電〕 self-induction ─과시 self-display ─관찰 self-observation ─기만 self-deception ─도취 self-absorption; narcissism; narcism ─동형 self-morphism ─모순 self-contradiction ─반성 self-reflection ─발견 self-discovery ─방식 *one's* own way [style] ─방위 self-defense ─방전 self-discharge ─변호 self-justification; self-vindication ─보존 self-preservation ─부담 paying *one's* own expenses: 비용은 자기 부담이다 Everyone must pay his own expenses. ─분석 self-analysis ─비판 self-criticism ─소개 self-introduction : 자기 소개를 하다 introduce *one*-

자기

self ―수양 self-culture; self-discipline ―숭배 self-worship ―억제 self-restraint; self-control ―용량 self-capacity ―자금 funds on hand ―자본 owner's equity ―자신 one's own self ―주장 self-assertion ―포기 self-renunciation ―희생 self-sacrifice

자기 自記 〈자신의〉 writing by oneself; 〈자동장치의〉 self-register ―기압계 barograph ―습도계 hygrograph ―온도계[우량계] a self-registering thermometer [rain gauge]

자기 瓷器 porcelain; china(ware) ■ 고려― Koryŏ ceramics [pottery, porcelain]

사기 磁氣 〔物〕 magnetism ◆자기의[를 띤] magnetic / 자기를 띠게 하다 magnetize; make a magnet of 《steel》 / 자기를 띠다 be magnetized / 자기를 없애다 demagnetize

■ 지구(地球)― terrestrial magnetism; geomagnetism ■ ―권 magnetosphere ―극 magnetic pole ―기뢰 a magnetic mine ―나침반 a magnetic compass ―녹음 magnetic recording ―녹음기 a magnetic (tape) recorder ―량 quantity of magnetism ―렌즈 magnetic lens ―력 magnetic force; magnetism ―력선 a line of magnetic force ―력선속 magnetic flux ―북극 the magnetic north ―유도 magnetic induction ―자오선 the magnetic meridian ―작용 magnetic action ―폭풍 a magnetic storm ―학 magnetics ―학자 a magnetist ―화 〔物〕 magnetization

자기류 自己流 〈자기 방식〉 one's own style [way, fashion] ◆자기류의 of one's own style / 자기류로 after one's own style [fashion]; (in) one's own way

자기만족 自己滿足 self-content(ment); self-satisfaction; complacence ◆자기 만족의 self-satisfied; complacent / 자기만족을 하다 satisfy [gratify, content] oneself

자기본위 自己本位 egocentricity; egoism; egotism ◆자기 본위의 egocentric; an egoist; an egotist / 자기 본위의 egotistic(al); egocentric; selfish
▶그는 자기 본위로 말한다 He speaks as he pleases [likes].

자기선전 自己宣傳 self-advertisement ―자기선전하다 advertise [sell] oneself

자기암시 自己暗示 〔心〕 autosuggestion; self-suggestion ◆자기 암시에 걸리기 쉬운 autosuggestible / 자기 암시에 걸리다 be subjected to autosuggestion

자기앞수표 自己―手票 a cashier's check; a bank [banker's] check

자기장 磁氣場 〔物〕 a magnetic field ■ ―의 세기 intensity of a magnetic field

자기중심 自己中心 egocentricity
◆자기 중심적(인) self-centered; selfish
▶그는 자기 중심적인 사람이다 He is a self-centered person. ⇌ He is an egoist [egotist]. ⇌ His motto is "self first."
■ ―주의 egocentricism

자기최면 自己催眠 autohypnotism; autohypnosis ◆자기최면에 걸리다 become autohypnotic; subject oneself to hypnotism

자기혐오 自己嫌惡 self-hatred; self-aversion; self-hate

◆자기 혐오에 빠지다 yield to self-hatred

자깜스럽다 〈조숙하다〉 hatefully [saucily] precocious

자꾸 1 〈잇 따라 서〉 frequently; repeatedly; again and again; 〈늘〉 incessantly; constantly
◆자꾸 같은 말을 하다 harp on a [on the same] string / 자꾸 울다 do not stop crying / 자꾸 걸어가다 walk on and on
▶비가 자꾸 왔다 It kept on raining.
▶아기는 자꾸 울었다 The baby went [kept] on crying.

2 〈열심히〉 eagerly; intently; hard
◆자꾸 알고 싶어하다 be eager for knowledge / 얼굴을 자꾸 보다 look hard at sb
▶나는 그 일을 자꾸 생각했다 I kept thinking hard about it.
▶그는 내게 술을 자꾸 권했다 He strongly urged me to drink.

자나깨나 waking or sleeping; awake or asleep; night and day; in sleep or wake; all the time
▶그는 자나깨나 일 생각뿐이다 He spends all his time on his work, nothing else.
▶그녀는 자나깨나 행방불명된 아들 생각만 하고 있다 She worries constantly about her missing son.
▶그는 자나깨나 그 일만을 생각하고 있다 Waking or sleeping, it's on his mind.
▶나는 이 일을 자나깨나 잊을 수가 없다 I cannot forget this waking or sleeping.

자낭 子囊 〔植〕 an ascus (pl. -ci)
■ ―균 ascomycete ―포자(胞子) an ascospore

자네 ◆자네들 you fellows; you people; you chaps
▶아, 자네인가 Oh, is that you?
▶어이, 자네 Hey, you.

자녀 子女 sons and daughters; children; offspring ◆양가의 자녀 children of good families / 자녀 교육 the education of one's children

자늑자늑하다 graceful; elegant; gentle; airy; limber; supple; suave
◆자늑자늑하게 gracefully
▶그 여자는 몸가짐이 자늑자늑하다 Her manner and movements are gentle and graceful.

자는 범 코침 주기 (속담) Let sleeping dogs lie.

자닝하다 《a sight》 too miserable [pitiful] to look at; 〈서술적〉 be in a miserable [piteous, sorry] plight

자다 1 〈잠자다〉 sleep; 〈잠들다〉 get [go] to sleep; fall asleep; 〈잠깐〉 take a nap; 〈졸다〉 nod; 〈잠자리에 들다〉 go to bed
◆잘 자다 sleep well; have a good sleep / 한 잠 못자다 do not sleep a wink / 푹 자다 sleep soundly [deeply]/ 옷을 입은 채 자다 sleep with one's clothes on / 잠 자지 못하다 sleep badly [poorly] / 밤 늦도록 자지 않고 있다 sit [stay] up till late at night; keep vigil / 잠 안자고 기다리다 wait up (for) / 밤 늦도록 자지 않고 공부하다 burn the midnight oil / 잠 안자고 생각하다 take counsel of [consult with] one's pillow
▶잘 시간이다 It is time for you to go to bed.

⇒ It is time you went to bed.
▶ 話「너는 대개 몇 시에 자니?」「10시에 자」 "What time [When] do you usually go to bed?" "At ten (o'clock)."
▶ 나는 그날 오전 내내 잤다 I slept away the whole morning that day.
▶ 나는 매일 밤 8시간 잔다 I sleep eight hours every night.
▶ 그는 일찍[늦게] 자고 일찍[늦게] 일어난다 He keeps early [late] hours.
▶ 그녀는 앓는 아이를 밤새 자지 않고 간호했다 She sat [stayed] up all night to look after her sick child.
2 〈바다가〉 become calm; calm down; 〈바람이〉 abate; drop; fall; subside; lull; 〈기계가〉 run down; stop
▶ 마침내 바람이 잤다 The wind has fallen at last.
▶ 파도가 좀 잤다 The sea has gone down a little.
▶ 시계가 잔다 The clock stops [runs down].
3 〈결이〉 get smoothed down; take a set
♦ 머리가 자다 one's hair sets nicely

자단 紫檀 〔植〕 a red sandalwood; a rosewood; a ruby wood

자담하다 自擔— take care [charge] of one's own share; 〈비용을〉 pay one's own expenses; pay oneself

자당 自黨 one's (own) party [faction]
자당 慈堂 your [his, her] esteemed mother
자당 蔗糖 cane sugar; sucrose; saccharose
자독 自瀆 masturbation; self-pollution; self-gratification; onanism
자동 自動 automatic action [movement, operation]; automatism ♦ 자동의 automatic ─자동하다 move automatically
■ ─감지기 an automatic sensing device ─개찰기 an automatic turnstile [ticket gate] ─경보수신기 an automatic alarm receiver ─금전출납기 an automatic cash register ─기계 an automatic machine; an automaton ─데이터처리 automatic data processing(略 ADP) ─문 an automatic door ─방위측정기 an automatic direction finder(略 ADF) ─변속기 an automatic transmission ─변압기 an automatic transformer ─소총 an automatic rifle ─열차제어장치 an automatic train control (略 ATC) ─예금출납기 an automatic teller (machine)(略 AT(M)) ─장치 an automaton (pl. ~s, -ta) ─제어 automatic control; servomechanism ─조작 automatic operation; 〔機〕 automation ─조정 self-adjustment ─조정기 an automatic regulator ─조정장치 automatic gears; 〔空〕 an auto(matic) pilot; a gyropilot ─판매기 a vending machine; a slot machine; an automat ─화기 automatic firearms ─화재경보기 an automatic fire alarm

자동사 自動詞 〔文法〕 an intransitive verb (略 v.i.) ■ ─불완전[완전]─ an incomplete [a complete] intransitive verb

자동승인 自動承認 automatic approval
■ ─제 the automatic approval system
자동식 自動式 ♦ 자동식의 automatic / 반자동식의 semiautomatic

■ ─권총[소총] an automatic pistol [rifle]
■ ─문 an automatic door
자동적 自動的 automatic; self-moving; self-operating; self-operative
♦ 자동적으로 움직이다 move automatically; move of itself; 〈기계적으로〉 work mechanically / 자동적으로 기록하다 register (automatically)
▶ 이 문은 자동적으로 열린다 This door opens automatically.
▶ 온도계는 자동적으로 영하 5도를 기록했다 The mercury registered five degrees of frost.
자동차 自動車 a car; a motorcar; (美) an automobile; (口) an auto
▶ 자동차에[를] 타다 ride in a motorcar / 자동차에 태워주다 give [offer] sb a lift / 자동차에서 내리다 get off [alight from] a car / 자동차로 가다 go by car / 자동차로 여행하다 make a motor trip
▶ 자동차 좀 태워줘 Give me a ride [lift] in your car.
▶ 나는 자동차를 운전하지 못한다 I can't drive.
▶ 그녀는 자동차 운전을 잘한다 She is a very good driver.
▶ 그는 자동차로 통근한다 He drives to work every day.
▶ 이 자동차는 승차감이 좋다 This car rides well [is comfortable].
▶ 제 자동차로 모셔다 드리지요 I'll take you home in my car.
■ ─고물 a jalopy; a flivver 영업용─ motorcars for business use; trade cars 임대─ a rent-a-car; (美) a rental 장갑─ an armored car 전기─ an electromobile; an electric car 포장형─ a convertible 화물─ a truck; (美) a motortruck; (英) a (motor) lorry ■ ─공업[산업] the auto [automotive] industry ─도로 a motor road ─메이커[제조업자] an auto maker; an automobile manufacturer ─번호판 a number [license] plate ─보험 car insurance; (美) automobile insurance; (英) motorcar insurance ─부대 (軍) a motorized unit ─사고 a motorcar accident ─세 a private auto [an auto] tax ─속도계 a speedometer ─수리공장 an auto-repair shop ─승용자 a motorist; an owner-driver ─여행 a car [motor] trip ─운전면허증 a driver's license ─운전사 an automobile [a motor] driver; 〈자가용의〉 a chauffeur ─전시회 an automobile show ─전용도로 an expressway; (英) a motorway ─주차장 a parking place; (美) a parking lot; (英) a car park ─차고 a garage ─판매업자 an automobile dealer ─학원 a driving school; a driver training school ─회사 an automobile company

자동차경주 自動車競走 a motor [an auto] race ─선수 a racing driver ─장[코스] an auto [motor] race course; a speedway; a motordrome
자동휴회 自動休會 an automatic [a spontaneous] recess
♦ (국회가) 자동휴회에 들어가다 enter [have] a spontaneous recess
자두 〔植〕 a plum; 〈말린〉 a prune

자동차에 관한 표현

1. 여러가지 자동차

▶ 대형차 a large-size car; a full-sized car / 중형차 a medium-size car / 소형차 a compact car; a baby car; a pony car / 준(準)소형차 a subcompact car (▶소형차보다 조금 더 작음)

▶ 승용차 a car; a passenger car / 4도어 세단 [설룬] a 4-door sedan [saloon] / 하드톱 a hardtop (▶도어 부분에 센터 필러(center pillar)가 없는 차) / 쿠페 a coupe; a coupé / 리무진 a limousine; (口) a limo / 운전석을 칸막이한 호화 대형차) / 스테이션 왜건 (美) a station wagon (▶뒷좌석이 접는식 의자 (fold-down seat)인 화물 겸용차); (英) a estate (car) / 컨버터블 a convertible; (英) a drophead; a ragtop (▶지붕이 천임)

▶ 자가용차 a private car; one's own car / 렌터카 a rent-a-car; a rental car (▶미국에서는 Avis사, Hertz사가 유명); (英) a hire car / 택시 a taxi; a cab (▶미국에서는 Yellow Cab Company가 유명) / 경주용차 a racing car; a racer / 순찰차 a police [patrol] car; a squad car; (美) a cruiser (▶빛깔이 흑백이어서 a black-and-white라고도 함) / 구급차 an ambulance / 소방차 a fire engine / 영구차 a hearse

▶ 버스 a bus; a coach / 2층 버스 a double-decker / 장거리 버스 a long-distance bus; a (motor) coach (▶미국의 2대 회사는 Greyhound Lines와 Continental Trailways Bus Systems) / 관광 버스 a sight-seeing bus / 전세 버스 a chartered bus / 스쿨 버스 a school bus / 리무진 버스 a limousine bus / 트롤리버스 a trolleybus / 셔틀[순환] 버스 a shuttle bus / 마이크로버스 a microbus / 미니버스 a minibus

▶ 트럭 a truck; (英) a lorry / 대형 트럭 a heavy-duty truck / 소형 트럭 a pickup / 트레일러 a trailer (▶18개의 차바퀴가 있는 대형 트레일러는 an 18-wheeler라고 함) / 덤프 트럭 a dump truck / 청소차 (美) a garbage truck [wagon]; (英) a dust cart / 살수차 a water cart [wagon] / 급수차 a water wagon / 탱크 로리 a tank truck [lorry] / 냉동차 a refrigerator truck / 이삿짐 트럭 a moving truck / 캠핑 카 a motor home; a camper; (英) a caravan

▶ 새차 a new model car / 중고차 a used car / 자동 기어차 an automatic (transmission) car / 1998년형 차 a 1998 model (car) / 경제형차 an economy car (▶「값이 싼 차」라는 뜻도 되고 「유지비가 적게 드는 차」라는 뜻도 됨) / 고성능차 a high-performance car / 불량차 a lemon (▶a lemon에는 「불량품」이라는 의미가 있는데 주로 차를 가리킴) / 해치백 a hatchback / 스포츠카 a sports [sport] car / 슈퍼 카 a super car

▶ 디젤차 a diesel (car) / 디젤 트럭 a diesel truck / 전기 자동차 an electric [a battery] car / 전륜 구동차(前輪驅動車) a front-wheel-drive car / 후륜 구동차(後輪驅動車) a rear-wheel-drive car / 4륜 구동차 a four-wheel-drive car / 트윈캠 a twin-cam (engine)

▶ 모터사이클 a motorbike; a bike; a motorcycle / 스쿠터 a scooter

2. 운전·사고·위반

▶ 운전자 a driver; a motorist; 〈고용 운전사〉 a chauffeur / 운전 면허증(을 갱신하다) (renew) a driver's license / 국제 운전 면허증 an international driving permit / 가면 허증 (英) a provisional license

▶ 교통 사고 a traffic accident / 충돌사고 a collision / 정면 충돌사고 a head-on collision / 연쇄 충돌사고 a multiple collision [pile-up] / 구멍 a flat tire; a puncture

▶ 주차 위반 illegal parking / 신호 위반 ignoring a traffic light; driving through the red light / 속도 위반 speeding / 음주 운전 driving while intoxicated (略 D.W.I.) / 음주 검사 a balloon test / 운전 부주의 inattentive driving

3. 도로

▶ 교통 표지 a traffic sign / 교통 법규 traffic regulations / 안전지대 a safety zone / 막다른 골목 a dead end / 일방 통행 one way traffic / 우회로 a detour / 추월 금지 No passing / 양보 표지 a yield sign / 유턴하다 make a U-turn / 횡단 보도 a crosswalk / 교차점 an intersection / 건널목 a railroad crossing / 인터체인지 an interchange / 고속도로 an expressway; (英) a motorway; a freeway / 사설 도로 a private road / 포장 도로 a pavement / 간선 도로 a highway / 유료 도로 a turnpike; a toll road

---

━━나무 a plum tree

자득 自得 1 〈만족〉 self-complacency; self-satisfaction ━━자득하다 be self-complacent; be self-satisfied
2 〈터득〉 apprehension; self-acquirement ━━자득하다 apprehend; grasp; understand; acquire by *oneself*

자디잘다 very small; tiny; petty; fine; minute
▶ 저 자디잔 오렌지 같은 노란 과일은 금귤이라 부른다 The yellow fruit which looks like a tiny orange is called kumquat.

자라 〖動〗 a snapping [mud, soft-shelled] turtle; a alligator tortoise; a terrapin

자라다¹ 1 〈발육하다〉 grow (up); 〈양육되다〉 be brought up; be bred
▶ 잘 자라다 grow well; thrive / 호강스럽게 [가난하게] 자라다 be bred in luxury [poverty] / 귀하게 자라다 be brought up like a tender plant / 무럭무럭 자라다 grow up fast [rapidly] / 키가 자라다 grow taller / 너무 자라다 be overgrown; overgrow *oneself* / 한창 자라는 아이 a growing child
▶ 이 토양에는 장미가 자라지 않는다 Roses do not grow in this soil.

▶ 그녀의 아기는 모유[분유]로 자랐다 Her baby was breast-fed [bottle-fed].
▶ 그녀의 아들은 훌륭한 젊은이로 자랐다 Her son has grown into a fine young man.
▶ 이 아이는 한창 자랄 때라 하루하루 커지는 것 같다 He is growing so fast that he seems to be taller every day.
▶ 그 소년은 자라서 옷이 작아졌다 The boy has outgrown his clothes.
▶ 나는 부산에서 태어나 서울에서 자랐다 I was born in Pusan and brought up in Seoul.
▶ 그는 다 자랐다 He has reached his full growth.
▶ 대나무는 이 지역에서는 잘 자라지 않는다 Bamboo plants do not thrive [won't grow well] in this area.
2 〈늘다〉 increase; gain; grow
자라다² **1** 〈족하다〉 enough; sufficient
▶ 1만원 정도면 자랄게다 Ten thousand won or so will do [answer our needs].
2 〈미치다〉 reach; get [attain] to; come up to (the standard)
♦ 힘이 자라는 데까지 to the best of *one's* ability / 손이 자라는 곳에 within *one's* reach / 힘이 자라다 be within *one's* power [influence] / 會話 「저 가지에 손이 자라겠니?」「안돼, 너무 높아서」 "Can you reach that branch?" "No, I can't reach that high."
▶ 힘이 자라는 데까지 시도해 보았지만 허사였다 I did every possible try that lay in my power, but (it was) in vain.
자라 보고 놀란 가슴 소댕 보고 놀란다 (속담) Once bitten, twice shy. ⇌ The burnt child dreads the fire.
자락 the skirt; the dress hem; 〈한복 등의〉 the bottom; 〈여성복의〉 the train
♦ 스커트 자락 the hem of a skirt / 치맛자락을 끌다 trail the skirt / 치맛자락을 걷어올리다 tuck up the skirt
자락자락 impertinently; impudently; saucily
▶ 그는 친절히 해 주면 자락자락 더 한다 He becomes more and more impertinent, presuming on your good nature.
자란 紫蘭 〔植〕 a bletilla; a red sandalwood
자란자란 to the brim; brimfully; to the full; overflowingly
♦ 잔에 포도주를 자란자란 따르다 fill a glass (up) to the brim with wine
자랑 pride; boast; self-conceit; self-praise
♦ 자랑 삼아 for show [display]; for *one's* boast
▶ 그 애는 우리 학교의 자랑입니다 He [She] is a pride of our school.
▶ 나는 이 나라에 태어난 것을 자랑으로 생각한다 I am proud of the fact that I was born in this country.
—**자랑하다** boast [brag] of; make a boast of; boast it; be boastful
♦ 자랑하는 사람 a braggart; a boaster / 자랑하지 않는 사람 a modest person / 자랑하는 물건 *one's* proud possession / 솜씨를 자랑하다 brag [vaunt] of *one's* skill / 자랑해 보이다 make a display [show] of
▶ 그것은 자랑할 만한 것이 못된다 That's nothing to be proud of [to boast about].
▶ 그는 우리 나라가 자랑하는 과학자중 한 사람이다 He is one of our best scientists.
자랑거리 a credit 《to》; something to brag about [of]; a feather in *one's* cap; a source of pride; a pride; a boast
▶ 그 여배우는 예쁜 얼굴이 자랑거리다 The actress is vain about her pretty face.
▶ 그 공원은 이 도시의 자랑거리다 The park is the pride of this city.
▶ 그는 그 가문의 자랑거리다 He is a credit to his family.
자랑 끝에 불 붙는다 (속담) Pride will have a fall. ⇌ Pride goes before destruction.
자랑스럽다 proud; boastful; brag
♦ 자랑스럽게 boastingly; braggingly; proudly / 자랑스럽게 여기다 be vain of [about]; pride *oneself* on; be proud of; take pride in / 자랑스럽게 말하다 speak boastingly of
▶ 그는 자기의 정원을 자랑스럽게 바라보았다 He looked with pride at his garden.
▶ 네가 성공했다는 소식을 들으면 네 아버님도 자랑스러워할 것이다 It will make [do] your father proud to hear of your success.
▶ 나는 아들이 자랑스러웠다 I felt proud of my son.
자력 自力 *one's* own strength [efforts, exertions] ♦ 자력으로 by *one's* own ability [efforts, exertions]; by [for] *oneself*; singlehanded / 자력으로 하다 do single-handed; do by *oneself* / 자력으로 출세하다 rise from one class to another on *one's* own merits / 자력 갱생하다 work out *one's* salvation by *one's* own efforts
자력 資力 means; (financial) resources; funds
♦ 자력에 따라 according to *one's* means [resources] / 자력이 있는 사람 a man of means / 자력이 없는 사람 a man of no means / 자력이 없어서 for want [lack] of money / 자력이 충분하다 have enough funds
▶ 그는 자력이 있다 He is a man of wealth [means].
▶ 나는 자력이 없다 I don't have much money.
▶ 우리는 그 계획을 실행할 자력이 없다 We don't have enough funds to carry out the plan.
자력 磁力 〔物〕 magnetic force=자기(~력)
■ —계(計) a magnetometer —선 =자기(~력선)
자료 資料 materials 《for》; data 《on, for》
♦ 자료를 모으다 collect [gather] materials [data] 《for》 / 자료를 뒤지다 hunt up materials / 자료를 제공하다 furnish [afford] data 《to, for》
■ 연구[통계]— materials for study [statistics]; research [statistic(al)] materials [data]
■ —실 a morgue
자루¹ 〈부대〉 a bag; a sack; 〈작은〉 a pouch
♦ 쌀 자루 a rice bag / 자루같이 baggy / 자루를 비우다 empty a bag
▶ 이것을 자루에 담아주십시오 Will you put it [them] in a bag?
▶ 그는 자루에서 무언가를 꺼냈다 He took something out of the bag.

▶ 나는 밀가루를 한 자루 샀다 I bought a sack of flour.

자루² 〈손잡이〉 a handle; 〈기계·무기의〉 a grip; 〈단도의〉 a hilt; 〈칼의〉 a haft; 〈도끼의〉 a helve; a stick
♦ 빗자루 a broomstick / 도끼 자루 the helve [shaft] of an ax / 자루가 긴 국자 a long-handled ladle / 자루를 달다[대다] put a handle [haft] to... / 자루를 갈다 change a handle
▶ 칼자루가 빠졌다 The handle of the knife came off.

자루³ 〈세는 단위〉 one; a piece [stick] 《of chalk》; a pair 《of scissors》; 〈총의〉 a stand
♦ 붓 두 자루 two writing brushes / 연필 다섯 자루 five pencils / 총 세 자루 three pieces [stands] of rifles / 칼 한 자루 a sword

자르다¹ 1 cut (off); chop; sever; saw (off); clip; shear
♦ 둘로 자르다 cut sth in [into] two / 목을 자르다 cut off sb's head; behead / 짧게 자르다 cut sth into short lengths / 잘라내다 cut away [off, out] / 나뭇가지를 잘라내다 cut [trim] branches off a tree
▶ 이 케이크를 둘로 잘라 주십시오 Please cut the cake in two [into two halves].
▶ 당근은 크게 자르고 파는 잘게 썹니다 Chop carrots and mince spring onions.
2 〈해고하다〉 fire; (口) give sb the sack

자르다² 〈동여매다〉 tie [bind] (tight); tighten; fasten

자리 1 〈좌석〉 a seat; one's place
♦ 자리에 앉다 take [(美) have] one's seat; seat oneself; sit in one's seat / 자리에 앉아 있다 be seated / 자리에 앉게 하다 place sb in a seat; seat / 자리에서 일어나다 rise from one's seat / 자리로 돌아오다 resume one's seat; return to one's seat / 자리를 양보하다 offer one's seat to 《an old man》 / 자리를 떠나다 leave one's seat / 자리를 비우다 vacate the seat / 자리를 잡다[잡아 놓다] get [secure] a seat (for sb); reserve [book] a seat / 자리를 맡아 놓다 keep [hold, save] a seat for sb / 자리를 바꾸다 change one's seat; 〈남과〉 change seats with sb / 자리를 같이하다 sit (side by side) together / 남의 자리를 빼앗다 take another's seat / 자리를 빼앗기다 lose one's place [seat] / 자리를 다투다 scramble [rush] for a seat
▶ 會話 「이 자리 비어 있습니까?」「아니오, 사람이 있어요」 "Is this seat vacant [free]?" "No, it's taken [occupied]."
▶ 그는 화가 나서 자리를 떠났다 He got angry and left his seat.
▶ 會話 「김선생님 자리에 계십니까?」「김선생님은 지금 자리를 비우셨어요, 곧 돌아오실 겁니다」 "Is Mr. Kim in?" "No, he is not at his desk right now, but he'll be back soon."
▶ 그는 버스 안에서 그 노인에게 자리를 양보했다 He gave his seat on the bus to the old person.
2 〈장소〉 (a) place; (a) room; space ♦ 자리를 너무 차지하다 occupy [take up] too much space
▶ 그는 두 사람 몫의 자리를 차지하고 있다 He occupies enough space for two (persons).
▶ 접는 식 침대는 별로 자리를 차지하지 않는다 A folding bed takes little room [space].
▶ 이 자리에서는 말할 수 없다 I can't speak of it here.
3 〈현장〉 the (actual) spot; the scene; 〈경우〉 an occasion ♦ 화재가 난 자리 the scene of fire / 그 자리에 있던 사람들 the people on the spot 《of murder》
▶ 범인은 그 자리에서 체포되었다 The offender was arrested [caught] on the spot.
▶ 경찰은 사고가 난 자리로 달려갔다 The police rushed to the scene of the accident.
4 〈터〉 a seat; a site; a place ♦ 공장이 설 자리 the site (assigned) for the projected factory / 절이 있었던 자리 the place where a temple formerly stood
5 〈위치〉 a position; a situation; a location ♦ 자리가 좋다[나쁘다] be well [badly] situated; be in a good [bad] position / 자리를 잡다 〈사람이〉 station oneself; place oneself; take one's position; 〈사물이〉 be situated [located] / 자리를 바꾸다 change [shift] (one's) position
▶ 자리가 좋아야 장사가 잘 된다 The locality brings a great deal of business.
▶ 책상이 제자리에 있지 않다 The desk is not in place.
6 〈직책〉 a position; a place; a situation; a post; 〈빈 자리〉 an opening; a vacancy
♦ 일할 자리 a job; a post / 자리를 노리다 have an eye to a post
▶ 그녀는 그 회사에서 아르바이트 자리를 얻었다 She got a part-time job with that firm.
7 〈정착지〉 ♦ 자리가 잡히다 settle down; establish oneself; get in the saddle; get on the (tight) track
▶ 내 사업은 자리가 잡혔다 My business has gained its footing [ground].
8 〈흉터〉 a mark ♦ 개에게 물린 자리 a scar from a dog bite
9 〈깔개〉 a mat; a mattress; 〈침구〉 a bed; bedding
♦ 자리에 들다 go into bed; go [retire] to bed / 자리를 보다 make [lay, prepare] a bed / 자리를 펴다 spread a mat; make a bed
10 〈병석〉 a sickbed
♦ 자리에서 일어나다 leave one's sickbed / 자리에 몸져눕다 be bedridden
▶ 그는 지난 2개월간 자리를 보전하고 있다 He has been sick in bed (for) the last two months.
11 〈숫자의〉 a position 《of a figure》; a digit; 〈소수점 이하의〉 a place
♦ 네 자리 수 a number of four figures [digits] / 1 [10, 100]의 자리 the unit's [ten's, hundred's] place
▶ 소수점 이하 세 자리까지 구하라 Calculate down to three decimal places.

자리 自利 one's own interests [advantage]; self-interest; personal profit
♦ 자리적(인) self-interested; self-seeking; selfish / 자리를 꾀하다 consult [follow] one's own interests

자리끼 nighttime drinking water; drinking water by bedside

자리보전하다 —保全— lie in *one's* bed ♦ 자리보전하고 눕다 fall ill

자리옷 nightclothes ⇨ 잠옷

자리자리하다 prickly; tingling; prickling ▶ 내 다리가 자리자리하다 I have pins and needles in my feet.

자리잡다 1 〈좌석을 잡다〉 take a [*one's*] seat; seat *oneself* (at a table); sit down ♦ 상석에 자리잡다 take the top seat / 넓게 자리잡다 take up much room ▶ 모두들 자리잡고 앉았다 Everybody took a seat. 2 〈위치하다〉 be situated; be located; lie (도시가); stand (건물이) ▶ 시청은 시의 중앙에 자리잡고 있다 The city hall is situated [located] in the center of a city. 3 〈정착하다〉 settle (down); make *one's* home; establish *oneself* ♦ 서울에 자리잡다 settle down in Seoul / 호텔에 자리잡다 put up at a hotel ▶ 너는 언제나 자리잡고 가정을 가질거니? When are you going to settle down and have a family?

자린고비 玼吝考妣 〈인색한 사람〉 a skinflint; a very stingy person; a notorious miser; (口) a cheapskate; (俗) a tightwad

자립 自立 〈독립〉 independence; self-reliance; 〈자활〉 self-support —**자립하다** become independent; establish *oneself*; rely on *oneself*; stand [get] on *one's* own legs [feet]; 〈자활하다〉 support *oneself* ♦ 자립하여 independently; on *one's* own account; for *oneself* / 자립할 수 있다 be able to stand alone ▶ 자립할 수 없는 사람들이 있다 Some people are not able to stand by themselves. ▶ 그는 자립하여 장사를 하고 있다 He is doing business on his own account. ▶ 그는 충분히 자립해 나갈 수 있다 He can get on very well by himself. ■—경제 self-supporting economy; autarky

자릿세 —貰 (俗) protection racket

자릿수 —數 a cipher [digit] ♦ 다섯 자릿수 a number of five ciphers [digits]

자릿자릿하다 〈저리다〉 benumbed; 〈쑤시다〉 tingling; 〈마음졸이다〉 thrilling; suspenseful; thrilled

자릿조반 —早飯 light breakfast in bed

자마구 〔植〕 pollen [farina] (of cereals)

-자마자 as soon as; no sooner...than...; hardly [scarcely]...when [before]...; directly; immediately; the very moment [instant]... ▶ 그녀는 대학을 나오자마자 결혼했다 She married directly she left the university. ▶ 그는 그 소식을 듣자마자 떠났다 He left as soon as he heard the news. ▶ 그는 도착하자마자 병이 들었다 He had no sooner [No sooner had he] arrived than he fell ill. ▶ 소년들은 내가 등을 돌리자마자 온갖 장난을 쳤다 The boys did all sorts of mischief immediately my back was turned.

자막 字幕 〔映〕 a title; a caption ♦ 한국말 자막이 있는 프랑스 영화 a French film with Korean subtitles / 영화에 자막을 넣다 superimpose a caption [dialogue] on a film; title a film; add titles to movies ■설명[보조]— a cut-in; a subtitle; an insert title

자막대기 a measuring stick; a foot rule; a yardstick

자만 自慢 self-conceit; conceit —**자만하다** be conceited [self-conceited]; be puffed up with conceit [vanity]; think highly of *oneself*; boast; brag ▶ 자만하지 마라 Don't be conceited [vain].

자만심 自慢心 self-conceit; self-opinion; vanity; vainglory ♦ 자만심이 강하다 be full of conceit; be self-opinionated

자매 姉妹 sisters; a sibling ♦ 자매의[같은] sisterly; sororal ■ 친(親)— sisters-german ■—기관 sister agencies —도시 a sister city —선[함] a sister ship (to) —편 a companion volume (to) —학교 a sister school —회사 an affiliated company; an affiliate

자매결연 姉妹結緣 establishment of sisterhood [sistership] ♦ 자매결연을 맺다 establish [set up] sisterhood relationship 《with》

자맥질 ducking ⇨ 무자맥질

자메이카 〈나라 이름〉 Jamaica ■—사람 a Jamaican

자멘호프 〈에스페란토어의 창안자〉 Zamenhof, Lazarus Ludwig (1859-1917)

자멸 自滅 〈제 탓으로 망함〉 self-destruction; self-ruin; suicide; 〈자연히 멸망함〉 natural decay ♦ 자멸을 초래하다 lead to self-destruction / 정치적 자멸을 초래하다 commit political suicide ▶ 그의 태만이 자멸을 가져왔다 His idleness resulted in self-ruin. ▶ 그것은 자멸 행위다 That is self-defeating behavior. ⇒ That will lead to your own destruction. —**자멸하다** destroy [ruin] *oneself*; commit suicide; 〈망하다〉 perish ▶ 조만간 그들은 자멸할 것이다 Sooner or later they will ruin themselves. ▶ 사실상 적은 자멸한 셈이다 In effect, the enemies destroyed themselves. ▶ 그 팀은 수비 에러로 자멸했다 The team brought defeat to itself by some errors in fielding. ■—책 a suicidal policy

자명 自明 self-evidence —**자명하다** self-evident; self-explaining; self-explanatory; axiomatic(al) ♦ 자명한 이치 a self-evident truth; a truism; an axiom

자명종 自鳴鐘 an alarm (clock) ♦ 자명종 소리에 잠을 깨다 wake to the alarm ▶ 나는 자명종을 5시 30분에 울리도록 맞춰 놓았다 I set the alarm clock for [to ring at] half past five.

자모 字母 1 〈글자〉 an alphabet; a letter (of

자모 the alphabet); a syllabic **2** 〈활자〉 a matrix 《pl. -trices, ~es》
자모 慈母 an affectionate mother; a loving mother
자모음 子母音 〔言〕 consonants and vowels
자못 〈매우〉 very (much); ever so much; greatly; awfully; 〈적잖이〉 not a little
▶그에 대한 기대가 자못 크다 I expect much from him.
▶그 일은 자못 어렵다 It is an exceedingly hard job.
▶내가 그에게 진 신세가 자못 크다 I owe him a great deal.
자문 自問 asking *oneself*
―자문하다 ask [question] *oneself*
자문 諮問 a consultation; an inquiry
◆자문에 응하다 provide advice and suggestions as requested
―자문하다 consult (with) *sb*; ask *sb's* counsel [opinion]; take counsel 《with》; inquire; submit 《a problem》 to *sb*
■―기관 an advisory organ [body] ―안 a draft submitted for deliberation ―위원회 a consultative committee; a trial board
자문자답 自問自答 a soliloquy; a monologue
―자문자답하다 answer *one's* own question; talk to *oneself*; soliloquize
자물쇠 a lock; 〈맹꽁이 자물쇠〉 a padlock; 〈자동 자물쇠〉 a snaplock
◆자물쇠를 달다 put a lock on / 문의 자물쇠를 열다 unlock a door / 자물쇠를 비틀어 열다 force a lock; wrench away [open] a lock / 자물쇠를 채우다 fasten a lock; lock (up)
▶이 문은 자물쇠가 잘 안 잠긴다 This door won't lock.
자바 〈인도네시아의 주된 섬〉 Java
◆자바의 Javanese; Javan
―말 Javanese ―사람 a Javanese; a Javan ―원인 the Java man ―커피 Java coffee
자바라 啫哰囉 〈타악기〉 small cymbals
자박 〈생금 덩어리〉〔鑛〕 a gold nugget
자반 salted fish
▶고등어 자반 a salted mackerel
자반 紫斑 〈자줏빛 멍〉 a purple spot
■―병 〔醫〕 purpura ―열 purpuric fever
자반뒤집기 a restless tossing of the body (in disease); writhing in agony ―자반뒤집기하다 toss restlessly about in bed
자발성 自發性 spontaneity; spontaneousness
자발없다 〈경솔하다〉 restless; impatient; rash; hasty
자발적 自發的 spontaneous; voluntary
◆자발적인 원조 voluntary aid / 자발적으로 행동하다 act spontaneously / 자발적으로 사직하다 resign voluntarily
▶나는 자발적으로 그 일을 맡았다 I undertook the work of my own accord.
자방 子房 〈씨방〉〔植〕 an ovary
자배기 an earthenware tub
자백 自白 confession; 〈자인〉 admission
▶고문 또는 강요에 의한 자백은 증거가 되지 않는다 Confessions extracted by torture or coercion cannot be accepted as evidence.
▶그에게서 자백을 얻어내지 못했다 We failed to produce confession from him.
―자백하다 confess 《to a crime》; own (up); make a confession; admit
▶그는 범행 일체를 자백했다 He confessed all his crimes. ⇒ He made a full confession of his crimes.
▶그는 그 집에 불을 질렀다고 자백했다 He confessed that he had set fire to the house.
자벌레 〔昆〕 a looper; a measuring worm; an inchworm
자복 子福 ◆자복이 많은 사람 a person blessed with many children
자본 資本 (a) capital; a fund
◆자본의 부족 lack of funds / 외국 자본의 도입 [유입] the introduction [inflow] of foreign capital / 자본의 축적 an accumulation of capital / 자본의 집중 centralization of capital / 자본의 수출 capital export / 자본의 회전 circulation of capital / 자본과 경영의 분리 separation between capital and administration / 자본을 대다 provide capital (for); furnish [supply] *sb* with capital [funds]; finance 《an enterprise》 / 자본을 투입하다 invest [lay out] capital 《in an enterprise》 / 자본을 변통하다 raise funds; employ [rotate] capital / 자본을 놀려 두다 let capital lie idle
▶그는 2천만원의 자본으로 장사를 시작했다 He started business with a capital of twenty million won.
▶그들은 외국 자본 유치에 열을 올리고 있다 They are working hard to attract foreign investment(s).
▶건강이 내 유일한 자본이다 Health is the only asset I have at my disposal.
▶나는 가게를 낼 만한 자본이 없었다 I didn't have enough capital to open my own store.
■―가변[불변]― variable [constant] capital 고정[유동]― fixed [circulating] capital 공칭[납입]― nominal [paid-up] capital 금융― financial capital 독점― monopolistic capital 매판(買辦)― comprador capital 사회― social overhead capital 산업[상업]― industrial [trading] capital 영세― a small [petty] capital 외국― foreign capital 운전― working capital [fund] 유휴― unemployed [idle] capital 의제(擬制)― fictitious [watered] capital 자기[타인]― owned [borrowed] capital 주식― share capital 준비― reserve capital 차입― loan capital 투하― invested capital 회전― revolving capital [fund] ■―거래 capital transaction ―계정 capital account ―과세 capital levy ―구성 composition of capital ―도피 flight of capital ―론(論) *The Capital*; (독) *Das Kapital* ―시장 the capital market ―잉여금 capital surplus ―재(財) capital goods ―주 a financier; a financial supporter ―초과 overcapitalization ―투자 capital investment ―회전율 capital turnover
자본가 資本家 a capitalist; a financier
◆자본가와 노동자 capital and labor
■―계급 the capitalist classes
자본금 資本金 (a) capital; (美) capital stock; (英) a share capital
▶이 회사의 자본금은 10억원이다 The com-

pany is capitalized at [has a capital of] one billion won.

자본주의 資本主義 capitalism
♦ 자본주의의 capitalistic
■ 국가— state capitalism 독점— monopolistic capitalism 수정— modified [revised] capitalism ■ —경제 capitalistic economy —국가 a capitalist country [nation] —자 a capitalist —제도 the capitalistic system —진영 the capitalist camp

자본화 資本化 capitalization —자본화하다 capitalize

자볼기 a whipping [verbal lashing] from *one's* wife
♦ 자볼기 맞다 be whipped [verbally lashed] by *one's* wife

자봉틀 自縫— a sewing machine ⇨ 재봉틀

자부 子婦 〈며느리〉 a daughter-in-law; *one's* son's wife

자부 自負 self-conceit
—자부하다 be (self-)conceited; be self-confident; think highly of *oneself*
▶ 그는 체력에서는 아무한테도 뒤지지 않는다고 자부하고 있다 He flatters himself that he is second to none in physical strength.

자부 慈父 a compassionate father; a loving father; an affectionate father

자부심 自負心 self-conceit; self-confidence; self-importance; self-esteem; pride
♦ 자부심이 있는[강한] self-conceited 《person》; self-confident; self-important; proud
▶ 그는 자부심이 대단하다 He has a very high opinion of himself. ⇌ He thinks highly of himself.

자북 磁北 magnetic north
■ —극 자기 (〜북극)

자비 自費 *one's* own expense [charge]
▶ 그는 자비로 논문집을 출판했다 He published a book of collected papers at his own expense.
■ —생 a private [self-paying] student —유학생 a student studying abroad at his [her] own expense

자비 慈悲 〈인정〉 mercy; benevolence; 〈연민〉 compassion; pity; clemency; 〈자선〉 charity
♦ 자비를 빌다 beg for mercy; beseech charity / 아무에게 자비를 베풀다 show mercy [clemency] to *sb*; do *sb* an act of charity
—자비롭다, 자비스럽다 merciful; charitable (to the poor); compassionate
■ —심 a merciful [benevolent] heart; mercy: 그는 자비심이라고는 없는 인간이다 He is a stranger to (pity or) mercy.

자빠뜨리다 〈사람을〉 make *sb* fall on 《his》 back [fall backward]; knock [throw, push] *sb* down on 《his》 back; 〈물건을〉 knock [push, pull, throw] *sth* down

자빠지다 1 〈뒤로 넘어지다〉 fall on *one's* back; fall backward; tumble down; fall (down)
♦ 빙판 위에 자빠지다 fall down on the ice / 미끄러져 자빠지다 slip and fall backward / 큰대자로 자빠지다 fall flat [full length] on *one's* back / 자빠진 놈 꼭뒤 차다 kick *sb* when he's down
2 〈손을 떼고 물러나다〉 drop away [off]; fall away
3 〈눕다〉 lie down; lay *oneself* down; 〈빈둥거리다〉 live in idleness; lounge
▶ 방에만 자빠져 있지 마라 Don't idle your time away in your room.

자빡 〈단호한 거절〉 flat [definite] refusal ♦ 자빡대다 decline definitely; refuse flatly / 자빡맞다 be refused point-blank; be given a brush-off

자산 資産 property; a fortune; 〈법인 등의〉 assets
♦ 자산과 부채 assets and liabilities / 자산의 동결 freezing of 《foreign》 assets
■ 고정— fixed assets 무형[유형]— intangible [tangible] assets 유동— circulating [floating] assets; current assets; liquid assets ■ —계정 assets account —목록 a statement [an inventory] of assets —상태 financial standing —소득 income from property —재평가 revaluation of property

자산가 資産家 a man of property [fortune, means]
■ —계급 the propertied classes

자살 自殺 suicide
▶ 그는 음독 자살을 꾀했다 He attempted suicide by taking poison.
▶ 사건은 타살이 아니라 자살로 판명되었다 It was found to be a case of suicide, not of murder.
▶ 그것은 자살 행위다 It is a suicidal act.
—자살하다 kill *oneself*; commit suicide; take *one's* own life; put *oneself* to death
♦ 권총으로 자살하다 shoot *oneself* to death; shoot *oneself* with *one's* pistol [revolver]/ 목을 매어 자살하다 hang *oneself* (to death)
■ 집단— mass suicide 투신— suicide by drowning : 강에 투신자살하다 jump in(to) the river to kill *oneself* —미수 an attempted suicide —미수자 a would-be suicide —방조 aiding and abetting suicide —방조죄 the crime of aiding self-destruction —자 a suicide

자상 自傷 self-inflicted injury
■ —행위 self-injury; a self-wounding act; injuring *oneself*

자상 刺傷 a stab; a pierced wound

자상하다 仔詳— 〈자세하다〉 minute; detailed; full; 〈찬찬하다〉 cautious and careful; thoughtfully kind; considerate
♦ 자상한 배려 attentive consideration / 자상하게 minutely; in detail; at (full) length; in full / 자상하게 가르치다 teach kindly
▶ 그 간호사는 환자들을 아주 자상하게 돌본다 That nurse is very attentive to (the needs of) her patients.

자새 〈얼레〉 a reel
■ —질 reeling

자색 姿色 a fair [beautiful] face; good looks; personal beauty ♦ 자색이 뛰어난 여인 a woman of rare personal beauty / 자색이 곱다 [아름답다] be beautiful; have a graceful figure / 자색이 뛰어나다 surpass 《others》 in beauty

자색 紫色 purple ⇨ 자주, 자줏빛
자생 自生 spontaneous generation; autogeny; abiogenesis; 〈야생〉 natural [wild] growth
♦자생의 autogenous; spontaneous; native —자생하다 grow wild [naturally]
♦산야에 자생하는 식물 native [wild] plants in mountains and fields
■—식물 native [wild] plants; self-sown plants

자서 自序 the author's preface
자서 自敍 writing one's own story
—자서하다 write one's own story
자서 自署 a signature; an autograph
—자서하다 sign (one's name); affix one's signature; autograph (a book)
♦자서한 사진 a signed photograph

자서전 自敍傳 an autobiography
♦자서전적인 소설 an autobiographical novel / 자서전체의 autobiographic(al) / 자서전을 쓰다 write one's life story; write the story of one's own life
■—작가 an autobiographer

자석 磁石 a magnet ♦자석의 인력 magnetic attraction / 자석의 magnetic
▶자석은 철을 끌어당긴다 A magnet attracts iron.
■말굽[막대]— a horseshoe [bar] magnet 영구[일시]— a permanent [temporary] magnet 천연— a natural magnet; a loadstone —발전기 a magnetogenerator; a magneto —식 교환기 a magneto switchboard —식 전화기 a magnetotelephone set

자석영 紫石英 amethyst ⇨ 자수정
자선 自選 self-selection —자선하다 select 《some》 out of one's own works ■—시집 a collection of poems selected by the author
자선 慈善 charity; benevolence; beneficence; philanthropy; 〈구휼〉 almsgiving
♦자선의 charitable; benevolent / 자선을 목적으로 for charitable purposes / 가난한 사람에게 자선을 베풀다 give alms to the poor; render aid to the poor in charity
■—가 a charitable person; a philanthropist —기금 a charity fund —냄비 a charity pot 《of the Salvation Army》 —단체 a charity institution [organization]; a charity —바자 a (charity) bazar —병원 a charity hospital —사업 philanthropic [charitable] work: 수익을 자선 사업에 기부하다 give [make over] the proceeds to charitable work —심 a charitable disposition [spirit] —음악회 a charity [benefit] concert —행위 an act of charity; charities

자설 自說 one's own view [opinion]
♦자설을 고집하다 stick [hold fast] to one's opinion / 자설을 굽히다 give up one's view; change one's opinion

자성 自省 self-examination; reflection; introspection
♦자성적인 introspective / 아무에게 자성을 촉구하다 ask sb to reflect on 《himself》 —자성하다 examine oneself; reflect on oneself; introspect

자성 資性 character; disposition; nature
자성 磁性 〔物〕 magnetism ♦자성의 magnetic / 자성을 띠게 하다 magnetize ■—체 a magnetic body [substance]

자세 姿勢 a posture; a pose; a stance; 〈몸가짐〉 a carriage; 〈태도〉 an attitude
♦앉은[선] 자세로 in a seated [standing] posture / 자세가 흐트러지다 lose one's balance / 강경한 자세를 취하다 assume a stance of toughness 《toward》 / 도전적인 자세를 취하다 assume a challenging attitude 《toward》 / 방어 자세를 취하다 assume a posture of defense / 차려 자세를 취하다 stand at attention / 자세를 바르게 가지다 keep a straight posture / 자세를 편히 하다 relax one's position
▶자세를 바로 하시오 Straighten yourself.
▶너는 자세가 좋다[나쁘다] Your posture is good [bad]. ⇌ 〈몸가짐이〉 You have a fine [poor] carriage.
▶그녀는 편안한 자세로 앉아 있었다 She was sitting in a comfortable position.
▶바른 자세는 건강에 필수적이다 Good posture is essential to health.
▶사진사는 그녀에게 그 자세를 흐트러뜨리지 말라고 당부했다 The photographer asked her to hold that pose.
■고[저]— a high [low] attitude [posture]

자세하다 子細— detailed; minute; full
♦자세한 이야기 a full [detailed] account / 자세한 내용-[것, 일] details; particulars; further information; the whole circumstances [story] / 사건의 자세한 전말을 보고하다 give a full account [all the circumstances] of the event
▶자세한 것은 모릅니다 I don't know the details.
▶이 책이 저 책보다 설명이 자세하다 This book gives a fuller explanation than that.
▶시간이 없어 자세한 이야기는 못 한다 I have no time to tell you the full of it.
▶자세한 것은 만나 뵙고 말씀 드리겠습니다 I'll tell you the details when we meet.
▶자세한 것은 설명서를 읽어 보시기 바랍니다 For further particulars [details], please read the explanatory note.

자세히 子細— in full; in detail; minutely; fully; closely
♦자세히 말하다 talk minutely; give a full [detailed] account 《of》 / 자세히 설명하다 explain sth in detail / 자세히 알다 know in full 《about》 / 자세히 조사하다 examine minutely / 자세히 보고하다 make a detailed report 《of》
▶그는 그 이유를 자세히 설명했다 He explained the reason in full. ⇌ He gave a full and detailed account of the reason.
▶참 자세히도 알고 있네 그려 You certainly are well informed about the matter. ⇌ You talk like a book.

자손 子孫 sons and grandsons; a descendant; an offspring; 〈총칭〉 posterity; offspring; progeny; issue
♦…의 자손이다 be a descendant of…; be descended from… / 자손에게 전하다 hand down sth to one's offspring
▶그의 빛나는 위업은 자손 대대로 전해질 것이

다 His brilliant achievement will be handed [transmitted] down to posterity.

자수 自首 self-surrender; self-denunciation; (voluntary) confession
—**자수하다** give *oneself* up (to the police); deliver [surrender] *oneself* to justice; surrender voluntarily to the police

자수 自修 self-teaching ⇨ 자습(自習)

자수 刺繡 embroidery —**자수하다** embroider; do [lay] embroidery ((on))
♦손으로[기계로] 자수한 스웨터 a hand-embroidered [machine-embroidered] sweater
■—본[무늬] embroidery designs —실 embroidery thread —틀 an embroidery frame; a tabo(u)ret

자수성가 自手成家 making *one's* own fortune
—**자수성가하다** make *one's* fortune by *one's* own efforts
♦자수성가한 사람 a self-made man

자수정 紫水晶 amethyst; violet quartz

자숙 自肅 self-discipline; self-control
—**자숙하다** discipline [control] *oneself*; practice self-control [self-discipline]
▶좀 더 자숙하기 바란다 I want you to exercise [practice] stricter self-discipline.

자습 自習 self-teaching
—**자습하다** teach *oneself*; study for [by] *oneself*; study without a teacher
■—문제 homework; home task [exercises]; (an) assignment —시간 study hours —실 a study (hall)

자습서 自習書 a self-teaching [teach-yourself] book [manual]; a book for self-study; a key; (美俗) a horse; a pony; (英俗) a crib
♦영어 자습서 a key to an English reader
▶자습서의 사용은 금지되어 있다 The use of cribs is prohibited.

자승 自乘 a square ⇨ 제곱

자승자박하다 自繩自縛— fall into a trap set by *oneself*; be caught in *one's* own trap
▶그는 자신의 고집 때문에 자승자박했다 He has fallen into [been caught in] his own trap because of his stubbornness.

자시하 慈侍下 〈어머니만 모심〉 having *one's* widowed mother to support

자식 子息 1 a child 《*pl.* children》; offspring (▶단수·복수 동형); sons and daughters
♦자식이 많다 have a brood of children / 자식을 낳다 give birth to a child; bear a child / 자식이 없다 be childless; have no child [issue] / 자식 복이 많다 be blessed with children / 자식 없이 죽다 die without issue; leave no issue / 자식이 태어나다 a child is born; have a visit from the stork
▶그녀는 자식이 셋이나 있다 She is blessed with three children.
▶귀한 자식 매로 키워라 (속담) Spare the rod and spoil the child.
▶자식 알기를 부모만한 사람 없다 The parents are the best judges of their son.
2 〈욕〉 a fellow; a chap; (美口) a guy; (卑) a bastard; 〈꼬마〉 a kid; an urchin; (蔑) a brat; an imp
▶이 개자식 You son of a bitch [gun]!

▶이 후레 자식 You son of a whore!
▶저 자식은 사기꾼인지도 몰라 That fellow might be a damn impostor.

자신 自身 《*one's*》 self; *oneself*
♦나 자신 myself / 너 자신 yourself / 자신이 by *oneself*; 〈자기 힘으로〉 for *oneself*; 〈몸소〉 in person; personally / 자기 자신을 위해 for *one's* own sake / 자신의 나아갈 길을 개척하다 make *one's* way in the world / 자신의 목숨을 걸다 risk *one's* (own) life
▶너 자신을 알라 Know yourself [thyself].
▶나 자신은 거기에 반대하지 않는다 Personally [For myself] I'm not against it.
▶나 자신에게 실망했다 I am disappointed with myself.
▶왜 내가 그런 짓을 했는지 나 자신도 모르겠다 Even I don't know why I did such a thing.

자신 自信 (self-)confidence; (self-)assurance
♦자신있는 태도[사람] a (self-)confident manner [person] / 자신만만한 청년 a young man of unbounded assurance / 자신을 가지고 confidently / 자신을 얻다[잃다] gain [lose] confidence
▶그는 자신이 만만하다 He is full of confidence.
▶성공에 항상 자신을 가지시오 Always be sure of your success.
▶자신을 가지고 행동하시오 Act with confidence.
▶그녀는 아주 자신이 강하다 She has great confidence in herself.
▶그는 자기의 역량에 대한 자신이 없다 He lacks confidence in his own ability.
▶나는 시험에 합격할 자신이 있다 I am confident [sure] of passing the examination.
▶나는 너를 설득할 자신이 없다 I'm not confident of persuading you.

자실 自失 〈명하니 있음〉 abstraction

자심 滋甚 aggravation
—**자심하다** aggravated; more serious

자아 自我 self; ego; the "I"
♦자아의 형성 the formation of *one's* ego / 자아의 주장 self-assertion / 자아가 강한 egotistic; egoistic; self-willed; selfish / 자아에 눈뜨다 become conscious of *oneself* / 자아를 몰각하다 efface *oneself* / 자아를 만족시키다 gratify *one's* ego
■—관념 the sense of self —보존 self-preservation —비판 self-criticism —실현 self-realization —억제 self-repression —의식 self-consciousness —주의 egoism; egotism —주의자 an egoist

자아내다 1 〈실을〉 draw out; reel off; spin
♦고치에서 실을 자아내다 reel silk off cocoons / 솜에서 실을 자아내다 spin thread [yarn] out of cotton
2 〈액체·기체를〉 draw (liquid) from; suck out; pump out
3 〈느낌 등을〉 draw out; evoke; provoke; create; arouse
♦눈물을 자아내다 draw tears from *one's* eyes / 동정심을 자아내다 evoke *sb's* sympathy / 분위기를 자아내다 produce [create] an atmosphere / 슬픔을 자아내다 make *sb* feel

sad
자아올리다 suck [draw] up 《water》; pump up ♦펌프로 우물에서 물을 자아올리다 pump water (up) from a well
자애 自愛 〈자신을 아낌〉 self-love; self-regard; 〈이기적임〉 selfishness; egoism
—자애하다 take care of *oneself*; look after *oneself* [*one's* health]
▶아무쪼록 자중 자애하시기 바랍니다 Please [I hope (that) you will] take good care of yourself.
자애 慈愛 affection; kindness; love; benevolence ♦어머니의 자애 motherly love [affection] / 자애로운 affectionate; loving; tender; benevolent / 자애가 넘치다 be full of affection / 자애로운 눈으로 보다 look with affection
자약하다 自若— self-possessed; calm; composed
자양 滋養 nourishment; nutrition; alimentation ♦—가치 nutritive value —물 nourishing [nutritious] food; nourishment; nutriment; nutrient —제 a tonic
자양분 滋養分 a nutritious [nutritive] element; nutritive material; nutriment
♦자양분이 많은 nutritious; nutritive; nourishing / 자양분이 적은 lean; innutritive; innutritious / 자양분을 섭취하다 take nutritious food
자업자득 自業自得 the natural consequences of *one's* own deed [misdeed]; a well-deserved punishment
▶자업자득이다 You've brought it on yourself. ⇒ As one sows, so one reaps. ⇒ As you make your bed, so you must lie on it. ⇒ It serves you [him] right!
—자업자득하다 reap the fruits of *one's* actions; reap the harvest of *one's* own sowing
자연 自然 **1** 〈천연의 모습〉 nature
♦자연의 힘 the force of nature; the natural [elemental] forces / 자연의 법칙 the law of nature; the natural laws / 자연의 natural / 자연으로 돌아가다 return to nature / 자연을 벗삼다 make a companion of nature; live with nature / 자연의 품에 안기다 be (nestled) in the bosom of nature
▶자연은 가장 좋은 의사다 Nature is the best physician.
▶여름은 자연과 친해지기에 좋은 기회다 Summer is a good chance to commune [be in close contact] with nature.
▶그는 생전에 자연을 벗삼아 지냈다 In his life, he used to take nature for a friend [live as a friend of nature].
2 〈저절로〉 spontaneously; naturally; of itself; of its own accord; in spite of *oneself*
♦자연히 생겨나다 come of itself / 병이 자연히 낫다 recover spontaneously from (an) illness
▶그건 자연히 알게 될 거야 It will speak for itself.
▶상처는 자연히 아물었다 The wound healed of itself.
▶그는 과묵하니까 자연히 친구도 적다 He is so reserved that naturally he has few friends.
■—계 a natural world; (the realm of) nature —공원 a natural park —과학 natural science —묘사 a description of nature —미 natural beauty; the beauty of nature —발생 spontaneous generation; 〔生〕 abiogenesis —발화〔연소〕 spontaneous combustion —법 the natural law —보전구역 nature-preservation district —생태 보호 지역 a natural ecology protection area —석(石) a living [native, natural] rock —선택 natural selection —수 〔數〕 a natural number —시인 a nature poet —요법 a nature cure; naturopathy; physiotherapy —인 a natural man; 〔法〕 a natural person —자원 natural resources —재해 a natural disaster —지리 (학) physical geography —현상 a natural phenomenon —환경 natural environment : 자연환경 보호지구 (designate as) natural environment preservation district
자연 紫煙 〈담배 연기〉 tobacco smoke; 〈보랏빛 연기〉 blue smoke
자연력 自然力 〈자연계의 작용〉 (a) natural agency; 〈풍력·수력 등〉 the forces of nature; elemental forces
♦자연력을 이용하다 harness nature 《for》
자연보호 自然保護 conservation of nature; protection of the natural environment; wildlife conservation
■—단체 a conservation group —운동 a (nature-)conservation movement; a nature-protection campaign —운동가 a nature conservationist
자연사 自然死 (a) natural death
—자연사하다 die a natural death
자연소멸 自然消滅 natural extinction
—자연소멸하다 die out [go out of existence] in the course of time
자연숭배 自然崇拜 nature worship [cult]
■—자 a nature worship(p)er
자연스럽다 自然— natural; unaffected; unstudied
♦자연스럽게 행동하다 behave naturally / 자연스럽게 이야기하다 speak unaffectedly
▶그의 말하는 태도는 아주 자연스럽다 His way of speaking is very natural.
▶그의 행동은 자연스럽지 않다 His behavior is unnatural [affected].
자연주의 自然主義 naturalism ♦자연주의적 naturalistic
■—자 a naturalist
자연증가 自然增加 natural increase [increment]
■—율 a rate of natural increase; a natural increasing rate
자엽 子葉 〈떡잎〉 〔植〕 a seed leaf
자영 自營 self-management; self-sustenance
♦자영의 self-supporting; self-sustaining
—자영하다 do (business) independently [on *one's* own account]
■—사업 an independent enterprise —업자 an independent businessman
자오선 子午線 〔天〕 the meridian (line)
■본초— the prime [first] meridian —경과 〔통과〕 (meridian) transit
자오의 子午儀 a transit instrument
자외선 紫外線 ultraviolet rays [light]

■—램프 an ultraviolet lamp —요법 the ultraviolet light therapy
자우 滋雨 a beneficial [welcome, fertile] rain
자욱하다 dense; thick; heavy
▶ 마을에 아침 안개가 자욱했다 The morning mist hung (low) over the village.
▶ 안개가 자욱해졌다 The fog thickened.
▶ 차내는 담배 연기로 자욱했다 The inside of the train was heavy with tobacco smoke.
자웅 雌雄 **1** 〈암수〉 male and female; the sex
◆ 자웅 양성의 bisexual / 자웅을 감별하다 determine the sex 《of》; sex 《a chicken》
2 〈승패〉 victory or defeat
◆ 자웅을 결하다 fight a decisive battle 《with sb》; fight it out; fight to the finish / 자웅을 겨루다 vie 《contend, strive》 《with sb》 for supremacy [hegemony]
■—도태[선택] sexual selection —동주(同株) monoecism —동체(同體) hermaphrodite —이주(異株) dioecism
자웅눈 雌雄— a pair of eyes that are not the same size ■—이 a person whose eyes do not match
자원 自願 volunteering
—**자원하다** volunteer 《for》 ◆ 자원하여 of one's own accord; voluntarily / 종군을 자원하다 volunteer for military service
■—봉사자 a volunteer (worker)
자원 資源 resources
◆ 유한한 자원 finite resources / 자원이 풍부하다 be full of resources; be rich [abundant] in natural resources / 바다의 자원을 개발하다 exploit [develop] the resources in the sea / 자원을 보호[절약]하다 conserve [economize] natural resources
▶ 한국은 천연 자원이 빈약하다 Korea is poor in natural resources.
▶ 그 업계에서는 인적 자원이 부족하다 There is a shortage of manpower in that industry.
▶ 전쟁은 국가의 자원을 고갈시킨다 A war is a great drain upon the country's resources.
■—광물— mineral resources 물적— material resources 미개발— undeveloped [dormant] resources 석유— oil resources 수— water resources 지하— underground resources
■—개발 resource development —보호 conservation of resources —부국[빈국] a resource-rich [resource-poor] country
자위¹ 〈알의 흰[노른] 자위 the white [yolk] of an egg / 눈의 검은[흰] 자위 the iris [white] of the eye
자위² 〈무거운 물건의〉 a fixed position; 〈태아의〉 the fixed position of a fetus
◆ 자위 뜨다 《a heavy thing》 move a little from 《its》 place; be dislodged; 〈태아가〉 (begin to) quicken; 《the baby》 change position
자위 自慰 **1** 〈자기 위로〉 self-consolation
—**자위하다** console [solace] oneself
▶ 나는 팔자려니 생각하고 자위했다 I consoled myself with the thought [by thinking] that it was the way of all flesh.
2 〈수음〉 masturbation
자위 自衛 self-defense; self-protection

▶ 자위상 그렇게 하지 않을 수 없었다 I could not help doing that in self-defense.
—**자위하다** defend [protect] oneself
■—대 the self-defense forces —본능 the instinct of self-protection —수단 a measure of self-defense: 테러 조직에 대한 자위수단을 강구해야 한다 We should adopt a measure of self-defense against a terrorist organization.
자위권 自衛權 the right of self-defense [self-protection]
◆ 자위권의 발동 invocation of self-defense power / 자위권을 주장하다 claim the defense right 《of the nation》
자위책 自衛策 a self-protecting policy
◆ 자위책을 강구하다 think over the means of self-preservation; devise a means of self-protection
자유 自由 freedom; liberty; 〈방종〉 license

> 解說 *freedom*과 *liberty*는 흔히 같은 뜻으로 쓰이나 freedom은 구속·장애 등이 없다는 것을 뜻하는 말이며 liberty는 속박·강제로부터의 해방이나 행동 선택의 자유를 암시한다. *license*도 행동·언론·사상 등의 자유를 뜻하지만 흔히 경멸하는 투로 방종의 자유를 가리킨다.

◆ 자유의 여신상 the Statue of Liberty / 자유의 집 the Freedom House / 자유의 땅 a land of freedom/ 자유의 몸이 되다 be set free; become free; be liberated / 자유를 위해 싸우다 fight for freedom [liberty]/ 자유를 목숨보다 중히 여기다 prize freedom more than life
▶ 자유 아니면 죽음을 달라 Give me liberty or give me death.
▶ 선택은 네 자유다 The choice rests with you.
▶ 떠나든 남든 그것은 네 자유다 You are free to leave or stay. ⇌ It's up to you whether you leave or stay.
▶ 언론[종교]의 자유는 헌법으로 보장되어 있다 Freedom of speech [religion] is guaranteed by the Constitution.
▶ 자유는 자칫하면 방종으로 흐른다 Liberty often degenerates into lawlessness.
▶ 개인의 자유를 존중하는 것이 민주주의의 원칙이다 It is the principle of democracy to prize personal liberty.
▶ 나는 행동의 자유를 잃었다 I was tied hand and foot.
■—결혼 free marriage [union]; common-law marriage —경쟁 free [open] competition —경제 free economy —계약 a free contract: 자유계약 선수 [野] a free agent —교육 liberal education —국가 a free state [country] —권 civil liberties —기업 a free enterprise —당 (英) the Liberal Party; the Liberals: 자유당원 a Liberal; a member of the Liberal Party —도시 a free city —민 free people —민권 democratic rights —세계 〈공산권에 대한〉 the free world —업 a liberal profession —연애 free love —왕래 〈국경 등의〉 free cross-border travel —의지 free will [volition]; spontaneity —인 a freeman —작문 free composition —종

자유노동

목 〈체조의〉 free exercises —진영 the free world; the Western Camp —투 〈농구 등의〉 a free throw —항 a free port —화(畵) a free drawing

자유노동 自由勞動 free [casual] labor
■—자 a free [casual] laborer —조합 a free trade union : 국제 자유노동조합 연합회 International Confederation of Free Trade Union

자유로이 自由— freely; at liberty [will]; as one likes [pleases, wishes]; at one's pleasure; without restraint [reserve]
♦자유로이 사용하다 make free use of sth / 자유로이 행동하다 behave as one pleases / 자유로이 활동하다 have free play
▶그는 영어를 자유로이 말할 수 있다 He is fluent in [at] English.
▶새처럼 하늘을 자유로이 날아 봤으면 I wish I could fly in the sky as freely [easily] as a bird.

자유롭다, 자유스럽다 自由— free; liberal; unrestrained
♦자유롭게 해주다 〈풀어주다〉 make sb free; liberate / 자유로워지다 become [get] free; be set free / 자유로운 행동을 하다 take [go] one's own way

자유무역 自由貿易 free trade
■—주의자 a free trader —항 a free port

자유방임 自由放任 noninterference; 〔經〕 laissez-faire; laisser-faire
■—주의 the principle of laissez-faire; a non-interference [let-alone] policy

자유사상 自由思想 liberal ideas; free [liberal] thought
■—가 a free thinker; a liberal thinker

자유선택 自由選擇 free choice
■—과목 an optional subject; (美) an elective subject

자유의사 自由意思 free will; one's voluntariness
▶그것은 그의 자유의사에 따른 것이다 He did it of his own free will. ⇒ It was purely voluntary on his part.
▶네 자유의사에 맡긴다 You may do as you please.

자유자재 自由自在 ♦자유자재로 freely; with perfect freedom; at one's pleasure; at will
▶그는 3개 국어를 자유자재로 구사한다 He can speak three languages freely. ⇒ He has a good command of three languages.
—자유자재하다 free; unrestricted

자유재량 自由裁量 latitude; discretion; a free hand ♦아무의 자유재량에 맡기다 leave sth to the discretion (of sb); give sb a free hand (in)

자유주의 自由主義 liberalism ♦자유주의의 liberal; liberalistic
■—경제 liberalistic economy —자 a liberalist; a liberal

자유행동 自由行動 free [independent] action; a free hand
♦자유행동을 취하다 act for oneself [at one's own discretion]/ 자유행동을 할 수 있다 have a free hand / 자유행동을 허락하다 allow [give] sb a free hand

자유형 自由型 〈수영의〉 (100 meter) free-style; 〈레슬링의〉 catch-as-catch-can

자유화 自由化 liberalization; freeing (of trade)
♦중학생의 두발과 교복의 자유화 the liberalization of hair styles and the abolition of school uniforms for middle school
—자유화하다 liberalize; free

자율 自律 self-control; self-regulation; 〔哲〕 autonomy
♦학생들의 자율적 학습 independent work on the part of students / 자율적인 self-controlling; self-regulating; autonomous
—규제 self-imposed control

자율신경 自律神經 an autonomic nerve
■—계 the autonomic nervous system —실조증 autonomic imbalance

자음 子音 〔聲〕 a consonant (sound)
♦자음의 consonantal ■무성[유성]— a voiceless [voiced] consonant

자음 字音 the sound of a word; 〈한자의〉 the pronunciation of a Chinese character

자의 字義 the meaning [sense] of a word
♦자의대로 해석하다 a literal interpretation / 자의대로 해석하다 interpret a word literally / 자의를 밝히다 ascertain [define] the meaning of a word

자의 自意 one's own will [volition]
♦자의로 of one's own will [accord, volition]; voluntarily

자의 恣意 arbitrariness; self-will; wantonness
♦자의적인 arbitrary; self-willed / 자의로 arbitrarily; willfully / 자의로 행하다 act willfully; have one's own way

자의식 自意識 self-consciousness ▶그는 자의식이 강하다 He is very self-conscious.

자이로스코프 a gyroscope

자이로컴퍼스 a gyrocompass; a gyroscopic compass

자인 自認 (self-)acknowledgment; admission
—자인하다 acknowledge 《oneself beaten》; own 《oneself to be inferior》; admit
▶그는 패배를 자인했다 He owned his defeat.
▶그녀는 자기의 잘못을 자인했다 She admitted that she was wrong. ⇒ She acknowledged her mistake.

자일 a (climbing) rope; (독) a Seil
▶그들은 자일로 몸을 묶고 있었다 They were on the rope. ⇒ They were roped together.

자임 自任 pretension
—자임하다 have pretensions

자자손손 子子孫孫 one's children and grandchildren; generation after generation; posterity; descendants; offspring
♦자자손손 전하다 hand sth down to posterity / 자자손손 전해지다 go down to posterity
▶이 이야기는 자자손손 전해질 것이다 This story will be handed down from generation to generation.

자자하다 藉藉— 〈서술적〉 be widely spread; be spread abroad; be on everybody's lips
♦명성이 자자한 소설가 a renowned writer / 칭찬이 자자하다 win wide admiration

▶그 오페라는 비평가 사이에서 칭찬이 자자하다 The opera is highly reputed among art critics.
자작 子爵 a viscount ■—부인 a viscountess
자작 自作 one's own making [work]
♦자작의 of one's own making [writing, composing]/ 자작 자연(自演)하다 act in a play of one's own writing [in one's own play]
—자작하다 make sth by [for] oneself; 〈농지를〉cultivate one's own farm
■—농 an independent [owner] farmer; a landed farmer —소설 a novel of one's own pen [writing] —시 one's own poem
자작 自酌 pouring wine for oneself; self-service in drinking —자작하다 pour 《wine》 for oneself; drink liquor by self-service
자작나무 〔植〕a birch
자잘하다 《all are》 small [tiny, little, fine]
자장 磁場 〔物〕a magnetic field ⇨ 자기장
자장가 一歌 a lullaby; a nursery song; a cradlesong ♦자장가를 불러 아기를 재우다 sing a lullaby to make a baby go to sleep; lullaby a baby to sleep
자장자장 hushaby ▶자장자장 잘도 잔다 Hushaby, baby [my dear].
자재 自在 unrestrictedness
♦자재로 〈자유로이〉 freely; 〈마음대로〉 at will; 〈쉽사리〉 with ease
자재 資材 materials
■—건축— building [construction] materials
—난 shortage of materials
자재 資財 property; means
자저 自著 one's own work
자적 自適 self-satisfaction —자적하다 be self-satisfied; be (self-)complacent
♦유유자적한 생활을 하다 lead a life of ease and contentment
▶아버지께서는 퇴직 후에 유유자적한 생활을 하고 계시다 My father has been enjoying a free life since he retired.
자전 字典 a dictionary; a lexicon
자전 自傳 an autobiography ⇨ 자서전
자전 自轉 rotation
▶지구의 자전으로 밤과 낮이 생긴다 The rotation of the earth causes day and night.
—자전하다 turn [revolve, rotate] on its axis
▶지구는 지축을 중심으로 자전한다 The earth rotates on its axis.
▶지구는 서쪽에서 동쪽으로 자전한다 The earth rotates from west to east.
자전거 自轉車 a bicycle; a cycle; (口) a bike
♦자전거를 타다 ride (on) a bicycle; 《俗》 bike / 자전거로 가다 go on a bicycle; go by bicycle / 자전거에서 내리다 get off a bicycle
▶너 자전거 탈 줄 아니 ? Can you ride a bicycle?
▶그는 자전거로 통학한다 He goes to school on a [by] bicycle.
▶자전거를 타고 고갯길을 내려오는 것은 재미있다 It is fun coasting on a bicycle down a slope.
▶그는 자전거를 잘 탄다[못 탄다] He is a good [bad] bicyclist.

▶자전거 타기는 이런 노인에게는 힘드는 일이다 It is tough work for this old man to pedal a bicycle.
—경주용— a racing bicycle ■—경주[경기] cycle racing; cycling; a bicycle [bike] race —선수 a bicycle racer; a cyclist —여행 a bicycle trip; a cycling tour; biking : 자전거 여행을 하다 take a bicycle trip [cycling tour] —포〈팔거나 수리하는 가게〉a bicycle shop
자전기 磁電氣 〔物〕magnetoelectricity
자정 子正 midnight ♦자정에 at midnight; in the middle of the night / 자정까지 till late at night
자제 子弟 sons; children; young ones
자제 自制 self-control; self-restraint; 〈참음〉 continence —자제하다 control [restrain] oneself; check oneself 《from doing》
♦자제하지 못하다 lose control of oneself; lose self-control
▶의지가 약한 사람은 자제할 수 없다 A man of weak will cannot be master of himself.
■—심 self-control : 자제심을 잃다 lose one's self-control
자제 自製 one's own manufacture [making]
♦자제의 of one's own making; made by oneself
자제력 自制力 the power of self-control [self-restraint] ♦자제력을 잃다 lose one's self-control; fly off the handle
자조 自助 self-help; self-reliance
—자조하다 help oneself; rely on oneself
—정신 the spirit of self-help : 그와 같은 엄격함이 자조정신을 기르는 데 도움이 된다 Such severity serves to cultivate the spirit of self-reliance.
자조 自嘲 self-scorn —자조하다 scorn oneself
자족 自足 〈스스로 만족함〉 self-satisfaction; self-contentment; 〈자급자족〉 self-sufficiency —자족하다 be self-satisfied; be self-sufficient
■—경제 a self-sufficient economy; autarky
자존 自存 self-existence —자존하다 exist of [by] itself
자존 自尊 self-respect; self-esteem; self-importance; pride
—자존하다 respect [esteem] oneself; have self-respect; be proud
자존심 自尊心 self-respect; pride
♦자존심이 없는 사람 a prideless man / 자존심이 있는 사람 a self-respectful [self-respecting] man / 자존심을 잃다 lose one's self-respect / 자존심을 누르다 swallow one's pride
▶그녀는 자존심이 강하다 She has great self-respect.
▶남의 자존심을 상하게 해서는 안된다 You should not hurt other people's pride.
▶누구든지 자존심이 상하는 것은 싫어한다 Nobody likes to have his pride hurt.
▶자존심을 잃지 마라 Don't hold yourself cheap.
자 주 often; frequently; repeatedly; many times; over and over again
♦자주 찾(아가)다 visit often [frequently]/ 자주 해보다 try again and again
▶그는 자주 지각한다 He is often late.

자주 ▶나는 그녀에게 자주 책을 빌린다 I have borrowed books from her frequently. ▶그는 그 사전을 자주 참고한다 He refers to the dictionary frequently. ▶학창시절에는 그 박물관에 자주 갔다 I frequented the museum in my school days. ▶자주 귀찮게 해드려서 죄송합니다만, 전화 좀 또 빌려 주시겠습니까? I am sorry to bother you so often, but may I use your phone again? ▶이맘때는 불이 자주 난다 Fires are frequent at this time of (the) year.

자주 自主 independence, autonomy ■—국 an independent state —국방 self-reliance of national defense —권 autonomy : 관세 자주권 tariff [customs] autonomy / 자주권의 상실 loss of autonomy —독립 sovereign independence —성 independence: 행동에 자주성이 없다 lack independence in *one's* own behavior —정신 an independent spirit; the spirit of independence

자주 紫朱 purple ⇨ 자줏빛

자주적 自主的 independent; autonomous ♦자주적인 independent; 〈자치의〉 autonomous; 〈자유로운〉 free; active / 자주적으로 independently; voluntarily; of *one's* own (free) will / 자주적으로 방침을 정하다 decide upon a course of action on *one's* own will ▶너는 벌써 자주적으로 행동할 나이가 돼 있다 You are old enough to act on your own judgment. ■—외교 an independent policy; voluntary diplomacy

자주포 自走砲 a self-propelled gun; (총칭) self-propelled artillery

자줏빛 紫朱— purple (color); amethyst ♦짙은 자줏빛 deep [dark] purple / 자줏빛을 띤 purplish; purply / 자줏빛이 되다 purple; become [turn] purple / 자줏빛으로 물들이다 dye sth (in) purple

자중¹ 自重 prudence; caution; deliberation; self-respect; self-love —자중하다 take care of *oneself*; be cautious; be prudent ▶분주한 생활 속에서도 자중하고 또 자중해야 한다 You must take good care of yourself in spite of your busy life.

자중² 自重 empty [dead] weight; dead load

자중지란 自中之亂 a fight among themselves; (an) internal strife

자지 the penis; (卑) the cock

자지러뜨리다 shrink; frighten; give sb a chill [shudders] ♦무서워서 몸을 자지러뜨리다 shrink with fear / 위경련으로 몸을 자지러뜨리다 double up with stomach cramps

자지러지다¹ cringe; shrink; cower; crouch ♦자지러지게 놀라다 shrink with fright; be frightened out of *one's* wits / 자지러지게 비명을 지르다 give a shrill cry / 자지러지게 웃다 hold [split] *one's* sides laughing; double up with laughter

자지러지다² 〈정교하다〉 elaborate; exquisite; refined

자진 自進 willingness; voluntariness —자진하다 volunteer *oneself*; volunteer to 《do》; be ready to 《do》 ♦자진하여 of *one's* own free will; voluntarily ▶그는 자진해서 책임을 맡았다 He took the responsibility on his own will. ▶그는 자진해서 어려운 일을 하겠다고 제의했다 He volunteered to do a difficult work. ▶그들은 자진해서 입대했다 They volunteered for military service. ▶그는 자진해서 사임했다 He resigned voluntarily. ■—신고 a voluntary report : 자진 신고 기간 the voluntary reporting period

자질 measuring —사실하다 measure (with a rule)

자질 資質 〈천성〉 nature; 〈기질〉 a temperament; 〈재능〉 a gift ▶그녀에게는 시인의 자질이 전혀 없다 She has no poetical temperament. ▶그에게는 외국어에 대한 자질이 없다 He has no gift for foreign languages. ▶공무원의 자질을 향상시키지 않으면 안된다 We have to improve the quality of government employees.

자질구레하다 all in small size; evenly small; petty; trifling; slight ♦자질구레한 물건 small articles; 〈부속품〉 a gadget / 자질구레한 일 sundry jobs; trifling matters

자찬 自讚 self-praise; self-admiration —자찬하다 praise *oneself*; blow *one's* own trumpet

자책 自責 self-reproach —자책하다 reproach *oneself* ■—감 a guilty conscience; pangs [pricks] of conscience; 〈후회〉 remorse : 그는 언제나 자책감에 사로잡혀 있다 He always has [suffers from] a guilty conscience. —점(點) 〔野〕 an earned run (略 ER)

자처 自處 1 〈자결〉 suicide 2 〈체함〉 pretension —자처하다 pretend; consider [fancy] *oneself* 《as, to be》; look upon *oneself* 《as》 ♦비평가로 자처하다 have pretensions as a critic / 위인으로 자처하다 pretend to be a great man ▶그는 스스로 시인으로 자처하고 있다 He considers himself to be a poet. ⇒ He looks on himself as a poet.

자천 自薦 self-recommendation ▶응모자의 대다수는 자천이었다 The greater part of the applicants were those who recommended themselves. —자천하다 recommend [offer] *oneself* 《for》

자철광 磁鐵鑛 〔鑛〕 magnetite

자청하다 自請— volunteer (for); offer *oneself*

자체 自體 oneself; itself ♦그 자체는 in itself ▶사고 그 자체는 작은 것이었다 The accident itself was a minor one. ▶그 계획 자체는 나쁘지 않다 The plan itself is not bad. ▶그의 의견 그 자체는 설득력이 있는 것은 아니다 His opinion, as such, is not persuasive [convincing]. ▶그 자체는 좋은 것이라도 쓰는 방법에 따라 나

빠지기도 한다 A thing good in itself may become bad by its use.
▶ 그런 말을 하는 것 자체가 잘못이다 You are absolutely wrong to say such a thing.
■ —감사 self-inspection

자체 字體 the form of a character; 〈활자의〉 type ♦ 큰 자체로 인쇄된 책 a book printed in large type

자초지종 自初至終 all the details; the whole story; 〈부사적〉 from beginning to end
♦ 자초지종을 듣다 hear the whole story 《of》
▶ 그는 그것에 대해 자초지종을 알고 있다 He knows everything about it.
▶ 그는 그 사건의 자초지종을 이야기했다 He gave a detailed account of the incident.

자초하다 自招— bring upon *oneself*; incur 《blame》; court 《danger》
♦ 화를 자초하다 bring misfortune on *oneself*
▶ 내가 자초한 실수니 누구를 탓하랴 I have none to blame but myself, for the blunder was of my own making.

자축 自祝 celebration by *oneself* —**자축하다** celebrate by *oneself* ♦ 생일을 자축하다 celebrate *one's* own birthday

자축거리다 limp [hobble] 《along》; walk lame

자취 〈흔적〉 a track; a mark; a trace; a vestige; signs; 〈행방〉 *one's* whereabouts
♦ 옛 성의 자취는 흔적도 없다 remain nothing of an old castle / 자취를 감추다 disappear without a trace / 자취를 남기지 않다 leave no trace behind
▶ 그는 자취도 없이 사라졌다 He disappeared like smoke.

자취 自炊 self-cooking —**자취하다** cook for *oneself*; do *one's* own cooking; board *oneself*
▶ 형은 자취하고 있다 My brother cooks his own food [meals].
■ —생 a self-boarding student

자치 自治 self-government; autonomy
♦ 대학의 자치 university autonomy / 읍면의 자치 the self-government of towns and villages / 자치의 self-governing; autonomous / 식민지에 자치를 인정하다 allow the colonies to govern themselves
—**자치하다** govern *oneself*
■ —권 the right of self-government; autonomy: 자치권을 지키다[빼앗다] defend [deprive of] the right of self-government —체 ⇨ 자치단체 —행정 self-governing administration —회 〈학생의〉 a student council; 〈단지 등의〉 a self-government association

자치기 tipcat ♦ 자치기 나무토막 a tipcat / 자치기를 하다 play tipcat

자치단체 自治團體 a self-governing community; an autonomy ■ —지방 a local self-governing [autonomous] body [entity]; a corporate town

자치령 自治領 a self-governing dominion
■ —해외 the dominions beyond the sea

자치제 自治制 the self-governing system
■ —지방 a municipal corporation

자친 慈親 *one's* mother; a loving mother

자침 磁針 a magnetic needle

자침하다 自沈— scuttle *one's* own boat

자칫 ♦ 자칫 잘못하면 if the worst happens; if things go wrong
▶ 자칫 잘못하면 너는 해고야 If the worst comes to the worst, you will be dismissed.

자칫하면 〈까딱하면〉 (very) nearly; barely; almost; at the slightest slip [provocation]
▶ 그런 일은 자칫하면 등한히 하기 쉽다 One is apt to be negligent in such matters.
▶ 그의 차는 자칫하면 다른 차와 정면 충돌할 뻔했다 His car barely escaped a head-on collision with another car.
▶ 자칫하면 죽을 뻔했다 I came within an inch of being killed.
▶ 자칫하면 기차를 놓칠 뻔했다 I almost missed the train.

자칭 自稱 〈형용사적〉 self-styled; self-appointed
♦ 자칭 만물박사라는 괴짜 an eccentric who calls himself a walking dictionary
▶ 자칭 김박사라는 남자분이 안계신 동안에 찾아 왔었습니다 A man who calls himself Dr. Kim came to see you in your absence.
—**자칭하다** profess *oneself*; call [style] *oneself*; represent *oneself*
▶ 그는 소설가를 자칭하고 있다 He represents [describes] himself as a novelist.
■ —시인 a would-be poet —신사[학자] a self-styled gentleman [scholar]

자카르타 〈인도네시아의 수도〉 Djakarta; Jakarta

자키 〈경마의 기수〉 a jockey

자타 自他 *oneself* and others; 〔哲〕 subject and object
▶ 그가 한국이 낳은 가장 위대한 학자라는 것은 자타가 공히 인정하는 바다 It is commonly acknowledged [generally admitted] that he is one of the greatest scholars that Korea has ever produced.

자탄하다 自歎— complain of *oneself*; lament *oneself*

자태 姿態 〈모습〉 a figure; 〈자세〉 a pose

자택 自宅 *one's* house; *one's* home; a private residence
♦ 자택 전화 번호 *one's* home telephone number / 자택 주소 *one's* home address / 자택에서 at *one's* home / 자택에 있다[없다] be [be not] (at) home; be in [out] / 자택에 연금하다 place *sb* under house arrest
▶ 그는 자택에서 기다리고 있었다 He was waiting at his home.
▶ 나는 그녀를 자택으로 방문했다 I visited her at her house.
■ —연금 house arrest; domiciliary confinement —요양 home treatment [remedy]

자퇴 自退 leaving voluntarily; voluntary resignation [withdrawal]
—**자퇴하다** leave 《*one's* post》 of *one's* own accord; resign voluntarily
♦ 입후보를 자퇴하다 withdraw *one's* candidacy of *one's* free will

자투리 odd ends 《of yardage》; remnants 《of dress goods》; cuttings; pieces
▶ 그녀는 자투리로 예쁜 인형을 만들었다 She made a beautiful doll with remnants of cloth.
■ —땅 a small piece of land

자파 自派 one's own party [faction]
자판 自辦 〈스스로 처리함〉 self-disposal
―**자판하다** manage [dispose of] 《matters》 by oneself; handle 《things》 by oneself
2 〈자비로 부담〉 payment of the expenses oneself ―**자판하다** pay one's own expenses; pay oneself
자판기 自販機 a vending machine ⇨ 자동 (~판매기)
♦ 커피― a coffee vending machine
자폐증 自閉症 〔心〕 autism
♦ 자폐증에 걸린 아동 an autistic child
자포자기 自暴自棄 desperation; despair; self-abandonment ♦ **자포자기의** desperate; self-abandoned / **자포자기가 되다** become desperate; abandon oneself (to despair)
▶ 그는 시험에 떨어져서 자포자기가 되었다 Failure in examination drove him to despair.
―**자포자기하다** become desperate; give oneself up to despair; abandon oneself to despair
♦ **자포자기하여** in [out of] despair; in 《one's》 desperation
▶ 그녀는 자포자기하여 자살했다 In desperation, she killed herself.
자폭 自爆 suicidal [self-blasting, suicide] explosion ―**자폭하다** 〈배가〉 scuttle oneself; self-blast; blow up one's own ship; 〈비행기가〉 crash one's plane against the target; self-destroy
자필 自筆 one's own handwriting; an autograph; 〔法〕 a holograph ♦ **자필로** in one's own hand [handwriting]; autographically
▶ 이것은 유명한 작가의 자필 원고다 This is the original handwritten manuscript of a famous author.
▶ 그는 자필로 서명했다 He signed his autograph.
―**자필하다** write by oneself; write with one's own hand; autograph
■ ―**이력서** one's personal history in one's own handwriting : 자필 이력서를 첨부하여 신청하시오 Please apply with your curriculum vitae in your own handwriting. ―**증서** a holograph deed
자학 自虐 self-torment; self-torture; masochism
▶ 그녀는 자학성이 강하다 She is masochistic [a masochist].
―**자학하다** torment [torture] oneself; be cruel to oneself
■ ―**증** masochism ―**행위** a cruelty to oneself
자해 自害 1 〈자기 몸을 해침〉 self-wrong; self-injury ―**자해하다** do self-wrong; injure [hurt] oneself **2** 〈자살〉 suicide
자해 字解 a glossary
자행 恣行 waywardness; willfulness; self-indulgence ―**자행하다** indulge; do as one pleases; have one's own way
♦ 폭력행위를 자행하다 commit [resort to] violence / 살육을 자행하다 kill recklessly; massacre brutally
자형 字形 the form of a character; 〈활자의〉 type
자형 姉兄 one's elder sister's husband; one's brother-in-law

자혜 慈惠 charity; benevolence
자화 磁化 〔物〕 magnetization ―**자화하다** magnetize ♦ 강철봉을 자화하다 magnetize a bar of steel
자화상 自畫像 a self-portrait
▶ 아버지는 자화상을 그리고 돌아가셨다 Father had painted his own portrait before he died.
자화수분 自花受粉 〔植〕 self-pollination ⇨ 자가(~수분)
자화수정 自花受精 〔植〕 self-fertilization ⇨ 자가(~수정)
자화자찬 自畫自讚 self-praise; self-admiration ―**자회자찬하다** praise oneself; sing one's own praises; blow one's own trumpet
▶ 세상에는 자화자찬하는 사람이 많다 There are lots of people in the world who praise themselves [blow their own trumpets].
자활 自活 self-support ♦ 자활의 길을 찾다 seek a living for oneself / 자활의 길을 터주다 put sb in the way of getting 《his》 living
―**자활하다** support [maintain] oneself; earn one's (own) living
▶ 나는 어쨌든 자활할 수 있다 I can shift [provide] for myself somehow.
▶ 그는 스무살에 자활하기 시작했다 He began to support himself at twenty.
자회사 子會社 a subsidiary company; an affiliated company
자획 字畫 the strokes in a Chinese character
작 作 〈저작·작품〉 a (piece of) work; a production
♦ 피카소 작 a work by [of] Picasso; a Picasso / 그린의 최근작 Greene's latest novel
▶ 이 소설은 누구 작입니까? Who wrote this novel?
▶ 이 바이올린은 스트라디바리 작입니다 This violin is a Stradivarius.
작 爵 a degree of nobility; peerage
♦ 작의 5등급 the five degrees of peerage
■ ―**세습** hereditary nobility
―**작 作** 〈수확·경작〉 a harvest; a crop; farming
▶ 금년은 풍작[평년작]이다 We have a bumper [an average] crop this year.
■ ―**이모** double-cropping; two crops a year
작가 作家 a writer; an author; a novelist
■ ―**신진** a new writer; a rising [young] novelist **여류―** a lady [woman] writer; an authoress **인기―** a popular writer
작고하다 作故― decease; die; pass away
♦ 작고한 사람 the deceased; the dead
▶ 그들은 작고한 사람들을 위한 추도식을 가졌다 They conducted a memorial service for the dead [those who had died].
작곡 作曲 composition
▶ 이 노래는 그의 자작곡이다 He wrote both the words and music for this song.
―**작곡하다** compose; write music
♦ 노래를 작곡하다 〈가사에 곡을 붙이다〉 set music to words; write a music to words
■ ―**가** a composer
작금 昨今 these days; recently; lately; nowadays
♦ 작금의 기온 the recent [present] tempera-

ture / 작금의 사건 a recent event / 작금의 학생들 present-day students / 작금의 present; recent / 작금은 lately; nowadays; these days ▶ 환경오염은 작금에 시작된 것이 아니다 The environmental pollution is not of recent origin.

작년 昨年 last year ♦ 작년 봄 last spring / 작년 4월 19일에 on April 19 (of) last year ▶ 나는 작년에 대학을 졸업했다 I graduated from a university last year.

작다 1〈크기가〉small; little; tiny

> [解說] *small*은 다른 것과 비교하여 작다는 뜻의 객관적인 말. *little*은 작으면서 귀엽다고 하는 감정적인 뜻을 포함한 주관적인 말. *tiny*는 구어적인 말로 아주 작은 것에 대해 말하는 사람의 놀람을 암시한다.

♦ 작은 아이들 little ones; young children / 작은 집 a small [little, tiny] house / 세계에서 제일 작은 나라 the smallest country in the world / 무를 작게 썰다 cut a radish into small pieces ▶ 이 웃옷은 내게 작다 This coat is too small for me. ▶ 그 지우개는 닳아서 곧 작아졌다 The eraser became smaller soon. ▶ 그 고화에는 무수히 작은 균열이 나 있었다 There were a lot of tiny cracks in the old painting.

2 〈수·정도·소리 등이〉small; low ♦ 작은 수 a small number / 작은 소리로 말하다 talk in a low [small] voice; 〈속삭이는 소리로〉talk in whispers [a whisper] / 라디오 소리[가스불]를 작게 하다 turn down the radio [gas] ▶ 소음은 점점 작아지더니 드디어는 사라졌다 The noise became less and less until it finally died out. ▶ 좀 작은 소리로 말씀해 주십시오 Please speak in a little lower voice.

3 〈보잘것없다〉small; little; trivial; trifling; slight ♦ 작은 잘못을 저지르다 make a slight [trifling, small] error (in) ▶ 싸움은 작은 일에서 비롯되는 수가 많다 Many quarrels have a petty beginning.

4 〈도량이 좁다〉narrow-minded; small-minded ♦ 마음이 작은 인물 a small-minded man

작다리 a person of small stature; a short person; (蔑) a shorty

작달막하다 short and thick; rather small; stumpy; stocky

작달비 a pouring [driving] rain; a downpour; a drenching shower

작당 作黨 forming a gang —작당하다 form a group [gang]; band together ♦ 작당하여 (raid) in a group; in a league

작대기 1〈긴 막대기〉a stick; a rod; a staff; a pole ♦ 작대기를 휘두르다 wield a stick

2 〈표〉the mark of failure (in a test); a cross; an "X" marking a mistake

♦ 시험지에 작대기를 긋다 put a failing mark on an exam paper ■ —바늘 a big [darning] needle

작도 作圖 1〈그리기〉drawing figures —작도하다 draw a figure [chart]

2 〔數〕construction —작도하다 construct ■ —문제 〔數〕a problem for construction —법 drawing; draftsmanship

작동 作動 functioning; working —작동하다 operate; work; move ▶ 드디어 엔진이 작동했다 The engine started at last. ▶ 추기 때문에 엔진을 작동시키는 데 시간이 많이 걸렸다 It took a lot of time to get [set] the engine going because of chillness.

작두 斫— a straw [grass] cutter; a fodder-chopper ■ —질 chopping fodder; cutting

작렬 炸裂 (an) explosion —작렬하다 explode; burst ■ —탄 an explosive

작명 作名 naming; 〈세례명의〉christening —작명하다 name; christen

작문 作文〈글짓기〉composition; writing; 〈문장〉a composition; a theme ♦ 작문을 짓다 make [write] a composition; (美) write a theme / 작문을 연습하다 practice the art of composition ▶ 나는 가족에 관해 작문을 지었다 I wrote a composition [an essay] about my family. —작문하다 make a composition; write composition ■ 영— English composition: 나는 날마다 영작문 연습을 한다 I do exercises in English composition every day. ■ —시간 a composition lesson ■ —제목 a subject for composition; a theme

작물 作物 the crops ▷ 농작물 ▶ 이 지방의 주된 작물은 쌀이다 Rice is the principal crop in this area. ■ 특용— a crop for a special use; a cash crop ■ —학 crop science

작법 作法 how to write [compose, make] ■ 소설[시나리오]— how to write novels [scenarios]

작벼리 the pebbly sands on the waterside

작별 作別 good-by; leave-taking; a farewell ♦ 작별을 고하다 say good-by (to); bid *sb* farewell / 작별을 아쉬워하다 be loath to part; express regret at parting —작별하다 part (from, with); take leave; bid farewell; say good-by ♦ 친구와 작별하다 take leave of *one*'s friends ▶ 그는 친구에게 손을 흔들어 작별했다 He waved a farewell to his friend. ■ —인사 parting words; a farewell greeting: 작별 인사를 하다 wish [bid, say] *sb* good-by

작보 昨報 the yesterday's [previous] report

작부 作付 planting —작부하다 plant 《seeds》; put in a crop ■ —면적 the area under cultivation

작사 作詞 writing songs —작사하다 make a song; write words ■ —자 a songwriter

작살 a fish spear; a harpoon ♦ 작살로 고기를 찌르다 spear a fish / 고래에 작살을 쏘다 harpoon a whale

작성 作成 drawing up; framing; preparation ―**작성하다** draw up; write [make] out 《a document》; frame; prepare
♦ 유언장을 작성하다 make [draw up] one's will [testament] / 프로그램을 작성하다 prepare a program 《for》 / 리스트를 작성하다 make out [up] a list
▶ 우리는 계약서를 2통 작성했다 We drew up the contract in duplicate.
▶ 나는 연설 초안을 작성하는 데 하룻밤이 걸렸다 I spent a whole night preparing the draft of the speech.

작시 作詩 versification; verse writing ―**직시하다** compose a poem; write a verse; versify ■―**법** the art of verse making; versification; prosody

작신거리다 〈조르다〉 tease sb for sth; badger [pester] 《sb to do》

작심 作心 resolve; (a) resolution; determination ―**작심하다** resolve; be determined; make up one's mind ―**삼일** a short-lived resolution; a resolution good for only three days

작약 芍藥 〔植〕 a peony

작약하다 雀躍― 〈날뛰어 기뻐하다〉 dance for joy; leap with joy; exult over

작업 作業 work; operations; 〈군대의 사역〉 fatigue duty
♦ 시계를 조립하는 정교한 작업 a delicate operation in watchmaking / 작업중(에) while at work; while working / 작업을 개시[정지]하다 begin [suspend] operations
▶ 슬슬 작업을 시작할까 Let's start working, shall we?
▶ 그는 작업중에 다쳤다 He got hurt while at work [working].
♦ 작업중 (게시) Men working [at work].
―**작업하다** work; conduct operations
■―**구조**― rescue operations ■―**계획** a work project ―**교대** a work shift ―**능률** operation [work] efficiency ―**대** a workbench; a worktable ―**량** amount of work done ―**명령** a job order ―**모** 〔軍〕 a fatigue cap ―**반** a work [working] party; 〔軍〕 a fatigue party ―**복** overalls; working clothes; a jumper ―**비**(費) operation [working] expenses ―**시간** working hours ―**시간표** a time card ―**실** a workroom ―**원** a worker ―**일** a workday; a working day ―**장** 〈공작소〉 a workshop; 〈공사장〉 a job site ―**전표** a job slip ―**조건** working conditions ―**화**(靴) work shoes ―**환경** working environment

작열 灼熱 incandescence; red [torrid] heat ―**작열하다** become red-hot
♦ 작열하는 태양 the scorching [burning] sun

작용 作用 (an) action; an operation; process; 〈기능〉 a function; 〈영향〉 an effect
♦ 산(酸)의 작용 the action of an acid / 심장의 작용 the function of the heart / 바위에 대한 파도의 작용 the action of water on rocks / 식물에 대한 빛의 작용 the effects of light on plants / 작용과 반작용 action and reaction / 부작용 side [ill] effect / 열의 작용으로 by [through] the agency of heat / 인력의 작용으로 under the influence of gravity

―**작용하다** operate 《on》; act 《on》; work 《on》; 〈불리하게〉 affect
▶ 그 독은 신경계에 작용하여 10분쯤이면 죽게 됩니다 The poison operates on [acts on, works on, affects] the nervous system, bringing death in about ten minutes.
■―**동화**― the process of assimilation **상호**―(an) interaction **심리**― a psychological [mental] process **정신**― operation [action] of the mind **호흡**― the operation of breathing **화학**― chemical action ■―**범위** the working realm

작위 作爲 artificiality; 〔法〕 commission; feasance
♦ 작위적인 deliberate; intentional / 작위적으로 행동하다 behave in an artificial way
▶ 이 작품은 작위적인 흔적이 역력하다 This piece is too artificial.
■―**동사** 〔文法〕 a factive verb ―**범** 〔法〕 a crime of commission

작위 爵位 a peerage; a title ▶ 그에게 작위가 수여되었다 He was graced with a title.

작은곰자리 〔天〕 the Little [Lesser] Bear; Ursa Minor

작은북 a small [snare] drum; a side drum

작은아버지 one's father's younger brother

작은어머니 the wife of one's father's younger brother

작은집 1 〈따로 사는 아들·동생의 집〉 one's son's [younger brother's] house; a branch [collateral] family
2 〈첩의 집〉 the house of one's concubine

작인 作人 a tenant (farmer); 《美》 a sharecropper; 〈총칭〉 tenantry

작자 作者 1 〈위인〉 a fellow; a guy
▶ 그 작자 갔니? Has the guy gone away?
2 〈저자자〉 an author; a writer
♦ 작자 불명의 시 an anonymous poem / 작자 불명의 of unknown authorship; anonymous
▶ 이 책의 작자는 누구냐? Who wrote this book? ⇒ Who is this book by?
▶ 그건 작자 불명이야 It is anonymous. ⇌ The author is unknown.
3 〈물건을 살 사람〉 a buyer; a needy person; a purchaser
♦ 작자가 없다 find no buyer; have no demand / 작자가 나서다 find a buyer
4 〈소작인〉 a tenant (farmer)

작작 〈적당히〉 not too much; properly; moderately
▶ 술 좀 작작 마셔라 Don't drink too much.
▶ 바보같은 소리 좀 작작 해라 Don't be silly.
▶ 농담도 작작 해라 You're always joking. ⇌ 《美》 No kidding!
▶ 담배 좀 작작 피워라 Don't smoke too much.
▶ 고집 좀 작작 부려라 No more of your selfishness.

작작하다 綽綽― ample; more than enough; 〈태도가〉 free and easy; leisurely
♦ 여유 작작하다 be free and easy; be calm and composed; 〈금전상〉 have enough and to spare

작전 作戰 military operations; maneuvers; 〈전체적인〉 strategy; 〈개개 전투의〉 tactics
♦ 작전상 중요한 of strategic importance / 작

전상 strategically; tactically; operationally / 작전을 짜다[세우다] elaborate a plan of operations; map out a plan (of operations); plan *one's* strategy
▶우리는 작전은 예정대로 진행됐다 The operations went ahead as scheduled.
▶우리는 명백한 작전 실수로 졌다 We lost apparently because of a tactical error.
▶그렇다면 작전을 변경하지 않으면 안된다 Then we might have to change our tactics.
▶그렇게 하는 것은 작전상 좋지 않다 It is strategically unwise to do so.
—작전하다 launch maneuvers; carry out military operations
■공동— concerted [combined] operations 공세[수세]— offensive [defensive] operations 양동— a feint operation ■—개시일 the D-day —계획 a plan of operations : 작전계획을 세우다 map out a plan of operations —기지(基地) a base of operations —명령 an operation order —목표 the objective of operations —지 a field of operations —회의 a strategy meeting; a council of war

작정 作定 〈결정〉 a decision; 〈결심〉 determination; resolution; 〈의향〉 an intention; a plan; a design; an idea; a thought; a notion; 〈목적〉 a purpose; a goal
▶나는 다음 주에 그들을 방문할 작정이다 I think I will visit them next week.
▶나는 도착하는대로 곧 너에게 편지를 쓸 작정이다 I will write you as soon as I arrive.
▶나는 그녀를 화나게 할 작정은 아니었는데 화나게 했다 I didn't mean to get her angry but I did.
▶나는 당신을 다치게 할 작정은 아니었다 I did not mean to hurt you.
▶그가 어떤 작정으로 그런 짓을 했는지 모르겠다 I don't know what made him do it [why he did such a thing].
▶나는 내일 돌아올 작정이다 I intend [I am planning] to come back tomorrow.
—작정하다 decide; determine; plan; intend to (do); resolve to (do)
▶그는 직장을 그만두기로 작정했다 He made up his mind to resign from his job.
▶그는 어른이 되면 선생님이 되기로 작정했다 He is determined to be a teacher when he grows up.

작차다 fill (up); become full (of); be filled up (with)

작태 作態 a conduct; a practice
♦점잔빼는 작태 airs and graces / 과거의 못된 작태 the evil practices of the past

작파하다 作破— cease; cancel; put an end (to); give up (trying); leave off; abandon

작폐하다 作弊— cause *sb* annoyance; make trouble [nuisance]; embarrass

작품 作品 a work; a piece; a product; a production; [樂] an opus (*pl.* opera, ~s)
♦피카소 작품 a work (of) Picasso / 초등학교 아동의 작품 works by elementary school children / 하이든 작품 76번을 연주하다 play Haydn's opus 76
▶「무기여 잘 있거라」는 헤밍웨이의 작품이다 "A Farewell to Arms" is Hemingway's work [is (a novel) by Hemingway].
▶그는 스타인벡의 작품은 거의 다 읽었다 He has read almost all of Steinbeck's works.
■문학— literary works 예술— works of art ■—집 the works: 김동인 작품집 the works [writings] of Kim Dong-in

작풍 作風 a (literary) style; 〈음악·미술의〉 idiom
♦드가의 작품 the idiom of Degas / 독자적인 작품이 있다 have *one's* own (unique) style
▶그는 플로베르의 작품을 모방하고 있다 He models his style on [after] Flaubert's. ⇒ He imitates Flaubert's style.

작황 作況 a harvest; a crop; a yield
♦쌀의 작황이 좋다[나쁘다] have a good [bad] rice crop
▶금년의 쌀 작황은 평년작일 것 같다 We expect an average rice crop this year.
■—보고 a crop report

잔 盞 a cup; a glass; 〈찻잔〉 a teacup; 〈술잔〉 a wineglass
♦맥주 한 잔 a glass of beer / 차 두 잔 two cups of tea / 잔을 비우다 empty [drain] *one's* wine glass / 잔을 돌리다 pass the glass round / 잔을 주고 받다 exchange glasses / 커피를 잔에 따르다 fill a cup with coffee / 잔을 가득 채우다 fill the cup to the brim

잔가시 small [fine] bones (of fish)

잔가지 a twig; 〈꽃·잎이 달린〉 a sprig; a spray 《of cherry blossom》 ♦잔가지를 치다 lop off twigs

잔걸음 frequent walking within a short distance; walking around the house [room]
♦잔걸음치다 walk with short steps

잔고 殘高 〔簿〕 the balance ⇨ 잔액

잔고기 small fish; 〈치어〉 fry

잔교 棧橋 a pier; a jetty; 〈선창〉 a wharf; a quay ♦상륙용 잔교 a landing pier

잔글씨 fine letters; small characters; 〈인쇄된〉 fine print; small type ♦잔글씨로 쓰다 write small characters

잔금 殘金 〈남은 돈〉 the balance; (the) surplus (money); (the) money left (over)
♦부채의 잔금 the balance of the loan; arrears / 잔금을 치르다 pay the balance [remainder]
▶잔금은 이것 뿐이다 This is all the money left.

잔기 殘期 〈남은 기간〉 the remaining period [time]; the unexpired period

잔기침 a hack; a hacking [slight] cough —잔기침하다 hack; have a hacking cough

잔꾀 (petty) tricks; wiles; artifice
♦비열한 잔꾀 a dirty trick / 잔꾀를 부리다 play cheap tricks (on); resort to petty tricks
▶잔꾀를 부리지 마라 None of your cheap tricks!

잔다르크 〈프랑스의 애국 소녀〉 Jeanne d'Arc; Joan of Arc (1412-31)

잔당 殘黨 〈남은 무리〉 the remnants of a defeated party ♦반란군의 잔당 the remnants of the rebel army

잔돈 (small) change; petty cash; small money;

잔돈푼 loose coins [cash, change]; broken money
♦ 잔돈 지갑 a change purse / 잔돈이 없다 have no small change / 잔돈으로 지불하다 pay 《a bill》 with small money [in small change] / 만원권을 잔돈으로 바꾸다 break a 10,000-won note into small money
▶ 나는 만원권을 지불하고 잔돈 2,500원을 받았다 I paid with 10,000-won note and got 2,500-won change.

잔돈푼 petty cash; a small sum of money; odd money; a mere pittance
♦ 잔돈푼깨나 벌다 save a petty sum
▶ 나는 가지고 있던 잔돈푼을 다 썼다 I spent all the petty cash I had.

잔등이 the back ⇨ 등

잔디 〔植〕 a lawn; grass; turf; sod
♦ 잔디 깎는 기계 a lawn mower; 〈수동식〉 a hand mower; 〈동력식〉 a power [motor] mower / 정원에 잔디를 심다 turf a garden; lay the garden with turf / 잔디를 깎다 cut [mow] the grass
—**구장** a lawn soccer field; a lawn ground

잔디밭 a grassplot; a lawn; a turf; a patch of grass ♦ 잔디밭에 물을 뿌리다 sprinkle over the lawn
▶ 잔디밭에 들어가지 마시오 《게시》 Keep off the grass.

잔뜩 1 〈많이〉 plentifully; in plenty; copiously; abundantly; amply; 〈충분히〉 full; to the full; to capacity
♦ 잔뜩 먹다 have [eat] one's fill / 잔뜩 마시다 drink one's fill / 할 일이 잔뜩 있다 have a lot of work to do; have one's hand full 《with work》 / 옷을 잔뜩 껴입다 be heavily clothed
▶ 그는 빚이 잔뜩 있다 He is deeply [heavily] in debt.
▶ 그는 책을 잔뜩 가지고 있다 He has got a lot of books.
2 〈몹시〉 intensely; heavily; extremely; exceedingly; 〈단단히〉 hard; steadily; firmly
♦ 술에 잔뜩 취하다 be heavily [dead] drunk; 《美俗》 be quite boozy / 잔뜩 골이 나다 become [get] hot with anger [rage] / 잔뜩 의심을 품다 cast grave doubt 《on》 / 아무의 얼굴을 잔뜩 노려보다 stare sb in the face; look straight at sb

잔루 殘壘 1 〔野〕 〈베이스에 남은 주자〉 runners left [stranded] on base
—**잔루하다** be left on base; strand
2 〈남아 있는 보루〉 a remaining fort

잔류 殘留 remaining; staying behind
—**잔류하다** remain; stay behind
■—**감각** 〔心〕 aftersensation —**물**(物) a residue; remnants; dregs —**부대** remaining forces —**자기** residual magnetism

잔말 useless talk ⇨ 잔소리

잔무 殘務 remaining [unsettled] business [work] ♦ 잔무를 정리하다[끝내다] settle [clear up, wind up] the remaining business [work]
▶ 잔무를 끝내기 위해 시간외 근무를 하였다 I worked overtime to wind up the remaining business.

잔물결 ripples; rippling waves; wavelets
♦ 잔물결이 일다 ripple / 잔물결을 일으키다 ripple [ruffle] 《the surface of the water》
▶ 호수의 수면에는 잔물결이 일고 있었다 The surface of the lake was covered with ripples.
▶ 미풍이 못 수면에 잔물결을 일으켰다 A faint breeze rippled the surface of the pond.

잔뼈 〈약한 뼈〉 a small [fine] bones
▶ 그는 이 회사에서 잔뼈가 굵었다 He grew up to be a respectable man at this company.

잔병 —病 a minor [slight] sickness [illness]; a minor indisposition; a minor ailment
♦ 잔병이 잦다 be frequently sick; be habitually ailing; be sickly
■—**꾸러기** a sickly [weak] person; a person disposed to illness —**치레** getting sick frequently

잔상 殘像 〔心〕 an afterimage

잔서 殘暑 〈늦더위〉 the lingering summer heat; the heat of late [lingering] summer
▶ 금년은 잔서가 대단하다 The lingering summer heat this year is very severe.

잔설 殘雪 〈안 녹고 있는 눈〉 the remaining [unmelted] snow; lingering snow
▶ 계곡에는 아직도 잔설이 남아 있었다 There was still some unmelted snow in the valley.

잔셈 〈자질구레한 셈〉 a small [trifling] account
♦ 잔셈을 치루다 settle small accounts

잔소리 1 〈나무람〉 (a) scolding
♦ 잔소리를 듣다 be scolded; get [receive] a scolding / 잔소리를 퍼붓다 give sb a good scolding [talking-to]; give sb a long lecture
—**잔소리하다** scold; chide; rebuke; read sb a lecture; lecture sb; take [call, bring] sb to task 《for》
▶ 그 학생에게는 잔소리해도 소용없었다 All my scolding fell flat on the student.
2 〈잔말〉 small [useless] talk; idle talk; empty prattle; tittle-tattle
♦ 잔소리가 많은 사람 a prattler; a chatterbox / 잔소리가 많은 prattling; talkative; chattering; gossipy
—**잔소리하다** talk idle; say useless things; tittle-tattle
▶ 그는 계속 잔소리하고 있었다 He was constantly chattering.
3 〈쫑알거림〉 nagging; faultfinding; carping; 〈불평〉 a complaint; grumbling
♦ 잔소리가 심한 여자 a nagging woman; a shrew; a termagant
—**잔소리하다** 〈쫑알거리다〉 nag 《at sb》; cavil 《at, about》; find fault 《with》; 〈불평하다〉 complain 《about, at, that》; grumble 《at, over》
▶ 잔소리하지 말고 시키는대로 해 Stop complaining. Do as I tell you.
■—**꾼** a chatterbox; a nag(ger); a carper; a faultfinder

잔손 fine [elaborate, detailed] hand work; a little touch ♦ 잔손이 가는[드는] 일 laborious [troublesome] handwork / 잔손질하다 work in detail [with much care]; give [add] the finishing touches; use elaborate processes / 잔손이 많이 들다[가다] take [require] much manual effort; take a lot of trouble [elaborate processes]

잔술 盞— liquor in a glass; a glassful of liquor; liquor by the cup [glass] ■—집 a pub [tavern] that sells liquor by the glass

잔심부름 sundry errands; odd jobs; miscellaneous services

잔악 殘惡 cruelty; atrocity —**잔악하다** cruel; atrocious; brutal; savage; inhuman; outrageous ◆잔악하게 cruelly; atrociously / 잔악하게 다루다 treat sb cruelly

잔액 殘額 the balance; the remainder
◆잔액을 지불하다 〈잔금을〉 pay the remainder of the money; 〈잔금을〉 pay the balance
▶예금 잔액은 50만원이다 The balance of the deposit is five hundred thousand won.
■—조회(照會) reference to [inquiry about] the balance of sb's bank account

잔업 殘業 overtime work; extra work
—**잔업하다** work overtime; work extra hours
■—수당 overtime pay

잔여 殘餘 the remainder; the remnant; the residue; the rest ◆잔여의 residual; residuary
■—액 the balance; the remainder —재산 remaining assets; a residuary estate; residual property

잔인 殘忍 atrocity; (a) brutality; (a) cruelty; savageness; cold-bloodedness
—**잔인하다** brutal; cruel; truculent; hardhearted; coldhearted; ruthless; heartless; inhuman; cold-blooded
◆잔인한 짓을 하다 do a cruel thing; commit cruelties [atrocities]/ 잔인하게 다루다 treat sb harshly [with brutality]
■—무도 abominable cruelty; inhumanity —성 one's brutal nature

잔일 petty jobs; chores; sundry jobs

잔입 a dry mouth in the morning before eating or drinking anything

잔잔하다 still; quiet; calm; tranquil; placid; peaceful; serene; smooth
◆잔잔한 물결 rippling waves / 잔잔한 바다 a calm [smooth, serene] sea / 잔잔한 호수 a placid lake / 잔잔히 quietly; calmly; softly / 잔잔한 목소리로 말하다 speak in a gentle [quiet] voice
▶잔잔한 물이 깊다 (속담) Still waters run deep.
▶바람이 잔잔해졌다 The wind died down.
▶오늘은 바다가 잔잔하다 The sea is calm today.

잔재 殘滓 leavings; leftovers; remnants; 〈흔적〉 a vestige; 〈액체의〉 dregs; 〔化〕 a residuum 《pl. -dua》; residue
◆봉건주의의 잔재 vestiges of feudalism / 권위주의의 잔재 vestiges of authoritarianism

잔재미 a bit of pleasure [amusement]
◆잔재미를 보다 have a nice little time (of it); 〈성공〉 make a hit in a small way; 〈이익〉 turn a tidy profit; 〈낚시질 등에서〉 fish up a nice bit of catch [take]

잔재주 —才— a petty artifice; a trick; a device ◆잔재주를 부리다 resort to petty tricks; employ petty shifts ▶잔재주를 부리지 마라 None of your petty tricks!

잔적 殘敵 〈적의 패잔병〉 stragglers; enemy remnants; the remaining [surviving] enemy
■—소탕군 a mopper-up 《pl. moppers-up》
—소탕전 a mopping-up operation

잔존 殘存 〈남음〉 survival
—**잔존하다** survive; be extant; be still existent [in existence, alive]; remain; subsist
◆잔존하는 surviving; extant
■—감각 〔心〕 a residual feeling —생물[종(種)] a relict —자 a survivor

잔주름 fine [little] wrinkles [crinkles, lines]; 〈눈가의〉 crow's-feet
◆잔주름이 진 얼굴 finely wrinkled face
▶그 여자는 눈가에 잔주름이 있다 She has crow's-feet.
■—살 fine wrinkles [lines]

잔지바르 〈탄자니아 공화국의 일부〉 Zanzibar
◆잔지바르의 Zanzibari
■—사람 a Zanzibari

잔챙이 the smallest one

잔치 a banquet; a feast; a party
◆돌잔치 a birthday party for one-year old baby / 생일 잔치 a birthday party / 혼인 잔치 a wedding feast [party, banquet]/ 환갑 잔치 a banquet on one's sixtieth birthday / 잔치를 베풀다 give [hold] a feast [banquet]/ 잔치에 손님을 초대하다 invite guests to a feast
■잔칫집 a banqueting house

잔털 fine [delicate] hairs; 〈솜털〉 down

잔품 殘品 remnants; the stock left; the dead stock; the remaining stock(s); unsold goods; (美俗) plugs ■—정리[매출] a clearance sale; a remnant [rummage] sale

잔학 殘虐 (an) atrocity; (a) brutality; (a) cruelty; inhumanity; outrage; (a) barbarity; cold-bloodedness
—**잔학하다** cruel; atrocious; outrageous; heartless; brutal; savage; barbarous; inhuman; cold-blooded
◆잔학한 행위 a brutality; an atrocity
▶전쟁은 잔학하다 War is cruel.

잔해 殘骸 the remains 《of》; 〈사체〉 a corpse; a carcass; 〈폐허〉 ruins; debris; 〈배·비행기 등의〉 the wreck [wreckage] 《of》
◆비행기의 잔해 the wreck [wreckage] of an airplane; the remains of a wrecked plane

잔허리 the lower [slender] part of the back [waist]; the small of the back

잔혹 殘酷 〈잔인·포악〉 (a) brutality; (an) atrocity; (a) cruelty; mercilessness; ruthlessness
—**잔혹하다** atrocious; brutal; brutish; cruel; ruthless; merciless; hard; heartless; coldhearted; inhuman; harsh
◆잔혹한 사람 a cruel [brutal] person / 잔혹한 형벌 a cruel punishment / 잔혹하게 cruelly; brutally; heartlessly / 잔혹하게도 be cruel enough to do

잘 1 〈훌륭히〉 aptly; well; excellently; nicely; finely; superbly; skillfully; cleverly
◆잘 처신하는 사람 a fine behaver / 잘 해내다 manage sth successfully; make a go of it; make a good [clean, fine] job of it / 잘 맞히다 make a (good) hit / 말을 잘 하다 talk well
▶잘했다 Well done! ⇌ Splendid! ⇌ That's

잘가닥

fine! ⇌ Capital!
▶그는 글을 잘 쓴다 He is a good [talented] writer.

2 〈자세히〉 closely; exactly; thoroughly; well; for certain; carefully; with care
◆잘 알다 know well / 잘 모르다 do not know well [for certain]; be uncertain 《of, about, as to》/ 잘 듣다 listen carefully to / 잘 생각하다 think 《a matter》 over; give much thought to 《a matter》/ 잘 보다 look at *sth* carefully
▶나는 그의 행동에 관해서는 잘 모른다 I am quite uncertain as to his movements.
▶내 말을 잘 기억해둬 Remember well what I say.

3 〈좋게〉 favorably; well; good; nice
◆아무에 대해 잘 말하다 speak well [favorably] of *sb*; say good things about *sb* /아무에게 잘 하다 be good [kind, nice] to *sb*; do *sb* a good turn /아무에게 잘 보이다 win the good opinion of *sb*; find favor in the eyes of *sb*

4 〈만족히〉 satisfactorily; thoroughly; fully; well; luckily; smoothly; fortunately; favorably; successfully
◆잘 먹다 eat well / 잘 자다 sleep well; have a good sleep / 잘 못 자다 sleep badly [poorly]; be wakeful / 잘 지내다[살다] live well; be well off
▶잘 먹었습니다 I have enjoyed my dinner very much.

5 〈탈없이〉 safely; in safety; well; all right
◆잘 있다[지내다] get along well [all right]; live in good health
▶잘 가[있어] 〈작별 인사〉 Good-by(e)! ⇌ So long!

6 〈멋지게〉 beautifully; smartly
◆잘 생기다 handsome / 잘 차려입다 be in *one's* (Sunday) best; wear [put on] fine clothes

7 〈많이〉 much; a lot; 〈보통〉 usually; generally; 〈자주〉 (very) often; frequently; 〈걸핏하면〉 readily; easily
◆잘 믿다 be too credulous / 잘 웃다 laugh readily / 잘 성내다 be apt to get angry; get angry readily / 잘 …하곤 했다 used to 《do》; would 《do》/ 남하고 잘 싸우다 be apt to pick quarrels with others / 학교를 잘 빠지다 be often absent from school

8 〈적절히〉 well; properly; suitably
▶그 건을 잘 부탁합니다 I leave it to your best judgment. ⇌ I trust it to your discretion [good offices].

9 〈몸에 맞는〉 well; nicely
◆잘 어울리다 match well; harmonize well 《with each other》/ 〈옷 등이〉 몸에 잘 맞다 [맞지 않다] fit *sb* well [ill]
▶이 장갑은 나에게 잘 맞는다 These gloves fit me well.
▶그 드레스는 너에게 잘 어울린다 That dress becomes [fits] you well. ⇌ You look nice in that dress.

10 〈마침〉 well; timely; at a good time
▶자네 마침 잘 왔네 You've come at just the right moment.

잘가닥 with a click [clink]; with a snap [crack]
◆사진을 잘가닥 찍다 snap picture / 문을 잘가닥 잠그다 lock the door with a click
—**잘가닥하다[거리다]** click; give a click [snap]; snap [click] away; 〈총의 방아쇠를〉 snick; 〈카메라를〉 snap off (pictures)

잘가당 with a clang [clank, clink]
—**잘가당하다** clank; clang; clink

잘게 finely; fine; closely; to [in] pieces; 〈좀스럽게〉 narrow-mindedly; pettily
◆글씨를 잘게 쓰다 write small [fine] characters, write microscopically / 잘게 자르다 cut *sth* to pieces [fragments]/〈고기 등을〉 잘게 썰다 mince 《meat》

잘그랑 with a clang [clink]; clinking

잘나다 **1** ⇨ 잘생기다
2 〈당당하다〉 stately; imposing; commanding
▶그 사람 잘났는 데 He is quite stately.
3 〈뛰어나다〉 distinguished; great; eminent; extraordinary; remarkable; excellent; superior ◆잘난 사람 a great man; an extraordinary character
4 〈반어적〉 trashy; useless; worthless; trifling; unworthy
▶잘난 소리 하지 마 Don't talk big.
▶그 잘난 생각을 왜 믿어? How come you believe such a trashy idea?

잘난체하다 assume an air of importance; assume [put on] airs; give *oneself* airs; look big; think *oneself* somebody; think highly of *oneself* ◆잘난 체하는 사람 a self-important fellow; a snob; a braggart

잘다 **1** 〈작다·미세하다〉 small; fine; tiny; minute ◆잔 글씨 a small character
2 〈성질이 좀스럽다〉 small; petty; narrow-minded; small-minded; meticulous; 《be》 of small caliber
▶저 교장은 사람이 잘다 That schoolmaster is a small-minded man.
3 〈정밀하다〉 strict; close; particular; 〈금전에〉 stingy; closefisted; miserly
4 〈소액의〉 small ◆잔 돈 small change

잘되다 **1** 〈출세하다〉 make a success in life [the world]; make *one's* way [get on] in life; 〈승진하다〉 be promoted [advanced] 《to》
▶그는 잘되었다 He has risen to a high positions.
2 〈일이〉 go well [right]; go on smoothly; 〈결과가〉 come [turn] out all right; come off well [fine]; succeed 《in》; be [prove] successful; work out (nicely)
◆잘되면 if things go well / 잘되지 않다 go wrong [amiss, awry]; be unsuccessful; come to no good
▶만사가 잘되어 가고 있다 Everything is going well.
3 〈장사·사업이〉 thrive; prosper; be prosperous; flourish
◆장사가 잘되다 be doing a good [prosperous, thriving] business / 장사가 잘되지 않다 be dull [heavy, quiet, stagnant]; be in a bad way
▶그가 손댄 사업은 뭐든지 잘되었다 Every business he did prospered with him.

4 〈작품·솜씨가〉 be done [made] well; be of fine make; be of excellent workmanship
▶ 수프가 잘되었다 The soup is done well.
▶ 이 장식은 잘되었다 This decoration is superbly done.
5 〈농사가〉 have a good [fine] crop; 〈과실이〉 be fruitful; 〈성장이〉 be growing [doing] well
▶ 올해는 사과가 잘되었다 This is a fruitful [bumper] year for apples.
▶ 쌀은 온난한 기후에서 잘된다 Rice grows well in a warm climate.
6 〈철저·완전하다〉 be thorough; be perfect [complete]
▶ 이 공장은 오락 시설이 잘되어 있다 This factory has complete recreation facilities.

잘되면 제탓, 못되면 조상탓 《속담》 One puts credit [merit] upon oneself when things go well and blames one's ancestors when they do not.

잘라내다 cut off; cut out [away]; lop (off); cleave; whittle down; tear off
▶ 그는 그 나무의 죽은 가지를 잘라내었다 He lopped the dead branches off the tree.
▶ 의사는 그녀의 편도선을 잘라내었다 The doctor cut out her tonsils.

잘라말하다 say [state] flatly [positively, definitely]; affirm; assert; make an assertion
▶ 그는 그런 세속적 명예는 안중에 없다고 잘라 말한다 He states flatly that such worldly fame is beyond his scope.

잘라먹다 1 〈동강을 내어 먹다〉 cut [tear] and eat; take a slice and eat it; bite [eat] off
2 ⇨ 떼먹다

잘랑거리다 clink; jingle; tinkle
▶ 방울을 잘랑거리다 jingle [tinkle] a bell

잘랑잘랑 jingling; tinkling; clinking

잘래잘래 shaking *one's* head 《from side to side to show denial》
▶ 그 어린 소녀는 거절의 표시로 머리를 잘래잘래 흔들었다 The little girl shook her head from side to side to show denial.

잘록하다 constricted [compressed] 《in the middle》; narrow; slender
♦ 잘록한 허리 a narrow [slender] waist; a wasp waist / 허리가 잘록한 여자 a wasp-waisted woman / 호리병박의 잘록한 곳 the narrow part of a bottle gourd
▶ 이 병은 중앙이 잘록하다 This bottle is narrow in the middle.

잘리다 1 〈끊어지다〉 be cut (off); be chopped; be severed; 〈나무가〉 be felled [hewed]; be cut down ♦ 둘로 잘리다 be cut in [into] two / 목이 잘리다 be decapitated [beheaded]
2 〈해고되다〉 be dismissed [discharged]; 《美口》 be fired [decapitated]
3 〈떼어 먹히다〉 be bilked; become irrecoverable
♦ 잘린 빚 a bad [an irrecoverable] debt

잘못¹ 〈오류〉 a mistake; an error; 〈과실〉 a fault; a misstep; a slip; a lapse; a wrong; 〈죄과〉 a blame
♦ 잘못을 저지르다 commit [make] an error [a fault, a mistake]; err; 《美口》 bobble / 잘못을 인정하다 admit [acknowledge] *one's* fault [error, mistake] / 잘못을 깨닫다 find out *one's* mistake; be convinced of *one's* error / 잘못을 고치다 correct a fault; remedy [amend] a fault; 〈틀린 데를〉 correct an error / 자신의 잘못을 고치다 mend *oneself* [*one's* ways] / 남의 잘못을 들추어내다 find out another's faults / 아무의 잘못을 덮어주다[호도하다] gloss over *sb's* fault
▶ 그것은 네 잘못이다 It is your fault. ⇌ You are to blame for it.
▶ 그녀는 자신의 잘못을 시인하여 사과했다 She admitted her mistake [fault] and apologized for it.
▶ 잘못이 있으면 고치시오 Correct errors, if any.
▶ 누구에게나 잘못은 있는 법이다 To err is human. ⇌ Every man is liable to err. ⇌ No mortal is infallible.

잘못² 《부사적》 **1** 〈틀리게〉 in error; by mistake; by accident; through *one's* fault; mistakenly; wrong
♦ 잘못 듣다 hear 《it, him》 wrong [amiss]; mishear / 잘못 알다 confuse 《A with B》 / 잘못 보다 〈오인하다〉 mistake [take] 《A for B》; 〈빠뜨리다〉 miss 《seeing》; fail to see / 사람을 잘못 보다 〈다른 사람으로〉 take one person for another; 〈잘못 평가하다〉 misjudge; make a wrong estimation [estimate] 《of》 / 잘못 쓰다 〈글자를〉 write incorrectly; miswrite; make a mistake in writing; 〈철자를〉 misspell / 잘못 계산하다 miscalculate / 잘못 발음하다 mispronounce / 기차를 잘못 타다 take a wrong train
▶ 네가 잘못 생각한 거야 You are wrong in your judgment [conjecture].
▶ 내가 너를 잘못 보았어 I have made a mistake in my estimate of you. ⇌ I was deceived in you.
▶ 잘못 거셨습니다 〈전화에서〉 You're calling a wrong number. ⇌ Wrong number.
2 〈서툴게〉 poorly; awkwardly; clumsily; unskillfully

잘못되다 go wrong [amiss]; 〈실패하다〉 fail; be botched; be bungled
♦ 잘못된 생각 〈오해〉 a misunderstanding; 〈오판〉 a misjudgment; a wrong idea; a false notion / 잘못된 정책 the wrong policy
▶ 뭔가 틀림없이 잘못되었다 Something must have been wrong [amiss].
▶ 너는 사고방식이 잘못되어 있다 You are wrongheaded.

잘못하다 err; mistake; make [commit] a mistake [an error] (in); be mistaken (in); blunder; do wrong; 〈실패하다〉 fail (in)
♦ 잘못하여 by [through] mistake; in error; by accident / 잘못하면 if luck turns against *one*; if things go wrong; if *one* is not careful
▶ 제가 잘못했습니다 I am sorry for what I have done.
▶ 그는 운전을 잘못하여 사고를 냈다 He had an accident because of his careless driving.

잘박 with a splash [splosh] ♦ 얕은 물을 잘박 밟다 step in a watered place with a splosh / 잘박 소리를 내다 make [cut] a splosh

잘생기다 good-looking; beautiful; handsome;

pretty; comely; fair
♦ 잘생긴 남자 a handsome man / 잘생긴 여자 a beautiful [good-looking] woman / 얼굴이 잘생긴 소녀 a girl with a comely face

잘잘 1 〈끓는 모양〉 boilingly; bubblingly; piping; simmeringly
♦ 잘잘 끓다 boil; simmer; seethe; stew; bubble
▶ 그는 열 때문에 몸이 잘잘 끓는다 His body is very hot [has a high temperature] with fever.
2 〈분주한 모습〉 bustlingly; busily ♦ 잘잘 쏘다니다 bustle [hustle] about; dash around
3 〈끄는 모양〉 draggingly
▶ 그녀의 긴 치맛자락이 잘잘 끌리고 있다 Her long skirt is trailing (along) behind her.
4 〈흔드는 모양〉 shakingly ♦ 우유병을 잘잘 흔들다 shake a bottle of milk
5 〈윤기 도는 모양〉 glossily; 〈얼굴 등에〉 sleekly; slickly; 〈기름기가〉 oilily; greasily
♦ 윤이 잘잘 도는 머리 sleek [slick] hair
6 ⇨ 절래절래

잘잘못 right and [or] wrong ♦ 잘잘못을 가리다 distinguish between right and wrong; tell right from wrong / 잘잘못을 따지다 discriminate the rights and wrongs (of)

잘츠부르크 〈오스트리아의 도시〉 Salzburg

잘하다 1 〈능숙하게 하다〉 be skillful (in); be clever (at); be expert (in, at); be good [great] (at); be a good hand (at)
♦ 스케이팅을 잘하다 be at home on ice skates / 계산을 잘하다 be good at figures / 프랑스어를 잘하다 be proficient [strong] in [be good at] French / 남보다 잘하다 do sth better than the others
▶ 그녀는 요리를 잘한다 She is a good cook.
▶ 나는 수학을 잘한다 I am strong in mathematics.
2 〈올바르게 하다〉 do a right thing; do right
▶ 네가 그렇게 한 것은 참 잘한 일이었다 It was quite right of you to do so.
3 〈훌륭히 하다〉 do well; make a success of
▶ 야아 잘한다 Bravo! ⇌ Wonderful! ⇌ Good for you!
▶ 정말 잘했다 Capital! ⇌ Well done!
4 〈만족하게 하다〉 satisfy; gratify; please
♦ 부모에게 잘하다 be dutiful toward one's parents / 아무에게 잘하다 be good [kind, nice] to sb
▶ 그는 우리에게 잘해준다 He is very nice to us.
5 〈자주 하다〉 used to; do often; do a lot
6 〈기타〉 ♦ 잘해야 at best; at the very best [most]; at (the) most
▶ 이 사업은 잘해야 본전이다 This business will make even at best.

잠 1 〈수면〉 (a) sleep; 〈숙면〉 (a) slumber; 〈졸기〉 a nap; a doze
♦ 잠투정 children's grouching habits before or after sleep / 잠버릇 one's sleep habit / 깊은 잠 a deep [sound] sleep / 얕은 잠 a light sleep / 잠이 오다 become [feel] sleepy [drowsy] / 잠이 부족하다 do not get [have] enough sleep; want sleep / 잠을 깨우다 arouse [awake] sb from his sleep [slumber]; wake (up) / 잠을 설치다 cannot sleep well; have a bad sleep / 잠을 못이루다 cannot get to sleep; lie [be kept] awake; be wakeful
▶ 그녀를 생각하느라 어젯밤 잠을 이루지 못했다 Last night I have lain awake thinking of her.
▶ 잠을 자야 꿈을 꾸지 No sleep, no dream.
2 〈누에의〉 the dormant state 《of the silkworm》
3 ⇨ 잠자다 2

잠결 ♦ 잠결에 while asleep; in one's sleep / 잠결에 듣다 hear while one is half asleep
▶ 나는 잠결에 누가 고함치는 소리를 들었다 When I was half asleep, I heard somebody's shouting.

잠귀 one's hearing while asleep
♦ 예민한 잠귀 sensitive ears in a sleep / 잠귀가 밝은 사람 a light sleeper / 잠귀가 밝다 be easily awakened; be a light sleeper / 잠귀가 어둡다 be a heavy sleeper

잠그다¹ 1 〈문을〉 lock (up); fasten 《with a lock [latch]》
♦ 자동차 문을 밖에서 잠그다 lock the car door from the outside of the car / 문을 잠그다 lock [fasten] a door
2 〈수도 등을〉 turn off
♦ 수도를 잠그다 turn off the tap [water] / 가스를 잠그다 turn off the gas; turn the gas out

잠그다² 1 〈액체 속에〉 sink; soak; immerse; submerge; put under water
♦ 옷을 물에 잠그다 soak clothes in water
2 〈투자하다〉 invest in; lay [put] out 《one's money》 in; sink in
▶ 나는 그 사업에 내 돈을 잠그어 둘 생각은 없다 I don't want to invest my money in that business.

잠기다¹ 〈문·자물쇠가〉 be locked; lock; be fastened
▶ 이 문은 자동으로 잠긴다 This door locks automatically. ⇌ This is a self-locking door.
▶ 그 문은 잠겨 있었다 The door was locked.
▶ 그 집은 안으로 잠기어 있었다 The house was locked from the inside.

잠기다² 1 〈물 속에〉 soak (in); be immersed (in); be soaked (in); be steeped (in); 〈수물하다〉 be submerged (in); be flooded 《with water》
▶ 우리 집은 마루[지붕]까지 물에 잠겼다 My house was flooded floor-deep [roof-deep].
2 〈몰두하다〉 be absorbed [engrossed, immersed] in; be intent [bent] on; give oneself to; be given to; devote oneself to
♦ 생각에 잠기다 be lost [sunk, buried] in thought; be absorbed in deep meditation / 슬픔에 잠기다 give [abandon] oneself to grief; be buried in grief / 공상에 잠기다 indulge in reverie
▶ 마을이 고요 속에 잠겨 있었다 Silence brooded over the village.
3 〈목이 쉬다〉 get [become, grow] hoarse [husky, harsh]; hoarsen; have a frog in the throat
▶ 그는 너무 소리를 질러서 목이 잠겼다 He shrieked himself hoarse.
▶ 나는 목이 잠겨서 말을 할 수가 없다 I am so

hoarse that I can't speak.
4 〈돈이 부동산에〉 be locked up; be tied up
▶ 내 돈은 토지에 잠겨 있다 My money is locked up in land.

잠깐 just a minute; (just) a moment; a while; a short time; briefly
◆ 잠깐 동안 for a moment; for an instant / 잠깐 사이에 in a minute [moment]; in no time / 잠깐 생각해 보고 나서 after a moment's thought
▶ 잠깐 쉬자 Let's rest a bit [moment].
▶ 잠깐 기다리십시오 Wait a bit [moment], please. ⇌ Just a moment, please.
▶ 잠깐 시간 좀 내주시겠습니까? Could you spare me a few moments?

잠깨다 **1** 〈잠에서 깨다〉 wake (up, from); awake (from, *one's* sleep)
▶ 잠깨서 커피 마셔라 Wake up and drink the coffee.
▶ 나는 자명종 소리에 잠깼다 I woke to the alarm.
2 〈깨닫다〉 wake (to, up); awake 《to》
◆ 실제 상황에 잠깨다 wake to the true situation

잠꼬대 talking in *one's* sleep; somniloquy; 〈사리에 닿지 않는 말〉 silly talk; nonsense
―**잠꼬대하다** talk in *one's* sleep; 〈사리에 닿지 않는 말을 하다〉 talk nonsense [rubbish]
◆ 잠꼬대하는 버릇 somniloquence / 잠꼬대하는 사람 a somniloquist
▶ 그는 가끔 잠꼬대를 한다 He often talks in his sleep.
▶ 잠꼬대 같은 소리 하지 마라 Don't talk nonsense.

잠꾸러기 a late riser; a lie-abed; a heavy sleeper

잠두 蠶豆 〔植〕 a broad bean; a horsebean; a fava bean

잠들다 〈잠자다〉 fall [drop] asleep; drop [go] off to sleep; sink [fall] into a slumber [sleep]
◆ 깊이 잠들다 fall fast asleep; sink into a sound sleep; sleep like a log / 쉽게 잠들다 get to sleep easily / 울면서[흐느끼며] 잠들다 cry [sob] *oneself* to sleep
▶ 그는 눕자마자 잠들었다 As soon as he lay down, he fell asleep.
▶ 어젯밤엔 좀처럼 잠들 수가 없었다 It took a lot of time for me to get to sleep last night.
2 〈사망하다〉 die; pass away
◆ 영원히 잠들다 go to *one's* long sleep; sleep the final [eternal] sleep
▶ 영혼이여, 고이 잠드소서 May the soul rest in peace!

잠란 蠶卵 a silkworm egg [seed]
―**지**(紙) a silkworm-egg card

잠망경 潛望鏡 a periscope

잠바 a jumper ⇨ 점퍼

잠방이 knee breeches

잠복 潛伏 **1** 〈숨기〉 concealment; hiding; ambush; latency
―**잠복하다** conceal *oneself*; be hidden; lie concealed [hidden]; hide (out); hide [lie] in concealment; lurk 《in, under》
2 〈병의〉 〔醫〕 incubation
―**잠복하다** be [lie] dormant; be latent
■―**근 무** (be on the) ambush (sentry) duty ―**장소** a hiding [lurking] place; a shelter; 〈사냥꾼의〉 a blind ―**초소** an ambush sentry box

잠 복 기 潛伏期 〔醫・動〕 the incubation [latent] period ◆ 긴[짧은] 잠복기 a long [short] incubation period

잠복성 潛伏性 latency ■―**보균자** a latent [subclinical] carrier ―**비타민 결핍증** a subclinical vitamin deficiency ―**질환** a latent disease

잠비아 Zambia; 〈공식 명칭〉 the Republic of Zambia ◆ 잠비아의 Zambian
■―**사람** a Zambian

잠사 蠶絲 silk yarn [thread]
■―**업** the sericultural industry

잠세력 潛勢力 latent force [power, strength]; potentiality

잠수 潛水 diving ―**잠수하다** dive; go under water; make a dive; submerge
◆ 깊이 잠수하다 dive deep; make a deep dive / 오랫동안 잠수하다 make a long dive; remain long under water
■―**공작원** 〔軍〕 a frogman ―**기구** a diving apparatus ―**모**(帽) a diving helmet ―**모함**(母艦) a submarine tender [carrier, depot ship] ―**병** caisson disease; the bends ―**복** a diving dress [suit] ―**부** a diver; a frogman ―**어업** diving fisheries

잠수함 潛水艦 a submarine; (俗) a sub; an underwater boat
◆ 잠수함으로 습격하다 submarine
■ **원자력―** an atomic(-powered) submarine; a nuclear-powered submarine; an N-submarine; an N-sub ■―**승무원** a submariner ―**전**(戰) submarine warfare ―**탐지기** a sonar; (英) an asdic

잠시 暫時 for a (little) while; for a moment; for some time; for a (period of) time; for a spell
◆ 잠시 후에 after a (little) while; after a (short) time; a little later (on) / 잠시 후면 in a short time; in a little while
▶ 잠시만 기다려 주세요 Wait a moment [minute], please.
▶ 잠시도 그것을 잊지 마라 Do not forget it even for a moment.
▶ 잠시 후에 그가 올 것이다 He will come in a few minutes [before long].

잠식 蠶食 encroachment; an inroad; invasion
―**잠식하다** encroach 《on, upon》; make an inroad 《into, on, upon》; gain on [upon]
◆ …의 영토를 잠식하다 encroach on [upon] the territory of… / 유럽 시장을 잠식하다 make inroads into European markets
▶ 수입품이 국내 시장을 잠식했다 Imports took over the domestic market.

잠실 蠶室 〈누에 치는 방〉 a silkworm raising [rearing] room

잠아 蠶蛾 〈누에나방〉 a silkworm moth

잠언 箴言 〈훈계나 경계가 되는 말〉 an aphorism; maxim; a proverb; 〔聖〕 〈구약 성서의 잠언편〉 The Book of Proverbs (略 Prov.)

♦솔로몬의 잠언 the Proverbs of Solomon
잠업 蠶業 sericulture ⇨ 양잠(~업)
■—시험장 a sericultural laboratory
잠열 潛熱 〔物〕 latent heat;〈인체의〉 dormant temperature
잠옷 nightclothes; a nightgown;〈여자·어린이용〉 a nightdress;〈남자용〉 pajamas
♦잠옷 바람으로 in [wearing] one's nightclothes [nightdress]
▶나는 잠옷 바람으로 뒤뜰을 산책했다 I took a walk in the backyard, wearing my nightgown.
잠입 潛入〔軍〕 infiltration;〔天〕〈하나의 천체가 다른 천체에 가리워지는 것〉 immersion
—잠입하다 filter [sneak, steal] into 《a place》; infiltrate into; slip in [into]; smuggle oneself into 《a country》
♦방에 잠입하다 steal [sneak] into a room
■—자 an infiltrator
잠자다 1 ⇨ 자다 1
2〈솜 등 부푼 것이〉 lie down; be smoothed [pressed] down
▶이불 솜이 잠잤다 The wadding in bedquilt is pressed down.
3〈상품이〉 remain unsold 《on the shelf》;〈자본 등이〉 lie idle
♦잠자고 있는 자본 dead capital
잠자리[1] 〔昆〕 a dragonfly
잠자리[2] 〈침소〉 a bed; a bedstead
♦잠자리에서 하는 이야기 a talk in bed / 잠자리가 편하다 be comfortable to sleep in / 잠자리를 보다 prepare a bed; make a bed / 잠자리를 같이 하다 sleep with; sleep in the same bed; share the same bed 《with》 / 잠자리에 들다 go to bed / 잠자리에서 일어나다 get out of bed; get up (from the bed)
▶그 아이는 잠자리에 들자 곧 잠이 들었다 The child fell asleep as soon as he touched the pillow.
▶나는 잠자리가 아주 뒤숭숭했다 I slept very badly. ⇌ I had a very bad night.
잠자코 in silence; silently; dumbly; without a word; without comment;〈무단히〉 without leave [permission]; without notice;〈순순히〉 without objection; without question
♦잠자코 있다 keep silence [silent]; remain silent; keep mum / 잠자코 앉아 있다 sit mum / 잠자코 서 있다 stand mum [tongue-tied] / 잠자코 명령에 따르다 obey an order without asking questions / 잠자코 모욕을 당하다 take an insult lying down
▶잠자코 있어 Be quiet! ⇌ Shut up! ⇌ Hold your tongue! ⇌ Hush (your mouth)! ⇌ Silence!
▶그 일은 그 사람한테는 잠자코 계세요 Please don't say anything about it to him.
▶이런 처사를 당하고야 잠자코 있을 수 없지 I cannot put up with such unjust treatment.
▶왜 여태 잠자코 있었지? Why haven't you told it to me? ⇌ Why have you kept it from me?
▶잠자코 보고만 있어 Just look and be silent.
잠잠하다 潛潛— silent; (deathly) quiet; still; hushed ♦잠잠해지다 〈조용해지다〉 become quiet; [still]; be hushed; calm [quiet] down;〈평온해지다〉 subside; become tranquil; quiet [die] down
▶오늘은 바다가 잠잠하다 The sea is calm today.
▶바람이 잠잠해졌다 The wind has died down.
잠재 潛在 potentiality; latency; dormancy
♦잠재적(인) potential; latent; dormant
—잠재하다 be latent; be [lie] dormant; lurk; lie behind
■—구매력 latent purchasing power —능력 latent faculties; potential capacities; potentiality —력 potential energy, latent force : 잠재력을 발달시키다 develop the powers latent within one —수요 a latent [potential] demand —실업 latent [potential, invisible] unemployment —실업자 the potentially jobless —위협 a latent threat —전력(戰力) war potentials —주권(主權) residual sovereignty —통화 latent currency
잠재우다 make sb sleep; put sb to sleep ⇨ 재우다
잠재의식 潛在意識〔心〕 subconsciousness
♦잠재의식의 subconscious
잠적 潛跡 concealment —잠적하다 conceal oneself [one's whereabouts]; lurk 《in, under》; cover (up) one's traces [tracks]
잠정 暫定 provisionality
♦잠정적인 provisional; temporary / 잠정적으로 provisionally; temporarily; tentatively; for the time being
▶그 건은 잠정적으로 김선생님께 맡기자 Let's leave the matter to Mr. Kim for the time being.
■—안 a tentative plan —예산 a provisional budget —조약 a provisional treaty —조치 a temporary step; a stopgap [tentative] measure —협정 a provisional agreement
잠종 蠶種〈누에씨〉 silkworm species
—개량 silkworm species improvement
잠투정 a baby's habit of being fretful [peevishness] before or after sleeping
—잠투정하다 get peevish [fret] before or after sleeping
▶이 아이는 잘 때마다 잠투정한다 This baby is always fighting sleep.
잠함 潛函 a caisson ■—공법 the caisson method —기초 caisson disease —병 the caisson disease; aeroembolism; air bends; (口) the chokes; the bends
잠항 潛航 a submarine [submersed] voyage; underwater navigation; an underwater cruise
♦72시간의 잠항기록 a submersion record of 72 hours
—잠항하다 cruise [navigate, go] underwater;〈물속으로〉 submerge
■—시간 underwater time —정 a submarine
잠행 潛行 traveling in disguise
—잠행하다 travel incognito [in disguise]
■—성 질병 an insidious disease
잡가 雜歌 a vulgar song; a folk song
잡감 雜感 miscellaneous impressions [feelings]
잡거 雜居 mixed residence [living]

—잡거하다 live [reside, dwell] together
■ —구금 associate confinement —지(地) a mixed-residence quarter
잡것 雜— 1 〈물건〉 miscellaneous things [junk]; odds and ends; 〈불순물〉 impurities
2 〈사람〉 a low [loose] fellow
잡계정 雜計定 〔簿〕 sundry [miscellaneous] accounts
잡곡 雜穀 minor cereals [grains]; miscellaneous cereals; 〈美〉 grain; 〈英〉 corn
—밥 boiled rice and cereals —상 a dealer in cereals [grains]; a corn merchant
잡귀 雜鬼 minor demons [fiends]; sundry evil spirits
잡균 雜菌 various [sundry] germs
잡기 雜技 various arts and crafts; miscellaneous games; 〈노름〉 gambling
잡기 雜記 miscellaneous notes; miscellanea
■ —장 a notebook; an exercise book
잡년 雜— a loose woman; a lady [woman] of easy virtue; a slut
잡념 雜念 idle [stray] thoughts; earthly [worldly] thoughts
♦ 잡념을 버리다 put all other thoughts out of *one's* mind; banish [dismiss] worldly thoughts from *one's* mind; get rid of worldly thoughts
▶ 너는 잡념을 버리고 공부에 열중해야 한다 You must put all other thoughts out of your mind and devote yourself to studying.
잡놈 雜— a loose [dissolute] man; a fast liver; (口) a no-good
잡다 1 〈손으로〉 seize; hold; catch; take (up); take hold of
▶ 멱살을 잡다 seize *sb* by the neck [lapels of his coat] / 덜미[소매]를 잡다 catch *sb* by the neck [sleeve]/공을 잡다 catch a ball / 소매를 잡으려 하다 catch at *sb's* sleeve
▶ 그는 소녀의 손을 잡았다 He took the girl by the hand.
▶ 꽉 잡고 놓지 마라 Don't release [let go] your hold [grip] on it.
2 〈포획하다〉 catch; get; take
♦ 고기를 잡으러 가다 go fishing
▶ 고양이는 쥐를 잡는다 Cats catch mice.
3 〈체포하다〉 arrest; round up; 〈사로잡다〉 capture; catch; get
♦ 도둑을 잡다 arrest [catch, get, capture] a thief
4 〈차를〉 pick up; take; get
♦ 택시를 잡다 pick up [take] a taxi
5 〈권력·기회 등을〉 take; seize; assume; wield
♦ 정권을 잡다 take power; come [get] into power / 정권을 잡고 있다 be in power / 기회를 잡다 catch [take] an opportunity [occasion]; seize upon a chance
6 〈증거를〉 seize; hold; secure; grasp
▶ 경찰측에서는 증거를 잡고 있다 The police are in possession of evidence.
7 〈담보로 맡다〉 secure ♦ 담보로 잡다 receive *sth* as security / 담보를 잡다 take security / 담보를 잡고 돈을 빌려주다 lend money on security [mortgage] / 저당 잡고 있다 hold *sth* in mortgage

8 〈떠나지 못하게하다〉 keep; prevent *sb* from going [leaving]
9 〈결정하다〉 decide; settle; fix; 〈선정하다〉 choose; 〈예약하다〉 reserve; book
♦ 날을 잡다 fix the date 《for》 / 방향을 잡다 take *one's* course / 호텔에 방을 잡다 reserve a room at a hotel
10 〈확보하다〉 get; obtain; secure ♦ 일자리를 잡다 get a job; find a position; obtain employment / 한 밑천 잡다 amass a sizable fortune
11 〈결점을 잡다〉 ♦ 흠을 잡다 find the faults 《of》; find fault 《with》; pick a hole [flaw] 《in》 / 약점을 잡다 get [find] *sb's* sore spot; find [get] the length of *sb's* foot
12 〈물가 등을〉 check; stop; curb; halt
♦ 인플레이션을 잡다 check [curb] an inflation
13 〈파악하다〉 grasp; comprehend; seize
♦ 문제의 핵심을 잡다 seize the essence of the matter
14 〈차지하다〉 occupy; take (up)
♦ 장소를 많이 잡다 occupy [take up] much room
▶ 그 일에는 넉넉하게 시간을 잡아야 한다 You must take your time over the work.
15 〈요량·어림잡다〉 put 《the expenses》 at; value 《at》; rate 《at》; calculate 《at》
♦ 대충 잡다 make a rough estimate; estimate roughly / 지나치게 비싸게[싸게] 잡다 overestimate [underestimate] / 많이 잡아도 at the (very) outside; at most / 최소로 잡아서 at (the very) least
▶ 많이 잡아도 10명 이상은 아니었다 There weren't more than ten at the outside.
16 〈가축을〉 butcher; slaughter; kill (off)
♦ 돼지를 잡다 butcher a hog
17 〈모함하다〉 plot against *sb*; slander; ensnare; entrap
▶ 사람 잡을 소리 그만해 Stop slandering me!
18 〈불을〉 끄다 put out 《a fire》; extinguish; bring [get] 《a fire》 under control
♦ 물[모래]로 불을 잡다 quench a fire with water [sand]
19 〈마음을〉 take [get] a grip on *oneself*; steady 《*one's* mind》; settle down; bring [get] 《*one's* passion》 under control; collect *oneself*
♦ 들뜬 마음을 잡다 pull *oneself* together; recover [regain] *one's* composure / 마음을 잡고 공부하다 settle down to *one's* studies
20 〈(굽은 것을) 바로잡다〉 straighten out [up]; make straight; unbend; 〔印〕 〈틀린 것을〉 correct ♦ 굽은 바늘을 바로잡다 make a bent needle straight
▶ 틀린 것이 있으면 잡아라 Correct errors, if any.
21 〈주름을〉 fold [arrange] 《in pleats》
♦ 주름을 잡다 pleat; crease; pucker; tuck / 치마에 주름을 잡다 crease *one's* skirt
잡다하다 雜多— various; miscellaneous; sundry; of various kinds
♦ 잡다한 사람들 all sorts of people; all sorts and conditions of men
잡담 雜談 idle [small, random] talk; a chat; a gossip; chitchat; tittle-tattle

▶ 나는 그와 잡담을 좀 나눴다 I exchanged some small talk with him.
—**잡담하다** gossip; chat; have a chat 《with》
▶ 그들은 잡담하고 있다 They were enjoying a chat.

잡도리 precaution; a strict control; supervision —**잡도리하다** exercise [keep] a strict control 《over》; supervise

잡동사니 rubbish; trash; odds and ends; (口) junk; sundries

잡되다 雜— 〈천하다〉 vulgar; low; mean; indecent; 〈난잡하다〉 obscene; dissolute; licentious, immoral
♦ 잡된 생각 wanton [lewd] thoughts / 잡된 소리를 하다 say obscene things; tell a dirty [filthy] joke

잡목 雜木 miscellaneous wood; small trees and shrubs; 〈하찮은〉 scrubs; scrub trees
■—림 a thicket of small trees or shrubs
—솎아내기 cleaning cutting

잡무 雜務 miscellaneous business [tasks]
♦ 가정의 잡무 household [domestic] chores
▶ 교사는 수업 외에 잡무가 너무 많다 Teachers have too many things to do besides teaching.
▶ 저는 요즈음은 여러 잡무에 시달리고 있습니다 I am occupied with trivial routine duties these days.

잡문 雜文 a literary miscellany

잡물 雜物 1 〈잡것〉 miscellaneous things [articles] 2 〈불순물〉 impurities; foreign matter

잡배 雜輩 vulgar people; a low fellow

잡범 雜犯 all kinds of crime except political crime

잡병 雜病 various diseases; 〈가벼운〉 a slight [mild] illness

잡보 雜報 general [miscellaneous] news
■—기자 a miscellanist —란 the general news column

잡부금 雜賦金 miscellaneous fees [charges]; sundry fees

잡비 雜費 sundry [miscellaneous, petty] expenses; general expenses; 〈임시비〉 incidental expenses; 〈용돈〉 petty cash
▶ 잡비가 꽤 많은 금액이 되었다 The miscellaneous expenses mounted up to quite a sum.
■—계정 a petty expenses account

잡상인 雜商人 miscellaneous traders; small tradesmen; peddlers

잡색 雜色 〈빛깔〉 various colors; multicolor; 〈사람〉 all kinds of people ♦ 잡색의 multicolored; parti-colored; motley

잡서 雜書 miscellaneous books; 〈여러 내용의〉 books on various subjects

잡석 雜石 broken [crushed] stones; rubble; stones of all sizes

잡설 雜說 〈갖가지 의견〉 all kinds [sorts] of opinions [views]; various theories; 〈잡소리〉 idle talk; nonsense

잡세 雜稅 miscellaneous taxes

잡소득 雜所得 odd incomes

잡소리 雜— 1 〈잡담〉 silly talk; idle talk; nonsense; small talk 2 〈잡된 소리〉 an obscene [a dirty] talk

잡손질 雜— 〈손장난〉 idle fingering; 〈손질〉 an unnecessary touch; meddling —**잡손질하다** play with one's fingers; meddle; tamper [mess] with; give an unnecessary touch

잡수다 eat ⇨ 먹다 ♦ 점심은 무엇을 잡수시겠습니까? What would you like (to have) for lunch?

잡수입 雜收入 〈개인의〉 miscellaneous [odd] income; 〈공공 단체의〉 miscellaneous [sundry] revenue

잡스럽다 雜— vulgar ⇨ 잡되다

잡식 雜食 a mixed diet (of various kinds of meat and vegetable)
—**잡식히다** live on a mixed diet
■—성 〔動〕 polyphagia; omnivority: 잡식성 동물 an omnivore; a polyphagous animal / 잡식성의 omnivorous; polyphagous / 곰은 잡식성이다 The bear is omnivorous [an omnivorous animal].

잡아가다 take; take [drag] off 《a suspect to a police station》

잡아내다 1 〈밖으로〉 take sth out; 〈쫓아내다〉 turn sb out of doors
2 〈잘못을〉 pick at; point out; indicate; 〔印〕 correct
♦ 원고에서 오자(誤字)를 잡아내다 find spelling mistakes in the manuscript

잡아당기다 pull; draw; 〈길게〉 stretch; 〈갑자기〉 jerk; 〈세게〉 drag [tug] 《at》
♦ 밧줄을 잡아당기다 pull at a rope; haul at [upon] a rope / 커튼을 잡아당겨 열다 draw the curtains open
▶ 불이 나면 이 지렛대를 잡아당기시오 Pull this lever in case of fire.
▶ 화살을 쏘려고 그는 활을 잡아당겼다 He drew his bow to shoot an arrow.

잡아들이다 take [haul, bring] sb in; place under arrest; arrest ♦ 범인을 잡아들이다 bring a criminal in / 경찰서에 잡아들이다 take [haul] sb to a police station

잡아떼다 1 〈물건을〉 tear off [up]; peel off [from]; draw [pull, set] apart
♦ 벽지를 잡아떼다 peel off the wallpaper
2 〈부인하다〉 deny flatly; pretend not to know; feign [affect] ignorance
▶ 그는 그런 말을 한 적이 없다고 잡아뗐다 He flatly denied having said so.

잡아매다 〈한데〉 tie up [together]; bind up; lash together; 〈고정된 곳에〉 bind [tie, fasten, lash] 《to》
♦ 구두끈을 잡아매다 fasten shoestrings [shoelaces] / 기를 깃대에 잡아매다 fasten a flag to a pole

잡아먹다 1 〈사람이 동물을〉 butcher [slaughter] and eat; 〈동물이 동물을〉 devour; prey on
♦ 서로 잡아먹다 devour one another; feed [prey] on each other
▶ 사자가 얼룩말을 잡아먹었다 A lion ate [devoured] the zebra.
2 〈괴롭히다〉 trouble; be hard on; torment; torture
▶ 그는 늘 나를 못 잡아먹어 야단이다 He treats me very harshly all the time.
3 〈요하다〉 take; take up; 〈차지하다〉 occupy
♦ 시간을 잡아먹다 take 《so much》 time / 많은

장소를 잡아먹다 occupy [take up] much room [space]
▶ 이 일은 시간과 비용을 많이 잡아먹는다 This job takes much time and money.
잡어 雜魚 small fish of various kinds; mixed small fish
잡역 雜役 odd jobs; miscellaneous work
━━**부**(夫) an odd man; a handyman; an odd jobber ━━**부**(婦) a maid of all work; 〈날품팔이〉〈英〉a charwoman
잡음 雜音 1〈소음〉noise;〔醫〕〈청진할 때의〉souffle; murmur
♦ 심장의 잡음 a heart souffle
2〈라디오・텔레비전 등의〉noise; jarring and grating; 〈혼선〉jamming
▶ 라디오에 잡음이 들린다 The radio picks up noise. ⇒ 〈고장 등으로〉 The radio program is hampered [disturbed] by noises. ⇒ 〈공중장애로〉 The radio is affected by atmospherics.
3〈부당한 간섭〉 interference; (an) irresponsible criticism (of an outsider)
▶ 남이 얘기하는데 괜히 잡음 넣지 마라 Don't interfere in our conversation.
■ ━계 a noise meter ━발생기 a noise oscillator ━제한기 a noise limiter
잡인 雜人 an outsider
잡일 雜— miscellaneous work [matters]; odd jobs; 〈일상의〉routine work; chores
잡제 雜題 miscellaneous subjects
잡종 雜種 〈튀기〉 a mixed-blood; a crossbreed; a hybrid; 〈접목의〉 a graft hybrid
♦ 잡종의 crossbred; half-bred; hybrid;〈잡다한〉miscellaneous / 잡종의 개 a mongrel / 잡종을 만들다 cross two breeds; cross one breed with another; interbreed; produce a hybrid
▶ 노새는 말과 당나귀 사이의 잡종이다 The mule is a cross between a horse and a donkey.
━━강세〔生〕heterosis; hybrid vigor ━불임성 hybrid sterility
잡주 雜株 〔證〕miscellaneous [minor] stocks
잡지 雜誌 〈일반적인〉 a magazine; 〈전문의〉 a journal; 〈정기적인〉 a periodical
♦ 월 2회 발행하는 잡지 a semimonthly / 격주로 발행되는 잡지 a fortnightly / 연 4회 발행하는 잡지 a quarterly (magazine) / 잡지를 구독하다 subscribe for a magazine; take (in) a magazine / 잡지를 편집[발행]하다 edit [publish] a magazine / 잡지에 기고하다 write for a magazine; contribute (an article) to a magazine
▶ 어떤 잡지를 구독하고 계십니까? What kind of periodicals do you subscribe to?
■ ━대중 a popular magazine 문예━ a literary magazine 여성━ a woman's magazine 여행━ a travel magazine 월간━ a monthly; a monthly magazine [journal] 의학━ a medical journal 종합━ a general magazine (of quality) 주간━ a weekly; a weekly magazine 패션━ a fashion magazine 평론━ a review (magazine) ■ ━기사 an article in a magazine; a magazine article ━기자[편집자] a magazine reporter [editor]; a journalist ━꽂이 a magazine rack

잡지출 雜支出 miscellaneous [sundry, incidental] expenditures [expenses]
잡채 雜菜 a mixed dish of vegetables and sliced meat
잡초 雜草 weeds
♦ 뜰의 잡초를 뽑다 weed a garden; pluck up [out] weeds from the garden
▶ 뜰에 잡초가 무성하다 Weeds have overrun the garden. ⇒ The garden is overgrown [overrun, covered] with weeds.
▶ 그들은 잡초처럼 끈질기다 They are (as) tough as weeds.
잡치다 spoil; ruin; damage; botch; make a mess of; mess up; upset
♦ 기분을 잡치다 hurt *sb's* feeling; offend *sb*
▶ 큰 눈이 와서 작물을 잡쳐 놓았다 A heavy snowfall damaged the crops badly.
▶ 비 때문에 모처럼의 소풍을 잡쳤다 The rain has spoiled [ruined] the much-awaited picnic.
▶ 나는 시험을 잡쳐버렸다 I've failed [〈美口〉flunked] (in) the examination.
▶ 조그마한 오산이 그의 장래를 잡쳐버렸다 A small miscalculation ruined [wrecked] his future.
잡칙 雜則 miscellaneous [minor] rules and regulations
잡탕 雜湯 1〈음식〉a hotchpotch; a hodgepodge; an olio 《pl. ~s》; a hotpot dish by stewing a mixture of meat, fish and vegetables
2〈뒤범벅〉a medley; (utter) confusion; chaos;〈프〉a mélange; a jumble
♦ 잡탕의 medley; mixed / 잡탕이 되다 be confused; be mixed up; be jumbled together
잡학 雜學 knowledge on a wide variety of subjects [matters]
잡혼 雜婚 mixed marriage; intermarriage; 〈난혼(亂婚)〉 (sexual) promiscuity
━━잡혼하다 intermarry
━━번식〔植〕panmixia ━제(制) promiscuity; (a system of) communal sexual relationships
잡화 雜貨 general merchandise [goods]; miscellaneous [sundry] goods; sundries; 〈식료품〉groceries
▶ 그들은 모든 잡화를 두루 취급하고 있다 They trade widely in all kinds of (sundry) goods.
■ ━점 a general store; convenience store; 〈식료품 중심의〉 a grocer's (shop); a grocery (store)
잡화상 雜貨商 〈장사〉 grocery business; 〈상인〉 a general dealer; a grocer
잡히다[1] 1 〈손에〉 be held; be seized; be caught; be taken (up); be grabbed
▶ 이 물고기는 미끈미끈해서 잘 잡히지 않는다 This fish is too slippery to hold.
2 〈붙잡히다〉 be caught; be captured
▶ 어제 이상한 물고기가 여기서 잡혔다 A strange fish was caught here yesterday.
3 〈검거되다〉 be arrested; be caught
♦ 소매치기[사기]로 잡히다 be arrested for pickpocketing [fraud]
▶ 그 도둑은 경찰에 잡혔다 The thief was caught [arrested] by the police.

4 〈사로잡히다〉 be captured; be seized; get taken in; 〈포로로〉 be taken prisoner
▶ 그는 적에게 잡혔다 He was captured [was made prisoner] by the enemy.
5 〈불 등이〉 go out; be held [put, brought] under control; be extinguished
▶ 불이 저절로 잡혔다 The fire burnt itself out.
6 〈결정되다〉 be decided [fixed]; 〈마음이〉 settle [calm] down; be under conrtol
♦ 마음이 잡히지 않다 feel uneasy [restless]; be ill at ease / 일이 손에 잡히지 않다 be in no mood for work
▶ 날짜가 잡히는 대로 알려 드리겠습니다 I'll tell you when the date is fixed.
▶ 결혼식은 5월 10일로 잡혔다 The wedding was fixed [arranged] for May 10.
7 〈반듯하게〉 be straightened out; 〈주름이〉 get [be] pleated [creased]; get [be] wrinkled
♦ 주름이 잘 잡힌 바지 well creased trousers
▶ 이 옷감은 주름이 잘 잡힌다[잡히지 않는다] This material [cloth] wrinkles easily [is wrinkle-free].
▶ 그녀의 눈가에 주름이 잡히기 시작했다 She has begun to develop wrinkles around her eyes.
8 〈증거가〉 be secured; be confirmed
▶ 여러 가지 증거가 잡혔다 Various proofs have been secured.
9 〈조도(賭租)가〉 get estimated at; be rated
10 〈기타〉 ♦균형이 잡혀 있다 be kept in an equilibrium; be equally balanced / 모양이 잡히다 take a form; take shape / 질서가 잡혀 있지 않다 be in disorder; be out of order / 한 밑천이 잡히다 make [build up] a fortune
▶ 연못에 살얼음이 잡혔다 A thin coat [layer] of ice formed on the pond.
▶ 나무에 꽃망울이 잡혀가고 있다 The trees are budding [coming into bud].

잡히다² **1** 〈담보로〉 give (as security); pawn; mortgage
♦ 땅을 잡히고 천만원을 빌리다 mortgage [take out a mortgage on] *one's* land for ten million won
2 〈약점·탈을〉 ♦약점을 잡히다 be found fault with / 흠을 잡히다 be spoken ill of; be caviled at
▶ 그에게 약점이 잡혀 있으니, 나는 그를 따를 수밖에 없다 He has something on me, so I have to obey him.

잣 big-cone pine nuts [seeds]
잣나무 〔植〕 a big-cone pine; a Coulter pine
잣눈¹ 〈눈금〉 a graduation on a ruler; a division on a scale
잣눈² 〈척설〉 a snowfall of one foot (deep); a foot-deep snow
잣다 **1** 〈실을〉 spin; make yarn
♦ 솜에서 실을 잣다 spin cotton into yarn [thread]; spin thread [yarn] out of cotton / 양털에서 실을 잣다 spin wool into threads
2 〈물을〉 draw up 《water》; 〈펌프로〉 pump up [out] 《water》
잣새 〔鳥〕 a crossbill ⇨ 솔잣새
장 長 **1** 〈길이〉 length
2 〈우두머리〉 the head; the chief; the boss; the commander; the leader
♦ 일가의 장[가장] the head of a family / 그 부족의 장 the chief [leader] of the tribe
3 〈장점〉 a merit; *one's* strong point; an advantage
장 將 **1** 〈군대의〉 a general; a commander
2 〈장기의〉 the king
▶ 장이야 Check! ⇌ Checkmate!
장 章 **1** 〈책의〉 a chapter
♦ 제2장 the second chapter; Chapter 2
2 〈기장〉 a badge; an emblem
장 場 **1** 〈시장〉 a market
♦ 장이 서는 날[고을] a market day [town] / 장로서 sell [buy] *sth* in the market / 장 보러 가다 go to market / 장에 나오다 appear in [come into] the market / 장에 내놓다 take [bring] 《*one's* produce》 to market / 장에서 생선을 사다 buy fish at the market
▶ 어머니는 장에 가셨다 Mother is at the market.
▶ 다음 장은 5일에 선다 The next fair is on the 5th.
2 〈장소〉 a place; a spot; a site; a ground; 〔物〕 a field
♦ 토론의 장 a place for debating [discussion] / 중력장 a gravitational field / 장 이론 field theory
3 〈연극의 장면〉 a scene
♦ 3막 2장 Act III, Scene ii
4 〔證〕 a session ▶ 오전 장이 섰다 The morning session was held.
장 腸 bowels; 〈장의 일부〉 a bowel; 〔解〕 the intestines; the guts
♦ 장의 intestinal; enteric / 장의 병[질환] a bowel disease; an intestinal trouble; an enteropathy / 장이 나쁘다 have an intestinal disorder; have a bowel trouble
장 醬 〈간장〉 soy sauce; 〈된장〉 soybean paste; 〈고추장〉 Korean hot pepper paste
장 欌 a chest of drawers; a cabinet; a closet; 〈옷의〉 a wardrobe; 〈식기의〉 a cupboard; a sideboard
♦ 단층 [2층]장 a single [double] chest of drawers / 붙박이 장 a built-in wardrobe / 서랍이 여러 층으로 달린 장 a chest-on-chest; a tallboy
장 張 〈책의〉 a leaf; 〈쪽〉 a page; 〈종이〉 a sheet
♦ 100원 짜리 우표 다섯 장 five one-hundred-won stamps / 종이 다섯 장 five sheets [pieces] of papar / 표 두 장 two tickets / 천원짜리 다섯 장 five one-thousand-won notes [bills] /《책을》 한 장 한 장 넘기다 turn over the pages [the leaves] (of a book)
-장 丈 〈존칭〉 an esteemed elder
♦ 노인장 an elderly person; an elder / 주인장 the owner; the proprietor / 춘부장 your father
장가 a marriage; taking a wife
♦ 장가 들려는 남자 a marrying man / 장가 가다[들다] get married 《to a woman》; marry; take a wife; take 《a woman》 for *one's* wife / 장가 보내다[들이다] marry 《a son》 to 《a woman》; get 《a son》 married
▶ 그는 장가를 일찍[늦게] 들었다 He married

장가스 腸— gas in the bowels; 〈방귀〉 wind; (鄙) fart

장갑 掌匣 (a pair of) gloves; 〈벙어리 장갑〉 (a pair of) mittens; 〈승마·검도용의 긴 장갑〉 a gauntlet
♦ 고무장갑 rubber gloves / 오른쪽 장갑 one's right glove [mitten]/ 권투 장갑 a boxing glove / 장갑 낀 손 a gloved hand / 장갑을 끼다 put on gloves / 장갑을 벗다 pull [take] off gloves / 장갑을 끼고 있다 have gloves on; wear gloves / 장갑을 낀 채 악수하다 shake hands with one's gloves on / 장갑을 뜨다 knit a glove
▶ 나는 장갑 한 짝을 잃어버렸다 I lost one of my gloves.

장갑 裝甲 armoring —**장갑하다** armor
♦ 장갑한 armored; armor-clad[-plated]
■ —부대 an armored corps —사단 a panzer division —인원수송차 an armored personnel carrier (略 APC) —자동차 an armored car —차 an armored car; a panzer —철판 an armor plate —함 an armored ship; an armor-clad ship

장강 長江 〈긴 강〉 a long river

장거리 長距離 a long distance; a long range
♦ 장거리의 long-distance; long-range
■ —경주 a long-distance race; a marathon (race) —달리기 a long-distance run —버스 a long-distance (touring) coach —비행 a long-distance flight; a long-range flight —선수 a long-distance runner —여행 a long journey —유도탄 a long-range guided missile —직통전화방식 the direct distance dialing system; the DDD system —탄도탄 a long-range ballistic missile —포 a long-range gun [cannon] —폭격기 a long-range bomber

장거리전화 長距離電話 a long-distance telephone
♦ 장거리전화를 걸다 call sb by long distance; make a long-distance call (to sb); (英) put a trunk call through / 장거리전화가 걸려오다 have a long-distance call (from)

장검 長劍 a long sword ♦ 장검을 차다 wear a long sword 《at one's side》

장결석 腸結石 〔醫〕 enterolite

장결핵 腸結核 〔醫〕 intestinal tuberculosis

장고 長考 a long meditation ▶ 장고 끝에 그는 결론에 이르렀다 After thinking it over for a long time, he finally arrived at a decision.
—**장고하다** think about sth for a long time; ponder

장골 壯骨 〈사람〉 a robust [strong, sturdy, stalwart] man; 〈골격〉 stout build; a robust constitution

장과 漿果 juicy fleshy fruit; 〔植〕 a berry

장관 壯觀 a grand sight; a magnificent spectacle [view]
♦ 그랜드캐니언의 장관 the amazing grandeur of the Grand Canyon / 장관을 보이다 present [provide] a grand sight [spectacle]
▶ 대해상의 일몰은 일대장관이다 The sun setting on the ocean is a grand sight.

장관 長官 (美) a secretary; (英) a minister; a Cabinet minister
♦ 장관이 되다 become [be appointed] a (state) minister; enter the Cabinet / 장관을 사임하다 resign from the Cabinet; leave the ministry
■ 국무—〈미국의〉 the Secretary of State 국방 [외무, 교육]— the Secretary [Minister] of Defense [Foreign Affairs, Education] —비서실 the minister's [ministerial] secretariat —직[자리] ministership; a Cabinet position; secretaryship

장관 將官 〈육군의〉 a general (officer); 〈해군의〉 an admiral; a flag officer

장광설 長廣舌 eloquence; volubility; a long-winded talk; a lengthy speech
♦ 장광설을 늘어놓다 make [give] a long speech; wag one's glib tongue

장교 將校 an officer; a commissioned officer
♦ 육군[해군, 공군, 해병대] 장교 a military [naval, air force, marine] officer / 장교로 임관되다 be commissioned; receive [get one's] commission / 장교와 사병 officers and men
■ 고급— a high-ranking officer; a high-ranker; (口) the brass ■ —단 an officer corps —식당 an officers' mess hall

장구 〔樂〕 a changgu

장구 長久 eternity; permanence
—**장구하다** eternal; (ever)lasting; long-ranged
♦ 장구한 시일을 요하다 require a long period of time
▶ 그 전설은 장구한 옛날부터 전래되어 왔다 The legend has been handed down from ancient times [the remote past].

장구 葬具 〈장례 제구〉 funeral equipment; funeral items

장구 裝具 〈사람의〉 an outfit; equipment; a rig; 〈실내의〉 fittings; 〈말의〉 harness; trappings
▶ 우리는 설중 캠핑 장구를 갖추고 있다 We have the right equipment [are properly equipped] for camping in the snow.

장구머리 a projecting head ⇨ 짱구머리

장구벌레 a wiggler; a wriggler; a mosquito larva

장국 醬— 〈맑은 국〉 clear soup; 〈간장을 탄〉 (beef) soup flavored with soy sauce
■ —밥 rice in beef soup

장군 a wooden or earthenware barrel [cask]
♦ 오줌— a urine barrel

장군 將軍 1 〔軍〕 a general; a commander
♦ 동장군 General Winter
2 〔장기〕 a check; a checkmate ♦ 겹장군 a double check
▶ 장군! Check! ⇌ Checkmate!

장궤양 腸潰瘍 〔醫〕 an intestinal ulcer

장기 長技 one's strong point; one's forte; one's speciality
♦ …이 장기다 be good [clever] at; be proficient [at home] in; be well versed in
▶ 그는 수학이 장기다 He is good at [strong in] math. ⇌ Mathematics is his strong point [speciality].
▶ 자기 장기를 살리도록 하여라 Try to develop your strong points.

장기 長期 〈장기간〉 a long term; 〈장시일〉 a long (period of) time
♦장기의 long; long-term; long-range; of long duration / 장기에 걸치다 extend over a long (period [space] of) time; be protracted; be prolonged
▶그 분쟁은 장기에 이르렀다 The dispute extended over a long period.
▶장기적으로는 그것이 우리에게 유리할 것이다 It will turn out to our advantage in the long run.
■―거래 long-term transaction ―결근 a long absence from work ―계획 a long-range plan ―공채 a long-term (public) bond ―금융 long-term finance ―대출 a long-term loan ―부채 long-term liabilities ―신용 long-term credit ―어음 a long-term bill ―예보 a long-range forecast ―임대 a long-term lease ―전 a prolonged [long-drawn-(out)] war ―정책 a long-range [long-term] policy ―집권 a prolonged one-man rule ―채무 a long-term debt ―체류 a long stay ―흥행 a long run

장기 將棋 *changgi*; 〈서양장기〉 chess
♦장기를 두다 play *changgi* (with); have a game of chess (with) / 장기에 이기다[지다] win [lose] a game of chess
▶장기 둘줄 알아요? Do you know how to play *changgi*?
■―짝 a *changgi* piece; a chessman; a man ―판 a chessboard

장기 臟器 〈내장 기관〉 internal organs; viscera; 〈내장〉 intestines; bowels
♦인공장기 artificial (internal) organs

장기근속 長期勤續 long service; years of labor
♦장기근속하다 serve for long years; be in continuous service
▶그는 장기근속 표창을 받았다 He was honored in recognition of his long service.
■―자 a worker [laborer] serving for long years

장김치 醬― *kimchi* pickled in soy sauce

장꾼 場― 〈상인〉 a marketeer; 〈떠돌이〉 a peddler; a hawker; 〈고객〉 a marketer; a shopper

장끼 a cock pheasant

장나무 長― a supporting timber; a long stick [rod]; a pole

장난 1 〈짓궂은〉 mischief; a practical joke; a prank; a trick; a hoax
♦운명의 장난 a trick of fortune [fate] / 장난 전화 prank [hoax] phone call
▶당신 장난이 지나쳤소 You carried your practical joke a bit too far.
▶장난에도 정도가 있는 것 아니에요? You should know that some types of mischief is unallowable?
―장난하다 do mischief; be mischievous; do a naughty thing; play [pull] a trick [prank] (on *sb*); play a (practical) joke (upon)
♦장난하기 좋아하는 mischievous; naughty; prankish; impish
▶사내아이들은 장난하기를 좋아한다 Boys like mischief [playing tricks]. ⇌ Boys are fond of mischief.
▶아이들이 방에서 장난하다 유리창을 깨뜨렸다 The childern broke the windowpanes when they were romping (about) in the room.
2 〈놀이〉 fun; amusement; 〈오락〉 a pastime; 〈도락〉 a hobby
♦장난삼아 half in fun; for [in] fun; for the fun of it [the thing]; in jest; 〈오락으로〉 as a pastime [hobby]
▶난 장난삼아 해본 말이야 I did it merely for the fun of it.
▶그 항아리는 내가 장난으로 구운 것이오 I baked that pot just for fun [half in fun].
3 〈가지고 놀기〉 ―장난하다 play (with); toy (with); (口) monkey (with)
♦불 장난하다 play with fire

장난감 a toy; a plaything; 〈노리개〉 the sport
♦장난감 자동차[권총] a toy car [gun] / 장난감 같은 집 a toy [match box] of a house; a toy(like) house / 장난감을 가지고 놀다 play with a toy / 장난감으로 삼다 make a toy [plaything] of; make fun [sport] of; sport [trifle] with
▶이 카메라는 장난감같은 싸구려다 This camera is no more than a toy.
■―가게 a toyshop ―상자 a toy box [chest] ―장수 a toy dealer

장난기 mischievousness; mischief
♦장난기가 많은 사람 a person full of fun and mischief / 장난기가 있는 playful; sportive; full of play [fun]; mischievous; impish / 장난기 어린 눈으로 with mischievous [impish] eyes

장난꾸러기 a practical joker; a rogue; 〈아이〉 a mischievous [naughty] boy; an urchin; a mischief; a joker
♦장난꾸러기의 mischievous; impish; naughty
▶어렸을 때 난 장난꾸러기였지 As a boy I used to do all kinds of mischief [used to play all sorts of prank].

장난꾼 a practical joker ⇨ 장난꾸러기

장난치다 do mischief ⇨ 장난(～하다)
▶초인종을 가지고 장난치지 마라 Don't play [fool] with the doorbell.
▶우리 안의 동물에게 장난치면 안된다 Don't tease the animals in the cage.

장날 場― a market day
▶5일마다 장날이다 Markets are held here every five days [fifth day].

장남 長男 the [*one's*] oldest [(英) eldest] son; the firstborn son

장내 場內 the inside of the hall [grounds, premises] ♦장내에(서) 〈회장내〉 in the hall; 〈부지내〉 in the grounds; on the premises; in the enclosure
▶장내에서는 금연입니다 No Smoking allowed in the hall.
▶장내가 더욱 혼잡해졌다 The place got more and more crowded.
■―방송 (an announcement over) the public address system ―정리 crowd control in the hall [on the premises]

장녀 長女 the [*one's*] oldest [(英) eldest] daughter; the firstborn daughter; 〈두 자매일 때〉 *one's* older [elder] daughter

장년 壯年 the prime of manhood
♦장년의 남자 a man in his prime / 장년기에 in one's manhood; at [in] the prime of one's life / 장년이 되다 reach manhood; attain the prime of manhood
▶그는 이미 장년이 지났다 He is already past his prime.

장뇌 樟腦 camphor; 〈방충제 알약〉 a camphor ball; mothballs ■—연고 camphor ice —유 camphor oil —정(精) spirit of camphor

장님 a blind [sightless] person; 〈총칭〉 the blind
♦눈 뜬 장님 〈문맹자〉 an illiterate (person) / 장님인 blind / 장님이 되다 become [go] blind; become sightless; lose one's (eye)sight / 장님으로 태어나다 be born blind

장다리 〈무·배추의〉 a flower stalk 《of radishes, cabbages, etc.》 ♦장다리가 나다 go [run] to seed ■—무 a seed radish

장단 長短 1 〈길이〉 (relative) length
♦두줄의 장단을 재다 measure the relative length of two strings
2 ⇨ 장단점
3 〈박자〉 time; rhythm
♦장단에 맞게[틀리게] 노래하다 sing in [out of] tune / 장단을 맞추다 〈박자〉 keep [beat] (good) time with [to]; 〈기분〉 attune oneself (to); play in another's key
▶그녀는 음악에 장단을 맞추어 춤을 추었다 She danced in time [rhythm] to the music.
▶그들은 손으로 장단을 맞추며 춤추었다 They danced beating time with their hands.
▶그들은 서로 장단이 척척 맞는다 They get along [hit it off] well with each other.

장단점 長短點 good and bad points; strengths and weaknesses; merits and demerits [faults]; 〈득실〉 relative merits [importance]
♦도시 생활의 장단점 the advantages and disadvantages of city life
▶사람마다 장단점이 있다 Every man has his merits and demerits.

장담 壯談 〈자신있게 하는 말〉 assurance; guarantee; vouching; assertion; affirmation
—장담하다 assure; vouch; vouch 《for》; affirm; commit oneself; warrant
▶내 기억이 정확한지는 장담할 수 없다 I can't vouch for the accuracy of my memory.
▶〔會話〕「확실한가?」「장담하지」 "Are you sure?" "Yes, I'm (dead) positive."
▶그 점은 내가 장담한다 I give [You may take] my word for it.
▶나는 어떻다고 장담할 수 없다 I cannot commit myself either way.

장대 壯大 〈크고 당당함〉 magnificence; 〈크고 훌륭함〉 grandeur
—장대하다 big and strong; stalwart; strapping; 〈美口〉 husky
♦정상에서의 장대한 전망 a grand [a magnificent] view from the top of the mountain / 장대한 체격 a large and robust build [frame] / 기골이 장대한 사람 a strapping person; 〈口〉 a strapper; a husky

장대 長— a pole; a rod ♦대나무 장대 a bamboo pole

장대높이뛰기 長— a pole vault ♦장대높이뛰기를 하다 pole jump; pole vault ▶아버지는 장대높이뛰기 선수였다 My father was a pole vaulter [jumper].

장대로 하늘 재기 〈속담〉 attempting the impossible; an attempt never to be realized

장대하다 長大 — 〈큰〉 big; large; 〈대규모의〉 large-scale; 〈긴〉 long; 〈훌륭한〉 great; 〈거대한〉 huge; 〈광대한〉 immense

장도 壯途 〈사명을 띠고 떠나는 길〉 an important mission; 〈용감히 떠나는 길〉 a heroic [valiant] departure; an ambitious course
♦탐험의 장도에 오르다 make a heroic departure on an expedition / 세계 일주의 장도에 오르다 start valiantly on a round-the-world trip ▶그는 혼자 북극 탐험의 장도에 올랐다 He started on an ambitious the Arctic expedition by himself.

장도 粧刀 an encased ornamental knife (hung at the belt)

장도리 〈망치〉 a hammer; 〈노루발장도리〉 a claw hammer
♦장도리 대가리 a hammerhead / 장도리 자루 the handle of a hammer / 장도리로 치다 hammer; work one's hammer / 장도리로 못을 박다 hammer a nail in; drive in a nail 《into a board》 with a hammer; hammer a nail 《into a board》 / 장도리로 못을 뽑다 extract [pull out] a nail with a claw hammer

─── 장도리 ───

헤드 / head
못뽑이 / claw
손잡이 / grip
두들기는 면 / face
자루 / handle

장독 醬— a crock [jar] of soy sauce ■—간 a place to keep jars of soy sauce —대 a terrace where soy sauce crocks are placed

장돌림 場— an itinerant market trader [dealer]; a roving marketeer

장돌뱅이 場— a roving marketeer ⇨ 장돌림

장두 長頭 〈머리가 길고 폭이 좁은 사람〉 a longhead; a dolichocephalic person

장두 檣頭 〈돛대의 맨 꼭대기〉 a masthead; the head of a mast

장두하다 〈거리를〉 compare 《two routes》 to see which is the shorter

장딴지 〔解〕 the calf

장래 將來 1 〈명사적〉 the future; the time [days] to come; 〈미래의 전망〉 (future) prospect(s); 〈사람·나라 등의 전도〉 a future
♦어두운[밝은] 장래 a dark [bright, rosy] future; gloomy [brilliant] prospect / 먼 장래 the remote future
〈장래의〉 장래의 아내 one's future [prospective] wife / 장래의 future / 장래의 계획을 세우다 make one's plan for the future; plan one's future

▶자네도 이제 곧 장래의 계획을 세워야 돼 You will soon have to make some plans for your future.
〈장래가[는]〉 장래가 유망한 청년 a promising youth; a young man of great promise
▶그의 전도에는 밝은 장래가 있다 He has a bright future ahead of him.
▶아무래도 그 아이의 장래가 염려된다 I cannot help feeling anxious about the future of that child.
▶그의 장래는 보장되어 있다 His future is assured.
▶그녀는 가수로서의 장래가 밝다 She has a bright [great] future (ahead of her) as a singer. ⇒ She is a (very) promising singer.
〈장래를〉 인류의 장래를 예상하다 foretell the future of mankind / 아들의 장래를 걱정[비관]하다 be anxious [feel gloomy] about *one's* son's future
▶그 결정은 신중하고도 장래를 내다본 것이었다 The decision was discreet and far-sighted.
〈장래에〉 가까운 장래에 in the near future / 먼 장래에 in the remote [distant, far-off] future
▶그는 먼 장래에 눈을 돌렸다 He looked far ahead into the future.
▶남자는 자기 가족의 장래에 대비하지 않으면 안된다 A man should provide for the future of his family.
▶가까운 장래에 누구나 달에 갈 수 있게 되겠지요 In the near future, anyone will be able to go to the moon.
2〈부사적〉 in the future; 〈앞으로〉 in (the) future; 〈언젠가〉 someday; one day; 〈가까운 장래에〉 in the near future; in the not too distant future; in the time [days, years] ahead [to come]
▶장래 무슨 일이 일어날는지 아무도 모른다 No one can tell [There is no knowing] what will happen in the future.

장래성 將來性 〈전도〉 future
♦장래성 있는 promising
▶그는 장래성이 있을 법한 소년이다 He seems a promising boy. ⇒ He seems a boy who has prospects.
▶그는 예술가로서 크게 장래성이 있다 He has a great [bright] future as an artist.

장려 壯麗 〈장대하고 화려함〉 magnificence, grandeur; 〈화려〉 splendor(s)
♦장려한 magnificent; splendid; grand; imposing
▶언덕 위에 장려한 성이 있다 A magnificent castle stands on the hill.

장려 奬勵 encouragement; 〈촉진〉 promotion; stimulation; incitement.
♦사회 봉사의 장려 the encouragement of social service
—장려하다 encourage; give encouragement (to); 〈촉진하다〉 promote; stimulate; incite
♦장려하여 …하다 encourage *sb* to 《do》
▶아버지는 나에게 저축을 장려했다 My father encouragd me to save.
▶우리 학교에서는 클럽 활동 참가를 장려하고 있다 Our school encourages us to participate in club activities.

■—급 incentive wages
장려금 奬勵金 《give》 a bounty; 《grant》 a subsidy; a grant in aid ■수출— an export bounty

장렬 壯烈 heroism; bravery —장렬하다 〈영웅적인〉 heroic; 〈용감한〉 brave; gallant
▶그는 그 전투에서 장렬한 최후를 마쳤다 He died a heroic death in the battle.

장렬 葬列 a funeral procession [train]
장례 葬禮 〈장례식〉 a funeral (ceremony); a funeral [burial] service (▶service 는 종교적 의식의 뜻); funeral [burial] rites
♦불교식 상례 a funeral in Buddhist rites / 장례에 참례하다 attend a funeral; be (present) at a funeral / 장례를 치르다 hold a funeral (for); perform [conduct] a funeral service [the last offices] 《for》
■—비 funeral expenses —위원 a funeral committee —위원장 the chief of a funeral committee —차 a funeral car; a hearse

장례식 葬禮式 a funeral (service [ceremony]); 〈매장〉 a burial
▶장례식은 엄수되었다 The funeral (service) was solemnly held [performed, conducted].
■—장 a funeral hall

장로 長老 〈연장자〉 an elder; a senior; 〈교회의〉 an elder; a presbyter
♦정계의 장로 an elder statesman / 마을의 장로 village seniors [elders]
■—교회 the Presbyterian Church

장롱 欌籠 a chest (of drawers); a cabinet; a wardrobe; a dresser; a bureau
장루 檣樓 〔海〕 a top; a roundtop; a crow's nest
장르 〔프〕 a genre; a category; a kind
장마 the rainy spell in summer; a long spell of rainy weather; the rainy [wet] season
▶장마가 들다 The rainy season sets in.
▶장마가 걷히다 The rainy season is over.
▶긴 장마로 넌더리 났다 The long spell of rain depressed me.
■—비 rain in the wet season —전선 a seasonal rainy front

장마철 the rainy [wet] season
▶올 장마철은 예년보다 빨리 들었다 This year the rainy season set in earlier than usual.
▶장마철로 접어들었다 The rainy season has set in.

장막 帳幕 a curtain; hangings; 〈천막〉 a tent
♦밤의 장막 the veil of night [darkness] / 철[죽]의 장막 the iron [bamboo] curtain / 신비의 장막에 싸이다 be wrapped [shrouded] in (a veil of) mystery
▶온 마을이 밤의 장막에 싸였다 The whole village was covered with a mantle [veil] of darkness.

장만 preparation; arrangement; acquirement
—장만하다 prepare; provide *oneself* 《with》; make; get ready; buy
♦자금을 장만하다 raise the fund / 옷을 새로 장만하다 have a new suit made; buy a new suit / 집을 장만하다 get a house / 땅을 담보로 돈을 장만하다 raise money on *one's* land
▶나는 장만해둔 돈이 없다 I have no money

prepared.
▶ 그녀가 5시까지는 저녁 식사를 장만할 것이다 She will get dinner ready by five o'clock.
장면 場面 〈연극〉a scene; 〈배경〉setting; 〈장소〉a place; 〈광경〉a spectacle; a sight
◆ 연극 장면의 설정 the setting of the scene of a play
▶ 장면이 바뀌다 The scene changes [shifts].
▶ 이 연극 장면은 술집이다 The setting of the play is a pub.
▶ 그것은 감동적인 장면이었다 It was a touching sight.
▶ 연인들의 헤어짐은 감동적인 장면이었다 The parting of the lovers was a very moving sight.
장모 丈母 the wife's mother; a man's mother-in-law
장문 長文 〈문장〉a long sentence; 〈기사·논문〉a long article; 〈편지〉a long letter
■ —전보 a long [lengthy] telegram
장물 贓物 〈훔친 물품〉stolen goods; a stolen article; (俗) hot goods; (俗) a swag
◆ 장물을 은닉하다 secrete stolen goods
■ —고매(故買) buying [purchasing] goods with full knowledge that they are stolen goods —아비 a dealer in stolen goods; a hot goods broker; (俗) a fence
장미 薔薇 〈꽃〉a rose; 〈나무〉a rosebush; a rose tree; 〈별명〉the queen of the prairie
◆ 장미꽃 장식[매듭(술)] a rosette
▶ 가시없는 장미는 없다 〈속담〉 No rose without a thorn. ⇒ Roses have thorns.
■ —들 a wild rose ■ —열 [醫] rose cold [fever] —전쟁 〈史〉 the Wars of the Roses —향수 rose water
장밋빛 薔薇 — rose color; rose pink
◆ 장밋빛 입술 rose-red[-pink] lips / 장밋빛 미래 a rosy future / 장밋빛의 rosy; rose-colored; roseate / 장밋빛으로 roseately
장바구니 場 — a shopping basket
장바닥 場 — a market place; the market ground [area]
장발 長髮 long hair
◆ 장발의 젊은이 a long-haired young man
▶ 그는 장발이다 He wears his hair long.
▶ 우리 학교에서는 장발이 금지되어 있다 Long hair is forbidden in our school.
■ —족 longhairs
장방형 長方形 a rectangle ⇒ 직사각형
장벽 腸壁 〈장자벽〉the intestinal wall
장벽 障壁 〈벽·울타리〉a fence; a wall; 〈장애물〉a barrier; an obstacle
◆ 장벽이 되다 constitute a barrier 《to》; be an obstacle 《to》 / 장벽을 쌓다 build [erect, set up] a barrier 《between》; raise a barrier / 장벽을 제거하다 remove [demolish, break down] a barrier 《between》
▶ 말이 다른 것이 그들의 장벽이 되었다 Their language differences became a barrier [an obstacle, a wall].
■ —비관세 — non-tariff barriers —언어 — a language barrier
장변 場邊 market interest; interest on a loan for a period of five days (from one market to the next)
장병 長病 〈오랜 병〉a long [protracted] illness; a lingering disease
▶ 그는 장병을 앓고 있다 He has been ill (in bed) for a long time. ⇒ He has been suffering from a long illness.
장병 將兵 〈장교와 사병〉officers and men
◆ 일선 장병을 위문하다 comfort officers and men on the front line
장보다 場 — 1 〈시장 가다〉 do *one's* marketing
◆ 장보러 가다 go shopping [marketing] 《to》; go to market
2 〈장사하다〉 open a booth at a market
장복 長服 constant [habitual] use 《of a medicine》 — 장복하다 take 《a medicine》 for a long time
장본 張本 1 〈발단의 근원〉 a (main) cause; the origin; the root
▶ 그 사건이 그의 사임의 장본이 되었다 The incident led to his resignation.
2 ⇒ 장본인(張本人)
장본 藏本 a collection of books ⇒ 장서
장본인 張本人 〈주모자〉the ringleader; 〈선동자〉the instigator; 〈교사자〉the author 《of a plot》
▶ 그 장난의 장본인 the author of the mischief
▶ 이 소동의 장본인은 누구냐? Who is the ringleader of this riot? ⇒ Who started this riot?
장부 〔建〕 a tenon; a pivot; a cog; 〈열장장부촉〉a dovetail ■ —촉 이음 a mortise and tenon joint 장붓구멍 a mortise
장부 丈夫 〈장성한 남자〉a full-grown man; a fully grown man; a manly man; a man (of spirit); a reliable man ▶ 장부 일언 중천금 A man's word is as good as a bond.
장부 帳簿 a book; 〈회계장부〉an account book; 〈원장〉a ledger; 〈호적 등의〉a register
◆ 장부를 매기다 keep accounts [books] / 장부를 정리하다 adjust the accounts / 장부(끝)을 속이다 falsify books [accounts]; cook [doctor, manipulate, juggle] the accounts / 장부를 검사하다 examine [inspect] the books; audit the accounts / 장부를 맞추다 make the accounts balances / 매상을 장부에 기입하다 enter the proceeds in the account book
▶ 장부상으로는 얼마간 이익으로 되어있다 The books show a slight profit.
▶ 나는 장부에서 부정을 발견했다 I found false entries in the books.
▶ 우리는 3월 말에 장부를 마감한다 We close our books at the end of March.
▶ 장부에 달아 놓으세요 Charge this against me [to my account].
▶ 장부는 꼭 맞아 떨어진다 The books balance exactly.
■ —상업 — trade books 외상 — a charge account 이중 — double bookkeeping ■ —가격 book value —감사 auditing —정리 adjustment of accounts —조직 ledger organization
장부끝 帳簿 — the balance of accounts; a balance (account)
▶ 가까스로 장부끝을 맞추어 놓았다 I managed to make the accounts balance.

장비

▶ 도무지 장부끝이 맞지 않는다 I'm afraid the accounts don't balance. ⇌ I can't make these come out right.

장비 裝備 equipment; outfit; 〈식구〉 rigging
♦ 중장비의 heavily equipped 《division》 / 배에 항해를 위한 장비를 하다 equip a ship for a voyage
▶ 그 등산자들의 장비는 불충분했다 The equipment of the climbers was imperfect.
▶ 그들은 충분한 장비로 북극탐험에 나섰다 Properly [Well] equipped, they set off on the expedition to the North Pole.
—**장비하다** equip 《oneself》 with》; furnish 《a boat with》; fit out 《an expedition with》; rig 《a ship with》; mount 《a gun》

장사 〈무역〉 trade; 〈상업 활동〉 business; commerce; 〈거래〉 a transaction; a deal; 〈직업〉 an occupation; a line; 〈전문직업〉 a profession
♦ 수지가 맞는[맞지 않는] [nonpaying] business / 장사가 쪼그라들다 business diminishes [dwindles, drops off] / 장사가 되다[안되다] pay [do not pay]; be [be not] a paying business / 장사를 잘하다 have a good head for business / 집안의 장사를 이어받다 take over [carry on, succeed to] the family business / 장사를 확장[축소]하다 extend [reduce] one's business / 장사를 시작하다[그만두다] go into [go out of] business
▶ 會話「장사는 어떻습니까?」「그저 그만 합니다」 "How's business?" "So-so."
▶ 요즘은 장사가 한산하다[한창이다] Business is slack [brisk] these days.
▶ 會話「무슨 장사를 하고 있습니까?」「식료품점을 하고 있습니다」 "What is your line (of business)?" ⇌ "What (line of) business are you in?" "I run a grocery store." ⇌ "I'm in the grocery business [line, trade]." 〈도매상으로서〉 "I deal in groceries."
▶ 우리 가게는 장사가 아주 잘된다 We are having brisk trade [a great rush of business].
▶ 그는 장사를 잘[잘못] 한다 He is a good [bad] businessman.
—**장사하다** 〈매매하다〉 deal in; trade in; 〈경영하다〉 engage in trade; run a business

장사 壯士 a strong man; a man of great strength; a powerful man; a Hercules
▶ 그는 힘이 천하장사다 He is as strong as Hercules. ⇌ He is a very powerful man.

장사 葬事 a funeral; a burial ♦ 장사를 지내다 hold a funeral; 〈매장하다〉 bury; inter; entomb; inhume ■ **장삿날** a funeral day

장사꾼 a merchant; a trader; a dealer; 〈점포주인〉 《美》 a storekeeper; 《英》 a shopkeeper; 〈총칭〉 the trading class
■ —**기질[근성]** a mercenary spirit

장사진 長蛇陣 a long line [file, row]; 〈차례를 기다리는 줄〉 a long queue
♦ 미술관 앞에는 입장을 기다리는 사람들이 장사진을 이루고 서 있었다 People were standing in a long line [queue] in front of the art museum awaiting their turn to be admitted.

장사치 a trader ⇨ 장사꾼
장삼 長衫 〈중의 웃옷〉 a Buddhist monks' robe
장삿속 〈장사꾼의 잇속〉 a commercial spirit; a mercantile mind
▶ 장삿속을 떠나서 from a noncommercial [disinterested] motive; apart from gain
▶ 장삿속을 떠나서 합니다 I will do it apart from interest.
▶ 그는 매사에 장삿속이다 He always acts from mercenary motives.

장색 匠色 a craftsman ⇨ 장인(匠人)
장생불사 長生不死 eternal life; immortality
♦ 장생불사의 영약 the elixir of life
▶ 그것은 장생불사의 샘으로 알려져 있다 That is known as a fountain of eternal youth.
—**장생불사하다** enjoy eternal life; share immortality

장서 藏書 〈소장본의 전부〉 a library; a collection of books; 〈도서관〉 the book stock
▶ 그는 3천 권의[많은] 장서를 가지고 있다 He has a library of 3,000 volumes [a large library].
■ —**가** the owner of a well-stocked [large, fine] library; a book collector : 김 교수는 장서가다 Professor Kim has [owns] a large library [great many books]. —**광** a book-aholic —**목록** a library catalog(ue) —**벽** bibliomania; bibliophilism —**인(印)[기호]** an ownership stamp [mark] —**표** a bookplate; a book label; 《라》 an ex libris

장석 長石 〔鑛〕 feldspar; 《英》 felspar
사 — plagioclase
장성 長成 〈어른이 됨〉 growth; maturity
—**장성하다** grow up; grow to manhood [maturity]
▶ 그는 장성하여 훌륭한 젊은이가 되었다 He grew up to be [into] a fine young man. (▶ to be 의 경우 up 은 생략할 수 없음)

장성 將星 generals ■ **육해군** — army and navy celebrities

장성 長城 a long wall
■ **만리** — the Great Wall of China

장소 場所 **1** 〈곳〉 a place; 〈특정한 지점〉 a spot; 〈현장〉 a scene; a point; a section; 〈고장〉 a place; a locality; a district; an area; a region; 〈경우〉 an occasion; a case
♦ 끊임없이 분쟁이 일어나는 장소 a trouble spot / 회합하는 장소 a place of [for] meeting / 장소를 가리지 않고 regardless of where one is; regardless of the occasion / 잇달아 장소를 바꾸다 move from place to place
▶ 會話「저봐, 위병 교대를 하고 있어」「빨리! 좋은 장소를 잡자」 "Look, they're changing the guard!" "Quick! Let's get a good place."
▶ 원래 있던 장소에 두어라 Put it where you found it.
▶ 장소를 가려서 말을 해라 Suit your words to the situation.
2 〈위치〉 a position; a situation; a location
♦ 장소가 좋다[나쁘다] be well [badly] situated; be conveniently [inconveniently] located / 장소를 알아내다 locate; localize
▶ 그 호텔이 있는 장소를 알고 있습니까? Do you know the location of the hotel [where the hotel is]? (▶ [ ] 의 표현이 구어적임)
▶ 장소가 좋아야 장사가 잘 된다 The locality brings a great deal of business.

3 〈소재지〉 a seat; 〈터·자리〉 a site
♦병원이 세워질 장소 the site for the projected hospital / 행방 불명이 된 아들이 있는 장소를 찾아내다 locate *one's* missing son / 장소를 고르다 select a site 《for》
▶그 호텔은 바다가 보이는 멋진 장소에 있다 The hotel has a fine location overlooking the sea.
4 〈현장〉 a scene; a site
▶이곳은 큰 화재가 있었던 장소다 This is the scene of a big fire.
5 〈여지〉 room; space; 〈좌석〉 a seat; a place
♦좁은 장소 limited space / 장소를 차지하다 take up much room; occupy a good deal of space
▶저희 집에는 그랜드 피아노를 둘 충분한 장소가 없습니다 There isn't enough room for a grand piano in my house.
▶그렇게 하면 장소가 절약된다 That will save space.

장손 長孫 the eldest son of the eldest son
장송 長松 〈큰 소나무〉 a tall pine tree; 〈널〉 a long pine board
장송 葬送 attendance at a funeral ─**장송하다** attend [be present] at a funeral; escort a funeral
─**─(행진)곡** a funeral [dead] march
장수 〈상인〉 a trader; a dealer; a seller; a tradesman; a merchant; 〈도붓장수〉 a peddler; a hawker; a vendor
♦모피 장수 a fur trader; a trader in fur
▶그는 목재 장수다 He is a timber merchant.
─**땅콩─** a peanut vendor **생선─** a fishmonger
장수 長壽 long life; longevity
♦장수의 비결 the secret of longevity
─**장수하다** live long; enjoy longevity; live to a great [ripe old] age ♦장수하는 혈통[집안] a long-lived family
▶그는 장수하는 혈통이다 He comes from a long-lived family.
▶조부님은 93세까지 장수하셨다 My grandfather lived to be ninety-three.
▶여자는 흔히 남자보다 장수한다 Most women live longer than men. ⇌ Women often outlive men.
─**─약** the elixir of life
장수 將帥 〈군사의 우두머리〉 a commander; a commandant; 〈장군〉 a general
장수 張數 the number of leaves [sheets]
▶필요한 표의 장수를 말하세요 Please tell me how many tickets you want.
장수로 長水路 〔泳〕 a 50-meter [long] course
장수벌 將帥─ a queen bee＝여왕(~벌)
장승 1 〈마을어귀의 목상·석상〉 a devil post; a road idol **2** 〈키다리〉 a tall man; (美) a gangling fellow
장시간 長時間 〈몇 시간이나〉 for many hours; 〈오랫동안〉 for a long time; long; for long
▶장시간 텔레비전을 보는 것은 눈에 좋지 않다 It is bad for the eyes to watch TV for a long time.
▶우리는 장시간에 걸친 토의 끝에 합의에 이르렀다 We reached an agreement after many hours of discussion.
장시일 長時日 a long period of time; years
♦장시일의 연구 long years of research; a long-time research / 장시일에 걸치다 extend over a long space of time / 장시일을 필요로 하다 require a long period of time
장식 裝飾 decoration; ornament; ornamentation; (an) adornment; (an) embellishment
♦장식용 꽃병 an ornamental [decorative] vase / 크리스마스 장식 Christmas decorations / 장식이 없는 simple; plain; unadorned; bare / 다이아몬드를 장식으로 박아넣다 stud (it) with diamonds for ornament
▶그녀는 가게의 쇼윈도에 크리스마스 장식을 하고 있다 She is dressing the store window for Christmas.
▶이 도자기는 실용적이 아닌 단순한 장식이다 This china is only for show and not for use.
─**장식하다** decorate; ornament; adorn; deck out; bedeck; dress

解說 ***decorate***는 주로 「장소·건물」 등에 대해 쓴다. ***ornament***는 특히 「장식품을 써서 물건을 장식하다」의 뜻. ***adorn***은 다소 문어적이고 「지금의 아름다움을 더욱 아름답게, 내재하는 아름다움을 표출하다」의 뜻으로 특히 사람에 대해 쓰는 경우가 많다.

▶방을 무엇으로 장식할까? What shall we decorate the room with?
■**─머리** headdress **무대─** stage decoration **실내─** interior decoration: 실내장식이 멋이 없다 The room decorations lack taste. ■**─단추** an ornamental button; a fancy button **─법** ornamentation; decoration **─예술** (a) decorative art **─유리** ornamental glass **─음〔樂〕** ⇒ 꾸밈(~음) **─조명** decorative illumination **─품** an ornament; a decoration; 〈장신구〉 an accessory
장식용 裝飾用 ♦장식용 전구 a decoration light bulb / 장식용의 for ornamental purposes; for decoration
장신 長身 a tall figure; high stature ♦장신의 남자 a tall man; a man of high stature / 장신의 (美) rangy
장신구 裝身具 personal ornaments [outfitting, adornments]; 〈남성용〉 furnishings; haber-dashery; 〈여성용〉 accessories; trinkets
장심 掌心 〈발바닥 한가운데〉〔解〕 the plantar arch; 〈손바닥 한가운데〉 the center of the palm
장아찌 sliced vegetables preserved in soy sauce [pepper paste]
장악 掌握 〈손안에 거머쥠〉 hold; grasp; seizure; 〈권력을 잡음〉 command
─**장악하다** hold; seize; grasp; command; dominate ♦(사람을) 장악하다 get [have] control 《over》 / 정권을 장악하다 assume [take (over)] the reins of government; come into [be in] power / 제해권을 장악하다 secure [hold] the command of the sea; command the sea
장안 長安 the capital; the metropolis

장애

♦온 장안에 throughout the capital (city)
♦서울 Seoul, the capital city

장애 障礙 1〈방해물〉an obstacle; 〈방해하기〉an obstruction; an impediment; 〈방해〉a hindrance; 〈차폐물〉a barrier; a stumbling block; 〈걸림·얽힘〉a difficulty; a hitch; a snag
♦뜻밖의 장애 an unexpected [unforeseen] obstacle 《to》/ 장애가 되다 be an obstacle 《to》; hinder; impede; be [come] in the way 《of》/ 장애를 극복하다 get over a barrier; overcome [tide over] a difficulty; overcome [surmount] an obstacle [a difficulty] / 장애를 돌파하다 break through an obstacle; demolish [break down] a barrier
▶수입 제한은 무역의 장애가 된다 Import restrictions are barriers to trade.
▶나는 많은 장애에 부딪쳤으나 가까스로 그것을 극복했다 I ran into [met with] a lot of difficulties, but managed to get them over.
2〈신체의 병〉trouble; 〈조직·기능의〉defect; 〔醫〕a lesion
♦심장— heart trouble 언어—〔醫〕a speech defect [disorder]; an impediment in *one*'s speech 위장— gastroenteric trouble [disorder] 정서— an emotional disturbance

장애물 障礙物 ♦〈방해물〉an obstacle; an obstruction; 〈차폐물〉a barrier
♦장애물을 뛰어 넘다 jump [clear] an obstacle [a hurdle] / 장애물을 없애다 get obstacles out of the way
■—경주〈경마〉a steeplechase; 〈운동회〉an obstacle race; 〈장애물 달리기〉a hurdle race; 〈스키회전 활강〉a slalom —통과 훈련장 obstacle course

장액 腸液 〈소화〉intestinal juice
장액 漿液 〔生〕serous fluid
장어 長魚 an eel; a common eel
♦장어 덮밥 a bowl of eel and rice / 장어 요릿집 an eel restaurant / 장어 구이 boiled eels; a spitchcock / 민물 장어 a freshwater eel / 장어를 먹다 eat eel / 장어 구이를 하다 (split and) broil 《an eel》

장엄 壯嚴 ♦ grandeur; solemnity; sublimity; magnificence; majesty
—장엄하다 sublime; solemn; impressive; grand; 〈장대한〉magnificent; majestic; stately
♦장엄한 궁전 a mgnificent palace / 장엄한 일몰 a glorious sunset / 장엄한 음악 solemn music / 장엄하게 solemnly; with solemnity
■—미사〈가톨릭〉Solemn Mass; (라) Missa Solemnis

장염 腸炎 〔醫〕〈창자의 염증〉enteritis
장염전(증) 腸捻轉(症) 〔醫〕〈창자의 뒤틀림·꼬임〉a twisting of bowel
장옷 長— a lady's veil; a cloak
장외 場外 ♦장외 마련 매장 an off-track betting place / 장외의 outside the hall / 장외(서) outside the hall [arena, grounds] / 장외 홈런을 치다 hit an out-of-the-park homer; hit a homer out of the (ball) park
▶장외에 있었던 사람들은 다치지 않았다 No one outside the hall was hurt.

장원 壯元 〈수석 합격〉passing a state examination first on the list; 〈사람〉the first place winner in a state examination
—장원하다 pass the civil service examination first on the list; head the list in a contest

장원 莊園 a manor ■—영주 the lord of a manor: 장원 영주의 저택 a manor house [seat] —제도 the manorial system

장유 長幼 〈어른과 어린이〉young and old
▶장유 유서하다 The younger should give precedence to the elder. ⇌ Elders first.

장음 長音 〈길게 나는 소리〉a prolonged sound; 〔音聲〕〈장모음〉a long vowel [syllable]; 〔通信〕a dash; a long tone

장음계 長音階 〔樂〕the major scale

장음부 長音符 〔音聲〕a macron; a long vowel mark ♦장음부를 붙이다 put a macron 《over a vowel》

장의 葬儀 a funeral ⇨ 장례 (葬禮)
■—사 an undertaker's (office); (美) a funeral home [parlor]

장의자 長椅子 a bench; a couch; a divan; 〈소파〉a sofa

-장이 a man who does…; a professional doer of…

장인 丈人 the wife's father; a man's father-in-law

장인 匠人 an artisan; a crafts man
장일 葬日 a funeral day
장자 長子 〈맏아들〉the *one*'s oldest [eldest] son [child]; the firstborn (child)
■—상속권 the right of primogeniture —상속법 primogeniture

장자 長者 1〈거부〉〈백만장자〉a millionaire; a rich [wealthy] person; 〈억만장자〉a billionaire; a multimillionaire
2〈덕망이 있는 어른〉an elder of virtue; a man of moral influence; 〈윗사람〉*one*'s superior; 〈연장자〉*one*'s elder; *one*'s senior

장작 長斫 firewood; wood (for fuel)
♦장작을 패다 chop [split] wood / 장작을 지피다 feed a fire with firewood; burn wood
■—개비 a piece of (fire)wood; a billet —단 a fag(g)ot —불 wood fire

장장 長長 ♦ very long; lengthily
♦장장 4시간에 걸친 시합 a game that went on for [lasted, took] as long as four hours
▶나는 장장 3시간이나 그를 기다렸다 I waited for him for as long as three hours [for three long hours, for three mortal hours].
■—추야(秋夜) the long nights of autumn —하일(夏日) the long days of summer

장전 裝塡 〈탄약을 잼〉a charge; loading —장전하다 load; charge 《a gun with a cartridge》
♦장전한 총 a loaded rifle
▶그는 총에 탄환을 장전했다 He loaded his gun with bullets.

장점 長點 〈특기〉a strong [good] point; forte; 〈공덕〉a merit; 〈미덕〉a virtue; a point of excellence; 〈강점〉an advantage
♦장점과 단점 merits and demerits; strong and weak points; strength and weakness; 《*one*'s》forte and foible / 장점을 살리다 make use of *one*'s strong point
▶그[계획]의 장점은 무엇입니까? What are his good points [the merits of the plan]?

▶누구나 장점과 단점이 있다 Everybody has his merits and demerits.
▶조작이 아주 쉽다는 것이 이 기계의 장점이다 The advantage of this machine is that it is very easy to operate.
▶능변은 정치가로서의 그의 장점의 하나다 Eloquence is one of his merits [good points] as a politician.
▶그것은 장점인 동시에 단점이기도 하다 What is its strength is also its weakness. ⇌ This is at once its strength and weakness.
▶그것은 값이 싸다는 장점이 있다 It has the advantage of cheapness.

장정 壯丁 〈성년 남자〉 a man; 〈징병 적령자〉 a man of enlistment [military] age; 〈징집자〉 a conscript ■—명부 a list of conscripts

장정 長征 a long march; 〈중공군의〉 the Long March

장정 裝幀 〈책의 제본〉 binding; getup; get-up; 〈책 의장〉 design ◆가죽 표지로 장정된 책 a book in leather binding
▶이 책은 장정이 훌륭하다 This book is beautifully bound. —장정하다 bind; get up

장조 長調 〖樂〗 major; maggiore; Dur ◆다장조 교향곡 a symphony in C major / 라장조 바이올린 협주곡 a violin concerto in D major

장족 長足 a great stride; a strong pace
◆장족의 진보를 하다 progress with rapid [giant] strides; make long strides; make rapid [great] progress; advance by strides
▶제2차 세계대전후 전자공학은 장족의 진보를 했다 Rapid [Fast] progress has been made in electronics since the Second World War.

장죽 長竹 a long (smoking) pipe

장중 莊重 〈장엄함〉 solemnity; impressiveness; gravity —장중하다 solemn; sublime; majestic; impressive; grave
▶오르간 음악이 장중하게 울렸다 The organ music sounded grave [solemn].

장중보옥 掌中寶玉 ▶그는 장중 보옥을 잃었다 He lost his most precious thing [the apple of his eye].

장지 葬地 a burial [burying] place [ground]; 〈묘지〉 a graveyard; 〈공동묘지〉 a cemetery; a churchyard

장지 障— a paper sliding door
◆장지를 열다[닫다] open [shut] a paper sliding door / 장지를 바르다[갈아 붙이다] paper [repaper] a paper sliding door

장차 將次 in the future; some day; in (due) time
▶장차 어떤 일이 일어날 것인가는 아무도 모른다 Nobody can tell [We never can tell] what will happen in the future.

장천 長天 the boundless sky

장총 長銃 a (long-barreled) rifle

장축 長軸 major diameter ⇨ 긴지름

장출혈 腸出血 〖醫〗 enterorrhagia; enterostaxis

장치 裝置 〈설비〉 a installation; 〈무대 장치〉 setting; 〈기계 부품〉 a device; 〈고안품〉 a contrivance; 〈한 벌의 기구〉 an apparatus (pl. ~, ~es); 〈기계 장치〉 a gadget; 〈조립식 장치〉 system
◆건물에 냉방 장치를 하다 air-condition a building —장치하다 equip [fit, furnish] (with); install
◆시한 폭탄을 장치하다 set a time bomb / 장치되어 있다 be equipped [fitted] (with)
▶그들은 그 배에 새 엔진을 장치했다 They equipped [fitted] the ship with new engines.
▶문은 자동으로 여닫히도록 장치되어 있다 The door is so made as to open and close automatically.
■급수— a feeding apparatus 난방[냉방]— a heating [an air-conditioning] apparatus 무대— (stage) setting; scenery 무전— a wireless installation 방화— fire prevention equipment [device] 스테레오— a stereo equipment 안전— a safety device 조명— a lighting system

장침 長枕 〈팔꿈치를 괴는 베개〉 a long pillow that serves as an armrest

장침 長針 **1** 〈긴 바늘〉 a long needle **2** 〈분침〉 the long [minute] hand

장카타르 腸— 〖醫〗 〈창자의 염증〉 intestinal catarrh

장쾌하다 壯快— stirring; thrilling; exciting

장타 長打 〖野〗 a long hit
◆장타를 날리다 make a long hit
■—력 the power to hit a long-distance ball —자 a long-ball [long-distance] hitter

장탄식 長歎息 a long [heavy, deep] sigh —장탄식하다 give [draw, heave] a long [deep, heavy] sigh
▶그는 하늘을 우러러보며 장탄식했다 He sighed deeply [gave a deep sigh] looking up at the sky.

장터 場— 〈장이 서는 곳〉 a market place

장티푸스 腸— typhoid; typhoid fever; typhoid abdominalis ■—균 a typhoid bacillus —보균자 a typhoid carrier —완친 typhobacterin

장파 長波 a long wave
■—라디오 수신기 a long-wave radio set

장판 壯版 a paper(ed) floor
—장판하다 paper the floor of a room; cover the floor with oilpaper ■—방 a oilpaper floor room —지 a (sheet of) oiled floor paper

장편 長篇 a long piece [work, article]
■—기록영화 a long documentary film [picture] —소설 a long [full-length] novel —영화 a long film [picture]; a feature (film)

장편(소설) 掌篇(小說) a short story; a short-short; a conte

장폐색(증) 腸閉塞(症) 〖醫〗 ileus; intestinal obstruction

장하다 壯— 〈훌륭하다〉 splendid; grand; magnificent; glorious; 〈가륵하다〉 praiseworthy; admirable; 〈놀랍다〉 wonderful
◆장한 어머니 a respectable [an honorable] mother / 장한 공적 a deed of high glory; a brilliant achievement / 장한 일을 하다 achieve [do] a great thing
▶우승을 했다니 너 참 장하다 It is splendid of you taking first prize.

장하다 長— 〈능하다〉 proficient [adept] (in); 〈서술적〉 excel (in); be clever [good] (at); be skilled [accomplished] (in); be a good hand (at); be at home (in)

장학 獎學 〈학문을 장려함〉 encouragement

[promotion] of learning / —장학하다 encourage learning ■ —기금 ⇨ 장학자금 —제도 a scholarship

장학관 獎學官 a school inspector [commissioner] ■ 도[시]— a provincial [municipal] school inspector

장학금 獎學金 a scholarship; fellowship
♦ 장학금을 설정하다 found [create] a scholarship / 장학금을 주다 offer [award] a scholarship / 대학 진학 장학금을 신청하다[받다] apply for [win, gain, get] a scholarship to the university / 장학금을 받고 있다 be on a scholarship; be supported by a scholarship
▶ 그는 장학금으로 대학을 나왔다 He got through the university [He finished his university education] on a scholarship.

장학생 獎學生 a student on a scholarship; a scholarship student; a scholar ♦ 장학생이 되다 gain [get, obtain] a scholarship

장학자금 獎學資金 a scholarship fund
♦ 장학자금을 설정하다 create [establish, found, set up] a scholarship fund

장해 障害 an obstacle ⇨ 장애 (障礙)

장형 長兄 one's oldest brother

장화 長靴 boots; 〈무릎까지 올라 오는〉 top boots ♦ 장화를 신다[벗다] pull on [off] one's boots ■ 고무— elastic boots

장황하다 張皇 lengthy; long-winded; long and boring; tedious; wordy; redundant
♦ 장황한 설명 a long-winded [tedious] explanation / 장황한 연설 a long boring speech / 장황하게 lengthily; at great length / 장황하게 이야기하다 enlarge [dwell] on (a subject); speak of sth at full length
▶ 조부님은 얘기 상대가 있으면 좋았던 옛 일을 장황하게 얘기하신다 My grandfather will tell in detail of the good old days whenever he has someone to talk to.

잦다[1] 〈액체가〉 dry up; boil [simmer] down; 〈바람 등이〉 sink; go down; subside; fall

잦다[2] 〈뒤로 기울다〉 lean [bend] back(ward)

잦다[3] 〈빈번하다〉 frequent; incessant; repeated; quick; rapid
♦ 잦은 기침 a hacking cough / 잦은 방귀 frequent farts / 잦은 걸음으로 with a quick [rapid] step; at a brisk pace; at a trot
▶ 이 길은 사람이나 차량의 왕래가 잦다 This is a busy [bustling] street with heavy traffic.
▶ 겨울에는 화재가 잦다 Fires are frequent in wintertime.
▶ 6월에는 비가 잦았다 Rainy weather prevailed in June.

잦뜨리다 throw 《one's head》 back; bend [pull] 《one's shoulders》 back
▶ 그는 머리를 잦뜨리고 앉아 있었다 He was sitting with his head thrown back.

잦아들다 run dry; keep sinking [going down]
▶ 우물물이 잦아들었다 The water in the well has got low.

잦아지다 dry up; be boiled down [dry]; boil down ▶ 수프가 잦아지지 않도록 불을 약하게 해라 Turn down the fire so that the soup will not boil down.

잦추다 〈잇달아 재촉하다〉 urge incessantly; press 《for》; hurry (up)

잦혀놓다 1 〈뒤집어 놓다〉 lay [place] sth face down [upside down]
2 〈열어 놓다〉 leave [keep] 《a window》 open
3 〈제쳐놓다〉

잦혀지다 1 〈뒤집히다〉 be turned over [upside down]; be overturned
2 〈뒤로〉 be pulled back
3 〈열리다〉 be flung [thrown] open
▶ 책이 잦혀져 있다 A book lies open.

잦히다[1] 1 〈뒤집다〉 turn sth upside down; turn over; lay sth face down
♦ 책상을 잦히다 turn over the leaves of a book; turn the pages of a book / 접시를 잦히다 turn a plate over [upside down]
2 〈뒤로〉 pull back; lean [bend] oneself backward
♦ 몸을 잦히다 straighten oneself up; stick out one's chest / 어깨를 잦히다 pull back one's shoulders
3 〈열다〉 fling [throw] open; open wide
♦ 문을 잦히다 fling a door open

잦히다[2] 〈밥을〉 steam boiled rice; allow boiled rice to settle by its own heat

재[1] 〈고개〉 a (mountain) pass; a ridge
♦ 무악재 the Muak Pass / 재를 넘다 cross (over) a pass; pass over the peak

재[2] 〈타고 남은〉 ash(es)
♦ 〈핵 폭발로 인한〉 죽음의 재 the lethal ash; the atomic dust; the lethal (radioactive) fallout 《from an atomic test》 / 재투성이의 full of ashes; ashy / 재가 되다 convert into ash; ash / 죽어서 재가 되다 be cremated / 재를 뿌리다 sprinkle ashes; ash
▶ 난로의 재를 청소해 주시오 Please clear the ashes from the fireplace.
▶ 이 석탄은 재가 많이 남는다 This coal leaves much ash.
▶ 그 화재로 인해 모든 것이 재로 변했다 Everything was burned [reduced] to ashes in the fire.
■ 연탄[석탄]— briquet [coal] cinders

재 齋 〖佛敎〗 a Buddhist memorial service; a Buddhist mass [service]
♦ 재를 올리다 hold a Buddhist service for the dead; have a mass read [said] for the repose of sb's soul

재- 再- re-; again; once more
♦ 재조사 reexamination / 재발견하다 rediscover / 재투자하다 reinvest; invest again

재가 在家 being (at) home; staying at home; 〖佛敎〗 leading the ascetic life of Buddhism at one's home
—**재가하다** be (at) home; be in; keep [stay] at home; 〖佛敎〗 lead the ascetic life of Buddhism at one's home
■ —승 a secular [married] Buddhist monk

재가 再嫁 remarriage 《of a woman》 ⇨ 개가 (改嫁)

재가 裁可 sanction; approval
♦ 대통령의 재가를 바라다 submit sth to Presidential sanction / 국왕의 재가를 얻다 obtain royal sanction
—**재가하다** sanction; approve; give sanction to

재간 才幹 ability; talent; capability; resources ◆이렇다 할 재간이 없는 사람 a person with no particular skill / 재간이 있는 able; talented; capable; gifted; resourceful ▶나는 아무 재간도 없다 I am good for nothing. ▶그는 재간이 많은 사람이다 He is a man of great resources. ⇌ He is an able man. ▶그는 학식과 재간이 남보다 뛰어나다 He excels both in talent and in attainments. ■말— oratorical talent [skill]; eloquence; (口) the gift of the gab 손— workmanship; handicraft; manual skill; dexterity; deftness

재간 再刊 republication; reprint; reissue —재간하다 republish; reprint; reissue

재갈 〈말의〉a bit; 〈입가개〉a gag ◆말에 재갈을 물리다 bit a horse / 재갈을 물다 take the bit ▶새로운 검열법은 언론에 재갈을 물리려는 시도다 The new censorship laws are an attempt to gag the press.

재감 在監 〔法〕 imprisonment; being [staying] in prison ◆재감중이다 be in prison [jail] ■—자 a prisoner; a prison inmate; (총칭) the criminal population

재감염 再感染 reinfection

재강 〈술 찌끼〉(brewer's) grains; liquor lees ■—장 soysauce made from liquor lees —죽 gruel made from liquor lees and rice

재개 再開 reopening; resumption —재개하다 reopen; hold 《a meeting》 again; resume ◆경기를 재개하다 resume play / 교섭을 재개하다 reopen [resume] negotiations ▶점심을 먹고 나서 토론을 재개합시다 Let's continue the discussion after lunch. ▶수업은 9월에 재개된다 School reopens in September. ▶회의는 오후 2시에 재개되었다 The meeting resumed at 2 p.m. ⇌ We resumed the meeting at 2 p.m.

재거 再擧 another [a second] attempt; 〈군대 등의〉a rally ◆재거를 꾀하다 try to find the next chance 《to do》; plan a comeback —재거하다 make another [a second] attempt; renew one's attempt

재건 再建 rebuilding; reconstruction —재건하다 reconstruct; rebuild ◆폐허가 된 성을 재건하다 reconstruct a ruined castle / 전쟁으로 황폐한 도시를 재건하다 rebuild a town devastated by the war ■산업[경제]— industrial [economic] reconstruction 전후— the postwar rehabilitation ■—비 rebuilding expenses

재검사 再檢査 reexamination; reinspection ▶당신의 위는 재검사가 필요합니다 Your stomach must be examined again. —재검사하다 recheck; reexamine; reinspect

재검토 再檢討 reexamination; reappraisal; review —재검토하다 reexamine; reappraise; review; take a new look 《at》; examine 《it》 all over again ▶우리는 그 문제를 재검토해야만 한다 We must take a new look at the problem.

재결 裁決 (a) decision; (a) judgment; a ruling; 〈중재의〉arbitrament; arbitration ◆재결에 따르는 abide by a decision / 재결을 내리다 pass judgment 《on》 / 의장의 재결을 청하다 ask for the chairman's decision —재결하다 give [pass] decision [judgment] 《on》; arbitrate; decide ■—권 authority to decide; a casting vote —서 a written verdict [decision]

재결합 再結合 reunion; recombination —재결합하다 reunite 《with》; recombine; rejoin together ◆전남편과 재결합하다 be reconciled [reunited] with her former husband

재경 在京 staying in Seoul ▶나는 그가 재경중이라고 들었다 I hear he is now in Seoul. ■—동창생 alumni in Seoul —외국인 foreign residents in Seoul

재경 財經 finance [financial administration] and economy

재계 財界 〈금융계〉the financial world; financial circles; 〈경제계〉the economic world; economic circles; 〈실업계〉the business world; business circles ◆재계의 거물 a leading financier; (口) a tycoon; a business magnate / 재계의 안정[불안] financial stability [unrest] / 재계의 불황 business depression ▶재계가 활기를 띠고 있다 The financial world shows signs of activity. ■—인(人) a financier; a businessman

재계 齋戒 purification (⇨ 목욕재계) —재계하다 purify oneself; perform purification

재고 再考 reconsideration ◆재고 끝에 on reflection; on second thought(s) / 재고를 촉구[요청]하다 urge [ask] sb to reconsider / 재고를 요함(라) ad referendum ▶재고의 여지가 없다 There is no room for reconsideration. —재고하다 reconsider; rethink; think over again ▶재고한 끝에 그 모임에는 나가지 않기로 했다 On second thought, I decided not to attend the party. ▶재고해 보겠습니다 I will consider it once more. ⇌ Let me think it over again.

재고 在庫 stock; the stockpile ▶주문하신 책은 재고가 있습니다[없습니다] The book you have ordered is in [out of] stock. ▶설탕의 재고는 많습니다 We keep [have] a large stock of sugar. ▶석유의 재고가 부족합니다 The stock of oil at our shop has run short. ▶통조림은 재고가 거의 바닥났다 The stock of canned goods has nearly run out. ■—과잉 overstock; surplus stocks: 시장은 재고 과잉이다 The market is overstocked. —대장 a stock book —량 the total stock —부족 a dearth [shortage] of goods in stock —정리 clearance; inventory adjustment: 재고정리 대매출 a clearance [stocktaking, rummage] sale

재고조사 在庫調査 stocktaking; an inventory; inventory-taking

재고품

◆재고조사를 하다 take [check] stock (of); take account of stock; make [conduct] inventory of (supplies); take inventory

재고품 在庫品 goods [stock] in store; stock [goods] on [in] hand; stored goods
◆재고품이 많다[적다] have a large [small] stock
■—목록 a stock list; an inventory: 재고품 목록을 작성하다 make [draw up] an inventory; inventory

재교 再校 the second proof; the second revision ◆재교를 보다 read the second proof
▶재교를 요함 Second proof required.

재교부 再交付 (a) reissue; (a) renewal
◆여권의 재교부를 신청하다 apply for reissuance of a passport —**재교부하다** reissue (a passport); renew

재교육 再教育 reeducation; retraining; reorientation; 〈재직자의〉 in-service training
◆재교육 받다 be reeducated; be retrained
—**재교육하다** reeducate; retrain; reorient

재구속 再拘束 (a) remand —**재구속하다** remand; send sb back into custody

재군비 再軍備 rearmament; remilitarization
◆재군비에 찬성[절대 반대]하다 be for [absolutely against] rearmament / 재군비에 광분하다 be mad about remilitarizing (a country)
—**재군비하다** rearm; remilitarize (a country)
■—계획 a remilitarization [rearmament] program

재귀 再歸 recurrence; return
■—대명사[동사] a reflexive pronoun [verb]
—열(熱) [醫] recurrent [relapsing] fever

재규어 (動) a jaguar; an American leopard

재기 才氣 talent ◆재기 발랄한 사람 a brilliant [very clever] man / 재기가 있는 clever; witty; talented; gifted

재기 再起 a comeback; recovery; rising again
▶회사는 재기 불가능하게 되었다 The company was damaged beyond recovery.
▶그는 재기가 불가능하다는 선고를 받았다 His recovery was pronounced as hopeless.
—**재기하다** come back; rise again; recover; be restored
▶그녀는 무대 배우로 재기했다 She made a comeback as a stage actress.
▶그가 재기할 가망은 전혀 없다 There is no earthly chance for him to come back.

재깍¹ 〈빨리〉 quickly; speedily; with dispatch; instantly; on the spot; at once
◆일을 재깍 해치우다 be prompt in one's work; do a thing with dispatch

재깍² 〈소리〉 with a click [clack, snap, snick]
◆자물쇠가 재깍 잠겼다 The lock clicked shut.
▶시계가 재깍재깍 소리를 내고 있다 Click, click, click...goes the watch.

재깍거리다 make a clicking [snapping] sound
◆시계가 재깍거린다 The clock is ticking.

재깔거리다 talk garrulously; babble; gabble; chatter; prattle

재깔재깔 garrulously; chattering; babbling

재난 災難 〈재앙〉 a disaster; a calamity; 〈불행〉 a misfortune; a mishap; woes; 〈돌발 사고〉 an accident
◆재난의 연속 a continuous series of calamities; a series [spell] of misfortunes / 재난을 초래하다 invite [court] a disaster; 〈스스로〉 bring a calamity upon oneself / 재난을 당하다 have an accident; meet (with) a misfortune [calamity]
▶이것은 재난의 전조다 This bodes disaster.
▶그녀에게 무슨 재난이 일어날 것만 같다 I'm afraid something bad is going to happen to her.
▶그의 경우 재산이 재난의 씨가 되었다 In his case, his estate proved a curse to him.
▶작년은 재난의 연속이었다 I had a run of bad luck last year.
▶그는 가까스로 재난을 모면했다 He narrowly escaped a disaster [an accident].
▶예정을 바꾸어 앞편의 비행기를 탔기 때문에 그는 재난을 당했다[피했다] Since he changed his plans and took the preceding flight, he met with [escaped] the disaster [accident].

재능 才能 ability; talent; gift; genius

> 解說 가장 일반적으로 선천적·후천적인 능력을 나타내는 말이 ***ability***인데, 「재능」의 의미로는 복수형인 abilities를 많이 쓴다. 선천적이며 특히 예술·예능 등 어떤 종류의 특별한 것에 대한 재능이지만, 그것을 훈련함으로써 비로소 개발되는 재능은 ***talent***. 천부의 재능으로 어떠한 노력도 필요 없이 자연적으로 발휘되는 재능은 ***gift***. 창조적인 일에 발휘되는 비범한 재능은 ***genius***.

◆재능 있는 사람 a talented [gifted] person; an able man; a man of talent [ability] / 재능을 타고나다 be endowed [gifted] with talent / 재능을 닦다 cultivate one's talents; improve one's ability / 재능을 발휘하다 display [show, exhibit] one's ability [talent]
▶그녀는 재능이 다양하다 She has various talents.
▶이 학생은 어학에 재능이 있다 This student has a linguistic talent [a talent for languages].
▶그 일이라면 그도 십분 재능을 발휘할 수 있을 것이다 In that work, he will be able to show his ability.

재다¹ **1** 〈측정하다〉 〈넓이·길이를〉 take measure of; 〈도량을〉 measure; gauge; 〈무게를〉 weigh; 〈측량하다〉 survey; 〈수심·마음을〉 fathom; sound
◆자로 재다 take measurement with a rule / 저울로 재다 weigh sth in the balance [on the scales] / 키를 재다 measure [take] sb's height / 몸무게를 재다 weigh oneself; take one's weight / 체온을 재다 take one's temperature / 각도를 재다 take [measure] the angle (of) / 강우량을 재다 gauge (the amount of) rainfall / 강의 수심을 재다 sound [fathom] the depth of a river
▶시간은 시, 분, 초로 잰다 Time is measured by the hour, minute and second.
▶나는 거리를 쟀다 I measured the distance.
▶야드는 길이를 재는 단위다 A yard is a unit in measuring length.

▶나는 양복의 치수를 쟀다 I was measured for a suit.
2 〈헤아리다〉 calculate; look before and after; give careful consideration; take every possible consequence into consideration
♦앞뒤를 재다 take every possible consequence [situation] into consideration; look before and after / 여러 각도로 재보다 view *sth* from various angles / 일을 재어서 하다 carry out *one's* plan with discretion
3 〈장전하다〉 load; charge ♦총에 탄환을 재다 load a gun
4 〈염탐하다〉 spy upon *sb*; search *sb* on a subject; feel out *sb's* view
♦형세를 재다 feel out the situation / 회사의 내정을 재다 investigate the inside affairs of a company / 남의 의중을 재다 sound (out) *sb*; tap *sb's* opinion
5 〈으스대다〉 put on airs; give *oneself* airs; assume an air of importance; wear a high hat; 《俗》 be high-hatted
▶그렇게 재지 말게 Don't be so puffed up.
▶그것은 전혀 잴 만한 일이 못된다 That is nothing to be proud of.
재다² **1** ⇨ 쟁이다
2 ⇨ 재우다
재다³ **1** 〈빠르다〉 quick; nimble; agile; alert; fast
♦몸이 잰 사람 a nimble person / 걸음이 재다 be quick [swift, fleet] of foot; have quick steps; be light-footed / 손이 재다 have nimble fingers; be skillful [smart] with *one's* hand
2 〈쉬이 더워지다〉 easy [quick] to warm up
3 〈입이 가볍다〉 talkative; voluble; glib
▶그는 입이 재서 탈이다 His tongue wags too freely.
재단 財團 a foundation
♦포드[록펠러] 재단 the Ford [Rockefeller] Foundation / 재단을 설립하다 establish an endowment [a foundation]; found a fund
■─법인 a juridical foundation; a foundational juridical person
재단 裁斷 1 〈마름질〉 cutting; a cut
♦재단이 잘 되어 있다 be well tailored [cut]; be a very good cut / 재단이 신통찮다 be ill tailored [cut]
─재단하다 cut out 《a dress》
♦상의를 치수에 맞추어 재단하다 cut (out) a coat to measure
2 ⇨ 재결(裁決)
■─기 a cutter; a cutting machine ─법 cutting; a cut ─사 a cutter
재담 才談 a witty remark; a quirk; 《美俗》 a wisecrack ─재담하다 make a witty remark; 《美俗》 crack wise
재당숙 再堂叔 a male second cousin of *one's* father
재당질 再堂姪 a son of *one's* male second cousin
재덕 才德 virtue and talent
♦재덕 겸비의 of [with] virtue and talent; virtuous and talented / 재덕을 겸비하다 be both talented and virtuous
재독 再讀 a second reading

─재독하다 read again; reread
재돌입 再突入 〈로켓의〉 (a) reentry
─재돌입하다 make a reentry 《into》; reenter
▶우주선은 무사히 지구 대기권에 재돌입했다 The spaceplane made a successful reentry into the earth's atmosphere.
재떨이 an ashtray; 〈스탠드식〉 a smoking stand ♦재떨이에 담배를 비벼 끄다 put out *one's* cigarette in an ashtray / 재떨이를 쓰레기통에 비우다 empty an ashtray into a dustbin
재래 在來 ♦재래의 usual; ordinary; common; traditional; customary; conventional; native / 재래의 방식을 바꾸다 change the conventional [traditional] method
■─식 a conventional type; a customary style: 재래식 무기 conventional arms [weapons] ─종 a native kind [species]; a local [home] breed: 재래종 딸기 native strawberries
재래 再來 a second coming ⇨ 재림 ─재래하다 come again─
재래하다 齎來─ 〈가져오다〉 bring; 〈초래하다〉 bring about [on, forth]
재량 裁量 discretion
♦자기의 재량으로 at *one's* own discretion / 재량에 맡기다 leave *sth* to *sb's* discretion; give *sb* a free hand 《in a matter》 / 자유 재량권이 없다 have no discretionary power [authority]
▶일체를 의장의 재량에 맡겼다 Everything is left to the president's discretion.
▶어느 길로 가느냐는 네 재량에 달려 있다 It is within your discretion [up to you] to decide which way to take.
▶네 재량대로 해라 Do it as you think fit.
■─처분 《法》 discretionary disposition
재력 財力 〈금력〉 financial power [ability]; competence; 〈재산〉 means; wealth ♦재력이 있는 사람 a man of means [wealth]
재론 再論 reargument; rediscussion
▶이 문제는 재론의 여지가 없다 This problem leaves no room for rediscussion.
─재론하다 reargue; rediscuss; argue [discuss] again
재롱 才弄 (baby's) cute tricks ♦재롱(을) 부리다 act cute; do cute things; give [make] sweet gestures ■─둥이 a cute baby; a sweet baby doing cute things
재롱스럽다 才弄─ cute; sweet
재료 材料 (a) material; matter; stuff; 〈원료〉 raw material(s); ingredients; 〈자료〉 data
♦케이크의 재료 the ingredients of a cake / 소설의 재료가 되다 be made the material for a novel / 재료가 떨어지다 be [run] out of resources [stock] / 재료를 모으다 amass [collect] materials 《for》
▶이 집은 좋은 재료를 써서 지었다 This house is built of good materials.
▶밀가루와 버터는 케이크의 재료다 Flour and butter are the ingredients of a cake.
■─건축─ building [construction] materials 실험─ materials for experiments: 생물학의 실험 재료 materials for biological experiments ■─고갈 exhaustion of materials ─비 the

cost of materials; the material cost ―시험 material testing

재류 在留 residence ―재류하다 reside; stay; live
♦ 워싱턴에 재류하는 한국인 the Korean residents in Washington, D.C. / 재류하는 resident; living
―민[교포] Korean residents abroad ―외국인 foreign residents 《in, at》; resident aliens 《in》

재림 再臨 a second coming [advent]
♦ 그리스도의 재림 the (Second) Advent of Christ / 그리스도 재림설 Adventism
―재림하다 come again

재목 材木 wood; (美) lumber; (英) timber
♦ 쌓아놓은 재목 piled lumber / 재목을 베어내다 (美) lumber; (英) cut down timber / 재목을 건조시키다 season the wood
▶ 소나무는 재목이 무르다 Pine is a soft wood.
―상 (美) a lumberman; (英) a timber dealer
―적재장 (美) a lumberyard; (英) a timberyard

재무 財務 financial affairs
▶ 그는 재무 담당이다 He is in charge of financial affairs.
―감사 financial audit ―고문 a financial adviser ―관 a financier; a finance secretary; a financial commissioner [agent] ―관리 financial management ―보고서 a financial report ―위원회 《국회의》 the finance committee ―제표(諸表) 〔經〕 financial statements ―행정 financial administration

재무장 再武裝 rearmament; remilitarization
―재무장하다 remilitarize 《a country》; rearm 《itself》

재물 財物 property; goods; *one's* valuables
♦ 재물에 눈이 어두워지다 be dazzled by riches / 아무의 재물을 빼앗다 rob *sb* of 《his》 property

재미 1 〈흥미〉 interest; 〈즐거움〉 fun; pleasure; enjoyment; amusement
♦ 독서의 재미 the pleasure of reading / 인생의 재미 the pleasure [joy, enjoyment] of life / 재미있는 경기 an exciting [a lively] game / 재미있는 사람 a man of humor; a jolly guy / 재미있는 생각 a good [happy] idea; an interesting idea / 재미있는 이야기 an amusing [a good] story; an entertaining [interesting] talk / 재미없는 경기 a dull [slow, joyless] game / 재미없는 사람 a matter-of-fact man; a prosaic person / 재미로 in [for] fun; out of fun; just for fun; for amusement / 그것이 재미가 나서 for the fun of it [the thing] / 재미있게 놀다 enjoy *oneself*; play merrily; have a fine [good] time / 재미있게 살다 live [lead] a pleasant life / 함께 하루를 재미있게 보내다 have a happy day together / 이야기를 아주 재미있게 하다 tell a story in a very amusing way / 재미를 보다 have a good time 《of it》; have fun; enjoy *oneself* / 재미를 붙이다 be interested 《in》; find pleasure 《in》; take pleasure [interest] 《in mathematics》 / 재미(가) 있다[나다] be interesting [amusing, jolly, entertaining, pleasant, enjoyable]; be full of interest [fun] / 재미(가) 없다 be uninteresting [dull, flat, insipid, unpleasant, unamusing]; be devoid of interest / 재미없는 화제त를 끄집어내다 bring up unpleasant subjects
▶ 이 바위 모양이 재미있다 The shape of this rock is interesting.
▶ 그는 일하는 것을 재미로 알고 있다 He is doing his job happily. ⇌ He is working for the fun of it.
▶ 그것 재미있을 것 같은데 It sounds like fun, doesn't it?
▶ 재미있었니? Did you have a good time? ⇌ Did you enjoy yourself?
▶ 뭐 재미있는 일 없어? Is there anything new [any news]?
▶ 그 소설 아주 재미있더라 I found the novel very interesting. ⇌ I enjoyed the novel very much.
▶ 재미없는 이야기는 그만 합시다 Let's drop this sore subject.
▶ 요즘은 일이 예전만큼 재미가 없다 I'm not as much interested in the job as I used to be.
2 〈형편·돈벌이 등의〉 favorableness; satisfactoriness; 〈이익〉 profit; good
▶ 이 장사는 별로 재미를 못 본다 This business doesn't pay much.
▶ 사태는 점점 재미없어졌다 The situation became less favorable to us.
▶ 너 그러면 재미없어 You'll pay for it!
▶ 이 품목으로 아주 재미보고 있다 This article is selling exceedingly well.

재미 在美 ♦ 재미중에 during *one's* stay in America; while in America / 재미중이다 be [reside] in America
―교포 Korean residents in America ―유학생 Korean students studying in America

재발 再發 1 〈질병·전쟁 등의〉 a relapse [return]; recurrence
♦ 전쟁의 재발 the recurrence of war / 병의 재발을 막다 prevent a disease from returning
▶ 이제 재발의 염려는 전혀 없습니다 There's no fear now that you will have a relapse.
―재발하다 〈병이 주어〉 recur; return; 〈사람이 주어〉 relapse 《into》; have [suffer] a relapse 《of》; have a second attack 《of》
▶ 중동 전쟁이 재발했다 The Arab-Israeli War broke out again.
▶ 그는 류머티즘이 재발했다 He had a return of rheumatism.
▶ 그는 퇴원하고 이내 재발했다 He relapsed soon after he got out of (the) hospital.
▶ 통증이 재발하면 이 약을 드십시오 If the pain returns, take this medicine.
2 〈재발송〉 resending; reforwarding
―재발하다 resend; reforward; send (out) again

재발견 再發見 rediscovery ―재발견하다 rediscover

재발급 再發給 reissuance; (a) reissue ―재발급하다 reissue ♦ 증명서를 재발급하다 reissue a certificate 《to》

재발행 再發行 reissue ―재발행하다 reissue

재방송 再放送 rebroadcasting; a rebroadcast ―재방송하다 rebroadcast
▶ 시청자의 요청에 따라서 재방송해 드립니다

We'll rebroadcast the program in response to the viewers' request.

재배 再拜 1〈절〉 bowing twice **―재배하다** bow twice **2**〈편지 끝에〉 Sincerely yours; Yours respectfully; As ever

재배 栽培 cultivation; culture; growing; raising ▶ 이 지방은 차 재배에 적합하다 This part of the country is suited for tea culture.
―재배하다 cultivate; grow; raise; rear
♦ 장미를 재배하다 grow [raise, cultivate] roses / 뜰에 국화를 재배하다 grow [cultivate] chrysanthemums in the garden / 딸기를 온실에서 재배하다 grow strawberries in a greenhouse
▶ 그는 취미로 토마토를 재배한다 He grows [raises] tomatoes as a hobby.
▶ 그들은 겨울에는 비닐하우스에서 토마토를 재배한다 They grow [raise] tomatoes in vinyl greenhouses during the winter.
■ 과수― fruit growing; pomiculture 담배― tobacco farming [raising] 속성[촉성]― forcing [intensive] culture; forcing; 촉성 재배한 야채 forced vegetables 수경― hydroponics
■ ―법 a method of cultivation ―자 a grower; a cultivator; a farmer

재배치 再配置 relocation; reassignment
♦ 군의 전국적인 재배치 the relocation of army units throughout the country
―재배치하다 relocate; reassign

재벌 財閥 a financial group [clique]; a great financial conglomerate; 〈부유 계층〉 the plutocracy; the plutocrats; 〈사람〉 a big businessman; a plutocrat
♦ 카네기 재벌 the Carnegie financial group [clique]; the Carnegie interests / 재벌의 횡포 plutocratic despotism
■ ―기업 a (business) conglomerate; a business group

재범 再犯 repetition of an offense; a second offense [conviction] **―재범하다** repeat an offense; commit a second offense ■ ―자 a second offender

재 보 財 寶 treasure(s); valuables; precious things; riches

재보험 再保險 reinsurance
―재보험하다 reinsure; 《英》 reassure
■ 의 무― obligatory reinsurance 임 의― facultative reinsurance ■ ―금 reinsurance claims [money] ―자 a reinsurer: 피재보험자 the reinsured ―중개인 a reinsurance broker

재복무 再服務 〈군인의〉 renewed enlistment; reenlistment **―재복무하다** reenlist

재봉 裁縫 sewing; needlework; tailoring
♦ 재봉이 잘 된 옷 a well-tailored suit / 재봉을 배우다[가르치다] take [give] lessons in sewing [needlework] / 재봉을 잘[못]하다 be good [poor] at needlework [tailoring]; be clever [awkward] with the needle
―재봉하다 do needlework; sew
■ ―공임[삯] sewing charges ―도구 sewing things [requisites] ―사 a tailor; 〈여자〉 a tailoress; a dressmaker ―실 a sewing room

재봉틀 裁縫― a sewing machine; a machine
♦ 재봉틀로 박다 sew 《a dress》 by machine; stitch 《a curtain》 on a sewing machine / 솔기를 재봉틀로 박다 run up a seam on the machine
▶ 이것은 손으로 꿰맨 거냐 재봉틀로 박은 거냐? Was the sewing done by hand or by machine? = Is this hand-sewed or machine-sewed?
■ ―기름 sewing-machine oil ―바늘 a sewing-machine needle

재분배 再分配 redistribution; reallotment
―재분배하다 redistribute; reallot

재빠르다 quick; swift; alert; nimble; agile; speedy; fleet
♦ 재빠른 동작 an agile movement / 재빠른 응답 a prompt answer; a quick reply / 재빠르게 ⇨ 재빨리
▶ 그는 손놀림이 재빠르다 He has nimble fingers.
▶ 그는 기회를 포착하는 데는 재빠르다 He is quick at seizing an opportunity.

재빨리 quickly; promptly; nimbly; alertly; rapidly; with dispatch ♦ 일을 재빨리 해치우다 finish one's work quickly; dispatch one's work; make short work of sth
▶ 그녀는 재빨리 대답했다 She answered promptly.
▶ 그는 재빨리 그것을 알아차렸다 He was quick to notice it.
▶ 그는 재빨리 일어나 노인에게 자리를 양보했다 He immediately stood up and gave his seat to the old man.

재사 才士 a man of talent; a man of (good, excellent) parts; a talented [clever] person
▶ 재사다병(多病)이라 Men of genius are often of delicate health.

재산 財産 property; means; a fortune; 〔法〕 an estate; 〈자산〉 assets
♦ 상당한 재산 a considerable [sizable] fortune; a competence / 수십억원의 재산 several billion won's worth of property / 한 재산 장만하다 amass [pile up] a fortune; (口) make up a pile / 재산을 만들다[모으다] make [accumulate, amass, pile up] a fortune / 재산을 상속하다 inherit [succeed to, come into] a fortune / 재산을 축내다 [까먹다] reduce [eat into] one's fortune / 재산을 낭비하다 waste one's wealth / 재산을 탕진하다 squander [run through] one's fortune; spend all one's wealth 《on》 / 재산을 보고 결혼하다 marry sb for 《his [her]》 fortune; marry a fortune; marry for money
▶ 내겐 재산이라고 할만한 것이 없다 I have no property to speak of.
▶ 우리에겐 먹고 살만한 재산이 있다 We have enough to live on.
▶ 그녀는 아버지로부터 막대한 재산을 물려받았다 She inherited a vast fortune from her father.
▶ 그는 재산이 있어 편히 살 수 있다 His means permit him to live comfortably.
▶ 그에겐 5억원의 재산이 있다 He has five hundred million won to his name.
▶ 그는 맨손으로 막대한 재산을 모았다 He built up a big fortune out of nothing.

▶ 그는 재산과 지위를 얻었다 He rose to fortune and rank.
▶ 건강은 큰 재산이다 Good health is a great asset.
▶ 국민의 생명과 재산을 보호하는 것이 그들의 임무다 It is their duty to protect the life and property of people.
■ 개인[공공]— individual [public] property 국유[사유]— state-owned [private] property 부부공유— community property 세습[상속]— hereditary [heritable] property 유형[무형]— tangible [intangible] property 증여— a settlement ■ —가 a man [person] of wealth [fortune, property]; a wealthy [rich] person —계정(簿) a property account; an assets and liabilities account —관리 property management; administration [custody] of property —관리인 an administrator [a custodian] of property —권 property right; the right to own or to hold property —목록 an inventory (of property); a list of property —법 (法) the law of property —분여 distribution of property —상속 succession to *sb's* property —상태 *one's* financial conditions [position]; the financial status [standing] 《of a firm》 —세 property tax —압류 attachment [seizure] of property —양도 conveyance of an estate —양도세 a tax on transfer of properties —양도인 an assignor; a transferer —양수인(讓受人) an assignee; a transferee —처분 disposition of property —취득세 tax on purchasing property —평가 property valuation [appraisal] —형(刑) a pecuniary punishment —형성 저축 build-up savings; funds installment savings; (worker's) property accumulation savings

재삼 再三 〈여러번〉 again and again; over and over again; more than once
♦재삼 시도하다 try again and again; try and try again / 재삼 경고하다 give repeated warnings
▶ 재삼 말해도 그는 듣지 않는다 He turns a deaf ear to my repeated warnings.

재상 宰相 the premier; the prime minister

재상영 再上映 a rerun; a repeat
—재상영하다 rerun; repeat
▶ 그 영화는 재상영되었다 The film was rerun [put on the screen again].

재색 才色 wit and beauty
▶ 그녀는 재색을 겸비하고 있다 She combines [has both] wit and beauty. ⇒ She is both beautiful and talented.

재생 再生 1 〈소생〉 revival; a return to life
—재생하다 return to life; revive
2 〈다시 태어남〉 rebirth; a second birth; regeneration
—재생하다 be reborn; be born again
3 〈폐품의 재생산〉 reclamation; regeneration; reproduction
▶ 헌 신문은 재생을 위해 수집된다 Old papers are gathered for reproduction.
—재생하다 reclaim; regenerate; reproduce; recycle
♦고무를 재생하다 reclaim rubber / 종이를 재생하다 remanufacture [remake] paper
4 〈녹음·녹화의〉 (a) playback; reproduction
—재생하다 play back; reproduce
▶ 그 녹음 테이프를 잠시만 재생해 주십시오 Please play back the (recorded) tape just a while.
5 〔生〕 regeneration; regrowth
♦털의 재생 regrowth of hair
—재생하다 regenerate; reproduce; renew; restore
■ —가능 에너지 a renewable [recycled] energy —고무 reclaimed [regenerated] rubber —로(爐) a regenerative furnace —법 a reproduction process —산업 the reproductive industry —섬유 regenerated fiber —양모 reworked [reclaimed] wool; mungo —유 reclaimed oil —장치 〈녹음·녹화의〉 playback equipment —지 recycled paper —품 reclaimed [made-over] articles; recycled products

재생산 再生産 reproduction —재생산하다 reproduce ■ 축소[확대]— reproduction on a regressive [progressive] scale

재선 再選 reelection
—재선하다 reelect
▶ 그는 이 시의 시장에 재선되었다 He was reelected mayor of this city.

재선거 再選擧 (a) reelection; a recall election
—재선거하다 reelect

재선적 再船積 reshipment
—재선적하다 reship; ship back; reexport

재세 在世 ♦재세의 living; in life / 재세시에 during [in] *one's* lifetime; while alive
—재세하다 live; be in life

재소자 在所者 a prisoner ⇨ 재감(∼자)

재수 再修 —재수하다 prepare for the entrance examination after *one* failed in the examination
▶ 그는 1년을 재수하여 원하던 대학에 들어갔다 He spent one year preparing for the entrance examination after he had left the high school and entered a university that he wanted.
■ —생 a student who failed a college entrance exam and has been cramming to try again; 〈유급생〉 (美) a repeater : 그는 대입 재수생이다 He is a high school graduate waiting for another chance to be admitted to a college.

재수 財數 luck; fortune
♦재수가 있다[좋다] be lucky; be in luck; be fortunate; have [be blessed with] a good luck / 재수가 없다 be unlucky; be unfortunate; be out of [off *one's*] luck; have no luck / 재수가 트이다 be in luck's way; fortune begins to smile (upon *one*); luck turns in *one's* favor
▶ 오늘은 재수가 좋을 것 같다 Today is going to be my lucky day! ⇒ Fortune seems to smile on me today.
▶ 자네는 요즈음 재수가 아주 좋구먼 You have been very lucky these days.
▶ 그런 소리 하지마라. 재수 없게 Don't say things like that. It might bring bad luck.

재수입 再輸入 reimport; reimportation —재수입하다 reimport ■—면장 a reimport permit —신고서 a reimport declaration —품 reimports; reimported articles

재수출 再輸出 reexport; reexportation —**재수출하다** reexport ■ —**품** reexports; reexported articles

재스민 〔植〕 a jasmin(e); a jessamine; 〈향수〉 jasmin(e)

재시합 再試合 rematch 《of a game》; a return game [match]

재시험 再試驗 (a) reexamination; retesting ♦ **재시험을 치르다** take an examination again; 《美口》 make up an examination —**재시험하다** reexamine; retest; examine again

재심 再審 reexamination; (a) review; 〔法〕 a retrial; a new trial; (a) renewal of procedure ▶ 그 서류는 재심을 위해 반송되었다 The papers were sent back to be reexamined. ▶ 그들은 그 사건의 재심을 청구했다 They demanded a retrial to the affair. ⇌ They applied for a new trial to the affair. —**재심하다** try a second time; review; retry

재심사 再審査 (a) reexamination; (a) review —**재심사하다** reexamine; examine again; review

재앙 災殃 〈재난〉 a disaster; a calamity; a fatality; woes; 〈불행〉 a misfortune; evils ♦ **거듭되는 재앙** a series [spell] of misfortunes / **재앙을 당하다** meet with a calamity [misfortune] / **재앙을 부르다[자초하다]** bring a calamity upon *oneself* / **재앙을 면하다** escape a disaster; be untouched by a disaster ▶ 이것은 재앙의 전조다 This bodes disaster. ▶ 그에게 재앙이 내릴 것만 같다 I'm afraid something bad is going to happen to him. ▶ 그에게 재앙이 닥쳤다 Misfortune befell him. ▶ 그의 부주의가 재앙을 몰고 왔다 His carelessness invited [brought on] the disaster.

재야 在野 ♦ **재야의** out of office [power]; in opposition / **재야 시절에** when [while] 《one is》 out of power / **재야의 명사들** distinguished men out of office —**재야하다** be in private life; remain out of public office; be out of office [power]

재연 再演 a second [repeat] performance; a rerun —**재연하다** perform [present] 《a play》 again; repeat 《the same play》; show 《a picture》 again; replay; rerun ♦ **범행을 재연하다** reconstruct *one's* crime

재연 再燃 a fresh outbreak; recurrence; revival; recrudescence —**재연하다** flare up again; come to the fore again; rekindle; revive ▶ 학생 운동이 재연됐다 The student movement came to the fore again.

재예 才藝 talent and accomplishments

재외 在外 ♦ **재외의** abroad; overseas —**공관** diplomatic establishments [missions] abroad; embassies and legations abroad —**교포[동포]** Korean residents [nationals] abroad; overseas Koreans —**자산** overseas [external] assets

재욕 財慾 desire for wealth; desire after riches

재우 promptly; quickly; nimbly; agilely; alertly

재우다 **1** 〈잠자게 하다〉 send [put] 《a child》 to sleep [bed]; let 《a child》 go to sleep ▶ 아이들을 재울 시간이다 It's time to put the children to [in] bed. ▶ 할머니는 요람을 흔들어 아기를 재웠다 The grandma rocked the baby to sleep. **2** 〈묵게 하다〉 lodge (and board) sb; give sb a bed; 〈여관 등이〉 accommodate sb with a lodging; put sb up; take ▶ 우리는 하룻밤 재워 달라고 부탁했다 We asked for a night's lodging. **3** 〈부픈 솜 등을〉 press; 〈머리 등을〉 smooth (down); settle ▶ 그는 들뜬 머리를 재웠다 He smoothed his fluffy hair down.

재우치다 rush [speed] up 《one's work》; dispatch 《work》; finish up quickly

재원 才媛 a talented girl; an accomplished young lady; a woman with literary talent

재원 財源 a source of revenue; 〈자금〉 funds ▶ 그 도시는 재원이 풍부[빈약]하다 The city is resourceful [resourceless]. ⇌ The city abounds [is poor] in resources. ▶ 급여를 인상시킬 재원이 없다 We have no means to finance the raise in the wages. ▶ 나는 새 집을 지을 만큼 재원이 없다 I do not have enough funds to build a new house. ▶ 우리는 그럭저럭 새로운 재원을 확보했다 We managed to obtain a new source of revenue.

재위 在位 ♦ **왕의 재위중에** during [in] the reign of the King / **재위 20년만에** after a reign of 20 years —**재위하다** be on the throne; reign ▶ 그 왕은 40년 이상이나 재위했다 The King reigned [was on the throne] for more than forty years. ■ —**기간** the period of 《King Sejong's》 reign

재음미 再吟味 (a) reexamination; a review —**재음미하다** reexamine; review

재의 再議 reconsideration; rediscussion ♦ **재의에 부치다** submit 《a matter before the committee》 for reconsideration —**재의하다** reconsider; discuss again

재인 才人 〈재능 있는 사람〉 a man of talent [ability]; 〈광대〉 an acrobatic tumbler; a performer

재인식 再認識 a new understanding; reappraisal —**재인식하다** have a new understanding [appreciation] 《of》; recognize [appreciate] anew ▶ 나는 외국을 여행하면서 영어 실력의 중요성을 재인식하게 되었다 I fully realized [realized clearly] how important a good knowledge of English was [is] when I traveled overseas.

재일 在日 residing in Japan ■ —**교포[동포]** Korean residents in Japan: 재일동포의 법적 지위 향상 the improvement of the legal status of Korean residents in Japan —**한국 거류민단** the Korean Residents Association in Japan

재임 在任 being in office ♦ **재임중에** during *one's* term [tenure] of office; during *one's* service —**재임하다** hold office [a post]; be in office ■ —**자** an incumbent

재임 再任 reappointment
—재임하다 get reappointed; reappoint
▶ 그는 외무부 장관에 재임되었다 He was reappointed Foreign Minister.

재입국 再入國 reentry 《into a country》
—재입국하다 reenter 《into a country》
■—허가서 a reentry permit

재입학 再入學 readmission 《to a college》; reentrance ◆재입학을 허가하다 readmit 《sb to a school》

재자 才子 a man of talent [parts]; a clever man; a wit
■—가인 a wit and a beauty

재작년 再昨年 the year before last
◆재작년 여름 (in) the summer before last

재작일 再昨日 the day before yesterday ⇨ 그저께

재잘거리다 chatter; prattle; gibber; jabber; wag one's tongue [jaw]
▶ 네가 그렇게 재잘거리면 나는 무슨 소린지 알아들을 수가 없어 I can't understand you when you jabber like that.

재잘재잘 chatteringly; tattlingly; volubly; glibly ▶ 그 여자 재잘재잘 잘도 지껄이네 What a glib tongue she has!

재재작년 再再昨年 two years before last

재적 在籍 enrol(l)ment
—재적하다 be on the register [roll]
▶ 그는 재적하고 있지 않다 He is no longer enrolled [on the register].
▶ 그 대학에는 많은 외국인 학생이 재적하고 있다 The university has a large enrollment of foreign students.
■—자〈학생〉 a registered person [student] —증명서〈학교의〉 an enrollment certificate; 〈단체의〉 a membership certificate

재적 材積 the volume of a piece of lumber [building stone]

재정 再訂 a second revision
—재정하다 revise again [a second time]
■—판 a second revised edition

재정 財政 finance(s); financial affairs 《of a company》; economy
◆재정의 핍박 financial straits [pressure, stringency] / 재정상의 위기 financial crisis / 재정이 곤란하다 be in financial difficulties; be in straitened circumstances / 재정이 풍부하다 be well off; be in abundant [easy] circumstances
▶ 이 회사는 재정이 넉넉하다 The finance of this firm is very good.
▶ 그런 사치는 나의 재정상 허락치 않는다 I cannot afford such luxury.
▶ 무엇보다도 먼저 나라의 재정을 재건하지 않으면 안된다 First of all, we must reconstruct the national economy.
▶ 시는 재정상의 어려움에 처해 있다 The city is in financial difficulties.
■건전[흑자]— sound [balanced] finance 국가— national finance 시(市)— the city finance [purse] 적자— red-ink [deficit, unbalanced] finance 지방— local (government) finance ■—가 a financier; a financial man —난 financial difficulties; pecuniary embarrassments: 재정난에 빠지다 get into financial trouble —면 financial aspects —문제 a financial question [problem] —법안 a finance bill —보증인 a financial guarantor —상태 the financial condition [status, situation]: 이 학교의 재정 상태는 개선되지 않으면 안된다 The finances of this school should be improved. —연도 a fiscal [financial] year —정책 a financial [fiscal] policy: 긴축 재정정책 a tight money policy; a tight-financing policy —증권 a treasury bill —통계 finance statistics —혼란 financial derangement

재정 裁定 (a) decision; a ruling; arbitration; adjudication ◆위원회의 재정에 따르다 accept [obey] the decision of the committee
—재정하다 decide; adjudicate; adjudge
■—거래 arbitrage —서 an award —안(案) an arbitration draft [proposal] —자 an adjudicator —조항〈노사간의〉 an arbitration clause —환 arbitrated exchange

재정적 財政的 financial; fiscal
◆재정적 원조 (a) financial support [help] / 재정적인 이유로 on financial grounds / 재정적으로 건전하다 be financially solvent
▶ 그는 재정적으로 어려움에 처해 있다 He is in a bad way financially. ⇌ He is hard up.

재정학 財政學 the science of finance; (public) finance ■—자 a financier

재제 再製 remanufacture; reproduction
—재제하다 remake; remanufacture; reproduce
■—염 refined salt —품 reclaimed [rebuilt, reprocessed] articles

재조 在朝 ◆재조 재야의 명사들 noted people in and out of official life

재조사 再調査 reexamination; reinvestigation
—재조사하다 reexamine; reinvestigate
▶ 그는 정부에 대해 그 사건을 재조사할 것을 촉구했다 He urged the Government to reexamine the case.

재조직 再組織 reorganization
▶ 파벌의 재조직이 현재 진행중이다 Reorganization of factions is now going on.
—재조직하다 reorganize

재종 再從 a second cousin
■—간 second-cousinship —고모 a female second cousin of one's father —매 one's younger female second cousin —숙 a male second cousin of one's father —제 one's younger male second cousin —질[질녀] a son [daughter] of one's second cousin —형 one's elder male second cousin

재주 才— 〈재능〉ability; talent; gifts; genius; aptitude; wit;〈재간·솜씨〉skill(fulness); dexterity;〈기예〉an art; a craft; an (artistic) accomplishment;〈곡예〉a feat; a trick; a stunt
◆재주 있는 사람 a talented [clever] man; a man of talent [ability] / 재주 있는 talented; gifted; clever / 재주 없는 talentless; dull / 손재주가 있다 be smart [clever] with one's hand / 재주를 부리다 exercise one's talent; perform a trick / 재주를 충분히 발휘하다 give full play to one's ability / 한 가지 재주에 통달하다 acquire an accomplishment [a skill]; be

재주 ▶그는 재주가 비상하다 He has eminent talents.
▶그는 동시에 두 가지 일을 하는 재주가 있다 He has a faculty for doing two things at once.
▶그녀는 문필에 재주가 있다 She has a talent [gift, genius] for writing. ⇌ She is a born [gifted] writer.
▶자기 재주를 과신하지 마라 Don't have too much confidence in your (own) talent.
▶나는 재주라고는 아무것도 없다 I have [can boast of] no accomplishment.
▶나는 재주가 몹시 서툴다 I am all thumbs.
▶나는 우리집 개에게 몇 가지 재주를 가르쳐 주었다 I have taught my dog some tricks.
▶재주는 곰이 넘고 돈은 되놈이 번다 (속담) One beats the bush and another catches the bird.

재주 在住 residence ━**재주하다** live 《in》; reside 《in》 ━**―자** a resident

재주 齋主 〔佛敎〕 the sponsor for a Buddhist requiem mass

재주껏 才― to the best of one's ability [skill]; as much as one can do

재주꾼 才― a person of high talents; a skillful person; a resourceful man

재주넘기 才― a somersault; a somerset

재주넘다 才― turn [make, do] a somersault; somerset

재중 在中 ◆견본 재중 (표시) Sample(s). / 사진 재중 (표시) Photos (only). / 인쇄물 재중 (표시) Printed matter only.

재즈 〔樂〕 jazz (music)
▶나는 시끄러운 재즈 소리를 좋아하지 않는다 I don't like clamorous sound of the jazz.
▶우리는 자주 재즈에 맞춰 춤을 추었다 We would often dance to jazz.
▶그녀는 피아노로 재즈를 연주했다 She played jazz on the piano.
■**―광** a hepster; a hipster ━**밴드[팬]** a jazz band [fan]

재지 才智 talent and wisdom; wit; intelligence

재직 在職 tenure of office
▶재직 10년 이상인 사람이 5명 있다 There are five people who have served [have been in service] for over ten years.
▶그 사건은 그의 재직중에 일어났다 The trouble happened during his tenure of office.
━**재직하다** hold office [a post]; be in office [service]
▶그 교사는 본교에 재직한 지 10년이 된다 The teacher has served this school for ten years.
■**―기간[연한]** the period of one's service; one's tenure of office ━**―자** an incumbent; the holder of a position

재질 才質 natural gifts [endowments]; talent; excellent fiber
◆재질이 풍부하다 be highly gifted [richly endowed] / 재질을 살리다[발휘하다] make the best use of one's talent

재질 材質 the quality of the material [lumber]

재차 再次 a second time; twice; again; for the second time ◆재차 방문하다 pay a [one's] second visit / 재차 시도하다 try again; make another [a second] attempt

재채기 sneezing; a sneeze ━**재채기하다** sneeze; do one's sneezing; have a fit of sneezing

재천 在天 existing in Heaven ◆재천의 in heaven; blessed; heavenly ▶인명은 재천이다 Life and death are providential.

재청 再請 〈재차의 청〉 a second request; an encore; 〈동의에 대한〉 seconding
◆재청을 받다 receive an encore
━**재청하다** request a second time; encore; 〈동의에〉 second 《a motion》

재촉 pressing; urging
▶어머니의 재촉을 받고 나는 자리를 떴다 At my mother's urging [Urged by my mother], I left my seat.
━**재촉하다** urge; press; prompt; quicken
◆걸음을 재촉하다 hurry one's way; quicken one's pace [steps] / 대답을 재촉하다 press sb for an answer / 아무에게 결정하도록 재촉하다 hurry [rush] sb into (making) a decision; urge [press] sb to make a decision / 성화같이 재촉하다 make an urgent request 《for》; press sb hard 《for》
▶그는 내게 빚을 갚으라고 재촉한다 He duns me for payment of a debt.
▶그는 재촉하지 않으면 아무 일도 안한다 He will not do anything unless he is pressed.

재출발 再出發 a fresh start; a restart
━**재출발하다** make a restart; make a fresh start; start again

재취 再娶 a second marriage; remarriage; 〈후처〉 a second wife ◆재취로 맞이하다 take 《a woman》 for [as] a second wife
━**재취하다** remarry (after the death of one's first wife); marry again

재치 才致 wit; quick wit; tact
◆재치있는 사람 a quick-witted person; a tactful man; a man of sense / 재치있는 농담 a nimble jest / 재치가 있다 be quick-[ready-]witted; be tactful [smart]
▶그는 언제나 재치있는 말을 한다 He always says smart [witty] things.
▶그의 이야기는 재치가 넘쳤다 His speech sparkled with wit.
▶그녀는 재치있게 화제를 바꿨다 She tactfully changed the subject.

재침략 再侵略 a reinvasion
◆적의 재침략에 대비하다 provide oneself against the enemy's reinvasion
━**재침략하다** reinvade

재칼 〔動〕 a jackal

재탕 再湯 〈다시 달임〉 a second decoction (of medicinal herbs); 〈재이용〉 a rehash; an adaptation
▶이 프로그램은 작년에 방송된 것의 재탕이다 This program is a rehash of a program (from) last year.
━**재탕하다** decoct again; make a second decoction 《of》; make a rehash 《of》
▶그 연사는 전에 했던 강연을 재탕했을 뿐이다 The speaker only rehashed some lectures he

had made before.
■ —차 the second brew of tea

재투자 再投資 reinvestment —재투자하다 reinvest; plow back 《the profits of a business》

재투표 再投票 revoting —재투표하다 take a vote again

재티 fine ashes; cinders; ash dust ◆ 재티가 눈에 들어가다 get cinders in *one's* eyes

재판 再版 reprinting; 〈제2판〉 a second edition [impression]; 〈되풀이〉 (a) repetition 《of a past event》
◆ 책의 재판을 찍다[발행하다] print [publish] a second edition of a book
▶ 그 책은 재판 중이다 The book is reprinting [being reprinted].
▶ 그 책의 재판이 곧 발행될 것이다 A second edition of the book will soon be issued.
▶ 우리는 그것이 1950년의 재판이 되지 않을까 걱정이다 We are anxious that it may be 1950 over again.
—재판하다 reprint ◆ 재판하게 되다 run into a second impression

재판 裁判 justice; 〈공판〉 a trial; a hearing; 〈판결〉 judgment; decision
◆ 재판의 공시 publication of a judgment / 재판에 부치다[회부하다] put 《a case》 on trial; bring 《a matter》 to trial [judgment] / 재판 일정을 정하다 assign a day for trial / 재판을 받다 be tried; face a trial; stand *one's* trial; be on trial / 재판에 이기다[지다] win [lose] a suit [case]
▶ 재판이 열리고 있다 The court is now sitting.
▶ 그 사건은 현재 재판 중이다 The matter is pending in court. ⇒ The case is now on trial.
▶ 그녀는 위증죄로 재판을 받았다 She was put on trial for perjury.
—재판하다 judge [try] 《*sb*, a case》; administer justice; stage a trial; decide on 《a case》
■ 결석[궐석]— judgment by default 모의— a mock trial 약식— a summary trial 인민— (美口) a kangaroo court 정식— a formal trial: 정식 재판을 청구하다 demand [appeal to the court for] a formal trial 확정— final judgment ■ —관 a judge; a justice; 〈총칭〉 the court; the bench —권 jurisdiction: 재판권이 있다 have jurisdiction 《over》 —비용 judicial costs —일 a court day —장 the chief [presiding] judge —절차 legal procedure [proceedings]

재편성 再編成 reorganization; reformation; rearrangement 《of classes》 —재편성하다 reorganize; reform; revamp ◆ 학급을 재편성하다 rearrange classes

재평가 再評價 revaluation; reassessment; reappraisal —재평가하다 revalue; revaluate; reassess; reappraise
■ 자산— revaluation [reassessment] of property: 자산재평가법 the Assets Revaluation Law —액 a revaluation amount —적립금 revaluation reserves

재포장 再包裝 repacking —재포장하다 repack

재학 在學 being in school
▶ 그는 대학에 재학 중이다 He is an undergraduate. ⇒ He is a college student.
—재학하다 be in [at] school [college]; be enrolled at [in] school; be a student 《at》
■ —기간 the period of attendance at school; the enrolling period at school —생 a (registered) student; 〈대학의〉 an undergraduate —증명서 a school certificate; a student registration certificate; a certificate of studentship

재할인 再割引 a rediscount 《of a bill》
—재할인하다 rediscount 《a bill》
■ —어음 a rediscount bill —율 a rediscount rate

재해 災害 a disaster; a calamity; an accident
◆ 자연 재해 a natural disaster / 홍수에 의한 재해 a flood disaster / 재해의 연속 a series of accidents; a spell of ill luck / 재해를 입다 suffer from a disaster / 재해를 당하다 meet (a) disaster / 재해에 대처하다 cope with (a) disaster
▶ 금년엔 여러 가지로 재해가 많았다 We have suffered many disasters this year. ⇒ This year has been remarkable for frequent disasters.
■ —방지 disaster prevention —보상 accident compensation —보험 accident [casualty] insurance —복구비 natural disaster relief expenditure [fund] —지 a stricken [suffering] district

재해대책 災害對策 countermeasures against calamities
◆ 중앙 재해 대책 본부 the Central Anti-Calamity Headquarters (略 CACH) / 재해대책을 세우다 take measures [precautions] against disasters
■ —위원회 the (national) anti-calamity measures committee

재행 再行 a bridegroom's post-marriage first visit to the bride's home
—재행하다 《a bridegroom》 pay (his) post-marriage first visit to the bride's home

재향군인 在鄕軍人 an ex-soldier; an ex-serviceman; a reservist; (美) a veteran
■ —회 an association of reservists; (美) the American Legion: 대한민국 재향군인회 the Korean Veterans Association

재현 再現 reappearance; reemergence; reproduction —재현하다 reappear; reemerge; appear again; reproduce
▶ 경찰관들은 그 사고 현장을 재현시켰다 The policemen reproduced the accident scene.
▶ 이것은 당시의 주거를 재현한 것이다 This is a reproduction of the house at that time.

재형저축 財形貯蓄 (worker's) property accumulation savings ⇨ 재산(～형성 저축)

재혼 再婚 a second marriage; remarriage
—재혼하다 marry again
■ —자 a remarried person

재화 災禍 a disaster ⇨ 재난

재화 財貨 money and goods; 〈부(富)〉 wealth; 〈재산〉 property

재확인 再確認 reaffirmation; reconfirmation
—재확인하다 confirm once more; reaffirm

재활용 再活用 the recycling [reuse] 《of waste

materials); the utilization (of waste materials) ◆재활용 휴지 recycled tissue paper / 재활용 비누 recycled soap —재활용하다 recycle; reuse; reutilize

재회 再會 meeting again; reunion
◆이산 가족의 재회 the reunion of the separated families / 재회를 약속하다 promise to meet again / 재회를 기약하고 헤어지다 part in the hopes of meeting again
—재회하다 meet again
▶그는 5년만에 아버지와 재회했다 He met his father for the first time in five years.

재흥 再興 revival; restoration; resuscitation; reestablishment; rehabilitation
—재흥하다 revive; restore; reestablish; rehabilitate

잭 1 〔機〕〈기중기〉a jack ◆잭으로 차를 들어 올리다 jack the car up; lift the car with a jack **2** 〈트럼프의〉the knave; the jack

잭나이프 a jackknife (*pl.* -knives)

잼 jam ▶나는 점심으로 빵에 잼을 발라 먹었다 I ate bread and jam for lunch.
▶빵에 잼을 발라라 Spread jam on your bread.

잼버리 a jamboree

잽 〔拳〕a jab ◆상대방에게 잽을 먹이다 jab *one's* opponent
▶그는 턱에 잽을 맞고 비틀거렸다 He reeled after being jabbed on the chin.
■라이트— a right(-hand) jab 레프트— a left(-hand) jab

잽싸게 quickly; swiftly; nimbly; agilely
◆잽싸게 달아나다 escape [run away] quickly / 일을 잽싸게 해치우다 rattle a piece of business through
▶소매치기는 잽싸게 모습을 감추었다 The pickpocket disappeared in a flash.

잽싸다 quick; swift; active; agile; nimble
▶이 아이는 동작이 잽싸다 This child is quick in his movements.

잿더미 (a heap of) ashes ◆잿더미가 되다 be reduced [burnt down] to ashes / 잿더미에서 일어서다 rise from the ashes
▶그 집은 하룻밤 사이에 잿더미로 변했다 The house was burnt to ashes overnight.

잿물 1〈재를 우려낸 물〉lye ◆잿물을 받다[내리다] render lye from ashes
2 ⇨ 양잿물
3〈유약〉glaze; enamel ◆도자기에 잿물을 올리다 put glaze on pottery

잿밥 齋— (boiled) rice offered to Buddha

잿빛 ash color; gray; 〈英〉grey
◆잿빛이 도는 grayish; ashy

쟁 箏 〈악기〉a thirteen-silk-stringed harp

쟁 鉦 a gong ⇨ 꽹과리

쟁강 with a clink ⇨ 쨍그랑

쟁권 爭權 contention of power; a struggle for supremacy [power] —쟁권하다 contend for supremacy [power]

쟁기 a plow; 〈英〉a plough ◆쟁기로 밭을 갈다 plow [plough] the fields ―꾼 a plowman ―질 plowing: 쟁기질하다 plow

쟁단 爭端 the beginning of a quarrel [dispute, discord]

쟁론 爭論 a dispute ⇨ 논쟁

쟁반 錚盤 a tray; a server; a salver

쟁의 爭議 a dispute; a strife; a trouble
◆쟁의를 일으키다 start [initiate] a dispute; beget [cause] a dispute [strife] / 쟁의를 해결 [조정]하다 settle [mediate] a dispute
▶대학 당국과 학생자치위원회 사이에 쟁의가 일어났다 A dispute arose between the University Administration and Student Council.
▶쟁의는 오래 끌었다 The dispute has dragged on.
■노동— a labor dispute ■—권 the right to strike —위원회 a dispute committee —점 the point at issue [in dispute]

쟁이다 heap (up); pile up; stack; put [lay] one thing on another; make a neat pile
◆김을 쟁이다 lay pressed laver sheets one on top of another

쟁쟁하다 錚錚— 〈출중하다〉prominent; eminent; outstanding; distinguished
◆쟁쟁한 학자들 prominent [distinguished, eminent] scholars / 각계의 쟁쟁한 인물들 outstanding people from various fields of life

쟁쟁하다 琤琤— 〈구슬 소리가〉clear; sonorous; resonant; 〈귀에〉ringing [lingering] (in *one's* ears)
▶그의 말이 지금도 귀에 쟁쟁하다 His words still ring in my ears.

쟁점 爭點 the point at issue [in dispute]; a point of contention; a disputed point; an issue
◆법률상의 쟁점 a legal dispute; an issue of law / 쟁점에서 벗어난 발언 remarks off the point

쟁취하다 爭取— win; gain; obtain; secure; score
◆독립을 쟁취하다 win *one's* independence / 승리를 쟁취하다 gain [win] a victory

쟁탈 爭奪 a scramble; a contest; a struggle; a contest
◆예산의 쟁탈 claimings for bigger shares in the budget
—쟁탈하다 scramble [struggle, contest, contend, fight] (for *sth*)

쟁탈전 爭奪戰 a scramble; a struggle; a fight
◆진지의 쟁탈전 a struggle for a position / 선수권 쟁탈전을 벌이다 play for the title
▶양자의 정권 쟁탈전은 본성 사나워졌다 The struggle for political power between them became quite dirty.
▶선수권 쟁탈전이 시작된다 A contest for the championship is going to start.

쟁패전 爭霸戰 a struggle [contest] for supremacy; 〈경기의〉a championship game [tournament]; a pennant race

저¹ 〔악기〕a flute; a traverse flute; a fife
◆저를 불다 play (on) the flute

저² 1〈나〉I; me ◆저의 my / 저를 me
▶저는 고등학생입니다 I am a high school student.
▶저는 커피입니다, 당신은요? Coffee for me, and you?
2〈자기〉oneself; self; he; himself
▶저 하고 싶은 대로 놓아둬라 Let him do as he pleases. = Let him go his own way.

저³ 〈저기의〉that (*pl.* those); the

▶ 저 건물을 보세요 Look at the building over there.
▶ 저 소리는 뭐지? What's that sound I hear?
▶ 저 사람들은 누구지요? Who are those people?

저⁴ 〔감탄사〕 Well; Let me see; By the way; If you please; please; I say; er-r-r; uh
♦ 저, 말씀드리기 미안합니다만 I hesitate to say it, but..
▶ 저, 어디로 갈까요? Well, where shall we go?
▶ 저 실례지만 부탁 하나 해도 될까요? Excuse me, but may I ask you a favor?

저 著 *one's* writings; written by ♦ 김박사 저 a book written by Dr. Kim

저 箸 (a pair of) chopsticks ⇨ 젓가락

저가 低價 a low price ♦ 저가의 cheap; inexpensive; low-priced ━주 low-priced stocks

저각 底角 〔數〕 a base angle=밑각

저간 這間 then; that time [occasion]; 〈요즈음〉 recent [these] days
▶ 그들이 어떻게 결혼하게 되었는지 저간의 사정은 나는 모른다 I have no exact knowledge of the circumstances leading to their marriage.

저감 低減 〈줄어짐〉reduction; decrease; 〈경감〉 mitigation ♦ 생산량의 저감 decrease in production ━저감하다 reduce; decrease; mitigate

저같이 such a; so; like that; (in) that way; that extent [degree]
▶ 나는 저같이 예쁜 소녀를 본 적이 없다 I have never seen such a beautiful girl.
▶ 저같이 큰 집에 살 수 있다면 좋겠다 I wish I could live in such a large house.

저개발 低開發 underdevelopment ♦ 저개발의 underdeveloped
■━국 〈후진국〉 underdeveloped countries ━지역 the underdeveloped areas

저것 〈사물〉 that (one); that thing (over there); 〈사람〉 a man like that; that fellow; that guy; that one
♦ 저것들 they; those / 이것 저것 this or [and] that; one thing and another

저격 狙擊 sniping; sharpshooting
♦ 저격용 소총 a sniper rifle
━저격하다 shoot [fire] at; snipe (at)
■━대 a sharpshooting squad ━병 a sniper; a sharpshooter ━자 a shooter; a sniper

저고리 a jacket; a coat ♦ 치마저고리 a skirt and jacket / 저고리를 입고[벗고] with *one's* jacket on [off] / 저고리를 입다[벗다] put on [take off] *one's* jacket

저공 低空 a low sky [altitude] ♦ 저공으로 비행하다 fly low; fly at a low altitude ■━비행 a low(-altitude) flight; low(-level) flying ━폭격 low-altitude bombing

저금 貯金 〈저금액〉 savings; 〈예금〉 a deposit; 〈저축하기〉 saving (money)
♦ 저금을 찾다[인출하다] draw [withdraw] *one's* savings
▶ 그는 은행에 저금이 많다 He has considerable [much] savings in the bank.
━저금하다 save money; deposit; lay [put] by money; lay aside money
▶ 그녀는 차를 사려고 저금하고 있다 She is saving (up) for [to buy] a car.
■━우편━ postal savings 은행━ a bank deposit 적립━ installment savings ━통 a savings box; a (piggy) bank ━통장 a bankbook; a (deposit, savings) passbook

저금리 低金利 low interest (rate)
♦ 저금리로 at a low rate of interest
■━정책 a cheap money policy

저급 低級 low grade; low class; inferiority ♦ 저급의 low-grade; low-class; inferior; vulgar; cheap

저기 that place; (over) there; yonder
♦ 여기저기에 here and there; all over / 여기서 저기까지 from here to there
▶ 강은 저기에 있다 The river is that way.
▶ 저기 높은 건물이 남산 타워다 That tall structure over there is Namsan Tower.

저기압 低氣壓 1 〔氣〕 cyclone; a low pressure
♦ 저기압의 중심 the center of a depression
♦ 저기압대가 동지나해를 동남으로 이동하고 있다 A low pressure area [zone] is traveling southeast across the East China Sea.
2 (비유) a bad temper; sullenness
♦ 오늘은 선생님이 저기압이시다 Our teacher is in a bad temper [mood] today.
■━열대━ a tropical cyclone 온대━ an extratropical cyclone; polar-frant cyclone

저까짓 such a; so trivial; that kind of; like that ♦ 저까짓 것 so trivial thing [matter]
▶ 저까짓 게 대수냐? That's no trouble at all.
▶ 저까짓 일로 허둥대지 마라 Don't get upset over such a small thing.

저나마 although it is (nothing more than) that; even that; considering
▶ 저나마 꽤 나아진 편이다 It is a considerable improvement as it is.
▶ 저나마 그는 잘 하는 편이다 He does well considering the circumstances.

저냐 panfried food; fried meat [fish]; a sautéed dish

저냥 (in) that way; (in) the same way as that; as it is [stands]
♦ 저냥 내버려두다 leave *sth* as it is; leave *sth* intact [untouched]
▶ 내 방은 저냥 놔두시오 Leave my room as it is [untouched].

저널 a journal

저널리스트 a journalist

저널리즘 journalism

저네(들) those people (over there); they; them ▶ 그는 저네들을 범인으로 의심하고 있다 He suspects them as the criminals.

저녁 1 〈때〉 evening; dewfall; nightfall; dusk
♦ 가을 저녁 an autumn evening / 저녁 7시쯤에 about seven in the evening / 일요일 저녁에 on Sunday evening; on the evening of Sunday / 저녁마다 every evening / 내일 저녁까지는 by tomorrow evening
▶ 그는 오늘[내일] 저녁 한국을 떠난다 He leaves Korea this [tomorrow] evening.
▶ 저녁 무렵에 철도사고가 있었다 Toward evening there was a railway accident.

2 〈저녁밥〉 supper; dinner; an evening meal
♦ 저녁거리 foodstuff for supper / 저녁(식사) 전[후]에 before [after] supper / 저녁을 먹다 take [have] supper; sup / 저녁을 준비하다 prepare supper; get dinner ready
▶ 저녁을 일찍 먹기로 하자 Let's have an early supper.
▶ 저녁으로 무엇을 먹을까요？ What shall we have for supper?

저녁놀 an evening [a sunset] glow; the afterglow of the sunset
♦ 저녁놀이 진 하늘 the sky aglow with the setting sun; the sky at sunset
▶ 서쪽 하늘에 저녁놀이 타고 있다 The western sky is glowing with the setting sun.

저녁때 evening; dewfall
♦ 저녁때에 in the evening / 저녁때가 지나서 after nightfall [sunset]
▶ 오늘 저녁때까지 이 시계를 고쳐 주세요 I'd like this watch fixed by this evening.

저녁바람 an evening breeze

저녁밥 supper; the evening meal ⇨ 저녁 2
▶ 그는 저녁밥도 먹지 않고 잤다 He went to bed without supper.

저녁안개 an evening mist

저녁풍경 an evening scene

저놈 that guy (over there); that fellow [chap, brute]; he ▶ 저놈은 고약한 녀석이다 He is a disgusting [nasty] fellow [guy].

저능 低能 low intelligence; feeblemindedness; mental deficiency; imbecility —**저능하다** feebleminded; deficient in mental ability; imbecile

저능아 低能兒 a mentally deficient child; a weak-minded child ■—교육 the education of the mentally deficient (children)

저다지 so; so much; like that; to that extent
▶ 저다지 양심적인 사람은 없다 Few people are more conscientious than he (is).

저당 抵當 mortgage; security; pledge
♦ 저당잡다 take [accept] sth as security 《for a loan》 / 주택을 저당잡혀 돈을 빌다 borrow money [secure a loan] on one's house; offer one's house as security / 저당을 잡고 돈을 빌려주다 lend money on security [mortgage] —**저당하다** mortgage; give [put, lay] sth in pledge
▶ 나는 이 집을 저당해서 돈을 마련해야 한다 I have to raise money on a collateral for this house.
▶ 이 땅은 5천만원으로 저당되어 있다 There is a mortgage of fifty million won on the land. ⇌ The land is mortgaged for fifty million won.
■—근— fixed collateral; a collateral security 동산— chattel mortgage 이중— double mortgage 1번[2번]— first [second] mortgage
■—대부금 a loan on security; a mortgage [secured] loan : 무저당 대부금 an unsecured loan; a loan without security —물 a collateral; a security; a pledge —증서 a mortgage; 〈채권 등〉 a mortgage bond

저당권 抵當權 mortgage; right of pledge
■—설정 settlement of mortgage —설정자 a mortgager; a mortgagor —자 a mortgagee

저대로 as it is [stands]; like that; in that condition ♦ 저대로 두다 leave 《a matter》 as it is; leave [let] 《a matter》 alone

저도모르게 in spite of oneself; unconsciously; without knowing it
♦ 저도 모르게 눈물을 흘리다 shed tears involuntarily [in spite of oneself] / 저도 모르게 죄를 짓다 commit a crime in spite of oneself

저돌 猪突 recklessness; foolhardiness
♦ 저돌적인 사람 a reckless [foolhardy] man / 저돌적인 reckless; rash; headlong; foolhardy / 저돌적으로 headlong; recklessly; foolhardily —**저돌하다** rush recklessly; make a reckless [headlong] rush

저들 those people (over there); they
▶ 저들이 누군지 가볼께 I'll go and see who they are.

저따위 a thing [person] of that sort [kind]; such; so; that sort of
♦ 저따위 남자 a man like that
▶ 뭐 저따위가 다 있어？ What a man! ⇌ That guy is impossible.

저락 低落 fall; depreciation; 〈시세의〉 decline
▶ 주가가 저락하고 있다 Stock prices are falling [declining].

저래 like that; so; that way
▶ 저래서는 그녀에게 너무 하는 것 아니니？ That would be treating her too harshly.
▶ 저래 가지고는 누구나 그를 싫어하는 것도 당연하다 The way he is, it's natural that everyone thinks him a nuisance.

저런[1] 〈저러한〉 such; like that; that (sort of)
♦ 저런 집 that sort of house / 저런 식으로 like that; (in) that way
▶ 이런저런 일로 나는 아주 바쁘다 I am terribly busy with this and that [one thing and another].
▶ 그가 저런 짓을 했을 리가 없다 He can't have done such a thing.

저런[2] 〈감탄사〉 Dear me!; Oh, dear!; Good Heavens!; Oh, God!; What a …!; Why!
▶ 저런, 웬일이냐？ Well, what's the matter?
▶ 저런！ 참 안됐구나 Dear, dear! What a pity!

저렇게 like that; (in) that way
▶ 나는 그가 저렇게까지 유명한 줄은 몰랐다 I did not know he was so [that] famous.
▶ 저렇게 말하면 안되는데 He shouldn't say it like that [(in) that way].

저렇다 like that; that way
♦ 이렇다 저렇다 말이 많다 say this and that; be critical (about); criticize
▶ 지금에 와서 이렇다 저렇다 해본들 무슨 소용이 있어 It is too late to make a fuss about it.
▶ 그녀는 오랫동안 이렇다 저렇다 말이 없었다 She remained silent [said absolutely nothing] for a long time.

저력 底力 latent [potential] energy [power]; underlying strength
▶ 그것은 그의 저력을 보여줄 좋은 기회였다 It was a good chance to show his real ability [his true potential].

저렴하다 低廉— cheap; low [moderate] (in

저류 price); inexpensive ♦저렴한 가격으로 중고차를 사다 buy a used [secondhand] car cheap [at a low price]

저류 底流 an undercurrent; an underflow ♦의식의 저류 the subconscious current / 저류를 이루다 be present as an undercurrent; underlie; lie [exist, flow] beneath

저리 1〈저렇게〉so; like that; (in) that way; to that extent ▶그가 저리 심한 말을 할 줄은 정말 몰랐다 I never thought he would say a terrible thing like that. ▶우리는 저리 많은 손님이 올 줄 몰랐다 We did not expect to have so many visitors. 2〈저곳·저쪽으로〉to that place; there; to that direction ♦이리 저리 둘러보다 look this way and that ▶저리 좀 비키시오 Step aside please. ▶저리 가요 Go away!

저리 低利 low interest; a low rate of interest ♦저리의 대부금 a low-interest loan / 저리로 돈을 빌려주다[빌리다] lend [borrow] money at low interest ■―금융 cheap credit; low-interest money ―자금 low-interest funds [loan]; (美) easy money

저리다 1〈마비되다〉become [go] numb; be numbed; be asleep ▶발이 저려 일어날 수 없었다 My feet went to sleep and I could not stand up. ▶다리가 찌르듯이 저린다 I have pins and needles in my legs. 2〈쑤시다〉feel pain in the joints ▶무릎이 저린다 My knee hurts [pains me].

저마다 each; every one; respectively ▶그들은 저마다 자기 방이 있다 Each of them has his or her own room. ▶그들은 저마다 자리에 앉았다 They sat in their respective seats. ▶그들은 저마다 다른 길을 갔다 They went their own ways. ▶사람은 저마다 생각하는 방식이 다르다 Each person has his own way of thinking.

저만큼 〈그렇게〉so; so much; that much;〈그 정도〉to that [such a] degree ▶저만큼은 누구라도 알고 있지 Everybody knows that much. ▶그녀가 저만큼이나 돈을 썼어요? Did she spend that much money? ▶저만큼 노력했는데도 그는 실패했다 For [In spite of] all his efforts, he failed.

저만하다 be that much; be as much [many] as that; be to that degree [extent] ♦저만한 인물 a man of that personality [caliber] ▶저만하면 충분할 거야 That much may be enough. ▶저만한 피해는 어쩔 수 없다 That much damage cannot be helped.

저맘때 about [around] that time; at that time of (the) day [night, year] ▶아이들은 저맘때에는 아직 낯가림을 한다 Children are still bashful [shy] in front of strangers at about that age.

저면 底面〔數〕the base (plane) ⇨ 밑면

저명 著名 eminence; prominence; distinction; celebrity ―**저명하다** famous; well-known; prominent; eminent; distinguished; celebrated ♦저명한 학자 a celebrated scholar ■―인사 a famous person [figure]; a celebrity

저물가 低物價 low prices ■―정책 a low price policy

저물다 1〈해가 지다〉get [grow] dark ♦날이 저물도록 till dark; till [until] sunset; till late ▶날이 서물고 있다 It's getting [growing] dark. ▶그녀는 날이 저문 후[저물기 전]에 돌아왔다 She came back after [before] dark. ▶날이 저물자 바람도 멎었다 The wind stopped with the coming of night. ▶겨울에는 여섯시경에 날이 저문다 It gets [grows] dark around six in winter. 2〈한 해가 지나다〉end; come to an end [a close] ▶이삼일이면 올해도 저문다 Only a few days are left before the year is out. ▶해가 저물고 새해가 되었다 The old year has gone and the new year has come.

저미다 cut [chop] into pieces; cut (thin); slice; mince; chop ♦고기를 얇게 저미다 cut meat into thin slices [small pieces]

저버리다 go back on 《one's promise》; disappoint;〈돌보지 않다〉desert; forsake ♦약속을 저버리다 break [go back on] one's promise(s) / 처자식을 저버리다 forsake [desert] one's wife and children ▶그는 우리의 기대를 저버지지 않았다 He met [came up to] our expectations. ▶그녀의 연기는 우리의 기대를 저버렸다 Her performance disappointed us. ⇌ Her performance fell short of our expectations.

저벅 with a crunch [thud]; with a heavy footstep; ploddingly

저벅거리다 walk with heavy footsteps; walk with a thud; crunch [plod] 《one's way》; trudge heavily ♦언덕길을 저벅거리며 올라가다 trudge wearily up the slope

저벅저벅 crunchingly; thuddingly ♦저벅저벅 걷다 walk with a thud; plod one's way ▶아이들은 눈에 파묻힌 길을 저벅저벅 걸어서 학교로 갔다 Children trudged their way to school through deep snow. ―**저벅저벅하다** make a crunching sound; crunch

저번 這番 (the) last time; the other day ♦저번의 last; previous; recent; of the other day / 저번 시장 the former mayor; the ex-mayor / 저번 일요일에 last Sunday; on Sunday last ▶저번에 한 약속을 잊지 말게 Don't forget what you promised the other day. ▶저번에 말한대로 이번 여름에는 뉴욕에 안 간다 As I said before [mentioned previously], I won't go to New York this summer.

저변 底邊〔數〕〈밑변〉a base ♦사회의 저변 사

람들 people at the lower levels of society

저부 底部 the bottom; the bottom portion [part]; the base

저상 沮喪 〈기운을 잃음〉 depression (of spirits); dispiritedness; demoralization
―**저상하다** (one's spirits) droop; be dejected [depressed, dispirited]
♦ 의기 저상하다 be depressed; be in low [out of] spirits / 의기를 저상시키다 damp(en) [depress] sb's spirits; dishearten sb
▶ 우리는 그 소식으로 의기가 저상되었다 We were discouraged [disheartened] at the news. ⇒ We lost heart at the news.

저서 著書 a book; a literary work [production]; one's writings
▶ 그는 한국사에 관한 저서가 많다 He has written many books on Korean history.

저세상 ―世上 the other [next] world; the afterlife ♦ 저세상에 가다 go to the other world; 〈죽다〉 die; pass away

저소득 低所得 a low [small] income
■ ―층 the lowincome brackets [group]

저속 低俗 vulgarity; baseness
―**저속하다** vulgar; base; low, lowbrow; lowbrowed
♦ 저속한 소설 a vulgar novel / 저속한 잡지 a low(er)-class [pulp] magazine / 저속한 취미 low taste; lowbrow [vulgar] tastes / 저속한 TV프로그램 a vulgar TV program

저속 低速 (a) low speed ♦ 저속으로 자동차를 운전하다 drive a car at low speed
■ ―기어 a low gear

저수 貯水 storage of water; reservoir water
―**저수하다** keep water in store; store water 《in》
▶ 빗물은 탱크에 저수된다 Rainwater is (collected and) stored in a tank.
■ ―량 the volume of water kept in store; pondage ―탱크 a (water) tank

저수지 貯水池 a reservoir; an irrigation pond
■ ―관개용― an irrigation reservoir

저술 著述 〈쓰기〉 writing (of books); 〈저작물〉 a book; a literary work; one's writings
▶ 이책은 그분의 저술이다 This is a book (written) by him.
―**저술하다** write a book; author 《a book》
▶ 그녀는 여러 권의 문학작품을 저술했다 She wrote [produced, published] many [a lot of] literary works.
■ ―가 a writer; an author; 〈여성〉 an authoress ―업 the literary profession

저습하다 低濕― low(-lying) and damp

저승 the other [next] world; the world of the dead; the underworld
♦ 저승으로 가다 go to the next world; die; pass away / 저승길을 떠나다 go on a journey to the next world; depart this life

저압 低壓 〈압력〉 low pressure; 〔電〕 low tension [voltage]
■ ―전선[케이블, 코일, 회로] a low-tension wire [cable, coil, circuit]

저액 低額 a small amount [sum]
■ ―소득자 a person with a low income; low-income earner; underpaid people

저어새 〔鳥〕 a blackfaced spoonbill

저어하다 fear; be afraid of [that]…; hesitate
♦ …하지 않을까 저어하여 for fear of 《doing》; fearful of 《getting infected》
▶ 그는 그런 말 하기를 저어했다 He hesitated to say that.

저온 低溫 a low temperature
■ ―냉동 low temperature refrigeration ―물리학 cryophysics ―살균 pasteurization ―수송 refrigerated transport ―처리[포장]법 〈통조림의〉 cold pack ―학 cryogenics

저온계 低溫計 a cryometer

저울 a balance; 〈천칭〉 a pair of scales [balances]; 〈대저울〉 a steelyard; lever [beam] scales; 〈접시 저울〉 a platform balance; 〈자동저울〉 a dial scale; 〈대형 계량기〉 a weighing machine
♦ 저울에 달다 weigh sth in the balance [on the scales] / 저울을 후하게 달아 주다 give good weight
■ ―대 a balance [scale] beam [arm] ―추 a weight ―판 a scale; a pan

저울눈 the notches of a beam; scale notches; 〈눈금〉 a division on a scale; a graduation
♦ 저울눈을 속이다 cheat weight; give short weight

저울질 weighing; scaling; putting on the scales
―**저울질하다** weigh sth in the balance [on the scales]; scale; put on the scales; 〈비교하여〉 weigh sth against [with]; compare sth with
▶ 그는 제안 수락의 득실을 저울질했다 He weighed the advantages and disadvantages of accepting the offer.

저위 低位 a low position [rank]; a low degree
▶ 그 팀은 줄곧 10위라는 저위에 있었다 The team was all the way down in the tenth place.

저위도 低緯度 〔地〕 a low latitude

저유 貯油 storage of oil
■ ―소 an oil reservoir ―탱크 an oil tank

저율 低率 a low rate; a low ratio
♦ 저율의 low-rate; low / 저율의 이자로 at low interest / 일천명중 한 사람의 저율로 at the low rate of one person out of one thousand

저음 低音 **1** 〔樂〕 bass
♦ 저음으로 노래하다 sing bass [in a low voice]
2 〈낮은 소리〉 a low tone
♦ 저음으로 말하다 speak in a low-pitched voice
■ ―가수 a low-voiced singer; a bass; 〈여성의〉 a contralto ―부 bass; the lower keys

저의 底意 a secret [true] intention; an underlying [ulterior, real] motive
♦ 아무의 저의를 간파하다 see through sb's underlying motive
▶ 그의 저의를 알 수가 없다 I don't know what he really means [what he is really plotting].
▶ 그에게는 어떤 저의가 있다 He has a secret intention. ⇒ (口) He has something up his sleeve.

저이 that gentleman [lady]; that man [person]; he; she
▶ 저이를 나는 잊을 수 없다 I cannot forget him [her].

저인망 底引網 a dragnet; a trawlnet
◆저인망으로 고기를 잡다 trawl
■—어선 a trawler; a dragnet fishing boat —어업 trawl [dragnet] fishery

저임금 低賃金 low wages
■—노동 cheap labor —노동자 a low-wage earner —정책 a low-wage policy

저자 〈가게〉 a market stand [booth]; 〈장〉 a market; a fair

저자 著者 an author; a writer; 〈여자〉 an authoress ◆저자불명의 동화집 an anonymous book of fairy tales
▶그가 이 소설의 저자다 He is the author of this novel. ⇒ He wrote this novel.

저자세 低姿勢 a low posture; a low profile
◆저자세를 취하다 take a low posture
▶그는 언제나 저자세다 He always humbles himself.
■—외교 low-profile diplomacy

저작 咀嚼 〈씹음〉 chewing; mastication; 〈소화〉 digestion; 〈이해〉 comprehension
—저작하다 chew; masticate; 〈이해하다〉 comprehend; appreciate

저작 著作 〈저술〉 writing; literary work; authorship; 〈저서〉 a (literary) work; a book; one's writings
◆그의 주요한 저작 his major writings / 저작에 종사하고 있다 be engaged in literary work / 저작으로 생활하다 live by one's pen
—저작하다 write a book; do writing for books
■—가 a writer; an author; 〈여류〉 a woman writer; an authoress —물 a book

저작권 著作權 (a) copyright; literary property
◆저작권을 소유하다 hold [own] the copyright 《of》 / 저작권을 침해하다 infringe the copyright 《of》
■국제— international copyright ■—법 〖法〗 the Copyright Act —사용료 a royalty; royalties on a copyright —소유 ownership of copyright; 〈표시〉 All rights reserved. (▶책에 인쇄됨) —소유자 a copyright holder —침해 an infringement of (a) copyright; (a) (literary) piracy —침해자 a (literary) pirate

저장 貯藏 storage; storing; preservation
—저장하다 store; lay up; lay by; keep sth in storage; preserve
◆겨울에 대비하여 연료를 저장하다 store [stock] up fuel for winter / 생선을 절여서 저장하다 keep fish salted
▶지하실은 물건을 저장하는데 쓰인다 The cellar is used for storing goods.
■냉동— cold storage; refrigeration —고(庫) a storehouse; a storage house —량 the amount of stock —물[品] stores; stored goods; stock; supplies —소 a storing place; storage —실 a storeroom

저적거리다 drag oneself along; shuffle [drag] one's weary feet ◆저적거리며 걷다 plod one's way; trudge along

저절로 by itself; of itself; of its own accord; spontaneously; 〈자동적으로〉 automatically
▶바람도 없는데 촛불이 저절로 꺼졌다 Although there was no breeze, the candle flame went out by itself.
▶그 상처는 저절로 나을 것이다 The wound will heal by itself.
▶그 정문은 앞에 서면 저절로 열린다 The front door opens automatically when you stand in front of it.

저조 低調 **1** 〈소리의〉 a low tone; an undertone —저조하다 low-toned; low-pitched; low-keyed
2 〈침체〉 dullness; 〈경제의〉 weakness; 〈운동선수의〉 a slump
—저조하다 weak; dull; inactive; sluggish; in a slump
◆저조한 기록 a poor record / 저조한 시황 dull [sluggish, slack] market
▶시황이 저조하다 The market is sluggish [dull].

저조 低潮 (a) low tide; low water
■—선 a low-water mark

저주 詛呪 cursing; a curse; (an) execration; 〈신의〉 damnation
—저주하다 curse; wish ill of sb
◆저주받은 사람 a person (who is) cursed [under a curse] / 세상을 저주하다 curse the world / 저주받다 be cursed by
▶그녀는 그를 저주했다 She cursed him. ⇒ She called down curses on him.

저주파 低周波 〖電〗 low frequency(略 L.F.)

저지 低地 lowland; low(·lying) ground; 〈지역〉 lowlands ◆시내의 저지대 the low-lying sections of a city

저지 沮止 obstruction; interception; blocking
—저지하다 obstruct; hinder; hamper; impede; retard; check; hold [set] back; block
◆법안 통과를 저지하다 block [prevent] passage of a bill / 적의 공격을 저지하다 check the enemy's attack
▶다수의 경찰관이 가두시위를 저지하려고 했다 A large number of policemen tried to stop [check, block] the street demonstration.

저지 〈심판원〉 a judge

저지난 before last time; the one before last
◆저지난달[해] the month [year] before last / 저지난밤 the night before last / 저지난번 the time before last

저지르다 〈잘못하여 그르치다〉 commit a fault [an error]; make a mistake
▶네가 기어이 일을 저질렀구나 What an awful thing you have gone and done! ⇒ You've really gone and done it now, haven't you?
▶그녀석은 혼자 놔두면 무슨 일을 저지를지 모른다 There is no telling what he will do if left alone.

저질 低質 low quality
◆저질의 신문 a gutter press / 저질의 인간 a crooked [vicious, vulgar] person / 저질의 low; low-grade; of inferior [poor] quality
▶저질 상품에 주의하세요 Be careful of goods of bad quality.
■—탄 coal of low quality —품 an article of poor [inferior] quality

저쪽 1 〈방향〉 that side [direction]; over there; 〈반대쪽〉 the other [opposite] side

[direction]
♦저쪽에 보이는 마을 the village you see over there / 저쪽에 on the other [far] side; over there; yonder / 강 저쪽에 on the other side of the river; across the river
▶강은 저쪽입니다 The river is that way [〈반대쪽〉 the other way].
▶전화는 저쪽에 있습니다 The telephone is over there.
▶저쪽으로 갑시다 Let's go to the other side.
2 〈상대방〉 the other party; he; she; they; him; them
▶저쪽은 당신이 매우 마음에 든다고 합니다 I hear they like you very much.

저러럼 〈저렇게〉 like that; in that way; so; 〈저 정도로〉 to that extent [degree]
▶나는 그가 저러럼 괴짜인 줄 몰랐다 I did not know he was so perverse.

저촉 抵觸 conflict; infringement; violation; collision
—**저촉하다** 〈충돌하다〉 conflict with; be in conflict with; 〈모순되다〉 be contradictory to; be contrary to
♦교통 법규에 저촉되는 짓을 하다 violate [break, be against] traffic regulations
▶나는 법에 저촉되는 짓은 아무것도 안했다 I have done nothing against [that contravenes] the law.
▶그것은 그 조항에 저촉된다 It is in conflict with the provisions.

저축 貯蓄 saving; 〈저금〉 savings; 〈비축〉 storing up
♦저축이 있다[없다] have some [no] savings; have some [no] money saved / 저축을 장려하다 encourage savings
—**저축하다** save (up); save money; store up; put [set] by [aside]
▶그는 월수입의 10퍼센트를 정규적으로 저축한다 He regularly puts aside ten percent of his monthly income.
▶만일의 경우에 대비하여 저축해야 한다 We should save for [against] a rainy day.
■—액 the amount of *one's* savings —예금 a savings deposit —운동 a savings campaign —채권 a savings bond

저축심 貯蓄心 thriftiness ♦저축심이 있는[없는] 사람 a thrifty [thriftless] person

저탄 貯炭 a stock of coal
♦—량 the quantity of coal stored —소[장] a coal yard [depot]; a coaling station; 〈배의〉 a bunker

저택 邸宅 a residence; a mansion
♦으리으리한 저택 a lordly [stately] mansion; a fine house

저편 —便 that side ⇨ 저쪽

저하 低下 a fall; a drop; a decline; 〈품질의〉 deterioration; 〈가격의〉 depreciation
—**저하하다** fall; drop; go down; deteriorate
▶요즈음 아이들은 체력이 저하되고 있다 Children today have less physical strength than they used to (have).

저학년 低學年 the lower classes [grades]
♦저학년의 아동 schoolchildren in the lower grades

저항 抵抗 1 〈대항〉 (a) resistance; defiance; 〈반대〉 (an) opposition ♦저항을 받다 meet with [run into] resistance
—**저항하다** resist; offer [make] resistance (to); defy; stand [struggle, fight] against
♦완강하게 저항하다 put up [make, offer] a stubborn [stout] resistance (to); oppose stubbornly
▶그녀의 유혹은 저항하기 어렵다 Her temptation is irresistible.
▶운명에 저항해도 소용없다 It's no use resisting [struggling against] destiny.
2 〔物·電〕 resistance
♦전기저항 electrical resistance
♦차는 공기의 저항을 줄이기 위하여 유선형으로 되어 있다 Cars are streamlined to lessen [reduce] air resistance.
■마찰— frictional resistance ■—기 〔電〕 a resistor —운동 the resistance movement; 〈제2차대전의〉 the Resistance —자 a resistant; a resister

저항력 抵抗力 (power of) resistance; resisting power [force]
▶아기들은 병에 대해 저항력이 적다 Babies have little resistance to diseases.
▶적절한 영양섭취는 바이러스에 대한 저항력을 향상시킨다 Proper nutrition makes us more resistant to virus.

저해 沮害 a check; an obstruction; an impediment; a hindrance
—**저해하다** check; hinder; impede; obstruct
♦나라의 발전을 저해하다 hinder [impede] the development of the country

저혈압 低血壓 low blood pressure; hypotension
♦저혈압이다 have low blood pressure; suffer from low blood pressure

저희 〈우리〉 we; 〈저 사람들〉 they; those people
♦저희들 we; they / 저희들의 희망 our [their] hope
▶왼쪽 방이 저희 방입니다 The room on the left is ours [theirs].

적 1 〈때〉 the time (when); (on) the occasion; as; while ♦옛날 옛적에 once upon a time; long, long ago
▶그가 거기 갈 적에는 언제나 비가 온다 When he goes there, it (always) rains. ⇌ Every time [whenever] he goes there, it rains.
2 〈경험〉 —전에 어디서 뵌 적이 있지 않아요? Haven't we met somewhere before?
▶영국에 가 본 적이 있습니까? Have you ever been to England?
▶나는 거기에 가 본 적이 없습니다 I have never been there.

적 敵 1 〈원수〉 an enemy; a foe; (총칭) the enemy
♦인류의 적 an enemy of mankind / 자유[민주주의]의 적 an enemy of freedom [democracy] / 불구대천의 적 a sworn [bitter] enemy / 적의 공격 an enemy attack / 적과 싸우다 fight with [against] the enemy / 적이 되다 become an enemy; turn against 《another》
▶그를 적으로 돌리면 무섭다 If you should antagonize him, he would make a fearful

적 enemy.
▶ 어제의 적이 오늘의 친구가 될 수 있다 Yesterday's enemies could be today's friends.
2 〈싸움의 상대〉 an opponent; an antagonist; 〈경쟁자〉 a rival; a competitor; 〈필적하는 상대〉 a match; an equal
♦사업상의 적 one's business rival; a rival [competitor] in business
▶ 그는 네 적이 못된다 He is no match for you.

적 積 〔數〕 the product ⇨ 곱¹ 3

적 籍 1 〈호적〉 one's family register; 〈본적〉 one's domicile; 〈선적〉 registry
♦적에 올리다[에서 빼다] have [get] sb's name entered in [removed from] the family register
▶ 내 적은 대전에 있다 Taejŏn is the place where my family records are registered.
▶ 그 배는 파나마적이다 The ship is of Panamanian registry. ⇒ The ship sails under the Panamanian flag.
2 〈단체의 적〉 membership
♦적을 두다 〈협회 등에〉 become [be] a member (of); 〈학교에〉 be enrolled (at a university)

-적 -的 -ic; -ical; like
♦귀족적 태도 an aristocratic manner / 경제적 economic; economical / 심적 mental / 정치적 political / 일반적으로 in general; as a (general) rule; on the whole / 금전적으로 monetarily; financially / 교육적 견지에서 from an educational point of view
▶ 그는 논리적으로 생각한다 He thinks logically.
▶ 이 지방 기후는 대륙적이다 The climate of this area is like that of continent.

적갈색 赤褐色 reddish brown; brownish red

적개심 敵愾心 a hostile feeling; hostility; enmity
♦적개심에 불타다 be influenced by a hostile feeling / 적개심을 부채질하다[불러 일으키다] arouse [excite, provoke] sb's hostility (against); 적개심을 품다 feel enmity (toward); be hostile to sb

적격 適格 (a) proper qualification; eligibility; competence
♦적격의 properly qualified; competent; eligible / …에 적격이다 be the very person for; be cut for
▶ 그는 교사로서 적격이 아니다 He is not cut out to be a teacher.
■ーー자 a qualified [competent] person; the right [very] person: 그는 그 일의 적격자다 He has the right [necessary] qualifications for the job. ⇒ He is qualified [eligible] for the job.

적교 吊橋 〈현수교〉 a suspension bridge
♦강에 적교를 놓다 construct a suspension bridge over a river

적국 敵國 a hostile country [power]; the enemy country ♦가상 적국 a hypothetical [potential] enemy

적군 敵軍 a hostile army [force]; enemy troops

적권운 積卷雲 〔氣〕 an altocumulus ((pl. -li))= 고적운

적극 積極 positiveness; positivism
■ーー외교 a positive diplomacy ーー정책 a positive policy

적극성 積極性 positiveness; aggressiveness; enterprising spirit
♦적극성이 있는 positive
▶ 그는 적극성이 대단하다 He is very aggressive. ⇒ He is really self-motivated.
▶ 그녀는 적극성이 없다 She never takes the initiative.

적극적 積極的 positive; active; aggressive
♦적극적인 사람 an active [a positive] person / 적극적으로 positively; actively / 적극적으로 참가하다 take an active part; participate actively / 적극적인 태도를 취하다 take a positive attitude
▶ 그녀는 지역사회의 일에 적극적이다 She is active in community affairs.

적금 積金 installment savings; an installment deposit
▶ 그녀는 월급의 일부를 결혼비용으로 적금을 붓는다 She saves up by installments a part of her salary for her marriage.

적기 赤旗 〈붉은 기〉 a red flag; 〈공산당의〉 the Red Flag; 〈위험 신호의 기〉 a red flag of warning

적기 適期 a suitable [fit, proper] time; a season (for)
♦적기의 well-timed; timely; opportune / 적기에 at an appropriate time
▶ 이 사업은 지금이 적기다 The timing is right for this enterprise.
▶ 나는 아주 적기에 취직을 했다 I found a job at just the right time [(口) just in the nick of time].

적기 敵機 an enemy [a hostile] plane

적꼬치 炙ー a skewer; a spit; a thin pick or rod for sticking meat and vegetables during cooking

적나라 赤裸裸 1 〈발가벗음〉 nakedness; nudity ーー적나라하다 (stark-)naked; nude; bare
2 〈솔직함〉 frankness; plainness; straightforwardness ーー적나라하다 frank; plain; outspoken
♦적나라한 사실 a plain [bald, bare] fact / 적나라하게 frankly; outspokenly; candidly
▶ 그녀는 자기 생각을 적나라하게 말했다 She spoke plainly about her real feeling. ⇒ She laid bare her inner feelings frankly.

적다¹ 〈쓰다〉 write [note, put] down; record; make [take] a note [notes] of [(美) on]
♦이름을 적다 sign [write down] one's name / 관찰 결과를 노트에 적다 write [put] down one's observations in one's notebook
▶ 여기에 좀 적어주시오 Just put it down here.
▶ 나는 그 연설의 요점을 적어놓았다 I took [made] notes on the speech.

적다² 〈수가〉 few; 〈양이〉 little; 〈수·양이〉 small; 〈부족하다〉 scarce; wanting; short of; 〈불충분하다〉 not sufficient [enough]
♦적지 않은 not a few
▶ 참석한 사람은 적었다 Few people attended.
▶ 작년에는 비가 적었다 We didn't have much

rain last year.
▶ 그는 말수가 적다 He doesn't talk much. ≒ He is a man of few words.
▶ 이 음식물은 칼로리가 적다 This food is low in calories.
▶ 나는 수입이 내 누이보다 적다 I earn less money than my sister. ≒ My income is smaller than my sister's. ≒ I don't earn as much money as my sister.
▶ 이 방법은 위험이 적다 This method is less risky.

적당 適當 1 〈알맞음〉 fitness; suitability; suitableness; appropriateness; propriety
—**적당하다** suitable; proper; appropriate; adequate; fit; right; good; 〈온당하다〉 reasonable; fair; 〈지나치지 않다〉 moderate; temperate
♦ 적당한 양 an adequate amount / 적당한 운동 moderate [a proper amount of] exercise / 아이들에게 적당한 책 a book right [fit] for children / 6명의 가족이 살기에 적당한 집 a house adequate for a family of six / 적당히 suitably; adequately; appropriately; properly; duly; reasonably; moderately / 적당한 기회에 on a suitable occasion; at an appropriate time / 적당한 가격으로 at a reasonable [moderate] price / 적당한 때에 at a proper [good] time; at the right moment
▶ 당신께 맡길테니 적당히 해주시기 바랍니다 I'm going to leave it to you. I hope you'll do as you see [think] fit.
2 〈얼버무림〉 —**적당하다** 〈애매하다〉 vague; 〈태도가 분명치 않다〉 noncommittal ♦ 적당히 vaguely; noncommittally
▶ 그 여자는 적당히 다루면 된다 You needn't deal with her seriously.
▶ 나는 적당히 몇 명의 이름을 댔다 I mentioned a few names at random.
▶ 그녀는 언제나 대답을 적당히 해버린다 She always gives a noncommittal [vague] answer.

적당주의 適當主義 expedience; expediency

적대 敵對 hostility; antagonism
—**적대하다** be hostile to; fight against; oppose; turn against [on]
▶ 그를 적대해도 소용이 없다 It is no use to turn against [oppose] him. ≒ There's no point in fighting him.
■ —국 a hostile country

적대시 敵對視 —**적대시하다** be hostile to; regard sb with hostility; have [feel] hostility to [toward]
♦ 적대시하는 태도 a hostile attitude
▶ 양국은 서로 적대시하고 있다 Both countries are hostile to each other.

적대행위 敵對行爲 a hostile act [action]; hostile activities
♦ 공공연한 적대행위 open hostilities / 미국에 대하여 적대행위를 하다 take hostile actions against America; behave in a hostile manner to America

적도 赤道 the equator; (L) the line
♦ 적도의 equatorial / 적도 바로 아래에 directly [right] under the equator
▶ 그 다음날 우리는 적도를 횡단했다 The next day we crossed the equator [the line].
▶ 적도 부근은 매우 덥다 It is very hot at around the equator.
■ 지구[천구]— the terrestrial [celestial] equator —면 the equatorial plane —무풍대 the doldrums —반류 the Equatorial Countercurrent —의(儀) an equatorial telescope —제(祭) the ceremony of crossing the equator —해류 equatorial currents

적도 賊徒 rebels; a rebel group [army]

적도기니 赤道— 〈나라 이름〉 the Equatorial Guinea; 〈공식명〉 the Republic of Equatorial Guinea

적동 赤銅 an alloy of copper and gold
♦ 적동색의 brown; tanned

적란운 積亂雲 〈쎈비구름〉〔氣〕 a cumulonimbus

적량 適量 a proper quantity; 〈약의〉 a proper dose ♦ 적량을 넘기다 take too much; eat [drink] to excess; 〈약의〉 overdose *oneself*
▶ 다음에 적량의 초를 칩니다 Then add a suitable [proper] amount of vinegar.

적령 適齡 a proper [fit] age
♦ 징병 적령의 젊은이들 young men of draft age / 징병 적령자 a person liable to military service
■ 결혼— the marriageable [nubile] age

적령기 適齡期 ♦ 결혼 적령기를 지나다 pass the marriageable age / 결혼 적령기에 달하다 reach [attain] the marriageable age; be old enough to marry

적례 適例 a good example; a case in point
♦ 적례를 들다 give a good example; cite an apt example
▶ 그는 적례로서 그 사건을 들었다 He referred to that incident as a case in point.

적리 赤痢 〈이질〉〔醫〕 dysentery
■ —균 a dysentery bacillus —환자 a dysentery [dysenteric] patient

적립 積立 saving —**적립하다** lay by [aside]; reserve; accumulate; save (up)
▶ 그녀는 여행비용으로 다달이 급료의 일부를 적립하고 있다 She saves [lays aside, sets aside] a part of her salary for the trip every month.
■ —배당금 an accumulated dividend —저금 〈저금〉 installment savings

적립금 積立金 a reserve (fund); an accumulated fund; (英) the rest
■ 별도[법정]— a special [legal] reserve

적막 寂寞 loneliness; solitude —**적막하다** lonely; lonesome; solitary; deserted; desolate ♦ 적막한 산중 lonely [desolate] mountain recesses / 적막한 광경을 이루다 present a dreary [desolate] sight
■ —감 a feeling of loneliness; a lonely feeling: 적막감이 들다 feel lonely

적멸 寂滅 death; (산) Nirvana —**적멸하다** 〈죽다〉 enter [attain] Nirvana; die; pass away

적반하장 賊反荷杖 carrying the war into the enemy's camp [country]; turning the tables; a false charge
▶ 우리는 적반하장으로 비난을 받게 되었다 We had the tables turned on us and had to face

criticism.

적발 摘發 exposure; disclosure ─**적발하다** expose; disclose; unmask; lay bare
▶그 은행의 금융 부정 사건이 적발되었다 The financial irregularities at that bank were exposed [laid bare].
▶마약범이 경찰에 의해 적발되었다 A drug dealer was unearthed by the police.

적법 適法 legality; lawfulness
◆적법의 legal; lawful
─적법하다 lawful; legal
▶경찰관들이 취한 조치는 적법하지 않았다 The measures the policemen took were illegal [unlawful].
─조치 a lawful measure ─행위 a legal [lawful] act

적병 敵兵 an enemy; an enemy soldier; (총칭) the enemy (troops)

적부 適否 fitness; propriety; suitability; 〈적성〉 aptitude
◆적부를 판단하다 judge whether a thing is proper or not
▶그들 행위의 적부에 대하여 논란이 일어났다 The propriety of their action was disputed.
▶먼저 그 수단의 적부를 논해야 한다 First of all we have to discuss whether the measure is proper or improper.
─심사 review of the legality

적부적 適不適 fitness; suitability; aptitude; propriety
▶이 방법의 적부적은 우리가 해보기 전에는 알 수가 없다 We can't tell whether this method is suitable or not until we try it.

적분 積分 〔數〕 integral; integration
─적분하다 integrate
─정(定)[부정]─ a definite [an indefinite] integral ■─곡선 an integral curve ─기호 the integral sign ─방정식 an integral equation ─법 integration ─학 integral calculus ─함수 an integral function

적빈 赤貧 extreme [dire] poverty; destitution
◆적빈에 시달리다 suffer from dire poverty [utter destitution]
▶그는 적빈여세(如洗)하다 He is [lives] in extreme poverty. ⇌ He is as poor as a church mouse.
─적빈하다 very poor; desperately poor

적산 敵產 enemy property ◆적산을 몰수하다 confiscate [seize] enemy property

적산 積算 addition; adding up ◆적산 전력계 a watt-hour meter; an integrating wattmeter

적삼 an unlined jacket (for summer clothes)

적색 赤色 1 〈붉은 색〉 a red color; red
◆적색 리트머스 시험지 a red litmus paper / 적색의 red
2 〈공산주의〉 communism
■─분자 a Red ─테러 Red terrorism ─혁명 a Red revolution

적선 敵船 an enemy ship [vessel]

적선 積善 1 〈선행〉 accumulation of virtuous [good] deeds ─적선하다 do virtuous [good] deeds
2 〈자선〉 alms; almsgiving; charity
─적선하다 render benevolence (to); give alms (to); practice charity

적설 積雪 snow (on the ground); snowfall
▶호남고속도로는 많은 적설로 불통이 되었다 The Honam Expressway was closed due to (the) heavy snowfall.
▶적설이 1미터에 달했다 The snow was [lay] one meter deep.
─량 a snowfall

적성 適性 aptitude; fitness
◆…의 적성을 보이다 show an aptitude for… / 적성을 개발시키다 develop one's aptitude
▶그는 음악에 대한 적성이 있다 He has musical aptitude [an aptitude for music].
■─직업─ vocational aptitude ■─검사 an aptitude test : 직업[진학] 적성 검사 a vocational [scholastic] aptitude test

적성 敵性 inimical character
─국가 a hostile country ─행위 a hostile act; hostilities

적세 敵勢 the enemy's strength [forces]; 〈기세〉 the morale of the enemy [foe] ◆적세를 꺾다 shatter the enemy's morale

적소 適所 the right [proper] place [position]
◆적소를 얻다 find one's niche
▶인재를 적소에 배치하시오 Place men of quality in the right positions.

적손 嫡孫 grandchildren by the legal wife

적송 積送 〔商〕 shipment; consignment
─적송하다 ship; consign; send
◆샌프란시스코로 화물을 적송하다 ship the cargo for San Francisco / 기선으로 적송하다 send by steamer
■─철도─ shipment [forwarding] by rail ■─인 a shipper; a consignor; a consigner; a sender ─품 consigned [consignment] goods; a consignment

적쇠 炙─ a grid ⇨ 석쇠

적수 赤手 〈맨손〉 a bare [an empty] hand; naked fists
◆적수 공권으로 〈혼자 힘으로〉 single-handed; without any financial support [backer]/ 적수로 장사를 시작하다 open a business on a shoestring
▶그는 적수 공권으로 거부가 되었다 He made an enormous fortune starting with nothing.

적수 敵手 〈경쟁 상대〉 a rival; a competitor; 〈시합 등의〉 an opponent; an antagonist; an adversary
▶나는 그의 적수가 못된다 I am no match for him.
▶너는 내 적수가 못 돼 You are not worth contending with me.
▶그는 내 좋은 적수다 I find a good match in him.

적습 敵襲 〈적의 습격〉 an enemy's raid [attack]
◆적습을 받다 be raided by the enemy

적시 適時 〈적시의〉 timely; opportune ■─안타〔野〕 a timely hit

적시다 wet; 〈축이다〉 moisten; dampen; make wet; 〈잠깐〉 dip; 〈함빡〉 saturate; 〈상당한 시간〉 soak
◆옷을 적시다 get one's clothes wet / 눈물로 소매를 적시다 wet one's sleeves with tears / 흠뻑 적시다 make thoroughly wet; drench;

soak / 손을 물에 적시다 dip *one's* hand in water
▶ 그녀는 다림질하기 전에 그 천을 축축히 적셨다 She dampened the cloth before ironing it.
▶ 컵의 물을 엎질러서 식탁보를 적시고 말았다 I knocked over [overturned] a glass of water and wet [wetted] the tablecloth.

적신호 赤信號 a red (traffic) light; a danger signal; a stoplight
♦ 적신호를 무시하고 길을 건너다 cross a street against the (red) light / 적신호를 보고 차를 멈추다 stop [brake] the car for a red light
▶ 그 여인은 적신호를 무시했다 The lady ignored the stoplight.
▶ 저 차는 적신호에서 멈추지 않았다 That car went through [didn't stop at] the red light.

적심 摘心 picking the buds

적십자 赤十字 〈휘장〉 a red cross on a white ground; 〈단체〉 the Red Cross ⇨ 적십자사
♦ 남북적십자회담 Talks between the South and North Korean Red Cross Societies
■ 청소년— the Red Cross Youth (略 R.C.Y.) ——구호반 a Red Cross relief squad —기 a Red Cross flag —병원 a Red Cross hospital —사업 Red Cross work —조약 the Red Cross Convention

적십자사 赤十字社 the Red Cross (Society) (▷정식명은 the International Red Cross Society)
■ 국제— the International Committee Red Cross ■—간호사 a Red Cross nurse

적어도 at (the) least; in the least; at the lowest; at a minimum; to say the least (of it)
▶ 적어도 한 달에 한 번은 소식 전해줘요 Write to us at least once a month.
▶ 적어도 그 정도는 해도 괜찮지 않겠니? It's the least you can do.
▶ 적어도 5만원은 들걸 It will cost you at least fifty thousand won.

적역 適役 a fit post; a suitable office; 〈연극의〉 a fit [suitable] role [part]
▶ 그녀는 이 일에는 적역이 아니다 She is not suitable [not the right person] for this job.
▶ 그 일에는 누가 적역일까? Who'll be the right man for the work?
▶ 그 일에는 그가 제일 적역이다 He is the (right) man for the work.

적역 適譯 〈정확한 번역〉 an exact translation; 〈가장 적절한 번역〉 the most appropriate translation; an exact rendering; a proper [good] translation
▶ 이 말의 적역이 영어에는 없다 There is no exact English equivalent to this word.
—적역하다 render exactly (into Korean); give a good [an exact] translation (of)

적온 適溫 〈중간의 온도〉 moderate temperature; 〈적절한 온도〉 proper temperature

적외선 赤外線 infrared rays
■—램프 an infrared lamp —복사 infrared radiation —분광계 an infrared spectrometer —사진 〈찍은 것〉 an infrared photograph; 〈사진술〉 infrared photography —암시(暗視) 장치 a night vision devise; noctovision —요법 infrared therapy —카메라 an infrared camera —필름 infrared film

적요 摘要 a summary; an epitome; a synopsis; a digest; an outline
♦ 조사의 적요 a summary of the investigation / 이 이야기의 적요 the gist of the story
—적요하다 summarize; sum up; epitomize; outline; give a summary ((of))
■—란 the remarks column

적요하다 寂寥— 〈고요하다〉 lonely; lonesome; desolate; deserted

적용 適用 application
♦ 법률의 적용 the application of the law
▶ 그것은 적용 범위가 넓다 It is of wide application.
▶ 그는 이론의 적용을 잘못했다 He made a wrong application of the theory.
—적용하다 apply
♦ 적용할 수 있는[없는] applicable [inapplicable] ((to)) / 이론을 실천에 적용하다 apply a theory to practice
▶ 이 규칙은 모든 경우에 적용할 수 있다 This rule applies to all cases.
▶ 그 규칙은 모든 사람에게 적용된다 The rule holds for everyone. ⇌ The rule is applicable to everyone.
▶ 이 규칙은 외국인에게는 적용할 수 없다 We cannot apply this rule to foreigners.

적운 積雲 〖氣〗 a cumulus (*pl.* -li)

적응 適應 adaptation; accommodation; adjustment; fitness
—적응하다 adapt [accommodate, adjust, acclimate] *oneself* ((to)); be adapted ((to, for)); be suitable ((for)); be fitted ((to))
♦ 새 환경에 적응하다 acclimate [acclimatize] *oneself* to a new environment / 적응시키다 fit; adapt; accommodate
▶ 그는 쉽게 새로운 생활에 적응했다 He quickly adapted himself to his new life.
▶ 그는 곧 군대 생활에 적응했다 He soon adjusted to army life.
■—설 an adaptation theory —성 adaptability; flexibility: 그녀는 새로운 환경에 놀라운 적응성을 보였다 She showed amazing adaptability to the new surroundings.

적의 適宜 suitableness; appropriateness
—적의하다 〈적절하다〉 suitable; proper; fitting; 〈목적·조건에 맞다〉 appropriate; discretionary
♦ 적의한 조치 a proper [suitable] measure [step]/ 적의한 조치를 하다 take proper measures; 〈자신의 판단으로〉 manage ((a matter)) at *one's* discretion

적의 敵意 a hostile feeling; hostility; enmity
♦ 적의있는 hostile; antagonistic / 아무에게 적의를 품다 have [feel] hostility toward *sb*; be [feel] hostile to *sb*
▶ 양국간의 적의는 언제 전쟁으로 발전할지 모른다 The hostility [enmity] between the two countries may at any moment develop into war.
▶ 나는 그에게 아무런 적의도 품고 있지 않다 I have no hostility [enmity] toward him. ⇌ I bear him no malice.

적이 〈다소〉 somewhat; to some extent; in some measure [degree]; a little; rather; quite ▶ 오늘 아침은 적이 기분이 좋다 I'm feeling a little better this morning. ⇌ I'm feeling a (little) bit better this morning.

적이나 〈다소라도〉 a little at (the) least; if any; at the very least

적임 適任 fitness; suitability; competence
♦ 적임이다 be fit [suitable] ((for)); be suited ((to)); be well qualified ((for))
▶ 그는 그 역에 적임이다 He is the right man [is perfect] for the role. ⇌ He is suitable [competent enough, a very good choice] for the role.

적임자 適任者 a person fit for the post [place]; a fit [suitable] person; a well-qualified man
▶ 그는 그 자리에 최적임자다 He is the best man for the position.

적자 赤字 〈부족액〉a deficit; 〈빨간 숫자〉red figures; red ink; a loss
♦ 무역 (수지의) 적자 a trade deficit / 적자가 나다 have a deficit / 적자를 내다 show [suffer] a loss [deficit]; go [get, fall] into the red; run into red figures
▶ 우리집 가계는 적자가 났다 Our family budget went into the red.
▶ 장사는 적자다 Business is in the red.
▶ 그 상품은 50달러의 적자를 내고 팔렸다 The goods were sold at a loss of 50 dollars.
▶ 적자를 메우도록 해봐라 Try to cover [make up] the deficit.
▶ 그는 적자를 내지 않도록 했다 He kept out of the red.
■ ─공채 a deficit(-covering) bond; a deficit loan; a red-ink bond ─국채 a deficit-financing bond: 적자 국채를 발행하다 issue a deficit-financing bond ─보전(補塡) a deficit covering ─생활 red-ink living ─예산 an unbalanced [adverse] budget; a deficit budget: 적자 예산을 짜다 make a deficit budget ─요인 a deficit-causing factor ─재정 red-ink finance; deficit finance; a financial deficit ─재정지출 deficit spending

적자 嫡子 a legitimate child [son]

적자생존 適者生存 the survival of the fittest
♦ 적자생존의 법칙 the law of the survival of the fittest

적장 敵將 the enemy's general; the enemy commander

적재 適材 a man fit for the post; the right [proper] man

적재 積載 〈실음〉loading; 〈나름〉carrying
─적재하다 load; lade; carry; 〈선박에〉take in
♦ 배에 화물을 적재하다 load [lade] a ship with goods
▶ 그 배는 밀을 적재하고 출항했다 The ship set sail with a cargo of wheat.
■ ─능력 carrying [loading] capacity; stowage ─량 loadings; loadage ─배수량 load displacement ─톤수 capacity [freight] tonnage ─하중 live load ─화물 cargo on board

적재적소 適材適所 the right man in the right place [for the right job]
♦ 적재적소에 두다 put the right man in the right place / 적재적소가 아니다 be a case of a square peg in a round hole

적적하다 寂寂 〈외톨이여서〉lonely; 〈친한 사람과 헤어져〉lonesome; desolate; 〈인적이 없어서〉deserted; dreary; solitary
♦ 적적한 곳[밤] a lonely place [evening] / 적적해 하다 feel lonely / 적적하게 살다 lead a lonely [solitary] life; live in loneliness [solitude]
▶ 아이들이 없으니 집안이 적적하다 The house is lonely without children.
▶ 당신이 없어서 몹시 적적했소 I was very lonely [I missed you so much] with you away.

적전 敵前 ♦ 적전의[에, 에서] in front [the face] of the enemy; before the enemy; facing the enemy / 적전에서 도망치다 escape under the enemy's fire [in the face of the enemy]; turn one's back to the enemy; be a deserter under fire
■ ─도하 a forced crossing of a river (against an enemy) : 적전 도하하다 cross a river under the enemy's fire ─상륙 landing in the face [presence] of the enemy; opposed [forced] landing : 적전 상륙하다 land in face of the enemy

적절 適切 〈타당함〉pertinence; relevance; 〈목적·조건 충족〉appropriateness; aptitude; propriety
─적절하다 fitting; proper; pertinent; fit; appropriate; adequate; apposite; happy; well-fitted; relevant; 〈시기가〉well-timed; timely
♦ 적절한 말 a happy [an apt] remark [expression] / 적절한 비유 a fitting comparison / 이 경우에 적절한 예 an instance apposite to the case; a case in point / 적절한 조언을 하다 give good [timely, relevant, pertinent] advice
▶ 적절한 조치를 취해 주시기 바랍니다 Please take proper [gentle] measures.
▶ 그의 인사는 결혼 피로연에는 적절하지 않았다 His greetings were not appropriate for a wedding reception.
▶ 그의 연설은 그 경우에 적절한 것이 아니었다 His speech wasn't suitable [good, fit, appropriate, proper] for the occasion.
▶ 교사는 항상 학생에게 적절한 조언을 해주어야 한다 Teachers should always give good advice to their students.

적정 滴定 titration ─적정하다 titrate

적정 適正 propriety; appropriateness; rightness; reasonableness
─적정 하다 〈적절하다〉proper; appropriate; 〈정당하다〉right; 〈공정하다〉just; 〈비싸지 않다·알맞다〉reasonable; 〈공평하다〉fair
▶ 재산의 적정한 배분은 어렵다 It is difficult to make a just [fair] distribution of property.
▶ 그의 판단은 적정했다고 생각한다 I think his judgment was right [reasonable].
■ ─가격 the just [reasonable, fair] price : 적정 가격으로 매매하다 buy and sell ((goods)) at reasonable prices ─이윤 reasonable profit ─통화량 optimum [adequate] money supply

적정 敵情 the movements [conditions, situation, circumstances] of the enemy
♦적정을 살피다 spy on the enemy's movements [positions]; feel the enemy out
적조 赤潮 a red tide; red water
적조 積阻 silence; being remiss in writing
—적조하다 be silent; be remiss in writing; be a poor correspondent
▶오랫동안 적조했습니다 Excuse me for not contacting you for a long time. ⇌ I must apologize for my long silence. ⇌ Excuse me for my long silence.
적중 的中 〈목표에 들어맞음〉 a (good) hit
—적중하다 hit (the mark); hit the bull's eye; make a good hit; 〈예상이〉 guess right; 〈계략이〉 take; work
♦적중하지 않다 miss [be wide of] the mark; 〈예상이〉 guess wild [wrong]
▶그녀의 예언이 적중했다 Her prediction came true.
▶수뢰가 적중했다 The torpedo hit the target.
▶그의 경제 예측이 적중했다 His forecasts about economy proved right.
적지 敵地 the enemy's country [territory, land]
♦적지에 깊숙이 들어가다 penetrate deep into the enemy's territory
적지않은 〈많은〉 not a few [little]; no small; many; much
♦적지않은 돈 no small amount of money; a considerable [a good, not a little] sum of money; no small sum of money; a sizable amount [sum] of money / 적지않은 수입 a handsome income
▶적지않은 책이 분실되고 있었다 Not a few [Quite a few, A good few] books were missing.
적지않이 not a little; 〈크게〉 greatly; 〈대단히〉 very much; 〈많이〉 a great [good] deal
♦적지않이 수고하다 take no little pains
▶그 광경을 보고 적지않이 놀랐다 I was not a little [was greatly] surprised at the sight.
▶그에게 적지않이 신세를 지고 있습니다 I owe a great deal [a lot] to him.
적진 敵陣 〈적의 진영〉 the enemy [enemy's] camp; 〈적의 진지〉 the enemy's position; the enemy line
♦적진을 공격하다 attack the enemy's position / 적진을 빼앗다 carry [capture] the enemy's position / 적진을 돌파하다 break through the enemy's line / 적진에 돌입하다 rush into the enemy camp
적철광 赤鐵鑛 〔鑛〕 hematite
적체 積滯 accumulation; (美) backlog
—적체하다 accumulate; pile up; form a backlog
적출 摘出 **1** 〈집어 냄〉 extraction; removal
—적출하다 pick out; take out; extract; remove
▶의사는 상처에서 총알을 적출했다 The doctor extracted [drew out, pulled out] a bullet from the wound.
2 〈들추어 냄〉 exposure; disclosure
—적출하다 expose; disclose; reveal

적출 嫡出 legitimacy (of birth)
♦적출자 a legitimate [lawful] child
▶그는 적출자다 He is born in lawful wedlock.
적출 積出 〈출하〉 shipment; forwarding
♦석탄 적출항 a coal loading port / 목재 적출지 a shipping point for lumber
—적출하다 ship 《a cargo》; send [ship] off; forward
■—인 a shipper
적탄 敵彈 〈총의〉 the enemy's bullets; 〈포의〉 the enemy's shells
♦적탄을 무릅쓰고 in the face of the enemy's fire
▶그는 적탄에 쓰러졌다 He was killed by the enemy's bullet.
적토 赤土 red clay [earth]; red soil
적평 適評 〈알맞은 비평〉 a just criticism; a (happy) hit; an appropriate [an apt, a pertinent] comment
♦적평을 내리다 criticize justly; make a just criticism [an appropriate comment]
적폐 積弊 〈오래 뿌리 박힌 폐단〉 long-standing [old] evils
적포도주 赤葡萄酒 red [purple] wine
적함 敵艦 an enemy [a hostile] ship; (총칭) hostile craft
적합 適合 〈들어맞음〉 fitness; suitability
—적합하다 fit; suitable; proper; befitting; adequate; appropriate
♦장미 재배에 적합한 흙 a soil congenial to roses / 체질에 적합한 음식 food suitable to one's constitution / 목적에 적합하다 serve [suit] one's purpose
▶그는 그 자리에 적합하다 He is suited for the post.
▶그는 자기의 안을 새로운 사태에 적합시켰다 He adapted his plan to the new situation.
적혈구 赤血球 〔解〕 a red corpuscle; a red blood cell [corpuscle]; an erythrocyte
■—생성 erythropoiesis —침강 속도 the erythrocyte sedimentation rate —침강 속도 검사 an erythrocyte sedimentation test
적화 赤化 bolshevization
♦적화 운동 the Red movement / 적화 위협 the red menace
—적화하다 make 《sb, a country》 communistic; bolshevize; turn [become] red [communist, Bolshevik]
▶그는 급속히 적화되었다 He became a communist rapidly.
적화 積貨 〈차·배에 실음〉 loading; shipping; shipment; 〈화물〉 a load; 〈특히 철도·도로 운송 화물〉 (美) a freight; (英) goods; 〈배·비행기 운송 화물〉 a cargo
▶그 트럭의 적화는 곡물이었다 The truck had a load of [was loaded with] grain.
—적화하다 load; take in [(美) on] cargo; ship goods
■—계수 stowage factor —량 〈중량〉 intake weight; 〈용적〉 intake measurement —목록 〈세관용〉 a manifest; an invoice —보험 cargo insurance —비용 loading [cargo] costs —수령서 a shipping receipt —안내장 an advice of

shipment —용적 cargo capacity —중량 manifest weight —항 a port of shipment [loading]

적확 的確 〈치밀하고 정확함〉 precision; 〈정확함〉 accuracy; 〈꼭 그대로임〉 exactness; 〈절대 확실함〉 infallibility
—**적확하다** precise; accurate; exact; infallible
♦ 말의 적확한 뜻 the exact meaning of a word / 적확한 보고 a precise report
▶ 그는 언제나 적확히 대답한다 His answers are always accurate.
▶ 그의 지시는 참으로 적확했다 His directions were very precise.

적흑색 赤黑色 reddish black; a reddish black color

적히다 be written [noted, put] down; be recorded; be put on record; 〈기술되다〉 be mentioned; be described
♦ 이름이 적히다 have *one's* name noted down
▶ 그 사건은 역사에 적혀 있다 The incident is recorded in history.
▶ 성경에 다음과 같이 적혀 있다 The Bible says [reads] as follows.

전 〈컵 등의〉 a brim; a rim; an edge
♦ 컵의 전 the rim of a glass / 물을 컵의 전까지 채우다 fill to the brim with water

전 前 1 〈전기〉 the first; the preceding; the last; 〈앞부분〉 the front; the fore part; 〈상기의·선행하는〉 above; preceding
2 〈이전의〉 former; past; ex-; previous; one-time; 〈퇴직한〉 retired
♦ 이 도시의 전 시장 the ex-mayor [the former mayor] of this city / 전 국무총리 an ex-prime minister; the former prime minister / 전 국회의원 an ex-member of the Nationl Assembly / 전 남편 *one's* former husband
3 〈시간〉 (ten minutes) to (ten); 〈일찍〉 prior to; (a little) before; earlier than
▶ 2시 15분 전입니다 It's a quarter to two.
▶ 그는 여름 방학 2일 전에 출발했다 He (had) left two days before the summer vacation started.
▶ 그는 아직 40전이다 He is yet under forty.
4 〈과거〉 before; ago; since; previous; earlier; back; former; past
♦ 이틀 전의 신문 a newspaper of two days ago / 전에 previously; formerly; before/ 2, 3일 전에 〈지금부터〉 a few days ago; 〈그때부터〉 a few days before / 전에 말한 바와 같이 as previously stated / 전부터 for some time (past) / 오래 전부터 since a long time [while] ago; from long ago; from way back
▶ 나는 전에 거기 갔던 적이 있다 I have been there once.
▶ 그가 죽기 사흘 전에 그렇게 말했다 He said so three days before he died.
▶ 이 골동품은 백년 전의 것이다 This antique is one hundred years old.
▶ 그는 전보다 더 열심히 공부하고 있다 He is working much harder than before [than he used to (do)].
▶ 그것은 오래 전의 일이다 It happened a long time ago.
5 〈…하기 전〉 before; prior to; earlier than; previous

♦ 출발하기 전에 before [prior to] *one's* departure / 해지기 전에 before the sun sets / 어둡기 전에 before dark

전 煎 panfried food ♦ 전을 부치다 prepare a panfried dish

전 廛 〈점포〉 (美) a store; (英) a shop; 〈노점〉 a stall; a booth

전 錢 〈돈〉 money; a coin; 〈화폐 단위〉 a *chŏn*

전 全 whole; entire; all; full; total; complete; pan-
♦ 전국 [전국민] the whole country [nation] / 전세계 the whole [entire] world / 전인류 all mankind; the whole [entire] human race

-전 傳 〈…의 전기〉 a life [biography] of…
♦ 링컨전 a life [biography] of Lincoln / 위인전 the lives of great men

-전 殿 a palace; a (Buddhist) temple
♦ 대웅전 the main building of a temple / 불전 a Buddhist temple / 신전 a shrine

-전 戰 1 〈전쟁〉 warfare; a war; 〈전투〉 a battle
♦ 국지전 a localized war / 소모전 a war of attrition / 근대전 modern warfare / 시가전 a street fighting / 육박전 a hand-to-hand fight; a close combat
2 〈경기의〉 a game; a match; a contest
♦ 연장전 an extended game / 1회전 the first game; 〈토너먼트의〉 the first round

전가 傳家 〈살림을 물려줌〉 ♦ 전가의 보도(寶刀) a sword treasured in the family for generations / 전가지보(之寶) an heirloom / 전가의 hereditary; ancestral; successive

전가 轉嫁 imputation
—**전가하다** transfer; impute 《a crime to *sb*》; lay [throw] 《the blame on *sb*》; shift [shuffle] 《a responsibility on(to) *sb*》
▶ 남에게 당신의 책임을 전가해서는 안되오 Do not transfer [shift] your responsibility to others.
▶ 그는 그 죄를 내게 전가했다 He laid [threw] the blame on me.

전각 殿閣 〈궁궐〉 a (royal) palace

전각 篆刻 seal engraving —**전각하다** engrave a seal

전갈 全蠍 〔動〕 a scorpion ■—**자리** 〔天〕 the Scorpion

전갈 傳喝 a verbal message
♦ 전갈을 보내다 send word [a message] / 전갈을 받다 receive a message; get word
▶ 저는 그분에게서 선생님에게 드릴 전갈을 가져왔습니다 I have brought a message from him [his message] for you.
—**전갈하다** send word [a message] 《to》; give a (verbal) message

전개 展開 unfolding; 〈진전함〉 development; 〔劇〕 discovery; 〈군대의〉 deployment; 〔數〕 expansion
♦ 국면의 전개 the development of the situation
—**전개하다** unfold; develop; 〈펴지다〉 spread [open] out; unfold itself; 〈군대가〉 deploy; fan out; 〔數〕 expand
♦ 새 국면을 전개하다 take a new turn / 이론을 전개하다 unfold [state] *one's* theory

▶웅대한 경치가 눈 아래에 전개되기 시작했다 A magnificent landscape began to unfold [spread out] under our eyes.
▶이야기는 의외의 결말로 전개했다 The story developed into an unexpected ending.
■—도 a development figure [view, drawing] —부《樂》the development (section) —식《數》an expansion

전거 典據 〈근거〉 authority; 〈출전〉 source
♦믿을 만한 전거 reliable authority / 전거가 있는 authentic; authorized; authenticated / 전거가 확실한 of good [right] authority / 전거가 없는 unauthorized; unauthenticated; without authority / 성서를 전거로 하여 on the authority of the Bible / 모든 인용문의 전거를 밝히다 cite the sources of [authorities for] all the quotations / 전거를 들다[밝히다] name [give, cite] the authority (for); indicate the source 《of》 / 명백한 전거를 보이다 give chapter and verse 《for》

전거 轉居 (house) moving ⇨ 이전(移轉)
전건 電鍵 a (telegraph) key; a tapper
전게 前揭 ♦전게의 above mentioned; shown above [before]
전격 電撃 〈전기 충격〉 an electric shock; 〈갑자기 공격함〉 a lightning attack; a blitz
♦전격적인 lightning; blitz / 전격을 당하다 be blitzed; be attacked with a blitz
■—작전 blitz tactics —전 a lightning war [attack]; a blitzkrieg

전경 全景 a complete view; a panorama 《of》; a panoramic view; 〈조감 경치〉 a bird's-eye view
▶이 다리에서 폭포의 전경이 보인다 From this bridge we can get [enjoy] a complete view of the waterfall.
■—사진 a panoramic photograph —사진기 a pantoscopic camera; a panoramic camera

전경 前景 〈풍경·그림의〉 the foreground
전고 典故 an authentic precedent
전곡 田穀 dry-field grain
전곡 〈—녹음〉(a) full-length recording —연주 a full-length play 《of》
전곡 錢穀 money and grain
전골 beef [pork] stew [casserole]
■—틀 a casserole; a stewpan

전공 專攻 one's specialty [field]; 《英》 one's speciality; one's major
—전공하다 《美》 major 《in》; specialize 《in》; study specially; make a special [an exclusive] study 《of》; make a specialty of; 《英》 read
▶나는 대학에서 생물학을 전공했다 I majored in [read] biology at (the) university.
▶대학에서 무엇을 전공했습니까? What did you major in at the university?
■—과목 a subject of special study; 《美》 a major —분야 a major field of study

전공 電工 an electrician
전공 戰功 meritorious services [exploits] in war; military merit [exploits]; distinguished war services
♦전공을 세우다 render distinguished services in war; distinguish oneself in war

▶그는 전공에 의해 무공훈장을 받았다 He was decorated with the Order of Military Merit for his distinguished services in war.

전과 全科 the whole [full, complete] course [curriculum]; all lessons; 〈참고서〉 a study-aid book for primary schoolchildren ♦전과를 이수하다 complete the whole course

전과 前科 a previous offense [conviction]; a criminal record
♦전과 4범인 사람 a person with four (previous) convictions / 전과가 있다 have been previously convicted; have a criminal [police] record
▶그는 전과가 있다[없다] He has a [no] criminal record.
▶그는 전과 3범이다 He is a man with three previous offences.
■—자[범] a man with a criminal record; an ex-convict; 《俗》 an ex-con; a former convict; an old offender

전과 戰果 war results; military achievements
♦혁혁한 전과를 올리다 achieve brilliant war results; make marked military achievements
▶우리는 그 작전에서 큰 전과를 거두었다 We made a great military advance in the operation.

전과 轉科 change of one's course —전과하다 change one's course 《to》; be enrolled in another course
▶그는 법학과로 전과했다 He changed departments and became a law major.

전관 前官 〈전임자〉 the predecessor 《in a post》; 〈자신의 전직〉 one's former post
▶그는 전관 예우를 받고 있다 He is granted the privileges of his former post.

전관 專管 exclusive jurisdiction [control, management] —전관하다 have the exclusive jurisdiction 《over》; have power 《over》
■—구역 an exclusive jurisdiction —(어업)수역 an exclusive fishing zone

전광 電光 〈전기 등의 불빛〉 electric light; 〈번갯불〉 (a flash of) lightning; a bolt
♦전광 석화(石火)와 같이 like (a flash of) lightning; in a flash [shot]; with lightning speed [swiftness]
▶그는 전광 석화와 같이 울타리를 뛰어 넘었다 He jumped over the fence as quick as lightning [with lightning speed].
■—간판 an electric sign 《of a store》 —게시판 an electric bulletin board 《경기장의》 an electric(al) scoreboard —뉴스 an electric news tape; an illuminated news display; 〈광고용의〉 a sky sign

전교 全校 the whole [all the] school
▶전교가 축구팀의 승리를 기뻐했다 The whole school rejoiced over the victory of its soccer team.
■—생 the whole student body; all the students of the school

전교 傳教 propagation (of religion) ⇨ 포교(布教)
전교 轉交 〈남을 거쳐서 받게 함〉 sending 《a letter》 in care of someone; delivery [transfer] through sb; care of 《略 c/o》
♦K씨 전교 M씨 귀하 Mr. M, care of [c/o]

Mr. K
▶그것을 회사 전교로 그에게 보내시오 Send it to him (in) care of [c/o] his office.
—전교하다 send 《a letter》 in care of [to the care of] *sb*

전구 前驅 the lead ⇨ 선구(先驅)

전구 電球 an electric [a light] bulb; an electric-light bulb
♦60촉짜리 전구 a 60 watt bulb / 끊어진 전구 a burnt-out light bulb / 전구를 갈다[끼우다] change [put in, screw in] a light bulb / 전구를 소켓에 끼우다 screw a lamp into its socket
▶전구가 끊어졌다 The filament has burnt out [broken]. = The light bulb has gone [burned out, blown out].
■—가스 a gas-filled bulb 반투명[젖빛]— a frosted bulb 백열— an incandescent light bulb 색— a colored bulb 섬광[플래시]— a flash bulb 소형[꼬마]— a miniature bulb 알— a naked light bulb 탄소선— a carbon-filament bulb

전국 술 undiluted liquor; soy sauce
■—간장 pure soy sauce —술 raw spirit

전국 全國 the whole country [land]; the whole of a country
♦전국의 national; nationwide; countrywide / 전국에(서) throughout [all over] the country
▶일본 뇌염이 전국에 퍼졌다 Japanese encephalitis has spread all over [around] the country.
▶한파가 전국을 덮쳤다 A cold wave hit the whole country [land].
▶대통령의 연설은 오늘밤 전국에 걸쳐 방송된다 The President's speech [address] will be broadcast nationwide tonight.
■—대회 〈정당의〉 a national convention; 〈스포츠의〉 a national athletic meet —중계(방송) a nationwide hookup —지 a national [nationwide] newspaper

전국 戰局 the military situation; the state [aspect] of the war; the war situation; the tide of war
▶전국은 일진일퇴를 거듭하고 있다 The war situation hangs in the balance [is very uncertain].
▶전국이 아군에게 유리[불리]해졌다 The (tide of) war turned in our favor [against us].

전국 戰國 ■—시대 the age of wars; 〔史〕 the Age [Period] of the Warring States

전국구 全國區 the national [nationwide] constituency
■—의원 a member of the Assembly elected from the national constituency —제 the national constituency system

전국민 全國民 the whole [entire] nation ♦전국민의 소리[여론] the voice of the whole nation

전국적 全國的 national; nationwide; countrywide
♦전국적인 규모로 on a nationwide scale / 전국적으로 all over [across] the country; all the country over; throughout the land / 전국적인 운동을 일으키다 start a nationwide movement / 전국적으로 행하여지다 be undertaken on a nationwide scale [throughout the land]; 《美》 go national
▶독감이 전국적으로 번졌다 Influenza spread all over the country [throughout Korea].
▶날씨는 전국적으로 좋겠습니다 The weather will be nice all across the country.

전군 全軍 the whole army [force]; 〈스포츠의〉 the whole team

전권 全卷 〈한 권의〉 the whole volume [book]; 〈한 질의〉 the whole set of books [volumes]; 〈영화의〉 the whole reel
♦전권을 통하여 from cover to cover; throughout the book / 전권을 통독하다 read the book from cover to cover; read through the book
▶그 고아에 대한 주인공의 애정이 전권을 통해서 상세히 서술되어 있다 The hero's love for the orphan is described in detail from cover to cover [throughout the book].

전권 全權 full [plenary] power; full [absolute] authority
▶그는 회사의 전권을 쥐고 있다 He has [holds, possesses] full [absolute] power in the company.
▶그들은 그 교섭의 전권을 그에게 위임했다 They invested him with full power to carry out [on] the negotiations.
■—공사 a minister plenipotentiary —대사 an ambassador plenipotentiary : 특명전권대사 an ambassador extraordinary and plenipotentiary —위원 a plenipotentiary —위임장 a commission of full power

전권 前卷 the preceding volume

전극 電極 an electrode; a pole; a [an electric] terminal ♦양[음]전극 the positive [negative] pole

전근 轉筋 a cramp; 《美口》 a charley horse

전근 轉勤 transfer; transference
—전근하다 be transferred 《to another office》
♦부산 지점으로 전근되다 be transferred to the Pusan branch
▶그는 서울 본사로 전근되었다 He was transferred to the head office in Seoul.

전근대적 前近代的 〈근대 이전의〉 premodern; 〈구태 의연한〉 old-fashioned

전기 前記 ♦전기의 foregoing; aforesaid; aforementioned; above-mentioned; the said 《person》 / 전기의 금액 the said sum; the sum mentioned above / 전기와 같이 as said [mentioned] above; as above-mentioned
▶전기의 장소로 지난 6월에 이전했습니다 We moved to the above address last June.
—전기하다 mention [say, refer to] above

전기 前期 〈한 해의 상반기〉 the first half (year); 〈2학기제의 전반〉 the first term [《美》 semester]; 〈시대의 초기〉 an early period
♦ (대학의) 2학년 전기에 in the first semester of the second year
■—결산 settlement for the first half year —국회[총회] the last session of the National Assembly [the general assembly] —이월금 the balance brought [carried] over from the previous [last] account

전기 傳奇 **1** 〈소설〉 a romance; a novel **2** 〈일사·기담〉 a strange [a curious, an

amazing] matter [story]
전기 傳記 a life; a biography; a life [biographical] story
▶나는 채플린의 전기를 읽고 감동했다 I read a biography [life] of Charlie Chaplin and was very impressed.
■―물[문학] biographical writings [literature] ―작가 a biographer
전기 電氣 electricity; 〈전등〉 an electric light; 〈전류〉 an electric current
♦전기의 electric; electrical
〈전기가〉 그 전선은 전기가 통하지 않았다 The wire wasn't charged with electricity. ⇌ The wire wasn't live [was dead].
▶여기 히말라야의 마을에는 전기가 들어오지 않는다 There is no electricity in this Himalayan village.
▶엊저녁부터 그의 방에는 전기가 죽 켜져 있었다 The light has been on in his room since last night.
〈전기를〉 전기를 켜다[끄다] switch [turn] on [off] the electric light / 전기를 통하게 하다 turn on an electric current [the juice] / 전기를 끌다 install electricity / 전기를 절약[낭비]하다 save [waste] electricity / 전기를 켜 놓은 체 자다 sleep with the light on
▶이 히터는 전기를 너무 잡아먹는다 This heater uses too much electricity.
▶나는 플러그를 뽑아 전기를 껐다 I turned off the electricity by pulling out the plug.
〈전기로〉 전기로 움직이는 창 electrically operated windows / 전기로 움직이다 be electrically operated
▶이 기계는 모두 전기로 움직이고 있다 These machines all run on [are all worked by] electricity.
■―수력― hydroelectricity 양[음]― positive [negative] electricity 정(靜)― static electricity ■―감응 electric induction ―검침원 an electricity checker [inspector] ―계기(計器) an electric meter ―공(工.) an electrician ―공사 electric work ―공업 the electric(al) industry ―공학 electrical engineering ―기계 an electric machine ―기관차 an electric locomotive ―기사 an electrical engineer; an electrician ―난로 an electric heater [stove] ―난방(법) electric heating ―냉장고 an electric refrigerator [freezer] ―다리미 an electric iron ―담요 an electric blanket ―도체 an electric conductor ―료 electric(al) charges [rates]; electricity [power] rates; 〈전등료〉 electric-light rates ―마사지 electromassage ―면도기 an electric razor; a [an electric] shaver ―밥솥 an electric rice-cooker ―방석 a heating pad ―사업 the electric(al) enterprise [industry] ―상 〈상점〉 an electric(al) appliances store; 〈상인〉 an electrician ―설비 electric installation [equipment] ―세탁기 an electric washing machine [washer] ―스탠드 a desk [reading] lamp ―야금(법) electrometallurgy ―역 학 electrodynamics ―요 법 electrical treatment; electropathy; electrotherapy ―유도 electric induction ―의료 기 계 an electromedical apparatus ―이발기 an electric (hair) clipper ―자동차 a battery car; an electric automobile [car]; an electromobile ―저항 electric resistance ―저항계 an ohmmeter ―전도 electrical conduction ―절연 electric insulation ―절연체 an electric insulator ―제어 electric control ―제품 an electric appliance [apparatus] ―조명 electric(al) illumination; electric lighting ―(진공)청소기 an electric vacuum cleaner ―철도 an electric railroad ―충격 〈公 전격(電擊)―침 〈외과용〉 an electric needle ―토스터 an electric toaster; a toaster ―통신 telecommunication; electric communication ―판(印) an electrotype; an electroplate ―풍로 an electric cooking stove ―학 the science of electricity; electric science ―화학 electrochemistry ―회로 an electric circuit ―회사 an electric(al) company 전깃줄 an electric wire [cord]
전기 電機 electrical machinery; electric appliances
■―중― heavy electrical equipment ■―공업 electrical machinery industry ―회사 an electrical manufacturing [engineering] company
전기 戰記 a record [an account] of war; a military history
♦『태평양 전기』 *A History of the Pacific War*
전기 戰機 the time for opening hostilities
▶전기가 무르익었다 The time is ripe for opening fire.
전기 轉記 〔簿〕 posting ―전기하다 post (an item); transfer (an entry to another account)
♦원장에 전기하다 post 《an item》 in the ledger
전기 轉機 a turning point; a point of change
♦인생의 전기 the turning point in *one's* life / …을 전기로 하여 with... as a turning point / 전기에 서다 be at a turning point 《in》 / 전기를 만들다[마련하다] make a turning point
▶이 사건이 그의 인생의 전기가 되었다 This event marked a turning point in his life.
전기기구 電氣器具 an electric(al) device [appliance]; (총칭) electric(al) apparatus
♦가정용 전기기구 household electric appliances
전기도금 電氣鍍金 electroplating; galvanization ―전기도금하다 electroplate; galvanize
전기분해 電氣分解 electrolysis; electrolytic analysis
―전기분해하다 electrolyze
전기용접 電氣鎔接 electric welding
■―기 an electric welder
전기의자 電氣椅子 an electric chair; (俗) the chair; (美俗) a hot seat
♦전기의자에 의한 사형 electrocution / 전기의자에 앉히다 [전기의자로 처형하다] execute 《a criminal》 in the electric chair; send 《a culprit》 to the (electric) chair; electrocute
전기자 電機子 an armature
전기장치 電氣裝置 (an) electric apparatus
♦전기장치가 되어 있다 be provided with electric apparatuses
전깃불 電氣― an electric light ⇨ 전등(電燈)
전나무 〔植〕 a fir (tree)
전날 前― the previous [preceding] day; the

day before; 〈과거의 어느 날〉 the other day; some time [days] ago
♦불이 난 전날 밤에 on the evening before the fire broke out
▶그는 전날 호텔 예약을 취소했다 He canceled his hotel reservations (on) the day before [preceding day].
▶출발 전날 당신 편지를 받았소 I received your letter (on) the day before my departure.
▶전날은 고마웠습니다 Thank you for the other day.

전남편 前男便 one's former [divorced] husband; one's ex-husband

전납 全納 full payment ━전납하다 pay in full

전납 前納 〈선납〉 advance payment; payment in advance; prepayment
━전납하다 pay (the rent) in advance; prepay
▶수업료는 전납입니다 You are requested to pay the tuition in advance.

전내기 全─ pure [undiluted] liquor

전내기 廛─ 〈날림치〉 goods for the market; ready-made articles [goods]

전년 前年 〈어느 해의 전해〉 the previous [preceding] year; 〈지난해〉 former [past] years; the other year; 〈작년〉 last year
♦그 전년 the year before / 전쟁이 일어난 전년 the year before the war broke out
■━도 the preceding [fiscal] year

전념 專念 concentration of mind; undivided attention
━전념하다 concentrate (on); devote oneself [one's time] (to); occupy oneself [be occupied] (with, in); be absorbed (in)
▶그는 암 연구에 전념하고 있다 He is applying himself diligently to the study of cancer.
▶그는 하루종일 그 일에 전념했다 He concentrated on the work all day long.
▶나는 휴일에 독서에 전념했다 I devoted the holiday to reading.
▶그녀는 그 소설의 집필에 전념하고 있다 She is occupied (in) [is bent on] writing the novel.

전뇌 前腦 〖解〗 the prosencephalon; the forebrain

전능 全能 omnipotence
━전능하다 omnipotent; almighty; all-powerful ♦전능하신 하느님 Almighty God; the Almighty; the Omnipotent (God)
▶하느님은 전능하시다 God is almighty. ⇌ All things are possible to God.

전단 全段 〈신문의〉 a whole page; the whole space ♦전단을 스포츠 기사로 메우다 devote a whole page to sports news
■━표제 a banner (headline); a bannerline

전단 專斷 arbitrary decision; arbitrariness
♦전단적 조치 an arbitrary measure / 전단으로 arbitrarily; at one's own discretion / 전단적 조치를 취하다 act arbitrarily [on one's own authority]
▶그는 재임 중에 전단적 처사를 남용했다 He abused his authority while in office.

전단 傳單 a bill; a handbill; (美) a handout; a leaflet ♦전단을 뿌리다 distribute handbills; drop leaflets (from a plane)
▶나는 집집마다 전단을 뿌리고 다녔다 I distributed leaflets to every door.

전단 戰端 the cause of war; hostilities; hostile operations
♦전단을 열다 〈선전하다〉 declare war on [upon, against]; 〈교전 상태에 들어가다〉 open [commence] hostilities (with); go to war (with)

전달 前─ 〈과거를 기준으로〉 the preceding [previous] month; 〈이달의〉 last month
♦전전달 the month before last / 전달 5일에 on the fifth of last month / 전달의 마지막 월요일에 on the last Monday (of) last month
▶나는 전달에는 몹시 분주했다 I was very busy last month.

전달 傳達 transmission; conveyance; communication; delivery; propagation
━전달하다 transmit; convey; communicate; deliver; propagate
▶그 메시지는 잘못 전달되었다 The message was transmitted incorrectly.
▶우리는 언어를 써서 사상이나 감정을 전달한다 We communicate ideas and feelings by (means of) language.
▶소리는 빛보다 늦게 전달된다 Sound travels slower than light.
■━경로 an avenue of communication ━속도 velocity of propagation; propagation velocity ━수단 a means of communication

전담 全擔 full [entire, whole] responsibility [charge]
━전담하다 assume [take] full responsibility [charge]; be wholly responsible (for)
♦비용을 전담하다 bear [shoulder] the whole expenses / 사업의 운영을 전담하다 assume full charge of a business

전담 專擔 exclusive responsibility [charge]
♦마약 전담반 the narcotics squad
━전담하다 take [bear, assume] exclusive responsibility (of); be exclusively responsible (for)

전답 田畓 paddy fields and dry fields

전당 典當 hocking; pawning; pawnage; pledge
♦전당잡다 take sth in pawn; hold sth in pledge / 전당잡히다 pawn; pledge; put sth in pawn / 만원에 전당잡히다 pawn sth for ten thousand won / 전당잡혀 있다 be in [at] pawn; (美俗) be in hock
▶그는 전당포에 있던 카메라를 찾았다 He got his camera out of hock.
▶그녀의 옷들은 생계를 위해 거의 모두 전당잡혔다 She hocked nearly all her clothes for her living.
▶그는 있는 것 없는 것 다 전당잡혀 먹었다 He is up to his ears in hock.

전당 殿堂 a palace; a hall; a sanctuary; a shrine; a temple ♦학문의 전당 a sanctuary of learning / 영예의 전당 the Hall of Fame

전당대회 全黨大會 the national convention (of); a party convention

전당포 典當鋪 a pawnbroker's shop; a pawnshop; (口) a hock shop; (英俗) a popshop
▶그는 자주 전당포에 드나든다 He visits a

pawnshop often.
■공설— a public [municipal] pawnshop —업 pawnbroking; the pawnbroking business —업자 a pawnbroker

전당표 典當票 a pawn ticket

전당품 典當品 a pawn; a pawned article; an article in pawn ◆전당품을 유질하다 forfeit a pawn / 전당품을 찾다 redeem [recover] a pawn [pawned article]

전대 前代 〈지나간 시대〉 former ages; 〈지나간 세대〉 a former generation

전대 戰隊 〈해군의〉 a squadron

전대 轉貸 〈토지의〉 underlease; sublease; 〈가옥의〉 underletting; subletting
—전대하다 sublet [subrent] 《a house》; sublease [underlease] 《land》
▶ 해외 여행을 하는 동안 방을 일년간 전대하고 싶다 I want to sublease [sublet] my room for a year while I make a foreign trip.
—인 a sublessor

전대 纏帶 〈허리에 차는〉 a money belt

전대미문 前代未聞 ◆전대미문의 unprecedented; unheard-of; unparalleled in history / 전대미문의 대참사 an unheard-of calamity / 전대미문의 일 a most sensational event
▶ 그것은 전대미문의 사건이었다 It was an unheard-of [unprecedented] accident.
▶ 그것은 전대미문의 스캔들이다 That's an unheard-of scandal. ≒ I've never heard anything like that scandal.

전대야 a projecting-brimmed washbowl

전도 全島 the entire [whole] island
◆전도에 throughout [all over] the island

전도 全道 the whole province
◆전도에 all over [throughout] the province

전도 全圖 a complete map [drawing]
■대한민국— a complete map of Korea 세계— a world map

전도 前途 〈장래〉 one's future; 〈가망〉 prospects; 〈여행의〉 the journey before one
◆유망한 전도 a bright future / 전도가 밝다 have a bright future [prospects] 《before one》 / 전도가 요원하다 〈사람이 주어〉 have a long [far] way to go; 〈일이 주어〉 be far [a long way] off / 전도를 걱정하다 be anxious about one's future / 전도를 그르치다 spoil one's future [career] / 전도를 축복하다 wish sb a happy future / 전도를 내다보다 look ahead into the future
▶ 외국 무역의 전도는 어둡다 The outlook for foreign trade is [The prospects for foreign trade are] gloomy.
▶ 전도를 비관하기에는 아직 이르다 It's too early to be [become] pessimistic about the future.
▶ 우리의 전도는 다난하다 Various difficulties are [lie] ahead of us [in our future, in our way].

전도 前渡 payment [delivery] in advance
—전도하다 pay in advance [beforehand]; prepay
■—금 advanced money; an advance; an advancement

전도 前導 guidance
—전도하다 guide; lead (the way); conduct
—자 a guide; a leader —함 a guide ship

전도 傳道 gospel preaching; missionary work; missions; evangelism
◆전도(사업)에 종사하다 engage in mission [missionary] work
—전도하다 evangelize; gospelize; propagate one's religion; preach the gospel
▶ 그는 한국 곳곳에 기독교를 전도했다 He preached Christianity throughout Korea.
■—사[자] an evangelist; a preacher; a missionary —서〔聖〕 (The Book of) Ecclesiastes

전도 傳導 〔物〕〈열·전기의〉 conduction; 〈빛·소리 등의〉 transmission
—전도하다 conduct; transmit
▶ 구리는 전기를 잘 전도한다 Copper conducts electricity well.
■열— heat conduction ■—도[율] conductivity —성 conductivity; conductibility —체 a conductor : 부전도체 a nonconductor

전도 顚倒 **1** 〈엎드러짐〉 a fall; an upset
—전도하다 fall down; overturn; tumble
2 〈거꾸로 됨〉 upside-downness; inversion; topsy-turvy —전도하다 invert; reverse
◆본말을 전도하다 put the cart before the horse; mistake the means for the end / 상하가 전도되어 있다 be upside down
▶ 이제 그들의 지위는 전도되었다 Their positions are now reversed.

전동 箭筒 〈화살통〉 a quiver

전동 電動 electromotion ◆전동(식)의 electromotive; electric-powered ■—력 electromotive force [power] —발전기 a motor generator —타자기 an electric typewriter

전동 傳動 gearing; transmission; drive
—전동하다 gear; drive —톱니바퀴— a gear drive —나사 a drive screw

전동기 電動機 an electromotor; an electric motor; a motor ■교류— an AC [alternating current] motor 직류— a DC [direct current] motor —회로 a motor circuit

전동자 電動子 an armature (of a motor)
■평판(平板)— a disc armature

전두 前頭 〔解〕 the sinciput
■—골 the frontal (bone) —부 the front; the forehead —엽(葉) the frontal lobe

전두리 a projecting rim [brim]

전등 電燈 an electric light [lamp] ◆전등을 켜다 turn [switch] on an electric light / 전등을 끄다 switch [turn] off an electric light
▶ 이 방은 밝은 전등이 필요하다 We need a bright light in this room.
▶ 전등이 어둡다 The electric light is dim.
▶ 전등이 꺼졌다 The electric light went out.
■꼬마— a fairy lamp [light] 장식— a decoration (electric) lamp 회중— an electric torch; 《美》 a flashlight ■—갓 a lamp shade —코드 a lamp cord

전라 全裸 total nudity; stark nakedness
◆전라의 stark-naked; nude; with no clothes on / 전라의 사진 a nude photograph / 전라가 되다 be stripped stark naked

전락 轉落 **1** 〈굴러 떨어짐〉 a fall
—전락하다 fall 《from》; roll [tumble] down

전란

▶ 그는 3위로 전락했다 He slid down to third place.
2 〈타락〉 degradation; 〈영락〉 ruin; downfall
―**전락하다** degrade; be ruined; go to ruin
▶ 그는 출세가 너무 빨랐다. 그것이 전락한 원인이었다 He was a success too soon. It was [caused] his downfall.
▶ 그녀는 거리의 여자로 전락했다 She degraded to the status of a woman of the streets.
■―자 a ruined person

전란 戰亂 the disturbances of war ◆전란의 유럽 war-torn[-shattered] Europe / 전란의 도가니 the scene of war [a battle]

전람 展覽 exhibition; show ◆전람중이다 be on show [view] ―**전람하다** exhibit; display
■―실 a showroom ―자 an exhibitor ―품 an exhibit

전람회 展覽會 an exhibition; an exhibit; a show
◆전람회를 개최하다 hold an exhibition
▶ 그는 그 전람회에 그림을 출품했다 He showed his painting at the exhibition.
■국화― a chrysanthemum show 미술― an art exhibition 학생 작품― an exhibition of the pupils' works ■―장 an exhibition gallery [hall]

전래 傳來 transmission; introduction
◆조상 전래의 가보 one's family treasure / 조상 전래의 의업 the family [hereditary] profession of medicine / 중국 전래의 의술 traditional Chinese medicine [medical practices]
―**전래하다** be transmitted; be handed down; descend 《from fathers》; 〈도입되다〉 be imported [introduced]
▶ 불교는 4세기에 한국에 전래됐다 Buddhism found its way [was introduced] into Korea in the fourth century.
▶ 이 검은 조상 전래된 것이다 This sword has been handed down [transmitted] from my ancestors.

전략 前略 omission of what precedes
―**전략하다** omit the preface
◆전략하옵고 〈편지에서〉 I hasten to inform you that...; Just a line to tell you that...

전략 戰略 strategy; a stratagem
◆전략상(으로) strategically / 전략상의 목적으로 for strategic purposes / 전략으로 이기다 outgeneral; outmaneuver / 전략을 세우다 map [work] out a strategy
▶ 그 섬은 전략상 중요하다 The island is strategically important [important from the strategic point of view].
■―가 a strategist ―공군 a strategic air force ―공군사령부 《美》 the Strategic Air Command (略 SAC) ―목표 a strategic target ―무기 strategic arms ―무기 삭감 조약 the Strategic Arms Reduction Treaty ―무기 제한 협정 the Strategic Arms Limitation Talks (略 SALT) ―물자 strategic goods [materials] ―수립자 a strategy-maker ―폭격 strategic bombing ―폭격기 a strategic bomber ―핵무기 strategic nuclear weapons [arms] ―회의 a strategy meeting

전략적 戰略的 strategic
◆전략적 지점 a strategic point / 전략적 후퇴 a strategic retreat [withdrawal]

전량 全量 the whole quantity

전량 錢糧 〈돈과 곡식〉 money and provisions; supplies

전량계 電量計 a coulometer; a voltameter

전력 全力 〈온힘〉 all one's power [strength, energies, might]; one's best [utmost]
◆전력을 다하여 with all one's strength [might]; at full strength; to the best of one's ability / 전력을 다하다 do one's best [utmost]; do everything in [within] one's power / 그 일에 전력을 기울이다 devote [apply] all one's energy [energies] to (doing) the task / 전력으로 달리다 run at full speed [strength]; run as fast [hard] as one can / 전력으로 로프를 잡아당기다 pull a rope with all one's strength [might]; use all one's strength to pull a rope
▶ 그들은 그녀를 설득하는 데 전력을 다했다 They did their best to persuade her. = They did all they could do to persuade her.
▶ 그는 목적을 달성하기 위해 전력을 다했다 He did his best to achieve his goal.
▶ 전력을 다해 자네를 돕겠네 I'll do my utmost to help you.
▶ 그는 이 사업에 전력을 기울였다 He gave his all energies to this undertaking.
▶ 김교수는 연구에 전력을 기울였다 The professor Kim devoted all his energies to his study.

전력 前歷 one's past [personal] record [history]; one's past (life)
◆전력을 조사하다 check [trace] sb's past record
▶ 그의 전력을 알고 계십니까? Do you know anything of his past [personal record]?
▶ 그의 전력은 관리다 He once served in a government office.

전력 專力 concentration of one's energies
―**전력하다** concentrate one's energies 《on》; devote oneself to

전력 電力 electric power; electricity
◆10만 마력의 전력 100,000 electrical horsepower / 전력의 낭비[절약] waste [economy] of electric power / 전력을 공급하다 supply electric power
■공업용― industrial electric power ■―개발 electrical power development ―계 a wattmeter ―공급 the supply of electric power [electricity]; the power supply ―공사 power supply works ―부족 an electric power shortage ―사업 the (electric) power industry ―사정 the electric power condition ―선 a power line ―소비 power consumption ―요금 electric power rates ―제한 power restrictions

전력 戰力 war potential; fighting strength; military power
◆전력 없는 군대 troops [an army] without war potential / 전력의 유지[상실, 증강] the maintenance [loss, buildup] of war potential
■―원(源) 〈재정적・물질적인〉 the sinews of war

전력 戰歷 a war experience; one's combat

career ◆전력이 혁혁한 군인 a soldier of many campaigns
전령 傳令 a [an official] message; 〈사람〉 a messenger; an orderly ◆전령을 보내다 send a message [an orderly] ■—근무 orderly duty —병(兵) an orderly
전령 電鈴 an electric bell
◆전령을 누르다 ring an electric bell
전례 典禮 a ceremony; a ritual
전례 前例 a precedent; a previous instance; a previous example
◆전례가 없는 unprecedented / 전례가 없는 일 an unprecedented matter; an unheard-of affair / 역사상 전례가 없다 be without precedent [parallel] in history / 전례가 되다 become [give] a precedent / 그 전례를 따르다 follow the precedent; follow previous instance / 전례를 만들다 set [make, create] a precedent / 전례를 깨뜨리다 depart from [violate] precedent / 전례로 삼다 take *sth* as a precedent
▶ 그것은 전례가 없다 There is no precedent for it. ⇌ It has no precedent. ⇌ It is unprecedented.
전로 電路 an electric(al) circuit; a circuit
전로 轉爐 〔冶〕 a revolving furnace; a converter ■—강(鋼) converter steel
전류 電流 an electric current; a voltaic current
◆전류의 세기 yield of current / 전류의 세기 current intensity / 전류의 역류 reversal of current / 전류의 galvanic; voltaic / 전류가 흐르고 있지 않는 모터 dead motor / 전류가 흐르고 있는 전선 a live wire / 전류를 끊다[통하다] turn off [on] electric current
▶ 이 전선에는 강한 전류가 흐르고 있다 There is a powerful electric current running through the wire.
■—고압[저압]— (美) a high-[low-]tension current 교류— an alternating current (略 A.C.) 직류— a direct current (略 D.C.) ■—계(計) a galvanometer; an amperemeter; an ammeter —단위 a current unit —량 amperage —밀도 current density —전환기 a commutator —제한기 a current limiter —증폭기 an electric current amplifier —차단기 a contact breaker —측정(법) galvanometry —표시기 an electric current indicator —학 galvanism —회로 a current circuit
전륜 前輪 a front wheel
■—구동(驅動) front-wheel drive: 전륜 구동차 a front-wheel drive car
전리 電離 electrolytic dissociation; ionization —전리하다 ionize ■—층 the ionosphere
전리품 戰利品 a (war) trophy; booty; a prize; spoils (of war)
전립선 前立腺 〔解〕 the prostate (gland)
◆전립선의 prostate; prostatic
■—비대 enlargement of the prostate gland —비대증 prostatomegaly —염 prostatitis —절제(수술) prostatectomy
전마선 傳馬船 a lighter; a flat-bottomed barge
전말 顚末 〈자세한 설명〉the full account; 〈사정〉the whole circumstances; 〈상세〉the particulars; the details; 〈경위〉the course of events
◆전말을 말하다 give the full account of; enter into particulars / 그 전말을 알고 있다 know everything about it; know all the details; have the whole story
▶ 그는 그 사건의 전말을 보고했다 He reported all the details of the event.
■—서 an account; a report
전망 展望 1 〈조망〉 a view; a sight; a prospect; a vista; an outlook

|解說| *view*는 특정 장소에서 눈에 보이거나 시야에 들어오는 경관을 나타내며 *sight*는 눈에 보이는 하나의 풍경을 가리키는데, 특히 주의를 끄는 것에 쓰인다. *prospect*는 멀리 바라볼 수 있는 장소에서 본 넓은 전망을 이르며 보통 단수형이다. *vista*는 가로수 길·거리 등 길게 내다보이는 경관이다.

◆전망이 좋다 have a fine view of / 전망을 가로막다 obstruct the view
▶ 옥상에 올라가면 전망이 더 좋다 You can get a better view from the rooftop.
▶ 새 건물이 들어서서 전망이 망쳐졌다 The new building spoils the view.
▶ 〖會話〗「난 전망이 좋은 방을 갖고 싶어」「정말이야」 "I'd like a room with a beautiful view." "Certainly."
—전망하다 have [command] a view of; look over ◆멀리 바다를 전망하다 have [command] a distant view of the sea
2 〈장래를 내다봄〉 a prospect; an outlook
◆경제적 전망 the prospects [outlook] for the economy / 밝은[암담한] 전망 a bright [gloomy] outlook / 사업의 전망 *one's* business outlook [prospects] / 전망이 좋다[밝다] have a bright prospect / 장기적 전망에 따른 에너지 정책 a far-seeing energy policy
▶ 과감한 개혁을 행하지 않는 한 새로운 전망은 열리지[나타나지] 않는다 Unless we make some drastic changes, new prospects won't open up [be opened].
▶ 금후 정계의 전망은 어떻습니까? Tell me your views on the future of the political sphere.
—전망하다 survey; make a survey 《of》
◆정치 상황을 전망하다 survey [make a survey of] the political situation
■—대 an observatory —차 an observation car —탑 〈잠수함의〉 a conning tower
전매 專賣 monopoly; monopolization —전매하다 monopolize; have complete marketing control; have a monopoly of [in, (美) on]
▶ 담배는 정부가 전매한다 The sale of tobacco is a government monopoly.
■—권 monopoly 《for》 —사업 the monopoly enterprise —제도 the monopoly system —청 the Office of Monopoly; the Monopoly Office —품 monopoly goods; monopolies
전매 轉賣 (a) resale —전매하다 resell
전매특허 專賣特許 a patent ⇨ 특허
전면 全面 the whole [entire] surface
◆호수의 전면 the entire [whole] surface of

the lake / 전면에 걸쳐 all over the surface
▶일면의 전면이 그 뉴스로 메워졌다〈신문의〉 The whole of the front page has been covered with the news.
▶이 문제는 전면에 걸쳐 조사가 이루어지고 있다 This question is being considered from all sides. ⇌ The matter is being studied in all its aspects.
■—강화 an overall [a world-wide] peace —공격 (launch) an all-out attack —광고 a full-page advertisement —전(쟁) an all-out [a total] war; a full-scale war; a global war —파업 an all-out [a general, a total] strike —핵전쟁 an all-out nuclear war

전면 前面 the front; the frontage; the facade
◆건물의 전면 the front of a building / 전면의 front; frontal; in (the) front / 전면에 in front (of); in the foreground
▶그 집의 전면은 희게 칠해져 있었다 The front of the house was painted white.

전면적 全面的 all-out; overall; general; full-scale; complete
◆전면적인 통제 full control / 전면적인 지지 one's entire support / 전면적으로 completely; entirely; generally; wholeheartedly / 전면적으로 개정하다 make a sweeping [an overall] revision (of)
▶위원회는 그 규약을 전면적으로 개정했다 The committee made an overall revision of the rules. ⇌ The committee revised the rules completely.
▶그는 우리 계획에 전면적인 지지를 약속했다 He promised to support our plan wholeheartedly [heartily]. ⇌ He promised a wholehearted [hearty] support to our plan.
▶그 호소는 사람들의 전면적 지지를 받았다 The appeal was supported wholeheartedly by the people.

전멸 全滅 annihilation; complete [total] destruction; extinction
▶한국의 많은 야생동물은 전멸의 위기에 직면해 있다 Many wild animals are on the verge of extinction in Korea.
—**전멸하다** be annihilated; be completely [totally] destroyed; be wiped out
◆전멸시키다 annihilate; destroy totally [completely]; wipe out
▶돌림병으로 마을 사람들이 전멸했다 The plague wiped out all the villagers. ⇌ The plague annihilated the whole (population of the) village. ⇌ None of the villagers survived the plague.
▶서리로 옥수수가 전멸했다 The frost spoiled the corn crop completely.
▶적은 우리 부대의 공격을 받고 전멸했다 The enemy has suffered a crushing defeat under the attack of our unit.

전모 全貌 the whole aspect; a full view (of); the whole [entire] picture (of)
◆사건의 전모를 밝히다 give [clarify] the whole picture of the case
▶그 계획의 전모가 밝혀졌다 Every detail of the project was made known.
▶사건의 전모를 밝히는 것은 결국 불가능했다 It was impossible, in the end, to bring the whole affair to light.

전몰 戰歿 death in battle ⇨ 전사(戰死)
■—용사[장병] a fallen soldier; (총칭) the war dead: 전몰 용사 기념비 a war memorial

전무 全無 total lack [absence]
—**전무하다** wholly lacking [wanting]
▶나는 그 주제에 대한 예비지식이 전무하다 I have no previous knowledge of the subject.
▶그들이 생존해 있을 가망은 전무하다 There is no hope of their being still alive.

전무 專務 〈사무〉 special duty; principal business; 〈사람〉 a managing director; an executive director ■여객— [鐵] a (chief) conductor —이사 ⇨ 전무

전무후무하다 前無後無— unparalleled; unheard-of; unprecedented; record-breaking; epoch-making
◆전무후무한 기록 (美) an all-time record / 전무후무한 대사업 the greatest enterprise which has never been made and probably will never be attempted
▶그것은 전무후무한 쾌거다 It is the first and probably the last brilliant achievement.

전문 全文 a whole sentence; a whole statement; the full text
◆조약의 전문 the full text of a treaty / 보고서의 전문 the whole statement of a report / 전문을 인용하다 quote the whole sentence / 전문을 게재하다 give (a letter) in full
▶전문을 국역하시오 Put [Translate] the whole passage into Korean.

전문 前文 〈법률·조약 등의〉 a preamble (to, of); 〈앞에 쓴 글〉 the above sentence; the foregoing statement ◆전문에서 언급한 바와 같이 as mentioned [stated] above

전문 前門 a front gate

전문 專門 a special object of pursuit; a specialty; (口) one's line; one's field; (美) a major
◆…의 전문 메이커 manufacturers specialized in the production of... / 전문의 special; technical; professional / 역사학을 전문으로 하다 specialize in history; make a specialty of history
▶당신은 무엇이 전문입니까? What is your major [specialty]? ⇌ What are you majoring in? ⇌ What do you specialize in?
▶이 음식점은 프랑스 요리 전문이다 This restaurant specializes in French cuisine. ⇌ The specialty of this restaurant is French cuisine.
▶그는 한국사를 전문으로 하고 있다 He is majoring [specializes] in Korean history. ⇌ Korean history is his major [specialty].
▶그것은 내 전문이 아니다 It is not in my line. ⇌ It is outside my (specialized) field.
▶이 회사는 농기구를 전문으로 제작하고 있다 This company specializes in making agricultural machines.
■—과목 a special(ized) subject [study] —교육 technical [professional] education —기술 expert skill —병원 a special hospital —서 one's field —서(적) a technical book —용어 a technical term; (총칭) terminology —위원 〈국회 등의〉 an expert committee (전체); a specialist (개인) —점 a specialty store —지(誌)

a technical journal [magazine] —지식 specialized [special, technical] knowledge —학교 a college; a special [professional, vocational] school —화 specialization: 전문화하다 specialize

전문 電文 〈전보〉 a telegram; a telegraphic message; 〈문구〉 the wording of a telegram; 〈해외로부터의〉 a cablegram

전문 傳聞 (a) report; (a) rumor; hearsay
▶ 나는 전문으로 알고 있을 뿐이다 I know about it only from [by] hearsay.
—전하다 hear [learn] from others; hear at second hand; be told ◆ 전문한 바로는 from what I hear; according to a rumor [report] —증거 hearsay evidence —증인 a hearsay witness

전문가 專門家 a specialist 《in》; an expert 《in, on》; a master hand ◆ 전문가의 의견을 듣다 take professional advice
▶ 그는 요리에 있어서 전문가 뺨칠 정도다 He puts even a professional to shame in cooking.

전문어 專門語 a technical term; (총칭) (technical) terminology ◆ 전문어를 쓰다 use technical language

전문의 專門醫 a medical specialist
■ —소아과 a pediatrician 안과— an eye specialist; an oculist

전문적 專門的 specialized; special; expert; technical; professional ◆ 전문적 지식 expert [technical] knowledge —전문적으로 specially; technically; professionally
▶ 그것은 전문적인 관점에서 보면 잘못돼 있다 It is wrong from a technical point of view.
▶ 변호사는 전문적인 일을 하는 사람이다 A lawyer is a professional man.
▶ 그 일은 상당히 전문적이다 The work is highly specialized.
▶ 그의 강의는 너무 전문적이어서 우리에게는 이해되지 않는다 His lecture is so technical that we can't understand it.

전물 奠物 offerings 《to gods, to Buddha》

전미 全美 all America; the whole of America
◆ 전미 선수권 an all-American championship

전박 前膊 the forearm ⇨ 하박(下膊)

전반 全般 the whole
◆ 사회[국민] 조직 전반 the world [people] at large / 조직 전반 the whole organization / 학생 전반 students in general / 전반의 whole; general; overall / 전반에 걸쳐 generally / 정세 전반을 내다보다 take an overall view of the situation
▶ 그것은 학생 전반의 문제다 It is a problem of students in general.

전반 前半 〈앞의 절반〉 the first half; 〈럭비 등의〉 the first period
▶ 그녀는 지금 50대 전반이다 She is in her early fifties now.
■ —기 the first half year —전 the first half of the game

전반사 全反射 [物] total reflection

전반적 全般的 general; 〈전체에 걸쳐〉 overall
◆ 전반적으로 in general; generally / 전반적으로 고찰하다 consider 《a matter》 by and large
▶ 금년에는 전반적으로 비가 많다 On the whole we have had a lot of rain this year.

전방 前方 **1** 〈앞쪽〉 the front
◆ 전방의 건물 the building ahead (of us) [in front (of us)] / 전방의 front; forward / 전방에 in front; ahead; forward
▶ 그것은 3백미터 전방에 있다 It's 300 meters ahead.
▶ 50미터 전방에 교통 신호등이 있다 There is a traffic signal fifty meters ahead.
2 〈제일선〉 the front (line)
◆ 전방의 병사들 the men on the front line / 군대를 전방지역 가까이 이동시키다 move troops close to front-line areas
■ —기지 an advanced base; an outpost —부대 a unit on the front line —위문공연 (美) a fox-hole circuit

전방 廛房 (美) a store; (英) a shop

전배 前杯 drinks *one* has taken previously ⇨ 전작(前酌)

전번 前番 the last time [occasion] ⇨ 지난번

전범 戰犯 〈전쟁 범죄〉 war crimes; 〈전쟁 범죄자〉 a war criminal ■—법정 a war crimes court —용의자 a suspected war criminal

전법 戰法 tactics; a plan of campaign; strategy

전변 轉變 mutation; change; vicissitude
◆ 전변무상한 vicissitudinous; ever-shifting; ever-changing; changeful —전변하다 change constantly; mutate

전별 餞別 giving a farewell party; a send-off —전별하다 hold a farewell party 《for》; give *sb* send-off ■ —금 a parting [farwell] money —연(宴) a farewell party [dinner] —주(酒) a parting drink

전병사 戰病死 death from a disease contracted at the front —전병사하다 die from a disease contracted at the front
■ —자 the dead from diseases contracted at the front

전보 電報 〈전문〉 a telegram; a telegraphic message; (口) a wire; 〈해외로부터의〉 a cable; a cablegram
〈전보를〉 전보를 치다 send [dispatch] a telegram 《to》; telegraph 《to》; (口) wire 《to》; cable / 전보를 배달하다 deliver a telegram
▶ 그는 내게 비행장에 마중나와 달라고 전보를 쳤다 He telegraphed me to meet him at the airport.
▶ 당신 어머니께 전보를 쳤습니까? Have you sent a telegram to your mother? ⇌ Have you telegraphed [(口) wired] to your mother?
▶ 아버지의 중환을 알리는 어머니의 전보를 받았다 I got a telegram from my mother saying (that) my father was very sick. ⇌ My mother telegraphed [wired] me that my father was very sick.
▶ 나는 형에게 곧 돌아오라고 전보를 쳤다 I telegraphed [(口) wired] my brother to come back as soon as possible.
〈전보로〉 전보로 by telegram [(口) wire, cable]
▶ 결과를 전보로 알려주시오 Please let me know the results by telegram [(口) wire cable].

전보 ■국내— a domestic telegram 발신— an outgoing telegram 서신— a letter telegram (略 LT) 수신— an incoming telegram 시간외— a late telegram [message] 신문— a press telegram [cable] 암호— a code telegram 지급— an urgent [a rush] telegram 해외[외국]— a foreign telegram; a cable ■—국 a telegraph office —료 a telegraph charge —배달원 a telegraph messenger —사무 telegraph service —업무 the cable and telegraph services —용지 a telegraph form; (美) a telegraph blank —환 ⇨ 전신환

전보 塡補 compensation; making up; filling —**전보하다** fill; compensate for; supply; make up for; replenish; complete; make good
♦ 결손[손실]을 전보하다 make up for [cover] the deficit

전보 戰報 war intelligence [news]; a war report

전보 轉補 transference; shuffling —**전보하다** transfer ♦ 전보되다 be transferred (to another position)

전복 全鰒 〔具〕 an ear shell; (美) an abalone

전복 顚覆 a turnover; an overturn; an overthrow; an upset; subversion; 〈배의〉 capsizal
♦ 급행열차의 전복을 꾀하다 attempt to wreck an express
—**전복하다** be overturned [overthrown, upset]; 〈배가〉 be capsized
♦ 정부[내각]를 전복시키다 overthrow [overturn] the government [the cabinet] / 열차를 전복시키다 overturn a train
▶ 그 보트는 큰 파도에 밀려 전복했다 The boat was capsized by [capsized in] high waves.

전봇대 電報— 〈전선용〉 an electric pole; 〈전신용〉 a telephone pole

전부 全部 〈모두〉 all; 〈전체〉 the whole; 〈합계〉 the total; 〈하나하나 모두〉 every; everything; 〈부사적〉 all; wholly; entirely; altogether; in all ♦ 거의 전부 nearly all
▶ 이것이 전부냐? Is this [Are these] all?
▶ 전부해서 얼마요? How much is it altogether?
▶ 그것들을 전부 샀다 I bought all of them.
▶ 학생들이 전부 거기에 갔던 건 아니다 Not all the students [Not every student] went there.
▶ 내가 할 수 있는 일은 전부 해봤다 I have tried every possible means.
▶ 너에게 말한 것은 전부 진실이야 Everything [All] I've told you is true.
▶ 하룻밤에 그 책을 전부 읽었다 I read the whole book [the whole of the book] in one evening.
▶ 신혼여행 비용은 전부 80만원 들었다 The overall [total] cost of our honeymoon was 800,000 won. ⇒ Our honeymoon cost was 800,000 won in all.
▶ 그는 가지고 있는 돈 전부를 써버렸다 He has spent all of his money.
▶ 이것이 내가 가지고 있는 돈 전부다 This is all the money I have.
▶ 사과는 전부 썩고 말았다 All (of) the apples have gone bad.

전부 前夫 one's former husband ♦ 전부의 자식 a child by one's former husband

전부 前部 the front [fore] part; the fore; the front; 〈대열의〉 forward ranks; 〈전반(前半)〉 the first half ♦ 기차의 전부 the front [fore] (part) of the train
▶ 엘리베이터는 건물의 전부에 있었다 The elevator was at the front [in the front part] of the building.

전분 澱粉 starch; 〔化〕 dextrin(e) ⇨ 녹말

전비 前非 〈이전의 허물〉 one's past error [folly, sin] ♦ 전비를 깨닫다 see the error of one's own ways / 전비를 뉘우치다 repent of one's past error [sin, misdeed]

전비 戰費 war expenditure(s); war funds; the cost of war

전비 戰備 preparations for war; war preparations ♦ 전비를 갖추다 prepare for war; make preparations for war

전사 全史 a complete history

전사 戰士 〈전투하는 병사〉 a fighter; a warrior; a soldier; 〈제일선에서 활약하는 사람〉 a frontline worker
♦ 무명전사의 묘 the tomb of the unknown soldier / 자유의 전사 a champion of liberty
■ 산업— an industry worker

전사 戰史 the history of a war ♦ 전사에 남다 be recorded [mentioned] in war history
■ —록(錄) a record [an account] of war; a military history

전사 轉寫 transcription; copying —**전사하다** transcribe; transfer; copy ■ —기 a transcriber —잉크 transfer ink —지 transfer paper

전사 戰死 death in battle [on the battlefield] —**전사하다** die [fall] fighting; be killed in battle [action]; fall on the battlefield
♦ 해전에서 전사하다 be killed in a naval battle / 명예롭게 전사하다 meet glorious death in action

전사자 戰死者 a person killed in battle [action]; a fallen soldier; (총칭) the war dead; combat fatalities
▶ 그 전투에서 다수의 전사자가 발생하였다 The battle took a heavy toll of lives.
■ —명부 a roll of honor —유족 a family bereaved by war; the war bereaved

전산 電算 calculation [computation] by computer ■ —기 ⇨ 전자(~계산기) —사식조판시스템 a computer typesetting system (略 CTS) —화 computerization

전상 戰傷 a war [battle] wound
—**전상하다** be wounded in battle [action]
■ —병 a wounded soldier —자 a wounded veteran; a person wounded in a war; (총칭) the war wounded

전색맹 全色盲 total color blindness; achromatopsia ▶ 그는 전색맹이다 He is totally color-blind.

전생 前生 〔佛敎〕 a former life; a previous [former] existence
♦ 전생의 인연 karma from a former life; a predestined relation; fate / 전생의 죄 sins committed in one's previous birth [existence]
▶ 우연한 사귐도 전생의 인연이다 Even a chance acquaintance is due to the karma in a

전생애 全生涯 one's whole life
♦전생애를 통하여 throughout one's life; from cradle to grave / 전생애를 바쳐 devoting one's whole life (to)

전서 全書 a complete book; 〈개설서〉 a compendium (*pl.* ~s, -dia)
■백과— an encyclopedia 육법— a compendium of laws; a statute book

전서 前書 one's last [previous] letter
■고린도— The First Epistle of Paul the Apostle to the Corinthians

전서구 傳書鳩 a carrier [homing] pigeon
♦전서구를 날려 보내다 fly [release] a carrier pigeon ■—통신[서신] a pigeon message; a pigeongram

전선 全線 〈모든 선로〉 the whole line; all lines; 〈모든 전선(戰線)〉 the entire battle line
♦중앙선 전선에 걸쳐 all along [the whole length of] the Chung-ang line
▶전선이 개통되려면 1주일은 더 걸릴 것 같다 It will probably be a week before the line is completely opened to service.
▶적군은 전선에 걸쳐서 활동을 개시했다 The enemy began activities all along the line [all up and down].

전선 前線 1 〈제일선〉 the front (line)
♦병력을 전선으로 보내다 send troops up to the front line / 전선에서 싸우다 fight in the front line
2 〔氣〕 a front
♦전선의 발생 frontogenesis
■강우— a rain front 한랭[온난]— a cold [warm] front ■—기지 a front-line base; an advanced base; an outpost —돌파 a breakthrough

전선 電線 (an) electric(al) wire; an electric cord; a power line; 〈해저의〉 a cable; 〈전화선〉 a telephone wire
♦전선을 가설하다 lay (on) electric wires / 새로 지은 집에 전선을 끌다 put up electric wires in a new house; wire a new house (for electricity)
▶태풍이 지나간 뒤 여러 곳의 전선이 끊어져 있었다 When the typhoon had passed, electric wires were down in several places.
▶그 로켓 엔진에는 모두 100킬로미터의 전선이 들어가 있다 The rocket engine contains 100 kilometers of electrical wiring altogether.

전선 戰船 a war vessel; a fighting ship

전선 戰線 the (battle) front; the fighting line
♦전선으로 보내다 send 《troops》 into battle / 적의 전선을 돌파하다 break through the enemy line / 전선을 축소하다 shorten the line / 전선에 나가다 go to the front; take part in the front / 통일[공동] 전선을 펴다 form a united [common] front 《against》
■노동— a labor front 인민— the popular [people's] front

전설 前說 one's former [previous] opinion [statement] ♦전설을 뒤집다 take back one's former opinion

전설 傳說 a legend; a tradition; 〈민화〉 a folk tale
♦아서왕 전설집 the Arthurian cycle / 전설상의 괴물 a fabulous monster / 전설적인 인물 a legendary person / 전설로 전해 내려오다 be handed down by tradition
▶전설에 따르면 이 호수에는 용이 살고 있었다고 한다 According to (a local) legend [Legend says that, There is a legend that] a dragon lived in this lake.
■—시대 the legendary age [period]

전성 全盛 the height [zenith] of prosperity
▶당시는 조씨 가문의 전성이 극에 달했다 In those days the Cho family were at the peak of their form.
■—시대[기] the [one's] heyday; one's best [palmy] days; the golden age

전성 展性 malleability
♦전성이 있는 금속 a malleable metal

전성관 傳聲管 a speaking tube; a voice pipe

전세 前世 1 ⇨ 전생
2 〈전대〉 former time [ages]; past ages

전세 專貰 charter; (美) reservation; (英) booking ♦전세내다 (美) reserve; (英) book
▶전세 (게시) Reserved.
▶그들은 관광을 하기 위해 버스를 전세냈다 They chartered a bus for sightseeing.
■—버스[비행기] a chartered bus [plane] —자동차 (美) a rental car

전세 傳貰 the lease of a house [room] on a deposit basis ♦전세 놓다 lease a house [room] on a deposit basis / 전세 들다 take a lease of a house [room] on a deposit basis
■—금 deposit money for the lease of a house [room] —방 a room which is leased on a deposit basis

전세 戰勢 the war situation
▶전세가 시시각각 악화되고 있었다 The military situation was continuing to deteriorate.

전세계 全世界 the whole world
♦전세계의 사람들 people throughout the world / 전세계에 (걸쳐서) all over [throughout] the world; across [around] the globe / 전세계로부터 《come》 from all parts [corners] of the world / 전세계를 여행하다 travel all over the world / 전세계를 놀라게 하다 astonish the whole world

전세기 前世紀 the preceding century; the past centuries

전소 全燒 total destruction by fire
—소하다 burn down; be burnt down; be totally destroyed by fire
▶건물의 내부가 전소했다 Fire totally destroyed the inside of the building.

전속 專屬 exclusive belongingness
▶그는 그 악단의 전속이다 He belongs exclusively to the band.
—속하다 belong exclusively to; be attached to; be under the exclusive contract 《of》
■—가수[여배우] a singer [an actress] attached to [under exclusive contract with] 《the production》 —부관 an aide-de-camp

전속 轉屬 transfer 《to》
—속하다 be transferred 《to》; be transferred 《to》

전속력 全速力 full [top] speed
♦전속력으로 at full throttle [speed]

▶ 나는 전속력으로 달렸다 I ran as fast as I could.
▶ 보트는 전속력을 냈다 The boat put on full steam.

전손 全損 〔商〕 total loss
♦ 전손을 보다 suffer a total loss
━추정— constructive total loss ■—담보 total loss only (略 TLO)

전송 電送 electrical transmission
—전송하다 transmit; telegraph; wire
♦ 사진을 전송하다 send [transmit] a picture by radio [wireless]; radio a photo
■사진— telephoto service; 사진 전송 장치 a telephotograph; a telephoto apparatus
■—사진 a telephotograph; (口) a telephoto (pl. ~s); a radio photo(graph) ━사진술 telephotography

전송 傳送 transmission; delivery; conveyance
—전송하다 transmit; convey; deliver

전송 餞送 a send-off; seeing off; a farewell
♦ 우리는 성대한 전송을 받았다 We were given a hearty send-off.
▶ 그는 아내의 전송을 받으며 김포 공항을 떠났다 He flew off from Kimpo Airport with his wife seeing him off.
—전송하다 see sb off; give sb a send-off; see sb's departure
▶ 나는 형을 전송하러 역에 갔다 I went to the station to see my brother off.
■—객 persons present for a send-off ━회 a farewell party

전송 轉送 forwarding; transmission
▶ 전송 요망 〈우편물에서〉 Please forward.
—전송하다 transmit; 〈우편물을〉 forward; send on [forward]
▶ 나에게 보내는 편지는 모두 이 주소로 전송해 주십시오 Please forward all the letters for me to this address.
■—처 a forwarding address

전수 全數 the whole [total] (number); 〈부사적〉 all; in all; totally

전수 專修 specialization
—전수하다 specialize [major] in; make a special study [speciality] (of); major in
■—과(科) a special course ━학교 a special-vocational school

전수 傳受 receiving; inheriting
—전수하다 be handed down [over]; receive; inherit; be initiated into 《mysteries》
■—자 an initiate

전수 傳授 transmission; instruction; initiation
—전수하다 hand down [over]; transmit; convey; instruct; initiate ♦ 비법을 전수하다 initiate sb into the secrets [mysteries]
▶ 그 비법은 대대로 전수되어 내려왔다 The secret (teaching) has been handed down from generation to generation.
■—자 an initiator

전술 前述 the above-mentioned; the foregoing
♦ 전술한 논거 the above(-mentioned) argument / 전술한 above-mentioned; aforesaid; said / 전술한 바와 같이 as mentioned [stated] above; as aforesaid

전술 戰術 tactics; strategy; the art of war
♦ 교묘한 전술 sharp tactics; a clever piece of tactics / 전술상의 요령 a tactical point / 전술적으로 tactically / 전술로 이기다 outmaneuver; outgeneral
▶ 야당의 지연 전술은 성공했다 The opposition party's delaying tactics were a success.
■고등— grand tactics ━가 a tactician ━용 핵무기 a tactical nuclear weapon ━전환 a change of tactics ━지정학 geostrategy

전술공군 戰術空軍 tactical air forces
■—사령부〔美軍〕 the Tactical Air Command (略 TAC)

전습 傳襲 inheritance
—전습하다 inherit 《one's father's habits》; follow 《the traditions》

전승 全勝 a clean score [record]
—전승하다 win [sweep] all the games; make a clean score [record]
▶ 우리 팀은 전승했다 Our team won all its games [finished with a perfect record].

전승 傳承 transmission; 〈전설〉 (an) oral tradition; a legend
—전승하다 hand down; transmit; tell 《a story》 from generation to generation
■민간— folklore; a folk story ■—문학 oral literature ━서사시 an oral epic

전승 戰勝 a victory; a triumph ♦ 전승을 축하 [기원]하다 celebrate [pray for] (a) victory
—전승하다 win [gain] a victory 《over》; carry the day
■—국 a victorious country [nation] ━기념일 an anniversary of the victory; a victory day

전시 全市 the whole city
♦ 전시에 걸친 축제 a citywide gala

전시 展示 exhibition; display; show
—전시하다 exhibit; put 《sth》 on display
♦ 학생의 작품을 교실에 전시하다 exhibit [display] the students' works in a classroom
▶ 그 미술관에 그의 그림이 전시되어 있다 His paintings are on exhibition [display, view] at the gallery.
■—관 a pavilion ━물 an exhibit; (총칭) exhibition; 〈특별 출품〉 a showpiece ━장 an exhibition hall [room] ━효과 display effect

전시 戰時 wartime; a time of war
♦ 전시의 wartime / 전시중 during the war; in wartime / 전시나 평화시를 가리지 않고 whether in peace or in war
■—경기 a war boom ━경제 wartime economy ━공채 a war loan ━국제법 international law in time of war ━금제품 contraband of war ━내각 a war cabinet ━배상 위원회 〈UN 의〉 the War Reparations Committee ━보상 war indemnity [compensation] ━보험 war risk insurance ━산업 the wartime industry ━수당 war bonus ━재정 wartime finance ━편성 war organization [footing]

전시대 前時代 former ages [times]; past generations

전시상태 戰時狀態 a state of war; belligerency ♦ 준전시상태 a quasi-state of war / 전시상태에 돌입하다 enter into a state of war

전시체제 戰時體制 wartime structure [organization]

◆전시체제에 있다 be on a war footing

전시회 展示會 a show; an exhibition; a display ◆전시회를 열다 hold a show [an exhibition, 《美》an exhibit]
■도서— a book exhibition [fair, show] 사진— a photo exhibition ■—장 an exhibit hall [room]

전신 全身 the whole body; 〈사진 등의〉the full length ◆전신에 상처를 입다 be covered with wounds / 전신에 화상을 입다 get burns over *one's* whole body
▶ 찬 바람에 전신이 떨렸다 The cold wind made me shiver all over.
■—불수 total paralysis —사진 a full-length photograph —운동 exericise of the whole body: 전신운동을 하다 exercise [take exercise for] every part of the body —초상화 a full-length portrait

전신 前身 *one's* antecedents; *one's* past life [history]; the predecessor
▶ 그녀의 전신은 가수였다 She used to be a singer.
▶ 그의 전신을 아는 사람은 거의 없다 Few people know his past history.
▶ 이 회사의 전신은 작은 유리 공장이었다 This company was originally a small glass factory. ⇌ This company started as a small glass factory.

전신 電信 telegraph; wire; telegraphic communication; 〈해외로부터의〉a cable
◆전신으로 by telegraph
▶ 태풍으로 전신이 끊어졌다 Telegraphic communication has been interrupted by the typhoon.
▶ 인천과의 전신이 회복되었다 Telegraphic service with Inch'ŏn has been reopened [resumed].
■무선— wireless telegraph(y) ■—국 a telegraph office [station] —기 a telegraph (apparatus); a telegraphic instrument —기사 a telegraph operator; a telegrapher —부호 a telegraphic code —사무 telegraphic service —술 telegraphy —암호 a telegram code —약호 a telegraphic [cable] address —주 a telegraph pole [post]

전신 轉身 turnover; changing *one's* position [job]
▶ 그는 전신이 빠르다 He is quick to change [in changing] his opinion.
—전신하다 turn over; change *one's* position [job]
▶ 그는 회사를 그만 두고 가수로 전신했다 He left the office and became a singer.

전신마취 全身痲醉 〔醫〕general anesthesia
◆전신마취를 시키다 put *sb* under general anesthesia

전신상 全身像 a full-length figure [portrait]
▶ 나는 그녀의 전신상을 그렸다 I painted a full-length portrait of her.

전신환 電信換 a telegraphic money order; a telegraphic transfer [remittance]
◆전신환으로 송금하다 remit money 《to *sb*》by telegraphic transfer

전실 前室 *one's* former wife ◆전실 자식 the children of *one's* former wife

전심 全心 *one's* whole heart [mind, soul]
▶ 그는 전심 전력을 다해 일에 몰두했다 He devoted himself to his work.

전심 專心 concentration of mind; undivided attention; the whole heart
◆전심으로 wholeheartedly; with *one's* whole heart; with all *one's* heart and soul
▶ 그는 연구에 전심하고 있다 He applies himself in his researches.

전아 典雅 refinement; elegance
—전아하다 refined; elegant; graceful
◆전아하게 gracefully; elegantly

전압 電壓 voltage; tension; electric pressure
◆높은[낮은] 전압 high [low] voltage / 120볼트 전압 (have) a voltage of 120 / 전압을 높이다[낮추다] increase [drop] voltage
■—계 a voltmeter —량 voltage —전류계 a volt-ammeter —조절기 a voltage regulator

전액 全額 the total [full] amount; the (sum) total
▶ 내주에 전액을 지불하겠습니다 I will pay in full next week.
▶ 전액을 내 외상으로 달아주십시오 Please charge the whole expense to my account.
▶ 소년들은 모금한 전액을 자선단체에 기부했다 The boys donated the entire sum of the raised money to charity.
■—담보 full coverage —불입[지불] full payment

전야 前夜 〈그 전날 밤〉the previous night [evening]; the night [evening] before; 〈축제일·사건 등의〉 the eve
◆크리스마스 전야 Christmas Eve
▶ 나는 그 사건 전야에 그와 만났다 I met him on the evening before the accident.
■—제 an eve: 전야제를 지내다 celebrate the eve 《of》

전약 煎藥 〔韓醫〕a (medical) decoction

전어 錢魚 〔魚〕a gizzard shad

전언 前言 〈이전에 한 말〉*one's* previous words [remarks, statement]
▶ 그는 전언을 취소했다 He withdrew what he had said.
▶ 그는 전언을 자주 번복한다 He often goes back on his word.

전언 傳言 〈전하는 말〉a message
◆전언을 남겨놓다 leave word [a message] 《with》/ 전언을 부탁받다 be charged with a message
▶ 그에게서 당신에게 온 전언이 있습니다 I have [There's] a message for you from him.
—전언하다 send *sb* word; send a message 《that...》
■—판 a message board

전업 專業 a special [principal] occupation; a speciality; a profession ◆…을 전업으로 하다 make a speciality of...; specialize in...
▶ 그는 화초 재배를 전업으로 하고 있다 He is a floriculturist by profession.

전업 電業 the electrical industry

전업 轉業 (a) change of trade [occupation, employment, career] —전업하다 change *one's* occupation [job, profession]

전역

■—자 a person who changed his occupation [trade] —자금 funds for occupational change

전역 全域 the whole [entire] area; ((through)) all the area; (in) all parts (of)
♦호남 지방 전역에 걸쳐서 throughout [all over] the Honam districts

전역 全譯 a complete translation (of)
—전역하다 translate the whole of 《Shakespeare》; translate 《Hamlet》completely (into Korean)

전역 戰役 a war; a battle; a campaign ⇨ 전쟁

전역 戰域 a war area; the theater of war
♦전역을 확대[축소]하다 extend [reduce] the area of operations

전역 轉役 〔軍〕 transfer 《from active service to the first reserve》; 〈제대〉 discharge from military service
—전역하다 discharge service; be transferred 《from the active list to the reserve list》

전연 全然 not at all ⇨ 전혀

전열 前列 the front rank [row]
▶나는 극장의 전열 오른쪽에서 세번째 자리에 앉았다 I took a seat on the third chair from right in the front row at the theater.

전열 電熱 electric heat
■—기(器) 〈난방용〉 an electric heater; 〈취사용〉 an electric range [stove]; a hot plate; an electric cooker

전열 戰列 a battle line; a line of battle
♦전열에 참가하다 join the line of battle / 전열을 벗어나다 leave the battle line

전염 傳染 contagion; infection ♦전염을 예방하다 prevent [keep off] infection
—전염하다 〈병이 주어〉 be contagious [infectious, catching]; infect; 〈사람이 주어〉 be infected with; catch
♦전염시키다 carry infection; communicate 《a disease》
▶그 병은 전염할 위험이 있다 There's danger that the disease is contagious.
▶웃음[하품]은 전염된다 Laughter [Yawning] is infectious [contagious].
▶이 병은 전염하지 않는다 This disease is not communicable [infectious, contagious].
공기— aerial [airborne] infection 접촉— contact infection 직접[간접]— direct [indirect] infection ■—성 contagiousness : 전염성의 contagious; infectious / 그 병은 전염성이 강하다 The disease is contagious. —원 a source of infection

전염병 傳染病 a contagious disease; an infectious disease; an epidemic
■법정— an epidemic designated by law 제1[2]종— the first [second] class communicable disease ■—병동 an isolated ward —연구소 the Infectious Disease Research Institute [Laboratory] —환자 a case epidemic; an infectious case: 전염병 환자는 격리된다 People with contagious diseases are isolated.

전와 轉訛 a turmoil [maelstrom] of war
♦전와에 휩쓸리다 be engulfed in a maelstrom of war

전와 轉訛 corruption (of a word) —전와하다 corrupt into; be corrupted 《from》

■—어 a corrupted word; a corruption

전완 前腕 the forearm ⇨ 하박(下膊)

전용 專用 exclusive [private, personal] use
♦전용의 exclusive; private; for exclusive use
▶자동차 전용도로 (게시) Motor Vehicles only. ⇌ Pedestrians and Bicycles Prohibited.
▶여성[회원] 전용 (게시) Ladies [Members] only.
▶이 선박은 화물 전용이며 승객을 취급하지 않습니다 This ship carries only freight [no passengers].
—전용하다 use 《a thing》 all for oneself; have sth for one's exclusive use
■ 한글— the exclusive use of Hangŭl ■—기 a plane for one's personal use: 대통령 전용기 a presidential plane [jet] —차 a private car; a car for one's personal use: 대통령 전용차 a presidential limousine

전용 轉用 diversion
—전용하다 use 《a thing》 for another purpose; divert; 〈공금을〉 convert
▶이것을 무엇에든 전용할 수 없을까 ? Isn't there any other use for this?
▶낡은 공장을 전용하여 새 쇼핑센터로 만들었다 The old factory was converted into a new shopping center.

전우 戰友 a comrade(-in-arms); a war comrade; (口) a war buddy

전운 戰雲 a war cloud
▶중동에 전운이 감돌고 있다 War clouds [The threat of war] hang over the Middle East.

전원 田園 farms and fields; 〈시골〉 the country; rural districts
♦전원의 rural; pastoral
■—곡 〔樂〕 a pastorale 《pl. -li》 —도시 a garden [rural] city —문학 idyllic [pastoral] literature —시 an idyl(l); a pastoral (poem) —시인 an idyllist; a pastoral poet —풍경 a rural landscape —화(化) ruralization

전원 全員 all the members; the entire staff; 〈배 등의〉 the whole crew; all hands
♦전원 일치의 unanimous / 전원 일치로 unanimously / 전원 출동하다 be sent out in full force
▶위원회 전원이 그것에 반대했다 All the members of the committee were against it. ⇌ The whole committee was against it.
▶전원 이상 무 All are safe and sound.
▶제트기가 바다에 추락하여 승무원 15명을 포함한 360명 전원이 사망했다 The jet crashed into the sea, killing all 360 persons aboard including a crew of 15.

전원 電源 a source of electricity; a power source [supply] ♦전원을 끄다 shut off the power
■—개발 development of power resources

전원생활 田園生活 (a) country [rural, pastoral] life ♦전원생활을 하다 lead a rural life; live in the country
▶그는 은퇴 후 전원생활을 즐기고 있다 He is enjoying country [rural] life since his retirement.

전월 前月 last month ♦전월 팔일에 on the eighth of last month

전위 前衛 〈군대의〉 an advance guard; the van-(guard); 〈테니스의〉 an up-player; a forward (player); 〔蹴〕 a forward; 〔美蹴〕 a lineman; 〈예술의〉 (프) avant-garde
■ 전위를 맡다 play forward
■ ─문학[미술, 음악] avant-garde [vanguard] literature [art, music] ─영화 avant-garde pictures ─파 the avant-garde

전위 電位 electric potential
■ 양[음]─ positive [negative] potential
■ ─강하 a potential drop ─계 an electrometer ─차 potential difference

전위 轉位 (a) transposition; 〈원자의〉 (a) dislocation; 〈태아의〉 version; 〔數〕 inversion; 〔遺〕 transposition; 〔化〕 rearrangement
■ ─생성물 a rearranged product

전위대 前衛隊 〔軍〕 the vanguard; an advance guard

전유 全乳 whole milk

전유 專有 exclusive [sole] possession; sole ownership
─전유하다 monopolize; take [have] sole possession; appropriate 《a thing》 to *oneself*
■ ─권 an exclusive right; monopoly: 전유권을 가지다 have [possess] an exclusive right ─자 a sole [private] owner

전율 戰慄 shivering; a shiver; a shudder
─전율하다 shudder; thrill; tremble with fear
♦ 전율할 광경 a horrible [bloodcurdling] sight / 전율케 하다 make *sb* shudder; give *sb* a shiver; freeze [curdle] *sb's* blood / 전율을 느끼다 feel a shudder of fear [horror]

전음 顫音 〔樂〕 a trill; a tremolo

전의 戰意 the intention [will] to fight; a fighting spirit; fight; morale
♦ 전의의 앙양 enhancement of fighting spirit / 전의를 잃다 lose *one's* fighting spirit
▶ 처음부터 그들은 전의가 없었다 From the beginning they had no intention of fighting spint [no will to fight].

전의 轉義 a transferred [figurative] meaning
♦ 전의의 figurative

전이 轉移 change; transition; 〈병의〉 transfer; metastasis; 〔物〕 transition; 〈결정의〉 transformation; 〔精神分析〕 transference
─전이하다 change; metastasize; spread (by metastasis)
▶ 위암이 폐로 전이했다 The stomach cancer has spread [transferred] to the lungs.

전인 全人 ■ ─교육 all-round education; education for the whole man

전인 前人 a predecessor; 〈옛 사람들〉 former people ♦ 전인 미답의 untrodden; unexplored; unprecedented; unheard-of; virgin / 전인 미답의 원시림 a trackless primeval forest

전인격 全人格 *one's* whole personality

전일 前日 〈전날〉 the previous [preceding] day; the day before; 〈일전〉 the other day; some days [time] ago; formerly
♦ 결혼식 전일의 the day before the wedding
▶ 전일에 한 약속을 잊지 마세요 Don't forget what you promised the other day.

전일제 全日制 〔敎〕 the full-time schooling system ♦ 전일제 고등학교 a full-time high school

전임 前任 〈사람〉 a former official ⇨ 전임(~자); 〈임무〉 the post previously occupied; a previous appointment
■ ─자 the predecessor; a former official: 바로 앞의 전임자 *one's* immediate predecessor / 당신의 전임자는 누구였나요? Who preceded you in the post? ─직 *one's* former [last] post

전임 專任 exclusive duty; full service
♦ 회사의 전임 고문 a full-time adviser to a company / 전임의 full-time
■ ─강사 a full-time lecturer; (美) 〈대학의〉 an instructor ─교사 a full-time teacher

전임 轉任 change of post; a tranference
─전임하다 be transferred to another post
▶ 그는 부산지점으로 전임했다 He (was) transferred to the Pusan branch (office).
■ ─자 a person transferred ─지 *one's* new post

전입 轉入 moving in [into]; transference
─전입하다 be [get] transferred 《from》; move into; 〈학교에〉 enter another school
▶ 김선생 가족은 서울에서 일산으로 전입했다 The Kims moved to Ilsan from Seoul.
■ ─생 a student transferred from another school ─신고 a moving-in notification

전입학하다 轉入學 be transferred to a school from another ♦ 사립 고등학교에 전입학하다 transfer [change] to a private high school

전자 前者 1 〈후자에 대한〉 the former; 〈this에 대한〉 that
♦ 전자… 후자… the one [former]… while the other [latter]…
▶ 저 두 기계중 전자는 국산이고 후자는 미제다 Of those two machines, the former is of Korean make and the latter is of American make.
2 〈전번〉 the other day; some time [days] ago
▶ 전자엔 협력해 주셔서 감사합니다 Thank you very much for your cooperation the other day.

전자 電子 〔物〕 an electron
♦ 전자의 electronic
■ ─계산기 a [an electronic] computer ─공업 electronics industry ─공학 electronics ─광학 electron optics ─기기(機器) electronic equipment ─레인지 a microwave oven ─렌즈 an electron lens ─망원경 an electron telescope ─볼트 an electron volt (略 EV, ev) ─산업 electronics industry ─설 the electron theory ─오르간 an electronic organ ─우편 electronic mail (略 EM) ─음악 electronic [electrophonic] music ─장치 an electronic device [gadget] ─총〔컬러TV〕 an electron gun ─현미경 an electron microscope

전자 電磁 ♦ 전자의 electromagnetic ■ ─석 an electromagnet ─장(場) an electromagnetic field ─파 electromagnetic waves ─학 electromagnetism

전자 篆字 a seal character; a [the] Chinese character mainly used for seals

전자기 電磁氣 electromagnetism

전작

♦ 전자기의 electromagnetic
■ —학 electromagnetism; electromagnetics

전작 田作 〈농사〉 farming done in non-paddy field; dry-field farming; 〈작물〉 farm products [crops]; crops grown in non-paddy fields

전작 前酌 drinks taken before to attending
▶ 저는 전작이 있습니다 I had a few drinks before I came here.

전장 全長 the full [total] length; an overall length
▶ 그 다리의 전장은 600미터다 The total length of the bridge is six hundred meters. ⇒ The bridge is six hundred meters long.

전장 前章 〈in〉 the foregoing [preceding] chapter; 〈바로 앞의〉 the last [prior] chapter

전장 前場 〔證〕 the morning market [session]

전장 電場 〔物〕 an electric field

전장 戰場 a battlefield; a battleground
▶ 그는 전장에서 죽었다 He fell [died, was killed] on the battlefield. ⇒ He died [was killed, fell] in battle.
▶ 그 도시는 전장화되었다 The city turned into a battlefield [a scene of battle].

전재 戰災 war damage; war devastation
♦ 심한 전재를 당하다 suffer great damage in a war
■ —고아 a war orphan —민 war(-damage) sufferers; war victims [refugees]; victims of war —지구[도시] a war-damaged[-devastated] area [city]

전재 轉載 reproduction; reprinting
▶ 전재불허 (표시) Reproduction forbidden. ⇒ All rights [Copyright] reserved. ⇒ No part of this book may be reproduced in any form (without permission).
—전재하다 reproduce; reprint
▶ 본 기사는 타임지에서 전재한 것이다 This article was reprinted from *the Time*.

전쟁 戰爭 (a) war; warfare
♦ 전쟁의 확대 expansion [escalation] of a war / 전쟁의 참화 the calamity of war; war calamities / 전쟁중의 at war (with); belligerent / 전쟁중에 during the war; in wartime 〈전쟁이[은]〉 전쟁이 양국간에 일어났다 A war broke out [started] between the two countries.
▶ 그 전쟁은 상당히 장기화되었다 The war was long drawn out.
〈전쟁을〉 전쟁을 계속[방지]하다 carry on [prevent] war / 전쟁을 수행[시작]하다 conduct [start] war / 전쟁을 야기하다 provoke [give rise to] war / 전쟁을 종결시키다 bring the war to an end; put an end to the war
〈전쟁에〉 전쟁에 개입하다 intervene in a war / 전쟁에 대비하다 prepare for war / 전쟁에 반대 [찬성]하다 be against [for] war / 전쟁에 이기다[지다] win [lose] a war / 전쟁에 지치다 be war-weary; be warworn / 전쟁에 휩쓸리다 be involved in a war
〈전쟁으로〉 그 정치문제가 전쟁으로 발전했다 The political problem developed into [led to] war.
▶ 전쟁으로 많은 사람이 죽었다 Many were killed in [by] the war.
—전쟁하다 make war 《with》; go to war 《with》; wage (a) war 《against》; war 《with》; open hostilities 《against》
▶ 연합국은 그 나라와 전쟁했다 The Allies made [waged] war on [against] the country. ⇒ The Allies went to war.
■ —국지 the local war 무역 — a trade war 세계 — a global [world] war 전면 — a total [an allout] war 제한 — a limited war 침략 — a war of aggression 핵 — (a) nuclear war —경기 a war [wartime] boom —고아 a war orphan —놀이 playing at soldiers —도발자 a warmonger —문학 war literature —물 〈서적〉 a war book; 〈소설〉 a war novel; 〈영화〉 a war film —미망인 a war widow —범죄 war crimes —범죄자 a war criminal —이야기 a war story; an account of a battle —재판 a war-criminals trial —재판소 a war-criminals court —터 ⇨ 전장(戰場) —포기 renunciation of war —행위 an act of war; warfare —희생자 war victims; victims of war

전쟁상태 戰爭狀態 a state of war; belligerency ♦ 전쟁상태를 종결하다 terminate a state of war
▶ 양국은 전쟁상태였다 The two countries were at war with each other.
■ —종결 선언 a declaration of the termination of the state of war

전적 典籍 books

전적 戰跡 an old battlefield

전적 戰績 〈전쟁의〉 a war record; 〈경기의〉 results; a record; a score ♦ 빛나는 전적 a brilliant (war, military) record
▶ 그 팀은 지난해에 좋은 전적을 남겼다 The team had a fine record in the past year.

전적 轉籍 transfer of *one's* (permanent) domicile —전적하다 transfer *one's* domicile [family register]

전적 全的 whole; complete; the full; overall
♦ 전적인 신뢰 full confidence / 전적으로 wholly; on the whole; totally; entirely / 전적으로 지지하다 give full support (to) / 전적으로 동의하다 give blanket consent (to)
▶ 조직을 전적으로 개혁해야 한다 The whole system must be reformed.

전전 戰前 prewar days
♦ 전전의 prewar / 전전에는 in prewar days; before the war
■ —세대 the prewar generation

전전 前前 former times; long time ago
♦ 전전날 two days ago [earlier]; 〈그저께〉 the day before yesterday
▶ 그것은 전전 회의에서 결정되었다 It was decided at the meeting before last.

전전긍긍하다 戰戰兢兢— be terribly [dreadfully] afraid; be trembling with in great fear [dread] ♦ 전전긍긍하여 with fear and trembling; nervously
▶ 그는 전전긍긍하고 있다 He is filled with trepidation.
▶ 그는 그녀의 복수에 전전긍긍하고 있다 He is living in constant fear of her revenge.
▶ 그는 부정행위가 탄로날까봐 전전긍긍하고 있다 He is terribly afraid that his dishonest

deed might come to light.

전전하다 轉戰 fight in one place after another; take part in various battlefields

전전하다 輾轉 ―〈헤매다〉 wander from place to place; roam about
♦직장을 여기저기 전전하다 change jobs many times
▶그 다이아몬드는 여러 사람의 손을 전전했다 The diamond passed from hand to hand [through many hands]. ≒ The diamond changed hands many times.

전절 前節 〈앞절〉 the foregoing [preceding] paragraph

전정 前庭 **1** ⇨ 앞뜰
2 〔解·動〕 the vestibule
■―기관 a vestibular organ

전정 剪定 pruning ―전정하다 prune; trim
♦장미를 전정하다 prune rose bushes
■―가위 (a pair of) pruning shears

전제 前提 (an) assumption; 〔論〕 a premise; 〈필요조건〉 a prerequisite
♦…을 전제로 하여 on the assumption [premise] that...; assuming that...; on condition that...
▶그는 잘못된 전제로 주장하고 있다 He is arguing from false premises.
▶그들은 결혼을 전제로 해서 교제하고 있다 They're dating with marriage in mind [with the intention of getting married].
―전제하다 set sth forth as a premise; premise
■대[소]― a major [minor] premise ■―조건 a prior condition; a precondition

전제 專制 despotism; autocracy
♦전제적(인) autocratic; despotic
■―군주 an absolute monarch; an autocrat; a despot ―군주 정체 an absolute monarchy ―정치 despotic [autocratic] government; autocracy ―주의 absolutism; despotism

전조 前兆 an omen ⇨ 징조(徵兆)

전조 前條 the preceding [foregoing] article [clause]

전조등 前照燈 〈차의〉 a headlight; a headlamp

전족 纏足 〈옛 풍습〉 foot-binding; 〈발〉 bound feet ―전족하다 bind one's feet

전주 前奏 a prelude; an introduction
▶그것은 뒤따르는 대사건의 전주에 지나지 않았다 It was a mere prelude to the great event that followed.
■―곡 〔樂〕 an overture; a prelude: 쇼팽의 전주곡 Chopin's Preludes / 가극의 전주곡 an overture to an opera

전주 前週 〈지난 주〉 last week; 〈그전 주〉 the preceding week; the week before
♦전주(의) 금요일 last Friday / 전주의 오늘 a week ago today; (美) today [this day] last week; (英) today [this day] week; (英) (a) week today

전주 電柱 〈전신의〉 a telephone [telegraph] pole; 〈전기의〉 an electric light pole; a utility pole
▶전주는 30미터 간격으로 서 있다 The poles stand at intervals of thirty meters.

전주 錢主 〈자본주〉 a financier; a financial supporter [backer]; 〈빚을 준 사람〉 a creditor
♦전주가 되다 finance; give sb financial support

전중 典重 courtesy; civility
―전중하다 courteous; civil ♦전중한 부인 a woman of graceful carriage

전지 田地 rice fields [paddies] and dry fields; farmland

전지 全知 omniscience ⇨ 전지전능

전지 全紙 the whole space of paper; 〈온전한〉 a whole [full] sheet (of paper)

전지 剪枝 pruning; trimming; lopping ―전지하다 prune [lop, trim] (the branches of a tree) ■―가위 pruning shears

전지 電池 a [an electric] cell; a battery
♦전지를 충전하다 charge a battery
▶이 장난감은 전지로 움직인다 This toy works on [by] batteries.
▶전지가 닳았다 The batteries are dead [finished, have run down].
■건― a dry cell [battery] 수은― a mercury battery 알칼리― an alkaline battery 축― a storage battery 태양― a solar battery [cell] ―개폐기[회로] a battery switch [circuit] ―충전 battery charging

전지 戰地 the (battle) front; a battlefront
♦전지로 가다 go to the front
■―근무 field [active] service

전지 轉地 a change of air ―전지하다 go 《to some place》 for a change of air; 〈경기 팀이〉 change a training camp
■―요양[요법] treatment by change of air; a change of air for health

전지전능 全知全能 omniscience and omnipotence ―전지전능하다 omniscient and omnipotent [all mighty]
♦전지전능하신 하느님 Almighty God; God Almighty; the Almighty

전직 前職 one's former occupation; the post [office] held previously ♦전직 외무 장관 an ex-foreign minister

전직 轉職 a change of occupation
―전직하다 change one's occupation; take up another job; switch jobs 《to》
♦교사에서 회사원으로 전직하다 quit being a teacher and become an office worker

전진 前進 an advance; a forward movement; progress
♦적의 전진을 저지하다 check the advance of the enemy
▶전진(口令) Forward!
―전진하다 advance; march [move] forward; go ahead; 〈배가〉 make headway
♦일보 전진하다 take a step forward
▶부대는 그 도시로 전진했다 The troops advanced toward [on] the town.
▶눈 때문에 우리는 전진하지 못했다 We could not go ahead [forward] because of the snow.
■―기지 an advance(d) base; an outpost ―력 driving power ―명령 orders to march [advance]; marching orders ―부대 the foremost troops (of an army) ―운동 a forward movement

전진 戰陣 〈전장〉 a battlefield; the front; 〈진영〉 a camp; 〈진형〉 battle formation

◆ 전진의 병사들 soldiers on the battlefield [at the front]
전진 戰塵 the dust of combat [the battlefield]
◆ 전진을 셋다 wash off the dust of combat / 전진을 피하여 산중에 은거하다 lead a secluded life in the mountains far from the tumult of war
전진 轉進 change of one's course ━전진하다 change one's course [direction]
전질 全帙 a complete set [series] of books; complete [collected] works
전집 全集 one's complete [collected] works
◆ 세계 문학[미술] 전집 the complete series of world literature [art]
━셰익스피어━ the complete works of Shakespeare ━물 a complete works series ━붐 a boom (in publication) of collected works
전차 前借 an advance ━전차하다 borrow [draw] money in advance; get an advance
━금 money borrowed in advance
전차 電車 a train (▶ 기차와 구분하지 않음); 〈시내 전차〉 an electric car; (美) a streetcar; (英) a tram(car)
◆ 전차를 타다[내리다] get on [off] a streetcar / 전차를 운전하다 run [operate] a train / 전차를 놓치다 miss the train / 전차로 가다 go by streetcar [tram]
▶ 오는 전차마다 만원이었다 Train after train [Car after car] was overcrowded (with passengers).
━ 교외━ a suburban train 꽃━ an illuminated [a decorated] car 통근━ a commuter train ━선로[궤도] a streetcar line [track]; (英) a tramway ━역 a train [railroad] station ━요금 a train fare ━운전사 a motorman ━정류장 (美) a streetcar stop ━차고 (美) a carbarn; (英) a tram shed ━차장 a streetcar conductor
전차 戰車 a tank
■ 경[중]━ a light [heavy] tank 수륙 양용━ an amphibian tank ■ ━대 a tank corps [unit]; a soldier assigned to a tank corps ━부대 tank forces [corps]; a fleet of tanks ━전 a tank battle; tank warfare ━포 a tank gun : 대(對)전차포 an antitank gun ━호 a tank trap; an antitank trench
전차 轉借 subtenancy; a sublease
━전차하다 〈책을〉 borrow a book secondhand [at second hand]; 〈방을〉 rent a room secondhand; 〈땅을〉 sublease land
━인 an undertenant; a subtenant; a sublessee
전차후옹하다 前遮後擁━ guard the van and protect the rear
전채 前菜 (프) an hors d'oeuvre
전채 戰債 war debts; war bonds
전책임 全責任 full responsibility ◆ 전책임을 지다 take [assume, bear] full responsibility
전처 前妻 one's former wife; one's ex-wife
◆ 전처의 소생 a child by a former wife
전천후 全天候 all-weather
■ ━기[전투기, 사진기] an all-weather airplane [fighter, camera] ━농업 all-weather agriculture ━비행 all-weather flying ━정구장 an all-weather tennis court
전철 前轍 the track [ruts] of a preceding wheel; a precedent
◆ 전철을 밟다 follow [tread] in another's steps; follow in the same wake
▶ 전임자의 전철을 밟지 않도록 조심해라 Be careful not to repeat the mistakes [errors] of your predecessors.
전철 電鐵 an electric railroad [(英) railway]
■ ━회사 an electric railroad company
전철 轉轍 [鐵] switching
━전철하다 switch [(英) shunt] (a train)
■ ━기 a (railroad) switch; a shunt: 자동 전철기 an automatic switch ━수 (美) a switchman; (英) a postman
전첩 戰捷 a victory; a triumph
━전첩하다 win [gain] a victory (over)
━기념일 an anniversary of a victory
전체 全體 the whole (body)
◆ 유럽 전체 the whole of Europe; all Europe / 전체와 부분 the whole and the parts / 전체적인 경향 the general tendency / 전체적인 문제 an overall problem / 전체의 whole; all; entire; general / 전체적으로 generally; in general; as a whole; on the whole / 전체에 걸쳐서 in entirely; all over / 전체를 합쳐서 in all; all told
▶ 마을 전체가 고요했다 The whole [entire] town was hushed and still.
▶ 항구 전체에 안개가 끼어 있었다 Fog hung all over the harbor [over the whole harbor].
▶ 전체적으로 이번 행사는 성공적이었다 On the whole, this event was successful.
■ ━집합 [數] a universal [a total] set ━회의 a plenary session; (총회) a general meeting
전체주의 全體主義 totalitarianism
◆ 전체주의의 totalitarian
■ ━국가 a totalitarian state [country]
전초 前哨 an outpost; an advanced post
━기지 an advanced base ━부대 an outpost unit ━선 the outpost [scouting] line ━전 a (preliminary) skirmish: 선거 운동은 이미 전초전에 들어가 있다 The election campaign has already entered its preliminary stages.
전축 電蓄 an electric phonograph [(英) gramophone]
◆ 라디오 겸용전축 a radiophonograph; (英) a radiogram; a radio gramophone
■ ━스테레오[하이파이]━ a stereophonic [highfidelity] phonograph
전출 轉出 〈이주〉 moving out; 〈전임〉 transfer(ence)
━전출하다 move out
◆ (근무처에서) 전출되다 be transferred / 서울에서 시골로 전출하다 move from Seoul to the country
▶ 그는 자회사로 전출되었다 He was transferred to a subsidiary company.
■ ━신고 a report of moving-out; a moving-out notification ━증명 certification of moving out ━지 a place of moving out ━처 a new address
전충 塡充 filling up [in] ⇨ 충전
전취 前娶 one's former wife ⇨ 전처

전취하다 戰取— gain by fighting
전치 全治 a complete cure
▶ 그는 전치 2주의 부상을 입었다 He suffered an injury which would take [require] two weeks to heal completely.
전치사 前置詞 〔文法〕 a preposition
♦전치사적 용법 a prepositional use
▶ 이 동사에는 어떤 전치사가 필요한가? What preposition is required after this verb?
■—구 a preposition [prepositional] phrase
전칙 典則 a law; a rule
전칭 全稱 〔論〕 ♦전칭의 universal; generic ■—명사(名辭) a general term —명제 a universal proposition —부정 a universal negative —판단 a universal judgment
전토 田土 the field =전답(田畓)
전토 全土 the whole land [country]
♦유럽 전토에 걸쳐서 all over Europe; throughout Europe
▶ 피해가 전토에 이르렀다 The whole country suffered damage.
전통 傳統 (a) tradition; 〈유산〉(a) heritage; 〈인습〉 a convention
♦오랜 전통이 있는 대학 an old university rich in tradition; a university with a long and honorable tradition / 80년의 전통을 가진 대학 a university with eighty years' tradition / 전통을 중시하다[무시하다] value [ignore] (a) tradition / 전통을 따르다 follow (a) tradition / 옛부터의 전통을 지키다 stick [adhere] to time-honored traditions / 전통을 버리다[깨뜨리다] relinquish [violate] a tradition / 전통에 매인 생각 a tradition-bound way of thinking
▶ 그들은 자기 민족의 전통을 유지하려고 한다 They try to keep up [maintain] the traditions of their race.
■—문화 a cultural heritage
전통 箭筒 〈화살통〉a quiver =전동(箭筒)
전통적 傳統的 traditional; conventional
♦전통적인 의상 traditional costumes / 전통적인 중국 축제 a traditional Chinese festival / 전통적으로 traditionally
▶ 이 학교는 전통적으로 규칙이 엄하다 They are traditionally [by tradition] strict in their discipline at this school.
전퇴 電堆 〔電〕a pile
전투 戰鬪 a battle; a fight; a combat; an action; an engagement
♦전투를 개시하다 go into battle [action]; commence hostilities / 전투를 중지하다 break off a battle; suspend hostilities; cease fire / 전투에 참가하다 take part in a battle; see action [combat]
—전투하다 fight (a battle); engage 《an enemy》
■야간— night fighting ■—경찰대 a combatant police unit —교련 combat drill —모(帽) a (field) service cap; a field cap —복 (a) combat uniform; (美) battle fatigues —부대 fighting forces [troops]; a combat unit [troop] —비행 combat flying —지역[구역, 지구] a combat zone; a battle area [zone] —지휘관 a combat commander [leader] —태세 combat readiness —폭격기 a fighter-bomber —행위 (combat) action; a hostile act —화(靴) combat shoes
전투기 戰鬪機 a fighter; a combat plane
■ 요격— a fighter-interceptor
전투대형 戰鬪隊形 (a) battle formation
♦전투대형의 in battle order / 전투대형을 이루다 form in fighting order
전투력 戰鬪力 fighting power [capacity, strength] ♦전투력을 상실하다 lose one's fighting [combat] power
전투원 戰鬪員 a combatant; (총칭) combat personnel ■비— a noncombatant; a civilian
전투적 戰鬪的 militant; combatant; aggressive ♦전투적인 부족 a militant tribe / 전투적으로 militantly; aggressively
전투준비 戰鬪準備 preparation for action; 〈군함의〉 clearing for action
♦전투준비를 갖추다 complete preparations [prepare] for action
▶ 전투 준비! (口令) To arms!
전파 全破 complete destruction
—전파하다 destroy completely; demolish
▶ 태풍으로 이 마을의 집 여섯채가 전파되었다 Six houses in this village were completely destroyed by the typhoon.
■—가옥 a completely destroyed [razed] house
전파 電波 an electric wave; a radio wave
♦전파를 통해서 through radio; over the radio / 전파를 타다 be broadcast; be [go] on the air
—감시 monitoring of radio waves —계 a [an electric] wavemeter; a cymometer —관리 radio regulation; radio wave control —망원경 a radio telescope —방해 jamming —수상경(受像鏡) 〔레이더의〕 a radarscope —장애 radio interference —조종 radio control —탐지기 a radar
전파 傳播 spread; transmission; propagation; circulation; diffusion
♦병원균의 전파 dissemination of disease germs / 열의 전파 transmission of heat / 서양 문명의 전파 the spread of Western civilization / 지식의 전파 the diffusion of knowledge
—전파하다 spread; propagate; be propagated [disseminated]; get abroad; circulate spread
▶ 열은 동선을 통해 전파된다 Heat is conveyed by [travels through] copper wire.
▶ 음파는 공기 속을 전파한다 Sound waves travel through the air.
■—속도 propagation velocity
전파수신기 全波受信機 an all-wave receiver [radio set]
전판 全— all; the whole; the entire lot
▶ 사과는 전판 상해버렸다 All (of) the apples have gone bad.
▶ 맹화가 도시를 전판 태워버렸다 Raging flames burned down the whole town.
전패 全敗 a complete defeat ⇨ 완패
전편 全篇 the whole book [volume]
♦전편을 통해서 from cover to cover; from title page to colophon / 전편에 이르는 반일 감정 the anti-Japanese feelings pervading the whole story

전편 前篇 the first volume [part] ◆이야기의 전편 the first part [volume] of a story

전폐 全廢 (total) abolition
▶그들은 핵무기의 전폐를 요구했다 They demanded the total abolition of nuclear weapons.
—**전폐하다** abolish totally [completely]; do away with

전포 廛鋪 (美) a store; (英) a shop; a stall

전폭 全幅 the overall [full] width; 〈배의〉 the whole breadth; 〈비행기의〉 the wing span
▶이 비행기는 전폭이 삼십육미터다 This plane has a wing span of thirty-six meters.

전폭기 戰爆機 a fighter-bomber

전폭적 全幅的 all; full; utmost
◆전폭적인 신뢰 complete [full] confidence / 전폭적으로 to the full; fully / 전폭적으로 지지하다 give sb full [wholehearted] support
▶그들은 자기들의 지도자를 전폭적으로 신임하고 있다 They put [place] full confidence in their leader. ⇌ They trust their leader wholeheartedly.
▶나는 그에게 전폭적 신뢰를 두고 있다 I trust him completely. ⇌ I have complete [full] confidence in him.

전표 傳票 a chit; a slip; a voucher; a ticket
◆전표를 떼다 issue a slip [chit]; write out a voucher / 전표와 교환하여 지불하다 pay money in exchange for a voucher
■대체— a transfer slip 매출— a sales check 수납[입금]— a receiving [receipt] slip 주문— an order slip ■—지불 a payment voucher [slip]

전풍 癜風 〔韓醫〕 〈어루러기〉 a white macula

전하 殿下 〈2인칭〉 Your (Royal) Majesty (▶동사는 3인칭); 〈3인칭〉 His [Her] (Royal)
◆동궁전하 His Royal Highness; the Crown Prince

전하 電荷 〔電〕 an electric charge
■양[음]— (a) positive [negative] charge

전하다 傳— 1 〈전달하다〉 tell; inform; convey; report; deliver; communicate; notify
◆소식을 전하다 bear news / 안부를 전하다 send one's compliments [regards] [(to) / 허위 보도를 전하다 spread [circulate] a false report / 비보를 가족에게 전하다 break the sad news to the family / 외신이 전하는 바로는… Foreign reports say that…; According to foreign reports
▶그에게 내가 말한대로 전해다오 Tell him just as I said.
▶내 의사는 이미 그에게 전했다 I have already told him my intentions [informed him of my intentions].
▶편지로는 제 감사의 마음을 전할 수가 없을 지경입니다 I cannot fully convey my gratitude to you in a letter.
▶아버님께 안부 전해 주십시오 Please give [send] my best regards [love] to your father.
▶그에게 무슨 전하실 말씀이 있습니까? Do you want me to tell him anything for you? ⇌ Do you have a message for him?
2 〈전수하다〉 teach; pass on; impart; initiate
◆지식을 전하다 impart knowledge to sb / 비법을 전하다 teach sb the mysteries of an art
▶중국에서 온 사람이 우리 조상에게 이 기술을 전했다 The people from China taught this art to our ancestors.
3 〈전승하다〉 hand down; transmit; bequeath
◆대대로 전하다 hand down [transmit] from father to son [from generation to generation]
4 〈전도하다〉 transmit; conduct
▶금속은 전기(電氣)를 전하지만 유리는 그렇지 않다 Metal conducts electricity, but glass doesn't.
▶공기는 소리를 전한다 Air conveys sound.
5 〈전파하다〉 introduce 《into》
▶기독교를 한국에 전하다 introduce Christianity into Korea

전학 轉學 change of schools
—**전학하다** remove from one school to another; change one's school
▶그는 한국대학에서 미국대학으로 전학했다 He changed [transferred] from a college in Korea to one in the United States.
■—생 a transfer (student); a new comer from another school

전학급 全學級 the whole class

전함 戰艦 a battleship; a warship

전항 前項 the preceding clause; the foregoing paragraph; 〔數・論〕 the antecedent

전해 前— the preceding [previous] year; the other year ⇨ 전년

전해 電解 electrolysis
—**전해하다** electrolyze
■—로 an electric furnace —용액 an electrolytic solution —조(槽) an electrolytic cell; an electrolyzer —질 an electrolyte: 전해질의 electrolytic

전해듣다 傳— hear from others; learn [know] by hearsay; hear at second hand
◆전해들은 말 a hearsay / 전해들은 바로는… According to what I've heard…
▶그것은 전해들었을 뿐이다 I know it only from hearsay.
▶전해들은 바로는 그는 10년전에 죽었다고 한다 I hear that he died ten years ago.

전해지다 傳— 1 〈전송되다〉 be handed down; be transmitted; come down 《from》; go down 《to》
◆대대로 전해지다 be transmitted [handed down] from generation to generation
▶이 가보는 조부때부터 전해지는 것이다 This family treasure has come [has been handed] down from our grandfather's time.
▶그 관습은 예로부터 전해져 왔다 The custom has come down to us from remote antiquity.
2 〈전달되다〉 be conveyed [transmitted]; 〈퍼지다〉 spread; go about; get abroad [about]; circulate; be circulated; be reported [told]
▶그 뉴스는 순식간에 온 도시에 전해졌다 The news spread rapidly [traveled fast, circulated quickly] throughout the town.
3 〈전래하다〉 be introduced; be brought; come
▶한자는 중국에서 한국으로 전해졌다 Chinese characters were introduced [brought] into Korea from China.

전향 轉向 〈방향 전환〉 changing directions; switching courses; a turnover; 〈주의의〉 a conversion; (美) an about-face
―전향하다 turn [swing] 《to》; be converted 《to》; switch over; shift
♦ 급진에서 보수로 전향하다 turn from Radical to Conservative
▶ 그는 사회주의에서 전향했다 He abandoned [was converted from] Socialism.
■―자 a convert; a turncoat ―점 a turning point

전혀 全― quite; wholly; totally; utterly; entirely; completely; altogether; hardly; (not) at all
♦ 전혀 모르는 사람 an utter [a total] stranger / 전혀 쓸모가 없다 be quite [utterly] useless; of no use at all
▶ 나는 전혀 배가 고프지 않다 I am not hungry at all.
▶ 그녀는 그런 것은 전혀 개의치 않고 있다 She is not in the least concerned [worried] about it.
▶ 그는 그 일을 전혀 모른다 He doesn't know anything [knows absolutely nothing] about the matter.
▶ 우리는 전혀 모르는 사이는 아니다 We are not entire strangers to each other.
▶ 그때부터 그에게서는 전혀 소식이 없다 I have heard nothing from him.
▶ 그것은 내가 들은 바와는 전혀 달랐다 It was entirely different from what I had heard.
▶ 나는 그 사건과는 전혀 무관하다 I have no connections whatever with the affair.
▶ 나는 전혀 짐작이 가지 않는다 I haven't the slightest [faintest] idea.

전형 典型 a model; a type; a pattern
♦ 부덕(婦德)의 전형 a model of female virtue / 미국의 전형 a typical American
▶ 그는 영국 신사의 전형이다 He is a typical English gentleman. ⇌ He is a fine specimen of an English gentleman.

전형 銓衡 (a) selection; screening
♦ 전형에서 떨어지다 be left out of selection
▶ 그녀는 서류전형으로 응모자 중에서 채용되었다 She was selected from among the applicants after a screening of documents.
―전형하다 select; make choice; screen
■―기준 criterion for selection ―시험 a screening test ―위원회 a selection [screening] committee

전형적 典型的 typical; representative; model
♦ 전형적인 미국인 a typical American / 전형적인 예 a typical example

전호 前號 the preceding number; the last issue [number]
♦ 전호까지의 줄거리 an outline of the story up to the preceeding number
▶ 전호에서 계속 (표시) Continued (from the last issue).

전호 電弧 〔電〕 an (electric) arc

전화 電化 electrification ♦ 철도의 전화 the electrification of railroads
▶ 농장의 전화가 급속히 진행되고 있다 The farms are being electrified at a rapid pace.
―전화하다 electrify
■―농촌― rural electrification ■―계획 an electrification scheme [program] ―구간 an electrified section ―사업 an electrification work

전화 電話 telephone; (口) phone; 〈통화〉 a call; a (tele)phone call; (美) a ring

|解說| **telephone, phone**은「통신 방식[업무]으로서의 전화 (telephone system [service])」의 뜻으로는 불가산명사 (不可算名詞)이고「전화기 (telephone set)」의 뜻으로는 가산명사다. telephone과 phone은 보통 같은 뜻으로 쓰이나 phone 쪽이 스스럼없는 말이다. 또 복합어에서는 phone을 많이 쓴다.

♦ 장난[잘못 걸려온, 협박] 전화 a prank [wrong, threatening] call / 전화 목소리 a voice heard over the telephone
〈전화가〉 전화가 울리고 있다 The phone is ringing.
▶ 전화가 왔어요 You're wanted on the phone. ⇒ You have a phone call. ⇒ There's a telephone call for you.
▶ 런던의 전화가 통하지 않는다 I can't get through to London.
▶ 누이 동생은 언제나 전화가 길다 My sister always talks for a long time when she makes a phone call.
▶ 전화가 갑자기 끊어졌다 Suddenly the phone went dead.
▶ 전화가 멀군요. 좀더 크게 말씀하세요 I can't hear you. Speak a little louder, please.
〈전화를〉 전화를 받다 answer the phone; (美) take a call / 전화를 받고 있다 be on the phone / 전화를 걸다 ⇨ 전화하다 / 전화를 잘못 걸다 ring sb up by mistake; misdial / 전화를 끊다 ring off; hang up / (교환원이) 전화를 연결하다 put sb through
▶ 전화(를) 좀 써도 되겠습니까? May I use this phone?
▶ 전화를 끊지 말고 기다리세요 Will you hold the phone [line] for a minute? ⇌ Hold [Hang] on a minute, please.
▶ 그는 내 이야기가 끝나기도 전에 전화를 딱 끊었다 He hung up [slammed down the receiver] before I finished speaking.
▶ 전화를 잘못 거셨습니다 You have the wrong number.
〈전화로〉 전화로 by (tele)phone; over the phone; through the telephone / 전화로 신청하다 apply by telephone / 전화로 불러내다 call [get] sb on the phone
▶ 나는 어젯밤 그와 전화로 이야기했다 I spoke to him on the phone [over the phone, by phone] last night.
―전화하다 phone; call (up); make a phone call; (英) ring up; telephone
▶ 전화해 주셔서 감사합니다 Thank you for calling (me).
▶ 내일 회사로 전화해 주십시오 Please call [telephone, phone] (me at) the office tomorrow. ⇌ Please give me a call at the office tomorrow.

▶ 나는 그에게 몇분 늦어질지 모른다고 전화했다 I called [phoned] him to say (that) I might be a few minutes late.
▶ 곧 경찰에 전화해라 Call [Dial] the police immediately!
▶ 나중에 또 전화하겠습니다 I'll call [ring you] back later.
▶ 지금 어디서 전화하고 있니? Where are you calling from?
▶ 會話 「몇번에 전화하셨습니까?」「303-1996번을 걸었습니다」 "What number did you dial?" "I dialed three-o-three one-double nine-six."
■ 공동— a party line 교환— an extension (tele)phone 구내—〈내부전화〉an interphone; a house phone;〈교환전화〉an extension telephone 국제— an international [overseas] telephone service 누름 단추식— a push-button (tele)phone 다이얼식— a dial telephone 도청 방지— a scrambler telephone 무선— a radio phone 시내— a local [city] call 이동— a mobile telephone 자동— an automatic telephone; a pay phone 직통— a direct phone; the direct communications link; the hot line 탁상— a desk (tele)phone 휴대—, a cellular [portable] telephone ■—가설료 the telephone installation cost —가입자 a telephone subscriber —교환국 a telephone exchange —교환대 a telephone switchboard —교환수 a telephone [switchboard] operator —국 a telephone office —기 a telephone (set) —도수제 (度數制) the message rate system of the telephone —번호 a (tele)phone number: 전화번호가 틀립니다 You have the wrong number./ 전화번호가 몇번입니까? What is your phone number? ⇌ Tell [Give] me your phone number. —번호부 a telephone directory [book]: 전화번호부를 찾다 consult the telephone directory —선 a telephone wire [line] —수화기 a (telephone) receiver —요금 telephone charges —주문 an order by telephone

—— 전화 ——

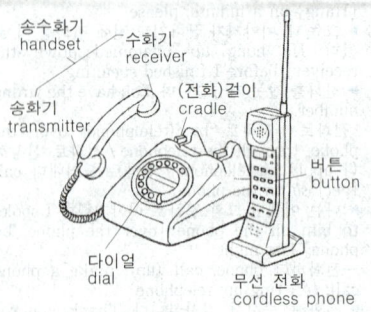

송수화기 handset
수화기 receiver
송화기 transmitter
(전화)걸이 cradle
버튼 button
다이얼 dial
무선 전화 cordless phone

전화 戰火 war fire [flames]; (the) sword and fire; war
▶ 전화는 중동지역으로 번졌다 The flames of war spread to the Middle East.
▶ 마침내 전화가 가라앉았다 At last the war came to an end.
전화 戰禍 the afflictions [horrors, ravages, disasters] of war; war damage
♦ 전화를 입다 suffer the ravages of war
♦ 우리는 전화를 몸소 겪었다 We learned the horrors of war firsthand.
전화 轉化 change; transformation
—전화하다 change; be transformed
—당(糖)〔化〕invert sugar
전화위복 轉禍爲福 good out of evil
▶ 전화위복의 기회로 삼읍시다 Let's turn the misfortune to our advantage.
—전화위복하다 turn a misfortune into a blessing
전환 轉換 1〈바뀜〉(a) changeover; conversion;〈방향 전환〉a switch; a turn; a turnabout;〈변환〉turnover; switchover
♦ 수출지향적 경제 정책의로의 전환 a changeover to export-oriented economic policy / 외교 방침의 전환 a turnabout of diplomacy / 군수산업의 평화산업으로의 전환 the switchover of war industries to peace industries
—전환하다 convert; change [switch] over (to)
♦ 180도 전환하다 execute a 180-degree turn; make a complete about-face
2〈마음의〉diversion
—전환하다 divert; turn
♦ 노래를 불러 기분을 전환하다 divert oneself in singing
■—기(器)〔物〕a commutator; a converter; a switch —로(爐)〔物〕a converter (reactor) —점 a turning point
전환기 轉換期 a turning point; a transition period
♦ 국민경제적 전환기 a turning point in national economy / 전환기의 한국 Korea in transition
▶ 교육제도는 전환기에 있다 The education system is in transition.
전황 戰況 the war [military] situation
♦ 전황을 보고하다 report on the military situation
▶ 전황은 아군에게 유리하게 전개되고 있다 The war is going in our favor.
■—뉴스 war reports [news]
전회 前回 the last time [occasion, session]; the preceding [previous] time
♦ 전전회(前前回)의 모임 the meeting before last; the last meeting but one / 전회까지의 줄거리 the outline of the story up to the last installment [issue] / 전회의 last; previous; preceding
전회 轉回 a rotation; a turnabout; a revolution;〔樂〕〈자리바꿈〉(an) inversion
—전회하다 rotate; revolve;〔樂〕〈자리바꿈하다〉invert
전횡 專橫 arbitrariness; high-handedness;〈압제〉despotism; tyranny
♦ 전횡적인 high-handed; arbitrary; despotic; tyrannical / 전횡을 부리다 act arbitrarily [in an arbitrary manner]; manage (a matter)

전화에 관한 표현

⟨Dialog⟩
미희: 여보세요, 스미스씨 댁입니까? Hello, is this Mr. Smith's home [residence]?
스미스: 네, 그렇습니다 Yes, it is.
미희: 김미희입니다만, 존을 좀 바꿔주십시오 This is Mi-hŭi Kim speaking. May I speak to John?
스미스: 예, 잠깐 기다리세요. 존, 미희양한테서 전화왔다 Yes, just a moment, please. John, there's a phone call for you from Miss Mi-hŭi Kim.
존: 미희구나. 잘 있었니? Hi, Mi-hŭi. How are you doing?
미희: 잘 있어, 그런데… 부탁이 있어. 지금 말해도 돼? Fine, thanks. Er… I have a favor to ask (of) you. Can I talk to you now?
존: 물론이지. 뭔데? Sure. What is it?

1. 전화에 쓰이는 주요한 표현들
▶ 존을 좀 바꿔주세요 May I speak to John? ⇌ I'd like to speak to John.(▶「존 있습니까?」Is John (at) home [in]? 이란 말투나 좀 쉽게 Is John there? 라는 표현을 쓸 수도 있음)
▶ 여보세요, 미희입니다만 Hello, this is Mi-hŭi (speaking).
▶ 누구십니까? Who's calling, please? ⇌ Who's this please? (▶ Who are you? 라고 하면 너무 거치른 말투)
▶ 잠시 기다려주십시오 Just a minute [One moment], please. ⇌ ⟨교환원 등이⟩ Please hold the line.
▶ 미안합니다만, 그는 지금 외출중입니다 Sorry, he is not in right now.
▶ 전화를 걸라고 할까요? Shall I have him call you back?
▶ 괜찮습니다. 나중에 다시 걸겠습니다 Thank you, but I'll call back later.
▶ 뭐 전할 말씀 없습니까? Would you like to leave a message? ⇌ Can I take a message? ⇌ Any message?
▶ 전화 잘못 거셨습니다 Sorry, you have the wrong number.
▶ 말씀이 좀 멀게 들립니다만 좀더 크게 말씀해 주시겠습니까? I'm sorry. I can't hear you very well. Could you speak a little louder?
▶ 아직 끊지 마십시오 Don't hang up yet.

2. 구내・외선, 국제 전화
▶ 구내 2045를 부탁합니다 Extension 2045, please.(two-o [ou]-four-five로 읽음)
▶ 연결되었습니다, 말씀하십시오 Your party is on the line. Please go ahead.
▶ 외선을 부탁합니다. 번호는 526-4458입니다 Give me an outside line, please. The number is 526-4458.
▶ 지금 통화중입니다 The line is busy.
▶ 이 전화로 국제 전화를 걸려면 어떻게 하면 됩니까? How can I make an overseas call on this phone?
▶ 다이얼의 0077을 돌리면 국제전화의 교환원이 연결시켜줍니다 (You) dial 0077 and the overseas operator will put the call through.

3. 부재중 전화 메시지
◆ (부재시의) 전화 자동 응답 장치 an answering machine
▶ 예, 김입니다. 지금 부재중입니다. 삐하는 발신음이 난 다음에 성함, 전화번호, 메시지를 말씀해 주세요. 나중에 연락드리겠습니다 Hello, this is the Kims'. Sorry, we cannot come to the phone right now. Please leave your name, phone number and message after the tone. We'll return your call as soon as possible. Thank you.(▶ 우리는 「지금 부재중입니다」라고 흔히들 말하지만 (美)나 (英)에서는 방법상의 이유에서 위에 말한 바와 같이 「지금 전화를 받을 수 없습니다」라고 한다. 또 여기서는 가족 단위로 살고 있는 경우고 혼자 사는 경우에는 "Hello, this is In-ho Lee."등의 성명으로 대답한다)

4. 전화 번호 문의
▶ 강남구 현대백화점의 전화번호를 알고 싶습니다 I'd like to know the number of Hyundai Department Store in Kangnam-gu.
▶ 문의하신 번호는 552-2233입니다 The number is five-five-two, two-two-three-three. (▶ 전화번호는 원칙적으로 숫자를 한자 한자 읽음)

---

arbitrarily; have *one's* own way; carry matters with a high hand
—**전횡하다** be despotic; tyrannize; act arbitrarily
전후 前後 1 ⟨앞과 뒤⟩ ◆ (글의) 전후 관계 the context / 전후 모순 [당착] self-contradiction / 전후 사정[사연] the circumstances [details] 《of an affair》/(배가) 전후 좌우로 흔들리다 pitch and roll
2 ⟨순서・질서⟩ order; sequence
▶ 전후가 뒤바뀌어 있다 The order is inverted [reversed].
3 ⟨가량・무렵⟩ about; around; toward(s); or so; nearly; approximately
▶ 그는 30세 전후의 남자다 He is about of about [around] thirty.
▶ 그것은 제 2차 대전말 전후의 일이었다 It happened around [before or after] the end of the World War Ⅱ.
▶ 그녀는 8시 전후해서 왔다 She came about [around] eight.
전후 戰後 the postwar period [days]
◆ 전후 수년간 for several years after the war / 전후의 postwar / 전후에 after the war
전훈 電訓 ⟨전보 훈령⟩ telegraphic instructions
절[1] a (Buddhist) temple ◆ 절에 불공드리러 가다 go to worship at a temple
절[2] ⟨인사⟩ a bow; a curtsy; an obeisance
◆ 큰절 a (ceremonial) deep bow
—**절하다** bow (to); bow down (to); make a bow [an obeisance] 《to》
◆ 공손히 절하다 bow politely / 꾸벅 절하다

bob / 무릎 꿇고 절하다 bow down upon *one's* knees / 서로 절하다 exchange bows / 고맙다고 절하다 bow *one's* thanks / 부모님에게 절하다 bow to [salute] *one's* parents
♦ 그는 우리에게 공손히[가볍게] 절했다 He bowed politely [slightly] to us. ⇒ He made a polite [slight] bow to us.

절 節 1 〈문장의〉 a paragraph; a passage; a part; a section; 〈시의〉 a stanza; a verse
♦ 제5장 제2절 Chapter V, Paragraph Ⅱ
2 〔文法〕 a clause ♦ 형용사절 an adjective clause / 종속절 a dependent clause

-절 -折 folding ♦ 12절 duodecimo; 12mo / 2절로 하다 fold in two [half]

-절 -節 〈명절〉 a festival; 〈철〉 a season
♦ 삼일절 Independence Movement Day / 성탄절 Christmas

절간 —間 a temple ⇨ 절¹

절감 節減 curtailment; reduction; retrenchment —**절감하다** curtail; cut (down); reduce; retrench
♦ 예산을 절감하다 cut down the budget
♦ 경비— the retrenchment of expenditure

절감하다 切感— feel strongly [acutely, keenly]
♦ 영어 회화의 필요성을 절감하다 feel keenly the necessity of English conversation

절개 切開 〔醫〕 (an) incision; (a) section; an operation
—**절개하다** cut open; open; operate (on); incise; make an incision (in)
♦ 종기를 절개하다 incise a tumor / 환부를 절개하다 cut out the affected parts
■ 제왕— a Caesarean section [operation]
■ —수술 a surgical incision [operation]: 위절개수술 〔醫〕 gastrotomy

절개 節概 principle; fidelity; integrity; chastity; morality; faith
♦ 절개있는 여자 a woman of principle / 절개 없는 inconstant; unprincipled / 절개를 지키다 keep [remain faithful to] *one's* principles; 〈여자가〉 maintain *one's* chastity
▶ 그는 절개가 없다 He has no principles.

절검 節儉 thrift ⇨ 검약

절경 絕景 a superb [wonderful] view; picturesque [fine] scenery; a scenic masterpiece
♦ 천하 절경 scenery unparalleled in the world; the sweetest view in the world
▶ 참으로 절경이다 What a grand sight this is!
▶ 금강산은 천하 절경이다 The scenery of Kŭmgangsan is unparalleled in the world.

절골 折骨 a fracture ⇨ 골절

절교 絕交 —**절교하다** break off (friendship) (with); renounce [rupture] friendship (with); be done [through] with *sb*; break with *sb*
♦ 친구와 절교하다 break (off) with a friend
▶ 너와는 이제 절교다 I will have nothing to do with you.
■ —장 a letter breaking off with *sb*

절구 a (stone, wood) mortar ♦ 절구에 찧다 pound (rice) in a mortar
■ —질 pounding grain in a mortar ■ —통 a mortar: 절구통 같은 몸매 a body with no curves [waist]

절구 絕句 1 〈한시의 4행 연시〉 a Chinese quatrain 2 〈말이 막힘〉 —**절구하다** break off (short) (in *one's* speech); find no words to say

절굿공이 a pestle; a pounder
♦ 절굿공이로 찧다 pound (rice) with a pestle; crush (grains) with a pounder

절규 絕叫 screaming; a scream; (an) exclamation —**절규하다** scream; exclaim; cry out; shout ♦ 절규하는 듯한 연설 an exclamatory speech

절그렁 with a clink [clank, clinking sound]
♦ 철판의 절그렁하는 소리 the clank of an iron plate

절그렁거리다 jingle; jangle; clink; clank

절기 絕技 〈뛰어난 기술〉 an excellent craft [technic]; 〈연기〉 an admirable performance; a miraculous feat; 〈기능〉 wonderful skill

절기 絕奇 〈매우 기묘함〉 exquisiteness; wonderfulness —**절기하다** very strange; wonderful; miraculous; 〈절묘하다〉 exquisite; excellent

절기 節氣 〈음력의 절기〉 a seasonal subdivision
▶ 음력에는 각 계절마다 6절기가 있으므로 1년은 24절기다 Each of the four seasons has six seasonal subdivisions in the lunar calendar. Therefore, there are 24 seasonal subdivisions in a year.

절꺼덕 with a snap [click, clank]
♦ 문을 절꺼덕 닫다 shut the door with a snap
▶ 문이 절꺼덕 잠겼다 The door clicked shut.
—**절꺼덕하다** snap; click; clank

절꺼덕 with a snap ⇨ 절거덕

절다¹ 〈소금에〉 get salted; be salted to the core; be seasoned with salt
▶ 김치는 절인 배추로 한다 Salted (Korean) cabbages are used in *kimchi*.
▶ 이 청어는 잘 절었다 This herring is well salted.

절다² 〈다리를〉 limp; hobble (along, about); walk lame; hitch (along)
♦ 왼쪽 다리를 절다 be lame in the left leg / 절면서 걷다 limp along; walk lame [with a limp]; hobble (along)

절단 切斷 cutting; severance; abscission; section; 〈손발의〉 amputation
♦ 팔 절단 환자 an arm amputee
—**절단하다** cut; cut off; chop; sever; 〈손발을〉 amputate
♦ 둘로 절단하다 cut (a thing) in two
■ —기 a cutting machine; a cutter; a shredder
■ —면 a section ■ —수술 amputation

절대 絕對 absoluteness
♦ 절대의 absolute; positive; unconditional; categorical / 절대불변의 immutable; permanent
■ —값 〔數〕 an absolute value ■ —고도[습도] absolute altitude [humidity] ■ —공간 absolute space ■ —군주 an absolute monarch; an autocrat ■ —군주제 absolute [despotic] monarchy ■ —금주 total abstinence ■ —단위 〔物〕 an absolute unit ■ —명사 〈名辭〉 〔論〕 an absolute term ■ —번지 〔電算〕 absolute address ■ —영도 〔物〕 absolute zero (degree) ■ —오차 〔物〕 absolute

error —온도 〔物〕 absolute temperature —음악 absolute music —자 〔哲〕 the Absolute; the absolute being —주의[론] 〔哲〕 absolutism —항(項) 〔數〕 an absolute term

절대권(력) 絶對權(力) absolute authority [right, power] 《over》
■—자 a despot; an autocrat; an absolutist

절대다수 絶對多數 an absolute majority
◆절대다수를 차지하다 get [win, gain] an absolute majority

절대량 絶對量 the absolute quantity
◆절대량이 많다[적다] be large [small] in absolute quantity

절대로 絶對— absolutely; positively; unconditionally; 《not》 by any means
◆절대로 필요[불가능]하다 be absolutely necessary [impossible] / 절대로 금하다 prohibit positively
▶그런 일은 절대로 하지 않겠습니다 I swear I will never do such a thing.
▶나는 절대로 가르쳐 줄 수 없다 I can't tell you for the life of me.
▶나는 절대로 가지 않겠다 I positively decline to go. ⇌ Blame me if I go.

절대반대 絶對反對 ▶그는 절대반대의 입장을 취했다 He took an attitude of positive opposition.
▶나는 그 제안에 절대반대다 I am positively [dead] against the proposal.

절대복종 絶對服從 absolute [unconditional] obedience
▶내 명령에 절대복종해라 Obey my orders unconditionally [without question].

절대안정 絶對安靜 a complete [an absolute] rest
▶환자는 절대안정을 요합니다 The patient must be kept absolutely at rest.

절대적 絶對的 absolute; unconditional; positive; imperative; categorical ◆절대적으로 absolutely; unconditionally; positively
▶신은 절대적 존재다 God is the absolute being. —실업 absolute unemployment

절도 節度 moderation
◆절도있는 moderate / 절도없는 immoderate; extravagant / 절도를 지키다 be moderate; use [exercise] moderation 《in》 / 절도가 없다 be rampant; be extravagant

절도 竊盜 〈行爲〉 (a) theft; pilferage; 〔法〕 larceny; 〈犯人〉 a thief (pl. thieves); a larcener; a larcenist
◆절도혐의로 on the suspicion of larceny [theft]
■—죄 theft; larceny: 절도죄로 체포되다 be arrested on a theft charge —행위[질] a larcenous act: 절도질을 하다 commit a theft; steal; pilfer; filch

절뚝거리다 walk lame ⇨ 절다²

절량농가 絶糧農家 a starving farm family; a farm(ing) family whose provisions have run out ◆절량농가를 구호하다 give relief to starving farmers

절로 1 ⇨ 저절로 **2** 〈저리로〉 that way [direction]; over there

절룩거리다 limp ⇨ 절다²

절류 絶倫 peerlessness; uniqueness
—절륜하다 peerless; matchless; unparalleled; unequaled; unique; wonderful
▶그는 정력이 절륜한 사람이다 He is a man of indefatigable energy.

절름거리다 walk lame ⇨ 절다²

절름발이 a lame person; a cripple
◆절름발이의 lame; limping; crippled / 절름발이가 되다 become lame; become crippled; go [fall] lame

절망 切望 an earnest desire; an eager wish [hope]; longing; (a) yearning 《for》
—절망하다 desire earnestly; wish eagerly; long [hunger, thirst, crave, hanker] 《for, after》; be anxious [mad] 《for, to do》
▶그는 귀국을 절망하고 있었다 He was anxious to return to his country.

절망 絶望 despair; hopelessness
◆절망적인 hopeless; desperate; despaired of / 절망상태에 빠져 있다 be in a desperate situation
▶사태는 절망적이다 The situation is hopeless [beyond hope].
—절망하다 despair of sth; be driven to despair; be plunged in despair; give up all hope; surrender all hope
◆절망하여 in despair; out of despair; despairingly / 절망시키다 throw sb into despair; drive sb to despair
▶그는 절망한 나머지 자살했다 Despair drove him to suicide. ⇌ He took his own life out of despair.

절멸 絶滅 extinction; extermination; extirpation; annihilation; eradication
▶많은 야생 조류들이 절멸 위기에 처해 있다 Many species of wild birds are in danger of extinction.
—절멸하다 become extinct; go out of existence; die out; cease to exit

절명 絶命 death —절명하다 die

절묘 絶妙 exquisiteness
—절묘하다 miraculous; exquisite; superb; excellent; 〈미묘한〉 delicate
◆절묘한 재주[솜씨] a superb [consummate] performance; a miraculous feat / 절묘한 필치 an exquisite touch

절무 絶無 〈아주 없음〉 nothing; nought; complete absence —절무하다 be wholly lacking; be none at all

절미 節米 rice saving; economy in rice consumption —절미하다 economize (in) rice
■—운동 a campaign for rice saving

절박 切迫 〈가까이 닥침〉 urgency; imminence; impendence; pressure; 〈긴박〉 acuteness; tensity
—절박하다 urgent; pressing; impending; imminent; acute; tense
◆절박한 문제 an urgent question / 절박한 위기 an imminent [overhanging, immediate] crisis
▶시간이 절박하다 Time presses.
▶총선이 절박해 있다 The general election is close [near] at hand.
▶상황이 절박하다 The situation has become

acute [tense, urgent].

절반 折半 a half
♦ 절반의 크기[값] half the size [price] / 절반 씩 나누다 go halves [shares]; share sth half and half 《with sb》
▶ 일은 절반 밖에 끝나지 않았다 I have finished only half of the job. ⇌ I am only halfway through the job.

절벅 with a splash [plash]
절벅거리다 splash; plash
절벅절벅 with a splash; with a plash; with splashing
♦ 얕은 시냇물을 절벅절벅 걸어가다 slosh [splash] through the shallow stream

절벽 絕壁 a cliff; 〈강·바다에 면한〉 a bluff; a precipice
♦ 절벽 끝에 서다 stand on the edge of a precipice [cliff] / 절벽을 기어 오르다 scale [clamber up] a cliff / 절벽에서 떨어지다 fall over a precipice

절상 切上 〔經〕〈화폐의 대외 가치를 높임〉(a) revaluation ♦ 원화의 평가 절상 a revaluation of the Korean won

절색 絕色 a rare beauty; a paragon of beauty; a woman [lady] of matchless [peerless] beauty

절세 絕世 〈뛰어남〉♦ 절세 미인 ⇨ 절색 / 절세 의 peerless; matchless; unrivaled; unequaled; nonpareil

절수 節水 〈물을 아낌〉 economization of water; water saving ━절수하다 save water; economize (in) water consumption

절식 絕食 a fast ⇨ 단식

절식 節食 temperance [moderation] in eating; an abstemious [a spare] diet
━절식하다 be temperate in eating; eat sparingly [moderately]; 〈미용·병 등 때문에〉 be on a diet

절실 切實 earnestness
━절실하다 acute; earnest; important; keen; fervent; poignant
♦ 절실히 keenly; deeply; fully; poignantly; 〈진심으로〉 heartily; sincerely; earnestly
▶ 내 차의 필요성을 절실히 느낀다 I feel keenly the necessity of my own car.

절약 節約 saving; economy; frugality; thrift; husbandry

> 解説 *saving*은 장래를 위해 돈 등을 예치하는 것. *economy*는 노력·돈·시간 등을 낭비하 지 않은 것. *frugality*는 특히 식품·비용 등 을 절감하는 것. *thrift*는 돈이나 물건을 낭비 하지 않는 것을 나타낸다.

━절약하다 economize (in); be frugal; practice economy (in); dispense (with); spare; save; 〈절감하다〉 curtail; cut (down)
♦ 경비를 절약하다 cut (down) expenses / 전기 를 절약하다 save [economize in] (electric) power
■ 비용— economy in expenditure : 그것은 비 용 절약이 된다 It saves us money. 시간— the saving of time 일광— daylight saving ■ 一가

〈家〉 a thrifty [frugal, saving] person; an economist; a man of economy

절연 絕緣 1 〈인연·관계의 단절〉 separation; dissolution of a tie; disconnection
━절연하다 cut [sever] *one's* connection 《with》; break 《with sb》; break off relations 《with》
2 〔電〕〈전류의 차단〉 insulation; isolation
━절연하다 insulate; isolate
♦ 절연한 insulated; isolated
━기(器) an insulator; a (cut-off) switch ━선 an insulated wire ━유(油) 〔電〕 insulating oil ━저항(抵抗) 〔電〕 insulation resistance ━체 an insulator; an isolator ━테이프 friction [insulating] tape

절연 節煙 〈담배를 줄임〉 temperance [moderation] in smoking ━절연하다 be temperate [moderate] in smoking

절의 節義 faithfulness [fidelity, sincerity] to *one's* principles; constancy; honor
♦ 절의를 지키다 adhere to *one's* principles

절이다 pickle; preserve in [with] salt; cure; salt (down); souse; corn 《meat》
♦ 〈소금에〉 절인 생선 cured fish / 소금에 절인 salted; cured / 생선을 소금에 절이다 salt fish; preserve fish in salt

절전 節電 economy in power consumption; power saving ━절전하다 economize (in) power; save electricity
■ 一운동 a power-savings campaign

절정 絕頂 the summit; the top; 〈정점〉 the peak; the zenith; the meridian; the height; the climax; the acme [ǽkmi]
♦ 인기 절정의 crest [peak, zenith] of *one's* popularity / 절정에 이르다 reach [make, gain] the summit; 〈정점의〉 reach [attain] the acme [climax]

절제 切除 excision; 〈외과의〉 erasion; a surgical removal; a resection ♦ 신경 절제(술) neurotomy / 폐 절제(술) pneumonectomy
━절제하다 excise; cut off; resect

절제 節制 temperance; abstinence; moderation; 〈성욕의〉 continence
━절제하다 be moderate [temperate] 《in》; use [exercise] moderation; practice temperance; restrain *oneself*; be continent
♦ 술을 절제하다 be temperate in drinking
■ 一가 a man of temperate habits; a temperate person 一생활 temperate living

절조 節操 〈지조〉 constancy; fidelity; integrity; honor; 〈정조〉 chastity; faith ♦ 절조있는 사람 a man of principles

절족동물 節足動物 〔動〕 an arthropod = 절지 동물

절주 節酒 moderation in drinking; temperance ━절주하다 be temperate; drink moderately

절지동물 節肢動物 〔動〕 an arthropod

절차 節次 (a) procedure; (a) process; proceedings; 〈정해진 형식〉 formalities; 〈조치〉 steps
♦ 정식 절차 the usual [regular, established] procedure / 절차상의 procedural / 절차를 밟다 comply with a formality; go through due formalities; perform formalities; take proceed-

절차 ...ings; take steps / 절차를 생략하다 dispense with the formalities
▶ 지원 절차는 알고 계십니까? Do you know how to apply?
■소송— legal procedure; legal [judicial] proceedings 수입— import procedure 입학— the entrance procedure ■—법 [法] the law of procedure; procedural law; an adjective law —위반 deviation from the procedure; violation of the procedure

절차탁마 切磋琢磨 〈학덕의 연마〉 studying hard to heighten the level of one's arts [craft, mental culture]
—절차탁마하다 study hard for the better standards of one's arts [craft, mental culture]

절찬 絶讚 acclamation; the highest admiration [praise]
▶ 그의 작품은 사람들의 절찬을 받았다 His work won the highest praise from the public.
—절찬하다 extol; express great admiration (for); praise [laud] sb highly [to the skies]

절창 絶唱 〈뛰어난 노래, 시〉 a superb song [poem]; 〈명창〉 a superb singer

절충 折衷 a compromise
—절충하다 make [arrange, manage, work out] a compromise
▶ 이 법안은 현행법과 구법을 절충한 것이다 This bill is a compromise between the existing laws and the old laws.
■—가격 a compromise price —법 an eclectic method —설 eclecticism; a compromise on conflicting views —안 a compromise; a compromise plan [suggestion, proposal] —주의 [哲] eclecticism

절충 折衝 negotiation(s); a parley
▶ 그는 절충의 명수다 He is a good negotiator.
▶ 우리의 임금 인상 문제는 현재 절충 중이다 The matter about our wage hike is now under negotiations.
—절충하다 negotiate; carry on negotiations; parley 《with》

절취 竊取 〈훔침〉 theft; larceny; stealing
—절취하다 steal

절취선 切取線 the line along which to cut 《a part》 off; 〈점선〉 a dotted line; 〈바늘 구멍〉 a perforated line

절친 切親 〈아주 친함〉 intimacy; familiarity; a close friendship
—절친하다 intimate; familiar; close
♦ 절친한 사람 an intimate (acquaintance); a close [confidential] friend
▶ 나는 그와 절친한 사이다 I am intimate [friendly] with him.
▶ 그 두 사람은 절친한 사이다 The two were close friends.

절판 絶版 going out of print —절판하다 print no more copies of 《the book》
♦ 절판된 책 an out-of-print book / 절판되다 go [pass] out of print
▶ 그 책은 절판입니다 The book is out-of-print.

절품 切品 absence of stock ⇨ 품절
절품 絶品 〈아주 좋은 물건〉 a nonpareil; an article without a rival

절필 絶筆 1 〈마지막 글(씨)〉 one's last writing 2 〈글쓰기를 그만둠〉 —절필하다 give up writing; break the pencil

절하 切下 (a) cut [reduction] 《in price》
—절하하다 cut; cut down 《to》; reduce 《to》; lower; slash
■평가— [經] 〈화폐가치의〉 devaluation 《of the dollar》: 평가절하하다 devaluate [devalue] 《the won currency》

절해 絶海 〈육지에서 멀리 떨어진 바다〉 a far-off [distant] sea
♦ 절해 고도 a solitary [lonely] island in a distant sea
▶ 그는 절해 고도에 표류했다 He was washed ashore on an isolated island in a far-off sea.

절호 絶好 the best
♦ 절호의 기회 a golden [rare] opportunity; an excellent [a rare] opportunity; an excellent [a rare] chance / 절호의 best; excellent; splendid; first-rate; golden
▶ 이것은 네게 절호의 기회다 This is your best chance.

젊다 1 〈나이가〉 young (in years); juvenile; youthful
♦ 젊은 부부 a young (married) couple / 나이보다 젊어 보이다 look young for one's age / 마음이 젊다 have a youthful spirit; be young in spirit
▶ 그는 젊어서 죽었다 He died young.
▶ 너는 언제 보아도 젊다 You always look young.
▶ 그녀는 무대에 서면 20살은 젊어 보인다 She looks twenty years younger on the stage.
▶ 그는 나이는 젊지만 생각은 깊다 He has an old head on young shoulders.
2 〈손아래〉 younger; junior
▶ 그는 나보다 세 살 젊다 He is three years younger than I. ⇌ He is three years my junior. ⇌ He is my junior by three years.

젊어지다 grow [get] younger; be [become] rejuvenated; be restored to youth; become [grow] young again
▶ 그는 10년은 젊어진 것 같다 He looks ten years younger.
▶ 젊은 사람들 속에 사니까 젊어지는 것 같다 Living among the young people makes me feel younger.

젊은이 a young person [man]; a youth; a youngster; 〈남자〉 a lad; (총칭) the young; the youth; young people
♦ 젊은이에게 어울리는 옷 dress fitted [suited] for young persons / 요즈음의 젊은이 young people (of) today; young folks nowadays
▶ 우리 할아버지는 젊은이 못지 않게 원기 왕성하시다 My grandfather is (as) strong as a young man.

젊음 youth; youthfulness
♦ 젊음을 유지하다 keep one's youth; retain one's youthfulness; remain [stay] young
▶ 젊음은 보배다 Youth is a treasure.
▶ 선생님께서 젊음을 유지하시는 비결은 무엇입니까? What is the secret of keeping your youth?
▶ 젊음도 한때다 We are young only once. ⇌

Young days will not come again.

점占 divination; fortune-telling; soothsaying; augury ◆점을 치다 divine
▶점은 맞기도 하고 안맞기도 한다 Fortune-telling is a hit-or-miss sort of thing.

점點 1 〈반점〉 a spot; a dot; a speck; a speckle; 〈얼룩〉 a blot; a stain
◆태양의 흑점 a sunspot / 점이 있는 spotted; dotted; specked; speckled
▶푸른 하늘에 흰 구름 몇점이 보인다 We can see a few specks of white clouds in the blue sky.
▶오늘 아침에는 바람 한 점 없다 There is not a breath of air this morning.
2 〈피부의〉 a mole; a macula (*pl.* -lae, ~s); 〈모반(母斑)〉 a birthmark; a mother('s) mark
◆애교점 a beauty spot / 점을 빼다 remove a mole
3 〈數〉 a point; a dot; a mark; 〈소숫점〉 a decimal point; 〈주사위 등의〉 a pip; 〈종지부〉 a period; 〈구두점 등〉 a point; a dot
◆4.6 four point six / 점과 선〈모스 부호〉 dots and dashes; dits and dahs / 점을 찍다 mark with a dot [point]; dot; point; spot
▶문장 끝에 점을 찍어라 Stop [Put a period to] a sentence.
▶i자에 점을 찍으시오 Put the dots on the i's. ⇌ Dot your i's.
4 〈평점〉 marks; (美) grades
◆80점으로 합격하다 pass an examination with 80 marks / 90점을 따다 get [gain] 90 marks
▶내 영어 점수는 90점이었다 My mark [grade] in English was 90.
▶내 영어 점수는 몇 점입니까? How many marks did I get in English?
5 〈경기의〉 a point; a score; 〈야구·크리켓의〉 a run
◆1점을 따다 score [make] a point; 〈야구에서〉 score a run; 〈농구에서〉 score a basket
6 〈논점〉 a point; a score; 〈사항〉 a respect; a detail; a particular; 〈견지〉 a standpoint; a point of view
◆어려운 점 the difficult [hard] point / 좋은 점 a strong [good] point; a merit / 나쁜 점 a weak point; a defect / 어떤 점에 있어서는 in some points [respects]; in certain details; in a way / 그 점에 있어서 on that point [score]; in that respect / 여러 가지 점에서 in many ways / 이 점에서 보면 in view of this; from this viewpoint / 어느 점으로 보나 in all points [respects]; in every respect; in all senses
▶미심쩍은 점을 검토합시다 Let's examine doubtful points.
▶남의 좋은 점을 보시오 See the good in others.
▶그 점은 안심하십시오 You may be easy on that score.
▶이 점에 관해 아는 바 없다 I have never had any idea on this point.
7 〔樂〕 a dot
8 〔物〕 a point
◆끓는점 the boiling point / 어는점 the freezing point / 녹는점 the melting point

9 〈지점〉 a point; 〈정도〉 a degree; a point
◆출발점 the starting point / 어느 점까지는 to a certain degree [point]
10 〈물품의 수〉 an item; a piece
◆가구 몇 점 several pieces [articles] of furniture / 옷가지 15점 fifteen pieces [items] of clothing
11 〈고기 등의〉 a piece 《of meat》; a cut; a slice
◆고기 한 점 a piece [slice] of meat
12 〈바둑의〉 a stone
◆한 점 두다 put [place] a stone

점가 漸加 〈점점 더해감〉 a gradual increase
─점가하다 increase gradually; make a gradual increase

점감 漸減 〈차차 줄어듦〉 a gradual decrease; (a) diminution ─점감하다 diminish [decrease] gradually; dwindle

점거 占據 occupation; exclusive possession
─점거하다 hold; occupy; take; capture
■불법─ unlawful [illegal] occupation
─자 an occupant ─지 an occupied territory

점검 點檢 1 〈물건〉 a check; inspection; (an) examination; overhauling; checking
◆점검을 받다 undergo [have] an inspection
▶나는 자동차 점검을 받았다 I had my car checked.
─점검하다 check; inspect; examine; overhaul; scrutinize; scan
2 〈인원〉 roll call
─점검하다 call the roll; muster
◆인원을 점검하다 roll-call; take roll call
◆불시(不時)─ a spot check 엔진─ an engine checkup

점고 漸高 〈점점 높아짐〉 a gradual rise [elevation] ─점고하다 rise gradually

점괘 占卦 a divination sign
◆점괘가 좋다[나쁘다] have a good [an ill] divination sign; have a good [bad] omen

점그래프 點─ 〔數〕 a dot graph

점근 漸近 〈점점 가까워짐〉 a gradual approach
─점근하다 approach gradually
─급수 〔數〕 an asymptotic series ─선 an asymptotic line ─원 an asymptotic circle

점대 占─ 〈점칠 때 쓰는 댓개비〉 divining rods [sticks]

점도 粘度 〈끈끈한 정도·성질〉 viscosity; 〈점도의 비율〉 a coefficient of viscosity

점두 店頭 a store [shop] front; a counter; 〈진열창〉 a show window; 〈가게〉 a shop; (美) a store
■─거래 〔證〕 over-the-counter [OTC] transaction ─광고 a (shop) window advertisement ─매매 〔證〕 over-the-counter [OTC] dealings [trade] ─매매 주식 over-the-counter stocks ─장식 window dressing [trimming] ─장식가 a window dresser [trimmer]

점동이 點─ a person with a birthmark ⇨ 점박이 1

점등 漸騰 〈점점 올라감〉 a gradual rise
─점등하다 rise gradually

점등 點燈 〈등불을 켬〉 lighting ◆점등시간 lighting-up time ─점등하다 light (a lamp); light up; switch [turn] on a light

점락 漸落 1 〈점점 내려감〉 a gradual fall ─점락하다 fall [decline] gradually
2 〈證〉〈시세 하락〉 a gradual decline; sagging; a droop ─점락하다 ease off; recede; sag

점령 占領 occupation; occupancy; capture; possession
♦ 마을의 점령 the capture of a town / 점령하에 있다 be under occupation
─점령하다 capture; take; seize; occupy; 〈탈취〉 carry; hold; take possession of
♦ 요새를 점령하다 carry a fortress
■ ─국 an occupying power [nation] ─군 the occupation army [troops, forces] ─자 an occupant ─정책 an occupation policy ─지 a territory under occupation; an occupied territory [area] ─지대 an occupation zone; a zone of military occupation

점막 店幕 an inn; a tavern ⇨ 여인숙

점막 粘膜 〔解〕 a mucosa (*pl.* -sae, ~s, ~); a mucous membrane ■ ─분비물 rheum

점멸하다 點滅─ 〈등불을 켰다 껐다 함〉 turn [switch] on and off; 〈등불이 켜졌다 꺼졌다 함〉 go [come] on and off ■ ─기(器) a switch ─등 an on-and-off light; a flasher

점묘 點描 〔美術〕 a sketch ♦ 인물─ personal sketches; the (personal) profile (of) ■ ─화가 a pointilliste ─화법 pointillisme

점박이 點─ 1 〈사람〉 a person with a birthmark [mole]; 〈동물〉 a spotted [speckled, piebald, dapple(d)] animal
2 〈손가락질받는 사람〉 a blot on the escutcheon [landscape]

점보 〈거대한 것〉 a jumbo (*pl.* ~s)
■ ─제트기 a jumbo jet plane

점서 占書 〈점술에 관한 책〉 a book on divination; a fortune book

점선 點線 〔數〕 a dotted line; 〈절취선〉 a perforated line ♦ 점선을 긋다 draw a dotted line
▶ 점선을 자르시오 Cut the paper along the dotted line.

점성 占星 〈별점〉 horoscope; astrology ■ ─가 an astrologist; an astrologer; a horoscopist ─술 astrology; horoscopy

점성 粘性 〈끈끈한 성질〉 viscosity ■ ─계수 viscosity coefficient; coefficient of viscosity

점수 點數 1 〈성적의〉 marks
♦ 점수가 좋다 [나쁘다] have good [bad] marks / 점수가 박하다 [후하다] be severe [liberal, generous] in marking / 점수를 매기다 give marks; award points / 좋은 [나쁜] 점수를 받다 get [gain] good [bad] marks
2 〈경기 등의〉 points; a score; 〈야구의〉 runs; 〈당구의 연속 득점〉 a break
♦ 점수를 많이 따다 make a good score

점술 占術 the art of divination [fortune-telling]; prognosticator's [fortune-teller's] arts

점신세 漸新世 the Oligocene ⇨ 올리고세

점심 點心 lunch; luncheon ♦ 점심을 먹다 lunch; luncheon; take [eat, have] lunch / 점심 먹으러 가다 go to lunch / 점심을 싸가다 take [carry] a lunch with *one* ■ ─때 [시간] lunchtime

점안 點眼 1 〈안약을 넣음〉 dropping eyewash [eyewater] in the eyes ─점안하다 apply eyewash (to); drop eyewash
2 〈눈동자를 그려 넣음〉 ▶ 불상을 만들고 나면 점안을 해야 한다 After finishing the Buddhist image, the pupils of the eyes must be drawn.
■ ─기 an eyedropper ─수[약] eyewash

점액 粘液 musin; mucus; mucilage ♦ 점액 같은 mucous; mucilaginous
■ ─변(便) mucous stool [evacuation] ─분비 secretion of mucus ─선 mucous gland ─세포 mucilage cell ─소(素) 〔生化〕 mucin

점액질 粘液質 〈끈기 있는 기질〉 phlegmatic temperament
♦ 점액질인 사람 a person of phlegmatic temperament; a phlegmatic person

점역 點譯 〈점자로 고침〉 translation into braille
─점역하다 translate into braille

점원 店員 a (store) clerk; a salesclerk; a shop assistant; a shopboy; a shopgirl ♦ 점원이 되다 [으로서 일하다] be employed as a clerk; clerk (for a store)

점유 占有 〈차지함〉 occupancy; occupation; possession ─점유하다 occupy; possess; take possession of
■ 불법─ 〔法〕 detention; deforcement; detinue ─물 a thing possessed; a possession ─율 (率) 〈시장의〉 a (market) share ─자 an occupant; a possessor; a seizor; an occupier

점유권 占有權 a possessory right ♦ 점유권을 획득하다 acquire possession (of) ■ ─토지─ a possessory title to land ■ ─대역 occupied band

점음표 點音標 〔樂〕 a dotted note

점입가경 漸入佳境 ▶ 그 사랑의 삼각관계는 점입가경이다 The triangular love affair is getting more interesting.
─점입가경하다 approach a climax; get more and more interesting; get to the best part
▶ 이야기는 점입가경했다 We reached [got into] the most interesting part of the story.

점자 點字 braille points [type]; braille; raised letters
♦ 점자 읽는 법 finger reading / 점자를 읽다 read braille type / 점자로 발행하다 publish in braille [raised type]
■ ─도서관 a braille library ─번역자 a braille transcriber ─법 the braille ─악보 braille music ─책 a book in braille [raised letters]; a book in embossed type for the blind

점잔 a dignified air; an air of importance
♦ 점잔 빼는 목소리 a genteel tone of voice / 점잔 빼다 [부리다, 피우다] assume [give *oneself*, put on, acquire] airs; look demure [grave]; do the genteel
▶ 그는 항상 점잔을 빼는 통에 상종할 수가 없다 He always puts on airs, and I can't get along with him.

점잖다 〈고상하다〉 decent; demure; gentle; genteel; gentlemanly; respectable; 〈의젓하다〉 dignified; grave; decorous; 〈수수하다〉 quiet; sober; sedate
♦ 점잖은 사람 a decent man; a fine gentleman / (옷감의) 점잖은 무늬 a genteel [refined] pat-

tern / 점잖지 못한 농담 a broad joke / 점잖지 못한 〈상스러운〉 indecent; low; vulgar; 〈고상하지 못한〉 ignoble; base; mean / 점잖은 말을 쓰다 use refined [elevated] language / 옷차림이 점잖다 be decently [elevated] dressed / 점잖게 굴다 behave *oneself*; behave like a gentleman
▶우리 사장은 언제나 점잖지만 술을 마시면 난폭해진다 My boss is usually well-mannered, but he gets rowdy when he drinks.

점재 點在 scattering
―점재하다 be dotted [studded] with
◆양들이 점재하는 들판 a field dotted with sheep / 섬들이 점재하는 바다 an island-studded [-dotted] sea / 점재하는 dotty; sporadic
▶야자수들이 해안에 점재해 있었다 Palm trees dotted the seacoast.

점쟁이 占― a fortune-teller; a diviner; a prognosticator ▶나는 어제 점쟁이를 찾아가 점을 쳤다 I visited a fortune-teller yesterday and had my fortune told.

점적 點滴 1 〈물방울〉 a falling drop of water; waterdrops; 〈빗방울〉 raindrops
2 〈정맥 주사〉 〔醫〕 an intravenous drip (injection); an instillation
▶그녀는 (정맥) 점적(법)을 받았다 She was put on an intravenous drip.
―점적하다 administer *sth* dropwise
■―기 〈혈관에의〉 an instillator; 〈안약 등의〉 a (medicine) dropper; an eyedropper

점점 漸漸 1 〈차차〉 gradually; by (slow [small]) degrees; little by little
◆점점 나아지다 show gradual improvement
◆그 노인은 식사가 점점 줄었다 The old man ate less and less.
2 〈더욱 더〉 increasingly; growingly; 〈더하다〉 more and more; 〈덜해지다〉 less and less
◆점점 어려워지다 become increasingly difficult / 점점 커지다 gradually grow in size / 점점 나빠지다 go from bad to worse
▶하루낮이 점점 길어진다 The day is getting longer (and longer).
▶소음은 점점 커졌다 The noise became louder and louder.

점점이 點點― 〈여기저기 하나씩〉 here and there; sporadically; scatteringly
▶하늘에는 깜박이는 별이 점점이 빛나고 있다 The sky is studded [strewn] with twinkling stars.
▶동산에는 진달래가 점점이 피어 있다 The hill is dotted with blooming azaleas.

점주 店主 a shopkeeper; 〈美〉 a storekeeper; a store owner; the proprietor of a shop
◆식료품 점주 a grocery store owner

점증 漸增 〈점점 늘어남〉 (a) gradual increase [increment]; a steady increase ―점증하다 increase gradually [by degrees]; be on the increase

점지하다 〈자식을 갖게 해줌〉 bless *sb* with a baby ◆점지해 준 아이 a godsent [heavensent] child

점진 漸進 〈차차 나아감〉 gradual progress; steady advance
◆점진적인 gradual; gradational / 점진적으로 gradually; step by step; by gradual degrees

―점진하다 progress gradually; make gradual progress; advance steadily

점진주의 漸進主義 moderatism; gradualism; the slow and steady principle
■―자 a moderatist; a gradualist

점찍다 點― mark out; 〈하나를 고르다〉 single [pick] out; spot; fix *one's* choice on; 〈마음속에 지목하다〉 select *sth* as desirable
◆범인으로 점찍다 suspect *sb* of a crime; throw [cast] suspicion 《on》 / 점찍어 놓은 좋은 사람 a man [girl] of *one's* heart; the choice of *one's* heart

점차 漸次 gradually; by (slow) degrees; step by step; little by little
◆점차 진보하다 make gradual progress / 점차 회복되어 가다 be gradually getting better

점착 粘着 〈달라붙음〉 adhesion; viscosity
―점착하다 stick (fast) 《to》; be glued 《to》; adhere 《to》 ■―력 adhesive [cohesive] power; 〔物〕 viscosity ―제 an adhesive; a gluing agent; an agglutinant

점착성 粘着性 〈끈끈함〉 stickiness; adhesion; viscosity; viscidity
◆점착성의 sticky; adhesive; viscous / 점착성이 없는 nonsticky; inadhesive

점철 點綴 〈하나씩 이어맺음〉 interspersion
―점철하다 《…을》 intersperse; dot; stud; 《…이》 be dotted [studded] 《with》
▶잔디밭에는 꽃들이 점철해 있다 The grass is dotted with flowers.

점치다 占― tell *sb's* fortune; divine; forecast; augur ◆길흉화복을 점치다 tell fortunes

점토 粘土 clay
◆점토질의 clayey; clayish 《soil》 / 점토로 만들다 make *sth* of clay
■―내화(耐火)― refractory clay; fireclay ―광물 clay mineral ―세공 〈물건〉 clay works; 〈공작〉 clay modeling ―암 〔鑛〕 claystone ―층 a clay layer

점판암 粘板岩 〔地球物〕 (clay) slate

점퍼 a jumper; a jacket

점포 店鋪 a shop; 〈美〉 a store
◆점포를 갖다 keep a store / 점포를 열다 open the store; 〈개업하다〉 open [start] a store; open [start] business / 점포를 닫다 close a store; 〈폐업하다〉 〈美〉 close up the store; 〈英〉 shut up shop; close down [wind up] business
■―광고 a store advertising ―정리 판매 a winding-up sale

점프 〈뜀질〉 a jump ―점프하다 jump

점하다 占― occupy; hold; take (up) ⇒ 차지(~하다) ▶한국인의 식자율(識字率)은 1990년에 96.3%를 점했다 The literacy rate of Koreans occupied 96.3% in 1990.

점호 點呼 (a) roll call; (a) call-over; rollcalling; calling over
◆점호 때에 at roll call
―점호하다 take roll call; call the roll 《of》; roll-call; call (over) the names 《of》

점화 點火 ignition; lighting ―점화하다 ignite; light; kindle; fire (up) 《an engine》
■―장치 an ignition system ―플러그 a spark plug

접 〈과실·야채의 백 개〉 a [one] hundred

접접 [植] grafting ♦접을 붙이다 graft ⇨ 접목(~하다)
접각 接角 〈인접한 각〉〔幾〕an adjacent angle
접객 接客 entertaining [receiving, serving] guests —접객하다 receive [entertain] a guest
접객업 接客業 the service trade; the entertainment business; the hotel and restaurant business ♦접객업에 종사하다 engage [be] in the service trade —자 hotel and restaurant keepers [businessmen]
접견 接見 an interview; a reception; an audience
—접견하다 receive *sb* 《in audience》; have an interview 《with》; give [grant] an interview [audience] 《to》
▶대통령은 어제 주한 외국사절을 접견했다 The president received foreign envoys in Korea yesterday.
■—실 a reception room [hall] —일 a reception day
접경 接境 a border; a boundary
—접경하다 border 《on》; abut 《on》
접골 接骨 bonesetting; coaptation
—접골하다 coapt; set 《a broken leg》
—사(師) a bonesetter : 접골사에게 부러진 왼쪽 다리를 접골했다 I had my broken left leg set by a bonesetter. —술 bonesetting
접근 接近 1 〈가까이 함〉 approximation; access; approach; 〈국제관계의〉〔프〕 rapprochement
—접근하다 approach; come [draw, get] near; come [get] close 《to》; approximate 《to》; make an approach 《to》; adjoin
♦접근하기 쉬운 accessible; easily approachable / 접근하기 어려운 inaccessible; unapproachable; difficult of access [approach]
▶개에 접근금지 Keep away from the dog!
2 〈밀접한 관계〉 intimate relations
♦선진국과의 접근을 꾀하다 bring about better relations with advanced countries
—접근하다 become intimate 《with》; be intimately related 《with》
▶이상과 현실을 더욱 접근시키다 bring the ideal and the real
■—전(戰) a close combat; 〔拳〕 infighting
접다 〈겹치다〉 fold up; double up; turn down
♦접는 우산 a foldaway [telescopic] umbrella / 접는 의자 a folding [collapsible] chair / 부채를 접다 shut a fan / 우산을 접다 fold [close, furl, shut] an umbrella / 종이를 접다 fold a piece of paper / 책장의 귀퉁이를 접다 fold down the corner of a leaf; dog's-ear / 텐트를 접다 strike a tent
▶그 아이는 종이로 학을 접었다 The child folded the paper into the shape of a crane.
접대 接待 1 (a) reception; a welcome
—접대하다 receive 《a guest》; 〈돌보다〉 attend to; welcome
♦손님을 극진히[정중히] 접대하다 receive a guest [visitor] cordially [with courtesy]
2 〈대접〉 entertainment; 〈상점 등의〉 service
—접대하다 entertain; serve
♦극진히 접대하다 give *sb* warm hospitality; entertain *sb* cordially / 손님을 잘 접대하다 〈고객에게〉 give a good service to a customer
■—부 a waitress; a service girl; a barmaid; a hostess —비 reception expenses —원 a receptionist —위원 a reception committee
접대 接臺 a host plant ◇ 접본(接本)
접두사 接頭辭 〔文法〕 a prefix 《to》
접때 some time [a few days] ago; the other day; not long ago ♦접때부터 for some days [time] past / 접때 편지에 in *one's* last letter / 접때 만났을 때 when I saw 《him》 last
접목 接木 〈접붙이기〉 grafting; 〈접붙인 나무〉 a grafted tree
—접목하다 graft [ingraft, engraft] 《in, into, onto, upon》; put a graft into 《a stock》
—법 grafting; engrafting
접미사 接尾辭 〔文法〕 a suffix
접바둑 〈하수가 미리 몇 점 놓고 두는 바둑〉 a *paduk* game which the lower grader plays with some outnumbered *paduk* stones
접변 接變 〔言〕 assimilation 《of sounds》
—접변하다 be assimilated 《to, with》
접본 接本 〈접붙일 때 뿌리 쪽 나무〉 the stool; a parent plant; a host plant
접붙이다 接— graft ⇨ 접목(~하다)
♦접붙이는 사람 a grafter
접사 接辭 〈단어나 어간에 첨가되는 말〉 an affix
▶unkind의 un- 같은 접두사와 careless의 -less 같은 접미사는 모두 접사다 The prefix such as un- in unkind and the suffix such as -less in careless are both affixes.
접사다리 〈높이를 연장하는 사다리〉 a stepladder
접선 接線 1 〔數〕 a tangent; a tangential line 2 〈접촉〉 contact; touch
—접선하다 make contact 《with》; contact; touch; come in [into] contact [touch] 《with》
접속 接續 connection; joining; junction; 〔電〕 a joint; splice; splicing
—접속하다 connect; join; conjoin; adjoin; link
▶이 기차는 포항행과 접속된다 This train connects [makes connection(s)] with one for P'ohang.
■—곡 〔樂〕 a medley; 〔프〕 a potpourri —선 a connecting line —역 〈연결역〉 a junction station; 〈합동역〉 a union station
접속사 接續詞 〔文法〕 a conjunction; a connective ■등위[종속]— a coordinate [subordinate] conjunction
접수 接收 seizure; requisition; take-over
—접수하다 requisition; take over; impound; 〈징발하다〉 commandeer
♦철도를 접수하다 take over a railway / 접수되다 be under requisition; be taken over 《by》
■—가옥 a requisitioned house —해제 derequisition
접수 接受 reception; acceptance; receipt
—접수하다 receive 《a petition, an application》; accept 《an application》; be in receipt of; pick up; take up 《an appeal》
▶원서는 1일부터 접수합니다 Applications will be accepted on and after the first.
■—국(國) a recipient country —기한 the time for application —번호 the application number; the receipt number —자 a recep-

tionist; a reception [an information] clerk; an usher —처 a reception [an information] desk [office]; 〈창구〉 a receiving window

접시 1 〈평평한〉 a plate; 〈우묵한〉 a dish; 〈큰 것〉 a platter; 〈받침 접시〉 a saucer; 〈총칭〉 flatware
♦고기 한 접시 a dish of meat / 접시에 음식을 담다 dish out food / 접시에 담아서 내놓다 serve (food) in a dish [on a plate] / 접시를 닦다 wash [《美》 do] dishes; scrub a dish
2 〈저울의〉 a scale; a bowl
■ —닦기 dish-washing; 《英》 washing-up —저울 a platform balance

접시꽃 〔植〕 a hollyhock; a rose mallow

접안 接岸 〔海〕 anchoring alongside the pier —**접안하다** come alongside the pier [quay, berth]

접안렌즈 接眼— 〈눈에 대는 쪽의 렌즈〉 an eyepiece; an ocular eyepiece

접어넣다 fold in; turn [tuck] in; make a tuck in

접어들다 1 〈다가오다〉 begin; head for [toward]; set in
▶그 회사는 파산의 길로 접어들었다 The firm headed toward bankruptcy.
▶여름철로 접어든다 The summer season draws near.
▶장마철로 접어들었다 The rainy season has set in.
2 〈들어서다〉 come to; enter
♦숲속으로 접어들다 take to the woods

접어주다 1 〈바둑에서〉 give [lay] odds (of); give (one stone) advantage (over sb) ♦다섯 점 접어주다 give a five-stone handicap
2 〈너그럽게 봐주다〉 shut [close] one's eyes to (sb's mistake); overlook

접원 接圓 a tangent circle

접자 摺— 〈접었다 폈다하는 자〉 a carpenter's rule; a jointed measuring rule; a zigzag rule; a folding scale [rule]

접전 接戰 〈싸움의〉 a close [tight] battle; a close combat; 〈경기의〉 a close contest [game, race]; a seesaw game
▶접전 끝에 톰이 이겼다 Tom won in a close contest.
—**접전하다** 〈싸우다〉 fight hand to hand; fight at close quarters; fight [engage in] a close fight; come to close combat [quarters]; 〈경쟁하다〉 be in keen competition (with); 〈경기에서〉 have a close contest [game] (with)

접점 接點 〔數〕 a point of contact [tangency]

접종 接種 〔醫〕 inoculation; vaccination
—**접종하다** inoculate; vaccinate
♦병균을 접종하다 inoculate sb with viruses
■ 비시지— inoculation of BCG 예방— preventive inoculation ■ —요법 a vaccine cure

접종 接踵 〈왕래[사건]의 계속〉 occurring in succession; following
—**접종하다** follow heel after heel; follow [step, tread] on the heels of sb; occur one after another (in quick succession)

접지 接地 〔電〕 earthing; an earth; grounding
—**접지하다** earth; ground
■ —선 an earth wire

접지 接枝 〈접본에 나뭇가지를 꽂음〉 grafting; 〈가지〉 a graft; a slip —**접지하다** graft

접지 摺紙 〈종이접기〉 paper folding; 〔製本〕 folding (of printed sheets) —**접지하다** fold printed sheets (to bind a book) ■ —공 a folder —기 a folding machine; a folder

접착 接着 adhesion; gluing —**접착하다** bond; adhere to; stick to —력 adhesive force —제 adhesives —테이프 adhesive tape

접촉 接觸 contact; touch; 〔電〕 (electrical) contact; 〔數〕 tangency
♦접촉을 유지하다 keep in touch [contact] (with); keep touch / 접촉을 피하다 avoid contact with / 접촉을 끊다 get out of contact [touch] (with); 〈전류의〉 break contact
▶나는 그 사람과 개인적인 접촉이 있다[없다] I am in [out of] personal contact with him.
—**접촉하다** touch; contact; make contact with; come in [into] contact [touch] with
▶이 두 가닥의 전선이 접촉하면 기계가 움직이기 시작한다 When these two wires touch [come into contact], the machine starts.
■ —각 an angle of contact —감염[전염] 〔醫〕 contagion; contact infection: 콜레라는 접촉감염으로 확산된다 Cholera spreads by contagion. —기(器) 〔電〕 a contactor —면 a contact surface —법 〔化〕 the contact process —부 〈기계 등의〉 a contacting part —비행 〔空〕 contact flying; a contact flight —사고 a near collision; a minor collision; a scrape with another vehicle: 접촉사고를 일으키다 have a minor collision (with) —산화 catalytic oxidation —원 〔數〕 an osculating circle —전기 contact electricity —제 〔化〕 a contact agent —촉매반응 〔化〕 (a) contact catalytic reaction

접촉성 接觸性 contagiousness ■ —알레르기 contact allergy —질환 a contagious disease

접촉작용 接觸作用 〔化〕 catalysis
♦접촉작용을 하다 catalyze

접치다 1 ⇨ 접다 2 ⇨ 접치이다

접치이다 get folded; be doubled (up) ⇨ 접히다

접칼 〈접는 칼〉 a clasp knife; a pocketknife

접피술 接皮術 skin grafting ＝ 피부(~이식(術))

접하다 接— 1 touch
♦많은 사람과 접하다 come in(to) contact with many people
2 〈인접하다〉 adjoin; be adjacent (to); be contiguous (to); border (on); abut (against, on)
♦하천에 접한 땅 the land abutting on the river
▶캘리포니아는 멕시코와 접하고 있다 California is contiguous with [to] Mexico.
3 〈받다〉 get; come to hand; hear; receive; be in receipt of
♦부음에 접하다 receive a notice of sb's death; hear of sb's death
▶귀하의 팩스를 접하였습니다 Your fax has come to hand.
4 〈일에 부닥치다〉 meet with; come across; encounter; experience
▶위급한 사고에 접해서는 침착성을 잃지 마라

When you meet with an urgent accident, do not loose your presence of mind.

접합 接合 connection; joining; union; junction; 〈혈관 등의〉 inosculation; 〈생식세포의〉 conjugation
―**접합하다** join; unite; connect; put together; 〈혈관을〉 inosculate; 〈生〉 conjugate
―**자(子)[체][生] a zygote; 〔植〕〈접합포자〉 a zygospore ―재(材) a binder ―제 glue

접히다 1 〈종이 등이〉 be [get] folded; fold; be doubled (up)
♦ 네 겹으로 접히다 be folded in four
2 〈바둑에서〉 have 〈one stone〉 advantage 〈over sb〉; receive odds
♦ 두점 접히다 receive a two-stone handicap

젓 salted [soused] fish [shrimps]
♦ 멸치젓 salted [soused] anchovies / 새우젓을 담그다 salt [souse] shrimps

젓가락 (a pair of) chopsticks
♦ 젓가락으로 먹다 eat with chopsticks / 젓가락도 대지 않다 leave (the food) untouched
■ ―**통** a chopstick case [stand]

젓갈 salted fish ⇨ 젓
젓갖 two leather string to tie hawk's legs
젓국 salted-fish juice
젓다 1 〈노를〉 row (a boat); scull; paddle; work at (oars); pull [ply] an oar
♦ 배를 젓다 row a boat / 한 번 젓다 row a stroke / 힘껏 젓다 row with all one's might; bend to [strain at] the oar / 크게 젓다 row (with) a long stroke / 노를 잘[잘못] 젓다 pull a good [bad] oar
2 〈액체를〉 stir (up) (coffee); churn (milk); beat up (cream); 〈뒤섞다〉 mix up
♦ 수저로 젓다 stir (one's tea) with a spoon / 달걀을 저어 거품을 내다 whip [beat] an egg
3 〈손을〉 wave (one's hand); 〈머리를〉 shake (one's head); 〈손짓하다〉 gesture; gesticulate; give a hand signal
▶ 그는 고개를 저었다 He shook his head.
▶ 그는 손을 저어 조용히 하라고 했다 He waved his hand for silence.

정[1] 〈연장〉 a burin; a chisel; a graver
정[2] 〈정말로〉 really; truly; actually; quite; indeed; very
♦ 정 그렇다면 if that's really the case

정 丁 1 〈십간의〉 the fourth; of the 10 Heven's Stems 2 〈등급의〉 the fourth grade; grade D
정 正 1 〈올바름〉 right; righteousness; rectitude; justice
2 〈사본·부본에 대해〉 the original
♦ 정본 the original copy
3 〈준(準)·부(副)에 대한〉 ♦ 정 교수 a full professor
4 〈부(負)·음(陰)에 대한〉 〔數〕 정수(正數) a positive number
5 〈정확한〉 due ♦ 정남으로 가다 go due south

정 疔 〔醫〕 a carbuncle; a furuncle
정 情 1 〈동정〉 sympathy; compassion; pity; 〈자비〉 mercy; charity; 〈친절〉 kindness; 〈감정〉 feeling(s); 〈정서〉 sentiment; emotion(s); 〈심정〉 heart
♦ 연민의 정 pity; compassion / 정이 많다 be kindhearted; have a kind [warm] heart / 정이 가다 feel friendly 《toward》 / 정이 들다 grow [be] intimate 《with》 / 정에 약하다 be susceptible; be tenderhearted
▶ 오는 정이 있어야 가는 정이 있지 《속담》 Claw me, and I'll claw thee.
2 〈애정〉 affection; attachment; devotion; a tender feeling; tender sentiment; love
♦ 부부의 정 conjugal affection / 부모의 정 parental affection / 부모 자식 사이의 정 the affection between parent and child / 정이 들다 feel affection 《toward》; have a tender feeling 《for》; feel tender 《toward》 / 정을 쏟다 give sb great affection / 정을 통하다 have a liaison [an affair, an amour, an intrigue] with sb; become intimate with 《a man, a woman》
▶ 나는 그 아이에게 정이 쏠렸다 My heart went (out) to the child.
3 〈사정〉 circumstances; 〈사실〉 the truth; the facts

정 精 1 ⇨ 정수(精髓)
2 〈정령〉 a spirit; a sprite
3 ⇨ 정수(精水)

정 町 unit of distance; a jeong (약 110m); unit of area; a jeong (약 9,900m²)
-정 -整 net [neat] amount
♦ 만원정 10,000 won flat
-정 -錠 a tablet

정가 〔植〕 a pigweed; a goosefoot
정가 正價 a (net) price
♦ 정가로 사다 buy sth at a net [fair] price
♦ 공(公)― a net [fair] price
정가 定價 a fixed [labeled, list, set, definite, marked] price
♦ 정가를 매기다 set a price on (an article) / 정가로 팔다 sell at a fixed price / 정가를 올리다 raise [put up] the price / 정가를 내리다 reduce [lower, cut down] the price
■ 공(公)― ⇨ 공정가격(公定價格) ■ ―표(票) a price tag: 물건에 정가표를 붙이다 fix a price tag to an article

정가극 正歌劇 〔樂〕 a grand opera
정각 正刻 the exact time ♦ 3시 정각에 just [exactly, punctually] at three; at three sharp
정각 定刻 the appointed hour; the time appointed 《for》; the fixed [regular] time [hour]
♦ 정각에 도착하다 arrive duly [on schedule, on time] / 정각보다 늦다[늦게 닿다] be behind time [schedule]; be later than due / 정각에서 10분 늦다 be ten minutes behind time

정각 頂角 〔數〕 〈꼭지각〉 a vertical angle
정간 停刊 prohibition [suppression, suspension] of publication
▶ 당국은 잡지의 정간을 해제했다 The authority released the suspension of a magazine.
―**정간하다** prohibit [suppress, suspend] publication
정간당하다 be suspended
정갈스럽다 clean ⇨ 정갈하다
정갈하다 clean; neat; dapper; tidy; trim
♦ 옷차림이 정갈하다 be neatly dressed / 방을 정갈하게 해두다 keep a room neat and clean
▶ 이 음식점은 정갈한 요리 솜씨로 유명하다

This restaurant is famous for its clean culinary art.

정감 情感 humane feelings; emotion; sentiment ◆ 정감있는 humane / 정감있게 말하다 speak with emotion [feeling]; speak soulfully [feelingly]

정강 政綱 〈정치의〉 a political principle [platform, program]; 〈정당의〉 a policy; a (party) platform
◆ 신당의 정강 the platform of a new party

정강이 the shank; the shin
◆ 정강이가 까지다 have *one's* shin barked / 정강이를 걷어치다 give *sb* a kick on the shin; kick *sb* in the (right) shin
▶ 그는 정강이를 바위에 부딪쳤다 He hit his shin against a rock.
■—받이 leggings; 〈경기용의〉 leg [shin] guards —뼈 the shinbone; 〔解〕 the tibia (*pl.* ~s, -ae)

정객 政客 a politician; a statesman

정거 停車 a stop ⇨ 정차(停車)
■—급 a sudden stop: 버스가 급정거했다 The bus came to a sudden stop.

정거장 停車場 〈기차역〉 a (railway) station; 〈美〉 a railroad station; 〈버스 정류소〉 a bus stop
◆ 〈열차가〉 정거장을 떠나다 leave [go out of, get clear of] the station
▶ 거기까지는 한 정거장밖에 안된다 It is only a station off.

정격 正格 regularity ◆ 정격의 regular; correct; orthodox; 〔樂〕 authentic
■—선법(旋法) 〔樂〕 an authentic mode —활용 〔言〕 a regular conjugation

정격 定格 〔電〕 rating ◆ 정격의 rated
■—마력 a rated horsepower (略 r.h.p.) —전류 a rated current —전압 rated voltage

정견 定見 a fixed opinion; a definite view [opinion]; 〈지론〉 a settled [firm] conviction
◆ 정견이 없는 사람 a man without settled convictions
▶ 그는 정견이 없다 He has no definite opinion of his own.

정견 政見 *one's* political views [opinions]
◆ 정견의 차이 political differences; differences in political opinions / 정견을 발표하다 state [give out, set forth, publish] *one's* political views / 정견을 달리하다 have different political views
■—발표회 a campaign meeting —방송 a (TV, radio) broadcast of political opinions [views] (by election candidates)

정결 淨潔 cleanliness; neatness; purity
—정결하다 clean; neat; undefiled; pure
◆ 정결한 물 clear [pure] water / 몸을 정결하게 하다 keep *oneself* (neat and) clean
▶ 네 방을 정결하게 해라 Keep your room clean (and tidy).

정경 政經 politics and economics
◆ 정경 분리의 원칙 the principle of separation of political matters from economic matters
■—학부 the department of politics and economics; the politico-economic department

정경 情景 〈광경〉 a scenery; a sight
◆ 눈물겨운 정경 a pathetic scene

정계 政界 the political world [arena]; the world of politics; political circles [quarters]
◆ 정계의 동향 the trend in political circles / 정계의 거물 a prominent [big] leader in politics; a great political figure / 정계의 정화 a cleanup of political circles / 정계의 사정에 정통하다 be familiar with political affairs / 정계로 진출하다 enter the political world; go in for politics
▶ 아버지는 70세에 정계에서 은퇴하셨다 My father retired from political life at the age of seventy.

정곡 正鵠 the point; the mark; the bull's-eye
◆ 정곡을 찌르다 be to the point; hit the mark / 정곡을 벗어나다 be not to the point
▶ 그 남자의 대답은 정곡을 찌른 것이었다 His answer was to the point.

정골 整骨 bonesetting ⇨ 접골

정공법 正攻法 the standard tactics for attack
◆ 정공법을 쓰다 employ [adopt] the standard tactics for attack

정과 正課 the regular course; a regular curriculum

정관 定款 the articles of association [incorporation]; 〈美〉 the certificate of incorporation; 〈英〉 the memorandum of association; a statute ◆ 정관 제1조 Art. 1 of the articles of association

정관 精管 〔解〕 the spermatic duct ⇨ 수정관
■—수술[절제(수)술] vasectomy

정관 靜觀 contemplation
—정관하다 contemplate; calmly watch
◆ 사태를 정관하다 calmly watch the development of the situation
■—주의 a wait-and-see policy

정관사 定冠詞 〔文法〕 the definite article

정교 正敎 1 〈바른 종교〉 orthodoxy
2 ⇨ 정교회
■—그리스— the Greek Orthodox Church

정교 政敎 〈정치와 종교〉 religion and politics; church and state; 〈정치와 교육〉 politics and education
■—분리 the separation of religion and politics [church and state] —일치 the unity of church and state

정교 情交 1 〈친교〉 friendship; intimacy
—정교하다 have friendly relations with
2 〈남녀의 색정〉 illicit (sexual) intercourse; a liaison; connection
—정교하다 have sex 《with》; have sexual intercourse 《with》; establish a liaison 《with》; have connection 《with》

정교 精巧 elaborateness; exquisiteness; delicacy —정교하다 elaborate; exquisite; delicate; ingenious
◆ 정교한 솜씨 exquisite workmanship / 정교한 작품 an elaborate work; a work showing elaborate workmanship

정교사 正敎師 a regular [full] teacher

정교회 正敎會 the Orthodox Church
◆ 그리스[동방] 정교회 the Greek [Eastern] Orthodox Church / 러시아 정교회 the Russian Orthodox Church

정구 庭球 (lawn) tennis
♦정구를 하다 play tennis
■ 경식(硬式)[연식(軟式)]— regulation-ball [soft-ball] tennis ■—공 a tennis ball —선수 a tennis player: 정구선수권 a tennis championship —시합[대회] a tennis match [tournament] —코트[장] a tennis court —화 tennis shoes

정국 政局 a political situation
♦정국의 안정[불안정] the stability [instability] of a political situation / 정국의 위기 a political crisis / 정국을 안정시키다[수습하다] stabilize the political situation / 정국을 담당하다 assume [take, be at] the helm of state affairs / 정국의 교착상태를 타개하다 break a political deadlock
▶그는 정국을 담당할 자격이 없다 He is not the right person to take over the government.

정권 政權 political [administrative] power
♦정권을 잡다[쥐다, 장악하다] take [win, attain] power; take [assume, be at] the helm of state affairs / 정권을 잃다 get [go] out of power; drop the reins of government / 정권을 이양하다 turn over the reins of government (to) / 정권을 연장하다 prolong the life of one's regime / 정권을 유지하다 stay in power / 정권욕에 불타다 burn with ambition [lust] for political power
▶영국은 현재 노동당이 정권을 잡고 있다 In Britain the Labor party is now in power.
■괴뢰— a puppet [dummy, robot] government [regime] 군사— a military regime; a junta ■—교체 the change of regime; a power change —다툼 a struggle [scramble] for political power —수립 the establishment of a government —이양 a transition [transfer] of power (to) —타도 the overthrow of a government —획득 accession to power

정규 正規 formality; regularity
♦정규의 regular; formal; proper
■—과정 the regular course: 정규 과정을 밟다 go through the regular course —교육 regular [formal] school education: 정규 교육을 받다 have regular school education —군 a regular army —병 regulars

정규 定規 1 〈규칙〉 fixed regulation; a definite rule 2 ⇨ 자

정근 精勤 diligence; industry; good [regular] attendance
♦15년간의 정근 one's fifteen-year faithful service
—정근하다 attend 《office》 regularly
■—상 a prize for good attendance; a diligence award —자 a regular attendant

정글 the jungle(s)
■—전 jungle fighting —짐 〈아동용 운동구〉 a jungle gym

정금 正金 1 〈순금〉 pure [solid, true] gold 2 〈금화·은화〉 specie
■—수송점 [經] a specie [gold] point —은행 a specie bank

정기 丁幾 tincture ⇨ [藥] 팅크
정기 定期 a fixed period; a stated term
♦정기의[적인] regular; periodic(al) / 정기로, 정기적으로 regularly; periodically; at a fixed period; at regular intervals
■—간행 a periodical (publication): 정기간행물 periodicals —건강진단 a routine [periodical] medical checkup —검사 periodical inspection —국회 an ordinary [a regular] session of the National Assembly —권 ⇨ 정기승차권 —여객기 a scheduled airliner; an airliner —연금 a terminable annuity —운행 a regular run —총회 a regular general meeting —편 a regular service [run, flight] —항공기 an [a scheduled] airliner —항공로 an air route [line]; an airway —항로 a regular line —항해 a regular service —휴일 a regular holiday [day off]; 〈상점의〉 a shop-holiday

정기 精氣 1 〈정력〉 energy; vigor; vitality 2 〈정신과 기력〉 spirit and vigor; 〈순수한 기운〉 essence (and feeling); ether

정기선 定期船 a (regular) liner; a packet (boat) ♦유럽 항로 정기선 a European liner

정기승차권 定期乗車券 a pass; (美) a commutation (commuting, commuter's) ticket; (英) a season ticket [pass] ♦정기승차권으로 다니다 〈통학·통근하다〉 commute

정기예금 定期預金 a fixed deposit; a time deposit
—자 a time depositor

정나미 情— attachment; affection; love
♦정나미가 떨어지다 be disgusted 《with, at, by》; fall out of love 《with》; be disaffected 《to, toward》
▶너한테는 이제 정나미가 떨어진다 I'm quite out of patience with you.

정남(방) 正南(方) due south

정녀 貞女 1 〈동정녀(童貞女)〉 a virgin 2 〈정부(貞婦)〉 a faithful wife

정년 丁年 (one's) majority; full age
♦정년에 달하다 attain [reach] one's majority; come [become] of age / 정년 미달이다 be under age; be in one's minority
■—미달자 a minor; a person under age —자 a major; an adult

정년 停年 the age limit; (mandatory) retirement age
♦정년에 달하다 reach the retirement age
▶우리 회사에서는 60세가 정년이다 Sixty is the retirement age in our company.
▶그는 내년에 정년이다 He is due to retire next year.
■—제 the retirement [age-limit] system —퇴직 retirement under the age limit : 그는 작년에 정년 퇴직했다 He retired at the retirement age last year.

정념 情念 1 〈느낌과 생각〉 one's feeling(s) [emotion(s)]; feeling and thought
♦애국적 정념 patriotic feelings
2 〈애정〉 affection(s); passion(s)
♦그녀에 대해 정념을 품다 conceive a passion for her

정녕 丁寧 certainly; surely; for certain; to be sure; for sure; without fail; without [beyond, out of] question
♦정녕코 certainly; surely

▶ 정녕 그러냐? Are you sure? ⇌ You bet?
▶ 정녕 그렇습니다 I assure you it is so. ⇌ 《美口》 I can bet you. ⇌ You bet!

정다각형 正多角形 〔數〕 a regular polygon
정다면체 正多面體 〔數〕 a regular polyhedron
정담 政談 a discourse on politics; a political talk
정담 情談 〈다정한〉 a friendly talk; 〈남녀의〉 a tête-à-tête; lover's talk
정담 鼎談 three-man [tripartite] talks; a three-way conversation
정답다 情— affectionate; loving; tender; intimate; friendly; 〈화목하다〉 harmonious 《life》; happy 《family》

◆ 정다운 인사 warm greetings / 정다운 말 affectionate words / 정다운 친구 a good [great, close] friend; 《口》 a chum / 정답게 살다 live happily together; be happy with / 정답게 맞이하다 give a warm reception; receive with warm hands
▶ 저 부부는 정말 정답게 지낸다 That couple gets on very well together.

정당 政黨 a political party
◆ 정당을 초월한 외교정책 supraparty foreign policy / 정당에 가입하다 join [enter] a political party; affiliate *oneself* with [to] a political party / 정당을 만들다 form [organize] a political party / 2대 정당제도 a two-party system
■ 기성— the existing political parties 보수[혁신]— a conservative [reformist] party 진보[급진]— a progressive [radical] party ■ —강령 《美》 a party platform; 《英》 a party programme —내각 a party cabinet —법 〔法〕 the Political Party Law —색 a political coloring —원 a member of a political party; a party man —정치 party politics [government] —조직 party organization

정당 精糖 〈설탕 정제〉 sugar refining; 〈정백당〉 refined sugar
정당하다 正當— just; justifiable; warrantable; right; due 《formalities》; proper; fair; reasonable 《excuse》; 〈합법적인〉 legitimate; lawful

◆ 정당한 보상 just compensation / 정당한 이유 없이 without good [sufficient] reason; without justification / 정당하게 justly; rightly; properly; duly; fairly; justifiably; warrantably; reasonably; 〈합법적으로〉 lawfully; legitimately / 정당하다고 평가하다 do *sb* justice; set due value on; duly appreciate
▶ 그녀가 그것을 거절하는 데는 정당한 이유가 있다 She has good reason to turn it down. ⇌ She is fully justified in rejecting it.
▶ 이 절차는 법률적으로 정당하다고 인정할 수 없다 This procedure is not warrantable by the law.
■ —방위 (legitimate) self-defense; legal defense; 《라》 〔法〕 se defendendo : 정당방위로 사람을 죽이다 kill a man in self-defense

정당화 正當化 justification
—정당화하다 justify; warrant
▶ 그는 자신의 행동을 정당화하려고 했다 He tried to justify himself.

▶ 그 사정은 이런 조치를 정당화했다 The circumstances warrant such measures.
▶ 목적이 수단을 정당화하는 경우가 있다 It sometimes happens that the end justifies the means.

정도 正道 the right path [track]; the path of righteousness [virtue]; the straight path
◆ 정도에 어긋나는 행위 an unrighteous [unjust] from the right path / 정도를 걷다 live [conduct *oneself*] honestly / 정도로 이끌다 guide sb into the right path / 정도에서 벗어나다 deviate from the right path

정도 程度 (a) degree; 〈범위〉 extent; measure; proportions; rate; 〈등급〉 (a) grade; 〈표준〉 (a) standard; a level; 〈한도〉 a limit
◆ 발달의 정도 the stage of development / 지능 정도 the intellectual standard / 어느 정도까지 to some [a certain] degree [extent]; to what extent [degree]; how far / 대학 정도의 교육을 받다 receive instruction of university standard / 정도를 지키다 keep within bounds; use moderation; be moderate (in drinking) / 정도를 지나치다 be excessive; go beyond bounds; go too far; go [run] to extremes / 정도를 높이다 [낮추다] raise [lower] the standard
▶ 이것은 정도의 문제다 It's a matter of degree.
▶ 그의 강의는 내게는 정도가 너무 높아 이해하기 힘들었다 His lecture was too difficult for me to follow.
▶ 그들의 생활 정도는 높다[낮다] Their standard of living is high [low].
▶ 매사에 정도라는 것이 있다 Everything has its limit.
▶ 그의 보고는 어느 정도는 맞는다 His report is in a [some] measure true.
▶ 추운 정도가 아니다 Cold is not the word.

정독 精讀 perusal; attentive [careful, intensive] reading —정독하다 peruse; read carefully [attentively, with care]

정돈 停頓 a deadlock; a standstill; a stalemate; a setback
◆ 정돈 상태에 있다 be at a deadlock [standstill]; be in a stalemate
▶ 휴전회담이 정돈 상태에 빠졌다 The truce talks came to [at] a deadlock.
—정돈하다 come to a standstill; be held up; reach a deadlock; bog down

정돈 整頓 proper arrangement; (good) order; adjustment
—정돈하다 put in order; put [set] to rights; arrange properly
◆ 정돈된 orderly; in (good) order; shipshape / 방을 정돈하다 put a room to rights [in order]; straighten up a room / 정돈해 두다 have [keep] in good order / 정돈되어 있지 않다 be in disorder; be out of order
▶ 그의 방은 잘 정돈되어 있었다 His room was shipshape.
■ —선반 〔軍〕 a kit shelf

정동 正東 due east
정동 精銅 refined copper
정동사 定動詞 〔文法〕 a finite verb
정들다 情— 〈사람에게〉 become familiar [ac-

quainted] 《with》; get intimate 《with》; become attached 《to》; 〈이성에〉 fall in love 《with》; 〈장소 등에서〉 get used to 《a place》
♦ 정든 님 〈남자〉 one's lover; her (young) man; 〈여자〉 one's love [sweetheart]; one's (best) girl / 정든 집 one's dear old house; one's beloved home / 여자에게 정들다 fall in love with [become fond of] a girl

정떨어지다 情― get [be] disaffected 《with》; be disgusted 《with》; be sick 《of》
♦ 정떨어지는 일[이야기] a disgusting affair [story]
▶ 그녀의 얼굴을 보면 정떨어진다 Her face quite puts me off.

정략 政略 1 〈정치상의 책략〉 political tactics; a political maneuver [move]; a policy
♦ 정략적인 political
2 〈책략〉 an artifice; 〈방편〉 an expedient
♦ 정략을 쓰다 use artifice; resort to an expedient
■ ―가 a clever political tactician ―결혼 a marriage of convenience; a marriage for political reasons

정량 定量 a fixed [determinate] quantity; 〈내복약의〉 a dose ♦ 정량의 quantitative
■ ―분석 [化] quantitative analysis

정력 精力 energy; vigor; vitality; hustle
♦ 정력의 소모 loss of energy / 정력적인 energetic; vigorous / 정력을 기울이다 put all one's energies 《into》 / 정력이 떨어지다 lose one's energy / 정력을 북돋우다 energize; invigorate
▶ 그는 그 연구에 온 정력을 쏟았다 He put all his energies into the research.
■ ―가 a man of (great) energy [vigor]; an energetic person

정련 精練 1 〈연습〉 good training [drill] ―정련하다 train [drill] well
2 〈섬유의〉 scouring ―정련하다 scour

정련 精鍊 refining; refinement; smelting ―정련하다 refine; smelt 《copper》
■ ―소 a (re)finery; a smelter(y) ―업 the refining industry ―업자 a refiner

정렬 整列 standing in a row; an array; a line-up ―정렬하다 stand in a row; form (a line); form in to a line; line [be lined] up; be drawn up; 〔軍〕 fall in
♦ 4열 횡대[종대]로 정렬하다 stand in four rows [files] / 6열로 정렬하다 be drawn [lined] up six deep [in six lines] / 정렬해서 기다리다 wait in 〔美〕 on] line / 군(군인을) 정렬시키다 get (soldiers) fallen in; fall (soliders) in
▶ 군인들이 2열 횡대[종대]로 정렬하였다 The solidiers stood in two rows [files].
▶ 정렬! 〈口令〉 Fall in!

정령 政令 a government ordinance [decree]; a cabinet order
■ ―위반 violation of a government ordinance

정령 精靈 〈혼백〉 the spirit of a dead person; 〈영혼〉 the spirit; the soul; the ghost; 〈초목 등의〉 deities; a spirit; a genius (*pl.* genii)
■ ―설 animism; spiritualism ―숭배 spiritism; animism

정례 定例 usage; a custom
♦ 정례의 regular; ordinary; usual / 정례에 따라[의하여] according to usage [practice]
■ ―각의[국무회의] an ordinary [a regular] Cabinet meeting [conference, council] ―기자회견 a regular press conference [interview]

정론 正論 a just [sound, fair] argument

정론 定論 an established [a fixed] opinion; an established theory

정론 政論 political arguments [discussion]

정류 停留 stoppage; a stop ―정류하다 stop; halt

정류 精溜 〔化〕 rectification; refinement ―정류하다 rectify; purify; refine
■ ―알코올 rectified alcohol [spirit]

정류 整流 〔電〕 rectification; commutation; 〔電子〕 detection ―정류하다 rectify; commute; commutate; detect
■ ―관 a rectifying tube [valve] ―기(器) a rectifier ―자(子) a commutator

정류장 停留場 a station; a stopping place; 〈버스의〉 a stop ■ 버스― a bus stop 지하철― a subway station

정률 定律 〔物・化〕 a fixed law; 〔樂〕 a fixed rhythm

정률 定率 a fixed rate
■ ―세 proportional tax

정리 定理 〔數〕 a theorem; a proposition
♦ 피타고라스의 정리 Pythagorean theorem
■ 다항[2항]― the multinomial [binomial] theorem

정리 情理 reason and sentiment [feeling]; heart and mind
♦ 그와의 친한 정리를 고려해서 considering the reason and feeling of intimate terms with him

정리 整理 1 〈가지런하게 바로잡음〉 arrangement; adjustment; regulation; 〈통합정리〉 consolidation
―정리하다 (re)arrange; put in order; put *sth* to rights; (re)adjust; regulate; consolidate
♦ 자료를 정리하다 arrange data; pigeonhole data / 서류를 정리하다 sort out papers / 원고를 정리하다 copy-edit / (은행의) 장부를 정리하다 adjust accounts / 회의장을 정리하다 restore order in the chamber / 유고를 정리하다 edit *sb*'s posthumous works
2 〈해체・해소〉 liquidation; disorganization; reorganization; 〈완불〉 full payment; settlement
―정리하다 liquidate; disorganize; wind up; 〈완불하다〉 clear [pay] off; pay in full; settle [pay] 《*one*'s debts》
♦ 채무를 정리하다 settle *one*'s debts / 회사를 정리하다 liquidate a company
3 〈감원〉 retrenchment; curtailment; a shake-up 〈대규모의〉; 〈매각〉 disposition; clearance
―정리하다 retrench; curtail; cut; 〈팔아버리다〉 dispose of; sell
♦ 폐품을 정리하다 dispose of waste / 가재를 정리하다 dispose of *one*'s household goods and furniture
■ ―경지 readjustment of arable land 인원― a personnel cut [reduction]; curtailment of the personnel ■ ―공채 〔英史〕 consolidated annuities; consols ―부(部) 〈신문사의〉 the

정립 copydesk: 정리부원 a copyreader; a deskman —안 a readjustment plan —위원회 an adjustment committee —자금 consolidated capital —장 a chest of drawers; 《美》 a commode —함 〔상자〕《서류의》 a filing cabinet

정립 鼎立 a triangular position
—정립하다 take a triangular position; be in a three-cornered [triangular] contest; stand in a trio
▶ 그 당시 3대 강국은 정립 상태에 있었다 The three big countries were opposed to one another at that time.

정말 正- **1** 〈명사적〉 the truth; a fact; reality
♦ 정말같은 거짓말 a plausible [specious] lie / 정말은 in fact; in reality [actuality]; to speak [confess] the truth; the truth (of the matter) is 《that...》 / 정말로 여기다 take 《a thing》 for truth; take 《a joke》 seriously; accept 《a remark》 (as true [truth]); believe 《a statement》 (to be true)
▶ 그 소문은 정말이냐? Is there any truth in the rumor?
▶ 정말은 내가 혼자서 했다 As a matter of fact, I did it [by] myself.
▶ 그의 말은 정말같이 들린다 His words ring [sound] true [like truth]. ⇌ He seems to be telling the truth.
2 〈감탄사적〉 indeed; really; really and truly
3 〈부사적〉 really ⇨ 정말로
▶ 정말 감사합니다 Thank you very much.
▶ 이것 정말 큰일이군 This is really a serious matter.
▶ 우리는 공원에서 정말 즐거운 하루를 보냈다 We spent a really pleasant day in the park.

정말로 正- 〈참으로〉 really; truly; indeed; 〈확실히〉 certainly; surely; to be sure; 〈진심으로〉 heartily; sincerely; from the bottom of *one's* heart; 〈매우〉 very; much; quite; greatly; extremely; 《口》 awfully; 《口》 terribly
▶ 정말로 지독한 추위다 Very cold indeed.
▶ 정말로 아름답다 It is really beautiful.
▶ 정말로 미안합니다 I'm terribly sorry.
▶ 우리는 단지 말로만이 아니라 정말로 도움이 필요하다 We need actual help, not just promises.
▶ 정말입니다 Believe me. ⇌ Take my word for it.
▶ 정말로 하는 말이냐? Do you really mean it?
▶ 그 사건의 증거를 이렇게 많이 모았다면 그는 정말로 무혐의가 될 것이 틀림없다 Since we have gathered this much evidence for the case, he must be really innocent.

정맥 精麥 scoured barley; cleaning barley [wheat]; cleaned [polished] barley [wheat]
—기 a barley-[wheat-]cleaning machine

정맥 靜脈 〔解〕 a vein
♦ 정맥의 venous [venose] 《blood》
■경(頸)— the jugular (vein) 안면— the facial vein ■경화증 〔醫〕 phlebosclerosis —계통 the venous system —류(瘤) 〔醫〕 a varix 《*pl.* varices》 —염(炎) 〔醫〕 phlebitis —주사 an intravenous injection —혈 venous blood

정면 正面 the front; 〈건물의〉 the facade; the frontage; the front part
♦ 정면의 frontal; front / 정면에 in front 《of》; just [right] opposite 《to》 / 정면에서 보다 take a front view 《of》 / 정면으로 공격하다 attack frontally [in front]; make a frontal attack on; 〈공공연하게〉 attack *sb* openly / 정면으로 벽에 부딪치다 run face into a wall
▶ 이 건물의 정면 입구는 어디입니까? Where is the front entrance of this building?
▶ 우리집 정면에 공원이 있다 There is a park in front of my house.
▶ 그는 선생님에게 정면으로 반대하였다 He directly opposed his teacher.
■—공격 a frontal attack —도(圖) a front view 《of》

정면충돌 正面衝突 a head-on collision; a frontal clash
—정면충돌하다 collide [clash] head-on 《with, against》; come into a head-on collision 《with》; run [go] smash 《into》

정모 正帽 〈정장 모〉 a full-dress hat; 〈예모〉 a ceremonial hat; 〈제모〉 a regulation cap

정묘 精妙 exquisiteness; elaboration
—정묘하다 exquisite; elaborate; fine; subtle; delicate

정무 政務 political affairs; state affairs
♦ 정무를 보다 administer the affairs of state
—장관 (First) Minister of State for Political Affairs —차관 《英》 a parliamentary secretary

정문 正文 the (official) text
정문 正門 the front [main] gate; the main entrance ♦ 정문으로 들어가다 go in at the front gate; enter by the main gate

정문 頂門 the crown (of the head) ⇨ 정수리
■—일침(一鍼) giving *sb* a touch on the sore place [spot]; a home thrust; a piercing reproach : 정문일침을 하다 give an admonition to the point

정문 正文 the original text

정물 靜物 **1** 〈움직이지 않는 물건〉 an object at rest; an inanimate object; 〈총칭〉 still life
2 ⇨ 정물화
■—사진 a still

정물화 靜物畫 a (picture of) still life ■—가 a still-life painter

정미 正味 net ♦ 세금 공제 후 정미 1천 달러 a clear [net] one thousand dollar after taxes / 정미 3일의 휴가 a clear [net] three days of vacation / 정미의 net; clear
■—가격 a net price —마력 net horsepower —중량[수량] the net weight [quantity]

정미 精米 rice cleaning [polishing]; 〈쌀〉 polished [cleaned] rice —정미하다 clean [polish] rice —기 a rice-cleaning machine —소 a rice(-cleaning) mill

정밀 精密 〈상세〉 minuteness; 〈정확〉 precision; accuracy
—정밀하다 minute; close; detailed; precise; exact; accurate
♦ 정밀한 지도 a detailed map / 정밀한 계획을 세우다 map out a program 《of》; make a blueprint 《of》 / 정밀하게 〈상세하게〉 minutely;

closely; in detail; 〈정확하게〉 precisely; exactly; accurately / 정밀하게 검사하다 examine closely; overhaul 《a machine》
■—검사 close examination 《of》; an overhaul —계기 a precision gauge —공업 the precision industry —공학 precision engineering —과학 an exact science —기계[기구] a precision machine [instrument] —도(度) precision —선반 a precision lathe —폭격 precision [pinpoint] bombing —화학(제)품 fine chemicals

정박 碇泊·淳泊 anchorage; anchoring; mooring ♦정박중인 선박 vessels at anchor [on the berth]
—정박하다 anchor; lie; berth; come to anchor; bring to moor; 〈닻을 내리다〉 cast [drop, let go] anchor; 〈기항하다〉 stop [call, touch, put in] at
♦정박하고 있다 be [lie, ride] at anchor; be in port [harbor]; be on the berth; be moored 《at the pier》; stay in port
■—기간 lay time —등 an anchor light; a riding lamp [light] —료[세] anchorage (dues); berthage; (英) groundage —시설 harbor accommodation(s) —지 an anchorage; a moorage; a berth —항 an anchorage harbor

정반대 正反對 the direct opposite [contrary]; the exact [perfect] opposite; the exact [very] reverse; just the opposite
♦정반대로 in direct opposition 《to》; directly opposite 《to》; diametrically / 정반대다 be just the opposite 《of》; be diametrically [diagonally, directly] opposite [opposed] 《to》; be quite contrary 《to》/ 정반대 방향으로 가다 go in the opposite [reverse] direction
▶그들의 성격은 전혀 정반대다 Their characters are completely opposite.
▶「덥다」는 「춥다」의 정반대다 'Hot' is opposite [contrary] to 'cold.' ⇌ 'Hot' is the (exact) opposite of 'cold'.
▶그는 그 뜻을 정반대로 해석했다 He interpreted the meaning in the opposite way.

정반응 正反應 〔化〕 forward reaction
정반합 正反合 〔哲〕 thesis-antithesis-synthesis
정방 精紡 (fine) spinning
■—기 a (fine) spinning machine
정방형 正方形 a (regular) square ⇨ 정사각형
정백 精白 1〈순백〉 pure white **2**〈정제〉 refinery; polishing ■—당 refined sugar —미 polished [cleaned] rice
정벌 征伐 conquest; subjugation; 〈원정〉 an expedition —정벌하다 subjugate; conquer; suppress; send an expedition 《to》
♦적을 정벌하다 conquer the enemy
■—군 an expeditionary force
정범 正犯 〔法〕 the principal offense
■—자 the principal offender
정법 定法 a fixed [an established] law [rule]
정변 政變 a political change; a change of government; a coup d'état
정병 精兵 crack [elite] troops; picked men; proved soldiers
♦정병 3만 a crack troop of 30,000 strong
정보 情報 《a piece of》 information 《about, on》; intelligence 《of》; a report; 〈외교·거래상의〉 advice(s); news
♦확실한 근거가 있는 정보 information from a reliable source / 귀중한 정보 a valuable piece [bit] of information / 최신 정보 the latest information [news] / 정보의 누설 a leakage of information / 모처에서 입수한 정보에 의하면 according to information received in certain quarters
▶정보가 외부로 누설되었다 The information leaked out.
▶정보가 아직 들어오지 않았다 No information has been received.
▶그가 한국에 온다는 정보를 퍼뜨려라 Release information that he will come to Korea.
▶나는 그것에 관해서는 아무런 정보도 갖고 있지 않다 I don't know anything about it.
▶우리는 그 책에서 많은 귀중한 정보를 얻을 수 있다 We can get [obtain] a lot of valuable information from the book. ⇌ The book gives us [provides] a lot of valuable information.
▶너는 그 정보를 어디서 입수했니? What's the channel [source] of your information?
▶그건 쓸 만한 정보다 That's a useful piece of infomation.
■—허위 a false [wrong] tip ■—경로[루트] a channel of information; 〈기밀의〉 a pipeline —과 the information division; the Public Information Section —과다 (a) surfeit of information —과학[공학] information science [engineering] —관리 시스템 information management system —국 the information [intelligence] bureau; the (Cabinet) Information Board; the Public Information Division (외무부 등의) —기관 the secret (intelligence) service; a counterintelligence corps (대첩보부대) —망 an intelligence network: 그들은 전세계에 정보망을 가설했다 They set up an intelligence network all over the world. —부대 an intelligence unit [organization] —산업 the information [communication] industry —원(員) an informer; an (intelligence) agent —원(源) a news [information] source; a source of news —장교 an intelligence officer —정치 tip-off politics —제공자 an informant; an informer —처리 information processing —혁명 information revolution —화 사회 an information-oriented society —활동 intelligence activities

정복 正服 formal attire; a formal dress; a uniform
■—경찰관 a policeman in full dress
정복 征服 (a) conquest; subjugation; mastery
♦인류에 의한 자연의 정복 man's conquest over nature
—정복하다 conquer; subjugate; overcome; master 《English》; subdue
♦정복할 수 없는 unconquerable; invincible / 정상을 정복하다 conquer the summit; climb to the mountain top / 자연을 정복하다 subdue nature
▶그는 겨울에 에베레스트산을 정복했다 He conquered the summit of Mount Everest in winter. ⇌ He succeeded in reaching the sum-

정본

mit of Mount Everest in winter.
▶그는 마침내 취약한 과목을 정복했다 At last he has mastered his weak subjects.
■—욕 desire for conquest —자 a conqueror; a subjugator; a vanquisher

정본 正本 〈문서의 원본〉 the original (text, copy); 〈공문서의 등본〉 an officially certified copy; an exemplified [attested] copy
◆정본과 부본 the original and a copy; original and copy [duplicate]

정부 正否 right or wrong
◆정부를 확인하다 ascertain whether it is right [correct] or wrong [not]

정부 正負 〔數〕 positive and negative; plus and minus

정부 正副 〈지위〉 principal and vice; 〈서류〉 original and duplicate [copy]
◆정부 2통의 서류를 작성[제출]하다 prepare [submit] (a document) in duplicate
■—의장 the speaker and vice-speaker; the chairman and vice-chairman —통령 the president and vice-president

정부 政府 the government; 〔美〕 the Administration; 〈내각〉 the cabinet; 〔英〕 the ministry
◆정부의 governmental / 한국정부 the Korean Government / 클린턴 정부 the Clinton Administration / 현 정부 the present government / 당시의 정부 the then government / 정부를 수립하다 establish [set up] a government / 정부를 지지하다[공격하다] support [attack] the Government
▶정부는 예산안을 승인했다 The government has approved the budget.
▶이번 선거 결과로 새 정부가 탄생했다 As a result of the recent election, a new government has come into power.
■세계— the World Government 연립— a coalition government [cabinet] 연방— the Federal Government 임시— a provisional government 중앙[지방]— the central [local] government ■—간행물 government [official] publications —고관 a high-ranking government official —기관 a government agency —당국 the government authorities —대표 a government representative —미(米) government-stock rice —보조금 government subsidies —보증 government guarantee —수반[소재지] the head [seat] of government —안(案) a government bill [measure]; 〔美〕 an Administration measure —자금 government funds —조직법 〔法〕 the National Government Organization Act —종합청사 the Unified [Integrated] Government Building

정부 情夫 a lover; a paramour; a beau 《pl. ~s, beaux》 ◆정부를 두다 walk out with a man

정부 情婦 a sweetheart; a mistress; a lady-love; a love; a paramour; a fancy woman [lady]; (口) one's girl ◆정부를 두다 get a mistress

정북방 正北方 due north
▶그 온천은 마을의 정북방에 있다 The spa lies due north of the town.

정분 情分 intimacy; affection; familiarity
◆정분이 두텁다 be on good terms 《with》; have a close relation 《with》

정비 正比 〔數〕 direct ratio

정비 整備 adjustment; maintenance; complete equipment; servicing
◆도로의 정비 the maintenance of roads
—정비하다 set sth in good condition [working order]; service 《an airplane》; fix 《a machine》; fit out 《a ship》; fully equip 《a factory》 with 《machinery》
◆기업을 정비하다 readjust [consolidate] an enterprise / 야구장을 정비하다 put a baseball ground in good condition / 인원을 정비히디 reshuffle the personnel / 자동차[기계]를 정비하다 fix a car [machine]
■기업— business reorganization; readjustment of enterprise 환경— (the) improvement of the environment; environment improvement —공 〈자동차의〉 a car [an automobile] mechanic; 〈기계의〉 a repairman; 〈경기장의〉 a ground(s)keeper; 〈비행기의〉 a ground crew; 〔英〕 a groundsman

정비례 正比例 〔數〕 direct proportion (↔ inverse proportion)
—정비례하다 be in direct proportion 《to》
◆…에 정비례하여 in direct proportion to...
▶X는 Y에 정비례할까 아니면 반비례할까? Is X directly or inversely proportional to Y?

정비례 定比例 〔化〕 constant [definite] proportion

정사 正史 authentic history [records, chronicles]

정사 正邪 right and [or] wrong; good and evil ◆정사를 구별하다 know [tell] right from wrong; discriminate between right and wrong

정사 正使 a senior envoy; the chief delegate

정사 政事 political [governmental] affairs; administrative business
◆정사를 보다 manage the administrative business

정사 情死 a love [double] suicide; a suicide for love
—정사하다 die together for love; commit a love [double] suicide
■강제— a forced double suicide ■—미수 an attempted double suicide

정사 情事 a love affair; lovemaking; an amour; a romance; 〈간통〉 an intrigue; a liaison ◆정사 장면을 연출하다 perform a love scene ■—혼외 extramarital intercourse

정사 精査 (a) close inspection; (a) minute investigation; a careful survey; scrutiny
—정사하다 investigate minutely; examine carefully; look closely into; scrutinize

정사 각뿔 대 正四角-臺 〔數〕 a truncated pyramid with square bases

정사각행렬 正四角行列 〔數〕 square matrix

정사각형 正四角形 a regular square [quadrilateral] ◆정사각형 탁자 a square table / 정사각형으로 자르다 cut square

정사면체 正四面體 a regular tetrahedron

정사영 正射影 〔數〕 an orthogonal projection ■—법 orthography

정사원 正社員 a regular member [employee];

a full member of the staff

정사투영도법 正射投影圖法 〔地〕 an orthographic projection

정산 精算 an accurate account; exact calculation; accurate reckoning;〈차감 계산〉adjustment;〈결산〉settlement of accounts
―정산하다 〈정밀히 계산하다〉settle accounts; calculate exactly; keep an account;〈조정하다〉adjust 《differences》
♦ 운임을 정산하다 adjust the traffic fares / 개찰구에서 정산하다 pay the adjusted fare at the ticket barrier
▶ 지금은 내가 지불할테니 나중에 나와 정산하자 I'll pay it now and you can settle with me [pay me back] later.
■ ―서 a settlement of accounts ―소 a fare adjustment office ―액 an adjusted amount ―표 a working sheet

정삼각형 正三角形 an equilateral [a regular] triangle

정상 正常 normalcy; normality ♦ 정상적인 normal; right / 정상이 아닌 abnormal; irregular; exceptional
▶ 우리의 관계는 곧 정상으로 돌아왔다 Soon our relation returned [was restored] to normal.
▶ 그가 정상이라는 것은 의심할 여지가 없다 His sanity is beyond doubt.
■ ―가격 a normal price ―궤도 the right track ―능률 normal efficiency ―상태 the normal condition [state] ―속도 a normal speed ―수심 normal depth ―아 a normal child

정상 定常 regularity; constancy
♦ 정상적으로 steadily
■ ―상태 〔物〕a stationary state; a steady state ―파 〔物〕a standing wave; a stationary wave

정상 頂上 〈산꼭대기〉the top; the summit; the crest; the peak ♦ 정상을 정복하다 conquer the (very) summit
▶ 그 산의 정상은 여름에도 눈으로 덮여 있다 The top of the mountain is covered with snow even in summer.
▶ 그들은 드디어 산의 정상에 올랐다 At last they got to the mountain peak.
■ ―회담 《hold》 a summit conference [meeting]

정상 情狀 conditions; circumstances
♦ 정상을 참작하다 make allowance for circumstances; take the circumstances into consideration
▶ 그의 범죄는 정상을 참작할 여지가 없었다 Nothing could extenuate his crime.

정상배 政商輩 businessmen with political [party] affiliation

정상화 正常化 normalization
―정상화하다 normalize; be normalized
♦ 외교 관계를 정상화하다 normalize diplomatic relations 《between, with》
■ ―국교― normalization of the diplomatic relations

정색 正色 〈안색〉a serious [solemn, grave] look; a serious countenance;〈엄정함〉seriousness; earnestness; gravity
―정색하다 become serious; look serious [grave]; assume a serious look [countenance]
♦ 정색하고 충고하다 give warning 《to sb》 with a solemn air
▶ 그 소녀는 정색하고 방안에 들어섰다 The girl came into the room with a grave [serious] look.

정색 呈色 coloration

정서 淨書 neat writing; a fair [clean] copy
―정서하다 make a clean copy 《of》; copy [write out] fair

정서 情緖 (an) emotion; feeling; heartstrings; sentiment
♦ 정서적으로 불안정한 emotionally unstable / 정서가 풍부한 full of artistic effect; charming; appealing
■ 이국― an exotic mood; exoticism ■ ―교육 culture of aesthetic sentiments [appreciation] ―장애아동 an emotionally disordered child

정서(방) 正西(方) due west

정석 定石 **1**〔바둑·將棋〕set moves in the game of *paduk* [chess]
▶ 그는 정석대로 둔다 He plays by the book.
2 〈일정한 방식〉a cardinal principle; a formula 《*pl.* ~s, -lae》
▶ 그것은 조사의 정석이다 That is only the ABC's of investigation.

정선 停船 〈항행 정지〉stopping of a ship;〈검역 정선〉quarantine ♦ 정선을 명하다 stop a ship; order a ship to heave to
―정선하다 stop; heave to; lie to; quarantine
▶ 배는 짙은 안개 때문에 정선했다 The ship was held up in a thick fog.

정선 精選 careful selection
―정선하다 select carefully [with care]; single [pick] out carefully; handpick
♦ 정선된 well-selected; choice; select 《fruit》; picked
■ ―품 choice [select] goods

정설 定說 〈학리상의〉an established theory;〈개인의〉a settled [definite] opinion;〈일반의〉an widely accepted opinion ♦ 정설을 뒤엎다 overthrow an established theory

정성 精誠 *one's* true heart; sincerity; devotion; earnestness
♦ 정성을 다하다 pour out *one's* soul; exert *oneself* to the utmost; make every effort; spare no pains / 정성을 쏟아 일하다 devote *oneself* to *one's* work; work with *one's* whole heart [devotion]
▶ 그녀는 환자를 정성껏 돌봤다 She looked after the patient devotedly.
▶ 그녀는 정성들여 아이를 길렀다 She brought up her child with great care.
▶ 이 작품은 내가 정성을 쏟은 것이다 I have given my whole mind to this work.
▶ 이것은 당신을 위해 정성들여 짠 스웨터입니다 This is the sweater that I knitted for you with my love.
―정성스럽다 sincere; heartfelt; truehearted; cordial; devoted

정성분석 定性分析 〔化〕 qualitative analysis

정세 情勢 the situation; circumstances; the state of things [affairs]; conditions; 〈형세〉 the appearance
♦ 수습할 수 없는 정세 an unmanageable [uncontrollable] situation / 정세의 변화 a change in the situation / 지금의 정세로는 under the present situation [circumstances, state of affairs]; judging by the present conditions; as matters [things] stand now / 현재의 정세에 비추어 in view of the situation; as the situation now stands / 긴박한[미묘한] 정세에 있다 be in a tense [delicate] situation / 정세(가 어떻게 진전되는지)를 살피다 see how the situation develops / 정세를 분석하다 analyze the situation / 정세에 밝다[어둡다] (ㅁ)be in [out of] the swim
▶ 그것으로 정세가 일변했다 That changed the whole situation.
▶ 전반적인 정세는 어떻습니까? What is the general situation?
▶ 정세는 심각해지고 있다 The situation is becoming serious.
■ 국제[국내]— the international [domestic] situation 세계— the world situation 일반— the general drift of affairs (in Asia) ■ —판단 (a correct) analysis (and judgement) of the situation

정세포 精細胞 〔生〕 a sperm cell

정소 精巢 a testis; a testicle; a spermary

정수 正手 〈바둑·장기의〉 the proper move

정수 正數 〔數〕 a positive number

정수 定數 1 〈일정수〉 a fixed [stated] number; the full number; 〈정족수〉 a quorum
♦ 정수에 달하다 make up the fixed number; make [get] a quorum / 정수를 넘다 exceed the number / 정수에 모자라다 fall short of the quorum; lack a quorum / 정수를 채우다 fill the necessary quorum
▶ 출석자수는 정수에 미달했다 Attendance fell below [short of] the quorum.
2 〈정해진 운수〉 fate; destiny
3 ⇨ 상수(常數)

정수 淨水 clean water ■ —기 a water purifier —장 a water purification plant; a cleaning bed

정수 精髓 1 〈골수〉 the bone marrow; the marrow (of a bone)
2 〈정화(精華)〉 the essence; the quintessence; the pith; the cream; the choice; the best
♦ 문학의 정수 the essence [quintessence] of literature / 정수를 골라내다 take essence of

정수 靜水 still water ♦ 정수의 hydrostatic ■ —역학 hydrostatics

정수 整數 〔數〕 an integer; an integral [a whole] number ■ —론 the theory of number

정수리 頂— the crown (of the head); (俗) the pate

정수식물 挺水植物 an emerged plant; an emergent

정수지 淨水池 clear well

정숙 貞淑 chastity; female virtue; feminine modesty —정숙하다 chaste; virtuous; modest
♦ 정숙한 아내 a virtuous [chaste] wife
▶ 그녀는 정숙한 여인이다 She is a chaste woman [a woman of virtue].

정숙 靜肅 silence; stillness; quietness; hush —정숙하다 silent; still; quiet; hushed
♦ 정숙하게 silently; quietly; in silence
▶ 정숙해 주십시오 Be [Keep] quiet. ⇌ Don't make a noise.
▶ 연주하는 동안 방안은 정숙했다 The room was perfectly quiet during the performance.

정승 政丞 a minister of State; a prime minister (in the Yi dynasty)

정시 正視 〈똑바로 봄〉 looking straight; 〔生理〕 stigmatism —정시하다 look *sb* in the face; look straight [square]《at》; 〈직면하다〉 confront; face
■ —렌즈 an orthoscopic lens —안(眼) emmetropia

정시 定時 regular [fixed] time; a fixed [stated] period
♦ 정시의 regular; periodical; ordinary / 정시에 regularly; periodically; on schedule / 정시를 지나서 past [beyond] the time (for)
▶ 열차는 정시에 출발했다 The train left at the scheduled time.
▶ 정시까지 그 일을 끝내주세요 Please finish the job by the fixed time.
▶ 그는 매일 정시에 출근한다 He comes to work on time every day.
▶ 그녀는 언제나 정시에 퇴근한다 She always observes regular (office) hours.
■ —제 〔教〕 the part-time (schooling) system

정식 正式 formality; due [regular] form
♦ 정식의 formal; regular; due; full-dress / 정식으로 formally; officially; regularly; duly; in due [proper] form
▶ 정식 절차를 밟아주세요 Go through due formalities.
▶ 나는 정식으로 그를 방문했다 I paid a formal visit [call] to him.
▶ 그들은 정식으로 결혼하지 않고 있다 They are not legally [properly, formally] married.
▶ 정식 통지가 오지 않는 한 안심할 수 없다 I won't feel at ease until formal notification arrives.
▶ 할머니는 정식 학교교육을 받지 않았다 My grandmother had very little formal schooling.
■ —결혼 legal [formal] marriage —식사 a regular [full-course] dinner —인가 a formal authorization —재판 (apply for) a formal trial

정식 定式 a formula (*pl.* ~s, -lae); an established [a prescribed] form

정식 定食 〈끼니〉 a regular meal; 〈정찬〉 a table d'hôte; a dinner; (英) an ordinary ♦ 정식을 먹다 have a set [regular] meal

정신 艇身 a boat's length
♦ 1 [2, 반] 정신의 차로 이기다 win《the race》 by a (boat's) length [two lengths, half a length]

정신 精神 1 〈마음〉 spirit; 〈지성〉 (a) mind; 〈넋〉 a soul; 〈의지〉 (a) will; 〈집중력〉 attention; 〈정신상태〉 mentality
♦ 숭고한 정신 a noble spirit / 비열한 정신 a mean spirit / 귀중한 정신 유산 the valuable

spiritual asset / 정신차리다 recover *one's* senses; recover consciousness; come round / 까무러쳤다가 정신차리다 recover from a faint
▶ 그는 정신이 수양되어 있다 He has a cultivated mind.
▶ 그건 정신 나간 짓이다 It's sheer madness.
▶ 나는 정신 없이 걸어다녔다 I walked about like a man in a trance.
▶ 나는 아침까지 정신없이 잤다 I slept like a log [soundly] until morning.
〈정신이[은]〉 정신이 나가다 grow absent-minded; become foolish / 정신이 없다 have a poor memory; have no spirit / 정신이 들다 come to *oneself*; recover consciousness / 정신이 말짱하다 be in *one's* right mind / 정신이 팔리다 be silly over 《a woman》; be absorbed in; be intent on
▶ 그녀는 겨우 정신이 들었다 She came to her senses at long last.
▶ 난 정신이 멀쩡해 I am sane enough.
▶ 너무 정신이 없어 우산을 놓고 왔다 I was so careless as to leave my umbrella behind.
〈정신을〉 정신을 가다듬다 brace *oneself* up; pull *oneself* together / 정신을 쏟다 concentrate *one's* attention on; devote *oneself* entirely to 《a job》; put *one's* soul into / 정신을 잃다 faint (away); lose consciousness; swoon / 정신을 차리다 collect *one's* mind
▶ 그는 정신을 못차릴 정도로 취했다 He is so drunk (that) he is out of his senses. ⇌ He is dead drunk.
▶ 정신을 어디다 빼놓고 있는거야 You're forgetting yourself!
▶ 그는 그 일에 온 정신을 쏟았다 He put his heart and soul into the work. ⇌ He devoted himself heart and soul to the work. ⇌ He did the work heart and soul.
▶ 공부하는데 좀더 정신을 집중시켜라 Concentrate [Focus] more attention on your studies.
▶ 나는 실패하고 난 뒤에야 정신을 차렸다 My failure brought me to my senses.
〈정신에〉 정신에 이상이 있다 be [get] mentally deranged; have a mental breakdown; become insane; go mad
〈정신으로〉 제 정신으로 그런 소리 하니? Do you say so in earnest?
2 〈근본 이념〉 the spirit
♦ 헌법의 정신을 존중하다 respect the spirit of the constitution / 헌법의 정신에 어긋나다 be contrary to the spirit of constitution / 기본 정신에 어긋나다 run counter to the fundamental spirit 《of》
■ 독립— the spirit of independence 입법— the spirit of legislation ■ —감응 psychomancy; (mental) telepathy —감정 a psychiatric test —계(界) the mental [moral, spiritual] world —과(科) 〈병원의〉 the department of psychiatry : 정신과 의사 a psychiatrist; a mental specialist —과학 the science of mind; mental science —교육 moral education —구조 *one's* mental makeup [structure] —무장 mental [spiritual] armament —문명[문화] moral [spiritual] civilization [culture] —병리학 psychopathology : 정신병리학자 a psychopath-ologist —분열증 schizophrenia; split personality : 정신분열증 환자 a schizophrenic; a schizophrene —생활 spiritual [inner] life —수양[단련] mental [moral] culture [training] : 정신수양[단련]을 하다 cultivate [train] *one's* mind —신경증 [醫] psychoneurosis : 정신신경증 환자 a psychoneurotic —안정제 (a) tranquilizer —연령 mental age : 다섯살짜리 정신연령 상태다 have a mental age of five —위생(학) mental hygiene —의학 psychiatry; mental [psychologic] medicine —작용 mental action; mentation —장애 a mental disorder —착란 a mental storm —통일 concentration of mind; mental concentration —현상 a mental phenomenon

정신노동 精神勞動 brain [mental] work
■ —자 a brain [mental] worker

정신대 挺身隊 a group of women entertainers for Japanese soldiers during the World War Ⅱ

정신박약 精神薄弱 mental deficiency [retardation]; mental weakness; feeble-mindedness; low intelligence
■ —아 a mentally deficient [defective handicapped] child; a feebleminded child; a mental defective —아 시설 a home for feeble-minded children —자 a feebleminded person; an intellectually handicapped person; (총칭) the mentally handicapped

정신병 精神病 a mental disease [trouble]; a psychosis 《*pl.* -ses》; psychopathy; insanity
■ —동(棟) a psychiatric [psychopathic] ward; a mental ward —의사 a psychiatrist; a psychopathist —의 mental specialist —자 a mental patient; a mentally deranged person; an insane [a demented] person; a lunatic; a psychopath; a psycopathic; (口) a psycho —학 psychiatry —학자 a psychiatrist; a psychiater —환자 a mental [psychopathic] patient

정신병원 精神病院 a mental asylum; a mental home [hospital]; a sanatorium for the insane; a madhouse; a lunatic [an insane] asylum
♦ 정신병원에 수용되다 be confined to [put into] a madhouse

정신분석 精神分析 psychoanalysis
♦ 정신분석학상의 psychoanalytic(al) / 정신분석을 하다 psychoanalyze
■ —학자 a psychoanalyst

정신상태 精神狀態 a mental condition [attitude]; a state of mind; mentality
♦ 정신상태를 의심하다 doubt *sb's* sanity

정신외과 精神外科 psychosurgery
■ —의사 a psychosurgeon

정신요법 精神療法 psychotherapy; spiritual cure [healing]; mental healing ■ —자 a psychotherapeutist; a psychotherapist

정신이상 精神異狀 mental derangement [disorder, aberration]; psychosis
■ —자 a mental patient

정신적 精神的 spiritual (↔ material); mental (↔ physical); moral; psychical
♦ 정신적 건강 mental health / 정신적 성장 mental development / 정신적 사랑 Platonic love / 정신적 유산 spiritual [mental] heri-

tage / 정신적 지지[압박] moral support [pressure] / 정신적 타격 a mental blow [shock] / 정신적인 삶을 영위하다 lead a spiritual life / 정신적 피로로 괴로워하다 suffer from mental fatigue / 정신적 쇼크를 받다 experience an emotional disturbance [upset] / 정신적 승리를 얻다 win a moral victory / 정신적으로 지원하다 give one's moral support / 정신적으로 지쳐버리다 be mentally tired out; suffer from a nervous breakdown

▶ 그녀는 육체적으로도 정신적으로도 지쳐 있다 She is physically and mentally [emotionally] tired out.

정신주의 精神主義 idealism; spiritualism
■—자 an idealist; a spiritualist

정실 正室 〈본처〉 a lawful [legal] wife; one's (legally) wedded wife

정실 情實 〈개인 사정〉 private circumstances; 〈편애〉 favoritism; personal [private] considerations

♦ 정실에 흐르다 be influenced by personal considerations / 정실을 배제하다 set aside all personal considerations

▶ 이번의 인사이동이 정실에 좌우되었다는 것은 분명하다 It is clear that the latest personnel reshuffle has been influenced by favoritism.
▶ 그는 지원자 선발에 일체의 정실을 배제했다 He rejected all personal considerations in selecting the applicants.
■—인사 personnel changes through favoritism; the spoils system

정압 定壓 〔物〕 constant pressure
정압 靜壓 〔物〕 static pressure
정액 定額 a fixed amount [sum]; the required amount; a flat sum ♦ 정액에 달하다 come up to the required amount

▶ 클럽의 비용은 정액 부담으로 합니다 The expense of our club shall be charged at a flat rate.
■—등 a fixed-rate lamp —보험 insurance of fixed sums —소득 a fixed [regular] income —예금 a fixed deposit —임금 a fixed wage —저금 fixed amount savings —환급제 imprest refund

정액 精液 〔生理〕 semen; sperm; spermatic fluid ♦ 정액의 spermatic; seminal

정양 靜養 (a) rest; (perfect) repose; 〈요양〉 recuperation ♦ 정양을 위해 for one's health; for recuperation
—정양하다 recuperate oneself

▶ 진단에 의하면 그는 한달 동안 정양하도록 되어 있다 The diagnosis is that he will require one month's rest.

정어리 〔魚〕 a sardine ■—통조림 canned [tinned] sardines —포 dried sardines

정언적 定言的 〔論〕 categorical
■—명제 a categorical proposition —삼단논법 a categorical syllogism —판단[명령] categorical judgment [imperative]

정역학 靜力學 〔物〕 statics ♦ 정역학적(인) static(al)

정연하다 整然— orderly; regular; systematic; well-ordered; well-regulated

♦ 정연하게 in good [shape] order; regularly; in a regular manner; systematically / 질서가 정연하다 be in good [perfect] order

정열 情熱 passion; enthusiasm; passionate emotion

♦ 종교적 정열 religious fervor / 정열적인 사랑 a passionate love / 정열적인 passionate; ardent; impassioned; full of ardor / 정열적으로 passionately; ardently; enthusiastically / 정열적으로 말하다 speak passionately [warmly] 《of, about》; give a glowing account 《of》 / 창작에 정열을 불태우다 have a passion for creative writing / 정치에 정열을 쏟다 be enthusiastic about politics

▶ 그녀는 음악에 대한 정열이 있다 She has a passion for music. ⇒ She is enthusiastic over [about] music.
■—가 a passionate [an ardent] person

정염 情炎 burning passion; flaming desire
♦ 정염을 불태우다 kindle the passions / 정염에 불타다 burn with passion

정예 精銳 an elite; the pick; 〈정병(精兵)〉 picked troops [men]; the choice [flower] 《of an army》

♦ 정예의 picked 《members》; elite; crack / 5천의 정예 a troop of 5,000 strong
▶ 우리 팀은 정예로 편성돼 있다 Our team has the best players.
■—부대 an elite troop [corps]; a crack contingent [unit]

정오 正午 (high) noon; noontime; midday
♦ 정오에 at (high) noon; at midday
▶ 정오의 태양이 그들에게 내리 쬐있다 The midday sun glared upon them.
▶ 가게에 도둑이 든 것은 정오였다 It was high noon when the store was broken into.

정오 正誤 correction; correction [rectification] of errors
■—표 a (list of) corrigenda [errata]

정온 定溫 a fixed temperature
■—기(器) the thermostat —동물 〔動〕 a homoiothermal animal

정욕 情慾 passions; sexual desire; carnal appetite; lust

♦ 정욕의 노예 a slave of 《one's》 passions / 정욕을 억제하다 restrain [subdue] one's passions [sexual appetite]; keep one's passions under control / 정욕을 채우다 gratify one's lust / 정욕에 사로잡히다 indulge in sexual desires

정원 定員 1 〈정한 인원〉 a fixed [prescribed] number; the regular number; the numerical limit; 〈정족수〉 a quorum; 〈할당된 인원수〉 a quota

♦ 정원의 배치 allocation of the authorized strength / 정원의 증가[감축] an increase [a decrease] in the fixed number / 정원 외의 supernumerary 《tourist》 / 정원에 이르다 be full (up); have [form] a quorum

▶ 지원자의 수는 정원에 달했다 The number of applicants reached the fixed [prescribed] number.
▶ 위원회는 정원에 차지 않았다 The committee lacked a quorum.
▶ 정원 미달로 모임은 연기되었다 The meeting

was adjourned for want of a quorum.
▶우리는 정원 외의 근로자를 고용하지 않으면 안된다 We have to employ the supernumerary workers.
2 〈수용력〉(a) (seating) capacity
◆정원 삼백명의 극장 a theater with a seating capacity of 300
▶이 버스는 정원이 마흔명이다 This bus has a capacity of forty passengers.
▶이 배는 정원을 초과하고 있다 This boat is carrying more passengers than the seating capacity allows. ⇌ This boat is overloaded.

정원 庭園 a garden; 〈넓은〉 a park
◆정원을 꾸미다 make [lay out] a garden; engage in landscape gardening
■—사(師) a landscape gardener; a gardener; 〈임시 고용된〉 a jobbing gardener —석 a garden stone [rock] —수 a garden plant [tree]: 정원수를 손질하다 trim garden trees

정월 正月 January (略 Jan.); the first month of the year ◆정월 초하루 New Year's Day / 정월 보름 the 15th of the New Year according to the lunar calender

정위치 定位置 *one's* regular position

정유 精油 1〈식물 정제유〉an essential oil
2〈정제 석유〉refined oil;〈정제〉oil refining
■—공장[소] an oil refinery

정육 精肉 meat; dressed meat —점 a butcher [meat] shop; (英) a butcher's

정육면체 正六面體 〔數〕 a regular hexahedron; a cube

정은 正銀 pure silver ⇨ 순은(純銀)

정의 正義 justice; righteousness; right
◆정의의 just; righteous / 정의의 싸움 a righteous war; fighting for justice / 정의의 옹호자 a champion of right
▶힘은 정의다 Might is right.
▶그는 자유와 정의를 위해 싸우다 죽었다 He was killed in the war for freedom and justice.
■—감 a sense of justice: 그는 정의감이 강하다 He has a strong sense of justice. —사회 a just society: 정의사회의 구현 the realization of a just society

정의 定義 (a) definition
◆정의를 내리다 give [formulate, frame, lay down] a definition (of); define
▶이 단어의 정의를 가리켜 줄 수 있습니까? Can you give me a definition of this word?
—정의하다 define
◆정의하기 어렵다 be indefinable; be hard to define; defy a definition
▶이 사전은 「죽음」을 생명의 끝이라고 정의하고 있다 This dictionary defines the word "death" as the end of life.
■—역 domain (of definition)

정의 情誼 friendly feelings; friendship; intimacy; good-fellowship
◆친구끼리의 정의로 for friendship's sake / 정의가 두텁다 be very friendly; be kind and warmhearted
▶나는 오랜 동안의 정의 때문에 그에게 거절 할 수 없었다 Because of our long-standing friendship, I could not say no.

정자 正字 a correct letter; the correct form of a Chinese character ■—법 〔文法〕 orthography

정자 亭子 an arbor; a bower; a summerhouse; a pavilion ▶저기 저 정자에서 점심을 먹읍시다 We'll have lunch in that arbor over there.

정자 精子 〔動〕 a spermatozoon (*pl*. -zoa); a sperm cell; (총칭) a sperms; 〔植〕 a spermatozoid
◆정자의 spermous; spermatozoal / 정자 모양의 spermatic
■—세포 a spermatid —은 행 a sperm bank —형성[발생] spermatogenesis

정자각 丁字閣 a T-shaped shrine in front of a royal tomb

정자형 丁字形 a T-shape; the shape of the letter T; the form of a T

정작 reality; actuality; practice;〈부사적〉really; actually; practically
▶정작 출발할 때가 되자 그는 병이 나버렸다 At the moment when he was actually to start, he became sick.
▶이것은 간단한 규칙이지만 정작 응용해보면 그리 간단치 않다 This is a simple rule, but, in practical application, it is far from simple.

정장 正裝 full [formal] dress;〈제복〉a full-dress uniform ◆정장을 요하는 모임 a dress affair; a white-tie function
▶이것은 정장을 입어야 하는 행사는 아니다 This is not a dress affair.
—정장하다 dress (*oneself*) up; be in *one's* best clothes
▶정장하실 필요는 없습니다〈초대장에서〉No dress. ⇌ Don't dress up.
▶아버지는 결혼식에 가셔야 하므로 정장하셨다 Father dressed (himself) up for a wedding.

정장 整腸 intestinal regulation
■—제 medicine for intestinal disorders

정장석 正長石 〔鑛〕 orthoclase

정쟁 政爭 a political strife [dispute]; political warfare ▶교육을 정쟁의 도구로 삼아선 안된다 You should not make a political issue of education.

정적 政敵 a political opponent [enemy, rival, foe, antagonist]

정적 靜寂 silence; stillness; quiet(ness) ◆정적을 깨뜨리다 break the silence

정적 靜的 static; statical; still ◆정적으로 statically

정적분 定積分 〔數〕 definite integral

정전 停電 (a) power failure [stoppage]; (a) power cut; a stoppage of [in] power supply; power suspension
▶어젯밤 폭설로 곳곳에서 정전이 있었다 The power supply was cut off in many places due to the heavy snow last night.
▶전 지역에 정전이 되었다 The whole block was blacked out by a power failure.
—정전하다[되다] (the electricity) be cut off; (the power) be gone off [give out]

정전 停戰 a cease-fire; an armistice; a truce; the suspension [cessation] of hostilities
—정전하다 cease fire; stop fighting; suspend hostilities
■—명령 a cease-fire [stop fire] order —위원

정전기 회 〈유엔의〉 the cease-fire committee —협상 [협정] an armistic [a cease-fire] agreement —회담 a cease-fire conference; cease-fire talks

정전기 靜電氣 〔電〕 static electricity ■—단위 an electrostatic unit —력 electrotatic force —유도 electrostatic induction —학 electrostatics —현상 an electrostatic phenomenon

정절 貞節 〈절개〉 fidelity; faithfulness;〈정조〉 chastity; womanly virtue
♦ 정절을 지키다 maintain chastity

정점 定點 〔數〕 a given point; 〔氣〕 a specific point at sea; an ocean station

정점 頂點 **1**〈맨꼭대기〉 the top; the peak; the summit
2〈꼭지점〉〔數〕 a vertex; an apex 《pl. ~es, apices》 ♦ 삼각형의 정점 the vertex [apex] of a triangle
3〈절정〉 the zenith 《of fame》; the climax 《of popularity》; the acme 《of prosperity》
♦ 정점에 달하다 reach [attain] the peak [acme] 《of》; come to a climax

정정 政情 a state of poitical affairs; a political situation [condition]

정정 訂正 (a) correction; rectification; revision —정정하다 correct; put [set] right; rectify; revise ♦ 틀린 것을 정정하다 correct [rectify] errors

정정당당하다 正正堂堂— fair and square; open and aboveboard
♦ 정정당당한 승부 a fairly contested match / 정정당당히 싸우다〔승부하다〕play fair [square, on the square]; fight openly and squarely
▶ 그의 태도는 언제나 정정당당하다 His manner is fair and square all the time.

정정법 政淨法 the Political Purification Act

정정하다 亭亭— **1**〈우뚝하다〉 lofty; tall; towering
2〈강건하다〉 vigorous; hale and hearty
♦ 정정한 노인 a man in his green old age; a hale old man
▶ 우리 할아버지는 지금도 정정하시다 My grandfather is still going strong.

정제 精製 **1**〈깨끗이 만듦〉 refining; purification —정제하다 refine; purify ♦ 정제한 refined; purificatory
2〈정성들여 만듦〉 careful manufacture —정제하다 manufacture carefully
■—공장 a refinery —당 refined sugar —법 a refining process —품 a refined article

정제 整除 〈나누어 떨어짐〉〔數〕 divisibility
—정제하다 can be divided (exactly); be exactly divisible
♦ 정제할 수 있는 divisible / 정제할 수 없는 indivisible
■—수(數) an aliquot part; an exact divisor

정제 整齊 regularity; symmetry —정제하다 make regular [symmetrical]; arrange in regular order ♦ 의관을 정제하다 dress oneself properly; adjust one's dress

정제 錠劑 a tablet; a pill; a lozenge; a pastille; (商標) a Tabloid

정조 貞操 〈절조〉 chastity; faithfulness; feminine virtue; (female) honor;〈처녀성〉 virginity
♦ 정조가 굳은 여자 a woman of virtue; a chaste woman / 정조를 지키다 remain chaste [faithful]; lead a chaste life / 정조관념이 희박하다 have a weak sense of virtue; be a woman of easy virtue / 정조를 중히 여기다 prize chastity / 정조를 잃다 lose one's chastity [virtue]; lose one's virginity / 정조를 유린하다 defile a girl's chastity; seduce [dishonor, ruin] a girl / 정조를 팔다 sell [sacrifice] one's chastity; prostitute oneself / 정조를 바치다 surrender one's chastity to 《a man》; give oneself to 《a man》
■—대(帶) a chastity belt —유린 a violation of chastity

정조 情調 a mood; an atmosphere; a tone; a spirit; a flavor

정조 情操 (a) sentiment
■—교육 culture of (aesthetic) sentiments; cultivation of artistic sentiments

정족 鼎足 〈솥발〉 the legs of a tripod
■—지세(之勢) a triangular position; a three-cornered [triangular] contest

정족수 定足數 a quorum ♦ 정족수에 이르다 constitute [form] a quorum / 정족수에 미달하다 fail to meet the quorum

정종 正宗 refined rice wine

정좌 正坐 sitting up straight
—정좌하다 sit upright; sit up straight

정좌 靜坐 sitting quietly; sitting in meditation
—정좌하다 sit quietly; sit in meditation

정주 定住 domiciliation; settlement; one's fixed residence; a settled existence
—정주하다 domicile [domiciliate] oneself 《in, at》 ♦ 서울에 정주하다 settle down in Seoul
■—자 a permanent resident; a settler —지 a fixed [permanent] abode

정중 正中 the very middle ♦ 정중의 median
■—동맥 a median (artery) —선 〔齒〕 a median line —신경 a median (nerve)

정중하다 鄭重— polite; courteous; civil; respectful; reverent
♦ 정중한 환영 a cordial [warm] reception / 정중한 편지 a courteous letter / 정중한 말씨를 쓰다 use polite language / 정중한 대접을 받다 receive [meet with] courteous treatment; be received with much courtesy / 정중한 태도를 취하다 assume a reverent attitude / 정중히 인사하다 give sb a polite greeting
▶ 그들은 서로 정중한 인사를 나누었다 They exchanged courteous greetings with each other.

정지 停止 〈멎음〉 a stop; a halt; a standstill;〈금지〉 suspension; stoppage; temporary prohibition; ban ♦ 정지를 명하다 call a halt
—정지하다 stop; halt; come to a standstill;〈금지하다〉 suspend; prohibit for a time
♦ 교차로에서 일단 정지하다 stop before crossing the intersection / 자격을 정지하다 disqualify sb from 《driving》
▶ 그 은행은 지급을 정지했다 The bank suspended payment.
▶ 회사는 가스 공급을 정지했다 The company cut off the gas supply.

▶그는 3개월간 운전 면허를 정지당했다 He was suspended [disqualified] from driving for three months.
▶그 선수는 1개월간 출장 정지당했다 The player was suspended for one month.
■ 발행[영업, 지급]— suspension of publication [business, payment]: 신문의 발행 정지를 해제하다 release the suspension of a newspaper ■—가격 a pegged [stopped] price —기간 the period of suspension —선 a stop line; 〈철도의〉a clearance post —신호 a stop signal —조건 〔法〕a condition precedent

정지 静止 stillness; repose; rest; a standstill
◆정지 상태 a stationary state
▶그 인공위성은 정지 상태에 있다 The artificial satellite is stationary state.
—정지하다 rest; stand still; come to a standstill ◆정지한 자세 the posture of repose
—궤도[위성] a geostationary orbit [satellite]

정지 整地 〈건축을 위한〉leveling of ground; land readjustment; 〈경작을 위한〉soil preparation
—정지하다 level the ground 《for construction》; prepare the soil 《for planting》

정직 正直 honesty; uprightness; 〈성실〉integrity; sincerity; 〈솔직함〉frankness; candor
▶정직은 최선의 방책이다 《속담》Honesty is the best policy.
—정직하다 honest; upright; sincere; frank; candid; straightforward
▶그는 정직한 소년이다 He is an honest boy.
▶무슨 일을 했는지 정직하게 말해라 Tell me honestly what you did.
▶정직하게 말해서 그는 신뢰할 수 없다 To tell the truth [To be frank with you], he cannot be trusted.

정직 定職 a regular occupation; a fixed employment; a steady job ◆정직이 없다 lead an idle life; have no regular occupation [employment]; be at a loose end

정직 停職 suspension from office [duty]

정진 精進 concentration of mind; close application; assiduity; devotion
—정진하다 devote *oneself* 《to》; apply *oneself* closely 《to》; be assiduous 《in》
▶그는 학문에 정진했다 He devoted [applied] himself to his studies.
▶그는 불도에 정진하고 있다 He devotes himself to Buddhism.

정차 停車 a stop; (a) stoppage; halt
—정차하다 stop 《at》; make a stop; 〈사고로〉be held up
◆역마다 정차하는 열차 a local train; (美) an accommodation [a slow] train / 정차하지 않고 달리다 run (on) without a stop; go nonstop
▶택시가 갑자기 정차했다 The taxi came to a sudden stop. ⇌ The taxi pulled up sharply.
▶나는 운전사에게 정차해 달라고 했다 I told [ordered] the driver to stop.
▶열차는 이번 역에서 3분간 정차합니다 The train makes a three-minute stop at this station.

▶다음에 정차하는 역은 어디입니까? What is the next stop? ⇌ What is the next station we stop at?
■—시간 stoppage time —신호 a stop signal

정착 定着 settlement; fixation; 〔寫〕fixing
—정착하다 settle 《down》; fix; (비유) take [strike] root; come to stay
▶이 지역에는 1세기 전부터 이민들이 정착했다 This area was settled by immigrants over a century ago.
▶몇년이나 떠돌아다닌 끝에 우리는 이곳에 정착하기로 결정했다 After years of travel, we decided to settle here.
▶그는 3루수로 정착했다 He got the regular position as third baseman.
▶새로운 풍습이 이 마을에도 정착했다 The new custom has taken root in this village.
■—금 resettlement funds —물 a fixture —생활 settled life —액〔寫〕a fixing solution; a fixative; a fixer

정찬 正餐 a dinner

정찰 正札 a price label [tag]
▶그는 가게에 있는 상품마다 정찰을 붙였다 He marked the price on every article in his store.
▶우산에는 7천원의 정찰이 붙어 있었다 The umbrella was marked [priced at] 7,000 won.
■—가격 a fixed [labeled] price

정찰 偵察 scouting; patrol; reconnaissance; spy
▶그는 정찰 나가 있다 He is out scouting.
▶그는 지금 적의 동태를 정찰 중이다 He is now on the scout for the enemy's movements.
—정찰하다 scout; spy; reconnoiter; patrol
◆적정을 정찰하다 feel [reconnoiter] the enemy; spy upon the enemy / 정찰하러 가다 go scouting [reconnoitering]
■ 공중— aerial reconnaissance ■—기 a spy [scout] plane; a reconnaissance plane: 사진정찰기 a photo-reconnaissance plane —대 a patrol; a reconnoitering party; scouts —병 [자] a reconnoiterer; a scout —비행 a reconnaissance flight: 정찰 비행을 하다 make [go on] a scouting [reconnoitering] flight —장비 reconnaissance equipment

정찰제 正札制 a fixed price system; a price-tag system
◆정찰제를 실시하다 enforce a price-tag system; put a price-tag system in operation [practice]
■—판매 sale at a fixed [set, labeled] price

정책 政策 a policy
◆한국의 대 중국 정책 Korea's policy toward China / 정책상의 문제 a matter of policy; a policy issue / 산업[사회] 정책을 세우다 shape [work out] an industrial [a social] policy / 정책을 결정하다 fix [decide on] a policy / 정책을 심의하다 deliberate on a policy / 정책을 수정하다 modify a policy / 정책을 실행에 옮기다 carry out a policy / 정책을 지지하다 support a policy
■ 경제— an economic policy 문호개방— the open-door policy 비동맹— the policy of non-alignment 선린— a good-neighbor policy 외교[대외]— a diplomatic [foreign] policy ■—강령〈정당의〉a (party) platform —결정 a pol-

정처 icy decision —수립[입안] policy-making —수립자[입안자] a policy maker [planner] —위원회 a policy planning committee —전환 policy switch

정처 定處 a fixed place [abode]; a definite destination; *one's* dwelling place
♦ 정처 없는 나그네 a wandering traveler / 정처 없이 떠돌아 다니다 wander [roam] about aimlessly; wander from place to place

정청 政廳 a government office

정체 正體 〈본성〉 *one's* true character [colors]; 〈본디의 모양〉 *one's* natural shape [original form]; identity 《of》
♦ 정체 불명의 사람 a mysterious man; a perfect stranger; 정체를 알 수 없는 병 an unidentified [a nondescript] disease / 정체를 감추다 wear [put on] a mask; disguise *oneself* / 정체를 폭로하다 unmask; (口) debunk / 정체를 드러내다 show *oneself* in *one's* true colors
▶ 그는 마침내 정체를 드러냈다 He has finally revealed his true character.
▶ 그것이 그의 정체다 That's what he really is.

정체 政體 the form of government; a government system; a regime; a polity
♦ 정체를 변경하다 change the form of government
■ 공화— a republican system of government 군주— monarchy: 입헌 군주 정체 a constitutional [limited] monarchy / 절대 군주 정체 an absolute [a despotic] monarchy 민주— democracy

정체 停滯 〈경기의〉 stagnation; 〈화물의〉 accumulation; 〈자금의〉 a tie-up; 〈지불의〉 falling into arrears; arrearage
♦ 교통의 정체 the congestion of traffic / 우편물의 정체 the pile-up of mail
—정체하다 pile up; accumulate; stagnate; be tied up; fall into arrears
▶ 폭설로 우편물이 정체되었다 Mail has piled up owing to the heavy snow. ⇌ The heavy snowfall caused postal delays.

정초 正初 the first ten days of January
♦ 정초에 early in January

정초식 定礎式 the laying of the cornerstone [foundation stone] ♦ 정초식을 올리다 lay the cornerstone 《of a building》

정충 精蟲 〔動〕 a spermatozoon 《*pl.* -zoa》⇨ 정자(精子)

정취 情趣 〈느낌〉 sensitive feeling; 〈기분〉 sentiment; mood; 〈아취〉 artistic flavor [taste]
♦ 정취 있는 뜰 an elegant [a tasteful] garden / 정취가 풍부한 rich in artistic flavor; full of artistic effect; tasteful / 정취를 맛보다 taste [experience] a mood [an atmosphere]
▶ 그의 그림에는 독특한 정취가 있다 In his paintings there is something peculiar which appeals to our artistic sentiment.
■ 이국— an exotic mood; exoticism

정치 定置 〈일정한 장소에 놓음〉 fixing; stationing —망어업(網漁業) fixed-net fishing; stationary net fishery

정치 政治 government; politics; administration; statecraft; political affairs
♦ 깨끗한 정치 clean politics / 정치를 논하다 talk [discuss] politics / 정치를 하다 administer [conduct] the affairs of state / 정치에 관여하다[손대다] engage in [take up] politics; meddle [dabble] in politics / 정치에 관여하지 않다 let [leave] politics alone; keep out of politics
▶ 정치의 빈곤이 화제가 되고 있다 Lack of proper [good] government is much talked about. ⇌ Much is said about lack of political ingenuity.
▶ 깨끗한 정치가 되도록 모두가 노력해야 한다 Everyone should make efforts to make politics clean.
▶ 현재 필요한 것은 강력한 정치다 What is needed at present is a strong government.
▶ 그에게는 안심하고 나라의 정치를 맡길 수 있다 We can fully entrust him with the government of our country.
■ 과두— oligarchy 관료— bureaucratic government 금권— plutocracy 독재[전제]— despotism 무단— the rule of the saber 정당— party politics 우민[폭민]— mobocracy; ochlocracy 지방— local politics [government] —감각 a political sense —결사 a political organization [association] —계 political circles —공작 political maneuvering; politicking —광(狂) politicomania; 〈사람〉 a politicomaniac —권력 political authority —기관 the political machinery; an organ of government —기구 (a) political structure [organization] —기자 a writer on political affairs; a political writer [correspondent] —깡패 political hoodlums; a political henchman —단체 a political body [organization] —도덕 political morality [ethics] —력 political power [influence] —범 〈범죄〉 political offense; 〈사람〉 a political offender [prisoner] —보복 political retaliation —사 a political history —사상 a political idea [thought] —사찰 political surveillance —생활 a political life [career] —소설 a political novel —안정 a political stability —열 political fever —위원회 a political committee —자금 money for political activities —정화 the political cleanup; the purification of politics —조직 a political system; (a) political organization —체제 a political structure —테러 political terrorism —투쟁 a political struggle; politics strife —평론가 a commentator on political [public] affairs; a political journalist [columnist]; a publicist —헌금 a political donation —협상 political negotiations —형태 a form of political organization; (a) polity

정치 精緻 exquisite fineness; delicacy; minuteness; subtlety
—정치하다 nice; fine; minute; subtle

정치가 政治家 a politician; a statesman

〔解說〕 ***politician***과 ***statesman***이 대조적으로 쓰이면 전자는 당리당략을 일삼아 사리를 꾀하는 정치꾼이라는 나쁜 뜻으로, 후자는 훌륭한 정치가라는 좋은 뜻으로 쓰이는 수가 있다. 그러나 보통 직업적인 정치가를 가리킬 때는 중립적인 의미로 전자를 쓴다.

■직업— a professional [career] politician

정치문제 政治問題 a political issue [problem] ◆정치문제로 삼다 make a political issue ((of a matter)) / 정치문제로 발전하다 develop into a political issue
▶ 교과서 개정이 정치 문제가 되었다 They made a political issue (out) of the revision of textbooks.

정치운동 政治運動 a political movement [campaign]

정치적 政治的 political
◆정치적 망명 political asylum / 정치적 수완 political ability [ingenuity]; statecraft / 정치적 해결 settlement (of a problem) through the political channel / 정치적인 무관심 political apathy / 정치화하다 politicize
▶ 그 사건은 정치적으로 해결되었다 The case was settled politically.
▶ 이 문제는 양국간에 정치적 해결을 보았다 The two countries came to a political settlement over this dispute.

정치철학 政治哲學 political philosophy; philosophy of politics ■—자 a philosopher of politics; a political philosopher

정치풍토 政治風土 the political climate
■—쇄신 the renovation of the political climate

정치학 政治學 politics; political science; the science of government ■—박사 a doctor of political science; 〈학위〉 Doctor of Political Science —자 a political scientist

정치활동 政治活動 political activity; politicking ◆정치활동을 하다 engage in politics [political activity]; politick

정칙 定則 an established rule; a law

정크 〈중국의 배〉 a junk

정탐 偵探 spying; scouting; espionage
—정탐하다 spy out ((a region)); spy into ((a secret)); feel ((out))
◆적정을 정탐하다 spy on the enemy's movements; feel the enemy / 회사의 내정을 정탐하다 investigate the inside affairs of a company ■—꾼[객] a spy; a scout; a secret agent

정태 靜態 stationariness ■—경제학[통계학] static economics [statistics]

정토 淨土 〔佛敎〕 the Pure Land; Paradise; the Buddhist Elysium

정통 正統 legitimacy; orthodoxy
◆정통적인 방법 the orthodox approach / 정통의 legitimate; orthodox
■—극 a legitimate drama —주의 legitimism —(학)파 an orthodox school

정통하다 精通— be well versed ((in)); be well informed ((about)); have a thorough knowledge ((of)); be conversant ((with)); be thoroughly; be well acquainted ((with)); be at home ((in, on)); have *sth* at *one's* fingers' ends [fingertips] ◆정통한 소식통 a well-informed source [person]
▶ 그는 고전에 정통하고 있다 He has classical literature at his fingertips.
▶ 그는 라틴어에 정통하다 He is well versed in Latin.

정판 整版 〔印〕 makeup; justification
—정판하다 make up; justify
—공(工) a maker-up; a justifier

정평 定評 an established [a good] reputation; a settled [fixed] opinion
▶ 그는 명의로서 정평이 있다 He enjoys an established reputation as a skilled physician.
▶ 그는 거래가 공정하기로 정평이 나 있다 He has an excellent reputation for fair dealing.
▶ 이 책은 입문서로서 정평이 있다 This book has a good reputation as an elementary text.
▶ 그 호텔의 서비스는 정평이 나 있다 That hotel enjoys a good reputation for excellent service.
▶ 그 고등학교는 야구가 세기로 정평이 나 있다 Everybody knows (that) that high school has a strong baseball team.

정표 情表 a love token; a keepsake; a memento ◆애정의 정표 a token of *one's* love and affection / 감사의 정표로서 in token [as a token] of *one's* gratitude

정풍 整風 rectification ■—운동 the rectification campaign

정하다 定— 〈결정하다〉 decide ((on)); determine; fix ((up)); 〈낙착시키다〉 settle; 〈협정하다〉 arrange; agree ((to do, on *sth*)); 〈일시를〉 set; appoint; 〈선정하다〉 choose; 〈결심하다〉 make up *one's* mind ((to do)); set *one's* heart on *sth*; resolve [be resolved] to do; 〈규정하다〉 lay down ((a law)); prescribe; provide; establish
◆값을 정하다 fix the price / 거처를 정하다 make *one's* home ((at, in)); fix [take up] *one's* abode / 규칙을 정하다 make [lay down] a rule; establish regulations / 날짜를 정하다 fix [appoint, set] a date / 목표를 정하다 set up a goal / 태도를 정하다 determine *one's* attitude ((toward))
▶ 출발 날짜는 정했습니까? Have you settled on a date for leaving?
▶ 우리는 다음 모임의 장소와 시간을 정했다 We appointed the place and time for the next meeting.
▶ 우리가 함께 정한 약속은 지켜 주기 바라네 I want you to keep the promise which we have made together.
▶ 그는 서울을 생활 근거지로 정했다 He decided that Seoul (should) be the base and center of his life.

정하다 淨— clear; pure; clean
◆옷을 정하게 입다 keep *oneself* neat and trim; be neat in *one's* dress

정학 停學 suspension from school [college]; 〈대학의〉 **(英)** rustication
▶ 그는 1개월의 정학 처분을 받았다 He was suspended from school for a month.
▶ 그는 정학이 풀렸다 He was allowed back to school from suspension.
■무기— indefinite suspension from school; suspension of attendance for an indefinite period

정해 正解 a correct [right] answer; a correct solution; 〈해석의〉 a correct interpretation
—정해하다 answer right; give a right answer; solve correctly; interpret correctly

정해 ■—자 one who gives a correct answer

정해 精解 detailed [minute, precise] explanation —**정해하다** explain minutely [in detail, precisely]

정해지다 定— 〈결정되다〉 be decided; be settled; be determined; be fixed; 〈합의되다〉 be arranged; be agreed upon; 〈규정되다〉 be laid down; be prescribed; be stipulated
▶ 이미 정해진 것을 바꿀 수는 없다 I cannot change what has already been decided.
▶ 내 방침은 아직 정해지지 않았다 My course has not yet been determined.
▶ 모임은 토요일 저녁에 갖기로 정해졌다 The meeting has been arranged for Saturday evening.

정향 丁香 〔韓醫〕 dried clove buds
■—나무 〈교목〉 a clove (tree); 〈관목〉 a kind of lilac bush —유 clove oil

정현 正弦 〔數〕 a sine (略 sin) ⇨ 사인²
■—곡선 a sine curve

정형 定形 a fixed form; a regular shape
■—동사 a finite verb

정형 定型 a type; a definite form; standard
◆ 정형적인 typical
■—시 rhymed verse; a fixed form of verse —화 standardization: 정형화하다 standardize

정형 整形 restoration of bone structures that are defective or damaged by injury or disease
■—수술 an orthopedic operation; orthopedic treatment: 정형수술을 받다 have [undergo] orthopedic surgery —외과 plastic [orthopedic] surgery; orthopedics —외과의사 an orthopedic surgeon; an orthopedist

정혼 定婚 betrothal; affiance —**정혼하다** betroth oneself 《to sb》; become betrothed 《to》

정화 正貨 〈본위 화폐〉 specie
◆ 정화의 유출[유입] an outflow [inflow] of specie / 정화로 in specie
■—결핍 shortage [lack] of specie —보유고 specie holdings —수송점 a gold [specie] point —준비 specie [gold] reserve —지급 specie payment

정화 淨化 purification; purgation; a cleanup —**정화하다** purify; cleanse; deterge; clean up
▶ 이것은 물을 정화하는 장치다 This is a device to purify water.
▶ 현재의 정계를 정화하는 데는 과감한 개혁이 필요하다 Drastic reforms are needed to clean up the present political world.
■—운동 a cleanup movement [campaign, drive]; a purge —장치 a purifier; an apparatus for purifying —조(槽) 〈먹는 물의〉 a purification tank; 〈하수의〉 a septic tank

정화 精華 the essence; the quintessence; the flower; the glory
◆ 기사도의 정화 the flower of chivalry

정화수 井華水 water drawn from the well at daybreak

정확 正確 correctness; accuracy; exactness; precision —**정확하다** correct; accurate; exact; precise; right
◆ 정확한 시간 correct [exact] time / 정확한 원 a perfect circle / 정확한 조준 폭격 pinpoint bombing / 정확한 지도 an accurate map / 정확한 측정 precise measurements / 정확한 판단 a correct judgment / 말의 정확한 뜻 the exact meaning of a word
▶ 정확한 시간은 몇시입니까? Do you have the correct [exact] time?
▶ 내 시계는 항상 정확하다 My watch is always correct [right]. ⇌ My watch keeps good time.
▶ 그는 계산이 빠르고 정확하다 He is quick and accurate at figures.
▶ 정확한 것은 모른다 I don't know for certain.

정확히 正確— correctly; accurately; exactly; precisely; 〈시간적으로〉 punctually
◆ 정확히 말하면 exactly [precisely] speaking; to be exact / 시간을 정확히 지키다 be punctual《to the moment》 / 정확히 대답하다 give a correct answer; answer right
▶ 무슨 일이 있었는지 정확히 말해다오 Tell me exactly what happened.
▶ 나는 정확히 10시간을 잤다 I slept for ten clear [full] hours.
▶ 그녀는 정확히 시간을 맞춰서 왔다 She came exactly on time.
▶ 정확히 말하면 지진은 오후 5시 3분에 일어났다 To be exact, the earthquake occurred at 5: 03 p.m.

정황 情況 the state of things [affairs]; conditions; a situation; circumstances
◆ 현재의 정황으로는 as matters stand; in the present situation; under these circumstances
▶ 현재의 정황으로 보아 큰 변화는 없을 것 같다 Judging from the present situation there will not be great change.
■—증거 〔法〕 circumstantial evidence

정회 停會 suspension of a meeting; 〈휴회〉 adjournment; 〈의회의〉 prorogation —**정회하다** suspend a meeting; adjourn; prorogue

정회원 正會員 a full [regular] member
◆ 정회원의 자격 full membership

정훈 政訓 troop information and education (略 TI&E) ■—요원 TI&E personnel

정히 正— surely; certainly; no [without] doubt ▶ 김선생에게서 일금 100만원을 정히 영수함 Received from [of] Mr. Kim the sum of 1,000,000 won.

젖 1 〈유즙〉 milk; 〈유방〉 the breast(s)
◆ 소젖 cow's milk / 어머니 젖 mother's milk / 젖과 꿀이 흐르는 땅 land of milk and honey / 소의 젖을 짜다 milk a cow / 젖을 달라고 울다 cry for the breast / 아기에게 젖을 빨리다[먹이다] suckle a baby; give the breast to a baby; give a baby suck; nurse a baby / 젖을 메다 wean a child
▶ 이 소는 젖이 잘 난다 This cow milks well. ⇌ This cow produces a lot of milk.
▶ 젖이 불었다 The breast is swollen. ⇌ The breasts fill.
▶ 그녀는 아기에게 젖을 물리고 있었다 She was suckling [nursing] her baby.
▶ 아기는 어머니의 젖을 빨고 있다 The baby is sucking milk from its mother's breast. ⇌ The baby is at its mother's breast.
▶ 그녀는 젖이 말랐다 Her breasts have run dry [gone off milk].

2 〈식물의 진·수액〉 milk; latex

젖가슴 the bosom; the breast

젖꼭지 a nipple; a teat; 〔解〕 mammilla (*pl.* -lae) ♦ 젖꼭지 모양의 nipplelike; mastoid

젖내 the smell of milk ▶ 갓난아기는 젖내가 난다 Babies smell of milk. ▶ 그는 아직도 젖내가 난다 He is still green. ⇌ He is still wet behind the ears.

젖니 a milk [deciduous, baby, calf's] tooth

젖다 **1**〈축축해지다〉get [be] wet [drenched]; become damp [moist]; moisten

♦ 젖은 옷 wet clothes / 눈물 젖은 뺨 cheeks wet with tears / 비에 젖다 get wet in the rain; be moistened by rain / 이슬에 젖다 get wet with dew / 흠뻑 젖다 be drenched [soaked] to the skin / 젖은 걸레로 닦다 wipe with a wet [damp] cloth

▶ 내 셔츠가 땀에 흠뻑 젖었다 My shirt was thoroughly soaked with sweat.

▶ 그녀는 탁자를 젖은 걸레로 닦았다 She wiped the table with a wet [damp] cloth.

▶ 그녀의 얼굴은 눈물에 젖어 있었다 Her face was bedewed [wet] with tears.

▶ 풀은 저녁 이슬에 흠뻑 젖어 있었다 The grass was heavily moist with evening dews.

2〈빠지다〉be addicted (to); indulge (in); be steeped [immersed] (in); give *oneself* up (to)

♦ 행복에 젖다 swim in bliss / 술에 젖어 살다 be [become] the slave of drink; give *oneself* over to drink

3〈귀에 익다〉get used to hearing; be accustomed to hear; become familiar with

♦ 귀에 젖은 목소리 a familiar voice / 귀에 젖도록 듣다 be sick [tired] of hearing *sth*; hear more than enough of *sth* / 귀에 젖도록 타이르다 admonish again and again; drum a lesson into *sb's* head

젖당 ─糖 〔化〕 milk sugar; lactose

젖동생 ─同生 a foster brother [sister]

젖떨어지다 be [get] weaned

♦ 젖떨어진 아이 a weaned child; a weanling

젖떼기 a child [an animal] of the weaning age

젖떼다 wean; cease to suckle

젖뜨리다 throw [bend] back(ward); lean backward

젖먹이 a suckling (child); a nursing (child)

젖멍울 mastitis ♦ 젖멍울이 서다 suffer [fill out] from mastitis; get mastitis

젖몸살 mastitis ♦ 젖몸살을 앓다 have inflamed mammary glands; suffer from mastitis

젖병 ─瓶 a baby [nursing, feeding] bottle; a nurser

젖비린내 the smell of milk ⇨ 젖내

젖빛 milk white ♦ 젖빛의 milk-white

젖산 ─酸 〔化〕 lactic acid ■─균 〔植〕 lactic acid bacteria ─염 〔化〕 a lactate ─음료 lactic acid drink

젖샘 〔解〕 the mammary gland ⇨ 유선(乳腺)

젖소 a milch [milking] cow; (총칭) dairy cattle

젖어머니 a wet nurse ⇨ 유모

젖통이 the cup of the breasts; the breast(s) ⇨ 유방(乳房)

젖히다 turn over ⇨ 잦히다¹

제¹ 1〈나·저〉▶ 제가 인수입니다 I'm In-su.

2〈자기〉self; oneself

♦ 제가 좋아서 하는 일 a self-imposed work / 제 생각만 하다 think of *oneself* only; be self-centered

제² there ⇨ 저기

제³ 1〈나의·저의〉my; my own

♦ 제 집 my house / 제 생각으로는 for my part; as for me

▶ 이쪽은 제 아내입니다 This is my wife.

▶ 처음에는 제 생각도 그랬습니다 I thought so myself at first.

2〈자기의〉one's own; personal; private

♦ 제 멋대로 of *one's* own free will / 제 이익만 생각하다 look to *one's* own interests

▶ 제 일은 제가 해야 한다 One should mind [look after] his own business.

제 諸 〈많은〉many;〈여러 개의〉several; various;〈모든〉all ♦ 제 문제 various problems / 제 단체 many parties

제題 a subject ⇨ 제목

제- 第- ♦ 제1[2, 3] the first [second, third] / 제3자 a third party [person] / 제4조 제5항 Clause Ⅳ, Article Ⅴ; the fifth clause of Article four / 제9 교향곡 The Ninth Symphony; Symphony No. 9

-제 -制〈제도〉a system

♦ 8시간제 the eight-hour system / 4년제 대학 a four-year college [university] / 2년제 대학 a junior college / 전일제 (全日制) a full-time course

▶ 그 공장은 2부제다 The factory is under the two-shift system.

-제 -祭〈의식〉a ceremony; a sacrifice;〈축제〉a festival; a fete

♦ 기념제 an anniversary; a commemoration / 예술제 an art festival / 위령제 a memorial service / 50년제 a semi-centennial; a jubilee / 백년제 a centennial (anniversary); a centenary / 2백년제 a bicentennial; a bicentenary

-제 -製 make; manufacture

♦ 외국제 물품 articles of foreign make [manufacture] / P사제의 만년필 a fountain pen made [manufactured] by P company / 특제 셔츠 a specially made shirt / 강철제의 made of steel; steel

▶ 이것은 이탈리아제 가방이다 This is an Italian-made bag. ⇌ This bag is of Italian make.

-제 -劑 a medicine; a drug; a dose

♦ 소화제 a digestive / 진통제 an anodyne

제가하다 齊家─ govern *one's* family wisely; manage [regulate] *one's* household

제각기 ─各其 1〈각자〉each; each one; each for *oneself*

▶ 모두 제각기 불평을 털어놨다 Everybody complained in his own way. ⇌ Everyone voiced their discontent.

▶ 아이들은 제각기 자리에 앉았다 Each of the children took his (own) seat.

▶ 모두는 제각기 그의 용기를 칭찬했다 Everybody unanimously praised his courage.

▶ 사람에게는 제각기 장점과 단점이 있다 Each

man has his merits and demerits.
2 〈따로따로〉 separately; severally; respectively; individually
♦제각기 살다 live separately 《from》
▶막이 내리자 그들은 자리를 떠서 제각기 극장 식당으로 갔다 When the curtain fell, they left their seats and went to the theater's restaurants as the fancy took them.

제강 製鋼 steel manufacture; steelmaking
■—법 a steel-making process —소 a steel mill; a steelworks —업 the steel industry —업자 a steelman; a steelmaker

제거 除去 removal; exclusion; elimination
—제거하다 get rid of; clear *sth* of; remove; exclude; eliminate
♦장애물을 제거하다 remove obstacles out of the way; clear the way of obstacles
▶의사는 그녀에게 식사에서 염분을 제거하라고 일렀다 The doctor told her to cut out all salt from her diet.
▶탐탁지 않은 회원은 제거되었다 Undesirable members were weeded out [eliminated].
▶나는 셔츠의 얼룩을 제거했다 I removed the stain from my shirt.

제격 —格 ♦제격이다 be suitable 《for, to》; be proper 《for》
▶이 일은 네게 제격이다 This job is just the thing [very suitable] for you. ⇒ You are just the [the ideal] person for the job.
▶이 장소는 쉬어 가기에 제격이다 This is a likely place to stop.

제고장 a home ⇨ 본고장

제곱 〈數〉 a square
▶5의 제곱은 25이다 The square of 5 is 25. ⇒ Five squared makes twenty-five.
—제곱하다 square 《a number》; multiply 《a number》 by itself
■—법 involution —비(比) 《a》 duplicate ratio —수 a square number —표 table of squares

제곱근 —根 a square root
♦제곱근을 구하다[풀다] extract [find] the square root 《of》
▶4의 제곱근은 2다 The square root of 4 is 2.
■—표 the table of square roots —풀이 extraction of the square root

제공 提供 an offer; a tender
▶이 프로그램은 주식회사 나라의 제공으로 보내드렸습니다 This program has been sponsored by the Nara Corporation.
—제공하다 offer; supply; give; present; tender; furnish; produce
▶그는 많은 돈을 제공받았다 He accepted an offer of a lot of money.
▶그녀는 자기 집을 회의장으로 제공했다 She offered her house as a meeting place.
▶그는 우리에게 귀중한 자료를 제공해 주었다 He supplied valuable data to us.
■실비— offered at cost —가격 the price offered —자 an offerer; a donor: 적십자 병원은 혈액 제공자를 구하고 있다 The Red Cross Hospital is looking for blood donors.

제공권 制空權 the command [mastery] of the air; air domination [supremacy]
▶미공군이 태평양상의 제공권을 장악하고 있다 The U.S. Air Force has command of the air over the Pacific Ocean.

제과 製菓 confectionery
—제과하다 make confections
■—업 the confectionery industry —업자 a confectioner —점 a confectioner's shop; a confectionery —회사 a confectionery company

제관 製罐 can manufacturing; canning; tinning ■—공장[업] a can manufacturing plant [industry]

제관 祭官 a priest; an officient at rites; 〈참례자〉 celebrants at rites

제구 祭具 〈제사도구〉 implements used in religious rites; ritual implements

제구력 制球力 〈野〉 control (of the ball)
▶저 투수는 제구력이 있다[없다] The pitcher has [lacks] good control.

제구실 1 〈마땅히 해야 할 일〉 one's function; one's duty [obligation]; one's part [share]; what is expected of one
♦제구실을 하다 do one's duty; play [do] one's part; be worth one's salt / 제구실을 못하다 fail in [fail to do] one's duty; be not worth one's salt
▶그는 제구실을 충분히 했다 He has fully performed his duties.
2 〈으레 치러야 할 홍역 등〉 children's epidemic diseases
♦제구실을 하다 have measles [smallpox]

제국 帝國 an empire ♦제국의 imperial
■—대영— the British Empire 로마— the Roman Empire

제국 諸國 various [many] countries
▶유럽 제국 European countries / 해외 제국 foreign countries

제국주의 帝國主義 imperialism
♦제국주의적 imperialistic
■—반— anti-imperialism: 반제국주의 감정 anti-imperialist sentiment —자 an imperialist

제군 諸君 gentlemen; my friends; you ⇨ 여러분

제금 〈樂〉 〈자바라의 하나〉 small cymbals

제금 提琴 〈樂〉 a violin; (口) a fiddle ⇨ 바이올린

제기¹ 〈놀이기구〉 a shuttlecock kicking on the sole; 〈놀이〉 a kicking shuttlecock game
♦제기를 차다 play shuttlecock with the feet

제기² 〈제기랄〉 Damn it!; Hang it!; Confound it!; God darn it!
▶제기 또 비가 오네 Gee, it's raining again!
▶제기 비싸기도 해라 It's damn expensive.

제기 祭器 ritual [sacrificial] vessels

제기 提起 presentation; 〈소송〉 institution; 〈항의〉 lodging; 〈제언〉 suggestion
▶새로운 정책의 제기가 물의를 일으켰다 The presentation of the new policy has given rise to criticism.
—제기하다 present; institute; lodge; submit; bring forward; raise 《a question》; bring up
♦이의(異議)를 제기하다 raise an objection 《to》
▶그는 드디어 소송을 제기했다 He instituted [lodged] a law suit at last.

제기다¹ **1**〈알제기다〉 have a white speck in the pupil of *one's* eye
2〈빠져 달아나다〉 sneak away from 《company》; steal [slip] out of 《a room》
제기다² **1**〈지르다〉 kick [nudge] with the heel [elbow]; heel; elbow
2〈깎다〉 whittle at 《a piece of wood》; trim
3〈붓다〉 pour 《water》 a little at a time
4〈맞히다〉 hit *one's* target coin in a money-tossing game

제기랄 Damn it! ⇨ 제기²

제깐에 in *one's* own thought [estimation, opinion]; to *one's* own mind [thinking]
▶그녀는 제깐에는 미인으로 알고 있다 She fancies herself beautiful. ⇒ She is beautiful in her own conceit.

제 꾀에 넘어간다〈속담〉 A schemer is caught in [deceived by] his own scheme.

제너〈영국의 의사, 종두법(種痘法)의 발견자〉 Jenner, Edward (1749-1823)

제너레이션〈세대〉 a generation

제네바〈스위스 남서부의 도시〉 Geneva
◆ 제네바의 Genevan; Genevese
■ —사람 a Genevan; a Genevese —협정 Geneva Conventions

제 논에 물대기〈속담〉 Every miller draws water to his own mill.

제 눈에 안경이다〈속담〉 Beauty is in the eye of the beholder. ⇒ Love blinds us to all imperfections. ⇒ Love is blind.

제단 祭壇 an altar ◆제단을 설치하다 prepare an altar ▶그는 제단으로 걸어올라가 꽃을 바쳤다 He walked up to the altar and decorated it with flowers.

제당 製糖 sugar manufacture
—제당하다 make sugar
■ —공장 a sugar mill [refinery] —업 the sugar-manufacturing industry —회사 a sugar-manufacturing company

제대 除隊 discharge from military service
—제대하다 leave the army; be (honorably) discharged from military service
▶그는 제대했다 He was discharged from military service.
■ 만기[명예]— an honorable discharge 불명예— a dishonorable discharge 의가사[의점]— a discharge from service by family hardships [of illness] ■ —군인 a discharged soldier; a dischargee; a veteran —명령 discharge orders —휴가 terminal [英] demobilization] leave

제대 梯隊〔軍〕 an echelon

제대로 1〈있는 그대로〉 as it is [stands]; intact; untouched ◆제대로 놔두다 leave 《a thing》 as it is [stands]
2〈바르게〉 in regular order; normally; regularly; properly; favorably; well; all right ◆만사가 제대로 되면 if everything [all] goes well; if nothing goes amiss / 외국어를 제대로 배우다 study a foreign language systematically
▶내겐 제대로 되는 일이 하나도 없었다 Everything went wrong with me.
3〈충분히〉 well; enough; fully; properly
◆제대로 생각지도 않고 without due consideration
▶그는 편지 하나 제대로 못쓴다 He can't even write a letter properly.
▶나는 간밤에 제대로 잠자지 못했다 I didn't get enough sleep [sleep well] last night.
▶제대로 살피지도 않고 그것을 사버렸다 I bought it without looking at it well.

제도 制度〈조직적인〉 a system;〈관습적인〉 an institution;〈기구〉 an organization
◆제도상의 결함 a defect in a system / 구[새] 제도하에 under the old [new] system / 제도를 마련[채용, 폐지]하다 establish [adopt, abolish] a system / 제도를 시행하다 put a system in operation
▶아이입양은 중요한 사회의 제도가 되고 있다 Child adoption is becoming an important social institution.
■ 교육— an educational system 결혼— the institution of marriage 문물— culture and institution 사회— a social system; a regime 의회— the parliamentary system [regime] 현행— the existing system

제도 製陶 pottery manufacture; porcelain making ■ —술 pottery —업 the pottery manufacturing industry

제도 製圖 drawing; drafting;〈지도의〉 cartography —제도하다 draft; draw
■ —가 a draftsman; a cartographer —기 a drawing instrument; draft equipment; drawing set —실 a drawing [drafting] room —연필 a drawing pen —용구 a draftsman's outfit —용지 drawing paper —판 a drawing [drafting] board

제도 諸島 (a group of) islands; an archipelago《*pl*. ～es, ～s》
▶하와이제도 the Hawaiian Islands / 말레이제도 the Malay Archipelago / 영국 제도 the British Isles

제도 濟度 salvation; redemption
—제도하다 save; redeem
◆제도할 수 없는 사람 a lost soul; an incorrigible person / 중생을 제도하다 work the salvation of all creature
▶그는 제도하기 어려운 사람이다 He is beyond redemption.
■ 중생— salvation of the world

제독 提督 an admiral; (美) a commodore
◆넬슨제독 (Fleet) Admiral Nelson

제 독주다 制毒—〈기운을 꺾다〉 humble [humiliate] *sb*; take *sb* down a notch or two; cut *sb's* comb

제독하다 除毒— neutralize the poison

제동〔機〕braking;〔電〕damping;〈스키〉 stemming
◆제동을 걸다 apply [put on] the brake
■ —레버 a safety lever —수 (美) a brakeman —자(子)〔電〕 a damper —장치 a damping [braking] device; a brake gear;〔空〕 an arresting gear —차〔鐵〕 a brake van —활강〔登山〕 glissade —회전 a stem turn

제동기 制動機 a brake ⇨ 브레이크

제등 提燈 a (paper) lantern
■ —행렬 a lantern parade: 제등 행렬을 하다 hold a lantern procession

제딴은 in *one's* own opinion

제때 a right [an appointed, a fixed, a scheduled] time; the right occasion
♦ 제때에 at a good time; just at the right moment / 제때에 끝내다 get *sth* done by the time appointed
▶ 김장은 제때에 담가야 한다 You have to make your *kimchi* at the right season.
▶ 제때의 예방은 때 늦은 치료보다 낫다 (속담) An ounce of prevention is better than [worth] a pound of care. ⇌ A stitch in time saves time.

제라늄 〔植〕 a geranium 《*pl.* ~s》

제련 製鍊 refining; refinement; smelting
♦ 제련용 용광로 a smelting furnace
─제련하다 refine (minerals); smelt (copper)
■ ─소 a refinery; a smelting works ─업 the refining industry ─업자 a refiner; smelter

제령 制令 laws and institutions

제례 祭禮 religious ceremonies; memorial services

제로 zero 《*pl.* ~s, ~es》; 《英》 (a) nought
♦ 시계 (視界) 제로에서 전진하다 go on in zero visibility
▶ 지침은 제로를 가리키고 있었다 The indicator on the scale pointed to zero.
▶ 그의 화학 점수는 제로였다 He got a zero in chemistry.
▶ 나의 물리 지식은 제로에 가깝다 I know practically nothing about physics.
▶ 100에 제로를 곱하면 제로다 Multiply 100 by nothing, and the result is nothing.
■ ─게임 〔테니스〕 a love game

제록스 《商標》 Xerox
♦ 편지를 제록스하다 make [take] a xerox of the letter; xerox the letter

제마 製麻 〈삼의 제조〉 hemp dressing; manufacture of hemp
─제마하다 dress [spin] hemp
■ ─회사 a hemp-dressing company

제막 除幕 (an) unveiling
─제막하다 unveil (a statue)
─식 the unveiling ceremony (of a statue): 그들은 고 김 박사의 기념비 제막식을 거행했다 They unveiled the monument of the late Dr. Kim.

제멋 *one's* own taste [way, fancy]
▶ 사람은 모두 제멋에 산다 All men live after their ways.

제멋대로 at will; as *one* pleases [likes]; at *one's* own pleasure
♦ 제멋대로 하다 [굴다] have (everything) *one's* own way; go [have] *one's* own way; do as *one* pleases / 제멋대로 살다 live to *oneself*; live selfishly
▶ 나는 네가 제멋대로 구는 것을 내버려 둘 수가 없다 I cannot let you have your own way.
▶ 아이들을 제멋대로 하게 내버려 둬서는 안됩니다 You shouldn't let your children have their own way.
▶ 그 아이들은 제멋대로 두어서 버릇이 없다 The children know no manners, for they are left to take care of themselves.

제면 製綿 cotton carding ─제면하다 〈씨를 빼다〉 gin cotton; 〈솜을 틀다〉 card cotton
■ ─기 a cotton carding machine

제면 製麵 noodle-making ─제면하다 make noodles ■ ─기 a noodle-making machine

제명 除名 expulsion; striking off a name
─제명하다 expel (*sb* from a club); take *sb's* name off the list [roll] / strike *one's* name off a list
▶ 그는 노동조합[팀]에서 제명되었다 He was expelled from [(口) was kicked out of] the labor union [team].

제명 題名 a title
♦ 「사랑」이라는 제명의 시집 an anthology of poems entitled *The Love* / 책에 제명을 붙이다 entitle a book / …라는 제명으로 출판되다 be published under the title…

제모 制帽 〈일반적으로〉 a regulation cap; 〈학생모〉 a school cap; 〈전투모〉 a combat hat

제목 題目 a subject; a theme; 〈표제〉 a title; a heading; 〈사진·만화 등의〉 a caption
♦ 제목을 붙이다 [달다] give a title; entitle; headline / 책에 제목을 붙이다 entitle a book
▶ 그는 우정이라는 제목으로 글을 썼다 He wrote a composition entitled [on the subject of] Friendship.
▶ 윌리엄 박사는 새로운 에너지라는 제목으로 강연했다 Dr. William spoke on the subject [theme] of The New Energy.
▶ 이 연극의 제목은 「햄릿」이다 The title of this play is *Hamlet*.
▶ 그의 책 제목은 뭐냐? What is the subject [theme] of his book?

제문 祭文 a funeral message; 〈제사 때의〉 a written address to the deities
♦ 제문을 낭독하다 read *one's* message of funeral; make a memorial address

제물 1 〈우러난 국물〉 gravy 《from meat》; 〈처음부터 둔물〉 the original water in which food was boiled
2 〈순수한 것〉 genuine [pure] stuff

제물 祭物 an offering; a sacrifice
♦ 신에게 제물을 바치다 make an offering to God [the gods]; offer a sacrifice to a deity; sacrifice to idols / 동물을 제물로 바치다 offer an animal in sacrifice / 제물로 삼다 (비유) victimize *sb*; make a scapegoat of *sb*

제물낚시 a fly; an artificial fly
♦ 제물낚시로 낚다 fish [angle] with a fly; fly-fish

제물로 of itself ⇨ 저절로
▶ 내 충치가 제물로 빠졌다 My decayed tooth has come out of itself.

제바람 ♦ 제바람에 of itself; by itself; under its own steam

제반 諸般 〈형용사적〉 various; several; all
♦ 제반 정세 all circumstances; the general state of things / 제반 준비를 갖추다 make every preparation (for) / 제반 사정을 고려하다 take all the circumstances into consideration
▶ 제반 사정으로 요구를 들어 줄 수 없습니다 Circumstances do not allow us to accept your request. ─사 various matters [affairs]

제반미 祭飯米 rice offered in memorial ser-

vice
제발 please; for God's [Heaven's] sake; kindly; pray
▶ 제발 문 좀 닫아주세요 Kindly oblige me by closing the door.
▶ 제발 열흘만 기다려 주십시오 For pity's sake, please wait ten days more.
제발덕분에 ─德分─ for mercy's sake; I beg of you; I pray you
▶ 제발덕분에 이 부탁을 들어주십시오 I entreat [pray] this favor of you.
제방 堤防 〈美〉 a levee; a bank; an embankment; a dike; 〈둑길〉 a causeway
♦ 제방을 쌓다 construct [build] a bank; put up a (confining) levee
▶ 제방이 터졌다 The bank gave away [collapsed]. ⇌ The dike has broken. ⇌ The embankment has collapsed.
▶ 강이 범람해서 제방이 유실되었다 The river overflowed and its bank was washed away.
제백사하다 除百事─ lay everything aside; set aside everything
▶ 제백사하고 오늘 이것을 하거라 Do this (the) first thing today.
▶ 제백사하고 아버님을 찾아 뵙겠습니다 I'll let everything else go and visit father.
제 버릇 개 줄까 〈속담〉 It is difficult for a man to give up his old bad habits. ⇌ Once a user forever a custom.
제번하다 除煩─ be without trouble
♦ (편지에서) 제번하옵고 I hasten to inform that...; Without ceremony...
제법 fairly; rather; pretty; quite; considerably; 〈생각 이상으로〉 beyond one's expectation
♦ 제법 시간이 걸리다 take a great deal of time
▶ 저 여학생은 제법 영어를 잘한다 That girl student speaks English fairly well.
▶ 제법 덥다 It is quite [rather] hot.
▶ 그는 제법이다 He is better than expected.
▶ 우리는 산꼭대기에 오르는 데 제법 시간이 걸렸다 We took a lot of time to go up the mountaintop.
▶ 소년은 테니스도 제법 친다 The boy is not half bad at tennis.
제법 除法 〔數〕 division ⇨ 나눗셈
제법 製法 a method [process] of manufacture; 〈요리 등〉 a recipe 《for》
▶ 이 빵의 제법을 알고 싶어요 I'd like to know the recipe for this bread.
제복 制服 a uniform; a livery
♦ 학교의 제복 a school uniform / 제복 차림의 경찰관 a uniformed policeman / 제복을 입다 [입고 있다] put on [wear] a uniform
▶ 여러분은 제복을 입고 등교해야 합니다 You should come to school in uniform.
제복 除服 〈거상 (居喪)을 벗음〉 going out of mourning ─**제복하다** go out of mourning; leave off mourning
제복 祭服 sacrificial robes; (liturgical) vestments
제본 製本 bookbinding
♦ 제본이 잘 되어 있다 be well bound / 가제본 (假製本)을 하다 make up a dummy book / 논문 제본을 하게 하다 have a treatise bound
▶ 이 사전은 제본이 잘 돼 있다 This dictionary is well bound.
─**제본하다** bind a book
♦ 3권을 1책으로 제본하다 bind (up) three volume into one
▶ 그 책은 지금 제본하는 중입니다 The book is binding [being bound] now.
■ ─소 a (book)bindery ─업 the bookbinding industry ─업자 a (book)binder
제분 製粉 milling
─**제분하다** grind 《grains》 to powder
■ ─기 a (flour) mill ─소 a flour mill ─업 the milling industry ─업자 a miller
제붙이 one's blood relatives [relations]
제비[1] 〈추첨〉 a lot; a lottery
♦ 제비 뽑다 draw [cast] lots / 제비를 뽑아 짝을 정하다 decide partners by lots / 제비로 차례를 정하다 draw lots for turns
▶ 내가 제비에 당첨됐다 The lot fell upon [to] me.
▶ 제비가 꽝이 나왔다 I drew a blank.
▶ 제비로 순번을 정하자 Let us draw lots and decide who's first.
▶ (경기의) 대진은 제비로 결정되었다 The pairings were drawn by ballot.
제비[2] 〔鳥〕 a swallow
▶ 제비 한 마리 왔다고 여름이 된 건 아니다 One swallow does not make a summer.
■ ─집 a swallow's nest
제비꽃 〔植〕 a violet
제비족 ─族 a gigolo
제빙 除氷 deicing; defrosting ─**제빙하다** deice; defrost ■ ─장치 a deicer
제빙 製氷 ice manufacture
■ ─공장 an ice plant ─기 an ice (making) machinery ─접시 〈냉장고의〉 an ice (cube) tray
제사 祭司 a [an officiating] priest; an officiant
제사 祭祀 〈종교적인〉 a religious service; (a) sacrifice; sacrificial rites; 〈조상에 대한〉 ancestral rites
♦ 제사를 지내다 perform an ancestral sacrifice; make sacrifices 《to》
▶ 우리는 추석에 조상의 영전에 제사 지낸다 We worship our (deceased) ancestors during ch'usŏk [the Korean (version of) Thanksgiving Day].
▶ 제삿날 a (memorial) sacrifice day; the anniversary of sb's death
제사 製絲 silk reeling 〈방적〉 spinning; 〈생사의〉 filature
■ ─공장 a filature; a silk mill ─기계 a reeling machine ─업 the silk-spinning industry ─업자 a silk-manufacture
제사 題詞 an epigraph; a prefatory motto
제사 第四 the fourth; number [No.] 4
■ ─계급 〈무산계급〉 the proletariat; 〈언론계〉 the fourth estate; journalists
제사기 第四紀 〔地質〕 the Quaternary period
제사날로 as one wants; of one's own accord; on [upon] one's own initiative
제산제 制酸劑 an antacid; an antiacid (agent)

제살붙이 *one's* blood relatives [relations]
제삼 第三 the third; number [No.] 3
◆ 제삼의 third; tertiary
■ 一계급 the third estate; the bourgeoisie 一기(期) the third term 一세력 a third force; 〈당파의〉 the third partisan group 一의불 atomic energy; nuclear power 一인칭 〖文法〗 the third person 一자 a third person [party]; an outsider 一제국 the Third Reich
제삼국 〈당사국 이외의 국가〉 a third power
■ 一인 third (power) nationals
제삼기 第三紀 〖地質〗 the Tertiary (period)
제삼자 〈삼자〉 a third person [party]; a disinterest person; 〈국외자〉 an outsider
◆ 제삼자의 위치에 서다 take *one's* position as a third party; stand outside
제상 祭床 a sacrificial table; a table spread with ritual food
제석 帝釋 〖民俗〗 the Harvest God ⇨ 제석천
■ 一풀이 the shamanistic rite celebrating the Harvest God: 제석 풀이하다 celebrate the Harvest God
제석 祭席 a prayer mat (used for a sacrifice)
제석천 帝釋天 (산) Sakra devanam Indra
제설 除雪 snow removing [removal]; snow clearing 一기 a snowplow 一작업 snow-removing work; snow clearing work
제설 諸説 〈여러가지 의견〉 various views [opinions, theories]
▶ 그 문제에 관해서는 제설이 분분하다 Various views are being expressed on the matter. ⇌ The opinion is divided on the matter.
제세 濟世 salvation of the world
一제세하다 save the world
■ 一안민(安民) promotion of social welfare and people's relief
제소 提訴 instituting a lawsuit
一제소하다 bring an action (against *sb*); bring...before the court; 〈고소하다〉 sue; appeal to...; institute (a lawsuit)
◆ 그 사건을 제소하다 bring the case before the court; present the case to the court
▶ 그 나라는 ILO에 제소했다 The country appealed to the ILO (=International Labor Organization).
▶ 그 분쟁은 결국 법원에 제소되었다 Finally the dispute was brought into court.
■ 一자 a suitor; a complainant
제수 弟嫂 *one's* younger brother's wife ⇨ 계수 (季嫂)
제수 除數 〖數〗 a divisor = 나눗수
■ 피一 a dividend
제수 祭需 offerings for a sacrifice; ritual food
제스처 〖몸짓〗 (a) gesture
◆ 제스처를 쓰다 make a gesture
▶ 그의 거절은 외교적[정치적]인 제스처에 지나지 않는다 His refusal is a mere diplomatic [political] gesture.
■ 一게임 charade
제습 除濕 dehumidification 一제습하다 dehumidify ■ 一기(器) a dehumidifier
제시 提示 presentation
一제시하다 present; show; 〖法〗 exhibit
◆ 실례를 차례로 제시하다 trot out examples

▶ 여권을 제시해 주십시오 Please show me your passport.
■ 一부 (樂) exposition
제시간 一時間 the regular [scheduled, fixed] time
◆ 제시간에 on time; at the appointed time / 제시간에 도착하다 arrive on schedule [time]; arrive duly
▶ 우리는 제시간보다 5분 늦었다 We are five minutes behind schedule.
▶ 그는 제시간까지 오지 않았다 He did not come by the appointed time.
제식교련 制式教鍊 〖軍〗 close-order drill
제씨 弟氏 your younger brother
제씨 諸氏 gentlemen; you; Messrs
◆ 독자 제씨 my readers
제안 提案 a proposal; a proposition; a suggestion ◆ 제안을 설명하다 enunciate the proposition (that)
一제안하다 propose; suggest; move; make overtures
▶ 나는 위원회에 다른 계획을 제안했다 I suggested another plan to the committee.
▶ 시의회는 그의 제안을 가결[부결]했다 The municipal assembly [city council] adopted [rejected] his proposal.
▶ 그는 계획을 변경할 것을 제안했다 He proposed a change of plan.
■ 반대一 a counterproposal 一설명 the description [enunciation] of a proposition 一이유 a reason for a proposal 一자 a proposer; a proponent; a suggester
제암 制癌 cancer inhibition; cancer prevention ■ 一제 an anti-cancer drug [medicine]
제압 制壓 control; suppression; ascendancy; supremacy; mastery
一제압하다 control; dominate; gain ascendancy [supremacy] over
◆ 바다를 제압하다 gain control of the seas; bring the sea under *one's* control / 반란을 제압하다 suppress a revolt
제야 除夜 〈섣달 그믐날〉 New Year's Eve
◆ 제야의 종소리 the watch-night bell; the bells that ring out the old year
▶ 제야의 종이 울리고 있다 The bells are ringing out the old year.
제약 制約 〈사람·행위 등을 제한함〉 (a) restriction; 〈행위 등의 한정·제한〉 (a) limitation; 〈속박·구속〉 (a) restraint; 〈조건〉 a condition
◆ 엄격한 제약을 받다[받고 있다] come [be] under strict restrictions / 유형무형의 제약을 받다 be restricted physically and mentally
▶ 우리 사회는 많은 제약이 있다 Our society is hampered by a lot of restrictions.
▶ 이 계약에는 아무 제약도 붙이지 않습니다 I will make no conditions on this contract.
▶ 나는 시간에 제약을 받으며 그것을 해야 한다 I must do it with a limited length of time.
▶ 이 나라에는 많은 수입 제약이 있다 There are a lot of limitations on imports in this country.
一제약하다 restrict; restrain; limit
◆ 정치적인 활동을 제약하다 restrict [put restrictions on] political activities

제안·요구·권유 등의 표현

1. …하면 어떨까라고 말하다 (시사·제안)
suggest *sb* + **that...** 동사의 원형
▶ 나는 그에게 중고차를 사는게 어떻겠느냐고 말했다 I suggested that he buy a used car.
▶ 선생님은 그녀에게 전공을 바꾸어 보는 것이 어떻겠느냐고 말씀하셨다 The teacher suggested that she change her major.
▶ 나는 톰에게 더 싼 아파트로 옮기면 어떻겠느냐고 말했다 I suggested to Tom that he move to a cheaper apartment.
[어법]
that clause에 동사의 원형을 쓰는 것은 (美)의 용법이다. (英)에서는 should + 동사의 원형을 쓴다.
[보기] (美) I suggested that he buy a used car./ (英) I suggested that he should buy a used car. (▶이것은 다음 1에서 8까지의 모든 항에 해당됨)

2. …하면 어떨까하고 제안하다
propose + **that...** 동사의 원형
▶ 그녀는 그들의 휴가를 하와이에서 보내면 어떻겠느냐고 제안했다 She proposed that they spend their holidays in Hawaii.
▶ 그는 김군을 서기로 임명하면 어떨까하고 제안했다 He proposed that Mr. Kim be appointed secretary.
▶ 몇몇 위원은 회의를 연기할 것을 제안했다 Several members of the committee proposed that the meeting be postponed.

3. …할 것을 요구하다[요청하다]
demand + **that...** 동사의 원형
▶ 선생님은 그녀에게 월요일까지 리포트를 내라고 말씀하셨다 The teacher demanded that she hand in her report by Monday.
▶ 야당이 한씨의 사임을 요구했다 The opposition demanded that Mr. Han resign.
▶ 그는 그 돈을 즉각 반환해 달라고 요구했다 He demanded that the money be repaid promptly.

4. …할 것을 주장하다[고집을 부리다]
insist + **that...** 동사의 원형
▶ 나는 몸이 좋지 않았다. 어머니는 나더러 곧 쉬어야 한다고 하셨다 I wasn't feeling well. Mother insisted that I go to bed at once.
▶ 그의 양친은 그가 충분한 휴식을 취해야 한다고 했다 His parents insisted that he take plenty of rest.
▶ 나는 그를 파티에 초대해야 한다고 주장했다 I insisted that he be invited to the party.

5. …할 것을 동의[제의]하다
move + **that...** 동사의 원형
▶ 그는 휴회할 것을 제의했다 He moved that the meeting be adjourned.

▶ 김여사는 그 돈을 도서비로 돌릴 것을 제의했다 Mrs. Kim moved that the money be used for library books.

6. …하도록 권하다[권고하다]
recommend + **that...** 동사의 원형
▶ 나는 그에게 새 차를 사는게 좋을 것이라고 권했다 I recommended that he buy a new car.
▶ 시의회는 고등학교를 신설하라고 권고했다 The city council recommended that a new high school be built.
[어법]
같은 내용을 recommend + 목적어 + to do 로도 표현할 수 있다.
[보기] I recommended him to buy a new car./ The city council recommended the mayor to built a new high school.(▶the mayor를 보충함)

7. …하는 것이 필요하다[꼭 필요하다, 중요하다]
It is necessary [essential, important] that... 동사의 원형
▶ 우리는 석유를 절약할 필요가 있다 It is necessary that we economize oil. ≒ It is necessary that oil be economized.
▶ 이 일은 무슨 일이 있어도 즉각 할 필요가 있다 It is essential that this work be done immediately.
▶ 우리는 서로 잘 아는 일이 중요하다 It is important that we know each other well.
[어법]
① 위 형용사 외에 better, advisable, desirable 등도 같은 구문으로 쓰인다.
② 위의 구문 외에 It is necessary [essential, important, etc.] for *sb* to do로도 같은 뜻을 나타낼 수가 있다.
[보기] It is necessary for us to economize oil. ≒ It is essential for this work to be done immediately.

8. …라는 시사[제안·요구 등]
a [*one's*] suggestion [demand, recommendation, etc.] that... 동사의 원형
▶ 영화를 보러 가면 어떨까 하는 것이 그의 제안이었다 It was his suggestion that we go to the movies.
▶ 그녀가 그만둬야 한다는 제안은 최종적으로 부결되었다 The suggestion that she resign was finally rejected.
▶ 그의 사임이 요구되고 있었다 There have been demands that he resign.
▶ 시의회는 학교를 5년 이내에 신설하라고 권고했다 The city council made a recommendation that a new school be built within five years.

제약 製藥 medicine [drug] manufacturing [making]; 〈제약술〉 pharmacy ■—**공장** a pharmaceutical factory —**업** the pharmaceutical industry —**업자** a medicine manufacturer; a pharmacist —**화학** pharmaceutical chemistry —**회사** a pharmaceutical company

제어 制御 control; governing —**제어하다** control; govern; manage; bridle (*one's* passion) ♦**제어 가능한[불가능한]** controllable [uncontrollable]; manageable [unmanageable];

docile [indomitable] / 제어할 수 없게 되다 lose control 《of》
■—기 a controller; a regulator —량 controlled variable —봉[막대] 〈원자로의〉 a control rod; rod cluster —작용 control action —장치 controller

제염 製鹽 salt making [manufacture]
■—소 a saltern; a salina —업 the salt (-making) industry —업자 a salt-worker

제오 第五 the fifth; number [No.] 5
■—공화국 the Fifth Republic: 제5공화국 정부 the Fifth Republic Government of Korea. —성병 the fifth venereal disease

제오열 第五列 the Fifth Column
■—분자 a Fifth Columnist

제왕 帝王 an emperor; a sovereign; a monarch
■—신권설 the theory of the divine right of kings —절개(술) 〔醫〕 a Caesarean operation [section]; 이 아기는 제왕절개로 태어났다 This child was born by Caesarean operation [section]. —학 a study of regal principles

제외 除外 exclusion; exemption; exception
—제외하다 except 《sth from the list》; exclude; 〈면제하다〉 exempt 《sb from a study》
♦ …를 제외하고 except; save; but; with the exception of / 소수를 제외하고 with a few exceptions / 여기에 있는 사람들을 제외하고 the present company excepted / 제외되다 be ruled out [off]
▶ 우리는 어린이를 제외하고 모두 10명이다 We are ten in all, excluding children.
▶ 그를 제외하고 누가 그걸 할 수 있을까? Who can do it except him?
▶ 나를 제외하고는 아무도 대답하지 못할 것이다 No one will reply but me.
▶ 이 법률은 미성년자를 제외한 전 시민에 적용된다 This law is applied to all the citizens except minors.
▶ 우리는 토요일을 제외하고 매일 영어 공부를 한다 We have an English lesson every day except Saturdays.

제요 提要 a gist; a summary; an epitome; a compendium ♦「윤리학 제요」 A Manual of Ethics / 생물학 제요 an outline [a survey] of biology ■—서 a manual; a handbook

제욕 制慾 the control of passion; suppression of one's desire —제욕하다 control one's passion; control oneself; suppress one's desire

제우스 〔그神〕 Zeus

제웅 〔民俗〕 a straw effigy

제위 帝位 the (imperial) throne; the crown
♦ 제위에 오르다 accede [ascend, mount] the throne; be crowned / 제위를 잇다 succeed to the throne / 제위를 넘겨주다 hand the crown to; abdicate the throne 《in favor of the crown prince》 / 제위를 빼앗다 usurp the throne / 제위를 다투다 pretend to [fight for] the throne

제위 祭位 the enshrined deity; a spirit to whom sacrifices are made

제위 諸位 〈여러분〉 gentlemen; all; everyone

제유 製油 oil manufacture ■—공장 an oil factory [refinery] —업 oil industry

제육 pork; hog meat [flesh]
■—구이 roast pork

제육감 第六感 a sixth sense ▶ 나는 제육감으로 그것을 알았다 I knew that by intuition. ⇌ My sixth sense told me that.

제의 提議 a proposal; a proposition; an offer; an overture; a suggestion
♦ … 의 제의로 at the instance [motion] of…/ 제의에 응하다 accept sb's offer / 제의에 동의하다 agree to sb's proposal / …의 제의를 거절하다 decline sb's offer
▶ 그 강에 다리를 놓자는 제의가 있었다 There was a proposal [suggestion] that we (should) build a bridge over the river. ⇌ There was a proposal [suggestion] to build a bridge over the river.
—제의하다 propose; offer; suggest; make a proposition; make overtures; suggest; move
▶ 나는 다른 방법을 제의한다 I'd like to suggest a different plan.
▶ 나는 아침에 출발할 것을 제의한다 I propose leaving [that we (should) leave] in the morning.
▶ 그는 내게 집을 사면 어떻겠느냐고 제의했다 He suggested (to me) that I buy the house. ⇌ He suggested my buying the house.
■—자 a proposer; a proponent

제이 第二 the second; 〈2차적인〉 secondary; number [No.] 2; 〈또 하나의〉 another
♦ 제이의 것[문제] a matter of secondary importance
▶ 그는 제이의 아인슈타인이 되고 싶어한다 He wishes to be a second [another] Einstein.
▶ 서울은 나의 제이의 고향이다 Seoul is my second [adopted] home.
▶ 그는 은퇴한 후 작가로서 제이의 인생을 시작했다 He started a new life as a writer after he retired.
■—국민역 disqualified conscription status —당 the second largest party —독회 the second reading —보충역 retired replacement status —인칭 〔文法〕 the second person —주제 〔樂〕 the subsidiary (theme)

제이차 第二次 ■—산업 the secondary industry —세계대전 World War Ⅱ; the Second World War —제품 secondary products —집단 〔社〕 a secondary group

제일 除日 New Year's Eve; the last day of the year

제일 祭日 a sacrifice day ⇨ 제사 (제삿날)

제일 第一 1 〈첫째의〉 the first; number [No.] 1; 〈중요한〉 primary; 〈으뜸의〉 the best; 〈선도적인〉 leading; 〈선두적인〉 the foremost; 〈전체중에서 주된〉 main
♦ KBS 제일방송 KBS 1 / 제일장 the first chapter; chapter 1 / 신문의 제일면 the front page of a newspaper / 심장질환의 제일인자 the leading authority on heart disease; the foremost heart disease specialist / 제일야당 the chief opposition party / 제일의 목표 the prime target / 세계제일의 부자 the richest man in the world / 재계 제일의 세력가 the most influential of all financiers
▶ 건강이 제일이다 Nothing is more important

than health. ⇌ Health is the most important of all.
▶성공에는 끈기가 제일이다 Perseverance is the first essential to success.
2 〈가장〉 most; best
♦제일 아름답다 be most beautiful of all
▶나는 이것이 제일 좋다 I like this best (of all).
▶나는 이것이 제일 어렵다 This troubles me (the) most.
▶그게 제일 좋은 방법이다 That's the best way.
■―강산 the first-class scenery ―과(課) the first lesson; lesson one; 〈회사 등〉 the first section ―국민역 eligible conscription status ―당 the leading party ―보충역 standby replacement status ―야당 the major opposition party ―차 세계대전 World War Ⅰ; the First World War

제일기 第一期 the first period [term]; 〈병등의〉 the first [initial] stage
■―불입 payment of the first installment ―졸업생 a first-time graduate

제일보 第一步 the first step; 〈발족〉 a start
♦제일보를 내딛다 start; make a start; take the first step
▶노력은 성공으로 가는 제일보다 Making an effort is the first step to success.

제일선 第一線 the forefront; 〈전선〉 the front
▶우리 아버지는 아직 제일선에서 활약중이시다 My father is still active in the forefront.
▶그는 제일선에서 물러났다 He has retired from active life.

제일성 第一聲 one's first speech
▶그는 국회에서 귀국 제일성을 피력했다 In the National Assembly he made his first (public) speech after returning from abroad.

제일심 第一審 the first trial [hearing]
♦제일심에서 무죄가 되다 be acquitted at the first trial
▶그는 제일심에서는 승소했으나 제이심에서는 패소했다 At the first hearing he won the case, but was defeated at the second.

제일인자 第一人者 the first man [person] 《in》; a leading person
▶그는 이 분야의 제일인자다 He is the leading [foremost] man in this field.
▶그녀는 자기 분야에서 제일인자다 She is at the top of her profession.

제임스 〈미국의 소설가〉 James, Henry (1843-1916); 〈미국의 심리학자〉 James, William (1842-1910)

제자 弟子 a pupil; a student; a disciple follower; an adherent; 〈도제〉 an apprentice
♦제자가 되다 become a pupil of
♦아버지는 그를 제자로 삼았다 Father took him as an apprentice.
▶그는 그 목수의 제자가 되었다 He was apprenticed to the carpenter.

제자 諸子 **1** 〈여러분〉 you **2** 〈자식들〉 one's sons **3** 〈중국의〉 masters; sages
■―백가 all philosophers and scholars; all classes of philosophers

제자 題字 a title; a heading; an inscription

제자리 〈마땅한 자리〉 the proper place; 〈본래 자리〉 the original [former] place
▶다 읽은 책은 제자리에 갖다 놓으시오 Put the book back in its place [to where it was] when you're through.
▶제자리에 〔競〕 On your marks!
■―멀리뛰기 a standing long jump

제자리걸음하다 1 〈나아가지 않고 걷는 동작을 하다〉 mark time ♦음악에 맞춰 제자리걸음하다 〈행진에서〉 mark time to the music
2 〈정체되어 진보하지 않다〉 come to a standstill; make no progress [headway]; be in a stalemate
♦제자리걸음하는 상태에 있다[가 되다] be at [come to] a temporary standstill
3 〈물가 등이〉 peg; remain stationary; mark time
▶물가는 4월 현재 제자리걸음하고 있다 The prices are pegged on the April basis.

제자리표 ―標 〔樂〕 a natural

제작 制作 a product; a work ―**제작하다** make; produce

제작 製作 manufacture; production
♦제작 중이다 be in the work
―**제작하다** manufacture; make
♦텔레비전프로그램을 제작하다 produce [make] a TV program
▶그들은 기계를 제작한다 They manufacture machines.
■―공동― (a) coproduction ―비 the cost of production; production cost ―실 a studio ―품 a manufactured product; a product

제작소 製作所 a factory; a plant; a works
■―국립영화― the National Film Production Center 영화― a movie studio [lot]

제작자 製作者 a maker; a manufacturer; 〔映〕 a producer
■―공동― 〔映〕 a coproducer

제잡담하다 除雜談― leave off [cut out] idle talk
▶제잡담하고, 본제로 돌아갑시다 Now, idle chatter aside, let's return to our topic.

제재 制裁 punishment; sanction(s)
♦경제[사회, 군사]적인 제재 economic [social, military] sanction / 법의 제재 legal sanction / 제재를 가하다 take sanction / 제재를 풀다 lift sanctions
▶범인은 법의 제재를 받았다 The criminal was brought to justice [punished according to the law].
―**제재하다** take [apply] sanction 《against》; punish; inflict punishment 《upon》

제재 製材 sawing; 〈美〉 lumbering ―**제재하다** saw up 《logs》; lumber ―**소** a sawmill; a lumbermill ―**업** the lumbering industry

제재 題材 a subject; a theme; the subject matter; 〈자료〉 (a) material
♦역사적 사실을 제재로 삼다 use historical material for one's subject matter; get one's material from historical facts

제적 除籍 〈호적에서〉 removal from the register; 〈학적에서〉 expulsion from school
―**제적하다** remove sb's name from the register; expel; dismiss

제적당하다 be expelled from school
▶그의 이름은 회원 명단에서 제적되었다 His name was struck off [dropped from] the membership.

제전 祭典 a festival; festivities
◆스포츠 제전 a sports festival / 제전을 치르다 hold [celebrate] a festival

제절 諸節 all your family; all of you
▶댁내 제절이 무고하신지요 How are your people [family]? ⇒ How is [are] your family?

제정 制定 enactment; establishment; institution
―**제정하다** establish; enact; formulate ⟨a rule⟩; institute ⟨an order⟩
◆국기를 제정하다 decide on the national flag / 새헌법을 제정하다 establish [set up, enact] a new constitution / 법률을 제정하다 enact laws
■―법 a statute law ―자 a legislator

제정 帝政 imperial government [rule, regime]
―러시아 Czarist Russia

제정 祭政 the church and the state
■―분리 the separation of church and state ―일치 the unity of church and state; ⟨제도⟩ theocracy

제정 提呈 presentation ―**제정하다** present; submit ◆신임장을 제정하다 present one's credentials (to)

제정신 ―精神 **1** ⟨실신 상태에 대한⟩ consciousness; one's senses
◆제정신을 잃다 faint; lose consciousness [one's senses] / 제정신이 들다 recover [regain] consciousness; come to one's senses / 제정신이 들게 하다 bring sb to ⟨himself⟩; bring sb round
▶그녀는 3분 후에 제정신이 들었다 She became conscious [came to her senses, regained consciousness] after three minutes.
2 ⟨미친 상태에 대한⟩ sanity; one's right mind
◆제정신의 sane / 제정신이 아니다 be out of one's senses; be not in one's right mind / 제정신을 잃다 lose one's wits [sanity]; go mad
3 ⟨취한 상태에 대한⟩ soberness
◆제정신의 sober / 제정신으로 in soberness

제제다사 濟濟多士 a galaxy of intellects; many talented men and women
▶이 협회에는 기라성 같은 제제다사가 있다 A galaxy of distinguished people are on the membership of this society.

제조 製造 manufacture; production; making
◆자동차[무기] 제조 the production of automobiles [arms]
―**제조하다** manufacture; produce; make; turn out
▶그는 정밀 기계를 제조하고 있다 He is a maker of precision instruments.
▶이 기계는 독일에서 제조한 것이다 This machine is made in Germany [of German make].
▶많은 기업들이 해외에서 상품을 제조하기 시작했다 Many companies have begun to manufacture goods abroad.
▶이 공장은 월 만대의 텔레비전을 제조하고 있다 This factory produces [turns out] ten thousand television sets a month.
■―(공)업 the manufacturing industry ―능력 manufacturing [production] capacity ―법 ⟨공정⟩ a manufacturing process; ⟨기술⟩ a manufacturing technique ―업 경쟁력 manufacturing competitiveness ―업자 a manufacturer; a maker; a producer ―원가 the cost of production ―일자 the date of manufacture ―장[소] a factory; a manufactory; a plant; a mill ―지시서 a production order ―품 products; manufactured articles [goods] ―회사 a manufacturing company

제주 祭主 ⟨맏상제⟩ the chief mourner; ⟨주재자⟩ the master of religious rites

제주 祭酒 sacrificial wine; sacred beverage; libation ◆제주를 올리다 offer wine in sacrifice

제중 濟衆 salvation [redemption] of the people; saving the (distressed) masses

제지 制止 (a) restraint; (an) inhibition; control; a check
―**제지하다** stop; restrain; control; check; curb; keep sb from; hold back sb
◆군중을 제지하다 control [keep back] the crowd / 제지할 수 없다 be beyond [out of] one's control; be out of hand
▶경찰은 군중을 제지할 수 없었다 The police could not hold back the crowd. ⇒ The crowd wouldn't be controlled by the police.
▶폭력은 제지할 수 없는 상태에 이르렀다 Violence has gone beyond our control.

제지 製紙 paper manufacture
―**제지하다** make [manufacture] paper
■―공장 a paper mill [manufactory] ―기 a paper machine ―업 the paper(-manufacturing) industry ―업자 a paper manufacturer ―용 펄프 paper pulp ―회사 a paper manufacturing company

제차 諸車 various [all] kinds of vehicles
▶제차 통행금지 ⟨게시⟩ Closed to all vehicles [traffic].

제창 提唱 ⟨제의⟩ proposal; ⟨창도⟩ advocacy
―**제창하다** advocate; put forward; propose
◆개혁을 제창하다 call for reforms / 새로운 학설을 제창하다 bring forward [advocate] a new doctrine
■―자 an advocator; a proponent

제창 齊唱 ⟨樂⟩ unison; homophony
―**제창하다** sing in unison
◆애국가를 제창하다 sing the national anthem in unison

제철 the right [best] season
◆제철인[의] seasonable / 제철이 아닌 out of season; unseasonable / 제철이다 be in season
▶사과는 지금이 제철이다 Apples are now in season.
▶포도는 제철이 아니어서 무척 비싸다 Grapes are out of season and very expensive.
▶이런 복숭아는 8월이 제철이다 This type of peach is in season in August. ⇒ This kind of peach is ripe enough to eat [is ripe and ready for eating] in August.

제철 製鐵 steel making

―제철하다 manufacture iron
■**―소** an iron mill; an ironworks **―업** the iron industry **―업자** an iron manufacturer **―회사** an iron manufacturing company

제철 蹄鐵 a horseshoe ⇨ 편자

제쳐놓다 1 〈치워 놓다〉 put aside; lay away
▶이 문제는 당분간 제쳐놓읍시다 Let's put aside this question for a while.
 2 〈따로 골라 놓다〉 lay aside; set apart
♦후일을 위해 따로 제쳐놓다 lay aside for some future occasion / 자기가 쓸 몫으로 제쳐놓다 keep [put aside] for *one's* own use
 3 〈빼놓다〉 leave out; set aside
▶당신을 제쳐놓고 그 일을 할 사람이 없소 No one but you can do the job.
 4 〈미루어 놓다〉 let *sth* wait; put off; hold over
♦만사 제쳐놓고 before everything [anything else]; first of all; above all

제초 除草 weedkilling
―제초하다 weed (out)
▶그는 정원에서 제초하고 있었다 He was weeding the garden. **―기** a weeder **―제** a weedkiller; a weedicide

제출 提出 presentation; introduction
―제출하다 〈의안 등을〉 present; introduce; submit; lay [bring] 《a bill》; 〈의견을〉 offer; advance; 〈항의를〉 lodge [file] 《a protest with the authorities》; 〈사표를〉 tender; 〈증거를〉 produce; bring forward; 〈원서·담안을〉 give [send, hand] in
♦상사에게 사표를 제출하다 tender *one's* resignation to the chief / 시장에게 청원서를 제출하다 submit a petition to the mayor; present the mayor (with) a petition / 불신임안을 제출하다 move a vote for nonconfidence
▶필요한 서류를 될 수 있는대로 빨리 제출하시오 You must submit the necessary forms as soon as possible.
■**―자** a presenter; an introducer; 〈동의의〉 a mover

제충 除蟲 **―제충하다** get rid of worms; cure of worms; worm 《a dog》

제취 除臭 deodorization
―제취하다 deodorize; absorb the odor of

제치다 remove; get rid of; put *sth* out of the way; pull [take] away

제칠 第七 the seventh; number [No.] 7
♦제칠 천국 the Seventh Heaven / 제칠 함대 the Seventh Fleet

제키다 be grazed [abraded, chafed]
▶내 무릎이 제켜졌다 My knee was grazed [skinned].

제트 a jet
―기 a jet (plane): 제트기로 가다 go by jet; jet / 제트기로 여행하다 jet-hop **―기류** a jet stream **―엔진** a jet engine **―여객기** a jet airliner; a jetliner **―폭격기[전투기]** a jet bomber [fighter]

제파 諸派 various parties [factions, sects]
―연합 a federation of minor parties

제판 ♦제판으로 놀다[굴다] have everything *one's* own way; be the sole master of the situation / 제판처럼 떠들다 keep rattling away [on]

제판 製版 〔印〕 plate making **―제판하다** make plate (for printing)
■**사진―** photoengraving **―소** a platemaker's [engraver's] shop

제팔 第八 the eighth; number [No.] 8

제패 制覇 (a) conquest; domination; supremacy; mastery
―제패하다 conquer; dominate; gain supremacy
▶전국 고교 야구 대회를 제패하는 것이 그들의 꿈이다 They dream [have a dream] of winning the National High School Baseball Tournament.
■**공중[해상]― 세계―** the mastery of the air [sea] world conquest [hegemony]; domination of the world: 그들은 배구에서 3년 연속 세계 제패를 이룩했다 They won the championship in the world volleyball games for three consecutive years. ■**―전** a struggle for supremacy

제퍼슨 〈미국의 대통령〉 Jefferson, Thomas (1743-1826)

제풀로 of itself

제품 製品 a product; manufactures; manufactured goods [articles]
♦한국 제품 Korean(-made) goods / 실크 제품 silk manufactures [goods, things] / 신제품 a new product; a new line (of products)
▶우리 회사 제품은 잘 팔린다 The products of our company sell well.
■**공업―** industrial products **국내―** home [domestic] products **외국―** foreign-made articles ■**―계획** product planning

제하다 除― 1 〈나누다〉 divide
♦100을 25로 제하다 divide 100 by 25
 2 〈없애다〉 exclude
 3 〈공제하다〉 subtract [deduct, subduct] 《from》; take off
♦세금을 제하고 100만원의 수입 an income of one million won after tax
▶그 비용은 내 봉급에서 제하여졌다 The cost was taken off my pay [was deducted from my pay].

제한 制限 (a) restriction; (a) restraint; (a) limitation; a limit
♦제한 없이 freely; unrestrictedly; without limitation [restriction] / 제한 내[밖]에 within [beyond] the limits / 수에 제한이 있다 be limited in number / 제한을 가하다 place [put, impose] restrictions 《on》; set limits 《to》 / 제한을 완화하다 relax restrictions 《on trade》 / 제한을 철폐하다 lift [withdraw] restrictions
▶회원이 되는 데는 연령의 제한이 있다 There is an age limit on membership.
―제한하다 restrict; limit; confine
♦식사를 제한하다 place [put] *sb* on a diet / 행동을 제한받다 be restricted in *one's* movements
▶나는 담배를 하루 10개로 제한했다 I restricted my smoking to ten cigarettes a day. ⇌ I restricted [limited] myself to (smoking) ten cigarettes a day.
▶연설은 15분으로 제한되었다 Speech was lim-

■군비— armament limitation 산아— birth control 수입— import restrictions 연령— an age limit 한자— a limitation [restriction] on the use of Chinese characters ■—속도 a speed limit : 제한속도를 지키시오 Keep within the speed limit. —시간 the restricted [limited] hours; the time limit

제한적 制限的 restrictive
◆제한적[비제한적] 용법 the restrictive [non-restrictive] use 《of relative pronouns》

제해권 制海權 the command of the sea; naval supremacy
◆제해권을 잡다[잃다] secure [lose] command of the sea
▶그들은 인도양의 제해권을 쥐고 있었다 They ruled the Indian Ocean.

제행 諸行 all earthly [worldly] things
▶제행무상 All things flow and nothing is permanent [certain] in this world. ⇌ Everything is transient. ⇌ All is vanity.

제헌 制憲 establishment of the constitution
—제헌하다 establish the constitution
—절 Constitution Day

제혁 製革 leather manufacturing; tanning
—제혁하다 tan hides; make hides into leather
—공장 a tannery —업 the tanning industry

제현 諸賢 gentlemen
제형 諸兄 (my) dear friends
제호 題號 the title (of a book)
▶그는 자기 소설에「푸른 대지」라는 제호를 붙였다 He entitled his novel "The Green Earth."

제화 製靴 shoemaking
■—공 a shoemaker —공장 a shoemaking factory —업 the shoe industry

제후 諸侯 feudal lords

제휴 提携 cooperation; coalition; (口) a tie-up
▶시장은 양당의 제휴로 당선됐다 The mayor was elected through a two-party coalition.
—제휴하다 cooperate with; tie up with; join together; go hand in hand with
◆…와 제휴하여 일하다 work in concert [cooperation] with...
▶우리 회사는 미국 회사와 제휴하고 있다 Our company is tied up with an American firm.
▶우리는 귀사와 제휴하기를 원합니다 We hope to link up [affiliate] with your company.
■기술— a technical cooperation [tie-up] : …와 기술제휴하고 있다 be technically tied up with... ■—회사 an affiliated concern

젠장 Oh no!; Oh dear!; Damn [Dash, Hang] it!; Hell!
▶젠장, 또 지각이다 Oh dear! I'm late again.

젠체하다 make an affected pose; assume airs [an air of importance]; act big; be proud [arrogant]
◆젠체하는 사람 an affected [arrogant] person; a snob / 젠체하며 affectedly; with an air of importance
▶그렇게 젠체하지 마라 Don't give yourself such airs.

젠틀맨 a gentleman
젤라틴 gelatin(e) ◆젤라틴의 gelatinous
젤리 jelly; 《과자》 (a) jelly ◆젤리처럼 하다[되다] jelly; jellify
■—롤 a jelly roll

젯날 祭— a sacrifice day ⇨ 제사(제삿날)
젯메 祭— (cooked) sacrificial [sacred] rice
젯밥 祭— (cooked) rice that has been offered in sacrifice

조[1] 〖植〗 foxtail millet
조[2] that ⇨ 저[3]

조 兆 〖數〗《美》a trillion; 《英》a billion

조 條 1 〈조목〉 a provision; an article; a clause; an item
◆제1조 Article [Section] 1 / 헌법 제9조에 의거하여 under Article 9 of the Constitution
2 〈어떤 조건으로〉 ◆…조로 as; for; by way of
◆계약금조로 일금 20만원을 정히 영수함 I acknowledge receipt of the sum of 200,000 won as the down [initial] payment.

조 組 a company; a party; a band; a group; a team
◆이인조 a pair; a duet; a duo / 삼인조 강도 a trio of robbers / 이인 일조로 in pairs

조 朝 〈왕조〉 a dynasty; 〈치세〉 a reign
◆조선조 the Chosun Dynasty; the Yi Dynasty

조 調 1 〈음조〉 a tone; 〈가락〉 tune; 〈운율〉 a meter; 《英》a metre
◆장조 a major key / 다장[단]조로 in C major [minor] (▶이 경우에는 key를 쓰지 않는 것이 보통)
2 〈어조〉 a tone; 〈방식〉 a way; a manner; 〈태도〉 an air; an attitude
◆연설조로 in an oratorical tone / 농담조로 jokingly; half in jest / 시비조로 in a defiant attitude

-조 -造 made; built
◆연와조의 집 a house built of brick; a brick house

조가 弔歌 a dirge; an elegy
조가비 a shell
◆바닷가에서 조가비를 줍다 gather [pick, collect] shells on the beach
■—세공 shellwork

조각 a (broken) piece; a bit; a fragment; a slip; a strip; a slice; a scrap; a cut
◆유리 조각 pieces [fragments] of broken glass; splinters of glass / 종잇조각 bits [scraps] of paper / 깨진 꽃병 조각 fragments of a broken vase / 파이 한 조각 a cut [piece, slice] of pie / 조각으로 in pieces [scraps] / 두 조각으로 깨지다 break [be broken] in two
■—달 a crescent [decrescent] (moon); a waxing [waning] moon —보(褓) patchwork wrapping-cloth

조각 組閣 formation [organization] of a cabinet [ministry]
▶조각은 난항을 거듭하고 있다 Difficulties are being felt in the formation of the new cabinet.
—조각하다 form [organize] a cabinet

조각 彫刻 sculpture; carving; engraving
◆조각처럼 뚜렷한 얼굴 (finely) chiseled features
—조각하다 carve; sculpture; engrave; 〈금속에〉 chase; 〈끌로〉 chisel; cut

♦나무에 조각한 상 an image carved in wood / 대리석을 깎아 상을 만들다 carve marble into a statue / 대리석으로 조각한 상 a statue carved out of marble
■—가 an engraver; a sculptor —도 a chisel; 〈동판의〉 a graver; a burin —술 engraving; sculpture; sculptural art; 〈조소(彫塑)의〉 the plastic art —품 a sculpture; a carving; an engraving

조각나다 〈갈라지다〉 split 《in [into] pieces》; cleave; splinter; break; be broken to pieces; 〈의견이〉 differ; have a split in opinion
♦산산이 조각나다 break [be broken] to pieces; smash [be smashed] to pieces [into fragments]
▶정당은 작은 파벌로 조각났다 The political party split into petty factions.

조각조각 in [to] pieces; in fragments; in strips
♦조각조각이 되다 become broken to pieces / 조각조각 부수다[찢다] break [tear] sth in [to, into] pieces
▶그 소녀는 헝겊을 조각조각 이어 방석 커버를 만들었다 The girl pieced together a patchwork cushion cover.

조간 朝刊 a morning paper; 〈석간에 대하여〉 a morning edition ♦런던타임스의 조간 the morning edition of *the London Times*

조갈 燥渴 a (raging) thirst; a parched throat
♦조갈이 나다 suffer from thirst ■—증 a morbid thirst

조감도 鳥瞰圖 a bird's-eye view; an airscape; 〈공중 부감도〉 an aeroview

조감독 助監督 〔映〕 an assistant director

조갑 爪甲 nails; claws

조강지처 糟糠之妻 one's wife married in [who shared his] poverty; one's old [faithful, devoted] wife

조개 a shellfish; 〈대합조개〉 a clam; 〈쌍각조개〉 a bivalve
♦조개를 캐다 dig out shellfish
▶우리는 조개를 구워 먹었다 We baked the clams and ate them.
■—관자 the adductor (muscle); 〈식품의〉 the eyes of scallops —구름 (俗) a cirrocumulus —껍질 a shell; a clamshell —무지[더미] ⇨ 패총(貝塚) —볼 full [plump] cheeks —탄 a briquet(te)

조객 弔客 a caller [visitor] for condolence
■—록 a guest book for condolers

조갯살 the flesh of a clam; clam meat; shucked [stripped] shellfish

조건 條件 1 〈조항〉 an item; a stipulation 2 〈제약 사항〉 a term; 〈제한〉 a qualification
♦지불 조건 the condition [terms] of payment / 계약 조건 the terms of a contract / 조건을 약정하다 stipulate for certain terms 3 〈필요 요건〉 a condition
♦세계 평화의 첫째 조건 the first conditions for world peace / 무조건의 unconditional 〈조건이〉 근무 조건이 좋은 일자리 a job with good working conditions
▶돈은 반드시 행복의 조건이 아니다 Money is not necessarily a condition of happiness.
▶네 과오를 눈감아주겠지만 한 가지 조건이 있다 I will overlook your mistake, but there's one condition.
〈조건을〉 조건을 받아들이다 accept a condition / 조건을 붙이다 attach a condition 《to one's proposal》; saddle sb with conditions
▶이 대학에 들어가려면 다음 조건을 충족시켜야 한다 You must meet the following requirements [have the following qualifications] to enter this university.
▶더 좋은 조건을 다른 구매자가 신청해 놓고 있다 Better terms are offered by other buyers. 〈조건에〉 조건에 맞다 meet the conditions [requirement] / 조건에 응하다 accept the terms
▶이 조건에 맞는 사람이면 누구든 채용하겠다 We'll employ anyone who meets these conditions [requirements].
▶수목은 기후 조건에 따라 서로 다르게 키가 자란다 The trees may reach various heights depending upon climatic conditions. 〈조건으로〉 좋은 조건으로 고용되다 be employed on favorable conditions [terms] / …라는 조건으로 on condition of... [that...]; provided [on the understanding] that...
▶그는 급료의 선불이라는 조건으로 그 일을 맡았다 He took the job on condition (that) [provided (that)] he got paid in advance.
▶너는 어떤 조건으로 승낙했느냐? On what terms did you accept it?
▶네가 도와준다는 조건으로 그것을 맡겠다 I will undertake it on condition that you help me.
■노동— labor conditions 부대— a collateral condition 전제— a precondition 필수— a sine qua non (condition) —문 〔文法〕 a conditional (sentence) —반사 〔生〕 a conditioned reflex —절 〔文法〕 a conditional (clause)

조건부 條件附 ♦조건부의 conditional; qualified; 〈조건이 붙은〉 with some strings attached 《to it》 / 조건부로 conditionally; with conditions attached; with (a) proviso / 조건부로 승낙하다 give a qualified consent
▶그는 그것을 조건부로 승인했다 He approved of it on certain conditions [conditionally]. ⇌ He gave a conditional approval of it.
■—계약 a conditional contract

조건표 早見表 a chart; a table ♦계산[이자] 조건표 a ready reckoner

조경 造景 landscape architecture
■—가 a landscape architect [gardener] —설계 landscape design

조계 早計 a premature scheme; rashness; prematurity; hastiness ♦조계의 premature; too hasty; rash

조계 租界 〈조차지〉 a settlement; a concession
♦외국 조계 a foreign settlement

조고 祖考 one's deceased grandfather

조곡 弔哭 wailing in mourning; keening
—조곡하다 wail in mourning; keen; lament

조곡 組曲 〔樂〕 a suite

조공 朝貢 tribute 《to a country》 ♦조공을 바치게 하다 lay a tribute on (a country [king]); lay (a country [king]) under tribute

조관

■—국 a tributary state
조관 條款 a stipulation; a provision; an article; a clause
 ■최혜국— a most favored nation clause
조관 朝官 a courtier; 〈총칭〉 the court
조광 躁狂 〈미쳐 날뜀〉 (a) delirium; (a) frenzy; raving madness
조교 助敎 an assistant teacher [instructor]
조교 照校 〈대조 검토〉 collation
 —조교하다 collate
조교 調敎 〈승마 훈련〉 horse breaking —조교하다 break (in); train
 ■—사 a horsebreaker
조교수 助敎授 an assistant [associate] professor
조국 祖國 one's homeland [fatherland, motherland]; one's mother [native] country ♦조국을 지키다[위해 싸우다] defend [fight for] one's fatherland / 조국을 떠나다 leave one's native country
 —근대화 modernization of one's fatherland
조국애 祖國愛 love of [for] one's fatherland [country]; patriotism ♦조국애에 불타다 burn with love for one's country
조규 條規 〈조문의 규정〉 a stipulation; provisions [regulations] (of a law)
조그마하다 smallish ⇨ 자그마하다
조그만큼 just a little [few]; to a slight degree
조금 1 〈양〉 a small quantity; a little; a bit ♦쇼핑[산책]을 조금 하다 do some shopping [walking] / (선거에서) 조금의 차이로 지다 be defeated by a small [narrow] majority / 아주 조금 just a little [bit] / 조금 더 a little [bit] more / 돈이 조금이라도 있으면 if one has any money / 저녁식사를 조금 하다 have a bite of supper / 소금을 조금 쳐서 간을 맞추다 season 《food》 with a dash of salt
 ▶그녀에게 폐를 조금 끼쳤다 I gave her a little [some] trouble.
 ▶돈이 조금 필요하다 I want some money.
 ▶시간은 조금밖에 남지 않았다 There is very little [only a little, hardly any, a little] time left.
 2 〈수〉 a small number; a few; some ♦아주 조금 just a few / 조금 더 a few more
 ▶시험에서 조금밖에 틀리지 않았다 I made very few [only a few, hardly any, a few] mistakes on the test.
 ▶이 작문에는 오류가 조금 있다 There are some mistakes in this composition.
 3 〈정도〉 something; somewhat; a bit; a little; a trifle; slightly; a shade
 ♦조금 쓴 partially used 《match-book》 / 조금이라도 친절한 마음이 있다면 if you have a spark [touch, drop] of kindness in you
 ▶〈會話〉「이 칼로는 안 되겠어」「내건 조금 나을까?」 "This knife's hopeless." "Well, would mine cut any better?"
 ▶오른쪽으로 조금 움직여 주시오 Move a little to the right.
 ▶나는 조금 속력을 내어 운전하고 있었다 I was driving rather fast.
 ▶창문을 조금만 열어둬라 Open the window a crack.

▶조금만 더 노력해라 Make one more effort.
▶오늘은 기분이 조금 좋다 I feel a little [slightly, rather, somewhat] better today.
4 〈시간〉 a moment; a minute; a second
 ♦조금 전에 a little while ago / 조금 있으면 [지나면] in a little while; in a short time; soon
▶그는 조금 있으면 돌아온다 He'll be back in a little while.
▶우리는 5시 조금 전에 도착했다 We arrived shortly before five.
▶아직 조금은 시간이 있다 You still have a little time left.
5 〈거리〉 a little way; a short distance
 ♦조금 떨어져서 a little way off / 강을 따라 조금 가다 go a little way along the river
▶조금 가니까 다리가 나왔다 A little way on, we came to a bridge.
▶역은 조금만 가면 됩니다 It is only a short distance [a little way] to the station. ⇒ It is but a short way from here to the station.
조금 潮— the neap tide
조금도 not the least; not in the least; not at all; not a bit; not the slightest
 ♦조금도 쓸모가 없다 be of no use at all; be good for nothing / 조금도 효과가 없다 take no effect whatever [at all] / 조금도 허점을 보이지 않다 allow sb no opportunity to seize
▶나는 조금도 상관하지 않는다 I don't care twopence [a straw] about it.
▶그런 일이 일어나리라고는 조금도 생각하지 않았다 I didn't in the least expect such a thing would happen.
▶그 일에 대해서는 조금도 알지 못한다 I don't know anything about it. ⇒ I know nothing about it.
▶이건 저것에 비하여 조금도 못하지 않다 This is every bit as good as that.
▶파티는 조금도 즐겁지 않았다 I didn't enjoy the party at all [in the least]. ⇒ The party wasn't at all [in the least, a bit] enjoyable.
조금씩 〈양〉 little by little; bit by bit; in tiny amounts [quantities]; 〈찔끔찔끔〉 sparingly; 〈정도〉 gradually
 ♦돈을 조금씩 쓰다 use one's money sparingly [stingily] / 조금씩 나아가다 advance inch by inch / 조금씩 떼어 갚다 mince one's pay for
▶쥐는 치즈를 조금씩 갉아 먹는다 Mice nibble at the cheese.
▶청중이 조금씩 모여들었다 The audience began to come in by twos and threes.
조급증 a quick [hot, short] temper; impatience; hastiness
조급하다 躁急— quick-tempered; impatient; impetuous; hasty
 ♦조급한 남자 a hot-tempered man; a man of impetuous temper / 조급함을 가라앉히다 control oneself; hold one's horses / 성질이 조급하다 be eager 《to do》; be driven by impetuosity
▶그렇게 일을 조급히 결정하는 것이 아니다 You should not decide matters so hastily [impetuously].
조기 〈魚〉 a croaker; a yellow corbina
 ■—젓 salted [pickled] croakers

조기 弔旗 a flag draped in black; 〈반기〉 a flag at half-mast [half-staff] ◆조기를 달다 half-mast; hang out [hoist] a flag half-mast high

조기 早起 early rising —**조기하다** rise [get up] early (in the morning); rise with the sun [lark]

조기 早期 an early stage
▶암은 조기에 발견 한다면 치유될 수 있다 Cancer can be cured if found early enough [in its early stage].
▶그 문제는 조기에 해결할 가망이 없습니다 The problem is unlikely to be solved soon.
■—교육 early-childhood education —**발견** 〔醫〕 early detection: 조기 발견하다 detect [spot] 《a disease》 in its early stage —**사용** an early use; advance use —**상환** advanced redemption —**암** early cancer —**진단** 〔醫〕 early diagnosis —**치료** early treatment —**환급** early refund

조깅 〈천천히 달리기〉 jogging
—**조깅하다** jog 《one's mile and a quarter》
◆공원에 조깅하러 가다 go jogging [go for a jog] in the park
▶나는 매일 아침 30분씩 조깅한다 I jog for half an hour every morning.

조끼 〈옷〉〈美〉a vest; 〈英〉a waistcoat
—**적삼** a sleeved vest [waistcoat]

조난 遭難 a disaster; an accident; 〈a〉 shipwreck; distress —**조난하다** meet with a disaster [an accident]; be wrecked; be shipwrecked; be in distress
▶어젯밤 스키어의 일행이 산에서 조난됐다 A group of skiers met with an accident [got lost] in the mountains last night.
■—**구조대** a rescue party [team] —**구조선** a rescue boat —**선** a ship in distress; a wrecked ship —**현장** the scene of a disaster [an accident]: 구조대가 조난 현장으로 달려갔다 The rescue team rushed to the scene of the accident [disaster].

조난신호 遭難信號 a distress signal [call]; an SOS
◆조난 신호를 보내다[받다] send [pick up] a distress call [an SOS]

조난자 遭難者 a victim; a sufferer ◆철도 사고의 조난자 a victim of a railway accident

조달 調達 supply; 〈필수품〉 procurement; 〈식료품〉 provision; 〈英〉 purveyance; 〈자금〉 raising
▶나는 주택 구입자금 조달로 바쁘다 I'm busy making the money to buy a house.
—**조달하다** supply; provide; furnish 《sb sth》; 〈英〉 purvey [cater] 《provisions》; raise 《a fund for》
▶토지를 저당잡혀 돈을 조달하다 raise money on one's land
▶체재지에서 필요한 물품은 조달할 수 있다 You can buy the goods you need at the place where you'll stay.
■**해외**— offshore procurement ■—**과** a supplies [procurement] section —**기관** a procurement agency —**청** the Office of Supply

조당 粗糖 〈막설탕〉 raw [crude] sugar

조대 〈담뱃대〉 a clay [bamboo] pipe

조도 照度 intensity of illumination; illuminance ⇨ 조명도

조동사 助動詞 〔文法〕 an auxiliary verb

조라떨다 bungle by a rash [hasty] act

조락 凋落 〈시들어 떨어짐〉 withering; 〈몰락〉 decline; decay; downfall; comedown
◆자연주의 문학의 조락 the decline of the naturalism in literature
—**조락하다** wither; decline; decay; fall

조력 助力 help; aid; assistance ⇨ 도움
◆조력을 청하다 seek assistance 《from a sb》; ask sb for (his) help / 남의 조력을 받지 않고 unaided; without another's help
▶나는 네 조력이 필요하다 I need your help [assistance].
—**조력하다** help; aid [assist] 《in sb's work》; give [render] sb aid 《in doing, to do》
▶나는 그의 일에 조력했다 I helped [aided, assisted] him with [in] his work.
—**자** a helper; an assistant

조력발전 潮力發電 a tidal electric power generation

조련 調練·操鍊 1 ⇨ 교련
2 〈강박함〉 —**조련하다** torment; harass; afflict; torture

조령모개 朝令暮改 frequent change [alteration] of regulations; lack of principle; an inconsistent policy ◆조령모개의 정책 a fickle [an inconstant] policy

조례 弔禮 condolatory etiquette

조례 條例 regulations; rules; a law; an act; an ordinance ■**시**(市)— a municipal ordinance

조례 朝禮 a morning gathering [meeting]

조로 早老 a premature decay; 〔醫〕 premature senility age ◆조로의 prematurely aged [old]

조로 朝露 〈아침이슬〉 the morning dew
▶인생은 조로와도 같다 Man's life vanishes like the dew. ⇒ Life is but a span.

조로아스터교 —教 Zoroastrianism
■—**도** a Zoroastrian

조롱 嘲弄 mockery; ridicule; derision; raillery
—**조롱하다** make a fool 《of》; make sport [fun] 《of》; mock at; ridicule; deride; scoff [jeer] at
◆조롱당하다 be ridiculed; be sneered at; be held in derision; be treated with scoff
▶나는 조롱당하고서는 못 참는다 I can't afford to be fooled.

조롱박 〔植〕 〈호리병박〉 a bottle gourd; 〈바가지〉 a (dipping) gourd

조루 早漏 〔醫〕 premature ejaculation

조류 鳥類 〔動〕 birds; fowls; bird life; the feathered tribe ◆수류와 조류 fur and feather
■—**보호** bird protection —**학** ornithology —**학자** an ornithologist

조류 潮流 1 〈해류〉 a tide; a (tidal) current
▶조류가 밀려오고[빠지고] 있다 The tide is making [ebbing].
▶조류는 여기서 방향을 바꾼다 The tidal current runs in a different direction here.
2 〈경향〉 a tendency; a current; a trend
◆시대의 조류에 따르다[거스르다] go with [against] the current [tide, times]

조류 藻類 〔植〕 algae 〔ǽldʒi:〕; algas; 〈해조〉 seaweeds ■—학 phycology; algology —학자 an algologist; a phycologist

조륙 造陸 〔地質〕 ■—운동 epeirogenic movements; epeirogenesis

조르기 〔柔道〕 choking techniques; a strangle hold

조르다 1〈단단히 죄다〉 tighten; constrict; choke; strangle
♦안전띠를 조르다 tighten one's seat belt / 그의 목을 조르다 grip him by the throat / 목을 졸라 죽이다 strangle sb to death / 졸라매다 bind [fasten] tightly; tie up / 구두끈을 졸라매다 lace (up) one's boots
2〈끈덕지게 요구하다〉 tease (importune, press) 《sb for》; ask sb importunately 《for》
▶동생은 어머니에게 자전거를 사달라고 졸랐다 My brother teased mother to buy him a bicycle.

조르르 1〈가는 물줄기〉 trickling; dribbling; 《flow》 in a thin [small] stream
▶수도 꼭지에서 물이 조르르 흐르고 있다 Water is trickling (down) from the tap.
▶길을 따라 작은 시내가 조르르 흐르고 있다 A small stream trickles along the path.
2〈잽싼 걸음새〉《walk》 with short; quick steps
▶쥐 한마리가 방을 조르르 질러갔다 A mouse ran quickly across the room.

조르륵 ♦조르륵 거리다[대다] make dribbling [dripping] sounds

조리 笊籬 a (bamboo) strainer; a meshwork ladle

조리 條理 logical sequence; logic; reason
♦조리 있는 reasonable; logical; consistent / 조리 없는 unreasonable; illogical; incongruous / 조리 없는 말 an incoherent account [remark] / 조리있게 설명하다 make a logically consistent statement / 조리에 맞다 stand to reason; square with reason
▶네 주장은 조리에 닿는다 Your claim is reasonable.

조리 調理 1〈조섭〉 care of health —조리하다 take care of one's health; nurse oneself
2 ⇨ 요리 —조리하다 cook 《food》; prepare 《a dish》; dress 《fish》
3〈처리〉 appropriate disposal [handling] of a matter —조리하다 deal with sth properly
■—기구 cookware —대 a mixing center —사 a cook

조리개 〈사진기의〉 a stop; an iris; a diaphragm ♦조리개 5.6으로 셔터를 누르다 shoot at F 5.6

조리다 boil down ♦생선을 간장에 조리다 boil fish down in soy / 과일을 설탕으로 조려서 잼을 만들다 boil fruit with sugar into jam

조리돌리다 lead 《a malefactor》 along the streets to expose 《him》 to public shame

조림 food boiled down in soy; hard-boiled food
♦생선조림 fish boiled in soy with spices

조림 造林 afforestation; forestation —조림하다 afforest 《a mountain》; plant trees ■—지 an afforested land; 〈삼림〉 a plantation ■—사방 — afforestation for erosion control

조립 組立 constructing; fabrication; 〈기계의〉 assembling; assembly; assemblage
♦조립식의 fabricated; knockdown
—조립하다 construct; fabricate; assemble; fix up; erect; put [fit, piece] together
♦자동차를 조립하다 assemble a motorcar / 시계를 조립하다 assemble watches / 부품을 조립하여 완성품으로 만들다 assemble the parts into a complete unit
■—공 an assembler; 〔機〕 an erector —공장 an assembly shop [plant, factory] —(식)가옥 〔주택〕 a prefabricated house; a prefab —(식)책장 a knockdown bookshelf

조릿조릿하다 be held [kept] in (great) suspense; be impatient and anxious; be on the edge

조마 調馬 horse training [breaking] —조마하다 train [break (in)] a horse
■—사(師) a horsebreaker; a horsetrainer —장 a riding ground; a paddock

조마조마하다 〈서술적〉 feel nervous [timid, uneasy]; be in fear (of); be kept in suspense; be in a fidget [flutter]
♦조마조마하면서 〈불안으로〉 in fear; in thrilling suspense; 〈기대 등으로〉 with breathless interest / 조마조마하게 하다 put sb into a flutter; keep sb in suspense; make [drive] sb nervous
▶나는 선생님이 화내실까봐 조마조마했다 I was nervous at the thought that my teacher might get angry.

조막 〈작은 주먹〉 a fist size ♦조막만하다 be about the size of a fist; be very small

조막손 a hand with unfoldable fingers; a clubhand ■—이 a clubhanded person

조만간 早晚間 sooner or later; (at) some time or other; in (the course of) time; by and by
▶조만간 네가 거기 가야 할 것이다 You will have to go there sooner or later.
▶조만간 우리도 그 일을 할 수 있게 될 것이다 We shall be able to do the work sooner or later.

조망 眺望 a view; a prospect; a lookout; an outlook ♦조망이 좋은 집 a house with a fine view / 조망이 좋다 have a nice view
▶나무 숲이 조망을 가로막고 있다 The cluster of trees shuts out [obstructs] the view.
▶언덕에서 보는 조망은 아주 좋다 The prospect from the hill is superb.
■—창 a view window

조망 鳥網 〈새 잡는 그물〉 a fowling [bird] net; a fowler's net

조매 嘲罵 〈조롱하며 꾸짖음〉 taunt; reviling; railing —조매하다 taunt; revile; rail at

조면 繰綿 〈일〉 cotton ginning; 〈솜〉 ginned cotton ■—공장 a ginnery —기 a (cotton) gin

조명 助命 lifesaving ⇨ 구명 (救命)

조명 照明 illumination; 〈무대의〉 lighting ♦조명이 잘 된[안 된] well-lit [ill-lit] / 조명이 부족하다 be poorly illuminated —조명하다 light up; illuminate
■—무대— stage lighting 직접[간접]— direct [indirect] illumination ■—기구 an illuminator;

〈총칭〉 lighting apparatus ━탄 a flare (bomb); a light bomb ━효과 lighting effects

조명나다 嘲名 ━〈좋지 않은 소문이 나다〉 have a bad reputation; have an ill name

조명도 照明度 illuminance; intensity of illumination ━계 illumination meter; illuminometer

조모 祖母 a grandmother

조목 條目 an article; a clause; an item
♦조목조목 item by item / 조목별로 심의하다 discuss article by article / 조목별로 쓰다 itemize
▶그것은 이 조목에 해당한다 It comes under this clause.

조무래기 〈어린 아이들〉 small children; little kids; small fry; 〈자질구레한 물건〉 small articles; petty goods; sundries; odds and ends

조문 弔文 a funeral address; a letter of condolence; a tribute to the memory of *sb*
▶그는 침통한 음성으로 고(故) 존슨씨에 대한 조문을 읽었다 In a mournful tone he read a funeral address for the late Mr. Johnson.

조문 弔問 a call of condolence
━조문하다 call 《on *sb*》 to express *one's* condolences; make a call of condolence 《on *sb*》
■━객(客) a caller for condolence

조문 條文 〈본문〉 the text 《of the law》; the letter 《of the statute》; 〈조항〉 a provision
♦헌법의 조문 the provisions of the Constitution / 조문에 있는 바와 같이 as stipulated in the text / 조문을 두다 provide / 조문에 명기되어 있다 be expressly stated in the provision 《of the statute》

조물주 造物主 the Creator (of the Universe); the Maker; the Great Artificer [Architect]; God

조미 調味 seasoning; flavoring ━조미하다 season; flavor; spice; give flavor to
■━료 a seasoning; a flavoring; 〈총칭〉 spice: 화학 조미료 a chemical condiment

조밀 稠密 density ━조밀하다 dense; crowded; thick; close ♦인구가 조밀한 지방 a congested district; a densely [thickly] populated district.
▶그 도시에는 인가가 조밀하다 Houses are closely crowded in that city.

조바꿈 調━ 〔樂〕 modulation; transition

조바심[1] 〈조의 타작〉 millet threshing
━조바심하다 thresh millet

조바심[2] 〈마음졸임〉 worrying; anxiety
♦조바심이 나게 하다 worry; fret *sb's* heart; keep [hold] *sb* in suspense
▶우리 딸이 무사하다는 것을 알기까지 몹시 조바심이 났다 We had a very anxious time until we knew that my daughter was safe.
━조바심하다 worry 《*oneself*》; be anxious [nervous] 《about》; bother 《*oneself*》 《about》; fidget [jitter] 《about》
▶나는 그의 귀국을 조바심하며 기다렸다 I waited in anxious suspense for his returning home.

조박 糟粕 〈술찌꺼기〉 draff; lees; grains; 〈학문의〉 dregs; lees; leavings
♦사회의 조박 〈인간 찌끼〉《비유》 the dregs of society / 고인(古人)의 조박을 핥다 imitate the styles of old masters

조반 朝飯 breakfast ♦조반을 먹다 eat [take] breakfast; breakfast

조발 調髮 〈머리를 땋음〉 plaiting hair; 〈이발〉 a haircut; hairdressing ━조발하다 〈땋다〉 plait [braid] *one's* hair; make *one's* hair into a plait; 〈이발하다〉 get a haircut

조발성치매 早發性癡呆 〔醫〕 schizophrenia ⇨ 정신(~분열증)

조밥 boiled millet; boiled rice with millet

조방농업 粗放農業 extensive agriculture

조백 早白 premature growth of gray hair
━조백하다 have premature gray hair while 《*one* is still》 young

조복 朝服 a court suit; a (full) court dress
♦조복을 입다 wear a court suit

조부 祖父 a grandfather

조부모 祖父母 grandparents

조분 鳥糞 bird droppings; 〈바다새의〉 guano
━석(石) guano

조붓하다 〈서술적〉 be somewhat narrow; be a bit narrow; be on the narrow side

조비 祖妣 *one's* deceased grandmother

조사 弔詞 words [a letter] of condolence; a funeral [memorial] address
♦조사를 하다 express *one's* condolence
▶내가 학급대표로 조사를 했다 I made a funeral address as the representative of my class.

조사 早死 〈젊어서 죽음〉 a premature [an early] death ━조사하다 die young; die an early death; die at an early age

조사 助詞 〔文法〕 a postpositional particle

조사 助辭 a particle ⇨ 어조사 (語助辭)

조사 祖師 the founder of a religious sect [a school]

조사 照射 irradiation ━조사하다 irradiate
♦엑스선을 조사하다 apply X-rays 《to》; X-ray 《*sb's* chest》 / 방사선을 가슴에 조사하다 apply radioactive rays to *sb's* chest

조사 調査 (an) investigation; (an) examination; (an) inquiry; research; (a) survey
♦조사를 받다 be examined 《by》; undergo an investigation / 조사를 시작하다 start [begin] an investigation / 조사를 실시하다 conduct [carry on] an investigation [examination]; carry out a survey; make a study
▶그 건은 현재 조사 중이다 That problem is now under investigation.
▶조사 결과 그 소문은 사실 무근으로 밝혀졌다 The investigation proved that the rumor was groundless.
━조사하다 investigate; examine (into); inquire [look, search] into; survey; look [go] over
♦조사해보니 on [upon] inquiry [investigation] / 철저히 조사하다 make a thorough [an exhaustive] investigation; investigate [examine into] 《a matter》 thoroughly; probe 《a matter》 to the bottom / 물건을 일일이 조사하다 look over the articles one by one / 사실을 조사하다 investigate the facts
▶그의 발언이 사실인지 조사해 주십시오

Please check up his remark.
▶이 연못의 수질을 조사하고 싶습니다 We want to examine the water of this pond.
■시장— a market research ■—결과〈판명된 일〉findings —단 an investigation committee —보고 a report of investigation —부 an inquiry section;〈신문사의〉the filing department —서 a written investigation —용지[표] a questionnaire —위원 an examiner; an investigator —위원회 a commission of inquiry —자료 data for investigation; research data

조산 早產 a premature birth [delivery] —조산하다〈산모가 주어〉be prematurely delivered of a child;〈아이가 주어〉be born prematurely ■—아 a premature; a premature baby

조산 助產 midwifery —사(師) a midwife

조산 造山 an artificial [a miniature] hill; a mound —대 an orogenic belt [zone] —운동 an orogenic movement; orogeny

조삼모사 朝三暮四 swindling by a clever trick

조상 弔喪 condolence ⇨ 문상(問喪)

조상 祖上 an ancestor; a forefather; fathers; the [a] progenitor;(총칭) ancestry
♦인류의 조상 the progenitor of the human race / 조상 대대로 내려오는 ancestral; hereditary / 조상 전래의 것이다 have been handed down to *one* from *one's* ancestors / 조상의 이름을 욕되게 하다 bring disgrace upon the good name of *one's* fathers
▶이 토지는 조상 전래의 것이다 This land has been handed down to us from our ancestors.
▶이것은 조상 대대로 내려오는 보물이다 This is our family heirloom.
▶안되면 조상 탓이다 A fool blames others if something goes wrong for him.

조상 彫像 a (carved) statue
♦대리석 조상 a statue in marble

조색 調色 mixing colors ■—판 ⇨ 팔레트

조생종 早生種 〈農〉a precocious species; an early(·ripening) variety ♦조생종 벼 an early variety of rice; an early rice

조서 詔書 an Imperial [a Royal] edict [rescript]

조서 調書 〔法〕a protocol; a record; a report; a written evidence ♦조서의 작성 drawing up of a report [protocol] / 조서를 꾸미다 put (a deposition) on record
▶경찰은 용의자를 심문하여 조서를 작성했다 The police drew up a report by questioning the suspect.

조석 朝夕 〈때〉morning and evening;〈밥〉morning meal and evening meal
♦조석으로 in the mornings and evenings;〈밤낮〉day and night;〈늘〉day in, day out
▶조석으로 많이 쌀쌀해졌다 We have much cooler mornings and evenings now. ⇌ It has become fairly cool in the mornings and evenings.

조석 潮汐 〈간만〉ebb and flow;〈조수〉a tide —수 ⇨ 조수 —운동 a tidal movement

조선 造船 shipbuilding
■—계획 a shipbuilding program —공 a shipbuilding worker; a shipwright —기사 a shipbuilder; a marine engineer; a naval architect —능력 shipbuilding capacity —대(臺) a shipway;〈경사진〉a slip; a slipway —소 a dockyard; a shipbuilding yard; a shipyard —업 the shipbuilding industry —업계 the shipbuilding world [circles] —업자 a shipbuilder —학 naval architecture —회사 a shipbuilding company

조선 朝鮮 〔史〕Chosŏn

조섭 調攝 care of health ⇨ 조리(調理)

조성 助成 fostering; furtherance; aid
—조성하다 further; foster; promote; conduce [contribute] to; assist; aid

조성 造成 creation; development; preparation (of a housing site) —조성하다 create (land); clear; develop land (for housing) ♦교사 부지를 조성하다 develop land for a school house ■택지— development of residential sites

조성 組成 composition; constitution; formation; makeup —조성하다 compose; constitute; form; make [set] up
■—물 a composite; a composition —성분 a component; a constituent

조성금 助成金 a bounty; a subsidy; a grant; a grant-in-aid ♦조성금을 지급하다 grant a bounty [subsidy] —수출— the bounty on exports 주택— housing subsidies

조세 租稅 taxes; taxation
♦조세를 부과하다 tax; impose a tax (on *sb*) / 조세를 면제하다 exempt *sb* from taxes / 조세를 경감하다 reduce taxes
■—부담 the burden of taxation; a tax burden —수입 tax revenues —징수 the collection of a tax —체납 tax delinquency

조소 彫塑 〈소상(塑像)으로 새김〉carving and modeling;〈소상〉a clay model

조소 嘲笑 derision; a derisive [sardonic] smile; a scornful laugh; a ridicule; a sneer
♦조소거리가 되다 make a laughingstock of *oneself* / 조소를 사다 incur [excite] ridicule; bring ridicule upon *oneself* / 세인의 조소를 사다 incur public ridicule
—조소하다 laugh [sneer, scoff, mock, jeer] at; deride; ridicule

조속기 調速機 〔機〕〈속도 조정기〉a governor; a speed regulator

조속히 早速— as soon as possible; at the earliest possible moment; at your earliest convenience

조수 助手 a helper; a help; an assistant
♦조수 노릇을 하다 be a helper to (a superior); serve as an assistant
■외과— a surgeon's mate; a surgical assistant 운전— an assistant driver

조수 鳥獸 birds and beasts; fur and feather
■—보호 wildlife conservation —보호 구역 a wildlife sanctuary —보호론자 a wildlifer

조수 潮水 the tide; tidewater
♦조수의 간만 the ebb and flow of the tide —표(標) a tidemark

조숙 早熟 early maturity; precocity; prematurity —조숙하다 grow [ripen] early; mature young [early]; be precocious [premature]
♦조숙한 아이 a precocious child

조식 粗食 〈검소한 음식〉 coarse [plain] food [fare]; a plain [simple] diet; a frugal meal
♦조식에 익숙해지다 become accustomed to plain fare
—조식하다 eat plain food; live on coarse fare [a frugal diet]

조신 朝臣 a courtier; (총칭) court

조실부모 早失父母 losing *one's* parents early in life —조실부모하다 lose *one's* parents early in life ▶그는 조실부모했다 He lost his parents at an early age.

조심 操心 〈주의〉 care; carefulness; heed; 〈경계〉 caution; (a) precaution; guard; vigilance; 〈신중〉 prudence; discretion; circumspection
▶개 조심 (게시) Beware of the dog.
—조심하다 take care 《of》; be careful [cautious]; take precautions 《against》; beware 《of》; guard 《against》; be watchful 《against》; use prudence; be circumspect
♦조심하여 carefully; cautiously; with care [caution] / 감기 들지 않도록 조심하다 be careful not to catch cold / 말을 조심하다 be cautious of *one's* tongue / 언행을 조심하다 be discreet in words and deeds / 조심스럽게 걷다 walk gingerly / 조심하지 않다 be imprudent / 조심해서 행동하다 behave prudently
▶발밑을 조심해라 Watch [Mind] your step!
▶차 조심해라 Watch out for cars!

조심성 操心性 cautiousness; carefulness; discretion; prudence; circumspection
♦조심성이 많은 thoughtful; careful; scrupulous; cautious; alert; prudent; circumspect / 조심성이 없다 be careless [thoughtless]; be imprudent

조아리다 prostrate *oneself* 《before》; kneel 《before, to》; bend *one's* head reverently; kowtow 《to》; knock head

조아팔다 〈헐어서 조금씩 팔다〉 sell in small lots; break up into small lots to sell

조악 粗惡 coarseness; crudeness —조악하다 coarse; crude; bad; inferior ■—품 an inferior article; a product of poor quality

조암광물 造岩鑛物 rock-forming minerals

조야 粗野 boorishness; coarseness; rusticity; rudeness; vulgarity
—조야하다 rustic; boorish; rude; rough; coarse; vulgar

조야 朝野 〈조정과 민간〉 the government and the people; the (whole) nation
♦조야의 명사 men of distinction both in and out of the government

조약 條約 a treaty; a pact; an agreement
♦조약상의 의무[권리] treaty obligations [rights] / 조약의 개정 the revision of a treaty / 조약의 발효 the effectuation of a treaty / 조약에 조인하다 sign a treaty / 조약을 맺다 conclude [make up, enter into] a treaty 《with》 / 조약을 지키다[어기다] observe [violate] a treaty / 조약을 폐기하다 denounce [annul] a treaty
♦불가침— a nonaggression pact [treaty] 상호 원조— a mutual assistance pact [treaty] 통상— a treaty of commerce 평화— a peace treaty ■—가맹국 signatory countries [powers] —규정 the treaty provisions [stipulations] —비준 the ratification of a treaty

조약돌 a pebble(stone); a small stone; a shingle

조어 造語 〈말〉 a coined word; a coinage
▶최근엔 조어가 많이 쓰이고 있다 Many coined words are used recently.
▶이것은 김박사의 조어다 This word was coined by Dr. Kim.

조언 助言 advice; counsel; a suggestion
♦조언을 구하다 ask advice 《of sb》; seek counsel 《from sb》/ 조언을 얻다 get counsel 《from sb》
▶그에게 조언을 해주었다 I aided him with advice.
—조언하다 advise; counsel; give *sb* advice [counsel]
■—자 an adviser; a counselor

조업 操業 operation; work
♦조업을 단축하다 curtail [reduce] operation / 조업을 개시[중단]하다 start [stop] operation
—조업하다 operate; run; work
♦조업하는 중이다 be in operation
■완전— full operation : 그 공장은 완전 조업을 하고 있다 The plant is in full operation.
■—단축 reduction [curtailment] of operation; short-time operation —일수 days operated —중지 a [the] shutdown of operations

조역 助役 an assistant; 〈철도역장의〉 an assistant stationmaster

조연 助演 〈역할〉 supporting performance; 〈사람〉 a supporting actor [actress]
▶가장 감동적인 것은 조연의 연기였다 The most impressive was the performance of the supporting actor.
—조연하다 assist [support] 《the leading actor》; play support
■—상 an award for the best supporting actor [actress] —자 a supporting actor [actress]

조영 造營 〈건물 축조〉 building; erection; construction —조영하다 build; erect; construct
■—물 buildings; structures —비 building expenses

조예 造詣 attainments; knowledge; scholarship
♦조예가 깊다 have a profound [deep] knowledge 《of》; be high in the attainment 《of》; be well [deeply] versed 《in》 / 음악에 조예가 깊은 사람 a man of profound knowledge in music
▶외국인이면서 존슨씨는 한국 현대 문학에 조예가 깊다 Being a foreigner, Mr. Johnson has a profound knowledge of modern Korean literature.

조용하다 〈잠잠하다〉 quiet; still; silent; 〈고요하다〉 calm; placid; serene; tranquil; 〈얌전하다〉 soft; gentle

|解說| ***quiet***는 움직임이나 소음이 그다지 없는 안정되고 지속적인 조용함을 강조한다. ***still***은 움직임이 없어서 소리가 나지 않는 것으로서 quiet보다 일시적인 조용함을 말한다. ***silent***는 음성도 소리도 없는 완전한 조용함을 말한다.

♦조용한 태도 quiet [calm] manners / 조용한 밤 a quiet night / 조용한 시골 a tranquil country place / 조용한 음악 soft music / 말소리가 조용한 사람 a quiet-spoken person / 쥐죽은 듯이 조용하다 be as silent as death [the grave] / 조용해지다 〈정국·치안 등이〉 become peaceful [quiet]
▶나는 조용한 음악을 좋아한다 I like soft music.
▶그녀는 조용한 음성으로 말한다 She speaks in a soft [gentle] voice.
▶거리는 쥐죽은 듯이 조용했다 There was dead silence in the streets.
▶밤이 깊어 감에 따라 주위는 더 조용해졌다 All became [went] more quiet as the night went on.

조용히 quietly; silently; calmly; softly; gently
♦조용히 하다 keep quiet [still] / 조용히 자고 있다 sleep quietly [in peace] / 조용히 살다 live in quiet [peace]
▶조용히 해 Hush! ⇌ Keep still! ⇌ Be silent [quiet]!
▶조용히 자게 놔둬라 Let him sleep undisturbed.
▶아기는 조용히 자고 있다 The baby is sleeping peacefully [quietly].

조우 遭遇 1 〈우연한 만남〉 an encounter
─조우하다 encounter; meet with; come across; be confronted with
2 〈임금의 신임〉 winning royal confidence
─조우하다 win royal confidence
■─전(戰) an encounter action; an incidental operation

조운 漕運 〈선박 수송〉 transportation by ships

조울병 躁鬱病 manic-depressive psychosis [insanity]
■─환자 a manic-depressive (psychotic)

조원 造園 landscape gardening ─조원하다 lay out [make] a garden; landscape; do the landscaping
■─가 a landscape gardener [architect]

조위 弔慰 condolence; sympathy ─조위하다 condole 《with sb》; offer [express] one's condolence(s) 《to》
■─금 condolence money; a solatium

조율 調律 tuning
─조율하다 tune (up)
▶이 피아노는 조율해야겠다 This piano needs tuning.
▶나는 피아노를 1년에 한번 조율한다 I have my piano tuned once a year.
■─기 a regulator ─료 a charge for tuning 《a piano》 ─사 a 《piano》 tuner

조음 調音 〈목소리의〉 articulation; modulation; 〈악기의〉 tuning
─조음하다 tune 《a piano》; articulate 《sound》

조음 噪音 〈소음〉 (a) noise; (a) discord

조의 弔意 condolence; mourning; sympathy
♦조의를 표하다 offer [tender] one's condolence 《to》
▶삼가 조의를 표합니다 Please accept my sincere condolence.

조인 調印 signature; signing; sealing ♦조약의 정식 조인 the formal signing of a treaty
─조인하다 affix [set] one's seal 《to》; put one's seal 《on》; seal 《a deed》; 〈서명하는〉 affix [put] one's signature 《to》; sign 《a treaty》
■─국 a signatory (power) ─식 a ceremony of signing; a signing ceremony ─자 a signatory ─장소 the place of signature

조작 造作 〈제작〉 making; manufacturing; 〈날조〉 fabrication; fake; invention; concoction; frame-up
▶이 기사는 완전한 조작이다 This article is a pure fabrication [mere fake].
─조작하다 〈제작하나〉 make, manufacture; 〈날조하다〉 make up; fabricate; concoct; invent 《a story》; fake; forge; (美) cook up
♦조작된 것 a made-up story; (美口) a build-up; a fabrication

조작 操作 (an) operation; (a) manipulation; handling
♦인위적 조작 artificial manipulation
─조작하다 operate [work] 《a machine》; manipulate 《the market》; handle
■시장[금융]─ market [monetary] manipulation

조잡하다 粗雜─ coarse; rough; crude; gross
♦조잡한 계획 a crude scheme / 조잡하게 만든 집 a roughly-built house / 조잡하게 만들어져 있다 be roughly made; be of crude [cheap] make

조장 助長 promotion; furtherance
─조장하다 promote; further; encourage; foster
♦교육의 발전을 조장하다 foster [promote] the development of education / 악폐를 조장하다 aggravate [promote] evils / 국제간의 친선을 조장하다 promote international friendship

조장 組長 the head [leader] of a team; a boss; a foreman

조전 弔電 a telegram of condolence; a condolatory telegram
♦조전을 치다 send a telegram of condolence 《to》; telegraph one's condolence

조절 調節 regulation; adjustment; control; 〈악기의〉 tuning; 〈라디오의〉 tuning in; 〈음성·음조의〉 articulation; modulation
─조절하다 regulate 《a machine》; adjust; control; fix; 〈음조 등을〉 modulate 《one's voice》; tune 《a piano》; tune in 《the radio》
♦실내 온도를 자동으로 조절하다 automatically regulate the temperature of a room / 하프의 음조를 조절하다 put a harp in tune
■─기 a regulator; 〔電子〕 a modulator ─판(瓣) a control valve

조정 朝廷 the (Royal, Imperial) Court

조정 漕艇 rowing; boating ♦조정을 잘 한다 pull a good oar ─조정하다 row a boat
■─경기 a boat race; a regatta ─술(術) oarsmanship; boatmanship

조정 調停 mediation; arbitration; intercession; peacemaking
♦…의 조정으로 through the mediation [intercession] of… / 분쟁 조정의 수고를 맡다 take upon oneself the trouble of mediating a dispute / 조정에 부치다 resort to mediation; sub-

mit 《a matter》 to arbitration / 조정으로 해결하다 settle by arbitration
—**조정하다** mediate; arbitrate; intercede; intervene 《in a dispute》; make peace
◆**분쟁을 조정하다** mediate a quarrel
◆**강제—** compulsory arbitration ■**—안** a mediation [compromise] plan; an arbitration proposal **—위원회** a mediation committee **—인[자]** a mediator; an arbitrator **—재판** court arbitration **—재판소** a court of arbitration

조정 調整 regulation; adjustment; control; coordination; 〈음조 등의〉 modulation; tuning
◆**물가 조정** the regulation [control] of price / **노사 관계의 조정** labor-management adjustment
▶ 선생들 사이의 의견 조정에 시간이 걸렸다 It took some time to adjust the differences of opinion among the teachers.
—**조정하다** regulate; adjust; control; coordinate; fix up; 〈음조 등을〉 modulate; tune
◆**가격을 조정하다** adjust the prices
▶ 정부는 수입 억제로 국제수지를 조정하려고 했다 The government attempted to regulate the balance of payments by controlling imports.
■**—기**(器) a regulator **—위원회** a coordinating committee

조제 粗製 crude [coarse] manufacture ◆**조제의** coarse; crude **—조제하다** manufacture roughly ■**—품** a crude article; an article of inferior [poor] quality

조제 調製 making; manufacture; 〈약의〉 preparation; 〈주문품의〉 execution **—조제하다** make; prepare; execute 《an order》
■**—법** a recipe **—품** a preparation

조제 調劑 〔藥〕 compounding [preparation] of medicines **—조제하다** prepare [compound] medicines; 〈처방대로〉 fill [make up, dispense] a prescription
◆**약을 잘못 조제하다** compound a medicine in a wrong way
▶ 나는 약방에 가서 감기약을 조제했다 I had my prescription for the cold filled in the drugstore.
■**—법** pharmacy **—실** a dispensary **—약** a mixture; a preparation **—학** pharmaceutics

조조 早朝 early morning
■**—할인영화** a movie shown at reduced admission fees for 《early》 morning

조종 弔鐘 a funeral bell; a death knell
조종 祖宗 the royal ancestors; forefathers of a king
조종 釣鐘 a hanging [temple] bell
조종 操縱 piloting; operation; steering; management; manipulation; handling; control
—조종하다 manage; work 《puppets》; operate 《a machine》; handle; control; pilot 《a plane》; steer 《a ship》
◆**막후에서 조종하다** pull 《the》 wires / **여론을 조종하다** manipulate public opinion / **물가를 조종하다** rig prices / **교묘히 조종하여 …하게 하다** maneuver sb into 《doing》
▶ 그의 어머니가 그를 배후에서 조종했다 His mother manipulated him.
■**—간** a control stick [lever] **—석** a cockpit **—자** a manipulator; an operator **—장치** controls; a controlling gear

조종사 操縱士 a pilot ■**부—** a copilot
조준 照準 aim; sight ◆**조준을 맞추다** adjust the sight(s) **—조준하다** aim 《at》; take aim [sight] 《at》; sight 《a target》; lay 《a gun》
■**—각** an elevation 《of a gun》 **—기** a sight : **폭격조준기** a bombsight **—선** a line of sight **—수** 〈군함의〉 (英) a gunlayer **—연습사격** a sighting shot **—폭격** (美) precision bombing

조지다 〈호되게 단속하다〉 control strictly; tighten the screws; 〈단단히 맞추다〉 screw up; tighten up; fix tightly

조지아 〈미국의 주〉 Georgia (略 Ga.)

조직 組織 1 〈결성〉 (an) organization; formation; construction; 〈구성〉 constitution; 〈구조〉 (a) structure; 〈계통〉 a system
◆**사회의 조직** the structure of society / **클럽의 조직** the organization of a club / **현재의 경제[산업] 조직** the present economic [industrial] system / **조직이 탄탄한[허술한] 정당** a well-[badly-]organized party
—조직하다 form; organize; set up; 〈회사 등을〉 incorporate; 〈구성하다〉 compose; constitute
◆**내각을 조직하다** organize [form] a Cabinet / **강팀을 조직하다** get together a strong team
▶ 그들은 새 정당을 조직했다 They organized [formed] a new political party.
2 〈생물의〉 tissue; texture
◆**근육[신경]—** muscular [nervous] tissue **세포—** cellular texture **인체—** human anatomy
■**—력** capacity for organization **—망** a network of system **—위원회** an organizing committee **—자** an organizer **—학** histology **—학자** a histologist

조직적 組織的 systematic; methodical
◆**조직적 연구** a systematic study / **조직적으로** systematically; methodically
▶ 이 문제에 관해서는 조직적인 연구가 바람직하다 A systematic study of this problem is desirable.

조직화 組織化 systematization
—조직화하다 systematize; organize

조짐 兆朕 〈징후〉 symptoms; signs 〈전조〉 an omen; a foreboding
◆**불길한 조짐** an evil [a bad] omen / **회복의 조짐** indications [signs] of recovery / **폭풍의 조짐** an indication of a storm / **조짐을 보이다** 〈유행 등의〉 show [exhibit] signs; 〈병의〉 develop symptoms / **풍년의 조짐이다** augur a good harvest
▶ 이것은 풍년이 들 조짐이다 This foretells a good harvest.
▶ 세계 경제는 회복의 조짐을 보이고 있다 The world economy shows signs of recovery.

조차 租借 a lease 《of territory》 ◆**조차 기한을 연장하다** extend the lease **—조차하다** lease; hold 《land》 by lease; obtain a lease 《on》
■**—지** a leased territory; a leasehold
조차 潮差 the range of the tide; tide range
조차 操車 〔鐵〕 marshaling

—조차하다 marshal 《locomotives》
　■ **—계원** a train dispatcher **—장** a marshaling yard; 《美》 a switchyard

-조차 〈…도〉 even; 〈게다가〉 besides; in addition
　◆ 이름조차 못쓰다 cannot so much as write one's own name
　▶ 그 사람은 만나기조차 힘들다 It's difficult even to get to see him.
　▶ 그것은 아이조차 알 수 있다 Even a child could understand it.
　▶ 그는 작별인사조차 안 하고 떠났다 He left without so much as saying goodbye.
　▶ 선생님조차 그 문제를 풀지 못하셨다 Even the teacher could not solve the question.
　▶ 강풍에다 비조차 오기 시작했다 Rain began to fall in addition to [on top of] strong winds.

조차권 租借權 (a) lease; leasehold
　◆ 100년간의 조차권을 얻다 obtain a 100 years' [100-year] lease on the territory

조찬 朝餐 breakfast
　—기도회 a breakfast prayer meeting

조처 措處 a measure ⇨ 조치 (措置)

조청 造淸 〈물엿〉 starch syrup

조촉 弔燭 a funeral candle

조촐하다 neat; neat and fresh; tidy; trim; smart; spruce
　◆ 조촐한 집 a neat [snug] house / 옷 맵시가 조촐하다 be neatly dressed / 조촐하게 차려 입다 spruce [tidy] *oneself* up / 조촐하게 살다 live in a small way

조총 弔銃 a volley of rifles at a funeral service
　◆ 조총을 발사하다 fire a volley for the dead

조총 鳥銃 〈새총〉 a fowling piece

조춘 早春 early spring

조치 措置 a measure; a step; 〈처리〉 management; arrangement; disposal
　◆ 강경한 조치를 취하다 take strong measures [action] 《against》
　—조치하다 take a step [measure]; take action; 〈처리하다〉 manage; arrange; dispose 《of》; conduct; settle
　◆ 적절히 조치하다 take a proper step; deal with *sth* properly / 쌍방에 공평하게 조치하다 take fair measures for both parties
　▶ 그 일은 적당히 조치해 주시오 Arrange the matter as you think best [fit].

조칙 詔勅 a Royal edict ⇨ 조서 (詔書)

조카 a nephew ◆ …의 조카 a nephew to…
　■ **처—** a wife's nephew [niece] ■ **—딸** a niece **—며느리** a nephew's wife **—사위** a niece's husband

조커 〈트럼프의〉 a joker

조크 〈농담〉 a joke

조타 操舵 steerage; steering **—조타하다** steer; helm ■ **—수** a steersman; a helmsman **—실** a steering house; a pilothouse

조탁 彫琢 〈보석 등의〉 carving and polishing; 〈문장의〉 elaboration
　—조탁하다 carve and polish; elaborate

조탄 粗炭 low-grade coal

조토 디 본도네 〈이탈리아의 화가〉 Giotto di Bondone (1266 ? -1337)

조퇴 早退 leaving office [school] early
　—조퇴하다 leave the class before it is dismissed; leave office earlier than usual
　◆ 한 시간 일찍 조퇴하다 leave office one hour early

조판 組版 〔印〕 composition; typesetting
　◆ 가조판으로 짜다 set type in a galley
　—조판하다 set up in type; compose 《type》
　▶ 그 책은 조판되어 있다 The book is in type.
　—공 a maker-up **—대** a composing stand [frame] **—료** composing charge

조폐 造幣 coinage; mintage ◆ 한국조폐공사 the Korea Mint Corporation **—조폐하다** mint **—국** the Mint Bureau **—국장** the Director [《美》 Treasurer] of the Mint Bureau

조포 弔砲 a salute of minute guns
　◆ 조포를 쏘다 fire a salute of minute guns

조포 粗暴 violence ⇨ 난폭

조품 粗品 〈변변치 못한 물품〉 an article of inferior quality; 〈남에게 보내는 선물의 겸칭〉 my small gift [present]

조하다 躁— quick-[hot-]tempered; impatient; hasty

조함 造艦 naval construction; naval shipbuilding **—계획** a naval construction program **—능력** naval shipbuilding capacity

조합 組合 an association; a society; a league; a fraternity; 〔商〕 a partnership; 〈동업의〉 a guild
　◆ 조합에 가입시키다 admit *sb* into an association / 조합에 가입하다 join an association / 조합을 만들다 form an association [a guild]; 〈근로자가〉 organize a union
　■ **공제—** a benevolent society **노동—** a labor union **산업별—** an industrial union **소비—** a consumers' cooperative society **신용—** a credit association **직업별—** a craft [horizontal] union ■ **—간부** a union official [leader] **—규약** a union charter [constitution] **—비** union dues **—운동** a union movement **—활동** union activities

조합 調合 **1** ⇨ 조미(調味)
　2 〈섞음〉 compounding; mixing; preparation
　—조합하다 compound [make up] 《a medicine》; mix 《together》; prepare; concoct
　◆ 처방대로 조합하다 fill [dispense] a prescription
　—물〔劑〕 a mixture; a preparation

조합원 組合員 a partner; a copartner; a union member
　■ **비—** a nonunion man [worker]

조항 條項 articles (and clauses); 〈항목〉 a provision
　◆ 법 조항을 존중하다 respect the provisions of a law / 유언장의 조항을 실행하다 follow out the provisions of *sb*'s will
　■ **계약—** a contract clause

조행 操行 behavior; conduct; deportment

조혈 造血 blood making; hematosis; hematogenesis ◆ 조혈의 hematogenic **—조혈하다** make blood ■ **—제** a blood-making medicine; a hematinic **—조직[기능]** hematogenous tissues [functions]

조형 造形 mo(u)lding; modeling
— 조형하다 mo(u)ld; model; shape
■ —예술[미술] formative [plastic] arts

조혼 早婚 (an) early marriage
▶ 옛날에는 조혼이 성행하였다 Early marriage prevailed in the old days.
— 조혼하다 marry young

조홍 潮紅 flush in the face ⇨ 홍조(紅潮) 1

조화 弔花 funeral flowers; floral tributes; an offering of flowers
▶ 조화 사절 〈부고란 등에서〉 No flowers.

조화 造化 〈자연의 힘과 재주〉 creation; nature
♦ 신의 조화 work of God; divine work / 조화의 신 the Creator; the Maker (of Nature) / 조화의 묘 the wonder(s) of nature

조화 造花 an artificial [an imitation] flower

조화 調和 harmony; accord; agreement; symphony; 〈균형〉 symmetry
♦ 색채의 조화 harmony of colors / 음의 조화 consonance of sounds / 조화를 깨뜨리다 impair [break] harmony
▶ 전체의 조화가 중요하다 It is important to have a good balance throughout.
— 조화하다 harmonize 《with》; be in harmony 《with》; match 《with》; agree [accord] 《with》; be harmonious 《with》
♦ 조화된 harmonious; well-matched / 조화되지 않다 be inharmonious [discordant] 《with》; be out of harmony [keeping] 《with》 / 조화시키다 harmonize
▶ 이것은 색채가 잘 조화된 작품이다 This work is a splendid harmony of colors.
■ —비례[수열] 《數》 a harmonic proportion [sequence] —중항[평균] 《數》 the harmonic means [mean]

조회 朝會 a morning gathering [meeting]

조회 照會 (an) inquiry; (a) reference
— 조회하다 inquire 《of sb about sth》; make inquiries 《as to》; refer [make a reference] to 《sb for sth》; apply 《to sb》 for information
♦ 조회한 결과 on inquiry / 인물을 조회하다 inquire about sb's character
▶ 조회한 모든 것을 지배인 앞으로 보내주시기 바랍니다 All inquiries should be addressed to the manager.
■ —장(狀) a letter of inquiry —처 〈신원 등의〉 a reference

족 足 1 〈발〉 the foot (of a cow); 〈양·돼지 등의〉 trotters; 〈돼지의〉 pettitoes 2 〈켤레〉 a pair (of socks)

-족 族 1 〈종족〉 a race; a tribe
♦ 티베트 족 the Tibet tribe
2 〈족속〉 a class; a tribe
♦ 사양족 a declining upper-class family; impoverished aristocrats / 피그미족 the Pygmies
3 〈원소 등의〉 a group
♦ 백금족 the platinum group

족대기다 torment; badger; harass; put the screw(s) on; force 《on》
♦ 채무자를 족대겨 돈을 (억지로) 받아내다 put the screws on a debator for his money / 아무를 족대겨 일을 시키다 force sb to work

족두리 a bride's headpiece; a bridal crown

■ —하님 a bride's maidservant

족발 足— 〈돼지의〉 pettitoes; 《pig's》 trotters

족벌 族閥 a clan; a clique
■ —정치 clan government —주의 nepotism

족보 族譜 a clan register; a genealogy; a pedigree; a genealogical table
♦ 족보를 캐다 trace [look into] one's genealogy / 족보를 만들다[편찬하다] draw up [compile] a genealogy (of)

족생 簇生 gregarious growth ⇨ 총생(叢生)

족속 族屬 〈겨레붙이〉 kinsmen; a clan; clansmen; 〈패거리〉 a party; a set

족쇄 足鎖 leg irons; fetters; shackles
♦ 족쇄를 채우다 fetter; shackle; put sb in the stocks

족인 族人 clansmen

족자 簇子 a hanging scroll [picture]; 《hang》 a scroll

족자리 〈손잡이〉 ears 《on a pot》; handgrips (of a pot)

족장 族長 a tribal head; a patriarch; 〈여자〉 a matriarch; the head of a family [clan]
■ —시대 the patriarchal age —정치 patriarchy

족적 足跡·足迹 〈발자국〉 a footprint; a footmark
♦ 족적을 남기다 leave one's footmarks [an impress, footprints] 《on one's age》 / 아무의 족적을 더듬어[뒤쫓아] 가다 follow (up) sb's footsteps

족제비 〔動〕 weasel; 〈한국산〉 a Siberian mink

족족[1] 〈마다〉 whenever; every time 《occasion》; as often as
♦ 오는 족족 whenever [as often as] one comes; each [every] time one calls / 하는 족족 실패하다 fail in every attempt
▶ 그녀는 사람을 만나는 족족 그 얘기를 한다 She tells the story to everybody she meets.
▶ 그는 입을 벌리는 족족 말이 다르다 First he says one thing, then another.
▶ 그는 하는 족족 잘 되어간다 Everything he does goes well.
▶ 케이크는 굽는 족족 먹어버렸다 Cakes were eaten up as fast as they were made.

족족[2] in rows [lines] ⇨ 죽죽

족집게 (a pair of) tweezers; nippers
♦ 족집게로 뽑다 tweeze 《a thorn out of the finger》; pluck 《a hair》 out with tweezers

족척 族戚 kindred; relatives; kin(s)folk

족치다 1 〈줄이다〉 waste ♦ 가산을 족치다 waste away one's patrimony
2 〈결딴내다〉 break; destroy ♦ 탁자를 족치다 break a table
3 ⇨ 족대기다

족하다 足— 〈충분하다〉 enough; sufficient; suffice; 〈충족하다〉 serve; 〈가치있다〉 (be) worth 《worthy of》; 〈만족하다〉 satisfied 《with》; content 《with》
♦ 천 명을 수용하기에 족한 호텔 a hotel large enough to accommodate a thousand people; a hotel with a capacity of a thousand / 마음에 족하다 be satisfactory
▶ 그 만큼의 빵이면 4인분으로 족하다 That much bread will be enough for four people.

▶ 5천원으로 족하겠니? Can you make five thousand won do?
▶ 차비는 2만원이면 족하다 Twenty thousand won will be enough [sufficient, do] for the fare.
▶ 그것으로 족해 That's enough. ⇒ That will do.

족히 足— 〈충분히〉enough; sufficiently; full(y); well
♦ 족히 볼[읽을] 만하다 be well worth seeing [reading] / 족히 그 직무를 감당하다 be adequate to one's post
▶ 그의 재산은 족히 100억원 이상이나 되었더 His assets amounted to [were] well over ten billion won.
▶ 거기에 가는데 족히 2시간 걸렸다 It took a good two hours to get there.
▶ 그와는 족히 정치를 논할 만하다 He is well worth talking politics with.

존 a zone
■ 스트라이크—〔野〕 the strike zone: 투구는 스트라이크존을 벗어났다 The pitch wasn't in the strike zone. ■ —디펜스〔籠〕 zone defense

존경 尊敬 respect; esteem; reverence; veneration; deference
—존경하다 respect; esteem; revere; venerate; hold sb in respect [esteem]; have respect for
♦ 노인을 존경하다 pay respect to the aged; have respect for age / 존경하는 마음을 갖다 feel respect 《for》 / 존경할 만한 respectable; venerable; worthy of respect / …을 존경하여 out of respect for; in deference to / 존경받다 win [gain] the respect 《of》; command 《another's》 respect
▶ 그는 노교수를 매우 존경하고 있다 He has (a) great respect [reverence] for the old professor. ⇒ He respects the old professor greatly.
▶ 그는 구국의 지사로 존경받았다 He was looked up to [regarded] as the savior of his country.
▶ 그는 이웃사람들 모두로부터 존경받고 있다 He is respected [is looked up to] by all his neighbors.

존귀 尊貴 nobility —존귀하다 high and noble

존대 尊待 treatment with respect —존대하다 treat with respect; hold sb in esteem
♦ 존대받다 be held in esteem 《by》; be highly thought of 《by》

존대어 尊待語 〈경어〉 an honorific (expression [word]); a term of respect
♦ 존대어를 써서 말하다 use polite expressions [honorifics]

존립 存立 existence; subsistence
▶ 그것은 국가의 존립을 위협하는 대사건이었다 It was a great event that threatened the existence of the nation.
—존립하다 exist; subsist

존망 存亡 life or death; existence; fate; destiny
▶ 이것은 국가 존망에 관한 문제다 This is a life-or-death question for the nation. ⇒ This is a serious national crisis.

존부 存否 existence and inexistence

존비 尊卑 high and low; the upper and the lower classes; aristocrats and plebeians
♦ 존비 귀천의 구별없이 without distinction of rank; high and low alike

존속 存續 continuance; continuation; duration
—존속하다 continue (to exist); endure; 〈지탱하다〉 last
▶ 이 관습이 현재까지 존속되어 왔다니 이상하다 It's strange that this practice has continued to the present.
■ —기간 a period of life; a term of existence

존속 尊屬 〔法〕 an ascendant; an ancestor
■ —직계— a lineal ascendant ■ —살해 the killing [homicide, murder] of a lineal ascendant; 〈부모 살해〉 a parricide; the murder of one's parent(s); 〈부친 살해〉 patricide; 〈모친 살해〉 matricide —친(親) 〔法〕 a lineal ascendant

존안 尊顔 your face ♦ 존안을 뵈옵다 have the honor [pleasure] of seeing you

존엄 尊嚴 dignity; majesty; sanctity
♦ 인간의 존엄 the dignity of man / 존엄을 유지하다[손상하다] maintain [impair] the dignity 《of》 / 법의 존엄을 지키다 uphold the majesty [dignity] of the law
—존엄하다 dignified; majestic; august

존영 尊影 your [his] portrait [picture]

존자 尊者 〔佛教〕 a (Buddhist) priest of eminent virtue; a saint

존장 尊長 one's elder ⇨ 손윗사람

존재 存在 existence; being; presence
♦ 불쌍한 존재 wretched being / 존재의 의의 the significance of the existence 《of》 / 존재를 무시하다 ignore the existence 《of》 / 존재를 의심[부정]하다 take no notice of sb / 존재를 의심[부정]하다 doubt [deny] the existence 《of》
▶ 그녀는 그 당시 평론가로서는 존재를 인정받지 못했다 She was not recognized as a critic in those days.
▶ 그는 기회 있을 때마다 자신의 존재를 주장했다 He asserted himself at every opportunity.
—존재하다 exist; be in existence [being]
▶ 그것이 어떻게 존재하게 되었는지 모르겠다 I don't know how it came into existence [being].
▶ 그는 가공인물로 역사상으로는 존재하지 않는다 He is a fictitious character that has no existence in history.
■ —론 〔哲〕 ontology —이유 reason for being; justification for existence; (프) raison d'être

존절 節 〈⇨ 절약〉 ♦ 돈을 존절히 쓰다 make economical use of money

존존하다, 쫀쫀하다 〈피륙의 발이 곱다〉 fine- [close-] wove; (be) close [fine] in texture

존중 尊重 respect; esteem; deference
▶ 개인의 권리 존중은 민주주의의 기초다 Respect for individual rights is the basis of democracy.
—존중하다 respect; esteem; hold sb in respect [esteem]; value; prize; set store by; pay (high) regard to; think much [highly] of
♦ 존중할 만한 respectable; estimable / 신의를 존중하다 set store by faith / 법을 존중하다 respect [have a regard for] the laws / 학문을 존중하다 hold learning in esteem / 다년간의

교우 관계를 존중하다 value a friendship of longstanding / 목숨보다 명예를 존중하다 value [put] honor above life
▶ 그는 남의 사생활을 존중하지 않는다 He doesn't respect [has no respect for] other's privacy.
존체 尊體 your esteemed health [self]
존치 存置 maintenance (of a system)
―존치하다 retain; maintain
존칭 尊稱 an honorific (title); a title of honor
존폐 存廢 maintenance or abolition
▶ 현행 제도의 존폐에 대해 토의합시다 Let's discuss whether to continue with the present system or abolish it.
존함 尊啣 your name
▶ 존함은 김선생으로부터 익히 듣고 있습니다 I have heard of you from Mr. Kim.
졸 〔장기〕 a pawn ♦ 졸을 잡다 take a pawn
졸 〔化〕 a sol; a colloidal solution
졸가리 1〈잎이 진 가지〉 dry bits of twig
2〈줄기〉 a stripped stalk [stem]
3〈골자〉 an outline; a summary
졸경치(르)다 卒更― have bitter experiences; have a hard time of it (with *sb*); pay dearly (for)
졸계 拙計 a poor policy ⇨ 졸책(拙策)
졸깃졸깃하다 gummy; sticky; chewy
▶ 이 해파리는 씹으면 졸깃졸깃하다 This jellyfish is hard to chew.
졸년 卒年 〈죽은 해〉 the year of *sb's* death
졸다¹ doze; nap; drowse; snooze; slumber; fall asleep
♦ 꾸벅꾸벅 졸다 doze off [over]; fall [drop (off), go off] into a doze; nod [rock] in a doze; nid-nod / 수업중에 졸다 sleep [fall asleep] in class / 회의중에 (깜박) 졸다 doze [(口) drop, nod] off during the meeting / 운전중에 졸다 doze off at the wheel / 일을 하면서 졸다 nod off over *one's* work
▶ 그녀는 앉아서 꾸벅꾸벅 졸았다 She sat nodding.
졸다² boil down ⇨ 졸아들다
졸도 卒倒 a faint; a swoon; a fainting fit
―졸도하다 faint (away); fall down in a swoon; fall into a swoon; swoon
▶ 아버지는 오늘 아침 뇌빈혈로 졸도하셨다 My father fainted from cerebral anemia this morning.
졸들다 be stunted [dwarfed]; be hindered from the growth ♦ 졸든 나무 a stunted tree
졸때기 1〈작은 일〉 a petty job
♦ 졸때기 장사 small trade
2〈지위가 낮은 사람〉 a petty person; (총칭) small fry
졸라 〈프랑스의 문호〉 Zola, Emile(1840-1902)
졸라대다 badger [pester] (*sb* do); press [tease, importune] (*sb* for)
▶ 그의 아들은 용돈을 더 달라고 졸라댔다 His son asked [pressed] him for more money.
▶ 그 남자는 의사에게 진실을 말해 달라고 졸라댔다 The man pressed the doctor for the truth.
졸라매다 fasten tight(ly); bind; tie; lace (up)
♦ 허리띠를 졸라매다 draw a belt tighter / 헌 잡지를 끈으로 졸라매다 tie old magazines together with string / 허리를 끈으로 졸라매다 lace *one's* waist in / 꽉 졸라매다 bind [tie] (things) fast
졸랑거리다 〈까불대다〉♦ 졸랑거리는 행동[말] frivolous [flippant] behavior [remarks]
▶ 졸랑거리지 마라 Don't act hastily [rashly].
졸래졸래 flippantly; frivolously
♦ 졸래졸래 돌아다니다 gad about
졸렬 拙劣 clumsiness; awkwardness; maladroitness
―졸렬하다 clumsy; awkward; bungling; unskillful; inexpert; maladroit; poor
♦ 졸렬한 수단 a bungling step; a clumsy measure / 졸렬한 연기 a poor play [performance]; a boner / 졸렬한 짓을 하다 act foolishly
졸론 拙論 a poor opinion [view]; a clumsy argument
졸리다¹ become [feel, get] sleepy; drowsy; have a sleepy spell
♦ 졸린 눈 sleepy [heavy] eyes; drowsy eyes / 졸리는 강의 a dull (and monotonous) lecture / 졸려 죽겠다 feel dying with sleep; be overcome by drowsiness
▶ 간밤에 늦게까지 일어나 있었더니 오늘은 몹시 졸리다 I'm very sleepy today because I stayed up late last night.
▶ 그 영화를 보고 있으니 졸린다 I get sleepy [drowsy] while I was seeing that movie. ⇌ That movie made me (feel) sleepy [drowsy].
졸리다² 1〈조름을 당하다〉 be badgered; get pestered [pressed, importuned]
2〈단단하게 매어지다〉 be [get] tightened
▶ 이 칼라는 너무 빳빳해서 목이 졸린다 This collar is so stiff it is strangling me.
졸막졸막하다 various in size
졸망졸망 1〈울퉁불퉁한 모양〉 bumpily; unevenly ―졸망졸망하다 bumpy; uneven
2〈자질구레한 모양〉 ―졸망졸망하다 small and irregular in size
♦ 졸망졸망한 아이들 a bunch of children of all sizes
졸문 拙文 poor writing; a poor composition; my writing
졸병 卒兵 a (common) soldier; a private
♦ 졸병들 the ranks; the rank and file
졸부 猝富 sudden riches; a new rich; a moneyed upstart ▶ 그는 토지로 졸부가 되었다 Land made him a rich man.
졸사 猝死 a sudden death
―졸사하다 die suddenly; pop off
졸사간에 猝乍間― 〈짧은 동안에〉in a moment; in an instant
졸속 拙速 ♦ 졸속의[한] done fast and sloppily; rough-and-ready; knocked-up
――주의 in raw ready method [rule]: 졸속주의로 in raw haste / 그의 일은 언제나 졸속주의다 His work is always rough-and-ready.
졸아들다 be boiled down [dry]; boil down
▶ 육수가 졸아들어 한 숟가락이 되었다 The gravy boiled down to a spoonful.
졸아붙다 be boiled dry; boil down to nothing
▶ 수프가 졸아붙지 않도록 불을 낮추어라 Turn down the fire so that the soup won't boil

away.
졸아지다 be boiled away [down]; gradually reduce [contract]
졸업 卒業 graduation; completion of a course (of study)
◆ 대학 졸업자 a college graduate
—**졸업하다** graduate [be graduated] from (Oxford); complete the whole course (of a school)
◆ 중학교를 졸업하다 complete the middle school course; finish middle school / 대학을 졸업하다 graduate from [at] a university / 수석으로 졸업하다 graduate first on the list [in one's class] / 우등으로 대학을 졸업하다 graduate with honors / 고학하며 대학을 졸업하다 work one's way through college
▶ 그는 1990년 서울대학교를 졸업했다 He graduated from Seoul National University in 1990.
■ —논문 a graduation thesis —반 the graduating class —시험 a graduation examination: 졸업 시험을 치르다[에 합격하다, 에 떨어지다] take [pass, fail] a graduation examination —예정자 a graduate-to-be —장 a diploma (of graduation); a certificate of the completion of a school course
졸업생 卒業生 a graduate; 〈남자〉 an alumnus (*pl.* -ni); 〈여자〉 an alumna (*pl.* -nae)
▶ 이 학교는 2만명의 졸업생을 냈다 This school turned out twenty-thousand boys [girls].
◆ 대학— a university graduate [man] ■—명부 alumni [alumnae] directory; a list of graduates
졸업식 卒業式 〈hold〉 a graduation ceremony; (美) the commencement
◆ 졸업식을 거행하다 hold a graduation (ceremony) [(美) a commencement]
■—날 the graduation day; (美) the commencement day
졸업정원제 卒業定員制 the graduation quota system
졸연하다 猝然— 〈갑작스럽다〉 sudden; abrupt; unexpected
◆ 졸연히 abruptly; suddenly; unexpectedly
▶ 우리는 그의 졸연한 죽음에 놀랐다 We were surprised at his sudden [unexpected] death. ⇌ We were surprised that he died suddenly [unexpected].
졸음 sleepiness; drowsiness; a sleepy spell
◆ 졸음이 오는 sleepy; drowsy / 졸음이 오다 become [feel] sleepy [drowsy] / 졸음을 쫓다 shake off sleepiness
▶ 나는 몹시 졸음이 왔다 I became very sleepy.
▶ 잔뜩 먹으면 졸음이 온다 A hearty meal will make you feel drowsy.
▶ 나는 졸음을 쫓기 위해 커피를 한 잔 마셨다 I drank a cup of coffee to get rid of my sleepiness [keep myself awake].
졸이다 1 〈졸아들게 하다〉 boil down; boil (salt) dry
2 〈조바심하다〉 worry (*oneself*); feel anxious [uneasy, nervous]
◆ 마음을 졸이다 worry [bother] (*oneself*)

(about); be anxious (about); fidget [jitter] (about); be in great fear (of); be kept in suspense / 돌아오기를 마음졸이며 기다리다 wait in anxious suspense for *sb's* return
▶ 그 일로 마음졸이지 말게 Don't worry about it.
▶ 시험보는 일로 너무 마음졸이지 마라 Don't worry too much [be so nervous] about the exams.
졸자 拙者 a petty [narrow-minded] fellow
졸작 拙作 a poor work; 〈자기 작품의 낮춤말〉 my poor [humble] work
▶ 이 작품은 졸작이다 This work is poorly done.
졸장부 拙丈夫 a small-minded man; a petty fellow; an unmanly man; a sissy
졸저 拙著 〈자기 저작의 낮춤말〉 my poor [humble, unworthy] work
졸졸 1 〈끊이지 않고〉 ◆ 졸졸 흐르는 시냇물 a murmuring brook / 수돗물이 졸졸 나오다 water trickles down (from the faucet)
▶ 시냇물이 바위 사이로 졸졸 흘렀다 A stream trickled through rocks.
▶ 시냇물이 돌멩이 위로 졸졸 흐르고 있다 The brook is murmuring [flowing with a murmuring sound] over the pebbles.
2 〈뒤를 줄곧〉 ◆ 졸졸 따라다니다 tag at *sb's* heels; tag [tail] after
▶ 그녀의 뒤를 졸졸 따라가는 개를 봐라 Look at the dog tagging at her heels.
졸중 卒中 〔韓醫〕 apoplexy
◆ 졸중에 걸리다 have a fit [stroke] of apoplexy; be seized with apoplexy
졸지에 猝地 〈갑자기〉 abruptly; suddenly; all of a sudden; out of the blue / 졸지에 사고를 당하다 have an accident all of a sudden
졸책 拙策 a poor plan [policy]; an imprudent [impolitic] measure; impolicy; 〈자기 계책의 낮춤말〉 my humble plan
졸필 拙筆 〈악필〉 poor (hand)writing; a poor hand; 〈자기 필적의 낮춤말〉 my clumsy writing
◆ 졸필이다 write a poor hand
졸하다 卒— 〈죽다〉 die; pass away; decease
졸하다 拙— 〈졸렬하다〉 unskillful; poor; clumsy; 〈옹졸하다〉 narrow-minded; petty
좀[1] 〔昆〕 a clothes moth; a bookworm; a silverfish ◆ 좀을 방지하는 mothproof (stuff) / 좀 먹은 moth-eaten (book)
▶ 나는 그 소식을 모두에게 알리고 싶어 좀이 쑤셨다 (비유) I was itching to tell everybody the news.
좀[2] 1 ⇨ 조금
◆ 좀 아는 사이 a slight acquaintance / 좀 전에 a little time [while] ago / 상점에서 물건을 좀 사다 make a small purchase at [in] a store
▶ 오늘 아침은 좀 춥다 It's a little cold this morning.
▶ 나는 5시가 좀 못되어 귀가했다 I returned home a little before five.
▶ 배가 좀 고프다 I am kind of hungry.
▶ 개한테 케이크를 좀 줘라 Give the dog a small piece of cake.
▶ 너 오늘 좀 이상하구나 Something is wrong

with you today.
▶자네와 할 얘기가 좀 있는데 I want to have a word with you.
▶그는 말투가 우리와는 좀 달랐다 His way of speaking was somewhat different from ours.
▶생각 좀 해봅시다 Let me think a while. ⇌ I will think about it a bit.
2 〈부디〉 (if you) please; pray; just
▶이것 좀 보시오 Just look at this.
▶좀 보여 주시오 Let me have a look.
▶문 좀 닫아 주세요 May I trouble you to shut the door?
▶말씀 좀 묻겠습니다 Excuse me, but may I ask you a question?

좀³ 〈그 얼마나〉 how; what; how much [many]
▶좀 걱정하셨겠어요 You must have felt very anxious.
▶좀 상심하셨습니까? I can well imagine your grief.
▶해외 유학을 할 수 있으면 좀 좋을까 How I wish I could study abroad!

좀- 〈좀스러움〉 petty; 〈소형〉 small
좀것 a petty person [thing]; small things; (총칭) small fry
좀꾀 little [shallow, cheap] tricks; petty wiles
♦좀꾀를 부리다 play cheap tricks; resort to petty wiles
좀노릇 a petty job; trifling work; a chore
좀놈 a petty fellow
좀더 〈분량〉 a little more; 〈수효〉 a few more; 〈시간〉 a little longer
▶좀더 천천히 말씀해 주세요 Please speak a little more slowly.
▶좀더 기다려 보겠다 I'll wait a little longer.
좀도둑 a sneak [petty] thief; a pilferer
▶집을 비운 사이에 좀도둑이 들었다 We had our house robbed in our absence.
━질 petty theft [larceny]; pilfering; filching; 좀도둑질을 하다 pilfer; filch; (口) sneak
좀말 small talk; a trivial remark
좀먹다 〈좀에 쏠리다〉 be worm-eaten [motheaten]; be eaten by worms; 〈은연중 손해를 입히다〉 gnaw at 《one's life》
♦좀먹은 책 a moth-eaten book / 마음을 좀먹는 근심 a gnawing anxiety / 동심을 좀먹다 spoil the child's heart
▶근심은 생명을 좀 먹는다 Care preys upon life.
▶부정부패가 나라를 좀먹고 있다 Corruption is gnawing at our country.
좀생원 a narrow-minded person; a petty poltroon
좀스럽다 〈성질이〉 small-minded; petty; 〈사물의 규모가〉 small; trifling; insignificant
♦좀스러운 사람 a petty person / 좀스러운 일 a trifling matter; a petty job / 좀스럽게 굴다 be too meticulous
▶좀스럽게 별것을 다 알려고 하는구나 Why are you so curious to know about such petty matters?
▶남자는 좀스러우면 못쓴다 A man should not trouble himself with small matters.
좀약 ━藥 a mothball
좀처럼 〈여간해서는〉 seldom; rarely; hardly; scarcely; 〈쉽사리〉《not》 easily; 《not》 readily
▶문이 좀처럼 안 열린다 The door will not open.
▶그는 좀처럼 책을 읽지 않는다 He seldom or never reads a book.
▶우리는 요즘 좀처럼 그를 볼 수가 없다 We rarely see him nowadays.
▶그녀가 술을 마시는 일은 좀처럼 없다 It is rarely that she drinks.
▶요즘은 좀처럼 가정부를 구할 수 없다 Nowadays you cannot readily get a maid.
▶그것은 좀처럼 얻기 어려운 기회다 It is a rare chance. ⇌ It is the chance of a lifetime.
좀쳇것 〈웬만한 물건〉 a so-so thing; a common [an ordinary] thing
♦좀쳇것으로는 마음에 안 들다 be dissatisfied with *sth* of any ordinary type
좀팽이 a petty person [thing] ⇨ 좀것

좁다 〈폭이〉 narrow; 〈면적이〉 small; 〈범위가〉 limited; 〈옹색하다〉 close; tight; 〈도량·소견이〉 narrow-minded
♦좁은 길[문] a narrow path [gate] / 좁은 방 a small room / 좁은 소견 a narrow [small] mind / 좁은 활동 무대 a limited sphere of activity / 교제 범위가 좁다 have a small circle of friends
▶그는 도량이 좁다 He is narrow-minded. ⇌ He has a narrow [small] mind.
▶그녀는 시야가 좁다 She has a narrow view of things.
▶이 외투는 품이 좁다 This coat is tight under the arm.
▶그들은 정치적 시야가 좁다 They are narrow in their political outlook.
▶그 이론은 적용 범위가 좁다 The theory has a limited range of application.
▶세상 참 좁구나 It's (such) a small world!
좁다랗다 narrow and close; narrowish
좁쌀 〈낱알〉 hulled millet; (비유) a tiny [petty] thing ━뱅이 a petty person ━영감 a petty old man
좁아지다 narrow; become [get] narrow
♦끝으로 갈수록 좁아지다 narrow toward the end; taper 《off》
▶길이 갑자기 좁아졌다 The road suddenly narrowed.
▶골짜기는 점점 좁아졌다 The valley narrowed more and more.
▶식구가 불어나서 집이 좁아졌다 Our family has outgrown our house.
좁히다 narrow; make narrow; 〈사이를〉 close; make compact
♦열[대오] 사이를 좁히다 close the ranks [files] / 좁혀 앉다 sit close [closely]
▶자리를 좀 좁혀 주십시오 Please crush up a little.
▶그 논의는 대리점 선정 문제로 좁혀졌다 The discussion boiled down to the choice between agencies.

종¹ 〈마늘 등의 꽃대〉 (the end of) a stalk 《of garlic》
종² 〈노비〉 a slave; a servant
▶계집 종 a slave girl; a female slave / 종으로 삼다 enslave; make a slave 《of》 / 종으로 팔리

다 be sold for a slave / 종같이 부리다 put *sb* to a practical slave labor; use *sb* like a slave / 종같이 일하다 work like a slave; drudge
■—노릇 slavery; servitude: 종노릇하다 serve as a slave; be a slave 《to》

종 種 1 〈생물 분류상의 단위〉 a species (▶단수·복수 동형)
♦종의 기원 〈다윈의〉 *The Origin of Species*
2 〈씨앗〉 a seed; a grain; 〈품종〉 a breed; a stock; a variety
♦몽고 종의 말 a horse of Mongolian breed
3 〈종류〉 a sort; a kind; a class; a type
♦여러 종의 꽃 every variety [sort] of flowers / 3종 우편 third-class mail

종 縱 length ⇨ 세로

종 鐘 a bell
♦시간을 알리는 종 the time bell / 하학(下學)을 알리는 종 the closing bell / 저녁 기도의 종 vesper bells / 종의 추 a clapper / 종치는 사람 a bell ringer / 종을 달다 put a bell 《on》 / 종을 울리다 ring [sound] a bell / 종을 치다 strike [toll] a bell
▶종이 울린다 A bell tolls [rings].
▶교회의 종이 11시를 알리고 있었다 The church bell was ringing out eleven.
▶저녁 종소리가 들린다 I hear an evening bell ringing.
▶누구를 위하여 종은 울리나 For whom does the bell toll?

종- 從- 〈촌수〉 ♦종형 one's (elder) cousin
-종 宗 〈불교·도교의 종파〉 a (religious) denomination [sect] ♦선종 the Zen sect
종가 宗家 the head family [house]
종가래 a small spade
종가세 從價稅 an ad valorem duty [tax]
종각 鐘閣 a bell pavilion
종간 終刊 〈신문·잡지의〉 cessation of publication ―호 the final number
종개념 種概念 〔論〕 species; specific concept
종견 種犬 a breeding dog
종결 終結 a close; a conclusion; an end; a termination
♦종결에 가까워지다 draw to a close
―종결하다 end; terminate; be concluded; come to a close [an end]
▶그들은 가능한 빨리 전쟁을 종결시키려고 노력했다 They tried to bring the war to an end as soon as possible.
▶우리는 파업을 종결시키려고 애썼지만 허사였다 We made efforts to bring the strike to an end, but without success.
종고모 從姑母 a female cousin of *one's* father
종곡 終曲 〔樂〕 the finale = 피날레
종관 縱貫 traversing; running through
―종관하다 run through; traverse
▶산맥이 반도를 종관하고 있다 A range of mountains runs through the peninsula.
―철도 a railroad running through 《the land》
종교 宗敎 (a) religion
♦신흥 종교와 기성 종교 the new and the established religions / 종교적 자비심 religious feeling / 종교적 의식 a religious ceremony / 종교(상)의 religious; spiritual / 종교에서 위안을 찾다 seek solace [consolation] in religion
▶그는 종교에 전연 관심이 없다 He is quite indifferent to religion.
▶그녀는 종교에서 구원을 얻었다 She attained salvation through religion.
▶그는 지금 어떤 종교에 빠져있다 He has become a religious fanatic. ⇌ He has become a fanatical adherent of a certain religion. ⇌ He is now devoted to a certain religion.
▶당신은 어떤 종교를 믿고 있습니까? What religion do you profess [believe in]?
▶나는 종교가 없습니다 I do not follow any particular religious belief.
■—가[인] a man of religion; a religionist
—개혁 religious reformation; 〔史〕 the Reformation —계 the religious world —광 a religious maniac [fanatic, enthusiast] —교육 religious education —극 a religious drama; 〈기적극〉 a miracle play —단체 a religious body [organization] —문학 religious literature —박해 religious persecution —서 a religious book; a book on religion —열 religious enthusiasm —음악 sacred music —재판 the Inquisition —철학 philosophy of religion —학 the science of religion —화 a religious picture; a picture of a sacred subject —회의 a religious conference; an ecclesiastical meeting
종교심 宗敎心 a religious sentiment
♦종교심이 있는 religious(-minded); pious / 종교심이 없는 irreligious; impious
종구라기 〈조그만 바가지〉 a small gourd
종국 終局 an end; a close; a conclusion; a finale
♦비참한 종국 a tragic end; a sad denouement / 종국에 가서는 after all; ultimately; in the long run / 종국을 고하다 come [be brought] to an end [a close, a conclusion]; be concluded
▶사건은 종국에 가까워지고 있었다 The case was drawing to a close.
종군 從軍 service in a war
♦종군을 지원하다 petition [apply] for permission to go to war
▶그는 제2차 세계 대전 종군 중에 죽었다 He died as a soldier in World War II.
—종군하다 follow [join] the army; go to the front; serve in the war
♦종군하고 있다 be at the front; be in active service
―간호사 a war nurse ―기자 a war correspondent ―기장 a war medal
종극 終極 finality; the ultimate
종기 終期 the end; the close; the termination
종기 腫氣 a boil; a tumor; an abscess; a swelling ♦종기를 삭히는 약 a resolvent; a resolutive / 종기가 나다 have a boil 《on》
▶내 등에 종기가 났다 A swelling has come out on my back.
종내 終乃 to the last ⇨ 끝끝내, 마침내
종내기 種— a breed; a stock; a strain; a variety; a species ♦종내기가 같다 [다르다] be of the same [a different] breed

종년 (卑) a woman slave
종놈 (卑) a slave
종다래끼 a small creel; a (small) fishing basket
종다리 〔鳥〕 a skylark; a lark
종다수 從多數 following the majority
―**종다수하다** agree to the views of the majority ■―결 decision by majority: 종다수결하다 abide by the decision of the majority
종단 宗團 a religious order; an order
종단 縱斷 vertical section; 〈분할〉 a division; a split ―**종단하다** cut [divide] sth vertically [longitudinally]; 〈국토 등을〉 run through 《the land》; travel [run] across; traverse
▶ 록키 산맥이 북미 대륙을 종단하고 있다 The Rockies run through North America.
■―면 a longitudinal section
종달거리다 grumble ⇨ 중덜거리다
종달새 a skylark ⇨ 종다리
종답 宗畓 clan fields ⇨ 종중(~답)
종당 從當 as a matter of course; from the very nature of things; after all; in the end
▶ 그는 종당 자신의 과오를 인정했다 He admitted his mistakes in the end.
종대 the stalk 《of garlic》
종대 縱隊 a column; a file
♦ 2열 종대로 in double file [column] / 4열〔분대, 소대, 중대〕 종대로 in columns of fours [sections, platoons, companies] / 종대를 짓다 form a column / 1열 종대로 행진하다 march in single file; defile
■―행진 a march in a column
종댕기 a pigtail ribbon
종돈 種豚 〈수컷〉 a boar; 〈암컷〉 a breeding pig; a brood sow
종두 種痘 vaccination for smallpox; vaccine inoculation ▶ 종두가 잘 되었다 The vaccination has taken.
―**종두하다** vaccinate; inoculate with vaccine
종람 縱覽 (general) inspection; 〈열람〉 reading ―**종람하다** inspect; visit; 〈열람하다〉 read
종래 從來 hitherto; heretofore; up to now [this time]; so far
♦ 종래의 건물 the old [former] building / 종래의 생각 a traditional notion [idea] / 종래의 악계를 뿌리뽑다 make away with the existing evils
▶ 종래는 이런 문제를 어떻게 처리했습니까? How have you dealt with problems like this in the past?
▶ 종래의 방식으로는 안된다 The traditional [conventional] method will not work any more.
▶ 입시는 종래대로 11월에 시행한다 Entrance examinations will be held as usual in November.
종량세 從量稅 a specific duty
■―율 a specific tariff
종려나무 棕櫚― 〔植〕 a (hemp) palm
■―유 palm oil
종렬 縱列 a column; a file; a train
♦ 분대〔소대, 중대〕 종렬로 in a column of sections [platoons, companies] / 종렬을 짓다 form a file; queue up / 종렬 행진을 하다 defile

종료 終了 an end; a close; (a) conclusion; 〈완료〉 completion; 〈기간・권리의〉 expiration
―**종료하다** 〈마치다〉 end; close; finish; conclude; complete; terminate; 〈끝나다〉 come to an end; be completed; expire
♦ 작업을 종료하다 finish [complete] the work
종루 鐘樓 a belfry; a bell tower; a campanile
종류 種類 a kind; a sort; a variety; a class; a species 《▶단수・복수 동형》; a description; 〈형태〉 a type; 〈성질〉 nature
♦ 여러 종류의 것 things of various kinds / 온갖 종류의 사람들 all sorts and conditions of people / 온갖 종류의 자동차 motorcars of every description / 이런 종류의 범죄 crimes of this nature / 이런 종류의 물품 articles of this kind / 온갖 종류의 all sorts [kinds] of; of every kind [description] / 같은 종류의 of the same kind [sort] / 종류가 다르다 be different in kind
▶ 어떤 종류의 소설을 좋아하십니까? What kind [sort] of novels do you like?
▶ 이것은 내가 찾고 있는 종류의 것이 아니다 This is not the sort of thing I am looking for.
▶ 그런 종류의 것에는 흥미가 없다 I am not interested in that sort of thing.
종류별 種類別 classification; assortment 《⇨ 종별》 ♦ 종류별로 하다 classify; assort
종마 種馬 a stallion; a studhorse; (美) a stud
종막 終幕 an end; a close; 〈연극의〉 a curtainfall; the finale; 〈대단원〉 (프) the dénouement
♦ 종막이 다가오다 draw to a close [an end] / 종막을 고하다 come [be brought] to an end
종말 終末 an end; a close; a conclusion
♦ 종말을 고하다 come [be brought] to an end
▶ 전쟁도 종말에 가까워지고 있다 The war is drawing to a close.
종매 從妹 a younger female cousin
종목 種目 an item; 〈경기의〉 an event ▶ 그는 두 종목에 출전했다 He took part in two events. ■ 영업― items of business
종묘 宗廟 the ancestral temple of the royal family; the Royal Ancestors' Shrine
종묘 種苗 seeds and saplings; seedlings
■―장 a field for seedling; a nursery
종무 宗務 religious affairs
■―소 a temple office
종무 終務 the closing of offices for the year
■―일 the last business day of the year at the offices
종무소식 終無消息 hearing nothing from
▶ 그후로 그에게서는 종무소식이다 Nothing has been heard [I haven't heard a word] from him since then.
종반 終盤 〈선거 등의〉 the last [final] stage [phase]; 〈바둑・장기 등의〉 the end game
▶ 선거전은 벌써 종반에 접어들었다 The election campaign has already entered [got into] the [its] final stage.
■―전 the end game
종발 鐘鉢 a small bowl
종범 從犯 〈범죄〉 participation in a crime; 〈범죄자〉 an accessory
♦ 살인죄의 종범 an accessory to murder
■ 사전[사후]― an accessory before [after]

the fact ■—자 an accessory (to a crime)
종별 種別 (a) classification; (an) assortment —종별하다 classify; assort
종복 從僕 a servant; an attendant; a valet
종사 宗嗣 the heir of the head family
종사 從死 self-immolation on the death of sb —종사하다 immolate *oneself* on the death of sb; follow sb to the grave
종사 從事 devoting *oneself* to an object —종사하다 〈전념하다〉 devote *oneself* to (an object); 〈일삼다〉 engage (*oneself*) in (business); be engaged [employed] in; be occupied with
♦ 암 연구에 종사하다 engage (*oneself*) in the study of cancer / 교육[저술]에 종사하다 employ *oneself* on education [in writing] / 무역[실무]에 종사하고 있다 be engaged in trade [business]
▶ 그는 무슨 업종에 종사하고 있습니까? What business is he engaged in?
▶ 나는 인쇄업에 종사하고 있다 I am in the printing business.
▶ 나는 전에는 육체노동에 종사하고 있었다 I used to do physical work.
종사 縱射 〖軍〗 a raking fire; an enfilade —종사하다 enfilade; rake (with fire); sweep ■—포 a raker
종산 宗山 a clan [an ancestral] graveyard
종서 縱書 vertical writing —종서하다 write vertically [in vertical lines]; write from top to bottom
종선 縱線 a vertical [longitudinal] line; 〖樂〗 a bar ⇨ 세로(~줄)
종성 終聲 〖言〗 a final consonant
종소리 鐘— the sound [ringing] of a bell
종속 從屬 subordination; dependency
♦ 종속적인 subordinate; dependent; auxiliary —종속하다 be subordinate [subject] (to); depend [be dependent] (upon, on)
♦ A를 B에 종속시키다 subordinate A to B
■—관계 subordinate relationship —국 a vassal state; a dependency; an appanage —절 〖文法〗 a subordinate clause —접속사 〖文法〗 a subordinate conjunction
종손 宗孫 the eldest grandson of the head family
종손 從孫 the grandson of *one's* brother; a grandnephew
종손녀 從孫女 the granddaughter of *one's* brother; a grandniece
종수 從嫂 the wife of *one's* cousin
종숙 從叔 a male cousin of *one's* father
종숙모 從叔母 the wife of *one's* father's cousin
종시 終始 from first to last ⇨ 시종(始終)
종시속 從時俗 conforming to the times —종시속하다 conform to the times; follow the customs of the day
종식 終熄 cessation; an end; eradication —종식하다 cease; end; come to an end; be brought to a close
♦ 전쟁을 종식시키다 put an end to war
종신 宗臣 a veteran [an elder] statesman; 〈벼슬하는 종친〉 a minister from the royal family

종신 終身 〈일생〉 a whole life; *one's* life; 〈죽음〉 the end of life; *one's* death; 〈임종〉 being at *one's* parent's deathbed
♦ 종신의 life; lifelong
—종신하다 〈죽다〉 end [finish, live out] *one's* life [days]; 〈임종하다〉 be on [at] *one's* parent's deathbed
■—고용제도 the life(long) employment system —생명보험 ordinary life insurance —연금 a life pension —직 a life office; an office for life —징역 a life imprisonment; a life sentence : 종신 징역을 살다 serve a life sentence —형 imprisonment for life : 종신형을 언도 받다 be sentenced to imprisonment for life —회원 a life member
종실 宗室 the royal family; a member of the royal clan
종심 終審 〈최후 심리〉〖法〗 the final [last] examination [trial] ■—법원 the court of last instance
종씨 宗氏 a clansman; a person of the same surname
종아리 the calf (*pl.* calves)
♦ 종아리를 때리다 whip sb on the calf / 종아리를 맞다 get whipped on the calf
■—뼈 a fibula; a splint bone —채 a switch; (美) a cane
종알거리다 mutter; murmur; grumble; mumble
▶ 그 어린 소녀는 혼자 종알거렸다 The little girl mumbled to herself.
종야 終夜 all night; the whole night
종양 腫瘍 〖醫〗 a tumor; a neoplasm
♦ 뇌— a cerebral tumor 양성[악성]— a benign [malign, malignant] tumor ■—학 oncology; phymatology
종언 終焉 〈죽음〉 the end of life; death; 〈종말〉 an end; a close; expiration; completion
♦ 종언을 고하다 come to an end; be brought to a close
종업 從業 work in service
—종업하다 be employed; be in the service; be in employment; work
종업 終業 the close of work [school]
—종업하다 end *one's* work
■—시간 the closing hour —식 the closing ceremony —일 〈학년말·학기말의〉 the last day of school; the breaking-up day
종업원 從業員 a worker; an employee; (총칭) the staff; the working men
▶ 이 회사의 종업원은 몇 명입니까? How many people work for this company? ⇌ How many employees do you have?
■—대표 the spokesman of the working men —명부 a name-list of employees —전용 출입구 service entrance —조합 a workers' union —퇴직 수당 적립금 a reserve for employees' retirement allowance
종연 終演 the end of a performance [show]
▶ 〖會話〗「종연은 몇 시입니까?」「종연은 오후 10시입니다」 "What time does the curtain fall?" "The curtain falls at 10 p.m."
—종연하다 end; finish; close (a theater, the performance); be over

종용 慫慂 〈권고〉 advice; suggestion; instance; 〈설득〉 persuasion; 〈유도〉 inducement
▶ 나는 친구의 종용으로 생명보험에 들었다 I bought [took out] a life insurance policy at my friend's suggestion.
—**종용하다** advise; suggest; counsel; persuade; prevail upon
▶ 그는 친구들을 종용하여 동행케 했다 He prevailed on his friends to go with him.

종우 種牛 a seed bull

종위접속사 從位接續辭 〔文法〕 a subordinate conjunction

종유 種油 〈씨의〉 seed oil; 〈평지의〉 rape oil; rapeseed oil; colza oil

종유동 鐘乳洞 a stalactite grotto [cave]

종유석 鐘乳石 〔鑛〕 a stalactite

종이 paper
♦ 종이 한 장 a sheet of paper / 종이 한 장의 차이 a very slight difference 《between》; 《by》a paper-thin majority [margin] / 종이로 만든 paper-made / 종이에 싸다 wrap [do up] *sth* in paper / 종이에 쓰다 write [put down] on paper / 종이를 뜨다[만들다] make paper / 벽에 종이를 바르다 paper the wall / 종이를 접어 배를 만들다 fold a piece of paper into the figure of a boat
▶ 천재와 미치광이는 종이 한 장 차이다 Genius is but one remove from insanity. ⇌ There's only a very fine line between a genius and a madman.
■ —색— colored paper ■ —꾸러미 a paper parcel [package] —냅킨 a paper napkin [serviette] —제품 paper products —집게 a paper holder [clip] —쪽 a piece [scrap, strip, slip] of paper —컵[잔] a paper cup; 《商標》a Dixie Cup —테이프 〔電算〕 a paper tape —표지 a paper cover —호랑이 a paper tiger

종일 終日 all day (long); the whole day; for a whole day; throughout [all through] the day; from morning till [to] night
▶ 어제는 종일 비가 왔다 It rained yesterday from morning till night.
▶ 나는 종일 서 있어서 피로했다 I was exhausted, having been on my feet all day.
▶ 오늘은 종일 연하장만 썼다 I spent the whole day writing New Year's cards today.

종자 從者 a follower; an attendant; a valet; 〈중세 기사의〉 a squire; 〈수행원들〉 a retinue; a suite; a following

종자 種子 a seed; a stone; a pip ⇨ 씨
■ —식물 a seed plant

종자매 從姉妹 female cousins

종작없다 pointless; desultory; senseless; nonsensical; rambling; loose; incoherent; absurd
♦ 종작없는 말[의견] a pointless [rambling] remark / 종작없는 생각 a loose idea
▶ 그는 종작없이 말한다 He speaks incoherently. ⇌ He talks in a rambling way.

종잡다 get the gist 《of》; grasp [catch] the point 《of》; get a rough idea 《of》; roughly understand
▶ 그 사람의 말은 통 종잡을 수가 없다 I can't make head or tail of what he is saying. ⇌ I can't see what he's driving at. ⇌ There is no logic in his remark.

종장 終章 〈시조·노래의〉 the last of the three verses of a *shijo*; the last part of a song

종장 終場 〔證〕 closing ■ —가격[시세] the closing price [quotations]

종적 蹤迹 traces; tracks; vestiges; whereabouts
♦ 종적을 감추다 cover *one's* traces [tracks]; conceal *one's* whereabouts; leave no trace behind; disappear

종적 縱的 longitudinal; lengthwise; 〈수직의〉 vertical ♦ 종적 연결 vertical contact

종전 從前 〈종전의 관계〉 *one's* past connections 《with *sb*》 / 종전의 previous; former / 종전(는) hitherto; heretofore; formerly; before / 종전과 같이 as usual; as before; as heretofore; as hitherto; as ever; as of old
▶ 우리의 일은 종전대로 한다 We'll do our work as before.

종전 終戰 the end [termination] of the war; the cessation of hostilities
♦ 종전 후의 혼란 postwar confusion / 종전 당시에 at the time of the war's end
▶ 종전이 되었다 The war came to an end.

종점 終點 the terminal (station); the last stop; the terminus
▶ 우리는 종점까지 갑니다 We are riding as far as the terminal (station) [end of the line].
▶ 자, 종점이다 Now we are at the last stop.

종제 從弟 a younger (male) cousin

종조모 從祖母 a grandaunt; a great-aunt; the wife of *one's* granduncle [great-uncle]

종조부 從祖父 a granduncle; a great-uncle

종족 種族 〈인종〉 a race; 〈부족〉 a tribe; 〈동식물의〉 a family; a species
♦ 종족 보존의 본능 the instinct of preservation of the species / 종족간의 분쟁 intertribal strife; conflicts between the tribes

종종 種種 1 〈가지가지〉 various [diverse, different] kinds
2 〈가끔〉 now and then; from time to time; 〈흔히〉 often; frequently
▶ 종종 놀러 오십시오 Come and see us often.
▶ 그에게서는 종종 소식이 있다 I hear from him once in a while.
▶ 그것은 종종 있는 일이다 It is a matter of no uncommon occurrence.

종종거리다 walk with quick, short steps

종종걸음 quick, short steps; mincing steps
♦ 종종걸음으로 걷다 walk with quick and short steps; walk hastily with short steps

종주 宗主 a suzerain
■ —국 a suzerain (state) —권 suzerainty

종주하다 縱走— run through; traverse; 〈능선을 따라 걷다〉 walk along the (mountain) ridges
▶ 태백산맥은 한반도를 종주하는 산맥 중의 하나다 The T'aebaek Range is one of the mountains that run through Korean Peninsula.

종중 宗中 a clan; a family
■ —답 the paddy fields owned by a clan; clan fields

종지 a small bowl [cup]

종지 宗旨 〈종문의 교리의 취지〉 the tenets [doctrines] of a religious sect; 〈근본이 되는

요지〉 the main purport; the fundamental meaning
♦종지가 다르다 embrace a different the main purport; belong to a different sect
종지 終止 an end; a stop; termination; cessation ―**종지하다** cease; stop; end; terminate; come to an end [a close]
종지부 終止符 〈마침표〉 a full stop; a period
♦종지부를 찍다 put an end [a period] 《to》
종지뼈 a kneecap; a kneepan ⇨ 슬개골
종진 縱陣 a column; a line ahead
♦종진으로 in a line ahead; in a single file / 종진을 싯다[펴다] form a column
종질 從姪 a son of a male cousin
―녀 a daughter of a male cousin
종짓굽 1 〈종지뼈 언저리〉 the rim of the kneecap ♦종짓굽이 떨어지다 〈젖먹이가 걷다 건다〉 《a baby》 start toddling; find its feet
2 〈쟁기의〉 the part that protrudes from the end of the under ridge of a plow
종착역 終着驛 a terminal station; a (railway) terminus; 《美》 a railroad terminal ♦인생의 종착역 the terminus [end] of *one's* life
▶이 열차는 여기가 종착역입니다 This train does not go any further.
종축 種畜 breeding stock
■―장 a breeding stock farm
종축 縱軸 a vertical [longitudinal] axis; 〔數〕 the axis of ordinates ⇨ 세로(~축)
종친 宗親 〈일가〉 clansmen; kindred 〈종실〉 a royal family; relatives [kindred] of the king
■―회 a clan [family] meeting
종탑 鐘塔 a bell tower; a campanile; a belfry
종파 宗派 1 〈종가의 계통〉 the main branch of a family [clan]
2 〈교파〉 a (religious) sect [denomination]
♦종파 싸움[다툼] a sectarian strife / 각 종파의 목사 clergy of all denominations / 같은 종파에 속하다 be of the same denomination
종파 縱波 a longitudinal wave
종피 種皮 〈씨껍질〉 〔植〕 a seed coat; a testa 《*pl.* -tae》
종합 綜合 (a) synthesis 《*pl.* -ses》; generalization; 〔論〕 colligation
―**종합하다** put together; synthesize; colligate
♦이런 말들을 종합해 보면 putting these talks together / 각 종목의 득점을 종합하다 total [add up] the points scored in individual events
■―개발 overall [comprehensive] development ―경기 combined exercises: 개인[단체] 종합경기 individual [team] combined exercises ―계획 an all-out plan; a comprehensive program [plan] ―대학 a university ―무역상사 a general trading company ―병원 a general hospital; a polyclinic ―비타민제 a multivitamin pill ―선수권 the all-round championships ―소득세 a composite income tax ―예술 a composite art ―잡지 a general magazine ―철학 synthetic philosophy ―청사 the Integrated Government Building ―판단 (a) synthetic judgment
종합적 綜合的 general; overall; synthetic; composite; all-around

▶라틴어는 종합적인 언어인 반면 영어는 분석적인 언어다 Latin is a synthetic language, while English is analytic.
종형 從兄 an elder (male) cousin
종형제 從兄弟 (male) cousins
종회 宗會 a clan [family] meeting
♦종회를 열다 hold a clan meeting
종횡 縱橫 length and breadth
♦종횡으로 달리는 철도망 a network of railways / 종횡의 교차로 a crisscross of streets / 종횡으로 lengthwise and breadthwise; vertically and horizontally; in all directions
종횡무진 縱橫無盡 ♦종횡무진의 기지 a wealth of wit / 종횡무진으로 freely; at will; right and left
▶그는 종횡무진으로 싸웠다 He fought his enemies right and left.
▶그는 종횡무진의 대활약을 했다 He played a remarkable [very active] part in it.
좆 the penis
좇다 follow; run after; conform to; obey; abide by
♦순서를 좇아 in order / 지시를 좇아 in accordance with [according to] *sb's* instructions / 법을 좇아 in accordance with the law / 관습을 좇아 in conformity with custom; according to custom / 원칙을 좇아 행하다 act on a principle / 남이 하는 대로 좇아 하다 follow another's example; follow in another's steps / 관습을 좇다 follow [conform to] the custom; toe the line / 대세를 좇다 follow the general trend / 뒤를 좇다 follow; run after / 명령을 좇다 obey *sb's* order / 유행을 좇다 follow the fashion [mode]
좋다¹ 1 〈즐겁다〉 well; good; glad; agreeable; joyful
♦기분 좋은 일 a glad [delightful] thing / 듣기 좋은 be agreeable [pleasant] to the ear/ 기분이 좋다 feel well [good]; be in good humor [mood]; be comfortable / 너무 좋아서 말을 못하다 be speechless with joy
▶오늘 아침에는 기분이 좋다 I'm feeling good [well] this morning.
▶시골길을 걸으면 기분이 좋다 It's pleasant walking along a country road.
▶남에게 칭찬 받는 것은 기분 좋은 일이다 It is sweet to hear one's own praises.
▶모차르트의 음악은 언제 들어도 좋다 The music of Mozart always gives me great joy.
2 【마음에 들다】 〈경치가〉 beautiful; nice; 〈날씨가〉 fine; bright; lovely; 〈냄새・맛・소리 등이〉 sweet; good; pleasing; agreeable
♦좋은 목소리 a sweet voice / 좋은 향기 a nice [sweet] smell / 경치가 좋은 곳 a place of scenic beauty; a beauty [scenic] spot
▶이차는 맛이 참 좋군요 This tea tastes excellent [very good].
▶오늘 날씨 참 좋다 What a lovely [fine] day (it is) today!
▶여기는 참으로 경치가 좋다 This is a place of scenic beauty. ⇌ This district has truly lovely scenery.
3 〈양호하다〉 good; nice; well; fine; 〈착하다〉

good-natured; 〈총명하다〉 bright; clever; smart
♦ 좋은 그림[길, 책] a good picture [road, book] / 마음자리가 좋은 사람 a good-natured [nice] person / 머리가 좋은 소년 a bright [clever, smart] boy / 건강이 좋다 be in good health / 좋지도 나쁘지도 않다 be neither good nor bad; be just tolerable
▶ 그는 좋은 녀석이다 He is a nice fellow.
▶ 그는 작업 성적이 좋았다 He has made a good showing in his work.
▶ 그것 참 좋은 생각이다 That's a good idea.
4 〈귀하다〉 valuable; precious; 〈훌륭하다〉 noble; good
♦ 좋은 자료 valuable [precious] materials / 좋은 소식 good news
▶ 이것은 특별히 좋은 물건이다 This is a very good one.
▶ 그것이 그의 좋은 점이다 That's one good thing about him.
▶ 그는 품행이 좋다 He behaves [conducts] himself well.
▶ 그는 좋은 집안 태생이다 He comes of a noble family.
▶ 우리는 그 제도의 좋은 점을 받아들여야 한다 We should take in the good points of the system.
5 〈길하다〉 good; lucky; fortunate; auspicious
♦ 좋은 전조 a good [lucky] omen / 좋은 번호 a lucky number / 좋은 날을 고르다 choose a lucky [an auspicious] day
6 〈유효·유익하다〉 good 《for》; efficacious; beneficial
♦ 몸에 좋다 be good for the health; do *sb* good / 천식에 좋다 〈약이〉 be efficacious [good] for asthma
▶ 아침 일찍 일어나는 것은 당신 건강에 좋습니다 Early rising is good for the your health.
7 〈알맞다〉 proper; right; good; suitable; fitting; 〈유리하다〉 profitable; favorable
♦ 좋은 기회 a good opportunity [chance] / 좋은 사업 a profitable [paying] business / 좋은 실례 a good [proper] example / 좋은 조건 remunerative terms
▶ 너는 마침 좋은 때에 도착했다 You arrived just in time [in the nick of time].
▶ 이것은 그리스 건축의 좋은 예다 This is a good example of Greek architecture.
8 〈괜찮다〉 good; well; all right; enough; 〈해도 좋다〉 may 《do》; be welcome to 《do》; might as well 《do》; 〈상관·지장 없다〉 do not mind 《doing》; do not care 《if》
▶ 재미있기만 하면 어떤 책이라도 좋다 Any book will do, so long as it is interesting.
▶ 내주라면 언제든지 와도 좋다 If it's next week, you may come and see me (at) any time.
▶ 내일은 오지 않아도 좋다 You need not [don't have to] come tomorrow.
▶ 둘 중 어느 것을 택해도 좋다 You may choose either of the two.
▶ 어느 쪽이든 좋다 I don't care which.
▶ 會話「창문을 열어도 좋습니까?」「네, 좋습니다」"Do you mind if I open the window?" ⇌ "Do you mind my opening the window?" "No, not at all."
9 〈소망하다〉 wish; hope
▶ 내일 비가 오면 좋을텐데 I hope it will rain tomorrow.
▶ 우산을 가지고 왔더라면 좋았을 걸 I wish I had brought my umbrella with me.
▶ 당신이 그런 일을 안 했으면 좋았을텐데요 You should not have done such a thing.
10 〈바람직하다〉 desirable; preferable; 〈좋아하다〉 like 《*sth* better than…》; love; prefer 《*sth* to》; choose
▶ 좋을대로 하세요 Do as you like.
▶ 무엇이 좋아서 그런 짓을 했니? Why did you choose to do such a thing?
▶ 꾸짖기 좋아서 꾸짖는 것이 아니다 I am not scolding you for my own pleasure.
▶ 네가 갈 수 있다면 그보다 좋은 일은 없다 If you can go, that would be the best possible thing.
▶ 그는 좋아서 그녀와 결혼한 것이 아니었다 It was not of his own accord [of his own free will] that he married her.
11 〈낫다〉 better; superior 《to》; 〈…하는 편이 낫다〉 had better 《do》
▶ 그는 예전엔 형편이 좋았던게 분명하다 He is sure to have seen better days.
▶ 그 환자는 오늘 다소 좋은 편이다 The patient is a little better today.
▶ 그런 짓은 하지 않는 것이 좋다 You had better not do such a thing.
12 〈친하다〉 intimate; good; friendly
♦ 사이가 좋다 be on good [intimate] terms 《with》 / 좋은 사람이 생기다 get [win] a lover
13 〈능숙·능란하다〉 skillful; good; clever; expert
♦ 말 솜씨가 좋다 be a good talker / 사격 솜씨가 좋다 be good with a rifle
좋다² Good!; Well!; All right!; O.K.!; 〈환성〉 Whoopee!; Goodie!; Oh boy!; Whee!; 〈찬성〉 Agreed!
▶ 좋아, 이제 결정됐어 Good, it's been settled.
▶ 좋아, 가자 Well, let's go.
좋아지내다 be on intimate terms 《with》; be good friends 《with》 ▶ 그 둘은 서로 좋아지낸다 The two of them are hand and [in] glove with each other.
좋아지다 1 〈좋게 되다〉 become [get] better; improve; take a turn for the better; take a favorable turn
♦ 날씨가 좋아지다 the weather clears up; the weather improves [becomes better] / 경기가 좋아지다 《the market》 pick up [look up]; perk up 《after depression》
▶ 그 환자의 병세는 좋아졌다 The patient has taken a turn for the better.
▶ 빚을 갚고 나니 기분이 좋아졌다 I felt better after repaying the debt.
2 〈좋아하게 되다〉 get [come, learn] to like *sth*; become fond 《of》; take a fancy 《to》; 〈사이가 가까워지다〉 become intimate 《with》
좋아하다 1 〈기호〉 like; 〈사랑〉 love; be fond 《of》; have a liking [fancy, taste] 《for》; 〈특별히〉 be partial 《to》; 〈주로 음식을〉 have a weakness 《for apples》; 〈주로 부정문·의문문

에서〉 care (for *sth*, to do)
♦좋아하는 작가[요리] *one's* favorite author [dish] / 좋아하는 이 *one's* lover; a sweetheart / 좋아하든 싫어하든 whether one likes (it) or not / 독서를 좋아하다 be fond of reading / 서로 좋아하다 love each other / A보다 B를 좋아하다 like B better than A; prefer B to A / 별로 좋아하지 않다 do not care much (about, for, to do)
▶그녀는 음악을 좋아한다 She likes [is fond of] music.
▶네가 좋아하는 가수는 누구냐? Who is your favorite singer?
▶그는 스포츠를 무엇보다도 좋아한다 He is partial to sports.
▶나는 술을 무척 좋아한다 I have a weakness for wine [liquor].
▶그는 어려서부터 공부를 좋아했다 He took kindly to books [was fond of study] from his childhood.
▶나는 혼자 있기를 좋아한다 I like to be alone. ≒ I enjoy being alone.
▶나는 그런 종류의 그림은 별로 좋아하지 않는다 I don't care much for that kind of painting.
2 〈즐거워하다〉 be pleased (with); be delighted [take delight] 《in doing》; rejoice [be rejoiced] 《about, to do》; be glad (to do)
♦장난치며 좋아하는 아이들 boys taking delight in doing mischiefs / 껑충껑충 뛰며 좋아하다 jump for joy
▶그는 그 말을 듣고 무척 좋아했다 He was much pleased to hear that.
▶그 소식에 모두들 좋아했다 All were delighted at the news.
▶그는 그의 아내가 거기 가는 것을 좋아하지 않는다 He doesn't like the idea of his wife going there.
좋이 well (enough); nicely; fully; full; fairly
▶역까지 좋이 3마일은 된다 It is a good three miles to the station.
▶그는 60세는 좋이 넘었겠다 He must be well over [past] sixty.
▶그 스타디움은 5만명은 좋이 수용할 만큼 크다 The stadium is large enough to seat fifty thousand people easily.
좋지않다 〈질이〉 bad; evil; wrong; 〈마음에 안 들다〉 disagreeable; unpleasant; 〈불길하다〉 ill; ominous; unlucky; 〈바람직하지 않다〉 undesirable; 〈부적합하다〉 improper; unfitting; unsuitable
♦좋지않은 소문 an unsavory rumor / 좋지않은 징조 a bad [an ill] omen / 위가 좋지않다 have a weak stomach / 안색이 좋지않다 look pale; have a bad complexion / 눈에 좋지않다 be bad for [be injurious to] the eyes
▶동물을 학대하는 것은 좋지않다 It is not good to maltreat animals.
▶오늘 아침은 기분이 좋지않다 I feel rather out of sorts this morning.
▶형세가 좋지않다 The prospects are not encouraging.
좌 左 (the) left ♦좌에서 우로 from left to right / 좌로 돌다[향하다] turn left

▶좌향좌 《口令》 Left face [turn]!
좌 座 a seat; 〈지위〉 a position; a status
♦권좌에 오르다 come to [into] power
-좌 -座 《天》 a constellation ⇨ 별자리
좌경 左傾 an inclination [a tendency] to the left; radicalization
♦좌경 색채를 띤 잡지 a journal of leftist coloring / 좌경적이다 radical; leftist; Red
▶그의 사상은 좌경적이다 His ideas lean toward the left.
—좌경하다 lean toward the left; incline to the left; become leftist [left-wing]
■—문학 leftist literature —분자 a radical [leftist] element —사상 radical thoughts —운동 a left movement —학생 a radical [Red] student
좌고 坐高 〈앉은키〉 *one's* sitting height
좌고우면하다 左顧右眄— 〈두리번거리다〉 look this and that way; look to left and right
좌골 坐骨 〔解〕 the hucklebone; the hipbone; the ischium (*pl.* -chia)
■—신경 the sciatic nerve —신경통 sciatic neuralgia; sciatica; hip gout
좌기 左記 the undermentioned (statement); the following ♦좌기와 같이 as undermentioned [underwritten]; as follows
좌담 座談 a conversation; a talk; 〈식탁에서의〉 a table talk
♦좌담에 능하다 be a good talker [conversationalist] / 좌담식으로 이야기하다 talk 《about a matter》 informally
좌담회 座談會 a round-table talk; a discussion meeting; a symposium
♦텔레비전의 정치 좌담회 a TV symposium on politics / 좌담회를 갖다 have a round-table talk [hold a symposium] 《on》
좌대 座臺 a pedestal
좌뜨다 〈생각이 남보다 뛰어나다〉 excel by far; surpass others
♦생각이 좌뜨다 have a far better idea than anyone else
▶그는 동료들보다 학식이 훨씬 좌뜬다 He towers high above his colleagues in scholarship.
좌르르 with a rush [splash]; pouring down; rushing
▶물이 좌르르 쏟아졌다 Water came rushing out.
▶콩이 탁자 위에 좌르르 쏟아졌다 The beans spilled on the table with a rattling sound.
좌변 左邊 the left side
좌불안석 坐不安席 being unable to sit comfortably 《from anxiety, etc》
▶그와 함께 있으면 나는 좌불안석이 된다 I feel ill at ease in his company.
—좌불안석하다 cannot sit still [idle]; be restless; be fidgety; be nervous; fidget
좌상 坐商 〈앉은 장사〉 keeping a shop; storekeeping
좌상 坐像 a seated [sitting] figure [image]; a sedentary statue [image]
좌상 座上 〈좌중〉 the company; the party; all those present; 〈연장자〉 the elder in a company

좌상 挫傷 1 〈상심〉 discouragement; disheartenment 2 〈좌창〉 a sprain; a contusion
▶ 그는 시합하다 손에 좌상을 입었다 He had his wrist sprained during the game.

좌서 左書 〈왼손으로 쓰는 글씨〉 lefthand(ed) writing ━**좌서하다** write lefthanded

좌석 坐席·座席 a seat; 〈계단식의〉 a tier; 〈조종사의〉 a cockpit; 〈교회의〉 a pew
♦ 차의 뒷[앞]좌석 rear [front] seat of a car / 버스의 좌석을 잡다 take [secure] a seat in a bus / 열차의 좌석을 예약하다 reserve a seat on the train / 창쪽[통로쪽] 좌석을 확보하다 secure a window [an aisle] seat / 좌석을 떠나지 않다 keep *one's* seat
▶ 이 강당의 좌석수는 2천개다 This hall seats [has a seating capacity of] two thousand.
▶ 당신의 좌석은 이쪽입니다 Your seat is over here.
▶ 나는 좌석을 좋은 데로 바꿨다 I changed my seat for a better one.
▶ 좌석을 지정받은 후 입장하십시오 Please get seat assignment before entering.
▶ 내 좌석을 한 할머니에게 양보했다 I offered [gave (up)] my seat to an old woman.
▶ 좌석을 잡아두지[예약하지] 않으면 일요일에는 그 영화는 볼 수 없다 You won't be able to see the film on Sunday if you don't reserve a seat [make reservations].
▶ 그는 좌석에 앉았다 He took his seat. ⇌ He seated himself.
━**-권** a place card ━**버스-** a seat bus ━**번호** the seat number ━**일람도** the plan of seats ━**정원(수)** seating capacity [accommodation] ━**지정권** a reserved-seat ticket ━**표** a seating chart

좌선 坐禪 〔佛教〕 Zen meditation; religious meditation ━**좌선하다** sit in (religious) meditation

좌시 坐視 watching idly ━**좌시하다** look on unconcernedly [idly, with indifference]; remain an idle spectator
▶ 나는 그녀의 곤경을 좌시할 수 없었다 I could not leave her in the lurch.

좌안 左岸 the left bank 《of a river》
좌안 左眼 the left eye
좌약 左藥 〔醫〕 a suppository; a bougie
좌완투수 左腕投手 〔野〕 a southpaw; a left-handed pitcher; (口) a lefty; a leftie; a lefthander
좌욕 坐浴 (take) a sitz [hip] bath
좌우 左右 1 〈왼편과 오른편〉 (the) right and left
♦ 좌우로 right and left; on the right and the left; on either side; on both sides
▶ 배가 좌우로 흔들렸다 The ship rolled from side to side.
▶ 길을 건널 때는 좌우를 살펴보아라 Look right and left when you cross the street.
2 〈측근〉 *one's* attendants; people in attendance
♦ 좌우를 물리치고 밀담을 하다 keep *one's* attendants away and have a closed-door conference (with)
3 〈영향〉 ━**좌우하다** 〈지배하다〉 control; dominate; sway; 〈영향을 미치다〉 influence; command; govern; gain control of; have 《a thing》 under *one's* control
♦ 시장을 좌우하다 control [gain control of] the market / 나라의 운명을 좌우하다 hold sway over the destinies of a nation / 감정에 좌우되다 be swayed by sentiment [passion]
▶ 그의 충고가 내 운명을 좌우했다 His advice decided my destiny.
▶ 수확은 기후에 좌우된다 The crop depends on [upon] the weather.

좌우 座右 〈좌석의 오른쪽〉 *one's* right side; 〈옆〉 *one's* side
♦ 좌우에 by *one's* side; at *one's* elbow; at hand / 좌우에 간직하다 keep 《a book》 at *one's* elbow [at hand]; have 《a dictionary》 by one [*one's* side]
━**-명(銘)** a favorite motto; a maxim

좌우간 左右間 at any rate; in any event; at all events; anyhow; anyway
▶ 좌우간 그것을 해봅시다 Now let's try it, shall we?
▶ 좌우간 나는 그런 짓을 하지 않겠다 I'm not going to do it at any rate.
▶ 좌우간 정오까지는 그를 기다릴 것이다 Well, at any rate, I will wait for him till noon.

좌우익 左右翼 1 〔軍〕 the left and right wings of an army
2 〈사상의〉 the left and right wings; the leftists and the rightists

좌익 左翼 1 〈대형의〉 the left wing [flank]
♦ 적의 좌익을 공격하다 attack the enemy's left wing
2 (총칭) 〈주의상의〉 the left (wing); a left-winger; 〈개인〉 a leftist
♦ 좌익적 사상 left-wing [leftist] idea / 좌익의 leftist; left-wing; leftish
3 〔野〕 left field
4 ⇨ 좌익수
━**-분자** the left-wing elements; the leftist faction ━**사상** Leftism : 좌익 사상에 물들다 be tinctured with radicalism ━**운동[단체]** a leftist movement [organization] ━**작가** a leftist writer

좌익수 左翼手 〔野〕 a left fielder
좌장 座長 the president; the senior person present (in a seated group)
좌절 挫折 a frustration; a setback; 〈실패〉 (a) failure; a breakdown; collapse; 〈용기의〉 discouragement
♦ 좌절을 극복하다 get over *one's* frustration [failure]
━**좌절하다** miscarry; fail; get ruin; be frustrated; break down; collapse; suffer a setback
♦ 좌절시키다 frustrate; discourage / 공격이 좌절되다 an attack is frustrated
▶ 우리의 계획은 좌절되었다 Our plan broke down [collapsed]. ⇌ Our plan fell through [failed, met with a setback].
━**-감** frustration: 좌절감을 맛보다 feel a sense of failure; feel [be] frustrated

좌정하다 坐定━ sit; be seated
좌중 座中 ♦ 좌중을 둘러보다 look over the whole assembly 《of people》

▶ 좌중이 모두 감동하여 눈물을 흘렸다 The whole company was moved to tears.

좌지우지하다 左之右之— turn [twist, twirl, wind, wrap] *sb* round *one's* little finger; control; take the lead (in)
▶ 그는 우리 학급을 좌지우지한다 He has our school class at his beck.

좌천 左遷 demotion; degradation; relegation
—**좌천하다** relegate (to); demote (to); consign [degrade] *sb* to an inferior [a lower] position
▶ 그는 지방의 지점으로 좌천되었다 He was demoted to a post in a provincial branch.
▶ 그는 음주 때문에 좌천되었다 He was degraded [relegated, transferred] to an inferior post for drunkenness.

좌초 坐礁 stranding; grounding; running aground
—**좌초하다** go [run, strike] aground; run [go] on a rock; strike [run against] a rock
♦ 좌초한 배 a stranded ship; a ship aground
▶ 그 배는 해안에 좌초되었다 The ship was stranded [ran] ashore.
▶ 화물선은 암초에 좌초되었다 The cargo ship ran upon [struck] a sunken rock.
▶ 폭풍우가 지나간 뒤 세 척의 배가 좌초되어 있었다 After a storm we found three ships (were) aground.

좌충우돌하다 左衝右突— dash this way and rush that; plunge forward on this side and dash in on that

좌측 左側 the left(-hand) side
♦ 좌측에 on the left (side)
▶ 병원은 길 좌측에 있습니다 The hospital stands on the left (side) of the road.
▶ 미국의 자동차 핸들은 보통 좌측에 있다 Steering wheels of American cars are usually on the left.
■ —통행 (게시) Keep (to the) left.

좌파 左派 〈사람〉 the left wing; the left-wingers; 〈정당 내부의〉 the left faction
♦ 좌파의 leftist; left-wing
▶ 그는 프랑스의 사회당 좌파에 속해 있다 He is affiliated with the left wing of the Socialist Party of France.

좌표 座標 〔數〕 coordinates
▪ 가로— the abscissa 공간— coordinates in space 극— polar coordinates 세로— the ordinate 직교— orthogonal [rectangular] coordinates ■ —계 coordinate system —기하학 coordinate geometry —변환 coordinate transformation —축 a coordinate axis —평면 coordinate plane

좌향 左向 ▶ 좌향좌 (口令) Left turn [face]!
▶ 좌향 앞으로 가 (口令) Left wheel!
▶ 반 좌향좌 (口令) Half-face!

좌향 坐向 〔民俗〕 the lay of a site; geomantic aspect; a prospect
♦ 묘의 좌향을 잡다 determine the exact direction in which a grave must face
▶ 이 묘는 좌향이 나쁘다 This grave has a bad aspect.

좌현 左舷 〔海〕 port (↔ the starboard); 〈좌현 쪽〉 the port side

♦ 좌현의 port / 좌현에 on the port side; aport / 좌현으로 향하다 port; turn a ship to port / 좌현으로 기울다 list to port
▶ 우리는 좌현에 배를 발견했다 We sighted a ship to port.

좌회전 左回轉 left(-hand) turn; rotate left
▶ 좌회전 금지 (게시) No left turn.
—**좌회전하다** turn (to the) left; make a left (at)

좌흥 座興 amusement; entertainment
♦ 좌흥으로 for [in] fun; by way of joke; to entertain the company
▶ 나는 좌흥으로 만담을 했다 I told a funny story to amuse the company.
▶ 좌흥으로 하더라도 그런 말을 해선 안된다 You shouldn't say a thing like that even for fun [a joke].

좍 1 〈퍼지는 모양〉 far and wide; widely
▶ 소문이 좍 퍼졌다 The rumor has spread in a flash [like wildfire].
2 〈거침없이〉 fluently; with ease
♦ 좍 외다 recite fluently
3 〈흐르는 모양〉 in a quick stream; with a splosh [splash]

좍좍 1 〈비 등이〉 heavily; in torrents
♦ 잔디에 물을 좍좍 끼얹다 pour [shower] water on [over] the grass
▶ 비가 좍좍 쏟아진다 It rains heavily [hard, in torrents, cats and dogs].
2 〈거침없이〉 easily; with ease; fluently
♦ 시를 좍좍 외다 recite a poem fluently [easily]

좔좔 (flow) freely [forcibly]; with a swilling sound
▶ 홍수로 시냇물이 좔좔 흐른다 The brook flows with a lively current by a flood.

좨기 a cake of cooked vegetables [flour]
쟁이 a casting net; a cast net

죄 罪 〈종교・도덕상의〉 (a) sin; 〈법률상의〉 a crime; 〈규칙위반 등에 대한〉 (美) an offense; (英) an offence; 〈과오〉 a fault; 〈책잡〉 blame; charge; 〈악덕〉 a vice
♦ 죽을 죄 a grave offense; a crime deserving of death / 극악한 죄 a crime of the deepest dye / 중대한 죄 a grave sin; a serious [grave] crime / 신체와 재산에 대한 죄 crimes against person and property / 죄 없는 innocent; not guilty; blameless; crimeless; free from guilt / 죄 많은 guilt; blamable; sinful
〈죄가[는]〉 그에게는 죄가 없다 He is innocent [not guilty].
▶ 그는 죄가 없다고[있다고] 인정되었다 He was found innocent [guilty].
▶ 그것은 사고였기 때문에 아무에게도 죄가 없다 It was an accident, so no one is to blame [is to be blamed, is responsible] (for it).
▶ 죄는 미워해도 사람은 미워하지 마라 Condemn the offense and not its perpetrator.
〈죄를〉 죄를 범하다[짓다] commit a crime [sin]; sin; be guilty of 〈murder〉 / 죄를 받다 meet with punishment / 죄를 밝히다[규명하다] inquire into *sb's* crime / 죄를 감추다 cloak a sin / 죄를 묻다 accuse *sb* of a crime; bring a charge against *sb* / 죄를 용서하다 forgive

[condone] an offense / 죄를 면하다 escape punishment / 죄를 뒤집어씌우다 make a false charge against *sb*; put the blame on *sb*; put [lay] the blame on *sb* 《for》 / 죄를 인정하다 admit an offense; plead guilty; submit to a sentence / 죄를 자백하다 confess *one's* guilt / 죄를 감하다 mitigate *sb* punishment / 죄를 뒤집어 쓰다 take *sb's* crime
▶ 죄를 범하면 벌을 받는다 Those who commit a crime will receive their punishment.
▶ 그는 자기 죄를 경찰에 자백했다 He confessed himself crime to the police. ⇌ He confessed to his guilt to the police.
▶ 그는 애인의 죄를 뒤집어 썼다 He took the blame for his girlfriend.

죄과 罪科 a crime; 〈종교·도덕상의〉 a sin; an offense; blame; guilt
♦ 죄과가 없는 사람을 처벌하다 punish *sb* for nothing
▶ 그 소년에게는 죄과가 없다 The boy is free from blame [fault].

죄과 罪過 an offense; 〈과오〉 a fault; 〈죄악〉 a sin

죄다[1] **1** 〈느슨한 것을〉 tighten; make tight(er); strain; draw in; stretch; 〈수축시키다〉 contract; 〈조르다〉 strangle; wring; 〈나사로 죄다〉 screw ♦ 고삐를 죄다 tighten [pull up] the rein / 느슨한 줄을 죄다 tighten [strain] a loose rope; stretch a loose rope tight
2 〈사이를 좁히다〉 put [place] close; 〈자리를〉 sit up; sit close [closely]
♦ 자리를 더 죄어 앉다 sit up a little closer; sit closer together
3 〈마음을〉 feel anxious [uneasy, nervous] 《about》; be fidgety; be worried 《about》; worry *oneself* 《about》
▶ 그 여자는 몹시 마음을 죄며 남편이 도착하기를 기다렸다 She waited in great suspense for her husband's arrival.

죄다[2] 〈전부〉 all; wholly; entirely; everything; every one 《of them》
♦ 용돈을 죄다 써버리다 spend the last penny of *one's* pocket money / 가지고 있는 것을 죄다 주다 give *sb* everything that *one* has
▶ 내가 알고 있는 것은 죄다 말했습니다 I have told you all I know.

죄명 罪名 a charge; charge the name of a crime [an offense]
▶ 그는 사기의 죄명으로 기소되었다 He was indicted on a charge of fraud. ⇌ He was charged with fraud.
▶ 그는 절도의 죄명을 썼다 He was charged with theft.

죄목 罪目 〈과과〉 a charge; 〈혐의〉 suspicion
▶ 그는 살인의 죄목으로 체포되었다 He was arrested on a charge of murder.

죄밑 罪— 〈죄의식〉 a guilty conscience; 〈죄의 진상〉 the fact of wrongdoing
♦ 죄밑을 느끼다 have a guilty conscience; suffer from a guilty conscience
▶ 그는 죄밑이 있어서 나를 피한다 He avoids me because of the wrong he has done to me.

죄받다 罪— suffer [incur] punishment [a penalty]; be punished ♦ 죄받을 짓을 하다 do a cruel thing ▶ 그런 짓을 하면 죄받는다 Heaven will punish you for it.

죄벌 罪罰 the punishment of crime; (a) punishment for a crime

죄상 罪狀 a crime; guilt
♦ 죄상을 자백하다 confess *one's* crime / 죄상을 시인하다 plead guilty
▶ 그는 죄상이 명백해져 5년의 징역에 처해졌다 His guilt became clear, so he was sentenced to five years at hard labor.
▶ 그는 죄상을 부인했다 He pleaded not guilt.
▶ 수사관은 그의 죄상을 문초했다 The investigator inquired into his guilt.

죄송하다 罪悚— sorry; regrettable
♦ 죄송스럽다 sorry / 죄송해 하다 be [feel] sorry 《for》; regret; 〈송구해 하다〉 feel small; be ashamed / 죄송하지만[합니다만] I am sorry to trouble you, but...; Excuse me, but...; I beg your pardon sir, but...
▶ 오래 기다리시게 해서 죄송합니다 I am very sorry to have kept you waiting so long.
▶ 공부를 방해해서 정말 죄송합니다 I am very sorry to trouble your studies.
▶ 죄송합니다만 버스 정류장이 어디에 있습니까? Excuse me, but where is the bus stop?
▶ 죄송합니다만 좀 천천히 말씀해 주시겠습니까? Would you mind speaking a little more slowly?

죄수 罪囚 〈복역자〉 a prisoner; a prison inmate; 〈유죄 선고를 받은 사람〉 a convict; (口) a jailbird
■—복 a prisoner's uniform ■—호송차 a patrol wagon; a police wagon; (口) a Black Maria; (美俗) a paddy [pie] wagon

죄악 罪惡 〈종교·도덕상의〉 a sin; 〈법률상의〉 a crime; a vice
♦ 죄악의 소굴 a sink of iniquity / 죄악을 범하다 commit a sin [crime]
▶ 시간의 낭비는 일종의 죄악이다 Waste of time is a sort of sin.
■—감 a sense of guilt; guilty feelings

죄어들다 become narrower [tighter]; get tightened [drawn up]; contract; shrink
♦ 수사망이 죄어들다 the dragnet moves in
▶ 양손을 묶은 밧줄이 살에 죄어들었다 The rope with which his hands were tied cut into the flesh.

죄업 罪業 〖佛敎〗 a sin; a sinful act
♦ 죄업을 거듭하다 live a sinful life; commit on sin after another

죄이다 〈물건이〉 tighten; be tightened; be constricted; 〈마음이〉 feel anxious [uneasy, nervous]
♦ 가슴이 죄이는 느낌 a constriction in the chest

죄인 罪人 〈형법상의〉 a criminal; an offender; 〈기결의〉 a convict; 〈죄수〉 a prisoner; 〈종교·도덕상의〉 a sinner; a transgressor

죄장 罪障 〖佛敎〗 sins; sin and retribution ♦ 죄장을 소멸하다 expiate *one's* sin(s)

죄적 罪迹 evidence [traces] of crime; proofs of guilt
♦ 죄적을 감추다 cover the traces of guilt
▶ 그 형사는 용의자의 죄적을 들춰냈다 The

detective traced out the suspect's crime.

죄주다 罪— punish; give a punishment [penalty]; subject sb to punishment

죄질 罪質 the nature of a crime [an offense]

죄짓다 罪— 〈법률상으로〉 commit a crime [an offense]; 〈종교·도덕상으로〉 commit a sin; sin; trespass 《against》

죄책 罪責 the liability for a crime
♦ 죄책을 묻다 accuse sb of a crime / 죄책감을 느끼다 feel guilty; have a guilty conscience

죄형법정주의 罪刑法定主義 the principle of "nulla poena [nullum crimen] sine lege"; the principle of legality

죔쇠 a buckle; a clasp; a clamp ♦ 죔쇠로 죄다 [죔쇠를 풀다] buckle [unbuckle]

죔틀 a vise; a press
♦ 죔틀에 걸어 죄다 put to a press

주 主 1 〈주인〉 one's master; one's employer; 〈임금〉 one's lord; 〈하나님〉 the Lord; God; 〈그리스도〉 our Lord
2 〈주요 부분〉 the chief [principal, main] part; the primary [prime] object
♦ 주 목적 one's main [primary] object / 주된 동기 the prime motive / 주된 principal; chief; main; primary / 주로 mainly; chiefly; primarily; principally

주 朱 vermilion; cinnabar

주 州 〈미국의〉 a state; 〈영국의〉 a shire; 〈캐나다 등의〉 a province
♦ 오하이오 주 the State of Ohio / 주로 되다 (美) attain statehood / 주립 대학 (美) a state university
■—의회 (美) a state legislature [assembly]

주 住 a dwelling; (a) shelter ♦ 의식주(衣食住) food, clothing and shelter

주 周 〈둘레〉 a circumference

주 洲 1 〈사주〉 a sandbank; a (sand)bar
♦ 삼각주 a delta
2 〈대륙〉 a continent ♦ 아시아 주 the Asian Continent

주 株 1 〈주식〉 (美) stocks; (英) shares
♦ 종업원 주 소유제도 employee stock ownership plan; ESOP / 주를 사다 buy stock(s) / 주를 갖다 hold [have] stocks (in a company) / 주를 모집하다 invite subscriptions for stocks; offer stocks for subscription / 주를 처분하다 liquidate stocks
2 〈그루〉 a root
♦ 밤나무 3주 three chestnut trees
■ 보통— common stock; (美) common share; ordinary stock [(英) share] 성장— growth [special] stock [(英) share] 우량— blue-chip [gilt-edged] stocks 우선— preference [preferred] stock [(英) share] 인기— active [leading, popular, favorite, glamor] stocks 투기— speculative stocks

주 週 a week
♦ 이번[다음, 지난]주 this [next, last] week / 2주간 two weeks; (英) a fortnight / 주초에 at the beginning of the week / 주중에 at midweek / 다음다음주 the week after next / 지지난주 the week before last
▶ 그 회사는 주 5일 근무제를 실시하고 있다 The firm has established a five-day work week.

주 註 〈주석〉 an annotation; (explanatory) notes; a commentary
♦ 난외(欄外)의 주 a marginal note / 주를 달다 annotate; add [annex] notes (to a book); make [write] notes (on) / 주가 붙어 있다 be annotated
▶ 이 책에는 손교수의 주가 붙어 있다 This book is annotated by Prof. Son.

주- 駐- resident [staying] (in) ♦ 주한의 resident in Korea / 주미 한국대사 the Korean Ambassador to [in] the United States

주가 酒家 a wineshop, a winehouse

주가 株價 the price of a stock; a stock price
♦ 주가가 오르다 one's stock (price) rises / 주가가 내리다 one's stock falls [goes down]
■—지수 the price index of stocks

주간 主幹 a chief; a head
♦ 편집 주간 the chief editor; the editor in chief —주간하다 manage sth as a chief [head]

주간 晝間 the daytime; day
♦ 주간에 in the daytime; in [during] the day; by day; days / 주간에는 일하고 야간에 학교에 다니다 work days and go to school nights
■—근무 day-duty; daywork —인구 the daytime population

주간 週刊 weekly publication; 〈간행물〉 a weekly (periodical)
■—지(誌) a weekly (magazine) : 시사주간지 a weekly newsmagazine; a newsweekly / 여성주간지 a women's weekly

주간 週間 a week
♦ 1주간의 휴가 a [one] week's holiday
■ 독서— (Read-a-) Book Week

주객 主客 host and guest; 〈사물〉 principal and auxiliary; the primary and the subordinate
♦ 주객간(에) between host and guest
▶ 그것은 주객전도다 It is the opposite of the usual order. ⇒ That is putting the cart before the horse.

주객 酒客 a drinker; a tippler

주거 住居 a dwelling (house); a residence; an abode; living
♦ 주거를 정하다 take up [make] one's abode [residence]; settle (down) / 주거를 옮기다 move one's residence (to)
■—공간 residing space —비 housing expenses [expenditure] —지(址) 〔考古〕 a dwelling site —지역 a residential district [area] —침입 homebreaking; violation of domicile

주거니받거니 giving and taking
♦ 주거니받거니하며 마시다 drink exchanging wine glasses; hobnob [have a hobnob] (with)

주걱 a spatula; a scoop ♦ 구둣주걱 a shoehorn
■ 밥— a rice scoop —상(相) a pushed-in face —턱 a spoonlike [protruding] chin

주검 a (dead) body; a corpse; one's remains; death
▶ 격전 직후 약 10구의 주검이 그 전장에서 발견 되었다 Right after the fierce fight, about ten bodies were found on the battle field.

주격 主格 〖文法〗 the nominative [subjective] (case)

주견 主見 main opinion; one's own opinion [view]; one's own firm conviction; one's own fixed opinion
♦주견이 없다 have no fixed views [definite opinion] of one's own

주경야독 晝耕夜讀 farming [working] by day and reading [studying] by night
―주경야독하다 farm [work] by day and read [study] by night

주고받다 give and take reciprocally; interchange; exchange; reciprocate
♦편지를 주고받다 exchange letters / 선물을 주고받다 give presents each other

주관 主管 supervision; superintendence; management
―주관하다 superintend; supervise; manage; have [be in] charge of
■―사항 matters [affairs] in one's charge
―자 a superintendent; a supervisor; a manager

주관 主觀 subjectivity; 〈주체〉 the subject; 〈자아〉 the ego
♦주관에 치우치다 be too subjective
■―론〖哲〗 subjectivism ―성 subjectivity

주관적 主觀的 subjective
♦주관적으로 subjectively / 주관적으로 보다 take a subjective view of 《things》

주광 酒狂 drunken madness; a crazy drunk; an alcoholic maniac

주광성 走光性 〖生〗 phototaxis; phototaxy
♦주광성의 phototactic

주교 主敎 1 〈가톨릭〉 a bishop; a pontiff 2 〈주장으로 삼는 교〉 a dominant [major] religion
■대― an archbishop; a primate ―구[관구] a bishopric; a diocese ―미사 a pontifical mass ―제도 episcopalian system; episcopacy ―제주의 Episcopalianism ―직 episcopate; bishopric

주교 舟橋 a pontoon bridge ⇨ 배다리

주구 走狗 1 〈사냥개〉 a hunting dog; a hound 2 〈앞잡이〉 a tool; a cat's-paw

주구 誅求 extortion ⇨ 가렴(~주구)

주권 主權 sovereignty; sovereign authority; supremacy
♦주권을 존중하다 respect the sovereignty / 주권을 잡다 hold sovereignty; reign supreme / 주권을 포기하다 yield [give up] (one's) sovereignty 《over an island to another country》 / 이웃나라의 주권을 침해하다 violate the sovereignty of the neighboring country / 주권을 회복하다 regain [restore] sovereignty
■―국(가) a sovereign nation [power] ―자 the sovereign; the ruler ―националь [국민] the sovereign power lies [rests] with the people ―재민론(在民論) the doctrine that sovereignty rests with [resides in] the people ―침해 the infringement of sovereignty

주권 株券 〈美〉 a stock (certificate); 〈英〉 a share (certificate)
♦주권의 명의를 바꾸다 transfer a stock [share] certificate / 주권을 현금으로 바꾸다 cash stocks / 주권으로 백만원 가지고 있다 have one million won in stock [share] certificates
■―기명― a registered stock [share] 무기명― a stock certificate to bearer

주근깨 freckles; flecks
♦주근깨가 낀 소녀 a freckle-faced girl
▶그녀의 얼굴은 주근깨투성이다 Her face is covered with freckles.

주금 株金 capital (stock)
■―계정 capital account

주금류 走禽類 〖鳥〗 cursorial birds; runners

주급 週給 weekly wages [pay]
▶그의 주급은 삼백 달러다 His weekly pay is three hundred dollars.
■―제도 the weekly payment system: 저 가게는 주급제도다 They are paid weekly [by the week] in that store.

주기 酒氣 the smell [odor] of wine [liquor]; an alcoholic smell
▶그는 주기를 띠고 있다 He smells of liquor. ⇌ He is drunk.

주기 周忌 an memorial day of sb's death
♦아버지의 1주기 the first memorial day of father's death / 할아버지의 3주기 the third memorial day of grandfather's death

주기 週期 a period; a cycle
♦천체의 주기적 운동 the periodic motion of a heavenly body / 주기적으로 periodically; in cycles
▶그때부터 그는 주기적으로 아팠다 From that time he became periodically ill.
■―성(性) periodicity ―운동 periodic motion ―율(律)〖化〗 the law of periodicity; the periodic law ―율표〖化〗 the periodic table; the periodic chart ―함수 periodic function ―혜성 a periodic comet

주기도문 主祈禱文 the Lord's Prayer; 《say》 a Pater; a Paternoster

주낙 a fishing reel with longline; a longline
♦주낙으로 고기를 잡다 fish with a reel and longline

주년 周年 a whole year; an anniversary
♦10주년 the tenth anniversary / 2백 주년 축제 the bicentennial festival

주눅 diffidence; timidness; timidity; backwardness
♦주눅(이) 들다 become [be] diffident; lose one's nerve; be [feel] daunted 《at, by》; feel timid [small]
▶많은 사람 앞에서 말할 때는 주눅이 든다 I suffer acute embarrassment when speaking before a group.

주니어 a junior ■―스타일 a junior [teenage] style ―웨어 junior wear

주다¹ 1 〈제공하다〉 give; present; let sb have sth
♦먹을 것을 주다 give sb sth to eat; feed 《a child》 / 거저주다 give sb sth without charge / 남몰래 주다 slip into sb's hand
▶그녀는 아이들에게 사과를 한 개씩 주었다 She gave each of her children an apple [an apple to each of her children].
▶대학은 그에게 장학금을 주었다 The univer-

주다²

sity awarded him a scholarship [a scholarship to him]. ⇒ He got a scholarship from the university.
▶ 정부는 난민에게 옷을 주었다 The government supplied the refugees with clothing. ⇒ The government supplied clothing to [for] the refugees.
▶ 내가 가지고 있으라고 준 돈은 어떻게 했니? What have you done with the money I gave you to keep?
▶ 이 다이아몬드는 누가 달라고 해도 절대로 주지 마라 Don't give this diamond to anybody whoever may ask.
▶《會話》"그에게 무엇을 주었니?" "책을 주었어" "What did you give him?" "I gave him a book."

2 〈수여·부여하다〉 give;〈상 등을〉 award;〈명예·칭호 등을〉 bestow;〈학위 등을〉 confer;〈금품·권리 등을〉 grant
♦아무에게 훈장을 주다 confer [award] a decoration [an order] on sb / 기회를 주다 afford [give, allow] an opportunity (of); give sb a chance [(口) break]
▶ 선생님은 그에게 조퇴를 허락해 주었다 The teacher allowed [permitted] him to go home early. ⇒ The teacher gave [granted] him permission to go home early.

3 〈공급하다〉 give; supply
▶ 태양은 우리에게 빛과 열을 준다 The sun gives us light and heat [warmth].
▶ 그녀는 개에 먹을 것을 주었다 She provided the dog with food. ⇒ She provided food for the dog.
▶ 학생들에게는 도서관의 책을 자유롭게 사용하는 편의가 주어졌다 There are lots of books in the library for the students to use.

4 〈대다〉 give (rations to); provide; furnish
♦일[일거리]을 주다 provide sb with work / 월급 100만원을 주다 pay a monthly salary of one million won

5 〈할당·부과하다〉 allot [assign] 《work to sb》; impose 《a task on sb》; set 《a pupil a problem》
♦아무에게 주어진 일 a task imposed on sb / 각자에게 몫을 주다 allot a share to each
▶ 그는 그녀에게 일거리를 주었다 He assigned her to the task.
▶ 선생님은 그 학급에 숙제를 내주었다 The teacher gave an assignment to the class.
▶ 주어진 제목으로 리포트를 쓰시오 Write a report on the subject you were given.

6 〈끼치다·가하다〉 cause; occasion 《anxiety to...》; 〈영향을〉 exert, exercise; inflict 《an injury on...》
♦아무에게 큰 영향을 주다 exert a great influence on sb / 타격을 주다 give a blow 《to sb's business》 / 모욕을 주다 insult sb
▶ 내 행동은 그에게 나쁜 인상을 준 것 같다 My conduct may have given him a bad impression.
▶ 그 태풍은 농작물에 큰 피해를 주었다 The typhoon caused [did, gave] a lot of damage to the crops.
▶ 그의 연설은 청중에게 큰 영향을 주었다 His speech had a lot of influence on the audience.

7 〈마음을〉 ♦마음을 주다 trust [confide in] sb; admit [take] sb into confidence
8 〈(줄을) 풀리게 하다〉 let loose; pay out
♦연줄을 주다 let loose [pay out] the string of a kite
9 〈박다〉 drive [knock] in 《a nail》
♦침을 주다 apply acupuncture / 주사를 주다 inject / 벽에 못을 주다 drive [hammer] a nail into a wall

주다² 〈베풀다〉 do sth for sb; do a favor for sb
♦부탁[청]을 들어 주다 grant [allow, comply with] sb's request / 문을 열어주다 open the door for sb
▶ 아이에게 인형을 만들어 주었다 I made a doll for the child.
▶ 여동생의 숙제를 거들어 주었다 I helped my sister with her homework.
▶ 내가 들어다 주지 I'll carry it for you.
▶ 내가 가서 표를 사 주겠다 I'll go get a ticket for you.
▶ 누님이 나에게 책을 사 주셨다 My (elder) sister bought the book for me.
▶ 물리학자는 알기 쉬운 말로 이론을 설명해 주었다 The physicist explained the theory for us in simple language.
▶ 그는 내 말을 들어 주지 않았다 He wouldn't listen to me.

주단 紬緞 silks and satins; silk fabrics [goods, stuff]
주당 酒黨 a drinker; a bacchant; a son of Bacchus
주도 主導 leading; initiative ♦민간 주도의 경제 private-initiated economy
―주도하다 lead 《a movement》; take the lead 《in educational reform》
▶ 그가 그 그룹을 주도하고 있다 He was the leader of the group. ⇒ The group was under his thumb.
■―자 the leader; the prime mover
주도 酒道 a drinking manner; a drinker's etiquette
주도권 主導權 leadership; initiative; hegemony
♦주도권을 잡다[쥐다] take the leader / 주도권을 빼앗다 wrest [take] away the initiative (from) / 교섭에서 주도권을 잡다[잃다] take [lose] the initiative in negotiations / 주도권 싸움을 벌이다 vie for the 《party》 leadership
▶ 그는 모든 주도권을 잡고 있다 He takes leadership [the initiative] in everything.
■―다툼 a struggle for leadership; a leadership struggle
주도하다 周到— scrupulous; attentive; cautious; careful; circumspect ♦주도면밀한 계획 a carefully worked-out plan
주독 酒毒 alcohol poisoning ♦주독이 오르다 have a blotchy face due to alcohol
■―코 a coppernose; a whisky nose
주동 主動 leadership ♦주동이 되다 take the lead [leadership] (of)
―주동하다 take the lead [leadership] (of)
■―자 the leader; the prime mover
주되다 主— be chief; be principal; be main;

be major; be prime; lead; be important
♦주된 산업 the chief industry / 주된 생산물 principal produce / 주된 사업 one's main business / 주된 회원 leading members / 보고의 주된 점 the chief points of the report / 주된 요리 the main dish(es); main course / 주된 원인 a major cause ⦅for⦆
▶이 부품이 사고의 주된 원인이다 This part is the major cause of the accident.
▶이 계획의 주된 목적은 무엇입니까? What is the main [chief] purpose of this plan?

주둔 駐屯 stationing; posting; staying; a stay
—**주둔하다** be stationed ⟨in, at⟩; stay; ⟨점령하다⟩ occupy
♦한국에 주둔하고 있는 미군 the United States troops stationed in Korea / 군대를 주둔시키다 station [post] troops
■—군 stationary troops; ⟨수비의⟩ a garrison; ⟨점령지의⟩ an occupation army; an army of occupation —지 a post; an army post

주둥이, 주둥아리 a mouth; ⟨개 등의⟩ a muzzle; ⟨새의⟩ a bill; ⟨육식조의⟩ a beak; ⟨물건의⟩ a mouthpiece; a mouth; a spout; ⟨주전자의⟩ a nozzle
♦주둥이가 싸다 be a glib (talker); be talkative; be a chatterbox / 주둥아리만 까다 talk volubly; talk one's mouth off / 주둥아리를 놀리다 wag one's chin [tongue, jaw]

주라통 朱螺筒 the gullet (of a cattle); the esophagus ⦅pl. ~es, -gi⦆

주란 酒亂 drunken madness ⇨ 주광

주람 周覽 a tour of inspection; a round-trip of observation —**주람하다** go on [make] a round-trip of observation

주랑 柱廊 a parvis(e); a colonnade

주량 酒量 one's drinking capacity; one's capacity for liquor
♦주량이 많다 drink much; be heavy drinker / 주량이 늘다[줄다] come to drink more [less] than before [one used to]
▶나는 주량이 별로 많지 않다 I am not very much of a drinker.
▶너는 주량을 줄이는 게 좋겠다 You'd better cut down on your drinking.
▶나는 요즈음 주량이 늘었다 I drink more liquor lately.

주렵 1 ⟨피로⟩ fatigue; exhaustion
2 ⇨ 주접

주렁주렁 in clusters; in full bearing
♦열매가 주렁주렁 열린 나무 a tree in full bearing / 주렁주렁 열리다 grow in clusters
▶정원에 있는 감나무에 감이 주렁주렁 열렸다 The persimmon tree in my garden has borne abundant [is loaded with] fruit.
▶그에게는 식솔이 주렁주렁 딸려 있다 He has a large family to feed.

주력 主力 the main force [body, strength]
▶여름방학 동안에는 약한 과목에 주력을 기울여라 Concentrate your energy on your weak subjects during the summer vacation.
■—멤버 leading member —부대 main-force [hard-core] units —전(戰) a major engagement —주(株) leading stocks [⦅英⦆] shares] —함 a capital ship —함대 the main fleet

주력 注力 concentration one's efforts; putting forth one's strength [effort]
—**주력하다** concentrate [focus] one's efforts [energies] ⦅on⦆; throw energy into
▶그는 과외공부에 주력했다 He concentrated all energy on learning out-of-school studies.

주렴 珠簾 a bead curtain; a beaded hanging screen

주례 主禮 ⟨일⟩ officiating at a wedding ceremony; ⟨사람⟩ an officiator
♦주례를 서다 officiate at a marriage
▶그들은 목사님의 주례로 결혼식을 했다 Their wedding ceremony was conducted by the minister.

주로 走路 ⟨경기장의⟩ a track; a course
♦주로 100 마일의 자동차 경주 a wild car race over a hundred mile course [run, drive]

주로 主 mainly; principally; chiefly; primarily; ⟨대체로⟩ in the main; ⟨대개⟩ mostly; for the most part; generally
▶관객은 주로 여성이었다 The audience consisted most of women.
▶그 사고는 주로 너의 부주의 때문에 일어났다 The accident happened mainly [chiefly, largely] because you were careless. ⇌ The accident is due largely to [largely due to] your carelessness.
▶아버지는 주로 운동을 위해 테니스를 하신다 My father plays tennis chiefly [mainly] for exercise.
▶그 회사는 주로 종이제품을 취급하고 있다 The company deals principally in paper products.
▶그 상품은 주로 해외로 보낸다 The goods are mostly sent abroad.

주루 走壘 ⦅野⦆ baserunning ♦주루를 잘하다 be good at baserunning / 주루를 방해하다 interfere with ⦅a base runner⦆

주룩주룩 1 ⟨주름이⟩ with wrinkles [rumples, folds] ♦주룩주룩 주름이 가다 become full of wrinkles [lines]
2 ⟨비 등이⟩ sprinklingly; patteringly; pitter-patter; pit-a-pat
♦(비가) 주룩주룩 오다 sprinkle; patter; fall pitter-patter on

주류 主流 the main current; the mainstream
♦한국 문학의 주류 the main current of Korean literature
■—파 the leading [mainstream, maincurrent] faction; the faction in power

주류 酒類 liquors; alcoholic beverages; intoxicating drinks; spirits
■—판매 허가증 a liquor license

주륙 誅戮 death punishment [penalty]
—**주륙하다** punish sb with death; put sb to death as a penalty

주르르 1 ⟨액체가 흘러내리는 모양⟩ tricklingly; dribblingly; runningly
▶상처에서 피가 주르르 흐르고 있다 Blood is oozing from the wound.
▶눈물이 그녀의 뺨을 주르르 흘러내렸다 Tears streamed [rolled] down her cheeks.
2 ⟨미끄러지는 모양⟩ slidingly; slipperily
♦주르르 미끄러져 내리다 slide [slip] down;

slip / (끈이) 주르르 풀리다 slip off
3 〈빠르게 내닫는 모양〉 at a dash; with one rush ♦주르르 달려가다 make a dash 《for》; go off at a dash

주르륵 gurglingly ♦주르륵 소리가 나다 gurgle / 주르륵 멈추다 suddenly stop dribbling

주름 1 〈피부의〉 wrinkles; lines; furrows
♦주름진 얼굴 a wrinkled [furrowed] face / 이마의 주름 wrinkles [lines] on one's forehead / 주름투성이의 full of wrinkles / 얼굴에 주름이 지다[잡히다] one's face is wrinkled [furrowed]
▶ 그녀의 얼굴에는 주름이 많다 She has a lot of wrinkles [lines] on her face. ⇌ Her face is full of wrinkles.
▶ 그녀는 화가 나면 이마에 주름이 생긴다 She gets wrinkles in her brows when she gets angry.
2 〈종이・의복 등의〉 creases; rumples; a wrinkle; a pleat; a fold; a pucker; gathers
♦주름투성이의 코트 a wrinkled coat / 치마의 주름 the pleats of a skirt / 주름을 잡다 crease; pleat; fold; crimple / 옷에 주름이 지다 one's clothes are wrinkled / 포장지의 주름을 펴다 smooth (down [out]) the creases in the wrapping paper / 다려서 바지의 주름을 펴다 press [iron] out the wrinkles in the trousers; press [iron] the wrinkles out of the trousers
▶ 리넨은 주름이 잘 간다 Linen wrinkles [gets wrinkles] easily.
▶ 재킷은 걸어놓지 않으면 주름이 잡힌다 Your jacket will crease [You will get creases in your jacket] unless you hang it.
■잔— fine wrinkles [lines]; 〈눈가의〉 crow's-feet —치마 a pleated [shirred] skirt

주름잡다 1 〈주름지게 하다〉 pleat; plait; crease; crimple
2 〈세력을 떨치다〉 overwhelm; dominate; predominate; sway
♦전국을 주름잡다 sway the whole nation / 금융계를 주름잡다 have a firm grip on the banking business
▶ 그는 당대를 주름잡는 정치가다 He is a most powerful [influential] politician today.

주리 the leg-screw torture ♦주리 틀다 impose the leg-screw torture

주리다 〈배곯다〉 be [go] hungry; starve; famish; be famished; 〈갈망하다〉 be hungry 《for, after》; hunger [hanker, thirst] for [after]
♦배를 주리다 go hungry; starve / 애정에 주리다 be hungry for affection / 지식에 주리다 be thirsty for [after] knowledge / 주린 배를 채우다 gratify one's hunger

주립 州立 〈형용사적〉 state-established; state-founded ■—대학[병원, 공원] a state university [hospital, park]

주릿대 1 〈고문 도구〉 (a pair of) leg-screw sticks ♦주릿대를 안기다 inflict a cruel punishment on sb
2 〈행실이 나쁜 사람〉 a wicked person; a villain; an outlaw

주마 走馬 〈달리는 말〉 a running [galloping] horse —주마하다 drive [gallop] a horse
■—가편 (加鞭) whipping an already galloping horse; urging [inspiring] sb to further efforts —간산 (看山) seeing the hills while passing on horseback; giving a hurried glance 《to, over》 —창 (瘡) 〔韓醫〕 boils that spread all over the body

주마등 走馬燈 〈등〉 a revolving lantern; 《비유》 kaleidoscopic change
♦주마등같은 kaleidoscopic; ever-changing; ever-shifting / 주마등처럼[같이] kaleidoscopically / 주마등처럼 변하다 make a kaleidoscopic change

주막 酒幕 an inn; a tavern ♦주막에 들다 put up at an inn ■—거리 a street lined with inns —쟁이 an innkeeper

주말 週末 a weekend
♦지난 주말 last weekend / 주말에 《美》 on [《英》 at] the weekend (▶「주말마다」의 뜻일 때는 on [at] weekends; every weekend) / 주말을 시골에서 즐겁게 보내다 spend a lovely weekend in the country
▶ 좋은 주말 보내세요 Have a nice weekend!
▶ 그는 주말이면 자주 골프를 친다 He often plays golf on weekends.
■—여행 a weekend trip —여행자 a weekender

주맥 主脈 1 〈주가 되는 산맥〉 the main range
2 〈가장 큰 잎맥〉 the main vein

주머니 1 〈돈・물건을 넣는 것〉 a bag; a sack; a pouch
♦주머니에 넣다 put sth into a bag / 주머니에서 시계[편지]를 꺼내다 take a watch [letter] out of a bag; draw a watch [letter] from a bag
2 〈호주머니〉 a pocket
♦주머니를 톡톡 털다 empty one's purse to the last penny [cent]
▶ 그는 언제나 주머니에 손을 넣고 다닌다 He always walks with his hands in his pockets.
▶ 그 책은 주머니에 넣을 수 있는 크기다 The book is pocket-sized.
▶ 나는 언제나 바지 주머니에 시계를 넣고 있다 I always carry my watch in my trouser pocket.
▶ 많은 물건을 사서 주머니가 가벼워졌다 I bought so many things (that) I have a lighter purse.
■—돈 a purse 뒷—〈바지의〉 a hip [back] pocket 신(발)— a shoe pocket ■—끈 purse strings —사정 one's financial [pecuniary] circumstances; one's finances [funds]: 나는 지금 주머니 사정이 좋지 않다 I'm hard up just now. / 주머니 사정이 좋다[나쁘다] have a heavy [light] purse —칼 a pocketknife; 〈큰 것〉 a jackknife

주먹 a (clenched) fist; the knuckles; 《俗》 dukes
♦주먹을 쥐다 clench one's fist; make a fist / 주먹으로 때리다 hit [strike] sb with one's fist / 주먹을 휘두르다 shake one's fist 《at》
▶ 갑자기 그는 나를 주먹으로 때렸다 Without warning [All of a sudden] he struck me with his fist.
■—밥 a rice ball; 〈손으로 밥먹기〉 eating with one's finger —심 the power of one's fist;

〈완력〉 physical strength ━싸움 a fist fight ━질 blows with the fists; fisting; fisticuffs

주먹구구 ━九九 1 〈손가락셈〉 finger counting
♦주먹구구로 셈하다 count [number] on one's fingers
2 〈어림〉 rule of thumb; a rough estimate [calculation]
♦주먹구구로 어림잡다 estimate by rule of thumb; make a rule-of-thumb estimate

주먹다짐 1 〈주먹질〉 blows with the fists; fisting; fisticuffs
▶ 그들은 마침내 주먹다짐을 벌였다 At last they got into a fistfight.
━주먹다짐하다 strike sb with one's fist; fisticuff sb; give sb (hard) blows with one's fist
2 〈윽박지르기〉 threats with one's fists; intimidation
▶ 그는 주먹다짐에 못이겨 돈을 빌려줬다 He was coerced into lending him money.
▶ 의붓아버지는 주먹다짐으로 그녀를 그 남자와 혼인시켰다 The stepfather coerced her into marrying the man.
━주먹다짐하다 threaten with one's fists; intimidate

주명곡 奏鳴曲 〔樂〕 a sonata ⇨ 소나타

주모 主謀 taking the lead (in a scheme); heading [leading] a conspiracy
━주모하다 lead [head] a conspiracy [plot, movement]; organize; stir up
■━자 a leader; a ringleader : 그는 이 쿠데타의 한 주모자였다 He was one of the principal architects of this coup d'état.

주모 酒母 1 〈술파는 여자〉 the hostess of an inn; an innkeeper
2 〈술밑〉 an admixture of malt and steamed rice

주목 注目 〈주의〉 attention; observation; heed; notice; note
♦주목을 할 만한 책 a noteworthy book; a book worthy of note / 세인의 주목을 끌다 attract public attention / 주목(을) 받다 be watched; attract [draw] sb's attention
▶ 그 선수는 이제 사람들의 주목의 대상이다 The athlete is now the focus of public attention. ⇌ The athlete is now in the limelight [public eye].
▶ 그의 새 소설은 일반 대중의 주목을 끌었다 His new novel attracted [drew] public attention.
━주목하다 take note [notice] of; pay [give] attention to; direct [turn] one's attention to; observe; watch; keep one's eye on
♦수업중 선생님을 주목하다 pay attention to one's teacher [what one's teacher says] in class
▶ 이쪽을 주목해 주세요 Let me have your attention, please.
▶ 존의 의견은 주목할 만하다 John's opinions are worthy of note [worth noticing].
▶ 당시의 비평가들은 아무도 이 시인을 주목하지 않았다 No critics took notice of this poet in those days.
▶ 그 일의 귀추가 매우 주목된다 The development is being watched with keen interest.

주무 主務 chief control of an affair
━주무하다 be in charge of; have [take] charge of; have competence over a matter
■━관청[장관] the competent authorities [Minister] ━부 the competent Ministry ━자 a person in charge; the chief official ((in charge of the affairs)); a supervisor

주무르다 1 〈만지다〉 finger; rub and press with the fingers; fumble with
♦흙을 주무르다 play [finger] with mud
2 〈안마하다〉 massage; 〈근육을〉 knead
♦어깨[다리]를 주무르다 massage sb's shoulders [legs] / 어깨를 주무르게 하다 have one's shoulder massaged
3 〈농락하다〉 make sport [a plaything, a fool] of
▶ 그녀는 그를 마음대로 주무른다 She carries [has] him in her pocket. ⇌ She turns him around her little finger.

주무시다 sleep ⇨ 자다

주문 主文 〈판결문의〉 the text of a judgment; 〈문장의〉 the main [principal] clause

주문 注文 1 〈맞춤〉 (an) order; 〈주문하는 일〉 ordering
♦책 주문 an order for a book / 견본 주문 a sample order / 급한 주문 a rush [an urgent] order / 주문이 쇄도하다 have a rush of orders; be flooded with orders / 대량의 주문이 들어오다 have a large order / 전화 주문을 받다 accept telephone orders / 해외에서 주문받다 get [receive] order from abroad / 주문을 취소하다 cancel [withdraw, recall] an order / 주문을 이행하다 supply [execute] an order / 주문에 따르다[응하다] fill [accept] an order / 주문에 따라 하다 make sth to order
▶ 주문에 쫓기고 있다 We have more orders than we can execute.
▶ 주문이 점점 줄어 들고 있다 Orders are falling off.
━주문하다 order; give an order
▶ 〔會話〕「무엇을 주문하시겠습니까?」「커피를 주세요」 "May I have [take] your order?" "Yes, (I'd like a cup of) coffee, please."
▶ 이것은 주문해서 만든 구두다 This pair of shoes are made to order.
2 〈요구・의뢰〉 a request; 〈강한 요구〉 a demand; 〈부탁〉 a favor; 〈조건〉 a condition; a desire
♦어려운 주문 a delicate request
▶ 그것은 무리한 주문이다 That's asking too much.
▶ 그에게 무리한 주문을 하지 마라 Don't make an unreasonable request of [demand on] him.
▶ 너한테 한 가지 주문이 있어 I have a favor to ask of you. ⇌ Will you do me a favor?
━주문하다 request; demand; ask; desire; wish
━구두━ a verbal order 대량[소량]━ a large [small] order 재[추가]━ a reorder ■━서 an order sheet; 〔商〕 an indent ━승낙서 a order receipt ━용지 an order blank [form] ━자 an orderer ━장(帳) an order book ━처 〈주문자〉 the orderer; 〈인수자〉 the receiver of an order ━품 goods ordered

주문 呪文 a spell; a charm; an incantation; a

conjuration; 〈액막이〉 an exorcism; magic words
♦개운의 주문 a good luck charm; a charm to bring in good luck / 액막이 주문 an incantation against bad luck / 주문을 외다 chant a spell; make an incantation / 주문으로 병을 고치다 charm away [off] a disease

주물 鑄物 (a) casting; (a) molding; an article of cast metal ■—공 a caster; a cast-iron worker; a founder —공장 a foundry

주물럭거리다 finger; knead; massage; work and press with the hands; fumble with

주물럭주물럭 kneadingly; fumblingly
—주물럭주물럭하다 finger ⇨ 주물럭거리다

주미 駐美 ♦주미의 resident [stationed] in America ■—한국 대사 the Korean Ambassador to the United States

주민 住民 inhabitants; residents; citizen; 〈전체〉 the population
■—등록 resident registration —세 residents' tax —투표 the inhabitants' poll [vote]: 주민투표로 결정하다 decide by the inhabitants' vote

주밀 周密 〈두루 세밀함〉 thoroughness; cautiousness; prudence; carefulness
—주밀하다 thorough; thoroughgoing; scrupulous; meticulous ♦주밀한 설계 thoroughgoing design

주반 酒飯 1 〈술과 밥〉 wine and rice 2 〈술밥〉 steamed rice for brewing rice wine

주발 周鉢 a (brass) bowl
■—뚜껑 the lid of a (brass) bowl

주방 廚房 a kitchen; a room for cooking
■—용품 kitchen utensils; kitchenwares —장 a head cook; a chef

주번 週番 weekly duty ▶금주는 내가 주번이다 I am on duty this week.
■—사관 〔軍〕 an officer of the week

주벌 誅伐 〈죄인을 침〉 a punitive expedition
—주벌하다 send a punitive expedition (to)

주벌 誅罰 〈벌 줌〉 punishment; chastisement
—주벌하다 punish; chastise

주범 主犯 〈사람〉 the principal offender; the main criminal; 〈죄〉 a principal offense

주법 主法 the substantive [principal] law; major laws

주법 走法 a way [form] of running

주법 奏法 〔樂〕 a style of rendition; execution
♦바이올린 주법 a way of playing the violin

주벽 酒癖 a drinking habits; *one's* behavior when drunk
▶그는 고약한 주벽이 있다 He is a terrible [vicious] drunk.

주변 initiative; resourcefulness; 〈융통성〉 versatility
♦주변이 좋은 resourceful; versatile / 주변이 없는 clueless; resourceless; not adaptable
▶그는 말주변이 좋다 He is fairspoken. ⇌ He is glib tongued.
▶그는 돈도 없고 주변도 없다 He is neither rich nor versatile.

주변 周邊 〈주위〉 the circumference; the surroundings; the periphery; 〈도회의〉 the outskirts; the environs
♦그 호수 주변 지역 the area around the lake / 서울과 그 주변에 in and around Seoul; in Seoul and the surrounding areas
▶학교 주변에는 많은 집이 들어서 있다 There are a lot of houses in the vicinity of the school.
▶그 과격파 학생들은 국회 주변을 시위 행진했다 The radical students staged a demonstration around the Assembly building.

주병하다 駐兵— station [keep] troops (at, in)

주보 酒甫 〈술에 걸신 사람〉 a heavy drinker; a drunkard

주보 週報 〈신문〉 a weekly (paper); 〈공보〉 a weekly (bulletin); 〈보고〉 a weekly report

주복 主僕 master and servant; valet and master

주봉 主峰 〈최고봉〉 the main [principal] peak; the highest peak

주부 主部 〈주요 부분〉 the main [principal] part; 〔文法〕 the subject
♦주부와 술부 (the) subject and predicate

주부 主婦 〈한 집안의〉 a housewife; a mistress; a homemaker; 〈안주인〉 the hostess
♦알뜰한 주부 a practical housewife / 주부가 되다 manage [run] *one's* household
▶그녀는 주부이자 세 아이의 어머니다 She is a housewife and mother of three children.

주부코 a bulbous nose with red blotches

주비 籌備 〈계획하여 준비함〉 arrangement; preparation —주비하다 arrange; prepare
■—위원회 a preparatory committee; an arrangements committee

주빈 主賓 the guest of honor ♦…을 주빈으로 하여 만찬회를 열다 give a dinner in honor of…
■—석 (take) the seat of honor

주뼛 hesitantly; timorously; nervously
—주뼛주뼛하다 shy and hesitant; nervous; timorous

주사 主事 1 〈관리의〉 a junior official; (총칭) the clerical staff 2 〈경칭〉 Mr.; Esq.

주사 走査 〔TV〕 scanning —주사하다 scan
■—기 a scanner —면 a scanning area —밀도 scanning density —선[판] a scanning line [disk] —장치 a scanner —진폭 scanning frequency

주사 注射 (an) injection; 〔口〕 a shot; 〈예방주사〉 inoculation
♦그 병을 주사로 치료하다 cure the disease by injection
—주사하다 inject; give [apply] an injection; syringe; inoculate
♦포도당을 주사하다 administer an injection of glucose
▶의사는 그녀의 팔에 페니실린을 주사했다 The doctor injected penicillin into her arm. ⇌ The doctor injected her arm with penicillin.
■—근육[정맥]— (an) intramuscular [intravenous] injection: 나는 팔에 정맥주사를 맞았다 I have had an intravenous injection in the arm. 모르핀— an injection of morphine 예방— a preventive injection [shot] 〈against〉: 나는 감기 예방주사를 맞았다 I was inoculated against (the) flu. ⇌ I was given a preventive

injection against (the) flu. 피하— (a) subcutaneous [hypodermic] injection ■—기 an injector; a syringe —액 an injection 주삿바늘 an injection syringe; a needle

주사 酒邪 a drunken frenzy [rampage]
◆주사가 있는 사람 a mean [vicious] drinker ▶그는 주사가 있다 He is an obnoxious drunk. ⇒ He is a bad drinker.

주사위 a die 《pl. dice》; (口) bones
◆주사위의 눈 the spots on [of] a die; the pips 《on a die》 / 주사위를 던지다 cast [throw] dice [a die]
▶주사위는 던져졌다 The die is cast [thrown].
—놀이 a diceplay; dicing

주산 珠算 calculation [computation] on the abacus ◆주산을 잘하다 be good at abacus calculation
—주산하다 reckon [count] on the abacus
■—경기대회 an abacus calculation contest

주산물 主産物 staple prouducts; main [chief, principal] products

주산지 主産地 a chief producing district [center]

주상 主上 〈왕〉 the King; His [Your] Majesty
주상 主喪 the chief mourner
주색 朱色 a vermilion color; vermilion
주색 酒色 wine and women; sensual pleasure; wine and debauchery
◆주색에 빠지다 be addicted [given] to sensual pleasure; abandon [yield] *oneself* to wine and women
■—잡기 wine, sex, and gambling

주서 〈과즙 짜는 기구〉 a juicer
주서 朱書 rubrication —주서하다 write in red 《ink》; rubricate

주석 主席 〈사람〉 the head; the chief; 〈자리〉 the top seat; the head seat

주석 朱錫 tin ◆주석의 tin; (made) of tin / 주석을 입히다 tin
■—광석 tin ores —도금 tinning —박(箔) tinfoil —제품 tinware

주석 柱石 1 〈기둥과 주추〉 pillars and cornerstones
2 〈사람〉 a pillar; a mainstay; a (main) prop; a cornerstone
◆국가의 주석 the main prop [cornerstone] of the state

주석 酒石 (化) (crude) tartar
◆주석을 함유한 tartarous ■—영(英) cream of tartar

주석 酒席 a banquet; a feast; a drinking party
◆주석을 베풀다 give a drinking party; hold a banquet

주석 註釋·注釋 explanatory notes; a commentary; 〈주석 붙이기〉 an annotation; explanation
◆주석이 있는 책 an annotated book / 주석을 달다 annotate; add [annex, append] notes 《to a book》
▶이 영어 교재에는 권말에 많은 주석이 있다 This English textbook has plenty of notes at the end.
—주석하다 annotate; comment (on)
■—서 an annotated edition; a book with annotations —자 an annotator; a commentator

주선 周旋 〈알선〉 good offices; kind offices; 〈중개〉 mediation; agency
◆친구의 주선으로 through the good offices [agency] of a friend
▶선생님의 주선으로 지금의 이 직업을 갖게 됐다 I have got this job through the good offices of my teacher.
▶이 모임은 김 선생님의 주선으로 이루어졌다 This meeting came about as a result of Mr. Kim's leadership.
—주선하다 〈알선하다〉 use *one's* influence; exercise *one's* good offices; 〈중개하다〉 mediate 《between》; act as an agent [intermediary]
■—료 brokerage; commission —업 brokerage; 〈고용인의〉 employment agency —인 an agent; an intermediary

주선 酒仙 〈술꾼〉 a son of Bacchus; a heavy [hard] drinker

주섬주섬 (picking them up) one by one
◆주섬주섬 줍다 pick up piece by piece [one by one]; gather / 옷을 주섬주섬 싸다 pack *one's* clothes one by one

주성 走性 (生) (a) taxis (pl. taxes); (a) tropism
◆주성의 tactic
■—운동 tactic movement

주성분 主成分 the principal [chief] ingredient; the main component(s); the chief element
▶이 약의 주성분은 요오드다 The chief ingredient of this medicine is iodine.

주세 酒稅 the liquor tax
■—법 〔法〕 the Liquor Tax Law

주소 住所 〈사는 곳〉 *one's* dwelling (place); 〈번지〉 *one's* address; *one's* residence [abode]; 〔法〕 a domicile
◆주소가 일정하지 않은 남자 a man of [with] no fixed address [abode]; a floater; (a) vagrant / 주소를 정하다 take up *one's* residence; fix *one's* abode (at); settle down (at) / 주소를 변경하다 change *one's* domicile [address] / 겉봉에 주소를 쓰다[적다] address an envelope [a letter] (to *sb*)
▶그의 주소[회사의 주소]는 어디입니까? What [Where] is his address [his office address]?
▶주소와 성명을 알려주십시오 Give [Tell, Teach] me your name and address, please.
▶주소가 어디시죠? What's [May I have] your address?
▶그의 주소를 알 수가 없다 I cannot obtain his address.
▶그녀는 내 주소를 알고 있습니다 She has my address.
■현— *one's* present address : 현주소를 쓰다 write down *one's* present address —록 an address book; a directory —변경통지 a change-of-address note —불명 (표시) the address unknown —성명 *one's* name and address: 이 용지에 주소 성명을 써주십시오 Write your name and address on this form,

please.

주술 呪術 incantation; enchantment; the black art ♦주술로 병을 고치다 charm [conjure] away an illness; cure an illness by a charm

주스 juice ■과일— fruit juice 깡통— canned juice 오렌지— orange juice

주시 注視 a steady gaze; close observation —주시하다 gaze steadily (on); observe sb closely; watch [look at] sth carefully ▶사람들은 모두 그 낯선 사람을 주시했다 All the people watched the stranger closely. ≒ All the people looked closely at the stranger. ▶그는 그녀를 주시했다 He fixed his eyes on [upon] her.

주식 主食 the staple [principal] food; the chief article of food ♦주식 대용품 a substitute for staple food ♦한국인은 쌀을 주식으로 한다 Rice is the staple food for Korean people.

주식 株式 (美) stocks; (英) shares ♦주식 발행 issue of stocks [shares] / 주식의 액면 the face-value of a stock [share] / 주식의 청약[응모] subscription for stocks [shares] / 주식을 매매하다 deal in stocks ▶나는 주식을 김선생님에게 양도했다 I transfered stocks to Mr. Kim. ▶우리는 주식을 모집한다 We offer stocks for subscription. ▶나는 주식 모집에 응한다 I take up [subscribe for] stocks. ■—매매 dealing in stocks [shares]; 〈부정한〉 stockjobbing —발행가액 the issue prices of stocks [shares] —발행액 issued stocks —배당 stock dividend —시세표 (美) a stock list; (英) a share list —시장 a stock market —자본 stock [share] capital; 〈미불입의〉 capital (stock) —중매(업) stockbroking; stockbrokerage —중매인 (美) a stockbroker; (英) a sharebroker —청약금 application money for stocks —투자 stock investment; investment in stocks

주식 酒食 food and drink; wine and refreshments

주식 畫食 lunch; luncheon; a midday meal ■—시간 lunch time [hour]

주식회사 株式會社 a company; (美) a stock company; (英) a joint-stock company

주심 主審 〈심사의〉 the chief judge; 〈야구의〉 the chief umpire; 〈축구·권투 등의〉 the (chief) referee

주악 奏樂 a musical performance —주악하다 play [perform] music

주안 主眼 〈주목표〉 the prime [principal] object; the chief end; 〈요점〉 the (main) point ♦…에 주안을 두다 aim at…; have an eye to… / 인격 양성을 주안으로 하다 have an eye to character-building ▶그것은 정치 발전에 주안을 두고 있다 It aims principally at political development. ■—점 the main [essential] point; the keynote : 학교교육의 주안점 the main object of school education

주안 酒案 a drinking table ⇨ 술상

주야 晝夜 night and day; 《for》 twenty-four hours ♦1주야 《for》 twenty-four hours; twice around the clock / 2주야 two days and nights / 주야로 일하다 work day and night / 주야로 가동하다 set 《a machine》 on the 24-hour job ▶그들은 주야 겸행으로 터널을 팠다 They worked night and day to build the tunnel. ▶우리는 주야 교대로 일했다 We worked in double shifts [shifts day and night]. ■—장천 〈밤낮으로〉 day and night; without a break; always; unceasingly

주어 主語 〔文法〕 the subject (of a sentence)

주역 主役 1〈주인공의 역할〉 the leading part; the principal [starring] role; the principal; 〈주연 배우〉 the leading actor [actress]; a star player ♦주역을 맡다 play the leading part; play the featured role; play [have] the lead 2〈중심인물〉 the leader ▶그녀는 깨끗한 선거운동의 주역이었다 She was the leader of the clean-elections campaign.

주역 周易 the Book of Changes

주연 主演 starring; playing the leading part ♦해리슨 포드 주연의 영화 a film starring [featuring] Harrison Ford ▶그녀는 많은 영화에 주연을 맡아왔다 She has starred in many pictures. —주연하다 play the leading part [role] (in); star (in) ▶그 영화는 그 여자가 주연했다 She (was) starred in the movie [film]. ≒ The movie [film] starred [featured] her. ■—남자배우[여자배우] a leading actor [actress]

주연 酒宴 a banquet; a feast; a drinking bout ♦주연을 베풀다 hold a banquet; give a feast / 주연을 벌이다 go on a drunken frolic [spree]

주영 駐英 ♦주영의 resident in Great Britain ■—한국대사 the Korean Ambassador to the United Kingdom

주옥 珠玉 〈보석〉 a gem; a jewel; (총칭) jewelry ♦주옥같은 글[작품] a literary gem ; a writing of rare beauty ■—편 a jewel of a literary work; a masterpiece

주요 主要 the principal; the important; the main; the essential ♦금주의 주요 행사 main events of the week / 그 전쟁의 주요 원인 the chief [main, principal] cause of the war —주요하다 principal; chief; main; major; leading; important; staple ▶미국의 주요한 도시의 이름을 들어보시오 Name the chief [major] cities of the United States. ▶그는 그 분쟁의 해결에 주요한 역할을 했다 He played a leading part [role] in settling the dispute. ▶울산은 한국의 공업도시로서 주요한 역할을 하고 있다 Ulsan fulfills an important role as a modern industrial Korean city.

—도시 principal cities —목적 the primary purpose —부 the principal part; the head and front —산물 staple products —산업 major [key] industries —성분 the main [principal] ingredients —수입품 the main [principal] imports —수출품 the principal exports —시장 a primary market —식품 staple article of food —인물 ⟨영화·연극의⟩ the leading characters; ⟨소설의⟩ the principal figure —점 the main points

주워내다 pick out; sort out; take out
주워담다 pick [take] up; put ⟨them⟩ in
▶ 그녀는 흩어진 사과를 바구니에 다시 주워담았다 She picked up scattered apples and put them back in a basket.
주워대다 quote [mention] this and [or] that; enumerate glibly ♦ 이유를 주워대다 pick excuses [reason] from the air / 거짓말을 주워대다 make up lies
주워듣다 happen to hear ⟨of, about⟩; learn *sth* by chance; pick up ⟨a bit of information⟩ ♦ 주워들은 정보 information picked up from others / 남에게서 이야기를 주워듣다 pick a story up from others
주워먹다 pick up and eat; take and eat; grab a bite to eat
♦ 아무거나 주워먹다 grab a bite of anything
주워모으다 gather; collect; ⟨이삭을⟩ glean
주워섬기다 chatter; narrate; spiel; rattle on [away]

주위 周圍 ⟨둘레⟩ (a) circumference; the girth; ⟨주변의 상황⟩ surroundings; ⟨환경⟩ (an) environment; ⟨부근⟩ environs; neighborhood ⟨**주위의**⟩ surrounding; neighboring; circumferential
▶ 주위의 눈을 마음에 두지 마라 Don't care what others think.
▶ 그는 주위 영향을 쉽게 받는다 He is liable to be influenced by the surroundings.
▶ 그들은 주위의 사람들을 전혀 아랑곳하지 않고 떠들어댔다 They made a lot of noise, without thinking about anyone else.
⟨**주위가[는]**⟩ 주위가 어두워지고 있었다 It was getting dark.
▶ 나는 가고 싶은데 주위가 가지 못하게 한다 I want to go, but those around me won't let me.
▶ 이 연못은 주위가 얼마나 됩니까? What is the circumference of this pond?
▶ 이 나무는 주위가 3 미터다 This tree is [measures] three meters around [in circumference].
▶ 그 마을은 주위가 아름답다 The town has beautiful surroundings.
▶ 주위는 무척 조용했다 It was very quiet all around (us).
⟨**주위를**⟩ 그는 주위를 둘러보았다 He looked around [round, about] (him).
▶ 호수 주위를 산책하자 Let's walk around (the edge of) the lake.
⟨**주위에(는)**⟩ 주위에 울타리를 치다 fence around [about]
▶ 주위에는 아무도 없었다 There was nobody around [about].

▶ 이 주위에는 아는 사람이 전혀 없다 I'm a complete stranger here.
▶ 그 집 주위에는 높은 담장이 처져 있다 The house is surrounded by [with] a high fence.
▶ 그 소리는 주위에 울려퍼졌다 The sound resounded in the neighborhood.

주유 舟遊 boating ⇨ 뱃놀이
주유 注油 ⟨급유⟩ oil supply; oiling; lubrication
—**주유하다** feed [supply] ⟨a machine⟩ with oil; oil ⟨an engine⟩; lubricate
■—기 an oiler; a lubricator —소 an oil station; ⟨美⟩ a gas station; a filling [service] station

주유 周遊 ⟨돌아다니며 유람함⟩ a (circular) tour; ⟨英⟩ a round trip (▶⟨美⟩에서는 「왕복여행」의 뜻); an excursion
—**주유하다** make a circular tour ♦ 세계를 주유하다 go [trip] round [⟨美⟩ around] the world; make a round-the-world trip

주의 主義 ⟨생활·행동 등의⟩ a principle; ⟨종교상의⟩ a doctrine; ⟨개인의 습관⟩ a rule; (口) an ism; ⟨방침⟩ a line; a system; a basis
♦ 주의가 있는[없는] 사람 a man of principle [no principle] / 주의를 지키다 be true [faithful] to one's principles; stick [hold fast] to one's principles / 주의를 버리다 abandon [desert] one's principles / 주의에 충실하다 be true [faithful] to principle / 안전 제일주의로 일하다 work on the principle of "Safety First" / 현금주의로 장사하다 do business on a cash basis
▶ 거짓말하는 것은 내 주의에 반하는 것이다 Lying is against my principle(s) [rule]. ⇌ It is against my principle(s) to tell lies.
▶ 돈을 빌리지 않는 것이 그의 주의다 He makes it a rule never to lend money. ⇌ It is his rule [a rule with him] never to lend money.
▶ 나는 주의가 없는 사람은 싫다 I hate men of no principles.
▶ 그녀는 자기의 주의를 굽히지 않았다 She stuck to [stood by] her principles.
■객관— objectivism 보호무역— protectionism

주의 注意 1 ⟨유의⟩ attention; observation; note; ⟨주목⟩ notice; heed; ⟨경계·조심⟩ care; watch; caution
♦ 주의를 환기시키다 call [awaken] one's attention ⟨to⟩ / 주의가 부족하다 be careless [inattentive, incautious] / 주의를 기울이다 pay attention ⟨to⟩ / 주의를 …로 돌리다 turn [direct, give] attention to… / 주의를 끌다 draw [attract, catch, command] sb's attention
▶ 그는 내 충고에 조금도 주의를 기울이지 않았다 He didn't pay any attention [heed] to my advice. ⇌ He took no notice [heed] of my advice.
▶ 이 사건은 많은 사람들의 주의를 촉구했다 This affair called the attention of many people.
▶ 주의를 게을리하면 안된다 You must not relax your attention.
▶ 그 장난감은 그의 주의를 끌었다 The toy

attracted [caught, drew, got] his attention.
▶ 공부에 주의를 집중해라 Concentrate (your attention) on your study.
─**주의하다** give attention [heed] to; take care of; be careful of; beware of; be cautious [watchful] of; look out for
▶ 교통 신호에 주의해라 Look [Pay attention] to traffic signals.
▶ 내가 하는 말을 주의해 들어라 Listen carefully [attentively] to what I say. ⇌ Listen to me carefully.
▶ 건강에 특히 주의해 주세요 Please take good care of yourself [your health].
▶ 앞으로 주의하겠습니다 I will be more careful in future.
2 〈충고〉 (a piece of) advice; counsel; 〈경고〉 (a) warning
▶ 나는 주차위반으로 경찰관에게 주의를 받았다 The policeman gave me a warning against [a caution for] illegal parking. ⇌ I was cautioned for illegal parking by the policeman.
▶ 이렇게 된 것은 네가 선생님의 주의를 무시했기 때문이다 This is because you neglected [didn't follow, didn't take] your teacher's advice.
─**주의하다** advise; counsel; give advice to; 〈경고하다〉 warn; give warning; caution sb against
▶ 어머니는 그에게 사탕을 너무 먹지 말라고 주의했다 His mother warned him about eating too much candy.
3 〈일깨움〉 suggestion; 〈타이름〉 admonition
♦ 남의 잘못에 주의를 주다 remind sb of (his) error
─**주의하다** remind sb of; admonish sb
4 〈규칙〉 rules; hints
♦ 위생상의 주의 sanitary rules / 여행자를 위한 주의점 hints to [for] travelers
─**력** attentiveness: 주의력이 부족하다 be careless [not attentive] ─**보** 〔氣〕 a advisory; a warning: 홍수[폭풍] 주의보 a flood [storm] warning ─**사항** matters to be attended to ─**인물** a suspicious character; a blacklisted person: 그는 요주의 인물이다 He is (a man) on the blacklist.

주익 主翼 the wings (of an aircraft)
주인 主人 1 〈집안 어른〉 the master of a house; the head of a family; 〈손님에 대해〉 the host; the hostess (여자)
♦ 주인과 손님 host and guest / 주인노릇을 하다 play the host; act as host
▶ 주인이 우리를 소개했다 Our host introduced us.
2 〈임자〉 the owner; the proprietor
▶ 이 집 주인은 누굽니까? Who owns this house?
3 〈고용주〉 an employer; a master; 〈경영주〉 the proprietor
♦ 호텔 주인 the proprietor of a hotel / 주인 행세를 하다 behave like a master
▶ 개는 주인에게 순종한다 A dog obeys his master.
4 ⇨ 남편(男便)

─**공** 〈소설 등의〉 a hero; a heroine (여자): 그가 사건의 주인공이다 He is the central figure in the affair.
주인 主因 the primary [principal] cause
▶ 지연의 주인은 악천후였다 The delay was mainly due to the bad weather.
▶ 불황의 주인은 생산 과잉에 있다 The trade depression is mainly due to overproduction.
주일 主日 the Lord's day; Sunday
주일 週日 a weekday; a week
♦ 매주일 week after [by] week / 이번[지난, 다음] 주일 this [last, next] week / 지난 주일의 오늘 a week ago today / 다음 주일의 오늘 a week from now / 지지난주일 the week before last / 일주일 걸러 week and week about; a week about
▶ 그 회사는 일주일에 5일 근무했다 The firm has established a five-day work week.
▶ 그는 한 주일에 200달러 번다 He earns 200 dollars a week.
▶ 나는 그 주일 내내 바빴다 I was busy all the week.
▶ 위원회는 한 주일에 한 번씩 열립니다 The committee meets weekly [once a week, every week].

주일 駐日 ♦ 주일의 resident [stationed] in Japan ─**한국 대사** the Korean Ambassador to the Japan
주임 主任 a chief; the person in charge (of); a manager; a head
─**수사** a chief investigator 영어과─ the head of the English department 홍보부─ the public relations [P.R.] manager 회계─ a chief treasurer ─**교사** the teacher in charge ─**교수** a head professor ─**기사** a chief engineer ─**변호인** chief [leading] counsel
주입 注入 pouring; 〈약액 등의〉 injection; 〈신사상 등의〉 infusion; instillation; 〈교육의〉 cramming
─**주입하다** 〈부어넣다〉 pour [put] 《water》 into; 〈약액을〉 inject; 〈사상 등을〉 infuse 《an idea》 into sb
♦ 정맥에 약을 주입하다 inject medicine into a vein; inject a vein with a drug / 지식을 (머리에) 주입하다 cram knowledge into one's head; force knowledge into one's head / 주입식 시험 공부를 하다 cram for an entrance exam(ination)
─**구** pouring basin ─**식 교육** the cramming system of education ─**식 수업** grinding
주자 走者 a runner; 〔野〕 a (base) runner
▶ 주자를 내보내다 send a runner (to) / 주자를 일소하다 clear the bases (of runners)
■ 단거리─ a sprinter 일루─ 〔野〕 a first-base runner 제일─ 〈릴레이의〉 the first runner 최종─ an anchorman
주자 奏者 a player ⇨ 연주자
주자 鑄字 typefounding; typecasting; 〈활자〉 a metal (printing) type
■ ─기 a typecaster ─소 a typefoundry
주장 主將 〈팀의〉 the captain; 〈군대의〉 the commander-in-chief; the supreme commander; a chief general ♦ 야구팀 주장 the captain of a baseball team

주장 主張 insistence; persistence; 〈권리의〉 (an) assertion; 〈논점〉 one's contention; one's point; 〈지론〉 one's opinion [stand, doctrine]
♦ 주장을 관철하다 carry [gain] one's point / 주장을 굽히다 concede one's point; compromise / 끝까지 주장을 굽히지 않다 stick to one's opinion to the last
▶ 그의 무죄 주장은 기각되었다 His claim of innocence [to be innocent] was rejected.
—주장하다 insist on [upon]; persist (in); assert; 〈역설하다〉 emphasize; press; stress
♦ 권리를 주장하다 claim one's right(s) (to) / 무죄를 주장하다 plead not guilty [one's innocence] / 정당방위를 주장하다 plead self-defense
▶ 그는 개혁을 주장했다 He advocated reform.
▶ 그는 그 일을 전부 자기 혼자 했다고 주장했다 He claimed to have [that he had] done all the work by himself.
▶ 콜럼버스는 서쪽으로 가면 인도에 도달한다고 주장했다 Columbus argued that he could reach India by going west.
■ —자 an assertor; a claimant; an advocate

주재 主宰 superintendence; supervision
♦ 송 선생의 주재하에 under the superintendence [supervision] of Mr. Song
—주재하다 superintend; supervise; preside
♦ 민 박사가 주재하는 계간 잡지 a quarterly magazine edited [run] by Dr. Min / 모임을 주재하다 preside over a meeting
■ —자 the president; the leader; the chairman

주재 駐在 residence; stay
—주재하다 reside 《at, in》; be resident 《at, in》; be stationed 《at, in》; stay
♦ 런던에 주재하는 외교관 a diplomat residing in London
▶ 그는 신문기자로 파리에 주재하고 있다 He is stationed in Paris as a newspaper reporter.
■ —관 a resident officer [official] —국 the country of residence —원 〈신문사의〉 a resident reporter: 뉴욕에는 한국 상사 주재원이 많다 There are many resident representatives of Korean firms in New York.

주저 躊躇 hesitation; reluctance; indecision
—주저하다 hesitate 《at, to do》; scruple 《at》; think twice 《about doing》; waver; be irresolute [hesitant]; hang back
♦ 주저하면서 hesitatingly; with hesitation; irresolutely / 주저하지 않고 without hesitation [scruple]; unhesitatingly
▶ 나는 한번 결정하면 주저하지 않는다 Once I have decided, I never waver.
▶ 그녀는 주저하면서[주저하지 않고] 내게 다가 왔다 She approached me hesitantly [without hesitation].
▶ 그는 그 차 사는 것을 주저하고 있다 He's having second thoughts about buying the car.
▶ 내가 그에게 입회를 권했지만 그는 주저했다 I invited him to join the society, but hung back.

주저앉다 1 〈맥없이 앉다〉 fall [sink] down; drop 《on one's knees》; sit down plump
♦ 바닥에 털썩 주저앉다 sink [drop] on the floor; slump [plop down] on the floor
▶ 그는 의자에 주저앉았다 He dropped [slumped] into a chair.
2 〈내려앉다〉 sink; fall [cave] in; collapse
▶ 벽이 주저앉았다 The wall fell [caved] in.
▶ 쌓인 짐이 주저앉았다 The pile of cargo collapsed.
3 〈머물다〉 stay on; sit on; settle down; remain
▶ 그는 현직에 주저앉기로 결정했다 He has decided to remain in his present office.
4 〈포기하다〉 give up; abandon; shrink from
▶ 그는 위험에도 주저앉지 않는다 He never shrinks [recoils] from danger.

주저앉히다 〈의자 등에〉 cause [make] sb to sit down; sit sb down (hard); 〈떠나지 못하게〉 make sb stay on
▶ 가려는 그를 우리는 주저앉혔다 As he was leaving, we stopped [detained] him.

주전 主戰 1 〈전쟁을 주장함〉 advocacy of war; pro-war argument 2 〈주력〉 fighting as the main force
■ —투수 an ace pitcher [hurler]

주전 鑄錢 〈주조〉 minting; mintage; coinage; 〈돈〉 a coin; 〈총칭〉 coinage
—주전하다 mint; coin; strike coins

주전거리다 eat [gobble] snacks between meals

주전론 主戰論 advocacy of war; jingoism; a bellicose [pro-war] argument ♦ 주전론을 펴다 advocate war; clamor for war
■ —자 a war advocate; a jingo 《pl. ~es》; a jingoist; a militant

주전부리 the habitual snacking; eating light meals frequently
—주전부리하다 ⇨ 주전거리다

주전자 酒煎子 a kettle; a teakettle
♦ 주전자의 주둥이[손잡이, 뚜껑] the spout [bail, lid] of a kettle / 주전자에 물을 끓이다 boil water in a kettle / 불위에 주전자를 얹어 놓다 put a kettle over the fire

주절 主節 〔文法〕 the main [principal] clause
주점 酒店 a wineshop; (美) liquor store [shop]; 〈술집〉 a barroom, a saloon; a tavern; (英) a pub

주접 〈발육부진〉 stunting; dwarfing; incomplete development; 〔生〕 ateliosis; 〈사는 형편〉 poverty

주접들다 1 〈발육이〉 get stunted [dwarfed]; 〈생기가〉 languish
♦ 주접든 나무 a stunted [scrubby] tree
2 〈살림살이가〉 be reduced to poverty; become poor; 〈몰골이〉 get [become] shabby [slovenly]

주접스럽다 greedy; ravenous
♦ 주접스럽게 먹다 eat greedily; gobble; wolf down one's food; make a pig of oneself

주정 舟艇 a boat; a craft
■ 상륙용— a landing boat [craft]

주정 酒酊 drunkenness; drunken frenzy; disorderly behavior caused by liquor
▶ 그는 주정이 심하니 너무 술을 권하지 마라 Don't press him to drink too much because he loses control of himself once he is drunk.
—주정하다 lose control of oneself in drink; become a bother to others in one's cups

주정 ■―꾼[뱅이, 쟁이] a troublesome drunkard; a bad drunk

주정 酒精 spirits (of wine); alcohol; an alcoholic solution
■공업용― industrial alcohol ■―분(分) alcoholic content [strength] ―(비중)계 an alcoholometer ―음료 alcoholic drinks [beverages]

주정설 主情說 〔哲〕 emotionalism; emotivism

주제 1 〈몰골〉 shabby [humble] appearance [looks]
◆주제사납다 be shabbily [poorly] dressed
▶ 주제가 사나우면 푸대접 받는다 You don't get service when you are so poorly [ill] dressed.
2 〈처지·형편〉 풋내기인 주제에 though (one is) only a beginner [novice]
▶ 그는 아무것도 모르는 주제에 아는체 말한다 He talks knowingly without knowing a thing.

주제 主題 a subject (matter); 〈작품 등의〉 a theme ◆음악적 주제 a (leit)motif / 사랑을 주제로 한 시 a poem on the subject of love / 주제의 thematic
―가 a theme song (of a movie)

주제넘다 forward; cheeky; presumptuous; impertinent; impudent; saucy; pert
◆주제넘은 녀석 an impertinent [a saucy, a presumptuous] fellow; an officious person / 주제넘게 presumptuously; forwardly; impertinently; impudently / 주제넘은 말을 하다 talk impudently [fresh, smart]; make impertinent remarks
▶ 그녀는 주제넘은 짓은 하지 않는다 She never pushes herself forward.
♦ 주제넘게 굴지 마라 Don't be so forward. ⇌ Mind your own business.
▶ 그녀는 주제넘게도 비평가로 자처한다 She is presumptuous enough to call herself a critic.

주조 主調 the dominant note(s); the keynote ▶ 이 그림의 주조는 청색이다 Blue is predominant in this painting.

주조 主潮 the main current ◆근대 음악의 주조 the main current of modern music

주조 酒造 making [the production of] alcoholic beverages; 〈양조주의〉 brewing; 〈포도주의〉 wine making; 〈증류주의〉 distilling
―주조하다 brew; distill (whisky)
■―가 a (liquor) brewer; a wine-maker; a vintner; a distiller ―업 the brewing [winemaking, distilling] industry [business] ―장 a brewery; a winery; 〈위스키 등의〉 a distillery

주조 鑄造 casting; founding; molding; 〈화폐의〉 minting; mintage; coinage
―주조하다 cast; found; mold [(英) mould]; 〈화폐를〉 coin; mint; strike
◆청동상을 주조하다 cast a statue of bronze / 새 주화를 주조하다 mint [strike] a new coin / 활자를 주조하다 cast [found] metal types
■―소 a foundry; 〈화폐의〉 a mint ―업 foundry ―자 a founder; a caster; a minter ―화폐 metallic currency; a struck coin

주종 主從 master and servant [man]; employer and employee; 〈주체와 종속〉 the principal and the subordinate [accessory]
◆주종 관계 the relationship between master and servant; the master-servant relationship

주주 株主 (美) a stockholder; (英) a shareholder
▶ 그는 그 회사의 대주주들중 한 사람이다 He is one of the large stockholders on that company.
■―명부 a stockholders' list; a list of shareholders; a stock ledger ―총회 a general meeting of stockholders; a general shareholders' meeting

주지 主旨 the main point; the (general) purport; the gist
◆그의 연설의 주지 the point [purport, drift] of his speech
▶ 그는 그런 주지로 내게 편지를 썼다 He wrote me to that effect.

주지 周知 common knowledge ◆주지의 사실 a well-known fact; a matter of common knowledge / 주지의 known to all [everybody]; universally [widely] known
▶ 그것은 주지의 사실이다 It is a well-known fact [a matter of common knowledge].
―주지하다 everybody knows; be known to everybody
◆주지하는 바와 같이 as everybody knows; as is generally known

주지사 州知事 the governor of a state; a state governor
―선거 a gubernatorial election

주지육림 酒池肉林 a sumptuous feast [banquet]; obscene orgies; a debauch
◆주지 육림에 빠지다 be immersed [have given oneself over] in a life of pleasure

주지주의 主知主義 〔哲〕 intellectualism
■―자 an intellectualist

주차 駐車 parking
◆길가에 주차중인 차가 있었다 There was a car parked [A car parked] on the side of the road.
◆주차 금지 (게시) No Parking.
―주차하다 park (a car)
▶ 이 근처에 주차할 데가 있습니까? Is there any parking space around here?
■―금지구역 (美) a no-parking zone; (英) a no-stopping zone ―미터 a parking meter ―위반 illegal parking; parking violation ―장 a parking zone [lot]; 〈건물〉 a parking building [structure]

주차 駐箚 residence; stay ⇨ 주재 (駐在)

주착 主着 a definite view ⇨ 주책

주창 主唱 advocacy; promotion
―주창하다 advocate; promote
▶ 그는 남녀 동등의 임금제도를 주창해왔다 He has long advocated equal pay for men and women.
■―자 an advocate; a promoter

주책 a definite view [opinion]; a fixed opinion ■―바가지 a wishy-washy [spineless] person; an irresponsible person

주책없다 frivolous; scatterbrained; shameful; immodest
◆주책없는 짓을 하다 behave disgracefully [indecently] / 여자에게 주책없이 굴다 take

liberties with a woman
주철 鑄鐵 cast iron
■—소 an iron foundry
주체 主體 the main [principal] body; 〔哲〕 the subject
♦주체적 행동 an independent action / 주체적 subjective; independent
■—성 individuality; independence : 그에게는 주체성이 결여되어 있다 He lacks self-direction. —세력 the main group [body] —의식 a sense of sovereignty
주체 酒滯 dyspepsia caused by (too much) drinking; a hangover
주체못하다 be burdensome; do not know [have no idea] what to do 《with》; find sb unmanageable; be at a loss; be beyond [out of] *one's* control; be unmanageable [uncontrollable]
♦주체못할 만큼 돈이 많다 have more money than *one* can spend
▶부모도 그 아이를 주체못하고 있다 That child is beyond his parents' control. ⇒ His parents can't manage that child.
▶사태는 내가 주체못할 지경이다 I can't deal with [handle] the situation.
주체스럽다 unmanageable; troublesome; burdensome
▶갠 날에 우산을 들고 다니자니 주체스럽다 It's a bother to carry an umbrella on a fine day.
▶가게 일이 그에게 주체스러워지고 있다 Running the store is becoming a burden to him.
주체하다 cope with [take care of] *one's* job [work]
주쳇덩어리 a bother; a burden; a white elephant; worry
주최 主催 auspices; sponsorship
♦…의 주최로 under the sponsorship [auspices] of…
—주최하다 host; sponsor; organize
♦파티를 주최하다 organize [host] a party
▶이 전람회는 누가 주최했습니까? Who organized this exhibition?
■—국 the host nation [country] : 월드컵 주최국 the host country for the World Cup —단체 the host organization —자 the sponsor; the promoter; the organizer
주추 柱— a foundation stone; a cornerstone
주축 主軸 the principal [main] axis 《pl. axes》; the main shaft [spindle]
주춤거리다 hesitate; be hesitant; waver; hang back 《from》; shy 《away》
♦주춤거리면서 hesitatingly; hesitantly; waveringly / 주춤거리며 말하다 speak in a halting way; stammer out / 나아갈까 되돌아갈까 주춤거리다 hesitate [waver] between going on and turning back / 명확히 대답하지 못하고 주춤거리다 hesitate to give a definite answer
▶그는 홀에 들어가기 전에 잠깐 주춤거렸다 He hung back momentarily before entering the hall.
주춤주춤 hesitatingly; hesitantly; falteringly
♦주춤주춤 걷다 walk with gingerly steps

주춧돌 柱— 〈주추〉 a cornerstone; a foundation stone
주치 主治 being in charge of the treatment of a patient —주치하다 take charge of 《the treatment》
■—의 the physician in charge 《of》; *one's* (family) doctor
주택 住宅 a house; (美) a home; 〈고급주택〉 a residence; 〈총칭〉 housing
♦김씨의 주택 (美) the Kim home; (英) Mr. Kim's (house) / 목조 주택 a wooden (frame) house / 한국주택공사 the Korea Housing Corporation / 한국주택은행 the Korea Housing Bank / 신흥주택지 a new housing area / 주택사정을 개선하다 improve housing [the housing situation]
▶그 건물은 주택으로는 적합하지 않다 The building is not fit to live in.
▶그 도시는 주택[2만호의 주택]이 부족하다 There is a shortage of housing [twenty-thousand houses] in the city.
■공영(公營)— a unit of public housing; public housing 모델— a model house 문화— a modern dwelling 분양— a house to be purchased on an easy payment plan 조립식— a prefabricated house; (口) a prefab 호화— a luxurious house; a palatial mansion
■—문제 the housing problem —부족 housing shortage —비 housing expenses —산업 the housing industry —수당 a housing allowance —시설 residential facilities —융자 a home [housing] loan —지역[지구] a residential quarter [zone]; (美) uptown : 그들은 주택지역에 살고 있다 They live in a residential area [quarter, district]. —행정[정책] the housing administration [policy]
주택난 住宅難 (a) shortage of house; housing shortage [trouble]
▶도시의 주택난이 큰 사회문제가 되고 있다 The housing shortage [trouble] in town poses [forms] a big social problem.
주파 周波 〔物〕 a cycle
■고[저]— a high [low] frequency 장[단]— a long [short] wave —계 ⇨ 파장(~계)
주파수 周波數 〔物〕 frequency ♦550 킬로헤르츠의 주파수로 방송하다 broadcast at [on] a frequency of 550 kilohertz
■가청— 〔通信〕 audible frequency; audio frequency (略 A.F., a.f.) ■—대 a frequency band —변조 frequency modulation (略 FM) —조정 amplitude modulation —증폭기 a frequency amplifier
주파하다 走破— run [cover] the whole distance ▶그는 1킬로미터를 3분에 주파한다 He covered one kilometer in three minutes.
주판 籌板 an abacus ⇨ 수판(數板)
주포 主砲 the main [principal] gun; the main battery
주폭도 走幅跳 〈멀리 뛰기〉 〔競〕 a broad [long] jump
주피터 〔로神〕 Jupiter
주필 主筆 the (chief) editor; the editor in chief
■—부— an assistant editor; (英) a subeditor

주필 朱筆 a red-writing brush; 〈주서〉 writing in red ◆교정지에 주필을 대다 make corrections on a proof in red ink
주한 駐韓 ■─미국 대사 the United States [American] Ambassador to Korea [in Seoul] / ─미군 U.S. armed forces (stationed) in Korea
주항 周航 circumnavigation
▶그 배는 세계를 주항중이다 The ship is sailing around the globe.
주해 註解 〈전체〉 (an) annotation; 〈개개의〉 comments; (explanatory) notes; a commentary ◆주해를 단 책 an annotated book; a book with notes
▶그 책은 상세한 주해가 달려 있다 The book is fully annotated.
—주해하다 annotate; comment 《on》; make [give] notes 《on》
◆한시에 주해하다 annotate Chinese poems
■─서 a reference book; 〈학생용〉 a key; (學俗) a crib; (美俗) a horse ─자 an annotator; a commentator
주행 舟行 going by boat; sailing; navigation
—주행하다 go by boat; sail along; navigate
▶이 강은 주행할 수 있다 This river is navigable.
주행 走行 traveling; covering
◆주행중인 차 a moving car
—주행하다 travel 《from A to B》; cover 《100 miles in an hour》
▶이 열차는 서울-부산 간을 4시간에 주행한다 This train covers the distance between Seoul and Pusan in four hours.
■─거리 the distance covered; 〈마일수〉 mileage ─시간 time taken in traveling; 〈기차의〉 rail time
주행성 晝行性 ◆주행성의 diurnal; active during daylight hours; daytime
주형 鑄型 a mold; 〈활자 등의〉 a matrix
◆주형을 뜨다 cast a mold / 금속을 주형에 붓다 cast [pour] metal into a mold / 주형으로 꽃병을 만들다 cast a vase in a mold
─공 a molder; a caster
주호 酒豪 a heavy drinker
주홍 朱紅 vermilion; crimson
주화 鑄貨 〈화폐〉 a coin; minting; mintage; coinage
◆5백원짜리 주화 3개 three 500-won coins / 주화를 만들다 mint coins / 주화로 지불하다 pay in coin / 자동판매기의 투입구에 주화를 넣다 put a coin in a slot of a vending machine
주화론 主和論 advocacy of peace
─자 a peace advocate; a pacifist
주황 朱黃 reddish yellow; orange color
주효 奏效 efficacy; an effect
—주효하다 〈약 등이〉 be effectual; be effective; take effect; work well; succeed
▶그 시도는 주효했다[하지 않았다] The attempt was [proved] effective [ineffectual].
주효 酒肴 wine and eatables; food and drink
주휴 週休 a weekly holiday
▶우리 회사는 주휴 2일제다 We are on a five-day workweek in this company.
주흥 酒興 entertainment at a drinking party; hilarity from drink; merrymaking
◆주흥에 겨워 merry with drink; exhilarated [elated] by wine / 주흥을 돋우다 enhance [heighten] the conviviality [festivity] / 주흥을 깨다 dampen [wet-blanket] the conviviality [festivity]

죽¹ 〈열 개〉 ten pieces; ten ◆접시 한 죽 (a set of) ten plates
죽² in a row ⇨ 쭉
죽 竹 (a) bamboo ■─의 장막 the Bamboo Curtain
죽 粥 (rice-)gruel; porridge; 〈유아용의〉 pap
◆죽 두 그릇 two bowls of rice-gruel / 죽을 먹다 eat gruel / 죽을 쑤다 boil rice into gruel / 죽도 못 먹을 지경이 되다 be reduced to a crust
▶그것은 식은죽 먹기다 (속담) That's very easy. ⇌ That's a piece of cake. ⇌ That's (as) easy as pie. ⇌ It's mere child's play.
▶죽이 되든 밥이 되든 해보겠다 Sink or swim, I will try.
죽기 竹器 bamboo ware
죽는소리 1 〈엄살〉 exaggeration of one's pain [hardship]
▶그들은 그녀의 죽는소리에 넘어갔다 They were taken in by her crocodile tears.
—죽는소리하다 exaggerate pain [hardship]
▶그 일로 내게 죽는소리해도 소용없다 It's no use whining about it to me.
2 〈비명〉 a scream; a shriek
◆죽는소리를 지르다 utter [give] a scream [shriek]; scream; shriek / 아파서 죽는소리를 지르다 give a cry of pain; shriek [shout] with pain
▶그 아이는 의사 앞에서 죽는소리를 질렀다 The child howled [screamed] in front of the doctor.
죽다 1 〈사망하다〉 die; pass away; be gone; be killed
◆죽은 사람 a dead person; (총칭) the dead / 60세에 죽다 die at the age of sixty / 죽은 것으로 치다 give up sb for lost [dead] / 노쇠하여 죽다 die of old age / 굶어 죽다 be starved to death / 물에 빠져 죽다 be drowned to death / 독약을 먹고 죽다 kill oneself by taking poison / 불타[얼어, 맞아] 죽다 be burnt [frozen, beaten] to death / 폐렴으로 죽다 die of [from] pneumonia / 젊어서[늙어서] 죽다 die young [old] / 갑자기 죽다 die suddenly; meet a sudden death / 웃으면서 죽다 face [meet] one's death with a smile / 평온하게 죽다 die peacefully [in peace]; die a peaceful death / 재직중에 죽다 die in office / 나라를 위해 죽다 die for one's country; lay down one's life for one's country / 남의 손에 죽다 die by another's hand(s); be killed by another / 죽도록 사랑하다 be desperately in love with sb / 죽도록 두들겨 패다 beat sb nearly to death / 심심해[피곤해] 죽을 지경이다 be bored [tired] to death / 죽은거나 다름없다 be almost [nearly] dead / 죽을 뻔하다 narrowly miss death; be nearly killed / 죽은 체하다 feign death; play dead / 죽기를 각오하다 stand prepared for death / 다 죽어가다 be dying; be at death's door

▶ 그는 죽은 거나 마찬가지다 He is as good as dead.
▶ 죽은 자는 말이 없다 Dead man tells no tale.
▶ 그 애는 죽은 아버지를 빼닮았다 The boy is the spitting image of his dead father.
▶ 그는 암으로 죽었다[죽어가고 있다] He died of cancer [is dying of cancer]. ⇌ Cancer killed him [is killing him].
▶ 그는 총상으로 죽었다 He died of [from] a gunshot wound.
▶ 내 아내는 교통사고로 죽었다 My wife was killed [died] in [by, of] a traffic accident.
▶ 그는 비참하게 죽었다 He died a miserable death.
▶ 그는 술 때문에 죽었다 Drinking cost his life.
▶ 돈이 없어 죽을 지경이다 I'm very hard up for money.
▶ 이것은 죽을 때까지 잊지 않겠다 I will remember this all my life. ⇌ I will remember this as long as I live.
▶ 그가 죽은지 10년이 된다 It's been [It's] ten years since he died. ⇌ He died ten years ago. ⇌ He has been dead for ten years.
▶ 방안에 남자가 한 명 죽어 있다 There's a dead man in the room.
▶ 나는 배가 고파 죽겠다 I'm dying [almost die] of hunger.
▶ 나는 커피 마시고 싶어 죽겠다 I'm dying for [to drink] some coffee.
▶ 죽겠다 죽겠다 하는 동안은 결코 죽지 않는다 He will never die so long as he continues to talk of dying.
▶ 더워 죽겠다 The heat is killing me.
▶ 나는 죽고 싶다 I wish I were dead.
▶ 죽기로 작정하면 못할 일이 없다 You can do anything if you're not afraid of death.
▶ 사람은 죽게 마련이다 Man is mortal.
▶ 돈 떨어지는 날이 죽는 날이다 Money gone, friends gone.
▶ 그들은 죽자 사자 사랑하는 사이다 They are desperately in love with each other.
2 〈초목이〉 wither; die; perish
♦ 죽은 withered; dead
▶ 이 나무는 물이 없어서 죽어 가고 있다 This tree is dying for want of water.
▶ 분재의 나무가 모두 말라 죽었다 All the potted plants withered and died.
3 〈기가〉 be discouraged [disheartened, dispirited]; feel depressed; get out of spirits
▶ 그는 기가 죽어 돌아왔다 He came back looking dejected [downhearted].
▶ 액자 때문에 그림이 완전히 죽어버렸다 That frame totally killed the picture.
▶ 이 말을 빼면 이 문장은 죽어버린다 The sentence falls flat if you cross that word out.
4 〈불이〉 go out; die out; be put out
♦ 죽어 가는 불 a dying fire / 불이 죽지 않게 하다 keep the fire alive [going]
5 〈동작이 멎다〉 stop; run down
▶ 팽이가 죽었다 The top stopped spinning.
▶ 시계가 죽었다 The clock has stopped [run down].
6 〔장기·바둑〕 be captured; be killed; 〔野〕 be (put) out

죽담 stone-studded earthen wall
죽데기 an outside piece cut from a log; a slab; slabwood
죽도 竹刀 a bamboo sword
죽마 竹馬 〈대말〉 a bamboo horse; stilts
♦ 죽마를 타다 walk [play] on stilts
■ 一고우(故友) a friend from childhood; an old playmate
죽물 粥— watery gruel
죽방울 a diabolo ♦ 죽방울을 받다 play with a diabolo; (비유) make fun of 《a boy》 by praising and dispraising by turns
죽살이 (a matter of) life and [or] death
♦ 죽살이 치다 make desperate [frantic] efforts; struggle for dear life [(口) like hell]
죽세공 竹細工 bamboo work ■ 一品 bamboo ware; a piece of bamboo work
죽순 竹筍 a bamboo shoot [sprout]
♦ 우후죽순처럼 나오다 spring [grow] up like mushrooms after rain; increase rapidly (in number)
▶ 새 건물이 우후죽순처럼 들어서고 있다 New buildings are sprouting up like mushrooms after rain.
죽술 粥— a few spoonfuls of gruel; meager food ♦ 죽술 연명하다 eke out a precarious living; scratch a living
죽어라하고 desperately; frantically; (口) like hell; for dear life; for one's life; with utmost effort
♦ 죽어라하고 도망치다 run for one's (dear) life / 죽어라하고 일하다 work away like one possessed
▶ 죽어라하고 뛰었지만 버스를 놓쳤다 I ran as fast as possible, but I couldn't catch the bus.
죽어지내다 〈위압되어〉 live under oppression [control]; 〈가난으로〉 live a life battered by privation; be desperately poor
▶ 그는 아버지 앞에서 죽어지낸다 He is under his father's thumb.
▶ 그는 아내 앞에서 죽어지낸다 He has completely been henpecked.
죽은목숨 a life [person] as good as dead; a living corpse
▶ 너는 이제 죽은목숨이다 You are a dead man now.
죽을둥살둥 desperately; frantically; like hell ⇨ 죽어라하고 ♦ 죽을둥살둥 덤비다 go at [attack] it like hell / 죽을둥살둥 싸우다 fight at the risk of one's life
죽을병 —病 a fatal disease ♦ 죽을병에 걸리다 suffer from a fatal disease
죽을뻔살뻔 with bare life; for one's (dear) life; by the skin of one's teeth; at the risk of one's life ♦ 죽을뻔살뻔 살아남다 escape from (the jaws of) death
죽을상 —相 an agonized look; a desperate look; a deathly look
▶ 그는 그 광경을 보고 죽을상이 되었다 He turned deadly pale at the sight.
죽을힘 ♦ 죽을힘을 다해 desperately; frantically; (口) like hell / 죽을힘을 다하다 make desperate efforts / 죽을힘을 다해 싸우다 fight desperately fight to the death

죽음 death; decease; 〈귀인의〉 demise
♦ 위암으로 인한 죽음 (a) death from [caused by] stomach cancer
〈죽음의〉 죽음의 공포 the fear of death / 죽음의 재 (radioactive) fallout; radioactive dust / 죽음의 행진 a death march / 죽음의 고통 the agonies of death
〈죽음이[은]〉 죽음이 다가오다 be near [approach] one's death [end]
▸ 죽음이 임박해 있다 Death is near at hand [approaching].
▸ 죽음은 만인을 평등하게 하다 Death equals [equalizes] all men.
〈죽음을〉 죽음을 무릅쓰고 at the risk of one's death / 그의 딸의 죽음을 애도하다 mourn (for) his daughter; mourn his daughter's death [the death of his daughter] / 죽음을 당하다 meet one's end; lose one's life; suffer death; be killed; die / 반 죽음을 당하다 be half-killed / 죽음을 각오하고 싸우다 fight to the death / 죽음을 초래하다 court [occasion] death / 죽음을 두려워하지 않다 challenge [defy] death; do not fear to die / 죽음을 예상하다 foresee one's end / 치욕적인[영광스러운] 죽음을 맞다 die a shameful [glorious] death
▸ 그 사건이 그의 죽음을 재촉했다 The event quickened [hasten] his death.
▸ 사람은 죽음을 면할 수는 없다 Man cannot escape death. ⇌ Man is mortal.
▸ 그는 그때 죽음을 각오하고 있었다 He was ready to die then.
▸ 그는 죽음을 무릅쓰고 그녀의 생명을 구했다 He saved her life at the risk of his own life.
▸ 이것은 죽음을 눈앞에 둔 젊은이의 이야기다 This is a story about the young man who faced death [was (on the point of) dying, (口) was at death's door].
〈죽음에〉 죽음에 임하여 in one's last moments; on one's deathbed / 죽음에 이르게 하다 cause sb's death; cause sb to die / 태연히 죽음에 임하다 face death with a smile; meet one's death with serene composure
▸ 그는 죽음에 임하여 아내에게 무슨 말인가 하려고 했다 He was trying to say something to his wife just before he died [on his deathbed].
〈죽음에서〉 죽음에서 다시 살아나다 rise from the dead; resurrect
〈죽음으로〉 죽음으로 속죄하다 atone for 《one's crime》 with death
▸ 그의 갑작스런 죽음으로 가족은 몹시 곤궁해졌다 His sudden [unexpected] death left his family without support.

죽이다 1 〈목숨을 빼앗다〉 kill; slay; put sb to death; take another's life; put an end to another's life; make [do] away with; 〈의도적으로〉 murder; 〈잔학하게〉 slaughter 《a bull》; butcher 《a hog》; 〈대량으로〉 massacre; 〈암살하다〉 assassinate
♦ 때려 죽이다 beat to death / 목졸라 죽이다 strangle to death / 어버이[왕, 아버지, 어머니, 형제, 유아]를 죽이다 commit parricide [regicide, patricide, matricide, fratricide, infanticide] / 죽이려고 하다 make an attempt on another's life / 죽이려고 계획을 짜다 plot the death 《of》; have designs upon another's life / 아무도 죽인다고 위협하다 threaten sb with death / 남을 죽이고 사형당하다 be executed [hanged] for murder
▸ 그 남자는 대통령을 죽이려고 했다 The man attempted to kill [assassinate] the President.
▸ 죽이든 살리든 마음대로 해라 I am at your mercy.
▸ 이 죽일 놈아 Damn you! ⇌ Be damned to you! ⇌ Death!
▸ 한 걸음이라도 움직이면 죽여 버린다 Stir a step, and you shall die.
2 〈잃다〉 suffer the death [loss] of; lose 《a son, a chessman》
♦ 졸 하나를 죽이다 lose a pawn / 돌림병으로 많은 돼지를 죽이다 lose many hogs from an epizootic
3 〈억제하다〉 hold back; deaden; restrain; muffle
♦ 숨을 죽이고 with bated breath; breathlessly / 목소리를 죽이고 in a suppressed tone of voice; in a whisper [low tone] / 발소리를 죽이다 muffle one's footsteps
▸ 그는 잠시 숨을 죽였다 He held his breath for a moment.
4 〈동작을 중지시키다〉 stop 《a timepiece, a top, a motor》; allow 《it》 to stop
5 〈기세를 꺾다〉 cause to lose 《courage》; damp(en) 《sb's spirits》; cast a damp over
♦ 기를 죽이다 depress sb's spirit; discourage
6 〈꺼지게 하다〉 put out 《a fire, a light》; let 《it》 go out
7 〈모서리를 깎아내다〉 round off [rub off] 《the corners》; chip 《an edge》

죽자꾸나하고 at the risk [peril] of one's life; for one's 《dear》 life; neck or nothing; frantically; resolutely; against all obstacles
♦ 죽자꾸나하고 노력하다 make desperate efforts

죽장 竹杖 〈대지팡이〉 a bamboo cane [stick]

죽장기 —將棋 a poor chess-player's hand
♦ 죽장기를 두다 play a poor game of changgi

죽젓개질 粥— interfering; stirring up trouble; getting in the way
—죽젓개질하다 stir porridge; interfere with; interrupt; stir up trouble

죽죽 1 〈줄줄이〉 in rows [lines]; row after row; in streaks
♦ 물건을 죽죽 늘어놓다 make an array of articles / 흰줄이 죽죽 그어져 있다 be banded with white strips; be streaked with white
2 〈거침없이〉 briskly; rapidly; steadily; 〈비가〉 in sheets [showers]
♦ 죽죽 나아가다 go ahead at a rapid pace / 키가 죽죽 자라다 grow taller and taller / 나뭇잎을 죽죽 훑다 strip off leaves briskly / 주스를 빨대로 죽죽 빨다 suck up juice through a straw
▸ 비가 죽죽 내린다 It rains fast [in sheets].
3 〈갈기갈기〉 to pieces; into shreds
♦ 죽죽 찢다 tear [rend] to pieces [shreds]

죽지 a shoulder blade; a scapula; the shoulder joint ■ 날갯— the joint of a wing 어깻— the shoulder joint 팔— the upper arm

죽지떼다 1 〈활을 쏘고나서〉 lower one's shoul-

der after shooting an arrow
2 〈배후를 믿고〉 act arrogantly [put on airs] through borrowed authority; be stuck-up [imperious]

죽창 竹槍 a bamboo spear

죽치 inferior articles sold by the tens; mass-produced goods of low quality

죽치기 wholesale ♦죽치기로 팔다 sell wholesale

죽치다 confine *oneself* to [in] *one's* house; shut *oneself* up; keep (to) the house; keep indoors
▶ 그는 성탄절 이후로 감기로 죽치고 있다 He has been laid up [been confined to bed] with a cold since Christmas.
▶ 그는 방에 죽치고서 생각했다 He shut himself (up) in [confined himself to] his room to think.

죽침 竹針 a bamboo (knitting) needle

죽통 粥筒 〈구유〉 a cow-[horse-]feed tub; a feeding trough

죽피 竹皮 a bamboo sheath

준- 準- quasi-; semi-; associate ♦준계약 a quasi-contract / 준독립국 a quasi-sovereign state / 준사법권 quasi-judicial power

준거 準據 〈의거〉 conformity; 〈표준〉 authority cited; standard referred to; referring to a precedent [rule]
—준거하다 be based upon 《sufficient grounds》; follow 《up-to-date lines》; conform to 《local customs》
▶ 이 책은 새로운 학습지도 요령에 준거해서 만들어졌다 This book was edited in accordance [conformity] with the new course of study.

준걸 俊傑 a great man; an outstanding figure; a hero

준결승(전) 準決勝(戰) a semifinal (game [英] match) ♦준결승에 진출하다 advance to [reach] the semifinals; advance [(口) make it] to a semifinal; go on to the semifinals
■—출전자 a semifinalist

준공 竣工 completion
—준공하다 be completed [finished]; be brought to completion
▶ 새 체육관이 준공되었다 The new gymnasium has been completed [finished].
■—시기 the time of completion **—식** a ceremony for the completion 《of》: 준공식을 거행하다 hold an inauguration [a completion] ceremony

준교사 準教師 a teaching assistant; an assistant teacher

준금속 準金屬 〔化〕 metalloid
♦준금속의 metalloid

준금치산 準禁治産 quasi-incompetence ⇨ 한정(~치산)

준급행(열차) 準急行(列車) a local express (train)

준동 蠢動 〈벌레의〉 wriggling; squirming; 〈사람의〉 activities; maneuvering
♦빨치산의 준동 activities of the partisans
—준동하다 wriggle; writhe; squirm; stir; be active; maneuver

준령 峻嶺 a high rugged mountain; an alp; a lofty range

준마 駿馬 a swift [fine] horse; an excellent horse; a fleet steed

준말 an abbreviation; an abbreviated word; a shortening
▶ Oct.는 October의 준말이다 Oct. is an abbreviation of October.
▶ P.T.A.는 무엇의 준말입니까? What does P.T.A. stand for?

준법 遵法 obeying the law; law observance; law-abiding **—준법하다** obey [observe, abide by] the law
■—정신 the spirit of obeying laws; the law-abiding spirit: 그들은 준법 정신으로 가득차 있었다 They were full of a law-abiding spirit.
—투쟁 〔勞〕 a work-to-rule struggle; a slow-down strike; a law-abiding labor struggle

준봉 峻峰 a steep peak

준봉 遵奉 observance ⇨ 준수(遵守)

준비 準備 preparation(s) (▶「준비한 것」의 뜻일 때는 보통 복수형으로 씀); arrangements (▶보통 복수형으로 씀); 〈예비〉 provision; reserve
♦마음의 준비 readiness of mind; preparedness / 준비없는 연설 an offhand(ed) [impromptu] speech / 연방준비은행 (美) the Federal Reserve Bank / 준비중이다 〈사람이〉 be getting ready 《for a party》; 〈일이〉 be in (course of) preparation / 출발준비를 하다 prepare [make ready] for departure / 여행준비를 하다 get 《oneself》 ready for a journey / 환영준비를 하다 make arrangements for the reception 《of a guest》 / 식사준비를 하다 prepare a meal; set the table for dinner / 전투준비를 하다 get ready for battle / 월동준비를 하다 prepare for (the) winter / 만일의 경우에 대한 준비를 하다 provide against an emergency [a rainy day]
▶ 會話 「출발 준비는 다 됐습니까?」「네, 됐어요」 "Are you ready to start?" "Yes, I am."
▶ 우리는 시험 준비가 되어 있다 We are ready for the test.
▶ 만반의 준비가 되었다. 우리는 화요일 9시에 출발한다 It's all set [We're all set, Everything's ready]. We leave on Tuesday at nine.
▶ 준비는 벌써 다 돼 있어 Arrangements have already been made, you know.
▶ 그는 시험준비를 하느라고 바쁘다 He is busy preparing for [getting ready for, preparing to take, with preparations for] the exam. (▶교사가 문제를 준비하는 경우는 prepare the exam)
▶ 준비는 잘 했는데 그녀가 실행할 수 있을지 모르겠다 The program is fine, but I wonder if she can carry it out.
—준비하다 prepare 《oneself》 《for the test》; arrange 《for departure》; make preparations [arrangements] 《for the meeting》; get ready 《for a meeting》; 〈대비하다〉 provide for 《a rainy day》; reserve 《a fund》
♦모임을 위해 방에 의자를 준비하다 provide the room with chairs for the meeting
▶ 모든 것이 다 준비되었다 All [Everything] is ready.

▶어머니는 저녁 식사를 준비하고 계신다 Mom is preparing [fixing] dinner. ⇌ Mom is getting dinner ready.
▶얼마간의 돈을 준비해 두었다 I had some money available [ready].
■시험[여행]— preparations for an examination [a journey] 외화— foreign currency reserves ■—기간[단계] a preparatory period [stage] —시간 make-ready time —운동 warming up; warming-up exercises; warm-up: 준비운동을 하다 warm up; have [go through] a warm-up —위원[위원회] a preparatory [an arrangement] committee —자본 unemployed [reserve] capital

준비금 準備金 a reserve fund
■법정— a legal reserve

준사관 准士官 〔軍〕 a warrant officer (略 WO)

준사원 準社員 a junior employe(e)

준설 浚渫 dredging
—준설하다 dredge (a harbor, a channel)
▶그들은 강을 준설하여 더 깊게 했다 They dredged the river to make it deeper.
—기 a dredge; a dredging machine —선 a dredger; a dredging vessel —작업 dredging operations [work]

준수 俊秀 superiority in talent and elegance
—준수하다 excellent [outstanding] in talent [personal appearance]; brilliant (mind)
♦준수한 젊은이 a young man of outstanding talent; 〈풍모가〉 a well-set, handsome youth

준수 遵守 observance; obedience; compliance
♦법률의 준수 law observance
—준수하다 observe; obey; adhere [conform] to; follow; abide by
▶법률을 준수하지 않으면 안된다 We must obey [observe, abide by, keep] the law.
▶우리는 법률을 준수하는 국민이다 We are a law-abiding people.

준엄 峻嚴 strictness; sternness; rigidity
—준엄하다 strict; stern; rigorous; severe; austere; rigid ♦준엄한 태도 a stern attitude
▶영화는 준엄한 검열을 받는다 The films were subjected to the strictest censorship.

준열 峻烈 severity; sternness; rigor; trenchancy —준열하다 severe; rigorous; stern; relentless; trenchant; sharp; incisive ♦준열한 비평 a sharp [trenchant] criticism
▶검사의 논고는 아주 준열했다 The prosecutor's address was most unsparing.

준용 準用 applying (a rule) correspondingly (to a case); adaptation; adapting
—준용하다 apply (provisions) correspondingly (to other cases); apply (the law) with necessary modifications
▶이 규칙은 다른 케이스에 준용될 수 있다 This rule can be applied to other cases.
▶그들은 그 규정을 이 경우에 준용했다 They applied that regulation correspondingly to this case.

준우승 準優勝 a victory in the semifinals
▶그녀는 웅변대회에서 준우승했다 She took second place in the speech contest.
■—자 a winner of the second prize [the semifinals]

준위 准尉 a warrant officer (略 WO)

준장 准將 〈육군〉 a brigadier general; 〈해군〉 a commodore; 〈공군〉 〈美〉 a brigadier general; 〈英〉 an air commodore

준재 俊才 〈재주〉 outstanding talent; 〈사람〉 a man of talent; a brilliant [talented, sharp] man

준족 駿足 〈준마〉 a swift horse; a fleet steed; 〈발빠른 사람〉 a fast runner [moving man]
♦준족의 swift-footed / 준족이다 be swift [fleet] of foot; be a fast runner

준준결승(전) 準準決勝(戰) a quarterfinal (game, match) ♦준준결승에 진출하다 advance to [reach] the quarterfinals
■—진출자 a quarterfinalist

준칙 準則 〈규칙〉 a standing rule (to act upon); working rules; 〈기준〉 a criterion (pl. -s, -ria); a standard ▶법률은 행위의 준칙이다 Law is the rule to action.

준평원 準平原 〔地質〕 a peneplain

준하다 準— 〈준용하다〉 apply correspondingly; 〈좇다〉 follow (the rule); conform to (the law); act on (a precedent); go by; 〈의거하다〉 be based upon (sufficient data)
♦…에 준하여 in accordance with (the rules)
▶그는 정회원에 준한 대우를 받았다 He was treated in the same way as a regular member.
▶이하 이에 준함 This applies correspondingly [in the same way] to the following cases.

준행 準行 conformity; following in accordance with the rule —준행하다 act on; go by; follow [act] in accordance with

준험 峻險 steepness; precipitousness
—준험하다 steep; precipitous

준회원 準會員 an associate member

줄¹ **1** 〈끈〉 a string; a cord; a rope; a line
♦줄을 매다[풀다] tie [untie] the strings
▶이 줄은 너무 가늘어요. 더 굵은 것을 주세요 This rope is too thin. I want a thicker one.
▶그는 기둥 사이에 줄을 팽팽하게 쳤다 He stretched a cord tight between the poles.
▶나는 그것을 줄로 묶었다 I tied it with a rope.
2 〈현악기의〉 a chord; a string
♦기타에 줄을 달다 string [restring] a guitar / 줄을 죄다 tighten the string / 줄을 퉁기다 twang the strings
▶줄이 끊어졌다 The string snapped.
3 〈선〉 a line
♦가는[굵은] 줄 a thin [thick] line
▶그는 종이에 굽은[곧은] 줄을 한 줄 그었다 He drew a curved [straight] line on the paper.
4 〈글의 행〉 a line
♦한 줄씩 건너 쓰다 write on every other line
▶여기서 줄을 바꾸는 것이 좋다 You should begin a new line here.
5 〈열〉 a row; a line; a file; a rank
♦한 줄로 늘어선 나무들 a line of trees / 두 줄로 서다 stand in two rows
▶줄을 서서 기다려라 Wait in (a) row.

▶ 나는 앞에서 다섯째 줄에 앉았다 I sat in the fifth row.
▶ 우리는 줄을 지었다 We formed a line [queue].
6 〈무늬〉 a stripe; a streak; a band
♦ 줄진 바지 striped trousers / 흰 바탕에 파란 줄이 있는 striped in blue on a white ground
7 〈관계〉 a connection; relations
▶ 그는 줄을 찾고 있다 He is looking for an introducer [intermediary].
8 〈나이〉 ♦ 30줄의 남자 a man in his thirties / 60줄에 접어들다 enter the sixties
9 〈광맥〉 a vein (of ore)
♦ 줄이 풀리다 strike a better vein of ore
10 〈쾀·엮음〉 a string (of)
♦ 건어 한 줄 a string of dried fish

줄² 〈연장〉 a file; a rasp ♦ 줄로 쓸다 file; rasp (off, away) / 줄로 쓸어 미끈하게 하다 file *sth* smooth / 줄로 쓸어 까슬까슬한 데를 없애다 file away roughnesses

줄³ **1** 〈방법〉 how to (do); the way
♦ 헤엄칠 줄 알다 know how to swim; can swim / 글을 쓸 줄 모른다 do not know how to write
▶ 그녀는 프랑스어를 좀 할 줄 안다 She has some knowledge of French.
▶ 앞으로는 컴퓨터를 다룰 줄 모르면 출세할 수 없다 From now on, we cannot succeed without a knowledge of computers [unless we know how to use computers].
▶ 그는 아무것도 할 줄 모른다 He is good for nothing.
2 〈셈속〉 (the fact) that
▶ 난 네가 자는 줄 알았다 I thought you were sleeping.
▶ 널 여기서 만날 줄이야 Little did I dream [expect] that I should see you here.
▶ 네가 올 줄은 미처 몰랐다 I had no idea that you would come.
▶ 네가 이것을 만든 줄을 내가 어찌 알겠니? How should I know that you made this?
▶ 그 사람이 간첩일 줄이야 To hear that he is a spy!
▶ 하도 추워서 얼어 죽는 줄 알았다 It was terribly cold, and I thought I would be frozen to death.
▶ 누구나 제 똥 구린 줄은 모른다 People are blind to their own defects.

줄거리 **1** 〈줄기〉 a bare stalk [stem]
2 〈골자〉 an outline; a plot; a summary; a synopsis (*pl.* -ses)
♦ 연극의 줄거리 the plot of a play / 〈연재 소설의〉 전회까지의 줄거리 the story so far / 줄거리가 복잡한[간단한] (a novel) of a complicated [simple] plot
▶ 그 영화의 간단한 줄거리는 신문에서 읽었다 I read a brief plot of the film in the newspaper.
▶ 그녀는 소설의 줄거리를 말했다 She gave an outline of the novel.

줄걷다 〈광대가〉 walk (on) a tightrope
줄걸리다 〈줄을 타게 하다〉 have 《a funambulist》 walk a tightrope
줄곧 all the time [way]; (all) through; throughout; all along; all during 《the vacation》; continuously; ceaselessly
♦ 줄곧 서 있다 stand [keep standing] all the time
▶ 나는 오전 중 줄곧 공부했다 I worked all through the morning.
▶ 열차는 대구까지 줄곧 만원이었다 The train was crowded all the way to Taegu.
▶ 지금까지 줄곧 어디 있었니? Where have you been all the time [all this while]?
▶ 그의 비밀을 줄곧 알고 있었다 I knew his secret all along.
▶ 나는 여름 휴가 동안 줄곧 미국에 있었다 I stayed in the U.S. throughout the summer vacation.

줄긋다 〈줄을 치다〉 draw a line; 〈괘선을〉 rule [draw] lines 《on》; rule 《paper》 with lines; 〈밑줄을〉 underline; 〈줄을 그어 지우다〉 line through
▶ 다음 문장의 틀린 데를 줄그어 지워라 Put a line through the mistakes in the following sentence.

줄기 **1** 〈나무의〉 a trunk; 〈초목의〉 a stalk; a stem; a cane; a haulm
2 〈물의〉 a course; a stream; a watercourse
♦ 강줄기 the course of a river
3 〈산의〉 a range ♦ 산줄기 a range of mountains
4 〈소나기의〉 a shower; a downpour
▶ 소나기가 한 줄기 올 것 같다 It looks like we're in for a bit of a downpour.
5 〈줄〉 a line; a stripe; a streak; a column 《of smoke》
♦ 한 줄기의 광선 a streak [ray] of light

줄기줄기 〈냇물이〉 in streams [streamlets]; 〈산이〉 in ranges [chains]
▶ 물이 줄기줄기 흐른다 The water flows in streamlets.
▶ 산이 줄기줄기 뻗어 있다 The mountain spreads out in ranges.

줄기차다 〈억세다〉 vigorous; exuberant; 〈끈질기다〉 tenacious; untiring; 〈끊임없다〉 incessant; continuous
♦ 줄기차게 vigorously; tenaciously; incessantly / 줄기차게 비가 내리다 rain hard; pour down / 줄기차게 노력하다 persevere in *one's* efforts / 줄기차게 항거하다 offer a stubborn [stout] resistance 《to》
▶ 그의 줄기찬 노력이 성공으로 이어졌다 His steady effort(s) led to his success.
▶ 소문이 줄기차게 나돌고 있었다 Wild reports flew thick and fast.

줄나다 〈표준 수량보다 덜 나다〉 be produced in less than estimated quantity; fall short of the production goal off

줄넘기 〈줄을 돌리는〉 rope skipping; 〈줄을 치고 하는〉 rope jumping
—**줄넘기하다** skip [jump] (a) rope; turn a skipping rope
▶ 나는 아이들과 줄넘기를 했다 I skipped rope with the children.
■ —줄 a skipping [jump] rope

줄눈 〔建〕 a joint 《of a wall》
줄다 〈양이〉 become less; lessen; 〈수가〉 become fewer; 〈조금씩 감소하다〉 decrease;

〈저하하다〉 fall off; 〈쇠약해지다〉 decline; 〈차츰 줄다가 없어짐〉 dwindle; 〈점점 작아지다〉 diminish; be reduced; go down; run low; abate; subside; 〈의복 등이〉 shrink; 〈단축되다〉 be shortened [abbreviated]
♦가치[수, 양]가 줄다 decrease in value [number, quantity] / 3분의 1로 줄다 be reduced to one-third / 체중이 줄다 lose weight / (빨아도) 줄지 않는 unshrinkable
▶ 사고 횟수가 줄었다 Accidents have decreased in number [become fewer].
▶ 인구는 점점 줄고 있다 The population is decreasing [on the decrease].
▶ 우물물이 줄었다 The water in the well has got low.
▶ 강물이 준다 The river sinks.
▶ 나는 체중이 4킬로그램 줄었다 I have lost weight by four kilograms. ⇒ I have lost four kilograms (in weight).
▶ 자동차의 수출이 1할 줄었다 The export of cars has decreased [fallen off] by 10 percent.
▶ 이것은 빨아도 줄지 않는다 This won't shrink in the wash.

줄다리기 a tug of war
―**줄다리기하다** play at a tug of war

줄달다 continue; occur in succession; follow one after another ⇨ 연달다
♦ 줄달아 continuously; without intermission [a break]; successively; in a row [line]
▶ 나는 8년간 줄달아 이 일을 하고 있다 I have been doing this work [job] for eight (consecutive) years.
▶ 주식 시장은 줄달아 활황이다 The stock market continuously shows signs of activity.
▶ 손님이 줄달았다 We received a cascade [stream] of visitors.

줄달음질 running fast; dashing; darting
―**줄달음질 하다**[치다] run fast [hard]; rush; dash; dart
▶ 불이야 하고 누군가 소리지르자, 사람들은 입구를 향해 줄달음질쳤다 "Fire!" someone cried, and people rushed [dashed] for the door.

줄대다 continue; go on; keep on; follow one after another; run [follow] without intermission [interruption]
♦ 줄대어 서다 stand in a row [line, queue]
▶ 사건이 줄대어 일어났다 Accidents occured one after another.
▶ 사흘을 줄대어 비가 내리고 있다 It's been raining for three straight [consecutive, successive] days. ⇒ It's been raining for three days straight [on end, in a row].

줄드리다 1 〈늘어뜨리다〉 hang down a rope
2 〈꼬다〉 make [twist, strand] a rope; twist threads into a string

줄띄우다 stretch (out) a rope (to measure the height [distance, angle]) 《of》

줄먹줄먹하다 of various sizes; various in size

줄멍줄멍 unevenly ⇨ 졸망졸망

줄모 〈農〉 rice seedlings transplanted in check rows

줄목 the key [essential, vital] point

줄무늬 stripes; a striped pattern
♦ 줄무늬 바지[천] striped trousers [cloth] / 줄무늬가 있는 striped

줄무더기 〈잡동사니〉 a medley; a motley (of colo(u)rs); a patchwork; 〈연줄〉 a kite string pieced together

줄밑걷다 inquire into 《the origin》; follow up 《a clue》; trace (up)

줄바둑 an unskillful *paduk* playing; (play) a poor game of *paduk*
■―꾼 a poor [unskillful] player of *paduk*

줄밥 〈줄질할 때의 부스러기〉 filings

줄방귀 a succession of flatuses; successive farts

줄방석 ―方席 a rush cushion [scat mat]

줄불 a string of (fire) crackers

줄사닥다리 a rope ladder

줄어들다 shrink; contract; shorten; dwindle (away); diminish (in size) ⇨ 줄다
▶ 모직을 뜨거운 물에 빨면 줄어든다 Wool shrinks when washed in hot water.
▶ 이 금속은 냉각되어도 줄어들지 않는다 This metal won't contract in cooling.
▶ 근년에 지원자의 수가 현저히 줄어들었다 The number of applicants has decreased [fallen off] sharply in recent years.
▶ 강물이 줄어들었다 The water in the river has gotten low. ⇒ The river has sunk.

줄이다 reduce; decrease; diminish; lessen; shorten; cut short; cut (down); curtail; economize; contract; boil down; abbreviate; abridge
♦ 목숨을 줄이다 shorten *one's* life / 기간을 줄이다 reduce the term / 예산을 줄이다 make a retrenchment in the budget / 생산량을 줄이다 curtail productions / 비용을 줄이다 reduce [cut down] expenses / 생활비를 줄이다 take in *one's* living cost / 옷의 기장을 줄이다 take in [shorten] a garment / 문장의 길이를 3분의 1로 줄이다 condense [cut down] a passage to a third of its length
▶ 그는 담배의 양을 줄였다 He has cut down on [reduced the number of] the cigarettes he smokes.
▶ 우리는 금년에는 쌀의 생산을 줄이지 않을 수 없었다 We had to reduce [cut back on] the production of rice this year.
▶ 체중을 줄이고 싶으면 간식을 먹지 마라 If you want to lose weight, don't eat between meals.

줄자 a tape (measure); a tapeline

줄잡다 make a conservative [moderate] estimate 《of》; estimate 《a cost》 low; underestimate
♦ 줄잡아서 on a conservative estimate; at a moderate estimate; moderately / 아무리 줄잡아도 at the lowest estimate / 줄잡아 평가해서 on a conservative basis (of appraisement)
▶ 그의 재산은 줄잡아 평가해도 1억원 쯤은 된다 A conservative estimate of the value of his property is about a hundred million won.
▶ 비용은 아무리 줄잡아도 100만원이 된다 The expenses will come to one million won at the most conservative [lowest] estimate.
▶ 손해는 줄잡아 천만원이다 The amount of damage is conservatively estimated at ten

million won.

줄줄¹ 〈계속 흐르는 모양〉 in streams; running ♦땀을 줄줄 흘리다 perspire profusely / 침을 줄줄 흘리다 drivel freely; dribble ▶지붕에서 물이 줄줄 샌다 The roof leaks badly. ⇒ The roof has a bad leak. ▶그의 얼굴에서 땀이 줄줄 흐른다 His face is dripping with perspiration. ▶상처에서 피가 줄줄 흘렀다 Blood trickled from the wound.

줄줄² 〈막힘없는 모양〉 smoothly (and easily); without a hitch; fluently; flowingly ♦시를 줄줄 외다 recite a poem fluently

줄줄이 in row after row; in rows; all lines [rows]

줄짓다 stand in (a) line [row]; form in (a) line; line up; rank ♦노점이 줄지어 선 거리 a street lined with stalls / 일렬로 줄짓다 stand in a line / 두 줄로 줄짓다 form [stand in] two lines / 줄지어 서다 stand in a row; 〈차례를 기다려〉 queue [line] up ▶그 거리에는 건물들이 줄지어 있다 A row of buildings lines the street. ▶많은 노점들이 그 거리에 줄지어 있다 A lot of stalls line the street. ▶많은 사람이 버스를 타려고 줄지어 기다리고 있었다 A lot of people were waiting in line for [to get on] the bus. ▶좋은 자리를 잡으려면 일찍부터 줄지어 서야 한다 We must queue up early in order to get a good seat.

줄치다 1 draw a line ⇨ 줄긋다 2 〈밧줄 등을〉 stretch a rope 《around a place》; 〈거미가〉 weave a web

줄타기 rope dancing [walking]; a tightrope feat [act] ♦줄타기를 하다 ⇨ 줄타다 / 위태위태한 줄타기를 하다 run a risk; make a risky attempt; engage in a touch-and-go business ▶원숭이는 줄타기를 잘한다 Monkeys are very good at walking on a tightrope. ▶위험한 줄타기는 그만두는 것이 좋아 You'd better not take a risk. ■―광대[곡예사] a funambulist; a tightrope walker [dancer]

줄타다 walk a tightrope; walk [dance] on a tightrope

줄팔매질 (stone-)slinging; a sling (of a stone) ―**줄팔매질하다** sling a stone

줄표 ―標 dash

줄행랑 ―行廊 1 〈행랑채〉 the front wing of a house; the servants' quarters 2 〈도망〉 abscondence; decampment; bolt ♦줄행랑치다 abscond; decamp; run away [off]; make off; take flight ▶범인은 해외로 줄행랑치기 직전에 잡혔다 The criminal was arrested just before he ran away overseas [fled the country].

줌 1 〈주먹〉 a fist 2 〈움큼〉 a handful; a fistful ♦소금 한 줌 a handful of salt 3 ⇨ 줌통

줌렌즈 〈가변 초점 거리 렌즈〉 a zoom lens

줌밖에나다 get out of sb's hands [control, power]; become uncontrollable [unmanageable, ungovernable] ♦아무의 줌밖에 나다 be freed from [slip out of] sb's grasp

줌벌다 be too big to take [hold] in one handful; be too many [much] to take [get] hold of

줌안에들다 fall into sb's hands [possession, control, power]; slip into sb's grasp [clutches]; be at the mercy 《of》 ▶그는 내 줌안에 들어 있다 I have him in my clutches.

줌통 a handgrip (of a bow)

줍다 pick up; 〈채집하다〉 gather 《shells》; 〈발견하다〉 find 《a purse》 ♦주운 물건 a thing picked up [found]; a find / 떨어진 이삭을 줍다 glean; gather ears of corn / 거리에서 지갑을 줍다 find a purse on the street / 정원에 흩어져 있는 종잇조각을 줍다 pick up the scraps of paper scattered about in the garden / 밤 주우러 가다 go chestnutting [gathering chestnuts] ▶소녀는 몇 개의 조가비를 주웠다 The girl picked up [gathered] several seashells. ▶이 지갑을 문 앞에서 주웠다 I found this wallet in front of the gate.

줏대 主― 〈확고히 정해진 의견〉 fixed opinion; 〈명확한 생각〉 a definite views; 〈지론〉 firm convictions; 〈기개〉 (the) backbone; moral fiber; firmness of character ▶그녀는 줏대가 있는 사람이다 She has firm convictions. ▶그는 줏대가 없다 He has no [lacks] backbone [moral fiber].

중 a Buddhist priest; a bonze; a monk ♦중이 되다 become a priest [monk]; enter the priesthood

중¹ 中 1 〈중앙〉 the center; the middle 2 〈중위〉 medium; average ♦중키의 사람 a man of medium [middle] height / 중 이상이[이하가] 되다 rise above [fall below] mediocrity ▶그녀의 학력은 중상[중하] 정도다 She is a little above [below] average in academic ability.

중² 中 1 〈…가운데〉 in; between; among; of; amidst; out of ▶셋 중에 누가 제일 나이가 많으냐? Who is the oldest of the three? ▶이것들 중에서 하나를 택해라 Choose one from among these. ▶나는 월급 중에서 저금하고 있다 I save out of my wages. ▶십중 팔구 그녀는 오지 않을 것이다 In nine cases out of ten she won't come. ▶20명 중 5명이 시험에 합격했다 Five out of twenty people passed the test. ▶열명이 합격했는데 나도 그 중의 하나다 Ten have passed, myself among the rest [number]. ▶그들은 모두 많은 학생 중에서 뽑힌 우수한 학생이다 They are all outstanding students chosen from among many. 2 〈…의 속〉 in; through ♦공중을 날다 fly in [through] the air. 3 〈…동안에〉 during; in (the course of); throughout; while; for

-중 ▶ 당신 부재 중에 이 편지가 왔소 This letter arrived in [during] your absence. ⇌ I received this letter while you were away. ▶ 오전 중에 죽 집에 있었다 I was at home all through [in] the morning. ▶ 그들은 수업 중이다 They are in class. **4** 〈…의 상태에 있다, 진행 중이다〉 under; in process [course] of ♦ 건설 중인 도로 a road under construction ▶ 그는 새 소설을 집필 중이다 He is at work on a new novel. ▶ 그 다리는 지금 건설 중이다 The bridge is now under construction. ▶ 그것은 아직 쓰는 중이다 I have not yet finished writing it. ▶ 통화 중입니다 The line is busy. ⇌ (英) The number is engaged.

-중 -重 fold ♦ 2중의 twofold; double / 3중의 threefold; treble; triple / 2중으로 겹치다 put one above the other ▶ 화병을 2중으로 포장하게 했다 I had a double wrapping put around the vase.

중가 重價 a high price ⇨ 중값

중간 中間 the middle; midway ♦ 중간의〈위치가 한 가운데의〉middle; mean; 〈거리가〉halfway; 〈장소·정도가〉intermediate; 〈시기가 잠정적으로〉interim / 중간에 in [at] the middle (of); halfway; midway / …의 중간에 있다 lie (midway, halfway) between… / …의 중간에 서다[들다] mediate between…; act as go-between for 《two parties》 ▶ 우리 학교는 그 두 지점의 중간쯤에 있다 Our school lies somewhere in between the two places. ▶ 그는 언제나 중간 입장을 취한다 He always takes [holds] the middle position. ━ 노선 a middle-(of-the-)road line; neutrality: 중간 노선을 걷다 take [follow] the middle-road course; steer a neutral course ━ 무역 intermediate trade ━ 보고 an interim report ━ 상인 a middleman; a broker ━ 선거 (美) an off-year election ━ 숙주 intermediary host ━ 시험[고사] a midterm examination ━ 역 an intermediate station; (美) a way station ━ 음 (樂) an intertone; an intermediate tone ━ 이득 intermediary profiteering ━ 정책 a middle-(of-the-)road policy ━ 착취 intermediary exploitation; kickback ━ 층 the middle class(es); the middlebrows ━ 파 neutrals; the middle-(of-the-)roaders ━ 휴식 a rest; a recess; a break; 〈경기의〉half time: 중간 휴식을 하다 take a rest; have a recess

중간 重刊 〈거듭 간행함〉republication; reprint; reissue ━ 하다 republish; reprint; reissue

중간색 中間色 neutral tints

중간자 中間子 〔物〕 a meson; a mesotron ♦ 중간자의 mesonic; mesotronic

중간치 中間— 〈중치〉medium [in-between] things [sizes, prices, quality]; a medium

중갈이 中— 〔農〕 〈푸성귀〉vegetables out of season

중갑판 中甲板 the middle deck

♦ 중갑판에 나가다 go on the middle deck

중값 重— 〈비싼 값〉a high [great, prohibitive] price ♦ 사치품의 중값 prohibitive prices on luxuries

중개 仲介 intermediation; 〈조정〉mediation; agency ▶ 변호사가 노사의 중개 역할을 했다 The lawyer mediated [acted as a mediator] between the union and the company. ▶ 강선생의 중개로 우리는 화해했다 We compromised by [through] the good offices of Mr. Kang. ━ 중개하다 mediate [intermediate] (between two parties) ■ ━ 국 a mediating power ━ 무역 merchant [commission, intermediary] trade ━ 물 a medium; a channel ━ 수수료 brokerage (commission) ━ 업 brokerage (business); agency ━ 자 ⇨ 중개인 ━ 판매 sale on commission

중개인 仲介人 a mediator; an intermediary; a go-between; 〈주선인〉an agent; a commission agent [broker]; a broker; a middleman ♦ 중개인을 통하여 through an agent / 중개인을 통하지 않고 without [minus] a middleman

중거리 中距離 ■ ━ 경주 a middle-distance race ━ 선수 a middle-distance runner ━ 탄도탄 an intermediate range ballistic missile 《略 IRBM》

중견 中堅 〈중심 세력〉the backbone; the mainstay; the nucleus; 〈의지가 되는 기둥〉pillar; 〔軍〕the main body; 〔野〕center field ▶ 40대는 이 회사의 중견이다 Those in their forties are [form] the backbone of this company. ▶ 그의 형은 회사의 중견이 되었다 His brother proved himself the backbone of his company. ■ ━ 간부 a leading [principal] member 《of a company》 ━ 수 〔野〕a center fielder ━ 인물 the nucleus; a leader; an animating spirit; a leading figure ━ 작가 a writer of medium standing

중경상 重輕傷 〈중상과 경상〉a serious or slight injury [wound]; 《suffer》a major or minor injury ▶ 10명이 중경상을 입었다 Ten people were injured either slightly or seriously.

중계 中繼 〈중간에서 이어줌〉relay; 〈라디오·텔레비전의〉relay broadcasting ⇨ 중계방송; 〔電〕translation ━ 중계하다 relay; rebroadcast; translate ▶ 서울 올림픽은 위성 중계되었다 The Seoul Olympic Games were televised by satellite transmission. ▶ 그 콘서트는 런던에서 위성 중계되었다 The concert was broadcast from London by [via] satellite. ■ ━ 무대 a stage relay broadcast; a drama relayed from the stage ━ 실황 ━ 실황방송 주 ━ 《via》the space relay 현장 ━ relay from the spot ■ ━ 국 a relay station ━ 무역 transit [intermediate] trade ━ 선 a junction line ━ 항 a transit port; a port of transit; an intermediate port ━ 회로 a junction circuit

중계방송 中繼放送 relay broadcasting; re-

broadcasting; a relay broadcast; a rebroadcast; (美) hookup
▶이 프로는 중계방송으로 보내드리고 있습니다 This program comes to you by relay broadcast.
—중계방송하다 relay; rebroadcast; translate ■전국— broadcasting over a nationwide hookup [network]: 텔레비전의 전국 중계방송에서 총리는 소신을 피력했다 Speaking to a nationwide TV audience [On a nationwide TV hookup], the prime minister made a speech on his general policy.

중고 中古 1 the Middle Ages; medieval times
♦중고의 medieval
2 〈중고품〉 secondhand [(slightly) used] goods
♦중고의 slightly used [old]; secondhand / 중고 옷가지 worn clothes / 신품이나 다름없는 중고 an article slightly used but almost brand-new [as good as new] / 중고를 사다 buy *sth* secondhand [at second hand]
▶나는 벼룩시장에서 중고 바이올린을 샀다 I bought a used [secondhand] violin at the flea market.
■—사[문학] medieval history [literature]
—차 a used car

중공 中共 Communist China ⇨ 중국
중공 中空 〈중천〉 midair; 〈내부가 비어있음〉 hollowness ♦중공의 hollow; empty; fistulous / 중공에 in midair; in the air

중공업 重工業 heavy industries
♦중공업 도시 a city with heavy industry / 중공업 회사 a heavy industry company

중과 衆寡 〈수효의 많음과 적음〉 large and small numbers ▶우리는 중과 부적이다 We are outnumbered [overcome in number]. ⇌ There is no contending against such heavy [big] odds.

중과실 重過失 〔法〕 gross negligence
중구 中歐 〈중부 유럽〉 Central Europe
중구 衆口 〈뭇입〉 popular criticism; public rumor ▶중구난방이다 You can't shut the doors of people's mouths. ⇌ There is no silencing Mrs. Grundy. ⇌ Grundyism is an annoying thing indeed.

중국 中國 China; 〈중화민국〉 the Republic of China; 〈중화 인민공화국〉 the People's Republic of China; (古·詩) Cathay
♦두 개의 중국 the two Chinas / 중국을 좋아하는[싫어하는] 사람 a Sinophile [Sinophobe]
▶자유— the Nationalist China; Free China —공산당 the Chinese Communist Party; 〈당원〉 the Chinese Communists —어 Chinese; the Chinese language —옷 a China dress; a Chinese suit [robe] —인 a Chinese; (총칭) the Chinese —인가(街) a Chinatown; the Chinese quarter —통(通) an authority on Chinese affairs; a person versed in things Chinese —학 sinology; study of things Chinese [Chinese culture]

중궁(전) 中宮(殿) 〈왕후의 높임말〉 the Queen
중권 中卷 〈가운데 권〉 the middle [second] volume [book] (of a set of three)
중근동 中近東 the Middle and Near East
중금속 重金屬 〔化〕 a heavy metal

중금주의 重金主義 〔經〕 the mercantile system
중급 中級 an intermediate grade
♦중급의 medium; of the middle class [intermediate rank] / 중급 코스 the intermediate course
▶나는 프랑스어의 중급 강의를 택했다 I took the intermediate course in French.
■—품 fair average quality; an article of medium quality; middlings

중기 中期 〈중간의 시기〉 the middle period; 〔生〕〈세포분열의〉 the metaphase
▶15세기 중기 the mid-fifteenth century

중기 重機 1 〈중공업용의 기계〉 heavy machinery 2 ⇨ 중기관총
중기관총 重機關銃 〔軍〕 a heavy machine gun
중길 中— middlings
중남미 中南美 Central and South America
♦중남미 음악 Latin-American music

중년 中年 〈청년과 노년 사이의 나이〉 middle age [life]; *one's* middle years
♦중년을 넘은 여자 a woman past middle age; an elderly woman / 중년의 middle-aged; in middle life
▶그는 중년을 넘어 있다 He is past his middle age.
■—기 the middle years of *one's* life —부인 a woman in middle age; a middle-aged woman —신사 a middle-aged gentleman —층 the middle-aged; the middle generation

중노동 重勞動 heavy [hard] labor
♦중노동을 하다 engage [be engaged] in heavy labor
▶그는 중노동 2년의 형을 받았다 He was sentenced to two years at hard labor.
■—자 a heavy worker

중노인 中老人 an elderly man ⇨ 늙은이
중농 中農 a middle-class[-scale] farmer
중농정책 重農政策 an agriculture-first policy
중농주의 重農主義 〔經〕 physiocracy; physiocratism ■—자 a physiocrat
중뇌 中腦 〔解〕 the midbrain; the mesencephalon (*pl.* -la)

중늙은이 中— an elderly man; a person in advanced middle age ♦중늙은이의 elderly / 중늙은이 신사 an elderly gentleman

중단 中段 〈상·하단에 대하여〉 the middle tier; 〈계단의〉 the middle of the stairs; 〈배·열차 등의 침대의〉 the middle berth [bunk]; 〈글의〉 the middle part of a writing [book]

중단 中斷 interruption; discontinuance; suspension; a break
♦대화[교통]의 중단 a lull in the conversation [traffic]
—중단하다 〈멈추다〉 stop; 〈계속하고 있는 것을〉 discontinue; 〈방해하다〉 interrupt; 〈일시적으로〉 suspend; 〈중지하다〉 break (off)
♦평화교섭을 중단하다 break off peace negotiations / 중단되다 be interrupted [suspended, discontinued]
▶그 프로는 임시 뉴스 속보 때문에 중단되었다 The program was interrupted by a special news flash.
▶그 소란으로 연주는 중단되었다 The concert

was interrupted by the uproar.
■ 시효— 〔法〕 interruption of prescription
중대 中隊 a company ♦ 보병 중대 an infantry company / 공병 중대 an engineer company / 포병 중대 an artillery battery / 비행 중대 a squadron ■—장 a company commander; a squadron leader
중대 重大 importance; gravity; seriousness; magnitude
—중대하다 important; serious; grave; (a matter) of great [vital] importance
♦ 중대한 과실 gross negligence; a gross mistake; a vital error / 중대한 결과 grave consequences / 중대한 문제 an important problem; a serious [vital] question; a grave issue [subject] / 중대한 결과를 가져오다 lead to a grave consequence
▶ 살충제의 남용은 중대한 문제가 되었다 The overuse of insecticides has become a serious problem.
▶ 그는 중대한 사명을 띠고 있다 He is charged with an important mission.
■—관심사 a matter of the utmost [gravest] concern —사(건) a serious affair [happening, case]; an important [a grave] matter —성 importance; gravity; seriousness —성명 an important statement [announcement]; 중대 성명을 발표하다 announce [make public] a serious statement —책임 grave responsibility
중대가리 〈빡빡 깎은 머리〉 a shaved [shaven] head; 〈사람〉 a shaven-headed person
중대문 中大門 〈중문〉 an inner gate
중대시하다 重大視— attach great importance to; take a serious view of; regard sth as serious ▶ 그는 그녀의 행동을 중대시하고 있다 He is taking a grave view of her conduct.
중대화하다 重大化— become serious; aggravate; assume great importance
중덜거리다 〈불평하다〉 grumble (at, about, over); complain (of); mutter (at, against); murmur (at, against); 〈美口〉 grouch
▶ 노인은 무엇가 아내에게 중덜거렸다 The old man grumbled at his wife, muttering something.
중도 中途 halfway; midway; midcourse
♦ 중도에서 halfway; midway; unfinished; in the middle
▶ 물건을 잊어버리고 와서 중도에서 되돌아 왔다 As I left something behind, I turned back halfway.
▶ 우리는 일단 일을 시작하면 중도에서 그만두어서는 안된다 Once we begin [set about] some work, we must not leave it unfinished [half done].
■—퇴학 leaving school in midcourse: 중도퇴학하다 give up school; leave school in midcourse [without finishing the whole course] —퇴학자 a school dropout
중도 中道 〈가던 길의 중간〉 the middle of a road; the middle path; 〈중용〉 the golden mean; the middle road (between two extremes); mean; 〈온당함〉 moderation
♦ 중도를 걷다[지키다] take [follow] the golden [happy] mean; take the middle-of-the-road [a moderate] course
▶ 그는 중도를 걷는다 He is a middle-of-the-roader.
■—정치 (美) middle-of-the-road politics —파 a Centrist; (美) a middle-(of-the-)roader
중독 中毒 〈독물·가스 등의〉 poisoning; toxication; 〈마약 등의 상습벽〉 addiction; 〔醫〕 intoxication
♦ 중독성의 poisonous; toxic / 중독 증세를 나타내다 develop [present, show] toxic symptoms / 중독되다 be [get] poisoned
▶ 그는 마약 중독이다 He is a drug addict. ⇒ He is suffering from narcotic poisoning [drug addiction].
▶ 코카인을 상용하면 중독이 된다 Habitual use of cocaine causes toxicosis.
■ 수은— mercurial [mercury] poisoning; hydrargyrism 식— food poisoning; poisoning from eating 아편— opiumism; opium poisoning 알코올— alcoholism; addiction to alcohol; alcoholic poisoning ■—사 death from poisoning —증 toxicosis (pl. -coses)
중동 中 〈사물의 중간 부분〉 the middle part (of a thing); the central part; the middle; 〈허리 부분〉 the waist (of the garment) ♦ 중동을 두 토막으로 자르다 cut in two in the middle / 생선의 중동 the center out of fish / (옷이) 중동이 긴[짧은] long-[short-] waisted
—끈 〈허리띠〉 a waistband; a waist sash
중동 中東 the Middle East; the Mideast
♦ 중동의 Middle Eastern; Mideastern / 중동 제국 the countries in the Middle East; the Mideastern countries
■—사태 the Middle East situation —전쟁 the Middle East war
중동 仲冬 〈한겨울〉 the eleventh lunar month; midwinter
중동무이 中 〈중간에서 흐지부지함〉 stopping halfway; leaving sth half done [unfinished]
♦ 중동무이의 half-finished; unfinished; halfway; incomplete
—중동무이하다 do sth by halves; leave sth unfinished [half done]; stop [give up] (working) halfway
중등 中等 〈가운데 등급〉 the middle [second] class; the secondary grade; 〈가운데 질〉 medium [average] quality; 〈중위〉 common standard; mediocrity; the average
♦ 중등의 middle(-class); medium; moderate; middling; mediocre; average / 〈성적 등이〉 중등 이상[이하]이다 be above [below] mediocrity [the average]
■—교원 a secondary school teacher —교육 secondary education —품 an article of medium [average] quality; medium(-quality [-grade]) goods; middles —학교 a secondary school; a school of secondary grade; a middle [high] school
중략 中略 〈글의 중간을 줄임〉 an ellipsis (pl. -lipses); an omission (of interior parts); 〔文法〕 a syncope; syncopation
—중략하다 omit part of a sentence [passage, paragraph]; omit; skip; syncopate
중량 重量 weight

◆중량이 모자라다 be short of weight; be underweight; weigh less than (it) should / 중량을 속이다 give short weight [measure]; cheat on weight / 중량을 속이지 않다 give honest weight
▶이 상자는 중량이 5킬로그램 나간다 This box weighs [The weight of this box is] five kilograms.
■총[정미]— gross [net] weight ■—감각 weight sensation —부족[초과] short weight [overweight] —제한 weight [美] load] limits —톤 a deadweight ton —화물 weight cargo; heavy [hard] goods

중량급 中量級 〔競〕the middleweight division [class]

중량급 重量級 〔競〕the heavy weight division [class]
—권투 선수 a heavyweight boxer

중력 重力 〈지구 인력〉gravity; 〈중력의 작용〉(terrestrial) gravitation
◆중력의 법칙 the law of gravity [gravitation] / 무중력상태 a state [the condition] of nongravitation [weightlessness]; a gravity-free state
▶그는 우주의 무중력 상태에서 거꾸로 떠 있다 He is suspended upside down in the weightlessness of space.
■—가속도 the acceleration of gravity —계 a gravimeter —단위 a gravitational unit —장 (場) the gravity field —전지 a gravity cell [battery] —파 a gravity [gravitational] wave

중령 中領 〈육군·해병〉(美) a lieutenant colonel; (英) a lieutenant-colonel; 〈해군〉 a commander; 〈공군〉(美) a lieutenant colonel; (英) a wing commander

중로 中老 an elderly man ⇨ 중늙은이

중론 衆論 〈여러 사람의 의논〉consultation; public discussion; 〈여러 사람의 의견〉a majority opinion; a consensus of opinion
◆중론에 따르다 act according to a majority opinion / 중론에 묻다 refer (a matter) to public discussion

중류 中流 1〈강의〉midstream; 〈상류·하류에 대한〉the middle reaches [courses]; the middle of a river
▶그 강은 중류가 얕다 The river is shallow in midstream.
2〈사회의〉the middle class(es)
—가정 a middle-class family —계급 the middle classes

중립 中立 neutrality; neutralization; 〈국외 중립·불개입〉indifference
◆중립의, 중립적인 neutral; 〈의원 등의〉independent / 중립적인 사람 a neutral person; a neutral; a fence-sitter / 중립을 지키다 observe [keep, maintain] neutrality / 중립노선을 따르다 follow [take] the neutral [neutralist] line / 중립적인 태도를 취하다 stand neutral; take a neutral attitude / 그 문제에 중립적 태도를 취하다 take a neutral attitude toward the problem; stand neutral in the problem
■무장[엄정, 우호적]— armed [strict, friendly] neutrality ■—선언 a declaration of neutrality —의원 an independent; a neutral member; (英) a crossbencher —정책 a neutrality [neutralist] policy —조약 a neutrality pact —지대 a neutral zone —파 a neutral party; middle-(of-the-)roaders

중립국 中立國 a neutral power [state, country]; a neutral; a neutralist [an unaligned, a noncommitted] nation
■—감시위원회 the Neutral Nations Supervisory Commission (略 NNSC) —기[선박] a neutral flag [ship]

중립주의 中立主義 neutralism ◆중립주의의 neutralist ■비무장[적극적]— disarmed [positive] neutralism ■—자 a neutralist

중립화 中立化 neutralization —중립화하다 neutralize; 〈국가가〉turn neutralist
■비— deneutralization

중망 衆望 〈여망〉popularity; 〈신임〉public confidence; 〈기대〉popular expectation
◆중망에 부응하다 meet [live up to] the expectations of the people / 중망을 얻고 있다 be popular (among, with); enjoy popularity [public confidence] (with, among)

중매 仲媒 matchmaking
◆…의 중매로 through sb's good offices; through the good offices of... / 남에게 중매를 부탁하다 ask another to act as (a) go-between / 중매들다, 중매서다 arrange a match ⇨ 중매하다
—중매하다 arrange a match (between); act as (a) go-between [a middleman]; go between (two parties)
■—결혼 a marriage made up by a go-between; an arranged match —인[쟁이] a matchmaker; a go-between; a middleman

중매 仲買 〈업(業)〉brokerage; 〈사람〉a broker; a commission merchant [agent]
—중매하다 act as a broker
—구전[수수료] (a) brokerage (on bills); a commission —인 a broker; a middleman; a commission merchant [agent] —점 a brokerage house [firm]

중문 中門 〈대문 안의 문〉an inner gate

중문 重文 〔文法〕a compound sentence

중미 中美 Central America ◆중미의 Central American / 중미의 나라 a Central American country / 중미의 사람들 Central Americans

중반전 中盤戰 〈선거 등의〉the middle phase (of an election campaign); 〈바둑·장기의〉the middle of the game
▶대통령 선거도 이제 중반전에 들어갔다 The presidential election is now at its height.

중방 中枋 a horizontal wall strut ⇨ 중인방(中引枋)

중배 中— 1〈중복(中腹)〉the bulging part (of); the belly; the bilge
◆독의 중배 the belly of a pot / 통의 중배 the bilge of a barrel / 중배(가) 부르다 be bulged out [swollen] in the middle; have a bulge [swelling] in the middle; be potbellied
2〈맏배 다음 새끼〉a middle litter (of pigs)

중배엽 中胚葉 〔生〕the mesoderm; the mesoblast

중벌 重罰 〈무거운 징벌〉a heavy [severe] punishment ◆중벌에 처하다 punish sb severe-

ly; inflict a severe punishment 《on *sb*》
▶ 그런 일은 중벌에 처해 마땅하다 A thing like that deserves severe punishment.

중범 重犯 1 〈중대 범죄〉 a major offense; a serious crime; 〔法〕 felony **2** 〈죄를 거듭 저지름〉 repetition of crimes; committing a crime again
♦ 중범인 경우에는 in the case of a repeated offense; for a repetition of the offense
■—인 〈중대범〉 a felon —자 〈거듭된〉 a perpetrator of several crimes; an old offender

중병 重病 〈중환〉 a serious [severe] illness [disease]; a disease of a serious nature
♦ 중병에 걸리다 get [fall, be taken] seriously ill
▶ 그는 중병을 앓고 있다 He is very [seriously, dangerously, critically] ill.
▶ 그는 중병으로 이달 내내 입원하고 있다 He has been in the hospital all through this month with a serious illness.
■—환자 a serious case

중복 中伏 the second 10-day period of the three dog days; the mid dog days

중복 中腹 〈산의 중턱〉 the mountain's breast; the midslope of a mountain
♦ 산 중복에 halfway up [down] a hill
▶ 산 중복에 넓은 목장이 있다 There is an extensive ranch halfway up the mountain.

중복 重複 duplication; overlap(ping); 〈되풀이〉 repetition; 〈군말〉 redundancy
♦ 중복을 피하다 avoid duplication [overlapping]
—중복하다 duplicate; overlap; double; repeat; be repeated; be redundant
♦ 중복된 duplicate; overlapping; repeated; redundant; 〈어구 등의〉 tautological; pleonastic
▶ 이 책에는 몇 군데 중복된 부분이 있다 The same passages are repeated several times in this book.

중복부 中腹部 〔解〕 the mesogastrium 《*pl.* -ria》; the middle abdomen

중부 中部 〈중심부〉 the central part; 〈중앙 부분〉 the middle part; the center; the middle; the heart
■—고속도로 the Chungbu [Central] Highway —전선(前線) the central forward area [region]; the central front-line area —지방 the central districts [area, region] —태평양 the mid-Pacific; the Central Pacific

중부하 重負荷 〔機〕 heavy loading

중불 中佛 〈프랑스와 중국(간)의〉 Sino-French

중뿔나다 〈참견하고 나서다〉 intrusive; officious; forward; meddlesome; pert; impertinent; self-assertive; presumptuous
♦ 중뿔난 사람 a nosy person / 중뿔나게 나서다 butt in on 《another's affair》; push [thrust] *oneself* forward; poke [thrust] *one's* nose into / 중뿔나게 말하다 make an uncalled-for [uninvited] remark; break [cut, butt] in; interfere in [meddle with] 《another's business》
▶ 중뿔나게 나서지 마라 This is no business of yours. ⇌ None of your business!

중사 中士 〈英〉 a sergeant; 〈美俗〉 a sarge; 〈육군〉〈美〉 a sergeant first class; 〈해군〉〈美〉 a chief petty officer; 〈공군〉〈美〉 a master sergeant

중산계급 中産階級 the middle class(es); the (petite) bourgeoisie; 〈사람들〉 the middle classes; middle-class people ♦ 중산계급의 시민 middle-class citizens [people]; a bourgeois

중산모 中山帽 〈높은 예장 모자〉 〈美〉 a derby (hat); 〈美俗〉 a pot hat; 〈英〉 a bowler (hat)

중상 中傷 〈말에 의한〉 (a) slander; 〈문서에 의한〉 (a) libel 《on, against》; calumniation; defamation; 〈정계의〉 mudslinging; aspersion
♦ 중상적(인) slanderous; libelous; calumnious; defamatory
—중상하다 slander; libel; calumniate; malign; injure *sb's* reputation; defame; stab *sb* in the back; put a slur upon *sb's* fair name; sling mud at *sb's* reputation; traduce
▶ 그의 발언은 나에 대한 중상이다 What he said is (a) slander against me.
▶ 그는 종종 너를 중상한다 He often slanders you.
■—자 a slanderer; a calumniator; a maligner; a scandalmonger; a mudslinger

중상 重喪 〈탈상 전에 부모상을 거듭 당함〉 double mourning; losing *one's* parents one after another within three years

중상 重傷 a serious [severe, heavy, major, mortal] wound [injury]
♦ 중상을 입다 receive [sustain] a serious wound; be badly [seriously, mortally] wounded [injured] / 머리에 중상을 입다 get a serious injury to [wound in] the head; be seriously wounded in the head / 중상을 입히다 inflict a severe [serious] injury 《upon another》
▶ 그는 중상으로 목숨을 잃었다 He succumbed to a severe wound.
▶ 그 사고로 3명이 중상을 입었다 Three were severely wounded in the accident.
■—자 a severely wounded [seriously injured] person

중상주의 重商主義 〔經〕 the mercantile system; mercantilism ■—자 a mercantilist

중생 衆生 〔佛教〕 〈일체의 생물〉 living things [creatures]; 〈지각력이 있는 생물〉 sentient beings; 〈인간〉 the people; mankind; the world
♦ 일체 중생 all sentient beings; all creatures; all life / 중생을 제도하다 save the world; deliver mankind

중생대 中生代 〔地質〕 the Mesozoic (era)
♦ 중생대의 Mesozoic (life) / 중생대 초기[후기] the early [late] Mesozoic
■—층 a Mesozoic formation

중서부 中西部 〈미국의〉 the Middle West; the Midwest ■—사람 a Middle Westerner; a Midwesterner

중석 重石 〔鑛〕 tungsten

중석기시대 中石器時代 〔考古〕 the Mesolithic period [era]; the Middle Stone Age
♦ 중석기 시대의 mesolithic

중선거구 中選擧區 a medium constituency [electoral district] ■—제 the medium constituency [electorate] system

중성 中性 〔文法〕 the neuter gender; 〔化〕 neutrality; 〔植〕 sterility; 〔生〕 sexlessness
♦ 중성의 〔文法〕 neuter; 〔化〕 neutral; 〔電〕 indifferent; 〔植〕 sterile
■ ―명사 〔文法〕 a neuter noun ―반응 neutral reaction ―세제 a (synthetic) detergent; soapless soap; neutral cleanser ―염(鹽) neutral salts ―화(花) a neutral flower

중성 中聲 〔言〕 the medial vowel of a Korean orthographic syllable; the vowels (and semivowels) of a Korean syllable

중성미자 中性微子 〔物〕 a neutrino (pl. ~s)
■ 반(反)― an antineutrino

중성자 中性子 〔物〕 a neutron
■ 광― a photoneutron 반― an antineutron 열― a thermal neutron 중(重)― a dineutron ―로[원자로] a neutron reactor ―성 a neutron star ―폭탄 a neutron bomb

중세 中世 the middle ages; the medieval times ♦ 중세의 medieval / 중세 유럽 Europe in medieval times / 중세의 건조물 medieval buildings
■ ―기 the Middle Ages ―사 (the) medieval history ―암흑시대 the Dark Ages ―영어 Middle English

중세 重稅 〈무거운 세금〉 a heavy tax; 〈관세〉 a heavy duty (▶종종 duties); 〈무거운 과세〉 heavy [excessive] taxation; overtaxation
♦ …에 중세를 과하다 impose heavy taxes on 《the people》; impose heavy duties on 《imports and exports》 / 중세에 시달리다 labor 《groan》 under a heavy load [burden] of taxation; suffer from heavy taxes
▶ 내년에도 정부는 우리 근로자들에게 틀림없이 중세를 부과할 것이다 There is no doubt that the government will impose heavy taxes on us wage earners next year, too.

중소기업 中小企業 small-and-medium(·sized) businesses [corporations, enterprises, firms] (▶「기업[회사]」에 해당하는 정식 단어는 corporation, 약식 표현은 business, firm); 〈작은 기업〉 minor [small] businesses
■ ―경영자 minor enterprisers ―자금 bank loans for medium and small enterprises [industries]

중소상공업자 中小商工業者 medium and small traders and manufacturers

중속환이 ―俗還― an ex-monk
중송아지 中― a half-grown ox
중수 重水 〔化〕 heavy water; deuterium oxide
중수 重囚 〈중죄를 지은 죄수〉 a felon
중수 重修 〈개수〉 repairing 《a building》; improvement; remodeling ―중수하다 repair; improve 《a road》

중수소 重水素 〔化〕 heavy hydrogen; deuterium
중순 中旬 the middle [second] ten days of a month
♦ 이달 중순경 about the middle of this month / 9월 중순에 during the second [middle] third of September; in mid-September
▶ 그 배는 9월 중순에 출항한다 The ship sails in the middle of September [mid-September].

중시 重視 〈중요시〉 taking a serious view 《of》
―중시하다 attach (great, much) importance to sth; take a serious view of; lay stress on; make [think] much of sb; make great [much] account of
♦ 중시되다 be accounted much of; be of importance; count for much; carry weight; go a long way / 중시하지 않다 make little [take no] account of; pay little [no] attention to
▶ 그것은 중시할 거리가 못된다 It is of little account.
▶ 나는 무엇보다도 건강을 중시한다 I value health above everything else.
▶ 나는 그의 충고를 중시한다 I attach importance to his advice.
▶ 그 학교는 과학교육을 중시하고 있다 The school lays stress on science.

중시하 重侍下 serving [looking after] both parents and grandparents ⇨ 층층시하

중신 重臣 a senior statesman; 〈봉건시대의〉 a chief [key] vassal [retainer]
■ ―회의 a conference of senior statesmen

중심 中心 1 〈한가운데〉 the center; the heart; the middle; 〈중추〉 the pivot [hub]; 〈중핵〉 the nucleus (pl. ~es, ·clei); the core
♦ 원의 중심 the center of a circle / 중력의 중심 the center of gravity / 금융 활동의 중심 a pivot of financial operation / 산업의 중심 a hub of industry / 이야기의 중심 the main subject / 중심의 〈중심이 되는〉 central; middle; 〈주요한〉 leading; main; major; principal; key / …을 중심으로 하여 with sb as the central figure / 중심을 피해서 말하다 talk around the subject / 중심을 벗어나 있다 be out of focus / 주어진 점을 중심으로 하여 원을 그리다 draw a circle round a given center
▶ 그가 중심이 되어 일한다 He plays a most active part in it.
▶ 파리는 유행의 중심이다 Paris is the center of fashion.
▶ 한국에서는 가족이 사회의 중심이다 In Korea the family is the nucleus of the community.
▶ 지구는 태양을 중심으로 돌고 있다 The earth revolves round the sun as a center.
2 〈균형〉 balance
♦ 중심이 잡혀 있지 않다 be out of balance; be ill-balanced / 중심을 잡다[잃다] keep [lose] one's balance / 한 발로 서서 몸의 중심을 잡다 balance oneself on one leg
■ ―가(街) the main street; the midtown area ―각 〔數〕 a central angle ―경향 〔統〕 central tendency ―사상 the dominating thought; the central idea ―세력 central force ―점 the central [center] point ―축 the central axis

중심 重心 〔物〕 the center of gravity; the centroid

중심인물 中心人物 the central [focal] figure; a key man; the leading [guiding] spirit; the leader; the brain; the ringleader

중심지 中心地 the center; the metropolis; the omphalos ♦ 세계 무역의 중심지 a center of the world trade / 해운[철도]의 중심지 a shipping [railroad] center

중압 重壓 (heavy) pressure; a heavy [great] burden ▶ 그것이 그에게는 상당한 중압이었다 It was a great burden for him.

중압감 重壓感 an oppressive feeling ♦중압감을 느끼다 have an oppressive feeling; be overwhelmed by ▶나는 그의 위엄에 중압감을 느꼈다 I was overwhelmed by his dignity.

중앙 中央 the center; the heart; the middle; 〈중앙 정부〉the central government ♦읍의 중앙에 있는 병원 a midtown hospital / 중앙의 central; middle / 시의 중앙에 in the center [heart] of the city / 중앙으로 집중시키다[모이다] concentrate; centralize ■ ─공무원교육원 the Central Officials Training Institute ─난방 central heating ─문단 literary circles in the metropolis ─분리대 a median [medial] strip ─선거관리위원회 the Central Election Management Committee ─아메리카 Central America ─아시아 Central Asia ─우체국 the Central Post Office (略 CPO) ─지(紙) a metropolitan newspaper ─집행위원회 the central executive committee ─행정 the central administration

중앙아프리카공화국 中央─共和國 〈나라이름〉 the Central African Republic

중앙집권 中央集權 centralization of government [administrative power] ♦중앙집권화하다 centralize; get centralized ■ ─제 centralism

중양(절) 重陽(節) the ninth day of the ninth lunar month

중언부언 重言復言 repeating [repetition of] the same words; reiteration
─중언부언하다 say over again; repeat [reiterate] the same words; rub (it) in; harp on the same string ▶그것은 중언부언할 필요가 없다 It needs no reiteration.

중얼거리다 mutter; murmur (at, against) ♦중얼거리는 소리[말] a murmur; a mutter / 무어라고 혼자 중얼거리다 mutter something to *oneself* / 저주의 말을 중얼거리다 mutter an oath

중얼중얼 muttering; murmuring; grumbling ─중얼중얼하다 mutter ⇨ 중얼거리다

중역 重役 a (company) director; 〈전체〉 a board of directors; the directorate ♦중역의 지위[자리] directorship / 중역의 한 사람 a member of the directorate / 중역의 직위에 있다 hold an executive post (in a firm) ▶마침내 그는 중역이 되었다 He obtained a seat on the board of directors. ─회 the board of directors ─회의 a directors' conference

중역 重譯 (a) secondhand translation; retranslation ─중역하다 retranslate; translate a translation

중엽 中葉 1 〈시대의 중간〉 the middle part of a period ♦19세기 중엽 the mid-nineteenth century / 고려 중엽 about the middle of the period of the Koryŏ dynasty / 1930년대 중엽에 in the mid-1930s
2 〈중간엽〉〔解〕 the middle lobe

중외 中外 〈나라 안팎〉 the inside and outside of the country; home and abroad ♦중외의 domestic [home] and foreign; internal and external / 중외에 (at) home and abroad; inside and outside the country; to the world / 중외에 독립을 선언하다 declare independence to the world

중요 重要 importance; consequence; magnitude ♦역사상의 중요 사건 some highlights [salient events] of history / 지정학상의 중요 지점 places of geopolitic importance
─중요하다 important; significant; crucial; essential; key; major; vital; material

[解說] ***important***는 가치·효과·영향력이 있어서 중요한 것. ***significant***는 특히 의의가 깊고 우수하여 남의 눈에 띄고, 장래에 영향이 미칠 가능성이 있음을 암시한다. ***crucial***은 장래나 생사를 걸 만큼 중요하여 없어서는 안될 결정적인 것. ***essential***은 어떤 것에 대해 근본적으로 없어서는 안되는 핵심적인 것. ***key***는 남이 의존할 만큼 중요하여 요체라고 할 만한 것. ***major***는 다른 것과 비교하여 중요성이나 중대성이 더한 것. ***vital***은 전체가 기능을 발휘하는 데에 기본적으로 필수 불가결한 것. ***material***은 법률용어로서 재판의 판결에 중대한 영향을 미칠 만큼 중요한 것.

♦중요한 일 an important task; 〈사항〉 an important matter; a matter of importance [significance] / 중요한 지위 an important position; a position of importance / 극히[가장] 중요한 일 a matter of great account [significance] / 그 회사의 중요한 위치 a key post in the company / 국가적으로 중요한 문제 a question of national magnitude / 중요하지 않은 unimportant; of little [no] importance; of no consequence; inessential; immaterial / 중요한 역할을 하다 play an important role ▶그런 것은 별로 중요하지 않다 It is of no great importance. ▶사업에 있어서 가장 중요한 것은 신용이다 What is most important in business is credit. ▶나에게는 무엇보다도 시간이 중요하다 Time is the most important to me. ─기사 important articles; news of value; front page news; the highlights (in today's paper) ─도시 principal cities ─문제 an important [a serious] question ─물자 critical materials ─법안 important bills; 〈俗〉 must bills ─사항 an important matter [affair]; a matter of consequence ─산물 staple products ─산업 the key industry; the staple industries ─상품 principal merchandise; staple commodities ─서류 important [valuable] documents [papers] ─인물 an important person; (口) a VIP (*pl.* ~s); a prominent person; a leading [key] figure

중요성 重要性 importance; gravity; materiality ♦중요성이 있다[없다] be of [of no] importance / 그 대책의 중요성을 강조하다 urge the importance of the measure

중요시하다 重要視─ think much of; regard [look upon] *sth* as important; attach importance to; set importance on; take seriously; value highly ♦매우 중요시하다 attach great importance

to; place great importance on
▶나는 시간을 무엇보다도 중요시한다 I value time above everything else.
중용 中庸 1 〈중정(中正)〉 the mean; a golden mean; a happy medium [mean]; the middle course [path, way]; (美) the middle-of-the-road; 〈알맞음〉 moderation
◆중용의 mean; medium; moderate; (美) middle-of-the-road / 중용을 취하다 take the golden mean; take the middle course; go middle / 중용을 얻다 strike an average; hit the happy mean / 중용을 지키다 follow the golden mean; keep to the middle path; exercise [use] moderation; take the middle-of-the-road course
▶무슨 일에나 중용이라는 것이 있다 There is a happy medium in everything.
2 〈경서의 하나〉 the Doctrine of the Mean
▶경서의 하나인 「중용」은 모든 인간 생활에서 중용을 강조하고 있다 "The Doctrine of the Mean", one of the Chinese classics of Confucianism emphasizes "Moderation" in human life.
중용 重用 promotion to a responsible post
—중용하다 promote *sb* to a responsible post; give *sb* an important position; appoint *sb* to a position of trust
◆중용되고 있다 hold an important position 《in a company》
중우 衆愚 the ignorant [vulgar] crowd [masses]; the blind populace; the mob
■—정치 mobocracy; mob rule; ochlocracy
중원 中元 the fifteenth day of July of the lunar calendar
중원 中原 〈들판의〉 the center of a field; 〈나라의〉 the central districts 《of a country》; 〈중국의 황하 유역〉 around the basin of the Hwang Ho
◆중원의 패권을 다투다 compete for supremacy in a country
중위 中位 medium; average
◆중위의 middle; medium; middling; moderate; average; indifferent / 중위 이상[이하]이다 be above [below] the average
▶그의 성적은 중위다 He has an average school record.
중위 中尉 〈육군〉(美) a first lieutenant; (英) a lieutenant; 〈해군〉(美) a lieutenant junior grade; (英) a sublieutenant; 〈해병대〉(美) a first lieutenant; 〈공군〉(美) a first lieutenant; (英) a flying officer
중위 中衛 〔排〕 the middle guard; 〔蹴〕 the halfback
중유 重油 heavy oil ■—기관 a heavy oil engine
중음 中音 a normally-pitched voice; 〔樂〕〈성악의〉 baritone (남성); contralto (여성) ◆중음으로 말하다 speak in a normally-pitched voice
중음 重音 〔言〕 a double sound
중의 衆意 a majority opinion; a consensus of opinion ◆중의에 따르다 act according to a majority opinion
중의 衆議 a general consultation; public discussion ◆중의에 부치다 refer *sth* to public discussion
▶이 문제는 중의로 결정되어야 한다 This problem should be decided by public opinion.
중이 中耳 〔解〕 the middle ear; the auris media 《*pl.* ~s, -na》 ■—염 〔醫〕 otitis media; tympanitis
중이 미우면 가사도 밉다 (속담) Hate a priest, and you will hate his very surplice.
중이 제 머리 못 깎는다 (속담) You cannot scratch your own back.
중이층 中二層 a mezzanine floor story
중인 中印 China and India; Sino-India
◆중인 국경 분쟁 Sino-India border dispute
중인 衆人 the people; the public ◆중인 환시리에 in public; in the presence of many people
중인방 中引枋 〔建〕 a horizontal strut in a wall
중일 中日 China and Japan
◆중일의 Chinese-Japanese; Sino-Japanese
■—관계 the relations between China and Japan —전쟁 the Sino-Japanese War (1894-95)
중임 重任 1 〈중대 임무〉 an important duty [mission]; 〈중책〉 a heavy responsibility [trust]; 〈요직〉 a responsible post [position]; an important post of duty
◆중임을 맡다 take a heavy trust on *oneself*; take upon *oneself* an important task; shoulder a heavy responsibility / 중임을 띠고[맡고] 있다 have a heavy responsibility on *one's* shoulders; be entrusted [charged] with an important mission
2 〈재임〉 reappointment; 〈재선〉 reelection
—중임하다 reappoint; reelect
▶광주 시장에는 이선생이 중임되었다 Mr. Lee has been reappointed Mayor of Kwangju.
중입자 重粒子 〔物〕 a baryon
중장 中章 the middle verse [line, stanza] of a poem [song]
중장 中將 〈육군〉(美) a lieutenant general; (英) a lieutenant-general; 〈해군〉(美) a vice admiral; (英) a vice-admiral; 〈해병대〉(美) a lieutenant general; 〈공군〉(美) a lieutenant general; (英) an air marshal
중장비 重裝備 heavy equipment ◆중장비의 heavily equipped 《division》 ■—공장 a heavy construction machinery shop
중재 仲裁 arbitration; mediation; intervention; intercession; peacemaking
◆중재를 기다리다 wait for arbitration / 중재를 부탁하다 ask for arbitration; ask *sb* to intercede [make an intercession] 《for *sb*》 / 중재에 부치다 refer [submit] 《a matter》 to arbitration / 중재로 분쟁을 해결하다 settle a dispute by arbitration
—중재하다 arbitrate; mediate [intervene, intercede] 《between》; act as (a) peacemaker
◆싸움을 중재하다 arbitrate a quarrel; make peace between two quarreling parties
■—결정 an arbitration award —역할 the role of mediation: 중재 역할을 하다 perform the part of mediator 《between》 —위원회 an arbitration committee; 〈정당 등의〉 a trouble-shooting committee —인[자] an arbitrator;

an arbiter; a peacemaker; a mediator ━조약 an arbitration treaty

중재계약 仲裁契約 arbitration agreement

중재재판 仲裁裁判 arbitration ◆중재재판에 부치다 submit 《a case》 to arbitration ■━소 an arbitration tribunal [court]; a court of arbitration

중전 中殿 〈왕비〉 the Queen ━━마마 Her Majesty the Queen

중전기 重電機 heavy electric apparatus [equipment]

중전차 重戰車 a heavy tank

중절 中絶 interruption; discontinuance; intermission; stoppage; suspension; abeyance ━중절하다 interrupt; discontinue; intermit; stop; suspend ■임신━ (an) artificial abortion; interruption of pregnancy

중절모(자) 中折帽(子) a soft [felt] hat; a homburg; 《美》 a fedora (hat); 《英》 a trilby (hat)

중점 中點 〔數〕 the middle point; the midpoint; 〔印〕 a centered period

중점 重點 an important point; 〈강조〉 emphasis; stress; 〈중요〉 importance; 〈우위〉 priority ◆중점적으로 preponderantly / …에 중점을 두다 lay [put, place] emphasis [stress] on; keep [throw] the accent on; give priority to 《the tourist industry》 ▶이 학교에서는 중국어 수업에 중점을 두고 있다 Special importance is attached to the teaching of Chinese in this school. ■━배급 priority rationing; rationing on priority basis ━생산 production on priority basis ━주의 a priority system [policy, principle]

중정 中正 impartiality; fairness ━중정하다 fair; impartial; unbiased

중정석 重晶石 〔鑛〕 barite; barytes; a heavy spar

중조 重曹 〔탄산수소나트륨〕 〔化〕 bicarbonate of soda; bicarb; sodium bicarbonate; baking soda; 〈요리용〉 saleratus

중죄 重罪 〔法〕 (a) felony; a grave [capital, major] offense [crime] ◆중죄를 범하다 commit a serious crime ■━인 a felon

중주 重奏 〔樂〕 a duet(t)

중중거리다 grumble; complain; mutter; murmur (with discontent); 《美口》 grouch

중증 重症 an advanced disease ■━환자 a patient with an advanced disease; 〔醫〕 an advanced case

중지 中止 stoppage; discontinuance; discontinuation; suspension; abeyance; interruption; 《美口》 a holdup ━중지하다 discontinue; suspend; interrupt; stop; call off 《a game》; break off 《a meeting》; leave off 《work》 ◆회담을 일시 중지하다 recess the talks / 중지되다 be discontinued [suspended, interrupted, stopped]; be called off; fall into abeyance ▶그 일은 중지된 상태에 있다 The business is in a state of abeyance. ▶그 경기는 비 때문에 중지되었다 The match [game] was called off owing to the rain. ⇌ The match was rained out.

중지 中指 the middle finger

중지 衆智 wisdom of many ◆중지를 모으다 seek counsel [ask advice] of many people

중지상 中之上 the higher class of the medium grade; B plus ▶그녀의 학력은 중지상이다 Her scholarship is above the average.

중지중 中之中 the middle class of the medium grade; B

중지하 中之下 the lower class of the medium grade; B minus

중직 重職 an important [a weighty] office; a responsible post [position]

중진 重鎭 a prominent [leading] figure; a leader; 〈학계 등의〉 an authority ◆한국 영문학계의 중진 a leading scholar of [an authority on] English in Korea / 문단의 중진 the most prominent figure in the literary circles / 재계의 중진 a tycoon in the financial world

중진국 中進國 a developing country [nation]; a semideveloped country [nation]

중질 中帙 an article of medium quality

중창 中— 〈구두의〉 an insole

중창 重唱 〔樂〕 part-singing; singing in plural parts

중책 重責 a heavy responsibility; an important mission [duty] ◆중책을 지다[맡다] assume [take] a heavy responsibility

중천 中天 midair; the midheaven; the middle sky ◆중천에 midair ▶달이 중천에 걸려 있다 The moon is [hangs] in midair [high up in the sky]. ▶그가 눈을 떴을 때 해는 중천에 떠있었다 When he awoke, the sun was high up in the sky.

중첩하다 重疊— 〈중복되다〉 be repeated [duplicated]; overlap; 〈겹치다〉 be piled one upon another; be heaped up

중추 中樞 the center; the hub; the backbone; the pivot; the nucleus; 〈인물〉 the central [a leading] figure; the main prop; a mainstay; a key man ◆사회의 중추 the mainstay of a society; a mainstay of society / 중추적인 central; pivotal; key ■━신경━ 〔解〕 a nerve center ━산업 a pivotal industry ━신경 the central nerve ━신경계통 the central nervous system ━신경조직 a central nervous tissue ━통 the central pain

중추 仲秋 midautumn; August the fifteenth of the lunar calendar ■━명월 the Harvest Moon; Midautumn Full Moon ━절(節) Ch'usŏk; Harvest Moon Day; Midautumn Festival; Korean Thanksgiving Day

중축 中軸 the axis; the pivot; 〈인물〉 the central [leading] figure; a key man

중층 中層 the middle stratum [layer]; 〈건물의〉 the middle story [floor]; 〈해저〉 the middle depths; the middepths; 〈중류〉 the middle class(es)

중층운 中層雲 〔氣〕 middle clouds
중치 中— ◆중치의 〈크기가〉 of medium size; medium-sized; neither large nor small; 〈품질이〉 middling; of medium quality; 〈정도가〉 moderate; middling; passable
중침 中針 〈중간치의 바늘〉 a medium-sized needle; a needle of medium size
중크롬산 重—酸 〔化〕 dichromic acid ■—소다[나트륨] sodium bichromate ■—염[칼륨] a bichromate; a dichromate ■—전지 a bichromate cell
중키 中— average [middle, medium] height; middling [mean, medium] stature ◆중키의 medium tall; 《a man》 of mean [middle] stature [height]
중탄산 重炭酸 〔化〕 bicarbonate ■—소다[나트륨] bicarbonate of soda; sodium bicarbonate; 《俗》 baking soda ■—염 bicarbonate
중탕하다 重湯— heat sth in boiling water
중태 重態 〔醫〕 〈위독상태〉 a critical condition; 〈중증〉 a grave [serious] condition ◆중태다 be seriously ill; be in a critical [serious] condition ▶ 그는 과도한 출혈로 중태다 He is seriously ill with excessive loss of blood. ▶ 그녀는 중태에 빠졌다 She fell into a critical condition. ⇌ Her disease has taken a serious turn.
중턱 中— 〈산의〉 the mountain's breast; the mid-slope of a mountain; a hillside; a mountainside ◆언덕의 중턱에 《서》 있다 be [stand] halfway up [down] the hill ▶ 산장은 산 중턱에 있다 The villa is located halfway up the hill.
중토 重土 〔化〕 baryta; barium oxide ■—수 baryta water
중퇴 中退 leaving school in mid-course; dropping out of school ■—하다 leave school in mid-course; leave 《a university》 without graduating [taking a degree]; drop out 《of school》; leave school halfway ▶ 그는 가정 형편으로 중퇴했다 He left school in midcourse owing to family circumstances [for family reasons]. ■—자 a dropout: 대학 중퇴자 a university dropout
중파 中波 〔通信〕 medium waves ■—방송 medium-wave broadcasting ■—수신기 a medium-wave receiver
중파장 中波長 a medium wave length
중판 重版 a reprint; a second printing; a reissue; 〈개정판〉 a second [revised] edition ▶ 그 책은 중판에 중판을 거듭했다 The book went into many editions.
중편 中篇 the second part [volume]; 〈제2권〉 〈중편 소설〉 a short novel; a novelette; a medium-length story; a long short story
중평 衆評 public [general] opinion ▶ 그가 적임자라는 것이 중평이다 Public opinion says he is just the man for the post.
중포 重砲 a heavy gun; (총칭) heavy artillery ■—병[대] heavy artillery; 〈한 사람〉 a heavy artilleryman

중포격 重砲擊 a heavy bombardment [fire] ■—중포격하다 bombard heavily
중폭 中幅 1 〈직물의 폭이 중치인 것〉 medium breadth [width] ◆중폭의 직물 cloth of medium width 2 〈변동 폭이 중정도인 것〉 moderate limits ◆임금인상을 중폭으로 억제하다 keep a wage increase within moderate limits
중폭격 重爆擊 a heavy bombing attack [raid] ■—중폭격하다 bomb heavily; make a heavy bombing raid ■—기 a heavy bomber
중품 中品 〔商〕 fair average quality; an article of medium quality
중풍 中風 〔韓醫〕 palsy; paralysis ◆중풍에 걸린 paralytic; palsied / 중풍에 걸리다 be stricken with paralysis; suffer an apoplectic fit [stroke]; have a stroke of paralysis ■—환자 a paralytic
중하 仲夏 midsummer; the fifth lunar month
중하 重荷 〈짐〉 a heavy burden [load]; 〈부담〉 a burden; an encumbrance
중하다 重— 1 〈중대하다〉 important; weighty; serious; grave; momentous ◆중한 문제 an important problem; a serious question; a grave issue [subject] / 극히 중한 일 a matter of the utmost magnitude 2 〈소중하다〉 valuable; of 《great, much》 value; valued; precious ◆중한 물건 a valuable article / 중한 단골 손님 a valued customer 3 〈무겁다〉 severe; serious; grave; weighty ◆중한 벌 a severe punishment / 중한 죄 a grave crime; (a) felony / 중한 책임 a heavy [grave] responsibility 4 〈위중하다〉 serious; critical; bad ▶ 아버님 병환이 중하다 Father is seriously [critically] ill.
중학 中學 a middle school ⇨ 중학교 ■—과정 a junior high school course ■—생 a middle-school [junior high school] student [boy, girl]
중학교 中學校 a middle school; a lower secondary school; (美) a junior high school ◆중학교 시절에 in one's middle school days / 중학교에 다니다 attend [go to] a middle school / 중학교를 졸업하다 finish [graduate from] a middle school; complete the middle school course
중합 重合 〔化〕 polymerization; polymerism ■—중합하다 polymerize ■—도[률] the degree [rate] of polymerization ■—체 a polymer
중항 中項 〔數〕 a mean; the middle term ■—비례— a mean proportional; a geometric mean
중핵 中核 the kernel; the core; the nucleus ▶ 불교는 고대 신라 문화의 중핵이었다 Buddhism was the nucleus of the civilization of Shilla Dynasty of ancient Korea.
중형 中型 a medium [middle] size ◆중형의 medium-[middle-]sized ■—차(車) a medium-sized car
중형 重刑 a severe punishment; a heavy penalty ◆아무를 중형에 처하다 sentence sb to a severe punishment; inflict a heavy penalty

중혼 重婚 bigamy; double marriage ◆중혼의 bigamous —**중혼하다** commit bigamy; marry sb bigamously ■—자 a bigamist —죄 bigamy

중화 中和 〔化〕neutralization; 〈독 등의〉counteraction ◆중화성(性)의 counteractive —**중화하다** neutralize; counteract; antagonize ◆독성을 중화하다 neutralize the effects of poison / 산을 염기로 중화시키다 neutralize an acid with a base
▶알칼리는 산을 중화한다 Alkalis neutralize acids.

중화 中華 ■—민국 the Republic of China; the Nationalist China —사상 Sinocentrism —요리 Chinese dishes [food] —요리점 a Chinese restaurant; (美) a chop suey house —인민공화국 the People's Republic of China

중화기 重火器 heavy weapons [firearms]

중화학공업 重化學工業 the heavy (and) chemical industry

중환 重患 a serious [severe] illness [disease] —자 a serious case

중후하다 重厚— grave; serious; dignified; solemn; profound; imposing
◆중후한 태도 a grave and serious attitude / 중후하게 weightily; seriously; gravely; with an important air; with profoundness [depth]
▶그는 중후한 느낌을 주는 인물이다 He impresses one as being a man of depth.

중흥 中興 restoration; revival ◆민족 중흥의 주역 the leader of the national restoration —**중흥하다** restore; revive

중히 重— carefully; with (much) care; with caution [respect]
◆중히 여기다 attach (great [much]) importance to; take a serious view of; lay stress on; make great [much] account of; 〈존중하다〉respect; value; set value on; esteem; hold sth [sb] in (high) esteem / 법률을 중히 여기다 respect [have a regard for] the laws / 무엇보다도 건강을 중히 여기다 value health above everything else / 학문을 중히 여기다 hold learning in esteem / 중히 여기지 않다 have no regard for; make little [light] of; slight; think slightly of
▶나는 생명보다도 명예를 중히 여긴다 I value [prize, esteem, put] honor above life.

쥐[1] 〔動〕a rat; 〈생쥐〉a mouse ((pl. mice))
◆쥐들이 천장에서 찍찍 운다 Rats [Mice] are squeaking in the ceiling.
▶쥐들이 벽에 구멍을 뚫었다 Rats [Mice] gnawed a hole in the wall.
▶이 낡은 빌딩에는 쥐가 들끓고 있다 This old building is full of [infested with] rats.
▶이제 범인은 독안에 든 쥐다 Now the culprit is like a rat in a trap.
▶그는 살며시 왔다가 쥐도 새도 모르게 없어졌다 He disappeared as stealthily as he had appeared.
■들— a field mouse 시궁— a sewer rat; a gutter rat 집— a house rat —잡기운동 an anti-rat drive

쥐[2] 〈근육의 경련〉(a) cramp; (美口) charley horse
◆다리에 쥐가 나다 be seized with (a) cramp in the calf; get cramped in one's leg
▶수영중에 왼발에 쥐가 났다 I had a cramp in the left leg while swimming.

쥐구멍 rathole; a mousehole
▶나는 창피해서 쥐구멍이라도 찾고 싶은 심정이었다 I was so embarrassed [ashamed] that I wished the earth would swallow me up [that I wished I could sink through the floor].

쥐구멍에도 볕들 날이 있다 〔속담〕Every dog has his day. ⇒ Everything comes to him who waits. ⇒ It is a long lane that has no turning.

쥐꼬리 a rattail
◆쥐꼬리만한 급료 a very small salary; a paltry [pitiful] pay / 쥐꼬리만 하다 be very small / 쥐꼬리만한 월급으로 일하다 [생활하다] work for [live on] a meager salary
■—톱 a compass [pad] saw

쥐노래미 〔魚〕a greenling

쥐다 1 grasp; clasp; grip; clutch; clench; hold; seize; take [get] hold of
◆주먹을 쥐다 clench one's fist / 밧줄을 양손으로 쥐다 grasp a rope with one's hands / 차의 핸들을 쥐다 grip the steering wheel of a car / 단단히 쥐다 take a firm grip (of)
▶그 남자는 내 손을 꼭 쥐었다 He clasped [grasped, gripped] my hand firmly.
▶그는 손을 쥐었다 폈다 했다 He clasped and unclasped his hand.
▶그는 큰돈을 쥐었다 He got a lot [a great deal] of money.
2 〈권력 등을〉◆권력을 쥐다 seize [get, come into] power / 정권을 쥐고 있다 be in power; hold the reins of government
▶그가 살인사건의 열쇠를 쥐고 있는 것같다 He seems to hold [have, possess] the key to the murder case.
▶그 회사의 실권은 그의 아버지가 쥐고 있다 The real power over the company is in his father's hands.

쥐덫 a rattrap; a mousetrap; a trap for rats
◆쥐덫을 놓다 set a mousetrap [rattrap] / 쥐덫으로 쥐를 잡다 catch a rat by a trap

쥐똥나무 〔植〕a privet

쥐며느리 〔動〕a pill bug; a wood louse

쥐방울 〔植〕a Dutchman's-pipe

쥐뿔 a trifling thing; trivial [wretched] stuff
▶그는 가진 게 쥐뿔도 없다 He is penniless. ⇒ He is as poor as a rat.
▶그는 그 건에 대해서 쥐뿔도 모르면서 큰소리 친다 He brags about [talks big] knowing absolutely nothing about the matter.

쥐새끼 a young rat
◆쥐새끼같은 놈 a mean rat; you dirty rat

쥐색 —色 dark gray; mouse-[rat-]colored
◆쥐색의 dark gray / 쥐색 모자 a dark-gray hat

쥐손이풀 〔植〕a herb Robert

쥐약 —藥 rat poison; rodenticide
▶그녀는 쥐약을 먹고 자살했다 She killed herself by taking rat poison.

쥐어뜯다 tear; tear [rip] off; rend; scratch off; pluck off

♦새털을 쥐어뜯다 pick [pluck] a fowl / 갈기갈기 쥐어뜯기다 be scratched to frazzles
▶그 여자는 화가 나서[절망한 나머지] 머리를 쥐어뜯었다 She tore her hair in rage [despair].

쥐어박다 hit [knock, strike] *sb* with *one's* fist; give [deal, deliver] *sb* a blow with *one's* fist
♦머리를 쥐어박다 hit (a blow) on the head; give *sb* a punch on the head
▶나는 그 남자의 볼을 쥐어박았다 I struck [knocked] him on the cheek.

쥐어주다 〈돈을〉 slip 《money》 into *sb's* hand [pocket]; 〈팁을〉 tip; 〈뇌물을〉 bribe; grease *sb's* palm; oil *sb's* hand
♦아무에게 백만원을 쥐어주다 give *sb* one million won bribe
▶그에게는 10만원만 쥐어주면 모두 말하게 할 수 있어 A 100,000 won bribe will make him tell everything.

쥐어지르다 smash *sb* with the fist; punch
♦머리를 쥐어지르다 give *sb* a hard punch on the head

쥐어짜다 1 〈액체를〉 press [squeeze] out; wring
♦수건을 쥐어짜다 wring a towel; wring water from a towel / 레몬을 쥐어짜다 squeeze juice out of a lemon
▶그 소녀는 젖은 수영복을 쥐어짰다 The girl wrung out her wet bathing suit.
2 〈머리 등을〉 press out; squeeze
♦머리를 쥐어짜다 rack *one's* brains 《about, over, to do》; strive hard to think out / 목소리를 쥐어짜다 strain *one's* voice; raise *one's* voice to the highest possible pitch
▶그는 쥐어짜는 목소리로 그렇게 말했다 He said so in a forced whisper.
3 〈착취하다〉 extort; exploit; squeeze
♦아무의 돈을 쥐어짜다 extort [squeeze] money from *sb*
4 〈몹시 조르다〉 importune [press] *sb* (for money); ask *sb* importunately (for money)

쥐엄나무 〔植〕 a honey locust

쥐엄발이 〈발〉 a shriveled foot; 〈사람〉 a person with a shriveled [shrunken] foot

쥐여지내다 be under the control of *sb*; live under *sb's* thumb; live in the grips of *sb*
♦아내에게 쥐여지내는 남편 a henpecked husband
▶그는 아내에게 쥐여지낸다 He is dominated by his wife. ⇒ He is tied to his wife's apron strings.

쥐오줌풀 〔植〕 a valerian

쥐잡듯(이) 1 〈철저히〉 thoroughly; out and out; all over
▶그것을 찾으려고 쥐잡듯이 뒤졌으나 허사였다 We searched every nook and cranny for it, but in vain.
2 〈거칠게〉 rudely; roughly; violently
♦아무를 쥐잡듯하다 treat *sb* roughly

쥐정신 —精神 forgetfulness ▶그는 쥐정신이다 He is forgetful. ⇒ He has a short [poor, bad] memory.

쥐젖 〈사마귀〉 a small wart

쥐죽은듯 ♦쥐죽은듯 고요하다 be (as) silent as the grave —쥐죽은듯하다 silent (as the grave); (deathly) quiet and still
▶주위는 쥐죽은듯했다 It was very quiet all around.
▶온 집안은 쥐죽은듯 고요하였다 A dead silence reigned throughout the house.

쥐치 〔魚〕 a filefish; a leatherjacket

쥘부채 a folding fan

쥘손 〈손잡이〉 a handle; a handgrip; a grip; 〈주전자 등의〉 a catch; an ear
♦쥘손을 달다 attach [add] a handle

즈런즈런 〈살림살이가〉 richly; abundantly; in affluency [opulence]; amply
♦살림이 즈런즈런하다 be wealthy; be well-to-do; be well [comfortably] off; live in plenty [abundance, comfort]

즈봉 (a pair of) trousers; 〈주로 반바지〉 pants; breeches; slacks
♦즈봉을 입다[벗다] put on [take off] *one's* trousers
▶반— (a pair of) breeches; shorts

즈음 when...; about the time when...
♦요즈음 these days; lately; recently; nowadays / 그 즈음 in those days; at that time; (back) then / 매년 이 즈음에는 at this time of (the) year

즈음하여 when; at the time 《of》; in case 《of》; on the occasion 《of》
♦국난에 즈음하여 at a national crisis / 이 책의 간행에 즈음하여 on the occasion of the publication of this book
▶폐회에 즈음하여 한말씀 드리겠습니다 Please allow me to say a few words to close this meeting.

즈크 canvas; duck ■—신 〔화〕 (a pair of) canvas 《duck》 shoes

즉 卽 1 〈곧〉 namely; that is (to say); i.e. (▶id est의 약자)
♦1파운드 즉 100펜스 one pound, or one hundred pence
▶노력이 즉 성공은 아니다 Effort does not lead directly to success.
2 〈바로〉 just; precisely; exactly; 〈다름아닌〉 nothing but
▶그것이 즉 내가 말하고자 하는 것이다 That's just [exactly] what I want to say.

즉각 卽刻 instantly; immediately; in no time; at once; on the spot [instant]; without delay; (口) right away [off]
♦즉각적인 행동 a prompt act / 즉각적인 immediate; instant; prompt / 즉각 효험이 나타나다 take immediate [instant, instantaneous] effect; work at once
▶나는 즉각 행동을 취했다 I took an immediate action.
▶나는 그들에게 즉각 정보를 쳤다 I cabled them immediately.

즉결 卽決 a prompt [an immediate] decision; 〈재판의〉 a summary decision; (美) a snap judgment
—즉결하다 decide promptly [immediately, on the spot]; 〔法〕 try summarily
■—처분 summary conviction

즉결재판 即決裁判 a summary decision [trial]
♦ 즉결재판을 하다 decide summarily on a case; pass summary judgment; try a case summarily
—권 summary jurisdiction —소 a summary court

즉낙 即諾 a ready [immediate] consent [approval, acceptance] —즉낙하다 give a ready [immediate] consent ⟨to⟩

즉납 即納 ⟨지급⟩ immediate [ready] payment; ⟨납입⟩ prompt delivery —즉납하다 pay immediately [on the spot]; deliver promptly

즉답 即答 a ready [an immediate, a prompt] answer [reply]
♦ 즉답을 요구하다 ask for a prompt reply; ask *sb* to answer immediately / 즉답을 피하다 avoid answering a question immediately; choose to answer later
—즉답하다 give a ready answer [reply]; answer offhand; reply immediately

즉매 即賣 a spot sale; a sale on the spot
—즉매하다 sell on the spot

즉사 即死 (an) instantaneous [instant] death; (a) death on the spot
—즉사하다 be killed instantly; be killed outright [on the spot]; die on the spot
▶ 승객 5명이 즉사했다 Five passengers were killed on the spot.
—자 a person killed instantly

즉석 即席 ♦ 즉석의 extempore; impromptu; improvised; offhand; ⟨美口⟩ ad lib; ⟨美口⟩ off-the-cuff / 즉석에서 instantly; promptly; at once; outright; ⟨美⟩ rightly away [off]; impromptu; offhandedly; on the spot / 즉석에서 시를 짓다 improvise a poem
▶ 그는 즉석에서 대답했다 He gave a ready answer. ⇌ He made an immediate reply.
▶ 나는 그의 초대를 즉석에서 승낙하였다 I accepted his invitation on the spot.
▶ 그녀는 즉석에서 의견을 말했다 She gave an offhand opinion.
▶ 나는 즉석에서 지급했다 I paid there and then.
—복권 an instant lottery ticket —식품 fast food —연설 an impromptu speech; an off-the-cuff speech —요리 a light, quickly prepared dish; an improvised meal

즉시 即時 at once; immediately; directly; without delay; instantly; on the spot [instant]; promptly; ⟨美口⟩ right away [off]
♦ …하자 즉시 as soon as…; no sooner…than; directly after…; scarcely [hardly]…when [before] / 즉시 행동하다 take immediate action; act immediately [promptly]
▶ 거기 도착하면 즉시 알릴게요 I'll tell you as soon as I arrive there.
▶ 즉시 답장을 주십시오 I'm expecting your prompt [immediate] answer. ⇌ Please answer this letter as soon as you can.
—인도 spot delivery —통화 direct dialing system

즉시불 即時拂 spot [immediate] payment; cash on the spot —어음 a sight bill [draft]

즉위 即位 accession to the throne; enthronement; coronation
—즉위하다 ascend [accede to] the throne; ⟨왕이⟩ become king; ⟨여왕이⟩ become queen
—식 an enthronement ceremony; a coronation (ceremony)

즉응 即應 conformity; agreement; adaptation
—즉응하다 ⟨즉시 응하다⟩ conform to; agree with; adapt *oneself* to; ⟨대처하다⟩ cope with; meet
♦ 시대에 즉응한 교육 education adapted to the times / …에 즉응하여서 in conformity [alignment] with…; in response to… / 시대적 요구에 즉응하다 meet the needs [demands] of the times
▶ 예기치 못한 진전에 그는 즉응하지 못했다 He was unable to deal with [handle] the unexpected development.

즉일 即日 ♦ 즉일에 on the same day; the very day / 투표는 선거 즉일 개표된다 The ballots are counted on the day of the election.

즉전즉결 即戰即決 an intensive [all-out] surprise attack —전법 blitz tactics

즉효 即效 an immediate effect
▶ 이 약은 치통에 즉효가 있다 This medicine has an immediate effect on toothache. ⇌ This is a quick remedy for a toothache.
—약 a quick remedy (for); a quick acting medicine: 오랜 악습에 대한 즉효약은 없다 There are no quick cures for long-standing abuses.

즉흥 即興 ♦ 즉흥적인 연설 an impromptu speech / 즉흥적인 improvisatorial; extempore; impromptu; offhand; ad lib / 즉흥적으로 시를 짓다[곡을 만들다] improvise a poem [melody] / 즉흥적으로 연주하다 ad-lib
▶ 즉흥적으로 말해서는 안된다 You shouldn't talk off the top of your head.
—곡 an impromptu; an improvisation

즉흥시 即興詩 an impromptu [improvised] poem; extempore verse [poetry]
—인 an improvisator

즐거움 joy; delight; pleasure; enjoyment; ⟨행복⟩ happiness
♦ 독서의 즐거움 the pleasure of reading / 인생의 즐거움 the pleasure [joy, enjoyment] of life / 즐거움을 만끽하다 enjoy *oneself* to the full [to *one's* heart's content] / …으로 즐거움을 삼다 delight in; take pleasure [delight] in…
▶ 음악을 듣는 것이 그의 큰 즐거움이었다 Listening to music was a great pleasure to him. ⇌ He took great pleasure in listening to music.
▶ 이것이 도예의 즐거움이다 This is the charm of ceramic art.
▶ 그 노부인의 유일한 즐거움은 딸이 때때로 찾아오는 것이었다 The old woman found her sole comfort in her daughter's occasional visits.
▶ 나는 인생의 즐거움도 슬픔도 겪은 바 있다 I have tasted the joy and sorrows of life.

즐거이 merrily; happily; pleasantly; delightfully; cheerfully
♦ 하루를 즐거이 보내다 have [pass] a nice [pleasant] day

즐겁다 merry; pleasant; happy; cheerful; delightful; enjoyable; joyous; joyful; sweet
♦즐거운 우리집 one's sweet [happy] home / 즐거운 추억 a pleasant [happy, sweet] memory / 괴로울 때나 즐거울 때나 in pain or pleasure / 즐거워하다 be pleased [delighted] 《with, at》; delight [take delight] 《in》; be happy with
▶어젯밤 파티는 정말 즐거웠다 We enjoyed ourselves very much at the party last night.
▶오늘은 참 즐거웠다 I had [have had] a very good time today.
▶그는 즐거운 얘기 상대다 It is pleasant to talk with him. ⇌ He is pleasant to talk with. ⇌ He is a nice person [is a pleasant person, is fun] to talk with.

즐겁게 joyously; joyfully; cheerfully; merrily; pleasantly; happily
♦즐겁게 이야기하다 have a pleasant chat [talk] with / 즐겁게 놀다[보내다] have a good [pleasant, fine] time (of it); (口) have a ball / 즐겁게 하다[해주다] amuse; entertain [delight] sb with sth; give pleasure to / 눈을 즐겁게 하다 〈사람이 주어〉 feast one's eyes 《on》; 〈사물이 주어〉 delight [please, regale] the eye
▶아이들은 정원에서 즐겁게 놀고 있다 The children are playing happily in the garden.
▶나는 여생을 즐겁게 보내고 싶다 I want to spend the rest of my life happily. ⇌ I want to enjoy the rest of my life.
▶그는 남을 즐겁게 하는 데 열심이다 He is eager to please others.
▶그는 마술로 우리를 즐겁게 해 주었다 He entertained [amused] us with magic tricks.

즐겨 1 〈소망하여〉 willingly; by [from] choice; be preference; 〈자진하여〉 willing to 《do》; of one's (own) free will
♦즐겨 걷는 길 one's favorite walk
▶그녀는 언니의 아이들을 즐겨 돌보아 주었다 She looked after her sister's children willingly [gladly].
2 〈종종〉 often ♦즐겨 그림을 그리다 draw a picture very often; paint a picture frequently

즐기다 1 〈즐거워하다〉 enjoy; enjoy oneself; like; love; have good [pleasant, fine] time (of it); take pleasure [delight] in; have fun
♦고독을 즐기다 love one's own company / 독서를 즐기다 enjoy oneself by reading [with books] / 드라이브를 즐기다 enjoy driving; enjoy oneself by driving / 쇼를 보고 즐기다 be entertained by a show / 인생을 즐기다 enjoy life
▶그는 그 일을 아주 즐기고 있다 He takes great pleasure in (doing) that job. ⇌ That job is his pleasure.
▶그는 커피를 별로 즐기지 않는다 He doesn't like [care for] coffee very much.
▶영시를 즐기려면 영어를 충분히 알지 않고서는 안된다 You can't appreciate English poetry without a thorough mastery of the language.
2 〈재미로 하다〉 amuse oneself; make sport of
♦낚시를 즐기다 enjoy 《oneself》 angling

즐비하다 櫛比— 〈서술적〉 stand in a row
▶길 양쪽에는 고층빌딩이 즐비하게 늘어서 있다 Tall buildings line the street on both sides. ⇌ The street is lined on both sides with tall buildings.

즙 汁 〈과일의〉 juice; 〈초목의〉 sap; 〈액체〉 liquid
♦즙내는 기구 a juicer / 〈과일·채소가〉 즙이 많은 juicy; succulent; watery / 즙이 나(오)다 run juice / 즙을 짜다[내다] extract [squeeze] juice; (美) juice
■고기— meat juice 레몬— the juice of a lemon; lemon juice

즙액 汁液 juice ♦즙액이 많은 juicy

증 症 symptoms ♦경증 a slight illness; a mild case / 중증 a serious illness / 자각증 subjective symptoms / 중독증 toxic symptoms

증 贈 presentation ♦저자증 〈책에 서명하여〉 "With the Compliments of the Author"

증 證 〈증서〉 a certificate; a warrant; a bill
♦면허증 a license / 영수증 a receipt / 학생증 a student (identification) card

증가 增加 (an) increase; (an) increment; (a) gain; (a) rise; (an) augmentation
♦인구의 급격한 증가 a sudden increase [growth, rise] in population / 인구의 폭발적 증가 a population explosion / 체중의 증가 a gain in weight
▶생산량은 지난달에 비해서 10퍼센트 증가를 보이고 있다 The production shows a 10 percent increase [an increase of 10 percent] over last month.
▶범죄는 증가 일로에 있다 There is a steady increase in crime.
—**증가하다** increase; grow; rise; augment; swell
▶회원수가 30퍼센트 증가했다 The membership has increased (by) 30 percent.
▶65세 이상의 인구가 꾸준히 증가하고 있다 The number of people over sixty-five is rising steadily.
■자연— (a) natural increase ■—액 the amount increased; the increment —율 a rate of increase; an increasing rate

증간 增刊 an extra number [issue, edition]
♦춘계 증간호 a special number of spring; a special [an extra] issue for spring

증감 增減 increase and [or] decrease; variations
♦인원의 증감 fluctuations [change(s)] in the number of personnel / 체중의 증감 variation in one's weight; gains and losses in weight
—**증감하다** increase and [or] decrease; add and [or] reduce; vary; fluctuate

증강 增强 reinforcement; strengthening; (an) increase; (a) buildup
♦군사력의 증강 the buildup of the military forces; military buildup
—**증강하다** reinforce; increase; build up
♦병력을 증강하다 reinforce troops; build up [美口) beef up] the military forces / 생산력을 증강하다 increase [boost (up)] production / 체력을 증강하다 build up one's strength; strengthen oneself

증거 證據 evidence; proof; 〈구체적일 때〉 a piece of evidence; a proof
♦ 범죄의 증거 evidences of a crime / 산 증거 a living witness 《to》 / 확실한 증거 certain [convincing, trustworthy] evidence / 충분한[불충분한] 증거 sufficient [insufficient] evidence
▶ 그는 불충분한 증거로 무죄가 언도되었다 He was declared not guilty on the ground of insufficient [weak] evidence [for lack of evidence].
▶ 그의 표정이 굳은 것은 긴장하고 있는 증거다 His stiff look is the proof [shows, bears witness] that he is tense.
〈증거가[는]〉 증거가 되다 evidence; prove; testify to; attest 《to》
▶ 증거가 없으니 넌 그를 어떻게 할 도리가 없다 In absence of evidence [proof], you can't do anything to him.
▶ 그의 진술을 믿을 만한 충분한 증거가 있습니까? Do you have enough evidence to believe his statement?
▶ 그 증거는 그에게 유리[불리]하다 The evidence is in his favor [is against him].
▶ 충분한 증거가 없는 이상 그가 범행했다고는 단정할 수 없다 Without sufficient evidence, we cannot blame the crime upon him.
〈증거를〉 증거를 가지고 판단하다 judge a case on the evidence / 증거를 들다 give evidence; cite *sth* as (a) proof 《of》 / 증거를 수집하다 collect [gather] evidence; accumulate proofs / 증거를 잡다 hold [secure] proofs; obtain evidence / 증거를 인멸하다 destroy the evidence of / 결정적인 증거를 제출하다 give [produce] conclusive evidence
▶ 증거를 조금이라도 보여 주면 너를 믿겠다 Show me a scrap of evidence [proof] and I'll believe you.
〈증거로서〉 …의 증거로서 in [as] evidence 《of》; as (a) proof 《of》
■ 간접[내적]— indirect [internal] evidence 물적— material evidence 반대— counter-evidence 상황— circumstantial evidence ■ —금 guarantee money; deposit money; a deposit —물[물건] a piece of evidence; an exhibit —보전 preservation of evidence —서류 documentary evidence —수집 the gathering [collecting] of proofs [evidence] —인 a witness —인멸 destruction of evidence —자료 corroborative facts —조사 the taking of evidence

증권 證券 〈유가증권〉 a security; 〈증서〉 a bill; 〈채권〉 a bond; 〈주식 증권〉 a certificate of stock [share]; 〈보험증권〉 an insurance policy
♦ 한국증권거래소 the Korea Stock Exchange
■ 국고— (美) a treasury bond 대용— a collateral security 선하— a bill of lading (略 B/L) 유가— securities; stocks and bonds 유통— a negotiable instrument 정부발행— government securities ■ —거래법 the Securities and Exchange Act —거래소 a securities [stock] exchange —거래위원회 (美) the Securities and Exchange Commission (略 SEC) —시세 stock quotations [prices] —시장 a security [stock] market —투자 investment in securities; securities investment —회사 a stock company; a (stock) brokerage firm; a securities firm

증권업 證券業 stock broking; stockbrokerage; securities business
■ —자 a stockbroker; (英) a sharebroker : 증권업자의 수수료 bill brokerage

증급 增給 an increase in salary [wages, pay]

증기 蒸氣 steam; vapor
▶ 이 배는 증기로 간다 This ship is driven by steam.
■ —관 a steam pipe —기관 a steam engine —기관차 a steam locomotive —난방 steam heating —난방장치 a steam heating system [apparatus] —력 steam power —선 a steamship; a steamboat —압 steam [vapor] pressure [tension] —욕 a steam bath —터빈 a steam turbine

증답 贈答 —증답하다 exchange presents [gifts] 《with》 ■ —품 a present; a gift: 증답품 매장 a gift corner

증대 增大 (an) enlargement; (an) increase
♦ 생산의 증대 a step-up in production / 수요의 대폭적 증대 a large increase in [of] demand —증대하다 〈커지다〉 become [grow] larger; 〈크게 하다〉 enlarge; increase; step up; gather
♦ 수요가 증대하다 be more in demand / 세력이 증대하다 increase in power / 국제 경쟁력을 증대시키다 increase international competitive edge

증량 增量 (an) increase in quantity —증량하다 increase the quantity 《of》

증류 蒸溜 distillation —증류하다 distill
▶ 브랜디는 포도주를 증류해서 만든다 Brandy is distilled from wine.
■ —기 a distiller; a still —수 distilled water —액 a distillate; a distillation —장치 distillatory [distillation] apparatus [equipment] —주 distilled liquor; spirits

증명 證明 (a) proof; evidence; (a) testimony; 〈증언〉 attestation; 〈논증〉 demonstration; certification; 〈입증〉 verification
—증명하다 prove; testify to; attest 《to》; witness; bear [give] witness [testimony] to 《a fact》; evidence; demonstrate; substantiate; certify; verify; authenticate
♦ 신분을 증명하다 prove [establish] *one's* identity; identify *oneself* / 무죄를 증명하다 〈일이 주어〉 establish [prove] *sb's* innocence / 학설을 증명하다 demonstrate a theory / 정직함을 증명하다 〈일이 주어〉 prove *sb* (to be) honest; show [testify, witness] that *sb* is honest
▶ 신원을 증명할 것이 있습니까? Do you have anything to prove [establish] your identity?
▶ 이 이론은 아직 과학적으로 증명되지 않았다 This theory is not yet scientifically established.
▶ 이 사실이 그의 정직함을 증명한다 This fact proves [shows, testifies] his honesty. ⇌ This fact is proof of his honesty.
■ —자 a witness; a testifier; a demonstrator; a certifier; a verifier

증명서 證明書 a certificate; 〈인물·자격 등의〉 a testimonial

♦증명서를 교부하다 grant a certificate 《to》; confer a certificate 《on *sb*》/ 증명서를 발급하다 issue a certificate 《to》
■ 건강— a (medical) certificate of health; a health certificate 사망— a death certificate 신분— an identification [identity] card; an ID card 출생— a birth certificate

증발 蒸發 1 〈액체의〉 evaporation; vaporization ♦증발성의 vaporable; volatile
—증발하다 evaporate; vaporize
▶열은 물을 증발시킨다 Heat evaporates water.
▶휘발유는 쉬 증발한다 Gasoline is volatile.
2 〈사람의〉 mysterious disappearance
—증발하다 disappear mysteriously
■ —계 an evaporimeter; an atmometer —기 an evaporator —력 the evaporative power —열 the heat of evaporation; evaporation heat —접시 an evaporating dish [basin]

증발 增發 1 〈열차의〉 operation of an extra train —증발하다 operate an extra train; increase the number of trains ♦임시 버스를 증발하다 operate extra buses
2 〈통화 등의〉 an increased issue ▶국채를 증발하다 issue additional national bonds

증배 增配 〈배당의〉 an increased dividend; 〈배급의〉 a ration increase; an increased [extra] ration
—증배하다 〈배당을〉 pay a larger [an increased] dividend; 〈배급을〉 increase the rations; distribute extra rations
▶회사의 이익이 늘었으니 차기 주식 배당을 증배할 것이다 As the company's profits have risen, it will pay a larger dividend on stocks next term.

증병 增兵 reinforcement; an increase (in the number of) soldiers

증보 增補 enlargement; supplement
♦개정 증보판 a revised and enlarged edition
—증보하다 enlarge; supplement 《a book》

증봉 增俸 an increase in salary; 《美》 a salary [英》 rise] in salary [pay]; 《美口》 a pay hike [boost] —증봉하다 increase [raise] *sb*'s salary [pay]

증빙 證憑 evidence; (a) proof; (a) testimony
■ —서류 documentary evidence; papers [documents] submitted as evidence: 증빙서류를 제출하다 submit [give, produce] documentary evidence

증산 增産 an increase in production; a production increase; increased production; 〈농산물의〉 an increased yield
—증산하다 increase [boost, step up] production; increase the yield; produce more
♦쌀을 증산하다 increase the yield of rice / 자동차를 증산하다 increase the production of cars
■ —운동 a production increase campaign; a drive for production increase

증상 症狀 symptoms ⇨ 증세(症勢)
■ 자각— subjective symptoms 중독— toxic symptoms

증서 證書 〈증명서〉 a certificate; 〈채무 등의 문서〉 a bond; 〈양도 등의 문서〉 a deed; 〈증거 서류〉 a document
♦증서에 조인하다 put [affix] *one's* signature to a bond / 증서에 서명하다 sign (and seal) a deed / 증서를 작성하다[쓰다] prepare [draw out, write out] a deed; execute a deed
■ 신탁— a trust deed 예금— a certificate of deposit; a deposit certificate [note, receipt] 졸업— a diploma 차용— a bond of debt [loan]; an IOU (*pl.* ~s); 《美》 a due bill

증설 增設 (an) increase 《of buildings》; extension; enlargement
—증설하다 build [establish] more; increase; extend; enlarge; install more 《telephones》
▶도시들은 학교를 증설하기에 매우 바쁘다 Cities are very busy increasing their schools.

증세 症勢 〈증후〉 symptoms; 〈병세〉 the condition of disease [a patient]
♦병의 초기 증세 initial symptoms of a disease / 감기 비슷한 증세 cold-like symptoms
▶그 환자는 콜레라 증세를 보이고 있다 The patient has [presents] symptoms of cholera.
■ 자각— subjective symptoms 중독— toxic symptoms

증세 增稅 a tax increase [(口) hike, boost] increase of taxation [taxes] ♦작년보다 10%의 증세를 제안하다 suggest a 10 percent increase in taxation over last year
—증세하다 increase taxes
■ —계획 an increased taxation plan —안 a tax increase bill

증손 曾孫 a great-grandson; a great-grandchild (*pl.* -children)
■ —녀 a great-granddaughter

증수 增水 the rise [rising] of a river; flooding
—증수하다 rise; swell
▶큰 비로 강이 증수했다 The heavy rains made the river rise [swelled the river].
■ —기 a flooded season; an annual flooding period —표(標) a floodmark; a high-water mark

증수 增收 〈농작물의〉 an increase yield; 〈수입의〉 increased income [receipts, revenue]; an increase [increment] of [in] income [revenue]
♦증수 대책을 세우다 take measures to increase receipts
—증수하다 increase (in) income [receipts]
▶이달 수입은 작년 같은 달에 비해 약 10퍼센트 증수했다 This month's income shows an increase of about 10 percent over the same month last year.

증수회 贈收賄 bribery; (offical) corruption; jobbery
■ —사건 a bribery case

증식 增殖 multiplication; increase; proliferation ♦세포의 이상 증식 hyperplasia of cells
—증식하다 increase; multiply; proliferate
■ —로 〈원자로의〉 a breeder (reactor); 〈발전용의〉 a power breeder (reactor)

증액 增額 the increased amount; (an) increase
♦국방예산의 증액 an increase in the national defense budget
—증액하다 increase; raise
▶가족 수당이 5% 증액되었다 The family

증언 證言 〈진술〉 testimony
♦법정에서 피고에게 유리한[불리한] 증언을 하다 testify in favor of [against] the accused in court
—**증언하다** testify 《to, that...》; give testimony; witness; bear witness 《to》
▶ 그녀는 용의자가 그 집에 들어가는 것을 보았다고 증언했다 She testified [witnessed] that she had seen the suspect enter the house.
■—서 a written testimony —자 a witness

증여 贈與 donation; presentation
—**증여하다** give; present 《*sth* to *sb*》
♦학교에 5천만원을 증여하다 donate [present] fifty million won to the school
■—물 a gift; a present; a donative —세 a donation [gift] tax —자 a giver; a donator; a donor —재산 a donated property

증오 憎惡 hatred; detestation; abhorrence
♦증오심을 품다 hate; have feelings of hate [hatred] —**증오하다** hate; detest; loathe

증원 增員 an increase in (the number of) personnel
—**증원하다** increase the staff [personnel]
▶ 우리 과는 8명에서 10명으로 증원되었다 The staff of eight in our section has been increased to ten.

증원 增援 reinforcement —**증원하다** reinforce
■—부대 reinforcements: 증원부대를 파견하다 dispatch reinforcements 《to》

증인 證人 〈목격자〉 an eyewitness; 〈증언자〉 a testifier; 〈선서증인〉 a deponent; 〈증서 작성의〉 an attestor; 〈보증인〉 a surety
♦증인이 되다 〈사건의〉 stand witness for *sb*; depose [testify] to *sth*; bear witness to *sb*; 〈신원의〉 stand [go] surety for *sb* / 증인을 소환하다 call [summon] a witness / 증인을 신문하다 hear [examine] a witness / 증인으로 세우다 call [take] *sb* to witness
▶ 변호사는 증인을 반대심문했다 The lawyer cross-examined the witness.
▶ 그는 증인으로 소환되었다 He was called as a witness in court [at the trial].
■—피고[검사]측— a defense [prosecution] witness —대 the witness box; 《美》 the witness stand: 증인대에 서다 take the witness stand

증자 增資 〈일반적으로〉 (an) increase of capital; (a) capital increase —**증자하다** increase the capital; 〈주식회사가〉 increase its [their] (capital) stock [《英》 shares]

증적 證迹 〈증거〉 evidence; 〈흔적〉 traces; marks
▶ 그 범인은 그녀의 방에 증적을 남겼다 The criminal left traces [marks] in her room.

증정 增訂 enlargement [supplement] and revision
—**증정하다** enlarge [supplement] and revise
■—판 a revised and enlarged edition

증정 贈呈 presentation; proffering
—**증정하다** present 《*sb* with *sth*, *sth* to *sb*》; make a present [gift] of *sth*; donate
♦증정할 〈서적에 서명하여〉 "With the Compliments of the Author" / …선생님께 증정하는 바입니다 "To [Presented to] Mr.…."
▶ 협회는 그녀에게 메달을 증정했다 The association presented her (with) a medal [a medal to her].
■—본 a presentation [complimentary] copy —식 a presentation ceremony —자 a presenter; a giver; a donor —품 a present; a gift

증조모 曾祖母 a great-grandmother
증조부 曾祖父 a great-grandfather
증지 證紙 a certificate stamp; 〈검사필〉 an inspection stamp [sticker]

증진 增進 increase; promotion; improvement
♦문화교류의 증진 the promotion of cultural exchanges / 사회복지의 증진 extention of social welfare services
—**증진하다** increase; promote; further
♦건강을 증진하다 promote health; improve [reinforce, build up] *one's* health / 능률을 증진하다 increase [improve] efficiency / 체력을 증진하다 build up *one's* strength

증축 增築 (an) enlargement [extension] of a building
—**증축하다** extend [enlarge, add to] a building; build an annex [extension] to
▶ 우리는 집을 조금 증축하고 있다 We are putting an addition on our house.
▶ 서점을 증축하는 중이다 The bookstore is being enlarged [expanded].
■—공사 extension work —비 the cost of extending a building

증파 增派 reinforcement; additional dispatch
—**증파하다** 〈병력·군함을〉 dispatch [send] more (troops [warships]) ♦함대를 증파하다 send naval reinforcements 《to》

증편 蒸— steamed rice-cake
증폭 增幅 〔電〕 amplification —**증폭하다** amplify
■—기(器) an amplifier
증표 證票 a voucher
증회 贈賄 bribery; (口) graft
—**증회하다** bribe *sb*; give *sb* a bribe; practice bribery; grease [gild, tickle] *sb's* palm; oil *sb's* hand [palm]
▶ 업자가 관리에게 천만원을 증회했다 The businessman gave a bribe of ten million won to the official.
■—사건 a bribery case —자 a briber —죄 bribery: 증회죄로 고발되다 be charged with bribery / 증회죄를 범하다 commit bribery / 그는 증회죄로 기소되었다 He is charged with [is caused of] bribery.

증후 症候 a symptom ⇨ 증세(症勢)
■—군(群) a syndrome: 다운증후군 Down's syndrome

지 〈동안〉 since…; from (the time when)…
▶ 한국에 오신 지 얼마나 됩니까? How long have you been in Korea?
▶ 그가 죽은 지 10년이 된다 He has been dead for ten years. = It is ten years [Ten years have passed] since he died.

지 知 〈지각〉 sense; 〈지성〉 intelligence; 〈지식〉 knowledge
지 智 〈지혜〉 wisdom; 〈지력〉 intellect; intelligence; sense

지- 至-〈까지〉till; until; to ◆ 자(自)오전 9시 지 오후 5시 from nine a.m. to five p.m.

-지 1〈의문〉what; if; whether
▶ 이것은 무엇이냐 What's this?
▶ 어떻게 그런 것을 알 수 있지 ? How do you know that, may I ask?
▶ 그는 어디론지 가버렸다 He has gone somewhere.
2〈부정〉◆ 좋지 않다 not good
▶ 덥지도 춥지도 않다 It is neither hot nor cold.
▶ 나는 가고 싶지 않다 I don't want to go.
3〈나열〉and; besides; moreover; what with..., and (what with)...
▶ 감기는 들었지, 배는 아프지, 나는 혼이 났다 I had a terrible time with a cold and stomachache.
4〈종결어미〉▶ 너도 가는 거지? You are going, aren't you?
▶ 너도 그렇게 생각하지? You think so too, don't you?
▶ 내일은 그가 오겠지 He will probably come tomorrow.
▶ 그녀는 이제 도착했겠지 She ought to have arrived by this time.
▶ (일을) 그만하고 좀 쉬지 Let's knock off our work here and have a rest.
▶ 내가 바보지 Fool that I am!

지가 地價 〈매매의〉the price of land; land prices; 〈대장의〉the value of land; land value
◆ 지가의 등귀[하락] the rise [fall] of land prices
▶ 지가가 올랐다 Land rose in price.
■ 법정— the assessed value of land

지가 紙價 the price of paper

지각 地殼 the crust (of the earth); the earth's crust; the lithosphere
■ —변동 diastrophism; crustal movements [disturbances] —운동 crustal activity; movement of the earth's crust —평형 isostasy

지각 知覺 1〈인식〉perception; sensory [sense] perception; consciousness
—지각하다 perceive; feel; sense
◆ 지각할 수 없는 imperceptible; incognizable
2〈철〉discretion; prudence; wisdom; good sense
◆ 지각 있는 discreet; prudent; thoughtful; understanding / 지각 없는 indiscreet; imprudent; injudicious; thoughtless; rash / 지각 없이 imprudently; rashly; indiscreetly; thoughtlessly / 지각이 들다 attain *one's* years of discretion; cut *one's* wisdom teeth
▶ 그는 아직도 지각이 없다 He doesn't have sense enough to know better.
▶ 정말 지각 없는 짓을 했구나 How imprudent he is [you are] to have done such a thing!
■ —기관 the organs of perception —동사〖文法〗 a verb of perception —력 perceptibility; perceptivity; sensibility —마비 stupor —상실 stupefaction; an(a)esthesia —신경 a sensory nerve (system) —연령〖法〗 age of discretion

지각 遲刻 lateness; late coming; being late
—지각하다 be [come] late; be behind time
◆ 30분 지각하다 be thirty minutes late / 학교에 지각하다 be late for [at] school; come late to school / 회사에 지각하다 come [go] late to office / 지각하지 않고 학교에 가다 go to school in time; be in time for school / 지각한 평계를 대다 make an excuse for being late
■ —일수 the number of days late —자[생] a latecomer: 지각자를 조사하다 check (off) the latecomers [those who have come late]

지갑 紙匣 a purse; (美) a billfold; a pocketbook; a wallet
◆ 가죽 지갑 a leather purse / 두둑한 지갑 a well-lined purse; a plump [fat] purse / 지갑이 가볍다 have a light purse / 지갑 사정을 알아보다 consult *one's* purse / 지갑을 톡톡 털다 empty *one's* purse to the last penny [cent]; spend *one's* last penny / 지갑을 꺼내다 draw out *one's* purse / 돈을 지갑에서 꺼내다 take money out of *one's* purse
▶ 나는 지갑을 도둑 맞았다 I had my wallet stolen. ⇒ Someone took my wallet.

── 지갑 ──

프레임 frame
지갑 bill compartment
잠금쇠 knob closure
카드꽂이 credit card slots

지검 地檢 a district public prosecutors' office
■ —검사 a district public prosecutor; (美) a district attorney

지게 1〈짐 지는 기구〉a coolie rack (for carrying things); a carrying frame; an A-frame (carrier) ◆ 지게를 지다 carry an A-frame on *one's* back / 물건을 지게에 얹다[싣다] load things on an A-frame; load an A-frame with things / 지게로 나르다 convey *sth* on an A-frame
2 ⇨ 지게문
■ —꾼 an A-frame coolie; a burden carrier 지 겟다리 the legs of an A-frame 지겟작대기 a prop for an A-frame

지게문 a sliding door

지게미 1〈술의〉wine lees; (brewer's) grains; draff 2〈눈의〉eye mucus; gum 3 ⇨ 비듬

지게질 carrying things on an A-frame —지게 질하다 carry things on an A-frame

지겹다 〈싫증나다〉boring; tedious; tiresome; 〈지긋지긋하다〉disgusting; loathsome; nauseous / 지겨운 일 a boring [an irksome] job; an ugly job; drudgery / 지겨워하다 be (quite) disgusted 《with, at, by》; get sick (to death) 《of》; be bored up 《with, by》; become fed up 《with》
▶ 나는 비참한 생활이 지겹다 I am tired of my miserable life.
▶ 그녀의 불평은 이제 지겹다 I'm fed up with her complaints.

지경 地境 1 〈경계〉 a boundary; a border ◆인접 토지와의 지경 the boundary with the neighboring land / 지경을 정하다 fix the boundary
2 〈형편〉 a situation; conditions; circumstances ◆어려운 지경에 처해 있다 be in needy circumstances; be badly off
▶배가 고파 죽을 지경이다. 뭐 먹을 것 있니? I'm starving to death. Is there anything to eat?

지계 地階 〔建〕 a basement; a cellar
지고 至高 supremacy; sublimity
—**지고하다** highest; supreme; most sublime
지골 肢骨 〔解〕 bones of the extremities
지골 指骨 〔解〕 a phalanx (pl. ~es, -langes); a phalange
지공품 紙工品 paper wares
지구 地球 the earth; the globe
◆지구의 공전[자전] the revolution [rotation] of the earth / 지구의 인력 terrestrial gravitation ; the earth's gravity / 지구의 표면 the surface [face] of the earth / 지구상에서 on earth; on the face of the earth
▶지구는 태양 주위를 돈다 The earth moves [goes] around the sun.
—**과학** earth science —**관측위성** an earth survey satellite —**궤도** the earth's orbit —**물리학** geophysics —**물리학자** a geophysicist —**본**[**의**] a (terrestrial) globe; a world globe —**역학** geodynamics —**중심설** the geocentric theory; geocentricism —**촌** a global village —**화학** geochemistry
지구 地區 a district; an area; a region; a zone
◆도시를 9지구로 분할하다 zone a city into nine districts [zones]
—**공장**[**주택**]— an industrial [a residential] area [zone] 상업— a business section [center, quarter]; a commercial district 오락— an amusement quarter ■—제(制) 〈도시의〉 zoning
지구 地溝 〔地質〕 a graben; a rift valley
지구 持久 endurance; sustenance; persistence
—**지구하다** hold out; endure; persevere; persist; sustain
지구당 地區黨 a (electoral) district party chapter; (a party's) constituency chapter ◆지구당 위원장 the chairman of a district party chapter; (美) a district leader / 지구당을 개편하다 reorganize a district party chapter; reorganize a provincial branch
지구력 持久力 sustaining [staying] power; endurance; tenacity; stamina
▶그는 지구력을 기르려고 날마다 줄넘기를 한다 He is skipping rope everyday to strengthen himself [get stamina].
지구전 持久戰 〈전투〉 a war of attrition; a drawn-out [protracted] struggle [war]
▶그들은 지구전의 태세를 갖추고 있다 They are prepared to hold out (in the war).
2 〔스포츠〕 an endurance contest [game]
지구책 持久策 a plan for a game of endurance ◆지구책을 세우다[강구하다] form a plan for holding out
지국 支局 a branch (office) ■—**장** the head [manager] of a branch; a branch manager
지그시 1 〈슬그머니〉 quietly; gently; lightly; softly ◆눈을 지그시 감다 close one's eyes gently / 지그시 누르다 press down softly
2 〈참는 모양〉 patiently; with perseverance; tenaciously ◆모욕을 지그시 참나 bear [endure] an insult stoically
지그재그 zigzag ◆지그재그로 in zigzags / 지그재그로 나아가다 (go) zigzag; follow [trace] a zigzag course / 지그재그로 행진하다 have [hold] a zigzag parade
지극하다 至極— 〈더할 나위 없다〉 utmost; extreme; 〈대단하다〉 tremendous; 〈극진하다〉 most faithful [devoted]; utterly sincere [loyal] ◆지극한 정성을 쏟다 put one's whole heart and soul (into)
▶그는 효성이 지극하다 He is very faithful to his parents. ⇒ He is a very faithful [filial] son.
지극히 至極— very; most; quite; exceedingly; extremely; to the utmost degree
◆지극히 가난하다 be awfully poor / 지극히 유감스럽다 be most regrettable
▶그것은 지극히 중대한 문제다 It is a problem of vital importance.
▶그 시합을 못봐서 지극히 유감이다 It is extremely regrettable that I missed the game.
지근 支根 〔植〕 a rootlet; a radicle
지근 至近 —**거리** the point-blank range; the shortest range —**탄(彈)** a shot fired at close range
지근거리다 1 〈귀찮게 굴다〉 annoy; bother; harass; tease; 〈졸라대다〉 importune [tease] (sb for sth)
◆여자에게 지근거리다 dangle after a woman; hang around a woman
2 〈머리가〉 have a throbbing pain (in one's head); have a headache
3 〈씹다〉 chew softly
지글거리다 sizzle; frizzle; simmer; bubble up
지글지글 with a sizzling sound; sizzling; simmering; frizzling; bubbling up
◆미움으로 지글지글 타는 마음 the mind seething with hatred / 지글지글 끓(이)다 simmer / 지글지글 튀기다 frizzle
▶고깃국이 지글지글 끓고 있다 The meat soup is boiling (furiously).
지금 只今 1 〈현재〉 the present; the present time [day]; this time [moment]; now
◆지금의 〈현재의〉 present; 〈오늘날의〉 of today; present-day; current / 지금의 여왕 the present Queen; the reigning Queen / 지금의 상황 present [existing] conditions (circumstances) / 지금의 학생 students (of) today; present-day students; students nowadays / 바로 지금 this very minute / 지금껏 ⇨ 지금까지 / 지금에 이르기까지 until [up to] now; down to this day [the present time] / 지금부터 10년전 ten years ago / 지금부터 50년 후 fifty years hence [from now]
▶지금부터 10일전 일이다 It was about ten days ago.
▶바로 지금이다 Now is the time [chance]. ⇒ Now or never.

▶ 지금은 가을이다 It is autumn [fall] now.
▶ 그는 해고되어 지금은 실직중이다 He was fired and is now [presently] out of work.
▶ 지금은 옛날같지 않다 Things are not what they used to be.
▶ 지금은 너무 늦다 It's too late now.
▶ 하이킹하기에는 지금이 가장 좋을 때다 This is the best time to go out on a hike.
▶ 그는 지금 전화중이다 He is on the line now [at the moment].
2 〈방금〉 now; at present; just (now); but [even] now; a moment ago; 〈이제 곧〉 soon; at once; right now; immediately
▶ 그들은 지금 출발했어요 They have just left.
▶ 지금 지불해 주시오 Pay me this very instant. ⇒ Pay right down.
▶ 지금 가요 I am coming right now.
▶ 지금 당장 오너라 Come here this very minute.
▶ 지금 당장은 안됩니다 It can't be done at a moment's notice [《美》in short order].

지금 地金 〈귀속 재료〉 metal; 〈원광〉 ore; 〈토대의〉 ground metal; 〈도금의〉 the metal underneath; 〈화폐의〉 bullion

지금거리다 chew gritty; be gritty to the teeth
▶ 밥이 지금거린다 The rice is gritty.

지금까지 只今— until [up to] now [the present]; by this time; so far; till [by] now
◆ 지금까지는 thus [so] far; as yet
▶ 지금까지는 만사가 순조롭다 So far all has gone well.
▶ 지금까지 어디에 있었느냐? Where have you been all this while?
▶ 지금까지 이렇게 재미있는 책은 보지 못했다 This is the most interesting book I have ever read. ⇒ I have never read a book so interesting as this.

지금쯤 只今— (about) this time; at this time of day [night, (the) year] ◆내일[어젯밤] 지금쯤 about this time tomorrow [last night]
▶ 지금쯤은 이미 부산에 도착했을 거야 He must have arrived in Pusan by this time.

지급 支給 payment; provision; supply; allowance; furnishment; 〈배급〉 an issue
◆ 지급이 늦다 be behind(hand) with one's payment / 지급을 거절하다 refuse payment; 〈어음의〉 dishonor a bill / 지급을 독촉하다 press sb for payment / 지급을 보증하다 guarantee payment / 지급을 연기하다 postpone [put off] payment / 지급을 정지하다 stop [suspend] payment / 지급을 청구하다 ask for payment [settlement]
—**지급하다** give; provide [supply, furnish]《sb with sth》; grant; issue; 〈급료를〉 pay
◆ 급료를 지급하다 pay wages / 여비를 지급하다 allow sb money for the traveling expenses / 연금을 지급하다 grant a pension
▶ 재단에서는 우수한 학생에게 학비를 지급한다 The foundation supplies excellent students with school expenses.
▶ 월급은 25일에 지급된다 We are paid on the 25th day every month. ⇒ Our monthly salary is given on the 25th.
▶ 그녀는 장학금을 지급받고 있다 She is supported by a scholarship.
■ 전액— payment in full 현금— cash payment
■ —거절 refusal of payment —계획 a payment plan —능력 solvency —명령 an order 《on a bank》 for payment —불능 insolvency —액 the amount paid [payable] —어음 a bill payable —인 a payer; 〈어음의〉 a drawee —일 〈월급의〉 a payday —전표 a payment [debit] slip —조건 the terms of payment —준비금 a reserve fund for payment —준비 제도 a reserve requirement system —지 the paying-teller's window —협정 a payment agreement

지급 至急 ◆「지급 친전」이라고 적힌 편지 a letter marked "private and urgent" / 지급의 urgent; pressing / 지급으로 urgently; promptly; immediately; at once; without delay; as quickly as possible
▶ 그 일은 지급을 요한다 The matter is pressing.
■ —전보[전화, 편지] an urgent telegram [call, letter]

지급기일 支給期日 the date of payment
▶ 지급기일이 지났다 The deadline for payment has passed. ⇒ Payment is overdue.

지급보증 支給保證 certification of payment
■ —수표 a certified check

지급우편 至急郵便 express mail ◆편지를 지급우편으로 부치다 send a letter by express

지급유예 支給猶豫 postponement of payment; 〈법령에 의한〉 a moratorium (pl. -ria)
■ —기간 days of grace; a grace period

지급정지 支給停止 suspension of payment
■ —은행 a bank in suspension

지급청구 支給請求 a demand for payment
◆ 지급 청구를 하다 demand [ask for] payment —서 a written application for payment

지긋지긋하다 **1** 〈지겹다〉 disgusting; detestable; loathsome; vexing; damned
◆ 지긋지긋한 광경 a frightening sight
▶ 듣기만 하여도 지긋지긋하다 It makes me sick even to hear.
2 〈넌더리나다〉 tedious; tiresome; 〈서술적〉 get sick (to death) 《of》; become tired [bored] (to death) 《of》
◆ 지긋지긋한 일 a boring [an irksome] job
▶ 그녀는 지긋지긋하다는 듯이 돌아섰다 She turned away with a fed-up look.

지긋하다 elderly; rather old; somewhat advanced in life;《be》well up in years
◆ 나이가 지긋한 사람 an elderly person; a person well advanced in years / 지긋한 나이 elderly age; elderliness

-지기[1] 〈논밭의 넓이〉 a stretch [plot, patch] of paddy good for planting ◆석 섬 지기 a stretch of paddy good for planting three sŏm of seed / 닷 되지기 a field that takes five toe of seed

-지기[2] 〈지키는 사람〉 a keeper; a watchman; a guard ■등대— a lighthouse keeper 문— a gatekeeper; a doorkeeper; a doorman 산— a (forest) ranger

지기 地氣 vapour of the earth; spirit of the

지기 earth; air in soil

지기 地祇 〈땅의 신령〉 the gods of earth ■천신— the gods of heaven and earth

지기 志氣 will and spirit; spirit ◆지기 상합(相合)하다 be of congenial spirit; find a kindred [congenial] spirit in *sb*

지기 知己 〈아는 사람〉 an acquaintance; 〈친한 친구〉 a bosom friend; an intimate (friend) *one's* bosom friend ◆지기가 많다 have a wide circle of acquaintances; know many people

지기 紙器 paper ware

지기지우 知己之友 an acquaintance ⇨ 지기(知己)

지꺼분하다 1 〈눈이〉 dirty; gummy ◆ 안질로 지꺼분한 눈 gummy eyes 2 〈물건이〉 disorderly; messy; littered; untidy; slovenly

지껄이다 talk garrulously; wag *one's* tongue; chatter; jabber; gibber; gabble
◆ 잘 지껄이는 사람 a chatter-box; a great talker; a rattler / 허튼 소리를 지껄이다 talk nonsense; talk rot / 쉴새없이 지껄이다 talk and talk; talk without ceasing; rattle on / 함부로 지껄이다 talk too freely; shoot off *one's* mouth
▶ 도대체 무슨 소리를 지껄이는 거야 What the deuce are you talking about?
▶ 그녀는 숨도 쉬지 않고 지껄여댔다 She rattled on [kept talking] without pausing for breath.

지끈 with a snap; snappingly —**지끈하다** snap; give a snap; crack; crash ◆ 지끈하고 부러지다 break with a snap; snap; crack / 막대를 지끈하고 부러뜨리다 snap a stick in two

지끈지끈 1 〈부러지는 소리〉 with a snap; snappingly ◆ 지끈지끈 부러지다 snap in [to] pieces
2 〈머리가 아픈 모양〉 ◆ 머리가 지끈지끈 아프다 have a splitting [racking] headache

지나가다 go [run] past; go [pass] by; go [pass] along [through]; pass (a place); 〈세월이〉 pass
◆ 지나가는 사람 a passerby / 우연히 지나가다 happen [chance] to pass (by); pass by casually / 지나가는 길에 as *one* passes; on the way; when passing
▶ 버스는 15분마다 지나간다 The buses run every 15 minutes.
▶ 태풍은 지나갔다 The typhoon has passed.
▶ 좀 지나갑시다 Let me by [pass, through], please.
▶ 인생은 꿈처럼 지나간다 Life is fleeing by.

지나다 1 〈통과하다〉 pass (by); go [run] past; go through
◆ 문전을 지나다 pass *sb's* door / 숲속을 지나다 pass through a wood / 폭풍우가 지나는 것을 기다리다 wait for the storm to pass / 수원을 지나서 가다 go beyond Suwon
▶ 지나는 길에 들렀습니다 I have just dropped in as I was passing.
▶ 벌써 신갈 인터체인지를 지났습니다 We have already passed Shingal interchange.
▶ 지나는 길에 그들이 말하는 것을 들었소 I caught what they said when I happened to pass by.

2 〈경과하다〉 pass; pass by [away]; elapse; 〈기한이〉 expire; be out
◆ 1, 2년만 지나면 in a year or two / (그로부터) 사흘 지나서 three days later [after that] / 시간이 지남에 따라 as time goes by [passes]; with the lapse [passage] of time / 몇 년 지나는 사이에 in the course of the years / 10년 기한이 지나다 exceed the limit of ten years; be over a period of ten years
▶ 그는 40세를 지났을 것이다 He must be over forty.
▶ 서울에 와서 3년이 지났다 It is three years [Three years passed] since I came to Seoul.
▶ 며칠이 지나도 그에게서는 소식이 없다 Days passed without a line from him.
▶ 지난 일은 다 잊어버리자 Let bygones be bygones.
▶ 너의 운전 면허증은 기한이 지났다 Your driver's license has expired.

3 〈초과하다〉 go beyond; exceed; go too far [to excess] ◆ 도가 지나면 if carried to excess [to the extreme]

지나새나 night in (and) day out; day and night; all day long; all the time
▶ 그녀는 지나새나 그의 생각 뿐이었다 Asleep or awake she was thinking of him.
▶ 그는 지나새나 담배만 피우고 있다 He is smoking all the time.

지나오다 1 〈통과하다〉 pass (by); pass through; come by [along, through]
▶ 기차는 벌써 대구를 지나왔다 Our train passed Taegu already.
2 〈겪다〉 experience; go through
◆ 지나온 일을 생각하다 think of [think back to] the past [bygone days]

지나지 않다 be nothing but...; be no more than...; only; merely
▶ 그는 이름뿐인 사장에 지나지 않는다 He is nothing but [no more than] a figurehead [nominal] president.
▶ 청중은 30명에 지나지 않았다 The audience consisted of only thirty people.
▶ 그것은 추측[소문]에 지나지 않는다 It is a mere [only a] guess [rumor]. ⇌ It is no more than a guess [rumor].

지나치다 1 〈정도를 넘다〉 go too far [to excess]; be too much; exceed (in)
◆ 말이 지나치다 say too much; go too far in talk; criticize too severely / 지나치게 일하다 work too hard [much]; overwork *oneself* / 지나치게 일해서 병이 나다 fall ill from overwork; overwork *oneself* ill / 술을 지나치게 마시다 drink too much; overdrink (*oneself*)
▶ 지나친 공부는 몸에 해롭다 Too much study is bad for your health.
▶ 지나치게 먹지 마라 Don't eat too much. ⇌ Don't overeat.
▶ 자네가 그런 말을 하다니 좀 지나치네 It is rather forward of you to say a thing like that.
▶ 농담이 좀 지나치군 You carry your joke a bit too far.
▶ 내 말이 지나쳤나? Did I put it too strongly?

2 〈지나가다〉 go [walk] past; pass by; 〈내려야 할 곳을〉 ride past [be carried beyond] 《*one's* destination》
♦ 두세 집 지나치다 go past two or three doors beyond
▶ 방심하다가 역을 지나쳤다 I was so absent-minded that I went right past the station.
▶ 그녀를 길에서 만났으나 모른체 지나쳐버리더라 When we met on the street, she passed [went by] me with no sign of recognition.

지난 last; past ♦ 지난 일들 (things of) the past; bygones / 지난 겨울 last winter / 지난 10월 20일 October 20 last; last Oct. 20

지난 至難 extreme difficulty
─**지난하다** most [extremely] difficult
♦ 지난한 일 a task of extreme difficulty
▶ 그를 설득하기는 나로서는 지난한 일이다 It is almost [next to] impossible for me to persuade him.

지난날 the past [old] days; the past; (the) bygone days; (the) days gone by
♦ 지난날의 일들 things of the past / 지난날을 생각하다 think of bygone days [the past]
♦ 지난날이 그립다 I long for the days past.
▶ 그녀의 얼굴에는 지난날의 모습이 어려 있었다 There was still something in her features which reminded me of her younger days.

지난달 last month; ultimo (略 ult.)
♦ 지난달 7일에 on the 7th (of) last month

지난번 ─番 the last time [occasion]; 〈부사적〉 last; last time; previously
♦ 지난번의 the last; preceding; previous / 지나번에 알려드린 바와 같이 as I let you know last time; as previously announced
▶ 그녀는 지난번보다 좋아보였다 She looked better than last time.
▶ 지난번 그에게 전화했더니 외출했더라 (The) last time I called him he was out. ⇌ When I called him last time, he was out.
▶ 지난번에 너에게 말하지 않았던가? Haven't I told you before?

지난주 ─週 last week ♦ 지난주의 오늘 this day (last) week; a week ago today

지난호 ─號 a back issue of a magazine

지날결 〈부사적〉 as *one* passes; when passing; on the way
▶ 지날결에 들렸습니다 I have just dropped in [stopped by] as I was passing.
▶ 나는 지날결에 슬쩍 본 것 뿐이다 I had only glanced at it as I passed by.

지남음 ─音 〔樂〕 passing note [tone]

지남철 指南鐵 〈자석〉 a magnet; 〈자침〉 a magnetic needle

지내다 **1** 〈시간·세월을 보내다〉 pass; spend; pass *one's* time
♦ 하루를[하룻밤을] 지내다 pass a day [night] / 하는 일 없이 지내다 waste time; idle [dawdle] *one's* time away / 휴가를 해변에서 지내다 spend *one's* holidays by the seaside
▶ 나는 에어컨 없이는 여름을 지낼 수 없다 I cannot go through the summer without an air-conditioner.
▶ 저녁에는 텔레비전을 보면서 지낸다 I spend my evenings watching television.

2 〈살아 나가다〉 live; get on [along]; lead [live] a life
♦ 편안히 지내다 live comfortably [in comfort]; be comfortably [well] off / 어렵게 지내다 make a poor [bare, scanty] living; be badly off / 행복하게 지내다 live happily [a happy life] / 가정부 없이 지내다 get along without a housemaid
▶ 〖會話〗「요즈음 어떻게 지내십니까?」「잘 지내고 있습니다」 "How are you getting along these days?" "We are (getting along) quite well, thank you."
▶ 그는 평범한 일생을 지냈다 He lived an uneventful life.
▶ 그녀는 자랄 때 유복하게 지냈다 She was brought up in affluent circumstances.
▶ 그는 적은 수입으로 그럭저럭 지내고 있다 He gets along on his scanty income.

3 〈교제하다〉 associate 《with》; keep company 《with》; mix [mingle] 《with》
▶ 그녀는 새 동료들과 잘 지내고 있는 것 같다 She seems to be getting along all right with her new colleagues.

4 〈어떤 지위를 누리다〉 serve 《as》; hold 《a post》; follow a career
♦ 오랫동안 외교관을 지낸 사람 a man of long diplomatic career
▶ 그는 한때 장관을 지냈다 He was once [at one time] a member of the Cabinet.

5 〈치르다〉 hold; celebrate; observe
♦ 장례를 지내다 hold a funeral service / 제사를 지내다 perform ancestral rites

지내보다 keep company with; associate with; get on [along] with
▶ 지내보니 그는 좋은 친구였다 On further acquaintance I found him a nice fellow.
▶ 사람은 지내봐야 안다 It takes time to really get to know a person.
▶ 그는 지내볼수록 좋은 사람이다 He is the sort of man who improves on acquaintance [intimacy].

지네 〔動〕 a centipede

지네고사리 〔植〕 a wood fern

지노 紙─ a twisted-paper string; a twisted piece of paper ♦ 지노를 꼬다 twist paper into a string; make a paper string / 지노로 철하다 file with a paper string

지느러미 a fin ♦ 지느러미 모양의 finny
■ 등[가슴, 배, 꼬리]─ a dorsal [pectoral, ventral, caudal] fin

지능 知能 intelligence; intellect; intellectual [mental] faculties; mental capacity

〖解說〗 *intelligence*는 「이해의 빠르기, 슬기로움」 등을 뜻하며 교육과는 관계없이 타고난 능력의 뜻이 내포되어 있다. *intellect*는 「이해력, 사고력」 등 교육이나 훈련에 의해 길러지는 것을 말한다. 따라서 「지능」이라함은 intelligence 쪽이 가깝다.

♦ 지능이 높은 아이 a child of high intelligence / 지능이 보통인 사람 a man with average intelligence / 지능이 뒤떨어지는 학생 a backward [(mentally) retarded] pupil / 지능

적인 intellectual / 지능을 계발하다 develop intellectual faculties [the intellect]
▶그녀는 지능이 우수하다 She has great mental ability.
▶이것은 어린이의 지능 발달에 중요하다 This is important for the development of a child's mental powers [intellectual faculties].
━범 an intellectual [a mental] offense [crime]; 〈범인〉 an intellectual [a mental] offender [criminal] ━연령 ⇨ 정신(~연령) ━정도 an intellectual standard [level]

지능검사 知能檢査 an intelligence test; an I.Q. test ♦지능검사 하다 give an intelligence test 《to》

지능지수 知能指數 an intelligence quotient (略 IQ, I.Q.) ♦그는 지능지수가 130이다 He has an IQ of 130.

지니다 〈휴대하다〉 carry; wear; have sth with [about] one; (美) have sth along; 〈가지다〉 have; possess; keep; own; 〈간직하다〉 hold; retain; bear; 〈품다〉 cherish; entertain
♦흉기를 지닌 강도 an armed robber / 무기를 지니다 carry [be armed with] a weapon / 비밀을 지니다 cherish a secret / 어떤 의미를 지니다 bear a meaning / 나쁜 감정을 지니다 have [bear] ill feelings 《against》 / 몸에 권총을 지니다 carry a pistol with one
▶인간은 이성을 지니고 있다 Man is endowed with reason.
▶그는 아직도 젊음을 지니고 있다 He still keeps [retains] his youthfulness [youth].
▶그는 절대로 많은 돈을 지니고 다니지 않는다 He never carries much money with him.
▶그녀는 화가로서 큰 재능을 지닌 사람이다 She has great talent as a painter.
▶이 사전은 지니고 다니기 편하다 This dictionary is handy to carry.

지다¹ 1 〈어떤 상태가 되다〉 ♦그늘이 지다 be shaded / 홍수가 지다 be flooded [inundated]
▶그 나무 때문에 집에 그늘이 너무 진다 The tree shades the house too much.
▶장마가 졌다 The rainy season has set in.
▶이렇게 비가 계속 오다가는 홍수가 지겠다 If it goes on raining, there will be a flood.
2 〈없던 것이 새로 생기다〉 ♦얼룩이 지다 become stained [blotted, smudged]
▶네 옷깃에 얼룩이 져 있다 Your collar has a stain on it.
▶천장은 비가 새어 얼룩이 져 있다 The ceiling was patched with damp.
3 〈기타〉 ♦원수지다 incur an enmity; make an enemy of sb / 모가 지다 be angular [stiff]; be harsh
▶그는 모가 지지 않은 사람이다 He has well-rounded corners.
▶그 둘은 서로 원수진 사이다 They are enemies to each other.

지다² 1 〈해·달이〉 sink; set; go down
♦지는 해 the setting sun / 해질 무렵 at dusk [nightfall]; toward evening / 해가 지기 전에 before (it is) dark; before sundown [sunset] / 해가 지고 나서 after dark [sunset]
▶달은 이미 졌다 The moon has already set [gone down].

▶해는 동쪽에서 떠서 서쪽으로 진다 The sun rises in the east and sets in the west.
2 〈꽃·잎이〉 fall; scatter; be scattered [shed]; be strewn 《to the ground》
▶곧 꽃이 지겠지 The blossoms will soon be gone.
▶나뭇잎은 모두 졌다 The leaves have all fallen from the trees.
▶단풍잎은 지금쯤 모두 졌을 것이다 The maple leaves must have all fallen by now.
3 〈때 등이〉 come out; be taken off [out]; be removed
▶이 잉크 얼룩은 빨아도 잘 지지 않는다 This ink stain will not wash out.
▶아무리 빨아도 때가 지지 않는다 The dirts will not come out, however hard I may try to wash them off.

지다³ 1 〈패배하다〉 be defeated; be beaten; be outdone; lose
♦경쟁에 지다 lose in a contest [competition] / 시합[소송, 전쟁]에 지다 lose a game [lawsuit, war] / 일부러 져 주다 throw a match [game, race] 《to one's opponent》 / 깨끗이 지다 be a good loser / 큰 점수차로 지다 be beaten by a large score
▶내가 졌다 I am beaten! ⇒ You win! ⇒ The game is yours.
▶어쩐지 우리 팀이 질 것 같다 I'm afraid our team will lose.
▶토끼도 때로는 거북한테 진다 The hare is sometimes outstripped by the tortoise.
▶이것은 지는 싸움이다 We are fighting a losing battle.
▶그는 아무한테도 져본 일이 없다 He has never met his match yet.
▶지는 것이 이기는 것일 수도 있다 I should say it is a case of stooping to conquer.
▶우리는 그 (야구) 시합에서 2대 1로 졌다 We were defeated in the (baseball) game by two to one. ⇒ We lost the (baseball) game by two to one.
2 〈굴하다〉 yield; give in; give way 《to》; be overcome 《with》
♦감정에 지다 give way to one's feelings; be overcome with emotion / 더위에 지다 succumb to the heat; be affected [upset] by hot weather / 유혹에 지다 yield [succumb] to temptation
▶자네의 열성에 졌네 Your enthusiasm leaves me standing.
▶어떤 어려움에도 지지 말고 연구를 계속해 주시오 Please carry on your research no matter what difficulties [obstacles] you encounter.
3 〈뒤지다〉 be second [inferior] 《to》; fall behind; yield 《to》; play second fiddle 《to》
♦수적으로 지다 be overwhelmed in number; be outnumbered
▶그의 재주는 누구에게도 지지 않는다 As far as talent is concerned, he is second to none.
▶그는 아직도 젊은이에게 지지 않는다 He can still keep up with young people.

지다⁴ 1 〈등에〉 carry on one's back; bear; shoulder
♦짐을 지고 with a load on one's back / 지게

를 지다 carry an A-frame on *one's* back / 무거운 짐을 지다 bear a heavy burden
2 〈빚을〉 fall [run, get] into (debt); incur [contract] 《a debt》
▶ 그는 막대한 빚을 지고 있다고 한다 He is said to have borne the burden of heavy debts.
▶ 그녀에게 진 빚을 갚을 방도가 없었다 I didn't have the means to pay for what I owed to her.
▶ 너는 그녀에게 얼마나 빚을 졌니? How much money do you owe her?
3 〈신세를〉 owe; be indebted to sb for sth
▶ 나는 그에게 신세를 많이 지고 있다 I owe him much. ⇌ I am under a heavy debt to him.
▶ 신세 많이 졌습니다 I am indebted to you for kindness.
4 〈책임 등을〉 undertake; assume; bear; take; be charged 《with》
♦ 책임을 지다 assume the responsibility 《of》 / …할 의무를 지다 be obliged to 《do》; be under obligation to 《do》
▶ 책임지고 그것을 하겠습니다 I will take the responsibility of doing it.
▶ 그 책임은 그가 져야 한다 The blame lies at his door.
▶ 사장은 사고의 책임을 지고 물러났다 Called to account [Held responsible] for the accident, the president resigned.

지다[5] 〈어떻게 되어가다〉 become; grow; get; come to 《be, do》
▶ 날씨가 아주 따뜻해지고 있다 It [The weather] is getting quite warm.
▶ 이제는 수학이 좋아졌다 Now I've come to like mathematics.
▶ 그는 그녀가 싫어졌다 He has fallen out of love with her.
▶ 폭풍우는 점점 더 심해졌다 The storm grew more and more severe.

지당하다 至當— proper; just; reasonable; fair
▶ 그것은 지당한 방법이라고 생각한다 I think it is a reasonable method.
▶ 지당한 말씀이오 You are (quite) right. ⇌ Your opinions are right enough.
▶ 지당하신 질문입니다 You may well ask that.
▶ 그의 말이 지당한 것인지 의심스럽다 I question the fairness of his statement.

지대 支隊 a detachment; a detached force [troop]

지대 地代 land [ground] rent; 〈지대 수입〉 rental
♦ 지대가 비싼[싼] 토지 a high-rented [low-rented] land / 지대를 거두다 collect ground rents / 지대를 올리다 raise ground rents / 지대로 생활하다 live on revenue from land

지대 地帶 a zone; a region; an area; a belt
■ 공업— an industrial area 구릉— a hilly district 녹(綠)— a green belt [zone] 비무장— a demilitarized zone (略 DMZ) 산악— a mountainous area 삼림— a forest area [region]; a woodland 안전— a safety zone 완충— a buffer zone 요새— a fortified [strategic] zone 위험— a danger spot [zone, area] 중립— a neutral zone

지대공 地對空 ♦ 지대공의 ground-to-air
■ —미사일 a ground-[surface-]to-air missile

지대지 地對地 ♦ 지대지의 ground-to-ground
■ —미사일 a ground-to-ground [surface-to-surface] missile

지대하다 至大— very great; immense; enormous
♦ 지대한 관심사 a matter of great interest / 평화에 지대한 공헌을 하다 make a great contribution towards peace; do much for peace
▶ 근대 과학에 끼친 아인슈타인의 영향은 지대하다 Einstein has a tremendous impact on modern science.

지덕 知德 knowledge and virtue

지도 地圖 a map; 〈도시의〉 a plan; 〈해도〉 a chart; 〈약도〉 a sketch; 〈지도책〉 an atlas
♦ 간단한[상세한] 지도 a rough [detailed] map / (벽에) 거는 지도 a wall map / 5만분의 1 지도 a map on a scale of 1 to 50,000 / 지도를 보다 consult a map / 지도에서 찾다 search a map for 《a place》; look up [out] 《a place》 on a map / 지도에 나와 있다 be (shown) on maps [the map] / 지도 보는 법을 배우다 take lessons in map-reading / 지도 보는 법을 잘 알고 있다 be good at reading maps
▶ 지도를 그려 주시겠습니까? Will you draw a map for me?
▶ 지도를 의지해서 그를 찾아갔다 I visited him with the help [aid] of a map.
▶ 지도로 지름길을 찾으시오 Study [Look on] the map for a shortcut.
■ 구면투영— a globular chart 등고선— a contour map 모형— a model map; a relief map 백— a blank map 역사— a historical map [atlas] 접— a folding map; a folder 항공— an air map; an aeronautical map; an aerial chart
■ —제작 cartography —제작자 a cartographer

지도 指導 guidance; lead; leadership; instruction; direction
▶ 탁구부는 정 코치의 지도를 받고 있다 The ping-pong club is under coach Chŏng's guidance.
▶ 그녀에게 우리 아들의 수영 지도를 부탁했다 I asked her to teach my son how to swim.
▶ 우리는 민교수님의 지도하에 연구하고 있다 We are doing research under the guidance [direction, leadership] of Prof. Min.
▶ 그는 이 프로젝트에서 지도적 역할을 하고 있다 He is playing a leading part in this project.
—지도하다 guide; lead; take the lead; direct
♦ 학생의 공부를 지도하다 guide a student in his studies / 잘못 지도하다 misguide; misdirect
▶ 앞으로도 잘 지도해 주시기 바랍니다 We are looking forward to your continued support.
■ 개인— personal guidance ■ —교사 a guidance teacher; 〈개인 지도 교사〉 a tutor —교수 an academic adviser —법 a method of guidance; how to guide 《*one's* pupils》 —부 a guidance division —서 a guide (book); 〈교과서의〉 a teacher's manual —안 a guidance plan; a teaching plan —원리[방침] a principle of guidance; a guiding [governing] principle

—위원(회) a direction [steering] committee; 〈정당의〉 a guidance committee —정신 a guiding spirit —체제 the leadership system: 단일[집단] 지도체제 a one-man [a collective] leadership system —층 the leadership

지도력 指導力 leadership; the ability to lead; the capacity as a leader ♦ 대단한 지도력이 있다 have great leadership / 지도력을 발휘하다 exercise *one's* leadership

지도리 〔建〕 pivots; hinges

지도자 指導者 a leader; a guide; a director; a pilot; a coach; a rudder ♦ 지도자가 되다 become a leader; assume leadership 《of, in》

지독하다 至毒— severe; awful; bitter; intense; terrible; harsh
♦ 지독한 구두쇠 an awful miser / 지독한 게으름뱅이 a hopeless idler / 지독한 냄새 a bad [nasty, nauseous, repulsive] smell; an offensive smell / 지독한 더위 intense heat / 지독한 추위 severe [intense, bitter] cold / 지독하게 추운 겨울 a bitter winter / 지독한 감기에 걸리다 catch a nasty cold / 지독한 말을 하다 use strong language / 지독하게 공부하다 study awfully hard / 지독하게 춥다[덥다] be terribly [awfully, bitterly] cold [hot]
▶ 그는 지독한 근시다 He is dreadfully near-sighted.
▶ 지독하게 붐비는군 What a crowd [crush]! ⇌ Hell of a crowd, isn't it?

지동설 地動說 the heliocentric theory; the Copernican theory

지둔하다 遲鈍— stupid; dull-witted; thick-headed; slow to understand

지드 〈프랑스의 소설가·비평가〉 Gide, André (1869-1951)

지드럭거리다 tease; harass; vex; pester; (俗) needle

지딱지딱 hurriedly; cursorily; hastily
♦ 일을 지딱지딱 해치우다 get through with *one's* work rather hurriedly

지라 〔解〕 the spleen; the milt

지란지교 芝蘭之交 sweet and noble friendship

지랄 1 ⇨ 간질
2 〈미친 짓〉 (an act of) madness; insanity; a crazy [frantic, wild] action; 〈난폭한 짓〉 outrageous [riotous] behavior
—**지랄하다** go crazy; run [go] wild; do violence; behave rudely [outrageously]; commit an outrage
■ —쟁이 〈간질병 환자〉 an epileptic; 〈못된 놈〉 a wild fellow; a rowdy; a madcap

지랄병 —病 epilepsy ⇨ 간질

지략 智略 resources; practical ingenuity; artifice ♦ 지략이 풍부한 사람 a resourceful mind; a man of resources / 지략이 풍부하다 be resourceful; be full of resources

지러지다 get stunted; wither; wilt; shrivel
♦ 지러진 나무들 stunted trees

지런지런 1 〈넘칠 듯한 모양〉 full to the brim; brimfully **2** 〈닿을락말락한 모양〉 close to 《the ground》; almost touching 《the bottom》

지렁이 〔動〕 an earthworm; 〈뉴싯밥〉 an angleworm; a fishworm

지렁이도 밟으면 꿈틀한다 (속담) Even a worm will turn. ⇌ Tread on a worm and it will turn. ⇌ The ant and the worm even have their wrath.

지레¹ 〈지렛대〉 a lever; a handspike
♦ 지레의 작용 the action of levers; leverage / 지레로 들어올리다 raise *sth* with a lever; lever up; (英) prize; prise
▶ 우리는 지레를 이용해서 길위의 돌을 치웠다 We removed the rock from the road with a lever.

지레² 〈미리〉 beforehand; in advance; prematurely; 〈성급하게〉 overhastily; without due consideration
♦ 지레 판단하다 make a hasty conclusion; jump at [rush to] a conclusion

지레질 levering —**지레질하다** lever up; raise *sth* with a lever

지레짐작 guess(work); (a) conjecture; a hasty conclusion [deduction]
—**지레짐작하다** guess [conjecture] (hastily); presuppose; form [come to] a hasty [rash] conclusion; make a hasty deduction
♦ …이라고 지레짐작하다 run off [away] with the idea that...

지렛대 a lever ⇨ 지레¹

지렛목 a fulcrum 《*pl.* ~s, -cra》

지력 地力 fertility of soil —**체감** decreasing [diminishing] fertility

지력 智力 intellect; mental [intellectual] power ♦ 지력이 발달한 intellectually [mentally] developed

지력선 指力線 〔物〕 line of force=역선

지령 指令 an order; instructions
▶ 나는 그들에게 그곳에 머물러 있으라는 지령을 보냈다 I gave them instructions to stay there.
▶ 조합원들은 파업을 결행하라는 지령을 받았다 The union members were ordered to go on strike.
▶ 우리는 본부의 지령에 따라 행동한다 We act upon orders of the headquarters.
—**지령하다** order; issue an order; instruct; give instructions

지론 至論 a most reasonable opinion

지론 持論 *one's* fixed [cherished] opinion [view]; a pet opinion [theory]; a stock argument
▶ 그는 한번 말을 시작했다 하면 절대로 지론을 굽히지 않는다 Once he begins to speak, he always sticks to [persists in] his opinion.
▶ 절대 권력은 반드시 부패한다는 것이 나의 지론이다 My opinion is [I am of the opinion] that absolute power corrupts without fail.

지뢰 地雷 a (land) mine
♦ 지뢰를 묻다 lay [charge] a mine / 지뢰를 밟다 strike a mine / 지뢰를 제거[회수]하다 remove [retrieve] (unexploded) mines / 적의 지뢰를 폭파하다 spring a mine laid by the enemy
■ —공병 〔軍〕 a miner —밭[원(原), 지대] a minefield —탐지기 a mine detector

지루하다 bored; tedious; tiresome; wearisome; 〈서술적〉 have a dull time

♦지루한 장마 a long and tiresome rainy season / 지루한 강의[설교] a tedious lecture [sermon] / 지루한 여행 a monotonous [tedious] journey / 지루한 줄 모르게 without any sense of boredom / 지루하게 만들다 bore; tire; weary
▶지루한 얘기였다 It was such a boring talk.
▶그는 지루하게 그 일을 이야기했다 He spoke of it tediously.
▶나는 지루해서 죽을 지경이었다 I was bored to death.
▶나는 지루한 나머지 산책에 나섰다 I went for a walk to kill time.
▶우리는 전혀 지루한 줄 몰랐다 We never had a dull moment.
▶하루가 가고 이틀이 지나니 점점 지루해졌다 After a day or two time began to hang heavy on my hands.

지류 支流 a branch; a tributary
▶아마존강에는 많은 지류가 있다 The Amazon has many tributaries [tributary streams].
▶한탄강은 임진강의 지류다 The Hant'angang is a branch [tributary] of the Imjingang.

지르다[1] 〈소리를 크게 내다〉 ♦고함을 지르다 yell; shout; bawl; give a loud cry / 비명을 지르다 utter [give] a shriek; scream; shriek
▶소리를 지르면 죽이겠다 Don't say a word, or you're a dead man.
▶그녀는 비명을 질러 도움을 청했다 She cried [screamed] for help.
▶군중은 기뻐서 환성을 질렀다 The crowd yelled with delight.

지르다[2] 1 〈치다〉 beat; strike; hit; punch; kick 〈at〉; 〈박아넣다〉 drive in; hammer; wedge in ♦못을 지르다 drive [hammer] a nail into 《a wall》 / 발로 정강이를 지르다 kick sb into the shin / 주먹으로 한 대 지르다 give a blow; strike [hit] sb with one's fist
2 〈불을〉 ♦불을 지르다 set fire to 《a shed》; set 《a house》 on fire
3 〈꽂다〉 pass [run, put] sth through; insert; put into ♦빗장을 지르다 bar [bolt] the gate / 머리에 비녀를 지르다 stick an ornamental hairpin in the hair
4 〈길을〉 ♦질러 가다 take a shortcut [shorter way]; cut across
5 〈자르다〉 cut off; clip; nip; snip 《off》 ♦순을 지르다 nip the bud
6 〈기운을 꺾다〉 crush; damp; cast a damp over ♦적의 예기를 지르다 break the brunt of the enemy
7 〈걸다〉 bet; stake; wager ♦판에 돈을 지르다 lay 《down》 a bet 《on the gambling table》; put money down

지르되다 grow slowly; be of slow growth; be slow to mature

지르르 1 〈번드럽게 흐르는 모양〉 greasily
▶그는 얼굴에 기름이 지르르 흐른다 Grease exudes on his face. ⇌ His face is sleek. ⇌ He has a well-fed look.
2 〈저린 느낌〉 ♦전기가 지르르 오르다 get an electric shock

지르박 〈사교춤〉《dance》 the jitterbug

지르신다 wear 《shoes》 half-on; slip 《shoes》 halfway

지르잡다 wash (only) the soiled part 《of a frock》 ♦얼룩을 지르잡다 wash the stain out

지르코늄 〖化〗 zirconium

지르콘 〖鑛〗 zircon ■—산 〖化〗 zirconic acid

지르퉁하다 sullen; sulky; huffy
▶무엇 때문에 지르퉁해 있니 ? What makes you so sulky?

지름 〖數〗 a diameter ♦지름이 3인치 3 inches in diameter / 지름이 2미터인 원을 그리다 draw a circle two meters across [in diameter] ■—반 a radius; a semidiameter

지름길 a shorter way; a shortcut
♦성공에의 지름길 a shortcut to success / 역으로 가는 지름길 a shortcut to the station / 지름길로 가다 take a shortcut [shorter way]
▶이쪽이 지름길입니다 This way is shorter than that.

지릅뜨기 (a person with) upturned eyes
지릅뜨다 cast an upward glance; turn up the eyes ♦눈을 지릅뜨고 with one's eyes turned up

지리 地利 1 〈이점〉 geographical advantages; advantages of a locality [situation]
▶지리를 차지하다 secure vantage ground
2 〈산물〉 profits from land; production

지리 地理 〈지리학〉 geography; 〈지세〉 geographical features; topography
♦지리적 위치[분포, 조건] geographical position [distribution, conditions] / 지리적으로 geographically
▶그는 이 일대의 지리에 훤하다 He is well acquainted [quite familiar] with this place. ⇌ He knows his way around in this neighborhood.
▶나는 이곳의 지리에 어둡다 I am a stranger 《around》 here.
■—책 a geography 《book》

지리다[1] 〈조금 싸다〉 wet [soil] one's pants
지리다[2] 〈냄새가〉 urinous; smelling of urine

지리멸렬 支離滅裂 〈부조리〉 incoherence; inconsistency; 〈사분오열〉 disruption; chaos
♦지리멸렬한 incoherent 《argument》; inconsistent 《policy》; incongruous / 지리멸렬이 되다 become incoherent; go to pieces; fall into a chaotic condition
—지리멸렬하다 split [divide] into many small fractions; be torn asunder; break up
♦지리멸렬한 대열 a disordered line
▶그의 집안은 지리멸렬했다 His family was broken up [torn asunder].
▶그의 말은 지리멸렬하다 What he says is incoherent [inconsistent].

지리하다 支離— bored ⇨ 지루하다
지리학 地理學 geography
■—인문[정치, 자연, 상업]— human [political, physical, commercial] geography ■—자 a geographer

지린내 the smell of urine; a urinous stink
-지마는, -지만 but; however; though; although; still; (and) yet; nevertheless
♦결점은 있지마는 with all one's faults / 나이는 어리지마는 though young; young as one

지리 용어

1. **지리학** geography
   ▶ **자연지리학** physical geography / 인문지리학 human geography / 정치지리학 political geography / 지정학(地政學) geopolitics / 지명학(地名學) toponymy / 지지(地誌) a geographical description; a local topography / 지세(地勢) geographical features; topography

2. **지구** the earth; the globe
   ▶ **지각** crust / 핵 core / 내핵 inner core / 외핵 outer core / 맨틀 mantle
   ▶ **대륙** a continent / 아대륙 a subcontinent / 신[구]대륙 the New [Old] Continent / 해양 the ocean / 태평양[대서양] the Pacific [Atlantic] Ocean

3. **산악** mountains
   ▶ **산** a mountain / 산봉우리 a peak / 표고 an altitude; an elevation; a height / 해발 above sea level / 산맥 a mountain range / 대지·고원 a tableland / 고지·고대 a height; heights
   ▶ **화산** a volcano / 활화산 an active volcano / 휴화산 a dormant volcano / 사화산 an extinct volcano / 화구(火口) a crater / 화구호 a crater lake / 외륜산 a somma / 분화 an eruption / 해저 화산 a submarine volcano / 온천 a hot spring; a spa / 간헐천 a geyser
   ▶ **동굴** a cave; a cavern; a grotto / 종유동 a limestone cave; a stalactite cave
   ▶ **삼림** a forest / 밀림 a jungle / 원시림 a virgin forest / 교목한계선 a timberline
   ▶ **협곡** a valley; a ravine; a canyon / 그랜드 캐니언 the Grand Canyon / 빙하 a glacier / 크레바스 a crevasse

4. **하천** rivers
   ▶ **강** a river; a stream / 시내 a brook / 주류 a main channel / 지류 a tributary; a branch / 상[하]류 the upper [lower] reaches (of a river) / 상류의[로] upstream / 하류의[로] downstream / 급류 rapids / 폭포 a waterfall / 나이아가라 폭포 Niagara Falls / 하구 a rivermouth / 삼각주 a delta / 운하 a canal
   ▶ **호수** a lake / 늪 a swamp; a marsh / 습지·소택지 marshy ground; a marsh land

5. **평지** flat land
   ▶ **평야** a plain / 경작지 arable [cultivated] land / 농장 a farm / (대규모) 농원 a plantation / 목장 a pasture; a ranch; 〈마·소 목장〉 a stock farm; 〈미국의 관광 목장〉 a dude ranch / 무논 a paddy field / 벼농사 짓는 논 a rice field / 대초원 〈북아메리카〉 a prairie; 〈남아메리카〉 pampas, 〈중앙아시아〉 a steppe; 〈아프리카〉 a savanna / 동토대 a tundra / 분지 a basin / 사막 a desert / 오아시스 an oasis

6. **바다와 섬** the sea and islands
   ▶ **해안** the (sea) coast / 반도 a peninsula / 곶 a cape; a promontory / 만 a bay / 큰 만 gulf / 후미 an inlet / 석호(潟湖) a lagoon / 내해 an inland sea / 지협(地峽) an isthmus / 피오르드 a fjord / 해협 a strait; a channel / 영국 해협 the English channel / 도버 해협 the Strait(s) of Dover / 사구(砂丘) a sandhill; a dune
   ▶ **작은 섬** an islet [áilət]; an isle / 맨 섬 the Isle of Man / 열도·군도 an archipelago; islands / 환초(環礁) an atoll / 산호초 a coral reef / 해류 an ocean current / 해구(海溝) a deep / 대륙붕 a continental shelf / 빙산 an iceberg
   ▶ **공해** high seas; the open sea / 영해 territorial waters / 연안국 a coastal country / 내륙국 a landlocked country / 섬나라 island [insular] country / 해양 국민 a maritime people / 해양 자원 marine resources / 해저 자원 seabed resources

7. **촌락과 도시** villages and cities
   ▶ **농촌** a farming village / 어촌 a fishing village / 읍 a town / 도시 a city / 전원 도시 a garden city / 위성 도시 a satellite city / 수도 a capital / 수도권 the metropolitan area / 대도시 a metropolis / 거대 도시 a megalopolis / 교외 주택지 a bedroom suburb 《of Seoul》 / 임해(臨海) 공업도시 a seaside industrial district

---

is / 오기야 오겠지마는 be sure to come, all right, but... / 그렇기는 하지만 for all that; nonetheless; nevertheless / 유감스럽지만 I'm sorry, but...; to my regret
▶ 가고는 싶지만 시간이 없다 I should like to go, but I don't have time.
▶ 돈은 많지마는 행복하지 못하다 I am rich but not happy.
▶ 완쾌는 되었지만 조심해야 한다 You have completely recovered, still you must be careful.
▶ 얼마 되지는 않지만 나도 기부할게 I will contribute my humble share to it.
▶ 형은 호담하지만 동생은 좀 소심하다 The elder brother is daring, while the younger is a little too timid.
▶ 그는 최선을 다했지만 실패했다 Though he did his very best, he still failed.

지망 志望 wish; desire; aspiration; ambition; 〈선택〉 choice
— **지망하다** wish; desire; aspire 《to》; choose
♦ 지망한대로 as *one* wishes
▶ 교사를 지망하는 사람은 거의 없다 Few people wish to be a teacher.
▶ 내가 일차로 지망한 학과는 법학과다 The course of my first choice is the law.
▶ 그는 지망한대로 외교관이 되었다 He has become a diplomat as he wished.
■제1[2]— *one's* first [second] preference [choice] ■ 학과 the desired course [subject of study] —학교 the school of *one's* choice
지망자 志望者 an applicant 《for》; a candidate

(for); an aspirant 《to》
▶ 그 대학에는 지망자가 많다 There are many applicants for entrance to the university.
■문학— a literary aspirant 여배우— a woman aspiring to a screen career; a would-be actress

지망지망 carelessly; heedlessly; thoughtlessly

지맥 支脈 a spur; an offset; an offshoot; a veinlet; feeder

지맥 地脈 the contiguous line of a stratum

지면 地面 the ground; the earth; land
♦ 지면에서 50센티미터 가량 떨어져 about fifty centimeters above the ground / 지면에 쪼그리고 앉다 squat on the ground
▶ 지면이 얼어붙었다 The ground is frozen.
▶ 지면이 말라 먼지가 잘 난다 Dust rises easily because the ground is dry.
▶ 지면에는 눈이 30센티미터나 쌓여 있었다 The snow lay thirty centimeters deep on the ground.

지면 知面 acquaintance ⇨ 면식

지면 紙面 space
♦ 할당된 지면 the space assigned 《to one》 / 지면이 허락하면 if space allows [permits] / 지면을 늘리다 increase the printed columns 《of a paper》
▶ 그 기사는 지면 관계로 삭제되었다 The article was cut for lack of space.
▶ 이 문제는 지면 관계로 자세히 밝힐 수 없습니다 Space does not allow me to dwell on this problem.
▶ 그 신문은 많은 지면을 할애하여 그 사건을 상세히 보도했다 The newspaper gave a lot of space to the affair and reported 《on》 it in detail.

지면 誌面 the space of a magazine [journal, periodical] ♦ 지면을 통해 through a magazine

지멸있다 steady (and honest); solid; faithful

지명 地名 a place name; a geographical name
■—사전 a geographical dictionary; a gazetteer

지명 知名 prominence; eminence; distinction
♦ 지명도가 낮은 사람 a person of little note
■—인사 a man of fame [distinction]; a noted [well-known] person; a notable

지명 知命 〈천명을 앎〉 knowing the decrees of Heaven; knowing one's own destiny

지명 指名 nomination; designation ♦ 지명순으로 in the order of the persons called
▶ 나는 선생님한테 지명을 받았지만 대답할 수가 없었다 I was called on by the teacher, but I couldn't answer.
—지명하다 nominate; designate
▶ 대통령은 그를 차기 국무총리로 지명했다 The President has designated him as the next Prime Minister.
■—입찰 a tender by specified bidders; a private tender —자 a nominator : 피지명자 a nominee —타자〔野〕a designated hitter —통화 a person-to-person call —투표 a roll-call vote —해고 a dismissal of workers by designation

지명수배 指名手配 arrangements for the search of an identified criminal
♦ 지명수배중인 wanted by the police
—지명수배하다 put sb on the wanted list
▶ 경찰은 범인을 전국에 지명수배했다 The police started an open search for the criminal throughout the country.
■—자 a most wanted criminal

지모 智謀 resources; resourcefulness
♦ 지모가 풍부한 사람 a resourceful mind; a man of resources / 지모가 풍부하다 be resourceful; be full of resources

지목 地目 land classification; the classification of land category
▶ 그 토지는 지목이 「산림」으로 되어 있었다 The land belonged to the category of "mountains and forests."
■—변경 reclassification of land; a change in the category of land : 지목 변경 신고 declaration of change of land category

지목 指目 pointing out; indication
—지목하다 point out; indicate; designate; spot; put the finger on
▶ 형사는 그를 범인으로 지목했다 The detective spotted him as the offender.

지문 地文 physiography ⇨ 지문학(地文學)

지문 指紋 a fingerprint; a finger mark
♦ 지문을 남기다 leave one's fingerprints 《on sth》/ 지문을 대조하다 identify 《a criminal's》 fingerprints
▶ 도어에 지문이 남아 있었다 There were some fingerprints left on the door.
▶ 경찰은 그의 지문을 채취했다 The police took his fingerprints.
■—채취 fingerprinting —학 dactylography

지문학 地文學 physiography; physical geography ■—자 a physiographer

지물 紙物 paper goods
■—포 a paper goods store [shop]

지미 地味 (the nature of) the soil
♦ 비옥한 지미 rich [fertile] soil

지미 至美 supreme beauty
—지미하다 supremely beautiful

지반 地盤 1〈지면〉the ground; 〈기초〉the base; the foundation
▶ 이 집은 지반이 단단하다〔무르다〕This house stands on firm [soft] ground.
▶ 이 일대는 지반이 매년 2, 3인치씩 가라앉고 있다 The ground around here [in this neighborhood] has been sinking [subsiding] by two to three inches a year.
2〈발판〉footing; foothold; position
♦ 확고한 지반 a firm foothold / 지반을 닦다〔굳히다〕establish [solidify] one's footing
▶ 그는 그 회사에서 확고한 지반을 닦았다 He made a firm position in the company.
3〈세력범위〉a sphere of influence; 〈선거의〉a constituency
♦ 사회당의 지반 the Socialists' constituency / 농촌을 지반으로 입후보하다 run for the National Assembly with agricultural districts for the constituency
▶ 그는 황선생의 지반을 파고 들어갔다 He has encroached upon Mr. Hwang's sphere of influence.
■—침하 subsidence of ground

지반자 紙— 〔建〕 a papered ceiling
지발중성자 遲發中性子 〔物〕 a delayed neutron
지방 地方 〈지구〉 a region; a district; a locality; an area; a part; a section; 〈시골〉 the country; 〈수도 이외의〉 the provinces; 〈부근〉 neighborhood; vicinity

> 解說 **region**은 지리적·사회적·문화적으로 주변에 대해 뚜렷한 특징을 지닌 지방. **district**는 행정적으로 구분된 것으로 어떤 특색이나 기능을 갖는 지방. **area**는 명확한 경계가 없는 지방으로 넓은 범위나 좁은 범위를 모두 가리킨다. **part**는 나라나 한 지방 중의 일부분을 뜻하며 복수형으로 쓰기도 한다.

◆ 서울 지방 Seoul and its vicinity [neighboring districts] / 영동 지방 the Yŏngdong area [districts] / 지방 사람들 country people [folks] / 지방의 provincial; local; regional / 지방에[으로] 가다 go to [into] the country / 지방을 여행하다 make a provincial tour ▶ 이것은 이 지방에서 유명한 건물이다 This building is famous in this area. ▶ 지방에 따라서는 5월에도 춥다 It is cold even in May in some parts of the country. ■—거래처 a local client —검사 (美) a district attorney (略 D.A.) —검찰청 a district public prosecutor's office —경찰 the local police —계획 local planning —공공 단체 a local public entity [body] —공무원 a local public service [employee] —공연 a provincial tour; (美) a road show —관청 a local [provincial] government —기사 local news —단체 a local [regional] body —도시 a provincial city [town]; a non-major city —법원 a district court : 지방법원 판사 a district judge —분권 decentralization of power —사투리 a local accent; a brogue : 지방 사투리가 심하다 speak with a brogue —선거 a local election —세 local taxes [(英) rates] —시(時) local time —신문 a local newspaper —은행 a local [provincial] bank —의회 a local assembly : 지방의회 의원 a local assemblyman —자치 local autonomy —자치단체 a local autonomous entity —장관 a provincial governor —재정 local finance —정책 a local policy —판 〈신문의〉 a provincial edition —행정 local administration —화 localization
지방 脂肪 fat; grease; 〈돼지의〉 lard
◆ 지방이 많은 (고기) fatty (meat) ▶ 지방을 빼려면 운동을 하시오 Exercise if you want to get rid of fat. ■—과다 excess of fat; obesity —분해효소 lipase —선(腺) ⇨ 피지(～선) —세포 a fat cell —조직 adipose tissue —층 a layer of fat
지방 紙榜 an ancestral paper tablet
지방색 地方色 local color
▶ 이 소설은 지방색이 짙다 This novel is full of [strong in] local color.
지방순회 地方巡廻 a provincial tour (of a theatrical troupe)
◆ 지방순회를 하다 make a country tour; (美) be on the road

지방질 脂肪質 fat; sebaceous constitution
◆ 지방질의 fatty; sebaceous / 지방질이 많다 be fatty
지배 支配 〈통치〉 rule; government; sway; 〈관리〉 control; superintendence; 〈처리〉 management; 〈지휘〉 direction
◆ 법의 지배 the reign of law / 강대국에 의한 약소국의 지배 the domination of a weak country by a strong one / …의 지배하에 있다 be under the control [dominion] of… ▶ 이 나라는 전에 영국의 지배를 받았다 This country was once subject to [under the rule of] Great Britain
—지배하다 rule; govern; dominate
◆ 백인이 지배하는 사회 a white-dominated society / 우주를 지배하는 법칙 the laws which regulate the universe / 세계를 지배하다 dominate the world / 여론을 지배하다 sway public opinion / 운명을 지배하다 control one's destiny / 자연의 법칙에 지배되다 be subject to the laws of nature / 환경에 지배되다 be at the mercy of one's circumstances
◆ 공포가 그의 행동을 지배했다 Fear ruled his actions.
▶ 바다를 지배하는 자가 세계를 지배한다 Those who have command of the seas have control of the world.
▶ 이런 생각이 여론을 지배하고 있다 This thought sways [leads] public opinion.
지배 遲配 ◆ 우편물의 지배 a delay in mail delivery
지배인 支配人 a manager; an executive ◆ 호텔의 지배인 the manager of a hotel; a hotel manager ■ 총[부]— a general [an assistant] manager —대리 an acting manager
지배적 支配的 dominant; overriding
▶ 그 생각이 지배적이다 The idea is dominant over all the others.
지벅거리다 stumble along; walk with difficulty
지벅지벅 stumblingly ◆ 지벅지벅 걷다 stumble along
지번 地番 a lot number
지벌 —罰 〔民俗〕 divine punishment; an evil spell; a curse ◆ 지벌(을) 입다 incur the divine wrath; be cursed (with)
지벌 地閥 one's pedigree; one's social standing in a community
지변 地變 a terrestrial upheaval; a natural calamity; a convulsion of nature
지병 持病 a chronic disease; an old complaint ▶ 지병인 신경통이 도졌다 I have had a return of my old complaint of neuralgia. ⇌ I have had attack of my chronic disease of neuralgia again.
▶ 천식이 그의 지병이다 Asthma is chronic with him.
지보 至寶 a most valuable asset; a cherished treasure
◆ 나라의 지보 a great national asset / 학계의 지보 the pride of academic circles / 한국 문단의 지보적 존재 the most prominent figure in Korean literary circles
지복 至福 supreme bliss; beatitude

지부 支部 a branch (office); ⟨클럽 등의⟩ ⟨美⟩ a chapter; ⟨노동조합 등의⟩ ⟨美口⟩ a local
♦ 본협회의 수원 지부 the Suwon branch [chapter] of this association

지부럭거리다 peck at; annoy; vex; bother; tease; make sport [fun] of

지부티 ⟨나라 이름⟩ Djibouti; ⟨공식명⟩ the Republic of Djibouti ♦ 지부티의 Djiboutian ■ ―사람 a Djiboutian

지분 脂粉 rouge and powder; cosmetics
■ ―내 an odor of cosmetics

지분거리다 peck at ⇨ 지부럭거리다

지불 支拂 payment ⇨ 지급(支給)

지붕 a roof
♦ 세계의 지붕 the roof of the world / 지붕이 새다 the roof leaks / 기와로 지붕을 이다 roof a house with tiles; tile the roof
▶ 지붕 위로 올라가는 것은 위험하다 It is dangerous to climb up on the roof.
▶ 도둑은 지붕을 타고 달아났다 The burglar fled along the roofs [from roof to roof].
▶ 그런 여자와 어떻게 한 지붕 밑에서 같이 살 수 있니? How can you live with that woman under the same roof?

지브롤터 ⟨이베리아 반도 남단의 영국령 항구 도시⟩ Gibraltar ■ ―해협 the Strait(s) of Gibraltar

지빠귀 〔鳥〕a thrush

지사 支社 a branch (office)

지사 地史 geological history

지사 志士 a patriot; a noble-minded patriot

지사 知事 a (provincial) governor
♦ 강원도 지사 the governor of Kang-won-do
■ ―직 governorship ―회의 a gubernatorial conference

지상 至上 supremacy ♦ 인생의 지상 목적 the supreme end of life / 예술 지상주의 the (doctrine of) art for art's sake
▶ 그는 백인 지상주의자다 He is a white supremacist.
■ ―권 supremacy; supreme power ―명령 a supreme order; 〔哲〕a categorical imperative ―선(善) the supreme [highest] good

지상 地上 ⟨지면⟩ the ground; ⟨지표⟩ the earth's surface
♦ 지상의 earthly; terrestrial; surface / 지상의 생활 an earthly existence / 지상 10층, 지하 2층의 빌딩 a building with ten stories above ground and two below / 지상에서 on [above] the ground; on (the) earth / 지상에서 모습을 감추다 disappear off the face of the earth / 지상에서 20미터되는 곳에서 뛰어내리다 jump [leap] down from a point 20 meters above (the) ground
▶ 상처 입은 새가 지상에 떨어졌다 The injured bird fell to the ground.
■ ―관제소 a ground control station ―국 an aeronautic(al) station ―군 a ground forces ―권 〔法〕surface rights: 지상권 설정 creation of superficies ―근무 ground service ―근무자 a ground crew member; ground personnel ―낙원 an earthly paradise ―병력 ground strength [force] ―부대 a ground unit; ground forces ―유도착륙 방식 〔空〕a ground control approach [GCA] method ―작전[공격] a ground operation [attack] ―전투 ground fighting ―정비원 a groundman; (총칭) a ground crew ―포화 ground fire ―핵실험 aboveground nuclear testing

지상 紙上 ♦ 지상에 on paper; in the newspaper / 지상의 논쟁 paper warfare / 본 지상에서 in our columns
▶ 나는 그 기사를 오늘의 지상에서 읽었습니다 I read the article in today's paper.
▶ 나는 지상에서 두들겨 맞았다 I was attacked in the press.
▶ 당신의 수필은 다음달 지상에 나올겁니다 Your essay will appear in print next month.
■ ―계획 a paper plan ―상담란 a personal advice column

지상 誌上 ♦ 지상에(서) in a magazine
▶ 다음 호 지상에 제 입장을 발표하겠습니다 I will make my position public in the next number [issue].

지새다 the day dawns [breaks]; it dawns

지새우다 pass a night without sleep; stay [sit] up all (through the) night
♦ 뜬 눈으로 지새우다 do not sleep a wink; be wakeful all night / 독서로 지새우다 sit up all night reading / 술로 지새우다 drink all night long; drink the night away / 이야기로 밤을 지새우다 talk the night away; talk all (through) the night / 눈물로 지새우다 pass a whole night in tears; weep the night away

지서 支署 branch (office); a substation; a police box [substation]

지석 誌石 a memorial stone

지석묘 支石墓 〔考古〕a dolmen; a cromlech

지선 支線 ⟨철도의⟩ a branch line; a feeder (line); ⟨지방 철도⟩ a local line; ⟨전주의⟩ a supporting wire

지선 至善 the highest [supreme] good

지성 至誠 (absolute) sincerity; devotion; wholeheartedness; one's true heart
♦ 지성으로 faithfully; heart and soul; wholeheartedly; with [in all] sincerity
▶ 당신의 지성을 보여줄 좋은 기회다 It is a good chance to show your sincerity.

지성 知性 intellect; intelligence; mentality
♦ 인간의 지성 human intelligence / 지성적 (인) intellectual; intelligent / 지성에 호소하다 appeal to the intellect
▶ 그는 높은 지성을 갖고 있다 He is highly intellectual.
■ ―미 beauty enhanced by intellect ―인 an intellectual; a highbrow

지성소 至聖所 〔聖〕the sanctuary; the holy of holies

지성이면 감천이라 ⟨속담⟩ Sincerity moves heaven. ⇌ Faith will move a mountain.

지세 地稅 a land tax

지세 地貰 ground [land] rent

지세 地勢 geographical features ⇨ 지형(地形) ♦ 한국의 지세 the physical aspect of Korea

지세븐 G-7; Group of Seven; Major Industrial Nations

지소 支所 a branch (office); a substation

지소사 指小辭 〔文法〕 a diminutive
지속 持續 duration; continuance; continuation; maintenance
　◆ 지속적(인) continuous; lasting; sustaining; durable
　―지속하다 〈계속하다〉 continue; last; keep up; 〈지탱하다〉 maintain; sustain; endure; 〈견디다〉 hold [stand] out
　◆ 전쟁을 지속하다 keep up [continue] a war
　▶ 그는 무엇을 하든 별로 지속하지 못한다 He can't stick at [to] anything very long.
　■ ―기간 duration ―력 endurance; sustaining power ―성 durability. 지속성이 있는 durable
지수 指數 〔數・經〕 an index (number); 〈거듭제곱의〉 an exponent
　■ 물가― a price index 불쾌― a discomfort index 생계비― an index of living costs 지능― intelligence quotient (略 IQ) ―방정식[함수] an exponential equation [function]
지스러기 refuse; waste; trash; odds and ends
　◆ 헝겊 지스러기 waste pieces of cut cloth; cuttings / 지스러기 실 waste threads
지시 指示 indication; 〈상세한〉 instructions; denotation; directions
　◆ 상사의 지시를 받다 receive directions from the boss / 의사의 지시를 청하다[바라다] ask a doctor for advice; ask for a doctor's advice
　▶ 추후 지시가 있을 때까지 기다리시오 Wait for further instructions.
　▶ 본사에서 아무 지시도 없었다 I've received no instructions from the head office.
　▶ 지시에 따라 대답하라 Answer the questions according to the directions.
　▶ 우리는 그의 지시대로 움직였다 We acted according to his directions.
　―지시하다 indicate; denote; show; point to; instruct; direct; give instructions
　■ ―대명사[형용사] 〔文法〕 a demonstrative pronoun [adjective] ―서 an order; directions ―약 (化) an indicator ―인 〈지시하는 사람〉 a director; 〈지정된 사람〉 a designated person ―판 a notice board; a finger post
지식 知識 knowledge; 〈학식〉 learning; 〈견문〉 information; 〈전문 기술〉 know-how
　〈지식이〉 많은 사람 a well-informed person / 지식이 늘다 advance [grow] in knowledge / 영어 지식이 다소 있다 have some knowledge of English
　▶ 그는 법률에 관한 많은 지식이 있다 He has a good knowledge of law. = He knows law well. = He knows quite a lot about law.
　▶ 나는 물리 지식이 전혀 없다 I have no knowledge of physics. = I know nothing of physics. = I am totally ignorant of physics.
　▶ 그 일에는 전문적 지식이 필요치 않다 No professional knowledge is needed for the work.
　▶ 지식이 힘이다 (속담) Knowledge is power.
　〈지식을〉 넓히다 [widen] one's knowledge / 지식을 쌓다 accumulate [store up] knowledge / 지식을 얻다 get [acquire, gain] knowledge / 지식을 향상시키다 improve one's mind [knowledge] / 지식을 뽐내다 parade [air] one's knowledge
　▶ 이 책은 영국에 관한 유익한 지식을 가르쳐 준다 This book gives us useful (piece of) information about Britain.
　■ 기초― a basic knowledge 전문― an expert [a professional] knowledge ―계급 the educated class; the intelligentsia ―산업 the knowledge industry ―인 an intellectual; (口) 〈학식이 있는〉 a person of knowledge [learning]; 〈교양이 있는〉 a cultured person
지식욕 知識慾 a desire to learn; an appetite for knowledge; intellectual appetite
　◆ 지식욕이 왕성하다 have a voracious appetite for knowledge; have a thirst for knowledge / 지식욕을 만족시키다 gratify one's thirst for knowledge
지신 地神 the god of the earth
지실 〈재난〉 (a) disaster; (a) misfortune; evil caused by ill luck
지실 知悉 〈죄다 앎〉 complete knowledge [information] ―지실하다 have a thorough knowledge (of); be fully informed (of)
지심 地心 〈지구의 중심〉 the center [core] of the earth
지싯거리다 ask sb importunately for; importune sb for; press sb for
지아비 a [one's] husband
지악하다 至惡― 1 〈극악〉 heinous; atrocious; most wicked; brutal; villainous
　◆ 지악한 놈 a devil; an accomplished villain; a fiend / 지악한 수단 knavish tricks; villainous measures
　2 〈억척〉 ―지악스럽다 assiduous; sedulous; hellbent
　◆ 지악스럽게 assiduously; sedulously; like hell [the devil] / 지악스럽게 일하다 toil and moil; work hard
지압요법 指壓療法 a finger-pressure therapy; manual therapeutics; acupressure ◆ 지압을 받다 get acupressure / 지압을 하다 practice [perform] the finger-pressure treatment
　■ ―사 a chiropractor
지양 止揚 〔哲〕 sublation; (獨) Aufheben
　―지양하다 sublate; (獨) aufheben
지어내다 make; turn out; produce; create; devise; frame up; fabricate
　◆ 지어낸 이야기 a made-up story; a build-up; a fabrication / 이야기를 지어내다 make up a story
　▶ 그것은 지어낸 이야기임에 틀림없다 That is without doubt a make-up story.
지어먹다 〈작심하다〉 gather one's wits; apply [gather] one's mind
지어미 〈아내〉 a [one's] wife
지언 至言 〈당연한 말〉 a wise saying [saw]
　▶ 시간이 돈이라는 것은 지언이다 It is rightly [well] said that time is money.
지엄 至嚴 extreme strictness [sternness]
　―지엄하다 extremely strict [stern, rigorous]
지업상 紙業商 〈상점〉 a paper store; 〈상인〉 a dealer in paper
지엔피 GNP [*gross national product*]
지역 地域 an area; a region; 〈지대〉 a zone
　◆ 광대한 지역 a vast area; a large tract of land / 지역적 local; regional / 지역적으로

locally; regionally / 지역별로 by regional groups / 지역에 따라 다르다 vary in different localities
▶ 피해는 넓은 지역에 미치고 있다 The damage covers a wide area.
▶ 호수를 맑게 하는 데는 지역 전체가 협력해야 한다 The whole community should cooperate to clean the lake.
■ 개발 유보— reserved development district 개발제한— limited development district 개발촉진— development-promoted district 공업—a manufacturing area 방화(防火)— fire zone 자연보존— nature-preservation district ■—간 격차 regional disparity —구 〈선거의〉 local [district] constituencies [electorates] —단체 a local [regional, territorial] society —대표 the delegation [delegates] of a district [region]; 〈조합의〉 local union delegates —대표 regional representation; territorial [regional] representation system —방언 a regional dialect —사회 a community —사회개발 community development —수당 an area allowance —안보체제 a system of regional security —이기주의 ⇨ 님비주의 —재개발 계획 an area redevelopment program —주민 a local resident; (총칭) local citizenry [populace] —특성 the (province's) regional characteristics

지역차 地域差 regional differences; provincialities ♦ 지역차를 없애다 iron out regional differences

지연 地緣 regional relation; regionalism
♦ 지연, 혈연을 따지다 stick to regionalism and kinship / 지연, 학연 및 혈연을 배격하다 reject regionalism, school relations, and kinship
■—사회 a territorial society

지연 遲延 delay; postponement; retardation
—지연하다 be delayed; be retarded; be late; be behind time
♦ 지연시키다 delay; retard; cause delay / 지불이 지연되다 be behindhand with payments / 예정보다 10분 지연되어 도착하다 arrive ten minutes behind schedule
▶ 열차는 폭설 때문에 2시간 지연되었다 The train was delayed [behind time] (for) two hours by the heavy snow.
■—작전 delaying tactics —책 a dilatory measure

지열 止熱 〈열기가 내림〉 the abatement of temperature (in sickness); dropping of temperature
—지열하다 〈열이 내리다〉 one's temperature falls [goes down]; 〈열을 내리게 하다〉 lower the temperature; bring down the fever

지열 地熱 the subterranean heat; the heat of the earth ♦ 지열의 geothermal / 지열 에너지의 개발 development of geothermal energy
■—발전 geothermal electric power generation —발전소 a geothermal power plant

지엽 枝葉 1 〈가지와 잎〉 branches and leaves 2 〈중요치 않은 일〉 minor details; a digression; side issues (of a story)
♦ 지엽적인 minor; unessential / 지엽으로 흐르다 enter into unimportant details; deviate from the subject [main issue] / 지엽적인 문제에 구애되다 be particular about minor importance
▶ 지배인은 너무 지엽적인 일에 신경 쓴다 The manager pays too much attention to trifling details.

지옥 地獄 hell; Hades; the inferno
♦ 생지옥 a hell on earth; a living hell / 지옥같은 infernal; hellish / 지옥에 떨어지다 go to hell; descend into hell
▶ 지옥에서 부처를 만난 기분이다 I felt as if I had found "a friend in need."
■—교통— a (terrific) traffic jam 입시— the torture of (entrance) examination

지온 地溫 〈지면의〉 ground temperature; 〈땅의〉 soil temperature

지용 智勇 wisdom and courage
▶ 그는 지용을 겸비한 명장이다 He is a great general who has both wisdom and valor.

지우 知友 an acquaintance; a bosom [close] friend

지우 知遇 favor; warm friendship
♦ 지우를 입다 enjoy sb's favor; be favored with sb's recognition [warm friendship] / 지우에 보답하다 requite sb's favor

지우개 an eraser; a rubber ♦ 지우개로 지우다 erase; rub (it) out with a rubber
■ 고무— an eraser; an india rubber; a rubber 칠판— a chalk [blackboard] eraser; a wiper

지우다¹ 〈형성하다〉 form; shape; make
♦ 그늘을 지우다 shade; cast shade upon / 그림자를 지우다 cast [throw] (its) shadow

지우다² 1 〈떨어지게 하다〉 cause to fall; scatter (flowers); 〈낙태하다〉 have a miscarriage 2 〈눈물을 떨어지게 하다〉 bring tears to sb's eyes
3 〈숨을 거두다〉 die; expire; breathe one's last

지우다³ 〈삭제하다〉 cut; delete; cross out; 〈문질러 없애다〉 rub out; wipe away [out]; erase; efface

解說 cut이 일반적인 표현. delete는「쓴 것이나 인쇄한 것을 삭제하다」, cross out는「낱말 등의 위에 선을 그어 지우다」의 뜻.

♦ 명부에서 아무의 이름을 지우다 strike sb's name off the list / 발자국을 지우다 cover (up) one's tracks / 칠판의 글자를 지우다 erase the words on the blackboard / 한 자를 지우다 cross out a word; erase a word / 페인트를 지우다 remove the paint (from)
▶ 나는 화장을 지웠다 I removed my makeup.
▶ 그녀는 드레스의 얼룩을 지웠다 She took the stain out of the dress.
▶ 세월이 그 쓰라린 기억을 지워주었다 The passage of time erased the bitter memory.

지우다⁴ 1 〈짐을 지게 하다〉 put sth on sb's back; make sb carry [bear]
♦ 짐을 지우다 burden sb; lay a burden upon sb / 말에 짐을 지우다 load a horse up
2 〈부담시키다〉 charge (sb with a duty); lay (a duty on sb); put (the responsibility for sth) on

지우다⁵

♦ 비용을 지우다 make sb bear the expenses
▶ 그는 자기 책임을 나에게 지웠다 He shuffled off his responsibility upon [onto] my shoulders.

지우다⁵ 〈이기다〉 beat; defeat; vanquish; get the better [upper hand] of sb
♦ 경주[경기]에서 지우다 beat sb in a race [at a game] / 토론에서 지우다 beat sb in argument; argue sb down
▶ 우리는 홈런을 쳐서 상대팀을 지웠다 We defeated our opponents with home runs.

지우산 紙雨傘 an oiled paper umbrella

지원 支援 support; aid
♦ 적극적 지원 active [positive] support / 정신적 지원 moral support / 지원을 청하다 ask sb's support (in)
━지원하다 support; back [bolster] up
♦ 평화운동을 지원하다 support the cause of peace
■━부대 backup [support] forces ━연설 a campaign speech 《for a candidate》 ━자 a supporter; a patron

지원 志願 〈지망〉 desire; aspiration; 〈신청〉 application; 〈자발적 봉사〉 volunteering
━지원하다 desire (for); aspire (to); apply (for); volunteer (for)
♦ 간호사를 지원하다 volunteer (to work) as a nurse / 병역을 지원하다 volunteer for military service
▶ 그는 서울대학에 입학을 지원했다 He applied for entrance [admission] to Seoul National University. ⇒ He applied to Seoul National University.
▶ 그 일을 지원하는 사람은 아무도 없었다 There was no volunteer for (doing) the job. ⇒ No one volunteered for the job.
■━병 a volunteer: 지원병 제도 the volunteer system ━서 a written application ━자 〈응모자〉 an applicant; 〈자발적인 신청자〉 a volunteer: 대학입학 지원자 an applicant for entrance [admission] to a university

지위 地位 〈신분〉 a position; status; (social) standing; 〈계급〉 (a) rank; 〈직업상의〉 a position; a post; a situation
〈지위가[는]〉 사회적 지위가 높다[낮다] have a high [low] social positon / 지위가 다르다 differ in social standing / 지위가 올랐다[낮아졌다] be advanced [reduced] in rank
▶ 소설가로서 그의 지위는 독특하다 His status among novelists is unique.
〈지위를〉 지위를 얻다 gain [get] a position; be given a place (in the government) / 유리한 지위를 차지하다 occupy a vantage ground; be on favorable ground / 지위를 남용하다 abuse one's position [authority] / 좋은 지위를 버리다 throw up a good place / 지위를 되찾다 recover [regain] one's lost position / 지위를 다투다 try [compete] for a position / 지위를 잃다 lose one's position [place] / 지위를 튼튼히 하다 consolidate one's position / 여성의 사회적 지위를 향상시키다 improve the social status of women
▶ 그는 지위를 유지하려고 애썼다 He made efforts to maintain [preserve] his position

[place].
〈지위에〉 사장의 지위에 있다 take a position [post] as president / 지위에 앉다 occupy [take] a position (as) / 높은 지위에 있다 hold a high rank 《among》
▶ 그는 높은 지위에 올랐다 He rose to a higher position.
▶ 나는 지금의 지위에 만족한다 I am very well where I am.

지위지다 1 〈쇠약해지다〉 be exhausted; be emaciated; be enfeebled; be weakened
♦ 병으로 몹시 지위지다 become worn-out from illness
2 〈살림이 줄다〉 fall (away); decline; be reduced
▶ 주인이 죽은 후로 가게는 지위졌다 Since the proprietor's death, the store has declined.

지육 智育 intellectual [mental] training; mental culture

지은이 an author ⇒ 저자(著者)

지의 地衣 〔植〕 lichen

지인 知人 an acquaintance; a friend

지인용 智仁勇 wisdom, benevolence, and valor

지일 至日 〔天〕 the solstices; 〈동지〉 the winter solstice; 〈하지〉 the summer solstice

지자 知者 a man of intellect; a learned and experienced man; a well-informed person; (총칭) the intellect

지자 智者 a wise man; a man of wisdom; a sage; (총칭) the wise
▶ 지자불혹(不惑) A wise man knows his own mind.

지자기 地磁氣 〔物〕 terrestrial magnetism; geomagnetism

지장 支障 〈장애〉 a hindrance; an obstacle; 〈곤란〉 (a) difficulty; 〈방해〉 interference; 〈불편〉 inconvenience
♦ 지장이 없는 한 if nothing interferes / 지장이 되다 hinder; obstruct; be a hindrance (to) / 지장이 있을 harmful (to); have sth happen; 〈곤란하다〉 have trouble; be engaged (볼일·선약으로); 〈불편하다〉 experience inconvenience / 지장이 없다 〈불편이 없다〉 experience no inconvenience; 〈곤란하지 않다〉 have no difficulty [trouble] (in doing); 〈없어도 되다〉 can do without; 〈선약이 없다〉 be disengaged; be free; be at liberty; 〈해가 없다〉 be harmless / 지장을 초래하다 hinder one; cause one inconvenience; impede; interfere with...
▶ 저는 내일 오후에는 지장이 없습니다 I will be free tomorrow afternoon.
▶ 이 문을 닫아도 지장이 없겠니? Do you mind my closing the door?
▶ 나침반이 없어도 우리는 지장이 없다 We can do without the compass.
▶ 잠이 부족하면 내일 일에 지장이 있다 Lack [Want] of sleep will interfere with your work tomorrow.
▶ 그 거래는 지장없이 행해졌다 The transaction was carried on without hindrance [a hitch].
▶ 지장이 없으시다면 저와 같이 가지 않으시겠습니까? If it is not too much trouble, will

you go with me?

지장 指章 a thumbprint ◆ 지장을 찍다 seal 《a document》 with the thumb ▶ 나는 서류에 지장을 찍었다 I put my thumbprint on the papers.

지장 智將 a resourceful general

지장보살 地藏菩薩 a guardian deity of children and travelers

지저 地底 the bowels [depths] of the earth

지저귀다 〈새가〉 sing; chirp; twitter; warble ◆ 지저귀는 새소리 a bird's twitterings [chirpings]

지저깨비 a chip (of wood); a splinter

지저분하다 1 〈불결하다〉 dirty; unclean; filthy; foul; smutty
◆ 지저분한 거리 a dirty street
▶ 지저분한 얘기지만 나는 치질을 앓고 있다 It is an indelicate thing to mention, but I have piles.
▶ 그의 말투는 지저분했다 He was vulgar in his speech.
2 〈어수선하다〉 scattered about; in disorder; messy; untidy
◆ 지저분하게 어지르다 scatter (about); put 《a room》 in disorder
▶ 방이 지저분하다 The room is untidy [in disorder].
▶ 사무실 안은 지저분하게 어질러져 있었다 The office was in a mess.

지적 地積 〈땅의 면적〉 acreage
■ —측량 a cadastral survey

지적 地籍 a land register
■ —도[부] a cadastral map [book]

지적 指摘 indication
—지적하다 point out; indicate
◆ 오류를 지적하다 indicate an error; point out a mistake / 위에 지적한 바와 같이 as pointed out above
▶ 그 길을 지도에 지적해 주세요 Please indicate the route on the map.
▶ 선생님은 몇 군데 잘못을 지적하셨다 The teacher pointed out some mistakes.

지적 知的 intellectual; 〈정신적〉 mental
▶ 그는 아주 지적인 얼굴을 하고 있다 He looks very intelligent.
■ —교류 intellectual interchange —노동 brain work —능력 mental faculties —생활 (an) intellectual life —직업 a profession; an intellectual occupation —활동 mental [intellectual] activity

지전 紙錢 paper money [currency]; a bank note; 《美俗》 soft money; 《英俗》 a bill
◆ 만 원짜리 지전 ten thousand won note [bill]

지전류 地電流 〈物〉 an earth current

지점 支店 a branch (office [shop, store])
◆ 지점을 개설하다 open [establish] a branch (office) / 지점에 전근되다 be transferred [assigned] to a branch office.
■ 해외— overseas branches [offices] ■ —망 a branch network —장 the manager of a branch office; a branch manager

지점 支點 〔物〕〈지렛대의〉 a fulcrum 《pl. ~s, -cra》; 〔建〕 a bearing

지점 地點 a spot; a point; a place
◆ 출발 지점 The starting point / 예정된 지점 the intended spot / 중추적인 [유리한] 지점 a pivotal [vantage] point

지정 至情 1 〈아주 가까운 정분〉 close intimacy [friendship] ◆ 지정이 있는 친구 true-hearted friend
2 〈충정〉 one's sincere heart; sincerity
3 〈아주 가까운 친척〉 close relative

지정 指定 appointment; specification; designation; assignment
—지정하다 appoint; designate; specify
◆ 미리 지정하다 designate beforehand; specify in advance / 지정한 대로 as specified / 지정한 시간에 그곳에 가다 go there at the appointed time / 면접할 시간과 장소를 지정하다 appoint [specify, designate] the time and place for an interview
▶ 그 지역은 국립공원으로 지정되었다 That area was designated (as) a national park.
▶ 다음의 회합을 위해 일시, 장소를 지정하지 않으면 안된다 We must appoint the time and place for the next meeting.
■ —가(격) the limits —대리인 an authorized agent —석 a reserved seat —인 an appointor —일 a designated day; a specified date —좌석권 a reserved-seat ticket —후견인 a designated guardian

지정거리다 loiter on the way; waste one's time on the road; linger

지정의 知情意 intellect, emotion and volition

지정지밀 至精至密 utmost minuteness
—지정지밀하다 detailed; minute; precise

지정학 地政學 geopolitics
■ —자 a geopolitician

지조 地租 a land tax; the tax on land
■ —미 rice paid as land tax

지조 志操 purpose; principle; 〈절조〉 constancy; fidelity; integrity; honor
◆ 지조가 없는 inconstant; unprincipled / 지조를 지키다 keep [remain faithful to] one's principles
▶ 기회주의자는 많은데 지조있는 사람은 드물었다 There were many opportunists and few men of principle.

지족 支族 a branch family [tribe]

지존 至尊 〈더없이 존귀함〉 the Most Reverend; 〈임금〉 His Majesty; the King

지주 支柱 a support; a stay; a prop
◆ 지주를 대다 prop [shore] up
▶ 그는 한 집안의 지주다 He is the prop and stay of his home. ⇌ He is supporting his family.

지주 地主 a landowner; a landholder; 〈남자〉 a landlord; 〈여자〉 a landlady
■ 대— a large [great] landowner 소— a small landowner ■ —계급 the landed class

지주 持株 〈소유주〉 one's stock holdings; one's shares
◆ 종업원 지주제도 a stock-sharing plan for the employees 《of a company》
■ —회사 a holding company

지중 地中 ◆ 지중의 subterranean; underground / 지중에 under the ground; in the earth
■ —선 a subterranean line —송전선 an underground transmission line —한랭계 an under-

ground thermometer

지중해 地中海 the Mediterranean (Sea)

지지 〈더러운 것〉 dirty ▶ 지지, 아가야 만지지 마 Oh, it's dirty. Don't touch it, baby.

지지 支持 support; backing
♦ 일반 대중의 지지 popular support / 현 내각의 지지율 the approval rate of the present cabinet / 그의 지지를 받다 get [have] support from him; get [have] his support / 국민의 지지를 잃다 lose the support of the public
▶ 그 새 정책은 국민의 지지를 받고 있다 The new policy has the support of the people.
▶ 그의 성책은 여론의 지지를 받지 못했다 His policy failed to win public backing.
—**지지하다** support; give support 《to》; stand by; back (up); uphold
♦ 모두 지지하다 line up behind *sb* / 전폭적으로 지지하다 throw *one's* full support behind *sb* / 남의 주장을 지지하다 support [second] *sb's* claim / 지지받다 have *sb* at *one's* back; get [gain] support 《from》
▶ 그는 그 계획을 지지하는 연설을 했다 He made a speech in support of the plan.
▶ 새 대통령을 지지하는 사람들이 많다 Many people support the new president.
▶ 나는 그 제안을 지지한다 I am for [in favor of] the proposition.
—**자** a backer; a supporter

지지 地誌 a topography
■—**학** (the science of) topography

지지난달 the month before last
지지난밤 the night before last
지지난번 —番 the time before last
지지난해 the year before last

지지다 1 〈끓이다〉 stew
♦ 생선을 지지다 stew fish
▶ 내 손가락에 장을 지져라 Broil me!
2 〈번철 등에〉 panfry; grill; sauté
♦ 저녁을 지지다 make fish sauté / 고기를 기름에 지지다 panfry meat
3 〈인두 등으로〉 cauterize; sear; scorch; brand
4 〈머리를 파마하다〉 frizzle; crinkle; curl; wave; singe
♦ 지진 머리 curly [frizzled] hair; frizz; curls / 머리를 지지다 singe [curl] *one's* hair

지지랑물 rancid drippings from a thatched roof

지지러지다 cringe ⇨ 자지러지다¹

지지르다 1 〈기운을 꺾어 누르다〉 keep down; repress; crush; daunt; depress (*sb's* spirit)
♦ 기를 지지르다 discourage; damp / 부대의 사기를 지지르다 depress [sap] the morale of the troops
2 〈무거운 것으로 누르다〉 press *sth* under [with]; put a weight on *sth*
♦ 돌로 지지르다 press *sth* with a stone

지지리 terribly; dreadfully; awfully; unbearably ♦ 지지리 못나다 〈못생기다〉 be awfully ugly(-looking); 〈어리석다〉 be downright stupid / 지지리 고생하다 go through unbearable hardships

지지부진하다 遲遲不進— make very slow progress; progress at a snail's pace
▶ 건설공사는 지지부진하고 있다 The construction work is making slow progress.

지지하다 遲遲— slow; tardy
♦ 지지하게 slowly; tardily; at a snail's pace

지지하다 worthless; trivial; rubbishy
♦ 지지한 책 [소설] a trashy book [novel] / 지지한 일 trash; garbage / 지지한 소리를 하다 talk nonsense [rubbish]; say silly things / 〈작가가〉 지지한 것을 쓰다 write trash

지진 地震 an earthquake; a shock; (口) a quake; 〈작은〉 a tremor (▶미〔약, 강, 격〕진은 a slight [weak, strong, severe] shock라고 함)
♦ 지진의 중심 a seismic center; 〈진원지〉 the epicenter / 지진의 seismic; seismal / 지진이 잦다 be subject to frequent earthquakes / 지진의 대책을 세우다 take anti-earthquake procedures [measures] / 지진을 예보하다 predict an earthquake
▶ 지진이 일어났다 An earthquake happened [occured].
▶ 오늘 아침 약한[강한] 지진이 있었다 We had [We felt, There was] a slight [strong] earthquake this morning. ⇌ A slight [strong] earthquake occurred this morning.
▶ 어제 밤의 지진은 현지에서 강도 6이었다 The earthquake we had here yesterday was of magnitude 6.
▶ 대부분의 집은 지진으로 파괴되었다 Most of the houses were destroyed by the earthquake.
▶ 지진으로 집이 흔들리는 것을 느꼈다 I felt the house shake from the earthquake.
■—**대**— a big [severe, great] earthquake 해저—a submarine [an undersea] earthquake 화산—〔함락, 단층〕— a volcanic [downfall, dislocation] earthquake ■—**계** a seismograph; a seismometer —**관측** seismological observation; seismometry —**관측소** a seismological observatory —**국** an earthquake(-ridden) country —**대**(帶) an earthquake zone [belt] —**도**(圖) a seismogram —**연구소** the Earthquake Research Institute —**파** a seismic [an earthquake] wave —**학** seismology —**학자** a seismologist

지진아 遲進兒 a (mentally) retarded [backward] child

지질 地質 geology; 〈토질〉 the nature of the soil ♦ 지질상의 geological
■—**도** a geological map —**분석** a soil analysis —**시대** the geological age; geologic eras —**연구소** the Geological Survey Office —**조사**(도) a geological survey (map) —**학** geology; 지질학상의 geologic(al); 지질학상[적으로] geologically —**학자** a geologist

지질 紙質 the quality of paper
▶ 이 종이는 지질이 좋다 [나쁘다] This paper is of good [poor] quality.

지질리다 〈무거운 것에 눌리다〉 be weighted; be pressed under [with]; 〈기가 꺾이다〉 be crushed [daunted]; be held down

지질지질하다 watery; soft

지질펀펀하다 1 〈평평하다〉 flat; broad and even 2 〈땅이 질척하고 펀펀하다〉 broad [wide] and marshy

지질하다 1 〈따분하다〉 tedious; dull; wearisome; tiresome

♦지질한 것[사람] a bore / 지질한 소설 a boring novel
2 〈번번치 못하다〉 worthless; poor; good-for-nothing; wretched
♦지질한 놈 a good-for-nothing (fellow) / 지질한 소리를 하다 talk nonsense; say silly things
지짐거리다 it rains off and on
▶이번 달은 지짐거리는 날이 많았다 We have had many rainy days this month.
지짐이 (a) stew ■고기— meat stew
지짐지짐 —지짐지짐하다 it rains off and on ⇨ 지짐거리다
지짐질 panfrying; making griddlecakes
—지짐질하다 panfry
지참 遲參 〈지각〉 late attendance —지참하다 come [arrive] late; be behind time
■—자 a latecomer
지참금 持參金 a dowry; (a) dower; a dot; a marriage portion
▶그는 지참금이 있는 여자와 혼인했다 He married a girl with a dowry.
▶그는 지참금이 탐나 그녀와 혼인했다 He married her for her dowry.
▶그는 딸에게 지참금을 딸려 보냈다 He dowered [endowed] his daughter at marriage.
지참 持參 —지참하다 〈가져오다〉 bring *sth* with *one*; 〈가져가다〉 take *sth* with *one*
▶비가 올 것 같으니 우산을 지참하는게 좋겠다 You had better take an umbrella with you, because it is likely to rain.
▶내일 시험에는 연필과 지우개를 지참할 것 For your examination tomorrow, be sure to bring your pencils and eraser with you.
■—인 a bearer
지척 咫尺 a very short distance; an inch
♦지척을 분간할 수 없는 어두운 밤 a pitch-dark night / 지척지간이다 be very close; be within a foot
▶안개가 짙어서 지척을 분간할 수 없었다 The fog was so dense that nothing was to be seen an inch ahead.
지척거리다 shuffle along; plod; drag *one's* way
지척이 천리다 (속담) Though it is closeby, the lack of news makes one feel as if it were a thousand miles away.
지천 至賤 **1** 〈많음〉 abundance
♦지천으로 ever so much [many]; in great abundance
▶그는 옷이 지천으로 많이 있다 He stinks of clothes.
▶그 지역에는 광물이 지천이다 The district is abundant in minerals.
2 〈천함〉 the most base
—지천하다 most vulgar [humble, base, mean]
▶그는 지천한 집안에서 태어난 사람이었다 He was a man of very humble birth.
지청 支廳 a branch (government) office
지청구하다 grumble without good reason; murmur; carp; find fault 《with》; complain needlessly
지체 〈문벌〉 lineage; birth; pedigree; the (social) standing of a family
♦지체가 높은[낮은] 사람 a person of high [low] birth; a person of high [low] standing
지체 肢體 the limbs; a member; 〈몸과 수족〉 the body and the limbs
■—부자유아 a physically handicapped child; a crippled child
지체 遲滯 (a) delay
♦지체없이 without delay; promptly; immediately / 지체없이 보고하다 lose no time in reporting *sth*
—지체하다 delay; be retarded; defer; 〈밀리다〉 be overdue
♦도중에서 지체하다 be delayed on the road
▶시민들은 지체하지 않고 세금을 납부했다 The citizens paid their taxes without delay.
▶이 일은 어떤 지체도 허용되지 않는다 This matter admits of no delay.
지촉 紙燭 paper and candles; an obituary gift
지축 地軸 the earth's axis
지출 支出 〈비용〉 expenses; expenditure; 〈지급〉 payment; disbursement; (an) outgo
▶나는 수입과 지출의 균형을 이루기가 어렵다 I find it hard to meet my expenses.
▶전달에는 그의 지출이 수입을 초과했다 His expenses exceeded his income last month.
▶이달에는 내 지출이 많아질 것이다 My expenses will run up considerably this month.
▶이것은 방대한 지출을 요한다 This involves a heavy outlay of money.
■총[경상, 임시] 지출을 삭감할 필요가 있다 It is necessary to curtail [retrench, cut down] total [ordinary, extraordinary] expenditure.
—지출하다 disburse; expend; pay; defray
♦국고에서 지출하다 disburse from the national treasury
■부당— an unjust disbursement 예산외— defrayment unprovided for in the budget 정부[재정]— government expenditure ■—담당자 a paying teller [cashier] —액 expenditure; the sum [amount] expended
지층 地層 〔地質〕 a stratum 《*pl*. -ta》; a layer; a bed
지치 〔植〕 a gromwell
지치다¹ 〈피로하다〉 be [get] tired (▶be tired [weary, fatigued]는「지쳐 있다」고 하는 상태를 나타내며,「지치다」라고 하는 변화를 나타내는 것은 be 대신 get, become, grow를 사용함); be fatigued
▶그녀는 완전히 지쳐 있다 She is tired [worn] out.
▶그는 심신이 모두 지쳐 있다 He is exhausted both in mind and body.
▶그는 노령으로 지쳐 있다 He is worn out with age.
▶나는 철야로 지쳐서 녹초가 됐다 I am worn out from staying up all night.
▶그녀는 지칠대로 지쳤다 She was exhausted.
▶오늘은 지쳤다 I've had a tiring day today.
▶그는 지칠줄 모르고 목표를 추구했다 He pursued his purpose with unflagging energy.
▶그는 지쳐버려서 더 이상 가지 못했다 He was too tired to go any farther.
▶그녀는 너무 지쳐서 의자에 주저앉았다 She dropped into a chair, utterly worn out.
지치다² 〈얼음을〉 slide [skate] on the ice; do

지치다³ 〈문을〉 close (a door) without locking it; close (a door) softly; leave (a door) unlocked but closed

지친 至親 1 〈아주 친함〉 very close relationship —**지친하다** most intimate
2 〈부자지간 등〉 near relationship by blood
♦ 지친이다 be *one's* very near relative

지침 指針 1 〈자석의〉 a compass needle; an index (*pl.* ~es, -dices); a pointer; 〈계기의〉 an indicator
2 〈길잡이〉 a guide
♦ 수험의 지침 a guide to examinations / 생애의 지침 a guide principle in *one's* life

지칭하다 指稱— call; name; designate

지키다 1 〈수호하다〉 defend; 〈보호하다〉 protect; 〈경호하다〉 guard; 〈비호하다〉 shield
▶ 마을 사람들은 스스로를 지키기 위해 무기를 들었다 The villagers took up arms to defend themselves.
▶ 그는 골을 지키고 있다 〈축구에서〉 He is the goalkeeper.
▶ 그것은 고양이에게 생선가게를 지키라고 하는 격이다 It is a case of setting the wolf to guard the sheep.
▶ 그녀는 적의 공격에 대항해서 조국을 지켰다 She defended [protected] her own country against the enemy's attack.
2 〈약속·비밀 등을〉 keep (*one's* word); obey (the law); observe (a custom)
▶ 약속은 지켜야만 한다 You must keep your word [promise]. ⇌ You must not break your word.
▶ 넌 비밀을 지킬 수 있니? Can you keep a secret?
▶ 그분은 시간을 잘 지키시니까 늦지는 않을거다 He is always very punctual, so I doubt if he will be late.
▶ 그는 약속을 지켰다 He was faithful to his promise.
▶ 그녀는 신념을 굳게 지켰다 She held firm to her belief.
▶ 그들은 협정을 굳게 지켰다 They adhered to the contract.
3 〈유지·보존하다〉 keep; maintain
▶ 스위스는 중립을 지키고 있다 Switzerland remains neutral.
▶ 그녀는 거기에 앉아 침묵을 지키고 있었다 She sat there and kept silent.
▶ 자연을 지킵시다 Let's protect [preserve] nature.
▶ 건강을 지키려면 규칙적으로 운동을 해라 If you want to stay healthy, you should take regular exercise.
▶ 체면을 지키려면 돈이 있어야 한다 You need money to keep up your appearances.
▶ 법과 질서를 지키는 것은 우리의 의무다 It is our duty to maintain law and order.
▶ 언제까지나 젊음을 지킬 수는 없다 You cannot retain your youth forever.
4 〈규칙 등을 따르다〉 keep; observe; follow
▶ 학교의 규칙은 지키지 않으면 안된다 You should keep [follow] the regulations [rules] of your school.
▶ 그 아이는 부모님의 말씀을 잘 지켰다 The boy obeyed his parents well.

지탄 指彈 1 〈손끝으로 튀김〉 fillip; flick
2 〈비난〉 (an adverse) criticism; blame; (a) reproach; rejection
▶ 그는 세상의 지탄을 받았다 He fell into disgrace with all the others.
▶ 그의 처사는 불공평하다는 지탄을 면치 못하고 있다 The step he has taken is open to the charge of favoritism.
—**지탄하다** 〈비난하다〉 criticize unfavorably; censure; 〈경멸하다〉 snap *one's* fingers (at)
♦ 지탄받다 incur a censure; lay *oneself* open to censure; be blamed [censured] (for)

지탱하다 支撐— 〈버티다〉 prop; bolster up; 〈유지하다〉 maintain; support; sustain; hold; keep; bear up
♦ 건강을 지탱하다 preserve *one's* health / 목숨을 지탱하다 support life / 지붕을 지탱하다 hold up the roof; receive the weight of the roof / 집안을 지탱하다 maintain *one's* family
▶ 내 봉급으로는 생활을 지탱해 나갈 수가 없다 I cannot make a living on my salary.
▶ 이 학교는 기부금으로 지탱해 나가고 있다 This school is supported by subscriptions.

지통 止痛 allaying [relieving, killing] pain
—**지통하다** allay [relieve, kill] pain
■ —제 an anodyne; a painkiller

지파 支派 a branch of a family; 〈부족〉 a branch tribe; 〈분파〉 a branch; an offshoot; 〈종파〉 a sect; 〈당내의〉 a faction

지팡이 a stick; a walking stick
♦ 마법의 지팡이 a magic wand / 등산용 지팡이 an alpenstock / 지팡이를 들고 다니다 carry [take] a cane / 지팡이를 짚다 use a stick / 지팡이를 짚고 걷다 walk with a cane / 지팡이에 의지하다 lean on *one's* cane
▶ 노인은 지팡이를 짚으며 걷고 있었다 The old man was walking with a cane.
▶ 그는 언제나 지팡이를 들고 다닌다 He always carries a stick.
▶ 노부인은 지팡이에 의지해 걸어왔다 An old woman came along the road leaning on her staff.
▶ 그는 다리가 나을 때까지 지팡이를 짚고 다니지 않으면 안되었다 He had to use a cane until his leg got better.

지퍼 a zipper; a zip fastener; a (slide) fastener ♦ 지퍼달린 가방 a bag with a zipper; zippered bag
▶ 그는 점퍼의 지퍼를 채웠다[풀었다] He zipped up [unzipped] his jacket.
▶ (등의) 지퍼를 좀 채워 주시겠어요 Zip me up, will you?

지평 地平 1 〈땅의 평면〉 the surface of the earth 2 ⇨ 지평선

지평선 地平線 the horizon; the skyline
♦ 지평선 위에 above the horizon / 지평선 위로 떠오르다 rise above the horizon / 지평선 아래로 가라앉다 sink below the horizon

지폐 紙幣 paper money; (美) a (bank) note
♦ 1만원권 지폐 a ten thousand-won bill / 지폐 뭉치 a roll of bills / 지폐의 남발 an excessive

issue of paper currency / 지폐 다발을 세다 count a wad of bills / 지폐를 발행[회수]하다 issue [recall] paper money / 지폐를 남발하다 inflate paper currency

▶ 그는 금액의 일부를 지폐로 지불했다 He paid part of the sum in bills.

▶ 이 지폐좀 바꿔주세요 Please change this bill.

■ ─불환 an inconvertible note ─위조 a counterfeit [forged] note ─태환 a convertible note ─ ─발행 note issue; issue of paper money ─발행고 a note issue ─발행은행 a bank of issue ─본위(제) the paper standard

지폭 紙幅 the width of paper
지표 地表 the surface of the earth
■ ─수 surface water
지표 指標 an index; a guideline; [數] a character(istic)
■ ─경기 a business indicator [barometer]
지푸라기 bits of straw; a straw
지프 (商標) a jeep
지피다¹ 〈신의 영이 내리다〉 be possessed; get inspiration from a divine power; be inspired
지피다² put [throw] *sth* on the fire; make a fire; feed (a fire with coal)

▶ 난로에 석탄을 좀더 지펴라 Feed the stove with some more coal.

지필 紙筆 paper and pens [writing brushes]
■ ─묵 paper, pens and ink
지하 地下 1〈땅속〉 ◆ 지하 세력 an underground influence / 지하 1층[2층]에 on the first [second] underground floor; 〈방 등〉 in the first [second] basement / 지하 10미터에 at ten meters underground [below ground] / 지하에 묻다 bury [lay] underground / (비밀 조직이) 지하에 잠입하다[숨다] go underground; go into hiding / 지하에서 일하다 work underground / 지하 3층 지상 10층 건물 a building with three stories below and ten above the ground

▶ 석탄 갱부는 지하에서 일한다 Coal miners work underground.

▶ 이 건물은 지하 3층이다 This building has three floors below ground level.

▶ 많은 범죄자는 경찰에 쫓겨 지하에 잠복했다 Many criminals went underground while hunted by the police.

2〈무덤〉 a grave; 〈저승〉 Hades; the other world; the underworld

◆ 지하에 잠들고 있는 전몰 희생자 many war victims sleeping in the grave [resting in peace] / 지하에 묻어[매장되어] under the sod; in *one's* grave / 지하에 잠들다 sleep in the grave

■ ─갱도 an underground tunnel ─경 〔植〕 a subterranean stem; 〈근경〉 a rhizome ─공작 underground activities ─근 a subterranean root ─도 (美) an underpass; (英) a subway; 〔軍〕 a gallery ─상가 an underground market ─선 an underground wire [cable]; a subterranean line ─수 underground [subterranean] water ─실 a basement; a cellar ─자원 underground resources ─정부 an underground government ─조직 an underground organization ─핵실험 an underground nuclear test ─활동 underground activities

지하운동 地下運動 underground activities; an underground movement
■ ─자 an undergrounder
지하철 地下鐵 (美) a subway; (英) an [the] underground (railway); 〈런던의〉 the Tube; 〈파리의〉 the Metro

◆ 지하철을 타다 take a subway train / 지하철로 가다 take the subway; go by subway

▶ 내 사무실은 지하철로 30분 걸리는 곳에 있다 My office lies only a half hour away by subway.

▶ 지하철로 10분 걸린다 You can get there in ten minutes by subway.

■ ─공사 subway construction work ─역 (美) a subway stop [station]; (英) an underground station ─이용자 an undergrounder ─입구 a subway entrance

지학 地學 earth science; geology; physical geography
지한 知韓 pro-Koreanism ■ ─파 the pro-Korean (group): 그는 지한파다 He is pro-Korean.
지함 紙函 a carton; a cardboard box
지해제 止咳劑 a cough medicine [lozenge]
지핵 地核 〔地質〕 the earth's nucleus; the centrosphere
지행 知行 knowledge and conduct [deed]
지향 志向 intention; an aim; inclination

◆ 권력 지향 an innate respect for authority / 미래 지향형의 future-oriented

▶ 요즘에는 가족 지향의 젊은이가 늘고 있다 We have more and more family-oriented young men these days.

─지향하다 intend [aspire] ((to do)); aim (at, to do)

▶ 우리가 지향하는 것은 스포츠의 대중화다 We aim at the popularization of sports.

지향 指向 ─지향하다 point ((to))
■ ─성(性) directivity ─성 안테나 a directional [directive] antenna
지혈 止血 arrest of bleeding [hemorrhage]; stanching
─지혈하다 stop blood [bleeding]

▶ 나는 손수건으로 지혈했다 I checked the bleeding with a handkerchief.

■ ─대(帶) a tourniquet ─법 stanching; styptic treatment; a hemostatic method ─제(劑) a hemostatic; a styptic

지협 地峽 an isthmus (*pl.* ~es, -mi); a neck of land ■ 파나마[수에즈]─ the Isthmus of Panama [Suez]

지형 地形 topography; the lay of the land; geographical features; 〔軍〕 terrain

◆ 지형의 이용 use of ground / 지형(학)상의 topographical

■ ─답사 〔地質〕 reconnaissance; survey ─도 (圖) a topographical map [chart] ─측량 a topographical survey ─판단 estimation of ground ─학 topography; morphology

지형 紙型 a paper [papier-mâché] mold
◆ 지형을 뜨다 make [take] a papier-mâché mold; make a paper mold

지혜 智慧 wisdom; 〈기지〉 wits; (a) brains; 〈지능〉 intelligence; an idea; 〈사려분별〉 sense
♦ 생활의 지혜 wisdom for living [of life] / 옛사람의 지혜 the wisdom of the ancients / 지혜로운 be wise [sagacious] / 지혜가 있는 wise; intelligent; witty; sagacious; resourceful / 지혜가 없는 dull; unwise; 〈우둔한〉 stupid / 지혜가 모자라는 shallow-brained; half-witted; slow-witted / 지혜를 빌다 consult [ask advise of] *sb*; ask *sb* for advice / 지혜를 짜내다 draw on *one's* resources; rack *one's* brains / 지혜를 발휘하다 show wisdom
▶ 그에게는 그것을 할만한 지혜가 없다 He is not wise enough [doesn't have the wisdom] to do it.
▶ 사람은 나이가 들수록 지혜가 생긴다 Man gains wisdom with age.
▶ 나는 지혜를 짜냈다 I have racked my brain.
▶ 나는 이 아이가 눈에 띄게 지혜로워진 것 같다 I think this child has grown remarkably intelligent.

지호 指呼 〈손짓해 부름〉 beckoning
♦ 지호지간에 있다 be within hail [call, hailing distance] —**지호하다** beckon (to *sb*)

지화 指話 talking with the hands; sign language ⇨ 수화(手話)

지휘 指揮 command; 〈지시〉 direction(s); instructions; 〈감독〉 superintendence; supervision; [樂] conducting
♦ 아무의 지휘로 [樂] conducted by *sb*; under the baton of *sb* / 아무의 지휘하에 under the command [direction] of *sb* / 아무의 지휘를 받다 be under the direction [command] of *sb*; take orders [command] of *sb*; take orders [instructions] from *sb*
▶ 너희들은 내 지휘에 따르기만 하면 된다 You only have to do as I order.
—**지휘하다** command; lead; direct; 〈악단 등을〉 conduct (a band)
▶ 나폴레옹이 지휘하는 군대 the army under Napoleon's command / 베토벤의 작품을 지휘하다 conduct Beethoven
▶ 그는 그 병단을 지휘했다 He commanded [took command of] the corps.
■ —**계통** a chain of command —**관** a commander; an officer in command —**권** (the right of) command —**대(臺)** [樂] a podium (*pl.* ~s, -dia); a raised platform —**법** [樂] conducting technique —**봉** [樂] a baton

지휘자 指揮者 a commander; a director; a leader; [樂] a conductor: 관현악단의 지휘자 an orchestral conductor

직 〈발작〉 an attack; a fit
♦ 학질을 한 직 앓다 have a fit of malaria

직 直 〈당직〉 duty; watch; guard
♦ 일직 day duty

직 職 〈관직〉 an office; a post; 〈직업〉 an occupation; a profession; a calling; a trade; 〈직책〉 (a) duty; an office

직- direct; straight; right
♦ 직수입 direct import / 직선 a straight line / 직각 a right angle

직각 直角 [數] a right angle
♦ 직각의 rightangled; rectangular / …과 직각으로 at a right angle to… / 직각으로 교차하다 〈two lines〉 cross [meet] at right angles / 직각을 이루다 make a right angle 〈with〉
▶ 이 선은 저 선과 직각을 이룬다 This line makes a right angle with that line.
▶ 하나의 선이 다른 선과 직각으로 만난다 One line meets another at right angles.
▶ 도로는 거기서 직각으로 구부러진다 The road makes a right angle turn there.
■ —**기둥** [數] a right prism —**삼각형** a right(-angled) triangle —**이등변삼각형** an isosceles right triangle

직각 直覺 intuition; insight
♦ 직각적 intuitive; intuitional / 직각적으로 알다 know intuitively [by intuition]
—**직각하다** know intuitively; intuit
■ —**력** intuitive power —**설** intuition(al)ism —**판단** intuitive judgment

직간 直諫 〈직언〉 personal remonstrance [admonition] —**직간하다** reprove *sb* face; remonstrate directly

직감 直感 intuition; 〈美口〉 hunch
♦ 직감적으로 intuitively; by intuition / 직감에 의지하다 rely (up)on *one's* intuition / 직감으로 알다 learn [perceive] intuitively
▶ 그의 직감이 들어맞았다 His intuition proved to be right. ⇌ He guessed right.
—**직감하다** know by intuition [intuitively]; feel *sth* in *one's* bones
▶ 나는 위험이 다가오고 있음을 직감했다 I knew by intuition [felt in my bones] that danger was approaching.

직거래 直去來 a direct deal; a direct [spot] transaction —**직거래하다** carry on direct transaction 〈with〉; make a direct deal 〈with〉

직격 直擊 direct hit
■ —**탄** a direct hit [shot, bomb]: 직격탄에 맞다 be hit directly by a bomb

직결 直結 direct connection
—**직결하다** connect [link] directly 〈with〉
♦ 직결되다 be connected directly 〈with〉
▶ 이것은 생사에 직결된 문제다 This is a vital question. ⇌ It is a matter of life and death.

직경 直徑 a diameter ⇨ 지름

직계 直系 a direct line [descent]
♦ 직계의 자손 a direct descendant; a descendant in a direct line
▶ 그는 대정치가의 직계 자손이다 He is a direct descendant of the great statesman.
■ —**가족** family members in a direct line —**존속[비속]** a lineal ascendant [descendant] —**혈족** a lineal relation —**회사** a directly affiliated concern [firm]

직계 職階 the class of *one's* position
■ —**제** a position classification system; 〈관직의〉 a classified civil service system —**조직** a line organization

직고 直告 —**직고하다** inform [report] truthfully; tell the truth

직공 職工 a workman; a worker; a (factory) hand; a mechanic; an artisan
♦ 양복점 직공 a tailor's man
■ —**기질** an artisan [a craftsman] spirit

직관 直觀 intuition ⇨ 직각(直覺)

직─력 intuition; intuitive power ─**주의** 〔哲〕 intuition(al)ism

직구 直球 〔野〕 a straight ball

직권 職權 authority; official power
♦직권에 의하여 in [by] virtue of *one's* office / 직권 밖이다 be beyond *one's* authority
▶ 그는 직권을 행사[남용]했다 He exercised [abused] his authority.
▶ 그런 경우에는 경찰이 직권을 행사할 수 없다 The police cannot exercise power [authority] on such occasions.
■─**남용** misfeasance; abuse of *one's* authority

직기 織機 a weaving machine; a loom

직녀성 織女星 〔天〕〈별자리〉 Vega

직능 職能 a function
■─**급(給)** wages based on performance [job evaluation] ─**대표제** vocational [professional] representation (system) ─**별 조합** a craft union

직답 直答 〈즉답〉 a ready [prompt] answer; 〈직접 대답한〉 a direct [personal] answer
─**직답하다** give a ready answer; answer personally

직력 職歷 *one's* business career [experience]; *one's* professional experience

직렬 直列 〔物〕 series
■─**연결** series connection ─**회로** a series circuit

직류 直流 〔物〕 direct current(略 DC); continuous current ■─**발전기** a direct current dynamo [generator] ─**전동기** a DC motor; a direct current motor ─**회로** a DC circuit

직립 直立 ♦직립부동 자세를 취하다 stand at attention; come to atter.tion
─**직립하다** stand erect [straight, upright]
♦직립하여 uprightly; erectly; in an erect posture; in an upright position
─**면[선]** a perpendicular plane [line] ─**원인(猿人)** Pithecanthropus erectus

직매 直賣 direct sales ─**직매하다** sell direct (to) ♦직매하는, 직매제의 directselling
─**소[점]** a direct sales depot[store]

직면하다 直面─ face (up to); confront; be confronted with [by]; be faced with; come face to face with; be up against
♦위험에 직면하여 in (the) face of danger / 죽음에 직면하다 be confronted by death; face [confront] death / 파산에 직면해 있다 be on the verge of bankruptcy
▶ 이것들이 우리가 직면하고 있는 문제다 These are the problems that we are confronted with.
▶ 그는 파멸에 직면하고 있다 Ruin stares him in the face.

직명 職名 〈직업명〉 (the name of) *one's* occupation; 〈직책명〉 an official title

직무 職務 (a) duty; an office; a function; a job
♦직무상의 비밀 a secret in respect of *one's* duties / 직무상의 official
▶ 그는 그의 직무에 충실하다 He is faithful to his duties [job].
▶ 그는 그의 직무를 태만히 한다 He neglects his duties.
▶ 나는 직무를 수행하지 않으면 안된다 I must perform [do] my duties, no matter what.
▶ 그는 직무가 태만하다는 이유로 해고당했다 He was dismissed on the ground of neglect of duty.
■─**규정** office regulations ─**내용** job specifications ─**방해** interference with *one's* work ─**분담** distribution of (office) duties ─**수당** a service allowance ─**유기** dereliction [delinquency] of *one's* duty ─**정지** suspension of performing *one's* duties ─**집행** performance of *one's* duties ─**태만** neglect of duty

직물 織物 cloth; textile; a (textile) fabric; woven stuff [goods]
─**공업** textile industry ─**공장** a textile factory ─**류** soft [woven, (美) dry] goods; textile fabrics; drapery ─**상** a draper ─**시장** the cloth market ─**업** drapery; dry-goods business; 〈제조〉 textile manufacture

직배 直配 direct delivery [distribution]
─**직배하다** deliver [distribute] directly

직분 職分 *one's* duty
♦직분을 다하다 do [discharge] *one's* duty / 직분을 지키다 be true [faithful] to *one's* duty
▶ 당신은 공무원으로서의 직분을 망각해선 안됩니다 You must not neglect your duty as a public servant.

직불카드 a debit card

직사 直射 〈총포의〉 direct [frontal] fire; 〈광선의〉 direct rays (of the sun)
♦포화의 직사를 받고 under direct fire
─**직사하다** 〈포화를〉 fire direct (upon); fire point-blank (at); 〈광선이〉 shine [fall] directly (on)
─**포** a direct-firing gun

직사각형 直四角形 〔數〕 a right-angled tetragon; a rectangle

직사광선 直射光線 a direct ray of the sun
▶ 여름에는 직사광선을 쪼이지 마라 Don't expose your skin to the summer sunlight.
▶ 이 꽃은 직사광선을 피하시오 Shelter this flower from direct sunlight.

직삼각형 直三角形 〔數〕 a right(-angled) triangle

직선 a straight [right] line; a beeline ⇨ 일직선
♦직선으로 in a straight line / 직선으로 늘어서다 line up in a straight line / 직선을 긋다 draw a straight line
▶ 그는 직선적이다 He is thoroughly straight.
= He is straightforward.
■─**기선(基線)** a straight baseline ─**미** lineal beauty ─**운동** 〔物〕 a straight line motion ─**코스** a straight course

직선거리 直線距離 a lineal distance
♦직선거리로 in a straight line [a beeline].

직설 直說 a straight talk ⇨ 직언(直言)

직설법 直說法 〔文法〕 the indicative mood

직성 直星 ♦직성이 풀리다 be satisfied [gratified]; feel relieved
▶ 나는 아직 직성이 풀리지 않는다 I am not fully satisfied yet.

직세 直稅 a direct tax ⇨ 직접(~세)

직소 —과 the direct tax section
직소 直訴 a direct appeal [petition]
—직소하다 make a direct appeal 《to》; appeal direct 《to》
직속 直屬 —직속하다 be under the immediate [direct] control 《of》
■ —부하 a subordinate under *one's* direct control: 내 아들은 그의 직속 부하다 My son is under his direct [immediate] control.
직손 直孫 a direct [lineal] descendant
직송 直送 direct delivery
—직송하다 send direct《ly》《to》
직수굿하다 〈고분고분하다〉 submissive; obedient; acquiescent; docile
♦ 직수굿하게 따르다 submit tamely 《to》; obey passively
직수입 直輸入 direct import [importation]
—직수입하다 import 《goods》 direct《ly》《from abroad》
■ —무역 direct import trade —상 a direct importer —품 direct imports; articles [goods] imported direct 《from abroad》
직수출 直輸出 direct export [exportation]
—직수출하다 export 《goods》 direct《ly》《to》
■ —상 a direct exporter —품 direct exports
직시 直視 looking *sb* in the face
—직시하다 look *sb* in the face; look squarely [straight] at *sb*
♦ 사실을 직시하다 face facts as they are / 현실을 직시하다 face (up to) the reality
직시류 直翅類 〔昆〕 Orthoptera
직신거리다 tease 《*sb* for *sth*》 ⇨ 작신거리다
직심 直心 honesty; right-mindedness; uprightness ♦ 직심스럽다 honest [upright, right-minded]
직언 直言 plain speaking; a straight talk; outspoken advice
—직언하다 speak plainly [frankly]; speak without reserve; speak *one's* mind; speak out
—가 a plainspoken [free-spoken] person
직업 職業 an occupation; a profession; a trade; a vocation; a career; a job; a work; a business

〔解說〕 *occupation*은 직업을 가리키는 가장 일반적인 말로 공식 문서 등에도 쓰이는 약간 형식적인 말이다. *profession*은 의사·변호사·교사 등 지적인 전문 지식이나 훈련을 요하는 직업이고 *trade*는 손을 쓰는 숙련을 요하는 직업이다. *vocation*은 이해를 떠나 사회에 공헌하는 직업, *career*는 일생 종사하는 직업, *job*은 임금을 받고 하는 일, 일자리란 뜻. *work*는 「일」이란 추상적인 개념을 나타내는 평이한 말이고, *business*는 상업에 관련된 직업이다.

♦ 직업이 없는 jobless; unemployed / 직업적 professional / 반(半)직업적인 semiprofessional / …을 직업으로 삼다 be 《a lawyer》 by profession; be 《a driver》 by trade / … 직업에 종사하다 follow [engage in] an occupation 《of…》 / 직업을 가지다 take up an occupation; adopt 《painting》 as a profession / 직업을 바꾸다 change *one's* occupation
▶ 그녀는 직업을 전전했다 She worked at a variety of occupations.
▶ 그는 형의 직업을 계승했다 He succeeded his brother in his occupation.
▶ 그의 직업은 무엇입니까? What is his occupation?
▶ 그의 직업은 의사다 He is a doctor by profession.
▶ 직업에는 귀천이 없다 All legitimate trades are equally honorable.
■ —경력 *one's* business career [experience] —교육 vocational education —군인 a professional [(美) career] soldier —병 an occupational disease —분야 fields of work —선수 a professional player; (口) a pro 《*pl.* ~s》 —소개소 an employment [(美) a placement] agency —안내란 〈신문 등의〉 a Help-wanted column —안정소 a public employment stabilization office —여성 a working [career] woman; a woman worker —외교관 (美) a career diplomat —윤리 vocational ethics —의식 professional consciousness; professionalism —적성검사 a professional [vocational] aptitude test —전환 (a) change of *one's* occupation —정치가 a professional politician —학교 a vocational [trade] school —화 professionalization —훈련 vocational training
직업별 職業別 ♦ 직업별로 정리하다 arrange according to occupations; group by occupation
■ —전화번호부 a classified telephone directory
직업보도 職業輔導 vocational guidance [training]
■ —소 a Public Vocational Training Center
직업야구 職業野球 〈프로 야구〉 professional baseball ■ —단[선수] a professional baseball team [player]
직역 直譯 a literal [verbatim, word-for-word] translation —직역하다 translate literally [word for word]
▶ 이 문장을 영어로 직역하시오 Translate this sentence into English word for word. ⇒ Make a literal translation of this sentence.
▶ 그녀는 그 영문을 직역하려고 했다 She tried to translate the English sentence word for word.
직영 直營 direct management [control]
♦ 직영 식당 a restaurant under direct management / 정부의 직영사업 an enterprise under government management / …의 직영이다 be under direct management of…
—직영하다 manage [control] directly
직원 職員 〈전체〉 the staff; the personnel; 〈교직원〉 the faculty; 〈개인〉 a member of the staff
▶ 나는 그 회사 직원이다 I am on the staff of the company
▶ 그의 회사는 직원이 충분하다 His office is sufficiently staffed.
■ —명부 a staff list; a personnel directory —실 〈교무실〉 a teachers' [faculty] room —일동 all the members of the staff; all the staff —회의 〈교직원〉 a staff meeting —훈련 staff training
직유 直喩 〔修〕 〈직유법〉 a simile

♦직유를 쓰다 similize
직인 職印 an official seal
직장 直腸 〔解〕 the rectum ♦직장의 rectal
■—경(鏡) a rectoscope —염(炎) rectitis; proctitis —탈(脫) rectal prolapse
직장 職長 a foreman
직장 職場 〈일터〉 one's place of work; one's job (site); one's post; 〈공장〉 a workshop
♦직장을 알선하다 help sb (to) find a job / 직장을 구해주다 find sb a place [situation] / 직장을 찾았다[구하다] seek employment; look for a position [place] / 직장을 그만두다 quit [throw up] one's job / 직장을 잃다 lose one's job / 직장을 얻다 obtain employment; get a job; find a place
■—결혼 marriage of [between] a man and a woman working in the same place —대표 〈노동쟁의의〉 a shop deputy —복귀령 a back-to-work order —포기[이탈] desertion of one's post [job]
직장내훈련 職場內訓鍊 a training within the industry (略 TWI)
직재 直裁 1 〈즉석 재결〉 (give) a prompt decision 2 〈직접 재결〉 (give) a personal [direct] decision
직전 直前 ♦직전에 just [right] before; immediately before; just prior to
▶ 나는 입시 직전에 심한 감기에 걸렸다 I caught a bad cold just [immediately] before the entrance examination.
직접 直接 immediate; direct(ly) ♦직접의 direct; immediate; personal; firsthand /직접으로 directly; immediately; at firsthand; firsthand; 〈몸소〉 personally / 직접 간접으로 directly or indirectly / 직접 듣다 hear at firsthand / 직접 말하다 tell (it) with one's own lips / 직접 만나 보다 see sb personally / 직접 …에 영향을 미치다 have direct influence on... / 직접 …와 관계가 있다 have direct connection with...
▶ 그의 직접 사인은 심부전이었다 The immediate cause of his death was heart failure.
♦당신을 직접 뵙고 말씀 드리고 싶습니다 I'd like to talk with you personally.
▶ 그 정보는 확실한 소식통으로부터 직접 입수한 것이다 The information was obtained firsthand [straight] from a reliable source.
■—거래 ⇨ 직거래 —매매 direct [spot] sales —목적어 〔文法〕 a direct object —선거 a direct election —세 a direct tax —원인 an immediate cause [occasion] —조명 direct illumination —행동 (a) direct action —화법 〔文法〕 direct narration [speech]
직접담판 直接談判 a direct negotiation; direct [personal] negotiations; a personal interview [talk]
—직접담판하다 negotiate 《with a person》 in person; make direct negotiations 《with》; have a personal interview [talk] 《with》
직제 職制 the organization [setup] of an office ♦직제를 개편하다 reorganize an office
직조 織造 weaving —직조하다 weave
■—공 a weaver —공장 a weaving shop; a textile mill —기 a loom; a weaving machine
직종 職種 a type [kind, sort] of occupation; an occupational category
♦직종별로 분류하다 classify by occupation
■—분류 occupational classification
직직 1 〈끄는〉 shuffling; scuffing
♦신을 직직 끌다 scuffle one's shoes
2 〈찢는〉 tearing; rending; rippingly
♦종이를 직직 찢다 tear[rend] paper to pieces
3 〈긋는〉 with (repeated) random strokes
♦직직 그어 지우다 scratch out
직직거리다 〈신발을〉 scuff; scuffle; shuffle
직진하다 直進— go straight on; make straight for; advance in a beeline
▶ 빛은 직진한다 Light travels straight.
직책 職責 one's duty; duties; (official) responsibility
▶ 나는 직책을 다해야 한다 I have to do [perform, discharge] my duties.
▶ 그는 직책을 중시하는 사람이다 He has a strong [keen] sense of duty [responsibility].
■—수당 an allowance for the post attached
직통 直通 〈바로 통함〉 direct communication; 〈직행〉 through service [traffic]
▶ 이 열차는 런던까지 직통입니다 This train goes direct [through] to London.
—직통하다 communicate directly 《with》; 〈도로가〉 lead directly 《to》; 〈탈것이〉 go direct [through] 《to》
■—열차 a through train —운행 through operation —전화(선) a direct telephone line; 〈정부 수뇌간의〉 a hot line
직필 直筆 〈실록〉 uncolored writing; straight reporting —직필하다 write plainly 《on a matter》; write in frank language
직하 直下 1 〈바로 아래〉 ♦적도직하 right under [below] the equator / 직하의[에] directly under 《a thing》; directly below
2 〈수직 강하〉 a vertical descent; a perpendicular fall
▶ 다년간의 현안이 급전직하 해결되었다 A long-pending question has come to a sudden solution.
—직하하다 fall perpendicularly; fall plumb down; descend vertically
♦급전 직하하다 take a rapid turn
-직하다 it is probable [possible]; likely
♦있음직한 이야기 a likely story / 먹음직하다 look delicious; be tempting [appetizing]
▶ 그는 믿음직하다 He is reliable. ⇒ He is trustworthy.
직할 直轄 direct control [jurisdiction]
♦…의 직할로 옮기다 transfer 《a matter》 to the direct control of... / …의 직할이 되다 come under the direct control of...
—직할하다 control directly; hold under direct jurisdiction
■—파출소 a police box under the direct control (of the police station)
직함 職銜 a title; (口) a handle
♦어마어마한 직함 a high-sounding title / 직함이 있는 with a title [handle] to one's name; titled / 직함이 없는 untitled; without any title
직항 直航 〈배의〉 a direct voyage [service]; 〈비행기의〉 a nonstop flight
—직항하다 〈배가〉 sail direct [straight] 《for,

to); 〈비행기가〉 make a nonstop flight (to); fly nonstop (to, for)
■ —로 a direct line —선 a direct steamer [boat]
직행 直行 going straight [direct]; through running; 〈정차하지 않음〉 nonstop
—**직행하다** go straight [direct] (to); 〈기차가〉 run [go] through (to)
♦ 집으로 직행하다 rush straight home / 갈아타지 않고 직행하다 go [run] through without making a change
▶ 그는 비행기로 런던으로 직행했다 He flew straight to London.
■ —버스 a nonstop bus —열차 a through train —운행 through operation

직후 直後 ♦ 직후에 immediately [directly, right] after; soon after… / 경기 직후에 immediately after the game
▶ 그 직후 폭발이 있었다 A bomb went off right after that.

진 津 〈수액〉 resin; gum; sap; 〈분비물〉 secretion; 〈담배진〉 nicotine; tar
♦ (나무에서) 진이 나오다 exude [excrete] gum [resin]

진 陣 〈진형〉 battle [camp] formation; battle array; 〈대열〉 lines; ranks; 〈진영〉 a camp; 〈진지〉 a position
♦ 진을 치다 take up a position; encamp; pitch [make] a camp / 진을 철수하다 break up [strike] a camp; break camp; evacuate a position
■ —교수 the teaching staff (of a university) —보도 a news front; (美) a press corps

진 〈술〉 gin —드라이— dry gin

진- 眞- real; true; genuine; original ♦ 진면목 one's true self [character] / 진짜 a genuine article

진가 眞價 real [true, intrinsic] value; real worth; true merit
▶ 그의 작품은 한국에서는 그 진가를 알아주지 않았다 The real worth [true value] of his work was not appreciated in Korea.
▶ 그는 실업계에서 그의 진가를 발휘했다 He proved his real worth in the business world.

진간장 —醬 old soy sauce

진갈이하다 plow a wet [watered] field

진갑 進甲 the 61st anniversary of one's birth
■ —잔치 a feast on one's 61st birthday

진객 珍客 a least-expected visitor; a welcome guest
♦ 아무리 진객이라도 사흘이 지나면 귀찮아진다 The best fish smells when they are three days old.

진걸레 a wet dustcloth [floorcloth]

진격 進擊 〈진군〉 a march onward; 〈공격〉 a charge; a drive; an advance; an attack
—**진격하다** charge (at, on); attack; make a drive [push] (on, upon); march (upon)
■ —명령 an order to advance —부대 a storming party; an attacking force

진공 眞空 a vacuum (pl. ~s, vacua)
♦ 진공의 vacuous / 진공이 되다 make vacuous / 진공이 되다 form a vacuum
■ —건조기 a vacuum drier —계 vacuum gauge —청소기 a vacuum cleaner [sweeper]

진공관 眞空管 a vacuum tube
■ 라디오— a radio tube 4극— a tetrode 5극— a pentode 2[3]극— a two-[three-]electrode vacuum tube

진구렁 a mud hole; a bog; a slough; a quagmire; a morass ♦ 진구렁에서 빠져나오다 find a way out of the swamp / 진구렁에 빠져들다 bog (down); be [get] bogged; (비유) be bogged down; get stuck in a bog

진국 眞- 〈전국〉 pure [undiluted] liquor; 〈사람〉 a true [truthful, an honest] person

진군 進軍 (a) march; (an) advance
♦ 진군 나팔을 불다 sound the march; bugle a march / 진군을 명하다 order the advance (to)
—**진군하다** march [advance] ((on against))
■ —가 a marching song

진귀 珍貴 —**진귀하다** rare and precious; valuable; priceless ♦ 진귀한 보석 a rare gem

진급 進級 (a) promotion; 〈학년의〉 remove
▶ 그는 진급이 빠르다[늦다] He is rapid [slow] in promotion.
—**진급하다** be promoted
♦ 상병으로 진급하다 be promoted to (be) corporal; make corporal / 진급시키다 promote ((sb to a higher position))
▶ 나는 내년에 4학년으로 진급한다 I'll be moved up to the fourth grade next year.
■ —상신 a recommendation for promotion —시험 an examination for promotion

진기 珍奇 novelty; rarity; curiosity; queerness —**진기하다** rare; novel; curious; 〈기이하다〉 queer; strange; singular
▶ 그것은 아주 진기한 보물이다 The treasure is a singular one.

진날 a rainy [wet] day

진노 震怒 wild rage; wrath; fury
—**진노하다** burst with anger; be enraged; be inflamed with rage

진눈깨비 sleet
♦ 진눈깨비가 내리는 날 a sleety day
▶ 진눈깨비가 내린다 It sleets. ⇒ Sleet is falling.

진단 診斷 (a) diagnosis ((pl. -ses))
♦ 진단을 잘못하다 make a wrong diagnosis / 진단을 내리다 pronounce a diagnosis; diagnosticate / 의사의 진단을 받다 consult [see] a doctor
—**진단하다** diagnose
♦ 바르게 진단하다 make a correct diagnosis
▶ 의사는 그녀의 병을 암으로 진단했다 The doctor diagnosed her illness as cancer.
■ —건강 (have) a medical [physical] examination; (get) a (physical) checkup 조기— (make) an early diagnosis (of) ■ —서 a medical certificate; a medical examination report; a diagnosis —테스트 a diagnostic test

진달래 〔植〕 an azalea

진담 珍談 a strange tale; an interesting story; a funny story; an episode; an anecdote

진담 眞談 a serious [an earnest] talk
♦ 농담을 진담으로 듣다 take a joke seriously
▶ 내 말은 진담이다 I mean business.
▶ 너 그 말 진담이냐? Do you really mean it?

⇌ Are you serious?
진도 進度 progress ◆이런 진도로 간다면 if things go at this rate
▶ 반에 따라 영어의 진도가 다르다 Progress in English is different from class to class.
▶ 이 반은 수학 진도가 늦다[빠르다] This class is slow [advanced] in mathematics.
■ 학과— progress of classwork ■—표 〈학교의〉 a teaching schedule (for the term); 〈일의〉 a progress chart
진도 震度 seismic intensity ◆진도 5의 지진 a tremor of the 5th degree on the seismic scale ■—계 a magnitude scale
진동 振動 oscillation; vibration; a swing —진동하다 oscillate; swing; vibrate
■—계 a vibration gauge; a vibrograph; a vibroscope —기 a vibrator —수 the number of vibrations; (an oscillation) frequency; a pitch —시간 the oscillation time —전류 〔物〕 oscillating electric current —파 an oscillating wave —판 〔物〕〈전화기 등의〉 a diaphragm —회로 an oscillating circuit
진동 震動 a shake; a shock; (a) vibration; a quake; a tremor; (a) concussion
▶ 그 버스는 진동이 심했다 The bus bumped horribly.
—진동하다 shake; quake; tremble; vibrate; quiver
◆진동시키다 shake; vibrate; convulse; jar
▶ 트럭이 지나가면 집이 진동한다 The house shakes [trembles] when the trucks pass [go by].
▶ 그 가스 폭발로 건물이 진동했다 The gas explosion made the building shake.
■—시간 the duration of the shock [vibration] —파 〈지진의〉 an earthquake wave
진두 陣頭 the head of an army
◆진두에 서다 lead the van; be at the head
진두지휘 陣頭指揮 command exercised by the head of an army —진두지휘하다 act as the leader of an army
진드기 〔動〕 a tick; a mite; an acarid; an acarus(*pl.* -ri) ◆진드기에 물리다 be bitten by a tick / 진드기 처럼 달라붙다 fasten on [cling to] *sb* like a tick
진득거리다 〈들러붙다〉 be (moist and) sticky; be tacky [clammy, dauby, glutinous, viscid]
▶ 페인트가 아직 진득거린다 The paint is still sticky [wet and smeary].
진득이 sedately; soberly; quietly; patiently; gravely; in earnest ◆한 곳에 진득이 머무르다 stay in one place for a long time
진득진득 1〈끈적끈적〉stickily; adhesively
◆진득진득 달라붙다 stick to [on]; adhere to
—진득진득하다 〈끈적끈적하다〉 sticky; adhesive; tacky; glutinous; viscous; viscid; pasty; 〈기름기로〉 greasy
2〈고집스럽게〉 stubbornly; unyieldingly; 〈검질기게〉 tenaciously; persistently
—진득진득하다 tenacious; persistent; stubborn; unyielding
진득하다 sedate; staid; settled; sober; earnest; quiet; patient; self-composed[-possessed]
◆진득한 성격 a staid character

▶ 그는 언제 보아도 진득하다 He always appears dignified. ⇌ He is a deep-seated person.
진디 〔昆〕 an aphid; an aphis (*pl.* aphides); a plant louse; an ant cow
■—등에 a gnat; a sandfly
진땀 津— sweat of anxiety; sticky sweat
◆진땀나다 sweat hard / 진땀(을) 빼다 have a hard [bad] time (of it) 《with *sb*》/ 시험을 치르느라 진땀 빼다 sweat out an exam
진력 盡力 effort; help; assistance
◆그의 진력으로 through [thanks to] the kind [good] offices of him
—진력하다 make an effort [efforts]; help; assist; do *one's* best
▶ 그녀는 나를 위해 진력하겠다고 약속했다 She promised to do her best [make every possible effort] for me.
진력나다 盡力— 〈물리다〉 be sick [sick and tired] (of); grow weary (of); be bored (with, by); 〈口〉 be fed up (with)
◆진력나는 a boring [tedious, tiresome, wearisome] / 진력나게 하다 bore; weary; sicken
진로 進路 a course; *one's* future course [career]
◆진로를 열다[헤치다] cut [cleave] *one's* way (through) / 진로를 정하다 lay a course; shape [set] *one's* course
▶ 졸업후의 진로는 결정했습니까? Have you decided what to do [on your future course] after graduation?
▶ 우리의 진로는 험난하다 We will have a lot of difficulties in the future [ahead of us].
진료 診療 medical examination and treatment
—진료하다 examine and treat 《a patient》
◆진료 받다 have *oneself* examined and receive treatment
■—소 a clinic; a medical office; a dispensary; an infirmary —시간 consultation hours —실 a consultation room; a medical office
진루 進壘 〔野〕 —진루하다 advance; move on
진리 眞理 (a) truth
◆과학적 진리 scientific truths; the truths of science / 영원한[절대적인] 진리 an eternal [absolute] truth / 진리의 추구 pursuit of truth / 진리를 탐구하다 seek (after) truth
▶ 네 말에도 일면의 진리가 있다 There is some truth in what you say.
진맥 診脈 feeling the pulse (for diagnosis)
—진맥하다 feel the pulse (of)
진면목 眞面目 *one's* true character
◆진면목을 발휘하다 show [exhibit] *one's* true character; give full play [justice] to *one's* ability [gifts]
진멸 殄滅 annihilation; extermination
—진멸하다 exterminate ; annihilate
진무 鎭撫 pacification; placating
—진무하다 pacify; placate; quell; calm
진문 珍聞 extraordinary news; a curious story
진문 陣門 a camp gate
진물 — watery discharge from a sore
◆진물이 흐르다 run with discharge
진물진물하다 sore; inflamed; 〈눈이〉 blear; bleary; 〈코가〉 rheumy
진미 珍味 a delicacy; 〈음식〉 a food of

진미 delicate flavor; a dainty; a choice delicacy; 〈맛〉 delicate flavor [taste]; a dainty (food); a feast
♦계절의 진미 the delicacies [dainties] of the season
▶이것 진미로구나 What a delicacy this is!
■산해— all sorts of delicacies; a sumptuous feast: 산해진미를 먹다 dine on delicacies; have a sumptuous meal

진미 眞味 true taste; genuine appreciation
♦음악의 진미 the charm of music / 동양화의 진미를 감상하다 appreciate what Oriental painting is all about

진배없다 (be) as good as; equal (to); tantamount (to)
♦죽은 거나 진배없다 be as good as dead / 새 것이나 진배없다 be as good as new
▶그의 말은 모욕이나 진배없다 His remark is equivalent to an insult.

진버짐 eczema
♦진버짐이 난 얼굴 an eczematous face

진범(인) 眞犯(人) the real [true] culprit; the real offender [criminal]
▶진범은 아직 안 잡혔다 The real criminal is still at large.

진법 陣法 the disposition (of troops); a plan of campaign; battle formation [array]
■방어[공격]— defensive [offensive] disposition

진보 進步 progress; (an) advance; advancement; (an) improvement; evolution
♦과학의 진보 the progress [advancement] of science / 급속한 진보 rapid [fast] progress [advance] / 의학의 진보 the progress in medical science / 지식의 진보 advance [improvement, progress] in knowledge / 큰 진보 great progress / 진보가 빠르다 make rapid [fast] progress / 진보가 더디다 make low progress; progress at slow pace / 진보를 방해하다 hinder [blockade, impede, retard, stunt] progress / 진보를 조장하다 further [facilitate] the advance [progress]
—진보하다 progress; advance; improve; make progress [headway]; get on [forward] (with); go forward
♦진보한 국민 an advanced nation / 진보한 병기 a sophisticated weapon / 현저하게 진보하다 make remarkable progress; make a marked advance / 꾸준히 진보하다 make steady progress; advance [progress] steadily / 그다지 진보하지 않다 make little [poor] progress
▶너는 영어가 꽤 진보했다 Your English has much improved.
▶그 나라에서는 교육이 꽤 진보해 있다 Education is greatly advanced in that country.
■—주의 progressionism; progressivism —주의자 a progressionist; a progressivist

진보적 進步的 progressive; advanced
♦진보적인 사람 a man of progressive ideas [advanced views]; a forward-thinking [-looking] man / 진보적인 사상 a progressive idea

진본 珍本 a rare (old) book

진본 眞本 an original book [writing, painting]; an authentic book [copy]; a genuine [real, sterling] piece of writing [painting]

진부 眞否 truth or falsehood
♦진부를 확인하다 ascertain whether it is true or not; ascertain the truth (of)

진부 陳腐 banality; commonplaceness; platitude; triteness; threadbareness
—진부하다 old-fashioned; antiquated; commonplace; conventional; banal; trite; hackneyed; hack; stale; worn-out; threadbare
♦진부한 격언 a hackneyed saying; a copybook maxim / 진부한 문구 a hackneyed phrase; a tag / 진부한 생각[사상] an old-fashioned [out-of-date] idea / 진부한 익살 a stale [threadbare] joke / 진부한 말을 하다 make a commonplace [trite] remark

진분수 眞分數 〔數〕 a proper fraction

진사 陳謝 an apology —진사하다 apologize to *sb* (for); express *one's* regret (for)

진상 眞相 the truth; facts; the true state of things; the real situation; (口) what's [what was] what
♦진상을 규명하다 find out the truth of an affair / 진상을 밝히다 disclose [reveal] the truth (of); give [provide] a true account (of) / 진상을 파악하다 grasp [take in] the real situation / 일의 진상을 알다 come at a true knowledge of an affair
▶진상은 이렇다 I'll tell you what's what.
■—조사단[위원회] a fact-finding mission [committee]

진상 進上 the presentation (of *sth*) to the king —진상하다 present *sth* to the king
■—물[품] (a list of) donation to the palace; a present to the king

진서 珍書 a rare (old) book=진본(珍本)

진선미 眞善美 truth, good and beauty; the true, the good and the beautiful

진설 珍說 a novel story [opinion]

진성 眞性 genuineness ♦진성의 genuine; authentic; true; real ■—뇌염[콜레라] true [genuine] encephalitis [cholera]

진세 陣勢 〈형세〉 the position of troops; the disposition of forces; 〈세력〉 military strength

진세 塵世 this (dusty) world; this mortal life
♦진세의 번거로움 worldly cares; this mortal coil / 진세를 버리다 renounce the world / 진세를 벗어나다 seclude *oneself* from the world; keep aloof from the world

진수 眞數 〔數〕 antilogarithm (略 antilog)

진수 眞髓 the essence; the quintessence; the pith (and marrow); the spirit; the soul
♦기사도의 진수 the soul of chivalry / 민주주의의 진수 the essence of democracy / 시의 진수 the essence [quintessence] of poetry

진수 進水 launching —진수하다 〈배를〉 launch; 〈배가〉 be launched; take (the) water
▶이 배는 지난 4월에 진수했다 This ship was launched last April.
■—대 the launching platform [ways] —식 a launching ceremony

진수성찬 珍羞盛饌 a sumptuous meal [feast, repast]; regalement

♦진수성찬을 먹다 dine on all kinds of delicacies / 진수성찬을 차려내다 serve a handsome entertainment [banquet]

진술 陳述 testimony; a statement; a declaration; 〈증인의〉 a deposition ♦거짓없는 진술을 하다 make a true statement / 허위 진술을 하다 make a false statement / 진술을 취소하다 withdraw [retract] one's statement
―진술하다 state (one's case); set forth; give [make, present] a statement; declare
♦의견을 진술하다 state [set forth] one's views [opinion]
■―서 a (written) statement [declaration]

진실 眞實 〈사실〉 truth; reality; fact; 〈성실〉 sincerity; faithfulness
♦진실로 truly; really; in reality / 진실을 말하다 tell [speak] the truth / 진실을 왜곡하다 bend the truth
▶진실은 결국에는 이긴다 Truth will prevail.
―진실하다 true; real; veracious; veritable; 〈성실하다〉 sincere; faithful
♦진실한 친구 a true [real, sincere] friend / 진실하지 않은 insincere; untruthful; dishonest / 진실하게 truly; really; sincerely; faithfully / 진실하게 행동하다 act in good faith

진실성 眞實性 fidelity; truth; veracity; authenticity; credibility; sincerity
♦진실성을 의심하다 doubt the truth [veracity] of (a report)
▶그의 말에는 진실성이 없다 There is no truth in his statement.

진심 眞心 sincerity; a true heart; earnest
♦진심에서 우러나오는 감사 warm [cordial, heartfelt] thanks; thanks from the bottom of one's heart / 진심으로 sincerely; heartily; earnestly; from (the bottom of) one's heart; wholeheartedly / 진심어린 sincere; hearty; heartfelt; wholehearted; cordial; warm / 진심을 토로하다, 진심을 밝히다 speak (out) one's mind; unbosom oneself (to); open [bare] one's heart (to) / 진심으로 이야기하다 speak from one's heart / 진심으로 성공을 바라다 sincerely hope for one's success
▶너 진심이냐? Are you in earnest?
▶진심으로 말하는 거냐? Do you mean what you say?
▶진심으로 환영합니다 We welcome you with whole heart.

진압 鎭壓 suppression; repression; subjugation
―진압하다 suppress; repress; subjugate; subdue; put down; quell
♦폭동을 진압하다 quell [put down] a riot
■―책 a repressive measure

진앙 震央 the seismic epicenter

진액 津液 resin; gum; sap; milk; 〈점액〉 mucus
♦진액이 많은 resinous; gummy; sappy / 진액을 받다 sap [tap] (a tree)

진언 進言 advice; counsel; 〈건의〉 a proposal; a suggestion ―진언하다 advise; counsel; suggest; propose

진열 陳列 exhibition; show; display
♦진열중인 상품 wares on show [display]
―진열하다 exhibit; display; put on show; place on exhibition [view]; lay out; expose
♦팔려고 진열하다 lay (articles) out for sale; expose [display] (wares) for sale / 진열되어 있다 be (placed) on show [display, exhibition]; be exhibited
■―관 a museum; an exhibition hall ―대 a display stand [counter] ―실 a show [display] room ―장 a showcase; a display rack ―품 an exhibit; an article on show [display]

진열창 陳列窓 a show [store] window; a display window; a shopwindow
♦진열창을 구경하고 다니다 window-shop / 진열창에 진열되어 있다 be on display in a show window

진영 陣營 a camp; an encampment; quarters
♦동서 양 진영간의 긴장 the tension between the East and West camps / 동서 어느 쪽 진영에도 속하지 않는 나라들 nonaligned nations / 진영을 치다 encamp; pitch a camp / 양 진영으로부터 중립하다 stand aloof from both camps
▶지금의 세계는 양대 진영으로 대별할 수 있다 Now the world may be divided into two major camps.
■민주― the democratic camp 반공― the anti-Communist camp 보수[혁신]― the conservative [progressive] camp

진용 陣容 battle array [formation]; disposition; 〈美俗〉 lining; a lineup
♦진용을 정비하다 array the formation of troops; array troops for battle; marshal an army in battle

진원(지) 震源(地) **1** the seismic [earthquake] center [focus]; a centrum (pl. ～s, -tra); the focus (of an earthquake); 〈진앙〉 the epicenter
2 (비유) the center of the disturbance

진위 眞僞 truth (or falsehood); genuineness; authenticity
♦진위를 조사하다 examine [look into, ascertain] the genuineness (of an article) / 진위를 분간하다 distinguish the true from the false; discriminate truth from falsehood / 소문의 진위를 확인하다 confirm (the truth of) a report
▶나로서는 그 진위를 보장할 수 없다 I cannot vouch for the truth of the matter.

진의 眞意 **1** 〈본심〉 one's real intention; one's true motive
▶내 진의는 거기에 있다 That is what I really mean.
2 〈참된 의미〉 the true meaning [sense, signification, conception] ♦말의 진의를 헤아리다 go behind (sb's) words

진의 眞義 the true meaning ⇨ 진의(眞意) 2

진일 housework involving wetting the hands
♦진일로 손이 거칠어지다 get dishpan hands
―진일하다 do chores involving wetting the hands

진입 進入 penetration; entry (into a place)
♦지상 관제 진입 방식 the ground controlled approach system (略 G.C.A.)
―진입하다 penetrate (into); enter; go (into); make [find] one's way (into)
♦궤도에 진입하다 achieve [go into, enter into] orbit

■—등(燈) 〔空〕 an approach light —로 an access road; 〈고속도로의〉 a ramp (비탈길); 〔英〕 a slip road; 〔機〕 an admission passage —밸브 an admission valve —지시기 〔鐵〕 an approach indicator

진자 振子 a pendulum; a bob

진자리 1 〈출산한〉 the spot where a baby has just been born; 〈죽은〉 the place where a person has just died
2 〈오줌·똥을 싼〉 the soaked [soiled] part of a baby's bed
3 〈그 자리〉 the very place; the very spot

진작 〈그 낭상에〉 then and there; on the spot; 〈일찌감치〉 earlier; long ago [since]; a long time ago
▶ 왜 진작 알려주지 않았느냐? Why didn't you let me know earlier?
▶ 진작 그렇게 말할 것이지 You should have said so long ago [then and there].
▶ 진작부터 그를 만나고 싶었다 I have long wanted to see him.

진작 振作 promotion; enhancement; rousing; awakening —**진작하다** promote; arouse; awaken; encourage; enhance ◆사기를 진작시키다 stir up the morale (of troops)

진재 震災 an earthquake disaster

진저리 1 〈몸의 떨림〉 a shiver; a shudder; a tremble; a quiver ◆진저리[치다] shiver (after urinating); shudder; tremble; quiver
▶ 전쟁이라는 말만 들어도 진저리가 쳐진다 The mere mention of a war makes me shake [shiver] in my shoes.
2 ⇨ 진절머리

진저에일 ginger ale

진전 進展 〈발전〉 development; 〈진보〉 progress; advance; 〈전개〉 evolution; evolvement ◆전국(戰局)의 진전과 더불어 with the progress of the war / 진전이 빠르다[느리다] make rapid [slow] progress / 큰 진전을 보다 make great progress / 사건의 진전을 지켜보다 watch the development of the affair
—**진전하다** develop; progress; advance; evolve ◆원활하게 진전되다 go on smoothly [without a hitch]
▶ 교섭이 전혀 진전되지 않고 있다 The negotiations make no progress at all.

진절머리 disgust; repugnance; aversion ◆진절머리나는 일 a boring [an irksome] job / 진절머리(가) 나다 become (thoroughly, quite) disgusted (with); get sick (to death) (of); have enough (of); become fed up (with); become tired [bored] (to death) (of)
▶ 그것은 이제 진절머리가 난다 I have had [seen, heard] more than enough of it.
▶ 매일같이 국수만 먹었더니 이제 진절머리가 난다 I'm sick and tired of eating noodles every day.

진정 眞正 genuineness; authenticity —**진정하다** true; real; veritable; genuine; authentic
◆진정한 사랑 true love / 진정한 친구 a true [genuine] friend / 진정한 의미에서 in the true [truest] sense (of the word [term])

진정 眞情 〈애틋한 마음〉 one's true feelings [heart]; one's genuine sentiment; 〈진심〉 sincerity
◆진정의 true; sincere; earnest; faithful / 진정으로 heartily; from the bottom of one's heart; with one's whole heart / 진정을 토로하다 express one's genuine feelings; speak from one's heart / 진정으로 걱정하다 be anxious heartily

진정 陳情 a representation; a petition; an appeal
◆진정을 받아들이다 grant a petition; recognize a representation / 진정을 각하하다 reject [spurn, turn down] a petition [representation]
—**진정하다** 〈청원하다〉 make a representation ((to, against)); lay (the case) before ((the authorities)); petition ((the authorities)); make a plea (for); make a petition [an appeal] ((to)); appeal ((to the authorities))
■—단 〈국회의〉 a group of lobbyists; a lobby —자 a petitioner

진정 進呈 presentation
▶ 견본 무료 진정 〔廣告〕 Write for free samples. ⇒ Samples sent free on application.
—**진정하다** give; present sb with sth; present sth to sb; make a present of sth to sb
■—자 a presenter

진정 鎭定 suppression; repression; subdual
—**진정하다** suppress; repress; subdue; pacify; quell; tranquil(l)ize

진정 鎭靜 calm; quiet; tranquil(l)ity; appeasement; pacification
—**진정하다** calm; quiet; 〈고통 등을〉 soothe; allay; appease; abate; make less; 〈소동 등을〉 tranquil(l)ize; pacify
◆마음을 진정하다 calm oneself (down) / 노여움을 진정하다 〈자기의〉 quell [appease] one's anger; 〈남의〉 calm [appease] sb's anger
▶ 사태가 진정될 때까지 기다립시다 Let's wait until things cool off.
▶ 제발 진정하게 Calm down. ⇒ Take it easy. ⇒ Don't be [get] so excited.
■—작용 〔醫〕 sedation —제 〔醫〕 a sedative; a calmative; a tranquil(l)izer

진정서 陳情書 a (written) petition ◆진정서를 제출하다 present [submit] a petition ((to the Government)); send [hand] in a petition

진종일 盡終日 all day (long) ⇨ 종일

진주 眞珠 a pearl
◆진주를 박은 반지 a ring set with a pearl / 진주같은 pearly / 진주를 채취하다 fish [dive] for pearls; pearl / 돼지 앞에 진주를 던지다 〔聖〕 throw [cast] pearls before swine
■ 모조[양식]— an imitation [a culture(d)] pearl 인조— an artificial [a false, an imitation] pearl 흑[핑크색]— a black [pink] pearl
■—목걸이 a pearl necklace —빛[색] pearl gray —세공 pearl work —양식 pearl culture; the culture of pearls —양식장 a pearl farm [bed] —잡이 〈채 취〉 pearl fishery; pearling; 〈채취자〉 a pearl diver [fisher]; a pearler —조개 a pearl oyster [shell]

진주 進駐 stationing; stay; 〈진입〉 an entry (into) —**진주하다** stay; be stationed ((at)); advance (into); make an (armed) entry (into)

■—군 stationary troops; 〈점령지의〉 occupation forces

진중 陣中 ◆진중의[에] in camp; in the ranks; in the field; at the front / 적의 진중으로 돌격하다 rush (bravely) into the ranks of the enemy
―근무 duties in the field; field duty

진지 a meal; dinner
▶진지 잡수셨습니까? Have you had your breakfast [dinner, supper]?

진지 陣地 〔軍〕 a position; an encampment
◆아군 진지 one's own position [encampment] / 진지를 사수하다 defend a position to the last / 진지를 점령하다 occupy [carry] a position / 진지를 잃다 lose the field / 진지를 철수하다 evacuate [withdraw from] a position; decamp; break camp / 진지를 탈환하다 recover a position
▶아군이 적의 진지를 빼앗았다 We dislodged the enemy from their position.
―전 position warfare; stabilized [stationary] warfare

진지하다 眞摯— serious; earnest; sober; sincere; grave
◆진지한 사람 a sincere [serious(-minded)] person / 진지한 노력 an earnest effort / 진지한 얼굴 an intense [a serious] face / 진지한 태도 a sincere attitude / 진지하게 sincerely; in earnest; earnestly; seriously; soberly / 진지하게 생각[고려]하다 give (a matter) a serious consideration; take (a matter) seriously
▶그것은 진지하게 생각할 필요가 있다 It requires grave [sober] reflection.

진진하다 津津— 〈맛이 좋다〉 tasteful; delicious; 〈솟아나듯 많다〉 overflowing; brimful
◆맛이 진진하다 be tasteful / 흥미 진진하다 be highly interesting; be full of interest

진짜 眞— a genuine [real] article; the real thing [stuff]
◆진짜 고려자기 an authentic piece of Koryŏ pottery / 진짜 바보 a confirmed [regular] fool / 진짜 진주 a natural pearl / 진짜 커피[버터] honest coffee [butter] / 진짜와 가짜를 분간하다 tell the real from the false; distinguish [tell] the imitations from the originals / 진짜같이 만들다 imitate to the life
▶그는 그것을 진짜라고 속여 팔았다 He played it off as genuine.
▶이 박제 새는 진짜보다 훨씬 비싸다 This stuffed bird costs much more than its living counterpart.
▶그는 진짜로 화를 냈다 He flew into a genuine rage.

진찰 診察 (a) medical examination
◆의사의 진찰을 받다 consult a physician; see a doctor (for his medical advice) / 세밀한 진찰을 받다 have oneself carefully examined
▶진찰을 받는 것이 좋겠다 You had better consult a doctor.
▶무료 진찰 (게시) Consultation free.
―진찰하다 examine [see, have a look at] (a patient)
―권 a consultation ticket ―료 a doctor's [consultation] fee ―시간 consultation hours ―실 a consultation [consulting] room

진창 mud; a muddy place [spot] 《in a road》; mire; a quagmire
◆진창 속을 걷다 trudge in the mud / 진창에 발이 빠지다 fall in the mire / 진창에서 빠져 나오다 pull oneself out of the mire
―길 a muddy road; a sloppy road

진척 進陟 progress; (an) advance
◆진척 중이다 be under way; be in progress / 현저한 진척을 보이다 show marked progress / 별 진척이 없다 make little progress; be slow in progress
―진척하다[되다] advance; progress; make (good) progress; make headway
◆잘 진척되다 go on smoothly [without a hitch] / 진척시키다 hasten; expedite 《a negotiation》; promote; speed [rush] up; accelerate
▶공사는 잘 진척되고 있다 The works are well forward [under way].
▶일이 순조롭게 진척되었다 Things made good headway.
▶건축 공사가 잘 진척되지 않아 비용이 늘어났다 The construction work progressed very slowly and costs mounted up.

진출 進出 advance; march; 〔軍〕 debouchment
◆여성의 사회 진출 participation of women in public affairs / 한국 제품의 해외 진출 the advance of Korean-made goods into foreign markets
▶그 기업은 해외[영화계]로의 진출을 계획하고 있다 The company is planning to branch out into foreign countries [the film industry].
―진출하다 advance (into); go [launch] (into); find one's way (into); branch out (into); 〔軍〕 debouch
◆결승에 진출하다 move into [advance to] the finals / 정계에 진출하다 enter [go into] politics / 해외 시장에 진출하다 find a larger market abroad; make inroads into [on] the foreign markets
▶그녀는 이 작품으로 문단에 진출했다 With this work, she made her debut in literary circles.

진취 進取 ◆진취적인 기상 (be endowed with) an enterprising [a go-ahead] spirit; (show) (a spirit of) enterprise / 진취적인 progressive; enterprising; (美口) go-ahead
―진취하다 progress; advance; go [move] ahead (with)

진치다 陣— 〈진지〉 take up one's position; 〈진영〉 encamp; pitch [make] a camp; 〈진용〉 form in [make] battle array

진탕 震盪 concussion; a shock
■뇌―〔醫〕 concussion of the brain

진탕 —宕 to one's heart's content; heartily; as much as one likes; to the full
◆진탕 먹다[마시다] eat [drink] one's fill

진토 塵土 dust and dirt

진통 陣痛 labor (pains); travail; throes
◆진통의 발작 the onset of labor pains / 진통을 겪다 suffer throes [pangs] (of childbirth); feel pains / 진통중이다 be in travail [labor]
▶그 나라는 지금 혁명의 진통기에 있다 The country is now in the throes of revolution.

진통 鎭痛 alleviation of pain —**진통하다** alleviate [relieve, soothe, lessen] pain
■—제 an anodyne; a lenitive; a balm; a painkilling drug; a pain-killer

진퇴 進退 **1** 〈운동〉 advance or retreat; movement
♦진퇴의 자유를 잃다 be unable to move / 진퇴양난[유곡]이다 be driven to the wall [corner]; be in a dilemma [fix]; be on the horns of a dilemma; find *oneself* between two fires
2 〈행동〉 *one's* course of action; 〈태도〉 *one's* attitude
♦진퇴를 같이하나 cast [throw] in *one's* lot (with); act [move] in line (with) / 진퇴를 결정하다 decide on *one's* course of action; define [clarify] *one's* attitude / 진퇴를 그르치다 take a wrong course (of action); act improperly [unwisely] / 진퇴가 바르다 act properly [wisely]; take the right course of action
3 〈사임이나 유임이냐의〉 resigning or remaining in office
▶ 나의 진퇴는 오로지 이 시도의 결과 여하에 달려 있다 Whether I must resign or I can continue in my office all depends on the result of this attempt.

진폭 振幅 〔物〕 amplitude (of vibration)
■—변조 〔變調〕〔物〕 amplitude modulation (略 AM)

진폭 震幅 a seismic amplitude; the amplitude of an earthquake

진품 珍品 a rare article; a rarity; a curio; a curiosity

진품 眞品 a genuine article; a real thing

진피 pertinacity; stubbornness; wilfulness
♦진피부리다 act stubbornly [wilfully]

진피 眞皮 〔解·動〕 the thick skin; the true [inner] skin; the derm(is)

진피아들 an extremely ugly-looking person

진필 眞筆 an autograph; a genuine writing; *one's* own handwriting

진하다 津— **1** 〈빛깔이〉 dark; deep; saturated
♦진한 색 dark (and vivid) color / 진한 파랑 deep blue; navy blue / 진하게 화장한 여자 a thickly painted woman
2 〈액체가〉 thick; heavy; strong(맛이)
♦진한 국물 thick soup / 진한 차[커피] strong tea [coffee] / 차를 진하게 하다 make tea strong / 커피를 진하게 마시다 drink coffee strong

진학 進學 entrance into a school of higher grade ♦대학 진학 코스 a college-preparatory course —**진학하다** enter a school of higher grade ♦대학에 진학하다 go on to a [the] university
■—적성검사 an academic [a scholastic] aptitude test —지도 〈고교의〉 counselling on choice of college —지망자 a student wishing to go on to a school of higher grade

진항 進航
—**진항하다** sail; steam; make headway [seaway]; proceed ♦시속 20노트로 진항하다 do 20 knots an hour

진해제 鎭咳劑 a cough remedy [mixture]

진행 進行 progress; an onward movement; advance; march
♦진행중인 기차 a running [moving] train; a train in motion (under way) / 진행이 빠르다 [느리다] make rapid [slow] progress / 진행을 계속하다 〈배 등이〉 continue in *one's* course; 〈의사(議事) 의〉 proceed with 《the business》 / 진행을 방해하다 hinder [impede] the progress 《of》 / 진행중이다 be in progress; be on the move; be going on; be under way
▶ 일의 진행 상황을 알려 주시오 Let me know how you are coming along [getting on] with your work
▶ 장마로 인해 건축 공사의 진행이 지연 되었다 A long rain delayed the progress of the construction work.
—**진행하다** advance; progress; make progress, proceed; go on [forward]; make headway
♦순조롭게 진행하다 progress favorably [smoothly] / 착실히 진행하다 make steady progress; make a steady advance / 의사를 진행시키다 expedite the proceedings
▶ 교섭은 어느 정도까지 진행됐습니까? How far have the negotiations progressed?
▶ 그는 열차가 진행하는 방향과 반대로 앉아 있었다 He sat with his back to the engine.
■—신호 〔鐵〕 a proceed signal —자 a program director; 〈사회자〉 the master of ceremonies —파 〔物〕 a traveling [advancing, progressive] wave

진행형 進行形 〔文法〕 the progressive form
■현재[과거, 미래]— the present [past, future] progressive form

진형 陣形 (battle, camp) formation; battle array ♦방비[공격]— a defensive [an offensive] disposition

진혼 鎭魂 repose of souls
■—곡 a Requiem —제 a service for the repose of the deceased [departed soul]

진홍(색) 眞紅(色) crimson; cardinal (red); (deep) scarlet ♦진홍색의 crimson; cardinal / 진홍색 옷을 입다 wear scarlet; be dressed in crimson [scarlet]

진화 鎭火 extinguishment of a fire
♦진화에 힘쓰다 fight a fire
—**진화하다** put out; extinguish; bring [keep] under control; get under (control)
♦진화되다 be put out [extinguished]

진화 進化 〔生〕 evolution; development
♦인류의 진화 human evolution; the evolution of man / 진화적인 evolutional; evolutionary / 진화의 과정을 거쳐 evolutionally
—**진화하다** evolve [develop] 《from... into...》
▶ 생물은 모두 진화한다 All living things evolve.
▶ 사람은 원숭이로부터 진화했다고 한다 Man is said to have evolved from the ape.

진화론 進化論 〔生〕 the theory [doctrine] of evolution; the evolution(ary) theory
♦진화론적[상의] evolutionistic; evolutionary / 진화론적으로 말해서 evolutionarily speaking
■—자 an evolutionist

진흙 1 mud; dirt; mire

解說 **mud**는 진흙을 말하는 가장 일반적인 말. **dirt**는 진흙뿐 아니라 먼지 (dust) 등 전반적인 오물을 의미한다.

◆진흙 속의 연꽃 a lotus flower in the mud; a rose among nettles / 진흙 투성이의 muddy; miry / 진흙 투성이가 되다 be covered with mud [dirt]; get muddy / 진흙에 빠지다 stick in the mud
2 〈점토〉 clay
◆진흙 덩어리 a lump of clay / 진흙으로 만든 상(像) a figure in clay; a clay figure / 진흙같은 clayey

진흥 振興 promotion; furtherance; rousing; awakening
◆경제 진흥 계획 a program of economic buildup / 산업[수출]의 진흥을 꾀하다 promote the development of industry [exports]
―**진흥하다** 〈조성하다〉 promote; help forward; further; advance; encourage; 〈진작하다〉 arouse; awaken; stir up; inspire
■ 무역― the promotion of foreign trade
■ ―책 measures for the promotion [advancement, furtherance] (of)

질 帙 1 〈책갑〉 a folding case for books; a book wrapper
2 〈책의 한 벌〉 a set of books
▶ 이 책은 10권이 한 질이다 This book is complete in ten volumes.

질 質 1 〈품질〉 quality
◆질이 좋다 be of good [superior] quality / 질이 나쁘다 be of poor [inferior] quality / 질이 다르다 differ in quality / 질을 높이다[떨어뜨리다] improve [debase] the quality (of)
▶ 이것은 견본과는 질이 다른 것 같다 This seems to be different from the sample in quality.
▶ 양보다 질이 중요하다 Quality matters more than quantity.
2 〈자질〉 nature; disposition; 〈체질〉 constitution; 〈특질〉 characteristic; 〈본질〉 property; 〈품성〉 character
◆질이 나쁜 장난 a mean trick / 질이 나쁜 범죄 a vicious crime / 질이 좋은[나쁜] good-[ill-]natured; well-[ill-]disposed; 〈일의〉 of good [bad] character [nature]; 〈병 등의〉 benignant [malignant] / 질이 다르다 be cast in different molds; be cast in another [a different] stamp / 질이 같다 be cast in the same mold
▶ 금년 입학자 중에는 질이 나쁜 학생이 여럿 있다 Among those who entered this school this year, there are several students who are poor in scholastic ability.
3 〈성분〉 matter
◆식물[동물, 광물]질 vegetable [animal, mineral] matter

질 膣 〔解〕 the vagina (*pl.* ～s, -nae)

-질 (the act of) doing
◆손가락질 pointing *one's* finger / 서방질 adultery / 톱질 sawing / 바느질 sewing

질겁하다 stagger back in surprise; be startled; be stunned; be thunderstruck; *one's* heart leaps [comes] into *one's* mouth; have *one's* heart in *one's* mouth [throat]
◆질겁하여 말을 못하다 be struck dumb with surprise
▶ 나는 그 소식을 듣고 질겁했다 I was startled by the news.
▶ 그 소리에 그녀는 질겁했다 The noise brought her heart into her mouth.

질겅질겅 chewingly; gnawingly
◆껌을 질겅질겅 씹다 chew chewing gum

질경이 〔植〕 a (broad-leaved) plantain

질곡 桎梏 fetters; bonds; a yoke
◆질곡을 벗어나다 break [shake off] the fetters [bonds] (of); cast [fling, shake, throw] off the yoke (of); break away from the yoke (of)

질권 質權 the right of pledge ◆질권을 설정하다 establish the right of pledge ■ ―설정자 〔法〕 a pledger; a pledg(e)or; a pawner; a pawnor ―자 a pledgee; a pawnee

질그릇 a pottery (ware); (총칭) unglazed pottery; earthenware

질근질근 1 〈새끼 꼬는 모양〉 twist (a strand, a rope) slowly [loosely] **2** ⇨ 질겅질겅

질금거리다 trickle; dribble; fall [run down] off and on

질기다 1 〈고기 등이〉 tough; leathery; sinewy
◆질긴 쇠고기 tough beef
2 〈내구성이〉 durable; lasting; enduring
◆질긴 천 durable cloth [material]
3 〈성질이〉 tenacious; resilient; persistent; persevering; tough
◆성질이 질긴 녀석 (口) a tough customer

질기와 an earthen (roofing) tile

질깃질깃하다 tough; tenacious; strong and resilient

질깃하다 rather [somewhat] tough; toughish

질끈 tight(ly); firmly; fast; securely
◆꾸러미를 끈으로 질끈 동이다 tie up a package securely with a piece of string

질녀 姪女 a niece＝조카(～딸)

질다 1 〈반죽·밥이〉 soft; watery **2** 〈땅이〉 muddy; marshy ◆진 길 a muddy road

질량 質量 1 〔物〕 mass ◆그 물체의 질량 the mass of the body / 질량 불변[보존]의 법칙 the law of conservation of mass [mass conservation]
2 〈질과 양〉 quality and quantity
■ ―단위 〈원자의〉 a mass unit ―분석계 a mass spectrometer ―분석기 a mass spectroscope ―수(數) mass number ―스펙트럼 a mass spectrum

질러가다 take a short way [a shortcut]; cut across (a field) ◆길을 질러가다 go by a shorter way [route]

질러오다 come by a short way [a shortcut]

질레 〔服〕 (프) a gilet; a vest

질리다¹ 1 〈진력나다〉 be bored [disgusted] (with); be sick and tired (of); be fed up (with); 〈혼나다〉 have a bitter experience
▶ 그녀를 상대하는 것은 이제 질렸다 I have had enough of her company. ⇌ I'm fed up with her company.
▶ 결혼이라면 이제 질렸다 I've had a bitter experience with marriage.

▶그 문제에는 질렸다 The problem beat me.
2 〈기가 막히다〉 be amazed [stunned, dumfounded]; be overawed; turn (ghastly) pale
♦무서워서[화가 나서] 파랗게 질리다 turn deadly pale [as white as a sheet] with fright [rage] / 질려서 말도 못하다 be (struck) dumb with amazement; be dumfounded 《at》
3 〈물감이〉 dye unevenly
♦옷감에 물이 질리다 a cloth gets [is] dyed unevenly
4 〈값이〉 cost *one*; set *one* back

질리다² 〈채다〉 be struck; be hit; get a kick; get kicked
♦옆구리를 질리다 get a kick on the side

질문 質問 a question; an inquiry; an interrogation; 〈국회에서의〉 an interpellation
♦날카로운 질문 a pointed [poignant] question / 급소를[정곡을] 찌르는 질문 a home [very pertinent] question / 질문의 연발 a barrage [volley] of questions / 질문을 받다 be questioned / 질문을 퍼붓다 fire [shoot] questions at *sb* / 질문을 종결짓다 bring interpellation to a close / 질문을 받아 넘기다 〈얼버무리다〉 parry a question / 질문에 답변하다 answer a question
▶질문이 있습니다 I have a question [something] to ask (you).
▶질문이 있으면 하세요 (If you have) any questions (, please ask them).
▶시장은 질문 공세를 당했다 The mayor faced [met with] a barrage of questions.
▶위원 전원이 그에게 질문을 퍼부었다 All the committee members rained questions on him.
—**질문하다** ask *sb* a question; ask a question of *sb*; put [address] a question to *sb*; question; interrogate; 〈국회에서〉 interpellate
♦성가시게 질문하다 pester [plague] *sb* with questions
▶질문해도 좋습니까? May I ask you a question? ⇒ May I trouble you with a question?
▶우리는 많은 것을 그에게 질문했다 We asked him a lot of questions. ⇒ We put a lot of questions to him.
■긴급[일괄, 일반]— 〈국회에서의〉 an emergency [an overall, a general] interpellation
■—서 a letter of inquiry; a written inquiry; 〈조사용의〉 a questionnaire —자 a questioner

질물 質物 a pawn; a pawned article; a pledge

질박 質朴 simplicity; unsophisticatedness
—**질박하다** 〈간소하다〉 simple and unadorned; 〈마음이〉 simple (and honest); simple-hearted [-minded]; unsophisticated

질병 疾病 a disease; a sickness
♦질병의 예방 prevention of a disease / 질병과 싸우다 combat [fight] a disease
▶어린이는 여러 가지 질병에 걸리기 쉽다 Children are susceptible to various illnesses.

질부 姪婦 the wife of a nephew

질빵 shoulder straps (of a pack); 〈총 등의〉 a sling

질산 窒酸 〔化〕 nitric acid
■—염 nitrate —은 silver nitrate; nitrate of silver —제거 denitration

질색 窒塞 disgust; detestation; abhorrence; abomination; dismay; shock; horror
▶그런 녀석은 딱 질색이다 I cannot endure [put up with] such a guy.
▶나는 담배 연기가 질색이다 I hate cigarette smoke.
—**질색하다** be disgusted; loathe; be appalled [shocked, dismayed]

질서 秩序 (public) order; 〈규율〉 discipline; 〈체계〉 system; method
♦법과 질서 law and order / 사회 질서 social [public] order / 새 질서 a new order / 질서있는 orderly; systematic / 질서없는 disorderly; disordered; unsystematic; unorganized / 질서 정연하다 be in good [perfect] order / 질서를 지키다 keep [maintain, preserve] order / 질서를 문란케 하다 disturb order / 질서를 확립하다 establish order / 질서를 회복하다 restore [reestablish] order
▶그는 일을 빠르고 질서있게 처리한다 He does his work speedily and systematically [methodically].

질소 窒素 〔化〕 nitrogen
♦질소를 함유한 nitrogenous; nitric; nitrous / 질소와 화합시키다 nitrify / 질소를 제거하다 denitrify
■공중— air [atmospheric] nitrogen ■—가스 nitrogen gas —고정 nitrogen fixation —공업 the nitrogen industry —비료 nitrogenous fertilizer [manure] —산화물 nitrogen oxide —순환 nitrogen cycle —폭탄 a nitrogen bomb

질식 窒息 suffocation; asphyxiation; (a) choke
♦질식성(性)의 suffocative; asphyxiating
—**질식하다** be suffocated [choked, smothered, stifled]
♦질식하여 죽다 be suffocated [choked] to death; die from [by] suffocation / 질식시키다 suffocate; choke (off); smother
▶나는 연기 때문에 질식할 뻔했다 I was almost suffocated [choked, stifled] by the smoke.
■—사 death from [by] suffocation; 질식사하다 die from suffocation; choke to death

질염 膣炎 〔醫〕 vaginitis; colpitis

질의 質疑 a question; an inquiry; 〈국회에서의〉 (an) interpellation
♦질의 응답 questions and answers / 질의에 답하다 answer a question
▶이것으로 질의를 끝내겠습니다 With this, we'll bring the questions to an end.
—**질의하다** ask *sb* a question; ask a question of *sb*; question; interrogate; 〈국회에서〉 interpellate
■—응답시간 a question period [session] —자 a questioner; an interpellator

질의연설 質疑演說 〈국회에서의〉 an interpellation ♦질의연설을 하다 address an interpellation 《on a matter to a minister》

질의전 質疑戰 〈국회에서의〉 interpellations
♦질의전을 벌이다 open a volley of interpellations 《on》

질적 質的 qualitative
♦질적으로 qualitatively; in quality / 질적으로 다르다 differ in quality; be cast in different

molds / 질적으로 우수하다 be superior in quality

질정 叱正 (a) correcton; pointing out errors

질주 疾走 running rapidly; speeding; a scamper; a scud; a scuttle
— 질주하다 run at full speed; dash; scuttle; scamper; scud
♦ 질주하는 차 a speeding car

질질 1 〈끄는 모양〉 draggingly; trailingly
♦ 질질 끌다 drag (along) [draggle] 《a heavy thing》/ 지친 발을 질질 끌다 drag [shuffle] *one's* weary feet / 긴 스커트를 질질 끌다 trail *one's* long skirt / 통나무를 땅에서 질질 끌다 drag [pull] a log along the ground
2 〈오래 끄는 모양〉 long; lingering
♦ 질질 끄는 병 a lingering disease / 〈시간·행사 등이〉 오래 질질 끌다 trail on; drag on / 일을 질질 끌다 work inefficiently
▶ 그녀는 밤 늦게까지 일을 질질 끌었다 She lingered over her work till late at night.
3 〈흐르는 모양〉 tricklingly; dribbling
♦ 기름기가 질질 흐르는 얼굴 an oily face / 땀을 질질 흘리면서 with sweat running down / 침을 질질 흘리다 drivel freely; drool; dribble (at the mouth)

질책 叱責 (a) scolding; (a) reproof; reproach; reprimand
— 질책하다 scold; reprove; rebuke; reprimand
▶ 그는 아들을 엄하게 질책했다 He scolded his son severely. ⇌ He gave his son a sharp reprimand.

질척거리다 be wet and soft; be muddy
♦ 길이 질척거려서 가까스로 목적지에 도착했다 The roads were so muddy that we could reach our destination only with great difficulty.

질척질척하다 muddy; sloppy; sludgy; slushy
♦ 눈이 녹아 질척질척하다 be slushy with melting snow

질척하다 soppy; mushy; muddy; sludgy; slushy; sloppy

질타 叱咤 scolding — 질타하다 give *sb* a scolding; reprimand

질탕하다 佚宕— ♦ 질탕하게 놀다 indulge in noisy merrymaking; go on a racket

질투 嫉妬 jealousy; envy
♦ 그의 명성에 대한 심한 질투 fierce jealousy for his fame / 질투로 인한 싸움 a quarrel caused by jealousy / 질투가 많은 jealous; envious; green-eyed / 질투가 나서, 질투 끝에 from jealousy; in a fit of jealousy
— 질투하다 be [feel] jealous 《of, over》; envy; be green with envy
▶ 아내는 내 비서를 질투하고 있다 My wife is jealous [envious] of my secretary.

질투심 嫉妬心 jealousy ⇨ 질투
♦ 질투심이 나다 feel jealous 《of, over》/ 질투심을 갖게 되다 become envious 《of》/ 질투심을 일으키다 arouse envy / 질투심에 불타다 burn with jealousy; be eaten up with envy
▶ 그는 질투심에 사로잡혀 죄를 짓게 되었다 He was driven by jealousy to commit a crime.

질퍽질퍽하다 sloppy; soppy; slushy; sloshy
♦ 질퍽질퍽한 길 a sloppy road

질펀하다 1 〈넓다〉 broad and open; wide and even ♦ 질펀한 들 a broad expanse of fields; an extensive [a spacious] field
2 〈게으르다〉 sluggish; slovenly; lazy
♦ 질펀하게 의자에 앉다 loll back in a chair languidly

질풍 疾風 a gale; a strong [swift] wind; 〔氣〕 a fresh breeze
♦ 질풍노도의 시대 a stormy age / 질풍같이 like a whirlwind; as quick as lightning

질화물 窒化物 〔化〕 a nitride

질환 疾患 a disease; an ailment; a disorder
■ 흉부— a trouble in the chest: 흉부 질환이 있다 have a chest trouble

질흙 1 〈진흙〉 mud 2 〈질그릇을 만드는 흙〉 (potter's) clay

짊어지다 1 〈등에〉 take *sth* on *one's* [the] back; shoulder; bear
♦ 등에 짊어지다 carry on *one's* back
2 〈부담 등을〉 shoulder; bear; be saddled 《with》
♦ 성가신 일을 짊어지다 be saddled with an encumbrance / 무거운 책임을 짊어지다 shoulder [assume] the heavy responsibility
▶ 그는 빚을 짊어지고 있다 He is deeply in debt.
▶ 너희는 우리나라의 운명을 짊어지고 있다 The destiny of our country rests upon you.

짐 朕 We ♦ 짐의 Our

짐 a load; a burden; 〈뱃짐〉 a cargo 《*pl.* ~es, ~s》; a freight; 〈화물〉 goods; 〈美〉 a freight; 〈수화물〉 〈英〉 luggage; 〈美〉 baggage; a package
♦ 무거운 [가벼운] 짐 a heavy [light] load / 마음의 짐 a load [weight] on *one's* mind / 짐이 되다 be a burden to *sb* / 짐을 벗다 unburden; be relieved [ease *oneself*] of a burden; discharge a burden / (남에게) 짐을 지우다 impose a burden [heavy charge] on *sb* / 짐을 꾸리다 pack up; package / 짐을 싣다 load; 〈배가〉 take in cargo / 짐을 부리다 unload 《a ship, a cart》; unpack 《a horse》; clear 《a ship》; 〈배가 주어〉 discharge her cargo / 짐을 부치다 send [consign] goods 《to *sb*》/ 짐을 덜다 lighten the load / 짐을 풀다 unpack 《a package, a box》/ 짐을 등에 지다 bear a load on *one's* shoulders
▶ 그 임무는 그에게는 과중한 짐이다 The mission is too much for him. ⇌ He is not equal to the mission.
▶ 이런 것을 갖고 가면 짐이 된다 Such things will encumber me.
▶ 내 짐을 호텔까지 갖다 주세요 Will you take my baggage [luggage] to the hotel?
▶ 어디에 짐을 맡깁니까? Where can I check [leave] my baggage [luggage]?
▶ 이제 마음의 큰 짐을 벗었습니다 Now I have a load off my mind.

짐꾼 a carrier; a porter; a burden-bearer; a cooly [coolie]

짐마차 —馬車 a wagon; a cart ♦ 짐마차를 끌다 draw a cart / 짐마차로 나르다 carry *sth* in a cart; cart

짐바리 a load (on a pack animal); a pack
♦ 노새의 짐바리 a mule's pack

짐바브웨 Zimbabwe; 〈공식명〉 the Republic of Zimbabwe

짐배 〈화물선〉 a freighter; 〈거룻배〉 a barge; a lighter

짐수레 〈손수레〉 a cart; 〈짐마차〉 a wagon; a van ◆짐수레로 건초를 나르다 carry hay in a cart [wagon]

짐스럽다 burdensome; cumbersome; troublesome
◆짐스럽게 여기다 find 《it》 burdensome
▶이 일은 내게 짐스럽다 The job is too much for me. ⇒ I am not up to the job.
▶그녀의 친절이 점점 심스러워진다 Her kindness is gradually becoming a burden.

짐승 a beast; an animal
◆짐승같은 행위 a brutal act; a brutality / 짐승같은 인간 a beast of a man; a brute / 짐승같은 bestial; brutal; animal
▶그는 짐승만도 못하다 He is worse than a beast.
▶이 짐승같은 놈아 You brute! ⇒ You rat!

짐싣기 loading; 〈선적〉 shipment

짐작 〈어림〉 guess; discretion; (a) presumption; conjecture; 〈판단〉 judgment
◆눈짐작 eye measure; measuring by (the) eye / 손짐작 measuring roughly with one's hands / 내 짐작에는 in my estimation; in my judgment; as near as I could guess / 짐작이 가다 can guess 《口》 imagine》; happen to know / 짐작이 가지 않다 cannot imagine; have no idea 《of》; do not have an idea
▶네 짐작대로다 You have guessed right. ⇒ You are right in your conjecture.
▶이제 대충 짐작이 간다 I have formed some idea of it. ⇒ I've got the rough idea of it.
—**짐작하다** guess; conjecture; estimate; 〈판단하다〉 judge
▶무척 바쁘시리라 짐작합니다 I suppose you must be very busy.
▶어디서 그것을 잃었는지 짐작할 수 있습니까? Do you have any idea where you lost it?

짐짐하다 1〈맛이〉 salty and tasteless; salty without any flavor 2 ⇨ 찜찜하다

짐짓 purposely; deliberately; intentionally; on purpose
▶그는 짐짓 아무렇지도 않은 투로 그렇게 말했다 He said so in a carefully casual tone.
▶그녀는 짐짓 모른 체했다 She pretended not to know anything about it. ⇒ She affected ignorance.

짐짝 a bundle; a package; a pack; a parcel; a piece of baggage [luggage]; an item of freight
◆무거운 짐짝을 어깨에 메고 나르다 carry a heavy load on one's shoulders / 짐짝 3개를 부치다 send three pieces of baggage [luggage]
▶짐짝을 조사당했다 I had my baggage examined.

짐차 —車 1〈화물차〉《美》 a freight car; a truck; 《英》 a goods wagon [van]; lorry 2〈수레〉 a cart; a wagon

집 1〈가옥〉 a house; 《美》 a home; 《口》 a place; 〈총칭〉 housing
◆기와집 a tile-roofed house / 목조[벽돌] 2층집 a two-story[-storied] wooden [stone] house / 넓은[좁은] 집 a large [small] house / 빈집 an unoccupied [untenanted] house; a vacant [an empty] house / 자기 집 a house of one's own; one's own house / 아담한 집 a modest house / 집 없는 homeless; houseless; shelterless; vagrant / 집 밖에(서) out of [outside] the house; out-of-doors; outdoors / 집 안에(서) inside the house; indoors / 집 없는 신세가 되다 be rendered homeless / 집 밖에서 놀다 play outside [outdoors]

〈집이[은]〉 그에게는 살 집이 없다 He has no house to live in [place to live (in)]. ⇒ He is homeless.
▶그의 집은 강가에 있다[세워져 있다] His house is [stands] by a river.

〈집을〉 집을 나가다 〈출근〉 leave the house; 〈독립해서〉 leave home / 집을 뛰쳐나가다 〈가출〉 run away from home / 집을 비우다 leave one's house empty / 집을 보다 take care of [look after] the house 《during sb's absence》 / 집을 헐다 take a house to pieces; pull down a house / 집을 빌리다 rent a house; take a house 《for the summer》
▶집을 안내하겠습니다 Let me show you around our house.
▶나는 (내가 살) 집을 지었다 I had my house built. ⇒ I built my house.
▶그녀는 집을 잘 비운다 She is seldom at home. ⇒ She is usually out.

〈집에(서)〉 집에 있다 stay [sit, be] at home; be in / 집에 없다 be out [not at home]; stay [be] away from home / 한 집에 살다 live in the same house; live under the same roof / 삼촌 집에[살다] live with one's uncle
▶박선생 집에서 파티를 벌였다 We had a party at Mr. Park's house.
▶언제 전화해도 그는 집에 없다 Every time I call him up, he is not in.
▶집에 놀러오세요 Please come and see me at home.
▶누가 나를 찾거든 집에 없다고 해라 If anyone calls, say that I am out.

2 〈가정·가족〉 a [one's] family; a household
◆우리집 사람 my (good) wife / 우리집 양반 my good man; my husband / 즐거운 집 a cheerful family
▶내 집보다 좋은 곳은 없다 There's no place like home.
▶너네 집에서 누가 제일 일찍 일어나니? Who gets up (the) earliest of your family?
▶집은 아내에게 맡기고 있습니다 I let my wife keep house.
▶그는 가난한 집에서 태어났다 He was born poor [into a poor family]. ⇒ He comes from a poor home [family].
▶집으로 돌아가게 I advise you to go home.

3 〈영업장소〉 a place; a house; 〈상점〉 a store; 《美》 a shop; 〈음식점〉 a restaurant
◆빵집 a bakery / 술집 a bar; a saloon; a tavern; 《英》 a public house / 국숫집 a noodle restaurant [shop] / 중국집 a Chinese restaurant / 일식[왜식]집 a Japanese restaurant

4 〈동물의〉 a nest; a roost; 〈벌의〉 a comb;

wasps' nest 〈말벌의〉; a beehive 〈꿀벌의〉; 〈거미의〉 a (cob)web; 〈우리〉 a den
♦ 개집 a kennel; a dog house / 새집 a bird's nest / 〈꿀벌의〉 벌集에 들다 hive / 집으로 돌아오다 fly home to roost
5 〈케이스〉 a box; a case; a protector; a sheath ♦ 안경집 a glasses case / 칼집 a sheath; a scabbard
6 〈바둑의〉 captured territory ♦ 열 집 이기다 [지다] win [lose] by ten crosses
7 〈수용소〉 a home
♦ 노인의 집 a home for the aged / 여성의 집 a woman's home / 선원의 집 a sailors' home
-집 -集 〈시가·문장 등의〉 a collection
♦ 단편(소설)집 collected short stories; a collection of short stories / 수필집 a collection of essays / 서간집 collected letters; a collection of letters

집 輯 a series ♦ 제1집 the first series

집게 tongs; flat pliers; pincers; nippers
♦ 집게로 집다 pick up with tongs / 집게로 못을 뽑다 pull a nail out with pliers

집게발 〈집게벌레의〉 forceps; claws; nippers; pincers ♦ 〈게가〉 집게발로 집다 nip with its claws

집게벌레 〔昆〕 an earwig

집게손가락 a forefinger; a index finger

집결 集結 concentration; collection; 〈군대의〉 assembly; buildup
—집결하다 〈모으다〉 collect; 〈군대가〉 build up; assemble
▶ 국경에 대군이 집결하고 있다 A large army is gathering near the border.
▶ 무장한 시민들이 광장에 집결했다 Armed citizens massed [rallied] in the public square.
■ **—지[장소]** an assembly place; a marshaling area

집계 集計 totalization
▶ 기부금의 집계가 3천만원이었다 The contributions totaled [amounted to] thirty million won.
—집계하다 totalize; combine into a total; total
♦ 투표지를 집계하다 add up (the) votes
■ **—표** a tabulation; a summary sheet: 최종결과 집계표 the final tabulation

집광 集光 〔光〕 **—집광하다** gather [condense] rays of light ■ **—기(器)** a condenser **—렌즈** a condensing lens; a condenser

집괭이 a house [domestic] cat

집구석 ♦ 집구석에 inside the house; indoors; within doors
▶ 집구석에 틀어박혀 있지 말고 밖으로 나가라 You shouldn't shut yourself up in [confine yourself to] the house and go out doors.

집권 執權 coming into power [office]
♦ 집권 중에 while in power
—집권하다 assume [take (over)] the reins of government; take [win, attain] power
■ **—당** the ruling party; the party in power [office]

집권 集權 ■ **중앙—** centralization of power [authority]: 중앙집권주의[제도] centralism; the centralizing system; centralized administration

집금 集金 **—집금하다** 〈수금하다〉 collect money [bills] ■ **—원** a (bill) collector

집기 什器 〈하나〉 an article [a piece] of furniture; 〈총칭〉 household furniture [articles] (and utensils); 〈고정시킨〉 fixtures
♦ 사무(실)용— office fixtures

집념 執念 〈집착〉 a deep attachment (to); tenacity; 〈복수심〉 spite; vindictive feeling
♦ 집념이 강한 tenacious; persistent
▶ 그는 집념이 강한 사람이다 He doesn't give up easily.
—집념하다 〈집착하다〉 be deeply attached (to); 〈전념하다〉 be intent (on); keep [have] one's mind (on)

집다 pick [take] up *sth*
♦ 모자를 집다 pick up one's hat / 손가락〈핀셋〉으로 유리조각을 집다 pick [take] up bits of glasses with one's fingers [tweezers]
▶ 나는 신문을 집으려고 손을 뻗혔다 I reached out for the newspaper.

집단 集團 a group; a band; a mass

〔解說〕 ***group***은 어떤 연줄이 있는 사람끼리의 작은 집단이고, ***band***는 지도자 밑에 모인 집단, ***mass***는 많은 사람이나 물체가 모여있는 것이다. group과 band는 전체를 한덩어리로 볼 때에는 단수로 취급되는 것이 원칙이지만, 하나하나의 멤버에 중점을 둘 때는 〈英〉에서는 복수 취급하고 〈美〉에서는 단수 동사, 복수 대명사로 받는 것이 보통이다.

♦ 집단으로 in a group / 집단적으로 collectively; as a group / 집단을 이루다 form a group; group together
▶ 식중독이 집단적으로 발생했다 There was a mass outbreak of food poisoning.
■ **—강도** a gang of burglars [robbers] **—검거** a mass arrest **—검진** a group medical examination **—결혼** a group marriage **—경기** 〔體操〕 a mass game **—농장** a collective farm; 〈이스라엘의〉 a kibbutz (*pl*. -zim) **—발생** a mass outbreak **—생활** living in a group **—심리학** group [crowd, mob] psychology **—의식** group consciousness **—이민[소개(疏開)]** collective [mass] emigration [evacuation] **—지도** collective leadership **—폭행** mob violence

집단안전보장 集團安全保障 collective security ■ **—제도** the collective security system

집달관 執達官 〔法〕 a bailiff

집대성하다 集大成— compile into one book; make [give] a comprehensive [complete] survey of ♦ 한국의 민간 설화를 집대성하다 compile all the folktales in Korea into a book [a single work]

집도 執刀 performance of an operation
—집도하다 perform [conduct] an operation
▶ 수술은 손박사가 집도했다 The operation was performed by Dr. Son.
■ **—자** 〈수술의〉 an operator

집들이하다 give [have] a housewarming (party)

집무 執務 performance of one's official duties; office work

집무 중이다 be at *one's* desk; be on work
▶**집무 중엔 금연입니다** Don't smoke during office hours [while you are at work].
▶**집무 중 면회사절 (게시)** Visitors declined during office hours.
—**집무하다** attend to *one's* business [duties]; work
♦**오전 아홉시부터 오후 다섯시까지 집무하다** work from nine a.m. to [till] five p.m.
■—**시간** office [business, working] hours —**지침[편람]** a guide to office [work] routine

집문서 —**文書** a house deed; a title deed; deed [title] papers ♦**십문서를 집히고 돈을 차용하다** make a loan with the deed for security; borrow money on *one's* house

집배 集配 collection and delivery
♦**우편 집배원** a postman; (美) a mailman / **집배 센터** a distribution center
—**집배하다** collect and deliver

집비둘기 a domestic pigeon

집사 執事 〈집의〉 a steward; a butler; 〈교회의〉 a deacon; 〈여자〉 a deaconess

집산 集散 collection and distribution
—**집산하다** collect [gather, receive] and distribute —**지** a distributing [trading] center

집산주의 集産主義 collectivism
♦**집산주의의** collectivistic
—**주의자** a collectivist —**화(化)** collectivization : **집산주의화하다** collectivize

집세 —**貰** a (house) rent; a rental
♦**비싼[싼] 집세** a high [low] rent / **밀린 집세** back rent; rent in arrears / **집세가 오르다[내리다]** the rent rises [falls] / **집세를 올리다[내리다]** raise [lower] the rent / **집세를 내다[치르다]** pay the rent; pay for the house / **집세를 내지 않고 살다** live rent-free (in a house); live (in a house) free of rent
▶**그는 집세가 밀려 있다** He is behind with his rent.
▶**이 집은 집세가 한 달에 30만원이다** The rent for this house is three hundred thousand won a month.

집시 a gypsy; (英) a gipsy
■—**족** the Gypsies —**춤** a gypsy dance

집안 1 〈가정〉 a family; a household; a [*one's*] home
♦**온 집안** the whole family; all the family / **집안 사람들[식구]** *one's* family; members of a family; (口) *one's* folks / **집안의 기둥** the support of a family / **집안의 보배** an heirloom; a household treasure / **집안의 명예** an honor [a credit] to *one's* family / **집안의 화목** domestic harmony / **집안의** family; domestic; household / **집안을 꾸려나가다** manage a household; keep house / **집안을 빛내다** raise the reputation of *one's* family / **집안의 수치를 드러내다 [감추다]** wash *one's* dirty linen in public [at home]
2 〈일가〉 a family; a clan; 〈친척〉 *one's* relative; 〈가문〉 the (social) standing [status] of a family
♦**유서깊은 집안** a family of a pedigree / **집안이 좋다** come of (a) good stock [a good family]; be of good lineage [birth] / **집안이 좋지 않다** be of low birth; come of a poor family
▶**그의 집안은 유명한 집안이다** He is from a well-known family.
3 〈집 내부〉 the inside of a house
♦**집안에 틀어박히다** keep [stay] indoors; keep to *one's* house; confine *oneself* in *one's* house / **집안에서 놀다** play indoors / **집안을 치우다** clean the house up
■—**사정** *one's* family circumstances [reasons] —**일** a family [domestic] affair; household matters : **나는 집안 일은 모두 아내에게 맡기고 있다** I leave all my household affairs to my wife.

집안싸움 a family trouble [discord]; a family quarrel [dispute]; 〈내분〉 an internal trouble [discord]
♦**집안싸움을 하다** have a family quarrel / **집안싸움을 일으키다** cause [give rise to] an internal trouble

집알이 a courtesy call on *sb* in his new house
—**집알이하다** call on *sb* to celebrate the occupancy a new home

집약 集約 ♦**집약적(인) 방법** an intensive method / **집약적인** intensive / **자본집약적인** capital-intensive —**집약하다** put together
■—**농업** intensive agriculture

집어넣다 put [take] in; throw [cast] in [into]
♦**컴퓨터에 자료를 집어넣다** feed data into a computer / **휴지통에 집어넣다** throw *sth* into the wastebasket / **교도소에 집어넣다** throw [cast] *sb* into prison
▶**호주머니에 손을 집어넣고 다니지 마라** Don't walk with your hands in your pockets.

집어등 集魚燈 a fish-luring [fish-gathering] light; a fishing lamp

집어먹다 1 〈음식을〉 pick up and eat
♦**손으로 집어먹다** eat greedily with the [*one's*] fingers [hands]
2 〈착복하다〉 embezzle; pocket
♦**공금을 집어먹다** embezzle official money

집어삼키다 1 〈삼키다〉 swallow
2 〈가로채다〉 embezzle; swallow up
♦**아무의 재산을 집어삼키다** misappropriate *sb's* property

집어주다 1 〈건네주다〉 pass; hand (over) (to)
▶**소금 좀 집어주십시오** 〈식탁에서〉 Pass me the salt, please.
2 〈돈을〉 slip (money) into *sb's* hand [pocket]; 〈팁을〉 tip (a porter); 〈뇌물을〉 grease *sb's* palm; bribe
♦**돈을 집어주고 입막음하다** bribe *sb* into secrecy

집어치우다 give [throw] up; quit; leave [lay] off
♦**공부를 집어치우다** give up *one's* studies / **장사를 집어치우다** quit *one's* business / **직장을 집어치우다** throw up *one's* job
▶**그런 이야기는 집어치워** Cut it out!
▶**그는 하던 연구를 집어치우고 여행을 떠났다** He gave up [laid aside] his research and went on a trip.

집어타다 take; get on; jump on
▶**택시를 집어타다** pick up [grab] a taxi / **자**

집오리 a (domestic) duck; 〈수컷〉 a drake
▶ 집오리가 꽥꽥거리고 있다 Ducks are quacking.

집요하다 執拗 obstinate; stubborn; tenacious; persistent ◆ 집요하게 stubbornly; obstinately; persistently
▶ 그들은 우리 계획을 집요하게 반대했다 They offered a resistance to our plan.

집적 集積 accumulation; 〔物〕 integration
—**집적하다** accumulate; pile (up); amass
—**회로** 〔物〕 an integrated circuit (略 IC)

집적거리다 1 〈간섭하다〉 meddle with [in]; have a hand [finger, concern] in ◆ 쓸데없이 집적거리다 have a finger in the pie
▶ 남의 일에 집적거리지 마라 Mind your own business.
2 〈건드리다〉 tease; harass; peck at *sb*; (俗) needle ◆ 개를 집적거리다 tease a dog / 누이를 집적거리다 needle *one's* sister
▶ 여자에게 집적거리지 마라 Don't flirt with [make passes at] girls.

집정 執政 administration; governing; government; 〈사람〉 an administrator; 〔史〕 〈프랑스 혁명 정부의〉 a director; 〈제1공화정 시대의〉 a consul
—**집정하다** rule [reign] over; govern [administer]; be in power
—**관** 〈로마의〉 〔史〕 a consul

집주인 —主人 1 〈가장〉 the master of a house; the head of a family
2 〈집임자〉 the owner of a house; a house owner; a landlord (남자); a landlady (여자)

집중 集中 concentration; centralization
◆ 도시로의 인구 집중 concentration of population in cities; urban concentration / 집중을 요하는 일 work that requires concentration
—**집중하다** 〈모으다〉 concentrate (upon); focus [center] (on); centralize (upon); 〈모이다〉 converge (into, on)
◆ 그가 하는 말에 주의를 집중하다 concentrate *one's* attention on what he says / 목적에 온힘을 집중하다 bend all *one's* energies on *one's* aim
▶ 질문은 그 점에 집중되었다 Questions centered on that point.
▶ 나는 공부에 집중할 수가 없다 I cannot concentrate my attention on studying.
■—**강의** an intensive course —**안타** 〔野〕 an avalanche [a rally] of hits —**포화**〔사격〕 concentrated [converging] fire —**폭격** (美) saturation bombing 《on Baghdad》 —**호우** a localized torrential rain; a concentrated heavy rain —**훈련** intensive training : 그들은 해외출장 전에 영어를 집중 훈련 받았다 They were given intensive training in English before going abroad on business.

집진기 集塵機 a dust collector

집집이 〈집집마다〉 at every door [house]; house to house; from door to door
◆ 집집이 방문하다 make a door-to-door visit; visit from door to door

집착 執着 〈애착〉 (a) deep attachment (to, for); 〈끈덕짐〉 persistence (in); tenacity
◆ 강한 집착을 가지다 be strongly attached (to)
—**집착하다** be attached (to); adhere [stick, cling] (to)
■—**심** attachment (to, for); tenacity of purpose

집찰 集札 collection of tickets
—**원** a ticket collector [taker]

집채 (the bulk of) a house
◆ 큰 집채 a house of huge size / 집채만한 파도 a mountainous wave; a mountain of a wave / 집채만하다 be of great size [bulk]

집치장 —治粧 the (interior) decoration of a house ◆ 집치장이 잘 되어 있다 be nicely decorated —**집치장하다** decorate [upholster] a house; do the interior decoration

집터 a house [home, building] site; a building site [lot]; 〈여러 주택의〉 land for housing
◆ 집터를 닦다 level the ground for a house / 집터를 물색하다 look for a site for a building / 집터를 사다 buy a lot for a building

집토끼 a house rabbit

집파리 a housefly

집필 執筆 writing —**집필하다** write; do writing; pen
◆ 잡지에 집필하다 write for a magazine; contribute to a magazine
■—**료** payment for writing; a contribution fee —**자** 〈저자〉 the writer; the author; 〈기고가〉 a contributor

집하 集荷 collection of cargo

집합 集合 (a) gathering; (a) meeting; (an) assembly; 〔數〕 a set; (a) concurrence
◆ 집합 나팔을 불다 bugle a muster call; sound a bugle call
—**집합하다** 〈모이다〉 gather; collect; assemble; meet; flock; rally; get together; 〈모으다〉 gather (together); collect; assemble; summon; rally; muster; call [get] together
▶ 집합 (口令) Fall in! ⇌ Close in! ⇌ Rally!
▶ 학생들은 9시에 교정에 집합했다 The students gathered in the playground at 9.
■**무한**〔유한〕— 〔數〕 an infinite [a finite] set —**나팔** a muster call —**론** 〔數〕 the theory of sets; the set theory —**명사** 〔文法〕 a collective noun —**장소** a place of meeting; a rendezvous (point); a roll call point —**점** 〔數〕 a concurrence —**체** an aggregate

집행 執行 execution; enforcement; performance; conduct
▶ 그는 누이에게 유언의 집행을 부탁했다 He asked his sister to execute his will.
—**집행하다** execute; discharge; perform; hold; enforce; carry into effect [execution]; carry out; exercise; conduct
◆ 공무를 집행하다 perform [carry out, do] *one's* official duty / 형을 집행하다 execute a sentence
▶ 대통령은 의회가 제정한 법률을 집행한다 The President executes what the Congress legislates.
■**강제**— compulsory [forcible] execution; 〈차압〉 distraint; seizure **영장**— commitment ■—**관** an executor —**기간** the term for execution

—기관 an executive organ [body] —기일 the date of [fixed for] execution —명령 an order of execution —부 the executives —수속[절차] execution proceedings —영장 a writ of execution —위원 a member of the executive committee; an executive committee man —자 an executor; 〈사형의〉 an executioner; 〈회사 업무의〉 (美) an executive —정지 suspension of execution —처분 an executive measure

집행유예 執行猶豫 〔法〕 probation; a stay of execution; suspension of a sentence (during good behavior)
♦ 집행유예 중인 피고인 a probationer / 집행유예가 되다 be granted a stay of execution / 집행유예 중이다 be on probation / 징역 2년, 집행유예 3년의 선고를 받다 be sentenced to two years in prison with a three-year stay of execution

집현전 集賢殿 〔史〕〈조선 시대〉 Chip'yŏnjŏn; the Hall of Worthies

집회 集會 a meeting; a gathering; an assembly; a rally; 〈종교적〉 a congregation
♦ 집회의 자유 freedom of assembly
▶ 학생들은 항의 집회를 열었다 The students held a meeting of protest.
—집회하다 assemble; gather; meet (together); get together; hold a meeting [rally]
■ 불법— an unlawful assembly 옥외[야외]— an open-air meeting; an out-of-door gathering ■ —소 a meeting [gathering] place; 〈회관〉 an assembly hall [room] —신고 a notice of an assembly

집히다 get picked up; be held [picked up] between *one's* fingers [thumb and fingers]
▶ 그녀는 책상 위의 것을 집히는 대로 그에게 내던졌다 She picked up whatever came to hand on the desk and threw it at him.

짓 〈행위〉 an act; a deed; behavior; conduct; 〈일〉 work; *one's* doings
♦ 대담한 짓 a deed of daring / 미치광이같은 짓을 하다 act [behave] like a madman / 나쁜 짓을 하다 do wrong [an evil deed]
▶ 이것은 누가 한 짓이냐 Who has done it?
▶ 그는 그런 짓을 할 사람이 아니다 He is not the kind of man to do such a thing.

짓거리 a gesture [an act] out of merriment; *one's* sportive doings; a bit of fun

짓궂다 mischievous; prankish; ill-natured; cross(-grained); spiteful; nasty
♦ 짓궂은 짓[장난] a prank; a mischievous act [trick]; a practical joke; harassment / 짓궂은 장난꾼 a practical joker / 짓궂은 전화질 pestering telephone calls / 짓궂은 질문 nasty [embarrassing] questions / 짓궂은 비 the cursed rain / 짓궂게 굴다 be cross with *sb*; harass

짓누르다 weigh down; press down; press upon *sth*; push [thrust] against; 〈억누르다〉 put down; 〈마음을〉 weigh heavily on 《*one's* mind》

짓눌리다 be weighed [pressed, put] down; be crushed [squashed]; be flattened ♦ 슬픔에 짓눌리다 be crushed with grief 《over》
▶ 나는 가슴을 짓눌린 느낌으로 깨어났다 I woke up feeling pressure on my chest.

짓다[1] **1**〈만들다〉 make; manufacture; sew; 〈옷을〉 tailor
♦ 잘 지은 옷 well-tailored[-cut] clothes / 구두를 짓다 make shoes
▶ 그 옷은 어디서 지었습니까? Where did you get your clothes made?
▶ 어머니가 내 스커트를 지어주셨다 Mother made me a skirt. ⇌ Mother made a skirt for me.
2〈건물을〉 build; construct
♦ 벽돌로 지은 집 a house built of brick; a brick house / 집을 짓다 build [put up, construct] a house
▶ 새가 집을 지었다 The bird has built a nest.
▶ 거미는 비단같은 집을 짓는다 A spider weaves a silken web.
3〈책·글을〉 write; compose
♦ 책을 짓다 make [write] a book / 시를 짓다 write [compose] a poem / 이름을 짓다 name; christen / 작문을 짓다 write a composition
▶ 시를 짓기는 글을 짓기보다 어렵다 It is more difficult to write poetry than prose.
4〈밥을〉 cook; prepare
♦ 밥을 짓다 cook [boil] rice / 저녁을 짓다 prepare [cook] supper
▶ 어머니께서 아침을 지어주셨다 Mother got breakfast ready for us. ⇌ Mother cooked [prepared] breakfast for us. ⇌ Mother cooked [prepared] us breakfast.
5〈열을〉 form; make
♦ 가게 앞에 열을 짓다 form a line [(英) queue] in front of a store / 줄을 지어 기다리다 wait in a queue
▶ 그들은 행렬을 지어 행진했다 They marched in procession.
6〈농사를〉 grow; farm; crop
♦ 농사를 짓다 do farm work; engage in farming / 벼농사를 짓다 grow [raise] rice; till a paddy field / 밀농사를 짓다 raise [grow] wheat
7〈죄를〉 commit; do
♦ 죄를 짓다 commit a crime [sin]
8〈표정 등을〉 show; express; wear
♦ 미소를 짓다 smile; wear a smile / 이상한 표정을 짓다 make a strange expression
▶ 그녀는 억지 웃음을 지었다 She forced a smile. ⇌ She gave a forced laugh.
9〈결말 등을〉 settle; solve
♦ 결말을 짓다 settle [wind up] 《a matter》; bring 《a matter》 to an end [a conclusion] / 결론을 짓다 draw [form] a conclusion / 해결을 짓다 bring 《a matter》 to a settlement
10〈약을〉 prescribe 《medicine》; prepare; dispense; 〈처방전대로〉 fill [make up] a prescription
11〈허구를〉 make up; invent; fabricate
♦ 지어낸 이야기 a made-up [an invented] story

짓다[2] 〈유산하다〉 miscarry; abort ♦ 아이를 짓다 have a miscarriage

짓무르다 be sore [inflamed]; become blistered ♦ 빨갛게 짓무른 살 an inflamed raw skin
▶ 상처가 짓물러 있다 The wound is inflamed.

짓밟다 1 〈발로 밟다〉 trample [stamp, tread] down; crush under *one's* feet
♦꽃을 짓밟다 trample (down [upon]) flowers / 잔디를 짓밟다 trample the grass flat / 불을 짓밟아 끄다 stamp [tread, trample] out a fire
2 〈유린하다〉 trample upon [down]; tread down; override
♦남의 감정을 짓밟다 trample on [hurt] *sb's* feelings / 남의 권리를 짓밟다 ride over [trample on] the rights of others / 법과 질서를 짓밟다 trample law and order under foot / 국토를 짓밟다 overrun a country

짓밟히다 be trampled [trodden] down [on]; get trampled under foot; be downtrodden; get overridden ♦짓밟혀 죽다 be trampled [trodden] to death 《by》

짓씹다 chew thoroughly; masticate

짓이기다 mash; squash; grind and knead; knead to (a) mash; 〈밟아서〉 stamp down (to the ground); tramp [trample] down
♦감자를 짓이기다 mash potatoes / 진흙을 짓이기다 knead mud / 포도를 밟아 짓이기다 trample grapes

징¹ 〈악기〉 a gong ♦징을 치다 strike a gong
징² 〈구두의〉 a clout nail; a hobnail; 〈장식용의〉 a stud ♦구두에 징을 박다 put [get] heel and toe plates on *one's* shoes / 징을 박은 구두 hobnailed boots

징거두다 1 ⇨ 징그다
2 〈일을〉 make advance preparation; arrange in advance ♦내일 할 일을 징거두다 make preparations for tomorrow's work

징건하다 feel heavy on the stomach; remain undigested in the stomach

징검다리 stepping stones ♦징검다리를 건너다 walk over the stepping stones
▶실패를 성공의 징검다리로 삼아라 Make your failure a stepping stone to success.

징계 懲戒 a disciplinary punishment; an official reprimand; discipline —**징계하다** punish for delinquency; reprimand; reprove
■—면직[파면] a disciplinary dismissal [discharge]: 징계파면이 되다 be dismissed on disciplinary reasons; be dismissed in disgrace —위원회 a disciplinary committee —조치 (take) a disciplinary measure

징계처분 懲戒處分 disciplinary action; a disciplinary measure ♦징계처분을 받다 be submitted to disciplinary punishment

징그다 〈듬성듬성〉 sew loosely [with long stitches] (for reinforcement); 〈접어서 호다〉 make a tuck 《in a dress》

징그럽다 creepy; disgusting; loathsome; revolting; detestable; repulsive; 〈서술적〉 feel a chill creep over one
♦징그러운 녀석 a disgusting fellow; (美俗) a creep / 징그럽게 웃다 give a sinister grin; grin a gruesome smile
▶뱀은 보기에 징그럽다 The sight of a snake makes my flesh creep.
▶지렁이가 징그럽다면 정원의 풀도 못뽑겠다 If you are revolted by earthworms you can't even weed the garden.

징글징글하다 very creepy [crawly]; very disgusting [detestable]

징두리 [建] the foundation of a house ■—널 a wainscot; a skirting board

징모 徵募 enlistment; recruitment; recruiting
♦징모에 응하다 enroll *oneself*
—**징모하다** enlist; enroll; recruit; raise
▶그들은 의용군을 징모했다 They recruited [enlisted] volunteer soldiers.

징발 徵發 requisition; commandeering; levy; 〈마초 등의〉 forage
—**징발하다** commandeer; requisition; put [bring] *sth* under requisition
♦징발된 토지 commandeered land / 군용으로 물자를 징발하다 requisition supplies for troops / 군대 숙소를 위해 민가를 징발하다 requisition private houses for billeting troops / 징발당하다 be requisitioned; be placed under requisition
■식량— requisition for provisions ■—권(權) (the right of) requisition —대 a foraging party —령 a requisition order —선(船) a requisitioned ship

징벌 懲罰 discipline; a disciplinary [punitive] measure; punishment; chastisement
▶그는 규칙위반으로 징벌을 받았다 He was disciplined for breaking [violating] the rule.
—**징벌하다** punish; discipline; castigate

징병 徵兵 conscription; enlistment; recruitment; (美) (military) draft
♦징병으로 나가다 serve in the army / 징병을 기피하다 evade conscription [military service]; (美) evade the draft / 징병을 면제받다 be exempted from military service
—**징병하다** conscript; enlist; recruit; (美) draft; enroll; call up
■—관 a conscription [recruiting] officer; a recruiter —구 a recruiting [conscription] district —제도 the conscription system

징병검사 徵兵檢査 an examination for conscription ♦징병검사를 받다 be examined for conscription / 징병검사에 합격하다 pass an examination for conscription; be found eligible for conscription

징병기피 徵兵忌避 evasion of conscription [military service]; (美) evasion of the draft; draft evasion [dodging] ■—자 (口) a slacker; (美) a draft evader [dodger]

징병적령 徵兵適齡 conscription [military] age; (美) draft age ■—자 a young man of conscription [draft] age

징세 徵稅 tax collection —**징세하다** collect [levy, impose] taxes ■—목표 a tax collection goal

징수 徵收 〈세금 등의〉 collection; 〈과세〉 levy —**징수하다** 〈모으다〉 collect; 〈부과하다〉 levy; impose; charge
♦세금을 징수하다 collect [levy] taxes
■원천— collection at the source ■—료 a collection fee —액 the amount collected

징역 懲役 penal servitude; imprisonment with [at] hard labor
♦징역 가다 be sent to prison; go to jail / 징역 살다 serve a sentence in jail; serve a prison

term / 징역에 처하다 sentence [condemn] *sb* to penal servitude / 5년 징역을 살다 serve a sentence of five years' penal servitude; serve five years' sentence / 3년 징역을 마치다 finish *one's* three years' prison term
▶그에게는 징역 2년의 판결이 내려졌다 He was sentenced to two years' imprisonment.
■무기— a life sentence —꾼[수] a convict; a prisoner —살이 a life behind the bars; a prison life

징용 徵用 drafting; commandeering; requisition ◆징용가다 be drafted
—**징용하다** draft; commandeer
▶나는 징용되어 공장에서 일했다 I was forced to work in a factory as a conscript laborer.
■—선 a requisitioned ship —자 a drafted worker; a draftee —해제 derequisition

징조 徵兆 an omen (of disaster); a precursor; a presage; a premonitory sign [symptom]; a foreboding; a premonitor
◆좋은[나쁜] 징조 a good [an evil] omen / 회복의 징조 indications [signs] of recovery / 지진의 징조 premonitory symptoms of an earthquake
▶이것은 한국의 장래를 위해서 좋은 징조다 This augurs well for the future of Korea.
▶그것은 새 시대의 징조였다 That was the sign of a new area.
▶달무리가 생기는 것은 비가 올 징조다 A halo around the moon signifies [foretells] rain.

징집 徵集 enlistment; enrollment; (美) draft; conscription; recruitment; recruiting
—**징집하다** enlist; conscript; enroll; recruit; call up [out]
▶그는 군대에 징집되었다 He was recruited [drafted] into the army.
■—연기 postponement of enlistment —연도 a conscription year —영장 a draft card

징집면제 徵集免除 exemption from conscription [enlistment]; (美) exemption from the draft ◆징집면제의 특전 the privilege of exemption from conscription / 징집면제가 되다 be exempted from the draft

징크스 a jinx ◆징크스를 깨다[믿다] break [believe in] a jinx

징후 徵候 ⟨병의⟩ a symptom; ⟨일반적인⟩ a sign ▶오한은 감기의 징후다 If you feel chilly, it is a symptom of a cold.

짖다 ⟨개가⟩ bark; yelp; yap; ⟨늑대·개가⟩ howl; ⟨맹수가⟩ roar; ⟨까막까치가⟩ caw; croak
◆짖는 소리 a bark; a bay; a howl; a roar
▶멀리서 사냥개 짖는 소리가 들렸다 We could hear the distant barking of the hound.
▶지난 밤 개가 몹시 짖는 바람에 나는 잠을 설쳤다 I wasn't able to sleep last night because a dog was barking terribly.
▶짖는 개는 물지 않는다 (속담) Barking dog seldom bites. ⇌ Great barkers are no biters.
▶그 개가 나를 보고 짖어댔다 The dog barked at me.

짙다 1 ⟨색이⟩ dark; deep; rich
◆짙은 색 dark color / 짙은 갈색 a dark [deep] brown (color); a dark shade of brown / 짙은 파랑 deep blue; navy blue
▶그녀는 화장이 너무 짙다 Her make-up is too thick [heavy]. ⇌ She wears too much make-up.
2 ⟨안개·구름 등이⟩ dense; thick; turbid
◆짙은 안개 a thick [dense, heavy] fog
▶안개가 갑자기 짙어졌다 The fog was thickening [getting thick] quickly.
3 ⟨조밀하다⟩ thick; heavy
◆짙은 눈썹 thick eyebrows / 짙은 숲 a thick forest
4 ⟨액체가 진하다⟩ thick; heavy; strong
◆짙은 수프 thick [rich] soup / 짙은 차[커피] strong tea [coffee] / 커피를 짙게 타서 마시다 drink coffee strong
▶피는 물보다 짙다 (속담) Blood is thicker than water.
5 ⟨농후하다⟩ deep
◆패색이 짙다 Defeat seems certain.
▶그의 수뢰 혐의가 짙어졌다 There were strong suspicions that he had taken bribes.

짙푸르다 deep blue; azure ◆짙푸른 하늘 deep blue sky / 짙푸른 호수 a sapphire lake

짚 (a) straw
◆밀[볏]짚 wheat [rice] straw / 짚으로 싸다 wrap up in straw / 짚을 갈다 spread straw / 짚을 묶다 bundle straw; tie up straw in sheaves / 짚을 썰다 cut straw into the chaff; chaff
▶이 모자는 짚으로 되어 있다 This hat is made of straw.

짚가리 a pile [stack] of straw; a rick
◆짚가리를 쌓다 pile straw (sheaves) in a stack; heap up in a rick; rick

짚다 1 ⟨지팡이·손을⟩ rest (on); lean (on); place [put] *one's* hand (on a cane) for support
◆지팡이를 짚다 use a cane / 지팡이를 짚고 다니다 walk with a stick [cane] / 목발을 짚고 다니다 walk on crutches / 테이블을 손으로 짚다 place *one's* hand on the table
▶그는 다리가 나을 때까지 지팡이를 짚어야 했다 He had to use a cane until his leg got better.
▶목발을 짚으면 걸을 수 있어요 I can walk if I use crutches.
▶땅 짚고 헤엄치기다 Nothing is easier. ⇌ (美俗) That's a cinch.
2 ⟨대다⟩ touch; feel; pat
◆맥을 짚다 take [feel, examine] *sb's* pulse; have *one's* fingers on *sb's* pulse / 글자를 짚다 point out [finger] a letter
▶그녀는 그의 어깨를 가볍게 짚었다 She put her hand tenderly on his shoulder. ⇌ She touched his shoulder [him on the shoulder] softly.
3 ⟨헤아려보다⟩ count on the fingers
◆날수를 짚다 count the days on *one's* fingers
4 ⟨짐작하다⟩ guess; give [take, make] a guess (at); have a shot
◆옳게 짚다 guess right; make a good guess; hit the mark / 잘못 짚다 guess wrong; miss *one's* guess
▶누가 그랬는지 나는 짚어 말할 수가 없다 I have no idea yet who did it.

짚단 a sheaf of straw ◆ 짚단을 만들다 tie up straw in sheaves
짚둥우리 a hanging basket of straw
짚북데기 a heap of straw refuse
짚불 straw fire ◆ 짚불을 놓다 make a fire with straw
짚신 straw sandals [shoes]
◆ 짚신을 신다 wear [put on] straw shoes / 짚신을 삼다 make straw shoes
짜금거리다 chew [eat] loudly; munch with relish
짜깁기 invisible mending —짜깁기하다 mend (the trousers) invisibly
짜깁다 〈짜깁기하다〉 mend invisibly; darn (socks)
짜다¹ 1 〈만들다〉 put [piece, fit] together; assemble; construct; make
◆ 책상을 짜다 make a desk / 나무로 궤작을 짜다 make a box of wood
2 〈조직·편성하다〉 form; organize; compose
◆ 독서 클럽을 짜다 form a reading club [circle] / 배구팀을 짜다 form a volleyball team / 조를 짜다 form [make up] a group / 편을 짜다 〈축구 등의〉 choose sides
▶ 편을 짜서 놀자 Let's play sides.
3 〈직조하다〉 weave
◆ 무명[모직]을 짜다 weave cotton [woolen] cloth / 실로 천을 짜다 weave thread into cloth / 베틀로 짜다 work [weave] at the loom
▶ 이 천은 면과 폴리에스테르로 짠 것이다 This cloth is made from [woven of] cotton and polyester.
4 〈뜨개질하다〉 knit; crochet
◆ 기계로[손으로] 짜다 knit by machinery [hand] / 털실로 스웨터를 짜다 knit a sweater out of wool
5 〈입안·구성하다〉 form; frame; 〈안출하다〉 hammer [work] out (a plan)
◆ 계획을 짜다 frame a plan / 새해 예산을 짜다 make [draw] up the New Year's budget / 일정을 새로 짜다 rearrange the schedule
6 〈조판하다〉 compose; set (up) in type; set type
7 〈공모하다〉 collude; conspire 《with》; plot together 《with》; arrange; be in collusion 《with》
◆ 짜고 하는 시합 a collusive contest; a fixed match / …과 짜고서 in league [conspiracy] with… / 미리 짜다 make a previous agreement; prearrange
▶ 그녀는 정부와 짜고 남편을 죽이려 했다 She conspired with her lover to murder her husband.
짜다² 1 〈물기를 빼다〉 wring; squeeze
◆ 수건을 짜다 wring a towel; wring water from a towel / 젖은 옷을 짜다 wring wet clothes
▶ 어머니는 젖은 수건을 짜고 계셨다 My mother was wringing out the wet towel.
▶ 그의 옷은 짜야 할 만큼 젖어 있었다 His clothes were wringing wet.
2 〈액체를 내다〉 squeeze; press; extract
◆ 즙을 짜다 press the juice out 《of an apple》; squeeze the juice from 《a lemon》 / 우유를 짜다 milk a cow / 기름을 짜다 press oil 《from》; extract oil by pressing / 고름을 짜다 force out pus / 눈물을 짜다 squeeze out a tear / 관객의 눈물을 짜내다 move the audience to tears
3 〈억지로 내다〉 press out; squeeze
◆ 지혜를 짜다 strain *one's* wits / 머리를 짜다 rack [cudgel] *one's* brains 《about, over》
4 〈착취하다〉 extort; squeeze; exploit; sweat
◆ 농민의 고혈을 짜다 squeeze [sweat, exploit] the farmers / 돈을 짜내다 extort [squeeze] money from *sb*
짜다³ 1 〈맛이〉 salty; salt; briny; saline
◆ 짠 맛 a salty [saline] taste / 조금 짜다 taste a little salty / 짠 것을 좋아하다 have a salty tooth
2 〈달갑지 않다〉 unpleasant; displeased
◆ 마음에 짜다 feel unpleasant; be displeased 《with *sb*》
3 〈인색하다〉 grudging; stingy; 〈점수 등이〉 strict; severe
◆ 점수가 짜다 be severe in marking / 짜게 굴어 돈을 모으다 pinch and save
짜드락나다 be found out; be revealed [discovered, exposed]; come [be brought] to light
짜디짜다 very salty [briny]
-짜리 1 〈…값어치의 것〉 《a thing》 worth…
◆ 5천원짜리 〈지폐〉 a 5,000-won bill / 〈물건〉 an article worth 5,000 won
2 〈…한 수·양의 것〉 《a thing》 weighing [measuring, containing]…
◆ 20킬로그램짜리 쌀부대 a twenty-kilogram bag of rice / 두 뼘짜리 물고기 a fish two spans long / 백 마력짜리 발동기 a 100-horsepower motor
3 〈나이 뒤에〉 ◆ 세 살짜리 a three-year-old 《child》
4 〈…입은 사람〉 《a person》 in [wearing]…
◆ 양복짜리 a person in western clothes
짜릿짜릿하다 thrilling; tingling
◆ 영화를 보고 짜릿짜릿해지다 get thrills from a movie
▶ 줄타기는 짜릿짜릿해서 볼 수가 없다 Tightrope dancing [walking] is so thrilling that I cannot watch it.
짜부라뜨리다 crush; crumple
짜부라지다 be [get] crushed; collapse
▶ 모자가 납작하게 짜부라졌다 My hat was crushed flat.
▶ 그 집은 지진으로 짜부라졌다 The house collapsed in [was flattened by] the earthquake.
짜이다 1 〈피륙이〉 be woven; 〈편물이〉 be knitted [crocheted]
▶ 그 천은 면사로 짜여 있다 The fabric is woven of cotton.
2 〈규격·규모 등이〉 be put [fitted, pieced] together; be assembled [constructed, composed, fabricated, made]; 〈조직 등이〉 be formed [framed, structured, organized]
◆ 잘 짜인 소설 줄거리 the well-constructed plot of a novel / 잘 짜인 팀 a close-knit team / 조직이 잘 짜이다 be well organized
▶ 이 연극은 잘 짜여 있다 The play is well got up.

짜임 〈조직〉 system; organization; 〈구성〉 composition; 〈구조〉 structure; framework; make-up
♦ 프로그램의 짜임 the drawing [getting] up of a 《TV, radio》 program

짜임새 structure; make; makeup; texture
♦ 짜임새 있는 보고 a well-organized report / 짜임새가 거칠다 be open [loose] in weave

짜장 really; truly; indeed; in (good) sooth

짜증 —症 fret; irritation; vexation; anger; annoyance
♦ 짜증나다[내다] fret; be vexed [irritated, chafed]; be fretful [peevish]; show temper / 짜증나게 하다 fret; vex; irritate; ruffle; annoy; put out of temper
▶ 그는 걸핏하면 짜증을 낸다 He is very irritable.
▶ 뭐가 그렇게 짜증이 나니? What are you sore at?

짜하다 widespread 《rumor》; spread abroad
▶ 소문이 짜하게 퍼졌다 The rumor spread like wildfire.

짝¹ 〈쌍 중의 하나〉 one of a pair [couple]; a counterpart; 〈사람의〉 one's pal [partner, mate, fellow]
♦ 양말[구두, 장갑] 한 짝 an odd sock [shoe, glove] / 짝이 없는 unpaired 《gull》; mateless / 짝을 맞추다 pair; make a pair of; match / 짝을 잃다 lose [be bereaved of, be deprived of] one's mate
▶ 구두 한 짝이 안 보인다 I can't find the other shoe. ≒ The mate to the shoe is missing.
▶ 그 게임에서 나는 그 여자와 짝이 되었다 I was her partner of the game.
▶ 새가 짝을 부르고 있다 The bird is calling its mate.

짝² 〈갈비의〉 a side 《of beef [pork] ribs》; 〈짐의〉 a pack 《of loads》; a bale 《of dried fishes》

짝³ 1 〈찢는 소리〉 ♦ 종이를 짝 찢다 tear up paper; rip paper
2 〈활짝〉 ♦ 입을 짝 벌리다 open one's mouth wide; gape

짝귀 (a person with) mismatched ears

짝눈 mismatched eyes ■ —이 a person with mismatched eyes

짝맞다 match with another; pair

짝맞추다 make a pair of 《two things》; pair; match

짝사랑 unreturned [unanswered, one-sided] love
▶ 결국 그의 사랑은 짝사랑으로 끝났다 His love was not requited after all.
—**짝사랑하다** be in love without success [return]; love one-sidedly

짝수 —數 an even number
♦ 짝수의 even

짝신 an odd pair of shoes; mismatched [mismated] shoes

짝없다 incomparable; matchless; extreme
♦ 기쁘기 짝없다 be delighted beyond measure / 괘씸하기 짝없다 be most outrageous
▶ 미안하기 짝없습니다 I'm ever so sorry for what I did.
▶ 음주 운전은 위험하기 짝없다 Drunken driving is extremely dangerous.

짝짓다 pair; mate; match; make a match [pair]
♦ 새를 짝짓게 하다 mate a bird / 짝지우다 pair off / 남녀를 짝지어 주다 mate a man with a woman / 둘씩 짝지어 일하다 work in pairs / 둘씩 셋씩 짝지어 오다 come by twos and threes

짝짜꿍 a baby's hand-clapping (game); pat-a-cake

짝짜꿍이 〈밀계〉 a clandestine scheme; a secret plot; 〈다툼〉 a quarrel; a fight

짝짝 1 〈찢는 소리·신발 끄는 소리〉 ♦ 옷을 짝짝 찢다 rip up one's clothes / 신을 짝짝 끌다 scuff; shuffle
2 〈끈끈한 것이〉 stickily
▶ 엿이 이에 짝짝 붙는다 A taffy sticks on the teeth.
3 〈입맛을〉 with smacking
♦ 입맛을 짝짝 다시다 smack one's lips; lick one's chops [lips]

짝짝거리다 1 〈혀로 소리내다〉 smack 《one's lips》
2 〈신발 등을〉 scuff; shuffle
3 〈찢다〉 rip; tear up

짝짝이 an odd [unmatched] pair 《of shoes》
♦ 짝짝이 양말을 신다 wear unmatched socks
▶ 이 신은 짝짝이다 These shoes are not a pair [do not make a pair].
▶ 그는 눈이 짝짝이다 One of his eyes is bigger than the other.

짝채우다 make a set [match]; match; mate
♦ 찻잔 하나를 사서 짝채우다 buy a teacup to match the set

짝하다 become a partner [mate]; partake; mate 《with》

짠물 salt water; brine; seawater
■ —고기 a saltwater fish

짠지 radish preserved with salt

짤끔거리다 1 〈액체가〉 drop; fall in drops; drip; trickle; dribble 2 〈조금씩 주다〉 ⇨ 찔끔거리다

짤끔짤끔 1 〈액체가〉 in drops; dribbly 2 〈물건을 주는 모양〉 ⇨ 찔끔찔끔

짤랑거리다 clink; jingle

짤막짤막하다 all shortish [short]; all brief
♦ 짤막짤막한 단어들 short words / 오이를 짤막짤막하게 썰다 cut cucumbers in small pieces / 글을 짤막짤막하게 쓰다 write choppy sentences

짤막하다 shortish; rather [somewhat] short
♦ 굵고 짤막한 손가락 a stubby finger / 짤막한 연설 a short address [speech]

짤짤이 a bustling fellow

짧다 1 〈시간·길이 등이〉 short; brief
♦ 짧은 기간 a brief [short] period of time / 짧은 생애 a short life; a brief span of life / 짧은 이야기 a brief talk; a short story / 짧은 여행 a short trip / 수명이 짧은 short-lived; ephemeral / 2미터나 짧다 be two meters too short; be too short by two meters / 짧게 하다 shorten; make short; abbreviate 《a sentence》; curtail; cut short / 머리를 짧게 깎다 have one's hair cut short / 손톱을 짧게 깎다 cut

one's fingernails close
▶ 설명은 될 수 있는 한 짧게 해주십시오 Please make your explanation as briefly as possible.
▶ 기예의 길은 멀고 인생은 짧다 (속담) Art is long, life is short.
▶ 이 스커트가 나에게는 3센티미터나 짧다 This skirt is about three centimeters too short for me.
▶ 그는 만찬회에서 짧은 연설을 했다 He made a short speech at the dinner party.
2 〈부족하다〉 wanting; short; lacking; insufficient; poor
♦ 짧은 밑천 a small capital; (美口) a shoestring / 밑천이 짧다 be short in funds / 짧은 영어로 말하다 speak in poor [broken] English
3 〈식성이 까다롭다〉 particular 《about》; fastidious 《about》
♦ 입이 짧다 be particular about one's food; be a small [light] eater

짧아지다 shorten; become [get] short
▶ 해가 점점 짧아지고 있다 The days are gradually getting shorter.

짬 **1** 〈겨를〉 an interval 《of, in, between》; 〈여가〉 spare [odd] moments; leisure (time hours); free [spare] time
♦ 짬이 없다 have no time to spare / 짬을 내다 make time 《to do》
2 〈틈〉 a chink; an interstice

짬짜미 a secret promise [agreement, pact]; undercover negotiations
―**짬짜미하다** promise secretly; indulge in undercover negotiations

짬짬이 〈틈틈이〉 at odd moments; at intervals; between whiles

짭짤하다 **1** 〈맛이〉 nice and salty; somewhat salty; 〈서술적〉 have a good salty taste 《to》
♦ 짭짤한 고기 반찬 a nicely salted meat dish
2 〈쏠쏠하다〉 fairly good 《at》
♦ 짭짤한 글 a sapid [pointed] article / 짭짤한 부자 a quite well-to-do person / 솜씨가 짭짤하다 be quite good 《at》
3 〈구격에 맞다〉 acceptable; respectable; decent; honorable; worthy 《of》

짱구머리 a projecting [bulging, protruding] head; 〈사람〉 a person with a bulging head

짱짱하다 stout; sturdy; strong

째 〈그대로·통째로〉 and all; together with; inclusive of; plus ♦ 생선을 뼈째 먹다 devour a fish, bones and all
▶ 태풍으로 나무가 뿌리째 뽑혔다 The tree was rooted up by the typhoon.

-째 〈순서·등급·시간〉 ♦ 첫[둘]째 (the) first [second]; the first [second] class 《rank, grade》 / 두번째 결혼 a second marriage / 오른쪽에서 세번째 남자 the third man from the right / 일곱째 날 저녁에 on the evening of the fifth day / 일곱째로 떨어지다 drop to the seventh place
▶ 「會話」「넌 반에서 몇 째냐?」「셋째입니다」 "How do you stand in your class?" "I stand third in my class."
▶ 그는 양친이 한국에 온지 3년째되는 해에 태어났다 He was born in the third year after his parents came to Korea.

째다¹ 〈찢다〉 rip; cut open; cleave; lance; incise ♦ 배를 째다 rip the belly open / 종기를 째다 incise a tumor; lance a boil / 칼로 호주머니를 째다 cut one's pocket open with a knife

째다² **1** 〈꼭 끼다〉 be tight; be pinched; be too small ♦ 옷이 째서 거북하다 feel uneasy in tight clothes
▶ 신이 째다 My shoes pinch 《my feet》.
▶ 이 모자는 너무 쩬다 This hat is too tight for me.
2 〈부족하다〉 be insufficient; be in want 《of》; be short 《of》
♦ 살림이 째다 be hard up; be in want [need] / 일손이 째다 be short of help [hands]; be shorthanded

째보 〈언청이〉 a harelipped person; 〈팔삭둥이〉 a stupid; a half-wit

째(어)지다 split; be [get] torn; tear; rip 《open》; be rent [riven]
♦ 째(어)진 곳 a tear; a split; a torn place; a rent 《in a shirt》 / 옷이 째(어)진 곳을 꿰매다 mend a rent [tear] in one's clothes

짹짹거리다 chirp; chirrup; chirr; cheep; twitter
▶ 새들이 짹짹거리고 있다 Birds are chirping.

쨍 with a clink [clank] ▶ 칼과 칼이 쨍하고 부딪쳤다 The swords clanked.

쨍그랑 with a clink [clank, clang] ―**쨍그랑하다** clink; clank; clang ♦ 쨍그랑하고 깨지다 《a windowpane》 break with a crack

쨍그랑거리다 clink; clank; clash; jingle

쨍그랑쨍그랑 with a clink ⇨ 쨍그랑

쨍쨍 **1** 〈볕이〉 glaringly; blazingly; brightly
▶ 해가 모래 위에 쨍쨍 내리쬐었다 The sun glared down upon the sand.
―**쨍쨍하다** glaring; blazing; bright
2 〈얼음 등이〉 with a crack; with a clink
♦ 쨍쨍 갈라지는 얼음 cracking ice

쩌렁쩌렁하다 resonant; sonorous; full and ringing

-쩍다 -ish; like; feel like; give [have] a feeling of
♦ 겸연쩍다 abashed; ashamed; embarrassed / 미심[의심]쩍다 doubtful; questionable

쩍쩍거리다 smack one's lips; lick one's chops
♦ 껌을 쩍쩍거리며 씹다 chew a stick of gum audibly

쩍하면 on the slightest movement [provocation]; easily; readily
▶ 그는 남의 말을 쩍하면 믿는다 He is too [all] ready to believe others.

쩔쩔매다 be nonplused [perplexed]; be completely puzzled; feel embarrassed
♦ 바빠서 쩔쩔매다 be too busy to know the left from the right / 부인들 앞에서 쩔쩔매다 feel embarrassed in the presence of ladies
▶ 이 문제는 선생님도 쩔쩔매실 정도로 어렵다 This problem is hard enough to perplex even the teacher.
▶ 나는 어찌해야 좋을지 몰라 쩔쩔맸다 I was at a loss what to do.

쩝쩝 with smacking ♦ 입맛을 쩝쩝 다시다 smack one's lips ―**쩝쩝하다[거리다]** smack 《at》; smack the [one's] lips

쩡쩡 1 〈소리가〉 with a crack
♦ 쩡쩡 울리는 sonorous / 얼음이 쩡쩡 갈라지다 the ice breaks with a crack; the ice cracks
2 〈권세가〉 resoundingly; powerfully; mightily ♦ 세력이 쩡쩡 울리다 enjoy resounding influence

쩨쩨하다 〈인색하다〉 stingy; niggardly; miserly; close-[tight-]fisted; 〈치사하다〉 mean; petty; poor; shabby
♦ 쩨쩨한 놈 a niggard; a stingy fellow; a miser / 쩨쩨한 생각 a narrow-minded idea; a petty contracted idea / 쩨쩨하게 stingily; niggardly
▶ 그만한 부자가 그것 밖에 안 내놓다니 정말 쩨쩨하다 It is mean in a man of his wealth to give so little.
▶ 그는 그런 쩨쩨한 짓은 결코 하지 않는다 He never descends to such meanness.

쪼개다 split (up); cleave; rend; splinter; divide ♦ 둘로 쪼개다 split [divide] *sth* in two / 나무[대나무]를 쪼개다 split wood [bamboo] / 땅을 쪼개어 팔다 sell *one's* land in lots

쪼개지다 split; be split; cleave; rend; splinter; divide ▶ 이 나무는 잘 쪼개진다 This wood cleaves easily.

쪼그랑할멈 a crone; a withered old woman

쪼그리다 1 〈몸을〉 crouch; squat down; hunker (down)
♦ 쪼그리고 앉다 squat [sit] on *one's* heels; squat (oneself); squat on *one's* hams / 몸을 쪼그리고 불을 쬐다 crouch over the fire
2 ⇨ 쭈그러뜨리다

쪼글쪼글하다 wrinkled ⇨ 쭈글쭈글하다

쪼다 1 〈새 등이〉 pick; pick up; peck
2 〈정 등으로〉 chisel
♦ 돌을 쪼아 이름을 새기다 carve *one's* name in a stone

쪼들리다 be in narrow [straitened] circumstances; be hard up [pressed]
♦ 돈에 쪼들리다 be pressed for money / 가난에 쪼들리다 be pinched with poverty / 빚에 쪼들리다 be harassed with debts / 생활에 쪼들리다 be in straitened circumstances; be hard up for living

쪼아먹다 peck; pick
▶ 닭이 마루에 흩어진 쌀을 쪼아먹고 있었다 The hens were pecking [picking] at the rice scattered on the floor.
▶ 새들이 옥수수를 쪼아먹고 있다 The birds are pecking at the corn.

쪽¹ 〈머리의〉 a chignon
쪽² 〈조각〉 a piece; a cut; a slice ♦ 마늘 한 쪽 a clove of garlic / 빵 한 쪽 a slice of bread
쪽³ 〈방향〉 a direction; a way; 〈측면〉 a side; 〈곳〉 a quarter
♦ 다른 쪽 the other way / 이쪽을 보다 look my [our] way
▶ 나도 그쪽으로 간다 I am going that way, too.
▶ 그는 가리킨 쪽을 보았다 He looked in the direction indicated.
▶ 당신 쪽 이야기를 들읍시다 Let me hear your side of the story.

쪽다리 a single-plank bridge
쪽마루 a narrow wooden veranda(h)
쪽매 a (wood) marquetry; a parquetry; a parquet; a wooden mosaic
♦ 쪽매질하다 make a marquetry; make (a wooden vessel) by fitting together pieces of wood / 쪽매붙임하다 do marquetry; inlay marquetries; decorate in marquetry
쪽문 —門 a side door [gate]; a wicket
쪽박 a small gourd
쪽발이 1 〈외발 달린 것〉 a one-legged thing
2 〈갈라진 발굽〉 a cloven foot [hoof]
쪽빛 indigo (blue); indigotin
쪽소매책상 —冊床 a desk with a tier of drawers on one side only
쪽잘거리다 pick (a meal); chew by bits
쪽지 a slip of paper; a note
♦ 쪽지를 남기다 leave a note (behind) (for *sb*) / 쪽지에 몇 자 적다 jot a few words down on a slip
쪽찌다 do *one's* hair in a chignon
쫀득거리다 be sticky [gummy]; be tough and clammy
쫄딱 completely; utterly; wholly; altogether; thoroughly ♦ 쫄딱 망하다 be completely ruined; go to the dogs
쫄래둥이 a flippant child [boy]
쫑그리다 〈귀를〉 cock [prick up] (its) ears
▶ 개가 귀를 쫑그렸다 The dog cocked its ears.
쫑긋거리다 1 〈입을〉 move the lips; 〈내밀다〉 purse (up) *one's* lips 2 ⇨ 쫑그리다

쫓겨나다 〈내쫓기다〉 be expelled; be turned [got, put, sent, driven] out; be kicked out (of); be turned out of doors; 〈해고되다〉 be dismissed; (美) be [get] fired
♦ 동네에서 쫓겨나다 be driven out of a village; be ostracized / 직장에서 쫓겨나다 be dismissed [fired] from *one's* post; be forced [compelled] to leave *one's* position
▶ 그들은 집세를 내지 않아 그 집에서 쫓겨났다 They were kicked out of the house because they didn't pay the rent.
▶ 그는 품행이 나빠서 학교에서 쫓겨났다 He was expelled from school because of his misconduct.

쫓기다 〈내쫓기다〉 be kicked out; 〈뒤쫓기다〉 be pursued [chased] (after); be run after; be trailed
♦ 일과에 쫓기다 be overtasked [too busy] with *one's* daily work
▶ 그는 시간에 쫓기고 있다 He is pressed for time.
▶ 그는 일에 쫓기고 있다 He is pressed [is very busy] with work [business].
▶ 그는 경찰에 쫓기고 있다 He is hunted by the police.

쫓다 1 〈쫓아버리다〉 drive away; shoo away
♦ 파리를 쫓다 drive [shoo] away flies / 악령을 쫓다 drive out [away] evil spirits / 졸음을 쫓다 shake off sleepiness
▶ 모기를 쫓아라 Keep off mosquitoes.
2 〈뒤쫓다〉 pursue [chase] (after); go [run] after; trail
♦ …을 쫓아서 in pursuit of… / 순서를 쫓아서

in order / 범인을 쫓고 있다 be on the track [trail] of a criminal
3 〈따르다·추구하다〉 follow; pursue
♦ 유행을 쫓다 follow [run after] the fashion / 쾌락을 쫓다 pursue [seek] pleasure

쫓아가다 **1** 〈뒤를〉 go in pursuit; chase; run [go] after 《another》; follow (up); pursue
♦ 쫓아가서 부르다 call after *sb*
▶ 그녀는 쭉 그의 뒤를 쫓아갔다 She followed a long way behind him.
2 〈추종하다〉 follow suit; follow in *sb*'s footsteps; take [copy] after; go with
♦ 남이 하는 대로 쫓아가다 do the same as others do / 당의 방침에 무조건 쫓아가다 toe a party line without protest
3 〈앞선 것을〉 catch up with [to]; overtake; close up with
▶ 먼저 가시오, 곧 쫓아갈테니 You go on, I will catch you up.
4 〈필적하다〉 be match for; match; equal; rival
♦ 영어는 그를 쫓아갈 자가 없다 No one matches him in English.

쫓아내다 **1** 〈몰아내다〉 expel; turn [get, put, send, drive] out; kick [run] *sb* out 《of the house [company, army]》; turn *sb* out of doors
▶ 매니저는 광적인 팬들을 문밖으로 쫓아냈다 The manager turned away fanatical fans from the door.
▶ 기동 경찰이 강제로 학생들을 건물에서 쫓아냈다 The riot police forcibly evicted the students from the building.
2 〈해고하다〉 discharge; dismiss; 《美口》 fire
♦ 하녀를 쫓아내다 dismiss [fire] a maid

쫓아다니다 〈뛰어다니다〉 run about [round]; 〈붙어다니다〉 follow about [around]; dangle about [after]
♦ 여자 뒤를 쫓아다니다 dangle after girls

쫓아버리다 drive [run] *sb* away; turn [send] away [off, out]; disperse [scatter] 《the crowd》
▶ 경찰이 군중을 쫓아버렸다 The police scattered the crowd.

쫓아보내다 〈돌려보내다〉 drive back [out]; 〈방문자 등을〉 send away; turn *sb* from the door

쫓아오다 **1** 〈바싹 뒤따르다〉 come in pursuit; follow at *sb*'s heels
▶ 누군가 나를 쫓아오는 소리가 들렸다 I heard somebody following me.
2 〈필적하다〉 be match for; match; rival; equal

쬐다[1] 〈볕이 비치다〉 shine on [over]; beat [strike] (down) on
♦ 쨍쨍 내리쬐는 햇볕 아래 in the fierce heat of the sun / 볕이 내리쬐다 burn; beat down on

쬐다[2] **1** 〈불에〉 warm *oneself* (at [by] the fire); take warmth; put *sth* over the fire; hold up to the heat
♦ 손을 불에 쬐다 warm *one's* hands over the fire / 젖은 옷을 불에 쬐어 말리다 dry wet clothes over [at] the fire
▶ 난로 앞에 앉아서 불을 쬐어라 Sit at the stove and have a warm.
2 〈볕을〉 expose *sth* to the sun; bathe [bask] in the sun
♦ 햇볕을 쬐다 bask in the sun; sun (*oneself*)
▶ 고양이는 한낮의 따뜻한 햇볕을 쬐고 있었다 The cat was basking in the warmth of the noon sun.

쭈그러뜨리다 press [squeeze] *sth* out of shape; crush; batter ♦ 모자를 쭈그러뜨리다 crush [batter] a hat

쭈그러지다 **1** 〈우그러지다〉 get [be] pressed; be squeezed out of shape; be crushed
♦ 쭈그러진 모자 a battered hat / 쭈그러진 깡통 a crushed can
2 〈쭈글쭈글해지다〉 wrinkle; be wrinkled; shrivel; be shriveled ♦ 고생으로 쭈그러진 얼굴 a face wrinkled with cares

쭈그렁이 〈물건〉 a thing battered out of shape; a shriveled thing; 〈늙은이〉 a withered old person

쭈그리다 **1** 〈물건을〉 ⇨ 쭈그러뜨리다 **2** 〈몸을〉 ⇨ 쪼그리다

쭈글쭈글하다 crumpled; wrinkled; crinkled; 〈시들시들하다〉 withered; shriveled
♦ 쭈글쭈글한 노파 a withered old woman / 쭈글쭈글한 얼굴 a wrinkled face / 쭈글쭈글한 손 a shriveled hand / 쭈글쭈글해지다 be wrinkled [rumpled]; become creased

쭈뼛하다 hair-raising; bloodcurdling
♦ 머리 끝이 쭈뼛해지는 이야기 a thrilling [hair-raising, bloodcurdling] story / 머리끝이 쭈뼛해지다 *one's* hair stands on end [bristles up] (at)

쭉 **1** 〈한 줄로〉 in a row [line]
♦ 쭉 늘어서다 stand in a row / 쭉 늘어놓다 make an array of 《toys》; display
▶ 자동차가 쭉 늘어서 있었다 There was an array of motorcars.
▶ 그 거리의 한쪽에는 점포가 쭉 늘어서 있다 On one side of the street is an unbroken succession of shops.
▶ 연도에는 경찰이 쭉 늘어서 있었다 The route was lined with policemen.
2 〈계속하여〉 all the time; (all) through; throughout; all along (the line)
♦ 아침부터 쭉 all through the morning / 그날부터 쭉 from that day on / 1년 동안 쭉 all the year round / 두시간 동안 쭉 가르치다 teach two hours at a stretch / 쭉 손해만 보다 suffer a series of losses
▶ (지금까지) 쭉 기다리고 있었다 I have been waiting all this while.
▶ 이 길은 다리께까지 쭉 자갈이 깔려 있다 This road is graveled as far as the bridge.
▶ 휴가동안 쭉 하와이에 있었다 I stayed at Hawaii (all) through the holidays.
▶ 안산서부터 쭉 서서 왔다 I was kept standing all the way from Ansan.
3 〈대강〉 roughly; briefly
♦ 쭉 훑어보다 glance through [over] 《a letter》; look [go] over 《the flat》 / 청중의 얼굴을 한번 쭉 둘러보다 sweep the faces of the audience with a glance
4 〈찢는 모양〉 with a rip

♦편지를 쭉 찢다 tear a letter across / 손수건[옷]을 쭉 찢다 rip (up) a handkerchief [dress] / 달력을 한 장 쭉 찢어내다 tear off a leaf from a calendar with violence
5 〈모조리〉 utterly; completely; entirely; all
▶큰물이 쭉 빠졌다 Flood waters have sunk [gone down] completely.
▶힘이 쭉 빠져버렸다 All my strength is gone.
6 〈곧게〉 straight; direct(ly)
▶풀이 무성한 길이 그들 앞에 쭉 뻗어 있었다 A grassy path led straight ahead of them.
7 〈단숨에〉 at a gulp [draught]; 〈빠는 모양〉 (suck) hard
♦한 잔 쭉 들이켜다 have a long drink [draught] of 《wine》
8 〈한꺼번에 빠지는 모양〉 gauntly
♦살이 쭉 빠지다 grow very thin; lose much flesh
쭉정이 empty [blasted] ears
쭝그리다 cock (its) ears ⇨ 쫑그리다
-쯤 1 〈정도〉 about; around; almost; some; something like; ...or so; ...or thereabouts
♦세 시간쯤 about three hours / 10마일쯤 about [some] ten miles; ten miles or so [thereabouts]; around ten miles / 만 원 쯤 something like [in the neighborhood of] 10,000 won / 쉰 살쯤된 남자 a man somewhere around fifty; a man about [around] fifty; a man who is fifty or thereabouts
▶그는 내 나이쯤 된다 He is about my age.
▶그쯤 해두자 Let's leave it about there.
▶자동차로 한 시간쯤 걸리는 곳이다 It is an hour's car ride, more or less.
2 〈무렵〉 about; around; toward(s); about the time when...
♦다섯시쯤 about [around] five o'clock / 15세기말쯤 toward the end of the 15th century / 매년 이맘때쯤 at this time of (the) year / 다음 일요일쯤 about next Sunday / 재작년쯤 the year before last or thereabouts / 집에 돌아갈 때쯤까지는 by the time you get home
▶열흘쯤 전의 일이었다 It was [happened] around 10 days ago.
▶내 생각에 그는 다음 토요일쯤 올 것이다 I think he will come around [about] next Saturday.
3 〈비교〉 as...as; so...as ♦높이가 남산쯤 되다 be as high as Namsan
4 〈적어도〉 at least
▶차 한잔쯤은 대접할 법도 한데 They might at any rate give us a cup of tea.
쯧쯧 tut, tut!; sucks!
▶「쯧쯧」하고 그는 혀를 찼다 "Tut, tut!" he clicked his tongue.
찌¹ 〈부전〉 a tag; a slip; a label ♦찌를 붙이다 tag; label
찌² 〈낚시의〉 a float; a bob; a quill ♦찌를 달아 tie a float (at)
찌개 stew ♦고기[생선] 찌개 meat [fish] stew
찌그러뜨리다 crush; smash; squash; distort; contort; twist ♦메달을 찌그러뜨리다 break up a medal
찌그러지다 be crushed [smashed, squashed, distorted]; be contorted; be battered

♦찌그러진 얼굴 a wry [distorted] face / 납작하게 찌그러지다 be crushed flat
찌긋거리다 1 〈눈을〉 wink (significantly) (at) **2** 〈옷을〉 pull sb by the sleeve (to call (his) attention)
찌꺼기 1 〈앙금〉 dregs; lees; draff; grounds; grouts; sediments; settlings; residuum ♦술 찌꺼기 wine lees
2 〈불용물〉 leftovers; leavings; remains; remnants; scraps; refuse; 《table》 waste
♦밥 찌꺼기 leftover rice [food]; the leftover (from a dinner) / 팔다 남은 찌꺼기 remainders; remnants; goods left unsold; a dead [an old] stock
찌끼 dregs ⇨ 찌꺼기
찌다¹ 〈살이〉 put on [gain] flesh; grow in flesh; put on weight; get [grow] fat; fatten
▶그는 살이 좀 더 쪄야겠다 He needs more flesh on him.
▶그녀는 살이 너무 쪘다 She is overweight.
찌다² 〈날씨가〉 swelter; be sultry ♦찌는 듯한 더위 the sweltering [simmering] heat
▶오늘은 푹푹 찐다 It is boiling [steaming] hot today.
찌다³ 〈김으로〉 steam; heat with steam
♦찐 감자 a steamed potato / 갓 쪄낸 fresh from the oven / 감자를 찌다 steam potatoes
▶쌀을 10분간 쪄야 한다 The rice must be steamed for ten minutes.
찌다⁴ 〈베다〉 cut; mow; 〈솎다〉 thin [cull] (out) 《plants》; 〈모를〉 pick
♦모를 찌다 pick rice seedlings
찌다⁵ 〈흙탕물이〉 overflow a field
찌득찌득하다 tough 《beef》; hard; stiff (to cut)
찌들다 1 〈더러워지다〉 become dirty; be smudged; 〈퇴색하다〉 be tarnished; fade
2 〈고생으로〉 be careworn
찌르다 1 〈뾰족한 것으로〉 prick; prickle; stab; thrust; pierce; transfix
♦단도로 찌르다 stab sb with a dagger / 창으로 찌르다 transfix [pierce] 《a tiger》 with a spear / 바늘로 찌르다 prick 《one's finger》 with a needle / 목을 찌르다 stab sb in the throat / 푹[쿡] 찌르다 stab through; plunge [thrust] 《a dagger》 home 《into》 / 찔러 죽이다 stab [thrust] sb to death
2 〈막대기 등으로〉 poke; prod; 〈팔꿈치로〉 nudge; elbow ♦옆구리를 쿡쿡 찌르다 poke [dig, nudge] sb in the ribs / 팔꿈치로 쿡쿡 찌르다 nudge sb with one's elbow
3 〈습격하다〉 attack; assail; 〈마음을〉 strike; touch; come home to sb
♦적의 배후를 찌르다 attack the enemy in the rear / 아픈 데를[약점을] 찌르다 touch sb on a sore [tender] place / 정곡을 찌르다 hit the (right) nail on the head / 마음을 찌르다 go to one's heart; come home to one [one's bosom]
▶그는 나의 아픈 데를 찔렀다 He touched me on a sore spot. ⇌ His words stung me to the quick.
4 〈코를〉 be pungent
▶고약한 냄새가 코를 찔렀다 An offensive smell assailed my nostrils.

5 〈닿을 듯하다〉 strike against
♦ 하늘을 찌를 듯한 skyscraping 《building》; cloud-kissing 《peak》
6 〈밀고하다〉 inform 《on, against》; report [tell] 《on *sb*》; betray; 〈俗〉 squeal [squeak] 《on *sb*》
♦ 경찰에 찌르다 denounce *sb* to the police / 공범자를 찌르다 betray *one's* accomplices
7 〈밑천을 들이다〉 lay [put] out 《*one's* money》 in; invest in ♦ 광산에 많은 돈을 찌르다 invest heavy in a mine

찌르레기 〔鳥〕 a starling
찌르르 greasily ⇨ 지르르
찌르륵 with a slurp ━찌르륵하다 make a slurp
찌르릉 ♦ 찌르릉하고 초인종을 울리다 ring the doorbell / 찌르릉찌르릉 소리나다[울리다] tinkle; jingle
찌무룩하다 ill-humored; sullen; sulky; 〈美口〉 grouchy
찌부러뜨리다 crush; squash; smash; batter; distort ♦ 모자를 찌부러뜨리다 smash [crush, batter] a hat
찌부러지다 be crushed [smashed, battered]; come [go] to smash ♦ 찌부러진 모자 a battered hat / 찌부러진 코 a bashed-in nose
▶ 내가 앉으면 이 의자는 찌부러질 거야 This chair will collapse under my weight.
찌뿌드드하다 1 〈서술적〉 feel uncomfortable; be out of sorts ♦ 몸이 찌뿌드드하다 be unwell; feel uncomfortable **2** 〈날씨가〉 heavy; lowering; overcast
찌지 ━紙 a tag; a label; a slip; 〈美〉 a sticker
찌푸리다 1 〈찡그리다〉 frown; let 《*one's* face》 cloud over
♦ 찌푸린 얼굴 a grimace; a scowl; a frowning [wry] face / 고통으로 찌푸린 얼굴 a face drawn [twisted] with pain / 눈살을 찌푸리다 knit the brows / 얼굴을 찌푸리다 grimace 《at》; frown 《at, on》; scowl 《at, on》; make [pull] a (wry) face / 얼굴을 잔뜩 찌푸리고 있다 be as sour as vinegar
▶ 그는 대답을 않고 그저 얼굴만 찌푸렸다 He made no reply, but simply scowled.
▶ 그녀는 눈부신 햇살에 얼굴을 찌푸렸다 She frowned in the bright sunlight.
2 〈날씨가〉 become cloudy [overcast]; cloud 《over》; cloud up
♦ 찌푸린 하늘 a sullen [an overcast] sky / 찌푸린 날씨 gloomy weather
찍 1 〈미끄러지는 모양〉 ♦ 찍 미끄러지다 get a slip; slip **2** 〈긋는 모양〉 ♦ 선을 찍 긋다 draw a line with a (vigorous) stroke **3** 〈찢는 소리〉 ♦ 찍 찢다 rip up 《*one's* clothes》; tear up 《paper》 **4** 〈쥐 등의 울음소리〉 ♦ 찍 하고 울다 squeak
찍다 1 〈인쇄물을〉 print; put 《a book》 in print ♦ 돈을 찍다 print money / 원색으로 찍다 print in colors
▶ 이 잡지는 몇 부나 찍습니까? How many copies of this magazine are issued?
2 〈도장 등을〉 stamp; seal; impress
♦ 서류에 도장을 찍다 affix [put] *one's* seal to a document / 편지에 소인을 찍다 imprint a postmark on a letter
3 〈묻히다〉 put on; dip 《into》
♦ 펜에 잉크를 찍다 dip a pen in ink / 붓을 먹에 찍다 dip a writing brush in Chinese ink / 설탕에 찍어 먹다 eat *sth* with sugar / 코에 분을 찍어 바르다 apply some powder to *one's* nose
4 〈점 등을〉 place; mark ♦ 점을 찍다 mark with a dot [point]; place a dot / 문장에 점을 찍다 spot [put a period to] a sentence
5 〈작살 등으로〉 thrust; pierce; spear
♦ 작살로 물고기를 찍다 spear a fish / 갈고리로 얼음덩이를 찍어 당기다 hook in a block of ice
6 〈사진을〉 ♦ 사진을 찍다 〈자기가〉 photograph; take a photograph 《of》; 〈자기 사진을〉 have *one's* photograph taken
7 〈도끼로〉 cut (down); chop 《with an ax》; hew; hack ♦ 도끼로 나무를 찍어 넘기다 cut [chop] a tree down with an ax
▶ 열번 찍어 안 넘어가는 나무 없다 〈속담〉 Little strokes fell great oaks.
8 〈차표 등을〉 punch 《a ticket》; clip
찍소리 ♦ 찍소리 없이 in silence; without (saying) a word; without complaining / 찍소리 없이 순종하다 obey without a whimper [murmur] / 찍소리도 못하다 be silenced; be in blank surprise / 찍소리도 못하게 하다 silence; floor; put *sb* to silence
찍어매다 sew (up); stitch 《two pieces of cloth》 together lightly; stitch *sth* onto; tack 《a ribbon to a hat》 ♦ 터진 데를 찍어매다 stitch up a tear [rip]
찍찍 〈울음소리〉 ♦ 찍찍 울다 〈새 등이〉 twitter; tweet; chirp; 〈쥐 등이〉 squeak
찍찍거리다 〈새가〉 tweet; twitter; chirp; 〈쥐가〉 squeak
찍히다 1 〈인쇄되다〉 be printed ♦ 잘 [선명하게] 찍히다 be well [clearly] printed
2 〈도장이〉 be [get] sealed [stamped, impressed]; 〈차표가〉 get punched
♦ 시드니 소인이 찍힌 편지 a letter postmarked from Sydney
3 〈지목받다〉 be marked out [down] for; be spotted ♦ 범인으로 찍히다 be suspected as the offender
4 〈사진이〉 be taken; come out
▶ 이 사진은 잘 찍혔다 This photo has come out well.
찐쌀 rice processed by steaming unripe grains
찔끔찔끔 〈액체가 흐르는 모양〉 dribbly; oozily; 〈물건을 주는 모양〉 by [in] driblets; in small doses [quantities] ♦ 찔끔찔끔 주다 give by [in] driblets
찔끔하다 startle 《at》; become startled; start; get a start [turn]
▶ 그녀는 살금살금 걷다가 나뭇가지 하나가 발에 밟혀 딱 부러지자 찔끔했다 She stepped stealthily, and started when a twig snapped underfoot.
찔레(나무) 〔植〕 a multiflora rose; a brier
찔름거리다 〈넘치다〉 brim over 《with》; run [flow] over the brim; 〈조금씩 주다〉 give by [in] driblets
찔름찔름 oozily ⇨ 찔끔찔끔

찔리다 be pierced [stuck, stabbed, thrust, pricked]; (비유) go home to *one's* heart
♦ 가시에 손을 찔리다 get a hand pricked by a thorn / 목을 찔리다 be stabbed in the throat
▶ 그의 말에 가슴이 찔렸다 I had a prick of conscience at what he said.

찜 〈요리〉 a smothered [steamed] dish ♦ 닭찜 smothered [steamed] chicken ─찜 하 다 smother 《meat》; steam

찜질 fomentation; applying a poultice
♦ 더운[찬] 찜질을 하다 apply a hot [cold] compress [pack]
─찜질하다 foment [poultice] 《an affected part》; apply a poultice [compress] 《to》
■ 모래— 《taking》 a 《hot》 sand bath; treatment by the sand bath 얼음— applying an ice pack ■—약 a fomenting lotion; a poultice; a cataplasm

찜찜하다 〈서술적〉 feel embarrassed [awkward]; feel uneasy 《about》; feel ill at ease
▶ 돈 문제는 말하기가 찜찜하다 It is awkward to speak about money matters.

찡그리다 distort [contort, twist] 《*one's* face》; knit [bend] 《the brows》
♦ 찡그린 얼굴 a wry face; a sour look; a sullen countenance; a scowl; a grimace / 얼굴을 찡그리다 frown; make a grimace [wry face]; give a scowl; distort [contort] *one's* face 《with pain》
▶ 늦게 귀가했더니 아버지가 얼굴을 찡그리셨다 My father frowned when I came home late.

찡긋거리다 contract [raise] *one's* eyebrows; frown at; wink at

찡얼거리다 fret; be peevish; be cross; be fussy; be fractious; (英) grizzle

♦ 찡얼거리는 애를 달래다 soothe a fretful [whining] child

찡찡거리다 grumble; murmur; whimper; whine

찡찡하다 1 ⇨ 찜찜하다 2 〈코가〉 (be) bunged [stuffed, stopped] up

찢기다 get torn [rent, ripped]
♦ 갈가리 찢기다 be torn up; be torn to ribbons [tatters, pieces] / 잘 찢기지 않다 do not tear easily
▶ 그의 옷이 가시철사에 찢겼다 His clothes were rent on barbed wire.

찢다 tear; rend; rip; split; rive; pull apart
♦ 편지를 길가리 찢다 tear a letter to pieces [fragments] / 자루를 찢어서 열다 tear open a bag / 사지를 찢어 죽이다 tear [rip] *sb* limb from limb

찢어지다 tear; become torn; rend; rip; split; burst
♦ 가슴이 찢어지는 듯한 heart-rending / 둘로 찢어지다 split in two / 갈가리 찢어지다 be torn in [to] pieces; be rent asunder / 찢어지게 가난하다 (비유) be as poor as a church mouse
▶ 입이 찢어져도 그건 말할 수 없다 For the life of me I cannot tell you about it.
▶ 가슴이 찢어지는 느낌이었다 It was enough to rend my heart.
▶ 못에 걸려 스커트가 찢어졌다 I've torn my skirt on a nail.

찧다 pound 《rice》; hull 《rice, barley》; beat [knock] 《*one's* head》 against; ram 《against》
♦ 절구에 쌀을 찧다 pound [hull] rice in a mortar / 코방아 찧다 fall flat on *one's* face / 엉덩방아를 찧다 fall (heavily) on *one's* backside [buttocks] / 문에 머리를 찧다 knock *one's* head against [on] the door

차 此 〈(이)것〉 this; these; present; current
차 次 1〈…하는 김에〉 when; while; on the occasion; by the way
♦ 서울 가는 차에 on the way to Seoul
2〈…하려던 참에〉 time; moment; just as
▶ 막 나가려던 차에 그녀가 왔다 I was just going out, when she came to see me.
차 車 〈탈것〉 a vehicle; a conveyance; 〈자동차〉 a car; a motorcar; an automobile; 〈짐차〉 a cart
♦ 차를 타다 take a car; get in a car / 차로 가다 go by car / 차를 세우다 〈주행 중에〉 stop a car; 〈주차하다〉 park a car / 차에서 내리다 get out of a car / 차를 끌다 pull [draw] a cart / (도로가) 차로 붐비다 be crowded with (auto) traffic
▶ 길을 건널 때 차 조심해라 When you cross a street, watch for the passing traffic.
▶ 차를 불러 주시오 Call me a taxi.
▶ 역까지 차를 태워 주시겠습니까? Could you give me a lift [drive me] to the station?
▶ 그가 차에 타라고 하자 그녀는 마지못해 탔다 When she was told to get in his car, she reluctantly got into it.
▶ 집에서 사무실까지 차로 20분 거리다 It takes twenty minutes from my house to the office by car.
▶ 이 길은 특히 차의 왕래가 많다 The traffic is especially heavy [bad] on this road.
차 茶 tea (▶보통 tea라고 하면 '홍차'를 가리킴); 〈녹차〉 green tea; 〈홍차〉 black tea; 〈커피〉 coffee; 〈차나무의 잎〉 tea-leaves; 〈차나무〉 a tea plant; a tea tree
♦ 진한[묽은] 차 strong [weak] tea / 갓 우려 낸 차 fresh-drawn tea / 차 거르는 기구 a tea strainer / 차 찌꺼기 tea grounds [dregs] / 차의 산지 a tea-growing district; a tea-producing center / 차를 따다 pick tea / 차를 끓이다 make [brew, draw, prepare] tea; fix tea
▶ 차 한 잔 할까? How about a cup of tea?
▶ 차 한 잔 더 하시었어요? Would you like another cup of tea?
▶ 이 차는 잘 우러난다 This tea draws well.
▶ 그녀가 차를 따라 주었다 She poured tea for me.
▶ 그녀는 나에게 차를 대접했다 She made tea for [served tea to] me.
▶ 우리는 차를 마시면서 즐겁게 이야기를 나누었다 We had a pleasant chat over (a cup of) tea.
차 差 1〈차이〉 (a) difference; 〈격차〉 (a) disparity; a gap; 〈가격의〉 a margin; 〈임금의〉 a differential; 〈득표의〉 a majority; a plurality (차점자와의); 〈차액〉 (a) balance
♦ 견해차 a difference in view / 세대차 a generation gap / 남녀의 차 the difference between man and woman / 신분의 차 disparity in social standing / 능력의 차 discrepancy in ability / 연령의 차 difference [disparity] in [of] age; age difference / 기온의 차 changes of temperature; variation in temperature / 품질의 차 difference in quality / 근소한 차로 이기다 win by a narrow margin [small majority] / 1점 차로 지다 lose the game by one point / 압도적인 차로 당선되다 be elected by an overwhelming margin / 남녀간에 급여의 차를 두다 make a difference in payment between men and women
▶ 빈부 차가 심하다 There is a tremendous gap between the rich and the poor.
▶ 그 두 의견 사이에는 큰 차가 있다 There is a big difference between the two opinions.
▶ 그들의 연령 차는 여섯살이다 The difference in their ages is six years.
▶ 그는 2위와 50미터 차를 두고 달렸다 He ran ahead of the second runner by fifty meters.
2 〖數〗 the difference
♦ 차를 구하다 find the difference
-차 -次 1〈목적〉 for the purpose 《of》; with the intention 《of》; with the object 《of》; by way 《of》
♦ 연구차 for the purpose of studying / 휴양차 for (the benefit of) one's health / 인사차 방문하다 call on sb to pay one's respect / 관광차 서울에 오다 come to Seoul for sightseeing
▶ 그는 사업차 일본에 갔다 He went to Japan for his business.
2〈순서〉 order; sequence; 〈횟수〉 time; 〖數〗 degree
♦ 일차 방정식 a linear [simple] equation; an equation of the first degree / 1[2]차 코일[전지] a primary [secondary] coil [battery] / 제2차 발표 the second announcement / 제2차 세계대전 World War Ⅱ
차가 借家 〈세든집〉 a rented [hired] house; 〈세듦〉 renting a house ━**차가하다** rent [hire, take] a house ■━료 a house rent ━인 a tenant
차간 거리 車間距離 the distance between (two) cars (going in the same direction)
♦ 차간거리를 지키다 observe the proper distance between cars
▶ 그는 추돌을 피하기 위해 차간거리를 충분히 확보했다 He left enough room between the two cars in order to avoid running into the car ahead.
차감 差減 〈빼기〉 (a) deduction; (a) subtraction; 〖法〗 (a) recoupment; 〈계정의〉 a balance; a margin ━**차감하다** balance 《an account》; 〖法〗 recoup
♦ 손익을 차감하다 balance the profit and loss
■━잔액 the balance

차갑다 cold; freezing; frigid; frosty; icy; 〈매정하다〉 cold-hearted; cold-blooded
♦ 차가운 날씨 cold weather / 차가운 바람 a chilly [cold] wind / 차가운 대접 a cold reception [treatment] / 차가운 태도 a cold [frosty, frigid] manner / 얼음처럼 차가운 icy; as cold as ice; ice-cold / 차가워지다 become [get] cold [chilled]; 〈태도가〉 cool off 《toward one's lover》
▶ 북풍은 살을 에일 듯이 차갑다 The north wind is cutting [biting] cold.
▶ 그는 마음이 차가운 사람이다 He is a cold-hearted man. ⇒ He has a cold heart.
▶ 처음 만났을 때 그녀는 나에게 아주 차가웠다 She was very cold to me [treated me very coldly] when we first met.
▶ 그의 손은 점점 차가워졌다 His hands grew colder and colder.

차고 車庫 a car shed; a carbarn; a (carriage) shed; 〈전차의〉 a tram depot [shed]; 〈자동차의〉 a garage; 〈지붕만 있는〉 a carport
♦ 차가 두 대 들어가는 차고가 딸린 집 a house with a two-car garage / 차를 차고에 넣다 put [park] one's car in the garage; garage one's car

차곡차곡 in orderly fashion; in a neat pile; 〈lay〉 one thing on another
♦ 벽돌을 차곡차곡 쌓다 lay one brick on another / 접시를 차곡차곡 쌓다 stack the dishes into neat piles / 침구를 차곡차곡 개다 fold bedding up in piles

차관 次官 a vice-minister; an undersecretary; (美) a deputy secretary
♦ 차관급의 sb of the vice-minister class
■ 교육부― the Vice-Minister of Education 사무― a permanent vice-minister 〔英〕 secretary] 정무― a parliamentary vice-minister 〔英〕 secretary] ―보 an assistant secretary

차관 借款 a loan
♦ 차관을 신청하다 ask [apply] for a loan / 차관을 얻다 obtain a loan [credit] / 차관을 제공하다 grant [extend, give] a credit (to) / 3억 달러의 차관을 체결하다 contract a loan of three hundred million dollars
■ 개발― a development loan [credit] 공공[재정]― a public [financial] loan 단기[장기]― a short-term [long-term] loan 대기― a stand-by credit 상업[민간]― a commercial [private] loan 연불― a delayed payment loan 현금― a cash loan; loans in cash ―계약 a loan contract ―단 a consortium (pl. ~s, -tia) ―업체 a firm using foreign loans ―협정 a loan agreement

차광 遮光 shading [shielding] the light
―차광하다 shade [shield] the light
―막 〈창문의〉 a blackout curtain; 〈등불 주위의〉 a shade; 〔TV〕〈카메라용의〉 a flag ―장치 shading ―판 〔機〕 a douser

차근차근 methodically; systematically; carefully; scrupulously; step by step
♦ 일을 차근차근 처리하다 dispose of a matter carefully [step by step] / 어려운 문제를 차근차근 해결하다 settle (up) a difficult problem by going at it systematically
―차근차근하다 methodical; scrupulous; slow and careful; slow but steady

차금 借金 a debt ⇨ 빚

차기 次期 the next term [period]
■ ―국회 the next session of the National Assembly ―대통령 the president for the next term; 〈대통령 당선자〉 the president-elect ―이월 〈전기에서〉 brought down from last term's account; 〈부기에서〉 carried forward (略 c/f); 차기 이월 이익금[손실금] balance [loss] to be carried forward ―정권 the next administration ―회의 the following [next] meeting

사깔하다 close [belt] 《a door》 tight; shut 《a door》 fast [securely]; keep 《a door》 shut tight

차꼬 shackles; fetters ♦ 차꼬를 채운 죄수 a convict in fetters / 차꼬를 채우다 shackle; fetter

차꼬막이 〔建〕〈용마루의〉 concave antefixes fixed at both ends of a ridge roof; 〈박공머리의〉 a square rafter and tile fitted to the edges of a bargeboard

차끈차끈하다 〈서술적〉 feel freezing cold; feel chilled

차끈하다 very cold; freezing

차남 次男 one's [the, a] second son
▶ 저 애는 내 친구의 차남이다 That is my friend's younger son.

차내 車內 the inside of a car
♦ 차내에서 〈자동차의〉 in a [the] car; 〈기차의〉 in [on] the train; 〈전차의〉 in the tram
▶ 차내에서는 금연입니다 (게시) No smoking in the car. ⇒ Smoking is prohibited in the car. ⇒ Please don't smoke in the car.
■ ―등 a room lamp [light] ―회견 an interview aboard a train

차녀 次女 one's [the, a] second daughter

차다¹ 1 〈가득하게 되다〉 fill (up); become full (of); be filled [replete] (with); brim (with)
♦ 독에 물이 차다 a jar is filled (up) with water / 배가 차다 one's stomach is full / 꽉 차다 be jammed; be tightly packed; be overcrowded; be packed full / 활기[희망]에 차 있다 be full of vigor [hope]
▶ 대합실은 사람으로 꽉 찼다 The waiting room was packed with people.
▶ 이상한 공기가 온 마을에 가득 찼다 A strange atmosphere pervaded [prevailed over] the whole town.
▶ 그는 자신에 차 있다 He is full of [filled with] confidence.
▶ 그는 아침부터 밤까지 스케줄이 꽉 차 있다 His schedule is jam-packed from morning to night.
▶ 會話「벌써 찼니?」「아냐, 더 넣을 수 있어」 "Is it already jam-packed?" "No, you can put in some more."

2 〈흡족하다〉 be satisfied [pleased] 《with》; be content 《with》; 〈사물이 주어〉 be satisfactory
♦ 마음에 차다 meet with satisfaction; prove satisfactory; be satisfied 《with》; be content 《with》
▶ 나는 웬일인지 마음에 차지 않았다 I felt

somehow dissatisfied.
▶ 아버지는 아들이 마음에 차지 않았다 The father was not satisfied with his son.
3 〈일정 수량에 달하다〉 measure up to 《a certain quantity》; come (up) to; amount to; be as much as
♦ 되가 차다 it is one *doe* full; it is one whole *doe* / 정원에 차다 reach the regular number / 일정 액수에 차지 않다 be short of a certain amount
4 〈기한이〉 expire; 〈어음 등이〉 mature; reach maturity; fall [be, become] due
♦ 임기가 차다 one's term of office expires / 어음의 기한이 차다 a bill matures [is due for payment]
▶ 그는 형기가 차서 출감했다 On the expiry of the term he was discharged from prison.
▶ 그녀는 달이 차서 사내아이를 낳았다 Her time came and she gave birth to a boy baby.
5 〈달이 둥글게 되다〉 wax; 《美》 full
▶ 달이 찼다 The moon is (at the) full.
▶ 달도 차면 기운다 Every flood [tide] hath its ebb.

차다² **1** 〈몸에 달다〉 attach; fasten on; carry; put on; wear
♦ 칼을 차다 wear [carry] a sword at one's side / 시계를 차다 put on a watch; wear a watch / 패물을 차다 wear trinkets / 허리에 차다 carry sth by one's side
2 〈수갑 등을〉 be handcuffed [manacled]
♦ 수갑을 찬 죄수 a handcuffed prisoner / 수갑을 차다 have one's hands handcuffed

차다³ **1** 〈발로〉 kick 《at》; give sb a kick
♦ 공을 차다 kick a ball / 정강이를 차다 give sb a kick on the shin / 되받아 차다 kick back; return a kick / 서로 차다 kick each other / 문을 난폭하게 차다 kick the door violently; give the door a violent kick / 차 넣다 kick in / 차 올리다 kick up; give an upward kick; send sth up with a kick / 차서 넘어뜨리다 kick sb down; kick 《a thing》 over / 문을 발로 차서 열다 kick a door open
2 〈거절하다〉 reject; refuse; turn down; 《美口》 kick 《a request》; 〈애인 등을〉 jilt; discard; throw sb over
♦ 애인을 차버리다 jilt one's lover
3 〈혀를〉 click
♦ 혀를 차다 click [clack] one's tongue; tsk
4 〈채뜨리다〉 snatch away 《from, off》

차다⁴ **1** 〈온도·날씨가〉 cold; freezing; frosty; icy; chilly; cool
♦ 찬 물 cold water / 찬 바람 a cold [chilly] wind / 찬 날씨 cold [chilly] weather / 차게 하다 cool; 〈얼음으로〉 ice; 〈냉장 장치로〉 refrigerate / 차게 되다 become [get] cold [chilled]; go cold / 얼음장같이 차다 be ice-cold; be (as) cold as ice
▶ 바깥 날씨가 몹시 차다 It is freezing cold outside.
▶ 산의 공기는 몹시 차다 There is a nip in the mountain air.
♦ 우유는 냉장고에 넣어 차게 해 두어라 Keep milk cool in the refrigerator.
2 〈마음·태도가〉 cold; frigid; cold-hearted; cold-blooded
♦ 찬 사람 a cold-hearted person

차단 遮斷 interception; isolation; 〈방역을 위한〉 quarantine
━**차단하다** intercept; isolate; cut off; shut off; quarantine; 〔電〕 break
♦ 광선을 차단하다 intercept [shut out] the light / 교통을 차단하다 cut off traffic; 〈전염병 발생지로부터〉 perform quarantine / 보급로를 차단하다 block the supply route / 퇴로를 차단하다 cut off the 《enemy's》 retreat; block the way of retreat
▶ 산사태 때문에 교통이 차단되었다 Traffic was blocked (off) by a landslide.
▶ 그 분지는 산에 막혀 바깥 세계로부터 차단되어 있다 The valley is shut off by the mountains from the rest of the world.
■**교통—** roadblocking; 〈방역을위한〉 quarantine ■**—기** 〈전류의〉 a circuit breaker; 〈건널목의〉 a crossing gate; a lifting gate ■**—장치** a cutoff; 〔船〕 a cutout gear

차대 車臺 a car body; a chassis 《pl. ~》
■ 앞[뒤]— 〔鐵〕 the front [rear] platform

차도 車道 a roadway; a carriageway; 《美》 a driveway
▶ 차도를 건널 때는 잘 살피고 건너라 Take good care in crossing the roadway.

차도 差度 improvement 《of illness》
♦ 차도가 있다 get better; improve (in health); take a turn for the better; take a favorable [better] turn
▶ 환자는 완연히 차도를 보이고 있다 The patient is well on toward recovery.

차돌 〈석영〉 quartz; quartzite; 〈야무진 사람〉 a tough fellow; a man of steadfast character
■**—모래** 〈규사〉 quartz [silica] sand

차동 差動 〔物·機〕 differential (motion)
■**—기어 장치** differential gear system ■**—도르래** a differential pulley ■**—전동기** a differential motor ■**—톱니바퀴** a differential gear

차드 〈나라 이름〉 Chad; 〈공식명〉 the Republic of Chad ♦ 차드의 Chadian ■**—사람** a Chadian

차등 此等 these (things)

차등 差等 gradation; graduation; (a) difference ♦ 차등이 있다 be different in grade(s) / 차등을 두다 grade; graduate; discriminate

차디차다 very cold; icy; freezing; frigid; as cold as ice ♦ 차디찬 사람 a cold-hearted [an icy] person

차라리 rather 《than》; better 《than》; sooner 《than》; before; preferably
▶ 노예로 사느니 차라리 죽는게 낫다 I would rather [sooner] die than live in slavery.
▶ 차라리 학교를 그만둬 버릴까? I wonder if I had(n't) better leave school.
▶ 너는 거기 가지 않는 편이 차라리 낫다 You had better not go there.
▶ 그는 가게를 걷어치우는 편이 차라리 낫다 He might as well close down his store.
▶ 나는 차라리 이 편을 택하겠다 I'd rather take this one. ⇒ I prefer this one.

차란차란 brimfully ⇨ 치런치런

차랑거리다 **1** ⇨ 치렁거리다 **2** 〈소리나다〉

clink; tinkle; jingle
♦ 열쇠 뭉치를 차랑거리며 걷다 walk along clinking a bunch of keys

차랑차랑 1 ⇨ 치렁치렁 2 〈소리〉 ting-a-ling; with a tinkle; with a clink ──**차랑차랑하다** ⇨ 차랑거리다

차랑하다 hanging loosely

차량 車輛 〈탈것〉 a vehicle; 〈기차의〉 (美) a car; (英) a carriage
♦ 한 차량 분의 화물 a carload 《of goods》 / 차량의 수송 wheeled transport
▶ 차량 통행 금지 《게시》 No thoroughfare for vehicles. ⇌ Closed to all vehicles.
■ ─검사 vehicle (maintenance) inspection; vehicle safety inspection ─격일제 운행 an alternative-day driving ban ─고장 a car trouble; a vehicular accident; a breakdown ─도선 《渡船》 a car ferry ─등록 vehicle registration ─번호판 〈자동차의〉 a licence plate ─부족 car shortage ─십부제 운행 (the) every-ten day limit on auto usage ─정비 vehicle maintenance: 차량 정비 불량 poor maintenance of the vehicles ─중량 the deadweight 《of a freight car》 ─회사 a rolling stock 《manufacturing》 company

차려 《口令》 Attention!; 'Shun!
♦ 차려 자세를 취하다 come to attention; stand at [to] attention / 벌떡 일어나 차려 자세를 취하다 spring to attention

차력 借力 boosting one's physical strength by taking medicinal or spiritual tonic

차례 1 〈순서〉 order; 〈순번〉 a turn
♦ 내[네] 차례 my [your] turn / 차례로 in (regular) order; in turn; by turns; by [in] rotation; one by one; one after another / 차례를 따라 in due order [course, succession]; in regular sequence; through regular grades / 나이 차례로 by priority of age; according to seniority / 자기 차례가 되어 in one's turn / 차례가 뒤바뀌다 be out of order; be in wrong order / 차례를 기다리다 await [wait (for)] one's turn / 차례를 앞당기다 move up sth in order / 차례를 바꾸다 change the order / 차례로 서다 stand in order; 〈줄지어〉 stand in a queue / 키 차례로 서다 stand in order of height / 술잔을 차례로 돌리다 pass the winecup around
▶ 차례가 아닌데 노래해서는 안된다 You must not sing out of (your) turn.
▶ 다음은 누구 차례입니까? Whose turn is it next?
▶ 마침내 내 차례가 돌아왔다 At last my turn came. ⇌ Finally it came to my turn.
▶ 이번에는 내가 읽을 차례다 It's my turn to read now.
2 〈횟수〉 time; round
♦ 한 차례 once / 두 차례 twice / 세 차례 thrice; three times / 한 차례 이기다 win one round of a game / 책을 여러 차례 읽다 read a book several times
3 〈목차〉 a table of contents
♦ 책에 차례를 달다 attach a table of contents to a book

차례 茶禮 ancestor-memorial rites
♦ 차례를 지내다 observe a worship service for family ancestors 《on Ch'usŏk morning》

차례차례 one by one; one after another; 〈순서대로〉 in turn; 〈연이어〉 in succession; successively
♦ 사람을 차례차례 불러들이다 call in men one after another / 그들에게 차례차례 물어보다 ask them one after another / 일을 차례차례 처리하다 dispose of matters in due order; settle things one by one
▶ 소년들은 차례차례 물속으로 뛰어들었다 The boys jumped into the water one after another. ⇌ One boy after another jumped into the water.

차렛걸음 proceeding in due order [course, succession]; orderly management; a regular process

차륜 車輪 a wheel ⇨ 차바퀴 ■ ─제동기 a wheel brake

차르랑 with a clink [tinkle] ──**차르랑하다** ⇨ 차르랑거리다

차르랑거리다 clink; tinkle; make a tinkling sound

차리다 1 〈마련하다〉 give; set; spread; get ready; 〈새로 갖추다〉 make; set up
♦ 밥상을 차리다 spread [set] the table (for dinner); lay covers 《for three guests》 / 술상을 차리다 prepare dishes for drink; set a drinking table / 잔치를 차리다 give [spread] a feast [banquet]; give [hold] a party / 살림을 차리다 make a new home 《at, in》 / 점포를 차리다 set up a store / 제단을 차리다 prepare [set up] an altar
▶ 차린 것이 별로 없습니다 It is not much of a dinner.
2 〈정신을 가다듬다〉 come to 《one's senses》; collect 《oneself》; concentrate 《one's mind》; keep; recover
♦ 의식을 차리다 recover [regain] consciousness / 정신을 바짝 차리다 preserve one's consciousness; keep one's senses / 정신을 차려 일하다 do the job carefully; be intent upon one's work; devote one's attention to the task at hand
▶ 정신을 차리고 보니 내가 시궁창에 누워 있었다 When I came to, I found myself lying in a ditch.
3 〈외관을 갖추다〉 dress 《oneself》 up; be dressed up; be in one's (Sunday) best; 《美俗》 fix oneself up
♦ 화려하게 차려입다 be gaudily dressed
▶ 그는 항상 잘 차려입는다 He always wears his clothes properly [attractively].
4 〈할 일의 준비를〉 prepare; make oneself ready 《for》
♦ 길 떠날 채비를 차리다 make oneself ready for the start on a trip; prepare [make preparations] for a journey; equip [outfit] oneself for a trip
5 〈예의 등을〉 keep; maintain; save; preserve; observe; pay attention (to)
♦ 인사를 차리다 observe decorum; keep up the common civilities of life / 체면을 차리다 keep up appearances

▶ 친한 사이에도 예의는 차려야 한다 There should be courtesy even among intimates.
6 〈욕심을〉 ♦ 제 욕심만 차리다 be self-interested; put *one's* own interests above everything else / 허울을 버리고 실속을 차리다 discard the shadow for the substance
7 〈알아차리다〉 sense; catch up

차림 〈행색·옷차림〉 (personal) appearance; guise; dress; attire; an outfit
♦ 행상인 차림의 남자 a man looking like a peddler / 나그네 차림으로 fitted out as a traveler; in a traveling outfit / 여자 차림으로 in the (dis)guise of a woman; disguised in female attire / 뱃사람 차림이다 be rigged out as a sailor
▶ 이런 차림이라 미안합니다 Pardon me for being in this dress.
▶ 직공 차림의 남자를 보셨습니까? Did you see a man looking like a workman?

차림새 1 〈옷의〉 *one's* manner of dressing; *one's* garb [getup, clothes, attire]
♦ 차림새가 말쑥하다[야하다] be neatly [loudly] turned out; be neat [loud] in *one's* dress / 차림새가 초라하다 dress shabbily; be shabbily dressed; be humbly clad
▶ 차림새만 보고도 그녀의 성격을 알 수 있었다 Her appearance betrayed her character. ⇒ You could judge her character through her outfit.
2 〈살림의〉 household effects [things]; furnishings; installation; 〈장식〉 decoration; 〈규모〉 setup

차림표 —表 a menu; a (menu) card

차마 ♦ 차마 견딜 수 없는 모욕 an intolerable [unpardonable] insult / 차마 …하지 못하다 do not have the heart (to punish him); cannot bear (to see *one's* grief); be loath (to leave)
▶ 나는 그의 부탁을 차마 거절할 수 없었다 I couldn't find it in my heart to refuse his request.
▶ 그것은 차마 눈뜨고 볼 수 없는 참상이었다 It was too miserable [cruel] to look at.

차마 車馬 horses and vehicles ♦ 차마의 통행 vehicular traffic ▶ 차마 통행 금지 (게시) No thoroughfare for horses and vehicles.

차멀미 車— car sickness **—차멀미하다** get [be] carsick

차명 借名 borrowing a name
—차명하다 borrow [assume] *sb's* name; use *sb's* name; masquerade under *sb's* name; impersonate (another)
♦ 차명하여 in the name of; under the (assumed) name of

차밍하다 charming; attractive

차바퀴 車— a wheel; a rundle
♦ 차바퀴에 깔리다 be run over by a car / 차바퀴에 기름을 치다 put oil on the wheels
▶ 차바퀴가 빠졌다 The wheel has come off.
■ **—자국** a (wheel) track; a rut; the print of a wheel

차반 茶盤 a tea tray [server, board]

차버리다 refuse ⇨ 차다³ 2

차변 借邊 the debit [debtor] (略 Dr, dr.); the debit [debtor] side
♦ 차변에 기입하다 debit (a sum) against [to] *sb*; enter (an item) to *sb's* debit [to the debit of *sb's* account]
■ **—계정[전표, 잔고]** a debtor account [note, balance] **—기입** an entry on the debtor side of an account; a debtor entry **—항목** a debit item

차별 差別 (a) discrimination; (a) distinction
♦ 차별적인 discriminative; discriminatory; preferential; differential / 남녀의 차별 없이 irrespective of sex; men and women (all) alike / 신분의 차별 없이 without distinction of rank / 차별을 두지 않고 indiscriminately; without distinction [discrimination]
—차별하다 draw [establish, set up] a distinction (between); differentiate (one from another); discriminate (against) ♦ 여성[외국인]을 차별하다 discriminate against women [foreigners] / 사람에 따라 차별하다 discriminate against certain persons
▶ 그 회사는 사람을 고용할 때 외국인을 차별한다 That company discriminates against foreigners when they hire them.
▶ 그 미용실은 단골과 그렇지 않은 손님을 차별한다 At that beauty parlor they discriminate [distinguish] between regular customers and strangers.
■ **계급—** class distinction **남녀—** sex(ual) discrimination; sexism **인종—** racial discrimination; 〈미국 흑인에 대한〉 segregation; 〈남아프리카의〉 apartheid : 인종 차별을 하다 discriminate against race **—관세** differential [discriminating] duties **—세율** a discriminative [differential] tariff **—임금** differential wages **—철폐** 〈인종의〉 abolition of racial discrimination

차별대우 差別待遇 discriminative [discriminating, preferential] treatment; discrimination in treatment; inequality of treatment; differentiation
♦ 차별대우를 하다 give discriminative [preferential] treatment (to); treat *sb* with discrimination; discriminate against / 차별대우를 받다 receive [be given] discriminatory treatment; be treated discriminately

차부 車夫 a driver; a cabman; 〈짐수레의〉 a carter

차분하다 calm; quiet; tranquil; placid; serene; subdued; sedate; collected; self-possessed
♦ 차분한 기분 a quiet mood / 차분한 빛깔 a sober [subdued] color / 차분한 태도로 in a calm [graceful] manner / 아주 차분한 목소리로 in a skilled, severely controlled voice / 차분히 생각하다 think over (a matter); ponder (over the plan) / 차분히 공부하다 settle [set] down to *one's* studies / 마음을 차분히 가라앉히다 calm [compose] *oneself*; keep cool; gather *one's* wits
▶ 그는 차분히 홀을 둘러보았다 He looked around the hall quite composedly [calmly].
▶ 그는 차분히 생각하는 법이 없다 He never stops to think.
▶ 아이들이 떠드는 통에 차분히 책을 읽을 수가 없다 The children are so noisy that I cannot

settle down to my reading.
차비 車費 the railroad [railway] fare; 〈전차 등의〉 the (car) fare; 〈운반료〉 freight; carriage; cartage
♦차비를 내다 pay the fare / 차비를 할인해주다 discount [reduce] the fare (for students) ▶부산까지 왕복 차비는 얼마입니까? What is the fare to Pusan and back?
차비 差備 preparations ⇨ 채비
차사 差使 〔史〕 an emissary (with the police power) ♦함흥— a lost messenger
차석 次席 the next seat [position]
♦차석의 next; ranking next / 자석이다 rank next to 《the captain》
■—자 〈관리 등〉 an official next in rank; an associate; 〈수상자 등〉 the second winner
차선 次善 the second best
■—책 (take) the second [next] best policy : 차선책이 있다 have two strings to one's bow
차선 車線 a (traffic) lane
♦4차선 도로 a four-lane road / 차선을 지키다 keep one's lane; stay in one lane
■—분리대 a divisional strip [island] —분리선 a lane-dividing line; a stripe
차세대 次世代 the next [coming] generation
♦차세대를 이끌어갈 젊은이들 the young who are to lead the coming generation
차손 差損 〔商〕 a loss from the difference of quotations
차송 差送 dispatch —차송하다 dispatch; despatch; send; detach
차수 次數 〔數〕 degree
차수 差數 difference (in number); balance; disparity
차아 次兒 one's [the] second son
차압 差押 〔法〕 attachment ⇨ 압류(押留)
차액 差額 the difference; the balance; a margin ♦큰[작은] 차액 a wide [narrow] margin / 무역 차액 the balance of trade / 차액을 지불하다 pay the difference
차양 遮陽 **1** 〈차일〉 a sunshade; a sunscreen; 〈지붕의〉 a penthouse; a pent roof; 〈창·문의〉 an awning; a (Venetian) blind
2 〈모자의〉 a visor; a peak; 〈운동모 등의〉 an eyeshade; an eye shield
♦차양이 있는 모자 a visored [peaked] cap / 차양이 넓은 모자 a broad-brimmed hat
차용 借用 borrowing; loan
—차용하다 〈무료로〉 borrow; have a loan; 〈유료로〉 rent
♦백만원을 차용해 달라고 부탁하다 ask sb for a loan of a million won; apply to sb for an advance of a million won
■—금 borrowed money; a loan; a debt —어 a borrowed word; a loanword; a loan —인 a borrower; 〈돈의〉 a debtor —증(서) a bond of debt [loan]; an IOU 《pl. ~s》; a due bill: 백만원에 대한 차용증을 쓰다 write an IOU for a million won
차원 次元 **1** 〔數〕 a dimension
♦3차원 the third dimension / 2차원의 of two dimensions; two-dimensional
2 〈입장·수준〉 ♦차원이 낮은[높은] 생각 a vulgar [an elevated] notion / 차원이 다르다 be on a different level [sphere]; belong to a different level [category]
차월 借越 a debt balance; 〈당좌예금의〉 an overdraft; overdrawing
—차월하다 overdraw
차위 次位 the second rank [place, position]
차이 差異 (a) difference; (a) divergence; disagreement; 〈구별〉 (a) distinction; 〈불일치〉 (a) discrepancy; 〈불균형〉 (a) disparity; 〈같지 않음〉 (a) dissimilarity; a gap
♦신분 차이 (a) disparity in social standing / 외관의 차이 a difference in appearance / 의견 자이 a difference [divergence] of opinion [views] / 취미의 차이 (a) disparity of tastes / 시와 산문의 차이 the distinction between poetry and prose / 세 살 차이인 형[아우] a brother three years older [younger] than 《one》/ 큰 차이가 있다 differ greatly 《from》; there is a wide difference 《between》/ 큰 차이가 없다 differ little 《from》; make little difference
▶그 두 언어 사이에는 별 차이가 없다 There are not many differences [There is not much difference] between the two languages.
♦양자 사이에는 하늘과 땅의 차이가 있다 They are poles asunder.
▶보는 것과 듣는 것과는 엄청난 차이가 있다 There is all the difference in the world between seeing and hearing.
▶야구와 크리켓의 차이를 모르겠다 I can't tell the difference [make a distinction] between baseball and cricket. ⇒ I can't tell [don't know, can't distinguish] baseball from cricket.
▶〔會話〕「택시를 타면 어떨까?」「전연 차이가 없어」"What if we take a taxi?" "It doesn't make any difference."
■—법〔論〕the method of difference —점 a point of difference; a differentia 《pl. -tiae》: 차이점을 밝히다 clarify the distinction 《between》; make clear the difference 《between》
차익 差益 marginal profits; a margin
차인꾼 差人— an employee (of a merchant)
차일 遮日 a sunshade; a tent; an awning; a blind; a marquee
♦차일을 치다 pitch a tent; fix a marquee
차일피일 此日彼日 ♦일을 차일피일 미루다 put the work off from day to day
—차일피일하다 delay 《a matter》 from day to day; put off [leave over] 《a matter》 day by day; procrastinate
♦차일피일하고 빚을 갚지 않다 defer payment on the debt time and again / 차일피일하다가 기회를 놓치다 procrastinate until an opportunity is lost
▶차일피일하다가 오늘에 이르렀다 And it has thus been delayed until now.
차임 a chime
차입 借入 borrowing; loaning —차입하다 borrow; obtain 《money》 on loan
■—금 a loan (of money); borrowed money; a debt
차입 差入 —차입하다 send in 《a thing》 to a

prisoner ■ —물 a thing sent in to a prisoner; outside supplies for a prisoner —식사 a meal sent in to a prisoner

차자 次子 one's [the, a] second son ⇨ 차남

차작 借作 〈대작(代作)〉 vicarious writing [making]; ghostwriting; writing [making] for 《another》; 〈작품〉 a vicarious work
—하다 write [compose, make] for 《another》; ghostwrite

차장 次長 a vice-chief; a vice-director; a deputy chief; an assistant director (general)
■ —편집 a subeditor ■ —검사 the deputy prosecutor general

차장 車掌 〈버스·전차의〉 a conductor; 〈기차의〉 a conductor; 〈美〉 a guard
▶ 차장이 표를 검사하러 왔다 The conductor came to check tickets.
■ —실 the conductor's compartment

차점 次點 the second largest number 《of votes》
▶ 그는 그 선거에서 차점으로 패했다 He was a runner-up in the election. (▶「차점」은 그 자체에 「패했다」는 뜻을 포함함)
■ —자 the second winner; 〈낙선자의 제1위〉 the runner-up

차제 此際 ♦ 차제에 now; on this occasion; at this juncture [time]; under [in] these circumstances
▶ 차제에 여러분께 감사의 말씀을 드립니다 Let me take this opportunity of thanking you.

차조 〔植〕 glutinous millet

차조기 〔植〕 a beefsteak plant

차좁쌀 polished glutinous millet

차주 車主 a car owner; the owner of a car [bus]

차주 借主 a borrower; a hirer; 〈부동산의〉 a renter; a tenant; a lessee

차중음 次中音 〔樂〕 tenor ⇨ 테너

차지 occupancy; occupation; possession
♦ 자기의 차지가 되다 〈물건이 주어〉 come [fall] into one's hands; pass into one's possession; 〈사람이 주어〉 come into possession of sth
▶ 이것은 네 차지다 This is for you. ⇌ This is your share (of it).
▶ 이만큼이 내 차지다 This much has fallen to my lot.
—차지하다 occupy; hold; have; possess; get; take (up); make 《a thing》 one's own; take possession of; 〈경기 등에서〉 gain; obtain; secure; score; win; 〈비율을〉 account for; amount to
♦ 〈국회의〉 의석을 차지하다 hold a seat in the National Assembly / 좋은 자리를 차지하다 get [occupy] a good seat / 높은 지위를 차지하다 hold [occupy] a high position / 윗자리를 차지하다 take the top seat / 수석을 차지하다 [sit] at the top [head] 《of one's class》; stand first 《in one's class》 / 과반수를 차지하다 get a majority / 절대다수를 차지하다 command an overwhelming [absolute] majority 《in the National Assembly》 / 제일 좋은 몫을 차지하다 take the lion's share
▶ 금메달은 존이 차지했다 The gold medal went to John. ⇌ John won the gold medal.
▶ 그는 그 지위를 6년 동안 차지하고 있었다 He had held [occupied] the position for six years.
▶ 침대가 방의 절반을 차지하고 있다 The bed occupies [takes up] half the room.
▶ 여성 참가자가 전체의 6할을 차지했다 Women participants occupied [took up, amounted to, made up] sixty percent of all.
▶ 신당은 총선에서 30석의 의석을 차지했다 The new party won thirty seats [places] in the general election.

차지 借地 〈행위〉 lease of land; 〈토지〉 leased land; rented ground; a leasehold
■ —권 a lease; a leasehold —료 (a) rent; (a) ground rent —법 the Land Lease Law —인 a leaseholder; a tenant; 〔法〕 a lessee —증서 a lease of land

차지다 glutinous; sticky; viscid

차질 蹉跌 〈실족〉 stumbling; 〈실패〉 a failure; a frustration; a miscarriage; a fiasco 《pl. -(e)s》; a setback; a deadlock; a snag
♦ 일에 차질이 생기다 fail in one's attempt; things go wrong 《with one》
▶ 그가 결석하는 바람에 우리 계획에 차질이 생겼다 His absence upset our plan.
▶ 증정식은 차질없이 진행되었다 The ceremony of presenting it was smoothly performed [was performed without a hitch].

차질다 stickily wet; clammy; viscous

차차 次次 **1** 〈조금씩〉 gradually; by degrees; little by little; step by step; 〈점점〉 increasingly; growingly; 〈더하여〉 more and more; 〈덜하여〉 less and less
♦ 차차 좋아지다 show gradual improvement / 차차 더워지다[추워지다] be getting warmer [colder]
▶ 그는 차차 높은 지위로 올라갔다 He advanced to a higher position step by step.
▶ 처음엔 쉬웠지만 차차 어려워졌다 It was easy in the beginning, but it gradually became harder.
▶ 그는 차차 수학에 재미가 붙었다 He has become more and more interested in mathematics.
▶ 그는 차차 그녀가 좋아졌다 He gradually got [came] to like her.
▶ 그는 새로운 방식에 차차 익숙해졌다 He became gradually accustomed [used] to the new method.
2 〈조만간〉 by and by; in due time; later; in (cause of) time; as time passes
▶ 차차 아시게 될 겁니다 You will come to understand it by and by.

차착 差錯 a mistake; an error; fallacy

차창 車窓 a car [train, bus] window
♦ 차창에 비치는 경치 the scenery seen from a car [train] window / 차창 밖을 내다보다 look out 《of》 a car window

차체 車體 a car body; the body 《of a car》; the chassis 《of a carriage》; 〈자전거의〉 the frame
▶ 2년마다 자동차의 차체 검사가 있다 Every two years we have an automobile inspection.
■ —중량 the tare

차축 車軸 a wheel axle; an axle
차츰차츰 little by little; inch by inch; by inches; step by step; slowly and [but] steadily; gradually; by degrees; (by) inchmeal
♦차츰차츰 나아가다 advance gradually; inch [edge] one's way forward
차치하다 且置— let alone; set aside [apart]
♦농담은 차치하고 joking [jokes] aside [apart] / 이 문제는 차치하고 apart from [setting aside] this question
▶ 비용은 차치하고 시간이 많이 걸릴 것이다 Aside from the expenses it will take a lot of time.
▶ 만사 차치하고 쓰레기 더미부터 치워야겠습니다 First of all [Before anything else], we must clear a pile of rubbish away.
차탄 嗟歎 〈탄식〉 lamentation; deploration; sigh —**차탄하다** lament; deplore; sigh
차탈피탈 此頉彼頉 one excuse and another; some excuse or other; all sorts of excuses —**차탈피탈하다** make [give] an excuse and another; make all sorts of excuses; be full of excuses
차터 charterage; the hiring of a ship
♦배를 차터하다 charter a ship (for a voyage)
차트 〈도표〉 a chart ♦차트로 만들다 make a chart (of); chart
차표 車票 a (public) conveyance; (by way of) a vehicle
♦차편을 이용하다 avail oneself of a vehicle / 차편으로 여행하다 travel by (a) vehicle
▶ 거기 가려면 어떤 차편이 있습니까? What kind of conveyance is available to go there?
차폐 遮蔽 cover; shelter; 〖軍〗〈축성의〉 defilade; 〖電〗 shielding
—**차폐하다** cover; shelter (oneself); screen; defilade
■—물 a cover; a shelter: 온갖 차폐물을 이용하여 making use of everything available for shelter —된 진지 a covered position —포대(砲臺) a masked battery
차표 車票 a (railroad [bus, subway]) ticket
♦차표를 사다 get [buy, take] a ticket (to Seoul); book (for Seoul) / 차표를 찍다 〈개찰하다〉 punch [clip] a ticket / 차표를 조사하다 examine tickets
▶ 이 차표는 3일간 유효하다 This ticket is valid for three days.
▶ 부산행 1등 차표 한 장 주십시오 (Please give me) one first-class ticket to Pusan.
▶ 차표를 보여 주세요 Ticket please.
■왕복—(美) a round-trip ticket; (英) a return ticket 편도—(美) a one-way ticket; (英) a single ticket 할인— a cheap ticket ■—판매소 a ticket window [office]; (英) a booking office —판매원 (美) a ticket agent; (英) a booking clerk
차필하다 借筆— have sb write for one
차하다 insufficient; short (of); not enough (for)
차하지다 差下— be inferior to; be worse than; be below; fall behind; be second to; yield to; compare unfavorably with
차호 次號 〈잡지 등의〉 the next number [issue]
차회 次回 next time; the following sequence; 〈경기의〉 the next round
차회 此回 this time; (on) this occasion
차후 此後 〈앞으로〉 after this; hence(forth); hereafter; 〈장차〉 in future; for the future; from this time on; from now on
▶ 차후로는 절대 거짓말을 않겠습니다 I will never tell a lie again.
▶ 그것은 차후의 문제다 That remains to be solved in the future.
착 1 〈붙는 모양〉 closely (and firmly); fast; tight(ly)
♦착 붙다 stick to [on]; cling to / 몸을 벽에 착 붙이다 stand [hold one's body] close to the wall; hug the wall / 땅에 착 엎드리다 keep close to the ground
▶ 옷은 젖으면 살에 착 붙는다 Wet clothes cling to the skin.
2 〈늘어진 모양〉 ♦착 가라앉은 목소리(로) (in) a subdued voice / 착 늘어지다 dangle; hang limply
-착 -着 1 〈도착〉 arrival; reaching
▶ 열차는 5시 30분착입니다 The train is due at 5:30.
▶ 점원이 신착의 잡지류를 늘어놓고 있었다 The clerk was arranging the newly-arrived periodicals.
2 〈도착 순위〉 ♦제1[2]착 the first [second] to finish [arrive, come in] / 제1[2]착이 되다 finish [come in] first [second]
▶ 그는 100미터 경주에서 1착으로 들어왔다 He came in first in the 100-meter dash.
착각 錯角 alternate-interior angles ⇨ 엇각
착각 錯覺 an illusion; a hallucination; misunderstanding; a wrong guess
♦눈의 착각 an optical illusion / 착각을 일으키다 be hallucinated; have [be under] an illusion; be confused into thinking (that...)
▶ 나는 내 방에 있는 듯한 착각에 사로잡혔다 I was under the false impression that I was in my own room.
—**착각하다** mistake; misunderstand; make a mistake; be hallucinated; be under an illusion
♦아무를 도둑으로 착각하다 mistake sb for a robber / (…이라고) 착각하고 있다 cherish [be possessed with] the illusion (that...)
▶ 빨간 색을 보면 따뜻한 것으로 착각한다 Red gives [creates] an illusion of heat.
▶ 그 문제를 그는 착각하고 있다 He is under an illusion on the matter.
착검 着劍 〖口令〗 Fix bayonets! ♦착검하고 with a fixed bayonet; with bayonets fixed
착공 着工 starting work —**착공하다** start [begin] (construction) work
▶ 학교의 건축 공사는 내년에 착공할 예정이다 The construction of the school will start next year. ■—식 a groundbreaking ceremony
착념하다 着念— bear [keep, have] sth in mind; be mindful of; take [lay] sth to heart
착란 錯亂 distraction; derangement; confusion —**착란하다** go distracted; go [run] mad; be in a confused state of mind; be (mentally) deranged

♦정신을 착란시키다 〈사물이 주어〉 drive sb distracted; derange one's mind
■정신— distraction; mental derangement —상태 a state of dementia

착륙 着陸 (a) landing; touchdown; 〈로켓의〉a blastdown
♦공항의 착륙용 활주로 the landing strip at an airport
—착륙하다 land 《at, on》; make a landing; reach the ground; ground; touch down
▶야간 착륙하다 make a night landing / 중도 착륙하다 make a stop on the way; stop off [over] 《at》/ 비행기를 강제로 착륙시키다 force an airplane down
▶비행기는 공항에 무사히 착륙했다 The plane landed safely at the airport.
▶헬리콥터가 착륙하려 하고 있다 A helicopter is coming in to land.
■계기[맹목]— blind landing 동체— (a) belly [a crash] landing: 비행기는 동체착륙했다 The plane belly-landed. ⇌ The plane landed on its belly. 비상[불시]— a forced [an emergency] landing 야간— a night landing 연— a soft landing 지상 유도— the ground-controlled landing ■—장 a landing field [ground, place] —지시기 a landing indicator —지점 a touchdown point

착륙장치 着陸裝置 landing gear; an undercarriage ■자동— automatic landing gear

착륙지 着陸地 a landing zone; 〈낙하산 부대의〉 a jump area ■중도— a way [an intervening] station; a staging post

착모하다 着帽 put on a hat [cap]; get a hat [cap] on

착발 着發 1 〈발착〉 arrival(s) and departure(s)
—착발하다 arrive and depart
2 〈격발〉 percussion; detonation by impact
—착발하다 detonate [be detonated] by impact
■—신관 a percussion fuse —탄 a percussion shell

착복 着服 1 〈착의〉 clothing oneself
—착복하다 clothe [dress] oneself 《in》; put on clothes
2 〈금품의 횡령〉 embezzlement; misappropriation; appropriation; peculation
▶은행원들의 착복이 자주 신문에 보도되고 있다 Embezzlements of bank clerks are often reported in newspapers.
—착복하다 pocket (secretly); embezzle; peculate
▶그는 모금한 돈을 착복했다 He pocketed the money that he had collected.
▶그는 주인의 돈을 착복했다 He embezzled his master's money. ⇌ He appropriated his master's money to his own use.
—자 an embezzler

착살맞다 mean; petty; stingy; illiberal

착상 着床 〔生〕 〈수정란의〉 implantation —착상하다 become implanted 《on the uterine wall》

착상 着想 an idea; a conception
♦좋은 착상 a happy thought [idea]; a good [capital, splendid] idea / 재미있는 착상 an interesting [a fascinating] idea

▶이 연극은 착상이 아주 좋다 The ideas contained in this play are very good.
▶그가 쓰는 글들은 착상이 기발하다 His writings are marked by originality of ideas.

착색 着色 coloration; coloring
—착색하다 color; paint; tint
▶인공 착색한 식품이 시장에 많이 나와 있다 A lot of artificially colored foods are on the market.
■—법 coloring —사진 ⇨ 컬러(~사진) —유리 colored glass; stained glass —제 a coloring agent: 인공 착색제 함유 《표시》 Artificially colored.

착석 着席 taking a seat
♦착석순으로 in the order of seats
—착석하다 take one's seat [place]; take a chair; sit (down)
▶착석해 주십시오 Please be seated. ⇌ Please take a chair.

착선 着船 〈배의 도착〉 the arrival of a ship 《in a harbor》; 〈도착한 배〉 a ship which has arrived

착수 着水 〔空〕 landing on the water; 〈우주선의〉 (a) splashdown
—착수하다 land on the water; 〈우주선이〉 splash down

착수 着手 start; commencement; outset
—착수하다 start; commence; begin; set about; get to 《work》; undertake; set [put] one's hand to; enter upon 《one's work》; embark on 《an enterprise》; launch 《upon》
♦현재 착수하고 있는 일 the work in hand / 일에 착수하다 start [begin] to work / 새로운 사업에 착수하다 start [make a start] on a new business / 내각의 개편에 착수하다 set about reshuffling the Cabinet
▶곧 일에 착수하겠다 I'll launch out on my work at once.
▶공사는 아직 착수하지 않고 있다 No start has yet been made with the work.
▶일단 착수하기만 하면 간단히 될 일이다 It's not at all a difficult job once you get started.

착수금 着手金 a deposit; an earnest money; deposit money; 〈변호사 등의〉 a retaining fee
♦착수금을 주다 make [leave] a deposit; place money on deposit; pay earnest money

착시 錯視 〔心〕 an optical illusion

착신 着信 arrival of the post [mail]; 〈전신〉 a message received

착실하다 1 〈견실하다〉 steady-going; slow but steady; trustworthy; sound
♦착실한 사람 a steady person; a trustworthy [reliable] man / 착실한 생각 a solid [sober] view / 착실한 성격 a stable [steady] character / 생활수준의 착실한 향상 a steady improvement in living standards / 착실히 일하다 be steady in one's work
▶그 회사는 착실한 영업을 하고 있다 That firm is run on a sound business principle.
▶그녀의 영어는 착실히 늘고 있다 She is making steady progress in (the study of) English.
▶우리는 계획을 착실하게 추진했다 We put the plan into action step by step.
2 〈알차다〉 solid; substantial; meaty

♦내용이 착실한 저술 a substantial work / 착실한 부자 quite a rich person; a well-heeled person
▶그는 돈푼깨나 착실히 모았다 He amassed quite a lot of money.

착안 着眼 aim; notice; observation; conception
♦착안이 좋다[나쁘다] be right [wrong] in one's way of looking at the matter
—착안하다 notice; perceive; aim at; pay [turn] one's attention to; have an eye to; fix one's eyes upon
▶좋은데 착안했구나 Your observation is very good. ⇌ Your aim is right.

착안점 着眼點 the point aimed at; the point of one's observation; 〈견지〉 a point of view; one's viewpoint
▶이것이 문제의 착안점이다 This is the aspect [point] of the question which we must consider.
▶사람마다 그 문제에 대한 착안점이 다르다 Everybody views the matter from different angles [sees the matter differently].

착암기 鑿岩機 a rock drill; 〈손에 드는〉 a jackhammer

착염 錯鹽 〔化〕 complex salt

착오 錯誤 a mistake; an error; a slip
♦착오가 생기다[나다] go wrong [misfire] / 착오를 내다 make a mistake
—착오하다 mistake; make [commit] a mistake; err
■시대— anachronism: 그의 생각은 시대 착오에 지나지 않는다 His ideas are nothing but an anachronism. 시행— trial and error

착용 着用 putting on; wearing
—착용하다 put on; wear; have (a coat) on
▶학생들은 등교시에 제복을 착용할 것 The students must attend school in uniform.
▶당일은 예복을 착용할 것 A dress suit is to be worn on the occasion.
■—품 (wearing) apparel; habiliments

착유 搾油 oil expression —착유하다 press [express] oil (from); extract oil by pressing
■—공장 an oil mill —기 an oil press [mill]

착유 搾乳 milking
■1회의 착유량 a milking
—착유하다 milk 《a cow》
■—기 a milker; a milking machine —자 a dairyman; 〈여자〉 a milkmaid; a dairymaid —장 a dairy (farm)

착의 着衣 clothing oneself; getting dressed
—착의하다 put on clothes; dress; dress 《clothe》 oneself; get dressed

착이온 錯— 〔化〕 a complex ion

착임 着任 arrival at one's post
—착임하다 arrive at one's post

착잡 錯雜 complication; complexity —착잡하다 complicated; intricate; knotty; entangled; complex; involved
▶그 여자의 표정은 착잡한 심정을 나타내고 있었다 Her face betrayed a mixture of emotions within.

착전 着電 〈도착한 전신〉 a telegram received; 〈전신의 도착〉 the arrival of a telegram

착정 鑿井 〈우물을 팜〉 well drilling [sinking]; digging a well —착정하다 drill [bore, dig, sink] a well

착종 錯綜 complication entangling ⇨ 착잡

착지 着地 〈비행기·도약 등의〉 (a) landing
▶그 체조 선수는 멋진 착지를 보여 주었다 The gymnast made a superb landing.
—착지하다 land; touch down 《on》

착착 readily ⇨ 척척 2

착착 着着 steadily; step by step
♦착착 진행되다 progress steadily; make steady progress [headway]
▶준비는 착착 진행되고 있다 The preparations are well under way.

착취 搾取 1〈짜냄〉 expression; extraction
—착취하다 squeeze; extract; press
2〈고혈의〉 exploitation; sweating; extortion; squeezing
♦자본가의 착취 capitalist exploitation
—착취하다 exploit; sweat 《one's employees》; squeeze 《money out of sb》; extort
▶소작인을 착취하다 squeeze [exploit] the peasants / 백성의 고혈을 착취하다 exploit [bleed] the people; grind the people down
▶그 악덕 고용주가 고용인을 착취하고 있다 The vicious employer sweats his workers.
■중간— intermediary exploitation —계급 the exploiting class: 피착취계급 the exploited class —공장 a sweatshop —노동 a sweated labor; sweatshop labor

착탄 着彈 〈미사일 등의〉 impact
■—지점 an impact area

착탄거리 着彈距離 the range 《of a gun》; gunshot; shooting [firing] distance
♦착탄거리 안[밖]에 있다 be in [out of] range / 착탄거리 안으로 들어오다 [밖으로 나가다] come within [go out of] range

착하 着荷 〈도착〉 arrivals; receipts; 〈화물〉 goods received; an incoming delivery [shipment]
■—신규 new arrivals —인도[불 (拂)] delivery [payment] on arrival

착하다 〈아이가〉 good; nice; 〈마음씨가 곱다〉 good(-natured); kind-hearted; kind; 〈온 순 하다〉 meek; 〈고분 고분하다〉 obedient; docile
♦착한 사람 a good(-natured) person / 착한 아이 a good child; a good [nice] (little) boy [girl] / 착한 일 a good thing; a good deed; a kindness / 마음이 착하다 be kind-hearted; be kind; be of good [nice] disposition; have a sweet temper / 착한 일을 하다 do something good; do (what is) good; practice virtue
▶그는 마음은 착하지만 분별력이 모자란다 He has a good heart but poor sense.
▶착한 일 하는 셈치고 내 심부름 좀 하렴 Be an angel [a good soul] and do an errand for me.
▶참 착하기도 해라 That's a good boy [girl]!

착함 着艦 〈비행기의〉 deck-landing; 〈귀함〉 rejoining [returning to] one's ship —착함하다 land 《on a carrier, on the deck of a ship》

착항 着港 arrival (in port) —착항하다 make port [harbor]; arrive in port [harbor]
■—가격 landed terms

착화 着火 〈점화〉 ignition; combustion —착화

하다 ignite; begin to burn ■—점〈발화점〉the ignition [combustion] point
찬 贊·讚 praise(s); a eulogy; a legend; a panegyric ◆ 그림에 찬을 쓰다 write a legend on a picture
찬 饌 a side dish ⇨ 반찬
찬가 讚歌 a song in praise (of); a paean
찬가게 饌— a pickle shop; a grocer's (store)
찬간 饌間 a kitchen; a pantry where side dishes are prepared
찬간자 〖動〗 a white-faced bluish horse
찬국 〈냉국〉 cold soup
찬기 —氣 cold; chill; 〈찬 공기〉 cold air
◆ 찬기가 돌다 be chill with cold air; have a cold fit / 찬기를 느끼다 feel chilly; feel a chill / 찬기를 쏘이다 be exposed to cold air
▶ 물을 찬기를 가시게 한 다음에 마셔라 Drink the water after taking off the chill.
찬동 贊同 (a) consent; (an) approval; support
◆ 찬동을 얻다〈사람이 주어〉obtain sb's consent (to);〈사물이 주어〉meet with sb's approval / 계획에 대한 찬동을 구하다 ask sb's approval of a plan
—**찬동하다** approve of; support; give one's approval (to); endorse (a plan)
찬란하다 燦爛— bright; brilliant; shining; glittering; lustrous; radiant; resplendent; dazzling
◆ 찬란한 별 glittering stars / 찬란한 보석 a brilliant [radiant] jewel / 찬란한 업적 a splendid [brilliant] achievement / 찬란하게 brightly; brilliantly; radiantly / 광채가 찬란하다 have bright [resplendent] colors; be lustrous / 찬란하게 빛나다 shine brightly [brilliantly]
▶ 햇빛이 찬란하게 비치고 있었다 The sun was shining brightly.
찬립 簒立 〈왕위를 빼앗음〉 usurpation of the throne —**찬립하다** usurp [seize] the throne
찬모 饌母 a female kitchen helper
찬무대 a cold current ⇨ 한류(寒流)
찬물 cold water
◆ 찬물을 끼얹다 pour [throw] cold water upon [over]; douse sb with cold water; dash cold water over; get shower with cold water; (비유) discourage (sb from); put a damper (on)
찬물에도 위아래가 있다 〈속담〉 There is an order in doing everything.
찬미 讚美 praise; admiration; adoration; glorification
—**찬미하다** praise; admire; adore; glorify; extol
◆ 신을 찬미하다 praise God; sing the praises of God / 인생을 찬미하다 sing [chant] the praises of life / 극구 찬미하다 extol sb to the skies
■—가 ⇨ 찬송가 —자 an admirer; an adorer
찬바람 a cold [chilly, bleak] wind
◆ 살을 에는 듯한 찬바람 a cutting [biting, piercing, nipping] wind / 찬바람을 쐬다 expose oneself to a cold wind
찬반양론 贊反兩論 pros and cons; arguments for and against a matter ⇨ 찬부(~양론)
▶ 그 안에는 찬반양론이 있었다 There were arguments pro and con regarding [about] the plan.
찬밥 cold rice
찬방 饌房 a service room; a pantry
찬부 贊否 approval or disapproval; yes or no; for and against; ayes or noes; yeas or nays; (라) pro et contra
◆ 찬부를 묻다 put (a question) to a vote; submit (a measure) to a ballot / 투표로 찬부를 결정하다 vote on (a proposal); take a vote on (a matter)
▶ 찬부가 반반이다 The ayes and noes are equally divided.
■—양론 pros and cons; arguments for and against: 그 의안에 대해서는 찬부 양론이 있다 They are arguing for and against the bill.
찬비 a cold [chilly] rain
찬사 讚辭 a eulogy; praise(s); words of praise; a compliment; laudatory remarks
◆ 아낌없는 찬사 unstinted praise / 찬사를 보내다[드리다] speak words of praise ((to)); pay a compliment ((to, on)); pay sb a compliment ((on his deed)); pay tribute ((to)) / 찬사를 아끼지 않다 be unsparing of [in] one's praise
찬성 贊成 〈동의〉agreement;〈시인〉approval; 〈호의·지지〉favor;〈지지〉support;〈동의에 대한〉seconding
▶ 내 계획에 찬성이요 반대요? Are you for or against my plan?
▶ 나는 그 정책에 전적으로 찬성이다 I am quite in favor of the policy.
▶ 그는 그 계획에 찬성의 뜻을 표했다 He showed [expressed] his approval to the plan.
▶ 그는 이 계획에 찬성도 반대도 하지 않았다 He did not approve or disapprove this plan.
▶ 그 결정은 위원회의 과반수의 찬성을 얻었다 The decision won [met with] the approval of the majority of the committee.
▶ 투표 결과는 원안에 대한 찬성 10표, 반대 5표였다 The result of the voting was 10 for and 5 against the original bill.
▶ 〖會話〗「좀 쉬었다 합시다」「찬성이오」 "Let's have a break, shall we?" "Yes, let's. ⇌ All right. ⇌ OK. ⇌ Sure."
—**찬성하다** agree; approve ((of)); support; second; fall in with

---

〖解説〗 **agree**를 쓸 때 「제안·계획」에 대한 찬성에는 **agree to**를, 「남의 의견」에 대한 찬성에는 **agree with**를 쓴다. agree to에는 「…을 (전폭) 지지하다」「…에 관하여 스스로도 행동으로 옮기겠다」는 등의 뜻이 함축되어 있는 데 대하여 agree with는 그냥 「…과 같은 의견이다」「…을 인정한다」는 뜻이다.

◆ 만장일치로 찬성하다 be unanimous in (their) approval [consent]; consent unanimously / 머리를 끄덕여 찬성하다 nod in agreement [approval]
▶ 찬성하시는 분은 일어서 주십시오 Those (who are) in favor [who approve], please stand up.
▶ 나는 그의 제안에 즉각 찬성했다 I agreed to his proposal at once.

▶그 건에 대한 당신의 의견에 전적으로 찬성할 수 없습니다 I can't entirely agree with you [your opinion] on the matter.
■—론 a supporting argument —연설 《make》 a speech in support of 《a measure》 —의 a member in favor 《of a bill》 —측 the consenting party; 〈토론에서의〉 the affirmative side —투표 a vote in favor of 《a bill》; an approval ballot: 찬성투표를 하다 vote for [in favor of] 《a bill》; cast a favorable [an aye] vote for 《a measure》

찬성자 贊成者 an approver; a supporter; 〈동의에 대한〉 a seconder; a standby
▶찬성자가 많다 The ayes have it.

찬송 讚頌 glorification 《of God》; praise 《to God》

찬송가 讚頌歌 a hymn; a psalm ◆찬송가를 부르다 sing a hymn ■—작가 a hymnist; a hymnodist; a psalmist —집[책] a hymnal; a psalmody

찬술 撰述 〈저술〉 writing; composing
—찬술하다 write 《a book》; compose

찬술 纂述 〈편찬〉 compilation; editing
—찬술하다 compile; edit

찬스 a chance; an opportunity
◆절호의 찬스 a capital chance; a golden opportunity / 찬스를 잡다 seize a chance / 찬스를 놓치다 lose [pass up] a chance
▶자, 지금이 찬스다 There! Now's your chance.

찬양 讚揚 praise; admiration; laudation; applause; commendation
▶그녀는 모든 사람으로부터 찬양을 받았다 She was the admiration of everyone.
—찬양하다 praise; admire; laud; applaud; extol; commend
◆찬양할 만한 admirable; laudable; praiseworthy / 신을 찬양하다 praise God; give glory to God; sing [chant] the praises of Him / 아무의 용기를 찬양하다 praise sb for 《his》 courage / 아무를 극구 찬양하다 extol [laud] sb to the skies
▶그는 공자를 찬양하는 연설을 했다 He gave an address of homage to Confucius.
■—대 a choir —대원 a chanter; chorister

찬역 簒逆 《high》 treason; rebellion; usurpation —찬역하다 rebel against the king; usurp

찬연하다 燦然— brilliant; radiant; resplendent ◆찬연히 빛나는 보석 a brilliant gem / 찬연히 빛나다 shine brilliantly
▶그의 용맹은 역사에 찬연히 빛나고 있다 His valor shines on in history. ⇌ His valor remains a brilliant spot in history.

찬위 簒位 usurpation ⇨ 찬탈《簒奪》

찬의 贊意 approval
◆찬의를 표하다 express [show, give, nod, voice] one's approval 《to, toward》

찬이슬 chill [cold] dew ◆찬이슬 맞는 놈 a night thief

찬장 饌欌 a cupboard; a sideboard; a dresser; a buffet

찬조 贊助 support; backing; patronage; approval
◆김선생의 찬조로 under the support [auspices] of Mr. Kim; supported by Mr. Kim / 찬조를 청하다 solicit sb's support / 찬조를 얻다 obtain sb's patronage [support]
—찬조하다 support; back 《up》; patronize
■—금 a contribution: 찬조금을 내다 make a contribution; contribute 《500,000 won to the project》 —연설 a supporting speech; a campaign speech for a candidate: 찬조 연설을 하다 speak for a candidate —자 a supporter; a patron —출연 appearance as a guest star [artist]: 그는 그 연극에 찬조 출연했다 He appeared in the play as a guest star. —회원 a supporting member

찬찬 round and round ⇨ 친친

찬찬하다 1 〈꼼꼼하다〉 meticulous; attentive; staid; careful; prudent; cautious; scrupulous
▶그녀는 성격이 아주 찬찬하다 She has a very steady character.
2 〈느리다〉 slow; leisurely; deliberate

찬찬히 1 〈침착하게〉 staidly; deliberately; calmly; quietly; 〈꼼꼼하게〉 carefully; cautiously; attentively
◆찬찬히 겨냥하다 take deliberate aim / 찬찬히 준비하다 make thoroughgoing preparations 《for》 / 무슨 일이나 찬찬히 하다 be cautious in doing anything / 남의 얼굴을 찬찬히 뜯어보다 get a good look into sb's face; take a close look at sb
2 〈천천히〉 slowly; leisurely; deliberately; 《wait》 with patience
◆찬찬히 하다 take one's time 《in doing, over sth》

찬칼 饌— a kitchen knife; a carver

찬탄 贊嘆·讚嘆 praise; admiration
—찬탄하다 admire; extol; speak highly of; be filled with admiration 《at》
◆찬탄할 만하다 be worthy of the highest admiration; merit the highest praise / 찬탄하여 마지 않다 be lost in admiration 《for》

찬탈 簒奪 usurpation ◆왕위의 찬탈을 꾀하다 plot to supplant the king —찬탈하다 usurp; seize ■왕위를 찬탈하다 usurp [seize] the throne ■—자 a usurper

찬평 讚評·贊評 a favorable criticism ⇨ 호평

찬합 饌盒 a nest of boxes; a tub 《with a lid》 for cooked rice
◆찬합에 담다 pack 《food》 in a nest of boxes

찰- 〈차진〉 glutinous; gluey; 〈지독한〉 extreme; deadly

찰가난 extreme [dire, abject] poverty; penury
■—뱅이 a needy [destitute] person; a pauper

찰거머리 〔動〕 a leech
◆찰거머리같은 사람 a barnacle; a hanger-on; a leech / 찰거머리처럼 달라붙다 cling to sb like a leech; fasten on sb like a tick

찰것 food made of glutinous grain

찰과상 擦過傷 an abrasion; a chafe; a scratch; a skin-deep wound; a brush burn
◆찰과상을 입다 sustain a scratch [an abrasion]
▶그는 나무에서 떨어졌지만 찰과상도 입지 않았다 He fell down from a tree, but didn't get even the slightest injury [scratch].

찰교인 —敎人 a firm [fanatic] believer 《in

Christianity)
찰그랑 with a clink ⇨ 절그렁
찰기 —氣 glutinousness; glutinosity; stickiness
♦ 찰기가 있다 be sticky [glutinous]
▶ 수입 쌀은 밥을 지었을 때 찰기가 없다 Imported rice doesn't hold together very well when cooked.
찰기장 〔植〕glutinous (Chinese) millet
찰깍 with a snap [click, crack]; snap; crack
♦ 수갑을 찰깍 채우다 snap the handcuffs on sb's wrists / 셔터를 찰깍 누르다 click the shutter
찰깍거리다 〈단단한 것이〉 click; clack; 〈시계가〉 ticktack
찰깍쟁이 〈지독한 깍쟁이〉 a nasty miser; a scrooge
찰깍찰깍 click-clack; ticktock; ticktack
♦ 사진을 찰깍찰깍 찍다 snap off pictures / (시계가) 찰깍찰깍 가다 tick away [off] (the time)
찰나 刹那 a moment; an instant; a trice
♦ 찰나의 momentary; transient / 찰나의 기쁨 a momentary joy / 아무가 문을 연 찰나에 the instant [minute] sb opened the door / 그 때에 at that very moment / 찰나적으로 살다 live on (momentary) impulses; live in the present; live for the moment
▶ 그는 찰나적인 향락에 빠져 있었다 He was addicted to momentary [passing, fleeting] pleasures.
━주의 the principle of living only for (the pleasure of) the moment; impulsiveness
찰담장이 〈불치의 매독환자〉 an incurable syphilitic (person)
찰딱거리다 cling [stick] to; keep clinging round 《the limbs》; hang on to
찰떡 a glutinous-rice cake
찰락거리다 〈물이〉 lap; lip; splash gently; 〈쇠붙이가〉 clatter; jingle
찰락찰락 lapping; splashing; clattering
찰랑거리다 lap; splash; slop; slosh
♦ 찰랑거리는 잔물결 laughing wavelets / 해변에 찰랑거리는 파도 waves lapping on the beach
▶ 독의 물이 찰랑거린다 The water in a jar is slopping from side to side.
▶ 뱃전에 물이 찰랑거렸다 The water lapped against the boat.
찰랑찰랑 to the brim; brimfully; to the full; overflowingly
━찰랑찰랑하다 brimful; overflowing
♦ 물이 찰랑찰랑한 대야 a basin filled to the brim with water / 술잔에 술을 찰랑찰랑하게 따르다 fill a glass (up) to the brim with wine; pour a glass full of wine; brim a cup with wine
▶ 독에 물이 찰랑찰랑하게 차 있다 The jar is filled with water to the brim.
찰밥 boiled glutinous rice
찰벼 〔植〕glutinous rice
찰부꾸미 a glutinous-rice pancake
찰상 擦傷 an abrasion ⇨ 찰과상(擦過傷)
찰쇠 a metal ring fitting around a gate pivot

찰싹 with a splash ⇨ 철썩
찰쌈지 a tobacco pouch carried on one's side
찰짜 a meticulous person; a stickler
찰찰 overflowingly ⇨ 철철
찰찰하다 察察— too meticulous; overscrupulous; finicky
찰카닥, 찰칵 with a snap ⇨ 잘가닥, 찰칵
찰카당 with a clank ⇨ 잘가당
찰흙 clay ⇨ 점토(粘土)
참¹ 〈진실〉 truth; reality; verity; genuineness
참² **1** 〈정말로〉 really; truly; indeed; quite; very
▶ 참 덥네 How hot it is!
▶ 참 이상도 하지 How strange!
▶ 그것 참 좋다 That's quite good.
▶ 그것 안 됐다 Indeed, that's too bad.
▶ 파티는 참 재미있었다 We had a mighty good time at the party.
▶ 참 반가운 소리구나 I am glad to hear it.
▶ 참 난처하게 되었다 This is a nice kettle of fish. ⇌ It's really annoying. ⇌ What an awful mess.
▶ 나는 참 운이 좋았다 I had capital luck.
2 〈감탄사적〉 well; oh; what; really; by the way
▶ 참 별소리 다 듣겠네 Just what do you mean talking to me that way?
▶ 참 별사람 다 보겠네 Really now, I have never seen such a dreadful person!
▶ 참 오늘이 일요일이지 Oh, it's Sunday, isn't it?
▶ 참 자네한테 물어볼 것이 있어 Well, now, I have something to ask you.
참- true; real; veritable; genuine
♦ 참사랑 a true love / 참뜻 the true meaning [sense] / 참말 a true remark [story] / 참모습 the true picture; one's true colors / 참사람 a true man
참 站 **1** 〈역참〉 a post; a station; a stage
2 〈쉬는 곳〉 a stop; a resting place
♦ 층계참 a halfpace; a (mean) landing
3 〈휴식〉 a (short) rest 《from work》; a recess; a (coffee) break; 〈참 때의 식사〉 a snack taken during a recess
4 〈계제〉 the occasion; 〈찰나〉 the instance; the moment
♦ …하려는 참에 just as [when] one is about to 《do》; the moment one is going to 《do》; on the point of 《doing》
▶ 막 떠나려던 참에 그녀가 왔다 She came just as I was leaving.
▶ 너를 부르러 사람을 보내려던 참이었다 I was just on the point of sending for you.
참가 參加 participation; joining; entry
♦ 참가를 신청하다 send an entry for 《a game》
▶ 한 학교의 참가 선수는 세 명으로 제한되어 있다 The entries for any one school are limited to three players.
━참가하다 participate in; take part in; join; enter
♦ 토론회에 참가하다 take part [participate, join] in a discussion / 클럽 활동에 적극적으로 참가하다 take an active part [be actively involved] in club activities / 테니스부의 여름 합숙에 참가하다 go to the summer training

참가자

camp of *one's* tennis club
▶ 퀴즈 게임에는 누구나 참가할 수 있다 The quiz game is open to all competitors. ⇒ The quiz game welcomes volunteers.
▶ 60개국이 그 조약에 참가하고 있다 Sixty countries are parties to the treaty.
▶ 우리는 전쟁에 참가하지 않을 것이다 We will not enter the war.
―교 an entrant school ―국 a participating nation ―료 an entry fee

참가자 參加者 a participator; a participant; 〈경기 등의〉 an entrant; (총칭) the entry
―명부 a list of participants

참게 〔動〕 a horseshoe crab; a king crab

참견 參見 1〈간섭〉 interference; meddling; 〈관여〉 participation
―참견하다 meddle [interfere] in; put [poke, thrust] *one's* nose into; put in *one's* oar; intrude *oneself* (into another's affair); butt [break] in (on another's affair); 〈관여하다〉 participate (in); take part (in)
▶ 남의 일에 참견하지 마라 Don't poke your nose in other's business.
▶ 그녀는 남의 일에 지나치게 참견한다 She meddles in other people's affairs too much.
▶ 그녀는 무슨 일에나 참견한다 She puts her nose into everything.
▶ 그것은 네가 참견할 일이 아니다 That's none of your business! ⇒ Mind your own business!
▶ 그의 일에 참견하면 안된다 You shouldn't interfere [meddle] in his affairs. ⇒ Keep your nose out of his affairs. 〈이미 참견하고 있는 경우에〉 Stop poking your nose into his affairs.
2 ⇨ 참관

참경 慘景 a terrible sight 《of a disaster》; a disastrous scene

참고 參考 reference; consultation; information
▶ 참고로 몇 말씀 드리겠습니다 I will make some suggestions for your reference.
▶ 앞으로 참고 자료로 활용하기 위해 이 책을 보관해 두는 것이 좋습니다 You had better keep the book for future reference.
▶ 그것은 그들의 사고 방식을 이해하는 데 참고가 될 것입니다 It will help you (to) understand their ways of thinking.
▶ 이 책은 당신한테 별 참고가 되지 않을 겁니다 This book is of little help to you. ⇒ This book is not a good reference book for you.
▶ 그의 조언은 크게 참고가 되었다 His advice was of much help to me. ⇒ His advice was a good guide [reference].
▶ 참고 되는 말씀을 해주셔서 고맙습니다 Thank you for your suggestion.
―참고하다 refer to; consult
◆ 주석을 참고하다 consult [refer to] the notes / 문헌을 참고하다 refer to literature; consult a document
▶ 여러 사람의 의견을 참고하여 계획을 세웠다 I consulted (the views of) several people before setting the plan up.

참고서 參考書 a reference book; a book of reference
◆ 영어 참고서 a reference book for the study of English / 참고서류 books for reference

참관 參觀 a visit; inspection; 〈입회〉 witnessing
―참관하다 visit; inspect; 〈입회하다〉 witness
◆ 공장을 참관하다 walk through a factory; pay a visit of inspection to a factory / 수업을 참관하다 visit a class at work; go to see classwork / 투표[개표]를 참관하다 witness the voting [ballot counting] / 참관할 수 있다 [없다] 〈사물이 주어〉 be open [closed] to visitors
▶ 어머니는 오늘 우리의 수업을 참관하셨다 Mother visited our class today.
―일 a visiting day

참관인 參觀人 a visitor; 〈선거의〉 a witness
■개표― a ballot-counting witness 투표― a voting witness; a referee of voting ■―명부 a visitors' book

참괴 慙愧 shame; humiliation; 〈회한〉 compunction
―참괴하다 feel shame (at); be ashamed (of, to)
◆ 참괴하여 마지 않다 be overwhelmed [burning] with shame; be quite ashamed of 《*oneself*》 / 참괴시키다 put *sb* to shame [the blush]; overwhelm *sb* with shame

참극 慘劇 a tragedy; a tragic event
◆ 참극의 현장 the scene of the tragedy / 참극을 빚어내다 enact a tragedy
▶ 참극은 여기서 일어났다 This was the scene of the tragedy. ⇒ The tragedy occurred here.

참기름 sesame oil

참깨 〔植〕 sesame; sesame seeds; a gingili (plant)

참깨가 기니 짧으니 한다 〈속담〉 There is little to choose between them.

참나리 〔植〕 a tiger lily

참나무 〔植〕 an oak (tree)

참녜 參 participation ⇨ 참여(參與)

참다 1〈인내하다〉 be patient; 〈견디다〉 bear 《with》; endure; forbear; stand; suffer; tolerate; put up with; persevere (in, with)
◆ 고통을 참다 endure [stand] pain / 굴욕을 참다 suffer humiliation; eat dirt [humble pie]; pocket [stomach] an insult / 더위를 참다 stand [bear] the heat / 모욕을 참다 put up with insults / 졸음을 참다 withstand sleepiness / 잘 참고 견디다 bear and forbear / 참을 수 있는 데까지 참다 bear to the best of *one's* capacity
▶ 아프겠지만 잠시 참아라 It must hurt, but just hang on for a minute.
▶ 참는 것도 한도가 있지 My patience is worn out. ⇒ There is a limit to my patience. ⇒ Human patience has its limits.
▶ 아파서 도저히 참을 수 없다 I cannot bear the pain any longer. ⇒ The pain is beyond my endurance.
▶ 그는 어린데도 용감하게 그 고통을 참았다 Although he was young, he was brave enough to endure the pain.
2 〈억제하다〉 control *oneself*; restrain *oneself*; stifle; repress; suppress; keep [hold, choke] back; contain 《*one's* passion》; gulp

down 《one's sobs》; subdue *oneself*
♦눈물을 참다 repress [keep back, force back] one's tears / 웃음을 참다 stifle [suppress] one's laughter; swallow a laugh / 화를 참다 repress [suppress, keep down] one's anger; contain one's passions / 변(이 마려운 것)을 참다 repress the movement of the bowels; resist the call of nature; 〈소변을〉 contain one's urine; hold one's water
▶나는 웃음을 참을 수가 없었다 I could not help laughing.
▶그 아이는 슬픔을 참다 못해 울음을 터뜨렸다 The child burst out crying, unable to repress his sorrow.

참담하다 慘憺— 〈가엾다〉 pitiful; pitiable; 〈비참하다〉 wretched; miserable; terrible; horrible; disastrous
♦참담한 광경 a frightful [dreadful, horrible] sight / 참담한 상태 《be in》 a wretched plight / 참담한 실수 a terrible [miserable] mistake / 참담한 결과로 끝나다 end in disaster
▶그는 선거에서 참담한 패배를 당했다 He suffered [met] a terrible defeat in the election.
▶그는 고심 참담하여 그 일을 완성했다 He took great pains to finish the project.

참답다 true; real; genuine; honest; sincere; faithful; truthful; right-minded; upright
♦참다운 친구 a true friend / 참다운 영웅 a hero worthy of the name / 참다운 뜻에서 in the true sense of the word [term]

참대 〔植〕 a common Korean bamboo
참돔 〔魚〕 a red sea bream; porgy
참되다 true; real; genuine; honest; sincere; faithful; truthful
♦참된 용기 true [genuine] courage / 참되게 honestly; faithfully; truthfully

참따랗게 truly; faithfully; sincerely; honestly; truthfully; really; genuinely

참뜻 the true meaning [sense]; 〈진의〉 one's real intention

참람 僭濫 〈외람하다〉 presumptuousness; presumption; forwardness; audacity
—**참람하다** presumptuous; arrogant; audacious; insolent

참례 參禮 attendance; presence
—**참례하다** attend; be present 《at》; present *oneself* 《at》; sit 《at》 ♦장례식에 참례하다 attend a funeral (ceremony)
■—자 an attendance; 〈총칭〉 those present: 참례자가 많았다 There was a large attendance.

참말 a true remark [story]; an authentic story; the truth; a (real) fact
♦참말을 하다 tell [speak] the truth / 참말로 받아들이다 believe; take 《it》 seriously; accept 《an account》 as true / 남의 말을 참말로 믿다 take *sb* at 《his》 word
▶그게 참말이야? Is that true? ⇒ Do you mean what you say?
▶그게 참말일까? Can that be true? ⇒ I wonder if it is true.
▶그 소문이 참말일까? Is there any truth in the rumor?
▶누가 그런 말을 참말로 믿는담 Who would believe it?
▶참말인지 아닌지 모르는 말은 입 밖에 내지 마라 Never say anything which you do not know to be true.
▶그의 말은 참말인 것 같다 He seems to be telling the truth.
▶너 참말로 잘 왔다 It is a jolly good job that you came.
▶참말이지 유감입니다 It is really a matter for regret.

참망하다 僭妄— 〈분수에 넘치다〉 presumptuous; audacious; assumptive; unreasonable; absurd

참매미 〔昆〕 a robust cicada
참먹 an ink stick of high quality
참모 參謀 〈군대의〉 a staff officer; 《총칭》 the (general) staff; 〈상담역〉 an adviser; a brain truster 《to *sb*》; 《총칭》 a brain trust; 〈선거운동 등의〉 a strategist
▶그 사람은 사장의 참모다 The man is a member of the president's brain trust. ⇒ The man is a brain truster to the president.
▶그는 사령관의 참모로 일했다 He served on the staff of the commander-in-chief.
■일반— the general staff ■—본부 the General Staff Office —장 the chief of staff —총장 [차장] the Chief [Vice-Chief] of the General Staff —회의 a council of war; a war council

참밀 wheat ⇨ 밀
참바 a rope; a hawser
참배 參拜 worship; a visit —**참배하다** 《go and》 worship at 《a temple》; pay reverence at 《a tomb》; visit [pay a visit to] 《a temple》
■—자 a visitor 《to a temple》

참벌 a honeybee ⇨ 꿀벌
참변 慘變 a calamity; a disaster; a disastrous [tragic] accident; 〈암살〉 assassination
♦참변을 당하다 suffer a disastrous accident

참빗 a fine-toothed bamboo comb
참사 參事 a secretary; a councilor
■—관 《대사관 등의》 a councilor [counselor] 《of an embassy》

참사 慘死 a tragic [miserable] death —**참사하다** meet with a tragic [miserable] death; come to a violent end
♦교통사고로 참사하다 be killed in a traffic accident ■—체 a mangled body

참사 慘事 a disaster; a disastrous [terrible] accident; a tragic incident; a catastrophe
♦철도 참사 a terrible railway accident / 참사를 빚다 cause a terrible accident
▶그의 부주의로 인해 그 참사가 일어났다 His carelessness caused the terrible accident.

참사람 an honest man; a good citizen
♦참사람이 되다 become a new man; turn over a new leaf; reform *oneself*

참살 斬殺 decapitation; beheading; decollation ⇨ 참수(斬首)

참살 慘殺 murder; slaughter; butchery; massacre —**참살하다** murder cruelly; slaughter; massacre; butcher
■—사건 a murder case

참상 慘狀 a terrible [disastrous] scene; a miserable state; a pitiable condition; misery
♦참상을 드러내다[보이다] present a terrible

참새

sight [spectacle] / 재해의 참상을 목격하다 witness the terrible sights of a disaster
▶ 이번 화재의 현장은 말할 수 없는 참상이었다 The site of the recent fire was devastating.
▶ 그 나라의 참상은 차마 눈뜨고 볼 수 없었다 We couldn't look squarely at the wretched condition of the country.

참새 〔鳥〕 a sparrow
◆ 참새떼 a flock of sparrows / 참새처럼 재잘거리다 chatter like a sparrow
▶ 참새가 짹짹 울고 있다 A sparrow chirps [twitters].

참서 讖書 a book of prediction; a prophetic book

참석 參席 attendance; presence; participation
—참석하다 attend (a meeting); be present (at); present *oneself* (at); participate in; take part in
▶ 내일 저녁 축하 파티에 참석해 주시렵니까? Won't you attend the celebration party tomorrow night?
▶ 그의 결혼식에는 많은 친구와 지기가 참석했다 Many friends and acquaintances attended his wedding.
▶ 전국 각 대학의 대표자가 그 회합에 참석했다 All the universities of the country were represented at the meeting.
▶ 친척들이 모두 결혼식에 참석했다 All the relatives attended the wedding.
▶ 나도 참관인으로 회견에 참석했다 I was also present at the interview as an observer.
■ —자 guests; an attendant; (총칭) attendance; those present; 〈참가자〉 a participator: 참석자가 많았다[적었다] There was a large [small] attendance.

참선 參禪 meditation in Zen Buddhism; 〈수행〉 practices of [in] Zen meditation
—참선하다 practice Zen meditation

참섭 參涉 meddling; inteference —참섭하다 meddle in [with]; intefere in; pry into; put [poke, push, shove, stick] *one's* nose into
◆ 남의 일에 참섭하다 meddle in another's affairs

참소 讒訴 a false charge; (a) slander; calumny
—참소하다 make a false charge (against); slander; calumniate
■ —자 a slanderer; a calumniator

참수 斬首 〈목을 벰〉 decapitation; beheading
—참수하다 behead; decapitate; cut the head off *sb*; cut *sb's* head off ◆ 참수당하다 have *one's* head cut off; be beheaded

참숯 hardwood charcoal

참신 斬新 novelty; originality; freshness
—참신하다 new; novel; original; fresh; up-to-date
◆ 참신한 디자인 a novel design / 참신한 발상 an original [a novel] idea / 참신함이 결여되다 be lacking in freshness / 참신한 맛을 내다 strike a fresh note; show (much) originality (in)

참억새 〔植〕 eulalia

참언 讒言 a false charge; (a) slander ⇨ 참소

참언 讖言 (a) prediction; (a) prophecy

참여 參與 participation (in)
—참여하다 participate [join] in; take part in; play *one's* part in; have *one's* share in; be concerned [associated] in
◆ 경영에 참여하다 have a voice in the management (of)

참예 參詣 a visit to a temple [shrine]; worship; a pilgrimage
—참예하다 visit [pay a visit to] (a temple); worship before (a temple); make a pilgrimage (to)
■ —자 a visitor (to a temple); a worshipper; a pilgrim

참외 〔植〕 a melon ■ —넝쿨 a melon vine —밭 a melon field [patch]

참월 僭越 presumption ⇨ 참람

참으로 〈정말〉 really; truly; in truth; indeed; 〈매우〉 very; (very) much; 〈감탄〉 how; what
▶ 그는 참으로 위대한 정치가였다 He was a truly great politician.
▶ 그는 어리기는 하지만 참으로 빈틈이 없다 Indeed he is young, but he is prudent.
▶ 참으로 뻔뻔한 놈일세 What a nerve he's got!
▶ 참으로 아름다운 꽃이로군 What a beautiful flower it is! ≒ How beautiful the flower is!

참을성 —性 patience; endurance; perseverance; forbearance; tolerance
◆ 참을성 있는 patient; forbearing; persevering; long-suffering / 참을성 없는 impatient; lacking perseverance / 참을성 있게 patiently; perseveringly; with patience
▶ 그는 참을성이 있다 He is patient.
▶ 개한테 재주를 가르치려면 참을성이 있어야 한다 You must be patient with a dog in order to teach him tricks.
▶ 나는 참을성이 없다 I can stick to nothing.
▶ 그는 참을성 있게 기다렸다 He waited patiently.

참의원 參議院 〈상원〉 the Upper House; 〈영국의〉 the House of Lords; 〈미국의〉 the Senate
—의원[의장] a member [the President] of the House of Councilors

참작 參酌 consideration; allowance(s); deliberation; reference
—참작하다 consider; allow for; make allowance(s) for; take *sth* into consideration [account]
◆ 정상을 참작하여 in extenuation of; in consideration of extenuating circumstances; allowing for circumstances
▶ 그가 젊다는 점을 참작해야 합니다 You should allow [make allowance(s)] for his youth. ≒ You should take his youth into consideration [account].
▶ 여러 가지 점이 참작되었다 Various considerations were taken into account.

참전 參戰 participation in a war; entry into a war
—참전하다 participate in [enter into] a war; 〈전쟁을 시작하다〉 go to war (against)
◆ 참전하지 않다 stand [stay] out of a war

참정 參政 participation in government
—참정하다 participate in government

참정권 參政權 suffrage; franchise; the right to vote; voting right
♦ 참정권을 부여하다 give the franchise [suffrage] (to) / 참정권을 획득하다 acquire the franchise
■ 여성— woman [women's, female] suffrage: 여성참정권 운동 a movement for female suffrage

참조 參照 reference; consultation; comparison
▶ 제1권 제3장 참조 See [Cf.] Volume I, Chapter 3.
—**참조하다** refer to; consult; see; compare 《with》
♦ 참조하라 see; confer (略 *cf*.); (라) vide (略 v., vid.) / 사전을 참조하다 consult [refer to] a dictionary
▶ 30쪽의 15행을 참조할 것 Refer [Make reference] to page 30, line 15.
■ 앞뒤— cross-reference

참조기 〔魚〕a yellow croaker

참주 僭主 a usurper (of the throne); a tyrant; a despot

참참 站站 〈쉬는 시간〉 rests; breaks; stops;〈각역참〉 every stage
♦ 참참이 (rest) at (frequent) intervals; (travel) by easy [short] stages

참척 慘慽 〈아들·손자가 앞서 죽음〉 the loss [bereavement] of *one's* child [grandchild]
—**참척보다** be bereaved of *one's* child [grandchild]

참척하다 〈몰두하다〉 be absorbed [lost] in; devote *oneself* to; be deeply engaged in; give *oneself* up entirely to

참칭 僭稱 assumption of a title; an unjustified title —**참칭하다** pretend to 《a throne》; claim the title 《to》; assume the title 《of》; arrogate 《a title》 to *oneself* ♦ 왕을 참칭하다 be a pretender to the throne

참패 慘敗 a crushing [complete, heavy, severe] defeat; a dismal failure;〔野〕〈영패〉 a shutout
♦ 군사적 참패 a total military defeat
—**참패하다** suffer [sustain, go down to] a crushing defeat; be crushingly defeated; be beaten (all) hollow;〈경기에서〉 be crushed; 〔野〕〈영패하다〉 be shut out

참하다 1 〈생김새가 곱다〉 nice; fair; charming; good-looking; good; pretty; comely;〈말쑥하다〉 neat; tidy; trim;〈맵시가〉 smart; stylish
♦ 참한 아가씨 a pretty [nice-looking] girl / 옷차림이 참하다 be neatly dressed; be dressed in style
2 〈성품이〉 quiet and gentle; mild; modest
♦ 참해 보이는 mild-looking; modest-looking

참하다 斬— 〈목을 베다〉 behead; decapitate; decollate; slay with a sword

참학 慘虐 cruelty; atrocity; brutality; inhumanity; outrage —**참학하다** cruel; outrageous; atrocious; brutal; savage; inhuman; cold-blooded

참한하다 —限— wait till the due date

참해 慘害 heavy [severe] damage; havoc; disaster; ravages; (a) calamity
♦ 전쟁의 참해 the horrors [evils] of war; the calamity of war / 작물에 참해를 입히다 work havoc with the crops; cause severe damage to the crops
▶ 우리는 태풍으로 참해를 입었다 We suffered heavy [severe] damage from the typhoon. ⇌ The typhoon brought us a great disaster.

참형 斬刑 (execution by) beheading
♦ 참형을 당하다 have *one's* head cut off; be beheaded / 참형에 처하다 punish by beheading; decapitate; behead

참형 慘刑 a cruel punishment; a merciless penalty

참호 僭號 a self-assumed title

참호 塹壕 a trench; a dugout; a sap
♦ 참호를 파다 dig a trench; open a trench; entrench; trench
▶ 적은 견고한 참호에 틀어박혔다 The enemy was [were] strongly entrenched.
■ —공사〈생활, 전〉 trench work [life, warfare] —자 a trencher —선 a trench line; entrenchments —열〔病理〕 trench fever —진지 trenches

참혹 慘酷 〈비참〉 misery; wretchedness; pitiableness;〈잔인〉 cruelty
—**참혹하다** miserable; wretched; tragic(al); pitiable; cruel; horrible; shocking
♦ 참혹한 광경 a grim scene [picture]; an appalling [a gruesome] sight; a cruel [bloody] sight / 참혹한 사건 a tragic accident; a disaster / 참혹한 생활 a wretched life; a life of misery / 참혹한 짓을 하다 do a cruel thing; commit cruelties [atrocities]
▶ 그것은 정말 눈뜨고 못 볼 참혹한 광경이었다 It was a really pitiable sight to see.

참화 慘禍 (an) evil; (a) calamity; a terrible effect; disaster; havoc; destruction
♦ 원자폭탄의 참화 the great damage [ravage] by the atomic bomb / 전쟁의 참화를 입다 suffer the ravages [evils, horrors] of war

참회 參會 attendance ⇨ 참석

참회 懺悔 〈뉘우침〉 penitence; repentance; contrition;〈고백〉 (a) confession
♦ 참회의 눈물 penitential tears / 참회의 생활 a penitential [penitent's] life
—**참회하다** repent 《of *one's* sins》; be penitent; 〈고백하다〉 confess; make (a) confession
♦ 참회시키다 draw a confession from *sb*
▶ 그는 자기의 죄를 사제에게 참회하기로 결심했다 He was determined to confess [make a confession] to the priest.
■ —담 a confession —록 *Confessions* —자 a penitent; a repentant sinner;〈고백하는 사람〉 a confessant

참획 參劃 participation in planning
—**참획하다** have a share [take part, participate] in a plan

찹쌀 glutinous rice ■ —가루 glutinous rice flour —떡 (a) glutinous rice cake

찹찹하다 1 〈쌓인 모양〉 neatly piled [heaped] up; (be) stacked in good order 2 〈침착하다〉 calm; quiet; serene; self-composed

찻간 車間 〈차내〉 the inside of a car [train]; 〈구획된〉 a compartment
♦ 찻간에서 in [on] a train; in a car

찻감 茶— tea material

찻길 車— **1** 〈궤도〉 a track; a railroad; (英) 〈전차의〉 a tramway
2 〈차도〉 a roadway; a driveway

찻물 茶— tea (to drink) ♦ 찻물이 잘 우러나다 tea draws [brews] well
▶ 찻물이 더는 우러나지 않는다 This tea will not draw any more.

찻삯 車— (a) (car) fare; 〈운반료〉 carriage

찻숟가락, 찻숟갈 茶— a teaspoon
♦ 찻숟갈로 하나 a teaspoonful (of sugar)

찻잎 茶— tea leaves

찻잔 茶盞 a teacup

찻장 茶欌 a tea cabinet; a cupboard for tea-things; a buffet

찻종 茶鍾 a teacup; a teabowl
♦ 차를 찻종에 따르다 pour tea into a cup

찻주전자 茶— a teapot; a teakettle

찻집 茶— a teahouse; a tearoom; a coffee-house

창¹ 〈구두의〉 sole leather; a sole
♦ 창이 나가다 (shoe) soles are [get] worn out / 창을 갈다 put a new sole (on); have (one's shoes) resoled (by)
■ 구두— a shoe sole 밑— an outer sole 속— an inner sole 안— a liner

창² 〈구멍〉 a hole (in cloth); a tear
♦ 저고리에 난 창 a hole in the coat

창 窓 a window; 〈내리닫이의〉 a sash window; 〈좌우로 여닫는〉 a casement (window); 〈배·비행기의〉 a port; a porthole
♦ 창가의 자리 a seat by the window; a window seat / 창가에(서) at the window / 창가에 서다 stand at a window / 창 밖을 내다보다 look out (of) a window / 창 안을 들여다 보다 look into [in through] a window / 창 밖으로 몸을 내밀다 lean out of a window / 창 너머로 보다 look through a window / 창을 열다 open a window; raise [pull up] a window / 창을 열어놓다 leave a window open / 창을 닫다 shut [close, let down] a window / 창을 닫아 놓다 keep a window shut [closed, down] / 창으로 들어가다 get in by a window
▶ 창 좀 열어(닫아) 주시겠습니까? Could you please open [close] the window?
▶ 창 밖은 경치가 좋다 The window commands a very fine view.
▶ 도둑은 창으로 침입했다 The thief entered by the window.
▶ 눈은 마음의 창이라고 한다 They say the eyes are the windows of the soul.
■ 이중— a double window 유리— a windowpane 턱 a windowsill 틀 a window frame; 〈내리닫이 창의〉 a (window) sash

창 槍 a spear; a spike; 〈투창용〉 a javelin; 〈기병의〉 a lance
♦ 창을 쓰다 wield [brandish] a spear / 창을 꼬나잡다 couch [tilt] a spear / 창을 고쳐 잡다 grip one's spear more firmly / 창으로 찌르다 lance; spear; tilt (at sb); thrust a spear
▶ 그는 그 사내를 창으로 찔러 말에서 떨어뜨렸다 He tilted the man out of the saddle.
■ —끝 a spearhead; a lance point: 창끝을 겨누다 point one's spearhead (at) —대〔자루〕 a spear handle [shaft]; the handle [shaft] of a spear

창가 娼家 a brothel; a house of ill fame; a bawdy house

창가 唱歌 〈노래하기〉 singing; 〈노래〉 a song
—창가하다 sing
■ —대 a choir —집 a collection of songs

창간 創刊 the first publication [edition]; foundation [of a periodical]
▶ 1962년 창간 (표시) First published in 1962.
—창간하다 start (a new magazine); launch (a newspaper); issue the first number
▶ 이 잡지는 1965년에 창간되었다 This magazine was started [was first issued] in 1965.
▶ 이 잡지는 20년 전에 창간되었다 This magazine was started [made its first appearance] twenty years ago.
■ —호 the first issue [number]; the initial [inaugural] number: 창간호를 내다 issue (its) initial number

창갈이 resoling; sole-repairing
—창갈이하다 resole (shoes); put a new sole (on); 〈시켜서〉 have one's shoes resoled (by)

창건 創建 foundation; establishment

창고 倉庫 a warehouse; a storehouse; 〈군수품의〉 a magazine
♦ 창고에 보관하다 put [store] (goods) in a warehouse; warehouse [store] (goods)
■ 사설[보세]— a private [bonded] warehouse —료 storage charges —업 warehousing (business) —업자 a warehouseman (pl. -men) —증권 (美) a warehouse bond —지기 a warehouse keeper —회사 a warehouse company

창공 蒼空 a blue [an azure] sky; the vault of heavens

창구 窓口 a window; a wicket
♦ 창구에서 사무를 보다 attend at the window / 창구의 서비스를 개선하다 give better service at the window
■ 매표— a ticket window 은행— a bank window 출납— a cashier's [teller's] window

창구 創口 a cut; a gash; the lips of a wound; a slit

창구 艙口 〔海〕 a hatch; a hatchway

창궁 蒼穹 the firmament; a blue sky; the vault of heaven

창궐 猖獗 fury; rage; rampancy; violence
—창궐하다 rage; be rife [rampant]
▶ 홍수 뒤에 전염병이 창궐했다 The epidemic raged in all its fury after the flood.

창극 唱劇 a Korean classical opera

창기 娼妓 a prostitute

창나무 〈키의 자루〉 a tiller; a helm

창난젓 salted guts of a walleye pollack; salt-pickled walleye pollack guts

창녀 娼女 a prostitute; a harlot; a whore; a woman of the streets [town]
♦ 창녀가 되다 become a prostitute; enter into prostitution / 창녀 노릇하다 sell oneself as a prostitute; prostitute oneself / 창녀로 팔리다 be sold for prostitution / 창녀와 놀다 consort with a whore; go to bed with a prostitute

창달 暢達 fluency; briskness; liveliness; advancement; development; growth; progress;

창달 暢達 promotion
♦ 언론의 창달에 공헌하다 contribute to the promotion of the freedom of speech
―**창달하다** develop; make progress; advance; promote

창당 創黨 the formation of a political party
―**창당하다** form [organize] a political party
■―**당원** a charter member of a party ―**이념** founding ideology of a party ―**정신** the spirit underlying the formation of the party

창던지기 槍― the javelin (throw) ―**창던지기하다** throw a javelin ■―**선수** a javelin thrower

창도 唱導 advocacy
―**창도하다** advocate; preach; advance [introduce] 《a new doctrine》
♦ 자유주의를 창도하다 advocate [preach] liberalism / 사회적 평등을 창도하다 advocate social equality
▶ 그들은 생활 개선을 창도하고 있다 They uphold the improvement of their lives.
■―**자** an advocate; a proponent; an exponent; an apostle

창독 瘡毒 〔韓醫〕 the virus of a boil [an abscess]

창립 創立 foundation; establishment; organization
♦ 새로운 회사의 창립 the foundation [establishment] of a new company
▶ 그들은 어제 회사의 창립 50주년을 축하했다 They celebrated the 50th anniversary of the foundation [founding] of the company yesterday.
―**창립하다** found; establish; organize

〔解說〕 **found**는 자금을 마련하여 설립하는 것, **establish**는 found할 뿐만 아니라 영속할 수 있도록 확립하는 것, **organize**는 창립할 뿐만 아니라 하나의 조직 기관을 설치하여 기능을 수행하도록 조치를 취하는 것을 뜻한다.

♦ 대학을 창립하다 found [establish, set up] a college
▶ 하버드 대학은 1636년에 창립되었다 Harvard University saw the light of day in 1636.
▶ 그 회사는 창립된지 얼마 안된다 It is not very long since the company was established.
■―**기념일** the anniversary of the founding [establishment] 《of a school》 ―**위원회** 〔사무소〕 an organizing committee [office] ―**자** the founder; the builder ―**총회** the inaugural general meeting ―**취지서** a prospectus

창만 脹滿 〔韓醫〕 abdominal dropsy

창망 滄茫·蒼茫 a boundless [vast] expanse 《of ocean》 ―**창망하다** boundless; vast; extensive

창문 窓門 a window ⇨ 창(窓)

창받다 〈신바닥에〉 sole; put a sole 《on a shoe》; 〈버선에〉 patch; put a patch 《on a sock》

창백하다 蒼白― pale; pallid; wan; livid; as white as a sheet
♦ 얼굴이 창백한 사람 a pale-looking [pale-faced] person / 그 장면을 보고 얼굴이 창백해지다 turn (deadly) pale [go white, lose color] at the scene
▶ 그는 안색이 창백하다 He has a pallid complexion.
▶ 어디 불편하니? 안색이 창백하구나 Is there something wrong? You look pale (as a ghost).

창법 槍法 spearmanship

창병 槍兵 a spearman; a lancer

창병 瘡病 〔韓醫〕 syphilis ⇨ 매독(梅毒)

창부 倡夫 an actor

창부 娼婦 a prostitute ⇨ 창녀(娼女)

창살 窓― 〈살 한개〉 a bar [rib] of a window; 〈뼈대〉 latticework; (a) lattice; a grid
♦ 창살 없는 감옥 a prison without bars

창상 創傷 a cut; a wound; a gash

창생 蒼生 the people; the populace; the masses

창설 創設 foundation; establishment
―**창설하다** found; establish
▶ 이 학술단체는 30년 전에 창설되었다 This academic institute was founded thirty years ago.
■―**자** the founder; the father 《of》

창성 昌盛 prosperity; flourishing; thriving
―**창성하다** prosper; thrive; flourish; be prosperous

창세 創世 the creation of the world ■―**기** 〔聖〕 (the Book of) Genesis (略 Gen.)

창술 槍術 spear practice; the art of using the spear; spear(s)manship
■―**가**(家) an expert spearman; a lancer

창시 創始 origination; creation; foundation
―**창시하다** originate; create; found; institute
■―**자** the founder; the originator

창안 創案 an original idea; invention
▶ 이것은 누구의 창안이지? Whose idea [plan] is this?
▶ 이것은 당신의 창안입니까? Is this your original [own] idea? ⇌ Are you the originator of this idea?
―**창안하다** originate; devise; invent
▶ 이것은 그가 창안한 것이다 The idea originated with him.
■―**자** the originator; the inventor

창알거리다 fret ⇨ 칭얼거리다

창애 〈덫〉 a trap; a gin
♦ 창애에 치다 be [get] caught in a trap

창업 創業 〈사업의〉 inauguration of an enterprise; 〈창립〉 foundation; establishment
▶ 내년에 우리 회사는 창업 50주년을 맞는다 Next year our company will celebrate the fiftieth anniversary of its foundation [establishment].
▶ 창업은 쉬우나 이를 지키기는 어렵다 The difficulty is not to start an enterprise, but to carry it to final success.
―**창업하다** 〈사업을〉 inaugurate [start] an enterprise; 〈창립하다〉 found; establish
▶ 회사는 창업한지 50년이 됩니다 It is fifty years since the company was established.
■―**비** origination expense ―**자** the founder

창연 蒼鉛 〈비스무트〉 bismuth ♦ 창연의 bismuthal

창연하다 悵然― sad; sorrowful

창연하다
♦창연히 sadly; sorrowfully; mournfully

창연하다 愴然— 〈푸릇푸릇하다〉 dark blue; 〈어둑어둑하다〉 dim; gloomy; gray; shady; somber; 〈고색이〉 antiquated
♦고색이 창연하다 be hoary with antiquity; look hoary; look very old

창유리 窓琉璃 window glass; 〈끼우는〉 a (window)pane
♦창유리를 깨(뜨리)다 break a windowpane / 창유리를 끼우다 glaze a window
▶나는 창유리를 양쪽 다 닦았다 I cleaned both sides of the windowpane.
■—닦개 〈자동차의〉 a windshield washer [cleaner]

창의 創意 an original idea; originality
♦창의적인 original; inventive; creative; ingenious / 창의력을 발휘하다 use one's originality; exercise one's ingenuity / 창의력이 부족하다 lack originality
▶그는 창의력이 풍부하다 He is a man of ideas. ⇌ He has a creative mind.
▶그것은 전적으로 그의 창의에 의한 것이다 It is entirely original with him. ⇌ That comes entirely from his originality.

창이 創痍 a wound ♦만신창이가 되다 be thoroughly hurt [injured]; be covered all over with wounds; have cuts all over one's body

창일 漲溢 〈물이 넘침〉 overflow; inundation
—창일하다 overflow; inundate; flood

창자 the intestines; the bowels; the entrails; 〈동물의〉 the guts
♦생선의 창자를 빼내다 gut a fish; take the guts out of a fish
▶나는 창자가 끊어지듯 아프다 I have a splitting stomachache.
▶그 이야기를 듣고 나는 창자가 뒤틀리는 기분이었다 The story made my blood boil. ⇌ I was boiling with anger [rage] to hear the story.

창작 創作 〈창조〉 creation; 〈제작〉 production; 〈소설의〉 story writing; 〈창작품〉 a creation; an original [a creative] work; a production; 〈소설〉 a novel
♦창작에 종사하다 engage in story writing
▶그는 아직 소설 창작에 종사하고 있다 He is still writing novels.
—창작하다 create; 〈소설을 쓰다〉 write a novel [story]
■—가 a storywriter; a novelist —력 creative power [imagination] —무용 creative dance —욕 an appetite for writing; will to write —활동 creative activity

창제 創製 (an) invention; creation
—창제하다 invent; create

창조 創造 creation ♦창조적 creative / 창조의 재능 creative genius / 창조적 예술[예술가]a creative art [artist] / 창조적 진화 creative evolution / 천지 창조 이래 since the creation of the world
▶신은 만물의 창조주시다 God is the creator of all nature.
—창조하다 create; make
▶태초에 하나님이 천지를 창조하셨다 〔聖〕In the beginning God created the heaven and the earth.
■—력 creative power; creativity; originality: 그는 창조력이 굉장히 풍부하다 He is a man of great originality. —물 a creature; (총칭) creation —설 creative theory —자 a creator; 〈신〉 the Creator

창졸 倉卒 suddenness; abruptness; precipitation; hurry

창졸간 倉卒間 ♦창졸간에 in the midst of great hurry; at a moment of precipitation [rush]
▶창졸간의 질문이라서 그의 물음에 대답도 제대로 못했다 In the hurry of the moment I couldn't answer his question properly.

창증 脹症 〔韓醫〕 abdominal dropsy; tympanites

창창하다 蒼蒼— 1 〈새파랗다〉 deep blue [green]; azure
♦창창한 바다 the blue sea; the deep / 창창한 하늘 a deep blue sky; an azure sky
2 〈멀다〉 far; distant; far off [away]; remote; 〈끝없다〉 vast; boundless; 〈앞길이 밝다〉 rosy; bright; prosperous
♦창창한 장래 a bright [rosy, great] future / 장래가 창창한 젊은이 a young man who has the world before him; one who is in the prime of youth
▶그는 앞길이 창창하다 He is still young. ⇌ He has a long [bright] future before him.
▶우리는 갈길이 아직도 창창하다 We still have a long way to go.

창천 蒼天 a blue [an azure] sky

창출 創出 creation ♦새로운 문화의 창출 creation of a new culture —창출하다 create
♦새 유행을 창출하다 create a new fashion

창칼 〈작은 칼〉 a small knife; 〈공작용〉 a pointed knife

창틀 窓— a window frame

창파 滄波 sea waves; billows; big waves
♦만경— the billowy sea; the endless waves; the boundless expanse of water

창포 菖蒲 〔植〕 an iris (pl. ~es, irides); a (sweet) flag; a sweet rush [sedge]; a sweetroot; a calamus

창피 猖披 shame; disgrace; dishonor; ignominy
♦큰 창피 a burning disgrace; a crying shame / 창피를 알다 be sensible to shame; have a sense of shame [dishonor] / 창피를[창피한 꼴을] 당하다 disgrace oneself; be put to shame; be disgraced; be put out of countenance; lose one's honor / 아무에게 창피를 주다 put sb to shame; humiliate; disgrace; put sb out of countenance / 창피를 모르다 be dead [lost] to (all sense of) shame; be shameless
▶그게 무슨 창피니 What a disgrace! ⇌ Shame on you!
▶나는 창피를 무릅쓰고 그에게 돈을 꾸어달라고 했다 I swallowed my pride and asked him for money.
—창피하다[스럽다] shameful; dishonorable; ignominious; disgraceful; scandalous

〔解說〕 영미인이 「창피하다」고 생각하는 것은 보통 양심에 비추어 「꺼림칙하다」고 말하는

경우지, 우리들처럼 잘못을 저질러서 남의 비웃음을 받기 때문에 창피하다고 생각하는 경우는 아니다.

♦창피한 일 a shameful thing; a shame / 창피한 짓[패배] a shameful conduct [defeat] / 창피하여 얼굴을 붉히다 blush for [with] shame / 창피하여 얼굴을 못 들다 hang *one's* head for shame /…하는 것을 창피하게 여기다 think [feel] shame to 《do》
▶ 모든 사람이 나를 보고 웃는 바람에 창피했다 Everyone laughed at me and I was humiliated.
▶ 시험에서 영점을 맞았을 때 창피했다 I was ashamed when I got zero on the test.
▶ 이런 친구를 둔 것이 창피하다 I am ashamed of having such a fellow among my friends.
▶ 그런 거짓말을 하다니 창피한 줄 알아라 You should be ashamed to tell such a lie. ⇌ Shame on you for telling such a lie.

창하 倉荷 warehouse goods ■―증권 《英》 a warrant
창해 滄海 a vast blue sea; a blue expanse of waters ―일속(一粟) a drop in the ocean [bucket]
창호 窓戶 windows and doors
■―지 window [door] paper; paper for sliding doors: 창호지를 바르다 paper a sliding door
창황 蒼黃·倉皇 〈몹시 급함〉 hurry; haste; flurry; precipitation
―창황하다 hurried; hasty; flurried; precipitated; 〈서술적〉 be in a great hurry [flurry]; be in a rush; be in (hot) haste
♦창황히 〈몹시 급히〉 with precipitation; hurriedly; hastily; in a flurry; in a great hurry / 창황히 달아나다 run away helter-skelter; beat a hasty retreat
■―망조(罔措) a flurry: 창황망조하다 be panic-stricken; be upset; lose *one's* head

찾다 1 〈사람·물건 등을〉 look for; seek (for); search (for); hunt (for)

解說 **look for**는 사람·물건을 찾는 것을 나타내는 가장 일반적인 말. **seek**는 시간·노력을 들여 찾는 일. **search**는 면밀히 찾는 것이고, **hunt**는 사냥감처럼 잡기 힘든 것을 필사적으로 쫓아가는 것을 뜻한다.

♦행방 불명된 친구를 찾다 search for a missing friend / 그리스 문화의 기원을 찾다 trace the origins of Greek culture
▶ 누구를 찾으십니까? Who [Whom] are you looking for?
▶ 어디를 찾아도 그 아이는 보이지 않았다 The child was nowhere to be found.
▶ 그는 셋집을 찾고 있다 He is looking [hunting] for a house for rent [《英》 to let].
▶ 찾는 책이 안 보인다 I can't find the book I want.
▶ 그것은 아무리 찾아도 없다 It is nowhere to be found [seen].
▶ 마침 찾으시는 물건이 없군요 〈상점에서〉 Sorry, but we don't have what you want.
▶ 이것이 내가 찾고 있던 모자다 This is the hat (which) I've been looking for [trying to find].
▶ 會話 「사장이 자네를 찾네」「사장이 날 왜 찾을까?」 "You're wanted by the boss." "What is he wanting me for, I wonder?"

2 〈찾아내다〉 find (out); 〈물색하다〉 locate; 〈발견하다〉 discover; detect
♦범인을 찾다 trace a criminal / 아무의 거처를 찾아내다 locate [find out] *sb's* whereabouts / 잃어버린 반지를 찾다 find *one's* lost ring / 우연히 보물을 찾아내다 find a treasure by accident
▶ 시체는 아직 찾지 못했다 The body is still missing.

3 〈되돌려오다〉 take [get] back; draw [take] out; have 《it》 back; regain; retake; resume; recover; restore; reclaim; redeem; retrieve
♦전당포에서 시계를 찾다 redeem [recover] a pawned watch / 빌려준 돈을 다시 찾다 get back the money which had been lent / 잃었던 영토를 (다시) 찾다 regain a territory which had been lost / 은행에서 예금을 찾다 draw *one's* money [deposit] from *one's* bank

4 〈방문하다〉 call on *sb*; call at 《*sb's* house》; come to see; visit; pay a visit to; pay *sb* a call
♦그들은 단풍을 보러 설악산을 찾았다 They visited Sŏraksan to see the autumn leaves.
▶ 그는 찾아오는 사람도 없이 외롭게 살고 있다 He lives in unvisited loneliness.
▶ 떠나기 전에 찾아볼 사람이 몇 사람 있다 I have a few calls to make before I leave.
▶ 언제쯤 찾아뵐까요? When shall I call at your house [call on you]?
▶ 오후에 찾아 뵙겠습니다 I'll call on you in the afternoon.

5 〈사전 등을〉 consult [use, refer to] 《a dictionary》; 《美》 look up 《a word in a dictionary》
♦낱말의 뜻을 알기 위해 사전을 찾다 consult a dictionary for the meaning of a word / 인명록에서 남의 이름을 찾다 look a name up in a directory
▶ 사전에서 이 단어를 찾아 보시오 Look up the word in the dictionary.
▶ 그 단어의 철자를 모르거든 사전을 찾아보아라 Refer to the dictionary if you cannot spell the word.
▶ 나는 사전 찾는 법을 모른다 I do not know how to use a dictionary.

찾을모 worth; (a) merit; value; a good point
♦찾을모 없는 사람 a good-for-nothing fellow / 찾을모 없다 be destitute of merit; be worthless; be good for nothing

채[1] 〈길이〉 the length 《of hair》
채[2] 〈수레·가마의〉 poles; shafts
■―가마― palanquin poles 상여― the pallbearers' poles on a funeral bier
채[3] 1 〈채찍〉 a whip; a rod; a switch; a cane
2 〈악기의〉 a drumstick; a plectrum; a pick
■―종아리― a switch to use on the legs 파리― a fly flap
채[4] 〈얼룩진 염색〉 unevenly dyed color; blotches ♦채가 지다 be dyed unevenly

채[5] 〈집의 구분〉 a building; a house; a wing
♦ 집 세 채 three houses / 우리집에서 여러 채 떨어져 several doors away from my house; several doors away from me
▶ 이 마을에는 서른 채 안팎의 집이 있다 This village [hamlet] consists of about thirty houses.

채[6] 〈가늘고 잘게 썰기〉 cutting in thin strips; 〈가늘고 잘게 썬 것〉 thin strips 《of a vegetable》

채[7] 〈그대로〉 as (it is [stands])
♦ 신발을 신은 채 with *one's* shoes on; in *one's* shoes / 전등을 켠 채 자다 sleep with the electric light on
▶ 간밤에 우리는 모두 옷을 입은 채로 잤다 Last night we all slept with our clothes on.
▶ 책은 펼쳐진 채였다 The book was lying open.
▶ 그는 등을 벽에 기댄 채 서 있었다 He stood with his back against the wall.
▶ 그들은 곰을 산 채로 잡았다 They caught [captured] a bear alive.
▶ 모자를 쓴 채로 남한테 인사하는 것은 실례다 It's rude of you to greet other people with your hat on.
▶ 누군가 물을 틀어놓은 채로 두었다 Somebody has left the water running.

채[8] 〈아직〉 (not) yet; as yet; so far; still
♦ 날이 채 밝기도 전에 before light / 1분도 채 못 되어 in less than a minute / 그의 말이 채 끝나기도 전에 before he could finish his sentence
▶ 사과가 채 익지 않았다 Apples are not ripe yet.
▶ 1킬로도 채 가기 전에 소나기를 만났다 I had not gone a kilometer before I was caught in a shower.
▶ 이 건물은 지은지 한 달도 채 안 된다 It is less than a month that [since] this building was built.

채 菜 a vegetable dish; vegetable salad
■ 무[오이]— a cold dish of sliced radishes [cucumbers]

채결 採決 ballot taking; a vote; 《美》 a roll call; 《英》 a division
—채결하다 vote (on); take a ballot 《for》; put 《a matter》 to (the) vote; 《美》 take a roll call; 《英》 go into division
♦ 가부를 채결하다 take the ayes and noes

채고추 thin strips of red peppers

채광 採光 lighting
♦ 채광이 좋은[나쁜] 방 a well-lighted [poorly-lighted, an ill-lighted] room / 채광이 좋다[나쁘다] be well [ill] lighted
—채광하다 light; let in light; admit light
■ —창 a skylight; a loophole

채광 採鑛 mining —채광하다 mine; work 《a mine》; dig for 《minerals》 ■ —권 a mining right —학 mining engineering —학자 a mining expert

채굴 採掘 mining; digging; exploitation
—채굴하다 mine (gold); work; exploit
♦ 금광을 채굴하다 work [exploit] a gold mine / 석탄을 채굴하다 mine [dig] coal

▶ 석탄을 채굴하고 있을 때 낙반 사고가 일어났다 The roof of the mine caved in when they were mining coal.
■ —권 a mining right [concession] —량 outturn; output —료 mining rent —장 a stope —출원자 a digging applicant

채권 債券 a bond; 〈사채〉 a debenture
♦ 채권의 상환 redemption of bonds [securities] / 채권을 사다 buy a bond / 채권을 상환하다 redeem bonds
▶ 그 철도회사는 5푼[퍼센트] 이자의 채권을 발행했다 The railroad company issued a five percent (loan) bond.
■ —개발 a development bond 국고 — a treasury bond 기명 — a registered bond 무기명 — a bond to bearer 무담보 — a plain bond 보증 — a guaranteed bond 유통 — a negotiable bond 장기[단기] — a long-term [short-term] bond 저축 — a savings debenture 투자 — an investment bond 할증금[프리미엄]부 — a premium-bearing debenture ■ —소유자 a bondholder —액면 the face value of a bond

채권 債權 an obligatory right; credit; a claim
♦ 채권 확정의 소송 an action for setting claims
▶ 나는 그에게 채권이 있다 I have a claim against [on] him. ⇒ I am his creditor.
■ —국 creditor power [nation] —담보 security for an obligation —법 the law of obligations —순위 the order of credit —신고기간 the period for reporting obligations —압류 garnishment —압류인 a garnisher —양도 cession of an obligation —자 a creditor; an obligee

채귀 債鬼 a dun; a creditor; a debt collector
♦ 채귀에 시달리다 be dunned; be tormented by *one's* creditors; have many duns at *one's* heels

채그릇 a wicker vessel; wickerware

채근하다 採根— 〈뿌리를〉 dig up roots; 〈근원을〉 trace *sth* to its origin; 〈재촉하다〉 press *sb* for; urge *sb* to (do)

채금 採金 gold mining
—채금하다 mine [dig] gold

채꾼 a boy cowhand; a young cowboy

채끝 〈쇠고기 부위〉 a flank of beef

채널 a channel
♦ 채널 11에서 on Channel 11 / 채널을 맞추다 select [pick up] a channel / 채널 9를 켜다 turn on Channel 9 / 채널을 딴 데로 돌리다 change the channel
▶ 아이들이 텔레비전의 채널권을 쥐고 있다 Our children have [hold] a monopoly of the TV channels.
▶ 제7 채널에서는 무엇을 하고 있지? What is on Channel 7?

채다[1] 〈값이 오르다〉 (the price) rise [advance, go up] a little ▶ 쌀값이 또 챌 모양이다 There are indications that the price of rice will advance [go up] again.

채다[2] 1 〈낚아채다〉 snatch [catch] away; carry off; swoop off; 〈가로채다〉 seize *sth* by force; steal
♦ (솔개 등이) 병아리를 채다 pounce away

with a chicken / 남의 단골을 채다 intrigue with another's customer / 손에서 핸드백을 채가다 snatch a handbag out of *sb*'s hand
2 〈홱 당기다〉 pull *sth* with a jerk; jerk
♦ 낚싯대를 채다 jerk *one's* fishing rod out / 소매를 잡아 채다 jerk *sb* by the sleeve

채다³ 〈눈치를〉 sense; suspect; smell; scent out; get wind [scent] of; become aware 《of, that》

채다⁴ 1 〈걷어채다〉 get kicked; get a kick
♦ 당나귀에 채다 get kicked by a donkey / 옆구리를 채다 get a kick [get kicked] on the side
▶ 나는 돌부리에 채어 넘어졌다 I tripped on [over] a stone.
2 〈뺏기다〉 have *sth* taken [snatched, stolen] away ♦ 핸드백을 채다 have *one's* handbag snatched
3 〈퇴짜맞다〉 be rejected [rebuffed]; get the mitten; be kicked out

채다⁵ ⇨ 채우다¹,²,³
채단 采緞 silk stuffs; silk(s)
채도 彩度 chroma ▶ 이 색은 채도가 낮다 This color has a low chroma.
채독 a large jar-shaped wicker box; a deep wicker container
채독 菜毒 a vegetable-borne disease; 〈십이지장충병〉 hookworm disease ♦ 채독에 걸리다 get [suffer from] a vegetable-borne disease
채둥우리 a round wicker basket
채뜨리다 snatch away ⇨ 채다²
채련 donkey leather
채록 採錄 recording in a book
— **채록하다** select [extract] 《a passage》 and put 《it》 on record; record
♦ 채록되어 있다 〈사전이 주어〉 contain 《a word》; 〈어구 등이 주어〉 be given [found] 《in a dictionary》
채롱 一籠 a box-shaped wicker basket; a hamper
채료 彩料 coloring materials; colors; pigment; paint ♦ 채료를 칠하다 paint; color 《a picture》
■ 수채화 — water colors 유화 — oil colors; oils
— 상자 a color box
채마 菜麻 vegetables ⇨ 남새
■ —밭[전] a kitchen [vegetable] garden
채무 債務 a debt; an obligation; liabilities
♦ 채무가 있다 be liable for debts; owe *sb*; be [stand] in *sb's* debt / 채무를 이행하다 perform *one's* obligation; meet [discharge] *one's* liabilities / 채무를 면제하다 release *sb* from a debt
▶ 나는 그에게 백만원의 채무가 있다 I owe him a million won.
▶ 그는 내게 채무의 이행을 독촉했다 He urged me to pay my debt to him.
■ —연대 a joint obligation ■ —국 a debtor power [nation] —불이행 default of an obligation —상환 redemption of a debt —소멸[면제] expiration [waiver] of an obligation —이행 fulfillment of an obligation —자 a debtor; a loanee; 〔法〕 an obligor —증서 a bond; an obligation
채문 彩文·彩紋 a design; 〈지폐의〉 a watermark

채반 —盤 1 〈그릇〉 a wicker tray
2 〈진미〉 delicacies 《which a bride takes to her parents》
채반상 —盤相 a flat and round face
채받이 〈쇠고기 부위〉 rump
채발 long shapely feet; slender feet
채벌 採伐 felling ⇨ 벌채(伐採)
채변 reserve; polite hesitancy
▶ 채변 말고 많이 드십시오 Please help yourself without ceremony.
채비 —備 preparations; arrangements; a getup; (an) outfit; equipment
♦ 아무 채비도 없이 without any preparation / 외출할 채비를 하다 fix *oneself* for going out / 길 떠날 채비를 하다 equip *oneself* [fit *oneself* out] for a trip
▶ 나는 캐나다로 여행갈 채비를 했다 I prepared for my trip to Canada.
▶ 나는 환영회에 나갈 채비를 했다 I got myself ready for the reception.
▶ 그녀는 무도회에 갈 채비를 하고 나왔다 She came out dressed for the ball.
— **채비하다** prepare *oneself* 《for》; arrange 《for》; make preparations [arrangements] 《for》; get *oneself* ready 《for, to do》; equip *oneself* 《for》
채산 採算 profit; gain
♦ 독립 채산제 the self-supporting accounting system / 채산이 맞는 장사 a paying [going] business / 채산만 따지다 be given to calculation; be calculative / 채산이 맞는 조건으로 거래하다 make transactions on a commercial basis
▶ 이 일은 채산이 맞지 않는다 This work is unprofitable. ⇌ This job doesn't pay.
▶ 우리는 채산을 무시하고 값을 매겼다 We priced it with no thought of profit.
■ —가격 a remunerative price —성 payability
채색 彩色 coloring; painting; coloration; 〈배합〉 a color scheme
— **채색하다** color; paint
♦ 지도에 채색하다 color a map / 벽을 파란 색으로 채색하다 color the wall blue; put a blue color on the wall
▶ 서쪽 하늘은 석양으로 아름답게 채색되어 있었다 The western sky was beautifully colored by the setting sun.
■ —도판 a colored plate —인쇄 color [chromatic] printing —토기 a colored earthen vessel —화 a colored picture; a painting
채색 菜色 〈푸성귀의 빛깔〉 a green color; green; 〈굶주린 사람의 얼굴빛〉 a starved look; a haggard [sallow] complexion
채석 採石 quarrying
— **채석하다** quarry 《marble》
▶ 그들은 채석장에서 대리석을 채석하고 있다 They are quarrying out marble at the stone pit.
■ —공 a quarryman —권자 an owner of stone quarrying rights —기 a quarrying machine —장 a quarry; a stone pit
채소 菜蔬 vegetables; greens; greenstuff; garden products; 《美》 (garden) truck
♦ 채소를 가꾸다 grow [raise] vegetables; 《美》

〈시장에 내려고〉 grow garden truck ■—가게 (美) a vegetable store —밭 a vegetable [kitchen] garden; (美)〈시장 판매용〉 a truck farm [garden] —요리 a vegetable [vegetarian] dish —장수 a greengrocer; (美) a vegetableman

채송화 菜松花 〔植〕 a sun plant; a rose moss; a garden portulaca

채식 菜食 a vegetable [vegetarian] diet; living on vegetables
—**채식하다** live on vegetables
■—동물 a herbivorous [grass-eating] animal —주의 vegetarianism —주의자 a vegetarian

채약 採藥 digging [gathering] medicinal plants —**채약하다** dig [gather, collect] medicinal plants [herbs]

채용 採用 1 〈임용〉 appointment;〈고용〉 engagement; employment
—**채용하다** employ; engage; hire; take *sb* into service
♦ 여러 명의 졸업생을 채용하다 engage several graduates / 임시로 채용하다 take *sb* on trial / 채용해 달라고 부탁하다 offer *one's* service(s); apply for a position
▶ 그 회사는 대졸자를 5명 채용한다 That company employs five college graduates.
▶ 그는 서기로 채용되었다 He was employed [engaged] as a clerk.
2 ⇨ 채택(採擇)
■—임시— trial employment ■—시험 an examination for service [employment] —조건 hiring requirements [specifications, qualifications] —통지 a notification of appointment

채우다¹ 1〈몸에 물건을〉 make [let, have] *sb* wear [put on]♦ 칼을 채우다 make *sb* wear [carry, gird on] a sword
2〈자물쇠·단추 등을〉 fasten; lock;〈형구(刑具)를〉 shackle; fetter
♦ 자물쇠를 채우다 fasten a lock; lock (up) / 단추를 채우다 fasten (a coat) with buttons; button (up) (*one's* coat) / 혹을 채우다 hook (up) (a dress) / 수갑을 채우다 handcuff; shackle *sb's* hands
▶ 코트 단추가 채워지지 않는다 My coat won't button (up). ⇌ I cannot button my coat.

채우다² 〈식히다〉 cool; chill;〈찬물에〉 put [keep] *sth* in cold water;〈얼음에〉 ice;〈냉장고에〉 refrigerate
♦ 얼음에 채운 생선 iced fish; fish in ice / 맥주[수박]를 찬물에 채우다 keep beer [watermelon] cool in cold water

채우다³ 1〈수량을〉 complete (a number); make good; make up for; fill up
♦ 수를 채우다 make up the number / 백을 채우다 make (it) 100; make a round hundred / 부족액을 채우다 replenish a shortage; make up a deficit / 결원을 채우다 fill up a vacancy
2 〈가득하게 하다〉 fill (up);〈꽉〉 pack (in); cram; charge
♦ 책장을 만화로 채우다 fill (up) bookshelves with comic books / 물을 채우다 contain water / 배를 채우다 fill the stomach; eat *one's* fill / 술잔을 채우다 fill a glass [cup] with wine / 사복(私腹)을 채우다 stuff *one's* own pocket
▶ 만원 인파가 홀을 가득 채웠다 Capacity crowds packed the hall.
▶ 그녀는 욕조에 물을 채웠다 She filled the bathtub with water.
▶ 나는 작은 뜰을 화초로 꽉 채웠다 I engulfed my tiny garden with plants and flowers.
3〈기한을〉 complete (a period, a term); see (it) through
♦ 임기를 채우다 complete *one's* term of service / 계약 기간을 채우다 fulfill the period [term] of a contract
4 〈만족시키다〉 satisfy; gratify; answer; meet; fulfill; fill
♦ 수요를 채우다 supply [meet] the demand / 욕망을 채우다 gratify [satisfy] *one's* desire / 조건을 채우다 meet the conditions
▶ 그들의 욕구를 전부 채워줄 수는 절대로 없다 It is impossible to satisfy all their desires.

채유 菜油 rape(seed) oil; colza oil

채유 採油 〈석유 채굴〉 drilling for oil; oil extraction
—**채유하다** drill for oil; extract oil (from olives)
■—권 an oil concession; drilling right

채이다 sense; get a kick ⇨ 채다³,⁴

채자 採字 〔印〕 type picking
—**채자하다** pick types

채잡다〈주관하다〉 take [assume] charge (of); take the lead [a leading part] (in)

채전 菜田 a vegetable garden

채전에 〈훨씬 전에〉 a long time [while] ago; beforehand; in advance
▶ 그의 결심을 채전에 알고 있었다 I had advance knowledge of his decision.
▶ 왜 그런 말을 채전에 하지 않았느냐? Why didn't you tell me so beforehand?

채점 採點 marking; grading; scoring; (美) rating
▶ 그는 채점이 후하다 [박하다] He is generous [severe] in marking. ⇌ He is a good [bad] marker.
▶ 우리는 출석을 채점에 반영한다 We consider attendances in awarding marks.
▶ 선생님은 지금 채점 중이시다 The teacher is grading [marking] the exams [exam papers] now.
—**채점하다** give [award] marks; mark examination papers; grade; (美) rate; score (a test)
▶ 답안은 백점 만점으로 채점되고 있다 The papers [exams] are graded [marked] on a scale of 100 points.
▶ 선생님은 해답을 색연필로 채점하셨다 The teacher marked the answers with a colored pencil.

채종 採種 〈씨앗 받기〉 seed-gathering
—**채종하다** gather the seeds

채주 債主 a creditor; an obligee

채지다 〈염색이 고르지 않다〉 be uneven [streaky] in dyeing; be dyed unevenly

채질 whipping; lashing; flogging
—**채질하다** whip; lash; flog

채집 採集 collection; gathering
—**채집하다** collect; gather

♦ 곤충을 채집하다 catch insects for specimens / 광물을 채집하다 collect rocks and minerals / 해중의 플랑크톤을 채집하다 gather marine planktons / 식물을 채집하러 가다 go botanizing
▶ 여름 방학에는 고산식물을 채집하러 갑니다 During the summer vacation, I go to collect alpine plants.
■ 곤충— insect collecting; (口) bugging; bug hunting: 곤충 채집망 a butterfly catcher 약초— gathering medicinal herbs ■ —가 a collector —상자 a vasculum (pl. ~s, -la)

채찍 a whip; 〈말의〉 a horsewhip
♦ 말을 채찍으로 때리다 whip [lash] a horse / 채찍을 휘두르다 wield a whip / 채찍을 울리다 crack [swish] a whip
■ —끈 a whipcord; a (whip) lash —소리 the sound [crack] of a whip —자국 a wale; a wheal; a welt

채찍질 〈매질〉 whipping; 〈격려〉 urging [spurring] on; encouragement
—채찍질하다 〈매질하다〉 whip; lash; 〈격려하다〉 spur [urge] on; encourage
♦ 달리는 말에 채찍질하다 urge on a willing person; make sb redouble his efforts / 채찍질하여 말을 달리게 하다 whip up one's horse; whip a horse on

채취 採取 picking; gathering
—채취하다 pick; gather; collect; harvest
♦ 지문을 채취하다 take sb's fingerprints; fingerprint sb / 진주를 채취하다 fish pearls / 해초를 채취하다 gather seaweeds
■ —진주— pearl fishery; pearling ■ —자 a picker; a gatherer; a collector

채치다¹ 〈채질하다〉 whip; lash; flog; flagellate; 〈독촉하다〉 press; urge; dun

채치다² 〈당기다〉 tweak; jerk; 〈잡아채다〉 snatch (from, off)
♦ 팔을 채치다 jerk at sb's arm / 손에 든 핸드백을 채치다 snatch a handbag from sb's hand

채치다³ 〈잘게 썰다〉 cut (a radish) into fine strips; cut fine; chop fine; shred ♦ 샐러드감으로 오이를 채치다 shred a cucumber for salad

채칼 菜— a knife for shredding vegetables; a chef's knife; a frenching tool

채탄 採炭 coal mining
—채탄하다 mine [extract] coal
■ —량 the output of coal —부 a pitman; a collier —소 a colliery; a coal mine

채택 採擇 〈선택〉 choice; selection; 〈채용〉 adoption
♦ 교과서의 채택 the choice of textbooks / 새로운 교수법의 채택 the adoption [introduction] of a new method of teaching / 채택 여부를 아무에게 일임하다 leave sth to sb's option
—채택하다 choose; select; accept (a proposal); adopt (a plan); use (a textbook)
▶ 그 원고는 채택되지 않았다 The manuscript was not accepted.
▶ 그 나라는 한층 더 자주적인 외교 정책을 채택했다 The country adopted a more independent foreign policy.
▶ 결국 나의 의견은 채택되지 않았다 After all my opinion was not accepted.

■ —원고 manuscripts accepted

채편 —便 〈장구의〉 the right-hand side of a changgu

채플 〈예배당〉 a chapel

채플린 〈영국 태생의 미국 희극배우〉 Chaplin, Charles Spencer (1889-1977)

채필 彩筆 a paintbrush; a painter's brush

채혈 採血 blood-gathering; blood-collecting; drawing of blood
—채혈하다 gather [collect] blood 《from a donor》; draw blood 《from a vein》
■ —기관 a blood-gathering agency —차 a blood-donation car; a bloodmobile

채화 彩畫 a colored picture; a painting

채화 菜花 flowers on vegetables

책 冊 a book; a volume; 〈작품〉 a work; 〈읽을거리〉 reading
♦ 책을 쓰다 write a book / 책을 내다 publish [bring out] a book / 책을 매다 bind a book / 책을 읽어 주다 read to sb / 책을 읽다가 잠이 들다 read oneself to sleep / 한 권의 책으로 엮다 collect (essays) into a single volume; compile (data) into a book / 책으로 출판하다 publish in book form
▶ 그 책은 품절입니다 We haven't got any copies of the book on hand now.
▶ 그는 책을 많이 읽었다 He is well-read.
▶ 그는 책을 많이 소장하고 있다 He has a large library.

— 책 —

천, 위 head of page
커버 jacket
타이틀 title
끈, 실 tassel
옆 fore edge
지, 아래 foot of page
홈 joint, hinge
표지 cover
등 spine

책 柵 1 〈울〉 a picket fence; a stockade; a paling; a railing; a palisade; a corral
♦ 책을 두르다 set (up) [put up] a fence round; fence round [around, about]
2 〈둑〉 a stockade; a log dike [dyke]

책 責 1 ⇨ 책임(責任) 2 ⇨ 책망(責望)

—**책 —策** a step; a measure; a scheme; a policy
♦ 궁여지책 a shift; the last expedient / 대응책 a countermeasure / 해결책 a solution

책가위 冊— a (book) jacket; a dust cover
—책가위하다 jacket; lay [put] a dust cover on a book

책갑 冊匣 a bookcase; a case for books [a

책값 册— the price of a book; a book price
책권 册卷 a volume; a book ▶ 그는 책권깨나 갖고 있다 He has a good many books.
책궤 册櫃 a book box
책 글 씨 penmanship used for handwritten books; a handwriting style used for books
책꽂이 册— a bookstand; a bookrack; a bookshelf
책동 策動 maneuvers; machination; scheming
—책동하다 maneuver; machinate; scheme
♦ 뒤에서 책동하다 maneuver behind the scenes; pull the wires (from behind)
■—가 a schemer; a wirepuller; a maneuverer; a machinator
책뚜껑 册— a (book) cover
책략 策略 a stratagem; a trick; an artifice; tactics; maneuvers; a scheme
♦ 책략을 써서 with stratagem [artifice] / 책략을 쓰다 resort to artifice; use tricks / 책략을 꾸미다 contrive [devise] a stratagem / 책략이 풍부하다 be resourceful; be full of resources ▶ 나는 책략을 써서 그에게서 돈을 우려냈다 I got money from him by a trick.
—가 a tactician; a schemer
책력 册曆 an almanac; a book calendar
책망 責望 blame; charge; (a) censure; (a) reproach; (a) rebuke; (a) reproof
♦ 책망을 듣다 be reproved [rebuked]; be called to task; receive a reproof (from); catch [get] it (from)
—책망하다 call sb to task [account]; blame; censure; charge; reproach; rebuke; reprove
♦ 부주의를 책망하다 reproach sb for his carelessness / 태만을 책망하다 blame sb for his negligence
▶ 그는 그녀가 약속을 지키지 않았다고 책망했다 He reproached [censured] her for not keeping her word.
▶ 남을 책망하지 말고 자신을 책망하라 Find fault with yourself rather than with others.
책모 策謀 (a) stratagem
책무 責務 (a) duty; (a) responsibility ⇨ 책임
♦ 국가에 대한 책무를 다하다 do one's duty to his country
책받침 册— a desk pad; a plastic sheet; a celluloid board
책방 册房 a bookseller's; (美) a bookstore ⇨ 서점(書店)
책 벌 責罰 〈견책〉 a reprimand; (a) censure; 〈처벌〉 a punishment
—책벌하다 〈견책하다〉 reprimand; censure; 〈처벌하다〉 punish
책벌레 册— 〈벌레〉 a bookworm; 〈사람〉 a bookworm
책보 册褓 a book wrapper; 〈책을 싼 보통이〉 a package of books
책사 策士 a tactician; a schemer; a machinator
책상 册床 a desk; a (writing) table
♦ 책상에서 하는 일 desk work / 책상에 앉다 sit at a desk
▶ 책상이 이렇게 어질러져 있는데 왜 치우지 않는 거냐? Why don't you clear [straighten] up the top of your desk; it is so messy?
■ 양소매— a kneehole desk ■—보 a table cloth
책상다리 册床— 1 a leg of a desk
2 〈앉음새〉 sitting on crossed legs; sitting with one's legs crossed
—책상다리하다 sit cross-legged; sit with one's legs crossed; sit down tailor-fashion
책상물림 册床— a naive academic; a novice from the ivory tower
책송곳 册— a bookbinding [bookbinder's] awl
책실 册— bookbinding thread
책싸개 册— a (book) jacket ⇨ 책가위
책씻이 册— an end-of-term party
—책씻이하다 hold an end-of-term party
책임 責任 responsibility; charge; blame; fault; duty; liability; obligation

> 解說 ***responsibility***는 자신의 일이나 의무 등을 수행하는 책임. ***charge***는 사람이나 조직을 관리하고 돌보며 보살피는 책임. ***blame***은 실패 같은 좋지 않은 일에 대한 책임. ***fault***는 과실에 대한 책임. ***duty***는 법률상의 (채무) 의무. ***liability***는 특히 차용금의 지불·손해 배상 등 법률적으로 생기는 의무.

♦ 전체의 the whole responsibility / 책임을 묻다 call sb to task (for) / 책임을 지우다 place [put] the responsibility (for sth) on sb; saddle sb with the responsibility (for) / 책임을 지다 bear [assume, take, shoulder] the responsibility (for, of); hold oneself responsible (for) / 책임을 다하다 fulfil(l) one's responsibility; discharge one's obligation(s) / 책임을 전가하다 shift the responsibility (for sth) on to sb; pass the buck to sb / 책임을 같이지다 share the responsibility (for sth) with sb
▶ 책임의 소재가 분명치 않다 I can't clearly determine where the responsibility lies.
▶ 버스 기사는 승객의 안전에 대해 책임이 있다 The bus driver is responsible for the safety of the passengers.
▶ 난 책임이 없다 I am not responsible.
▶ 아무도 책임을 지려고 하지 않는다 Nobody cares to take the blame.
▶ 자기의 책임을 회피해서는 안된다 You must not shirk your responsibility.
▶ 그는 모든 책임을 한 몸에 졌다 He took it upon himself to bear the whole burden.
▶ 그들이 늦어진 것은 네 책임이다 It was your fault that they were delayed.
▶ 좋아, 그것은 내가 책임지겠어 All right, I will see to it.
■ 무— irresponsibility 연대[공동]— collective responsibility; joint liability 유한[무한]— limited [unlimited] liability
■ —내각 a responsible cabinet —자 a responsible person; a person in charge (of) —전가 shifting of responsibility; (美口) buck-passing —해제 release from responsibility —회피 evasion [shirking] of responsibility
책임감 責任感 a sense of responsibility
▶ 그는 책임감이 강하다 He has a strong sense

책자 冊子 a booklet; a pamphlet
책잡다 責— find fault with sb; call sb to account (for); take sb to task; blame [reproach] (for)
  ♦ 실언을 책잡다 take sb to task for a slip of the tongue / 직무태만을 책잡다 denounce sb for his neglect of duty
책잡히다 責— be called to account [task]; be taken to task; be blamed [reproached]
  ♦ 약속을 위반했다고 책잡히다 be blamed for having broken one's promise / 직무 태만으로 책잡히다 be accused of having neglected one's work
  ▶ 그 장관은 언제나 책잡히지 않을 답변만 한다 The minister always gives only noncommittal answers.
책장 冊張 a leaf of a book; the pages
  ♦ 책장을 넘기다 turn over the leaves of a book; turn [thumb] the pages of a book; leaf through a book
책장 冊欌 a bookshelf (pl. -shelves); a bookcase
책정 策定 〈예산 등의〉 appropriation; 〈가격 등의〉 fixing
  —책정하다 appropriate; allot; earmark (for)
  ♦ 가격을 책정하다 fix a price
  ♦ 봉급의 arrangement of a salary scale
책치레 冊— make-up of a book
책하다 責— blame ⇨ 책망(~하다)
챔피언 a champion
  ♦ 복싱 챔피언 a boxing champion; a champion boxer / 챔피언이 되다 win [gain] a championship / 챔피언 자격이 있다 be entitled to become a champion
  ■—벨트 a champion belt —십 (a) championship
챗국 a cold soup prepared with shredded radish
챗열 〈채찍 끝의〉 a whiplash; a lash
챙 a blind ⇨ 차양(遮陽)
챙기다 put (things) in order; set (things) in (good) order; tidy up
  ♦ 서류를 챙기다 get papers in order / 소지품을 챙기다 get one's things together; gather up one's belongings / 책상 위의 것들을 챙기다 clear up one's desk / 제 물건을 잘 챙기다 take good care of one's (own) things
  ▶ 그 아이는 너무 어려 제 몸 하나 챙길 줄 모른다 The child is too young to take care of himself.
처 妻 a wife (pl. wives); one's better half; 〔法〕 a feme ⇨ 아내
  ♦ 내연의 처 a common-law wife
처 處 〈정부기구〉 an office
  ♦ 법제처 the Office of Legislation / 국가 보훈처 the Ministry for Patriots and Veteran Affairs
-처 -處 〈곳〉 a place ♦ 근무처 one's place of employment; one's office
처가 妻家 one's wife's home
  ■—살이 living in one's wife's home

처결 處決 settlement; disposal; disposition; decision —처결하다 settle; dispose of; decide
처깔하다 〈문을〉 close tight ⇨ 차깔하다
처남 妻男 one's wife's brother; one's brother-in-law
처넣다 〈마구 넣다〉 press [thrust, jam, stuff, force] in; 〈감금하다〉 lock sb up [in]; confine
  ♦ 감옥에 처넣다 cast [throw] (a culprit) into a prison / 전재산을 증권에 처넣다 put all one's fortune into stocks
처네 〈덧이불〉 a coverlet; a counterpane
처녀 處女 a virgin; a maiden
  ♦ 처녀다운 maidenlike; maidenly; virginal / 처녀답게 like a maiden; in a maidenlike manner / 꽃다운 처녀 시절에 in the flower of maidenhood; in virginal bloom
  ■—숫— an immaculate virgin ■—기[시대] maidenhood; virginhood —림[봉] a virgin forest [peak] —막 〔解〕 the maidenhead; the hymen —연설[출판, 비행, 항해] a maiden speech [publication, flight, voyage] —자리 〔天〕 the Virgin; Virgo —작 a maiden work —지 a virgin soil
처녀가 애를 낳아도 할 말이 있다 (속담) Every evildoer has his reasons.
처녀성 處女性 virginity; virginhood; maidenhood
  ♦ 처녀성을 잃다[빼앗기다] lose [be deprived of] one's virginity; be deflowered / 처녀성을 지키다 keep [retain] one's virginity
처녑 the manyplies; an omasum (pl. -sa)
처단 處斷 〈결단〉 decision; 〈처치〉 disposition; 〈처벌〉 punishment —처단하다 〈결단하다〉 decide; 〈처치하다〉 punish; deal with
  ♦ 범법자를 엄히 처단하다 punish [deal with] an offender severely
처대다 1 〈불사르다〉 put [throw] sth into a fire; burn on a fire
  2 〈대 주다〉 keep supplying [providing] thoughtlessly
처덕 妻德 〈아내의 덕행〉 the virtue of one's wife; 〈아내의 내조〉 one's wife's assistance [help]
  ♦ 처덕으로 by one's wife's help; thanks to one's wife
처덕거리다 1 〈빨래를 두들겨 소리내다〉 keep beating with a paddle; paddle; slap; flap; pound
  ♦ 빨래를 처덕거리다 paddle the laundry
  2 〈함부로 바르다〉 paste [affix, stick] at random [haphazardly]
처덕처덕 1 〈빨래를〉 paddling; beating; slapping 2 〈바름〉 (paste) at random [haphazard]; thick(ly) ♦ 담에 전단을 처덕처덕 붙이다 paste bills all over a wall
처든지르다 devour ⇨ 처먹다
처때다 heap fuel on a fire
처뜨리다 hang down; suspend; droop
  ♦ 어깨를 처뜨리다 droop one's shoulders / 긴 머리를 뒤로 처뜨리다 have one's long hair flowing down one's back
처란 〈탄알〉 a pellet; (총칭) bird shot; a pellet-like thing
처량하다 凄凉— 1 〈쓸쓸하다〉 desolate; dreary;

bleak; deserted
♦처량한 풍경 a desolate and forlorn scene / 처량한 벌판 a wind-swept [desolate] plain; a wilderness
2 〈구슬프다〉 sad; sorrowful; doleful; plaintive; melancholy; mournful; depressed
♦처량한 노래 a plaintive song / 처량한 느낌 a feeling of wretchedness / 처량한 모습 a wretched [lonesome] look / 처량한 신세 a pitiable condition / 처량한 이야기 a pathetic story / 처량해지다 feel miserable [wretched]
▶그녀는 처량해 보인다 She looks depressed [lonely].
◆처량한 소리 집어치우고 기운 좀 내 Cheer up! Don't be fainthearted.

처럼 〈…와 같이〉 like; (the same) as; as...as; (not) so...as; as if; as though
♦여느때처럼 as usual / 전처럼 as before; as in the past / 아무일도 없었던 것처럼 as if nothing had happened / 돈을 물처럼 쓰다 spend money like water / 가족처럼 대하다 treat *sb* as one of the family / 친자식처럼 사랑하다 love (a child) like *one's* own / 대낮처럼 밝다 be as bright as (noon) day / 우후죽순처럼 나타나다 spring up like (so many) mushrooms after rain
▶나도 그처럼 센 권투 선수가 되고 싶다 I wish to be a strong boxer like him.
▶벌이 꿀을 좋아하는 것처럼 프랑스인은 프랑스 포도주를 좋아한다 French people love their wine (just) as [(口) like] bees love honey.
▶너처럼은 못하겠다 I cannot do it like you do.
▶그는 무엇이나 다 아는 것처럼 이야기한다 He talks as if [as though] he knew everything.
▶싸움은 끝이 없을 것처럼 보였다 It seemed as if the fight would never end.
▶나도 영어를 그 사람처럼 잘 할 수 있었으면 좋겠다 I wish I could speak English as well as he.
▶음식이 몸의 영양이 되는 것처럼 책은 마음의 영양이 된다 As food nourishes our body, so books nourish our mind.

처리 處理 〈취급〉 management; handling; transaction; 〈처분〉 disposal; disposition; 〈화학적인〉 treatment; 〔電算〕 processing
▶나는 그 사건의 처리를 위임받았다 I was entrusted with the conduct of the affair.
—**처리하다** manage; handle; dispose of; deal with; transact; treat; 〔電算〕 process
♦일을 처리하다 manage [dispose of, deal with, take a care of] a task / 어려운 문제를 처리하다 deal with a difficult problem / 열로 처리하다 treat (metals) by heating; heat-treat (metals)
▶그 사건은 원만히 처리되었다 The case is settled amicably. ⇌ The case is brought to an amicable settlement.
▶이 문제부터 처리합시다 Let's settle this problem first.
▶그는 자기 일을 잘 처리하고 있다 He is in control [on top] of his job.
▶그는 오전중에 많은 일을 척척 처리했다 He got through a lot of work briskly in the morning.
▶이 문제는 신중히 처리할 필요가 있다 We must handle [treat] this problem carefully.
■ **열—** heat treatment

처마 the eaves
♦처마의 홈통 the eaves gutter
▶나는 그 집 처마 밑에서 비를 그었다 I took shelter from rain under the eaves of the house.
▶처마 끝에 매달린 풍경이 댕그렁거리고 있다 The wind-bell hanging from the eaves is tinkling.

처매다 bind up 《a wound》; bandage 《a wound》 up
▶그녀는 붕대로 상처를 처맸다 She wrapped a bandage around the wound.

처먹다 devour; cram 《food》 into *one's* mouth; shove [shovel] down; eat greedily

처먹이다 feed immoderately; stuff *sb* with food

처방 處方 (a) prescription; a recipe
♦처방을 쓰다 write a prescription 《for a disease》 / 처방대로 조제하다 prepare a medicine as prescribed [according to a prescription] / 처방을 잘못하다 make out a wrong prescription 《for》
▶이 약은 의사의 처방 없이는 팔 수 없습니다 We cannot sell you this medicine without a doctor's prescription.
▶처방 조제 (표시) Prescription filled.
—**처방하다** prescribe 《to a patient for a complaint》
■ —**전(箋)** a (medical) prescription

처벌 處罰 punishment; (a) penalty
♦처벌을 면하다 escape the penalty 《of》
▶그는 교통위반으로 처벌을 받았다 He was punished for breaking the traffic regulations.
—**처벌하다** punish 《*sb* for a crime》; inflict a penalty on 《*sb* for an offense》
♦엄중히 처벌하다 punish severely; inflict severe [heavy] punishment on / 처벌받다 be punished; incur a penalty / 처벌받을 만하다 deserve the punishment 《of》 / 처벌받지 않고 넘어가다 go unpunished; get off scot-free

처부모 妻父母 the parents of *one's* wife; a man's parents-in-law

처분 處分 〈처치〉 disposal; disposition; dealing; a measure; 〈처벌〉 punishment
♦쓰레기의 처분 garbage disposal; the disposal of garbage
▶우리는 모든 것을 그의 처분에 맡겼다 We left everything to his own discretion [judgment].
—**처분하다** dispose of; deal with; make a clearance of 《unsold goods》
♦토지[재산]를 처분하다 dispose of *one's* land [property] / 관대히 처분하다 deal leniently with
▶그는 토지를 처분했다 He disposed of [sold] the land.
▶이 집을 어떻게 처분하느냐가 문제다 The question is how to dispose of [what to do with] this house.
▶헌 옷은 어떻게 처분하십니까? What do you do with your old clothes?

■ 공매— (disposition by) public sale 매각— disposal by sale 부당— an unwarrantable proceeding [measure] 체납— disposition for failure to pay (taxes) —품 clearance goods

처사 處士 a retired scholar

처사 處事 treatment (of an affair); dealing [handling] (with a matter); conduct; disposal; action; 〈조치〉 a measure; a step
♦ 적절한 처사 an appropriate [adequate] measure; a proper step / 처사를 잘하다 take a proper step; deal with a matter properly
▶ 네 처사는 현명했다 You acted wisely.

처삼촌 妻三寸 one's wife's uncle; an uncle-in-law

처상 妻喪 one's wife's death; mourning for one's wife

처서 處暑 one of the 24 seasonal divisions (about August 23rd to September 7th)

처세 處世 conduct of life
♦ 처세에 능한 사람 a worldly-wise person
▶ 그는 처세에 능하지 못하다 He is lacking in worldly wisdom.
—**처세하다** get on in the world; walk through the world; get along with people; conduct oneself
■ —술 the secret of success in life; the art of living; how to get on in the world: 그는 처세술이 능하다 He knows well how to get on in the world. —훈(訓) the (guiding) motto for one's life

처소 處所 〈장소〉 a place; 〈거처〉 a living [dwelling] place; one's residence; one's abode; 〈주소〉 one's address
■ 임시— one's temporary residence

처시하 妻侍下 a henpecked husband; a man tied to his wife's apron strings ⇨ 엄처시하

처신 處身 behavior; conduct; deportment; demeanor
—**처신하다** behave [conduct, deport, demean] oneself
♦ 훌륭하게[의젓하게] 처신하다 behave fine [well, handsomely]
▶ 그는 늘 신사답게 처신한다 He always behaves [conducts himself] like a gentleman.
▶ 그는 마침내 어떻게 처신할 것인지를 결정했다 At last he decided how to dispose of himself.

처우 處遇 treatment
♦ 처우를 개선하다 improve treatment; give better treatment to 《workers》
▶ 그는 부당한 처우를 받았다 He was not fairly treated.
■ —개선 better treatment

처음 〈시작〉 the beginning; the start; the opening; the outset; commencement; 〈최초〉 (the) first; the first time; 〈기원〉 the origin
♦ 맨 처음 the very first [beginning] / 처음부터 끝까지 from (the) beginning to (the) end; from start [first] to finish [last]; throughout; all the way / 처음은[에는] at first; at the start [outset, beginning]; 〈본디는〉 originally; primarily / 처음으로 for the first time / 책을 처음부터 끝까지 읽다 read a book from cover to cover / 처음부터 다시 하다 do all over

again; begin afresh; make a new start

解說 (1) 「처음 뵙겠습니다」에 해당하는 가장 일반적인 표현은 **How do you do?**로 상대방도 How do you do?라고 대답한다.
(2) 이 응답에 잇따라 「뵙게 되어 영광입니다」, 「잘 부탁드립니다」의 뜻으로 (**I'm) glad to meet you.** 나 **Nice [Pleased] to meet you.** 라고 한다. 어느 경우에도 meet을 강하게 발음한다. 이런 말을 들은 쪽은 **The pleasure is mine.** 이라든가 (**It's) nice to meet you.** 등으로 대답한다. 이 경우 mine, you을 각각 강하게 발음한다.
(3) 형식을 차릴 필요가 없는 경우에는 How do you do?를 생략하고 **How are you? Hello!** 등의 말을 교환한다. 특히 젊은이들 사이에서 이런 경향을 볼 수 있다.

▶ 매사는 처음이 중요하다 A good beginning makes a good ending.
▶ 이것이 처음이자 마지막이다 This is the first and the last.
▶ 이런 그림은 생전 처음 보았다 I have never seen such a painting in my life.
▶ 처음에는 회원이 단 세명이었다 We had only three members to start with.
▶ 처음에는 부탁조더니 막판에는 협박조로 나왔다 He began with soft entreaties and ended with threats.
▶ 나는 처음에는 교사가 될 생각이 아니었다 Teaching was not my original intention.
▶ 그 회사는 처음에는 보잘 것 없었다 The company began in a small way.
▶ 처음부터 다시 시작해 Begin at the beginning.
▶ 그건 처음부터 알고 있었다 I knew it all along.
▶ 계획은 처음부터 실패하게 되어 있었다 The plan was foredoomed to failure.
▶ 연단에 선 것은 이번이 처음입니다 This is the first time that I have ever stood on the platform.
▶ 부산에 온 것은 이번이 처음이다 This is my first visit to Pusan.
▶ 외국인으로서는 그가 처음으로 한라산에 올랐다 He was the first foreigner to climb Hallasan.

처자 妻子 one's wife and children; one's family ♦ 처자를 부양하다 support [provide for] one's family / 처자를 버리다 desert [discard] one's wife and children / 처자를 돌보지 않다 have no regard for one's wife and children
▶ 그녀는 처자가 있는 남자와 사랑에 빠졌다 She fell in love with a married man who had children.

처재 妻財 one's wife's property [dowry]

처쟁이다 pile [heap] up; make a pile

처절 悽絶 extreme sadness [sorrow]; ghastliness
—**처절하다** extremely sad [melancholy, wretched, miserable]; heartbreaking; 〈처참하다〉 ghastly; gruesome
♦ 처절한 광경 a sorrowful [heartbreaking] sight; a gruesome scene

처제 妻弟 one's wife's younger sister; one's sister-in-law

처조모 妻祖母 one's wife's grandmother

처조부 妻祖父 one's wife's grandfather

처조카 妻— one's wife's nephew [niece]

처족 妻族 one's wife's relatives [family]

처지 處地 1 〈형편〉 a situation; a condition; circumstances; one's lot; one's 《financial》 status; 〈입장〉 a standpoint; a position; one's standing; 〈신분〉 a station in life
♦ 곤란한 처지 a difficult [an awkward] situation; a delicate position; a dilemma / 처지의 변화 a change in one's circumstances / 남의 처지가 되어 생각하다 put [place] oneself in another's place [shoes] / 편안한[어려운] 처지에 있다 be in easy [needy] circumstances / 자기의 처지에 만족하다 be contented with one's lot / 같은 처지에 있다 be in the same circumstances / 남의 딱한 처지에 동정하다 sympathize with sb's sad plight / 남의 처지를 부러워하다 envy sb's lot / 자기 처지를 모르다 do not know where one stands [is]
▶ 우리는 각기 처지가 다르다 We are all differently circumstanced.
▶ 현재의 나로서는 그렇게 할 처지가 못된다 My present circumstances will not allow me to do so.
▶ 우리는 하인을 둘 처지가 못된다 Our circumstances do not allow us to keep a servant.
▶ 나는 그들 사이에 끼어서 어색한 처지가 되었다 Placed between them, I find my position awkward.
▶ 당신 처지가 부럽소 I wish I were in your shoes.
2 〈사이〉 relations; terms
▶ 우리는 서로 말을 놓고 지내는 처지다 We are on thee-and-thou terms with each other.

처지다 1 〈늘어지다〉 hang (down); droop; sag
♦ 처진 어깨 drooping shoulders / 귀가 처진 개 a dog with button [drooped] ears / 가지가 처진 나무 a tree with drooping branches
▶ 천장이 처졌다 The ceiling has sagged.
▶ 사과가 많이 열려서 가지가 처져 있다 The branches are drooping under the weight of the apples.
2 〈뒤지다〉 fall [drop] behind; fall back; trail; be outstripped 《by》
♦ 혼자 뒤에 처지다 fall [remain] behind all alone / 경주에서 처지다 drop [fall] behind in a race / 행군중에 처지다 fall out while on the march

처지르다 lay [put] plenty of 《wood》 on (the fire)

처질 妻姪 one's wife's nephew [niece]

처참 處斬 execution by decapitation [beheading] —**처참하다** cut off sb's head; execute sb by beheading

처참하다 悽慘— ghastly; grim; gruesome; appalling; lurid; miserable; wretched
♦ 처참한 광경 a gruesome scene; a ghastly [an appalling] sight / 처참한 생활 a wretched [miserable] life / 처참한 전투 a bloody battle
▶ 처참한 사고 현장에서 얼굴을 돌리지 않는 사람이 없었다 There were none but turned their faces away from the dreadful scene of the accident.

처창하다 悽愴— desolate; dreary, pathetic; miserable; tragic

처처 處處 several [various] places
♦ 처처에(서) (here, there, and) everywhere

처첩 妻妾 one's wife and concubine

처치 處置 1 〈처분〉 disposal; disposition; management; 〈조치〉 a measure; a step
♦ …이 처치 곤란이다 do not know what to do with 《an affair》; be at a loss how to deal with 《a matter》
—**처치하다** dispose of; deal [do] with
2 〈제거〉 removal; clearance; elimination; liquidation
—**처치하다** remove; get rid of; clear [take] away; do away with; eliminate; liquidate
♦ 반당 분자를 처치하다 eliminate anti-party elements
▶ 우리는 그를 처치하기로 했다 We marked him for death.

처칠 〈영국의 정치가〉 Churchill, Sir Winston (Leonard Spencer) (1874-1965)

처하다 處— 1 〈놓이다〉 be placed (in); be [get] faced with
♦ 역경에 처하다 be in adversity; be under unfavorable circumstances / 불리한 입장에 처하다 be in a disadvantageous position / 위기에 처하다 face [be confronted with] a crisis
2 〈처벌하다〉 sentence; condemn
♦ 구류에 처하다 order detention for sb / 사형에 처하다 sentence [condemn] sb to death / 3일간의 구류에 처해지다 be sentenced to three days' detention
▶ 그는 엄벌에 처해야 한다 He deserves severe punishment.

처형 妻兄 one's wife's elder sister; one's sister-in-law

처형 處刑 〈처벌〉 punishment; 〈사형집행〉 execution —**처형하다** punish; execute
▶ 그는 전범으로 처형되었다 He was executed as a war criminal. ■—장 a place of execution

척¹ make-believe

척² 1 〔機〕 a chuck 2 〈지퍼〉 a zipper

척³ 1 〈붙는 모양〉 closely; tightly; hard; fast
♦ 척 들러붙다 stick fast 《to one's hand》
2 〈선뜻〉 without hesitation [delay]; readily; 〈즉각〉 instantly; quickly; offhand; right away [off]
♦ 척 보고 at first sight; at the first glance / 대답을 척하다 answer 《questions》 readily / 돈을 척 내걸다 bet one's money without hesitation
▶ 한 번 척 보고 그의 사기임을 알아보았다 One glance was enough to see through his fraud.
3 ⇨ 축²
4 〈의젓하게〉 imposingly; with dignity
♦ 안경을 척 쓰다 put on one's glasses imposingly

척 尺 〈자〉 a chuk (=0.994 ft., 30.3 centimeters) ♦ 척수가 짧다[모자라다] be wanting in length; be short of measure / 척수를 재다 measure (the length of)

척 隻 number of vessels

♦ 배 한 척 a [one] vessel [ship, boat] / 거룻배 한 척 분의 석탄 a lighterload of coal

척결하다 剔抉— gouge [hollow] out ((the eyes)); scrape out ♦ 부정사건을 척결하다 expose a scandal

척골 尺骨 〔解〕 the ulna ((pl. ~s, -nae))

척골 脊骨 〔解〕 the backbone; the spine; the spinal column

척골 蹠骨 〔解〕 a metatarsal (bone)

척도 尺度 a (linear) measure; a scale; a gauge; a yardstick; 〈기준〉 a standard; a criterion ((pl. ~s, -ria))
♦ 문명의 척도 an index [a barometer] of civilization / …을 재는 척도가 되다 be a measure [a barometer, an index] of…; be a yardstick for…
▶ 재산이 행복의 척도는 아니다 You cannot measure a man's happiness by his wealth. ≒ Wealth is no criterion of a man's happiness.

척량 脊梁 〔解〕 the spinal [vertebral] column; (the ridge of) the spine
■ —산맥 the main mountain range

척박 瘠薄 sterility; barrenness ((of land))
—척박하다 sterile; barren; infertile; poor
♦ 척박한 땅 barren [poor, unproductive] soil; sterile [infertile] land / 땅을 척박하게 하다 impoverish the soil

척분 戚分 kinship; (ties of) relationship

척살 刺殺 〈찔러 죽임〉 stabbing to death; 〔野〕 touching-out; a put-out —척살하다 stab sb to death; 〔野〕 put [touch] ((a runner)) out

척수 隻手 one arm [hand]
♦ 척수인 사람 a one-armed person

척수 脊髓 〔解〕 the spinal cord [marrow]; pith
■ —마비 spinal paralysis —마취 spinal anesthesia —병 a spinal disease —신경 the spinal nerves —액 the spinal fluid —염 myelitis —주사 a spinal injection

척식 拓植 colonization; exploitation —척식하다 colonize; settle ■ —은행 a colonial bank —자 a colonist —회사 a colonization company

척신 隻身 singleness; celibacy; 〈남자〉 bachelorhood; 〈여자〉 spinsterhood
♦ 척신의 single; sole; unmarried; celibate / 척신으로 alone; single-handed

척주 脊柱 〔解〕 the spinal [vertebral] column; the spine
■ —측만증 〔醫〕 scoliosis; spinal curvature

척지 尺地 〈작은 땅〉 a (single square) foot of land; a small strip of land; 〈가까운 곳〉 a place a foot away [at a stone's throw]

척지다 隻— come to hate each other

척짓다 隻— earn sb's grudge; incur grudge [ill will]

척척 1 〈들러붙는 모양〉 close(ly); tightly; adhesively; fast
♦ 척척 들러붙다 stick fast ((to)); adhere ((to))
2 〈서슴없이〉 without hesitation [delay]; readily; 〈얼른얼른〉 quickly; promptly; rapidly; speedily; with dispatch; briskly; right off; 〈수월하게〉 easily
♦ 척척 대답하다 give ready answers / 어려운 문제를 척척 풀다 solve hard problems easily /

일을 척척 하다 be prompt in one's work; do it businesslike
▶ 일이 척척 진척되었다 The matter went on swimmingly.

척척하다 wet; damp ⇨ 축축하다

척추 脊椎 〔解〕 the backbone; the spine; the spinal column; the vertebra ((pl. ~s, -brae))
■ —골 a vertebra —동물 a vertebrate; Vertebrata: 무척추 동물 an invertebrate; Invertebrata —마취 spinal anesthesia; rachianesthesia —염 spondylitis —카리에스 spinal caries

척축 斥逐 expulsion; ouster; ejectment
—척축하다 drive [turn] out; expel; oust; eject

척출 斥黜 ouster; ousting; expulsion; dismissal; discharge —척출하다 dismiss [discharge] sb from office; oust [expel] sb from a position

척출 剔出 extraction; removal; excision
—척출하다 extract; excise; remove; cut out
■ —난소 removal of an ovary; ovariotomy
■ —기 an extractor

척탄 擲彈 a (hand) grenade
■ —병 a grenade thrower

척토 尺土 a foot of land [territory]; an inch of land [territory] ⇨ 촌토 (寸土)

척후 斥候 〈정탐〉 scouting; patrol duty; reconnaissance; 〈척후병〉 a scout; a patrol; a reconnoitering soldier
♦ 척후로 나가다 go out scouting / 척후를 내보내다 send out scouts
—척후하다 scout; reconnoiter
■ —전투[정찰]— a combat [reconnaissance] patrol ■ —대 a reconnoitering party —대장 a patrol leader —전 skirmishes of scouts; a patrol encounter

천 (plain) cloth; woven stuff; texture; (textile) fabrics
♦ 고급 천 quality cloth / 나일론 천 nylon cloth / 좋은[나쁜] 천 good [bad] stuff / 얇은 [두꺼운] 천 a piece of thin [thick] cloth / 천을 짜다 weave cloth / 천을 재다 measure a piece of cloth / 천을 끊다[사다] buy a piece of cloth
▶ 그 레인코트는 방수 천으로 만들었다 The slicker was made of waterproof texture.
▶ 이 천은 질깁니다 This stuff wears well.

천 千 a thousand
♦ 천에 하나 one in a thousand / 천 분의 1 a [one-]thousandth / 수천의 thousands of ((people)) / 천 단위로 계산되다 be counted by the thousand
▶ 그 축제에 매일 수천명의 사람들이 몰려들었다 People flocked in their thousands to the festival every day.
▶ 내 마음은 천 갈래 만 갈래로 찢어졌다 My heart was deeply disturbed.

천 薦 recommendation ⇨ 추천

천개 天蓋 〈관 뚜껑〉 a coffin lid; the lid of a coffin ♦ 천개를 덮다 put on [shut down] the lid of a coffin

천거 薦擧 〈추천〉 recommendation —천거하다 recommend; say [put in] a good word for

천격 賤格 〈품격〉 mean [low] character; 〈사람〉 a man of mean [low] character; a low-minded person; a mean countenance ♦ 천격스

천견 淺見 a shallow view; a superficial idea
천계 天界 the celestial world ⇨ 천상(天上) (～계)
천계 天啓 (divine) revelation; revelation [a sign] from Heaven
천고 〈태고〉 remote antiquity; 〈영원〉 eternity; all ages ♦ 천고의 명언 an unchangeable maxim; an eternal truth / 천고 불멸의 everlasting; eternal; immortal
천고마비 天高馬肥 ♦ 천고마비의 계절 the season of "high sky and plump horses"
천골 賤骨 (a person with) a mean physiognomy
천공 天功 Nature's work; work [wonders of] Nature ♦ 천공의 미 natural [scenic] beauty
천공 天空 the sky; the air; the heavens
♦ 천공을 날다 fly high in the air
천공 穿孔 perforation; boring; punching —천공하다 drill; perforate; bore; punch —기 a drill; a perforator; 〈컴퓨터 카드의〉 a key punch —카드 [電算] a punch(ed) card
천공해활 天空海闊 ♦ 천공해활의 기질 a spacious [an oceanic] mind / 천공해활이다 be serene as the sky and open as the sea; be magnanimous
천구 天球 the celestial sphere
—도(圖) a celestial map —의(儀) a celestial globe —적도 the celestial equator
천국 天國 the kingdom of Heaven [God]; Heaven; Paradise; the blessed land ♦ 천국의 heavenly / 천국에 가다 go to Heaven
■ 지상— a terrestrial [an earthly] paradise
천군만마 千軍萬馬 thousands of troops and horses ♦ 천군만마간을 왕래하다 fight [be in] many battles
천궁도 天宮圖 a horoscope ♦ 천궁도를 펼쳐 별점을 치다 cast a horoscope
천극 天極 〔天〕 the celestial poles
천금 千金 a thousand pieces of gold; 〈많은 돈〉 a lot of money
▶ 그것은 천금을 주고도 못 산다 It is a priceless treasure.
▶ 천금을 준다 해도 그것은 못하겠다 I would not do that for anything [the world].
천기 天氣 the weather ⇨ 일기(日氣), 날씨
■ 一도 a weather map [chart]
천기 天機 1 〈하늘의 기밀〉 the profound secret of Nature [Heaven]; the hidden plans of Providence 2 〈큰 기밀〉 a profound [top] secret; 〈국가의〉 a state secret
천기 喘氣 a light [mild] case of asthma
천녀 天女 a celestial nymph; a heavenly maiden
천녀 賤女 a woman of humble [low] birth
천년 千年 a thousand years; a millennium
♦ 천년만년 〈부사적〉 forever; for all eternity
천단 淺短 shallowness; superficiality
—천단하다 shallow; superficial
천단 擅斷 arbitrary decision; arbitrariness ⇨ 전단(專斷) —천단하다 decide arbitrarily; decide at *one's* discretion [on *one's* own authority]
천당 天堂 Heaven; the palace of Heaven; Paradise; the kingdom of Heaven
♦ 천당가다 go to glory [Heaven]; die
천대 賤待 (a) contemptuous [cold] treatment —천대하다 treat *sb* [*sth*] contemptuously [with contempt] ♦ 천대받다 be treated contemptuously; get the cold shoulder
천더기 賤— a despised person; a child of scorn; a poor wretch
♦ 사회의 천더기 a pariah; an outcast; an untouchable / 천더기 노릇을 하다 be treated as a child of scorn
▶ 그는 동네의 천더기다 He is the scorn of his neighbors.
천덩거리다 keep dripping messily
천덩천덩 dripping messily
—천덩천덩하다 ⇨ 천덩거리다
천도 天桃 a heavenly peach
천도 天道 1 〈천지 자연의 도리〉 the way of Heaven; Providence; the way of Providence 2 〈천체의 길〉 the orbits of heavenly bodies
천도 遷都 the transfer of the capital (to) —천도하다 transfer [remove] the capital (to); move [remove] the seat of government (to)
천도교 天道敎 the Cheondo-kyo
천동설 天動說 the Ptolemaic theory [system]; geocentricism
천둥 thunder ♦ 천둥소리 a peal [roar, roll] of thunder; cracks of thunder / 천둥치다 thunder; roll; 〈멀리서〉 grumble
▶ 멀리서 천둥 소리가 울려왔다 Rolls of thunder were heard in the distance.
▶ 밖에는 천둥 번개가 치고 있다 It is thundering and lightning outside [outdoors].
▶ 정말 대단한 천둥소리군 What a (terrific) clap of thunder!
천둥벌거숭이 a wild [reckless] fellow; an impetuous daredevil
천둥지기 paddies dependent on rain water; rain-dependent farmland
천랑성 天狼星 〔天〕 the Dog Star; Sirius
천래 天來 ♦ 천래의 heavenly; divine; inspired; heaven-sent
천량 money and food; supplies
천려 淺慮 indiscretion; thoughtlessness; lack of prudence
천려일실 千慮一失 an oversight of a wise man; a mere slip
천렵 川獵 river-fishing; fishing in a river —천렵하다 fish in a river [brook]
천루 賤陋 baseness; meanness; lowness; abjectness; vulgarity —천루하다 base; mean; low; abject; vulgar; nasty
천륜 天倫 Natural Law; the natural relationships of man; moral law ♦ 천륜에서 벗어난 짓을 하다 transgress Natural Law
천리 千里 a thousand *ri*; 〈비유〉 a long distance ■ 一마 a fine [swift] horse
천리 天理 natural laws; the laws of nature
♦ 천리에 어긋나다 violate the laws of nature; go against nature
천리안 千里眼 〈투시〉 clairvoyance; 〈통찰력〉 an insight; penetration
♦ 천리안을 가진 사람 〈남자〉 a clairvoyant;

〈여자〉 a clairvoyante / 천리안을 가지고 있다 have [possess] clairvoyant powers; be gifted with second sight

천릿길도 한 걸음부터 〈속담〉 A journey of a thousand miles starts with but a single step. ⇌ Step after step the ladder is ascended. ⇌ He who would climb the ladder must begin at the bottom.

천마 天馬 〈나는 말〉 a flying horse; 〔그神〕 Pegasus; 〈명마〉 a fine steed

천막 天幕 a tent; 〈배의〉 an awning; (총칭) tentage ◆ 천막을 치다 pitch [set up] a tent / 천막을 걷다 strike [pull down] a tent
■ 一生活 camping; camping-out: 천막 생활을 하다 camp out —존 a tent [camp] village

천만 千萬 〈1천만〉 ten million; 〈무수〉 a countless number; a myriad; 〈매우〉 exceedingly; extremely; very much
◆ 수천만의 tens of millions of (locusts) / …은 유감 천만이다 it is really regrettable that…; it is much to be regretted that…; it is a thousand pities that…
▶ 유감 천만이었으나 그 제의를 사절했다 I declined the offer with much regret [many regrets].
■ 一古(古) remote [great] antiquity; most ancient times; 〈영원〉 eternity —金 ⇨ 천금 —년[세(歲)] ten million years; myriad years; a long long time —사(事) ⇨ 만사 —세(世) / 만세(萬世) —인 millions of people; so many people —장자 a billionaire; a multimillionaire

천만 喘滿 〔韓醫〕〈천식〉 asthma; 〈헐떡거림〉 pursiness; panting

천만다행 千萬多幸 great good fortune [luck]; a stroke of good luck — 천만다행하다 extremely fortunate; very lucky ◆ 천만다행히 very fortunately [luckily]; by good fortune [luck]
▶ 천만다행히도 내 시도는 성공했다 I was fortunate enough to succeed in my attempt.

천만뜻밖 千萬— being quite unexpected
◆ 천만뜻밖의 일 the last thing that one thinks of [expects]; a great surprise; a bolt from the blue / 천만뜻밖의 quite unexpected; least expected; unlooked-for; unforeseen; unanticipated; never dreamed of / 천만뜻밖에 quite unexpectedly; beyond [contrary to] one's expectation; surprisingly enough; 〈갑자기〉 (all) of a sudden
▶ 너를 여기서 만나다니 천만뜻밖이다 It's quite a surprise to see you here.
▶ 그가 성공하다니 천만뜻밖이다 His success is really surprising.

천만번 千萬番 ten million times; 〈부사적〉 ever so many times; over and over again
▶ 너 따위는 천만번 죽어 마땅하다 Thousands of death are too good for the likes of you.

천만부당 千萬不當 being utterly [absolutely] unjust ◆ 천부당만부당 (千不當萬不當)

천만의말씀 千萬— 〈당찮은〉 an inappropriate remark; a remark wide of the mark; 〈과분한〉 an undeserved compliment [courtesy]
▶ 천만의 말씀입니다 Not at all. ⇌ Oh! Don't mention it. ⇌ You're welcome.

천만층 千萬層 all classes [strata, levels]; every kind [sort, variety]
▶ 세상이란 천만층이다 It takes all sorts of people to make the world.

천명 天命 1 〈하늘의 뜻〉 God's will; Heaven's decree; 〈운명〉 fate
◆ 천명을 알다[좇다] submit to Heaven's will; resign oneself to one's fate / 최선을 다하고 천명을 기다리다 do one's best and leave the rest to Heaven
▶ 이렇게 된 것도 천명이다 It has been ordained by Providence.
2 〈수명〉 one's natural span of life
◆ 천명이 다하다 come to one's journey's end; pay out the debt of nature

천명 闡明 clarification; elucidation —천명하다 make clear; explain; elucidate; clarify ◆ 안팎에 천명하다 affirm before [declare to] the world

천문 天文 〈현상〉 astronomical phenomena; 〈천문학〉 astronomy; 〈점성술〉 astrology
◆ 천문을 보다 make astronomical observations; study the stars; 〈점성술로〉 cast a horoscope
■ 一년[일, 시, 조석(潮夕)] astronomical year [day, time, tide] —단위 an astronomical unit —대 an astronomical observatory —도(圖) an astronomical chart

천문동 天門冬 〔韓醫〕 the root of a kind of asparagus

천문학 天文學 astronomy ◆ 천문학적 숫자에 달하다 reach into astronomical figures
■ 一자 an astronomer

천민 賤民 (총칭) lowly [humble] people; the lowly; the humble; low-class people

천방지축 天方地軸 rashness; recklessness; harum-scarumness; 〈덤벙댐〉 rashly; recklessly; harum-scarum; headlong; foolhardily
◆ 천방지축 덤비다[날뛰다] rush recklessly; make a headlong [foolhardy] rush

천배 千倍 a thousand times; a thousandfold
◆ 천배로 하다 increase sth a thousandfold

천벌 天罰 Heaven's vengeance [judgment]; divine punishment [retribution]; the punishment of Heaven; the wrath [scourge] of God; divine wrath ◆ 천벌을 받다 incur the wrath of Heaven; be punished by Heaven
▶ 그는 천벌을 받아 싸다 He deserves divine punishment.
▶ 그것은 거짓말을 한 천벌이다 It is a judgment on you for having lied.

천변 川邊 a riverside; a streamside; a riverbank ◆ 천변에(서) at the side of a river [stream]; at the riverside [streamside]

천변만화 千變萬化 innumerable [kaleidoscopic] changes; an endless series of changes; immense variety
—천변만화하다 change endlessly; make kaleidoscopic changes
◆ 천변만화하는 ever-changing / 천변만화하는 세상 the kaleidoscopic world

천변지이 天變地異 extraordinary phenomena in heaven and earth; a natural disaster [calamity]; a convulsion of nature

천병만마 千兵萬馬 a great host of mounted and foot soldiers; a mighty army; horse and foot

천보 賤— (a) mean nature; low behavior; bad manners

천복 天福 Heaven's blessing; benediction
♦ 천복을 받다 be blessed by Heaven

천부 天賦 natural; native; inborn; innate; inherent / 천부의 인권 natural [inherent] rights of man / 천부의 재능 a natural gift; an inherent talent; a gift of nature
▶ 그녀는 음악에 천부의 재능이 있다 She is endowed with musical talent. ⇒ She has a natural talent [gift] for music.

천부 賤夫 a man of lowly [humble] birth

천부당만부당 千不當萬不當 being utterly [absolutely] unjust
—천부당만부당하다 utterly [absolutely] unjust [unreasonable, unjustified]
♦ 천부당만부당한 소리 an absolutely [unreasonable] remark; an utterly inappropriate remark
▶ 그것은 천부당만부당한 비난이다 The reproach is quite unjust.

천분 天分 one's natural gifts [talents, endowments]
♦ 천분이 있는 사람 a talented [gifted] man / 천분이 있다 be talented [gifted]; be endowed with talents (for) / 천분이 없다 be untalented; be endowed with no genius / 천분을 타고나다 be born with talents / 천분을 발휘하다 give full play to one's natural endowments / 천분을 개발시키다 develop one's natural talent

천사 天使 an angel; a herald of God; (총칭) hierarchy
♦ 천사같은 소녀 an angel of a girl / 천사 같은 웃음 an angelic smile / 천사의 무리 a flight of angels; the host of heaven / 천사의 계급 the angelic order / 천사같은 angelic; seraphic
■ 대— an archangel 수호— a guardian angel
■ —장 an archangel

천사슬 天— leaving sth to take [run, follow] its own [natural] course; letting nature take her course; doing things nature's way

천산갑 穿山甲 (動) a pangolin; a scaly anteater

천산물 天産物 natural products; (총칭) natural produce ♦ 갖가지 천산물이 풍부하다 be rich in natural products of all kinds

천산지산 lengthily excusing oneself; with all sorts of excuses ♦ 핑계를 천산지산 늘어 놓다 make [produce, invent, come out with] all sorts of excuses (for)

천상 天上 the heavens ♦ 천상의 heavenly; celestial; etereal / 천상으로부터 from above [heaven, on high]
▶ 천상천하 유아독존 I am my own Lord throughout heaven and earth.
■ —계 the celestial [heavenly] world

천상 天象 an astronomical phenomenon; the aspect of the heavens
■ —의(儀) a planetarium

천상바라기 天上— a person with an upturned face

천생 天生 1 〈타고남〉 nature ♦ 천생의 natural; born / 천생의 음악가 a born musician
2 〈부사적〉 by nature; naturally; 〈두고두고〉 as [for] ever
▶ 그는 천생 학자가 될 운명이었다 He was destined [fitted] from birth for the scholar.
■ —배필 a match made in Heaven; a Heaven-made match; a predestined couple —연분 predestined [Heaven-ordained] relation

천석꾼 千石— a wealthy farmer (who harvests 1,000 sŏk of rice)

천성 天性 (one's) nature; one's innate disposition [character, temperament]
♦ 인간의 천성 human nature / 천성적인 쾌활성 one's native cheerfulness / 천성의[적인] natural; inborn; innate / 천성이 정직하다 be honest by nature
▶ 그녀는 천성이 누구에게나 친절하다 She is kind to everybody by nature.
▶ 그의 게으름은 천성이다 His idleness is bred in the bone.
▶ 그는 천성이 나쁜 사람은 아니다 He is not really bad at heart [bottom].
▶ 습관은 제2의 천성이다 (속담) Habit is (a) second nature.

천세 千歲 a thousand years; a millennium; eternity ♦ 천세만세까지 forever and ever; through all ages / 천세에 이름을 남기다 win (an) immortal fame; immortalize one's name
■ —력(曆) a perpetual calendar

천세나다 be much in demand; become scarce; run short

천수 天水 rainwater ■ —답 ⇨ 천둥지기

천수 天壽 one's natural span of life (⇨ 천명 (天命)) ♦ 천수를 다하다 live out one's life; complete the natural span of life; die a natural death

천수 天數 1 one's natural span of life ⇨ 천명 (天命) 2 〈천운〉 fate; destiny

천시 天時 1 〈기회〉 a heaven-appointed time; a time of providence [Heaven] ♦ 천시를 기다리다 wait upon such times as Heaven should appoint
2 〈자연현상〉 the times and seasons

천식 喘息 (醫) asthma
■ —환자 an asthmatic (patient)

천신 天神 the heavenly gods ■ —지기(地祇) the gods of heaven and earth

천신 薦新 〈신에게 올림〉 offering the first harvest of the season to gods; 〈굿〉 a shamanist rite in spring [autumn]
—천신하다 offer the first harvest [crop, fruits] of the season to gods; have a spring [an autumn] shamanist rite

천신만고 千辛萬苦 indescribable hardships; intense application
▶ 그는 다년간의 천신만고 끝에 그 발명을 완성하였다 He has consummated his invention after years of intense application.
—천신만고하다 experience [go through] all kinds of hardships; make intense application

천심 天心 1 〈하늘의 복판〉 the zenith
▶ 달이 천심에 걸렸다 The moon is at [has reached] its zenith.

2 〈하늘의 뜻〉 the will of Heaven
▶민심은 천심이다 The voice of the people is the voice of God.

천안 天顔 the King's visage; the Emperor's [Imperial] countenance
◆천안을 뵙다 〈배알하다〉 be received in audience by [be presented to] the King [Emperor, His Majesty]

천안문 天安門 〈중국 북경의〉 *Tienanmen* Gate; Gate of Heavenly Peace
■—광장 *Tienanmen* Square

천앙 天殃 Divine retribution; Heaven's punishment

천애 天涯 **1** 〈하늘 끝〉 the horizon
2 〈먼 곳〉 a far-off country; a remote region; a distant land ◆천애의 고아 a lonely orphan / 천애 고아의 신세다 have no relatives

천야만야하다 天野萬野— 〈높다〉 lofty; sky-high; 〈깊다〉 unfathomable ◆천야만야한 계곡 an unfathomable ravine; an abyss

천양 天壤 heaven and earth
■—지간 the space between heaven and earth; the whole universe —지판 ⇨ 천양지차

천양지차 天壤之差 a world of difference; extreme opposition; poles apart
◆천양지차(가 있)다 there is a world of difference (between); be poles apart; be (as) different as light from darkness [as day from night, as chalk from cheese]
▶그들 사이에는 천양지차가 있다 There is all the difference (in the world) between them.

천언만어 千言萬語 innumerable [countless] words; endless expressions

천업 賤業 a discreditable [mean] occupation; a dishonorable [shameful] calling [trade]

천여 天與 a gift of Heaven; a heaven's gift; a godsend ◆천여의 Heaven-sent; godsent; providential / 천여의 자원이 풍부하다 be rich in natural resources

천역 賤役 a mean job [service]; dishonorable work

천연 天然 **1** 〈자생〉 spontaneity
◆천연의 natural; unartificial; native; 〈자생의〉 spontaneous; 〈야생의〉 wild; 〈타고난〉 natural; innate; inborn; congenital / 천연의 아름다움 natural beauty; the beauty of nature / 천연(적)으로 naturally; unartificially; in nature; spontaneous
▶금은 천연으로 산출된다 Gold occurs in nature.
2 〈부사적〉 just [exactly] (like); much [nearly] as; as if
▶그는 천연 제 아버지다 He is the very [exact] image of his father.
■—가스 natural gas: 액화 천연가스 liquefied natural gas (略 LNG) —기념물 a natural monument —물 a natural object [substance]; the natural form (of *sth*) —석 native rock —수 natural water —자원 natural resources

천연 遷延 delay; postponement —천연하다 delay; put off; postpone ◆일을 천연하다 delay *one's* work

천연두 天然痘 (the) smallpox ⇨ 마마²
■—균 a smallpox germ [virus] —환자 a case of smallpox

천연색 天然色 (a) natural color; (商標) [映] technicolor ■—사진 a color photograph —영화 a color [technicolor] movie —텔레비전 a color television

천연스럽다 天然— **1** 〈자연스럽다〉 natural; unartificial; 〈꾸밈이 없다〉 unaffected; 〈그럴싸하다〉 looking like the truth
◆천연스러운 자세 a natural posture / 천연스레 거짓말하다 tell a clever lie; tell a lie that sounds like truth
2 〈태연하다〉 calm; cool; unmoved; 〈무관심하다〉 unconcerned; indifferent
◆천연스럽게 calmly; coolly; as if nothing had happened; with an innocent look; unconcernedly
▶그는 천연스럽게 그렇게 말했다 He said so as if nothing had been the matter with him.

천엽 千葉 **1** 〈복엽〉 a compound leaf ◆천엽의 double(-petaled) **2** ⇨ 처녑
■—벚꽃 double cherry blossoms

천왕성 天王星 〔天〕 Uranus

천왕지팡이 天王— a tall lank man; a lamppost; (美) a gangling fellow; (美俗) a high-pockets

천우신조 天佑神助 God's [providential] help; special Providence; heavenly assistance; the grace of Heaven [God]
◆천우신조의 providential / 천우신조로 by the grace of God [Heaven]
▶내가 다치지 않은 것은 천우신조였다 There was Providence in my getting off unhurt.
▶네가 살아난 것은 정말 천우 신조다 You must bless your stars that you have escaped!

천운 天運 fate; destiny; the will of Heaven; Providence ◆천운으로 여기고 체념하다 resign *oneself* to fate / 천운에 맡기다 trust to Providence [Heaven]; leave *one's* fate to Heaven / 천운을 감사하다 thank [bless] *one's* stars 《for》

천은 天恩 **1** 〈하느님 은혜〉 the grace of God [Heaven]; divine grace [favor]; heavenly blessing ◆천은으로 by the grace of Heaven
2 ⇨ 성은(聖恩)

천의 天意 the will of Heaven; the divine will; Providence; Heaven's decree [will]
◆천의에 따르다 obey [follow, bow to] the will of Heaven [Providence]

천의무봉 天衣無縫 perfect beauty with no trace of artifice ◆천의무봉이다 be natural and flawless; 〈사람이〉 be a man of artless and unaffected character

천인 天人 〈하늘과 사람〉 God and man
▶그는 천인공노할 죄를 저질렀다 He has sinned against God and man.

천인 賤人 a lowly man; a person of humble [low] birth [origin]

천일야화 千一夜話 *The Thousand and One Nights*; *The Arabian Nights' Entertainments*

천일염 天日鹽 bay salt; sun-dried salt

천일초 千日草 〔植〕 a globe amaranth

천자 天子 a son of Heaven; an emperor

천자 天資 nature; natural constitution; a natural endowment ◆천자가 영매하다 be endowed with great talents [high intelligence]; be highly gifted

천자만태 千姿萬態 an endless variety of forms; multifariousness
♦ 천자만태의 multifarious

천자만홍 千紫萬紅 a dazzling variety of beautiful flowers
▶ 정원에는 꽃들이 천자만홍으로 피어 있다 The garden is a riot of colors with a variety of flowers in full glory.

천자문 千字文 the Thousand-Character Text; a primer of Chinese characters

천잠 天蠶 〔昆〕 a wild silkworm ■ 一사(絲) tussah

천장 天— the ceiling
♦ 둥근 천장 a vault; a dome / 천장 모르게 뛰어오르는 물가 skyrocketing prices / 천장이 높다[낮다] be high-[low-]ceil(ing)ed; have a high [low] ceiling / 천장에 매달려 있다 be hanging from the ceiling
■ 반자— a boarded ceiling ―등(燈) an overhead [a ceiling] light ―선풍기 a ceiling fan

천재 天才 〈재능〉 genius; natural gift [talent, endowment]; 〈사람〉 a (man of) genius; a prodigy; (口) a wizard
♦ 세상에서 인정 받지 못한 천재 an ignored genius / 수학의 천재 a genius in mathematics / 천재의 번득임 a flash of genius / 천재(적인) 화가 a born artist; an artistic genius / 천재적인 talented; gifted / 천재를 십분 발휘하다 bring *one's* genius into full play; give full play [swing, scope] to *one's* genius
▶ 그녀는 어학의 천재였다 She was a born linguist.
▶ 그는 천재적인 데가 있다 He has a touch of genius.
▶ 그의 천재는 어려서 이미 드러났다 His genius early asserted itself.
▶ 천재는 노력이다 Genius is a capacity for taking pains. ⇒ Genius means hard work.
▶ 천재와 바보는 종이 한 장 차이다 (속담) Extremes meet.
■ 一교육 genius education; the education of gifted children ―아 an infant prodigy; a gifted child; (美) a boy [girl] wonder; a budding genius

천재 天災 a natural calamity [disaster]; 〈불가항력〉 an act of God ♦ 천재를 당하다 be visited [hit] by a natural calamity; meet with disaster
■ 一지변 a natural disaster [calamity]; the disturbances of the elements

천재일우 千載一遇 the chance of a lifetime; a very rare opportunity ♦ 천재일우의 호기를 놓치다 throw away a golden [rare] opportunity; lose the chance of a lifetime

천적 天敵 〔生〕 a natural enemy

천정 天頂 〔天〕 the zenith; the vertex
■ 一거리 the zenith distance ―의(儀) a zenith telescope ―점 the zenith

천정부지 天井不知 skyrocketing ♦ 천정부지의 시세 a soaring [skyrocketing] price
▶ 물가가 천정부지로 오르고 있다 Prices are being boosted to sky. ⇒ Prices are skyrocketing.

천제 天帝 the Lord of Heaven; God; Heaven; the Creator

천조 天助 Heaven's [providential] help; help from above [Heaven]; special Providence

천조 踐祚 accession (to the throne) ♦ 천조식을 거행하다 perform an accession ceremony ―천조하다 ascend [accede to] the throne

천주 天主 the Lord of Heaven; God; (라) Deus ―경(經) the Lord's Prayer; 《say》a pater [paternoster] ―삼위 the Trinity ―십계 the Ten Commandments, the Decalog(ue)

천주 天誅 〈천벌〉 Heaven's punishment; punishment from on high; 〈하늘을 대신하는 벌〉 well-deserved punishment
♦ 천주를 가하다 inflict just punishment 《on *sb*》 / 천주를 받다 be punished by Heaven

천주교 天主敎 (Roman) Catholicism; Romanism ■ 一국(國) a Catholic nation ―도 a (Roman) Catholic ―신부 a (Roman) Catholic father ―회 the (Roman) Catholic Church

천지 天地 1 〈하늘과 땅〉 heaven and earth; the heavens and the earth; 〈우주〉 the universe; 〈자연〉 nature
♦ 천지의 of heaven and earth; universal; mundane / 천지의 진동 a convulsion of nature; the disturbances of the elements / 천지를 진동시키다 〈위업 등으로〉 shake the sphere [heaven and earth]; make the whole world wonder; 〈음향 등이〉 rend the air
▶ 양자 사이에는 천지의 차가 있다 They are poles asunder [worlds apart]. ⇒ There is a world of difference between the two.
▶ 천지를 뒤흔드는 함성이 일어났다 There arose a tumultuous shouting, seeming to rend the very sky.
2 〈장소·세계〉 a land; a world; a realm; a sphere; a stage
♦ 새 천지 a new world / 자유의 천지 a free land; the land of freedom / 새 천지를 개척하다 open up a new field [sphere] of activity; break new [fresh] ground
▶ 그곳은 아주 별천지다 The place makes a world of its own.
3 〈많음〉 (an) abundance; (a) plenty; (an) opulence; richness
▶ 그곳은 관광객 천지다 The place swarms with tourists. ⇒ The district is overflowing [crowded] with tourists.
■ 一만물 universal [all] nature; the universe; the creation; all creatures ―창조 the Creation

천지개벽 天地開闢 1 〈창조〉 the Creation (of Heaven and Earth); the beginning of the world
♦ 천지개벽 이래의 사건 an unprecedented event / 천지개벽 이래 since the beginning [creation] of the world; since the dawn of history
―천지개벽하다 create heaven and earth
2 〈대변혁〉 a cataclysmic change; an upheaval; a revolution ―천지개벽하다 undergo a cataclysmic change; revolutionize

천지신명 天地神明 the gods of heaven and

earth ♦천지신명께 맹세하다 swear by the gods of heaven and earth

천직 天職 a mission; a vocation; a calling; one's divinely appointed work in life
♦목사를 천직으로 알다 feel a call to the ministry / 천직을 찾아내다 find out one's mission
▶이것이 내 천직이다 Heaven has called me to this work.
▶사람마다 천직이 있다 God has a plan for every life.

천진난만 天眞爛漫 naiveté; naivety; simplicity; artlessness; innocence
—천진난만하다 naive; unaffected; artless; innocent; simple-hearted[-minded]; unsophisticated; ingenuous
♦천진난만한 미소 an innocent smile / 천진난만한 어린이 a simple and innocent child / 천진난만한 태도 an unaffected air; an unsophisticated attitude
▶그녀에게는 어딘지 천진난만한 데가 있다 She has something innocent about her.
▶그녀는 항상 천진난만하게 말한다 She always talks like a child.

천차만별 千差萬別 infinite variety
♦천차만별의 multifarious; motley; of various kinds; an infinite variety of; in a thousand different ways / 천차만별의 계급 infinite gradation of ranks / 천차만별의 사람 all sorts of people; various kinds of people
▶사람의 마음은 천차만별이다 So many men, so many minds.

천착 穿鑿 〈학문 등의〉 digging into; inquiry; search; pursuit; scrutiny
—천착하다 dig [pry, delve] into; inquire into; make inquiries into; search; seek [look] for; pursue; scrutinize; rake; ransack; poke and pry

천착스럽다 舛錯— crooked; mean ⇨ 천착하다 ♦천착스러운 사람 a disagreeable [a nasty, an odious] fellow; a low-minded person

천착하다 舛錯— 〈심정이〉 crooked; crabbed; perverse and disorderly; untoward; cross-grained; ill-natured; 〈생김새·행동이〉 vulgar; low; indecent; ugly; base; mean; sordid
♦천착한 얼굴 an ugly face; vulgar features / 천착한 말씨 a vulgar (way of) expression

천창 天窓 a skylight; a scuttle; 〈갑판의〉 a companion

천천하다 slow; tardy; unhurried; leisurely

천천히 〈느리게〉 slowly; without haste [hurry]; 〈한가롭게〉 leisurely; deliberately; in a leisurely manner [way]; at (one's) leisure; by easy stages
♦(일을) 천천히 하다 take one's time (in doing) / 천천히 걷다 walk leisurely; walk at a leisurely pace / 천천히 이야기하다 speak slowly; speak leisurely / 천천히 식사하다 eat leisurely; take one's time with the meal / 천천히 여행하다 make a leisurely trip; travel by easy stages
▶열차는 천천히 출발했다 The train started slowly.
▶교통 혼잡 때문에 차들은 천천히 움직였다 Because of the traffic jam vehicles were moving at a snail's pace.
▶그 일은 천천히 생각해도 좋습니다 You may think over the matter at your leisure.

천첩 賤妾 1 〈첩〉 a concubine of low birth [origin] **2** 〈부인의 자칭〉 I

천체 天體 a heavenly [celestial] body; a celestial sphere [object]; an orb
♦천체를 관측하다 observe (the) heavenly bodies; make an astronomical observation; survey the starry heavens
■—관측 an astronomical observation —도(圖) a celestial map —망원경 an astronomical telescope —물리학 astronomical physics; astrophysics —물리학 관측소 an astrophysical observatory —물리학자 an astrophysicist —사진 the photograph of a star [heavenly body] —사진술 astrophotography; stellar photography —역학 celestial mechanics —운동 the movements of heavenly bodies —측량 uranometry —학 uranography; uranology

천추 千秋 〈천년〉 a thousand years; 〈긴 세월〉 many years
♦천추의 한(恨) a matter of great regret / 이름을 천추에 남기다 win (an) immortal fame / 하루가 천추같이 기다려지다 wait impatiently for sb; look eagerly forward to sth; await 《sb's arrival》 on tiptoe

천축 天竺 〈인도〉 India

천출 賤出 a child born of a concubine of low birth [origin]

천치 天癡·天痴 an idiot; an imbecile; a moron; a natural ▶이 바보 천치야 You damned [champion] idiot! ⇌ You big [bloody] fool!

천칭 天秤 a balance ⇨ 천평칭(天平秤)

천칭 賤稱 a derogatory term; a depreciatory term [word, name] —천칭하다 call by a depreciatory term

천태만상 千態萬象 all sorts of forms and figures; a great diversity in form and figure; multifariousness

천트다 薦— **1** 〈추천받다〉 be [get] recommended [commended] 《for》
2 〈손대다〉 turn one's hand to; attempt; embark on 《a new business》

천편일률 千篇一律 monotony; humdrumness; lack of variety ♦천편일률의 dull; monotonous; humdrum; stereotyped / 천편일률적이 되다 get [fall] into a groove
▶그녀는 천편일률적인 말만 한다 She always harps on one [the same] string.

천평칭 天平秤 a balance; a pair of scales
♦천평칭에 달다 weigh sth in the balance [on the scale] ■—비중— a specific-gravity balance 화학— a chemical balance

천품 天稟 〈성품〉 nature; 〈재질〉 a natural endowment; natural talents
♦천품이 뛰어나다 be endowed with high intelligence [great talents] / 천품을 발휘하다 display one's natural talents

천하 天下 〈세계〉 the world; the universe; the earth; 〈전국〉 the whole country [land, realm]; 〈세상〉 the public; the world

♦천하 없어도 whatever happens; under [in] any circumstances / 천하 없이 without parallel; unrivaled / 천하 무적이다 have no rival [be unrivaled] in the world
▶지금은 그의 천하다 He is now in power.
▶천하가 태평하다 Peace reigns over the land. ⇒ Peace is everywhere.
▶천하 없는 학자도 그것은 모른다 The best scholar does not know it.
〈천하의〉 천하의 공론 public opinion / 천하의 대세 the general situation of the world; the trend of the international affairs / 천하의 영웅 the greatest hero ever known
▶그는 천하의 형세를 살폈다 He observed the situation [trend] of public affairs.
〈천하를〉 천하를 다스리다 govern [reign over] the whole country / 천하를 호령하다 dictate to the world / 천하를 얻다 conquer [rule, reign over] the whole country; 〈정권을 잡다〉 come to power; get into power; hold the reins of government; become the ruler of the country / 천하를 잃다 be out of power; drop the reins of government / 천하를 통일하다 unify a country; bring the whole country under *one's* rule [sway]; make *oneself* master of the realm
▶그가 천하를 얻은 것은 300년도 훨씬 전의 일이였다 It was as long as three hundred years ago that he conquered [subdued] the whole country.
〈천하에〉 천하에 under the sun; under heaven; in the world; on earth / 천하에 둘도 없는 unique; beyond comparison / 천하에 이름을 떨치다 make a noise [name] in the world; spread *one's* name around the world; become world-famous
▶그는 천하에 이름을 떨쳤다 He made a name in the world.
▶그는 그때 자기를 당할 자는 천하에 없다고 호언했다 He then boasted that he had no rival in the world.
♦이 산은 아름답기로 천하에 알려져 있다 This mountain is world-famous for its beauty.
■—명창 one of the greatest [most excellent] singers in the world; a world-famous [world-renowned] singer —일색 a woman of matchless [peerless] beauty; the fairest of the fair

천하다 賤— **1** 〈비천하다〉 humble; low; lowly; ignoble; obscure; low-born
♦천한 직업 a mean [humble] occupation / 천한 몸 a person of humble [ignoble] birth / 천한 신분 a lowly [humble] station in life; a low social position [standing, status]
2 〈비열하다〉 base; mean; despicable; vile; bastard(ly); low-minded; dirty; ignoble
♦천한 짓 a mean [an ignoble] action
3 〈상스럽다〉 vulgar; base; mean; low; gross; rude; beastly
♦천한 말씨 a vulgar (way of) expression / 천한 티 a vulgar streak / 천한 풍속 base manners / 근성이 천한 mean-spirited
4 〈혼하다〉 plenty; superfluous; 〈값 싸다〉 cheap; low(-priced)

▶요즈음은 천한 것이 수박이다 Watermelons are very cheap these days.

천하장사 天下壯士 the strongest man in the world; a man of Herculean strength; a Hercules; an Atlas
▶그는 힘이 천하장사다 He is a pillar of strength [a very powerful man]. ⇒ He has strength of a horse [lion].

천학 淺學 shallow learning; superficial knowledge
♦천학비재(菲才) 하오나 though I make no account of myself; although I have no pretensions either to learning or ability; in spite of my lack of knowledge and ability

천행 天幸 the blessing [grace, help] of Heaven [God]; (a piece [stroke] of) good luck [fortune]; a godsend
♦천행으로 by (a stroke of) good luck; as good luck would have it / 천행으로 …하다 have the (good) fortune to 《do》; be lucky enough to 《do》

천험 天險 a natural stronghold [barrier for defense]

천형 天刑 divine punishment ■—병 leprosy

천혜 天惠 Heaven's blessing; a gift of nature; natural advantage; God's favor ♦천혜가 풍부한 나라 a country blessed with [rich in] natural resources

천후 天候 the weather ♦전천후 비행기 an all-weather airplane

철¹ 〈계절〉 a season; the time of the year
♦철 따라 피는 꽃 flowers of the season / 철 늦은 사과 late apples; apples behind the season / 철 이른 사과 early apples / 제철이 아닌 unseasonable; out of season; off-season / 철에 상관없이 in all seasons; all the year (round); in and out of season / 철이 바뀔 때 a change [turning point] of season / 철이 바뀌다 a season changes; the seasons change / 제철을 만나다 〈사람이〉 be in *one's* heyday [prime]; be in *one's* palmy days; be in *one's* element
▶경치는 철 따라 바뀐다 The scenery varies from season to season.
▶굴은 지금이 제철이다 Oysters are now in season (for the table). ⇒ It is the season for oysters now.

철² 〈분별〉 discretion; judgment; prudence; wisdom; good sense
♦철이 들 나이 the age of discretion / 철이 들고 나서부터 from *one's* earliest recollection; ever since *one* could remember / 철이 들다 [나다] know better; become possessed of discretion; attain [reach] the age of discretion; cut *one's* wisdom teeth / 철도 들기 전에 아버지를 여의다 lose *one's* father while still a little child
▶그는 아직 철이 덜 들었다 He is still immature in his way of thinking. ⇒ He has not yet arrived at the age of discretion.
▶이젠 좀 철이 나야지 You ought to know better now.

철 鐵 iron; 〈강철〉 steel ♦철의 ferrous; ferric / 철을 함유한 containing iron; ferrous; ferriferous (rocks, soil)

-철 綴 a file ◆서류철 a file of documents [papers] / 신문철 a newspaper file; a file of newspapers

철각 鐵脚 iron legs ◆철각을 자랑하는 선수 a runner of the iron legs

철갑 鐵甲 〈갑옷〉 iron armor; 〈칠갑〉 a coating; a crust ■—선 an ironclad (ship)

철갑상어 鐵甲— 〔魚〕 a sturgeon ◆철갑상어의 알젓 caviar(e)

철강 鐵鋼 steel ■—업 the steel industry —제품 steel manufactures

철거 撤去 removal; demolition; dismantlement ◆빈민굴의 철거 the clearing of slums / 무허가 판잣집의 철거 the removal of illegally built shacks
—철거하다 remove; clear (away); demolish; pull [take] down; dismantle
◆장애물을 철거하다 remove the obstacles; clear (the passage) of obstacles / 시설을 철거하다 dismantle [take away] facilities

철겹다 be behind the season; be out of season; be unseasonable; be off-season
◆철겹게 핀 꽃 a blossom out of season; a flower coming out unseasonably / 철겨운 날씨 unsettled [crazy] weather

철골 a skinny [bony, thin, meager, emaciated] appearance ◆철골이 되다 become emaciated [skinny]; be reduced [waste away] to a mere skeleton [skin and bones]

철골 鐵骨 〈철근〉a steel [an iron] frame; a steel skeleton; 〈튼튼한 몸〉 a strongly-built physique ◆철골로 조립하다 build with an iron frame
■—건축물 a steel-frame[-skeleton] building —공사 steel-frame work —구조 a cage; steel-frame structure; skeleton construction

철공 鐵工 an ironworker; an ironsmith
—소[장] an ironworks: 철공소 주인 an ironmaster

철관 鐵管 an iron tube [pipe] ◆철관이 터지다 an iron pipe bursts / 철관을 묻다 lay iron pipes

철광 鐵鑛 〈광석〉 iron ore; 〈광산〉 an iron mine

철교 鐵橋 an iron bridge; 〈철도의〉 a railway bridge ◆철교를 놓다 construct [build] a railway bridge (over)

철군 撤軍 withdrawl [removal] of troops; military withdrawal; evacuation
◆철군의 규모와 일정 the size and timetable of the pullout (of the troops)
—철군하다 withdraw troops 《from a place》; evacuate 《a place》; pull troops out 《of a place》; pull out

철권 鐵拳 a (clenched) fist
◆철권을 먹이다 fist; strike sb with one's fist; use one's fists (on) / 철권을 휘두르다 shake one's fist 《at sb, in another's face》
—정치 ironfisted rule

철권제재 鐵拳制裁; 〈英俗〉toco
◆철권제재를 가하다 administer fist-law [toco] to sb

철궤 鐵軌 an iron rail; a rail

철근 鐵筋 〔建〕 a [an iron] reinforcing rod [bar] ■—콘크리트 ferroconcrete; reinforced concrete: 철근 콘크리트 건물 a ferroconcrete building

철기 鐵器 ironware; hardware; ironmongery ■—시대 the Iron Age

철끈 綴— a binding string [strip]

철도 鐵道 a railway; 《美》 a railroad; a railroad line
◆철도의 운행 operation of railways; 《美》 railroading / 철도를 부설하다 construct [build, lay, make] a railway (line) / 철도로 여행하다 travel by rail [train]
▶ 서울에서 목포까지 철도가 통해 있다 A railroad runs from Seoul to Mokp'o.
▶ 10년 전까지는 이 도시에 철도가 없었다 There was no railraod service in this town until ten years ago.
▶ 이 도시에는 불원간 철도가 통하게 된다 The city will soon be brought into railway communications.
—경편— a light railway 고가— an elevated [overhead] railroad 고속— a high-speed railroad 관광— a scenic railway 광궤[협궤]— a broad-gauge [narrow-gauge] railroad 교외— a suburban railway 국유— a government [state] railway 군용— a military [strategic] railway 단선[복선]— a single-track [double-track] railroad 사설— a private railroad 전기— an electric railway 증기— a steam railway ■—경비대 a railway (guard) corps; railway guards —공사 railway (construction) work —공안원 a railway public peace officer; (총칭) the railway police —기관사 《美》 a locomotive engineer; 《英》 an engine driver on the railway —기사 (技師) a railway engineer —망 a network [system] of railways; a railway network —병원 a hospital for railroad employees —사고[참사] a railway accident [disaster] —수송 transportation by rail; railway transportation; 《美》 railroading —왕 a railway magnate —우편 the railway post service —운임[요금] 〈여객의〉 railway fare; 〈화물의〉 freight [goods] rates; freight-age —인도 (引渡) ex rail —청 (Korean) National Railroad Administration —행정 railway administration —화물 (貨物) railway goods; 《美》 freight

철도부설 鐵道敷設 the construction [building] of railways; 《美》 railroading —권 a railway charter; railway building concession

철도선로 鐵道線路 a railway [railroad] track; a (railway) line; (총칭) trackage —보수공 a trackman; a linesman

철도여객 鐵道旅客 a railway [railroad] passenger —운임 a railway [railroad] fare —운임표 a railroad tariff

철도여행 鐵道旅行 railway traveling; a railway journey; 《美》 railroading ■—자 a rail traveler

철도종업원 鐵道從業員 《美》 a railroader; 《美》 a railroad man [worker, employe(e)]
—조합 a rail [railroad] union

철도편 鐵道便 transportation by rail ◆철도편으로 per [by] rail; by train; by freight

철도

1. 미국·영국의 철도

　영국의 철도는 런던 주변의 일부 지하철(tube)을 제외하고는 국유이고 영국 국철은 British Rail이라고 한다. 미국에는 사철(私鐵)이 많은데 철도의 만성적 적자를 해소하기 위해 정부 주도로 전미 철도여객 수송 공사(National Railroad Passenger Corporation), 통칭 암트락(Amtrak) (▶American travel by track의 약어)을 설립하여 전국의 주요 여객 수송을 담당케 하고, 동부·중서부의 화물·통근 수송은 콘레일(Conrail) (▶Consolidated Rail Corporation의 약어)을 설립하여 반관 반민의 경영을 하고 있다. 국토가 넓은 미국에서는 철도의 주체는 여객보다는 화물 수송에 있다. 플랫폼은 영국에서는 「5번선」이면 Platform 5라고 하는데, 미국에서는 근교선·지하철 등을 제외하고는 대개 플랫폼이 없기 때문에 「5번선」하면 선로란 뜻의 track을 써서 Track No.5라고 한다.

2. 역의 시설

　▶역 a train station / 매표소 a ticket window (▶창구에는 TICKETS라고 쓰여 있다) / 승차권 자동 발매기 a ticket machine / 운임표 〈여객의〉 a fare table; 〈화물의〉 a freight list / 대합실 a waiting room / 전언판 a message board / 코인 로커 a coin locker / 유실물 보관소 Lost and Found / 신문·잡지 판매대 a newsstand; a kiosk / 중앙 홀 a concourse / 행선지 표시 an indicator; a destination sign / 열차 시간표 a (train) timetable / 개찰구 a gate (▶미국에서는 근거리 열차·지하철을 제외하고는 집찰을 차내에서 하므로 한국이나 영국과 같은 개찰구(a ticket barrier)는 없고 열차 타러 가는 입구(a gate)가 있을 뿐이다)

3. 열차

　▶보통 열차 a local train / 급행 열차 an express (train); a through (train) (▶직행 열차의 의미로도 쓰인다) / 준급행 a semi-express (train) / 특급 a limited express (train) / 초특급 a superexpress / 통근 열차 a commuter train / 귀성 열차 a train for homecoming passengers / 장거리 열차 a long-distance train / 대륙횡단 열차 a transcontinental train / 유럽 국제급행열차 Trans-Europe-Express (略 TEE) / 오리엔트 특급 Orient Express (▶Paris와 Istanbul 간을 잇는 호화 열차)

　▶첫차 the first train / 막차 the last train / 10량 편성 열차 a ten-car train / 상[하]행 열차 an up [down] train (▶an up train이라고 하면 보통 북쪽으로 가는 열차, a down train이라고 하면 보통 남행열차를 의미하므로 서울행 열차를 상행, 서울을 떠나는 열차를 하행이라고 하는 우리말과는 다르다. 서울행 열차는 a train for Seoul; a Seoul bound train과 같이 구체적으로 지명을 쓰는 것이 좋다)

　▶객차 〈美〉 a (passenger) car; 〈英〉 a coach / 차장 〈美〉 a conductor; 〈英〉 a guard / 1등차 a first-class train; 〈美〉 a Pullman (car) (▶미국인 Pullman이 고안한 호화 객차. 야간에는 침대로 된다고 하여 「침대차」라는 별명으로도 불린다) / 2등[보통]차 a coach / 식당차 a dining car / 간이 식당차 a buffet car / 2층 전망차 a vista-dome car / 침대차 a sleeping car; 〈美〉 a Pullman (car) (▶침대는 bed라 하지 않고 berth라고 한다. 위 침대는 an upper berth, 아래 침대는 a lower berth라고 한다)

4. 차표

　▶편도 차표 〈美〉 a one-way ticket; 〈英〉 a single ticket / 왕복 차표 〈美〉 a round-trip ticket; 〈英〉 a return ticket / 지정 좌석권 a reserved seat ticket / 유람권 an excursion ticket (▶외국인용 주요 유람권에는 Amtrak의 어떤 열차든 승차할 수 있는 미국의 USRAIL Pass, 영국의 Britrail Pass, 그리고 영국을 제외한 서유럽 16개국에서 통용되는 Eurailpass 등이 있다) / 정기권 〈美〉 a commuter ticket [pass]; 〈英〉 a season (ticket) / 회수권 a coupon ticket

철두철미 徹頭徹尾 **1** 〈명사적〉 thoroughness; completeness; exhaustiveness
2 〈부사적〉 thoroughly; completely; through and through; out-and-out; in every way; every inch; at all points; in every particular; to the core; from top to bottom; from beginning to end; from first to last; all the way [time]
　◆철두철미하다 반대하다 be dead set against; oppose 《anything》 tooth and nail / 철두철미 애국자다 be a patriot to the core
─**철두철미하다** thorough; complete; exhaustive; thoroughgoing; out-and-out
　◆철두철미한 연구 a thorough [an exhaustive] study / 철두철미한 조사 a thoroughgoing investigation / 철두철미한 학자 a scholar to the core [bone]; a scholar through and through [to the last inch]
　▶그 후보자는 철두철미한 개혁주의자였다 The candidate was an out-and-out reformist.

철떡거리다 be dripping wet and clinging to 《one's body》; keep clinging round 《the limbs》
철리 哲理 the philosophy; the philosophical principles; the metaphysics
철마 鐵馬 a (railway) train
철망 鐵網 **1** 〈철사로 엮은〉 (총칭) wire netting; a wire net; 〈그물코가 촘촘한〉 a (wire) gauze; 〈난롯가의〉 a fireguard
　◆철망을 친 창 a wire-mesh window / 철망을 치다 cover *sth* with wire netting
2 ⇨ 철조망
철매 soot ●철매 투성이의 sooty; sooted; soot-covered
철면 凸面 a convex surface; a convexity
　──경 a convex mirror ──렌즈 a convex lens [glass]; a convex
철면피 鐵面皮 brazenness; shamelessness; impudence; audacity; effrontery; 〈俗〉 cheek
　▶그는 철면피다 Nothing can abash him.

▶자기 부모한테 그런 말을 하다니 그는 정말 철면피구나 He has got a lot of cheek to say that to his parents.

철모 鐵帽 a steel helmet; a trench [shrapnel] helmet; a battle helmet ♦철모를 쓴 군인 a helmeted soldier

철모르다 〈분별이 없다〉 lack judgment [discretion]; be imprudent [indiscreet, thoughtless, injudicious]; 〈천진하다〉 be simple-minded [innocent, untutored]
♦철모르는 어린아이 a thoughtless [an innocent] child
▶어린애라 철모르고 한 짓이니 용서하십시오 Please forgive his behavior, he is only a child.

철문 鐵門 an iron door [gate]

철물 鐵物 ironware; ironwork; hardware; 〈英〉 ironmongery; 〈쇠장식〉 metal fittings
■―상[상인] an ironmonger; 〈美〉 a hardwareman ―전〈美〉 a hardware store [shop]; 〈英〉 an ironmonger's (shop)

철바람 a seasonal [periodic] wind; 〈인도양의〉 a monsoon

철버덕 with a splash ―**철버덕하다[거리다]** ⇨ 철벅거리다

철버덩 with a plop [dull splash]
♦물속에 철버덩 뛰어들다[떨어지다] splash [fall plop] into the water

철벅거리다 splatter; paddle; 〈물 속에서〉 splash about in the water ♦철벅거리며 내를 건너다 splash across a stream

철벅철벅 splashing(ly); paddling
♦철벅철벅 물을 튀기다 splash water about

철벽 鐵壁 an iron wall; 〈견고한 성벽〉 an impregnable fortress ♦철벽같은 진을 치다 take up an impregnable position
♦금성― an impregnable fortress

철병 撤兵 withdrawal of troops ⇨ 철군
♦철병을 거부하다 refuse to withdraw the army; refuse evacuation / 철병을 강요하다 press for the withdrawal of the troops

철봉 鐵棒 1 〈쇠막대〉 an iron bar [rod]; 〈곤봉〉 an iron club
2 〈체조용의〉 a horizontal bar; gallows; 〈경기 종목의〉 the horizontal bar; gymnastics on the bar ♦철봉을 하다 exercise on the horizontal bar
▶그는 철봉에서 1위를 차지했다 He got (the) first place in horizontal bar exercise.

철부지 ―不知 〈철없는 사람〉 a person of immature judgement; an indiscreet [a thoughtless] person; 〈어린애〉 a mere child; just a child ♦철부지 노릇을 하다 behave like a mere child; play a fool
▶나는 철부지가 아니다 〈깔보지 마라〉 I was not born yesterday.
▶그는 아직 아무것도 모르는 철부지다 He is just a child who does not know his mind as yet.

철분 鐵分 iron (content) ♦철분을 함유한 containing iron; ferric; ferrous; ferruginous / 철분이 많다[적다] be rich [poor] in iron
▶그 온천에는 다량의 철분이 함유되어 있다 That hot spring contains a lot of iron.

철빈 鐵貧 extreme poverty; destitution; indigence; pauperism
―**철빈하다** very poor; destitute; indigent; 〈서술적〉 be in dire poverty

철사 鐵絲 (a) wire; (총칭) wiring
♦철사의[같은] wiry / 철사 한 가닥 a (piece of) wire / 철사를 감다 reel wire / 철사로 묶다 wire together
■―게이지 a wire gauge ―그물 a wire net ―세공 wirework

철삭 鐵索 a cable

철상 撤床 clearing the (offertory) table
―**철상하다** 〈상을 치우다〉 clear the table; remove [draw] the cloth

철새 a migrant; a migratory [passage] bird; a bird of passage; (총칭) migrants

철색 鐵色 iron blue; reddish-black

철석 鐵石 〈쇠와 돌〉 iron and stone; being hard and strong
♦철석같은 adamantine; firm as a rock / 철석같은 마음 an iron [adamantine] will; a steadfast resolution / 철석같은 언약 a solemn promise / 남을 철석같이 믿다 pin one's faith [hope] upon another's sleeve

철석간장 鐵石肝腸 a hard heart; an iron [adamantine] will; a steadfast resolution
♦철석간장이 녹다 one's firm purpose gives way; one's steadfast resolution is shaken / 철석간장을 녹이다 disarm sb's hard-heartedness; make sb's firm purpose waver; captivate 《a man》

철석영 鐵石英 〈鑛〉 ferruginous quartz

철선 鐵線 iron [steel] wire ⇨ 철사

철설 鐵屑 scrap iron; iron scaps; 〈줄밥〉 iron filings

철수 撤收 withdrawal; removal; evacuation
―**철수하다** withdraw (from); remove; evacuate 《a place》; draw off; pull out
♦군대를 철수하다 pull the troops out of 《Cuba》; call (the armed forces) home
▶미국은 베트남에서 군대를 철수했다 America withdrew [evacuated] the troops from Viet Nam.
■―전면― a total withdrawl

철시하다 撤市― close all shops; close the market; close up shops [stores]; suspend business ♦철시한 상가(商街) a closed shopping street; a shopping street in suspension

철심 鐵心 1 〈철석 같은 마음〉 an iron [adamatine] will; a steadfast resolution
2 〈쇠로 박은 심〉 an iron core
■―판 (리액터) an ironcore disk (reactor)

철썩 1 〈물소리〉 with a splash [splosh, swash]; with a dash; with spattering noise
―**철썩하다** splash; plash; swash
▶파도가 바닷가에 철썩하고 부딪친다 The waves splash on the beach.
2 〈때리는 소리〉 with a slap [spank, crack]
♦따귀를 철썩 때리다 slap sb on the cheek; slap sb in [on] the face / 어린애의 볼기를 철썩 때리다 spank a child; paddle a child's bottom ―**철썩하다** make a spanking sound; slap; clash; slam

철썩거리다 splash; swash; plash
♦철썩거리는 파도 소리 the plash of the

waves; the splosh of the surf
철썩철썩 〈파도 소리〉 splashing; dashing; with splashes [plashes]; 〈때리는 소리〉 with slaps [snaps, spanks]
 ▶파도가 뱃전에 철썩철썩 부딪쳤다 The waves slapped against the side of the boat.
철야 徹夜 〈밤샘〉an all-night vigil [sitting]
 ◆철야로 회의하다 have an all-night conference / 철야로 시험 공부하다 sit up all night over *one's* texbooks for examination
 ▶이 읍에는 철야로 영업하는 약방이 있다 There is an all-night drugstore in this town.
 —철야하다 sit [stay, be] up all night; keep vigil ◆섣달 그믐날 철야하다 sit out New Year's Eve
 ▶그녀는 환자의 머리맡에서 철야했다 She kept vigil at a patient's bedside.
 —운행〈버스 등의〉all-night service —작업 all-night work; 철야 작업하다 work all night —회담 an overnight conversation [talk]
철없다 indiscreet; imprudent; thoughtless; reckless; rash; 〈서술적〉 have no sense [discretion]; lack judgment
 ◆철없는 어린아이 a mere child; a greenhorn of a boy / 철없는 짓을 하다 commit a rash act; do something rash; behave like a mere child
철옹(산)성 鐵甕(山)城 an impregnable fortress ◆철옹성같다[이다] be impregnable; be very [ever so] strong; be hard of approach
철완 鐵腕 a strong arm
 ◆철완의 투수 a pitcher with an iron arm; an iron-armed [a strong-armed] pitcher
철음 綴音 the sound of a syllable
철의 장막 鐵—帳幕 〈구소련〉 the Iron Curtain
 ◆철의 장막 안의 inside (of) [behind] the Iron Curtain / 철의 장막을 쳐부수다 tear down the Iron Curtain / 철의 장막에서 망명해 오다 defect [flee] from behind the Iron Curtain
철인 哲人 a wise man; a sage; a philosopher
 —정치가 a philosopher-statesman
철인 鐵人 an unyielding man; an iron(-bound) man
철자 綴字 spelling; orthography
 ◆정확한 철자 the exact spelling / 철자의 잘못 misspelling; cacography / 철자가 틀린 단어 a misspelt word / 철자가 틀리다 misspell; be misspelled / 이름을 철자를 생략하지 않고 정식으로 쓰다 spell (out) *one's* name in full
 ▶그 단어의 철자를 가르쳐 주십시오 Please tell me how to spell the word. ⇌ How do you spell that word?
 —철자하다 spell
 ▶그의 이름은 그렇게 철자하지 않는다 That is not the way to spell his name.
철자법 綴字法 〈文法〉the system [rules] of spelling; how to spell (a word) ⇨ 맞춤법
철재 鐵材 iron (material); an iron frame
 ◆철재를 써서 집을 짓다 build a house with iron frames
철저하다 徹底— through(going); exhaustive; complete; perfect; utter; out-and-out; all-out; downright; drastic; radical
 ◆철저한 에고이스트 an out-and-out [a dyed-in-the-wool] egoist / 철저한 조사 a thorough investigation / 철저한 해결 a final solution [settlement] / 고대 유적의 철저한 연구 an exhaustive study of ancient ruins
 ▶그는 매사에 철저하다 There is nothing half-and-half about him. ⇌ He is always thorough about anything.
철저히 徹底— thoroughly; thoroughgoingly; completely; exhaustively; downright; all-out; through and through; (up) to the hilt
 ◆철저히 조사하다 make a thorough [an exhaustive] investigation of *sth*; search *sth* to the bottom / 자기 뜻을 철저히 이해시키다 have *oneself* fully understood
 ▶이왕 공부를 하려면 철저히 해라 If you study at all, be sure to master your subject.
철제 鐵製 ◆철제의 (made of) iron ▶이 철제 문은 삐걱거린다 This iron gate creaks.
 —기구 an iron tool; ironwork; ironware
철제 鐵蹄 〈편자〉 a horseshoe; 〈말〉 a swift horse; a fleet steed
철제 鐵劑 iron; an iron preparation; a ferric medicine
철조망 鐵條網 barbed wire entanglements; 〔軍〕a hedgehog ◆철조망을 치다 set [stretch, construct] wire entanglements / 철조망에 걸리다 get entangled in barbed wire
 ▶전차들은 철조망을 부수고 전진했다 The tanks broke through the wire entanglements.
철주 掣肘 〈제재〉(a) restraint; restriction; control; a check; interference
 ◆철주를 받다 be restricted; be under [subjected to] restraint
 —철주하다 restrain; restrict; put [impose, place] restrictions 《on》; check; curb; interfere 《with *sb*》
철주자 鐵鑄字 an iron [metal] type; 《총칭》iron type
철쭉 〔植〕a royal azalea; a rhododendron
 —꽃 a royal azalea
철창 鐵窓 a steel-barred [an iron-barred] window; prison bars; the bars; a prison
 ◆철창 신세가 되다 be placed behind prison bars; be cast into prison; be imprisoned; be a prisoner / 10년간 철창 생활을 하다 pass ten years in prison
 ▶그 음주 운전자는 철창 안에서 하룻밤을 보내지 않으면 안되었다 The drunken driver had to spend a night behind bars.
철찾다 suit [fit] the season; be seasonable
철책 鐵柵 an iron railing [paling, fence]
 ◆철책이 쳐져[둘려] 있다 be enclosed with an iron railing / 잔디를 철책으로 보호하다 protect the lawn by iron railings / 철책을 쳐서 사람들을 못 들어오게 하다 keep people away with an iron railing [fence]
철천지한 徹天之恨 a lasting regret; a bitter [deep] grudge; deep-rooted enmity; an inveterate resentment
 ◆철천지한을 품다 bear [have, nurse] *sb* a deep(-rooted) grudge; cherish an implacable hosility 《toward》/ 철천지한을 풀다 vent *one's* bitter spite; satisfy *one's* inveterate grudge
철철 overflowingly; brimmingly

♦ 철철 넘치도록 to the brim; brimfully; to the full / 철철 넘치다 overflow 《the bank》; brim over 《with》 / 잔에 철철 넘치도록 술을 따르다 fill a glass 《up》 to the brim with wine; brim a cup with wine

철철이 each 《and every》 season; from season to season ♦ 경치는 철철이 달라진다 Scenery changes from season to season.

철청이 —聽— a horse with dark-blue dapples

철칙 鐵則 an iron rule; a hard and fast rule; an invariable principle ♦ 철칙을 정하다 lay down immutable laws; make strict rules
▶ 우리는 민주주의의 철칙을 지켜야 한다 We should keep an iron(bound) rule of democracy.

철커덕 with a snap; with a click [clink]; rattling ♦ 문을 철커덕 잠그다 lock the door with a rattling sound [click]

철탑 鐵塔 a steel tower; 〈고압선용의〉 a pylon

철통 鐵桶 a steel tub
♦ 철통같은 방어진 an impenetrable defense cordon / 철통같은 방비 impregnable fortification / 철통같은 경계망을 펴다 throw [lay] a tight cordon / 철통같이 경계하다 be on strict watch; guard rigorously
▶ 적은 그 도시를 철통같이 에워쌌다 The enemy surrounded the city like a ring of iron.

철퇴 撤退 (a) withdrawal; (an) evacuation; 〈후퇴〉 a retreat
—**철퇴하다** withdraw [draw off] 《troops》; evacuate 《a place》; pull out 《of place》
■ **부분—** a partial pullout; a thinout **전면—** the total withdrawal; a general pullout **—명령** an evacuation order: 그 도시로부터의 철퇴 명령을 받다 be ordered out of the city **—자** an evacuee

철퇴 鐵槌 an iron hammer; an iron mace
♦ 철퇴를 내리다[가하다] give [deal] a hard [heavy, crushing] blow 《to》

철판 凸版 letterpress; relief [anastatic, surface] printing
■ **아연—** a zinc relief **—인쇄** letterpress; anastatic [relief, surface] printing **—잉크** letterpress [typographic] ink

철판 鐵板 an iron [a steel] plate [sheet]; sheet iron; a sheet of iron; 〈번철〉 a griddle; a hot plate ♦ 고기를 철판에 굽다 grill meat on an iron plate

철편 鐵片 〈쇳조각〉 a piece [scrap] of iron
♦ 얇은 철편 taggers

철편 鐵鞭 an iron whip

철폐 撤廢 abolition; removal
—**철폐하다** abolish; remove; do away with; repeal; annul; lift 《a ban》
♦ 제한을 철폐하다 remove [take away] the restriction / 계급차별을 철폐하다 do away with [obliterate] class distinctions
▶ 링컨은 미국의 노예제도를 철폐했다 Lincoln abolished slavery in the United States.

철폐 鐵肺 〈인공 호흡 기계〉 an iron lung; a Drinker respirator

철필 鐵筆 〈펜〉 a pen; 〈등사판용의〉 a steel pen; a stencil pen; an iron stylus; a metallic pencil; 〈새김칼〉 a burin; a seal graver
▶ 전에는 철필로 원지를 긁었다 We used to cut the stencil paper with a steel pen.

철하다 綴— bind 《a book》; file ♦ 서류를 철하다 file papers / 신문을 철해 두다 keep newspapers on file / 철해져 있다 be on file

철학 哲學 philosophy
♦ 철학적인 philosophical / 철학적으로 philosophically / 철학을 논하다 talk philosophy / 철학적으로 생각하다 philosophize 《about》
▶ 그는 철학에 심취해 있다 He is much imbued with philosophic ideas.
▶ 그것은 그 사람 특유의 철학이다 That is a philosophy all his own.
▶ 나에게는 내 나름의 철학이 있다 I have a philosophy of my own.
■ **경험[귀납]—** empirical [inductive] philosophy **독단[도덕, 연역]—** dogmatic [moral, deductive] philosophy **동양[서양]—** Oriental [Occidental, Western] philosophy **법—** philosophy of law **분석—** analytic philosophy **비판—** 〈칸트의〉 critical philosophy **사변[자연]—** speculative [natural] philosophy **사회—** social philosophy **선험(先驗)—** a priori philosophy 《of Kant》 **실존—** existential philosophy; existentialism **실증—** positive philosophy; positivism **실험—** experimental philosophy **역사—** philosophy of history **인생—** philosophy of life **종교—** philosophy of religion **처세—** a philosophy of living ■ **—개론** an introduction to [an outline of] philosophy **—과** the philosophy department **—박사** 〈사람〉 a doctor of philosophy; 〈학위〉 Doctor of Philosophy (略 Ph. D., D. Ph(il).) **—자** a philosopher; a man of philosophy **—체계** a system of philosophy

철혈 鐵血 blood and iron **—재상** 〈비스마르크〉 the Iron Chancellor **—정책** a blood-and-iron policy

철형 凸形 convexity ♦ 철형의 convex

철회 撤回 withdrawal; revocation; retractation; repeal; relinquishment
—**철회하다** withdraw; take back; repeal; revoke; recall; retract; relinquish [recede from] 《one's demand》; forgo 《one's claim》
♦ 사표를 철회하다 withdraw one's resignation / 요구를 철회하다 withdraw [forgo] one's claims; relinquish [recede from] one's demands / 앞서 한 말을 철회하다 withdraw [take back] one's words

첨가 添加 addition; annexing
♦ 첨가 기입하다 add sth in writing
—**첨가하다** add 《to》; annex 《to》; append 《to》; affix 《to》; attach 《to》
♦ 덤으로 첨가하다 throw in; flag in
■ **—물** an annex(e); an appendix; an addition; an additive: 식품 첨가물 an [a food] additive **—어** an agglutinative language

첨단 尖端 1 〈뾰족한 끝〉 a pointed end [head]; a fine point; a tip; a cusp
2 〈앞장〉 the spearhead; the vanguard
♦ 첨단적인 ultramodern; up-to-date; up-to-the-minute; up-to-the-second / 유행의 첨단 the ultrafashionable mode [style] / 유행의 첨단을 걷다 set [lead] the fashion / 시대의 첨단을 가

첨대

다 be in the van of the era
▶ 그녀는 유행의 첨단을 걷는 옷을 입고 있다 She wears the latest fashion.
■—기술 high technology —산업 a high technology industry

첨대 籤― **1** 〈댓조각〉 a bamboo bookmark(er) **2** ⇨ 접대(尖一)

첨벙 with a splash [plop]; splosh
♦ 물속으로 첨벙 떨어지다 fall plop into the water / 물속으로 첨벙 뛰어들다 plunge [splash] into the water

첨병 尖兵 a point (of an advance guard); an advance guard point

첨부 添附 appending; annexing
—첨부하다 attach 《sth to another》; append; annex; be accompanied 《by》
▶ 원서에 이력서를 첨부하여 제출할 것 File an application along with a curriculum vitae.
—물 an appendix; an annex(e); a supplement —서류 appended papers; accompanying documents; an annex(e)

첨삭 添削 correction
♦ 작문의 첨삭을 받다 have *one's* compositions looked over and corrected 《by》
—첨삭하다 correct; look over; touch up
—료 a correction fee

첨서 添書 an addition 《to》; an additional note; 〈편지의〉 a postscript 《略 P.S.》
—첨서하다 add *sth* in writing; write in; 〈행간에〉 interline; 〈편지에〉 write [add] a postscript to 《a letter》

첨예 尖銳 〈날카로움〉 being sharp [acute]; 〈급진적임〉 being radical
—첨예하다 sharp; acute; radical
■—분자 radicals; extreme [radical] elements; the radical part

첨예화하다 尖銳化― **1** 〈분쟁 등이〉 become [get] acute [tense]; be aggravated
♦ 첨예화하는 분쟁 a sharpening conflict
2 〈사상 등이〉 be radicalized; become more radical

첨자 籤子 **1** 〈장도집의〉 a knife clasp
2 ⇨ 접대

첨작 添酌 an extra sacrificial libation
—첨작하다 pour an extra libation

첨지 籤紙 a paper bookmark

첨차 檐遮 〔建〕 an ancon 《*pl.* ancones》; a bracket; a corbel piece

첨첨 heap upon heap; layer on layer; pile after pile ♦ 돌[벽돌]을 첨첨 쌓다 heap up stones [bricks]; lay one stone [brick] upon another

첨탑 尖塔 a pinnacle; a spire; a steeple

첨하 檐下 ♦〈처마밑〉 첨하에(서) under the eaves / 첨하에서 비를 긋다 take shelter from (the) rain under the eaves

첨 妾 a (kept) mistress; a concubine
♦ 첩의 소생이다 be born of a concubine / 첩살림을 하다 live with a concubine; keep a second [separate] establishment / 첩이 되다 become a mistress; serve as a concubine / 첩을 두다 keep [set up] a mistress [concubine]

첩 貼 a paper (of medicine); 〈가루약의〉 a chartula 《*pl.* -lae》; 〈복용량〉 a dose 《of》
♦ 약 한 첩 a paper [wrapper] of medicine
♦ 이 약은 식후에 한 첩씩 들도록 하시오 Take a dose of this medicine after each meal.

-**첩** ―帖 an album; a (note)book
♦ 견본첩 a sample book / 사진첩 a photograph [photo] album

첩경 捷徑 **1** 〈지름길〉 a shortcut 《to》; 〈손쉬운 방법〉 a shorter way; a royal road
♦ 외국어를 배우는 첩경 the shortest way to learn foreign languages / 지식을 얻는 첩경 a shortcut to knowledge
2 most likely; in all probability; easily; readily

첩모 睫毛 eyelashes; lashes ⇨ 속눈썹
■—난생(亂生) 〔醫〕 introverted eyelashes
—난생증 〔醫〕 trichiasis

첩박다 board up 《a door》; shut up 《a house》 by boarding the front of it
♦ 대문을 첩박다 board up the gate

첩보 捷報 news of a victory; the tidings of victory

첩보 牒報 a written report to *one's* superior
—첩보하다 report to *one's* superior; let *one's* superior know by a written report

첩보 諜報 secret information; intelligence
■—기관 an intelligence office [organization, agency]; a secret service —망 a spy net [ring]; an intelligence [espionage] network —부 an intelligence department [bureau]; 〈방첩의〉 a counter-intelligence office —원 an intelligence man; a secret agent —활동 espionage activities

첩부 貼付 pasting [sticking] on
—첩부하다 ⇨ 붙이다

첩실 妾室 a concubine ⇨ 첩(妾)

첩약 貼藥 a pack of prepared herb medicine; medicinal herbs in packages

첩자 諜者 a spy; an informer; an agent; a secret agent; an emissary
♦ 첩자 노릇을 하다 be engaged in espionage; act as a spy / 첩자를 보내다 send (out) a spy 《to》; send a spy 《into》/ 첩자를 침투시키다 plant [infiltrate] spies

첩지 an ornamental hairpin; a ceremonial hairpin

첩지머리 1〈첩지를 쓴 머리〉 a hairdo with a ceremonial hairpin **2** 〈머리 모양〉 a girl's ear-covering plait style

첩첩산중 疊疊山中 ♦ 첩첩산중에 deep in the mountains; far up (in) the mountain; in the inmost [deepest] recesses of mountains

첩첩수심 疊疊愁心 a flock [lot] of worries
♦ 첩첩수심에 싸이다 have a lot of worries [anxieties]; have worries upon worries

첩첩이 疊疊― heap on heap; fold upon fold; layer upon layer; in heaps; in piles
▶ 길에 낙엽이 첩첩이 쌓였다 The street was heaped with the fallen leaves.

첩출 妾出 a child by a concubine; being born of a concubine

첩출 疊出 repeated [frequent] occurrence; a succession [series] 《of events》
—첩출하다 occur [happen] repeatedly; come [come out, crop up] again and again

♦첩출하는 사건 a rash [close sequence] of events / 불행한 일이 첩출하다 have one misfortune after another; have a series of misfortunes

첫 the first; new; maiden; starting; the beginning ♦ 첫 글자 the first letter (of a word); 〈이름의〉 an initial (letter) / 첫비행 the inaugural flight / 첫차 the first train [bus]

첫가을 early autumn [fall]; the beginning of autumn

첫걸음 the first step (to, toward); an initial step; a start; 〈초보〉 the rudiments [elements, ABC] (of); a beginners' course (in)
♦첫걸음을 내딛다 take [mark] the first step; make [get] a start / 첫걸음을 그르치다 make a false start; start in the wrong way
▶ 그는 예술가로서 인생의 첫걸음을 내디뎠다 He started out in life as an artist.

첫겨울 early winter; the beginning of winter

첫고등 〈첫 기회〉 the first chance; the outset; the start; the beginning

첫공개 —公開 the first public exhibition

첫공연 —公演 the premire [first public] performance

첫국밥 〈산모의〉 the first seaweed soup and rice taken after childbirth

첫기제 —忌祭 the first anniversary of (one's father's) death after the three-year mourning period

첫길 1 〈초행길〉 an unfamiliar road; an unaccustomed course; one's first trip (to)
2 〈신행길〉 (on) the way to one's wedding

첫나들이 one's first outing
—첫나들이하다 〈갓난아이가〉 go out for the first time after one's birth; 〈신부가〉 make her first post-marriage outing; (비유) have sth smeared on one's face

첫날 the first [opening] day; 〈연극의〉 the premire ♦ 학기[학년]의 첫날 the opening day of the school year [term] / 경기의 첫날 opening day of the games

첫날밤 the bridal night; the first night (after marriage)

첫낯 an unfamiliar face; the first meeting (with)

첫눈[1] 〈처음 봄〉 the first sight [look]; the first glance [glimpse]
♦첫눈에 at first sight [look, glance]; at a glance; at the first meeting / 첫눈에 반하다 love [fall in love with] (a girl) at first sight; be struck [captivated] (by a girl) at first sight

첫눈[2] the first snow(fall) of the season

첫더위 the first spell of hot weather (of the season); the first heat of the season

첫돌 〈아기의〉 the first birthday (of a baby); 〈행사의〉 the first anniversary [memorial day]

첫딸 one's first(born) daughter; a daughter as one's first child ♦ 첫딸을 낳다 give birth to a girl as one's first child

첫마디 an opening word [remark]; the first word [remark]
♦첫마디를 꺼내다 open one's mouth; 〈하기 거북한 말을〉 break the ice / 첫마디부터 욕을 퍼붓다 abuse sb as soon as one opens one's mouth
▶ 선생님의 첫마디는 「왜 지각했니?」하는 것이었다 The teacher's first word to me was "Why are you late?"

첫머리 〈필두〉 the head [top]; 〈시작〉 the opening; the beginning; the start; the outset
♦명단의 첫머리 the first on the list [in a roll] / …의 첫머리에 at the beginning of…; at the head [top] of… / 책을 첫머리부터 끝까지 읽다 read a book from cover to cover

첫무대 —舞臺 one's first appearance (on the stage); one's debut ♦ 첫무대를 밟다 make one's debut (on the stage)

첫물 the wearing period before the first wash
♦첫물옷 a new suit before the first wash
▶ 내 옷이 첫물에 못쓰게 됐다 My clothes are worn out before they got laundered.

첫밭 the beginning; the ouset; the start
♦첫밭에 at the start [outset]

첫발 the first step (to, toward); an initial step
♦첫발을 내디디다 take [make] the first step; make [get] a start

첫밥 the first feeding (of silkworms) ♦ 첫밥을 주다 feed (silkworms) for the first time

첫배 the first litter [hatch, brood]; the firstling
▶ 내 개가 첫배에 강아지를 네 마리 낳았다 My dog farrowed four puppies at the first litter.
■—돼지 the first litter of pigs —병아리 the first hatch [brood] of chickens

첫봄 early spring; the beginning of spring

첫사랑 one's first love; 〈풋사랑〉 calf [puppy] love; 〈사람〉 one's first lover [sweetheart]
♦첫사랑의 추억 recollection of one's first love / 첫사랑에 실패하다 lose [be disappointed in] one's first love

첫새벽 early dawn [morning]; daybreak; (美) the crack of dawn [day]
♦첫새벽에 before dawn; at daybreak; at the peep [crack] of day; at the early dawn / 첫새벽을 기다리다 wait for the light of day
▶ 첫새벽이어서 아직 어두웠다 It was before dawn and the light was poor.

첫서리 the first frost of the season

첫선 〈등장〉 the first puplic appearance; a debut; 〈공개〉 the first public exhibition [presentation] ♦ 가수로서 첫선을 보이다 make one's debut as a singer

첫소리 1 〔言〕 an initial sound [consonant]
2 ⇨ 첫마디

첫솜씨 one's skill tried for the first time
♦첫솜씨를 보이다 show off one's skill for the first time

첫술 the first spoonful of food [rice]
♦첫술을 뜨다 take one's first spoonful of food at a meal

첫술에 배부르랴 〈속담〉 You can hardly expect to be perfect from the outset.

첫아기 one's firstborn (child); the first child

첫아들 one's first(born) son

첫얼음 the first freeze of the season

첫여름 the beginning of summer; early summer

첫이레 〈아기의〉 the seventh day after birth

첫인상 —印象 the first impression
♦첫인상이 좋다 make [produce, have] a favorable [good] first impression 《upon, on》 ▶그녀의 첫인상이 어땠습니까? What was your first impression of her?

첫잠 the early stage of sleep ♦첫잠에서 깨어나다 be woken up just after dozing off

첫정 —情 the first love [affection, attachment, devotion] ♦첫정을 바치다 give one's first love 《to》; devote one's first affection / 첫정을 못 잊다 cannot get over one's first attachement at all / 서로 첫정이 들다 fall in love each for the first time

첫째 the first; number one; No. 1; the first [top] place; the head; the top; the foremost ♦첫째의 first; foremost; top; second to none; primary / 첫째 권 the first volume; the book one / 첫째로 first; firstly; in the first place; first of all; to begin [start] with; at the first [initial] step; above anything else / 첫째가는 부자 the wealthiest person / 첫째로 오다 come first; be the first to come / 첫째로 합격하다 pass an examination first on the list / 첫째를 하다 secure [take, win, get] (the) first place; stand [rank] first 《in, among》; be at the head [top] 《of》; head [top] the list 《of》; finish [come in] first; come out first [top]
▶성공에는 건강이 첫째다 Health is the first essential to success.
▶첫째 난관은 돌파했다 We have managed to overcome the first obstacle.
▶그는 우리 반에서 첫째다 He is at the head [top] of our class. ⇌ He stands [is] first in our class.
▶첫째 돈이 부족하다 To begin with, we do not have sufficient funds.
▶첫째로 그는 잘 생겼다 He is handsome in the first place.

첫차 —車 the first train [bus] 《of the day》

첫추위 the first spell of cold weather; the first cold of the season ♦첫추위가 닥치다 the first cold weather sets in

첫출발 —出發 a start; a beginning
♦인생의 첫출발 one's start in life / 첫출발이 좋다[나쁘다] begin [start] well [ill]; make a good [bad] start; make a successful [an unsuccessful] beginning

첫출사 —出仕 entering on an official career for the first time

첫판 the first round [game, bout]; 〈첫시작〉 the beginning; the opening ♦첫판에 지다 get beaten in the first bout 《of wrestling》

첫판 —版 the first edition ⇨ 초판(初版)

첫항해 —航海 〈배의〉 a maiden voyage; 〈사람의〉 one's first voyage

첫해 the first year ♦미국에 간 첫해 the first year one was in America
■—권농(勸農) 〈처음이라 서투름〉 being clumsy because of inexperience; a greenhorn

첫해산 —解産 one's first childbirth [confinement]; a woman's first delivery [parturition] 《of a child》

첫행보 —行步 1〈처음 감〉 one's first visit [going] 2〈첫 행상〉 one's first peddling (tour) ♦첫행보에 상당한 이익을 보다 make a considerable profit on one's first peddling

첫혼인 —婚姻 one's first marriage

첫회 —回 the first time; 〈野〉 the first inning

청 〈막〉 a membrane; a film; a pellicle
♦귀청 〈고막〉 the drum membrane / 대청 the white film inside a bamboo

청 青 blue; azure ⇨ 청색(青色)

청 請 a request; a favor; one's wishes; 〈간청〉 an entreaty; a solicitation
♦간절한 청 an earnest [importunate] request / 긴한 청 an urgent [important] request / …의 청에 따라 at sb's request; in compliance [accordance] with sb's request / 청을 들어주다 comply with [grant, accede to] sb's request; oblige sb / 청을 들어주지 않다 refuse [turn down] request; turn a deaf ear to a request
▶청이 하나 있습니다 I have a favor to ask 《of》 you. ⇌ Allow me to make you a request.
▶청이라니 무슨 청인가요? What is your request? ⇌ What is that you would have me do?
▶네 청이라면 무엇이든 들어주마 I can refuse you nothing.

청 廳 1〈관청〉 an office; a board; an agency; a ministry; an administration
♦국세청 National Tax Administration
2 ⇨ 대청

청가뢰 青— 〔昆〕 a green blister beetle; a Spanish fly; a cantharis 《pl. -rides》

청각 聽覺 (the sense of) hearing; hearing sense; auditory [acoustic] sense; audition
♦청각의 인상 an auditive impression / 청각으로 aurally / 청각을 잃다 lose one's hearing / 청각에 호소하다 appeal to the ear
▶그녀는 청각이 예민하다 She has a keen sense of hearing. ⇌ She has acute hearing.
■—과민(증) hyperacusis —기관 a hearing [an auditory] organ —신경 the auditory [acoustic] nerve —심상(心象) an acoustic image —형 the auditory type

청각채 青角菜 〔植〕 a glue plant

청강 聽講 attendance at a lecture; 〈美〉 audit
♦청강을 허락하다 grant sb admission
▶청강 무료 (게시) Attendance [Admission] (is) free.
—청강하다 attend (a lecture); listen to 《a lecture》; 〈美〉 audit 《a course》
▶나는 작년에 김교수의 강의를 청강했다 I audited Prof. Kim's lectures last year.
■—료 an admission (fee) —생 an irregular [a special] student; 〈美〉〈대학의〉 an auditor —증 an attendance [admission] ticket

청강자 聽講者 an auditor; a listener; 〈총칭〉 audience; attendance
▶청강자가 많았다[적었다] There was a large [small] audience.

청개구리 青— 〔動〕 a tree [green] frog; a hyla

청결 清潔 cleanness; cleanliness; neatness; purity —청결하다 clean; neat; pure

♦청결히 하다 clean (up); make clean
▶부엌은 항상 청결히 해 두시오 Always keep the kitchen clean.
▶그는 심신이 다같이 청결한 사람이다 He is pure in body and mind.
청경우독 晴耕雨讀 (a life of) working in the fields when the weather is fine and reading at home when it's rainy
▶그 뒤로 그는 청경우독의 생활을 해왔다 Since then he has led a life of working in the fields when fine and reading at home in wet weather.
—**청경우독하다** work in the field in fine weather and read at home in wet weather
청계 〖民俗〗〈잡귀〉 a plague demon
청고 淸高 purity and loftiness
—**청고하다** pure and noble [lofty]
청공 靑空 a blue [an azure] sky; the blue heavens
청과 靑果 vegetables and fruits
—**상[시장]** a vegetable and fruit dealer [market] —**점** a green-grocery
청관 聽管 〖解〗 the organs of hearing; the auditory organs
청교도 淸敎徒 a Puritan ♦청교도적인 puritanical; puritan ■—**주의** Puritanism
청구 請求 a demand; a request; a claim
♦청구대로 as requested [demanded] / 청구에 응하다 comply with [accede to] sb's request; meet sb's demand / 청구를 들어주다 concede a demand; grant a request / 청구를 거절하다 deny [reject, refuse, decline, turn down] a request
—**청구하다** ask [apply] for; request; demand (of, from); claim; call upon 《sb to do》; 〈대가·요금을〉 charge
♦대금의 지급을 청구하다 claim [demand] payment 《from sb》 / 책값을 청구하다 demand payment for a book / 손해 배상을 청구하다 claim damages; demand reparation for injury / 견본을 청구하다 ask for a sample
▶그 수리 대금으로 그에게 10만원을 청구했다 I charged him a hundred thousand won for the repair.
▶청구하시는대로 견본을 보내 드리겠습니다 We will send you a sample on [at your] request.
■**손해배상[상환]—** a claim for damages [reimbursement] **지급—** a demand for payment ■**—불** ⇨ 요구불(要求拂) **—액** the amount claimed [asked] **—인** an applicant; a demandant; a claimant
청구권 請求權 a (right of) claim
♦청구권을 포기하다 waive [abandon, give up] one's claim 《for》; disclaim
■**대일(對日)—** a claim to Japan 《for war damages》
청구명 請— 〈연줄〉 a pull; (an) influence; connections; contacts ♦좋은 청구멍을 가지고 [the right] connections / 청구멍이 있다 have a pull 《with the firm》
청구서 請求書 a bill; an account
♦청구서를 내다 render [send in] an account; submit a bill 《to》 / 청구서를 쓰다 write [make] out a bill
■**손해배상—** a written claim for damages 지급— a bill (for payment)
청구자 請求者 a claimant; a demandant; an applicant ♦청구자 없는 은행 예금 an unclaimed [a dormant] bank account
청국 淸國 China under the Ch'ing dynasty
청국장 淸麴醬 fermented soybeans
청기와 靑— a blue [green] tile
■**—장수** a man who keeps the tricks of his trade secret
청꾼 請— an influence middleman; a five-percenter
청널 廳— a floor board; (총칭) flooring
청년 靑年 a youth; a young man; (총칭) the youth; young people; the younger [rising] generation
♦전도 유망한 청년 a promising youth / 청년 실업가 a young businessman / 혈기 왕성한 청년 (총칭) young blood(s); vigorous youth
▶그의 아들은 훌륭한 청년이 되었다 His son has grown into a fine young man.
▶마을 청년들은 모두 도회로 일하러 갔다 All the village youngsters have gone to the cities to work.
■**—기** adolescence **—남녀** young men and women; young people **—단** a young men's association **—시절** youth; one's younger [youthful] days **—운동** a youth movement **—회의소** the Junior Chamber
청녹두 靑綠豆 tiny green peas [chickpeas]
청담 淸淡 1 〈맛·빛깔의〉 lightness
—**청담하다** light; plain; simple ♦청담한 색 a light color / 맛이 청담한 lightly seasoned
2 〈마음의〉 integrity; probity; uprightness; purity and honesty
—**청담하다** honest; upright; cleanhanded; 〈깨끗하다〉 clean; pure ♦청담한 사람 a man of integrity; an upright man
청담 晴曇 clearness and cloudiness (of the sky)
청대 〖植〗 a short-jointed variety of bamboo
청대콩 靑— beans not quite ripe; green beans [peas]
청동 靑銅 bronze ♦청동의 bronze / 청동색의 bronzy ■**—세공** bronze work; a bronze **—화로** a bronze brazier
청동기 靑銅器 bronze ware; a bronze tool ■**—시대** 〖考古〗 the Bronze Age
청동호박 a full-ripe pumpkin
청등롱 靑燈籠 a blue-silk lantern
청등홍가 靑燈紅街 gay quarters; (美) a red-light district
청람 晴嵐 〈아지랑이〉 shimmering of heated air; heat haze [shimmer]
청랑하다 晴朗— clear; fair; fine; serene
▶날씨가 청랑하다 The weather is fine. ⇌ It is a fine day.
청량 淸凉 being clear and cool; being cool and refreshing —**청량하다** clear and cool; cool and refreshing
♦청량한 날씨 nice cool weather
■**—제** a refrigerant; a refresher; a cooler
청량음료 淸凉飮料 a cold drink; a refreshing

[cooling] drink [beverage]; a refrigerant; a pop; (美) a soft drink; (英) mineral water
■—점 a soft drink stand; a soda fountain

청력 聽力 (the power [sense] of) hearing; hearing ability; audition
♦청력이 좋다 have a keen sense of hearing / 청력을 잃다 lose *one's* hearing
—검사 a hearing test —계 an audiometer —측정 audiometry

청렴(결백) 淸廉(潔白) integrity; probity; uprightness; purity —청렴(결백)하다 upright; cleanhanded; incorruptible; pure
♦청렴결백한 사람 a man of integrity; a man of pure heart and clean hands

청록색 靑綠色 a bluish green color; bluish green

청료 靑蓼 〔植〕 a kind of persicaria [smartweed]

청룡도 靑龍刀 a Chinese broadsword; a falchion

청루 靑樓 a brothel; a house of ill fame; a whorehouse

청류 淸流 a (clear) limpid stream

청매 靑梅 an unripe plum

청맹과니 靑盲— 〈못보는 눈〉 an eye that is blind though it looks perfect; 〔醫〕 amaurosis; 〈못보는 사람〉 an amaurotic [a bat-blind] person

청명 淸明 1 〈맑음〉 fineness; fairness; brightness —청명하다 clear and bright; fine; fair
♦청명한 날씨 clear [fair, fine] weather / 청명한 하늘 a clear [crystalline] sky
2 〈절기〉 one of the 24 seasonal divisions (about April 5)

청문 聽聞 audience; audition
—회 a (public) hearing: 미 의회 청문회 the U.S. Congressional hearing

청밀 淸蜜 honey ⇨ 꿀

청바지 靑— blue jeans ♦청바지를 입은 in blue jeans; jeaned (teenager)

청백 靑白 blue and white
■—전 a contest [tourney] between two groups [the white and blue teams]

청백리 淸白吏 a cleanhanded government officer

청병 請兵 requesting (the dispatch of) troops —청병하다 request (the dispatch of) troops

청부 請負 a contract (for work)
♦청부로 under [by] contract / 청부(를) 주다 give out a contract (for the work); put (the work) out to contract / 청부(를) 맡다 contract (for the work); receive a contract (for the work from *sb*)
■—살인 a contract murder —살인자 a hired assassin [killer, murderer]

청빈 淸貧 honest [honorable] poverty —청빈하다 poor but honest ♦청빈한 생활을 하다 live [carry] a poor but honest life

청사 靑史 history; annals ♦청사에 빛나다 be noted in history / 청사에 길이 남다 remain long [be recorded, live] in history

청사 廳舍 a Government building

청사 靑絲 blue yarn [thread]

청사등롱 靑紗燈籠 a red-and-blue gauze lantern

청사진 靑寫眞 a blueprint
♦청사진을 만들다 make a blueprint 《of》; blueprint 《a plan》 / 아직 청사진 단계다 be still in the blueprint stage
▶그들은 한국의 장래를 위한 청사진을 작성했다 They drew up a blueprint for Korean future.

청산 靑山 green mountains [hills]; blue mountains
▶인간 도처 유청산(有靑山) You can seek your fortune anywhere in the world. ⇌ Fortune awaits you everywhere.

청산 淸算 〈회 사 의〉 liquidation; winding-up; 〈지급의〉 clearing; 〈사업의〉 dissolution; settlement —청산하다 liquidate; wind up; clear off [up] 《*one's* debts》; balance [settle, square] 《*one's* accounts》
♦과거를 청산하다 bury the [*one's*] past / 빚을 청산하다 clear off [pay back] *one's* debt / 부채를 청산하고 해산하다 〈사람이 주어〉 liquidate [wind up] 《a company》 / 〈회사가 주어〉 go into liquidation / 자살로써 죄를 청산하다 commit suicide in atonement for *one's* crime; atone for *one's* sin with *one's* life
■—거래 〔證〕 future transaction —계정 an open account —사무 liquidative affairs —사무소 a liquidation office —사원 a liquidation partnership —서 a statement of liquidation; 〈결산서〉 a balance sheet —소득 liquidation income —인 a liquidator; 〈청산서 작성자〉 a balancer —회사 a company in liquidation

청산유수 靑山流水 eloquence; fluency
♦청산유수로 with great fluency [volubility]; very fluently; glibly
▶그녀는 청산유수로 말했다 She spoke very fluently. ⇌ She talked glib(ly).
▶그는 말이 청산유수다 He is a fluent speaker.

청상과부 靑孀寡婦 a young widow

청상아리 靑— 〔魚〕 a mako (shark)

청새치 靑— 〔魚〕 a spearfish

청색 靑色 a blue color; blue ♦짙은 청색 deep [dark] blue
▶청색과 황색을 섞으면 녹색이 된다 Mix blue with yellow and you get green.

청서 靑書 a blue book

청서 淸書 a fair [clean] copy ⇨ 정서(淨書)

청소 淸掃 cleaning; 〈비질〉 sweeping; 〈먼지 떨기〉 dusting; 〈문질러 닦기〉 scrubbing; 〈도로의〉 street cleaning
—청소하다 clean; sweep; dust; scrub; scavenge ♦실내를 청소하다 clean (up [out]) a room / 거리를 청소하다 clean [scavenge] a street
■—대— a general house cleaning ■—도구 dusting [scrubbing] things —주간 a clean-up week —차 〈쓰레기차〉 a refuse cart; a garbage wagon [truck]

청소기 淸掃機 a cleaner
■진공[전기]— a vacuum cleaner: 거실 양탄자를 진공청소기로 청소하다 run a vacuum cleaner over the carpet in the sitting room

청소년 靑少年 youth; young people; juveniles;

the younger [growing] generation
■ ―범죄 juvenile delinquency

청소부 淸掃夫 《英》 a dustman; 《美》 an ashman; 〈쓰레기의〉 a garbageman; a garbage collector / 굴뚝― a chimney sweep(er) 도로― a scavenger; a street cleaner [sweeper]

청송 靑松 a green pine

청수 淸水 clear [pure] water

청순 淸純 purity ―청순하다 pure; innocent
♦ 청순한 처녀 a pure and simple girl

청술레 靑― an early-ripening (variety of) greenish pear

청승 a pitiable condition; a pitiful lot; a miserable [wretched] look ♦ 청승 떨다 excite (another's) pity [sympathy]
■ ―꾸러기 a miserable-looking man

청승맞다 pitiable; pitiful; piteous; miserable; wretched; poor; sorrowful
♦ 청승맞게 말하다 have a plaintive way of speaking / 청승맞게 울다 wail piteously

청신 淸新 being new and fresh ―청신하다 new and fresh ♦ 청신한 작품 a new and fresh style in literature / 청신한 맛 freshness / 청신한 맛이 없다 lack freshness; be stale
▶ 그의 작품에는 청신한 맛이 조금도 없다 We find nothing new [fresh] in his work.

청신경 聽神經 〔解〕 the auditory [acoustic] nerve

청신남 淸信男 a male Buddhist

청신녀 淸信女 a female Buddhist

청신호 靑信號 a green traffic signal; a green light
▶ 청신호다 The signal [light] is green. ≒ The light is on for "Go."

청실 靑― blue thread [yarn]

청아 淸雅 elegance; grace(fulness); purity; clarity ―청아하다 elegant; graceful; pure; clear ♦ 청아한 목소리 a clear [silvery] voice

청야 淸夜 a serene [clear] night

청약 請約 subscription (for stocks); offer ―청약하다 subscribe (for bonds); send a subscription
■ ―금 subscription money ―기한 a time limit for subscription ―서 a written subscription; 〈용지〉 《美》 a subscription blank [《英》 form] ―순 the subscription order ―자 a subscriber ―처 a place where the subscriptions are accepted

청어 靑魚 〔魚〕 a herring

청옥 靑玉 〔鑛〕 sapphire

청올치 the inner bark of arrowroot; arrow-root bark ■ ―끈 a string made of arrowroot bark

청와대 靑瓦臺 the Blue House; the (Korean) Presidential residence

청요리 淸料理 〈중국 요리〉 Chinese cooking [food]; a Chinese dish ■ ―집 a Chinese restaurant

청우 晴雨 fair or rainy [foul] weather; sunshine and rain
♦ 청우에 관계 없이 rain [wet] or shine; whether it may rain or not; in all weathers
■ ―계 a barometer; a weatherglass; a rain glass: 청우계가 올라가다[내려가다] barometer rises [falls, drops]

청운 靑雲 〈구름〉 blue clouds; 〈높은 벼슬〉 high offices
♦ 청운의 뜻을 품은 청년 an aspiring youth / 청운의 뜻을 품다 aspire after greatness [distinction]; have [entertain, harbor] a high [great, lofty] ambition
▶ 그는 청운의 뜻을 품고 고향을 떠났다 He left his hometown with lofty ambitions.

청원 請援 asking help; calling for aid ―청원하다 ask for [seek, invoke] sb's assistance; seek sb's help; call in sb's aid; appeal [make an appeal] 《to sb》 for help

청원 請願 a petition (for); an application (for) ♦ 청원을 들어주다 grant a petition / 청원을 각하하다 reject [throw out, turn down] a petition
―청원하다 petition 《the government for sth》; make a petition 《to》; present [submit] a petition 《to》; file [lodge] a petition 《with the National Assembly》; hand [send] in a petition 《to》; apply (for)
♦ 감형을 청원하다 petition [send a petition to] 《the authorities》 for a commutation of a sentence
▶ 정부에 청원해 보자 Let's present our petition to the Government.
■ ―경찰(관) a policeman on special guard assignment ―권 (exercise) the right of petition

청유 淸遊 a pleasure excursion [trip]
♦ 하루의 청유 a day's outing
―청유하다 go on a pleasure excursion

청음 淸音 〈맑은 소리〉 a clear voice; 〈안울림소리〉 a voiceless sound

청음기 聽音機 a sound locator [detector]; 〈수중의〉 a hydrophone

청이불문 聽而不聞 turning deaf ears 《to》 ―청이불문하다 turn a deaf ear to [be deaf to] 《sb's request》

청일 淸逸 purity; loftiness; noble-mindedness ―청일하다 pure; lofty; noble-minded

청일전쟁 淸日戰爭 the Sino-Japanese War (of 1894-95)

청자 靑瓷·靑磁 celadon ■ 고려― Koryo celadon ―색 celadon (green); jade green

청장 請狀 a letter of invitation ⇨ 청첩장

청장 廳長 the Administrator

청재 淸齋 purification ⇨ 재계(齋戒)

청전 靑田 green paddy fields; unripe rice fields

청정 淸淨 purity; immaculateness; cleanness; immaculacy
―청정하다 pure; immaculate; clean
■ ―수역 blue belt ―액 a cleaning solution ―야채 clean vegetables ―작용 cleaning action ―재배 sanitary [germ-free] culture

청조 靑鳥 〈반가운 사자〉 a messenger (bearing good news)

청조 淸朝 〈중국의〉 the Ch'ing dynasty

청종 聽從 obeying; listening 《to》; following ―청종하다 obey; follow [listen to] 《sb's advice》

청주 淸酒 refined rice wine

청죽 靑竹 〈대나무〉 a green bamboo; an unseasoned bamboo (마르지 않은)

청중 聽衆 an audience; an attendance; hearers
♦많은[적은] 청중 a large [small] audience [attendance] / 수만 명의 청중 an audience of tens of thousands / 청중을 끌다 attract [draw] an audience / 청중을 열광케하다 move [arouse] one's audience to enthusiasm
▶오늘 저녁엔 청중이 형편없이 적었다 We had a very small attendance [audience] this evening.
▶청중은 물을 끼얹은 듯 조용했다 Silence reigned over the audience.
▶청중으로부터 우레와 같은 박수갈채가 터져 나왔다 Thunderous applause arose among the audience.
■—석 an auditorium; an audience seat

청지기 廳— a steward; a chamberlain; an attendant to a high official

청직 淸直 integrity; probity; uprightness; honesty —청직하다 honest; upright

청진 聽診 〔醫〕 auscultation; stethoscopy —청진하다 auscultate; stethoscope; examine with a stethoscope
■—법 auscultation; stethoscopy

청진기 聽診器 a stethoscope ♦청진기를 대다 apply a stethoscope ((to)) / 청진기로 진찰하다 stethoscope; examine with a stethoscope
▶의사는 환자의 가슴에 청진기를 대었다 The doctor placed a stethoscope on the patient's chest.

청질 請— solicitation; entreaty
♦청질하다 entreat [implore] sb to exercise his influence ((in favor of)); solicit sb for his good offices; implore aid ((from sb))

청참외 靑— 〔植〕 a green melon

청처짐하다 〈느리다〉 slow; tardy; sluggish; 〈느슨하다〉 loose

청천 靑天 a blue [an azure] sky; the blue heavens

청천 淸泉 a clear [crystal] spring

청천 晴天 fine [fair] weather; a cloudless [clear, bright] sky

청천백일 靑天白日 1 〈맑게 갠 날〉 a clear day; a bright blue sky
2 〈무죄가 됨〉 innocence
▶그는 무죄 판결을 받아 청천백일의 몸이 되었다 He was given a decision of "not guilty" and completely cleared of the charge.

청천벽력 靑天霹靂 a bolt from [out of] the blue; a thunderbolt from a clear sky
▶그 소식은 나에게는 청천벽력이었다 The news was a bolt from the blue to me.

청첩 請牒 〈초대장〉 a letter of invitation; an invitation (card)
♦청첩을 내다 send [issue] an invitation (card) ((to)) / 청첩을 받다 have [receive] an invitation ((from sb)); be invited
■결혼— a wedding invitation

청청하다 靑靑— freshly [vividly] green; fresh and green; verdant
▶산들은 초록으로 청청하다 The hills are robed in green [covered with verdure].

청초 靑— 〈연〉 a blue kite with a white top

청초 靑草 〈푸른 풀〉 green grass; 〈담배〉 green tobacco

청초 淸楚 neatness —청초하다 neat and clean; tidy; trim ♦청초한 옷차림을 하고 있다 be neatly dressed.

청추 淸秋 〈가을〉 a bright autumn [《美》 fall]; fine autumn weather; 〈음력 팔월〉 the eighth lunar month

청춘 靑春 the springtime [springtide] of life; the bloom [heyday] of youth; youth
♦꽃다운 청춘 the bloom of (one's) youth / 청춘시절에 in the days of one's youth; in one's youthful days [years] / 청춘의 고민 mental struggle of youth / 청춘의 꿈 a dream of youth / 청춘의 정열 ardor of youth; youthful ardor / 청춘의 피가 끓다 burn with youthful ardor / 청춘의 피를 끓게 하다 stir up one's young [youthful] blood / 청춘을 즐기다 enjoy one's youth
■—기(期) adolescence; puberty —남녀 young boys and girls; 〈총칭〉 young men and women

청출어람 靑出於藍 a disciple outstanding one's master

청취 聽取 listening; hearing; audition; 〈라디오의〉 listen-in —청취하다 listen to; hear; 〈라디오〉 listen (in) ((to the radio))
♦증언을 청취하다 hear sb's testimony; hold a hearing ((on)) / 무선을 청취하다 pick up wireless message
▶라디오로 그의 강연을 청취했다 I heard [listened to] his lecture on [over] the radio.
■—자 〈라디오의〉 a radio [wireless] listener; a radio audience; a listener-in: 청취자 참가 프로그램 a participation program

청취 테스트 聽取— an audition; a listening comprehension test
♦청취 테스트를 하다 audition sb; give an audition ((to)) / 청취 테스트를 받다 audition

청치 靑— 1 〈쌀〉 unripe [green] grains of rice
2 〈소〉 a bluish mottled cow

청칠 靑漆 blue lacquer [paint]

청컨대 請— (if you) please; I pray; I beg; I hope [wish]; It is to be hoped ((that))...

청코너 靑— 〔拳〕 the challenger's corner

청탁 淸濁 〈맑음과 흐림〉 purity and impurity 2 〈선인과 악인〉 (the) good and (the) bad; 〈선악〉 good and evil
♦청탁을 가리다 discriminate good and bad / 청탁을 가리지 않다 be so broad-minded as to be tolerant of all sorts of men

청탁 請託 〈부탁〉 a request; a favor; 〈의뢰〉 trust; commission
♦간절한 청탁 solicitation; entreaty; supplication / 청탁을 들어주다 grant [concede, comply with] a request / 청탁을 거절하다 reject [refuse] sb's request / 청탁을 받다 be asked [solicited] ((to do))
▶청탁이 하나 있습니다 I have a favor to ask (of) you.
—청탁하다 request; ask 《sb to do》; beg; 〈의뢰하다〉 entrust 《sb with sth》; commission 《sb to do》 ♦취직자리를 청탁하다 ask sb to get a job ((for))

청태 青苔 **1** 〈이끼〉 (green) moss [lichen] ♦ 청태가 낀 돌 stones covered with green moss **2** 〈김〉 green laver
청파 青— green scallion; a Welsh onion which passed the winter
청편지 請便紙 a letter of solicitation; a letter asking a favor; a written request
청포 青布 bluish hemp cloth
청포 青泡 green gram [mung bean] curd
청풍 清風 a cool [refreshing] breeze ■—명월 a cool breeze and a bright moon
청하다 請— **1** 〈부탁하다〉 ask; request; beg; call on [upon] sb to 《do》; pray for; entreat; supplicate 《sb for pardon》; solicit 《for》; demand; plead for ♦ 가르침을 청하다 ask for instruction / 도움을 청하다 ask sb's assistance; call for help / 면회를 청하다 ask for [request, seek, solicit] an interview 《with》/ 용서를 청하다 ask [seek] sb's forgiveness; beg [implore] forgiveness / 연설을 해 달라고 청하다 call on [upon] sb to make a speech / 하룻밤 자고 가기를 청하다 ask for a night's lodging / 노래를 한 곡 청하다 ask for a song from sb; call (up)on sb to sing **2** 〈달라다〉 beg; solicit ♦ 물건을 청하다 ask [beg, solicit] sb for sth; apply to sb for sth **3** 〈부르다〉 invite; dsk; call in; send for
청향 清香 fragrance; perfume
청허 聽許 permission; sanction; approval; grant —청허하다 accept; assent to; allow; approve; sanction; grant
청혼 請婚 a proposal [an offer] of marriage 《to》; courtship; addresses ▶ 그녀에게는 많은 청혼이 들어오고 있다 She has had a dozen offers of marriage. —청혼하다 propose (marriage) 《to a girl》; make an offer of marriage to 《a girl》; court; ask [sue] for 《a lady's》 hand; pay one's addresses to 《a lady》 ♦ 김씨 가문에 청혼하다 propose marriage to the Kim family; ask to marry a girl of the Kim family ▶ 그가 그녀에게 청혼했다는 소문이 있다 It's rumored that he proposed marriage to her. ▶ 아직까지 그녀에게 청혼하는 사람이 없다 No man has asked for her hand. ■—자 a suitor 《for a woman's hand》
청혼 請魂 〔佛教〕 invocation of the spirit (of a dead person) —청혼하다 invoke [summon] the spirit
청홍 青紅 blue and red ■ —실 blue and red threads —치마 blue and red skirts 《worn by a bride》
청훈 請訓 a request for instructions —청훈하다 ask 《the home government》 for instructions
청흥 清興 an elegant [a refined] amusement
체[1] 〈체질하는〉 a sieve; a sifter; 〈굵은〉 a riddle; a mesh strainer; a bolter; 〈석탄 고르는〉 a screen; 〈네모틀에 메운〉 a grate; 〈선광용의〉 a jig; a griddle ♦ 체로 친 자갈 screened gravel / 체를 메우다 fix a sieve / 체로 치다, 체질하다 put [pass, powder] sth through a sieve [sifter]; sift 《the flour from the bran》; screen; bolt; riddle / 쌀을 체질하다 sift rice
체[2] 〈꾸민 태도〉 (false) show; make-believe; pretense; affectation —체하다 pretend to 《be, do》; affect; feign; make believe; put on a show of 《doing》; set up for 《a gentleman》; pose as 《a wise man》; make a pretense 《feint, show》 of 《doing》; make as if; assume [put on] an air of 《a scholar》 ♦ 믿는 체하다 affect to believe / 못들은 체하다 pretend [make believe] not to hear sb / 아는 체하다 pretend to know; assume an air of wisdom; set up for a wise man / 모르는 체하다 pretend 《affect, feign》 ignorance 《about》; put on a show of ignorance; act innocent; 〈사람을 만났을 때〉 look the other way; cut sb (dead); turn one's back on sb / 보고도 못 본 체하다 pretend not to see; blink [wink] at 《a fault》; connive at 《an offense》/ 귀가 먼 체하다 feign deafness; pretend to be deaf [not to hear] / 미친 체하다 feign madness; pretend to be insane / 죽은 체하다 feign [sham, simulate] death / 아픈[자는] 체하다 pretend to be ill [asleep]; make a pretense of illness [sleep] / 달아나는 체하다 make as if one were going to run away / 무서운 체하다 dissemble [simulate] fear / 화난 체하다 put on a semblance of anger / 학자인 체하다 assume an air of a scholar; set up for a scholar / 시인인 체하다 pose as a poet / 안보는 체하며 보다 look through one's fingers 《at》/ 친절한 체하며 남을 속이다 cheat sb under pretense [color, the mask] of friendship ▶ 자는 체하지 말고 어서 일어나 Don't play possum. Now get up! ▶ 그는 어리석은 체하고 사람을 속인다 He fools [deceives] people by pretending to be a fool.
체[3] 〈감탄사〉 Tut!; Shucks!; Phew!; Pshaw!; Fie!; Tsk!; Hang it all!
체 體 a style; a form; a fashion ♦ 체를 모방하다 imitate sb's style / 체가 잡히다 take [get into] shape; take form
체 滯 〔漢醫〕 indigestion; dyspepsia
—체 -體 **1** 〈몸〉 the body; physique; build; frame; constitution ♦ 건강체 a healthy body / 기업체 an enterprise **2** 〔數〕 a solid (body) ♦ 4면체 a tetrahedron
체가름 sieve analysis
체감 遞減 successive [gradual] diminution; decrease in order; gradual decrease ♦ 수확 체감의 법칙 the law of diminishing returns —체감하다 decrease gradually [in order]; diminish successively ■ —률 successive diminution ratio
체감 體感 bodily sensation ■ —온도 effective temperature
체격 體格 (a) physique; (physical) constitution; frame; (physical) make; (a) (physical) build; physical features; structure of body; setup

◆가냘픈 체격 a slight build; a delicate physique / 강철같은 체격 an iron constitution / 튼튼한 체격 a compact [well-knit, well-set] frame / 체격이 좋은 남자 a fine-built man / 체격이 건장한 사람 a man of sturdy [stalwart] build / 체격이 좋다[나쁘다] have a good [weak] constitution; have a fine [poor] physique
▶아들은 체격이 튼튼한[호리호리한] 것이 그 아버지를 닮았다 The son resembled his father in his strong [weedy] build.

체격검사 體格檢査 a physical [medical] examination ⇨ 신체검사

체결 締結 conclusion ◆평화 조약의 체결 the conclusion of a peace treaty
—체결하다 conclude; contract ◆조약을 체결하다 conclude [enter into] a treaty 《with》 / 차관을 체결하다 contract a loan

체경 滯京 stay in Seoul
◆체경중에 during *one's* stay [sojourn] in Seoul; while in Seoul
—체경하다 remain [stay] in the capital [Seoul]; make a stay in Seoul

체경 體鏡 a full-length [large] mirror; a large looking glass

체계 遞計 usury; loan-sharking
■체곗돈 money used for lending at a usurious rate of interest 체곗집 a money lender's; a loan office; a financial association

체계 體系 a system; an organization
◆체계적인, 체계있는 systematic(al) / 체계적으로 systematically / 체계가 없다 lack system; have no system / 체계를 세우다 formulate [erect, develop] a system / 완전한 체계를 이루고 있다 form a complete system / 체계화하다 systematize
▶이론 체계가 완벽한 학설이다 It is a theory with a complete system.
▶학문에는 온갖 이론의 체계화가 필요하다 In pursuit of learning, it's necessary to systematize all the theories.
■철학— a system of philosophy; a philosophical system

체공 滯空 staying [remaining] in the air
—체공하다 stay [remain] in the air
—기록 a flight record —비행 an endurance flight —시간 duration of flight

체관 諦觀 1 〈명확히 봄〉 clear vision —체관하다 see clearly
2 〈체념〉 resignation —체관하다 resign *oneself* 《to *one's* fate》; endure 《*one's* misfortune》 with philosophy

체구 體軀 1 〈몸〉 the body; 〈키〉 stature
2 〈체격〉 physique; physical constitution; build ◆체구가 우람하다 have a magnificent physique; be huge of limb
▶그는 체구가 건장하다 He is of sturdy build.

체급 體級 〈스포츠〉 weight
■—제한 weight limits

체기 滯氣 a touch of indigestion [dyspepsia]
◆체기가 있다 have a touch of indigestion; suffer from slight dyspepsia

체납 滯納 nonpayment; arrearage; default 《of payment》; failure to pay; delinquency 《in payment》
—체납하다 fail to pay; default; be remiss in *one's* payment; be delinquent in payment; be in arrear(s) with the payment; let 《taxes》 fall in arrears
◆세금을 체납하다 fail to pay [default in paying] *one's* taxes
▶나는 세금을 체납한 적이 없다 I have never had my taxes in arrears. ⇌ I have never failed to pay [defaulted in paying] my taxes.
■—금 arrears; arrearage; delinquency —상습자 a habitual delinquent —세금 taxes in arrears [default]; tax arrears; back [delinquent] taxes —액 an amount in arrears —자 a delinquent; a delinquent

체납처분 滯納處分 disposition for failure to pay 《taxes》; coercive collection
◆체납처분에 의한 압류 attachment for default / 체납처분을 하다 institute a process 《against *sb*》 for the recovery of taxes in arrears; make attachment 《on *sb's* property》 for unpaid taxes
■—비 the disposition fee for arrears

체내 體內 the interior of the body
◆체내에 in the body; internal / 체내의 당분 body [tissue] sugar
▶총알은 체내에 남아 있었다 The bullet remained in the body.
▶의사는 그의 체내에서 총알을 빼내었다 The surgeon took out the bullet from his body.
■—기생충 an endoparasite; an entoparasite; an entozoon 《*pl.* -zoa》 —수정 《受精》 internal [entosomatic] fertilization

체념 諦念 resignation; reconciliation; abandonment
▶인생 살이에서 제일 먼저 배워야 할 것이 체념이다 Resignation is the first lesson in life.
▶그는 체념을 잘 한다 He gives up readily.
—체념하다 give up; resign [reconcile] *oneself* to 《*one's* fate》; be resigned [reconciled] to 《*one's* loss》
◆아무를 실종한 것이라고 체념하다 give up *sb* for lost / 환자를 살지 못할 것으로 체념하다 give over a patient for dead / 도리없다고 체념하다 abide by [resign *oneself* to] the inevitable; submit to necessity / 세상이란 그건 것이라고 체념하다 take world as it is
▶그는 이것도 운명이려니 하고 체념했다 He met his fate with resignation.
▶그는 체념하고 그녀와 함께 살기로 했다 He reconciled himself [was reconciled] to living with her.

체능 體能 physical aptitude [ability]
■—검사 a physical aptitude test

체대하다 體大— large(-sized); big-bodied; of imposing [large] build
◆체대한 사람 a man of large build

체득 體得 1 〈체험〉 realization; experience
—체득하다 realize; learn from experience
2 〈습득〉 comprehension; 〈숙달〉 mastery
—체득하다 comprehend; master
▶그녀는 영어를 가르치는 요령을 체득하고 있다 She has (got) the knack of teaching English.

체력 體力 the strength of *one's* body; physical [bodily] strength; physical stamina
♦체력의 양성 physical training; development of physical strength / 체력을 검사하다 check up *one's* physical strength / 체력을 기르다 develop [build up] *one's* physical strength; build strength
▶그는 체력이 늘었다[줄었다] His strength increased [declined].
■─검정 an examination of physical strength ─시험[테스트] a test of strength ─장(章) the physical strength measurement

체류 滯留 stay; sojourn ♦미국 체류 중에 during *one's* stay in America; while *one* is in America
─체류하다 stay; make a 《long》 stay 《at》; remain; sojourn; 〈잠시 동안〉 stop
■─객〈호텔의〉 a (staying, resident) guest; 〈일반 가정의〉 a house guest; a sojourner ─기간 the length of *one's* visit [stay] ─지 a place of sojourn

체맹 締盟 conclusion of a treaty 《of alliance》 ─체맹하다 sign [conclude] a treaty ■─국 a treaty power; 〈조인국〉 a signatory (power)

체머리 spasmodic head-shaking; a shaky head ♦체머리를 흔들다 shake *one's* head chronically; have a shaky head; 〈싫증나다〉 be sickened 《of》; (口) be sick and tired 《of》; be fed up 《with》

체메 an unscrupulous [impertinent] person; a man of no scruples

체메다 fix a sieve screen on its frame; make a sieve

체면 體面 〈면목〉 face; honor; 〈품위〉 dignity; prestige; decency; 〈명성〉 reputation; a good name; 〈외관〉 appearances
♦체면에 관계되는 문제 a matter of dignity; a question of face / 체면이 서는 face-saving 《concession》 / 체면이 깎이는[손상되는] undignified; compromising; disgraceful / 체면을 무릎쓰고 without caring about decency / 체면에 관계되다 affect [reflect on] *one's* honor [prestige]; be compromising to *one's* reputation [fair name] / 체면을 지키다[유지하다] keep up [maintain] appearances; save the honor [face] of / 체면을 세우다[차리다] save [patch up] appearances; save 《one's》 face; put up a good front / 체면을 중시하다 respect *one's* honor; think much of *one's* reputation / 학교[집안]의 체면을 손상하다 throw [reflect] discredit upon *one's* school [family]
▶그것은 체면 문제다 It is a matter of "face." ⇌ It is a point of honor with me.
▶체면 따위를 생각하고 있을 때가 아니다 Maintaining appearance is now out of the question.
▶그렇다면 내 체면은 어떻게 되나? How can I save my face [honor] then?
▶자네 덕분에 우리의 체면이 섰네 You kept up our prestige [appearances]. ⇌ You saved our face(s).
▶체면 깎일 짓은 그만두어라 Stop that for decency's sake.

체면상 體面上 for appearance's [decency's sake; for honor's sake; for the sake of appearances; for *one's* reputation; (just) to save *one's* face [honor]
▶이 돈은 체면상 받을 수가 없다 I cannot, in honor, accept this money.
▶그는 체면상 그렇게 말하지 않을 수 없다 He is bound to say so to save his face.

체모 體毛 hair (of *one's* body)

체미 滯美 stay(ing) in America [the United States] ♦체미중 while staying in America; during *one's* stay in the (United) States ─체미하다 stay [make a stay] in America

체발 剃髮 shaving *one's* head; tonsure ─체발하다 take the tonsure; be tonsured; get [have] *one's* head shaved; tonsure

체벌 體罰 corporal [physical, bodily] punishment ♦체벌을 가하다 inflict corporal punishment 《on *sb*》 / 체벌을 받다 suffer corporal punishment
▶그는 순순히 체벌을 받았다 He meekly accepted the corporal punishment. ⇌ He resigned himself to receiving corporal punishment.

체법 體法 the style of penmanship and the technique of calligraphy

체불 滯拂 a delay in payment; delayed payment 《of wages》 ─체불하다 fall into arrears; be overdue; be delayed
■─임금 overdue wage; wage unpaid; wages in arrears; delayed pay: 체불 임금의 청산을 요구하다 call for clearance of overdue wages

체비지 替費地 an area of land secured by the authorities in recompense of development outlay

체색 體色 〈동물의〉 the color of the body

체선료 滯船料 demurrage

체세포 體細胞 〔生〕 a somatic [body] cell

체소하다 體小─ small(-sized); small in body [frame, build]; short ♦체소한 사람 a man of small build

체송 遞送 conveyance; forwarding

체스 chess ♦체스판 a chessboard / 체스의 말 a chessman

체신 遞信 transmission through stages; 〈통신〉 communications
■─사무 postal and telegraphic service

체액 體液 〔生理〕 body fluids; humors
■─병리학 humoral pathology

체약 締約 the conclusion of a treaty; 〈협정〉 a convention; a treaty; an agreement ─체약하다 conclude 《a treaty》

체언 體言 〔文法〕 indeclinable parts of speech in Korean grammar; the substantives

체열 體熱 body heat; 〈동물의〉 animal heat

체온 體溫 (bodily) temperature; body heat
♦체온의 변화 changes in *one's* temperature / 체온이 높다[낮다] have a high [low] temperature / 체온을 재다 take *one's* temperature
▶체온은 약간 오르내린다 The temperature shows some fluctuations.
▶나는 저녁 무렵에 체온이 올라갔다[내려갔다] My temperature rose [fell] toward the evening.
▶환자는 체온이 38도 2분이다 The tempera-

ture of the patient is 38.2 degrees.
▶ 그의 체온은 정상보다 조금 높다 His temperature is a little above the normal.
■ —계 a (clinical) thermometer —곡선 a temperature curve —표 a fever chart

체위 體位 1 〈체격〉 a physical standard; physical condition; physique
◆ 국민 체위의 저하 deterioration in the national physique / 체위를 향상시키다 improve the physique; elevate [raise] the physical standards 《of a nation》
▶ 당국은 국민 체위의 향상을 위해 모든 노력을 기울이고 있다 The authorities are making every effort to improve the physique of the people.
2 〈자세〉 a posture; a position of the body
■ 평균— the physical average 《in the country》 ■ —향상[저하] improvement [deterioration] of physical condition

체육 體育 physical training [culture]; the physical upbuilding 《of a nation》; 〈교과명〉 physical education; (口) gym; 〈체조〉 gymnastics; 〈운동〉 athletics ◆ 체육을 장려하다 encourage physical culture / 체육을 중시하다 stress [make much of] physical education; attach importance to physical education
■ —가 a physical educator; an athlete —관 the course of physical education —관 a gymnasium 《pl.》~s, -sia》; (口) a gym —단체 an athletic organization —대회 an athletic meeting —부 〈신문사의〉 the department of athletics; 〈대학의〉 an athletic club —선생 a physical education teacher —지도자 a physical director —특기생 a sports talent —회(會) an athletic association [club]: 대한 체육회 the Korea Amateur Athletic Association 《略 K.A.A.A.》

체읍 涕泣 weeping and wailing —체읍하다 weep and wail; shed tears

체인 a chain; 〈자동차의〉 a tire chain
■ —구동식 chain drive type —운반장치 chain delivery

체인 스토어 (美) a chain store; (英) a multiple shop [store]

체인지 〔野〕 a change ■ —오브 페이스 a change of pace

체재 滯在 a stay; a sojourn
◆ 2주일간의 체재 a week's stay [visit] / 미국 체재중에 during one's stay [visit, sojourn] in America; while (staying) in America
—체재하다 stay 《at, in》; make a stay; sojourn
◆ 장기간[잠깐 동안] 체재하다 make a long [short] stay

체재 體裁 form; style; 〈겉보기〉 appearance; show; 〈만듦새〉 format; (口) getup
◆ 체재가 좋다 be of good style; be seemly [presentable]; look nice [presentable] / 체재가 나쁘다 do not look nice; cut a sorry figure; be unsightly / 체재를 갖추다 have proper form [style]

체적 體積 〈부피〉 volume; cubic volume [content(s)]; cubage; solid measure; 〈용적〉 capacity ◆ 물체의 체적 the volume of a body / 체적을 구하다 find the volume 《of》; cube

■ —계 a stereometer; a volumeter —측정 stereometry; volumetry —팽창 volume [cubical] expansion

체제 體制 1 〈조직〉 (a) structure; a system; an order; a setup; organization ◆ 국내 체제를 강화하다 strengthen the internal structure of the nation
2 〈기성의 사회 제도〉 the Establishment
▶ 그는 체제 쪽의 사람이다 He belongs to [is a member of] the Establishment.
■ 경제— an economic structure 구— the old order [system, structure] 신— a new system 전시— a war footing 정치— a political system [dispensation] ■ —파 the Establishmentarians

체조 體操 gymnastics; physical [gymnastic] exercises; (美) gym work [exercises]; (英口) jerks; (口) physical jerks —체조하다 practice gymnastics; have gymnastic exercises
■ 기계— apparatus gymnastics 라디오— radio gymnastic exercises 맨손[도수]— gymnastic exercises without apparatus; 〈경기 종목〉 free standing exercises 미용— calisthenics; aesthetic gymnastics 율동— rhythmic gymnastics [calisthenics] ■ —경기 gymnastics competition —교사 a gymnastic(s) teacher; a gymnast; a drillmaster —기구 gymnastic appliances [apparatus, gear] —복 gym suit —선수 a gymnast —시간 a gymnastics hour [period] —팀 a gymnastic team —학교 a gymnasium

체중 體重 the weight 《of one's body》; one's body weight
◆ 체중의 증가 an increase in weight / 체중의 감소[저하] weight loss / 체중이 늘다 put on [gain, pick up] weight / 체중이 줄다 lose weight / 체중이 1킬로그램 늘다[줄다] gain [lose] a kilogram / 체중을 줄이다 reduce [lessen] one's weight / 체중을 재다 weigh oneself
▶ 너는 체중이 얼마나 되니? How much do you weigh? ⇌ What is your weight?
▶ 그는 체중이 70킬로그램 나갔다 He tipped the scales at seventy kilograms.
■ —검사 〈스포츠의〉 a weigh-in

체증 滯症 indigestion; dyspepsia
◆ 체증이 있다 suffer from indigestion
▶ 이 거리는 차의 체증이 심하다 This street is always congested.
■ 교통— (traffic) jam; traffic congestion; a traffic snarl [backup]: 나는 교통 체증 때문에 지각했다 I was late because of the traffic congestion [a traffic jam].

체증 遞增 gradual increase
—체증하다 increase gradually

체질 sieving; screening; sifting ⇨ 체¹
—체질하다 sieve; screen; riddle 《coal, sand, gravel》; sift (out)
◆ 모래에서 체질하여 자갈을 걸러내다 sift (out) pebbles from the sand

체질 體質 (physical) constitution; 〔醫〕 a diathesis; 〈소질〉 predisposition
◆ 병약한 체질 constitutional tendencies to disease / 체질적 결함 a constitutional defect

▶그는 체질적으로 강하다[약하다] He is of strong [weak] constitution.
▶나는 감기에 잘 걸리는 체질이다 I'm apt to catch cold.
▶그것은 내 체질에 맞지 않는다 That doesn't suit my constitution. ⇌ That doesn't agree with me.
■—개선 improving one's physical constitution; 〈단체·기업 등의〉 radical reform; revamping; overhauling

체체파리 〔昆〕 a tsetse

체취 體臭 1 〈몸의 냄새〉 body smell; the personal odor; 〈주로 겨드랑이 냄새〉 body odor (略 B.O.)
♦체취가 나다 give out [send forth] a body smell
2 〈독특한 느낌〉 something characteristic of the man
▶이 그림은 그 화가의 강한 체취를 담고 있다 This painting reveals the strong personality of the artist.

체코 Czech; 〈공식명〉 the Czech Republic
■—말 Czech —사람 a Czech

체크 1 〈수표〉 (美) a check; (英) a cheque
2 〈무늬〉 checks; checkers; (英) chequers; cross stripes
♦체크 무늬의 스커트 a checkered [cross-striped, check] skirt
3 〈검사대조〉 collation; check(up)
—체크하다 check [tick] (off); mark

체통 體統 《an official's》 dignity [prestige]; honor; face
♦체통이 서는 face-saving / 체통에 관한 문제 a matter of dignity; a question of face / 체통을 세우다 save (one's) face [one's honor]/ 체통을 잃다 lose (one's) face

체팽창 體膨脹 〔物〕 cubical expansion ⇨ 체적 (~팽창) ■—계수 coefficient of cubical expansion; cubic expansion coefficient

체포 逮捕 (an) arrest; apprehension; (a) capture
♦체포를 모면하다 escape arrest
—체포하다 arrest; place under arrest; make an arrest; apprehend; capture; catch; take sb into custody; keep sb in custody
♦살인 혐의로 체포하다 arrest sb for murder / 체포되지 않고 있다 be at large
▶당신을 체포합니다 You are under arrest.
▶그는 절도 혐의로 체포됐다 He was arrested for theft.

체포령 逮捕令 a mandate for an arrest; a warrant for [of] an arrest ♦…의 체포령을 내리다 issue a warrant for the arrest of…

체포영장 逮捕令狀 a warrant of arrest [apprehension]; an arrest warrant
♦체포영장을 발급하다 issue [put out] a warrant for the arrest (of)

체하다 滯— 〈음식이 주어〉 sit [lie] heavy on one's stomach; 〈사람이 주어〉 have an attack of indigestion
▶아침 먹은 것이 체했다 What I took for breakfast lies heavy on my stomach.

체한 滯韓 stay(ing) in Korea
♦체한중에 while staying in Korea; during one's stay in Korea
—체한하다 stay in Korea

체험 體驗 (personal) experience
♦값진[진귀한] 체험 a valuable [novel] experience / 체험을 살리다 make good use of one's experience / 체험으로 알다 learn by [from] experience
—체험하다 experience; have experience of; go through; undergo; feel actually; know
♦직접 체험하다 gain one's experience at first hand
■—담 the story of one's experiences; talk of one's personal experiences

체현 體現 embodiment; personification; impersonation —체현하다 embody; impersonate; personify; give concrete form to

체형 體刑 〈체벌〉 corporal [physical, bodily] punishment; 〈징역〉 penal servitude ♦체형을 과하다 inflict [impose] corporal punishment 《on sb》; sentence sb to penal servitude

체호프 〈러시아의 작가〉 Chek(h)ov, Anton Pavlovich (1860-1904)

체화 滯貨 〈화물의〉 accumulation of freights [goods]; freight congestion; (美) backlog; 〈시장의〉 accumulation of stocks [supplies]
♦체화를 일소하다 clear out the accumulated goods [commodities]
2 〈상품의〉 stockpiles of goods; a drug in [on] the market

첼레스타 a celesta

첼로 a cello 《pl. ~s》; a violoncello 《pl. ~s》
■—주자 (奏者) a cello player; a cellist; a violoncellist

쳄발로 a cembalo 《pl. -bali, ~s》

쳇다리 a fork-shaped sieve rails; a frame supporting a sieve 《over a tub》

쳇바퀴 a sieve-frame; the frame of a sieve
♦개미 쳇바퀴 돌 듯하다 go round and round

쳇불 a sieve-bottom; the bottom of a sieve
♦쳇바퀴에 쳇불을 메우다 fix [attach] sieve-bottom to the frame of a sieve

쳐가다 collect and take [carry] away 《garbage bags》; take away 《rubbish bags》
♦변소를 쳐가다 carry away night soil from a privy

쳐내다 take away; clear off [out]; remove 《from》; clean up
♦눈을 쳐내다 shovel away snow; clear 《a yard》 of snow / 변소를 쳐내다 remove night soil from a privy / 돼지우리를 쳐내다 clean out a pigsty

쳐넣다 throw [cast, fling] in [into]; dump into ♦감옥에 쳐넣다 cast [throw] sb into prison / 강에 쳐넣다 throw sth into the river

쳐다보다 look up 《at》; look upward; lift (up) [raise] one's eyes; cast up one's eyes 《to》
♦하늘을 쳐다보다 look up at the sky
▶위를 쳐다보면 한이 없다 Don't compare yourself with those above you.

쳐들다 1 〈올리다〉 lift (up); raise
♦높이 쳐들다 hold sth aloft / 고개를 쳐들다 raise one's head; (비유) gain strength
2 〈초들다〉 cite; point out; adduce 《proofs》

◆남의 결점을 쳐들다 point out [bring up] another's faults

쳐들어가다 invade; make inroads 《on, into》; penetrate 《into》; attack; raid [storm] into; 〈돌격하다〉 charge 《at, on》; rush [dash] at; break into 《a house》
◆적진으로 쳐들어가다 rush [charge] the enemy's position

쳐버리다 〈치우다〉 take [clear] away; remove; 〈쓸다〉 sweep away; clean up
◆쓰레기를 쳐버리다 clear refuse away

쳐주다 1〈값을〉 appraise; value; evaluate; set [put] a price 《on》; assess; estimate; rate
◆비싸게[싸게] 쳐주다 estimate high [low]; rate 《a thing》 high [low]
▶나는 그 집 값을 1억원 쳐줬다 I appraised the house at a hundred million won.
2〈간주하다〉 regard 《as》; consider; deem; reckon; count 《as, for》; look on [upon] 《as》; take 《for》
◆적임자로 쳐주다 regard sb as fit [suitable] for the post
3〈치워주다〉 take [clear] away; clean up; remove

쳐죽이다 strike [knock, beat, club] 《a dog》 to death; strike 《a cat》 dead; kill by a blow
◆돌로 쳐죽이다 stone sb to death

초 a candle; 〈가는 것〉 a taper
◆초의 심지 the wick 《of a candle》; a candle-wick / 초에 불을 붙이다[당기다] burn [light] a candle / 초를 불어서 끄다 blow out a candle

-초 -初 1〈처음〉 the beginning; (the) first; the early part
◆학기초 the beginning of (the school) term / 5월초에 early in May
2〔野〕 the first [upper] half; the top
◆9회초 the first half of the ninth inning

초 草 a rough copy; a draft ◆초를 잡다 make a draft 《of》; make a rough copy 《of》; draft

초 醋 vinegar ◆초간장 soy sauce mixed with vinegar / 초에 절이다 pickle in vinegar / 초를 치다 vinegar sth; put vinegar in [on]

초 秒 a second ◆천분의 1초 a millisecond / 백만분의 1초 a microsecond / 초를 다투다〈병 등이〉 require [call for] prompt treatment; 〈문제 등이〉 need a speedy solution
▶초를 다투는 문제다 There is no moment to loss.

초- 初- early ◆초봄 early spring / 초하루 the first (day) of the month

초- 超- super; ultra
◆초강대국 a superpower / 초특급 열차 a superexpress / 초자연적인 supernatural

초가 草家 a thatched house; a straw-thatched house ■─삼간 a three-room thatched house; a small cottage ─집 a thatched house

초가 樵歌 a woodcutter's [woodman's] song

초가을 初- early autumn [fall]; the beginning of autumn

초감각적 超感覺的 extrasensory; supersensible; pretersensual

초강초강하다 thin; lean
◆초강초강한 얼굴 a thin face; a haggard countenance / 얼굴이 초강초강하다 be thin in the face

초개 草芥 bits of straw; 〈하찮은 것〉 a worthless thing; rubbish; dirt
◆초개같은 worthless; valueless; unworthy / 초개같은 인생 a worthless life 《existence》; a humble life / 목숨[죽음]을 초개같이 여기다 think nothing of one's life; hold one's life as nothing

초거성 超巨星 〔天〕 a supergiant star

초겨울 初- early winter; the beginning of winter

초경 初更 the first watch of the night (about 8 o'clock p.m.)

초경 初耕 the first plowing
─초경하다 do the preliminary plowing

초경 初經 〔첫월경〕 menarche

초계 哨戒 patrol; patrolling ◆초계 중이다 be on patrol ─초계하다 patrol
■ 연안─ coastal patrol 해상─ sea patrol ─부대〔기, 선〕 a patrol force [plane, line] ─정 a patrol [vedette] boat; a picketboat

초고 草稿 a (rough) draft; notes; a manuscript (略 MS., ms.)
◆강의의 초고 notes for a lecture / 연설의 초고 a draft of a speech / 초고를 작성하다 make (out) a draft 《of》; draft (out) 《an address》; prepare notes 《for a lecture》

초고속 超高速 superhigh [ultrahigh] speed
■ ─도로〔美〕a superhighway;〔英〕a motorway ─카메라 a superhigh-speed camera

초고주파 超高周波 〔物〕 superhigh frequency (略 SHF)

초과 超過 excess; 〈잉여〉 surplus; (an) extra
◆중량 초과 overweight
▶이 소포는 200그램 중량 초과입니다 This parcel is 200 grams overweight.
─초과하다 exceed; be in excess 《of》; be above [over, more than]
◆예산을 초과하다 exceed the budget / 제한 연령[시간]을 초과하다 exceed the age [time] limit / 규정된 무게를 초과하다 exceed the fixed weight; overweigh; outweigh
▶저 차는 제한속도를 초과하고 있다 That car exceeds the speed limit.
▶공사비는 나의 당초 예상을 크게 초과했다 The construction expenses [cost of construction] exceeded my original estimate by a great deal.
▶이 배는 정원을 초과하여 손님을 태우고 있다 This ship is carrying more passengers than the seating capacity allows.
■ 수입[수출]─ an excess of imports [exports]; the unfavorable [favorable] balance of trade ─소득 excess income ─액 a surplus; an excess ─요금 〈차의〉 excess fare

초과근무 超過勤務 overtime work [service]; extra duties
◆초과근무를 하다 work overtime
■ ─수당 overtime pay(ment); an overtime premium [allowance]

초교 初校 the first proofing; the first revise
◆초교를 보다 read the first proof

초국가 超國家 a superstate ◆초국가적인 supranational ■ ─주의 ultranationalism ─주의

자 an ultranationalist
초군 超群 preeminence
─초군하다 preeminent;〈서술적〉be preeminent above the rest 《for》; excel 《others in》
초근목피 草根木皮 the roots of herbs [plants] and the barks of trees;〈악식〉coarse and miserable food
♦초근목피로 연명하다 barely keep alive with the aid of herb roots and tree barks
초급 初級 the first [beginner's] class; the junior course
■─대학 a junior college
초급 初給〈첫월급〉an initial salary [pay]
초기 初期 **1**〈한 시대의〉the early days [period, years]; the beginning
♦신라 초기에 early in the Shilla era
2〈병 등의〉the first [initial, incipient, early] stage
♦문명의 초기 the early stage of civilization / 소월의 초기 작품 Sowol's early works
▶이 병은 초기에 치료하면 나을 수 있다 The disease can be cured if treated in early stages.
▶그의 암은 아직 초기라고 한다 The doctor says that he is in the first stage of cancer.
■─결핵〔醫〕early [incipient] tuberculosis [T.B.] ─침윤〔醫〕primary infiltration
초김치 醋─ vinegared *kimchi*
초꼬지 a dried small abalone
초나흗날 初─ the fourth day of a month
초년 初年 **1**〈인생의〉one's youth; one's early years; one's younger days
♦초년에 when young; while in one's youth; in one's youth; at an early age
2〈첫 해〉the first year;〈초기〉the early years
■─병 a raw recruit; a new conscript ─생 a beginner; a novice; a greenhorn
초념 初念 one's original mind [intention]
초능력 超能力 supernatural power
초다짐하다 初─ eat just a bite to ease [assuage] one's hunger before mealtime; snack before mealtime
초단 初段〈바둑·유도 등의〉the lowest grade of the senior class 《in》; the first grade
♦바둑 초단인 a *paduk* player of the first grade / 유도 초단자 first-grader in judo
초단파 超短波 ultrashort waves; very high frequency 《略 V.H.F.,VHF,v.h.f., vhf》
■─극 a microwave; ultrahigh frequency 《略 U.H.F., UHF, u.h.f., uhf》 ─방송 frequency modulation [FM] broadcasting ─수신[송신]기 an ultrashort wave receiver [transmitter]
초닷새 初─ the fifth day of a month
초당 草堂 a straw hut; a little cottage
초당안보기구 超黨安保機構 a suprapartisan [nonpartisan] organization for national security
초당파 超黨派 ♦초당파의 suprapartisan; nonpartisan;《美》bipartisan
■─내각 a suprapartisan [coalition] cabinet ─외교 suprapartisan diplomacy; a bipartisan diplomacy ─정부 an all-party government
초대 初─〈초심자〉a greenhorn; a green

hand; a fledg(e)ling; a novice; a beginner; a cub
▶그는 골프에는 아직 초대다 He is still a beginner in golf.
초대 初大〈초급대학〉a junior college
초대 初代〈제 1 대〉the first generation;〈사람〉the founder ♦초대의 the first ─대통령 the first President
초대 招待 (an) invitation; (口) (an) invite
♦초대를 받다 be invited 《to》; have [receive] an invitation 《from *sb*》 / 초대를 사양하다 decline [refuse] an invitation / 초대에 응하다 accept an invitation
▶그녀는 록펠러 재단의 초대로 뉴욕에 갔다 She went to New York at the invitation of the Rockefeller Foundation.
▶초대에 기꺼이 응하겠습니다 I shall be glad to accept your invitation.
─초대하다 invite; ask; extend an invitation 《to *sb*》
♦만찬에 초대하다 invite [ask] *sb* to dinner
▶초대해 주셔서 감사합니다 I thank you for your kind invitation. ⇒ I am very much obliged for your kind invitation.
■─객 an invited guest ─권 an invitation card [ticket];〈우대권〉a complimentary ticket ─석 a seat reserved for a guest ─연 a dinner party; a feast; a banquet ─작가 an invited artist ─회〈시연·시사회 등의〉a trade show; a preview
초대면 初對面 the first meeting [interview] 《with》
▶우리는 초대면입니다 This is the first time we have met.
▶그들은 초대면의 인사를 나누었다 They exchanged formal greetings at the first meeting.
초대작 超大作 a super-production;〈영화의〉a superfilm; a supra-feature film
초대장 招待狀 a letter of invitation; an invitation (card); (口) an invite ♦초대장을 (보)내다 send [issue] an invitation (card) 《to》
초대형 超大型 ♦초대형의 extralarge; (口) outsize(d) ■─여객기 a jumbo (jet) ─여객선 a superliner
초도 初度〈첫번〉(for) the first time ■─순시 one's first tour [round] of inspection
초동 初冬 early winter; the beginning of winter
초동 樵童 a young woodcutter; a fuelgathering boy
초두 初頭〈첫머리〉the beginning; the opening; the start; the outset;〈애초〉(the) first
♦21세기 초두에 at the beginning [outset] of the 21st century
▶일이 초두부터 잘 되어 갔다 We made a successful beginning. ⇒ We made a good start.
초들다〈말하다〉mention; refer [allude] 《to》;〈인용하다〉cite (as an example); instance
♦과거사를 초들다 make reference to what had passed / 남의 단점을 초들다 bring up *sb's* failures
초등 初等 an elementary [a primary] grade; the lowest grade

■ —과 an elementary course; a beginner's class **—교육** elementary [primary] education **—기하** elementary geometry **—학교** an elementary [a primary, (美) a grade] school

초등학생 初等學生 a primary school pupil; a schoolboy; **(총칭)** schoolchildren

초라니 an exorcist who appears in woman's dress at a court rite

초라떼다 make a fool of *oneself*; be put to shame; be humbled; get taken [brought, let] down a peg (or two)

초라하다 〈겉모양이〉 shabby; poor-[shabby-] looking; mean; miserable; wretched
♦ 초라한 옷 shabby clothes / 초라한 음식 coarse [plain] food / 초라한 집 a humble [shabby] house / 옷차림이 초라하다 be shabbily [poorly] dressed; be ill-clad / 초라해 보이다 look shabby; cut [make] a poor [sorry] figure / 초라하게 살다 be poorly [badly] off

초래하다 招來— bring about; give rise to; lead to; bring [draw] on (*oneself*); court; invite; incur; cause; induce; produce
♦ 파멸을 초래하다 bring down ruin (on *sb*) / 화를 초래하다 bring calamity on *oneself*; court disaster / 좋은 결과를 초래하다 produce (good) results / 물가의 등귀를 초래하다 cause an advance in the prices of commodities / 죽음을 초래하다 court [occasion] death
▶ 그 법안은 당의 분열을 초래했다 The bill caused a split within the party.

초략 抄略 1 〈노략질〉 pillage; plunder; spoilage; spoliation; despoilation; despoilment
—초략하다 plunder; pillage; spoliate; despoil; loot
2 〈줄임〉 abbreviation; abridg(e)ment
—초략하다 abbreviate; abridge

초련 〈가을걷이 전의 풋바심〉 an early crop to be served until the regular harvest

초례 醮禮 a marriage [nuptial, matrimonial] ceremony; a wedding (ceremony)
♦ 초례를 지내다 hold [perform, celebrate, solemnize] a marriage [wedding]
■ **—청** a wedding hall

초로 初老 〈중년〉 middle age; 〈쉰 살〉 fifty years of age ♦ 초로의 middle-aged; elderly / 초로의 사람 a middle-ager

초로 草路 a path [lane] across a meadow [a field of grass]

초로 草露 dew on the grass
▶ 인생은 초로와 같다 The world is but a fleeting shadow. ⇒ Life is but a span.
■ **—인생** a life as evanescent as the dew; an ephemeral [a transient] life

초록 抄錄 an excerpt; an extract; 〈적요〉 an abstract; an epitome; a summary
—초록하다 abstract; excerpt; extract; make an abstract of (a book)
■ **—자** an abstracter; an excerpter

초록 草綠 green; verdure
♦ 초록의 green; grassy-green; verdant / 초록의 언덕 a green hill

초록은 동색이다 (속담) One devil knows another. ⇒ Like knows like.

초롱 a tin; a can

♦ 석유 한 초롱 a tin [can] of kerosene / 페트 다섯 초롱 five pails of paint

초롱 籠 a (paper) lantern

초롱꽃 〔植〕 a bellflower; a Canterbury bell

초름하다 〈불충분하다〉 insufficient; not enough; 〈미달하다〉 not up to the mark; less than due amount [quantity]; 〈모자라다〉 a bit short of
▶ 내 몫이 네 몫보다 초름하다 My share is [looks] smaller than yours.

초립 草笠 a straw hat ■ **—동(이)** a (married) youngster wearing a straw hat

초막 草幕 〈초가〉 a straw-thatched hut [cottage]; 〔佛敎〕 a Buddhist monk's cell (near the temple)

초만원 超滿員 being overly filled-up
♦ 초만원이다 be filled [full, packed] to overflowing; be crowded beyond capacity
▶ 아침 열차는 언제나 초만원이다 The morning train is always packed to overflowing.
▶ 강당은 그의 연설을 들으려는 사람들로 초만원이었다 The hall was overcrowed [congested, jammed] with people to hear his speech.

초매 草昧 〈미개〉 a primitive [primeval] state; primitiveness; 〈혼돈〉 chaos; confusion; disorder

초면 初面 the first meeting (with) ⇨ 초대면
♦ 초면의 사람 a person met for the first time; a stranger
■ **—인사** greeting on the first meeting: 그들은 초면인사를 나누었다 They introduced themselves to each other.

초면 炒麵 (美) chow mein; Chinese fried noodles

초멸 剿滅 extermination; extirpation; mopping up (a gang)
—초멸하다 mop up; exterminate; extirpate; rid

초모 醋母 〔植〕 〈아세트산균〉 acetic acid bacteria

초목 草木 trees and plants; grass and trees; plant life; vegetation
♦ 초목이 우거진 산 a thickly-wooded hill / 초목이 우거지다 have lush vegetation
▶ 그 섬에서는 초목이 전혀 자라지 못한다 There were no plant on the island.
■ **산천—** nature; natural scenery

초문 初聞 a thing heard of for the first time
▶ 그것은 금시초문이다 That's news [a revelation] to me. ⇒ It's the first time I've heard that.

초미 焦眉 〈위급함〉 ♦ 초미의 urgent; pressing; exigent; impending; crying ■ **—지급(之急)** an urgent [a crying, a pressing] need

초민 焦悶 impatience; sadness; worry **—초민하다** feel impatient (at); be sad at heart; be anxious (about)

초반 初盤 the opening part (of); an early stage (of)
▶ 시합의 결과는 초반에 결정되었다 The result of the game was decided in the early stages of it.

초밥 醋— vinegared fish and rice

초방 初枋 〔建〕 the first strut in the middle of a wall to be housed
초배 初褙 〈애벌 도배〉 lining; underlining ━초배하다 line [underline] ((a wall)) with paper ■━지 lining paper; a lining
초벌 初━ the first (stage) ⇨ 애벌
━김 the first weeding ━도배 ⇨ 초배
초벌구이 初━ 〈굽는 일〉 unglazed pottery; 〈도자기〉 unglazed earthenware
초범 初犯 〈죄〉 the first offense; 〈초범자〉 a first offender
초벽 初壁 〈바르기〉 rough coating; a first [rough] coat; 〈벽〉 a rough-coated wall
━초벽하다 give the wall a first coat ((of plaster))
초병 哨兵 a sentry ⇨ 보초 (步哨)
초병 醋瓶 a vinegar bottle ■━마개 (비유) a person with repulsive and nauseous manners
초보 初步 the [a] first step ((to, toward)); the rudiments ((of)); the elements ((of)); 〈기본적 사항〉 the ABC('s) ((of)); 〈초심자의〉 a beginner's course
◆산수의 초보 the rudiments [elements, ABC] of arithmetic / 초보를 가르치다 initiate sb into; give sb elementary lessons (in); teach sb the rudiments ((of)) / 초보를 배우다 learn the rudiments
▶그의 연구는 아직 초보단계에 있다 He is only at the first step of his study.
■경제학━ the ABC of economics ■━영어 elementary English ━지식 an elementary [a rudimentary] knowledge ((of))
초보자 初步者 a beginner; (美) an abecedarian; a new [green] hand; a novice; a greenhorn
◆초보자의 beginners' / 초보자의 영어 회화 beginners' English conversation / 초보자용의 (a book) for beginners
초복 初伏 the beginning of the dog days
◆초복이 들다 the dog days begin [set in]
초본 草本 〔植〕 a herb; (총칭) herbage
◆초본의 herbal; herbaceous
■━대 the herbaceous plant zone
초본 抄本 an extract; an abstract; an abridged transcript [copy]
◆호적━ an abstract of one's family register
초봄 初━ early spring; the beginning of spring
▶산불은 초봄에 자주 난다 Forest fires break out frequently in the early spring [at the beginning of spring].
초봉 初俸 an initial [a starting, a begining] salary [wages, pay]
◆초봉 100만원을 받다 start with a salary of one million won a month
초부 樵夫 〈나무꾼〉 a firewood cutter; a woodcutter; a woodsman; a lumberman; a lumberjack; (美) a logger
초분 初分 〈인생의 초년 운수〉 one's star [fortune, lot] in early days [years, life] ◆초분이 길하다[좋다] be lucky in one's early life
초빙 招聘 (an) invitation; a call; an engagement
◆초빙에 응하다 accept the offer of a position; accept the call ((to))
▶나는 그의 초빙에 응했다 I accepted [received] a call from him.
━초빙하다 invite ((a lecturer)); call in ((an expert)); call on ((sb to do))
▶그를 총지배인으로 초빙했다 Our company engaged him as a general manager.
▶우리는 전자 공학 전문가를 초빙하고 싶다 We want to call in an electronics specialist.
초사 焦思 worry; anxiety ⇨ 노심초사 (勞心焦思) ━초사하다 worry ((oneself)) ((about)); trouble oneself ((about))
초사흘날 初━ the third day of a month
초사흘 初━ the third day of a month=초사흘날
초산 初産 one's first childbirth [birth, confinement]
◆처의 초산 때에 at the time of one's wife's first confinement
▶아내의 초산은 순산[난산]이었다 My wife's first delivery was an easy [a difficult] one.
■━부 a primipara ((pl. ~s, -rae)); 〈초산할〉 a woman expecting (a baby) for the first time; 〈초산한〉 a woman having had her first baby
초산 硝酸 〔化〕 nitric acid ⇨ 질산 (窒酸)
초상 初喪 (a period of) mourning
◆초상나다 a death occurs ((in sb's family)) / 초상을 당하다 have a death in one's family
■━집 a house [family] in mourning
초상 肖像 a portrait; a likeness; 〈청동·대리석 등의〉 a statue ◆초상을 그리다 portray sb; take sb's likeness
▶이 초상은 누구를 그린 것입니까? Who does the portrait represent?
■━권 one's portrait rights
초상화 肖像畫 a portrait; 〈화법〉 portrait painting
◆초상화를 그리다 paint sb's portrait / 초상화를 그리게 하다 have [get] one's likeness [portrait] painted [drawn, taken] ((by an artist))
■━가 a portrait painter; a portraitist
초서 〈영국의 시인〉 Chaucer, Geoffrey (1343?-1400)
초서 草書 〈글자〉 grass [cursive] characters; 〈서체〉 the grass [cursive] hand [style]
◆초서(체)로 쓰다 write in grass characters
초석 草席 a straw mat
초석 硝石 〔化〕〈질산 칼륨〉 niter [náitər]; saltpeter
■━칠레━ Chile [cubic] saltpeter; niter
초석 〈표면에 나타나지 않은 돌〉 a sunken [submerged] rock; a reef
초석 礎石 〈토대가 되는 돌〉 a foundation stone; 〈귓돌〉 a cornerstone; a quoin; 〈토대〉 a foundation; a basis ((pl. -ses))
◆나라의 초석 the pillar [mainstay] of the state / 초석이 되다 be a cornerstone ((of)) / 초석을 앉히다 lay foundation stone
▶그는 나라의 초석이 되기를 바랐다 He wanted to become a pillar of the state.
초선 初選 ◆초선의 〈당선된〉 newly-elected
■━의원 a newly-elected member of the National Assembly

초설 初雪 the first snow=첫눈
초성 初聲 〔言〕 an initial sound [consonant]
초소 哨所 〈보초가 서있는 곳〉 a guard [sentry] post; 〈검문하는〉《美》 a checkpoint
초소형 超小型 ◆초소형의 subminiature
■—카메라 a subminiature (camera)
초속 初速 initial velocity ⇨ 초속도
초속 秒速 the speed [velocity] per second
◆초속 30미터로 at a speed of 30 meters per [a] second
▶소리는 수중에서 초속 약 1,400 미터로 전달된다 Sound travels at (a speed of) about 1,400 meters a [per] second in water.
초속 超速 super velocity ⇨ 초속도
초속 超俗 unworldliness
◆초속적(인) unworldly; supermundane
초속도 初速度 〈최초의 속도〉 initial velocity; 〈탄환의〉 muzzle velocity
초속도 秒速度 the velocity per second ⇨ 초속
초속도 超速度 〈굉장히 빠른 속도〉 superhigh [ultrahigh] speed; super velocity
초손 初孫 〈첫 손자〉 one's first grandchilld
초순 初旬 the first decade [ten days] of a month
◆12월 초순에 early in December
▶초순에 정례 회의가 개최된다 Our regular meeting is held at the beginning of [early in] the month.
초승 初— the first days [the beginning] of a month ■—달 a new [young] moon; a crescent (moon); the sickle [horned] moon: 초승달 모양의 crescent (shaped)
초시계 秒時計 a microchronometer; 〈스톱워치〉 a stopwatch
초식 草食 〈먹을〉 eating grass [vegetables]; living on grass [vegetables] ◆초식의 plant-[grass-]eating; graminivorous; herbivorous
—초식하다 eat grass [vegetables]; live on grass [vegetables]
■—동물 a plant-[grass-]eating animal; a grazer; a herbivorous animal; a herbivore; 〈초식의〉 〔動〕 Herbivora
초실 初室 1 〈새 집〉 a newly built house 2 〈첫 아내〉 one's first wife
초심 初審 〔法〕 the first trial [hearing]
초심 焦心 impatience; anxiety; worry
초심자 初心者 a beginner; a novice; a greenhorn; a neophyte
◆그는 초심자 치고는 골프를 잘한다 He plays golf pretty well for a beginner.
초아흐레 初— the ninth day of a month=초아흐렛날
초아흐렛날 初— the ninth day of a month
초안 草案 〈초잡은 글발〉 a (rough) draft; notes; a manuscript
◆법안의 초안 a draft bill / 초안을 기초하다 prepare [make out] a draft (for); draft [draw up] (a bill)
초야 初夜 1 〈초저녁〉 the first half part of a night 2 〈첫날밤〉 the bridal [first] night; one's wedding night
초야 草野 〈시골〉 an out-of-the-way place; the backcountry; a remote district
◆초야에 묻혀 살다 live in retirement [seclusion]; bury oneself in the country

초여드레 初— the eighth day of a month=초여드렛날
초여드렛날 初— the eighth day of a month
초여름 初— early summer; the beginning of summer
▶이 꽃은 초여름에 핀다 This flower comes out in the beginning of summer.
초역 抄譯 〈발췌 번역〉 an abridged [a summarized, an epitomized] translation; a selected translation
—초역하다 make an abridged [an epitomized, a summarized] translation 《of》; translate selected chapters [passages] 《from》
▶그는 오디세이를 초역했다 He translated selected passages from the Odyssey.
초연 初演 〈음악·연극의〉 the first performance; 〈영화·연극의〉 the premiere (▶후자는 전문적인 느낌을 주는 표현)
—초연하다 give the first perfomace 《of》; perform … first (▶전자는 다소 격식차린 표현); premiere (a play)
▶그 연극은 한국에서는 1990년에 초연되었다 The drama was first performed [staged] in Korea in 1990.
초연 超然 transcendence; 〈남과 관계하지 않음〉 aloofness; noninterference; standoffishness
—초연하다 transcendental; standoffish
◆초연한 detached; unconcerned; transcendental / 초연히 aloof; with a detached air; above the world / …에 초연하다 stand [hold, keep] aloof from; rise [be] above 《worldly matters》/ 속세에 초연하다 keep aloof from the crowd [masses]; rise above the world
▶그는 돈에 관해서는 초연하다 He is quite indifferent to money.
■—주의 a standoff policy [attitude]; a principle of noninvolvement
초연 硝煙 powder smoke
◆초연 탄우(彈雨) 속에 amid the smoke of powder and hail of bullets; in the thick of the fight
초열 焦熱 1 〈타는 듯한 더위〉 scorching heat 2 ⇨ 초열지옥
초열지옥 焦熱地獄 a burning hell; an inferno (pl. ~s). 〔聖〕 Gehenna
초열흘(날) 初— the tenth day of a month
초엽 初葉 the early days [years]; the beginning; the initial phase
◆20세기 초엽에 in the early part of the 20th century
초엽 蕉葉·草葉 〔建〕 〈까치발〉 a bracket; a corbel
초엿새 初— the sixth day of a month=초엿샛날
초엿샛날 初— the sixth day of a month
초오 草烏 〔植〕 a monkshood; a wolfsbane
초옥 草屋 a thatched cottage
초우라늄 超— transuranium
■—원소 the transuranic elements
초원 草原 a grassy [grass-covered] plain; grassland(s); 〈북미의〉 a prairie; 〈남미의〉 pampas; 〈중앙아시아의〉 a steppe; 〈아프리카의〉 a savanna

초월 超越 transcendence; transcendency
♦ 초월적인 transcendental / 초월적 태도 a transcendental attitude
━초월하다 transcend; rise above; stand aloof from; be superior 《to》
♦ 생사를 초월하다 disregard the peril of one's life / 속세를 초월하다 rise above the world; stand aloof from the world / 이해를 초월하다 be disinterested / 자기를 초월하다 be above *oneself*; rise above self
▶ 그는 세속적인 일에서 완전히 초월해 있다 He lives a quiet life quite free from worldly affairs. ⇌ He is quite aloof from [above] the world.
━수(數) a transcendental number ━주의 transcendentalism ━함수[곡선] a transcendental function [curve]

초유 初有 ♦ 초유의 first; initial; original; unprecedented; unexampled / 사상 (史上) 초유의 unprecedented [unparalleled] in history
▶ 그것은 항공사상 초유의 사고였다 It was an accident unprecedented in the history of aviation.

초유 初乳 〔醫〕〈해산부의〉 colostrum; foremilk; 〈암소의〉 beastings; beestings

초음속 超音速 supersonic speed ♦ 초음속의 supersonic / 극초음속의 hypersonic / 초음속으로 날다 fly at supersonic speed
▶ 이 로켓은 초음속으로 날아간다 This rocket travels at supersonic speeds.
━비행 a supersonic flight ━여객기 a supersonic transport [plane] ━제트기 a supersonic jet plane

초음파 超音波 ultrasonic; ultrasonic waves
━검사 〔醫〕 ultrasonography; 〔工〕 ultrasonic testing; ultrasonic inspection ━진동기 an ultrasonic oscillator ━탈지(脫脂) ultrasonic cleaning ━치료 ultrasonic therapy

초이레 初━ the seventh day (of a month)=초이렛날

초이렛날 初━ the seventh day (of a month)

초이튿날 初━ the second day (of a month)

초이틀 初━ the second day (of a month)=초이튿날

초인 超人 a superman ♦ 초인적(인) superhuman; preterhuman / 초인적으로 superhumanly
▶ 그는 세계 평화 유지를 위해 초인적인 노력을 했다 He made superhuman efforts to maintain world peace.
━주의 supermanism

초인종 招人鐘 a (call) bell; a doorbell; a buzzer; 〈숙박업소의〉 a service bell
♦ 초인종을 누르다 push a doorbell; give a doorbell a push / 초인종을 울리다 ring a (door)bell / 초인종을 울려 하인을 부르다 ring for a servant
▶ 초인종이 울리고 있다 There's the doorbell ringing. ⇌ I hear the bell ring.
▶ 필요하실 때는 이 초인종을 눌러 주십시오 《게시》 Ring this bell when you want me.

초일 初日 the first day ⇨ 첫날

초읽기 秒━ countdown ♦ 초읽기를 하다 count down
▶ 그 실험은 초읽기의 단계다 The experiment is in the (final) countdown stage.
▶ 로켓 발사 전의 초읽기가 시작되었다 The countdown has started for launching the rocket.

초임 初任 the first appointment ⇨ 신임(新任)
━급(給) an initial [a starting, a beginning] salary [pay]

초입 初入 1 〈어귀〉 an entrance; an approach; a way in ♦ 강 [길] 초입 an entry to a river [road] / 마을 [터널] 초입 an approach to a village [tunnel]
2 〈처음으로 들어감〉 entering for the first time; the first entrance

초자 硝子 〔化〕 glass ⇨ 유리(琉璃)

초자연 超自然 supernaturalness ♦ 초자연적인 supernatural; preternatural ━력 supernatural forces ━주의 supernaturalism

초잡다 草━ make a draft (of); draft ♦ 헌법을 초잡다 draft [draw out] a constitution
▶ 그가 그 평화 조약을 초잡았다 He made a draft of the peace treaty.

초장 初章 〈가곡의〉 the first part (of a song); the first movement; 〈시조의〉 the first of the three verses (of a *sijo* poem); 〈글의〉 the first chapter

초장 初場 〈시장의〉 the opening [morning] market [session, sale]; 〈일의〉 the outset; the start; the beginning
▶ 초장부터 시세가 높았다 The market opened higher.
▶ 초장에는 실패했다 I failed (in it) at first.

초장 醋醬 soy sauce mixed with vinegar and parched sesame, etc.

초장파 超長波 〔通信〕 very low frequency (略 V.L.F., VLF, v.l.f., vlf)

초재 草材 native medicinal herbs

초저녁 初━ (the) early evening
♦ 초저녁에 early in the evening; in the early part [hours] of the evening
▶ 아직 초저녁이다 The night is still young. ⇌ It is still early in the evening.
▶ 초저녁부터 그는 잠이 들고 말았다 He went to bed in spite of the early hour.

초적 草笛 a reed (pipe)

초전 招電 calling by telegraph; a summons by wire ♦ 초전을 내다 issue a summons by wire

초절 超絶 transcendence
━론[주의] transcendentalism

초점 焦點 a focus (*pl.* ~es, foci); a focal point
♦ 분쟁의 초점 the focus of trouble / 초점이 맞다 [안 맞다] be in [out of] focus / 초점을 맞추다 focus 《one's glasses on an object》; bring *sth* into focus / 현미경의 초점을 맞추다 focus the lens of a microscope / 적의 공격의 초점이 되다 bear the brunt of the enemy's attack
▶ 문제의 초점이 흐려졌다 The crucial point of the issue has been blurred.
▶ 교수는 그 문제에 초점을 맞추어 강의를 진행했다 The professor delivered his lecture focusing on that issue.
━고정━ a fixed focus ━거리 the focal length; focus length : 초점거리 측정기 a focometer; a focimeter ━면 a focal plane

―심도(深度) the focal depth

초조 初潮 〔生理〕 the first menstruation ⇨ 초경(初經)

초조 焦燥 fret; impatience; irritation; chafe ♦초조를 느끼다 feel impatient; fret 《about》 ―**초조하다** fretful; impatient; irritated; vexed; anxious; restless
♦초조한 기색 a worried look / 초조한 마음 an anxious [a nervous] state of mind / 초조해 보이다 seem impatient; look anxious [worried]/ 초조해하다 fret; worry; be impatient; show impatience / 초조해지다 get impatient; (美) get jittery
▶그녀는 하찮은 일로 초조해하고 있었다 She fretted over [about] trifles.
▶초조해 하지 마라 Take it easy. ⇌ Easy does it.

초종 初終 the whole procedure of mourning ⇨ 초종장사 ■―범절 customary procedure [due formalities] of mourning

초종장사 初終葬事 the whole procedure [period] of mourning (from beginning to end) ♦초종장사를 치르다 go through due formalities of mourning

초주검되다 初― be more dead than alive; be all but dead; be half-dead; 〈남의 손에〉 be half-killed; be nearly [all but] killed
▶그들은 초주검되어 그 장소에 당도했다 They came to the place half-dead.

초지 初志 one's original intention [purpose, aim, object] ♦초지를 이루다 realize [fulfill] one's long-cherished desire / 초지를 굽히다 [번복하다] give up one's original purpose
▶그 소년은 초지를 관철했다 The boy accomplished [carried out] his original purpose.

초지 草紙 a draft paper used in preparing a rough copy [draft]

초지 草地 grassland; pasture

초지니 初― a yearling falcon; a two-year old hawk

초진 初診 the first [initial] medical examination ■―료 the fee charged for a patient's first visit ―환자 a new patient [client]

초집 抄集·抄輯 a collection of extracts [excerpts, abstracts]; 〈선집〉 a selection ―**초집하다** make a collection of extracts [excerpts, abstracts] ―법안― extracts of bills; a copy of extracted bills

초집 草集 literary drafts; a collection of manuscripts ■―시문(詩文)― (a collection of) manuscripts of one's literary works

초창 草創 inauguration; initiation; inception; beginning

초창기 草創期 the initial stage(s); the early period; the pioneer days
♦인류의 초창기 the early days of mankind / 문예부흥의 초창기 the dawning of the Renaissance / 초창기의 회사 운영 the management of a company in its early stage
▶최대의 어려움을 겪은 것은 회사의 초창기였다 It was at the first stage that our firm encountered the greatest difficulty.

초청 招請 (an) invitation ♦초청을 받아들이다 [사절하다] accept [decline] an invitation ―**초청하다** invite [ask] 《sb to a party》
♦강사를 초청하다 invite [call in] a lecturer / 집에 초청하다 ask sb to one's home
▶그는 회의에 초청되었다 He was invited to the conference.
▶왜 너를 초청하지 않았을까? Why did they leave you out of the invitation?
―**경기** an invitation game ―국 an inviting country; 〈주최국〉 the host nation ―장 a letter of invitation; an invitation (card): 초청장을 보내다 send [extend] an invitation 《to》

초체 草體 〈글자체〉 a cursive character

초추 初秋 early autumn ⇨ 초가을

초춘 初春 early spring ⇨ 초봄

초출 抄出 extraction 〈발췌(拔萃)〉

초출 初出 the first bearing; the first fruiting
■―포도 the first grapes of the season; the earliest grapes of the season

초출 超出 excellence; preeminence; outstandingness; prominence ―**초출하다** excel 《in》; stand conspicuous; be preeminent [outstanding]; surpass 《others》

초췌 憔悴 haggardness; gauntness; emaciation ―**초췌하다** haggard; emaciated; gaunt; thin and worn
♦초췌한 얼굴 a haggard face; a worn-out look / 초췌해지다 get [become] haggard [gaunt, emaciated] 《from》; be worn out / 근심으로 초췌해지다 be careworn / 형편없이 초췌해지다 be worn to a shadow
▶그녀는 근심으로 아주 초췌해졌다 She is utterly worn out [exhausted] with worry.

초취 初娶 one's first [former] wife

초치 招致 summons; invitation ―**초치하다** 〈불러들이다〉 summon; invite; call; 〈유치하다〉 attract 《tourists》

초친놈 醋― 〈사람 구실할 여망이 없는 사람〉 a worthless playboy; a hopeless roué; a rake of no promise

초침 秒針 the second hand [sweepsecond] (of a watch)

초콜릿 chocolate; 〈과자〉 a chocolate; a stick [bar] of chocolate
♦초콜릿 색깔 chocolate brown

초크 〈분필〉 (a piece of) chalk; 〔地〕 〈백악〉 chalk ―**초크로 쓰다** write with [in] chalk / 초크로 잔뜩 써놓은 칠판 a blackboard covered with scribbles in chalk

초탈 超脫 trascendency; transcendence; detachment ―**초탈하다** transcend; stand aloof 《from》; rise above
♦세속을 초탈하다 rise above the world; stand aloof from the world; be in this world, but not of it / 이해를 초탈하다 be disinterested / 생사를 초탈하다 disregard the peril of one's life

초토 焦土 〈불탄 흙〉 scorched earth; burnt ground; 〈불탄 자리〉 the ruins [site] of a fire
▶전쟁 통에 전 도시가 초토화했다 The whole town was reduced to ashes [burnt to the ground] during the war.
■―전 술 scorched-land[-earth] strategy [tactics]

초특급 超特急 〈열차〉 a superexpress (train)

초특작(품) 超特作(品) a super production; 〈영화의〉 a superfilm
초파리 醋— 〔昆〕 a vinegar fly
초판 初— the first round [period, bout, scene]; the opening (of a game)
♦ 초판에 in [at] the beginning; at the outset; in the early stage / 초판에 잘 나가다 make a successful beginning; make a good start / 초판부터 다시 하다 do all over again; begin afresh; make a new start
▶ 나는 초판에서 잡쳤다 I began at the wrong end. ⇌ I made a false [wrong] start.
초판 初版 the first edition [impression]
♦ 초판을 3천부 찍다[발행하다] print [issue, publish] the first edition of 3,000 copies (of a book)
■ 一本(本) a copy of the first edition; a first edition; (총칭) the first edition
초피 貂皮 marten; sable
초하 初夏 early summer; the beginning of summer
초하다 抄— 〈추려 베끼다〉 make an extract 《from》; make an abstract 《of》; extract [excerpt, select, cull] 《from》
초하다 草— make a draft 《of, on, from》; draft [draw up] 《a bill》
♦ 연설문을 초하다 draft out an address
초하루 初— the first day of a month
▶ 내달 초하룻날 표 있습니까? Do you have any tickets for the first of next month?
초학 初學 〈처음 배움〉 learning first in one's life; the beginning of learning; 〈미숙한 학문〉 elementary learning
■ 一자 a beginner; a learner; a greenhorn; a novice; an abecedarian
초학 初瘧 〈처음 걸린 학질〉 one's first suffering from malaria; 〈하루거리〉 tertian malaria
초한 初寒 the first cold (of the season); the first spell of cold weather
초한 峭寒 piercing [biting, bitter] cold
초함 哨艦 a patrol boat; a picket warship
초항 招降 inviting sb to surrender; persuasion into surrender —초항하다 invite sb to surrender; persuade 《the enemy》 into surrender
초행 初行 going for the first time; one's first trip [journey]
▶ 제주도는 초행입니다 This is my first visit to Chejudo.
■ 一길 a road new to one; one's first trip [journey]
초현대적 超現代的 ultramodern
초현실주의 超現實主義 surrealism
■ 一자 a surrealist
초혜 草鞋 straw shoes ⇨ 짚신
초호 初號 1〈창간호〉 the first [initial, opening] number 2〈활자의 크기〉 No.1 type
■ 一활자 a 42-point type
초호 礁湖 a lagoon
초혼 初昏 (the evening) dusk; twilight ⇨ 황혼(黃昏)
초혼 初婚 one's first marriage
▶ 그녀는 서른 살에 초혼을 했다 She married for the first time at thirty.
초혼 招魂 invocation of the spirits of the dead —초혼하다 invoke the spirit of the deceased ■ 一제(祭) a memorial service 《for the war dead》
초화 草花 a flower of a herb; a herbaceous flower
초환 招還 recall; call back ⇨ 소환(召還)
초회 初回 the first time
촉 鏃 〈뾰족한 끝〉 the point; the nib 〈화살촉〉 an arrowhead; the point of an arrow; a gad
♦ 만년필 촉 the point of a fountain pen / 펜 촉 a penpoint; a nib
촉 燭 1 ⇨ 촉광
2 〈촛불〉 candlelight
촉각 觸角 a feeler; an antenna 《pl. -nae, ~s》; a tentacle; a horn ♦ 촉각을 내밀다 put out (its) feelers
■ 一선(腺) antennary gland
촉각 觸覺 the sense of touch; (a) tactual sense ■ 一기 a tactile organ
촉감 觸感 1〈느낌〉 feel; touch
♦ 촉감이 좋다 be pleasant [smooth] to the touch [feel]; feel smooth; have a smooth feel / 촉감이 나쁘다 be unpleasant to the touch / 촉감이 거칠다[부드럽다] be rough [soft] to the touch; feel rough [soft]
2 ⇨ 촉각(觸覺)
촉관 觸官 a tactile organ ⇨ 촉각(~기)
촉광 燭光 1〈物〉〈예전의 광도의 단위〉 candle-power; candle
2〈촛불의 밝기〉 candlelight
촉구하다 press sb for sth; urge 《sb to do》; call upon 《sb to do》
♦ 주의를 촉구하다 call [attract] sb's attention to sth / 진지한 반성을 촉구하다 demand sb's serious reflection / 사임을 촉구하다 urge sb to resign; insist upon sb's resignation
촉규(화) 蜀葵(花) 〈접시꽃〉 a rose mallow; a hollyhock
촉급 促急 urgency
촉노하다 觸怒— offend 《an elder》; incur 《one's superior's》 anger
촉대 燭臺 a candlestick ⇨ 촛대(一臺)
촉더레 鏃— the body [flange] of an arrowhead
촉돌이 鏃— an arrowhead vise
촉루 燭淚 guttered candle (wax) ⇨ 촛농(一膿)
촉루 髑髏 a skull; a death's-head
촉망 囑望 expectation; hope
▶ 그는 주위 사람들의 촉망을 받고 있다 He is the hope of those around him.
—촉망하다 fasten [hang, pin, put] one's hopes on sb; expect much of [from] sb
♦ 앞날이 촉망되는 청년 a promising youth; a young man (full) of promise; a young man with a great [rosy] future / 크게 촉망하다 expect very much of [from] sb; entertain great expectations of sb
▶ 그는 장래가 촉망되는 음악가다 He has a bright future as a musician.
촉매 觸媒 〔化〕 a catalyzer; a catalyst
■ 一반응 a catalytic reaction; catalyst 一작용 catalysis 一환원 catalytic reduction ■ 역— an anticatalyzer

촉모 觸毛 〔動·解〕 a cirrus (*pl.* cirri)
촉박하다 促迫— urgent; pressing; imminent
♦시간이 촉박하다 be pushed [pressed] for time
▶약속 기일이 촉박하다 The appointed day is now close [near] at hand.
촉발 觸發 detonation by contact; contact detonation; 〈감정의〉 being excited [moved]
—**촉발하다** detonate [be detonated] by contact; be touched off; be excited [moved]
▶그 문제는 국제 위기를 촉발할 우려가 있었다 The matter had the possibility of triggering an international crisis.
■—수뢰(水雷) a contact mine —장치 a contact-detonating device
촉새 〔鳥〕 a bunting
촉성 促成 **1** 〈동식물의〉 forcing **2** 〈일 등의〉 ⇨ 촉진(促進) ■—용 품종 forcing variety
촉성재배 促成栽培 forcing culture ♦촉성재배용 온실 a forcing house; a hothouse —촉성재배하다 force ⟨strawberries⟩ ♦촉성재배한 야채 forced vegetables
촉수 觸手 **1** 〔動〕 a tentacle ♦촉수를 뻗치다 put out a feeler; reach 《for》 **2** 〈손댐〉 touching
촉수 觸鬚 〔生〕 a palp; a palpus (*pl.* -pi); 〈물고기의〉 a barbel
촉언 囑言 ⟨dying⟩ words of entrusting ⟨another⟩ with future affairs; words of dying charge —**촉언하다** say words of entrusting ⟨another⟩ with future affairs
촉진 促進 promotion; advancement; acceleration; hastening; facilitation; furtherance
♦야당과의 대화 촉진 the encouragement of dialogue with opposition parties
—**촉진하다** hasten; promote ⟨an undertaking⟩; accelerate; expedite; facilitate; quicken; further; speed [step, gear] up ⟨a job⟩; give [lend] an impetus ⟨to⟩; give a boost ⟨to⟩
♦…의 실현을 촉진하다 quicken the realization of…/ 식물의 성장을 촉진하다 hasten [accelerate, force] the growth of a plant / 문명의 진보를 촉진하다 expedite [facilitate, further, quicken, accelerate, speed up] the progress of civilization / 양국의 우호를 촉진하다 promote friendship between the two countries
▶그 연구는 자연과학의 진보를 촉진했다 The research advanced natural science.
▶그 조약은 양국간의 무역을 촉진할 것이다 The treaty will give impetus to trade between the two countries.
■ 발아— hastening germination
촉진 觸診 〔醫〕 palpation —**촉진하다** palpate
촉처봉패 觸處逢敗 failure at every attempt [turn] —**촉처봉패하다** fail in every attempt [turn]
촉촉하다 ⟨slightly [moderately]⟩ wet; dampish; moist ⇨ 축축하다 ♦이슬에 촉촉히 젖다 get moist [become wet] with dew; be bedewed
촉탁 囑託 〈위촉〉 commission; entrusting; charge; 〈위촉 받은 사람〉 a part-time employee; a part-timer ♦관청[은행]의 촉탁 a part-time employee of a government office [a bank]
—**촉탁하다** entrust [charge] sb with ⟨a job⟩; commission ⟨sb to do⟩

촌 寸 **1** 〈친등의 단위〉 ⇨ 촌수 ♦사촌 a cousin; a relative in the fourth degree / 사돈의 8촌 a cousin forty times removed **2** 〈길이의 단위〉 ⇨ 치¹
촌 村 〈마을〉 a village; 〈특히 작은 촌락〉 a hamlet; a rural community; 〈시골〉 the country; a rural district; 〈美〉 the backcountry
♦빈민촌 a poor village / 색시 a country lass / 촌구석에서 살다 live in a secluded place
촌가 寸暇 a moment's leisure; a spare moment
♦촌가를 아끼다 utilize every odd moment / 촌가도 없다 have not a minute to call *one's* own; have no time to spare at all
촌가 村家 a village [country] house ⇨ 시골(~집) ♦촌가에서 자라다 be brought up in a country house
촌각 寸刻 a moment; a second ♦촌각을 다투다 〈병 등이〉 require prompt treatment; 〈문제 등이〉 need a speedy solution
촌거 村居 country life; rural living
—**촌거하다** ⇨ 시골(~생활)
촌극 寸劇 a playlet; a skit; a little dramatical performance [sketch]; a short play
촌극 寸隙 a spare moment ⇨ 촌가(寸暇)
촌길 村— a village road; a country path [road] ⇨ 시골(~길)
촌내 寸內 〈십촌 안쪽〉 a relative within the tenth degree; near relatives
촌놈 村— a rustic; a rube; 〈조롱적〉 a boor; a ⟨country⟩ bumpkin; a yokel; a clodhopper; 〈美〉 a backwoodsman; a hillbilly; 〈美俗〉 a hayseed
▶나는 말하자면 서울 촌놈이다 I am, so to speak, a Seoul rustic.
▶촌놈 수작 마라 Don't make you a boor!
—티 ⇨ 촌티
촌뜨기 村— a rustic; a countryman; a bumpkin ⇨ 시골(~뜨기)
촌락 村落 a hamlet; a village community
—공동체 a village community
촌로 村老 a village patriarch; 〈총칭〉 old folks of a village
촌목 寸— 〈소목 연장〉 a mortise ga(u)ge
촌민 村民 a villager; 〈총칭〉 villagers ⇨ 촌사람
촌백성 村百姓 country people [folk]
촌백충 寸白蟲 〔動〕 a tapeworm; a taenia (*pl.* -niae)=촌충(寸蟲)
촌보 寸步 a few steps
▶그는 촌보도 옮길 수 없다 He is unable to move [take] a step.
촌부 村婦 a country [village] woman
촌사람 村— a villager; a countryman; a rustic; 〈총칭〉 countryfolk ⇨ 촌놈
촌샌님 村— a narrow-minded [an obstinate] ⟨old⟩ villager
촌수 寸數 degrees; the degree of consanguinity [kinship, relationship ⟨by blood⟩]
♦혼인 금지의 촌수 ⟨the⟩ prohibited [forbidden] degrees ⟨of marriage⟩ / 촌수가 가까운 [먼] 친척 a person who is near [distant] in kinship; a near [distant] relative / 촌수를 따

촌스럽다 〈촌티나다〉 boorish; rustic; countrified; 〈세련되지 못하다〉 unfashionable ((clothes)); unrefined; unpolished; uncouth; ungainly ((figure))
♦촌스럽게 입다 be unfashionably [uncouthly] dressed

촌시 寸時 a moment; a minute=촌음(寸陰)

촌음 寸陰 a moment; a minute
♦촌음을 아끼다 skimp on time; grudge even a minute; cannot spare a moment / 촌음을 아껴 연구에 몰두하다 devote all *one's* time and energies to studies

촌장 村長 a village headman [chief]

촌전척토 寸田尺土 a tiny strip [patch] of land

촌지 寸地 an inch of land ⇨ 촌토(寸土)

촌지 寸志 a little token of *one's* gratitude [appreciation]; a small present; 〈봉투에 쓸때〉 With compliments
▶촌지니 받아 주십시오 This is just a token of my gratitude, please accept it.

촌철 寸鐵 1〈작은 무기〉 a small weapon 2〈경구(警句)〉 a pithy [terse, witty, short, sententious] saying; an epigram
♦촌철 살인의 경구 a saw coming home to *one's* heart; a pithy epigram that stings [cuts, pierces] *one* to the quick
▶그의 문장은 촌철 살인의 감동을 준다 His writing is full of pithy sarcasms.

촌촌걸식 村村乞食 begging around from village to village ―촌촌걸식하다 go (about) begging from village to village

촌충 寸蟲 a tapeworm; a taenia ((*pl*. -niae))
■―구제약 a taeniafuge; a taeniacide

촌탁 忖度 (a) conjecture; (a) surmise; a guess ―촌탁하다 conjecture; surmise; guess; judge; gauge ♦자기 마음으로 미루어 남을 촌탁하다 judge others in terms of *oneself*; measure another's corn by *one's* own bushel

촌토 寸土 an inch of land [territory]; a small strip of land ♦촌토도 양보하지 않다 do not yield [budge] an inch [a step]

촌티 村― rusticity; boorishness ⇨ 촌스럽다

촌평 寸評 a brief review ((of)); a brief comment ((on))

촐랑거리다 1〈까불거리다〉 behave frivolously; act flippantly; be frivolous [flippant]
♦촐랑거리며 돌아다니다 gad about; flit [flitter] about
2〈물이〉 lap

촐랑이 a frivolous [flippant] fellow

촐랑촐랑 1〈까불까불〉 frivolously; flippantly; lightly 2〈물소리〉 overflowingly

촐싹거리다 1〈경망을 떨다〉 act frivolously [flippantly] 2〈부추기다〉 incite; abet; instigate; egg on; stir up ♦촐싹거려 …하게 하다 set [needle] *sb* to do

촐싹촐싹 1〈경망스러운 모양〉 frivolously; flippantly 2〈부추기는 모양〉 inciting; abetting; instigating

촐촐 with an empty stomach ♦촐촐 굶다 go hungry ((all day)); starve ―촐촐하다 somewhat [rather] hungry; feel a bit empty

▶촐촐하니 어디 가서 요기나 합시다 Let's drop in somewhere to fill up our empty stomach, will you?

촘촘하다 close; compact; dense; fine
♦촘촘한 천 cloth of (a) close texture / 촘촘하게 쓰다 write closely / 촘촘하게 박다[꿰매다] sew with short stitches / 모를 촘촘하게 심다 set young rice plants close together

촛농 ―膿 guttered candle (wax); melted wax running down a candlestick ♦방울져 떨어지는 촛농 droppings from a candle
▶촛농이 흐르고 있다 The candle is running.
▶그는 책상 위에 촛농을 흘리고 그 위에 초를 세웠다 He stuck a candle in its own wax on the desk.

촛대 ―臺 a candlestick; a candlestand; a pricket; 〈대형 장식의〉 a flambeau ((*pl*. ~s, -beaux)) ♦촛대에 초를 꽂다 fix a candle in a candlestick

촛불 candlelight ♦촛불을 켜다 burn [light] a candle / 촛불을 끄다 put out a candle / 촛불에 책을 읽다 read by candlelight

총 〈말총〉 horsehair; the hairs of a horse's mane [tail]

총 銃 〈총포〉 a gun; (총칭) firearms; arms; 〈보병총〉 a musket; 〈선조총〉 a rifle; (총칭) small arms
♦총을 메다 shoulder a rifle / 총을 들이대다 [겨누다] point [level, aim] a gun ((at *sb*, against *sth*)) / 권총으로 위협하여 유괴하다 kidnap *sb* at gunpoint / 총을 쏘다 shoot [fire, discharge] a gun / 총 솜씨가 능하다[서투르다] be a good [poor] shot / 총으로 쏘아 죽이다 shoot *sb* dead
▶받들어 총 ((口令)) Present arms!
▶어깨 총 ((口令)) Carry [Shoulder] arms!
▶세워[걸어] 총 ((口令)) Order [Pile] arms!
▶총이 불을 뿜었다 The gun spat fire.
■―다발― a Russian automatic rifle 단발― a single-barreled gun; a single-loader 쌍발― a double-barreled gun ■―개머리 the stock; the butt of a rifle ―허리 the small of the butt

총 寵 favor; good grace ⇨ 총애(寵愛)

총― 總― whole; all; entire; general; gross; aggregate; combined; total; full
♦총본부 general headquarters; the center / 총예산 the total budget; the general estimate / 총재무 자원 all financial resources / 총중량 the gross weight

총가 銃架 an arm rack; a rifle stand; a gun rest [mounting]

총각 總角 a bachelor; an unmarried [a single] man; ((美口)) a bach
■처녀― unmarried (young) men and women ■―김치 pickled radishes ―무 a (whole) radish

총감 總監 〈치안〉 a Commissioner General

총감독 總監督 a general manager

총검 銃劍 〈총과 칼〉 firearms and swords; 〈총 끝에 꽂는 칼〉 a (sword) bayonet; side arms
♦총검으로 찌르다 bayonet *sb*; stab *sb* with a bayonet / 총검을 들이대어, 무력으로 at the point of the bayonet
■―술 bayonet fencing

총격 銃擊 rifle-shooting ◆총격을 가하다 direct fire 《toward》/ 총격을 받다 be under fire
—총격하다 shoot a rifle 《at a target》; 〈기관총으로〉 machine-gun; 〈저공에서〉 strafe
—전 a gunfight: 총격전을 벌이다 gunfight

총결산 總決算 1 〈결산〉 settlement of the whole accounts —총결산하다 settle the whole accounts; balance one's all accounts 2 clearing
■연말— the year-end settlement 《of the whole accounts》

총경 總警 a Senior Superintendent 《略 Sen. Supt.》

총계 總計 〈합계〉 the total; the total [whole] amount [sum]; the sum [grand, full] total 《소계(小計)에 대하여》; the aggregate; 〈부사적〉 in all; in total; all told; altogether; in the aggregate
▶ 총계가 얼마나 됩니까? What does the total come to? ⇌ How much is it altogether?
—총계하다 total; sum [count, add] up
—l법 the total count method

총고해 總告解 〔가톨릭〕 a general confession

총공격 總攻擊 an all-out [a general] attack; a full-scale offensive
◆…에 대하여 총공격을 개시하다 launch a mass attack against...
—총공격하다 make [open, launch] an all-out attack 《on, against》; attack 《the enemy》 in full force

총괄 總括 〈개괄〉 generalization; colligation; 〈요약〉 summarization; epitomization; recapitulation; summary; a résumé
—총괄하다 〈개괄하다〉 generalize; 〈요약하다〉 summarize; sum up; epitomize; recapitulate
◆총괄하여 말하면 generally speaking; to sum up / 모든 문제를 총괄하여 토론하다 discuss all the problems at one time
■—개념 a collected conception —보험 blanket insurance —성(化) a colligative property —운임 lump-sum freight —질문 a general interpellation

총괄적 總括的 all-inclusive; all-embracing; overall; blanket; lump-sum; omnibus
◆총괄적 의안 an omnibus [a blanket] bill / 총괄적으로 in the gross [mass, lump]; collectively; 《프》 en bloc [masse]

총구 銃口 the muzzle 《of a gun》 ⇨ 총부리

총급하다 忽急— 〈서술적〉 be in a great hurry

총기 銃器 〈총칭〉 small [fire] arms ⇨ 총(銃)
—실(고) a gun room; an armory

총기 聰氣 bright intelligence; brightness; cleverness; spark 《of intelligence》; sense; wit; a good memory; retentiveness
◆총기가 있다 be intelligent; be quick of apprehension / 총기가 없다 be dull [unintelligent] / 총기가 좋다 have a good [retentive] memory
▶ 그 아이는 총기가 있다 The boy has a clear head.
▶ 그는 총기라고는 전혀 없다 He hasn't a lick of sense about him.

총꾼 銃— a gunner; a hunter; a gunman; a rifleman

총냥이 a weasel-[fox-]faced person with popeyes

총담요 —毯— a horsehair blanket

총대 銃— the stock 《of a gun》; the gunstock

총대리점 總代理店 a general agency

총대우 a horsehair [an oxhair] crown 《of a Korean top hat》

총대장 總大將 a commander in chief; a general; a boss; a captain

총독 總督 a governor-general 《pl. governors-general, ~s》; a viceroy ■—부 the government-general

총동원 總動員 general [full] mobilization
▶ 일가 총동원으로 대청소를 했다 All the family joined in cleaning the whole house.
▶ 어느 나라나 전시에는 총동원을 한다 Every country mobilizes the entire army in war time.
—총동원하다 mobilize fully; mobilize all the resources 《of》
◆산업계를 총동원하다 mobilize all 《of》 the industrial world
▶ 그 사건을 수사하기 위해 경찰관이 총동원되었다 All the policemen were called out [mobilized] to investigate the case.
■국가— the national mobilization ■—령 orders for the mobilization of the entire army: 총동원령이 내렸다 General mobilization orders were given.

총람 總攬 superintendence; 《general》 control
—총람하다 preside over; superintend

총량 總量 the gross weight [volume]; the total [aggregate] amount

총력 總力 all one's energy [strength]; the aggregate power
▶ 우리는 총력을 기울여 싸웠다 We fought with all our energies [might, power, strength].
■—안보(태세) 《strengthen》 an all-out national security 《posture》 —외교 a total diplomacy —전 a total [an all-out] war

총렵 銃獵 hunting; shooting=총사냥

총론 總論 general remarks; an outline 《of》; an introduction 《to》 ◆총론에서 각론으로 들어가다 descend from the general to the particular ■민법— an introduction to the study of civil law

총론 叢論 a collection of treatises [essays]
■문학— a collection of essays on literature

총리 總理 1 〈수상〉 the prime minister; the premier 2 〈총관리〉 general overseeing [control]
—총리하다 preside over; oversee; control
■국무— the Prime Minister; the Premier 부— the Deputy Prime Minister ■—실 the Prime Minister's Office —직 premiership

총림 叢林 a dense wood [grove]; 〈덤불숲〉 a bush; a thicket

총망 忽忙 a great hurry; busyness
—총망하다 hurried; 《be》 in great haste [in a great hurry]; very busy 《doing, with work》
◆총망한 중에 by [owing to, on account of] pressure of work

총명 聰明 sagacity; cleverness; brightness;

총 wisdom; intelligence; 〈기억력〉 a good [sharp, retentive] memory
—**총명하다** bright; wise; clever; brilliant; sagacious; perspicacious; intelligent; 〈서술적〉 have a good memory (기억력이)
◆**총명한 사람** a man of sagacity; a wise [an intelligent] person

총목록 總目錄 a complete catalog(ue); a full list

총무 總務 〈업무〉 general affairs; 〈담당자〉 a manager; a director
—**원내—** (美) the floor leader; (英) the (party) whip; (英) the whipper-in ((pl. whippers-) ■**—과[국]** the general affairs section [bureau] —**부(장)** the (chief of) the general affairs department [division] —**처** the Ministry of Government Administration —**처장관** the Minister of Government Administration

총민 聰敏 brightness and shrewdness; cleverness and keenness; smartness and quickness
—**총민하다** bright and shrewd; clever and keen

총반격 總反擊 an all-out counterattack
—**총반격하다** make an all-out counterattack; mount a general counteroffensive

총부리 銃— 〈제일선〉 the foremost [fighting, first] line; the forefront (of the battle)

총보 總譜 〔樂〕〈모음악보〉 a full score

총복습 總復習 〈학과의〉 a general review of one's lessons

총본산 總本山 〈총본부〉 the (general) headquarters; 〔佛敎〕 the head temple of a Buddhist sect

총부리 銃— the muzzle (of a rifle) ◆ **총부리를 들이대고** at the point [end] of a gun; at gunpoint / **총부리를 대다** level [point] a gun (at sb); hold a gun (on the enemy)

총사냥 銃— hunting; shooting

총사령관 總司令官 the supreme commander; the commander in chief (略 C. in C., C in C)

총사령부 總司令部 the General Headquarters (略 GHQ)
■**유엔군—** the United Nations Command (略 UNC)

총사직 總辭職 a general resignation; resignation in a body [en bloc] —**총사직하다** resign in a body [en masse, en bloc]

총살 銃殺 shooting (to death); 〈처형〉 execution by shooting [by a firing squad]
—**총살하다** shoot sb dead [to death]; execute (a criminal) by shooting
▶ **범인은 총살되었다** The criminal was shot to death.
■**—대** a firing squad —**—형** execution by a firing squad; punishment of death by shooting

총상 銃傷 a bullet [gunshot] wound ◆ **가슴에 총상을 입다** be shot into the chest

총생 叢生 gregarious growth; growing in clusters; 〔植〕 fasciculation —**총생하다** grow in clusters; 〔植〕 be arranged in fascicles

총서 叢書 〈시리즈 간행서〉 a series (of English literature); a library; 〈갖가지의〉 a collection of books
◆ **총서로 출판되다** be published in a series

총선거 總選擧 a general election ◆ **총선거에서 승리하다** win in the general election
—**총선거하다** hold a general election; (英) appeal [go] to the country
■**—일** the general election day

총설 總說 general remarks ⇨ **총론**(總論)

총성 銃聲 a shot ⇨ **총소리**

총소리 銃— the report of a gun [rifle]; a gun [rifle] report; a shot ◆ **총소리가 들리다** a shot is heard; hear a shot

총수 總帥 〈총지휘관〉 the commander in chief ; 〈영도자〉 a supreme leader ◆ **재벌 총수** the head of a financial group

총수 總數 the total [aggregate] (number); the whole sum; 〈부사적〉 in all; in the aggregate; all told
▶ **총수가 얼마냐?** What does it amount to in all?
▶ **총수는 백이다** They are one hundred in all. ⇌ They total a hundred.

총수입 總收入 the total income; the gross revenue

총신 銃身 the barrel 《of a gun》 ⇨ **총열**

총신 寵臣 a favorite retainer [subject]; a court favorite

총아 寵兒 a favorite; a darling; a pet; (蔑) a minion
◆ **문단의 총아** a popular writer / **시대의 총아** the lion of the day; the man of the day / **운명의 총아** a fortune's favorite
▶ **그는 그 소설로 일약 문단의 총아가 되었다** He suddenly became a very popular writer by writing the novel.

총안 銃眼 a loophole; a crenel(le); an eyelet 《of a wall》; a gunport ◆ **총안벽** crenelated (wall) / **총안을 내다** crenelate

총알 銃— a ball; 〈소총탄〉 a bullet; 〈산탄〉 a shot; 〈납 탄환〉 a slug
◆ **빗나간 총알** a stray bullet / **총알처럼 빠르게** at rifle-bullet speed / **총알이 비오듯하다** bullets rain [shower (like hail)]; bullets come thick and fast / **총알을 재다** load (a gun) (with shot); charge (a gun) / **적에게 총알을 퍼붓다** rain bullets on the enemy; subject the enemy to fire / **총알에 맞다** be hit by a bullet; get [receive] a bullet (in one's arm)
▶ **총알이 그의 발에 박혔다** A bullet has lodged in his foot.
▶ **그가 쏜 총알은 표적 대신에 나무에 맞았다** His shot found a tree instead of the target.

총애 寵愛 favor; good graces; love; affection; patronage
◆ **총애를 받는 사람** a favorite; a pet / **총애를 받다[얻다]** win sb's favor; be a favorite with (one's master); be in sb's favor [good graces]; be patronized / **총애를 잃다** lose sb's favor; be in disgrace (with); fall into disfavor [disgrace] (with)
—**총애하다** favor; bestow favor upon; make a favorite of; love sb tenderly; fondle; coddle; pet (a child); patronize
◆ **총애하는** favorite; beloved; pet

총액 總額 the total amount [sum]; the sum total ◆ **총액 5천만원** 50,000,000 won in total [in the aggregate] ■수출— the total exports 예산— the total [overall] budget

총열 銃— the barrel ((of a gun)); the gunbarrel

총영사 總領事 a consul general ((*pl.* consuls general)) ■—관 a consulate general ((*pl.* consulates general))

총원 總員 the entire strength; the whole personnel; all the members; 〈배의〉 all hands; 〈부사적〉 in all; all told ◆총원 50명 fifty persons in all [all told] / 회사[군대]의 총원 the entire strength of a company [an army]

총의 總意 the collective [general] will [opinion] ((of the nation)) ◆국민의 총의 the consensus of the people / 국민의 총의를 묻다 〈총선거로〉 appeal [go] to the country

총이말 驄— a white horse with bluish-gray mane and tail

총자본금 總資本金 gross capital; 〈공칭의〉 nominal [authorized] capital; 〈등기필의〉 registered capital

총잡이 銃— a gunman; a (professional) killer; a gangster

총장 總長 the president ◆대학 총장 the president of a university; 〈英〉 the chancellor / 총장에 취임하다 assume the presidency ((of a university)); take [occupy] the presidential chair ((of)) ■사무— the secretary-general ((*pl.* secretaries-)) 참모— the Chief of the General Staff

총재 總裁 a president; a governor ◆총재가 되다 assume the presidency ((of)) ■당— the president of a party; a party chief 부— a vice-president

총점 總點 〈시험 점수〉 the (sum) total of one's marks; 〈경기의 득점〉 the total score ◆총점이 …이다 one's marks total...

총좌 銃座 a gun emplacement [position]

총죽 叢竹 a bamboo grove

총중 叢中 being amidst a crowd [throng] ◆만록 총중의 홍일점 the only member of the fair sex present; the only woman in the company; a woman in a men's party

총중량 總重量 gross weight

총지배인 總支配人 a general manager

총지출 總支出 gross [total] expenditure

총지휘 總指揮 the high [supreme] command —총지휘하다 take the supreme command of ((an army)) ■—관 ⇨ 총사령관

총질 銃— shooting; firing —총질하다 shoot [fire] a gun; fire at

총집 叢集 crowding around; swarming —총집하다 crowd; throng; flock together

총채 a dusting brush; a ((horsehair)) duster ■털— a feather duster

총첩 寵妾 one's (favorite) mistress [concubine]

총체 總體 the whole; all ◆총체적으로 on the whole; in general

총총 忽忽 hurriedly; hastily; in a hurry; in haste —총총하다 hurried; flurried ◆총총히 집으로 돌아가다 hurry home / 총총히 달아나다 run away helter-skelter

총총걸음 a quick pace; quick [short] steps; a trot ◆총총걸음으로 at a quick pace; with quick steps / 총총걸음치다 walk with quick steps; trot; hurry along

총총들이 葱葱— thickly; densely; closely; compactly

총총하다 葱葱— thick; dense; close ▶그 산에는 소나무가 총총히 들어서 있다 The mountain is densely wooded with pine trees.

총총하다 叢叢— dense; crowded; numerous ◆별이 총총한 하늘 the starry [star-spangled] sky / 총총히 densely; numerously ▶하늘에는 별이 총총하였다 The heavens were strewn [studded] with glittering stars.

총출동 總出動 general mobilization ((of the army)) —총출동하다 be all mobilized [called out] ▶경찰이 총출동했다 The police turned out in full force.

총칙 總則 general rules [provisions] ■민법— the general provisions of the civil code

총칭 總稱 a general term; a generic name —총칭하다 give a general name ((to)); name generically ▶이들 동물을 총칭하여 포유류라고 한다 Mammalia is a general term for these animals. ⇌ They are generally referred to as Mammalia.

총칼 銃— a gun and a sword; weapons ◆총칼로 다스리다 rule over with guns and swords [by force]

총탄 銃彈 a bullet; a shot ⇨ 총알

총톤수 總—數 gross tonnage ◆총톤수 1만톤의 배 a steamer of 10,000 tons gross / 총톤수가 5만 2천톤이다 have a gross tonnage of 52,000 tons; be 52,000 tons gross

총통 總統 〈나치스 독일의〉 the Führer; 〈대만의〉 the President; the Generalissimo

총퇴각 總退却 a general [full] retreat —총퇴각하다 make a general retreat

총파업 總罷業 ((go on)) a general strike

총판 總販 an exclusive sale; sole agency [trade] ◆총판 특약을 체결하다 enter into a special contract for the sole agency —총판하다 make an exclusive sale ((of))

총평 總評 a general survey [review, critique] ■문단— a general review of the literary world

총포 銃砲 firearms; guns; ((총칭)) gunnery —상 〈상점〉 a gun store; 〈상인〉 a dealer in firearms —화약류 단속법 the Firearms & Explosive Control Law

총할 總轄 general control ⇨ 총람(總攬)

총합 總合 the (sum) total; the total amount; the aggregate —총합하다 total; sum [add] up; gather [collect] together

총화 銃火 rifle [musket] fire; gunfire ◆총화를 무릅쓰고 under fire / 총화를 받다 come [be] under fire

총화 總和 the sum total ⇨ 총계

총회 總會 a general meeting [assembly]; a plenary session ◆총회에 부치다 submit ((a matter)) to the general meeting for discussion ■유엔— the United Nations General Assembly (略 UNGA) 정기[임시]— an ordinary [extraordinary] general meeting 주주— a general meeting of stockholders ■ —꾼 a professional trouble-maker at a shareholders' meeting; 〈회사가 고용한〉 hired toughs to keep order at a shareholders' meeting

총희 寵姬 a favorite mistress

촬영 撮影 photographing; picture-taking; a shot ◆ 촬영을 개시하다 crank in
▶ 촬영 금지 〈게시〉 No photographing within the zone.
—촬영하다 〈사진을〉 take a photograph [picture, (口) photo] of *sb*; photograph; 〈영화를〉 film [shoot] 〈a scene〉
▶ 그는 그 축구 시합을 영화로 촬영했다 He filmed the football game.
■ 실내[야간]— indoor [night] photographing 야외— shooting on location; 그들은 야외 촬영 중이다 They are on location. ■ —고도 flight height —기 a (movie) camera —기사 a cameraman (*pl*. -men); a cinematographer —기술 camera technique [work] —대본 a continuity —소 a studio; (美) a lot —속도 crankspeed —시간 shooting time

최- 最- the most; the maximum; the extreme; ultra- ◆ 최북단의 the northernmost / 최첨단의 ultramodern

최강 最强 the strongest ◆ 최강의 the strongest; the most powerful / 한국 최강의 팀 the strongest team of Korea

최고 最古 ◆ 최고의 the oldest
▶ 그 절은 세계 최고의 목조 건축물이다 The temple is the oldest wooden building in the world.

최고 最高 the highest; the uppermost; the maximum; the very best
◆ 최고의 the highest; the greatest; maximum; supreme; paramount; top(-rate); No. 1; A 1 / 최고의 기쁨 the utmost joy; the greatest pleasure
▶ 서울은 기온이 최고 39도에 달했다 In Seoul the temperature reached a maximum of 39℃.
▶ 오늘은 올 여름 들어 최고로 덥다 Today is the hottest weather we've had this summer.
▶ 그가 최고 득표를 했다 He polled the largest number of votes.
■ —간부 the executive —고문 a supreme advisor —권위 the highest [supreme] authority —기관 the highest organization [organ, institution] —기온 the maximum temperature —사령관 the supreme commander; the commander in chief —사령부 the high command; the supreme headquarters —속도 the maximum speed —수준 (be) the highest level —수훈선수 〔野〕 the most valuable player (略 MVP) —온도계 a maximum thermometer —음 〔樂〕 treble; soprano —임금제 the maximum wage system —최저 온도계 a maximum-minimum thermometer —한도 the highest limit; the maximum —회의 the supreme council; the top-level meeting

최고 催告 (a) notification; 〔法〕 a peremptory notice; 〈불입의〉 a call —최고하다 notify; call on *sb* to 〈do〉

최고가 最高價 the top [ceiling] price
◆ 최고가를 정하다 set the ceiling 《on》

최고급 最高級 the highest grade [class]
◆ 최고급의 of the highest grade; top-level; top-ranking; first-rate; of the best [highest, finest] quality; (口) choicest
■ —품 an article of the highest quality : 우리 회사 제품은 최고급품으로 꼽힌다 Our products are numbered [classed] among the best.

최고기록 最高記錄 the best record; (美) an all-time [a new] high
◆ 자신의 최고기록 *one's* best record / 최고기록을 내다 make [establish] the best record / 최고기록을 깨다 break [beat] the best record
■ 세계— a world record

최고도 最高度 the highest degree; the maximum; the climax
◆ 최고도로 to the highest degree; to the utmost / 재능을 최고도로 활용하다 make the utmost use of *one's* ability [talent]

최고득점 最高得點 the highest point ⇨ 최고점

최고봉 最高峰 the highest peak 《of》; (비유) the highest authority
◆ 한반도의 최고봉 the highest mountain in Korean peninsula / 현대문학의 최고봉 the highest authority of contemporary literature
▶ 그는 한국 화단의 최고봉으로 간주되고 있다 He is regarded as the most prominent in Korean painting circles.

최고위 最高位 the highest rank; the top place
◆ 최고위를 차지하다 hold (the) top place; rank first

최고위원 最高委員 a member of the supreme council ■ 대표— the chairman of the supreme council; the supreme representative

최고점 最高點 the highest point; 〈경기의〉 the highest score; 〈시험의〉 the highest mark(s); 〈투표의〉 the largest vote
▶ 그는 최고점으로 당선됐다 He was elected at the head of the polls. ⇒ He was elected with the highest poll [largest number of votes].
▶ 그녀는 이번 시험에서 최고점을 받았다 She gained the highest marks in the latest examination.

최고조 最高潮 〈조수점〉 a high-water mark; 〈정점〉 the climax; the peak; the acme
▶ 여행 붐이 최고조에 달했다 A traveling boom has come to its peak.
▶ 비틀즈의 인기는 1960년대에 최고조에 달했다 The popularity of Beatles reached its peak in the 1960's [1960s].

최고학부 最高學府 the highest institution of learning ◆ 최고학부를 나오다 graduate [be graduated] from a university

최근 最近 the latest date
◆ 최근에 지은 집 a house recently built / 최근의 유행 the latest fashion [mode] / 최근에 일어난 사건들 recent events / 최근의 recent; the latest; up-to-date / 최근에 recently; lately; of late / 아주 최근에 most recently / 최근 10년간에 in the last ten years
▶ 최근에 그녀를 만나 보셨습니까? Have you seen her lately?

▶그는 아주 최근에야 결혼했다 He got married only recently.
▶나는 최근까지 그것을 몰랐다 I didn't know it till recently.
▶최근 20년 사이에 그런 폭설은 없었다 There has not been such a heavy snowfall for the last twenty years. ⇌ This is the heaviest snowfall (we've had) in twenty years.
▶「타임」 최근호 있습니까? Do you have the latest issue of "the Time"?

최근세 最近世 recent times; the modern period ▶「한국 최근세사」 A History of Modern Korea

최급무 最急務 the most urgent matter [business]

최긴하다 最緊— very important; vital 《to》; essential 《to》; urgent; pressing
▶법관에게 최긴한 것은 공평무사함이다 Impartiality is absolutely essential to a judge.

최다 最多 the greatest [largest] in number
▶그는 최다 승리를 기록했다 He has won the most victories.
■—량[액] the greatest [largest] quantity [amount]; the maximum —수 the greatest [largest] number 《of》; the largest majority: 최다수의 인구 the largest population

최단 最短 being the shortest ■—거리[시일] the shortest distance [time]: 최단 거리를 가다 take the shortest course; go the nearest way

최대 最大 ◆최대의 the greatest [largest, biggest]; the maximum / 최대의 업적 the crowning achievement / 최대의 찬사를 보내다 pay one's highest tribute of admiration 《to》
▶셰익스피어는 영국이 낳은 최대의 시인이다 Shakespeare is the greatest poet that England has ever produced.
▶우리는 최소의 노력으로 최대의 효과를 거두려고 한다 We are trying to find the maximum of efficiency with the minimum of labor.
▶그는 최대 다수의 최대 행복을 신봉하고 있다 He believes in the greatest happiness of the greatest number.
■—강우량 the maximum rainfall —공약수 (數) the greatest common divisor (略 G.C.D.) —량 the largest [maximum] quantity —마찰력 the maximum frictional force —소비 전력 the maximum dissipation power —압력[장력] the maximum pressure [tension] —출력 the maximum output

최대값 最大— the maximum value

최대한(도) 最大限(度) the maximum
◆최대한의 능률 (put out, show) the maximum of efficiency / 최대한으로 to the highest degree; to the utmost / 능력을 최대한도로 발휘하다 give full play to one's abilities

최량 最良 ◆최량의 the best; superfine; the most excellent

최루 催淚 causing [producing] tears
■—가스 tear gas; lachrymatory gas; a lacrimator; a lachrymator —총 a tear-gas gun —탄 a tear(-gas) bomb [shell]; a lacrimatory shell

최면 催眠 hypnosis; hypnogenesis; somnolency ■—자기— self-hypnotism; self-hypnosis —요법 a hypnotic cure; hypnotic treatment; hypnotherapy —학 hypnology

최면상태 催眠狀態 a hypnotic state; hypnosis; hypnotism
◆최면상태에 빠지다 be hypnotized / 최면상태에서 깨어나다 be dehypnotized / 최면상태로 만들다 put sb into a state of hypnosis

최면술 催眠術 mesmerism; hypnotism
◆최면술의 mesmeric; hypnotic / 최면술에 걸린 사람 a hypnotic; a person under hypnosis / 최면술에 의하여 hypnotically; mesmerically / 최면술을 걸다 mesmerize sb; hypnotize sb; exercise a mesmeric power 《over》 / 최면술에 걸리다 be mesmerized; be hypnotized
■—사 a hypnotist; a mesmerist

최상 最上 the best ◆최상의 the best; the finest; the highest 《quality》; supreme; superb; superlative; (美) top-notch / 최상의 행복 the supreme happiness
▶부도 권력도 최상의 행복을 가져다 주지는 못한다 Neither wealth nor power produces the supreme happiness.
■—선(善) the supreme good —층 〈사회의〉 the uppermost class; 〈건축물의〉 the uppermost story; the top floor —품 ⇨ 최고급(~품)

최상급 最上級 1 〈등급〉 the highest grade; 〈학교의〉 the top [graduating] class
2 〈文法〉 the superlative 《degree》

최선 最善 the best; one's best ◆최선의 노력 the utmost [best] efforts / 최선을 다하다 do one's best [utmost]; do all one can
▶정직은 최선의 방책이다 Honesty is the best policy.
▶최선을 다해 도와 드리겠습니다 I'll do my best to help you.

최성기 最盛期 〈전성기〉 the prime; the golden age; the height of prosperity; 〈과일 등의 제철〉 the season
▶문화의 최성기에 이르다 reach the high watermark [zenith] of (its) culture
▶로마는 아우구스투스 시대가 최성기였다 Rome was in its prime during the age of Augustus.
▶사과는 지금이 최성기다 Apples are in season now. ⇌ Apples are at their best now.

최소 最小 the smallest; the minimum ◆최소의 the smallest; minimum; minimal / 위험을 최소로 줄이다 minimize the danger 《of》
▶그는 최소의 노력으로 최대의 효과를 거뒀다 He achieved a maximum of efficiency at a minimum of effort.
■—공배수 (數) the least common multiple (略 L.C.M.) —공통분모 (數) the least common denominator (略 L.C.D.) —량 the minimum quantity

최소 最少 ◆최소의 the fewest; the least; the minimum; minimal

최소한(도) 最小限(度) the minimum
◆최소한의 요구 the irreducible minimum of a demand / 최소한으로 at a minimum / 비용을 최소한도로 줄이다 reduce the expenses to the minimum
▶우리는 피해를 최소한도로 줄였다 We checked the damage to a minimum.

최상급의 표현

1. 제일…; 가장…; 최…
(1) 형용사
명사 앞에 둔다
▶ 세계에서 가장 큰 도시는 어디입니까? What is the largest city in the world?
▶ 에베레스트는 세계 최고봉이다 Mt. Everest is the highest mountain in the world.
▶ 한국에서 가장 놀랐던 일은 무엇입니까? What is the most surprising thing you have seen in Korea?
▶ 베토벤은 세계 최고의 작곡가 중의 한 사람이다 Beethoven is one of the world's finest composers.

(2) 보어로
▶ 에베레스트는 세계에서 가장 높다 Mt. Everest is (the) highest in the world.
▶ 어느 달이 가장 춥습니까? Which month is the coldest?
▶ 어느 과목이 가장 어렵습니까? Which lesson is the most difficult?

(3) 부사 (동사 뒤에 둔다)
▶ 그가 가장 열심히 일한다 He works (the) hardest.
▶ 나는 야구를 제일 좋아한다 I like baseball (the) most.
▶ 여기서 제일 먼 곳에 사는 사람은 누구니까? Who lives (the) farthest from here?

[어법]
① 최상급에는 the를 붙인다. 단, 부사의 최상급에는 the를 생략할 때가 많다. the 외에 my, your, his 등 인칭대명사의 소유격이나 명사의 소유격도 붙인다.
보기 This is my youngest daughter.
② 「훨씬」「단연」 등 최상급을 강조하는데는 much, by far, far and away를 쓴다.
보기 This is much [by far] the best. (이것이 단연 제일 좋다)
Baseball is by far the most popular sport in Korea. (한국에서는 야구가 단연 인기 스포츠다)
③ 동일인[동일물]에 관하여 말하며 두 사람[물건] 사이의 비교가 아닐 때에는 the는 생략한다.
보기 This road is widest at this corner. (이 도로는 이 모퉁이가 가장 넓다) (▶다른 도로와의 비교가 아니다)
I work best in the morning. (나는 아침에 일이 제일 잘된다) (▶타인과의 비교가 아니다)

2. ～중에서 제일 [가장] …
(1) the + 최상급 …of ～
(of 뒤에는 복수명사·집합명사 또는 복수의 뜻을 나타내는 말이 온다)
▶ 우리들 중에서는 그가 제일 헤엄을 잘 친다 He is the best swimmer of all of us. (▶of us all이라도 되지만 문어적이다. 구어에서는 all of us를 쓴다)
▶ 셋 중에서는 이것이 가장 좋다 This is the best of the three.
▶ 그는 우리들 중에서 제일 일을 열심히 한다 He works the hardest of all of us.
▶ 나는 학과 중에서 영어가 제일 재미있다 English is the most interesting of all the subjects I study.
▶ 일년 중에서 가장 긴 날은 언제입니까? Which is the longest day of the year?
▶ 내가 읽은 소설 중에서 이것이 제일 재미있다 Of all the novels I have read, this is the most interesting. (▶of ～ 가 문두에 오는 경우도 있음)
▶ 우리 세 사람 중에서 그의 영어가 가장 유창하다 Of the three of us, he speaks English (the) most fluently.
▶ 그 세 도시 중에서는 어디가 가장 큽니까? Which of the three cities is the largest?

(2) the + 최상급 …in ～
(in 뒤에는 주로 장소를 나타내는 말이 온다)
▶ 세계에서 가장 긴 강은 무슨 강입니까? What is the longest river in the world?
▶ 그 학급에서 제일 키가 큰 사람은 누구니까? Who is the tallest student in the class?
▶ 그는 시내에서 제일 가는 부자다 He is the richest man in town.

(3) the + 최상급… 그 밖의 전치사
(나타내는 뜻에 따라 여러 가지 전치사를 취한다)
▶ 그것은 이 근방에서 가장 높은 건물입니다 That is the tallest building on this block.
▶ 그녀는 시장에서 가장 싼 물건을 샀다 She bought the cheapest thing on the market.

(4) the + 최상급…
(that clause 에서 that 은 흔히 생략된다)
▶ 네가 공부하고 있는 과목 중에서 가장 재미있는 것은 무엇이니? What is the most interesting subject you are studying?
▶ 당신이 알고 있는 사람 중에서 가장 유능한 사람은 누구입니까? Who is the ablest person you know?
▶ 지금까지 보신 것 중에서 가장 아름다운 도시는 어디입니까? What is the most beautiful city (that) you have ever seen?

3. ～다음으로 제일 [가장]…, ～다음가는 대…
the + 최상급… + after [next to] ～
▶ 반에서 수남이 다음으로 키가 큰 것은 인호다 After Su-nam, In-ho is the tallest boy in the class.
▶ 부산은 서울 다음가는 대도시다 Pusan is the largest city in Korea after [next to] Seoul. (▶「두[세]번째로…」는 「the second [third] + 최상급」으로 나타낸다. 이 어법은 네[다섯, 여섯]번째 등 상당히 널리 쓰인다)
▶ 그것은 유럽에서 세번째로 높은 산입니다 It is the third highest mountain in Europe.

4. 제일[가장] …하지 않다
the least + 형용사의 원급
▶ 내가 읽은 책 중에서 이것이 제일 재미없다 This is the least interesting book I've ever read. ⇌ This is the most uninteresting book I've ever read.
▶ 형제 중에서 제일 영리하지 못한 것은 그다

He is the least intelligent of the brothers. ⇌ He is the dullest of the brothers.
[어법]
「the least + 형용사의 원급」대신에 반대의 뜻을 나타내는 형용사의 최상급을 써서 표현하는 것이 일반적이다.
5. 누구 [무엇, 어느 것] 가 제일 …라고 생각하니?
who [what, which] do you think… + 최상급?
▶ 반에서 제일 키가 큰 것은 누구라고 생각하니? Who do you think is the tallest boy in the class?
▶ 영국에서 제일 인기 있는 스포츠는 무엇이라고 생각합니까? What do you think is the most popular sport in Britain?
▶ 세 개 중에서 어느 것이 제일 좋다고 생각합니까? Which of the three things do you think is the best?
[어법]
① who, what, which가 글의 주어에 해당할 때는 who, [what, which] do you think the + 최상급…? 의 어순이 된다. 위의 예문에서는 모두 의문사가 주어다.
② 이 구문에서 동사는 think 외에 believe, suppose, say 등도 쓸 수 있다.
6. 이런 [저런] …은 처음이다; ~만이다
(1) **the + 최상급… in ~**
(in 뒤에는 연수를 나타내는 말을 쓴다)
▶ 금년 겨울은 10년만의 추위다 This is the coldest winter in ten years.
(2) **the + 최상급 (+명사) + that clause**
(that clause 안에는 현재완료형을 쓴다)
▶ 이렇게 맛좋은 포도주는 이것이 처음입니다 This wine is the best that I have ever tasted.
▶ 그런 심한 눈보라는 처음이었습니다 That was the worst snowstorm I have ever experienced.
▶ 그런 아름다운 정원은 처음 본다 That is the most beautiful garden I have ever seen.
▶ 금년 들어 이렇게 더운 날은 처음입니다 Today is the hottest day (that) we have had this year.
▶ 그렇게 맛있는 식사는 수주일만의 일입니다 That was the best dinner we have had in several weeks.
[어법]
① that clause 안에 ever가 없을 때에는 그에 대신하는 다른 표현(this year, in several years 등)을 쓴다.
「~만에」는 "the + 최상급… that + 주어 + 현재완료 + in + 때"로 나타낸다.
보기 The coldest winter that we have had in ten years.
② 「~만에」의 in 대신에 영국에서는 for을 쓴다.

최신 最新 up-to-dateness
◆최신 자료 an up-to-date material / 최신의 the newest; the latest; up-to-date / 극히 최신의 up-to-the-minute[-second]; ultramodern
▶ 그들은 해외로부터 최신 정보를 입수했다 They received fresh information from abroad.
■—형 the newly-made type : 이것은 최신형차다 This is a car of the latest [most up-to-date] model.
최신식 最新式 the latest [newest] fashion [style] ◆최신식 호텔 a hotel with the latest improvements
최신유행 最新流行 the latest fashion; the newest style ◆최신 유행의 모자[양복] a new-look hat [suit]
최심 最甚 the most extreme [excessive]; the severest; the heaviest; the worst
—최심하다 most extreme [excessive]; severest; heaviest; worst
◆피해가 최심하다 suffer the worst damage
최악 最惡 the worst ◆최악의 경우에는 in the worst case; at the worst; if [when] (the) worst comes to (the) worst
▶ 사태가 최악의 상태에 있다 Things are at the [their] worst.
▶ 최악의 사태를 각오해야만 합니다 You must prepare for the worst.
최우등 最優等 the top grade; the highest [greatest] distinction; top honors ◆최우등으로 졸업하다 graduate 《from a college》 with the highest [greatest] distinction
■—생 the highest honorsman; the top student
최우수 最優秀 the very best; an A 1; an ace
—선수 the best player

최음제 催淫劑 an aphrodisiac (medicine); a lascivious drug
최장 最長 ◆최장의 (the) longest ■—거리 the longest [greatest] distance
최저 最低 the lowest
◆최저의 lowest; lowermost; minimum
▶ 월급은 최저 70만원이다 The monthly salary is 700,000 won at the lowest.
■—기록 the lowest record; 《美口》 a new low —생활비[생활비] the minimum standard [cost] of living —온도계 a minimum thermometer
최저가 最低價 the lowest [bottom] price; 《美》 the floor (price); 〈낙찰 가격〉 a reserve ◆최저가에 달하다 reach [strike] (the) bottom; bottom out
최저임금 最低賃金 the minimum wages; a wage floor ■—제 the minimum wage system
최적 最適 ◆최적의 the most fitted [suitable]; optimum
▶ 그 일에는 그녀가 최적의 인물이다 She is the only person for the job.
■—온도[밀도, 속도, 규모, 기준] the optimum temperature [density, speed, size, standard] —조건 (生) the optimum
최전방 最前方 the front line ⇨ 최전선
최전선 最前線 the front line; the forefront
최종 最終 〈맨 뒤〉 the last; 〈끝〉 the end
◆최종의 the last; final; closing; ultimate / 최종까지 to the last [end]
▶ 우리는 활동의 최종 단계에 있다 We are on the last stage of our activity.
▶ 최종적으로는 내가 이 문제를 처리하지 않으면 안된다 I will have to deal with this problem finally.
■—결정 the final decision —목적 the ulti-

mate goal [object] —병기 an ultimate weapon —수요자[소비자] an end user —시험 the final [last] examination —안 the final program [plan] —용도 〖經〗 end use —회 〈시합의〉 the last inning [round]

최종일 最終日 the last day; the closing day
♦ 연극 공연의 최종일 the final [leave-taking] day of a theatrical performance

최초 最初 the first; the beginning; the commencement; 〈발단〉 the outset
♦ 최초의 the first 《doing》; initial 《attempt》; opening 《game》; original 《plan》; primary 《object》; the earliest 《visitor》/ 최초의 경험 one's first [new] experience
▶ 그 기획은 그런 형식으로는 최초의 것이었다 The planning was the first of its type.
▶ 최초에는 누구나 최선을 다하지만 끝까지 하는 사람은 거의 없다 Everybody does his best at first, but only a few can hold out to the end.

최하 最下 the lowest
♦ 최하로 싸게 해서 얼마입니까? What is the very lowest price you will go down to?
■—가격 the lowest price —층 〈사회의〉 the lowest stratum of society; the lowest class; 〈건물의〉 the lowermost story

최하급 最下級 the lowest grade [class]
■—생 a first-year student; 〈美〉〈대학·고교의〉 a freshman

최하등 最下等 the lowest grade
■—품 an article of the lowest quality

최하위 最下位 the lowest rank [position]
♦ 최하위 팀 the tailender / 최하위다 rank lowest; be lowest in rank; 〈경기에서〉 be in the cellar

최혜국 最惠國 a most favored nation
■—대우 most-favored-nation treatment —약관 the most-favored-nation clause

최활 a tenter; a temple

최후 最後 1 〈맨 끝〉 the last; 〈결말〉 the end
♦ 최후의 last; final; closing; concluding; conclusive; ultimate; terminal / 최후의 만찬 〖基〗 the Last Supper / 최후의 심판 the (Last) Judgment / 최후의 순간 the last [critical] moment / 최후의 일격 the last [a final] blow / 최후로 lastly; in conclusion; eventually; in the end / 최후까지 to the end [last] / 최후의 승리를 얻다 win the ultimate [final] victory; win in the long run
▶ 그것은 최후의 수단이다 That is the last resort.
▶ 그들은 최후의 한 사람까지 싸웠다 They fought to the last man.
▶ 최후의 5분이 중요하다 The last five minutes determines the issue.
▶ 어떤 일이 있어도 최후까지 버틸 작정이다 Whatever happens, I will hold out to the end. 2 〈죽음·임종〉 one's last moment; one's death; one's end
♦ 최후의 말 one's dying words / 최후를 장식하다 be [bring] the last glory to one's life
■—수단 (resort to) the last measure; one's [the] last resort —통첩 (send) an ultimatum 《pl. ~s, -ta》; a final note

추 錘 a weight; a poise; 〈시계추〉 a pendulum; a bob; 〈다림추〉 a plummet

추가 追加 an addition; an addendum 《pl. -da》; an appendix 《pl. ~es, -dices》; 〈보충〉 a supplement
—추가하다 add sth (to); supplement
♦ 예산을 추가하다 supplement a budget / 부록을 추가하다 add an appendix / 술을 추가하다 〈연회 등에서〉 order more bottles of wine
■—경정예산(안) a revised supplementary budget (bill) —비용 additional expenses —신청 additional application —예산(안) a supplementary budget (bill) —조항 an added [a supplementary] article; a rider —주문 an additional order —지출 a supplemental appropriation —징수 additional collection

추가시험 追加試驗 a supplementary examination; 〈美〉 a makeup (examination); 〈가진급 학생의〉 a condition
♦ 추가시험을 치르다 take a makeup

추간 追刊 additional publication —추간하다 publish in addition

추거 推擧 recommendation ⇨ 추천(推薦)

추격 追擊 pursuit; chase; a follow-up attack
♦ 적을 맹추격 중이다 be in hot pursuit [chase] of the enemy
—추격하다 pursue; chase; give chase to; run after
■—기 a pursuit plane [fighter]; a chase plane; a chaser —전 a pursuit battle; 〈해상의〉 a running fight

추격붙이다 追擊— 1 〈習陣(習陣)시키다〉 hold [carry out] maneuvers; do military exercise; hold a sham battle [fight]
2 〈이간질하여 싸우게 하다〉 make 《people》 quarrel; set 《people》 by the ears

추경 秋耕 autumn plowing ⇨ 가을갈이

추경 秋景 autumn(al) scenery

추계 秋季 autumn; 〈美〉 fall
■—운동회 an autumn athletic meet

추계 推計 (an) estimation —추계하다 estimate / …으로 추계되다 be estimated at…

추고 追考 retrospection; reminiscence; recollection —추고하다 look back upon [to] (the past); retrospect; reminisce

추곡 秋穀 autumn grain —수매(가격) the government purchase (price) of rice

추골 椎骨 〖解〗 a vertebra 《pl. -brae, ~s》

추괴 醜怪 ugliness; grotesqueness —추괴하다 ugly; grotesque

추교 醜交 an illicit [improper] connection [liaison] between a man and a woman
♦ 추교를 맺다 have a [an illicit] liaison (with)

추구 追求 pursuit; chase; search; follow-up
♦ 행복 추구 pursuit [quest] of happiness
—추구하다 pursue; seek after; chase; give chase to; follow after
♦ …을 추구하여 in quest [pursuit, search] of… / 쾌락을 추구하다 seek [pursue] pleasure; gather (life's) roses / 행복을 추구하다 conduct the pursuit of happiness / 어떤 목적을 추구하다 pursue an object
■—이윤— pursuit of profits

추구 追究 thorough investigation; close inquiry
♦진리의 추구 an inquiry into the truth
―추구하다 inquire into *sth* closely; follow up an inquiry; investigate *sth* thoroughly; probe *sth* to the bottom

추구 推究 inference ―추구하다 infer

추궁 追窮 pressing hard ―추궁하다 press hard; come down hard (on, upon)
♦책임을 추궁하다 call *sb* to account
▶그 이상은 추궁당하지 않았다 It was not pressed any further.

추근추근 tenaciously; persistently; pertinaciously, importunately
♦추근추근 여자를 쫓아다니다 dangle after [hang around] a girl with annoying persistence / 추근추근 묻다 pester [plague] *sb* with questions
―추근추근하다 persistent; tenacious; pertinacious; dogged; importunate; inquisitive
♦추근추근한 요구 an importunate demand

추급 追及 overtaking ―추급하다 overtake; catch [come, fetch] up with

추급 追給 (a) supplementary payment ―추급하다 pay in addition

추기 秋氣 autumnal air; a sign of autumn

추기 秋期 fall ⇨ 추계(秋季)

추기 追記 an additional writing; a supplement; an addendum (*pl.* -da); a postscript
―추기하다 add *sth* in writing; write an addendum; add 《to》; supplement

추기경 樞機卿 〔가톨릭〕 a cardinal
■―의 a consistory

추기다 〔꾀다〕 entice; tempt; allure; seduce; decoy; 〈구워 삶다〉 cajole; wheedle; 〈선동하다〉 incite; abet; instigate; stir up
♦노동자를 추겨서 파업을 시키다 instigate workers to go on strike

추깃물 secretion from corpses; cadaveric fluid

추남 醜男 a bad-looking [an ugly] man

추납 追納 supplementary payment ―추납하다 pay in addition

추녀 〔建〕 a hip rafter

추녀 醜女 a plain [an ugly] woman; 《美》 a homely [plain-looking] woman

추념 追念 commemoration; recollection
―추념하다 commemorate; recollect; cherish [honor] the memory of *sb*
■―사 a memorial address

추다¹ 〈춤추다〉 dance ♦남의 장단에 춤을 추다 dance to [after] *sb's* tune [pipe]
▶고고를 출 줄 압니까? Can you do the go-go?
♦함께 추실까요? May I have your next dance?

추다² 〈칭찬하다〉 praise ⇨ 추어주다

추다³ 1 〈들추다〉 ransack 2 〈채어올리다〉 pull up; draw up; lift up ♦멍석 한 구석을 추다 pull up a corner of a mat

추단 推斷 (an) inference; (a) deduction
―추단하다 infer [deduce] 《from》; conclude
▶이 사실로부터 다음과 같이 추단할 수 있다 From this fact we may safely infer as follows.

추담 醜談 a filthy [foul] talk; an obscene [indecent] talk; a dirty [smutty] story

추대하다 推戴― have *sb* as the president [head] of; have *sb* over 《a society》
▶그를 회장으로 추대하기로 결정했다 We have decided to have him as chairman.

추도 追悼 mourning; lamentation ―추도하다 mourn 《for the dead, over *sb's* death》
■―가〈歌〉 a dirge ―문 a memorial writing ―사 a memorial address ―식 〈hold〉 a memorial service ―회 〈hold〉 a ceremony in memory of *sb*

추돌 追突 a rear-end collision; 〔競漕〕 a bump ―추돌하다 dash [bump, crash] 《against *sth*》 from behind; collide 《with *sth*》 from behind
▶그는 과속으로 달리다 앞차에 추돌했다 He drove so fast (that) he crashed into the rear of a car.

추락 墜落 a fall; a drop; a crash
―추락하다 fall; drop; crash
▶비행기 한 대가 들판에 추락했다 An airplane crashed in the field.
▶제트기는 추락하여 조종사는 죽었다 The jet plane crashed and the pilot was killed.
▶차 한 대가 호수에 추락했다 A car plunged into the lake.
■―사 death from a fall: 그는 그 벼랑에서 추락사했다 He fell off the cliff and died.

추량 秋凉 cool [chilly] autumnal weather

추량 推量 (a) conjecture ⇨ 추측(推測)

추레하다 shabby; dirty; slovenly ♦〈늙어서〉 추레해지다 run to seed

추력 推力 (a) thrust; impellent [driving] force
■―실 a thrust chamber

추렴 joint contribution ♦추렴으로 at the joint expense of
―추렴하다 contribute jointly; collect money; pool 《funds》; club 《the expenses》
▶이 비용은 각자 추렴하자 Let us share the expenses. ⇌ Let's go Dutch.
▶그 소년들은 추렴해서 3만원을 만들었다 The boys raised thirty thousand won among them.
▶학생들은 돈을 추렴해서 공을 샀다 The students clubbed together [up] and bought a ball.

추렴새 1 ⇨ 추렴 2 〈각금〉 one's share 《in the expenses》; 〈술값〉 one's shot ♦추렴새가 많다 a 〈one's〉 share is large

추록 追錄 a postscript ⇨ 추기(追記)

추론 推論 reasoning; ratiocination; (an) inference; 〈귀납〉 induction; 〈연역〉 deduction
▶우리의 추론이 맞을 가능성이 더 크다 Our reasoning has a better chance to succeed.
―추론하다 reason; ratiocinate; infer 《from》; draw an inference 《from》; induce; deduce

추루하다 醜陋― filthy ⇨ 누추하다

추리 the hind flank 《of beef》

추리 推理 reasoning; ratiocination; (an) inference ―추리하다 reason; ratiocinate; infer 《from》
♦자료를 가지고 추리하다 deduce [infer, reason] from the data / 하나하나 추리해 나가다 follow out a train of reasoning
■ 연역적〔귀납적〕― deductive [inductive] inference 직접〔간접〕― immediate [mediate]

inference; direct [indirect] inference ■—력 reasoning power; the faculty of reasoning —소설 a detective [mystery] story; a mystery; 〈美俗〉 a whodunit (▶Who done it? 에서)

추리다 select; choose; pick out; sort; assort
◆여럿 중에서 추리다 choose from among many / 짚을 추리다 pick and trim straws (weeding out short ones) / 좋은 것만을 추리다 pick out the best ones / 수백명 중에서 추리다 single out of several hundred applicants

추맥 秋麥 〈가을보리〉 winter barley

추명 醜名 an ill name; ill repute [fame]; infamy; notoriety; 〈추문〉 a scandal ◆추명을 사다 earn [fall into] bad repute; become notorious (for)

추모 追慕 cherishing the memory of 《a deceased person》 —**추모하다** cherish *sb's* memory; look back upon the memory of 《a deceased person》 with respect and affection
◆선친을 추모하다 cherish [revere] the memory of *one's* late father
▶김선생을 추모하는 기념비가 세워졌다 A monument was erected to the memory of the late Mr. Kim.

추문 醜聞 a scandal; ill fame ◆추문을 일으키다 create [cause, give rise to] a scandal ■—거리 a scandalous affair; a source of scandal

추물 醜物 〈물건〉 an ugly [a dirty] object [matter]; 〈사람〉 an ugly [a bad-looking] person

추밀원 樞密院 〈英〉 the Privy Council

추방 追放 banishment; expulsion; purge; exile; deportation; 〈사회적〉 ostracism
—**추방하다** banish; exile; deport; expel; expatriate; ostracize
◆국외로 추방하다 banish [deport, exile] *sb* from the land; expatriate / 공직에서 추방하다 remove [oust] *sb* from public office; purge *sb* from public life / 현직에서 추방하다 evict *sb* from 《his》 present post
■빈곤— the elimination of poverty ■—령 a deportation order; 〈공직에서의〉 a purge directive —자 an exile; an evictee; 〈공직에서의〉 a purgee : 국외 추방자 an exile; an expatriate —해제 clearing of purge —해제자 a depurgee; 〈총칭〉 the depurged

추백 追白 a postscript (略 P.S.) =추신(追伸)

추병 追兵 a pursuing party [force]; soldiers in chase [pursuit]

추분 秋分 the autumnal equinox

추분점 秋分點 〈天〉 the autumnal equinoctial point

추비 追肥 topdressing=덧거름

추사 秋思 autumnal sentiment [thought]

추산 推算 calculation; a computation; an estimate —**추산하다** calculate; compute; reckon; estimate
▶우리는 수리비를 50만원으로 추산했다 We estimated the cost of repairs at five hundred thousand won.

추삼삭 秋三朔 the three autumnal month

추상 抽象 abstraction
—**추상하다** abstract 《from》
■—론 an abstract argument; generalities —명사 〈文法〉 an abstract noun —예술 abstract art —주의 abstractionism —표현주의 abstract expressionism

추상 秋霜 1 〈가을 서리〉 autumn frost
2 〈준엄〉 severity; sternness; rigidity; mercilessness
◆추상같은 명령 a stern order / 추상같은 논고 a most relentless argument 《against》
▶김 검사의 논고는 추상같았다 The final speech of prosecutor Kim was a scathing one.

추상 追想 recollection; retrospection ⇨ 추억
■—록 reminiscences; memoirs; recollections

추상 推想 conjecture; surmise; inference; guess
—**추상하다** conjecture; suppose; surmise; infer; guess

추상적 抽象的 abstract
◆추상적으로 abstractly; in the abstract / 추상적으로 말하다 speak in the abstract
■—개념 an abstract idea [notion]

추상파 抽象派 〈美術〉 the abstractionist school; abstractionism ■—화가 an abstractionist; an abstract painter

추상화 抽象畫 〈美術〉 an abstract painting [picture] ■—반— a semi-abstract painting

추색 秋色 autumnal scenery; autumnal tints; signs of autumn
◆추색을 즐기다 enjoy autumnal tints
▶추색이 완연하다 There is a definite sign of autumn in the air. ⇌ The autumnal tints are in full glory.

추서 追書 a postscript ⇨ 추신(追伸)

추서 追敍 posthumous honors
—**추서하다** confer posthumous honors on *sb*; be promoted to 《a rank》 posthumously

추서다 get well again; recover 《from illness》; be *oneself* again; be restored to health
▶그의 몸이 추서기까지는 오랜 시간이 걸렸다 He took a long time to come round.

추석 秋夕 *Ch'usŏk*; the Korean 《version of》 Thanksgiving Day; Harvest Moon Day
■—성묘 a visit to *one's* ancestral graves on the occasion of *Ch'usŏk*

추세 趨勢 a tendency; a trend; a drift
◆시대의 추세 the current of the times / 여론의 추세 the trend of public opinion / 물가의 추세 a price trend / 자연적인 추세 the course of natural tendency / 일반적인 추세 a general tendency / 시대의 추세에 따르다 follow the trend of the times / 〈자연의〉 추세에 맡기다 let things [matters] take their own course
▶세상 추세를 거스르는 것은 어리석은 일이다 It is unwise to row against the current.
▶세계의 추세는 평화를 지향하고 있다 The world is drifting toward peace.

추소 秋宵 an autumn evening [night]

추소 追訴 a supplementary action [suit, indictment] —**추소하다** bring a supplementary action 《against》

추속 醜俗 indecent [disgraceful] customs; mean [foul] manners

추수 秋收 harvesting; harvest
◆3백석의 추수 a harvest [crop] of three hundred bags of rice / 추수에 바쁘다 be busy har-

추수하다 harvest; reap (a harvest); gather [take] in 《crops》; crop
♦추수하는 사람 a harvester; a reaper / 논에서 곡식을 추수하다 harvest the paddy fields
■—감사절 Thanksgiving Day —기 harvesttime

추수 追隨 association; fellowship; intercourse
—추수하다 associate with; hold intercourse with; keep company with; mix with; get on [along] with

추스르다 1 〈치켜 올리다〉 pick up and put in place ♦ 업은 아이를 추스르다 jiggle a baby on one's back
2 〈수습하다〉 set (things) in order; manage
♦ 일을 추스르다 handle matters nicely

추습 醜習 a foul [vicious] habit; a vice; an indecent practice

추시 趨時 〈시속을 따름〉 keeping pace with the time; swimming with stream [current]
—추시하다 swim [go, float] with the stream [current]; follow the spirit of the times

추신 追伸 a postscript (略 P.S., PS, ps.)

추신하다 抽身— get oneself free 《from business》; disengage oneself; get away from work; manage to find time
♦ 잠시도 추신할 틈이 없다 have no time to spare; be fully occupied; be too busy

추심 推尋 collection
♦ 수표를 추심에 돌리다 put a check through for collection —추심하다 collect
■—금 money collected —료 a collection charge —어음 a bill for collection —위임 배서 (背書) endorsement for collection —은행 the collection bank —인 a 《bill》 collector

추썩거리다 〈어깨 등을〉 shrug 《one's shoulders》 repeatedly; 〈옷을〉 keep pulling up; rock up
♦ 업은 아이를 추썩거리다 rock the baby up on one's back / 바지를 추썩거리다 keep pulling up one's trousers

추썩추썩 shrugging 《one's shoulders》 repeatedly; pulling [hitching] up 《one's trousers》 repeatedly; rocking up

추악하다 醜惡— 〈흉하다〉 ugly; unsightly; 〈비루하다〉 abominable; mean; base; foul; filthy; repulsive; scandalous
♦ 추악한 인상 ugly features / 추악한 싸움 an abominable quarrel / 추악한 동기 a foul motive / 추악한 짓을 하다 behave unseemly; act dishonorably; 〈여자에게〉 take liberties with a woman

추앙 推仰 reverence; veneration; adoration; respect; worship
—추앙하다 revere; venerate; adore; respect; worship; look up to; hold sb in esteem
♦ 추앙받다 be held in respect [esteem]
▶ 모두가 그를 지도자로 추앙하고 있었다 They all looked up to him as their leader.
▶ 그는 세인의 추앙을 받고 있다 He stands high in public esteem.

추야 秋夜 an autumn night
♦ 추야장 긴긴 밤에 in the long nights of autumn; in autumn when the nights are long

추양 秋陽 autumn sunshine; the autumn sun

추어 鰍魚 a loach ⇨ 미꾸라지 ■—탕 loach soup

추어내다 dig up ⇨ 들추어내다

추어올리다 1 〈끌어올리다〉 pull up; lift (up); hoist 2 ⇨ 추어주다 ▶ 그렇게 추어올리지 말게 Spare my blushes.

추어주다 praise; applaud; compliment; speak highly of; sing sb's praise; flatter; say nice things (to); extol sb
♦ 부지런하다고 추어주다 praise sb for (his) diligence / 몹시 추어주다 praise sb sky-high; extol sb to the skies; speak very highly of sb / 빈말로 추어주다 offer one's lip service
♦ 추어주어 싫다는 사람은 없다 Nobody feels offended at compliments.
▶ 그는 조금만 추어주어도 곧 우쭐해 진다 A little flattery will fetch him.

추억 追憶 recollection; reminiscence; remembrance; retrospection; a retrospect; a memory
♦ 어린 시절의 추억 my reminiscence of childhood / 즐거운 추억 dear [happy] memories / 추억을 새롭게 하다 refresh one's memory
▶ 나는 잠시 추억에 잠겼다 I looked back on my past days. ≒ I spent some time indulging in reminiscence(s).
▶ 추억에 남을 여행이었다 It was a journey which would not easily be forgotten [an unforgettable journey].
—추억하다 recollect; reminisce; recall; look back upon [to] 《the past》; retrospect; review
♦ 옛날을 추억케 하다 make sb reminiscent of old times; remind sb of the old days
▶ 그 사진은 나로 하여금 옛날을 추억케 한다 That picture carries my mind back to old times [brings back old times to me].
■—거리 a remembrancer; a reminder; a memento

추억담 追憶談 a reminiscent talk; memoirs; reminiscences
♦ 추억담을 나누다 exchange memories

추업 醜業 a shameful calling; prostitution
♦ 추업에 종사하다 live a life of shame [prostitution]

추완 追完 [法] subsequent completion
—추완하다 complement; subsequently complete 《an act》

추요 樞要 importance —추요하다 pivotal; key; important; principal; cardinal

추우 秋雨 an autumn rain
■—전선 an autumnal rain front

추운 秋雲 an autumn cloud

추워지다 grow [get] cold(er); get chilly; cool down ▶ 날씨가 추워진다 The cold weather has set in.

추위하다 feel (the) cold; feel chilly; complain of the cold ▶ 그는 추위하는 것 같다 He looks cold.

추월 秋月 the autumn moon

추월 追越 passing; outrunning
▶ 추월 금지 《게시》 《美》 No passing
—추월하다 pass overtake; get ahead of; 〈배가〉 outsail; outsteam

■―금지구역 a no-passing zone ―차선 a fast lane; (美) a passing lane; (英) an overtaking lane

추위 coldness; (the) cold
♦심한 추위 the intense [bitter] cold / 살을 에는 듯한 추위 the biting [piercing] cold / 갑자기 닥치는 추위 a cold snap / 추위를 몹시 타는 사람 a cold-blooded person; a person exceedingly sensitive to cold / 추위를 견디다 stand [bear] the cold / 추위를 막다 keep off [out] the cold / 추위를 타다 be sensitive to cold; feel the cold readily; be easily chilled; have a cold constitution / 추위에 약하다 be easily affected by cold weather / 추위에 떨다 shiver with cold; quiver from cold / 추위에 익숙해지다 inure *oneself* to cold
▶금년 추위는 유난하다 The cold of this winter is quite unprecedented.
▶모두 혹독한 추위에 떨었다 Everybody shivered with intense [bitter] cold.
▶추위가 누그러졌다 The cold has decreased [relaxed] in severity.

추이 推移 (a) transition; (a) change
♦시대의 추이와 더불어[함께] with the change of times
▶그는 대통령선거의 추이에 관심을 가졌다 He interested himself in the progress of the presidential election.
―추이하다 change; undergo a change [transition]; shift

추인 追認 ratification; confirmation
―추인하다 ratify; confirm

추잠 秋蠶 an autumn breed of silkworms
♦추잠을 치다 raise silkworms in autumn

추잡하다 醜雜― dirty; filthy; nasty; foul; indecent; obscene; low; vulgar
♦추잡한 말 a filthy [a foul, an obscene, an indecent, a dirty] talk; four-letter words / 추잡한 농담 a broad joke; (俗) water-closet joke / 추잡한 소문 a scandal / 추잡한 꼴 a disgraceful [disgusting] state of things / 추잡한 소설 a novel with indecent suggestions; a lascivious novel
▶그런 추잡한 언사를 쓰지 마라 Don't use such bad [innocent, filthy] language.
▶그는 추잡한 농을 잘 했다 He often cracked vulgar jokes.

추잡하다 麤雜― coarse; crude; rough; gross

추장 酋長 a chief; a head; a chieftain

추장 推奬 recommendation; commendation
―추장하다 recommend; commend
♦추장할 만한 commendable / 크게 추장하다 recommend highly; give *one*'s hearty recommendation 《to》

추저분하다 醜― dirty; unclean; untidy; messy ♦추저분한 방 a dirty [messy] room

추적 追跡 pursuit; a chase; tracking
♦추적중이다 be in pursuit [chase] of; be on the track of
▶그는 경찰의 추적을 받으면서 도망쳤다 He ran off with the police following at his heels.
―추적하다 pursue; chase; give chase to; track; run [follow] after
♦추적해 오다 come in pursuit / 추적시키다

send *sb* in pursuit of; put *sb* on the track of
▶여기는 추적당할 염려는 없다 We are safe here from pursuit.
■―검사 a follow-up ―권 〈외국선박 등에 대해〉 the right of hot pursuit ―소 〈인공위성 등의〉 a tracking station ―원소 a tracer element ―자(子) 〔化〕 a tracer ―조사 a follow-up survey

추적자 追跡者 a pursuer; a chaser
♦추적자의 무리 a pursuing party; men in the chase

추절 秋節 autumn; (美) fall

추접스럽다 dirty; mean; base; low; sordid
♦추접스러운 생각 a mean [low-down] idea / 추접스럽게 굴다 behave in a mean [low-down] fashion
▶나는 그런 추접스러운 짓은 하지 않는다 I am above such meanness.

추접지근하다 somewhat dirty [unclean, untidy, messy]

추젓 秋― tiny shrimps salted in autumn

추정 推定 (a) presumption; an assumption; (an) inference; (an) estimation
♦추정에 의하면 it is estimated that...
―추정하다 presume; assume; infer; estimate
♦ 유죄로 추정하다 presume *sb* to be guilty
▶손해는 300만원으로 추정되고 있다 The loss is estimated at three million won.
■―가격 the presumed value 《of》 ―량 estimated volume ―상 속 인 〔法〕 an heir presumptive ―위치 the estimated position ―증거 presumptive evidence

추종 追從 following; 〈모방〉 imitation
♦타의 추종을 불허하다 be peerless; have no equal [second]; be unrivaled 《by》; have no superior 《in》; be inimitable
―추종하다 follow; be servile to; 〈굽신대다〉 ko(w)tow 《to》; imitate
♦상관에게 추종하여 출세하려고 하다 seek a chance of promotion by flattering *one*'s boss
■―자 a follower; 〈비굴한〉 a lackey

추증 追贈 the posthumous conferment of honors ―추증하다 confer honors [court rank] posthumously

추지 推知 a guess; (a) conjecture; (an) inference ―추지하다 guess; conjecture; surmise; infer 《from》; gather 《from》

추지다 moist; damp; wet ♦추진 수건을 이마에 대다 apply a damp towel to *one*'s forehead

추진 推進 propulsion; drive
―추진하다 propel; drive [thrust] forward; 〈촉진하다〉 push forward; promote; further
♦교섭을 추진하다 proceed [go on] with the negotiations / 계획을 추진하다 go ahead with a plan
▶그가 이 운동을 추진했다 He was the driving force of this movement.
■―기 a propeller; 〈배의〉 a screw ―력 a thrust; propulsion; driving [propulsive] force ―제[용 연료] a propellant

추징 追徵 an additional collection; supplementary charge
―추징하다 collect in addition; collect the balance 《of a tax》; make an additional collec-

추찰 推察 a guess; (a) conjecture; (an) inference; (a) surmise
—추찰하다 guess; conjecture; surmise; infer (from); gather (from)

추천 推薦 recommendation
♦ …의 추천으로 by [through] the recommendation of…; on [at] the recommendation of…
—추천하다 recommend; propose; say [put in] a good word for sb; 〈지명하다〉 nominate
♦ 후보자를 추천하다 nominate [put up] a candidate / 아무를 회장으로 추천하다 recommend [nominate] sb as chairman / 아무를 회원으로 [어떤 지위에] 추천하다 recommend sb for membership [for a position]
▶ 나는 그 사람을 추천할 수 없다 I have not a good word to say for him.
▶ 자네라면 내가 안심하고 추천할 수 있네 I can confidently recommend you.
■ —자 a recommender; 〈소개자〉 an introducer —작가 a recommended writer —장[서] a letter of recommendation; a recommendatory letter —후보 a recommended candidate

추천 鞦韆 a (rope) swing ⇨ 그네

추첨 抽籤 a lot; (lot) drawing; a lottery
▶ 그는 추첨에 당첨되었다[떨어졌다] He drew a winning [losing] number.
▶ 그녀는 추첨으로 1등이 되었다 She won the first prize by lot [drawing lots].
▶ 우리는 추첨으로 순번을 정했다 We drew lots for turns. ⇌ We settled the order of our turns by lot.
—추첨하다 draw lots; cast lots; hold a lottery
■ —권[번호] a lottery ticket [number] —기 a lottery wheel

추첨제 抽籤制 the lottery system
■ —중학입시 the lottery (and ward) system for middle school entrance

추축 樞軸 〈기계의〉 a pivot; an axle; an axis 《pl. axes》; 〈중추〉 a central point; the center (of power)
■ —국 〈제2차 대전 때의〉 the Axis powers

추출 抽出 abstraction, 〔化〕 extraction, 〔統〕 sampling
—추출하다 abstract; extract; sample; educe
♦ 무작위로 추출한 견본 a random sample / 사탕수수에서 설탕을 추출하다 extract sugar from cane
■ —물 an extract; an educt —법 a sampling process; 임의추출법 a random sampling method —조사 a sampling inspection; (美) a spot check

추측 推測 (a) conjecture; (a) surmise; (a) supposition; (a) presumption; (an) inference
♦ 근거있는 추측 a well-founded conjecture / 추측대로 as conjectured [supposed] / 내 추측으로는 in my guess / 추측이 맞다[틀리다] guess right [wrong]; be right [wrong] in one's conjecture / 아무의 추측에 맡기다 leave sth to sb's conjecture
■ —금 money collected in addition; an additional imposition; a forfeit —세 a tax penalty; a penalty tax —처분 punishment by imposing a penalty by tax

▶ 그것은 추측에 불과하다 It is a mere guess.
▶ 추측만으로 이러쿵저러쿵 해봤자 소용없다 It is of little use to talk in various ways merely by conjecture.
—추측하다 conjecture; surmise; presume; suppose; speculate; guess; infer 《from》
▶ 그에 대해 달리 추측할 길이 없다 I have no other conjecture to offer [make] on it.
▶ 말씨로 추측컨대 그는 목사인 것 같다 I presume from his speech that he is a pastor.
■ —기사 a speculative article [news story]

추켜들다 raise; hold up; lift (up); heave
♦ 어린애를 추켜들다 lift [pick up] a child

추켜잡다 lift (up); hold up
♦ 치맛자락을 추켜잡다 hold up one's skirt to keep it from dragging

추키다 raise; lift (up); hold up
♦ 바지를 추키다 hitch up one's trousers

추탕 鰍湯 loach soup ⇨ 추어(~탕)

추태 醜態 disgraceful behavior; shameful conduct; an unseemly sight; a scandalous condition
♦ 추태를 부리다 act disgracefully; behave oneself in a shameful manner; make a show of oneself; cut a ridiculous [sorry] figure

추토 追討 pursuing to subjugate
—추토하다 hunt down and kill; track down and dispose of
■ —군 punitive force —사(使) a general appointed to liquidate rebels

추파 秋波 an ogle; an amorous [a coquettish] glance ♦ 추파를 던지다[보내다] wink 《at》; cast an amorous [a coquettish] glance 《at》; make (sheep's) eyes 《at》; ogle 《at》

추풍 秋風 an autumn(al) wind [breeze]
■ —낙엽 leaves blown off by the autumn wind: 추풍 낙엽의 정객들 fallen politicians like so many leaves blown off by the autumn wind

추풍 醜風 indecent customs ⇨ 추속(醜俗)

추하다 醜— 1 〈아름답지 않다〉 ugly; bad looking; plain; ugly-looking; ill-favored
♦ 추한 여자 a plain [homely] woman (▶ 회화에서는 ugly라는 표현은 피하는 것이 좋음)
2 〈망측하다〉 unseemly; unsightly; indecent; 〈수치스럽다〉 ignoble; disgraceful; dishonorable; mean
♦ 추한 싸움 a scandalous dispute / 추한 짓 disgraceful [shameful, scandalous] conduct; a misdeed / 추한 관계를 갖다[맺다] have an illicit [improper] connection 《with》; have evil relations 《with》 / 추하게 굴다 behave in a shameful fashion; act dishonorably
▶ 부모와 자식이 싸우는 것은 정말 보기에 추하다 It is most unbecoming for parents and children to quarrel.

추하다 麤— 〈거칠다〉 coarse; crude; rough; gross; unpolished
♦ 추한 물건 unpolished [coarse] stuff

추한 醜漢 an ugly fellow [guy]; a mean fellow; a low-down type

추측의 표현

1. 조동사를 사용하여
(1) …일지도 모른다 **may, might**; …했을지도 모른다 **may [might] + have + 과거분사**
▶오후에는 비가 올지도 모른다 It may rain in the afternoon.
▶그녀는 건강이 좋지 않아서 누워 있을지도 모른다 She might be ill in bed.
▶그는 그 열차를 타지 못했을지도 모른다 He may [might] have missed the train.
(2) …일 것이 틀림없다 **must**; …했을 것이 틀림없다 **must + have + 과거분사**
▶저 부인이 우리의 새 담임일 것이 틀림없다 That lady must be our new homeroom teacher.
▶그에게 무슨 일이 있었음이 틀림없어. 벌써 사흘이나 학교를 쉬고 있으니까 Something must have happened to him. He's already been absent from school for three days.
(3) …일 것이다 **will, would**; …해 버렸을 것이다 **will + have + 과거분사**
▶그에게 말하는 것은 나중에 하세요. 지금 방에서 공부하고 있을테니까요 Talk to him later; he'll be studying in his room now.
▶2000년까지는 그 난치병도 극복되어 있을 것이다 By the year 2000, that incurable disease will have been conquered.
(4) (응당) … 할 것이다 **should, ought to**; (지금쯤은) …하고 있을 것이다 **should + have + 과거분사**; (응당) …했을 것이다 **ought to have + 과거분사**
▶그는 열 여덟 살이 넘었을 것이다. 운전 면허증을 가지고 있으니까 말이야 He should be over eighteen. He has a driver's license.
▶어젯밤에는 밤새 일어나 있었으니 몹시 졸릴 것입니다 You ought to be very sleepy after staying up all night.
▶김선생은 이미 부산에 도착해 있을 것이다 Mr.Kim should [ought to] have arrived in Pusan by now.
(5) …일 수 있다 **can, could**; …일리가 없다 **cannot**; …이었을 리가 없다 **cannot + have + 과거분사**
▶사고는 일어날 수 있다 Accidents can happen.
▶「会話」「전화 좀 받아주지 않을래.어쩌면 엄마일지도 몰라」「그럴리가 없어」 "Will you answer the phone? It could be my mom." "No, it can't be your mother."
▶그가 그런 말을 했을 리가 없어 He cannot have said such a thing.

2. 동사를 사용하여
(1) …라고 생각하다 **think, suppose** 등
▶아마 그는 늦을 거라고 생각해 I think he'll be late.
▶필시 그는 집에 없을 것이다 I don't suppose he's at home.
▶그는 틀림없이 무죄일 것이다 I believe (that) he is innocent.
▶그가 올지 어떨지 확실치 않아 I doubt whether he will come.
▶그는 그것에 대하여 무언가 알고 있는 게 아닌가 하고 생각해 I suspect (that) he knows something about it.
(2) …인 것 같다, …라고 생각된다 **seem, appear** 등
▶그는 좀 내향적인 사람처럼 생각된다 He seems rather introverted.
▶우리들 사이에는 오해가 있는 것 같다 There appears to be some misunderstanding between us.
▶「会話」「김선생님은 이제 곧 결혼한단다」「그래서 행복해 보이는군」 "Miss Kim's getting married soon." "No wonder she looks happy."
▶그의 요구가 나로서는 당연하다고 생각해 His request sounds reasonable to me.

3. 부사를 사용하여
아마 **probably, likely**; 어쩌면 **maybe, perhaps, possibly**
▶「会話」「우리 팀이 이길까요?」「이기겠지요. 최강의 팀이니까요」 "Do you think our team will win?" "We probably will. Our team is the strongest (of all)." (▶probably, likely는 우리말의「아마」보다 높은 확률의 뉘앙스가 있음)
▶어쩌면 그녀는 나의 주소를 알고 있을지도 모른다 Perhaps [Maybe] she knows my address.
▶어쩌면 그는 천재일지도 모른다 Possibly, he is a genius.

추해당 秋海棠 〔植〕a begonia; an elephant's-ear
추행 醜行 disgraceful conduct; shameful [scandalous] conduct; a misdeed ◆추행을 들춰내다 bring a scandal to light; expose a scandal
추호 秋毫 autumn down; a bit; a hair
◆추호도 (not) in the (very) least; (not) a bit; (not) at all; (not) in the slightest degree / 추호의 의심할 데가 없다 be above suspicion; there is no room (left) for doubt (as to)
▶내 말에는 추호도 거짓이 없다 I mean everything I say. ⇌ Cross my heart, I'm not telling a lie.
▶당신의 권리를 무시할 생각은 추호도 없다 I have not the slightest intention of ignoring your rights.
추화 秋花 an autumn flower
추확 秋穫 harvest in autumn
추회 追懷 recollection ⇨ 추상(追想), 추억
추후 追後 later (on); afterward; 〈이윽고〉by and by; in due (course of) time
◆추후 통지가 있을 때까지 till further notice
▶그것에 대해서는 추후에 이야기하기로 하자 We shall make mention of it further on.
추흥 秋興 autumn fun
축[1] 〈동아리〉a group; a set; a circle; a com-

축²

pany
♦…의 축에 끼이다 be grouped together with…; take *one's* place among…; rank with…; associate *oneself* with…; join (the circle of…) / 선진국 축에 들다 be numbered among the advanced nations / 축에도 들지 못하다 be insignificant; count for nothing [little]; be of no account; (俗) be off the map
▶ 열명이 합격했는데 나도 그 축에 끼었다 Ten passed, including myself [myself included].
▶ 그 사람에 비하면 나는 축에도 못 듭니다 I am a mere nothing before him.
▶ 그쯤 가지고는 컴퓨터를 아는 축에 끼이지 못하겠다 With that much knowledge, you can hardly be said to know computers.

축² 〈처진 모양〉 loosely; droopingly; languidly
♦ 축 늘어지다 dangle; hang loose [limply]; droop / 축 처지다 hang down / 지쳐서[피곤해서] 축 늘어지다 be dead tired; be dog-tired; be tired [fagged] out

축 祝 a ritual prayer ⇨ 축문(祝文)
축 逐 〔바둑〕 a ladder
축 軸 **1** 〈굴대〉 an axis 《*pl.* axes》; an axle; an arbor; a spindle; a shaft; a pivot
▶ 지구는 그 축을 중심으로 24시간에 1회전한다 The earth turns on its axis once in twenty-four hours.
2 〈한지(韓紙)의 단위〉 a ream (of ten quires); 〈집문의 한 두루마기〉 a roll
■ 수평[횡]— a horizontal [transverse] axis 수직[종]— a vertical [longitudinal] axis —마력 a shaft horsepower —바퀴 a wheel axle; wheel and axle

축縮 (a) lack; a deficit; a shortage ⇨ 축나다
축가 祝歌 a song of congratulation; a carol
♦ 결혼— a nuptial song
축가다 縮— diminish ⇨ 축나다 1
축감 縮減 reduction; decrease; lessening
—축감하다 decrease; lessen; be decreased [lessened, reduced]
축객 逐客 turning a guest out; driving a guest away
—축객하다 turn a guest out; drive a guest away
♦ 문전 축객하다 refuse to see *sb*; turn away *sb* at the door / 문전 축객을 당하다 be turned away at the door; be refused admittance
축견 畜犬 〈개를 기르기〉 keeping a dog; 〈기르는 개〉 a kept [domestic] dog
축구 蹴球 soccer; football
♦ 2002년 월드컵 축구 the 2002 World Cup Soccer / 축구를 하다 play football [soccer]
■ 러식— Rugby football 미식— American football 아식— association football; (口) soccer ■—공 a soccer ball; a football —선수 a soccer [football] player; a footballer —시합 [경기] a soccer [football] game —장 a football field [ground] —팀 a football team; the eleven
축나다 縮— **1** 〈수량이〉 decrease; diminish; be lacking; lessen; fall (off)
♦ 만원이 축나다 come short by ten thousand won / 자본이 축나다 have *one's* capital holed
▶ 천원이 축났다 There was a shortage of one thousand won. ⇌ One thousand won was found missing.
2 〈몸이〉 become [grow] weaker; lose (*one's*) weight; 〈병으로〉 lose flesh
♦ 병 때문에 축나다 languish under illness; become worn out from illness
▶ 나는 체중이 5킬로그램 축났다 I have lost weight by five kilograms.
▶ 걱정 근심은 고된 일보다 더 사람을 축나게 한다 Worries wear a man more than hard work.
축내다 縮— **1** 〈수량을〉 cause a loss; make deficient [lacking]; reduce a sum by 《a certain amount》; spend 《part of a sum》; 〈감소시키다〉 decrease; lessen; reduce
♦ 재산을 많이 축내다 cause a serious gap in *one's* finances / 은행 돈을 약 3백만원 축내다 appropriate about three million won of the bank's money 《for *one's* private use》 / 십만원에서 만원을 축내다 spend ten thousand won (out) of a hundred thousand won
2 〈몸을〉 make weak; reduce weight; weaken
축년 丑年 〔民俗〕 the Year of the Ox
축년 逐年 every year; 〈부사적〉 year by year; annually
축농증 蓄膿症 〔醫〕 ozena; empyema
축다 become damp [moist, wet]; dampen; moisten
♦ 옷이 밤이슬을 맞아 축다 *one's* clothes become wet [damp] with night dew
축대 築臺 an embankment (faced with stone)
♦ 위험축대 an embankment in dangerous conditions / 축대를 쌓다 erect an embankment / 축대가 무너지다 an embankment collapses
축도 祝禱 〔基〕 blessing ⇨ 축복(~기도)
축도 縮圖 a reduced drawing [copy]; a miniature (copy); an epitome
♦ 인생의 축도 an epitome of human life / 세계의 축도 the world in epitome / 축도를 그리다 represent [draw] on a smaller scale; miniature
■ —기(器) a pantograph
축록 逐鹿 〈각축〉 running for a high position; contending for the object of *one's* ambition; contending for mastery [supremacy]
■ —전 competition for dominance [supremacy, mastery]; an election campaign
축류 畜類 domestic animals; livestock
축문 祝文 a written [ritual] prayer; a form of invocation ♦ 축문을 읽다 read a ritual prayer
축발하다 蓄髮— let *one's* short hair grow long
축방 丑方 the direction of the Ox; northeast by north (略 NEbN)
축배 祝杯 a toast; a celebratory drink
♦ 축배를 들다 drink a toast 《for, to》; drink [toast] (to) *sb's* health [success] / 서로 축배를 들다 toast each other
▶ 축배를 듭시다 Bottoms up! Your health! ⇌ Here's to you!
▶ 그는 김박사를 위해 축배를 들자고 제의했다 He proposed a toast for [to] Dr. Kim.
축복 祝福 (a) blessing; (a) benediction
♦ 우리[그들]에게 축복이 있기를 May God

bless us [them]!
▶ 그 두 사람의 결혼은 모든 이의 축복을 받았다 That couple's marriage had the blessing of everybody.
―축복하다 bless; give *sb one's* blessing; pronounce [give] a benediction upon
◆ 축복받은 나라 a blessed country / 전도를 축복하다 wish *sb* a happy future / 축복을 받다 be blessed; be given [receive] a benediction
▶ 사제는 어린이를 축복했다 The priest blessed the child.
■―기도 《pronounce》 a benediction; a blessing

축사 畜舍 〈소의〉 a cattle shed [pen]; a barn; 〈돼지의〉 a pigpen; a pigsty; 〈양의〉 cot; sheep cote

축사 祝辭 a congratulatory address [speech]; a message of contgratulations; congratulations; felicitations
◆ 축사를 낭독하다 read (aloud) a congratulatory address
―축사하다 deliver a congratulatory address (at a ceremony); offer [tender] *one's* congratulations [felicitations] 《to》; congratulate 《*sb* on his success》
― 결혼 ― wedding congratulations

축사 縮寫 a reduced copy; a miniature reproduction
―축사하다 copy [draw] on a smaller scale; make a reduced copy 《of》
■―도 a reduced drawing: 1,000분의 1의 축사도 a drawing on the scale of one to one thousand ―사진 a small-size [reduced-size] photograph

축산 畜産 livestock farming [breeding, raising]; stockbreeding; animal husbandry; 〈축산업〉 livestock industry; 〈가축〉 domestic animals; livestock
■―물 stock farm products ―박람회 a livestock exhibition [fair, show] ―시험장 the Livestock Experiment Station ―식품 livestock products ―업자 stock raiser [farmer]; stockbreeder; (美) rancher ―자금 (government) loans for livestock industry ―장 stock farm ―장려 promotion of livestock farming ―조합 a stockbreeders' association ―학 animal husbandry; zootechny ―협동 조합 중앙회 the National Livestock Cooperatives Federation

축생 畜生 1 〈짐승〉 animals; beast
2 〈사람답지 못한 사람〉 a brute (of a man); a veritable beast
3 ⇨ 축생도

축생도 畜生道 〔佛敎〕 the tormenting purgatory; the World [Hell] of Beasts
◆ 축생도에 빠지다 degrade *oneself* to the level of the brute

축성 祝聖 〔가톨릭〕 consecration; sanctification ―축성하다 consecrate; sanctify; bless
◆ 축성된 consecrated; oblate

축성 築城 construction of a castle [wall]; fortification
―축성하다 fortify; build [construct] a castle
■―학[술] (the science [art] of) fortification

축소 縮小 reduction; curtailment; retrenchment; a cut
▶ 정부는 공공 지출비의 축소를 생각하고 있다 The government hopes to cut down on [reduce, curtail] public spendings.
▶ 미국은 군비축소에 관한 새 제안을 했다 The U.S. has made new proposals for military cutbacks [reductions in armaments].
―축소하다 reduce; curtail; retrench; cut [scale] down; 〈단축하다〉 contract
◆ 인원을 축소하다 cut [reduce] the personnel 《of》
■ 군비― (a) reduction of armaments; arms reduction; disarmament ■ ―판 ⇨ 축쇄판 ―형 a miniature

축쇄판 縮刷版 a reduced-size [smaller-size] edition; a pocket edition ◆ 축쇄판으로 내다 publish in reduced size

축쇄하다 縮刷― print in reduced size

축수 祝手 invocation by prayer; folding *one's* hands in prayer; wishing
―축수하다 pray with *one's* hands pressed together; pray with joined hands
◆ 하느님의 은총을 축수하다 pray to God for mercy [blessing]
▶ 그녀는 어머니의 병이 완쾌되기를 하느님께 축수했다 She prayed to God for her mother's recovery from illness.

축수 祝壽 wishing *sb* a long life
―축수하다 wish *sb* a long life

축승 祝勝 celebration of a victory; rejoicings over a victory ―축승하다 celebrate a victory

축시 丑時 〔民俗〕 the hour of the Ox; 〈십이시의〉 the 2nd of the 12 double hour periods (1:00-3:00 a.m.); 〈이십사시의〉 the 3rd of the 24 hour periods (1:30-2:30 a.m.)

축어 逐語 ◆ 축어적(인) word for word; literal; verbatim
■ ―역(譯) word-for-word [literal] translation: 축어역하다 translate literally [word for word]

축연 祝宴 a banquet ⇨ 축하연

축우 畜牛 a domestic cow [ox]; (총칭) cattle

축원 祝願 praying; (a) supplication; (an) invocation; (a) wish
―축원하다 pray 《for》; supplicate; invocate; wish
◆ 세계 평화를 축원하다 pray for the peace of the world
▶ 즐거운 여행이 되기를 축원합니다 (I hope you) have a nice trip.
▶ 나는 열심히 (하느님께) 축원했다 I prayed earnestly (to God). ⇌ I offered an earnest prayer (to God).
▶ 성공[행운]을 축원합니다 Good luck to you! (▸시합이나 일 등에 나서는 사람에게 말하는 구어적 표현)

축음기 蓄音機 (美) a phonograph; (英) a gramophone
◆ 축음기를 틀다 play [turn on] a phonograph; set a gramophone going / 축음기를 끄다[멈추다] turn off a phonograph / 판이 자동으로 바뀌는 축음기 a phonograph with an automatic record changer
■ 전기― ⇨ 전축(電蓄) ■ ―바늘 a stylus 《*pl.*

~es); a (gramophone) needle —음악 phonograph music; recorded music; canned music —판 a record; a disk

축의 祝意 congratulations; *one's* good [best] wishes
♦ 축의를 표하다 extend [offer] *one's* congratulations; express *one's* good wishes
▶ 나는 그의 사업 성공에 축의를 표했다 I congratulated him on his success in business.

축의 祝儀 a celebration; a festival; a commemoration; a congratulatory gift

축이다 wet; moisten; damp(en)
♦ 입술[목]을 축이다 moisten *one's* lips [throat] / 수건을 축이다 damp [wet] a towel / 혀로 마른 입술을 축이다 wet *one's* dry lips with *one's* tongue
▶ 우표를 축여서 떼어냈다 I wet the stamps and peeled them off.

축일 祝日 a festival (day); a feast (day); a gala [fête] day; a flag day; a legal holiday; a red-letter day

축일 逐一 one by one; one after another; minutely
♦ 축일 열거하다 mention one by one; enumerate / 법안을 축일 심의하다 discuss the bills one by one / 축일 보고하다 report in detail; make a detailed report (of)

축일 逐日 day by [after] day; every day
♦ 축일 회의하다 confer [hold conferences] day after day

축장 蓄藏 accumulation; storage; hoarding; stockpiling —축장하다 accumulate (wealth); amass; pile up; store (up)

축재 蓄財 accumulation of wealth; money-grubbing; a store of money; accumulated [piled-up] wealth; a hoard
▶ 그는 축재에 뛰어나다 He is clever at making money.
—축재하다 accumulate [store up, pile up] wealth; gather wealth; make money; save [hoard] up
■ 부정— illegal profiteering; property amassed by illegal means: 부정 축재자 an illicit fortune maker

축적 蓄積 storing up; hoard; accumulation; stockpiling
♦ 부(富)[자본]의 축적 accumulation of wealth [capital] / 지식의 축적 the accumulation of knowledge
—축적하다 accumulate; amass; store (up); stockpile; hoard up
♦ 축적된 지식 accumulated knowledge / 정력을 축적하다 store up energy
■ —물 accumulation —배당 an accumulated dividend —이자 accumulated interest —잉여금 accumulation surplus

축전 祝典 a celebration; a festival; a commemoration
■ 기념— a festival in commemoration; a commemoration (festival): 우리 학교는 창립 10주년 기념 축전을 올렸다 We held the celebration of the 10th anniversary of the foundation of the school.

축전 祝電 a congratulatory telegram; a (telegraphic) message of congratulations
♦ 축전을 치다 send a congratulatory telegram (to); telegraph a congratulatory message (to); wire *one's* congratulations (to)

축전 蓄電 accumulation [storage] of electricity —축전하다 store
■ —기(器) an electric condenser —지(池) a storage battery [cell]

축정 築庭 landscape gardening
—축정하다 garden; make a garden

축제 祝祭 a festival; a fete; a fête; a gala; a feast
♦ 축제 분위기 a festive mood [atmosphere] / 축제때에 on the occasion of a festival / 축제를 지내다 celebrate [keep, observe] a festival
▶ 그들은 축제 기분으로 들떠 있다 They are making merry in a festive [holiday] mood [spirit].

축제 築堤 embankment; (em)banking
—축제하다 construct [build (up)] a bank (for); embank; dike; (美) levee
■ —공사 embanking; embankment works

축제일 祝祭日 a national [public] holiday; legal holiday; a festival (day); a gala day; feast [fete, fête] (day); a red-letter day

축조 逐條 article by article; item by item; point by point; seriatim
■ —심의[토의] article-by-article [clause-by-clause, item-by-item] discussion: 그 법안은 축조 심의해야 합니다 The bill should be discussed article by article.

축조 築造 construction
—축조하다 build; construct (a dam)

축지다 縮— 1 〈사람의 가치가 떨어지다〉 fall [sink] in public estimation; discredit *oneself*; bring discredit on *oneself*; fall into discredit
▶ 그런 말을 하면 자네가 축지네 I think you degrade yourself by saying that.
2 ⇨ 축나다 2

축지법 縮地法 〔民俗〕 the art of having Seven-League Boots
♦ 축지법을 쓰다 contract space by magic

축짓다 軸— 〈추축을〉 make a pivot; 〈종이로〉 roll paper into a roll; 〈굴대로〉 fix an axle

축차적 逐次的 ♦ 축차적으로 〈하나씩〉 one by one; one after another [the other]; point by point; 〈차례로〉 in order; 〈연속적으로〉 successively; in succession; 〈서서히〉 gradually
▶ 이들 문제점은 축차적으로 해명될 것이다 These problems will be cleared one after another.

축척 縮尺 a reduced scale
♦ 축척 1,000분의 1의 지도 a map on the scale of one to one thousand

축첩 蓄妾 a kept woman; keeping a concubine [mistress]; concubinage
—축첩하다 keep a concubine [mistress]

축축 all drooping [dangling]; all sagging [hanging down] low; 〈맥없이〉 all limp(ly)
▶ 그녀의 머리는 어깨까지 축축 늘어져 있다 Her hair falls over her shoulders.
▶ 과일이 많이 열려 가지가 축축 늘어져 있다 The branches are drooping under the weight of the fruit.

축축하다 moist; damp; dampish; humid; wet
♦축축한 땅 moist ground / 축축한 지하실 a damp cellar / 축축해지다 become damp [moist, wet]; dampen; damp; moisten
▶나뭇잎이 가랑비에 축축하게 젖어 있다 The leaves are wet with the drizzling rain.
▶풀이 밤이슬로 축축해져 있었다 The grass was heavily moist with evening dews.

축출 逐出 expulsion; dismissal; ejection
♦반대파의 축출을 꾀하다 try to oust the objectors (from…)
―축출하다 expel; drive out; dismiss; eject; oust; kick sb out
▶그 학생은 비행 때문에 대학에서 축출당했다 The student was expelled from college for misconduct.

축판 縮版 a reduced-size edition ⇨ 축쇄판(縮刷版)

축포 祝砲 a salute (of guns); firing a gun as a mark of respect [pleasure] ♦축포를 쏘다 salute

축하 祝賀 (a) celebration; festivities; 〈말〉 congratulations; felicitations; rejoicings

〖解說〗 (1) 우리말의「축하하다」는 모든 경사에 쓰이지만 영어는 사항에 따라 표현을 달리한다. 입학·졸업·약혼·결혼·승진·성공 등의 경우는 *Congratulations*!가 일반적이다.
(2) 새해 인사나 생일 축하 등은 Congratulations!를 쓰지 않고 *Happy…*!를 쓴다.

♦축하 인사를 하다 offer sb one's congratulations 《on an event》
▶이것이 승리의 축하로 세워진 기념비입니다 This is a monument set up in celebration [commemoration] of the victory.
―축하하다 〈사람을〉 congratulate [felicitate] sb 《on》; 〈일을〉 celebrate 《a birthday》; commemorate 《a wedding》
♦축하할 일 a matter for congratulation [joy] / …을 축하하여 in celebration of…; congratulating…; / 승리를 축하하다 celebrate [rejoice over] a victory
▶성공[결혼]을 축하합니다 I congratulate you on your success [marriage]. (▶I congratulate your success. 라고는 하지 않음)
▶축하합니다 Congratulations! ⇌ I offer you my congratulations. ⇌ 〈결혼식 등에서〉 Good luck to you both. ⇌ 〈생일에〉 Happy birthday to you!
▶득남을 진심으로 축하합니다 Please accept my sincere congratulations upon the birth of your son.
■―객 a congratulator; a well-wisher ―선물 a congratulatory present [gift] ―장 a congratulatory letter; a note of felicitation ―주 a celebratory drink

축하다 縮― 〈생기가 없다〉 languid; limp; 〈신선하지 않다〉 stale; 〈서술적〉 lack freshness

축하연 祝賀宴 a banquet [feast] 《held in celebration of an event》
♦축하연을 베풀다 give a feast in honor of sb; hold a banquet in celebration of 《an event》
▶우리는 국회의원 당선 축하연을 베풀었다 We held a feast in honor of his being elected to a member of the National Assembly.

축하회 祝賀會 a celebration; a party [banquet] held in celebration of 《an event》
♦축하회를 열다 have [hold] a celebration; give a party [hold a banquet] in celebration of 《an event》

축합 縮合 〖化〗 condensation ―축합하다 condense ■―물 a condensate; a condensation product

축항 築港 harbor construction [improvement] ―축항하다 construct [improve] a harbor ■―공사 harbor works

춘경 春耕 spring plowing
―춘경하다 plow [till a field] in (the) spring

춘경 春景 spring scenery; a spring scene

춘계 春季 spring; springtime; springtide; spring season ―방학 the spring vacation ―운동회 a spring athletic meet

춘곤 春困 the lassitude of spring

춘광 春光 spring scenes ⇨ 춘색(春色)

춘궁 春宮 〈동궁〉 the Crown Prince; the Heir Apparent (to the Throne)

춘궁 春窮 spring poverty; the spring shortage of food ■―기 the spring lean season; the spring food-short season

춘기 春期 spring ⇨ 춘계(春季)

춘기 春機 sexual desire [passion]
■―발동 awakening of the spring; puberty ―발동기 (the age of) puberty; adolescence (▶adolescence는 남자 14세, 여자 12세부터 성년까지, puberty는 남자 13~16세, 여자 11~14세)

춘난 春暖 mild spring weather
■―지절(之節) the mild season of spring; warm spring weather

춘뢰 春雷 spring thunder

춘맥 春麥 spring barley

춘면 春眠 drowsiness in spring; sleep on a spring morning
▶춘면에 취하면 날 새는 줄 모른다 In spring one sleeps a sleep that knows no dawn [fast and sound].

춘몽 春夢 spring dreams; visionary fantasies; a vernal [springtime] fantasy
♦일장 춘몽으로 돌아가다 end in an empty; vanish like a dream
▶인생은 일장 춘몽이다 Life is but an empty dream.

춘복 春服 (a suit for) spring wear; a spring suit

춘부장 春府丈 your august [honored] father

춘분 春分 the spring [vernal] equinox
■―날 Vernal Equinox Day ―점 the vernal equinoctial point

춘사 春思 **1** 〈봄의〉 feelings [sentiments] in spring; spring(time) pensiveness [meditation, musing]
2 〈색정〉 thoughts of sex; sexual [carnal] desire [passion]; the sex urge; (a surge of) lust

춘사 椿事 an accident; a disaster; a tragedy; an unexpected event; 〈희귀한 일〉 a rare event; marvel

춘산

♦ 춘사의 희생자 the victims of the accident / ▶ 춘사가 일어났다 An accident happened.

춘산 春山 mountains [hills] in springtime

춘삼월 春三月 March of the lunar calendar ■一호시절(好時節) pleasant spring days; pleasant, warm weather of spring

춘색 春色 spring scenery; spring [vernal] tints; the vernal beauty of nature ♦춘색이 바야흐로 짙다 Spring is now in full glory.

춘설 春雪 spring snow

춘수 春水 springtime water [stream]; a stream in (the) spring; water scenes in (the) spring

춘수 春愁 spring(time) sadness [sorrow]; melancholy [anxiety] aroused in spring-(time)

춘신 春信 tidings of spring; signs [tokens] of spring; 〈꽃소식〉 tidings [news] of flowers

춘심 春心 sexual desire ⇨ 춘정(春情)

춘야 春夜 a spring night

춘약 春藥 an aphrodisiac; a love potion

춘양 春陽 spring [vernal] sunshine; the spring sun; the spring season; the springtide; springtime

춘우 春雨 spring rain [brizzle]; rain in spring-time

춘일 春日 a spring day

춘잠 春蠶 a spring breed of silkworms ♦춘잠을 치다 raise silkworms in spring

춘절 春節 spring; the spring season; the springtime; the springtide

춘정 春情 sexual [carnal] desire; sexual passion; the sex urge; lust ♦춘정을 자극하다 inflame [excite, arouse] one's sexual passion [carnal desire]

춘초 春初 early spring; the beginning [onset] of spring

춘추 春秋 1 〈봄과 가을〉 (in) spring and autumn ♦춘추복 spring-and-autumn wear; between-season wear
2 〈나이〉 years; age; one's honored age; winters ♦춘추 80의 노인 a man of eighty winters / 춘추가 높다 be very old / 80의 춘추를 누리다 attain the age of eighty; live to eighty (years of age) ▶춘추가 어떻게 되십니까? Venerable Sir, what may be your age?
3 〈오경(五經)의 하나〉 the Chronicles of Lu (722-481 B.C.) ♦춘추의 필법 the guiding principle of Confucius in writing the Annals

춘풍 春風 a spring [vernal] breeze [wind]

춘하추동 春夏秋冬 the four seasons; all the year round ♦춘하추동 사철을 통하여 throughout the year; all through the year

춘한 春寒 the lingering cold in spring

춘화 春花 spring [vernal] flowers

춘화(도) 春畫(圖) an obscene [indecent, erotic] picture; (총칭) pornography

춘화처리 春化處理 〔農〕 vernalization

출가 出家 〈불문에 듦〉 entering the priesthood —출가하다 (leave home and) become a bonze [Buddhist priest]; enter the (Buddhist) priesthood

출가 出嫁 a woman's being married ▶출가 외인이다 A married daughter is no better than a stranger. —출가하다 marry into (her groom's family); be married to (a man) ♦이씨 가문에 출가하다 be married to one of the Lees / 딸을 출가시키다 marry one's daughter off; give one's daughter away in marriage ▶내 딸은 출가할 나이다 My daughter is old enough to be [get] married. ▶양친은 나를 그 의사한테 출가시킬 작정이시다 My parents intend to make me marry the doctor.

출간 出刊 publication; issue —출간하다 publish; bring [put] out; issue ♦출간되다 be published; come out

출감 出監 release from prison —출감하다 be released [discharged] from prison ■一자 a released convict

출강 出講 lecturing —출강하다 lecture; give lectures (at); teach (at) ▶그녀는 이 대학에 시간 강사로 출강하고 있다 She lectures at this college as a part-time teacher.

출격 出擊 a sally; a sortie ▶그는 50회의 출격 기록이 있다 He has a record of 50 sorties. ▶사령관은 공군에 출격을 요청했다 The commander asked the air force for a sally. —출격하다 sally (forth [out]); make a sortie [sally]

출결 出缺 attendance (and [or] absence) ⇨ 출석(出席)

출경 出京 〈서울을 떠남〉 leaving Seoul [the capital] —출경하다 leave Seoul [the capital]; go to the country

출계하다 出系— be adopted into (a family); become sb's adopted heir; enter (a family) as an adopted heir ♦삼촌댁에 출계하다 be adopted into one's uncle's family

출고 出庫 delivery of goods from a warehouse [storehouse] —출고하다 deliver (goods) from a warehouse; take (goods) out of a warehouse ■一가격 a factory [store] price —지시(서) a delivery order

출관하다 出棺— carry [take] a coffin out of the house

출구 出口 1 〈나가는 곳〉 a way out; an exit; a gateway ♦극장의 출구 the exit of a theater / 시청 방면 출구 〈지하철에서〉 the way out toward the City Hall ▶출구가 어딥니까? Will you show me the exit? ▶출구는 이쪽입니다 This (is the) way out.
2 〈상품의〉 sending [taking] out of a port; clearing a port —출구하다 send [take] out of a port; clear a port ■一비상— an emergency exit [door]; a fire exit

출구 出柩 carrying a coffin out
출국 出國 departure from a country
━출국하다 leave [depart from, go out of] a country ■ ━허가서 an exit [a departure] permit
출근 出勤 attendance; presence
▶ 오늘은 오후 출근이다 I'm on the afternoon turn [shift] today.
▶ 그녀는 언제나 출근이 이르다[늦다] She is always early [late] at office.
▶ 그녀의 출근 성적은 아주 좋다 Her record of office attendance is very good.
▶ 그는 출근 상태가 좋지 않다 He is not regular in his attendance at his office.
━출근하다 attend one's office; go [come] to (one's) office [work]; report for work [duty]
▶ 나는 매일 전철로 출근한다 I take the subway train daily to my work [office].
▶ 나는 오전 아홉시에 출근한다 I come to office [report for work] at 9 a.m.
■ ━시간 (the) starting [clocking-in] time (for work) ━일 (non-)absentee rate [ratio] ━일 workday; a working day ━일수 the number of days attended; the number of attendances ━자 an attendant; (총칭) attendance
출근부 出勤簿 an attendance book
◆ 출근부에 도장을 찍다 register one's name in the attendance book
출금 出金 〈지출〉 defrayal; payment; 〈예금의〉 a withdrawal ━출금하다 〈지출하다〉 defray; pay; 〈예금을〉 make a withdrawal
■ ━전표 a paying-out slip
출납 出納 receipts and disbursements [expenses]; revenue and expenditure; incomings and outgoings
◆ 출납을 맡아보다 take [have, be in] charge of accounts; hold the purse strings
━출납하다 take in and pay out; receive and disburse; handle the cash accounts [transactions]
◆ 현금을 출납하다 handle cash; be a cashier
■ ━계 〈부서〉 the cashier('s section); the bursar('s office); 〈사람〉 a cashier; a treasurer; 〈은행의〉 a (paying and receiving) teller ━공무원 an accounting official ━부 a cashbook; an account book
출동 出動 going [starting] out; moving (out); 〈군대의〉 marching; mobilization; 〈함대의〉 sailing
◆ 출동을 명하다 order to move / 출동 준비를 하다 hold itself in readiness for action
▶ 그들은 경찰에 순찰차의 출동을 요청했다 They asked the police to send a patrol car.
▶ 그는 부하들을 구조 활동에 출동시켰다 He mobilized his men for the rescue work.
━출동하다 go [set, start] out; go into action; move out [in]; start moving; 〈군대가〉 be mobilized; be called out; 〈함대가〉 sail; 〈소방관 등이〉 turn out
◆ 출동시키다 dispatch; send; move
▶ 폭도를 진압하기 위해 기동대가 출동했다 A riot squad was sent to suppress the mob.
▶ 그 화재를 진압하기 위해 5대의 소방차가 출동했다 Five fire engines turned out to put out the fire.

출동명령 出動命令 an order to go into action; an order for moving [turning out]; 〈육군〉 marching orders; 〈해군〉 sailing orders
◆ 출동명령을 내리다 give an order for moving / 출동명령을 받다 be ordered to 《the front》; be called [ordered] out; be ordered to stand to / 출동명령을 받고 있다 〈육군이〉 be under orders for the front; 〈해군이〉 be under orders to proceed 《to》
■ 긴급━ a scramble order
출두 出頭 appearance; presence; attendance
━출두하다 appear 《at》; attend; present oneself 《at》; report oneself to; be present 《at》; make one's [put in an] appearance; turn [show] up; report oneself 《at》; report personally [in person] 《to sb, at an office》
◆ 법정에 출두하다 appear in court / 법정에 출두하라는 명령을 받다 be ordered to 《appear in》 court / 출두하라고 통고하다 serve notice to appear; summon to appear 《in court》
▶ 그는 경찰서에 출두하라는 통고를 받았다 He was told to report to the police.
▶ 그는 몸소 출두했다 He appeared in person.
■ 임의[자진]━ voluntary appearance: 임의 출두형식으로 in the form of voluntary appearance ━명령 〈법원에의〉 summons
출람 出藍 a disciple outstanding one's master ⇨ 청출어람(青出於藍)
출렁거리다 surge; roll; undulate; wave
출력 出力 〔機・電〕 generating power; output (of power)
◆ 출력 100만 킬로와트의 원자력 발전소 a nuclear power station that generates one million kilowatts / 출력이 크다[작다] have a large [small] output
▶ 이 엔진은 출력이 300마력입니다 This engine has the capacity of 300 horse power.
■ ━계 an output meter ━장치 an output device
출루 出壘 〔野〕 ━출루하다 get to 《first》 base; take one's base
▶ 그는 일루에 출루했다 He got to first base.
▶ 그는 포볼로 출루했다 He walked. ⇌ He took his base on balls.
▶ 두 명이 출루해 있다 Two men are on base.
출마 出馬 〈美〉 candidacy; 〈英〉 candidature
◆ 출마를 선언하다 declare one's candidacy 《for》
━출마하다 stand as a candidate for 《an election》; run for 《the National Assembly》; be a candidate for
◆ 국회의원에 출마하다 run for election to the National Assembly / 서울에서 출마하다 run as a candidate in Seoul
▶ 그는 다음 총선거에 출마할 것이다 He will run in the next general election.
▶ 그는 내년에 시장 선거에 출마할 것이 예상된다 He is expected to run [stand] for mayor next year.
출몰 出沒 appearance and disappearance; popping in and out
━출몰하다 appear and disappear; pop in and out; make frequent appearances; frequent;

출무성하다

haunt; infest; be often seen
▶그 산길에는 도둑이 출몰한다 The mountain path is haunted by robbers.
▶옛날에 그 섬 연안에는 일본 선박들이 출몰하곤 했다 In olden times Japanese vessels were often seen off the coast of the island.

출무성하다 1 〈굵기가 비슷하다〉(be) of almost equal in thickness
2 〈대가리가 가지런하다〉(be) of the same [equal] height; even; level
♦출무성한 묘목들 young trees of even height

출발 出發 departure; a start; leaving
♦출발에 즈음하여 at [on] one's departure 《to a place》/ 출발 직전에 just before departure / 인생의 출발을 잘하다 make a good start in life
▶출발 날짜가 정해지면 우리에게도 알려 주세요 Please tell us, too, when the date of your departure is fixed.
▶나는 1주일 정도 출발을 연기했다 I put off my departure for a week.
▶그 주자는 출발이 좋았기 때문에 100미터 경주에서 우승했다 The runner made a good [quick] start, so he won a 100-meter dash.
━출발하다 start 《from》; depart 《from》; leave 《a place》; set out 《on, for》;〈이륙하다〉take off; sail

[해설] *leave*는 어떤 장소에서 떠난다는 데, *start*는 이동하기 시작한다는 데 중점이 있다. *depart*는 leave의 딱딱한 표현이다.

♦일찌감치[느지막이] 출발하다 make an early [a late] start / 1시간 먼저 출발시키다 give *sb* an hour's start
▶그 비행기는 오전 10시에 서울에서 부산을 향해 출발한다 The plane takes off from Seoul for Pusan at 10 a.m.
▶종소리가 그치자마자 열차는 출발했다 As soon as the bell stopped ringing, the train started.
▶배는 내일 아침 출발한다 The ship sails tomorrow morning.
■━시간 the starting [departure] time: 출발 시간이 되었다 The time for our departure has come. ━신호 a starting [leaving] signal ━역 a starting station ━일 the departure day

출발점 出發點 the starting [take-off] point; the point [place] of departure;〈육상경기의〉the starting mark [line]
♦(경기에서) 출발점에 서다 toe the line [mark, scratch]

출범 出帆 sailing; departure (of a ship)
━출범하다 sail (out [forth]); set sail 《from》; leave 《for》; clear 《from》; put out to sea
■━기(旗) the Blue Peter ━명령 sailing orders ━시간 (ship's) sailing time ━일 the sailing day

출병 出兵 the dispatch of troops [an expeditionary force] (to)
♦한국군의 베트남 출병 the dispatch of Korean troops to Viet Nam
━출병하다 dispatch [send] troops [an expeditionary force] 《to》

▶해외로 출병하다 send troops overseas

출분 出奔 〈달아남〉abscondence; flight;〈남녀의〉(an) elopement ━출분하다 abscond; decamp; fly (the country); run away [off]; make off; clear out; flee;〈남녀가〉elope
■━자 an absconder; a runaway; an eloper

출비 出費 expenses ⇨ 지출(支出)

출사 出仕 going into government service [office] ━출사하다 go into government service [office]; enter on an official career

출사 出社 going [coming] to office ━출사하다 go [come] to office

출사 出師 dispatching troops ⇨ 출병(出兵)

출사 出寫 a photographer's visit (to a private house)

출산 出産 delivery; (a) childbirth; (a) birth ━출산하다 give birth to 《a child》; be delivered of 《a baby》 ■━율 a birthrate ━휴가 a maternity leave

출상 出喪 carrying the coffin out of the house
▶오전 9시 출상 예정이다 The hearse is to leave home at 9 a.m.
━출상하다 carry the coffin out of the house

출생 出生 (a) birth ━출생하다 be born
■━신고 a report [register] of a birth ━연월일 the date of one's birth ━증명서 a certificate of birth ━지 one's birthplace; one's native place

출생후 出生後 since one's birth; (in) all one's born days
♦출생후 처음으로 for the first time in one's life [since one was born]

출석 出席 attendance; presence; appearance
♦출석을 부르다 call the roll [names] / 출석을 요구하다 request [ask for] *sb's* attendance (at)
▶출석 여부를 알려 주시기 바랍니다 Please let me know whether you will be present or not.
━출석하다 attend; be present 《at》; present oneself 《at》
♦출석하지 않다 do not [fail to] attend; absent *oneself* 《from》
▶부디 출석해 주십시오 We request the pleasure of your company.
■━전원━ complete [perfect] attendance ━률 the percentage of attendance: 회원의 출석률은 극히 나빴다 The member's attendance was very small [poor]. ━부 a roll book; an attendance book ━일수 the number of one's attendances [days attended] ━정지 suspension of attendance ━카드 an attendance slip ━표 a table of attendance

출석자 出席者 a person present; an attendant (at); (총칭) attendance; those present
▶모임에는 출석자가 많았다[적었다] The meeting had a large [small] attendance.

출세 出世 〈입신〉success [advancement] in life; a successful career [life];〈영달〉distinction; eminence;〈승진〉promotion
▶그는 출세가 빨랐다 He got [won] speedy [rapid, quick] promotion.
▶그는 출세 가도를 달리고 있다 He is on the promotional track.
━출세하다 〈입신하다〉succeed in life; rise

[get on, go up] in the world; rise to a high position; 〈승진하다〉 win [get, obtain] promotion; be promoted 《to》; be advanced 《to》
♦ 출세한 사람 a successful man; a success / 빨리 출세하다 mark a rapid rise in the world; win [get, obtain] rapid [quick] promotion / 갑자기 출세하다 suddenly rise to a higher position; rise suddenly in the world
▶ 그는 출세하기 위해 상경했다 He came up to Seoul to rise in the world [make a name in the world].
▶ 너도 열심히 하면 출세할거야 If you try hard, you will succeed (in life) [get on in the world].
▶ 그의 아들은 크게 출세했다 His son achieved great success in life.
■ ―욕 ambition to make *one's* mark in the world

출세작 出世作 a work which has won the author distinction 《as a novelist》; *one's* initial success-piece
▶ 그것이 그의 출세작이다 The work started him on the road to success. ⇌ This is one of the works that made him famous.

출소 出所 release 《from prison》 ⇨ 출옥(出獄)
―출소하다 be released [discharged] from prison; leave [come out of] prison

출소 出訴 instituting a lawsuit ⇨ 제소(提訴)

출수 a flood; an inundation; 〈눈 등이 녹아서 나는〉 a freshet
―출수하다 〈강이 주어〉 overflow (its banks); 〈증수하다〉 swell; 〈지역이 주어〉 be flooded; be inundated

출수 出穗 coming out in ears
■ ―기 the earing season

출신 出身 origin; birth; stock
♦ 군인 출신 a former military man / 중국 본토 출신 a native to China proper / 민주당 출신의 장관 a minister from [affiliated with] the Democratic Party; a minister representing the Democrats / S대학 출신이다 be a graduate of S University / 도시[시골] 출신이다 be town-[country-]bred / 호남 출신이다 come [be, 《美》) hail] from Honam
▶ 이번에 온 사장은 K대 출신이다 The new president is a graduate of K University [a K University graduate].
▶ 〔會話〕「어디 출신입니까?」「제주도입니다」 "Where are you from?" "I come [am] from Chejudo."
▶ 우리 사장은 군인 출신이다 The president of our concern is a former military man.
▶ 그는 지체 높은 집안의 출신이다 He comes of a noble family [stock].
■ ―교 *one's* alma mater; the school [college, university] one graduated from ―지 *one's* native place; *one's* hometown; *one's* birthplace

출아 出芽 germination; sprouting; budding
―출아하다 germinate; sprout (out); bud (out); put forth buds

출애굽기 出―記 〔聖〕 (The Book of) Exodus 《略 Exod.》

출어 出漁 going out fishing
―출어하다 go out fishing; sail out for fish
■ ―구역 a fishing area ―기[권] the fishing season [right]

출연 出捐 contribution; subscription; donation
―출연하다 contribute 《money》 to 《a fund》; donate ■ ―금 a contribution; a donation ―자 a contributor; a donator

출연 出演 appearance on the stage; performance
―출연하다 appear on the stage; play; perform; take part in; 〈노래하다〉 sing
▶ 그는 지난 주 텔레비전에 출연했다 He appeared on television last week.
▶ 이것은 인기 스타가 총출연하는 영화다 This is a film with an all-star cast.
■ ―계약 booking ―료 a performance fee; an actor's [a singer's] fee

출연자 出演者 a performer; a player; 〈남자〉 an actor; 〈여자〉 an actress; 〈가수〉 a singer; 〈퀴즈 프로그램 등의〉 a panelist; 《총칭》 the cast 《of a drama》

출영 出迎 meeting; 〈영접〉 reception
♦ 출영을 받다 be met [greeted] 《at the station》 ―출영하다 receive; greet; meet; go [come] (out) to meet sb on arrival

출옥 出獄 release (from prison)
―출옥하다 be released [discharged] from prison; leave [come out of] prison
♦ 출옥시키다 release; discharge; set 《a prisoner》 free [at liberty]
▶ 그는 갓 출옥했다 He has just got(ten) out of prison.
■ ―자 a person released from prison; a released convict

출원 出願 (an) application
▶ 특허 출원중 Patent applied for. ⇌ Patent pending.
―출원하다 make [file] an application; apply (for)
♦ 특허청에 특허를 출원하다 apply to the Patent Office for a patent
■ ―기한[기일] the time limit for application ―번호 the application number ―자 an applicant ―절차 the procedure of application

출입 出入 1 〈드나들기〉 coming in and out; entrance and exit
♦ 경찰서 출입 기자 a newspaperman assigned to the police / 청와대 출입 기자 a reporter accredited to the Blue House / 출입을 허락하다 give sb the run [entrée] of 《a house》; allow sb access to 《one's house》 / 출입을 금하다 forbid sb to enter 《a place》
▶ 이 문으로는 출입을 금하고 있다 No entrance is allowed through this door.
▶ 저 집은 사람들의 출입이 잦다 They have a lot of visitors.
▶ 출입금지 (게시) Keep off [《美》 out]! ⇌ Off limits.
▶ 미성년자 출입금지 (게시) No minors.
▶ 무단 출입금지 (게시) No admittance except on business. ⇌ Unauthorized entry is forbidden. ⇌ No unauthorized entry allowed.
―출입하다 go [come] in and out; enter and leave; 〈자주〉 frequent; visit

출입국

♦…에 마음대로 출입할 수 있다 have free access to 《a house》; be given free admission ▶경찰은 그 방에 출입하는 모든 사람을 감시했다 The police watched everyone going in and out of the room.
2〈나들이〉going out for a visit
—**출입하다** go out for a short visit
■—**구** an entrance; an exit; a door(way); a gate(way) —**권(券)** an admission ticket —**처**〈신문기자의〉a beat

출입국 出入國 entry into, and departure from the country; emigration and immigration
■—**관리국** the Immigration Bureau —**관리법** the Immigration Control Law

출자 出資 (an) investment; financing
—**출자하다** invest 《one's money》 in; finance 《an enterprise》; contribute 《money》 to; make an investment in
♦주식에 출자하다 invest one's money in stocks/ 주식에 거액을 출자하다 make a large investment in stocks
▶그는 신규 사업에 1억원을 출자했다 He invested a hundred million won in a new enterprise.
▶그는 그 사업에 출자하기를 꺼렸다 He was reluctant to make an investment in the enterprise.
■—**공동**— a joint capital ■—**금** money invested; an investment —**액** the amount of investment 《money invested》 —**자** an investor; a financier

출장 出張〈공무원의〉an official trip [tour]; 〈회사원의〉a business trip;〈수리 등을 하기 위한〉a service call
♦아무를 뉴욕으로 출장보내다 send [dispatch] sb on business to New York
▶그는 업무차 런던에 출장중이다 He is now in London on business [on a business trip].
▶나는 1년간 해외출장을 명받았다 I was ordered (to go) abroad to work for one year.
—**출장하다[가다]** travel on official business (to); take an official trip 《to》; make a business trip 《to》
▶나는 한달에 한번씩 부산에 출장한다 I go to Pusan on business once a month. ⇌ I make an official trip to Pusan once a month.
■—**비** traveling expenses; a traveling allowance —**소** a branch [local] office; an agency —**지** the destination of one's business trip —**촬영** ⇨ 출사(寫)

출장 出場〈어느 장소에〉appearance 《in a place》;〈경기에〉participation 《in》; an entry 《for》
♦출장을 취소하다 withdraw [cancel] one's entry 《for》
—**출장하다** appear 《in a place》; take part 《in》; participate 《in》; enter 《for an event》

출장원 出張員〈공무원〉a dispatched official; 〈대리인〉an agent

출전 出典 the source; the authority
♦출전을 밝히다 indicate [name] the source 《of》; give [cite] the authority 《for》
▶이 문장은 출전을 살펴보는 게 좋겠다 You'd better check the source of this passage.

출전 出戰 1 ⇨ 출정(出征)
2〈경기 등에〉participation 《in》; an entry 《for》
—**출전하다** take part 《in》; participate 《in》; enter 《for an event》
♦경기에 출전하다 take part in a [an athletic] contest
▶그는 전국체전의 체조경기에 출전했다 He participated [took part] in the gymnastics competition in the National Athletic Meet.
■—**선수** a participating player [athlete]; an entrant; (총칭) the entry 《of a race》 —**자격** qualification 《for》

출정 出廷 (法) appearance in court
♦출정 명령을 받다 be ordered to (appear) in court
—**출정하다** appear in court; present oneself at the court
♦출정하지 않을 때에는 in case of nonappearance; in default of attendance / 출정해 있다 be in court

출정 出征 departure for the front; taking the field
▶그는 첫 출정에서 공을 세웠다 He distinguished himself in his first campaign [battle].
—**출정하다** go to war [the front]; take the field; go on an expedition
■—**군** an army in the field; troops at the front —**군인** a soldier at the front [going to the front] —**기(記)** a war account [journal, book]

출제 出題 setting a problem
—**출제하다** set sb a problem [question]; make questions for an examination; prepare an examination paper
▶선생님은 교과서에서 출제했다 Our teacher took the questions for the exam out of the textbook.
■—**경향** a tendency of questions —**범위** a range of possible questions: 기말 시험의 출제 범위 the range of possible questions in a term-end examination —**자** an examiner: 수학의 출제자는 김교수다 Professor Kim made questions in mathematics.

출중 出衆 preeminence; prominence
—**출중하다[나다]** preeminent; prominent; outstanding; conspicuous
▶학력면에서 그는 반의 누구보다도 출중하다 He far excels the other members of the class in scholastic ability.

출진 出陣 departure for the front ⇨ 출정(出征)

출차 出差 (天) evection

출찰 出札 issue of a ticket ■—**계(원)** (英) a booking clerk; (美) a ticket agent [clerk] —**구** a ticket [(英) booking] window

출처 出處 the origin; the source
♦출처가 분명한 이야기 information (drawn [collected]) from a sure [reliable] source / 출처가 분명치 않은 of doubtful origin; from an unreliable source / 출처를 밝히다〈정보 등의〉disclose [indicate, name] the source 《of》; 〈인용문 등의〉give chapter and verse 《for》

▶ 이 구절의 출처는 셰익스피어다 This phrase is quoted [a quotation] from Shakespeare.
▶ 경찰은 뉴스의 출처를 조사하고 있다 The police are looking into the source of news.

출초 出超 〈수출 초과〉 an excess of exports over imports; a favorable balance of trade
◆ 10억 달러의 출초 an excess of exports amounting to a billion dollars

출출하다 hungry; 〈서술적〉 feel a bit hungry; feel somewhat [rather] hungry [empty]

출타 出他 going out; an outing; leaving home
◆ 출타 중이다 be out —출타하다 go out; take an outing; leave home

출탄 出炭 coal production; production of coal
—출탄하다 produce [yield] coal
—량[액] output of coal; coal output

출토 出土 〔考古〕—출토하다 〈사물이 주어〉 be excavated [unearthed] 《at a site, from the ruins of...》; 〈장소가 주어〉 produce; yield
▶ 이 항아리는 논산 유적에서 출토된 것이다 This urn was excavated from the ruins of Nonsan.
■ —품 a [an archaeological] find

출판 出版 publication; publishing
◆ 출판의 자유 freedom of the press
◆ 그 책은 언제 출판 예정입니까 ? When is the book to be published?
—출판하다 publish; issue; bring [put] out a book
▶ 그는 그 책을 자비로 출판했다 He published the book at his own expense.
▶ 그 책은 이미 출판되었다 The book is already out.
▶ 그 책은 갓 출판되었다 The book is just off the press.
■ —자비 publication on one's own account 한정— limited publication ■ —계 the publishing world; publishing circles —권 the right of publication; publication rights —기금 publication fund —기념회 a party in celebration [honor] of the publication of a book —법 the Publication [Press] Law —부 a publishing department —사 a publishing company [house, firm]; a publisher; (美) a book concern —인 a publisher —협회 the publishers' association

출판물 出版物 a publication ◆ 출판물이 범람하다 have too many publications / 출판물을 단속하다 exercise control over publications

출판업 出版業 the publishing business; publishing ■ —자 a publisher

출품 出品 exhibition; show; display
—출품하다 exhibit; show; display; put [place] on exhibition [show]
◆ 그림을 전람회에 출품하다 send [submit] one's painting to an exhibition
▶ 그의 그림이 그 화랑에 출품되어 있다 His paintings are exhibited [are on exhibition] in the art gallery.
■ —국 an exhibiting country —물 an exhibit; an article on show [exhibition] —자 an exhibitor —점수[목록] the number [a catalog] of exhibits

출하 出荷 forwarding; shipment; shipping; consignment
—출하하다 forward; ship; consign
▶ 서울로 채소를 급행편으로 출하합니다 We ship vegetables to Seoul by express.
▶ 물품은 화차로 출하되었다 The goods were shipped by rail.
■ —안내[통지] an advice [a note] of shipment; a shipping advice —자 a shipper; a forwarder —지 the place of shipment

출항 出航 a takeoff; departure
—출항하다 leave; sail from; take off; depart

출항 出港 departure from a port
◆ 출항을 허가하다 give a ship clearance / 출항을 정지시키다 lay [put] an embargo on a ship
—출항하다 leave port; set sail 《from》; clear a port
■ —명령 an order for sailing —서 a clearance paper —세 a clearance fee; clearance dues —절차 clearance formalities —정지 an embargo —지 the outport; the clearance station —통지[허가장] a clearance notice [permit, certificate]

출향 出鄕 departure from one's hometown
—출향하다 leave [depart from] one's home [native place]

출현 出現 appearance; emergence; arrival; advent
◆ 구세주의 출현 the advent of the Savior
▶ 새 정당의 출현은 정계의 구도를 바꾸어 놓았다 The appearance of the new political party has changed the political climate.
—출현하다 appear; make one's appearance; emerge; turn [show] up; come in
▶ 간밤에 이상한 혜성이 출현했다 A strange comet made its appearance last night.

출혈 出血 1 〈피가 남〉 bleeding; hemorrhage; loss of blood
◆ 과다 출혈 profuse [copious] bleeding; excessive loss of blood
▶ 그 환자는 출혈이 심하다 The patient bleeds badly [copiously].
▶ 그는 과다 출혈로 죽었다 He died from excessive bleeding [loss of blood].
▶ 출혈이 멎었다 The bleeding stopped.
—출혈하다 bleed; lose blood
2 〈전쟁 등으로 인한 희생〉 casualties; sacrifices
◆ 막대한 출혈 many casualties
▶ 우리편의 다소의 출혈을 각오해야 한다 We must be prepared for some sacrifices on our side.
■ —내[뇌]— internal [cerebral] hemorrhage —경쟁 a cutthroat competition; a dumping war —수출 below-cost export —판매 a sacrifice [below-cost] sale: 출혈 판매를 하다 sell 《goods》 below cost [at a sacrifice]

출화 出火 an outbreak of fire; a fire
—출화하다 a fire breaks out [occurs]

출회 出廻 movement of commodities; flow of goods; supply
—출회하다 arrive [appear] on the market; be moving; goods flow out to the market
■ —고 〈농산물 등의〉 visible supply —기 a season for movement 《of crops》: 지금은 감자

춤¹

의 출회기다 The potato is in season.

춤¹ 〈무용〉 a dance; dancing; 〈俗〉 a step
♦춤을 추다 dance; have a dance; tread a (dainty) measure; (口) step it / 음악에 맞추어 춤을 추다 dance to [after] music / 남의 장단에 춤을 추다 dance to [after] another's tune; be made a puppet of another
▶그녀는 춤을 잘 춘다 She dances well. ⇌ She is a good dancer. ⇌ She is good at dancing.
■양— a Western dance; ballroom dancing 어깨— shoulder dancing 엉덩이— a hula dance ■—선생 a dancing master [mistress]

춤² 〈우두〉 the height of an upturned rim; 〈높이〉 height ♦춤이 높은[낮은] 구두 a high-[low-]cut shoe

춤³ inside the waist of *one's* trousers ⇨ 허리춤

춤⁴ 〈분량〉 a handful; a fistful
♦모 한 춤 a handful of rice seedlings

춥다 cold; chilly

[解說] *cold*는 「춥다」의 일반적인 말. *chilly*는 cold보다 좀 덜 춥고 으슬으슬한 불쾌한 느낌의 추위를 말한다.

♦추운 겨울 a severe winter / 추운 날씨 cold weather; a freezing [wintry] day / 추운 지방 a cold area / 추워지다 get [grow] cold; become chilly / 추워서 떨다 shiver with cold; quiver from cold / (사람이) 추워보이다 look cold / 추위하다 feel the cold; complain of the cold
▶날씨가 춥군요 It is cold today.
▶추위 죽겠다 I'm dying of the cold.
▶오늘 아침은 몹시 춥다 It is piercing [biting] cold this morning.
▶이번 겨울은 몹시 춥다 We have a severe cold this year.
▶10월이 되면 아침 저녁으로 꽤 추워진다 When October comes, it gets [becomes] quite cold in the morning and night.

충 蟲 〈벌레〉 an insect; a bug; a worm; a moth; (총칭) vermin; 〈회충〉 a roundworm

충간 忠諫 a loyal remonstrance; pleading with *one's* master from a loyal motive
—충간하다 plead with *one's* master from a loyal motive

충격 衝擊 an impact; a shock; an impulse; percussion; [原子物] bombardment
♦미래의 충격 future shock / 충격을 주다 give *sb* a shock; shock / 충격을 받다 get [have, feel] a shock; be shocked (at, by)
▶폭발의 충격으로 건물이 흔들렸다 The shock of the explosion rocked the building.
▶그가 죽었다는 소식은 우리 모두에게 큰 충격이었다 The news of his death gave a shock to all of us.
▶그의 사임은 정계에 큰 충격을 주었다 His resignation had a great shock on the political world.
■—력 shock power —시험 an impact [a percussion] test —요법 shock treatment —음 a crashing sound —파 a shock wave —파음(波音) 〈초음속기의〉 a sonic boom —하중 impul-

sive load

충견 忠犬 a faithful dog

충고 忠告 〈조언〉 (a piece of) advice; counsel; 〈경고〉 (a) warning; caution; 〈타이름〉 admonition
♦충고를 구하다 ask advice 《of *sb*》; seek the advice 《of *sb*》 / *sb*의 충고를 무시하다 disregard [give no heed to] *sb's* advice / 충고에 따르다 follow [act upon] *sb's* advice
▶그는 의사의 충고에 따라 담배를 끊었다 He gave up smoking on the advice of his doctor.
▶그 학생은 선생님의 충고를 귀담아 듣지 않았다 The student took no heed of his teacher's advice [counsel].
▶그는 내 충고를 기꺼이 받아들였다 [받아들이지 않았다] He took my advice in good [bad] part.
—충고하다 advise; give *sb* advice [counsel]; counsel; 〈경고하다〉 give *sb* warning; caution; 〈훈계하다〉 admonish; remonstrate 《with》
▶너에게 충고할 것이 하나 있다 Let me give you a piece of advice.
■—자 an adviser; a counselor

충군애국 忠君愛國 loyalty and patriotism

충군애민 忠君愛民 loyalty and love of the people

충근 忠勤 loyal [faithful, devoted] service; loyal discharge of *one's* duties

충나다 蟲— get infested with vermin

충당 充當 appropriation; devotion
—충당하다 apply [devote] (a sum to); appropriate (a sum for); earmark (a sum for)
▶예비비로 적자를 메우는 데 충당하지 않으면 안된다 We have to appropriate the reserve fund for the deficit.

충돌 衝突 1 〈물건의〉 a collision; a clash; a bump; an impact
▶호남선에서 열차의 충돌 사고가 있었다 There was a railroad collision on the Honamsŏn.
▶버스와 트럭의 충돌로 30분간 교통이 마비되었다 On account of a collision between a bus and a truck, the traffic was paralyzed for half an hour.
—충돌하다 collide 《with》; come into collision 《with》; run [smash, crash, bump] 《against, into》
♦정면 충돌하다 clash [collide] head-on
▶그녀의 차가 벽에 세게 충돌했다 Her car crashed [smashed] into the wall.
2 〈불일치·불화〉 a conflict; a clash; a collision; a discord; a quarrel
♦감정의 충돌 an emotional [a temperamental] clash 《between, with》 / 이해(利害)의 충돌 a conflict [clash] of interests 《between》 / 의견의 충돌 a conflict of opinions; a collision of views
▶학생과 경찰 사이에 충돌이 있었다 A collision [clash] took place between the students and the police.
—충돌하다 〈의견 등이〉 conflict [clash] 《with》; be in conflict 《with》; 〈불화하다〉 fall out 《with》; quarrel 《with》; be at strife [feud, variance, odds] 《with》
♦…으로 남과 충돌하다 clash [collide] with

sb over...
3 〈전투〉 an encounter; 〈사소한〉 a skirmish; a brush
━**충돌하다** encounter; have an encounter [a skirmish] 《with》
■**무력**━ an armed conflict 《with, between》 삼중━ a three-way collision 《among》 정면━ a frontal clash 《between》; a head-on collision 《with》

충동 衝動 1 〈순간적 욕구〉 an impulse; an impetus; an urge; 〔心〕 a drive
♦일시적[순간적] 충동 a sudden impulse / 순간적 충동으로 on the spur [impulse] of the moment / 일시적 충동에 이끌리다 be carried away by the impulse of the moment / 충동을 억제하다 inhibit [resist] an impulse 《to do》
▶ 나는 큰소리로 외치고 싶은 충동을 느꼈다 I felt [had] an impulse [urge] to cry out.
2 〈교사·선동〉 instigation; abetment; incitement
♦…의 충동으로 at the instigation of...; abetted by...
━**충동하다** instigate; abet; incite; stir up; egg [set] *sb* on 《to do》
■━**구매** impulse buying : 충동 구매를 하다 buy *sth* impulsively [on impulse]

충동적 衝動的 impulsive
♦충동적인 사람 a man of impulse; an impulsive man / 충동적(인) 행동 an impulsive act / 충동적으로 impulsively; on the spur of the moment / 충동적으로 행동하다 act on impulse
▶ 아이들의 행위는 대개 충동적이다 Children are usually impetuous.
▶ 그는 충동적으로 톰의 뺨을 때렸다 He hit Tom on the face on impulse.

충량하다 忠良━ loyal (to the throne); honest and virtuous

충렬 忠烈 unswerving loyalty
━**충렬하다** unswervingly [most] loyal

충류 蟲類 insects and worms

충만 充滿 repletion; fullness; abundance
━**충만하다** be full; be filled [pregnant, replete] 《with》; overflow 《with》

충매 蟲媒 〔植〕 entomophily; insect pollination
■━**화** an entomophilous flower

충복 忠僕 a faithful [loyal, devoted, dutiful] servant

충분하다 充分━ enough; sufficient; full; plentiful; plenty of; good; 〈만족스럽다〉 satisfactory; 〈완전하다〉 perfect; thorough; 〈알맞다〉 adequate
♦충분한 돈 enough money / 충분한 보수 satisfactory pay [remuneration]/ 충분한 식사[음료] a good meal [drink]/ 충분한 이유 every [good] reason; adequate reasons / 충분한 수입 an ample income
▶ 우리는 식량이 충분하다 We have sufficient food.
▶ 그것이면 충분하다 That's enough. ⇒ That will do.
▶ 만원이면 충분하다 Ten thousand won is enough.
▶ 시간은 아직 충분하다 There is still plenty of time left.
▶ 앞으로 한 시간이면 충분하다 One more hour will be enough.

충분히 充分━ enough; sufficiently; fairly; fully; in full; perfectly; adequately; 〈풍부하게〉 amply; copiously; plentifully; 〈만족하게〉 satisfactorily; to *one's* satisfaction; to *one's* heart's content
♦충분히 먹다 eat *one's* fill / 충분히 쉬다 take *one's* fill of rest / 충분히 자다 sleep well / 충분히 알고 있다 know well enough / 충분히 설명하다 explain in full / 충분히 이해하다 understand perfectly
▶ 이 책은 읽을 가치가 충분히 있다 This book is well worth reading.
▶ 증거는 충분히 갖췄다 We have gathered enough [sufficient] evidence.
▶ 시간[돈]이라면 충분히 있다 We have plenty of time [money].
▶ 한 시간은 충분히 기다렸다 I waited for a good hour.
▶ 그 그림은 볼만한 가치가 충분히 있다 The picture is well worth seeing.
▶ 이 병에 3리터는 충분히 들어간다 This bottle can hold a full measure of three liters.
▶ 그는 먹고 살아갈 만큼은 충분히 벌고 있다 He earns just enough to live upon.

충비 充備 completion ⇨ 완비(完備)

충빠지다 《an arrow》 quiver [vibrate] in flight

충사 忠死 a loyal death
━**충사하다** die for *one's* loyalty

충상 衝上 〔地質〕 thrust ■━**단층(斷層)** a thrust [an overthrust] fault

충색하다 充塞━ fill up; plug; stop (up); block; clog up; 〈막히다〉 be filled [stopped] up

충성 忠誠 loyalty; devotion; fidelity; fealty; allegiance
♦충성을 다하다 render [give] devoted service / 국가에 충성을 다하다 give *one's* fealty to the nation / 충성을 맹세하다 pledge loyalty [allegiance] 《to》
━**충성스럽다** loyal; devoted; faithful; dutiful
♦충성스러운 신하 a loyal [devoted] retainer
■━**과잉** excessive loyalty ■━**선서** 〈공무원 등의〉《美》 a loyalty oath

충수 蟲垂 〔解〕 the (vermiform) appendix
■━**염** 〔醫〕 appendicitis

충순 忠純 loyalty and sincerity; faithfulness and pureness [honesty]
━**충순하다** loyal and sincere; faithful and pure [genuine]; true and honest

충순 忠順 allegiance; loyalty; fealty; 〈순종〉 obedience ♦충순을 맹세하다 vow [pledge] *one's* allegiance 《to》 ━**충순하다** loyal; faithful; obedient

충신 忠臣 a loyal subject [retainer, vassal]; a loyalist
▶ 이기면 충신, 지면 역적 《속담》 Might makes [is] right.

충신 忠信 fidelity; loyalty; faithfulness

충실 充實 〈실질이 있음〉 substantiality; fullness; 〈충만·충족〉 repletion; replenishment;

〈완비〉 completeness; completion; perfection
◆군비[국방]의 충실 repletion [perfection] of armaments [national defense]/내용의 충실 meatiness [substantiality] in contents
▶우리는 국력의 충실을 기해야 한다 We should try to build up [consolidate] national power [strength].
—충실하다 full; replete; complete; rich;〈질·내용이〉 substantial (meal); solid (reading)
◆내용이 충실한 작품 a substantial work / 충실한 생활을 영위하다 live a full life; live to the full
▶그는 몸이 충실하다 He is in perfect health. ⇌ He has a sound body.
▶이 책은 내용이 충실하다 This book is full of useful information.
▶여름 휴가를 충실하게 보냈다 I enjoyed my summer vacation to the full.
충실 忠實 faithfulness; devotion; sincerity; integrity; honesty; fidelity; faith
—충실하다 faithful; honest; devoted; true; trusty; loyal; sta(u)nch
◆충실한 하인 a faithful [loyal] servant / 직무에 충실하다 be faithful to one's duties
▶그 번역은 원문에 충실하다 The translation is faithful to the original.
▶그 하인은 주인을 충실하게 섬겼다 The servant faithfully served his master.
충실도 忠實度〔通信〕 fidelity;〈텔레비전 영상의〉 linearity
◆고(高)충실도 수신기 a high-fidelity [hi-fi] receiver
충심 忠心 faithfulness; loyalty; allegiance; fidelity
충심 衷心 one's true heart; one's inmost feelings [heart]
◆충심으로부터의 환영 a hearty [cordial] welcome [reception]/충심에서 우러나오는 동정 hearty [heartfelt] sympathy / 충심으로 heartily; cordially; from the bottom of one's heart; in one's heart of hearts; with one's whole heart; wholeheartedly / 충심으로 감사하다 thank sb from (the bottom of) one's heart
▶졸업을 충심으로 축하한다 I sincerely congratulate you on your graduation.
충애 忠愛〈충성과 사랑〉 loyalty and love; devoted affection;〈충군애국〉 loyalty and patriotism
충양돌기 蟲樣突起〔解〕 the appendix ⇨ 충수(蟲垂)
충언 忠言 advice ⇨ 충고(忠告)
▶충언은 귀에 거슬린다 Good advice sounds harsh to the ear.
충욕 充慾 gratification of one's desire
—충욕하다 gratify [satisfy] one's desire
충용 充用 appropriation; application
—충용하다 appropriate (a sum) to [for]; apply ((sth to); earmark (some money for house repair)
충용 忠勇 loyalty and bravery [valor]
—충용하다 loyal and brave [courageous]
충원 充員 supplement of the personnel;〔軍〕 the reserves; recruits; drafts
—충원하다 supplement the personnel; call up [recruit] personnel; recruit ■—계획 a levy plan —소집 a general levy
충의 忠義 loyalty (and uprightness)
충이다 shake (a rice bag) up and down [from side to side] ((to put [pack] rice to the full); joggle (rice in a bag)
충일 充溢 overflow; affluence; exuberance; abundance —충일하다 overflow; be full (of); be affluent [abundant, exuberant]
충재 蟲災 damage from [done by] insects; vermin damage; a blight
충적 沖積〔地質〕◆충적이 alluvial
■—기[세] the alluvial epoch [period] —선상지(扇狀地) an alluvial fan —층 an alluvial bed —토 alluvial soil; alluvium —평야 an alluvial plain; a floodplain
충전 充電 charge; charging
—충전하다 charge (a battery, a shaver) (with electricity)
◆과— overcharge 재— recharging ■—기 a (battery) charger —(용)발전기 a charging dynamo [generator] —장치 charging equipment
충전 充塡 filling up [in]; replenishment;〈충치 등의〉 plugging;〈가스의〉 inflation
—충전하다 fill up [in]; stop (up); replenish; plug;〈가스를〉 inflate
◆충치를 충전하다 fill up a decayed tooth (with gum) / 치아를 충전하다 stop [plug] a tooth; fill a tooth (with gold)
■—기 a plugger; a filling machine —물 a filling; a plug; a tamping —제 fillers
충절 忠節 loyalty; allegiance; fidelity; fealty; devotion ◆충절을 다하다 serve with loyalty; be loyal to (one's lord)
충정 衷情 one's inmost feelings; one's true heart ◆충정을 털어놓다 open one's heart [mind] (to); unbosom oneself (to)
충정 衝程〔機〕 a stroke
충족 充足 sufficiency;〈만족〉 satisfaction
—충족하다 meet; fulfill; answer; satisfy
◆충족되지 않은 욕구 an unfilled desire / 욕망을 충족시키다 satisfy one's desire / 조건을 충족시키다 meet the qualifications [requirements]; satisfy the conditions
충직 忠直 faithfulness; honesty; uprightness
—충직하다 faithful; honest; upright; straightforward
◆충직한 마음 an honest mind; a true heart / 충직한 사람[하인] an honest [a faithful] man [servant] / 충직하게 일하다 be faithful to one's duty
충천하다 衝天— rise high toward the sky; soar high up to the sky; go sky-high
◆충천하는 기세 high [roaring, towering] spirits
▶노인은 노기 충천했다 A wave of fierce wrath rolled up in the old man.
충충거리다〈걸음을〉 walk with quick steps; walk fast; walk at a quick [brisk] pace
충충하다〈물·빛깔 등이 어둡다〉 depressingly dark [dusky]; gloomy; dull; leaden; somber
◆충충한 갈색 a dusky brown / 충충한 방 a

충치 蟲齒 a decayed [bad] tooth; a carious tooth
♦ 충치 구멍 a cavity in a tooth / 충치가 두개 있다 have two decayed teeth / 충치가 먹다 have a tooth decay; get a decayed tooth / 충치가 쑤시다[아프다] have an ache in one's carious [decayed] tooth / 충치를 뽑다 have a decayed tooth (pulled) out [extracted] / 충치를 예방하다 prevent teeth from decaying; prevent tooth decay / 충치를 치료[처치]하다 treat a decayed tooth; have a decayed tooth treated / 충치에 봉을 하다[박다] fill [stop] a decayed tooth

충해 蟲害 damage from [done by] insects; vermin damage; a blight
▶ 콩은 올해 충해를 입었다 The bean crop this year was damaged by insects.

충혈 充血 〔醫〕 congestion; hyperemia; engorgement
♦ 뇌충혈 congestion of the brain / 충혈성의 congestive / 충혈을 없애다 relieve (mucous membranes) of congestion; decongest
—충혈되다 be congested; be engorged; 〈눈이〉 be bloodshot
♦ 충혈된 눈 bloodshot [inflamed, injected] eyes

충혼 忠魂 〈정신〉 a loyal [faithful] soul [spirit]; 〈죽은 자〉 the loyal dead ♦ 충혼을 위로하다 propitiate the loyal dead —비 a monument to the loyal dead [war dead]

충효 忠孝 loyalty and filial piety

췌론 贅論 〈군더더기 이론〉 a redundant [superfluous] argument

췌액 膵液 〔生〕 pancreatic juice=이자액

췌언 贅言 〈군더더기 말〉 redundant [superfluous, unnecessary] words; (a) pleonasm; redundancy; tautology

췌장 膵臟 〔解〕 the pancreas ⇨ 이자 ■—결석 a pancreatic calculus —암 cancer of the pancreas —염 pancreatitis

취 〔植〕 an aster; a leopard plant

취 嘴 〔樂〕 the embouchure; a (woodwind) reed

취객 醉客 a drunken man [fellow]; a drunkard

취결 就結 〈어음의〉 drawing (of bills) —취결하다 draw ♦ 아무 앞으로 어음을 취결하다 draw a bill upon sb (for a sum)

취결례 取潔禮 〔가톨릭〕 purification ■ —첨례 (瞻禮) the Purification (of the Virgin Mary [Blessed Virgin]); Candlemas (Day)

취관 吹管 a blowpipe; a blast pipe ■ —분석 a blowpipe analysis

취광 醉狂 a frenzied drunk; 〈만취상태〉 drunken frenzy [madness]

취급 取扱 1 〈응대·대접〉 treatment; reception; dealing
♦ 공평한 취급 a fair [square] deal / 어린애 취급을 받다 be treated as [like] a child; be made a baby of sb
—취급하다 treat; deal with
♦ 개처럼 취급하다 treat sb like a dog / 공평하게 취급하다 deal justly [fairly] with sb / 부하 취급하다 treat sb as an underling / 죄인 취급하다 treat sb like a criminal / 손님처럼 취급받다 be treated as a guest

2 〈다룸〉 handling; manipulation; working
♦ 거친 취급 rough handling / 취급법 how to handle
—취급하다 handle; manipulate; work [operate] (a machine)
♦ 사회문제를 취급한 소설 a novel dealing with [treating of] social problems / 거칠게 취급하다 handle roughly; give (a thing) rough handling / 조심스럽게 취급하다 handle with care / 취급하기 쉽다[편리하다] 〈기계 등이〉 be easy to work [operate]; be convenient to handle [operate]
▶ 취급 주의(표시) Handle with care. ⇌ Fragile.

3 〈처리·거래〉 management; conduct; transaction
—취급하다 manage; deal in (foreign exchange); conduct; transact
▶ 저희 회사는 목재를 취급합니다 Our firm handles [deals in] lumber.
▶ 우체국에서도 전보를 취급합니다 Telegraphs are also handled [accepted] by the post office.
▶ 우리 가게에서는 조화는 취급하지 않습니다 This store does not carry artificial flowers.
■—량 the volume of business; the total of dealings —소 an office; an agency: 수화물 취급소 a baggage [(英) luggage] office / 화물 취급소 a freight [(英) forwarding] agency —시간 service hours; hours of attendance —인[자] a person in charge (of); an agent —점 a store dealing in (a particular item)

취기 醉氣 effects of drink; signs of intoxication; tipsiness
♦ 취기가 가시다 become sober; recover from one's intoxication / 취기가 돌다 grow [get, become] drunk [tipsy]; feel the effects of drink; show signs of intoxication

취담 醉談 speech [talking] under the influence of liquor [drink]; drunken words [talk]
▶ 그 사람 취담이니 개의치 마시오 Don't mind his words—he's drunk.
—취담하다 burble [babble] under the influence of alcohol

취대 取貸 〈꾸고 꾸어줌〉 borrowing and lending; a loan —취대하다 borrow and lend

취득 取得 (an) acquisition; 〈구득〉 (a) purchase
—취득하다 acquire; gain; get; obtain; take possession of (the new property); 〈구득하다〉 purchase
♦ 소유권을 취득하다 acquire the ownership (of)
■ —가격 acquisition cost —권 ownership: 선취득권 〔法〕 the right of priority —물 an acquisition —세 an acquisition tax: 부동산 취득세 a real estate acquisition tax —시효 acquisitive prescription —자 an acquisitor

취락 聚落 a settlement; a community; a colony

취렴 聚斂 〈착취〉 exploitation; exaction
　—취렴하다 exploit; sweat 《people》; squeeze 《money out of people》; exact 《taxes from people》; overtax; collect mercilessly

취로사업 就勞事業 a job-producing project

취로하다 就勞— set to work; work; find work [employment]

취리 取利 〈돈놀이〉 moneylending; usury
　—취리하다 lend [loan] money; run moneylending business; practice usury
　◆취리하여 돈을 모으다 make money by usury

취리히 〈스위스의 도시〉 Zurich

취목 取木 layering ⇨ 휘묻이

취미 趣味 (a) taste; a hobby; (an) interest; (a) liking
　◆고상한[저속한] 취미 refined [vulgar, loud] taste / 다방면의 취미 varied [various, manysided, wide] interests [tastes] / 취미가 고상한 사람 a person of refined [well-cultivated] taste / 취미가 다양한 사람 a person with many interests [hobbies] / 취미가 없는 사람 a man of few interests; a person who lacks taste / 취미에 맞는 직업 an occupation to one's liking / 취미가 고상하다 have (a) refined [well-cultivated] taste (in clothes) / 취미를 가지다 be interested (in); have a taste 《for》 / 취미를 붙이다 acquire [attain, develop] a taste 《for》 / 취미를 기르다 cultivate a taste 《for music》 / 취미를 잃다 lose one's interest (in); lose one's taste 《for》 / 취미에 맞다 suit one's taste; be to one's liking / 취미로 골동품에 손을 대다 dabble in curio as a hobby / 취미로 우표를 수집하다 collect stamps as a hobby
　▶ 그는 원예가 취미다 He has a taste for gardening.
　▶ 독서가 그녀의 유일한 취미다 Reading is her only pastime.
　▶ 그것은 취미의 문제다 It may be a matter of taste.
　▶ 이런 것에는 나는 별로 취미가 없다 I have little interest in these things.
　▶ 내 취미는 영화 감상이다 My hobby is watching films [movies].
　▶ 취미는 사람마다 다르다 Tastes differ. ⇌ Every man has his (own) taste. ⇌ So many men, so many tastes.
　▶ 그는 어려서부터 낚시에 취미를 갖고 있었다 From his childhood he was fond of angling.
　▶ 추상화는 내 취미에 맞지 않는다 The abstract painting is not to my taste.

취병 翠屛 a quickset gate [door, screen]
　◆취병 틀다 make a quickset door [screen]

취사 炊事 cooking; kitchen work
　—취사하다 cook; do cooking
　■—당번 the cook's duty —도구 cooking utensils; kitchenware —병(兵) (총칭) kitchen police

취사선택 取捨選擇 adoption (or [and] rejection); choice; option; selection
　◆취사선택의 자유 freedom of choice / 취사택에 망설이다 be at a loss which to take [choose] 《from among》
　—취사선택하다 adopt or reject sth; choose; select; make one's option [choice]
　—권 a right of selection; an option

취사장 炊事場 〈주방〉 a kitchen; (美) a cookery; 〈야외의〉 a cookhouse; a field kitchen; 〈배·비행기의〉 a galley
　■—공동— a common [communal] kitchen

취산꽃차례 聚繖— 〔植〕 centrifugal inflorescence; cyme ◆취산꽃차례의 cymose; cymous

취색 翠色 verdure; green; jade (green)

취생몽사 醉生夢死 idling one's life away
　—취생몽사하다 idle [slumber, sleep] one's life away; lead a befuddled life (as if drunk or in a dream)

취석 臭石 〔鑛〕 stinkstone

취선옹 醉仙翁 〔植〕 a rose campion

취소 取消 cancellation; 〈철회〉 withdrawal; 〈명령 등의〉 annulment; 〈약속·면허 등의〉 revocation ((of a license)); retraction
　◆의안의 취소 withdrawal of a measure / 판결의 취소 annulment [revocation] of a sentence
　—취소하다 cancel; revoke; withdraw; retract 《one's statement》; take back; recall; annul
　◆취소할 수 있는 retractable; recallable; revocable / 취소할 수 없는 irrevocable; beyond revoke [recall] / 앞서 한 말을 취소하다 take back what one has said; go back on [eat] one's word / 면허[결정]를 취소하다 revoke a license [decision] / 약속을 취소하다 recall [withdraw] a promise / 예약을 취소하다 cancel a reservation / 영업 허가를 취소하다 cancel a business license
　▶ 나는 그 상품의 주문을 취소했다 I canceled my order for the commodities.
　▶ 그저께 한 약속을 취소합니다 I'll take back the promise I made the day before yesterday.
　▶ 호텔 예약을 취소해야 되겠습니다 I have to cancel the hotel reservation.
　▶ 그것은 취소할 수 없는 발언이다 It's an irrevocable statement.
　—권 right of rescission; the right to rescind: 취소권부 신용장 a revocable letter of credit
　—명령 a countermand —소송 an action for nullity

취소 臭素 〔化〕 bromine ⇨ 브롬

취소불능 取消不能 ◆취소불능의 irrevocable; irreversible; indefeasible ■—신용장 an irrevocable letter of credit

취안 醉眼 drunken eyes; eyes dim [bleary] with drink
　◆취안이 몽롱하여 with one's eyes heavy [bleary] with drinking; sleepy from drink

취안 醉顔 a face flushed with liquor; a drunken face [look]

취약 脆弱 frailty; fragility; brittleness; delicacy —취약하다 fragile; frail; delicate; flimsy; brittle ■—지구[지점] 〔軍〕 a vulnerable area [point]

취업 就業 entering a profession; working; 〈취직〉 getting a job
　◆취업 중이다 be at work; be on duty
　—취업하다 enter a profession; take up an occupation; be employed
　■—야간— night work 해외— overseas employment ■—규칙 the rules of employment;

office [shop] regulations ―상태 the state of employment ―연령 working age ―인구 the working population ―일수 working days; days worked ―제한 restriction on employment ―지 the location [place] of employment

취업률 就業率 the percentage of employment
▶ 금년도 대학 졸업자들의 취업률이 좋다 The percentage of employment among the college graduates shows a favorable trend this year.

취역 就役 getting a commission
―취역하다 go into commission; be placed [put] in [into] commission; be commissioned ▶ 그 배는 태평양 항로에 취역했다 The ship was placed on the Pacific ocean line.
■―함(艦) a commissioned ship

취옥 翠玉 an emerald; green jadeite

취와하다 醉臥 lie in a drunken stupor; lie dead [blind] drunk

취용 取用 〈빌려 씀〉 borrowing ―취용하다 borrow 《sth from sb》

취우 驟雨 a shower ⇨ 소나기

취음 取音 〈음역(音譯)〉 transliteration
―취음하다 transliterate Korean words into [with] Chinese characters
■―자(字) a Chinese transliteration of a Korean word

취임 就任 assumption of office; inauguration; installation
―취임하다 take [assume] office 《as》; get into office 《as》; be inaugurated 《as》
♦ 내무부장관에 취임하다 take office as Home Minister / 대통령에 취임하다 be inaugurated [sworn in] as President / 공식으로 취임하다 take office formally
■―사[연설]〈대통령・주지사의〉《美》an inaugural (address) ―식 an inaugural (ceremony); an inauguration

취입 吹入 recording
―취입하다 record; blow in; put on a record [disk, tape]

취재 取才 picking out of talented persons; selecting a man of talent
―취재하다 select [choose, pick out, single out] talented persons

취재 取材 〈작품의〉 collecting data [materials]; 〈기사의〉 news gathering; coverage
▶ 그녀는 그 소설의 취재를 위해 런던에 갔다 She went to London to collect materials for the novel.
―취재하다 collect [gather, obtain] data [materials] 《on, for》;〈신문 기자가〉 collect [gather] news materials 《for, on》; cover 《a fire》
▶ 기자들이 그 사고를 취재하기 위해 현장으로 달려갔다 News reporters rushed to the scene to cover the accident.
▶ 그것은 현대의 미국에서 취재한 소설이다 That is a story based on modern America.
■―기자 an assignment man; a beat reporter; 《美俗》a legman ―담당 구역 one's newsbeat ―범위 coverage ―원(源) a news source ―활동 coverage activities;《美口》legwork

취조 取調 an inquiry ⇨ 심문(審問)

취종 取種 〈씨받기〉 gathering seeds
―취종하다 gather the seeds; breed from 《a stock》

취주 吹奏 playing; blowing; a blow ―취주하다 play [blow] 《the flute》
■―악 wind(-instrument) music ―악기 a wind instrument ―악 단[악 대] a brass band ―자 a player

취중 醉中 ♦ 취중의 싸움 a drunken brawl / 취중에 in a drunken state
♦ 취중에 실수하다 make a drunken slip; make a mistake while in one's cups
▶ 그는 취중에 운전하다 사고를 일으켰다 He drove his car when he was drunk and had an accident.
■―운전 ⇨ 음주(~운전) ―운전자 ⇨ 음주 (~운전자)

취중 就中 〈그중 특히〉 above all; first of all; in particular

취중에 진담이 나온다 《속담》 One tells the truth when drunk.

취지 趣旨 〈의미・요지〉 the meaning [purport]; the tenor; the point; 〈목적〉 an object; an aim; a purpose
♦ 담화의 취지 the drift [gist] of a discourse / 법의 취지 the intent of the law / 연설의 취지 the tenor [purport] of a speech / 질문의 취지 the point [tenor] of one's question / …이라는 취지의 편지 a letter to the effect that...
▶ 취지는 알겠습니다 I understand what you mean.
▶ 본 회의 취지를 설명드리겠습니다 Let me explain the object of our society.
▶ 그의 해석은 그 법률의 취지에 반한다 His interpretation is against the spirit of the law.
■―서(書) a prospectus: 취지서에 나와 있는 바와 같이 as is mentioned in the prospectus / 취지서를 작성하다 draw up [write out] a prospectus

취직 就職 finding employment; getting a job
♦ 취직을 부탁하다 ask sb for a job / 취직을 알선하다 help sb get a job [find a position]; help sb (to) find a job / 취직을 지망[신청]하다 apply for a position
▶ 그는 아직 취직을 못했다 He has not gotten [found] a job yet.
―취직하다 find employment [work]; get a job 《with a firm [newspaper]》; enter the service 《of》; secure [obtain, get] a position 《in, with》
♦ 관공서에 취직하다 enter government service / 보험 회사에 취직하다 take [get] a job with an insurance company / 취직해 있다 be in employment / 취직시켜주다 place sb in the service 《of a company》
▶ 會話 「졸업 후 어떤 직종에 취직할 거니?」「은행에 취직할 계획이야」"What kind of job are you going to get after you graduate?" "I'm going [planning] to get [find] a job [position] at a bank."
■―률 ⇨ 취업률 ―시험 an employment examination ―신청 an application for a position ―알선 (job) placement ―원서 a job application [bid] ―지망자 a job applicant

[candidate]

취직난 就職難 job shortage; difficulty in finding employment
▶취직난이 심각하다 It's very hard to find a job. ⇌ Jobs are very scarce.
▶그 대규모 사업이 취직난을 완화했다 The big scale project relieved the difficulty of finding employment.

취직운동 就職運動 job hunting; seeking employment
◆취직운동을 하다 seek employment [work] (at a bank); look [hunt] for a position [job, place] / 취직운동에 바쁘다 be busy seeking employment [hunting for a position]

취직자리 就職— a position; a situation; an opening
◆취직자리를 찾다 seek employment; look [hunt] for a position
▶삼촌께서 취직자리를 구해 주셨다 My uncle found me the job. ⇌ I got the job through my uncle's influence. ⇌ I got the job with the help of my uncle.

취진 驟進 〈고속의 승진〉 rapid elevation [promotion, advancement] 《in the official world》
—취진하다 be elevated [promoted] rapidly

취처 娶妻 taking a wife —취처하다 take a wife; marry 《a woman》

취체 取締 control ⇨ 단속(團束)

취침 就寢 going to bed [sleep]
◆취침 중에 while (one is) sleeping [asleep, in bed]
▶취침 중 (게시) Do not disturb.
—취침하다 go to bed; turn in; retire
■—시간 bedtime; time to go to bed: 이제 취침 시간이다 It's time for bed.

취태 醉態 drunkenness; intoxication; tipsiness
◆취태를 부리다 put on a drunken display; 《美俗》 hit the booze and become wild
▶그는 취태를 보였다 He was seen drunk.

취택 取擇 selection ⇨ 선택(選擇)

취하 取下 withdrawal; discontinuance
—취하하다 withdraw; drop; dismiss; abandon
◆소송을 취하하다 withdraw [call off, drop, abandon] a case / 신청을 취하하다 withdraw *one's* application

취하다 取— 1 〈가지다〉 take; 〈채택·채용하다〉 adopt; assume
◆공세를 취하다 assume [take] the offensive / 긴축 정책을 취하다 adopt a retrenchment policy / 연락을 취하다 get in touch (with); effect liaison (with) / 입장을 취하다 take the stand (that) / 조치를 취하다 take action; take a step [measure]; make a move / 강경한 태도를 취하다 assume [take] a firm attitude
▶그는 신중한 태도를 취했다 He took a cautious attitude.
▶하루 8시간은 수면을 취하여야 합니다 You must get 8 hours' sleep every night.
▶정부는 효과적인 대기 오염 방지 조치를 취하지 않으면 안된다 The government must take effective measures to prevent air pollution.
2 〈선택하다〉 prefer; choose; pick; take

◆중용을 취하다 go middle; take the (golden) mean [middle course] / 여럿 가운데서 하나를 취하다 choose [pick] one out of many / 죽음과 불명예 가운데 하나를 취하다 choose between death and dishonor
3 〈추가하다·얻다〉 ◆이(利)를 취하다 pursue gain; be bent upon gain / 많은 이윤을 취하다 gain a fair margin of profit
4 〈섭취하다〉 take; have
◆영양을 취하다 have some nourishment; take nourishing food
5 〈자세 등을〉 assume a posture (of); pose
◆방어 자세를 취하다 take [assume] a posture of defense / 총을 자세를 취하다 hold the rifle at the ready / 포즈를 취하다 pose (*oneself*) (as a model); strike [get into] a pose / 사진을 찍기 위해 포즈를 취하다 pose for *one's* picture; pose for a photography
▶그는 덤벼들려고 자세를 취했다 He stood ready for a fight [to strike at me].
6 〈꾸다〉 borrow
◆돈을 취하다 borrow money

취하다 醉— 1 〈술에〉 get drunk; become [get] intoxicated [tipsy]; be overcome with liquor; make *oneself* drunk on wine
◆취한 drunk; drunken; intoxicated / 취하여 under the influence of liquor [drink] / 맥주에 취하다 get drunk on [with] beer / 거나하게 취하다 be pleasantly intoxicated / 곤드레만드레 취하다 be dead [blind, beastly] drunk / 취하여 쓰러지다 fall dead-drunk / 취해서 자다 go off into a vinous sleep / 마셔도 취하지 않다 drink soberly
▶알코올은 사람을 취하게 한다 Alcohol intoxicates people.
▶오늘 저녁은 그를 취하게 합시다 Let's get him drunk this evening.
▶그는 취하면 기분이 좋아진다 When he gets drunk, he will be in a good humor.
▶그는 이미 꽤 취해 있었다 He was already far gone [as high as a kite].
▶얼근하게 취하는데요 I feel myself warm with the wine.
2 〈약물 등에 중독되다〉 be poisoned; get intoxicated
◆카페인에 취하다 be tipsy [poisoned] with caffeine
3 〈도취하다〉 be intoxicated; be elated; be exalted; be spellbound; be in raptures
▶그들은 성공[승리]에 취해 있었다 They were intoxicated [elated] by success [with victory].

취학 就學 entering school —취학하다 enter [attend, go to] school ◆취학시키다 put [send] (a boy) to school
■—률 the percentage of school attendance —아동 a schoolchild : 미취학 아동 a preschool child; a preschooler —연령 (attain, reach) the school age

취한 取汗 〈발한(發汗)〉 〔韓醫〕 diaphoresis; sweating —취한하다 sweat 《a patient》; induce perspiration ■—요법 sweating treatment

취한 醉漢 a drunkard ⇨ 취객(醉客)

취항 就航 commission; service; 〈배의〉 sailing
♦ 이라크 여객기의 취항을 금지하다 inhibit the operation of Iraquian airlines
─ 취항하다 go into commission; enter service; 〈배가〉 set sail
♦ 서울-제주간을 취항하다 be put into service [operation] between Seoul and Cheju / 미국 항로에 취항하다 be placed on the American line / 배를 취항시키다 place a ship in commission; commission a vessel in service / 유럽 항로에 여객기를 취항시키다 operate airliners on the European route
▶ 그 배는 유럽 항로에 취항했다 The ship has been put into service on the European line.
■ ─선 vessels in commission

취향 趣向 taste; liking; fondness; 〈경향〉 one's bent; inclination
♦ 옷에 대한 취향 one's taste in dress / 취향에 맞다 suit one's taste; please [suit, hit] one's fancy
▶ 누군가가 이것을 내게 주었지만 내 취향에 맞지 않는다 Somebody gave this to me, but it doesn't suit my taste.

취화 臭化 〔化〕 bromination ⇨ 브롬화

취흥 醉興 exhilaration due to alcohol; joviality [merriment] over one's cups; delight in intoxication
♦ 취흥에 겨워 excited [elated] under the influence of wine / 취흥이 일다 become cheerful in one's cups / 취흥을 못 이겨 춤을 추다 dance in drunken delight

-측 -側 the side
♦ 양측 both [the two] sides / 한국[유엔]측 the Korean [the UN] side / 노동자측의 요구 the demand on the part of workers / 사용자측의 태만으로 owing to neglect of duty on the part of the management

측간 廁間 a toilet shed ⇨ 뒷간
측거의 測距儀 a range finder
측근 側近 1 〈가까운 곁〉 the side; around sb
♦ 측근에서 모시다 attend [wait] on 《one's boss》
2 〈측근자〉 those close to 《the minister》; one's close associates [staff members]; (美) an aide (to)
♦ 대통령 측근 a presidential aide / 국무총리 측근 소식통에 의하면 according to sources close to the Prime Minister
측근자 側近者 those close to ⇨ 측근 2
측도 測度 measurement; gauging ─측도하다 measure; gauge
측량 測量 1 〈물건의〉 measurement; measuring; 〈토지의〉 a survey; surveying
♦ 항공 측량을 하다 make an aerial survey (of)
─ 측량하다 measure; take a measurement (of); survey; make a survey 《of》
♦ 바다의 깊이를 측량하다 sound the sea / 산의 높이를 측량하다 measure (the height of) a mountain
2 〈헤아림〉 estimation; guess; conjecture
─ 측량하다 estimate; measure; guess; fathom; sound; plumb
♦ 남의 마음을 측량하다 enter into another's feelings
■ 고저[수준]─ leveling 기선 a base line measurement 사진[항공]─ a photo [an aerial] survey 삼각─ triangulation 토지─ ⇨ 측지(測地) ─기 a surveying instrument ─기사 a (land) surveyor; a surveying engineer ─도 a survey map ─반 a surveying squad ─술 surveying (technique); mensuration

측면 側面 the side; the flank; a side [lateral] face
♦ 기계의 좌우 양 측면 the right and left sides of a machine / 측면의 side; flank; lateral / 재정적인 측면에서 in the financial aspect / 측면을 엄호하다 cover the flanks / 적의 측면을 찌르다 attack the enemy on the flank / 측면에서 보다 take a side view 《of》
▶ 그 집의 측면에는 창이 없다 There are no windows at [on] the sides of the house.
▶ 그의 성격에는 그런 측면도 있다 He has something like that in his character.
■ ─공격 a flank attack: 측면공격을 하다 make [launch] a flank attack 《against, on》; attack 《the enemy》 in the flank ─도 a side [lateral] view [elevation]; a profile ─방어 a flank defense

측문 仄聞 〈얻어 들음〉 learning by hearsay
─ 측문하다 learn by hearsay; hear casually [occasionally]; hearsay 《of, that...》
♦ 측문한 바에 의하면 from what I heard by chance; I hear [understand] 《that》

측백나무 側柏─ 〔植〕 an Oriental [a Chinese] arborvitae
측벽 側壁 a side wall
측보기 測步器 〈계보기(計步器)〉 a pedometer
측사 側射 a flanking fire
측사기 測斜器 〔物〕 a clinometer
측산 測算 calculation; estimation ─측산하다 calculate; estimate
측선 側線 〈철도의〉 a sidetrack; a siding; 〈어류 등의〉 a lateral line
♦ 열차를 측선에 넣다 sidetrack a train
측수 測水 sounding the depth ⇨ 측심
측심 測深 sounding the depth
─측심하다 measure the depth 《of》; fathom; sound 《the sea》
■ ─기[의(儀)] a (depth) sounder

측심연 測深鉛 a plumb (bob); a sounding lead; a plummet
♦ 측심연으로 수심을 재다 measure the depth (of the sea) by sounding (with a plumb); plumb
■ ─선 a sounding [lead, fathom] line ─수 lead(s)man

측열기 測熱器 a calorimeter
측우기 測雨器 a rain gauge; a pluviometer
측은 惻隱 pity ─측은하다 pitiful; pitiable; piteous; poor
♦ 측은한 이야기 a touching [moving] story / 측은한 마음이 들다 be overwhelmed with pity (for); feel compassion [pity] (for); be moved with pity / 측은히 여기다 have [take] pity (on); feel pity (for)
■ ─지심(之心) sympathy; compassion; com-

측음 側音 〔音聲〕 a lateral (sound)
측점 測點 a station
측정 測定 measurement; 〈토지의〉 survey; 〈수심의〉 sounding; 〈관측〉 observation
─측정하다 measure; survey; sound; gauge
♦강우량을 측정하다 measure the rainfall (in the region) / 거리를 측정하다 find [measure] the distance (to) / 태양의 고도를 측정하다 take the height of the sun / 차의 속도를 측정하다 measure the speed of a car / 풍력을 측정하다 gauge the strength of the wind
■ ─기 a measuring instrument ─법 a method [way] of measurement
측정기 測程器 〔海〕 (throw, heave) a log
측지 測地 〈토지측량〉 land surveying; a geodetic survey
─측지하다 survey (land); practice surveying
■ ─위성 a geodetic [an earth-mapping] satellite ─학 geodesy
측판 測板 〈측량용〉 a surveying table
측화산 側火山 〈기생화산〉 a parasitic volcano; an adventive [a parasitic] cone
측후 測候 〔氣〕 a meteorological observation
─측후하다 make a meteorological observation (of)
■ ─소 ⇨ 기상관측(~소)
츱츱하다 〈염치가 없다〉 shameless; brazen; cheeky
▶그는 츱츱하게 남의 물건을 자꾸 달라고 한다 He keeps asking me for things shamelessly.
층 層 1 〈건물의〉 a story; 〈英〉 a storey; a floor
♦1층 〈英〉 the first floor; 〈英〉 the ground floor / 2층 〈美〉 the second story [floor]; 〈英〉 the first floor / 20층 건물 a twenty-story [twenty-storied] building / 5층에 살고 있다 live on the fifth floor
▶〔會話〕「이 건물은 몇 층입니까?」「30층입니다」 "How many floors has [How many stories high is] this building?" "It has thirty stories."
▶그 건물은 지상 12층 지하 4층이다 The building has twelve floors above ground and four underground.
▶승강기는 각 층마다 선다 The elevator [lift] serves [stops at] every floor.
2 〈지층 등의〉 a layer; a stratum; a seam; 〈석탄 등의〉 a bed
♦대기(大氣)의 상층 the upper layers of the atmosphere / 암석층 rock stratification / 제3기층 the Tertiary formation / 석탄층 a coal bed [seam]; coal measures / 층을 이루다 be in layers; be in strata; be stratified
3 〈계층·단계〉 a class; a stratum
♦근로자층 the working class / 연령층 an age group [bracket] / 중산[중류]층 the middle class / 지식층 the intellectual class; the intelligentsia
4 〈등급〉 a grade; a class
▶배우에도 여러 층이 있다 There are various grades [classes] of actors.
5 〈정도〉 ♦한층 더 furthermore; moreover; still more; all the more
층각 層閣 a storied tower ⇨ 층루(層樓)

층계 層階 stairs; a staircase; a stairway; a flight (of stairs)
♦가파른 층계 a steep staircase / 층계 위[아래]에(서) at the top [foot] of the stairs / 층계를 올라가다 ascend [go up] the stairs; go upstairs / 층계를 내려가다 descend [go down] the stairs; go downstairs / 층계에서 굴러 떨어지다 fall downstairs
■ ─참 a landing (place); a (mean) landing
층계송 層階頌 〔가톨릭〕 gradual; (라) Graduale
층나다 層─ 〈층등이 생기다〉 be graded; be stratified into classes [grades]; show disparity 《in rank》
층널 層─ 〈서랍 밑의〉 a bottom board 《of a drawer》
층대 層臺 stairs ⇨ 층층대
층도리 層─ 〔建〕 a girth
층돌 層─ a touchstone; a Lydian stone
층등 層等 〈등급〉 a class; a grade
층루 層樓 〈누각〉 a storied tower; a tower of several stories
층류 層流 〔物〕〈층흐름〉 laminar [streamline] flow
층리 層理 〔地質〕 stratification; bedding
■ ─면 a stratification [bedding] plane
층면 層面 1 〈쌓인 물건의 겉〉 the surface 《of piled up things》
2 〈층리〉 ─면
층상 層狀 ♦층상의 stratiform; stratified / 층상을 이루다 be stratified; have a stratified formation
■ ─암 a stratified rock ─운 〈층운형 구름〉 a stratiform cloud
층새 層─ 〈황금의 품질〉 the quality [purity] of gold / 금의 층새를 가리다 assay gold; grade gold
층수 層數 the (total) number of layers [floors, stories] 《of a building》
층암절벽 層岩絕壁 a precipitous wall of stratified rock; a rocky cliff [precipice]
층애 層崖 〔地質〕 an escarpment; a stratified precipice [cliff]
층운 層雲 〔氣〕 a stratus 《pl. -ti》(略 S., St)
층적운 層積雲 〔氣〕 a stratocumulus; a roll cumulus 《pl. -li》
층지다 層─ be graded ⇨ 층나다
층집 層─ a house [building] of more than one story [level, floor]
층층 層層 all (the) strata [layers]; 〈각 층〉 every layer [stratum]; each floor [story]
♦층층으로 된 모래와 자갈 sand and gravel spread in alternate layers / 층층으로 in strata [layers, tiers]; layer upon layer / 돌을 층층이 쌓다 pile up stones / 벽돌을 층층이 쌓다 lay bricks course upon course / 건물 층층이 국기를 게양하다 put up national flags at every floor of a building
층층다리 層層─ a staircase
층층대 層層臺 stairs ⇨ 계단(階段)
층층시하 層層侍下 serving both parents and grandparents alive
♦층층시하의 며느리 a daughter-in-law who has to serve the parents and grandparents of her husband

층하하다 層下— 〈차별하다〉 discriminate against *sb* [*sth*]; treat *sb* with less respect [favor] than others
▶ 그는 사람을 층하하지 않는다 He treats every person just and fair. ⇌ He treats all alike.

치¹ **1**〈사람〉 a fellow; a guy; a chap
◆ 그[저] 치 that fellow [guy, chap] / 장사치 a peddler; a trader
2 〈물건〉 an article; a thing; goods
◆ 중간치 in-between things; 〈크기〉 an article of in-between [medium] size / 하치 coarse [low-grade] stuff
3 〈몫·분량〉 a share; a portion; a part
◆ 사흘치 약 medicine for three days / 이달치 임대료 [회비, 수업료] the rent [dues, fee] for this month / 하루치 식량 a day's ration

치² 〈길이의 단위〉 a *ch'i*
◆ 한 치 앞도 볼 수 없는 눈보라 a blinding blizzard / 한 치 앞도 못 보다 (비유) have no foresight
▶ 캄캄하여 한 치 앞도 보이지 않는다 It's pitch-dark and we cannot see an inch ahead of us.

치 値 〈값〉〈數〉 value

치가 治家 home management —**치가하다** manage a household; regulate the family

치가떨리다 齒— make [drive] *one* mad with vexation; be infuriated; be tense with indignation.
▶ 그의 말을 들으니 치가 떨린다 His remark makes me mad.
▶ 우리집 아이가 맞는 것을 보니 치가 떨려 죽겠다 It gets my goat to see our boy whipped.

치감 齒疳 〔韓醫〕 pyorrhea alveolaris; dentoalveolitis; Riggs' disease

치감 齒疳 wind [bind, coil] upward[ly] (around)

치강 齒腔 〔解〕 a dental cavity

치경 齒莖 〈잇몸〉 the gum(s); a gum; a gingiva (*pl.* -vae)

치고 〈예외없이〉 ▶ 여자치고 화장 안 하는 사람은 없다 Every woman makes up her face.
▶ 비밀치고 탄로 안 나는 것이 없다 There is nothing so secret but it comes to light.
▶ 사람치고 결점 없는 사람은 없다 There is no one but has some faults.
▶ 저 사람은 음식치고 못 먹는 것이 없다 He eats anything that is at all in the nature of food.
▶ 나는 이 나라 명찰치고 안 가본 데가 없다 I have been to every famous temple in this country.

치고는 considering; seeing; as; for
▶ 그는 나이치고는 늙어보인다 He looks oldish considering (that) he is so young.
▶ 그는 외국인치고는 한국어를 유창하게 한다 He speaks fluent Korean for a foreigner.
▶ 그는 신참치고는 꽤 잘 했다 Seeing [Considering] that he is new to the job, he has done very well.
▶ 그는 아마추어치고는 그림을 썩 잘 그린다 He paints very well as amateur painters go.
▶ 그 소년은 나이치고는 키가 크다 The boy is tall for his age.
◆ 여자아이치고는 행동이 거칠다 For a girl,

she behaves roughly.

치골 恥骨 〔解〕 the pubis (*pl.* pubes); the pubic bone

치골 齒骨 〔醫〕 (a) dentary bone

치골 癡骨 〈어리석은 사람〉 a fool; a numbskull

치과 齒科 dental surgery [service]; dentistry; 〈병원〉 a dentist's [dental] office
◆ 치과에 가다 go to (see) a dentist; go to the dentist's
■ —교정학 orthodontics; orthodontia —기공 dental technician —기구 a dentist's tool; a dental [dentist's] instrument —대학 a dental college —병원[의원] a dental hospital [clinic] —(의)학 dentistry; odontology —치료 dental treatment

치과의사 齒科醫師 a dentist; a dental surgeon
◆ 치과의사의 치료를 받다 consult a dentist; receive dental treatment

치관 齒冠 the crown (of a tooth)

치국 治國 governing a country —**치국하다** govern a country; rule over a country

치근 齒根 the root of a tooth; a dental root

치근거리다 harass; pester; importune [tease] 《*sb* for *sth*》
◆ 여자에게 치근거리다 molest [make advance to] a woman

치근치근 teasingly; harrassingly
—**치근치근하다** ⇨ 치근거리다

치긋다 〈올려긋다〉 stroke upwards; draw 《a line》 upwards; make an upward stroke 《in writing a Chinese character》

치기 稚氣 childishness; puerility
◆ 치기 어린 childish; puerile / 말하는 것이 치기를 띠다 talk like a child; say childish things

-치기 〈내기〉 a game (of) ◆ 돈치기 a kind of money-throwing game / 딱지치기 a game of slap-match

치다¹ 〈물결이〉 dash 《against》; roll; undulate; wave; 〈눈보라 등이〉 rage; bluster; 〈벼락 등이〉 strike; hit; thunder; lighten
◆ 천둥치는 소리 a peal [roar, roll] of thunder / 파도치는 해변 the shore washed by the waves / 바람이 세차게 치는 거리 a blustering street / 물결치는 대로 《drift about》 at the mercy of the waves / 벼락이 치다 thunder; the thunder rolls
▶ 들에는 눈보라가 치고 있었다 A blizzard was raging over the field.
▶ 가까이에서 벼락이 쳤다 The thunderbolt fell close by.

치다² **1**〈때리다〉 strike; hit; beat; knock; punch; give [deal] a blow
◆ 머리를 치다 hit [strike] *sb* on the head / 종아리를 치다 whip *sb* on the calves of the legs / 어깨를 톡 치다 pat *sb* on the shoulder / 어린애 궁둥이를 찰싹 치다 spank a baby / 주먹으로 치다 smash *sb* with the fist; punch; slug / 몽둥이로 치다 hit *sb* with a club / 서로 치고 받다 exchange [trade, bandy] blows 《with》

2 〈때려서 소리를 내다〉 beat 《a drum》; strike [ring] 《a bell》; clang 《a gong》; clap 《hands》
◆ 박수를 치다 clap *one*'s hands / 타이프라이터를 치다 pound [tap] a typewriter / 피아노를

치다³ play (on) the piano
3 〈시계가〉 strike
♦ 3시를 치다 strike three
▶ 會話「지금 몇 시를 쳤지?」「2시를 쳤어」 "What did it [the clock] strike?" "It has struck two."
4 〈공을〉 strike; hit ♦ 공을 치다 hit the ball / 홈런을 치다 hit [clout, slam] a home run 《over the left field fence》
5 〈놀이를 하다〉 play 《a game》 ♦ 테니스[탁구]를 치다 play tennis [ping-pong] / 골프를 치다 play (at) golf; golf / 당구를 치다 play (at) billiards; have a game of billiards
6 〈전보를〉 ♦ 전보를 치다 send a telegram; telegraph (to); wire (to sb)
▶ 그는 즉시 그녀에게 급전을 쳤다 He immediately sent an urgent telegram to her.
7 〈두드려 박다〉 drive in; hammer
♦ 못을 치다 nail; drive a nail
8 〈두들겨서 만들다〉 ♦ 떡을 치다 pound steamed glutinous rice; make rice cake
9 〈공격하다〉 attack; assault; assail; strike
♦ 적의 후방을 치다 take [attack] the enemy in the rear / 불시에 적을 치다 surprise the enemy / 쳐들어가다 invade; make an inroad 《on, into》 / 쳐서 빼앗다 take 《a fortress》 by storm [assault]
10 〈공박하다〉 attack; criticize; denounce; speak 《talk, write》 against sb
♦ 신문에서 남을 치다 write against sb; attack [pound] sb in the newspaper
11 〈자르다〉 ♦ 가지를 치다 prune 《off, down》 / 머리를 짧게 치다 cut [crop] one's hair short / 목을 치다 cut off sb's head; behead sb / 무채를 치다 cut a radish into fine strips
12 〈깎다〉 shave ♦ 밤을 치다 shave the skin of a chestnut 《with a knife》
13 〈체질하다〉 sift; sieve ♦ 밀가루를 치다 sift out flour

치다³ 1 〈설치하다〉 set; put up
♦ 그물을 치다 set [throw] a net; pitch [lay] a net / 모기장을 치다 put up [hang] a mosquito net / 두 기둥 사이에 밧줄을 치다 stretch a rope between the two poles / 병풍을 치다 set up a screen / 진을 치다 encamp; pitch a camp; take up (a) position / 천막을 치다 pitch [set up, put up] a tent
2 〈엮다〉 weave ♦ 돗자리[가마니]를 치다 weave a straw mat [bag]
▶ 큰 거미가 줄을 치고 있었다 A big spider was spinning its web.
3 〈감아 매다〉 tie; wear; put on
♦ 각반을 치다 put on spats / 대님을 치다 tie one's trousers-cuffs [trousers around the ankles]

치다⁴ 1 〈기르다〉 raise; rear; breed; keep; feed
♦ 누에를 치다 rear [raise, breed] silkworms / 돼지를 치다 raise hogs; breed pigs
2 〈낳다〉 procreate; propagate; bring forth the young; litter
♦ 1년에 5, 6회 새끼를 치다 have five or six litters yearly
3 〈이자가 붙다〉 draw [bear, yield] interest
♦ 이자가 새끼를 치다 bear double interest
4 〈벌이 꿀을〉 produce and store honey
▶ 벌이 꿀을 치다 Bees store honey.
5 〈나무가 가지를〉 spread; shoot out

치다⁵ 1 〈양념류를〉 put 《soy》 into [in, on]
♦ 양념을 치다 spice 《a dish》 / 생선에 소금을 치다 sprinkle salt on fish / 샐러드에 소스를 치다 put sauce on the salad / 설탕[소금]을 쳐서 먹을 치다 eat sth with sugar [salt]
2 〈기름을〉 apply 《a lubricant》 ♦ 기계에 기름을 치다 apply oil to a machine; grease a machine
3 〈술을〉 pour; fill ♦ 술을 치다 fill a glass with wine; serve wine

치다⁶ 1 〈계산에 넣다〉 count among; include
♦ 이자까지 쳐서 50만원 500,000 won, inclusive of interest
▶ 합격자는 나까지 쳐서 10명이었다 Ten applicants passed the examination, myself among the number.
2 〈평가하다〉 price; value
♦ 그림[집] 값을 천만원으로 치다 value the picture [house] at ten million won / 베토벤을 다른 모든 작곡가보다 높이 치다 place Beethoven above all others
3 〈가정하다〉 suppose; assume; presume; take it for granted that...
♦ 그것이 정말[사실]이라 치고 assuming that it is [it to be] true
4 〈간주하다〉 regard 《as》; consider; think of 《as》 ♦ 아무를 바보로 치다 consider sb (to be) a fool

치다⁷ 1 〈선·점(點) 등을〉 ♦ 줄을 치다 draw a line / 방점을 치다 mark with a side dot [point]
2 〈점(占)을〉 ♦ 점을 치다 have one's fortune told

치다⁸ 1 〈숙박시키다〉 lodge ♦ 하숙을 치다 run a lodging house
2 〈접대하다〉 entertain ♦ 손님을 치다 entertain guests
3 〈시험 등을〉 ♦ 영어 시험을 치다 〈시행하다〉 examine 《students》 in English; 〈응시하다〉 go [come] up for an examination in English / 자동차 운전 면허 시험을 치다 take one's test for a driver's license

치다⁹ 〈제거·청소하다〉 remove; take [clear, sweep] away
♦ 재를 치다 remove [clean out] ashes (from the fireplace) / 변소를 치다 remove [dip up] night soil / 우물을 치다 clean a well

치다¹⁰ 1 〈소리를 지르다〉 ♦ 고함을 치다 shout; cry [call] out / 호통을 치다 yell at; hurl words of thunder at; (美) bawl sb out
2 〈동작·행위를 하다〉 ♦ 물장구를 치다 paddle one's feet in the water / (개가) 꼬리를 치다 wag its tail / 활개를 치다 swing one's arms / 뺑소니를 치다 run away [off]

치다¹¹ 〈차에 깔리다〉 be run over ⇨ 치이다¹
치다¹² 〈정돈하다〉 put sth in order ⇨ 치우다¹
치다꺼리 1 〈치러내기〉 management; conduct; disposition; disposal; dealing 《with》
♦ 손님 치다꺼리 entertaining guests
—**치다꺼리하다** manage; conduct 《business》;

dispose of; deal with 《an affair》 ♦ 손님을 치다꺼리하다 entertain a guest; attend to a guest
2 〈바라지〉 help; aid; assistance; caretaking ♦ 아이의 치다꺼리를 하다 look after [take care of] a child / 환자의 치다꺼리를 하다 attend to [on] the sick; tend the sick
—치다꺼리하다 help; aid; assist; take care (of); look [see] after

치닫다 run [go] up 《a hill》; run uphill; run [dash] upstairs

치대다 **1** 〈위쪽으로〉 put [fix, fasten, stick] *sth* on the upper part ♦ 판자를 벽에 치대다 fix a board on the upper part of a wall ▶ (강가에서) 배를 좀더 치대시오 Moor the boat a bit upward.
2 〈문지르다〉 knead 《dough》; rub [scrub] 《laundry》

치도곤 治盜棍 a club (for the lash) ♦ 치도곤을 안기다 club [cudgel] 《a criminal》

치독 治毒 detoxification; detoxication
—치독하다 counteract [neutralize] the poison; remove the (effect of) poison 《from》; detoxify; detoxicate

치독 置毒 poisoning; administration of poison
—치독하다 put poison in [on] 《food》; poison 《the wells》; envenom

치둔 癡鈍 stupidity; imbecility
—치둔하다 stupid; dull-witted; doltish

치뜨다 cast an upward glance; turn up *one's* eyes ♦ 눈을 치뜨고 with *one's* eyes turned up

치뜨리다 toss up; throw up; fling [hurl, pitch] up ♦ 볏단을 마차에 치뜨리다 toss sheaves of rice up on the cart / 꼴을 치뜨려 뒤집어 말리다 toss hay about

치뜰다 mean; base; contemptible ♦ 치뜬 놈 a mean fellow; an ugly guy; a base wretch / 치뜬 짓 a mean conduct [deed]

치란 治亂 **1** 〈치세와 난세〉 peace and war; order and confusion **2** 〈평정〉 pacification; suppression of a rebellion —치란하다 restore order; put down a revolt

치런치런 1 〈넘칠듯 말듯〉 brimfully; to the full; overflowingly ♦ 컵에 술을 치런치런 따르다 fill a glass to the brim with wine ▶ 우물에 물이 치런치런 괴었다 The well is overflowing with water
2 〈스칠락말락〉 long; dragging; trailing ♦ 치런치런 늘어진 버들가지 drooping willow branches that almost sweep the ground
—치런치런하다 trailing; dragging
♦ 치런치런한 머리채 a long pigtail

치렁거리다 1 〈드리워진 것이〉 hang (and swing) loosely; dangle ▶ 긴 머리가 그녀의 등에서 치렁거리고 있다 Her long hair hangs loose(ly) down her back.
2 〈늦추어지다〉 be put off from day to day; be prolonged; trail on

치렁치렁 1 〈늘어진 모양〉 hanging [swinging] loosely; danglingly ♦ 허리까지 치렁치렁 늘어뜨린 머리 a pigtail that hangs down to *one's* waist
2 〈미적미적〉 ♦ 〈시일을〉 치렁치렁 끌다 prolong; protract; delay; draw [drag] out / 체류 일수를 치렁치렁 끌다 protract *one's* stay indefinitely

치레 embellishment; adornment; beautifying; prettifying; decoration; 〈옷의〉 dressing-up ♦ 체면 치레를 하다 save [keep up] appearances; put up a good front / 옷치레를 하다 dress [deck] up; sport fancy attire
—치레하다 embellish; adorn; decorate; deck [dress] up; smarten up; 〈꾸미다〉 affect

치료 治療 (medical) treatment; remedy; cure; medical care
♦ 치료를 받다 receive treatment; undergo [take] medical treatment; be treated; be given treatment; be placed under medical care / 응급 치료를 하다 give *sb* first aid / 치료를 게을리하다 neglect to have proper medical care / 치료중이다 be under medical treatment [the care of a physician] / 치료중에 절명하다 succumb under the treatment
▶ 나는 심장병 치료를 받고 있다 I am receiving medication for my heart trouble.
▶ 그는 지금도 신경통 치료를 받고 있다 He is still under treatment for neuralgia.
▶ 그녀는 민박사의 치료를 받고 있다 She is under the treatment [care] of Dr. Min.
▶ 나는 눈 치료를 받기 위해 안과에 갔다 I went to the eye doctor's to have my eyes treated.
▶ 그는 두 달 동안 의사의 치료를 받았지만 결국 죽고 말았다 Though he was given medical treatment for two months, he eventually died.
—치료하다 treat; give *sb* medical treatment; 〈상처 등을〉 dress; 〈고치다〉 cure 《*sb* of a disease》; remedy
♦ 치료하기 어려운 irremediable; incurable / 상처를 치료하다 dress [treat] a wound / 환자를 치료하다 treat [care for, attend to] a patient / 치료해 주다 treat 《a patient》; subject 《a patient》 to treatment
▶ 그 환자는 치료해 봤자 소용이 없다 The patient is past treatment [curing].
■ —대 a treatment table —법 ⇨ 요법(療法) —비 a doctor's fee; 〈배상하는〉 smart money —소 an infirmary; a clinic —자 a curer —학 therapeutics; iatrology —효과 remedial [therapeutic, curative] value

치루 痔瘻 [醫] an anal fistula 《*pl.* ~s, -lae》

치룽 a large round wicker basket ■ —장수 a peddler with wares in a round wicker basket

치룽구니 a stupid, good-for-nothing fellow

치르다 1 〈지급하다〉 pay (off) (for)
♦ 값을 치르다 pay for 《an article》; pay the price 《for》 / 셈을 치르다 pay a bill; settle *one's* account / 계약금을 치르다 advance money on a contract
▶ 셈을 치르고 나니 돈이 거의 남지 않았다 After paying the bill I had little money left.
2 〈겪다〉 undergo; go through; experience; 〈큰 일을〉 carry out; have; observe
♦ 시험을 치르다 undergo [go through] an examination / 제사를 치르다 observe the formalities of ancestor worship / 혼례를 치르다 have a wedding ceremony / 홍역을 치르다 〈혼이 나다〉 have a hard time of it; have a bitter experience

3 〈접대하다〉 entertain
♦ 손님을 치르다 entertain guests

치를떨다 齒— **1** 〈인색하게 굴다〉 grudge; begrudge; be stingy; be close-fisted
▶ 그는 한 푼 쓰는데도 치를 떤다 He has a fit every time he has to spend a penny. ⇒ He pinches a penny till it hurts.
2 〈분하여 이를 떨다〉 grind one's teeth with vexation; grit one's teeth

치마 a skirt ♦ 치마의 주름 a pleat [gather] on a skirt / 치마를 입다[두르다] put on [wear] a skirt / 치마를 벗다 remove [take off] one's skirt ■ —끈 a girdle of a skirt

치마분 齒磨粉 〈가루 치약〉 tooth powder

치마폭 —幅 the width of a skirt ♦ 어린애를 치마폭에 감싸다 tuck a child in a skirt

치맛바람 1 〈서슬〉 the swish of a skirt
2 〈차림새〉 informal dress
♦ 치맛바람으로 in informal attire
3 〈여성의 힘〉 female influence [power]

치맛자락 the hem of a skirt; the train
♦ 치맛자락을 걷어 잡다 tuck [pick up, hold up] a skirt / 치맛자락을 끌며 걷다 walk with a trailing skirt

치매 癡呆 〔醫〕 dementia
■ 노인성— senile dementia 조발성(早發性)— precocious dementia

치매기다 number [give numbers] in reverse sequence [ascending order]; assign numbers in reverse order
♦ 번지를 치매기다 number the houses in reverse order

치먹다 1 〈번호 등이〉 be numbered in reverse order; run upward (in order)
▶ (집) 번지가 치먹었다 The houses are numbered upward. ⇒ The house numbers run upward.
2 〈상품이〉 (local products) sell [be sold] in the metropolis

치먹이다 〈상품을〉 sell (local products) in the metropolitan area; supply (local products) to the capital ♦ 농산물을 서울로 치먹이다 supply [sell] agricultural products to Seoul

치먹히다 be numbered in reverse order ⇨ 치먹다

치면하다 almost full to the brim; brimful

치명상 致命傷 a fatal [mortal] wound
♦ 치명상을 입다 be fatally [mortally] wounded; suffer [receive] a mortal wound / 치명상을 입히다 give sb a mortal wound
▶ 그것이 그에게는 치명상이 되었다 It proved fatal to him.

치명적 致命的 fatal; mortal; deadly; lethal
♦ 치명적 타격을 주다 deal sb a fatal blow / 치명적인 타격을 입다 suffer a deathblow
▶ 그것은 한국의 해외 무역에 치명적인 타격이었다 It was a deathblow to Korea's foreign trade.

치명타 致命打 a fatal [mortal] blow; a deathblow; a disaster ▶ 선거 결과는 당에 치명타가 될지도 모른다 The election results may be a disaster for the party.

치목 治木 〈목재를 다듬고 손질함〉 trimming timber (for building purposes)

—치목하다 trim timber

치목 穉木・稚木 a young plant [tree]; a sapling ♦ 참나무의 치목 a young oak tree; an oak sapling

치민 治民 governing the people
—치민하다 govern [rule over] the people

치밀 緻密 precision; accuracy; minuteness
—치밀하다 precise; minute; fine; nice; elaborate; close; accurate; exact
♦ 치밀한 두뇌 a fine brain / 치밀한 관찰 a careful [close] observation / 치밀한 계획 a carefully thought-out plan / 치밀한 생각 close [careful] thinking / 머리가 치밀한 사람 a fine-thinking man / 치밀한 주의를 요하다 require a close attention; lack accuracy / 치밀하지 못하다 be lacking in precision; lack accuracy / 치밀하게 생각하다 think closely / 치밀하게 조사하다 investigate minutely [closely]
▶ 그 일을 하는 데는 치밀한 계획이 필요하다 Careful planning is needed for the work.

치밀다 1 〈위로 밀다〉 push [thrust, force] up
♦ 죽순이 흙을 치밀고 나오다 bamboo sprouts push up [out] through the earth
2 〈복받치다〉 surge (up); swell; have a fit (of) ♦ 분노가 치밀다 have a fit of anger / (감동으로) 뜨거운 것이 가슴에 치밀다 feel a lump rise in one's [the] throat

치받다 butt up; push up; thrust [stick, knock] up ♦ 머리로 치받다 give sb a butt of head; butt 《sb's chest》

치받이 an upward slope; an ascent; a rise; an up-grade; an uphill way
▶ 길은 거기서부터 치받이가 된다 There the road is running uphill.

치받잇길 an uphill road ♦ 치받잇길을 오르다 go up [ascend, climb (up)] a slope; go uphill

치받치다 1 〈버티다〉 prop (up); support; stick (식물을) ♦ 기둥으로 천장을 치받치다 support a ceiling with a post / 지붕을 치받치다 give support to a roof
2 〈세게 오르다〉 rise; go up; ascend
▶ 연기가 치받친다 Smoke rises.
▶ 불길이 치받친다 A flame flares [blazes] up.
3 ⇨ 치밀다 2
4 〈먹은 것이〉 retch; keck; feel nausea

치병 治病 treatment ⇨ 치료(治療)
—치병하다 cure a disease; treat a disease

치부 恥部 the private parts; the intimate parts of the body

치부 致富 amassment of fortune
—치부하다 make [amass] a fortune; amass [gather, pile up] one's wealth; attain (to) wealth ♦ 주식으로 치부하다 make a killing on the stock market
■ —꾼 one who makes money; a money-maker

치부 置簿 〈기입〉 bookkeeping; booking; 〈장부〉 a ledger —치부하다 keep books; keep accounts; enter in a book ♦ 금액을 아무 앞으로 치부하다 charge [put] 《a sum》 to sb's account
■ 외상— a credit account ■ —책 an account book; a ledger

치분 齒粉 tooth powder

치사 致死 being fatal [lethal] ◆치사의 fatal; mortal; deadly; lethal
■─과실─〖法〗 homicide [death] misadventure 상해─ a bodily injury resulting in death ■─량 a fatal [lethal] dose ─율 lethality

치사 致謝 extending thanks; gratitude; appreciation
─치사하다 thank; express *one's* gratitude; express *one's* appreciation
◆도와준 데 대하여 아무에게 치사하다 thank *sb* for 《his》 help

치사 恥事 shame; disgrace; dishonor; infamy; ignominy; meanness; baseness
─치사하다[스럽다] shameless; infamous; ignominious; disgraceful; mean; base; dirty
◆치사한 인간 a shameless [mean, base] fellow / 치사하게 여기다 be ashamed 《to do》; feel humiliated / 치사스럽게 굴다 behave meanly [shamefully]
▶나는 그런 치사한 짓은 안한다 I am above such meanness.

치산 治山 forestry conservancy [conservation, protection]; antiflood [flood control] afforestation ─치산하다 conserve [protect] the forests; afforest 《a mountain》
■─치수 conservation of rivers and forest: 치산 치수 사업 an anti-erosion project

치산 治産 〈가사의〉 management of household affairs; 〈재산의〉 management of *one's* property [estate] ─치산하다 manage *one's* property [estate]; manage household affairs
■─금─ incompetency 한정─ quasi-incompetency

치살리다 〈치켜세우다〉 laud [extol] *sb* to the skies; speak highly of; flatter
▶나를 너무 치살리지 마 Spare my blushes.

치상 治喪 performance of a funeral ceremony
─치상하다 perform a funeral ceremony; take charge of [attend to] the funeral rites

치상 齒狀 dentiform; tooth-shape
■─구조〖植・動〗 dentation

치석 治石 stone dressing
─치석하다 dress [shape] stone

치석 齒石 tartar 《on the teeth》; dental calculus ◆치석이 끼다 be coated with tartar / 치석을 제거하다 remove [scrape] tartar from *sb's* teeth; scale *sb's* teeth
■─제거 scaling 《of the teeth》 ─제거기 a scaler

치성 致誠 〈신령에의〉 devotions; a fervent prayer ◆치성을 드리다 devote *oneself* 《to spirits》; offer 《up》 a fervent prayer

치세 治世 a reign; a rule; a regime; 〈태평성대〉 peaceful times
◆세종의 치세 the peaceful era of King Sejong / 엘리자베스 1세 하에서 during [in, under] the reign of Elizabeth I

치소 嗤笑 〈빈정거리며 웃음〉 a despising [derisive] laugh
◆치소거리가 되다 be made a laughing stock 《of all》; become the butt of a ridicule
─치소하다 laugh at; ridicule

치솟다 1 〈솟아오르다〉 rise suddenly (and swiftly); skyrocket; shoot up; 〈비행기가〉 zoom ▶물가가 천정 부지로 치솟고 있다 Prices are skyrocketing. **2** ⇨ 치밀다 2

치수 ─數 measure; measurements; dimensions; size
◆치수대로 to measure; according to *one's* [its] measurements / 치수에 맞추어 to measure / 치수가 모자라다 be too short 《for》; be short of measure / 치수를 재다 take *sb's* measurements [measure] 《for a new suit》; measure 《*sb* for clothes》 / 치수를 잘못 재다 take a wrong measure
▶당신의 셔츠 치수는 얼맙니까? What size shirt do you wear? ⇌ What size do you take in shirts?

치수 治水 flood control; river [riparian] improvement; river training
▶그 강의 치수는 대성공이었다 The flood control of the river turned out to be a great success.
─치수하다 regulate rivers [watercourses]; control floods
■─계획 a water control project ─공사 embankment [riparian, flood prevention] works; 《美》 levee works ─공학 hydraulic engineering

치수 齒髓 〖解〗 the dental pulp; the pulp of a tooth
■─강 the pulp cavity ─염 pulpitis

치수내다 ─數─ measure the length 《of》
◆필목을 치수내다 measure the length of a piece of cotton

치술 治術 〈병의〉 the medical [healing] art; medicine; 〈정치의〉 administrative skill; statecraft; statesmanship

치신경 齒神經 〖解〗 the dental nerve

치신사납다 indecent; unbecoming; disreputable; unseemly; unsightly
◆치신사나운 꼴을 보이다 cut an awkward [a ridiculous] figure / 치신사납게 굴다 behave indecently; make a sight of *oneself*

치신없다 undignified; ungentlemanly; unbecoming; unseemly ◆치신없는 사람 a person with no dignity / 치신없게 굴다 behave unseemly [unbecomingly]

치아 齒牙 the teeth ⇨ 이¹ 1
■─학 odontology

치안 治安 (the) public peace (and order); security
◆치안을 어지럽히다 break [disturb] the peace / 치안을 유지하다 maintain public peace and order
■─감 the Senior Superintendent General (略 Sr. Supt. Gen.) ─경찰 the security police ─당국 law enforcement authorities ─문란행위 disorderly conduct ─방해 breach [disturbance] of public order ─방해자 a peace breaker ─유지 maintenance of (the) public order ─재판 a summary trial ─판사 a justice of the peace (略 J.P.)

치약 齒藥 〈연고 모양의〉 toothpaste; dental cream; 〈가루로 된〉 tooth powder; (총칭) dentifrice

치어 稚魚 a fry; the young of fish; a fingerling

치열 治熱 checking fever; 〈해열〉 removal of fever ─**치열하다** check fever; reduce fever ■ 이열(以熱)─ 〈속담〉 Like cures like.

치열 齒列 a row [set] of teeth; a denture ♦ 치열이 고르다[고르지 않다] have a regular [an irregular] set of teeth ■ ─교정 correction of irregularities of the teeth ─교정기 a brace ─교정술 orthodontics; orthodontia ─교정의(醫) an orthodontist

치열 熾烈 violence; severity; intensity; fierceness ─**치열하다** violent; severe; intense; acute; keen; fierce ♦ 치열한 경쟁 (a) keen [sharp, cutthroat] competition; a sharp [hot] contest / 치열한 논쟁 a heated [fiery] discussion / 치열한 전투 a fierce battle [fight]

치오르다 rise (up); go up ♦ 하늘로 치오르다 soar [go up] in the air

치올리다 toss [throw] up; lift [raise] up

치와와 〈멕시코 원산의 작은 개〉 a chihuahua [tʃəwɑ́ːwɑː]

치외법권 治外法權 〔法〕 extraterritoriality; extraterritorial rights; 〈영사 재판권〉 consular jurisdiction [rights] ♦ 치외법권상의 extraterritorial / 치외법권을 행사[철폐]하다 exercise [abolish, relinquish] extraterritoriality

치욕 恥辱 disgrace; dishonor; shame; humiliation; indignity ♦ 국가적인 치욕 a disgrace to the nation; a stain upon the national honor / …을 치욕으로 여기다 be ashamed of 《sb, doing》 / 가문에 치욕을 가져오다 bring disgrace [dishonor] upon (the name of) one's family / 치욕을 참다 bear disgrace; pocket an insult / 치욕을 씻다 wipe away [off] a disgrace; clear one's reputation [dishonor] ▶ 이런 치욕은 내 생전에 처음이다 I have never been disgraced as much as this.

치우 癡愚 imbecility; stupidity

치우다 1 〈정돈하다〉 put sth in order; tidy [straighten] up 〈a room〉; clean up ♦ 부엌을 치우다 straighten (out) the kitchen / 응접실을 치우다 put the parlor in order; tidy [fix] up the parlor / 책상 위를 치우다 clear up one's desk 2 〈옮기다〉 put [take] away 《the tea things》; clear away; get rid of; remove 《the dishes》; 〈방해물을〉 get [put] out of the way ♦ 거치적거리는 것을 치우다 remove an obstacle / 길의 돌을 치우다 remove stones from the road / 밥상을 치우다 remove the dinner table / 의자를 치우다 put the chairs back [set the chairs] in their places / 한 쪽으로 치우다 put sth aside [to one side] ▶ 방안의 잡동사니는 깨끗이 치워졌다 The odds and ends in the room were all cleared away. 3 ⇨ 해치우다 ♦ 먹어 치우다 eat up all / 책 한 권을 읽어 치우다 finish a book 4 〈간수하다〉 stow away; 〈옆으로〉 put away; 〈원래 있던 곳으로〉 put back ♦ 책을 책장에 치우다 put the books away in the bookcase / 물건을 광으로 치우다 store things in a godown / 안전한 곳으로 치우다 take sth into safe keeping 5 〈시집보내다〉 marry 《one's daughter》 off; give 《a man》 the hand of 《one's daughter》

치우치다 〈기울다〉 lean to [toward(s)]; incline toward; 〈편파적이다〉 be one-sided; be prejudiced; be biased; be partial (to); have a partiality (for, to) ♦ 치우친 생각[견해] a biased view; a partial [distorted] view; a prejudice / 서쪽으로 치우치다 lean to the west / 사치에 치우치다 be inclined to luxury / 사랑이 막내 아들에게 치우치다 be partial toward the youngest son ▶ 감정에 치우쳐서는 안된다 Don't be carried away by your emotions [feelings]. ▶ 자네의 치우친 의견은 듣고 싶지 않네 I won't listen to your partial opinion.

치유 治癒 healing; cure; recovery ─**치유하다** heal; cure; be cured; recover ♦ 치유할 수 있는[없는] curable [incurable] / 치유되지 않는 병 a stubborn disease which will yield to no remedy ■ ─기 convalescence ─력 healing power

치은 齒齦 〔解〕〈잇몸〉 the gum(s); the gingiva (pl. -vae) ─염 gingivitis; inflammation of the gums

치음 齒音 〔音聲〕 a dental (sound)

치이다¹ 1 〈무거운 것에〉 be pressed under 《a fallen tree》; be crushed [squeezed] ♦ 무너진 집에 치여 죽다 be crushed to death under a fallen house 2 〈차에〉 be run over (by a train); be hit (by a car) ♦ 차에 치여 죽다 be killed by a car 3 〈덫에〉 be trapped [entrapped]; be caught ♦ 쥐가 덫에 치였다 A rat was trapped [was caught in the trap].

치이다² 〈피륙의 올이 한쪽으로 쏠리다〉 lose (its) weave; 〈솜 등이 뭉치다〉 form into a lump; lump (up) ▶ 방석의 솜이 치여 거북하다 The cushion lumped up into uncomfortable hard wads.

치이다³ 〈값이〉 cost; amount to 《so much》; be priced; be valued ♦ 비싸게 치이다 come [prove to be] expensive / 싸게 치이다 come little; come cheap ▶ 그렇게 하는 것이 값싸게 치인다 It comes cheaper to do so. ▶ 그것은 한 개에 300원씩 치였다 It cost me three hundred won a piece.

치인 癡人 a simpleton; an idiot; a fool

치자 治者 a ruler; a governor

치자 梔子 a gardenia seed ■ ─나무 a Cape jasmine; a gardenia

치자 癡者 a fool ⇨ 치인(癡人)

치자다소 癡者多笑 〈속담〉 A fool laughs over nothing. ⇌ A fool is easily tempted to laugh.

치잡다 snatch up

치장 治粧 〈장식〉 ornamentation; decoration; adornment; embellishment; 〈화장〉 toilet; makeup ♦ 가게의 치장 shop decoration / 몸치장 personal adornment; dressing up ▶ 그녀는 장보러 가는 데도 치장에 많은 시간이 걸린다 She takes much time in dressing even

when she just goes shopping.
―치장하다 ornament; decorate; adorn; deck [trick] out [up]; bedeck; embellish; dress; 〈화장하다〉 make up
♦보석으로 치장한 귀부인 a lady glittering [bedecked] with jewels / 몸을 치장하다 dress up [out]; deck up 《with jewels》; adorn *oneself* /집을 치장하다 decorate [pretty up] *one's* house / 잔뜩 치장하고 나서다 go out all dolled up

치적 治績 (the results of an) administration
♦…의 치적을 기념하여 비를 세우다 erect a monument in commemoration of *sb's* remarkable executive services

치정 癡情 a foolish passion; blind love; infatuation ♦치정에 의한 범죄 a crime of passion / 치정에 빠지다[눈이 멀다] be blinded with [by] passion
▶ 두 사람 사이에 치정 관계가 있었던 것 같다 It is suspected that there was a liaison [amorous relationship] between the two.
―살인(사건) a sex [scandalous] murder (case)

치조 齒槽 〔解〕 an alveolus 《*pl.* -li》; the socket of a tooth ■―농루(膿漏) pyorrhea alveolarice

치졸 稚拙 clumsiness; artlessness ―치졸하다 clumsy; naive; (awkwardly) artless

치죄 治罪 punishment ―치죄하다 punish *sb* for 《his》 crime; punish a crime

치중 置重 attachment of weight [importance] [to, on] ―치중하다 attach weight [importance] to; stress; emphasize; lay stress [emphasis] on [upon]; put [set] value on
♦지나치게 치중하다 give undue value to / 교육에 치중하다 attach importance to education; value [make much of] education
▶ 이 학교에서는 영어에 치중하고 있다 Special importance is attached to the teaching of English in this school.

치중 輜重 〈군수품〉 military supplies [stores]; impedimenta; 〈말에 실은 짐〉 a pack [load] on a horse

치즈 cheese ♦치즈 덩어리 a chunk of cheese / 치즈 한 조각 a cheese / 치즈를 얹은 빵 bread and cheese

치지도외하다 置之度外― leave *sth* out of account [consideration]; ignore 《it》 utterly

치질 痔疾 piles; hemorrhoids
♦치질이 있다 have [suffer from] piles / 치질을 절제하다 remove hemorrhoids
■수― external hemorrhoids; blind piles 암― internal hemorrhoids ■―수술 hemorrhoidectomy ―환자 a victim of [a sufferer from] piles

치천하다 治天下― reign [rule] over the (whole) Empire; govern the whole country

치다 stroke [draw a line] upward ♦획을 치 치다 make an upward stroke (in writing)

치켜들다 〈올려 들다〉 raise; lift ♦칼을 치켜들고 with a sword raised overhead / 머리를 치켜들다 raise *one's* head; toss the head

치켜세우다 praise [extol] *sb* to the skies; pay *sb* a compliment; say pretty [nice] things 《to》; flatter ♦치켜세워서 우쭐하게 하다 get *sb* all puffed up with pride by praising 《him》 sky-high
▶ 그는 조금만 치켜세워도 우쭐해한다 A little flattery will fetch him.

치키다 raise; lift; heave; boost; pull [draw] up ♦치맛자락을 치키다 tuck up the skirt / 눈썹을 치켜 올리다 raise *one's* eyebrows / 머리를 치켜 깎다 trim *sb's* hair up; have *one's* hair cut short / 큰 돌을 치켜 들다 heave up a large stone

치킨 chicken ■―라이스 chicken and rice fried and seasoned with tomato catsup ―수프 chicken soup

치타 〔動〕 a cheetah

치태 癡態 foolery; silliness
♦치태를 부리다 make a fool of *oneself*; cut a ludicrous figure

치통 齒痛 (a) toothache; odontalgia; dentalgia
♦치통이 나다 have [suffer from] a toothache
▶ 주사를 맞았더니 치통이 좀 가라앉았다 The injection eased the toothache a little.

치평하다 治平― (be) peaceful by good [wise] government

치하 治下 under the rule [government, regime] 《of》
♦엘리자베스 여왕 치하의 영국 England under the reign of Queen Elizabeth / 공산당 치하의 Communist-ruled 《countries》/ 세종대왕 치하에서 during [in, under] the reign of King Sejong

치하 致賀 appreciation; compliment; 〈축하〉 congratulation; 〈칭찬〉 praise
―치하하다 appreciate; compliment; praise; admire; congratulate; felicitate
♦치하하는 연설 a complimentary address [speech] / 노고를 치하하다 show appreciation of *sb's* effort / 용기를 치하하다 compliment *sb* on 《his》 courage / 성공을 치하하다 congratulate [felicitate] *sb* on 《his》 success

치한 癡漢 a molester of women; 《俗》 a wolf; 《美俗》 a masher

치행 癡行 a folly; a foolish act [move]; foolery

치환 置換 transposition; 〔數·化〕 substitution; replacement ―치환하다 substitute; displace; replace; transpose ♦치환할 수 있는 〔化〕 displaceable / A로 B를 치환하다 substitute A for B

칙령 勅令 《issue》 a royal edict [decree, ordinance]

칙명 勅命 a royal order [command, commission, mandate] ♦칙명을 받들어 in obedience to a royal command

칙사 勅使 a royal envoy [messenger]

칙서 勅書 a royal letter [message]

칙선 勅選 royal nomination

칙어 勅語 a royal rescript [edict, message]

칙유 勅諭 royal instructions; a royal mandate

칙임 勅任 royal appointment

칙재 勅裁 royal decision [sanction]

칙지 勅旨 〈칙명〉 a royal order [mandate, wishes] ♦칙지를 받들어 in obedience to the royal wishes

칙칙폭폭 1 〈기차소리〉 chug-chug; chuff-chuff; puff-puff
♦ 칙칙폭폭 소리를 내며 지나가다 chug [chuff] along
2 〈기차〉 (兒) a choochoo (train)

칙칙하다 dark; somber; dull
♦ 칙칙한 빛깔 a dark [heavy] color / 칙칙해 보이다 look dark and dull

칙필 勅筆 a royal autograph; the king's own handwriting

칙허 勅許 royal sanction [grant, consent, permission]

친- 親 1 〈혈연의〉 own; full; whole; true; real; german
♦ 친어머니[아버지] one's own [true, real] mother [father] / 친형제[자매] one's own [full, whole, true, real, blood] brothers [sisters]; one's brothers-[sisters-]german
▶ 그애는 내 친자식이오 He is my own child.
2 〈친밀한〉 favoring; pro-
♦ 친서방의 pro-Western
3 〈몸소〉 (for) oneself; in person; personally

친가 親家 a woman's native home ⇨ 친정(親庭)

친경 親耕 royal plowing in person
—친경하다 (the king) plow in person

친고 親告 [法] a victim's complaint
—친고하다 make a criminal complaint
■—죄 an offense subject to complaint

친고 親故 relatives and acquaintances

친교 親交 (intimate) friendship; intimacy; good fellowship; friendly [intimate] relations
♦ 친교가 있다 be on friendly [close, intimate] terms 《with》; be good friends 《with》 / 친교를 도모하다 promote friendly relations 《with》 / 친교를 맺다 contract [form] a (warm) friendship 《with》 / 20년간 지속된 친교를 끊다 break off a friendship of twenty years' standing

친구 親舊 a friend; 〈동지〉 a companion; a mate; a fellow; a comrade; (口) a pal; (口) a chum; 〈교우〉 a circle; company
♦ 술[낚시] 친구 a boon [fishing] companion / 외국인 친구 one's foreign friend / 학교친구 a schoolmate / 오랜 친구 a long-time friend; an old friend / 좋은 친구 a good friend / 친한 친구 a close [an intimate] friend / 막역한 친구 a sworn [bosom] friend / 평생의 친구 a lifelong friend / 못믿을 친구 a fair-weather friend / 친구와의 우정을 생각해서 for friendship's sake / 못된 친구와 어울리다 get [fall] into bad company / 좋은[나쁜] 친구와 사귀다 keep good [bad] company / 친구가 되다 make friends 《with》; form a friendship 《with》 / 친구가 되고 싶어하다 seek the company [friendship] 《of》 / 친구가 되어 주다 keep company 《with them》 / 친구가 없다 have no friends; be friendless / 친구를 사귀다 make a friend
▶ 그는 친구가 아주 많다 He has a very wide circle of [a great many] friends.
▶ 친구는 얻기보다 잃기가 쉽다 A friend is easier lost than found.
▶ 어려울 때의 친구가 진짜 친구다 (속담) A friend in need is a friend indeed.
▶ 사귀는 친구를 보면 그 사람됨을 알 수 있다 People are judged by the company they keep.

친권 親權 parental authority ♦ 친권을 행사하다 exercise parental authority
■—자 a person in parental authority

친근 親近 intimacy; friendship; familiarity
—친근하다 intimate; friendly; close; familiar 《with》
♦ 친근한 사이 intimate relationship / 친근한 사이다 be on good [friendly] terms 《with》; be friends 《with》 / 매우 친근하다 be hand and [in] glove 《with each other》

친근감 親近感 a sense [feeling] of intimacy [familiarity]; friendly feeling; affection
♦ 부모 자식 간의 친근감 affection between parent and child / 친근감이 들다 entertain friendly sentiments 《toward》; feel friendly 《toward》

친기 親忌 the annual sacrifice to one's departed parent

친남매 親男妹 one's own brothers and sisters

친누이 親— one's own sister

친독 親獨 ♦ 친독의 pro-German
■—주의 pro-Germanism

친동기 親同氣 one's own brothers and sisters ⇨ 친남매(親男妹)

친동생 親同獨 one's own younger brother [sister] ⇨ 친아우

친등 親等 the degree of kinship [consanguinity, relationship (by blood)] ⇨ 촌수

친모 親母 one's own mother ⇨ 친어머니

친목 親睦 friendship; friendliness intimacy; amity ♦ 상호 친목을 도모하다 cultivate [promote, enhance] mutual friendship
▶ 회원의 친목을 도모하는 것이 우리의 첫째 목적입니다 Our first aim is to promote friendship [fraternity] among the members.
—친목하다 intimate; friendly
■—단체 a friendly society —회 an informal social gathering; a mixer; (美) a get-together meeting

친미 親美 ♦ 친미의 pro-American
■—노선 the pro-American line —정책 a pro-American policy —주의 pro-Americanism

친밀 親密 friendliness; close friendship; 〈단체·국가 간의〉 amity; intimacy
—친밀하다 friendly; familiar; close; (口) chummy; thick; intimate (▶intimate는 「성적 관계를 맺고 있다」는 뜻이 되는데 유의할 것)
♦ 친밀히 intimately; closely / …와 친밀하다 be on friendly terms 《with》; be very good friends 《with》; (口) be thick 《with》 / 친밀해지다 become intimate 《with》; make friends 《with》
▶ 그는 그 여배우와 친밀하다 He is on intimate [friendly] terms with the actress.

친부 親父 one's own father ⇨ 친아버지

친부모 親父母 one's own parents
▶ 친부모보다 길러준 부모가 낫다 The foster parent is dearer to one than the real parent.

친분 親分 acquaintance(ship); friendship; intimacy; familiarity
♦ 친분이 있다 be acquainted [familiar] 《with》 / 친분이 없다 have no acquaintance 《with》; be not close [intimate] 《with》 / 친분

이 깊다 be intimate 《with》; be on intimate terms 《with》 / 친분이 두터워지다 get more closely acquainted / 친분을 맺다 make *sb's* acquaintance; get [become] acquainted 《with》

친불 親佛 ◆ 친불의 pro-French
━━주의자 a pro-French

친불친 親不親 the relative degree of intimacy ⇨ 친소(親疎)

친사돈 親査頓 the parents of *one's* son-[daughter-]in-law

친산 親山 *one's* parents' graves

친상 親喪 mourning for *one's* parent; bereavement of *one's* parent ◆ 친상을 당하다 lose [be bereaved of] *one's* parent; have *one's* parent die

친생자 親生子 *one's* (real) child; a child of *one's* own

친서 親書 an autographed letter; a personal letter [message] ◆ 대통령의 친서 an autograph letter [a personal message] from the President / 친서를 휴대하다 carry a personal letter 《from》
━친서하다 write 《a letter》 in person

친선 親善 friendship; friendly relations [ties]; amity; goodwill
◆ 주변국들과의 친선 amity with surrounding nations / 한미 간의 친선을 강화하다 strengthen the ties of friendship between Korea and America / 국제 친선을 도모하다 cultivate [promote] international friendship / 국제 친선에 기여하다 contribute to a better international friendship
━━경기 a friendly match; a game [match] to promote goodwill ━━관계 friendly [amicable] relations 《between, among》 ━━방문 (pay) a goodwill visit 《to a country》 ━━비행 a goodwill flight ━━사절 a goodwill envoy; 〈사절단〉 a goodwill mission ━━조약 a treaty of amity

친소 親疎 the relative degree of intimacy
◆ 친소간에 whether intimate or not [near or distant]; regardless of relationship / 친소를 가리다 discriminate among *one's* friends according to their intimacy with *one*; show favoritism / 친소를 가리지 않고 사귀다 mix with everybody without discrimination

친속 親屬 a relative ⇨ 친족(親族)

친손녀 親孫女 a daughter of *one's* son; *one's* granddaughter

친손자 親孫子 a son of *one's* son; *one's* own grandson

친솔 親率 the members of *one's* family; *one's* family

친수 親受 personal receipt [acceptance]
━친수하다 receive [accept] in person [personally]

친수 親授 personal investiture ━친수하다 bestow in person; invest personally

친수성 親水性 〈化〉 hydrophile

친숙 親熟 familiarity; acquaintance; being familiar; intimacy
━친숙하다 close; familiar; well acquainted
◆ 친숙한 사이 a familiar acquaintance / 친숙한 사이다 be well acquainted 《with》 / 친숙해지다 become familiar [acquainted] 《with》; make friends 《with》

친아들 親— *one's* true [real] son; *one's* son by blood

친아버지 親— *one's* own father

친아우 親— *one's* own younger brother [sister]

친애 親愛 affection; love; intimacy
━친애하다 love; feel affection for
◆ 친애하는 벗 *one's* dear friend / 친애하는 상배군 my dear (Mr.) Sang-bae / 친애하는 dear; beloved
▶ 친애하는 신사 숙녀 여러분 Ladies and gentlemen!

친어머니 親— *one's* own mother

친언니 親— *one's* own elder sister

친영 親英 ◆ 친영의 pro-British ━정책 a pro-British policy ━주의 Anglophilism ━주의자 a pro-British; an Anglophil(e) ━파 the pro-British

친우 親友 a friend ⇨ 친구

친위대 親衛隊 the bodyguards 《to the Queen》; the royal guards

친의 親誼 acquaintance ⇨ 친분(親分)

친일 親日 ◆ 친일의 pro-Japanese
━━파 the pro-Japanese

친자 親炙 a close contact with *one's* teacher
━친자하다 have a close contact with *one's* teacher; be under the personal influence of *one's* master

친자식 親子息 *one's* true [real] child; *one's* child by blood

친전 親展 Confidential; Personal
━서 a confidential [personal] letter

친절 親切 kindness; goodness; goodwill; friendliness; hospitality; a favor
◆ 자그마한 친절 a small kindness / 친절을 핑계삼아 under the show [pretense] of kindness / 친절을 베풀다 be kind to *sb*; show *sb* kindness; do *sb* a good turn; be good to *sb* / 친절을 다하다 show *sb* every kindness / 친절에 보답하다 repay *sb's* kindness / 친절을 이용하다 take advantage of *sb's* kindness
━친절하다 kind; friendly; good; obliging; cordial; warm-hearted
◆ 친절한 말 kind words / 친절한 행위 a kind act; an act of kindness / 친절한 사람 a kind person / 친절한 마음에서 in [out of] kindness / 친절해 보이는 kindly-looking / 친절히 kindly; kindheartedly; with kindness; cordially / 친절하게도 …하다 be kind [good] enough to 《do》; be so kind as to 《do》
▶ 그는 친절하게도 시내 구경을 시켜 주었다 He was kind [good] enough to show me around the city. ⇌ He was so kind as to show me around the city. ⇌ He kindly showed me around the city.
▶ 그는 원래 친절하다 He is kindly by nature. ⇌ He was born a kind man.
▶ 그들은 모두 우리에게 아주 친절했다 They were all very friendly to us.
▶ 친절하신 말씀 고맙습니다 It is very kind of you to say so. ⇌〈여자에게〉 It's very sweet of

친정 親政 royal governing in person
―친정하다 (the king) rule [govern] in person
친정 親庭 a woman's native home; one's parents' [parental] home
▶ 집사람은 친정에 가 있습니다 My wife stays now with her parents.
친족 親族 a relative; a relation
■ 부계― an agnate 모계― a cognate 직계[방계]― a lineal [collateral] relative ■ ―관계 kinship; relationship by blood and marriage ―법 the Domestic Relations Law; the law of domestic relations ―회의 a family council; a conference of one's relatives
친지 親知 acquaintances; a friend; kith
▶ 그에게는 친지가 많다 He has a wide [large] acquaintance. ■ ―관계 acquaintanceship
친척 親戚 a relative; a relation; 〈남자〉 a kinsman; 〈여자〉 a kinswoman; 〈총칭〉 kinsfolk
♦ 아버지[어머니] 쪽의 친척 one's relative on the paternal [maternal] side / 촌수가 가까운 [먼] 친척 a near [distant] relative / 친척간이다 be of kinship (with) / 친척처럼 가까이 지내다 associate practically as relatives (with)
♦ 그분은 당신과 친척입니까? Are you related to him?
■ ―일가 one's kith and kin; all one's relatives ■ ―관계 kinship; relationship
친친 round and round (about); coil upon coil
♦ 밧줄을 친친 감다 wind a rope round sth / 친친 감기다 coil [wind itself] (a)round (a tree)
친친하다 unpleasantly damp [moist] and sticky; clammy ♦ 친친한 손 clammy hands
▶ 나는 땀이 나서 등이 친친했다 My back was clammy with perspiration.
친칠라 〈動〉 a chinchilla
친탁하다 親― take after [resemble] one's father's side of the family
친필 親筆 one's own handwriting; an autograph; 〈法〉 a holograph
♦ 친필로 in one's own hand [handwriting]; autographically
■ ―편지 an autograph letter (of)
친하다 親― 1 〈가깝다〉 familiar; close; friendly; near; intimate (▶intimate는 주로 남녀간의 성적 관계를 말할 때 쓰이므로 주의할 것)
♦ 친한 친구 a good [close] friend; a bosom [an intimate] friend / 친한 사이다 be on good [friendly] terms (with); be friends (with) / 친해지다 make friends (with); grow intimate (with); become familiar [intimate] (with); chum up (with) / 친하게 지내다 have a friendly [close] relation (with); associate on good terms (with)
▶ 그들은 무척 친한 친구다 They are very close friends.
▶ 두 사람은 우연히 친해졌다 Chance made them acquainted with each other.
▶ 친한 사이에도 예의는 지켜야 한다 There should be courtesy even between close friends.
2 〈가까이 하다〉 make friends (with); associate on good terms (with); familiarize oneself (with)

♦ 친하기 쉬운 사람 a genial and accessible person / 친하기 어려운 사람 an unfriendly and inaccessible person / 자연과 친하다 commune [hold communion] with nature
친할머니 親― one's own grandmother
친할아버지 親― one's own grandfather
친형 親兄 one's own elder brother
친화 親和 friendship; friendly relations
―친화하다 make [be] friends (with)
■ ―도 〈化〉 an affinity; an appetence
친환 親患 one's parent's illness ♦ 친환이 있다 one's parent [father, mother] is ill
친히 親― 1 〈친하게〉 intimately; in a friendly way
♦ 친히 사귀다 be on friendly terms (with); associate on good terms (with)
2 〈몸소〉 personally; in person
♦ 친히 보다 see with one's own eyes / 친히 지휘하다 take personal command (of) / 친히 방문하다 pay a visit in person
칠 七 seven ⇨ 제 칠 the seventh
칠 漆 1 〈옻칠〉 lacquering
2 〈도료〉 paints; daubs; varnishes; 〈칠하기〉 varnishing; painting
♦ 물감질 daubing colors on sth / 페인트칠 painting / 풀칠 pasting / 칠공사 a painter's work / 한 번의 칠 one coat (of paint) / 회칠 한 벽 a white-plastered wall / 벽에 흰 칠을 하다 paint [plaster] a wall white / 칠이 벗겨지다 the paint comes [peels] off
▶ 칠조심 (게시) 〈美〉 Wet 〈英〉 Fresh Paint.
3 〈얼룩〉 a stain; a blot; a smut; a smear
♦ 흙 칠 a mud stain; a smear of mud
칠각형 七角形 a heptagon
♦ 칠각형의 heptangular; heptagonal
칠거지악 七去之惡 the seven valid causes for divorce
칠기 漆器 1 wooden lacquer ware ⇨ 칠목기
2 lacquer(ed) ware; lacquer(-work)
칠대불가사의 七大不可思議 the seven wonders (of the world)
칠대양 七大洋 the Seven Seas
칠독 漆毒 〈옻독〉 poison by ivy
칠떡거리다 drag; draggle; trail ♦ 치마가 땅에 칠떡거리다 one's skirt drags on the ground
칠떡칠떡 draggingly; dragglingly; drably
칠뜨기 七― a half-wit ⇨ 칠삭동이 2
칠락팔락 七落八落 confusion ⇨ 칠령팔락
칠럼거리다 〈물이〉 spill [splash] over; slop over; brim over (with)
♦ 국이 칠럼거리게 휘정대며 나르다 carry the soup so unsteadily that it slops over
칠럼칠럼 spilling [splashing] over; brimming over ―칠럼칠럼하다 spill over
칠렁거리다 brim over; be brimful
칠렁칠렁 to the brim; brimfully
―칠렁칠렁하다 full to the brim; filled (with water) to the brim; brimful
▶ 물이 칠렁칠렁한 대야 a basin filled to the brim with water
칠레 〈나라 이름〉 Chile; 〈공식명〉 the Republic of Chile
♦ 칠레의 Chilean ■ ―사람 a Chilean; a Chilian ■ ―초석 Chile saltpeter [niter]

칠령팔락 七零八落 confusion; disorder; irregularity; muddly; pell-mell; mess; topsy-turviness
—칠령팔락하다 (utterly) confused; disorderly; disordered; irregular; pell-mell; jumbly; topsy-turvy; higgledy-piggledy; 《be》 at sixes and sevens

칠면조 七面鳥 1 〔鳥〕 a turkey
♦ 수칠면조 a male turkey; a gobbler; 《英》 a turkey cock / 암칠면조 a turkey hen / 칠면조 새끼 a turkey poult
▶ 칠면조가 운다 A turkey gobbles.
2 〈변덕쟁이〉 a man of moods; capricious person

칠목기 漆木器 wooden lacquer [japan] ware
칠박 漆— a large lacquered wooden bowl
칠변형 七邊形 a heptagon
칠보 七寶 〔佛敎〕 the seven treasures
■—자기 (프) cloisonné (ware)
칠보재 七步才 〈문재(文才)에 뛰어남〉 outstanding [excellent] literary talent [ability]; 〈시재(詩才)에 뛰어남〉 eminent [superb] poetic gift [genius]
칠분도미 七分搗米 seventy-percent polished rice
칠붓 漆— a lacquer brush
칠삭동이 七朔童— 1 〈조산아〉 an infant born in the seventh month of pregnancy
2 〈바보〉 a half-wit; a lackwit
칠색 七色 seven colors (of the rainbow)
칠서 七書 the Seven Chineses Classics
칠석 七夕 〈명절〉 the seventh day of the seventh lunar month ■—물 the rainfall on the seventh of the seventh lunar month —제(祭) the Festival of the Weaver [Vega]
칠성 七星 the Great Bear ⇨ 북두칠성
■—각[당] a shrine to the Great Dipper
칠성장어 七星長魚 〔魚〕 a lamprey
칠성판 七星板 a mortuary plank (containing seven holes representing the Dipper)
♦ 칠성판을 지다 〈죽다〉 die; 〈사지에 들다〉 risk death; enter the jaws of death
칠소반 漆小盤 a lacquer(ed) tray; a small lacquer dining table
칠순 七旬 1 〈일혼 날〉 seventy days
2 〈일혼 살〉 seventy years of age
■—노인 a septuagenarian; an old man [woman] at the age of seventies
칠십 七十 seventy; 〈인간의 수명〉 threescore (years) and ten ♦ 제칠십 the seventieth / 칠십대의 노인 a septuagenary old man
칠야 漆夜 a pitch-dark[-black] night
칠언절구 七言絶句 a quatrain with seven words to a [each] line
칠오조 七五調 the seven-and-five-syllable meter
♦ 칠오조의 시 a poem [verse] in seven-and-five-syllable meter
칠요일 七曜日 the seven days of the week
칠월 七月 July (略 Jul.)
■—혁명 the July Revolution (프랑스의)
칠일 漆— lacquering; lacquer work; 〈페인트 칠〉 painting
칠일장 七日葬 a burial on the seventh day after death; 《have》 a seven-day funeral

칠전팔기 七顚八起 indomitability
♦ 칠전팔기의 정신 an indomitable spirit; fortitude of mind
■—칠전팔기하다 fall down seven times and [but] get up eight (times); never give in to adversity; stand firm in difficulties
칠전팔도하다 七顚八倒— writhe in agony; toss *oneself* about in great pain; go through many hardships
칠정 七情 the seven feelings [emotions] (i.e. joy, anger, sorrow, fear, love, hate, lust)
칠창 漆瘡 〔韓醫〕an acute skin disease caused by lacquer poison
칠칠치못하다 slovenly; untidy 《dress》; dowdy; careless; loose; messy; draggletailed
♦ 칠칠치 못한 사람 a sloven; a sloppy person; (口) a slob / 칠칠치 못한 여자 a loose woman; a slattern; a slut
▶ 그는 모든 일에 칠칠치못하다 He does everything in a slovenly way [slipshod manner].
▶ 일하는 것이 칠칠치 못하다 He lacks method in his business.
칠칠하다 1 〈길차다〉 exuberant; fresh and crisp
♦ 칠칠한 배추 fresh and crisp cabbages
2 〈깔끔하다〉 decent; decorous; proper
3 〈민첩하다〉 brisk; smart; nimble; sharp
♦ 칠칠하게 일하다 work with alacrity
칠판 漆板 a blackboard
♦ 분필로 칠판에 쓰다 put down 《words》 on the board with chalk / 칠판을 지우다 wipe [erase, clean (off)] the blackboard
■—지우개 an [a chalk] eraser; a wiper
칠팔월 七八月 July and [or] August
칠팔월 수숫잎 〈속담〉 a (fainthearted) and capricious [whimsical] person; a timorous man of incalculable moods
칠팔월 은어 끓듯 한다 〈속담〉 One has a hard time to make a living because of a sudden drop [decrease] of income.
칠포 漆布 1 〈칠을 한 천〉 a lacquered (hemp) cloth **2** 〈관에 붙이는〉 lacquered cloth for covering a coffin
칠하다 漆— 〈유채 물감·페인트를〉 paint; 〈모르타르 등을〉 plaster; 〈니스를〉 varnish; 〈옻을〉 lacquer; 〈수채 물감·유약을〉 coat; 〈비누·페인트를〉 apply
♦ 갓 칠한 페인트 raw [fresh] paint / 처덕처덕 칠하다 daub (paint) all over *sth*; bedaub 《with》/ 새까맣게 칠하다 paint *sth* jetblack / 흰 에나멜을 두 번 칠하다 give [apply] two coats of white enamel 《to》/ 벽에 페인트를 칠하다 paint a wall; coat [cover] a wall with paint / 지도에 색을 칠하다 color a map / 테이블에 골고루 니스를 칠하다 varnish over a table / 칠하여 지우다 paint out (a signboard)
▶ 그는 벽을 녹색으로 칠했다 He has painted the wall green.
▶ 그는 표면에 페인트를 칠해서 마무리했다 He finished it up by coating the surface with paint.
칠함 漆函 a lacquered box [case, chest]
칠현 七賢 the Seven Sages (of ancient China)
칠현금 七絃琴 a seven-stringed lute; a hepta-

chord
칠화 漆畫 a lacquer painting
칠흑 漆黑 coal-black; pitch-black; jet-black
♦칠흑같은 밤 a pitch-dark [jet-black] night / 칠흑같은 어둠 pitch-darkness / 칠흑같은 머리 raven(-black) hair
칡 〔植〕 an arrowroot
■―가루〔전분〕 arrowroot starch ―덩굴 the vines of arrowroots
칡범 〈수범〉 a tiger; 〈암범〉 a tigress
칡소 a striped ox 〔cow〕
침 saliva; spit; spittle; sputum 《pl. -ta, ~s》
♦침을 뱉다 spit 《on, at》; salivate / 침이 마르도록 칭찬하다 be very loud in sb's praise; speak in the highest terms 《of》 / 침을 튀기다 froth at the mouth / 남의 얼굴에 침을 튀기다 spit in sb's face / 침을 삼키다 swallow one's saliva; 〈초조해서〉 catch [hold] one's breath; strain one's attention; 〈군침이 돌다〉 lust 《for》; gloat 《on, over》; be envious 《of》 / 손가락에 침을 묻혀서 책장을 넘기다 turn leaves with wet fingers [with fingers moistened]/ 침을 흘리다 drivel; slobber; salivate; slaver; 〈군침을 흘리다〉 slaver over
▶침을 뱉지 마시오 《게시》 No spitting.
▶보도에 침을 뱉으면 안된다 Don't spit on the sidewalk.
▶그에게 침이라도 뱉어주고 싶었다 I would have spat on [at] him.
■―샘 salivary gland ―샘염색체 salivary gland chromosome
침 針 1 〈바늘〉 a needle; 〈시계의〉 a hand 2 〈가시〉 a thorn; 〈벌 등의〉 a sting(er)
침 鍼 〈도구〉 a acus; a needle; 〈침술〉 acupuncture
♦침놓다〔주다〕 acupuncture; apply [treat with] acupuncture / 침을 맞다 get acupunctured; be treated with acupuncture
침감 沈― a persimmon sweetened in salt water
침강 沈降 〔地〕 subsidence; sedimentation; precipitation
―침강하다 precipitate; subside; settle 《down》
■―반응 precipitation reaction ―소(素) 〈혈액중의〉 precipitin ―속도 〈혈액의〉 sedimentation velocity ―장치 a sinking set ―해안 〔地〕 a plunging coast
침골 枕骨 the suboccipital bone
침공 侵攻 (an) invasion; a raid; an attack
―침공하다 invade; make an invasion 《upon》; raid 《into》; attack
침구 寢具 bedclothes; bed clothing; bedding
♦침구를 개다〔펴다〕 fold up [lay out] bedclothes [bedding]
침구 鍼灸 〔韓醫〕 〈침질과 뜸질〉 acupuncture and moxibustion
■―술 (the art of) acupuncture and moxibustion ―술사 an acupuncturist and moxacauterizer
침낭 寢囊 a sleeping bag
침노하다 侵擄― invade; raid; make an inroad upon 《a country》; encroach upon 《the territory of》
침담그다 沈― cure 《persimmons》 in salt water; remove the astringency 《of》
침대 寢臺 a bedstead; a bed; 〈열차·선박의〉 a (sleeping) berth
♦접는 침대 a folding [collapsible] bed / 침대겸용 소파 a sofa bed / 《침대칸의》 상단 [하단] 침대 an upper [a lower] berth / 침대칸을 예약하다 reserve [book] a berth
■―권 a berth ticket ―보[커버] a bedspread; a bedcover ―요금 a berth charge ―차 《美》 a sleeper; a sleeping car [carriage]

침대

베개 pillow
헤드보드 headboard
담요 blanket
매트리스 mattress
침대 다리 bedpost
시트 sheet
풋보드 footboard

침독 鍼毒 poisoning caused by improper practice of acupuncture
침략 侵掠 pillage; plunder; spoilage; spoliation
―침략하다 plunder; pillage; despoil; loot
침략 侵略 (an) aggression; (an) invasion; a raid; an inroad
♦바다로부터의 침략 a seaborne invasion / 침략적(인) aggressive / 공산군의 침략을 격퇴하다 repel Communist [Red] aggression
▶타국의 무력 침략을 피하기가 아주 어려웠다 It was very difficult to keep away from other countries' armed aggression.
―침략하다 invade; raid; make a raid 《on》; make an inroad 《into》; conquer
■―경제― an economic invasion 무력― an armed aggression 직접[간접]― a direct [an indirect] invasion ■―국 an aggressor nation; an aggressor ―군 an invading army ―자 an aggressor; an invader ―전쟁 a war of aggression; an aggressive war ―주의 a policy of aggression; an aggressive policy ―행위 an act of aggression
침례 浸禮 〔基〕 baptism by immersion; immersion
♦침례를 베풀다 immerse; baptize immersion
■―교도 a Baptist ―교회 the Baptist Church
침로 針路 a course
♦침로를 정하다 fix one's course 《for, toward》 / 침로를 바꾸다 turn [alter, change, shift] one's course 《toward》 / 침로에서 벗어나다 deviate from [go off] one's course / 침로를 북으로 잡다 steer one's course northward; take a northerly course / 침로를 잘못 잡다 take a wrong course 《in life》
침마취 鍼痲醉 anesthesia by acupuncture
♦침마취를 시키다 anesthetize by acupuncture
침맞다 鍼― get acupunctured; be treated

with acupuncture

침모 針母 a seamstress; a needlewoman
■난— a daily [live-out] seamstress 든— a resident [live-in] seamstress

침목 枕木 (美) a (railroad) tie; a crosstie; (英) a sleeper ♦ 침목을 갈다 renew the ties
■철도— a sleeper; a rail tie

침몰 沈沒 sinking; submersion; 〈침수에 의한〉foundering
▶ 배는 가까스로 침몰을 면했다 The ship managed to escape being submerged.
—침몰하다 sink; go down; be submerged; founder
♦ 수백 명의 승객을 태운 채 침몰하다 sink with hundreds of passengers on board / 침몰시키다 sink [submerge] 《a vessel》; send 《a ship》 to the bottom / 〈배밑·뱃전에〉구멍을 뚫어 침몰시키다 scuttle 《a ship》
▶ 배는 승무원 전원과 함께 침몰했다 The ship sank with all her crew.
▶ 배는 변산반도 앞에서 침몰했다 The ship sank off the Pyŏnsanpando.

침몰선 沈沒船 a sunken [submerged] ship
♦ 침몰선을 인양하다 salve a sunken vessel —인양 작업 salvage operations [work]

침묵 沈默 〈소리가 없음〉silence; 〈말이 없음〉taciturnity; reticence
♦ 깊은[무거운] 침묵 a deep [an oppressive] silence / 침묵을 지키다 keep silent; observe [keep, maintain, preserve] silence; remain silent [mute, dumb]; keep one's tongue quiet / 침묵을 깨다 break one's [the] silence
▶ 침묵은 금이다 (속담) Silence is gold(en).
▶ 무거운 침묵이 계속되었다 There continued weighted silence.
▶ 나는 그의 침묵을 묵인으로 받아들였다 I took his silence to be a tacit consent.
▶ 그는 오랜 침묵을 깨고 신작을 발표했다 He made a new work public after many years of silence.
—침묵하다 hold one's tongue; become silent; fall into silence
♦ 침묵시키다 silence; put [reduce] sb to silence; 〈설득으로〉argue sb into silence / 적의 포화를 침묵시키다 silence the enemy's fire
▶ 그의 한 마디에 상대는 침묵했다 One word he uttered silenced his opponent.

침방 寢房 a bedroom

침뱉다 spit 《on, at》; expectorate; salivate
♦ 남의 얼굴에 침뱉다 spit in sb's face; spit at sb; (비유) humiliate; insult / 자기 얼굴에 침뱉다 disgrace oneself

침 범 侵犯 1 〈침 입〉 (an) invasion; (an) aggression; (a) trespass
—침범하다 invade; raid; (en)trench on; encroach on
♦ 영해를 침범하다 invade 《a country's》 territorial waters / 사유지를 침범하다 trespass on a private land
▶ 국적 불명의 비행기가 우리 영공을 침범했다 An unidentified aircraft violated our territorial airspace.
2 〈침해〉infringement; violation; encroachment
—침범하다 violate; infringe on; 〈권리를〉disturb
♦ 권한을 침범하다 impinge upon sb's authority / 사생활을 침범하다 violate sb's privacy / 병이 침범하다 be attacked [smitten] with a disease
■국경— a border incursion; a frontier violation

침봉 針峰 〈꽃꽂이의〉a frog

침불안석 寢不安席 anxiety-disturbed sleep
—침불안석하다 cannot sleep well [at ease] because of anxieties

침사 沈思 meditation ⇨ 심사(深思)

침상 針狀 the acicula ♦ 침상의 aciculate; needle-shaped; pointed
■—엽(葉) a needle (leaf) —조직 a acicular structure

침상 寢林 a bed(stead) ⇨ 침대

침소 寢所 a sleeping place; a bedchamber; a bedroom

침소봉대 針小棒大 exaggeration; overstatement
—침소봉대하다 exaggerate; magnify; overstate; aggrandize; overdo; overshoot oneself
♦ 침소봉대하여 with exaggeration; exaggeratedly
▶ 그는 언제나 침소봉대하는 버릇이 있다 He always makes a mountain out of a molehill.

침수 浸水 inundation; flood(ing); submersion
—침수하다 be flooded [submerged]; be inundated with; be under water; 〈배가〉spring a leak; make water
▶ 폭우로 오백여 채가 마루까지 침수 되었다 Five hundred houses were flooded above [up to] floor(boards) by the heavy rain.
■—가옥 submerged houses; houses under water —지역 a flooded [submerged] area —식물 a submerged plant

침술 鍼術 〔韓醫〕acupuncture
■—사 ⇨ 침의 —요법 acupuncture therapy

침식 浸蝕 〔地〕erosion; corrosion
♦ 비[바람, 물]에 의한 침식 rain [wind, water] erosion / 침식으로 by erosion
—침식하다 erode; corrode; eat away; 〈물이〉wash out; 〈바다가 육지를〉gain [encroach] on
▶ 해안일대에 걸쳐서 바다가 육지를 침식하고 있다 The sea gains on the land along the coast.
▶ 그곳은 풍우에 침식되어 급사면을 이루었다 Eroded by wind and rain, it formed a steep slope.
■—대지(臺地) an eroded plateau —분지 an eroded basin —윤회 a cycle of erosion —작용 erosion process —토양 soil erosion —평야 a erosional plain

침식 寢食 food and sleep
♦ 침식을 잊고 without sparing oneself; devotedly / 침식을 잊고 공부하다 be absorbed [buried] in one's study / 침식을 잊고 간호하다 nurse sb devotedly
▶ 그는 독서에 침식을 잊고 있다 Reading is meat and drink to him.
▶ 우리는 오랜 세월 침식을 같이 했다 We lived under the same roof for many years.

침실 寢室 a bedroom; a bedchamber; a sleeping room ♦침실겸 거실 a bed-sitting room
▶어머니는 침식을 잊고 딸을 간호했다 Her mother was so busy nursing her daughter that she had no time to eat or sleep.

침염 浸染 1 〈염색의〉 dip-dyeing —침염하다 dip-dye《cloth》 2 〈감화〉 influence —침염되다 be influenced [inspired] with ■—식 날염 a dyed style printing

침엽 針葉 〔植〕 a needle (leaf); an acerose leaf; a needle-shaped leaf

침엽수 針葉樹 〔植〕 a needle-leaf[coniferous] tree ■—림 a coniferous forest

침울 沈鬱 melancholy; gloom; depression; 〈口〉 the blues
—침울하다 melancholy; dismal; gloomy; depressed; heavy-hearted
♦침울한 심정 a gloomy mind / 침울한 표정 a melancholy look / 침울한 얼굴을 하다 pull [make] a long face / 침울해 보이다 look gloomy [depressed, blue] / 침울한 기분을 씻어 버리다 dissipate melancholy; dispel gloom
▶그것을 생각하면 침울해진다 Melancholy seizes me when I think of it.

침윤 浸潤 saturation; permeation; infiltration
—침윤하다 permeate in [through]; infiltrate [soak]《into》
■폐— infiltration of the lungs

침의 寢衣 nightclothes ⇨ 잠옷
침의 鍼醫 〔韓醫〕 an acupuncturist
침입 侵入 (an) invasion; a raid; an inroad; 〈무단침입〉 (a) trespass; (an) intrusion
—침입하다 enter into; enter forcibly; invade; raid into; make an inroad into [upon]; march into; encroach on; penetrate into; trespass on; intrude [break] into; force an entrance [one's entry] into
▶적이 불시에 침입해 왔다 The enemy invaded our country all of a sudden.
■가택— housebreaking; burglary ■—로 an invasion route

침재 針才 skill [talent] in needlework [sewing]

침전 沈澱 〔化〕 precipitation; deposition; sedimentation; settlement
—침전하다 settle (to the bottom); precipitate; be precipitated [deposited]
▶바닥에 뭔가 침전되어 있다 Something is deposited at the bottom.
■—기(器) 〔物・化〕 a precipitator ■—농도 precipitation density ■—물 a deposit; a precipitate; a sediment; 〈찌꺼기〉 lees ■—반응 precipitation reaction ■—분석 precipitation analysis ■—제(劑) a precipitator; a precipitant ■—지(池) a settling tank [pond]

침전 寢殿 1 〈임금의 침실〉 the hall containing the king's bedchamber
2 〈정자각(丁字閣)〉 T shrine for royal tomb rites

침점 侵占 occupying by force
—침점하다 (invade and) occupy

침중 沈重 1 〈침착〉 composure; self-possession; serenity; presence of mind; calmness; coolness
—침중하다 composed; self-possessed; calm; cool; collected; sedate; serene
2 〈병세의 위중〉 seriousness; gravity
—침중하다 serious; critical

침지 浸漬 〔化〕 digestion; immersion
—침지하다 digest ■—기(器) a digester

침질 鍼— 〔韓醫〕 acupuncture —침질하다 perform acupuncture

침착 沈着 self-possession; presence of mind; calmness; coolness; composure
—침착하다 self-possessed; calm; cool; composed; have presence of mind
♦침착한 사람 a self-possessed person; a calm (and collected) person / 침착한 성격 a staid character / 침착한 태도 a calm attitude; a cool manner / 침착하게 calmly; coolly; composedly; with composure; with presence of mind / 침착한 태도를 보이다 bear *oneself* with coolness; show presence of mind / 침착하게 행동하다 act with composure
▶그는 매우 침착해 보였다 He seemed so collected.
▶그는 늘 침착하게 행동한다 He always acts with coolness [presence of mind].
▶그는 침착하게 판단하여 그곳에 모인 사람들을 안전한 곳으로 인도했다 He led the people, gathering them into a safe place by his self-possessed [calm] judgment.

침착성 沈着性 composure; equanimity; self-possession; presence of mind; poise
♦침착성을 잃다 lose *one's* presence of mind [*one's* self-possession] / 침착성을 되찾다 regain [recover] *one's* presence of mind; recover *one's* composure / 침착성을 잃지 않다 remain composed; be [remain] absolutely calm and self-possessed

침체 沈滯 dullness; stagnation; slackness; inactivity
♦한국의 경제적 침체 Korea's economic stagnation
▶주가는 수요부족으로 침체 상태에 있다 Stock prices are held in check for lack of sufficient demand.
—침체하다 stagnate; become sluggish [dull]
♦침체된 시장 a dull [slack] market / 침체해 있다 be stagnant [stagnating]; be dull [slack, inactive] / 침체시키다 depress《trade》; cause the stagnation《of》
▶침체된 공기가 감돌고 있다 A stagnant atmosphere prevails.

침침하다 沈沈— 1 〈어둡다〉 gloomy; somber; dim
♦침침한 방안 a dimly-lit [ill-lighted] room / 침침한 곳에서 in the gloom [semi-dark] / 침침한 등불 아래서 독서하다 read in the dim [poor] light of a lamp
2 〈흐릿하다〉 dim《med》; dimsighted; misty; blurred; 〈눈이〉 purblind
♦눈이 침침해지다 have dim eyes [sight]
▶나이가 들면 눈이 침침해진다 Our sight grows dim with age.

침탈 侵奪 〔法〕 〈부동산의〉 disseisin; disseizin
—침탈하다 disseise; disseize
■—자 a disseisor; a disseizor: 피침탈자 a disseisee; a disseisee

침통 鍼筒 a case for acupuncture needles; a needle case

침통하다 沈痛— grave; serious; anguished; sorrow-stricken; in a sad
♦침통한 어조로 in a sad [mournful] tone / 침통한 얼굴로 with a sad look / 침통한 얼굴을 하다 look grave [sorrowful]/ 침통해 하다 be distressed [anguished] 《at》; grieve 《at, over》; one's heart aches 《at》
▶아버지를 잃은 그녀의 마음은 침통했다 Her heart was heavy with sorrow because of the loss of her father.

침투 浸透 permeation; infiltration; penetration
♦공산주의의 침투 infiltration of Communism 《into》/ 무장간첩의 침투 infiltration of armed agents
—침투하다 permeate; infiltrate; penetrate; spread *itself* 《into, through》; seep
♦정계에 침투하다 infiltrate 《into》 political circles
▶물은 모래에 침투한다 Water percolates through sand.
▶면냅킨은 물이 잘 침투한다 Water will easily permeate a cotton napkin.
▶신사상이 사람들 마음속에 침투하기 시작했다 The new idea began to filter [infiltrate] into people's minds.
■경제— economic penetration —작전 infiltration operations

침팬지 〔動〕 a chimpanzee

침하 沈下 settlement; subsidence; sinking
—침하하다 subside; sink; 〈지층이〉 dip
▶이 지역의 지반은 작년부터 약 1 센치미터 침하했다 The ground in this area has sunk about one centimeter since last year.
■지반— ground sinkage

침해 侵害 infringement; violation; encroachment; trespass; invasion; obstruction; disturbance
—침해하다 infringe 《on》; encroach [trespass, trench] 《on》; violate; 〈권리를〉 disturb
♦침해할 수 없는 inviolable / 권한을 침해하다 impinge upon *sb's* authority
▶당신은 그녀의 사생활을 침해했소 You violated her privacy.
▶그는 내 인권을 침해했다 He trespassed on my human rights.
▶나는 기득권을 침해당하고 싶지 않다 I don't want my vested interests to be trespassed upon.
■저작권— an infringement of copyright : 그는 저작권을 침해했다 He infringed on the copyright. ——자 a trespasser

침향 沈香 〔植〕 〈나무〉 aloeswood; an agalloch; 〈그 향료〉 agallochum

침흘리개 a slobberer; a slaverer; a driveler

칩 〔電算〕 a chip

칩거 蟄居 keeping the house; seclusion
—칩거하다 keep the house; keep [stay] indoors; confine *oneself* in *one's* house; shut *oneself* up 《in a room》
♦종일 방안에 칩거하다 keep (in) *one's* room all day long

칩룡 蟄龍 〈숨은 용〉 a hidden dragon; a dragon in concealment; (비유) 〈숨은 영웅〉 a hidden hero; a great man in obscurity

칩복 蟄伏 〈동면〉 hibernation
—칩복하다 hibernate

칩수 蟄獸 hibernating animals; hibernants

칩충 蟄蟲 hibernating [hibernant] insects

칫솔 齒— a toothbrush
♦칫솔질하다 brush *one's* teeth

칭 稱 1〈명칭〉 a name; a title; an appellation 2〔文法〕〈인칭〉 person
♦1[2,3] 인칭 the first [second, third] person

칭동 秤動 〔天〕〈행성의〉 libration

칭병 稱病 malingering
—칭병하다 plead illness (as an excuse); pretend [feign] to be ill; malinger

칭사 稱辭 a eulogy ⇨ 찬사

칭송 稱頌 praise; applause; admiration; eulogy; laudation
—칭송하다 admire; applaud; laud; extol; commend; praise
♦고인의 덕을 칭송하다 eulogize the virtue of the deceased / 극구 칭송하다 be loud in *sb's* praises; extol [laud] *sb* sky-high [to the skies]; speak in highest terms of *sb*
▶세상 사람들은 그를 높이 칭송하였다 People were loud in his praises.

칭얼거리다 fret; be peevish [fussy]; whine; whinge; whimper

칭얼칭얼 fretfully; peevishly
♦칭얼칭얼 울다 cry peevishly

칭원하다 稱寃— say spiteful things 《of *sb*》; reproach [blame] 《*sb* for *sth*》; complain 《to *sb* of *sth*》; grumble 《at, about, over》

칭찬 稱讚 praise; applause; admiration; commendation; laudation
♦칭찬의 말 a word of praise 《for》; a eulogy / 이웃에 칭찬이 자자한 사람 the center of appreciation in the neighborhood
▶그의 책임감은 칭찬받을 만하다 His sense of duty is praiseworthy [worthy of praise].
—칭찬하다 praise; commend; admire; extol; applaud; eulogize; compliment; laud; pay a tribute of praise to; speak well [highly] of; speak in high terms of
♦칭찬할 만한 praiseworthy; laudable; commendable; commendatory; admirable / 극구 칭찬하다 speak very highly of; cry [praise, talk] up; sing [chant] the praises of / 아무의 근면함을 칭찬하다 praise *sb* for his diligence / 칭찬하여 격려하다 encourage *sb* with praise / 칭찬받다 be praised [complimented] 《by》; win [enjoy] the admiration 《of》; get *sb's* compliment
▶이루 다 칭찬할 수 없다 He is above praise.
▶별로 칭찬할 만한 것이 못 된다 There is not much to be said for it.
▶칭찬받고 싶은 것은 인지상정이다 Everybody wishes to win applause.
▶칭찬받고 화내는 사람은 없다 Nobody feels offended at compliments.
▶우리는 그의 용기를 칭찬했다 We praised his courage. ⇌ We admired him for his courage.

칭탁 稱託 〈핑계〉 an excuse; a pretext; a plea; a pretense

—**칭탁하다** make a pretense [pretext] of; make an excuse of
♦ …을 칭탁하여 under [on] the pretext of 《ill health》; under cover of 《charity》

칭탄 稱歎 admiration ⇨ 찬탄

칭탈하다 稱頉— make [find] an excuse [a pretext] 《in an accident》; make 《some circumstances》a 《good》pretext 《for》; plead 《a hitch》as *one's* excuse

칭하다 稱— **1** 〈부르다〉call; name; term; designate
♦ 놀부라고 칭하는 남자 a man who gives the name of Nolbu; a man of [by] the name of Nolbu
▶ 진정한 교육자라고 칭할 만한 사람은 극히 드물다 There are very few, if any, who really deserve the name of educationist.
2 〈사칭하다〉pretend; feign; 〈주장하다〉claim; 〈항변하다〉plead
♦ 왕이라고 칭하다 assume the title of king / 친척이라고 칭하다 claim to be *sb's* relative / 고흐의 그림이라고 칭하는 것 what purports to be a Gogh / …이라 칭하여 on [under] the plea [pretext] of 《illness》; under [on] 《the》 pretense of; representing *oneself* as

칭호 稱號 〈관직 등〉a title; 〈명칭〉a name; an appellation; a designation; 〈학위〉a degree
♦ 박사의 칭호 the degree of doctor; a doctorate / …의 칭호를 수여하다 confer the title [degree] of… 《on *sb*》

카 1 〈맛・냄새 등이 심할 때〉 Wow!; Ouch!; Phew!; Oh, my!
▶카, 맵다 Wow! It's hot.
2 〈곤히 잘 때〉 zzz

카 〈차〉 a car; an automobile ■—풀 a car pool

카나리아 〔鳥〕 a canary (bird)

카나리아 제도 the Canary Islands; the Canaries

카네기 〈미국의 강철왕・자선가〉 Carnegie, Andrew (1835-1919)
♦카네기 홀 Carnegie Hall

카네이션 〔植〕 a carnation

카누 〈통나무 배〉 a canoe ♦카누 젓는 사람 a canoeist / 카누를 젓다 canoe; paddle a canoe
▶그들은 카누를 타고 강을 내려갔다 They canoed down the river.

카니발 〈사육제〉 a carnival

카덴차 (이) 〔樂〕 cadenza

카드 1 〈두꺼운 종이〉 a card; 〈종잇조각〉 a slip (of paper)
♦빈 카드 a blank card / 영어 단어를 카드에 적다 put [note] down English words on cards
▶네 이름을 이 카드에 적어라 Write your name on this card.
2 〈크레디트 카드〉 a (credit) card
▶이 카드로 지불해도 될까요? Can I pay with this credit card? = Do you accept this credit card?
3 〈카드놀이의〉 a card; a playing card
♦카드 한 벌 a pack [deck] of cards / 카드를 도르다 deal the cards
4 〈연하장 등〉 a (greeting) card
♦회원카드 a membership card / 카드상자 a card case
■—목록 a card catalog [file] ■—번호[색인] a card number [index] ■—식 부기 bookkeeping on the card system

카드놀이 card playing; a card game

카드뮴 〔化〕 cadmium

카디건 〈앞이 트인 털스웨터〉 a cardigan

카라비너 〔登山〕 a carabiner; a snap ring

카라얀 〈오스트리아의 지휘자〉 Karajan, Herbert von (1908-89)

카라치 〈파키스탄의 도시〉 Karachi

카라카스 〈베네수엘라의 수도〉 Caracas

카랑카랑하다 1〈날씨가 맑고 차다〉 clear and cold 2〈목소리가〉 clear and high-pitched
▶그의 목소리는 카랑카랑하다 He has a high-pitched voice.

카레 curry ♦카레 가루 curry (powder) / 카레라이스 curry and rice; curried rice / 카레 요리 (a) curry; curried food / 점심에 카레를 먹다 have curry for lunch

카로사 〈독일의 작가・시인〉 Carossa, Hans (1878-1956)

카로틴 〔化〕 carotene

카르스트지형 —地形 〔地〕 karst

카르타고 〈고대 도시 국가〉 Carthage

카르테 〈〈독〉 Karte〕 〔醫〕 a medical card [record]; a chart; a history sheet; a file

카르텔 〈〈독〉 Kartell〕 〔經〕 a cartel
♦카르텔을 결성하다 form (into) a cartel; cartelize / 카르텔을 해체하다 decartelize

카리브해 —海 the Caribbean Sea

카리스마 charisma 《pl. ~s, -mata》 ♦카리스마적 charismatic

카리에스 〔醫〕 caries ■척추— caries of the vertebrae; spinal caries

카메라 a camera; 〈영화용의〉 a cinecamera; 〈英〉 a movie camera
♦자동초점 35밀리미터 카메라 an automatic 35 millimeter camera / 카메라에 담다 take a picture [photo, photograph] (of); photograph sb / 카메라에 필름을 넣다 load a camera (with a film); load a film into a camera / 카메라를 들이대다 point [aim] one's camera (at)
■소형— a miniature camera; a minicamera
■—앵글 a camera angle

카메라맨 〈영화・텔레비전의〉 a cameraman; 〈사진사〉 a photographer; 〈신문의〉 a newspaper photographer; 〈스포츠의〉 a sports photographer

카메룬 〈나라 이름〉 Cameroon; 〈공식명〉 the Republic of Cameroon ■—사람 a Cameroonian

카메오 〈돋을 새김 장신구〉 a cameo

카멜레온 〔動〕 a chameleon

카무플라주 〈위장・속임수〉 a camouflage
▶인간은 카무플라주를 자연에서 배웠다 Man borrowed the idea of camouflage from nature.
■—카무플라주하다 camouflage

카뮈 〈프랑스의 작가〉 Camus, Albert (1913-60)

카바레 a cabaret

카바이드 〔化〕 carbide

카보베르데 〈나라 이름〉 Cabo Verde; 〈공식명〉 the Republic of Cape Verde

카본 〔化〕 carbon ⇨ 탄소 ♦카본 복사 a carbon copy / 카본 블랙 carbon black / 카본지 (a sheet of) carbon paper; 〈한장〉 a carbon

카뷰레터 〈기화기〉 〔機〕 a carburet(t)or; a carburet(t)er

카비네판 —判 〔寫〕 a cabinet size photograph

카빈총 —銃 a carbine
♦자동 카빈총 a machine carbine

카사노바 〈이탈리아 작가〉 Casanova, Giovanni Giacomo (1725-98)

카사블랑카 〈모로코의 도시〉 Casablanca

카세인 〔化〕 casein

카세트 a cassette ■—녹음기 a cassette tape

카슈미르 〈인도·파키스탄의 북부 지방〉 Kashmir ◆카슈미르의 Kashmirian ■—사람 a Kashmiri

카스텔라 [〈(포) pão de Castella] sponge cake

카스트 〈인도의 신분 제도〉 a caste ◆카스트 제도 the caste system

카스트로 〈쿠바의 정치가〉 Castro, Fidel (1927-) ■—주의 Castroism

카스피해 —海 the Caspian Sea

카시오페이아자리 〖天〗 Cassiopeia

카약 〈배〉 a kayak

카우보이 a cowboy; 〈美口〉 a cowpuncher ─모자 a cowboy hat

카운셀링 〈상담〉 counseling

카운슬러 〈상담자〉 a counselor

카운터 〈상점 등의〉 a counter; a cash counter ◆카운터에서 지불하다 pay at the counter

카운터블로 〖拳〗 a counterblow

카운트 1 a count; counting
▶카운트가 어떻게 되니? What's the count?
▶카운트는 투 스트라이크, 원볼이다 One ball, two strikes is the count.
2 〖拳〗 ◆카운트 아웃하다 count (him) out / 카운트 아웃이 되다 be counted out
▶그는 카운트 에이트에서 일어났다 He got to his feet at eight. = He took a count of eight before getting up.
■풀— 〖野〗 a full count (of three and two)

카이로 〈이집트의 수도〉 Cairo ◆카이로 선언 the Cairo Declaration

카이저수염 —鬚髥 a Kaiser mustache

카지노 a casino

카카오 1 ⇨ 카카오 나무 2 ⇨ 카카오 열매 ─나무 〖植〗 a cacao (tree) ─열매 cacao beans

카키색 —色 khaki (color) ◆카키색 옷을 입고 있다 be in a khaki dress

카타르¹ 〈나라 이름〉 Qatar; 〈공식명〉 the State of Qatar

카타르² 〈점막 염증〉 〖醫〗 catarrh ◆카타르성의 catarrhal (pneumonia)
─비(鼻)— nasal catarrh

카타르시스 (a) catharsis (pl. -ses)

카타스트로프 〈파국〉 a catastrophe

카타콤 〈가톨릭〉 the Catacombs

카탈로그 〈목록〉 a catalog(ue) ◆카탈로그에 싣다 catalog; put (an item) in a catalog ▶카탈로그 무료 증정 Catalog offered free.

카터 〈미국의 제39대 대통령〉 Carter, Jimmy (1924-)

카턴 〈마분지〉 carton; 〈상자〉 a carton

카테고리 〖哲〗 a category ⇨ 범주

카테테르 [〈(독) Katheter] 〈도뇨관〉 〖醫〗 a catheter

카톨릭 Catholic ⇨ 가톨릭, 천주교

카투사 KATUSA; Katusa [*Korean Augmentation Troops to U.S. Army*]

카트리지 a cartridge ◆카트리지를 갈다 put a new cartridge (in)

카트만두 〈네팔의 수도〉 Kathmandu

카틀레야 〈양란〉 〖植〗 a cattleya

카페 a café; a coffee shop; a coffee house; 〈술집〉 a saloon; a barroom

카페리 a car ferry

카페인 caffeine ◆카페인 없는 커피 caffeine-free coffee

카페테리아 〈간이 식당〉 a cafeteria; a self-service restaurant

카펫 〈양탄자〉 a carpet; 〈깔개〉 a rug

카프리치오 〈광상곡〉 〖樂〗 a capriccio

카프카 〈오스트리아의 소설가〉 Kafka, Franz (1883-1924)

카프카스 〈흑해와 카스피 해 사이의 지역〉 Kavkaz

카피 〈복사(물)〉 a copy ◆카피하다 copy; take a copy (of); copy down; duplicate

카피라이터 〈광고 문안 작성자〉 a copywriter

칵칵 with repeated coughs (to clear *one's* throat) ─칵칵하다 keep coughing away

칵칵거리다 keep coughing (to clear *one's* throat)

칵테일 (have, drink) a cocktail ■—글라스 a cocktail glass ─드레스 a cocktail dress; an afternoon dress ─파티 a cocktail party

칸 1 〈칸살 수〉 a room (unit); *kan* ◆단칸집 a one-room house
2 〈칸막이〉 a partition; a compartment ◆방의 칸을 막다 partition a room
3 〈빈 칸〉 a blank (space); (a) space
▶맞는 답으로 빈 칸을 채워라 Fill (in) the blanks with correct answers.

칸 〈프랑스의 피한지〉 Cannes

칸나 〖植〗 a canna; an Indian shot

칸델라 1 〈광도 단위〉 〖電〗 a candela (略 cd.)
2 〈등〉 a lantern; a metal hand lamp

칸딘스키 〈러시아의 화가〉 Kandinski, Vasili (1866-1944)

칸막이 〈칸막기〉 partitioning; screening; 〈칸막이 재료〉 a screen; a partition ◆칸막이하다 partition; screen off ■—벽 a partition

칸살 1 〈칸의 면적〉 the size of a room ◆칸살이 넓은[좁은] 방 a large [small] room
2 〈거리〉 a space; distance; an interval

칸수 —數 the number of *kan*; the floor space of a house

칸초네 (이) 〖樂〗 a canzone 《*pl.* ~s, -ni》

칸칸이 〈방마다〉 (in) every [each] room; from room to room; room by room

칸타빌레 (이) 〖樂〗 cantabile

칸타타 (이) 〖樂〗 a cantata

칸트 〈독일의 철학자〉 Kant, Immanuel (1724-1804) ◆칸트학파의 사람 a Kantist; a Kantian / 신칸트학파 neo-Kantians; neo-Kantists / 칸트(학파)의 Kantian
─철학 Kantianism; Kantism

칼¹ 1 〈소형칼〉 a knife (pl. knives); 〈접는 칼〉 a clasp knife; 〈선원용〉 a jackknife; 〈주방용〉 a kitchen knife; 〈식탁용〉 a table knife; 〈단검〉 a dagger ◆잘드는[무딘] 칼 a sharp [dull] knife
2 〈검〉 a sword; 〈군도〉 a saber ◆칼날 the edge of a sword / 칼에 벤 상처 a

sword cut [wound]/ 칼을 차다 wear [carry] a sword 《at *one's* side》/ 칼을 뽑다 draw a sword
▶ 부부싸움은 칼로 물베기다 The couple are inseparably bound up by love.
■면도— a razor 주머니— a pocketknife; a penknife

칼² 〈서양 형틀〉a pillory; 〈중국·한국에서의〉a cang(ue) ◆칼을 씌우다 cangue / 칼을 쓰다 wear a cangue

칼깃 〈빳빳하고 긴 새깃〉a flight feather; a remex (*pl.* remiges); 〈총칭〉the pinion

칼끝 a sword [knife] point; the point of a sword

칼날 the edge [blade] of a sword [knife]
◆예리한 칼날 an sharp edge / 무딘 칼날 a blunt edge

칼데라 〔地質〕a caldera ■—호(湖) a caldera lake

칼등 the back of a sword [knife]

칼라 〈깃〉a collar ■소프트[더블]— a soft [turn-down] collar ■—단추 a collar button [stud]

칼라스 〈미국의 소프라노 가수〉Callas, Maria (1923-77)

칼라일 〈스코틀랜드 태생의 평론가·역사가〉Carlyle, Thomas (1795-1881)

칼럼 〈신문·잡지 등〉a column

칼럼니스트 a columnist

칼로리 a calorie (略 cal.)
◆칼로리 계산 calorie counting / 칼로리가 낮은[칼로리를 제한한] 식사 a low-calorie [calorie-controlled] diet / 하루에 2,500칼로리를 섭취하다 eat [take] 2,500 calories a day
▶ 이 요리는 칼로리가 높다 This dish is high in calories [has a high calorific value].
▶ 이 비프스테이크는 몇 칼로리나 될 것 같습니까? How many calories do you think there are in this beefsteak?
■킬로(그램)— a kilogram calorie; a kilo-calorie ■—가(價) calorific value —섭취량 caloric intake —표 a caloric chart —함유량 caloric content

칼륨 〔化〕potassium; kalium ⇨ 칼리

칼리 〔化〕potassium; potash; kalium
■—비누 potash soap ■—비료 (a) potassic fertilizer —염 potassic salt

칼리지 〈단과 대학〉a college

칼립소 〔樂〕〈음악〉calypso; 〈노래〉a calypso song

칼맞다 get stabbed; suffer a sword stroke

칼뱅 〈종교 개혁가〉Calvin, John (1509-64)
■—주의 Calvinism —파 the Calvinists: 칼뱅파의 a Calvinistic(al)

칼부림 wielding a knife [sword] (at)
—칼부림하다 wield [brandish, flourish] a sword at sb

칼새 〔鳥〕a salangane; a white-rumped swift; 〈북미산〉a chimney swift [swallow]

칼슘 〔化〕calcium
◆칼슘분을 함유하다 contain calcium
■염화[산화]— calcium chloride [oxide] 인산[황산, 탄산]— calcium phosphate [sulphate, carbonate] ■—시안아미드 calcium cyanamide; lime nitrogen —주사 an injection of calcium

칼자국 a sword wound [cut]

칼자루 the hilt 《of a sword》; the haft of a dagger; the handle 《of a knife》
◆칼자루를 쥐다 hold a sword by the hilt; (비유) control; lead; dominate; have the (final [last]) say

칼장수 a cutler

칼질하다 cut; chop; 〈다지다〉hash

칼집 a sheath; a scabbard; a case ◆칼집에서 칼을 뽑다 unsheathe [draw] a sword / 칼을 칼집에 넣다 sheathe [put up] a sword

칼춤 a sword dance ◆칼춤을 추다 perform a sword dance

칼침 —鍼 the thrust of a knife [sword]

칼칼하다 thirsty ⇨ 컬컬하다

칼코등이 the guard of a sword

캄보 〔樂〕a (jazz) combo (*pl.* ~s)

캄보디아 〈나라 이름〉Cambodia; 〈공식명〉the Kingdom of Cambodia ◆캄보디아의 Cambodian ■—사람 a Cambodian

캄브리아기 —紀 〔地質〕the Cambrian

캄차카반도 —半島 the Kamchatka

캄캄하다 1〈몹시 어둡다〉pitch-dark; 《as》dark as pitch; 〈암담하다〉dark; gloomy; dismal; somber
◆캄캄한 밤 a jet-black [pitch-dark] night
▶ 바깥은 캄캄했다 It was pitch-dark outside.
▶ 내 앞날이 캄캄하다 I can't see the future at all. ⇒ My future seems to be filled with gloom.
2〈전혀 알지 못하다〉be ignorant 《of》; know nothing about

캄팔라 〈우간다의 수도〉Kampala

캄프리 〔植〕a compressor

캉캉 〈춤〉(프) the cancan ◆캉캉을 추다 do the cancan

캐나다 Canada ◆캐나다의 Canadian
■—사람 a Canadian

캐내다 dig up [out]; grub up [out]; pry; unearth
▶ 나는 남편의 비밀을 캐냈다 I wormed [pried] a secret out of my husband.

캐다 1〈파내다〉dig up; grub; 〈감자 등을〉lift
◆땅콩을 캐다 dig (up) peanuts / 금을 캐다 dig gold / 감자를 캐다 lift [grub up] potatoes / 풀뿌리를 캐다 grub up grass roots
2〈밝혀내다〉examine closely; pry into 《*sb's* secret》; peck [pick] at 《*sb's* faults》
◆비밀을 캐다 pry into a secret; probe [trace] a secret / 사건의 근원을 캐다 go to the root of a matter / 꼬치꼬치 캐다 scrutinize; rake; ransack; poke and pry
▶ 그는 남의 일을 꼬치꼬치 잘 캔다 He often pries into other people's affairs.
▶ 나는 그 뜬소문의 출처를 캤다 I have traced the source of the rumor.

캐디 〔골프〕a caddie; a caddy ◆캐디로 일하다 caddie 《for a golfer》

캐딜락 (商標) a Cadillac (automobile)

캐러멜 〈과자〉a caramel ◆캐러멜을 먹다 chew a caramel

캐러밴 〈대상〉a caravan

캐럿 〈보석의 무게 단위〉 a carat; 〈순금의 함유도 단위〉 a karat
♦8캐럿의 다이아몬드 a diamond of 8 carats; a 8-carat diamond
캐리커처 〈회화·풍자화〉 (a) caricature
캐릭터 〈성격·등장 인물〉 (a) character
캐묻다 ask; examine; question closely; press [drive] a question home; cross-question
♦…의 사실을 캐묻다 ascertain the truth of…
캐비닛 a cabinet
캐비아 〔料〕 caviar(e)
캐비지 〈양배추〉〔植〕 a cabbage
캐빈 〈선실·객실〉 a cabin
캐스터 a caster; 〈해설자〉 a commentator; 〈뉴스 캐스터〉 an anchorman; a newsreader
캐스터네츠 〔樂〕 castanets
캐스트 〈배역〉 the cast (of a play)

解説 「배역」의 뜻인 「캐스트」는 영어의 *cast*와는 용법이 다르다. 즉 cast는 총칭적으로 배역 전체를 말한다. 따라서 배역 중의 한 사람은 a member of the cast다. 개개의 배역은 role 또는 part라고 한다. 메인 캐스트(주역)도 배역의 하나므로 a leading role [part]이다.

캐스트리스 〈세인트루시아의 수도〉 Castries
캐스팅보트 〈결정 투표〉 the casting vote
▶당신이 캐스팅 보트를 쥐고 있습니다 You hold the casting vote.
캐시 〈현금〉 cash ♦캐시로 지불하다 pay in cash
■—카드 a cash card
캐시미어 〈직물〉 cashmere; kashmir
캐주얼 casual
■—웨어 casual wear
캐처 〈포수〉〔野〕 a catcher ♦캐처를 맡(아보)다 catch; be (a) catcher
캐치 catching; a catch —캐치하다 catch (the ball) ♦어디서 그 정보를 캐치했니? Where did you pick up that information?
캐치볼 〈play〉 catch ♦캐치볼을 하다 play catch
캐치프레이즈 〈표어〉 a catchphrase
캐터펄트 a catapult
캐터필러 〈무한 궤도차〉 a caterpillar
캑 〈마른 기침〉 with a hack ♦캑캑거리다 give dry coughs; hack
캔 〈美〉 a can; 〈英〉 a tin; a canister ⇨ 깡통
캔디 (a) candy; sweets
▶그녀는 캔디를 좋아한다 She is fond of [likes] candy.
캔버라 〈오스트레일리아의 수도〉 Canberra
캔버스 (a piece of) canvas ■—틀 a (canvas) stretcher
캔슬 〈취소〉 cancellation
♦캔슬하다 cancel
캔자스 〈미국의 주〉 (the State of) Kansas (略 Kans., Kan.)
캔터베리 〈영국의 도시〉 Canterbury
캘리코 〈옥양목〉 calico
캘리퍼스 〈측정 양각기〉 (a pair of) cal(l)ipers ♦캘리퍼스로 재다 cal(l)iper
캘리포니아 〈미국의 주〉 California (略 Calif., Cal.)

캘린더 a calendar ♦캘린더를 떼다[찢다] tear a sheet off the calendar ■벽걸이[탁상]— a wall [desk] calendar
캘커타 〈인도의 항구 도시〉 Calcutta ■—체인 〔海〕 a Calcutta chain
캠 〔機〕 a cam
■—장치 cam mechanism
캠퍼 〈장뇌〉〔化·藥〕 camphor ■—주사 (a) camphor injection
캠퍼스 〈교정〉 a campus ♦캠퍼스에서 on the campus
캠페인 a campaign; a drive ▶그 단체는 흡연 반대 캠페인을 벌였다 The group launched an anti-smoking campaign.
캠프 〈야영〉 a camp
■—파이어 a campfire
캠핑 camping ♦캠핑 용구[용품] a camping outfit; camping equipment ■—카 a camper; a trailer; a mobile home
캡 a cap
캡션 〈사진의 설명문〉 a caption
캡슐 〈약·인공위성의〉 a capsule ♦캡슐로 싼 capsulated
■우주— a space capsule
캡틴 a captain ⇨ 주장(主將)
캥거루 〔動〕 a kangaroo (*pl*. ~s); (총칭) kangaroo
캥캥 〈강아지 등의 우는 소리〉 ▶강아지가 캥캥 운다 A puppy yelps [yips].
커녕 1 〈그 반대로〉 anything but; far from; not at all; instead of; none too
♦그렇기는커녕 far from it; on the contrary / 즐겁기는커녕 none too pleasant
▶이 문장은 잘 쓰기는커녕 무슨 소리인지 통 알 수가 없다 This sentence is anything but well written; it is a perfect jargon.
▶그는 기뻐하기는커녕 몹시 화를 냈다 Far from being pleased, he got very angry.
▶그는 저금을 하기는커녕 그날그날 살아가기도 어려운 형편이다 Far from saving money, he can hardly make his living.
2 〈…은 말할 것도 없이〉 not to mention; not to speak of; to say nothing of; not only…
▶그는 영어는커녕 국문도 제대로 못쓴다 He can not write good Korean, much less English.
커다랗다 huge; great; gigantic; enormous; monstrous; mammoth; colossal
♦커다란 탱커 a huge [gigantic] tanker
▶그 스캔들은 신문에 커다랗게 났다 The scandal was reported with large [big] headlines.
커다래지다 become larger [bigger]; get bigger; grow larger; increase in size; 〈자라다〉 grow; become taller; 〈늘다〉 swell; expand; be enlarged
♦눈이 커다래지다 open *one*'s eyes wide; 〈美俗〉 be pop-eyed
▶이 도시는 요 몇 해 동안에 급속히 커다래졌다 This city has grown bigger [larger] rapidly for the past several years.
커리어 〈경력〉 a career; 〈경험〉 experience
▶그는 외교관으로서 오랜 커리어를 가지고 있다 He has a long career as a diplomat.
커리큘럼 a curriculum (*pl*. -la, ~s); 〈교육 과

정〉 a course of study
커머셜메시지 a commercial message
커머셜송 a commercial song
커뮤니케이션 communication ◆매스 커뮤니케이션 mass communication / 커뮤니케이션갭 the communications gap
커뮤니티 〈지역 사회·집단〉 a community
커미션 〈수수료〉 a commission
♦10퍼센트의 커미션 a ten percent commission 《on the sale》/ 매상고의 십퍼센트의 커미션을 받다 get a commission of ten percent on the sales made
■—브로커 a commission broker
커버 1 〈덮개〉 a cover; a covering; 〈책의〉 a dust cover; a book jacket
♦커버를 씌우다 lay a cover; cover 《a sofa》; 〈책에〉 jacket / 커버를 벗기다 take off the cover 《from》
2 〈벌충〉 —커버하다 cover up 《a loss》; make up for 《a loss》; 〈경기에서〉 cover 《the first base》
▶그는 손해를 커버하려 했으나 허사였다 He tried to cover up a loss but in vain.
커브 1 〈곡선〉 a curve
♦커브를 틀다[돌다, 꺾다] bend 《to》; 〈자동차가〉 turn; make a turn
▶고속으로 커브를 도는 것은 위험하다 It is not safe to go round a bend at high speed.
▶커브를 돌 때는 조심해라 You should be careful in taking curves.
2 〔野〕 a curve (ball)
♦느린 커브 a slow curve / 날카로운 커브 a sharp-breaking curve
▶그는 느린 커브를 던졌다 He pitched a slow curve.
▶공이 손에서 미끄러지는 바람에 커브가 듣지 않았다 The ball slipped out, failing to curve.
■급— a steep [sharp] curve : 그 트럭은 교차로에서 급커브로 좌회전했다 The truck tried to turn sharp left at the intersection. 아웃— an outcurve 인— an incurve
커지다 get bigger; grow larger [bigger]; increase in size; 〈자라다〉 grow (up); become [grow] taller; 〈늘다〉 swell; expand; spread; 〈중대해지다〉 grow serious
♦부피가 커지다 increase [grow] in volume / 키가 1미터로 커지다 reach a height of one meter
▶화재는 삽시간에 커졌다 The fire spread in a moment.
커터 〈절단기〉 a cutter; 〔海〕 a cutter
커트 〈탁구 등의〉 a cut
—커트하다 cut
커튼 a curtain; 〈두꺼운〉 《美》 drapes
♦커튼을 치다 curtain 《the windows》; put up 《lace》 curtains; draw a curtain 《over》/ 커튼을 열다 open the curtains / 커튼을 닫다 close the curtains
▶그녀는 방으로 들어가 커튼을 닫았다 She went into the room and closed [drew] the curtains.
▶방의 그 부분은 커튼으로 칸막이가 되어 있다 That part of the room has been curtained off.
■—레일[로드] a curtain rail [rod]

커틀릿 〈튀김 요리〉 a fried cutlet
♦닭고기[돼지고기] 커틀릿 a fried chicken [pork] cutlet
커프스 cuffs ■—버튼[단추] sleeve [《美》 cuff] links
커플 〈한 쌍〉 a couple
♦잘 어울리는 커플 a well-matched couple
커피 (a cup of) coffee
♦짙은[엷은] 커피 strong [weak] coffee / 커피 우유 coffee-flavored milk
〈커피는〉나는 커피는 짙은 것이 좋다 I like my coffee strong.
〈커피를〉커피를 마시다 have [drink] coffee / 커피를 준비하다[내다] make [serve] coffee
▶커피를 두 잔 부탁합니다 Two coffees, please.
▶우리는 커피를 마시면서 2시간 동안 얘기했다 We talked about two hours over (a cup of) coffee.
▶[會話]「커피를 어떻게 드릴까요?」「블랙으로요.」 "How do you like your coffee?" "Black please."
■밀크— 〈프〉 a café au lait 블랙— black coffee 아이스— ice [iced] coffee 인스턴트— instant coffee ■—거르개 a coffee strainer —끓이개 〈여과식〉 a percolator; a coffeepot; 〈드립식〉〈商標〉 a Dripolator —나무 a coffee tree [plant] —세트 a coffee set —숍 a coffee shop —잔 a coffee cup —재배농장 a coffee plantation —콩 coffee beans —포트 a coffeepot
컨덕터 〈지휘자〉〔樂〕 a conductor
컨덕턴스 〔電〕 conductance
컨디션 condition
♦컨디션이 좋다 be [feel] well; be in (good) condition / 컨디션이 나쁘다 be [feel] unwell; be out of condition / 컨디션을 조절하다 tone up *one's* system
▶나는 컨디션이 좋다 I'm in good condition [shape].
▶주자는 최고의 컨디션이다 The runner seems to be in the best condition.
컨베이어 〔機〕 a conveyor; a conveyer
■—벨트 a conveyor belt —시스템 a conveyor system
컨설턴트 〈고문·자문〉 a consultant ◆경영 컨설턴트 a management consultant
컨소시엄 〈국제 차관단·협회〉 a consortium (*pl.* -tia, ~s)
컨테이너 a container ■—선 a container ship —차 〈트럭〉 a container truck; 〈열차〉 a container train
컨트롤 control
▶그 투수는 컨트롤이 좋다[나쁘다] The pitcher has good [poor] control. ⇌ The pitcher has good [no] pitching control.
—컨트롤하다 control 《*one's* feelings》
■—타워 ⇨ 관제(~탑)
컨트리클럽 a country club
컬 a curl (of hair); a curly [curled] hair
♦컬이 풀리다 go out of curl / 머리에 컬을 하다 curl *one's* hair
▶나는 머리를 감을 때마다 컬을 한다 I curl my hair every time I wash it.

컬러 (a) color; (英) colour ◆컬러로 풍경을 찍다 take the scene in color ■—사진 a color photograph; colored picture —슬라이드 a color slide —텔레비전 color television [TV]; 〈수상기〉 a color television (set) —필름 a color film

컬럼비아 〈미국의 도시〉 Columbia ■—특별구 the District of Columbia (略 D.C.)

컬렉션 〈수집품〉 a collection; 〈패션 발표회〉 a fashion collection

컬처쇼크 〈문화 충격〉 (a case of) culture shock

컬컬하다 〈목마르다〉 thirsty
▶껄껄한데 맥주 한 잔 했으면 좋겠다 I am thirsty for a glass of beer.

컬 클립 a curler

컴맹 —盲 computer illiteracy

컴백 〈복귀〉(口) a comeback
—컴백하다 come back (to); make one's comeback; return (to activity)
▷그의 아내는 영화배우로 기적적으로 컴백했다 His wife made a miraculous comeback as a movie [film] actress.

컴컴하다 1 〈어둡다〉 pitch-dark; dark; gloomy; somber; murky; 〈어두컴컴하다〉 dusky; dim
▷그 방은 컴컴했다 The room was completely dark.
▶정전으로 방이 컴컴해졌다 The room went black when the power failed.
2 〈음흉하다〉 blackhearted; sly; dark; black

컴퍼스 1 〈제도 용구〉 (a pair of) compasses
◆컴퍼스로 재다 measure with compasses
2 〈나침의〉 a mariner's compass; a compass
3 〈걸음나비〉 width of steps
▶그는 컴퍼스가 길다[짧다] He has long [short] legs.

컴퓨터 a computer
◆컴퓨터에 입력하다 put [feed] (data) into a computer / 컴퓨터로 처리하다 use a computer to process 〈information〉; process 〈information〉 with [in] a computer; computerize 〈information〉 / 컴퓨터 게임을 하다 play a computer game
▶우리 회사는 급여 부문을 완전히 컴퓨터화했다 Our company has completely computerized its wages department.
■아날로그[디지털]— an analog(ue) [a digital] computer 퍼스널— a personal [home] computer ■—그래픽스 computer graphics —마니아 a hacker —범죄 a computer crime —시대 the computer age —언어 (a) computer language —제어장치 a computer-controlled machine

컴프레서 〈공기 압축기〉〔機〕 a compressor

컵 a glass; 〈상배〉 a cup; a trophy
◆종이 컵 a paper cup / 일회용 컵 a disposable cup / 한 컵의 물 a glass of water / 컵을 비우다 [다 마셔버리다] drain [empty] a glass / 컵에 가득 따르다 fill the glass up (to the brim)

컷 〈삽화〉 an illustration; a cut; 〈필름 등의 편집〉 cutting ◆잔혹한 장면을 컷하다 cut brutal scenes

컷백 〔映〕 a cutback ◆컷백하다 cut back (to)

컹컹 ▶불독이 낯선 사람을 보고 컹컹 짖었다 A bulldog bayed at a stranger.

케냐 〈나라 이름〉 Kenya; 〈공식명〉 the Republic of Kenya
◆케냐의 Kenyan
■—사람 a Kenyan

케네 〈프랑스의 경제학자〉 Quesnay, François (1694-1774)

케네디 〈미국의 정치가〉 Kennedy, John Fitzgerald (1917-63) —국제공항 John F. Kennedy International Airport —라운드 the Kennedy Round

케라틴 〈각질〉〔化〕 keratin

케이매그 KMAG [Korean Military Advisory Group]

케이블 a cable ■—해저 a submarine cable : 해저 케이블을 가설하다 lay a submarine cable ■—카 a cable car

케이블 텔레비전 〈유선 텔레비전〉 cable TV; community antenna television (略 CATV)

케이비에스 KBS [Korean Broadcasting System]

케이스 〈상자〉 a case; 〈경우〉 a case
◆케이스에 넣어두다 keep sth in a case
■담배— a cigarette case

케이스 바이 케이스 case-by-case ▶우리는 이런 문제를 케이스 바이 케이스로 처리하겠다 We'll deal with questions of this kind separately on a case-by-case basis [depending on the circumstance].

케이스 워커 〈사회복지 지도원〉 a caseworker

케이슨 〈잠함〉 a caisson ■—병 caisson [diver's] disease; (口) the bends

케이에스 KS [Korean Standard] ■—마크 a KS mark —표시품 KS goods

케이오 KO; K.O. [knockout]
▶무명의 복서가 라이트급 챔피언을 케이오시켰다 The unknown boxer KO'd the lightweight champion.

케이오시 KOC [the Korean Olympic Committee]

케이크 a cake
◆나이프로 케이크를 자르다 knife a (wedding) cake
▶케이크를 너무 많이 먹지 마라. 그렇지 않으면 체중이 는다 Don't eat too much cake, or you'll put on weight.
■생일[크리스마스]— a birthday [Christmas] cake

케이프 a cape; a tippet

케인스 〈영국의 경제학자〉 Keynes, John Maynard (1883-1946) ■—학설 〔經〕 Keynesianism

케임브리지 〈영국의 도시〉 Cambridge ■—대학 Cambridge University : 케임브리지대학의 학생[졸업생] a Cantabrigian

케첩 ketchup; catchup; (美) catsup
■토마토— tomato ketchup

케케묵다 old; antiquated; 〈시대에 뒤지다〉 old-fashioned; stale; out of date; archaic; outdated; (美) old hat; 〈진부하다〉 stale; hackneyed; timeworn
◆케케묵은 이야기 an old story / 케케묵은 관습 a worm-eaten custom / 케케묵은 학설 a worn-out theory / 케케묵은 생각 a completely

outmoded idea / 케케묵은 수작 a hackneyed remark
▶ 그것은 케케묵은 생각이다 That's a moss-grown idea.
케플러 〈독일의 천문학자〉 Kepler, Johannes (1571-1630)
━망원경 Keplerian telescope; Kepler's telescope ━법칙 the Kepler's law
켄터키 〈미국의 주〉 Kentucky (略 Ken.)
켄트 〈영국의 주〉 Kent
켄트지 ━紙 kent paper
켈러 〈미국의 사회교육가〉 Keller, Helen Adams (1880-1968)
켈로이드 〔醫〕 keloid; cheloid
◆ 켈로이드(모양)의 keloidal
켈트 〈사람〉 a Celt; 〈민족〉 the Celts
━말 Celtic
켕기다 1 〈불안해지다〉 be afraid of 《failure》; feel guilty; have a guilty [bad] conscience; feel uneasy; feel ill at ease
◆ 조금도 켕기는 기색 없이 without (the slightest) compunction / 양심에 켕기다 feel the qualms of conscience; have an uneasy conscience
▶ 양심에 켕겨서 나는 도저히 그런 짓은 못한다 I cannot, in all conscience, do such a thing.
2 〈팽팽하게 당기다〉 strain; stretch; tighten
◆ 밧줄을 켕기다 tighten [strain] a rope; stretch a rope tight
▶ 그 줄을 너무 세게 켕기면 끊어진다 If you strain the rope too hard, it will break.
3 〈마주 버티다〉 vie each other; stand against [up to]; hold out against
켜 〈포개진 층〉 a layer
◆ 벽돌을 켜로 쌓다 pile up bricks; 〈한 장씩〉 put bricks one on top another / 켜를 이루다 form layers; be piled up; be on top of one another
▶ 여러가지 접시가 테이블에 켜로 쌓였다 Plates and dishes were piled up on the table.
켜다 1 〈불을 붙이다〉 light (up); 〈스위치 등을〉 turn [switch]...on
◆ 성냥을 켜다 strike a match / 불을 켜다 make a light
▶ 전등을 켜 주십시오 Please put [turn, switch] on the light.
▶ 라디오를 켜도 될까요? Do you mind if I have the radio on?
▶ 라디오를 켜둔채로 잠자지 마라 Don't sleep with the radio on.
2 〈톱으로〉 saw 《a log》
◆ 통나무를 켜서 널판지를 만들다 saw a log into boards
3 〈현악기를〉 play; sweep 《the strings》
▶ 당신은 바이올린을 켤줄 아십니까? Can you play [perform on] the violin?
▶ 그는 기타를 켜면서 노래를 불렀다 He sang to his accompaniment on the guitar.
켤레[1] 〈公約〉 〔數〕 a conjugate
━각[면, 초점, 축] a conjugate angle [plane, focus, axis] ━근(根) conjugate roots ━복소수 a conjugate complex number ━쌍곡선 a conjugate hyperbola ━지름 a conjugate diameter ━호(弧) a conjugate arc

켤레[2] a pair
◆ 구두 한 켤레 a pair of shoes / 양말 한 켤레 one pair of socks
코 1 〈사람·동물의〉 a nose; 〈개·말 등의〉 a muzzle; 〈코끼리의〉 a trunk; 〈돼지 등의〉 a snout
◆ 납작코 a short [flat, small] nose / 들창코 turned-up nose / 매부리코 a Roman nose / 코를 후비다 pick one's nose 《with a finger》 / 코를 쥐다 hold [pinch] one's nose / 코가 좋다[나쁘다] 〈후각이〉 have a good [bad] nose 《for》; have a good [bad] sense of smell / 코가 예민하다 have a sharp nose / 〈냄새가〉 코를 찌르다 be offensive to the nose
▶ 그는 코가 크다 He has a long [big, large] nose.
▶ 감기가 들어 내 코가 막혔다 My nose is stuffed up with my cold. ⇒ My nasal passages are blocked because of the cold.
▶ 실험실에 들어가니 암모니아 냄새가 코를 찔렀다 Ammonia assailed my nose as I entered the laboratory.
2 〈콧물〉 snivel; nasal mucus
◆ 코를 풀다 blow one's nose 《with a tissue》 / 코를 흘리다 snivel; drivel; run at the nose / 코를 훌쩍이다 snuff; snivel / 코를 닦다 wipe one's (running) nose
▶ 「자 코를 닦아라」하며 그녀는 아이에게 휴지를 주었다 "Here, wipe your nose," she said, handing the child a tissue.
▶ 너는 코를 풀어야겠다 Your nose wants blowing.
▶ 너는 코가 나온다 Your nose is running. ⇒ You have a running [runny] nose. ⇒ You are running at the nose.
3 〈물건의 코〉 the nose; the tip; the cap; the toe
◆ 버선코 the toe of a sock / 신코 the toe [cap] of a shoe
4 〈뜨개질 등의 코〉 a stitch; a link; 〈그물의〉 the knot
5 (비유) ◆ 코가 높다 be proud
코감기 ━感氣 (have) a cold in the nose [head]
◆ 코감기에 걸리다 have a head cold; have a cold in the head
코걸이 a nose ring
코골다 snore
◆ 코고는 사람 a snorer / 코고는 소리 snoring; a snore / 크게 코골다 give loud snores; snore loudly / 자기 코고는 소리에 잠을 깨다 snore oneself awake / 드르렁드르렁 코골다 sleep with a loud snore; snore loudly [terribly] / 코골기 시작하다 fall to snoring / 금방 코골며 잠들다 plunge into a noisy sleep
▶ 그는 몹시 코곤다 He snores loudly. ⇒ He is a terrible snorer.
▶ 그가 코고는 바람에 나는 잠을 잘 수가 없었다 His snore kept me awake.
코끝 the tip of a nose
코끼리 an elephant
◆ 수[암]코끼리 a bull [cow] elephant / 새끼 코끼리 a calf elephant / 코끼리의 코 the trunk of an elephant / 아프리카[인도] 코끼리

an African [Indian] elephant
▶코끼리는 코가 길다 The elephant has a long trunk.
코나크리 〈기니의 수도〉 Conakry
코납작이 a flat-nosed person; 〈기가 꺾인〉 a person who got a snub
코냑 〈브랜디의 일종〉 cognac
코너 〈구석〉 a corner; 〈매장의〉 a special counter (for the young) ■─킥 [蹴] a corner (kick)
코네티컷 〈미국의 주〉 Connecticut (略 Conn.)
코넷 〈악기〉 a cornet
♦코넷 연주자 a conet(t)ist
코높다 〈건방지다〉 (be) proud; arrogant; puffed-up
코다이 〈헝가리의 작곡가〉 Kodály, Zoltán (1882-1967)
코닥 〈商標〉 a Kodak
코담배 snuff
♦코담배를 맡다 take snuff
코대답 ─對答 an indifferent [a nonchalant] answer; a half-hearted [reluctant] answer ─코대답하다 answer indifferently [nonchalantly, reluctantly]
코데인 〈化〉 codein(e)
코듀로이 〈천〉 corduroy ♦코듀로이 바지 corduroy pants; (a pair of) corduroys
코드 1 〈끈〉 a cord; 〈전깃줄〉 a cord; (英) a flex; 〈연장 코드〉 an extension cord
2 〈부호·암호〉 a code
♦코드 북 a code book / 프레스 코드 a press code / 오산 검출 코드 an error-detecting code / 자동 검사 코드 a self-checking code
3 〈화음〉 〈樂〉 chord
코딱지 nose dirt [wax] ♦코딱지를 후비다 pick one's nose
코떼다 suffer [meet with] a rebuff; get a snub; 〈거절당하다〉 get rejected; 〈창피당하다〉 be put to shame
코뚜레 a nose ring ♦쇠코뚜레 a nose ring for cattle; a cattle leader
코란 〈宗〉 the Koran
코랄 〈樂〉 a choral(e)
코러스 〈합창대〉 a chorus ♦남성[여성] 코러스 a chorus of male [female] voices
코로 〈프랑스의 화가〉 Corot, Jean Baptiste Camille (1796-1875)
코로나 〈天〉 a corona (pl. ~s, -nae)
♦코로나 방전 corona discharge / 코로나 전압 corona voltage
코르네유 〈프랑스의 극작가〉 Corneille, Pierre (1606-84)
코르셋 a corset
코르시카 〈프랑스령의 섬〉 Corsica
코르크 cork; 〈마개〉 a cork
■─마개 a cork stopper : 코르크 마개를 하다 [뽑다] cork (up) [uncork] (a bottle) / 누가 그 병에 코르크 마개를 했습니까? Who corked the bottle? ─마개뽑이 a corkscrew
코르티손 〈藥〉 cortisone
코린트 〈고대 그리스의 도시〉 Corinth (▶성경에서는 「고린도」) ■─식 [建] the Corinthian order
코만치 〈아메리칸 인디언의 일족〉 a Comanche (pl. ~(s))
코맹녕이 a person with a twangy voice ⇨ 코맹맹이
코맹맹이 〈사람〉 a person with a twangy voice; a person who twangs ♦코맹맹이 소리 a nasal voice [tone]; a twang / 코맹맹이 소리하다 speak through the nose
코머거리 a person with a clogged [stuffed-up] nose
코메콘 COMECON [〈the Council for Mutual Economic Assistance〉]
코멘트 (a) comment 《on, upon》 ♦코멘트하다 make a comment 《on, upon》 ▶노 코멘트 No comment.
코모로 1 〈나라 이름〉 (the) Comoros; 〈공식명〉 the Federal Islamic Republic of the Comoros 2 〈섬〉 the Comoro Islands
코뮈니케 〈공식 성명〉 (프) a communiqué
♦공동 코뮈니케를 발표하다 issue a joint communiqué
코뮌 a commune ♦파리 코뮌 〔史〕 the Commune (of Paris)
코미디 〈희극〉 a comedy
코미디언 〈희극배우〉 a comedian
코민테른 the Comintern [〈Communist International〉]
코민포름 the Cominform [〈Communist Information Bureau〉]
코밑 ♦코밑에 under the nose ■─수염 (美) a mustache : 코밑수염을 기르다 wear a mustache
코바늘 a hook; 〈레이스의〉 a crochet needle
코발트 〔化〕 cobalt
♦코발트 블루 cobalt blue; azure blue / 코발트색 cobaltic color / 코발트 폭탄 a cobalt bomb; a C-bomb
코방귀 a snort; a pooh-pooh ♦제안에 코방귀 뀌다 spurn the proposal; (口) turn up one's nose at the proposal
코방아찧다 fall (down) on one's face
코번트리 〈영국의 도시〉 Coventry
코브라 〔動〕 a cobra
♦킹코브라 a king cobra
코뿔소 〔動〕 a rhinoceros; (口) a rhino
코사인 〔數〕 cosine (略 cos)
코사크(병) ─〔兵〕 a Cossack
코세다 hardnosed; stiffnecked; stubborn; headstrong
코스 1 a course; a route; a lane; 〈산 속의〉 a trail
♦하이킹 코스 a hiking route [trail, course] / 하루 코스 a one-day course of a trip / 인기있는 데이트 코스 a popular place for dating couples / 비행기가 코스를 벗어나서 날다 fly off course
▶이 코스가 관광에는 제일 좋다 This route is the best for sightseeing.
2 〔競〕〈골프 등의〉 a course; 〈경주·경영의〉 a lane

解說 우리가 흔히 쓰는 ***course***와는 다른 경우로, 수영이나 육상경기의 「코스」는 ***lane***이다. 풀의 「코스로프」는 lane rope다. 또 야구의 「인코스의 공」「아웃코스의 공」은 각각 inside pitch, outside pitch다.「퍼레이드의 코스」는 parade route가 올바른 표현이다.

♦ 제1코스를 달리다 have [run on] Lane No. one / 전 코스를 완주하다 stay the course
3 〈과정〉 a course
♦ 영어의 집중 코스를 택하다[배우다] take an intensive course in English / 박사학위 코스를 밟다 take the doctor's course
4 〈정식 요리에서〉 a course
♦ 코스요리 (美) a special; (英) a set dinner [lunch]
▶ 나는 다섯 코스의 요리를 주문했다 I ordered a five-course dinner.

코스모스 〔植〕 a cosmos
코스타리카 Costa Rica; 〈공식명〉 the Republic of Costa Rica
■ 一사람 a Costa Rican
코스터 〈활주용의〉 a coaster
코스트 〈원가〉 cost ▶ 우리는 생산 코스트를 낮췄다 We lowered the cost of production.
■ 一다운 a reduction in cost 一업 an increase in cost
코시컨트 〔數〕 a cosecant (略 cosec)
코싸쥐이 bury one's face in one's hands (for shame)
코안경 一眼鏡 (프) a pince-nez (▶ 단수·복수 동형)
코알라 〔動〕 a koala
코앞 ♦ 코앞에 under one's (very) nose; right before one
▶ 입시가 코앞에 닥쳤다 Now the entrance examination is near at hand.
코요테 〔動〕 a coyote
코웃음 scoffs; a jeer; a sneer ▶ 그는 내게 코웃음쳤다 He laughed [jeered, sneered] at me.
코일 〔電〕 a coil 一유도[감응]— an induction coil 2차— a secondary coil
코찔찔이 a habitual sniffer [sniffler]
코청 〔解〕 the nasal septum
코치 〈사람〉 a coach; 〈행위〉 coaching; training ♦ 농구[테니스]코치 a basketball [tennis] coach
―코치하다 coach (him, a team)
▶ 우리 형은 야구팀을 코치하고 있다 My brother coaches a baseball team.
■ 一박스 a coach's [coaching] box
코친 〈닭〉 a Cochin
코침 tickling sb's nose ♦ 코침주다 tickle sb's nose [through the nostrils]
코카서스인종 一人種 the Caucasian race
코카인 〔化〕 cocain(e) ■ 一중독 cocainism; cocaine poisoning 一중독자 a cocainist; (美俗) a coke addict
코카콜라 〔商標〕 Coca-Cola; (俗) Coke
코카타르 〔醫〕 nasal catarrh
코커스패니얼 〈개〉 a cocker spaniel
코코넛 〔植〕 a coconut
코코아 〈음료〉 cocoa ♦ 코코아를 마시다 have [drink] cocoa
■ 一나무 a cocoa tree 一열매 a cocoa bean; a cacao (pl. ~s)
코코야자 一椰子 〈나무〉 a coconut palm [tree]; 〈열매〉 a coconut

코콤 COCOM [〈the *Co*ordinating *Com*mittee for Export to Communist Area]
코크스 (a piece of) coke ♦ 코크스를 연료로 하다 use coke for fuel
코키유 (프) 〔料〕 coquille
코탄젠트 〔數〕 cotangent (略 cot)
코털 the hairs of [in] the nostrils ♦ 코털을 뽑다 pull out the hairs of the nostrils
코트 a (tennis) court ♦ 코트를 만들다 lay out a court
코트디부아르 〈나라 이름〉 Côte d'Ivoire; the Ivory Coast; 〈공식명〉 the Republic of Côte d'Ivoire
코트라 KOTRA [〈*Ko*rea *Tra*de Promotion *Corporation*]
코튼 cotton 一사(絲) (a reel of) cotton thread; sewing cotton
코팅 coating
코페르니쿠스 〈폴란드의 천문학자〉 Copernicus, Nicolaus (1473-1543)
■ 一설 the Copernican system 一지동설 the Copernican theory
코펙 〈러시아연방의 화폐단위〉 a copeck; a kopeck; a kopek
코펜하겐 〈덴마크의 수도〉 Copenhagen
코펠 〔(독)〕 Kocher) a camp stove
코프라 copra
♦ 코프라유 copra oil
코피 nosebleed(ing) ♦ 코피가 나다[를 흘리다] bleed at the nose; have a bloody nose; one's nose bleeds
코허리 the narrow part of the nose ♦ 코허리가 시큰하다 be moved with compassion; be touched with pity
코흐 〈독일의 의사·세균학자〉 Koch, Robert (1843-1910)
코흘리개 a snivel(l)ing young kid; a sniveler; a snot(nose)
콕¹ 〔機〕 a cock; 〈수도·가스 등의〉 a tap; (美) a faucet; a valve ♦ 비상 콕 an emergency handle
콕² **1** 〈찌르는 모양〉 pricking hard; piercing hard
♦ 가시[바늘]로 콕 찌르다 prick with a thorn [needle] / 벌이 콕 쏘다 a bee stings sharply / 〈냄새가〉 코를 콕 쏘다 assail one's nostrils
▶ 양심이 콕콕 찔린다 My conscience pricks me.
2 〈쪼는 모양〉 ▶ 닭들이 마당에 흘린 쌀알을 콕콕 쪼고 있다 The hens are pecking at the rice scattered on the yard.
콕토 〈프랑스 시인·극작가〉 Cocteau, Jean (1889-1963)
콘 a [an ice-cream] cone
콘덴서 〔電〕 a condenser
콘도르 〔鳥〕 a condor
콘도미니엄 a condominium
콘돔 a condom; (美) a rubber; (英俗) a French letter
콘래드 〈영국의 작가〉 Conrad, Joseph (1857-1924)
콘비프 corn(ed) beef ■ 一통조림 a canned corn beef
콘서트 a concert ■ 一마스터 a concertmaster

—홀 a concert hall

콘센트 〔電〕 an electric socket; (美) an [a wall] outlet; a plug receptacle; (英) a power electrical point

> 解說 전기 플러그를 꽂는 장치를 「콘센트」라고 하는 것은 우리말식 영어다. 「동심(同心) 플러그」의 뜻인 concentric plug가 어원이라는 설도 있으나 확실치 않다. 하여간 consent나 concent는 「전기 콘센트」는 아니다.
> 영어로는 **socket**이 일반적인 말인데 「전구 소켓」과 구별키 위해 **wall socket**이라고 하는 경우도 있다. (美)에서는 (***wall*** *outlet*; *plug receptacle*, (英)에서는 ***power electrical point***라고 한다.

콘스타치 (美) cornstarch; (英) cornflour
콘스턴트 〈상수〉 〔數〕 a constant
콘월 〈영국의 주〉 Cornwall
콘체르토 (이) 〔樂〕 a (piano) concerto (pl. ~s, -ti)
콘체른 〔(독) Konzern〕 a concern; a combine; a pool
콘크리트 concrete
♦콘크리트 건물 a concrete building / 콘크리트 기초공사 ground concrete work / 콘크리트 믹서 a concrete mixer / 콘크리트 바닥 a concrete floor / 콘크리트 블록 a concrete block / 콘크리트 포장 a concrete pavement / 둑에 콘크리트를 하다 concrete the bank; cover the bank with concrete
콘택트렌즈 a contact lens ▶ 그녀는 콘택트렌즈를 끼고 있다 She wears contact lenses.
콘테스트 a contest ♦미인 콘테스트 a beauty contest
콘트라베이스 〈악기〉 a contrabass; a double bass —연주자 a contrabassist
콘트라스트 〈대조〉 a contrast ▶ 이 집은 풍경과 두드러진 콘트라스트를 보이고 있다 The house is in a striking contrast with the scene.
콘트랄토 (이) 〔樂〕 a contralto (pl. ~s)
콘티넨털 continental ■—탱고 the continental tango
콘티(뉴이티) 〈촬영 대본〉 〔映〕 a continuity
콘플레이크 cornflakes
콜 〈독일의 정치가〉 Kohl, Helmut (1930-)
콜드게임 〔野〕 a called game ▶ 큰 비로 콜드게임이 되었다 The game was called off on account of heavy rain. ≒ The game was called because of heavy rain.
콜드미트 cold meat
콜드웰 〈미국의 작가〉Caldwell, Erskine (1903-87)
콜드체인 a cold chain (▶신선한 식료품을 냉동 유통시키는 조직)
콜드크림 〈화장용의〉 cold cream
콜드퍼머넌트 a cold wave [perm] ▶ 나는 콜드퍼머넌트를 하고 왔다 I've had my hair cold permed.
콜라 〔植〕 cola; kola
콜라주 (프) 〔美術〕 (a) collage
콜럼버스 〈이탈리아의 항해가〉 Columbus, Christopher (1451-1506)
♦콜럼버스의 아메리카 발견 Columbus' discovery of America / 콜럼버스의 달걀 an achievement that seems impossible until it has been actually tried and easily accomplished
콜럼븀 〔化〕 columbium
콜레라 cholera
♦콜레라의 유행 an epidemic of cholera / 콜레라에 걸리다 be infected with cholera / 콜레라 예방주사를 맞다 have a shot against cholera ▶ 그 항구 도시에서 콜레라 환자가 발생했다고 한다 A case of cholera has been reported from the port city.
—의사(擬似) false of cholera 진성— a genuine case of cholera; Asiatic cholera ■—균 a cholera germ [bacterium] —환자 a cholera patient; a case of cholera
콜레스테롤 〔生〕 cholesterol ♦저[고] 콜레스테롤 식품 low-[high-]cholesterol food ▶ 이런 식품은 네 혈액 속의 콜레스테롤치를 높일 거야 That sort of food will raise the cholesterol level in your blood.
콜레이트 〔經〕 a call rate (▶금융기관 상호의 단기 금리)
콜로니 a colony
콜로라도 〈미국의 주〉 Colorado (略 Colo.)
콜로라투라 (이) 〔樂〕 coloratura; colorature —소프라노 coloratura soprano —소프라노 가수 a coloratura (soprano)
콜로세움 〈대원형 경기장〉 the Colosseum
콜로이드 〔化〕 colloid ♦콜로이드성의 colloidal —용액 colloidal solution —이온 colloidal ion —입자 a colloidal particle
콜로타이프 a collotype ♦콜로타이프로 하다 collotype ■—제판 the collotype process —판 a collotype plate
콜록거리다 keep coughing [hacking] ▶ 그는 밤새 콜록거렸다 He was coughing badly all night long.
콜록쟁이 a person with a hacking cough; an asthmatic (patient)
콜록콜록 ♦콜록콜록 기침하다 give [have] a hacking cough
콜론[1] 〈이중점〉 a colon
콜론[2] 〔經〕 a call loan
콜롬보 〈스리랑카의 수도〉 Colombo ■—계획 the Colombo Plan
콜롬비아 Colombia; 〈공식명〉 the Republic of Colombia ♦콜롬비아의 Colombian ■—사람 a Colombian
콜리 (a) collie
콜리지 〈영국의 시인〉 Coleridge, Samuel Taylor (1772-1834)
콜리플라워 〈꽃양배추〉 (a) cauliflower
콜머니 〔經〕 call money
콜사인 〈호출 부호〉 a call sign; call letters
콜콜 zzz ⇨ 쿨쿨
콜타르 〔化〕 coal tar ♦콜타르를 칠하다 tar (a board)
콜택시 a call taxi
콜트 〈권총〉 〈商標〉 a Colt (revolver)
콜호즈 〈구소련의 집단농장〉 a kol(k)hoz (pl. ~es, -zy); a collective farm
콤마[1] 〈구두점〉 a comma
♦두 단어 사이에 콤마를 찍다 put [use, insert] a comma between the two words

2 〈소숫점〉〚數〛 a decimal point
♦ 콤마 이하의 below the decimal; (비유) below [beneath] the mark
▶ 콤마 이하는 버리시오 Drop the figures after the decimal point.

콤바인 〈수확기〉〚機〛 a combine; a harvester
콤비나트 〔(러) kombinat〕 an industrial complex
콤비네이션 〈조합〉 combinations
콤팩트 〈휴대용 화장분갑〉 a compact; 〈소형차〉 a compact (car)
콤퍼지션 〈작곡〉 (a) composition
콤플렉스 〚心〛 (have) an inferiority complex

> 解說 영어의 *complex*는 「강박관념, 이상심리, 복합(複合)」의 뜻으로 쓰이며 우리가 쓰는 「열등감」의 뜻으로는 *inferiority* (열등)를 붙여야 한다. 반대로 「우월감」은 superiority complex [feeling]다.

♦ 백인에 대한 콤플렉스를 없애다 rid *oneself* of [be rid of] *one's* inferiority complex toward the white

콧구멍 the nostrils; the nares (*sing.* naris)
♦ 콧구멍을 벌름거리다 flare *one's* noses
콧김 a snort; the breath from the nose
♦ 콧김이 세다 be influential
콧날 the ridge [line] of the nose ♦ 콧날이 서다 have a straight nose ▶ 그녀는 콧날이 오똑한 미인이다 She is a pretty girl with a shapely nose.
콧노래 a hum
♦ 콧노래를 부르다 hum a song [tune]; sing through the nose / 콧노래를 부르면서 일하다 do *one's* work humming a tune
▶ 그는 콧노래를 부르고 있었다 He was humming a song [tune] (to himself).
콧대 the nose bridge; the bridge [ridge] of the nose; self-assertion; haughtiness
♦ 콧대가 센 사람 a self-assertive [defiant] person / 콧대가 세다 be self-assertive [defiant, haughty, aggressive, conceited] / 콧대를 꺾다 make *sb* humble; (口) take *sb* down a peg (or two); snub *sb* down; knock *sb* off his perch / 콧대가 꺾이다 have *one's* nose put out of joint
▶ 저 녀석은 콧대를 좀 꺾어 놔야 해 That fellow needs to be taken down a peg.
콧등 the bridge [ridge] of the nose
콧마루 the ridge of the nose
콧물 snivel; nasal mucus
♦ 콧물을 훌쩍이다 snuff; snivel / 콧물을 흘리다 snivel; run at nose / 콧물을 닦다 wipe *one's* (running) nose
콧방울 the wings of the nose
콧병 —病 a nose disease
콧소리 **1** 〚音聲〛 a nasal (sound) **2** 〈코먹은 소리〉 a nasal voice [tone]; a twang ▶ 그녀는 콧소리로 말한다 She speaks through the nose [with a twang].
콧수염 —鬚髯 a moustache; (美) a mustache
콧숨 a snort; breathing through the nose
콩 〈두류〉 beans; 〈완두〉 peas; 〈대두〉 a soybean; a soya (bean); a soy (pea)

♦ 삶은 콩 boiled [cooked] beans / 볶은 콩 parched beans [peas] / 콩을 볶다 parch beans / 밭에 콩을 심다 sow beans in the field
콩가루 (soy)bean flour
콩고 〈나라 이름〉 the Congo; 〈공식명〉 the People's Republic of the Congo ♦ 콩고의 Congolese; Congoese ■ 一사람 a Congolese; a Congoese
콩고물 (soy)bean flour
♦ 콩고물떡 rice cake coated with soybean flour
콩국 soybean soup
콩기름 soy(bean) oil; (soya) bean oil
콩깍지 bean chaff; a bean hull [shuck]; 〈완두의〉 a peasecod ♦ 콩깍지를 까다 pod [hull] beans; shell peas
콩깻묵 bean cake; soybean (oil) meal
콩꼬투리 a bean [pea] pod; a legume
콩나물 bean sprouts
■ 一교실 an overcrowded classroom 一국 bean-sprout soup 一밥 boiled rice with bean sprouts 一시루 a jar in which bean sprouts are grown: 콩나물시루 같다 be packed [jammed] like sardines; (美俗) be jammed up
콩댐 treating with bean oil 一콩댐하다 treat (floor paper) with bean oil
콩밥 boiled rice and beans; 〈죄수의 밥〉 prison rations [food]
♦ 콩밥(을) 먹다 serve [do] time 《at》; serve a prison term / 콩밥을 먹이다 put [send] *sb* to prison [jail]; imprison
콩볶듯하다 crack; crackle; rattle; snap
♦ 콩볶듯하는 기관총 소리 the cracking [rattle] of a machine gun
콩새 〚鳥〛 a hawfinch; a grosbeak
콩설기 a rice cake with bean layers
콩소메 (프)〚料〛 consommé; clear soup
콩 심은 데 콩 나고 팥 심은데 팥 난다 《속담》 You cannot make a silk purse out of a sow's ear. ⇒ Like father, like son.
콩알 a grain of beans
콩엿 a taffy with beans
콩으로 메주를 쑨다 해도 곧이듣지 않는다 (속담) You've cried wolf too many times.
콩자반 beans boiled in soysauce
콩장 —醬 parched, seasoned beans
콩죽 —粥 rice and bean porridge
콩짜개 split beans [peas]
콩케팥케 〈뒤죽박죽〉 a hotchpotch; a jumble; a medley; a muddle ♦ 콩케팥케가 되다 be mixed up; be jumbled together [up]; get confused; go to pie
콩쿠르 a contest; a competition; (프) a concours (▶ 단수·복수 동형)

> 解說 「콩쿠르」는 「경쟁」 또는 「협력」이라는 뜻의 프랑스어 *concours*에서 왔다. 영어에서는 *contest* 또는 *competition*으로 나타내고 photo contest (사진 콩쿠르), piano competition (피아노 콩쿠르)과 같이 쓴다.

♦ 콩쿠르에 참가하다 enter a contest
♦ 음악— a musical contest
콩테 〈크레용의 일종〉 (프) conté (crayon)

콩튀듯팥튀듯하다〈몹시 화내다〉fly into a rage; boil with rage [anger]; hit the ceiling; be wild with rage

콩트¹〈프〉a conte; a short story; a short-short

콩트²〈프랑스의 철학자〉Comte, Auguste (1798-1857)

콩팔칠팔 pointlessly; incoherently
♦ 콩팔칠팔 지껄이다 talk in a rambling way; make a rambling [pointless] speech; talk wild

콩팥〈신장〉the kidney

콱 1〈세게〉violently; 〈갑자기〉suddenly
♦ 콱 잡아당기다 pull *sth* with a jerk; give a strong jerk / 옆구리를 콱 쥐어박다 give a strong thrust in the ribs
2〈세게 막히는 모양〉quite; strongly
♦ 숨이 콱 막히다 be choked; be stifled / 코가 콱 막히다 *one's* nose is bunged [stuffed] up / 말이 콱 막히다 be stuck for a word; be at a loss for words

콸라룸푸르〈말레이시아의 수도〉Kuala Lumpur

콸콸〈물 등이〉gushingly; gurglingly
♦ 콸콸 쏟아져 나오다 gush out 《of》 / 콸콸 솟아나다 gurgle up; well up with gurgle
▶ 그는 산허리에서 콸콸 솟아오르는 샘을 발견했다 He found a spring gushing up [out] on the hillside.

쾅 with a bang; with a bump
▶ 그녀는 문을 쾅 닫았다 She slammed the door.
▶ 나는 넘어져서 머리를 마루에 쾅 부딪쳤다 I bumped my head on the floor when I fell.
▶ 그는 벽에 머리를 쾅 부딪쳤다 He clashed his head against the wall.

쾌〈북어 세는 단위〉a string (of 20 dried pollacks) ♦ 북어 한 쾌 one string of twenty dried pollacks

쾌감 快感 a pleasant [an agreeable] feeling [sensation]
♦ 쾌감을 느끼다 feel pleasure; feel good [comfortable, agreeable, fine, nice]

쾌거 快擧 a remarkable deed; a heroic deed [feat]
▶ 그는 마침내 히말라야 등정의 쾌거를 성취했다 He finally achieved a splendid feat of gaining the summit of the Himalayas.

쾌남아 快男兒 a fine [spirited] fellow; a jolly (good) fellow; 《美》a regular guy [fellow]

쾌도 快刀 a sharp sword [blade]; a trenchant sword
♦ 쾌도로 난마(亂麻)를 자르다 solve a knotty problem readily; cut the Gordian knot
▶ 그는 쾌도난마식으로 그 어려운 문제를 풀었다 He solved the difficult problem as quickly and decisively as if he were cutting the Gordian knot.

쾌락 快樂 pleasure; 〈즐김〉enjoyment
♦ 육체적 쾌락 sensual [carnal] pleasures / 쾌락을 추구하다 seek [pursue] pleasure
▶ 그들은 관능적 쾌락에 빠졌다 They gave themselves up to enjoyment of sensual pleasures.
■—주의[설]〔倫〕hedonism; Epicureanism
—주의자 an Epicurean; a hedonist

쾌락 快諾 a ready consent
♦ 쾌락을 얻다 obtain *sb's* ready [willing] consent; be given a hearty consent
—쾌락하다 consent readily; agree willingly; give a ready consent
▶ 양친은 그 결혼을 쾌락했다 The parents gave their willing consent to the marriage.

쾌면 快眠 a sound [restful, nice] sleep

쾌변 快辯 eloquence; fluent speech
♦ 쾌변을 토하다 have a flow of words

쾌보 快報 good news; cheerful [welcome] news; glad tidings
♦ 쾌보를 전하다 convey the joyous news 《to》
▶ 그 쾌보를 접하고 온 시내는 들끓었다 The good news threw the whole city into a wild celebration.

쾌복 快復 complete recovery ⇨ 쾌차 ♦ 병의 쾌복 recovery from sickness

쾌사 快事 a pleasant matter; a joyful event

쾌속 快速 (a) high speed
♦ 쾌속의 high-speed; fast; swift; speedy
▶ 그 차는 쾌속으로 달렸다 The car ran at top [full] speed.
▶ 특급 열차는 시속 200킬로미터의 쾌속으로 달리고 있다 The super express is running at the high speed of two hundred kilometers an hour.

쾌승 快勝 a decisive [an overwhelming] victory 《over》 ♦ 쾌승을 거두다 win a sweeping [an overwhelming] victory 《over》; have an easy win; win easily

쾌유 快癒 complete recovery ⇨ 쾌차
▶ 당신의 빠른 쾌유를 빕니다 I wish you a speedy recovery.

쾌재 快哉 ♦ 쾌재를 부르다 yell with delight 《over》; shout for joy

쾌적하다 快適— comfortable; pleasant; cozy
♦ 쾌적한 방 a comfortable [cozy, pleasant] room
▶ 이 차는 승차감이 쾌적하다 This car is comfortable [pleasant] to ride in.

쾌조 快調 an excellent condition ♦ 쾌조를 보이다 go on smoothly ♦ 엔진은 쾌조로 작동되고 있다 The engine is running [working] smoothly.

쾌주 快走〈배가〉fast sailing —쾌주하다 run well; sail [run] fast [at an exhilarating speed]

쾌차 快差〈완쾌〉complete recovery 《from an illness》; the return [restoration] of health
—쾌차하다 be completely recovered; recover completely; be quite restored (to health); be perfectly well again
▶ 그 환자는 쾌차하였다 The patient is quite strong again.
▶ 어머니는 신경통이 쾌차되셨다 My mother made a complete recovery from neuralgia.

쾌척하다 快擲—〈희사하다〉generously throw out; make a generous contribution 《to, for, toward》; give 《a donation》willingly

쾌청 快晴 fine [good] weather; fair [splendid, bright] and clear weather
—쾌청하다 (very) fine; nice and fine
♦ 쾌청한 날 a clear day

쾌청한 ▶전국적으로 쾌청한 날씨가 될 것이다 Fair skies will prevail over the country.
▶내일은 쾌청한 날씨가 될 거야 It [The weather] will be fine [clear] tomorrow.

쾌투 快投 a good [nice] throw

쾌활하다 快活— cheerful; merry; cheery; jolly; gay; jovial; lively
♦쾌활한 성격 cheerful spirit / 쾌활한 사람 a jolly [lively] fellow / 쾌활하게 웃다 laugh merrily [cheerfully]
▶그 소녀는 쾌활하다 The girl is full of spirit [energy]. ⇒ She is a very cheerful kid.

쾌히 快— readily; willingly; 〈반갑게〉 gladly
♦쾌히 그에게 돈을 꾸어주다 lend him money willingly
▶그는 그것을 쾌히 승낙했다 He accepted it most willingly.
▶그는 이 안을 쾌히 승낙해주었다 He readily consented to this plan.
▶쾌히 제가 도와드리겠습니다 I'll gladly help you. ⇒ I'll be glad to help you.

쾨쾨하다 stinking ⇨ 퀴퀴하다

쾨헬번호 —番號 〈모차르트의 작품을 정리하여 매긴 번호〉 Köchel number (略 K.)

쾰른 〈독일의 도시〉 Cologne

쿠데타 〈프〉 a coup d'état
♦쿠데타를 일으키다 effect a coup d'état; pull (off) a coup ■군사[군부]— a military coup 무혈— a bloodless coup

쿠렁쿠렁하다 slack-filled ♦쿠렁쿠렁하게 채우다 slack-fill

쿠르베 〈프랑스의 화가〉 Courbet, Gustave (1819-77)

쿠릴해류 —海流 the Kurile [Okhotsk] Current

쿠바 Cuba; 〈공식명〉 the Republic of Cuba
■—사람 a Cuban —설탕 Cuban sugar

쿠베르탱 〈프랑스의 근대 올림픽 창시자〉 Coubertin, Pierre, Baron de (1863-1937)

쿠션 a cushion

> [解說] 소파 등에 놓는 장식용 쿠션을 *cushion* 이라고도 하지만 throw pillow 또는 간단히 pillow라고도 한다. 우리말로는 운동화 등의 탄력성을 「쿠션이 좋다」고 말하지만 실제는 「끼워넣는 것」의 탄력성이므로 cushion이 아니고 pad다. 카세트 테이프 등을 넣어서 보내는 「쿠션봉투」는 padded bag이라고 한다.

♦쿠션이 좋은 의자 a soft, comfortable chair / 쿠션을 대다 cushion (a seat)
▶이 차는 쿠션이 좋다 The seats in this car provide a good support.
■—스리— 〈撞球〉 three-cushion billiards [carom]; three cushions

쿠웨이트 Kuwait; 〈공식명〉 the State of Kuwait
♦쿠웨이트의 Kuwaiti
■—사람 a Kuwaiti

쿠키 〈과자〉 a cookie; a cooky
▶어머니는 언제나 손수 쿠키를 만들어 주신다 My mother usually bakes homemade cookies.

쿠페 〈소형차〉 〈프〉 a coupé; a coupe

쿠폰 a coupon ♦〈통신판매 등의〉 주문용 쿠폰 an order coupon / 주문식 쿠폰 판매법 a coupon system / 쿠폰으로 사다 purchase by means of coupon
■—권(券) a coupon ticket —제(制) a coupon system

쿡¹ 〈요리사〉 a cook

쿡² 〈찌르는 모양〉 violently; vigorously
♦옆구리를 쿡 찌르다 poke sb in the ribs

쿨러 〈냉방 장치〉 an air conditioner; 〈냉각기〉 a cooler
■카— a car cooler

쿨롬 〈電〉 a coulomb (略 C) ■—계 a coulomb meter; a coulometer

쿨리 〈〈중〉 苦力〉 a coolie; a cooly

쿨쿨 〈코고는 소리〉 snoring; zzz ♦쿨쿨 코를 골다 snore loudly / 쿨쿨 자다 sleep soundly; be fast asleep

쿵 with a bump
—쿵하다 ♦쿵하고 떨어지다 fall plump / 쿵하고 넘어지다 fall down with a thud / 쿵하고 놓다 flop [slam] *sth* down 《on the table》

쿵쾅거리다 romp about; make din; raise a racket

쿵쿵 1 〈무거운 것이 연이어 떨어지는 소리〉 with thumps [plumps, bangs]
2 〈북소리〉 bang, bang; boom, boom
3 〈발구르는 소리〉 stamp, stamp; thumping
4 〈찧는 소리〉 ♦방아를 쿵쿵 찧다 pound (grain) heavily with a pestle

쿵푸 〈〈중〉 功夫〉 kung fu

쿼터백 〔美蹴〕 (a) quarterback (略 q.b.)
♦쿼터백을 맡아보다 quarterback (for a team)

쿼털리 〈계간〉 quarterly

쿼텟 〔樂〕 a quartet

퀀셋 〔美〕 a Quonset hut; a Nissen hut

퀘벡 〈캐나다의 주〉 Quebec

퀘스천마크 〈물음표〉 a question mark

퀘이커 〔宗〕 a Quaker; a Friend ■—교파 Quakerism; the Society of Friends

퀭하다 cavernous; sunken; deep-set; hollow
♦퀭한 눈 sunken [cavernous, deep-set] eyes

퀴닌 〈항말라리아 약〉 quinine

퀴닌산 —酸 〔化〕 quininic acid

퀴륨 〔化〕 curium

퀴리 1 〈사람〉 Curie, Pierre (남편); Curie, Marie Sklowdowska (부인)
2 〈방사능 단위〉 〔物〕 a curie (略 c.)
■마이크로— a microcurie ■—법칙 〔物〕 the Curie's law —온도 the Curie temperature

퀴즈 a quiz; a quiz game ■—프로그램 a quiz program [show]; a panel show: 퀴즈 프로그램의 사회자 a quizmaster

퀴퀴하다 ill-smelling; foul-smelling; stinking; offensive ♦퀴퀴한 냄새가 나다 smell offensive [foul]; stink

퀸 a queen ♦다이아몬드의 퀸 〈카드의〉 the queen of diamonds

퀸텟 〔樂〕 a quintet(te)

퀼팅 〈수예〉 quilting ♦퀼팅 가운 a quilted gown

큐 1 〈당구채〉 a cue ♦큐를 잡다 play billiards 《with》
2 〈신호〉 a cue ♦큐를 주다 cue; give a cue;

큐비즘 〔美術〕 cubism ◆큐비즘(풍)의 그림 cubist(ic) picture
큐시 〈품질 관리〉 Q.C.; quality control
큐피드 〔로神〕 Cupid
쿨렉스모기 a culex mosquito 《pl. ~es, ~s》
크게 big; large; very; greatly; highly; 〈대대적으로〉 hugely; a great deal; 〈대규모로〉 on a large scale; in a large scale
  ♦글씨를 크게 쓰다 write large [in large letters] / 장사를 크게 하다 carry on a large [an extensive] business; do business on a large scale / 눈을 크게 뜨다 open one's eyes wide / 윗도리를 크게 하다 let out [enlarge] a jacket / 라디오 소리를 크게 하다 turn up (the volume) of [on] the radio / 크게 다르다 be very [much, far, widely] different (from) / 크게 환영하다 receive with open arms / 크게 놀라다 be greatly surprised (to hear) / 크게 기뻐하다 be very delighted; be highly pleased
  ▶내 작업복을 좀 크게 만들어 주세요 Make my overalls rather full.
  ▶다시 한번 크게 말씀해 주십시오 Please say it again louder [in a loud voice].
  ▶우리는 그 소식을 듣고 크게 놀랐다 We were greatly surprised to hear the news.
  ▶그 신문은 이 사건을 크게 보도했다 The paper played [written] up this incident [gave this incident front page attention].
  ▶그는 공부를 열심히 하지 않은 것을 크게 후회했다 He was very sorry he had not studied hard.
  ▶그는 크게 만족한듯 고개를 끄덕였다 He nodded with great satisfaction.
크기 size; dimension; 〈용적〉 volume; bulk; 〈양·형상의〉 magnitude
  ♦라이터 크기의 카메라 a camera (about) the size of a cigarette lighter / 실물 크기의 초상 a life-size portrait / 달걀 크기의 돌 a stone as big as an egg
  ♦온갖 모양과 크기가 갖추어져 있습니다 We have all sizes and shapes.
  ▶저 궤짝의 크기는 어느 정도인가? What size is that box?
  ▶나는 그 가스탱크의 크기에 놀랐다 I was surprised at the enormous size of the gas tank.
  ▶그 집들은 크기가 다 같다 Those houses are all of the same size.
  ▶이 집은 우리 가족에게 충분한 크기다 This house is big [large] enough for my family.
  ▶이 타이프라이터는 휴대하기에 알맞은 크기다 This typewriter is of a (conveniently) portable size.
크나크다 huge; gigantic; giant; enormous
  ♦크나큰 탱커 a huge [gigantic] tanker / 크나큰 손실 a tremendous [an enormous] loss / 크나큰 은혜 a great favor [obligation]
크낙새 〔鳥〕 a Korean redheaded woodpecker
크다[1] 〈자라다〉 grow (up); get bigger; become taller; grow larger; increase in size; 〈증대하다〉 swell; expand; spread
  ▶그는 작년보다 10센티미터가 컸다 He has grown ten centimeters taller than last year.
  ▶나는 서울에서 태어나 서울서 컸다 I was born and brought up in Seoul.
  ▶나는 커서 훌륭한 사람이 되고 싶다 I want to be somebody when I grow up.
  ▶서울의 위성 도시는 자꾸 커지고 있다 The satellite cities around Seoul are growing rapidly.
  ▶그는 시골에서 컸다 He grew up in the country.
크다[2] 〈형상·규모 등이〉 big; large; great

> 解說 물건에 대해 말할 때 big은 중량·부피가 큰 것에, large는 면적·넓이에 중점을 둔다.
> 수·양에 대해서는 large가 일반적으로 쓰인다. big은 구어적이고, 말하는 사람의 감정이 담겨 있는 경우가 많다.

  ♦큰 강 a big [large, major] river / 큰 보따리 a bulky package / 큰 기대 high hopes; great expectations / 큰 잘못을 저지르다 make a big [serious] mistake
  ▶그녀는 어머니보다 (훨씬) 크다 She is (much) bigger [taller] than her mother.
  ▶태풍은 작물에 큰 손해를 끼쳤다 The typhoon caused [did] a great [serious, severe] damage to the crops.
  ▶이 모양에 이 색깔로 더 큰 것이 있습니까? Do you have another one in this style and color, but a larger size?
  ▶그는 너무 커서 그 양복을 입지 못한다 He is too big to fit into that suit.
  ▶엊저녁에 큰 지진이 있었다 There was a big [a severe] earthquake last night.
  ▶우리는 승리를 위해 큰 희생을 치렀다 We paid heavy price for victory.
크라이슬러 〈자동차〉 (商標) a Chrysler
크라프트지 —紙 kraft (paper)
크래커 a cracker ◆크래커를 와작와작 먹다 crunch a cracker
크랭크 a crank ◆크랭크를 돌리다 crank (an engine); turn a crank / 크랭크인하다 〔映〕 start filming / 크랭크업하다 〔映〕 finish filming
  ■—축 a crankshaft
크레디트 a credit
  ◆크레디트로 사다 buy on credit
  ▶현금입니까, 크레디트입니까? Cash or charge? ⇒ (Will it be) cash or charge?
  ■—카드 a credit card: 크레디트 카드를 쓸 수 있나요? Do you accept a (credit) card?
크레바스 〈빙하 등의 갈라진 틈〉 a crevasse
크레센도 (이) 〔樂〕 crescendo (略 cres., cresc.)
크레용 (a) crayon
  ♦흰[빨간] 크레용 a stick of white [red] crayon; a white [red] crayon / 12색 크레용 twelve-colored crayons / 크레용으로 그림을 그리다 draw a picture in crayon(s); crayon (a portrait)
  ■—화 a crayon drawing; a picture in crayon(s) —화가 a crayonist
크레오소트 〔化〕 creosote
크레이터 a (lunar) crater

크기의 표현

1. 크다
「크다」에 해당하는 영어로 가장 일반적인 것은 large, big, great이다. 그밖에도 「아주 크다」의 뜻인 huge, enormous, gigantic, monstrous, massive, vast, immense 등이 있다.
▶ 인수는 나보다 훨씬 크다 In-su is much bigger than I (am) [me].
▶ 그 씨름 선수는 엄청나게 컸다 The wrestler was really gigantic.
▶ 그녀 집 부엌에는 대형 찬장이 놓여 있었다 There was a massive sideboard in her kitchen.
▶ 매년 무척 많은 사람들이 교통사고로 죽는다 A great number of people are killed in traffic accidents every year.

2. 보통이다, 중간 정도다
▶ 우리 집은 보통 크기다 My house is of medium size.
▶ 그 남자는 중키에 보통 몸집이었다 He was a man of medium build [average height and weight].
▶ 내가 사는 동네는 크지도 작지도 않은 보통 크기다 The town where I live is neither large nor small, just average size.

3. 작다, 어리다
「작다」를 나타내는 주요한 말로는 small과 little이 있다. small과 little은 대개의 경우 같은 뜻으로 쓸 수 있으나 small이 객관적으로 「작다」는 것을 말하는 데 대하여 little은 감정적인 뉘앙스가 있다.
▶ 내 동생은 나이에 비해 작다 My brother is small for his age.
▶ 많은 어린이들이 길거리에서 놀고 있었다 Many little children were playing in the street.
▶ 나는 그 아기의 조그만 손을 쥐었다 I held the baby's tiny hand.

4. 크기를 묻고 대답하는 방법
보통 how와 what을 사용해 묻는 두 가지 방법이 있는데, 일상적으로 how가 많이 쓰이고 what에는 기술적·과학적인 의미가 내포되어 있다.
(1) 길이
▶ 會話 「자네는 어느 정도나 헤엄칠 수 있나?」「500미터 정도 될거야」 "How far can you swim?" "I guess about five hundred meters."
▶ 會話 「이 차는 길이가 얼마나 됩니까?」「4미터 72센티미터입니다」 "What is the length of this car?" "It's 4 meters seventy-two centimeters long [in length]."
(2) 높이
▶ 會話 「자네는 신장이 얼마지?」「5피트 7인치야」 "How tall are you?" "I'm five feet seven inches tall."
▶ 會話 「설악산의 높이는 얼마지?」「가만 있자, 1,708 미터야」 "What's the height of Sŏraksan?" "Let me see. It is 1,708 meters."
(3) 넓이
▶ 會話 「이 도로의 넓이는 얼마나 될까?」「정확히 6미터야」 "I wonder how wide this road is?" ⇌ "What is the width of this road?" "It's just six meters."
(4) 깊이
▶ 會話 「이 호수의 깊이는 얼마입니까?」「가장 깊은 곳이 192미터입니다」 "How deep is this lake?" ⇌ "What's the depth of this lake?" "At its deepest, it's one hundred ninety-two meters deep [in depth]."
(5) 면적
▶ 會話 「이 운동장은 넓이가 얼마나 됩니까?」「33,000 제곱미터입니다」 "How large is this field?" "It's thirty-three thousand square meters."
(6) 속도
▶ 會話 「그는 100미터를 몇 초에 달립니까?」「최고 기록은 9.89초입니다」 "How fast does he run the one-hundred-meter?" "His record is nine point eight nine seconds."
(7) 온도
▶ 會話 「이 교실은 덥군. 몇 도나 되나?」「적어도 섭씨 30도는 될 거야」 "It's hot here in this classroom. I wonder how hot it is." "Probably it's thirty degrees or more centigrade."
(8) 인구·규모
▶ 會話 「서울은 인구가 몇 명입니까?」「약 천만 명입니다」 "What's the population of Seoul?" "It's about ten million."
▶ 會話 「이 학교의 규모는 얼마나 됩니까?」「학생 수 말입니까, 아니면 캠퍼스의 넓이 말입니까?」 "How big is this school?" "You mean the number of students or the size of the campus?"

크레이프 〈직물〉 crepe; crape
■ —셔츠 a crepe undershirt —지(紙) crepe paper
크레인 〈기중기〉〔機〕 a crane; a derrick
♦ 크레인으로 들어 올리다 lift [hoist] *sth* with a crane
■ 데릭— a derrick crane 지브— a jib crane
—선 a floating crane —차 a crane truck
크레졸 〔化〕 cresol ♦ 크레졸의 cresylic
■ —비눗물 a saponated cresol solution —수 cresol water
크레타섬 〈에게해의 섬〉 Crete ♦ 크레타섬의 Cretan ■ —사람 a Cretan
크레파스 a pastel crayon
크레펠린 검사 —檢査 〔心〕 Kraepelin's census [test]
크렘린 the Kremlin ■ —궁전 the Kremlin
크로네 〈덴마크·노르웨이의 화폐단위〉 a krone
크로노미터 〈정밀 시계〉 a chronometer
크로닌 〈스코틀랜드 출신의 의사·작가〉 Cronin, Archibald Joseph (1896-1981)
크로마뇽인 —人 〔人類〕 Cromagnon [Cro-Magnon] man
크로셰 ♦ 크로셰로 뜨다 crochet 《a shawl》

크로스레이트

■ —뜨개바늘 a crochet hook [needle] —뜨기 crochet work
크로스레이트 〈經〉 cross rate ◆영·미 크로스레이트 〈영·미 환시세〉 the Anglo-American cross rate
크로스워드퍼즐 a crossword puzzle ◆크로스워드퍼즐을 하다 do [work on] a crossword puzzle
크로스컨트리 a cross-country race; (a) cross-country
크로커스 〈植〉 a crocus 《*pl.* ~es, -ci》
크로켓 〈料〉 a croquette
크로키 〈프〉〈美術〉 a croquis; a rapid sketch; a rough draft
크로포트킨 〈러시아의 무정부주의자〉 Kropotkin, Pëter Alekseevich (1842-1921)
크롤 〈泳〉 the crawl (stroke) ◆크롤로 헤엄치다 swim the crawl
크롬 〈化〉 chromium; chrome
■ 염화[산화]— chrome chloride [oxide] ■ —강 chrome [chromium] steel —도금 chromium plating —산 chromic acid —철광 chromite; chrome iron [ore] —합금 chrome amalgam
크롬웰 〈영국의 군인·정치가〉 Cromwell, Oliver (1599-1658)
크리스마스 Christmas 《略 Xmas》; Christmas Day; Christmastide; Christmas time
◆크리스마스에 at Christmas; on Christmas / 크리스마스를 축하하다 keep [observe] Christmas / 크리스마스에 그에게 시계를 사주다 buy him a watch on Christmas
▶크리스마스를 축하합니다 (I wish you) A merry Christmas. ⇒ A merry Christmas to you!
■크리스마스 세일 (게시) Christmas Sale.
■ —선물 a Christmas present [gift]; 〈하인 등에게 주는〉 a Christmas box —실 a Christmas seal —이브[전야] 〈on〉 Christmas Eve —카드 a Christmas card: 크리스마스카드를 보내다[받다] send [get] a Christmas card 《to [from]》 —캐럴 a Christmas carol —케이크 a Christmas cake —트리 a Christmas tree —파티 a Christmas party —휴가 Christmas holidays
크리스천 a Christian (⇨ 기독교(~도))
■ —네임 a Christian name; a baptismal name
크리스털 〈수정〉 crystal ■ —글라스[유리] crystal glass
크리스티 〈영국의 추리작가〉 Christie, Agatha Miller (1891-1976)
크리스티아니아 〈스키〉 Christiania
크리켓 a cricket
◆크리켓을 하다 play cricket
■ —선수 a cricketer; a cricket player —팀 a cricket team
크릴 〈動〉 a krill (▶단수·복수 동형)
크림[1] 1 〈식품〉 cream ◆크림 모양의 creamy; creamlike
2 〈화장품〉 (facial) cream ◆얼굴에 크림을 바르다 apply cream to *one's* face
3 ⇨ 아이스크림
■ 배니싱[콜드]— vanishing [cold] cream 생— fresh cream 셰이빙— shaving cream 화장용— cosmetic [facial, face] cream —빛

cream (color) —빵 a cream bun
크림[2] 〈우크라이나의 크림반도〉 Crimea; the Crimean Peninsula ■ —전쟁 the Crimean War
크립톤 〈化〉 krypton
크메르 Khmer (⇨ 캄보디아) ■ —말 Khmer —족 a Khmer 《*pl.* ~ (s)》
크세논 〈化〉 xenon
큰가시고기 〈魚〉 a stickleback; a tittlebat
큰개자리 〈天〉 the (great) Dog; Canis Major
큰계집 a legal wife ⇨ 본처
큰고래 〈動〉 a finback (whale)
큰골 〈解〉 the cerebrum—대뇌(大腦)
큰곰 〈動〉 a brown bear
큰곰자리 〈天〉 the Great Bear
큰기침하다 clear *one's* throat loudly (to draw *sb's* attention); give a cough
큰길 a main street [road]; a thoroughfare; an avenue; a highway; a broad street
◆큰길을 활보하다 swagger along [strut on] the road
▶그 데모대는 큰길로 미어지게 행진했다 The demonstration parade shuffled along the main street.
큰누이 *one's* eldest [〈美〉 oldest] sister
큰달 〈긴달〉 a long month
큰대자 —大字 ◆큰대자로 눕다 lie at full length; stretch *oneself* / 큰대자로 넘어지다 fall flat [full length]
▶그는 침대에 큰대자로 누워 있었다 He was lying in full length on the bed. ⇌ He was stretching (himself) out on the bed.
큰댁 —宅 *one's* eldest brother's house ⇨ 큰집
큰돈 a large sum of money; a lot of money; 〈비용〉 a great cost
◆큰돈을 벌다 make a lot of money
▶100만원이면 내게는 큰돈이다 One million won is a lot (of money) to me.
▶그는 그 그림을 큰돈을 주고 샀다 He bought the painting at a great price.
큰따옴표 double quotes
큰딸 〈맏딸〉 *one's* eldest daughter
큰마누라 *one's* wedded wife; a legal [lawful] wife
큰마음 1 〈대망〉 a great desire; (an) ambition; (an) aspiration
◆큰마음을 품다 have [cherish, harbor] an ambition; be full of ambitions / 큰마음을 품고 남미로 가다 go over to South America with a great ambition [with high aspirations]
2 〈후한 마음〉 a big [large] heart; a generous heart
◆큰마음 써서 팁을 후하게 주다 tip 《a waiter》 generously; generously tip 《a waiter》; fork out a handsome gratuity (in a hotel)
▶나는 큰마음 먹고 고급 호텔에 묵었다 I went to the expense of putting up at a high-class hotel.
▶나는 큰마음 먹고 그것을 해보겠다 I'm going to risk [chance] it.
▶나는 큰마음 먹고 고급시계를 샀다 I treated myself to an expensive watch.
▶나는 큰마음 먹고 새옷을 맞췄다 I indulged in a new suit.

큰말 〔言〕 a heavy isotope of a word
큰물 a heavy flood; 〈대홍수〉 a deluge; 〈범람〉 an overflow
♦ 큰물지다 be flooded; be inundated
▶ 집중호우로 그 지방에 큰물이 졌다 A flood struck that area as a result of the localized downpour. ⇒ The localized downpour caused a flood in that area.
큰바늘 〈시계의〉 the long [minute] hand
큰북 a big drum; 〈오케스트라용의〉 a low [bass] drum
큰불 〈화재〉 a big [great] fire; a destructive [disastrous] fire; a conflagration; a holocaust
▶ 엊저녁에 우리집 가까이에 큰불이 났었다 There was a big fire [A big fire broke out] in my neighborhood last night.
큰비 a heavy rain; a big [heavy, torrential] rainfall; (口) a drencher ▶ 큰비가 왔다 There was [We had] a downpour [heavy rainfall].
큰사람 〈키가 큰〉 a tall man; 〈거인〉 a giant (of a man); 〈성인〉 an adult; a grown-up; 〈위대한〉 a great man; a great [master] mind
♦ 큰사람이 되다 attain greatness
큰사랑 —舍廊 a large guest room; the main guest room
큰사위 〈맏사위〉 one's eldest son-in-law
큰살림 a large [big] family ▶ 우리는 큰살림이다 I have a large family. ⇒ My family is large.
큰상 —床 a large feast table (for the guest of honor)
큰소리 1 〈음성〉 a loud voice
♦ 큰소리로 in [with] a loud voice; loudly; aloud / 큰소리로 부르다 call *sb* in a loud voice; call out / 큰소리로 외치다 shout in a loud voice [loud(ly)]; give a loud cry
▶ 큰소리로 말하지 마라 Don't shout [speak loud(ly)].
▶ 큰소리로 말해주시오 Please speak a little louder. ⇒ Louder, please.
2 〈야단〉 a roar; a yell; a shout; a bawl; a rawl
♦ 큰소리로 야단치다 call down; scold (severely); roar out
3 〈흰소리〉 a big talk; boasting; boastful words; bragging
♦ 큰소리치다 talk big; brag 《of》; boast 《of, that》
▶ 그는 늘 큰소리를 친다 He always talk big. ⇒ He always blows his own horn.
큰손 〈주요 업체〉 major dealers; the majors
큰손녀 —孫女 〈맏손녀〉 one's eldest granddaughter
큰손님 〈귀빈〉 an honored [a distinguished] guest; a guest of honor; 〈많은 손님〉 many [numerous] guests
큰손자 —孫子 〈맏손자〉 one's eldest grandson
큰솥 a large pot; a cauldron
큰아기 1 〈처녀〉 a grown-up girl; a maiden
2 〈맏딸〉 one's eldest [(美) oldest] daughter
큰아들 〈맏아들〉 one's eldest son
큰아버지 one's father's elder brother; one's elder uncle
큰어머니 the wife of one's father's elder brother; one's elder aunt
큰언니 one's eldest sister
큰오빠 one's eldest brother
큰일 1 〈대업〉 a great thing; a great task; a big [an important] job; 〈큰 기업〉 a great enterprise; a great achievement [deed]; a great [monumental] work
♦ 큰일을 이룩하다 achieve [do] a great thing [work] / 큰일을 계획하다 plan a big enterprise
▶ 이건 큰일입니다 This is no small undertaking. ⇒ This is a big job.
▶ 그 놈은 꼭 큰일을 할 걸세 He is sure to do something big some day.
▶ 지금부터가 큰일이다 We've got a long way to go yet.
2 〈중대사〉 an important matter [affair]; 〈재난〉 a great trouble; a disaster; 〈위기〉 a crisis (*pl.* crises); an emergency; 〈대사〉 an important event
♦ 큰일(이) 나다 assume alarming [serious] proportions; grow [get] serious; face a matter of grave [serious] concern; face disaster / 큰일을 저지르다 cause [invite] a disaster; cause a serious trouble
▶ 큰일났다 The worst has happened. ⇒ Here's a nice [pretty] go. ⇒ What a fine fix we're in! ⇒ What shall I do!
▶ 그런 짓을 하면 큰일난다 It may bring upon you serious consequences. ⇒ It will lead you to a grave consequence.
▶ 어머니가 큰일났어요 Something awful has happened to my mother.
▶ 실수하면 큰일난다 A miss, and all is up [over].
▶ 아버지가 들으시면 큰일난다 If it comes to my father's ear, I shall get into an awful row.
큰절[1] 〈예의를 갖춘 절〉 a deep bow ━ 큰절하다 make a deep bow; 〈초례청에서〉 make one's ceremonial deep bows
큰절[2] 〈큰사찰〉 a main temple; a head temple
큰집 1 〈커다란〉 a big [large] house; a mansion 2 〈맏형의〉 the house of one's eldest brother 3 〈정실의 집〉 the house [home] of the legal wife
큰처남 —妻男 the eldest brother of one's wife; one's eldest brother-in-law
큰체하다 act big; put on airs; act the big shot
큰춤 a full-dress dance; dancing in costume
♦ 큰춤추다 dance in costume
큰치마 a long trailing skirt
큰칼 〈형구〉 a large cang(ue); 〈검〉 a long sword
큰코다치다 get the worst of it; pay dearly; have bitter experiences; pay dearly 《for》; (俗) get [take] it in the neck
▶ 그런 짓을 하다가는 큰코 다칠걸 You will suffer if you do such a thing. ⇒ You shall smart for this.
▶ 그는 믿지 못할 사람을 믿었다가 큰코 다쳤다 He made the bitter experience of putting his faith in someone who couldn't be trusted.
▶ 그것 때문에 큰코 다쳤다 I paid dearly for it. ⇒ It cost me dear.

큰판 〈도박의〉 a high play (at cards)
큰할아버지 one's grandfather's elder brother; a granduncle
큰형 —兄 one's eldest brother; 〈호칭〉 big brother
큰형수 —兄嫂 the wife of one's eldest brother; one's eldest sister-in-law
클라리넷 〔樂〕 a clarinet
  ■ —주자(奏者) a clarinet(t)ist; a clarinet player
클라우제비츠 〈독일의 군사이론가〉 Clausewitz, Karl von (1780-1831)
클라이맥스 a climax
  ◆ 클라이맥스에 달하다 reach [come to] the climax 〈of a film〉
  ▶ 여기서 그 얘기는 클라이맥스에 달한다 Here the story reaches [comes to] the climax.
클라이스트 〈독일의 극작가〉 Kleist, Heinrich von (1777-1811)
클래스 〈학급〉 a class; 〈등급〉 a class

> [解說] 학교에서의 「클래스」는 「학급, 반」의 뜻으로 영어에서도 *class*를 (the) 6 B Class (6학년 B반), class 2D (2학년 D반)으로 쓴다. class는 또 math class, class in math (수학반)와 같이 과목별 「수업」도 나타낸다.
> (美)에서는 class를 「동기 졸업생(반)」의 뜻으로 class of 1997 (1997년도 졸업반)과 같이 쓴다 ; I was in the same class with her. ⇒ She and I were in the same class. (나는 그녀와 동기 졸업생이었다)

  ◆ 영어 클래스 an English class
  ▶ 이 클래스는 40명이다 This class is composed [consists] of forty students.
클래스메이트 〈동급생〉 a classmate ▶ 우리는 지난해에 클래스메이트였다 We were classmates last year.
클래식 a classic; 〈총칭〉 classics ■ —음악 classical music
클랙슨 a klaxon; a horn
  ◆ 클랙슨을 울리다 sound [toot] the klaxon [horn]; honk
  ▶ 클랙슨 금지 〈게시〉 No Horn Blowing.
클러치 〔機〕 〈자동차의〉 a clutch; 〈보트의〉 a rowlock; crutch
  ◆ 클러치를 넣다 shove the clutch in; throw in the clutch
  ▶ 그는 클러치를 풀었다 He let out the clutch.
클럽 **1** 〈골프채〉 a club; a playclub
  2 〈동호인〉 a club; 〈건물〉 a clubhouse
  ◆ 클럽에 들다 join a club; become a member of a club
  ▶ 그녀는 테니스 클럽에 들어 있다 She belongs to the tennis club.
  3 〈카드놀이〉 clubs
클레 〈스위스의 화가〉 Klee, Paul (1879-1940)
클레망소 〈프랑스의 정치가·총리〉 Clemenceau, Georges Eugène Benjamin (1841-1929)
클레오파트라 〈이집트의 여왕〉 Cleopatra (69-30 B.C.)
클레이사격 —射擊 trapshooting; clay pigeon shooting
클레임 〔經〕 a claim (for damages)

> [解說] 영어의 *claim*은 「요구, 청구」, 특히 돈에 관한 「배상」 등의 뜻으로 쓰이며 「불평, 반대」의 뜻은 아니다. 따라서 「클레임을 걸다」는 complain; make a complaint 또는 object; raise an objection 등으로 해야 한다 ; He complained [made complaints] about the hotel service. (그는 호텔 서비스에 클레임을 걸었다)

  ◆ 클레임을 붙이다 make [put in] a claim for compensation/ 클레임을 제기하다 advance a claim; make a claim on; send in a claim / 클레임에 응하다 meet a claim for damages
클렌저 〈洗劑〉 a cleanser; a detergent
클렌징크림 cleansing cream
클로델 〈프랑스의 시인·외교관〉 Claudel, Paul Louis Charles Marie (1868-1955)
클로렐라 〔植〕 a chlorella (algae)
클로로마이세틴 〔藥〕 chloromycetin
클로로벤젠 〔化〕 chlorobenzene
클로로포름 〔藥〕 chloroform ◆ 클로로포름으로 마취시키다 chloroform (a cat) ■ —중독 chloroformism
클로로필 〈엽록소〉 〔植〕 chlorophyll
클로르초산 —醋酸 〔化〕 chloroacetic acid
클로르칼크 〔〈독〉 Chlorkalk〕 〈표백분〉 chloride of lime
클로버 〈토끼풀〉 〔植〕 a clover ◆ 네잎클로버 four-leaf [leaved] clover
클로스 cloth; 〈책의 표지〉 book cloth
  ■ —제본 a clothbound book; (a book with a) cloth binding : 클로스 제본하다 bind (a book) in cloth
클로스게임 〈접전〉 a close game
클로즈업 〔映〕 〈근접촬영〉 a close-up (略 CU); a close shot
  —클로즈업하다 take [obtain] a close-up (of); bring into a close-up
  ◆ 클로즈업되다 be brought into a close-up; (비유) be highlighted; be in the limelight; 〈신문 등에서〉 be played up (by the papers)
  ▶ 이 문제가 크게 클로즈업되어 있다 This problem has attracted a lot of attention.
  ▶ 카메라맨은 가수를 클로즈업했다 The cameraman took a close-up of the singer.
클론 〔生〕 a clone ◆ 클론을 만들다 produce clones (of); clone (a mammal)
클리닉 〈의원·진료소〉 a clinic
클리닝 cleaning; laundry —클리닝하다 clean
  ◆ 클리닝시키다 have (one's coat) cleaned / 클리닝하러 보내다 send (one's suit) to the cleaner's; send (one's shirt) to the laundry
클리블랜드 **1** 〈미국 Ohio주의 도시〉 Cleveland **2** 〈미국의 제22, 24대 대통령〉 Cleveland, Stephen Grover (1837-1908)
클린업트리오 〔野〕 a cleanup trio; the third, fourth, and fifth batters (in a team's lineup)
  (▶ 클린업의 cleanup의 4번 타자)
클린치 〔拳〕 a clinch; clinching —클린치하다 clinch ◆ 클린치하고 있다 be in a clinch
클린턴 〈미국의 제42대 대통령〉 Clinton, William J. (1946-)
클린히트 〔野〕 a clean hit

> 解說 **clean hit**는 틀린 말은 아니지만 보통 single hit (단타), line drive (라이너) 등으로 쓴다. 이 밖에 clothesline, bullet-like hit와 같이 말한다.

♦ 클린히트를 치다 smash out a clean hit
클립 a (paper) clip; 〈킬용〉 a curling pin
♦ 서류를 클립으로 끼우다 clasp [fasten] papers with a clip; clip papers
▶ 그녀는 머리에 클립을 한 채 부엌일을 하고 있었다 She was doing kitchen work with curling pins in her hair.
▶ 그는 서류를 클립으로 물렸다 He clipped the papers together.
큼직이 big; large(ly); 〈대규모로〉 on a large [grand] scale; in a large [big] way; 〈도량이 크게〉 generously; liberally
♦ 집을 큼직이 짓다 build a house big / 마음을 큼직이 먹다 assume a generous attitude
큼직하다 quite [fairly] big [large]; good-sized; fair-sized; 〈도량이〉 quite generous [liberal]
♦ 신문에 큼직한 광고를 내다 place [put in] a large advertisement in a newspaper
쿵쿵 sniff, sniff; snorting
♦ 코를 쿵쿵거리다 snuffle; sniffle / 쿵쿵 냄새를 맡다 sniff 《at》; give a sniff 《at》
▶ 개는 코를 쿵쿵거리며 돌아다니고 있다 The dog is sniffing here and there.
키¹ 〈까부르는〉 a winnow; a winnowing basket; a winnowing fan; a winnower; a fan
♦ 키로 까부르다 winnow 《grain, chaff》 / 키로 까불러 겨를 없애다 winnow the chaff away [out] 《from the grain》
키² 〈신장〉 one's height; stature
♦ 키를 재다 measure one's height / 키가 삼 센티미터 크다 grow [become] three centimeters taller / 키가 크다[작다] be tall [short]
▶ 두 소년은 키를 대봤다 The two boys compared how tall they'd gotten.
▶ 나는 아버지하고 키를 대봤다 I compared my height with my father's.
▶ 우리 키 대볼까? Let's see which is taller.
▶ 도토리 키 재기다 《속담》 There's little [not much] to choose among them.
▶ 우리 선생님은 키가 6피트다 My teacher is six feet tall [in height].
▶ 그는 키가 약 180센티미터다 He stands about 180 centimeters.
키³ 〈조종타〉 a rudder; 〈조종장치〉 a helm; 〈타륜(舵輪)〉 a (steering) wheel
♦ 키를 잡다 ster; be at the helm; 〈조종하다〉 manage; control; handle; direct
▶ 배는 키를 북쪽으로 돌렸다 The ship steered north.
▶ 키가 말을 듣지 않는다 The ship doesn't answer.
▶ 이제 그같이 강력한 사람이 키를 잡았으니 형세는 좋아질 게 분명하다 Now that we've got a strong man as him at the helm, things are sure to improve.
■ ―머리 a rudder head ―받이 a pintle ―자루 a rudder tiller; a tiller

키⁴ 〈열쇠〉 a key; 〈피아노 등의 건(鍵)〉 a key
♦ 피아노의 키를 쾅쾅[가볍게] 두드리다 pound [touch] the keys of a piano ▶ 이 자물쇠에 맞는 키는 어떤 것입니까? Which is the key for this lock?
키갈리 〈르완다의 수도〉 Kigali
키내림하다 pour out grain in the winnowing process
키네마 a kinema; a cinema ⇨ 시네마
키다리 a very tall fellow; a spindly fellow; a lamppost; 《美》 a gangling fellow ▶ 그는 키가 전봇대 만한 키다리다 He is as tall as a lamppost.
키드 〈가죽〉 kid ■―구두 kid shoes ―장갑 kid gloves; kids
키르기즈 ■―말 Kirghiz; Kirghese; Kirgiz; Khirghiz ―사람 a K(h)irghiz (▶단수·복수 동형); a Kirghese; a Kirgiz
키리바시 〈나라 이름〉 Kiribati; 〈공식명〉 the Republic of Kiribati
키부츠 〈이스라엘의〉 a kibbutz 《pl. -zim》
키순 ―順 the order of stature [height]
♦ 키순으로 in order of [according to] stature / 키순으로 서다[줄다] stand [line up] in order of height
키스 a kiss
♦ 키스를 보내다[던지다] throw [blow] a kiss 《to》 / 잘 자라는[이별의] 키스를 하다 kiss 《him》 good night [good-by]
▶ 그 가수는 청중에게 키스를 던졌다 The singer threw a kiss to the audience.
―**키스하다** kiss; give sb a kiss
♦ 그녀의 이마에 쪽하고 키스하다 give her a smack on the forehead; smack a kiss on her forehead
▶ 그는 그녀의 볼에 키스했다 He kissed her on the cheek.
키신저 〈미국의 정치학자·국무장관〉 Kissinger, Henry Alfred (1923-)
키에르케고르 〈덴마크의 신학자·철학자〉 Kierkegaard, Sören Aabye (1813-55)
키예프 〈우크라이나의 수도〉 Kiev
키우다 1 〈크게 하다〉 make sth larger [bigger]; enlarge; 〈문제 등을〉 make serious
▶ 나는 내 가게를 키우고 싶다 I hope to enlarge my shop.
▶ 그는 사업을 키웠다 He extended his business.
▶ 그는 늘 문제를 키운다 He always aggravates the problem.
2 〈동·식물을〉 grow; raise; rear
♦ 화분의 화초를 키우다 grow [raise, nurse] a potted flower
3 〈양육하다〉 bring up; rear; foster; nurse 《a child》
♦ 어린애를 우유[모유]로 키우다 feed [raise] a child on the bottle [at the breast] / 아이를 훌륭히 키우다 breed 《a child》 a good boy [girl]
▶ 그녀는 다섯 아이들을 홀몸으로 키워냈다 She brought up her five children by herself.
▶ 아이는 부모가 키우기에 달렸다 A child is what his parents make it.
4 〈보호·육성하다〉 promote; protect; support; develop; 〈재능 등을〉 cultivate

♦음악적 재능을 키우다 foster musical ability / 두 사람의 우정을 키우다 foster friendly relations between the two
▶ 그 학교는 음악가들을 키워왔다 The school has trained [has turned out, has produced] musicians.
키위 〔鳥〕 a kiwi; an apteryx
키잡이 a helmsman; a steersman; 〈보트의〉 a coxswain
키질 winnowing ─**키질하다** winnow 《grain》
키츠 〈영국의 시인〉 Keats, John (1795-1821)
키친 〈부엌〉 a kitchen
키케로 〈고대 로마의 정치가·웅변가〉 Cicero, Marcus Tullius (106-43 B.C.)
키토 〈에콰도르의 수도〉 Quito
키퍼 a keeper ■ ─골── a goalkeeper
키펀처 a cardpuncher; a keypuncher
키펀치 a key punch
키포인트 a main point ♦ 키포인트를 파악하다 get [catch] the point [the main idea]
▶ 이것이 키포인트다 This is the most important point.
키프로스 〈나라 이름〉 Cyprus; 〈공식명〉 the Republic of Cyprus
키플링 〈영국의 작가〉 Kipling, Joseph Rudyard (1865-1936)
킥 a kick ─**킥하다** kick 《the ball》
■ 코너─ 〔蹴〕 a corner kick 페널티─ 〔蹴·럭비〕 a penalty kick
킥오프 〔蹴〕 a kickoff ─**킥오프하다** kick off
킥킥 ♦ 킥킥 웃다, 킥킥거리다 titter; chuckle; laugh to *oneself* / 뒷전에서 킥킥 웃다 laugh in *one's* sleeve

킥턴 〔스키〕 a kick turn ♦ 킥턴을 하다 make a kick turn
킨제이 〈미국의 동물학자·사회학자〉 Kinsey, Alfred (1894-1956)
킬로 a kilo; 〈킬로리터〉 a kiloliter (略 kl)
♦ 시속 백 킬로미터로 at velocity of 100 km [kilometers] per an hour
■ ─사이클 a kilocycle (略 kc) ─암페어 a kiloampere (略 kA) ─헤르츠 a kilohertz (略 kHz)
킬로그램 a kilogram [kilogramme] (略 kg)
킬로미터 ♦ a kilometer (略 km)
킬로수 〔數〕 〈킬로미터 수〉 the number of kilometers 《used to express length or distance》; 〈킬로그램 수〉 the number of kilograms 《used to express weight》; 〈킬로와트 수〉 the number of kilowatts 《used to express electrical power》
킬로와트 a kilowatt (略 kW) ■ ─시(時) a kilowatt-hour (略 kWh, kwhr, K.W.H., kwh)
킬리만자로 〈탄자니아의 산〉 (Mount) Kilimanjaro
킬킬 ♦ 킬킬 웃다, 킬킬거리다 giggle; titter; chuckle; snicker
킷값 behavior appropriate to *one's* height [stature] ♦ 킷값도 못하다 be unworthy of *one's* stature
킹 〈왕〉 a king; 〈카드의〉 a king
♦ 클럽의 킹 the king of clubs
킹스턴 〈자메이카의 수도〉 Kingston
킹콩 King Kong
킹킹거리다 〈아이가〉 fret; be peevish [fractious]; whine; blubber; 〈개가〉 whimper; whine

타- 他- 〈다른 것·사람〉 another; other(s); the other; the others; something [someone] else; 〈나머지 것·사람〉 the rest
  ♦타의 추종을 불허하다 be peerless; be unrivaled; be matchless
타 打 a dozen ⇨ 다스
타가수분 他家受粉 〔植〕 cross-pollination
타각증상 他覺症狀 〔醫〕 objective symptoms
타개책 打開策 a way out; a countermeasure
  ♦타개책을 강구하다 find a way out 《of》
타개하다 打開— 〈타파하다〉 break; 〈돌파구를 얻다〉 make a breakthrough 《in》; 〈타개책을 강구하다〉 find a way out 《of》
  ♦정체 국면을 타개하다 break the deadlock / 난국을 타개하다 overcome [get over, get out of] difficulties
타격 打擊 1 〈세게 치기〉 a blow; 〈정신적 타격·충격〉 (a) shock; 〈손해〉 damage
  ♦타격을 주다 give a blow 《to》; deal a blow 《to》 / 타격을 받다 be hit; suffer a blow; be shocked 《at, by》
  ▶화재로 그의 사업은 큰 타격을 받았다 His business suffered serious damage [a heavy blow] in the fire.
  2 〔野〕 batting; hitting
  ▶그 팀은 타격이 꽤 좋다 The team's batting average is pretty high. ⇌ The team is batting pretty well.
  ■─률 the batting [hitting] average ─부진 shortage of hits; poor batting ─상 the batting award ─순위 the batting order ─연습 batting practice ─왕 the leading hitter 《for the season》 ─전 a slugfest; a hitfest; a game with many hits and runs
타격력 打擊力 〔野〕 hitting [batting] power; 〈핵전략에서〉 striking power [capability]
타결 妥結 〈해결〉 settlement; 〈의견의 일치〉 an agreement
  ♦타결을 보다 reach an agreement 《with》; come to terms 《with》 / 타결을 짓다 make a compromise agreement 《with》
  ▶노사가 타결을 보았다 Labor and management reached an agreement.
  ─타결하다 reach an agreement 《with》
  ▶교섭은 타결되었다 The negotiations came to a settlement [an agreement].
  ■─점 a point of agreement ─조건 terms of agreement
타계하다 他界— 〈죽다〉 die; depart this life; depart from life; pass away
타고나다 be born 《with》; be gifted
  ♦타고난 지도자 a born leader / 타고난 음악가 a born musician / 타고난 born; inborn; inbred; inherent; natural; native; innate
  ▶그녀는 타고난 화가다 She is a born [natural] artist.

타고르 〈인도의 시인〉 Tagore, Rabindranath (1861-1941)
타고을 他— 〈다른 고장〉 another county [district]
타고장 他— another place [district]
타관 他官·他關 a foreign country [land]; a strange land ⇨ 타향
타구 打球 〔野〕 batting; 〈친 공〉 a batted ball
타국 他國 a foreign country
  ♦타국의 foreign; strange; alien / 타국 땅에 묻히다 die in a strange land; die far from home
  ■─인 a stranger; a foreigner; an alien; an outlander
타기 舵機 〔海〕 a helm ⇨ 키³
타기하다 唾棄— detest; hate; abominate; abhor; reject ♦타기할 detestable; disgusting; abhorrent
타내다 〈얻어내다〉 get 《from one's elder》; obtain; be given ♦아버지한테서 용돈을 타내다 get pocket money from one's father
타닌 〔化〕 tannin ■─산 tannic acid; tannin ─산염 tannate
타다¹ 1 〈연소하다〉 burn; 〈밝게 불꽃을 내며〉 blaze; 〈불꽃·연기를 내지 않고〉 glow
  ♦타기 쉬운 재료 inflammable 〔美〕 flammable〕 material / 타는 듯한 저녁 놀 a fiery [flaming] sunset
  ▶그 집은 타고 있었다 The house was burning [on fire, in flames].
  ▶난로에서 불이 타고 있다 A fire is burning in the fireplace.
  2 〈타버리다·타서 재가 되다〉 burn; be burned; 〔英〕 be burnt
  ▶그의 원고는 화재로 다 타버렸다 His manuscripts were all burned (up) in the fire.
  ▶그 큰 화재로 많은 집들이 타버렸다 A lot of houses (were) burned down.
  ▶다행히 그 건물은 타지 않고 남았다 Fortunately, the building remained unburned [survived the fire].
  3 〈햇볕에〉 (sun)burn; tan; get a (sun)tan
  ▶그녀의 피부는 햇볕에 잘 탄다 Her skin sunburns [tans] easily.
  ▶뜨거운 햇살에 내 등어리가 탔다 The hot sun burned my back. ⇌ My back (was) burned in the hot sun.
  ▶그는 볕에서 일하기 때문에 볕에 잘 탔다 Since he works in the sun, he has a good (sun)tan [is really tanned].
  4 〈눌다〉 be [get] scorched [charred]; be parched; be singed
  ♦탄 밥 scorched rice
  ▶밥이 탔다 The rice is scorched.
  ▶타지 않게 자꾸 저어라 Stir it constantly to prevent scorching.
  5 〈감정이 고양되다〉 ▶그는 명예욕에 불타고

있었다 He was burning for fame [to win fame].
▶그는 야심[정열]에 불타고 있다 He is burning with ambition [passion].
6 〈빛깔이〉 glow
▶산 허리는 붉은 단풍으로 불타는 듯하다 The hillside glows [flames] with red maples.
7 〈속이 · 애가〉 be anxious [worried] 《about》

타다² **1**【탈것을】take; 〈열차 · 버스 등을〉 get on; 〈차 · 택시 등을〉 get in...; 〈말 · 자전거 등을〉 ride (on); 〈배 · 비행기 등을〉 get [go] aboard [on board]; board; 〈차를 운전하다〉 drive; 〈택시 등을 잡다〉 catch; get; 〈엘리베이터 등을〉 step [go] into 《an elevator》

解説 *take*는 열차 · 전차 · 버스 · 비행기 등을 이용한다거나 또는 그것을 타고 간다는 것: take a taxi [train, plane, ship, the subway]. 타는 동작을 나타내는 경우는 *get on* [*in*]을 쓴다. 그 중에서 get on (↔ get off)은 버스나 열차 등 대형의 탈것이나 말·자전거를 타는 경우고, get in (↔ get out of)은 차·택시 등을 탈 때에 쓰인다. 올라타는 동작을 강조하려면 in, on 대신에 into, onto가 쓰인다: get into the car; get onto the bus. 그리고 *ride*는 말이나 자전거에 걸터앉아 탈 때에 쓰인다: ride (on) a horse [bicycle]. ride는 또 열차·버스·자동차 등에 승객으로서 탈 경우에도 쓰인다: ride (on) a bus; ride (in) a car. *get aboard* [*on board*], *board*는 배·비행기·열차·버스에 올라타는 경우에 쓰인다.
탈것의 수단을 강조하려면 by가 쓰인다: He came by train [bus, car]. 이 경우에는 관사가 안 붙지만 형용사로 수식되는 경우에는 관사가 붙는다: by a fast train; by the 2:20 train. '…을 타고'란 느낌을 강조할 때는 on이나 in이 쓰이는데 이 때는 관사가 붙는다는 것을 알아야 한다: Do you go to school on [in] a bus?

♦배를 타다 get [go] on board a ship; board a ship; take a ship / 비행기를 타고 런던에 가다 fly to London; go to London by plane
▶시청에 가려면 어떤 지하철을 타야 합니까? Which subway do I take for the City Hall?
▶그녀는 차를 타고 시동을 걸었다 She got in [into] the car and started the engine.
▶택시를 타고 집에 가자 Let's take a taxi home.
▶그 배에는 50명이 타고 있었다 There were fifty people aboard [on board] the ship.
▶그들이 어느 열차에 타고 있는지 우리는 알 수 없었다 We didn't know what train they'd be on.
▶그녀는 자전거를 못 탄다 She can't ride a bicycle.
▶이 버스를 타면 10분이면 역에 갈 수 있습니다 This bus will take you to the station in ten minutes.
2【올라가다】〈높은 데로〉 go up; climb
♦산을 잘 타는 사람 a good [an expert] climber / 산을 타다 go up [climb] a hill / 나무를 타다 climb (up) [be up in] a tree / 지붕을 타다 get on the roof / 밧줄을 타다 walk a rope [tightrope]
3【전파·매스컴·바람 등을】〈전파를〉 be broadcast; be on the air; 〈매스컴을 타다〉 receive much publicity from the press
♦전파를 타고 온 에어 on the air
4〈스키·스케이트 등을〉 ski; skate
♦스케이트 타러 가다 go for a skate
5〈기회·틈 등을〉 seize 《an opportunity》; seize on the situation; 〈기화로 삼다〉 take advantage of

타다³ 〈섞다·보태다·묽게 하다〉 mix; blend; mingle; 〈약품 등을〉 compound; 〈물 등으로 묽게 하다〉 dilute; 〈불순하게 하다〉 adulterate

解説 보통 두 가지 이상의 것을 혼합해서 균질이 되는 경우는 *mix*, 각성분의 조화로 바람직한 결과를 얻을 경우에는 *blend*를 쓴다. *mingle*은 원래의 성분을 분간할 수 있는 경우에 많이 쓴다.

♦물을 타다 dilute 《with》; water...down; mix 《with》/ 물에 소금을 타다 dissolve salt in water; salt the water / 물감을 타다 dissolve dye (in water) / 그림물감을 타다 mix [blend] the paints
▶이 위스키에 물을 타주십시오 Will you water down this whiskey? ⇌ I'd like a little water with my whiskey, please.
▶우유에 물을 타는 것은 법으로 금지되어 있다 It is against law to dilute [adulterate] milk with water.

타다⁴ 〈상 등을〉 be awarded 《a prize》; receive; win; 〈월급·용돈 등을〉 get 《a salary》; take
♦졸업장을 타다 receive a graduation diploma / 용돈을 타다 get an allowance [pocket money, spending money]
▶그는 노벨 평화상을 탔다 He received [was awarded] a Nobel Peace Prize.
▶나는 한 달에 1,500 달러를 탄다 I'm making $1,500 a month.

타다⁵ **1**〈맷돌에 갈다〉 grind
♦밀을 타서 밀가루로 만들다 grind wheat into flour
2〈쪼개다·켜다〉 split; divide; 〈반으로〉 halve
♦박을 타다 halve a gourd
3〈가르마 등을 가르다〉 part; divide
♦가르마를 타다 part *one's* hair

타다⁶ **1**【잘 느끼다】〈노염을〉 quick-[short-, hot-]tempered; irritable; touchy; 〈부끄럼을〉 shy; bashful; coy; 〈간지럼을〉 ticklish; sensitive to tickling
2【영향을 받다】〈옻 등을〉 be allergic to 《lacquer》; suffer easily from 《lacquer》; 〈더럼을〉 pick up dirt easily; 〈계절을〉 suffer from 《the summer heat》; be sensitive to 《cold》

타다⁷ 〈악기 등을〉 play; perform
▶당신은 바이올린을 탈 줄 압니까? Can you play [perform] (on) the violin?
▶그녀는 피아노로 쇼팽의 곡을 탔다 She played [performed] Chopin on the piano.

타다⁸ 〈솜을〉 beat 《cotton》 out; willow [whip] 《cotton》; 〈헌솜을〉 rewhip; whip [willow] again

타닥거리다 **1**〈무거운 걸음을 옮기다〉 trudge

along; trudge on; tread along [on]
2 〈어려운 살림을 하다〉 barely manage to live along; rub along; make a bare [scanty] living
3 〈살살 두드리다〉 thump; beat

타당성 妥當性 propriety; appropriateness; adequacy; soundness

타당하다 妥當— 〈적절한〉 proper; appropriate; right; fit; adequate; reasonable
♦타당한 결론 a valid [reasonable, sound] conclusion / 타당한 값에[으로] at a reasonable price / 타당한 조치를 취하다 take appropriate [proper] measure
▶그가 회장으로 뽑히는 게 타당하다 It is proper that he (should) be chosen chairman.

타도 打倒 overthrow
—**타도하다** overthrow; throw out; defeat; knock down; topple *sb* from power
▶공산주의(를) 타도하라 Down with communism!

타도 他道 another province; other provinces

타동 他洞 another dong [village]; other towns [villages]

타동사 他動詞 〔文法〕 a transitive verb (略 vt., v.t.)

타락 墮落 〈정치·도덕적 부패〉 corruption; 〈품행이 나빠짐〉 a fall (from grace); 〈품위를 떨어뜨림〉 degradation; degeneration; 〈문예 등의 퇴폐〉 decadence
▪경찰의 타락 the corruption of the police; police corruption / 인격의 타락 the degradation of character
—**타락하다** corrupt; 〈품위를 떨어뜨리다〉 degrade; 〈길을 잘못 들다〉 go astray; 〈퇴폐하다〉 degenerate 《into a narcotic》
♦타락한 정치가 a corrupt politician / 타락한 corrupt
▶그는 도시 생활 때문에 타락했다 He was corrupted by city life.
▶권력은 그것을 가지는 자를 타락시킨다 Power corrupts those who hold it.
▶돈 보고 결혼해서 몸을 타락시키지 말게 Don't degrade yourself by marrying into money.

타락줄 a hair-rope

타란텔라 〈무용·무곡〉(이) the tarantella

타래 〈실 등의 묶음〉 a hank; a skein; a bunch; a round; a coil; a coiled bundle (of)
♦실 한 타래 a skein of thread / 새끼 한 타래 a bunch [coil] of rope

타래박 〈두레박〉 a long-handled well bucket

타래버선 〈누비버선〉 children's quilted socks with decorations

타래송곳 **1** 〈나사송곳〉 a gimlet; an auger
2 〈마개뽑이〉 a corkscrew

타래타래 in coils [skeins]; in spirals
♦새끼를 타래타래 감다 coil the rope up

타력 打力 〔野〕 batting [hitting] power ⇨ 타격력

타력 他力 help from without; outside help; the power of another ▶타력에 의존치 마라 Don't rely upon others.

타력 惰力 〈타성〉(an) inertia; (a) momentum 《*pl.* -ta, ~s》; force of habit
♦타력으로 by the force of inertia

타령 打令 〈곡조의 하나〉 a kind of Korean tune; 〈민요〉 a Korean ballad

타로탄 —土卵 〔植〕 a taro 《*pl.* ~s》

타륜 舵輪 〔海〕 a steering wheel; the wheel; a helm
♦타륜을 잡다 be at the wheel

타르 tar ♦타르를 칠하다 tar

타르타르산 —酸 tartaric acid

타매하다 唾罵— insult; caluminate; slander

타면 他面 the other side
♦타면에 있어서 〈다른 한 편으로는〉 while; on the other hand

타면 打綿 〈솜타기〉 cotton beating; willowing
—**타면하다** beat cotton out; willow [whip] cotton ▪—기(機) a cotton gin; a willowing machine; a scutcher

타문 他聞 〈남이 들음〉 publicity
▶이것은 타문을 꺼리는 일이다 This is a confidential [secret] matter.

타박 faultfinding; blame; criticism; grumbling; complaint
▶그는 늘 음식에 타박을 한다 He is always grumbling at [about, over] the food.
—**타박하다** find fault 《with》; criticize; blame; accuse *sb* 《of》; grumble
▶우리의 계획을 타박하지 말아라 Don't throw cold water on our plan.
▪음식— grumbling at [about, over] food
▪—쟁이 a grumbler; a faultfinder

타박 打撲 〔매림〕 〈주먹·막대 등으로〉 a blow; 〈무기류로〉 a stroke

타박상 打撲傷 a bruise; a contusion
♦머리에 타박상을 입다 get a bruise [stroke] on the head
▶나는 다리에 타박상을 입었다 I got a bruise on the leg.

타박타박 **1** 〈걷는 모양〉 ♦타박타박 걷다 plod; 〈힘든 듯이〉 trudge; walk slowly
▶하루의 고된 일을 마치고 노동자들은 집으로 타박타박 돌아간다 Workers plod home after a hard day's work.
▶아이들은 깊은 눈 속을 헤치며 학교로 타박타박 걸어갔다 Children trudged their way to school through deep snow.
2 〈음식이〉—**타박타박하다** dry and hard
♦타박타박한 빵 dry bread
▶그 빵은 타박타박했다 The bread was dry and crumbling.

타방면 他方面 another side [place, quarter]; the other side [hand]

타봉 打棒 〔野〕 batting ⇨ 타격

타분하다 〈생선·육류·생각 등이〉 stale; musty; moldy; ill-[foul-]smelling ♦타분한 생선 stale fish / 타분한 생각 a musty idea

타블로이드 a tabloid
♦타블로이드판 신문 a tabloid (newspaper) / 타블로이드형[판]으로 in tabloid (form)

타사 他事 other matters

타산 打算 calculation; self-interest —**타산하다** calculate; consult *one's* own interests

타산적 打算的 ♦타산적인 생각 a selfish [an egocentric] idea / 타산적인 동기 〈금전면에서〉 a mercenary motive / 타산적인 〈금전면에서〉 mercenary; 〈빈틈없는〉 calculating; 〈이기적

인〉 selfish
▶ 그는 타산적인 사람이다 He is a calculating man.

타산지석 他山之石 〈실례에 의한 교훈〉 ▶ 그의 실패를 타산지석으로 삼아라 You should take his failure as an object lesson. ⇒ You should learn from his failure. ⇒ You should profit from his failure. ⇒ You should learn a good lesson from his failure.

타살 他殺 (a) murder
♦ 타살 시체 a murder victim

타살하다 打殺— strike sb dead; beat sb to death; kill sb with blows

타석 打席 〔野〕〈타수〉 at bat (略 ab.); 〈배터 박스〉 a batter's box
♦ 타석에 서다 be at bat; come to bat
▶ 그는 두번째 타석 때 홈런을 쳤다 He hit a home run when he was at bat the second time.
▶ 그는 3타석, 2안타를 쳤다 He was at bat three times and scored two hits.

타선 打線 〔野〕 the batting lineup [order]
♦ 강력한 타선 a powerful batting lineup / 상위[하위] 타선 the top [bottom] of the batting order

타선 唾腺 a salivary gland ⇨ 타액(〜선)
타성 他性 〔哲〕 otherness; differentness
타성 他姓 another [a different] surname
타성 惰性 inertia 〈타력(惰力)〉
♦ 타성으로 커피를 마시다 drink coffee out of [by, from force of] habit
▶ 공은 타성으로 굴러가고 있었다 The ball rolled on by the force of inertia.

타수 打手 a batter ⇨ 타자(打者)
타수 打數 〔野〕 ▶ 그는 4타수 2안타를 쳤다 He made two hits in four at bats.
타수 舵手 a helmsman ⇨ 조타(〜수)
타순 打順 〔野〕 a batting order
♦ 타순 4번 the fourth position
▶ 그는 타순이 어떻게 되지? Where [When] does he bat?

타스 〈구소련 통신사〉 TASS [〈*T*elegrafnoe *A*gentstvo *S*ovetskovo *S*oyuza*〉*]

타악기 打樂器 〔樂〕 a percussion instrument; 〈재즈의〉 the traps
■ 一연주자 a percussionist

타액 唾液 〈침〉 saliva; sputum
♦ 타액을 분비하다 salivate; secrete saliva
■ 一관[구] the salivary duct [corpuscle] —분비 salivation; flow of saliva —선 a salivary gland —소(素) 〔生化〕 ptyalin

타오르다 〈확 타다〉 burn [flare, blaze, flame] up; 〈갑자기 타기 시작하다〉 burst into flames
▶ 갑자기 불길이 확 타올랐다 Suddenly the fire flamed [flared, blazed] up.
▶ 목조 가옥은 확 타올랐다 The wooden house burst into flames.

타울거리다 〈애쓰다〉 strive hard 《to do, for》; make great efforts
▶ 그는 돈을 벌려고 타울거리고 있다 He strives hard to make money.

타원 楕圓 an ellipse; 〈타원형〉 an oval
♦ 타원의 oval; elliptic / 타원으로 ellipticaly
■ 一궤도 an elliptical orbit —운동 elliptic motion —율 ellipticity —주(柱) 〔數〕 a cylindroid; an elliptic cylinder —추(錐) an elliptical cone —컴퍼스 a trammel

타원체 楕圓體 〔數〕 an ellipsoid; an ovoid
♦ 타원체의 ellipsoidal; spheroidal

타원형 楕圓形 an oval
♦ 타원형의 oval; elliptical

타월 a towel; a washcloth; 〈英〉 a facecloth
♦ 타월로 닦다 towel *oneself*; wipe [dry] 《*one's* hands》 with a towel
▶ 손닦을 타월이 여기 있습니다 Here's towel to wipe [dry] your hands.
■ 一친 toweling

타율 他律 heteronomy; external or foreign laws [rules]
♦ 타율의 heteronomous

타율 打率 〔野〕 the batting average (略 bat. avg.) ▶ 그의 이번 시즌 타율은 2할 2푼 5리다 He is hitting .225 this season. (▶225는 two twenty-five로 읽음)

타의 他意 〈딴 생각〉 any other intention; 〈엉큼한 생각〉 an ulterior motive; 〈악의〉 malice; ill will; 〈남의 뜻〉 another person's will
▶ 그는 타의가 없음을 밝혀야만 했다 He had to show that he had no other intentions.

타이[1] **1** 〔競〕 ⇨ 타이기록, 타이스코어
♦ 타이를 이루다 tie the score
▶ 경기는 4대4 타이로 끝났다 The game ended in a 4-4 tie. (▶four to four로 읽음)
2 〔樂〕 a tie ♦ 타이로 연결하다 tie
3 〈넥타이〉 a tie; a necktie
♦ 보우 타이 〈나비 넥타이〉 a bow tie

타이[2] 〈泰國〉 Thailand; Thai; 〈공식명〉 the Kingdom of Thailand ♦ 타이의 Thai
■ 一말 Thai; Siamese —사람 a Thai; a Thailander

타이가 〈시베리아 등지의 침엽수림〉 a taiga

타이기록 —記錄 a tie record
♦ 세계 타이기록을 세우다 equal [tie] the world mark [record]

타이르다 reprove gently; admonish 《sb for his fault》; remonstrate 《with sb on a matter》; reason 《with sb on his folly》; persuade 《sb to do》
♦ 잘못을 타이르다 reason with sb on 《his》 mistake / 타일러 …시키다 persuade 《sb to do [into doing]》 / 타일러 그만두게 하다 dissuade 《sb from (doing) an attempt》
▶ 나는 그에게 자기 잘못을 간곡히 타일렀다 I tried hard to make him see that he was at fault.
▶ 나는 여러 가지로 타일렀으나 소용이 없었다 My admonitions fell on deaf ears.

타이밍 timing
▶ 타이밍이 참 좋았다 It was quite timely [well-timed]. ⇒ It came at just the right time.
▶ 그는 늘 타이밍을 놓치고 있다 His timing is always bad [off].

타이스코어 a tie score
♦ 타이스코어가 되다 tie the score

타이어 a tire; 〈英〉 a tyre
♦ 체인감은 타이어 a chained tire / 타이어에 바람을 넣다 pump up a tire / 새 타이어를 달다

tire; put on [fix] a new tire
▶ 내 차의 타이어가 구멍났다 I had a flat tire.
■고무— a rubber tire 공기— a pneumatic (tire) 예비— a spare tire ■—공장 a tire plant —자국 a tire track —체인 (tire) chains

타이어

- 사이드월 sidewall
- 브레이커 breaker
- 카커스 carcass
- 축(軸)받이 axle hole
- 휠 wheel
- 트레드 tread

타이츠 tights (▶복수 취급)
♦ 타이츠를 입은 소녀 a girl in tights
타이트스커트 a tight skirt
타이틀 〈표제〉a title; 〈선수권〉a title; a championship
♦ 그 책의 타이틀 the title of the book / 타이틀을 방어하다[잃다, 빼앗다] defend [lose, gain] a title
■—매치 〖拳〗a title match —페이지 a title page
타이프 a typewriter ⇨ 타이프라이터
타이프라이터 a typewriter
♦ 타이프라이터로 친 편지 a typewritten letter / 편지를 타이프라이터로 치다 type a letter; write a letter on a typewriter / 타이프라이터를 연습하다 practice typing
▶ 그녀는 타이프라이터를 빨리[잘] 친다 She types fast [well]. ⇌ She is a fast [good] typist.
■—국문[영문]— a Korean [an English] typewriter 휴대용— a portable typewriter ■—용지 typewriter paper —인쇄물 a typescript
타이피스트 a typist ♦ 타이피스트로 취직하다 find [get] a job as typist
■—국문[영문]— a typist in Korean [English]
타인 他人 1〈다른 사람〉another person; other people; 〈그〉others
2〈남〉an unrelated person; a stranger; 〈국외자〉an outsider
♦ 타인 취급을 하다 treat sb like a stranger; make a stranger of sb
▶ 타인은 참견하지 말아야 한다 A third party should not get a word in sideways.
타인 打印 punching
■—기(器) a punch; a punching machine
타일 他日 〈다른 날〉some other day; some other time; some day or other; 〈근일중〉one of these days; 〈훗날〉at some future date; in future; on some future occasion
♦ 타일을 기약하고 열심히 일하다 work hard, hoping for something better in the future / 타

일을 기약하고 서로 헤어지다 part from sb deferring the matter to some future occasion
타일 a tile
♦ 타일을 깔다 tile (the floor); cover (the floor) with tiles / 욕실에 타일을 붙이다 floor a bathroom with tiles; tile a bathroom
■—색[무늬]— an encaustic tile —공(工)a tiler; a tile-setter —공사 tiling; tiler's work; tile works —공장 a tilery
타임¹ 1〈시각〉time
♦ 주자의 타임을 재다 time [clock] a runner / 〈심판이〉타임을 선언하다 call the time
▶ 나의 100 미터 달리기의 최고 타임은 12초 4다 My best time in the 100-meter dash is 12.4 seconds.
2〈경기중의 휴식시간〉time out; (口) time
♦ 타임을 요구하다 call time out
■—리코더 a time clock [recorder] —머신 a time machine —스위치 a time switch; a timer —워치 a stop watch —터널 a time tunnel —캡슐 a time capsule —테이블 a timetable, 〖鐵〗a train schedule
타임² 〈신문명〉the New York Times
타임카드 a time card [sheet]
♦ 타임카드를 찍다 punch a time card; 〈출근시〉clock in; 〈퇴근시〉clock out
타입 〈형〉(a) type; (a) pattern
♦ 여러 타입의 사람 people of various types; various types of people
▶ 그녀는 내가 좋아하는 타입의 사람이다 She is the type [kind] of woman I like. ⇌ She is my type.
타자 打字 typing; typewriting
—타자하다 typewrite; type (out)
♦ 타자한 편지 a typed letter
▶ 이 편지를 타자해 주십시오 I want to have this letter typed.
■—연습 practice of typing —인쇄물 a typescript —학원 a typewriting [typing] school
타자 打者 〖野〗a batter; a batsman; a hitter
♦ 잘 치는 타자 a slugger / 대 타자 a pinch hitter
강— a heavy batter 3할— a three hundred hitter; a .300 hitter 왼손— a left-handed hitter 2번— the second batter 1번— a leadoff (man); the first batter
타자기 打字機 a typewriter ⇨ 타이프라이터
타자수 打字手 a typist ⇨ 타이피스트
타작 打作 thresh(ing); thrash(ing)
—타작하다 thresh; thrash
■—마당 a thrashing floor [ground]
타전 打電 sending a telegram; telegraphing
—타전하다 telegraph; wire; cable; send a telegram 《to》; 〈무선으로〉radio 《to》
♦ 구조 요청을 타전하다 flash [send out] an SOS
▶ 우리는 그들에게 즉시 귀환하라고 타전했다 We cabled [telegraphed] them to return home immediately.
타점 打點 1〈점을 찍음〉dotting; pointing
—타점하다 mark with a dot [point]; point; spot
2〈선택〉spotting
—타점하다 single [pick] out; fix; select

타조 3 〔野〕 run(s) batted in (略 an RBI)
♦타점왕 the RBI king
타조 駝鳥 〔鳥〕 an ostrich
타종 打鐘 striking [tolling] a bell
─타종하다 strike [ring] a bell; toll [ring] a gong
♦타종하여 사람들을 (교회로) 모으다 toll in the people / 송구영신을 타종하다 ring out the Old Year and ring in the New
타죄 他罪 〈다른 죄〉 other crimes [charges]
타죽다 burn to death; be burned to death; die by fire; perish in the flames [by fire]
▶그 화재로 여덟 사람이 타죽었다 Eight persons died [lost their lives] in the fire.
타진 打診 1 〔醫〕 percussion; tapping
─타진하다 examine 《a part of the body》 by percussion
▶의사는 내 가슴을 타진했다 The doctor sounded my chest.
2 〈탐색〉 sounding; tapping
─타진하다 sound (out) 《sb's feelings》; tap; feel out 《sb about sth》; put [throw] out feelers
▶그의 기분을 타진해 주게 Will you sound him out?
▶그것에 관한 그의 의향을 타진해 보자 Let's sound [feel] him out about the matter.
─기 a plexor; a plessor ─음 a percussion sound
타짜(꾼) 〈노름의〉 a hoodwinker (in card game); a humbug; a sharper; 《美俗》 a gyp
타처 他處 another place; some other place; any other place ♦타처에서 at [in] another [some other] place; somewhere else
타천 他薦 recommendation (of other people)
▶그 한 자리에 자천타천의 많은 후보자가 몰려왔다 For that one post, many candidates turned up, some on their own, and some recommended by others.
타타르 Tartary
■─말 Ta(r)tar ─사람 a Ta(r)tar
타파 打破 breaking; destruction
─타파하다 break down; defeat; do away with; get rid of
♦인습을 타파하다 do away with [abolish] old conventions; break down long-established customs / 미신을 타파하다 explode [kill] superstitions
■─계급─ the abolition of class distinctions
타합 打合 an [a previous, a preliminary] arrangement
♦타합이 되다 reach an arrangement
─타합하다 make (previous) arrangements 《as to time》; arrange 《a matter with sb, that...》; prearrange
타향 他鄕 a foreign country [land]; a strange land
♦타향의 foreign; alien / 타향살이를 10년 하다 be absent from home for ten years / 타향에서 살다 live away from home / 타향에서 떠돌다 [죽다] wander [die] in a strange land
타협 妥協 (a) compromise; understanding
♦타협적 태도 a compromising [conciliatory]

attitude / 비타협적인 사람 an uncompromising person
─타협하다 compromise; make [effect] a compromise; reach [arrive at] a compromise; come to terms [an understanding] 《with》
▶우리는 이점은 타협할 수 없다 We cannot compromise on this point.
▶타협할 여지가 없다 There is no room for compromise. ⇌ It admits of no compromise.
■─안 a compromise; a compromise plan [proposal]: 마침내 타협안이 마련되었다 A compromise agreement was finally reached [arrived at]. ─자 a compromiser
타협점 妥協點 a point of compromise [agreement] ♦타협점을 찾아내다 find out a point of compromise; hit upon compromise; come to an agreement
타화수분 他花受粉 〔植〕 cross-pollination
─타화수분하다 cross-pollinate
타화수정 他花受精 cross-fertilization
─타화수정하다 cross-fertilize
타히티(섬) Tahiti
■─말 Tahitian ─사람 a Tahitian
탁 1 〈부딪치는 모양〉 with a slap [snap, click, crack, bump, clunk]
♦문을 탁 닫다 slam [bang] the door / 무릎을 탁 치다 slap [smack] one's knee / 탁하고 부딪치다 run slap [smack] into
▶돌이 창문에 탁 맞았다 A stone plunked against the window.
2 〈드넓은〉 탁 트인 전망 an open view / 탁 트인 초원 an extensive [a spacious] meadow
탁견 卓見 〈의견〉 excellent views; a fine idea; 〈식견〉 farsightedness; clear-sightedness
♦탁견이 있는[을 가진] 사람 a man of great insight; a farsighted man / 탁견이 있다 have a broad vision
탁구 卓球 table tennis; ping-pong
♦탁구를 치다 play ping-pong
■─경기 a table-tennis tournament [match] ─공 a ping-pong ball ─대 a ping-pong table

─── 탁구 ───

라켓 racket, paddle
기둥 support post
공 ball
네트 net
탁구대 table
센터라인 center line

탁론 卓論 a lofty [superb] argument; excellent views
탁류 濁流 a muddy stream; turbid [dark] waters ▶탁류가 온 마을을 휩쓸었다 The muddy water rushed through the whole vil-

탁마 琢磨 〈옥석의〉 polish(ing); 〈학문・덕행의〉 cultivation; improvement
—**탁마하다** polish; give *sth* a polish; cultivate; improve; refine
♦ 정신을 탁마하다 cultivate *one's* mind

탁발 托鉢 religious mendicancy
—**탁발하다** go about [go from house to house] asking for alms
■ —승 a Mendicant

탁상 卓上 ♦ 탁상용 사전 a desk dictionary / 탁상에 on the table [desk]
■ —계획 a desk [paper] plan —공론 a desk [mere] theory; an impracticable proposition —시계 a table clock —연설 a table-speech —작전 연습 a war game —정치가[전략가] a closet politician [strategist] —컴퓨터 a desktop computer

탁선 託宣 an oracle; a divine message; a revelation ⇨ 신탁(神託)

탁설 卓說 an excellent opinion; excellent views ■ —명론 a sound, well-argued thesis

탁성 濁聲 a thick voice
♦ 탁성으로 말하다 speak in a thick [guttural] voice; speak thickly

탁세 濁世 〈더러운 세상〉 the corrupt [degenerate] world; 〈이 세상〉 this world

탁송 託送 consignment —**탁송하다** consign 《goods to a forwarding agency》; send *sth* by [through, under the care of] *sb*
■ —물[품] a consignment

탁아소 託兒所 a day-care center; a day [public] nursery; a children's home; a nursery school

탁언 託言 1 〈구실〉 a pretext; an excuse; a pretext
2 〈전언〉 a message

탁엽 托葉 〔植〕 a stipule

탁월 卓越 excellence; eminence; prominence
—**탁월하다** 〈형용사적〉 excellent; eminent; preeminent; distinguished; superb; 〈동사적〉 excel
♦ 탁월한 학자 a prominent [distinguished] scholar / 탁월한 업적 an outstanding [a brilliant] achievement / 인물과 기량이 모두 탁월하다 surpass others both in character and ability
▶ 그는 냉철한 판단력이 그들 중 탁월했다 He stood out among them for his cool judgment.
■ —풍 〔氣〕 the prevailing wind

탁음 濁音 〔音聲〕 a voiced sound; a sonant
■ —자음 a voiced consonant

탁자 卓子 a table; a desk
♦ 둥근 탁자 a round table / 탁자에 놓다 put *sth* on the table / 탁자에 둘러앉다 sit around a table / 탁자를 두고 마주앉다 sit facing each other with a table between
▶ 탁자에 앉은 사람 모두가 웃었다 The whole table laughed.

탁주 濁酒 raw rice wine ⇨ 막걸리

탁출 卓出 excellence ⇨ 탁월(卓越)

탁탁 1 〈부딪치는 소리〉 rattling; cracking; with cracks [pops]; with snaps
♦ 손가락을 탁탁거리다 crap [pop] *one's* knuckles / 탁자를 탁탁 치다 pound [beat] the table (with *one's* fist) / 먼지를 탁탁 털다 beat the dust off / 탁탁거리며 타다 burn crackling; burn with a cracking sound
2 〈쓰러지는 모양〉 《fall》 in succession; 《come down》 one after another
▶ 일사병으로 여러 학생이 탁탁 쓰러졌다 Affected by sunstroke, several students collapsed one after another.
3 〈일을 해치우는 모양〉 speedily; promptly; briskly
♦ 일을 탁탁 처리하다 do *one's* business efficiently [in a businesslike manner]; be prompt in *one's* work
4 〈침 뱉는 모양〉 spit-spit
♦ 침을 탁탁 뱉다 spit and spit again; go spit-spit-spit; spit all over the place
5 〈숨이 차는 모양〉 stifling; chocky; short [out of] breath
♦ 숨이 탁탁 막히다 be hard to breathe; be stifled

탁탁하다 1 〈피륙이〉 close-woven; close; thick and strong
2 〈살림이〉 be well-to-do; be well [comfortably] off; be abundant; live in plenty [ease, comfort]

탁하다 濁— 1 〈액체 등이〉 muddy; turbid; dull; 〈목소리가〉 thick; 〈발음이〉 voiced; sonant
♦ 탁한 공기 smoky [murky] air / 탁한 목소리 a thick voice / 탁한 물 muddy water / 탁한 세상 this corrupt [impure] world / 탁해지다 become muddy [turbid, impure, thick]
▶ 큰 비가 온 뒤로 강물은 탁해졌다 The river was muddy after the heavy rain.
2 〈얼굴이〉 dark and dull
♦ 표정이 탁하다 look glum [blue]; look unwell

탄 炭 coal ⇨ 석탄(石炭)

탄갱 炭坑 a coal mine shaft; 〈갱〉 a shaft; a pint; 〈횡갱〉 a gallery; 〈갱도〉 a coalpit; 《총칭》 a colliery ⇨ 탄광

탄고 炭庫 a coal bunker [bin, cellar]

탄광 炭鑛 a coal mine; a coalpit; 《총칭》 a colliery
■ —노동자 a coal(·mine) worker —도시 a coal town —부(夫) a coal miner —업 the coal-mining industry —주[업자] a coal-mine owner [operator] —지대 a coal-mining area [region] —폭발 a mine [colliery] explosion —회사 a coal mining [colliery] company

탄내 a burnt [scorched] smell
♦ 탄내나다 smell *sth* scorching [burning]; smell smoke
▶ 무슨 탄내가 난다 There's a smell of burning [scorching]. ⇌ I smell something burning.

탄내 炭— coal stench; a scorched smell of charcoal

탄대 彈帶 an ammunition [a cartridge] belt; a bandolier; a bandoleer

탄도 彈道 a trajectory; a ballistic trajectory
■ —곡선 a ballistic curve —비행 a trajectory [suborbital] flight —학 ballistics

탄도탄 彈道彈 a ballistic missile

◆공중발사— an air-launched ballistic missile (略 ALBM) 단거리— a short range ballistic missile (略 SRBM) 대륙간— an intercontinental ballistic missile (略 ICBM) 중거리— an intermediate range ballistic missile (略 IRBM)

탄두 彈頭 a warhead
◆미사일— a missile warhead 수폭[원폭]— an H-bomb [an A-bomb] warhead 핵— a nuclear warhead : 핵탄두 미사일 a nuclear-tipped missile

탄띠 彈— an ammunition belt ⇨ 탄대(彈帶)

탄력 彈力 elasticity; elastic force; resilience
◆탄력적인 태도 a flexible attitude / 탄력이 있는 : elastic; flexible; resilient / 탄력없는 inelastic; nonelastic
▶고무는 탄력이 아주 강하다 Rubber is very elastic. ⇌ Rubber has a lot of elasticity.
■—계 an elastometer —관세제 the elastic tariff system —률 the modulus of elasticity —성 elasticity; resilience; 〈융통성〉flexibility; adaptability —시험 an elasticity test

탄로 綻露 disclosure; exposure
◆탄로 날까봐 for fear of detection / 탄로나다 be found out; be discovered [exposed, disclosed, revealed]; be laid bare; come out
▶그의 지난날의 부정이 탄로났다 His past misdeeds have been exposed.
▶음모는 탄로났다 The plot has been laid bare.

탄막 彈幕 a barrage; an artillery barrage
◆탄막을 치다 lay down [put up, deliver] barrage
■고정— a standing barrage 엄호— a covering barrage ■—포화 curtain fire; a curtain of fire

탄말 炭末 charcoal dust; 〈분쇄한〉ground charcoal

탄맥 炭脈 a coal seam [vein]

탄명스럽다 muddle-headed; fuzzy-headed; thick-headed; 《look》 dumb [stupid]

탄미 嘆美 admiration; adoration
—탄미하다 admire; extol; adore; be filled with admiration
◆탄미할 작품 an admirable [a marvelous] work / 탄미하여 마지 않다 be wrapped in admiration
■—자 an admirer; an adorer

탄복 歎服 admiration
—탄복하다 admire; have [feel] a great admiration [esteem] for
◆탄복할 일 an admirable [a praiseworthy] deed
▶그의 깊은 통찰력에 우리는 탄복했다 We admired [were impressed by] the depth of his insight.
▶그의 용기에는 적도 탄복하지 않을 수 없었다 His bravery compelled applause even from his enemy.

탄사 歎辭 〈감탄의 말〉praise(s); an admiration; 〈탄식하는 말〉a lamentation
◆아무의 업적에 탄사를 아끼지 않다 be unstinting in one's praise of sb's work

탄산 炭酸 《化》 carbonic acid

◆탄산의 carbonic / 탄산을 제거하다 decarbonize
■—가스 carbonic acid gas; 〈이산화탄소〉carbon dioxide —기 carboxyl; the carboxyl radical [group] —나트륨 sodium carbonate; carbonate of soda —석회 carbonate of lime; calcium carbonate —소다 sodium carbonate; carbonate of soda; sal soda —수 soda (water); (美口) (soda) pop; fizz-water —암모늄 ammonium carbonate —염 a carbonate —음료 a carbonated drink; soda —천(泉) a carburetted spring —칼륨 potassium carbonate; carbonate of potash —칼슘 calcium carbonate; carbonate of lime

탄산증 呑酸症 〔醫〕 pyrosis; heartburn

탄산지 炭酸紙 carbon paper
◆탄산지로 복사한 카피 a carbon copy / 탄산지로 복사하다 take copies with carbon paper

탄상 歎賞 admiration; praise; laudation
—탄상하다 admire; praise highly
—자 an admirer

탄생 誕生 (a) birth; nativity
◆신교의 탄생 the birth of Protestantism
▶나는 그녀의 탄생축하로 시계를 선물했다 I gave her a watch for her birthday.
—탄생하다 be born; come into the world
■—석 a birthstone —일 one's birthday: 그의 20살 탄생일을 축하하다 celebrate his twentieth birthday —지 〈출생지〉one's birthplace; one's place of birth

탄성 彈性 elasticity ◆탄성이 있는 elastic; springy / 탄성이 없는 inelastic; nonelastic
■당김[비틀림, 굽힘]— elasticity of traction [torsion, flexure] ■—고무 elastic gum; gum elastic —곡선 elastics; an elastic curve —공학 elasticity engineering —률[계수] the modulus [coefficient] of elasticity —변형 elastic deformation —에너지 elastic [strain] energy —치 the value of elasticity —체 an elastic body

탄성 歎聲 〈한탄의〉a sigh; a groan; 〈감탄의〉a sigh of admiration; an exclamation ◆탄성을 지르다 heave a sigh; groan; admire with a deep sigh
▶그의 매혹적인 그림을 보고 모두가 탄성을 질렀다 Everybody uttered a cry of admiration at his entrancing picture.

탄소 炭素 《化》 carbon
◆수소와 탄소의 화합물 a compound of hydrogen and carbon / 방사성 탄소에 의한 연대 측정 radiocarbon [radioactive carbon] dating / 탄소의 carbonic / 탄소질의 carbonaceous / 탄소를 함유하다 be carbonaceous / 탄소화하다 carbonate / 탄소와 화합시키다 carburet; carburize / 탄소를 제거하다 decarbonize
■—강 carbon steel —동화 작용 carbon dioxide assimilation —마이크로폰 a carbon microphone —봉 a carbon —선 a carbon filament —섬유 carbon fiber —순환 carbon cycle —제거 decarbonization —지 carbon paper —화합물 carbon compounds

탄수 炭水 〈석탄과 물〉coal and water; 〈탄소와 수소〉carbon and hydrogen
■—차 a (locomotive) tender

탄수화물 炭水化物 〔化〕 a carbohydrate
♦ 탄수화물의 섭취를 줄이다 cut down (on) one's intake of carbohydrates

탄식 嘆息 a sigh; lamentation; grief ♦ 탄식으로 나날을 보내다 sigh away one's days ―**탄식하다** sigh; heave [draw, fetch] a sigh; 〈한탄하다〉 sigh for grief; lament; deplore
♦ 탄식하면서 with a sigh of grief; sighingly / 정계의 부패를 탄식하다 deplore the corruption of political circles
▶ 그는 자기의 불운을 탄식했다 He lamented [grieved over] his misfortune.
▶ 그 비보를 듣고 전원이 깊이 탄식했다 The sad news drew deep sighs of grief from all present.

탄신 誕辰 a birthday ♦ 제70회 탄신 the 70th birthday

탄알― 彈― a bullet ⇨ 탄환

탄압 彈壓 oppression; suppression; repression
♦ 탄압적인 oppressive; suppressive; repressive; coercive / 탄압을 받다 be subjected to pressure [suppression]; be suppressed
―**탄압하다** oppress; suppress; repress; crush; cramp down on
♦ 약자를 탄압하다 oppress the weak / 언론을 탄압하다 shackle speech and writing; place a gag on the freedom of speech / 사상의 자유를 탄압하다 suppress freedom of thought
▶ 정부는 소수파를 탄압했다 The government clamped down on the minority group.
■ 무력― military [armed] pressure 언론―suppression of the press ■―정책 a policy of suppression; an oppressive [a repressive] measure

탄약 彈藥 ammunition; 〔口〕 ammo
♦ 탄약 30발 thirty rounds of ammunition
■ ―고 a powder magazine [dump] ―공장 [제조소] an ammunition factory; a powder mill ―대 an ammunition [a cartridge] belt ―상자 an ammunition box [chest]; a cartridge box; a caisson ―차 an ammunition car [wagon]; a caisson ―창(廠) an ammunition depot ―통 a cartridge; a cartouch(e) ―합 (盒) an ammunition [a cartridge] pouch

탄우 彈雨 a shower [hail] of bullets
♦ 탄우 속을 amid a hail of bullets
▶ 선발대에 탄우가 날아왔다 The advancing troops were met with a hail of bullets.

탄원 歎願 a plea; (an) appeal; (a) petition; (an) entreaty ♦ 탄원을 들어 주다 grant a petition; listen to sb's entreaties
▶ 그는 그녀의 탄원을 거절했다 He turned down her supplication [plea].
―**탄원하다** appeal (to sb for sth); entreat; solicit; petition; beg ♦ 정부에 감세를 탄원하다 petition the government for decreasing a tax
▶ 학생들은 선생에게 그를 벌하지 말 것을 탄원했다 The pupils begged their teacher not to punish him.
■ ―자 a petitioner; a supplicant; a supplicator

탄원서 歎願書 a (written) petition
♦ 탄원서를 제출하다 present [send in] a (written) petition to; file a petition with

탄일 誕日 a birthday ⇨ 탄신(誕辰)

탄자니아 〈나라이름〉 Tanzania; 〈공식명〉 the United Republic of Tanzania ♦ 탄자니아의 Tanzanian ■ ―사람 a Tanzanian

탄저 炭疽 〔醫〕 anthrax

탄저병 炭疽病 〔植〕 anthracnose

탄전 炭田 a coalfield

탄젠트 tangent (略 tan)

탄지 burnt tobacco residue (in a pipe bowl)

탄진 炭塵 coal dust

탄질 炭質 the quality of coal
♦ 탄질이 좋다[나쁘다] The coal is of good [poor] quality.

탄주 彈奏 play; performance ♦ 그의 기타 탄주를 듣다 hear him play (on) the guitar ―**탄주하다** play (on) 〈the piano〉; perform; pluck [touch] 〈the string of〉 ■ ―법 〔樂〕 touch ―자 a player; a performer

탄차 炭車 a coal waggon [tram]; 〔美〕 a coal car; 〔英〕 a coal truck

탄착 彈着 hit; impact
■ ―거리 range; gunshot: 미사일의 탄착거리는 3천 킬로미터다 The missile has a range of 3,000 kilometers. ―관측 spotting ―점 the point of impact ―지역 the impact area

탄창 彈倉 a magazine (of a revolver)

탄체 彈體 〈유도탄의〉 the airframe

탄층 炭層 a coal bed; a coal seam ♦ 탄층이 깊은 탄광 a coal mine with a thick [deep] bed

탄탄대로 坦坦大路 a broad and level highway; 〈순탄한〉 a royal road ♦ 성공으로의 탄탄대로 the royal road to success
▶ 그의 일생은 탄탄대로였다 He led a peaceful [successful] life.

탄탄하다 strong ⇨ 튼튼하다

탄탄하다 坦坦― level; even; smooth
♦ 탄탄한 길 a smooth [level] road
▶ 강 양편으로는 탄탄한 들판이 펼쳐져 있다 There is an expanse of level, open land on either side of the river.

탄탈룸 〔化〕 tantalum

탄편 彈片 a shell splinter

탄폐 炭肺 anthracosis pulmonum

탄피 彈皮 an empty cartridge

탄하다 1 〈참견하다〉 meddle; make an uncalled-for [uninvited] remark; poke [put, stick] one's nose into 〈sb's affair〉
2 〈나무라다〉 blame; criticize; find fault with
♦ 실언을 탄하다 blame sb for his improper remarks

탄핵 彈劾 impeachment; denunciation
♦ 탄핵적[의] denunciatory / …에 대하여 탄핵 절차를 취하다 bring impeachment proceedings against sb
―**탄핵하다** impeach 〈sb of [with] sth〉; denounce; censure
▶ 대통령은 수뢰로 탄핵되었다 The President was impeached for taking a bribe.
■ ―연설 an impeachment [a denunciatory] address ―자 an impeacher; a denunciator ―재판소 a Court of Impeachment

탄핵안 彈劾案 an impeachment motion [resolution]; a vote of censure
♦ 정부 탄핵안을 제출하다 introudce a motion

of impeachment against the Government

탄화 炭化 〔化〕 carbonization; carburization; 〈탄소와의 화합〉 carburetion
—탄화하다 carbonize
■—강 carbonic steel —규소 silundum; silicon carbide —물 a carbide —불꽃 carburizing flame —수소 hydrocarbon —철 cementite —칼슘 calcium carbide; carbonized calcium

탄환 彈丸 〈소총탄〉 a bullet; a shot; 〈포탄〉 a shell; 〈유산탄〉 a shrapnel
♦탄환에 의한 부상 a gunshot wound / 탄환이 뚫지 못하는 bulletproof; shellproof / 빗발치는 탄환 속을 전진하다 advance under a shower [hail, rain] of bullets / 적에게 탄환을 퍼붓다 rain [shower] shells upon the enemy
▶이 총에는 탄환이 장전되어 있다 This rifle is loaded.
▶팔에 탄환을 맞았다 I got a shot [was shot] in the arm.
■—열차 a bullet train; a flier —저장실 a magazine; a depot

탄회 坦懷 frankness ⇨ 허심탄회(虛心坦懷)

탄흔 彈痕 a bullet mark [hole]; a shot hole
♦탄흔 투성이의 벽 a bullet-pocked wall

탈 〈가면〉 a mask
♦탈을 쓰다 put on [wear, assume] a mask; cover one's face with a mask; mask (one's face) / …의 탈을 쓰고 under the mask [cloak] of (friendship); under [in] the semblance of (a sage); under color of (religion) / 탈을 벗다 throw off [drop, pull out] one's mask / 탈을 벗기다 unmask; take off the mask of
▶그는 인간의 탈을 쓰고 있을 뿐이다 He is human only in appearance [shape].

탈 頉 1 〈사고〉 a trouble; an accident; an incident; a mishap; a hitch; a snag
♦탈없이 without accident [incident, mishap]; without a hitch; smoothly; 〈무사히〉 safely; in safety / 탈없이 진행되다 go on without a hitch [trouble]; go all right [well]; run smoothly / 탈없이 도착하다 arrive at safely; 〈것〉이 reach in good order
▶자금이 모자라는 것이 탈이다 The trouble is we don't have enough money.

2 〈병〉 illness; sickness
♦탈없이 free from sickness; in good health; safe and sound / 탈없이 지내다 be getting along very well
▶과식해서 탈이 나지 않도록 해라 Don't upset your stomach by eating too much.
▶그는 순환계통에 탈이 있다 He has circulatory trouble.

3 〈흠〉 a fault; a flaw
▶그는 소심한 것이 탈이다 Timidity is his weakness [defect].
▶그는 내가 하는 일에 일일이 탈을 잡는다 He picks holes in [finds fault with] everything I do.

탈각 脫殼 〔動〕〈껍질 벗기〉 exuviation
—탈각하다 exuviate; cast off a skin [shell]; slough

탈각하다 脫却— get rid of; rid [extricate] oneself of; free oneself from
♦악습에서 탈각하다 break away from [shake off] a bad habit
▶그는 마침내 망상에서 탈각하기에 이르렀다 He has finally awakened from his delusion.

탈것 a vehicle; a (public) means of transportation [transport]; 〈유원지의〉 a ride
♦탈것을 타다 ride [get a ride in] a vehicle
▶교외는 공기는 좋으나 탈것이 불충분하다 In the suburbs the air is fresh, but transportation facilities are inadequate.

탈격 奪格 〔文法〕 the ablative (case)

탈고 脫稿 completion of a manuscript
—탈고하다 finish writing; complete (a novel)
♦탈고되다 be completed
▶나는 마침내 백 쪽의 논문을 탈고했다 I finally managed to complete my hundred-page thesis.

탈곡 脫穀 threshing; thrashing —탈곡하다 thresh; thrash —기 a threshing [thrashing] machine; a thresher; a thrasher —장 a threshing [thrashing] floor

탈구 脫臼 〔醫〕 dislocation
—탈구하다 be dislocated
▶그는 오른팔을 탈구했다 He has had his right arm dislocated. ≒ His right arm is out of joint.
■—교정 extension —부전(不全) incomplete dislocation

탈나다 頉— 1 〈사고나다〉 an accident happens; have a hitch [mishap]; run into trouble [snag]; 〈고장나다〉 get out of order; go wrong [awry]; break down
▶에어 컨디셔너가 탈났다 The air conditioner has got out of order [has gone wrong].
▶그에게 뭔가 탈난게 틀림없어 Something [Some accident] must have happened to him.
2 〈병나다〉 fall [get, be taken] ill [sick] ♦과식하여 탈나다 overeat oneself sick / 과로하여 탈나다 work oneself ill

탈놀음 a mask(ed) show; a masque; a masquerade

탈당 脫黨 withdrawal from a party; defection; (美) bolt —탈당하다 leave [desert] a party; withdraw from a party; break with [break away from] a party; (美) bolt
■—성명(서) a (written) statement of one's secession from the party —자 a seceder; a defector; (美) a bolter

탈락 脫落 1 〈빠짐〉 falling [coming] off; 〈뒤짐〉 dropout; 〈깃털의〉 deplumation
—탈락하다 fall [slip] off [away]
▶이 새는 깃털이 탈락하기 시작했다 This bird is starting to lose its feathers.
2 〈누락〉 an omission; a lacuna; 〈제외〉 exclusion; 〈이탈〉 defection
—탈락하다 be omitted; be left out; be excluded; 〈이탈하다〉 fall away (from); drop out (of)
▶이 페이지는 한 절이 탈락되어 있다 A paragraph is missing from this page.
▶그들은 연속 두 게임에 져서 예선에서 탈락했다 They lost two games in succession and were eliminated.
▶그 경주에서 많은 사람이 탈락했다 Many people dropped out of the race.

■ —자 a dropout
탈락거리다 keep slapping ⇨ 털럭거리다
탈루 脫漏 an omission
　—탈루하다 be missing; be omitted
▶ 오류와 탈루는 제외됨 Errors and omissions excepted. (略 E.& O.E.)
탈륨 〔化〕 thallium
탈리 脫離 a secession ⇨ 이탈(離脫)
탈리도마이드 〔藥〕 thalidomide
■ —기형아 a thalidomide [seal] baby
탈린 脫燐 dephosphorization
　—탈린하다 dephosphorize
탈모 脫毛 〈빠짐〉 alopecia; falling-out[-off] of hair; loss of hair; 〈털〉 fallen hair
　—탈모하다 〈빠지다〉《one's hair》 fall out [off]; 〈사람이 주어〉 lose one's hair; 〈뽑다〉 remove the hair 《from》
▶ 그 치료를 받고 나서 그는 탈모했다 The (medical) treatment caused him to lose his hair [caused his hair fall out].
■ —로션 depilatory lotion —제(劑) a depilatory (agent) —증〔醫〕 alopecia: 원형 탈모증 alopecia areata
탈모 脫帽 taking [pulling] off one's cap [hat]
▶ 탈모 (口令) Hats off (please)! ⇌ Off with your hats!
　—탈모하다 take [pull] off one's hat [cap]; doff the hat; raise [lift, remove] one's hat [cap]
▶ 남자들은 탈모하고 서 있었다 The men stood bareheaded [with their heads uncovered].
탈무드 the Talmud　■ —학자 a Talmudic scholar; a Talmudist
탈바가지 a gourd mask; 〈탈〉 a mask
탈바꿈 〔昆〕 metamorphosis ⇨ 변태(變態)
탈법행위 脫法行爲 an evasion of the law
▶ 그것은 분명히 탈법행위다 That is a clear evasion of the law.
탈산 脫酸 〔化〕 deoxidization; deoxidation
　—탈산하다 deoxidize ■ —제(劑) a deoxidizer
탈상 脫喪 leaving off mourning; the end of mourning　—탈상하다 leave off [go out of] mourning; finish mourning
탈색 脫色 decoloration; bleaching; decolorization　—탈색하다 remove the color; decolorize; bleach　■ —제(劑) a decolorant; a decolorizer; a bleaching agent
탈선 脫船 running away from a ship; desertion from a ship　—탈선하다 run away from a ship; desert a ship; jump ship　■ —자 a runaway seaman; a deserter (from a ship)
탈선 脫線 1 〈열차의〉 derailment　—탈선하다 run off the rails [tracks]; be [get] derailed; derail; jump [leave] the track
▶ 화물열차가 탈선하여 쓰러졌다 A freight train derailed and fell on its side.
▶ 열차는 선로 위의 돌 때문에 탈선했다 The train was derailed because of a rock on the rails.
2 〈언행의〉 deviation; (a) digression; aberration; a ramble
　—탈선하다 〈행동이〉 deviate [go away] from the right path; get on the loose; go astray

[wild]; 〈이야기 등이〉 digress [go adrift] 《from the subject》; make a digression; go off the rails; go [run] off the (main) track; get sidetracked; get off the subject
■ —학생 an erratic student
탈세 脫稅 tax evasion; a tax-dodge
▶ 그는 탈세로 입건되었다 He was accused of tax evasion.
　—탈세하다 evade [dodge] (paying) tax
■ —수단[수법] a tax-dodge —액 the amount of the tax evasion —자 an evader of taxes; a tax-dodger; a tax evader —품 smuggled goods
탈속 脫俗 unworldliness; absence of vulgarity
◆ 탈속적 견해 an unworldly point of view
　—탈속하다 be liberated; be free from conventionality [vulgarity]; rise above the world
◆ 탈속하여, saintly / 탈속하여 도를 닦다 rise above [transcend] the world and cultivate one's moral sense
탈수 脫水 〔化〕 dehydration
　—탈수하다 dehydrate; desiccate; dry
■ —기 a dehydrator; a spin drier [dryer] —작용 dehydration —제(劑) a dehydrating [desiccating] agent —증〔醫〕 dehydration
탈수소 脫水素 〔化〕 dehydrogenation
탈습 脫濕 dehumidification; dehumidifying
　—탈습하다 dehumidify
■ —기(器) a dehumidifier
탈싹 with a plop [flop]; with a thud
탈싹거리다 keep plopping [plunking]; plop [plunk] repeatedly
탈쓰다 1 〈얼굴에〉 mask 《one's face》; wear [put on] a mask; 〈가장하다〉 disguise oneself; mask one's real character
◆ 탈쓴 masked / 종교의 탈을 쓰다 assume the mask of religion
2 〈닮다〉 be the very image 《of》; be an exact likeness [replica] 《of》
▶ 그 애는 아버를 탈썼다 The boy is the very portrait [a carbon copy] of his father.
탈염 脫鹽 desalinization; 〔化〕 desalting
　—탈염하다 desalt; desalinate; desalinize
■ —수 desalted [demineralized] water
탈영 脫營 desertion from barracks; decampment　—탈영하다 desert from barracks; desert from the army; 《美俗》 go over the hill
■ —병 a deserter; a runaway soldier
탈옥 脫獄 prison [jail] breaking; (a) prison breach [break]; jailbreak
◆ 탈옥을 기도하다 attempt an escape from jail; try [attempt] to break prison
　—탈옥하다 break (out of) prison; break jail; escape from prison
■ —수 a prison-[jail-]breaker; an escaped prisoner [convict]; a runaway
탈의 脫衣 divestiture; divestment; disrobing
　—탈의하다 undress 《oneself》; take off one's clothes
■ —장[실] a dressing [changing] room; 《美》 〈해수욕장의〉 bathing booth; a bathhouse; 〈체육관의〉 a locker room
탈자 脫字 an omitted word; an omission
▶ 탈자가 두 개 있다 Two words are missing

탈잡다 頂— find fault with; pick flaws with; (口) nitpick; blame; criticize
♦ 이러쿵저러쿵 탈잡다 criticize *sb* for one thing or another
▶ 그의 태도는 탈잡을 데가 없었다 His manner was above criticism. ≒ His manner left nothing to be desired.

탈장 脫腸 〔醫〕 hernia (*pl.* ~s, -ae); rupture
▶ 그는 탈장이 되었다 He has a hernia.
—**탈장하다** herniate; rupture
■—대(帶) a truss —봉합술 herniorrhaphy —수술 herniotomy

탈저 脫疽 〔醫〕 gangrene; sphacelus; necrosis (*pl.* -ses) ♦ 탈저에 걸리다 be attacked by [suffer from] gangrene; sphacelate

탈적하다 脫籍— have *one's* name removed [deleted, dropped] from the register; strike *one's* name off the register

탈주 脫走 (an) escape; flight; abscondence; a breakaway; (a) desertion
♦ 자유로의 탈주 a break for freedom / 탈주를 꾀하다 plan [attempt] an escape
—**탈주하다** flee; escape; run [make] away; make off (with *oneself*); bolt; (口) 〈탈옥·탈영〉 give [take] leg bail; desert; (美俗) 〈탈영〉 go over the hill
♦ 교도소에서 탈주하다 escape [run away] from prison; break out of prison
▶ 병사들은 집단으로 군에서 탈주했다 The soldiers deserted from the army in a group.
■—병 a deserter; a fugitive [runaway] soldier —자 a runaway; a fugitive

탈지 脫脂 removal of fat [grease]
♦ 양모를 탈지하다 remove grease from wool
—면 absorbent [sanitary] cotton; (英) cotton wool —분유 skim milk powder; dried skim milk —유 skim [nonfat] milk

탈진 脫盡 (total) exhaustion —**탈진하다** be utterly exhausted [fatigued]; be dead tired; be tired out ♦ 탈진하도록 일하다 exhaust *oneself* by overwork

탈출 脫出 (an) escape —**탈출하다** escape from 《a prison》; defect; get away 《from a place》; get out
♦ 다른 나라로 탈출하다 escape to another country / 불타는 집에서 탈출하다 escape from [get out of] the burning house / 비행기에서 낙하산으로 탈출하다 make a parachute jump [bail out] from a plane
▶ 마침내 그는 곤경에서 탈출했다 At last he got himself out of [extricated himself from] the difficult situation.
■—속도 〈로켓 등의〉 escape velocity

탈춤 a masked dance

탈취 脫臭 deodorization —**탈취하다** remove the unpleasant smell; deodorize; remove the odor (of) ■—제(a) deodorant; a deodorizer; a deodorizing agent

탈취 奪取 capture; seizure; wresting
—**탈취하다** carry off; capture; seize; snatch 《from, out of, away》
▶ 그들은 그의 가방을 탈취했다 They robbed him of his bag.
▶ 그 팀은 수위를 탈취했다 The team wrested the first position.

탈타리 a rattletrap ⇨ 털터리

탈탈 ploddingly ⇨ 털털

탈퇴 脫退 withdrawal; secession ♦ 탈퇴서를 내다 submit a written notice to quit 《to a society》 —**탈퇴하다** secede [withdraw] from; break (away) from
▶ 그는 그 회를 탈퇴했다 He withdrew from the society.
■—자 a seceder; a bolter

탈피 脫皮 1 〈곤충 등의〉 exuviation; molt(ing); ecdysis (*pl.* -dyses); casting —**탈피하다** cast off the skin; slough (off); exuviate; molt
▶ 뱀은 해마다 탈피한다 The snake sloughs annually.
2 〈벗어남〉 self-renewal; outgrowing; emergencing —**탈피하다** outgrow; emerge ♦ 인습에서 탈피하다 outgrow the convention
▶ 우리는 구습에서 탈피해야 한다 We must shake ourselves from convention.
■—억제 호르몬 molting inhibiting hormone

탈하다 頂— 〈핑계대다〉 plead; make an excuse of ♦ 병을 탈하고 결근하다 stay away from office under the pretext of being ill

탈함 脫艦 desertion from a warship
—**탈함하다** desert a warship; run away from a warship
■—자 a runaway sailor; a naval deserter

탈항 脫肛 〔醫〕 (suffer from) prolapse of the anus

탈환 奪還 recapture; recovery —**탈환하다** recapture; take back; win back; regain; recover; retake ♦ 고지를 탈환하다 recapture a fortress on a hill from the enemy

탈황 脫黃 〔化〕 desulfurization —**탈황하다** desulfurize; desulfur ■—기 a desulfurizer —제 a desulfurizing agent

탈회 脫會 withdrawal [secession] 《from a society》 —**탈회하다** withdraw [secede] from; give up *one's* membership 《in a club》; leave 《a society》; drop out; quit

탈회 奪回 recapture ⇨ 탈환(奪還)

탐 貪 〈탐욕〉 covetousness; avarice; greed; 〈욕심〉 desire —**탐하다** covet; crave; be greedy 《of, for》 ♦ 주색을 탐하다 give *oneself* up to wine and women

탐검 探檢 (a) probe; investigation; examination —**탐검하다** probe; sound; investigate; examine

탐관오리 貪官汚吏 a corrupt official ♦ 탐관오리의 숙청 a purge of corrupt officials

탐광 探鑛 prospecting —**탐광하다** prospect 《a region for gold》 ■—갱 a prospecting tunnel —자 a prospector

탐구 探究 research; study; investigation; inquiry —**탐구하다** research; do reseach(es) 《into》; study; investigate; inquire 《into》
—심 the spirit of inquiry; an inquiring mind —자 an inquirer; an investigator

탐구 探求 a quest; search; pursuit ♦ 진리의 탐구 pursuit of truth / 지식의 탐구 a quest of knowledge —**탐구하다** search (for); pursue 《truth》

탐나다 貪— 〈대상이 주어〉 be desirable; be appetizing; be tempting; 〈사람이 주어〉 be desirous [covetous] of; be envious of; desire; lust after [for]
♦ 탐나는 여자 a desirable woman / 탐나는 음식 appetizing [mouth-watering] food / 탐나는 듯이 wistfully; longingly / 돈이 탐나서 for love of money / 돈이 탐나다 be covetous of money
▶나는 명예 따위는 탐나지 않는다 I have no desire [don't care] for fame.

탐내다 貪— covet; crave; be greedy 《of》; be covetous 《of》
♦ 명예와 부를 탐내다 covet fame and fortune / 음식을 탐내다 devour; eat greedily; gorge 《of》/ 남의 재산을 탐내다 be covetous of another's property
▶누구든지 돈을 탐낸다 Love of money is common to all.

탐닉 耽溺 〈빠짐〉 indulgence; addiction; 〈방탕〉 dissipation; prodigality; debauchery
—탐닉하다 be indulged; indulge 《oneself》 in; be addicted to; be immersed in; give *oneself* up to; abandon *oneself* to 《the pursuit of pleasure》
♦ 주색에 탐닉하다 abandon *oneself* to liquor and sex; be addicted to sensual pleasures; lead a life of dissipation
▶그는 도박에 탐닉했다 He gave himself over to gambling.
▶그는 술에 탐닉하고 있다 He indulges (himself) in drinking.

탐독 耽讀 indulgence in reading; avid reading
—탐독하다 read avidly; be absorbed in reading; be immersed in a book; steep *oneself* in reading; pore over a book
▶그는 추리소설을 탐독하느라고 어머니가 부르는 소리도 못들었다 He was absorbed in [was poring over] a mystery story and didn't hear his mother call.
▶나는 소년시절에 모험소설을 탐독했다 I was very fond of [absorbed in reading] adventure stories in my boyhood.
■—자 an inveterate reader

탐리 貪吏 a greedy official
탐리 貪利 love of undue gain [profits]; greed of gain —탐리하다 covet undue profits; be greedy of gain

탐문 探問 indirect inquiry
—탐문하다 inquire about indirectly; sound (out) by indirect inquiry

탐문 探聞 obtaining information (by inquiry)
—탐문하다 obtain information (by inquiry); hear; 〈소문을〉 get wind of; 〈형사 등이〉 snoop [beat the bushes] for information
♦ 탐문한 바에 의하면 according to what I [we] have learned

탐미 耽美 (a)estheticism; love of beauty ♦ 탐미적인 (a)esthetic ■—주의 (a)estheticism —주의자 the (a)esthete —파 the (a)esthetic school; 〈단체〉 the (a)esthetes

탐방 splash ⇨ 텀벙
탐방 探訪 (private) inquiry; an interview
—탐방하다 make (private) inquiries; interview
■카메라— a photographic interview ■—기사 a report; reportage; an interview —기자 a reporter; an interviewer; a legman

탐사 探査 inquiry; investigation; probing
♦ 심해 탐사용 선박 a vessel designed for deep sea probes
—탐 사 하 다 make inquiries; investigate; inquire [look] into; probe into
♦ 고적을 탐사하다 visit a place of historical interest / 월면을 탐사하다 probe the surface of the moon / 철저히 탐사하다 make a thorough [rigid] inquiry
■ 달— a lunar [moon] probe

탐상 探賞 sight-seeing ⇨ 탐승(探勝)
탐색 探索 1 〈수색〉 search; hunt; quest
—탐색하다 search (for); look [quest] for; delve into; seek for; hunt up; probe
♦ 범인의 행방을 탐색하다 inquire into [look for] the whereabouts of the culprit
▶그들은 서로 속셈을 탐색하고 있다 They are sounding one another (out). ⇌ They are trying to read the thoughts of each other.

2 〈조사〉 (a) probe; inquiry; investigation; research —탐색하다 inquire into; investigate; probe
■—기구 (氣球) an observation [a sounding] balloon —전(戰) an engagement in reconnaissance; a reconnoitering skirmish —코일 a search coil; a exploring coil —행동 〔軍〕 a probing action

탐스럽다 貪— desirable; appetizing; coveted; attractive; tempting; charming ♦ 탐스러운 사과 an appetizing apple / 탐스러운 여자 a charming woman
▶나는 이것이 제일 탐스럽다 This suits my taste best.

탐승 探勝 sight-seeing; a sight-seeing trip
—탐승하다 go on a sight-seeing trip; do [see] the sights 《of》 ■—객 a sightseer; a visitor to scenic spots

탐식 貪食 voracity; edacity —탐식하다 eat voraciously [greedily]; eat avidly; devour; gormandize ■—가 a voracious person; a glutton; a gourmand(izer)

탐심 貪心 avarice; greed; cupidity
탐욕 貪慾 greed; avarice; rapacity; covetousness; cupidity ♦ 탐욕의 화신 (be) avarice itself; (be) the incarnation of avarice
—탐욕스럽다 greedy; covetous; avaricious
♦ 탐욕스럽게 avariciously; rapaciously; greedily; covetously
■—가 a shark; a harpy; a vulture

탐재 貪財 love of money; desire for wealth
—탐재하다 love money; desire wealth

탐정 探偵 〈행위〉 secret investigation; detection; detective work [service]; 〈군사상의〉 espionage; 〈사람〉 a detective; a spy; (口) a sleuth
▶한 탐정이 내 뒤를 밟았다 A detective was on my track.
—탐정하다 spy 《on, into》; trace; inquire into; detect
■군사— a military spy 비밀— a secret agent;

a secret (-service) detective 사설— a private detective; (口) a private eye ■—소설 a detective story [novel]; (총칭) detective fiction

탐조 探照 throwing [beaming] a searchlight —탐조하다 throw [beam] a searchlight (on) ♦해상을 탐조하다 flash over the sea

탐조등 探照燈 a searchlight ♦탐조등으로 비추다 turn [flash] a searchlight (on *sb*); sweep (the sea) with a searchlight / 탐조등을 켜다 switch on a searchlight

탐지 探知 detection —탐지하다 find out; detect; spy [search] out; trace out ♦비밀을 탐지하다 smell out a secret ▶범인의 행동은 모두 경찰에 탐지되었다 All the criminal's activities were detected by the police. ▶우리는 그 해역에 부설된 기뢰를 탐지하는데 성공했다 We succeeded in detecting the mines laid in that sea area.

탐지기 探知機 a detector; a locator ■방향— a direction finder 어군— a fish detector 전파— a radar; a radar set

탐측 探測 sounding; probing ■—기 a probe; a prober —기구 [氣] a pilot balloon

탐침 探針 a probe; an explorer ♦탐침을 넣다 probe (a wound); plunge a probe (into)

탐탁스럽다 nice ⇨ 탐탁하다

탐탁하다 nice; pleasant; agreeable; desirable; satisfactory; suitable ♦탐탁한 사람 a nice [good] person / 탐탁한 환경 desirable [delightful] surroundings / 탐탁치 않은 손님 an unwelcome guest ▶결과는 별로 탐탁치 않았다 The result was not as [so] good as we had expected.

탐탐 耽耽 with a vigilant eye ⇨ 호시탐탐(虎視眈眈)

탐폰 [醫] a tampon

탐해등 探海燈 a searchlight ♦탐해등으로 해면을 탐조하다 sweep the sea with a searchlight

탐해법 探海法 [海] creeping

탐험 探險 (an) exploration; an expedition ♦남아프리카 탐험 an expedition to [into] South Africa —탐험하다 explore; make an exploration ♦무인도를 탐험하다 explore an uninhabited island / 남극을 탐험하러 가다 go on an Antarctic expedition ▶그는 아마존강을 탐험하러 갔다 He went on an expedition to the Amazon River. ■우주— space exploration ■—가 an explorer ■비행 an exploratory flight (over the regions) —선 a research ship —여행 an expedition

탐험기 探險記 an account of an expedition (to) [explorations (in)]

탐험대 探險隊 an expeditionary [exploration] party ♦탐험대를 보내다 dispatch an expeditionary [exploration] party ♦남극[북극]— an Antarctic [Arctic] expedition ■—장 the leader [chief] of an expedition

탐호 貪好 fanatic love; great liking; indulgence —탐호하다 be very fond of; have a passion for; indulge in

탐혹 耽惑 indulgence; addiction; infatuation —탐혹하다 indulge in; be addicted [given] to ♦여자에게 탐혹하다 be infatuated [taken] with a woman; be smitten with [by] a woman's charms

탑 塔 a tower; 〈사찰의〉 a pagoda; 〈첨탑〉 a steeple; a spire; 〈방첨탑〉 an obelisk; 〈기념탑〉 a monument ♦5층 탑 a five-storied pagoda / 탑을 세우다 erect [build] a tower

탑본 搨本 a rubbed copy; a rubbing ♦비문의 탑본을 뜨다 make a rubbing of a monumental inscription; rub a copy from a monument —탑본하다 make a rubbing (of); rub

탑비 塔碑 pagodas and monuments

탑삭나룻 a thick and short beard; a short heavy beard

탑삭부리 a man with a short heavy beard

탑새기주다 spoil; ruin; damage; destroy; make a mess [muddle] of

탑승 搭乘 boarding; riding (a plane) —탑승하다 get into; board; 〈항공기에〉 get on (a plane); 〈함선에〉 go on board a ship ♦탑승시키다 embark; entrain; enplane ■—권 〈여객기의〉 a boarding card —원 a crewman; a crew —자 a passenger

탑재 搭載 loading; embarkation; entrainment —탑재하다 load; embark; carry ♦배에 화물을 탑재하다 load a ship with goods; get [take] goods on board ▶그 군함은 5문의 거포를 탑재하고 있다 The warship carries five heavy guns. ■—량 burden; (have) a carrying capacity (of 50,000 tons) —중량 weight on board

탑파 塔婆 a stupa; a pagoda

탓 〈잘못〉 fault; blame; responsibility; 〈이유〉 reason; cause; ground(s) ♦내 탓으로 through my fault / 나이 탓으로 because of [owing to] one's age / 남의 탓으로 돌리다 lay (a fault) at another's door / 실패를 불운 탓으로 돌리다 attribute [ascribe, impute] one's failure to bad luck ▶그것은 다 내 탓이다 It's all my fault. ▶그것은 네 탓이다 You're to blame for it. ▶지각한 것은 교통 정체 탓이었다 The delay was due to heavy traffic. ▶그는 실패를 남의 탓으로 돌리고 있다 He is putting the blame for his failure on others. ▶누구 탓도 아니다. 다 내 잘못이다 No one else is to blame. It's entirely my fault. ▶그들은 산불의 원인을 등산객들의 부주의 탓으로 돌렸다 They attributed the forest fire to the carelessness of hikers.

탓하다 〈책임을 물어〉 blame (for); 〈실망하여〉 reproach (for); 〈비난조로〉 reprove; 〈탈을 잡다〉 find fault (with) ♦자기를 탓하다 reproach *oneself* (for) / 하늘을 탓하다 quarrel with providence / 세상의 무정을 탓하다 accuse the hardness of the world ▶나만 잘못한다고 탓하지 마시오 Don't lay the blame upon me alone. ⇌ Don't make me the scapegoat. ▶나는 네가 지각한 것을 탓하지 않겠다 I don't blame [reproach] you that you came late.

탕 bang; boom ♦ 탕하고 문을 닫다 bang the door; slam the door closed [shut] / 주먹으로 책상을 탕하고 치다 bang one's fist on the table

탕 湯 1 〈국〉 soup; broth
2 〈한약〉 a (medical) decoction; an infusion
3 〈목욕탕〉 a (hot) bath; a public
♦ 남[여]탕 the men's [women's] section 《of a bathhouse》 / 탕에 들어가다 have a dip in the bathtub

탕감 蕩減 write-off; cancellation; remission ―탕감하다 write off 《debts》; cancel (out) ♦ 빚을 탕감해주다 remit [write off] sb's debt

탕개 a clamp; a tightening lever ♦ 탕개 틀다 twist the tightening lever; tighten 《ropes》 with a lever put between ■―목 a tightening wooden peg [bar] ―붙임 fastening with a tightening lever ―줄 ropes with a tightening lever put between

탕건 宕巾 a horsehair skullcap; a horse hair inner cap ♦ 탕건 바람에 with one's skullcap exposed

탕관 湯罐 a pipkin
탕기 湯器 a soup bowl
탕녀 蕩女 a dissolute woman ⇨ 탕부(蕩婦)
탕메― soup and rice (offered at ancestral rites)
탕면 湯麵 noodles in soup
탕반 湯飯 rice in broth [soup]
탕부 蕩婦 a dissolute [licentious, lewd, wanton] woman; a slut
탕산하다 蕩產― squander [dissipate] one's fortune; run [go] through one's fortune
탕솥 湯― a soup kettle
탕수 湯水 hot [boiling] water
탕수육 糖水肉 sweet and sour pork
탕심 蕩心 propensity to dissipation; salacious thinking; a lewd mind
탕아 蕩兒 a prodigal; a debauchee; a libertine
탕약 湯藥 a (medical) decoction; an infusion; herb tea [water]
탕자 蕩子 a prodigal [profligate] son
탕전 帑錢 the privy purse
탕제 湯劑 a decoction ⇨ 탕약(湯藥)
탕진 蕩盡 waste; squandering; dissipation; dilapidation ―탕진하다 waste; squander; run through 《money》 ♦ 가산을 탕진하다 squander [dissipate] one's fortune / 돈을 탕진하다 run through all one's money / 정력을 탕진하다 be drained of one's energy

탕치 湯治 a hot spring cure ―탕치하다 have the baths in hot spring for medical purposes; take a hot spring cure ■―객 visitors at hot springs cure ―요양 spa treatment; a hot spring cure ―장 a spa; hot springs

탕치다 蕩― 1 〈탕진하다〉 waste; squander [dissipate] one's fortune ♦ 노름으로 탕치다 gamble away one's fortune
2 〈탕감하다〉 write-off; cancel (out) ♦ 빚을 탕치다 write off a debt; remit sb's debt

탕탕 1 〈총포 소리〉 Bang! Bang!; crack; 〈두드리는 소리〉 with a rattat; thump ♦ 총을 탕탕 쏘다 blaze [bang] away / 탕탕 문을 두들기다 pound [bang at, thump at] the door
2 〈큰소리 치는 모양〉 with hot air; with big words ♦ 탕탕 큰소리 치다 boast; brag; talk big [tall]; tell a tall tale

탕탕거리다 bang [boom] away; bang [boom] repeatedly

탕파 湯婆 a foot warmer; a hot-water bottle; a foot [warming] pan; 《美》 a hot-water bag

태¹ 〈깨진 금〉 a crack; a fissure ▶ 이 컵은 태가 갔다 There is a crack in this cup. ⇄ This cup is cracked.

태² 〈새를 쫓는〉 a clap(ping) [cracking] whip

태 胎 the placenta and the umbilical cord ♦ 태(를)가르다 cut the navel [umbilical] chord

태 態 1 〈맵시〉 shapeliness; a form; an appearance; 〈태도〉 an air; bearing ♦ 귀여운 태가 있다 have a certain loveliness about one / 아는 태를 내다 pretend to know [put on an air of knowing] 《all the answers》
2 〈文法〉 voice ■―능동[수동]― active[passive] voice

태가다 crack; be cracked ♦ 태간 질그릇 a cracked pottery

태고 太古 ancient times; remote antiquity [ages]
♦ 태고적 사람들 ancient [primitive] peoples / 태고의 ancient; primeval; 〈원시의〉 primitive / 태고적부터 from [since] time immemorial ■―대 〔地質〕 the Archean Era [Group] ―림 primeval forests ―사 ancient history ―시대 ancient times; antiquity

태공망 太公望 an angler ⇨ 강태공(姜太公)
태교 胎敎 prenatal culture [education]; antenatal training ▶ 아름다운 음악을 듣는 것이 태교에 좋다고 한다 Sweet music is said to have a good effect on an unborn baby.

태권도 跆拳道 T'aekwŏndo; the Korean art of self-defense

태그 ■―레슬링 a tag wrestle ―매치 a tag match ―팀 a tag team

태극 太極 the Great Absolute 《in Chinese philosophy》; the entity of the cosmos ♦ 태극 무늬가 있는 기와 a two-comma-patterned roofing tile ■―선〔扇〕 a fan with a taegŭk design

태극기 太極旗 the T'aegŭkgi; the national flag of Korea

태기 胎氣 signs [indications] of pregnancy [conception]

태깔 態― 1 〈태와 빛깔〉 figure and color ♦ 태깔이 나다 look nice
2 〈교만한 태도〉 a haughty attitude ―태깔스럽다 haughty; proud; arrogant ▶ 그는 아랫사람들에게 태깔스럽게 군다 He behaves haughtily to his inferiors.

태껸 T'aekyŏn; the kicking and tripping art as a sport

태나다 be born ⇨ 태어나다
태낭 胎囊 〔動〕 an embryonic sac
태내 胎內 the interior of the womb ♦ 태내에 있는 아이 a child in the womb; an

unborn child; a fetus / 태내에서 죽다 die while in the (mother's) womb

태다수 太多數 〈썩 많은 수효〉 a multitude; a great number; too many [great] number

태도 態度 an attitude; a manner; bearing; deportment; an air; a stand
♦군인다운 태도 a military bearing / 심적 태도 one's attitude of mind / 젠체하는[점잔빼는] 태도 airs and graces
〈태도가〉그의 태도가 마음에 안 든다 I don't like his manner [attitude].
▶너는 식사 중의 태도가 아주 좋지 않다 Your behavior at meals is [Your table manners are] really bad.
▶요즘 그 사람 태도가 이상하다 He is not his usual self [not quite himself] these days.
▶그는 남들 앞에서는 태도가 변한다 He behaves differently in public.
▶[會話]「그는 태도가 어떠니?」「요즘은 이해심이 아주 많아졌어요」"How's he behaving?" "Recently he's been very considerate."
〈태도를〉태도를 바꾸다 change one's attitude [tune]; alter one's stand / 태도를 밝히다 define [clarify] one's attitude; make one's attitude clear / 쌀쌀한 태도를 보이다 behave oneself toward (another) like a stranger; wear a distant air / 강경한[냉정한, 약한] 태도를 취하다 take [assume] a strong [cool, weak] attitude (toward [to, on]) / 명백한 태도를 취하다 take a clear stand (on a problem) / 모호한 태도를 취하다 assume [maintain] an ambiguous attitude (toward a problem); sit on the fence / 거만한 태도를 취하다 strike a haughty attitude
▶미국은 그 문제에 대하여 강경한 태도를 취했다 America took a strong attitude toward the problem.
▶태도를 분명히 해라 Determine your attitude.
▶그는 친구에게 심한 태도를 취했다 He behaved badly to [toward] his friend. ⇌ He treated his friends badly.
▶이제 태도를 정했나요? Have you decided yet?
〈태도에〉그는 감정이 곧 태도에 나타난다 He easily shows his feelings in his attitude.
〈태도로〉결연한 태도로 in a determined attitude; with a determined air / 위협적인 태도로 나오다 take [assume] a threatening attitude
▶선생님께 그런 태도로 대해서는 안 된다 You shouldn't act like that toward your teacher.
▶그는 늘 소극적인 태도로 말을 한다 He always speaks in defensive manner.

태독 胎毒 [醫] eczema on a baby's head or face; congenital boils

태동 胎動 quickening; fetal movement; the movements of the fetus; 〈비유〉signs [indications] (of forthcoming activities)
▶부픈 봉오리가 봄의 태동을 알려주고 있다 Fat buds show signs of spring.
—**태동하다** quicken; 〈비유〉show signs (of)
▶민주화가 태동하고 있다 There is a quickening of democratization.
■—**기** the quickening period

태두 泰斗 an [a great] authority; a leading light; a luminary; a star
♦영문학의 태두 a great authority on English literature / 한국 의학계의 태두 a luminary in the medical profession of Korea

태령 太嶺·泰嶺 〈준말〉 a high and steep pass [ridge]; a sharp divide

태류 苔類 [植] the liverworts

태막 胎膜 a fetal [an embryonic] membrane

태만 怠慢 negligence; neglect; 〈의무 등의〉 default; delinquency; 〈게으름〉 idleness; laziness; 〈부주의〉 inattention; carelessness
▶태만은 모든 악덕의 근원이다 Idleness is the parent of all vice.
▶이 말썽은 그녀의 태만으로 인해 일어난 것이다 This trouble has happened through her default.
—**태만하다** negligent; neglectful; derelict; idle; lazy; 〈부주의하다〉 inattentive; careless; remiss (in one's duty)
♦직무를 태만히 하다 neglect [be negligent of] one's duties
▶그는 태만하여 해고되었다 He lost his job through [because of] negligence.
■**직무**— neglect [dereliction] of duty; culpable neglect; delinquency: 직무태만자 a defaulter; a delinquent / 직무 태만으로 해고되다 be dismissed for neglect of (one's) duty; be dismissed for being negligent [neglectful] of one's duty ■ —**죄** a sin of omission; criminal neglect

태몽 胎夢 a dream of forthcoming conception

태무하다 殆無— 〈거의 없다〉 very scarce [few, rare]; 《there is》 little; 〈서술적〉 be next to nothing
▶성공 가능성은 태무하다 There is not the remotest chance of success.
▶그 사건에 관하여 아는 사람은 태무하다 Hardly anyone knows [Almost no one knows, Very few people know] the incident. ⇌ The incident is almost unknown.
▶내가 얻은 것이라곤 태무하였다 I scarcely gained anything.

태반 太半 〈반 이상〉 the greater [most] part; the large portion; the majority; the bulk
♦태반이 mostly; for the most part; nearly all; generally
▶그 산봉우리는 1년의 태반이 눈으로 덮여 있다 The peak is covered with snow much of the year.
▶화재로 건물의 태반이 소실되었다 The bulk of the building was destroyed by fire.
▶일은 태반이 끝났다 We have broken the back of the work.
▶시험이 끝나서 학생들의 태반은 귀성했다 The examination being over, most of the students have returned home.
▶그는 1년의 태반을 해외에서 산다 He lives abroad for a great part [portion] of the year.

태반 胎盤 [解] the placenta (pl. ~s, -tae)
■—**염** placentitis (pl. -titides) —**잡음** a placental souffle —**형성** placentation

태백성 太白星 Venus; the evening [morning] star; the daystar

태벌 笞罰 flogging ⇨ 태형(笞刑)
태부족 太不足 〈많이 모자람〉 a great want [shortage, lack]
ㅡ**태부족하다** be greatly wanted; be in great shortage
태블릿 〈정제〉 a tablet
태산 泰山 〈큰 산〉 a great [high] mountain; (비유) a heap; a pile; a mountain 《of》
◆ 할 일이 태산같다 have lots [a heap] of things to do; have (ever) so many things to do / 태산처럼 쌓여 있다 be piled up mountain-high
태산 명동에 서일필 〈속담〉 Much [Great] cry and little wool. ≒ Much ado about nothing.
태상왕 太上王 an abdicated king; an ex-king
태생 胎生 **1**〈출생·출신〉 birth; origin
◆ 태생이 천한 사람 a person of mean parentage [humble origin] / 미국 태생의 한국인 a American-born Korean / 시골 태생의 countryborn / 태생이 좋은 wellborn; of noble [good] birth; gently born
▶ 어디 태생입니까? Where are you from?
▶ 그는 인천 태생이다 He was born in Inch'ŏn. ≒ His birthplace is Inch'ŏn.
▶ 그는 태생도 좋고 가정교육도 좋다 He is a man of birth and breeding.
2 〔動〕 viviparity
◆ 태생의 viviparous / 반태생의 semoviviparous ㅡ동물 a viviparous animal; (총칭) vivipara ㅡ학 〔醫〕 embryology ㅡ학자 an embryologist
태서 泰西 〈서양〉 the West; the Occident; the Western countries / ㅡ태의 European; Occidental 《civilization》; 《things》 Western
태선 苔癬 〔醫〕 lichen
◆ 태선의 lichenous
태세 態勢 a posture; setup; 〈준비〉 preparedness; 〈상태〉 a condition
◆ 만반의 준비 태세가 되어 있다 be prepared for anything / 반격 태세를 갖추다 prepare to counterattack / 철통같은 방위 태세를 견지하다 maintain an iron-tight defense posture / 방어 태세를 취하다 assume a posture of defense / 전투 태세를 취하다 hold battle position
▶ 신입사원의 수용 태세가 갖추어졌다 We have made all the preparations for receiving new employees.
▶ 그것에 관해서는 만반의 태세가 갖추어져 있다 All the necessary arrangements have been made for it.
▶ 우리는 언제라도 일을 시작할 태세에 있다 We are ready to start work(ing) at any time.
태수 太守 a governor; a viceroy
태심하다 太甚ㅡ 〈극심하다〉 very [exceedingly] severe; extreme; excessive; intense
태아 胎兒 an embryo 《pl. ~s》; 〈임신 3개월 이후의〉 a fetus
■ ㅡ교육 ⇨ 태교(胎敎) ㅡ기 the fetal [prenatal] life
태아 胎芽 〈싹〉〔植〕 a propagule; a bulbil
태양 太陽 the sun
▶ 지구는 태양의 주위를 돈다 The earth goes around the sun.
▶ 태양은 동쪽 하늘에서 떠올라 서쪽으로 진다 The sun rises in the east and sets [goes down] in the west.
■ ㅡ경(鏡) a solar eyepiece ㅡ계 the solar system ㅡ관측 solar observation ㅡ관측용 망원경 a helioscope ㅡ광선 the sun's rays; the sunlight; the rays of the sun: 인공 태양광선 artificial sunrays ㅡ년 the solar year ㅡ등 an artificial sunlight; a sun [sunray] lamp ㅡ력 the solar calendar ㅡ로 a solar furnace ㅡ복사 solar radiation ㅡ사진 a solar print : 분광 태양 사진 a spectroheliogram ㅡ상수 solar constant ㅡ숭배 heliolatry; sun worship ㅡ숭배자 a sun worship(p)er ㅡ스펙트럼 solar spectrum ㅡ시 solar time ㅡ신 the god of the sun; the sun god; 〔그神〕 Helios; 〔로神〕 Sol; 〔詩〕 Apollo ㅡ신경총(叢) 〔解〕 the solar plexus ㅡ신화 a solar [sun] myth ㅡ에너지 solar energy ㅡ연구[학] heliology ㅡ열량계 a heliothermometer ㅡ월 a solar month ㅡ의(儀) a heliometer ㅡ일 a solar day: 평균 태양일 a mean solar day ㅡ전지 a solar cell [battery] ㅡ잡음 a solar noise; solar radio-frequency radiation ㅡ중심설 the heliocentric theory; heliocentricism ㅡ증류기 a solar still ㅡ표면 the sun's surface ㅡ풍 a solar wind ㅡ흑점 a sunspot; a solar spot ㅡ흑점설 the sunspot theory
태양열 太陽熱 solar heat
◆ 태양열로 데운 sunwarmed 《water》
▶ 우리는 좀 더 효과적으로 태양 열을 이용하지 않으면 안 된다 We should utilize the heat of the sun more effectively.
■ ㅡ발전 solar power generation ㅡ온수기 a solar water heater ㅡ주택 a solar house
태어나다 be born; come into the world; come into being [existence]; see the light
◆ 태어난 곳 one's birthplace; the place of one's birth; one's (old) home / 갓 태어난 아기 a newborn baby; a newborn / 태어난 집 the house where one was born; the home of one's birth / 태어난 환경 one's natal environs / 곧 태어날 아이 the coming [expected] child / 태어난 날부터 from the day of birth / 세상에 태어나서 처음으로 for the first time in one's life [since one was born] / 부자로 태어나다 be born rich [to wealth, with a silver spoon in one's mouth] / 운을 타고 태어나다 be born under a lucky star
▶ 김 선생 댁에 딸이 태어났다 A baby girl was born to Mr. Kim.
▶ 그는 가난한 집안에서 태어났다 He was born poor [born into a poor family].
▶ 그는 태어날 때부터 병약했다 He has been delicate from (his) birth [since he was born].
▶ 나는 1980년 5월 20일 서울에서 태어났다 I was born in Seoul on May 20, 1980.
태업 怠業 〔勞〕 a work stoppage; deliberate idleness; (美) a slowdown (strike); (英) a ca'canny
◆ 태업 전술을 개시하다 begin slowdown tactics
ㅡ**태업하다** go on a slowdown strike; start a work slowdown
태연자약하다 泰然自若ㅡ perfectly calm; im-

태연하다 perturbable; self-possessed
♦태연자약하게 with perfect [great] composure; with imperturbable calm; quite composedly [calmly]; in a most imperturbable manner
▶그는 그 비보를 듣고도 태연자약했다 He kept his presence of mind [his countenance] at the sad news.

태연하다 泰然— calm; composed; collected; self-possessed
♦태연히 calmly; composedly; with (perfect) composure; with great presence of mind / 태연히 죽음에 임하다 face death calmly [with perfect composure]; meet death with fortitude
▶그는 부친의 사망 소식을 접하고도 태연한 체했다 He pretended calmness [to be calm, not to turn a hair] at the news of his father's death.

태열 胎熱 〔醫〕 congenital fever
태엽 胎葉 〈시계 등의〉 a spring
♦시계의 태엽 the spring of a watch / 태엽 장치를 한 장난감 a clockwork [windup] toy / 태엽이 풀리다 run down / 시계의 태엽을 감다 wind (up) a clock; wind a clock spring
▶이 장난감은 태엽으로 움직인다 This toy moves by clockwork.
큰[주(主)]— a mainspring

태우다¹ 1 〈연소시키다〉 burn; fire; set (the hay) on fire; 〈화재로〉 have [get] (one's house) burnt down
♦쓰레기를 태우다 burn rubbish
▶뜰의 낙엽을 긁어 모아 태워 주세요 Please rake the garden leaves together and burn them.
▶어제의 화재가 그의 집을 태워버렸다 He had his house burned [(英) burnt] (down) in the fire yesterday.
2 〈그을리다〉 burn; scorch; singe; char
♦밥을 태우다 burn [scorch] the rice / 새까맣게 태우다 char; burn to a cinder
▶그녀는 테라스에서 햇빛에 살갗을 태웠다 She tanned herself on the terrace.
▶다리미가 너무 뜨거워서 셔츠를 태웠다 The iron was so hot that I singed the shirt.
3 〈시체를〉 cremate; burn (a corpse) to ashes
4 〈마음을 졸이다〉 burn (one's soul); agonize; worry
♦속을 태우다 be worried [anxious, agonized]; burn with anguish / 남의 속을 태우다 make sb worry; make sb awfully anxious / 애를 태우다 worry oneself
▶그런 사소한 일로 애를 태우지 마라 Don't get so worried over such a little thing.

태우다² 1 〈탈것에〉 carry; take in; take sb on board; place (a man) in a train; pick up; 〈수용하다〉 accommodate
♦승객을 태우다 〈배가〉 take passengers on board; 〈기차·버스가〉 take in passengers / 도중에서 승객을 태우다 pick up passengers / 말에 태우다 put [set] sb on a horse; 〈도와서〉 help sb into (a car); put [place] (a child) on (a train)
▶그 배는 많은 승객을 태우고 있었다 The ship had a lot of passengers on board. ⇌ The ship was carrying a lot of passengers.
▶나는 그녀를 시내까지 태워주었다 I gave her a lift [a ride] to town.
▶자네 차에 좀 태워주지 않겠나? Will you give me a ride in your car?
2 〈비유〉 ♦비행기를 태우다 flatter immensely [grossly]
▶나를 비행기 태우고 있군 Oh, you flatter me immensely.

태우다³ 1 〈재산·상여금 등을 주다〉 divide; portion out; apportion
♦재산을 자녀들에게 태우다 divide one's property among one's sons and daughters; settle one's estate on one's sons and daughters
2 〈내기에서 돈 등을 지르다〉 place a bet (on); lay (a wager); bet; stake; wager
♦5천원을 태우다 lay a wager of five thousand won (on); stake five thousand won (on)
3 〈가리마를〉 have (one's hair) parted (on the left-hand)
4 〈맷돌에〉 have sth crushed
♦팥을 맷돌에 태우다 have sb crush [grind] red beans on a millstone

태우다⁴ 〈줄·그네를〉 put [let] in and out
♦그네를 태우다 let (a child) have a swing / 연줄을 태우다 let the string of a kite in and out

태위 胎位 〔醫〕 〈태아의 위치〉 presentation of the fetus
태음 太陰 the moon
—력(曆) the lunar calendar —시 the lunar time —일[월, 년] a lunar day [month, year] —태양력 a lunisolar calendar —표 lunar tables —학자 a selenologist
태자 太子 the Crown Prince ⇨ 황태자
■—궁(宮) the Crown Prince's palace
태조 太祖 〈시조〉 a founder; the first king (of the dynasty)
태중 胎中 ♦태중인[에] in pregnancy ▶그녀는 태중이다 She is pregnant. ⇌ She is going to have a baby.
태질 1 〈메어치기〉 throwing down
—태질하다 ⇨ 태질치다
2 〈타작〉 threshing against a block
—태질하다 thresh against a block
태질치다 ♦사람을 태질치다 throw a man down / 짐을 태질치다 fling one's pack down (on the ground)
태초 太初 the beginning of the world [all things]
♦태초에 in the beginning / 태초부터 since the beginning of things
태코미터 〈속도 표시기〉 a tachometer
태클 〔球〕 a tackle —태클하다 tackle
태평 太平 (perfect [profound, undisturbed]) peace; tranquility
♦태평 세월 peaceful times / 태평 세월에 in time of peace; in the piping times [days] of peace / 태평을 구가하다 enjoy the blessings of peace; sing the praises of undisturbed peace
—태평하다 peaceful; tranquil
▶천하가 태평하다 All the world is at peace. ⇌ Peace reigns over the land.

■―가(歌) a song of peace ―무드 a mood of tranquility and satisfaction ―성대(聖代) a peaceful reign; the most fortunate and happy age

태평 泰平 〈마음의〉 optimism; easygoingness ―**태평하다** free and easy; carefree; easygoing; 〈낙천적이다〉 optimistic; leisurely
♦ 태평한 사람 an easygoing person; a light-hearted person / 무사 태평한 얼굴 a carefree face
▶ 너 참 태평하구나 You look quite carefree.
▶ 네가 어떻게 그렇게 태평할 수 있는지 모르겠다 I wonder how you can take things [it] so easy.
▶ 태평한 소리만 하는구나 You are too optimistic [hopeful].
▶ 이런 판국에 내가 어떻게 태평하게 있을 수 있겠나? How can I take it easy in such circumstances?

태평스럽다 泰平― easygoing ⇨ 태평(~하다)
♦ 태평스러운 생각 an optimistic view; wishful thinking
▶ 그는 태평스러운 생활을 하고 있다 He lives in a happy-go-lucky fashion.

태평양 太平洋 the Pacific (Ocean) ♦ 북[남] 태평양 the North [South] Pacific
■―경제 협의회 the Pacific Basin Economic Council (略 PBEC) ―문제 the problems of Pacific relations ―안전보장조약 the Pacific Security Pact ―연안 the Pacific coast; 〈미국의〉 the West coast ―연안표준시 Pacific Standard Time (略 PST) ―전쟁 the Pacific War ―함대 the Pacific fleet ―항로 service on the Pacific; 태평양 항로에 취항하다 go into service on the Pacific ―회의 the Pan-Pacific Conference ―횡단 비행[항로] a transpacific flight [line]

태풍 颱風 a typhoon

> 解說 *typhoon*은 태평양에서 발생하는 것이며 인도양에서 발생하는 것은 cyclone, 서인도제도 부근에서 발생하는 것은 hurricane이라고 한다.

♦ 태풍의 눈[중심] the eye [center] of the typhoon / 태풍이 맹위를 떨치다 a typhoon rages / 태풍경보를 발하다 issue [give] a typhoon warning / 태풍권내에 있다 be within the typhoon area
▶ 태풍이 남태평양에서 발생했다 A typhoon has formed [was born] in the South Pacific.
▶ 태풍은 대만으로 상륙할 것이다 The typhoon will strike [hit] Taiwan.

태형 笞刑 flogging; the lash ♦ 태형을 가하다 lash *sb* on the buttocks

태환 兌換 conversion ―**태환하다** convert; redeem ♦ 태환할 수 있는[없는] convertible [inconvertible]
■―성 convertibility ―은행 a bank of issue ―제도 the conversion system ―준비 specie reserve ―지폐 ⇨ 태환권(兌換券)

태환권 兌換券 a convertible note [paper money] ♦ 태환권을 발행하다 issue convertible notes

태후 太后 an empress dowager ⇨ 황태후

택시 a taxi; a (taxi)cab
♦ 택시를 부르다 〈소리질러〉 hail a taxi; 〈전화로〉 call a taxi / 택시를 세우다 halt a taxi / 택시를 잡다 get a taxi; pick up a taxi / 택시를 타다 take a taxi
■―무선― a radio [a radio-dispatched] taxi ■―강도〈행위〉 taxi robbery; 〈사람〉 a taxi robber ―기사 a taxi driver; a cabdriver; a cabman; 〈口〉 a cabby [cabbie]; (英) a taximan; a cabette (여자) ―요금 taxi fare ―정류장 a taxi stand; a cabstand; a cab zone [line]; (英) a taxi rank

택일 擇― alternative ♦ 택일적으로 in an alternative way

택일 擇日 choice of an auspicious day ―택일하다 choose an auspicious [a lucky] day

택지 宅地 building land; a building lot; a site for building; a residential site; the grounds; 〔法〕a curtilage
♦ 택지를 조성하다 develop 《the land》 into home lots

택지 擇地 〈좋은 땅을 고름〉 selecting land [a lot] ―**택지하다** select a site [lot, ground]

택하다 擇― choose; prefer; pick; take
♦ 길일을 택하다 fix 《upon》 [choose] an auspicious day / 인품으로 남편을 택하다 choose [pick] one's husband for his (good) personality (▶for 는 「이유」를 나타냄) / 교육을 평생의 직업으로 택하다 choose education for one's career (▶for는「목적」을 나타냄)
▶ 우리는 왼쪽 길을 택했다 We took the road on the left.
▶ 이것과 저것 중 어느 것을 택하겠습니까? Which do you prefer, this or that?
▶ 그 두 학교 중에서 하나를 택해라 Choose [Make a choice] between the two schools. ⇄ Choose one (or the other) of the two schools.
▶ 치욕을 당하느니 차라리 죽음을 택하겠다 I choose death before disgrace. ⇄ I prefer death to dishonor.

탤런트 a talented person; (총칭) talent

> 解說 *talent*는「재능」의 뜻,「재능있는 사람」의 뜻도 있으나 주로 총칭적으로 쓰이며 한 사람을 가리키는 경우는 드물다. 영화나 TV에 나오는 유명 인사, 연예인을 우리는「탤런트」라고 하나, 이 뜻으로는 personality, celebrity, performer, entertainer, star 등을 쓴다.「TV [라디오] 탤런트」라고 할 때는 "TV [radio]"를 그 앞에 붙이면 된다.

탬버린 〔樂〕 a tambourine

탬퍼 〔物〕 a tamper

탭댄스 a tap dance ▶ 그는 탭댄스를 추고 있었다 He was tap-dancing.

탯줄 胎― the umbilical cord; the navel string [chord] ♦ 탯줄을 자르다 cut the navel cord

탱고 the tango 《pl. ~s》 ♦ 탱고를 추다 dance the tango

탱알 〔植〕 an aster; a Michaelmas daisy

탱자나무 〔植〕 a trifoliate orange

탱커 a tanker; 〈유조선〉 a tankship; a [an oil] tanker ♦ 초대형 탱커 a mammoth tanker; a supertanker

탱크 1 〈큰통〉 a tank; 〈수조〉 a water tank; a cistern 2 〈전차〉 a tank
■ 가스— a gas tank / ■—로리 a tanker; (美) a tank truck; (英) a tank lorry / —저장량[용량] the capacity of a tank; tankage

탱탱 tautly; tightly / —**탱탱하다** swollen up [out]; puffed up; distended; hard and taut [tense, tight]
▶ 종기가 부어 탱탱하다 A boil is swollen up.
▶ 밧줄을 탱탱하게 잡아 당겼다 I stretched [tightened] the rope taut.
▶ 타이어는 모두 탱탱하게 바람을 넣어두었다 All the tires are pumped up hard and tight.

터¹ 〈땅〉 a site; a (building) lot; land (for); a place; a plot; 〈공간〉 space; room; 〈일이 벌어지는 장소〉 an arena; a theater
◆ 빈터 a vacant lot / 장터 a marketplace / 옛날의 절터 the site of an ancient temple / 싸움터 the theater [seat] of war; a battlefield / 터를 돋우다 build up [fill in, raise] the land (for)
2 〈기초〉 the foundation; the ground; footing; foothold; groundwork; spadework
◆ 터가 잡히다 have a firm foothold; be well-grounded / 터를 다지다 solidify the foundation

터² circumstances ⇨ 터수

터³ 〈예정〉 a plan; an expectation; hope; 〈의도〉 intention / …할 터이다 be going to (do); plan to; will (do); be expected to
▶ 넌 어떻게 할 테냐? What are you going to do? ⇒ What do you intend to do?
▶ 지금쯤 도착했을 텐데 He ought to have arrived there by this time.
▶ 서둘렀으면 틀림없이 기차를 탈 수 있었을 텐데 You must [should surely] have caught the train if you had hurried.
▶ 아마 그럴 테지 I suppose so.
▶ 서울엔 얼마나 있을 텐가? How long do you plan to stay in Seoul?

터널 a (railway) tunnel; an excavation
◆ 터널을 파다[뚫다] build [bore, drive, cut, excavate, dig, pierce] a tunnel (through a mountain); tunnel (a hill, through a mountain)
▶ 열차는 터널을 빠져나갔다 The train passed through [went out of] the tunnel.
▶ 터널이 무너졌다 The tunnel caved in.
■ 해저— an underwater tunnel / ■—개통 the opening of a tunnel / —공사 tunneling work

터놓다 1 〈막은 물건을 치우다〉 lay [make] open; open (it) up; break; undam (a river)
◆ 둑을 터놓다 break [burst] a dam (on a river) / 물꼬를 터놓다 open a sluice / 두 방을 하나로 터놓다 throw [knock] two rooms into one
2 〈마음을 열다〉 open one's heart; open up one's mind; be frank [candid, open] (with sb); break down all reserve; throw [shake, cast] off all restraint
▶ 너와 한번 터놓고 이야기하고 싶다 I would like to talk frankly [have a heart-to-heart talk] with you.
▶ 그는 누구하고나 터놓고 이야기한다 He talks quite freely [frankly] with everybody.
▶ 그는 좀처럼 남에게 흉금을 터놓지 않는다 He would not come out of his shell.

터다지다 harden the earth by pounding; roll [level] the ground (for)

터닦다 1 〈고르고 다지다〉 build up [prepare] a site (for); level [smooth] a (building) lot; roll the land (for)
2 〈토대를 굳게 잡다〉 consolidate [solidify] the foundation

터닫다 harden the earth by pounding ⇨ 터다지다

터덕거리다 1 〈걸음이〉 walk wearily; plod; trudge
▶ 일행은 빗속을 터덕거리며 걸었다 The party trudged [plodded] along in the rain.
2 〈살림이〉 make a bare living
3 〈일을〉 struggle with hard work
4 〈두드리다〉 tap; pat; rap

터덜거리다 1 〈걸음이〉 walk wearily; trudge; jog (on); plod 2 〈빈 수레가〉 jolt; rattle along (a stony road)

터득 據得 understanding; comprehension; apprehension; realization; mastery
—**터득하다** understand; apprehend; comprehend; master; make out; grasp; have a grasp of; realize; learn
◆ 터득하기 쉬운 easy to learn [understand] / 터득하기 어려운 incomprehensible; hard to understand [learn]; puzzling / 요령을 터득하다 learn the knack (of a trade); get the hang (of)
▶ 그 말의 참뜻은 쉽게 터득할 수 있는 것이 아니다 One can hardly understand [grasp] (fully) the true meaning of the word.
▶ 이 기술을 완전히 터득하는 데는 시간이 걸린다 The [A] complete mastery of this technique requires [takes] time.
▶ 곧 요령을 터득하게 될 것이다 You will soon learn how to do it. ⇒ You will soon get the knack [hang] of it.

터뜨리다 1 〈막힌 것 등을〉 break; burst; tear; have sth break [burst, tear]
◆ 종기를 터뜨리다 break one's boil; have one's boil break / 풍선을 터뜨리다 break [burst] a balloon
2 〈폭발시키다〉 explode; burst; detonate
◆ 폭탄을 터뜨리다 explode a bomb / 다이너마이트를 터뜨리다 set [touch] off a dynamite / 울음을 터뜨리다 burst out crying; burst into (a flood of) tears / 웃음을 터뜨리다 explode with laughter; burst [break out] into (fits of) laughter
▶ 그녀는 그 슬픈 소식을 듣고 울음을 터뜨렸다 She burst into tears at the sad news.

터럭 hair ⇨ 털

터무니없다 〈근거없다〉 groundless; baseless; unfounded; 〈부당하다〉 unreasonable; 〈엉뚱하다〉 extraordinary; wild; preposterous; fabulous; 〈과도하다〉 exorbitant; 〈불합리하다〉 absurd
◆ 터무니없는 값 an exorbitant [an extravagant, an incredible, a fabulous] price / 터무니없는 거짓말 a damned [whopping] lie; a

whopper / 터무니없는 말 a pure fabrication; an unfounded report; nonsense / 터무니없는 오해 a gross misunderstanding / 터무니없는 생각 a wild idea; a fantastic notion / 터무니없는 요구 a wholly unacceptable demand; an unreasonable demand / 터무니없는 실수를 하다 make a fatal [an absurd, a big] mistake
▶ 터무니없는 일이 일어났다 A terrible [An awful, an unexpected] thing happened.
▶ 터무니없는 소리 마라 Don't talk nonsense. ⇒ That is absurd! ⇒ That is an exaggeration.

터무니없이 absurdly; exorbitantly; fabulously; unreasonably; ridiculously; incredibly
♦ 터무니없이 비싼[싼] ridiculously [fabulously] high [cheap] / 터무니없이 싸게 사다 get 《it》 at an absurdly low price; buy 《an article》 dirt cheap

터미널 a terminal (station); 《英》 a terminus 《pl. ~es, -ni》

> 解說 *terminal*은 「시발[종착]역(의 건물)」을 가리키며 bus terminal, air terminal 처럼 쓴다.

▶ 터미널은 내리고 타는 손님으로 혼잡했다 The terminal was crowded with passengers.

터벅터벅 trudgingly; ploddingly; wearily
♦ 터벅터벅 걷다 trudge along [one's (weary) way]; trudge on 《the street》; plod on; jog [pad] along
▶ 노인은 터벅터벅 걸어갔다 The old man plodded along.

터번 《wear》 a turban ♦ 터번을 두른 turbaned
터보제트엔진 a turbojet (engine)
터보프롭엔진 a turboprop; a turboprop(-jet) engine
터부 a taboo; a tabu ♦ 터부로 삼다 taboo; put *sth* under taboo / 터부로 되어 있다 be taboo; be under (a) taboo
▶ 그 이야기는 여기서는 터부다 The topic is taboo [tabooed] here.

터분하다 1 〈맛이〉 unpleasant; muddy-tasting
♦ 터분한 음식 untasty food; dull fare / 입이 터분하다 have a muddy [brown] taste in one's mouth 2 〈성미나 하는 짓이〉《be》 sloppy; untidy; messy

터빈 a turbine (engine) ♦ 터빈을 돌리다 spin a turbine
■ 가스[증기, 수력]— a gas [steam, water] turbine ■ —기관차 a turbine locomotive ■ —발전기 a turbine generator

터세다 《a site is》 ill-omened; unlucky; ill-fated; jinxed

터수 1 〈처지〉 circumstances; one's lot; a station in life; a condition of life
♦ 터수가 좋다 be well off; make a good [decent, fair, comfortable] living; earn a good [decent, handsome] livelihood / 터수가 나쁘다 be badly [poorly] off; earn a poor living / 터수를 알다 know one's station in life 2 〈관계〉 relationship; friendship; terms; a footing
▶ 그들은 서로 너나하이하는 터수다 They are on first-name basis with each other.

터울 a gap 《of three years》; the age gap (among siblings)
♦ 한살 터울의 아이 a child born within a year of another; children born in two successive years / 터울이 잦다 be frequent in having a baby
▶ 우리 아이들은 모두 두 살 터울이다 Our children are spaced two years apart.

터잡다 select [pick out, secure] a site [lot, ground]; 〈기초를〉 establish the foundation 《of》

터전 a site; a lot; the grounds; a base; a basis; a foundation ♦ 넓은 터전 a large lot
▶ 민주주의의 터전은 자유를 수호하겠다는 국민의 의지다 The foundation of democracy is the will of the people to preserve liberty.
▶ 그는 상인으로서 터전을 잡았다 He has established himself as a trader.

터주 —主 〔民俗〕 〈집터를 지키는 지신〉 the spirit of a house site

터주다 leave 《a way》 open; permit; allow; give leave [permission]; lift 《the ban》
♦ 길을 터주다 open a road 《for sb》; leave a road open; clear the way 《for sb》 / 외상을 터주다 let *sb* open a credit account; open a charge account 《for sb》

터지다 1 〈파열하다〉 burst (open); break; split; splinter
♦ 터진 데 〈옷 등의〉 a rip; a rent 《in a sleeve》; a tear; an open seam; 〈양말의〉 a run / 터진 손 chapped hands / 가슴이 터질 듯한 heart-rending; heart-breaking / 박수 갈채가 터지다 break into a loud applause / 둑이 터지다 a dike collapses [gives way] / 종기가 터지다 a boil bursts [breaks] / 입술이 터지다 one's lips crack / 풍선이 터지다 a balloon bursts [breaks]
▶ 타이어가 터졌다 The tire was punctured. ⇒ The tire had a blowout.
▶ 극장은 관객으로 터질 것 같았다 The theater was bursting with the audience.
2 〈폭발하다〉 explode; burst (out); go off; break out; blow up; 〈발생하다〉 occur [happen] suddenly
♦ 화약이 터지다 gunpowder explodes / 중대 사건이 터지다 a serious matter pops up / 울화통이 터지다 〈사람이 주어〉 fly into a passion; burst into a rage
▶ 전쟁이 터졌다 A war broke [burst] out.
▶ 평소의 울분이 터지고 말았다 Their smoldering resentment flared up.
3 〈탄로나다〉 get exposed; be [come] out; be found out; be disclosed; be revealed; come [be brought] to light
▶ 기밀문서가 신문에 터졌다 A classified document has leaked out to the press.
▶ 비밀이 터졌다 The secret is [comes] out (of the bag).
4 〈얻어맞다〉 get a blow; be beaten; be struck on

터치 a touch
▶ 그의 그림은 경묘한 터치로 그려져 있다 All of his pictures are painted with a light and

witty touch.
ー터치하다 touch; 〈손대다〉 touch on; 〈간여하다〉 have a hand 《in》
▶나는 그 문제에 터치하고 싶지 않다 I don't want to be concerned with [involve myself in] the matter.

터치다운 〔美蹴〕 a touchdown; 《美口》 a TD 《*pl*. TD's》 ー터치다운하다 make [score] a touchdown

터치라인 〔蹴〕 a touchline

터키 Turkey; 〈공식명〉 the Republic of Turkey ◆터키의 Turkish
■ー말 Turkish ー모자 a fez; a tarboosh ー사람 a Turk ー제국 the Turkish Empire; the Ottoman Empire ー황제 the Sultan of Turk

터프가이 《美俗》 a tough guy

턱¹ 〈입의 위아래〉 the jaws; the chops; 〈아래턱〉 the chin
◆아래턱 the lower jaw; the mandible; the chin / 위턱 the upper jaw; the maxilla / 이중턱 a double chin / 턱이 뾰족한 lantern-jawed (person) / 턱이 네모진 square-jawed / 너무 웃다가 턱이 빠지다 laugh one's jaw out of joint / 턱으로 가리키다 indicate *sth* with *one's* chin / 턱을 쓰다듬다 rub *one's* chin / 손으로 턱을 괴다 rest *one's* chin on [in] *one's* hand; cup *one's* chin in *one's* hands / 턱을 내밀다 stick out *one's* chin
▶장시간 이야기했더니 턱이 아팠다 I talked so long (that) my jaw ached.
▶그는 사람을 턱으로 부리고 싶어한다 He likes to have others at his beck and call [boss others around].

턱² 〈높은 데〉 a projection; an elevated place; a rise; a sill ◆고갯턱 the top of a pass [slope] / 문턱 a doorsill / 창턱 a windowsill / 턱지다 rise; swell; be raised

턱³ 〈음식 대접〉 a treat; a feast; an entertainment ◆한 턱 내다 stand treat for 《*one's* friend》; give *sb* a treat; treat *sb* to *sth*; stand 《*sb* dinner》
▶그가 우리에게 술을 한 턱 냈다 He stood us drinks.
▶이 술은 그가 한 턱 내는 것이다 This drink is his treat.
▶걱정말게, 이건 내가 한 턱 내는 거야 Don't worry. This is on me.

턱⁴ **1** 〈까닭〉 (a) reason; grounds
▶그가 도둑일 턱이 있나 He cannot be a thief. ⇌ It is impossible that he should be a thief.
▶네가 그것을 모를 턱이 있나 It is hardly possible that you do not know about it.
2 〈정도〉 extent ◆아직 그 턱이다 be still the same
▶그의 병세는 아직 그 턱이다 He has not been making any perceptible recovery.
3 〈능력〉 ability; power; faculty; capability ◆턱도 안 닿다 be beyond *one's* power [reach]; be not in [be out of] *one's* power
▶내 힘으로는 턱도 없다 It's beyond my power.

턱⁵ **1** 〈긴장이 풀리는 모양〉 at complete ease [rest] ◆마음을 턱 놓다 set *one's* mind at complete ease; make *one's* mind quite easy
2 〈손을 잡는 모양〉 affectionately
▶그녀는 내 손을 턱 잡고 만나서 반갑다고 말했다 She grasped my hands affectionately and said she was glad to see me.
3 〈의젓한 모양〉 with a grand air; composedly; without hesitation ◆앞에 턱 나와 한마디 하다 step forward composedly and speak a word 《about》 / 의자에 턱 앉다 install [settle] *oneself* comfortably in *one's* seat

턱걸이 **1** 〈철봉의〉 a chin-up; chinning exercises
◆턱걸이를 스무번 하다 do [perform] twenty chin-ups
ー턱걸이하다 chin *oneself*; do a chin-up [chinning exercises] 《at an iron bar》
2 〈씨름·싸움에서의〉 a chin hold [catch]
ー턱걸이하다 topple with a chin hold [catch]
3 〈기식(寄食)〉 parasitism; sponging
ー턱걸이하다 sponge [hang] on 《*one's* friends》; be parasitic on
▶대학 시절의 처음 2년간은 삼촌댁에 턱걸이하고 있었다 I lived with my uncle at his expense for the first two years of my college life.

턱밑 **1** 〈턱의 끝〉 the tip of the chin
2 〈가까운 곳〉 ◆턱밑에 두고도 못 보다 can't see [fail to find] what is right under *one's* nose [eyes]
▶그는 그 짓을 내 턱밑에서 했다 He did it under my very eyes [nose].

턱받이 a bib; a pinafore; 《英》 a feeder

턱뼈 a jawbone; a maxilla; a maxillary (bone)

턱수염 ー鬚髯 a (chin-)beard; 〈염소 수염〉 a goatee (beard)
◆턱수염을 기른 사람 a man with a beard / 턱수염을 기르다 grow [have] a beard

턱시도 《美》 a tuxedo 《*pl*. ~(e)s》; a tuxedo jacket; 《美口》 a tux; 《英》 a dinner jacket [coat]

턱없다 **1** 〈터무니없다〉 unreasonable; groundless; unfounded; exorbitant; immoderate; extreme; excessive
◆턱없는 기대 unfounded hopes / 턱없는 혐의 unfounded suspicions / 턱없는 거짓말 a whopping lie / 턱없이 키가 크다 be extremely tall
▶저 레스토랑은 턱없이 비싸게 받는다 That restaurant often charges unreasonable [exorbitant] prices.
▶나는 턱없이 비싸서 그 가구를 사지 못했다 I didn't buy the furniture, as it was ridiculously high.
2 〈신분에 맞지 않다〉 not suitable [proportionate] to *one's* means
◆턱없는 복장을 하다 dress above *one's* circumstances / 턱없는 생각을 품다 have ideas above *one's* station
▶그는 턱없는 고급차를 타고 돌아다니고 있다 He drives around in a luxury car unfit [unsuitable] for his means.

턱주가리 〈아래턱〉 the lower jaw; the chin

턱지다 〈언덕이 생기다〉 rise; be raised; swell; be hilly

턱짓 gesture with the chin; nodding
◆턱짓으로 부리다 have *sb* at *one's* beck (and call) / 턱짓으로 부르다 call *sb* by a nod

—턱짓하다 nod 《to, toward, into, out》
◆ 턱짓하여 방으로 들어오게 하다 nod sb into the room
턱턱 flapping ⇨ 탁탁
턴 〈수영 등의〉 a turn
▶ 그는 턴을 잘 한다 He makes a good turn.
—턴하다 turn; make [execute] a turn
◆ 50m 지점에서 턴하다 turn (around) at the 50-meter mark
턴파이크 《美》〈유료 고속도로〉 a turnpike road
털 1 〈사람의〉 hair
◆ 곱슬곱슬한 털 curly [crisp, kinky] hair / 부드러운 털 soft hair / 뻣뻣한 털 coarse [bristly] hair / 덥수룩한 털 disheveled [rumpled] hair / 헝클어진 털 matted [tangled] hair / 털투성이의 hairy; thick-haired; shaggy / 털이 있는 haired; hairy / 털이 성긴 thinly-[sparsely-]haired / 털이 없는 hairless; bald 《head》/ 털이 나다 hair grows [appears, comes out] / 털을 뽑다 pull out a hair; unhair / 털을 지지다 have one's hair frizzled and curled
▶ 내 머리털이 자꾸 빠진다 I am losing my hair.
2 〈짐승의〉 fur; 〈양의〉 wool; 〈깃털〉 feathers; 〈솜털〉 down
◆ 털 양말 woolen socks [stockings] / 털로 안을 댄 《a coat》 lined with fur; fur-lined / 닭털을 뽑다 pluck a chicken / 제 털 뽑아 제 구멍에 박다 be rigid [inflexible]; lack flexibility [resourcefulness] / 털도 안 뜯고 먹으려 하다 be hasty [impatient]; be out to get all sb's possessions
3 〈植〉〈잎·줄기 표면의〉 hair; trichome
◆ 털 같은 piliform
털가죽 a fur ⇨ 모피(毛皮)
털갈다 〈새 등이〉 molt; shed feathers
털갈이 〈새의〉 molting; 〈짐승의〉 coatshedding; shedding hair —털갈이하다 〈새가〉 molt; 〈짐승이〉 shed 《its》 hair
▶ 새는 깃털을 털갈이한다 The bird molts its feathers.
■—새 a molter —시기 the molting season; the molt
털게 [動] a hairy crab
털구멍 pores (of the skin)
털끝 1 〈털의 끝〉 the end of a hair; an end of hair; the tips of hair; hair tips
2 〈조금〉 a bit; a jot; a whit
◆ 털끝만큼도 (not) in the least; (not) a bit [whit]; (not) a fig [straw]; (not) a particle [an ounce, an atom] 《of》
▶ 그에게 동정심 같은건 털끝만큼도 없다 He has not an ounce [a particle] of sympathy.
▶ 그는 그 소식을 듣고도 놀라는 빛이 털끝만큼도 없었다 When he heard the news, he was not surprised in the least.
털내의 —內衣 woolen underwear
털다 1 〈먼지 등을〉 shake off [down]; beat off; dust (off)
◆ 먼지를 털다 dust sth; brush off dust 《from》; beat the dust out of 《carpet》; clear dust away / 구두 속에 들어간 모래를 털다 shake the sand from one's shoes / 파이프의 담뱃재를 두드려 털다 knock the ash off one's pipe / 모자의 먼지를 털다 flick the dust off one's hat / 옷의 눈을 털다 shake snow off one's clothes
▶ 그녀는 자루에 붙어 있는 설탕을 털어냈다 She brushed the sugar off the bag.
2 〈가진 것을 전부 써버리다〉 empty
▶ 나는 가진 돈을 몽땅 털어서 이것을 샀다 I spent all the money I had on me to buy this.
▶ 그녀는 지갑을 털어 오버코트를 샀다 She spent all the money she had [emptied her purse (to the last penny)] to buy the overcoat.
3 〈도둑질하다〉 rob sb of; strip sb of
◆ 금고를 털다 rob a safe / 은행을 털다 〈도둑이〉 break into [burglarize; 《俗》 burgle] a bank; 〈강도가〉 rob a bank
▶ 그는 그 집을 털었다 He burglarized [robbed] the house.
털럭거리다 keep slapping; flap; flop
▶ 열어 놓은 창문에서 커튼이 털럭거리고 있다 The curtains are flapping at the open window.
털리다¹ 1 〈먼지 등이〉 get brushed [dusted, shaken] off
▶ 잔 먼지는 잘 털리지 않는다 Fine dust is not easily swept up.
2 〈완전히 비우게 되다〉 be [get] emptied
▶ 자루가 다 털렸다 The bag was completely emptied.
▶ 노름에서 그는 몽땅 털렸다 He was cleaned out in gambling.
3 〈도둑맞다〉 get robbed [stripped] 《of》
◆ 금고를 털리다 have one's safe robbed / 소매치기한테 주머니를 털리다 have one's pocket picked 《of a purse》
▶ 집을 비운 사이에 털렸다 We had our house robbed in our absence. ⇌ Our house was robbed while we were away.
털리다² 〈털게 하다〉 have [make, let] sb shake [brush, knock, beat, dust] sth off
털모자 —帽子 a fur hat; a woolen cap
털목도리 a fur muffler; a comforter (털실로 짠); a boa (모피로 만든)
털방석 —方席 a fur cushion
털 배자 —褙子 a women's fur-lined vest [waistcoat]
털버덕거리다 keep splashing [dabbling, slopping] ▶ 우리는 내를 털버덕거리며 건넜다 We splashed our way across the stream.
털버선 fur outer-socks; woolen socks
털보 a hairy [thickly-haired] person; a hairy-faced person
털북숭이 a hairy person [animal]
◆ 털북숭이의 hairy; shaggy
털붙이 〈털가죽〉 furs; 〈털가죽 제품〉 fur goods [pieces]; 〈털옷〉 fur clothes
털셔츠 a woolen shirt
털스웨터 a jersey; 《美》 a sweater
털실 woolen yarn [thread]; worsted (yarn); 〈뜨개질용〉 knitting wool
◆ 털실로 어깨걸이를 짜다 knit wool into shawl; knit shawl out of wool
■—가게 a wool shop —뭉치 a knitting ball —장수 a woolman
털썩 flop; plump; with a thud [flump]

♦ 털썩 주저앉다 plump down 《into a chair》; sit down plump [with a flop]; fall flat on *one's* behind [rear] / 땅에 털썩 주저앉다 sit flat [exhausted] on the ground / 가방을 마루에 털썩 내려놓다 put down [drop] a suitcase on [to] the floor with a thud

털양말 一洋襪 woolen socks [stockings]

털어놓다 〈마음속을〉 confide in *sb*; confess; disclose; reveal
♦ 털어놓고 말하면 to be frank [candid] with you; frankly speaking / 계획을 털어놓다 show *one's* hand / 비밀을 털어놓다 confide [reveal, disclose] a secret to *sb* / 흉금을 털어놓다 open [bare, unlock] *one's* heart 《to》; speak (out) *one's* mind / 털어놓고 이야기 하다 talk without reserve [frankly]; have a heart-to-heart talk 《with》
▶ 그녀는 남편에게 그 비밀을 털어놓았다 She told [confided] the secret to her husband.
▶ 그는 자기가 결혼했음을 그녀에게 털어놓았다 He confessed (to her) that he was married.
▶ 그녀는 아무것도 털어놓으려 하지 않았다 She kept everything secret [to herself].

털어먹다 spend the last cent; run through; spend all 《*one's* money》; eat *oneself* up; 《口》 clean out
♦ 자기 재산을 털어먹다 run through *one's* fortune

털어서 먼지 안 나는 사람 없다 《속담》 No man is infallible.

털옷 a fur [woolen] robe [coat]

털외투 一外套 a fur [fur-lined] overcoat

털장갑 一掌匣 fur(-lined) gloves; 〈털실의〉 woolen gloves

털터리 1 ⇨ 털털이 2
2 ⇨ 빈털터리

털털 1 〈걷는 모양〉 ploddingly; trudgingly; tottering(ly) ♦ 털털 걷다 trudge along; plod *one's* way
2 〈소리〉 rattling; with a rattling noise
♦ 털털 소리가 나다 rattle; clatter / 〈짐차 등이〉 다리 위를 털털 지나가다 rattle over the bridge

털털거리다 1 〈걸음〉 plod [trudge] on [along]; jog [pad] along 2 〈소리〉 rattle
▶ 짐차가 털털거리며 지나갔다 A cart rattled as it went away. ⇌ A cart rattled away.

털털이 1 〈털털한 사람〉 an unassuming person; a free and easy person 2 〈몹시 낡은 탈것〉 a rattletrap; 〈헌 수레〉 《美》 a jerky; 〈고물 자동차〉 a rickety car; 《口》 an old heap; a jalopy

털털하다 1 〈사람이〉 unaffected; free and easy 2 〈맛이〉 somewhat puckery ♦ 시금털털하다 sourish

털토시 a fur-lined muff

텀벙 splash; with a splash [plop] ♦ 물속으로 텀벙 뛰어들다 jump into the water with a plop [splash]; splash [plop] into the water
▶ 그 소년은 텀벙 풀에 뛰어들었다 The boy dived into the pool with a splash.

텁석 with a snatch [snap]; 〈갑자기〉 suddenly; all at once ♦ 텁석 움켜쥐다 snatch; clutch; grab

▶ 물고기가 미끼를 텁석 물었다 The fish snapped at the bait.
▶ 그녀는 그의 팔을 텁석 쥐었다 She grasped [grabbed] him by the arm.

텁석부리 a man with a bearded [whiskered] face; a heavily bearded [whiskered] man

텁수룩하다 hairy; shaggy; bushy; disheveled
♦ 텁수룩한 머리 a mop of hair; long unkempt hair / 수염이 텁수룩하다 have a bushy beard; be heavily bearded / 구레나룻이 텁수룩하게 나 있다 have a shaggy growth of whiskers

텁텁하다 1 〈맛이〉 thick and tasteless; unpleasant-tasting; 〈서술적〉 have a muddy taste
♦ 텁텁한 된장국 thick and tasteless, bean-paste soup / 맛이 텁텁하다 have an uninviting taste
2 〈성미가〉 easy-going; casual; broad-minded
♦ 성미가 텁텁해서 누구하고나 잘 사귀다 be a good mixer and get along well with others
3 〈눈이〉 bleary; bleared; dim; dimmed

텃고사 一告祀 sacrifices for the spirit of a house site

텃도지 一賭地 site [lot] rent

텃세 一貰 rent for a site [place]; site rent

텃세하다 一勢— disregard a newcomer; treat a newcomer high-handedly [overbearingly]; pull *one's* rank 《on》

텅 ♦ 텅 빈 vacant; (quite) empty; hollow
▶ 그는 머리가 텅 비어 있다 He doesn't have any brains.
▶ 그녀의 방은 텅 비어 있었다 I found her room empty. ⇌ I found no one in her room.

텅스텐 〈化〉 tungsten; wolfram
■—강(鋼) tungsten steel —전구 a tungsten bulb [lamp]

텅텅 ♦ 텅텅 비다 be quite empty
▶ 그 상자는 텅텅 비어 있다 The box is quite empty. ⇌ There is nothing in the box.
▶ 지금은 주머니가 텅텅 비어 있다 I'm penniless now.
▶ 버스는 텅텅 비어 있었다 There were few passengers in the bus. ⇌ We had the bus almost to ourselves.

테[1] 1 〈매우는〉 a hoop
♦ 금속[대나무] 테 a metal [bamboo] hoop / 테를 메우다 put a loop 《on》; loop / 테를 벗기다 unhoop; take off hoops
▶ 테가 헐거워졌다 The hoop got loose.
▶ 통의 테가 벗겨졌다 The hoop of the barrel came loose.
2 〈모자 띠〉 a band; a stripe; 〈언저리〉 a brim; a rim ♦ 금테 두른 모자 a cap banded with gold stripes / 테가 넓은 모자 a broad-brimmed hat
3 〈안경 등의〉 a rim; a frame
♦ 테 없는 안경 (a pair of) rimless glasses / 검은 테의 안경을 쓰다 wear black-rimmed glasses
4 〈테두리〉 a border; a rim
♦ 장식 테 an ornamental border [rim]
5 〈機〉 〈축의〉 a collar; 〈철관의〉 a flange

테[2] 〈실의〉 a reel; a bunch; a skein
♦ 실 한 테 a reel of thread

테너 〔樂〕〈음악〉 tenor; 〈사람〉 a tenor (singer)
♦테너로 부르다 sing tenor

테네시 〈미국의 주〉 Tennessee (略 Tenn.); 〈속칭〉 Volunteer State ◆테네시 주의 Tennessean / 테네시 주의 사람 a Tennessean

테니스 (lawn) tennis ◆테니스를 하다 play tennis ■단식[복식]— a tennis match [game] of singles [doubles] —경기 a tennis match [tournament] —선수 a tennis player —코트 a tennis court

테두리 1 〈가장자리〉 the edge; the border; the hem; the fringe; 〈테〉 the brim; the rim; the frame
♦검은 테두리 black borders [edges]; 〈부고 등의〉 mourning borders / 테두리를 달다[붙이다] edge; rim; fringe; border; hem; frame
2 〈윤곽〉 an outline; a sketch
3 〈범위·한계〉 a limit; a framework; a boundary
♦테두리 안에서 within the limit [framework] 《of》 / 법의 테두리 안에서 within the legal limit; without infringement of the law / 테두리를 넘다[벗어나다] pass [exceed] the limit 《of》; overstep the boundary 《of》 / 월 100만원의 테두리에서 생활하다 live within the limits of 1,000,000 won a month / 테두리를 정하다 fix the limit; set limits [bounds] 《to》; set framework 《for》
▶지출이 예산의 테두리를 벗어날 것 같다 The expenses may run over the budget.

테라마이신 〔藥〕 terramycin

테라스 a terrace ◆테라스에(서) on the terrace —하우스 a terrace(d) house

테러 terror; terrorism ◆우익[공산당] 테러 right-wing [Communist] terrorism / 테러에 희생되다 fall a victim to terrorism
■백색[적색]— the white [red] terror ■—단 a gang of terrorists; the terrorists —전술 terrorist tactics —행위 (an act of) terrorism

테러리스트 a terrorist

테러리즘 terrorism

테레빈유 —油 turpentine (oil)

테르펜 〔化〕 terpene

테리어 〈개〉 a terrier ■스카치— a Scotch [Scottish] terrier 폭스— a fox terrier

테마 〔(獨) Thema〕 a theme; a subject
♦자연을 테마로 한 시 a poem with a nature theme / 좋은 테마를 잡다 find a good subject for writing
▶당신 논문의 테마는 무엇입니까? What is the subject of your thesis?
■—연구 a subject of study ■—송 a theme [title] song —음악 theme music [song]

테메(우)다 hoop; put a hoop on
♦통을 테메우다 hoop a tub [barrel]; put a hoop on a tub [barrel]

테석테석 rough(ly); coarse(ly)
—테석테석하다 uneven; rough; coarse

테스트 a test; an examination; a quiz; 〈배우·가수의〉 an audition
♦테스트를 받다 take [undergo] a test / 테스트에 합격하다 pass a test
▶지금 마이크 테스트중(입니다) Testing, one, two, three, four [ABC].
▶오늘 수학 테스트가 있었다 We had a test in math today.
—테스트하다 give a test; test (out); try (out)
♦음성을 테스트하다 test *one's* voice
■객관식[주관식]— an objective [a subjective] test 성능— a performance [an efficiency] test 지능[실력]— an intelligence [an (academic) ability] test 체력— a test of (physical) strength 학력— an achievement test ■—케이스 a test case —파일럿 a test pilot —패턴 〔TV〕 a test pattern

테이블 a table
♦4인용 테이블 a table for four / 테이블에 둘러 앉다 sit around a table / 테이블에 앉다 sit (down) at [to] table / 테이블을 사이에 두고 앉다 〈쌍방이 주어〉 sit across a table
▶테이블에 앉은 사람들이 모두 웃었다 The whole table laughed.
■—매너 table manners —보 a table cover; a tablecloth(식탁의); (美) a table spread —센터 a centerpiece

테이블스피치 an after-dinner speech; a luncheon speech; a speech at a party [dinner]
♦간단한 테이블스피치를 하다 make [give] a little after-dinner speech

테이프 1 〈종이·천 등의〉 (a) tape; 〈접착용〉 (adhesive) tape; 〈녹음·녹화용〉 a (recording) tape; 〈축하용〉 a paper streamer
♦45분 짜리 (녹음) 테이프 a forty-five-minute spool of tape / 테이프에 녹음하다 record on a tape; take a tape-recording of; tape-record / 테이프를 재생하다 play (back) a tape (on a deck) / 테이프를 붙이다 tape; scotch-tape; sellotape / 짐짝에 배달 꼬리표를 테이프로 붙이다 tape a delivery tag to a package / 테이프를 던지다 fling [throw] a paper streamer / 테이프를 끊다 〈육상경기에서〉 breast [break] the tape; 〈개통식에서〉 cut the tape 《for》; cut [snip] a ribbon (on a ceremony)
2 〈줄자〉 a tape
■골— 〈육상 경기의〉 the finish tape 스테레오— a stereotape ■—녹음 tape recording

테이프리코더 a tape recorder
♦음악을 테이프리코더로 녹음하다 record music on a tape recorder; tape-record music

테일라이트 a taillight; a tail lamp; (英) a rear light [lamp]

테일러 〈양복점 주인〉 a tailor ■—숍 a tailor shop

테일러시스템 〈생산 관리의〉 the Taylor system

테크니션 a technician

테크니컬러 〔映〕 technicolor

테크닉 〈기교〉 (a) technique; (a) technic

테헤란 〈이란의 수도〉 Teheran; Tehran

텍사스 〈미국의 주〉 Texas (略 Tex); 〈속칭〉 Lone Star State ■—리거[히트] 〔野〕 a Texas leaguer —사람 a Texan

텍스 texture ■—골든— the Golden-brand texture

텍스트 1 〈교과서〉 a textbook ◆수학 텍스트 a textbook on mathematics; a math text / 영어 텍스트 an English text(book)
2 〈원문·본문〉 a text

텐스 〔文法〕〈시제〉 the tense
텐트 a tent ⇨ 천막
♦텐트를 치다[거두다] pitch [strike] a tent
텔레그래프 telegraph
텔레마크 〔스키〕 telemark
—텔레마크하다 telemark
텔레미터 a telemeter
♦텔레미터로 전송(電送)하다 telemeter
■—장치 a telemetric system
텔레비전 television; TV; (英口) the telly; 〈수상기〉 a television [TV] (set); a teleset
♦24인치 텔레비전 a 24-inch television / 텔레비전을 보다 watch television [TV] / 텔레비전을 켜다[끄다] turn on [off] the television / 텔레비전에 초대손님으로 나오다 make a guest appearance on TV / 텔레비전에 달라붙어 있다 be glued to the TV / 텔레비전으로 보다 teleview; watch [see]... on TV
▶하루에 몇시간 텔레비전을 봅니까? How many hours do you spend watching TV every day?
▶그 농구 경기는 내주에 텔레비전으로 방송된다 The basketball match will be televised [be broadcast on television] next week.
▶저 가수는 텔레비전에 자주 나온다 That singer often appears on television.
■—유선 cable television 컬러[천연색]— color television 폐쇄회로— closed-circuit television 흑백— a black-and-white television
■—광(狂) a television fanatic; a vidiot —뉴스 telenews; television news —드라마 a teleplay; a television play —송신기 a television transmitter —수상기 a television (set); a TV set; a television [video] receiver —시청자 a (tele)viewer; (총칭) a television audience —연속(방송)극 a television serial drama; (美) a soap opera —영화 a television [a TV] film; a telefilm; a vidfilm —전화 a television [video] telephone; a TV phone; a videophone —카메라 a television [TV] camera; a telecamera —탑 a television pylon [mast] —프로그램 a television program; a TV show —화면 a television [a TV] screen; a telescreen
텔레비전방송 —放送 a television [TV] broadcast; a telecast ♦텔레비전방송을 하다 telecast; televise ■—국 a television [TV] station —자 a telecaster
텔레타이프 a teletype(writer); a teleprinter
♦뉴스를 텔레타이프로 보내다 teletype news; send news by teletype
텔레파시 〈정신감응〉 telepathy ♦텔레파시로 전하다 communicate by telepathy; telepath
텔렉스 (商標) Telex; 〈통신문〉 a telex
♦뉴스를 텔렉스로 보내다 telex news
텔루륨 (化) tellurium
텔스타 〈미국의 통신위성〉 Telstar
템페라 —화 〔美術〕 a tempera painting; a painting in distemper —화가 a tempera artist
템포 tempo (*pl.* ~s, -pi); speed
♦템포가 빠른[느린] 곡 a tune with a quick [slow] tempo / (음악에서) 반템포 더디다 be one beat behind [late] / 빠른[느린] 템포로 at quick [slow] tempo; rapidly [slowly] / 템포가 맞지 않다 be out of tempo / 템포에 맞추다 keep pace with the tempo
▶그는 하는 일이 남보다 한 템포 느리다 He is always one step slower than others in doing things.
토 1 〈한자에 다는〉 Korean sylables next to the end of a Chinese phrase to show the syntactical relationship
2 〔文法〕〈토씨〉 a particle; a postposition
토건업 土建業 civil engineering and (heavy) construction; construction work; the construction industry —자 a civil engineer (and building) contractor —회사 a construction company
토고 Togo ♦토고의 Togolese
—사람 a Togolese (▶단수·복수 동형)
토관 土管 an earthen pipe [tube]; a clay pipe
♦토관을 묻다 lay an earthen pipe
토굴 土窟 a cave; a dugout; 〈동물의〉 a burrow ♦토굴을 파다 dig a hole [pit] in the ground
토기 土器 an earthen(ware) utensil [vessel]; (총칭) earthenware
—장(이) an earthenware maker; a potter —점 an earthenware shop
토끼 〈집토끼〉 a rabbit; 〈산토끼〉 a hare
—고기 hare meat —굴 a rabbit hole; a rabbit burrow —사육장 a (rabbit) warren; a rabbitry —집 〈기르는〉 a rabbit hutch
토끼 둘을 잡으려다가 하나도 못 잡는다 (속담) If you run after two hares, you will catch neither. = Grasp all, lose all.
토끼뜀 (a) leapfrog; leapfrogging; jumping along in a squatting position —토끼뜀하다 hop forward in a squatting position; leapfrog; play leapfrog
■—식 작전 a leapfrog [an island-hopping] operation
토끼사냥 hare [rabbit] hunting ♦토끼사냥하러 가다 go hare hunting; go rabbiting
토끼풀 〔植〕 a white [Dutch] clover
토너먼트 a tournament; a tourney
▶그는 테니스 토너먼트에서 우승했다 He won the tennis tournament.
토닉 〈강장제〉 tonic (medicine)
—진— a gin and tonic 헤어— a hair tonic
토닥거리다 strike gently with a light blows; keep patting [tapping, beating]
♦어깨를 토닥거리다 tap sb on the shoulder / 아기를 토닥거려 재우다 put a baby to sleep by patting; pat [tap] a baby to sleep / 가슴을 토닥거리다 〈의사가〉 sound sb's breast
토닥토닥 patting; tapping; striking gently
토단 土壇 a terrace of earth
토담 土— a mud [an earthen] wall
—집 a mudwall hut
토대 土臺 1 〈건축의〉 the base; a foundation; 〈벽돌벽 등의〉 a plinth
♦토대를 놓다 lay the foundation [cornerstone] (of)
2 〈사물의 기초〉 a foundation; groundwork; the base; the basis (*pl.* bases)
♦…을 토대로 하여 on the basis of... / 오랜 경험을 토대로 한 지식 (a) knowledge based on

long expriences / 생활의 토대를 쌓다 establish the base for *one's* life; lay the foundation(s) of *one's* life
▶ 이 건물은 토대가 단단하다 This building has [is built on] a solid foundation.

토댄스 toe-dancing; toe dance
♦ 토댄스를 하다 toe-dance

토라지다 1 〈기분이〉 sulk; be [get] sulky [cross, peevish]
▶ 그녀는 잘 토라진다 She gets sulky [gets put out] at the least provocation.
2 〈음식이〉 lie [sit] heavy on *one's* stomach; 〈사람이 주어〉 have heartburn; have a sour stomach
3 〈일이〉 fail; go wrong [amiss]
♦ 계획이 토라지다 a plan misfires [miscarries]

토란 土卵 〔植〕 a taro 《*pl*. ~s》
■ —국 taro soup

토레아도르 〈기마 투우사〉 a toreador

토로하다 吐露— express; utter; speak out; voice
♦ 심중을 토로하다 speak out *one's* mind; lay bare *one's* heart
▶ 그는 일기에 자기 진심을 토로했다 He expressed his true feelings in his diary.
▶ 그녀는 나에게 자기 비밀을 토로했다 She confided her secret to me.

토록 to...; up to...; as much as; to the extent of; so much; so far
♦ 이토록 (많이) this much; thus much; so much / 종일토록 all day (long); throughout the day
▶ 그토록 그녀가 밉니? You hate her that much?
▶ 그토록 할 필요는 없어요 There is no need to go that far.

토론 討論 〈토의〉 (a) debate; (a) discussion; a talk; 〈논쟁〉 a contention; argumentation
♦ 텔레비전 토론 a TV debate / 활발한 토론 a living [hot] discussion / 토론의 명수 a good debater; a master of fence / 토론을 마치다 close [wind up] a discussion [debate] / 토론에 부치다 put (a question) to debate; bring (a question) up for debate / 토론에 참가하다 join the debate; 《美》 take the floor
▶ 신공항 건설 여부에 관한 격렬한 토론이 벌어졌다 Whether to build a new airport or not was hotly [heatedly] debated.
—**토론하다** discuss; debate; have [hold] a debate; 《美》 talk up
♦ 그 문제를 아무와 토론하다 debate on [about] the matter with *sb*; discuss (about) the matter with *sb*
■ 자유[집단]— free [group] discussion ■ —술 dialectic(s) —자 a debater; a disputant

토론종결 討論終結 《美》 cloture of debate; 《英》 closure of debate
♦ 토론종결을 동의하다 move the closure [cloture]
—**토론종결하다** cloture; closure

토론회 討論會 a forum 《*pl*. ~s, -ra》; a debate; a discussion
■ 공개— an open forum 텔레비전— a TV debate 패널— a panel discussion

토류 土類 earths
■ —금속 an earth metal

토륨 〔化〕 thorium

토르소 a torso 《*pl*. ~ (e)s, -si》

토마루 土— a mud floor

토마토 a tomato 《*pl*. ~es》
■ —소스 tomato sauce —케첩 tomato catsup [catchup, ketchup]

토막 1 〈물체의〉 a piece; a block; a slice; a chip
♦ 나무 한 토막 a piece [block] of wood / 토막 내다[치다] chop [cut] (up); cut into [to] pieces; hack (to pieces); 〈톱으로〉 saw
2 〈이야기・강연 등의〉 a passage; a part; a section; 〈영화의〉 a frame; 〈장면〉 a scene
♦ 네 토막 만화 a four-frame comic strip
3 〈한동안〉 a while; a moment
♦ 역사의 한토막 a page [scene] of history

토막 土幕 a mud hut; a cave

토막토막 into [to] pieces; piece by piece
♦ 무를 토막토막 썰다 cut a radish into cubes / 죽은 가지를 토막토막 쳐내다 chop [cut] the dead branches off the trees

토멸 討滅 conquest; extermination; destruction
—**토멸하다** conquer; crush; exterminate
♦ 적을 토멸하다 destroy [conquer] the enemy

토목 土木 〈공사〉 engineering [public] works
♦ 토목공사를 맡다 undertake public works
■ —건축업 the civil engineering and construction industry —공학 civil engineering —기사 a civil engineer —인부 a construction laborer [worker] —청부업자 a public works contractor

토민 土民 the natives; the aborigines

토박이 土— a native
♦ 순 서울 토박이 a true [genuine] Seoulite; a Seoulite born and bred

토박하다 土薄— barren; sterile; infertile
♦ 토박한 땅 barren [poor, unproductive] soil [land]

토벌 討伐 subjugation; suppression
—**토벌하다** subjugate; suppress; subdue
♦ 반란군을 토벌하다 put down a rebellion; subdue a rebel army / 게릴라를 토벌하다 suppress [subdue] the guerrillas
■ —군 a punitive force —전 (a) punitive expedition

토벌대 討伐隊 a punitive force [expedition]
♦ 토벌대를 파견하다 send a punitive expedition (against)

토벽 土壁 a mud [an earthen] wall

토병 土兵 native [local] troops

토비 土匪 rebellious natives; native insurgents; local rebels [guerrillas]

토비 討匪 suppression [subjugation] of bandits —**토비하다** suppress [subdue] bandits

토사 土砂 earth and sand
■ —붕괴 a landslide; a mudslide

토사 吐瀉 vomiting and diarrh(o)ea
—**토사하다** vomit; 《口》 throw up; suffer from vomiting fits and diarrh(o)ea
■ —곽란 〔韓醫〕 vomiting and diarrhea —물 a

토사견 一犬 a Tosa dog
토산물 土産物 (special) products of the district [place]; local produce
토성 土星 〔天〕 Saturn
♦토성의 고리 Saturn's rings
토성 土城 a mud rampart [fortification]
토속 土俗 local customs [manners]; folk customs ■—신앙 (a) folk belief —학 〈민속학〉 folklore; 〈민족학〉 ethnology —학자 〈민속학자〉 a folklorist; 〈민족학자〉 a ethnologist
토스 toss
▶저 배구 선수는 토스를 잘 한다 That volley ball player is good at setting the ball up.
—토스하다 toss 《a ball》
토스터 a toaster; an electric toaster
♦토스터로 빵을 굽다 toast (a slice of) bread [make toast] in a toaster
■자동식— a pop-up toaster
토스트 toast
♦버터를 바른[바르지 않은] 토스트 한 조각 a slice of buttered [dry] toast / 토스트에 마가린을 바르다 spread toast with margarine; spread margarine on toast / 토스트를 굽다 [만들다] make toast 《in a toaster》; toast bread
■프렌치— French toast
토시 a muff; a wristlet
토신 土神 a deity [spirit] of the soil
토실토실하다 plump; chubby; buxom
♦아기의 토실토실한 손 a baby's chubby hands / 토실토실한 아기 a plump [chubby] baby
토악질 토— 1 〈구토〉 vomit; vomiting
—토악질하다 vomit; throw up; spew
2 〈도로 내어 놓음〉 —토악질하다 disgorge
토양 土壌 soil ♦기름진 토양 rich [fertile] soil / 메마른 토양 barren [poor, sterile, infertile, unproductive] soil
■—개량제 a soil conditioner —오염 soil pollution —조사 an agronomical survey
토양학 土壌学 pedology; soil science
—자 a pedologist; a soil scientist
토어 土語 〈토박이의〉 a native language [tongue]; 〈사투리〉 local language; a dialect
토요일 土曜日 Saturday 《略 Sat.》
▶토요일은 반나절 영업입니다 We have a half day off on Saturday.
토의 討議 (a) discussion; (a) debate; (a) deliberation
♦토의를 종결하다 close a discussion / 개혁안을 토의에 부치다 submit a reform bill for debate; bring a reform bill up for discussion
▶지금은 격렬한 토의가 진행중이다 A heated discussion [debate] is now going on.
—토의하다 discuss; hold a discussion; debate on [about]; deliberate upon [over]
▶우리는 대책을 토의했다 We discussed countermeasures [what measures to take].
■—자유— free discussion —사항 items on the agenda —안 a subject for debate [discussion]
토인 土人 a native; 〈원주민〉 an aboriginal; 〈총칭〉 aborigines

토일릿 〈화장실·변소〉 a toilet; 〈美〉 a toilet room; toilet facilities; a bathroom; 〈공공의〉 a rest room
■—페이퍼 toilet paper [tissue]; a toilet roll; bathroom tissue
토제 吐劑 an emetic medicine; a vomit; a vomitory
토지 土地 1 〈지면〉 land; a piece [tract] of land 《셀때》; 〈소유지〉 a lot [plot] 《구획된》; 〈큰〉 an estate; a landed property [estate]; real estate《넓은》
♦토지를 개척하다 clear land; exploit the land [ground] / 토지를 매매하다 deal in real estate / 토지를 사다 buy [purchase] (a piece of) land; buy a lot / 토지를 소유하다 own [hold] land / 토지를 임차하다 lease [rent] land [a lot] / 토지를 임대해 주다 grant the lease of a piece of land / 토지에 투자하다 invest in land [real estate]
▶집은 비싸지 않으나 토지는 비싸다 The house is not expensive but the land is.
▶그는 시골에 큰 토지를 가지고 있다 He owns a large estate [a vast tract of land] in the country.
2 〈경작지〉 land; ground; 〈토양〉 soil
♦비옥[척박]한 토지 rich [poor] land / 토지를 경작하다 cultivate the land [ground] / 토지를 개량하다 improve [enrich] the soil
3 〈영지〉 territory
■—개혁 land reform —관리인 a land steward; 〈英〉 a land agent —구획정리 land readjustment [reallocation, (re)plotting] —국유 state ownership [nationalization] of land —대장[등기부] a land register [ledger]; a terrier; a cadastre —매매 land dealings in real estate —매매 중개업자 a real estate agent; 〈美〉 a land agent; 〈美〉 a realtor; 〈英〉 a land-jobber —불법 점거자 a squatter —소산 ⇨ 토산물 —전매 land-rolling; the quick buying and selling of real estate (intended to boost prices) —제도 the land system
토지가옥 土地家屋 land [estate] and buildings; houses and lands
■—소개[중개]업자 ⇨ 토지(~매매 중개업자)
토지개량 土地改良 land improvement —토지 개량하다 improve land
■—사업 land improvement projects
토지소유 土地所有 landholding
■—권 landownership; 〔法〕 a (possessory) title to land —권 이전등기 registration of the transfer of the ownership of the land —자 a landowner; 〈총칭〉 the landed interest
토지수용 土地収用 expropriation of land
■—권 (the right of) eminent domain
토지측량 土地測量 land surveying
—토지측량하다 survey land
토질 土質 soil quality; (the nature of) the soil; the fertility of soil
♦토질을 검사하다 analyze [test] the soil
■—분석 soil analysis
토착 土着 aboriginality
♦토착의 native(-born); indigenous
■—동식물 aborigines; autochthon(e)s —민 natives; the aborigines

토코페롤 [生化] tocopherol
토키 (口) a talkie; a talking film [picture]
■—대본 a talkie script —만화 an animated-cartoon
토털 the total
■—스코어 the total score
토테미즘 totemism
토템 a totem ♦토템의 〈토템신앙의〉 totemic
■—기둥 a totem pole [post] —신앙[숭배] totemism —연구가 a totemist
토플리스 〈옷〉 a topless suit
토픽 a topic; a subject ♦오늘의 토픽 current topics; the topics of the day
토하다 吐— 1 〈게우다〉 spit; throw up
♦토할 것 같다 feel like vomiting [throwing up]; (美) feel sick 《to [at] one's stomach》
▶그녀는 먹은 것을 전부 토해 버렸다 She has thrown up [vomited] everything she ate.
▶그는 횡령한 500만원을 토해냈다 He has disgorged the embezzled five million won.
▶그는 욕지기가 나서 토하기 시작했다 He felt sick [nauseous] and began to vomit [throw up].
2 〈내뿜다〉 send [give] out; belch forth [out]; emit; throw forth; puff out 《smoke》; breathe out
♦(화산이) 불과 연기를 토하다 belch (out) fire and smoke
▶크게 숨을 들이키고 천천히 토해내시오 Inhale [breathe in] deeply and exhale [breathe out] slowly.
3 〈토로하다〉 express; give vent 《to》; speak out 《one's mind》
토혈 吐血 vomiting [spitting] of blood —**토혈하다** spit [vomit, cough up] blood
토호 土豪 〈세력이 있는 사람〉 a wealthy landowner; 〈호족〉 a powerful local family [clan]
토후 土侯 an emir; a sheik
■—국 an emirate; a sheikdom
톡 1 〈불거져 오른 모양〉 protruding; protuberant; bulging; sticking out; popping; bulging out
♦눈이 톡 불거지다 have protruding [protuberant, bulging] eyes; (美俗) be pop-eyed
▶커다란 바위가 기슭에서 강으로 톡 튀어나와 있었다 A huge rock stuck [jutted] out from the bank into the river.
2 〈치는 모양·소리〉 with a pat [rap, tap]
▶어깨를 톡 치다 tap sb on the shoulder / 마루를 지팡이로 톡 치다 tap the floor with one's stick
3 〈부러지는·뱉을 꼴〉 ♦포도씨를 톡 뱉다 spit out grape seeds
▶전화가 도중에서 톡 끊어졌다 The call was suddenly cut off.
4 〈쏘는 모양〉 sharply; bitterly; spicily
▶나는 벌에 톡 쏘였다 A bee stung me.
톡탁 beating; tapping; patting; dabbing
—**톡탁하다** ⇨ 톡탁거리다
톡탁거리다 tap [rap, knock] at [on] 《the door》; pat; dab
톡톡 tap-tap ⇨ 톡
♦톡톡 문을 두드리다 tap [rap, knock] at [on] the door

톡톡하다 1 〈국이〉 thick; rich; strong; heavy
2 〈피륙이〉 close; close-woven; thick
♦톡톡한 천 cloth of close [firm] texture
톡톡히 1 〈심하게〉 harshly; severely
♦톡톡히 때려 주다 beat sb soundly / 톡톡히 꾸지람 듣다 get a round rating [scolding] / 톡톡히 즐기다 enjoy oneself to the full
2 〈많이〉 quite a lot; much
♦톡톡히 팁을 주다 tip handsomely / 돈을 톡톡히 가지고 있다 have enough [quite a lot of] money / 톡톡히 쉬다 have a good rest
3 〈진하게〉 thick; rich
♦국을 톡톡히 끊이다 prepare soup thick
4 〈배게〉 close; thick
♦베를 톡톡히 짜다 weave cloth thick
톤 a ton; 〈톤수〉 tonnage
♦미국〈작은〉 톤 an American [a short] ton / 미터 톤 a metric ton / 영국〈큰〉 톤 a British [long] ton / 10톤 짜리 덤프트럭 a ten-ton dump truck / 5천톤의 기선 a ship of 5,000 tons
톤세 —稅 tonnage dues
톤수 —數 tonnage
▶그 배의 톤수는 5천톤이다 The ship has a tonnage of 5,000 gross tons. ⇌ The ship displaces 5,000 tons.
■등록— registered tonnage 배수[순]— displacement [net] tonnage 재화(載貨)중량— deadweight capacity [tonnage] 적재— capacity tonnage 총— gross tonnage; the total tonnage
톨 ♦쌀 한 톨 a grain of rice / 밤 한 톨 a chestnut
톨스토이 〈러시아의 작가〉 Tolstoy, Leo Nikolaevich (1828-1910)
■—이즘 Tolstoyism
톱[1] a saw; a handsaw
♦가두리 톱 an edger / 기계 톱 a sawing machine / 내릴 톱 a ripsaw / 동가리 톱 a crosscut saw / 큰[대]톱 a large saw; 〈둘이 켜는〉 a pit saw / 판자를 톱으로 켜다 saw a board; cut a board with a saw / 나뭇가지를 톱으로 잘라내다 saw a branch off a tree
톱[2] 〈꼭대기〉 the top; 〈형용사적〉 top; first; best; leading
♦톱과 꼴찌 the top and the bottom / 자동차의 톱메이커 the leading car manufacturer / 톱을 끊다 lead; be at the top [head] (of); come to the top
▶그는 성적이 언제나 학급의 톱이다 He is always (at) the top of the class.
■—매니지먼트 top management —타자 [野] a lead-off (man) / 〈그 회〉 the first batter
톱기사 —記事 a front-page [lead] story; a lead ♦톱기사가 되다 make the front page
톱날 a sawtooth ⇨ 톱니
톱뉴스 top [front-page] news
▶모든 신문이 그 사건을 톱뉴스로 취급했다 Every newspaper treated the affairs as top news.
톱니 the tooth of a saw; a sawtooth
♦톱니꼴 [機] a tooth form [profile] / 톱니꼴의 dentiform; sawtoothed; serrate(d); serriform / 톱니꼴을 세우다 set (the teeth of) a

톱니바퀴 saw
▶ 이 스테이크용 칼은 톱니모양이다 This steak knife is serrated [has a serrated blade].

톱니바퀴 a toothed wheel
♦ 큰 톱니바퀴 a gear wheel; a cogwheel / 작은 톱니바퀴 a pinion / 톱니바퀴의 이 a cog; a tooth
▶ 이 기계는 톱니바퀴가 물려 있지 않다[있다] The machinery is out of gear [in gear].
■ 맞물림— a cogwheel 베벨[엇물림]— a bevel [skew] gear 중간— an intermediate [a mid] gear 평(平)— a spur wheel ■—장치 gear(ing); a train of gears

톱밥 sawdust

톱상어 〈魚〉 a saw shark

톱질 sawing
—톱질하다 saw
♦ 톱질하는 사람 a sawyer

톱클래스 ♦ 톱클래스의 top-class; first-rate; leading; foremost; (口) topflight; (美口) top-notch / 한국의 톱클래스 은행들 the top-ranking banks in Korea

톱톱하다 〈국물이〉 thick; heavy

톳 ♦ 김 한 톳 a 40-sheet bundle of laver

통¹ ♦ 〈배추의〉 a head, 〈박의〉 the body (of a gourd)
♦ 박 한 통 a gourd / 배추 세 통 three heads of cabbage
2 〈사람됨〉 caliber; 〈도량〉 magnanimity; 〈담력〉 boldness
♦ 통이 큰 large-[broad-]minded; liberal; 〈대담한〉 bold; daring / 통이 작다 be a person of small caliber
▶ 그는 통이 크다 He has guts.
3 〈피륙의〉 a roll; a bolt
♦ 옥양목 다섯 통 five rolls of calico
4 〈노름의〉 10 points obtained from 3 cards
5 〈바지의〉 the inside diameter; 〈넓이〉 width; breadth; 〈둘레〉 girth; 〈굵기〉 thickness
♦ 소매통이 좁다 a sleeve is rather tight
▶ 이 나무는 통이 2미터다 This tree is two meters around [in circumference].

통² **1** 〈복잡한 둘레·기세〉 influence (of something disturbing); confusion
♦ 북새통에 한물 보다 fish in troubled waters
♦ 넘어지는 통에 다리가 부러졌다 [지갑을 떨어뜨렸다] I broke my leg [dropped my wallet] when I fell down.
2 〈동아리〉 a gang; a group; a junto; cahoots
♦ 한통이 되다 be in cahoots [in conspiracy] with / 한통이 되어 사람을 속이다 conspire together to cheat sb
▶ 그들은 한통속이다 They were all in it together. ≒ They were in league with each other.

통 通 〈편지〉 a letter; 〈문서〉 a document; 〈증서〉 a bond
♦ 편지 세 통 three letters / 서류 세 통 three copies of a document
▶ 이 영수증을 두 통 복사해 주시오 Please make two copies of the receipt.

통 桶 〈물통 등〉 a pail; a (wooden) bucket; a tub; 〈술 등의〉 a cask; 〈큰〉 a barrel; 〈작은〉 a keg; 〈조(槽)〉 a tank; a vessel; 〈분뇨통〉 a soil pail
♦ 맥주 두 통 two casks [barrels] of beer / 두 통분의 물 two bucketfuls of water / 통을 열다 tap a barrel / 통을 메우다 hoop a tub / 통에 넣다 put sth in a barrel; tub; cask

통 筒 a pipe; a tube; a barrel; 〈원통〉 a cylinder; 〈기계의〉 a sleeve
♦ 대통을 꽃병으로 쓰다 use a bamboo cylinder as [for] a vase

통 統 1 〔地質〕 a series
2 〈행정구역〉 a tong; a subdivision of a dong
■—장 the head of a tong

통 〈전혀〉 quite; entirely; utterly; absolutely; completely; 〈조금도〉 (not) at all; 《not》 in the least; 《not》 a bit
▶ 나는 헤엄을 통 못 친다 I cannot swim a stroke.
▶ 나는 술을 통 못합니다 I can't drink at all.
▶ 그는 일에는 통 쓸모가 없다 As for work, he is utterly useless.
▶ 당신의 제안은 통 말이 안됩니다 What you propose is entirely out of the question.
▶ 그것이 무엇인지 나는 통 모르겠다 I don't have a slightest [faintest] idea what it is.

-통 -通 1 〈정통한 사람〉 an authority 《on》; an expert (in, at); a well-informed person
♦ 소식통 informed sources; well-informed quarters / 중국통 an authority on Chinese affairs
▶ 그는 대단한 경제통이다 He is very well informed [versed] in economics ≒ He is an expert in economics.
▶ 그녀는 영화통이야 She is very knowledgeable [(口) in the know] about movie.
2 〈거리〉 a street
♦ 해안 통 a waterfront street

통각 痛覺 a sense of pain
■ 무— 〔醫〕 analgesia : 무통각의 analgesic ■—계(計) an algometer; an algesimeter —공포증 algophobia —과민 hyperalgesia

통감 統監 1 〈관직명〉 a Resident-General
2 〈감독〉 supervision; 〈감독자〉 the commander
—통감하다 supervise; superintend

통감하다 痛感 feel strongly [deeply, acutely]; fully [keenly] realize
♦ 영어공부의 어려움을 통감하다 keenly realize the difficulty of learning English
♦ 우리는 우리의 사회적 책임을 통감하고 있습니다 We keenly realize our social responsibility.

통거리 the whole; all the stuff
♦ 통거리로 in a lump / 통거리로 팔다 sell things in a lump [in the gross]

통격 通格 〔文法〕 the common case

통계 統計 statistic(s); figures; a numerical statement
♦ 통계의[적인] statistical / 통계상으로는 statistically; in the statistics / 출생률의 통계를 잡다 compile [take] statistics of the birthrate
▶ 통계에 의하면 날마다 자동차 수가 증가하고 있다 According to statistics [The statistics show that] the number of cars is increasing day by day.
■ 사망[출산]— statistics of mortality [birth]

인구— population statistics; vital statistics; statistics of population ■—과[관] a statistics section [officer] —국(局) the Bureau of Statistics —도표 a statistical chart [graph] —보고 a statistical report —분석[해석] a statistical analysis 《*pl.* -ses》 —연감 a statistical yearbook —예보 statistical forecast —자료 statistical data —전문가 a statistician —조사 (a) statistical research [investigation]; statistics and research

통계표 統計表 statistics; a statistical table; a table of statistics

통계학 統計學 (the science of) statistics ♦통계학상의 statistical ■—자 a statistician

통고 通告 (a) notification; (a) notice
♦일방적인 통고 a one-sided [unilateral] notice / 최후의 통고 a last [final] notice; an ultimatum / 아무런 통고도 없이 without any advance notice [warning] / 통고를 하다 [받다] give [receive] notice
—통고하다 notify 《*sb* of [that]》; give *sb* notice 《of, that...》
▶퇴직시는 일주일 전에 통고해야 한다 You should give a week's notice (to your employer) when you quit the job. ⇌ You may quit the job on a week's notice.

통곡 痛哭·慟哭 lamentation; wailing
—통곡하다 weep bitterly; lament [grieve] 《over, for》

통과 通過 pass; passage; passing; transit; 〈의안의〉 carriage
♦법안의 통과 the passage of a bill / 통과의 자유 freedom of transit / 의안의 통과를 저지하다 block the passage of a bill
—통과하다 pass (through); go [get] through
♦서울 상공을 통과하다 fly [pass] over Seoul / 영국을 통과하다 pass through England
▶그것은 세관을 통과했다 It passed customs.
▶그녀는 제1차 심사를 통과했다 She passed the first screening.
▶예산안은 국회를 통과했다 The budget has passed the National Assembly. ⇌ The National Assembly has passed the budget.
▶특급열차가 본 역을 곧 통과합니다 A special express train will pass (through) this station shortly.
■—무역 transit trade —사 증 a transit visa —세 〈화물의〉 transit duty [tax]; 〈운하·교량 등의〉 tolls —여객 a transit passenger [traveler] —역 a local [non-express] station —의례 a rite of passage —화물 transit goods; 〈포장 표기〉 "Transit"

통관 通關 entry; (customs) clearance
—통관하다 clear customs; clear [pass] *sth* through the customs
—수수료 a customs clearance fee —신고서 a bill of entry —업자 a customs broker —절차(節次) customs formalities [procedure]; clearance; customs; customs clearance process: 통관절차를 마치다 go through customs formalities; clear [go through] customs —필(畢) cleared —항(港) a port of entry —허가서 a goods-clearance permit

통괄 統括 generalization ⇨ 총괄(總括)

통권 通卷 the consecutive number of volumes

통근 通勤 attending [going to] the [*one's*] office; commutation
▶나는 통근 시간이 약 한 시간이다 It takes me about an hour to come [go] to the office. ⇌ My commuting time is about an hour.
—통근하다 commute; attend [go to] (*one's*) [the]) office; go to work
▶나는 버스와 열차로 통근한다 I go to work by bus and train.
▶그는 자전거로 통근한다 He cycles to work.
■—거리 commute —비 transit expenses to and from *one's* place of work —수당 a commutation [commuting] allowance —시간 time spent in commuting —시간대 commuter rush hours —열차 a commuter [commuting] train; a train for commuters —자 a commuter —정기 승차권 a commutation ticket; a season ticket —제도 〈입주 제도에 대하여〉 a living out system

통금 通禁 the curfew ⇨ 통행금지(야간~)
♦통금을 실시하다 impose [order] a curfew
—사이렌 a curfew siren —시간 curfew hour —위반 a curfew violation —해제구역 a curfew-lifted area

통기 通氣 ventilation; draft; 《英》 draught; 〈공기 쐬기〉 airing; aeration
♦통기가 잘 되는 방 a well-ventilated room
■—자연[인공]— a natural [an artificial] draft —갱(坑) 〔鑛〕 an air pit —공(孔) a vent (hole); 〔機〕 an air hole —관 an air pipe —대 zone of aeration —성 permeability —성 breathability —실(室) a draft chamber —장치 a ventilator; an aerator —조직 〔植〕 aerenchyma

통김치 cabbages pickled whole

통나무 a log ♦통나무를 켜다 saw up a log
■—다리 a log bridge; 《美》 a footlog —배 a canoe; a dugout —집 a log cabin [house]

통념 通念 a common idea; a generally [commonly] accepted idea
▶저것은 오늘날 사회 통념으로는 용납되지 않을 것이다 That will not be generally accepted by society today.

통달 通達 1 〈정통〉 mastery; conversance; expertness —통달하다 be familiar 《with》; have a thorough knowledge 《of》; be well [deeply] versed 《in》
♦영어에 통달하다 be proficient in English; have a good [thorough] command of English
▶그는 법률에 통달하고 있다 He is familiar with law. ⇌ He is an expert [a specialist] in law.
2 〈통지〉 notification; (an) official notice
—통달하다 give an official notice

통닭 a (whole) chicken; a chicken cooked whole —구이 a roast chicken; a chicken roasted whole

통대구 —大口 a dried cod

통독 通讀 reading from beginning to end —통독하다 read through [over] 《a book》; read 《a book》 from cover to cover
▶그 책은 통독할 가치가 있다 The book is worth reading through.

통람 通覽 a general (re)view; a survey ―**통람하다** survey; look over; take a general view of
♦ 보고서를 통람하다 look over [glance over] a report

통렬하다 痛烈― severe; fierce; bitter; biting; sharp ♦ 통렬한 일격 a hard [terrible] blow / 그 연극을 통렬히 비판하다 criticize the drama bitterly [severely]

통례 通例 common [usual] practice; a (common) usage; a general rule
▶ 나는 통례를 따른 것 뿐이다 I just followed normal practice.
▶ 그렇게 하는 것이 통례로 되어 있다 It is the custom to do so.

통로 通路 a passage; a way; a path; 〈정원·공원의〉 a walkway; 〈좌석 사이의〉 an aisle; 〈동물의〉 a track
♦ 통로 옆의 좌석 an aisle seat / 통로를 열다 [막다] clear [block] the passage / 통로에 있다 lie [be] in one's way; be in the route (of) / 통로의 방해가 되다 be [stand, get] in sb's way
▶ 두 집 사이에는 좁은 통로가 있다 There's a narrow passage between the two houses.
▶ 이것은 종업원 전용 통로입니다 This passage is for the exclusive use of the employees [for the employees only].

통론 通論 an outline; an introduction
■ 문학― an introduction to literature 법학― an outline of law

통마늘 a whole bulb of garlic

통메(우)다 1 〈통데를〉 hoop a tub; put a hoop on a barrel
2 〈빽빽이 차다〉 be closely [tightly] packed; (口) be jam-packed (with); be full of

통메장이 桶― a hooper; a cooper

통발 筒― a fish trap; a weir; (英) a coop

통법 通法 1 〈통칙〉 a universal law
2 〔數〕 reduction to a single unit

통변 通辯 interpretation ⇨ 통역

통보 通報 reporting; information; a report; a bulletin ―**통보하다** report; notify; inform ♦ 그 일을 경찰에 통보하다 report the matter to the police; inform the police about the matter
■ 기상― a weather report

통보 通寶 〈옛 주화〉 a coin; currency

통분 通分 〔數〕 reduction (of fractions) to a common denominator
▶ 2/3와 1/4을 통분하여라 Reduce 2/3 and 1/4 to a common denominator.

통분 痛憤·痛忿 great [strong] indignation ―**통분하다** greatly indignant
▶ 그는 그들의 냉대에 통분했다 He strongly resented [was very indignant] at their cold treatment.

통비 通比 〔數〕 a common ratio (*pl.* ~s)

통사정하다 通事情― 1 〈사정을 구하다〉 tell frankly (about); unbosom [unburden] *oneself* (on); beg (for); appeal (for mercy); solicit earnestly
♦ 돈을 달라고 통사정하다 beg *sb* for money; plead with [appeal to] *sb* for money
2 〈사정을 알아주다〉 have [feel] compassion [sympathy] for; be sympathetic

통산 通算 summing up; 〈액수〉 the sum total
♦ 통산 20년간 이 도시에 살다 live in this city for a total of twenty years / 미결 30일 통산 1년의 금고 one year's imprisonment with credit for thirty days service as an unconvicted prisoner ―**통산하다** sum [add] up; total; 〈포함시키다〉 include
▶ 그 비용은 통산하여 300만원에 달했다 The expenses amounted [added up] to three million won

통상 通常 normally; usually; commonly; as a rule; in generel; under normal conditions
▶ 영업은 통상 9시부터 5시까지입니다 We are usually [generally] open from nine to five.
■ ―복 everyday clothes [wear] ―우편물 ordinary mail ―총회 an ordinary general meeting ―회원 an ordinary [a regular] member

통상 通商 trade; commerce ♦ 어떤 나라와 통상을 개시하다 open trade [commerce] with a country ―**통상하다** trade (with a country)
■ ―관계 trade relations ―마찰 trade friction ―무역 trade and commerce ―사절단 a trade delegation ―산업부 the Ministry of Trade, Industry and Energy ―촉진 acceleration of trade transaction ―항해 조약 a commerce and navigation treaty

통상조약 通商條約 a commercial treaty; a treaty of commerce ♦ 통상조약을 맺다 conclude [sign] a commercial treaty

통설 通說 a commonly-held opinion; a popular view
▶ 그의 발견은 통설을 뒤집었다 His discovery disproved the popularly-held view in the field.

통성 通性 1 〈공통의 성질〉 a common property [quality]; generality
▶ 그것은 조류의 통성이다 It is a habit common to birds.
2 〔文法〕 the common gender

통성명 通姓名 exchanging names ―**통성명하다** introduce (themselves) to each other; exchange [give] (their) names

통속 通俗 1 〈풍속〉 a common [popular] custom 2 〈성질〉 popularity; conventionality
■ ―문학[소설] popular literature [novels] ―어 (a) colloquialism; popular [familiar, colloquial] language ―음악 popular music

통속적 通俗的 popular; common; vulgar
♦ 통속적인 과학서 a popular book of science / 통속적인 생각 a layman's idea [view]; a common way of thinking / 통속적인 책 a book for the lay reader / 통속적으로 말하면 to use plain language
▶ 그의 연설은 통속적이었다 His speech was very commonplace.

통속화 通俗化 popularization ―**통속화하다** popularize

통솔 統率 command; leadership
―**통솔하다** command; lead
▶ 그는 부하를 잘 통솔한다 He leads his men well. ⇒ He exercises excellent leadership over his subordinates.

■—권 (the right of) command —력 leadership; ability to command

통솔자 統率者 a leader; a commander
◆통솔자가 되다 take the lead of; stand at the head of

통수 統帥 the supreme [high] command
—통수하다 command; have the supreme command (of) ◆삼군을 통수하다 command all the armed forces
■—권 the supreme command —부 the high command

통신 通信 correspondence; communication; news; a report
◆런던에서 들어온 통신에 의하면 according to a dispatch [message, news] from London; a London dispatch says 《that…》/ 통신을 시작하다 get into communication [correspondence] 《with》; enter into correspondence 《with》/ 통신을 계속하다 maintain a correspondence 《with》; keep in touch [communication] 《with》
▶그 항공기와는 통신이 두절되어 있다 The airplane is out of radio communication [contact].
—통신하다 communicate 《with》; correspond 《with》
■—강좌 a correspondence course —공학 telecommunication engineering —교수 instruction by correspondence; correspondence course [lesson] —기관 a means [an organ] of communication; facilities for communication —난 a correspondence column; 〈신문・잡지의〉 the "letter-to-the-editor" columns; 〈그림 엽서의〉 space for a message —대 a signal corps —망 a communications network [system] —방해 communication jamming —병 a signalman; a signal corpsman; a signaler —보도기관 vehicles of news —비 communication expenses —사(士) 〈유선의〉 a telegraph operator; 〈무선의〉 a wireless [radio] operator —사무 communication business [affairs] —사업 communication enterprise [service] —선(線) a line of communication(s); a communications line —속도 transmission speed —시설 the communication facilities —시스템 communication system —실 〔電信〕 an operation [a communications] room —연계 a communication link —위성 a communication(s) satellite; a news satellite —채널 a communication channel —통 a communication tube [cylinder] —학교 a correspondence school

통신교육 通信教育 correspondence education; education by correspondence; a correspondence course (of college) education
◆통신교육을 하다 teach by correspondence / 통신교육으로 번역 코스를 수강하다 do [take] a correspondence course in translation

통신사 通信社 a news agency; a news [《美》 wire] service ◆연합— the Yŏnhap News Agency

통신원 通信員 〈신문사 등의〉 a correspondent; 〈보도기자〉 a reporter; 〈회사의 통신 담당〉 a correspondence clerk ◆본사 뉴욕 통신원 our correspondent in New York ■특파[군사]— a special [war] correspondent

통신판매 通信販賣 mail order; mail-order sale [selling] ◆통신판매로 책을 사다 buy a book from a mail-order house ■—회사[점] a mail-order firm [house, store]

통약 通約 〔數〕 reduction to a common measure ⇨ 약분

통어 統御 〈지배〉 rule; reign; 〈제어〉 control; 〈관리〉 management
—통어하다 rule [reign] over; govern; control; bring [get] under one's control [girdle]; manage; keep under control
◆통어하기 어려운 ungovernable; uncontrollable; unmanageable / 통어할 수 없게 되다 be [out of] control; get out of hand

통역 通譯 〈일〉 interpretation; 〈사람〉 an interpreter ◆통역 없이 without an interpreter; without interpretation
▶나는 김선생의 통역으로 스미스씨와 회담했다 I talked with Mr. Smith through the interpreter, Mr. Kim.
▶그는 무역 회사에서 통역을 하고 있다 He works as an interpreter for a trading company.
▶나는 그에게 통역을 부탁했다 I asked him to interpret for me.
—통역하다 interpret; act as (an) interpreter
▶나는 그의 연설을 통역했다 I acted as an interpreter for his speech.
■동시— simultaneous interpretations ■—관 an official interpreter; a secretary-interpreter

통용 通用 popular [common] use; circulation; currency
◆지폐의 통용을 제한하다 restrict the currency of bank notes
—통용하다 be in common use; pass 《for》; circulate; be [pass, go, run] current; 〈표 등이〉 be available; be good; 〈규칙 등이〉 hold good [true]
◆국제간에 통용하다 have international currency / 일반적으로 통용되다 pass [go, run] current
▶그 이론은 지금도 통용된다 The theory holds good today.
▶그 지폐는 지금은 통용되지 않는다 We don't use that bank note any more [longer]. ⇌ The bank note is no longer used [current, in current use].
▶그런 사고 방식은 세상에서는 통용되지 않는다 Such a way of thinking won't be accepted in the world.
■—기한 a valid [stipulated] period [term]; 〈표의〉 the term for which a ticket is available [valid, good] —문(門) a side gate [door]; a service [back] entrance —어 a current word [language]; a word [language] in current use —화폐 currency; a current coin

통운 通運 transportation; transport; forwarding; express —통운하다 transport; forward; ship
■—업 forwarding business —업자 a forwarding agent —회사 a transport company; a forwarding agency; 《美》 an express agency [company]

통으로 all; wholly; altogether; bodily; collectively; in the gross [mass, lump]; (프) en bloc
◆통으로 삼키다 swallow *sth* whole / 통으로 팔다 sell by the lump / 나무를 통으로 때다 burn logs without splitting them

통음 痛飮 a swill; a swig; a carousal ―**통음하다** drink heavily [hard, deep]; (口) have a booze; swill; swig; go [have] on the spree; carouse

통일 統一 〈단일〉 unity; 〈단일화〉 unification; 〈통합〉 consolidation; coordination; 〈균일〉 uniformity; coherence; oneness; 〈표준화〉 standardization; 〈지배〉 rule, sway, dominance, 〈집중〉 concentration
◆통일 국가 a unified nation / 통일적인 unific / 통일이 된 [안된] 행동을 취하다 take united [divided] action
▶그러면 당내의 통일이 안 될 것이다 That would cause disunity among the party members.
―**통일하다** unify; consolidate; coordinate; 〈표준하다〉 standardize; 〈지배하다〉 rule; bring under sway
◆가격을 통일하다 standardize the prices / 나라를 통일하다 unify a nation; bring a country under unified rule / 통일된 unified; uniform; systematic; homogeneous / 통일되지 않은 diverse; incoherent
▶그는 12세기에 나라를 통일했다 He unified the country in the twelfth century.
■국내― national unity [unification] 남북― unification of North and South (Korea) 세계― federation of the world; confederation of the nations 재― reunification 정신― psychic [mental] concentration 평화― peaceful unification ■―정부[전선] a unified government [front] ―체 a unity; a whole

통일교 統一敎 〈교회〉 the Unification Church; 〈교리〉 Moonism ■―신자 a Moonie

통장 通帳 〈은행의〉 a bankbook; a passbook
통장 統長 the head of a *tong*

통절하다 痛切― keen; poignant; severe; acute; urgent
◆통절히 keenly; poignantly; severely; acutely / 결함을 통절하게 느끼다 feel the shortcomings severely / …의 필요성을 통절히 느끼다 keenly feel the necessity of [for]…
▶나는 건강의 중요함을 통절히 느끼고 있다 I've realized how important health is.

통점 痛點 〔醫〕 a pain spot

통제 統制 control; regulation; management
◆정부의 통제 governmental control / 통제가 없는 uncontrolled; noncontrolled
▶정부는 통제를 강화[완화, 해제]하였다 The government tightened [loosened, removed] the control.
▶전쟁중에는 검열에 의해 사상의 통제가 행해졌다 Thought control was exercised during the war through censorship.
―**통제하다** control; exercise control over [on]; hold under control; place *sth* under (government) control; regulate; govern; regiment
▶정부는 물가를 엄격히 통제하지 않으면 안된다 The government must impose strict price control(s).
■물가― price control ■―가격 controlled prices; price control ―경제 controlled economy ―계정 controlling account ―기관 a control organ [agency]; an organ for control ―무역 controlled [managed] trade ―장치 control unit ―철폐 decontrol ―품 controlled goods [articles] ―화폐 managed currency

통제부 統制府 〈해군의〉 a naval yard; a naval station; an admiralty port

통조림 桶― 〈제조〉 canning; (美) packing; (英) tinning; 〈제품〉 canned [(英) tinned] food [goods]
▶그 공장에서는 생선 통조림을 만들고 있다 The factory produces canned fish.
■고기― canned [(英) tinned] meat 쇠고기― canned [(英) tinned] beef; bully (beef) 연어 [생선]― canned [(英) tinned] salmon [fish] ■―공(工) a packer; a canner; (英) a tinner ―공업 the canning [(美) packing, (英) tinning] industry ―공장 a cannery; (美) a packinghouse; a canning plant [factory]; (英) a tinning works ―제조법 canning; (英) tinning

통증 痛症 a pain; an ache; 〈격통〉 a pang; 〈따끔따끔한〉 pricking
◆격렬한 통증 a severe [a sharp, a poignant, an acute] pain / 등[옆구리]의 통증 a (sharp) pain in back [side] / 통증이 심하다 feel a bad [severe] pain (in *one's* teeth) / 통증을 느끼다 feel [have, suffer] a pain
▶통증이 갑자기 가라앉았다 The pain suddenly stopped.
▶이 약을 마시면 통증이 즉시 멎습니다 This drug will kill [relieve] the pain at once.

통지 通知 〈통고〉 (a) notice; (a) notification; 〈공식의 보고〉 (a) report; information; 〈통신〉 communication; 〈상업상의〉 an advice
◆추후 통지가 있을 때까지 till further notice [advice]; until *one* hears further from *sb* / 통지를 받는 즉시 at a minute's notice; immediately on receipt of *one's* notice / 통지를 받다 be informed 《of, that…》; have [receive] notice 《of, that…》; be notified [advised] 《of, that…》; receive advices
▶나는 그런 통지를 받지 않았다 I have not received such (a) notice.
▶그는 정식으로 합격 통지를 받았다 He formally received (a) notice [was formally notified] that he had passed the exam. ⇌ He was formally notified of having passed the exam.
―**통지하다** notify 《*sb* that [of]》; inform 《*sb* that [of]》; let *sb* know 《that, of》; communicate 《news to, with *sb*》; advise [apprise] 《*sb* that [of]》; 〈주로 해약·해고 등의〉 give *sb* notice 《that, of》
◆미리 통지하다 give *sb* previous notice; send word beforehand / …임을 통지해 드립니다 This is to give notice [notify, inform you] that…
▶도착하시면 바로 통지해 주십시오 Please write to me immediately upon your arrival.
▶변경이 있을 때마다 통지해 드리겠습니다 We

will let you know whenever there is an alteration.
■발송— shipping advices 송금— a remittance advice 어음부도— a notice of dishonor 착하[이전, 해약]— a notice of arrival [removal, cancellation] ■—예금 a deposit at call [notice] —인 an informer —전표 an advice slip —표 a report; (美) a report card

통지서 通知書 a (written) notice; a written message; a letter of advice
■공식— an official notice 거절— a notice of protest 부도—〈어음의〉 a notice of dishonor [protest]

통짜 the whole mass [lump] 《of》
♦통짜로 whole ⇨ 통째(로)

통째(로) whole; altogether; bodily; entirely; in 《its》 entirety
♦통째로 삶다 cook 《a chicken》 whole / 통째로 먹다 eat *sth* whole / 고기 한 토막을 통째로 삼키다 swallow a piece of meat whole
▶금고 속에 든 패물을 통째로 도둑맞았다 The adornments of the safe were stolen in their entirety [en masse].

통찰 洞察 discernment; penetration; insight
—**통찰하다** discern; penetrate [see] into; see through; fathom [read] 《*sb's* heart》; gain [have] an insight into
▶그녀는 그 문제를 통찰하고 있었다 She had great insight into the problem.

통찰력 洞察力 an insight; penetration; vision; discernment
♦통찰력이 있는 discerning; penetrative; penetrating; perceptive; perspicacious / 통찰력이 있는 사람 a man of penetration / 통찰력이 있다 gain [have] an insight into / 예리한 통찰력이 있다 can see through [into] a brick wall
▶그는 인간성에 대한 통찰력이 없었다 He had no insight into human nature.

통첩 通牒 a note; a notification; a circular; instruction
▶정부는 대사에게 통첩을 보냈다 The government sent [issued] the ambassador a note [message].
—**통첩하다** notify 《*sb* of [that]》; give notice 《to》; communicate
■외교— a diplomatic note 최후— an ultimatum (*pl*. ~s, -ta)

통촉 洞燭 〈밝게 살핌〉 understanding; comprehension; judgment; discernment
—**통촉하다** (deign to) see; understand; comprehend; judge; discern; consider; realize
▶저의 흉중을 통촉하여 주시기 바랍니다 I hope you will be kind enough to understand my feelings.

통치 通治 curing all diseases [ills] —**통치하다** cure all diseases [ills]
♦만병통치약 a panacea; a cure-all; a heal-all; a catholicon
▶이 세상에 만병통치약은 없다 There is no cure-all in the world.

통치 統治 rule; reign; government; administration ♦국가의 통치 the administration of the state
▶그 나라는 당시 영국의 통치하에 있었다 The country was then under the rule of Great Britain.
▶국왕[여왕]은 군림하되 통치는 하지 않는다 The King [Queen] reigns, but he [she] does not rule.
—**통치하다** rule over [govern] 《a country, a people》; hold sway over; administer; guide
♦한 나라를 통치하다 rule (over) a country; reign over a country; govern [administer] a country
▶한때 군사 정권이 이 나라를 통치했었다 A military government once ruled this country.
■신탁— trusteeship 위임— mandatory rule [administration] ■—권 sovereign [supreme] power; sovereignty; majesty: 통치권을 행사하다 exercise the sovereign power —기관 government organs [machinery] —자 the ruler; the sovereign —제도 a ruling system

통치마 a seamless one-piece skirt

통칙 通則 general [common] rules [principles, provisions]

통칭 通稱 〈공통의 이름〉 a common designation [title]; 〈통용하는 이름〉 a popular [common] name; (an) alias
▶그는 통칭 짐이라고 한다 He is commonly called Jim. ⇌ He goes by the name of Jim.

통쾌 痛快 a keen pleasure; a thrill; piquancy
—**통쾌하다** awfully pleasant; extremely delightful; piquant ♦통쾌한 사나이 a jolly fellow / 통쾌한 문장[연설] an incisive [a trenchant] style [speech]
▶회의에서 그는 통쾌한 발언을 했다 He made an incisive observation at the conference.
▶그것은 실로 통쾌한 일이다 That's an awfully delightful event.
▶녀석이 졌다는 걸 들으니 정말 통쾌하다 I am thrilled [delighted] to hear that he was beaten.
■—감 smart [thrilling] feelings

통킹 〈베트남 북부 지방〉 Tonkin; Tongking
■—만 the Gulf of Tonkin —사람 Tonkinese

통탄 痛歎 —**통탄하다** lament [regret] deeply; grieve bitterly; deplore ♦통탄할 deplorable; lamentable; grievous; regrettable / 통탄할 일 a matter of great regret
▶그것은 실로 통탄할만한 사고였다 It was a deplorable accident.
▶나는 나의 불운을 통탄했다 I lamented over my misfortune.

통탕 stampingly ⇨ 퉁탕

통통¹ 〈몸피가 굵은 모양〉 plumply; full
—**통통하다** round; plump; chubby; buxom; full ♦통통한 아이 a chubby [plump] child / 통통한 젖가슴 an ample bosom / 통통하게 살찌다 become rounded; plump (up [out]) / 모습이 통통하다 look chubby
▶그 어린애는 볼이 통통하다 The baby has plump cheeks.
▶그녀는 너무 울어서 눈이 통통 부었다 Her eyes are all swollen [puffed up] with crying.
▶그녀의 몸매는 점점 통통해진다 Her form is rounding.

통통² 〈두드리는·구르는 소리〉 pound; stampingly; tramp; resoundingly; 〈발동기 소리〉 chug-chug (of a motorboat)

통통거리다 pound; beat; stamp; tramp
♦ 통로에서 통통거리는 발소리 the pound of feet in the passageway / 〈발동기〉 통통거리며 지나가다 chug away [along] / 〈발로〉 통통거리며 박자를 맞추다 (one's feet) tom-tom out a pattern of rhythm

통통배 a motorboat; a motor-powered boat

통틀다 lump [put] together; sum up; draw into one mass

통틀어 all put together; in total; (all) in all; (in) all told; in the gross [mass, lump]; in one lot; collectively; (프) en bloc [masse]
▶ 통틀어 열 개 in all; ten all told / 〈물건 값이〉 통틀어 6천원 6,000 won for the whole lot [in all told] / 통틀어 십만원이 되다 total up to 100,000 won
▶ 통틀어 백 달러 든다 It costs one hundred dollars in all [altogether].
▶ 통틀어 얼마입니까? What do you charge for them all? ⇌ How much does it cost altogether?

통폐 通弊 a common evil [abuse, weakness]
▶ 끈기가 없는 것이 도시 사람들의 통폐다 Lack of tenacity is a weakness common to city-dwellers. ⇌ People living in town are apt to lack tenacity.
▶ 우리는 시대의 통폐를 시정하는데 최선을 다해야 한다 We should do our best to reform evils prevailing in our own time.

통풍 通風 ventilation; airing; draft; draught
▶ 이 방은 통풍이 잘 된다[되지 않는다] This room is well [badly] ventilated.
▶ 이 굴뚝은 통풍이 잘 된다 This chimney draws well.
—**통풍하다** let (fresh) air in; admit air; ventilate
■ —갱도 〈광산의〉 an air pit —관 an air pipe [line]; a vent pipe; a ventiduct —구(口) a ventilation opening; an air hole; an airway; a vent; 〈건물의〉 a ventilator; an aerator —장치 a ventilator; a ventilation arrangement [device, apparatus] —창 a ventilation window [opening] —통(筒) a ventilator; an air duct

통풍 痛風 〔醫〕 gout; podagra ♦ 통풍에 걸리다 be afflicted with gout; be gouty

통하다 通— 1 〈길·차편 등이〉 run; lead (to, into); open (into a room, upon a corridor [garden]); communicate (with); 〈개통하다〉 be opened (to [for] traffic); 〈이어지다〉 be connected (by a railway)
▶ 이 길은 해변으로 통하고 있다 This road leads to the beach.
▶ 이 도시에서 그 마을까지 철도가 통하고 있다 A railway runs from this town to the village. ⇌ There is a railway service between this town and the village.
▶ 이 문은 응접실로 통하고 있다 This door opens into the parlor.
▶ 모든 길은 로마로 통한다 All roads lead to Rome.
2 〈공기가〉 vent (through a chimney); be ventilated; ventilate; 〈빛·열 등이〉 pass [run, get, go] through; penetrate; permeate; 〈혈액 등이〉 be circulated; circulate; 〈파이프 등이〉 draw; drain
♦ 공기가 잘 통하다 have a good ventilation [vent] / 담뱃대에 연기가 잘 통하다 a pipe draws well / 빛이 통하다 be penetrable to light / 피가 잘 통하다 have a good circulation of blood
▶ 그 하수도는 물이 잘 통한다 The sewer runs [drains] well.
3 〈전류가〉 transmit; flow ♦ 전기가 통하고 있는 전선 a live [an electrified] wire
▶ 금속류는 전기가 통한다 Metals transmit electricity.
▶ 이 전선에는 전류가 통하고 있다 This wire is charged with electricity. ⇌ This is a live wire.
4 〈전화가〉 be put [go, get] through; be on (the line); be working; get connected (with)
▶ 전화가 통하지 않는다 The phone [wire] is dead. ⇌ The line is out.
▶ 김박사에게 전화를 걸었으나 통하지 않았다 I could not get [reach] Dr. Kim on the phone. ⇌ I could not get through to Dr. Kim.
5 〈내용·사정 등에 환하다〉 be well [deeply] versed (in); be an expert (in, on); be (well) up (in); be familiar with; be proficient (in); be at home (in, on); be a master (of); be well acquainted (with); be well informed (of)
▶ 그는 중국의 사정에 잘 통한다 He is well informed about the Chinese affairs.
▶ 그는 한국사에 통해 있다 He is well versed in Korean history.
6 〈말·의사 등이〉 be understood; be comprehended; be spoken; make *oneself* understood; understand (each other); be congenial
♦ 일반적으로 통하는 말 a popular [common] word / 말이 서로 통하다[통하지 않다] be able [unable] to communicate with each other (in English) / 서로 기분이 통하다 understand each other's sentiments
▶ 나는 영어로 통할 수 있었다 I was able to make myself understood in English.
▶ 내 기분이 결국 그녀에게 통했다 She finally understood my feelings.
▶ 그에게는 농담이 통하지 않는다 He can't get a joke. ⇌ He has no sense of humor.
▶ 그와는 수월하게 이야기가 통했다 I could communicate with him easily.
▶ 암시를 주어도 그에게는 통하지 않았다 My hint was lost upon him.
7 〈글의 뜻이〉 make sense; be understandable
▶ 이 글은 뜻이 통하지 않는다 This sentence doesn't make sense.
▶ 저 문장으로는 네가 말하고 싶은 것이 통하지 않는다 That sentence won't convey what you mean.
8 〈비밀히 관계를 맺다〉 become intimate (with); have relations (with); form a liaison (with); commit misconduct [adultery] (with); intrigue (with)
♦ 유부녀와 통하다 have an affair with a married woman

▶그녀는 상사와 통하고 있다 She has relations with her boss.
9 〈내통하다〉 communicate secretly with; inrtigue 《with the enemy》; be in touch with 《the other party》
♦비밀히 적과 통하다 communicate secretly with the enemy; be in touch with the enemy
10 〈통용하다・알려지다〉 pass (for [as]); figure as; be known as; pass current; circulate
♦…의 이름으로 통하다 pass under the name of…; go [be known] by the name of… / 대가(大家)로 통하다 be reputed [acknowledged] as an authority
▶그녀는 구두쇠로 통하고 있다 She has a reputation for being stingy [stinginess]. ⇒ She has the reputation of being stingy.
11 〈허용되다〉 pass; be admissible; be admitted
▶너의 의견은 그들에게 통할 것 같지 않다 Your opinion will not go down with them.
▶잊어버렸다는 말 가지고는 통하지 않을 게다 To say, "I have forgotten it" will make no excuse.
12 〈유효하다〉 be valid; hold [stand] good; be available (차표 등이); 〈유통되다〉 pass; circulate
♦규칙이 통하다 a regulation holds good
▶이 돈은 어디서나 통한다 This money passes [can be used, goes] freely everywhere.
13 〈거치다〉 pass [go] through; go by way of
♦민선생을 통해 through Mr. Min; through Mr. Min's good offices / 중매인을 통해서 청혼하다 propose to 《a girl》 through a go-between
▶우리는 앵커리지를 통해서 파리로 날아갔다 We flew to Paris by way of [via] Anchorage.
14 〈시간・공간에 걸치다〉 ♦전국을 통하여 throughout [all over] the country; in the whole country / 일생을 통하여 throughout *one's* life
15 〈대・소변이〉 《*one's* bowels》 move
♦소변[대변]이 통하다 have regular urination [bowel movements] / 대소변이 통하지 않다 have excretory difficulties
16 〈관계가 있다〉 be concerned [connected] 《with》; have a relation [connection] 《with》
▶그 두 사건에는 서로 통하는 데가 있다 The two incidents are connected [related to] each other. ⇒ There is a connection [relation] between the two incidents.

통학 通學 attending school ─통학하다 attend [go to] school [classes]
♦걸어서 통학하다 walk to school; attend school on foot / 자기 집에서 통학하다 attend school from *one's* home
▶통학하는 학생들로 버스는 만원이다 The bus is crowded with [full of] boys and girls going to school.
▶나는 자전거로 통학하고 있다 I go to school by bicycle. ⇒ I cycle to school.
■─구역 a school district ─생 a day scholar [student]; an extern; 〈기숙학교의〉 a day boy [girl] ─차 〈버스〉 a school bus; 〈기차〉 a student train; a student commuter train

통할 統轄 (general) control; control and jurisdiction ─통할하다 control; supervise; preside over; govern; have [exercise] jurisdiction over ■─구역 the area under the direct control (of) ─자 the person in charge

통합 統合 integration; unification; unity; combination; synthesis ─통합하다 integrate; combine; unify; unite; consolidate; put [bring] together; make into one; synthesize
♦두 회사의 통합 the consolidation of two companies into one / 민족의 통합 the unity [unification] of the people / 여러 가지 기획의 통합 the integration of various projects / 통합의 상징 a symbol of the unity
■─계획 a plan for integrating

통항 通航 navigation; sailing; plying ─통항하다 navigate; sail; ply

통행 通行 passing; transit; traffic
♦통행이 많은 도로 a road with heavy [busy] traffic / 통행을 금하다 close (up) a road; seal a street to traffic; block a street / 통행을 방해하다 obstruct (the) traffic; block *sb's* passage; stand [get] in *sb's* way
▶일방 통행 (게시) One way only. ⇒ One-way traffic.
▶좌측 통행 (게시) Walk on the left. ⇒ Keep to the left.
▶그 길은 자동차 통행이 가능합니까? Can cars pass through that street?
▶자동차 통행이 금지되어 있다 Automobile traffic is closed.
─통행하다 pass (through); go [get] past; go through [along]
♦통행할 수 있는[없는] passable [impassable] / 거리를 통행하다 pass [go] along a street; walk down a street
■─권(權) a right of way [passing] ─료 passage money; a toll: 통행료 받는 곳 a tollhouse; a tollstation ─인 a passerby 《*pl.* passersby》; a foot passenger; a pedestrian ─증 a pass; a safe-conduct (pass)

통행금지 通行禁止 the suspension of traffic
▶이 도로는 공사 때문에 일시 통행금지다 This road is temporarily closed to traffic for construction work.
▶제차 통행금지 (게시) No thoroughfare for all vehicles.
■─야간─ the curfew ■─지역 a no passing zone

통혼 通婚 〈혼인 의사의 타진〉 making an offer [a proposal] of marriage; 〈혼인 관계를 맺음〉 entering into matrimony ─통혼하다 make an offer of marriage; enter into matrimony

통화 通貨 currency; current money [coins]; the medium of circulation
♦약한[강한] 통화 weak [strong] currency / 그 나라의 통화로 지불하다 pay the bill in the currency of the country
■─관리─ the managed [controlled] currency 불환(不換)─ inconvertible [irredeemable] currency ■─관리 currency management ─단위 a currency unit ─발행고 amount of currency in issue ─수축 deflation [contraction] of currency ─안정 stabilization of the cur-

rency ─위기 a monetary crisis ─위조 counterfeiting of currency ─유출[유입] the efflux [influx, inflow] of currency ─유통량 the total amount of money in circulation ─저락 depreciation of currency ─정책 a monetary policy ─제도 a currency [monetary] system : 통화제도 개혁 (a) monetary reform ─증발(增發) increased issue of currency ─팽창 currency inflation [expansion]; inflation [overissue] of currency

통화 通話 a (telephone [phone]) call; telephone conversation ◆ 요금 수신인 지급 통화 (美) (make) a collect call; (英) (make) a reverse-charge call / 통화 중이다 be on [talking over] the telephone
▶ 한 통화 3분간의 요금은 50원이다 The charge is fifty won for each three-minute call.
▶ 지금 통화중 (美) Line's busy. ⇌ (英) Number's engaged.
─**통화하다** speak [talk] over [upon] the telephone; speak by telephone
■ 시내─ a city [local] call 시외─ a long-distance call 지명─ a person-to-person call ■ ─구 the mouthpiece ─량 telephone traffic ─료 telephone charges ─신호 a busy signal ─횟수 the number of telephone calls

통회 痛悔 〈뉘우침〉 contrition ─**통회하다** be contrite

퇴각 退却 (a) retreat; (a) withdrawal
◆ 예정대로 퇴각을 하다 make a prearranged withdrawal [retreat]; retreat as prearranged / 퇴각을 엄호하다 cover a retreating army; protect the retreat
▶ 군의 퇴각은 질서정연하게 이루어졌다 The army retreated in orderly fashion.
─**퇴각하다** retreat (from, to); withdraw; give ground ◆ 서둘러 퇴각하다 beat a hasty retreat / 무사히 퇴각하다 make good one's retreat
■ 총─ a full [general] retreat ■ ─군 an army in retreat; a retreating army ─로 a route of retreat; a withdrawal route : 퇴각로를 차단하다 cut off [intercept] a retreat ─명령 an order to retreat; the retire ─선 a line of retreat

퇴거 退去 〈이전〉 leaving; quitting; 〈인도・철수〉 evacuation; withdrawal; 〈추방〉 deportation; 〈도망〉 an exodus (from a country)
◆ 퇴거를 명하다 order to leave (a place, a house); order sb out of a place [to quit a place]
─**퇴거하다** leave; depart; evacuate; withdraw [go away] (from a place); (美) move out
◆ 퇴거시키다 cause sb to withdraw (from)
■ ─명령 an order for departure; an expulsion order; an eviction [evacuation] order : 건물의 불법 점유자들은 퇴거 명령을 받았다 The illegal tenants [squatters] were ordered to leave the building. ─보상금 compensation for removal ─신고 a removal report

퇴고 推敲 〈글을 고침〉 polish; elaboration
─**퇴고하다** polish; elaborate (on); improve
◆ 퇴고한 글 an elaborate style / 퇴고할 여지가 있다 need more polishing; need to be improved
▶ 그는 거듭 논문을 퇴고했다 He worked hard to polish his thesis.

퇴골 腿骨 〈다리뼈〉 a leg [thigh] bone

퇴관 退官 retirement from office [the government service]
─**퇴관하다** retire from office; leave the government service ◆ 퇴관하여 연금생활을 하다 retire and be pensioned off

퇴군 退軍 retreat ⇨ 퇴각(退却)

퇴근 退勤 leaving one's office [desk, work]
◆ 퇴근길에 on one's way back [home] from the office ─**퇴근하다** come [go] home from work; leave the office ■ ─시간 the closing hour

퇴락 頹落 dilapidation ─**퇴락하다** dilapidate; fall [go] to ruin; collapse
◆ 퇴락한 성 a dilapidated castle / 퇴락한 broken and old

퇴로 退路 the path of retreat ◆ 적의 퇴로를 차단하다[끊다] intercept [cut off] the enemy's retreat

퇴맞다 退─ be rejected ⇨ 퇴박맞다

퇴물 退物 〈물려받은 물건〉 a hand-me-down; a used article; 〈퇴박맞은 물건〉 a thing rejected to accept
◆ 형의 퇴물을 받아 입다 wear hand-me-downs from one's brother

퇴박맞다 退─ be denied; be rejected [refused]; be turned down; meet with a refusal
◆ 면허 신청이 퇴박맞다 an application for a license is turned down
▶ 나의 제안은 퇴박맞았다 My proposal was turned down.

퇴박하다 退─ refuse; reject; deny; decline
▶ 그들은 그의 의견을 퇴박했다 They rejected [refused to adopt] his opinion.

퇴보 退步 retrogression; a step backward; a backward step; 〈퇴화〉 degeneration; deterioration
◆ 문명의 퇴보 the retrogression of civilization / 퇴보적인 retrogressive; backward
─**퇴보하다** go [move, fall] backward; slip back; retrocede; deteriorate
▶ 나의 계산 능력은 나이와 더불어 퇴보하고 있다 My computation(al) ability has declined with age.

퇴비 堆肥 compost; barnyard [farmyard] manure ◆ 퇴비를 만들다 compost (grass) / 땅에 퇴비를 주다 compost [manure] the land ■ ─더미 a compost heap [pile]

퇴사 退社 1 〈퇴직〉 retirement from a company ─**퇴사하다** retire from a company; leave a company
▶ 그는 일신상 사정으로 퇴사했다 He resigned for personal reasons.
2 〈퇴근〉 leaving one's office ─**퇴사하다** leave the office

퇴산 退散 dispersal; dismissal ─**퇴산하다** disperse; run away; flee; make off
◆ 퇴산시키다 disperse; break up (a mob); drive away

퇴색 退色 fading; faded color
─**퇴색하다** 〈색이 주어〉 go [come] off; fade

(away); 〈사물이 주어〉 lose color; discolor
♦퇴색하기 쉬운 색깔 a fugitive color / 퇴색한 옷 a faded [discolored] dress / 퇴색하지 않는 색깔 a fast [fadeless, standing] color
▶이 색은 빨아도 퇴색하지 않는다 This color will stand wash.
▶커튼은 햇빛 때문에 퇴색되어 있었다 The curtains were faded [discolored] by the sun (light).

퇴석 堆石 1 〈돌더미〉 a pile of stones 2 〔地質〕 a moraine

퇴석 退席 leaving one's seat —**퇴석하다** leave one's seat; retire; withdraw
♦급한 일로 퇴석하다 leave one's seat on urgent business

퇴세 頹勢 one's declining fortunes; a decline
♦퇴세를 만회하다 restore the declining fortunes 《of》
▶그들은 퇴세를 만회하려고 애썼다 They tried hard to reverse their declining fortunes [stop their slide from power].

퇴역 退役 retirement (from service) —**퇴역하다** retire (from service); leave office [the army]
♦퇴역시키다 decommission; put 《place》 (an officer) on the retired list; mothball 《a ship》
▶아버지는 60세에 퇴역하셨다 My father retired from service [left the army] at the age of sixty.
■—군인 (美) a veteran; (英) an ex-serviceman —장교 a retired officer —함(艦) a decommissioned battleship

퇴영 退嬰 retrogression; conservatism ♦퇴영적인 conservative; retrogressive —**퇴영하다** retrograde; retrogress

퇴원 退院 leaving (the) hospital
—**퇴원하다** leave (the) hospital; be discharged from (the) hospital
▶퇴원해도 좋다[하기에는 이르다] be [be not] well enough to leave (the) hospital
▶그 환자는 이번 주말까지는 퇴원하지 못할 것이다 The patient will not be discharged from (the) hospital until the end of this week.
▶그는 어제 퇴원했다 He left [got out of] (the) hospital yesterday.
■—환자 a discharged patient

퇴위 退位 (an) abdication —**퇴위하다** abdicate [step down from] 《the throne》 ♦퇴위시키다 depose; dethrone 《a king》

퇴일보하다 退一步— take a step backward; fall [draw] back
▶퇴일보해 보면 전체 상황을 더 잘 볼 수 있다 You can see the whole situation better if you step back a little.

퇴임 退任 resignation ⇨ 사임(辭任)

퇴장 退場 1 〈회의 등에서〉 leaving ♦퇴장을 명하다 order sb out of the room [hall]
—**퇴장하다** leave 《the place》; go away
▶투수는 퇴장당했다 The pitcher was thrown out of the game.
▶그들은 표결에 항의하여 퇴장했다 They walked out of [left] the meeting to show their opposition to the vote.
2 〔劇〕 〈한 사람의〉 exit; 〈두 사람 이상의〉 exeunt
♦샤일록 퇴장 〈희곡의 지시문〉 Exit Shylock
—**퇴장하다** make one's exit; leave the scene
■—총— a general walkout

퇴장 退藏 hoarding —**퇴장하다** hoard ♦창고에 수천권의 책을 퇴장하다 hoard thousands of books in the storehouse ■—물자 hoarded goods

퇴적 堆積 (an) accumulation; a pile; a heap; 〔地質〕 sedimentation —**퇴적하다** accumulate; pile [build] up
■—물 〔地質〕 sediment —암 〔地質〕 sedimentary rock

퇴조 退潮 the ebb [low] tide
♦퇴조시에 at low water [tide] / 퇴조를 보이다 be on the ebb
—**퇴조하다** ebb
▶경기가 퇴조하고 있다 The economy is in a downturn. ⇌ Business activity has slackened.
■—기(期) a period of ebb

퇴직 退職 retirement; resignation
—**퇴직하다** retire [withdraw] from office [the service]; be relieved of office; go out of office; go into retirement; (口) quit one's job
♦연금을 받고 퇴직하다 retire on a pension / 퇴직시키다 place sb on the retired list; retire sb / 연금을 주어 퇴직시키다 pension off sb
▶그는 60세에 그 회사를 퇴직했다 He retired from the company at (the age of) sixty.
■—공무원 a retired official —금 a retirement allowance [pay]; 〈해고시의〉 a severance pay; a discharge allowance —연금 a retirement annuity —연령 the retirement age —자 a retired employee; a retiree —적립금 a reserve fund for retirement allowance

퇴진 退陣 decampment; (비유) retirement; resignation
♦교육부장관의 퇴진을 요구하다 demand the resignation of the Minister of Education
▶아군은 퇴진이 불가피했다 Our army had to retreat.
—**퇴진하다** decamp; withdraw; (비유) retire 《from a position》; resign; exit; go out
♦곧 퇴진하는 수상 the outgoing premier

퇴짜 退— rejection; refusal; a turndown; a rebuff; a reject
♦퇴짜놓다 refuse (to accept); reject; deny; turn down; rebuff / 요구를 퇴짜놓다 reject [refuse] sb's demand / 퇴짜맞다 be rejected; be turned down
▶그의 제안은 여지없이 퇴짜맞았다 His proposal was turned down point-blank.
▶그녀는 돕겠다는 제의를 퇴짜놓았다 She rejected [declined] the offer of help.
▶그녀에게 데이트 신청을 했는데 그녀가 퇴짜를 놓았어 When I asked her for a date, she gave me the brush-off.

퇴치 退治 〈정복〉 subjugation; conquest; 〈박멸〉 eradication; elimination; extermination
—**퇴치하다** subdue; subjugate; suppress; wipe [stamp, root] out; clean up; eliminate; get rid of
♦괴물을 퇴치하다 slay [kill] a monster / 전염병을 퇴치하다 eradicate [stamp out] infec-

tious diseases
■문맹— a crusade against illiteracy
퇴침 退枕 a wooden pillow with drawers; a box pillow
퇴폐 頹廢 〈도덕·풍기 등의〉 corruption; degeneration; demoralization; decadence; 〈황폐〉 decay
♦도덕의 퇴폐 moral decadence; the corruption [decay] of morals / 퇴폐적(인) decadent; declining; corrupt / 퇴폐적 생활을 하다 lead a decadent [corrupt] life
—퇴폐하다 be corrupted [demoralized, degenerated]; decay; decline
♦퇴폐한 세대 the decadence [degeneration] of the age; the decadent world / 퇴폐한 corrupt(ed); degenerate(d)
■—기 a period of decadence —문학 decadent literature —영화 a decadent film —주의 decadence; decadentism —주의자 a decadent —풍조 decadent (and degenerating) trend : 퇴폐풍조 퇴치 운동 antidecadence drive
퇴하다 退— refuse to accept [receive]; reject; turn down; decline ♦뇌물을 퇴하다 refuse to accept a bribe; reject a bribe
퇴학 退學 〈학생 스스로의〉 leaving school; (a) withdrawal; 〈학교 당국의〉 expulsion from school —퇴학하다 leave school
♦가정 형편으로 퇴학하다 leave school for family reasons [owing to family circumstances] / 낙제하여 퇴학하다 flunk out of (a school) / 퇴학시키다 〈부모가〉 withdraw (a boy) from school; make (a boy) quit school; 〈학교가〉 dismiss [expel] (a student)
▶그는 열일곱살에 고교를 퇴학하였다 He left [(口) dropped out of] high school at seventeen.
▶그는 절도를 하여 퇴학당했다 He was expelled [dismissed] from school for stealing.
■—생 a school dropout —처분 expulsion of a student (from school)
퇴혼하다 退婚— break (off) [reject] engagement (with)
퇴화 退化 degeneration; degradation; retrogression; 〈기관 등의〉 atrophy
—퇴화하다 degenerate; degrade; retrograde
♦퇴화시키다 degrade; degenerate
▶근육은 사용하지 않으면 퇴화한다 Muscles, if not used, degenerate.
■—기관 〔生〕 ⇨ 흔적(~기관) —동물 a degenerate
툇마루 退— a narrow porch; a veranda (h)
투 套 1 〈버릇〉 a (peculiar) way; a manner; a habit ♦말투 one's way [manner] of speaking
▶이런 투로 써라 Write in this way [manner]. ⇌ Write like this.
2 〈법식〉 a form; a style
♦옛 투 an old style; a conventional form
투견 鬪犬 〈개싸움〉 a dogfight; 〈개〉 a fighting dog
투계 鬪鷄 〈닭싸움〉 cockfighting; 〈한번의〉 a cockfight; 〈싸움닭〉 a fighting cock ♦투계를 시키다 have [stage] a cockfighting match
■—장 a cockpit
투고 投稿 (a) contribution

▶투고 환영 All contributions are welcome.
—투고하다 contribute 《an article to a periodical》; write 《for》
▶그는 그 신문에 자주 투고한다 He is a frequent [regular] contributor to the newspaper. ⇌ He often contributes to [writes for] the newspaper.
■—규정 contribution rules [regulations] —란 the reader's column —자 a contributor
투과 透過 〈빛·소리 등의〉 penetration; transmission; 〈액체·공기 등의〉 permeation
—투과하다 penetrate; transmit; permeate
▶유리는 빛을 투과한다 Glass is pervious to [transmits] light.
▶방사능은 철판도 투과한다 Radioactivity can even penetrate an iron plate.
■—성 permeability; penetrability —율 transmissivity
투광기 投光器 a floodlight (projector)
투구 a helmet; a headpiece
♦투구끈 a helmet cord / 투구를 벗다 take one's helmet off / 투구를 쓰다 wear one's helmet
투구 投球 throwing a ball; a throw; 〔野〕 pitching; a pitch; hurling; delivery
♦왼손 투구 left-handed pitching
▶그의 투구에는 커브가 많다 His pitching is full of curves.
—투구하다 pitch; hurl; throw a ball; make a throw 《to second》 ♦잘 겨냥해 투구하다 make a well-aimed throw
—모션 a windup: 투구 모션을 취하다 wind up (for the first pitch)
투그리다 snarl [growl] at each other; say in an angry [bad-tempered] way
투기 投機 (a) speculation; a venture; an operation; gambling; stockjobbing
♦땅 투기 speculation in land / 투기적인 speculative; adventurous / 투기에 실패하다 fail in speculation / 투기에 손을 댔다가 큰 손해를 보다 lose heavily in speculation / 투기로 돈을 벌다[잃다] make [lose] money in speculation
▶투기가 성공[실패]했다 The speculation has turned out well [has failed, has gone wrong].
—투기하다 speculate 《in》; make a venture; gamble 《in stocks》; engage in speculation
♦주식[땅]에 투기하다 speculate in stocks [land]
■—꾼[업자] a speculator; 〈주식〉 a stockjobber —매매 speculative trading —매입 speculative buying [purchase]; buying on speculation —사업 a speculative business [enterprise]; a venture —시장 a speculative market —심 a speculative spirit [disposition] —열 a craze [mania] for speculation
투기 妬忌 jealousy; green envy
—투기하다 be jealous 《of》
▶아내는 내 비서를 몹시 투기하고 있다 My wife is extremely jealous of my secretary.
투기 鬪技 a competition; a contest ■—장 an arena; a ring
투덜거리다 grumble 《at, about》; complain 《of, about》; murmur (with discontent); nag at; (美俗) bitch; gripe

◆ 투덜거리는 사람 a grumbler / 대우가 나쁘다고 투덜거리다 complain of ill treatment
▶ 그는 혼자 투덜거리며 가버렸다 He went away muttering to himself.
▶ 투덜거리지 마라 Don't keep grumbling [complaining]. ⇌ (美) None of your gripes.
▶ 그는 무엇이 못마땅한지 밤낮 투덜거리기만 한다 I don't know what is biting him, but he keeps griping all the time.

투레질 《a suckling child》 blowing from the mouth ━투레질하다 blow from the mouth

투망 投網 a cast(ing) net ◆ 투망을 던지다 cast a net; throw a cast net ━투망하다 cast [throw] a net ◆ 투망하여 고기를 잡다 net fish

투매 投賣 dumping; a sacrifice (sale); 〈재고 정리〉 a clearance sale
━투매하다 dump; sell at a loss [sacrifice]; sell dog-cheap
◆ 의류를 시장에 투매하다 dump clothing on the market
■ ━출혈━ distress selling ■ ━가격 a bargain [sacrifice] price ━상품 distress merchandise; sacrifice goods

투명 透明 transparency; clarity
━투명하다 transparent; lucid; clear
◆ 투명한 물 clear water / 투명한 유리문 a transparent glass door / 반투명한 semitransparent / 불투명한 opaque / 무색 투명한 colorless and transparent 《liquid》 / 투명해지다 become transparent; clarify
■ ━도 (the degree of) transparency ━유리 plain (plate) glass ━체 [物] a transparent body

투묘 投錨 anchoring; an anchorage ◆ 항구에 투묘하다 be [lie] at anchor in the harbor
━투묘하다 anchor; cast [drop] anchor

투미하다 foolish; silly; dull; stupid; thickheaded

투박스럽다, 투박하다 〈물건이〉 unshapely; coarse; rough; crude; 〈사람이〉 unrefined; rustic; boorish; awkward
◆ 투박스러운 구두 unshapely shoes / 투박한 손 rough hands / 투박스러운 그릇 crudely made dishes / 투박한 성격 an unsophisticated [(口) unaffected] character / 투박한 솜씨 a clumsy hand / 투박한 천 coarse fabric
▶ 그들은 투박한 사람들이다 They are simple and good-natured people.

투베르쿨린 〔醫〕 tuberculin
◆ 투베르쿨린 검사를 받다 take a tuberculin test; be tuberculin-tested
▶ 나의 투베르쿨린 검사 결과는 양성[음성]으로 나타났다 My tuberculin test turned out to be positive [negative].
■ ━반응 a tuberculin reaction

투병 鬪病 a fight [struggle] against a disease
━투병하다 fight [struggle] against a disease
■ ━생활 one's life under medical treatment: 투병생활을 하다 live under medical treatment

투사 投射 projection; 〈입사〉 〔物〕 incidence
━투사하다 project 《on》
◆ 영상을 스크린에 투사하다 project an image on a screen
■ ━각 ⇨ 입사(入射)(~각) ━선 〈입사 광선〉 an incident ray ━영(影) ⇨ 투영(投影)

투사 透寫 tracing ━투사하다 trace (out) 《a writing, drawing》 ◆ 본[화면]을 투사하다 trace (out) a pattern [drawing] ■ ━지 tracing paper

투사 鬪士 a fighter; a champion
◆ 민주화 운동의 투사 a fighter for democratization / 자유의 투사 a champion of liberty / 노동조합의 투사들 the militants of the labor unions
■ 독립━ a leader of national independence movement 혁명━ a champion of revolution
■ ━형(型) 〔心〕 the athletic

투서 投書 〈익명의〉 an anonymous notice [letter]; 〈투고〉 a contribution; 〈신문의〉 a letter to the editor
◆ 경찰에 투서로 알리다 inform the police 《of a crime》 by sending an anonymous letter
▶ 투서 환영 Contributions are cordially invited.
━투서하다 contribute 《an article to...》; write (a letter) to 《the newspaper》
■ ━함 a suggestion [complaints] box

투석 投石 stone-throwing[-slinging]
━투석하다 cast [throw, hurl] a stone 《at》; stone 《at》 ◆ 기동대에 투석하다 throw [hurl] stones at the riot squad
■ ━기(器) a sling; a catapult

-투성이 covered with...; daubed (all over) with...; full of...
◆ 오식 투성이의 책 a book full of misprints / 피투성이의 bloodstained; bloody / 기름 투성이의 oil-[grease-]stained; oily / 먼지 투성이의 dust-covered; dusty / 땀투성이다 be all of [in] a sweat
▶ 그의 옷은 진흙 투성이가 되었다 His clothes got all covered with mud.
▶ 그의 얼굴은 피투성이었다 His face was all smeared with blood.
▶ 거리는 쓰레기 투성이었다 The streets were full of litter. ⇌ There were piles of litter on the street.
▶ 그녀는 상처 투성이었다 She was wounded all over.

투수 投手 〔野〕 a pitcher; a hurler; a moundsman
◆ 왼손잡이 투수 a left-handed pitcher; (口) a lefty; a southpaw (pitcher) / 투수와 포수 the battery / 속구 투수 a fastball pitcher / 투수를 보다 pitch; be a pitcher / 투수를 교대하다 change the pitcher
■ 구원━ a relief pitcher 선발(先發)━ the starting pitcher 승리[패전]━ a winning [losing] pitcher 주전━ a front-line pitcher ■ ━력 pitching strength ━전 a pitching [mound] duel; a 《tense》 pitchers' battle ━진 the pitching staff ━판(板) a pitcher's plate [box]; the mound

투숙 投宿 putting up [registering] 《at a hotel》 ━투숙하다 stay at [in] 《a hotel》; put up at 《a hotel》; lodge in 《a hotel》; check into 《a hotel》; register at 《a hotel》
◆ 함께 투숙하다 stay at the same hotel; 〈한방에〉 share a room 《with》

◆하룻밤 투숙하다 stop for the night ■―객 a guest (registered at hotel); a lodger

투시 透視 〈비치어 봄〉 seeing through; 〈꿰뚫어 봄〉 clairvoyance; second sight; 〈X선의〉 fluoroscopy; roentgenoscopy
◆X선에 의한 투시 X[x]-raying; an X[x]-ray examination ―투시하다 see through ―검사 fluoroscopy ―도 a perspective drawing ―도법 perspective; representation: 투시도법으로 그리다 draw in perspective ―력 clairvoyant power

투신 投身 **1** 〈자살행위〉―투신하다 plunge to death; drown *oneself*; 〈물에〉 throw *oneself* into the water [river]
▶그녀는 빌딩 옥상에서 투신했다 She killed herself [committed suicide] by jumping off the top of a building.
2 〈종사〉―투신하다 go into; enter upon; engage (*oneself*) in
◆실업계에 투신하다 go into business / 문단에 투신하다 make *one*'s debut in the world of letters
▶그는 혁명 집단에 투신했다 He joined a revolutionary group.
▶그녀는 여성 해방 운동에 투신했다 She devoted herself to the women's liberation movement.
■―자살 a death leap (from); committing suicide by jumping off [in]; suicide by drowning

투약 投藥 medication; prescription; dosage
◆과잉 투약 excessive dosing [medication]; overdosing ―투약하다 prescribe [administer] a (dose of) medicine
◆환자에게 투약하다 give [administer] medicine to a patient; prescribe for a patient

투어리스트 〈관광객〉 a tourist

투영 投影 **1** 〈그림자〉 a cast shadow
―투영하다 reflect; cast a reflection (on, in); throw an image on
2 〔數〕 projection ―투영하다 project
■―기 a projector ―도(圖) a projected figure ―면 a projected plane ―법 〔心〕 projective technique; the projective method ―화법 the method of projections

투옥 投獄 imprisonment
▶그는 투옥을 모면했다 He escaped imprisonment.
―투옥하다 throw *sb* into prison; put *sb* in prison [jail]; imprison; jail
◆투옥되다 be put in jail; be imprisoned; be jailed

투우 鬪牛 〈경기〉 bullfighting; a bullfight; 〈소〉 a fighting bull ◆투우를 시키다 have bulls fight (each other); fight a bull
■―사 a bullfighter; a matador ―장 a bullring

투원반 投圓盤 discus throw(ing); the discus
―투원반하다 throw a discus
■―선수 a discus thrower ―세계기록보유자 the world-record holder in the discus

투입 投入 〈던져 넣음〉 throwing [casting] in; injection; input; 〈투자〉 investment
―투입하다 throw [cast] into; order (troops) in; invest (money) in
◆투표함에 투표용지를 투입하다 deposit a ballot in the ballot box
▶그 나라는 그 전쟁에 5만의 병력을 투입했다 The nation committed 50,000 men to the battle.
▶그 회사는 공장과 설비에 다액의 돈을 투입했다 The company invested [sank] a lot of money into plant and equipment.
■―병력 committment ―자본 an investment

투자 投資 (an) investment
◆확실한 투자(물) a sound investment
▶네 교육은 장래에 대한 투자다 Your education is an investment in your future.
―투자하다 invest (in); make an investment (in); lay out 《*one*'s money in》
◆국채에 투자함 investment in national debts / 토지에 투자하다 invest *one*'s money in land
▶그는 새 사업에 대금을 투자했다 He invested heavily in the new project.
■―공공― public investment 민간― private investment 시설― investment in plant and equipment; equipment investment 주식― investment in stocks 총― gross investment 해외― overseas investment ―가 an investor ―계획 an investment program ―유인[동기] an investment incentive ―은행 an investment bank ―주식[채권, 증권] an investment stock [bond, security] ―회사 an investment company

투자신탁 投資信託 investment trust
■―회사 an investment trust company

투쟁 鬪爭 a fight; a struggle; a combat; (a) war; 〈운동〉 a campaign
◆투쟁적인 combative
―투쟁하다 fight; struggle
◆회사에 대하여 남녀 고용차별 철폐를 위해 투쟁하다 carry on a struggle with the company against sex descrimination in employment
■―계급― a class struggle [srtife, war] 권력― a power struggle; a struggle for power 무력― an armed struggle 임금인상― a fight for higher wages ■―방침 a struggle policy ―본능 fighting instinct ―심 a combative spirit ―위원회 a struggle [strike] committee ―의식 strike consciousness ―자금 struggle [strike] funds ―태세 a struggle setup ―파(사람) the militants

투전 投錢 chuck-farthing ⇨ 돈치기

투전 鬪錢 〈노름패〉 Korean playing cards; 〈놀이〉 a game of cards; 〈노름〉 gambling
◆투전 한벌 a pack [(美) deck] of cards
―투전하다 play cards; gamble
■―꾼 a cardplayer; a gambler

투정 complaining; grumbling.
◆음식 투정 grumbling over *one*'s food
―투정하다 fret; be fretful; be grouchy; grumble (at, over); complain (about, of); growl
◆과자를 사달라고 투정하다 clamor for candy / 투정하는 아이를 달래다 soothe a fretful child

투조 透彫 〔美術〕 openwork
◆투조의 openworked

투지 鬪志 combative [fighting] spirit; fight
♦투지가 없다 lack one's fight [fighting spirit] / 투지를 잃다 lose one's fight [fighting spirit] / 투지를 보이다 show fight
▶그는 아직도 투지 만만하다 He still has plenty of fight [fighting spirit] in him.

투창 投槍 〔競〕 the javelin (throw); 〈창〉 a javelin
▶그녀는 투창에서 80미터로 우승했다 She won the javelin with a throw of 80 meters.
━**투창하다** throw a javelin
━**선수** a javelin thrower

투척 投擲 throwing; a throw
━**투척하다** throw
♦수류탄을 투척하다 throw a hand grenade
━**경기** the distance throw

투철 透徹 penetration; lucidity; thoroughness
━**투철하다** clear; lucid; pure; thorough
♦투철한 민족주의자 a nationalist to the core / 투철한 책임감을 가진 사람 a person with a thoroughgoing sense of responsibility / 투철한 두뇌 clear brains; a clear head

투포환 投砲丸 〔競〕 the shot put ⇨ 포환(~던지기)
━**투포환하다** put a shot

투표 投票 〈결과〉 vote; suffrage; 〈투표하기〉 poll; ballot; voting; 〈한 표〉 a vote
♦투표를 실시하다 take [hold] a ballot / 투표를 마감하다 close polls / 투표를 매수하다 buy a vote / 법안을 투표에 붙이다 put a bill to the [a] vote / 투표로 결정하다 determine [decide] by ballot / 투표로 선출하다 elect by vote; vote by ballot / 제안을 투표로 부결하다 vote down the proposal
▶투표는 오전 6시부터다 Voting begins at 6 a.m.
▶투표결과는 찬성 15 반대 6이었다 The vote stood at fifteen ayes and six noes.
▶그 문제는 투표로 정해질 것이다 The matter will be decided by vote [ballot]. ⇌ A vote will be taken on [to decide] the matter.
▶그들은 투표로 회의를 연기했다 They voted to postpone the meeting. ⇌ They voted that the meeting [(英) should] be postponed.
━**투표하다** vote; ballot 《for》; cast a ballot; give one's vote [ballot]
♦민주당에 투표하다 vote Democratic / 투표하러 가다 go to the poll(s)
▶나는 김선생에게 투표했다 I gave my vote to Mr. Kim. ⇌ I voted (for) Mr. Kim. ⇌ My vote went to Mr. Kim.
▶나는 혁신 후보에게 투표할 작정이다 I intend to vote [cast my ballot] for the reform candidate.
━**결선**— a final [decisive] ballot; a showdown vote **결정**— a casting vote **국민**— a plebiscite; the referendum **기립**— a rising [standing] vote **기명**— an open vote; a singed ballot **단기**(單記)**[연기**(連記)**]**— a vote with single [plural] entry **대리**— voing by proxy **무기명[비밀]**— a secret vote; an unsigned vote **무효**— a spoiled vote **복식[단식]**— a plural [single] vote **부재자**— absentee voting **부정**— an illegal [unjust] ballot **불신임**— a vote of nonconfidence; a nonconfidence vote **신임**— a vote of confidence **1차**— the first ballot **지명**— a roll-call vote **직접**— a direct (popular) vote ■━**구** a polling district. ━**권** the (right to) vote; suffrage: 투표권이 없는 사람 a voteless person ━**기권자** a nonvoter ━**소[장]** a polling place [station]; (美) the polls ━**수** the number of votes ━**연령** voting age ━**용지** a ballot (paper); a voting slip ━**율** a turnout (of voters) ━**일** a voting [polling, election] day ━**자** a voter ━**참관인** a voting witness; a referee of voting ━**함** a ballot box

투피스 a two-piece dress [suit]

투하 投下 throwing down; dropping; 〈비행기에서〉 an airdrop (of supplies); 〈투자〉 investment
♦해외로의 자본투하 overseas capital investment
━**투하하다** throw down; drop; 〈비행기에서〉 airdrop; 〈투자하다〉 invest 《in》
♦수도에 폭탄을 투하하다 drop bombs on the capital city
■━**자본** invested capital ━**자본이익률** return on investment ━**탄[폭탄]** a dropped bomb; an aerial bomb

투하 投荷 〔海〕〈짐〉 jetsam; jettisoned cargo; 〈행위〉 jettison ━**투하하다** cast cargo overboard; jettison cargo

투함 投函 (美) mailing; (英) posting
━**투함하다** mail [(英) post] 《a letter》; drop 《a letter》 into a mailbox [(英) postbox]; put 《a letter》 in a mailbox

투항 投降 surrender
━**투항하다** surrender 《to》; lay down one's arms
♦적에게 투항하기를 권하다 urge [call on] the enemy to surrender
━**자** a surrenderer

투해머 投— 〔競〕 the hammer throw ⇨ 해머(~던지기) ━**투해머하다** throw a hammer

툭 with a snap ⇨ 톡

툭탁 tapping ⇨ 톡탁

툭탁거리다 tap at ⇨ 톡탁거리다

툭툭 with a pat ⇨ 톡톡

툭하면 (too) often; on [at] the slightest provocation; unexpectedly; ready to; always ⇨ 걸핏하면
♦툭하면 싸우다 pick a fight at the slightest provocation
▶그녀는 툭하면 운다 She will cry over nothing.
▶그는 툭하면 죽겠다고 한다 He constantly talks of dying.
▶그는 툭하면 화를 낸다 He flies into a rage.

툰드라 the tundra
▶툰드라 지대 the tundra area

툴륨 〔化〕 thulium

툴툴거리다 grumble 《at, over, about》; complain 《about》 ⇨ 투덜거리다

툽툽하다 thick ⇨ 톱톱하다

퉁¹ 〈질 낮은 놋쇠〉 inferior [low-quality] brass

퉁² 〈소리〉 with a boom; booming; ringing hollow
♦기타줄의 퉁하는 소리 the twang of a guitar

string / 북을 퉁 울리다 boom a drum; give a boom [beat] on a drum; bang (on) a drum
퉁겨지다 1 〈제자리에서〉 come off; get out of place; 〈뼈마디 등이〉 be dislocated; slip out of joint
▶ 책상 다리가 퉁겨졌다 The leg of a desk got disjointed.
▶ 그의 뼈마디가 퉁겨졌다 His joint came dislocated
2 〈숨겼던 것이〉 come [be] out; come to light; be revealed [exposed, disclosed]
퉁구스 a Tungus 《pl. ~ (es)》; a Tunguz 《pl. ~ (es)》
■—말 Tungus
퉁기다 1 〈버티어 놓은 것을〉 get (it) out of place; loosen (it); take (it) apart
2 〈악기를〉 pluck the strings; play with one's fingers
3 〈뼈 등을〉 put (it) out of joint; dislocate 《one's knee joint》
♦ 어깨의 관절을 퉁기다 put one's shoulder out
4 〈기회 등을〉 let (a chance) slip [missed]; miss 《an opportunity》
퉁명스럽다 blunt; brusque; curt; gruff; snappish; curt; unaffable
♦ 퉁명스럽게 bluntly; brusquely; curtly / 퉁명스럽게 대답하다 give a surly reply; reply brusquely [snappishly] / 퉁명스럽게 말하다 talk bluntly; be blunt of speech; speak stiffly
▶ 그는 누구에게나 퉁명스럽다 He is brusque with everyone.
퉁방울 a brass bell
■—눈 protruding eyes; pop-eyes —이 a lobster-eyed [pop-eyed] person
퉁소—簫 〈악기〉 a (six-holed) bamboo flute
♦ 퉁소를 불다 play the bamboo flute
퉁탕 〈구르는 소리〉 stampingly; pound; strikingly; 〈총소리〉 Bang, bang!
퉁탕거리다 1 〈두드리거나 밟다〉 pound; beat (loudly); tramp
♦ 계단을 퉁탕거리며 올라오다 come quickly upon the stairs with light steps / 복도를 퉁탕거리며 걷다 bounce along the passageway
2 〈총 소리가〉 keep banging away
▶ 총 소리가 퉁탕거린다 Guns are banging away.
퉁퉁 pounding ⇨ 통통
퉤 spitting
♦ 퉤퉤 spit-spit / 퉤하며 침을 마구 뱉다 spit all over the place
튀각 fried kelp [tangle]; flakes of fried tangle
튀기 a person [child] of mixed parentage; 〈잡종〉 a hybrid; a cross; a cross-breed
♦ 백인과 흑인의 튀기 a mulatto / 미국인과 아시아인의 튀기 an Amerasian (child) / 아메리칸 인디언과 백인의 튀기 a half-breed
▶ 그는 한국인과 프랑스인의 튀기다 He is half French and half Korean.
▶ 노새는 말과 나귀의 튀기다 A mule is a cross between a horse and an ass.
튀기다¹ 1 〈손가락으로〉 fillip; flip; snap; 〈주판알을〉 move 《counters》; 〈용수철 등을〉 spring
♦ 손가락으로 튀기다 flip sth away with one's finger / 기탓 줄을 튀기다 pluck (the strings of) a guitar
2 〈물 등을〉 splash; spatter; dabble; 〈침을〉 spit; sputter
♦ 책장에 잉크를 튀기다 splash a page with ink / 아무에게 흙탕물을 튀기다 splash sb with mud
▶ 나의 앞치마에 물이 튀겼다 My apron was splashed with water.
3 〈놀래서 달아나게 하다〉 start; rouse; scare away
♦ 토끼를 굴에서 튀기다 start a hare from its burrow
튀기다² 〈기름에〉 fry; deep fry; frizzle; 〈곡식을 불에〉 pop
♦ 기름에 튀기다 fry in oil / 새우를 기름에 튀기다 (deep) fry shrimps / 쌀[옥수수]을 튀기다 pop rice [corn]
튀김 〈음식〉 fried food; a fried dish; a fry
♦ 굴튀김 fried oysters / 튀김기름 frying oil / 튀김덮밥 a bowl of rice topped with fries
튀니지 Tunisie; 〈공식명〉 the Republic of Tunisie ♦ 튀니지의 Tunisian
■—사람 a Tunisian
튀다 1 〈공 등이〉 bound; rebound; bounce
▶ 이 공은 잘 튄다 This ball bounds well.
▶ 덫이 튄다 A trap springs.
2 〈불똥이〉 spark; sparkle; sputter; 〈장작 등이 타면서〉 snap; crack; crackle; 〈볶는 것이〉 burst [crack] open; pop open
▶ 밤이 불에 타면서 튀었다 The chestnuts cracked open in the fire.
3 〈물·침 등이〉 splash; spatter; get spattered; be splashed
▶ 흙탕물이 차의 앞유리까지 튀었다 The mud splashed up to the windshield.
4 〈달아나다〉 fly (away); run away; make off; take (to) flight
▶ 도둑은 창문으로 튀었다 The burglar ran away through the window.
튀밥 popped rice
튀어나오다 1 〈숨은 것 등이〉 spring out; jump [leap, bounce] out; rush out
♦ 거리로 튀어나오다 rush out into the street
2 〈돌출하다〉 protrude; jut (out)
▶ 못이 하나 벽에서 튀어나와 있다 There is a nail sticking out of the wall.
튀하다 ♦ 닭을 뜨거운 물에 튀하다 scald a chicken in hot water
튜너 〈라디오·텔레비전의〉 a tuner
튜바 〈악기〉 a tuba
튜브 a tube; 〈타이어 속의 고무관〉 an inner tube
♦ 튜브에 든 물감 tube colors / 튜브에서 그림물감을 짜내다 squeeze paint from a tube
튜턴 Teuton ♦ 튜턴의 Teutonic
■—말 Teutonic —족 the Teutons
튤립 〈植〉 a tulip
트다¹ 1 〈싹이〉 bud; sprout; shoot; spring up
2 〈피부가〉 chap; be [get] chapped; be cracked
♦ 튼 손 a chapped hand / 손이 트다 one's hands chap; 〈사람이 주어〉 get chapped hands / 피부가 트지 않게 하다 keep the skin from chapping

▶ 그녀의 피부는 겨울이면 튼다 Her skin chaps in winter.
3 ⇨ 동트다

트다² **1** 〈막힌 것을〉 break [slit] (it) open; cut; open
♦ 길을 트다 build [open] a road; cut a path / 아귀를 트다 make an opening; put in a slit / 두 방을 터서 한 방으로 만들다 throw two rooms into one
2 〈거래를〉 open; begin; initiate
♦ 거래를 트다 enter into a business relation with / 외상을 트다 open a charge account / 은행과 거래를 트다 open an account with [at] a bank

트라이앵글 〈악기〉 a triangle
트라코마 〔醫〕 trachoma
♦ 트라코마에 걸리다 suffer from trachoma
트래지코미디 a tragicomedy
트랙 a track ♦ 경주[자동차 레이스]용 트랙 a running [motor-racing] track
■ ―경기 track events [sports] ―경기 대회 track meet [meeting]
트랙터 a tractor
♦ 농업용 트랙터 a farm tractor
트랜스 a transformer ⇨ 변압(~기)
트랜지스터 〔物〕 a transistor ■ ―라디오[텔레비전] a transistor radio [televison]
트램펄린 〈체조 기구〉 a trampolin(e)
트랩 〈배의〉 a gangway (ladder); 〈美〉 an accommodation ladder; 〈비행기의〉 a ramp
♦ 트랩을 올라[내려]가다 go up [down] the ramp [gangway]
트러블 a trouble
♦ 트러블을 일으키다 cause trouble; make [stir up] trouble / 트러블에 휘말리다 get involved in trouble
트러스 〔土〕 a truss ■ ―교 a truss bridge
트러스트 〈독점적 기업합동〉 a trust ♦ 트러스트를 만들다[조직하다] organize a trust
■ ―금지법 an antitrust law [act]
트럭 a truck; an autotruck; 〈英〉 a (motor-)lorry
♦ 트럭 4대분의 화물 four truckloads of goods / 트럭으로 나르다 carry in a truck; transport by truck; truck
■ 소형― a pickup (truck) ■ ―수송 trucking; truck transport ―운전사 a truckdriver; 〈美〉 a truckman
트럼펫 〈악기〉 a trumpet ■ ―주자 a trumpeter
트럼프 (playing) cards
♦ 한 벌의 트럼프 〈美〉 a deck [pack] of cards / 트럼프의 으뜸패 a trump / 트럼프를 하다 play cards / 트럼프의 패를 떼다[도르다] cut [deal] the cards / 트럼프 놀이에서 따다 [잃다] win [lose] at cards
트렁크 **1** 〈가방〉 a trunk
2 〈자동차의〉 the trunk (compartment)
트레머리 swept-back hair with a chignon
트레몰로 〔樂〕 a tremolo 《*pl.* ~s》
트레바리 a perverse [weird] person; a habitual [regular] objector
트레이너 a trainer
트레이닝 training ■ ―하드― hard training

―셔츠 a sweat shirt ―캠프 a training camp ―팬츠 sweat pants
트레이싱페이퍼 tracing paper
트레일러 a trailer
■ ―버스 a trailer bus ―트럭 a trailer truck ―하우스 a (house) trailer
트렌치코트 a trench coat
트로이 〈소아시아의 옛 도시〉 Troy
♦ 트로이의 목마 the Trojan horse
■ ―전쟁 the Trojan War
트로이카 a troika
트로츠키 〈러시아의 혁명가, 정치가〉 Trotsky, Leon (1879-1940)
■ ―주의 Trotskyism ―주의자 a Trotskyist
트로피 a trophy
♦ 트로피를 타다 win a trophy
트롤 〈저인망〉 a trawl ■ ―망 a trawl; a trawl-net ―어업 trawling ―선 a trawlboat; a trawler
트롤리버스 a trolleybus
트롬본 〈악기〉 a trombone
■ ―주자 a trombonist
트롯 〈말의 속보〉 a trot; 〈사교 댄스〉 a (fox-)trot
♦ 트롯을 추다 fox-trot
트리니다드 〈서인도 제도의 섬〉 Trinidad
트리니다드토바고 〈나라 이름〉 Trinidad and Tobago; 〈공식명〉 the Republic of Trinidad and Tobago
트리밍 〈사진의〉 trimming; 〈의복의 장식〉 trimming(s) ♦ 레이스 트리밍이 있는 소매 a cuff with lace trimmings
―트리밍하다 trim
트리오 a trio 《*pl.* ~s》
♦ 트리오로 노래하다 sing in a trio
♦ 보컬― a vocal trio 현악― a string trio
트리코 〈프〉 〈직물〉 tricot ―재킷 a tricot jacket ―직조기 a tricot loom
트리코마이신 〔藥〕 trichomycin
트리플 triple
트릭 〈속임수〉 a trick; 〈영화 촬영의〉 a trick (work)
♦ 영화의 트릭 제작 the fabrication of faked pictures
▶ 그는 트릭에 정통으로 걸려들었다 He was completely taken in.
■ ―사진 a trick picture ―영화 a trick picture (film) ―촬영 a trick shot
트릴 〔樂〕 a trill ♦ 트릴로 노래하다 trill
트림 belching; a belch; (口) burp
―트림하다 belch; give a belch [burp]; (口) burp
트릿하다 〈가슴이〉 feel stuffed up; have congestion in the chest; 〈음식이〉 〈food〉 sit [lie] heavy; 〈사람이〉 dull; stupid; slow
트위스트 the twist ♦ 트위스트를 추다 twist; dance [do] the twist
트위드 〈직물〉 tweed ♦ 트위드 옷 tweeds
트윈베드 a twin bed
트이다 **1** 〈막힌 것이〉 get cleared; be open 〈길 등이〉 be cut; 〈운이〉 be in the ascendant
♦ 가슴속이 시원히 트이다 feel refreshed [relieved]
▶ 넓은 전망이 눈앞에 훤히 트였다 A broad

view opened out [spread out] before us.
▶ 두 도시간에 새 버스노선이 트였다 A new busline was opened between the two towns.
▶ 내 운이 트이기 시작했다 Luck is beginning to turn in my favor. ⇌ Luck is coming my way.
2 〈마음이〉 be open-minded; be liberal [generous]; 〈물정에 밝아지다〉 come to know much of the world
♦ 마음이 트인 사람 an open-minded person; a man [woman] of the world
▶ 그는 속이 트인 사람이다 He is an open-minded person.

트적지근하다 〈서술적〉 feel a tightness [be choked up] in the chest

트집 1 〈결점〉 a fault; a blemish; 〈까탈〉 a false charge
♦ 트집잡다 find fault 《with》; pick holes [flaws] 《in》; cavil at / 말 트집을 잡다 find fault with sb's remark / 사소한 일에도 트집을 잡다 trump up charges on the slightest pretext / 트집을 잡아 싸움을 걸다 pick a quarrel with sb; invent a pretext for a quarrel
▶ 그들은 트집을 잡아 나를 협박하려 했다 They tried to blackmail me on some pretext or other.
2 〈틈새〉 a crack; a fissure; a break
■ ―쟁이 a faultfinder; a caviler; a nag(ger)

특가 特價 a special [bargain] price; a specially reduced price
♦ 특가로 팔다 sell at a special [reduced, bargain] price / 정가의 60퍼센트 할인 특가로 사다 buy at the special price of sixty percent off the original price
■ ―본 a book reduced in price; a bargain-priced book ―제공 a special offer ―판매 ⇨ 특매 ―품 an article offered at a special price; a bargain(-priced) article [item]

특공 特功 a great achievement [performance]; distinguished services

특공대 特攻隊 a special attack unit; a suicide [commando] squad
▶ 그들은 인질들의 구출을 위해 특공대를 파견했다 They sent the commandos to rescue the hostages.

특과 特科 〈특수 과목〉 a special course [subject]; 〈군대의〉 an arm (of the army) other than infantry
■ ―병 a technical soldier

특권 特權 a privilege; a special [an exclusive] right; a prerogative
♦ 외교관의 특권 diplomatic privileges (and immunities) / 의회의 특권 the prerogatives of parliament / 특권이 있는[부여된] privileged / 특권을 주다 grant sb a privilege / 특권을 갖다 [누리다] possess a special right; hold [enjoy] a privilege / 특권을 행사[남용]하다 exercise [abuse] one's privilege
▶ 특권에는 항상 책임이 수반되어야 한다 Once you are given a privilege, you should always be prepared to accept the responsibility that goes with it.
■ ―계급[층] the privileged classes : 소수 특권 계급 a privileged minority [few] / 그는 특권 계급에 속한다 He belongs to [is a member of] the privileged classes. ―상실 lapse [loss] of privileges ―침해 breach of privilege

특근 特勤 〈시간외 근무〉 overtime work ―특근하다 work overtime
■ ―수당 overtime pay [allowance]

특급 特急 a limited [special] express
♦ 특급을 타다 take limited express

특급 特級 a special grade; the highest grade
■ ―포도주 the highest [best] quality wine ―품 a special grade article; the highest quality article [goods]

특기 特技 one's special ability [skill]; speciality

특기 特記 special mention ―특기하다 mention specially ♦ 특기할 만한 noteworthy; remarkable ▶ 이 사건은 특기할 만하다 This incident is worthy of special mention.

특대 特大 ♦ 특대의 outsize(d); extra large [big]; king-size(d) / 특대의 스커트 a queen-size(d) skirt ■ ―호 〈잡지 등의〉 a special enlarged issue [number]

특대 特待 (a) special treatment [attention]; distinction
♦ 특대를 받다 be treated with special attention ―특대하다 give a special treatment
■ ―생 ⇨ 장학생

특등 特等 the top grade
▶ 그는 추첨에서 특등을 뽑았다 He drew the top [special] prize in the lottery.
■ ―석 a special seat; 〈극장의〉 a box ―실 a special(-class) room ―품 an article of special quality; an A 1 [a deluxe] article

특례 特例 a special case; 〈예외〉 an exception
▶ 우리는 어떤 특례도 인정하지 않는다 We make [grant] no exceptions.
■ 전시― a wartime exception ■ ―법 a (special) exception law

특매 特賣 (a) special sale; sale at a special price
♦ 특매 가격으로 사다 buy at a special [bargain] price
―특매하다 sell at a special price
▶ 저 가게는 이번 주에 카메라를 특매한다 That store has a special sale on cameras this week.
▶ 특매한 물품의 교환은 안됩니다 Goods bought at the sales [《美》on sale] cannot be exchanged.
■ ―기간 the period for special sale ―일 a special bargain day ―장 a bargain counter ―품 articles for special sale

특면 特免 (an) amnesty ⇨ 특사(特赦)

특명 特命 a special order; a personal order; 〔軍〕 a mission
♦ 특명의 extraordinary / 특명을 띠고 on a special mission
―특명하다 give a special order
―전권 대사 an ambassador extraordinary and plenipotentiary

특무 特務 special duty [service]
■ ―공작원 a secret agent ―기관 the Special Service Agency; the secret (military) agency

특배 特配 special distribution; a special [an extra] ration ―특배하다 distribute specially

특별 特別 being special —**특별하다** special; especial; particular; peculiar; extraordinary; extra

> 解說 *special*은 「특수한, 특정의」라는 의미고 *especial*은 「유별난」이란 뜻인데 구어에서는 special이 이 뜻으로도 쓰인다. *particular*는 general의 반대어로서 special 보다도 개별성·특수성을 더욱 강조한다.

♦우리와 특별한 관계가 있는 사람들 those with whom we have a special connection / 특별한 이유 없이 for no particular reason / 특별한 배려로 by special grace / 특별한 사례를 인용하다 cite specific cases
▶그는 특별하다 He's an exception.
▶백합의 향기에는 뭔가 특별한 것이 있다 There's something special about the lily's fragrance.
■—계약 a specialty [special] contract —공채 [세, 지출, 가봉] a special loan [tax, grant, additional salary] —국회 a special session of the Assembly —규정 an express provision —기 a special plane —기금 a special fund —기획물 a (magazine) feature —대우 a special treatment —명령 (軍) special orders —배당 an extra [a special] dividend —법 a special law —보조금 a special grant —보좌관〈대통령〉 President's Special Adviser; Special Adviser (to the President) —상여금 a special bonus —석 a reserved [special] seat; a box —세 a special tax —수당 a special [an extra] allowance —시 a special municipality [city] —열차 a special train —예산 a special [an extraordinary] budget —요금〈할증의〉 an extra fee;〈할인의〉a specially reduced fee —위원 an extraordinary member of a committee —위원회 an ad hoc committee; a special committee —인출권 Special Drawing Rights (略 SDR) —전보 a special telegram —조치 special [emergency] measures —주문 a special order —프로그램 a special program —호 a special [an extra] number [issue, edition] —회계 special accounts —회원 a special member —훈련 special training

특별검사 特別檢事 an independent special prosecutor

특별임용 特別任用 special appointment
♦총영사로 특별 임용되다 be specially appointed Consul General

특별히 特別— specially; especially; particularly; in particular

> 解說 원칙적으로 *specially*는 「특정 목적을 위하여, 특별한 방법으로」란 뜻이다. *especially*는 「대단히, 그 중에서도」란 뜻으로 쓰이는데 especially 대신에 specially가 쓰이는 일도 흔히 있다. 또 especially는 딱딱한 문제에서 많이 쓰이며 특히 전치사나 접속사 앞에서 잘 쓰인다.

♦특별히 그날에 한하여 on that particular day / 특별히 주의하다 pay special attention 《to》; exercise special care
▶오늘은 특별히 안개가 짙다 It is especially foggy today.
▶내가 특별히 누구를 지칭하고 있는 것은 아니다 I am not referring [alluding] to anyone in particular.

특보 特報 a special report; special news; a (news) flash —**특보하다** flash the news; give a special report《on》
▶내각 총사직이 특보되었다 There was a news flash announcing that the Cabinet had resigned.
■뉴스— a news flash [bulletin]

특사 特使 a special envoy [messenger]
♦특사를 파견하다 dispatch a special envoy
▶정부는 미국에 그를 특사로 파견했다 The government dispatched [sent] him to the United States as its special envoy.
■대통령— a presidential envoy

특사 特赦 (an) amnesty; a particular [special] pardon ♦특사로 출감하다 be released from prison under an amnesty
—**특사하다** grant [give] an amnesty [a special pardon]《to》
■—령 an act of grace [amnesty]

특사 特賜 a special grant —**특사하다** give as a special grant; grant specially

특산 特産 a (local) specialty; a well-known [special] product ♦이 지방의 특산 the principal products of this district
▶제주도의 특산은 무엇입니까? What's the specialty of Chejudo?
■—물[품] a local product; a specialty —종 an endemic species (▶단수·복수 동형) —지 special production localities

특상 特上 ♦특상의 the finest [choicest, best]; superb; superfine ■—품 a choice article [item]; an extra superior one

특상 特賞 a special prize
▶김선생이 특상을 받았다 The special prize went to Mr. Kim. ⇌ Mr. Kim was awarded the special prize.

특색 特色 a specific character; a characteristic; a (specific) feature; a peculiarity; a distinction
♦특색 있는 special; characteristic; peculiar; distinctive; distinguishing / 특색 없는 indistinctive; featureless; common / 특색을 발휘하다 display *one's* characteristic feature / 특색 짓다 characterize; mark; distinguish
▶독일어의 특색은 긴 복합어를 만든다는 데 있다 The formation of long compound words is a marked characteristic of the German language.
▶이 지역의 지리적인 특색은 산이 많다는 점이다 As a geographical feature of this region, we can mention that it is mountainous.
▶이 마을에는 이렇다할 특색이 없다 This town has no special characteristics worthy of mention.
▶이것이 서양 문명의 한 특색이다 This is one of the characteristics [features] of Western civilization.
▶끈기가 이 민족의 특색이다 Perseverance marks this nation.

특선 特選 special selection [choice] ◆특선이 되다 be specially selected
▶그녀의 그림이 전람회에서 특선이 되었다 Her picture won the highest honors [was specially selected] at the exhibition.
■―品 a choice [deluxe] article

특설 特設 special establishment [installment]
―특설하다 set up [establish, install] specially
▶이 회의를 위해 구내에 우체국이 특설되었다 A special post office was opened on the premises to serve this congress.
■―도로 an accommodation road ―링 a specially prepared ring ―전화 a specially installed telephone ―학급 a special class

특성 特性 a characteristic; a special [distinctive] quality; a specificity; a peculiarity; a (peculiar) property; a feature; 〈個性〉 a trait of character
◆개인적[국민적] 특성 individual [national] peculiarities / 이 약의 특성 the peculiar properties of this drug / 특성을 갖추다 possess the characteristics (of) / 특성을 발휘하다 show a special quality / 특성을 살리다 make the most of 《its》 characteristics
▶디자이너는 이 소재의 특성을 충분히 살리고 있다 The designer has made the best use of the quality of this material.
▶전성(展性)은 모든 금속의 특성이다 Malleability characterizes [is characteristic of] all metals.

특수 特殊 ―특수하다 special; particular; peculiar; characteristic; specific; distinct; distinguishing; unique
◆특수한 목적 a particular object / 특수한 원인 a specific cause / 특수한 재능 an unusual talent / 특수한 경험을 하다 have a unique experience / 특수한 위치를 차지하다 hold a unique position
■―강(鋼) special steel ―교육 special education ―법인 a corporation [juridical person] having a special status ―병기 a super [special] weapon ―부대 《軍》 special forces ―사정 special circumstances ―성 peculiarity; speciality; special characteristics ―은행 a special [chartered] bank ―층[계급] a privileged class ―학급 special classes (for the education of physically or mentally handicapped children) ―화(化) specialization ―효과 〈영화·텔레비전의〉 special effect(s)

특수취급 特殊取扱 special treatment [handling] ◆특수취급을 하다 make discrimination in sb's favor; give sb special treatment
■―우편 mail for special handling

특약 特約 a special contract [agreement]
◆AP 특약 under a special contract with the AP
―특약하다 make a special contract [agreement] 《with》
■―사항 〈보험 등의〉 a clause containing special policy conditions ―점 a special agent; a chain store

특용 特用 (a) special use ―특용하다 use specially; use sth for a special purpose ■―작물 a crop for a special use; a cash crop

특유 特有 ◆특유의 characteristic 《of》; special 《to》; peculiar [proper] 《to》 / 한국 특유의 미술 Korea's characteristic arts / 이 지방 특유의 풍습 customs peculiar to this district
▶동물마다 그 동물 특유의 본능이 있다 Every animal has its proper instinct.
▶이 문체는 그사람 특유의 것이다 This style is peculiarly his own.
―특유하다 characteristic 《of》; unique; specific; peculiar 《to》

특이 特異 ―특이하다 unique; singular; peculiar
◆특이한 현상 a unique [singular] phenomenon / 특이한 재능의 소유자 a person of unique talent
▶이것은 특이한 경우다 This is a peculiar case. ⇒ This case is out of the ordinary.
―성 a singularity; a peculiarity; specificity
―체질 an allergy 《to》: 그는 돼지고기에 대해서는 특이체질이다 He is allergic [has an allegy] to pork.

특작 特作 a special production [work]; 〈영화의〉 a special film; a feature film ■―초― a super production; 〈영화의〉 a super picture

특장 特長 a strong [good] point; a merit

특전 特典 a special favor; a benefit; 〈특권〉 a privilege
◆회원의 특전 advantages of the members 《of》 / 도서관 자유출입의 특전 the privilege of free use of the library / 특전을 주다 grant a special favor [privilege]; privilege
▶이 보험에는 대단한 특전이 있다 This policy has a lot of wonderful benefits.

특전 特電 a special telegram; a telegraphic dispatch ◆CNN특전 CNN's special (service)

특점 特點 a characteristic ⇨ 특징(特徵)

특정 特定 ◆특정의 specific; specified; special; particular
―특정하다 specify; identify; pin sth down
▶현상태로는 범인을 특정하기 곤란하다 It is difficult to determine the offender under these circumstances.
■―계약 a specified contract ―물 a specific thing ―범죄가중처벌법 the Additional Punishment Law on Specific Crimes ―요금 a specified fare [rate] ―인 a specified person

특제 特製 special make [manufacture]
◆특제의 specially made [manufactured]; of special make; 〈제본의〉 specially bound
■―본 a book in a special [an extra] binding; a specially bound book ―품 specially made goods; special goods; an extra fine article

특종 特種 〈종류〉 a special kind [type]; 〈보도의〉 exclusive news; an exclusive (story); a scoop
◆특종을 잡다 get a scoop; scoop / 특종을 내다 [신다] publish an exclusive (on) / 특종으로 경쟁사를 따돌리다 scoop [get a scoop on] rival papers

특지 特志 1 〈특별한 뜻〉 special intention; special interest 2 ⇨ 특지가

특지가 特志家 a volunteer; a person interested

특진 特進 a special promotion of rank

♦2계급 특진 a double promotion of rank; promotion by two ranks

특질 特質 a characteristic; a specific character; a distinctive quality ♦고딕 건축의 특질 the characteristics of gothic architecture

특집 特輯 a special edition ♦특집을 만들다 prepare a special number; make up a special edition / 올림픽 특집을 내다 publish a special issue on the Olympic Games ▶이 잡지는 정계의 뇌물 사건을 특집으로 삼고 있다 This magazine features payoff scandals in political circles. ■—기사 a special feature article; a cover story; (美) a feature story —부록 a (special) supplement —호 a special number [issue]: 신년 특집호 a January number 《of a magazine》 with New Year features / 임시 특집호 an extra special issue

특징 特徵 a characteristic; a (special [distinctive]) feature; 〈인상 등의〉 identifying marks; a peculiarity; 〈개인의〉 a trait of character; a peculiarity; a quality ♦이 사전의 특징 the characteristics of this dictionary / 한국 지형의 뚜렷한 특징 the notable geographic features of Korea / 특징 있는 얼굴 a face with a distinctive [noticeable] feature / 특징적인 characteristic; distinctive; typical / 특징 없는 featureless; characterless / 특징짓다 characterize; distinguish; mark / …의 특징을 나타내다 be characteristic of; characterize; mark ▶그녀의 웃음은 특징이 있다 She has a peculiar manner [way] of laughing. ▶긴 코가 코끼리의 특징이다 The long nose is a peculiarity of the elephant. ▶이것은 멕시코 날씨의 가장 두드러진 특징의 하나다 This is one of the most remarkable features of the weather in Mexico.

특채 特採 special appointment [employment] —특채하다 employ specially

특청 特請 (a) special [urgent] request —특청하다 make a special request 《to sb》

특출 特出 prominence; distinction —특출하다 far better; outstanding; excellent; prominent; distinguished; striking; remarkable ♦특출한 수학자 a prominent mathematician / 역사상의 특출한 인물 a great [an outstanding] figure in history ▶그는 전교에서 성적이 특출하게 좋다 He is by far the best student in the whole school.

특칭 特稱 special designation; a special name —특칭하다 give a special name; designate in particular

특파 特派 dispatch —특파하다 dispatch [send] (specially) ♦사원을 런던으로 특파하다 dispatch [send] an employee to London for special purposes ■—대사 an ambassador extraordinary —사절 a special envoy [mission]

특파원 特派員 1 〈특별히 파견된 사람〉 a special envoy; a representative **2** 〈신문사의〉 a special correspondent ♦본지의 뉴욕 특파원에 의하면 according to our correspondent (stationed) in New York

특품 特品 an article of special quality; the best [top-quality] item [article]

특필 特筆 special mention —특필하다 mention [write] specially; make special mention of ♦대서 특필하다 write in large letters; single sth out for special mention ▶이것은 특필할 만한 사건이다 This is an incident worthy of special mention. ▶오늘은 나의 생애에서 대서 특필할 만한 날이다 Today's a very important day in my life. ▶그녀의 헌신적인 봉사는 특필할 만하다 Her self-sacrificing service deserves special mention.

특허 特許 1 〈특별 허가〉 a special permission [license] —특허하다 license 《sb to do》; grant sb a special permission **2** 〈정부가 허가하는〉 a charter; a concession —특허하다 charter **3** 〈발명 등의〉 a patent ♦특허를 얻다 obtain [get] a patent 《for, on》; have sth patented / 특허를 출원하다 apply for [file] a patent / 특허를 가지고 있다 hold a patent ▶특허를 출원 중 Patent pending. —특허하다 patent ♦특허된 기계 a patent machine ■—공보 a patent journal [gazette] —료 〈신청료〉 a patent fee; 〈사용료〉 a royalty —법 (法) the Patent Act —변리사 a patent agent —사무소 a patent attorney's office —심판[심사] patent judgment [examination] —장 a charter; a special license —증 letters patent [overt] —청 the Industrial Property Administration; the Patent Office —출원 a patent application —출원인 an applicant for a patent —품 a patented article; a patent

특허권 特許權 a patent right; the right to a patent ♦특허권을 가진 patent / 특허권을 침해하다 infringe (on) a patent right ■—사용료 (a) royalty —자 a patentee —침해 a patent infringement

특혜 特惠 a special favor; preference ♦특혜의 preferential; privileged / 특혜를 주다 [받다] extend [accept] a preference ■—관세 preferential duties —금융 preferential financing —대우 preferential treatment —융자 a privileged [preferential] loan —주의 favoritism; preferentialism

특효 特效 (a) special [miraculous] virtue [efficacy] 《for》 ♦특효가 있다 be specially good [efficacious] 《for》 ■—약 a specific (medicine) 《against》; a specific remedy 《for》; a miracle [wonder] drug: 두통의 특효약 a remedy that works wonders for headaches

특히 特— especially; specially; expressly; particularly; in particular; specifically; 〈무엇보다도〉 above all; before everything else ♦특히 중대한 일 a matter of special importance; an especially important matter / 특히 주의하다 pay special [particular] attention 《to》 ▶나는 쇼핑을 특히 좋아한다 I like shopping in particular.

튼실하다

▶이 책은 특히 젊은 독자를 위해서 쓰여졌다 This book was written especially [specially, particularly] for young readers.
▶그의 기여를 특히 언급해야 한다 Special mention should be made of his contribution.
▶나는 꽃을 좋아하는데, 특히 붉은 꽃을 좋아한다 I like flowers, especially red ones.

튼실하다 〈튼튼하고 실하다〉 strong and firm; solid; strong and healthy; sturdy

튼튼하다 〈견고하다〉 strong; strongly-built; firm; 〈건강하다〉 strong (and healthy); tough; sturdy; robust; healthy
♦튼튼한 철문 a solid iron gate / 든든한 집 a strongly-built house / 튼튼한 체질 a strong constitution / 튼튼한 기초 a strong [firm, sound] foundation / 튼튼한 자본 substantial capital / 튼튼한 회사 a sound [solid] business firm / 튼튼히[하게] strongly; stoutly; sturdily; firmly; solidly / 튼튼하게 하다 strengthen; make firm [solid]; solidify / 국방을 튼튼히 하다 strengthen the national defense / 튼튼해지다 become healthy; grow strong / 몸을 튼튼히 하다 improve [build up] *one's* health
▶나는 내 아들이 건전한 마음과 튼튼한 몸을 지니기를 바란다 I would like my son to be sound in mind and strong in body.
▶이 양말은 특히 뒤꿈치가 튼튼합니다 These socks are reinforced at the heels.

틀 1 〈테〉 a frame; (a) framework
♦사진틀 the frame of a picture; an embroidery frame; a picture frame / 자수틀 a tambour / 창틀 a window frame / 틀에 끼우다 frame (a picture); set [put] (a picture) in (a) frame
2 〈주형(鑄型)〉 a mold; a matrix; a cast
♦틀을 뜨다 make a model of / 납을 틀에 부어 넣다 pour lead into a mold / 이의 틀을 뜨다 make [take] an impression of *sb's* teeth
3 〈형태〉 a (definite) shape [form]
♦틀을 잡다 get *sth* into shape; give shape to *sth* / 틀이 잡히다 take shape; take a concrete [definite] form; materialize
4 〈형식〉 formality; a formula (*pl.* -lae, ~s); 〈모형〉 a model; pattern
♦틀에 박힌 생각 a stereotyped way of thinking / 틀에 박힌 stereotyped; conventional / 틀에 박히지 않은 unconventional; (口) offbeat; free / 틀에 박히다 harden into a set formula; be conventional
5 〈기계·기구〉 a machine; a device; an instrument ♦솜틀 a cotton gin; a (saw) gin; a willow (machine) / 재봉틀 a sewing machine / 형틀 an instrument of torture
6 〈인간의〉 caliber; capacity ♦틀이 큰[작은] 사람 a broad-minded [narrow-minded] man; a man of great [small] caliber

틀거지 a figure; an imposing manner [appearance]; a commanding presence ♦틀거지가 있다 be dignified / 틀거지가 없다 lack dignity

틀국수 machine-processed noodles

틀누비 machine-quilting

틀다 1 〈비틀다〉 twist; wrench; wring
♦팔을 틀다 wrench [twist] *sb's* arm
2 〈돌리다·작동시키다〉 turn; wind

♦라디오를 틀다 turn on the radio / 핸들을 오른쪽으로 틀다 turn a handle to the right / 병마개를 틀어 열다 screw the top off the bottle / 수도 꼭지를 틀다 turn the tap on
3 〈일 등을〉 thwart; counteract; work against ♦계획을 틀다 thwart [counteract] *sb's* plan
4 〈솜을〉 gin (out) [willow] 《cotton》
5 〈머리털을〉 tie [do] up 《*one's* hair》; dress ♦상투를 틀다 do *one's* hair up into a topknot

틀리다¹ 1 〈비틀리다〉 get twisted [wrenched]; grow warped
♦그의 마음은 틀려 있다 He has a twisted [warped] mind.
2 〈돌아가다〉 get turned [wound]; wind; turn ♦나사가 틀리다 a screw turns
3 〈솜이〉 get ginned [willowed]
4 〈머리털이〉 be done up; tie
♦상투가 잘 틀리지 않다 a topknot won't tie properly

틀리다² 1 〈잘못되다〉 be mistaken (in); be in the wrong; become wrong [erroneous, incorrect]; 〈잘못하다〉 mistake; make a mistake [an error]; do wrong
♦계산을 틀리다 make an error in calculation; miscalculate / 틀린 답을 하다 give a wrong [an incorrect, a false] answer / 틀리지 않다 be right [correct] / 틀리지 않도록 주의하다 guard against error; be cautious to prevent mistakes
▶그 답은 틀렸다 The answer is wrong [not right].
▶편지의 주소가 틀렸다 The letter was wrongly addressed.
▶틀린 곳이 있으면 고쳐라 Correct errors, if any.
2 〈나쁘다〉 be wrong [bad, evil]
♦틀린 생각 an evil intention; a wicked idea / 틀린 짓 an evil deed; a misdeed; a wrong; evildoing
3 〈끝장나다〉 be done for
▶그는 이제 다 틀렸다 He's done for now. ⇒ It's all up with him now.
▶일은 다 틀렸다 There's no help for it. ⇒ Nothing can be done about it.
▶그것 때문에 내 계획이 다 틀렸다 That upset all my plan.
4 〈심사가〉 become crooked [perverse, distorted] ♦심사가 틀리다 have a perverse mind; be in a crooked temper
5 〈불화하다〉 ⇨ 틀어지다 2

틀림 〈잘못〉 a mistake; an error; a fault; a discrepancy; incorrectness
♦틀림이 없는 correct; (all) right; sure; certain; trustworthy / 틀림이 없도록 to prevent mistakes / 내 관찰에 틀림이 없다면 unless I have erred in observation
▶그의 판단에는 틀림이 없다 He is infallible [unerring] in his judgment.
▶계산에는 하나도 틀림이 없었다 There were no mistakes [was not a single error] in the calculation.

틀림없다 〈잘못없다〉 correct; exact; (all) right; 〈확실하다〉 sure; certain; unfailing; infallible; 〈믿을 만하다〉 trustworthy

♦틀림없는 계산 a correct calculation / 틀림없는 사람 a reliable [trustworthy] person / 틀림없는 사실 a plain [an indisputable] fact
▶그것은 틀림없는 사실이다 It's a plain fact. ⇒ It is only too true.
▶내 기억이 틀림없다면, 그녀는 그 모임에 왔었다 If I remember right [rightly, correctly], she was present at the meeting.
▶그의 당선은 틀림없다 It is certain [sure] that he will win the election. ⇒ He will surely [is sure to] win the election.
▶그는 변호사임에 틀림없다 I'm sure he is [He must be] a lawyer.
▶그의 판단에 맡겨두면 틀림없을 거야 It may safely be left to his judgment.

틀림없이 〈어김없이〉 surely; certainly; without fail; unfailingly; 〈정확히〉 correctly; rightly
♦틀림없이…하다 do not fail [forget] to do / 일을 틀림없이 하다 do a job without fail
▶그녀는 틀림없이 올 것이다 She will surely [certainly] come. ⇒ She is sure [certain] to come. ⇒ I'm sure [certain] (that) she will come. ⇒ It is certain (that) she will come. ⇒ She won't fail to come.
▶틀림없이 도중에서 그에게 무슨 일이 일어난 모양이다 Something must have happened to him on his way.
▶틀림없이 그를 초청한 거지? You did invite him, didn't you?
▶틀림없이 내 눈으로 직접 보았다 I saw it with my own eyes.
▶나중에 틀림없이 와주시오 Be sure to come later. ⇒ Don't [Never] fail to come later. ⇒ Come later without fail.
▶틀림없이 알려주시오 Don't fail [Be sure] to let me know about it.

틀스럽다 imposing; dignified; commanding
틀어넣다 cram; stuff; squeeze (into); jam; crowd (into)
♦옷가방에 옷을 틀어넣다 cram *one's* clothes into a suitcase / 구멍에 종이를 틀어넣다 stuff a hole with paper; stuff paper in a hole
틀어막다 1 〈구멍을〉 stop (up); fill (up); stuff (up); plug (up); block
♦구멍을 틀어막다 stop [block] up a hole; fill [stop] a hole / 솜으로 귀를 틀어막다 stuff [fill] *one's* ears with cotton / 구멍을 흙으로 틀어막다 fill [plug up] a hole with earth / 병을 병마개로 틀어막다 stop a bottle with a cork
2 〈억제하다〉 stop; curb; put a stopper [gag] on ♦입을 틀어막다 stop *sb's* mouth; put a gag on *sb* / 돈을 주어 입을 틀어막다 buy *sb's* silence
틀어박다 1 ⇨ 틀어넣다
2 〈오래 두다〉 hoard; keep in long storage
틀어박히다 confine *oneself* to [in]; shut *oneself* up; seclude *oneself*; remain [keep] indoors
♦온종일 방안에 틀어박히다 keep (in) *one's* room all day long / 방을 걸어 잠그고 틀어박히다 lock *oneself* up in a room
▶집에만 틀어박혀 있지 말고 밖으로 나가라 You shouldn't shut yourself up in house. Go outdoors.

틀어지다 1 〈빗나가다〉 deviate; turn aside [away]; swerve; go wild [astray]
♦(이야기가) 옆길로 틀어지다 wander [digress] from the subject / 표적에서 틀어지다 go wide of the mark
▶우리의 기대가 틀어졌다 It fell short of our expectations.
2 〈불화하다〉 break 《with》; quarrel [fall out] 《with》; be estranged [alienated] 《from》
▶두 사람은 서로 틀어져 말도 하지 않는다 The two have fallen out with each other and aren't on speaking terms.
▶그것 때문에 식구들끼리 틀어졌다 That led to bad feelings between the members of the family.
3 〈어그러지다〉 go wrong [amiss]; break down; fail
♦일이 틀어지다 a plan goes wrong [fails] / 교섭이 틀어지다 negotiations break down / 다 틀어지다 end in failure; end up in a failure [fiasco]
▶우리가 하는 일이 모두 틀어졌다 Everything went wrong with us.
▶그의 실수로 우리 계획이 온통 틀어졌다 His blunder upset all our plans.
4 〈꼬이다〉 get [be] twisted; be distorted; go [be] awry ♦넥타이가 틀어지다 have *one's* tie twisted

틀지다 be imposing; be dignified; have dignity
틀톱 a frame saw; a pit saw
틈 1 〈갈라진〉 a gap; an opening; a crack; a crevice; a cleft; an aperture

> 解說 *gap*은 「막을 필요가 있는 틈」, *opening*은 「본래 닫혀 있어야 하는 것이 열려져 있는 것」, *crack*은 「살짝 갈라진 금」.

♦벽의 틈 a crevice in the wall / 문틈 an opening left by a door ajar; a chink in the door / 들여다 보는 구멍 a peephole / 문틈으로 들여다보다 peep in through a chink [crack] in the door / 틈을 막다[메우다] stop [fill] up a crevice; stuff *sth* into a crevice; chink / 틈이 나다 open; get a crack (in)
2 〈공간〉 space; room
▶내가 끼어들 틈도 없었다 I had no room to step [stand] in.
▶책상 하나 더 들어갈 틈이 있겠니? Is there room for one more desk?
3 〈불화〉 (a) discord; a split; an estrangement
♦틈이 생기다 be estranged [alienated] 《from》; fall out with 《each other》 / 틈이 생기게 하다 estrange 《them》; cause an estrangement [a rift] 《between》
▶왜 그들은 틈이 벌어졌니? What has come between them? ⇒ What has estranged them from each other?
4 〈여가〉 spare [leisure] time; time to spare; 〈기회〉 a chance; an opportunity
♦틈만 있으면 at all spare moments / 틈만 있으면…하다 take every opportunity to 《do》/ 틈이 나다 be disengaged; be at leisure; be

free / 틈이 없다 have no time to spare; be (too) busy / 틈이 있을 때 하다 do *sth* at *one's* leisure / 틈을 내다 make time (to do); find time / 도망칠 틈을 노리다 [wait] for a chance to escape / 방심한 틈을 타다 take advantage of *sb's* unguarded moment
▶ 그는 도망칠 틈이 없었다 He saw [had] no chance of escape.
▶ 편지를 쓸 틈이 없다 I'm so busy that I have no time to write a letter.
▶ 오늘은 전혀 틈이 없습니다 My hands are quite full today.
▶ 틈을 보아 그를 방문하겠다 I will call on him when I have time (to spare).
▶ 틈이 나면 이 서류를 들여다 보십시오 Look into these papers in your free [spare] time.
▶ 그녀는 틈만 있으면 독서를 했다 She read whenever she could snatch a moment.

틈바구니 1 〈벌어진 틈・사이〉 a crack; an opening; a crevice; a gap; an aperture; space ♦틈바구니가 생기다 crack; cleave; rift; split / 틈바구니를 메우다 stop [fill] up a crevice (with *sth*)
2 ⇨ 틈새기

틈새기 a narrow crack [opening, space]
♦두사람 틈새기에 끼이다 be squeezed [sandwiched, pinned] in between two people
▶ 눈이 틈새기로 불어닥쳤다 The snow sifted in through the door crack.

틈입 闖入 intrusion —틈입하다 intrude [force] into ♦좌익의 일단이 강연장에 틈입했다 A group of leftists broke into the lecture hall.

틈타다 〈이용하다〉 take advantage of; avail *oneself* of; 〈약점 등을 잡다〉 seize; take ♦어둠을 틈타다 under cover of darkness [night] / 방심을 틈타다 take advantage of *sb's* unguarded moment; take *sb* off his guard / 혼란을 틈타서 달아나다 make good *one's* escape in the confusion
▶ 그는 감시원이 잠든 동안을 틈타서 도망쳤다 He ran away while the guard was asleep.

틈틈이 1 〈틈마다〉 at each gap; in every opening
2 〈여가마다〉 in *one's* spare [free] time; 〈중간에〉 in the intervals (of); at intervals
♦일하는 틈틈이 in the intervals [intermission] of *one's* work / 틈틈이 공부하다 turn every odd moment to account for *one's* studies
▶ 그는 틈틈이 책을 읽는다 He spends his spare time in) reading.
▶ 그녀는 틈틈이 스웨터를 짰다 She made use of her leisure time to knit a sweater.
▶ 그는 틈틈이 나에게 들른다 Occasionally [Every now and then] he drops in on me.

티^1 1 〈먼지〉 dust; a mote; a particle; 〈이물질〉 a foreign element ♦눈에 티가 들어가다 have a mote in *one's* eye / 티를 없애다 remove [get rid of] impurities
2 〈흠〉 a flaw; a defect; a stain; a blemish ♦옥에 티 the flaw in a gem; a fly in the ointment [amber]; a flaw in an otherwise perfect thing / 티없는 clean; pure; unblemished; immaculate; innocent
3 〈기색・작태〉 bearing; an air; a look; a shade; a tinge; a touch; 〈태도〉 a manner; an attitude
♦거만한 티 an arrogant manner [bearing]/ 유식한 티를 내며 with a knowing air / 시골 티가 나다 have a rural appearance; look rustic; 〈사람이〉 look like a countryman / 학자티를 내다 assume an air of a scholar; have a scholarly air about (him)
▶ 그녀는 숙녀 티를 내고 있다 She behaves like a lady.
▶ 그는 되게 선배 티를 낸다 He doesn't have to put on such a superior air (even) if he is my senior.

티^2 〈골프〉 a tee

티^3 〈홍차〉 tea ■아이스— iced tea 레몬— lemon tea; tea with lemon / —컵 a teacup / —포트 a teapot

티격나다 break (with) ⇨ 틀어지다 2

티격태격 wranglingly; bickeringly —티격태격하다 quarrel [dispute, wrangle] (with); pick quarrels; bicker with each other

티끌 1 〈먼지〉 dust; a mote
♦티끌 하나 없는 방 a spotless room / 티끌을 털다 shake off the dust; dust
▶ 책상에는 티끌 하나 없었다 There wasn't a speck of dust on the desk.
2 〈아주 작은 것〉 a tiny bit ♦티끌 만큼도 개의치 않다 do not care a bit [straw] (about *sth*)
▶ 티끌 만큼의 값어치도 없다 It is not worth a snap of *one's* fingers).
▶ 그에게는 티끌 만큼의 성의도 없다 He has not an ounce [a particle] of sincerity in him. ■—세상 the tainted world we live in; this contaminating [dirty, filthy] world; 티끌세상에 물들다 be contaminated with the impurities of the world

티끌 모아 태산 〈속담〉 Many a little [pickle] makes a mickle. ⇌ Many drops make a shower [flood]. ⇌ Drop by drop the tub is filled.

티눈 a corn ♦발가락에 티눈이 생기다 have a corn on the toe ■—약 corn plaster

티뜯다 1 〈티를 뜯어내다〉 get rid of a foreign [an impure] element
2 〈흠잡다〉 find fault (with); cavil [carp] at *sb's* faults; pick holes (in); **(美口)** pick on *sb* [*sth*]

티롤 〈알프스 산중의 지역〉 the Tyrol; the Tirol

티룸 a tearoom

티베트 T(h)ibet ♦티베트의 T(h)ibetan ■—말 T(h)ibetan —사람 a T(h)ibetan

티보다 〈흠을 살피다〉 look over whether there is any flaw in (it); 〈티뜯다〉 find fault (with)

티석티석 coarsely; unevenly —티석티석하다 coarse; rugged; uneven ♦머리를 티석티석하게 깎다 cut *one's* hair unevenly

티셔츠 a T-shirt; a tee shirt

티슈페이퍼 tissue paper; 〈화장용〉 facial tissues

티스푼 a teaspoon

티엔티 〈폭약〉 TNT [〈*trini*tro*toluene*]

티오 〈인원 편성표〉 TO [〈*table of organiza*-

티자 a T [tee] square
티적거리다 〈흠을 잡다〉 find fault 《with》; pick holes [flaws] 《in》; 〈성가시게〉 tease; peck at *sb*; pick holes in others ♦머느리에게 티적거리다 be hard on *one's* daughter-in-law
티케이오 〔拳〕 a TKO; a T.K.O. [〈*technical k*nock*out*]
티켓 a ticket
티크 〔植〕 a teak ■─재(材) teakwood; teak
티탄 〔化〕 titanium
티티새 〔鳥〕 a dusky thrush ⇨ 지빠귀
티파티 a tea party; tea
티푸스 〈장티푸스〉 typhoid (fever); 〈발진티푸스〉 typhus (fever); 〈파라티푸스〉 paratyphoid (fever) ■─균 a typhoid bacillus [germ]
틴에이저 a teen-ager
▶ 그 여자애는 틴에이저다 She is a teen-ager [a teen-age(d) girl, in her teens].
틴에이지 teen age ♦틴에이지의 teen-age(d); of teen age
팀 a team ♦팀을 짜다 make a team
▶ 나는 야구팀에 들어 있다 I am in [on] our baseball team.
▶ 우리 학교팀이 이겼다 Our school team won.

■ 야구─ a baseball team; the nine 축구─ a football team; the eleven 혼성─ a combined team 홈─ the home team
팀워크 teamwork ♦팀워크가 좋다 exhibit fine teamwork; work well together as a team / 팀워크가 나쁘다 be poor in teamwork
팀파니 〈악기〉 timpani 《*sing*. -pano》; kettledrums ■─연주자 a kettledrummer; a timpanist
팁 1〈행하〉 a tip
♦팁 제도 the tipping system / 많은[적은] 팁 a large [small] tip / 팁을 주다 give *sb* a tip; tip *sb* / 팁을 1달러 주다 tip *sb* a dollar / 팁을 후하게 주다 give a generous tip; tip generously / 팁을 바라다 expect a tip / 웨이터에게 팁을 남겨두다 leave a tip for a waiter
▶ 팁 일체 사절 (게시) No tips accepted. ⇌ Tips declined.
▶ 그녀는 항상 팁에 짜다 She is always stingy with [about] her tips.
2 〔野〕 a tip
♦파울 팁 a foul tip
팅크 tincture ♦요오드[캠퍼]─ tincture of iodine [camphor]
팅팅 swollen ⇨ 탱탱

파

파¹ 〖植〗 a Welsh [spring] onion; a stone leek; 〈양파〉 an onion; a scallion; 〈골파〉 a shallot

> **[解説]** 우리나라의 파는 동양 원산으로 유럽·미국에는 없고, 이와 비슷한 *leek*도 우리나라의 것보다 굵다. *scallion*이나 *spring onion*은 실파에 가깝다.

파² 〖樂〗 fa ♦파음 F; f

파 派 **1**〈그룹〉 a group; 〈동인〉 a coterie
♦소장파(少壯派) a young group / 전후파 the postwar generation / 친미파 a pro-American group
2〈당파〉 a party; a faction
♦반대파 an opposition group / 지지파 a supporting group [faction] / 주류파 the mainstreamers / 중도파 the middle-of-the-roaders / 비주류파 the non-mainstreamers / 혁신파 the reformists / 강경파 the hard-line faction / 온건파로 the moderate faction; the moderates / 두 파로 갈리다 be divided into two factions [camps]
3〈유파〉 a school
♦고전파 the classical school / 낭만파 the romantic school / 한 학파를 이루다 found a school of *one's* own
4〈종파〉 a sect; a denomination
♦장로교파 the Presbyterian denomination

파 破 〈상한 물건〉 breakage; damage; injury; breakdown ♦파가 나다 be damaged

파가하다 罷家— wind up *one's* house; give up housekeeping

파격 破格 an exception; breaking the rules; 〖文法〗 a solecism
—**파격하다** break (the rules); make an exception; commit an offense against grammar; make a solecism
■—구문〖修〗 an anacoluthon (*pl*. -tha)

파격적 破格的 exceptional; unprecedented; special; abnormal; 〖文法〗 solecistic
♦파격적 승진〖get〗 an exceptional promotion / 파격적인 값으로 팔다 sell 〖an article〗 at an absurdly low price / 파격적인 대우를 받다 enjoy exceptionally good treatment

파견 派遣 dispatch; despatch
—**파견하다** dispatch; despatch; send
♦대표를 파견하다 send a representative / 군대를 파견하다 dispatch an army 〖to〗 / 대사를 파견하다 accredit an ambassador 〖to〗
■—군 an expeditionary force [army] —대 a contingent; a detachment

파경 破鏡 **1**〈깨진 거울〉 a broken mirror
2〈이지러진 달〉 a waned moon; halfmoon
3〈이혼〉 (a) divorce; separation
♦파경에 이르다 be divorced

파계 破戒 offense against the commandments; transgression of the 〖Buddhist〗 commandments; apostasy —**파계하다** violate the Buddhist commandments
■—승 a sinful priest; a depraved monk —자 a transgressor

파고 波高 the height of a wave; wave height

파고다 〈塔〉 a pagoda

파고들다 dig into 〖a problem〗; make a thorough investigation of 〖a matter〗; investigate; 〈침투하다〉 permeate; infiltrate; burn into (*one's* mind)
♦마음 속에 파고들다 eat into *one's* heart / 외국시장에 파고들다 make an inroad into foreign market
▶그 새로운 사상이 사람들 마음에 파고들었다 The new idea filtered into the people's mind.

파곡 波谷 a trough [furrow] between waves

파곳 〖樂〗〈목관악기〉 a bassoon; (이) a fagotto (*pl*. -ti) ■—주자 a bassoonist; a fagotto player

파과 破瓜 puberty of a girl; pubescence
■—기(期) (the time of) puberty

파괴 破壞 destruction; demolition; breakdown
♦대량 파괴 병기 a weapon of mass destruction
—**파괴하다** destroy; break; 〈집 등을〉 demolish; ruin; wreck; dilapidate; work havoc (upon); make havoc 〈of, among〉; ravage
♦가정의 평화와 행복을 파괴하다 destroy the peace and happiness of families / 파괴되다 be broken (down); be destroyed [smashed, demolished]
▶그들은 낡은 빌딩을 파괴했다 They demolished [pulled down] the old building.
▶홍수로 철도가 파괴되었다 The flood has destroyed the railway track.
■—계수(係數) a modulus of rupture —력 destructive power —병기 destructive weapons —분자 a subversive element; a subversive; a disrupter —자 a destroyer; a desolator; a devastator —작용 〈세포의〉 destructive metabolism —점 a breaking point —주의 destructionism; vandalism —주의자 a destructionist —활동 subversive activities: sabotage

파국 破局 collapse; catastrophe; a cataclysm
♦파국에 직면하다 be in the face of ruin / 파국을 막다 prevent a catastrophe
▶그들의 결혼생활은 파국에 직면해 있다 They are confronted by [with] the catastrophe of their conjugal life.
▶그들의 연애 관계는 파국적 결말로 끝났다 Their love affair ended in catastrophe.

파급하다 波及— extend 〈to〉; spread 〈to〉; influence; affect
♦파급되다 extend 〈to〉; influence / 전국에 파

급되다 extend to all over the country
▶ 손해는 이웃 마을에 파급되었다 The damage extended to the next village.
▶ 그 분쟁은 영국까지 파급되었다 The dispute spread to England.

파기 破棄 destruction; 〈무효화〉 annulment; 〈취소〉 cancellation; 〈약속의〉 breach; [法] 〈판결·계약의〉 reversal; recall
♦ 문서의 파기 the destruction of documents / 조약의 파기 the denunciation [abrogation] of a treaty
—**파기하다** destroy; tear *sth* to pieces and throw 《it》 away; 〈무효로 하다〉 annul 《a decision》; cancel 《a contract》; break 《a promise》
♦ 원심을 파기하다 annul the original decision; quash the original judgment [decision]

파김치 pickled scallion; 〈극도의 피로〉 exhaustion ♦ 파김치가 되다 get dead tired; be exhausted; be dog-tired; be worn-out

파나다 破— 〈못쓰게 되다〉 be damaged [destroyed, impaired, spoilt]; be broken 《down》
♦ 파난 그릇 a broken dish; a damaged dish
▶ 그릇이 파났다 The dish got damaged.

파나마 〈나라 이름〉 Panama; 〈공식명〉 the Republic of Panama
♦ 파나마의 Panamanian
■—모자 a Panama (hat) —사람 a Panamanian —운하 the Panama Canal —운하지대 the Panama (Canal) Zone —지협 the Isthmus of Panama

파나물 scallion salad

파내다 dig up [out]; dig open; unearth; excavate; disinter
♦ 땅 속에서 석탄을 파내다 mine coal out of the ground / 나무 뿌리를 파내다 grub up the roots of a tree / 금을 파내다 dig gold 《from a mine》

파노라마 a panorama
▶ 그것은 바로 파노라마같은 경치였다 It was quite a panoramic view.
■—사진기 a panoramic [pantoscopic] camera; a pantoscope

파니 idly; indolently

파다 1 〈구멍을〉 dig (up); excavate; 〈터널 등을〉 drive 《a tunnel》; 〈우물을〉 drill; sink; 〈후벼내다〉 scoop out
♦ 땅에 구덩이를 파다 dig a hole in the ground / 땅을 파다 delve [dig in] the ground; 〈농사짓다〉 till the soil; do farm work / 우물을 파다 sink [dig] a well / 산에 터널을 파다 [bore, cut] a tunnel through a mountain / 삽으로 파다 dig with a shovel
▶ 그는 갯벌을 파고 조개를 잡았다 He dug the beach for seashells.
▶ 그들은 해저 터널을 팔 계획을 세웠다 They made a plan to tunnel under the sea.
▶ 나는 뜰에 부엌 쓰레기 버릴 구덩이를 팠다 I dug a hole in the yard for the garbage.
▶ 그들은 보물을 찾아 이곳저곳을 팠다 They dug here and there for treasure.
▶ 그들은 우물을 파고 있었다 They were digging [sinking] a well.
▶ 그놈은 제 무덤을 팠다 He dug his own grave. ⇌ He brought on his own ruin.

2 〈새기다〉 carve 《in, on》; cut; engrave; chisel
♦ 도장을 파다 〈손수〉 engrave a seal; 〈남을 시켜〉 have *one's* seal engraved

3 〈이치·문제 등을〉 make a search [inquiry] into; delve [probe] into 《a problem》; dig 《into》
♦ 진상을 파다 inquire into the true state of things / 문제를 깊이 파다 get to the bottom of a matter
▶ 그는 사전을 파고든다 He goes heart and soul into the matter.

4 〈전력을 기울이다〉 study [work] hard; (口) dig in [into] 《*one's* subject》; (俗) bone [cram] up 《on》
♦ 공부를 들이 파다 study [work] in earnest; grind away at work

파다하다 頗多— 〈아주 많다〉 numerous; abundant; large in number
▶ 그러한 예는 파다하다 We have a good many such examples.

파다하다 播多— 〈널리 퍼진〉 widely rumored; widespread; 〈서술적〉 be widely known; be rife
▶ 그가 구속됐다는 소문이 파다했다 It was widely rumored that he has arrested.
▶ 그가 자살했다는 소문이 파다하게 퍼졌다 The news of his suicide is noised abroad.
▶ 그 현지에는 전쟁이 날 것이라는 소문이 파다했다 Rumors of war were rife in that part of the country.

파닥거리다 flutter; flap; splash; flop
♦ 새가 날개를 파닥거리다 a bird flutters 《its》 wings / 돛이 바람에 파닥거리다 a sail flutters in the wind / 파닥거리며 날아가다 fly with a flap of the wings
▶ 상처를 입은 새가 파닥거리며 땅에 떨어졌다 A wounded bird fluttered to the ground.
▶ 깃발이 바람에 파닥거렸다 The flag flapped in the breeze.
▶ 물고기가 갑판 위에서 파닥거렸다 The fish flopped helplessly on the deck.

파닥파닥 〈새 등이〉 flapping; fluttering; flip-flap; 〈물고기가〉 flopping

파담 破談 breaking off 《an agreement》; rejection —**파담하다** cancel; break off; 〈자동사〉 be broken off; be rejected

파도 波濤 wave; waves; billows; seas; surges; 〈밀려오는〉 surf; 〈부서지는〉 a breaker
♦ 파도 소리 the sound of waves / 파도치다 wave; undulate; roll / 파도치는 대로 떠다니다 drift on the waves / 파도에 휩쓸리다 be carried away by the waves / 파도와 싸우다 buffet the waves / 파도에 시달리다 be tossed about by the waves
▶ 파도가 가라앉았다 The sea has gone down.
▶ 아이가 밀려온 파도에 휩쓸려버렸다 A child has been washed away [been carried away] by the surging waves.
▶ 파도가 거칠다 The waves are rough.
▶ 오늘은 파도가 높다 The waves are high today.
▶ 파도가 해변을 찰싹거린다 The waves beat upon the shore.
▶ 파도가 보트를 삼켜버렸다 The waves swallowed up the boat.

파도타기

▶배가 거친 파도를 헤쳐 나갔다 The ship floundered in rough seas.

파도타기 波濤— surfing; surfboard-riding
—**파도타기하다** surf; ride the surfboard
◆파도타기하는 사람 a surfer; a surfie; a surf rider

파동 波動 a wave [an undulatory] motion; fluctuation; undulation
—**파동하다** fluctuate; undulate; wave
■**가격**— fluctuations in prices **경제**— an economic crisis **정치**— a political upheaval **증권**— a stock market crisis; wild fluctuations of the stock market ■—**설** the wave theory (of light) —**역학** wave mechanics

파두 巴豆 〔植〕 a croton (plant)
파두츠 〈리히텐슈타인의 수도〉 Vaduz
파라과이 Paraguay; 〈공식명〉 the Republic of Paraguay ◆파라과이의 Paraguayan ■—**사람** a Paraguayan
파라볼라 안테나 〈포물면 안테나〉 a parabolic antenna [aerial]
파라솔 a parasol
파라슈트 a parachute ⇨ 낙하산
파라오 〈고대 이집트왕의 칭호〉 a Pharaoh
파라티온 〈살충용 농약〉 parathion
■—**중독** parathion poisoning
파라티푸스 〔醫〕 paratyphus
■—**균** a paratyphoid bacillus
파라핀 〔化〕 paraffin(e)
■—**연고** poaraffin ointment —**유** paraffin [coal] oil; (美) kerosine —**지** wax paper

파란 波瀾 〈소동·분규〉 (a) disturbance; trouble(s); 〈성쇠〉 ups and downs; vicissitudes; a storm
◆가정의 파란 family [domestic] troubles / 파란만장한 eventful; stormy; full of ups and downs
▶그는 파란 많은 생애를 보냈다 He led a life marked by vicissitudes [full of ups and downs].
▶그녀는 비밀을 폭로해서 파란을 일으켰다 She disclosed the secret and caused [raised, made] a disturbance.
▶그 정치가의 파란만장한 일생이 끝났다 The stormy life of the statesman was at an end. ⇌ 그 정치가는 파란만장한 일생을 마쳤다 The statesman ended his eventful life.

파랄림픽 〈신체장애자 올림픽 대회〉 the Paralympics

파랑 blue; green; indigo; azure

[解說] 우리말의 「파랑」에는 **blue**(청색), **green** (초록), **indigo**(남색), **azure**(하늘빛) 등의 빛깔을 모두 포함하므로 주의. 예를들면 신호등의 「파랑」은 영어에서는 **green**이다.

파랑 波浪 〔氣〕 wave
파랑돌 〔樂〕〈춤곡〉 farandole
파랑새 1 〔鳥〕 a broad-billed roller
2 〈푸른 새〉 a blue bird; the Blue Bird (▶행복의 상징)
파랑이 a blue one; a blue stuff
파랗다 〈청색〉 blue; azure; 〈녹색〉 green; 〈창백하다〉 pale; pallid
◆파란 사과 a green apple / 파란 하늘 a blue [an azure] sky / 파란 나무라곤 혼적도 없는 공장지역 an industrial district without a trace of greenery / 파랗게 질린 얼굴 a pallid [wan, cadaverous] face / 파랗게 물들이다 dye blue / 파랗게 질리다 turn deadly pale
▶우리는 파란 하늘 아래에서 운동했다 We excercised under the blue sky [outside].

파래 〔植〕 green edible seaweed; green laver; (a) sea lettuce
파래지다 become blue; turn green; 〈얼굴이〉 turn pale [pallid]; go green
◆파래졌다 빨개졌다 하다 turn alternately pale and red; become pale and red by turns

파렴치 破廉恥 shamelessness; infamy; ignominy
—**파렴치하다** shameless; infamous; ignominious; disgraceful; scandalous
◆파렴치한 행위 a shameless act
▶파렴치한 사람에게는 보다 엄한 처분을 해야 한다 Shameless people should be dealt with [disciplined] more harshly.
■—**죄** a disgraceful offense; an infamous offense [crime] —**한**(漢) a shameless fellow

파로틴 parotin
파르나시앵 〈고답파(高踏派) 시인〉 (프) the Parnassians
파르르 trembling ⇨ 바르르
파르스름하다 〈빛깔이〉 bluish; greenish; 〈얼굴이〉 rather pale [pallid]
파르테논신전 —神殿 the Parthenon
파릇파릇하다 vividly green; freshly blue; fresh and green; verdant
◆파릇파릇한 신록의 계절 the season of fresh verdure [green]
▶나무에는 새싹이 파릇파릇하게 돋아나고 있었다 There were great bursts of verdant leaves growing on the trees.

파리¹ 〔昆〕 a fly
◆파리를 쫓다 whisk the flies off; 〈부채로〉 fan flies away / 파리가 꾀다 flies swarm 〈about, round〉 / 파리를 날리다 (비유) be dull; 〈one's business〉 be slack; fall off / 파리를 잡다 catch flies; 〈파리채로〉 flap [swat] a fly
▶증시는 파리를 날리고 있다 There is virtually no business done in the stock market.
■—**똥**(자국) a fly speck —**망** a fly net —**목숨** transient [ephemeral] existence; cheap life —**약** flypoison; 〈물약〉 fly water —**잡이** a fly catcher; 〈끈끈이〉 flypaper; 〈통〉 a flytrap; a fly bottle —**채** a flyflap [swatter]; a flapper

파리² 〈프랑스의 수도〉 Paris ◆파리(사람)의 Parisian ■—**사람** 〈남자〉 a Parisian; 〈여자〉 a Parisienne —**코뮌** 〔史〕 the Commune (of Paris)

파리모 玻璃母 a lump of hot [molten] glass
파리하다 〈창백하다〉 pale; thin; pallid; 〈해쓱하다〉 emaciated; gaunt
◆파리한 얼굴 a thin face; a pallid [drawn] face / 파리해지다 lose flesh; become thin
▶그녀는 오래 앓고 나서 얼굴이 파리해 보였다 Her face looked wan after her long illness.

파마 a permanent (wave) ⇨ 퍼머넌트
파먹다 1 〈파서 먹다〉 dig 《a thing》 out and eat 《it》; 〈좀먹어 들어가다〉 eat into [away,

out]
♦ 땅을 파먹다 live by farming
▶ 벌레가 과일을 파먹었다 A worm bored into the fruits.
▶ 부패는 나라의 심장부를 파먹는다 Corruption eats at the heart of the country.
2 〈놀고 먹다〉 eat idle bread; eat the bread of idleness; live an idle life; 〈재산 등을〉 eat away what *one* has
♦ 하는 일 없이 재산을 다 파먹다 run through *one's* fortune in idleness

파면 罷免 dismissal; discharge
—**파면하다** dismiss; discharge; (美口) fire
▶ 그는 파면되었다 He was dismissed [relieved of his post].
▶ 그녀는 직무 태만으로 파면되었다 She lost her position through neglect of duty.
■—권 the right of dismissal

파멸 破滅 ruin; destruction; downfall
♦ 파멸에 직면하고 있다 be on the brink of ruin
▶ 그는 스스로 파멸을 초래했다 He brought on his own destruction. ⇌ He brought (down) ruin upon himself. ⇌ He ruined himself.
▶ 술이 그의 파멸의 원인이었다 Drinking was the cause of his ruin [destruction].
▶ 그녀의 미모가 파멸의 원인이었다 Her beauty was her ruin.
▶ 그는 노름에 미쳐서 일신의 파멸을 초래했다 His mania for gambling has brought about his ruin.
—**파멸하다** ruin; go to rack and ruin; be ruined; go [come, fall] to ruin
♦ 파멸시키다 ruin; destruct; bring to ruin
▶ 막대한 손실 때문에 그는 파멸했다 The great loss brought down ruin upon him.
▶ 술과 여자가 그를 파멸시켰다 Liquor and women brought about his ruin.

파문 波紋 **1** 〈잔물결〉 a ripple; a water ring; a wavelet
♦ 파문이 퍼지다 waves ripple out in all directions
▶ 돌멩이가 연못에 파문을 그렸다 The stone started a water ring in the pond.
2 〈영향〉 a sensation; a stir; (a) repercussions
▶ 대통령의 발언은 경제계에 파문을 던졌다 The statement of the president caused a sensation [created a stir] in the economic world.

파문 破門 〈종교상의〉 (an) excommunication; 〈제자의〉 (an) expulsion
—**파문하다** expel; excommunicate
♦ 파문당하다 be excommunicated; be expelled
▶ 나는 제자를 파문했다 I expelled my pupil.
▶ 그는 이단자가 되었기 때문에 교회에서 파문당했다 He was excommunicated from the church because he became a heretic.

파묻다[1] 〈땅속 등에〉 bury (in, under); entomb; 〈매장하다〉 inter
♦ 땅 속에 깊이[얕게] 파묻다 bury *sth* deeply [lightly] in the ground / 죽은 새를 뜰에 파묻다 bury a dead bird in the yard / 땅속에 파이프를 파묻다[매설하다] sink [lay] a pipe in the ground
▶ 그는 머리를 이불에 파묻고 자고 있다 He is sleeping with his head (buried) under the covers.
▶ 그녀는 손수건에 얼굴을 파묻고 울었다 She was weeping in her handkerchief.

파묻다[2] 〈캐어묻다〉 ask inquisitively [closely]; press a question home; poke and pry
♦ 남의 계획을 파묻다 quiz *sb* about (his) plan
▶ 그들은 내 과거를 파묻기 시작하였다 They began poking around into my past.

파묻히다 be buried (under, in); be buried in oblivion
♦ 눈에 파묻히다 be buried in snow; be covered with snow; be snowed in [up, under] / 시골에 파묻히다 bury *oneself* [be buried] in the country / 파묻힌 인재를 찾아내다 find [unearth] hidden talent, discover new talent / 속세에 파묻혀 살다 sink into obscurity
▶ 그는 곧 군중 속에 파묻혀 보이지 않았다 The man soon disappeared in the crowd.
▶ 편지는 서류 밑에 파묻혀 있었다 The letter was buried under [was hidden under, was covered with] papers.
▶ 그의 작품은 여러 해 동안 세상에 파묻혀 있었다 His works remained unrecognized [unknown to the public] for many years.

파물 破物 a damaged [broken, defective] article; damaged goods

파미르 〈중앙 아시아에 있는 고원〉 Pamir
■—고원 the Pamirs

파발 擺撥 〈역참〉 a post station; a stage
■—꾼 an express messenger; a courier —마(馬) a post horse: 파발마를 띄우다 dispatch a messenger on a post horse

파방치다 罷榜— break up (*one's* home) to move; shut up (*one's* house)

파방판 罷榜— a close; the final scene ♦ 파방판이 되다 come to an end; get finished

파벌 派閥 a faction; a clique
▶ 그 당은 3개의 주요 파벌로 분열되어 있다 The party is split (up) into three (main) factions.
▶ 그들은 당내의 파벌을 해소시켜야 한다 They must dissolve the intraparty factions.
■—싸움 faction; a factional strife —주의 factionalism; cliquism

파별 派別 (a) division 《by schools [parties]》
—**파별하다** divide; split; branch

파병 派兵 〈군대를〉 the dispatch of troops [an army]
—**파병하다** dispatch [send] troops (to)
♦ 해외로 파병하다 send troops overseas

파브르 〈프랑스의 곤충학자〉 Fabre, Jean Henri (1823-1915)

파블로프 〈러시아의 생리학자〉 Pavlov, Ivan Petrovich (1849-1936)

파삭파삭하다 crisp; crumbly; friable
♦ 파삭파삭한 흙 crumbly soil / 파삭파삭한 비스킷 a crisp biscuit / 파삭파삭하게 구워지다 be burned to a crisp

파산 破産 bankruptcy; (financial) failure; (法) insolvency
♦ 파산의 위기에 처하다 be on the brink of bankruptcy / 파산을 선고하다 declare bankruptcy / 파산 직전에 있다 be on the verge

[brink] of bankruptcy
▶ 회사는 파산에 직면해 있다 The company is on the very [brink, edge] of bankruptcy.
▶ 법원은 그에게 파산을 선고했다 The court adjudicated a bankrupt to him.
—파산하다 become [go] bankrupt [insolvent]; go into bankruptcy; fail; be brought to ruin; (俗) go broke
▶ 가게에 불이 나서 그는 파산했다 He went bankrupt [was ruined, (口) went broke] after the fire in his shop.
▶ 사업 실패로 나는 파산했다 I went bankrupt [into bankruptcy, (俗) broke] because of my failure in business.
▶ 저렇게 사치하면 그녀는 머지않아 파산할 것이다 Such high living will ruin her before long.
■ —관재인 a trustee in bankruptcy; a receiver —법 (法) the Bankruptcy Act —선고 an adjudication of bankruptcy: 그 회사는 마침내 파산선고를 받았다 The company was finally declared bankrupt. —신청서 a petition in bankruptcy —자 a bankrupt; an insolvent —절차 bankruptcy procedure —채권 claims provable in bankruptcy —채무 debts provable in bankruptcy —청산인 an assignee in bankruptcy; a liquidator in bankruptcy

파상 波狀 wave; undulation
♦ 파상적인 wavy; undulating; wavelike / 파상을 그리다 be wavy; undulate

파상공격 波狀攻擊 an attack in waves
▶ 폭격기에 의한 파상공격 wave bombing; a [an air] raid in waves / 파상공격을 가하다 launch [make] a series of attacks (on, upon)

파상풍 破傷風 〈醫〉 tetanus; 〈턱뼈가 굳어지는〉 lockjaw
♦ 파상풍의 tetanic
—균 a tetanus bacillus (*pl.* -li) —항독소 혈청 an antitetanic serum (*pl.* ~s, -ra)

파생 派生 derivation
—파생하다 derive ((from)); be derived
♦ 파생된 사건 a matter incidental to a main issue
▶ 거기서 뜻밖의 사태가 파생되었다 An unexpected situation developed from it.
▶ 그것은 파생된 사건에 지나지 않는다 It's purely a secondary matter.
■ —어 a derivative —어미 a derivational suffix —형 a derived form

파선 波線 wave; a wavy [an undulating] line
파선 破船 〈난파〉 shipwreck; 〈난파선〉 a wrecked ship; a wreck
—파선하다 get [be] shipwrecked; be wrecked
♦ 파선한 배를 구하다 save a ship from wreck; salavage a ship in distress
파선 破線 〈제도의〉 a broken [dashed] line
파손 破損 breakage; breakdown; injury; damage
♦ 파손이 크다[작다] suffer a heavy [slight] damage / 파손을 면하다 be intact
—파손하다 break down
♦ 파손되기 쉬운 easy to break; fragile / 파손되다 be broken (down); be damaged [dilapidated, destroyed, impaired]

▶ 그들은 그것이 마치 파손되기라도 하는 것처럼 조심스레 다뤘다 They handled it as if it was made of porcelain.
—물 a fragile article; breakables —부분 a damaged [broken] part; a break(age); 〈제방 등의〉 a breach —품 damaged goods

파송 派送 dispatch ⇨ 파견
파쇄 破碎 breaking to pieces; crush; smash; fragmentation —파쇄하다 crush; smash; shatter; break [crack] to pieces; break up ■—기 a disintegrator; a crusher

파쇠 破— 〈헌쇠〉 scrap iron; iron scraps
—상 a junk dealer

파쇼 [〈이〉 Fascio] 〈주의〉 Fascism; 〈사람〉 a fascist; a Fascista; 〈운동〉 the Fascist movement
♦ 파쇼적 fascistic
■ —사상 Fascism; fascistic ideas —화 fascistization: 파쇼화하다 fascistize; go fascist

파수 把守 watch; lookout; guard
—파수보다 watch; guard; keep (a) watch ((for, against))
■ —꾼 a watchman; a guard; 〈보초〉 a sentry —막 (幕) a lodge; a sentry box; a watch box; a watchhouse —병 a sentry; a guard

파스 〔藥〕 PAS [*Para-Aminosalicylic Acid*]
파스너 a fastener; (美) a zipper; (英) a zip fastener; a zip; a snap fastener
♦ 점퍼의 파스너를 열다 zip down *one's* jumper / 파스너를 잠그다 zip up

파스칼 〈프랑스의 철학자·물리학자·수학자〉 Pascal, Blaise (1623-62)
파스테르나크 〈구소련의 작가〉 Pasternak, Boris Leonidovich (1890-1960)
파스텔 (a) pastel —컬러 a pastel; pastel shades —화 (畫) a pastel (drawing); a drawing in pastel —화가 a pastel(l)ist
파스퇴르 〈프랑스의 화학·생물학자〉 Pasteur, Louis (1822-95) —살균법 pasteurization —접종법 pasteurism —효과 〔生化〕 Pasteur effect [reaction]
파슬리 〔植〕 a parsley
파슬파슬 crumbling ▶ 과자가 파슬파슬 부스러진다 The cake crumbles into decay [to pieces]. —파슬파슬하다 crumbly
파시 波市 a seasonal fish market
파시스트 a fascist; a Fascista
파시즘 Fascism
—운동 the Fascist movement
파악 把握 〈잡아 쥠〉 grasp; seizing; gribbing; 〈이해〉 understanding
—파악하다 grasp; seize; understand
♦ 요점을 파악하다 grasp the point / 업무를 파악하다 understand *one's* business
▶ 이 글의 뜻을 파악하기가 퍽 어렵다 It is very difficult to get [grasp] the meaning of this sentence.
▶ 그만이 이 문장의 뜻을 제대로 파악했다 Only he was able to grasp the real meaning of this sentence.
▶ 나는 그의 논지를 파악하기가 어려웠다[힘들었다] I had difficulty in finding a valid point in his argument.
▶ 정황을 완전히 파악하지 않으면 간혹 실패하

는 수가 있다 Sometimes you fail if you don't size up the situation thoroughly.

파안 破顔 (breaking into) a broad smile
♦ 파안대소하다 give [show, smile] a broad smile; burst into laughter

파약 破約 a breach of contract [promise]
—파약하다 break an agreement [a promise]; break *one's* word
▶ 그 협약은 파약되었다 The agreement was broken off.

파업 罷業 1 〈폐업〉 a strike; (美口) a walkout
2 ⇨ 동맹 파업
♦ 파업중인 공장 a struck factory / 파업에 들어가다 go (out) on strike / 파업중이다 be on [(美) on] strike
▶ 노조원은 파업중이다 The union members are on a strike.
▶ 우리는 파업에 들어가기로 결정했다 We decided to go on strike.
▶ 파업은 해제[중지]되었다 The strike was called off [halted].
▶ 파업 결행중 (게시) On strike.
—파업하다 strike; turn out; (美) walkout
■ 동정— a sympathetic strike 무기한— an indefinite period strike 부분— a partial strike 시한— a strike for a limited number of hours 총— a general strike ■ —권 the right to stike: 파업권을 행사하다 exercise *one's* right to strike —기금[자금] a strike fund —자 a striker —중지명령 a stop-strike order —지령 a strike order —파괴자 a strike-breaker; (英) a blackleg; a rat

파열 破裂 explosion; blast; (a) bursting; 〈혈관 등의〉 (a) rupture; 〈화산의〉 (an) eruption
♦ 혈관의 파열 the rupture of a blood vessel
—파열하다 explode; burst; erupt; rupture; blow out; blow up
♦ 산산조각으로 파열하다 burst into fragments
▶ 올 겨울 혹한에 수도관이 파열하였다 The water pipes burst when we had the freeze this winter.
▶ 보일러가 큰 소리로 파열했다 The boiler burst [exploded] with a loud noise.
■ —음 〔音聲〕 a plosive; an explosive; 〈폭탄 등의〉 the crump(ing) —탄 an explosive; a bomb; a shell

파옥 破獄 (a) breach of prison; jailbreak
—파옥하다 break (from) *sb*; break jail

파운달 〔物〕 a poundal (略 pdl.)

파운데이션 foundation
■ —크림 foundation cream

파운드 1 〈무게 단위〉 a pound (略 lb.)
♦ 20파운드 twenty pounds; 20 lbs. / 파운드로 팔다 sell by the pound
▶ 몸 무게가 몇 파운드냐? How many pounds do you weigh?
2 〈화폐 단위〉 a pound (略 £); 〈영국 화폐〉 a pound sterling; (英俗) a quid
♦ 10 파운드 ten pounds; £10 / 5파운드 지폐 a five-pound note
▶ 그는 10파운드 지폐로 지급했다 He paid with a ten-pound note.
■ —(통용)지역[권] a sterling area [bloc] —환(換) the pound exchange

파울 〔競〕 a foul; (a) foul play
♦ 파울을 하다 foul; violate against the rules / 파울로 퇴장하다 foul out of the game / (야구에서) 파울을 치다 foul; hit a foul ball
▶ 그 선수는 커브를 두 번 파울했다 The player fouled off two curves.
■ —볼 a foul ball

파워 power ■ 블랙[흑인]— black power ■ —게임 power game —엘리트 the power elite —포지션 〔골프〕 a power position —폴리틱스 power politics

파이¹ 〈양과자〉 a pie; (美) a potpie; 〈주로 고기의〉 a meat pie
♦ 파이의 껍질 (a) piecrust; a pastry
■ 건포도— a raisin pie 고기— a meat pie 과일— a fruit pie; (美) 〈구운〉 a cobbler; (英) 〈과일을 넣은〉 a tart 민스— a mince pie 복숭아— a peach pie 소시지— a sausage pie 애플— an apple pie 크림— a cream pie 호박— a pumpkin pie

파이² 〔數〕 pi; π
■ —중간자 〔原子物〕 a π-meason (略 π)

파이버 (vulcanized) fiber
■ —관(管) a fiber pipe —보드 fiber board —유리[글라스] fiber [fibrous, spun] glass; (商標) Fiberglas

파이트 〔투지〕 fight; a fighting spirit
♦ 파이트에 불타고 있다 be burning to fight; be full of fight
▶ 난 파이트가 있는 사람이 좋아 I like people with guts.
■ —머니 fight money; a fighter's purse

파이프 1 〈관〉 a pipe; a tube
♦ 파이프로 물을 끌다 draw water through a pipe
2 〈담뱃대〉 a (tobacco) pipe; 〈궐련용〉 a cigarette holder; 〈엽궐련용〉 a cigar holder
♦ 파이프의 재를 털다 tap *one's* pipe out; knock the ashes out of *one's* pipe / 파이프를 빨다 pull at a pipe / 파이프에 불을 붙이다 light *one's* pipe / 파이프에 궐련을 끼우다 fit a cigarette into a holder / 파이프에 담배를 재다 fill *one's* pipe with tobacco / 파이프를 청소하다 clean a pipe
♦ 비닐— a vinyl pipe 수도— a water pipe
■ —라인[배관] a pipeline —렌치 〔機〕 a pipe wrench —오르간 a pipe organ

파인더 〔寫〕 a (view)finder

파인애플 〔植〕 a pineapple

파인트 〈액량의 단위〉 a pint (기호 pt.)

파인플레이 〔競〕 a fine play; 〔野〕 a fine fielding play
♦ 파인플레이를 하다 make a fine play; give a fine performance

파일 八日 〔佛敎〕 〈음력 4월 초파일〉 Buddha's birthday festival; the anniversary of the birth of Buddha
■ —등(燈) lanterns lighted on Buddha's birthday

파일 〈서류철〉 a file
♦ 신문 파일 a newspaper file
▶ 이 서류를 파일해 두세요 Keep this paper on file, please.

파일럿 a pilot
파자마 〈美〉 pajamas; 〈英〉 pyjamas

> [解說] 파자마는 영어로는 ***pajamas***로 복수형으로 쓴다. 다만 a pajama coat「파자마의 상의」, pajama trousers「파자마의 바지」처럼 형용사적으로 쓸 때는 단수형이다. 이것들은 각각 a pajama top, pajama bottoms로 말하는 경우도 있다.

 ♦ 파자마 바람으로 in *one's* pajamas
파장 波長 (a) wavelength
 ♦ KBS에 파장을 맞추다 tune in on KBS
 ━계 cymometer; a wavemeter ━대(帶) a wavelength range ━정조기(整調器) a tuner
파장 罷場 〈옛날 과거장의〉 the conclusion of state examination; 〈시장의〉 close of a marketplace
 ━파장하다 bring state examinations to a close [an end]; close a marketplace
 ■━시세 the closing quotation [price]
파적 破寂 diversion for idle moments; beguiling the tedium
 ━파적하다 divert *oneself* from idle moments; beguile [relieve] the tedium; mind from loneliness
 ■━거리 a kill-time; a timekiller; a pastime
파종 播種 sowing; seeding
 ♦ 파종의 계절 the planting season
 ━파종하다 sow; sow seed
 ♦ 봄에 파종하다 sow seed in spring / 밭에 보리[밀]를 파종하다 sow a field with barley [wheat]
 ■━기(期) the seedtime; the seeding [sowing] season ━기(機) a sower; a sowing [seeding] machine; a seeder
파죽지세 破竹之勢 irresistible [crushing, overwhelming] force
 ♦ 파죽지세로 with irresistible force; with progressive increase of force / 파죽지세로 나아가다 carry all [everything] before *one*; sweep away everything in *one's* way
 ▶ 그 군대는 파죽지세로 진격했다 The troops swept away everything in their path.
파지 破紙 wastepaper; a defective sheet of paper; paper scraps
파직 罷職 dismissal [removal] from office; discharge; deprivation of office
 ━파직하다 dismiss *sb* from (his) office; discharge *sb* from (his) duties; 〈美口〉 fire
파찰음 破擦音 〔音聲〕 an affricate
파천 播遷 royal flight from the palace; the evacuation of the capital
 ━파천하다 flee from the royal palace; evacuate the capital
파천황 破天荒 〈전대미문〉 unprecedentedness
 ♦ 파천황의 record-breaking; unheard-of
파철 破鐵 scrap iron ⇨ 파쇠
파초 芭蕉 〔植〕 a plantain
파출 派出 dispatch; derivation
 ━파출하다 dispatch; send out
 ■━부 a day housekeeper; a visiting housekeeper [maid]; 〈英〉 a charwoman: (유료)파출부 소개소 an employment agency for domestic help ━소 a branch office; 〈경찰의〉 a police box [stand]: 파출소에 신고하다 report to a policeman at the police stand
파충류 爬蟲類 the reptiles; creeping things; Reptilia ♦ 파충류의 reptilian / 파충류의 동물 a reptile
 ■━시대 the reptilian age ━학 herpetology
파치 破━ 〈손상품〉 a defective [damaged] article; unmarketable goods
 ♦ 파치가 되다 become odd
파키스탄 Pakistan; 〈공식명〉 the Islamic Republic of Pakistan ♦ 파키스탄의 Pakistani
 ■━사람 a Pakistani 《*pl.* ~(s)》
파킨슨법칙 ━法則 〔社〕 Parkinson's law
파킨슨병 ━病 〔醫〕 Parkinson's disease; 〈증후군〉 Parkinsonism
파킹 parking ━미터 a parking meter
파탄 破綻 1 〈불성립〉 failure; 〈교섭의〉 a rupture
 ▶ 계획한 일이 파탄 났다 The plan failed.
 ━파탄나다 fail; come to a rupture
 2 〈은행・회사의 지급정지〉 bankruptcy
 ♦ 은행의 파탄 a bank failure
 ━파탄하다 become [go] bankrupt; break down
 3 〈붕괴〉 breaking
 ♦ 인격 파탄을 가져오다 break up *one's* personality; lead to the bankruptcy of *one's* character
파트너 a partner
 ▶ 나는 그녀를 댄스의 파트너로 택했다 I chose her as my partner for the dance.
파트타임 a part-time employment
파티 a party; a meeting
 ♦ 파티를 열다 have [hold] a party; party / 남성[여성]만의 파티 a stag [hen] party
 ■댄스━ a dance [dancing] party 디너━ a dinner party 축하━ a celebration party 크리스마스━ a Christmas party 티━ a tea party
파파 〈兒〉 papa; pa; pop; dad(dy)
파파노인 皤皤老人 a very old person; a white-haired old man [woman]
파파야 〔植〕 a papaya
파편 破片 a broken piece; a fragment; a splinter
 ▶ 내 발에 파편이 박혔다 I've got a splinter in foot.
 ▶ 꽃병의 파편이 마루에 흩어져 있었다 The fragments of the vase were scattered on the floor.
 ▶ 그는 잘못해서 유리 파편에 손가락을 베였다 He accidentally cut his finger with a piece [fragment] of glass.
 ■강철━ (sharp) steel splinters 유리━ pieces of broken glass; fragments of glass 포탄━ splinters of a shell
파푸아뉴기니 the Papua New Guinea
 ■━사람 a Papua New Guinean
파피루스 〔植〕 a papyrus 《*pl.* papyri》; 〈종이〉 papyrus
파하다 罷━ close; be over; bring to an end
 ♦ 학교를 파하다 close the school; dismiss school / 회의를 파하다 bring the meeting to a close; end a meeting

▶ 회사가 파한 뒤에 만나자 Let's meet after office hours is over.
▶ 학교는 5시에 파합니다 School closes at five (o'clock).
파행 爬行 crawling; creeping —**파행하다** crawl; creep —**동물** a reptile
파행 跛行 〈절뚝거림〉 limping; (an) imbalance
♦ 파행적 운영 the crippled operation 《of》 —**파행하다** limp
— **경기(景氣)** an erratic ecomomy —**국회의 crippled operation of the National Assembly
파헤치다 〈땅을〉 dig up; dig 《the ground》 over; tear up 《a road》; 〈비유〉 rake up 《an old scandal》; bring 《a secret》 to light
▶ 도로가 몇 군데 파헤쳐져 있다 The road is torn up at several places.
▶ 우리는 진상을 파헤쳤다 We inquired into the true state of things.
파혼 破婚 breach of promise of marriage; breaking off a marriage engagement
—**파혼하다** break the engagement; undo a match
▶ 양친은 나에게 그녀와의 약혼을 파혼하도록 충고하셨다 My parents advised me to break [call] off my engagement with her.
파훼 破毀 destruction; demolition; 〔法〕 annulment; breach
—**파훼하다** destroy; demolish; breach
파흥 破興 spoilage of the fun [pleasure]
—**파흥하다** spoil the fun [pleasure]; dampen *sb's* enthusiasm; (口) throw a wet blanket 《over, on》; wetblanket
♦ 파흥케 하는 사람 a killjoy; (口) a spoilsport; (口) a wet blanket
▶ 파흥하는 소리 작작해 Don't be a spoilsport.
팍 1 〈찌르는 모양〉 with a thrust; violently; hot and strong
♦ 주먹으로 팍 쥐어박다 give *sb* a hard blow with *one's* fist
2 〈쓰러지는 모양〉 weakly; suddenly; all at once
♦ 팍 쓰러지다 fall with a flump; drop down (dead); collapse; break down
팍삭 1 〈주저앉는 모양〉 flopping down; with a flump; sinking
—**팍삭하다** 〈주저앉다〉 get flopped down; plump down; 〈지반 등이〉 sink; 〈지붕·벽 등이〉 cave in; fall in
2 〈부스러지는 모양〉 into pieces [fragments]
—**팍삭하다** be broken [smashed] to [into] fragments; come to pieces
판 〈일이 벌어진 자리〉 a place; a spot; a stage; a site; a scene; 〈판국〉 state of affairs; the situation; circumstances; 〈경우〉 an occasion; a case; 〈때〉 the moments
♦ 노름판 a gambling place / 난장판 a scene of utter confusion / 씨름판 a wrestling arena / 이 판에 on this occasion; at the present moment / 위급한 판에 in time of danger / 바둑을 한 판 두다 play a game of *paduk* / 세 판 내리 이기다[지다] win [lose] three games (straight)
판 板 a board; a plate; 〈널빤지〉 a plank; 〈원판〉 a disk [disc]

♦ 바둑판 a *paduk* board / 체스판 a chessboard / 축음기판 a record; a disk; a disc / 판유리 plate glass
판 版 1 〈판목(版木)〉 a (printing) block; a plate; a cast
♦ 사진판 a photo plate / 판에 박힌 말 a set [conventional] phrase; a stereotyped expression / 판에 박은 듯한 conventional; cut and dried; stereotyped; formal / 판에 박힌 인사말을 하다 give a conventionally worded address
2 ⇨ **활판**
3 〈책을 펴내는 일〉 printing; print; 〈발행 판수 (版數)〉 an edition; an impression
♦ 개정 증보판 a revised and enlarged edition / 〈신문의〉 시내판 the city [metropolitan] edition / 염가판 a cheap edition / 〈책이〉 판을 거듭하다 go through [run into] several editions / 판을 개정하다 publish a new [revised] edition
▶ 이 사전의 신판은 내달에 나올 예정이다 The new edition of this dictionary will be published [come out] next month.
▶ 초판 5,000부는 첫날 다 팔렸다 The first impression [printing] of five thousand copies sold out on the first day.
■ **지방** — the local [provincial] edition 초[재] — the first [second] edition [impression, printing] 포켓 — a pocket edition 해적 — a pirated edition 호화 — a deluxe edition
판 瓣 1 〔植〕 〈꽃잎의〉 a petal
2 〈기계의〉 a valve; 〈악기의〉 a ventil; 〈피리의〉 a reed
판 判 〈종이·책의 규격〉 size; 〈책의〉 format 《of a book》
♦ 대판의 종이 large-sized paper / 국판(菊版) a small octavo / 사륙(四六)판 duodecimo / 사륙배판 a large [royal] octavo / B6판 B6 size / B6판본(의 책) a B6-sized volume
▶ 이 책은 그것과 같은 판이다 This book is the same size as that.
판가름 judging sides (which side is right and which side is wrong); decision; a showdown
♦ 판가름나다 be decided; come to a conclusion
—**판가름하다** judge; sit in judgment 《on》; try
♦ 천하를 판가름하는 싸움 a decisive [life-and-death] battle / 우승의 행방을 판가름하는 시합 a big match [bout] which will greatly affect the final destination of the championship / 소송사건을 판가름하다 try a case
판각 板刻 engraving on woodblock; woodcutting; 〈판각한 것〉 a wood engraving; a woodcut; a xylograph
—**판각하다** engrave 《designs, letters》 on wood; make a print from a woodcut [woodblock]
■ — **본** a woodblock-printed [xylographic] book — **사(師)** a woodcutter; a wood engraver; a block cutter; xylographer — **술** xylography — **자(字)** a block letter — **화** a woodcut; xylograph
판검사 判檢事 judges and public prosecutors; judicial officers; (총칭) the bench

판결 判決 (a) judgment; a ruling; (a) decision; (a) sentence; 〈배심원의 평결〉 a verdict
♦ 판결의 집행 execution of judgment / 판결에 승복하다 accept [abide by] a decision / 판결에 불복하다 protest against [contest] the decision / 판결을 내리다 give a decision 《upon》; adjudicate 《on a case》; rule 《that...》; find 《*sb* guilty》; judge / 아무에게 판결을 언도하다 pronounce [pass] sentence on *sb* / 판결을 파기하다 reverse the judgment [ruling, decision] / 판결을 유예[연기]하다 reserve [suspend] judgment
▶ 판결은 원고의 패소[승소]로 돌아갔다 The case was decided against [in favor of] the plaintiff.
▶ 재판관은 그에게 유죄[무죄] 판결을 내렸다 The judge found the accused guilty [not guilty].
▶ 그는 징역 3년의 판결을 받았다 He was sentenced to three years in jail.
▶ 그는 사형 판결을 받았다 He was given [He received] a sentence of death. ⇌ He was sentenced to death.
—**판결하다** decide 《on a case》; give (a) decision 《on a case》; pass judgment 《on a case》; adjudicate [adjudge] 《on an action》; sentence *sb* to 《death》
■ 최종— the final decree ■—례 a judicial precedent —문 the decision: 판결문을 낭독하다 read the ruling; read out the decision —서 a judgment paper —이유 reasons for judgment —주문(主文) the text of a decision; formal adjudication

판공비 辦公費 expediency fund; 〈접대비〉 expense account; 〈예비비〉 extra-expenses; 〈기밀비〉 confidential money [account] for public service [official affairs]

판국 —局 a situation; the state of affairs [things] ♦ 위험한 판국 a critical situation / 수습할 수 없는 판국 an uncontrollable situation / 돌아가는 판국을 관망하다 watch the situation [the development of affairs]

판권 版權 copyright
♦ 판권을 획득하다 copyright 《a book》; secure [obtain] copyright 《for a book》 / 저서의 판권을 소유하다 hold [own] the copyright on a book / 판권을 침해하다 infringe a copyright
▶ 판권 소유 Copyrighted. ⇌ All rights reserved. ■—소유자 a copyright holder —양도 transfer of a copyright —장 colophon; imprint —침해 infringement of copyright —침해자 a copyright infringer; a copyright law violator

판금 板金 a metal plate; sheet metal
■—공 a sheet metal worker —공장 a sheet metal plant

판나다 1 〈판이 끝나다〉 get finished; come [be brought] to an end [a close, a conclusion]; be concluded; be over ♦ 〈분쟁 등이〉 원만히 판나다 be settled in peace
▶ 싸움은 이미 판났다 A fight is already finished.
2 〈다하다〉 be all gone; run out; be exhausted; be used up; be spent
▶ 인제 우리 식량이 판났다 We have run out of provisions.
3 〈망하다〉 be ruined; go [fall] crash; go bankrupt
▶ 그의 살림은 판났다 His family is ruined.
▶ 그의 회사는 벌써 판났다 His company is bankrupt long ago.

판다 〔動〕 a panda

판단 判斷 (a) judgment; 〈결정〉 (a) decision; 〈결론〉 conclusion; 〈해석〉 (an) interpretation
♦ 옳은 판단 fair judgment / 틀린 판단 a misjudgment / 종합 판단 (a) synthetic judgment / 판단을 내리다 make a judgment 《about, on, regarding》 / 내 판단으로는 in my own judgment; as I take it
▶ 답이 옳은지 (옳지 않은지) 판단이 서지 않는다 I cannot judge [tell] whether the answer is right (or not).
▶ 그녀는 이 일에 관해 판단을 잘못[올바로] 했다 She made a poor [the correct] judgment in this matter.
▶ 네 판단에 맡기겠다 I will leave it to your judgment.
▶ 내 판단으로는 그가 잘못이다 In my judgment [opinion, view], he is wrong. ⇌ My judgment is that he is wrong.
—**판단하다** judge; decide; conclude; interpret
♦ 잘못 판단하다 judge wrongly; make an error in judgment / 아무를 첫인상으로[겉모양으로] 판단하다 judge *sb* by first impressions [by *sb'* appearance]
▶ 스스로 판단하라 Judge for yourself.
▶ 그의 편지로 판단하건대 그는 성실한 사람인 것 같다 Judging from his letter, he seems to be a sincere person.

판단력 判斷力 judgment; discernment; sense
♦ 판단력이 좋다 have good judgment / 판단력이 없다 lacking [wanting] in judgment / 판단력을 발휘하다 use *one's* judgment 《in》 / 판단력을 잃다 lose *one's* judgment

판도 版圖 (a) territory; a dominion; a domain
♦ 영국의 판도 the British dominion / 판도를 넓히다 extend *one's* territory

판도라 〔그神〕 Pandora
♦ 판도라의 상자 (a) Pandora's box

판독 判讀 decipherment; interpretation; reading; making out
—**판독하다** decipher; read; make out; spell out
♦ 고문서를 판독하다 decipher an old manuscript
▶ 그의 필적은 판독하기 어렵다 I find it hard to read [make out] his handwriting. ⇌ His handwriting is hardly legible [readable].
▶ 그 봉투의 주소 성명은 판독할 수가 없었다 The address on the envelope was not legible.

판돈 stakes; money let upon the gambling table
♦ 판돈을 쓸다 rake in the stakes; sweep the board / 판돈을 떼다 divide up the stakes

판례 判例 〔法〕 a (judicial) precedent; a (leading) case
♦ 판례를 인용하다 cite a precedent; refer to a case
■—법 〔法〕 case law; judiciary law —위반

판세

contravention to judicial precedents ―집 law reports

판로 販路 a market for goods; an outlet
♦ 판로가 없다 be unmarketable [unsalable]; be in poor [little] demand; there is little [no] market [demand] / 판로를 찾다 seek a market [an outlet] 《for an article》/ 판로를 확장하다 extend [enlarge] the market 《for》
▶ 이 상품은 판로가 넓다[좁다] There is a good market [small demand] for these articles.
▶ 우리는 이들 제품의 새 판로를 개척하지 않으면 안된다 We have to find [open] a new market for these products.

판막 瓣膜 〔解〕 the valves (of the heart)
■ ―심장 [혈관]― valves of the heart [veins] 호흡― pulmonary valves ■ ―염 valvulitis ―절개(술) valvulotomy ―증 valvular [mitral] disease

판막음 〈그 판에서의 마지막 승리〉 bringing a game to an end by winning it ―판막음하다 bring a contest to a close by winning it

판매 販賣 (a) sale; selling; marketing
♦ 판매를 촉진하다 promote sales / 미성년자에게 주류 판매를 금지하다 prohibit the sale of alcoholic drinks to minors
―판매하다 sell; deal in; handle
♦ 판매되고 있다 be on sale; be on the market
▶ 이 가게는 구두를 판매하고 있다 They sell shoes at this store. ⇌ This store deals in [carries] shoes.
■ ―독점― an exclusive sale 신용― a credit sale; a sale on credit 예약― sale by subscription 외상― a credit sale; tick 월부― installment plan 위탁― consignment sale 통신― selling by mail 특가[염가]― a bargain sale; sale at a special reduction 할인― a discount [reduction] sale 현금― a cash sale; a sale for cash ■ ―가격― ―가격 ―선[sale] price ―개시 opening the sale ―과 a sales department ―대리점 a selling agency ―루트 a marketing route; a distribution channel ―망 a sales network ―부 a sales department; 〈군대·광산 등의〉 a commissary ―부장 a sales manager [chief]; a marketing executive; 〈신문·잡지의〉 a circulation manager ―수단 sales tactics ―수익 a margin ―술 the art of selling; salesmanship ―원 〈남자〉 a salesman; 〈여자〉 a saleswoman, a salesgirl; (총칭) a clerk; (英) a shop assistant ―인 a seller; a dealer; an agent ―전 (a) sales war ―점[소] (美) a store; (英) a shop ―정책 a sales policy ―조건 the condition of sale ―촉진 sales promotion

판명 判明 becoming clear ―판명되다 become clear [plain]; be known; be ascertained; be confirmed; be known; prove [turn out] (to be)
▶ 그 사고의 원인이 판명되었다 The cause of the accident has become clear.
▶ 아버지의 소재는 아직 판명되지 않았다 My father's whereabouts is still unknown.
▶ 그 소문은 허위임이 판명되었다 The rumor turned out [proved] to be false.
▶ 그 시체의 신원은 아직 판명되지 않고 있다 The body is not yet identified.

판목 版木 a (printing) block; a woodblock; a wooden printing block; a woodcut

판몰이 winning all the money that there is around a gambling place
―판몰이하다 win all the money

판무관 辦務官 a commissioner
■ ―고등― a high commissioner

판문점 板門店 Panmunjŏm; the Panmunjŏm truce village
■ ―공동 경비 구역 the Joint Security Area of Panmunjŏm ―군사 정전 위원회 회의 the Military Armistice Commission meeting (held) at Panmunjŏm ―중립국 감시 위원회 the Neutral Nations Supervisory Commission at Panmunjŏm

판박이 版― 1 〈판에 박아낸 책〉 a printed book 2 〈아이들의 장난감〉 a copy picture; 〈도자기·유리 등에 옮기는〉 a decalcomania; a decal 3 〈틀에 박힌 것〉 a fixed form; a stereotyped pattern
■ ―구 a set [conventional] phrase ―소리 a set [conventional] phrase; a stereotyped remark [phrase, expression] ―인사 conventional greeting

판별 判別 distinction; discrimination
―판별하다 distinguish 《between A and B》; tell 《A》 from 《B》; discriminate 《between A and B, one from the other》; judge
♦ 시비를 판별하다 discriminate between right and wrong / 진짜와 가짜를 판별하다 distinguish the real thing from false one [imitations]
▶ 문학을 공부하면 양서와 무가치한 책을 판별할 수 있게 된다 Studying literature enables us to discriminate good books from poor ones.
■ ―식(式) 〔數〕 a discriminant

판본 版本 a block [xylographic] book

판사 判事 a judge; a justice; (총칭) the judiciary
▶ 박 판사가 그 사건을 담당하고 있다 Judge Park presides over [is in charge of] the case.
■ ―배석― an associate [a puisne] judge 부장― a senior judge 주심― a presiding judge ■ ―석 a judgment seat; the bench ―직 judgeship; the bench

판상 辦償 compensation; indemnification
―판상하다 compensate 《sb's loss》; indemnify; repair

판서 判書 〔古制〕 a minister (in ancient times)

판서 板書 (make) a blackboard demonstration ―판서하다 write on a blackboard

판설다 unfamiliar 《with》; unaccustomed 《to》

판세 ―勢 〈형세〉 the situation; the state [condition] of affairs; 〈바둑 등의〉 the position; 〈전망〉 the prospects
♦ 유리[불리]한 판세 a favorable [an unfavorable] turn of the situation / 판세를 관망하다 watch the situation; see how the wind blows / 판세가 변하다 take a new turn; take on a new aspect
▶ 판세가 유리[불리]해졌다 The tide turned in favor of [against] us.

판소리 *pansori*; narrative musical form unique to Korea

판수 a blind fortuneteller; 〈소경〉 a blind man

판시 判示 judgment; (a) decision —**판시하다** decide 《on a case》; give (a) dicision

판연하다 判然— distinct; plain; evident; clear; explicit; 〈명확하다〉 definite; 〈확실하다〉 certain
♦**판연히** clearly; plainly; distinctly

판유리 板琉璃 〈두꺼운〉 plate glass; 〈얇은〉 sheet glass

판이하다 判異— entirely different 《from》; diametrically opposed 《to》
▶ 그 소설은 원작과는 판이하게 연극으로 각색되었다 The novel was adapted for the stage a quite different from the original.

판자 板子 a wooden board; 〈두꺼운〉 a plank; (총칭) boarding
♦판자를 대다 board; plank; lay boards 《on》 / 방을 판자로 막다 board up a room
■—문 a wooden door —벽 a board wall —울타리 a board(ing) fence; a wooden fence —조각 a small piece of a board —지붕 a shingle roof: 판자 지붕을 하다 cover the roof with shingles

판잣집 a barrack; a shack; a makeshift hut

판장 板牆 a wooden wall ⇨ 널판장

판정 判定 〈판단〉 (a) judgment; 〈결정〉 (a) decision; 〈재정(裁定)〉 a ruling
♦판정의 기준 a criterion for judging / 판정을 내리다 pass judgment 《on》; give a decision 《on》 / 심판의 판정에 따르다 obey the umpire's decision [ruling] / 피고에게 유리한 판정을 내리다 find for [against] the defendant
—**판정하다** judge; decide
▶ 나는 잘못 판정했다 I misjudged.

판정승 判定勝 a decision
—**판정승하다** 〔拳〕 win a decision; defeat [beat] 《one's opponent》 on points [by a decision]
▶ 그는 심판 전원 일치로 판정승했다 He won the match in a unanimous decision.
▶ 10회전 시합에서 조는 짐에게 판정승했다 In a ten-round bout Joe won by decision over Jim.

판정패하다 判定敗— 〈경기에서〉 lose on a decision; lose on points; be defeated [beaten] by a decision

판지 板紙 cardboard; pasteboard; paperboard; carton

판차리다 get a place ready for 《gambling》

판촉 販促 sales promotion ⇨ 판매(~촉진)

판치다 stand unchallenged [without a rival]; reign supreme; exercise great influence 《over》

판크레아틴 〔生化〕 pancreatin

판크레오지민 〔生理〕 pancreozymin

판타지아 〔樂〕〈환상곡〉 a fantasia; a fantasy

판탈롱 〈여성의 바지〉(a pair of) bell-bottoms; bell-bottomed trousers; pantaloons

판판이 every time; whenever; all the time
♦판판이 지다 defeated in every battle / 판판이 실패하다 fail in every attempt; fail at every step ▶ 그는 판판이 굶고 있다 He goes hungry.

판판하다 even; level; smooth; flat
♦판판한 땅 even [level] ground / 땅을 판판하게 하다 level [roll] the ground

판화 版畫 a print; 〈목판화〉 a woodcut; a wood-block print; 〈동판화〉 an etching; 〈판화술〉 (pictorial) wood printing
■—가 a woodblock artist

판히 判— clearly; plainly; distinctly

팔 an arm; 〈팔뚝〉 the forearm; 〈팔죽지〉 the upper arm
♦팔씨름 arm wrestling / 팔을 붙잡다 take [catch] *sb* by the arm / 팔을 걸어붙이다[걸어올리다] pull up [roll up] *one's* sleeves / 두 팔을 벌리다 spread out *one's* arms; open *one's* arms / 팔에 의지해 걷다 walk on *one's* arm
▶ 그는 팔힘이 세다 He has strong arms.
▶ 그 투수는 팔이 길다 The pitcher has long arms.
▶ 나는 팔이 부러졌다[팔을 뼈었다] I had my arm broken [sprained].
▶ 그 아이는 싸우다 팔이 부러졌다 The boy broke his arm in the fight.
▶ 그녀는 내 팔을 붙잡고 울었다 She caught me by the arm and cried.
▶ 그는 팔을 걸어올리고 장미 문신을 내게 보여 주었다 He rolled up his sleeves [bared his arm] and showed me the rose tattoo.
▶ 소녀는 팔에 시장바구니를 들고 있었다 The girl had a shopping basket on her arm.
▶ 환자는 간호사의 팔에 의지해 걸었다 The sick person walked leaning on the nurse's arm.
▶ 그녀는 팔에 책을 끼었다 She tucked a book under her arm.

─ 팔 ─

손 hand
상박 upper arm
손목 wrist
겨드랑이 armpit
앞팔 forearm
팔꿈치 elbow

팔 八 eight
♦제 팔 the eighth / 8분의 1 one-eighth

팔각 八角 eight angles; 〈팔각형〉 an octagon
♦팔각의 octagonal
■—당(堂)[정(亭)] an octagonal pavilion

팔걸이 an armrest
■—의자 an armchair; an elbow chair

팔괘 八卦 eight signs of divination

팔굽혀펴기 〔體操〕(美) a push-up; (英) a press-up ♦매일 팔굽혀펴기를 30번 하다 do 30

push-ups every morning

팔꿈치 an elbow
♦ 팔꿈치를 펴다 spread out [square] *one's* elbow / 팔꿈치로 밀어제치다 elbow *sb* aside / 팔꿈치로 치다 hit [poke, dig] *one's* elbow into 《another's side》; jog; jostle; 〈툭 치다〉 nudge
▶ 그는 팔꿈치로 사람을 밀어제치고 만원 버스에 올라탔다 He elbowed his way into the jam-packed bus.
▶ 그는 팔꿈치로 머리를 괴고 누웠다 He rested his head on his elbow.
■—관절 an elbow joint

팔다 1 〈판매하다〉 sell; deal in; carry
♦ 팔 집을 house for [on] sale / 과일을 팔러 다니다 carry fruits about for sale / 가재를 팔아버리다[치우다] dispose of the household goods / 한 개 1,000원에 팔다 sell 《a thing》 at one thousand won each [apiece] / 쌀을 킬로당 2,500원에 팔다 sell rice for two thousand five hundred won a kilogram / 비싸게[싸게] 팔다 sell *sth* dear [cheap] / 외상으로 팔다 sell on credit [tick, trust]; give *sb* credit / 미모를 팔다 trade [capitalize] on *one's* beauty / 지조 [명예]를 팔다 sell *one's* honor for money
▶ 우리 가게에서는 달걀을 팔고 있다 We sell eggs at this store. ⇌ This store sells eggs.
▶ 그는 톰에게 그 중고차를 팔았다 He sold Tom the used car. ⇌ He sold the used car to Tom.
▶ 밀은 킬로그램 단위로 판다 Wheat is sold by the kilogram.
2 〈노력 등을〉 ♦ 품을 팔다 do job work; do wage labor; work for wages / 날품을 팔다 work by the day; work as a day laborer
3 〈배신·배반하다〉 betray; deceive; delude; impose upon
▶ 그는 조국을 팔았다 He betrayed his country. ⇌ 《口》 He sold his native country down the river.
4 〈이름 등을〉 ♦ 아무의 이름을 팔다 assume [use] *sb's* name; make a fraudulent use of *sb's* name / 자기 이름을 팔다 〈빌려주다〉 lend *one's* name
▶ 그는 그 소설로 이름이 팔렸다 〈명성을 얻었다〉 He won fame by the novel.
5 〈곡식을 사다〉 ♦ 쌀을 팔다 buy [purchase] rice
6 〈정신·눈을〉 ♦ 한눈을 팔다 turn *one's* eyes away 《from》; avert *one's* eyes 《from》; look away 《from》 / 정신을 팔다 distract [divert] *one's* attention 《from》 / 독서에 정신이 팔리다 be absorbed in reading

팔다리 the arms and legs; the limbs
♦ 팔다리가 없는 limbless / 팔다리를 못쓰다 lose the use of *one's* limbs

팔도 八道 the eight provinces of Korea; 〈한국〉 Korea
■—강산 the land of Korea; all Korea

팔등신 八等身 a well-proportioned figure
▶ 그 여자는 팔등신이다 She has a well-proportioned figure.

팔딱거리다 1 〈맥박치다〉 pulsate; palpitate; throb; beat; leap
▶ 내 가슴이 심하게 팔딱거렸다 My heart throbbed heavily.
2 〈가볍게 뛰다〉 hop; leap; jump; spring; bound

팔딱팔딱 〈맥박치는 모양〉 pulsating; palpitating; throbbing; 〈뛰는 모양〉 hopping; jumping
■—팔딱팔딱하다 leap

팔뚝 the forearm; the wrist area

팔라듐 《化》 palladium

팔랑개비 1 〈장난감〉 a pinwheel 2 〈가볍게 구는 사람〉 a frivolous [flighty] fellow

팔랑거리다 flutter; flap; wave
♦ 바람에 팔랑거리다 flutter [wave] in the wind

팔랑팔랑 flutteringly; flappingly

팔레스타인 Palestine
♦ 팔레스타인의 Palestinian
■—게릴라 Palestinian guerillas ■—해방기구 〈독립되기 전의〉 Palestine Liberation Organization (略 PLO)

팔레트 《美》 a palette
■—나이프 a palette knife

팔리다 1 〈물건이〉 sell; be sold; be in demand [request]
♦ 잘 팔리다는 물건 a good seller / 잘 팔리다 sell well; be in good demand; have a good sale; 〈출판물이〉 have a large circulation / 비싸게 팔리다 sell dear; fetch a high price / 잘 팔리지 않다 do not sell well; be in poor demand; find no sale [market]; have a poor sale / 가장 잘 팔리다 be the best [top] seller
▶ 그 책은 곧 팔렸다 〈책 자체의 특질 때문에〉 The book sold quickly. ⇌ 〈적극적인 판매활동으로〉 The book was sold quickly.
▶ 그 넥타이는 잘 팔리고 있다 The tie sells [is selling] well. ⇌ 〈날개 돋친듯〉 The tie is selling [going] like hot cake [《口》 like crazy].
▶ 이 물건은 이제는 팔리지 않는다 There is no more demand for the article now.
2 〈사람이〉 go into bondage [slavery]; 〈미혼녀가〉 get married; 〈고용되다〉 get [obtain] employment
▶ 그 학교의 졸업생은 잘 팔린다 The graduates of that school are eagerly sought after.
▶ 그 여배우는 요즘 잘 팔리고 있다 The actress is very much in the public eye these days.
3 〈알려지다〉 become well-known; become popular; get around
♦ 잘 팔리고 있는 작가 a popular writer / 얼굴이 팔려 있다 be popular; be widely known
4 〈정신이 한쪽에 쏠리다〉 gaze upon *sth* in [with] rapture; look at *sth* else; be fascinated; be absorbed; lose *oneself* 《in》; go mad [crazy] 《after, over》
▶ 그는 여배우의 미모에 정신이 팔려 있다 He runs mad after pretty feature of an actress.
▶ 형은 낚시에 정신이 팔려 있다 My brother is given over to angling.

팔림새 sale; demand
▶ 이것 때문에 이 책의 팔림새가 나빠지지는 않을 것이다 This will not hurt the sales of the book.

팔만대장경 八萬大藏經 the Tripitaka Koreana 《consisting over eighty thousand blocks》

팔매 throwing; slinging; hurling
♦ 돌팔매 stone-throwing / 팔매치다[팔매질하다] throw; sling; hurl; fling 《a stone at》
▶ 그는 팔매질을 잘 한다 He throws well.

팔면 八面 eight sides; 〈팔방〉 all sides ♦ 팔면의 octahedral ■—부지 a complete stranger —체 an octahedron 《pl. -dra》: 정 8면체 a regular octahedron

팔모 八— eight angles ♦ 팔모의 octagonal ■—꼴 an octagon —살 〔建〕 octagonal lattice [latticework]

팔목 the wrist; 〔解〕 carpus
♦ 아무의 팔목을 잡다 take [catch] sb by the wrist
▶ 배팅에는 팔목 작용이 중요하다 It is the wrist action which is important in batting.
■—시계 ⇨ 손목시계

팔방 八方 〈팔방으로 in all directions; in every direction; on all sides / 〈사면〉 팔방에서 from all directions [quarters]; from every side

팔방미인 八方美人 a beauty in every respect; a person who is nice to everybody; a man of many talents

팔베개 ♦ 팔베개를 하다 rest one's head on one's elbow / 팔베개를 하고 자다 sleep with one's head (pillowed) on one's arm

팔변형 八邊形 〔數〕 an octagon
♦ 팔변형의 octagonal

팔분쉼표 八分— 標 〔樂〕 an eighth rest
팔분음표 八分音標 〔樂〕 a quaver; an eighth note
팔분의 八分儀 an octant
팔불용, 팔불출 八不用, 八不出 〈바보〉 a good-for-nothing fellow
팔삭둥이 八朔— 1 〈조산아〉 an infant born in the 8th month of pregnancy
2 〈얼뜨기〉 a half-witted person
팔색조 八色鳥 〔鳥〕 a fairy pitta
팔세토 〔樂〕 falsetto 《pl. ~s》 ♦ 팔세토로 in falsetto ■—가수 a falsetto (singer)
팔순 八旬 eighty years; fourscore years ♦ 팔순 노인 an octogenarian
팔시간 八時間 eight hours ■—노동제 the eight-hour day system
팔심 the strength of one's arm ▶ 그는 팔심이 세다 He has strong arms.
팔십 八十 eighty; a fourscore
♦ 제 팔십 the eightieth / 팔십대의 사람 an octogenarian / 팔십 노인 an 80-year-old man [woman]
팔싹 rising in a puff ⇨ 펄썩
팔씨름 Indian wrestling; arm wrestling
—팔씨름하다 armwrestle 《with》; wrestle with one's arms; have a hand wrestling
팔아먹다 1 〈팔아버리다〉 sell off [away]; dispose of by sale
♦ 가산을 다 팔아먹다 squander one's fortune / 〈값을 받고〉 ♦ 명예를 팔아먹다 sell [prostitute] one's honor for money / 지식을 팔아먹다 peddle one's knowledge
3 〈곡식을 사먹다〉 buy [purchase] grain
팔오금 the bend of the arm
팔월 八月 August (略 Aug.)

■—한가위 〈추석〉 the 15th day of the eighth lunar month
-**팔이** a seller; a peddler; a hawker
♦ 신문팔이 a newsboy
팔이 들이굽지 내굽나 〈속담〉 Blood is thicker than water.
팔일오 八一五 the Liberation Day of Korea; August 15th, 1945
♦ 팔일오 52주년 기념 the 52nd anniversary of Korea's Liberation
팔자 八字 〈운명〉 (a) destiny; fate; (a) lot; one's fortune; doom; one's star
♦ 기구한[사나운] 팔자 a hard [an evil] fate / 기이한 팔자 a curious fate / 팔자 좋은 사람 a lucky fellow / 팔자가 사나운 사람 a hapless person; an unfortunate [ill-fated] person / 팔자 사납다 be unlucky [unfortunate]; be out of luck / 팔자에 맡기다 leave one's fate to Heaven; trust to Providence / 팔자 소관으로 돌리다 resign oneself to one's fate; accept sth as fate; be reconciled to one's fate / 팔자가 늘어지다 be in easy circumstances; be comfortably off; be blessed with good fortune / 팔자를 잘못 타고나다 be born under an unlucky star / 팔자를 한탄하다 bemoan [bewail] one's ill fate / 팔자를 탓하다 grumble at one's lot / 팔자를 고치다 〈개가하다〉 marry again; remarry; 〈벼락 출세하다〉 rise suddenly in world; 〈벼락부자가 되다〉 gain quick riches; get [become] rich suddenly
▶ 그 남자는 팔자가 좋다[나쁘다] He is lucky [unlucky].
▶ 사람 팔자 시간문제다 (속담) No one can foretell his destiny.
팔자걸음 八字— toeing out
♦ 팔자걸음으로 걷다 toe out; walk with the toes turned out [outward]
팔자땜 八字— a compensation for one's doom
♦ 팔자땜으로 알고 체념하다 take it as the price for one's escape from misfortune
—팔자땜하다 suffer a minor misfortune in compensation for one's ill fate
팔재간 —才幹 〈씨름〉 skill in using one's arms
팔절판 八切判 〔寫〕 an octavo (略 8vo, oct.)
팔죽지 the upper arm
팔짓 arm gestures —팔짓하다 make gestures with one's arms
팔짝 hopping lightly (and nimbly); jumping suddenly ⇨ 펄쩍
팔짱 folding one's arms
♦ 팔짱을 끼다 fold one's arms (across one's chest [breast]) / 팔짱을 끼고 〈남과〉 lock arms with / 연인과 팔짱을 끼고 걷다 walk arm in arm with a lover
▶ 그는 팔짱을 끼고 방관했다 He looked on with folded arms. ⇌ He took a wait-and-see attitude.
▶ 그는 팔짱을 낀채 잠자코 앉아 있었다 He sat silent with his arms folded.
팔찌 a bracelet; a bangle; a wristlet; an armlet; 〈활 쏠 때의〉 a bracer
♦ 팔찌를 끼다 wear a bracelet
팔촌 八寸 〈촌수〉 the eighth degree (of consanguinity); 〈사람〉 a third cousin; a first

cousin twice removed
♦사돈의 팔촌 a cousin 40 times removed; an unrelated person; a stranger
팔팔 boiling ⇨ 펄펄
팔팔하다 1〈성질이 급한〉quick tempered; passionate; impatient
2〈생기 있는〉sprightly; snappy; full of life
♦팔팔한 소년 a young and lively boy
팜플렛 a pamphlet; a brochure;〈한장으로 된〉a leaflet

|解說| (1) 우리는 선전용의 한장짜리 종이에서부터 십수면의 작은 책자까지를 모두 팜플렛이라고 하지만 영어에서는 여러 면으로 된 책자로 꾸민 것을 ***pamphlet***이라 하고 한장짜리는 ***leaflet***이다.
(2)「팜플렛」중에서, 사진·삽화 등을 실은 상업적이며 pamphlet보다 고급인 것을 ***brochure***라고 한다.

♦팜플렛을 찍(어내)다 issue pamphlets; pamphleteer
■선전— a propaganda pamphlet
팝아트〈전위적 예술운동〉pop; pop art
팝콘 popcorn
팡파르〔樂〕a fanfare [fǽnfɛər]; a flourish (of trumpets); a tucket
팡파지다 get well-rounded ⇨ 펑퍼지다
팡파짐하다 gently curved ⇨ 펑퍼짐하다
팥 a red bean
■—고물 mashed red bean; red bean flour
—단자 a dumpling covered with red bean jam
—떡 rice cake coated with mashed red beans
—밥 rice boiled with red beans —빙수 red-bean sherbet
팥소 bean jam filling
♦팥소를 넣다 stuff 《a rice cake》 with bean jam
팥으로 메주를 쑨다 해도 곧이듣는다 (속담) You should sell him the Brooklyn Bridge.
팥죽 —粥 rice and red-bean porridge
—단— sweet red-bean soup with rice cake
패 牌 1〈표로 쓰는 나뭇조각 등〉a tag; a tab; a tablet; a plate; a tally
♦문패 a doorplate / 위패 a mortuary [memorial] tablet;〈조상의〉an ancestral tablet / 상패 a medallion / 명패 a name plate /「팔 것」이라는 패를 붙이다 put up a "For Sale" sign
2〈카드놀이·화투 등의〉a (playing) card; a suit(같은 종류의)
♦손에 든 패 the cards in a hand / 바닥에 깐 패 a lay card / 패를 도르다 deal the cards / 패를 떼다 cut the cards / 패가 좋다[나쁘다] have a good [bad] hand
▶그는 능숙한 솜씨로 패를 쳐서 돌렸다 He deftly shuffled and dealt the cards.
3〈한패〉a party; a company; a group; a set; a circle; a gang; a clique
♦우리 패 our group; our team / 젊은 패 young folks / 패를 짓다 form a party
▶나는 학생을 두 패로 나눴다 I divided the students into two groups.
패 覇〔바둑〕eternal alternation
패가하다 敗家— ruin *one's* family; a family is wrecked; a family goes to ruin; a family goes bankrupt
■—망신 ruining both *oneself* and *one's* family; *one's* ruin: 그는 노름으로 패가망신했다 He gambled himself out of house and home.
패각 貝殼 a shell ⇨ 조가비
패거리 牌— a party ⇨ 패 3
패검 佩劍〈칼을 참〉wearing a sword;〈차는 칼〉side arms; a sword worn —패검하다 wear [bear] a saber [sword] 《at *one's* side》
패군 敗軍 a defeated army ♦패군의 장군 a vanquished [defeated] general
패권 覇權 supremacy; domination; mastery; hegemony; leadership
♦패권을 쥐다 hold sway (over); assume [have] the hegemony (of the land); dominate; secure supreme power; hold supremacy
▶그 팀은 전국경기대회에서 패권을 차지했다 The team won the championship in the national meet.
▶강국들이 세계의 패권을 다투고 있었다 The great powers were struggling [striving] for the supremacy of world.
패기 覇氣 ambition; aspiration; an ambitious spirit ♦패기 없는 사람 a dull [an inert, an apathetic] person
▶그는 패기 있는 젊은이다 He is a young man of spirit.
▶그에게는 패기가 있다 He is full of an ambitious spirit.
패널〔建〕a panel ■—히팅 panel heating
패다¹〈이삭이〉come out
♦이삭이 패다 come into ears; ear (up) / 이삭이 패어 있다 be in ear
패다²〈마구 때리다〉beat; strike; knock; thrash; give 《deal, deliver》 *sb* a blow
♦늘씬하게 패다 give *sb* a sound beating; beat *sb* to a jelly / 멍이 들도록 패다 beat *sb* black and blue
패다³〈쪼개다〉break 《wood》 to pieces
♦장작을 패다 chop [split] firewood
패다⁴ 1〈패어지다〉sink; be dug; be hollowed
♦움푹 팬 볼 hollow [sunken] cheeks
▶빗방울 때문에 땅이 패었다 The raindrops have hollowed out the ground.
2〈파게 하다〉let [have] *sb* dig 《the ground》
패담 悖談 an unreasonable remark
—패담하다 talk unreasonably; say unreasonable things
패덕 悖德 immorality; demoralization; corruption ■—한(漢) an immoral man; a scoundrel —행위 immoral conduct [act]
패도 佩刀 wearing a sword ⇨ 패검(佩劍)
패도 覇道 ruling by force; military rule; the rule of might
패랭이 1〔古制〕a bamboo hat (worn by commoners) 2 ⇨ 패랭이꽃
패랭이꽃〔植〕a pink
패러그래프 a paragraph
패러다이스 a paradise
패러데이 1〈영국의 물리·화학자〉Faraday, Michael (1791-1867) ♦패러데이의 법칙 Faraday's Law 2〈전기량의 단위〉a faraday (略 F)

패러독스 a paradox
패러디 (a) parody ─**작가** a parodist
패럿 〔電〕 a farad (略 F)
 ♦ 백만 패럿 a megafarad / 100만분의 1 패럿 a microfarad
패류 貝類 shellfish
 ■ ─학 conchology ─학자 a conchologist
패륜 悖倫 immorality ♦ 패륜의 immoral
 ─아 an immoral person ─행위 immoral conduct
패리 悖理 irrationality; absurdity
 ─패리하다 irrational; unreasonable; absurd
패리디 〔經〕 parity ♦ ─가격 a parity price ─계산 a parity account [computation] ─지수(指數) a parity index
패망 敗亡 ruin; (a) defeat; rout; wreck
 ─패망하다 be ruined; be defeated; be routed; suffer [sustain] a defeat; fall crash
패멸 敗滅 ruin; decay; destruction; demolition
 ─패멸하다 fall into decay; fall; be ruined; go to ruin; collapse; be destroyed
패물 貝物 shell goods; shellware; things made of coral
패물 佩物 personal ornaments [outfittings]; accessories; trinkets
패배 敗北 (a) defeat; a loss; 〈패주〉 rout
 ♦ 패배를 맛보다 meet with defeat; taste defeat / 패배를 인정하다 admit *one's* defeat
 ▶ 마침내 그는 이 문제에 패배를 인정했다 He admitted defeat about this matter at last.
 ▶ 싸움은 그들의 패배로 끝났다 The battle ended in their defeat.
 ─패배하다 be defeated; be beaten; suffer a defeat; have the worst; lose a battle; 〈경기에서〉 lose a game; 〈패주하다〉 be routed
 ▶ 그는 선거에서 패배했다 He suffered [was defeated] in the election. ≒ He lost the election.
 ─자, a loser; a failure ─주의 defeatism ─주의자 a defeatist
패병 敗兵 a defeated army; routed soldiers [troops]
패보 敗報 the news [tidings] of defeat; a report of defeat
패사 稗史 an unofficial history [chronicle]; an unauthentic history
패산 敗散 a disorderly defeat
 ─패산하다 be defeated disorderly
패색 敗色 signs of defeat; unfavorable signs in battle
 ▶ 패색이 짙다 Defeat seems certain.
패석 貝石 a fossil shell
패설 悖說 an unreasonable remark ⇨ 패담
패설 稗說 a folktale; a folk story; a legend
패세 敗勢 a losing situation; the reverse tide of a war; signs of defeat
패션 (a) fashion
 ■ ─모델[디자이너] a fashion model [designer] ─산업 the fashion industry ─쇼 a fashion show ─잡지 a fashion journal
패소 敗訴 losing a case; a lost case
 ♦ 패소의 당사자 the party defeated
 ─패소하다 lose a case; fail in an action; be cast in a suit

─나는 손해 배상 소송에서 패소했다 I have lost my damage suit.
패스 1 〈합격〉 passing ─**패스하다** pass
 ♦ (물품이) 검사에 패스하다 pass muster; stand the test / 시험에 패스하다 succeed in [pass] an examination [a test]
2 〈무료 입장권·승차권〉 a pass; a free pass; 〈정기권〉 a commutation [〔英〕 season] ticket ─철도의 패스 a pass on the railroad
3 〈통과〉 passing ─**패스하다** pass
 ♦ (의안이) 국회를 패스하다 pass the National Assembly
4 〈球〉 a pass; passwork ─**패스하다** pass
 ♦ 아무에게 볼을 패스하다 pass a ball to *sb*
5 〈카드놀이〉 ─**패스하다** pass
 ─통근 a commutation ticket for workers ■ ─볼 a passed ball: 패스 볼로 득점하다 score on a passed ball
패스트 푸드 fast food
패스포트 〈통행증〉 a passport
 ♦ 패스포트를 신청하다 apply for a passport
패습 悖習 a bad habit; an evil custom
패싸움 牌 ─ a gang fight ─**패싸움하다** have a gang fight; fight in groups
패쓰다 覇 ─ 〔바둑〕 make a no-man's point
패악 悖惡 wickedness; viciousness
 ─패악하다 wicked; vicious
패업 覇業 supremacy; achievements of a conqueror; domination; hegemony
 ♦ 패업을 이룩하다 establish *oneself* as ruler of a country
 ▶ 이 팀은 10연패의 패업을 달성했다 The team has gained the supremacy by a 10-game winning streak.
패역 悖逆 immorality; revolt; uprising
 ─패역하다 rebellious; refractory
패연 沛然 raining in torrents ─**패연하다** heavy; violent
패용 佩用 wearing
 ─패용하다 wear 《a decoration》
패운 敗運 a bad luck to loss; *one's* declining fortune; adverse fortune; *one's* waning star
패인 敗因 a cause of defeat; a factor contributing to defeat
패자 敗者 a loser; the defeated (person); the vanquished
 ■ ─부활전 a repechage ─전 a consolation match [game, race, round]
패자 覇者 〈정복자〉 a supreme ruler; 〈우승자〉 a champion; a winner; a titleholder
패잔병 敗殘兵 remnants 《of a defeated troop》; stragglers; runaway troops ♦ 적의 패잔병 the (escaped) remnants of the enemy / 패잔병 소탕작전 a mopping-up operation
패잡다 牌 ─ get the deal; become the dealer [banker]
패장 敗將 a defeated [vanquished] general
패전 敗戰 defeat in war; defeat; (a) reverse
 ─패전하다 be defeated in a battle; lose a war [battle]
 ■ ─국 a defeated [vanquished] nation ─투수 〔野〕 a losing pitcher
패전트 a pageant; (총칭) (a) pageantry
 ♦ 공중 패전트 an air pageant

패주 敗走 flight; rout; debacle
♦패주중이다 be on the run
―패주하다 be routed; be put to rout; take to flight / 적을 패주시키다 put an enemy to rout; rout an enemy
■―자 a refugee; a fugitive

패총 貝塚 a shell mound; a shell heap; a kitchen midden

패킹 packing ―패킹하다 pack up; stuff up; fill 《a crevice with cotton》

패턴 a pattern

패퇴 敗退 (a) defeat; (a) setback
―패퇴하다 retreat; 〈지다〉 be defeated; lose a battle; 〈경기에서〉 lose a game; be out

패트런 a patron; a patroness (여자); (俗) an angel

패트롤 a patrol ―카 a (police) patrol car

패트리어트 미사일 a Patriot missile

패하다 敗― 1 〈싸움에서 지다〉 be defeated; be beaten; lose 《a game, a battle》
♦경기에 패하다 lose a game / 전쟁에 패하다 be defeated in a war; lose a war / 장기에 패하다 be beaten in a game of chess [*changgi*]
▶나는 불행하게도 패했다 I was defeated unfortunately.
2 〈살림이 거덜나다〉 go [become] bankrupt; (美口) go broke
♦그의 집안은 패했다 His family went to ruin.
3 〈야위다〉 become thin; be worn out
♦그는 결핵을 앓아서 몸이 패했다 Tuberculosis left him a wreck.

패혈증 敗血症 〔醫〕 blood [septic] poisoning; septicemia
■출혈성― hemorrhagic septicemia

팩 with a thud ⇨ 목 2,4

팩시밀리 a facsimile (〈단수·복수 동형〉)

팬 〈애호자〉 a fan; a lover; 〈열광자〉 an enthusiast; 〈숭배자〉 an admirer
♦열렬한 야구 팬 an ardent baseball fan [enthusiast]; a baseball devotee / 음악 팬 a lover of music; a music lover / 스포츠 팬 an enthusiast for sports; a sports enthusiast
▶그의 팬은 층이 넓다 He has fans of a wide variety.
■―레터 a fan letter; (총칭) fan mail

팬더 〔動〕 a (giant) panda

팬지 〔植〕 a pansy; a heartsease; a heart's-ease

팬츠 〈속옷〉 underpants; (英) pants; drawers; 〈남성용〉 briefs; 〈여성용〉 panties; 〈운동 선수의〉 trunks

〔解說〕 (1) *pants*는 (英)에서는 속옷의 팬츠를 가리키고, (美)에서는 바지를 가리키는 경우가 많으나 요즘은 (美)의 용법이 (英)으로도 쓰이게 되어 문맥에 따라서는 그 어느것도 가리키게 되었다.
(2) 더 명확히 구분하려면 속옷의 팬츠는 *underpants*로 하면 되며, *briefs*나 *shorts*라고도 하지만, 이것은 남성용 속옷이고, 여성용은 *panties*이다.

■쇼트― shorts; trunks 운동― athletic shorts 핫― hot pants

팬케이크 a pancake; a griddlecake; a flapjack ■―화장(품) pancake makeup

팬터그래프 〔電〕 a pantograph; pantagraph ■―집전기(集電器) a pantograph collector

팬터마임 ♦a pantomime; a dumb show ♦팬터마임을 하다 pantomime 《an act》; indicate by dumb show
■―배우[작가] a pantomimist

팬티 panties ■―스타킹 a pantihose; a panty hose

팻말 牌― 《put up》 a notice [bulletin] board

팽 1 〈한 바퀴 도는 모양〉 round; (美) around
♦소문이 팽 돌다 a rumor gets abroad / 자전거를 타고 마을을 한 바퀴 팽 돌다 go around the village on a bicycle
2 〈정신이 아찔한 모양〉 reelingly
♦(눈, 머리가) 팽 돌다 be [feel] dizzy; get giddy; spin; be stunned (맞아서)

팽개치다 1 〈내던지다〉 throw [cast] away; fling 《at》; hurl 《at》
♦마루에 책가방을 팽개치다 throw [fling] one's satchel down on the floor
▶그녀는 화를 내며 그에게 책을 팽개쳤다 Getting mad at him, she flung a book at him.
2 〈포기하다〉 give [throw] up; abandon; 〈내버려두다〉 leave off; leave untouched; neglect; desert
♦직무를 팽개치다 neglect *one's* duties
▶그는 그 운동을 위해 직업을 팽개쳤다 He threw up his job for that movement.
▶나는 일을 중도에서 팽개치지 않는다 I don't quit a job halfway.
▶그는 처음부터 시험을 팽개친 것 같아 보였다 He seemed to have given up (on) the exam from the beginning.

팽그르르 round quickly ⇨ 빙그르르

팽글팽글 round and round (quickly) ⇨ 빙글빙글

팽나무 〔植〕 a (Chinese) nettle tree; a (Chinese) hackberry
♦팽나무 열매 a (Chinese) nettle-tree nut

팽대 膨大 expansion; swelling
―팽대하다 expand; swell; bulky; massive; huge; vast

팽만 膨滿 eating enough of food; inflation
―팽만하다 be inflated; eat enough of food

팽배 澎湃 overflowing; surging; rampage; rage ―팽배하다 overflow; surge; rage; rise high ♦팽배한 민주 사상 the flood tide of democracy

팽압 膨壓 〔植〕 turgor pressure

팽이 a top ♦팽이를 치다 spin a top / 팽이를 쳐서 돌리다 whip a top to make it spin
▶팽이가 가만히 섰다 The top is sleeping.

팽창 膨脹 swelling; 〈통화 등의〉 inflation; 〈기체 등의〉 expansion; distension
♦인구의 팽창 the growth [increase] of population / 예산의 팽창 an increase in the budget / 도시의 팽창 the growth of a city
―팽창하다 swell; expand; inflate; grow
♦급속하게 팽창하는 인구 a rapidly expanding [increasing] population / 팽창시키다 expand; swell; inflate
▶가스가 팽창해 기구(氣球)가 터졌다 The gas in the balloon expanded [was expanded] and

팽패롭다
exploded.
▶ 나무는 물기를 머금으면 팽창한다 Woods swells when (it gets) wet.
▶ 수출량은 해마다 계속 팽창하고 있다 The export goes on increasing year after year.
■ 통화— inflation [expansion] of currency —계(計) a dilatometer —계수 〔物〕 the coefficient of expansion —력 expansive power [force]; tension —률 〔物〕 the rate of expansion —성 expansibility; extensibility —정책 expansionist policy —주의 expansionism —주의자 an expansionist

팽패롭다 cranky; particular; crotchety; fussy
팽패리 〈사람〉 a crank; a crosspatch; 《美俗》 a fuss-budget
팽팽 round and round (quickly) ◆ 팽팽 돌다 turn [go] round and round rapidly; spin
팽팽하다 1 〈켕기어서〉 tight; taut; tense; strained; stretched to the full
 ◆ 팽팽하게 tightly; tight; tensely; closely / 팽팽해지다 become tight / 밧줄을 팽팽하게 당기다 tighten [strain] a rope; stretch a rope tight
▶ 너무 팽팽하게 잡아당기면 끊어진다 If you strain it too hard, it will break.
 2 〈힘이〉 equally-balanced; well-matched; close; equal; even
 ◆ 팽팽한 경기 a close game; a well-matched game / 실력이 팽팽하다 be well-matched in power
▶ 양진영이 팽팽히 맞섰다 Two parties were in bitter tug-of-war.
 3 〈성질이〉 narrow-minded; rigid; strict; illiberal; strait-laced
 ◆ 팽팽한 사람 a strict [narrow-minded] person
팽하다 〈알맞다〉 suitable; just right; neither more nor less
퍅하다 愎— snappish; quick-tempered; cranky; peevish; touchy
퍼내다 bail [dip] out; 〈펌프로〉 pump out (a well)
 ◆ 연못 물을 퍼내다 evacuate water from a pond / 삽으로 모래를 퍼내다 dip out sand with a shovel
▶ 소년은 보트의 물을 퍼냈다 The boy bailed water out of the boat.
퍼니 idly; lazily; indolently
퍼덕거리다 flutter ⇨ 파닥거리다
퍼뜨리다 spread; disseminate; propagate; diffuse; popularize; 〈소문 등을〉 set (a rumor) afloat; circulate [spread] (a rumor)
 ◆ 불교를 퍼뜨리다 propagate Buddhism / 헛소문을 퍼뜨리다 spread [circulate] a false rumor
▶ 모기가 그 병을 퍼뜨린다 Mosquitoes spread [carry] the disease.
▶ 그는 결코 소문을 퍼뜨릴 만한 사람이 아니다 He is the last person to tell tales [spread scandal]. ⇒ He is no gossiper.
퍼뜩 suddenly; in a flash
 ◆ 퍼뜩 생각나다 it occurs to one (that); flash across one's mind
▶ 퍼뜩 그는 낚싯줄 끝을 무언가가 잡아당기고 있다는 것을 느꼈다 Suddenly he felt something pulling at the end of his fishline.
퍼렇다 blue ⇨ 파랗다
퍼레이드 a parade
 ◆ 우승 퍼레이드 a victory parade
▶ 그들은 화려하게 시내를 퍼레이드했다 They staged a colorful parade in the city.
퍼머넌트 a permanent (wave); 《口》 a perm
 ◆ 퍼머넌트를 하다 have [get] a permanent; have one's hair permed
 ◆ 그녀의 머리는 천연 퍼머넌트다 Her hair has natural curl.
퍼먹다 1 〈퍼서 먹다〉 dip [scoop, ladle] sth and eat (it)
 ◆ 손으로 밥을 퍼먹다 eat rice with fingers
 2 〈많이 먹다〉 bolt (one's dinner); shovel 《food》 into one's mouth
퍼붓다 1 〈퍼서 붓다〉 pour [throw] 《water》 on [over]; dash 《water》 over
 ◆ 사람에게 물을 퍼붓다 shower [pour] water on [over] sb
 2 〈비가〉 pour (down); pelt down
 ◆ 퍼붓는 비 a pouring rain; a downpour of rain
▶ 비가 억수같이 퍼붓는다 It's raining in torrents [cataracts, cats and dogs]. ⇒ The rain is pouring [coming down in torrents].
 3 〈욕설 등을〉 heap 《abuses》 on; 〈포화를〉 rain 《fire》 on; bring 《the enemy》 under 《fire》
 ◆ 욕설을 퍼붓다 curse and swear (at sb) / 질문을 퍼붓다 shower questions on sb; bombard sb with questions / 적에게 포화를 퍼붓다 rain shells on [upon] the enemy
▶ 변호사는 증인에게 질문을 퍼부었다 The lawyer fired questions at the witness.
▶ 사람들은 그녀에게 비난을 퍼부었다 People heaped [showered] abuse on her.
퍼블릭 public
 ■ —릴레이션 public relations —스쿨 〈영국의〉 a public school —코스 〈골프〉 a public course
퍼석하다 dry and crumbling
▶ 날씨가 가물어서 땅이 퍼석했다 The weather had been dry and the ground was crumbly.
퍼센트 《美》 percent; 《英》 a per cent; 〈백분율〉 (a) percentage (略 p.c., per ct.)

|解說| (1) 보통 앞에 수사가 올 때는 ***percent***를, what나 high, low, large, small 등의 형용사가 올 때는 ***percentage***를 사용하는데 (口)에서는 percentage 대신 percent를 쓰는 경우가 있다. %라는 기호는 보통 상업·기술관계의 문서에 쓴다.
(2) 보통 25% 보다는 a quarter가, 50% 보다는 (a) half를 쓴다.
(3) 0.5%는 point five percent라고 읽는 것은 딱딱한 어법. half of one percent, (口) half a percent 쪽이 보통이다.

 ◆ 백 퍼센트의 성공 a one-hundred percent success / 현금 지급에는 10퍼센트 할인하다 discount ten percent [make a ten percent discount] for cash
▶ 수입이 10퍼센트 줄었다 My income has gone down by ten percent.

▶ 이 직물은 울 50퍼센트, 화학섬유 50퍼센트이다 This fabric is half wool and half synthetic.
▶ 이 학교는 약 60퍼센트가 여학생이다 About sixty percent of the students are girls in this school.
▶ 졸업생의 취업률은 몇 퍼센트입니까? What percentage of the graduates of your school find employment?
▶ 효과는 100퍼센트다 It is certainly one-hundred percent efficiency.

퍼센티지 a (small, large) percentage
♦ 상당히 큰 퍼센티지를 차지하다 take up a considerably high percentage
▶ 수입에 대한 당신의 소득세 퍼센티지는 어느 정도입니까? What percentage of your income is paid in income tax?

퍼스널컴퓨터 a personal computer
퍼스트 〔野〕 〈1루〉 first base; 〈1루수〉 a first baseman
퍼스트레이디 the first lady
퍼올리다 draw up; scoop [dip] up; 〈펌프로〉 pump up
퍼즐 a puzzle ♦ 퍼즐을 풀다 solve a puzzle; work out a puzzle
  ■ 크로스워드— a crossword puzzle
퍼지다 1 〈넓어지다〉 widen; broaden; spread out; become wider [broader]
♦ 끝이 퍼지다 the tip spreads out / 쫙 퍼진 나뭇가지 spreading branches
▶ 그 강은 이 지점에서 퍼져 있다 The river widens at this point.
▶ 그 사막은 멀리까지 퍼져 있다 The desert stretches far and wide.
2 〈유포되다〉 spread (abroad); prevail; be wide-spread; pervade 《a city》; be circulated; 〈소문 등이〉 get about [abroad, around]; go around
▶ 나쁜 소식은 빨리 퍼진다 Bad news circulates quickly.
▶ 소문이 입에서 입으로[사람에게서 사람으로] 전해져 삽시간에 온 시중에 퍼졌다 The rumor went [passed] from mouth to mouth [from person to person] and went all around town in a flash.
▶ 재스민 향기가 주변에 퍼졌다 The odor of jasmine permeated [pervaded] the air.
▶ 유행성 감기가 마을에 퍼졌다 The flu epidemic ran through the village.
▶ 암은 그의 온몸에 퍼졌다 The cancer spread throughout his body.
▶ 불은 사방으로 퍼졌다 The fire spread in all directions.
3 〈불어서 커지다〉 swell up; 〈물을 먹어〉 become soaked; sodden; 〈밥이〉 be steamed (to a proper degree)
▶ 떡쌀이 잘 퍼졌다 Rice for cake got nice and soft.
4 〈유행하다〉 be in fashion; become popular; come into vogue
▶ 이 노래는 학생들 사이에 널리 퍼져 있다 This song is much in vogue [very popular] with the students.
5 〈번식하다〉 breed; multiply; flourish; propagate

♦ 자손이 퍼지다 have a flourishing progeny
6 〈분 등이 먹다〉 spread
▶ 이 분은 잘 퍼진다 This powder spreads well.
7 〈구김살이〉 smooth (down); become [get] smooth

퍼트 〈골프에서〉 a putt ♦ 퍼트를 연습하다 practice putting ─ 퍼트하다 putt
퍼티 putty ♦ 유리창 접합용 퍼티 glazier's putty / 퍼티를 바르다 apply putty 《to》
퍼펙트게임 〔野〕 a perfect game
퍼프 a (powder) puff
퍽¹ 〈매우〉 very much; pretty; quite; quite a bit [a lot]
♦ 퍽 많은 quite a number of 《cars》; a good many 《books》 / 퍽 잘 생긴 quite good-looking / 퍽 재미있다 be very interesting / 퍽 춥다 be pretty cold
▶ 환자가 퍽 좋아졌다 The patient is much better.
▶ 눈이 퍽 많이 왔다 It snowed heavily.
▶ 나는 퍽 시장하다 I'm very hungry. ⇌ (口) I'm simply starving.
▶ 날씨가 11월치고는 퍽 따뜻하다 The weather is quite warm for November.
▶ 그는 퍽 (많이) 변했다 He has changed greatly [so much].
▶ 올해는 물가가 퍽 내려갔다 Prices have come down very much [(口) a lot] this year. ⇌ Prices have become much [(口) a lot] lower this year.
퍽² 1 〈냅다 지르는 모양·소리〉 with a thrust; with great force; (good and) hard
♦ 칼로 퍽 찌르다 thrust with a knife
2 〈힘있이 거꾸러지는 모양·소리〉 with a thud; plump; flop
♦ 퍽 쓰러지다 fall with a thud; fall plump (on the ground)
퍽석 1 〈맥없이 주저앉는 모양·소리〉 limply; with a flump; heavily ♦ 의자에 퍽석 주저앉다 flop down into [on] a chair; sit limply in a chair
2 〈깨지는 모양·소리〉 《break》 easily; fragilely
펀둥거리다 idle *one's* time away ⇨ 빈둥거리다
펀처 a puncher
펀치 〔拳〕 (a) punch; 〈구멍 뚫는 가위·공구〉 a punch
♦ 펀치가 있는 선수 a puncher / 턱에 펀치를 먹이다 punch *sb* on the jaw; land a punch on *sb's* jaw
  ■ ―카드 a punched [punch] card
펀트킥 a punt kick ─ 펀트킥하다 punt
펀펀하다 flat; even; level
♦ 펀펀한 땅 flat ground
펄 1 〈개펄〉 a tideland 2 〈들판〉 a prairie; a vast plain (of lowland)
펄떡거리다 pulsate ⇨ 팔딱거리다
펄럭이다 flutter; wave; flap; fly; stream
▶ 깃발이 펄럭이고 있었다 The flag was fluttering.
펄럭펄럭 fluttering(ly); flapping; with a flutter ▶ 깃발이 바람에 펄럭펄럭 나부낀다 A flag

flaps in the wind.
펄렁거리다 flutter; flap; wave; fly; stream
펄렁펄렁 flutteringly; flappingly
펄스 〔電〕 a pulse; an electric pulse
♦펄스를 발생시키다 pulse 《a transmitter》
■—동작시간 pulse operating time —반복수 a pulse repetition rate —변조(變調) pulse modulation: 펄스 위상[밀도, 주파수, 진폭] 변조 pulse phase [number, frequency, amplitude] modulation —폭 pulse width [length]
펄썩 1 〈먼지 등이 이는 모양〉 rising in a puff
♦먼지가 펄썩 일어나다 a cloud of dust rises
2 〈주저앉는 모양〉 plump; heavily; with a thud
♦의자에 펄썩 주저앉다 plump down into [on] a chair; drop into a chair / 땅바닥에 펄썩 주저앉다 plump 《oneself》 down on the ground
펄쩍 1 〈갑자기 여는 모양〉 suddenly; abruptly
2 〈갑자기 뛰는 모양〉 nimbly; lightly
♦펄쩍 뛰다 make a sudden leap; jump [start, leap, spring] to *one's* feet / 펄쩍 뛰며 좋아하다 jump for joy
▶그는 놀라서 펄쩍 뛰었다 He jumped up with surprise.
펄펄 1 〈끓는 모양〉 simmeringly; seethingly
▶물이 펄펄 끓는다 Water is boiling hard.
2 〈나부끼는 모양〉 flappingly; flutteringly; 〈눈 등이〉 in flakes
♦눈이 펄펄 내린다 It snows in great flakes.
▶새가 펄펄 날고 있다 The birds are flying flapping their wings.
3 〈신열이〉 feverishly; 〈방 등이〉 broilingly; scorchingly
▶그의 몸이 펄펄 끓는다 He has a high fever.
펄펄하다 quick-tempered; lively
펄프 (wood) pulp
♦펄프로 만들다 pulp; reduce to (a) pulp
■대용— substitute for wood pulp 인견[목재, 제지]— rayon [wood, paper] pulp ■—공장 a pulp mill —재(材) pulpwood
펌블 〔野〕 a fumble —펌블하다 fumble 《a grounder》
♦볼을 펌블하다 fumble a ball
펌프 a pump
♦펌프의 손잡이[자루] a pump handle [brake] / 우물에서 펌프로 물을 퍼올리다 pump water up from a well / 펌프질하다 work a pump / 뱃바닥의 물을 펌프로 퍼버리다 pump the water out of a ship; pump out a ship
■공기— an air pump; 〈자전거의〉 a bicycle pump 급수— a feeding pump 배수— a drainage pump 소방— a fire engine 수동(式)— a hand pump; 〈소방용의〉 a manual fire engine 양수— a lift pump 증기[압력, 회전식]— a steam [pressure, rotary] pump 진공[배기]— a vacuum pump 흡인식— a suction pump
■—실 a pump room —우물 a pump well —차 〈소방용〉 a pumper
펌프스 〈여성의 구두〉 (a pair of) pumps
펑 pop; bang
펑퍼지다 well-developed; well-rounded
펑퍼짐하다 flat and round; gently curved; broad and roundish ♦펑퍼짐한 어깨 broad and well-developed shoulders / 펑퍼짐한 엉덩

이 well-rounded hips
평평 1 〈눈 등이 쏟아지는 모양〉 《pour forth, spout》 copiously; gushingly; spoutingly; 〈눈 이〉 《fall》 thickly
♦눈이 평평 쏟아지다 snow falls thick and fast / 눈물을 평평 흘리다 shed copious [a flood of] tears / 돈을 평평 쓰다 lavish *one's* money
2 〈거듭나는 총소리〉 bang! bang!; pop, pop; poppingly
▶폭죽이 평평 터졌다 Bang! bang! went off the fireworks.
페가수스 〔그神〕 Pegasus; the winged horse
■—자리 〔天〕 the Winged Horse; Pegasus
페넌트 〈삼각기〉 a pennant; 〈야구의 우승기〉 (美) a pennant; (英) a championship flag; 〈우 승〉 winning the pennant
♦페넌트를 다투다 compete for the pennant
■—레이스 〔野〕 a pennant race
페널티 〔競〕 (a) penalty ■—골 a penalty goal —에어리어 a penalty area —킥 a penalty kick
페놀 〔化〕 phenol; carbolic acid
■—수지(樹脂) phenolic resin
페놀프탈레인 〔化〕 phenolphthalein
페니 a penny 《略 p.》 《*pl.* -nies, pence》 《▶복수 형의 pennies는 화폐의 개수에 쓰이며, pence는 금액에 사용함》
♦반 페니 a halfpenny / 1 페니 반 three halfpennies [halfpence]
페니실린 〔藥〕 penicillin ♦10만 단위의 페니실 린 100,000 units penicillin
■—쇼크 a penicillin shock —연고 a penicillin ointment —주사 a penicillin shot [injection]
페니키아 Ph(o)enicia
♦페니키아(사람)의 Ph(o)enician
■—말 Ph(o)enician —사람 a Ph(o)enician
페달 a pedal; a treadle ▶나는 자전거의 페달을 밟았다 I pedaled my bicycle.
페더급 —級 〔拳〕 the featherweight
■—선수 a featherweight (boxer)
페디큐어 (a) pedicure
♦페디큐어를 하다 give 《*oneself*》 pedicure
페로몬 〔生〕 pheromone
페로시안화 —化 ■—나트륨 〔化〕 sodium ferrocyanide; yellow prussiate of soda —물 (物) ferrocyanide; prussiate —칼륨 potassium ferrocyanide; yellow prussiate of potash
페루 Peru; 〈공식명〉 the Republic of Peru
♦페루의 Peruvian ■—사람 a Peruvian
페르마타 〔樂〕 a fermata 《*pl.* ~s, -te》
페르미 〔物〕 〈10조분의 1센티미터〉 a fermi
페르시아 Persia ♦페르시아의 Persian
■—고양이 a Persian cat —만 the Persian Gulf —말 Persian —사람 a Persian —양탄자 Persian carpet [rug] —전쟁 the Greco-Persian War
페리 〈미국의 제독(提督)〉 Perry, Matthew Calbraith (1794-1858)
페리보트 a ferry; a ferryboat
페리클레스 〈그리스의 정치가·장군〉 Pericles (B.C. 495?-429)
페미니스트 a feminist 《▶남녀 양쪽에 씀》; 〈여성에게 친절한 남자〉 a chivalrous [a gallant] man; a man who is very kind to woman

페미니즘 feminism
페서리 〖醫〗 a pessary
페세타 〈스페인의 통화 단위〉 a peseta
페소 〈통화 단위〉 a peso 《pl. ~s》
페스탈로치 〈스위스의 교육개혁가〉 Pestalozzi, Johann Heinrich (1746-1827)
페스트 〖醫〗 (the) pest; the black plague ■―선(腺)― bubonic plague ■―바실루스― a plague bacillus 《pl. -li》
페스티벌 (a) festival
페시미스트 a pessimist
페시미즘 pessimism
페어 a pair
페어플레이 fair play
♦페어플레이를 하자 Let's play fair.
페이 pay
■―데이 (美) a payday; (英) a wage day
페이드아웃 〖映·TV〗 (a) fade-out
페이드인 〖映·TV〗 (a) fade-in
페이브먼트 〈포장한 도로〉 a paved road [street]; 〈보도〉(美) a sidewalk; (英) a pavement
페이소스 〈비애감〉 pathos
♦일말의 페이소스 a touch of pathos
▶그 소설에는 페이소스가 넘친다 The novel is full of pathos.
페이스 (a) pace

> 〖解說〗 영어의 *pace*는 「보조, 속도」를 나타내는 말인데 at *one's* own pace라고 하면 「자기에게 알맞는 속도로」라는 뜻이다. 「자기 나름대로 하나」의 「내 페이스대로 하다」는 do *sth one's* way이고 「남을 아랑곳하지 않고 나대로」의 「내 페이스대로」는 go *one's* own way 라고 표현한다.

페이지 a page 《略 p.》《pl. pp.》; 〈양면〉 a leaf 《pl. leaves》
♦페이지 수 the number of pages / 50페이지의 잡지 a magazine of fifty pages; a fifty-page magazine / 페이지의 위[한가운데, 아래] 쪽에 at the top [middle, bottom] of a page / 10페이지에서 15페이지까지 읽다 read pages ten to fifteen [pp. 10-15] / 페이지를 매기다 page 《a book》; paginate 《a book》; number the pages / 12 페이지를 열다[펴다] open 《the book》 at [to] page twelve; find page twelve
▶이 책 20페이지에 그 사진이 나 있다 You will find the picture on page 20 in this book.
▶페이지를 넘기시오 Turn (over) the pages.
▶교과서의 15페이지를 펼치세요 Open your textbook at [to] page fifteen.
▶이 책에는 4페이지의 낙장(落張)이 있다 There are four pages [two leaves] missing from this book.
▶앞 페이지에서 계속 Continued from the previous page.
페이퍼 〈종이〉 paper; 〈논문〉 a paper; 〈사포〉 sandpaper; emery paper [cloth] ♦페이퍼로 문지르다 polish with sandpaper; sandpaper
페이퍼백 a paperback (book); a paperbound (book); a papercover [soft-cover] (book)
페인트 paint
▶페인트가 벗겨졌다 The paint came off.
▶나는 문의 페인트를 문질러 벗겼다 I scraped the paint off the door.
▶페인트 주의(게시) Wet [(英) Fresh] Paint.
■―수성― water paint ■―공 a painter
페인트 〖競〗 a feint; feinting
페치카 〖〈러〉pechka〗 a Russian brick stove
페트 a pet ♦페트를 기르다 keep a pet
페트라르카 〈이탈리아의 시인·학자〉 Petrarch (1304-74) (♦이탈리아 이름은 Francesco Petrarca)
페티코트 a petticoat; an underskirt
페팅 petting
페퍼민트 peppermint
펜 a pen
♦굵은[가는] 펜 a broad [fine] pen / 펜 글씨 pen writing
▶이 펜은 잘 써진다 This pen writes well.
▶편지는 펜으로 써라 Write your letters with a pen.
▶그는 펜으로 싸웠다 He fought with the pen as his weapon.
▶펜은 칼보다 강하다 (속담) The pen is mightier than the sword.
■―라이트― 〖電算〗 a light pen 볼― a ball-point (pen) ■―네임 〈필명〉 a pen name ―대 a penholder ―습자 penmanship ―촉 a pen-point; a nib
펜더 〈자동차의〉(美) a fender; (英) a wing; a mudguard
펜던트 a pendant
펜맨십 penmanship; a copybook
펜스 pence ⇨ 페니
펜스 a fence ▶그 강타자는 펜스를 넘는 공을 쳤다 The slugger hit the ball over the fence.
펜실베이니아 〈미국 동부에 있는 주〉 (the State of) Pennsylvania 《略 Pa., Penn., Penna., PA》 ♦펜실베이니아의 Pennsylvanian
■―사람 a Pennsylvanian
펜싱 〖競〗 fencing; foils
♦펜싱 연습을 하다 practice fencing
■―교사 a fencing master ―도장 a fencing school ―선수 a fencer; a foilsman ―시합 a fencing match; a match at foils ―(용)칼 a (fencing) foil
펜치 (a pair of) (cutting) pliers; pinchers; pincers
펜클럽 the P.E.N. club 〖<the International Association of Poets, Playwrights, Editors, Essayists, and Novelists〗
펜타곤 〈미국 국방부〉 the Pentagon; the Department of Defense
펜팔 a pen pal; a pen-friend
▶많은 펜팔과 편지를 교환하고 싶다 I want to exchange letters with a lot of pen pals.
펜홀더그립 〖球〗 a penholder grip; the grip of a penholder
펜화 ―畫 〈화법〉 line drawing; 〈그림〉 a pen(-and-ink) picture [drawing]; a drawing in pen and ink
펠리컨 〖鳥〗 a pelican
펠트 felt ■―모자 a (soft) felt hat; (美) a soft hat
펩신 〖生化〗 pepsin ■―제(劑) a pepsin
펩톤 〖生化〗 peptone ♦펩톤의 peptonic

펭귄 〔鳥〕 a penguin ■—새끼 a penguin chick
펴내다 〈발행하다〉 publish; issue
♦펴낸이 a publisher
펴놓다 〈벌이어 놓다〉 spread; unfold; lay out; lay open; unroll 《a scroll》 ♦책을 펴놓은다 open a book / 상품을 죽 펴놓다 lay articles out for sale; display articles for sale
펴다 1 〈펼치다〉 spread; lay out; unfold; unroll; open
♦신문을 펴다 unfold a newspaper / 날개를 펴다 spread the wings / 이부자리를 펴다 make [prepare, spread] a bed
▶여기에 지도를 펴라 Spread [Unfold] the map here.
▶그녀는 내게 자기 우산을 펴주었다 She was kind enough to open her umbrella for me.
2 〈뻗다〉 stretch; outstretch; hold out; spread out
♦가슴을 펴다 throw [stick] out one's chest (to); make a long arm 《for》 / 팔다리를 펴다 stretch one's limbs; 〈편안히〉 make *oneself* comfortable / 등을 꼿꼿이 펴다 make your back straight
▶가슴을 펴라 《口令》 Chest out!
▶그는 허리를 폈다 He straightened up.
▶가슴을 펴고 걸어라 Walk with your chest thrown out [expanded].
3 〈굽은 것을〉 straighten; 〈말린 것을〉 uncoil; 〈금속판을〉 planish; roll; 〈구김살 등을〉 smooth out; 〈다리미 등으로〉 iron out
♦철사를 펴다 uncoil wire / 바지의 주름을 펴다 take creases out of the trousers
4 〈재능을〉 cultivate; develop 《one's talent》; realize
♦천부의 재능을 펴다 develop [display] one's natural abilities
5 〈수사(망) 등을〉 ♦전국에 수사망을 펴다 spread [set up] a dragnet [network of police cordon] all over the country
▶KBS는 전세계에 정보망을 펴고 있다 KBS has a world-wide network of news [intelligence].
6 〈세력 등을〉 extend [expand]; establish 《one's influence in a district》
7 〈기를〉 ease 《one's mind》; relieve; keep up
♦기를 펴다 keep his spirits up / 기를 못 펴다 〈공포 때문에〉 shrink; be timid; be in a funk
8 〈공포하다〉 promulgate 《a law》
펴이다 1 ⇨ 펴지다
2 〈형편이〉 become better; be changed for the better; improve; 〈일·어려움이〉 be smoothed (down, away); be eased
♦셈이 펴이다 become better off
▶금년에는 형편이 펴이시길 빕니다 I hope you'll better it this year.
펴지다 1 〈펼쳐지다〉 get unfolded [unrolled]; spread; unroll
▶책상 위에 지도가 펴져 있었다 A map lay spread out on the desk.
2 〈굽은 것·구김살 등이〉 be straightened; be flattened; get smoothed
♦옷의 주름이 펴지다 wrinkle in cloth smooth out / 굽은 허리가 펴지다 one's bent waist straightens up

▶할아버지 이마의 주름살이 펴졌다 Wrinkles on grandfather's brow were gone.
편 便 1 〈쪽〉 a side; 〈방향〉 a direction; a way; 〈패〉 a party; a team
♦우리편 our side [part]; our team [party] / 상대편 the other party; the opposite party / 이[저] 편에 this [that] way / 왼편에 on the left (-hand) side / 동편으로 eastward; to the east / 오른편에 앉다 sit on one's right side / 편을 짜다 make up a party; team up 《with》 / 적의 편에 붙다 go over to the enemy; take sides with the enemy / 자기 편에 끌어들이다 get [win, gain] *sb* over to one's side
▶그 여자는 작은 편이다 The woman is rather small.
2 ⇨ 인편(人便)
3 〈우편〉 《英》 post; 《美》 mail ♦항공편으로 부치다 send 《a letter》 by air mail
4 〈교통〉 facilities; service
♦교통 편 traffic [transportation] facilities; facilities for communication / 철도 편으로 per [by] rail; by train / 배 편으로 by ship [steamer, sea]
▶그 섬으로 가는 배 편이 있습니까? Is there (a) steamer service to the island?
▶그곳은 교통편이 좋다 The place is easy of access.
5 〈선택·경향〉 ▶그와 가느니 집에 있는 편이 낫다 I would rather [sooner] stay at home than go with him.
▶노름 같은 건 안하는 편이 좋다 You had better not gamble.
편 編 compilation; editing
♦이순신편 compiled [edited] by Yi Sun-shin
편 篇 1 〈권〉 a volume; a book
♦전편(前篇)[후편] the first [latter] volume
2 〈나눈 대목〉 a chapter; a section; a part; a canto ♦제1편 the first chapter; chapter Ⅰ; 〈시의〉 canto Ⅰ
3 〈수효〉 a piece ♦한 편의 시 a piece of poetry / 다섯편 five pieces
편가르다 便— divide (the men) in two teams; separate into groups [parties]
♦두 패로 편갈라 싸우다 divide into two groups and fight
편각 偏角 〔地〕 declination; 〔數〕 amplitude; 〔空〕 variation ■—계(計) a declinometer
편견 偏見 prejudice; a bias; a biased view
♦개인적 편견 a personal bias / 편견이 있는 prejudiced; biased; partial / 편견이 없는 unbiased; impartial; fair
▶그는 편견이 강한 사람이다 He is a man of strong prejudices.
▶나는 그에게 편견을 가지고 있었다 I had a prejudice against him.
▶인종적 편견을 버려라 Cast away your racial prejudice.
편곡 編曲 〔樂〕 arrangement
—편곡하다 arrange
▶그는 이 곡을 바이올린곡으로 편곡했다 He arranged this piece of music for the violin.
■—자 an arranger; an adapter
편광 偏光 〔物〕 polarized light; polarization (of light)

■—각 a polarization angle —계 a polarimeter —기 a polariscope —자 a polarizer —현미경 a polarization microscope

편년 編年 ■—사(史) a chronicle; annals —체 a chronological order [form]: 그 책에는 영・미 작가의 이름이 편년체로 짜여져 있다 The name of some English and American authors are arranged chronologically [in chronological order] in the book.

편달 鞭撻 1 〈채찍질〉 whipping; lashing —편달하다 whip; lash 2 〈격려〉 urging; encouragement ▶ 선생의 지도 편달을 바랍니다 I take to you for your guidance and encouragement. —편달하다 encourage [urge] 《sb to do》; spur on 《sb to industry》

편대 編隊 (a) formation ♦ 편대를 짜다 fly into formation; 〔美空軍〕 formate / 6기(機) 편대로 비행하다 fly in a six-plane formation ■—비행— flight formation ■—비행 a formation flight: 편대 비행을 하다 fly in formation; make a formation flight —장 a flight leader

편도 片道 one way; each way ♦ 편도를 택시로 가다 go by taxi one way ▶ 편도로 1,000원입니다 It costs you one thousand won one way. ■—승차권 《美》 a one-way ticket; 《英》 a single (ticket): 편도 승차권입니까, 왕복입니까? Do you want a one-way or a round-trip ticket? —요금 《美》 a one-way fare; 《英》 a single fare

편도 扁桃 〔植〕〈나무〉 an almond (tree); 〈열매〉 an almond ■—유(油) almond oil

편도선 扁桃腺 〔解〕 the tonsils; the amygdala (pl. -lae) ♦ 화농성편도선염 septic tonsillitis ▶ 당신의 편도선은 부어 있습니다 You have swollen tonsils. ⇒ Your tonsils are swollen. ■—비대 swollen [enlarged] tonsils —염 tonsillitis —절제술 tonsillectomy

편두통 偏頭痛 〔醫〕 (a) migraine; (a) megrim ♦ 편두통이 나다 have a migraine; suffer from a migraine

편들다 便— take sides with; side with; take sb's part; be on sb's side ♦ 아들을 편들다 side with one's son ▶ 그는 언제나 가난한 사람을 편든다 He always takes sides with the poor.

편람 便覽 a handbook; a manual ♦ 영문법 편람 a handbook of English Grammar

편력 遍歷 〈여담〉 travels; 〈순례〉 a pilgrimage ▶ 「나의 독서편력」이라는 제목으로 에세이를 쓰기로 했다 I am to write an essay on [under] the title of "My Life with Books." —편력하다 go on a pilgrimage; travel about; itinerate ♦ 전국을 편력하다 make a tour of the country; traverse the whole country ■—자 an itinerant; a pilgrim

편류 偏流 〔海・空〕 (a) drift; (a) deflection; 〈총알의〉 windage —각 a drift angle —계 a drift meter [indicator]

편리 便利 convenience; expediency; handiness ♦ 아무의 편리를 도모하다 consult [serve] the convenience of sb —편리하다 convenient; useful; handy ♦ 편리한 도구 a convenient [a handy, a useful] tool / 가지고 다니기에 편리한 사전 a handy [helpful] dictionary to carry / 생활에 편리한 여러가지 물건 various conveniences of life / 편리한 때에 at your convenience; whenever it suits you [it is convenient to you] ▶ 피크닉 갈 때는 종이 접시가 편리하다 Paper dishes are convenient [handy] on a picnic. ▶ 나는 버스로 가는 것이 아주 편리하다 It is very convenient [a great convenience] to me to go by bus. ▶ 우리 집은 역에서 가까워 편리하다 My house is convenient for [to] the station. ⇒ My house is conveniently [handily] located near the station. ▶ 이웃에 의사가 있다는 것은 아주 편리하다 It is a great convenience to have a doctor in one's neighborhood. ▶ 이 기계는 아주 편리하게 고안되었다 This machine is skillfully devised for convenient use.

편린 片鱗 〈사물의〉 a part; a glimpse ▶ 이로써 그의 성격의 편린을 엿볼 수가 있다 It enables us to get a glimpse of his personality.

편마암 片麻岩 〔地質〕 a gneiss

편만 遍滿 pervasiveness; diffusiveness; omnipresence —편만하다 diffuse; omnipresent; all-pervasive

편면 片面 one side ■—레코드 a single-faced record; a single-sided disk —인쇄기 a single-side (printing) machine

편모 偏母 one's widowed [lone] mother ■—슬하 having only one's mother to serve: 편모 슬하에서 자라다 grow up under widow-mother's care

편모 鞭毛 〔生〕 a flagellum 《pl. ~s, -la》 ♦ 편모가 있는 flagellate ■—운동 flagellar movement —충 a flagellate

편무 片務・偏務 a unilateral duty (responsibility) ♦ 편무적(인) 〔法〕 unilateral; one-sided 《treaty》 ■—계약 〔法〕 a unilateral [one-sided] contract

편무역 片貿易 one-way trade; unbalanced [lopsided, unilateral] trade

편물 編物 knitting; crochet; 〈뜨개질한 것〉 knitted goods; knitting; knit; 〈옷〉 knitted garment; knitwear ♦ 편물을 하다 knit; do knitting; crochet ■—기계 a knitting machine; a knitter

편발 編髮 plaiting the hair

편법 便法 a convenient [handy] method; an expedient; a shortcut; an expediency ♦ 편법을 쓰다 adopt [resort to] an expedient ▶ 그의 행위는 일시적인 편법에 지나지 않는다 His act is only a temporary expedient.

편벽 偏僻 eccentricity; one-sidedness; partiality; unfairness —편벽하다[되다] eccentric; one-sided; prejudiced; partial; bias(s)ed

편복 便服 an ordinary dress [attire]; plain

clothes; easy [informal] dress; home wear
편상화 編上靴 lace-up [laced] boots
편서풍 偏西風 〔氣〕 the (prevailing) westerlies
편성 編成 〈조직하고 형성함〉 organization; formation
▶지금은 예산편성으로 몹시 바쁜 때다 Now is the time we are extremely busy making up the budget.
—편성하다 organize; compose; compile; draw up; frame; embody
♦프로그램을 편성하다 draw up a program / 예산을 편성하다 draw up an estimate; make up a budget
▶우리 반은 50명으로 편성돼 있다 Our class consists of fifty students.
◆예산— the compilation of a budget 전시[평시]— a war [peace] footing [organization] 프로그램— 〔라디오·TV〕 program(m)ing
■—국 〈방송국의〉 the program(m)ing department
편수 編修 editing; compilation
—편수하다 edit; compile
■—관(官) an editorial officer; an (official) editor —국(局) 〈교육부의〉 the Textbook Compilation Bureau
편승 便乘 1 〈교통편을 얻어 탐〉—편승하다 get a lift
♦그의 차에 편승하다 get a lift in his car
2 〈기회를 틈타기〉—편승하다 take advantage of; avail *oneself* of
♦시세에 편승하다 〈이용하다〉 take advantage of the trend of the times
■—가격 인상 follow-up price hikes; me-too price raise —자 an opportunist; a man on the fence
편식 偏食 an unbalanced diet
▶아이들에게 편식 버릇을 들여선 안된다 Children should be kept from having unbalanced diets.
—편식하다 have an unbalanced diet
편심 偏心 〈마음〉 a one-sided mind; 〔機〕 eccentricity
■—력 eccentric force —륜 an eccentric (wheel) —봉 an eccentric rod —톱니바퀴 an eccentric gear
편쌈 便— a gang fight —편쌈하다 fight in groups; have a gang fight ■—꾼 a gang fighter
편안 便安 〈무사함〉 security; safety; 〈평온〉 peace; calmness; quietness; 〈안락〉 ease; comfort; carefreeness
—편안하다 secure; safe; peaceful; comfortable; quiet; calm; tranquil; restful; easy
♦편안한 생활 a quiet [peaceful] life; a comfortable living; an easy life / 편안히 safe(ly); peacefully; quietly; in comfort / 마음이 편안하다 feel at ease; be free from care / 집안에서 편안한 밤을 지내다 spend a quiet [a peaceful] evening at home / 편안히 지내다 get along well / 여생을 편안히 보내다 spend *one's* declining years in peace / 마음을 편안히 가지다 ease *one's* mind; take it easy
▶그 사람 옆에 있으면 마음이 편안해진다 I feel easy [at ease] when I am around him.

▶아기는 엄마 품에서 편안히 잠들어 있었다 The baby was sleeping peacefully in its mother's arms.
▶아무것도 그들의 마음을 편안히 할 수 없었다 Nothing could set their minds at rest.
편암 片岩 〔鑛〕 schist
♦편암(모양)의 schistose
편애 偏愛 favoritism; favor; partiality
▶막내딸에 대한 그의 편애가 그녀를 이기적으로 만들었다 His partiality to the youngest girl made her selfish.
—편애하다 be partial 《to》; show favoritism 《to》; favor
▶어머니는 그를 편애했다 The mother was partial to him.
편액 扁額 a framed picture; a (horizontal) tablet; a plaque
편영 片影 a speck; a sign; a shadow
편육 片肉 slices of boiled beef
편의 便衣 an ordinary dress ⇨ 편복(便服)
■—대(隊) 〈중국의〉 plain clothes soldiers; a partisan; snipers
편의 便宜 convenience; facility; accommodation; expediency; 〈교통 등의〉 facilities; 〈이익〉 advantage
♦연구의 편의 facilities for study / 편의상 as a matter of convenience; for convenience' sake / 서로의 편의상 for mutual convenience / 편의를 제공하다 offer [afford] convenience 《to *sb*》; provide [afford] facility; offer advantage 《to》 / 공중의 편의를 도모하다 [존중하다] promote [respect] the public convenience
▶나는 아버지의 편의를 위해 현재의 집으로 이사했다 I moved to the present house for the convenience of my father.
▶버스는 여행자의 편의를 위해 있다 Buses are for convenience of travelers.
♦신문은 편의상 많은 약어를 사용한다 The newspaper uses many abbreviations for the sake of convenience.
■—점 a convenience store —주의 opportunism —주의자 an opportunist —품 convenience goods
편이 便易 convenience; handiness; easiness
—편이하다 convenient; handy; easy; useful
편익 便益 〈이익〉 benefit; advantage; 〈편리〉 convenience; facility; profit
편입 編入 1 〈입학허가〉 admission; 〈합병〉 incorporation; 〔軍〕 enlistment; enrol(l)ment 《in》
—편입하다 〈부류에〉 class 《with, among》; include 《in》; 〈학급에〉 admit 《into》; place 《in a grade》; enrol(l) 《into》; 〈예산에〉 insert; 〈군대에〉 assign 《to the infantry》; enrol(l) [incorporate] 《into》; 〈예비역에〉 transfer 《to the reserve》
♦2학년에 편입되다 be admitted to the second grade; be accepted as a second grader
▶그 도시는 최근 울산시에 편입되었다 The town has recently been incorporated into Ulsan city.
2 〈짜 넣음〉 weaving —편입하다 weave 《in》
■—생 an enrol(l)ee —시험 a transfer admis-

편자 a horseshoe ♦말에 편자를 박다 shoe a horse
편자 編者 an editor; a compiler
편재 偏在 maldistribution; unfair distribution ♦부의 편재 the maldistribution of wealth ─**편재하다** be unevenly distributed; be maldistributed
편재 遍在 omnipresence; ubiquity ─**편재하다** be omnipresent; be ubiquitous; be widespread
편저 編著 compilation; redaction ♦스미스 편저 (a book) edited [compiled] by Smith
편전 便殿 the king's private quarters [living room]
편제 編制 formation; organization; composition ■전시─ war organization 평시─ peace organization
편중 偏重 undue emphasis 《on》; preponderance ▶이 회사는 학력 편중을 피하고 능력주의를 취하고 있다 This company does not make too much of school [academic] careers but takes merit [ability] system. ─**편중하다** preponderate; attach [give] too much importance; lay disproportionate emphasis 《on》 ♦학력에 편중하다 place undue [too much] emphasis on educational background ♦학력─ diplomatism
편지 片紙·便紙 a letter; a communication; a note; a line; 〈서간〉 an epistle; (총칭) mail ♦5월 4일자의 그녀의 편지 her letter dated [of] May 4 〈편지의〉 편지의 사연 the contents [purport, text] of a letter ▶나는 즉시 편지의 답장을 썼다 I answered the letter immediately. ▶이 편지의 우송료는 얼마입니까? What's the postage on [for] this letter? 〈편지가〉 그녀에게서 편지가 왔습니까? Have you received a letter from her? ▶모임의 세부 사항을 묻는 편지가 많이 왔다 A lot of poeple have written in (asking) about details of the meeting. ⇒ There were a lot of letters asking for details of the meeting. 〈편지를〉 나는 그에게 긴 편지를 썼다 I wrote him a long letter. ⇒ I wrote a long letter to him. ▶나는 런던으로 편지를 부쳤다 I sent a letter to London. ▶도착하면 간단한 편지를 주십시오 Please drop me a note [line] when you get there. 〈편지에〉 편지에 따르면 그는 머지 않아 미국으로 떠난다고 한다 He says in his letter [His letter says] that he is leaving for America before long. 〈편지로〉 답변은 편지로 해주십시오 Please answer [reply] by letter. ▶그는 편지로 내게 언제 오느냐고 물어왔다 He has written and asked (me) when I will come. ⇒ He has written asking [to ask] (me) when I will come.

▶그녀는 편지로 곧 결혼한다고 내게 알려왔다 She wrote (to) me that she was going to get married soon. ■**감사[사례]─** a letter of thanks; an appreciative letter **안부─** a letter inquiring after sb's health **연애─** a love letter **인사─** a letter of greetings ■**─봉투** an envelop; an envelope **─지** letter paper; notepaper **─통** a letter case; 〈대문의〉 (美) a mailbox; (英) a letterbox
편집 偏執 bigotry; obstinacy ─**편집하다** be begoted 《to, in》; be obstinate; stick to ■**─광** 〈상태〉 monomania; paranoia; 〈사람〉 a monomaniac **─병환자** a paranoid
편집 編輯 editing; compilation; redaction ▶이 책은 편집이 잘 돼 있다[있지 않다] This book is well [badly] edited. ─**편집하다** edit; compile ♦테이프를 편집하다 edit a tape / 안내서를 편집하다 compile a guidebook / 신문기사를 편집하다 edit; blue-pencil ▶이 책은 저명한 학자 셋이 편집했다 Three famous scholars edited this book. ■**─국** an editorial office [section]; a news office **─국장** a managing editor **─기** a editor **─마감** the editorial deadline **─방식** a edit mode **─방침** the editorial policy **─부** the editorial department **─부원** an editorial staff member; a member of the editorial staff **─부장[주간]** the chief editor; the editor in chief **─실** an editorial office [room]; (美) 〈신문사의〉 the desk **─자** an editor; a compiler **─장** the chief editor **─회의** an editorial [editors'] meeting; an editorial conference **─후기(後記)** the editor's note
편짓다 片─ 1 〈목재를〉 sort according to use; classify 《lumber》 into various uses **2** 〈인삼을〉 arrange 《ginseng》 to make a fixed number of pound lots
편짜다 便─ form [make up] a team; team up; 〈편 가르다〉 separate into groups ♦**편** 짜서 놀이를 하다 play (on opposite) sides (in a game)
편짝 便─·偏─ 〈한쪽〉 one side; one hand; 〈한편〉 a party ♦이[저] 편짝 this [the other] side / 우리[상대] 편짝 our [the other] party / 반대 편짝에 on the opposite side / 한편짝으로 기울다 lean to one side
편차 偏差 〔物〕 (a) deflection; (a) variation; 〔統〕 (a) deviation; 〔測〕 (a) declination; windage; 〔空·海〕 (a) drift; driftage ♦나침반의 편차 deflection [deviation] of the compass ■**자침─** magnetic declination [deviation] **표준─** 〔統〕 the standard deviation ■**─값** the deviation (value)
편찬 編纂 compilation; editing ♦사전 편찬 compilation of a dictionary ─**편찬하다** compile 《a dictionary》; edit 《an anthology》 ▶사전을 편찬하는데는 수년이 걸린다 It takes many years to compile a dictionary. ■**─물** a compilation **─위원** a compilation

committee —자 a compiler; an editor
편찮다 便— **1** 〈편하지 않다〉 uncomfortable; uneasy; inconvenient
♦편찮은 잠자리 an uncomfortable bed; a bed uncomfortable to sleep in
2 〈병을 앓고 있다〉 ill; sick; unwell
♦몸이 편찮다 be unwell; be [feel] out of sorts
▶어디 편찮으십니까? Is anything the matter with you?
▶나는 어저께 속이 편찮았다 I had something wrong with my inside yesterday. ≒ My stomach was out of order yesterday.
편충 鞭蟲 〔動〕 a (human) whipworm
편취 騙取 a swindle; a fraud; an imposture; a cheat; a defraudation
—편취하다 defraud; obtain by fraud; swindle; cheat; deceive
♦아무의 금품을 편취하다 swindle money out of *sb*; swindle *sb* out of money
■—자 a swindler; an impostor; a cheat; a crook
편친 偏親 one parent; an only parent
♦편친의 아이 a fatherless [motherless] child / 편친 슬하에서 사는 아이 a child with only one parent living
편파 偏頗 partiality; favoritism; 〈불공평〉 unfairness; (unfair) discrimination; 〈한쪽으로 치우침〉 one-sidedness
♦편파적인 재판 an unfair [unjust] trial / 편파적인 세제(稅制) an unfair tax system / 편파적인 판단을 내리다 pass an unfair [a partial] judgment 〈on it〉
▶그가 하는 말만 듣는다는 것은 편파적이다 Listening only to his side of the story is unfair.
—편파하다 partial; unfair; one-sided
편편하다 便便— easy; comfortable; free from care
♦편편히 지내다 lead a comfortable life; live at *one's* ease
편평족 扁平足 〔病理〕 flatfoot; splayfoot; 〈발〉 a flatfoot; a splayfoot
♦편평족이다 be flat-footed; have flatfeet
편평하다 扁平— even; level; flat; horizontal
편하다 便— **1** 〈안락하다〉 easy; comfortable; 〈걱정이 없다〉 carefree; free from care; easygoing
♦편한 잠자리 a comfortable bed / 편히, 편하게 easily; at ease; comfortably / 속이 편하다 feel comfortable in the stomach / 마음이 편하다 be carefree; feel at ease / 마음이 편하지 않다 be ill at ease; be uneasy / 잠시도 마음 편할 때가 없다 have no moment of ease / 편히 앉다 sit at ease; make *oneself* at home
▶마음을 편하게 가지십시오 Please make yourself at home [comfortable].
▶너는 편한 마음으로 시험을 치러야 한다 You should relax when taking an examination.
▶아저씨는 마음 편히 지내고 계신다 My uncle leads an easy life.
▶시골 생활은 마음이 편하다 Country life is free from care.
2 〈편리하다〉 convenient; handy; suitable; expedient

♦편한 물건 a handy thing / 쓰기에 편하다 be convenient of use; be easy to use / 교통이 편하다 have (good) facilities of communication
▶전기 기구로 인해 집안일이 편해졌다 Electric appliances have made homework easier.
3 〈쉽다〉 easy; light; simple; soft
♦편한 일 an easy task; light labor; a soft job
▶그 일은 옆에서 보는 것처럼 그렇게 편한 일은 아니다 It is by no means so easy as it seems.
4 〈고통이 없다〉 ♦편해지다 〈고통이〉 be mitigated; be alleviated; 〈사람이〉 feel relief; get rid of 《pain》
▶이 약을 먹으면 편해진다 This medicine will bring you relief.
편향 偏向 (an) inclination; a leaning; a propensity; a tendency; 〔物〕 (a) deflection
♦편향적인 의견 a partial [prejudiced, biased] opinion
—편향하다 incline; lean; tend; deflect; be deflected
▶그의 판단은 편향되어 있다 His judgment is partial [prejudiced, one-sided].
■—감도 deflection sensitivity —교육 deflected education
편협 偏狹 narrow-mindedness; illiberality; intolerance
—편협하다 narrow-minded; intolerant; 〈편견을 가진〉 prejudiced
▶나는 편협했다 I was narrow-minded.
편형동물 偏形動物 〔生〕 a flatworm; a platyhelminth
■—문 the Platyhelminthes
펼치다 unfold; spread [open] (out); lay out; unroll; develop; stretch
♦날개를 펼치다 spread the wings / 담요를 펼치다 spread [lay out] a blanket / 돛을 펼치다 unfurl a sail / 많은 관중 앞에서 열전을 펼치다 play an exciting game in front of [watched by] a huge crowd of spectators
펼침화음 —和音 a broken chord
폄론 貶論 disparagement; adverse criticism; censure
—폄론하다 disparage; censure; criticize
폄하다 貶— disparage; speak ill of; despise
♦아무를 폄하다 speak ill of *sb*; run *sb* down
평 評 (a) criticism; 〈비평〉 a comment; a review; 〈평판〉 (a) reputation
♦영화평 a film review / 서평 a book review / 평이 좋다[나쁘다] be well [ill] spoken of; have a good [bad] reputation
▶그의 행동은 그에게 나쁜 평을 초래했다 His actions had given him a bad name.
—평하다 criticize
평 坪 **1** 〈넓이〉 a *p'yŏng*; 〈부피〉 a *p'yŏng*
♦평당 per *p'yŏng*
▶이 집은 40평입니다 This house covers 40 *p'yŏng*.
2 〈유리・헝겊・벽의〉 a *p'yŏng*
3 〈조각・동판의〉 *p'yŏng*
평- 平- ordinary; common; plain
♦평교사 a common teacher / 평사원 a mere employee [clerk]
평가 平價 〔經〕 par; parity

◆실제 평가 real par of exchange / 평가의 par / 평가로 at par / 평가 이상[이하]이다 be above [below] par
■법정(法定)— mint par; par of exchange ─절상 upvaluation (of the won); upward evaluation ─절하 devaluation (of the won): 평가절하하다 devaluate; devalue

평가 評價 valuation; appraisal; estimation; 〈과세의〉 assessment; 〈성적의〉 evaluation
◆정당한 평가 a correct estimate / 재산의 평가 the assessment [rating] of one's property ─평가하다 evaluate; rate; estimate; value; assess; estimate
◆높게[낮게] 평가하다 rate 《a thing》 high [low]; put [set] high [low] value on 《a thing》 / 학생의 능력을 평가하다 evaluate student's abilities / 그 집을 9천만원으로 평가하다 estimate [value] the house at ninety million won; rate the house at [as worth] 90 million won / 자신의 기준으로 남을 평가하다 measure others by one's own standard
▶ 그들은 당신을 높이 평가하고 있소 They think highly of [have a high opinion of] you. ⇒ They regard you highly.
■ 과대— overestimation 과소— underestimation 재— revaluation; reappraisal ─교수단 a group of professors assigned to evaluate the government policies ─기준 a valuation basis; an appraisal standard ─액 appraised [estimated] value : 평가액 10억원의 토지 an estate with a value of a billion won ─익(益) [손(損)] an appraisal profit [loss] ─자[인] an appraiser; an assessor; a valuer

평각 平角 〔數〕 a straight angle

평결 評決 a decision; 〈배심원단의〉 a verdict
◆원고에게 유리한 평결 a verdict for [favorable to] the plaintiff
▶ 배심원은 유죄[무죄] 평결을 내렸다 The jury returned [brought in] a verdict of guilty [not guilty].
─평결하다 bring in [give, deliver, return] a verdict 《of》

평균 平均 1 〈고름〉 an average; 〔數〕 the (arithmetical) mean
◆한 사람 평균 per head / 월평균 강우량 the average monthly rainfall
▶ 그의 성적은 평균 이상[이하]이다 His school work is above [below] (the) average. ⇒ He is above [below] (the) average in school work.
▶ 3과 5와 7의 평균은 5다 The average of 3, 5, 7 is 5.
▶ 나는 기말시험에서 평균 70점을 받았다 I got an average grade of 70 on the terminal examination.
▶ 그는 평균 주5일 근무한다 He works for five days a week on (an [the]) average. ⇒ He averages five days' work a week.
▶ 이 나라의 인구밀도는 1제곱킬로미터에 평균 5명이다 In this country there are, on an average, five persons to the square kilometer.
▶ 소년들의 평균 신장은 170센티미터다 The average height of the boys is 170 centimeters.
─평균하다 average; strike [take] an average

◆평균하여 on an [the] average
2 〈균형〉 equilibrium; equipoise; balance
■산술[기하]— the arithmetical [geometric] mean 연[월]— the yearly [monthly] mean 조화—〔數〕 the harmonic mean ─값 the average [mean] value ─거리 the mean distance ─기온 the average temperature ─대〔體操〕 a balance beam ─속도 average [mean] velocity ─수 the mean number ─수명 the average [mean] life ─수위 mean water level ─여명 (餘命)〔保〕 average future lifetime; expectation of life; life expectancy ─연령 the average age ─오차 the mean error ─온도〔體操・舞〕 balance ─태양시 the mean solar time ─편차 mean [average] deviation ─해수면 the mean sea level

평기와 平— a plain roof tile

평년 平年 1 〈윤년이 아닌 해〉 a common year
2 〈예년〉 the normal [average] year
▶ 올해의 평균기온은 평년보다 2도 높다 The average temperature this year is two degrees higher than usual.
▶ 올해의 쌀 수확량은 평년 수준이 될 것이다 This year's rice crop will be normal.
─작 an average [normal] crop

평등 平等 equality; 〈공평무사〉 impartiality
◆민족(의) 평등 racial equality
─평등하다 equal; even; impartial
◆평등한 권리 equal rights / 평등하게 equally; evenly; 〈차별없이〉 impartially / 기회를 평등하게 주다 give equal opportunities 《to》
▶ 그는 그들에게 그 돈을 평등하게 분배했다 He divided the money equally among them.
▶ 그녀는 학생들을 평등하게 취급했다 She treated her students impartially [〈공평하게〉 fairy, 〈차별없이〉 without discrimination]. ⇒ She was impartial [fair] to her students.
▶ 법 앞에는 만인이 평등하다 All men are equal before [in the eye of] the law.
▶ 사람은 모두 나면서부터 평등하다 All men are created equal.
─론자 an equalitarian; an egalitarian ─주의 equalitarianism; egalitarianism ─주의자 an egalitarian; a leveler ─화 equalization

평란 平亂 suppression of a rebellion
─평란하다 suppress a rebellion; put down a revolt

평로 平爐 an open hearth; an open-hearth furnace
■─법 the open-hearth process

평론 評論 〈비평〉 (a) criticism; a comment; a commentary; a critique; 〈잡지・신문의〉 a review
◆야구 평론가 〈해설자〉 a baseball commentator / 영문학 평론가 a criticizer of English literature / 영화 평론가 a movie critic [reviewer]
─평론하다 comment; make comments 《on》; review; criticize
■문예— literary criticism; a critical essay: 문예평론가 a literary critic 시사— comments on current topics; a contemporary review ■─가 a critic; a commentator; a reviewer ─문(文)

a critical essay —(잡)지 a review
평맥 平脈 the normal [regular] pulse
평면 平面 a plane (surface); a level; a flat
♦ 평면의 plane; level; flat / 동일 평면상에 있다 be on the same plane [plane] 《with》; be in one plane
■—각 a plane angle —거울 a plane mirror —교차 (美) crossing at grade; grade crossing; (英) level crossing —교차점 a grade [(英) level] crossing —기하학 plane geometry —도 (圖) a plan; a flat; 〈건축의〉 a floor plan —도형 a plane figure —묘사 a plane delineation —배양 plate culture —삼각법 plane trigonometry —지도 a map on Mercator('s) projection; a Mercator('s) chart
평미레 平— a strickle; a grain leveler (used in measuring grain); a leveling stick
■—질 strickling: 평미레질하다 strickle; strike the measure
평미리치다 平— 〈고르게 하다〉 make even; smooth; place (all) on a footing of equality
평민 平民 a commoner; a plebeian; (총칭) the common people
▶ 그 왕은 평민적이었다 The King was democratic.
평방 平方 a square ⇨ 제곱
평범 平凡 commonness; commonplaceness; platitude; mediocrity
—평범하다 common; ordinary; commonplace; humdrum; banal; trite; 〈범용(凡庸)한〉 mediocre; 〈특색이 없는〉 featureless
♦ 평범한 체험 a common experience / 평범한 사람 a mediocrity; an ordinary [average] man / 평범한 얼굴 a common [featureless] face / 평범한 나날 uneventful days / 평범하게 살다 live a humdrum life
▶ 그는 평범한 작가가 아니다 He is no ordinary [mediocre] writer.
평복 平服 plain clothes; ordinary attire; ordinary dress; 〈군복에 대해〉 civilian clothes; (口) civ(v)ies; mufti
♦ 평복을 입은, 평복차림의 (dressed) in plain clothes; in everyday [ordinary] clothes [attire]
▶ 그는 평복으로 식당에 왔다 He came into the dining room in plain clothes.
—평복하다 wear plain clothes
평분 平分 equal division
♦ 주야 평분의 equinoctial / 주야 평분점 the equinoctial point / 주야 평분시 equinox
—평분하다 divide equally; divide into two equal parts
평사원 平社員 a mere [plain] clerk
평상 平床 a flat bench; a wooden bedstead
평상 平常 ordinary times ⇨ 평상시
■—복 ⇨ 평복(平服)
평상시 平常時 ordinary [normal] times; 〈평화시〉 peace time
♦ 평상시의 usual; ordinary; normal; common; everyday; 〈상습적인〉 customary; habitual / 평상시에 at ordinary [normal] times; 〈보통〉 ordinarily; commonly; usually; 〈상습적으로〉 customarily; habitually / 평상시와는 달리 unusually

▶ 나는 오늘 아침에 평상시보다 일찍 일어났다 This morning I got up earlier than usual.
▶ 업무는 평상시대로 한다 Business will be carried as usual.
평생 平生 one's [a] lifetime; one's (whole) life
♦ 평생의 사업 one's lifework [life's work] / 평생의 한(恨) a lifelong regret / 평생토록 변치 않는 우정 lifelong friendship / 평생을 독신으로 지내다 remain single through life
▶ 그의 평생은 불행의 연속이었다 His life was a series of misfortunes.
▶ 그 사전을 만드는데는 평생이 걸릴 것이다 It would take your (whole) lifetime to make the dictionary.
■—소원 one's lifelong desire; a desire cherished for life
평서문 平敍文 〔文法〕a declarative sentence; an assertive sentence
평석 評釋 an annotation; a commentary; a critical note —평석하다 annotate; make critical [explanatory] notes (on)
평소 平素 ordinary times
♦ 평소처럼, 평소와 같이 as usual / 평소의 소망이 이루어지다 one's long-cherished desire [wish] is realized
▶ 그의 태도는 평소와 조금도 다르지 않았다 His attitude was no different from usual.
▶ 나는 평소 6시에 일어난다 I usually get up at six.
평수 坪數 the number of p'yŏng area; 〈건평〉 floor space [area]; 〈넓이〉 space
▶ 가게는 평수가 20평이다 The store covers 20 p'yŏng.
평시 平時 normal times ⇨ 평상시
♦ 평시에는 in time of peace / 평시에도 전시에도 in peace and war
■—국제법 international law in time of peace —봉쇄 〔國際法〕pacific blockade —산업 peacetime [nonwar] industry —작전권이양 the transfer of peacetime operational control —편제 peace organization [establishment, footing]
평신도 平信徒 a lay believer; a layperson; 〈남자〉 a layman; 〈여자〉 a laywoman; (총칭) the laity
평안 平安 peace; calm(ness); quiet(ness); tranquility
—평안하다 peaceful; quiet; calm; tranquil
♦ 평안한 날을 보내다 lead a quiet life; live in peace / 평안하게 peacefully; quietly; calmly; in peace; at rest
▶ 평안하시기를 빕니다! Peace be with you!
▶ 평안히 잠드소서 〈비문〉 Rest in peace.
평야 平野 a plain; an open field
■ 호남— the Honam plain(s)
평열 平熱 the normal temperature
▶ 내 평열은 36.5도다 My normal temperature is 36.5 degrees.
평영 平泳 the breaststroke
▶ 나는 오늘 처음으로 평영을 할 수 있게 되었다 Today I was able to swim breaststroke for the first time.
■—선수 a breaststroker

평온 平溫 a normal temperature; an average [a mean] temperature

평온 平穩 calmness; quiet(ness); tranquility; serenity
―평온하다 quiet; peaceful; tranquil; serene
▸ 집회는 평온한 가운데 끝났다 The rally came to an end in peace.
▸ 폭풍 뒤에는 무척 평온해졌다 The storm was followed [succeeded] by a great calm.
▸ 아버지는 시골서 평온한 생활을 하고 계신다 My father is enjoying a quiet life in the country.

평원 平原 a plain; a champaign; (美)〈대초원〉 a prairie

평의 評議 conference; consultation; 〈토의〉 discussion; deliberations
▸ 우리는 그 건을 평의에 부쳐 결정하였다 We had a conference on the matter and decided.
▸ 그 건은 현재 평의중에 있다 The matter is now under discussion.
―평의하다 confer; consult (with sb); discuss (a matter)
■―원 a councilor ―회 a council; a conference

평이 平易 1 〈쉬움〉 easiness; facility
―평이하다 easy
♦ 평이한 영어로 쓰여진 책 a book written in plain [simple, easy] English
2 〈간명〉 plainness; 〈단순〉 simplicity
―평이하다 plain; simple
♦ 평이한 문체 a simple [plain] style / 설명을 평이하게 하다 simplify an explanation / 평이하게 하다 simplify

평일 平日 〈일요일 이외의 날〉 a weekday; 〈일하는 날〉 a workday; a business day; 〈평상시〉 ordinary times
♦ 평일처럼, 평일과 같이 as usual / 평일에는 on weekdays; on business days
▸ 평일에는 학교에 간다 We go to school on weekdays.
▸ 저 가게는 평일에는 9시에 연다 The store opens at nine on weekdays.

평자 評者 a critic; a commentator; a reviewer
평작 平作 a normal crop ⇨ 평년작
평전 平傳 a critical biography
평점 評點 〈점수〉 grades; marks; (美) rating; grading
평정 平定 subjugation; suppression
―평정하다 subjugate 《the whole country》; suppress; repress
♦ 반란을 평정하다 put down the uprising [rebels]
▸ 내란은 곧 평정될 것이다 The civil war will soon be terminated.

평정 平靜 calm; calmness; peace; serenity; 〈침착〉 composure
♦ 마음의 평정 presence [peace, serenity] of mind
▸ 그는 곧 평정을 되찾았다 He soon restored to tranquility.
▸ 그녀는 평정을 가장했다 She feigned calmness. ⇌ She pretended to be calm.
―평정하다 calm; quiet; composed; peaceful
평정 評定 rating; evaluation; valuation
―평정하다 rate; evaluate; valuate
■ 근무― efficiency rating

평준 平準 〈수준〉 level; 〈평균〉 equality
■ ―점 a level point ―화 leveling; equalization: 평준화하다 level; equalize; make equal

평지 〔植〕 a rape; a cole ■―씨 a coleseed; a rapeseed ―유 rape(seed) oil

평지 平地 the level land [ground]; 〈평원〉 a plain; a flat [level] country
▸ 적설은 평지에서 20센티미터였다 The snow lay twenty centimeters deep on the level ground.
■―풍파 an unnecessary disturbance [trouble]: 장모님은 이따금 평지풍파를 일으킨다 My mother-in-law sometimes causes a disturbance where everything is peaceful.

평직 平織 plain fabrics
평집 平― 〔建〕 a small house with only three or four crossbeams

평찌 an arrow flying low and level

평탄 平坦 1 〈지면이〉 flatness; evenness
―평탄하다 flat; smooth; plane; level
▸ 차는 평탄한 도로를 달렸다 The car ran on the plain road.
2 〈마음의〉 calmness; tranquility
―평탄하다 calm; placid; peaceful; tranquil; even
3 〈일이 순조로움〉 smoothness; favorableness
―평탄하다 favorable; smooth; uneventful

평토 平土 leveling the ground after burial
―평토하다 level off ■―장(葬) burying without making a mound on the grave

평판 平板 a flat board; a slat
평판 評判 (a) reputation; 〈정평〉 a (good) name; 〈명성〉 fame; 〈인기〉 popularity; the talk 《of》
〈평판이〉 평판이 나쁜 사람 a man of bad [evil] reputation / 평판이 대단한 가게 a store with a excellent reputation / 평판이 자자하다 be talked about; become popular
▸ 그는 의사로서 평판이 좋다 He has [enjoys] a good reputation as a doctor.
▸ 그 회사는 일이 조잡해 평판이 나빴다 The company had a bad reputation [name] for its poor work.
▸ 그 영화는 젊은이들 사이에서 평판이 좋다 The movie is popular with [among] young people.
▸ 그 이후 그는 평판이 올라갔다[떨어졌다] His reputation has risen [fallen] since then.

평판인쇄 平版印刷 lithography; planography; surface printing; lithoprinting ―평판인쇄하다 lithograph; planograph; lithoprint
■―공 a lithographer; a lithoprinter

평평하다 平平― 1 〈평탄하다〉 flat; level; even; smooth; horizontal; plane
♦ 평평한 땅 even [level, flat] ground / 평평히 하다 flat; flatten; level down [up]; even; smooth; make even [smooth]; 〈금속등을〉 roll
2 〈평범하다〉 common; ordinary; commonplace

평하다 評― criticize; comment 《on》
♦ 시사문제를 평하다 comment on the news of the day

▶ 사람들은 그를 골프광이라고 평한다 They speak of him as an avid golfer.

평행 平行 〔數〕 parallelism; parallel
♦ …와 평행으로 선을 긋다 draw a line parallel to…
—평행하다 parallel 《to, with》
▶ 그 철도는 고속도로와 평행하게 뻗어 있다 The railway runs parallel to [with] the superhighway.
▶ 선 A와 평행한 선을 그으시오 Draw a line parallel to line A.
■ —권(圈) a parallel circle —력 〔物〕 parallel forces —봉 〔體操〕 parallel bars —사변형 〔數〕 a parallelogram —선 〔數〕 parallel (lines) —운동 a parallel motion —자 a parallel ruler —절단 parallel cutting —체 parallel form

평형 平衡 balance; equilibrium; counterbalance; counterpoise; a state of perfect balance; poise
♦ 몸의 평형을 유지하다 keep *one's* balance [equilibrium]
▶ 스케이트 선수는 몸의 평형을 잃고 넘어졌다 The skater lost his balance and fell.
—평형하다 balanced; well-balanced; poised; (be) in equilibrium
■ 안정[불안정]— stable [unstable] equilibrium —감각 the sense of equilibrium; the static sense —력 〔物〕 a counterbalance; an equilibrant —상태 (a state of) equilibrium; equilibrium state —수준기(水準器) a balance level —시험 a balancing test —키 a balanced rudder

평형 교부금 平衡交付金 an equalization grant (to a local government)
■ 일반— a general equalizing subsidy

평화 平和 peace; 〈평정〉 quiet; 〈평온〉 tranquility
♦ 가정의 평화 domestic harmony [peace]/ 마음의 평화 peace of mind; (*one's*) inward peace / 40년간의 평화 forty years of peace; a peace of forty years
〈평화의〉 비둘기는 평화의 상징이라고 한다 A dove is said to be a symbol of peace.
〈평화가〉 그에게는 마음의 평화가 없다 He has no peace of mind.
▶ 세계 평화가 회복되었다 Peace returned to the world.
〈평화를〉 평화를 유지하다[사랑하다] maintain [love] peace / 영원한[영속적인] 평화를 확립하다 establish a permanent [an everlasting] peace / 평화를 깨뜨리다 disturb peace
▶ 그들은 평화를 사랑하는 국민이다 They are peace-loving people.
—평화롭다 peaceful; pacific; harmonious
♦ 평화로운 마음 a peaceful mind / 평화로운 방법 an amicable way / 평화로운 시대 a pacific era / 평화롭게 peacefully; in peace; quietly / 평화롭게 살다 live in peace; lead a peaceful life; enjoy a life of peace
▶ 우리는 평화롭게 살고 있다 We are living peacefully [in peace].
▶ 우리는 평화로운 세계를 원한다 We hope for a peaceful world.
■ 세계— world peace; the peace of the world;

universal peace 집단— collective peace
■ —공세 a peace offensive —공존 peaceful coexistence —교섭 peace negotiations —론자 a pacifist; a peacemonger —사절 a peace envoy —산업 (a) peaceful [peacetime] industry —선 the Peace Line —애호국가 a peace-loving nation —연구 peace studies —외교 peaceful diplomacy —운동 a peace [pacifist] movement [campaign] —유지군 〈유엔의〉 a peace [peacekeeping] force —정책 policy of universal peace —주의 pacifism; pacificism —주의자 a pacifist; a pacificist —회담 peace talks —회의 a peace conference [congress]

평화 봉사단 平和奉仕團 〈미국의〉 the Peace Corps ■ —원 a Peace Corpsman

평화조약 平和條約 a peace treaty; a peace
♦ 평화조약을 맺다 conclude a peace treaty 《with》

평활 平— a bow for practice

평활 平滑 —평활하다 smooth; level; even
♦ 평활하게 하다 make smooth; 〈기름을 쳐서〉 lubricate ■ —근(筋) 〔解〕 a smooth muscle —도 smoothness —회로 smoothing circuit

폐 肺 〔解〕 the lungs
♦ 폐의 pulmonary / 폐가 나쁘다 have a weak chest / 폐를 앓다 have lung trouble; have a lung [pulmonary] complaint
▶ 그는 오른쪽 폐가 나쁘다 His right lung is affected.
▶ 흡연은 폐에 나쁘다 Smoking is bad for the lungs.
■ —동맥[정맥] the pulmonary artery [vein] —절제(切除) pneumonectomy

폐 弊 1 ⇨ 폐단(弊端)
2 〈남에게 끼치는 괴로움〉 (a) trouble; (a) worry; a bother 《to *sb*》; 〈귀찮은 일〉 (an) annoyance
♦ 아무에게 폐를 끼치다 trouble [annoy] *sb*; give [cause] *sb* trouble; put *sb* to bother
▶ 〔會話〕「폐가 안될지 모르겠습니다」「아닙니다, 폐라니요」 "I'm afraid I'm disturbing you." "Oh, no. You aren't disturbing me at all."
▶ 폐를 끼쳐서 죄송합니다 I'm sorry to give you much trouble. ⇌ I'm sorry to trouble you.
▶ 폐가 많았습니다 I owe you very much. ⇌ I'm afraid I have caused you a great deal of trouble.

폐가 廢家 1 〈버려두어 낡은 집〉 a deserted house **2** 〈단절된 집안〉 an extinct family; an abolished house —폐가 하다 the family becomes extinct

폐간 廢刊 discontinuance 《of a publication》; ceased publication
—폐간하다 cease to publish; discontinue the publication 《of a newspaper》
♦ 폐간된 잡지 a defunct magazine; a magazine now defunct / 폐간되다 be discontinued; go out of print

폐갱 廢坑 an abandoned mine ⇨ 폐광

폐결핵 肺結核 〔醫〕 (pulmonary) tuberculosis (略 TB, T.B., t.b., tb); consumption
▶ 그는 폐결핵을 앓고 있다 He is suffering from tuberculosis of the lungs.

■―환자 a consumptive (patient)
폐경기 閉經期 〔生理〕 the climacteric; the menopause
◆폐경기의 여자 a woman at the menopause
폐관 閉管 a closed pipe; a closed tube
폐관 閉館 closing (its doors)
▶도서관은 10시에 폐관한다 The library closes at ten.
▶금일 폐관 (게시) Closed (For) Today.
폐광 廢鑛 an abandoned [an unworked, a disused] mine; a dead pit [mine]
―폐광하다 abandon a mine; disuse a mine
폐교 廢校 abolition [closing] of a school
―폐교하다 close [abolish] a school
▶경영난으로 이 학교를 폐교하기로 결정했다 Being in financial difficulties we decided to close this school.
폐기 廢棄 〈제도・풍습 등의〉 abolition; disuse; 〈법률 등의〉 (an) abrogation; repeal; 〈방기〉 abandonment; 〈조약의〉 denunciation
―폐기하다 abandon; scrap; 〈철폐하다〉 abolish; 〈법률 등을〉 repeal; abrogate
▶헌차를 폐기하고 새차를 샀다 We scrapped the used car and bought a new one.
▶이런 낡은 것들은 이제 다 폐기할 시기다 It's about time all these old things were done away with.
폐기물 廢棄物 (a) waste (matter)
■방사성― radioactive waste [products]; atomic waste 산업― industrial waste 플라스틱― waste plastic material(s) ■―처리 〈원자로의〉 disposal of (radioactive) waste matter; waste disposal : 방사성 폐기물 처리는 지금 큰 사회문제가 되어 있다 How to dispose of atomic waste is now a big social problem.
폐기종 肺氣腫 〔醫〕 emphysema of the lungs; pulmonary emphysema
폐농 廢農 giving up farming ―폐농하다 give up [abandon] farming
폐단 弊端 an evil; an abuse; an obnoxious custom; evil pratices ◆폐단을 고치다 remedy [correct] an abuse
▶젊은이들은 자칫 이런 폐단에 빠지기 쉽다 Young men are apt to fall into this evil.
폐디스토마 肺― 〔動〕 pulmonary distoma; lung fluke
폐렴 肺炎 〔醫〕 pneumonia; inflammation of the lungs ■급성― acute pneumonia
폐롭다 弊― **1** 〈귀찮다〉 bothersome; troublesome ◆폐롭게 여기다 grudge taking the trouble of (doing)
2 〈성미가 까다롭다〉 fussy; fastidious; particular ◆폐로운 사람 a man hard to please; a fussy person
폐립 廢立 enthronement and dethronement
―폐립하다 enthrone and dethrone (a king)
폐막 閉幕 a curtainfall; the falling of the curtain; a close
―폐막하다 close [bring down] the curtain; close; end; finish; bring to an end
▶공연은 10시에 폐막된다 The performance ends [closes] at 10 p.m.
폐문 肺門 〔解〕 the pulmonary hilum (*pl.* -la); the hilum of a lung

폐문 閉門 closing the gate
▶폐문 (게시) Closed up. ⇌ No entrance.
―폐문하다 close the gate; bar the gate
―시간 the closing time; lockup
폐물 廢物 waste material; a useless article [thing]; 〈부스러기・쓰레기〉 refuse; dregs; garbage; 〈낡은 것〉 an obsolete thing; a has-been
◆폐물이 되다 become useless; go to waste
―이용 the utilization of waste material
폐방 廢房 a deserted room ―폐방하다 put a room into disuse
폐백 幣帛 **1** 〈신부의〉 bride's gifts to her parents-in-law
◆폐백을 올리다 (a bride) make a deep bow and offer her gifts to her parents-in-law
2 〈신랑의〉 silks offered to the bride by the bridegroom
3 〈제자의〉 a present from a pupil on meeting his teacher for the first time
폐병 肺病 consumption; a lung disease; 〈폐결핵〉 tuberculosis
▶그 남자는 폐병에 걸렸다 His lungs were [became] affected.
■―환자 a consumptive (patient); 《美俗》 a lunger
폐부 肺腑 **1** ⇨ 폐 (肺)
2 〈마음의 깊은 속〉 the depths of *one's* heart; *one's* inmost heart; 〈급소〉 the key [vital] point
◆폐부에서 우러나오다 come from the heart / 폐부를 찌르다 give *sb* a home thrust
▶이것은 사람의 폐부를 찌르는 듯한 얘기다 This is a heart-breaking story.
폐비 廢妃 a deposed queen; a former queen; a deposal of a queen ―폐비하다 depose a queen; force a queen to abdicate
폐사 敝社 our company [firm]
폐사 廢寺 a ruined temple
폐색 閉塞 **1** 〈닫아 막음〉 blockade; stoppage; 〔鐵〕 a block; 〔醫〕 occlusion; obstruction
―폐색하다 blockade; block (up)
◆항구를 폐색하다 block up [blockade, bottle up] a harbor
2 〈운수가 막힘〉 coming to the end of *one's* luck
■장(腸)― 〔醫〕 ileus ―구간[신호] 〔鐵〕 a block section [signal] ―선(船) a blockader ―음 an occlusive ―전선 〔氣〕 an occluded front
폐석 廢石 〔鑛〕 muck; gob; goaf
폐선 廢船 a scrapped vessel; a hulk; a vessel retired from service ―폐선하다 scrap a vessel
폐소공포증 閉所恐怖症 〔精神醫〕 claustrophobia
폐쇄 閉鎖 a shutdown; (a) lockout; closing; closure ◆폐쇄적인 사회 a closed society
―폐쇄하다 close; close down; 〈일시적으로〉 shut down; lock out; wind up
◆공장을 폐쇄하다 close [shut] down the factory
▶공항은 안개 때문에 폐쇄되었다 The airport was closed because of (the) fog.
■공장― 〈노동자의 때의〉 《美》 a closedown; a

lockout ■ —음 a stop (sound); an implosive —혈관계(系) closed blood vascular system
폐수 廢水 waste water
■ 공장— liquid waste from a factory : 공장폐수에 의한 환경오염 environmental pollution caused by effluent from factories ■ —처리 waste-water treatment —처리시설 a waste-water disposal plant
폐수종 肺水腫 〔醫〕 a pulmonary edema (*pl.* -mata); an edema of the lungs
폐스럽다 弊— troublesome; bothersome; worrisome; annoying; cumbersome
폐습 弊習 a bad habit; an evil practice; a corrupt [an evil] custom
◆ 방치할 수 없는 폐습 a crying abuse / 폐습에 물들다 be tainted with a bad habit / 폐습을 고치다 remedy abuses / 폐습을 없애다 do away with evil customs
폐식 閉式 closing of a ceremony —폐식하다 break up a ceremony
폐안 廢案 a rejected bill; a draft withdrawn
◆ 폐안을 처리하다 withdraw a bill
폐암 肺癌 〔醫〕 cancer of the lungs; lung cancer; pulmonary carcinoma
폐어 肺魚 〔魚〕 a lungfish; a dipnoan
폐어 廢語 an obsolete [a disused] word
폐업 廢業 discontinuance [abolishment] of business
—폐업하다 give up [close, quit] one's business; 〈폐점하다〉 shut up one's shop; 〈의사・변호사 등이〉 close down one's store; give up one's practice; 〈배우 등이〉 retire (from the stage)
▶ 그는 장사를 폐업하지 않으면 안되었다 He was forced out of business.
■ —신고 a report of cessation of business : 폐업신고를 내다 report the cessation of business
폐엽 肺葉 〔解〕 a lobe of the lung; pulmonary lobe
■ —절제술 lobectomy
폐옥 廢屋 a house left in ruin ◆ 폐옥이 되다 fall into disrepair; become dilapidated
폐원 閉院 〈의회의〉 the closing of the National Assembly
—폐원하다 close [adjourn] (the session of) the National Assembly
■ —식 the closing ceremony of the National Assembly
폐위 廢位 dethronement —폐위하다 dethrone; depose (a sovereign)
▶ 백성은 왕을 폐위시켰다 The people took the crown from the king.
폐유 廢油 waste oil; rejected [defective] oil
폐인 廢人 a crippled [disabled] person; a cripple; a confirmed invalid; (俗) a crock
◆ 폐인이나 다름없이 되다 become as good as a living dead
폐일언하다 蔽一言— sum up (a story); boil down ◆ 폐일언하고 in a word; in brief [short]; to sum up; to be short
폐장 閉場 closing (of a place) —폐장하다 close; be closed ■ —식 a closing ceremony —후 〔證〕 after the close

폐장 肺臟 〔解〕 the lungs ⇨ 폐(肺)
폐점 閉店 〈가게를 닫음〉 —폐점하다 close a [the] shop; close one's doors; 〈폐업하다〉 shut up one's shop; close one's shop
▶ 그 가게는 9시에 폐점한다 The store closes at nine.
▶ 폐점시간입니다 〈손님에게〉 I'm afraid it's time to close.
▶ 금일 폐점 (게시) Closed (For) Today.
▶ 저 가게는 지난달에 폐점했다 That store went out of business last month.
■ —시간 the closing hour
폐점 弊店 my [our] store
폐정 閉廷 the adjournment of the court
▶ 재판장은 금요일까지 폐정을 선언했다 The presiding judge adjourned court till Friday.
—폐정하다 adjourn the court
▶ 1시간 쯤 뒤에 폐정했다 The court rose [adjourned] after an hour or so.
폐지 閉止 stoppage —폐지하다 stop; cease; close
폐지 廢止 abolition; disuse; 〈법률 등의〉 repeal; abrogation; 〈취소〉 annulment
▶ 노예제도의 폐지는 흑인들의 꿈이었다 The abolition of slavery was the dream of blacks.
—폐지하다 abolish; disuse; do away (with); repeal; abrogate; annul
◆ 폐지되다 be abolished; go out of use
폐질 廢疾 〈지체장애〉 disablement; an incurable disease ◆ 폐질이 되다 be disabled; be crippled for life
■ —자 a disabled person; a physically handicapped person
폐차 廢車 a scrapped vehicle [car]
◆ 폐차 처분하다 scrap a car ■ —장 an auto junkyard
폐창 廢娼 abolition of licensed prostitution —폐창하다 abolish licensed prostitution [white slavery]
폐첨 肺尖 〔解〕 the apex of a lung
■ —카타르 pulmonary apicitis; the catarrh of the apex of the lung
폐출혈 肺出血 〔醫〕 pneumonorrhagia; hemorrhage from the lungs
폐충혈 肺充血 〔醫〕 pneumonemia; congestion of the lungs
폐침윤 肺浸潤 〔醫〕 infiltration of the lungs
폐포 肺胞 〔解〕 an alveolus (*pl.* -li); pulmonary alveolus ■ —음(音) 〔醫〕 a vesicular murmur
폐품 廢品 waste articles; useless materials; junk
◆ 폐품을 회수[재생이용]하다 collect [recycle] waste articles
■ —수집 collection of waste articles [materials]; recovery of scrap —회수업자 a junk dealer; (英) a rag-and-bone merchant
폐풍 弊風 a bad habit ⇨ 폐습(弊習)
폐하 陛下 〈3인칭〉 His [Her] Majesty (略 H.M.); 〈2인칭〉 Your Majesty
◆ 영국 여왕 폐하 H.M. the Queen of England; Her Britannic Majesty (略 H.B.M.)
폐하다 廢— 1 〈제도 등을〉 abolish; abandon; discard

♦ 노예 제도를 폐하다 abolish slavery
2 〈법률 등을〉 repeal; annul; abrogate
3 〈일·사용을〉 discontinue; give up
♦ 허례 허식을 폐하다 do away with formalities / 이틀 동안이나 음식을 폐하고 go without meal for two days
4 〈임금을〉 dethrone; depose

폐학하다 廢學— discontinue one's studies; leave school [college]

폐함 廢艦 a ship out of commission; a decommissioned warship —**폐함하다** decommission a warship

폐합 廢合 abolition and amalgamation —**폐합하다** abolish and amalgamate; reorganize
▶ 그다지 중요하지 않은 부서는 폐합하자고 제안했다 I suggested the reorganization of [that we (should) reorganize] rather unimportant sections.
■ —정리 reorganization; rearrangement

폐해 弊害 an evil; a vice; evil practices; 〈악습〉 an abuse; 〈악영향〉 a harmful [bad] influence
♦ 폐해가 따르다 be attended by an evil / 폐해를 끼치다 exert an evil influence upon; have an injurious effect upon / 폐해를 고치다 remedy [correct] an abuse
▶ 흡연은 건강에 여러 가지 폐해를 가져온다 Smoking brings about a lot of bad effects on health.

폐허 廢墟 ruins; remains
♦ 폐허가 된 성 a castle in ruins; a ruined castle
▶ 성은 폐허가 되었다 The castle has fallen into ruins.
▶ 그 이집트 사원은 지금은 폐허가 되어 있다 The Egyptian temple is now a ruin [lie in ruins].

폐환 肺患 a lung disease ⇨ 폐병

폐활량 肺活量 lung [vital] capacity
▶ 그의 폐활량은 3,500이다 The capacity of his lungs is 3,500 cubic centimeters.
■ —계(計) a spirometer; a pulmometer; a pneumatometer —측정 spirometry; pulmometry

폐회 閉會 the closing; a close
♦ 폐회를 선언하다 declare the meeting closed
▶ 국회는 폐회 중이다 The National Assembly is not in session.
—**폐회하다** 《a meeting》 close; break up; 〈회가〉 be closed
▶ 위원회는 6시에 폐회했다 The committee adjourned at six.
■ —사 a closing address —식 a closing ceremony

포 苞 〔植〕 a bract
♦ 포가 있는 bracteate / 포가 없는 ebracteate

포 砲 a gun; 〈대포〉 a cannon; 〈야포〉 a fieldpiece; 〈총칭〉 gunnery; ordnance
♦ 12인치 포 twelve-inch gun / 포를 쏘다 fire a gun

포 脯 dry sliced meat ⇨ 포육(脯肉)

포 〈미국의 소설가·시인〉 Poe, Edgar Allan (1809-49)

-포 a period (of time)

♦ 달포 a period of about a month

포가 砲架 〔軍〕 a gun carriage; 〈군함용의〉 a naval gun mount ♦ 포가를 설치하다 set a gun carriage

포개다 put one upon another; lay over; pile [heap] up
♦ 포개놓은 쟁반 nested; a nest of trays / 벽돌을 포개다 pile up bricks

포갬포갬 one upon another; in piles [heaps, stacks]; in layers
♦ 물건을 포갬포갬 쌓다 pile things one upon another

포격 砲擊 bombardment; shelling; gunfire; a gunshot; a cannonade
♦ 포격을 개시하다 open fire 《on a fort》 / 포격을 받다 be bombarded 《by》; be [come] under fire 《from》
—**포격하다** bombard; cannonade; shell; fire on [at]
▶ 그들은 대포로 그 성을 포격했다 They battered down the castle with cannon.

포경 包莖 〔醫〕 phimosis 《pl. -ses》 ■ —수술 an operation for phimosis; phimosiectomy

포경 捕鯨 whaling; whale fishing
—**포경하다** whale; catch [capture] whales
■ —국제—관리조약 the International Whale Fishing Control Treaty 국제—위원회 the International Whaling Commission (略 IWC) 국제—협정 the International Whaling Agreement (略 IWA) ■ —금지 a ban on the hunting of whales —금지운동 an anti-whaling campaign —기간 the whaling season —기지 a whaling station —선 a whaling ship; a whaler —선단 the whaling fleet —업 the whaling industry —장 a whaling ground; a whale fishery —포 a whaling gun; a harpoon gun —포수 a harpooner —회사 a whale company

포고 布告 proclamation; declaration; announcement; notification
♦ 포고를 내다 issue [make] a proclamation
—**포고하다** proclaim; announce; declare; decree; notify
▶ 그것은 작년에 법령으로 포고되었다 It was declared by statute last year.
■ —선전— a declaration of war ■ —문 a decree; an edict; an ordinance; proclamation; a declaration

포괄 包括 inclusion; comprehension
♦ 포괄적인 [으로] inclusive(ly); comprehensive(ly)
▶ 우리는 이들 문제에 관한 포괄적인 의견을 필요로 한다 We require a general opinion of these problems.
—**포괄하다** include; comprehend; comprise
■ —범위 〈협약의〉 the coverage 《of an agreement》 —보험 (a) blanket insurance —보험증서 a blanket policy —승계인 a general successor —안 a package plan —유증(遺贈) a universal legacy

포교 布敎 propagation (of religion); missionary work; mission
♦ 포교에 종사하다 be engaged in missionary work
—**포교하다** preach; propagate; mission;

포구

propagandize; proselytize
■ ―구[지] a mission (field) ―단 a mission ―자 a propagator; a missionary (worker); an evangelist

포구 浦口 an inlet; a port

포구 砲口 〈포문〉 the muzzle of a gun

포구 捕球 〈野〉 a catch ◆ 멋진 포구 a nice catch ―포구하다 catch a ball

포근하다 1 〈따뜻하고 편안하다〉 comfortably warm; snug (and comfortable); 〈폭신하다〉 soft; downy; fluffy
◆ 포근한 이부자리 downy bedding / 어머니의 포근한 가슴 mother's warm breast
2 〈겨울 날씨가〉 mild; soft; genial
◆ 포근한 겨울 a soft [mild, green] winter

포금 砲金 gunmetal

포기 a plant; a head 《of cabbage》; a root
◆ 풀 한 포기 one clump of grass / 배추 열 포기 ten heads of cabbage / 포기가 실한 배추 a cabbage with a good head

포기 抛棄 abandonment; giving up; 〈권리 등의〉 renouncement; surrender; 〔法〕 release; 〈요구 등의〉 relinquishment
◆ 재판권의 포기 waiver of jurisdiction ―포기하다 give up; throw up; abandon; desert; 〈권리·요구 등을〉 renounce; lay aside; relinquish
◆ 계획을 포기하다 give up one's plan / 직장을 포기하다 give up one's job / 지위를 포기하다 throw up one's position [post, office] / 권리를 포기하다 resign the right / 일을 포기하다 give [chuck] up one's job / 불타고 있는 배를 포기하다 abandon a burning ship
▶ 그는 그 토지의 소유권을 포기하였다 He renounced the ownership of the land.
▶ 병 때문에 그는 학업을 포기할 수 밖에 없었다 He could not help laying aside his studies because of illness.

포달 an abusive tirade; naughty language
◆ 포달스럽다 naughty; perverse / 포달부리다 behave wickedly; use abusive language

포대 包袋 a sack ⇨ 부대(負袋)

포대 砲臺 (a gun) battery; a casemate
◆ 포대를 구축하다 build a fort; construct a battery

포대기 a swaddle; a quilt for little children

포도 葡萄 〔植〕 〈열매〉 a grape; 〈나무〉 a (grape)vine
◆ 포도 수확 a vintage / 포도를 재배하다 raise [grow] grapes
▶ 금년은 포도가 풍작[흉작]이다 This has been an excellent [a poor] year for grapes.
■ ―건 ― a raisin ■ ―당(糖) grape sugar; dextrose; 〔化〕 glucose ―덩굴 a grapevine ―밭 [원] a vineyard; a vinery; a grapery; a grape plantation ―색 dark grape purple ―송이 a bunch [cluster] of grapes ―씨 a grape seed; a grapestone ―재배 grape-growing; viticulture ―즙 grape juice

포도 鋪道 a pavement; a paved street

포도동 〈날개치는 소리〉 with a rapid flapping of the wings; flutteringly
―포도동하다 flap [clap, beat] the wings; flutter; beat the air

포도상구균 葡萄狀球菌 〔菌〕 a staphylococcus 《pl. -cocci》

포도주 葡萄酒 wine; vinous liquor
◆ 포도주 한 다스 a dozen bottles of wine
■ ―백 ― white wine; Rhenish wine; hock; sherry; (프) vin blanc 적(赤)― red [purple] wine; claret ―상(商) a vintner ―양조장 a winery

포동포동하다 plump; fleshy; round; well-fleshed; chubby
◆ 포동포동한 손 chubby hands / 포동포동한 아기 a plump baby / 포동포동하게 살이 찌다 be plump; be chubby

포드 1 (商標) 〈자동차〉 a Ford (car) 2 〈미국의 자동차 제조업자〉 Ford, Henry (1863-1947)

포란 抱卵 incubation ―포란하다 incubate
■ ―기(期) 〈새의〉 sitting

포로 捕虜 1 〈전쟁의〉 a prisoner (of war) 《略 P.O.W., POW》; a war prisoner; a captive
◆ 포로로 삼다 take sb prisoner; make a prisoner of sb / 포로를 수용하다 intern a prisoner
▶ 그들은 포로가 되었다 They were taken prisoner.
2 〈비유〉 a victim; a slave ◆ 포로가 되다 be a slave to; be enslaved; enslave oneself to
■ ―교환 an exchange of prisoners ―교환 협정 the Prisoners of War Exchange Pact ―송환 the repatriation of prisoners of war ―송환 관리 repatriation and custody of prisoners of war ―수용소 a prisoners' [POW] camp; 〈강제 수용소〉 a concentration camp ―인도 the delivery of prisoners

포르노 pornography; (口) porno
■ ―숍 a porn(o)shop ―영화 a pornographic film; (俗) a skin flick ―작가 a pornographer ―잡지 a porno(graphic) magazine

포르르 1 〈끓어오르는 모양〉 bubbly; boilingly ―포르르하다 bubble [boil] up; seethe
2 〈나는 모양·소리〉 ◆ 포르르 날다 flush
3 〈타는 모양〉 (burn) crisply
4 〈떠는 모양〉 tremblingly

포르말린 〔化〕 formalin ■ ―소독 formalin disinfection

포르테 (이) 〔樂〕 forte 《略 f.》

포르토노보 〈베냉의 수도〉 Porto Novo

포르토프랭스 〈아이티의 수도〉 Port-au-Prince

포르투갈 Portugal; 〈공식명〉 the Republic of Portugal ◆ 포르투갈의 Portuguese
■ ―말 Portuguese ―사람 a Portuguese

포르티시모 (이) 〔樂〕 fortissimo 《略 ff》

포마드 pomade; pomatum
▶ 그는 머리에 포마드를 발랐다 He applied pomade to his hair.

포만 飽滿 satiety; satiation ―포만하다 be satiated [sated] 《with》

포말 泡沫 a bubble; foam; froth
■ ―회사 a bubble company; a fly-by-night concern

포목 布木 linen and cotton (cloth); piece goods; (美) dry goods; (英) drapery
■ ―상(장수) a draper; a linen-draper; (美) a dry-goods dealer ―전(廛)[점] a draper's shop; (美) a dry-goods store

포문 砲門 〈포구(砲口)〉 the muzzle of a gun;

〈군함의〉 a gunport; a porthole; 〈성벽의〉 an embrasure
♦ 포문을 열다 open fire / 논쟁의 포문을 열다 (비유) broach a discussion; commence [start] a debate

포물면 안테나 抛物面— parabolic antenna
포물선 抛物線 〔數〕 a parabola
♦ 포물선을 그리다 describe a parabola
▶ 그 물체는 포물선을 그리며 머리 위로날아갔다 The object passed away overhead describing a parabola.
■ —운동 〔物〕 a projectile motion

포미 砲尾 the gun breech; the breech (of a cannon)
포박 捕縛 (an) arrest; apprehension; capture
—**포박하다** arrest; apprehend; catch; seize; nab ♦ 포박되다 be arrested; be apprehended
포배기 repetition; reiteration
포병 砲兵 an artilleryman; a gunner; (총칭) artillery
■ 사단[군단]— division [corps] artillery 중(重)[야전]— heavy [field] artillery ■ —과 the artillery arm —기지 an artillery base —대[단] an artillery corps [unit] —대대 (美) an artillery battalion; (英) an artillery brigade —사령관 an artillery commander —연대 an artillery regiment —전 an artillery duel [engagement] —중대 a battery —진지 an artillery [a gun] position —학교 the Artillery School

포복 匍匐 creeping
▶ 우리는 적군을 향해 포복 전진했다 We crept [crawled along] toward the enemy.
—**포복하다** creep; crawl; walk on one's hands and knees
▶ 열차는 산간의 급경사를 포복하듯 올라갔다 The train crawled up a steep slope between the mountains.
■ —경(莖) 〔植〕 〈기는 줄기〉 a creeping stem [shoot] —식물 a groundling; a creeping plant

포복절도하다 抱腹絕倒— laugh oneself into convulsions; be convulsed with laughter; die with laughing
▶ 그 코미디언은 청중을 포복절도케 했다 The comedian threw the audience into convulsions.

포부 抱負 (an) aspiration; 〈큰뜻〉 (an) ambition; wishes; 〈계획〉 a plan
♦ 포부가 있는 aspiring; ambitious; aspirant / 포부가 크다 be highly ambitious; have a great ambition; aim high / 포부를 말하다 talk about one's ambitions; tell 《us》 one's 《ambitious》 plan 《for》
▶ 젊을 때는 큰 포부를 가져야 한다 You should have a great ambition [aim high] when young.

포비즘 〔美術〕〈야수파〉fauvism
■ —화가 a fauvist

포살 捕殺 catching and killing
—**포살하다** catch and kill
포상 砲床 a gun platform [emplacement]
포상 褒賞 a prize; a reward
♦ 포상을 주다[받다] award [win] a prize
—**포상하다** give a prize 《to》; reward; praise

포석 布石 **1** 〈바둑의〉 the strategic placing of paduk-stones; the initial stage in a paduk match
2 〈장래에 대한 준비〉 preparations; precautions
▶ 그 경제위기에 대처하기 위해 온갖 포석이 마련되었다 Every strategic move had been made to cope with the economic crisis.
—**포석하다** prepare; arrange; take precautions 《against》

포석 鋪石 a flag(stone); a paving stone
♦ 포석이 깔려 있다 be paved [floored] with stone; be flagged

포섭 包攝 **1** 〈받아들임〉 winning sb over to one's side
♦ 포섭 공작을 하다 contrive to win sb over
—**포섭하다** win [gain] sb over to one's side; bring sb round
♦ 뇌물로 아무를 포섭하다 fix [bring round] sb by bribery
2 〔論〕 connotation; subsumption
—**포섭하다** connote; subsume

포성 砲聲 the sound of firing [gunfire]; the roaring of a gun; the boom of a cannon
▶ 멀리서 포성이 들렸다 We heard the distant boom of guns.

포수 砲手 a hunter
포수 捕手 〔野〕 a catcher
포술 砲術 gunnery; artillery ■ —교관 a gunnery instructor —연습 gunnery practice
포스아웃 〔野〕 a force-out ♦ 포스아웃시키다 force 《a runner》 out
포스터 〈미국의 작곡가〉 Foster, Stephen Collins (1826-64)
포스터 a poster; a placard
▶ 이 포스터를 붙여도[떼어도] 될까요? May I put up [take down] this poster?
■ 광고— an ad-poster ■ —광고 billing —선전 publicity [advertisement] with posters —컬러 poster colors

포스트 〈지위〉 a post; a position
포승 捕繩 a rope to bind a criminal with; a policeman's rope ♦ 포승을 묶다 bind up 《a criminal》; arrest 《a wanted person》 / 포승을 풀다 unbind sb

포식 捕食 predation; predatism —**포식하다** prey upon
▶ 여우는 토끼를 포식한다 Foxes prey on rabbits.

포식 飽食 gluttony; satiation; engorgement
—**포식하다** satiate oneself; be fed up 《with》; eat one's fill; eat to one's heart's content
▶ 나는 바닷가재를 포식했다 I ate a lot of lobsters.

포신 砲身 a gun barrel; the barrel of a gun
포실하다 well-off; rich; wealthy; comfortable
포악 暴惡 〈난폭〉 violence; 〈폭정〉 tyranny; 〈야만〉 savagery; 〈잔학〉 atrocity
—**포악하다** ruthless; atrocious; outrageous; barbarous
♦ 포악한 살인범 a ruthless murderer

포안 砲眼 a gun hole; 〔築城〕 an embrasure
포연 砲煙 the smoke of cannon; cannon [artillery] smoke; powder smoke

포열 砲列 a battery (line); a train of artillery ◆포열을 배치하다 lay a field battery; place guns in position

포옹 抱擁 an embrace; (口) a hug ―포옹하다 embrace; (口) hug; hold sb to *one's* breast ▶그는 그녀를 힘껏 포옹했다 He hugged her tightly.

포용 包容 tolerance; inclusion ―포용하다 comprehend; embrace; imply; include; tolerate; accept with magnanimity ▶때로는 저런 건방진 녀석도 포용하지 않으면 안된다 We should sometimes tolerate such an impudent guy [fellow]. ■―력 capacity; catholicity: 그는 포용력이 있는 사람이다 He is a broad-minded [magnanimous] person.

포워드 〔競〕〈전위〉a forward

포위 包圍 (a) siege; encirclement; besiegement; investment ▶군인들은 적진의 포위를 풀었다 The soldiers raised the siege of the enemy camp. ―포위하다 surround; encircle; invest; envelop; besiege; lay siege to 《a fort》; throw a cordon round 《a place》 ▶경찰은 그들의 은신처를 포위했다 The police closed in on their hideout. ■―공격 an enveloping [outflanking] drive [attack]; a siege ―군 an investing [a besieging] army; besiegers ―망 an encircling net ―사격 an enveloping [a converging] fire ―작전 an encircling [enveloping, outflanking] operation ―전 a battle of encirclement; besiegement ―태세 an encircling formation: 포위태세를 취하다 get into encircling formation

포유 哺乳 lactation; suckling; nursing ―포유하다 suckle; give suck to; nurse ■―동물 a mammal; a mammalian; a suckler ―류 〔動〕 Mammalia ―병 nursing [feeding] bottle

포육 脯肉 dry sliced meat; jerky; charqui; pemmican

포인터 〔개〕 a pointer

포인트 1 〈전철기〉 a (railway) switch; points; a point switch **2** 〈활자〉 point ◆9포인트의 활자 (a) 9-point type **3** 〈소수점〉 a (decimal) point **4** 〈경기의 득점〉 a point ◆포인트를 따다[얻다] win [get, score] a point **5** 〈요점〉 the point 《of a story》

포자 胞子 〔植〕 a spore; a sporule ■―낭(囊) a sporangium ―생식 spore reproduction; reproduction by spore; sporogenesis; sporogony: 무포자 생식 apospory ―엽 a sporophyll ―체 a sporophyte

포장 布帳 a linen screen [awning]; 〈수레·자동차 등의〉 a hood; a (folding) top ◆포장을 치다[걷다] pull up [let down] the top ■―마차 a covered carriage [wagon]; (美) a prairie schooner

포장 包裝 packing; wrapping ◆포장이 잘 돼 있다 be well packed / 포장이 허술하게 돼 있다 be poorly [defectively] packed / 포장을 풀다 unwrap 《a package》; unpack 《a box》 ―포장하다 wrap; pack (up); (美) package; wrap (it) up ◆종이로 포장하다 pack [wrap] up 《a thing》 in paper ▶이것을 선물용으로 포장해 주세요 Would you wrap this as a gift. ■―기계 a packing machine; a packer ―물 a package ―비 packing charges ―재료 packing (materials) ―지 packing sheet [paper]; 〈선물용의〉 a wrapper

포장 褒章 a medal (of merit)

포장 鋪裝 pavement; paving ―포장하다 pave; surface ◆아스팔트로 포장하다 lay 《a street》 with asphalt ▶이 길은 포장돼 있지 않다 This road is not paved. ■―공사 pavement work(s); paving ―도로 a pavement; a paved road ―재료 paving materials

포좌 砲座 a gun platform; a barbette; 〈포가〉 gun carriage

포주 抱主 a keeper of a brothel; a whoremaster; a pimp

포즈 〈자세〉 a pose ◆포즈를 취하다 pose (oneself) 《as a model》; take *one's* pose; posture ▶그녀는 카메라 앞에서 포즈를 취했다 She posed [made a pose] before the camera.

포지션 〈위치〉 (a) position ◆포지션을 지키다 stand [guard] *one's* position / 포지션이 바뀌다 be changed in *one's* position

포지티브 〔寫〕 a positive; 〔醫〕 positive

포진 布陣 the lineup (of); lines ―포진하다 take up *one's* position ▶경찰기동대는 그 바리케이드 앞에 포진했다 The riot police took up their position in front of the barricade.

포진 疱疹 〔醫〕 herpes ■―단순 herpes simplex; cold sores; fever blisters 대상(帶狀)― shingles

포집다 1 〈거듭 집다〉 pick up [take hold up] sth over again **2** 〈포개어 놓다〉 pile up; lay one upon another

포차 砲車 a gun carriage

포착 捕捉 capture; apprehension ―포착하다 catch; seize; take hold of; 〈이해하다〉 understand; 〈레이더가〉 pick up ◆기회를 포착하다 seize (on) an opportunity ▶레이더가 국적 불명의 비행기를 포착했다 A radar picked up a plane of unknown nationality. ▶나는 그 의미를 포착하기 어렵다 The meaning is beyond my understanding. ⇌ I can hardly grasp the meaning.

포촌 浦村 a waterside village ■―놈 waterside trash

포충망 捕蟲網 an insectnet; a butterfly net

포충엽 捕蟲葉 〔植〕 an insectivorous leaf

포츠담 Potsdam ■―선언[회담] the Potsdam Declaration [Conference] ―협정 the Potsdam Agreement

포츠머스 〈영국 남부의 항구 도시〉 Portsmouth; 〈미국 뉴햄프셔주의 항구 도시〉 Portsmouth
■ —조약 the Portsmouth Peace Treaty

포치 a porch

포커 (play) poker

포커스 a focus

포켓 a pocket
♦ 포켓이 없는 바지 pocketless trousers / 포켓을 달다 sew up a pocket 《on a coat》/ 포켓에 넣다 put 《a thing》 in [into] a pocket; drop 《a volume》 into one's pocket / 열쇠를 찾으려고 포켓을 뒤지다 fish in one's pocket for the key / 포켓에서 꺼내다 take 《a letter》 out of one's pocket; draw 《a newspaper》 from one's pocket
▶ 그는 포켓에 두 손을 찌르고 걷고 있었다 He was walking with his hands in his pockets.
■ —머니 pocket money —북 a pocket(-sized) book —판(版) a pocket edition —판 사전 a pocket dictionary

포크 1 〈식사용〉 a fork
♦ 나이프와 포크 knife and fork / 식탁용 포크 a table fork 2 〈돼지고기〉 pork
■ —소테 pork saute —촙 pork chop

포크너 〈미국의 소설가〉 Faulkner, William (1897-1962)

포크댄스 a folk dance; folk dancing

포크리프트 a forklift (truck)

포크볼 〔野〕 a fork ball

포크송 a folk song
■ —가수 a folk singer

포크커틀릿 a pork cutlet

포타슘 〔化〕 potassium

포타주 (프) 〔料〕 〈진한 스프〉 potage

포탄 砲彈 a shell; a cannonball
♦ 적에게 빗발치듯 포탄을 퍼붓다 rain shells on [upon] the enemy

포탈 逋脫 〈탈세〉 tax evasion; evasion of taxes
—포탈하다 evade [dodge] a tax; defraud the revenue
♦ 세금포탈액 the amount of the tax evasion / 세금포탈자 a tax dodger [evader, cheat]; an evader of taxes

포탑 砲塔 a gun turret; a cupola; a barbette

포터 a (baggage) porter; (美) a redcap

포터블 portable ■ —라디오 a portable radio —타이프라이터 a portable typewriter —텔레비전 a portable television

포토그래프 a photograph

포트 a pot ■ 커피— a coffee pot

포트모르즈비 〈파푸아뉴기니의 수도〉 Port Moresby

포트와인 port; port wine

포틀랜드 〈미국 오레곤주의 항구 도시〉 Portland

포퓰러 popular ■ —뮤직[음악] popular music; pop —송 a popular song

포프 〈영국의 시인〉 Pope, Alexander (1688-1744)

포플러 〔植〕 a poplar ▶ 우리는 키가 큰 포플러가 늘어선 길을 걸었다 We walked a long an avenue of high poplars.

포플린 〈직물〉 poplin ▶ 이것은 포플린 직물이다 This is a poplin fabric.

포피 包皮 〔解〕 the foreskin; the prepuce
♦ 포피의 preputial

포학 暴虐 (a) tyranny; (an) atrocity; (a) cruelty
—포학하다 tyrannical; cruel
♦ 포학한 군주 a tyrant
▶ 그 왕은 농민들에게 온갖 포학한 짓을 다했다 The king committed all sorts of atrocities on the peasants.
■ —무도 tyranny and injustice

포함 包含 inclusion; comprehension; implication
♦ 우송료 포함 1파운드 price one pound, postage included [including postage]
—포함하다 include; contain; 〈의미를〉 imply
♦ …을 포함하여 including; inclusive of… / …을 포함하지 않고 excluding; exclusive of… / 포함시키다 include; count (in); put into / …에 포함되다 be comprised in
▶ 모든 비용을 포함하여 10만원이다 The inclusive cost is one hundred thousand won.
▶ 네 이름도 명부에 포함돼 있다 Your name is included in the list.
▶ 그 계획은 몇가지 작업을 포함한다 The plan comprehends several projects.
▶ 그 보고서는 여러 가지 다른 문제들을 포함하고 있다 The report embraces various subjects.
▶ 그 가운데는 5명의 어린애가 포함되어 있다 Included among them are five children.
■ 세금— 〔商〕 duty paid 운임— 〔商〕 (美) freight prepaid; (英) carriage paid —량 the (amount of) content —률 the percentage of content

포함 砲艦 a gunboat

포합 浦合 〈껴안음〉 embrace
—포합하다 embrace

포핸드 〈테니스의〉 one's forehand; 〈탁구의〉 a forehand (stroke)

포화 砲火 (a) gunfire; (a) shellfire; (an) artillery fire; (a) fire
♦ 맹렬한 포화 a heavy fire; drumfire / 포화를 퍼붓다 rain fire on 《the enemy》/ 포화를 받다 be under fire; be subjected to fire / 서로 포화를 주고 받다 exchange fire / 포화를 집중시키다 concentrate fire 《on》
■ 십자— 〔軍〕 cross fire

포화 飽和 〔化〕 saturation
—포화하다 be saturated
♦ 포화시키다 saturate [charge] 《with》
■ 과(過)— 〔化〕 supersaturation ■ —곡선 a saturation curve —기(器) a saturator —도(度) a degree of saturation —온도 saturation temperature —용액[화합물] a saturated solution [compound] —점 a saturation point —증기 saturated steam —증기압 saturated vapor pressure

포화상태 飽和狀態 saturation
♦ 포화상태다 be in saturation; be saturated
▶ 서울의 교통사정은 포화상태다 Traffic in Seoul is at its peak of congestion.

포환 砲丸 a cannonball; a slug; 〔競〕 a shot; a

weight
▶ 그는 포환을 던졌다 He put the shot.
―던지기 the shot put; shot-putting ―던지기 선수 a shot-putter; a weight-putter

포획 捕獲 capture; seizure
―포획하다 catch; capture; seize
▶ 우리는 적의 배를 3척 포획했다 We captured three enemy ships.
■―고[량] a (good, poor) catch (of fish) ―물 a booty; a prize ―선[군함] a captured ship [warship] ―자 a captor

포효 咆哮 roar; roaring; howling; 〈소리〉 a roar; a howl; a bellow; a yell
―포효하다 roar; howl

폭¹ 〈셈·정도〉 about; ratio; rate
♦ 하루 40,000원 폭으로 at the rate of forty thousand won a day / 100명에 한 사람 폭으로 in the ratio of one to a hundred persons
▶ 홍수로 10억원 폭의 손실이 났다 The flood loss was estimated at about a billion (a thousand million) won.

폭² home ⇨ 푹

폭 幅 1〈너비〉 width; breadth
♦ 폭이 넓은 wide; broad / 폭이 좁은 narrow / 폭이 4 피트다 be four feet wide [in width] / 폭을 넓히다 widen; broaden
2〈도량·포용성〉 generosity; magnanimity; caliber; 〈범위〉 range
♦ 폭이 넓은 사람 a broad-minded [large-minded] person; a man of large caliber
▶ 그는 사업의 폭을 넓혔다 He widened his range [scope] of business.
▶ 그의 지식은 폭은 넓지만 깊이가 없다 His knowledge covers a wide range of subjects, but lacks depth.
3〈가격의 폭〉 difference (in price)
♦ 이익의 폭 a margin of profit
4〈그림·병풍 등의〉 a scroll; a strip; a piece (of)
♦ 두 폭 병풍 a double-leaf [double-folded] screen
▶ 배의 갑판에서 바라보는 여명(黎明)의 베니스는 마치 한 폭의 그림이었다 Venice at dawn, seen from the deck of the ship, looked like a picture scroll spread out.

폭거 暴擧 violence; 〈난폭〉 outrage; 〈폭동〉 a riot; 〈무모한 기도〉 a reckless attempt
▶ 그들은 폭거로 나왔다 They resorted to violence.
▶ 우리는 그의 폭거를 경계했지만 아무 소용이 없었다 We warned him against a reckless act in vain.

폭격 爆擊 (aerial) bombing; a bombing raid [attack]
▶ 그 폭격은 1시간 동안 계속되었다 The bombing lasted as long as an hour.
―폭격하다 bomb; drop a bomb (on); make a bombing raid
▶ 그 지역은 육지와 하늘에서 폭격해 잿더미가 되었다 The district was bombed [bombarded] from land and air, and reduced to a charred and smoldering waste.
■ 무차별― indiscriminate bombing 융단― carpet [pattern] bombing 전략― strategic bombing 정밀― precision bombing ―대 a bombing squad; an air strike force ―목표 a bombing target ―수 a bombardier

폭격기 爆擊機 a bombing plane; a bomber; (총칭) bombing craft ■ 전투― a fighter-bomber 중[경]― a heavy [light] bomber ■―대[단] a bomber [bombing] fleet

폭군 暴君 a tyrant; 〈전제군주〉 a despot

폭도 暴徒 rioters; a mob; mobsters
♦ 폭도의 무리 a mob of rioters / 폭도를 선동하다[쫓아 흩어버리다] stir up [disperse] a mob / 폭도에게 습격당하다 be mobbed / 폭도를 진압하다 put down rioters
▶ 그 시위대는 폭도로 돌변했다 The protest marchers turned into rioters.

폭동 暴動 a disturbance; rioting; a riot; an uprising; 〈군대내의〉 a mutiny; a rebellion
♦ 폭동이 일어나다 a riot arises [break out] / 폭동을 일으키다 raise a riot; start rioting; rise in riot [insurrection]; create a disturbance
▶ 인종문제로 폭동이 일어났다 A race riot broke out [arose].
▶ 그 폭동은 곧 진압되었다 The riot was put down quickly.
▶ 누가 폭동을 선동했나? Who incited rebellion?
■ 무장― an armed revolt ■―자 a rioter; an insurgent; a rebel; 〈군대의〉 a mutineer ―죄 a charge of sedition [rioting] ―진압경찰 riot police; a riot squad

폭등 暴騰 an abnormal [a sudden] rise; a jump; (美) a boom
―폭등하다 jump; soar; rise abnormally [suddenly]; (美) boom
♦ 폭등하는 물가 soaring prices; (美) boom prices
▶ 물가가 폭등하고 있다 Prices are skyrocketing.
▶ 땅값이 폭등했다 The land price has risen suddenly [skyrocketed, soared].
▶ 인플레이션으로 물가가 폭등하고 있다 Prices are soaring owing to the inflation.

폭락 暴落 a sudden [heavy] fall; a slump; a crash; a smash; sagging
♦ 주식의 폭락 a slump [plunge] in stocks
―폭락하다 decline heavily [sharply]; slump; fall suddenly; (美) 〈가치가〉 toboggan; 〈주식이〉 slump; plunge; plummet
▶ 그 회사의 주(株)는 어제 10,000원으로 폭락했다 The stock of that trading company slumped to ten thousand won yesterday.

폭력 暴力 violence; force
♦ 가정내 폭력 family [domestic] violence; violence in the family / 학교내 폭력 school violence
〈폭력이[은]〉 폭력이 난무하다 an act of violence prevails (on)
▶ 폭력은 또 다른 폭력을 가져온다 An assault would lead to another violence.
〈폭력을〉 폭력을 휘두르다[행사하다] use [employ] violence [force] 《on sb》; use one's fist; (美) employ strong-arm methods 《upon》/ 폭력을 가하다 cause [offer] violence; commit violence 《toward》; commit an

outrage ((to))
〈폭력에〉 어떤 경우에도 폭력에 호소해선 안된다 You should not make an appeal to violence [force] in any case.
〈폭력으로〉 폭력으로 by force [violence]; by recourse to violence / 폭력으로 강요하다 coerce ((sb to do it)) by violence; bulldoze ((sb to do it))
▶ 그들은 그에게서 폭력으로 돈을 빼앗았다 They took his money by force [violence].
■ 조직— violence committed by a criminal organization 집단— mass violence; organized violence ■ —단 a band of thugs; a goon squad —단원 a gangster; a goon —배 hoodlums; hooligans; (street) gangsters; street toughs: 폭력배의 단속을 강화하다 tighten control on hooligans —정치 Bolshevik terrorism in politics —행사 use of violence [force] —행위 an act of violence; gangsterism

폭로 暴露 exposure; disclosure; divulgence
—폭로하다 expose ((a secret plan)); disclose [reveal] ((a secret)); betray ((another's plot)); lay bare ((an evil design))
◆ 사기꾼의 정체를 폭로하다 expose an impostor
▶ 그는 그 계략을 폭로했다 He revealed the trick.
■ —기사 an exposé —소설 a telltale story —전술 exposure tactics

폭뢰 爆雷 a depth bomb [charge]

폭리 暴利 excessive profits; 〈고리(高利)〉 usury; exorbitant interest
◆ 폭리를 취하다 make undue [unreasonable] profits ((on)) / 폭리를 단속하다 control profiteering
▶ 그는 폭리를 취하고 있다 He is a profiteer.

폭민 暴民 rioters; a mob; insurgents ■ —정치 mob [mass] rule; mobocracy; ochlocracy

폭발 爆發 sudden discharge; explosion; detonation; burst(ing); blowing up; 〈화산의〉 eruption
—폭발하다 〈총이〉 go off; explode; burst (up); blow up; detonate; 〈화산이〉 erupt; burst into eruption
◆ 분노가 폭발하다 〈사람이 주어〉 fly into a passion; burst into a rage / 폭발시키다 explode; detonate; burst (up); set off; blow up; 〔鑛〕 shoot / 다이너마이트를 폭발시키다 set off a dynamite
▶ 그 가스 탱크가 폭발했다 The gas tank blew up.
▶ 그들의 쌓였던 울분이 폭발했다 Their smoldering resentment flared up.
■ 원자[핵]— atomic [nuclear] explosion 인구— a population explosion ■ —가스 explosive gas; firedamp —력 explosive power —물 an explosive (substance) —방지장치 〈보일러의〉 a hydrostat —성 explosiveness —신관 a detonating fuse —점 the point of an explosion; the flash(ing) point ((of an atomic bomb))

폭발적 爆發的 exlosive; tremendous
◆ 폭발적인 인기 tremendous popularity / 폭발적인 인구증가 a population explosion; an explosive increase of population / 폭발적으로 explosively

폭사 爆死 death resulting from bombing
—폭사하다 be bombed to death; be killed by a bomb

폭삭 〈온통〉 entirely; wholly; completely; thoroughly ◆ 곳간이 폭삭 주저앉았다 The shed collapsed completely.

폭서 暴暑 severe [torrid, intense] heat

폭설 暴雪 a heavy snowfall
◆ 폭설 지역 an area of high snowfall / 폭설에 파묻히다 be buried in a snowdrift

폭성 爆聲 an explosion ⇨ 폭음(爆音) 2

폭소 爆笑 a burst [roar] of laughter; an explosive laugh; uproarious laughter
—폭소하다 roar with laughter; burst out laughing; burst into laughter
▶ 우리는 그의 농담에 폭소했다 We burst into laughter at his joke.

폭스테리어 〔動〕 a fox terrier

폭스트롯 〔舞〕 a fox-trot

폭식 暴食 voracious eating; gluttony; gorging; voracity
—폭식하다 eat to excess [too much]; overeat ((oneself)); gorge
▶ 그는 폭음 폭식해서 건강을 해쳤다 He ruined his health by drinking and eating too much.
■ —가 a glutton; a great [an excessive] eater; a heavy eater

폭신폭신 all soft ⇨ 푹신푹신

폭심 爆心 an epicenter; the blast center
—지(점) the center of explosion; the blast center

폭압 暴壓 oppression; coercion; repression
—폭압하다 oppress; coerce

폭약 爆藥 an explosive compound; detonator; blasting powder
◆ 폭약을 장치하다 lay an explosive / 폭약에 점화하다 set off the blasting powder
■ 고성능— a high explosive

폭양 暴陽 the heat of the sun; blazing sunlight

폭언 暴言 violent [abusive] language; harsh [wild, strong] words
◆ 폭언을 해대다 use violent [abusive] language; utter wild words; speak vehemently; speak violently [abusively]
—폭언하다 abuse; use violent [strong] language

폭우 暴雨 a heavy rain [rainfall]; a downpour ◆ 폭우로 피해를 입다 be damaged by a heavy rain

폭위 暴威 tyranny; violence; abuse of power
◆ 폭위를 떨치다 tyrannize over; play havoc ((with))

폭음 暴飲 excessive [heavy] drinking; intemperance
▶ 폭음은 건강에 나쁘다 Heavy drinking is not good for the health.
—폭음하다 drink hard [heavily, deep]; drink like a fish; drink too much [to excess]; booze
▶ 폭음하지 마시오 Don't drink too much.
■ —가 a hard drinker; a soaker

폭음 爆音 1 〈비행기의〉 buzzing; a roar; bur-

ring; drumming; whizzing; 《내연기관의》 knocking
▶비행기가 폭음을 내며 날아갔다 The airplane flew away with a roar.
2 〈폭발음〉 an explosion; a detonation
▶동굴 속에서 큰 폭음이 났다 There was a loud explosion in the cave.

폭정 暴政 tyranny; tyrannic(al) government [rule]; despotic government; despotism
◆폭정을 펴다 tyrannize over a country / 폭정에 시달리다 groan under tyranny

폭주 暴走 〈자동차 등의〉 reckless driving; speeding; 〔野〕 a reckless run; 〈가축떼 등의〉 a stampede
━폭주하다 run recklessly
■━족 a group of rowdy [reckless] drivers; 〈모터사이클〉 hell's angel ━택시 a runaway taxi

폭주 暴酒 heavy drinking ⇨ 폭음(暴飮)

폭주 輻輳 overcrowding; 〈교통의〉 congestion
◆화물[우편물]의 폭주 congestion of goods [mail] / 교통의 폭주를 완화하다 relieve the congestion of traffic
━폭주하다 be crowded [congested] 《with》

폭죽 爆竹 a firecracker; a petard; a squib (cracker)
◆폭죽을 터뜨리다 set off firecrackers; fire squibs

폭침 爆沈 sinking by an explosion; blowing up
━폭침하다 〈가라앉히다〉 blow up and sink

폭탄 爆彈 a bomb; a bombshell
◆도시에 폭탄을 투하하다 drop [deliver] a bomb on a city / 폭탄을 싣다 bomb up / 기차에 폭탄을 던지다 throw [hurl] a bomb at a train / 다리에 폭탄을 설치하다 plant a bomb on the bridge
▶어젯밤 그 도시에 폭탄이 투하됐다 A bomb was dropped on the city last night. ⇌ The city was bombed last night.
■고성능━ a TNT bomb; a high explosive bomb 시한━ a time bomb 원자[수소]━ an atomic [a hydrogen] bomb 음향━ a scream bomb 초대형━ a superbomb; a blockbuster 화염━ a liquid-flame bomb ■━적재량 bomb carrying capacity ━투하 bombing; bombdropping

폭투 暴投 〔野〕 a wild throw; 〈투수의〉 a wild pitch; wild pitching
━폭투하다 pitch [throw] wild

폭파 爆破 blasting; blowing up; explosion
━폭파하다 blow up; blast; explode
▶그들은 열차를 폭파했다 They blew up [exploded] the train.
■━약 blasting powder [charge] ━작업 blasting operations

폭포(수) 瀑布(水) a waterfall; falls; 〈작은〉 a cascade; 〈큰〉 a cataract
▶나이아가라 폭포 the Niagara Falls
▶비가 폭포처럼 퍼부었다 The rain was pouring down in torrents.
▶그 노동자들은 폭포수같이 땀을 흘리고 있었다 The workers were sweating profusely [freely].

폭풍 暴風 a storm; a windstorm; a tempest
◆폭풍 전의 고요 the calm before a storm / 폭풍의 바다 〈달 표면의〉 the Ocean of Lunar Storms / 폭풍의 중심[눈] a storm center; the eye of storm / 폭풍의 진로 a storm lane
▶폭풍이 지나갔다 The storm is over [gone]. ⇌ The storm has blown over.
■━경보[주의보] a storm warning ━권 a storm zone [area] ━피해 storm damage; havoc wrought by storms

폭풍 爆風 a bomb blast; a blast 《from an explosion》

폭풍설 暴風雪 a snowstorm; a snowdrift; a driving snow; a blizzard

폭풍우 暴風雨 a rainstorm; a storm; a tempest
◆폭풍우를 만나다 be hit by a storm / 폭풍우로 파괴되다 be damaged by storm
▶폭풍우가 종일 맹위를 떨쳤다 The storm raged all day.
▶항해중 우리 배는 여러번 폭풍우를 만났다 Our ship met with [was caught in] a storm many times during our voyage.

폭한 暴寒 severe [intense, sharp] cold; cold snap

폭한 暴漢 a ruffian; a rowdy; 《美俗》 a roughneck
◆폭한에게 습격당하다 be assaulted by a ruffian

폭행 暴行 an outrage 《on, against》; (an act of) violence; riotous behavior; an assault
◆부녀자에게 폭행을 가하다 commit an outrage on [upon] a woman; attack [rape] a woman
▶사체에는 폭행의 흔적이 보이지 않았다 The body bore no marks of violence [violation].
━폭행하다 behave violently; act outrageously; assault (criminally); attack; use [do] violence to; commit an outrage on; 〈능욕하다〉 violate [outrage, rape, ravish] 《a woman》
■━자 an outrager; a rioter; an assaulter; 〈능욕자〉 a violator [rapist]

폰 〔物〕 〈소리 크기의 단위〉 a phon
▶그 교차점의 소음은 80폰이었다 The noise at the crossing registered eighty phons.

폴[1] 〔레슬링〕 a fall; win by a fall
◆폴로 이기다 win by a fall; beat [defeat] 《one's opponent》 by a fall
━승 a victory by a fall

폴[2] a pole ▶그들은 토지를 측량하기 위해 폴을 세웠다 They set up a pole for a survey.

폴라로이드 〔商標〕 a Polaroid

폴라리스 1 〈미사일〉 a Polaris
2 ⇨ 북극성

폴란드 Poland; 〈공식명〉 the Polish People's Republic ◆폴란드의 Polish ■━사람 a Pole; the Poles; (총칭) the Polish ━말 Polish

폴로 〔競〕 polo
■━경기자 a poloist; a polo player ━셔츠 a polo shirt

폴로네즈 〔樂〕 polonaise

폴로늄 〔化〕 polonium

폴리네시아 〈태평양 중서부의 작은 제도의 총칭〉 Polynesia

♦폴리네시아의 Polynesian ■—사람 a Polynesian
폴리스 〈고대 그리스의 도시 국가〉 polis
폴리에스테르 〔化〕 polyester
■—섬유[수지] a polyester (fiber)
폴리에틸렌 〔化〕 polyethylene
폴리오 1 ⇨ 소아마비
2 〔印〕 a folio (*pl.* ~s)
폴리프로필렌 〔化〕 polypropylene
폴카 〔舞〕 (a) polka
♦폴카를 추다 dance the polka; polka
폴트 〔테니스·배구〕 a fault
폼 1〈스포츠〉 (a) form ▶그의 피칭폼은 좋다 His pitching form is excellent.
2 ⇨ 플랫폼
폼페이 〈이탈리아의 옛도시〉 Pompeii
♦폼페이의 Pompeian ■—사람 Pompeian
폿소리 砲— the boom of a gun ⇨ 포성(砲聲)
퐁당 plop; plump; with a plop
♦물에 퐁당 빠지다 fall plop into the water; drop into the water with a plop / 물에 퐁당 뛰어들다 jump into the water with a plop; plump into the water
퐁당거리다 keep plopping [flopping]
퐁당퐁당 with splashes; with splash after splash
♦퐁당퐁당 헤엄치다 swim splashing the water
퐁퐁 1〈물이 쏟아지는 소리〉 pouringly
♦물이 퐁퐁 쏟아지다 water pours forth [out]
2〈작은 구멍이 터지는 소리〉 breaking open repeatedly
푄현상 —現像 〔氣〕 a foehn [föhn] phenomenon
표 表 1〈일람표 등〉 a table; a tabular statement;〈항목을 나열한〉 a list;〈예정표〉 a schedule; a diagram;〈도표〉 a chart
♦위의 표에 나타나 있는 것처럼 as listed above / 표에 나와 있다 be on the list; be listed / 표로 만들다 list; tabulate; tabularize; make into a table / 실험 결과를 표로 만들다 make the results of experiments into a table ▶세율은 표에 나타나 있다 The tax rates are shown in [on] the table.
▶나는 읽고 싶은 책 모두를 표로 작성했다 I made a list of [listed] all the books I'd like to read.
2〈표지〉 a mark; a sign
■시간— a timetable;〈학교의〉 a schedule 연— a chronological table 일람— a catalog 정가— a price list 통계— the tabulation of statistics
표 票 1〈각종 딱지〉 a card; a label;〈꼬리표〉 a tab; a tag;〈보관표〉 a receipt; a check;〈번호표〉 a number check;〈이름표〉 a name card;〈좌석표〉 a place card;〈전당표 등〉 a ticket;〈한장씩 떼어내는〉 a coupon; a chit
♦표를 붙이다 paste a card [label]; label (a bottle) / 표를 달다 label (a trunk); put a tag (on an article); ticket
2〈차권·입장권 등〉 a ticket; a coupon (ticket)
♦표받는 사람 a ticket [check] taker / 표파는 곳 a ticket office; (英) a booking office / 용산까지의 표를 사다 buy a ticket to [for] Yongsan / 표를 찍다 punch [clip] a ticket
▶표가 없는 사람은 입장할 수 없습니다 Admission by ticket only.
3〈선거의〉 a vote; a ballot
♦깨끗한 한 표 an honest [a fair] vote / 1인 1표 one man one vote / 표를 얻다[모으다] win [get, draw, gather, round up] votes / …에게 한 표를 던지다 cast a vote [ballot] (for)
▶그 제안에는 반대표가 많았다 There were a lot of votes against the proposal.
▶그 동의(動議)는 15표 대 31표로 부결되었다 The motion was rejected by a vote of 31 to 15.
■고정— a fixed vote 극장— a movie ticket 당일유효— a day ticket; a tickt available on the day of issue only 무료— a free ticket 반액— a half ticket 배— a steamboat [boarding] ticket 부동(浮動)— a floating vote 왕복— (美) a roundtrip ticket; (英) a return (ticket) 직행— a through ticket 편도— a one-way ticket; (美) a single (ticket)
표 標 1〈부호〉 a mark; a sign; a note
♦물음표 a question mark / 별표를 하다 mark *sth* with an asterisk [a star]
2〈징표〉 a symbol; an emblem
3〈휘장〉 a badge; a mark ♦회원표를 달고 있다 wear a membership badge
4〈증거〉 a proof (of); evidence (of, for); a testimony (to)
5〈마음의 표시〉 a token; a mark; a sign; a manifestation ♦감사의 표로서 in token [as a token] of *one's* gratitude; as a mark of *one's* appreciation
6〈상표〉 a trademark; a brand
♦코끼리표 the Elephant brand
7〈징후〉 a symptom; a sign; an indication
표결 表決 〈의결〉 a decision; a vote; voting a roll call; (英) a division
♦표결에 들어가다 vote / 표결을 요구하다 call for a division [vote]
—표결하다 decide; resolve; vote (on); take a vote (on); take a ballot (for); (美) take a roll call; (英) take a division; divide (on)
▶표결하여도 괜찮겠습니까? Is everybody ready for the ballot?
표결 票決 a vote on a bill; voting; a decision by vote
▶위원회의 표결에 따라 김선생이 선정되었다 Mr. Kim was elected by the vote of the committee.
—표결하다 take a vote (on); vote (on)
■—권 a vote; voting rights; the right to vote
표고 標高 (an) altitude
표구 表具 mounting —표구하다 mount (a picture); put (a picture) in a mount ■—사 a paper hanger; a mounter; a paperer
표기 表記 1〈겉에 표시해 씀〉 inscription on the face
▶나는 표기의 주소로 이전했다 I have moved to the address mentioned on the outside.
—표기하다 inscribe [mention] on the surface [outside]
2〈철자〉 spelling; transcription;〈내용을 적

기> declaration
―표기하다 〈철자를〉 spell; 〈다른 글로〉 transcribe; 〈내용물을〉 declare; insure
♦ 한글을 로마자로 표기하다 romanize Korean [*Hangŭl*]
■ ―가격 declared [insured] value: 표기 가격 우편물 mail with value declared; insured mail ―법 notation: 음성 표기법 phonetic notation
표기 標記 marking; a mark ―표기하다 mark
표나다 表― be conspicuous [obvious]; stand out; 〈겉으로 드러나다〉 show signs; be shown clearly
♦ 유난히 표나다[표날 짓을 하다] make (*oneself*) (too) conspicuous / 표나게 예쁘다 be strikingly beautiful
▶ 회색옷은 먼지가 묻어도 표나지 않는다 Gray clothes do not show the dust.
표독 慓毒 fierceness; ferocity
―표독하다[스럽다] fierce; ferocious; vicious; (口) shrewd
♦ 표독한 여자 a ferocious woman; a shrew; a she-devil / 표독스러운 말 stinging words / 표독한 성격 a prickly character / 표독스러운 얼굴로 with a look of venom / 표독하게 말하다 speak daggers (to *sb*)
표류 漂流 **1** 〈흘러 떠내려감〉 drift; drifting
―표류하다 drift about; drift with the current [on the tide]; be adrift
▶ 배는 파도치는 대로 표류했다 The ship drifted at the mercy of the waves.
2 〈유랑〉 wandering ―표류하다 wander aimlessly; drift; rove
■ ―물 driftage; flotsam ―선 a drifting ship; a castaway (ship); a derelict ―자 a person adrift on the sea; a castaway; a drifter
표리 表裏 〈속과 겉〉 inside and outside; obverse and reverse; 〈표면과 내심〉 appearance and mind [real intention]
♦ 표리가 없는 사람 an honest person / 표리가 부동한 사람 a two-faced person; a double-dealer; 〈위선자〉 a hypocrite
표면 表面 the surface; the face; the obverse; 〈외부〉 the exterior; the outside; 〈외견〉 the appearance; (a) show
♦ 지구 표면 the surface of the earth / 표면(상)의 이유 an ostensible reason; a plausible excuse / 표면상으로는 externally; outwardly; apparently; on the surface (of things) / (사람이) 표면에 나서다 appear in the limelight; show *oneself* in the public eye
▶ 책상의 표면은 사뭇 거칠었다 The desk had a rough surface.
▶ 그녀는 속으로 화가 나 있었지만 표면으로는 드러내지 않았다 Although she was angry inside, she didn't show it.
▶ 표면상으로는 순해 보이지만 그에게는 아주 고집센 면이 있다 He seems to be gentle, but there is a very stubborn side to him.
■ ―색 a surface color ―장력 (物) surface tension ―파(波) a surface wave ―활성제 [化] a surface-active agent; a surfactant
표면적 表面積 the surface [superficial] area
표면화하다 表面化― come [be brought] to the fore [front]; come out in the open; come up to the surface
♦ 표면화시키다 bring (a matter) to the surface [fore, front]; make (a matter) public / (문제가) 표면화되다 come to the surface / 표면화시키지 않고 해결하다 settle (a case) out of court / 표면화되지 않도록 하다 keep *sth* out of the public eye; keep *sth* under wraps
▶ 그 사건이 표면화되었다 The affair was brought to public notice.
▶ 그의 수뢰가 표면화되었다 His acceptance of a bribe has come to light.
표명 表明 expression; demonstration; manifestation
―표명하다 express; state; announce; demonstrate; show; manifest
♦ 사의를 표명하다 announce *one's* intention to resign / 그 제안에 반대[찬성]를 표명하다 declare against [for] the proposal
▶ 귀하의 후의에 대해 깊은 사의를 표명하는 바입니다 I would like to express my sincere gratitude for your kindness.
표박 漂泊 〈떠돎〉 wandering; roaming; tramp
―표박하다 wander about; vagabondize
표방하다 標榜― profess (*oneself* to be); adopt a slogan [motto] (of); advocate; champion; espouse; stand for
♦ 정의를 표방하다 be professedly for justice; champion the cause of justice
▶ 그는 인도주의를 표방하고 있다 He claims to stand for humanitarian principles.
표밭 票― a favorable voters' district
표백 漂白 bleaching; decoloration; decolorization
―표백하다 bleach; decolor; decolorize
♦ 시트를 표백하다 bleach a sheet
■ ―분 bleaching powder; chloride of lime ―액 a bleaching solution ―제(劑) a bleacher; a decolorant; a decolorizer
표범 豹― [動] 〈수컷〉 a leopard; a panther; 〈암컷〉 a leopardess; a pantheress
■ 아메리카― an American leopard; a jaguar 흑― a black leopard [panther] ■ ―나비 [昆] a fritillary
표변 豹變 a sudden change; a change of front; an about-face ―표변하다 change suddenly; 〈변절하다〉 turn *one's* coat
표본 標本 a specimen; 〈견본〉 a sample; 〈전형〉 a type; an example
♦ 월석의 표본 specimens of moon rocks / 임의[무작위] 표본추출 (統) random sampling / 곤충을 표본으로 만들다 mount insects
▶ 나는 곤충의 표본을 만들었다 I prepared some specimens of insects.
▶ 그는 그야말로 실업가의 표본이다 He is a typical businessman.
■ ―동물[식물]― a zoological [botanical] specimen 박제― a stuffed [mounted] specimen (of a bird) ■ ―실 a specimen room [gallery]; 〈식물의〉 a herbarium (*pl*. ~s, -ria) ―조사 a sample survey
표사 漂砂 [地質・土] drift sand
■ ―광상 [鑛] a placer (deposit)
표상 表象 **1** 〈상징〉 a symbol; an emblem
2 [心] (a) representation; (a) presentation;

표상 〔哲〕 an idea
—표상하다 symbolize; be symbolic(al) of; be a symbol of; emblematize
▶ 그 기장(記章)은 자유를 표상하고 있다 The badge symbolizes liberty.
■**부분—** a partial idea ■**—주의** presentationism

표석 表石 a tombstone; a grave marker

표석 漂石 〔地質〕 an erratic block; a (traveled) boulder

표석 標石 a stone marker ⇨ 푯돌

표수 票數 the number of votes

표시 表示 1 〈드러내 보임〉 (an) indication; (an) expression; (a) demonstration
◆ 의사 표시를 하다 indicate *one's* intention
—표시하다 indicate; show
▶ 그는 그 계획에 찬성 의사를 표시했다 He expressed his intention of approving the plan.
2 〈표적〉 a sign; a token; a mark; a manifestation
◆ 감사의 표시로 작은 선물을 하나 보냈습니다 I have sent you a little gift as a token of my gratitude.
■ **의사—** expression of *one's* intention
■ **—기 (器)** 〔계기의〕 an indicator

표어 標語 a motto; a slogan; a catchword; a watchword
◆ 적절한 표어 a fitting motto (for) /「안전 운전」이라고 하는 교통안전주간의 표어 the slogan "Drive Safe(ly)" for the traffic safety week / 표어를 모집하다 offer a prize for the best motto

표연히 飄然— 〈훌쩍〉 aimlessly; 〈뜻하지 않게〉 unexpectedly; casually
◆ 표연히 나타나다 appear unexpectedly
▶ 그는 표연히 여행에 나섰다 He went on a trip aimlessly.
▶ 그가 표연히 떠나가는 뒷모습이 잊혀지지 않는다 I will never forget the sight of his back as he walked casually away.

표음 表音 phonetic representation ■**—문자** a phonogram **—주의** phoneticism: 표음주의자 a phoneticist

표의 表意 ideography
■**—문자** an ideogram; an ideograph; an ideographic character

표일하다 飄逸— unconventional
▶ 그의 표일한 작풍이 많은 사람의 마음을 휘어잡았다 His unconventional technique attracted many people.

표장 標章 an ensign; a badge; an emblem; a mark

표저 瘭疽 〔醫〕 felon; whitlow; paronychia

표적 表迹 〈형적〉 traces; 〈부호〉 a mark; a sign; 〈증표〉 a proof (of); a manifestation
◆ 표적을 남기지 않다 leave no trace behind / 표적으로 한 책장을 접어두다 double over a leaf to mark the page / 제주에 갔던 표적으로 as a souvenir of *one's* visit to Cheju / 감사의 표적으로 in token [as a token] of *one's* gratitude

표적 標的 a target; a mark
◆ 표적을 벗어나다 fall beside [miss] the mark [target]

■**—사격** target shooting **—지역** 〈미사일 실험의〉 a target area **—함** 〈사격·폭격 훈련용〉 a target ship

표절 剽竊 plagiarism; literary piracy; crib
—표절하다 pirate; plagiarize ■**—물** a plagiarism; a crib **—자** a literary pirate; a plagiarist

표정 表情 (an) expression; a look
◆ 불만스러운 표정 a discontented look / 근심스러운 표정 a look of anxiety [worry] / 표정이 없는 얼굴 an expressionless face; (美俗) a poker face; (美俗) a dead pan / 표정이 굳어지다 harden *one's* face; freeze / 표정을 살피다 read *sb's* face
▶ 그녀는 (얼굴) 표정이 풍부하다[없다] Her face is expressive [expressionless].
▶ 슬픈 표정으로 그는 나를 보았다 He looked at me with a sad expression [look].

표제 標題·表題 〈책의〉 a title; 〈사진·만화 등의〉 a caption; 〈신문기사의〉 a headline; a head; 〈문장의〉 a superscription
◆ 표제를 달다 give a title [headline] to; headline [head] 《an article》; put a caption on 《a cartoon》
▶ 그는 「독서론」이라는 표제의 책을 썼다 He wrote a book entitled "On Reading."
■**부 (副)—** a subtitle; a subhead(ing) **2단—** a double head ■**—어** 〈사전 등의〉 a headword; an entry word; a vocabulary entry; 〈난외(欄外)의〉 a catchword; a guide [direction] word **—음악** program music

표주박 瓢— a small gourd

표준 標準 a standard; 〈작업량 등의〉 a norm; a criterion; a measure; 〈평균〉 a level
◆ 일정한 표준 a fixed standard / 표준이하의 substandard 《goods》; below standard / 표준에 미달하다 fall [come] short of the standard [mark] / 표준을 높이다[낮추다] level up [down]; raise [lower] the standard 《of》/ 표준을 정하다[세우다] fix [establish, set (up)] a standard
▶ 사물에 대한 판단은 사람에 따라서 표준이 다르다 People judge things by different standards.
▶ 그의 능력은 표준 이상[이하]이다 His ability is above [below] average.
■**—가격** a standard price **—계산서** an official form (of accounts) **—궤간 (鐵)** the standard gauge **—기록** the standard record; 〈예선 통과의〉 the qualifying standard [time, distance] **—상태 (物)** a normal state **—생활비** the standard [average] cost of living **—시계** a standard clock; a regulator **—액** a standard solution **—어** the standard language 《of a nation, in a country》; standard Korean [English, etc.] **—영어** standard English; (英) King's [Queen's] English **—편차 (統)** standard deviation **—항성 (天)** a standard star **—형** a standard type **—화** standardization: 표준화하다 standardize / 그것들은 모두 표준화되어 있다 They are all standardized.

표준시 標準時 (the) standard time; Greenwich (Mean) Time (略 G.M.T.)
■**만국[그리니치]—** universal time; Greenwich Mean Time **한국—** Korean Stan-

dard Time (略 KST)
표지 表紙 a cover; 〈제본〉 binding
♦ 〈종이로〉 책의 표지를 싸다 cover a book in paper; put the covers on a book
▪ 겉— a jacket; (英) a wrapper 뒤— a back cover 앞— a front [an upper, an obverse] cover 종이[가죽, 천]— a paper [leather, cloth] cover: 종이 표지의 책과 책 (bound) in paper covers; a paperback / 가죽 표지의 책 a book bound in leather; a leather-bound book ▪—도안[의장] a cover design —뒷면 the inside of cover

표지 標識 a sign, a mark; a signal; 〔쵸〕 a beacon; a guide
♦ 「우선 멈춤」의 표지 a stop sign; a sign saying "Stop" / 표지를 붙이다 put up a sign / 표지를 따라가다 follow a sign
▶ 표지를 따라 가시오 Follow the sign.
▪ 공중— 〈비행장의〉 a pylon 교통[도로]— a traffic [road] sign 수심(水深)— a depth mark 지상[항로]— a ground [channel] mark 항공— an air [aerial] beacon 해상— a sea mark; a beacon —등(燈) a beacon light

표징 表徵 a mark; a sign; a symbol
표차 表差 〔數〕 tabular difference; difference table
표차롭다 表— striking; conspicuous; standout; prominent
표착 漂着 drifting ashore
—**표착하다** be thrown [cast, washed] ashore; drift (ashore); be driven 〈to〉
▶ 그 사체가 해안에 표착했다 The body was washed ashore.
▪ —물 a drift; driftage

표찰 標札 a label; a bill; a sticker [nameplate]
▶ 나는 대문에 표찰을 붙였다 I put up a nameplate at the gate.

표창 表彰 (official) commendation; honoring; awarding
—**표창하다** commend (officially); award a prize 〈to sb〉; honor [do honor to] sb; make public recognition 〈of services〉
♦ 표창받다 win official commendation
▪ —식 a commendation ceremony; a ceremony of awarding an honor —장 a certificate of commendation; a testimonial: 그는 표창장을 수여받았다 He was awarded [given] a certificate of commendation.

표창 鏢槍 a dart; 〈단검〉 a dirk; a javelin
표출 表出 expression —**표출하다** express
♦ 감정을 표출하다 express one's feelings
표층 表層 the outer(most) layer [stratum]
표토 表土 topsoil; surface soil; regolith
표표하다 表表— conspicuous; famous; distinguished; noted
표피 表皮 1 〔解〕 the outer skin; the scarfskin; 〈동물의〉 the cuticle
2 〔植〕 the epidermis; the exterior coating; 〈수목의〉 the bark
▪ —세포 an epidermal cell —조직 epidermal tissue
표하다 表— express; show; manifest; demonstrate
▶ 나는 그들의 후의에 대해 감사의 뜻을 표했다 I expressed my gratitude for their kindnesses.
▶ 나는 경의를 표하기 위해 그를 방문했다 I called on him to pay my respects.

표하다 標— mark sth; put [place] a mark on sth
♦ 〈책의〉 읽은 곳을 표하다 mark the place that one has read (up to)

표현 表現 (an) expression; (a) representation; (a) manifestation
♦ 사상의 자유로운 표현 the free expression of thoughts / 눈에 보이지 않는 세계의 표현 representation of the invisible world / 교묘한 표현의 자유 freedom of expression / 교묘한 표현의 well-turned 《phrase》
▶ 예술은 자기 표현의 한 방식이다 Art is a form of self-expression.
—**표현하다** express; 〈말로〉 put (in, into); 〈그림 등으로〉 represent; manifest; 〈감정 등을〉 give expression to
♦ 표현할 수 없는 indescribable; beyond expression / 감상을 글로 표현하다 write one's impressions; express one's feelings in writing / 자기 생각을 영어로 표현하다 express oneself [put one's idea] in English
▶ 나는 그때의 즐거움을 말로는 표현할 수가 없다 I can't express (in words) [No words can express] how delighted I was at that time. ⇌ I can't put my delight at that time in [into] words.
▶ 내 기분을 반도 표현할 수 없다 I cannot tell half of what I feel.
▪ —력 (one's) power of expression —법 expression; how to express oneself —주의 〔藝〕 expressionism —파 the expressionist school; 〈사람〉 the expressionists

푯대 標— a (signal) post; a mark(ing) post; a signpost
푯돌 標— 〈길 표지〉 a stone marker; 〈경계를 나타내는〉 a boundary stone; 〈이정표〉 a milestone ♦ 푯돌을 세우다 set up a landmark stone
푯말 標— a post; a signpost ♦ 푯말을 세우다 set up a signpost
푸 1 〈내뿜는 소리〉 whew!; whoo!; with a light whistle 2 〈방귀 소리〉 with a light "poop"
푸가 (이) 〔樂〕 a fugue
푸근하다 comfortably warm ⇨ 포근하다
푸나무 풀과 나무 grasses and trees
푸나무서리 a place luxuriant with vegetation
푸념 1 〈무당의〉 the ravings of a shaman (transmitting the rage of a spirit while in a trance)
2 〈불평〉 an idle [a doleful] complaint; a grumble; grumbling
—**푸념하다** grumble 《at》; complain 《of, about》; make complaints 《to sb about sth》; whine 《about》; dwell on grievances; 〈美口〉 gripe 《at, about》
♦ 자기의 불운[손실]을 푸념하다 lament (over) one's misfortunes [loss]
푸다 〈물 등을〉 draw; 〈국자로〉 ladle; 〈뜨다〉 dip [scoop] up; 〈펌프로〉 pump
♦ 우물물을 푸다 draw water from a well / 국

을 푸다 ladle [spoon up] soup / 밥그릇에 밥을 푸다 serve rice in a bowl; serve out rice; fill a bowl with rice 《from the pot》/ 독에서 쌀을 푸다 scoop rice out of a jar

푸대접 an exorcism
—푸닥거리하다 perform an exorcism

푸대접 —待接 cold [unkind] treatment; 〈손님에 대한〉 a cold reception; inhospitality
♦ 푸대접을 받다 receive unkind treatment
—푸대접하다 treat [receive] coldly [with coldness, unkindly, in a cold way]; receive *sb* with indifference; be inhospitable 《to》; give *sb* a cold [frosty] reception; give [show, turn] the cold shoulder 《to》
♦ 푸대접받다 get a cold reception; be left out in the cold

푸두둥거리다 〈새가〉 flitter; flutter

푸드덕 flappingly; flutteringly ♦ 푸드덕 날개치다 flap [flutter] 《its》 wings

푸드덕거리다 〈새가〉 flap; flutter

푸들 〈개〉 a poodle

푸딩 (a) pudding

푸뜩푸뜩 all appearing suddenly; now and then; intermittently; occasionally ♦ 생각이 푸뜩푸뜩 나다 ideas pop up; an idea occurs to *one* now and then

푸르다 1 〈색이〉 blue; azure; green
♦ 푸른 들 a green field / 푸른 하늘 a blue [an azure] sky; the blue heavens / 싱싱하게 푸른 freshly [vividly] green; fresh and green
▶ 수목은 푸른 잎으로 덮여 있다 The trees are covered with green leaves.
2 〈서슬이〉 sharp(-edged)
♦ 서슬이 푸르다 〈날이〉 have a sharp edge; 〈체력이〉 be high and mighty

푸르데데하다 bluish; greenish; 〈얼굴이〉 somewhat pale [pallid]

푸르디푸르다 be blue as blue can be; be green as green can be; be ever so blue [green]; freshly [vividly] blue; fresh and green

푸르락붉으락하다 turn alternately pale and red ⇨ 붉으락푸르락하다

푸르르 〈끓는 모양〉 bubblingly; 〈타는 모양〉 《burn》 crisply; 〈떠는 모양〉 tremblingly

푸르스름하다 bluish; greenish; be tinged with blue

푸르죽죽하다 bluish ⇨ 푸르데데하다

푸른곰팡이 〔植〕 green mold; a penicillium 《*pl.* -lia》

푸릇푸릇 green [blue] here and there; all spotted green [blue]
♦ 푸릇푸릇 풀이 나다 grass sprouts out all green here and there / 온몸이 푸릇푸릇 멍들다 turn black and blue all over
—푸릇푸릇하다 green 《fields》; verdant; vivid
▶ 비온 뒤에는 나뭇잎들이 푸릇푸릇해 보인다 After the rain the leaves on the trees look bright green.

푸만하다 feel stuffy from overeating

푸새¹ 〈풀을 먹임〉 starching **—푸새하다** starch 《clothes》

푸새² 〈풀〉 grasses; weeds; pasturage

푸서리 bush; a weedy place

푸석돌 a crumbly stone; a loose rock

푸석푸석 all crisp; crumbly
♦ 푸석푸석 부서지다 crumble; break into crumbs
—푸석푸석하다 crumbling; crumbly; loose 《soil》; friable; 〈과일 등이〉 dry and tasteless [insipid]; 〈감자 등이〉 dry and crumbling
♦ 푸석푸석한 흙 crumbly soil / 〈나무가〉 푸석푸석해지다 become crumbly; undergo dry rot

푸석하다 crumbling; crumbly; friable

푸성귀 greens; green vegetables; greenstuff
■ **—장사** greengrocery **—장수** a greengrocer; a vegetable seller

푸슈킨 〈러시아의 시인·소설가〉 Pushkin, Aleksandr Sergeevich (1799-1837)

푸시폰 a touch-tone telephone

푸싱 〔球〕 〈미는 반칙〉 pushing

푸에르토리코 Puerto Rico; 〈공식명〉 the Commonwealth of Puerto Rico ♦ 푸에르토리코의 Puerto Rican ■ **—사람** a Puerto Rican

푸주 —廚 a butcher('s) shop; a butchery; 《美》 a meat market
■ **—한(漢)** a butcher; 《美》 a meatman

푸지다 abundant; plentiful; ample; lavish; profuse; generous
♦ 푸진 대접 liberal treatment / 푸지게 in (great) plenty [abundance]; abundantly; plentifully; 《美》 aplenty; amply; fully; lavishly; generously; liberally / 푸지게 먹다 eat plenty

푸짐하다 plentiful; abundant; copious; generous
♦ 푸짐한 성찬 an abundance of good cheer

푸치니 〈이탈리아의 작곡가〉 Puccini, Giacono (1858-1924)

푸푸 in puffs ♦ 푸푸 불다 puff and blow

푸하다 swollen; loose; puffy; bulging; untidy
♦ 푸한 머리 untidy hair / 푸한 짐 a loose bundle / 머리가 푸하게 일어서다 *one's* hair bristles up untidily

푹 1 〈찌르는 모양〉 home; hard; through
♦ 푹 찌르다 stab through; plunge; thrust 《a dagger》 home
▶ 그는 원수를 깊숙이 푹 찔렀다 He stabbed his enemy up to the hilt.
2 〈뒤집어 쓰거나 싸는 모양〉 completely; entirely
♦ 푹 싸다 wrap 《it》 all up carefully / 모자를 푹 눌러쓰다 pull [draw] *one's* hat over 《his》 eyes; wear *one's* hat pulled low over 《his》 eyes / 이불을 푹 뒤집어 쓰다 pull the bedclothes over *one's* head
3 〈잠자는 모양〉 fast; sound(ly)
♦ 푹 자다 sleep soundly; be sound asleep; sleep like a top [log] / 푹 잠이 들다 fall sound asleep
▶ 하룻밤 푹 자고 나면 회복될 겁니다 A good night's sleep will set you right.
4 〈쉬는 모양〉 thoroughly; completely; quite
♦ 푹 쉬다 rest up; rest completely; have a good slack
5 〈흠뻑〉 thoroughly; well; through
♦ 고기를 푹 삶다 do meat thoroughly / 푹 젖다 be wet [soaked] through [to the skin]
6 〈패거나 빠진 모양〉 deeply
♦ 푹 파다 dig deep(ly) / 진창에 푹 빠지다 be

caught [stuck] deep in the mud
▶ 비가 와서 땅이 푹 패였다 The raindrops have hollowed out the ground.
▶ 그는 고개를 푹 숙였다 His head sank forward on his breast.
7 〈쓰러지는 모양〉《fall》with a clash [thud]; plump; flop
◆푹 쓰러지다 fall with a clash [thud]; fall flat [plump]
8 〈갑자기 줄어든 모양〉sharply
◆푹 줄다 decrease [decline, fall off] sharply [remarkably]
9 〈내뿜는 모양〉in a puff
10 〈썩는 모양〉rotting completely

푹신푹신 softly; gently; lightly
―**푹신푹신하다** soft; downy; cottony; flossy; fluffy; spongy ◆푹신푹신한 소파 a soft, comfortable sofa

푹신하다 soft; downy; cottony; flossy; spongy
▶ 나는 푹신한 침대가 싫다 I don't like a soft bed.

푹푹 1 〈날씨가 더운 모양〉sultrily; (hot and) close; swelteringly
◆푹푹 찌는 더위 the sweltering [simmering, steaming] heat
2 〈찌르는 모양〉piercing [pricking] repeatedly
◆바늘로 푹푹 찌르다 prick《one's body》with a needle repeatedly
3 〈빠지는 모양〉sinking deep(ly)
◆발이 눈 속에 푹푹 빠지다 one's feet sink deep in the snow
4 〈썩는 모양〉decaying rapidly; rotting fast because of the hot weather
◆속이 푹푹 썩다 be sick at heart; feel mortified

푹하다 unseasonably warm; soft; mild
◆푹한 겨울 a soft [mild, green] winter

푼 〈돈 한 닢〉a *pun*; a Korean penny
◆돈 한 푼(도) 없다 be penniless; have not a penny [brass farthing, red cent] in the world; 《美》be utterly broke
▶ 한 푼의 값어치도 없다 It isn't worth a farthing. ⇒ That is utterly worthless.
▶ 그런 일에는 한푼도 낼 수 없다 I wouldn't give a plug nickel for that.
▶ 한푼도 깎을 수 없소 I won't take a cent less. ⇒ I wouldn't come down a cent.
2 〈무게 단위〉a Korean penny-weight
3 〈길이 단위〉a *pun*
4 〈백분비〉percentage; percent [%]
◆3할 3푼 thirty-three percent / 2푼 이자 2 percent interest

푼거리 buying [selling] firewood by the bunch [bundle]; dealing in a small way
―나무 firewood sold by bunches

푼거리질 buying one's firewood by the bunch; buying small faggots
―**푼거리질하다** buy one's firewood by the bunch
◆나무를 푼거리질할 만큼 가난하다 be so poor that one buys the firewood a bunch at a time

푼끌 a small narrow chisel

푼나무 buying firewood by the bundle ⇨ 푼거리(~나무)

푼내기 1 〈도박〉penny gambling; penny ante
2 ⇨ 푼거리
■―흥정 small-time business; penny ante business; business in a small way [on a small scale]

푼더분하다 1 〈얼굴이〉well-rounded; full-faced
◆푼더분한 얼굴 a full face
2 〈풍부하다〉ample; plentiful
◆푼더분한 보수 rich payment / 푼더분하게 대접하다 treat *sb* liberally

푼돈 odd [loose, broken] money; a trifling amount (of money); small change; a (mere) pittance
◆푼돈을 모으다 save money little by little; save pocket money [a petty penny] / 푼돈을 아끼다 be penny-wise

푼사 〈絲〉floss (silk); filoselle

푼수 〈얼마에 상당한 정도〉degree; extent; 〈율〉rate; 〈비〉ratio
◆이 푼수로 나간다면 (if things go on) at this rate / 세 사람 푼수를 일하다 do three men's work

푼어치 a pennyworth; a penny's worth

푼치 a small difference; a bit
◆한푼치의 양보도 하지 않다 don't yield a fraction of an inch; make no concession at all

푼푼이 penny by penny ◆푼푼이 모은 돈 money saved penny by penny [little by little]

푼푼하다 liberal; generous; abundant; plentiful ◆씀씀이가 푼푼하다 spend money liberally / 푼푼하게 liberally; generously; amply; abundantly

풀¹ 〈초본식물〉grass; a herb; 〈잡초〉a weed; 〈총칭〉herbage
◆풀 한잎 a blade of grass; a grass leaf / 한 포기의 풀 one clump of grass / 풀에 덮인 무덤 a grass-covered grave / 풀위에 드러눕다 lie down on the grass / 풀속에 숨다 hide in the grass / 풀이 무성하다 be overrun [overgrown, rank] with grass [weeds] / 풀을 베다 cut grass / 풀을 먹(고 살)다 feed on grass; graze / 소에게 풀을 뜯다 graze a cow / 정원의 풀을 뽑다 weed a garden
▶ 목초지에서 소가 풀을 뜯고 있다 Cattle are grazing in the pasture.
▶ 그는 밭에서 풀을 뽑고 있었다 He was pulling up weeds in the field.

━ 풀 ━

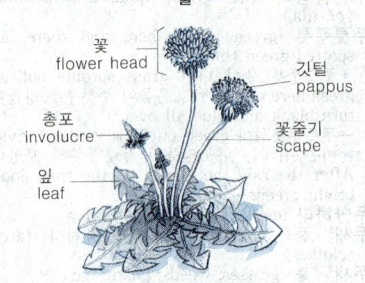

꽃 flower head
깃털 pappus
총포 involucre
꽃줄기 scape
잎 leaf

풀² **1** 〈밀가루로 만든〉 paste; 〈녹말로 만든〉 starch; 〈아교풀〉 glue; 〈고무풀〉 gum; 〈피륙에 먹이는〉 a size
 ♦풀이 잘 먹은 well-starched 《cloth》; starchy 《shirt》 / 풀을 쑤다 make paste / 풀을 개다 temper starch with water / 풀로 붙이다 paste; stick *sth* with paste
 ▶이 우표 뒷면에는 풀이 붙어 있지 않다 There is no gum on the back of this stamp.
 ▶옷깃에는 풀을 많이 먹여라 Please put a lot of starch on the collar.
 ▶그녀는 세탁물에 풀을 약간 먹여 다리미로 다렸다 She put a little starch on the laundry and ironed it.
 2 〈기운〉 spirit(s); heart; starch
 ▶그는 시험에 떨어져서 몹시 풀이 죽었다 Failing the examination made him thoroughly dejected. ⇌ He was quite blue over failing the examination.
풀³ **1** 〈수영장〉 a swimming pool; (英) a swimming bath
 2 〔經〕 〈공동출자〉 a pool
 ♦이익을 풀제로 하다 pool 《a group's》 profits
 ■실내— an indoor swimming pool ■—계산 a pool account
풀기 —氣 **1** 〈뻣뻣함〉 stiffness; starchiness
 ♦풀기가 있다 be starchy [starched, stiffened] / 풀기가 없다 be not starched; be unstarched [unstiffened]
 2 ⇨ 풀² 2
풀다 **1** 〈묶은 것·엉킨 것을〉 untie 《a string》; undo 《a bundle》; unbind 《a bandage》; loosen 《one's hair》; unpack 《a package》; unfasten 《a rope》; unravel 《a thread》; disentangle 《a knot》
 ♦밧줄을 풀다 unfasten [untie] a rope / 보따리를 풀다 undo [unwrap, untie] a package; unpack / 머리를 풀다 let down *one's* hair / 매듭을 풀다 undo [disentangle] a knot; unknot / 구두끈을 풀다 unlace the shoes / 여장을 풀다 take off *one's* traveling attire; 〈숙박하다〉 stop at an inn
 ▶그녀는 엉킨 실을 풀었다 She untangled the thread.
 2 〈문제 등을〉 solve 《a question》; work out 《a difficult problem》; answer 《a question》; explain; clear up 《the meaning》
 ♦방정식을 풀다 solve [reduce] an equation / 수수께끼를 풀다 solve [find out, undo] a riddle / 암호문을 풀다 decipher; decode / 점괘를 풀다 interpret [expound] *one's* divination sign
 3 〈해제하다〉 dissolve [cancel, rescind] 《a contract》; remove 《a prohibition》; lift 《a ban》; absolve 《sb from an obligation》; release; disengage
 ♦포위[봉쇄]를 풀다 raise a siege [blockade] / 자금의 동결을 풀다 thaw the frozen assets
 4 〈의심 등을〉 dispel 《doubts》; clear away [up]; remove 《a misunderstanding》
 ♦기분을 풀다 dispel [dissipate] the gloom; distract [divert] *oneself* / 의심을 풀다 clear *oneself* of the charge 《of theft》; dispel doubts / 원한을 풀다 pay off old scores 《with sb》 / 여행으로 기분을 풀다 go on a trip for a change [to relax, for relaxation]
 5 〈사람을 동원하다〉 call [send, draw] out 《troops》
 ♦증원 부대를 풀다 send out fresh troops; reinforce 《the guards》
 6 〈용해하다〉 dissolve; melt; 〈녹이다〉 thaw (out)
 ♦도료를 풀다 dissolve a paint / 물에 소금을 풀다 dissolve salt in water
 7 〈피로 등을〉 relieve; banish
 ♦피로를 풀다 relieve *one's* fatigue; freshen up / 잠을 자서 피로를 풀다 sleep off *one's* fatigue / 몸을 풀다 〈준비운동을 하다〉 warm up; limber up; 〈해산하다〉 deliver a child; give birth to a child
 8 〈긴장을〉 relieve; relax; ease; unwind
 ♦긴장을 풀다 relieve the tension / 마음을 풀다 ease *oneself*; ease *one's* mind
 9 〈화 등을〉 appease; calm; pacify
 ♦화를 풀다 quell [appease] *one's* anger / 갈증을 풀다 quench thirst / 시장기를 풀다 appease [alleviate] *one's* hunger
 10 〈소원을〉 realize; satisfy; gratify
 ♦소원을 풀다 realize *one's* desire; gratify *one's* wishes; have *one's* wish fulfilled
 11 〈코를〉 blow 《*one's* nose》
 ♦손수건으로 코를 풀다 blow *one's* nose into *one's* handkerchief
 12 〈논을〉 turn land into 《a paddy》; create 《a paddy》 out of land
 ♦개펄에 논을 풀다 turn shoreland into paddies
풀떡 lightly; nimbly; quickly
 ♦풀떡 뛰어 내리다 swing *oneself* down 《from》 / 개울을 풀떡 뛰어넘다 clear a brook in *one* vault
풀리다 **1** 〈매듭이〉 get [come] loose; come untied [undone]; 〈얽힌 것이〉 become disentangled; 〈구두끈이〉 become unlaced; 〈천의 가장자리가〉 fray; become frayed
 ♦구두끈이 풀리다 *one's* shoestrings get loose; *one's* shoes come untied [become unlaced] / 머리가 풀리다 *one's* hair gets loose / 실마리가 풀리다 (비유) find a clue 《to》
 ▶매듭이 풀렸다[풀리려 한다] The knot came [is coming] untied.
 2 〈누그러지다〉 be allayed; relent 《toward sb》
 ▶두 집안 사이의 불화는 오랫동안 풀리지 않았다 The two families were long at feud with each other.
 ▶그의 노여움은 풀렸다 His anger is gone. ⇌ His anger has been allayed [appeased].
 ▶이 때문에 그녀의 마음도 다소 풀렸다 She relented a little at this.
 3 〈의혹·의심 등이〉 be solved; be removed [cleared]; disappear; vanish
 ♦오해가 풀리다 a misunderstanding is removed / 혐의가 풀리다 be cleared of a charge
 ▶네 말로 내 의심이 모두 풀렸다 Your statement has dispelled all my doubts.

우리의 오해는 깨끗이 풀렸다 Our misunderstanding was cleared up.
4 〈문제 등이〉 work out; be [get] solved [unraveled]
♦ 풀리지 않는 문제 an unsoluble problem
▶ 문제[수수께끼]가 다 풀렸다 A problem [puzzle] is wholly solved.
5 〈해방되다〉 be released; be [get] freed
♦ 교도소에서 몸이 풀리다 be released from prison
6 〈해제·제거되다〉 be removed; be lifted [raised]
▶ 금지령이 풀렸다 The ban is removed.
▶ 포위가 풀렸다 The siege is raised [lifted].
7 〈유통되다〉 circulate; pass current
♦ 은행 돈이 풀리다 money in the bank is released
8 〈용해되다〉 dissolve; become dissolved; melt; 〈언 것이〉 be thawed out; thaw
♦ 물에 풀리다 be soluble in water
▶ 얼음이 풀리는 철이 되었다 A thaw has set in.
9 〈이루어지다〉 get realized; be fulfilled
♦ 소원이 풀리다 have one's wish realized; one's wish comes true
10 〈긴장 등이〉 become [get] remiss; remit; relax; slack(en)
♦ 마음이 풀리다 one's mind relaxes [becomes remiss]
▶ 학생들의 규율이 풀린 것 같다 Discipline seems relaxed among the students.
▶ 시합이 끝나자 긴장이 확 풀렸다 I found myself very relaxed after the game was over.
11 〈추위가〉 abate; moderate; go down
▶ 추위가 한결 풀렸다 The cold has remarkably abated.
12 〈피로가〉 be relieved (of one's fatigue); get over (from fatigue)
▶ 커피 한 잔에 피로가 풀렸다 A cup of coffee relieved my fatigue.

풀매 a hand mill
풀매듭 a slipknot
풀먹이다 starch (linen, one's shirt)
♦ 풀먹인 starched
풀무 (a pair of) bellows; a blower; a forge
■ ─손 a hand bellows ─질 blowing with bellows: 풀무질하다 blow with a bellows; work [blow] a bellows
풀밭 a grass field; a field of grass; a grassy land [plain]; a meadow ♦ 풀밭에 누워 뒹굴다 lie down on the grass
풀백 〔蹴〕 a fullback
풀브라이트법 ─法 the Fulbright Act
♦ 풀브라이트법에 따른 교환 교수 a Fulbright professor; (口) a Fulbrighter
풀빛 (dark) green; emerald green
풀세트 〔테니스〕 a full set
■ ─게임 a full-set game [match]
풀솜 floss (silk)
♦ 풀솜같은 구름 puffy clouds
풀솜나물 〔植〕 a cottonweed; a cudweed; an everlasting (flower)
풀숲 a cluster of grass; a bush; a grassy [weedy] place; a growth of weeds
풀스피드 full speed ♦ 풀스피드로 달리다 run (at) full speed
풀썩 rising in a puff [cloud]
♦ 먼지를 풀썩 일으키다 raise a cloud of dust
풀쐐기 〔昆〕 a hairy caterpillar
풀쑤다 1 〈풀을〉 make [prepare] paste
2 〈재산을〉 dissipate [squander] 《one's fortune [property]》
풀어내다 〈얽힌 것을〉 unravel; disentangle
♦ 얽힌 실을 풀어내다 unravel a thread / 밧줄을 풀어내다 pay out a rope
2 〈밝혀내다〉 clear up (the meaning); work out (a difficult problem); solve (a question)
♦ 힘든 문제를 풀어내다 solve [crack] a difficult problem / 수수께끼를 풀어내다 figure [make, work] out a puzzle; solve a riddle; solve [untangle] a mystery
풀어놓다 1 〈맨것을 끌러주다〉 untie; unfasten; free; set free; cast loose; release
♦ 탈옥수에 개를 풀어놓다 loose a dog on an escaping convict / 짐을 풀어놓다 undo a bundle; leave a bundle undone
2 〈여러 사람을〉 put; send; dispatch
♦ 형세를 알아보려고 사람들을 풀어놓다 dispatch men to feel the situation
풀어먹이다 1 〈사람에게〉 distribute (food) among the people **2** 〈귀신에게〉 perform an exorcism with sacrificial food to drive out evil spirits
풀어주다 free; set free; release; liberate
풀어지다 1 ⇨ 풀리다
2 〈국수 등이〉 become [turn] soft ♦ 국수가 풀어지다 noodles become [turn] soft
3 〈눈이〉 (one's) eyes become bleared; go [get] bleary
풀이 (an) explanation; elucidation; exposition; (an) interpretation
─**풀이하다** interpret; explain; construe; elucidate; expound
♦ 바르게[잘못] 풀이하다 interpret rightly [falsely]
─**풀이** removing; dispelling; exorcising; a shamanist [shamanisitic] performance
풀잎 a blade of grass; a grass leaf
■ ─피리 a reed (pipe)
풀죽다 1 〈의류가〉 lose (its) starch; get limp
♦ 풀죽은 옷깃 a limp collar
2 〈사람이〉 be [get] depressed [dispirited, disheartened]; lose one's starch [spunk]; be downcast; be down in [at] the mouth; be in the blues [dumps]; be out of spirits
♦ 풀죽은 얼굴을 하다 look blue [downcast]; be down (in the mouth)
▶ 선생님께 꾸지람 좀 들었다고 풀죽지 마라 Don't be so dejected just because you were scolded by the teacher.
풀질 pasting
─**풀질하다** paste; apply paste
풀쩍 (opening or closing the door) suddenly [unexpectedly]
♦ 문을 풀쩍 열다[닫다] open [close] the door suddenly
풀쩍거리다 keep opening and closing (the door); come in and go out all the time; keep

coming in and going out
풀쳐생각 unburdening *one's* mind; putting *one's* mind at ease; taking it easy; relaxing
—**풀쳐생각하다** unburden *one's* mind; put *one's* mind at ease; take it easy; relax

풀치 〔魚〕 a young hairtail

풀치다 pardon [forgive] generously
♦생각을 풀치다 put *one's* mind at ease

풀칠 1 〈풀질〉 pasting
—**풀칠하다** paste; spread [cover] 《paper》 with paste
2 〈끼니를 잇기〉 bare living [livelihood]
—**풀칠하다** make *one's* living; keep the pot boiling; eke out a living
♦겨우 입에 풀칠하다 eke out a scanty livelihood; live from hand to mouth / 입에 풀칠하기도 어렵다 have no means of livelihood; find it difficult to make a living

풀카운트 〔野〕 a full count
▶그는 풀카운트에서 홈런을 쳤다 He slammed a homer on a full count [3-2 pitch].

풀칼 a wooden paper-knife used to spread paste; a pasting spatula

풀포수 —泡水 starching 《paper》 before oiling
—**풀포수하다** starch 《cloth》 before oiling

풀풀 1 〈기운차게〉 in high spirits; full of vigor; lustily
2 〈흩날리는 모양〉 in flakes
♦먼지가 풀풀 나다 dust rises; it is dusty
▶일단의 트럭이 먼지를 풀풀 일으키며 달려갔다 A convoy of trucks rolled past, raising a cloud of dust.
3 〈끓는 모양〉 boiling hard

풀피리 a reed (pipe)《～피리》

품¹ **1** 〈옷의 폭〉 width 《of a coat》
♦앞[뒤] 품 the breast [shoulder] width / 품이 손 저고리 a coat cut too tightly
2 〈가슴〉 the bosom; the breast
♦산[대자연]의 품 the bosom of a mountain [of Nature] / 어머니의 품에 안겨 있는 갓난아이 an infant nestling in its mother's breast / 단도를 품에 품고 with a dagger in *one's* bosom / 지갑을 품에 넣다 tuck [put] a wallet into *one's* bosom

품² 〈수고·힘〉 trouble; labor; work
♦하루 품 a day's work [labor] / 품이 많이 드는 일 work that requires much labor / 품이 들다 require [cost] 《much》 labor; be troublesome / 품을 들이다 expend *one's* labor / 품을 덜다 save 《oneself》 labor / 품을 갚다 work in return

품³ 〈외양〉 (personal) appearance; 〈방식〉 a way; a fashion
♦생긴 품 (personal) appearance / 사람된 품 (a) personal character; (a) personality / 그가 말하는 품 *one's* way of talking; the fashion of *one's* speech

품1 1 〈물품〉 an article; a piece; an item
♦국산품 homemade [domestic] goods
2 〈품질〉 quality
♦상품(上品) a first-class article
3 〈품계〉 (official) rank; order
♦정[종] 2품 the senior [junior] grade of the second (court) rank

품값 pay for labor ⇨ 품삯

품값음 returning work for work
—**품값음하다** do return service to *sb's* help; work in return

품격 品格 (a) grace; character; dignity

품귀 品貴 a scarcity [paucity] of goods [supply]; a shortage of stock; an inadequate supply [an undersupply] of goods
♦품귀가 되다 〈상품이 주어〉 run short; become scarce; 〈가게 또는 상인이 주어〉 run short 《of an item》
▶유류는 지금 품귀 상태가 되어 간다 Oil in stock is running short [low]. ⇌ Oil is in short supply.

품다 1 〈안다〉 hold [take] 《a child》 in *one's* arms; embrace; hug
♦비수를 품다 hold a dagger 《in *one's* bosom》
▶그녀는 아이를 꼭 품고 있었다 She held her child tightly in her arms.
▶강도는 단도를 품고 있었다 The robber carried a dagger concealed. ⇌ A dagger was found on the robber's person.
2 〈마음에〉 entertain 《hope》; cherish 《a desire, an ideal》; harbor 《suspicion》; nourish 《an illusion》; bear 《malice》; hold 《a belief》; nurse [foster] 《an idea》; have
♦원한을 품다 bear a grudge 《against》 / 희망을 품다 cherish a hope
▶그녀는 그에게 앙심을 품고 있다 She has a grudge against him. ⇌ She bears him a grudge.
3 〈알을〉 brood; sit 《on eggs》
♦알을 품다 sit [brood] on eggs; brood / 알을 품게 하다 set 《a hen》 on eggs

품등 品等 〈등급〉 (a) grade; rating; 〈품질〉 quality

품명 品名 the name of an article [item]

품목 品目 a list of articles; an item
♦품목별로 by item
■수입— (a list of) the items imported 영업— business items; items of business 주요수출[제조]— the chief [principal] items of export [manufacture]

품사 品詞 〔文法〕 a part of speech
■ 팔(八)— the eight parts of speech ■—론 〔文法〕 accidence

품삯 pay [wages] for labor
♦품삯을 치르다 pay *sb* for (his) trouble [labor]; pay *sb* by the piece / 품삯을 받다 receive *one's* wages [pay] for the labor / 품삯을 일하다 work by the day; hire out

품성 品性 (a) character
♦품성이 훌륭한[비열한] 사람 a man of fine [low, mean] character / 품성을 도야하다 cultivate [build (up)] *one's* character

품성 稟性 nature; character

품속 the bosom; the breast
♦품속에 안다 hold [take] 《a child》 in *one's* arms [breast] / 자연의 품속에 안기다 be (nestled) in the bosom of Nature

품안 the bosom ⇨ 품속

품앗이 exchange of services; an exchange of labor —**품앗이하다** exchange services; work in turn for each other

품위 品位 1 〈품격〉 dignity; (a) grace; nobility ◆품위없는 사람 a man of coarse character / 품위있는 언사 vulgar language / 품위가 있다 be dignified; have grace / 품위를 떨어뜨리다 lose *one's* dignity; degrade *oneself* / 품위를 지키다 keep [maintain] *one's* dignity / 품위를 높이다 dignify [elevate] *one's* character; ennoble [refine] *sb*
▶ 그녀는 매우 품위가 있다 She has grace and dignity.
2 〈품등〉 (a) grade; 〈품질〉 quality; 〈금속의〉 a standard ◆품위가 낮은 광석 a low-grade ore / 품위가 낮다 be low in quality [grade]
3 〈품계〉 a (court) rank
◆품위가 높은 사람 a person of high rank

품의 稟議 consultation 《with a superior》
—품의하다 consult; confer 《with a superior》; report *sth* to a superior for decision

품절 品切 absence of stock
◆품절되다 be out of stock; be sold out; be exhausted / 품절이 되다 run out of stock; be sold out
▶ 품절 《게시》 All sold. ⇌ Sold out.
▶ 바나나는 지금 품절입니다 Bananas are out of stock [all sold out] now.

품종 品種 a kind; a sort; a species; 〈가축의〉 a breed; a description; 〈변종〉 a variety
◆새 품종을 만들다 produce new varieties / 같은 품종이다 be of the same kind
■—개량 improvement of breed [plants]; cattle [plant] breeding

품질 品質 quality
◆품질이 좋은[나쁜] of good [inferior] quality; good [bad, poor] in quality / 품질이 떨어지다 be inferior in quality / 품질을 개량하다 improve *sth* in quality; improve the quality 《of *sth*》
▶ 우리 가게는 품질본위입니다 Quality first is our motto.
▶ 이 물건은 품질이 떨어진다 This article is inferior in quality.
■—관리 quality control —보증 a guarantee of quality; 《게시》 Quality Guaranteed. —저하 deterioration —증명 a hallmark

품팔이 work for (daily) wages; work as a day laborer

품팔이 doing day labor
—품팔이하다 work for (daily) wages; do piecework [job work]; do odd jobs; work as a day laborer; be hired [《美口》 hire out] by the day; work by the day
■—꾼 a piecework man; a pieceworker; a day laborer; 〈여자〉 a charwoman

품평 品評 evaluation; estimation; criticism; comment; judgment
—품평하다 evaluate; estimate; criticize; comment 《on》; judge the merits [worth] 《of》

품평회 品評會 a competitive [prize] show; an exhibition; 《美》 a fair
■—농산물— an agricultural fair

품하다 稟— tell *one's* superior; submit 《a plan》 to a superior

품행 品行 conduct; behavior; demeanor; deportment; moral character; morals
◆품행이 나쁜 사람 a libertine; a man of loose conduct
▶ 그는 품행이 단정하다 He conducts himself well. ⇌ His conduct is exemplary.

풋— 〈덜 익은〉 green; unripe; 〈새로 나온〉 new; fresh; 〈미숙한〉 green; inexperienced

풋감 an unripe [a green] persimmon

풋것 〈처음 것〉 the first product 《of fruit, vegetables, etc.》 of the season [year]; 〈덜 익은〉 unripe grain [fruit, vegetables, etc.]

풋고추 an unripe hot pepper

풋곡식 —穀— new grain

풋과실 —果實 green [unripe] fruits

풋김치 *kimchi* prepared with young vegetables

풋나물 (a dish of) young herbs
◆풋나물 먹듯하다 eat liberally of…

풋내 smell of fresh young greens [herbs]
◆풋내나다 smell of greens; 《비유》 be green [unfledged, inexperienced, callow]

풋내기 1 〈미숙한 사람〉 a new [green, raw] hand; a beginner; a novice; a fledg(e)ling; a freshman; 《英》 a fresher; 《口》 a greenhorn
◆풋내기 문필가 a hack writer; a scribbler / 풋내기 기자 《美》 a cub [novice] reporter / 풋내기 야구 선수 a rookie
2 〈경솔한 사람〉 a rash person

풋담배 green tobacco

풋머리 the season when things are just ripening or coming to market

풋바심 harvesting unripe grain [crops]
—풋바심하다 harvest (rice) too early [before it is ripe]

풋밤 unripe chestnuts

풋배 green [unripe] pears

풋벼 unripe rice ■—바심 harvesting unripe rice

풋볼 football; 〈축구〉 soccer; association football; 〈럭비〉 rugger; rugby football; 〈공〉 a football

풋사랑 transient love; calf [puppy] love

풋솜씨 poor hand; undeveloped [imperfect] skill

풋워크 〔스포츠〕 footwork
◆풋워크가 흐트러지다 lose *one's* footwork
▶ 그는 풋워크가 좋다[나쁘다] His footwork is good [poor].

풋잠 a light sleep; a doze

풋장기 —將棋 a poor [bad] hand at chess [*changgi*] ◆풋장기를 두다 play a poor game of *changgi*

풋콩 unripe beans [peas]

풍 1 〈방귀 소리〉 with a poop
◆방귀를 풍 뀌다 break wind noisily
2 〈구멍 뚫리는 소리·모양〉 breaking open
◆크게 풍 뚫린 구멍 a large gaping hole

풍 風 1 ⇨ 허풍
▶ 그의 이야기에는 풍이 좀 섞였다 His statement is rather exaggerated.
2 〈바람〉 (the) wind
◆강풍 a strong [high] wind
3 〈중풍〉 paralysis

-풍 -風 〈차림〉 a look; appearance; 〈태도〉

bearing; manner; 〈유파·식·형〉a style; a fashion; a type; a mode; 〈풍습〉manners; customs; a custom; ways; 〈기질〉disposition; 〈종류〉a kind; a sort
♦도회지풍 town [urbane] manners; urbanity / 이탈리아 풍 an Italian style / 미국풍의 집 an American-style house / 호걸풍의 사람 a man of (a) heroic disposition

풍각쟁이 風角— a street singer [musician]; a strolling musician

풍간 諷諫 insinuative exhortation; exhortation by innuendo —**풍간하다** exhort by insinuation [innuendo]

풍격 風格 〈성격〉character; personality; 〈풍채〉appearance; 〈문예상의〉style; gusto; race; tone; color
▶ 그는 풍격이 있는 사람이다 He is a man of noble appearance.

풍경 風景 scenery; a landscape; a scene; 〈조망〉a view; a prospect; a sight
▶ 풍경의 아름다움 scenic beauty
▶ 이 근처는 풍경이 아주 좋다 The neighborhood has [presents] a very fine view.
▶ 그 섬은 풍경이 아름답기로 유명하다 The island is famous for its scenic beauty.
■ 거리— a scene on the street; a street scene [view] 전원— a rural landscape; a scene of the countryside

풍경 風磬 a wind-bell 《with a fishlike clapper》 ■ —소리 the tinkling [tinkle] of a wind-bell

풍경치다 風磬— go in and out continually

풍경화 風景畫 a landscape (painting, picture)
♦바다 풍경화 a seapiece; a seascape
♦—가 a landscape painter; a landscapist

풍광 風光 (beautiful) scenery; natural [scenic] beauty
♦풍광명미하다 have beautiful scenery; have great scenic beauty

풍구 風— 1 〈농기구〉a winnowing machine; a winnower 2 ⇨ 풀무

풍금 風琴 〈악기〉an organ; a harmonium; 〈손으로 돌리는〉a hand organ; 〈아코디언〉an accordion; 〈6각형의〉a concertina
♦풍금을 치다 play (on) the organ

풍기 風紀 〈도의〉public morals [decency]; 〈규율〉discipline; 〈풍속〉manners
♦풍기 문란[퇴폐] demoralization; the decay [corruption, relaxation] of public morals / 풍기 문란케 하다 corrupt public morals / 풍기를 단속하다 enforce discipline; watch over public morals
▶ 요즈음 풍기가 문란해졌다 Public decency has recently become corrupt [loose].

풍기다 1 〈냄새를〉 give out [off, forth] 《an odor》; send forth 《a scent》; 〈냄새가〉smell (of); hang [float] in the air [in midair]; 〈방향이〉be fragrant; 〈악취가〉stink; reek
♦향기를 풍기다 smell sweet; emit [give out] a sweet smell / 악취를 풍기다 stink; smell bad; give out [off] a bad smell
▶ 그녀는 향긋한 냄새를 풍기며 방으로 들어왔다 She came in the room, giving off a sweet smell.

▶ 그의 입에서는 술 냄새가 풍겼다 I could smell liquor on his breath.
▶ 하수도가 악취를 풍긴다 The ditch stinks (offensively).
2 〈낌새를〉have a smack [savor] of...
♦관리티를 잔뜩 풍기다 smack strongly of the bureaucrat
3 〈사람·짐승을〉start [flush (up), rise] 《a bird》; 〈새가〉flush; fly [start] out; rise in the air; take wings
4 〈곡식을〉winnow 《grain》; winnow away [out]; fan

풍년 豊年 a year of abundance [plenty]; a fruitful [rich] year; a banner year for crops; a bumper year; 〈풍작〉a good crop [harvest]
▶ 올해는 쌀이 풍년이었다 The rice crop bore a plentiful harvest this year. ⇌ We had a bumper rice crop this year.
▶ 올해는 풍년이 들 것 같다 We shall probably have a good harvest this year.
▶ 눈은 풍년의 징조다 Snow is the harbinger of a rich year.
■ —거지 a man who has an unlucky break while all his friends are lucky —축제 the celebration of a good harvest; a harvest festival

풍덩 with a plop [splash]
♦풍덩 떨어지다 drop (into the water) with a plop; fall plop into 《the water》 / 풍덩 뛰어들다 plunge 《into the water》 with a plop
—**거리다** keep plopping [splashing]

풍덩풍덩 with plops; plop

풍뎅이 a goldbeetle [goldbug]

풍도 風度 one's appearance and manners; one's bearing; deportment ♦대인의 풍도 the bearing [air] of a noble gentleman

풍동 風洞 〈物〉a wind tunnel; a wind channel
■ —시험 a wind tunnel test

풍랑 風浪 〈氣〉wind and waves; heavy seas
♦풍랑에 시달리다 be buffeted by [at the mercy of] the wind and waves / 풍랑과 싸우다 battle with [struggle against] the wind and waves
▶ 풍랑이 심하다 The waves are high. ⇌ The sea is running high.

풍력 風力 the wind force
■ —계 an anemometer; a wind gauge —계급 a wind scale —발전소 〔電〕a wind power plant [station]

풍로 風爐 a wind furnace

풍류 風流 1 〈운치〉elegance; taste; refinement
♦풍류적인 elegant; tasteful; refined; graceful; artistic(al); aesthetic(al); romantic / 풍류를 알다 appreciate poetry [beauty]; have a love of poetry / 풍류를 일삼다 indulge in romantic pursuits
2 〈음악〉music
■ —가[객, 인] a man of taste; a person of a romantic turn of mind

풍만하다 豊滿— plump; corpulent; voluptuous; buxom; well-developed 《breasts》; stout 《lady》
♦풍만한 가슴 a full [an ample] bosom / 풍만한 미인 a plump, voluptuous beauty; a

glamorous-looking girl
▶ 그는 그녀의 풍만한 육체미에 매료되었다 He was captivated by her plump and voluptuous beauty.

풍매 風媒 〔植〕 anemophily
◆ 풍매의 wind-pollinated; wind-fertilized; anemophilous
■ —식물 a wind-pollinated plant; an anemophile; an anemophilous plant —화 an anemophilous [a wind-pollinated] flower

풍모 風貌 〈용모〉 looks; features; 〈풍채〉 appearance
◆ 풍모가 좋은 사람 a fine-looking man / 풍모를 묘사하다 depict sb's personality
▶ 그는 당당한 풍모를 지녔다 He had a commanding [an imposing] presence.

풍문 風紋 a wind-wrought pattern on sand

풍문 風聞 a rumor; a report; hearsay
◆ 풍문에 듣다 hear from sb; know by [from] hearsay / 풍문을 퍼뜨리다 spread a rumor; set a rumor afloat / …라는 풍문이다 Rumor has it that...; It is said (that)...; There is a rumor (in the air) that...
▶ 그것은 풍문에 지나지 않는다 It's nothing but a rumor. ⇒ That is mere hearsay.
▶ 풍문으로 알고 있을 뿐입니다 I know this only by hearsay.

풍물 風物 1 〈경치〉 scenery; nature; a landscape; 〈풍속〉 scenes and manners
◆ 자연의 풍물 natural features / 한국의 풍물 things Korean / 시적인 풍물 things poetical
2 〈농악기〉 farmers' musical instruments
■ —시 poetic descriptions of natural scenery; natural poetry

풍미 風味 flavor; savor; taste; relish; 〈얼얼한〉 tang; 〈술 등의〉 bouquet
◆ 풍미가 있다 be delicious; taste good / 풍미가 없다 be insipid [tasteless, flat]; taste bad / 풍미를 내다 season; flavor; give a flavor to / 그 고장의 독특한 풍미가 있다 be racy of the soil

풍미하다 風靡— overwhelm; dominate; predominate; sway; sweep; carry all (before one)
◆ 일세를 풍미하다 take the world by storm; sway the whole nation; rule the time / 천하를 풍미하다 rule the whole world

풍병 風病 1 〔韓醫〕〈풍증〉 nervous disorders; palsy; paralysis
2 〈한센병〉 leprosy

풍부 豊富 abundance; opulence; affluence; plenty; wealth; richness
—풍부하다 abundant; plentiful; rich; ample; affluent; abound in [with]; be replete with; well-off (for)
◆ 풍부한 지식 a great stock of knowledge; a mine of information / 풍부한 천연자원 rich natural resources / 풍부한 식량 공급 an abundant supply of food / 경험이 풍부하다 have a large experience / 어휘를 풍부하게 하다 enrich [increase, enlarge] one's vocabulary
▶ 콩에는 단백질이 풍부하다 The bean comes high in protein.
▶ 그 나라는 물과 목재가 풍부하다 That country abounds [is rich] in water and wood. ⇒ That country has a rich [an abundant] supply of water and wood.
▶ 그녀는 육아 경험이 풍부하다 She has a lot of childcare experience.
▶ 이것은 확실히 내용이 풍부한 책이다 This is surely a work of rich contents. ⇒ This is surely a well-packed book.

풍비박산하다 風飛雹散— 〈날아 흩어지다〉 scatter [disperse, be scattered] (in all directions); 〈부서지다〉 break to [into] fragments

풍상 風霜 1 〈바람과 서리〉 wind and frost
2 〈많은 고생〉 hardships; troubles; sufferings
◆ 온갖 풍상을 겪나 go through all sorts of hardships; experience [taste] the bitters of life

풍선 風船 a balloon
◆ 풍선을 띄우다 fly [send up] a balloon / 풍선을 터뜨리다 break a balloon
▶ 풍선이 터졌다 The balloon burst.
◆ 고무[종이]— a rubber [paper] balloon
■ —껌 《a piece of》 bubble gum —폭탄 a balloon bomb

풍설 風說 rumor; a (current) report; hearsay
◆ 항간의 풍설 the talk of the town / 갖가지 풍설 various rumors

풍설 風雪 wind and snow; a snowstorm; a blizzard ◆ 대— a heavy snowstorm

풍성 風成 〔地質〕 ◆ 풍성의 aeolian
■ —암[분지, 층] an aeolian rock [basin, deposit] —토 aeolian soil

풍성하다 豊盛— plentiful; abundant; ample; affluent; exuberant; 〈부유하다〉 rich; wealthy
◆ 풍성한 수확 an abundant crop [harvest] 《of rice》

풍세 風勢 the force [velocity] of the wind; wind force [velocity]

풍속 風俗 〈풍습〉 manners; customs; 〈풍기〉 puplic morals
◆ 풍속을 문란케 하다 corrupt [be against] good manners; vitiate public morals
▶ 영어를 공부하는 사람은 반드시 영국의 풍속을 알아야 한다 Knowledge of English manners and customs is essential to a student of English.
▶ 풍속 습관은 나라마다 다르다 Every country has its own manners and customs.
■ —사범 an offense against public morals; a morals offense —소설 a light novel depicting social customs and manners; a genre novel —화 a genre picture: 풍속 화가 a genre painter [style]

풍속 風速 〔氣〕 wind velocity; the wind speed
◆ 최대 풍속 초속 25미터의 태풍 a typhoon with a maximum wind velocity [speed] of twenty-five meters per second / 풍속을 재다 gauge the wind speed
▶ 풍속 20미터의 바람이 불었다 The wind blew at twenty meters a second.
■ —순간최대— the maximum instantaneous wind velocity —계 an anemometer; a wind gauge

풍수 風水 〔民俗〕 1 〈학설〉 wind-and-water magic; geomancy

2 〈지관〉 a practitioner of geomancy; a geomancer
■ —설 the theory of geomancy —학 geomantic studies; geomancy

풍수해 風水害 wind and flood damage
■ —대책 measures against natural disasters

풍습 風習 manners and customs; practices
♦ 풍습의 customary / 풍습에 따르다 conform to custom / 옛 풍습을 지키다 keep to the good old ways
▶ 나는 이 지방풍습에 익숙하지 않다 I am not accustomed to the manners and customs here.

풍식 風蝕 〔地質〕 wind erosion; weathering
■ —력 force of wind erosion —작용 wind erosion

풍신 風神 **1** 〈바람의 신〉 the god of (the) wind **2** ⇨ 풍채

풍아 風雅 elegance; refinement; grace
—풍아하다 elegant; refined; artistic; graceful and cultured

풍악 風樂 Korean music
♦ 풍악을 잡히다 have music performed [played]
▶ 풍악이 울렸다 Music began.

풍압 風壓 wind pressure
■ —계 a pressure anemometer —계수 a wind pressure coefficient

풍어 豊魚 a heavy [good] catch; a good [rich] haul
♦ 풍어를 만나다 have a large [big] take of fish; make a good haul; have a successful haul
▶ 오늘은 정어리가 풍어였다 We got a big catch of sardine(s) today.

풍요 豊饒 fertility; richness; abundance; productiveness; fruitfulness
—풍요하다 fertile; rich; affluent; productive; fruitful; abundant
♦ 풍요한 사회 an affluent society / 풍요한 땅 a fertile land; 〔聖〕 a land flowing with milk and honey (민수기 14 : 13)

풍우 風雨 wind and rain; a rainstorm
♦ 풍우에 시달린 weather-beaten / 풍우를 무릅쓰고 in spite [in defiance, in the teeth] of the storm

풍운 風雲 **1** 〈바람과 구름〉 winds and clouds; elements
2 〈형세〉 the state of affairs; the situation
♦ 풍운의 뜻을 품다 cherish an ambition
■ —아 a lucky adventurer; a soldier of fortune

풍월 風月 the bright moon and cool breezes; beauties of nature; 〈시〉 poetry
♦ 들은 풍월 smatter / 풍월을 즐기다 enjoy the beauties of nature / 풍월을 벗삼다 converse [commune] with nature / 풍월을 짓다 compose a poem; make verses
■ —객 a person who dabbles in poetry —주인 a person who enjoys the beauties of nature

풍위 風位 the direction of the wind
♦ 풍위가 바뀌다 the wind shifts / 풍위를 재다 define the direction of the wind

풍유 諷諭 allegory; allegorization; a hint; insinuation

—풍유하다 use an allegory; allegorize; insinuate

풍자 諷刺 (a stroke of) satire; (a) sarcasm; an innuendo 《*pl.* ~s, ~es》; an irony; a squib; a lampoon
♦ 사회 풍자 a satire (on) society / 통렬한 풍자 a bitter [harsh, scathing] satire / 풍자적인 satirical; sarcastic; ironical
▶ 이 만화는 정치에 대한 풍자다 This comic strip is a satire on politics.
▶ 풍자가 지나쳤다 The sarcasm is overdone [too pungent].
—풍자하다 satirize; innuendo; lampoon; squib; pasquinade
▶ 그 영화는 오늘날의 한국을 통렬하게 풍자하고 있다 That movie severely satirizes Korea of today.
■ —가 a satirist; a lampooner; a lampoonist —문학 satire; satirical literature —소설 a satirical novel [story] —시 a satiric(al) poem [verse]; a lampoon; a satire; a pasquinade

풍자문 諷刺文 a prose satire; a satirical prose; a lampoon; a squib
■ —체 a satiric style

풍자화 諷刺畵 a satire in drawing; a caricature; 〈시사적인〉 a cartoon
■ —가 a caricaturist; a cartoonist

풍작 豊作 a good [an abundant] harvest [crop]; a heavy crop (of rice); a large yield 《of fruit》
▶ 쌀은 풍작이 확실시된다 There is every prospect of a large rice crop.
▶ 금년엔 쌀이 풍작일 것이다 We will have a good [rich] harvest this year. ⇌ The rice crop will be good [abundant] this year.

풍재 風災 wind damage; crop loss caused by the wind

풍전등화 風前燈火 a light before the wind; a candle flickering in the wind
▶ 국운이 풍전등화같다 The fate of the nation hangs by a thread.

풍조 風鳥 〔鳥〕 a bird of paradise; a king bird; a bee martin

풍조 風潮 **1** 〈조수〉 the lee(ward) tide
2 〈세태〉 a tendency; a trend; a genius; 〈비유〉 the tide; the current; the stream
♦ 시대의 풍조 the trend of the times / 세상 풍조에 따르다[거스르다] go with [against] the stream [current]
▶ 세상 풍조에 역행하는 젊은이가 많다 Many young people swim against the time.

풍족 豊足 (an) abundance; (a) plenty; (an) opulence; (an) affluence; (a) wealth; richness
—풍족하다 abundant; plentiful; rich; wealthy; opulent; affluent
♦ 풍족한 사회 the affluent society / 자금이 풍족하다 have ample funds; be well supplied with money / 풍족하게 살다 be well [comfortably] off; live in plenty [abundance, comfort]
▶ 우리는 식량이 풍족했다 We had an abundant supply of food.
▶ 그는 재정적으로 풍족하다 He is in good

풍진 風疹 〈라〉〔醫〕rubella; German measles
풍진 風塵 〈먼지〉dust; 〈세속적인 일〉worldly affairs; cares of life ━세상 this world of woe and tumult; troubles of life
▶그 나라는 천연자원이 풍족하다 The country is rich [abundant] in natural resources.
풍차 風車 a windmill
■━간 a windmill; a windmill shed
풍채 風采 (one's personal) appearance; air; mien; getup; presence; sb's bearing
◆풍채가 당당한 사람 a person of commanding appearance / 풍채가 좋다 have a fine presence; look fine
▶그의 풍채는 보잘 것 없다 He is a plain-looking man. ≒ He has a poor presence.
풍치 風致 taste; elegance; 〈풍경의〉scenic beauty
◆풍치없는 경치 dry and monotonous scenery / 풍치가 있다 have beautiful scenery / 풍치를 더하다 add charms to a view; enhance the beauty of scenery
▶그 고가도로가 풍치를 완전히 망쳐 놓았다 The highway has entirely spoiled the beauty of the scenery.
■━보안림 scenery forests ━전망 공원 a scenic outlook park ━지구 a scenic area
풍침 風枕 an air pillow; an air [a pneumatic] cushion
풍토 風土 natural features of a region; climate
◆풍토의[풍토적인] climatic; 〈지방특유의〉endemic / 풍토에 익숙해지다 acclimatize; get acclimated; (美) acclimate (oneself) (to)
■━기(記) a description of the natural features of a region; a topography ━병 an endemic (disease); a vernacular [local] disease; 〈가축의〉an enzootic (disease) ━학 climatology ━학자 a climatologist
풍파 風波 **1** 〈바람과 물결〉the wind and waves [seas]; rough seas
◆풍파가 높은 바다 a wind-whipped sea / 풍파를 만나다 be caught by a storm / 풍파를 무릅쓰다 brave the wind and waves
▶풍파가 일었다[가라앉았다] The wind and sea rose [went down].
2 〈인생의 고초〉a storm; hardships
◆인생의 풍파 the storm [rough and tumble] of life / 세상의 온갖 풍파에 시달리다 be buffeted by the waves of adversity
3 〈불화〉(a) discord; a quarrel; a trouble
◆가정의 풍파 family troubles; domestic discord / 평지 풍파를 일으키다 cause trouble where there is no cause; raise unnecessary trouble
▶그 가정에는 풍파가 끊이지 않았다 There were constant troubles in that family.
풍편 風便 〈소문〉a rumor; a report; hearsay
◆풍편에 듣다 hear of; know by hearsay; (口) hear tell [say] of (it)
풍해 風害 damage by wind; wind damage; wind hazard; wind injury ■━방비 보안림 wind damage prevention forests
풍향 風向 〔氣〕the wind direction

◆풍향을 살펴보다 see which way the wind is blowing
▶풍향이 동쪽으로 바뀌었다 The wind shifted round to [hauled into] the east.
━계 an anemoscope ━기(旗) a wind vane; a wind sock [sleeve, cone] ━지시기 a wind direction indicator; a wind vane
풍화 風化 〔地質〕weathering; 〔化〕efflorescence
◆풍화성의 efflorescent
━풍화하다 weather; effloresce
▶바위가 풍화하여 기이한 형태가 되었다 The rocks were weathered into fantastic forms.
■━물 efflorescence ━토 soil of weathered rock
퓨리턴 a Puritan
◆퓨리턴적인 puritanical
퓨마 〔動〕a puma; a cougar
퓨즈 a fuse
◆퓨즈를 달다 fit a fuse 《to》; fuse / 퓨즈를 교체하다 replace a fuse; put in a new fuse
▶퓨즈가 끊어졌다 The fuse is gone [has blown out].
퓰리처상 ━賞 the Pulitzer Prize
━수상자 a Pulitzer Prize winner; a Pulitzer laureate ━작(品) a Pulitzer Prize work
프놈펜 〈캄보디아의 수도〉Phnom Penh
프라우다 〈구 소련의 신문〉the Pravda
프라이 〈요리〉fry
━프라이하다 fry ◆프라이한 fried / 생선을 프라이하다 fry fish
◆새우— fried prawns; fried lobsters
프라이드 pride ◆프라이드가 강하다 be (very) proud
프라이버시 (the right of [to]) privacy
◆아무의 프라이버시를 침해하다 disturb [invade] sb's privacy
▶남의 편지를 뜯어보는 것은 프라이버시 침해다 Opening someone else's letter is an invasion of privacy.
프라이팬 a frying pan; (口) a frypan; a fryer; a skillet
프라하 〈체코의 수도〉Praha
프랑 〈프랑스의 화폐단위〉a franc 《略 F., f.》
프랑슘 〔化〕francium
프랑스 〈나라 이름〉France; 〈공식명〉the French Republic
◆프랑스의 French
■━국가 (프) La Marseillaise; the French national anthem [song] ━국기 the Tricolor ━빵 French bread ━어 French; the French language ━요리 French cuisine [cookery]; dishes à la Française ━인 a Frenchman; 〈여자〉a Frenchwoman; (총칭) the French ━혁명 the French Revolution
프랑코 〈스페인의 정치가〉Franco, Francisco (1892-1975)
프랑크푸르트 〈독일의 도시〉Frankfort; (독) Frankfurt
프래그머티즘 〔哲〕pragmatism
프랜차이즈 franchise
프랭클린 〈미국의 정치가・과학자〉Franklin, Benjamin (1706-90)
프러스트레이션 〔心〕〈욕구 불만〉frustration

프러시아 〈독일 북부에 있던 옛 왕국〉 Prussia
♦프러시아의 Prussian
■—사람 a Prussian
프런트 (美) 〈호텔〉 the front [reception] desk
프런티어정신 —精神 (美) the frontier spirit
프레스 1〈압축 기계〉 a press —프레스하다 press 《a coat》
2 〈신문〉 the press
■—캠페인 a press campaign
프레스코 fresco; wall painting ■—화 a fresco (*pl.* ~es, ~s); a mural (painting) in fresco —화가 a frescoer; a fresco painter
프레시 fresh ♦프레시한 느낌이 들다 find *sth* fresh 《in a picture》
프레올림픽 the Pre-Olympics; the Pre-Olympic Games
프레이즈 〈성구〉 a phrase
■ 캐치— a catch phrase
프레이즈반 —盤 〔機〕 a milling cutter; 〈소형의〉 a fraise
프레임 〈틀〉 a frame; a framework
프레젠트 〈선물〉 a present; a gift
프레파라트 〔《독》Präparat〕〈조직 표본〉〔生〕 a preparation
프렌치드레싱 〈소스〉 French dressing
프렌치토스트 French toast
프렐류드 〔樂〕 a prelude
프로 professional ⇨ 프로페셔널 ♦프로로 전향하다 turn professional
프로그래머 〔電算〕 a (computer) programmer
프로그래밍 〔電算〕 program(m)ing
프로그램 a program(me); (美口) a card
♦다채로운 프로그램 a varied [diversified] program / 프로그램을 짜다 arrange [prepare] a program; draw [get] up a program
▶그 프로그램은 몇 시부터 시작합니까? What time does the program come on?
▶프로그램대로 진행해 주십시오 Please go on with it as scheduled.
▶이것으로 오늘의 프로그램을 마칩니다 This concludes today's program.
■ 교양— an educational program 연극— a playbill; a theater program 청취자[시청자]참가— an audienceparticipation program [show] 특별— a feature [special] program
■—기억 방식 a stored program method —암호 a program password —제어 〔電算〕 program control —편성 program(m)ing —학습 program(m)ed learning
프로덕션 〔映〕 a production; a (movie) studio 《*pl.* -dios》
프로듀서 〔映·劇〕 a producer
프로레슬링 professional wrestling ■—선수 a professional wrestler
프로메테우스 〔그神〕 Prometheus
프로메튬 〔化〕 promethium
프로모터 a promoter
프로복싱 professional boxing ■—선수 a professional boxer; a ring professional; a prizefighter; a pugilist
프로세스 a process
프로야구 —野球 professional baseball
■—선수 a professional baseball player —팀 a professional baseball team —팬 a professional baseball fan
프로이트 〈오스트리아의 정신분석학자〉 Freud, Sigmund (1856-1939)
♦프로이트의 Freudian —학설 Freudianism
프로젝트 a project
프로카인 〔化〕 procaine; novocaine
프로타민 〔化〕 protamine
프로테스탄트 〔基〕〈신교〉 a Protestant
프로텍터 〈보신구〉 a (chest) protector; a (shine) guard
프로토콜 〔電算〕 a protocol
프로톤 〔物·化〕 a proton
프로탁티늄 〔化〕 protactinium
프로파간다 〈선전 (운동)〉 propaganda (work); publicity
프로판 〔化〕 propane
■—가스 propane [liquefied petroleum] gas; LP gas; propane
프로페서 〈교수〉 a professor
프로페셔널 〈일〉 professional (team); 〈사람〉 a professional (player); (口) a pro
프로펠러 a propeller; (英) an airscrew; (空俗) a prop
♦프로펠러 소리 the burr [roar] of a propeller / 프로펠러를 돌리다 spin the propeller
▶프로펠러가 돌기 시작했다 The propeller began whirling.
■—비행기 a propeller(-driven) plane; a prop plane; prop-driven plane —축 a propeller shaft
프로포즈 a proposal of marriage
—프로포즈하다 propose 《to a *sb*》
프로필 〈옆모습〉 a profile; 〈인물평〉 a brief character sketch; a brief biography
♦현대 예술가의 프로필 profile [sketches] of the present-day artists / 장관의 프로필을 신문에서 읽다 read a profile of the secretary in the newspaper
프록코트 a frock (coat)
프롤레타리아 the proletariat; a proletarian
♦프롤레타리아 독재 the dictatorship of the proletariat
■—문학[예술] proletarian literature [art] —혁명[작가] a proletarian revolution [writer]
프롤로그 a prologue 《to》
프롬프터 〔劇·TV〕 a prompter
프루스트 〈프랑스의 소설가〉 Proust, Marcel (1871-1922)
프루트 〈각종의〉 fruits; 〈총칭〉 fruit
■—주스 fruit juice —편치[칵테일, 샐러드] (美) a fruit cup [cocktail, salad]
프리 free ♦프리가 되다 become free and independent; 〈전속 계약이 해제되어〉 become a free lance
프리깃함 —艦 a frigate
프리랜서 a free-lancer
♦프리랜서가 되다 become a free-lancer / 프리랜서로서 집필하다 write as a free-lancer
프리마돈나 〈여자 주역〉 (이) a prima donna 《*pl.* ~s, prime donne》
♦가극의 프리마돈나 the prima donna in an opera
프리메이슨 a Freemason 《▶프리메이슨단

Free and Accepted Masons의 회원)

프리미엄 a premium
♦프리미엄부(附)로 at a premium (of ten per cent); above par / 프리미엄이 붙다 command a premium / 프리미엄을 붙이다 be [stand] at a premium; put a premium (on)

프리배팅 〔野〕 free batting

프리스로 〔籠〕 a free throw ♦프리스로를 넣다 sink a free throw

프리스타일 〔泳·레슬링〕 the freestyle; 〔레슬링〕 the catch-as-catch-can

프리웨이 〈고속도로〉 a freeway

프리저 a freezer
■아이스크림— an icecream freezer

프리즘 〔物〕 a prism
♦프리즘의 prismatic
■직각— a right-angled prism ■—굴절[반사] prismatic refraction [reflection] —쌍안경 a prism binocular(s)

프리지어 〔植〕 a freesia

프리킥 〔蹴〕 a free kick

프리토리아 〈남아프리카공화국의 행정 수도〉 Pretoria

프리패브 〔建〕〈조립식 주택〉 a prefab; prefabrication

프리패스 a free pass

프린세스 〈여왕〉 a princess

프린스 〈왕자〉 a prince

프린트 a print; 〈등사 인쇄물의〉 a mimeo; a mimeographed copy; 〈옷감〉 print; 〈英〉 calico
♦프린트로 하다 print; mimeograph
■—배선 〔電〕 a printed circuit [wire] —업자 a (mimeograph) printer ■—강의— a printed lecture; a printed synopsis of a lecture

프릴 a frill

프토마인 〔化〕 ptomaine
■—중독 ptomaine poisoning

프티부르주아 〈〔프〕 a petit bourgeois〉〈소시민〉 a petty bourgeois; a lower middle-class citizen; (총칭) the petty bourgeoisie; the lower middle class

플라네타륨 〔天〕 a planetarium (*pl.* ~s, -ia)

플라멩코 〈춤〉 flamenco
♦플라멩코를 추다 dance the flamenco

플라밍고 〔鳥〕 a flamingo (*pl.* ~es, ~s)

플라스마 〔物〕 plasma

플라스크 a flask; 〈소형〉 a flasket

플라스터 〔建〕 plaster

플라스틱 (a) plastic; plastics
■—제품 a plastic; plastic goods

플라이 〔野〕 a fly (ball)
♦플라이를 치다[쳐 올리다] fly (a ball); pop (up, out); hit a fly ball / 플라이를 잡다 catch a fly ■센터— a center fly 희생— a sacrifice fly

플라이급 —級 the flyweight
■—선수 a flyweight

플라자 a plaza

플라타너스 〔植〕 platanus; a plane (tree); a platan(e)

플라토닉러브 Platonic love

플라톤 〈고대 그리스의 철학자〉 Platon (427?-347B.C.)
■—철학 Platonism —학도 a Platonist

플란넬 flannel
■—셔츠 flannel underwear

플랑크톤 〔動·植〕 (a) plankton
■동물성— zoo-plankton; animal plankton 식물성— phytoplankton; plant plankton

플래시 1 〔映〕 〈순간 장면〉 a flash
2 〔寫〕 a flash; (a) flashlight
♦플랜시 세례를 받다 be in a flood [flares] of flashlights / 플래시를 터뜨리다 light a flashbulb; snap a flashlight
3 ⇨ 회중전등
■—백 〔映〕 a flashback : 플래시백하다 backflash (to the original scene) —전구 a flashbulb; a flash lamp

플래카드 a placard ♦플래카드를 들다 lift up a placard / 플래카드를 들고 행진하다 march with placards lifted up

플래티나 platina; platinum

플랜 a plan; a scheme
♦플랜을 짜다 make [form, map out] a plan; form [contrive, lay down] a scheme

플랜트 〈공정설비〉 a plant
■—수출 export of (industrial) plants

플랫 〔樂〕 a flat; 〔競〕 flat
▶내 백미터 기록은 15초 플랫이었다 I ran one hundred meters in fifteen seconds flat.

플랫폼 a platform
♦3번 플랫폼 No. three platform; platform No. 3 / 플랫폼에서 on the platform / 플랫폼으로 들어가다 enter the platform / 플랫폼에서 나가다 move [go] out of the platform

플러그 〔電〕 a plug
♦플러그를 꽂다 plug in
■연결— an attaching plug

플러스 plus; 〈이익〉 a gain (to *one*'s happiness); an advantage; an asset
▶마이너스보다 플러스 되는 면이 많다 The pluses outweigh the minuses.
▶플러스는커녕 오히려 마이너스가 되었다 Far from being a gain, it proved (to be) a loss.
▶2 플러스 3은 5다 Two and three are [make, equal] five. ⇒ Two plus three is [makes, equals] five.
▶그것은 도시 미관에 조금도 플러스가 되지 않는다 It would add nothing to the beauty of the city.
▶당신이 오시면 회사에 큰 플러스가 됩니다 You will be a great asset to our firm.
—플러스하다 〈더하다〉 add to; 〈기여하다〉 contribute to; do (much) for
—기호, a plus (sign) —마이너스 plus or minus —요소 a plus factor

플레밍진공관 —眞空管 a Fleming('s) valve

플레어스커트 a flared [flaring] skirt

플레이 a play
♦좋은 플레이를 보이다 perform [do] a fine play —플레이하다 play (in a game)

플레이백 〈녹음·녹화의〉 (a) playback
—플레이백하다 play back

플레이보이 a playboy

플레이볼 〔野〕 play ball

플레이스킥 〔蹴〕 a placekick; a placement kick —플레이스킥하다 make a placekick; placekick (a ball)

플레이어 〈선수·연주자〉 a player; 〈레코드의〉 a record player
플레이오프 a play-off
플레이트 1 〔寫〕 a plate 2 〔野〕 the (pitcher's) mound 3 〔電〕 a plate ■홈— 〔野〕 the home plate ■—전압[전류] plate voltage [current]
플로렌스 Florence ⇨ 피렌체
플로리다 〈미국의 주〉 Florida (略 Fla., Flor.) ◆플로리다의 Floridan; Floridian
플로베르 〈프랑스의 소설가〉 Flaubert, Gustave (1821-80)
플로어 a floor
플로어링 〔建〕 flooring
플로피디스크 〔電算〕 a floppy disk
플롯 a plot ◆소설의 플롯 the plot of a story
플루오르 〔化〕 [〈獨〉Fluor] fluorine ■—산 fluoric acid —산염 fluorate —(중독)증 fluorosis —처리 fluorination; fluoridization
플루오르화 —化 〔化〕 fluoridation ■—물 a fluorid(e) —수소 hydrogen fluoride —수소산 hydrofluoric acid —암모늄[칼슘] ammonium [calcium] fluoride
플루토늄 〔化〕 plutonium
플루트 〔樂〕 a flute ◆플루트를 불다 play (on) the flute ■—주자 a flutist; a flute player
피¹ 1 〈혈액〉 blood ◆피의 순환 circulation of the blood / 피묻은 셔츠 a bloodstained shirt; a shirt stained with blood / 코(에서) 피가 나다 bleed at the nose / 피가 멎다 stop bleeding / 피를 뽑다 draw blood / 피를 멎게 하다 stop the bleeding; check the flow of blood / 피를 흘리다 spill [shed] blood / 피를 토하다 〈기침하면서〉 spit (up) blood; eject blood; cough blood; 〈위에서〉 vomit blood
▶내 손가락 끝에서 피가 난다 My fingertip is bleeding.
▶그는 피 묻은 바지를 입고 있었다 He was wearing bloodstained trousers.
▶피가 용솟음친다 Blood spurts [spouts, gushes out].
▶잇몸에서 피가 나온다 The gums bleed.
▶상처에서 피가 흐르고 있었다 Blood was oozing [flowing] from the wound.
▶붕대에 피가 배어 들었다 The bandage is saturated [stained] with blood.
▶전쟁터는 피바다를 이루었다 The battlefield was flooded with blood.
▶그 사건은 끝내 피를 보게 됐다 The affair resulted in bloodshed.
2 〈혈통〉 blood (relation); 〈가계〉 lineage; 〈혈족〉 consanguinity
◆피를 나눈 형제 a blood brother; a brother by blood; a brother-german / 피를 나누다 be blood-related; be of the same blood / 피를 이어받다 descend 《from》; be blood-related (to)
▶그에게는 한국인의 피가 섞여 있었다 He had Korean blood in his veins.
▶피는 물보다 진하다 〈속담〉 Blood is thicker than water.
▶피는 어쩔 수 없다 Blood will tell.
3 (비유) 〈새발에 피 a drop in the bucket / 피도 눈물도 없다 be cold-blooded; be stonyhearted; be insusceptible to pity / 피가 끓다 one's blood boils [tingles, stirs] / 정의를 위해 피를 흘리다 bleed for a righteous cause
▶그것을 보고 온몸의 피가 끓어 올랐다 Every drop of blood in my body tingled at the sight.
▶그것을 보고 나는 피가 얼어붙는 것 같았다 The sight made my blood curdle.
▶그는 아직 머리에 피도 안 마른 녀석이다 He is wet behind the ears.
피² 〔植〕 a Deccan grass; a barnyard grass [millet]
피³ 〈비웃는 소리〉 pooh; pish; pshaw
▶피! 웃기지 마라 Pshaw! You're fooling me.
피검 被檢 being arrested ▶그는 선거법 위반으로 피검되었다 He was arrested for violation of the election law. ■—자 the arrested; a person in custody
피겨스케이팅 figure skating
◆피겨스케이팅을 하다 skate [cut] figures (on the ice) ■—선수 a figurer
피격 被擊 being attacked ◆피격당하다 be attacked [assailed, assaulted] 《by》
피고름 bloody pus
피고용자 被雇傭者 an employee; (총칭) the employed
피고(인) 被告(人) 〈민사상의〉 a defendant; 〈형사상의〉 the accused; a prisoner at the bar ■—대리인 a defendant's representative —(측)변호사 the counsel for the defense [accused] —석 the dock; the bar
피곤 疲困 exhaustion; weariness; tiredness —피곤하다 tired; weary; fatigued; exhausted ◆피곤한 느낌 tired feeling; the feeling of tiredness [languidness] / 서 있어서 피곤하다 be tired from standing
▶아아, 피곤해 Oh, I'm tired.
▶그 여자와 얘기하고 있으면 피곤해진다 Talking to her tires me.
피골 皮骨 skin and bones
◆피골이 상접하다 be reduced to a (mere) skeleton [bag of bones]; be all [just] skin and bones; be worn to a shadow
피그미족 —族 a Pygmy; a Pigmy
피근피근 obstinately; stubbornly; headstrongly
◆피근피근 말을 듣지 않다 stubbornly refuse to listen; turn a deaf ear to
—피근피근하다 obstinate; stubborn; headstrong; willful
피나무 〔植〕 a linden [lime] tree; a basswood
피난 避難 refuge; shelter; harborage; evacuation
▶그들은 우리 집으로 피난 왔다 They sought shelter at my house.
—피난하다 seek safety in flight; take [seek] refuge 《in a place, with sb》; take [find] shelter 《in》; flee 《to a place》 for safety; 〈다른 지방으로〉 evacuate
▶홍수 때문에 그들은 인근 초등학교 건물로 피난했다 They took refuge from the flood in the primary school building nearby.
■—민 refugees; evacuees; displaced persons —살이 refugee life —처 a place of refuge

피날레

[safety]; a shelter; a refuge; an asylum; a haven (of rest) —항 a harbor of refuge
피날레 〔樂〕 a finale
피낭 被囊 〔動·植〕 a cyst; 〔解〕 a capsule; a tunic
피넛 〈땅콩〉 a peanut
 ■ —버터 peanut butter
피눈물 tears of blood [great sorrow, pain]; bitter tears
 ♦ 피눈물 나는 심정 a breaking [bleeding] heart / 피눈물나게 번 돈 money raised by desperate means / 피눈물을 흘리다 shed tears of blood [bitter tears]; weep tears of pain
피니시 〈마무리〉 a finish
피닉스 〈불사조〉 a phoenix
피다 1 〈꽃이〉 bloom; blossom; flower; open; come out; come [open] into flowers
 ♦ 갓 핀 진달래 a newblown azalea / 빨리 피는 국화 early chrysanthemum flowers / 늦게 피는 꽃 a late flower / 봄에 피는 화초 plants blooming [flowering] in spring / 피기 시작하다 begin to bloom; come into blossom [bloom] / 활짝 피다 burst into blossom / 꽃이 피어나다 come into full bloom / 피어 있다 be in bloom [flower]; be out; be open / 꽃을 피게 하다[피우다] make flowers open [bloom]
 ▶ 꽃이 피었다 The flowers bloomed. ≒ The flowers are out.
 ▶ 내 정원에 꽃이 피기 시작했다 The flowers are peeping out in my garden.
 2 〈불이〉 begin to burn; get lively; be kindled; 〈연기가〉 go up; rise; ascend; trail
 ♦ 하늘로 피어 오르는 연기 smoke rising into the air
 ▶ 불이 피었다 The fire is made.
 ▶ 석탄불이 피어 있다 The coal is living.
 3 〈얼굴이〉 bloom; 〈형편이〉 thrive; flourish; prosper; get on well
 ♦ 활짝 피어 미인이 되다 bloom into a beautiful woman
 ▶ 그도 이제는 제법 형편이 피었다 He is now in quite comfortable circumstances.
 4 〈면이 평평하게〉 be flattened; flatten; be smoothed; smooth (down, out)
피담보인 被擔保人 a warrantee
피대 皮帶 a (leather) belt; (총칭) belting
피동 被動 passivity; passiveness
 ♦ 피동적(으로) passive(ly)
 ■ —사(詞) 〔文法〕 a passive verb —형 〔文法〕 the passive form
피둥피둥 1 〈몸이〉 ♦ 피둥피둥 살찐 사람 a plump person; a fatty
 —피둥피둥하다 fatty; fleshy; puffy; plump; 〈노인이〉 vigorous; hale and hearty; in green old age
 ▶ 나이[연세] 여든이신데 아직도 피둥피둥하시다 He wears his four score years lightly.
 2 ⇨ 피근피근
피드백 feedback
피딱지¹ 〈종이〉 coarse paper
피딱지² 〈피의〉 the crust formed by dried blood
피땀 blood and sweat; 〈진땀〉 greasy sweat
 ♦ 피땀흘려 번 돈 money raised by desperate means / 피땀 흘리며 일하다 sweat blood; toil and moil
피똥 bloody excrement [stool, feces]
피뜩 suddenly; quickly
 ♦ 피뜩 지나가다 pass quickly; flit (across the sky)
피라미 〔魚〕 a minnow
피라미드 a pyramid ♦ 피라미드 모양의 pyramidal ■ 인간— a human pyramid ■ —식 조직 a pyramid organization
피란 避亂 refuge ⇨ 피난(避難)
 ♦ 피란가다 get away from war; take [seek] refuge (in a place); flee (to a place) for safety; evacuate
피레네산맥 —山脈 the Pyrenees
피렌체 〈이탈리아의 도시〉 Firenze
피력하다 披瀝— express (one's opinion); give expression [vent] to (one's thoughts); make known; reveal
 ♦ 흉중을 피력하다 unbosom oneself (to); open [lay bare] one's heart (to)
피로 披露 (an) announcement; 〈소개〉 (an) introduction; 〈광고〉 (an) advertisement
 —피로하다 announce; introduce; advertise
 ■ —연(宴) a dinner for making an announcement: 결혼 피로연 (give) a wedding reception [dinner]; (hold) an after-wedding celebration
피로 疲勞 fatigue; weariness; exhaustion; languor; lassitude
 ♦ 눈의 피로 eye strain / 두뇌의 피로 brain fatigue / 긴 여행의 피로 the exhaustion of a long journey / 피로를 모르는 tireless; inexhaustible / 피로를 느끼다 feel fatigue [tired] / 피로를 풀다 relieve one's fatigue; rest oneself; rest from one's fatigue / 잠으로 피로를 풀다 sleep off one's fatigue / 피로가 풀리다 be relieved of one's fatigue; get over [recover from] one's fatigue
 ▶ 낮잠을 좀 잤더니 피로가 풀렸다 A short nap relieved my fatigue.
 ▶ 어머니는 피로로 쓰러지셨다 Mother fell down with exhaustion.
 —피로하다 tired; weary; fatigued; exhausted
 ♦ 피로한 기색도 없이 tirelessly / 녹초가 되도록 피로하다 be reduced to pulp; be dog-tired; be tired to death / 피로한 기색을 보이다 show signs of fatigue / 피로한 기색을 보이지 않다 show no trace of fatigue / 피로하게 하다 fatigue; tire; exhaust / 피로해지다 grow weary; become exhausted; be fagged; be knocked up / 몹시 피로해 보이다 look very tired
 ▶ 일을 끝냈을 때 나는 몹시 피로했다 I felt quite exhausted when I finished the work.
 ▶ 그는 가족을 부양하기 위해 피로한 줄도 모르고 일했다 He worked tirelessly to support his family.
 ■ —강도 〔工〕 fatigue strength —물질 〔醫〕 fatigue stuff —상태 fatigue; a fatigued condition
피뢰침 避雷針 a lightning rod [conductor]
 ▶ 피뢰침 덕분에 우리는 큰 피해를 모면할 수 있었다 Fortunately we were able to prevent a great deal of damage with a lightning rod.
피륙 piece goods; (美) dry goods; textiles

■—장수 a dealer in textile fabrics; 《英》 a draper

피리 a flute; a pipe; a fife
♦목동의 피리 a shepherd's pipe / 피리부는 사람 a flute player; a flutist; a piper / 피리를 불다 play (on) a flute; pipe
■—구멍 a stop [finger hole] of a flute —소리 the sound of a flute; piping (sound)

피리새 〔鳥〕 a bullfinch

피리어드 〈마침표〉 a period(.); a full stop
♦피리어드를 찍다 put a period 《to》

피마자 蓖麻子 〔植〕 a castor-oil plant ⇨ 아주까리

피막 皮膜 〔解〕 a membrane; a film; a tapetum 《pl. -ta》

피막 被膜 〔解·動〕 a tunic; 〔解〕 a capsule

피망 〔植〕 a green pepper; a pim(i)ento 《pl. ~s》

피맺히다 extravasate; get bruised

피명 被命 commission
—피명하다[되다] be commissioned; receive a commission; receive orders 《from》

피목 皮目 〔植〕 a lenticel

피배서인 被背書人 an endorsee; an indorsee

피보증인 被保證人 a warrantee; the principal debtor

피보험물 被保險物 an insured article [thing]; insured property

피보험자 被保險者 a person insured; an insurant; (총칭) the insured

피보호국 被保護國 a dependency; a dependent state

피보호자 被保護者 〈남자〉 a protégé; 〈여자〉 a protégée; a ward

피복 被服 clothes ⇨ 옷 ■—비 clothing expenses —창(廠) a clothing depot

피복 被覆 covering; coating —피복하다 cover; coat ■—선 a covered wire —재료 covering material

피부 皮膚 the skin
♦갈라진 피부 chapped skin / 피부로 느끼다 get the feel of 《political sentiment》 with the skin / 피부가 약하다[거칠다] have a delicate [rough] skin
■—감각 skin sensation —과 dermatology —과 의사 a dermatologist —병 a skin [cutaneous] disease —병학 dermatology —색 skin color; complexion —성형술 dermatoplasty; skin grafting —신경 cutaneous nerves —암 cutaneous cancer; cancer of the skin —염 dermatitis —이식(술) skin grafting —호흡 cutaneous [skin] respiration

피브리노겐 〔生理〕 fibrinogen

피브린 〔生理〕 fibrin

피비린내 ♦피비린내 나는 사건 a sanguinary incident / 피비린내 나는 광경 a bloody sight / 피비린내 나는 싸움 a bloody fight [battle] / 피비린내 나는 bloody; sanguinary

피사 〈이탈리아의 도시〉 Pisa
♦피사의 사탑 the Leaning Tower of Pisa

피사리 weeding —피사리하다 pick out [pluck] weeds; weed 《a rice field》

피사체 被寫體 a (camera) subject; an object (of shooting); a thing pictured

♦카메라에서 피사체까지의 거리 camera-to-object distance

피살 被殺 being killed
—피살되다 be killed [murdered]
■—체 the body of a murdered person; the body of the victim of a murder

피상 皮相 〈외관〉 an outward look; 〈표면〉 the surface; 〈깊이 없음〉 superficiality
♦피상적인 superficial; shallow / 피상적인 견해를 갖다 take a superficial view 《of》
▶그는 사물을 피상적인 면밖에 보지 못한다 He looks only at the surface of things.

피상 속인 被相續人 〔法〕 an ancestor; a predecessor; an inheritee

피새 〈성 잘내는 성미〉 a quick [short] temper
♦피새 내다 lose one's temper

피새놓다 〈훼방놓다〉 put a spoke in sb's wheel

피새나다 〈발각되다〉 be revealed [disclosed, exposed]

피서 避暑 summering
—피서하다 summer 《at, in》; pass [spend] the summer 《at, in》
▶그는 남해안으로 피서하러 갔다 He went to the south coast for the summer [to avoid the heat of summer days].
■—객 a summer visitor [resident] —지 a summer resort

피선 被選 being elected —피선되다 be elected
▶나는 의장으로 피선되었다 I was elected chairman. ⇌ I was elected to the chair.

피선거권 被選擧權 eligibility for election
♦국회의원의 피선거권이 있다 be eligible for election to a member of the National Assembly

피선거인 被選擧人 an eligible person

피스톤 〔機〕 a piston
■—로드 a piston rod —링 a piston ring

피스톨 a pistol ⇨ 권총

피습 被襲 ♦피습당하다 be attacked [assaulted]; be set upon

피승수 被乘數 〔數〕 a multiplicand

피신 避身 escape; flight; refuge
—피신하다 escape; get off [away]; flee; take refuge 《in》; 〈숨다〉 conceal [hide] oneself

피아 彼我 both sides; he and I; they and we; self and others; that and this
▶피아의 세력이 백중지세다 This side is nearly equal to that in strength. ⇌ Both sides are nearly equal in strength.

피아노 **1** 〈악기〉 a piano 《pl. ~s》
♦피아노를 치다 play (on) the piano / 피아노를 배우다 take piano lessons 《from》 / 피아노를 가르치다 teach sb the piano / 피아노를 연습하다 practice on the piano / 피아노에 맞춰 노래하다 sing to the piano
▶피아노 교수 (게시) Piano Lessons.
2 (이) 〔樂〕 〈여리게〉 piano
■그랜드— a (concert) grand piano 수형(竪型)— an upright piano 자동— a player piano; (商標) Pianola —독주 a piano solo 《by》 —선(線) piano wire —용 의자 a piano stool —조율사 a piano tuner —협주곡 a piano concerto

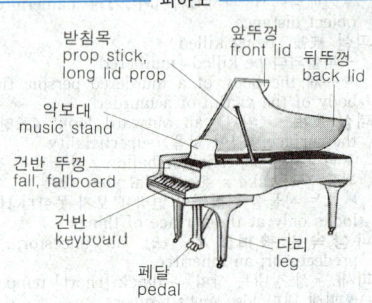

— 피아노 —
- 받침목 prop stick, long lid prop
- 앞뚜껑 front lid
- 뒤뚜껑 back lid
- 악보대 music stand
- 건반 뚜껑 fall, fallboard
- 건반 keyboard
- 다리 leg
- 페달 pedal

피아니스트 a pianist
피아르 public relations (略 PR)
―**피아르하다** publicize; advertise
■―영화 a PR film ―지 〈회사 등의〉 a house organ ―활동 public relations (activities); publicity activities
피안 彼岸 1 〈강의 건너편 기슭〉 the other shore [side] 《of》 2 〈내세〉 the other world
피압박민족 被壓迫民族 the oppressed people
피앙세 〈남자〉 one's fiancé; 〈여자〉 one's fiancée
피어나다 1 〈불이〉 light [blaze] up (again); burn up; get lively
▶ 숯불이 피어나다 The charcoal fire gets lively (again).
2 〈형편이〉 begin to prosper [flourish, thrive]
3 〈의식이〉 come to oneself; regain consciousness; revive; come back to life
피어오르다 go up; rise; ascend
♦ 뭉게뭉게 피어오르다 curl [roll] up
피에로 a pierrot; a 《circus》 clown
피엑스 〔美軍〕 a post exchange; a PX (pl. PXs)
피오르드 〔地〕 a fjord; a fiord
피우다 1 〈꽃을〉 make 《flowers》 open; make bloom
2 〈불을〉 kindle; burn; make (up)
♦ 석탄불을 피우다 burn coal / 숯불을 피우다 make fire with charcoal / 난로에 불을 피우다 make a fire in the stove / 향을 피우다 burn incense
3 〈담배를〉 smoke; puff
♦ 담배 피우다 smoke 《a tobacco》; smoke a cigarette / 한대 피우다 have [take] a smoke; smoke 《a pipe》
▶ 그는 술도 마시고 담배도 피운다 He both drinks and smokes.
4 〈냄새를〉 emit; give out [off]; send forth [out]
5 〈먼지를〉 raise [make, kick up] 《dust》
6 〈부리다〉 do; play; use; perform; display
♦ 난봉을 피우다 indulge in follies / 소란을 피우다 make [create] a commotion / 익살 피우다 play the fool; jest
피의자 被疑者 a suspected person; a suspect
♦ 피의자의 사진 the photograph of a criminal suspect
▶ 경찰은 피의자에게 임의 출두를 요구했다 The police asked the suspect to appear voluntarily.
피임 被任 being appointed ―**피임하다** be appointed; get [receive] an appointment
■―자 an appointee; an appointed person
피임 避姙 contraception; prevention of conception
―**피임하다** prevent conception; practice birth control
―기구 a contraceptive appliance ―법 a contraceptive measure [method]; a preventive method of conception; sterilization ―수술 a contraceptive operation; contraceptive treatment ―약[제] a contraceptive (pill): 경구 피임약 an oral contraceptive; the pill
피자 a pizza (pie)
피자식물 被子植物 an angiosperm
피장파장 evenness; equality; a tie
▶ 이제 피장파장이다 Now we are quits [all square].
피점령국 被占領國 an occupied country
피제수 被除數 〔數〕 a dividend
피조물 被造物 a created thing; a creature; 《총칭》 creation
피지 〈나라이름〉 Fiji; 〈공식명〉 Fiji
―사람 a Fijian ―제도 the Fiji Islands
피지 皮脂 〔生理〕 sebum; sebaceous matter
■―선(腺) a sebaceous gland
피지급인 被支給人 a payee
피진 皮疹 〔醫〕 an efflorescence; an exanthema (pl. -mata)
피질 皮質 〔醫〕 the cortex (pl. -tices)
♦ 피질의 cortical
피차 彼此 〈저것과 이것〉 that and this; 〈서로〉 each other; you [he] and I; they and we; between you and me; between both sides [parties]
♦ 피차간 each other; between you and me / 피차 사랑[미워]하다 love [hate] each other / 피차의 구별을 할 수 없다 be unable to tell friend from foe
▶ 우리는 피차간의 약점을 알고 있다 We know each other's weak points.
피차일반 彼此一般 both the same; equality between each other; no difference between us [him and me]
♦ 피차일반이다 be mutually equal [the same]
▶ 잘못하기는 피차 일반이다 They are both to blame.
피처 〔野〕 a pitcher
♦ 피처를 보다 pitch; be a pitcher / 피처를 맡아하다 play as a pitcher
■―플레이트 the pitcher's plate; the (pitcher's) mound
피천 the smallest sum (of money)
♦ 피천 한닢도 쪼개 쓰는 녀석 a pinch-farthing; a skinflint
피천 被薦 being recommended ―**피천하다** be recommended; get a recommendation
피청구인 被請求人 a claimee; a demandee
피초청국 被招請國 an invited country

■ ―대표 a visiting delegate

피층 皮層 the cortex (*pl.* -tices)

피치 1 〈노의 횟수〉 a stroke
2 〈작업 능률의 정도〉 a pace
♦ 급피치로 at high speed; speedily / 일의 피치를 올리다 speed up the pace of one's work; quicken one's pace / 피치를 늦추다 slacken one's pace; slow down the speed
3 〔樂〕 (a) pitch
4 〔化〕 pitch; 〈상하 요동〉 pitch; pitching
5 〔野〕 〈투구의〉 a pitch
♦ 나이스 피치 nice pitch

피치카토 (이) 〔樂〕 〈통기기〉 pizzicato

피침 被侵 being invaded
― 피침하다 be invaded; be raided [violated]

피칭 〔野〕 pitching
■ ―머신 a pitching machine

피켈 〈등산용〉 a pickel

피켓 〈노사 분규 등의〉 a picket; picketing
♦ 피켓을 치다 establish a picket line; picket (a place)
▶ 그들은 공장에 피켓을 쳤다 They placed pickets at [near] the factory. ⇌ They picketed the factory.
■ ―라인 a picket line

피콜로 〈악기〉 a piccolo (*pl.* ~s)
■ ―주자 a piccoloist

피크닉 a picnic ♦ 피크닉 가다 go (out) on a picnic; go picnicking ■ ―도시락 a picnic lunch

피크르산 ―酸 〔化〕 picric acid

피클 〈절인 서양 음식〉 pickles

피타고라스 〈그리스의 철학자·수학자〉 Pythagoras (582?-500?B.C.)
■ ―의 정리 the Pythagorean theorem

피탈 被奪 being robbed of
― 피탈하다 be robbed of (a thing); have sth taken away

피통치 被統治 being subject (to); being governed [ruled] ■ ―민족 a subject race

피투성이 ♦ 피투성이의 bloody; bloodstained; blood-soaked; gory / 피투성이의 싸움 a bloody fight; (비유) the hardest struggle / 피투성이가 되다 be smeared [covered] with blood; be bathed in blood; be spattered [covered] all over with blood
▶ 그는 피투성이가 되어 거기에 쓰러져 있었다 He was lying there covered with blood.

피트 feet (*sing.* foot) (略 ft.)
♦ 3피트 5인치 three feet five inches; 3 ft. 5 in.; 3′5″ / 10피트 길이의 장대 a ten-foot pole
▶ 그는 신장이 5피트 7인치다 He stands five feet seven inches high.

피티에이 〈사친회〉 a PTA [《a *P*arent-*T*eacher *A*ssociation》]

피펫 〔化〕 a pipet(te)

피폐 疲弊 exhaustion; impoverishment
♦ 재정의 피폐 financial exhaustion / 농촌의 피폐(상) the impoverished conditions of rural communities
― 피폐하다 become [be] impoverished [exhausted]
♦ 피폐해 있다 be in an exhausted condition / 피폐시키다 impoverish; exhaust

피폭 被爆 being bombed
― 피폭하다 be bombed; suffer from bombing
■ ―지구 a bombed block [area]

피하 皮下 ♦ 피하의 hypodermic; subcutaneous
■ ―선(腺) a hypodermal gland ―주사 a hypodermic [subcutaneous] injection: 피하주사를 놓다 inject (medicine) under the skin; inject hypodermically ―주사기 a hypodermic injector [syringe] ―지방 subcutaneous fat

피하다 避― 〈도피하다〉 avoid (the heat); escape; 〈모면하다〉 evade; 〈회피하다〉 elude (payment); 〈비키다〉 dodge [duck] (a blow); 〈막다〉 avert; 〈사람 눈을〉 put off; 〈비바람을〉 take [seek, find] shelter (from)
♦ 피할 곳 a shelter (from the enemy's fire); a place of safety / 피할 수 없는 unavoidable; unescapable; inevitable / 길을 피하다 get out of the way / 난을 피하다 find a refuge / 더위를 피하다 avoid the summer heat; get away from the heat / 자리를 피하다 leave [quit] one's seat; slip away (from) / 남의 눈을 피하다 avert people's eyes / 때리는 것을 피하다 dodge [elude] a blow / 잽싸게 피하다 make a swift dodge / 폭풍우를 피하다 take shelter [get away] from a storm
▶ 사고는 피할 수 있다 An accident could be averted.
▶ 그는 질문에 대한 대답을 교묘히 피했다 He skillfully evaded the question.
▶ 그들은 충돌을 피하려고 했다 They tried to head off the collision.
▶ 사람들은 나무 그늘에서 더위를 피하려고 했다 People sought relief from the heat in the shade of trees.
2 〈멀리하다〉 keep away from (danger); stand [keep] clear of (politics); keep aloof from (bad company); shun
♦ 암초를 피하다 steer clear of the rocks [reef] / 만나기 싫은 사람을 피하다 give sb a wide berth
▶ 그런 친구들은 피하는 것이 좋다 You had better keep clear of such company.
▶ 차는 노상의 아이를 피해서 갔다 The car veered away from the child in the road.
3 〈책임 등을〉 shirk (responsibility); evade (an answer)
♦ 책임을 피하다 shirk [evade, avoid] one's responsibility / 확인을 피하다 take care not to commit oneself

피한 避寒 wintering; hibernation
― 피한하다 winter (at, in); pass the winter (at, in); go to a place for the winter; hibernate (at, in)
■ ―지(地) a winter resort

피해 被害 〈무생물의〉 damage; 〈주로 사람의〉 (an) injury; harm
♦ 피해가 많다[적다] suffer heavily [lightly] (from) / 피해를 입다 be damaged (by); be injured; suffer damage (from a flood) / 피해를 모면하다 be intact; come out unhurt; 〈사람이〉 escape injury / 피해를 주다 〈농작물 등에〉 damage; do damage 《to》; 〈남에게〉 injure; do harm (to)
▶ 지진 피해는 그 도시가 가장 컸다 The city

suffered most from the earthquake.
▶ 우리 측은 인명 피해를 입지 않았다 We suffered no casualties.
▶ 그는 지난번 태풍으로 큰 피해를 입었다 He suffered a great deal of damage from the recent typhoon.
■ —액 the (amount of) damage; 〈범위·정도〉 the extent of damage —자 a victim; a sufferer; the injured person —지역[지구] the damaged [stricken, suffering] district

피해망상 被害妄想 a delusion of persecution
■ —자 a persecution maniac

피험자 被験者 〈실험의〉 a subject; 〈시험의〉 a testee; an examinee

피혁 皮革 〈가죽〉 hides and skins; 〈무두질한〉 leather
■ 인조[합성]— artificial [synthetic] leather ■ —공 a tanner —상(商) a dealer in hides and skins; a leather dealer; a pelterer —제품 leather articles

피후견인 被後見人 a ward

픽¹ 1 〈바람 빠지는 소리〉 hiss —픽하다 hiss
♦ 픽하는 소리 a hiss; a hissing sound; a swish; a whoosh
2 〈쓰러지는 모양〉 ♦ 픽 쓰러지다 fall down feebly [lightly]
3 〈웃는 모양〉 grinningly; sneeringly
♦ 픽 웃다 grin; sneer; let go a despising laugh

픽² 〈악기의〉 a pick; a (bone) plectrum (*pl.* ~s, -tra)

픽션 (a) fiction

픽업 1 〈건축의〉 a pickup
2 〈자동차〉 a pickup (truck)

픽픽 〈쓰러지는 모양〉 (fall) in rapid [quick] succession ♦ 픽픽 쓰러지다 fall down feebly again and again

핀 1 a pin ♦ 핀을 꽂다[뽑다] pin [unpin] (a thing) / 핀으로 고정시키다 pin (up); pin (cloth) together; fasten with a pin
2 〈골프의〉 a pin ♦ 홀에 핀을 꽂다 set the pin into the hole
3 〈볼링의〉 a pin
■ 넥타이— a tiepin 머리— a hairpin

핀란드 Finland; 〈공식명〉 the Republic of Finland ♦ 핀란드의 Finnish
■ —말 Finnish —사람 a Finn; a Finlander

핀볼 pinball

핀셋 (a pair of) tweezers; (프) a pincette
♦ 핀셋으로 집다 pick up *sth* with a pincette

핀업걸 (美) a pinup girl

핀잔 scolding; (口) a wipe; a snub; a rebuff
♦ 핀잔 주다 scold; give a rebuff (to *sb*) / 핀잔 먹다 catch it; get scolded; meet with a rebuff

핀치 a pinch; (野) a clutch
♦ 핀치에 몰리다 find *oneself* in a fix [pinch] / 핀치를 벗어나다 tide over a crisis
■ —러너[히터] a pinch runner [hitter]

핀트 〈초점〉 a focus; 〈요점〉 the point
♦ 핀트를 맞추다 focus *one's* camera on (an object); bring (an object) into focus / 핀트가 맞다[맞지 않다] be in [out of] focus; (비유) be to [off] the point

필 疋 a head 〈말[소]〉 세 필 three head of horses [cows]

필 疋 a roll of cloth
♦ 무명 세 필 three rolls of cotton cloth / 필로 사다[팔다] buy [sell] by the roll

-필 -畢 finishing; finished; completing; completed; done ♦ 지급필 Paid / 검사필 Examined

필가 筆架 a writing-brush rack

필갑 筆匣 a writing-brush [pen] case

필경 畢竟 after all; in the end; finally; in the long run; in the final [last] analysis
▶ 그는 돈을 낭비하여 필경에는 빈털터리가 되었다 He squandered his money until he became penniless.
▶ 그는 필경 오지 않을 것이다 He will not come after all.

필경 筆耕 copying; stencil-paper writing
—필경하다 copy; 〈등사하다〉 stencil
■ —료 a copying fee —사 a copyist; a scribe; 〈등사판의〉 a stenciler

필공 筆工 a (writing-)brush maker

필기 筆記 taking notes; notes
—필기하다 take a note [notes] of; write [note, put] down ♦ 연설을 필기하다 take down a speech / 요점을 필기하다 jot down the main points
■ —시험 a written examination [exam] —자 a copyist —장 a notebook

필담 筆談 conversation by writing
▶ 우리는 필담으로 대화를 했다 Our conversation was carried on in writing. ⇒ I talked with him in writing.
—필담하다 talk by means of writing; carry on a talk by writing

필답 筆答 a written answer [reply]
—필답하다 answer in writing
■ —시험 a written examination

필독 必讀 required reading
♦ 학생의 필독서 a book which every student must read; a must book for students

필두 筆頭 1 〈붓끝〉 the head [tip] of a writing brush
2 〈첫머리〉 the first on the list [in a roll]
▶ 그의 이름이 필두에 올라 있었다 His name was (the) first on the list. ⇒ His name headed the list.
3 〈우두머리〉 the head; the boss

필드 the field
■ —경기 field sports; 〈종목〉 a field event

필딩 (野) fielding

필라델피아 〈미국 Pennsylvania 주의 도시〉 Philadelphia (略 Phil., Phila.)

필라리아 (動) the filaria (*pl.* -iae)
■ —병 (醫) a filarial disease

필라멘트 (電) a filament

필래프 〈볶음밥의 하나〉 pilaf(f); pilau

필력 筆力 the power of the pen [brush]; the brush stroke; 〈문장의 힘〉 the force of style
▶ 그 여류작가는 80이 넘었는데도 필력이 쇠하지 않았다 Though the writer is over eighty now, her style of writing is still powerful.

필름 (a) film ♦ 필름 한 통 a roll [reel, spool] of film / 필름에 담다 film (a scene) / 필름을 현상하다 develop a film / 카메라에 필름을 넣다 load a camera
■ 네거티브[포지티브]— (a) negative [posi-

tive] film 컬러[흑백]― (a) color [black-and-white] film ■**―편집** cutting

필리핀 〈나라이름〉 the Philippines; 〈공식명〉 the Republic of the Philippines
 ◆필리핀(사람)의 Philippine; Filipino
 ■**―사람** a Filipino 《*pl.* ~s》; 〈여자〉 a Filipina ―**제도** the Philippine Islands (略 P. I.); the Philippines

필링 (a) feeling

필마 匹馬 one horse; a single horse
 ―**단기**(單騎) riding alone without servants [retinue] ―**단창**(單槍) fighting alone

필멸 必滅 mortality; being fated to perish
 ◆필멸의 perishable; mortal; doomed to decay
 ▶생자 필멸이다 All living things must die.

필명 筆名 a pen name; a name as a calligrapher ◆…의 필명으로 쓰다 write under the pen name of…

필묵 筆墨 brush and Chinese ink; pen and ink; writing materials

필법 筆法 〈운필법〉 a style of penmanship [hand-writing]; the technique of calligraphy; 〈문체〉 the guiding principle of a piece of writing; *one's* style of writing
 ◆힘찬 필법 a powerful stroke of the brush
 ―**춘추―** the guiding principle of Confucius in writing the Annals

필봉 筆鋒 **1** 〈붓의 위세〉 the power of a piece of writing
 ◆필봉이 날카롭다 be forcible [sharp] in *one's* argument [style]
 2 〈붓끝〉 the tip of a brush

필부 匹夫 〈한 남자〉 a man; 〈신분이 낮은 남자〉 an ordinary man; a man of low birth
 ―**지 용**(之勇) foolhardiness; brute courage
 ―**필부**(匹婦) humble men and women; common people; Jack and Jill

필부 匹婦 〈한 여자〉 a woman; 〈신분이 낮은 여자〉 an ordinary woman; a woman of low birth

필사 必死 〈반드시 죽음〉 inevitable death; 〈사력을 다함〉 desperation
 ◆필사의 공격 a desperate [frantic] attack

필사 筆寫 copying; transcription
 ◆필사의 잘못 a clerical error
 ―**필사하다** copy; transcribe

필사적 必死的 desperate; frantic
 ◆필사적(인) 노력 desperate [frantic] efforts / 필사적으로 desperately; frantically; in desperation; for dear life / 필사적이 되다 become [get] desperate; be driven to desperation / 필사적으로 일하다 work away like one possessed; work for *one's* life
 ▶그들은 필사적으로 싸웠다 They fought in desperation.
 ▶나는 필사적으로 그 자리를 도망쳐 나왔다 I fled (from) there for my life.

필산 筆算 calculation with figures; ciphering
 ―**필산하다** calculate with figures; cipher; figure with pen [pencil]

필생 畢生 ◆필생의 노력 *one's* lifelong efforts / 필생의 사업 *one's* lifework / 필생의 lifelong

필생 筆生 a copyist

필설 筆舌 writing and speech

▶그 경험은 필설로 다할 수 없다 The experience is beyond all description.

필세 筆勢 a stroke [dash] of the brush [pen]

필수 必須 essentiality; indispensability
 ◆필수의 indispensable; essential; requisite; mandatory
 ―**과목** a required [an obligatory] subject
 ―**조건** a precondition; an essential condition : 비자는 여러 나라에 있어서 아직 여행하는 데 필수 조건이다 A visa is still a prerequisite for travel in many countries. ―**조항** a mandatory clause

필수품 必需品 necessaries; necessities; a requisite; an essential
 ■**생활―** the necessaries [necessities] of life; living necessaries

필승 必勝 (a) certain [sure, unfailing] victory ◆필승의 신념 faith in certain victory / 필승의 신념을 가지고 with every confidence of victory / 필승을 기하다 〈자신〉 be sure [confident] of victory; 〈각오〉 resolve to secure a victory at any cost

필시 必是 surely; no doubt; certainly
 ▶그 여자는 필시 기뻐할거야 She'll be very pleased, I'm sure.

필연 必然 inevitability; necessity
 ◆필연적으로 inevitably; necessarily; naturally; as a necessity; in the nature of things / 필연적인 inevitable; necessary; certain / 필연적인 결과로서 as a necessary [an inevitable] consequence
 ▶그것은 역사적 필연이다 That is one of the inevitabilities of history.
 ■**―성** inevitability; necessity

필연 筆硯 pen and ink (stone); 〈문필업〉 literary work ◆필연을 벗삼다 be engaged in literary work

필요 必要 necessity; need; requirement
 ◆필요에 따라서 as occasion demands; at need / 필요에 의해서 out of (sheer) necessity; driven by necessity [need]; under the necessity [pressure] (of) / ―을 필요로 하다 need; be [stand] in need of; require; want / …할 필요가 있다 it is necessary 《to do》; must 《do》; have to 《do》 / ―할 필요가 있다 there is no necessity for 《doing》; need not 《do》; don't have to 《do》 / 필요를 충족시키다 meet the requirements; serve the [*one's*] need
 ▶너는 의사의 진찰을 받을 필요가 있다 You must see the doctor. ⇌ It is necessary for you to take medical advice.
 ▶이 일을 서두를 필요가 있습니까 ? Does this work need to be finished quickly? ⇌ Is there any need for this work to be done in a hurry?
 ▶난 그런 건 필요없다 I don't want it.
 ▶거스름돈은 필요없습니다 Keep the change.
 ▶아직 서두를 필요는 없다 You need not make haste yet. ⇌ There is no need to hurry yet.
 ▶우리 회사는 유능한 기술자의 필요를 통감하고 있다 We are in great need of able technical experts in the company. ⇌ The need for able technical experts is keenly felt in our company.
 ▶「필요는 발명의 어머니」라는 속담이 있다

There is a proverb which says "Necessity is the mother of invention."
—**필요하다** necessary; needful; needed; required; requisite; indispensable; essential
▶ 그것이 급히 필요하다 The need of it is pressing.
▶ 나는 꼭 만원이 필요하다 I must have ten thousand won.
▶ 그에게 필요한 것은 끈기다 What he needs is perseverance.
▶ 그 일에는 시간이 많이 필요하다 The job requires a lot of time.
▶ 필요하면 자금을 빌려 드리겠소 I'll lend you money if you need some.
■ —경비 necessary expenses —악 a necessary evil —조건 a necessary condition; a requirement —품 a necessary; a necessity; a requisite

필유곡절 必有曲折 There must be some reason for it.

필자 筆者 the writer; the author ◆ 이 글의 필자 〈자신을 가리켜〉 the present writer
▶ 이 글의 필자는 여성이다 This was written by a certain lady.

필적 匹敵 rival; a match
—**필적하다** equal; rival; be a match for; match; be equal to; compare with; stand comparison with
▶ 단단하기로는 다이아몬드에 필적하는 것이 없다 Nothing can compare with diamond in hardness.
▶ 조각가로서 그에 필적할 자는 없다 No one can equal him as a sculptor. ⇌ He stands alone [has no equal, is unrivaled] as a sculptor.
▶ 당시의 1원은 현재의 만원에 필적한다 One won in those days is equivalent to ten thousand won now.

필적 筆跡 〈쓴 글씨〉 a holograph; a calligraphic specimen; a specimen of handwriting; 〈글씨 솜씨〉 one's handwriting; penmanship; one's hand
◆ 남자[여자]의 필적 a masculine [feminine] hand / 유려한 필적으로 씌어 있다 be written in a beautiful, flowing hand / 필적이 좋다 [나쁘다] write a good [bad] hand / 필적을 흉내내다 copy sb's hand; imitate sb's handwriting
▶ 그 편지는 그의 필적이었다 The letter was written in his hand.
■ —감정 (an) analysis of sb's handwriting; handwriting analysis

필전 筆戰 paper warfare; a paper battle; a war of the pen —**필전하다** fight with one's pen; have paper warfare

필주 筆誅 denunciation in writing
◆ 필주를 가하다 denounce sb in writing

필지 必至 inevitability; necessity
—**필지하다** follow as a necessary [an inevitable] consequence

필지 必知 required knowledge
■ —사항 matters everyone must [should] know; indispensable information

필지 筆地 a lot [plot, piece] (of land)

■ —조사[측량] field by field land surveying

필진 筆陣 〈진용〉 the writing [editorial] staff; 〈포진〉 a maneuver in paper warfare
◆ 필진을 펴다 set forth one's argument 《for, against》

필치 筆致 〈필세〉 a stroke of the brush; a touch; 〈문체〉 a literary style
◆ 가벼운[거친] 필치 a light [rough] touch / 원숙한 필치 a mellowed style
▶ 그의 필치는 경묘하고 원숙하다 His style is easy and well mellowed.

필터 〈寫〉 a light filter; 〈컬러용〉 a color filter; 〈담배의〉 a filter tip
◆ 필티 딜린 깉런 a filter tip(ped) cigarette; a filter cigarette
■ —적외선— an infrared filter

필통 筆筒 〈꽂아두는〉 a pencil vase; a brush [pen] stand; 〈넣고 다니는〉 a pencil case

필하다 畢— end; finish; complete; get [be] through ◆ 검사를 필하다 stand the test; measure up to the standards / 대학 과정을 필하다 complete a [one's] university course

필하모닉 philharmonic; a philharmonic
◆ 런던 필하모닉 오케스트라 the London Philharmonic Orchestra

필화 筆禍 a serious slip of the pen
◆ 필화를 초래하다[입다] be indicted for one's article (in a newspaper)

필휴 必携 indispensableness; 〈안내서〉 a handbook; a manual ◆ 학생 필휴의 책 a book indispensable to students

필히 必— 〈꼭〉 certainly; surely; necessarily; by all means; at any cost
▶ 그 편지를 필히 부칠 것 Be sure to mail the letter.

핌피 a pimfy; a PIMFY [〈please in my front yard〉] (▶NIMBY의 반대 개념으로, 지역 발전에 유리한 편의 시설을 인근에 끌어들이려는 지역 이기주의를 뜻함)

핍박 逼迫 pressure (for money); stringency; tightness (of money) ◆ 재정의 핍박 stiffened [tight] financial conditions
—**핍박하다** be tight; get stringent
▶ 금융사정이 핍박해져 있다 Money is scarce [tight].

핍진 逼眞 verisimilitude; truthfulness to life

핏기 —氣 one's complexion; the color of the face
◆ 핏기없는 얼굴 a pale face; a face as white as a sheet / 핏기가 없다 be pale and bloodless; look pale; have a bad complexion / 핏기가 가시다 turn pale [white] 《with fear》
▶ 그녀는 몸이 아파서 얼굴에 핏기가 없다 Her cheeks are pale with sickness.
▶ 그의 얼굴에서 핏기가 가셨다 The color drained from his face.

핏대 (blue) veins ◆ 핏대를 올리다[세우다] turn purple with rage / 핏대를 올리고 다투다 have a hot dispute

핏덩어리 1 〈덩어리〉 a clot of blood; clotted blood; gore **2** 〈갓난아기〉 a newborn baby

핏발 congestion; a bloodshot condition ◆ 핏발선 눈 bloodshot eyes / 핏발이 서다 become bloodshot; become turgid with blood

핏빛 blood red ♦ 핏빛으로 물들다 be dyed in blood red
핏자국 a bloodstain; a blood mark
♦ 핏자국이 있는 bloodstained
핏줄 1 〈혈관〉 a blood vessel; a vein
♦ 핏줄이 붉어진 손 a veinous [veiny] hand
2 〈혈통〉 lineage; stock; blood (relationship)
♦ 좋은 핏줄 a good strain [stock] / 핏줄이 같다 be blood-related 《to》; be of the same blood; be related by blood 《to》
▶ 핏줄은 속일 수 없다 Heredity will out. ⇌ Blood will tell.
▶ 우리는 같은 성씨이지만 핏줄은 같지 않다 We have the same surname, but are not related (by blood).
핑 1 〈도는 모양〉 round; 《美》 around
♦ 한쪽 뒤꿈치로 핑 돌다 spin on *one's* heel
2 〈어쩔한 모양〉 dizzy; giddy
♦ 핑 돌다 feel dizzy; feel giddy
▶ 눈물이 핑 돌았다 Tears came to her eyes.
▶ 술기운이 핑 돌기 시작했다 The wine began to take its effect.
핑거볼 a finger bowl
핑계 an excuse; a pretext; a pretense; a plea

♦ 그럴듯한 핑계 a plausible excuse; a specious pretense / 좋은 핑계를 생각해내다 find good excuse 《for》
▶ 그것은 핑계에 지나지 않는다 It is nothing but a mere excuse [evasion].
▶ 핑계 좀 작작 대라 Stop making such excuses.
▶ 그런 핑계는 통하지 않는다 Such excuse will not serve you [go down with me].
ᅳ**핑계하다**[삼다] make a pretext [a pretense, an excuse] of; pretend 《to be ill》; use *sth* as pretext
♦ 병을 핑계 삼아 사직하다 resign (from) *one's* post under the pretext of ill health
핑계 없는 무덤이 없다 〈속담〉 A pretext is never wanting.
핑그르르 round ♦ 뒤꿈치로 핑그르르 돌다 spin on *one's* heel
핑글핑글 round and round ⇨ 빙글빙글
핑크 pink
핑퐁 〈탁구〉 ping-pong; table tennis
핑핑 round and round ♦ 핑핑 돌다 〈몸이〉 turn [revolve] rapidly; spin; 〈눈·머리가〉 feel dizzy [giddy]
핑핑하다 tight ⇨ 팽팽하다

하¹ 〈많이・크게〉 very; too (much); excessively
♦하 많은 집들 a great many houses
▶나는 하 피곤해서 일찍 잠자리에 들었다 I went to bed early because I was dead tired.
하² 〈입김〉 with a hot wet breath; Ha!
▶그는 내 얼굴에서 담배 연기를 하 하고 내뿜었다 He puffed smoke into my face.
하³ 〈감정을 나타내는 소리〉 Ha!; Huh!; Oh!
▶하 자네 아닌가 Well, well. If it isn't you!
하 下 1 〈하급〉 the low class [grade]
♦하의 하 the lowest (of the low)
▶그의 성적은 평균보다 하다 His grade is below the average.
2 〈하권〉 the last volume
3 〈아래〉 ♦…의 지휘[지도, 감독] 하에 under the command [direction, supervision] of...
하감 下疳 〔韓醫〕 chancre
■연성[경성]— soft [hard] chancre
하감 下瞰 〈내려다 봄〉 looking down
—하감하다 look down (upon)
하강 下降 a descent; a fall; a drop; 〈경기의〉 (a) decline
♦기온의 하강 a drop in temperature
—하강하다 descend; go down; drop; fall
▶시세가 하강하고 있다 The market is dropping.
■—곡선 a downward curve —기류 a descending current
하객 賀客 a well-wisher; a congratulator
♦신년 하객 a New Year's caller [visitor]
하게하다 address *sb* in a familiar style of speech without using honorifics
하계 下界 〈이 세상〉 the lower world; this world; 〈지상〉 the earth; 〈낮은 곳〉 the lower place [region]
♦하계의 earthly; mundane / 하계를 굽어보다 look down upon the earth
하계 河系 a river system
하계 夏季 summer ⇨ 하기 (夏期)
하고 〈및〉 and; 〈함께〉 with; along [together] with
♦너하고 나 you and I
▶나는 부모님하고 함께 산다 I live in the same house with my parents.
하고많다 plenty; plentiful; abundant; numerous
▶하고많은 곳 중에 내가 여기 살게 될 줄은 꿈에도 몰랐다 I never expected to live here of all places.
하곡 夏穀 summer crops [harvests]; barley and wheat ■—수매가(收買價) the government purchase price of barley
하관 下官 a minor [lower] official; a subordinate official
하관 下棺 taking down the coffin
—하관하다 lower a coffin into the grave; take down the coffin
하관 下顎 the lower part of the face; the jaws
♦하관이 빨다 have pointed jaws
하교 下敎 instructions; an order; directions; 〈전교〉〔史〕 orders from the king
—하교하다 deign to order [instruct]; direct
하구 河口 the mouth of a river; an estuary
■—항 an estuary harbor
하권 下卷 the last volume; 〈상・중・하권의〉 the third volume; 〈상・하권의〉 the second volume
하극상 下剋上 the lower [juniors] dominating the upper [seniors]; a revolt against seniors; a mutiny
♦하극상의 시대 a period of social upheaval
▶그것이 하극상이라는 것이다 That's an instance of the juniors dominating the seniors.
하급 下級 a lower [low] class [grade]
♦하급의 lower(-grade); low-level; junior; inferior; subordinate
■—관리[공무원] lower(-ranking) [petty, minor] official —관청 a subordinate agency [office] —반 a lower class; an underclass —법원 a lower [an inferior] court —생 a lower-class[-grade] student; 〈고교・대학 등의〉(美) an underclassman —선원 sailors and stokers —자 a subordinate; a lower-grade person —장교 a junior officer —품 lower-grade goods
하기 下記 the writing given below; the following; what is stated below
♦하기의 사항들 the following items / 하기와 같이 as in the following; as follows
▶이 제도의 특징은 하기와 같다 The features of this system are as follows: (▶as follows 다음에는 보통 colon (:)을 붙임)
하기 夏期 summer; summertime; summer-tide; the summer period
■—강좌 a summer lecture course —방학[휴가] the summer vacaton [holidays] —학교[강습회] a summer school; extension courses for the summer
하기는 indeed; in truth
▶하기는 그래 Yes, you are right.
▶하기는 예외라는 것도 있다 There are, indeed, some exceptions to this.
▶하기는 그렇게 되어야 하겠지 Indeed it has got to be that way.
하기식 下旗式 a flag-lowering ceremony; 〔軍〕 a retreat ■—나팔 a retreat
하기야 indeed; definitely
▶하기야 요즘 세상은 돈이면 다니까 It is safe to bet that money is everything nowadays.
하나¹ 1 〈어떤 것이나 다〉 ♦하나에서 열까지 from beginning to end; in everything; in every particular

▶그의 아들은 하나를 가르치면 열을 안다 His son is very quick to understand. ⇌ His son is so clever (that) one word is enough for him.
▶그 일이라면 그가 하나에서 열까지 알고 있다 He knows everything about the matter. ⇌ He knows the matter from A to Z.
▶너는 하나만 알지 둘은 모르는 구나 You look only on one side of the shield.
2 〈한 개〉 one; a piece
♦또 하나 one more; another / 하나씩 one by one; one at a time; by ones; piece by piece; separately / 하나도 남김 없이 all; without exception; to the very last / 하나 걸러 alternately
▶이 사과는 하나에 얼마 입니까? How much are these apples each?
▶수박 하나를 다섯이서 먹었다 One watermelon was eaten by five people.
▶하나는 붉고 하나는 노랗다 One is red, and the other is yellow.
▶좋은 걸로 하나 주시오 Give me a good one.
3 〈유일〉 a single one; only one
♦하나뿐인 친구 *one's* [the] one and only friend / 단 하나의 the only; the sole 《survivor》; single
▶이것 하나 밖에 없다 This is the only one.
▶하나도 틀린 데가 없었다 There wasn't even one mistake.
▶모든 것이 네 결심 하나에 달려 있다 It's all up to you. ⇌ Everything [The whole thing] depends upon your decision.
▶이 책을 읽은 사람은 너 하나 뿐이다 You are the only one that has read this book.
4 〈동일〉 the same
▶그의 말은 하나 같이 사실이 아니다 Nothing that he says is true.
▶우리 생각은 하나다 Our ideas are the same.
5 〈일체〉 one (body); one flesh
▶전 국민이 하나가 되어 국난에 임했다 The whole nation rose as one man in the national crisis.
6 〈조차〉 not even; not so much as
▶그는 편지 하나 제대로 못쓴다 He can't so much as write a letter properly.
하나² 〈그러나〉 but; however; still; (and) yet ⇨ 그러나
하나님 〔基〕 God; the Almighty; the Lord; the Supreme Being
♦전능하신 하나님 Almighty God; God Almighty / 하나님의 은총 the blessing [grace] of God; divine blessing [grace] / 하나님께 기도하나 pray to God 《for》 / 하나님께 맹세하다 swear before Heaven / 하나님을 공경하다 revere God; be pious / 하나님을 믿다 believe in God
하녀 下女 a maidservant; a (house)maid
하념 下念 gracious consideration
　—**하념하다** give gracious consideration to; deign to be considerate about
하노이 〈베트남의 수도〉 Hanoi
하느님 God ⇨ 신(神)
하느작거리다 flutter; quiver; tremble
♦미풍에 하느작거리는 갈대 reeds swaying in the breeze
하는수없이 unavoidably ⇨ 부득이
하늘 **1** 〈천공〉 the sky; the blue; the heavens; 〈공중〉 the air

|解說| 보통 *the sky*라고 단수형을 쓰지만 광대함을 강조하여 the skies라고 복수형을 쓸때도 있다. 또 하늘의 상태에 관한 수식어가 붙으면 보통 a가 붙는다. *the air*는 「공중」이란 뜻이다.

♦맑은[흐린] 하늘 a clear [cloudy] sky / 화창한[잿빛] 하늘 a bright [gray] sky / 파란 가을 하늘 a blue autumn sky / 하늘의 요새 a flying fortress / 하늘의 용사 a hero of the air / 하늘을 찌를 듯한 skyscraping; cloud-kissing / 하늘을 나는 새 a bird of the air / 하늘을 바라보다 look at the sky; look skyward / 하늘을 날다 fly in the air / 하늘로 날아오르다 soar up to the sky / 하늘로 사라지다 disappear into space [thin air]
▶수목들이 하늘 높이 자라고 있다 Trees are growing high up in the sky.
▶파란 하늘이 보인다 I see a blue sky.
▶하늘은 맑게 개어 있다 The sky is clear.
▶한국의 하늘은 어느 나라의 하늘보다 맑다 Korea has a brighter sky than any other country.
▶하늘에는 구름한 점 없었다 There was not a speck of cloud in the sky.
▶동쪽 하늘에 무지개가 나타났다 A rainbow appeared across [in] the eastern sky.
2 〈하늘나라·신〉 Heaven; God
♦하늘에 계신 우리 아버지 〈주기도문〉 our Father, who art in Heaven / 하늘의 선물 heavenly gift; a gift from Heaven [God] / 하늘에 맹세하다 swear by Heaven / 운을 하늘에 맡기다 trust to Providence / 하늘을 두려워하다 fear God
▶하늘의 응보는 더디나 반드시 온다 Heaven's vengeance is slow but sure.
▶하늘은 스스로 돕는 자를 돕는다 〈속담〉 Heaven helps those who help themselves.
▶하늘이 내려다 보신다 Heaven knows that.
하늘거리다 sway; tremble; waver; quiver; 〈불꽃이〉 flicker; flare
♦(나뭇잎 등이) 바람에 하늘거리다 tremble in the breeze; sway in the wind / 하늘거리는 불꽃 wavy flames
하늘다람쥐 〔動〕 a (white-cheeked) giant flying squirrel
하늘빛 sky blue; azure
하늘소 〔昆〕 a long-horned beetle; a longicorn
하늘이 무너져도 솟아날 구멍은 있다 〈속담〉 There is a way out of every situation, however bad.
하늘하늘 lightly; buoyantly
▶종잇조각이 하늘로 하늘하늘 올라갔다 A piece of paper rose buoyantly in the air.
　—**하늘하늘하다** light and flimsy 《cloth》
하다¹ **1** 〈행하다〉 do; perform; deliver; 〈공연하다〉 perform; 〈해보다〉 try; 〈실행하다〉 practice; execute; carry out [on]; 〈놀이를〉 play; have 《a game》

하다²

♦강의를 하다 do lecturing / 쇼핑을 하다 do the shopping / 실수를 하다 make [commit] a blunder / 해야 할 일을 하다 do what is due to one / 하는 일 없이 지내다 idle away one's time; live an idle life / …하게 되다 learn to 《do》; come to 《do》/ 해보다 try to do; have [make] a try 《at sth》/ 해버리다 get through 《a task》; get sth done; finish / …하기로 하고 있다 make it a rule to 《do》/ …할 생각이 있다 have a mind 《to do》; feel like 《doing》
▶ 무얼 하고 있니? What are you doing?
▶ 아무것도 할일이 없다 I have nothing to do.
▶ 하라는 대로 하기만 하면 돼 You've only to do as you are told.
▶ 그건 이렇게 하는 거니? Is this how [the way] to do it?
▶ 그것을 할 자신이 있어 I can do it.
▶ 그는 못 하는 것이 아니라 안 하는 것이다 Not that he cannot, but that he will not.
▶ 이런 일은 늘 해왔다 I am used to such things.
▶ 그런 일은 하고 싶지 않다 I don't feel like 《doing》 it.
▶ 너 좋을 대로 하면 돼 You may do as you please.
▶ 그 극장에서는 지금 무얼 하고 있니? What is on [playing] at that theater now? ⇌ What are they giving [showing] at that theater now?
▶ 그것을 어떻게 하든 네 마음이야 You can do what you like with it.
▶ 잡담이나 하고 있을 겨를이 없다 I have no time to engage in a chat [gossip, small talk].
2 〈먹다〉 eat; 〈마시다〉 drink; 〈피우다〉 smoke
♦점심을 하다 take [have] lunch [luncheon] / 한 잔 하다 have a drink
▶ 술을 하십니까? Do you drink?
▶ 그는 술, 담배를 일절 안 한다 He is a total abstainer from liquors and tobacco.
3 〈부르다〉 call; name; 〈주장하다〉 claim; 〈사칭하다〉 pretend; feign
♦김 아무개라고 하는 사람 a man named [called] a certain Kim / 피카소의 그림이라고 하는 것 what purports to be a Picasso / 친척이라고 하다 claim to be sb's relative
▶ 나는 김이라고 합니다 My name is Kim.
▶ 그는 위인이라 할 수는 있으나 선인이라 할 수는 없다 You may call him a great man, but you cannot call him a good man.
▶ 여기에는 공원이라 할만한 것이 없다 There is no park worth mentioning [worthy of the name] here.
4 〈소문에 듣다〉 they [people] say; it is said; I hear
▶ 그렇다고 하더군 So I understand.
▶ 그는 지금 앓고 있다고 한다 He is reported [said] to be ill.
▶ 그가 사직했다고 하던대 The story goes that he resigned his post.
5 〈알다〉 know; 〈배우다〉 study
♦영어를 꽤 하다 be pretty good at English; have a good [great] command of English
▶ 그는 대학에서 건축을 했다 He majored in architecture at the university.
6 〈종사하다〉 engage [be engaged] in; 〈경영하다〉 keep; run; work
♦변호사[의사]를 하다 practice law [medicine] / 문학을 하다 go in for [take to] literature / 중매장이 노릇을 하다 act as (a) go-between / 책방을 하다 run [keep] a bookstore
▶ 무슨 일을 하고 계십니까? What line (of business) are you in?
7 〈생각하다〉 consider; think (of, about, over)
▶ 누가 들어왔나 했더니 우리가 얘기하고 있는 바로 그 사람이었다 Who should come in but the very man we were talking about?
8 〈말하다〉 say; remark; talk; speak
♦남들이야 뭐라고 하든 whatever others may say 《about, of》
▶ 지금 뭐라고 했니? What did you say just now?
9 〈값이 얼마 나가다〉 cost; be worth
▶ 이 셔츠 얼마 합디까? How much did this shirt cost (you)? ⇌ How much did you pay for it?
▶ 사과는 한 개에 500원 한다 The apples are five hundred won each.
10 〈경험하다〉 experience; go through
♦고생을 많이 하다 go through hardships and privations
11 〈착용하다〉 wear; be dressed in
♦귀고리를 하다 wear earrings
▶ 그는 형편없는 옷차림을 하고 있다 He is shabbily [poorly] dressed.
12 〈정하다〉 fix; decide; make
▶ 위원회는 5명으로 한다 The committee shall consist of five members.
▶ 그 사람을 회장으로 합시다 Let's make [appoint] him president.
13 〈나타내다〉 look; have
♦슬픈 얼굴을 하다 look sad
▶ 망고는 어떤 색깔을 하고 있습니까? What colors are mangoes?
14 〈처리하다〉 do with
▶ 내 책을 어떻게 했지? What did you do with my book?

하다² 〈매우〉 really; quite; indeed
♦참 좋기도 하다 be quite beautiful / 아름답기도 하다 be really beautiful / 빠르기도 하다 be speedy indeed
▶ 참 춥기도 하다 How cold!

하다못해 〈심지어〉 so far as; to the extent of; even; 〈적어도〉 at (the) least; to say the least (of it); 〈별도리 없이〉 under the pressure of necessity; driven by necessity; 〈종국에는〉 in the end; finally
▶ 좋아서가 아니라 하다못해 한 것이다 I did it of necessity, not of choice.
▶ 하다못해 자식들까지 부모를 멸시하였다 Even his children despised their parents.
▶ 그들은 입씨름을 하다못해 나중에는 치고 받기까지 하였다 The quarrel ended in their coming to blows.
▶ 하다못해 성함이라도 알려 주실 수 없을지요? Can [Could] you let us know your name?

하단 下段 〈글의〉 the lowest column; 〈계단의〉 the lowest step; 〈침대차의〉 the lower berth

하단 下端 the lower end (of a pole); 〈페이지의〉 the tail

하단 下壇 leaving the platform
―**하단하다** leave [go down] the platform

하달 下達 notification (to an inferior); conveyance
―**하달하다** notify (to an inferior); convey (to the people); pass down (word); 〈명령을〉 issue (an order)
♦ 상의(上意)를 하달하다 convey the will and ideas of a superior officer to subordinate officials

하대 下待 1 〈낮은 대우〉 a disrespectable reception; inhospitability
―**하대하다** treat [receive] sb inhospitably; be inhospitable (towards)
2 〈말을 낮춤〉 using disrespectful words
―**하대하다** use disrespectful words; use low forms of speech (to); do not mister sb

하도 too; too [very] much; excessively; to excess
♦ 하도 기뻐서 in the excess of one's joy / 하도 보고 싶어서 in one's eagerness to see
▶ 하도 바빠 잠도 제대로 잘 수 없다 I am too busy to get enough sleep.
▶ 보석 반지는 하도 비싸서 못 사겠다 A jewel ring is too expensive for me to buy.

하도급 下都給 subcontracting; a subcontract
♦ 하도급을 주다 sublet; underlet
―**하도급하다** subcontract
■ ―업자 a subcontractor

하도롱지 ―紙 brown paper; sulfate paper

하드보드 hardboard

하드보일드 ♦ 하드보일드의 hard-boiled
♦ 하드보일드파의 소설 novels of the hard-boiled school

하드웨어 〔電算〕 hardware

하드트레이닝 hard training

하등 下等 〈하급〉 a low(er) class [grade]; 〈열등〉 inferiority
♦ 하등의 low; lower (plant); inferior
■ ―동물[식물] lower animals [plants] / ―인간 a mean(-spirited) fellow; a person of low character / ―품 an article of inferior quality

하등 何等 〈아무런〉 what; whatever; (not) any; no; (not) in any way
♦ 하등의 이유도 없이 without any reason; for no reason
▶ 하등 의심할 여지가 없다 There is no doubt whatever.
▶ 그것은 하등 이상할 게 없다 There is nothing strange about it.
▶ 그녀와는 하등의 관계도 없다 I have nothing to do with her.

하라레 〈짐바브웨의 수도〉 Harare

하락 下落 〈가격의〉 a fall [drop, decline] (in price); depreciation; 〈품질의〉 deterioration
♦ 물가의 하락 a fall in prices / 원화의 하락 the decline in the won rate / 하락을 예상하고 in anticipation of a decline [drop]
―**하락하다** fall (off); decline; come [go] down; depreciate; 〈가치가〉 deteriorate; degrade
♦ 물가가 하락하다 decline [drop, fall] in prices / 하락시키다 depreciate; lower; bring down (prices); degrade
▶ 인플레이션의 시기에는 돈의 가치가 하락한다 The value of money declines during the inflationary period.
▶ 물가가 평균 1할 하락했다 Prices have come down by 10 percent on an average.
▶ 경기후퇴 기간에 생산고가 하락했다 Production has dropped [sagged] during the recession.
■ ―경향 a downward movement; a falling tendency / ―시세 〔證〕 a bear [bearish] market

하략 下略 the rest [concluding part] omitted
―**하략하다** omit the rest [the concluding part]

하량하다 下諒― consider; take into consideration [account]; make allowance(s) (for); show consideration (for)

-하러 to; for; in order to [that...may]; so as to (do); for the purpose of
♦ 아무를 마중하러 가다 go to meet sb / 쇼핑하러 가다 go shopping / 낚시하러 가다 go fishing / 산책하러 나가다 go out for a walk

하렘 〈이슬람교국의〉 a harem; a haram

하례 賀禮 〈식〉 a congratulatory ceremony; a celebration; 〈축하〉 congratulation
♦ 신년하례 the New Year's ceremony / 하례를 받다 accept sb's felicitation
―**하례하다** hold a congratulatory ceremony; celebrate; congratulate

하롱거리다 act hastily [rashly]; be frivolous [flippant]

하롱하롱 frivolously; flippantly
♦ 하롱하롱 까불다 behave flippantly

하루 1 〈일수〉 a day
♦ 하루의 일 a day's work / 하루 세번[8시간] three times [eight hours] a day / 하루 걸러 every other [second] day / 하루 이틀에 in a day or two / 10년을 하루같이 for ten years as one day / 하루 세 끼를 먹다 take three meals a day
▶ 내일은 하루 쉽니다 I'm going to have a day off tomorrow.
▶ 거기 가는 데는 꼭박 하루 걸린다 It takes me a whole day to go there.
▶ 학교의 소풍은 비 때문에 하루 연기되었다 The school excursion (day) was postponed for one day because of rain.
▶ 교통 사고가 없는 날은 하루도 없다 Not a single day passes without some traffic accidents.
▶ 하루종일 열심히 일했다 I have worked hard all day (long).
2 〈초하루〉 the first day of a month
3 〈어느 날〉 one day
♦ 하루 저녁은 one evening

하루같이 the area for a day's plowing

하루거리 〈학질〉 〔醫〕 malignant [tertian] malaria ♦ 하루거리에 걸리다 be taken with malignant [tertian] malaria

하루바삐 without a day's delay; as soon as

하루바삐 …하다 lose no time in 《doing》
▶ 이 문제는 하루바삐 처리해야만 한다 This problem calls for [requires] prompt treatment.
◆하루바삐 기운 차리시기를 빕니다 I hope you will get well as quickly as possible.

하루살이 〔昆〕 a dayfly; a Mayfly; an ephemera
◆하루살이 같은 인생 《비유》 an ephemeral existence [life]

하루아침 one morning
◆하루아침에 overnight; in a day / 하루아침에 유명해지다 leap [flash] into fame
▶ 로마는 하루 아침에 이루어지지 않았다 《속담》 Rome was not built in a day.

하루치 a day's portion; 〈식량의〉 a ration
◆하루치 식량 a day's ration / 하루치 약 medicine for a day

하루하루 every day; daily; from day to day; day after [by] day
◆하루하루의 생활 everyday [day-to-day] life; one's daily life / 하루하루 나아지다 get better day by day / 하루하루 연기하다 put off 《a matter》 from day to day
▶ 날씨가 하루하루 더워진다 It is growing warmer day by day.
▶ 사태는 하루하루 악화되어 가고 있다 The situation is getting worse and worse every day.

하룻강아지 a (one-day-old) puppy
하룻강아지 범 무서운 줄 모른다 《속담》 Fools rush in where angels fear to tread.

하룻날 the first day (of a month)

하룻밤 〈한 밤〉 a [one] night; 〈온 밤〉 all night (long); 〈어느날 밤〉 one night
◆하룻밤 사이에 in one night; overnight / 하룻밤을 이야기로 지새다 talk a night away / 불안한 하룻밤을 지내다 pass an uneasy night
▶ 그의 집에서 하룻밤을 묵었다 I stayed overnight at his house.
▶ 나는 하룻밤을 기다리며 새웠다 I stayed up all night waiting.

하류 下流 1 〈강의〉 the downstream; the lower reaches [course] of a stream
◆한강 하류에 on the lower Hangang / 하류로 내려가다 go down the river
▶ 5킬로미터 하류에 큰 다리가 있다 There is a big bridge five kilometers down the river.
2 〈사회의〉 a lower social stratum
◆하류의 lower-class
━계급 the lower classes ━사회 the lower strata of society ━생활 (a) low life

하르르하다 〈천 등이 여리고 풀기가 없는〉 thin; flimsy; filmy 《cloth》

하르툼 〈수단의 수도〉 Khartoum

하리놀다 〈고자질하다〉 slander; calumniate; malign; scandalize

하리다¹ 〈마음껏 사치하다〉 indulge [roll] in luxury; be addicted to extravagance

하리다² not clear ⇨ 흐리다²

하리들다 〈방해가 생기다〉 be crossed; suffer from a cross; get thwarted

하리쟁이 a slanderer; a calumniator

하릴없다 〈어쩔 수 없다〉 inevitable; unavoidable; inescapable; 〈서술적〉 cannot help 《it》; 《it》 cannot be helped; cannot choose but 《do》; have no choice but 《to do》
▶ 그가 대학을 그만두고 싶다니 하릴없다 We cannot help his quitting college if he wants to.

하릴없이 〈어쩔 수 없이〉 unavoidably; inevitably; helplessly; as there is no help
▶ 하릴없이 그는 나를 따라왔다 He followed me against his will.

하마 下馬 dismounting
━하마하다 dismount from a horse; get off [alight from] a horse
■ ━비 (碑) a notice stone requiring riders to dismount ━석 (石) a horse block; a stepstone

하마 河馬 〔動〕 a hippopotamus 《pl. ～es, -mi》; 《口》 a hippo 《pl. ～s》

하마터면 almost; nearly; by a close shave
▶ 나는 하마터면 죽을 뻔했다 I came within an inch of being killed. = I narrowly escaped death.
▶ 나는 하마터면 빠져 죽을 뻔했다 I was on the verge of drowning.
▶ 나는 하마터면 택시에 치일 뻔했다 I narrowly [just] missed being run over by a taxi.
▶ 하마터면 우리는 기차를 놓칠 뻔했다 We almost [nearly] missed the train.

하마평 下馬評 an advance rumor; an appointment widely [conjecturally] rumored among the public

하명 下命 〈명령〉 orders; a command; 〈주문〉 an order ━하명하다 order; give orders to; issue a command; command
▶ 하명하여 주시기 바랍니다 We solicit your orders.

하모니 〈조화〉 harmony; 〔樂〕 (a) harmony
하모니카 a harmonica; a mouth organ
◆하모니카를 불다 play 《a tune》 on the harmonica

하묘 下錨 anchoring ⇨ 투묘

하물 荷物 〈짐〉 a load; a burden; 〈수하물〉 《미》 baggage; 《영》 luggage ⇨ 화물

하물며 〈긍정〉 much [still] more; 〈부정〉 much [still] less; not to mention; to say nothing of; let alone
▶ 그는 원수도 사랑하는데, 하물며 친구를 사랑하지 않겠는가 He loves his enemies, not to mention his friends.
▶ 아이들은 약도 싫어하는데 하물며 주사를 좋아할까? Children do not like medicine, and much less injections.
▶ 그는 독일어와 불어도 아는데 하물며 영어쯤이야 He knows German and French, to say nothing of [not to speak of, not to mention] English.

하미 下米 rice of inferior quality; low-grade rice

하민 下民 the common people; lower-class people

하박 下膊 the forearm ■ ━골 forearm bones

하반 下半 the lower half; the latter [second] half ━기 the latter half of the year ━신 the lower half of the body

하복 夏服 a summer suit; summer clothes; a summer uniform
하복부 下腹部 〔解〕 the abdominal [hypogastric] region; the underbelly; the hypogastrium
하부 下部 the lower part ■—기관 a subordinate office [agency] —조직 a substructure
하사 下士 〔軍〕〈육군·공군·해병〉 a staff sergeant; 〈해군〉 a petty officer second class
하사 下賜 a royal grant [donation, gift]
—하사하다 give; grant; bestow; 〈돈을〉 donate; make a donation ♦금일봉을 하사하다 grant a monetary gift 《to, toward》
■—품[金] a royal gift [grant, bounty, gratuity]
하사 何事 what; whatever
▶정신일도 하사불성 Nothing is impossible to a determined mind. ⇒ Where there is a will, there is a way.
하사관 下士官 〈육군·공군·해병〉 a noncommissioned officer 《略 NCO》; 〈해군〉 a petty officer
하산 下山 a descent from a mountain
—하산하다 descend [go down, come down] a mountain
하상 河床 a riverbed; the bed of a river
하선 下船 leaving a ship
—하선하다 leave a ship; go ashore
♦하선시키다 discharge; land
하선 下線 an underline; an underscore
♦하선을 그은 부분 an underlined part / 하선을 긋다 underline 《a word》
하세 下世 decease ⇨ 별세(別世)
하소 煆燒 〔化〕 calcination; calcining
—하소하다 calcine
■—기 a calciner; a calcinatory —로(爐) a calcining furnace; a calcinatory
하소연 an appeal; a petition; a complaint
♦하소연을 들어 주다 give sb a hearing
—하소연하다 make an appeal [a plea] 《for》; appeal 《to》; complain of; whine 《about》
♦서러운 사정을 하소연하다 complain of one's sad plight
▶그는 억울함을 하소연하였다 He complained of an injustice.
▶그는 내 동정심을 하소연했다 He appealed to me for my sympathy.
하수¹ 下手 〈솜씨〉 unskillfulness; 〈사람〉 a poor hand; 〈장기·바둑의〉 a lower grader
하수² 下手 〈살인〉 murder; killing
—하수하다 murder; kill; slay
■—인 the murderer; the killer; the slayer
하수 下水 sewage; sewerage; drainage; foul water
■—관 a cesspipe; a sewer pipe; a drainpipe —구 an outfall; a gully hole —조(槽) a cesspool —처리장 a sewage disposal plant
하수 下垂 drooping; hanging down
■—위 gastric ptosis; gastroptosis
하수구 下水溝 a ditch; a drain; a kennel; a sewer; a gutter ♦하수구를 치다 clear (out) a ditch; clean a drain
♦하수구가 막혔다 The drain is obstructed.
하수도 下水道 sewerage; drainage; a sewer
■—공사 drainage [sewerage] works

하숙 下宿 boarding; lodging; 《美》 board and lodging; room and board
♦하숙 생활을 하다 live in lodgings [a lodging house] / 하숙을 구하다 be on [have] a hunt for lodgings
▶학교 근처에 하숙을 잡았다 I have taken rooms near the school.
—하숙하다 lodge [board, room] 《at a house, with sb》; make [take (up)] one's lodgings
▶그는 학창 시절에 미국인 가정집에서 하숙했다 He stayed [boarded, lodged] with an American family during his school days.
■—방 a room for boarding; a lodger's [boarder's] room —비 board charge; the boarding expenses [charges]: 하숙비는 식사 포함 월 30만원이다 My room and board is three hundred thousand won a month. —생 a student boarder —인 a lodger; a boarder; 《美》 a roomer: 하숙인을 두다 take in [keep] lodgers [boarders]; run [keep, operate] a lodging house —집 (one's) lodgings; a boardinghouse; 《英》 a lodging house; 《美》 a rooming house
하순 下旬 the last ten days [the last third] 《of a month》 ♦6월 하순에 toward the end of June; late in June / 9월 하순 중에 during the last ten days of September
하시 下視 〈내려다봄〉 looking down; 〈업신여김〉 looking down on [upon]; despising
—하시하다 〈내려다보다〉 look down (from a height); 〈업신여기다〉 look down on; have contempt for; despise
▶그녀는 하시하는 듯한 눈으로 나를 보았다 She gave me a contemptuous look.
하악 下顎 〔解〕 the submaxilla 《pl. -lae》; the lower jaw —골 the submaxilla; the lower jawbone
하안 河岸 a riverside; a riverbank; a waterfront ■—단구 river terrace
하야 下野 retiring from public life
▶대통령은 하야를 결심했다 The president made up his mind to resign [leave] office.
—하야하다 retire [withdraw] from public life; resign office
하양 white; whiteness
하얗다 (pure) white; snow-white; (as) white as snow
♦하얀 시트 an immaculate sheet / 하얗게 칠하다 paint white
▶내가 일어나 보니 눈이 하얗게 쌓여 있었다 I awoke to find the ground silvery white with snow.
하얘지다 become (pure) white [snow-white]; 〈머리가〉 turn gray [white]
♦머리가 하얘지다 one's hair turns white [gray]
▶그의 얼굴이 하얘졌다 His face went pale [got white as a sheet].
-하여 as being; on the ground of [that]
▶그 책은 미풍양속을 해친다하여 발매 금지되었다 The book was suppressed as being injurious to public morals.
하여간(에) 何如間(—) anyhow ⇨ 하여튼
하여금 ♦아무로 하여금 무슨 일을 하게 하다

cause sb to do sth
▶그로 하여금 다시 한번 해보게 해라 Let him have another try. ⇌ Give him one more chance.
▶그로 하여금 그녀에게 편지를 쓰게 해라 Make him write a letter to her.

하여튼 何如— anyhow; in any case; anyway; at any rate
▶하여튼 시작합시다 Let's get started, anyway.
▶되든지 안 되든지 하여튼 나는 그것을 해 보고 싶다 Whether it's possible or not, I want to give it a try.
▶하여튼 나는 그녀석이 싫어 Anyhow, I don't like him.
▶하여튼 그 날은 반드시 온다 The day is sure to come at any rate.

하역 荷役 loading and unloading (of vessels); stevedoring
♦석탄 하역을 하다 load [unload] coal ―하역하다 load and unload (a ship); ship and discharge (cargo); do the cargo working
■―인부 a stevedore; (美) a longshoreman (pl. -men); a wharf laborer

하연 賀宴 a celebration banquet; a congratulatory feast

하염없다 1 〈아무 생각이 없다〉absentminded; vacant; blank; idle
♦하염없는 생활 a life without meaning; a hollow [an empty] life / 하염없는 나날 idle days
2 〈끝이 없다〉endless; ceaseless

하염없이 1 〈아무 생각 없이〉absentmindedly; blankly; vacantly; abstractedly; idly
♦하염없이 바라보다 look vacantly [blankly] (at); stare into space / 하염없이 생각에 잠기다 be in a brown study; be lost in reverie [in the clouds] / 하염없이 세월을 보내다 idle one's time away; loaf away one's time [days]
▶그는 하염없이 뜰의 단풍나무만 바라보고 있었다 Lost in thought, he kept gazing at the maple tree in the yard.
2 〈끝없이〉endlessly; ceaselessly; unceasingly
♦하염없이 눈물을 흘리다 give free vent to one's tears; be dissolved in tears; dissolve into tears

하염직하다 worth 《doing》;〈서술적〉be worthy of 《praise》
♦고려하염직한 문제 a matter worthy to be considered / 하염직한 일 a job worth doing

하오 下午 afternoon ⇨ 오후

하옥 下獄 〈투옥〉imprisonment; confinement ―하옥하다 put in jail; cast into prison; send [take] to prison; jail; lock up; imprison

하와이 Hawaii ♦하와이의 Hawaiian
■―말 Hawaiian ―사람 a Hawaiian ―제도 the Hawaiian Islands

하와이안기타 a Hawaiian guitar; a steel guitar

하원 下院 the Lower House [Chamber];〈영국의〉the House of Commons;〈미국의〉the House of Representatives;〈프랑스의〉the Chamber of Deputies
■―의원〈영국의〉a Member of Parliament (略 M.P.);〈미국의〉a Member of Congress (略 M.C.); a Representative; a Congressman ―의장 Speaker of the House of Representatives

하위 下位 a low(er) rank [grade]; a subordinate position
♦하위에 있다 occupy [hold] a subordinate position (to); be below (another) in rank / 하위로 떨어지다 sink in the scale

하의 下衣 (a pair of) trousers; (口) pants; pantaloons

하의 下意 〈아랫사람의 뜻〉the will and ideas [the wishes] of the lower-grade personnel;〈민의(民意)〉the will of the people

하이다이빙 high diving ■―선수 a high diver

하이델베르크 〈독일의 도시〉Heidelberg

하이라이트 a highlight

하이볼 (美) a highball; (英) a whisky and soda

하이스쿨 a high school ⇨ 고등학교

하이에나 〔動〕 a hyena; a hyaena

하이커 a hiker

하이킹 (a) hiking; a hike ♦하이킹 가다 go on a hike; go hiking; hike (to) ■―코스 a hiking trail

하이템포 a high [fast] tempo

하이틴 one's late teens
■―소년[소녀] a boy [girl] in his [her] late teens

하이파이 high fidelity; (口) hi-fi ♦하이파이의 hi-fi; high-fidelity ■―재생 장치 a high-fidelity sound reproduction system

하이픈 a hyphen ♦하이픈으로 이어진 단어 a hyphenated word / 하이픈을 넣다[으로 잇다] hyphen; hyphenate; hyphenize
▶이 단어에는 하이픈이 들어가야 한다 This word needs to be hyphenated.

하이힐 high-heeled shoes

하인 下人 a servant; a domestic (servant)
♦하인을 두다 keep a servant; have a servant in one's service ■―배(輩) servants; menials; a lowly fellow

하인 何人 〈누구〉who; what(ever) person
♦하인을 막론하고 whoever it may be; no matter who he may be
▶하인을 막론하고 여기는 들어갈 수 없다 Nobody is allowed to enter here.
▶종교의 자유는 하인을 막론하고 보장된다 Freedom of religion is guaranteed to all.

하인방 下引枋 〔建〕 a lower lintel

하자 瑕疵 〈흠〉a flaw; a blemish; a defect
♦하자 없는 flawless; immaculate; all-perfect

하잘것없다 insignificant; trifling; trivial; petty; worthless; poor
♦하잘것없는 선물 a trifling gift / 하잘것없는 일로 소란을 떨다 make a fuss about trifles; make much of a trifling matter
▶두 사람은 하잘것없는 일로 자주 다툰다 The two often quarrel over a trifle.

하장 賀狀 〈축하편지〉a congratulatory letter; a greeting card; greetings

하전 荷電 〔電〕 electric charge; charge
■―입자 charged particle

하절 夏節 the summer (season)

하정 賀正 New Year's greetings;〈연하장의 문구〉A Happy New Year!

하제 下劑 〈완하제〉〔藥〕 a purgative (medicine); a purge; a laxative; a cathartic ♦하제를 쓰다 use a purgative; purge the bowels

하주 荷主 the owner of goods ⇨ 화주(貨主)

하중 荷重 〔機〕 load; loading ■안전— safe load 유료— payload

하지 下肢 〔解〕 the lower limbs; the legs; nether extremities

하지 夏至 the summer solstice ■—선〈북회귀선〉 the Tropic of Cancer —점 the summer solstice (point)

하지만 but; however; though; still; yet; nevertheless
▶ 하지만 그는 나중에 그것을 포기하기로 했다 Later, however, he decided to give it up.
▶ 하지만 그는 위대하다 He is great, though.
▶ 하지만 그건 지나친 요구가 아니니? But it is asking too much, isn't it?

-하지않도록 (so as) not to 《do》; so that... may not 《do》; lest...should
▶ 취하지 않도록 해라 See (to it) that you do not get drunk.
▶ 시험에 낙제하지 않도록 열심히 공부해라 Work hard so as not to fail in the examination.
▶ 지각하지 않도록 서두르자 Let's hurry so we won't be late.

-하지않을수없다 cannot help doing; cannot but do; cannot help but do
▶ 그는 사직하지 않을 수 없게 되었다 He compelled to resign his post.
▶ 이 사실을 개탄하지 않을 수 없다 I cannot help deploring this fact.
▶ 그는 진실을 말하지 않을 수 없었다 He could not help telling the truth.

하지하 下之下 the lowest of its kind; the poorest [worst] of all

하직 下直 〈작별〉 leave-taking; (saying) good-by(e); a farewell
♦하직인사를 하러 가다 go for a parting call; pay *sb* a farewell visit
—하직하다 take (*one's*) leave 《of *one's* elder》; say good-bye 《to》; bid farewell
♦고향을 하직하다 leave *one's* hometown [native place]/ 이 세상을 하직하다 leave this world; depart this life; die

하차 下車 getting off; getting out; alighting
—하차하다 get off 《the train》; get down 《from a car》; alight 《from a train》; get out 《of a car》
♦종점에서 하차하다 get off 《the train》 at the terminal
▶ 나는 대전에서 하차합니다 I shall break my journey [stop off, stop over] at Taejŏn.
■도중— a stopover ■—역 the station where *one* gets off 《the train》

하찮다 〈대수롭지 않다〉 petty; insignificant; trifling; trivial; 〈무가치하다〉 worthless; valueless; good-for-nothing; poor; trashy
♦일상생활의 하찮은 근심 걱정 petty worries of everyday life / 하찮은 너석 a worthless fellow; a petty underling; a nothing / 하찮은 선물 a trifling gift / 하찮은 일 a matter of no importance [account]; a trifling thing; a trifle; a trivial affair [matter] / 하찮은 일을 크게 떠벌리다 make much of a trifling matter; make a mountain (out) of a molehill / 하찮은 일로 법석을 떨다 make a fuss about trifles / 하찮게 여기다 make light [little] of; think little [nothing] of; belittle
▶ 그는 하찮은 일로 화를 냈다 He lost his temper on a slight provocation. ⇌ He was offended by a trifling thing.

하천 河川 rivers
■—개수 river improvement —공사 river conservation work —부지 the dry riverbed —부지 사용 허가 a permit to use a dry riverbed —수위 river stage —오염 the river contamination: 공장 폐수에 의한 하천 오염 industrial pollution of a river —측량 river surveying

하청 下請 subcontracting ⇨ 하도급

하체 下體 the lower part of the body; the nether limbs

하초 下焦 the lower part of the abdomen

하층 下層 1 〈아래층〉 downstairs; 〈아래 켜〉 a lower layer [stratum]; an underlayer; a substratum 《*pl*. -ta》
2 〈사회의〉 a lower social stratum
♦하층의 lower-class
■—계급 the lower classes —민 the people of the lower classes; the great unwashed; (common [vulgar]) herd; the rabble —사회 the lower strata of society —운(雲) lower clouds

하치 下— low-grade goods; goods of inferior [poor] quality
▶ 이 물건은 하치다 This article is of inferior quality.

하치장 荷置場 a place to put *sth* in; a yard; a depository; a repository
♦목재 하치장 (美) a lumberyard; (英) a timberyard / 노천의 석탄 하치장 an open storage yard for coal

하키 〔競〕 hockey ♦하키를 하다 play hockey ■아이스[필드]— ice [field] hockey —선수 a hockey player —스틱 a hockey stick

하퇴 下腿 〈종아리〉 the calf; 〔解〕 the crus 《*pl*. crura》

하트 〈카드의〉 a heart; 〈마음〉 heart
♦하트의 에이스[퀸] the ace [queen] of hearts / 하트 모양의 heart-shaped

하편 下篇 the last volume ⇨ 하권(下卷)

하품 yawning; 〈1회의〉 a yawn; a gape
♦하품의 발작 the gapes / 하품을 참다 suppress [stifle] a yawn; bite down a yawn / 하품을 크게 하다 yawn a big long yawn; give a big yawn / 하품을 하며 기지개 켜다 stretch *oneself* with a yawn / 하품을 하면서 말하다 yawn out *sth*
▶ 하품은 잘 옮는다 Yawning is catching.
—하품하다 yawn; gape; give a yawn
♦하품하는 사람 a yawner; a gaper / 손으로 가리고 하품하다 hide a yawn behind *one's* hand / 자꾸 하품하다 have the gapes

하품 下品 low-grade goods ⇨ 하치

하프 〔樂〕 〈play〉 a harp ■—주자(奏者) a harpist; a harper

하프백 〈축구의〉 a halfback ♦하프백을 맡다 play halfback

하프시코드 〔樂〕 a harpsichord ■ —주자(奏者) a harpsichordist
하프타임 〔競〕 halftime
하필 何必 of all things (in the world); of all occasions [people]
▶ 그 많은 나라 중에서 왜 하필 인도에 가니? Why do you go to India of all countries?
▶ 하필이면 왜 내가 가야 하지? Why should I go of all persons?
▶ 다른 날도 많은데 하필 섣달 그믐날 밤이야 Of all the good days in the year, on New Year's Eve!
▶ 왜 하필 오늘이어야 하는거지? Why need it be today?
하하 〈웃음소리〉 haha; ha-ha
하학 下學 ending of the school day; coming home from school
— 하학하다 school ends for the day; school gets [lets] out; leave school
■ —시간 dismissal time — 종 the dismissal bell
하한 下限 the lowest limit; the greatest lower bound; the inferior limit
■ —점 the low trip point
하항 河港 a river port
하해 河海 rivers and seas
♦ 하해(와) 같은 은혜 a great debt of gratitude; great favor; unlimited grace
하행 下行 〈아래로〉 going down; 〈서울에서〉 going away from Seoul
— 하행하다 go down; go into the country
— 선 a downline — 열차 a downtrain
하향 下向 a downward look; looking [bending, facing] downward
♦ 하향 기미다 begin to decline [fall]; show a downward tendency
— 하향하다 look down; lower one's gaze [eyes]
■ —세 a downward [declining] tendency; a downtrend
하향 下鄕 〈시골로〉 going to the country; 〈고향으로〉 going back to one's country home
— 하향하다 go away from the capital; go to the country; go back to one's country home
하현 下弦 the last quarter of the moon
— 달 a waning [an old] moon
하혈 下血 discharging blood — 하혈하다 discharge blood (from the bowels); flux
하회 下回 〈다음 회〉 next time; 〈회답〉 a reply; an answer ♦ 하회를 기다리다 await sb's reply
하회하다 下廻— do not amount ⇨ 밑돌다
학 學 learning; study; science; scholarship
학 鶴 〔鳥〕 a crane
학계 學界 learned [academic] circles [world]
♦ 학계의 권위 an authority of the academic world / 학계에 크게 공헌하다 do much [render great services] for the cause of learning
학과 學科 〈과목〉 a school subject; a subject of study
▶ 네가 좋아하는 학과는 뭐니? What are your favorite subjects?
■ —과정 a course of study; a school course; a curriculum (pl. ~s, -la) — 시험 examinations in academic subjects — 주임 the head of a department
학과 學課 a lesson; school [class] work
♦ 학과를 복습하다 review one's lessons / 내일의 학과를 예습하다 prepare tomorrow's lessons ■ —시간표 a (teaching) schedule
학관 學館 〈학원〉 an educational institution; an academy; an institute ♦ 영수 학관 an English and mathematics institute
학교 學校 a school; an academy; 〈대학〉 a college
♦ 학교가 파하고 나서 after school (is over) / 학교를 그만두다[중퇴하다] leave [stop] school / 학교를 무단 결석하다 play truant (from school) / 학교를 세우다[설립하다] establish [found] a school / 학교를 조퇴하다 leave school early / 학교에 두고 오다 leave 《a notebook》 at school / 학교에 다니다 attend [go to] school / 학교에 들어가다 enter a school; go into school / 아이를 학교에 보내다 send a boy to school / 학교에서 돌아오다 come home from school / 학교에서 제적당하다 be expelled from school
▶ 내일은 학교가 쉰다 We have no school tomorrow.
▶ 학교는 8시에 시작한다 School begins at eight.
▶ 그녀는 어제 학교에 결석했다 She was absent from school yesterday.
▶ 형은 작년에 학교를 졸업했다 My brother graduated from [at] a school last year. ⇒ My brother completed his school last year.
▶ 그는 학교를 갓 졸업했다 He is fresh from school.
▶ 어느 학교에 다니니? What school do you attend [go to]? ⇒ What school are you at?
■ —교육 school education; schooling: 정규 학교 교육 regular [formal] schooling — 급식 school feeding; school lunch — 도서관 a school library — 방송 〔TV·라디오〕 the school hour — 법인 an educational foundation — 생활 school [college] life — 선생 a schoolteacher; (美) a schoolman — 성적 one's school [academic] record — 신문 a school paper — 일람 a school prospectus [(美) catalog] — 장 ⇨ 교장 — 차(差) scholastic disparity among schools : 학교차를 없애다 diminish the scholastic parity among schools
학구 學究 〈연구〉 study; learning; 〈학도〉 a scholar; a student
♦ 학구적인 생활 an academic [scholastic] life / 학구적인 정신 a scholastic spirit
학구 學區 a school district ■ —제 the school district system
학군 學群 a school group ■ —제 the school group system
학급 學級 a class; (美) a grade; (英) a form
♦ 학급을 편성하다 organize a class ■ —문고 a classroom library
학기 學期 a (school) term; (美) a session; 〈2학기제의〉 a semester
■ 신— a fresh [new] term 제1[2]— the first [second] term ■ —말 (at) the close [end] of a term — 말 시험 a term [terminal] examina-

학년 學年 a school [an academical, a scholastic] year; a class; (美) a grade; (英) a form
♦ 1[2, 3, 4]학년생 a first-year [second-year, third-year, fourth-year] student; (美) a first [second, third, fourth] grader; 〈고등학교 이상〉 (美) a freshman [sophomore, junior, senior]
▶ 그는 중학교 2학년이다 He is in the second year of a middle school.
▶ 〔會話〕「너는 몇 학년이냐?」「3학년이야」 "What grade [year] are you in?" "I'm in the third grade [third-year class]."
▶ 그녀는 고학년을 담임했다 She was in charge of a higher class.
■—말 the end of a school year —말 시험 an annual [a final] examination

학당 學堂 an educational institution; 〈학교〉 a school

학대 虐待 cruel treatment; ill-treatment; maltreatment; abuse; cruelty
♦ 동물 학대 방지협회 the Society for the Prevention of Cruelties to Animals / 정신적 학대 mental cruelty / 학대에 못이겨 being unable to bear the severity of the treatment / 학대를 감수하다 submit to ill-treatment
—학대하다 treat *sb* cruelly [ill, with cruelty]; be cruel to 《an animal》; use 《animals》 cruelly; ill-treat; maltreat
♦ 동물을 학대하다 be cruel to animals / 아내를 학대하다 treat *one's* wife cruelly / 약자를 학대하다 oppress [bully] the weak / 학대당하다 be ill-treated [maltreated]

학덕 學德 learning and virtue ♦ 학덕을 겸비하다 be eminent in both learning and virtue

학도 學徒 a student; 〈학문을 닦는〉 a scholar
■—병 a student soldier —호국단 the Students' National Defense Corps

학동 學童 a school child; a pupil; 〈남자〉 a schoolboy; 〈여자〉 a schoolgirl

학력 學力 scholarship; scholastic ability; scholarly attainments
♦ 학력이 뛰어난 사람 a person excellent in scholarship / 학력이 뛰어나다 be excellent in scholarship / 학력이 있다[없다] be a good [poor] scholar
▶ 학력의 저하가 현저하다 There has been a remarkable decline in academic achievement.
▶ 나는 학력으로는 그의 상대가 안된다 I am no match for him in scholarship.
■—고사 a scholastic ability test

학력 學歷 a school career; an academic background; schooling
♦ 전문대 졸업 이상의 학력이 있는 자 someone with at least a junior college education / 학력이 없는 사람 a person without any school education / 학력을 불문하고 irrespective of the academic background
▶ 그는 별다른 학력도 없이 박사가 되었다 He has been made a doctor, though he has pursued no regular studies.

학령 學齡 school age ♦ 학령이 되다 reach [attain] school age
■—미달 아동 a preschool child —아동 children of school age; school-aged children

학리 學理 a theory; a scientific principle
♦ 학리상(으로는) theoretically; in theory / 사회의 변화를 학리적으로 연구하다 study social changes theoretically

학명 學名 a scientific name [term]; a technical term
♦ 동물[식물]의 학명 a zoological [botanical] name / 학명을 붙이다 give a scientific name 《to》

학무 學務 school [educational] affairs ■—과 an educational affairs section —국장 the Chief of the Educational Bureau

학문 學問 〈학업〉 pursuit of learning; study; 〈지식〉 knowledge; learning; scholarship; scholarly attainments; 〈학술〉 a science
♦ 학문의 세계 the academic world / 학문의 자유 academic freedom / 학문이 없는 사람 an unlettered [uneducated] person / 학문을 위한 학문 learning for learning's sake / 학문이 깊다 be very learned; be a good scholar / 학문이 뛰어나다 stand high [be proficient] in *one's* studies / 학문이 있다 have learning [education]; be learned [educated] / 학문을 좋아하다 like [be fond of] learning / 학문을 하다 pursue learning; study; follow *one's* studies / 학문에 정진하다 devote *oneself* to studies
▶ 사회학은 사회 현상을 다루는 학문이다 Sociology is a science which treats of social phenomena.
▶ 학문의 진보가 대학의 궁극적 목표다 The advancement of learning is the ultimate aim of a university.
▶ 학문에는 왕도(王道)가 없다 《속담》 There is no royal road to learning.

학벌 學閥 school ties [affiliations]; an academic clique; academical cliquism [sectionalism]
♦ 학벌 싸움 rivalry between academic cliques / 학벌을 형성하다[타파하다] form [break down] an academic clique

학병 學兵 a student soldier

학보 學報 a school bulletin [newsletter]; a gazette

학부 學府 an educational institution; an academic center; a seat of learning ♦ 최고—the highest seat [institution] of learning

학부 學部 〈대학의〉 a department; a faculty; 〈종합대학의〉 a college

학부모 學父母 parents of students ♦ 학부모들의 대단한 교육열 the exceptional zeal for education among parents
■—회 a parents' association

학부형 學父兄 parents (and brothers) of students

학비 學費 school [educational] expenses
♦ 학비 면제의 특전을 받다 enjoy [be granted] the priviledge of tuition exemption; be exempt from paying school fees / 학생의 학비를 대어 주다 pay a student's educational expenses; supply a student with his [her] college expenses / 학비를 벌다 earn *one's* school expenses by working; work for *one's* education / 학비에 곤란을 받다 be hard up for

school expenses
▶ 그는 아르바이트로 학비를 벌어 대학을 나왔다 He worked his way through college.
▶ 그녀는 나의 대학 4년간의 학비를 대주었다 She paid my college fees for four years. ≒ She paid for my entire college education.

학사 學士 a (university) graduate; 〈학위〉a bachelor ━문 —〈학위〉Bachelor of Arts (略 B.A.); 〈사람〉a bachelor of arts ━학위 a bachelor's degree; a baccalaureate

학사 學事 school affairs; education(al) matters ■━보고 a report on education(al) matters ━시찰 (an) educational inspection

학살 虐殺 slaughter; massacre; carnage ━학살하다 slaughter; massacre; butcher ▶ 대량━ holocaust 민족━ genocide ■━자 a slaughterer; a slayer

학생 學生 a pupil; a student

解說 *pupil*은 주로 초·중등 학생을 가리킨다. 개인적인 레슨을 받는 학생도 이에 포함된다. *student*는 주로 대학생을 가리키는데, 미국에서는 고등학생에 대해서도 쓰지만 영국에서는 대학생만 가리킨다.

♦ 과격파 학생 a student extremist / 학생다운 태도 a manner proper to a student / 학생의 날 Students' Day / 남학생과 여학생 men and women students / 학생수 15,000명의 대학교 a university with a student enrollment of fifteen thousand
▶ 학생인 이상 학생답게 처신해라 As long as you are a student, behave like one.
▶ 그 대학의 학생수는 얼마입니까? How many students are there in the college? ≒ How many students does the college have?
▶ 그 노래는 학생들에게 인기가 있다 The song is popular with [among] the students.
■━기질 the students' way of thinking; the student spirit ━복 a school uniform ━생활 student [college] life ━시절 one's school [student] days ━운동 a student movement ━자치회 student government; (美) a student union ━증 a student's (identification) card ━처 the office of student affairs ━처장 the dean of student affairs ━특별 할인[요금] a special discount [rate, fare] for students ━회 a student council ━회관 a students' hall

학설 學說 a theory; a doctrine ♦ 새로운 학설을 세우다 set up [formulate, propound] a new theory

학수고대하다 鶴首苦待━ wait expectantly [anxiously, eagerly] (for); be on (the) tiptoe of expectation; eagerly look forward (to)
▶ 그녀는 그가 도착하기를 학수고대했다 She anxiously waited for his arrival.
▶ 나는 고향 소식을 학수고대하고 있다 I am dying for news from home.

학술 學術 〈학문〉learning; scholarship; 〈과학〉science; 〈학문과 예술〉art and science ♦ 학술의[적인] scientific; academic / 학술상의 연구 scientific research / 학술 연구를 진흥하다 promote scientific researches
▶ 이것은 학술상의 의의가 있는 문제다 This is a question of scientific significance.
■━강연(회) a scientific lecture (meeting) ━논문 a scientific essay; a treatise; a paper ━(용)어 a technical term ━잡지 a scientific journal

학술원 學術院 the Academy ■━한국━ the National Academy of Sciences ━회원 a member of the Academy

학습 學習 learning; study
▶ 그 학생은 학습 태도가 아주 진지하다 That pupil's attitude towards his studies is very serious.
━학습하다 study; learn
■━서 a study book ━자 a learner ━장 a workbook; a drill book ━지도 요령 a course of study

학승 學僧 a learned priest

학식 學識 learning; scholarship; scholarly attainments; knowledge
♦ 심오한 학식 profound knowledge [learning]; erudition / 학식과 경험이 많은 사람 a man of learning and experience / 학식이 있는 learned; erudite; educated
▶ 그는 학식이 없다 He lacks [has no] scholarship. ≒ He is uneducated.

학업 學業 schoolwork; studies; learning; scholarship
♦ 학업성적이 좋다 be a good scholar; do well at school / 학업을 게을리 하다 neglect one's schoolwork / 학업을 중단하다 [마치다] give up [complete] one's studies / 학업에 힘쓰다 study one's lessons with diligence; be attentive to one's studies

학예 學藝 arts and science [letters]; literary accomplishments
■━란(欄) the literary columns [page] ━부 〈신문사의〉a department of arts and science ━회 literary exercises [exhibition]

학용품 學用品 school things [supplies]

학우 學友 a schoolmate; a schoolfellow; a fellow student; a classmate ■━회 a student [students'] union; an old boys' [girls'] association

학원 學院 an (educational) institute; an academy; a private school
━자동차━ a drivers' school

학원 學園 an educational institution; a school; a campus
■━분쟁 a campus dispute ━사찰 inspection on campus activities ━생활 school [campus, student] life ━소요 campus unrest [disturbances] ━자율화 campus liberalization [autonomy]

학위 學位 a degree; an academic degree
♦ 학위를 갖고 있다 hold a degree / 예일 대학의 의학박사 학위를 갖고 있다 have one's M.D. from Yale university / 학위를 주다 grant a degree (to); confer a degree (on); award sb a degree / 학위를 받다 be granted [awarded] a degree / 학위에서 학위를 취득하다 take [obtain] a degree from a university
▶ 그는 하버드대학교에서 법학박사 학위를 받았다 He received the degree of Doctor of Laws from Harvard University.

명예— an honorary degree 박사— a doctor's degree; a doctorate ■ **—논문** a thesis for a degree **—수여식** the (ceremony of) conferment of a degree

학자 學者 a scholar; a learned man; a man of learning; a savant; a literary man
♦ 학자 기질의 scholarly; academic / 학자다운 scholarlike; scholarly
▶ 그는 학자 기질의 사람이다 He is of a scholarly turn of mind.
▶ 그녀는 학자연한다 She assumes an air of a scholar. ⇌ She is pedantic. ⇌ She is not much of a scholar.
▶ 그는 학자다운 데가 있다 He has something of the scholar in him.

학자 學資 school expenses ⇨ 학비(學費)
■ **—금** school expenses; an education fund **—보험** educational endowment insurance

학장 學長 a dean; a rector; a president; a chancellor ■ **—회의** the council of deans

학적 學籍 a school [college] register
♦ 학적에 올리다[에서 빼다] put a student's name on [strike a student's name off] the school register
▶ 학적에 올라 있는 학생수는 총 8,000명이다 The total registration of students is eight thousand.
■ **—부** a school [college] register

학점 學點 a unit; (美) a point; a credit
♦ 2학점 짜리 프랑스어를 수강하다 take a French course for two credits / 학점이 모자라다 do not have sufficient credits 《to graduate》 / 20학점을 따다 take 20 units
▶ 그는 학점이 모자라서 졸업하지 못했다 He hasn't got enough credits for graduation.
▶ 대학 졸업을 위해서는 140학점을 따야 한다 To complete the college course, it is required to take a hundred and forty credits.
■ **—제도** the credit [unit] system

학정 虐政 oppressive [tyrannical] government; tyranny; despotism
♦ 학정을 펴다 tyrannize 《over》; rule cruelly / 학정에 시달리다 groan under tyranny

학제 學制 an educational system ♦ 학제를 개혁하다 reform the system of education
■ **—개혁** a reform [reorganization] of the school system **—개혁안** the proposed educational system reform

학질 瘧疾 malaria ⇨ 말라리아
♦ 학질을 떼다 (비유) get [be] rid of a nuisance / 학질에 걸리다 be taken with malaria
■ **—모기** an anopheles (mosquito); a malaria mosquito

학창 學窓 〈학교〉 a school; a campus
♦ 학창을 떠나다 leave school
■ **—생활** school life **—시절** one's school days

학춤 鶴— the Crane Dance

학칙 學則 (apply) school regulations
♦ 학칙을 정하다 frame school regulations / 학칙을 지키다[어기다] observe [break] school regulations
▶ 그것은 학칙에 어긋난다 It's against the school regulations.

학파 學派 a school; a sect

♦ 에피쿠로스 학파 the school of Epicurus / 헤겔 학파의 철학 the Hegelian school of philosophy / 학파를 세우다 found a school / 두 학파로 갈라지다 be divided into two different schools

학풍 學風 academic traditions [features]; 〈교풍〉 school character ♦ 학풍을 세우다 set up the character of a school; establish academic traditions

학형 學兄 〈학우간에〉 you; 〈편지에서〉 Mr. ...

학회 學會 a learned society; an academic society; an institute; an academy
♦ 학회에서 연구 논문을 발표하다 read a paper at a meeting of the association [society]
■ **한국 영어 영문—** the English Literary Society of Korea **한글—** the Korean Language (Research) Society

한 1 〈하나의〉 one; a (single)
♦ 맥주 한 병 a bottle of beer / 밥 한 그릇 a bowl of boiled rice
2 〈같은〉 the same
♦ 한 하숙에 in the same boarding house
3 〈약〉 about; some; nearly
♦ 한 10킬로미터 about [some] ten kilometers / 한 열흘 about ten days
▶ 한 20명이 그 사고로 다쳤다 About twenty persons were injured in the accident.
4 〈온통〉 whole; entire; all
♦ 한 군(郡)을 차지하다 possess the whole county

한 恨 〈원한〉 a bitter [an ill] feeling; a grudge; a spite; a resentment; 〈한탄〉 a regret; a regrettable matter; a discontent; an unsatisfied desire; 〈증오〉 (a) hatred; hate; rancor; 〈적의〉 (an) enmity
♦ 천추의 한 a lasting regret / 한이 많다[없다] have much [nothing] to regret / 한을 품다 bear [cherish, nurse] sb a grudge; have a grudge [rancor] against sb / 한을 풀다 vent one's spite; satisfy [wreak] one's grudge; avenge [revenge] oneself 《on》 / 아무에 대한 한이 골수에 사무치다 have a deep-rooted grudge against sb
▶ 그 왕은 한 많은 일생을 보냈다 The king led a life full of tears and regrets.
▶ 그는 많은 사람의 한을 샀다 He incurred enmity from many people. ⇌ He invited the rancor of many people.
▶ 언젠가 이 한을 풀고야 말겠다 I will revenge myself upon you some day or other.

한 限 1 〈한계〉 a limit; limits; bounds; an end
♦ 한이 있는 limited; restricted; finite
▶ 인간의 힘에는 한이 있다 There is a limit to man's power [strength].
▶ 사람의 욕심에는 한이 없다 Avarice knows no bounds [limits].
▶ 위를 쳐다보면 한이 없다 Don't compare yourself with those above you.
2 〈범위 내〉 as [so] far as; as long as
♦ 가능한 한 as far [much] as possible / 사정이 허락하는 한 so far as circumstances permit / 달리 규정이 없는 한 unless otherwise provided
▶ 내가 살아 있는 한 네 마음대로는 못한다 So

long as I live, I won't let you have your own way.
▶내가 아는 한 그렇지 않다 Not that I know of.
3 〈기한〉 a term; a time limit; a period
▶세금은 이달 25일 한 납부할 것 The tax must be paid not later than the 25th of this month.
▶통용 기한 당일 한 〈표 등의 표시〉 Available on the day of issue only.
한 漢 〈중국의 옛 왕조〉 Han
한- 1 〈큰〉 large; big; great
♦한길 a main [broad] street [road] / 한시름 a big worry; a great anxiety
2 〈한창〉 the peak; right [just] in the middle (of); midmost (of)
♦한복판 the middle; the center / 한낮 midday; high noon / 한여름 midsummer / 한겨울 midwinter; the depth of winter
한가 閑暇 leisure; leisure [spare] time; time to spare
―**한가하다** free; disengaged; 〈서술적〉 be at leisure; have spare time [time to spare]; have leisure
♦한가한 때에 when *one* is free [at leisure]; in *one's* leisure hours; at *one's* leisure / 한가히 in a leisurely way; with leisure / 한가한 세월을 보내다 live quietly; lead a quiet life
▶마침내 나는 한가한 몸이 되었다 Finally I became a man of leisure.
▶그는 한가할 때엔 낚시를 간다 He goes fishing in his leisure time.
한가닥 a line; a stripe; a streak
♦한가닥의 광명 a thread of light / 한가닥의 희망 a ray [flash] of hope
▶그녀는 한가닥의 희망을 품고 있었다 She clung to her last hope.
▶환자는 아직 한가닥의 희망은 있다 There is still a ray of hope of the patient's recovery.
한가롭다 閑暇 free
▶오후는 추리 소설을 읽으며 한가로이 지냈다 I whiled away the afternoon by reading a detective novel.
한가운데 the middle; the center; the heart
♦상업지구의 한가운데에 in the heart of the business district / 과녁의 한가운데에 맞다 hit the target right in the center / 머리를 한가운데서 가르다 part *one's* hair in the middle / 방 한가운데에 눕다 lie right in the middle of the room
한가위 the Korean Thanksgiving Day ⇨ 추석
한가을 1 〈가을철〉 the depth [dead] of autumn; 〈추수기〉 the busy harvest time
2 〈가을 내내〉 the whole autumn; all autumn through
한가지 1 〈한 종류〉 a kind; 〈일〉 one thing
▶벼는 풀의 한가지다 The rice plant is a kind of grass.
▶그것도 한가지 방법이다 That's a good idea, as far as it goes.
▶이것 한가지만 보아도 그의 품행을 알 수 있다 This one instance is enough to show his moral character.
2 〈마찬가지〉 (one and) the same thing
▶그는 늘 한가지 말만 되풀이한다 He always repeats the same thing (over and over again).
▶영과 혼은 결국 한가지다 The spirit and the soul are one and the same after all.
한갓 only; merely; simply; solely; alone
▶그것은 한갓 시간 문제에 지나지 않는다 It is merely a question of time.
▶나는 한갓 장사꾼에 지나지 않는다 I am a mere tradesman.
▶그것은 한갓 아이들한테만이 아니라 부모에게도 중요한 일이다 It is important not only for children but also for their parents.
한갓지다 quiet; tranquil; restful; peaceful; leisurely ♦한갓진 시골 생활 peaceful [quiet] country life
한개 一個 one; a piece
♦사과 한개 an apple / 비누 한개 a cake of soap / 한개에 100원 one hundred won apiece [each] / 한개씩 one by one / 계란을 한개 얼마에 팔다 sell eggs by the piece
한거 閑居 a quiet [secluded, retired] life; a leisurely [an idle] life
▶소인 한거 위불선(爲不善) (속담) The devil finds mischief for idle hands to do.
―**한거하다** live in seclusion [retirement]; lead a retired life; live in leisure
한걱정 a great anxiety ⇨ 한시름
한걸음 a step
♦한걸음 한걸음 step by step / 한걸음 앞으로 나오다[물러서다] take a step forward [backward] / 한걸음 앞서가다 go a step ahead (of *sb*); leave a bit earlier
▶한걸음 차이로 그녀를 못 만났다 I missed her by a minute.
▶한걸음 먼저 떠나겠습니다 I'm going to leave a little before you.
▶천릿길도 한걸음부터 (속담) A journey of a thousand miles starts with but a single step.
▶피곤해서 한걸음도 더 못 걷겠다 I'm so tired (that) I cannot walk a step farther [another step].
한걸음에 at [on] a stretch; in a single spell; without rest
한겨울 (in) the depth [dead] of winter; (in) midwinter
한결 〈눈에 띄게〉 conspicuously; noticeably; markedly; remarkably; 〈한층〉 more; much [still] more; 〈특히〉 especially; particularly
♦한결 좋은 물건 a much [far] better article / 한결 돋보이다 stand out conspicuously
▶그녀는 한결 예뻐 보였다 She looked more beautiful than ever.
▶동생이 언니보다 인물이 한결 낫다 The younger sister is far [decidedly] more beautiful than her elder sister.
▶이것이 저것보다 한결 낫다 This is much better than that.
▶단풍이 비를 맞으니 한결 아름답다 Rain lends [adds] a special charm to the red-tinted autumnal leaves.
▶고치니까 보기가 한결 낫다 The change makes it look much nicer.
한결같다 constant; unchanging; consistent
♦한결같은 우정 constant [unwavering] friendship / 한결같은 사랑 steadfast love / 한

결같은 태도 a consistent attitude
한결같이 1 〈변함없이〉 constantly; invariably; as ever; 〈시종일관〉 consistently
♦한결같이 사랑하다 love *sb* as ever
▶그녀는 한결같이 매일 아침 6시에 일어난다 She gets up at six every morning.
▶우리는 한결같이 그것에 반대했다 We were against it first, last and all the time.
2 〈모두〉 all alike; every one of them; one and all
▶그 소식을 듣고 한결같이 기뻐한 것은 아니다 Not all of us [them] rejoyced at the news.
▶김선생의 딸들은 한결같이 수재다 Mr. Kim's daughters are all bright.
▶회원들은 한결같이 반대했다 The members opposed unanimously.
한겻 a quarter of a day ♦한겻일 a quarter-day('s) work
한계 限界 a boundary; bounds; limits; a limit; limitation(s); a margin
♦인간 능력의 한계 the limitations of human faculty / 한계를 두다 place a limit (upon); set limits (to) / 한계를 정하다 fix the limit / 한계를 넘다 pass [exceed] the limit (of); overstep the boundary (of)
▶나이가 들면 자기 능력의 한계를 알게 된다 As you grow older, you'll learn the limits of your ability [know your limitations].
━가격 a ceiling price ━생산력 marginal productivity ━속도 critical speed ━효용 marginal utility
한계점 限界點 the critical point; the uppermost limit ♦한계점에 도달하다 reach [be at] the top [uppermost limit]
한고비 a crisis ⇨ 고비¹
한교 韓僑 Korean residents abroad; overseas Koreans
한구석 a corner; a nook
♦한구석에 in a corner (of); in a nook (of) / 방 한구석에 앉다 sit in the corner of the room
▶그녀는 부엌 한구석에 소화기를 놔두고 있다 She keeps a fire extinguisher in a corner of the kitchen.
한국 寒菊 [植] a winter chrysanthemum
한국 韓國 Korea; 〈공식명〉 the Republic of Korea (略 ROK)
▶두 개의 한국 two Koreas / 한국의 Korean / 한국 사정에 밝다 be well-informed on Korean affairs
━말 ⇨ 한국어 ━문제 Korean problems ━사람 a Korean ━요리 Korean dishes ━전쟁 the Korean War ━제품 Korean products; products made in Korea [of Korean make]
한국과학기술원 韓國科學技術院 the Korea Advanced Institute of Science and Technology (略 KAIST)
한국무역협회 韓國貿易協會 the Korea International Trade Association (略 KITA)
한국어 韓國語 Korean; the Korean language
▶그것을 한국어로 뭐라고 합니까? What do you call it in Korean?
한국은행 韓國銀行 the Bank of Korea
━권 a Bank of Korea note ━법 [法] the Bank of Korea Act ━총재 the Governor of the Bank of Korea
한군데 1 〈한 곳〉 one place [spot]
♦책을 한군데에 쌓다 pile the books up in one spot
▶한군데도 탓할 데가 없다 There is not a point open to criticism.
▶한군데에 모이지 마시오 Don't crowd around one place.
2 〈같은 장소〉 the same place [spot]
▶그들은 일요일마다 한군데서 만나곤 했다 They used to meet together at the same place on every Sunday.
▶그들은 모두 한군데서 왔다 All of them came from the same part of the country.
한근심 a big worry ⇨ 한시름
한글 *Hangŭl*; the Korean alphabet
━날 *Hangŭl* Day ━맞춤법 *Hangŭl* orthography; the rules [system] of the spelling of *Hangŭl* ━전용 exclusive use of *Hangŭl*
한기 寒氣 〈추위〉 cold weather; 〈오한〉 a chill; chilliness ♦한기가 나다 feel a chill; feel chilly; have a chill
한길¹ 〈큰 길〉 a main [broad] street [road]; a high road; a street; a thoroughfare
♦한길에서 in the open street / 한길 복판에서 in the middle of the street / 한길에서 놀다 play on the street / 한길을 막다 block the street [road] / 한길에 나앉다 〈집을 잃다〉 become [be rendered] homeless; be thrown on the streets
한길² 〈깊이〉 one [a] fathom
▶그 웅덩이는 깊이가 한길이다 The pond is a fathom deep.
한꺼번에 1 〈한번에〉 at once; at a [one] time; 〈일거에〉 at a stretch [sitting, stroke, breath]; 〈일제히〉 all together; 〈동시에〉 simultaneously; at the same time
▶자, 한꺼번에 덤벼 봐 Come on all at a time.
▶한꺼번에 여러 가지 일에 손대지 마라 Don't have too many irons in the fire.
▶한꺼번에 두 가지 일은 할 수 없다 You can't do two things at the same time.
▶네 편지와 소포가 한꺼번에 도착했다 Your letter and package reached here at the same time.
2 〈한데 몰아서〉 altogether; in the lump [gross]
▶모두 한꺼번에 치면 얼마 듭니까? How much does it cost altogether?
▶나는 두 달치 급료를 한꺼번에 받았다 I received two months' pay in a lump.
한껏 1 〈힘껏〉 with all *one's* might; with might and main; to the best of *one's* ability; to the utmost (of *one's* power)
▶그는 한껏 일했다 He worked as hard as he could [possible].
▶저는 한껏 했습니다 I did my best.
2 〈한도껏〉 to the utmost limit; to the maximum
♦끈을 한껏 잡아당기다 draw a string out to its (full) length
3 〈실컷〉 to *one's* heart's content; to the full; to the fullest measure

한끝 **1** 〈한쪽 끝〉 an edge; one end ♦ 밧줄의 한 끝을 잡다 hold one end of a rope
2 〈맨끝〉 the (tail) end; the tip; the extremity ♦ 하늘 한끝 the (furthest) end of the sky / 줄의 한끝에 서다 stand at the end of a queue

한끼 a [one] meal ♦ 한끼를 거르다 miss a meal / 하루에 한끼밖에 못 먹다 have only one meal a day / 한끼는 빵을 먹다 take bread at one of the meals

한나절 half a day; a half day
▶ 그들은 한나절에 그 빌딩을 허물었다 They demolished the building in half a day.
▶ 어제는 한나절을 독서로 보냈다 I spent half of yesterday reading.

한낮 noontide; high noon; midday; 〈백주〉 broad daylight
♦ 한낮에 at noon; at midday; at high noon
▶ 우리는 한낮의 햇살을 받으면서 걸었다 We walked in the daytime sun.

한낱 mere; merely; only
▶ 그것은 한낱 핑계에 지나지 않는다 It is a mere excuse. ⇒ That's an excuse, and nothing more.

한눈 **1** 〈한쪽 눈〉 one eye
♦ 한눈이 안보이다 be blind of [in] one eye / 한눈으로 겨냥하다 aim 《at *sth*》 with one eye
2 〈한번 보기〉 a look; a glance; a glimpse
♦ 한눈에 at a look; at a glance; on sight; 〈첫눈에〉 at first sight
▶ 그는 그녀에게 한눈에 반했다 He fell in love with her at first sight.

한눈팔다 look away [aside, off]; take *one*'s eyes off; look at something else
▶ 일할 때 한눈팔면 안된다 Don't look away from your work.
▶ 그는 한눈 한 번 안 팔고 일에 전념했다 He devoted himself [gave himself up] solely to his work.
▶ 한눈팔지 말고 걸어가거라 Don't walk along gazing around.
▶ 그는 한눈팔고 있다가 차에 치었다 He was looking the other way when he was hit by a car.

한니발 〈카르타고의 장군〉 Hannibal (247-183 B.C.)

한다한 distinguished; eminent; celebrated; respectable
♦ 한다한 학자 an eminent scholar / 한다한 집안 a respectable family; a distinguished family / 정계에서 한다하는 사람 a celebrity in the political world

한닥거리다 shake; move (to and fro) ♦ 이가 한닥거리다 a tooth loosens [becomes loose]

한닥이다 shake ⇨ 한닥거리다

한단몽 邯鄲夢 a short dream of human prosperity

한달음에 at a run; without a rest; straight through
▶ 거기는 한달음에 갈 수 있다 You can get there at a run.
▶ 한달음에 가서 가져 오겠다 I will run for it.

한담 閑談 a chat; an idle talk; a gossip
♦ 한담으로 시간을 보내다 chat the time away; pass *one*'s time in a quiet talk
─한담하다 gossip; have a casual talk; chat (with); have a chat [gossip] (with)

한대 寒帶 the frigid [frozen] zones; the arctic regions ■─동물 a polar [an arctic] animal ─식물 a polar [an arctic] plant ─지방 the cold latitudes

한댕거리다 dangle; swing; sway (to and fro)

한더위 fierce [violent] heat; the midsummer heat

한데¹ one place ⇨ 한군데

한데² 〈노천〉 the open (air); the outdoors
♦ 한데서 in the open (air); outdoors; out of doors
▶ 그들은 한데서 하룻밤을 보냈다 They passed a night in the open air.

한도 限度 a limit; limits; bounds
♦ 최대[최소] 한도까지 to the utmost [bottommost] limit; to the maximum [minimum] / …을 한도로 within the limit(s)... / 최소 한도의 비용으로 at a minimum of expense / 한도를 정하다 fix the limit(s); set a limit / 한도에 이르다 reach the limit / 한도를 넘다 pass [go beyond] the limit; go over the line
▶ 우리는 50만원 한도내에서 생활한다 We live within the limits [framework] of 500,000 won.
▶ 참는 데도 한도가 있다 My patience is worn out. ⇒ There is a limit to my patience.
▶ 모든 일엔 한도가 있는 법이다 There is a limit to [in] everything. ⇒ Everything has its limit.
▶ 경비는 월 30만원을 한도로 한다 The monthly expenditure is limited to 300,000 won.
■ 신용─ a credit limit

한독 韓獨 Korea and German ♦ 한독의 Korean-German

한돌림 〈차례의〉 one [a] round; 〈둘레의〉 one circumference ▶ 술이 한돌림 돌자 주인이 의례적 인사말을 했다 When the wine had passed round, the host gave a formal address.

한동기 ─同氣 full [whole] brothers [sisters]; brothers [sisters] of the same venter [mother] ■─간(間) full [whole] brotherhood [sisterhood]

한동생 ─同生 full [whole] brothers [sisters] ⇨ 한동기

한동안 (for) quite some time; a while; (for) a good while
♦ 그후 한동안 for some time since / 한동안 있다가 after a long stretch [period] of time / 한동안 번영하다 flourish for a while / 한동안 머무르다 (I) stay quite a while
▶ 한동안 소식을 드리지 못해 죄송합니다 Excuse me for not contacting you for a long time. ⇒ I must apologize for my long silence.

한되다 恨─ regret; be sorry for; be regretful; 〈사물이 주어〉 be a matter for regret
▶ 나는 젊어서 공부 못한 것이 한된다 I regret that I could not study while young.
▶ 모르는 것이 한된다 I wish I knew.

한두 one or two; a few

♦한두 번 once or twice / 한두 해 one [a] year or two / 한두 사람 one or two persons / 한두 번이 아니고 again and again; time [once] and again; several times
▶네게 한두 가지 일러 주어야겠다 I'll tell you a thing or two.
한둘 one or two ♦사람이 한둘 one or two persons
한드랑거리다 dangle; swing; sway (to and fro) ▶나뭇잎이 바람에 한드랑거린다 Leaves are swaying in the wind.
한들거리다 sway; shake; tremble; swing; 〈불꽃이〉 flicker; flare
♦한들거리는 촛불 a flickering [wavering] candlelight
▶코스모스가 바람에 한들거리고 있다 The cosmoses are trembling in the wind.
▶촛불이 바람에 한들거렸다 The candlelights fluttered [quivered] in the breeze.
한들한들 swingingly; waveringly; swayingly; flickeringly
한때 〈한 시기〉 a time; 〈잠시〉 a while; a moment; a spell; 〈부사적〉 for a time; for a while; for a moment; 〈과거의〉 once; at one time
♦한때의 transient; transitory; temporary; passing; short-lived
▶그들은 한때의 쾌락만을 추구하고 있다 They are seeking only temporary pleasures.
▶그의 장사는 한때 잘 되었다 His business flourished for a time.
▶미모도 한때다 Beauty is evanescent. ⇌ Beauty lasts only for a time.
▶그의 인기도 한때 뿐이었다 He enjoyed a mere mushroom [transient] popularity.
▶우리는 저녁 식사후 즐거운 한때를 가졌다 We had a happy time after the evening meal.
▶크리스마스 이브에 나는 가족과 즐거운 한때를 보냈다 I had a good time with my family on Christmas Eve.
▶그 가방은 한때 유행했다 The bag was once in fashion.
▶그녀도 한때는 행복했었다 She had happy days at some time in her life.
한란 寒暖 heat and cold; 〈온도〉 temperature
♦한란의 차 difference in temperature
■―계 ⇨ 온도계
한랭 寒冷 cold; coldness; chilliness ―한랭하다 cold; chilly ■―전선 〔氣〕 a cold [polar] front
한량 限量 〈분량〉a limited [fixed] quantity; 〈한정〉 a limit; limits; bounds
♦한량없는 unlimited; limitless; boundless; endless / 한량없이 unlimitedly; boundlessly; endlessly; infinitely
▶사람의 욕심에는 한량이 없다 There is no limit to man's desire. ⇌ Avarice knows no bounds.
▶사막은 한량없이 계속되었다 The desert reached to the horizon.
한러 韓― Korea and Russia ♦한러의 Korean-Russian ■―관계 Korean-Russian relations ―국경 the Korean-Russian border
한류 寒流 a cold current
한마디 a (single) word; one word

♦한마디(만) 더 one more word / 한마디로 말해서 in a word; in short / 한마디 말도 없이 without saying a word / 한마디도 하지 않다 do not utter a word; say nothing
▶한마디 말씀드리겠습니다 I should like to say a word [to make a remark].
▶청중은 한마디도 놓치지 않으려고 귀를 기울이고 있었다 The audience were all ears so as not to miss a single word.
▶그는 인사 한마디 없이 떠났다 He left us without a single word of greeting.
―한마디하다 speak [say] a word 《about》; pass a remark
▶당신이 한마디해 주시면 그는 승낙할 것입니다 He will consent at a word from you.
한마음 one mind; a whole mind
♦한마음으로 with one accord / 한마음이 되어 일하다 act in concert 《with》; work in close cooperation
▶그들은 한마음 한뜻이다 They have one mind between [among] them.
한명 限命 the appointed limit of life; the destined duration of life
한모금 a draft; a draught; 〈약간〉 a drop; 〈담배의〉 a draw; a pull ♦한모금의 물 a draught of water / 한모금에 at a [one] draft
한목 〈한가번에〉 in the lump; in one lot; in one sum; by the gross
♦물건을 한목에 사다 buy things in the mass / 돈을 한목에 치르다 pay in a lump sum
한몫 a share; one's portion
♦한몫 끼다[들다, 타다] have a share 《in》; take one's share 《in》; share in 《the profits》; take part [participate] in / 한몫 잡다 make a profit 《from》; make money / 한몫 내다 pay one's share; take [bear] one's share of expense; 《俗》 chip in / 한몫 주다 give a share 《to》; 《美俗》 cut sb in 《on》
▶그는 그 계획에 한몫 끼었다 He has played a role in the scheme.
한문 漢文 Chinese writing
■―자 a Chinese character [ideograph] ―학 Chinese classics [(classical) literature]; 〈한문연구〉 study of Chinese classics ―학자 a scholar of Chinese classics
한물 〈채소·과일·어류 등의〉 the season; the best time 《for》; 〈최성기〉 the prime
♦한물 지다 be [come] in season; be at 《its》 best / 한물 가다 be out of season; be past 《its》 season
▶그 작가의 인기도 머지않아 한물 갈 것이다 The popularity of the writer will soon be on the wane.
한미 韓美 Korea and America
♦한미의 Korean-American
■―관계 the relations between Korea and the United States; Korean-American relations ―상호 방위 협정 the ROK-U.S. Mutual Defense Agreement ―연합군 사령부 the ROK-U.S. Combined Forces Command 《略 CFC》 ―원자력 협정 the ROK-U.S. Atomic Energy Agreement ―재단 the American-Korean Foundation 《略 A.K.F.》 ―행정 협정 the ROK-U.S. Administrative Agreement; the

ROK-U.S. Status-of-Forces Agreement; the ROK-U.S. Agreement on Status-of-Forces in Korea —협회 the Korean-American Association

한밑천 a sizable amount of capital ◆ 한밑천 잡다 make [amass] a (sizable) fortune

한바닥 the central part; the heart; the center ◆ 시장 한바닥 (in) the center [heart] of a market(place)

한바퀴 one [a] round; a turn; 〈경기장의〉 a lap
◆ 한바퀴 돌다 take a turn; go round; make a tour (of); 〈담당 구역을〉 go one's rounds / 도시의 상공을 한바퀴 돌다 circle over a town / 세계를 한바퀴 돌다 travel round the world
▶ 〔會話〕「차로 시내를 한바퀴 돌까요?」「아주 좋지요」 "How about driving around the city?" "That sounds great."
▶ 그들은 손을 맞잡고 연못을 한바퀴 돌았다 They walked around the pond, hand in hand.
▶ 신년 인사로 한바퀴 돌까 합니다 I am going to make a round of New Year's calls.

한바탕 a round; a bout
◆ 한바탕 연설하다 make a harangue / 한바탕 울다 have a good cry; cry for a spell / 한바탕 싸우다 make a (hard) fight (with)
▶ 아버지는 아들을 한바탕 야단쳤다 Father gave his son a good scolding.
▶ 눈이 한바탕 왔다 It snowed heavily for some time.

한반도 韓半島 the Korean peninsula
◆ 한반도에서의 평화와 안정의 유지 the maintenance of peace and stability on the Korean peninsula / 한반도에서의 긴장을 완화시키다 defuse tension on the Korean peninsula
▶ 대한민국은 한반도에서의 유일한 합법적 국가다 The Republic of Korea is the sole legitimate state on the Korean peninsula.

한발 a [one] step
◆ 한발 한발 step by step; gradually; by (slow) degrees
▶ 한발 앞으로 나오시오[뒤로 물러서시오] Take a step forward [backward].
▶ 나는 그보다 한발 앞서갔다 I went a step ahead of him.
▶ 우리는 한발 늦어 기차를 놓쳤다 We missed the train by a second.

한발 旱魃 〈가뭄〉 a (long) drought; (a long spell of) dry weather; want of rain
◆ 한발이 계속되다 have a long drought
▶ 우리 나라는 한발을 겪고 있다 Our country is suffering from want of rain.
▶ 계속되는 한발로 작물이 피해를 입었다 Crops have been damaged because of the long drought.
■—대책 measures against a drought —피해 damage from a drought

한발짝 a [one] step ⇨ 한발
▶ 온종일 한발짝도 밖에 나가지 않았다 I kept indoors all day long.

한밤중 —中 midnight; the middle [dead] of the night
◆ 한밤중에 at midnight; at dead of night; in the dead [middle, depth] of the night
▶ 우리는 한밤중까지 안 자고 얘기했다 We stayed up and chatted far into the night [until the middle of the night].

한방 —放 a (single) shot
▶ 밤의 어둠 속에서 한방의 총성이 들렸다 I heard a shot [the report of a gun] in the darkness of night.
▶ 사냥꾼은 한방에 곰을 잡았다 The hunter killed a bear with a single shot.

한방 —房 a [one] room; the same room; 〈전체〉 the whole room
◆ 한방에 거처하다 live in the same room with sb; share a room with sb
▶ 사람들이 한방 가득했다 The room was packed with people.

한방 韓方 ■—약 a herb medicine —의(醫) a doctor of Oriental medicine; a herbalist; a herb doctor

한방울 a drop ◆ 한방울씩 drop by drop

한배 1 〈동물〉 a litter (of pigs); a brood (of chickens) ◆ 한배의 강아지 a litter of puppies / 한배의 병아리 a brood of chickens
2 〈사람〉 ◆ 한배 형제 brothers of the same venter [mother]

한번 —番 once; a [one] time
▶ 나는 단 한번에 시험에 합격했다 I succeeded in an examination at my first attempt.
▶ 한번 엎지른 물은 주워 담지 못한다 (속담) It is of no use crying over spilt milk. ⇒ What is done cannot be undone.
▶ 한번만 보면 된다 One look is enough.
▶ 내가 한번 해보겠다 I will have a go at it.
▶ 그는 한번 만난 적이 있다 I have met him once.
▶ 나는 한번 말하면 알아듣는다 A word is enough for me to understand it.
▶ 부디 곧 한번 놀러 오십시오 Please come and see us soon.
▶ 너의 어릴적 사진을 한번 보고 싶다 I'd like to take a look at a picture of you when you were a child.
▶ 그런 일은 한번도 해본 적이 없다 I have never done such a thing.
▶ 그곳은 한번쯤 가볼 만한 곳이다 The place is worth a visit.

한벌 〈의복〉 a suit; 〈도구〉 a set; a suite
◆ 가구 한벌 a set [suite] of furniture / 여름옷 한벌 a suit of summer clothes; a summer suit / 식기 한벌 a table service

한복 韓服 Korean clothes [dress, costume]
◆ 한복을 입은 in Korean clothes [dress]
▶ 소녀는 한복을 입고 있다 The girl is in Korean clothes.

한복판 the middle; the center; the heart ⇨ 한가운데
◆ 한복판의 middle; central / 서울 한복판에 right in the heart [center] of Seoul / 길 한복판에 in the middle of the road
▶ 그 사수는 과녁 한복판을 맞혔다 The marksman hit the target right [fairly] in the center.
▶ 그 학교는 마을 한복판에 있다 The school is situated in the middle [center] of town.

한불 韓佛 Korea and France ■—사전 a Korean-French dictionary

한사 寒士 a poor [penniless] scholar
한사람 one person; one man
 ♦ 한사람씩 one by one; one at a time; one after another
 ▶ 한사람씩 방으로 들어오십시오 Please enter the room one by one.
한사리 the flood [spring] tide; the spring(s)
한사코 限死— to the death; at the risk of *one's* life; for [with] *one's* life; desperately, frantically; (口) like hell
 ♦ 한사코 반대하다 be dead set against; persist in *one's* opposition / 한사코 버티다 persist to the bitter end; hold on to it through thick and thin
 ▶ 우리는 한사코 싸웠다 We fought at the risk of our lives.
 ▶ 그녀는 한사코 그 일을 맡겠다고 한다 She insists on accepting the work.
한산 閑散 dullness; inactivity; slackness; leisure
 —한산하다 dull; inactive《market》; slack;〈한가하다〉leisurely; quiet
 ♦ 한산한 시장 a dull [flat] market
 ▶ 이 가게는 이 시간엔 한산하다 It is the slack hour now in this store.
 ▶ 거리가 이맘때는 한산하다 The traffic is light about this time.
한살〈나이〉one year of age ▶ 그는 나보다 한 살 위다[아래다] He is my senior [junior] by one year.
한살되다 1〈물건이〉be united; be incorporated **2**〈남녀가〉become one flesh; become man and wife
한색 寒色 a cold color
한서 寒暑 heat and cold;〈온도〉temperature
 ▶ 그 지방은 한서의 차가 심하다 The heat and cold are extreme in that part of the country. ⇌ There are great extremes [changes] of temperature in that region.
한서 漢書 a Chinese book; (총칭) Chinese classics [literature]
한선 汗腺〔땀샘〕〔解〕a sweat gland
한세상 —世上 **1**〈한평생〉a lifetime; *one's* (whole) life;〈부사적〉all [throughout] *one's* life; through life; as long as *one* lives
 ▶ 그는 한세상을 편안히 지냈다 He lived comfortably to the end of his life.
 ▶ 울며 살아도 한세상이요, 웃으며 살아도 한세상이다 Life is life, whether spent in tears or laughter.
 2〈한때〉*one's* bright [best] days; the heyday of *one's* life
 ▶ 한세상 만나다 have *one's* day
한속〈한마음〉one mind
 ♦ 한속이다 be of a [one] mind / 한속이 되다 act [be] in collusion《with》; (美俗) go (in) cahoots《with》
한손 one hand
 ♦ 한손만 사용하는 one-handed / 한손에 하나씩 one to each hand / 한손을 호주머니에 찔러넣다 thrust [stick] *one's* hand into *one's* pocket
 ▶ 그 신사는 한손에는 지팡이, 한손에는 모자를 들고 있었다 The gentleman held a stick in one hand and a hat in the other.

한손놓다〈(일)이〉come to an end for the time being;〈장편이〉be completed
 ▶ 일은 일단 이것으로 한손놓았다 This has brought the job to a pause for the present.
한수 —手〈바둑・장기의〉a move
 ♦ 한수 두다 make a move;〈한판〉play a game of《*paduk*》
 ▶ 그가 나보다 한수 위다 He is a cut above me.
한술 a spoonful《of food》;〈적은 음식〉a bite [morsel]《of food》
 ♦ 한술 뜨다 take a spoonful of food; have a bite / 수프를 한술 뜨다 spoon up *one's* soup
 ▶ 그는 한술 더 뜬다 (비유) He is superior in cunning [cleverness].
 ▶ 점심 한술 뜨자 Let's take a spot of lunch.
한숨 1〈호흡〉a breath;〈휴식〉a pause; a relief
 ♦ 한숨에 at a breath [stroke]; (all) in a breath; at a stretch / 한숨 돌리고 나서 after a pause / 한숨 돌리다 pause for breath; take [have] a rest; feel relieved / 한숨 자다 have [take] a nap; sleep a wink / 한숨 돌릴 여유를 찾다 seek a breather (in the cold war)
 ▶ 한숨 돌리고 다시 시작하자 Let's have a little rest, and start again.
 2〈탄식〉a sigh; a deep [long] breath
 ♦ 한숨을 쉬면서 with a (deep) sigh; sighingly / 한숨짓다[쉬다] sigh; heave [draw] a sigh
 ▶ 그녀는 한숨을 쉬며 슬퍼했다 She sighed out her grief.
한시 —時 ♦ 한시도 잊지 않다 do not forget (it) even for a moment; keep *sth* in mind all the time
 ▶ 그는 책을 한시도 손에서 떼지 않는다 He always carries books about [on] him.
한시 漢詩 a Chinese poem; (총칭) Chinese poetry
한시름 a (big) worry; an [a great] anxiety
 ♦ 한시름 놓다 have peace of mind [feel relieved] for a while
 ▶ 모두들 한시름 놓았다 Everybody gave a sigh of relief.
한식 寒食 〔民俗〕 the "Cold Food" day (which falls on the 105th day after the winter solstice); *hansik*
한식 韓式 Korean style ■ —집 a Korean-style house
한식 韓食 Korean-style food; a Korean meal
한심하다 寒心— 〈가엾고 딱하다〉pitiful; pitiable; wretched; miserable; sorry;〈통탄스럽다〉lamentable; deplorable; grievous; woeful
 ♦ 한심한 짓을 하다 do a shameful thing
 ▶ 한심한 녀석 What a wretched fellow! ⇌ You wretch!
 ▶ 그런 걸 못하다니 참으로 한심하구나 It is a great pity that you can't do such a thing.
 ▶ 내 신세가 정말 한심하다 Ah me! How miserable I am.
 ▶ 사회 기강이 이토록 문란하다니 참으로 한심하다 It is deplorable that the public morals should be so corrupt.
한쌍 —雙 a pair; a couple ♦ 잘 어울리는 한쌍의 부부 a well-matched pair [couple]
한아름 an armful《of》♦ 한아름의 볏짚 an

한약 薬薬 a herb medicine=한방(～약)
■一국[방] a dispensary of herbal medicine
한어 漢語 a Chinese word; a Chinese expression
한없다 限— unlimited; limitless; boundless; infinite; endless
♦한없는 바다 the boundless ocean / 한없는 기쁨 a limitless [boundless] joy / 한없이 unlimitedly; boundlessly; without limit [end]; endlessly; infinitely / 수가 한없이 많다 be infinite in number / 아들을 한없이 사랑하다 love one's son ever so much
▶그 사막은 한없이 펼쳐져 있었다 The desert reached to the horizon.
▶그녀는 딸을 한없이 신뢰하고 있다 She has complete trust in her daughter.
한여름 1〈한창〉 midsummer; high [full] summer ♦한여름의 midsummer / 한여름 더위 midsummer heat / 한여름에 in midsummer; in [at] the height of summer
2〈여름 내내〉 the whole summer; all the summer (long, through)
한역 韓譯 translation into Korean ♦영문 한역법 how to translate English into Korean —한역하다 translate [put] into Korean
한영 韓英 Korea and Britain ♦한영의 Korean-English ■一사전 a Korean-English dictionary
한옆 the [one] side ♦한옆으로 밀다(비키다) push [step] aside
한옥 韓屋 a Korean-style house
한움큼 a handful (of); a fistful; a grasp
♦한움큼 쥐다 make a grip (of)
한월 寒月 a winter moon
한은 韓銀 the Bank of Korea ⇨ 한국은행
한음 漢音 Han pronunciation of Chinese characters
한의사 韓醫師 a doctor of Oriental medicine; a herbalist; a herb doctor
한의학 韓醫學 Oriental medicine [medical science]
한인 閑人 a man of leisure; a leisured man; an idler ■一한담(閑談) idle thoughts of an idle fellow
한일 韓日 Korea and Japan ♦한일의 Korean-Japanese
■一각료회담 the Korea-Japan Ministerial Conference —사전 a Korean-Japanese dictionary —의원연맹 the Korea-Japan Parliamentarians League —회담 the Korea-Japan talks; the Korean-Japanese Conference
한일자로 一字— in a straight line; in a bee line ♦입을 한일자로 다물다 firmly close one's lips
한입 a mouthful; a bite
♦한입에 at a [in one] mouthful / 사과를 한입 먹다 take a bite out of an apple
한자 漢字 a Chinese character [ideograph] (▶a Chinese letter로는 쓰지 않음)
♦중고교에서 가르치는 기초 한자 the basic Chinese characters to be taught at middle and high schools / 한자로 쓰다 write in Chinese characters
▶이름을 한자로 써주십시오 Please write your name in Chinese characters.
■一상용— the Chinese characters in common [daily] use ■—어 a word written in Chinese characters —제한 restriction on the use of Chinese characters —철폐 abolition of Chinese characters
한자동맹 —同盟 〔史〕 the Hanseatic League
한잔 —盞 1〈분량〉 a cup (of tea); a glass (of beer); a cupful; a glassful
▶차 한잔 더 드시겠습니까? Won't you take one more cup of tea?
2〈음주〉 a drink (of liquor)
♦한잔 내다 treat sb to drinks / 한잔 권하다 offer sb a glass of liquor
▶그는 한잔 들어가 얼큰하게 취했다 He was a little drunk. ⇌ He was tipsy.
▶그는 한잔만 마셔도 얼굴이 빨개진다 A single cup of wine makes him flushed.
▶그는 한잔 들어가면 말문이 열린다 Wine loosens his tongue.
—한잔하다 have [take] a drink
▶한잔하면서 이야기하자 Let's have a talk over our cups.
▶오늘밤 한잔하세 Let's have a drink tonight. ⇌ How about having a drink tonight?
▶가끔 한잔합니다 I enjoy a glass now and then.
▶그는 한잔하면 시비조가 된다 He gets quarrelsome in his cups.
한잠 a sleep; a snatch [wink] of sleep; a doze; 〈졸기〉 a nap
♦한잠 자다 get a sleep; sleep [have] a wink; take a nap / 한잠 들다 fall into a sleep / 한잠 푹 자다 have a sound [deep] sleep
▶나는 어젯밤 한잠도 못잤다 I could not get a wink of sleep last night.
한적 閑寂 quiet(ness); tranquility
—한적하다 quiet; tranquil; secluded
♦한적한 곳 a quiet [secluded] place / 한적하게 살다 live a retired life
한절 寒節 the cold season
한점 —點 〈조금〉 a speck; a dot; 〈바둑의〉 a stone; 〈조각〉 a piece (of)
♦고기 한점 a piece of (roast) meat / 한점 따다 score a point / 한점 놓다 put a stone (in advance)
▶하늘에는 구름 한점 없었다 There was not a speck of cloud in the sky.
한정 限定 limitation; qualification; 〔論〕 determination
—한정하다 limit; restrict; set limits to; qualify; 〔論〕 determine
♦한정된 limited; defined / 시일을 한정하다 put [set] a time limit (to) / 수가 한정되어 있다 be limited in number
▶우리 클럽의 회원수는 20명으로 한정되어 있다 Our club membership is restricted to twenty.
▶연설 시간은 10분으로 한정되어 있다 Speeches are limited to ten minutes.
■—가격 the ceiling price; the (price) ceiling —사〔文法〕 a definitive (word); a determinative; a determiner; 〔論〕 a determinant —상속 qualified acceptance of heritage —전쟁 (a)

limited war —치산(治産) quasi-incompetence —치산자 a quasi-incompetent (person) —판 a limited edition : 1,000부 한정판 a limited edition [publication] of 1,000 copies

한제 寒劑 a freezing mixture; a cryogen

한조각 a piece; a bit; a fragment
♦ 빵 한조각 a piece [slice] of bread

한족 韓族 the Korean race

한족 漢族 the Han race

한줄기 〈한가닥〉 a line; a stripe; a streak; 〈한바탕〉 (for) a time [while]; (for) a spell
♦ 한줄기의 빛 a streak of light / 소나기가 한줄기 쏟아지다 have a (spell of) shower
▶ 벽에 난 구멍에서 한줄기의 빛이 새어들고 있었다 A ray of light came through the gap in the wall.

한줌 a handful (of); a fistful; a lock (of)
▶ 사람은 한줌의 흙에 지나지 않는다 Man is but a lump of clay.

한중 寒中 midwinter ■—훈련 midwinter exercises [training]

한중 韓中 Korea and China
♦ 한중의 Korean-Chinese; Sino-Korean ■—국교 수립 establishment of diplomatic relations between Korea and China —무역 a Korean-Chinese trade —사전 a Korean-Chinese dictionary

한즉 〈그러한즉〉 if so; then; in that case

한증 汗蒸 a sweating (steam) bath —한증하다 take a sweating bath ■—막 a sweating bathroom: 한증막하다 be sweltering; be sultry

한지 韓紙 Korean paper (handmade from paper mulberry)

한직 閑職 an easy [a leisurely] post; a sinecure ♦ 한직에 있는 사람 a sinecurist / 한직으로 좌천되다 be relegated to a less important post

한집 〈한채〉 a house; 〈같은 집〉 the same house
♦ 한집에 살다 live together; share [live in] the same house 《with》

한집안 1 〈한가족〉 one's family [people]; (美) one's folks
♦ 한집안 식구처럼 대하다 treat sb as a member of one's family / 한집안이나 다름없다 be in close relation with each other
2 〈친척〉 one's relatives; a clan; the same family [clan]

한짝 〈외짝〉 one of a pair; the fellow [mate, pair] 《to, of》
▶ 장갑 한짝을 잃어버렸다 I've lost one of my gloves.
▶ 구두 한짝이 어디 갔지? Where is the fellow [pair] to this shoe?

한쪽 〈방향〉 a quarter; 〈양쪽 중의〉 one side; 〈다른쪽〉 the other side; 〈상대편〉 a party
♦ 계약의 한쪽 당사자 a party to the contract / 한쪽에 치우치다 be one-sided / 한쪽 귀가 먹다 lean to one side / 한쪽 귀가 먹다 be deaf in one ear / 한쪽 말만 듣다 hear (only) one side of the story

한차례 one round; a turn; once; a time; 〈부사적〉 for a time [while]; for a spell
♦ 한차례의 비 a rainfall / 한차례 씨름을 하다 have a round of wrestling

▶ 비가 한차례 내리다가 그쳤다 After a short spell of rain it cleared up.
▶ 그는 서류를 한차례 훑어본 뒤 다시 비서에게 넘겨주었다 After looking over the paper, he handed it back to his secretary.

한참 1 〈노정〉 the distance between two stages
2 〈한차례〉 a break; a rest; a pause; a spell
♦ 한참의 일 a spell [stretch] of work; a sitting
3 〈한동안〉 (for) a good while; for a (long) time [while]
♦ 한참 있다가 after a good while / (시간이) 한참 걸리다 take long; take a long time
▶ 자네 한참만일세 It is a long time since we met [I saw you last].

한창 〈절정〉 the height; the climax; the summit; the peak; the zenith; (in) prime; flower; bloom; 〈부사적〉 in the midst [middle, thick] of; at the height of
♦ 한창 일할 나이의 젊은이들 youths of working age / 한창 젊은 시절에 in the prime of youth; in one's days / 한창 더위에 in the heat of the day / 전쟁이 한창일 때에 in the midst of the war / (꽃이) 한창이다 be in full bloom / (나이가) 한창이다 be in the prime [noon] of life
▶ 사과 [딸기]가 한창이다 Apples [Strawberries] are (now) in (season).
▶ 지금이 한창 더울 때다 It is at its height [peak] of the hot season.
▶ 그 아이는 한창 먹을 나이다 The boy has keen appetite at his age.
▶ 이곳도 마침내 봄이 한창이다 Spring is really here at last.
▶ 바야흐로 단풍이 한창이다 The autumnal tints are now in all their glory.
▶ 여름에 더위가 한창일 때 소나기만큼 시원한 것은 없다 Nothing is as [so] refreshing as a shower in the heat [at the height] of the summer.
▶ 그는 폭풍우가 한창 휘몰아칠 때 밖으로 나갔다 At the height of [In the midst of] the storm, he went out.

한창때 〈청춘〉 the prime [spring] of life; the bloom of youth; 〈왕성한 때〉 one's palmy [best] days; heyday; 〈과일 등의〉 the season; the best time (for)
♦ 한창때의 여자 a woman in her bloom / 한창때를 지나다 be past one's prime; go to seed

한천 旱天 dry weather

한천 寒天 1 〈우무〉 agar(-agar); Chinese isinglass 2 〈추운 겨울철〉 cold weather
■—배양기 an agar culture medium

한철 one season

한촌 寒村 a poor [deserted] village; an out-of-the-way hamlet

한추위 〈한차례의 추위〉 a spell of cold weather; a cold snap; 〈큰 추위〉 (the) intense [severe, bitter] cold

한층 一層 1 〈건물의〉 one story
2 〈더욱〉 more; still [much] more; (all) the more
♦ 한층 힘드는 일 (much) harder work / 한층

더 조심하다 take all the more care / 한층 더 노력하다 make greater efforts
▶ 나는 홀로 남게 되자 슬픔이 한층 더했다 Left alone, I felt all the more sad.
▶ 그녀가 그 드레스를 입으니 한층 더 매력적이다 Her dress makes her all the more attractive.

한치 an inch; a *ch'i* (⇨ 치²) ◆한치 앞도 볼 수 없는 눈보라 a blinding blizzard [snowstorm]
▶ 한치의 땅도 양보할 수 없다 We shall never cede an inch of ground.

한칼 a single stroke of the sword
◆한칼에 베다 cut down with [at] one [single] stroke of the sword

한탄 恨歎 lamentation; deploring; regret
—**한탄하다** lament; deplore; sigh; regret; grieve
◆한탄할 lamentable; deplorable; regrettable / 일신의 불행을 한탄하다 bewail *one's* misfortune / 자식이 없음을 한탄하다 regret that *one* is childless / 정치의 부패를 한탄하다 deplore the corruption of politics / 친구의 죽음을 한탄하다 lament over [for] the death of *one's* friend
▶ 참으로 한탄할 일이다 It is really a matter for regret.
▶ 자기의 불운을 한탄해 봤자 아무 소용이 없다 It's no use lamenting one's misfortune.

한턱 an entertainment; a treat; a feast
◆한턱거리 something happy to make a treat out of / 한턱 내다 give *sb* a treat / 불고기[술]를 한턱 내다 treat *sb* to *pulgogi* [a drink] / 한턱 얻어먹다 be feasted [treated]
▶ 이번엔 내가 한턱 낼 차례다 It is my treat now.
—**한턱하다** entertain; treat; stand treat for (*one's* friend)
◆돌아가며 한턱하다 provide a round of entertainment

한테서 from ⇨ 에게서

한통속 fellow adherents [conspirators]; a party (to a plot); a ring; a gang
◆한통속이 되다 conspire (with); act in collusion (with); plot together; (美) go (into) cahoots (with) / 한통속이 되어 속이다 conspire together to cheat *sb*

한통치다 put [group] together ◆한통쳐서 taking all (things) together; altogether; in the lump [gross]

한파 寒波 a cold wave [snap]
▶ 서울과 중부 일원에 금년 겨울 최대의 한파가 내습했다 The biggest cold wave hit [swept] Seoul and the central districts.

한판 a [one] game; a round; a bout; 〈레슬링의〉 a turn ◆씨름을 한판 하다 have a bout at wrestling / 바둑을 한판 두다 have a game of *paduk*
◆최후의 한판은 톰과 존 사이에 벌어졌다 The last bout was held between Tom and John.
—**한판 승부** a contest of single round

한팔 〈한쪽 팔〉 one arm

한패 —牌 one of the (same) party; 〈공범자〉 an accomplice; 〈일당〉 a confederate; 〈한 동아리〉 a company; a party; a set; 〈악당의〉 a gang
◆3인조 강도의 한패 one of the gang of three robbers / 한패가 되다 join (others in *sth*); participate [take part] in *sth*; mix *oneself* (among)

한편 —便 1 〈한 쪽〉 one side; one way; 〈자기편〉 friend; an ally; *one's* side
◆한편에 치우치다 be one-sided / 길의 한편을 걷다 keep to one side of the road / 한편이 되다 〈게임에서〉 partner; pair (with) / 한편으로는… 다른 한편으로는… on the one hand [side]… on the other (hand [side])…
▶ 나는 자네와 한편일세 I stand your friend.
▶ 의사는 한편으로는 치료하고 한편으로는 연구하지 않으면 안된다 Doctors have to treat sick persons on one hand and study on the other.
2 〈…한 외에〉 in addition to; while; but (at the same time); 〈다소·조금〉 somewhat; in a way; a bit; 〈이야기는 바뀌어〉 in the meantime; meanwhile; on the other hand
▶ 그는 본업은 의사지만 한편 식물 연구도 했다 Although a physician by vocation, he was a botanist by avocation.

한평생 —平生 a lifetime; *one's* (whole) life; 〈부사적〉 all [throughout] *one's* life; for life; through life; to the end of *one's* life
◆한평생 잊지 못할 일 a memory for life / 한평생 독신으로 지내다 remain single through life / 한평생 편히 지내다 live comfortably to the end of *one's* life

한푼 a penny; a coin; a copper; a farthing
◆동전 한푼 a single penny; (even) a penny / 한푼도 없는 penniless / 한푼의 값어치도 없다 be not worth a farthing / 한푼없는 빈털터리가 되다 become penniless
▶ 한푼 줍쇼 〈구걸할 때〉 Tip [Spare] us a copper.
▶ 한푼도 깎아드리지 못하겠습니다 I won't take a cent less.
▶ 한푼을 아끼려다 천냥을 잃는다 Penny-wise and pound-foolish.
▶ 한푼을 아끼면 한푼을 번다 A penny saved is a penny earned.

한풀꺾이다 be dispirited; be discouraged [disheartened, downhearted]; be downcast [cast down, crestfallen]
▶ 추위도 한풀 꺾인 것 같다 The cold seems to have decreased in severity.
▶ 그 실패로 그의 열의가 한풀 꺾였다 The failure damped his enthusiasm.

한풀다 恨— attain *one's* cherished object; realize the desire of *one's* heart; have *one's* cherished hope [desire] fulfilled
◆한풀어 주다 fulfill *sb's* desire; gratify [satisfy] *sb's* desire

한풀이 恨— realizing *one's* heart's desire
—**한풀이하다** vent *one's* spite; satisfy *one's* grudge; avenge [revenge] *oneself*; pay off old scores

한풍 寒風 a cold [chilly, bleak] wind

한하다 限— 〈제한하다〉 limit (to); restrict (to); confine (*sth* to)
◆성인에 한한 영화 a movie for adults only / 이번에 한하여 for this time only; for this

once / 정당한 사유가 있는 경우에 한하여 provided that there is just reason for it
▶1인 1매에 한함 〈입장권에 적힌 문구〉 Admission for one person only.
▶학생에 한하여 입장 가 〈게시〉 No admission except to students.
▶회원은 40세 미만에 한한다 Membership is limited to those who are under forty.

한학 漢學 study of Chinese classics ◆한학의 대가 an authority on Chinese classics
■─자 a scholar of Chinese classics

한한사전 漢韓辭典 a dictionary [lexicon] of classical Chinese explained in Korean

한해 旱害 damage from a drought; a drought disaster ◆한해를 입다 suffer from a drought
─지구 a drought(-stricken) area

한해 寒害 cold-weather damage; damage from cold weather ◆농작물을 한해로부터 지키다 protect crops from being damaged by cold weather

한해살이 〔植〕 an annual [a yearly] plant

한호 韓濠 Korea and Australia
◆한호의 Korean-Australian

한화 韓貨 〈한국의 화폐〉 Korean money

할 割 percentage; percent
◆연 1할 2푼의 이자 〈at〉 12 percent interest per annum / 정가의 7할로 팔다 sell sth at 70 percent of the price / 3할 할인해서 팔다 sell sth at 30 percent discount
▶나는 연 1할의 이자로 돈을 빌렸다 I borrowed money at an interest of ten percent [at ten percent interest] per annum.
▶현금이면 1할 할인해 드립니다 We make ten percent discount for cash.

할거하다 割據─ hold one's own ground; each holds (his) own sphere of influence
▶그 시대에는 군웅이 할거하고 있었다 In those days there were a number of local military leaders [barons] competing with each other for power.

할근거리다 pant; gasp (for breath); breathe hard; wheeze; rattle

할기족족 with reproachful eyes; with a displeased look from the corner of one's eyes
◆할기족족 쳐다보다 glare; look daggers 《at》; scowl from the corner of one's eyes

할긋거리다 cast sidelong glances of disapproval; look sidelong 《at sb》 ⇨ 흘깃거리다

할당 割當 assignment; allotment; allocation; apportionment; quota; 〈부과〉 assessment; 〈배급〉 rationing
─할당하다 assign; allot; allocate; apportion; 〈부과하다〉 assess; 〈배급하다〉 ration
◆각자에게 할당하다 allot a share to each / 방을 할당하다 assign rooms 《to persons》/ 역을 할당하다 assign a role 《to each actor》/ 일을 할당하다 assign sb for a task; assign a task to sb / 주를 할당하다 allot shares
▶그는 자기에게 할당된 일을 끝내기 위해 전력을 다했다 He did his best to finish the work assigned to him.
■─금[액] allotment; 〈부과금〉 assessment
─량 a quota ─제 a quota system: 수출 할당제 the export quota system ─제한 quota restrictions

할듯할듯하다 look as if one is going [ready] to 《do》; be on the point of doing sth
◆일을 할듯할듯하면서 안 하다 look about to do the work but never do it
▶그는 계속 대답을 할듯할듯했지만 끝내 하지 않았다 He kept looking as if he were going to come up with an answer but then he never did.

할딱거리다 pant ⇨ 헐떡거리다

할똥말똥 half-heartedly
─할똥말똥하다 cannot decide to 《do》; hesitate to 《do》

할렐루야 hallelujah

할례 割禮 circumcision ◆할례를 하다 circumcise sb

할로겐 〔化〕 halogen ■─화합물 a halide; a halogenide

할리우드 Hollywood ◆할리우드 (영화 산업) 의 Hollywoodian

할말 1 〈해야 할 말〉 one's say; what one has to say; 〈주장〉 one's claim
▶할말은 해야 한다 You should say what you have to say.
▶할말 있으면 해봐라 Say your say.
▶별로 할말이 없다 I have no say in the matter.
▶사람에게는 누구나 할말이 있다 Each has his own claims.
2 〈이의〉 an objection; 〈불평〉 a complaint
◆할말이 있다 have an objection 《to, against》; have sth to complain of; be dissatisfied 《with》
▶너한테 할말이 있다 I have a bone to pick with you.

할머니 1 〈조모〉 a grandmother; a grandma; a granny ◆할머니의[같은] grandmotherly 《love》 **2** 〈늙은 여자의 존칭〉 an old woman; a granny

할멈 〈노파〉 an old woman; a granny; 〈하녀〉 an old maid

할미 〈할머니·할멈의 낮춤말〉 a grandma; an old woman

할미꽃 〔植〕 a pasqueflower; a windflower

할미새 〔鳥〕 a wagtail

할복 割腹 disembowelment ─할복하다 disembowel oneself ■─자살 suicide by disembowelment

할부 割賦 ◆차를 할부(제)로 팔다 sell motor-cars on the installment plan
■─불입금 an installment (money) ─상환 amortization ─제(制) 〔美〕 the installment plan [system] ─지급 payment by [in] installment ─판매 selling on an installment basis

할선 割線 〔數〕 secant line; a secant (略 sec)

할쑥하다 haggard; worn-out and pale; drawn; emaciated ◆할쑥한 얼굴 a haggard [worn] face

할아버지 1 〈조부〉 a grandfather; a grandpa **2** 〈노인〉 an old man

할아범 an old man

할아비 〈할아버지·할아범의 낮춤말〉 a grandpa; an old man

할애하다 割愛— spare sth;〈내주다〉part with sth ◆바쁜 중에서도 시간을 할애하다 take time off *one's* busy work / 지면을 할애하다 allow space 《for》
할양 割讓 cession 《of territory》 —할양하다 cede 《territory》
할인 割引 (a) discount; (a) reduction ◆5퍼센트의 할인 5 persent discount —할인하다 discount; give a discount [reduction]; reduce ◆5퍼센트 할인하다 give a 5 percent discount 《on》; reduce the price by 5 percent / 어음을 할인하다 discount a bill / 은행에서 어음을 할인하다 get a bill discounted at a bank / 5퍼센트 할인하여 at 5 percent discount; at a reduction of 5 percent
▶ 현찰로 지불하면 얼마나 할인해 줍니까? Do you allow any discount for cash?
▶ 대량 주문이면 할인해 드립니다 We make a reduction on a big order.
▶ 단체에 한해서는 운임을 할인해 줍니다 A discount is allowed on party tickets.
■ 단체— a group reduction;〈여행시의〉a party-trip reduction 동업자— (a) trade discount 어음— bill discount 은행— bank [banker's] discount 재— rediscount 현찰— (a) cash discount ■—가격 a reduced price —권 a discount ticket [coupon] —기간 the term of discount —수수료 a discount commission —시간 reduced fare hours —어음 a discounted bill —율 a discount rate —은행 a discount bank

할일 a thing to do; work; business; *one's* duty ◆할일이 많다 have much to do; be busy / 할일이 없다 have nothing to do
할증 割增〈요금의〉an extra 《fare, charge》;〈주식 등의〉a premium; a bonus
▶ 그들은 채권을 할증부로 판매하고 있다 They are selling the bonds at a premium.
—할증하다 pay [give] (an) extra [a premium]
■ —금 a premium; a bonus —배당금 an extra dividend; a bonus —임금 extra [premium] wages
할쭉하다 haggard ⇨ 할쑥하다
할퀴다 scratch; claw ◆할퀸 상처 a scratch; a nail mark / 손톱으로 얼굴을 할퀴다 scratch *sb's* face with *one's* fingernails
▶ 그곳에는 전쟁이 할퀴고 간 자국이 아직도 남아 있다 There are still scars left by the war.
핥다 lick; lap
▶ 고양이가 제 발을 핥고 있다 The cat is licking its paws.
▶ 개가 내 손을 핥았다 The dog licked my hand.
▶ 그는 숟가락을 깨끗이 핥았다 He liked the spoon clean.
핥아먹다 1〈혀로〉lap (up); lick in
◆ 우유를 핥아먹다 lap (up) milk / 깨끗이 핥아먹다 lick (the plate) clean / 입술에 묻은 잼을 핥아먹다 lick the jam off *one's* lips
2〈빼앗다〉cheat *sb* of; swindle *sb* out of
핥이다 be [get] licked;〈핥게 하다〉have *sth* licked; have *sb* lick 《it》
함 函 a box; a chest; a case ◆서류— a filing cabinet 우편— a mailbox ■—진아비 a box bearer [carrier]
함교 艦橋 the bridge of a warship
함구 緘口 keeping *one's* mouth shut
◆함구불언하다 refuse to talk; shut *one's* mouth and remain silent
▶ 그는 함구 무언이었다 He would not open his mouth.
—함구하다 keep *one's* mouth shut; hold *one's* tongue; keep silent
함구령 緘口令 a gag law [rule] ◆함구령을 내리다 forbid mentioning 《a matter》; gag [muzzle] 《the press》
함기 艦旗 an ensign
함께 together; with; together [along] with; in company with
◆모두 함께 all (together); in a body / 함께 가다 go with *sb*; accompany *sb* / 함께 노래하다 sing in chorus [in unison]
▶ 부부가 함께 열심히 일한다 Both husband and wife work hard.
▶ 온 가족이 함께 외출했다 The whole family went out together.
▶ 그 방을 셋이서 함께 썼다 The room was shared by the three.
▶ 이 우표 전부를 친구와 함께 수집했다 I've collected all these stamps in cooperation with a friend.
▶ 나는 그와 운명을 함께 할 작정이다 I'm going to share my fate with him.
함대 艦隊 〈작은〉a squadron;〈큰〉a fleet
◆함대를 파견하다 dispatch a squadron [fleet] 《to》
■ 무적— [史] the Invincible Armada 연합— a combined fleet 주력— the main fleet ■—사령관 the commander of a fleet
함락 陷落〈땅의〉depression; collapse; cave-in; sinking;〈적진의〉fall; surrender
◆수도의 함락 the fall of the capital city
—함락하다 fall [cave] in; sink; be depressed; collapse; fall; surrender
◆요새를 함락시키다 take a fortress
▶ 적의 요새는 두달 동안의 포위 끝에 함락되었다 The enemy fortress fell to us after two months' siege. ⇌ The enemy surrendered their fortress to us after a siege of two months.
■—호 a depression [cave-in] lake
함량 含量 content ◆비타민 함량 vitamin content / 높은 지방 함량 a high fat content
함몰 陷沒 depression; collapse; cave-in; sinking;〈몰락〉ruin —함몰하다 sink; subside; be depressed; cave [fall] in; collapse ■—지진 a fallen earthquake —해 an ingression sea
함묵하다 緘默—〈입다물고 있다〉keep [remain] silent; keep *one's* mouth shut; hold *one's* tongue; be taciturn [reticent]
함미 艦尾 the stern 《of a warship》
—닻 the stern anchor —포 a stern chaser
함박꽃 [植] a peony 《flower》
함박눈 (feathery) snowflakes
◆함박눈이 내린다 The snow is coming down in large flakes.
함부로 1〈무분별하게〉thoughtlessly; careless-

ly; roughly; rashly; recklessly; indiscriminately; at random
♦함부로 지껄이다 make thoughtless remarks / 돈을 함부로 쓰다 spend money recklessly / 일을 함부로 하다 do a slipshod work / 짐을 함부로 다루다 handle a baggage roughly [carelessly] / 침을 함부로 뱉다 spit promiscuously
▶그는 함부로 입을 놀리지 않는다 He weighs [picks] his word.
▶남을 함부로 비판하지 마라 Don't blame others unreasonably [without due cause].
2 〈허가없이〉 without permission; 〈이유없이〉 without (good) reason
♦함부로 때리다 hit *sb* without reason / 나무를 함부로 베다 cut down trees without permission; fell trees indiscriminately

함부르크 〈독일의 도시〉 Hamburg

함빡 thoroughly; greatly; completely; all
♦얼굴에 웃음을 함빡 띠고 with *one's* face beaming with smiles / 함빡 젖다 be all wet; be wet through [to the skin]; be soaked to the bone [skin] / 땀으로 함빡 젖다 be dripping wet with perspiration
▶내 옷이 함빡 젖었다 My clothes were dripping [wringing] wet.

함상 艦上 ♦함상의[에서] aboard; on board (a warship)

함석 zinc; tin; galvanized iron ♦함석으로 지붕을 이다 roof with galvanized iron sheets ■—지붕 a zinc [tin] roof —판 sheet zinc; a tin plate

함선 艦船 warships and other vessels [crafts]

함성 喊聲 a shout; a battle [war] cry ♦승리의 함성 a shout of victory [triumph] / 함성을 지르다[올리다] raise [give, shout] a battle cry
▶함성이 크게 진동했다 A tremendous hubbub was heard.

함수 函數 〔數〕 a function ■미분[대수]— a differential [an algebraic] function ■—관계 functional relation —식 a functional formula

함수 鹹水 〈염수〉 salt water; brine; 〈해수〉 sea water ♦함수의 saline ■—호 a salt [saline] lake

함수 艦首 the bow (of a war vessel) ■—포 a bow chaser

함수초 含羞草 〔植〕 a mimosa ⇨ 미모사

함양 涵養 cultivation; culture; fostering —함양하다 cultivate; foster; develop (national power); build (up) (character)
♦덕성을 함양하다 cultivate moral character; foster *one's* moral sentiment / 독립 정신을 함양하다 foster [cultivate] the spirit of independence

함유 含有 containing —함유하다 contain; have (in); hold
▶이 채소에는 미네랄이 풍부하게 함유되어 있다 This vegetable contains abundant minerals.
■—량 content: 알코올 함유량이 많다 contain a high percentage of alcohol —성분 a component

함입 陷入 depression; subsidence —함입하다 be depressed; subside; sink; cave [fall] in; collapse

함자 銜字 〈성함〉 your [his, her] name; an honored name ▶선생님의 함자가 어떻게 되십니까? What is your name, sir?

함장 艦長 the captain (of a warship); 〈소형 함선의〉 the commander ■—실 the (captain's) cabin

함재 艦載 carrying aboard a warship; loading on a warship
■—기 a ship(-based) airplane; (美) a deck plane; (총칭) carrier-borne aircraft —보트 (land by) a ship's boat —수뢰정 a vedette (boat); a torpedo launch

함적 艦籍 the Navy list ♦함적에서 빼다 strike (a ship) off the Navy list

함정 陷穽 a pitfall; a pit; a trap
♦함정을 파다 lay [set] a trap [snare] (for) / 함정에 빠뜨리다 ensnare; entrap; catch (an animal) in a trap / 함정에 빠지다 fall in a pit; fall into a snare [trap]; be caught in a trap; fall a victim to *sb's* plot
▶우리는 방심하고 있다가 적의 함정에 빠졌다 As we were off our guard we were entrapped by the enemy.
▶남을 함정에 빠뜨리려고 하면 자기가 먼저 빠지는 법이다 He who digs a pit for others falls in himself.

함정 艦艇 war [naval] vessels; warships

함종 艦種 a category [class] of warships; a warship class [category]

함지 **1** 〈나무그릇〉 a wooden basin **2** 〈금을 잡는〉 a pan for gold panning **3** ⇨ 함지박

함지 陷地 low [depressed] ground; a basin; a sunken place; a depression

함지박 a wooden bowl

함체 艦體 the hull of a warship

함축(성) 含蓄(性) (an) implication; significance; suggestiveness
♦함축성 있는 말 a word full of hidden meanings [implications, suggestions] / 함축성 있는 significant; pregnant (sentence); suggestive
▶그가 하는 말은 함축성이 많다 What he says is very suggestive.
▶함축성 있는 표현이 직접적인 표현보다 중요한 경우가 종종 있다 An implication is often more important than a direct statement.
—함축하다 imply; bear; comprise; suggest
♦함축된 뜻 a hidden [a latent, an implied] meaning [significance]
▶그의 말은 항상 깊은 뜻을 함축하고 있다 What he says always has a deep meaning.

함치르르 sleekly; glossily ♦함치르르 윤이 흐르다 be smooth and glossy; be sleek
—함치르르하다 sleek; glossy

함포 艦砲 the guns of a warship
■—사격 bombardment from a warship [by naval guns]; naval bombardment; 함포사격을 하다 bombard (a city) from the sea; shell (a fort) by war vessels

함함하다 smooth; soft and glossy; lustrous (hairs) ▶고슴도치도 제 새끼는 함함하다고 한다 (속담) Everyman's goose is a gander.

함형 艦型 a type of a warship
함호 鹹湖 a salt [saline] lake ⇨ 함수(~호)
함흥차사 咸興差使 a lost [corbie] messenger
▶그는 미국에 가더니 함흥차사가 되어 버렸다 He has gone to America never to return [for good (and all)].
합 盒 a brass [brazen] bowl with a lid
합각 合閣 gable ■―지붕 a gable roof
합격 合格 success in an examination; passing an examination
▶합격을 축하합니다 I congratulate you on your success in the examination.
―합격하다 〈수험자가〉 pass an examination [a test]; succeed in an examination; 〈적합하다〉 come up to the standard [mark]; stand the test; pass inspection; 〈적임·적격이다〉 be found eligible; 〈채용되다〉 be accepted
♦신체 검사에서 갑종 합격하다 pass as A on one's physical examination / 전 과목에 합격하다 pass every subject / 가까스로 합격하다 barely pass 《the entrance examination》
▶그는 고려대학 입시에 합격했다 He passed [succeeded in] the entrance examination for Korea University.
■―률 the ratio of successful applicants ―자 a successful candidate [applicant]: 합격자 발표는 내일 오전 9시입니다 The results will be announced at 9:00 tomorrow morning. ―점 (get) a passing mark ―증 a certificate; 〈이수증〉 《美》 a credit ―통지 a notice of success ―품 tested goods
합계 合計 the sum total; the total (amount [sum]); an aggregate (of)
▶그가 쓴 돈은 합계 백만원에 달했다 His expenses reached a total of a million won.
―합계하다 add [sum] up; add together; total; count up
♦합계하여 in total; in the aggregate; altogether; all told
▶그녀는 비용을 합계했다 She summed [added] up the expenses.
합금 合金 an alloy; a compound metal
♦구리 3에 은 1의 비율로 섞은 합금 an alloy of three parts of copper to one of silver
―합금하다 alloy 《metals》; make an alloy of 《copper and zinc》
――강(鋼) alloy(ed) steel
합기도 合氣道 *hapkido*; an art of self-defense
합당 合當 adequacy; appropriateness; fitness; suitability ―합당하다 adequate; appropriate; fit; suitable; proper; befitting
♦그 경우에 합당한 조치 measures appropriate to the occasion / 합당한 가격으로 at a reasonable price / 합당하지 않다 be improper [unsuitable, inappropriate]
▶조건이 합당하면 받아들이겠다 I will accept your offer on fair terms.
합당 合黨 the merger [fusion] of political parties ―합당하다 merge the parties; the parties merge
합동 合同 combination; union; amalgamation; incorporation; merger; fusion; coalition; 〔數〕 〈도형의〉 congruence; congruent ♦합동의 joint; united; combined; (in)corporated
―합동하다 combine; unite (in one body, with others); amalgamate 《with》; merge (in *sth* greater); incorporate (in, with)
♦합동하여 unitedly; jointly; in combination 《with》 / 합동하여 일에 대처하다 make a joint effort; form a united front 《against》
■―기업 a trust; 《美》 a combine ■―결혼 (식) a joint wedding ―관리[경영] a joint control [management] ―사업 a joint undertaking ―식 〔數〕 a congruence equation ―위령제 a joint service for the (war) dead ―위원회 a joint committee (of both Houses) ―작전 concerted [united, combined] operations ―장례식 a joint funeral ―정견 발표회 a joint election speech [campaign] rally ―참모회의 의장 the Chairman of the Joint Chiefs of Staff; the JCS Chairman ―협의회 a joint council ―회의 〈상·하원의〉 a joint session [convention]
합력 合力 〈힘을 합침〉 collaboration; cooperation; a joint effort; 〔物〕 a resultant force
―합력하다 unite one's efforts 《with》; join forces 《with》; make united efforts; collaborate 《with》; cooperate 《with》
♦합력하여 by united efforts; in cooperation 《with》
합류 合流 1 〈강이 합침〉 confluence; conflux
―합류하다 join; flow [run] together
▶그 강은 한강에 합류한다 That river joins the Han-gang.
2 〈합동〉 joining; linking; union ―합류하다 join; unite [link up] 《with》; be merged (into)
♦민주당에 합류하다 join forces with the Democrats / 모임에 합류하다 join a party [meeting] / 운동에 합류하다 join in the movement
■―점 the junction [confluence] of two rivers; the meeting point (of two civilizations)
합리 合理 rationality; reasonableness
♦합리적인 rational; reasonable; logical / 합리적으로 rationally; logically
▶그것은 합리적인 생각이다 It is a rational [reasonable] idea.
▶오늘날의 젊은이들은 사고 방식이 합리적이다 Young people today think rationally [are amenable to reason].
■―론[주의] 〔哲〕 rationalism ―성 rationality
합리화 合理化 rationalization ♦경영의 합리화 the rationalization of management / 산업 합리화 industrial rationalization
▶국어 교육의 합리화가 필요하다 It is necessary to rationalize the education of the Korean language.
―합리화하다 rationalize; make (it) more

rational [reasonable]
♦ 자기의 행위를 합리화하다 rationalize *one's* behavior

합명회사 合名會社 an unlimited partnership; a general partnership

합반 合班 a combined class —**합반하다** combine 《two》 classes ■ —수업 combined classwork [teaching]

합방 合邦 〈병합〉 annexation of a country; 〈통합〉 unification of 《two》 countries —**합방하다** annex a country; unite 《two》 countries
♦ 합방되다 be annexed 《to》
■ 한일— the Japanese annexation of Korea

합법 合法 lawfulness; legality; legitimacy
♦ 합법적 투쟁 a law-abiding struggle / 합법적인 lawful; legal; legitimate / 합법적 수단으로 by lawful means / 비합법적으로 unlawfully; illegally; illicitly
▶ 합법적인 수단에 호소할 수 밖에 없다 We have to appeal to lawful means.
▶ 그 행위가 합법적임은 이론의 여지가 없다 The legality of the act cannot be disputed.
■ —성 lawfulness; constitutionality —정부 a legitimate government —주의 legalism

합법화 合法化 legalization; legitimation —**합법화하다** legalize; legitimate
▶ 한국에서는 총기의 소지가 합법화되어 있지 않다 The use of guns is not legal in Korea.
■ 비— outlawing: 비합법화하다 outlaw 《an organization》

합병 合倂 combination; union; amalgamation; consolidation; merger; coalition; fusion; affiliation; annexation; incorporation
—**합병하다** combine; unite; amalgamate; merge; affiliate; be incorporated with; annex
♦ 갑과 을을 합병하다 combine [unite] one thing with another / 영토를 합병하다 annex a territory 《into》 / 《큰 것에》 합병되다 be merged into; be annexed [affiliated] to
▶ 두 회사가 합병하여 큰회사가 되었다 The two companies were amalgamated [united] into a big enterprise.
■ 신설— consolidation 흡수— merger ■ —절차[조건] amalgamation procedure [conditions] —호(號) 〈잡지의〉 a combined number

합병증 合倂症 〔醫〕 a complication; complicating disease ♦ 합병증을 일으키다 develop a complication; a complication occurs [sets in]

합보시기 盒— a bowl with a lid

합본 合本 copies bound together in one volume; bound volumes 《of a magazine》
♦ 잡지의 일년[반년]치의 합본 the annual [semiannual] volume of a magazine
—**합본하다** bind 《copies》 together; combine in a single volume

합사 合絲 twisted thread [yarn]; twine —**합사하다** twist threads; twine threads into a string
■ —기 a twisting machine

합삭 合朔 the conjunction [conjuncture] of moon and sun

합산 合算 adding up
—**합산하다** add up; add [put] together; sum up; total
▶ 잡비를 합산하면 총지출은 천만원 이상이 된다 The total expenditure will amount to over ten million won when we add up miscellaneous [incidental] expenses.
■ —신고 joint returns —액 total (amount)

합석 合席 sitting together; sharing a table
▶ 《식당에서》 합석 좀 할까요? Would you mind sharing your table?
—**합석하다** sit together; sit with; sit in company with; share a table 《with》
♦ 음식점에서 다른 사람과 합석하다 share a table with another at a restaurant

합선 合線 〔電〕 (a) short (circuit) —**합선하다** make a short circuit; short-circuit
▶ 전선이 합선되면 대개 퓨즈가 끊어진다 A short circuit usually blows a fuse.

합성 合成 〔物〕 composition; 〔化〕 synthesis
♦ 힘의 합성 composition of forces / 합성의 compound; composite; 〔化〕 synthetic
—**합성하다** compose; compound; 〔化〕 synthesize
■ —고무 synthetic rubber —력 〔物〕 a resultant force —물 a compound; a composite thing; a synthetic 《product》; a synthesized product —분 a component (part) —비료 compound fertilizer —섬유 synthetic [chemical] fiber —세제 a synthetic detergent —수 〔數〕 a composite number —수지 synthetic resins; plastics —어 a compound 《word》 —운동 〔物〕 a resultant motion —음 a composite sound —주(酒) compound [synthetic] liquor —피혁 synthetic leather —화학 synthetic chemistry

합세 合勢 joining forces —**합세하다** join forces; form an alliance ♦ 운동에 합세하다 join in the movement

합수 合水 conflux ⇨ 합류(合流)1

합숙 合宿 joint billet; lodging together
—**합숙하다** lodge [board, stay] together; be billeted together [with]
▶ 우리는 매년 여름이면 합숙하여 야구 연습을 한다 We stay in the same dormitory to practice baseball every summer.
■ —소 a boarding house; a dormitory; 〈운동의〉 a training camp —훈련 camp training: 합숙 훈련을 하다 live together in a training camp

합승 合乘 riding together; sharing a vehicle; a shared ride
—**합승하다** ride together
♦ 택시에 합승하다 share a cab 《with》
■ —객 a fellow passenger —마차 a stagecoach; a diligence —택시 a jitney (cab)

합심 合心 union; unity; concert
—**합심하다** unite; be of one accord [mind]; be in union 《with》; cooperate in harmony
♦ 합심하여 with one accord
▶ 그들은 합심하여 일했다 They worked together in perfect accord.

합의 合意 mutual agreement; mutual [common] consent; concurrence
♦ 쌍방의 합의 하에 by mutual [common] agreement [consent] / 합의 하에 별거하다 live apart by mutual consent
▶ 모든 점에서 합의를 보았다 They reached an agreement [came to terms] on every

point.
　―**합의하다** come to [reach] an agreement [accord]; be agreed (on) ◆ …이라는 데 합의했다 it was agreed that…
　■ ―(문)서 a statement of mutual agreement; a written agreement ―사항 items of understanding ―이혼 a divorce by mutual agreement

합의 合議 consultation; conference; counsel ◆ 합의를 거쳐 after consultation; by mutual consent ―**합의하다** consult [counsel] together; confer 《with》; take [go into] counsel
　■ ―재판 collegial [collegiate] judgment ―제 a representative [council, parliamentary] system: 합의제 법원 a collegiate court

합일 合一 union; unity; oneness ◆영육(靈肉)의 합일 the union of soul and body ―**합일하다** unite; be united 《with, in one body》; be in accord 《with》

합자 合字 [印] a ligature; a double letter

합자 合資 partnership; joint capital [stock] ―**합자하다** enter into partnership 《with》; join stocks ◆ …와 합자하여 in partnership with…
　■ ―회사 a limited partnership: 동일 합자회사 Dongil & Co., Ltd.

합작 合作 collaboration; cooperation; a joint work; a joint venture; (美) a pool
◆ 회사를 한미 합작으로 경영하다 operate [run] a company under Korean-American joint management
　―**합작하다** collaborate with *sb* 《on a book》; produce [write] jointly; cooperate with *sb* 《in a work》
　■ ―물 a joint work [production] ―자 a collaborator; a joint author; a coauthor ―회사 a joint corporation

합장 合掌 joining *one's* hands
　―**합장하다** join *one's* hands; put *one's* hands flat together; clasp *one's* hands 《in veneration》 ◆ 합장하고 with folded palms
　■ ―배례 worshiping with joined [clasped] hands

합장 合葬 burying together ―**합장하다** bury [inter] together; bury 《husband and wife》 in one grave ◆ 부인을 남편과 합장하다 bury the wife's body with her husband's

합제 合劑 a medical mixture; a compound; 〔化〕 a flux

합주 合奏 (a) concert; (an) ensemble ―**합주하다** play in concert ◆ 결혼행진곡을 합주하다 play a wedding march in concert
　■ ―2[3, 4]부― a duet [trio, quartet] ■ ―곡 an ensemble (piece) ―단 a musical ensemble (group); a concert group

합주 合酒 home-brewed alcoholic beverage (made from glutinous rice for summertime drink)

합죽거리다 mumble toothlessly
합죽선 合竹扇 a folding fan
합죽이 a toothless person
합죽하다 toothless and puckered
합죽할미 a toothless old woman
합죽합죽 mumblingly
합중국 合衆國 a federal state ■ ―아메리카― the United States (of America)

합지 合紙 pasteboard

합창 合唱 singing together; chorus; ensemble ◆ 백 명의 합창 a chorus of 100 voices
　―**합창하다** sing together; sing in chorus
　■ ―2[3, 4, 5]부― a duet [trio, quartet, quintet] ―혼성(混聲)― a mixed chorus ■ ―곡 a chorus; a choral; a part-song: 남성 합창곡 a chorus for men's [male] voices ―단[대] a chorus; 〈교회의〉 a choir: 국립 합창단 the National Chorus ―대원 a chorus [choir] girl [boy]; a chorister ―대장 a chorus master ―자 a chorist; a chorister

합체 合體 union, incorporation; consolidation; amalgamation; merger ―**합체하다** unite; be united; incorporate; consolidate

합치 合致 agreement; coincidence; concurrence ―**합치하다** agree 《with》; accord 《with》; be in accord 《with》; concur 《with》; coincide 《with》; correspond 《with》; tally 《with》
▶ 양자의 의향은 완전히 합치했다 Both parties' wishes [intentions, views] were in complete agreement.
▶ 그의 이야기는 사실과 합치하지 않는다 His story does not agree with the facts.

합치다 合― 1〈하나로〉 put [join] together; combine; unite; amalgamate; merge; annex
◆ 두 강이 합치는 곳에 at the junction of two rivers / 힘을 합치다 join [unite] efforts / 두 회사를 하나로 합치다 merge [amalgamate] two companies / 도중에 일행에 합치다 join [rejoin] a party on the way
▶ 그들은 마음을 합쳐서 일했다 They worked together in close cooperation.
▶ 그 나라는 독일과 프랑스를 합친 것만큼 크다 The country is as large as Germany and France put together.
▶ 그는 양당을 합쳐 신당을 결성했다 He united the two factions into a new party.
2〈섞다〉 mix (up); compound; combine
◆ 크고 작은 것을 합쳐 모두 20개 twenty pieces altogether, large and small
3〈합산하다〉 sum up; add up; total; put together
▶ 모두 합쳐 얼마입니까? 〈총액〉 How much is it altogether? ⇌ 〈총수〉 How many are they in all?
▶ 전부 합쳐 50만원입니다 The total amounts to five hundred thousand won. ⇌ It sums up to 500,000 won.
▶ 반대자는 전부 합쳐 열명이었다 The dissenters totaled 10.
▶ 항공 운임과 그 밖의 모든 비용을 합쳐 여행 경비가 얼마나 듭니까? How much will the traveling expenses be including the airfare and all other items?
4〈겹치다〉 put together; overlap
◆ 종이 두 장을 합치다 put two sheets of paper together

합판 合板 plywood
합판 合版 joint publication ―**합판하다** publish jointly
합판 合辦 joint management; a joint venture; (美) a pool ⇨ 합작(合作)

합판화 合瓣花 〔植〕〈통꽃〉 a gamopetalous [compound] flower
합평 合評 a joint review [criticism]
■—회 a meeting for a joint review
합하다 合— 1〈하나가 되다〉 be put [joined] together; be brought together; be combined; be united; become one; 〈병합되다〉 be merged (into); be amalgamated (to)
2〈합당하다〉 (come to) fit; suit; 〈합의하다〉 agree 《with》; harmonize 《with》; be in tune 《with》
합헌 合憲 ♦합헌적(인) constitutional
—성 constitutionality
합환주 合歡酒 nuptial cups exchanged between the bride and bridegroom
핫— 1〈솜을 둔〉 wadded (garment) 2〈배우자가 있는〉 having *one's* spouse ♦핫아비 a married man / 핫어미 a married woman
핫것 (총칭) wadded clothes [bedclothes]
핫길 下— 〈하등 품질〉 inferior quality; a low grade [class]; 〈하등품〉 an article of inferior quality; low-grade goods
핫뉴스 hot news
핫도그 (美) a hot dog
핫두루마기 a wadded overcoat
핫라인 a hot line
핫머니 〔經〕 hot money
핫바지 1〈솜바지〉 (a pair of) padded trousers 2〈촌뜨기〉 a countryman; (蔑) a bumpkin; a clodhopper
핫반 〈겹솜반〉 double-layered cotton wool
핫옷 wadded clothes
핫이불 wadded bedclothes
핫저고리 a wadded jacket
핫케이크 a hot cake
핫코너 〔野〕〈삼루〉 the hot corner
핫퉁이 〈두툼한〉 thick-wadded clothes; 〈철 지난〉 wadded clothes worn out of season
항 項 1〈조항〉 a clause; 〈문장의 절〉 a paragraph; 〈항목〉 an item
♦제 3 조 제 5 항에 해당하다 come under Clause 5, Article 3 / 항으로 나누다 paragraph; itemize
▶이 항은 5페이지 하단에 계속됨 This paragraph is continued on the bottom of page 5.
2 〔數〕 a term
♦방정식의 일항 a term [member] of an equation / 이[삼, 다]항식 a binomial [trinomial, polynomial] expression
-항 -港 a port; a harbor

解說 port는 항구와 그 도시까지를 포함한 「항」의 뜻. harbor는 항구 그 자체만을 가리키며 비유적으로「피난처」의 뜻도 있음.

♦부산항 the port of Pusan; Pusan Port / 자유항 a free port
항간 巷間 ♦항간의 소문 a current rumor; the talk of the town / 항간에 떠도는 말에 의하면 a rumor has it that…; people say that…
▶항간의 소문에 의하면 그는 인천에서 입후보할거라고 한다 People say [It is said] that he will run as a candidate in Inch'ŏn.
항거 抗拒 resistance; defiance —항거하다 resist; disobey; defy; oppose; antagonize
■—죄 an offense of resisting lawful order
항고 抗告 〔法〕 a complaint; an appeal (from); a protest —항고하다 complain (against a decision); appeal (from a decision); file a protest (against)
▶피고는 판사의 판결에 불복하여 고등법원에 항고했다 The defendant appealed to the High Court against the judge's decision.
■—기간 the term for complaint —심 hearing of a complaint —인 a complainant; a complainer —장 a bill [memorandum] of complaint [exception] —재판 an appeal trial
항공 航空 aviation; flying; flight; aerial navigation
■—계(界) the aerial world; aviation circles —계기 aeronautical [aircraft] instruments —교통관제 air traffic control (略 ATC) —기록기〔空〕 a flight recorder —기사 an aeronautical engineer —기상학 aeronautical meteorology; aerology —대 the air force; a flying [an air] corps —등대 an airway beacon; an aerial lighthouse —로 an air route [line]; an airway; an air lane —모함 an aircraft [airplane] carrier; a carrier; (口) a flattop —물리학 aerophysics —병(兵) an airman; a military aviator —병(病) airsickness —력 an air force —보험 aviation [aerial] insurance —사업 air transportation business; air service —사진 an air [aerial] photo(graph) —사진기 an air camera —사진술 an aerophotography —서한 an aerogram(me); (美) an air letter —수송 air transportation [transport]; flight [air] service; (美) airlift —수송화물 airborne [airlift] goods —술 aeronautics; aviation —시대 the air age —시설 air navigation facilities —심리학 aviation psychology —역학 aeromechanics —요금 an air fare —우편 airmail; (英) aerial post: 항공우편으로 부치다 send (a package) by air; airmail —우편물 airmail matter —우표 an airmail stamp —의학 aviation medicine; aeromedicine —조약 an air treaty —지도 an air map; an aerial chart —측량 an aerial survey —편 (send a letter by) airmail —표지 a radio [an aerial, an air] beacon —학 aeronautics —화물 an air cargo —회사 an aviation company; an airline
항공기 航空機 an airplane; a plane; a flying machine; an aeroplane; (총칭) aircraft
■—경(輕)— lighter-than-air craft; an aerostat —중(重)— heavier-than-air craft; an aerodyne
■—승무원 (총칭) an aircrew; a flight crew; 〈한 사람〉 an aircrewman —조종술 (aircraft) pilotage; airmanship
항공우주국 航空宇宙局 〈미국의〉 the National Aeronautics and Space Administration (略 NASA)
항공우주산업 航空宇宙産業 the aerospace industry
항구 恒久 permanency; perpetuity; eternity
♦항구적(인) lasting; everlasting; permanent; eternal; perpetual / 항구적인 평화를 이룩하다 establish a lasting [permanent] peace
—항구하다 lasting; everlasting; permanent;

eternal
■—성 permanency; imperishability 《of the universe》 —화 perpetuation: 항구화하다 perpetuate
항구 港口 a harbor; 〈육지를 포함한〉 a port; a haven
♦항구를 떠나다 leave (a) port; clear [sail from] a port / 항구에 들어가다 enter (a) port; come into [arrive in] port / 항구에 들르다 call [touch] at a port
■—도시 ⇨ 항도
항균성 抗菌性 ♦항균성의 antibacterial
항내 港內 ♦항내에 within [in] the harbor; in port —설비 harbor facilities
항담 巷談 a town talk; a gossip
항도 港都 a port (town)
항독성 抗毒性 ♦항독성의 antitoxic
항독소 抗毒素 〔醫〕 an antitoxin
■—요법 antitoxin treatment
항등식 恒等式 〔數〕 an identity
항라 亢羅 silk gauze; gossamer; sheer silk
항렬 行列 generations of the clan ♦같은 항렬이다 be a collateral relative; be in the same generation of the clan —자(字) a generation character; one's generation name
항례 恒例 a common usage ⇨ 상례(常例)
항로 航路 a sea [sailing] route; a course; 〈정기 노선〉 a line; a service
♦항로를 열다 launch [inaugurate] a regular service / 항로를 정하다 lay a course / 《배가》 항로를 바꾸다 change one's course
■—안전— a fairway 외국— an ocean lane [route, service] 정기[부정기]— a regular [an irregular] service [line] —도 a track chart —목표 a seamark —변경 a deviation (of route) —신호 a marine signal —이탈 〈항공기의〉 deviation from the flight route —표지 a nautical mark; a beacon
항만 港灣 harbors ⇨ 항구(港口)
■—노동자 a port laborer; a longshoreman —시설 port [harbor] facilities —운송 transportation service in harbors; harbor express service —하역 harbor loading and unloading
항명 抗命 disobedience —항명하다 disobey sb's order ■—죄 〔軍〕 mutiny
항목 項目 a head; a heading; an item; a point; 〈조항〉 a clause; a provision 《in a will》
♦항목별로 나누다 itemize / 내용을 항목별로 검토하다 examine the contents item by item
▶항목별로 하는 것이 더 보기 쉽다 It is easier to understand when itemized.
■—별표(別表) an itemized list 《of》 —화 itemization; specification
항무 港務 harbor [port] service
항문 肛門 〔解〕 the anus; 〔動〕 a vent; 〈婉〉 the back passage
♦항문의 anal
■—경(鏡) an anoscope; a proctoscope —과 (學) proctology —괄약근 the anal sphincter —병 an anal disease —병전문의 a proctologist —부(部) the anal region
항법 航法 navigation
■—계기(計器)— instrumental navigation 극지 (極地)— polar navigation 무선[천문]— radio [celestial] navigation 지문(地文)— geo-navigation
항변 抗辯 〈피고의〉 a plea; (a) defense; 〈변박〉 a protest; (a) refutation; confutation; 〈이의〉 a demurrer; a demur
—항변하다 protest; make a plea; plead; defend oneself; refute; confute
♦상관에게 항변하다 remonstrate with one's superior / 소송에 항변하지 않다 file no answer to the suit
■ 방소(妨訴)— 〔法〕 a plea in abatement; a demurrer
항병 降兵 a surrendered soldier
항복 降伏 (a) surrender; 〈복종〉 submission; capitulation
—항복하다 surrender (oneself) 《to》; capitulate 《to the enemy》; 〈굴복하다〉 submit [yield, bow, give in] 《to one's rival》
♦무조건 항복하다 surrender at discretion / 항복을 권하다 summon 《the enemy》 to surrender / 항복시키다 cause [make] 《the enemy》 to surrender; bring 《the enemy》 under [to his knees]
▶일본은 무조건 항복했다 Japan surrendered unconditionally.
▶자, 항복해라 Admit you're beaten! ⇒ Give up, give up!
■조건부— a conditional surrender —권고(서) a summons to surrender —기(旗) a white flag; a flag of surrender; 〈휴전의〉 a flag of truce —문서 ⇨ 항서 —조건 terms of capitulation
항산 恒産 〈일정 재산〉 fixed property; 〈생업〉 regular occupation
▶항산이 없으면 항심(恒心)도 없다 A real property, a real purpose. ⇌ Competency is for constancy of mind.
항산성 抗酸性 ♦항산성의 acid-fast[-proof]
항산성균 抗酸性菌 an acid-fast bacterium
항상 恒常 always; at all times; constantly; usually; customarily; habitually ⇨ 늘, 언제나
■—성 〔生理〕 homeostasis
항상주거 杭上住居 a pile [stilt] dwelling [house]; a house on piles
항생 抗生 〔生〕 antibiosis
항생물질 抗生物質 〔生〕 an antibiotic (substance) —학 antibiotics
항서 降書 a capitulatory letter; an instrument of surrender
항설 巷說 a town talk; a talk of the town; a rumor; a street-corner gossip
▶그에 관한 항설이 분분하다 Wild rumors are in circulation about him.
항성 恒星 〔天〕 a fixed star
♦항성의 sidereal —시 sidereal time —일[년] a sidereal day [year] —주기 a sidereal period
항소 抗訴 〔法〕 an appeal to a higher court; an intermediate appeal ♦항소의 appellate; appellant / 항소를 기각하다[철회하다] dismiss [withdraw] an intermediate appeal
▶그의 항소는 기각되었다 His appeal was dismissed [was turned down].
—항소하다 bring an intermediate appeal 《in a higher court》; appeal to a higher court of

intermediate appeal; enter [lodge, file] an intermediate appeal / 판결에 대하여 항소하다 appeal against the decision
▶ 검사가 항소했다 The public prosecutor made the application for intermediate appeal. ■ 검사가 a public prosecutor's appeal ■─권 the right of appeal ─기각 dismissal of appeal ─기간 the time for appeal; the time allowed for appeal ─법원 a court of appeal(s); an appellate court ─심(審) a hearing of intermediate appeal ─이유 the grounds of appeal ─인 an appellant ─장 a notice of intermediate appeal; a petition of appeal

항속 航續 cruising; flight; flying
■─거리 a cruising [flying] radius [range] (of 2,000 km) ─력 a cruising [flying] power [capacity] ─시간 the duration of cruise [flight]; endurance

항습 恒習 〈버릇〉 one's habit [custom, wont]; an inveterate habit

항시 恒時 always ⇨ 항상(恒常)

항심 恒心 constancy; steadiness; steadfastness

항아리 缸─ an earthenware pot; a crock; a jar; a jug 물─ a water jar

항아리손님 缸─ 〔醫〕 parotitis; mumps ⇨ 이하선(~염)

항암제 抗癌劑 an anticancer drug

항언 抗言 a protest; a retort; (a) refutation; confutation ─항언하다 protest; make a protest; refute; confute

항오 行伍 〈줄〉 rank and file; the ranks; files
◆ 항오 정연하게 in regular ranks; in perfect order

항외 港外 ◆ 항외에(서) outside the port [harbor] / 항외에 정박해 있다 lie at anchor off the harbor / 항외로 나가다 get out [clear] of a port; leave (a) port ■─정박지 a roadstead

항용 恒用 〈보통〉 ordinarily; commonly; 〈항상〉 always; usually; all the times; constantly
◆ 항용 있는 일 a common affair / 학생에게 항용 있는 일로서 as is usual with students; as students will

항원 抗元・抗原 〔生理〕 an antigen ■─균 an antigenic germ ─항체반응 an antigen-antibody reaction

항의 抗議 a protest; 〈반대〉 an objection; 〈이의〉 an exception; 〈불평〉 a complaint
◆ 항의가 들어오다 have a complaint lodged against one 《from sb》/ 항의를 제기하다 lodge [file, enter] a protest 《with sb against sth》
▶ 그들은 심판의 판정에 대해 항의를 제기했다 They lodged a protest against the referee's decision.
─항의하다 protest [make a protest] 《to sb against sth》; object 《to》; offer [raise] an objection 《to》; remonstrate 《against》
▶ 국무장관은 그 전쟁에 항의하여 사임했다 The Secretary of State resigned in protest to the war.
■─정식─ 〔競〕 a protest 집단─ a mass protest ─데모 a protest demonstration [parade, march] ─서[문] a (written) protest; a note of protest ─자 a challenger ─집회 a protest meeting [rally]; an indignation meeting ─파업 a protest strike 《against》

항일 抗日 resistance to Japan
■─사상 anti-Japanese sentiments ─운동 the resistance to Japan; an anti-Japanese movement ─투사 an anti-Japan fighter ─투쟁 an anti-Japanese struggle [fight]

항쟁 抗爭 (a) contention; contending; (a) dispute; 〈투쟁〉 (a) struggle; 〈저항〉 resistance ─항쟁하다 contend; dispute; strive 《against, for》; struggle 《with, against》; resist

항적 抗敵 resistance
─항적하다 resist; fight against an enemy

항적 航跡 a wake (behind a sailing ship); a furrow; a track; 〔空〕 a flight path; 〔空〕 a vapor trail ◆ 다른 배의 항적을 따라가다 follow up the wake of another vessel

항전 抗戰 resistance
─항전하다 offer [make] resistance 《to, against》; resist; fight against an enemy
■─력 power of resistance

항정 1 〈짐승의 목덜미〉 the scruff of the neck **2** 〈쇠고기의〉 chuck beef

항정 航程 1 〈도정〉 the run [passage] (of a ship); the distance covered (by a ship); 〈항해〉 a sail; a voyage
◆ 하루의 항정 a day's sail 《from, between》
2 〈행정〉 a flight; a lap; (口) a leg
◆ 전 항정을 날다 fly [cover] the whole distance
─지시기 a distance recorder ─표 a logbook

항존 恒存 〔物〕 conservation
■─에너지─ conservation of energy [force]

항주 航走 sailing ─항주하다 sail; cruise; steam; run ─력 speed

항진 亢進 rise; 〔醫〕 exasperation; exacerbation
─항진하다 rise; accelerate; be exasperated [exacerbated]
■─심계(心悸)─ 〔醫〕 palpitation; heart acceleration 혈압─ 〔醫〕 a rise in blood pressure

항진 航進 sailing; cruising ─항진하다 sail; proceed; steam ◆ 매시 15해리를 항진하다 steam fifteen miles an hour

항차 much [still] more; much [still] less; to say nothing of ⇨ 하물며

항체 恒體 〔生理〕 an antibody ◆ …에 대하여 항체를 만들어내다 build up antibodies to sth ─형성 the antibody formation

항타기 抗打機 〈말뚝 박는 기계〉 a pile driver [mallet]

항풍 恒風 a constant [trade] wind

항해 航海 a voyage; navigation; (a) sailing; a passage (over the sea); a (sea) trip
◆ 항해중에 during the voyage / 항해길에 오르다 〈사람이〉 start [go] on a voyage; 〈사람・배가〉 set sail; 〈배가〉 put out to sea / 항해를 계속하다 〈사람이〉 continue the voyage; 〈배가〉 keep the sea; hold on her course / 항해 중의 무사[즐거운 항해]를 빌다 wish sb bon voyage [a pleasant trip] / 항해 중 병이 나다 fall ill while on a voyage [at sea, aboard a liner] / 항해에 견디다[견디지 못하다] 〈배가〉 be seaworthy [unseaworthy]; 〈사람이〉 be a good [bad] sailor

▶ 항해중 무사하시기를 빕니다 I wish you bon voyage. ⇌ Have a nice trip [voyage].
▶ 그들은 곧 세계 일주 항해를 떠난다 They will soon go on [take] a round-the-world cruise [voyage].
▶ 항해 중에는 바다가 잔잔했다 We had a calm voyage [passage]. ⇌ The passage was calm.
▶ 그는 지금 항해중이다 He is on a voyage [(out) at sea].
─항해하다 sail; make a voyage [to]; voyage; navigate; take a passage
▶ 그는 태평양을 항해했다 He sailed (across) the Pacific.
■ ─연안 coastwise sailings ─원양 ocean navigation; distant voyage ─처녀 a maiden trip [voyage]: 우리 배는 호주로 처녀 항해를 했다 Our ship made its maiden voyage to Australia. ■ ─권 the right of navigation ─도 a chart ─선 a service ship ─속력 sea [service] speed ─수당 a sea [service] allowance ─술 (the art of) navigation; seamanship ─일지 〈海〉 (keep) a (voyage) log; a logbook; a ship's journal [log] ─자 a mariner; a seaman; a navigator ─장 a chief navigator; a navigating officer ─천문학 nautical astronomy ─표 nautical tables

항해사 航海士 a mate; a navigation officer
■ 2[3]등─ the second [third] mate [officer] 1등─ the chief mate; the first mate [officer]

항행 航行 navigation; sailing; voyage; 〈순항〉 a cruise
─항행하다 navigate; sail; cruise
♦ 항행할 수 있는[없는] 강 a navigable [an unnavigable] river
▶ 많은 배가 부산과 인천 사이를 연중 항행한다 Many ships sail between Pusan and Inch'ŏn all (the) year round.
■ ─구역 a navigation area ─권 the right of navigation

항혈청 抗血清 〔醫〕 an antiserum (*pl.* ~s, -ra)
항히스타민제 抗─劑 〔藥〕 an antihistamine; an antihistaminic (medicine)

해¹ **1** 〈태양〉 the sun; 〈햇빛〉 sunshine; sunlight
♦ 해가 지기 전에 before dark [sunset, the sun sets] / 해가 진 뒤에 after dark / 해가 드는 곳에 in a sunny place; in the sun / 해가 들지 않는 곳에서 in a shady [sunless] place; in the shade / 해를 향하여 heliotropically / 해를 등지고 with the sun to *one's* back
▶ 해는 동쪽에서 떠서 서쪽으로 진다 The sun rises in the east and sets in the west.
▶ 해가 쨍쨍 빛나고 있었다 The sun was shining bright(ly).
▶ 그는 해가 지고 나서 이곳을 떠났다 He left here after sunset.
▶ 내 방은 해가 잘 든다[들지 않는다] My room gets a lot of [doesn't get much] sun [sunshine].
▶ 그가 눈을 떴을 때 해는 중천에 떠 있었다 When he awoke, it was broad daylight.
2 〈낮〉 (a) day; daytime
▶ 해가 짧다 The daytime is short.
▶ 해가 점점 짧아진다[길어진다] The days grow shorter [longer].
▶ 겨울에는 해가 짧다 The days are short in winter.
▶ 여름이 다가올수록 해가 길어진다 The days grow [get] longer as summer approaches.

해² 〈연〉 a year
♦ 올해 this year / 지난해 last year / 그 다음해 the following year / 해마다 every year; year after [by] year; every year to come / 해가 갈수록 as years go [pass] by / 해가 가기 전에 before the end of the year; within the year / 새해를 맞이하다 welcome [greet, ring in] the New Year / 묵은 해를 보내다 see the old year out; ring out the old year
▶ 새해가 밝았다 The new year has begun.
▶ 가까스로 빚 없이 해를 넘겼다 We managed to get through the year without a debt.
▶ 새해 복 많이 받으세요 (A) Happy New Year!

해³ 〈소유물〉 a possession ♦ 내 해 mine
해⁴ 〈웃는 모양〉 《smile》 with *one's* mouth open

해 害 〈위해〉 injury; harm; hurt; 〈손상〉 damage; 〈악영향〉 bad [ill, harmful] effects
♦ 담배의 해 the ill [bad] effects of smoking / 해가 없는 harmless; unharmful; innoxious / 해가 되는 harmful; injurious / 해가 되다 do harm; do harm to...; be injurious to; be bad for / 해를 입히다 do injury [harm] 《to》; inflict injury 《upon》; injure / 해를 입다 〈손상을〉 suffer damage [wrong]; be damaged; 〈해독을〉 suffer from evil effects
▶ 아이를 때리는 것은 유익하기보다 오히려 해가 많다 Beating a child will do more harm than good.
▶ 태풍은 벼 수확에 많은 해를 끼쳤다 The typhoon did [caused] great damage to the rice crop.
▶ 나는 너에게 해가 되는 말은 안한다 I say nothing to your disadvantage.

해- 該- 〈바로 그(것)〉 that; the very; the said; 《the matter》 in question
♦ 해사건 the very affair / 해인물 the man in question; the said person

-해 -海 〈바다〉 ♦ 동해 the East Sea

해갈하다 解渴- 〈갈증을〉 appease [quench, relieve] *one's* thirst; 〈가뭄을〉 wet dry weather; be relieved from drought

해감 silt; slime; ooze
♦ 해감내가 나다 smell of slime

해거름 sunset; 《美》 sundown; 〈황혼〉 dusk
♦ 해거름에 at sunset; at dusk

해결 解決 solution; settlement; resolution
♦ 원만한 해결 an amicable settlement / 그 문제의 두 가지 해결책 two solutions of [to] the problem / 해결책을 찾다 find a solution 《to [of] a problem》; find a way out / 노사 분규의 원만한 해결책을 찾아내다 reach [arrive at, come to] an amicable settlement of the labor dispute
▶ 우리는 에너지 문제의 조속한 해결을 기대한다 We expect a speedy solution of the energy problem.
─해결하다 solve; settle; effect a settlement;

bring 《a matter》 to a settlement; resolve 《an issue》; work out 《a problem》; 《美》 fix 《up》 《a problem》
♦ 해결할 수 없는 insoluble 《problem》; unsolvable / 원만히 해결하다 arrange [settle] 《an affair》 amicably; bring to an amicable settlement / 협상으로 해결하다 negotiate a settlement 《of a problem with sb》 / 해결되다 be solved; be settled; come to a settlement; reach [arrive at] a solution
▶ 돈으로는[가만히 앉아 걱정만 해서는] 문제를 해결할 수 없다 You can't solve the problem with money [by sitting and worrying].
▶ 싸움으로는 아무 일도 해결하지 못한다 Fighting won't settle anything. ⇌ Nothing will be settled by fighting.
▶ 그것은 너 자신이 해결해야 할 일이다 That's something you must work out for yourself.
▶ 회화 「깬 유리창을 내가 변상할 생각이야」「하지만 그걸로 일이 해결되니?」 "I'm going to pay for the broken window." "Will that be the end of it, though?"
▶ 그 문제는 시간이 해결할 것이다 Time will solve the matter.

해고 解雇 discharge; dismissal; 《美》 〈일시적〉 lay-off; 《口》 sacking; the sack
♦ 한달 전에 해고 통지하다 give one month's notice 《to》
―**해고하다** dismiss; 《口》 fire; 《英俗》 sack; give sb the sack [bag]; 〈일시적으로〉 lay sb off
▶ 종업원 한 사람이 음주 운전으로 해고되었다 One of the workmen was dismissed [fired, sacked] for drunk driving.
■ 집단― mass dismissal ■ ―기준 a criterion for personnel dismissal ―수당 a discharge allowance; dismissal pay ―자 a discharged person ―장 a dismissal notice ―통지 a dismissal notice; a notice of dismissal; a warning

해골 骸骨 〈뼈〉 a skeleton; bones; 〈유골〉 a skull; 〈두개골〉 a cranium 《pl. -nia, ~s》
♦ 해골처럼 여위다 become very thin [skinny]; 《口》 become 《all》 skin and bone(s)
▶ 그는 해골 같다 He looks like a skeleton.

해공전 海空戰 an air-and-sea battle

해관 海關 the (maritime) customs

해괴하다 駭怪― strange; queer; eccentric; mysterious; weird; outrageous; scandalous; monstrous
♦ 해괴한 소문 a wild rumor / 해괴한 행동 an eccentric behavior / 해괴망측하다 be extremely strange [outrageous, scandalous]

해구 海狗 〈動〉 a fur seal; a sea bear ⇨ 물개
―**신**(腎) the penis of a sea bear

해구 海寇 〈해적〉 pirates; sea robbers [marauders]

해구 海溝 〈地〉 a trench
■ 민다나오― the Mindanao Trench

해국 海國 〈섬나라〉 a seagirt country; a maritime power ―**민** a maritime nation [people] ―**주의** navalism

해국 海菊 〈植〉 a kind of aster

해군 海軍 the navy; the naval service; the naval forces ♦ 해군의 naval; navy ―**공창**(工廠) a naval dockyard [shipyard]; a naval yard ―**국** a sea [naval] power ―**군인** a naval [navy] man; a sailor; 〈총칭〉 the Navy ―**기**(機) a navy plane ―**기**(旗) the navy flag ―**기지** a naval base ―**력** naval power [strength] ―**무관** a naval attaché ―**복** a seaman's uniform ―**본부** the Navy Headquarters ―**부대** naval forces ―**사관**[장교] a naval officer ―**사관학교** the Naval Academy; 《英》 the Royal Naval College ―**사관학교생도** a naval cadet; a midshipman ―**연습** naval maneuvers ―**참모총장** the Chief of Naval Operations 《略 C.N.O.》 ―**헌병** 《美》 the shore patrol 《略 S.P.》

해굽성 ―性 〔植〕 (positive) heliotropism

해금 奚琴 〔樂〕 a Korean fiddle

해금 解禁 removal [lifting] of a ban [an embargo]; 〈사냥 등의〉 the opening 《of the shooting [fishing] season》
―**해금하다** remove [lift] an embargo 《on》 (▶embargo는 통상(通商) 등의 금지에 한정되어 있음); lift [remove] a ban 《on》
♦ 금의 수출입을 해금하다 lift the embargo on gold [gold embargo]
■ ―**기** 〈수렵의〉 the open season; the opening of the shooting seasnon

해기 海技 seamanship

해껏 〈온종일〉 till dark [sunset]; all day long
♦ 해껏 일하다 work till sunset [dark]

해꼬무레하다 whitish

해끔하다 whitish

해낙낙하다 satisfied; contented; pleased

해난 海難 a sea disaster; a shipwreck
▶ 그 배는 해난을 당했다 The ship suffered a sea disaster. ⇌ The ship was wrecked.
■ ―**구제소** a life saving station ―**구조** sea rescue; salvage; 〈해공 합동의〉 air-sea rescue 《略 ASR》 ―**구조선** a salvage boat [steamer] ―**구조신호** an SOS: 해난 구조 신호를 보내다 radio [flash] an SOS; flash a distress signal ―**구조원** a lifesaver; 〈총칭〉 the Lifesaving Service ―**구조작업** salvage work [operation] ―**심판법** 〔法〕 the Marine Accidents Inquiry Act ―**심판소** the Marine Accidents Inquiry Agencies ―**심판 위원회** the Marine Accidents Inquiry Committee ―**증명서** a wreck certificate; an extended protest

해납작하다 white and flat; whitish and broad

해내다 1 〈사람을 이겨내다〉 beat; defeat; vanquish; get [gain] the better of sb
2 〈일을 처러내다〉 complete; achieve; carry through [out]; finish; accomplish; fulfill
▶ 그는 그 일을 혼자서 해냈다 He completed the task by himself.
▶ 그는 마침내 그 일을 해냈다 At last he accomplished the task.
▶ 너는 무슨 일이나 한번 손댄 일은 끝까지 해내야 해 You must carry it through to the end whatever you set out doing.

해넘이 sunset; 《美》 sundown ♦ 해넘이에 at sunset

해녀 海女 a woman diver
▶ 해녀는 전복을 따려고 잠수했다 The woman diver dived for abalones.

해단 解團 disbanding ―**해단하다** disband 《an

expeditionary party》 ■—식 the ceremony of disbanding

해달 海獺 〔動〕 a sea otter ■—모피 a sea-otter fur

해답 解答 a solution 《of [to] a problem》; an answer 《to a question》
♦시험문제의 해답 a key [(a set of) answers] to examination questions
▶이 문제의 해답을 가르쳐 주십시오 Please tell me [let me know] the (correct) answer to the question.
—**해답하다** answer 《a question》; solve 《a problem》 ♦맞게[잘못] 해답하다 answer correctly [incorrectly]
■—자 a solver; an answerer; 〈퀴즈 프로그램 등의〉 a panelist

해당 該當 ♦해당 항목 the appropriate heading —**해당하다** come [fall] under; 〈적용되다〉 be applicable to; 〈(…에) 상당하다〉 correspond to; 〈충족시키다〉 fulfill
▶그것은 형법 3조에 해당한다 It comes [falls] under Article 3 of the Criminal Code. = Article 3 of the Criminal Code applies to it.
▶이 조건에 해당하는 사람은 아무도 없다 There is nobody who fulfills these conditions.
■—사항 pertinent [relevant] data

해당 解黨 the dissolution of a party
—**해당하다** dissolve a party

해당화 海棠花 〔植〕 a sweetbrier

해대다 fall [turn] upon; go at; attack; lash (out) 《at》; fly out 《at》 ♦찍소리 못하게 해대다 talk [argue] *sb* down; corner *sb* in argument

해도 海圖 a sea chart ♦해도에 없는 섬 an uncharted island / 해도에 나와 있지 않은 바다 a chartless sea
■—대 a chart table —실 a chart room —학 chartology

해독 害毒 evil; harm; an evil [a baneful] influence ♦사회에 해독을 끼치다 exert a baneful [harmful] influence on society; corrupt [poison] society

해독 解毒 〔醫〕 detoxication; detoxification
♦해독의 anti-poison; antidotal
—**해독하다** counteract [neutralize] the poison; detoxify; detoxicate
■—제 an antidote; a toxicide; a counterpoison

해독 解讀 decipherment; interpretation; decoding; understanding —**해독하다** break [crack] 《the enemy's code》; decipher; decode; decrypt ♦암호 전문을 해독하다 decipher a coded telegram
♦사진— photographic interpretation ■—기 a decoder

해돈 海豚 a dolphin=돌고래

해돋이 sunrise; 《美》 sunup ♦해돋이를 구경하다 see the sunrise 《from the mountaintop》

해동 解凍 thawing; a thaw ▶올해는 해동이 이를 것이다 This year the thaw will set in earlier. —**해동하다** thaw; defrost

해동갑 —同甲 〈부사적〉 until sunset; while it is light —**해동갑하다** do *sth* until sunset
♦해동갑하여 일하다 work till sunset

해동청 海東靑 〔鳥〕 a duck hawk ⇨ 송골매

해득 解得 understanding; apprehension; comprehension ♦해득이 빠르다 [느리다] be quick [slow] of apprehension —**해득하다** understand; apprehend; comprehend; grasp ♦해득하기 어려운 hard to understand

해뜨다 wear out ⇨ 해어뜨리다

해뜩거리다 get very dizzy ⇨ 해뜩거리다

해라하다 use the low forms of speech 《to an inferior》; talk down 《to *sb*》

해란초 海蘭草 〔植〕 a toadflax

해로 海路 a sea route; a seaway
♦해로로 울산에 가다 go to Ulsan by sea; take a sea route to Ulsan

해로 偕老 〈부부의〉 living together in wedlock; growing old together
—**해로하다** grow old together; live together in wedlock

해로동혈 偕老同穴 1 〈해로의 맹세〉 ♦해로동혈의 가약을 맺다 be united as husband and wife [a wedded pair]
—**해로동혈하다** grow old together [live together in wedded life] 《as man and wife》
2 〔動〕 a Venus's-flower-basket; a glass sponge

해롭다 害— harmful; injurious; bad
♦청소년에게 해로운 잡지 a magazine harmful to youth
▶담배는 건강에 해롭다 Smoking is bad for [harmful to, injurious to] the [our] health. ≒ Smoking damages our health.

해롱거리다 frolic ⇨ 희롱거리다

해류 海流 〔地〕 an oceanic current; a (marine) current
■—도(圖) a current chart —병(瓶) 〔地球物〕 a current bottle; a drift bottle —의 대순환 a general circulation of oceanic current

해륙 海陸 land and sea ♦해륙 양면 작전 amphibious operations / 해륙으로 by land and sea ■—풍(風) land and sea breeze

해리 海狸 〔動〕 〈비버〉 a beaver; a castor
■—향(香) castor; castoreum

해리 解離 〔化〕 dissociation —**해리하다** dissociate ■—곡선 a dissociation curve —상수(常數) a dissociation constant

해리 海里 〈해상의 거리 단위〉 a nautical [sea] mile; a knot 《→약 1,852m》

해마 海馬 1 〔魚〕 a sea horse 2 〔動〕 a elephant seal; a walrus

해마다 every year; yearly; annually; from year to year; year by [after] year ♦해마다 똑같은 일을 하다 do the same every year
▶그 가게는 해마다 커 간다 The store gets bigger every year [year by year].

해말갛다 fair ⇨ 희멀겋다

해말쑥하다 fair and clean ⇨ 희멀쑥하다

해맑다 white and clean

해망적다 slow-witted; stupid; dull

해머 a hammer ■—공기—an air [a pneumatic] hammer 증기— a steam hammer —던지기 hammer throw —던지기 선수 a hammer thrower

해먹 a hammock ♦해먹에서 자다 sleep in a hammock / 해먹을 치다[걷다] sling [lash] a hammock / 뒷마당의 야자나무 밑에 친 해먹 a hammock under the backyard palm tree

해먹다 1 〈만들어 먹어〉 cook and eat
2 〈횡령하다〉 embezzle; pocket; appropriate unlawfully
♦ 공금을 해먹다 embezzle public money
3 〈생업으로 삼다〉 earn a living by; live by; do

해면 海面 〈바다 표면〉 the surface of the sea; 〈표준 해면〉 the sea level
▶ 이 지역은 해면보다 낮다 This area is below sea level.
▶ 거울 같이 잔잔한 해면에 요트가 떠 있었다 Yachts were afloat on a glassy sea.
ー경정(更正) reduction to mean sea level ー기압 atmospheric pressure of sea level ー어업 sea level fishery ー온도 (a) sea-surface temperature

해면 海綿 〖動〗 a sponge ♦ 해면골의 spongy / 해면으로 빨아들이다 sponge up
■ー동물 a Porifera; sponges ー조직 spongy weave; 〖生〗 a spongy parenchyma ー질 spongy matter; spongin ー체 a spongy body; 〖解〗 a cavernous body

해면 解免 1 〈해제〉 release; absolution; discharge; acquittal ー해면하다 release; free; absolve; relieve; acquit 《sb of his responsibility》
2 ⇨ 면직(免職)

해명 海鳴 rumbling of the sea; sea noise

해명 解明 explanation; elucidation; explication ー해명하다 make clear; explain; clarify; elucidate; explicate ーー서 a letter of explanation; a written explanation

해몽 解夢 the reading [interpretation] of a dream; dream reading; oneirocritic; oneiromancy ー해몽하다 interpret [read] a dream
■ー가 a dream reader; an oneirocritic; an oneiroscopist

해무 海務 maritime affairs ⇨ 해사(海事)

해무 海霧 a sea fog; a fog on the sea

해묵다 be carried [brought] over from the previous year
♦ 해묵은 쌀 〈지난 해의〉 rice of the previous year's crop; 〈오래된〉 old rice; long-stored rice / 해묵은 골칫거리 an outstanding [a long-pending] trouble

해묵히다 carry over to next year

해물 海物 marine products ⇨ 해산물 ■ー상 a dealer in marine products

해미 a thick [dense, heavy] fog on the sea
▶ 바다에는 해미가 자욱했다 The sea was covered with a heavy fog.

해바라기 〖植〗 a (common) sunflower; a helianthus; 《美》 a combflower
ーー기름 sunflower oil

해박 該博 profundity
ー해박하다 extensive; profound; exhaustive
♦ 해박한 지식 profound learning; an exhaustive [extensive] knowledge; erudition / 해박한 지식을 가지고 있다 have [be possessed of] a vast stock of knowledge

해반닥거리다 goggle [roll] one's eyes; turn one's eyes up and down

해반드르르하다 fair and glossy

해반지르르하다 fair and glossy = 해반드르르하다

해발 海拔 above sea level
▶ 그 산은 해발 3,000미터다 That mountain is three thousand meters above sea level.
■ー고도 〖地〗 altitude

해방 解放 release; liberation; disengagement; emancipation
♦ 빈곤으로부터의 해방 freedom from poverty
ー해방하다 release; liberate; disengage; disenthral(l); emancipate; enfranchise; free sb from; rescue (a prisoner, a slave); extricate; deliver
♦ 노예를 해방하다 liberate [emancipate] a slave / 노예 신분에서 해방하다 release sb from slavery
▶ 죽음이 그를 고통으로부터 해방시켰다 Death released him from his torments.
▶ 이 지긋지긋한 잡일에서 하루 속히 해방되고 싶다 I want to get rid of this troublesome chore as soon as possible.
■ー노예 the emancipation of slaves 8·15ー the 1945 Liberation (of Korea) ■ー군 a liberation army ー운동 a liberation movement [campaign] ー자 an emancipator ー전쟁 a war of liberation ー지구 a liberated district [area]

해법 解法 a solution; a key to solution; how to solve (a problem)

해변 海邊 the seashore; the seaside; the beach
♦ 해변의 coastal; seaside / 해변에서 on the seashore; at the seaside / 해변에 살다 live by the sea / 해변을 산책하다 take a walk along the beach; stroll [ramble] about the beach
■ー도시 a coast [seacoast] town; a town along the coast ー식물 seaside plants; coast-grown floras [vegetables]

해병 海兵 a marine ■ー대 《美》 the (U.S.) Marine Corps ー대원 a marine; 《美俗》 a leatherneck ー사령관 the Marine Corps commandant

해보다 1 〈시도하다〉 try; make [have] a trial (of); have a try (at); attempt (to do); make an attempt (at)
♦ 처음 해보다 try (surfing) for the first time / 되든 안되든 해보다 do sth at a venture; try one's luck / 저항을 해보다 offer [put up] resistance / 최선을 다해보다 do [try, exert] one's best [utmost]; do all one can / 다시 한 번 해보다 try again; make another attempt
▶ 할 수 있으면 해봐라 Try and do it.
▶ 여하튼 한 번 해보기나 하자 Let us have a try anyhow.
▶ 그건 한 번 해볼 만하다 It is worth a try.
2 〈경험하다〉 experience; go through ♦ 고생을 해보다 experience [go through] hardships (of life) / 사랑을 해보다 experience love
▶ 나는 이런 일을 해본 적이 없다 I am quite new [an utter stranger] to this kind of work.
3 〈겨루다〉 fight (against); contend with; stand [rise] against
▶ 그와는 끝까지 해볼테다 I will never yield to him until he says [cries] uncle.

해부 解剖 1 〈의학상의〉 dissection; anatomy; 〈검시의〉 a postmortem (examination); autopsy
▶ 해부 결과 타살로 판명되었다 The postmortem examination showed that it was a case of murder.
━해부하다 dissect; cut up; 〈생체를〉 vivisect; 〈동물체를〉 anatomize; 〈사체를〉 hold a postmortem [an autopsy] (on); necropsy
2 〈분석〉 (an) analysis 《pl. -ses》
━해부하다 analyze
● 병리— pathological anatomy 생체— vivisection 시체— 〔醫〕 a postmortem examination; autopsy 인체— dissection of a human body —대[실] a dissecting table [room] —도(刀) a dissecting knife; a scalpel —도(圖) a dissecting chart —모형 an anatomical model —용 시체 a subject for dissection —자 a dissector; a prosector (표본 담당의) —현미경(生) an anatomy microscope

해부학 解剖學 〔醫〕 anatomy; anatomia
◆ 해부학(상)의 anatomical / 해부학상[적으로] anatomically
■ —동물 animal anatomy; zootomy 식물— plant anatomy; phytotomy 인체— human anatomy; anthropotomy ━—자 an anatomist

해빙 海氷 〔地〕 sea ice

해빙 解氷 thawing; a thaw ━해빙하다 (it) thaw; break (up)
▶ 압록강은 해빙됐다 The Yalu is now free from [of] ice.
■ —기 the thawing season

해사 maritime affairs [matters]
━—법 (法) the law of admiralty —위성 통신 a maritime satellite communication —재판소 (英) the Court of Admiralty —협회 a marine association

해사하다 clean and fair; fair-complexioned

해산 海産 marine products ⇨ 해산물(海産物)
◆ 해산의 marine
■ —동물 marine animals —식품 seafood —업 the marine products industry

해산 解産 (a) childbirth; (a) delivery ⇨ 분만(分娩)
◆ 해산의 고통을 겪다 go through labor; undergo the pangs of childbirth / (산모가) 해산 구완을 하다 attend a case of confinement; assist at a childbirth
▶ 그녀는 해산을 앞두고 있다 She is going to have a baby. ━ (口) She is expecting a baby.
━해산하다 be delivered of a child; give birth to a baby
▶ 그녀는 어젯밤 해산했다 She had a baby last night. ⇌ She was delivered of a baby last night.
■ —기 one's time; period of delivery —미역 seaweed for soup as postpartum diet

해산 解散 1 〈모임의〉 breakup; dispersion
◆ 해산을 명하다 order 《a crowd》 to disperse
━해산하다 break up; disperse
◆ 집회를 해산하다 break up a meeting / 군중을 해산시키다 disperse a crowd
▶ 우리는 역에서 해산했다 We broke up at the station.
▶ 경찰은 군중을 해산시켰다 The police broke up the crowd.
▶ 그 데모는 경찰에 의해 해산되었다 The demonstration was dispersed by the police.
2 〈회사·국회 등의〉 dissolution 《of a company》; disorganization
◆ 해산을 명하다 order 《an organization》 to be disbanded
▶ 국회의 갑작스런 해산은 혁신 정당들에게 타격을 주었다 The unexpected dissolution of the National Assembly was a great shock to the reformist parties.
━해산하다 dissolve《partnership, the National Assembly》; disorganize; wind up
■ 강제[임의] — compulsory [voluntary] winding-up ■ —권 the right to dissolve 《the National Assembly》

해산물 海産物 marine products; the yield of the sea ◆ 해산물이 풍부하다 be rich in marine products
■ —가공품 processed marine products

해삼 海蔘 〔動〕 a trepang; a sea cucumber

해상 海上 the sea
◆ 해상의 maritime; marine; on the sea / 해상에(서) on the sea; at sea / 해상에서 폭풍을 만나다 be overtaken by a storm at sea
▶ 그녀는 해상을 5시간이나 표류하고 있었다 She was floating on the sea for five hours.
■ —권 maritime [sea] power; the command of the sea —근무 seaservice; sea duty; service afloat —납치 a seajacking —무선 표지국 the maritime radio beacon station —무역 maritime [sea, floating] trade; overseas trade —법 (法) maritime law —보급로 a seaborne supply route —보험 ⇨ 해상보험 —봉쇄 a naval [sea] blockade —비행 an ocean (overseas) flight —생활 a seafaring life; ocean life; life afloat [at sea] —여행 a voyage on the sea; traveling by sea; seafaring —여행자 a sea traveler; a seafarer —운수[수송] marine transport(ation); sea-lift —이동 업무 maritime mobile service —인명 안전 협약 International Convention for the Safety of Life at Sea 《略 SOLAS》 —자위대 〈일본의〉 the Maritime Self-Defense Force —화재 a fire at sea; a fire on [in] a ship

해상 海床 the bottom of the sea ⇨ 해저(海底)

해상 海商 〈장사〉 marine commerce; 〈사람〉 a sea trader

해상 海象 1 〈바다코끼리〉 an elephant seal; a sea elephant; a morse 2 〈듀공〉 a sea pig; a dugong

해상보험 海上保險 marine insurance
◆ 해상보험에 들다 effect marine insurance; insure 《the cargo》 against sea perils
■ —대리업자 a marine insurance agent —업 underwriting —업자 an underwriter —증권 a marine (insurance) policy

해생 海生 ■ —동물[식물] a marine animal [plant]

해서 楷書 〈한자 서체〉 the printed style of writing; the print [square] hand ◆ 해서로 쓰다 write in the printed [square] style

해석 解析 analysis ◆ 해석적인 analytic(al)

ー해석하다 analyze
■ ー기 하 학 analytic geometry ー학 analysis ー함수 an analytic function
해석 解釋 (an) interpretation; construction; 〈설명〉 (an) explanation; elucidation; exposition
♦ 문법적 해석 a grammatical interpretation / 법의 해석 the construction of law / 영어의 해석 능력 ability of reading English; reading ability in English / 해석의 차이 a discrepancy in interpretation
▶ 같은 영화를 봐도 사람마다 해석이 구구하다 When people see a film, their interpretations vary [differ] widely from person to person.
ー해석하다 interpret; construe; put [place] a construction on; 〈설명하다〉 explain; elucidate; expound / 〈이해하다〉 take; make out 《the meaning》
♦ 선의[악의]로 해석하다 take 《sb's words》 in good [bad] part / 잘못 해석하다 misinterpret; misconstrue; misunderstand / 해석을 달리 하다 take the meaning differently / 여러 가지로 해석하다 interpret variously
▶ 이 문장은 여러 가지로 해석할 수 있다 This sentence can be interpreted in many [various] ways. ⇌ This sentence admits of several interpretations.
▶ 나는 그녀의 침묵을 동의로 해석했다 I took her silence for agreement.
▶ 내 말이 잘못 해석되었다 My talk was falsely interpreted. ⇌ My talk was misunderstood [misinterpreted].
해설 解說 (an) explanation; (an) interpretation; a commentary; exposition
ー해설하다 explain; comment on 《the news》; interpret; expound
♦ 그 규칙을 해설해 주시겠습니까? Will you explain the rule to us?
▶ 그는 시사문제를 해설했다 He commented on current events.
■ 뉴스ー a news commentary ー자 〈뉴스〉 a commentator; 〈서적〉 an expounder
해성 海成 ♦ 해성의 sea-formed
ー단계 〔地質〕 a marine terrace ー층 〔地質〕 the marine deposits
해소 咳嗽 a cough = 해수(咳嗽)
해소 海嘯 1 〈만조 때의 파도〉 a (tidal) bore; 〈썰물 소리〉 the sound of ebbing waves 2 〈해일〉 a tidal [storm] wave
해소 解消 1 〈해결〉 solution; settlement
ー해소하다 solve; settle
♦ 난관을 해소하다 iron out the difficulties / (…의) 부족을 해소하다 supply [cover, fill up, remedy] the shortage 《of》 / 주택난을 해소하다 solve the housing problem
2 〈소멸〉 annulment; (a) cancellation
ー해소하다 cancel 《a contract》; dissolve [annul] 《a marriage》
▶ 나는 계약을 해소했다고 벌금을 물게 되었다 I was fined for having canceled the contract.
3 〈해체〉 (a) dissolution; disorganization
ー해소하다 dissolve; disorganize
▶ 그는 파벌을 해소하자고 제안했다 He suggested that factionalism (should) be ended.
해소수 a little over [more than] a year
해소일 －消日 wasting time ー해소일하다 idle [dawdle] away *one's* time; lead an idle life
해손 海損 〔保〕 an average (loss)
■ 공동[단독]ー a general [particular] average ー계약[계서] an average agreement [bond] ー공탁금 an average deposit ー담보 with average(略 W.A.) ー정산 average adjustment ー정산서 an average statement ー정산인 an averager; an adjuster ー조항 an average clause ー화물 sea-damaged goods
해송 海松 1 〈총칭〉 a pine (tree) on the beach 2 〈흑송〉 a black pine
해수 咳嗽 a cough; coughing ■ ー약 a cough medicine; a remedy for cough; cough drops [syrup]
해수 海水 seawater; salt water; brine ♦ 해수의 침입을 막다 hold back the seawater / 해수에서 얻은 민물 desalted [desalinated] seawater
■ ー순환 circulation of seawater ー어 a saltwater fish ー온도 seawater temperature ー투명도 transparency of seawater
해수 海獸 a marine [sea] animal
해수욕 海水浴 sea bathing; a sea (water) bath ー해수욕하다 bathe in the sea; swim in the sea
♦ 변산에서 해수욕하다 bathe on the beach of Pyŏnsan / 해수욕하러 가다 go for a swim in the sea; go sea bathing; go bathing in the sea
■ ー객 a sea bather ー모자 a bathing cap ー복 a bathing suit [dress]; a swimsuit ー장 a bathing resort [place]; a (bathing) beach; a beach [seaside] resort
해시계 －時計 a sundial; a dial
해식 海蝕 〔地〕 marine erosion ー동굴 a marine cave ー작용 abrasion ー지형 marine topography
해신 海神 the god of the sea; the sea god; 〔로神〕 Neptune; 〔그神〕 Poseidon
해심 海深 the depth of the sea ♦ 해심을 재다 plumb [sound] the sea; take soundings
▶ 해심은 30피트다 The water is 30 feet deep.
해쓱하다 pale; pallid; wan; waxy ♦ 몹시 해쓱하다 deathly [ashy] pale / 얼굴이 해쓱해지다 turn pale [white] / 해쓱해 보이다 look pale
▶ 그는 앓고 나서 얼굴이 해쓱하다 His complexion is pasty from an illness.
해악 害惡 evil; harm; mischief; 〈악영향〉 an evil influence [effect]
♦ 사회의 해악 the ills of society / 전쟁, 역병 (疫病), 그 밖의 해악 war, pestilence and other evils / 세상에 해악을 끼치다 have a harmful influence on many people / 해악을 근절하다 eradicate [wipe out] the cause of evil
해안 海岸 the seashore; the (sea)coast; the seaside; the beach; 〈도시의〉 the waterfront
♦ (배에서 보아) 해안쪽에 coastwards / 해안의 경치 a coastal landscape / 해안의 호텔 a seaside hotel; a hotel by the seaside / 해안에 on the shore [beach]; by the sea; at the seaside / 해안을 산책하다 take [have] a walk along the beach / 해안을 따라 항해하다 sail coastwise

[along the coast]
▶ 큰 파도가 해안에 부딪쳤다 Great waves beat against the shore.
▶ 그는 해안에 아담한 별장을 가지고 있다 He owns a cozy cottage by the sea.
—가리[통] a sea road; a waterfront street —경비 coast defense —경비대 the coast guard —경찰 the shore patrol —기후(氣候) coastal climate —도시 a coast [seaside] town —사구(砂丘) coastal sand dune —상륙[양륙] beach landing —선 the shoreline; 〔鐵〕 a coast railway —지방 a seaside [coast] district; a coastal region —침식 coastal [beach] erosion —평야 a coastal plain —포대(砲臺) a coast-battery

해야하다 have to (do); must (do); should (do); ought to (do)
▶ 나는 곧 출발해야 한다 I must set out at once.
▶ 자녀는 부모님께 순종해야 한다 Children should obey their parents.
▶ 자기 일은 자기가 해야 한다 You ought to look after yourself.

해약 解約 cancellation [annulment] of a contract; 〔法〕 rescission
—해약하다 cancel [annul] a contract; call [break] off 《one's engagement》; surrender 《an insurance policy》; 〈구독을〉 discontinue
—반환금 〔保〕 cancel returns; 〈생명보험의〉 premium surrendered

해양 海洋 the sea(s); the ocean
♦ 해양의 자유 the freedom of the seas
—경찰대 the National Maritime Police —고고학 a nautical archaeology —관측선 a marine research ship —국가 a maritime power —기상대 a marine meteorological observatory —대학 a mercantile marine college —동물학 marine zoology —문학 sea literature —물리학 oceanophysics —박람회 an ocean(ic) exposition —법(法) law of the sea —생물 oceanic life —성 기후 oceanic climate —소설 a sea story —수산부 the Ministry of Maritime Affairs and Fisheries —수산부장관 the Minister of Maritime Affairs and Fisheries —식물 an oceanphyte —오염 방지 prevention of ocean pollution —지리학 ocean geography —측량 marine surveying —학 oceanography —학자 an oceanographer

해어 海語 nautical terms; sea-terms
—사전 a dictionary [nomenclature] of nautical terms

해어뜨리다 wear; wear (it) out [away, down]
♦ 구두를 구멍나도록 해어뜨리다 wear one's shoes (away) into holes / 바지 무릎을 실밥이 보이도록 해어뜨리다 wear one's pants threadbare at the knees

해어지다 wear; wear [get worn] out [away, down]; get tattered; become tattery
♦ 다 해어진 옷 (well) worn-out clothes; threadbare [tattered] clothes / 너덜너덜 해어지다 be reduced to [fall into] tatters; tatter; be worn to rags
▶ 사전이 너덜너덜 해어졌다 The dictionary has been worn to tatters.
▶ 스웨터의 팔꿈치가 해어졌다 The sweater has ravel(l)ed at the elbow.

해역 海域 a sea area
▶ 그 해역에서는 한국의 조업이 금지되어 있다 Korean fishing boats are not allowed to operate in the area.

해연 海淵 〔地〕 the deep

해연풍 海軟風 〔地〕 a sea breeze

해열 解熱 removal [alleviation, subsiding] of fever —해열하다 bring down one's fever; alleviate fever; break a fever
—제 a medicine for fever; an antifebrile; an antipyretic; a febrifuge

해오라기 〔鳥〕 a night heron

해오라기난초 —蘭草 〔植〕 a fringed orchis [orchid]

해왕성 海王星 〔天〕 Neptune

해외 海外 foreign countries
▶ 그는 해외 사정에 밝다 He has a thorough knowledge of foreign affairs. ⇒ He knows very well about foreign affairs.
▶ 이번 여름엔 해외로 나갑니다 I am going abroad this coming summer.
▶ 그는 작년에 특파원으로 해외에 파견되었다 He was sent abroad as a correspondent last year.
▶ 그의 이름은 해외에 널리 알려져 있다 He is well-known all over the world. ⇒ He has an international reputation.
▶ 우리는 해외에서 양모를 수입하고 있다 We get raw wool from abroad.
—공관 diplomatic establishments [offices] abroad; embassies and legations abroad —귀환자 a returnee [repatriate] from abroad —근무(수당) overseas service (allowance) —무역 overseas [foreign] trade —문학 foreign literature —발송 an overseas shipment —발전 overseas expansion —방송 overseas broadcasting [radio service]; an overseas radio broadcast —방송프로그램 the overseas programs —사절 an envoy sent abroad —시장 an oversea(s) [a foreign] market —여행 a foreign travel [trip]; a trip abroad —영토 overseas possessions —유학 study(ing) abroad —이민[이주] emigration —전보 a cable(gram); an overseas telegram —정보 information from abroad —진출 overseas expansion; 〈기업의〉 overseas ventures —통신 news from abroad —투자 overseas investment —파병 the overseas dispatch of troops —판 an overseas edition —홍보 활동 information activities

해우 海牛 〔動〕 a sea cow; a manatee; a dugong

해운 海運 marine [sea, ocean] transport(ation); shipping
—계 the shipping world; shipping circles —관리 control of marine transportation —국(國) a maritime power —국(局) the Maritime Transportation Bureau —업 marine transportation business; the shipping business [trade, industry] —업자 a shipping agent; (총칭) shipping interests —정책 a shipping policy —항만청 the Korea Maritime and Port

Administration(略 KMPA) —화물 seaborne goods
해원 海員 a seaman; a mariner; a sailor; (美) a crewman; (총칭) a crew
♦해원이 되다 become a seaman; go to sea
—명부 a crew list —생활 a seafaring life; a sailor's life —숙박소 a sailors' home —심판소 the Marine Court —양성소 a seamen's training school —용어 nautical terms —조합[협회] a seamen's union [association]
해읍스름하다 whitish
해이 解弛 relaxation; slackness; looseness
—해이하다 relax; be relaxed; slack (en) (up); grow lax; become remiss
♦해이한 규율 slack discipline / 마음이 해이해지다 one's attention [mind] relaxes [becomes remiss]
해인초 海人草 〔植〕 Corsican weed
해일 海溢 a tidal wave; a overflowing of sea
♦해일에 휩쓸리다 be washed [swept] away by a tidal wave / 해일을 만나다 be struck [hit] by a tidal wave
▶ 남해안에 해일이 일어났다 A tidal wave struck [visited, swept along] the south coast.
▶ 그 지진이 해일을 일으켰다 The earthquake caused a overflowing of sea.
—경보 a tidal wave warning
해임 解任 release from office; dismissal
—해임하다 release sb from office; relieve sb of (his) post; dismiss
♦해임되다 be released from [relieved of] one's office; be dismissed from service
■—장(狀) a letter [notice] of dismissal; a dismissal letter [notice] —제(制) the recall system
해자 垓字 a moat; a fosse
♦성에 해자를 두르다 moat a castle
해자 楷字 a printed-[square-]style character
해작질 playing with one's food —해작질하다 play [toy] with one's food; poke about
해장 drinking in the morning to relieve the hangover
—해장하다 have a morning drink (to relieve the hangover); (口) take a hair of the dog
■—국 broth [soup] to relieve the hangover —술 a drink of wine (on) the morning after; a morning drink; (口) a hair of the dog
해장 海葬 a burial at sea ⇨ 수장(水葬)
해저 海底 the bottom of the sea; the sea bottom; the seabed; the ocean floor [bed]
♦해저에 가라앉다[침몰하다] sink [go down] to the bottom of the sea
■—곡(谷) a submarine canyon —동식물 seafloor plants and animals; submarine organisms; the benthos —유전 a submarine oil field —전보 a cable (message); a cablegram —전선 a submarine cable (line): 해저전선을 부설하다 lay a submarine cable —전신 submarine telegraph; 〈기술〉 submarine telegraphy: 해저전신으로 by cable —지진 a submarine earthquake —침적물 a submarine deposit —탐험 an undersea [seabed] exploration —터널 an undersea [a submarine] tunnel —핵실험 an undersea nuclear test —화산 a submarine [submerged] volcano
해적 海賊 a pirate; a sea robber; a corsair
♦해적이 출몰하는 바다 a sea infested with pirates; pirate-infested waters / 해적질하다 commit piracy; pirate (a ship); rob at sea
■—기 a black flag; the Jolly Roger; the skull and crossbones —선 a pirate ship; a sea rover —판(版) a pirated edition [version, reprint] —행위 piracy
해전 —前 〈일몰 전〉 before sunset [sundown]
해전 海戰 a sea fight [battle]; a naval battle [engagement, action] ♦트라팔가르 해전 the Battle of the [Trafalgar]
해제 解除 1 〈풀어줌〉 release; absolution; discharge
—해제하다 release; free; absolve ((sb from an obligation); relieve (sb of responsibility)
♦무장을 해제하다 disarm; dismantle / 책무에서 해제되다 obtain release from an obligation / 공직 추방에서 해제되다 be released from purge
2 〈취소〉 cancelation; dissolution; removal (of a ban)
—해제하다 cancel (a contract); call off (an alert); lift (a ban); remove
♦「공습경보」를 해제하다 sound the "all clear" / 통제를 해제하다 remove control (on); decontrol / 금지가 해제되다 obtain the annulment of the ban
▶ 홍수 경보가 해제되었다 The flood warning was canceled.
▶ 계엄령이 해제되었다 Martial law was lifted.
■ 무장— disarmament; demilitarization 폭풍경보— lifting of a storm warning ■—조항[조건] a resolutive clause [condition]
해제 解題 a bibliographical introduction (to); bibliographical notes (of)
—해제하다 make a bibliographical introduction (to); annotate bibliographically
■ 한 서(漢書)— bibliographical notes of Chinese classics [literature] —목록[서목] an annotated catalogue [bibliography] —자 a bibliographer
해조 害鳥 an injurious [a harmful] bird
해조 海鳥 a sea bird; a seafowl ■—분(糞) guano (pl. ~s)
해조 海藻 seaweeds; marine algae [plants] ■—분(粉) kelp meal —회(灰) kelp (ash)
해조 諧調 〈조화〉 harmony; 〈가락〉 melody; euphony
해조음 海潮音 the sound [boom] of the sea [waves]
해좌 蟹座 〔天〕 the Crab ⇨ 게(~자리)
해주다 do sth for (another); help (with); do as a favor ♦숙제를 해주다 do a homework for (a boy) / 심부름을 해주다 run an errand for sb / 옷을 해주다 make sb new clothes
해죽 with an affable [a sweet] smile; smilingly
♦해죽 웃다 smile sweetly (at sb); break into a smile
해죽거리다[1] 〈웃다〉 grin (broadly) (at) ⇨ 히죽거리다
해죽거리다[2] 〈걷다〉 swing one's arms as one walks ⇨ 헤죽거리다

해중 海中 ♦해중의 submarine / 해중에[(으로)] in [into, beneath] the sea; underseas(s)
■一생물 sea life 一핵실험 ⇨ 해저(~핵실험) 一화산 ⇨ 해저(~화산)
해지 解止 cancelation of a contract; 〔法〕termination ♦파산 절차의 해지 the termination of bankrupt procedure
一해지하다 abandon; terminate; close
해지다¹ 〈저물다〉the sun sets [goes down, sinks]
해지다² wear out ⇨ 해어지다
해직 解職 release from office; dismissal; discharge
  해직히다 release sb from (his) office [position]; relieve sb of (his) post; dismiss; discharge; fire
♦해직되다 be relieved of one's post; be released from one's office [position]; be dismissed [fired]
■一수당 a discharge allowance 一통고 (hand) a dismissal notice
해질녘 sunset; (美) sundown ♦해질녘에 toward evening [nightfall]; at dusk [sunset]
해질무렵 sunset ⇨ 해질녘
해 질 성 一性 〔植〕negative heliotropism; apheliotropism
해쭉 smilingly ⇨ 해죽
해찰 〈해침〉mischief; spoiling things
一해찰하다 play [behave] mischievously; do mischief; spoil things; (口) monkey; 〈딴짓하다〉give one's attention to something else while one is at work
해 찰 궂 다 mischievous; meddlesome; rash; slapdash; frivolous; inconsiderate
해찰스럽다 mischievous ⇨ 해찰궂다
해체 解體 1〈해부〉dissection; 〈분해〉taking to pieces; dismantling; dismantlement
一해체하다 disjoint; dismantle (a machine); take to pieces; break up (a ship); pull down (a building); dissect
♦선박 해체업자 a ship breaker / 기계를 해체하다 take a machine to pieces; disjoint [knock down] a machine / 폐차를 해체하다 scrap [break up] a disused [an old] car
2〈해산〉(a) dissolution; disorganization; liquidation
♦조합의 해체 the dissolution of a partnership 一해체하다 dissolve; disorganize; disband; liquidate; break up
♦조직의 합리화를 위해 해체하다 be dissolved to form a better organization
해초 海草 seaweeds ⇨ 해조(海藻)
해초 海鞘 〔動〕an ascidian ■一류 Ascidiacea
해춘 解春 thawing; the beginning of spring; the spring thaw ♦해춘기에 in the spring thaw 一해춘하다 thaw; a thaw sets in; the spring thaw sets in
해충 害蟲 a noxious [harmful] insect; (총칭) vermin ♦사과의 해충 an insect injurious to apple trees / 해충의 피해 insect plague / 해충을 구제하다 exterminate vermin [noxious insects]; debug
■一구제 extermination of vermin
해치 〔海〕a hatch ♦해치의 뚜껑 a hatch cover

해치다 害— injure; harm; hurt; impair; spoil; damage; do damage [mischief] (to); inflict injury (upon)
♦감정을 해치다 hurt [injure] sb's feeling; hurt [offend] sb / 과음으로[과로로] 건강을 해치다 injure [impair, ruin] one's health by excessive drinking [overwork] / 미관을 해치다 mar [injure] the beauty (of)
▶질투가 그들의 우정을 해쳤다 Envy poisoned their friendship.
해치우다 〈일을〉finish up; get through; 〈지우다〉defeat; beat; 〈죽이다〉kill; do away with
♦일을 해치우다 get through with one's work; get a job finished / 상대를 간단히 해치우다 defeat an opponent with one hand
해커 (컴퓨터의) a hacker
해탈 解脫 deliverance (of one's sin); (Buddhist) emancipation; salvation
一해탈하다 be delivered from (sin, passions, attachments) ♦번뇌를 해탈하다 be delivered from earthly bondage; be cut loose from the ties of the earth
해태 a mythical unicorn-lion
해태 海苔 dried laver ⇨ 김²
해태 懈怠 laziness; idleness; indolence 一해태하다 lazy; idle; indolent
해토 解土 thawing (of the ground); a thaw 一해토하다 (the ground) thaw ■一머리 the beginning of a thaw
해트트릭 〔蹴·크리켓〕a hat trick
해파리 〔動〕a jellyfish; a sea jelly; a medusa (pl. ~s, -sae)
해판 解版 〔印〕distribution of printing type 一해판하다 distribute type
해포 a year or so
해포석 海泡石 〔鑛〕meerschaum; sepiolite
해표 海豹 〔動〕a seal ■一가죽 바다표범
해풍 海風 a sea wind [breeze]
해피엔딩 a happy ending ♦해피엔딩으로 끝나다 come to a happy ending; end happily
해하다 害— harm ⇨ 해치다
해학 諧謔 a jest; a joke; humor; (a) pleasantry ♦해학을 아는 사람 a man with a sense of humor / 해학적인 humorous; witty / 해학을 농하다 crack [let off] jokes
■一가(家) a humorist; a man of humor; a joker; a jester 一곡 (樂) a scherzo (pl. ~s, scherzi) 一극 a farce; a comedy 一소설 a humorous story
해항 海港 a seaport
해해거리다 keep laughing playfully [in fun]; laugh frolicsomely [silly]
해협 海峽 a strait; a channel; (美) a sound
♦해협을 건너다 cross a strait [channel]
■一대한— the Straits of Korea 도버— the Straits of Dover 영국— the (English) Channel 지브롤터— the Strait(s) of Gibraltar
해화석 海花石 〔動〕star coral
해후 邂逅 a chance [casual] meeting; encounter
一해후하다 meet by chance; happen [chance] to meet; come across sb; encounter
▶그 두 사람은 40년만에 해후했다 Chance brought the two together after a separation

of forty years. ⇌ The two happened to meet after forty years' interval.
핵 核 〈세포 등의〉 a nucleus 《*pl.* nuclei》; 〈과실의 심〉 a core; 〈과실의 씨〉 a kernel; a stone
—핵의 nuclear
■ —세포 a cell nucleus ■ —가족 a nuclear family —개발 nuclear development —경쟁 a nuclear race —공격 (make) a nuclear attack [strike] 《on a base》 —기지 a nuclear station —물리학[화학] nuclear physics [chemistry] —물질 nuclear materials —반응 nuclear reaction —보유국 ⇨ 핵무기(~보유국) —붕괴 disintegration of a cell nucleus; karyoclasis —시대 the nuclear age —에너지 nuclear energy —연료 nuclear fuel —우산 the (U.S.) nuclear umbrella: 핵우산의 보호하에 두다 put 《a nation》 under the protection of 《American》 nuclear umbrellas —융합 〔物〕 nuclear fusion; 〔生〕 fusion of cell nuclei; karyogamy —전력(戰力) (acquire) nuclear capacity [potential, force] —탄두 a nuclear warhead : 전략 핵탄두 a strategic nuclear warhead —탄두 미사일 a nuclear-tipped[-warhead] missile —폐기물 nuclear waste —폭탄 a nuclear bomb —항공모함 a nuclear-powered aircraft carrier —확산 nuclear proliferation —확산 방지 조약 a nuclear (weapons) non-proliferation treaty
핵과 核果 〔植〕 a stone fruit; a drupe
핵막 核膜 〔生〕 the nuclear membrane
핵무기 核武器 a nuclear weapon
♦ 소형 핵무기 a low-power nuclear weapon / 핵무기에 의한 파괴[보복] nuclear destruction [retaliation] / 핵무기의 확산을 방지하다 check the spread [dissemination] of nuclear weapons; prevent nuclear proliferation / 핵무기를 배치하다 deploy nuclear weapons
■ 전략[전술]— a strategic [tactical] nuclear weapon —보유국 a nuclear power [nation]: 비핵무기 보유국 a non-nuclear power —운반 로켓 a nuclear carrying rocket —폐기 total destruction [abolition] of nuclear weapons
핵무장 核武裝 nuclear armament(s)
♦ 비핵무장화 denuclearization / 핵무장을 금지하다 denuclearize 《a country》
—핵무장하다 be armed with nuclear weapons ■ —경쟁 competition in nuclear armaments —국 a nuclear-armed country; a nuclear power —금지지역 a denuclearized [nuclear-free] zone
핵분열 核分裂 〔物〕 (nuclear) fission(↔fusion); 〔生〕 nuclear division
—핵분열하다 fission; undergo fission
♦ 우라늄을 핵분열시키다 fission uranium
■ —물질 fissionable materials; fissionables —생성물 a fission product —연쇄반응 fission chain reaction —폭탄 a (nuclear) fission bomb
핵산 核酸 〔生化〕 nucleic acid
■ 디옥시리보— deoxyribonucleic acid (略 DNA) 리보— ribonucleic acid (略 RNA)
핵시설 核施設 nuclear facilities
▶ 북한은 핵시설에 대한 국제적인 사찰을 받아야 한다 North Korea should accept international inspection of its nuclear facilities.

핵실험 核實驗 nuclear testing; a nuclear test
♦ 핵실험의 중지[재개] a suspension [resumption] of nuclear test / 핵실험을 재개하다 resume nuclear weapons test
■ 고공(高空)— a high altitude nuclear test 대기권— a nuclear test in the atmosphere; an atmospheric nuclear test 지하— underground nuclear testing; an underground nuclear test
■ —경쟁 nuclear testing competition —금지 a ban on nuclear tests; a nuclear test ban —금지 협정 a nuclear test ban agreement —장 a nuclear testing ground
핵심 核心 the core; a kernel; 〈요점〉 the point
♦ 문제의 핵심 the heart [kernel] of a problem / 핵심을 찌르다 touch the core (of a subject); come to the point / 문제의 핵심을 파악하다 go [get] to the heart of a matter; tear the vitals out of a subject
핵원형질 核原形質 〔生〕 nucleoplasm
핵인 核仁 〔生〕 a nucleolus 《*pl.* -li》
핵자 核子 〔植〕 a stone; 〔物〕 a nucleon
— 중(重)— a hyperon
핵전쟁 核戰爭 a nuclear war ♦ 핵전쟁의 위협을 줄이다 reduce the threat of a nuclear war
핵질 核質 〔生〕 nucleoplasm; karyoplasm
핵클럽 核— the Nuclear [Atomic] Club
핵투명성 核透明性 the nuclear transparency
♦ 북한의 핵투명성 보장에 관한 문제를 제기하다 raise the question of guaranteeing North Korean nuclear transparancy
핵폭발 核爆發 a nuclear explosion [blast]
— 장치[실험] a nuclear device [test]
핵학 核學 〔生〕 karyology
핸드드릴 a hand drill
핸드백 a handbag
핸드볼 〔競〕 handball

—————— 핸드볼 ——————

골 라인 goal line
골 에어리어 goal area
사이드 라인 side line
골 goal
프리 스로 라인 free throw line
페널티 스로 라인 penalty throw line
골 에어리어 라인 goal area line
센터 라인 center line

핸들 〈손잡이〉 a handle; a pull; 〈자전거의〉 a handlebar; 〈자동차·비행기의〉 a (steering) wheel; 〈도어의〉 a doorknob
♦ 핸들을 우[좌]로 돌리다[꺾다] wheel right [left] / 핸들을 잡다 be [sit] at the wheel; take the wheel (of the car)

핸들링 〈蹴〉 a handling

핸디캡 a handicap
♦ 핸디캡 18의 골퍼 a 18-handicap player; a 18-handicapper / 신체적 핸디캡을 극복하다 overcome a physical handicap / 핸디캡을 주다 handicap *sb* / …에게 핸디캡 3을 주다 give three points to
▶ 그는 학력이 없는 것이 핸디캡이다 He is handicapped by his lack of formal education.

핸섬하다 handsome; good-looking

핼끗 with a sidelong glance ⇨ 흘끗 2

핼리혜성 —彗星 〔天〕 Halley's comet

핼쑥하다 pale; pallid; wan; waxy; pasty
♦ 핼쑥한 얼굴 a pallid [wan] face / 송장처럼 핼쑥하다 look ghastly / 앓고 나서 핼쑥하다 look thin after an illness / 몹시 핼쑥해지다 turn ghastly [deadly] pale

햄[1] 〈식품〉 ham
♦ 훈제(燻製)— smoked [cured] ham; gammon —샌드위치 ham sandwiches —샐러드 ham and salad —에그 ham and eggs

햄[2] 〈아마추어 무선사〉 a (radio) ham

햄릿 〈셰익스피어 희곡〉 *Hamlet*

햄버거 a hamburger

햄버거스테이크 a hamburger steak

햄족 —族 the Hamitic race

햄프셔 〈영국 남부의 주〉 Hampshire

햅쌀 new rice; the year's new crop of rice
■ —밥 rice cooked from the new crop

햇— new; 〈crop〉 of the year ♦ 햇감자 a new crop of potatoes / 햇콩[햇팥] new beans [red beans]; the year's new crop of beans [red beans]

햇것 the year's (new) crop; a new crop of the year)

햇곡식 —穀食 a new crop of the year; the year's new grain

햇귀 1 〈처음 솟는 햇빛〉 the first sunlight of the morning; the first streak of daylight
2 ⇨ 햇살

햇덧 a short autumn [fall] day

햇무리 the halo of the sun; the ring [corona] around the sun
■ —구름 〔氣〕〈권층운〉 a cirrostratus cloud

햇물 1 ⇨ 햇무리 2 〈샘물〉 a spring which gushes out only after the rainy season

햇발 sunbeams ⇨ 햇살

햇병아리 〈병아리〉 a chicken; a chick; 〈풋내기〉 a fledgling; a greenhorn; a new [green] hand; a novice; 〈俗〉 a tenderfoot
♦ 대학을 갓 나온 햇병아리 a new-fledged university man
■ —기자 a cub reporter

햇볕 the heat [warmth] of the sunbeams [sunlight]; the sun
♦ 내려쬐는 햇볕 glaring sunshine / 햇볕이 잘 드는 sunny (room) / 햇볕이 들다 shine in / 햇볕을 가리다 screen [shade] (a thing) from the sun / 햇볕을 쬐다 bask in the sun / 곡식을 햇볕에 널다 spread grain out beneath the sun / 햇볕에 말리다 dry a thing in the sun / 햇볕에 타다 be [get] sunburnt; be (sun)tanned
▶ 햇볕이 점점 따가워졌다 The sun was fiercer every minute.
▶ 그녀의 피부는 햇볕에 잘 탄다 Her skin sunburns [gets sunburnt] easily.

햇빛 sunshine; sunlight; sunbeams
♦ 강렬한 햇빛 glaring [hard] sunlight / 햇빛을 들이다 let the sun in / 햇빛을 보다 see the light of day; 〈계획 등이〉 be realized; materialize / 햇빛을 보지 못하다 keep indoors; 〈식물·장소 등이〉 be sunless; have no sunshine; 〈법안 등이〉 be shelved [tabled]
▶ 방은 햇빛이 나날이 더 잘들고 있다 The room gets more sunshine every day.
▶ 그의 계획은 마침내 햇빛을 보게 되었다 His plan materialized [was realized] at last.
▶ 그 책은 결국 햇빛을 보지 못했다 The book did not see the light after all.

햇살 beams [streaks] of sunlight; sunbeams; the rays of the sun
♦ 부드러운 햇살 soft beams [streaks] of sunlight / 나뭇가지 사이로 비치는 햇살 sunbeams shining through branches of trees / 햇살을 받다 be [bathe, bask] in the sun
▶ 햇살이 퍼지고 있다 The sun is spreading its beams.

햇수 —數 the number of years
▶ 뉴욕에 온 지 햇수로 10년이다 This is my tenth year in New York.

행[1] **行** 〈글의〉 a line; a row
♦ 시 한행 a line of verse; a verse / 위에서 셋째 행 the third line from the top / 1행씩 걸러 쓰다 write on every other line / 행을 바꾸다 begin a new line; start a new paragraph

행[2] **行** 〔佛敎〕〈수행〉 religious austerities; self-discipline; asceticism; 〈근행〉 a service

행 幸 fortune ♦ 행인지 불행인지 for better or for worse

-행 -行 ♦ 뉴욕행 비행기 an airplane for New York / 수원행 수하물 luggage destined [booked] for Suwon / 서울행 차표 a ticket to Seoul / 부산행 bound [destined] for Pusan; (an express) for Pusan
▶ 대전행 기차는 여기서 바꿔 타십시오 Change trains here for Taejŏn.

행각 行脚 1 〔佛敎〕〈수행〉 a pilgrimage
—**행각하다** go on (a) pilgrimage; make a pilgrimage
2 〈돌아다님〉 traveling; a walking tour
♦ 사기 행각을 하다 commit a fraud; practice a deception / 애정 행각에 나서다 go on an affection tour
—**행각하다** travel on foot; make a walking tour
■ —승 an itinerant monk [priest]; a priest on a pilgrimage

행간 行間 space between lines
♦ 행간의 여백 interlinear space / 행간을 넓히다[좁히다] leave more [less] space between the lines / 행간을 메다 leave space between lines; space out / 행간을 읽다 read between

the lines
행객 行客 a traveler; a wayfarer
행군 行軍 a (military) march; marching
▶무리한 행군으로 사망자가 나왔다 Some men died during the hard march.
─**행군하다** march
▶그들은 폭설을 무릅쓰고 태백산을 행군했다 They marched among the T'aebaek Mountains in the face of a heavy snowstorm.
■강─ a forced march 눈속─ a march in [through] the snow 무장─ an armed march 철야─ an overnight march ■─대형 a march formation ─명령 marching orders ─속도 a rate of march
행궁 行宮 a rural palace; the king's traveling lodge
행글라이더 a hang glider

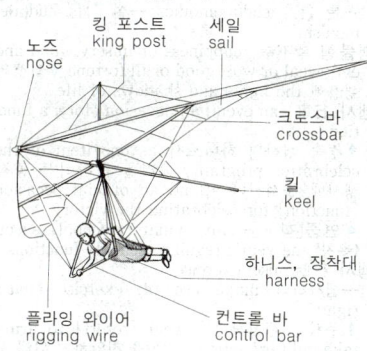
─ 행글라이더 ─

행낭 行囊 (美) a mailbag; a mail pouch; (英) a postbag
행내기 〈보통내기〉 an ordinary person; a mediocrity; the common run of men
♦행내기가 아닌 사람 a man of no common order; a smart [sharp] fellow / 행내기가 아니다 be not an ordinary man; be very hard to manage [deal] with
행동 行動 action; 〈1회의〉 an act; 〈행동거지〉 behavior; movement; conduct; 〈활동〉 activities; 〔軍〕 operations
〈행동의〉 행동의 자유가 허용되다 be allowed freedom of action [movement]; be allowed to go *one's* own way / 행동의 자유를 속박하다 restrain *sb's* freedom of action; tie *sb's* hands 〈행동이[은]〉 행동이 기민하다 be prompt in action / 행동이 수상하다 behave [act] suspiciously
▶말보다 행동이 더 잘 나타난다 Actions speak louder than words.
▶그의 행동은 용감했다 His act [action, behavior] was brave.
〈행동을〉 행동을 감시하다 watch [keep an eye on] *sb's* movements / 행동을 고치다 mend *one's* ways / 행동을 개시하다 start action; set to work / 행동을 취하다 act; behave; take action 《against》 / 곧 행동을 취하다 act immediately; take immediate action / 훌륭한 행동을 하다 do a good deed; behave *oneself* well
▶너는 어른이니까 거기에 걸맞는 행동을 해야 한다 You're an adult and should act [behave] accordingly.
▶우리는 온종일 행동을 같이했다 We spent the whole day together.
〈행동에〉 행동에 드러나다 show in *one's* manner / 행동에 들어가다 go [get] into action / 생각을 행동에 옮기다 put *one's* idea into action; translate an idea into action
▶자기 행동에 책임을 져야 한다 You should answer for your actions [what you do].
▶남들 앞에서는 행동에 조심해라 Be careful about your behavior in public.
▶그의 반응은 말뿐으로, 행동에 옮기지는 않았다 His response was merely verbal and he took no action.
─**행동하다** act; behave; move
♦경솔하게 행동하다 act [behave] rashly / 명령[충고]대로 행동하다 act on *sb's* order [advice] / 집단으로 행동하다 go around in group
▶앞으로는 좀더 신중하게 행동하도록 해라 You must be more prudent in future about what you do.
▶지금이야말로 행동할 때다 Now is the time for action [to act]. ⇌ We must act now.
■군사─ military movements; hostile operations 단독─ separate action 단체[개인]─ group [individual] action 자유─ free [independent] action; 《have, get》 a free hand 적대─ hostile operations 직접─ direct action ■─강령 a code of conduct ─거지 behavior; deportment; manner; conduct ─과학 behavioral science ─권(圈) 〔生態〕 the home range ─대 an action corps [group] ─력 acting power ─미술 action painting ─미술가 an action painter ─반경 a radius of action [operation]; a cruising [an action] radius ─방침 the course of action ─방향 a line of action ─범위 a sphere of action; elbowroom ─주의 〔心〕 behaviorism ─주의 (심리학)자 a behaviorist ─특성 a behavioral characteristic ─형〔양식〕〔心·社〕 behavior pattern
행동개시 行動開始 〔軍〕 deployment
─**행동개시하다** deploy 《an army》
■─시간 (the) H-hour; (the) zero hour ─(예정)일 the deployment day; D-day
행동통일 行動統一 action in concert 《with》; united action
▶회원들끼리 행동통일이 안 되고 있다 There is lack of unity among the members.
─**행동통일하다** act in concert 《with》
행락 行樂 pleasure; enjoyment; pleasure-making; holiday-making; a good time; fun; an outing
♦봄의 행락 pleasures of springtime; 〈나들이〉 a spring outing
─**행락하다** enjoy *oneself*; have a good time; have [go on] an outing
■─객 a weekender; a vacationist; a holiday-maker ─지 a pleasure resort; a (holiday) spot

행랑 行廊 a room on a side of the front gate; 〈하인들의 방〉 the servants' quarters (on both sides of the main gate)
■—살이 ((lead, live)) the life of a resident servant; servantship —아범[어멈] a man [woman] servant who sleeps in

행려 行旅 〈여행〉 travel; 〈사람〉 a traveler
■—병사자 a person dead from sickness on the road —병자 a person fallen sick on the road; an ill wayfarer

행렬 行列 **1** 〈행진하는〉 a procession; a parade; 〈늘어선〉 a line; a queue [kjúː]
♦ 행렬의 선두[후미] the head [tail] of a procession [queue] / 행렬의 끝에 붙다 be at the tail of a procession [queue] / 행렬의 선두에 서다 head a procession / 행렬을 짓다 stand in a line; 〈쇼핑 등의〉 form a queue; queue up / 행렬을 지어 가다 march in procession; parade / 행렬을 지어 버스를 기다리다 wait for a bus in a line [queue]; line up [((美)) queue up] for a bus / 행렬에 끼어 들다 join a (waiting) line
2 〔數〕 a matrix 《*pl*. ~es, -trices》
■가장— a masquerade parade; a costume procession 제등(提燈)— a lantern procession [parade] —식 〔數〕 a determinant

행로 行路 〈길〉 a path; a road; a course; 〈세상살이〉 one's path [course] in life
■ 인생— life's journey; the path [course] of life: 긴 인생 행로에는 때때로 큰 어려움을 만나게 된다 We will sometimes suffer great hardships on life's long journey.

행리 行李 a traveler's equipment ⇨ 행장(行裝)

행림 杏林 〈의원〉 physicians; medical men
■—계(界) medical circles

행망쩍다 careless; inattentive

행방 行方 one's whereabouts (▶단수 취급); one's traces
♦ 행방이 묘연한 missing / 행방을 감추다 cover one's traces; conceal oneself [one's whereabouts]; run away / 행방을 알아내다 locate sb; discover the trace of 《a missing man》; find out one's whereabouts / 행방을 찾다 trace; search [hunt, look] for sb
▶ 경찰은 범인의 행방을 쫓고 있다 The police are after [looking for] the criminal.
▶ 경찰은 마침내 그의 행방을 찾아냈다 The police have finally tracked him down.

행방불명 行方不明 ♦ 행방불명의 missing; lost / 행방불명이 되다 be [get] lost; be heard of no more
▶ 백방으로 알아 보았지만 그는 아직도 행방불명이다 Inquiries have been made in every likely place, but his whereabouts is still unknown.
■—자 a missing person; (총칭) the missing; the lost

행보 行步 walking; going on foot —행보하다 walk; go on foot

행복 幸福 happiness; felicity; well-being
♦ 인생의 행복 human happiness; happiness of life / 행복을 누리다 enjoy happiness / 행복을 빌다 pray for sb's happiness; wish sb every happiness / 행복을 추구하다 look for [seek] happiness / 행복을 위협하다 threaten one's happiness [well-being]
▶ 행복에 이르는 길은 여러 가지가 있다 There are different ways to happiness.
—행복하다 happy; blessed; fortunate
♦ 행복한 가정 a happy home / 더할 나위없이 행복하다 as happy as a king; as happy as one can be / 행복하게 happily; in happiness / 행복하게 살다 live [lead] a happy life; live happily
▶ 오늘만큼 행복한 적은 없었다 I'd never felt happier than I did today. ⇒ This is the happiest day of my life.
▶ 두 사람의 생활은 행복한 일만 있었던 것은 아니었다 It wasn't all just roses with them.
■—감 〔心〕 euphoria; the sense of well-being —론 〔哲〕 eud(a)emonics —설 〔哲〕 eud(a)emonism

행불행 幸不幸 happiness or misery; good and evil; weal or woe; good or ill fortune ♦ 인생의 행불행 the lights and shadows of life

행사 行事 an event; an occasion (for); a function
♦ 경축 행사의 하나로서 as one item of the celebration program / 승리를 축하하는 공식 행사에 출석하다 attend an official occasion [function] for celebrating the victory
■ 연중[학교]— an annual [a school] event; (총칭) the year's regular [school] functions

행사 行使 use; exercise
—행사하다 make use of; exercise 《one's rights》
♦ 무력을 행사하다 appeal [resort] to arms; take military action / 폭동을 진압하기 위해 무력을 행사하다 use (armed) force to put down a riot / 선거권을 행사하다 exercise one's right to vote / 실력을 행사하다 use [employ] force; resort to forced measures / 특권을 행사하다 exercise [employ] a [one's] privilege

행상 行商 〈장사〉 peddling; hawking; an itinerant trade; 〈상인〉 a peddler
—행상하다 peddle; hawk; engage in an itinerant trade ♦ 시골로 다니며 행상하다 peddle goods about the country
■—업 peddlery —인 a peddler; a pedlar; a hawker

행상 行賞 awarding sb (with a) prize; the conferment of rewards for services rendered; distribution of honors; the official recognition of distinguished services ⇨ 논공행상(論功行賞)
—행상하다 award a prize 《to sb》; reward

행색 行色 〈차림새〉 one's appearance [look]; 〈태도〉 demeanor; a manner; an attitude
♦ 거지 행색 the appearance of a beggar / 행색이 초라하다 look shabby

행서 行書 〈한자 서체의 하나〉 the semicursive style of writing Chinese characters

행선 行船 sailing —행선하다 sail

행선지 行先地 〈목적지〉 one's destination; the end of one's journey; the place where one is going; 〈행방〉 one's whereabouts

▶ 그의 행선지는 분명치 않다 I am not sure where he has gone [of his whereabouts].
▶ 행선지를 말하고 나가거라 Tell me where you are going before you leave.

행성 行星 a planet; a globe ♦ 행성의 planetary
■ 내— an interior planet 대— a major planet 소— a minor planet; a planetoid: 소행성설 the planetesimal hypothesis 외— an exterior [a superior] planet ■—광행차(光行差)[세차(歲差)] planetary aberration [precession] —로켓 an interplanetary rocket —(상)성운 planetary nebula —운동[환류] planetary motion [circulation]

행세 行世 1 〈행합〉 conduct of life; behavior; 〈태도〉 one's bearing [manners]
♦ 행세를 잘못하다 misbehave [misconduct] oneself
—행세하다 conduct [go] through life [the world]; behave [conduct] oneself
2 〈가장〉 show; pretense; affectation
♦ 주인 행세를 하다 assume [put on] a proprietary air
—행세하다 pass oneself off 《as》; pretend; affect; set up for; assume an air of
♦ 백만장자로 행세하다 pose as a millionaire / 학자로 행세하다 assume an air of a scholar

행세 行勢 〈세도를 부림〉 wielding special power; assuming political power
—행세하다 wield [exercise, exert] power [authority] 《over》; hold sway
♦ 행세하는 집안 a distinguished [an influential] family

행수 行首 the head of a group; a boss
행수 行數 the number of lines; linage
행습 行習 〈버릇〉 a habit; a practice
♦ 행습이 사납다 have [be in] a bad habit
—행습하다 make 《it》 a habit to 《do》; cultivate a habit

행실 行實 conduct; demeanor; behavior; deportment
♦ 좋은 행실 good conduct / 나쁜[못된] 행실 misconduct; misbehavior / 행실이 나쁜 여자 a woman of loose morals / 행실이 좋다 be well-behaved [well-conducted]; show good deportment [conduct] / 행실이 나쁘다 be ill-conducted; misconduct [misbehave] / 행실을 고치다 reform oneself [one's conduct]; amend one's ways [conduct]; turn over a new leaf / 행실을 조심하다 be careful [prudent, discreet] in one's conduct

행악 行惡 doing evil
—행악하다 do evil; do [use] violence; do a cruel thing; practice wickedness

행여(나) 幸— by (some) chance; by any chance [possibility]; possibly
♦ 행여나 하고 on the chance 《of finding sb》; 〈요행을 바라고〉 on the off chance 《of》
▶ 그녀는 행여나 하고 응모했다 She applied on the off chance.
▶ 나는 행여나 네가 오나 하고 기다렸다 I have waited in case you might drop by.

행운 幸運 good fortune; (good) luck; (美) a lucky [good] break

♦ 행운의 여신 the Goddess of Fortune / 행운을 타고나다 be born under a lucky star
▶ 우연히 그 이야기를 들은 것이 행운이었다 It was a stroke of luck that I happened to hear about it.
▶ 행운을 빕니다 Good luck (to you)! ⇌ Best of luck to you! ⇌ I wish you good luck.
■ —아 a lucky fellow [person]

행원 行員 〈은행원〉 a bank clerk [employee]; a clerk of a bank

행위 行爲 an act; (an) action; a deed; 〈행실〉 behavior; conduct; 〈소행〉 a work; doings
♦ 영웅적 행위 a heroic deed; a heroism / 정당한 행위 a justifiable [legitimate] act / 친절한 행위 an act of kindness
▶ 그의 행위는 신사답지 않다 His conduct is unworthy of a gentleman.
▶ 그의 행위는 꼭 미친 사람 같다 He behave himself exactly like a mad man.
■ 도덕(적)— a moral act 법률— a juristic act; a legal action 상(商)— a commercial [business] transaction 자선— an act of charity; charities 잔혹— a cruel act [action]; an act of cruelty —능력 (legal) capacity —무능력 (legal) incompetence —세 the service [act] tax —자 a doer; a performer 《of a deed》; 〔法〕 an actual offender; 〈상행위의〉 a transactor —지(地) 〔法〕 the place of an act

행음 行淫 committing adultery —행음하다 commit adultery

행인 行人 a passerby 《pl. passersby》; a foot passenger; 〈나그네〉 a wayfarer

행인 杏仁 〈살구씨 알맹이〉 an apricot stone —유 apricot-kernel oil

행자 行者 〔佛敎〕 an ascetic; an ascetic devotee; 〈이슬람교 등의〉 a fakir

행장 行狀 1 〈행적의 기록〉 records of a deceased person's life; a biography [life history] of a deceased person
2 〈수감자의 성적〉 the conduct mark

행장 行裝 〈여행의〉 travel gear; a traveling [traveler's] outfit [suit, kit]; a traveler's equipment
♦ 행장을 꾸리다[갖추다] make preparations [prepare] for a journey / 행장을 풀다 take off one's traveling attire; 〈숙박하다〉 stop at an inn; (美) check in at a hotel

행적 行績·行蹟 one's (lifetime) achievements [doings, work]; one's work

행전 行纏 leggings; uppers; 《a pair of》 gaiters; puttees ♦ 행전을 치고 with gaitered legs / 행전을 치다 wrap one's legs with puttees; put on leggings

행정 行政 administration ♦ 행정적인[상의] administrative; executive
▶ 그는 행정적 수완이 있다 He has administrative ability [talent].
■ —각부 administrative branches —감독[관리] administrative control [management] —개혁 an administrative reform —경찰 the administrative police —관 an executive [administrative] officer; an administrator; 《총칭》 the executive —관청 a government [an administrative] office [agency] —구획 an

administrative district [division, section]; a jurisdiction ―권 administrative [executive] power [authority] ―기관 an administrative organ [body]; an executive agency ―기구 administrative organization; an administrative structure: 기존의 행정기구를 간소화하다 simplify the administrative organization in existence ―명령 an administrative [executive] order ―법 (法) the administrative law ―법령 an administrative decree ―부(府) the Executive; the Administration ―사무 administrative affairs ―서사 an administrative scrivener ―소송 administrative litigation ―재판(소) (a court of) administrative litigation ―정리 administrative readjustment ―조직 ⇨ 행정(~기구) ―조치 an administrative measure [action] ―처벌 administrative punishment ―처분 an administrative measure [disposition] ―학 public administration ―협정 an administrative agreement; a status-of-forces agreement

행정 行程 **1** 〈거리〉 (a) distance; a march; 〈일정〉 an itinerary
▶ 여기서 하루 행정이다 It is a day's journey from here.
▶ 우리는 30마일의 행정을 답파했다 We covered a distance of 30 miles.
2 [機] a stroke; a throw (of a switch)
♦ 내향[외향]행정 an instroke [outstroke] / 상[하]행정 an up [a down] stroke / 4행정의 four-stroke (engine)

행주 a dishcloth; a dish towel ―질 wiping with a dish cloth: 행주질하다 [행주치다] wipe with a dishcloth ―치마 an apron

행중 行中 〈일행〉 a party; a company
♦ 행중에 끼다 join a party

행진 行進 a march; a parade
▶ 군인들이 행진 중이었다 The soldiers were marching [on the march].
―행진하다 march; parade; proceed
♦ 거리를 행진하다 march along [down] the streets
■―곡 a march: 결혼[군대] 행진곡 a wedding [military] march

행짜 mischief ⇨ 행티

행차 行次 an honored going [coming]; a visit of a high personage to a place
―행차하다 go (out); come; visit
▶ 행차 뒤에 나팔 (속담) That is the case of coming a day after the fair.

행커치프 a handkerchief (*pl.* ~s, -chieves)

행티 〈심술버릇〉 ill-willed behavior; mischief
♦ 행티 부리다 do (*sb*) *sth* wicked; show ill will / 행티 사납다 be cross(-grained); be perverse; be malicious

행패 行悖 misconduct; misbehavior; outrage; violence ♦ 행패를 부리다 resort to violence; commit an act of outrage (on)

행포 行暴 violence; riot; outrage ♦ (온갖) 행포를 (다) 부리다 commit (all sorts of) excesses ―행포하다 do violence; run riot; commit excesses [outrage]

행하 行下 a gift (of money from a master to his servant); 〈놀음차〉 a tip; a gratuity ♦ 행하를 주다 give *sb* a tip [gratuity]; tip (a porter)

행하다 行― **1** 〈행동하다〉 do; act; 〈처신하다〉 behave (oneself); conduct oneself
2 〈실행하다〉 do; practice (moderation); perform; 〈이행하다〉 discharge (one's duty); commit; carry out
♦ 기적을 행하다 work a miracle / 선을 행하다 do good; practice virtue / 악을 행하다 do wrong [evil]; commit vice
▶ 말하기는 쉬워도 행하기는 어렵다 (속담) Theory is one thing, practice is another. ⇌ Easier said than done.
3 〈실시하다〉 conduct (education); exercise (authority)
♦ 정의를 행하다 dispense justice
4 〈거행하다〉 hold (a meeting); give (an examination); perform (a ceremony)
♦ 의식을 행하다 perform a ceremony / 혼례를 행하다 hold [perform] a marriage [wedding]

행형 行刑 [法] the execution of a sentence; 〈사형의〉 execution ―행형하다 execute (a sentence) ―학 penology

행화 杏花 〈살구꽃〉 an apricot blossom

행흉 行凶 〈살인〉 murder; 〈암살〉 assassination ―행흉하다 commit murder

향 向 **1** 〈방향〉 a direction; a quarter; 〈방위〉 a situation
▶ 풍향이 바뀌었다 The direction of the wind has turned [shifted].
2 〈집 등의 앉음새〉 an exposure; an aspect
♦ 남향집 a house facing (the) south; a house with a southern aspect [exposure] / 서향이다 〈집이〉 look to the west; look [face] west; 〈창문이〉 open to the west

향 香 (an) incense; (a) perfume
♦ 향을 피우다 burn [offer] incense
■―갑[주머니] an incense case [pouch]

향가 鄕歌 old Korean folk songs [ballads]

향관 鄕關 〈고향땅〉 one's native place

향교 鄕校 a local old-time school annexed to the Confucian shrine

향국 鄕國 〈고국〉 one's native land; one's mother country; the country of one's birth [origin]; 〈고향〉 one's home (province)

향군 鄕軍 ex-service men ⇨ 재향군인

향긋하다 somewhat fragrant; 〈서술적〉 have a faint sweet smell [scent]
▶ 이 장작은 탈 때 향긋한 냄새가 난다 This wood gives off a fragrant smell as it burns.

향기 香氣 (a) fragrance; (a) perfume; a sweet smell [odor]; (a) scent; aroma
♦ 꽃향기 the fragrance of a flower / 커피의 향기 (inhale) the aroma of coffee / 장미 향기가 나는 비누 soap scented with roses; rose-scented soap / 향기있는 fragrant; aromatic; sweet-smelling; (sweet-)scented / 향기가 없는 inodorous; scentless / 향기가 나다 smell sweet; be fragrant; be sweetly scented / 향기를 풍기다 emit [send forth] fragrance [a sweet smell]; give out a sweet smell
▶ 이 차는 향기가 좋다 This tea smells good [nice].
▶ 라일락이 정원에서 향기를 내뿜고 있다 The

lilacs smelled sweet in the garden.
향기롭다 香氣— fragrant; aromatic; balmy; sweet-smelling; (sweet-)scented; sweet
♦ 향기로운 냄새 a fragrance; a sweet [fragrant] smell / 향기로운 꽃 a fragrant flower
향꽂이 香— an incense holder [burner]
향나무 香— 〔植〕 Chinese juniper;〈향기나는 나무〉an aromatic tree
향낭 香囊 an incense pouch [bag]; a sachet
향내 香— fragrance ⇨ 향기(香氣)
향년 享年 one's age at death ▶ 그는 향년 75세로 죽었다 He died at the age of seventy-five.
향당 鄕黨 one's village community; one's hometown; one's native village;〈사람들〉people of one's hometown
향도 嚮導 〈일〉guidance; conduct; leading;〈사람〉a leader; a guide;〔軍〕a fugleman
—**향도하다** guide; conduct; lead
■—**기(機)** a leader plane —**함** a flotilla leader; a guide ship
향락 享樂 enjoyment ♦ 향락적(인) pleasure-loving; given up to pleasure
—**향락하다** enjoy
▶ 그는 인생을 향락한다 He enjoys life. ⇌ He leads a gay life.
—**주의** epicurism; epicureanism; hedonism
—**주의자** an epicure; an epicurean; a hedonist
향로 香爐 an incense burner; a cassolette; a (bronze) censer
향료 香料 1〈식물의〉spice(s); spicery
♦ 향료를 넣다 spice; season with spice
2〈화장품 등의〉(a) perfume; aromatic; essence
■—**류** 〈식품의〉spicery;〈방향의〉perfumery
—**식물** aromatic plants —**제조소** a perfumery
향리 鄕里 〈고향〉the place where one was born and brought up; one's birthplace; one's hometown; one's native village
♦ 향리로 돌아가다 go [come] home
향미 香味 a flavor; smack
■—**료** spices; seasoning; condiments
향방 向方 a direction; bearings;〈진행하는〉a course [line];〈목적지〉a destination;〈집 등의〉an aspect
♦ 향방을 모르다 do not know the direction; do not know which way is up; lose one's way [bearings]; have no sense at all
향배 向背 for or against; pro or con;〈태도〉one's attitude ♦ 향배를 정하다[분명히 하다] define [clarify] one's attitude 《toward》
▶ 그것은 그의 향배에 달려 있다 It depends on his attitude.
향불 香— an incense fire; (a) burning incense
♦ 향불을 피우다 burn incense
향사 向斜 〔地質〕a syncline; a synclinal (fold)
향사 鄕士 a country gentleman
향상 向上 〈상승〉(a) rise;〈개선〉improvement; betterment;〈진보〉(an) advance; progress
♦ 지위의 향상 a rise in position (▶「승진」의 뜻으로는 보통 (a) promotion을 씀) / 생활 수준의 향상 the improvement of living standards / 생활 향상을 꾀하다 try to improve one's living condition; try to get [gain] a better life (for oneself)
▶ 여성의 지위 향상을 위하여 노력했다 We made efforts to raise [elevate] the status of women.
—**향상하다** rise; be elevated; become higher;〈개선하다〉improve; advance; progress;〈진보하다〉make progress
♦ 향상시키다 raise; elevate; improve; make better; better / 학문이 향상하다 improve [advance] in one's studies / 향상하려고 노력하다 struggle for betterment
▶ 정부는 노인 복지를 향상시키고 있다 The Government is promoting welfare for the old people.
▶ 여성의 사회적 지위가 향상됐다 Women's social status has risen [has been improved]. ⇌ Women have risen in their social status.
■—**심** a desire to improve oneself; ambition; aspiration
향선 香腺 〔動〕a scent bag [gland]
향속 鄕俗 rural [local] customs [ways]
향수 享受 enjoyment —**향수하다** enjoy; have; be given ♦ 건강을 향수하다 be in [enjoy, have] good health
향수 享壽 enjoying longevity —**향수하다** live long; enjoy longevity; live to a great age
향수 香水 a perfume; scent; perfumed [scented] water; (총칭) perfumery
♦ 장미 향수 rose water / 향수를 바른[넣은] perfumed; scented / 향수를 쓰다 use perfume / 몸에 향수를 뿌리다 perfume oneself
■—**병** a scent bottle —**분무기** an atomizer; a scent sprayer
향수 鄕愁 homesickness; nostalgia 《for》♦ 향수를 느끼다 feel homesick; feel nostalgic [nostalgia] 《for》/ 향수에 젖다 be nostalgic 《for》/ become homesick [nostalgic] / 향수를 느끼게 하다 make sb homesick; excite nostalgia
향습성 向濕性 〔植〕positive hydrotropism
향신료 香辛料 (cooking) spice(s) ♦ 향신료를 넣다 spice (food); season with spice
향심력 向心力 central force;〔物〕centripetal force ⇨ 구심(~력)
향악 鄕樂 Hyangak; Korean music (as opposed to Chinese music)
향연 香煙 1〈향 연기〉the smoke of incense 2〈향기로운 담배〉fragrant tobacco
향연 饗宴 a feast; a banquet; a dinner
♦ 향연을 베풀다 hold [give] a banquet
향유 享有 enjoyment; possession ♦ 인권의 향유 the enjoyment of personal rights
—**향유하다** enjoy; possess oneself of; be possessed of
▶ 우리는 자유를 향유할 권리가 있다 We have [hold] the right to enjoy liberty.
향유 香油 perfumed [scented] oil; balm
♦ 머리에 향유를 바르다 put perfumed oil on one's hair
■—**기** sperm oil
향유고래 香油— 〔動〕a sperm whale
향응 饗應 (an) entertainment; a treat;〈연회〉a banquet; a dinner; a feast

♦향응을 받다 be entertained at dinner —향응하다 entertain *sb* at dinner; invite *sb* to dinner; feast *sb*; give a (dinner) party
향응 響應 1 〈메아리〉 resonance; an echo 《*pl*. ~es》 —향응하다 echo; resonate; be resonant (with); respond 《to》
2 〈호응〉 acting in concert —향응하다 act in concert 《with》; follow suit; respond to
향의 向意 (an) intention ⇨ 의향(意向)
향일성 向日性 〔植〕 positive heliotropism
■—식물 a heliotropic plant
향자 向者 the other day; some days ago
향전 香奠 condolence money=부의(賻儀)
향점 向點 〔天〕 an apex 《*pl*. ~es, apices》
■—태양— the solar apex
향정신성 의약품 向精神性醫藥品 a psychotropic (medicine)
향지성 向地性 〔植〕 positive geotropism
향초 香草 〈향기나는 풀〉 fragrant [aromatic] grass [plants]; herbs; 〈향기로운 담배〉 fragrant tobacco
향촉 香燭 incense and candles (used in memorial [religious] service)
향촌 鄕村 〈시골〉 the country; 〈마을〉 a village; a rural community
향취 香臭 fragrance ⇨ 향기(香氣)
향토 鄕土 〈고향〉 one's native province; one's home country; 〈출생지〉 one's birthplace; 〈어떤 지방〉 local
▶그는 우리 향토의 자랑이다 He is the pride of our home town [province].
■—무용 a folk dance —문학 folk literature —민요 a folk song [ballad] —사가(史家) a student of the local history —색 local color; 향토색이 짙은 rich in local color; of rich local color —애 love for [of] one's home province —예비군 the homeland reserve forces —예술 folk art; local crafts —요리 a style of cooking peculiar to certain locality —음악 local [folk] music —지 a chronicle of a province; (a) local history
향하다 向— 1 〈대하다〉 face; look 《to》; front 《on》; turn 《on, toward》
♦바다를 향하다 look out on the sea / 이 쪽을 향하다 look this way / 벽쪽을 향해서 서다 stand facing to a wall
▶그 배는 남쪽을 향해 항해하고 있다 The ship is heading south.
▶그 창문은 길쪽을 향해 나 있다 The window opens on the street.
▶나는 그녀쪽으로 시선을 향했다 I cast an eye in her direction.
▶경찰은 공중을 향해 권총을 발사했다 The policeman fired a shot into the air.
2 〈가다〉 proceed 《to》; go 《to, toward》; start 《for》; leave 《for》; be bound 《for》; head 《toward》; take one's way 《toward》
♦전선으로 향하다 go to the front / 유럽으로 향하여 leave for Europe
▶배는 뉴욕을 떠나 홍콩으로 향했다 The ship set her course from New York to Hongkong.
3 〈지향하다〉 be inclined 《to, toward》; tend 《to》; lean [trend] 《toward》
♦민심이 향하는 바를 살피다 watch [see] the trend of popular feelings

향학심 向學心 love for learning; a desire to learn [for learning]
▶신입생은 모두 향학심에 불타 있다 All the freshmen are eager to learn.
향합 香盒 an incense case [container]
향화 香火 an incense fire ⇨ 향불
향후 向後 after this; from now on; hereafter; henceforth ♦향후 수년간 for a few years ahead [from now]
허 Oh!; O!; Alas!; Heavens!
▶허, 열쇠를 잃어버렸네 Oh, dear [my goodness]! I've lost my key.
▶허, 또 실수했군 Gosh, I've made a mistake again.
허 虛 1 〈공허〉 emptiness; void; 〈거짓〉 an untruth 2 〈방심〉 an unguarded moment; unpreparedness
♦허를 찌르다 catch *sb* off his guard [napping]; take advantage of *sb* at an unguarded moment / 허를 찔리다 be caught off one's guard / 허를 보이다 lay oneself open to attack; be off one's guard
▶아군은 적의 허를 찔렀다 Our army made a surprise attack on the enemy. ⇌ Our army took the enemy unawares.
허가 許可 〈허락〉 permission; leave; 〈승인〉 approval; sanction; 〈면허〉 a license; 〈입학·입장〉 admission
♦허가없이 without permission [leave] / 당국의 허가를 받다 get permission [(口) an OK] from the authorities / 허가를 신청하다 ask for permission; apply for a permit / 허가없이 외박하다 stay out without permission / 허가를 받고 영업하다 do business under license
▶허가없이 이 건물에 들어가면 안 된다 Don't enter this building without permission.
▶퍼레이드를 하기 위해서는 경찰의 허가가 필요하다 Police permission is necessary to hold a parade.
▶그는 선생님에게 조퇴 허가를 냈다 He asked his teacher for permission [asked his teacher's permission] to leave school early.
—허가하다 〈적극적으로〉 permit; 〈소극적으로〉 allow; let; 〈공식적으로〉 authorize
▶지사는 그 돈의 지불을 정식으로 허가했다 The governor authorized the payment of the money.
▶그는 입학을 허가받았다 He obtained [got, gained] admission (in)to this school. ⇌ He was admitted to this school.
■—상륙— shore leave 입학— admission to a school; 〈대학의〉 matriculation ■—제 a license [licensing] system: 수렵은 허가제다 Hunting is on a license system.
허가증 許可證 a permit; a written permission; a warrant; a license
♦허가증을 발행하다[받다] issue [obtain] a license / 허가증을 취소하다 revoke a license
▶주무 관청은 허가증을 발행한다 The competent authorities issue [grant, give] a license [permit].
■—건축— a construction [building] permit 수출[수입]— 〈통관 서류〉 an export [import]

permit 채광(採鑛)— a mining license
허겁 虛怯 faintheartedness; (口) funk
■—쟁이 a pudding heart; a (blue) funk; a coward
허겁지겁 in a hurry [flurry]; confusedly; hurry-scurry ⇨ 허둥지둥
♦허겁지겁 달아나다 run off helter-skelter; run away with the tail between the legs
허공 虛空 the (empty) air [sky]; empty space; the void ♦허공을 노려보다 stare into space [at nothing] / 허공에 뜨다 float in the air / 허공으로 사라지다 disappear into nothingness; vanish into the air
허구 虛構 (a) fabrication; (a) fiction; a falsehood; a lie; a fake
♦허구의 make-up; invented; fictitious; false / 순전한 허구 a pure [an out-and-out] fabrication; a perfect fake
허구렁 虛— 〈빈 구멍〉 empty hollow; a hole; a pit ♦허구렁에 빠지다 fall in a pit
허구리 one's sides; the sides of one's waist
허구하다 許久— very long; longtime
♦허구한 나날 day in (and) day out; so many days / 허구한 세월 a long (period of) time; a long stretch of time
▶우리는 허구한 날을 덧없이 보내고 있다 We are spending a long time in vain.
허근 虛根 [數] an imaginary root
허기 虛飢 〈배고픔〉 hunger; hungriness
♦허기를 느끼다 feel hungry [empty] / 허기를 달래다 appease [alleviate] one's hunger / 허기를 채우다 satisfy one's appetite 《with some food》; gratify one's hunger (on)
▶그는 물을 마셔서 허기를 달랬다 He drank water to keep off his hunger.
■—증 hungry feeling; a sense of hunger : 허기증이 나다 be [feel] hungry
허기지다 虛飢— **1** 〈배고과지다〉 go hungry; be famished; be exhausted with hunger
▶나는 허기져서 쓰러질 것 같았다 I was faint from hunger.
2 〈욕심 나다〉 be hungry for [after]; hunger [starve, thirst, hanker] after [for]
허깨비 〈환영(幻影)〉 a phantom; an apparition; 〈유령〉 a ghost; a specter; a spook
♦허깨비를 보다 see sth in a vision
허니문 〈신혼여행〉 a honeymoon
허다하다 許多— 〈많다〉 many; numerous; innumerable; 〈흔하다〉 (very) common; ordinary; 〈서술적〉 be met with everywhere
♦허다한 일 a common [familiar] affair; not an uncommon case
▶그런 일은 허다하다 That sort of things happen quite often. ⇌ We have a lot of examples of that sort.
▶정직한 사람이 손해보는 예는 허다하다 It often happens that honesty does not pay.
허닥하다 begin to spend one's reserve funds; eat [cut] into one's savings
허덕거리다 **1** 〈숨이 차서〉 pant; gasp (for breath); puff (and blow); breathe hard
▶그는 허덕거리면서 달려왔다 He came running out of breath.
2 〈애쓰다〉 fight hard 《with poverty》 ⇨ 허덕이다
허덕이다 〈피로워하다〉 suffer (from); be distressed 《by》; 〈애쓰다〉 struggle 《for bare existence》; fight hard 《with poverty》
♦가난에 허덕이다 suffer dire poverty; be poverty-stricken; be pressed by poverty / 생활에 허덕이다 live with one's nose at the grindstone; find it hard to make a living
▶그는 빚에 허덕이고 있다 He is troubled with debts.
▶국민은 과중한 세금 부담때문에 허덕이고 있다 The people groan under the heavy burden of taxes.
허덕지덕 〈숨차하는 모양〉 gasping and panting; 〈지친 모양〉 exhaustedly; 〈애쓰는 모양〉 desperately
▶전령은 허덕지덕 소식을 전했다 The messenger panted out the news.
허두 虛頭 the beginning 《of a speech》; the opening; the opening paragraph
허둥거리다 fluster oneself; be in a flurry [fluster]; be flurried [flustered]
▶나는 어쩔줄 몰라 허둥거렸다 I was so flustered that I did not know what to do.
허둥지둥 hurry-scurry; in a flurry; helter-skelter ♦허둥지둥 달아나다 run away [flee] helter-skelter; run away in a flurry
▶그는 허둥지둥 문밖으로 뛰어 나갔다 He bustled [hurried] out of the gate.
—허둥지둥하다 fluster oneself; be confused
허드레 odds and ends
■—꾼 an odd(-job) man; an odd-jobber; a handy man —옷 working dress [clothes] 허드렛물 water for sundry uses 허드렛일 odd jobs; chores
허드재비 odds and ends ⇨ 허드레
허든거리다 walk unsteadily; reel; stagger; wobble
허든허든 reelingly; staggeringly; falteringly
허들 〈경기〉 the hurdles; a hurdle race; 〈장애물〉 a hurdle ♦100미터 허들 경기 the 100-meter hurdles / 허들을 넘다 clear [leap] a hurdle —선수 a hurdler
허락 許諾 〈승락〉 consent; assent; approval; sanction; acceptance; (美口) an O.K.; 〈허가〉 permission; leave
♦허락을 받고 with sb's permission / 허락없이 without sb's permission / 허락을 얻다 get [obtain] permission 《to do》 / 허락을 청하다 ask for permission [leave] 《to do》
▶나는 아버지의 허락을 받아내야만 한다 I must obtain my father's consent.
▶우리는 교장의 허락을 받고 이 교실을 사용하고 있는 겁니다 We use this room by permission of the principal.
—허락하다 〈승낙하다〉 consent 《to》; assent 《to》; grant; 〈찬성하다〉 approve 《of》; 〈허가하다〉 permit; (美口) O.K.; 〈입학 등을〉 admit; 〈경제ая 사정 등이〉 can afford; 〈마음 등을〉 trust sb; confide in sb
♦시간[사정]이 허락하는 한 so far as time permits; so far as circumstances permit / 결혼을 허락하다 give sb permission to marry; consent to sb's marriage

허랑방탕 虛浪放蕩 looseness; indulgence; profligacy; dissipation —허랑방탕하다 loose; licentious; dissolute; profligate; dissipated
♦ 허랑방탕한 자식 a profligate son

허례 虛禮 dead [empty] forms; empty [useless] formalities; formalities; formal courtesy
♦ 허례에 빠지다 lapse into an empty formality / 허례를 없애다 dispense with empty forms; do away with useless formalities
▶ 나는 허례는 폐지되어야 한다고 생각한다 I think we should dispense [do away] with formalities.
■—허식 empty formalities and vanity

허룩하다 almost empty; more or less empty

허름하다 **1** 〈싸다〉 cheap; cheapish
♦ 허름한 물건 a cheap [low-priced] article
2 〈낡아서〉 shabby; humble; worn-out
♦ 허름한 옷 shabby [old] clothes / 허름한 집 a humble house

허릅숭이 an unreliable [untrustworth, undependable] person; a light [frivolous] fellow

허리 **1** 〈몸의〉 the waist; the hip; the small of the back; the loin; 〈짐승의〉 the haunch
♦ 호리호리한[굵은] 허리 a slender [thick] waist / 허리가 굽은 노인 an old man bent with age / 허리가 날씬하다 have a slender [slim] waist / 허리가 굽다 be bent (in the back) / 허리를 굽혀 인사하다 greet with a deep bow / 허리를 펴다 straighten [stretch] oneself / 허리를 삐다 have one's waist dislocated
▶ 그녀는 허리가 절구통 같다 She has no waist.
▶ 그 노파는 허리를 굽히고 걷는다 The old woman walks with her back bent.
▶ 물이 허리까지 찼다 The water rose to my hips.
▶ 이 혁대는 내 허리에 짧다 This belt won't meet round my waist.
2 〈옷의〉 the waist
♦ 치마 허리를 달다 attach the waist part of a skirt
■—둘레 one's waist measurement —뼈 the hipbone; the hucklebone —통 one's girth

허리끈 a belt ⇨ 허리띠

허리띠 a (leather) belt; a waistband; a waist sash; a girdle; (총칭) belting
♦ 허리띠를 매다[풀다] tie [untie] a belt / 허리띠를 조르다[느슨하게 하다] tighten [loosen] one's belt / 허리띠를 졸라매다 (비유) tighten (up) one's belt; gird (up) one's loins

허리세장 〈지게의〉 the waist strut [lowest crosspiece] of an A-frame

허리질러 (cut) in the middle (of); (run) across the middle (of)

허리춤 inside the waist of one's trousers
♦ 허리춤에 감추다 slip sth in the waist of one's trousers / 허리춤에 손을 찌르다[넣다] put one's hands into the waist of trousers

허리치기 [柔道] a hip throw; waist [loin] techniques; [레슬링] a cross-buttock
♦ 허리치기를 하다 have [get] sb on the hip

허리케인 a hurricane

허릿매 the shape of one's waist; the waistline
♦ 허릿매가 날씬하다 have a shapely waist

허릿심 the strength of one's waist
♦ 허릿심이 세다 have a strong waist

허망 虛妄 falsehood; untruth; a sham
—허망하다 false; untrue; groundless; fabulous; unreliable; vain
■—지 설(之 說) fallacious reasoning; a groundless view

허명 虛名 an empty name; a false reputation
♦ 허명무실한 vain; empty; unsubstantial; nominal

허무 虛無 emptiness; hollowness; futility; vanity; [哲] nothingness; nihility
♦ 허무적인 nihilistic
—허무하다 〈공허한〉 empty; 〈빈〉 void; 〈효과 없는〉 vain; fruitless; 〈쓸모 없는〉 useless; futile ♦ 허무하게 in vain ; uselessly; to no purpose; futilely
▶ 인생은 허무하다 All is vanity in life. ⇌ Life is but an empty dream.
■—감 a feeling of futility —주의 nihilism —주의자 a nihilist

허무맹랑하다 虛無孟浪— fabulous; groundless; wild; false
♦ 허무맹랑한 소문 a groundless rumor / 허무맹랑한 소리를 하다 say absurd things; talk wild

허물[1] 〈살갗〉 the skin; 〈뱀·매미 등의〉 a cast-off skin (of a cicada); an ecdysis 《pl. -ses》; a slough [slʌf]
▶ 뱀은 허물을 벗는다 The snake sloughs its skin [sloughs off, casts (aside) its slough].
▶ 햇볕에 타서 어깨의 허물이 벗겨졌다 The skin of my shoulders peeled off when I got sunburnt.

허물[2] 〈과실〉 a fault; an error; 〈잘못〉 a mistake; 〈죄과〉 a blame; 〈흠〉 a defect (in one's personality); a flaw; a blot (on one's character)
♦ 허물을 용서하다 forgive [overlook] sb's fault / 허물을 뉘우치다 repent one's fault / 허물을 깨닫다 see the errors (of) / 허물을 사과하다 apologize (to sb) for one's fault / 허물을 탓하다 blame sb for (his) fault / 허물을 들추어내다 find fault with sb
▶ 그는 자기 허물을 남의 탓으로 돌린다 He blames another for his fault.
▶ 허물이 없는 사람은 없다 No one is free from faults. ⇌ Every man is liable to err.

허물다 pull [tear] down; break up [down]; demolish; destroy
▶ 그들은 낡은 건물을 허물고 새 건물을 지었다 They pulled down the old building and built a new one.

허물벗다[1] 〈뱀·매미 등이〉 cast (off) the skin; shed the skin; slough (off); exuviate

허물벗다[2] 〈누명을〉 clear oneself of a false charge; cleanse one's dishonor

허물어지다 crumble (to the ground); fall (down); collapse; break (down); give way
▶ 그 건물은 와장창 허물어졌다 The building fell down with a crash.

허물없다 unreserved; free; open(-minded); candid; familiar ♦ 허물없이 without reserve; unreservedly; familiarly
▶ 그 사람하고는 허물없는 사이다 I am friendly

[on friendly terms] with him.
▶ 우리는 서로 허물없이 이야기할 수 있는 사이는 아니다 We are not on speaking terms with each other.
허밍 〈콧노래〉 humming
허발하다 voracious; ravenous 《for food》
허방 〈팬 땅〉 a hollow; a hole; a pit
♦ 허방을 디디다 step in a hollow; make a false step / 허방에 빠지다 fall in(to) a pit
허방다리 a pit(fall); a trap ⇨ 함정
허방짚다 〈실패하다〉 miscalculate; misjudge; shoot at the wrong mark
허벅다리 the thigh ♦ 허벅다리를 드러내다 expose [bare] one's thighs
허벅살 〈사람의〉 the flesh of the thigh; 〈소의〉 round; 〈돼지의〉 ham
허벅지 the inside [inner part] of a thigh
허벅허벅하다 〈무르다〉 soft and somewhat dry
허보 虛報 〈거짓 소식〉 a false report; false news ♦ 허보를 퍼뜨리다 circulate a canard; spread a false report
▶ 그 소식은 허보였다 The report has proved false.
허분허분 —허분허분하다 soft and juicy
허비 虛費 〈낭비〉 (a) waste; useless expenses; 〈사치〉 extravagance
♦ 에너지의 허비 (a) waste of energy
▶ 그렇게 하면 시간만 허비할 뿐이다 It is (a) waste of time to do so.
—허비하다 waste 《on》; throw away
▶ 그들은 자원을 허비하고 있다 They are wasting resources. ⇌ They are wasteful of [with] resources.
▶ 나는 10만원을 허비했다 I spent hundred thousand won for nothing.
허비다 pick ⇨ 후비다
허비적거리다 keep picking ⇨ 후비적거리다
허사 虛事 〈헛됨〉 futility; 〈헛된 일〉 a vain effort [attempt]; lost labor
♦ 허사로 돌아가다 come [go] to nothing; go for nothing; prove fruitless [all in vain]
▶ 그의 노력은 다 허사로 돌아갔다 All his efforts were in vain [proved fruitless, came to nothing].
허사 虛辭 1 〈文法〉 an expletive
2 ⇨ 허언(虛言)
허상 虛像 〈物〉 a virtual image
허설 虛說 a false news ⇨ 허보(虛報)
허섭쓰레기 rubbish; trash; odds and ends; odd ends; lumber
허세 虛勢 a bluff; a bluster; bravado; a show; a false show of courage
♦ 허세 부리다 bluff; show off; put on a bold front; make a bluff; make a false show of courage
▶ 겁쟁이일수록 허세를 부리게 마련이다 The weaker the man, the stronger the bluff.
▶ 그는 허세만 부린다 He is always bluffing. ⇌ He always acts big.
허송 虛送 —허송하다 idle one's time [life] away; pass one's time idly
▶ 나는 1주간의 휴가를 허송해버렸다 I have wasted [idled away] a week's vacation.

허송세월 虛送歲月 idling one's time away
허수 虛數 〔數〕 an imaginary (number)
허수아비 1 a scarecrow ♦ 허수아비를 세우다 set [put] up a scarecrow **2** (비유) a (mere) figurehead; a dummy; a puppet ♦ 허수아비 노릇을 하다 be a puppet
▶ 그는 허수아비에 지나지 않고 진짜 실력자는 그의 동생이다 He is just a figurehead. The real boss is his younger brother.
허술하다 1 〈초라하다〉 shabby; poorlooking; humble
♦ 허술한 옷 shabby clothes / 허술한 모습의 노인 a shabby old man / 허술한 작은 집 a miserable [shabby] little house / 옷차림새가 허술하다 be shabbily [poorly] dressed
2 〈부주의하다〉 careless; inattentive; neglectful; negligent; loose
▶ 이 곳 경비는 허술하다 The defenses are weak around here.
허식 虛式 〔數〕 an imaginary expression
허식 虛飾 〈겉치레〉 show; vanity; affectation; display; 〈멋부리기〉 foppery; dandyism
♦ 허식적(인) ostentatious; showy / 허식이 없는 인품 an unaffected personality
—허식하다 show off; affect; be ostentatious; cut a dash
허실 虛實 〈진위〉 truth and falsehood; 〈약점과 강점〉 weakness and firmness
♦ 적의 허실을 알아내다 discover the strong and weak points of the enemy / 허실을 밝히다 ascertain the truth 《of》
▶ 그 허실을 잘 알 수 없다 It is not certain whether it is true or not.
허심 虛心 an open mind; open-mindedness; impartiality
허심탄회 虛心坦懷 an open mind; frankness; candidness; open-mindedness
—허심탄회하다 open-minded; open-hearted; candid; frank; free and easy
♦ 허심탄회하게 frankly; candidly; with an open mind; without reserve [prejudice]
▶ 우리는 허심탄회하게 이야기를 나눴다 We discussed it frankly. ⇌ We had a frank discussion. ⇌ We had a heart-to-heart talk.
허심하다 許心— trust [confide in] sb; admit [take] sb into confidence; allow oneself 《to》
허약 虛弱 weakness; infirmity; feebleness
—허약하다 weak; infirm; delicate; feeble; frail; sickly
♦ 허약한 사람 a weakly [an infirm, sickly] person; (총칭) the feeble
▶ 운동이 부족하면 허약해진다 Lack of exercise will make you weak.
▶ 그녀는 몸이 허약하다 She is physically weak.
—아(동) (physically) weak children —체질 a weak constitution
허언 虛言 〈거짓말〉 a lie; a falsehood; an untruth **—허언하다** tell a lie; lie
허여멀걸다 〈액체 등이〉 whitish and thin; washy 《milk》; 〈피부 등이〉 nice and fair
허여멀쑥하다 white and clean
허영 虛榮 vanity ⇨ 허영심
♦ 허영의 vain / 여자의 허영 feminine vanity /

허영거리다

허영에 차 있다 be full of vanity
허영거리다 totter; falter; reel; wobble
허영심 虛榮心 vanity
♦허영심이 강한 여자 a vain woman / 허영심에 들떠서 driven by vanity; out of vanity / 영심을 만족시키다 satisfy *one's* vanity / 허영심을 자극하다 tickle *one's* vanity
▶저를 허영심이 많은 여자로 여기지 마세요 Don't take me for a vain woman.
▶그는 허영심이 몹시 강하다 He is really vain.
허영허영 totteringly; falteringly; shakily
허영다 very white; chalk-white; ashy pale
♦안색이 허영다 look very pale
허예지다 become [get] chalk-white; turn as white as a sheet; turn ashy pale
허욕 虛慾 greed; avarice
♦허욕이 많은 사람 a greedy person / 허욕이 많다 be blind with avarice; be avaricious
허용 許容 〈용인〉 permission; allowance; approval; admission; 〈용서〉 pardon; forgiveness
―허용하다 permit; approve; grant; allow; admit; 〈용서하다〉 pardon; forgive
♦허용할 수 있는 permissible; allowable
―량 an acceptable limit; a permitted level
―범위 a permitted limit ―시간 allowed time
―오차 an allowable [a permissible] error
―온도 allowable [permissible] temperature
―한계[한도] a tolerance limit: 방사능의 허용 한도 the maximum permissible exposure to radiation
허우대 stature; height
♦허우대가 크다 be high in stature; be of great stature
허우룩하다 〈서술적〉 miss *sb*; feel lonely
♦허우룩한 느낌 a sense of emptiness; (a feeling of) loneliness
허울 〈겉모양〉 appearance; looks
♦허울뿐이다 be not so good as it looks; be deceptive / 허울좋다 look nice; be seemly; make a good figure [appearance]; be nice-looking; 〈그럴듯한〉 be plausible; fair-spoken
허울좋은 하눌타리 〈속담〉 a person [a thing] only superficially attractive
허위 虛僞 (a) falsehood; an untruth; a deceit; fraud; a lie; 〔論〕 fallacy
♦허위의 false; sham; untrue; feigned
■―보고 a false report ―신고 a false return ―진술 〔法〕 misrepresentation: 허위진술을 하다 make a false statement 《of》; misrepresent; 〈증인이〉 give false testimony; commit perjury
허위넘다 〈애써 넘다〉 cross [go over] 《a mountain》 panting(ly)
허위단심 〈무척 애씀〉 a (hard) struggle; making strenuous efforts
♦허위단심으로 with great efforts; laboriously
▶그녀는 아들을 만나려고 허위단심 먼 길을 갔다 She struggled a long distance to see her son.
허위적거리다 struggle; flounder; paw the air
♦물에서 헤어나려고 허위적거리다 paw the air to get out of the water
▶고양이가 강물에 빠져 헤어나려고 허위적거리고 있었다 A cat fell in the river and was struggling to get out.
허위적허위적 strugglingly; flounderingly
허장성세 虛張聲勢 〈허세로 떠벌림〉 bluster; bluff; bravado; swashbuckling
―허장성세하다 bluster; bluff; swashbuckle
▶그는 허장성세하기 일쑤다 He is a bluffer. ⇌ He often bluffs.
허적거리다 〈들추어 헤치다〉 ransack; rummage 《in》; scatter; disperse
♦서랍속을 허적거리다 ransack [rummage in] a drawer 《for》
허적이다 ransack ⇨ 허적거리다
허전거리다 〈다리 힘이 빠져〉 walk with faltering [tottering] steps; falter (along)
허전하다 〈서술적〉 feel empty; feel lonely; feel something lacking; miss something
▶그 사람이 없으니 허전하다 I miss him (badly). ⇌ I feel lonely without him.
▶이 그림은 어딘지 허전하다 I feel that something is missing from this picture.
허점 虛點 〈약점〉 a blind spot [point]; an unguarded point; a weak [vulnerable] point; a sore [tender] spot
♦허점을 보이다 lay *oneself* open to attack
▶그는 법의 허점을 이용해서 큰돈을 벌었다 He made a huge sum of money by taking advantage of a blind point of the law [imposing on a loophole in the law].
허정 deceptive appearance; a mere show; emptiness
―허정하다 deceptive; showy but worthless; shoddy; unsubstantial; empty
허정거리다 walk with an unsteady gait; be unsteady on *one's* feet [legs]
허즈번드 a husband
허청대고 〈마구〉 rashly; recklessly; blindly; thoughtlessly
♦허청대고 돈을 쓰다 spend (*one's*) money recklessly
허초점 虛焦點 〔物〕 a virtual focal point; a virtual focus
허출하다 hungry; 〈서술적〉 feel [be] hungry
▶나는 허출하다 I'm hungry.
허탈 虛脫 〈명함〉 blankness (of mind); absent-mindedness; 〔醫〕 (physical) collapse; prostration
―허탈하다 collapsed; prostrated
■―상태 〈무기력〉 a state of lethargy; 〈명함〉 absentmindedness: 허탈상태에 빠지다 fall into a state of lethargy / 허탈상태다 be utterly absentminded
허탕 vain [fruitless] effort; vain attempt; lost labor
♦허탕치다 prove fruitless [abortive, all in vain]; come to nothing
▶모든 노력이 허탕이 되었다 All our efforts were in vain.
▶우리의 노력은 다 허탕으로 끝났다 All our efforts proved fruitless [abortive]. ⇌ All our efforts resulted in failure. ⇌ All our efforts came to nothing.
허투 虛套 (a) sham; (a) pretense; simulation; (a) semblance
허투루 carelessly; heedlessly; lightly; 〈아무렇

게나〉 negligently; in a slovenly way; roughly
♦ 허투루 보다 〈과소평가하다〉 underrate; make [think] light of; make little account of; slight [neglect] sb / 허투루 다루다 handle 《a thing》 roughly [carelessly] / 일을 허투루 하다 do a slapdash job; work in a perfunctory manner
▶ 상대를 허투루 보지 마라 Never underrate your opponent.
▶ 그의 실력을 허투루 보지 마라 You should not underrate [misjudge] his ability.

허튼계집 a loose woman; a slut; a slattern
허튼고래 a hypocaust supported by scattered columns (as opposed to flues)
허튼맹세 《make》 an unreliable pledge; a shaky [shifty] vow
허튼모 scatter-planted rice seedlings
허튼소리 nonsense; absurd remarks; a silly talk; 〈잡소리〉 idle gossip [talk]; an empty prattle
♦ 허튼소리(를) 하다 say silly things; talk nonsense
허튼수작 ─酬酌 〈말〉 silly talk; idle talk; nonsense; 〈짓〉 a foolish act
▶ 허튼 수작 부리지 마라 None of your tricks with me. ⇌ No, that won't do.
허튼톱 a rip-and-crosscut saw
허파 〔解〕〈폐장〉 the lungs; 〈가축의〉 lights
♦ 허파에 바람 들다 〈실없이 웃는 사람의 비유〉 be easily tempted to laugh; laugh over nothing; be giggly / 허팟줄이 끊어지다 〈시시덕이를 놀리는 표현〉 lose control and burst into laughter
허풍 虛風 a boast; a brag; tall [big] talk; a gasconade; exaggeration; 《美俗》 hot air
♦ 허풍 떨다 boast; brag; talk big [tall]; tell a tall tale
▶ 허풍 작작 떨어라 I have had enough of your big talk.
▶ 그는 늘 허풍을 떨기 때문에 아무도 곧이 듣지 않는다 He is always talk big [tall] and nobody takes him seriously.
▶ 그는 영국해협을 헤엄쳐 건널 수 있다고 허풍을 쳤다 He boasted [bragged] that he could swim across the English Channel.
▶ 그 허풍 대단하군 That is a pretty tall story.
─선이 〈사람〉 a boaster; a braggart; a windbag; 《俗》 a big talker; a gasbag; 《美俗》 a blowhard
허하다 許─ 〈허락하다〉 permit
허하다 虛─ **1** 〈속이 비다〉 hollow; empty; void; vacant
2 〈몸이 허약하다〉 〔韓醫〕 weak(ly); infirm; sickly; delicate; feeble; frail
♦ 기가 허하다 lack vitality [spirit]
▶ 그는 몸이 허하다 He is in delicate health. ⇌ He has a delicate [weak] constitution.
허한 虛汗 〈식은땀〉 (a) cold sweat
허행 虛行 making a fruitless visit
허허¹ 〈웃음 소리〉 ha! ha!
♦ 허허 웃다 laugh aloud
허허² 〈놀람〉 Oh!; Well!; Why!; Heavens!; Dear me!; 〈슬픔〉 Alas!; 〈낙심·낭패〉 Oops!; Damn it!

▶ 허허 이거 야단났네 Well, what a fine fix this is! ⇌ Oh, here's pretty go!
허허바다 a boundless (expanse of the) ocean; a waste of waters
허허벌판 〈광활한 들판〉 a vast stretch of land; a wild plain; 〈황야〉 a desert land
허허실실 虛虛實實 ♦ 허허실실로 regarding truth as truth and falsehood as falsehood; accepting failure as failure and success as success; recognizing reality; taking things as they come; leaving a matter to take its own course
▶ 허허실실의 싸움이다 Both contestants are full of wiles and tricks. ⇌ It is a game [match] of shrewdness.
허혼하다 許婚─ give sb permission to marry; permit sb to marry (to)
허화 虛華 vain glories; empty [outward] show
허황하다 虛荒─ absurd; nonsensical; fantastic(al); wild
♦ 허황된 소리를 하다 say absurd things; talk wild
▶ 그의 이야기는 아주 허황하다 His story is quite a nonsense [absurd].
헌 old; secondhand; used; worn-out; shabby
♦ 헌 차 a used car; a secondhand car / 헌 집 an old house / 헌 책 a secondhand [used] book; an old book
헌거롭다 軒擧─ 〈의기가〉 high-spirited; 〈풍채가〉 stately; imposing; dignified; 〈도량이〉 big-hearted
헌걸스럽다 high-spirited ⇨ 헌거롭다
헌걸차다 high-spirited ⇨ 헌거롭다
헌것 worn-out [used] things; a secondhand thing [article]
♦ 헌것으로 사다 buy 《a thing》 at secondhand
헌금 獻金 a contribution; a donation; 〈교회 등에서의〉 a collection; an offering
♦ 헌금을 모으다 collect contributions; make [take up] a collection
─헌금하다 contribute; donate; make a contribution [donation]; 《美俗》 kick in
■ 정치─ a political contribution [donation] / ─자 a contributor; a donor / ─함 a collection [contribution] box
헌납 獻納 presentation; offering; contribution; donation
─헌납하다 contribute; donate
■ ─자 a contributor; a donor / ─품 an offering; a present
헌당 獻堂 〈교회의〉 the dedication of a church; consecration
─헌당하다 consecrate a church
헌데 〈부스럼〉 a sore; a boil; a rash
▶ 아기의 목덜미에 헌데가 생겼다 The baby has got a boil on the back of its neck.
헌등 獻燈 a votive lantern
헌배하다 獻杯─ offer sb a cup of wine
헌법 憲法 the constitution; the constitutional law
♦ 헌법에 보장된 권리 one's constitutional rights / 헌법(상)의 constitutional / 헌법 상으로 constitutionally / 헌법을 제정하다 [발포하다, 시행하다, 개정하다, 옹호하다] establish

헌병

[promulgate, enforce, amend, defend] the constitution
■성문[불문]— a written [an unwritten] constitution ■—개정(改正) an amendment to the constitution; a constitutional amendment —기관 a constitutional institution —위반 a breach of the constitution: 헌법위반의 unconstitutional —재판소 the Constitutional Court —정신 the spirit of the constitution; constitutional principles —제도 a constitutional regime —제정 enactment of a constitution —학자 a scholar of constitutions

헌병 憲兵 〈육군〉 a military policeman (略 MP); (총칭) the military police (略 MP); 〈해군〉 a shore patrolman (略 an SP); (총칭) the shore patrol (略 SP)
■—대 〈육군〉 the military police; 〈해군〉 the shore patrol —장교 a provost officer —파견대 a detachment of the military police

헌사 獻詞 (a) dedication; a dedicatory letter
헌상 獻上 presentation
—헌상하다 present 《a thing to *sb, sb* with a thing》; make sb a present of 《a thing》

헌쇠 scrap iron; iron scraps

헌수하다 獻壽— offer *sb* a cup of wine for 《his》 longevity

헌시 獻詩 a dedicated poem
—헌시하다 present [dedicate] a poem 《to》

헌신 獻身 devotion; self-sacrifice; dedication
◆헌신적인〈사람·일이〉self-sacrificing; 〈사람이〉 devoted / 헌신적으로 devotedly; with devotion
▶그 간호사는 환자를 헌신적으로 간호했다 The nurse gave a self-sacrificing care to her patients.
—헌신하다 devote [dedicate] *oneself* 《to》; sacrifice *oneself* 《for》
▶그녀는 사회 복지 사업에 헌신했다 She devoted herself to social service.
▶그는 평생 빈민 구제에 헌신했다 He devoted his whole life to helping the poor.

헌신짝 a worn-out shoe; an old shoe
▶그는 그의 지위를 헌신짝처럼 버렸다 He threw up his office just as he would throw away an old hat [without any regret].

헌앙하다 軒昻— stately ⇨ 헌거롭다

헌옷 〈낡은〉 old clothes; 〈남이 입던〉 secondhand [used] clothing; (美口) a hand-me-down; (英口) a reach-me-down
■—가게 a secondhand clothes store —장수 an old-clothes dealer

헌작 獻爵 offering *sb* a cup of wine

헌장 憲章 a charter
■—대 the Magna C(h)arta; the Great Charter 대서양— the Atlantic Charter 어린이— the Children's Charter 유엔— the United Nations Charter 인민— the People's Charter

헌정 憲政 〈정체〉 constitutional government; 〈제도〉 constitutionalism
◆헌정의 정도 normal procedures in constitutional government / 헌정을 펴다 adopt constitutional government
■—옹호운동 a movement for safeguarding [defending] constitutionalism

헌정 獻呈 presentation; dedication
—헌정하다 present 《a copy》 to *sb*; dedicate; offer
■—본 a presentation copy

헌짚신도 짝이 있다 〈속담〉 Every Jack has his Jill [Gill].

헌책 —冊 a secondhand [used] book; an old book
◆헌책으로 사다 buy a book at secondhand
■—방 a secondhand bookstore

헌칠민틋하다 〈허우대가〉 tall and well-built [well-constructed]; have a good constitution

헌칠하다 tall and handsome

헌털뱅이 used things ⇨ 헌것

헌팅캡 〈사냥용〉 a hunting cap; 〈일반적인 것〉 a sports cap

헌혈 獻血 blood donation; donating blood
—헌혈하다 donate *one's* blood
■집단— group blood donation ■—운동 a blood (donation) drive [campaign] —자 a blood donor

헐값 歇— a giveaway price; a sacrifice
◆헐값의 dirt cheap; dog-cheap; cheap as dirt / 헐값에 사다 buy 《a thing》 cheap as dirt; get 《an article》 for a mere [an old] song [for a song] / 헐값에 팔다 sell at a low [slaughter] price; sell *sth* for 《its》 scrap value; sell 《an article》 dirt-cheap
▶그는 집과 땅을 헐값에 팔았다 He sold his house and lot practically for nothing.

헐겁다 loose(-fitting); baggy; too large
◆헐거운 바지 loose(-fitting) trousers

헐근거리다 pant ⇨ 할근거리다

헐다 1〈부스럼 등이〉 form [develop] a boil; break out in sores; be inflamed
▶내 무릎이 헐었다 I have got a boil on my knee.
▶상처가 헐었다 The wound was inflamed.
2〈무너뜨리다〉 break [pull] down 《a building》; demolish; destroy
◆담을 헐다 break down a wall / 집을 헐다 pull a house down
3〈돈을〉 break; change
◆만원짜리를 헐다 break [change] a ten thousand won note (into small money)
4〈헐뜯다〉 speak ill of; slander; defame
◆뒤에서 남을 헐다 speak ill of *sb* behind 《his》 back; backbite *sb*
5〈낡아지다〉 become old; wear [be worn] out
▶동생의 신발은 벌써 헐어서 누더기가 되었다 My brother's shoes were already worn out to rags.

헐떡거리다 〈숨이 차서〉 pant; gasp (for breath); breathe hard
◆헐떡거리며 gaspingly; pantingly; between gasps; out [short] of breath
▶그는 헐떡거리며 몇 마디 말했다 He gasped out [forth] a few words.
▶그는 헐떡거리며 뛰어왔다 He came running out of breath.

헐떡이다 pant ⇨ 헐떡거리다

헐떡하다 1〈핏기가 없다〉 pale; pallid; worn; emaciated

2 〈지쳐서 눈이〉 hollow; sunken
헐뜯다 speak ill of *sb*; revile; slander; disparage; paint *sb* black; backbite; belittle
♦뒤에서 아무를 헐뜯다 speak ill of *sb* behind (his) back / backbite *sb* / 남의 성공을 헐뜯다 belittle another's success
헐렁거리다 1 〈헐거워서〉 be loose; fit [work] loose
♦신이 헐렁거리다 one's shoes fit loose
2 〈행동이〉 act [behave] carelessly
헐렁이 a careless [frivolous] person; a harum-scarum; a scatterbrain
헐렁하다 loose(-fitting); baggy
헐렁헐렁하다 1 〈헐겁다〉 loose 《coat》; too large; baggy
♦헐렁헐렁한 바지 a baggy trousers
2 〈행동이 조심성이 없다〉 all unstable; terribly unstable
헐레벌떡 out of breath; 〈황급히〉 hurry-scurry; helter-skelter
♦헐레벌떡 달려가다 run along panting and puffing / 헐레벌떡 계단을 내려가다 hurry down the stairs
—**헐레벌떡하다[거리다]** puff and pant; gasp for breath; be out of breath
헐레이션 〔寫〕 halation
헐리다 be demolished [destroyed]; be pulled down
▶그 집은 헐렸다 The house was pulled down [cleared, removed].
헐리우드 Hollywood
헐벗다 1 〈누더기를 입다〉 be in need [want] of clothes
♦헐벗은 아이들 poorly clothed children
2 〈잎·나무가 없다〉 be bared [stripped] of leaves
♦헐벗은 산 a bare [bald] mountain
3 〈가난하다〉 be poor
헐변 歇邊 low interest; a low rate of interest
헐수할수없다 〈서술적〉 be driven to the wall; be at one's wit's end; be at the end of one's tether
♦헐수할수없어서 as there is no help; driven at a tight corner; at [in, on] a pinch
헐쑥하다 pale ⇨ 핼쑥하다
헐어지다 〈무너지다〉 collapse; crumble; 〈낡아지다〉 get old; wear out; be worn out; 〈옷 등이〉 become shabby
헐하다 歇— 1 〈값싸다〉 cheap; low
♦헐한 물건 low-priced goods; a (good) bargain / 헐하게 cheap; at a bargain
2 〈엄하지 않다〉 light; lenient
♦헐한 벌 a mild [lenient, light] punishment
3 〈쉽다〉 easy; simple; light
♦헐한 일 an easy [a light] task; a soft job / 헐한 상대 a poor [weak] rival
헐후하다 歇后— insignificant; unworthy; trivial; worthless
험객 險客 1 〈성질이 험악한 사람〉 a roughneck; a rowdy; a person of rough disposition; a man of violent temper
2 〈험구가〉 a foulmouthed person
험구 險口 an evil [a malicious, wicked] tongue; slander; abuse

—**험구하다** wag one's slanderous tongue 《at》; slander; speak ill of; abuse; curse
■—가 a foulmouthed person; a slanderer; a carper
험난 險難 danger; peril; steepness; precipitousness; hardship; difficulty
—**험난하다** rough; difficult; steep; rugged; hard; arduous; full of danger; perilous
♦험난한 길 a thorny path / 험난한 등산 코스 a dangerous course
▶전도가 험난하다 There is rocky going ahead.
험담 險談 (a) slander; abuse; calumny; 〈뒷전에서 하는〉 backbiting; gossip; scandal
♦험담을 잘 하는 사람 a scandalmonger; a backbiter / 험담을 하다 〈뒷전에서〉 talk about *sb* behind (his) back; backbite *sb*
—**험담하다** speak ill of *sb*; talk scandal about; slander; abuse; backbite
험로 險路 a rough [rugged] road; a breakneck road; a hard pass
♦아마존의 험로 a steep pass in the Amazon
험산 險山 a steep [precipitous] mountain
험상 險狀 a threatening look; a terrible look
험상궂다, 험상스럽다 險狀— terrible; ugly-looking; horrible; threatening
▶그는 험상스런 얼굴을 하고 있었다 He had a forbidding countenance.
험악하다 險惡— dangerous; perilous; 〈날씨 등이〉 threatening; stormy; 〈사태가〉 serious
♦험악한 하늘 threatening sky / 험악한 얼굴 a menacing look; an angry look / 험악한 길 a rugged road
▶그는 험악한 얼굴로 나를 보았다 He gave me a stern look.
▶형세는 날로 험악해져 가고 있다 The situation is getting more strained every day.
험준하다 險峻— steep; precipitous; rugged; sheer; perpendicular
♦험준한 산길 a steep [rugged] trail
▶산은 험준해 보였다 The mountain looked quite forbidding.
험하다 險— 1 〈험상궂다〉 savage-looking; sinister; grim
♦험한 표정 a grim look
▶그는 험한 얼굴을 하고 있다 He has a sharp look.
2 〈위태롭다〉 rugged; steep; rough; dangerous; perilous
3 〈날씨 등이〉 foul; stormy; rough; threatening
♦험한 날씨 rough weather
4 〈거칠고 힘겹다〉 rough; harsh
♦험하게 다루다 handle roughly
헙수룩하다 1 〈머리털이〉 untidy; unkempt; untrimmed; bushy
2 〈옷차림이〉 shabby; poor-looking; seedy
▶그날 따라 나는 헙수룩한 옷차림을 하고 있었다 I was shabbily dressed on that day.
헙헙하다 〈사람됨이〉 generous; liberal; 〈씀씀이가〉 wasteful; lavish
♦돈 씀씀이가 헙헙하다 be too free with one's money; be wasteful of money
헛가게 a booth; a stall

헛간 —間 a barn; a shed; an outhouse
헛걸음하다 go on an empty [a bootless] errand; make a visit 《on *sb*》 in vain; go somewhere for nothing
♦아무에게 헛걸음시키다 send *sb* on a fool's errand
헛구역 —嘔逆 a queasy feeling; [醫] vomiturition
♦헛구역나다 be queasy; have a queasy feeling / 헛구역질하다 try to vomit in vain
헛글 ineffectual [wasted] learning
♦헛글을 배우다 waste *one's* schooling; learn nothing
▶그는 말하자면 헛글을 배운 셈이다 He is, so to speak, a learned fool.
헛기침 a dry cough; a hacking cough
—헛기침하다 have a dry cough; 〈일부러〉 clear *one's* throat; give a cough; hawk; hem
헛김 leakage air [steam]; an air leak
♦헛김 나다 get an air leak; 〈맥빠지다〉 lose heart; be disappointed; be dispirited
헛노릇 a vain [fruitless, useless] effort; waste labor —헛노릇하다 make vain efforts; waste [lose] *one's* labor
헛다리짚다 make a false steps; guess wrong; make a wrong guess; misjudge
헛돈 money thrown away; wasted money
♦헛돈쓰다 waste [throw away] *one's* money 《on》
헛돌다 〈바퀴 등이〉 skid; race; 〈기계 등이〉 run idle; idle
헛되다 1 〈보람없다〉 fruitless; vain; ineffective; useless; 〈서술적〉 be in vain; come to nothing
♦헛된 꿈 an empty dream / 헛된 노력 a vain [fruitless] effort; lost labor / 헛된 죽음 useless death / 헛되지 않다 be worthwhile 《(to do)》; be worth 《(doing)》 / 헛되지 않게 하다 make good use of
▶내 노력은 헛되지 않았다 I have not labored in vain.
▶나는 헛된 일은 하고 싶지 않다 I do not want to exert myself in vain.
▶그의 노력은 헛되었다 His efforts proved ineffective.
▶말해 봤자 헛된 일이다 It's no use [There is no use (in)] saying anything.
2 〈허황하다〉 wild; groundless; false
♦헛된 소문 a groundless [wild] rumor; a canard
헛되이 uselessly; in vain; vainly; to no purpose; 〈보람없이〉 fruitlessly; futilely; to no [without] avail; 〈목적도 없이〉 aimlessly
♦헛되이 세월을 보내다 pass *one's* time idly; live in idleness / 헛되이 돈을 쓰다 spend money uselessly; waste *one's* money / 헛되이 일생을 보내다 loaf through life / 헛되이 죽다 die a useless death; die in vain
헛듣다 〈잘못 듣다〉 hear 《it, him》 wrong; mishear; misunderstand; 〈예사로 듣다〉 pay little [no] attention to 《*sb's* talk》
▶너무 뜻밖의 소식이어서 내가 헛듣지 않았나 생각했다 The news was such a surprise that I could hardly believe my ears.

헛디디다 miss *one's* foot [step]; lose *one's* footing; take a false step
▶나는 계단을 헛디디어서 아래로 떨어졌다 I slipped on the stairs and fell down. ⇌ I tumbled down the stairs.
헛맹세 a false pledge; an empty vow
—헛맹세하다 make a false [an empty] vow 《(that, to do)》
헛물켜다 exert *oneself* to no purpose; make vain efforts; get nothing for *one's* pains; labor for nothing; waste time and labor; plow the sand(s) [air]; catch at shadows; run after a shadow, draw water with a sieve
헛발 ♦헛발 디디다 take a false step; tread on air
헛방 —房 a lumber room; a storeroom; a room not in use
헛방 —放 1 〈빗맞음〉 a miss shot; a wrong hit; a mishit; 〈실탄 없는〉 a blank shot [cartridge]
♦헛방놓다 〈빗맞히다〉 miss *one's* shot [the mark]; fail to hit; 〈공포를 쏘다〉 fire blank cartridges [shots]
2 〈큰말〉 empty talk; (俗) gas; hot air
♦헛방 놓다 〈빈말하다〉 (美口) talk through *one's* hat; (美俗) shoot [sling, throw] the bull
헛방귀 a gentle fart; a silent odorless fart
헛배부르다 have gas in the stomach; feel flatulent; have a false sense of satiety
헛보다 miss seeing; mistake; 〈못보고 넘어가다〉 fail to see [notice]; 〈허깨비로 보다〉 see *sth* in a vision
♦신호를 헛보다 mistake a signal; fail to see a signal
헛불 a miss shot; a mishit; a wrong hit
♦헛불놓다 miss *one's* shot; fail to hit
헛소동 —騷動 a storm in a teacup; much ado [a great fuss] about nothing; much cry and little wool; all cry and no wool; more cry than wool
▶호기심 많은 구경꾼들이 헛소동을 일으켰다 Curious onlookers made a fuss [much ado] about nothing.
—헛소동하다 make a (great) fuss [make much ado] about nothing
헛소리 1 〈실속없는〉 a falsehood; idle words; nonsense
2 〈혼미중의〉 delirious utterances
▶그녀는 고열로 헛소리를 하고 있었다 She was delirious because of a high fever.
—헛소리하다 talk in (a) delirium; utter ravings
헛소문 —所聞 a groundless [false] rumor; a canard; idle gossip ♦헛소문을 퍼뜨리다 set a false rumor afloat
헛손질 pawing the air; a mishit
—헛손질하다 hit space; beat the air [wind]
헛수 —手 [바둑·장기] a wrong [an ineffective] move
♦헛수를 두다 make an ineffective move
헛수고 useless [fruitless, vain] efforts; waste of labor; lost labor
♦헛수고가 되다 prove fruitless; end in a waste of labor
▶그것은 헛수고였다 It proved fruitless.

—헛수고하다 make vain efforts; work [labor] in vain; lose one's labor
헛심 wasteful strength; a useless effort
♦ 헛심 쓰다 strain *oneself* in vain
헛애 useless efforts ⇨ 헛수고
헛웃음 a smirk; a simper; a feigned laugh; an affected smile
♦ 헛웃음 치다 affect [feign] a laugh; simper
헛일 useless work; a wasted effort; waste of labor; lost labor
♦ 헛일이다 be no use; be of no avail; be useless; be in vain; be no good
—헛일하다 do useless work; labor in vain; lose *one's* labor; labor for nothing
헛잠 〈자는 체하는 잠〉 pretended sleep; sham [feigned] sleep; a simulation of sleep; 〈선잠〉 a nap; a catnap; a doze
♦ 헛잠(을) 자다 sham sleep; play possum; 〈선잠을〉 take [have] a nap
헛잡다 miss catching; miss *one's* hold; fail to catch [grasp]
♦ 공을 헛잡다 miss a ball; fumble 《a grounder》/ 접시를 헛잡아 떨어뜨리다 let a plate slip from *one's* hand
헛장 a bluff; a bluster; a bold front; a big talk; 《俗》 hot air
♦ 헛장치다 bluff; talk big; blow *one's* own trumpet; make a bluff
헛청 —廳 a shed; an open shed; a (storage) barn; an outbuilding
헛총 —銃 a blank cartridge; a blank shot
♦ 헛총 놓다 fire blank cartridges [shots]
■ —질 blank firing
헛치다 fail to hit; miss 《*one's* aim》; strike at the air; 《俗》 whiff; 〔拳〕 swish the air; 〔골프〕 foozle
헛코골다 pretend to snore; feign sleep by snoring
헛턱 a Barmecide('s) feast; 《pay》 lip service; a mere verbal entertainment
헛헛증 —症 hungriness; chronic hunger
♦ 헛헛증이 있다 suffer from chronic hunger
헛헛하다 〈서술적〉 feel [be] hungry
헝가리 Hungary; 〈공식명〉 the Republic of Hungary
♦ 헝가리의 Hungarian
■ —말 Hungarian —사람 a Hungarian
헝거스트라이크 〈단식 투쟁〉 (a) hunger strike
♦ 헝거스트라이크를 하다 go on (a) hunger strike; hunger-strike
헝겁지겁 rapturously; in delight; in elation; leaping [jumping, flying] out of *one's* skin (for joy)
헝겊 a piece of cloth; a patch; a rag; a scrap
■ —신 cloth [canvas] shoes —조각 a small piece of cloth; a scrap of cloth
헝클다 tangle; entangle; dishevel
♦ 실을 헝클다 tangle thread / 머리를 헝클다 dishevel *one's* head
헝클어지다 tangle; become tangled; be entangled; be in a tangle
♦ 헝클어진 머리 disheveled [unkempt] hair / 헝클어진 실을 풀다 unloose [unravel] tangled thread

헤 agape; wide open
♦ 입을 헤 벌리고 with *one's* mouth wide open / 입을 헤 벌리다 open *one's* mouth wide; gape
헤게모니 hegemony
♦ 헤게모니 싸움 strife over hegemony / 헤게모니를 잡다 hold hegemony
헤겔 〈독일의 철학자〉 Hegel, Georg Wilhelm Friedrich (1770-1831)
헤근거리다 wobble; shake; be shaky [rickety, unstable]
헤다¹ 〈멋대로 행하다〉 have *one's* own way; do as *one* pleases
헤다² 〈헤엄치다〉 swim; have a swim
헤다³ rinse ⇨ 헹구다
헤대다 bustle about; run [move] about like a busy bee
헤덤비다 rush about; make needless haste
헤드라이트 a headlight
♦ 헤드라이트를 켜다[끄다] turn on [off] the headlight
헤드록 〔레슬링〕 a headlock
헤드폰 a headphone
헤딩 〔蹴〕 heading
—헤딩하다 head 《the ball》
헤뜨러지다 be dispersed; get [be] scattered; disperse ♦ 사방으로 헤뜨러지다 disperse in all directions
헤뜨리다 disperse; scatter; strew; put in disorder; clutter
♦ 닭이 모이를 헤뜨리다 chickens scatter their feed / 군중을 헤뜨리다 disperse a crowd / 방안에 노트와 책을 헤뜨리다 litter a room with books and notebooks
헤라클레이토스 〈그리스의 철학자〉 Heraclitus (540?-? B.C.)
헤로도토스 〈그리스의 역사가〉 Herodotus (484?-425? B.C.)
헤로인 〔藥〕 heroin
■ —중독 heroinism
헤르니아 〈탈장〉 〔醫〕 hernia 《pl. ~s, -niae》
헤르츠 a hertz 《略 Hz》
■ —파 a hertzian wave
헤르쿨레스자리 〔天〕 Hercules
헤매다 1 〈돌아다니다〉 wander [roam] about; hover 《about, around》; 〈길을 잃고〉 stray about
♦ 여기저기를 헤매다 wander from place to place / 길을 잃고 숲속을 헤매다 miss *one's* way and wander through the forest
▶ 나는 온 밤을 산속에서 헤맸다 I was roaming over the mountains all (through the) night.
▶ 그는 생사지경을 헤맸다 He hovered between life and death.
2 〈갈피를 잡지 못하다〉 be puzzled [perplexed]; be at a loss; be quite embarrassed
헤먹다 loose; loose-fitting
헤모글로빈 〔生〕 hemoglobin
헤무르다 soft; feeble; flabby; flaccid; weak; weak-kneed
♦ 헤무른 사람 a feeble person; a weak-spirited person
▶ 그는 헤무른 사람이다 He is feeble-minded.

헤묽다 watery; (wishy-)washy; sloppy; thin ((soup))

헤밍웨이 〈미국의 소설가〉 Hemingway, Ernest (1899-1961)

헤번드르르하다 fair and bright ⇨ 희번드르르하다

헤벌어지다 open wide; be opened wide; 〈입이〉 be agape (with joy)

헤벌쭉하다 〈입이〉 wide open; agape

헤브라이 Hebrew ⇨ 헤브루

헤브라이즘 Hebraism

헤브루 Hebrew

헤비급 —級 the heavyweight
■ —권투선수 a heavyweight (boxer)

헤살 interference; hindrance; disturbance
♦ 헤살놓다[부리다] thwart; interfere with; hinder; disturb; throw an obstacle in path / 계획을 헤살놓다 counteract [thwart] sb's plan / 공부하는데 아무에게 헤살부리다 disturb sb in his study
■ —꾼 an obstructionist

헤세 〈독일의 소설가·시인〉 Hesse, Hermann (1877-1962)

헤시오도스 〈그리스의 시인〉 Hesiod (8c, B.C.)

헤식다 〈무르다〉 weak; fragile; frail; feeble; tender; 〈탐탁지 못하다〉 unsatisfactory; undesirable

헤실바실 1 〈모르는 사이에〉 before one is aware; 〈조금씩〉 little by little
♦ 헤실바실 없어지다 run out before one is aware of it
2 〈건성으로〉 indifferently; halfheartedly
♦ 헤실바실 일하다 scamp [fudge] one's work

헤싱헤싱하다 loose; slack; lax

헤아리다 1 〈세다〉 count; calculate; estimate; amount to; come up to
♦ 헤아릴 수 없는 incomputable; immeasurable / 수천을 헤아리다 go [run] into the thousands; be counted by (the) thousands
▶ 그런 예는 헤아릴 수 없이 많다 There are countless [numerous] instances like that.
2 〈미루어 생각하다〉 consider (a matter); think over (a matter); guess; conjecture; infer [deduce] (from) ; ponder on (a problem); deliberate
♦ 앞뒤를 잘 헤아린 뒤에 after due [careful] consideration / 아무의 마음을 헤아리다 fathom sb's heart; enter into sb's feelings; read sb's mind; 〈동정하다〉 sympathize with sb
▶ 만일 그의 기분을 헤아렸다면 너는 그런 것은 말하지 않았을 것이다 If you had entered into his feelings, you would not have said such a thing.

헤어나다 〈벗어나다〉 escape from (danger); get out of (a difficulty); extricate oneself from (difficulties); free oneself from (a bondage); find one's way out of (a fix)
♦ 곤경[위기]에서 헤어나다 get through trouble [a crisis]

헤어네트 a hairnet

헤어브러시 a hairbrush

헤어스타일 a hairstyle

헤어지다 1 〈흩어지다〉 disperse; be dispersed; be scattered; scatter
▶ 연설이 끝나자 군중은 사방으로 헤어졌다 The crowd dispersed when the speech was over.
▶ 방안에 온통 헤어져 있는 장난감을 정리하거라 Tidy up the toys scattered all over your room.
2 〈이별하다〉 break up; part (from, with); be parted (from); separate; be separated (from); 〈이혼하다〉 divorce oneself [be divorced] (from)
♦ 아주 서로 헤어지다 leave each other forever / 헤어져 살다 live apart (from); live separately / 아내와 헤어지다 divorce one's wife
▶ 그와 헤어진지 꽤 오래 된다 It's such a long time since I saw him last.
▶ 나는 역에서 그와 헤어졌다 He and I left each other [parted] at the station.
▶ 나는 다섯살 때 부모와 헤어졌다 I was parted from my parents when I was five.
▶ 그는 부모와 헤어져 살고 있다 He lives away [apart] from his parents. (▶ live separately (from...)은 「(부부가) 별거하다」의 뜻)

헤어토닉 a hair tonic

헤어핀 a hairpin

헤엄 swimming; a swim
♦ 헤엄을 잘[못]치는 사람 a good [poor] swimmer / 헤엄을 잘 치다 swim well; be a good swimmer; be good at swimming / 헤엄을 잘 못 치다 be a poor swimmer; be poor at swimming
—**헤엄치다** swim; have a swim
♦ 강에서 헤엄치다 swim in a river / 옆으로 헤엄치다 swim on one's side / 헤엄치러 가다 go swimming (in a river); go (to a lake) for a swim / 헤엄쳐 거슬러 올라가다 swim upstream [against a stream] / 헤엄쳐 건너다 swim across (a river)
▶ 나는 조금도 헤엄칠 줄 모른다 I can't swim a stroke.
▶ 헤엄치는 법을 좀 가르쳐 다오 Teach [Show] me how to swim.
■ 개— swimming in dog fashion; the dog paddle 팔매— (swim by) the overarm stroke; hand-over-hand swimming

헤적이다 〈찾으려고 뒤지다〉 ransack; rummage (in); 〈파헤치다〉 stir [dig] up (the mud); 〈흩뜨리다〉 scatter (about); disperse
♦ 서류를 헤적이다 rummage among papers

헤죽거리다 swing one's arms as one goes [walks]

헤집다 dig up [over]; turn up; tear up
▶ 닭들이 벌레를 찾아 흙을 헤집고 있다 Hens are scratching the ground for worms.

헤치다 1 〈파헤치다〉 dig up; turn up
♦ 무덤을 파헤치다 dig a grave open; open a grave
▶ 그는 쓰레기를 헤치고 잃은 물건을 찾아냈다 He searched through the debris and found what he had lost.
2 〈흩어져 가게 하다〉 disperse; scatter; break up ♦ 군중을 헤치다 disperse a crowd
3 〈좌우로 물리치다〉 push [shove, thrust] aside [out of the way]; 〈팔꿈치로〉 elbow aside [off]

♦ 군중 속을 헤치고 나아가다 plow [work, push, force, elbow] *one's* way through the crowd / 파도를 헤치고 나아가다 cut [plow] *one's* way through the waves [water] / 헤치고 들어가다 make *one's* way into; push [force] *oneself* in [into]

헤프다 1 〈물건이〉 not durable; soon used up; 〈서술적〉 do not stand long use; do not last long; go fast
▶ 이 비누는 헤프다 This soap doesn't last long.
▶ 요새는 돈이 헤프다 Money doesn't go far these days.
2 〈씀씀이가〉 uneconomical; wasteful; prodigal; unthrifty
♦ 돈을 헤프게 쓰는 사람 an extravagant person; a spendthrift / 돈의 씀씀이가 헤프다 be too free with *one's* money; be wasteful of money / 돈을 헤프게 쓰다 be too free with *one's* money; be wasteful of money; be careless with money
3 〈몸가짐이〉 loose; dissolute; dissipated
♦ 몸가짐이 헤픈 여자 a loose woman
4 〈말이〉 talkative; voluble; glib-tongued
▶ 그는 말이 헤프다 He speaks too much.
헤피 uneconomically; unthriftily; wastefully
♦ 돈을 헤피 쓰다 spend money wastefully
헤하다 beam with delight; grin (broadly)
헤헤 ♦ 헤헤 웃다 laugh foolishly
헥타르 〈면적의 단위〉 a hectare
헨델 〈독일 태생의 작곡가, 후에 영국에 귀화〉 Handel, George Frederick (1685-1759)
헬레니즘 Hellenism
헬륨 〔化〕 helium
헬리오트로프 〔植〕 a heliotrope
헬리콥터 a helicopter; (口) a copter; (美俗) a chopper
♦ 헬리콥터로 가다 helicopter (to) / 헬리콥터로 운반되다 be transported by helicopter; be helicoptered (to)

─────── 헬리콥터 ───────

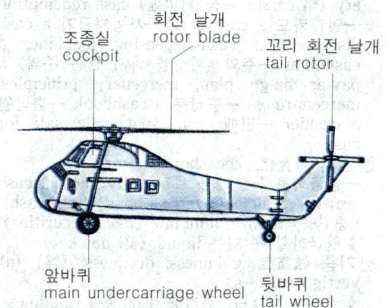

조종실 cockpit / 회전 날개 rotor blade / 꼬리 회전 날개 tail rotor / 앞바퀴 main undercarriage wheel / 뒷바퀴 tail wheel

헬리포트 〈헬리콥터 발착장〉 a heliport; a helidrome
헬멧 a helmet; a hard hat
헬스클럽 a health club
헬싱키 〈핀란드의 수도〉 Helsinki

헷갈리다 1 〈뒤섞이다〉 be mixed (confusedly)
♦ 서류가 헷갈리지 않도록 하다 see that the papers do not get mixed
2 〈깔피를 못잡다〉 be hardly distinguishable (from); hardly tell [discriminate] (A from B); 〈머리가 혼란하다〉 be thrown into confusion; be confused; be perplexed
▶ 나는 정신이 헷갈린다 I'm getting confused.
▶ 나는 어느 것이 어느 것인지 헷갈린다 I can't tell which is which.
헹가래 tossing; hoisting *sb* shoulder-high
♦ 헹가래 치다 toss; hoist *sb* shoulder-high
헹구다 wash out; rinse; give *sth* a rinse [swill]
♦ 빨래를 헹구다 rinse laundry in clean water after washing
헝글헝글 baggy; loose-fitting
─**헝글헝글하다** loose; baggy; loose-fitting (trousers)
혀 〈사람의〉 a tongue; 〈악기의〉 a reed
♦ 혀차는 소리 a tongue-clicking sound; a click [clack] of the tongue; 〈못마땅하여〉 Tut, tut / 혀가 잘 돌다 be oily-tongued; have a glib tongue / 혀가 잘 돌지 않다 be tongue-tied; be inarticulate in *one's* speech / 혀를 내밀다 put [stick, poke] out *one's* tongue; 〈개가〉 loll (out) the tongue / 혀를 깨물다 bite *one's* tongue / 혀를 차다 clack [click] *one's* tongue; tut / 혀를 내두르다 marvel (at); be astounded (at); be speechless with admiration (at)
▶ 그녀는 나를 보고 혀를 내밀었다 She stuck [put, poke] out her tongue at me.
▶ 개는 혀를 축 늘어뜨렸다 The dog let its tongue loll out.
혀꼬부랑이 an inarticulate person
혀끝 the tip of the tongue
혀 아래 도끼 들었다 〈속담〉 Least said, soonest mended.
혀짜래기 a lisper ⇨ 혀짤배기
혀짤배기 a lisper; a tongue-tied person
♦ 혀짤배기의 lisping (child); tongue-tied / 혀짤배기 말을 하다 lisp (out); speak with a lisp
혁대 革帶 a leather belt
■─고리 a buckle; a clasp; a clamp
혁명 革命 a revolution
♦ 혁명적(인) revolutionary (ideas) / 혁명을 일으키다 start a revolution (against)
▶ 그 나라에 혁명이 일어났다 A revolution broke out in the country.
▶ 그들이 혁명을 단행할 것은 틀림없다 It is certain that they will carry out a revolution.
▶ 컴퓨터는 과학 기술에 혁명을 가져왔다고 할 수 있다 It may be said that computers have revolutionized [have caused a revolution in] technology.
■ 명예— 〔史〕 the Glorious Revolution 무력— an armed revolution 무혈— a bloodless revolution 사회— a social revolution 산업— an industrial revolution; 〔史〕 the Industrial Revolution 평화— a pacific revolution 폭력— a revolution by force [violence] 프랑스— 〔史〕 the French Revolution ■─가(家) a revolutionist; a revolutionary ─가(歌) a revolutionary song ─군 a revolutionary army

혁신

—사상 revolutionary ideas —시대 an epoch of revolution —아(兒) a man of a revolutionary temperament —운동 a revolutionary movement —전쟁 a revolutionary war —정부 a revolutionary government

혁신 革新 (a) reform; (a) renovation; (an) innovation

◆정계의 혁신 a political reform [renovation] / 혁신적(인) innovative; progressive; reformist / 전술에 일대 혁신을 가져오다 bring about a revolution in the art of war

▶그는 교육제도의 혁신을 부르짖고 있다 He is clamoring for reform in the educational system.

—혁신하다 reform; make a reform 《in》; renovate; innovate

▶회사는 많은 기술을 혁신했다 The company has put through many technical improvements.

■—세력 the progressive force; the progressive political group —운동 a reform movement —자 a reformer; an innovator —정당 a reformist political party —파 the reformists; a reformist group

혁지 革砥 a strop; a razor strap

◆혁지에 갈다 strop; strap 《a razor》; sharpen 《a razor》 on a strop

혁혁하다 赫赫— splendid; brilliant 《victory》; glorious; distinguished 《service》 ◆혁혁한 공덕 a glorious exploit / 혁혁한 명성 a brilliant reputation / 혁혁한 전과를 거두다 achieve brilliant war results

현 弦 1 〔활시위〕 a bowstring
2 〔幾〕 a chord; 〔數〕 a subtense; 〈직각 삼각형의 빗변〉 a hypotenuse **3** 〔天〕 〈달의〉 a quarter

현 舷 the gunwale; the gunnel ⇨ 뱃전

현 絃 〈현악기의〉 a string; a chord

◆2현은 a two-stringed instrument / 현을 퉁기다 pluck [pick] the strings; twang the strings

현 縣 〈중국의〉 a district; 〈일본의〉 a prefecture

현— 現— present; existing; actual; incumbent

◆현내각 the present Cabinet / 현시장 the incumbent mayor / 현시점에서는 at present; at this point in [of] time

현가 現價 the current price

현격하다 懸隔— far [wide] apart 《from》; widely different 《from》

◆현격한 차이 a great disparity; a wide difference [gap] / …와 비교하여 현격한 차가 있다 bear [have] no proportion 《to》; there is a wide difference [unbridgeable gulf] 《between》

▶두 사람의 역량에는 현격한 차가 있다 As for their ability, there is a marked [distinct] difference between the two.

현관 玄關 〈입구〉 the entrance; the porch (way); the (front) door; 〈현관 홀〉 the vestibule; the hall (way); the entrance [front] hall; (美) the entry hall

◆현관으로 들어가다 enter at the front door / 자동차를 현관에 대다 drive a motorcar up to the door

▶현관에 누가 와 있습니다 There is someone at the front door.

▶그는 그녀를 현관까지 배웅했다 He saw her to the door.

현군 賢君 a wise lord [king]

현금 現今 the present time ⇨ 현재(現在)

◆현금의 상황 the existing [present, prevailing] state of things / 현금인 present(-day); current; of today / 현금에는 now; at the present time; today; nowadays; (in) these days

현금 現金 〈현찰〉 cash; 〈현재 있는 돈〉 actual [ready] money; 〈맞돈〉 prompt [spot] cash; ready funds

◆현금이 부족하다 be [run] short of cash / 현금이 없다 be out of cash / 현금인 경우에 1할 깎아주다 take ten percent off for cash / 현금으로 치르다 pay in cash; present ready money; (美) pay down / 현금으로 거래하다 deal in cash; conduct business on a cash basis / 현금으로 사다[팔다] buy [sell] *sth* for cash / (수표·채권 등을) 현금으로 바꾸다 cash 《a check》; have [get] 《a check》 cashed; convert 《a bond》

▶나는 무엇이나 현금으로 산다 I buy everything in cash. ⇒ I pay cash for everything.

▶대금은 현금에 한함 (게시) We sell only for cash.

▶지불은 현금도 되고 월부도 됩니다 Payment may be made either in cash or in monthly installments.

▶현금으로 사시면 5퍼센트 할인합니다 Goods are subject to five percent discount when paid in cash. ⇒ We shall take off five percent for cash.

■—가격 a cash [spot] price —거래 cash transaction [business]; cash-and-carry transaction; (美) spot transaction —구매 cash purchase; purchase with cash —등록기 a cash register —불 cash payment; (美) down payment —불 주문 cash with order (略 C.W.O., c.w.o.); a cash order —불 할인 cash discount —비율 cash ratio —상환(相換) cash on delivery (略 c.o.d.) —상환(償還) cash redemption —인출카드 a cash card —자동지급기 a cash dispenser; a cash-dispensing machine; a cashomat —주의 〈외상을 하지 않는 주의〉 a pay-as-you-go plan; mercenary principles; mercenariness —출납부 a cashbook —출납원 a cashier —판매 cash [spot] sale; sale for cash

현금화 現金化 encashment

—현금화하다 〈수표·채권 등을〉 encash; cash (in) 《a check》; convert 《a bond》 (into cash); 〈증권을〉 realize; liquidate 《one's securities》

◆현금화할 수 있는 liquid; (美) quick

현기증 眩氣症 giddiness; dizziness; 〔醫〕 〈an〉 vertigo (*pl.* ~s)

◆일어설 때 나는 현기증 dizziness [giddiness, vertigo] on standing up; 〔醫〕 orthostatic syncope / 현기증이 나는 높이에서 at a giddy [dizzy(ing)] height 《from the ground》 / 현기증이 나다[을 느끼다] be [feel] dizzy; get [feel] giddy; one's head swims / 때때로 현기증이 나다 have frequent dizzy spells; be sub-

ject to attacks of vertigo / 일어설 때 현기증이 나다 feel [get] dizzy [giddy] on standing up ▶ 会話 「어디 편찮으십니까?」「예, 현기증이 좀 납니다」 "Is anything wrong with you?" "Yes, I feel a little dizzy [woozy]."
━산후(産後)— puerperal vertigo

현대 現代 the present age [day, generation]; modern times; today
♦ 현대의 한국 modern [contemporary] Korea; (the) present-day Korea; Korea (of) today / 현대의 과학자 the scientists of the time / 현대의 present-day; contemporary; present / 현대에 (있어서) in our time; at the present day; in these modern days
▶ 현대는 스피드의 시대다 Now is the age of speed.
▶ 그런 낡은 이론은 현대에는 통용되지 않는다 Such an old theory cannot be applied today.
■━교육 modern education ━극 a modern play; a drama of present-day life ━문 current style ━문학 contemporary [current] literature ━사(史) contemporary history ━사상 modern ideas [thought]; modernism ━사조 current thought; 〈시대정신〉 the spirit of the times ━생활 present-day life ━식 a modern style [fashion]: 현대식 건물 a building in modern style ━어 a living [modern] language ━여성 a (young) woman of today; a modern girl ━영어 present-day [up-to-date] English ━인 a modern; (총칭) the moderns ━전(戰) modern war(-fare) ━주의 modernism ━주의자 a modernist ━판 a modern edition: 현대판 이솝 이야기 a modern version of the Aesop's Fables

현대적 現代的 modern(-type); modernistic; up-to-date; up-to-the minute; contemporary
♦ 현대적 건물 a building in modern style / 현대적으로 in a modern style; along [on] modern lines
▶ 그는 현대적 감각의 소유자다 He is modern in his feelings.

현대풍 現代風 the present [latest, up-to-date] fashion; the modern style [fashion]; modernism
♦ 현대풍의 건물 a building of modern style [fashion] / 현대풍의 of the modern style; up-to-date / 현대풍으로 in the present fashion [style]; fashionably

현대화 現代化 modernization; updating
━현대화하다 modernize; update; 〈현대풍으로 되다〉 be modernized
♦ 건축양식을 현대화하다 modernize a style of building / 완전히 현대화하다 be completely modernized

현란하다 絢爛— brilliant; gorgeous; dazzling; flowery; florid; gaudy
♦ 현란한 문체 a flowery [richly ornate] style / 눈부시도록 현란한 광경 a spectacle [sight] of dazzling gorgeousness
▶ 그녀는 현란한 의상을 입고 있었다 She was gorgeously [dazzlingly] dressed.

현명 賢明 〈지혜〉 wisdom; intelligence; sagacity; 〈분별〉 prudence; 〈양식〉 good sense; 〈상책〉 advisability
━현명하다 wise; intelligent; sagacious; judicious; sensible; prudent; discreet; well-advised
♦ 현명한 방책 a wise policy / 현명한 사람 a wise man; an intelligent person; a man of intelligence / 현명치 못한 illconsidered; injudicious; inadvisable; illadvised; unwise / 현명한 조치를 취하다 adopt a wise policy / 현명하게 처신하다 act wisely [sensibly]
▶ 그렇게 하는 것이 과연 현명할까 몰라 I can't help wondering if we are wise to do so.
▶ 그렇게 하는 것은 현명치 못한 방법이다 That is an unwise [a tactless] way of doing so.
▶ 우두커니 그를 기다린다는 것은 현명치 못하다 There is no sense in waiting for him idly.

현모 賢母 a wise mother
━━양처 a good wife and wise mother

현몽 現夢 appearing in one's dream
━현몽하다 appear in one's dream; appear [come] to one in a dream

현묘 玄妙 abstruseness; occultness
━현묘하다 abstruse; occult; recondite; mysterious; miraculous; 〈포착하기 힘들다〉 subtle 《meaning》
♦ 현묘한 사상 profound ideas

현무암 玄武岩 〔地質〕 basalt; whinstone
현문 舷門 (海) a gangway
현물 現物 the (actual) thing [article]; spot goods; spots
♦ 현물을 보지 않고 without seeing the goods / (세금 등을) 현물로 지불하다 pay 《taxes》 in kind
▶ 현물을 보기 전에는 뭐라 말할 수 없다 I cannot say either way before I inspect the article.
▶ 그녀는 돈이 아니라 현물로 빚을 갚았다 She paid the debt in kind rather than with money.
■━가격 spot prices ━거래[매매] spot trading; spot transaction ━급여 an allowance in kind ━배상 reparations in kind ━시장 the spot market ━인도 delivery of the goods ━인환 불(引換拂) pay(ment) [cash] on delivery 《略 P.[C.]O.D.》 ━출자(出資) investment in kind

현미 玄米 unpolished [uncleaned, unmilled] rice; brown rice
━━기(機) a (rice) huller; a husker ━빵 whole-rice bread

현미경 顯微鏡 a microscope
♦ 배율 1000배의 현미경 a microscope of one thousand magnifications / 현미경적 유기체 a microscopic organism / 현미경적(인) microscopic 《exactness》 / 현미경적으로 microscopically / 현미경의 초점을 맞추다 focus a microscope (on, upon) / 현미경으로 보다 see [look at] sth under [through] a microscope / 현미경으로 조사하다 examine sth with a [the] microscope; inspect sth microscopically / 현미경으로 연구[검사]하다 make a microscopic study [inspection] (of)
■━고배율(高倍率)— a powerful [high-power(ed)] microscope 복합(複合)— a compound microscope 쌍안— a binocular microscope 전자— an electron microscope ■━분석

현미분광기

microscopic analysis ―사진 a microphotograph; a photomicrograph ―사진기 a photomicroscope ―시험[검사] a microscopic test [examination, inspection]; microscopy ―자리 〔天〕 the Microscope; Microscopium

현미분광기 顯微分光器 a microspectroscope
현미해부 顯微解剖 〔生〕 microdissection
현부 賢婦 a wise [sagacious] woman
현부인 賢夫人 〈어진 부인〉 a wise wife; 〈남의 부인의 존칭〉 your wife; Mrs. ...
현사 賢士 a wise man [scholar]; a sage
현상 現狀 the present condition ; the existing state of things; the (present) situation [state]; the existing state [circumstances]; (라) the status quo

♦한국의 현상 the present state of affairs in Korea; Korea as she is [stands] / 경제계의 현상 the present [prevailing] economic situation [condition] / 현상으로는 in [under] the existing circumstances; as affairs [things, matter] now stand; as things stand [are] today; under the present conditions / 현상 그대로 in status quo; as (it) is / 현상을 유지하다 maintain [preserve] the status quo; keep things in status quo / 현상을 타파하다 break the situation; do away with the present state of things / 현상에 만족하다 be content with things as they are

▶이것이 중국의 현상이다 Such is the state of things in China.
▶나는 현상 그대로가 좋다 I am perfectly contented with the matter as it is.
▶당분간 현상 그대로 둡시다 Let's leave the matter as it is for the time being.
―유지 maintenance of the status quo ―유지 협정 a status quo [standstill] agreement ―타파 destruction of the status quo

현상 現象 a phenomenon (*pl.* -na); an appearance; a happening

♦전후(의) 현상 postwar phenomenon / 사회 발달에 있어서의 일시적 현상 a passing phase in the development of society / 진기한 현상을 나타내다 present an extraordinary phenomenon

▶현상과 실체는 다르다 A phenomenon is different from a substance.
▶이상한 현상이 일어났다 A strange phenomenon presented itself.
―물리 a physical phenomenon 사회― a social phenomenon 언어― the phenomena of language 자연― the phenomena of nature; a natural phenomenon ■―계 〔哲〕 the phenomenal world ―과학 a phenomenal science ―론 〔哲〕 phenomenalism; phenomenology ―학 phenomenology

현상 現像 〔寫〕 development
―하다 develop (negatives, films)
♦너무(덜) 현상된 overdeveloped [underdeveloped] (film, negative)
■―과도 overdevelopment ―반(盤) a developing tray ―부족 underdevelopment ―실[소] a processing laboratory ―액[제] a developing solution; a developer ―지(紙) developing-out paper (略 D.O.P.)

현상 懸賞 〈상을 걸기〉 a prize competition; an offer of a prize [reward]

♦현상 붙은 with a prize offered / 현상을 걸다 offer a prize [reward] 《for》; set a prize / 현상 모집을 하다 hold a prize (novel) contest
―광고 an advertisement for a prize contest; a prize ad ―논문 a prize essay ―당선자 a prize winner ―문제 a problem for a prize contest ―소설(-winning) novel; 현상 소설 모집 a prize novel competition

현상금 懸賞金 prize money; a reward; a prize 《on *sb's* head》

♦현상금을 걸다 offer a prize [reward] 《for》; 〈범인 등에〉 set [put] a price on 《an offender's head》 / 현상금을 타다 win [carry off] a prize 《in a contest》
▶지명 수배자에게 500만원의 현상금이 걸려 있다 A reward of five million won is being offered for the wanted man.

현상태 現狀態 the present state of things; the present circumstances; the existing condition [state]
♦현상태로는 as matters stand (now); as the case stands at present; in the present circumstances [state of things]; under the present conditions

현선 絃線 (cat)gut; a chord; a string
현세 現世 this world [life]; the transient life; 〔佛敎〕 the land of the living; 〔地質〕 the Recent
♦현세의 괴로움[즐거움] the hardships [pleasures] of life / 현세와 내세 this world and the next / 현세적(인) worldly; mundane; earthly; secular
■―사(事) the affairs of this transient life ―주의 secularism

현세기 現世紀 this century; the present century
현손 玄孫 a great-great-grandson
현수 懸垂 suspension; dangling; pendency
―근(筋) 〔解〕 a suspensory muscle ―대(帶) 〔醫〕 a suspensory bandage ―분사(分詞) 〔文法〕 a dangling [hanging] participle ―운동 〈철봉의〉 chinning exercises: 현수 운동을 하다 chin *oneself* (up); do chinning exercises 《at an iron bar》

현수교 懸垂橋 a suspension bridge
♦현수교를 놓다 construct a suspension bridge 《over a river》; suspend a bridge 《over a river》; span 《a river》 with a suspension bridge

현수막 懸垂幕 a hanging screen; a curtain; 〈무대의〉 a drop curtain; 〈플래카드〉 a placard
♦현수막을 내걸다 put up a placard

현숙하다 賢淑― good and virtuous
현시 現時 the present time; today
♦현시와 같은 때(에) in times like the present
현시 顯示 revelation; manifestation 《of God's power》; 〔가톨릭〕 exposure
―하다 show; unfold; be revealed; uncover; unveil; open out
■―성체 the exposure of the Host

현시대 現時代 the present age; modern times
현신 賢臣 a wise retainer [vassal]

현신 現身 presenting *oneself* before *one's* master
―현신하다 present *oneself* before *one's* master; put in *one's* appearance; appear

현실 現實 reality; actuality
◆ 가혹한 현실 grim [hard, harsh] realities / 답답한 현실 heavy actualities / 현실적(인) realistic; materialistic; matter-of-fact / 현실으로 actually; in actuality; practically / 현실이 되다 become reality / 현실을 직시하다 face the realities / 현실과 동떨어지다 become disconnected with reality; be divorced from reality / 현실에 맞게 계획을 세우다 plan realistically [on a realistic basis] / 현실에 맞지 않다 be at variance with the reality [real conditions, actual state of things]
▶ 이상과 현실을 혼동하지 마라 Don't confuse the ideal with the real.
▶ 현실에서 도피하려고 하면 안된다 You should not try to escape from realities.
▶ 그는 아주 현실적인 사람이므로 돈 버는 일 밖에는 생각하지 않는다 He is a very practical man and thinks only of making money.
▶ 현실에 적합한 해결책을 강구해야 한다 You should try to find a solution that is adapted to the realities.
■ ―감 the sense for the real ―도피 escape from reality ―론 a bread-and-butter theory ―성 actuality; reality ―주의 actualism; realism ―주의자 an actualist; a realist

현실화 現實化 actualization; realization; materialization
―현실화하다 actualize; realize; materialize; 〈물가 등을〉 readjust 《prices》 to a realistic level

현악 絃樂 string music
■ ―4중주 a string quartet(te) ―3중주 a string trio ―5중주 a string quinte(te) ―합주(단) a string ensemble [orchestra]

현악기 絃樂器 a stringed (musical) instrument; a string instrument; (총칭) the strings
■ ―주자 a string musician [player]

현안 懸案 a pending [an outstanding] problem [question]
◆ 양국간의 현안 문제 a question pending between the two countries / 현안으로 남겨두다 leave [hold] 《a matter》 pending [undecided]
▶ 그것은 다년간의 현안이다 It's a long-standing problem.
▶ 그 문제는 요 몇년 동안 현안이 되어 있다 The problem has remained unresolved for the past few years.

현애 懸崖 an overhanging cliff; a precipice

현양 顯揚 exaltation
―현양하다 gain fame; become famous; be widely known; exalt

현업 現業 work in the field; a work-site operation
■ ―원 a field [an outdoor] worker; (총칭) the outdoor staff

현역 現役 active service; 〈휴직에 대하여〉 service on full pay; 〈군함의〉 commission
◆ 현역의 〈군대〉 on the active list; 〈군함〉 in commission; commissioned / 현역중이다 be in active service; be on service; be on the active list / 현역을 마치다 serve *one's* full time in the army; go through active service; wind up *one's* service / 현역에 복무하다 enter active service / 현역에 복귀시키다 〈군함을〉 demothball / 현역에 머무르다 stay in uniform / 현역에서 물러나다[퇴역하다] retire from active service
■ ―군인 a soldier in active service; a serviceman on active duty; a soldier with the colors ―명부 the active list ―장교 an officer in active service [on the active list]; (총칭) the effectives ―함 a commissioned vessel; a vessel in commission [service]

현옹수 懸雍垂 the uvula ⇨ 목젖

현우 賢友 a wise [good] friend

현우 賢愚 wisdom or folly; 〈현자와 우자〉 the wise and the foolish

현월 弦月 a crescent (moon); a young moon ⇨ 초승(~달)

현유 現有 ◆ 현유 해군 세력 the fleet in being / 현유의 present; existing; 〔法〕 manual; actually possessed

현인 賢人 a wise man ⇨ 현자(賢者)

현임 現任 the present office [post]
■ ―수상 the present [incumbent] prime minister; the prime minister in office ―자 the present holder of the office [post]

현자 賢者 a wise man; a sage; a man of high intelligence

현장 現場 〈사건의〉 the (actual) spot; the scene 《of action》; 〈작업의〉 the scene of labor; a job site; 〈건축의〉 a (building) site; a construction field
◆ 사건 현장 the very spot where the accident took place / 조난 현장 the scene of a disaster / 현장에 있던 사람들 those who happened to be there; those present / 현장에서 on the spot [ground, scene]; then and there / 마침 현장에 있다 happen to be on the scene 《of an accident》 / 도둑질하는 것을 현장에서 붙잡다 catch *sb* in the act of stealing / 현장에서 체포되다 be arrested on the spot [then and there] / 현장에서 죽다 be killed on the spot / 현장에서 들키다 be caught red-handed [in the act] / 현장으로 달려가다 rush [hasten, hurry] to the scene 《of the rescue》 / 현장을 목격하다 be an eyewitness of the disaster [accident] / 사고현장을 조사하다 investigate the scene of the accident
▶ 범인은 현장에서 체포되었다 The criminal was arrested [caught] red-handed.
▶ 살인 현장에서 피묻은 수건이 발견되었다 A bloodstained towel was found on the scene of murder.
▶ 그는 그때 현장에 없었다 He was not on the spot at the time.
▶ 지금 현장에는 다섯명의 세일즈맨이 배치되어 있다 We now have five salesmen in the field.
▶ 그들은 현장 교사들의 소리를 존중하지 않으면 안된다 They should respect what active teachers have to say.
■ ―감독 a field overseer; an on-the-job super-

intendent: 현장 감독을 하다 supervise the work of construction in the field ―검증 an inspection of the scene 《of a murder》; an on-the-spot inspection [investigation] ―관리 field supervision ―근무 field service ―도(渡) [매매] spot delivery [sale] ―도가격 a loco price ―보고 a field [an on-scene] report ―부재 증명 《法》 an alibi ―사무소 a field office ―시찰 a spot inspection ―십장 a working foreman; a work leader ―조사 an on-the-spot survey; a field investigation ―주임 a foreman

현장감 現場感 〈레코드·테이프의〉 presence; realism; ambience

현재 現在 1 〈지금〉 now; presently; 《at》 the present time
♦ 현재의 남편[주소] one's present husband [address] / 현재 진행 중인 on-going 《summit conference》 / 현재의 present; existing; current / 현재로서는 at present; at this time; as of now; for the present; 〈당분간〉 for the time being; in the present state of things; under existing circumstances / 현재까지 up to now; up [down] to date / 현재 그대로 놔두다 leave 《a matter》 as it is
▶ 나는 현재의 위치에 만족한다 I am contented where I am.
▶ 이 도시의 4월 1일 현재의 인구는 20만입니다 The population of this city as of April 1 is two hundred thousand.
2 〔文法〕 the present tense
■ ―완료(시제) the present perfect (tense) : 그 동사는 현재 완료 (시제)다 The verb is in the present perfect (tense). ―원(員) the present members on the list [roll] ―회원수 the actual membership

현재 賢才 a man of ability [talent]; 《총칭》 talent

현저하다 顯著― notable; remarkable; noticeable; conspicuous; marked; distinguished
♦ 현저한 공적 distinguished [eminent] services / 현저한 사실 an obvious fact / 현저한 예 a striking [conspicuous] example / 현저한 차이 a sharp [striking] difference 《in》 / 현저히 다른 substantially different / 현저히 remarkably; considerably; strikingly; conspicuously / 현저한 발달을 하다 make marked [remarkable, conspicuous] progress / 더욱더 현저해지다 become more and more conspicuous [marked]

현정부 現政府 the present [existing] Government

현존 現存 ♦ 현존의 existing; living; actual; extant
―현존하다 exist; be in existence; be extant; subsist
▶ 현존하는 사람 중에 당시를 기억하는 사람은 적다 There are few persons living who remember those days.
■ ―작가 living writers

현주 現住 actual residence
―현주하다 reside [dwell, live] at present
■ ―민 present inhabitants [residents] ―자 a current occupant ―지 〈주소〉 one's present address [domicile, abode]; 〈장소〉 where one is living at present

현지 現地 the actual place; the (actual) locale
♦ 현지 사람들 the local people / 현지의 on-the-spot; in-the-field; field / 현지에서 촬영한 photographed on the actual location
■ ―로케이션 an on-the-spot location ―방송 an on-the-spot [a mikeside] broadcast; a broadcast from the scene ―보고 a spot [an on-the-spot, an onscene] report; a report from the spot; 〈르포르타주〉 reportage ―시간 local time; 현지 시간으로 오후 3시 (한국시간으로 일요일 오전 4시) at three p.m. local time (04:00 KST Sunday) ―시찰 여행 a field trip; a fact-finding tour ―인(人) the natives ―조달 self-subsistence [self-sufficiency] on the spot ―특파원 a correspondent on the scene

현지조사 現地調査 an on-the-spot [a field] survey [investigation, inquiry]; investigation on the scene; an on-site study
♦ 현지조사를 하다 study 《the question》 on the spot [scene]; conduct a spot investigation
■ ―반 a field investigation party

현직 現職 the present post [office]
♦ 현직에 있는 사람 an incumbent / 현직의 on the active list; in active service / 현직에 머무르다 remain [stay] in (one's present) office; stay on the job
■ ―경찰관 a policeman on the active list [in active service] ―국회의원 an incumbent National Assembly member ―대통령 the president in office; the incumbent president

현찰 現札 〈현금〉 (hard) cash; actual [ready] money; 〈지폐〉 a (bank) note
♦ 현찰로 백만원 a million won in notes / 현찰로 지불하다 pay in cash; present ready money

현찰 賢察 your discernment
▶ 귀하의 현찰을 바랍니다 I submit the matter for your discernment.

현창 舷窓 〔海〕 a porthole; a port; a side light

현책 賢策 〈현명한 계책〉 a wise policy
♦ …하는 것이 현책이다 it is well-advised [advisable] to do sth

현처 賢妻 an intelligent [a wise] wife

현철 賢哲 a sage; a wise man; 《총칭》 the wise
―현철하다 wise; intelligent

현충탑 顯忠塔 a memorial monument

현측 舷側 〈뱃전〉 the (ship's) side; 〈수면상의〉 the broadside
♦ 현측에 alongside 《the ship》 / 현측에 대다 come alongside 《of》 a ship
■ ―도(渡) free alongside ship 《略 F.A.S., f.a.s.》; overside delivery

현탁액 懸濁液 〔化〕 suspension

현판 懸板 a tablet; 〈그림으로 이루어진〉 a framed picture

현품 現品 the (actual) things; actual article; the article in question; 〔商〕 spots; spot commodities [goods]; merchandise on spot
▶ 전시된 현품에 한하여 반액 판매 Display items (sold at) half price.
▶ 현품은 견본보다 못하다 The article in question does not come up to (the) sample. ⇌ The goods are inferior to (the) sample.

▶ 현품을 보지 않고서는 뭐라 말할 수 없다 I cannot say either way before I inspect the actual article.
■ —급여 wages [an allowance] in kind —대장 a stock ledger —상환불(相換拂) cash on delivery (略 C.O.D.) —시장 the spot market

현하 現下 the present time; now
◆ 현하의 중대 과제 a serious problem of the hour / 현하의 present; existing; of the hour [day]; at the present moment
▶ 현하의 주택 사정을 어떻게 생각합니까? What do you think of the present housing situation?
▶ 현하의 국제 정세는 극히 불안정하다 The existing state of international affairs is very unstable.

현하 懸河 a stream flowing down a precipice
■ —지변(之辯)[구변, 웅변] an eloquent speech; fluency in speech

현학 衒學 〈학식을 뽐냄〉 pedantry; display [parading] of *one's* learning ◆ 현학적(인) pedantic —자 a pedant; a gerund-grinder

현행 現行 〈형용사적〉 existing; present; current; in force; in use; in operation
◆ 현행대로 the same as at present
▶ 현행의 임금률은 너무 낮다 The ruling rates of wages are too low.
▶ 현행의 영어 교과서는 몇 종류가 있습니까? How many kinds of English textbooks are now in use?
■ —교과서 the textbooks now in use —규정 the regulations (now) in force; the standing rules: 현행 규정은 그것에 관하여 아무 언급이 없다 The regulations now in force do not say anything about it. —맞춤법 the current system of spelling —제도 the present system in existence [force]: 현행 제도하에서는 under the present system / 현행 제도의 결점은 무엇입니까? What are the defects of the present system? —화폐 the current coins; the currency now in circulation

현행범 現行犯 [法] 〈행위〉 a flagrant delict [offense]; a crime committed in the presence of a policeman; 〈사람〉 a criminal taken in an act of crime; a flagrant delictor [offender]
▶ 그 사나이는 절도 현행범으로 잡혔다 The man was arrested (in the act of) [caught red-handed] stealing.

현행법 現行法 the existing [operative] law; the law (actually) in force
◆ 현행법에 따르면 according to the law now in force
▶ 그 범죄는 현행법의 적용을 받는다 The crime is subject to the existing laws.
▶ 현행법 하에서는 경찰이 그녀를 처벌할 수 없다 The police cannot punish her under the existing law.

현혹 眩惑 dazzlement; bewilderment; a daze
■ —하다 dazzle; daze; blind; make dizzy [giddy]; mystify; bewilder
◆ 현혹되다 be dazzled 《by》; be bewildered; be mystified
▶ 사나이들은 그녀의 미모에 현혹되었다 The men were dazzled [fascinated] by her beauty.

▶ 그의 말에 현혹되지 않도록 조심해라 Be careful not to be misled by his words.

현화식물 顯花植物 [植] a flowering plant; a phanerogamous plant; a phanerogam

현황 現況 the present condition [state, situation] ⇨ 현상(現狀)

현훈 眩暈 〈어지러움〉〔韓醫〕 vertigo; scotodinia; dizziness; giddiness

혈 穴 1 [民俗] a lucky site for a grave
2 〈침놓는 자리〉 a spot on the body suitable for acupuncture

혈거 穴居 cave dwelling; troglodytism
◆ 혈거의 cave-dwelling; troglodytic
—혈거하다 dwell in a cave
■ —생활 cave dwelling; troglodytism —시대 the cave [troglodytic] period [age] —인(人) a caveman; a cave dweller; a troglodyte

혈관 血管 [解] a blood vessel; a vascular tract; a vein
◆ 혈관의 vascular; hemal; hematal / 혈관밖의 extravascular
▶ 정맥은 혈맥을 심장으로 돌려 보내는 혈관이다 Veins are blood vessels that carry the blood back to the heart.
▶ 혈액은 혈관을 통해 체내로 흐른다 Blood flows in the body through blood vessels.
■ —경화(증) hardening of the walls of the blood vessels; sclerosis of the blood vessels; angiosclerosis —압박기 a compressor —압축 thlipsis —파열 the bursting [rupture, laceration] of a blood vessel

혈괴 血塊 a clot of blood; gore

혈구 血球 [解] a blood corpuscle [cell]; a hemocyte; a hematocyte
◆ 혈구를 측정하다 make a blood count
■ 백— a leucocyte; a white (blood) corpuscle [cell] 적— an erythrocyte; a red (blood) corpuscle

혈기 血氣 1 〈체력〉 vitality; strength; stamina
2 〈의기〉 hot blood (of youth); youthful vigor [ardor]; the sap of youth; animal spirits
◆ 젊은 혈기 youthful follies [indiscretion] / 혈기 왕성한 젊은이 a sanguine youth; a young man in full vigor / 혈기에 찬 hot-blooded; hot-headed; sanguine / 혈기 왕성한 시절에 in *one's* hot [raw, vigorous] youth / 혈기에 이끌리다 be driven [carried away] by youthful vigor
▶ 그는 혈기 왕성하다 He is full of youthful vigor [high spirits]. ⇌ He is young and hot-blooded.
▶ 나는 혈기에 날뛰는 젊은이들을 달랬다 I calmed down the hasty [impetuous] young people.

혈농 血膿 bloody pus [matter]

혈뇨 血尿 [醫] bloody urine; h(a)ematuria

혈담 血痰 [醫] bloody [blood] phlegm

혈당 血糖 blood sugar ◆ 혈당 검사를 받다 receive a blood sugar test

혈로 血路 a perilous way out; a difficult escape-route ◆ 혈로를 찾다 seek a way out
▶ 적의 혈로를 뚫고 탈출했다 We cut our way through the enemy's ranks and fled. ⇌ We found our way through the enemy's

ranks.
혈루 血淚 tears of blood; bitter tears ⇨ 피눈물
혈맥 血脈 1 ⇨ 혈관(血管)
2 〈혈통〉 lineage; blood; pedigree; consanguinity
◆ ━상통(相通) blood relationship [bond]: 혈맥상통하다 be related by blood (ties)
혈맹 血盟 〈약속〉 a blood pledge; 〈동맹〉 a blood alliance
혈반 血斑 a blood spot
혈변 血便 bloody excrement ⇨ 피똥
혈병 血餠 〈生〉 a clot of blood; a blood clot
혈색 血色 (a) complexion; color (of the face)
◆ 썩 좋은 혈색 a high color / 혈색이 좋은 사람 a person of healthy complexion / 혈색이 좋은 얼굴 a sanguine face
▶ 그녀는 혈색이 좋다 She is high in color. ⇌ She looks well. ⇌ She has a good [healthy] complexion.
▶ 그녀는 혈색이 나쁘다 She looks pale [unwell]. ⇌ She has a pale [wan, sallow] complexion.
혈색소 血色素 〔生化〕 h(a)emoglobin
혈서 血書 a writing in blood; a document written in one's own blood
◆ 혈서를 쓰다 write in blood / 혈서로 탄원서를 내다 send in a petition written in one's own blood
혈석 血石 〔鑛〕 bloodstone
혈세 血稅 a tax paid by the sweat of one's brow; unbearably heavy taxes
◆ 혈세를 과하다 tax (people) to the bone
▶ 국민의 혈세를 낭비하는 것은 용서할 수 없다 It is unpardonable to waste the money earned by taxpayers with the sweat of their brow(s).
혈소판 血小板 〔解〕 a thrombocyte; a blood platelet; a plaque
혈속 血屬 blood relation; blood relatives
혈손 血孫 one's (direct) descendants
혈안 血眼 a bloodshot eye
◆ 혈안이 되어 madly; frantically; desperately / 돈을 빌려고 혈안이 되다 feel mad about making money; make a frantic attempt to make money
▶ 그는 혈안이 되어 잃어버린 아이의 행방을 찾았다 He looked desperately [frantically] for his lost child.
혈암 頁岩 〔地質〕 shale
혈압 血壓 〔醫〕 blood pressure
▶ 정상인의 혈압은 80에 120 정도다 In normal man, the average blood pressure is 120 over 80.
▶ 나는 혈압이 높다[낮다] I have high [low] blood pressure.
◆ 혈압은 약으로 낮출 수 있다 Blood pressure can be lowered [reduced] with medicine.
▶ 혈압을 재주세요 I'd like to have my blood pressure checked [taken].
▶ 이 약을 드시면 혈압이 내려갈 겁니다 This medicine will lower your blood pressure.
━고━ high blood pressure; hypertension: 고혈압증의 hypertensive 저━ low blood pressure; hypotension: 저혈압증의 hypotensive 정상━ normal blood pressure; normotension: 정상혈압의 normotensive ━계 a tonometer; a sphygmomanometer; a hemadynamometer; a manometer ━저하제[항진제] a hypotensive [hypertensive] drug ━측정 sphygmomanometry
혈액 血液 blood
◆ O[AB]형의 혈액 blood of the O [AB] type / 혈액의 h(a)ematal; hematic; hemal / 혈액에 작용하는[포함되는] h(a)ematic / 혈액에 기생하는 sanguicolous; hematobic / 혈액을 맑게 하다 purify blood
━결핍 a deficiency of blood; an(a)emia ━과다 an excess of blood ━은행 a blood bank 〔institute〕 a blood donor
혈액검사 血液檢查 〔醫〕 a blood test
◆ 혈액검사용으로 피를 뽑다 take a blood sample / 혈액검사를 하다 examine the blood; conduct [institute] a blood test
▶ 나는 혈액검사를 받았다 I had my blood examined.
혈액순환 血液循環 the circulation of the blood; blood circulation
◆ 혈액순환을 돕다 promote blood circulation
▶ 운동을 하면 혈액순환이 좋아진다 Exercise causes a quick circulation of the blood.
혈액형 血液型 a type of blood; a blood type
◆ 혈액형의 분류 blood typing / 혈액형을 조사하다 examine the blood of sb's blood / 피를 뽑아 혈액형을 검출하다 take a blood sample and type it
▶ 내 혈액형은 B형이다 I have type B blood.
▶ 당신은 무슨 혈액형입니까? What's your blood type?
▶ 나와 그는 혈액형이 맞지 않는다 My blood type is incompatible with his.
혈연 血緣 blood relation; family ties [connections]
━관계 relationship by blood; blood relationship; consanguinity: 그와는 혈연관계다 I am related to him by blood. ━단체 a kinship society ━사회 blood society
혈온 血溫 blood heat; the temperature of blood
혈우병 血友病 〔醫〕 h(a)emophilia; bleeder's disease ━환자 a h(a)emophiliac; a bleeder
━━환자의[에 걸린] h(a)emophilic
혈육 血肉 〈피와 살〉 flesh and blood; 〈자녀〉 one's own children
◆ 혈육의 정 love for one's flesh and blood / 슬하에 혈육이 없다 be childless
▶ 그 애는 내 일점 혈육이다 He is the only son of my flesh and blood.
혈장 血漿 〔解〕 blood plasma; (a) serum
━건조━ dried plasma 인공━ a plasma substitute; dextran
혈전 血戰 a bloody battle; a desperate fight; a murderous [red] battle
◆ 혈전을 치르다 fight a bloody battle; fight desperately
━━지 a scene of desperate fighting
혈전 血栓 〔醫〕 a thrombus (pl. -bi)
혈전증 血栓症 〔醫〕 (a) thrombosis (pl. -ses)
◆ 혈전증의 thrombotic / 혈전증에 걸리다 thrombose

■관상동맥— coronary thrombosis 뇌— cerebral thrombosis

혈족 血族 a blood relative; a relative by blood; kinsfolk; one's (kith and) kin
■—결혼 (a) consanguineous marriage; (an) intermarriage —관계 kinship; relationship by blood; blood relationship

혈종 血腫 〔醫〕 a hematoma (pl. ~s, -mata)

혈청 血淸 〔醫〕 (a) (blood) serum (pl. ~s, sera)
■—예방— a preventive serum ■—간염 serum hepatitis —검사 serum test —반응 (a) serum reaction; (a) seroreaction —병 a serum disease; serum sickness —요법[치료] serum treatment [therapy]; serotherapy —주사 a serum injection —진단 serum diagnosis; serodiagnosis —학 serology

혈침 血沈 〈적혈구 침강 속도〉 precipitation of blood; blood sedimentation ◆혈침을 재다 measure the precipitation of sb's blood

혈통 血統 blood; lineage; pedigree; family line; descent
◆아버지[어머니]쪽의 혈통 the paternal [maternal] line; blood relationship on one's father's [mother's] side / 혈통이 좋다[나쁘다] come of a good [bad] stock; be of a good [bad] strain / 혈통을 조사하다 inquire into sb's lineage; trace back sb's family line; trace sb's descent (to)
▶이 말은 혈통이 좋다 This horse has a good line of descent [bloodline].
▶혈통이 끊어졌다 The line has died out.
▶혈통은 속일 수 없다 Blood will tell.
■—서(書) 〈소・양의〉 a herdbook

혈투 血鬪 a bloody fight; a desperate struggle [fight]
—혈투하다 fight a bloody fight; fight desperately; engage in a life-and-death [life-or-death] struggle

혈판 血判 〈도장〉 a seal of blood; 〈찍기〉 sealing with blood
—혈판하다 seal with (one's) blood
◆청원서에 혈판하다 seal a petition with one's blood
—장 a petition [pledge] sealed with blood

혈한 血汗 〔醫〕 a blood [bloody] sweat

혈행 血行 the circulation of the blood; blood circulation
◆혈행을 좋게 하다 improve [stimulate] blood circulation
■—계(計) a rheometer —장애 interruption in blood circulation

혈혈단신 孑孑單身 ◆혈혈단신으로 all alone in the world ▶나는 혈혈단신이다 I am [stand] all alone in the world.

혈흔 血痕 a bloodstain; a mark [spot, trace, smear] of blood
◆혈흔이 있는 bloodstained
—검사 the examination of bloodstains

혐기 嫌忌 dislike; aversion; abhorrence —혐기하다 dislike; abhor; hold sb in abhorrence

혐기 嫌氣 〔生〕 ◆혐기성의 an(a)erobic
■—균 an(a)erobic bacteria; an(a)erobes

혐오 嫌惡 hatred; dislike; disgust; aversion; abhorrence; repugnance ▶그는 뱀에 대하여 혐오감을 갖고 있다 He hates snakes. ⇌ He has a dislike [hatred] for [of] snakes.
—혐오하다 hate; dislike; abhor; abominate; detest; loathe

혐의 嫌疑 1 〈의심〉 suspicion; charge
◆간첩 혐의로 on the suspicion of being a spy / 살인 혐의로 on a charge of murder / 혐의를 받다 fall [come] under suspicion; be suspected 《of》/ 혐의를 받고 있다 be [lie] under suspicion 《of》/ 혐의를 두다 suspect 《sb of a crime》; throw [cast] suspicion 《on》; fix one's suspicion 《upon》/ 혐의를 품다 entertain [have, harbor] a suspicion 《that》/ 혐의를 풀다 dispel suspicion; clear 《oneself, sb》 of suspicion
▶그에게 살인 혐의가 씌워졌다 Suspicion of the murder fell upon him. ⇌ He was suspected of the murder.
▶증인의 증언으로 피고의 혐의는 풀렸다 The testimony of the witness cleared the defendant of suspicion.
▶그는 혐의를 받을 만한 사람이 아니다 He is above suspicion. ⇌ His character is quite above [beyond] suspicion.
▶그는 사기 혐의로 체포되었다 He was arrested on (the) suspicion of fraud.
2 〈미움〉 dislike; aversion

혐의자 嫌疑者 a suspected person; a person under suspicion; 〈범죄의〉 a criminal suspect

협 峽 a gorge; a ravine; a glen; 《美》 a canyon

협각 夾角 〔數〕 an included angle ⇨ 끼인각

협객 俠客 a man of chivalrous spirit; a chivalrous person; a knight of the town
▶그에게는 협객 기질이 있다 He has a touch of chivalry in his character.

협곡 峽谷 a gorge; a ravine; a glen; a gullet; a gully; 《美》 a canyon

협골 頰骨 〔解〕 the cheekbone; the zygomatic bone; the zygoma (pl. -ta)

협공 挾攻 an attack on both sides [flanks]; a pincer attack
▶우리는 적의 협공을 받았다 We were attacked on both sides by the enemy.
—협공하다 〈십자포화로〉 catch (the enemy) in a crossfire; 〈양면에서〉 attack (the enemy) from both sides; launch [make] a pincer attack against (the enemy)
◆협공당하다[받다] be attacked on both sides; find oneself between two fires
■—작전[전술] pincer operations [tactics]; pincers

협궤 狹軌 a narrow [small] gauge
■—철도[선로] a narrow gauge railway [track, line]

협기 俠氣 a chivalrous spirit; chivalry
◆협기가 많은 사람 a very gallant man; a chivalrous man / 타고난 협기로 out of one's inborn chivalrous spirit

협도 俠盜 a generous [chivalrous] robber; a Robin Hood

협동 協同 〈협력〉 cooperation; collaboration; 〈결합〉 union; combination; 〈제휴〉 partnership

◆협동의 communal; joint; concerted; united / 협동으로 in partnership 《with》; jointly; communally
─협동하다 〈협력하다〉 cooperate 《with》; collaborate (in); act in concert [union] 《with》; 〈힘을 모으다〉 join forces [hands] 《with》; team up 《with》
◆협동하여 in conjunction [cooperation, collaboration, concert, association, participation] 《with》; jointly
▶우리는 협동하여 난관에 대처해야 한다 We should be united against the trouble. ⇒ Let's be united against the trouble.
■-기업 a joint enterprise [undertaking] ─농장 a collective farm; 〈옛 소련의〉 a kolkhoz (pl. -zy, ~es) ─작전 concerted [united, combined] operations ─정신 a spirit of cooperation; a cooperative spirit

협동조합 協同組合 a cooperative association [society]; a cooperative; (口) a co-op
■-농업─ an agricultural cooperative association 생산─ a producers' cooperative (society) 소비자─ a consumers' cooperative (society) ■-원 a copartner

협동체 協同體 a community ⇨ 공동체

협량 狹量 narrow-mindedness ─협량하다 narrow-minded; ungenerous; meanspirited

협력 協力 cooperation; 〈협동〉 collaboration; 〈공동 작업〉 working together
◆긴밀한 협력 close cooperation; intimate collaboration / 협력적인 cooperative / 협력적으로 cooperatively / 협력을 구하다 ask [appeal to] sb for help [assistance] / …의 협력을 얻다 obtain cooperation from...; win [secure] the cooperation of...
▶협력을 부탁합니다 I would like to ask for your cooperation.
─협력하다 cooperate 《with》; work together; collaborate 《with》; unite one's efforts 《with》; make united [concerted] efforts; join forces [hands] 《with》; team up 《with》
◆긴밀히 협력하여 일하다 work in close cooperation [shoulder to shoulder]
▶기꺼이 협력하겠습니다 I am ready to give you my cooperation.
▶우리는 그들과 협력하여 이 일을 마쳤다 We completed this project in cooperation with them.
▶협력해 주셔서 감사합니다 Thank you for your cooperation. ⇒ Thank you for helping me. ⇒ I appreciate your cooperation.
■경제─ economic cooperation 상호─ mutual cooperation ■-자 a cooperator; a co-worker; a collaborator

협로 峽路 〈산길〉 a mountain path; a defile
협로 狹路 〈좁은 길〉 a narrow path
협만 峽灣 a fjord
협문 夾門 a small side gate [door]
협박 脅迫 a threat; a menace; blackmail; intimidation
◆협박적인 태도 a threatening attitude / 협박적인 threatening; menacing / 협박을 받아 under threat [menace, duress(e)]
▶나는 협박에 굴했다 I have surrendered [yielded] to intimidation.
─협박하다 threaten; intimidate; menace; blackmail
▶그는 나를 권총으로 협박했다 He threatened me with a revolver.
▶그는 그 남자를 죽이겠다고 협박했다 He threatened the man with death.
▶그는 고소하겠다고 나를 협박했다 He threatened me with a lawsuit.
▶그는 그녀를 협박하여 승낙하게 했다 He threatened her into consent.
■-자 an intimidator; a blackmailer ─장 a threatening [an intimidation] letter; a blackmail letter ─전화 (get) a threatening (telephone) call

협살 挾殺 〔野〕 a rundown
─협살하다 run down [touch out] 《a runner》

협상 協商 negotiation(s); bargaining; (a) conversation; an understanding; an agreement; 〔商〕 a conference; 〔外交〕 an entente
◆협상 중이다 be in [under] negotiations / 협상을 개시하다 open [start] negotiations 《with》 / 협상을 맺다 conclude an entente 《with》 / 협상을 재개하다 put negotiations back on track
▶협상이 결렬되었다 Negotiations broke down.
─협상하다 negotiate 《with》; bargain 《with》; confer 《with》; have a conference 《with》
◆직접 협상하다 negotiate directly with sb; enter into direct negotiations with sb
■비밀[비공개]─ a closed-door negotiation 삼국─ the Triple Entente 평화─ peace negotiations ■-국(國) a party to an entente; (총칭) an entente

협소하다 狹小─ 〈좁고 작다〉 narrow; confined; cramped; limited; small
◆협소한 방 a small room / 면적이 협소하다 be small [confined] in area
▶우리 학교 운동장은 협소하다 Our playground is small.

협심 協心 〈합심〉 unison; concert; cooperation
─협심하다 unite; be in union 《with》
◆협심하여 일하다 work in unison; work together

협심증 狹心症 〔醫〕 stricture of the heart; angina pectoris [cordis]; stenocardia; heart attack
▶그는 협심증으로 죽었다 He died of [from] heart attack.

협약 協約 an agreement; a convention; a pact; an entente; an understanding
◆구두 협약 a verbal agreement / 협약을 맺다 conclude [enter into] an agreement 《with》
■노동─ a labor agreement 단체─ a collective [(英) trade] agreement 신사─ a gentleman's [gentlemen's] agreement ─국 a party to an agreement [entente] ─서 a written agreement [understanding]

협업 協業 cooperation; cooperative work
─협업하다 cooperate; work together; work in cooperation

협의 協議 conference; council; consultation; deliberation; discussion

♦ 협의 아래[하에] by mutual agreement; upon deliberation 《with》 / 협의 후 결정하다 decide after due consultation [upon deliberation] / 협의에 부치다 bring 《one's》 plan up at a meeting; send [refer] 《a matter》 to conference
▶ 그 건은 협의중이다 The matter is under discussion [deliberation, consideration].
▶ 사장은 임원과 협의중이다 The president is in conference with the directors.
▶ 협의 결과 다음과 같이 결정되었다 As a result of the conference the following decision was made.
―협의하다 confer [consult] 《with》; deliberate 《on a matter》; discuss 《a matter》; talk 《with *sb*》 over 《a matter》; hold a conference [consultation] 《with》
♦ 면밀히 협의하다 deliberate fully 《on a matter》; have a long and careful consultation 《about a matter》
▶ 이 건에 관해서는 내일 협의합니다 This problem is to be discussed [talked about] at the meeting tomorrow.
▶ 오늘 회의에서는 다음 사항들을 협의합니다 Today we are going to talk over the following items in the meeting.
■ ―사항 a subject of discussion; a matter for consultation; an item on the agenda ―이혼 a divorce by agreement [consent] ―회 (hold) a conference [council (meeting), consultative meeting]

협의 狹義 a narrow sense
♦ 협의의 교육 education in a narrow sense / 낱말을 협의로 해석하다 take [interpret] a word in a narrow sense

협잡 挾雜 cheating; dishonest dealing; trickery; (a) fraud; a swindle; (an) imposture; (美) a fake
♦ 협잡의 tricky; fake; sham; bogus; false; spurious / 협잡에 걸리다 be imposed upon ; be cheated; be taken in
▶ 이건 순전히 협잡이다 This is all humbug. = It's all a trick [(美俗) do].
―협잡하다 cheat; deceive; swindle; take [let] *sb* in; play a trick 《upon》; juggle
▶ 그는 카드놀이에서 협잡했다 He cheated in cards.
■ ―꾼 a trickster; a cheat(er); an impostor; a swindler; a crook; (美) a faker; a humbug: 그는 엄청난 협잡꾼이다 He is one hell of a good impostor. ―물 an adulterated [impure] thing; a fraudulent [an adulterated] article; a fraud; dirty gains

협장 脇杖 〈목다리〉 (a pair of) crutches
♦ 협장을 짚고 걷다 walk [go] on crutches

협정 協定 an agreement; a convention; a pact
♦ 협정을 이행하다 fulfill [carry out, act up to] an agreement / 협정을 파기하다 break an agreement / 협정에 조인하다 sign an agreement
▶ 그들은 협정을 맺었다 They concluded an agreement.
▶ 양자간에는 협정이 성립되었다 The two parties arrived at [came to, entered into] an agreement.
▶ 군사 협정이 체결되었다 A military convention was concluded.
―협정하다 agree upon ; make arrangements 《with》; make [conclude, arrive at, enter into] an agreement 《with》
♦ 가격을 협정하다 make an agreement with *sb* on prices
■ 관세― a customs agreement 국제― an international agreement; an accord 상호― a bilateral [reciprocal] agreement 신사― a gentlemen's agreement 어업― a fisheries agreement [pact] 운임(군사)― a freight [military] convention 잠정― a provisional agreement; (라) a modus vivendi 《*pl.* modi vivendi》 정전(停戰)[휴전]― a cease-fire [an armistice] agreement; a truce accord 편무― a unilateral agreement 평화― a peace accord 항공― a civil aviation agreement [pact] 행정― an administrative agreement ■ ―가격 a price agreed upon; an agreed price ―안(案) a draft agreement ―임금 wages agreed upon; agreed wages

협정서 協定書 a written agreement
♦ 협정서를 작성[기초]하다 prepare [draft] an agreement / 협정서를 교환하다 exchange copies of an agreement 《between, with》

협조 協助 〈조력〉 help; aid; assistance; 〈후원〉 support; 〈협력〉 cooperation
♦ 협조를 바라다 ask for help; turn [look] to 《another》 for assistance
▶ 너의 협조가 필요하다 I need your help.
―협조하다 help 《*sb* in his work》; aid [assist] 《in *sb's* work》; render [give] *sb* aid [assistance] 《in doing》
▶ 그에게 협조하려는 자는 없었다 There was nobody to support him [back him up].
■ 상호― mutual help [aid] ―자 a helper; an assistant; a supporter

협조 協調 cooperation; 〈조화〉 harmony; 〈타협〉 conciliation
♦ 협조적 태도 a conciliatory attitude / 협조적(인) cooperative; conciliatory; harmonious
▶ 노사의 협조가 없으면 우리 회사는 무너집니다 But for conciliation of capital and labor, our company would fail.
▶ 그녀는 협조적인 사람이다 She is cooperative.
―협조하다 cooperate; act in concert [union, alignment] 《with》; act harmoniously 《with》
♦ 협조하여 in cooperation 《with》; in concert [alignment] 《with》; in concert [alignment] 《with》
▶ 우리는 서로 협조하여 일했다 We worked in cooperation with each other.
■ ―심 a spirit of cooperation

협주곡 協奏曲 〔樂〕 a concerto 《*pl.* ~s》
♦ 바이올린― a violin concerto

협죽도 夾竹桃 〔植〕 an oleander; a rosebay

협착 狹窄 〔醫〕 stricture; strangulation; stenosis 《*pl.* -ses》
―협착하다 narrow; confined; limited
■ 요도(尿道)[직장(直腸)]― stricture of the urethra [rectum] ■ ―부 an isthmus 《*pl.* ~es,

-mi) —사격 miniature cartridge practice; morris tube practice —탄 a miniature cartridge

협찬 協贊 〈찬성〉 approval; 〈지지〉 support; 〈협력〉 cooperation
♦ 국회의 협찬을 받다 be approved by the National Assembly
▶ 그 웅변대회는 A사 주최, B사 협찬으로 개최되었다 The speech contest was sponsored by company A with the cooperation of company B.
▶ 자선 바자가 마을 사람들의 협찬으로 개최되었다 A charity bazaar was held with the co-operation of the people of the neighborhood.
—**협찬하다** 〈찬성하다〉 approve of; 〈지지하다〉 support; give one's support 《to》; 〈돕다〉 aid; assist; help; 〈협력하다〉 cooperate 《with》; join hands 《with》

협화 協和 1 〈화합〉 harmony; concord; concert —**협화하다** be in harmony [concord] 《with》; act in concert 《with》
2 〔樂〕 consonance
—음 a consonance; a concord

협회 協會 an association; a society; 〈학술상의〉 an institution; 〈연맹〉 a league
♦ 협회를 조직하다 form [organize] an association
■ 방송— the Broadcasting Corporation 저작가— the Authors' League

혓바늘 a rash on the tongue ♦ 혓바늘이 돋다 have eruption on one's tongue ▶ 혓바늘이 돋았다 My tongue broke out in a rash.

혓바닥 the flat of the tongue
♦ 혓바닥 모양의 tongue-like / 혓바닥으로 핥다 lick with one's tongue / 혓바닥을 굴리다 wag one's tongue / 혓바닥을 내밀다 put [stick, poke, thrust] out one's tongue 《at》

혓소리 〔舌聲〕 a lingual (sound)

형 兄 1 〈형제간의〉 an elder [older] brother; a big brother; 〈부를 때〉 Brother!

〔解說〕 영어에서는 특별히 필요치 않은 한 형제자매를 부를 때 **elder, younger**는 붙이지 않고 그저 one's brother, one's sister라고만 한다. 영미에서는 나이가 많고 적음에 관계없이 형제자매는 John, Mary와 같이 이름을 부르는 것이 보통이다.

▶ 우리 큰 형은 지난 주에 결혼했다 My eldest brother got married last week.
2 〈친구간에〉 Mr. …; 〈당신〉 you
♦ 김형 Mr. Kim / 형〈씨〉 Hey, pal!; Young man!; 《俗》 Buddy!
— 맏— one's eldest brother; the eldest of one's (elder) brothers 매〔자〕— a brother-in-law 처— a sister-in-law 친— a full [whole] brother

형 刑 〈벌주기〉 (a) punishment; a penalty; 〈형의 선고〉 a sentence
♦ 형의 집행을 유예하다 suspend the execution of a sentence / 형을 언도하다 pronounce [pass] a sentence on sb / 징역 5년형에 처하다 sentence [condemn] 《a prisoner》 to five years at [《英》 with] hard labor / 형을 치르다 serve [submit to] a sentence / 2년 형을 언도받다 get [be sentenced to] two years
▶ 그는 살인죄로 무거운 형에 처해졌다 He received a heavy [long, severe] sentence on a charge of murder. ≒ He was severely punished for murder.
■ 재산— a pecuniary punishment 종신— a life sentence; imprisonment for life

형 形 1 〈형상〉 shape; 〈형식〉 (a) form
♦ 달걀형의 얼굴 an egg-shaped face / V자 형의 반지 a ring in the shape of a letter V
2 〈만듦새〉 (a) cut; (a) make; 〈크기〉 (a) size
♦ 포켓형의 사전 a dictionary of pocket size; a pocket-size(d) dictionary / 대〔중, 소〕형의 of large [medium, small] size; large-sized [medium-sized, small-sized]

형 型 〈모형〉 a model; 〈주형(鑄型)〉 a mold; 〈양식〉 (a) style; (a) type; a pattern; a make; 〈형식〉 form; mode; a pattern
♦ B형 Model B; 〈혈액의〉 blood type B / 여러 가지 형이 다른 자동차 cars of different makes / 새로운 형의 모자〔코트〕 a new-look hat [coat] / 1997년형의 자동차 a 1997 model (of a) car / 형이 다르다 be of another type
▶ 나는 석고로 흉상의 형을 떴다 I made a model for a bust in plaster.
▶ 그 시계는 새로운 형이다 The watch is (of) a new type.

형 桁 〈건물의〉 a beam; a crossbeam; 〈교량의〉 a girder; 〈총칭〉 girderage

형강 形鋼 section [shape] steel
—압연기 a rolling mill for section steel

형광 螢光 〔物〕 fluorescence ♦ 형광을 발하다 fluoresce; be fluorescent; generate fluorescence
■ —도료〔염료〕 (a) fluorescent paint [dye] —등 a fluorescent light [lamp] —물질〔재료〕 a fluorescent material —조명 fluorescent lighting —판 a fluorescent screen

형구 刑具 an implement of punishment [torture]

형국 形局 1 〈형세〉 the situation; the state of things [affairs] 2 〈관상·풍수지리의 겉모양〉 a phase; a facet; an aspect; a facies; how the land lies

형극 荊棘 a bramble; a thorn ♦ 형극의 길 〈가시밭 길〉 a thorny path; a brambly way; 〈수난의 길〉 the way of the Cross

형기 刑期 a term of imprisonment [penal servitude]; a prison term; 《口》 time
♦ 3년의 형기를 마치다 serve three years (in prison); serve out a sentence of three years' imprisonment / 형기가 만료되어 출감하다 leave prison [be set free] at the expiration of one's term
▶ 그는 형기를 다 치렀다 He served his term in prison. ≒ He did time in prison.

형기 衡器 〈저울〉 a balance; scales

형률 刑律 criminal law ⇨ 형법

형리 刑吏 an executioner; 〈교수형의〉 a hangman

형명 刑名 the denominations [designations] of penalties

형무소 刑務所 a prison ⇨ 교도소

형벌 刑罰 a punishment; a penalty
♦ 무거운[가벼운] 형벌을 과하다[에 처하다] inflict a heavy [mild] punishment [penalty] on *sb* / 형벌을 받다 receive (a) punishment; be punished / 형벌을 면하다 escape punishment / 형벌을 면제해 주다 let *sb* off a penalty; indemnify
▶ 운전자는 엄한[가벼운] 형벌을 받았다 The driver was punished severely [lightly].

형법 刑法 〔法〕 criminal law; penal code; 〈좁은 뜻의〉 the Criminal Law Act; 〈형법전〉 the Criminal [Penal] Code
♦ 형법상의 죄 a criminal [penal] offense / 형법에 따라 처벌하다 deal with *sb* according to the provisions of the criminal code
■ 국제— the international criminal law ■ —위반 a penal offense —학 criminal jurisprudence —학자 a scholar of [an expert in] the criminal law

형부 兄夫 one's [a girl's] elder sister's husband; one's brother-in-law

형사 刑事 1 〈사건〉 a criminal [penal] case
♦ 형사상의 책임 penal responsibility
2 〈경찰〉 a (police) detective; 〈美〉 an operative; 〈美俗〉 a gumshoe; 〈수사계의〉 an investigator; 〈첩보담당〉 a secret service man
♦ 그 살인 사건을 담당하고 있는 형사 a detective on the murder case
■ 사복— a plainclothesman ■ —범(犯) a criminal [penal] offense; an indictable offense —법원 a criminal court —보상법 〔法〕 the Criminal Indemnity Act —사건 a criminal case; a penal offense: 형사사건 전문 변호사 a criminal attorney [〔英〕 lawyer] —실 detectives' quarters; a detective squad room —재판 a criminal trial: 형사재판권 criminal jurisdiction —처분 (suffer) a criminal punishment —피고인 a prisoner at the bar; the accused: 형사피고인석 a dock —학 criminology; penology

형사소송 刑事訴訟 a criminal action [suit]
♦ …을 상대로 형사소송을 제기하다 proceed against *sb* criminally
■ —법 〔法〕 the Criminal Procedure Act [Code] —절차 criminal proceedings

형삭반 形削盤 〔機〕 a shaping machine; a shaper

형상 形狀·形相 shape; form; configuration 《of the sea bed》
♦ 악마의 형상 a diabolical look / 형상대로 in due form; formally / 형상이 여러가지다 be various in form [shape]; be of varied forms

형상 形象 a shape; a figure; an image; a phenomenon 《*pl.* -mena》; (a) figuration

형색 形色 〈형상과 빛깔〉 form [shape] and color; 〈용색〉 features; looks; appearance

형석 螢石 〔鑛〕 fluorite; fluorspar; Derbyshire spar; 〔英〕 fluor

형설 螢雪 hard study under great adversity
♦ 형설의 공(功) the fruits of diligent study / 형설의 공을 쌓다 apply *oneself* closely to one's studies; burn the midnight oil

형성 形成 formation; making; molding ♦ 좋은 습관의 형성 the formation of good habits / 형성중이다 be in the making
—형성하다 form; mold; give form to; shape; make up; build up ♦ 인격을 형성하다 form [mold, shape] one's character
▶ 그의 인격은 아직 형성되지 않았다 His character is not yet fully developed.
■ 인격— character building [formation]; the formation of character ■ —기 the formative period 《of a nation》; the formative years 《of *sb*》 —물질 a formative substance —소(素) a plastic material [element]; formation [formative] stuff —층 〔植〕 the formative layer; the cambium 《*pl.* ~s, -bia》

형세 形勢 〈정세〉 the situation; the state of affairs [things]; 〈대세〉 the tide; the current; 〈전망〉 the prospects; an outlook
♦ 형세를 관망하다 watch the situation [the development of affairs]; see how the land lies; see how [which way] the wind blows / 현재의 형세로는 as matters stand; as things are [stand]
▶ 형세가 호전되었다 The situation has improved [has taken a favorable turn].
▶ 형세가 악화되었다[협악해졌다] The outlook went bad [became threatening].
▶ 형세가 일변했다 The tables [tide] turned.
▶ 형세가 희망적[비관적]이다 The prospects are bright [gloomy].
▶ 형세가 역전했을지도 모른다 The shoe might be on the other foot.
▶ 형세는 10대 1로 우리 팀에게 유리[불리]하다 The chances are ten to one for [against] our team.

형수 兄嫂 an elder brother's wife; a sister-in-law

형식 形式 (a) form; (a) formality; 〔哲〕 a mode; form
♦ 형식상 formally; in form; for form's sake; as a matter of form / 희곡 형식으로 in the form of a drama / 갖가지 형식으로 under varied forms / 어떤 형식으로든 in any form / 정당한 형식을 밟다 go through the proper formalities / 형식을 배제하다 do away with all formalities / 형식에 구애되다 stick to forms; adhere to formality / 형식에 빠지다 degenerate into formalism
▶ 형식에 너무 치우치면 오히려 목적을 그르칠 염려가 있다 Too much adherence to form will defeat its own end.
▶ 그것은 단지 형식상의 문제지만 우리는 그것을 해야만 한다 It's merely a matter of form, but we have to do it.
■ —가 a formal man —논리 formal logic —도야(陶冶) 〔敎〕 formal building of character —미〔藝〕 the beauty of form; formal beauty —법 formal law —주의[론] formalism: 형식주의자 a formalist

형식적 形式的 formal; perfunctory 《inspection》
♦ 형식적인 예의 formal courtesy / 형식적으로 formally; perfunctorily; for form's sake; for the sake of formality; as a matter of form
■ —의례(儀禮) formality 《at a wedding [funeral]》

형안 炯眼 a sharp [keen, quick] eye; a penetrating eye

형언 形言 description; expression
—**형언하다** describe; express (by words)
♦ 형언할 수 없는 아름다움 indescribable [exquisite] beauty / 형언할 수 없다 baffle [be beyond] description
▶ 그 참상은 도저히 형언할 수 없는 것이었다 The terrible scene was beyond description.

형용 形容 qualification; 〈수식〉 modification; description; 〈비유〉 a metaphor; a figure of speech; a figurative expression
—**형용하다** 〈수식하다〉 qualify; modify; 〈비유적으로 말하다〉 express sth figuratively
♦ (무어라) 형용할 수 없다 baffle [be beyond] description; be too 〈beautiful〉 for words
▶ 그 경치의 아름다움을 형용할 말이 없었다 I couldn't find a word to describe the beauty of the scenery. ⇒ The beauty of the scenery was beyond description.
■ —동사 〔文法〕 an adjective verb —어 epithet —어구 an attribute; 〔修〕 a trope

형용사 形容詞 〔文法〕 an adjective; 〈형용어〉 an epithet ♦ 과장된 형용사 a high-flown epithet / 형용사의 adjective / 형용사적인 adjectival
■ 명사 용법— an adnoun 제한적— a limiting adjective ■ —구[절] an adjective phrase [clause]

형이상 形而上 ♦ 형이상의 metaphysical / 형이상의 문제 a metaphysical matter; an abstract matter
■ —학 metaphysics; metaphysical philosophy: 형이상학적인 metaphysical —학자 a metaphysician —학적 유심론[결정론] metaphysical idealism [determinism]

형이하 形而下 ♦ 형이하의 physical; concrete
■ —학 a concrete [physical] science

형장 兄丈 〈상대방의 존칭〉 you

형장 刑場 a place of execution; an execution ground ♦ 형장의 이슬로 사라지다 be executed; die on the scaffold

형적 形迹 〈흔적〉 traces; marks; vestiges; 〈증거〉 signs; indications; evidence(s)
♦ 형적을 남기지 않다 leave no trace behind / 형적을 없애다 cover up one's traces; destroy all evidence
▶ 사슴이 지나간 형적이 있었다 I found the tracks [traces] of a deer.
▶ 고대 도시의 형적은 무엇 하나 남아 있지 않다 There remain no traces [vestiges] of the ancient city.
▶ 섬 어디에도 사람이 살았던 형적은 없었다 In the island there was not a sign of life anywhere.

형제 兄弟 a sibling brothers; 〈동포〉 brethren
♦ 피를 나눈 형제 a blood brother; a brother by blood / 형제의 brotherly; fraternal / 형제(의 의)를 맺다 swear to be brothers
▶ 나는 5형제의 막내다 I'm the youngest of five brothers.
▶ 그들은 형제처럼 사이가 좋다 There is brotherly friendship between them.
■ 사촌— cousins; cousin brothers 의— sworn [pledged] brothers 이복— a half brother; a brother on the father's [paternal] side 이부— a half brother; a uterine brother; a brother on the mother's [maternal] side 친— full [whole] brothers ■ —간 brotherhood; brotherly ties; fraternity —애 fraternal love; brotherly affection —지의(之誼) a Damon and Pythias friendship

형제자매 兄弟姉妹 brothers and sisters; 〈동포〉 brethren

형조 刑曹 〔史〕 the Ministry of Justice
■ —판서 the Minister of Justice

형지 型紙 a paper pattern (for a dress); a dress pattern (for a suit)

형질 形質 1 〈형태와 성질〉 form and nature 2 〔生理〕 a character ■ 유전— an inherited character —세포 a plasma cell

형찰하다 詗察 investigate secretly; make confidential [secret] inquiries

형체 形體 (a) form; (a) shape; (an) appearance; 〈모습〉 a figure; bodily appearance; 〈몸〉 the body
♦ 사람의 형체를 한 인삼 a ginseng in human shape / 형체를 알아 볼 수 없게 beyond [out of] recognition / 형체를 갖추다 be given a form; be embodied / 형체를 부여하다 give form (to); embody

형태 形態 (a) form; (a) shape; 〔心〕 configuration
♦ 진귀한 형태의 돌 stones of unusual forms / …의 형태를 취하다 assume the form of... / 형태를 바꾸다 transform; transfigure
▶ 민주주의는 정치의 한 형태다 Democracy is a form of government.
▶ 그 형태는 공과 비슷하다 It resembles a ball in shape.
■ —론 〔言〕 morphology; morphemics; —accidence —변화 〔言〕 modification —심리학 Gestalt [form] psychology; configurationism —음운론(音韻論) 〔言〕 morphophonemics

형태소 形態素 a morpheme ♦ 형태소의 morphemic ■ —론 morphemics

형태학 形態學 〔生〕 morphology
♦ 형태학상의 morphological / 형태학상(으로) morphologically
■ 사회— social morphology ■ —자 a morphologist

형통하다 亨通— go well [fine, smoothly, all right]; progress favorably
▶ 만사가 형통한다 Everything goes well with them.

형틀 刑— 〈고문대〉 a rack; 〈형구〉 an implement of punishment; a chair in which a criminal is fastened to be interrogated

형편 形便 1 〈상태〉 a condition; a state; 〈사정〉 circumstances
♦ 국내 형편 domestic situation [affairs] / 일이 되어가는 형편 the course [run, development] of events [affairs]; the turn of events / 형편상 in view of circumstances / 형편상 부득이 from the force [by force] of circumstances / 형편의 여하를 불문하고 in any circumstances; regardless of circumstances
▶ 나는 형편상 갈 수 없다 Circumstances do

not permit (of) my going.
〈형편이〉 형편이 허락하면 if circumstances permit [favor] / 형편이 이러하므로 such being the case; in [under] these [such] circumstances
▶ 지금은 형편이 많이 달라졌다 Things have changed greatly.
〈형편에〉형편에 따라 owing to circumstances; in view of [to meet] changed circumstances; for certain reasons; for reason of *one's* own / (그때의) 형편에 따라서 according to circumstances; according to the development of the situation; according as things go
〈형편으로(는)〉 경제적 형편으로 owing [due] to economic circumstances / 여러 가지 형편으로 for many reasons combined / 부득이한 형편으로 for some unavoidable reasons; under unavoidable circumstances / 지금 형편으로는 under the present circumstances; in the present state of things; as the matters stand now; for the time being; as of now
2 〈살림살이의 형편〉 living conditions; *one's* circumstances; living
◆ 가정 형편 *one's* family circumstances [reasons] / 가정형편으로 on account of family affairs; for family reasons
〈형편이〉 형편이 넉넉하다[좋다] be well [comfortably] off; be in easy circumstances; be well-to-do / 형편이 어렵다[옹색하다] be badly [poorly] off; be in needy [narrow, bad] circumstances; find it hard to make a living / 형편이 말이 아니다 live a wretched [dog's] life; lead a miserable existence
▶ 그는 형편이 나보다 낫다 He is better off than I am.
3 〈편의〉 convenience; 〈계제〉 an occasion; time; 〈기회〉 an opportunity; a chance
〈형편이〉 형편이 닿으시면 if (it is) convenient (to you); if it suits your convenience / 형편이 닿는대로 at the first opportunity; at *one's* earliest convenience / 형편이 좋다[나쁘다] be convenient [inconvenient] / 형편이 좋아지다 [나빠지다] become convenient [inconvenient]; make a good [an evil] case for...
▶ 형편이 좋으시다면 5시에 만납시다 If you are agreeable we will meet at five o'clock.

형편없다 形便— 〈시시하다〉 useless; trifling; unworthy; poor; 〈터무니없다〉 unreasonable; exorbitant; absurd; nonsensical
◆ 형편없는 근시안 a dreadful nearsighted person / 형편없는 오류 a serious mistake / 형편없는 놈 an impossible fellow / 형편없이 terribly; exorbitantly / 형편없이 고생하다 suffer terribly; go through many hardships / 형편없이 지다 be beaten all hollow / 형편없이 취하다 be heavily drunk; drink *oneself* dead drunk
▶ 그는 형편없는 구두쇠다 He is an awful miser.
▶ 그 집은 수리하지 않아서 형편없이 되었다 The house was in very bad repair.

형평 衡平 balance; equilibrium ◆형평의 원칙을 무시하다 ignore the principle of equity
■ **—법** 〔法〕 equity: 형평법 재판소 a court of equity; an equity court; (美) a (court of) chancery —**운동** a social equality movement; a leveling movement: 형평운동가 a (social) leveler

형해 形骸 〈뼈대〉 the body; a frame; skeletal structure ◆ 형해화한 민주주의 a mere shell of democracy; democracy that had become a dead letter; democracy stripped of all its contents
▶ 그 성문은 지금 형해만이 남아 있다 All that remains of the castle gate is its frame.

형형색색 形形色色 the various colors; many sorts and kinds
◆ 형형색색의 물건 articles of every sort and kind; a great variety of things; all sorts of things / 형형색색의 various; varied; sundry; multifarious; of all kinds [sorts] / 형형색색으로 in many [various] ways

형형하다 炯炯— glaring; glittering; penetrating ◆안광(眼光)이 형형하다 have piercing [penetrating] eyes; have a piercing look [gaze]

혜고 惠顧 〈왕림〉 a gracious visit; 〈보살펴줌〉 (your, his) kind regards [attention]
—**혜고하다** kindly [graciously] visit
▶ 혜고해 주시기 바랍니다 We request the honor of your presence at the meeting.

혜람하다 惠覽— kindly read; deign to read [peruse]

혜림하다 惠臨— kindly visit

혜사하다 惠賜— give; present 《sb with sth》; bestow 《sth on sb》; favor 《sb with sth》

혜서 惠書 your kind letter
▶ 혜서는 잘 받아 보았습니다 Your letter has been noted with thanks. ⇒ We are in receipt of your kind letter. ⇒ Thank you very much for your kind letter.

혜성 彗星 〔天〕 a comet
◆ 혜성의 꼬리[광망] the tail [trail] of a comet / 정계의 혜성 a dark horse in politics / 혜성같이 나타나다 be brought into sudden prominence; make a meteoric rise from obscurity
■ **핼리—** Halley's comet ■**—군** a comet group **—년** a comet year

혜시 惠示 your kind instruction
—**혜시하다** kindly show [instruct, inform]

혜안 慧眼 a keen [sharp] eye; 〈통찰력〉 a keen insight; good judgment; acumen
◆ 혜안의 quick-sighted; keen-sighted; perceptive; keen-eyed; sharp-eyed

혜존 惠存 〈증정본에〉 "With the compliments of (the author)"

혜택 惠澤 (a) favor; (a) benefit; (a) benefaction
◆ 문명의 혜택 the benefits of civilization / 혜택을 입다 owe sth to sb; be indebted 《to sb for sth》; benefit [profit] 《by sth》 / 혜택을 주다 bestow a favor 《on》 / 문명의 혜택을 받다 share in the benefits of civilization; be benefited by civilization
▶ 우리는 현대 과학의 혜택을 누리고 있다 We enjoy the benefits of modern science.

혜한 惠翰 your kind letter ⇨ 혜서(惠書)

혜함 惠函 your kind letter ⇨ 혜서(惠書)

호 with a whiff [puff] ◆등불을 호하고 불어서 끄다 blow out a lamp with a puff

호 戶 a house; a door; a family
◆50호 되는 마을 a village of fifty houses

호 弧 〔數〕 an arc ◆호를 그리다 draw [describe] an arc

호 湖 a lake

호 號 1 〈아호〉 a pen name; a pseudonym; 〈명칭〉 a title ◆소월이라는 호를 가진 작가 a writer with the pen name of Sowol
2 〈번호〉 a number; 〈잡지·신문의〉 an issue ◆제5호 No. 5; number five / 제 3호실 Room No. 3 / 지난 호 a back number / 다음 호 the next number [issue]
3 〈항목〉 an item; a head ◆제1조 제3항 제2호에 해당하다 come under Paragraph 2, Subsection 3, Section 1
4 〈장신구의 크기〉 size; 〈실의 굵기〉 count ◆12호의 방적사 12-count cotton / 2호 더 큰 모자 a hat two sizes larger
5 〈배·기차 등의〉 "the..." ◆통일호 the Tongil / 퀸엘리자베스 호 the Queen Elizabeth / 마산 호 the S.S. Masan

호 壕 〈참호〉 a trench; 〈방공호〉 an underground air-raid shelter; a dugout

호- 好 good; favorable
◆호적수 a good rival [match] / 호재 good news; an encouraging factor

호가 呼價 〔商〕〈부르는 값〉 a nominal price [quotation]; the price asked; a bid; the asking price; 〈살 사람이 부르는 값〉 the price offered; 〈경매의〉 a bidding
━호가하다 ask [bid, offer] a price (for)
◆엄청나게 호가하다 ask [name, demand] an extravagant price (for)

호각 互角 equality; evenness; par; a good match
◆호각의 승부 a close [well-matched] game / 호각의 equal; even; evenly-matched / …와 호각이다 be equal with…; stand even with… / 호각을 이루다 get even (with); draw level (with) / 호각으로 싸우다 meet sb [contest with sb] on even terms

호각 號角 a (signal) whistle ◆호각을 불다 blow a whistle

호감 好感 (a) good feeling; goodwill; 〈좋은 인상〉 a good [favorable] impression
◆호감이 가는 amiable; attractive; pleasing / 호감이 가지 않는 unaffable; unattractive; repulsive / 아무에게 호감을 주다 impress sb favorably; make a favorable impression on sb; have [entertain] a friendly feeling toward sb / 남의 호감을 사다 win [find] sb's favor [good will]; be in sb's favor
▶그에게는 어딘지 모르게 호감 가는 구석이 있다 He has something attractive about him.
▶그녀는 내게 호감을 가지고 있다 She feels kindly [friendly] toward me.
▶그는 심사원에게 호감을 주었다 He favorably impressed the examiner.

호강 comfort; luxury; pomposity; sumptuousness ━호강하다 live in luxury [comfort]; live in easy circumstances; be comfortably off
◆호강하며 자라다 be bred [brought up] in (the lap of) luxury; grow up in well-off circumstances
━호강스럽다 easy and comfortable; luxurious
◆호강스러운 살림 a luxurious life; comfortable [high] living; a life of luxury

호객 呼客 touting
━호객하다 tout; solicit patronage
■─꾼 a tout(er); (美) a (hotel) runner; 〈구경거리의〉 (俗) a barker; (美俗) a spieler; 〈매춘의〉 a pander; a pimp

호걸 豪傑 a hero; a great man; an extraordinary man ━호걸스럽다 heroic; gallant
■─남아 a heroic man ━─풍 a heroic [gallant] air

호격 呼格 〔文法〕 the vocative case

호경기 好景氣 good business; a prosperous condition; a wave of prosperity; a brisk market; good times; 〈벼락 경기〉 a boom
◆전시의 호경기 a war boom / 호경기의 prosperous; lively; good; active (market); booming (town)
▶요즘 백화점은 호경기다 The department store has been active recently.

호곡 號哭 wailing; weeping aloud; (wild) lamentation ━호곡하다 wail; weep aloud; bewail; weep [cry] bitterly

호광 弧光 〔電〕 an (electric) arc

호구 戶口 the number of houses and inhabitants; population

호구 好球 〔野〕 a good pitch
◆호구를 놓치다 miss a good pitch

호구 虎口 1 〈위험〉 the tiger's mouth; danger
◆호구를 벗어나다 escape from the tiger's jaws; escape from the jaws of death; get out of danger / 호구에 들어가다 put one's head into the lion's mouth; get into a perilous place
2 〈바둑의〉 a cross surrounded by three white [black] stones

호구 糊口 〈입에 풀칠하기〉 bare [scanty] livelihood; 〈살아나가기〉 living; livelihood; subsistence
━호구하다 gain a bare livelihood; eke out a living; make one's living
■─지책(之策) a means of livelihood [living]; a living; 당장의 호구지책으로 슈퍼마켓에서 일했다 I worked in a supermarket as a stopgap measure.

호구조사 戶口調査 census taking ◆호구조사를 하다 take a census ■─기록부 a census register ━─원 a census taker; a census enumerator

호국 護國 defense of the fatherland
◆호국 영령 a guardian god [spirit] of the state
━호국하다 defend the fatherland

호궁 胡弓 〔樂〕 a Chinese [an Oriental] fiddle

호기 好期 a good [right] time (of one's life); a good [favorable] season

호기 好機 a good [golden] opportunity; a good [an excellent] chance; a good time [occasion); a most appropriate moment
◆호기를 잡다[포착하다] take [seize] an opportunity; take time by the forelock / 호기

를 놓치다 miss [lose, let slip] a golden opportunity; let the chance go [slip by] / 호기를 기다리다 wait and see; gain time; 〈가만히〉 lie low
▶너무 망설이면 이 호기를 놓치고 말 것이다 If you hesitate too long, you will miss this golden opportunity.
▶이런 호기는 두 번 다시 오지 않을 거야 Such a chance will never come again.

호기 豪氣 **1**〈씩씩한 기상〉a heroic temper; a sturdy spirit; a stout heart
♦호기부리다 make a show of *one's* sturdy spirit; display *one's* gallantry / 호기있게 팁을 주다 give a generous tip
━호기롭다 of a heroic temper; brave; daring
2〈뽐냄〉pride; haughtiness; arrogance; pomposity ♦호기를 부리다 bear *oneself* haughtily; hold *one's* head high

호기성 好氣性 〔生〕aerotropism
♦호기성의 aerotropic; aerobic
■─생물 an aerobe; an aerobium (*pl*. -bia) ─세균 aerobic bacteria (*sing*. -rium)

호기심 好奇心 curiosity; an inquisitive mind
♦호기심이 강한 사람 a curious person; a person who has (an) intense curiosity 〈about〉 / 호기심이 생기다 become [feel] curious / 호기심을 일으키다 arouse [excite] *sb's* curiosity / 호기심을 만족시키다 gratify [satisfy] *one's* curiosity
▶호기심이 신세를 망친다 Curiosity killed the cat.
▶그는 호기심에 끌려 창문 안을 들여다 보았다 He peeped through the window out of curiosity.
▶소년들의 모험담은 친구들의 호기심을 돋우었다 The stories of the boys' adventures intrigued their friends.

호까나무 〔植〕a raisin tree
호남 湖南 〈지방〉the Honam district [area]; the Chŏlla-do provinces
■─고속도로 the Honam Expressway ─선 the Honamsŏn (Railroad [Railway]) Line ─평야 the Honam Plains

호남아 好男兒 〈멋진 사내〉a fine fellow; a nice fellow [chap]; (美) a regular guy; 〈미남자〉a handsome man; a good-[fine-]looking man; an Adonis

호놀룰루 〈미국 하와이주의 주도〉Honolulu
호농 豪農 〈부농〉a wealthy [rich] farmer; a gentleman farmer
호다 sew 〈seams〉with large stitches; broadstitch
호담 豪膽 boldness; dauntlessness; intrepidity; fearlessness; a stout heart ━호담하다 bold; fearless; daring; stout-hearted; dauntless; 〈서술적〉be stout of heart
▶그는 아주 호담하다 He is very dauntless.
호도 胡桃 a walnut ⇨ 호두
호도 糊塗 temporizing; a makeshift; a stopgap
▶그것은 호도책에 불과하다 That is only a stopgap measure.
━호도하다 patch up; temporize; gloss (over); make (a) shift 〈with〉

♦과실을 호도하다 gloss over *one's* errors
호되게 severely; harshly; soundly; violently; roughly; mercilessly; (口) terrible; terribly; cruelly
♦호되게 야단치다 scold *sb* unsparingly; give *sb* a good scolding [talking-to] / 호되게 때리다[치다] beat *sb* soundly; (美口) give *sb* a good hiding / 호되게 얻어 맞다 suffer a heavy blow; be hard-hit
▶그 교사는 학생들을 호되게 다뤘다 The teacher dealt roughly with his students.
호되다 severe; harsh; rough; (口) terrible; cruel
▶그는 아이들 다루는 것이 호되다 He is very severe with his children.
호두 胡— a walnut
♦호두 까는 기구[집게] (a pair of) nutcrackers / 호두를 까다 crack a walnut
■━까기 인형 〔樂〕*The Nutcracker* (*Suite*) ─껍질 a walnut shell ─나무 a walnut (tree) ─속(살) the kernel of a walnut ─유 walnut [nut] oil

호드기 a reed pipe [flute]
호드득거리다, 호드득대다 〈콩·깨 등을 볶을 때〉crackle; crepitate; decrepitate; snap; 〈옥수수 등이〉pop; 〈총이〉bang
▶마른 나무가 탈 때 호드득거렸다 The dry wood snapped and crackled as it burned.
▶콩은 볶으면 호드득거린다 Beans crackle when parched.
2 〈방정떨다〉act frivolously [rashly]
호드득호드득 1 〈튀는 소리〉crackling; crepitating; decrepitating; snapping; popping
2 〈방정맞게〉rashly; imprudently; frivolously
호들갑떨다 make a great fuss about trifles; make much ado about nothing; act rashly [hastily]
▶호들갑떨지 마라 Don't act hastily. ⇌ Be prudent.
호들갑스럽다 〈경망스럽다〉flippant; 〈부주의하다〉careless; thoughtless; frivolous; 〈야단스럽다〉fussy; hasty; rash; precipitate
♦호들갑스런 여자 a flippant woman / 호들갑스럽게 행동하다 act in a flippant [frivolous] manner
호등 弧燈 an arc lamp [light]
호떡 胡— a Chinese pancake
호떡집에 불난 것 같다 〈속담〉Running around like chickens with their heads cut off.
호락질 raising crops single-handed(ly); a family farming
━호락질하다 raise crops single-handed(ly)
호락호락 〈쉽사리〉easily; readily; with ease
♦호락호락 속아넘어가다 be deceived easily
▶내가 호락호락 속을 줄 아니? Is there [Do you see] any green in my eye?
▶그는 호락호락하지 않다 He is hard to deal with. ⇌ He is an ugly customer.
호랑나비 〔昆〕a swallowtail (butterfly)
호랑이 虎狼— **1**〈범〉a tiger; a tigress 〈암컷〉
♦호랑이 새끼 a tiger kitten [cub] / 호랑이 담배 먹을 적에 〈옛날에〉in ancient [old] time [days]; a long time ago
▶호랑이를 그리려다가 고양이가 되었다 It is a

호랑이굴

bungling work.
2 〈무서운 사람〉 a cruel [merciless] person; an inhumanly sharp person
♦호랑이 형사 a crack detective
■벵골— a Bengal tiger
호랑이굴 虎狼一窟 a tiger's den
♦호랑이굴에 들어가다 (비유) put [run] one's head into [in] the lion's mouth
호랑이굴에 들어가야 호랑이를 잡는다 (속담) Nothing venture, nothing have [win]. ⇌ Nought venture, nought have.
호랑이도 제 말하면 온다 (속담) Talk of the devil, and he is sure to [will] appear. ⇌ Speak of the wolf and you will see his tail. ⇌ Talk of angels, and you will hear the flutter of their wings.
호랑이 없는 골에는 토끼가 스승이라 (속담) When the cat is away, the mice will play.
호래아들 an ill-bred [ill-mannered, a rude] fellow; a boor; a clown; a clodhopper; 〈욕〉 a bastard; a son of a bitch
호렴 胡— Chinese halite [rock salt]; crude [unrefined, rough] salt
호령 號令 〈명령〉 a (word of) command; an order —호령하다 command; order; give an order; give a (word of) command; 〈구령하다〉 shout a command (to)
호로 葫蘆 〔植〕 a gourd
호로병 葫蘆瓶 a gourd bottle ⇨ 호리병
호롱 the base of a kerosene lamp
호루라기 a whistle ⇨ 호각(號角)
호르르 **1** 〈타는 모양〉 rapidly; lightly
▶낙엽이 호르르 타오른다 The fallen leaves burn up lightly in a flame.
2 〈나는 소리〉 flapping; fluttering
♦호르르 날아가 버리다 fly away with a flap of the wings
3 〈호루라기 소리〉 warbling; trilling ♦호루라기를 호르르 불다 blow a whistle loudly
호르몬 〔生〕 hormone ♦호르몬의 hormonal; hormonic ■남성[여성]— male [female] hormone ■—결핍증 hormone deficiency —제 a hormone drug [preparation]
호른 〔樂〕 a horn ♦호른을 불다 play [sound, toot] a horn ■—취주자 a horn player; a hornist
호리 〔農〕 a one-ox plow ■—질 plowing [working] with a one-ox plow: 호리질하다 plow [turn up the soil] with a one-ox plow
호리 毫釐 〈극소량〉 the slightest amount; a modicum; a bit; a whit; a jot
■—불차(不差) be exactly the same; there is not the slightest difference 《between A and B》 —지차 a narrow [slim] margin; a slight difference; a shade of difference
호리다 〈매혹하다〉 charm; bewitch; enchant; fascinate; attract; 〈유혹하다〉 seduce; allure; entice; 〈속이다〉 cheat; deceive
♦여자를 잘 호리는 남자 a woman-killer; a Don Juan / 남자를 잘 호리는 여자 a vamp; (俗) a man-killer
호리병 葫—瓶 a gourd [calabash] bottle
호리병박 葫—瓶— 〔植〕 a gourd; a calabash
♦호리병박 모양의 gourd-shaped

2442

호리호리하다 slim; slender; thin; lean; lanky
♦호리호리한 여자 a slim girl
▶그녀는 호리호리한 미인이다 She is pretty and slender.
호마 胡馬 a Manchurian horse
호마 胡麻 〔植〕 a sesame; a gingili
■—유 sesame oil; gingili
호마노 縞瑪瑙 〔鑛〕 onyx
호머¹ 〈그리스의 시인〉 Homer
호머² 〔野〕 a homer; a home run ⇨ 홈런
호면 湖面 the surface of a lake ♦잔잔한 호면 the tranquil waters
호명 呼名 calling sb by name; 〈점호〉 roll call ♦호명에 대답하다 answer to one's name —호명하다 call sb by name; 〈점호하다〉 make a roll call; call the roll; take a roll call (of)
호모 〈동성애〉 homosexuality; 〈사람〉 a homo
▶그는 호모 성향이 있다 He has a homosexual tendency.
호모사피엔스 〔人類〕 Homo sapiens
호모에렉투스 〔人類〕 Homo erectus
호무하다 毫無— not in the least; not at all; not a bit; not in the slightest degree
호미 a weeding hoe (with a short handle)
♦호미로 땅콩을 캐내다 dig out [up] peanuts with a weeding hoe
호미로 막을 것을 가래로 막는다 (속담) A stitch in time saves nine.
호미씻이 〈논매기 끝낸 뒤의〉 a farmer's feast after the final weeding of rice paddies; a hoe-washing holiday —호미씻이하다 have [enjoy] a "hoe-washing" holiday
호미자락 〈끝부분〉 the lower part of a hoe blade; 〈길이〉 the depth of the tip of a hoe blade ♦비가 호미자락만큼 오다 have a rain enough to soak into the soil an inch deep
호밀 胡— 〔植〕 rye ■—빵 rye bread
호박 a pumpkin; 〈호리병박 모양의〉 a squash
▶호박이 굴렀다 It is a piece of good luck [a godsend, a windfall].
■—고지 dried slices of pumpkin —밭 a pumpkin plantation [patch] —씨 a pumpkin seed
호박 琥珀 〔鑛〕 amber
♦호박의 succinic
■—인조— artificial amber; amberoid ■—단(緞) taffeta —산 succinic acid —색 amber (color) : 호박색의 amber(-colored) —유 amber oil —잠(簪) an amber hairpin
호박개 〔動〕 a stout hairy dog
호박벌 〔動〕 a carpenter bee
호반 虎班 〔史〕 the military nobility
호반 湖畔 a lakeshore; a lakeside; a lakefront
♦호반의 별장 a villa by the lake; a lakeside villa / 호반의 lakeside / 호반에(서) by [on] the lake
■—시인 (one of) the Lake Poets
호반새 湖畔— 〔鳥〕 a Korean ruddy kingfisher
호발 毫髮 〈잔털〉 the tiniest [most minute] hair; (비유) 〈잔물건〉 a single iota
♦호발 부동(不動)하다 do not budge an inch; don't move at all; be quite immovable [motionless]

호방하다 豪放— noble-minded; manly and large-minded [broad-minded]; unrestrained; vigorous; virile

호배추 胡— 〔植〕a Chinese cabbage

호별 戶別 〈각 집〉each house
 ♦ 호별의 door-to-door; house-to-house / 호별로〈집집마다〉from house to house; from door to door
 ■ —조사 a house-to-house investigation; a door-to-door inspection

호별방문 戶別訪問 a house-to-house [door-to-door] visit; 〈선거유세〉a house-to-house canvass
 —호별방문하다 make a door-to-door visit; visit from door to door; 〈유세하다〉make a house-to-house canvass

호복 胡服 a Manchu [Chinese] garment [gown]

호봉 號俸 a pay step; a salary class ♦ 이호봉 a second-class salary

호부 好否 good and [or] bad; likes and [or] dislikes ♦ 호부간에 〈좋든 싫든〉whether *one* likes it or not

호부 豪富 a man of (great) wealth and power; a plutocrat

호부 護符 a charm ⇨ 부적(符籍)

호불호 好不好 good and bad ⇨ 호부(好否)

호비다 pick ⇨ 후비다

호비작거리다 keep picking ⇨ 후비적거리다

호비칼 a hooked router

호사 豪奢 luxury; extravagance; grandness; magnificence
 —호사스럽다 〈호화롭다〉luxurious; 〈사치하다〉extravagant; 〈성대하다〉magnificent; grand
 ♦ 호사스러운 생활을 하다 live in (great) style; live in luxury; repose on a bed of down [roses]
 —호사하다 〈호강하다〉repose in the lap of luxury; roll in luxury

호사 好事 a busybody; a go-getter; a dilettante (*pl.* ~s, -ti); a curiosity seeker; a curious person

호사다마 好事多魔 〈속담〉Lights are usually followed by shadows. ⇌ There's many a slip [Many things fall] between the cup and the lip.

호사바치 豪奢— a dandy; a gallant; a fop; a coxcomb; a dude; a beau (*pl.* beaux, ~s)

호산성 好酸性 〔生〕acidophil(e) ♦ 호산성의 acidophilic; acidophil(e) ■ —균 an acidophilic bacterium

호상 好喪 a propitious mourning (of a person dying old and rich)

호상 弧狀 ♦ 호상의 arc(-shaped); arcuate
 ■ —열도 〔地〕arcuate islands

호상 湖上 ♦ 호상의[에서] on [in] the lake / 호상의 lacustrine
 ■ —가옥 a lake dwelling; lacustrine dwellings
 —생활시대 the lacustrine age [period] —생활자 a lake dweller

호상 壺狀 ♦ 호상의 potlike; urceolate ■ —화관(花冠) an urceolate corolla

호상 豪商 a wealthy merchant; a merchant prince; a business magnate; (美口) a baron

호상 護喪 〈초상 차지〉the master [a man in charge] of a funeral ceremony
 —호상하다 manage funeral arrangements; take charge of a funeral ceremony
 ■ —소 the office in charge of a funeral ceremony

호색 好色 sensuality; amorousness; lewdness; lust; lechery; eroticism
 ♦ 호색적인 sensual; amorous; lewd; lustful; lecherous; erotic; indecent
 ■ —가[꾼, 한] a lewd [lustful] man; a lecher; a sensualist; a Don Juan —문학 pornographic [erotic] literature; pornography; erotica

호생 互生 〔植〕♦ 호생의 alternate
 ■ —엽 alternate leaves (on a plant)

호선 互先 〔바둑〕have the first move in alternate games; play on an equal footing
 ■ —바둑 an unhandicapped match of *paduk*

호선 互選 mutual election
 —호선하다 elect 《the chairman》by mutual vote; elect from among 《themselves》
 ▶ 사무총장은 회원 중에서 호선되었다 The secretary-general was elected from among its members.
 ■ —투표 mutual vote

호선 弧線 an arc

호성적 好成績 good grades (in *one's* studies); good 《business》results [showing]
 ♦ 호성적을 올리다 obtain [gain, attain] good [excellent] results

호세아 〔聖〕(The Book of) Hosea (略 Hos.)

호소 呼訴 〈불평·고충〉a complaint; 〈상소〉an appeal; a petition
 ♦ 대중에 대한 호소력이 약하다 be of little appeal 《to people》
 —호소하다 〈불평하다〉complain of; 〈의존하다〉appeal to; resort to 《arms》; have recourse to 《violence》; 〈애원하다〉appeal 《to》; wring *sb's* heartstrings; 〈간청하다〉plead 《for》
 ♦ 아픔[두통]을 호소하다 complain of a pain [a headache] / 법에 호소하다 appeal to the law; bring an action [a suit] 《against *sb*》/ 힘에 호소하다 resort [go] to force [violence]; use force / 폭력에 호소하다 have recourse to violence / 이성에 호소하다 appeal to *one's* reason / 여론에 호소하다 appeal to public opinion

호소 湖沼 lakes and marshes; 〔地〕lake ♦ 호소의 lacustrine —어업 lake fishery —학 limnology

호손 〈미국의 소설가〉Hawthorne, Nathaniel (1804-74)

호송 護送 escort; convoy
 ♦ …의 호송하에 under escort of… / 군대의 호송을 받다 be under the convoy of troops
 —호송하다 escort; convoy 《a merchant ship》; send *sb* under due escort; 〈죄수를〉send *sb* under guard
 ♦ 죄수를 호송하다 send a prisoner under guard
 ■ —선 a convoy —차 〈죄수의〉(美) a patrol

호수 [police] wagon; 《俗》 a paddy wagon; 《英》 prison van; 《口》 a Black Maria
호수 戶數 〈가옥수〉 the number of houses; 〈가구수〉 the number of families
호수 好手 [바둑·장기] a good move
호수 湖水 a lake
 ◆호수의 lacustrine 《dwellings》 / 호수에(서) 사는 [나는] 〔生〕 lacustrine / 호수가 많은 laky
호수 號數 number; a register [serial] number
 ◆집의 호수 the number of a house
호스 a hose; a hosepipe ◆호스로 물을 뿌리다 hose water 《over, on》; water 《the garden》 with a hose; hose 《a burning building》
 ◆소화용— a fire hose
호스텔 a hostel ■유스— a youth hostel
호스티스 a hostess; 〈여급〉 a barmaid
호승지벽 好勝之癖 love of beating others; a competitive spirit
호시기 好時期 a good chance ⇨ 호기(好期)
호시절 好時節 a good season 《for》; a favorable season [time]
호시탐탐 虎視眈眈 with a vigilant eye; vigilantly; gloatingly
 ◆호시탐탐 기회를 노리다 watch for an opportunity [a chance]
 ▶그는 호시탐탐 공격할 기회를 노렸다 He watched thirstily for a chance to attack.
호신 護身 self-protection; self-defense
 ◆호신용의[으로] for self-protection; for use in self-defense / 호신용 권총 a pistol for self-protection
 —호신하다 protect oneself; defend oneself
 ■—부(符) an amulet; a talisman 《pl. ~s》
 —술 the art of self-defense
호심 湖心 the heart [center] of a lake
호심경 護心鏡 〈가슴받이〉 a breastplate
호안 好顔 a happy face; a bright look
호안 護岸 〔土〕 a revetment; shore [bank] protection
 ■—공사 shore [bank] embankment; 《美》 a levee protection works: 호안 공사를 하다 carry out the shore protection works
호안석 虎眼石 〔鑛〕 a tigereye; a tiger's-eye
호양 互讓 〈서로 양보함〉 mutual concession; compromise; 〈주고 받기〉 give-and-take
 ▶호양의 정신에 입각하여 교섭을 진행했다 We conducted the negotiations in the spirit of compromise.
 —호양하다 make a mutual concession 《on a matter》; compromise 《on, with》
호언 豪言 tall [big] talk; a brag; a boast
 —호언하다 talk tall [big]; brag 《about, of》; boast 《about, of, that...》; talk boastfully
호언장담 豪言壯談 tall talk ⇨ 호언(豪言)
호연 好演 good acting; an excellent performance 《of a play》 —호연하다 put up a good show; perform [act] well
 ▶신인이 햄릿을 호연했다 The new actor gave an excellent performance as Hamlet.
호연지기 浩然之氣 a vast-flowing spirit
 ◆호연지기를 기르다 revive one's exhausted [spent] energy; refresh [recreate] oneself 《with》; enliven [nourish] one's spirits
 ▶우리는 시원한 고원에서 호연지기를 길렀다 We refreshed ourselves in mind and body on the cool height.
호열자 虎列剌 cholera=콜레라
호염 好鹽 ◆호염성의 halophilic; halophilous; halophile; halophil
 ■—성 halophilism —성균 halophilic bacteria; halophiles
호염 胡鹽 crude salt=호렴
호오 好惡 one's likes and dislikes; partiality
 ▶그는 호오의 감정이 심하다 He has strong likes and dislikes.
호외 戶外 the open air ⇨ 야외(野外)
호외 號外 〈신문·잡지〉 an extra [a special] (edition) 《of a newspaper》, a special
 ◆호외를 발행하다 publish [issue] an extra
 ▶호외요 호외요 Extra, Extra!
호우 豪雨 〔氣〕 a heavy rain [rainfall]; a torrential rain; a downpour; 《口》 a drencher
 ▶굉장한 호우였다 It rained heavily [in torrents]. ⇌ The rain fell in sheets.
 ◆호우로 하천이 범람했다 The heavy rain caused rivers to overflow.
 ■집중— a localized torrential downpour
 —주의보 a torrential [heavy] rain warning
호운 好運 good fortune ⇨ 행운(幸運)
호위 護衛 guard; bodyguard; escort; convoy
 ◆경찰의 호위 아래[를 받고] under the escort of police
 —호위하다 guard; 〈경호하다〉 escort; 〈호송하다〉 convoy 《a ship, supplies》
 ◆요인을 호위하다 guard an important person
 ■—경관 a policeman on guard; a police escort —병 a guard; a military escort —자 an escort —전투기 an escort fighter —함 a convoy; a naval escort; an escort 《(war)ship》
호음 豪飮 heavy [deep] drinking; a carouse
 —호음하다 drink heavily [deep, hard]; 《口》 soak
호읍 號泣 wailing; moaning; (wild) lamentation
 —호읍하다 weep [cry] bitterly; moan; wail; bewail; lament aloud
호응 呼應 1 〈부름에 대답함〉 hailing (to) each other
 —호응하다 hail (to) each other
 2 〈기맥 상통〉 acting in concert
 —호응하다 act in concert [unison] 《with》; be in sympathy 《with》; respond 《to》
 ◆호응하여 in concert [cooperation]; in response 《to》; in collusion 《with》
 ▶그들은 호응하여 일어나서 적을 무찔렀다 They rose in concert [unison] and beat the enemy.
 3 〔文法〕 〈일치〉 concord; agreement
 ◆시제의 호응 sequence of tenses
호의 好意 favor; goodwill; good will; 〈친절〉 kindness; 〈친애〉 friendliness; 〈주선〉 good offices
 ◆호의로[에서] with good intentions; out of kindness [goodwill] / 김 선생님의 호의로 through the kindness [courtesy] of Mr. Kim / 호의에 보답하다 return sb's favor
 ▶그는 우리에게 커다란 호의를 보였다 He showed great favor [goodwill] toward us.

▶호의는 결코 잊지 않겠습니다 I shall never forget (all) your kindness.
▶선생님의 호의에 감사드립니다 Thank you for your kindness [favor]. ⇌ I am grateful for your sympathy.
▶그의 호의를 물리치지 마라 Don't reject his kind offer.
▶그녀는 네게 호의를 가지고 있다 She means by [to, toward] you.
▶호의로 그런 것이니 화내지 말게 Don't be angry because I did it out of goodwill.

호의적 好意的 favorable; kind; friendly
◆호의적 제안 a kind offer / 호의적인 대답 a favorable answer / 호의적인 미소 a friendly [kind] smile / 호의적으로 in a friendly way; out of good will; with good intentions; with a good will / 아무를 호의적으로 다루다 treat sb with favor [kindness]; treat sb favorably [kindly]

호의호식 好衣好食 a luxurious living; high living; comfort; pomp; luxury
—호의호식하다 live in luxury

호인 好人 a good-natured person; a good [nice] fellow; a nice chap; 《美》 a regular guy

호재(료) 好材(料) good material; excellent data; 〖證〗 bullish [favorable, encouraging] factors; favorable news

호저 湖底 〈호수밑〉 the bottom of a lake
호저 豪猪 〖動〗 a porcupine
호적 戸籍 〈등록〉 census registration; 〈장부〉 a census [family] register
◆호적에 올리다[에서 빼다] have sb's name entered in [deleted from] the family register / 호적을 조사하다 inquire into sb's family register / 호적의 정정을 신청하다 apply for the rectification of one's family register
▶그는 호적상으로는 내 아들이 아니다 He is not my son on the register.
▶그녀는 아직 남편의 호적에 올라있지 않았다 She has not yet had her name entered on her husband's family register.
—담당자 a registrar —법 〖法〗 the Family Registration Act —증명서 a birth certificate; one's identity paper [card] —초본[등본] an extract [a copy] of one's family register

호적 好適 suitability
◆호적지 an ideal place
—호적하다 suitable; right; good; best; ideal
◆…에 호적하다 be suitable [suited] for…; be right fit for…

호적수 好敵手 a good match [rival]; a worthy opponent
▶그는 내 호적수다 I find my match in him. ⇌ He is a match for me.

호전 好戰 bellicosity ◆호전적인 국민 warlike nation / 호전적(인) bellicose; warlike; pro-war

호전 好轉 a favorable turn [move]; a turn [change] for the better; improvement
◆식량 사정의 호전 improvement in the food situation
—호전하다 get [become] better; change [take a turn] for the better; 〈시황 등이〉 improve; look up
▶사태는 곧 호전될 것이다 Things will be better [improve] soon.
▶당분간 경기는 호전되지 않을 것이다 Business will not be looking up for a while.
▶그의 병세는 꽤 호전되었다 His condition has improved considerably.

호접 胡蝶 a butterfly ⇨ 나비¹

호젓하다 〈고요하고 쓸쓸하다〉 still; quiet; calm; hushed; deserted; lonely; solitary
◆호젓한 산길 a lonely [lonesome] mountain path / 호젓한 해변 a deserted seaside
▶그 등산가는 산막에서 호젓하게 살고 있다 The mountaineer lives solitarily in a mountain hut.
▶해변은 9월이면 호젓했다 The seaside was deserted in September.

호정 糊精 〖化〗 dextrin(e)
호조 戸曹 〖古制〗 the Ministry of Finance
호조 好調 (a) good condition; a favorable tone [tendency, trend]; 〖證〗 improvement
◆호조의 good; favorable; satisfactory / 호조다 〈건강 상태가〉 (口) be in the pink; 〈선수 등이〉 be in good condition [shape]; 〈사업 등이〉 go [get] on [along] swimmingly
▶만사는 호조였다 Everything went well.

호족 豪族 a powerful family [clan]
호졸근하다 wet and limp ⇨ 후줄근하다
호종 扈從 attendance
—호종하다 attend on 《a dignitary》; be in attendance on 《a prince》; follow

호주 戸主 the head of a family; a householder; the master of a house
◆호주와의 관계 one's relation to the head of the family
—권 the headship of a family; the leadership of a household —상속 succession to (the headship of) a house

호주 好酒 love of drink —호주하다 like [love, be fond of, be given to] drinking; have a liking for wine
—객 a heavy drinker

호주 濠洲 (the Commonwealth of) Australia ⇨ 오스트레일리아
◆호주의 Australian
—사람 an Australian; 《英俗》 an Aussie

호주머니 1 〈주머니〉 a pocket
◆호주머니가 없는 pocketless / 호주머니에 들어가는 pocket(-size(d)); pocketable 《handphone》; vest-pocket 《walkman》 / 호주머니에 넣다 pocket; put 《a thing》 in [into] one's pocket / 호주머니에 손을 넣다 reach in one's pocket / 호주머니에 손을 넣어 더듬다 feel [fumble, dip] in one's pocket 《for sth》 / 호주머니에서 꺼내다 take sth out of one's pocket / 호주머니를 뒤지다 fish in one's pocket 《for》; search over *s pocket
▶네 호주머니가 불룩하다 Your pockets are bulging.
▶그 사람은 한손을 호주머니에 넣고 서 있었다 The man was standing with his hand in his pocket.
2 〈돈지갑・돈사정〉 one's pocket; one's purse; one's finances

◆호주머니가 두둑하다 have a long [heavy, fat] purse / 호주머니가 텅 비다 have an empty purse
▶그는 장사가 잘 돼서 호주머니가 두둑해졌다 The business prospered and his purse grew fat.
■바지— a trouser(s) pocket: 바지 뒷호주머니 a hip-pocket 스커트— a placket 안— an inside pocket 옆— a side pocket 조끼— a vest pocket

호주머니사정 —事情 one's finances [funds]; one's purse
▶지금 나는 호주머니 사정이 좋지 않다 I am hard up just now.

호초 胡椒 black pepper ⇨ 후추

호출 呼出 〈불러냄〉 a call; calling out; 〈소환〉 a summons; citing; 〈법원의〉 a subpoena
◆호출에 응하다[응하지 않다] answer [ignore] a summons
—**호출하다** 〈불러내다〉 call sb out; 〈전화로〉 ring sb up on the phone
◆원고[피고]를 호출하다 cite the plaintiff [defendant] (before the judge)
▶그는 법정에 호출되었다 He was summoned to the court.
■자동— an automatic calling 장거리 전화 (의)— a trunk [long-distance] call ■부호 (通信) a call sign; call letters —신호 a call signal —장 〈소환장〉 a (writ of) summons; a subpoena

호치 皓齒 〈흰 이〉 white [pearly] teeth

호치민 〈베트남 민주공화국의 초대 대통령〉 Ho Chi Minh (1890-1969)

호치키스 a stapler; (商標) a Hotchkiss (paper fastener)
◆호치키스 알 a staple / 호치키스로 철하다 staple 《sheets》 together
▶서류를 호치키스로 철해 주세요 Please staple the documents together.

호칭 互稱 〈서로 일컬음〉 the name [title] that each calls the other; mutual designations

호칭 呼稱 a name; a title; a designation; an appellation
—**호칭하다** 〈부르다〉 call; name; designate

호콩 胡— a peanut ⇨ 땅콩

호쾌하다 豪快— dynamic; superb; exciting; heroic
◆호쾌한 인물 a large-hearted man

호타 好打 〔野〕 a good [nice] hit; a swat
—**호타하다** make a good [nice] hit
■—자 a good [nice] hitter

호타순 好打順 the top of the batting order

호탕 豪宕 grandeur; magnanimity
—**호탕하다** magnanimous; large-minded
◆호탕한 웃음 a hearty laugh

호텐토트 〈남아프리카에 사는 종족〉 a Hottentot

호텔 a hotel; 〈자동차 여행자용의〉 a motel; 〈여관〉 an inn
◆조선 호텔에 묵다 stay at the Chosun Hotel / 호텔에 방을 예약하다 reserve [make reservation for] a room at the hotel; book a hotel room / 호텔에 도착하다 arrive at a hotel; 〈체크인하다〉 check in at a hotel / 호텔에서 나오다 leave a hotel; 〈체크아웃하다〉 check out of a hotel
▶어느 호텔에 묵을 예정이십니까? Which [What] hotel are you going to stay in [at]?
■—보이 a bellboy —시설 hotel facilities —업자 a hoteman

호통 〈노하여 꾸짖음〉 hurling words of thunder; a roar; a yell
◆호통치다 hurl words of thunder 《at》; storm [thunder, roar] 《at sb》; give sb a good scolding

호투 好投 〔野〕 good [fine, nice] pitching
—**호투하다** pitch well [expertly]

호패 號牌 〔古制〕 an identity tag

호평 好評 〈좋게 받아들여짐〉 a favorable [good] reception; 〈인기〉 popularity; 〈책·영화 등의〉 a favorable [good] review; public favor
◆호평의 of good repute; well-reputed / 호평이다 be popular; be highly [favorably] spoken of; enjoy [win, gain] popularity / 호평을 받다 meet with [get, have] a favorable reception; win popularity; be well received; gain public favor
▶그 연극은 호평이었다 The play was well received.
▶당신의 요리는 호평이었소 Everyone has enjoyed the meal you cooked.
▶그 책은 학생들 사이에 대단한 호평이다 The book is popular with [among] the students.

호포 號砲 a signal [watch] gun
◆호포를 쏘다 fire a signal gun

호풍 胡風 1 〈만주인의 풍속〉 Manchu customs 2 〈바람〉 the north wind

호피 虎皮 〈호랑이 가죽〉 a tiger skin
■—방석[융단] a tiger-skin cushion [rug]

호학 好學 〈학문을 좋아함〉 love of learning; intellectual appetite [thirst]
—**호학하다** love [be fond of] learning

호한 好漢 〈의협심 있는 남자〉 a nice [jolly] fellow; 《美俗》 a regular guy; 《俗》 a brick

호항 湖港 a lake harbor

호헌 護憲 protection of the Constitution
■—운동 a movement for the defense of the Constitution; a movement opposing revision of the Constitution

호혈 虎穴 a tiger's den ⇨ 호랑이굴

호협 豪俠 bravery; chivalrousness; gallantry
—**호협하다** brave; chivalrous; gallant ◆호협한 기상 gallantry; chivalrous disposition

호형 弧形 an arc

호형호제 呼兄呼弟 〈가까운 친구 사이〉 close friendship
—**호형호제하다** be good friends; call each other brother; be intimate with each other; associate 《with another》 like brothers

호혜 互惠 reciprocity; mutual benefits
■—관세율 a reciprocal tariff —무역협정 a fair [reciprocal] trade agreement —조약 a reciprocal treaty —주의 a principle of reciprocity —통상 reciprocal trading [trade] —통상조약 a reciprocal trade pact

호호 戶戶 〈집집마다〉 every [each] house ⇨ 가가호호

호호¹ 〈입김 내는 소리〉 in puffs [whiffs]
♦추워서 손을 호호 불다 warm one's hands with one's breath; breathe upon one's hands to keep them warm

호호² 〈웃음 소리〉 ha-ha; haw-haw

호호백발 皓皓白髮 〈머리〉 hoary hair; snow-white hair; 〈사람〉 a white-headed [white-haired] old man

호화 豪華 splendor; pomp; gorgeousness; luxury
—호화하다, 호화롭다 splendid; gorgeous; most luxurious; deluxe 《car》
♦호화로운 생활을 하다 live in luxury; live in grand style
■—선《船》 a luxury [deluxe, palatial] liner; a luxury ship —제본 luxury binding —주택 a palatial mansion —판《版》 a deluxe edition: 이건 정말 호화판이군 This is really wonderful.

호화찬란하다 豪華燦爛— brilliant; gorgeous; splendorous; gaudy; dazzling; pompous

호환 虎患 a disaster caused by a tiger; the ravages of tigers

호황 好況 〈번창〉 prosperity; 〈장사〉 booming business; a (business) boom; 〈좋은 시황〉 good (prosperous) times
♦호황의 favorable; prosperous; brisk 《market》; thriving 《business》 / 호황이다 be booming [flourishing, thriving] / 호황을 보이다 show signs of prosperity; present a favorable aspect
▶ 제조업은 호황으로 돌아서고 있다 Manufacturing industry is picking up [taking a turn for the better].
■—시대 prosperous days [times]; 《美》 boom days; flush times

호흡 呼吸 1 〈숨〉 a breath; breathing; respiration
▶ 그는 호흡이 곤란하다 He breathes hard. ⇌ He has difficulty in breathing.
▶ 그는 호흡이 끊겼다 He stopped breathing. ⇌ He breathed his last.
▶ 그의 호흡은 정상이다 His respiration is normal.
—호흡하다 breathe; respire; draw one's breath
♦거칠게 호흡하다 〈호흡이 곤란하다〉 breathe hard; pant for breath
▶ 사람은 1분 간에 열 여덟번 호흡한다 A man breathes eighteen times a minute.
2 〈장단〉 tone; time
♦호흡을 맞추다 keep time 《with》 / 호흡이 맞다 be in rhythm; tune 《with》; be in harmony 《with》
▶ 그들은 호흡이 잘 맞았다 They were getting along well [《口》 hitting it off] with each other. ⇌ They were in perfect harmony.
■—심[복식(腹式)]— deep [abdominal] breathing 인공— artificial breathing [respiration]
■—곤란 difficulty in breathing; difficult breathing; laboring breath; dyspn(o)ea —근《根》 a respiratory root; a pneumatophore —기능 respiratory function —작용 [動·植] respiration —중추 respiratory center

호흡기 呼吸器 the respiratory organs
■—질환 a chest complaint; a respiratory disease [trouble]; a disease of the respiratory organs

호흡운동 呼吸運動 1 〈폐의〉 breathing; [動] a respiratory movement
2 〈체조의〉 breathing exercise
■—기록기 a spirograph; a pneumograph; a pneumatograph

혹 1 〈피부의〉 a wen; a lump; 〈매맞아 생긴〉 a bump; a swelling; a protuberance; 〈낙타의〉 a hump
♦얼굴에 혹이 있다 have a wen on one's face / 눈두덩에 혹이 생기다 get a bump over one's eye / 혹을 떼다 cut away a wen
▶ 나는 공에 맞아서 혹이 생겼다 I got a bump [lump] on my head when I was hit by a ball.
2 〈나무의〉 a knot 《on a tree》; a knob; a gnarl; a node
♦혹투성이의 knotty; knurly; knurled; gnarled

혹² 1 〈후룩〉 ♦죽을 혹 들이마시다 slurp up one's soup
2 〈입김〉 with a blow [puff, whiff]
♦촛불을 혹 불어 끄다 blow out a candle

혹 或 1 〈혹시〉 possibly; perhaps; maybe
2 〈간혹〉 occasionally; at times; once in a while; now and then
♦혹 있는 일 a rare occurrence / 혹 가다가 찾아오는 손님 an occasional visitor
3 〈더러〉 some
▶ 혹은 희고 혹은 검다 Some are white, others black.

혹간 或間 sometimes ⇨ 간혹(間或)

혹독 酷毒 severity; harshness; cruelty; rigor 《of winter》
—혹독하다 〈모질다〉 severe; hard; harsh; cruel; 〈엄하다〉 strict; rigorous; rigid
♦혹독한 처사 cruel treatment / 혹독한 말 harsh [bitter] remarks / 혹독한 더위 violent [intense, terrible] heat / 혹독한 바람 a violent [strong] wind / 혹독하게 cruelly; severely; harshly / 혹독하게 다루다 treat sb harshly [cruelly]; deal harshly 《with》

혹 떼러 갔다 혹 붙여 온다 《속담》 Go for wool and come home shorn.

혹벌 a gall wasp; a gallfly

혹부리 a person with a wen (on his face)

혹사 酷似 (a) close resemblance
—혹사하다 〈서술적〉 be very [extremely] like sth; be very [strikingly] similar 《to》; bear a close resemblance [a strong likeness] 《to》; be the very picture of sb

혹사 酷使 rough use; driving sb hard; abuse; working sb hard
▶ 이 기계는 혹사에 견딘다 This machine stood rough use [rough handling].
—혹사하다 work [drive] sb hard; overwork sb; sweat 《one's workers》
♦두뇌를 혹사하다 overwork one's brain / 눈을 혹사하다 overwork one's eyes / 종업원을 혹사시키다 work [drive] the employees hard; 《口》 push the employees around
▶ 그는 수주일간 몸을 혹사했다 He worked too much for several weeks.

혹서 酷暑 (the) intense [severe] heat; fierce [violent, torrid] heat of summer

◆혹서의 계절 the hot season; the hottest weather
▶이 혹서 중에 몸조심하십시오 Please take good care of yourself in this intense heat [heat of midsummer].

혹설 或說 〈어떤 이의 말〉 one opinion; a certain view [argument]

혹성 惑星 a planet ⇨ 행성(行星)

혹세무민하다 惑世誣民 delude the world and deceive the people

혹시 或是 **1** 〈어쩌면〉 possibly; by some possibility; maybe; by (some) chance
▶혹시 그의 주소를 알고 계신지요? Do you happen to know his address?
▶너 혹시 그 일을 잊은 게 아니냐? Could you possibly have forgotten it?
▶혹시 무슨 일이 생기거든 바로 나를 부르게 In case anything happens, call me immediately.
▶혹시 그는 외출했는지도 모른다 He may possibly have gone out.
2 〈행여나〉 if; 〈걱정하여〉 lest...should...; for fear of... [that...may...]
▶혹시나 하고 걱정했던 일이 사실이 되었다 My fear has come true. ⇌ The worst that we feared has happened.

혹심 酷甚 severity; harshness
—**혹심하다** severe; hard; terrible; harsh; intense; extreme; violent
◆혹심한 추위 severe [intense] cold / 혹심한 피해를 입다 suffer heavy losses

혹야 或也 possibly ⇨ 혹시(或是)

혹염 酷炎 (the) intense heat ⇨ 혹서(酷暑)

혹위 —胃 〈반추 동물의〉 a rumen (pl. ~s, ·mina); a paunch

혹은 或 or ⇨ 또는

혹자 或者 〈어떤 사람〉 someone; some; somebody; a certain [some] person
◆혹자는 가로되 Somebody says...

혹평 酷評 (a) severe [harsh, bitter, sharp] criticism; a cruel remark ◆혹평을 받다 〈저서가〉 be subjected to severe criticism
—**혹평하다** criticize sharply [bitterly, severely]; speak bitterly [badly] of sb; say harsh things about 〈an opposition party〉; hypercriticize
▶그의 신작소설은 혹평당했다 His latest novel was subjected to severe [harsh] criticism.

혹하다 惑— **1** 〈반하다〉 be charmed by; be tempted; be seduced; be infatuated with; be captivated [fascinated] by 〈a woman's beauty〉
▶그녀는 그의 인품에 혹했다 She was charmed with his personality. ⇌ The charm of his personality won her heart.
▶그는 물욕에 혹했다 He was blinded by love of gain.
2 〈미혹되다〉 be deluded; be misled; be led into error; be trapped

혹한 酷寒 〈추위〉 severe [bitter, intense] cold; 〈겨울〉 a hard [severe] winter
◆혹한에 견디다 endure [stand] the intense cold

혹형 酷刑 a severe [cruel] punishment [penalty] ◆혹형을 과하다 inflict a severe punishment 《on》

혼 魂 a soul; a spirit; 〈혼령〉 the spirit of the dead; sb's departed soul; 〈귀신〉 a ghost
◆혼을 부르다 call back the spirit of the dead

혼가 婚家 〈혼인집〉 the house where there is a wedding

혼구 婚具 〈혼인 제구〉 wedding equipment

혼구멍내다 魂— 〈심히 혼내다〉 give sb a hard time; do [serve] sb a bad turn; 〈징계하다〉 teach sb lesson; 〈몹시 꾸짖다〉 give sb hell; give it hot

혼기 婚期 the marriageable age ◆혼기가 되다 be of [reach] marriageable age
▶그녀는 혼기를 놓쳤다 She is past marriageable age. ⇌ She (has) missed the chance to get married.

혼나다 魂— have a terrible [dreadful] experience; have a hard [rough] time (of it); pay dearly 《for》
▶나는 어저께 아주 혼났다 I had a hard time (of it) yesterday.
▶이런 짓을 했으니 혼나봐라 You will have to pay for this.
▶개가 짖어서 혼났다 The dog gave me a bad time.

혼내다 魂— treat sb cruelly [badly]; give sb a hard [rough] time; do sb a bad [an ill] turn; teach sb a lesson
▶이런 짓을 했으니 너를 혼내줄테다 You will pay (dearly) for this.

혼담 婚談 a proposal [an offer] of marriage; a (marriage) proposal
◆많은 혼담이 들어오다 have a lots of proposals [offers] of marriage / 혼담을 성사시키다 arrange [make up] a marriage / 혼담을 거절하다 refuse [decline] an offer of marriage
▶그 혼담은 깨졌다 The match has been broken.

혼도 昏倒 a swoon; a faint
—**혼도하다** swoon; fall into a swoon; faint (away); have a fainting fit; fall [drop] unconscious

혼돈 混沌·渾沌 chaos; confusion
◆혼돈 상태에 있다 be in a chaotic state; be in (a state of) chaos
▶정세는 혼돈 상태에 있었다 The political situation was in a state of chaos.
—**혼돈하다** chaotic; confused

혼동 混同 confusion 《of, between》
◆「study」와 「learn」의 혼동 the confusion of "study" and "learn"
—**혼동하다** confuse [confound, mix up] 《A with B》; mistake 《A for B》
◆그 쌍둥이를 혼동하다 confuse [mix up] the twins
▶꿈과 현실을 혼동하지 마라 Don't confuse dreams with [and] facts.
▶공과 사를 혼동해서는 안된다 We shouldn't mix up public and [with] private affairs.
▶자유와 방종을 혼동하지 마라 Don't confuse liberty with license.

혼란 混亂 (a) confusion; 〈순서·질서의〉 disorder; 〈무질서 상태〉 (a) chaos; (口) a mix-up

♦ 장내의 혼란 the confusion in the hall / 혼란을 틈타 달아나다 escape in the confusion / 혼란 상태에 있다 be in (a state of) confusion / 혼란에 빠지다 fall [be thrown] into confusion [disorder]; turn to chaos
▶ 화재가 나자 혼란이 일어났다 There was a panic when the fire broke out.
▶ 시 전체가 혼란 상태였다 The whole city was in a state of confusion.
—혼란하다 confused; disorderly; chaotic; messy; 〈서술적〉 be in confusion [disorder]
♦ 혼란된 생각 confused ideas / 회의를 혼란시키다 put [throw] a meeting into confusion
▶ 그는 머리가 혼란하여 어찌할 바를 몰랐다 He got so confused [mixed up] that he didn't know what to do.
▶ 그 회의는 혼란스런 가운데 끝났다 The conference ended in confusion.
▶ 사고 때문에 교통이 일시 혼란했다 The traffic was snarled for a time owing to an accident.

혼령 魂靈 the spirit (of the dead); *sb's* departed soul; the soul

혼례 婚禮 a wedding ceremony; a wedding; a marriage rites
♦ 혼례를 올리다 solemnize a marriage; celebrate a wedding / 혼례에 초대하다 invite *sb* to a wedding / 혼례에 초대받다 be invited to a wedding / 혼례에 참석하다 attend [be present at] a wedding

혼문 混文 〔文法〕 a compound-complex sentence; a mixed sentence

혼미 昏迷 〈명함〉 stupefaction; 〈혼란 상태〉 bewildering confusion; 〈혼수〉 〔醫〕 stupor
♦ 혼미상태에 빠지다 be thrown into confusion
—혼미하다 stupefied; confused; 〈서술적〉 be stupefied; lose *one's* consciousness; lose control of *oneself*
혼미하게 하다 stupefy; bewilder; confuse; fuddle
▶ 정국은 갈수록 더 혼미해지고 있다 The political situation is getting more and more chaotic.

혼방 混紡 mixed [blended] spinning
♦ 혼방 직물 mixed(-spun) fabrics / 나일론 20% 혼방의 면직물 cotton cloth with a 20% nylon mix
■ —사(絲) mixed yarn

혼백 魂帛 〈임시 신위〉 a temporary spirit tablet
■ —상자 a spirit box

혼백 魂魄 the soul; the spirit; the ghost

혼비백산하다 魂飛魄散— 〈몹시 놀라다〉 be frightened out of *one's* wits; be terrified out of *one's* senses ♦ 혼비백산하여 with *one's* heart in *one's* mouth

혼사 婚事 a matrimonial [marital, nuptial] matter; (a) marriage

혼색 混色 〈색을 섞기〉 mixing colors; a color blend; (a) mixture of colors; 〈섞은 색〉 compound [mixed] colors
—혼색하다 mix colors

혼선 混線 〈전화의〉 cross; entanglement of wires; 〈혼란〉 confusion
—혼선하다 get entangled [crossed]; be mixed up
▶ 전화가 혼선되었습니다 The lines [wires] are crossed.
▶ 만사가 혼선되어 있다 Everything is in confusion.
▶ 우리 이야기는 자꾸 혼선된다 Our talks often get mixed up.

혼성 混成 mixture; composition
♦ 혼성의 mixed; composite
—혼성하다 mix; mingle; combine; compound
■ —곡 〔樂〕 a medley —물 a mixture; a compound; a medley —어 a hybrid (word); a blend —열차 a composite train —팀 a combined team

혼성 混聲 〔樂〕 mixed voices
■ —합창 a mixed chorus : 4부 혼성 합창 a mixed chorus in four voices

혼수 昏睡 〈의식 불명〉 a coma; 〈실신〉 a trance; stupor; 〔醫〕 lethargy
♦ 혼수 상태에 있다 be in a state of coma
▶ 그는 혼수 상태에 빠졌다 He fell into a coma. ≒ He became unconscious.

혼수 婚需 〈물건〉 necessary articles for marriage; 〈비용〉 marriage expenses

혼식 混食 mixed food
—혼식하다 eat mixed food

혼신 渾身 the whole body
♦ 혼신의 힘을 다하여 with all *one's* might; by using all *one's* strength; with might and main
▶ 그는 혼신의 힘을 다하여 보트를 저었다 He rowed his boat with all his might [might and main].

혼신 混信 〈라디오의〉 interference; 〈방해에 의한〉 jamming

혼약 婚約 an engagement; a betrothal ⇨ 약혼

혼연 渾然 wholly; in perfect harmony ♦ 혼연 일체가 되다 constitute [form] a harmonious [perfect, complete] whole; be jointed [united] together
▶ 과학자들은 혼연 일체가 되어 연구중이다 Scientists are doing research in perfect cooperation.

혼외 婚外 ♦ 혼외의 extramarital ■ —정사 extramarital intercourse

혼욕 混浴 mixed bathing
—혼욕하다 《men and women》 bathe together

혼용하다 混用— mix; use (A) together with (B); mix (A and B); mingle
▶ 영국식 영어와 미국식 영어를 혼용하는 것은 바람직하지 않다 It is not advisable to mix British English and American English.

혼인 婚姻 a wedding ⇨ 결혼
■ —날 a wedding day

혼인신고 婚姻申告 registration of *one's* marriage
—혼인신고하다 register *one's* marriage

혼입 混入 mixing; mixture; admixture; blending
—혼입하다 mix; mingle; intermix; blend; adulterate

혼자 〈한사람〉 one person; 〈홀몸〉 a single person; 〈홀로〉 alone; by *oneself*; 〈혼자 힘으로〉 for *oneself*

혼자말

♦혼자 살다 live alone; 〈독신으로〉 be unmarried; remain single / 혼자서 고민하다 suffer by *oneself* / 혼자 여행하다 travel alone
▶ 그녀 혼자 진상을 알고 있다 She alone knows the truth.
▶ 나는 혼자 있을 때 공부가 제일 잘 된다 I work best when I'm by myself.
▶ 제발, 혼자 있게 해줘 Please, leave me alone.
▶ 저 사람은 마흔이 되었건만 아직 혼자다 Although he has reached forty, he is still single.
▶ 내 아기는 이제 혼자 걸을 수 있다 My baby can now walk by itself.
▶ 그 아기는 아직 혼자 걷지 못한다 The baby cannot walk by itself [himself, herself] yet.
▶ 그녀는 여기서 혼자 살고 있다 She lived here by herself.
▶ 밤에 혼자 나다니지 마라 Don't go out alone at night.

혼자말 a soliloquy; a monologue; talking to *oneself*
♦혼자말처럼 말하다 say half to *oneself*
▶ 저 남자는 늘 중얼중얼 혼자말을 하고 있다 That man is always muttering to himself.
―혼자말하다 say [speak, talk] to *oneself*

혼작 混作 〈섞어 갈기〉 mixed cultivation
―혼작하다 grow [cultivate] together

혼잡 混雜 〈붐빔〉 congestion; a jam; din and bustle; a rush; 〈혼란〉 confusion; disorder
♦도시 생활의 혼잡 the din and bustle of city life / 교통 혼잡을 완화하다 relieve the traffic jam
▶ 그 가게는 일요일 오후 혼잡의 절정에 이른다 Congestion in the store reaches a peak on Sunday afternoons.
―혼잡하다 confused; disordered; crowded; congested; bustling; jammed
♦혼잡한 시간 rush hour
▶ 기차 역은 사람들로 무척 혼잡했다 The train station was very crowded with people.
■―통행료 congestion fees

혼잣손 single-handedness
♦혼잣손으로 일하다 do *sth* single-handed; work single-handed

혼재 婚材 a suitable candidate for marriage; a marriageable person

혼전 混戰 a confused fight
―혼전하다 fight in confusion
▶ 금년의 페넌트 레이스는 혼전 상태였다 This year's pennant race has been in confusion.

혼절 昏絕 〈기절〉 fainting; a swoon
―혼절하다 faint; swoon; fall into a swoon

혼쭐나다 魂― 1 〈황홀감으로〉 be transported; be struck with admiration
2 ⇨ 혼나다

혼처 婚處 a marriageable family or person
♦마땅한 혼처를 구하다 look around for some suitable candidates for

혼취 昏醉 dead-drunkenness; intoxication
―혼취하다 get dead drunk

혼탁 混濁 impurity; muddiness; turbidity
―혼탁하다 get [become] muddy; turbid; thick; dull

♦혼탁한 공기 foul air / 혼탁한 물 polluted water; dirty water / 혼탁한 세상 the corrupt world / 물을 혼탁하게 하다 muddle water
▶ 그의 의식은 혼탁해졌다 His consciousness grew dim [faded].
▶ 포도주가 혼탁해졌다 The wine has become cloudy.

혼합 混合 mixing; mixture; admixture
―혼합하다 mix; mingle; blend; compound; intermix
♦혼합된 mixed; compound / 혼합하기 쉬운 mixible; easy to mix / 물과 술을 혼합하다 mingle wine and water
▶ 그것은 마치 물과 기름을 혼합하려고 하는 것과 같다 It's like trying to mix oil with water.
■―경기 a mixed competition [race] ―물 a mixture; a blend; a compound; a medley ―비 the mixture ratio ―비료 compound manure; mixed fertilizer; compost ―색 mixed color

혼혈 混血 mixed blood; racial mixture
♦혼혈의 of mixed blood; half-blood(ed)
■―아 a child of mixed parentage; a half [mixed] blood; an interracial child; 〈흑인과 백인의〉 a mulatto (*pl*. ~ (e)s); 〈유럽인과 아시아인의〉 a Eurasian : 혼혈아문제 the problem of mixed blood

혼화 混化 combination; compound; blend
―혼화하다 compound (with); blend into; be made into a compound

혼화 混和 mixture; mingling ―혼화하다 mix (with); blend; mingle (with); compound

혼효 混淆 mixing; mixture; confusion; a medley; a tangle; a jumble ―혼효하다 mixed; mingled; confused; jumbled; tangled
■―옥석(玉石)― (a medley of) chaff and corn; thread and thrum

홀― 〈짝없음〉 single

홀 笏 a [an official] mace; a scepter

홀¹ a hall; a saloon; 〈댄스홀〉 a dancing hall; (美) a dance hall
♦콘서트 홀 a concert hall / 댄스홀에 드나들다 frequent a dance hall

홀² 〈골프의〉 a hole; a cup
♦공을 홀에 넣다 hole a ball
―인원 (make) a hole in one

홀가분하다 light; free and easy; lighthearted
♦홀가분한 복장 casual clothes / 홀가분한 마음으로 with a light heart / 마음이 홀가분해지다 be lightened in heart / 몸이 홀가분하다 be unencumbered / 홀가분하게 차려입다 be lightly dressed / 홀가분하게 혼자 살다 enjoy a carefree life alone
▶ 빚을 갚고 나니 홀가분하다 The load is off my mind now that I have cleared off my debts.
▶ 시험이 끝나니 마음이 홀가분하다 I feel a load off my mind when the exam was over.

홀대 忽待 〈푸대접〉 unkind treatment; neglecting; slighting ―홀대하다 treat *sb* unkindly; neglect ♦아무를 홀대하다 treat *sb* unkindly

홀딩 [排·籠] holding

홀딱 1 〈옷을 벗는 모양〉 (removing it) completely; entirely; quickly
♦옷을 홀딱 벗다 strip *oneself* bare; strip *one*-

self of all *one's* clothes
2 〈뒤집는 모양〉 (turning a thing) inside out
◆주머니를 홀딱 뒤집다 turn *one's* pocket inside out
3 〈반하는 모양〉 deeply; dead; madly
◆홀딱 반하다 be deeply [dead, madly] in love 《with》; lose *one's* heart 《to》
▶내 친구는 내 동생에게 홀딱 반했다 My friend is awfully struck on my sister.
4 〈여지없이〉 completely; thoroughly
◆홀딱 속아 넘어가다 be nicely [fairly] taken in / 돈을 홀딱 날리다 become (quite) penniless
홀란드 Holland ⇨ 네덜란드
홀랑 1 ⇨ 홀딱 1,2 **2** 〈헐거운 모양〉 loosely; easily ◆홀랑 들어가다 slip into place; slip in loosely
3 〈벗어진 모양〉 ▶그는 머리가 홀랑 벗어졌다 His head was as bald as an egg.
홀로 alone; single; singlehanded(ly)
홀리다 1 〈귀신 등에〉 be possessed 《with》; be obsessed 《by》; be bewitched 《by》
◆홀린 사람처럼 like *one* possessed / 마치 무엇에 홀린 듯이 as if possessed by some devil or other / 여우에 홀리다 be bewitched by a fox / 귀신한테 홀리다 be possessed by a demon
2 〈현혹되다〉 be tempted; be seduced; 〈이성 등에〉 be infatuated 《with》; be captivated 《by》
◆여자에게 홀리다 fall under the spell of a girl's charms; be infatuated with a woman / 돈에 홀려 나쁜 짓을 하다 be tempted by money to do wrong; commit a crime for money
홀맺다 tie [knot] *sth* firmly; tie securely [hard]
홀몸 〈단신〉 a single person; 〈독신〉 an unmarried person; a bachelor (남자); a spinster (여자)
▶그녀는 평생 홀몸으로 지냈다 She remained single all her life.
홀뮴 〔化〕 holmium
홀소리 〔音聲〕 a vowel (sound)
홀수 —數 an odd number
홀스타인 〈젖소의 품종〉 a Holstein
홀씨 〔植〕 a spore ⇨ 포자
홀아비 a widower ◆홀아비로 살다 live in widowerhood ■—살림 the life of a widower; a single life
홀아비는 이가 서말 (속담) A widower cannot keep things tidy.
홀알 an unfertilized egg
홀앗이살림 a small household; a small family
홀어미 〈과부〉 a widow
홀연 忽然 suddenly; all of a sudden; unexpectedly
◆홀연(히) 사라지다 vanish as if by magic
▶그는 홀연(히) 나타났다 홀연히 사라졌다 He disappeared as suddenly as he had appeared.
홀짝 1 〈단숨에 들이마시는 모양〉 at a gulf; sipping; in a sip; supping; slurping
◆술을 홀짝 마시다 gulf down liquor; take a sip of whiskey
▶나는 뜨거운 커피를 홀짝 마셨다 I drank hot coffee in sips.
2 〈뛰거나 날아오르는 모양〉 at a jump [bound]; with a jump; lightly
◆홀짝 뛰다 leap lightly / 새가 홀짝 날아오르다 a bird suddenly takes wing
▶소년은 개울을 홀짝 뛰어넘었다 The boy leaped over a brook with a jump.
3 〈콧물을〉 sniffling; sniveling
◆콧물을 홀짝 들이마시다 sniff; sniffle; snivel
홀짝거리다 1 〈액체를 연해〉 keep sipping [supping]
◆차를 홀짝거리다 sip *one's* tea
2 〈콧물을〉 sniffle; snivel
3 〈우는 모양〉 weep [cry] with sniffling
◆소녀가 홀짝거리다 a girl cries and sniffles
홀쭉이 a lanky person
홀쭉하다 1 〈가늘고 길다〉 lank; lanky; spindly; slender; spindling; 〈야위다〉 lean
◆홀쭉한 사내 a lanky man / 얼굴이 홀쭉하다 be thin in the face / 허리가 홀쭉하다 have a slim waist / 근심으로 홀쭉해지다 become thin from worries
2 〈뾰족하다〉 pointed; tapering
◆한쪽 끝이 홀쭉하다 one end tapers
홀쳐매다 tie firmly ⇨ 홀맺다
홀치기(염색) dyeing with uncolored spots
홀태 1 〈생선〉 a slim fish without spawn
2 〈물건〉 a slim thing
홀태바지 slender-legged trousers
홀태질 stripping grain from the ear on a threshing machine; hackling; threshing
—홀태질하다 hackle (rice); thresh
홀 하 忽— 1 〈경솔·소홀하다〉 careless; thoughtless; inconsiderate; hasty; rash
◆대접이 홀하다 be careless in treating *sb* / 행동이 홀하다 behave rashly
2 〈대수롭지 않다〉 be of little importance
홀홀 fluttering(ly); nimbly ⇨ 훌훌
홈¹ 〈길게〉 a groove, a furrow; 〈세로 긴〉 a flute; 〈쇠시리의〉 a quirk ◆홈을 파다 cut [hollow out] a groove; groove
홈² **1** 〈가정〉 *one's* home
2 ⇨ 홈베이스
◆홈인하다 get [reach, go] home; score
홈걸이 〈홈통 받치는〉 a gutter hook
홈그라운드 a home ground
◆홈그라운드의 경기 a home game
홈런 〔野〕 a home run; a homer; a circuit clout; a round-tripper; a four bagger
◆홈런을 치다 hit [clout, slam] a home run ■굿바이— a home run to end the game; a clinching homer 단독[솔로]— a solo homer 만루— a bases-loaded homer; a grand slam [slammer] 장외(場外)— an out-of-the-park homer ■—왕 a home-run king [leader]
홈룸 a homeroom
◆홈룸 교사 〈담임교사〉 a homeroom teacher
홈베이스 〔野〕 a home base [plate]
홈스트레치 〔競〕 the homestretch
◆홈스트레치에 들어서다 get on the homestretch
홈스펀 homespun
◆홈스펀의 homespun (cloth)

홈질 tacking; tacks —**홈질하다** sew with large stitches; tack (together, to)

홈착거리다 1 〈더듬어 뒤지다〉 grope [fumble] for *sth*
♦호주머니 속을 홈착거리다 fumble in *one's* pocket /
▶그는 캄캄한 어둠 속에서 홈착거려 손전등을 찾았다 He groped for a flashlight in the utter darkness.
2 〈눈물을 씻다〉 wipe away
♦눈물을 홈착거리다 wipe *one's* tears away

홈처때리다 give *sb* a good whaling; dust [thrash] *sb's* jacket

홈타기 〈갈라지는 오금〉 a fork; a crotch
♦바지[나무] 홈타기 the crotch of trousers [a tree] / 나무 홈타기에 앉다 sit in the crotch of a tree / 홈타기지다 be forked

홈통 一桶 a conduit (pipe); a spout; an aqueduct; a gutter
♦대나무 홈통 an aqueduct of bamboo pipes / 빗물받이 홈통 a gutter at the eaves; an eave(s) trough / 집에 홈통을 달다 gutter a house

홈팀 the home team
홈파다 hollow out ⇨ 움파다
홈패다 be hollowed out ⇨ 움패다
홉¹ 〈용량의 단위〉 a hob
홉² 〔植〕 a hop; 〈암꽃〉 hops
♦홉으로 맛을 내다 hop

홉뜨다 turn up the whites of *one's* eyes
홉스 〈영국의 철학자〉 Hobbes, Thomas (1588-1679)

홋홋이 without encumbrances; with few dependents
▶그 부부는 딸린 식구 없이 홋홋이 산다 The couple leads a carefree life with no one else to worry about.

홋홋하다 unencumbered; carefree; 〈서술적〉 have no dependents [ties]
♦홋홋한 살림 a carefree household with few encumbrances

홍 紅 red ⇨ 홍색
홍기 紅旗 a red flag
홍꼭지 紅— a kite with a round piece of red paper at its top
홍당무 紅唐— a red radish; 〈당근〉 a carrot
♦얼굴이 홍당무가 되다 become red; turn as red as a turkey cock; be flushed

홍대 洪大・鴻大 hugeness; immensity
—홍대하다 huge; immense; vast; tremendous
홍도 紅桃 〈나무〉 a red-blossoming peach tree; 〈꽃〉 a red peach blossoms
홍두깨 1 〈다듬잇감 도구〉 a round wooden stick for fulling clothes
♦아닌 밤중에 홍두깨 a startling surprise; a bolt from the blue
2 〔農〕 soil which an inexpert plowman has neglected
3 〈소의 홍두깨살〉 rump
■—질 fulling cloth on a wooden roller
홍등 紅燈 a red lantern; a red light
■—가 gay quarters; 〈美〉 a brothel area
홍련 紅蓮 a red lotus flower
■—지옥 〔佛敎〕 one of the Eight Icy Hells

홍루 紅淚 1 〈미녀의 눈물〉 tears of a fair 2 〈피눈물〉 bloody tears
홍매 紅梅 〔植〕 red plum blossoms
홍모 鴻毛 wild goose down
♦목숨을 홍모같이 여기다 (比喻) make [think] nothing of *one's* life
홍반 紅斑 red spots; 〔醫〕 erythema
홍백 紅白 red and white
■—전(戰) ⇨ 청백—전
홍보 弘報 public information; publicity; public relations
■—과 a public relations section —지(誌) a public relations magazine —책자 a publicity booklet [pamphlet] —활동 public relations (略 P.R.) (▶단수 취급)
홍삼 紅蔘 ginseng steamed red
■—근 a red ginseng —정(精)[차] red ginseng extract [tea]
홍색 紅色 red; a red color
♦홍색을 띤 reddish; pinkish
■—짜리 a bride (dressed in a red skirt)
홍소 哄笑 loud laughter; a roar of laughter; a guffaw
—홍소하다 laugh loudly; roar with laughter; guffaw
홍수 洪水 1 a flood; 〈대홍수〉 a deluge; an inundation; 〈홍수의 물〉 floodwaters
♦노아의 홍수 the Deluge; the Flood; the Noachian deluge / 홍수를 만난 사람들 flood victims; people suffering from the flood / 홍수를 만난 가옥 flooded houses; houses under water
▶큰비가 1주일 동안 계속 내리더니 홍수가 났다 The heavy rain that continued for a week caused a deluge.
▶집중호우로 그 지방에 홍수가 났다 A flood struck that area as a result of that localized downpour. ⇌ The localized downpour caused a flood in that area.
▶다리가 홍수에 떠내려 갔다 The bridge was washed [carried] away by the flood.
▶빈번한 홍수로 많은 사람이 집을 잃었다 Frequent floods left a lot of people homeless.
2 〈많은 사물의 비유〉 ♦정보의 홍수 a flood of information / 질문의 홍수 a shower of questions
▶도로는 자동차의 홍수다 There is a stream of cars on the streets. ⇌ The streets are crowded with cars.
■—경보[예보] a flood warning [forecast]: 홍수 경보를 발하다 issue a flood warning 《for an area》 —막이[방어] flood prevention [protection] —조절 flood control —지[구역] a flooded area [district]
홍수 紅樹 〔植〕 a mangrove tree
■—림 a mangrove forest
홍순 紅脣 1 〈여자의 붉은 입술〉 cherry [red] lips
2 〈반쯤 핀 꽃송이〉 a half-open flower
홍시 紅柿 a ripe (and soft) persimmon
홍실 紅— (a) red thread
홍안 紅顔 a rosy [ruddy] face; pink cheeks
♦홍안의 미소년 a fair youth; a handsome rosy-cheeked youth / 백면 홍안의 milk-and-

roses
홍어 洪魚 ·[魚] a skate; thornback
홍업 洪業·鴻業 a glorious achievement; great work [exploit]
홍역 紅疫 [醫] the measles; rubeola
  ♦홍역을 하다 catch [have] the measles / 홍역을 치르다 (비유-) have bitter experiences; have a hard time (of it)
홍연광 紅鉛鑛 [鑛] crocoite; crocoisite; red lead ore
홍염 紅焰 1〈붉은 불꽃〉red blazes of flame 2〈天〉〈태양의〉prominence
홍엽 紅葉 〈단풍이 든〉red leaves; autumn colors [tints];〈단풍나무의〉red maple foliage
홍예 虹霓 1 ⇨ 무지개
  2 ⇨ 홍예문 ♦홍예를 틀다 span with an arch; arch (a gate) ■ ─다리 an arch(ed) bridge
홍예문 虹霓門 the arch of a gate
홍옥 紅玉 1 [鑛] a ruby
  2〈사과의 품종〉a Jonathan
홍위병 紅衛兵 〈중국의〉the Red Guard
홍은 鴻恩 great benevolence [grace]
홍익인간 弘益人間 devotion to the welfare of mankind
  ♦홍익인간의 이념 the humanitarian ideal
홍인종 紅人種 the red race; the American Indian race
홍일점 紅一點 the only member of the fair sex (among); the only woman in the company
  ▶그녀는 홍일점이었다 She was the only woman present among male members.
홍적세 洪積世 [地質] the Pleistocene; the diluvial epoch
홍적층 洪積層 [地質] a diluvium (pl. ~s, -via); a diluvial formation
홍적토 洪積土 diluvial deposits
홍조 紅潮 1〈붉어진 얼굴〉flushing; a glow
  ♦홍조를 띠다 flush (up)
  2〈붉게 보이는 바다〉the seascape aglow with the rising sun
  3 ⇨ 월경(月經)
홍조류 紅藻類 [植] red algae
홍진 紅塵 1〈티끌〉dust in the air; thick dust
  2〈번거롭고 속된 세상〉the troublesome affair of the mundane world
  ♦홍진을 피하다 keep away from the din and bustle of the world
홍차 紅茶 black tea
  ♦홍차를 끓이다 make black tea
홍채 虹彩 [解] the iris (pl. ~es, irides)
  ■ ─염 iritis
홍학 紅鶴 [鳥] a flamingo (pl. ~(e)s) ⇨ 플라밍고
홍합 紅蛤 [貝] a hard-shelled mussel
홍해 紅海 the Red Sea
홑 〈겹이 아님〉one layer
  ♦홑이다 be one-layered
홑- 〈한겹·외톨〉single; onefold
홑겹 one layer; a single layer
홑눈 [動] a stemma (pl. ~s, -mata); an ocellus (pl. -lli) ♦홑눈의 ocellar
홑몸 1 ⇨ 홀몸
  ♦홑몸으로 살다 live single; lead a bachelor's life
  2〈임신하지 않은 몸〉a (married) woman who has not become pregnant yet
  ▶그녀는 홑몸이 아니다 She is with child [in the family way].
홑바지 unlined trousers; (Korean woman's) undergarment
홑반 a single layer of cotton wool
  ■ ─뿌리〈옷〉garment with a single layer of cotton padding
홑벌 1〈한겹으로 된 물건〉single-ply [onefold] thing 2 ⇨ 단벌
홑벌사람 〈속이 얕은 사람〉a shallow-minded person
홑소리 [音聲] a single sound; a monosyllabic sound
홑실 a single-ply thread; singles
홑옷 unlined clothes
홑으로 〈적은 수효로〉merely; just; no more than; in small numbers;〈단순히〉simply
  ▶홑으로 한두 개만이 아니다 It isn't just a mere one or two of them.
홑이불 a (bed) sheet; a single-layer quilt
홑잎 1〈홑꽃잎〉a single petal
  2〈한 잎새로 된 잎〉a simple leaf
홑지다 〈홋홋하다〉unencumbered; without family encumbrances;〈복잡하지 않다〉simple; uncomplicated
홑집 [建] a single-wing house; a shack
홑창 一窓 [建] a sliding window without an inner one
홑치마 a skirt worn without an underskirt;〈겹겹으로 된〉an unlined skirt
화 火 1〈성〉anger; ire; rage; wrath; indignation
  ♦화를 잘 내는 hot-tempered; quick-tempered; irritable / 홧김에 in a fit of anger
  ▶아버지는 머리 끝까지 화가 나셨다 Father burned with anger.
  ▶왜 그렇게 화가 났니 ? What are you angry about?
  ▶그는 화를 잘 낸다 He gets angry [offended] easily. ⇌ He has a short temper.
  2 ⇨ 오행(五行)
화 禍 〈불행〉(a) misfortune; (a) mishap; (an) evil; trouble;〈재앙〉(a) disaster; one's [the] ruin
  ♦화를 당하다 meet with a calamity;〈살해되다〉be killed / 화를 자초하다 bring a calamity upon oneself / 화를 모면하다 escape a disaster
  ▶입은 화의 근원이다 (속담) Out of the mouth comes evil. ⇌ Better the foot slip than the tongue.
-화 化 -ization ♦-화하다 -ize
  ▶그의 소설은 영화화되었다 His novel was made into a film.
  ▶한국의 근대화는 놀라울 정도로 빨랐다 The modernization of Korea was astonishingly fast.
-화 畫 〈그림〉a picture; a drawing; a painting
  ♦서양화 a Western painting / 한국화〈동양화〉a Korean painting; an Oriental painting / 인물화 a figure painting
-화 靴 〈신〉shoes; boots

♦스키화 ski boots / 신사[숙녀]화 men's [ladies] shoes / 운동화 sports [gym] shoes
화가 畫架 an easel ⇨ 이젤
화가 畫家 a painter; an artist
♦화가가 되다 enter upon a painting career
• 동양[서양]— an artist of Oriental drawing [Western painting] 인물[풍경]— a portrait [landscape] painter 한국— an artist of Korean painting
화간 和姦 fornication —화간하다 fornicate 《with》
화강암 花崗岩 granite ♦화강암의 granitic
화경 火鏡 a burning glass; a sunglass
화경 花梗 〔植〕 a flower stalk ⇨ 꽃자루
화공 火攻 a fire attack; an attack by fire —화공하다 attack with fire
화공 畫工 〈직업 화가〉 a painter
화관 花冠 1 ⇨ 꽃부리
2 〈관〉 a coronet; an ornamental crown
화교 a Chinese residing abroad; 〈총칭〉 overseas Chinese
화구 火口 1 〈아궁이의〉 a fire hole; 〈총포의〉 a muzzle 2 〈화산의〉 a crater ■—구(丘) a volcanic cone
화근 禍根 the root of evil; a source of calamity
♦화근을 없애다 cut off the evil at its root
▶그의 경우는 재산이 화근이 되었다 In his case, his estate proved a curse to him.
▶그녀는 미모가 화근이 되었다 Her personal beauty was her ruin.
화급 火急 urgency; emergency; exigency
—화급하다 urgent; pressing; exigent; imminent
▶그는 화급한 용무로 대구에 갔다 He left for Taegu on an urgent business.
화기 火氣 1 〈불기운〉 fire; the heat of fire
♦화기엄금 〈게시〉 No Fire. ⇌ Caution, flammables.
2 〈가슴이 답답한 기운〉 a stifling sensation in the chest
3 ⇨ 화증(火症)
화기 火器 〈병기〉 firearms
■경[소]— light firearms; small arms 자동[중]— automatic [heavy] firearms
화기 和氣 〈날씨〉 mild [genial, agreeable] weather; 〈화목〉 geniality; peacefulness; harmoniousness
화기애애하다 和氣靄靄— 〈온화한 기색〉 harmonious; peaceful; happy
♦화기애애한 가정 a happy [harmonious] family / 화기애애하게 harmoniously; peacefully
화끈 with a sudden flush [glow]; with a burning sensation
♦부끄러워서 얼굴이 화끈 달다 feel one's face burning with shame
—화끈하다 hot; burning; flushing; glowing
화끈거리다 feel hot [warm]; burn; blush; glow
▶열이 나서 몸이 화끈거린다 I feel hot with fever.
▶부끄러워서 얼굴이 화끈거렸다 I flushed with shame.
화나다 火— be angered; get [become] angry 《with, at》
♦화난 얼굴을 하다 look angry [mad]; have an angry look / 화나서 소리치다 shout in anger
▶그를 화나게 하지 마라 Don't make him angry [mad].
▶그는 늘 그녀에게 놀림받는데 화났다 He was irritated by her constant teasing.
▶그런 사람에게 무시당하다니 화난다 I hate to be looked down on by a man like him.
화내다 火— get [become] angry 《with, at》; take offense 《at》; 〈美〉 get mad; lose one's temper
♦벌컥 화내다 flare up; flash up; blow one's top; burst into a fit of anger [rage]
▶그는 걸핏하면 화낸다 He gets angry [offended] easily. ⇌ He loses his temper easily. ⇌ He has a short temper.
▶그가 그것을 알면 벌컥 화낼 걸 He will be very angry to know it.
▶그는 여간해서 화내지 않는다 He always keeps his temper. ⇌ He is slow to get angry.
화냥년 an adulteress; an adulterous 〈unfaithful〉 wife; a woman of easy [loose] morals; a slattern; a slut
화냥질 adultery ⇨ 서방질
화농 化膿 maturation; suppuration
♦화농성의 suppurative; festering; maturating; purulent / 화농 방지의 antipyic
—화농하다 〈곪다〉 be ripe; come to a head; become infected; fester; suppurate
♦화농한 상처 a purulent sore / 화농시키다 suppurate; maturate
■—균 suppurative germs —작용 pyogenesis
화다닥 suddenly ⇨ 후다닥
화단 花壇 a flower bed [garden]
화단 畫壇 the artists' world; painting circles
화답 和答 〈시·노래에 대한 응답〉 a response
—화답하다 respond 《in singing》
화대 花代 〈팁〉 a charge for entertainer's service; a entertainer's fee
화덕 火— 1 ⇨ 화로(火爐)
2 〈솥 거는〉 a cooking stove; an oven
화동 和同 〈화합〉 unison; harmony; 〈재화합〉 reunion
—화동하다 get in unison; be in harmony
화두 話頭 〈말머리〉 a topic [subject] of conversation
♦화두를 돌리다 change the topic [subject] of conversation
하드득 〈묽은 똥이 갑자기 나오는 소리〉 with a slosh; 〈총포 등이 터지는 소리〉 with a crackling sound; 〈경망스런 모양〉 foolishly; giddily
하드득거리다 slosh repeatedly; crackle [whizz] repeatedly
화라지 〈옆으로 길게 뻗은 나뭇가지〉 a long spread-out branch; a bough
화락 和樂 peace and harmony
—화락하다 harmonious; peaceful; happy; 〈서술적〉 be at peace with each other
화랑 花郞 〔史〕 an elite youth corps of Silla; a warrior caste of noble youths of Silla
■—도(道) the code of Silla chivalry
화랑 畫廊 a (picture) gallery; an art gallery

화려 華麗 splendor; magnificence; gorgeousness
—**화려하다** splendid; gorgeous; magnificent; flowery
◆화려한 문체 flowery style / 화려한 무늬 a showy pattern / 화려한 일생 a brilliant career / 화려한 의상 a gay costume; 《a lady in》 gala dress / 화려한 연기 a splendid [brilliant] performance / 화려하게 splendidly; gorgeously; gaudily
▶ 우리는 그 극장의 화려함에 놀랐다 We were amazed at the splendor of the theater.
▶ 그녀의 연기는 화려하다 Her performance is magnificent.

화력 火力 heat; heating [thermal] power; 〈불길의〉 the force of the fire; 〈총포 등의〉 firepower
◆화력의 우세 a firepower advantage / 화력이 세다[약하다] have strong [weak] caloric force / 화력에서 우세하다 surpass 《the enemy》 in firepower; outgun 《the enemy》
▶ 이 가스 버너는 화력이 세다 This gas burner has strong heating power.
■—**발전** thermal power generation —**발전소** a thermal power plant [station] —**증강** 〔軍〕 increase in [of] firepower

화로 火爐 a charcoal brazier; a fire pot
◆화롯불을 쬐다 warm *oneself* [*one's* hand] at [over] a brazier

화룡점정 畫龍點睛 〈중요 부분의 완성〉 giving the finishing; the finishing touches

화류 花柳 ─병 ⇨ 성병 ─장(場) a resort for pleasure and dissipation

화류계 花柳界 the gay quarters [world]; the frivolous community
■—**여자** a woman of a certain character [of the gay world]; a gay lady; a prostitute

화면 畫面 a picture; 〈영화・TV의〉 screen; a scene
◆화면이 넓은 wide-screen / 화면에 들어오다 〈영화・TV에서〉 enter [get into] the picture; come on / 화면에서 사라지다 go [get] out of the picture; go off the screen

화목 和睦 harmony; concord; peace
◆가정의 화목 family concord; peace within a family
—**화목하다** peaceful; harmonious; 〈서술적〉 be in harmony [concord]; be at peace with each other
◆화목한 가정 a peaceful family / 화목하게 harmoniously; happily; affectionately / 화목하게 살다 live in perfect harmony [concord, union]
▶ 그의 집안은 아주 화목하다 His family live very happily [in harmony]. ⇌ Perfect peace reigns in his family.

화무십일홍 花無十日紅 〈속담〉 Pride will have a fall.

화문 花紋 〈꽃무늬〉 a floral pattern [design]
─**석** ⇨ 꽃돗자리

화물 貨物 〈운송 화물〉《美》freight; 《英》goods; 〈뱃짐〉cargo; 〈상품〉commodities; merchandise; 〈수화물〉《美》baggage; 《英》luggage
◆화물을 탁송하다 consign goods 《to》 / 철도편으로 화물을 발송하다 send goods by rail
▶ 저 배는 화물을 운송한다 That ship carries freight. ⇌ That is a freighter.
▶ 그 물품을 항공 화물로 보냈다 The goods were sent (by) air cargo [freight].
■**중량**— hard goods **철도**— rail freight
■—**담당자** a freight clerk; a freightman —**상환증** a bill of lading —**선** a cargo boat; a freight vessel; 《美》a freighter —**수송기** a cargo [freight] plane; a freighter —**열차**《美》a freight (train); 《英》a goods train —**운송** freight; 〈탁송〉forwarding; 《美》shipment —**운임** freight; freightage; 〈철도의〉railway freight charges —**자동차**《美》a truck; 《英》a (motor) lorry —**차**《美》a freight car; 《英》a goods van —**취급소** a forwarding agency; 〈역의〉 a freight office —**칸** 〈기차의〉 a goods car; 〈항공기의〉 a cargo compartment

화물환 貨物換 〔商〕 a documentary bill [draft]

화미 華美 splendor ⇨ 화려

화밀 花蜜 〈꿀〉〔植〕 (floral) nectar

화반 花盤 〈자기 화분〉 a flowerpot

화방 花房 〈꽃집〉 a flower shop

화방 畫房 〈화실〉 a studio; 《프》an atelier; 〈재료점〉 an art store

화방수 —**水** 〈소용돌이〉 a whirl current; a whirlpool; an eddy

화백 畫伯 〈화가〉 an [a great] artist; a (master) painter

화법 話法 〔文法〕 narration; speech ■**직접[간접]**— the direct [indirect] speech

화법 畫法 the art of drawing; the canons of painting ◆화법에 맞다[맞지 않다] be in [out of] drawing ■**산수**— landscape painting

화변 禍變 〈큰 재난〉 a great disaster [calamity]

화병 火病 〈울화병〉 a nervous disorder caused by *one's* pent-up resentment

화병 花瓶 a vase ⇨ 꽃병

화보 花譜 an album [a catalog] of flowers

화보 畫報 a pictorial; a graphic; 〈보도를 겸한〉 pictorial news; a picture report; 〈잡지〉 an illustrated magazine ■**시사**— news in pictures

화보 畫譜 a picture book [album]; a catalog of pictures

화복 禍福 〈재앙과 복록〉 weal or [and] woe; good or [and] evil; fortune and [or] misfortune; prosperity or adversity
◆인생의 화복 the haps and mishaps [ups and downs] of life; the sweets and bitters of life

화본과 禾本科 〔植〕 Graminaceae ■—**식물** (true) grasses

화부 火夫 〈불때는〉 a stoker; 《美》a fireman; 〈화장터의〉 a corpse man; a cremator

화분 花盆 a flowerpot ◆화분에 심은 장미 a potted rose

화분 花粉 〔植〕 pollen (⇨ 꽃가루) ■—**증** hay fever; pollinosis

화불단행 禍不單行 Misfortunes never come alone. ⇌ Misfortunes come in succession. ⇌ Bad things (always) come in threes.

화사 華奢 〈화려〉 splendor; pomp; gaudiness; 〈사치〉 luxury —**화사하다** splendid; pompous;

화사첨족 畫蛇添足 redundancy ⇨ 사족(蛇足)

화산 火山 a volcano (*pl.* ~(e)s)
♦화산의 폭발 the eruption of a volcano; a volcanic eruption
▶화산이 활동하고 있다 The volcano is now active.
▶화산이 폭발했다 The volcano erupted [burst into eruption].
■—사[활, 휴]— an extinct [an active, a dormant] volcano 해저— a submarine volcano ■—국 a volcanic country —군(群) a volcanic group —대(帶) a volcanic zone —도 a volcanic island —맥 a volcanic chain [range] —분출물 ejecta —사(砂) volcanic sand —석[암] (a piece of) volcanic rock —열도 volcanic islands —작용 volcanism; volcanic action —재 volcanic ash —탄(彈) a volcanic bomb —학 volcanology —학자 a volcanologist —현상 a volcanic phenomenon; volcanism —활동 volcanic activity

화살 an arrow; 〈굵은〉 a bolt
♦공격의 화살 the aim of attack / 빗발치듯 하는 화살 a shower [barrage] of arrows / 질문의 화살을 던지다 fire questions (at *sb*) / 화살을 시위에 메기다 fix [notch, fit] an arrow to the string / 화살을 쏘다 shoot [send, let fly] an arrow (at)
▶화살이 그의 어깨에 박혔다 An arrow lodged in his shoulder.
▶그는 과녁을 향해 화살을 쏘았다 He shot the arrow at the target.
▶세월은 화살처럼 빠르다 (속담) Time flies (like an arrow).
■—대 the shaft of an arrow; an arrow shaft —자리 〔天〕 the Arrow; Sagitta —촉 an arrowhead —통 a quiver —표 an arrow

화상 火床 〈보일러의〉 a firebed
화상 火傷 〈불에 덴〉 a burn; 〈김·물에 덴〉 a scald
♦가벼운[심한] 화상 a slight [serious, deep] burn / 화상 자국 a scar of burn; a burn (scar) / 손에 화상을 입다 get burnt in the hand; burn *one's* hand / 화상으로 죽다 be scalded to death (▶be burned to death는 「타 죽다」)
▶나는 뜨거운 물로 손가락에 화상을 입었다 I scalded my fingers with hot water.
—화상입다 be [get] burnt [scalded]; have [suffer] a burn; burn [scald] *oneself*
■ 제1[2, 3, 4]도— a first-degree [second-degree, third-degree, fourth-degree] burn

화상 和尙 〔佛敎〕 a Buddhist priest
화상 華商 〈중국 상인〉 a Chinese merchant (residing abroad)
화상 畫商 a picture dealer
화상 畫像 a portrait; 〔TV〕 a picture; 〈얼굴〉 (俗) a face ■—면적 〔TV〕 a picture area

화색 和色 〈온화한 표정〉a mild complexion; a peaceful countenance; 〈혈색〉 a healthy [ruddy] complexion ♦화색이 돌다 regain color

화생방전 化生放戰 〔軍〕 chemical, biological and radiological warfare; CBR warfare
화서 花序 〔植〕 an inflorescence ⇨ 꽃차례
화석 化石 a fossil ♦나무[물고기]의 화석 a fossil tree [fish] / 뼈[조가비, 발자국]의 화석 a fossil bone [shell, footprint]
■—식물[동물] a fossil plant [animal] —연료 fossil fuel —인류 fossil men —층 fossiliferous strata —학 fossilology —학자 a fossilologist; a fossilist —화(化) petrification: 화석화하다 petrify; fossilize

화선지 畫宣紙 Chinese drawing paper
화섬 化纖 chemical [synthetic] fiber=화학 섬유 ■—직물 synthetic textiles
화성 化成 〈생장〉 growth; 〈변화〉 transformation; change; 〔化〕 chemical synthesis —화성하다 transform; change
■—공업 the chemical (and synthetic) industry —비료 a compound [complex] fertilizer

화성 火星 〔天〕 Mars ♦화성의 Martian 〈atmosphere〉 ■—인(人) a Martian
화성 和聲 〔樂〕 harmony; concord; a chord
♦화성적[의] harmonic ■—법 the law of harmony —학 harmonics
화성 畫聖 〈대화가〉 a master painter; a great master in painting
화성 火成 〔地質〕 ♦화성의 igneous; pyrogenous; pyrogenic
■—광물 a pyrogenetic mineral —광상 igneous (ore) deposits —암 igneous rock: 심성(深成) 화성암 Plutonic rock

화세 火勢 〈불기운〉 the force of the fire [flames]
화수 花穗 〔植〕 a spike; an ear
화수분 an inexhaustible (fountain of) wealth [treasury]; a golconda; a widow's cruse
화수회 花樹會 〈일가 친목회〉 a convivial society of the members of a clan; a family [clan] gathering
화술 話術 the art of conversation [narration]; narrative skill
♦화술에 능한 사람 a good talker; a master storyteller; a brilliant conversationalist
▶그는 화술이 좋다 He has the gift of the gab.
화승 火繩 〈화약심지〉 a fuse [match] ■—총 a matchlock (gun); a firelock
화식 火食 〈eating〉 cooked food —화식하다 eat 《fish》 cooked; make a diet of cooked food
화식 貨殖 moneymaking —화식하다 make money
화식도 花式圖 a flower [floral] diagram
화식조 火食鳥 〔鳥〕 a cassowary
화신 化身 (an) incarnation; (an) embodiment 《of valor》; (a) personification
▶그 놈은 악마의 화신이다 The villain is a fiend incarnate.
▶그는 탐욕의 화신이다 He is the picture [incarnation] of avarice.
화신 花信 〈꽃소식〉 tidings of flowers; information about flowers for viewing
■—풍(風) a spring breeze (presaging blossoms)
화실 火室 〈기관차 등의〉 a fire box [chamber]

화실 畫室 a studio 《pl. ~s》; (프) an atelier
화심 花心 1〈植〉the center [central part] of a flower 2〈미인의 마음〉the heart of a beautiful woman
화심 禍心 malice; an evil intention; malicious intent; treacherous designs
화씨 華氏 Fahrenheit (略 F.) ♦화씨 90도 90 degrees Fahrenheit; 90°F. ■—온도계 a Fahrenheit (thermometer)
화압 花押〈수결〉a signature; a written seal
화약 火藥 gunpowder; powder ♦대포에 화약을 재다 load a gun / 화약을 폭발시키다 blow up [explode] explosives
■면— guncotton 무연— smokeless gunpowder 합성— compound powder 흑색— black gunpowder —고 an explosive warehouse; a (powder) magazine —공장 a powder mill [plant] —류 explosives —류 단속법 [法] the Explosives Control Act —취급 면허장 gunpowder license —통 a powder flask
화엄경 華嚴經 〖佛敎〗the Avatamska Sutra
화열 火熱 caloric heat
화염 火焰 a flame; a blaze ♦화염에 휩싸이다 be enveloped [wrapped] in flames; be in a blaze
■—방사기 a flame thrower [projector] —병 a (glass-)bottle grenade; a fire bottle; (俗) a Molotov cocktail
화엽 花葉〈꽃잎〉a petal; a floral leaf;〈꽃과 잎〉flowers and leaves
화예 花蘂〈꽃술〉〖植〗a pistil and a stamen
화요일 火曜日 Tuesday (略 Tues.)
화용월태 花容月態 a fair face and graceful carriage
화운 和韻 composing a verse in response —화운하다 respond in verse to a poem
화원 花園 a flower garden
화음 和音 〖樂〗a chord; an accord ♦화음의 chordal ♦기초— a fundamental chord 주— a tonic chord
화음 華音〈중국음〉the Chinese pronunciation of Chinese characters
화응 和應 response; agreement
—화응하다 respond 《to》; agree 《with》
화의 和議 1〈평화협상〉negotiations for peace; peace conference;〈화해〉reconciliation
♦화의를 맺다 make peace; conclude peace 《with》/ 화의를 제의하다 make overtures of [for] peace; extend [hold out] the olive branch
—화의하다 negotiate for peace; make overtures of peace; effect a reconciliation 《with》2 〖法〗composition
▶채권자들과의 화의가 성립되었다 We made a composition with the creditors.
—화의하다 make a composition 《with》
■—법 the composition law —사건 a composition matter; a case of composition —신청 application [petition] for composition —절차 〈상법의〉composition proceedings;〈화의법의〉procedures of composition
화이트소스 〖料〗white sauce
화이트칼라 an office worker; a white-collar worker ♦화이트칼라의 white-collar(ed)

화이트하우스 〈백악관〉the White House
화인 火印 1〈낙인〉a brand (mark) 2〈되〉a stamped grain measure
화인 火因 the origin [cause] of a fire
♦화인 불명의 화재 a fire of unknown origin / 화인을 조사하다 inquire into the cause of the fire
화인 禍因 the cause [root] of evil [trouble, disaster] ♦화인을 남기다 sow the seeds of evil
화잠 花簪 a bride's ornamental hairpin; a bridal hairpin inlaid with jewels
화장 —長 〈소매 길이〉the length of a sleeve; the sleeve length
▶이 웃은 화장이 짧다 This coat is short in the sleeves. ⇒ This coat has short sleeves.
■—걸음 leisurely steps; a gentlemanly gait
화장 化粧 (a) makeup; (a) toilet; dressing
♦짙은[엷은] 화장 heavy [thin] toilet; a thick [light] makeup / 화장을 안한 얼굴 an unpowdered face / 화장용의 for toilet purposes; cosmetic; toilet / 화장 중이다 be at one's toilet / 화장을 고치다 touch up [adjust] one's makeup / 화장을 거의 안하다 wear little makeup / 화장을 마치다 finish [fix] up one's toilet; complete one's makeup / 화장을 지우다 remove one's makeup / 엷은 화장을 하다 powder one's face lightly; do a little makeup / 짙은 화장을 하다 paint one's face thick with makeup; wear (too) much makeup; be heavily powdered [made up]; be thickly painted
▶그녀는 눈물에 화장이 지워졌다 Her tears washed away the paint from her face.
▶그녀는 화장을 너무 짙게 한다 She uses too much makeup.
—화장하다 make up 《one's face》; put on makeup; make one's toilet; paint [powder] one's face
♦엷게 화장한 얼굴 a lightly-powdered face / 짙게 화장한 아가씨 a girl with a thick makeup; a painted girl / 화장하지 않아도 아름다운 여자 a woman who has natural beauty / 공들여 화장하다 give much time and care to one's toilet
▶그녀는 나이보다 젊어 보이려고 화장한다 She makes herself up to look younger than she really is.
▶그녀는 화장하는 데 한 시간이 걸린다 It takes her an hour to make herself up [put on her face].
▶그녀는 화장하면 몰라볼 정도로 예뻐진다 When she puts on makeup, she becomes so beautiful that you may not recognize her.
■기초— makeup base; a foundation —대 a dressing [toilet] table; (美) a dresser —도구 a toilet set —비누 《a cake of》toilet soap —수 (beauty) wash; toilet water [lotion] —실 a lavatory; a bathroom; a toilet (room); a rest room —지 《a roll of》toilet paper [tissue] —크림 facial cream
화장 火葬 cremation
—화장하다 cremate 《the remains》; burn 《the body》to ashes
▶시신은 화장되었다 The body was cremated

[burnt to ashes].
■—인부 a cremator; a burner at a crematory —장[터] a crematory

화장품 化粧品 cosmetics; a toilet article
▶월급 받아 봐야 몽땅 화장품값 밖에 안 돼요 My whole income goes just to cover my beauty expenses.
■남성용— men's toiletries ■—점 a cosmetic store

화재 火災 a fire; 〈대화재〉 a conflagration
♦누전으로 인한 화재 a fire started by a short circuit / 원인 불명의 화재 a fire of unknown origin / 화재를 감시하다 watch for an outbreak of fire; guard against fire / 화재를 당하다 suffer from [have] a fire / 화재로 집을 잃다 become homeless by fire / 화재를 일으키다 cause [start] a fire / 화재로 타버리다 be burnt in a fire; be destroyed by fire
▶겨울에는 화재가 많다 We have frequent fires in winter.
▶어젯밤 이 부근에서 화재가 났다 Last night there was a fire around here.
▶화재는 우체국에서 났다 The fire started [broke out] in the post office.
▶화재는 이내 진화되었다 The fire was soon put [brought] under control. ⇌ The fire was soon overcome.
▶다행히 그의 집은 화재를 면했다 Fortunately his house escaped the fire.
▶그 화재로 집 다섯 채가 타버렸다 Five houses were destroyed by the fire.
▶어제 화재로 두 사람이 타 죽었다 Two were burned to death by the fire yesterday.
■—감시인 a fire watchman —경보 a fire alarm —경보기 a fire alarm (box); a firebox; a signal box: 화재경보기를 울리다 sound a fire alarm; ring a firebox —예방주간 Fire Prevention Week —원인 the cause of a fire —현장 《rush to》 the scene of a fire

화재 畵才 talent for art; artistic genius

화재보험 火災保險 fire insurance
♦화재보험에 들다 insure 《a house》 against fire
▶그 집은 2억원의 화재보험에 들어 있다 The house is insured against fire for two hundred million won.
■—료 a fire-insurance premium —업자 a fire underwriter —회사[계약, 증서] a fire insurance company [contract, policy]

화적 火賊 bandits ⇨ 불한당(不汗黨)

화전 火田 a slash-and-burn field
▶그들은 화전에 메밀을 심었다 They planted buckwheat after they burned off the fields.
■—농업 slash-and-burn farming —민 slash-and-burn farmers

화전 火箭 an incendiary [a fire] arrow; a rocket

화전 和戰 1〈화친과 전쟁〉peace and [or] war
▶정부는 화전 양면의 대비를 하고 있다 The government is prepared for both war and peace.
2〈강화〉making peace
—화전하다 make [conclude] peace 《with》
■—양면 정책 stick-and-carrot strategy

화제 畵題 〈그림 제목〉the subject [title] of a painting; 〈시문〉a legend over [on] a picture

화제 話題 a topic [subject] (of conversation)
♦오늘의 화제 current topics; the topics of the day / 세간의 화젯거리다 be the talk of the town / 화제가 떨어지다 find one's topics of conversation exhausted; have nothing more to talk about
▶우리는 곧 화제가 궁해졌다 We soon ran out of topics of conversation.
▶그는 화제가 풍부한 사람이다 He always has an ample stock of topics.
▶그는 화제가 무궁무진하다 He has no end of things to talk about.
▶그 사건이 세간의 화제다 The event is the talk of the town. ⇌ The event has become the topic of our conversation.
▶화제를 바꿉시다 Let's change the subject.

화조 花鳥 〈꽃과 새〉flowers and birds; 〈새〉 birds flying about from flowers to flowers; 〈그림·조각〉a painting [sculpture] of flowers and birds
♦화조 풍월을 벗삼다 converse [commune] with nature

화주 火酒 hard [strong] liquors; (ardent) spirits; (美俗) firewater

화주 花柱 〈암술대〉(植) a style

화주 貨主 the owner of goods; a shipper; a consignor
♦화주의 손실부담 조건으로 화물을 보내다 consign goods at the owner's risk

화중 華中 Central China

화중지병 畵中之餠 〈그림의 떡〉an unattainable object; a prize beyond one's reach

화증 火症 〈울화〉fury; anger; (a) passion; ire
♦화증이 나다 get angry [mad]; lose one's temper; get out of temper

화집 畵集 a book of paintings; a picture album ♦피카소 화집 (A Collection of) Picasso Paintings

화차 貨車 a goods wagon [van]; (美) a freight car ♦화차로 (美) by freight; (英) by goods wagon [van]
■무개[유개]— an open [a covered] wagon; (美) a flat [freight] car ■—인도 (美) free on board (略 f.o.b.)

화창하다 和暢— beautiful; balmy; bright; sunny
♦화창한 날씨 beautiful [bright] weather / 화창한 봄날 a beautiful spring day

화채 花菜 honeyed juice mixed with fruits as a punch

화첩 畵帖 a picture album [book]; an album

화초 花草 a flowering plant; a flower ♦화초를 가꾸다 cultivate [grow] flowering plants
▶그녀는 정원에 화초를 많이 가꾸고 있다 She grows many flowers in her garden.
■—밭 a flower garden —장이 a flower man; a florist; a floriculturist —재배 floriculture; cultivation of flowers —전시회 a flower show

화촉 華燭 〈혼례〉a wedding; a marriage ceremony; 〈양초〉a colored candle ♦화촉을 밝히다 celebrate a wedding; hold a marriage ceremony
■—동방(洞房) the bridal room for the wed-

ding night —지전(之典) a wedding ceremony
화축 花軸 〈꽃대〉[植] a flower stalk; a floral axis
화친 和親 friendly relations; amity —화친하다 contract [form] a friendship 《with》; make peace 《with》 —조약 a peace treaty
화탁 花托 〈꽃턱〉[植] a receptacle; a torus 《pl. -ri》
화톳불 a bonfire; a split-log fire ♦ 화톳불을 놓다[피우다] make a bonfire
화통 [建] a cross groove at the top of a pillar
화통 火筒 a smokestack; a funnel
화투 花鬪 Korean playing cards; flower cards —화투하다[치다] play flower cards; play Korean cards
■—을 playing flower cards; card playing
화판 花瓣 [植] a petal ⇨ 꽃잎
화판 畫板 a drawing [drafting] board
화편 花片 a fallen petal
화평 和平 peace; 〈마음의〉 placidity ♦ 화평을 제의하다 make a peace offer; make an overture of peace
■—공작 a peace move —교섭 peace negotiations [talks]
화폐 貨幣 money; currency; 〈경화〉 a coin; 〈총칭〉 coinage
♦ 화폐의 교환가치 the exchange value of a currency / 화폐의 구매력 purchasing power of money / 화폐를 발행하다 issue coins / 화폐를 주조[위조]하다 mint [forge] coins
■ 대용— token money [coin] 법정— legal tender 보조— a subsidiary coin 본위— a standard coin 위조— counterfeit money ■—가치 the value of money; value of currency: 화폐 가치가 낮다 be low in monetary value / 인플레이션으로 화폐 가치가 떨어졌다 The value of money has declined because of inflation. —개혁 monetary reform —경제 monetary economy —교환소 an exchange house [shop] —단위 a monetary unit —법 the Coinage Act —본위 a monetary standard —소득 a monetary income —위조 coining —위조자 a coiner; a counterfeiter —유통량 the volume of coins in circulation; the amount of currency —제도 the coinage [monetary] system —주조 coinage; mintage
화포 火砲 a gun; a firearm
화포 花布 dark-blue cloth with white flower patterns; figured cotton cloth
화포 花苞 [植] a bract ⇨ 포(苞)
화포 畫布 canvas ⇨ 캔버스
화폭 畫幅 〈그림〉 a picture; a drawing; a painting
화풀이 火— venting one's anger [wrath]; letting off steam
♦ 화풀이로 out of spite
▶ 그것으로 어느 정도 화풀이가 되었다 That is some consolation to me.
▶ 그는 화풀이를 아내한테 했다 He vented his ill humor upon [his anger on] his wife.
—화풀이하다 give vent to one's anger; satisfy one's resentment [grudge]; vent one's anger; 〈口〉 let off steam
♦ 엉뚱한 사람에게 화풀이하다 snarl at a wrong person; vent one's anger without reason upon sb
▶ 그녀는 남편에게서 꾸중을 들으면 하인에게 화풀이한다 When scolded by her husband, she works off her vexation on her servant.
화품 畫品 artistic merit of a picture [drawing]
화풍 和風 a balmy [mild] breeze
화풍 畫風 a style of painting [drawing] ♦ 피카소의 화풍 the brush of Picasso; Picasso's brushwork
화피 花被 [植] the perianth; the floral envelope
화필 畫筆 a paintbrush; an artist's [a painter's] brush
화하다 化— change [turn] 《into, to》; convert 《into, to》; transform 《into》; be transformed
♦ 돌로 화하다 change [turn] into a stone; petrify / 타서 재로 화하다 be reduced to ashes / 죽어서 흙으로 화하다 die and turn to clay
▶ 마을은 잿더미로 화했다 The whole town was reduced to ashes [burned to the ground].
화학 化學 chemistry
■ 농예— agricultural chemistry 무기[유기]— inorganic [organic] chemistry 분석— analytical chemistry 실용— practical chemistry 열— thermal chemistry 응용— applied chemistry 이론— theoretical chemistry ■—결합 chemical combination; a chemical bond —공업 chemical industry —공학 chemical engineering —기구[기기] chemical instruments [appliances] —기호 a chemical symbol —기호법 chemical notation —무기 chemical weapons [arms] —반응 a chemical reaction —반응식 a chemical reaction formula —방정식 a chemical equation —변화 a chemical change —분석 chemical analysis —비료 chemical fertilizer —선(線) chemical [actinic] rays —식 a chemical formula: 물의 화학식은 H_2O이다 The (chemical) formula for water is H_2O. —약품 chemicals —요법 chemotherapy —요법제 a chemotherapeutic agent —자 a chemist —작용 chemical action —전 chemical warfare —제품 chemical goods [products] —조미료 chemical seasoning —처리 a chemical treatment —합성 chemical synthesis
화학섬유 化學纖維 chemical [synthetic] fiber
화학적 化學的 chemical ♦ 화학적 성질 chemical property / 화학적으로 추출하다 chemically extract [recover]
■—산소요구량 chemical oxygen demand (略 COD)
화합 化合 [化] chemical combination
—화합하다 combine 《with》
▶ 수소와 산소는 화합하여 물이 된다 Hydrogen combines with oxygen to form water.
▶ 질소는 수소와 화합하여 암모니아가 된다 Nitrogen combines with hydrogen [Nitrogen and hydrogen combine] to form ammonia.
■—량 chemical equivalent —력 combining power —물 a (chemical) compound
화합 和合 harmony; concord; union; unity
♦ 부부의 화합 conjugal [marital] harmony /

국민의 화합과 단결 national reconciliation and unity
▶부부 화합의 비결을 좀 가르쳐 주십시오 Please teach me the secret of harmonizing as man and wife.
—화합하다 harmonize 《with》; be harmonious; agree 《with each other》; be in accord 《with》
▶그 집안은 화합하여 살고 있다 The family live in harmony.
▶부부는 서로 화합해야 한다 Man and wife should live together in unity.

화해 和解 reconciliation 《between A and B》; amicable [friendly, peaceful] settlement; accommodation; compromise
▶그 분쟁은 화해가 되었다 The quarrel has been amicably settled.
▶양자간에 화해가 성립했다 A reconciliation has been effected between the two.
—화해하다 make peace 《with》; come to terms 《with》; be [become] reconciled 《with》; reconcile *oneself* 《with》; accommodate [compromise] 《with》
♦화해할 수 있는[없는] reconcilable [irreconcilable] / 화해시키다 conciliate; reconcile; make peace 《between》; mediate a settlement 《between》
▶그는 누이와 화해했다 He was [became] reconciled with his sister.
▶대통령은 양국을 화해시키는데 성공했다 The President succeeded in making peace between the two countries.
▶그들을 화해시킬 방법은 없다 There is no way of reconciling them.

화현 和絃 〔樂〕 a chord; a concord=화음

화형 火刑 (burning at) the stake; (fire and) faggot
♦화형시키다 burn *sb* at the stake; burn *sb* alive / 화형을 당하다 be burnt at the stake; be condemned at [to] the stake

화호불성 畫虎不成 failing to succeed in imitating another person

화환 花環 a garland; a wreath; 〈목에 거는〉 a lei
♦화환을 만들다 wreathe flowers into a garland / 화환을 목에 걸다 wear a wreath around *one's* neck / 무덤에 화환을 바치다 place [lay] a wreath at the grave.

화환어음 貨換— a documentary bill [draft]
♦화환어음을 발행하다 draw a documentary bill 《on》

화훼 花卉 〔植〕 a flowering plant ■—산업 floricultural industry —재배[원예] floriculture —재배가 a floriculturist —품평회 a flower show

확¹ 1 〈절구의 구멍〉 the hollow of a grain mortar ▶그 절구는 확이 넓다 The mortar has a large bowl.
2 〈돌절구〉 a stone mill [mortar]

**확² **〈갑자기〉 suddenly; 〈잽싸게〉 in a flash; alertly; 〈힘차게〉 with a jerk
▶그녀는 촛불을 확 불어 껐다 She blew out a candlelight.
▶그는 밧줄을 확 당겼다 He pulled the rope with a jerk.
▶불꽃이 확 타올랐다 The flames flared up.
▶벚꽃이 일시에 확 피었다 Cherry blossoms come out at once.
▶문이 확 열렸다 The door flew open.
▶바람이 확 불었다 There was a gust of wind.
▶개 한 마리가 확 달려들었다 A dog suddenly sprang at me.

확고 確固 firmness; determination
♦확고부동의 unshakable; unwavering
▶우리 회사에서의 그의 지위는 확고부동하다 His position in our company is absolutely secure.
—확고하다 firm; definite; resolute; fixed; steady; determined
♦확고한 신념 a firm [an unshakable] belief / 확고한 지위 a secure position / 확고한 태도 a determined [resolute] attitude / 확고하게[히] firmly; resolutely; determinedly
▶그의 결의는 확고하다 His resolution is firm [unshakable]. ⇒ He stands firm in his resolution.

확답 確答 a definite answer [reply]
♦확답을 얻다 secure [gain] a definite answer / 확답을 피하다 evade any definite answer / 확답을 주지 않다 give no definite answer; be noncommittal
▶장관은 확답을 피했다 The minister evaded committing himself in his answer. ⇒ The minister avoided giving a definite answer.
—확답하다 answer [reply] definitely; give a definite answer

확대 擴大 expansion; extension; enlargement; magnification; escalation
▶이 복사기는 확대 축소가 가능하다 This copying machine is capable of enlargement and reduction.
▶그는 법 규정을 확대 해석했다 His interpretation involved a stretching of the provisions.
▶대통령은 전쟁의 확대를 피하겠다고 약속했다 The president promised to avoid a wider war.
—확대하다 magnify; scale up; 〈퍼지다〉 spread; expand; 〈사건 등이〉 assume serious proportions 《…의 크기로 확대하다 magnify to the size of…
▶이 현미경은 물체를 1,000배로 확대한다 This microscope magnifies (an object) 1,000 times.
▶그는 연구를 새 분야에까지 확대시켰다 He extended his research into a new field.
▶내란은 더욱 확대될 전망이다 The rebellion is likely to escalate still further.
■—경 a magnifying glass [lens]; a magnifier —기(器) an enlarger —복사(물) enlarged photocopy —율 magnifying power; 〔寫〕 an enlargement ratio —회의 an expanded [extended] meeting

확률 確率 probability
♦확률의 법칙 the law of probability / …할 확률이 크다 there is every probability that [of]…
▶주사위를 던져 짝수의 눈이 나올 확률은 2분의 1이다 In tossing dice there is a fifty percent probability of an even number turning up.
■—론 a probability theory; a theory of probability

확립 確立 establishment; settlement
♦세계 평화의 확립 the establishment of world peace
―**확립하다** establish; build up; fix; settle
♦기초를 확립하다 set up a (firm) foundation / 명성을 확립하다 establish one's reputation / 방침을 확립하다 fix a policy
▶이 이론은 아직 학문적으로 확립되지 않았다 This theory is not yet scientifically established.

확보 確保 security; insurance; guarantee
▶다음 선거에서 20석 확보가 우리의 목표다 Our goal is to win twenty seats in the next [upcoming] election.
―**확보하다** secure; make good (one's position); ensure; assure; guarantee; maintain
♦교두보를 확보하다 secure [establish] a bridgehead / 안정성을 확보하다 ensure against risks
▶내 좌석을 확보해주시오 Please keep [save] a seat for me.
▶우리 당은 이번 선거에서 10석을 확보했다 Our party won ten seats in this election.
▶그는 호구지책을 확보하고 있다 He is secure of his livelihood.

확보 確報 a definite [reliable, confirmed] report; authentic [definite] news

확산 擴散 spread; dissemination; proliferation; 〔物·化〕 diffusion (of light, gas)
♦빛의 확산 the diffusion of light / 핵무기의 확산에 반대하다 oppose the spread of nuclear weapons
―**확산하다** spread; disseminate; scatter; proliferate; diffuse
■핵― spread of nuclear arms; nuclear proliferation: 핵 확산 금지조약 a nuclear non-proliferation treaty

확성기 擴聲器 a (loud)speaker; a megaphone; a speech amplifier; a speaking trumpet; 〈휴대용의〉 (美) a bullhorn
♦확성기로 말하다 speak through a megaphone; speak on [over] a loudspeaker

확신 確信 a conviction; a firm belief; assurance; confidence
♦성공에 대한 큰 확신 great confidence of success / 확신을 주다 carry conviction ((to, with)) / 확신을 얻다 gain confidence / 성공할 확신이 없다 be not confident of success
▶이것만큼은 확신을 가지고 말할 수 있다 This much I can say with certainty.
▶충분한 확신을 가지고 그를 추천합니다 I recommend him with every confidence.
▶나는 그가 살아있다는 확신을 굳혔다 I was confirmed in my belief that he was alive.
―**확신하다** believe firmly; be convinced [confident] ((of, that)); be sure ((of)); feel certain ((of, that)); have a firm belief ((that))
♦확신시키다 convince
▶우리는 승리를 확신하고 있다 We are sure to win.
▶나는 그가 결백하다고 확신한다 I firmly believe that he is innocent.
▶그는 신의 존재를 확신하고 있다 He is positive as to the existence of God.
▶그녀는 만사가 잘 될것으로 확신하고 있다 She is confident that everything will get on well.
■―범 a convinced crime

확실 確實 certainty; trustworthiness; reliability; authenticity; sureness
―**확실하다** 〈틀림없다〉 certain; sure; secure; positive; 〈믿을 만하다〉 reliable; trustworthy; 〈확정되다〉 definite
▶우리의 승리는 확실하다 I'm sure we'll win. ⇒ Our victory is a certainty.
▶그 보도는 확실합니까? Is that news reliable?
▶확실한 증거가 있다 There is positive proof.
▶확실한 것은 말할 수 없다 I cannot say for certain.
▶그가 성공할 것은 확실하다 He is sure to succeed.
▶그는 당선이 확실하다 His being elected is a sure thing. ⇒ He is sure to be elected.
▶확실한 숫자를 알고 싶다 I want to know the correct figure.
■―성 certainty; reliability

확실히 確實― certainly; surely; for certain; to be sure; positively; definitely; no doubt; doubtlessly; beyond doubt; decidedly
♦확실히 하다 ensure; make sure ((of))
▶그녀는 확실히 별난 여자다 She is a funny girl, and that's the truth.
▶그 병이 무엇인지 확실히 아는 의사는 아무도 없었다 None of the doctors were sure what the trouble was.

확약 確約 a strict [definite] promise
―**확약하다** promise positively; make a definite promise; give one's word ((to)); commit oneself ((to))
▶그 점은 확약할 수 없습니다 I cannot give you my word on the matter [for it].

확언 確言 a positive [definite] statement; assertion; affirmation
▶그녀는 확언을 피했다 She avoided making a definite statement.
―**확언하다** state [say] positively [definitely]; assert; affirm; commit oneself
▶나는 그가 거기 있었다고 확언할 수 없다 I cannot affirm that he was there.

확연하다 確然― definite; positive; sure; certain ♦확연히 definitely; positively; surely; certainly
▶그가 코치가 된다는 건 이제 확연히 드러난 사실이다 It's now definite that he will become the coach.

확인 確認 confirmation; affirmation; certification; validation
♦무효의 확인을 청구하다 〔法〕 call for the affirmation of the nullity of resolution
―**확인하다** confirm; affirm; certify; validate; identify; ascertain; make sure ((of, that))
♦사실 여부를 확인하다 ascertain whether [if] it is true / 사실을 확인하다 make certain of the truth of the matter
▶방에 아무도 없는 걸 확인했다 I made sure that there was nobody in the room.
▶그 남자의 신원을 확인할 만한 것은 아무것도

없었다 There was nothing to identify the man.
▶ 손님이 도착했는지 확인하기 위해 집에 전화를 걸었다 I telephoned home to make sure that the guest had arrived.
■ ―사항 items confirmed ―서 a (written) confirmation ―신용장 a confirmed letter of credit ―자 (法) a confirmer; an identifier ―통지서 a confirmation note

확장 擴張 extension; expansion; enlargement; aggrandizement; dilation
▶ 판로의 확장에 전력을 다합시다 Let's do our best to enlarge [extend] the market for our goods.
―확장하다 extend; expand; enlarge; aggrandize; increase; dilate
♦ 도로를 확장하다 widen a street / 사업을 확장하다 expand [extend] business / 판로를 확장하다 extend the market 《for》
▶ 사업을 확장하고 싶다 I want to expand my business.
▶ 그녀는 가게를 확장할 계획을 하고 있다 She is planning to enlarge the store.
■ 군비― the expansion of armaments 영토― territorial expansion: 영토확장론자 an expansionist ■ ―공사 extension work ―기(器) (醫) a dilator

확전 擴戰 escalation (of the war) ―확전하다 escalate

확정 確定 decision; settlement
♦ 확정적인 definite / 확정적으로 definitely; conclusively
▶ 그의 승진은 거의 확정적이다 It is almost definite [certain] that he will be promoted.
―확정하다 decide upon 《a matter》; settle; fix; confirm
♦ 확정되다 be decided 《upon》; be settled; become definite [certain]; be fixed 《upon》
▶ 그들은 4층 건물을 짓기로 확정했다 They decided on a four-story building.
▶ 파티 날짜가 확정됐습니까? Has the day [date] for the party been set [fixed] yet?
▶ 방침은 아직 확정되지 않았다 The course to be taken is not yet decided upon.
▶ 날짜가 확정되면 알려 드리겠습니다 I'll let you know when the date is fixed.
■ ―사항 a definitely settled matter ―신고 a final return [declaration]: 소득세 확정신고(서) a final income tax return 《for the year》 ―안 a final draft ―일자 a fixed date ―주문 a firm order ―판결 (法) an irrevocable judgment

확증 確證 a sure [positive] proof; conclusive evidence; corroboration; confirmation
♦ 확증적(인) confirmatory; corroborative / 확증을 잡다 secure positive evidence 《of》
▶ 그가 유죄라는 확증은 없다 There is no positive proof that he is guilty. ≒ We have no conclusive evidence of his being guilty.
―확증하다 prove [show] positively; corroborate; confirm; verify; give positive proof of; be corroborative of
▶ 그의 이론이 맞는다는 것은 실험에 의해 확증되었다 The validity of his theory was confirmed experimentally.

확집 確執 〈주장을 고집함〉 adherence to one's own opinion
―확집하다 adhere [stick, cling] to one's own opinion [view]

확청 廓淸 purification; expurgation; a purge; a cleanup ―확청하다 purify; purge; expurgate; clean up

확충 擴充 (an) expansion; (an) amplification; (論) distribution; (物) generalization
♦ 생산력 확충 the expansion of productivity
―확충하다 expand; amplify
♦ 교육 시설을 확충하다 expand [enlarge] educational facilities

확호 確乎 firmly; determinedly
―확호하다 firm; determined; inflexible

확확 1 〈바람·연기 등이〉 with great puffs; with [in] gusts
♦ 바람이 확확 불다 have gust after gust of wind / 연기를 확확 내뿜다 send out puffs of smoke
2 〈불길이〉 briskly; in flare-ups; in blazes; 〈햇볕이〉 broilingly; scorchingly
♦ (불이) 확확 타오르다 burn hot [briskly, furiously]
3 〈손으로〉 strongly; with jerks
♦ 확확 당기다 pull [drag] sth with jerk / 확확 밀다 push with jerks

환 〈마구 그린 그림〉 a poor drawing; a wretched painting; a daub ♦ 환(을) 치다 draw [paint] poorly; daub

환 丸 a pill ⇨ 환약

환 換 a money order; exchange; (商) transfer
♦ 10만원을 환으로 송금하다 remit 100,000 won by money order / 아무에게 20만원의 환을 치결하다 draw a money order on sb for 200,000 won / 환을 현금으로 바꾸다 have a money order cashed
■ 내국― domestic exchange 소액― a postal note 송금― remittance by draft 외국― foreign exchange 우편― a postal money order 원[달러]― won [dollar] exchange 전신― a telegraphic transfer ■ ―관리 (商) exchange control ―관리법 the Exchange Control Law ―발행인 a drawer ―수취인 a payee ―시장 an exchange market ―어음 a bill of exchange: 외국 환어음 a foreign bill of exchange

환 環 〈고리〉 a ring

환가 換價 conversion (into money); realization
―환가하다 convert into money; cash; sell; realize
♦ 재산을 환가하다 realize property
■ ―불능자산 unrealizable assets ―성 marketability ―율 a conversion rate ―하중 (空) payload

환각 幻覺 a hallucination; an illusion
♦ 환각을 일으키다 hallucinate; have hallucinations
■ ―예술[음악] psychedelic art [music] ―제(劑) a hallucinogen ―제 상용자 a psychedelic ―증(상) hallucinosis

환갑 還甲 〈회갑〉 the 60th anniversary of one's birth; one's 60th birthday
■ ―노인 an old person of sixty; a sexagenar-

ian —잔치 a banquet on *one's* 60th birthday

환경 環境 environment; surroundings; circumstances

♦ 환경의 변화 a change in *one's* circumstances / 환경의 영향 the influence of environment / 건전한 환경 healthy surroundings / 환경에 지배되다 be influenced by *one's* environment / 환경에 순응하다 adapt *oneself* to circumstances / 좋은 가정 환경에서 자라다 be raised [brought up] in a perfect home environment

▶ 우리 학교는 조용하고 좋은 환경에 있다 Our school has a nice quiet environment.

▶ 그녀는 새로운 환경에 쉽게 적응한다 She can adapt herself readily to new surroundings.

▶ 사람은 환경에 좌우되기 쉽다 A man is easily influenced by his surroundings. ⇒ Man is a creature of circumstances.

▶ 너는 새로운 환경에 순응하지 않으면 안된다 You have to adapt yourself to the new environment.

■ 가정— home environment 사회— social environment 생활— *one's* living environment 자연— natural environment ■ —공학 environmental engineering —교육 education from *one's* environment —권 the right to protect [preserve] *one's* environment —기준 an environmental standard —문제 an environmental problem —보전 environmental safeguard —보전운동 ecoactivity —보호 environmental protection [conservation]; the protection of environment —보호론자 an environmentalist —보호운동가 a Green; a green activist; an ecoactivist —부 the Ministry of Environment —오염 environmental pollution —위생 environmental hygiene [sanitation] —의학 environmental medicine —친화 ecofriendliness —친화국 an ecofriendly nation —친화사회 an ecofriendly society —친화정책 an ecofriendly policy —파괴 environmental disruption

환곡 換穀 the exchange of cereals [grain]
—환곡하다 exchange cereals [grain]

환골탈태 換骨奪胎 being recasted; becoming beautiful —환골탈태하다 become beautiful; be adapted wonderfully; be recasted

환관 宦官 〈내시〉 a eunuch

환국 還國 returning home from abroad ⇨ 귀국(歸國)

환군 還軍 withdrawal of troops
—환군하다 withdraw troops 《from》

환궁 還宮 return(ing) to the Royal Palace
—환궁하다 return to the Royal Palace

환금 換金 1 〔商〕〈물건의 현금화〉 realization; conversion 《of goods》 into money
—환금하다 realize; convert 《goods》 into money; cash 《a check》

♦ 증권을 환금하다 realize *one's* securities

▶ 저 외국인이 여행자 수표를 환금하고 싶답니다 That foreigner wants to have his traveler's check cashed.

2 〈환전〉 exchange
—환금하다 exchange
■ —작물 a cash crop

환급 還給 refund ⇨ 환불

환기 喚起 awakening; evocation
—환기하다 awaken; rouse; arouse; excite; evoke

♦ 여론을 환기하다 rouse [stir up, excite] public opinion / 주의를 환기하다 call *sb's* attention 《to》

환기 換氣 ventilation; a change of air

♦ 창을 열어 환기를 하다 open the windows to let fresh air in / 환기가 잘 되다[안되다] be well [badly, ill] ventilated

▶ 이렇게 환기가 안되는 방에서 잘도 지내는 구나 How can you stay in such an ill-ventilated room?

—환기하다 ventilate; air

♦ 방을 환기하다 air [ventilate] a room

■ —갱(坑) a ventilating shaft —장치(裝置) a ventilator; ventilation facilities [equipment] —창 a vent; a window for ventilation

환난 患難 trouble; distress; misfortune

환납 還納 return(ing) 《public goods》; restoration —환납하다 return; restore; give back

환담 歡談 a pleasant chat [talk]; a confabulation —환담하다 have a pleasant chat [talk] 《with》; confabulate 《with》

환대 歡待 a hospitable [warm, cordial, hearty] reception; hospitality; hospitable treatment; welcome

—환대하다 give *sb* a warm reception; entertain warmly; receive warmly [cordially]; treat hospitably

♦ 환대받다 be warmly received; be received cordially

환도 環刀 a military sword; a saber
■ —뼈 〔解〕 the hipbone

환도 還都 the return of the government 《to》; returning to the capital
—환도하다 《an evacuated government》 return; return to the capital

환등 幻燈 a filmslide; a color slide; a magic lantern ■ —기 a slide projector; a stereopticon —필름 a filmstrip —화(畵) a slide

환락 歡樂 pleasure(s); merriment; mirth; merrymaking; enjoyment; gaieties

♦ 인생의 환락 the pleasures of life / 환락에 빠지다 indulge in pleasure; give *oneself* up to pleasure / 환락을 쫓다 pursue [seek] pleasure; gather (life's) roses; lead a gay life

■ —가(街) an amusement center [quarter]; gay quarters

환롱질 幻弄— cheating *sb* by switching objects —환롱질하다 ⇨ 환롱치다

환롱치다 幻弄— cheat *sb* by switching 《objects》; switch 《objects》 while *sb* is unaware

환류 還流 a return current; a back flow; flowing back; (a) reflux

♦ 자금의 환류 the reflux of capital

—환류하다 flow back; return; be refluxed

▶ 미국은 해외로 유출된 달러를 환류시키려고 노력해 왔다 The U.S. has been trying to attract the return of the overseas dollars.

■ —냉각기 a reflux condenser

환매 換買 〈물물교환〉 barter —환매하다 barter; 《美》 trade; truck

환매 還買 〔商〕 redemption; repurchase; 〔證〕 covering ―환매하다 buy back; repurchase; redeem; cover shorts
  ■―계약 a repurchase agreement ―권 the right of repurchase; the redemptive right
환멸 幻滅 disillusion; disillusionment; disappointment
  ◆환멸을 느끼다 〈환멸을 느끼게 하다〉 disillusion; 〈낙담시키다〉 disappoint; be disillusioned; be disappointed
  ▶그의 불성실에 환멸의 비애를 느꼈다 I was sadly disillusioned at [with] his dishonesty.
  ▶나는 존경하던 지도자들에게 환멸을 느끼고 있다 I am disillusioned with the leaders I respected.
  ▶나는 그 진실을 알고 환멸을 느꼈다 I was disappointed when I learned the truth.
환몽 幻夢 a fantasy; an empty dream; a daydream
환문 喚問 〔法〕 a summons (*pl.* ~es)
  ―환문하다 summon (*sb* for examination)
환물 換物 conversion of money into goods
  ―환물하다 convert money into goods
환부 患部 the affected [diseased] part; the seat of a disease
  ◆환부를 차게[따뜻하게] 하다 cool (down) [warm (up)] the affected part
환부 還付 return; restoration; restitution; retrocession ―환부하다 return; give back; restore; retrocede; refund (a tax)
  ―금 a refund
환불 還拂 (a) refundment; (a) refund; (a) drawback; (a) repayment
  ―환불하다 pay back; repay; refund; rebate; reimburse
  ◆관세를 환불하다 draw back the duties paid / 대금을 환불하다 return the price paid
  ―금 a refund; a repayment
환산 換算 conversion; change; exchange
  ―환산하다 convert (won into dollars); change (into)
  ◆미터로 환산하여 calculated in terms of meters / 달러를 원으로 환산하다 convert dollars into won / 에이커를 제곱킬로미터로 환산하다 turn acres into square kilometers
  ▶그것은 원으로 환산하면 얼마가 됩니까? How much is it in won [Korean money]?
  ▶그의 작품을 돈으로 환산할 수는 없다 His work cannot be calculated in (terms of) money.
  ■―율 the exchange rate ―표 a conversion table
환상 幻想 a fantasy; an illusion; a vision; a (day)dream; a reverie; a phantasm
  ◆즐거운 환상 a sweet illusion / 환상적인 음악 dreamy music / 환상적인 visionary; dreamy / 환상에서 깨어나다 wake from *one's* reverie
  ■―가 a fantast; an illusionist; a dreamer ―곡 a fantasy; a fantasia
환상 幻像 a phantom; a phantasm; a vision; an illusion; an apparition ◆환상을 보다 see a vision / 환상을 쫓다 pursue phantoms
환상 環狀 a ring shape; annulation
  ◆환상의 ring-shaped; annular; loop; circular

  ■―도로 a loop [ring] road; 〈도시의〉 a belt-line avenue ―선 a loop (line); 〈美〉 a belt line ―성운 〔天〕 the Ring Nebula
환생 還生 〈되살아남〉 revival; resuscitation; renascence; 〈다시 태어남〉 rebirth; regeneration
  ―환생하다 revive; be resuscitated; be [get] reborn; be restored to life; be born again
환성 歡聲 a cheer; a shout of joy [jubilation]; a hurrah
  ◆아이들은 환성을 올렸다 The children shouted for [gave shouts of] joy.
  ▶그가 무대에 등장하자 관객은 환성을 올렸다 The audience cheered as he appeared on (the) stage.
  ▶갑자기 환성이 터져 나왔다 Suddenly a great cheer arose.
환속 還俗 return to secular life
  ―환속하다 return to secular life [to the laity]; quit the priesthood
환송 還送 sending back ⇨ 송환
환송 歡送 sending off; a send-off; a farewell
  ―환송하다 give *sb* a hearty [good] send-off; farewell
  ■―식 a farewell [send-off] ceremony ―회 a send-off [farewell] party: 김선생을 위해 환송회를 열다 give a farewell party in honor of Mr. Kim
환술 幻術 magic (arts); the black art; sorcery; witchcraft
환시 幻視 a visual hallucination
환시 環視 concentration of attention
  ◆중인(衆人) 환시리에 in full view of the public; in the presence of the whole company
  ▶그는 중인 환시리에 추태를 부렸다 He cut a ridiculous figure in public [with all eyes fixed upon him].
환시세 換時勢 the exchange rate ⇨ 환율(換率)
환심 歡心 good graces; favor
  ◆환심을 사다 win *sb's* favor; ingratiate *oneself* with *sb* / 환심을 사려고 알랑거리다 curry favor with *sb*; curry *sb's* favor
  ▶그녀는 나의 환심을 사려고 그랬다 She did it to win my favor.
  ▶그는 그녀의 환심을 사기 위해 모피 코트를 사주었다 He bought her a fur coat to win her heart.
환약 丸藥 a (medicinal) pill; a globule
  ◆환약을 만들다 make a pill; pill
환어음 換― a bill of exchange (略 B.E., B/E, b.e.); a draft
  ◆3천 달러의 환어음을 발행하다 draw a bill of exchange (on *sb*) for 3,000 dollars
  ■―일람불― a bill at sight; a sight bill 청구불― a draft on demand; a demand draft
환언하다 換言― say [put, express] in other words; put [say] in other way
  ◆환언하면 in other words; that is (to say); namely
환영 幻影 a vision; a phantom; a phantasm; 〔心〕 an illusion; a fancy; a fantasy; imagination
  ◆환영을 보다 see a vision / 환영을 쫓다 be lured by an illusion

환영 歡迎 (a) welcome; (a) reception; an ovation
♦ 환영 준비를 갖추다 kill the fatted calf / 따뜻한 환영을 받다 receive [get] a warm welcome / 아무의 환영회를 열다 give a welcoming party for sb; 〈정식으로 성대하게〉 hold a reception for [to welcome] sb / 환영의 말을 하다 say a few words of welcome 《to him》; give a welcoming address 《to him》; make an address [a speech] of welcome 《in honor of him》
▶ 환영 런던 교향악단 《게시》 Welcome! London Symphony Orchestra.
▶ 투고 환영 Contributions are cordially invited.
—환영하다 welcome; give sb a welcome; give a welcome to sb; receive warmly [favorably]; give the glad hand
♦ 따뜻하게[성대히] 환영하다 give a warm [hearty, cordial] welcome; receive sb with open arms / 대대적으로 환영하다 stage a festive welcome 《for》 / 신입생[신입사원]을 환영하다 welcome newcomers / 충고[제안]를 환영하다 welcome advice [a suggestion]
▶ 우리는 그를 환영했다 We welcomed him. ⇒ We gave him a welcome.
▶ 나는 크게 환영받았다 I was heartily welcomed. ⇌ I met with a cordial [friendly] reception.
▶ 언제든지 환영합니다 You shall always be welcome.
▶ 우리는 그들을 충심으로 환영했다 We welcomed [received] them heartily [cordially]. ⇌ We gave them a hearty [cordial] welcome.
▶ 그는 어디를 가나 환영받았다 He was welcomed wherever he went.
▪ —대— a hearty [cordial] welcome ▪ —만찬회 a reception dinner —사 《give》 an address of welcome 《in honor of》; a welcoming speech —아치 a welcome arch —위원회 a reception committee —자 a welcomer

환영회 歡迎會 a welcome [welcoming] party; a reception (dinner) ♦ 환영회를 열다 give [hold] a reception (dinner) 《in honor of》

환우 換羽 molting ⇨ 털갈이
▪ —기 the molting season

환원 還元 1 〈복귀〉 restoration; return
—환원하다 restore 《to its original state》; 〈환원되다〉 be restored to 《the former condition》
▶ 그 사업에서 생긴 이익은 사회에 환원해야 한다 The profit made from the business should be returned to the community.
2 〔化〕 reduction; 〈분해〉 resolution; 〈산화물의〉 deoxidization; deoxidation
—환원하다 be reduced 《to》; 〈원소로〉 resolve 《itself》 into its elements; 〈산화물을〉 deoxidize
▶ 화합물은 그 원소로 환원된다 The compound resolves itself into its elements.
▪ —력 reducing power —성불꽃 a reducing flame —작용 a reducing process —제 a reducing agent; a reducer

환율 換率 the (foreign) exchange rate; the rate of exchange
♦ 1달러 900원의 환율에서 at the exchange rate of 900 won to the (U.S.) dollar
▶ 당장의 급선무는 환율을 안정시키는 일이다 The pressing need of the hour is to stabilize exchange rate.
▪ 고정— a fixed exchange rate 대미(對美)— the exchange rate on the United States; the won-dollar rate ▪ —변동 exchange fluctuations —인상 a raise in the exchange rates —표 a list of exchange quotations

환자 患者 a patient; a sufferer; 〈특정한 병상의〉 a case; a subject 《of operation》; a client; 〈의사의 환자 전체〉 a practice
♦ 중증 환자 a seriously ill patient; a serious case / 절망적인 환자 a hopeless [fatal] case / 환자를 진찰하다 see [examine] a patient
▶ 저 의사는 환자가 많다 That doctor has a large practice.
▶ 에이즈환자가 늘어나고 있다 Cases of AIDS are increasing.
▶ 환자는 경과가 좋다 The patient is progressing favorably.
▶ 식중독 환자가 많이 생겼다 Many cases of food poisoning occurred.
▪ 내과[외과]— a medical [surgical] subject 무료— a charity-patient; a free patient 수술— a subject to be operated on; a surgical patient 외래— an outpatient 입원— an inpatient 콜레라— a cholera patient [case] ▪ —명부 a sick list

환장하다 換腸— become [go] mad [crazy]; go off [out of] one's mind; lose one's mind [reason] ▶ 그는 아주 환장했다 He's gone stone crazy.

환쟁이 a dauber; a wretched painter

환전 換錢 exchange (of money); money changing
—환전하다 exchange; change
▶ 이 만원권을 환전해 주십시오 Please change [break] this ten thousand won bill.
▶ 호텔의 현금출납원이 달러를 원화로 환전해 줄 것입니다 The hotel cashier will exchange dollars into won.
▪ —상 a money changer —수수료 a commission for exchanging money

환절 換節 〈철이 바뀜〉 a change of seasons
▪ —기 a change [turning point] of season: 환절기에 at the change [turn] of season

환절 環節 〔動〕 a segment; an annulated segment

환지 —紙 drawing paper

환지 換地 replotting; land substitution; 〈토지〉 a substitute lot ▪ —설계[지정, 처분] the design [designation, disposal] of replotting

환짓다 丸— make a pill; pill

환청 幻聽 an auditory hallucination

환초 環礁 an atoll; a coral island

환치다 daub; raw [paint] poorly [unskillfully]

환태평양 環太平洋 ▪ —구상 the Pan-Pacific Concept —지진대 Circum-Pacific seismic zone [belt] —화산대 Circum-Pacific volcanic zone [belt]

환택 還宅 returning to one's honored home; going home

환표 換票 1 〈표를 바꿈〉 change of tickets

2 〈선거에서의〉 switching of votes; voting irregularities
―**환표하다** switch ballots; commit voting irregularities

환표 換標 〔史〕 a bill of exchange

환품 換品 exchange of goods [articles]
―**환품하다** exchange goods

환풍기 換風機 a ventilation [ventilating] fan

환하다 **1** 〈탁 틔다〉 open; clear; unobstructed
♦ 환히 보이다 be open to the eye; be fully exposed to view
▶ 길이 환하다 A road is wide open. ⇌ A road is clear.
2 〈밝다〉 bright; light
♦ 환한 방 a well-lighted room / 환한 색 light color; bright [vivid] colors / 대낮 같이 환하다 be as bright as day / 환해지다 lighten; grow [get] light / 환하게 하다 brighten; lighten; light up
▶ 날이 환히 밝는다 The day dawns bright.
▶ 그는 환할 때 집에 돌아왔다 He went [came] home while it was still light.
▶ 이 전등은 환하다 This lamp is bright.
▶ 그 여자는 환한 색의 옷을 입고 있다 She is dressed in bright (colored) clothes.
3 〈잘 생긴〉 fine-looking; handsome; bright; radiant
♦ 환한 얼굴 a handsome face; a bright [radiant] face / 환히 웃는 얼굴로 with a bright [cheerful] smile
▶ 그 소식을 듣고 그녀의 얼굴이 환해졌다 Her face brightened (up) to hear the news.
4 〈명백하다〉 clear; plain; evident; obvious; patent; explicit
♦ 환한 사실 a plain truth; an obvious fact / 환히 밝히다 make clear; clarify; manifest / 불 보듯 환하다 be as clear as day; be as plain as the sun
5 〈정통하다〉 know...very well; be familiar (with); be well versed (in); be well up (in)
▶ 그는 이 근처 지리에 환하다 He knows his way around here.
▶ 그녀는 사무에 환하다 She is well versed in business methods.
▶ 그는 법률에 환하다 He knows law very well. ⇌ He is familiar with law. ⇌ He is an expert [is a specialist, is at home] in law.
▶ 그는 그 방면에는 환하다 He is in the know about it.

환향 還鄕 return(ing) home; return to one's native place ―**환향하다** go [come] home; return (to one's old) home
■ 금의(錦衣)― returning home loaded with honors; returning home in glory

환형 環形 a ring shape
♦ 환형의 looped; ring-shaped
■ ―동물 an annelid; Annelida

환호 歡呼 a cheer; an acclamation
♦ 환호 속에 amid (hearty) cheers
―**환호하다** cheer; give cheers; shout for joy; acclaim
▶ 관중은 열광적으로 환호했다 The spectators cheered wildly.
▶ 많은 사람이 그 영웅을 환호하여 맞이했다 Thousands of people hailed the hero.
■ ―성 a shout of joy; a cheer: 환호성을 올리다 give a shout of joy; shout for joy; send up rousing cheers

환희 歡喜 (great) joy; delight; gladness; glee; ecstasy

활 **1** 〈무기〉 a bow; 〈궁술〉 archery
♦ 활과 화살 bow and arrow / 활을 쏘다 shoot an arrow / 활로 쏘다 shoot with a bow (and arrow) / 활에 화살을 메기다 put [fix] an arrow to the bow / 활에 시위를 걷다 string a bow / 활을 잔뜩 잡아당기다 draw a bow to the full
▶ 그는 활의 명수다 He is a good archer.
2 〈현악기의〉 a (fiddle) bow ♦ 활쓰기 bowing / 활을 켜다 manage the bow (in playing a violin); bow
3 〈무명활〉 a bow

활강 滑降 〔스키〕 a descent
■ ―경기 downhill (competition) ―선수 a downhiller

활개 **1** 〈새의 날개〉 the wings of a bird
♦ 활개치다 flap [beat] the wings; flutter
2 〈사람의 양팔〉 one's arms; one's limbs
♦ 활개치며 걷다 walk swinging one's arms / 네 활개치다 walk with a swaggering gait; strut; swagger about

활갯짓 swinging one's arms in walking; swagger; strut ―**활갯짓하다** swing one's arms; swagger; strut

활고자 the ends of a bow

활공 滑空 〔空〕 gliding; a glide; a volplane
―**활공하다** glide; volplane
■ ―각 gliding angle ―거리 a gliding distance ―경로 glide path [slope] ―기 a glider ―비행 gliding flight ―속도 gliding speed

활극 活劇 a stormy fighting scene; 〈영화〉 an action film [picture, movie]; an action-packed drama
♦ 활극을 벌이다 make a scene; enact a stormy scene
■ 서부― a Western (film); (口) a horse opera

활기 活氣 vigor; energy; spirit; liveliness; animation; activity
♦ 활기 있는 active; vigorous; lively / 활기 없는 inactive; dull; spiritless / 활기있는 청년 a young man full of vigor [life]; a lively young man / 활기 있는 토론 a spirited [an animated] debate / 활기 있는 시장 an active market / 활기 없는 생활 a dull life / 활기찬 도시 a city vibrant with life and energy / 활기를 띠다 become active [enlivened]; liven [brighten, quicken] up; grow lively / 활기를 띠게 하다 give life to; animate; activate; enliven
▶ 그는 언제나 활기에 넘쳐 있다 He is always full of vigor [life].
▶ 거리는 쇼핑객으로 활기를 띠고 있었다 The streets were busy [alive] with shoppers.
▶ 이 도시에는 활기가 없다 There is little life in this town. ⇌ This town looks dull.
▶ 장사가 활기를 띠어 가고 있다 The business is quickening up [becoming brisk].
▶ 그녀의 출현은 파티에 활기를 띠게 했다 Her

appearance animated the party.

활꼴 〔數〕 cresent; segment ■ **—각** angle of segment

활달 豁達 generosity; magnanimity; liberality **—활달하다** generous; magnanimous; liberal; broad-minded
♦ 활달한 태도 broad-minded manners; a spirit of generosity

활대 〈돛의〉 a (sail) yard; a stick

활동 活動 〈활약〉 activity; action; 〈작업〉 a operation; 〈기능〉 function; working
♦ 구조 활동을 하다 carry out a rescue operation / 학급[클럽] 활동을 하다 take part in classroom [club] activities
▶ 그는 활동 범위가 넓다 He is active in many areas.
▶ 구조 활동은 밤새 계속되었다 The rescue operation continued throughout the night.
▶ 그는 한때 정치적 활동을 했다 He was once involved in political activities.
▶ 화산이 다시 활동을 개시했다 The volcano has become active again.
—을하다 be active; work; lead an active life; play [take] an active part (in); (口) be on the go; function
▶ 배구는 전신을 활동시키는 스포츠다 Volleyball is a sport that exercises the whole body.
■ **과외—** extracurricular (activities): (학교에서) 과외활동을 하다 take part in extracurricular activities **교내—** school activities; classroom activities **정신—** mental activity **정치—** political activities ■ **—가** an active [energetic] person; a man of action [energy]; an activist; (口) a go-getter; (美口) a rustler **—력** energy; vitality **—무대** one's field [stage] of action [activity] **—분야** one's sphere [field] of activity **—사진** motion picture; moving picture **—전류** action current **—전위** action potential

활동적 活動的 energetic; active; dynamic; (美口) rustling; go-getting
▶ 그 여자는 활동적인 여성이다 She is an active [energetic] woman.

활딱 1 〈벗어진 모양〉 clear(ly); completely; entirely
♦ 머리가 활딱 벗어지다 get all bald and shiny on top / 옷을 활딱 벗기다 strip sb of all (his) clothes; strip sb naked
2 〈끓어 넘치는 모양〉 overflowing; boiling

활량 1 〈활 쏘는 사람〉 an archer
2 〈무위도식자〉 an idler; a drone; 〈난봉꾼〉 a prodigal; a playboy; 〈협협한 사람〉 an open-handed man

활력 活力 vitality; vital power; energy
▶ 그 선생은 활력이 넘쳐 있었다 The teacher was full of vitality.
—설 〔哲〕 vitalism **—소** a tonic; a vitamin

활로 活路 a means of escape; a way out (of the difficulty)
♦ 활로를 찾다[열다] find a means of escape (from); find a way (out of); cut one's way (through)

활무대 活舞臺 a sphere of activity; the field of action

활물 活物 a living being [creature]
■ **—기생**(寄生) 〔生〕 a parasitism on living things

활발 活潑 liveliness; activity; briskness; sprightliness; vivacity; animation
—활발하다 active; lively; animated; brisk; sprightly
♦ 동작이 활발하다 be brisk [quick] in one's movement; move briskly [quickly] / 활발해지다 be enlivened; become active / 활발하게 actively; briskly; lively; with animation / 활발하게 움직이다 move lively [briskly]
▶ 그 그룹은 활발히 활동하고 있다 The group is now very active.
▶ 그 애는 여자아이치고 너무 활발하다 She is too active for a girl.
▶ 그 소년은 동작이 활발하다[활발하지 않다] The boy is quick [slow] in action.
▶ 시황[시장]은 활발해졌다 The market has been brisk [active].
▶ 그들은 활발하게 토론을 했다 They had a lively [an animated] discussion.

활보하다 闊步— stride; stalk; strut; swagger; walk with a swaggering gait
♦ 거리를 활보하다 strut down [stride along] a street

활불 活佛 1 〈생불〉 a living Buddha; an incarnation of Buddha
2 〈라마교의 수장〉 the grand Lama

활빈당 活貧黨 chivalrous robbers; (a band of) Robin Hoods

활빙 滑氷 skating **—활빙하다** skate (on the ice); do skating

활살 活殺 life and death ⇨ 생살(生殺)

활석 滑石 〔鑛〕 talc; talcum
■ **—가루** talcum (powder)

활성 活性 〔化〕 activity
♦ 활성의 active; activated / 비활성의 inert / 계면(界面)활성제 a surface active agent
■ **—부위** 〔生化〕 active site **—비타민제** an activated vitamin preparation **—오니** activated sludge **—탄** active carbon **—화 상태** activated state **—화에너지** activated energy

활수하다 滑手— liberal; generous; open-handed; have an open hand
▶ 아내는 씀씀이가 활수하다 My wife is free with her money.

활시위 a string; a bowstring ♦ 활시위를 메우다[풀다] string [unstring] a bow

활안 活眼 〈사리를 밝게 보는 눈〉 a quick eye; piercing [penetrating] eyes; insight

활액 滑液 〔解〕 synovia
■ **—낭**(囊) a bursa 《pl. ~s, -sae》

활약 活躍 activity; action
—활약하다 be active (in); take [play] an active part (in); participate actively (in); be actively engaged (in)
▶ 그는 그 시합에서 대활약했다 He did a very good job in the game.
▶ 그는 실업계에서 활약하고 있다 He is active [plays an active part] in business circles.
▶ 그는 정계에서 활약하고 있다 He is active [a leading figure] in politics.

활어 活魚 live fish

활연 ―선 a live fish transport (ship) ―조 a corf; a crawl; a preserve; 〈어선의〉 a well

활연 豁然 1 〈탁 터진 모양〉 extensively ―**활연하다** extensive; open; wide; sweeping **2** 〈깨닫는 모양〉 with a sudden flash [burst]; in a flash
♦ 활연 깨닫다 be awakened with [come to] a sudden flash; a truth bursts upon *one*

활엽수 闊葉樹 a broadleaf [broad-leaved] tree; a latifoliate tree
■―림 a broad-leaved forest

활용 活用 1 〈응용〉 practical use; application ―**활용하다** put (the data) to practical use; take advantage of; make use of
♦ 기회를 충분히 활용하다 make full use [take full advantage] of the opportunity / 능력을 최대한으로 활용하다 make the best use [make the most] of *one's* talents / 자료를 활용하다 put the data to practical use / 인재를 활용하다 put the right man in the right place
2 〈文法〉 〈동사의 어미변화〉 conjugation; 〈어미의〉 inflection; 〈격변화〉 declension ―**활용하다** conjugate; inflect; decline
♦ 〈동사가〉 활용되다 be conjugated
■―어 an inflected [inflective] word ―형 conjugation (of verbs)

활유어 蛞蝓魚 〈動〉 〈창고기〉 a lancelet; an amphioxus (*pl.* -oxi, ~es)

활인화 活人畵 a living picture; (프) a tableau vivant

활자 活字 (a) printing type; (총칭) type
♦ 큰 [작은] 활자로 인쇄한 책 a book in large [small] print / 작은 활자로 짜다 set up in small type / 활자로 인쇄되다 be printed by movable type
▶ 이 사전의 활자는 아주 선명하다 The printing type in this dictionary is very clear.
▶ 의사는 내게 가는 활자는 읽지 말라고 했다 The doctor told me not to read fine print.
■―고딕― Gothic type (face) 볼드― boldface; fullface 악보― a font of music type 1호― No. 1 type 포인트― point type 표음― a phonetic sign; a phonotype ■―금 type metal ―면 typeface ―본 a printed book ―인쇄 type-printing; typography ―주조 typefounding; typecasting ―주조소 a typefoundry ―체 print: 활자체로 쓰다 write in block letters ―케이스 a case ―화 printing; putting (a manuscript) into print: 활자화하다 print [put] (an article) in type; put into print / 그녀의 책은 아직 활자화되지 않았다 Her book hasn't been printed [in print] yet.

활주 滑走 gliding; a glide; 〈빙상의〉 slide; 〈비행기의〉 planing; taxiing
―**활주하다** glide; slide; taxi; volplane
▶ 비행기는 활주하여 이륙했다 The plane taxied and took off.
■―공중 gliding; volplane 선회― a spiral glide 이륙― a takeoff run 지상― 〈비행기의〉 taxiing; taxying 착륙― a landing run ■―각 a gliding angle ―기 a glider ―로 a runway; a runfield; an airstrip ―속도 planing speed ―지시 taxi instruction

활죽 the prop stick of a sail

활집 a bow case

활짝 1 〈한껏 열린 모양〉 wide(ly); broad(ly); openly; extensively
▶ 나는 창문을 활짝 열었다 I threw open the window.
2 〈날씨가〉 clearly; brightly
♦ 활짝 갠 하늘 a bright and clear sky
▶ 날씨가 활짝 갰다 It has cleared up.
3 〈웃음·꽃 등이〉 brightly; radiantly; happily
♦ 활짝 웃다 beam (upon, at); smile radiantly / (꽃이) 활짝 피다 bloom in all their glory

활차 滑車 〔機〕 a pulley; a block; a tackle ⇨ 도르래
■―신경 a trochlear nerve ―장치 (a) tackle; a whip; a pulley block

활촉 ―鏃 an arrowhead; the barb of an arrow

활터 an archery ground [range]

활톱 a hacksaw

활판 活版 printing; 〈활판술〉 typography
♦ 활판으로 인쇄하다 print with type
■―인쇄 type printing

활하중 活荷重 live load

활화 活畵 a picturesque [charming] scene

활화산 活火山 an active volcano

활활 1 〈부채질하는 모양〉 briskly; vigorously
♦ 활활 부채질하다 fan *oneself* vigorously
2 〈불타는 모양〉 in (fierce, tall) flames; in a blaze; vigorously
▶ 장작이 활활 탄다 Firewood burns vigorously.
▶ 벽난로에서 불이 활활 타고 있다 A fire is blazing in the fireplace.
3 〈새가 나는 모양〉 with great flaps of the wings
4 〈옷을 벗는 모양〉 (taking off) briskly
♦ 옷을 활활 벗다 slip off *one's* clothes

활황 活況 activity; briskness; prosperity
♦ 활황을 띠다 show (signs of) activity; present animated [brisk, lively] appearance; become active
▶ 거래는 활황이었다 The market was lively.

홧김 火― the influence of anger
♦ 홧김에 under the influence of anger; in a fit of anger [rage]; spurred by anger / 홧김에 술을 마시다 drink liquor in anger

홧술 火― liquor drunk in anger
♦ 홧술을 마시다 drown *one's* anger in drink; drink out of anger

홧홧 hot(ly); fierily; feverishly
♦ 얼굴이 홧홧 달아오르다 flush up (hotly); feel *one's* face burning / 몸이 홧홧 달다 be feverish
―**홧홧하다** (feel) hot; fiery; feverish
▶ 숯불이 홧홧하다 Charcoal burns hot.
▶ 술을 마셔서 얼굴이 홧홧하다 I feel my face burning from the drink.

황 黃 1 yellow ⇨ 황색
2 〔化〕 sulfur

황갈색 黃褐色 yellowish brown; light brown; tan; tawny ♦ 황갈색의 yellowish brown; tan; tawny

황감 惶感 deep [reverent] gratitude ―**황감하다** exceedingly thankful; deeply grateful

황겁 惶怯 awe; fear ―**황겁하다** afraid; awed;

awestruck; awestricken; frightened; fearful; 〈서술적〉 be filled with fear
황경 黃經 the celestial longitude
황공 惶恐 awe; fearfulness
　─**황공하다** awed; awestruck; awestriken; frightened; fearful; overwhelmed with awe
황구 黃狗 a yellow dog ─**신(腎)** the penis of a yellow dog ─**피(皮)** skin of a yellow dog
황국 黃菊 〔植〕 a yellow chrysanthemum
황금 黃金 〈금〉 gold; 〈돈〉 money
　◆**황금의 나라** an El Dorado / **황금의 gold**; auric; golden / **황금빛의 golden**
　─**률(律)** 황금빛의 ─**문서 the Golden Bull** ─**분할 the golden section** [mean] ─**빛** [색] a gold color; golden [bright] yellow ─**숭배 plutolatry**; mammon-worship ─**시대 the golden age**; 〈전성기〉 the palmy days: 그 때가 그 작가의 황금시대였다 The writer was then at his [her] zenith.
황금만능 黃金萬能 ◆**황금만능의** devoted to the pursuit of wealth; mammonistic
　▶**황금 만능이다** 〈돈만 있으면 귀신도 부린다〉 A golden key will open most locks. ⇌ Money makes the mare (to) go.
　─**시대** a mammonish age ─**주의** mammonism ─**주의자** a mammonist
황급 遑急 extreme urgency [haste]
　─**황급하다** urgent; pressing; hurried
　◆**황급히** hastily; in great haste; hurry-scurry / **황급히 귀가하다** hurry home
황기 黃旗 a yellow flag
황기끼다 ─氣─ be seized with fear; be overcome with fright; get intimidated [cowed]; get awestruck
황달 黃疸 〔醫〕 jaundice; icterus
　■**신생아**─ jaundice of the newborn ■─**환자** an icteric
황답 荒畓 a barren paddy field
황당 荒唐 absurdity; nonsense
　─**황당하다** absurd; nonsensical
　─**객(客)** a windbag; a braggart; a wild talker; an unreliable person
황당무계 荒唐無稽 absurdity; nonsense
　─**황당무계하다** absurd; nonsensical; fantastic; wild; fabulous
　◆**황당무계한 이야기** an absurd story; a cock-and-bull (story)
　▶**그의 얘기는 정말 황당무계하다** His story is quite a nonsense [absurd].
황도 黃道 〔天〕 the ecliptic
　─**경사** the obliquity of ecliptic ─**광 (光)** the zodiacal light ─**대** the zodiac ─**면** the plane of the ecliptic
황동 黃銅 brass
　─**광(鑛)** copper pyrites; chalcopyrite ─**도금** brass plating ─**색** brass yellow ─**전(錢)** a brass coin
황락 荒落 desolation; desertion; bleakness
　─**황락하다** desolate; deserted; bleak
황랍 黃蠟 yellow wax [beeswax]
　─**촉** a yellow-beeswax candle
황량 荒凉 desolateness; dreariness; bleakness
　─**황량하다** desolate; dreary; bleak; deserted; wild
　◆**황량한 벌판** a desolate plain; wilderness
황로 荒路 a rough road
황록색 黃綠色 yellow-green; olive
황룡 黃龍 a yellow dragon
황린 黃燐 yellow phosphorus; white phosphorus ■─**성냥** a lucifer [yellow phosphorus] match; a lucifer
황림 荒林 a deserted woods; a neglected grove
황마 黃麻 〔植〕 a jute ■─**자루** a jute [gunny] bag
황막 荒漠 wildness; vastness
　─**황막하다** vast; wild; desolate; waste; 〈넓다〉 extensive; boundless ◆**황막한 벌판** a vast wilderness; the boundless wilds
황망 慌忙 being in haste; rush; hurry; flurry
　─**황망하다** hurried; bustling; flurried
　◆**황망히** hurriedly; flurriedly; in a flurry
황망 遑忙 busyness ─**황망하다** very busy
황모 黃毛 〈족제비 꼬리털〉 hairs from a weasel's tail ■─**필** a writing brush made of weasel's tail hair
황무 荒蕪 wildness; barrenness; desolation
　─**황무하다** wild; waste; desolate; barren; uncultivated
황무지 荒蕪地 waste [wild, barren] land; a wilderness; a waste ◆**황무지를 개간하다** reclaim [break up] wild land
황민 荒民 famine-stricken people; famine sufferers
황반 黃斑 yellow spot; macula lutea
황밤 黃─ a dried-shelled chestnut
황비 皇妃 an empress; a queen
황사 黃砂 yellow sand
　■─**현상** sandy dust phenomena
황사등롱 黃紗燈籠 a yellow-gauze lantern
황산 黃酸 〔化〕 sulfuric [〔英〕 sulphuric] acid; (oil of) vitriol ◆**황산의 sulfur**; vitriolic / **황산을 뿌리다** throw vitriol (at, on, over)
　■─**구리** sulfate of copper; copper sulfate ─**나트륨** sodium sulfate ─**아연** zinc sulfate ─**암모늄[칼륨, 마그네슘]** ammonium [potassium, magnesium] sulfate ─**염(鹽)** a sulfate ─**지(紙)** parchment [sulfate] paper ─**철** iron sulfate; ferrous sulfate ─**화** sulfation
황새 〔鳥〕 a stork
　◆**뱁새가 황새를 따라가려 하다** try to do what is beyond one's capacity
황새걸음 the gait of a stork; a long stride
　◆**황새걸음으로 걷다** take [walk with] long steps [strides]
황새치 〔魚〕 a swordfish; a broadbill ■─**자리** 〔天〕 the Swordfish; the Dorado
황색 黃色 yellow ■─**신문** 〈옐로 페이퍼〉 a yellow paper [journal]; 〈총칭〉 the yellow press ─**인종** the yellow race; the Mongoloid ─**토** yellow soil
황석 黃石 yellow calcite
황설 荒說 an absurd story; (sheer) nonsense; a balderdash
황성 荒城 a ruined castle
황소 a bull ◆**황소같이 일하다** work like a horse ■─**자리** 〔天〕 the Bull; the Taurus
황소걸음 黃─ 〈황소의〉 the gait of a bull; 〈느

런〉 a snail's [slow] pace
♦황소걸음을 치다 walk slowly
황소바람 黃— a heavy draft (of air); a big blow
황송 惶悚 awe ⇨ 황공 ♦황송하게도 graciously; obligingly / 말씀드리기 황송하오나… May I humbly inform you that…?
황숙하다 黃熟— ripen yellow
황실 皇室 the Imperial Household; the Royal Family
황아 荒— 〈잡다한 생활 용품〉 variety goods; miscellaneous [sundry] goods; sundries; notions ━장수 a peddler of sundries ━전(廛) 〈가게〉 a notions [variety] store
황야 荒野 a wilderness; a waste; wasteland; wild land
♦황야를 헤매다 wander in the wilderness
황어 黃魚 〔魚〕 a dace 《pl. ~ (s)》; a chub 《pl. ~(s)》
황열(병) 黃熱(病) 〔醫〕 yellow fever [jack]; black vomit
황옥 黃玉 〔鑛〕 (a) topaz; 〈보석〉 true [precious] topaz
황위 黃緯 celestial latitude
황육 黃肉 beef
황음 荒淫 carnal excesses; sexual indulgence; dissipation ♦황음무도하다 lustful; dissipated and depraved
황의 黃衣 1 〈누런 옷〉 yellow clothes
2 〈누룩〉 wheat malt
황인종 黃人種 the yellow race ⇨ 황색(~인종)
황잡 荒雜 incoherence; desultoriness; looseness ━황잡하다 incoherent; desultory
♦황잡한 지식 unsystematic knowledge / 황잡한 주장 an incoherent argument / 황잡한 사고 방식 a loose way of thinking
황적색 黃赤色 yellowish red
황전 荒田 uncultivated fields; a deserted field; overgrown land [fields]
황제 皇帝 an emperor; an Imperial
♦황제의 imperial / 황제의 자리에 오르다 ascend [accede to] the throne; be raised to the purple
━신성로마— the Roman Emperor ━폐하 His [Your] Majesty the Emperor
황조 皇朝 1 〈황제의 조상〉 imperial ancestors
2 〈돌아가신 할아버지〉 one's own revered dead grandfather
황조 皇祚 the (imperial) throne
황조 黃鳥 〔鳥〕 a golden oriole
황조근정훈장 黃條勤政勳章 〈제2등급 근정훈장〉 the Order of Service merit, Yellow Stripes
황조롱이 〔鳥〕 a kestrel
황족 皇族 the imperial [royal] family; royalty; royal persons; a member of the imperial family
황지 荒地 wasteland; barren land; desert [desolate] land; a wilderness
황진 黃塵 1 〈흙먼지〉 dust in the air; 〔氣〕 a dust storm
2 〈속세의 일〉 the mundane affairs

━만장(萬丈) 《raise》 a cloud of dust
황차 況且 much more ⇨ 하물며
황채 荒菜 a dish of sliced ripe cucumber
황천 皇天 1 〈하늘〉 High Heaven; Heaven on High; god's Heaven
2 〈하느님〉 god; Heaven
▶ 황천은 굽어 살피소서 God [Heaven] be my witness! ⇌ So help me heaven!
━후토(后土) the gods of heaven and earth
황천 荒天 〈악천후〉 stormy weather
♦황천의 항해 a rough voyage
황천 黃泉 Hades; Sheol; the shades; the region [land] of the dead; the netherworld
♦황천길을 떠나다 leave this world; start on a journey to the next world
━객 a dead person: 황천객이 되다 join the majority; depart (from) this life; go down to the shades
황철광 黃鐵鑛 〔鑛〕 (iron) pyrites
황청 黃淸 yellow honey
황체 黃體 〔解〕〈난소의〉 a corpus luteum 《pl. corpora lutea》
━형성 호르몬 luteinizing hormone ━호르몬 corpus luteum hormone
황촌 荒村 a deserted [desolate] village
황치마 黃— 〈연〉 a kite which is white in the upper half and yellow in the lower half
황칠 黃漆 a yellow lacquer
황탄 荒誕 absurdity ⇨ 황당(荒唐)
황태자 皇太子 the Crown Prince; the Prince Imperial; the Heir Apparent to the Throne; 〈영국의〉 the Prince of Wales
♦황태자를 책봉하다 proclaim the Heir Apparent to the Throne
━비(妃) the Crown Princess ━전하 His Imperial Highness the Crown Prince
황태후 皇太后 the Empress Dowager; the Queen Mother
━폐하 Her Imperial Majesty the Empress Dowager
황토 荒土 barren land; a waste; 〈전쟁으로 인한〉 war-devastated land
황토 黃土 〔地質〕 loess; (yellow) ocher; löss; yellow soil
황통 皇統 the imperial line
♦황통을 잇다 accede to the throne
황파 荒波 raging waves; rough seas; a heavy [high] sea
황폐 荒廢 waste; ruin; desolation; devastation; dilapidation
━황폐하다 go to ruin; be devastated; be laid waste
♦황폐한 ruined; devastated / 황폐한 집 a dilapidated house / 황폐한 뜰 an utterly neglected garden / 황폐한 땅 desolate [desert] land
▶ 그 절은 황폐해져 있다 The temples lay in ruins.
▶ 그 지역은 전쟁으로 황폐해졌다 The area is war devastated.
▶ 전염병으로 그 마을은 황폐해졌다 Plague desolated the town.
━삼림— forest denudation
황포 黃袍 the imperial [royal] robe

황하 黃河 the Yellow River; the Huang He [Ho]; the Hwang Ho
황하다 荒— rough; careless; sloppy
♦황한 사람 a slipshod person
황해 黃海 the Yellow Sea
황혼 黃昏 dusk; twilight; gloaming
♦황혼에 on the dusky evening; in the twilight; at dusk; at twilight / 인생의 황혼기에 in *one's* twilight years
▶황혼이 되었다 Dusk fell.
황홀 恍惚 rapture; ecstasy
―황홀하다 enraptured; enchanted; fascinated; (be) in ecstasies [raptures]
♦황홀해지다 be in raptures [ecstasies] (over); be enraptured [entranced] (by, with, at); be carried away (by) / 황홀하게 하다 enrapture; enchant; fascinate / 황홀할 정도로 아름다운 bewitchingly beautiful
▶우리는 황홀해져서 그녀의 노래를 들었다 We listened to her song in ectasy [with rapture, spellbound].
▶그는 그 그림을 황홀하게 바라보았다 He gazed on the picture with rapture.
황화 荒貨 variety goods ⇨ 황아
황화 黃化 (化) sulfuration; (英) sulphuration; sulfurization
―황화하다 sulfurate; sulfurize
■—고무 vulcanized India rubber —구리 copper sulfide —물 a sulfide —물감 sulfur dyes —수소 sulfuret(t)ed hydrogen; hydrogen sulfide —알릴 allyl sulfide —암모늄 ammonium sulfide
황화 黃禍 〈황색 인종에 의한 화〉 the Yellow Peril
황후 皇后 an empress; a queen; an empress [a queen] consort
―폐하 Her (Imperial) Majesty the Empress
홰¹ 1 〈새장의 가로 막대〉 a perch; a roost
♦닭이 홰에 올랐다 A hen went to roost.
▶닭이 홰에 앉아 있다 A hen is on the perch.
2 〈새벽닭이 우는 소리〉 crow
♦닭이 두 홰 울었다 The cock crowed twice.
홰² 〈햇불〉 a torch; a flambeau (*pl.* -beaux, ~s)
♦홰에 불을 붙이다 kindle a torch / 홰를 들고 가다 carry a torch in *one's* hand
홰³ a clothes rack ⇨ 횃대
홰나무 a pagoda tree ⇨ 회화나무
홰치다 flap the wings; flutter
▶닭이 홰친다 A hen flaps its wings.
홰홰 〈계속해서 내두르는 모양〉 round and round (about); in circles
▶노인은 지팡이를 내게 홰홰 내둘렀다 The old man brandished a stick at me.
획 1 〈갑자기〉 suddenly; 〈잽싸게〉 quickly; with dispatch; nimbly
♦획 돌아보다 turn right round / 획 지나가다 pass quickly; flit (across the sky) / 몸을 획 비키다 dodge (a blow) nimbly / 모퉁이를 획 돌다 whip round the corner
▶딕은 창 밖으로 얼굴을 획 내밀었다 Dick popped his head out of the window.
2 〈힘차게〉 vigorously; with a jerk

♦획 던지다 throw [fling, hurl] *sth* at *sb* / 획 잡아당기다 pull with a (sudden) jerk; tweak; twitch; yank; give (it) a jerk / 팔을 획 뿌리치다 pull free from *sb's* grasp; jerk *one's* arm loose
▶소년은 내 손을 획 뿌리치고 도망쳤다 The boy tore himself away from my grasp.
▶그녀는 문을 획 열었다 She flung [threw] the door open.
▶어머니는 아이의 손을 획 잡아당겼다 The mother jerked her child by the hand.
3 〈때리는 모양〉 with a whack [swish]
♦채찍으로 획 갈기다 whack [give a whack] with a whip
획획 1 〈날쌔게〉 snap-snap; with dispatch; quickly ♦일을 획획 해치우다 finish *one's* job quickly
2 〈갑자기〉 swish-swish; fast; speedily
▶차가 획획 지나갔다 Cars zoomed by.
3 〈던지는 모양〉 flinging repeatedly
♦책을 획획 던지다 bang books away
4 〈뿌리치는 모양〉 with shove after shove; with jerk after jerk
♦획획 팔을 뿌리치다 keep jerking *one's* arm loose; keep shoving *sb* away with *one's* arm
횃대 a clothes rack; a clotheshorse
횃불 a torch; a flambeau (*pl.* -beaux, ~s); a torchlight; a link
♦횃불을 켜다 kindle a torch / 손에 횃불을 들다 carry a torch in *one's* hand / 횃불로 길을 밝히다 light *one's* way with a torch
―행렬 a torchlight procession [parade]
횅댕그렁하다 hollow; empty; deserted; look bare [empty, hollow]
♦횅댕그렁한 방 an empty room
▶가구가 없어서 방이 횅댕그렁하다 The room looks bare without furniture.
횅하다 1 〈서술적〉 be familiar (with); be well versed (in); be well acquainted (with); be well informed (of); know well (about)
▶형님은 영어에 횅하다 My elder brother is proficient in English.
▶그는 그 내부 사정을 횅하게 알고 있다 He is well informed of the inside facts.
▶그는 이곳 지리에 횅하다 He knows the lay of the land around here.
2 ⇨ 횅댕그렁하다
회 灰 lime ⇨ 석회 ♦회를 바르다 plaster
회 蛔 a mawworm ⇨ 회충
회 會 1 〈모임〉 a meeting; an assembly; a gathering; a party; (美) a get-together; a conference
♦회를 소집하다 call a meeting / 회를 개최하다 hold [have, give] a party; hold a meeting / 회에 참석하다 attend [be present at] a meeting / 회에 불참하다 fail to attend a meeting; be absent
▶회는 연 2회 회장이 소집한다 The meeting shall be called by the president twice a year.
▶회는 유회되었다 The meeting fell through.
▶회는 9시에 산회했다 The meeting broke up at nine o'clock.
2 〈조직〉 a society; an association; a club
♦문학회 a literary society [club] / 회에 가입

하다 join [enter] a society; associate oneself with a society / 회를 조직하다 form [organize] a society

회膾 〈생선회〉 slices of raw fish; sliced raw fish; 〈육회〉 minced raw beef
♦ 다랑어회 slices of raw tuna; sliced raw tuna / 생선을 회를 치다 slice raw fish; prepare sliced raw fish

회 回 〈횟수〉 a time; 〈경기의〉 a round; a game; (美) [野] an inning
♦ 1회 once / 2회 twice; two times / 3회 three times / 4회 초[말] the first [second] half of the fourth inning / 3회 승부 a match of three games / 경기가 회를 거듭함에 따라 as the game advances [progresses] / 회를 채우다 play the full game; finish the round
▶ 그는 동남아시아에 2,3회 다녀왔다 He has been to Southeast Asia two or three times.
▶ 그녀는 응시 첫회에 합격했다 She passed the examination on her first try.
▶ 다저스는 5회 말에 3점을 냈다 The Dodgers scored three runs in the second half of the fifth inning.
▶ 나는 몇 회나 거듭 해봤지만 실패했다 I tried again and again but I did not succeed.

회갑 回甲 one's 60th birthday

회개 悔改 repentance; penitence
―회개하다 repent (of one's sins); renounce one's former sins; be [become] penitent; reform oneself; turn over a new leaf
▶ 회개하면 죄가 사하여진다 Repentance wipes out sin.

회견 會見 an interview
♦ 회견을 청하다 ask for an interview (with)/ 회견을 허락하다 grant [give] an interview (to a journalist)
―회견하다 have an interview (with); interview; meet [(美) meet with] sb; have a talk with; give an interview to (the pressmen)
■공식[비공식]― a formal [an informal] interview 기자― a press conference : 기자 회견을 하다 meet the press; hold [host] a press conference 단독― a single interview; an exclusive interview (with) ■―기[담] an interview ―자 an interviewer

회계 會計 1 〈출납〉 accounts; finance 2 〈계산서〉 a bill; 〈지불〉 payment
♦ 회계를 하다 pay [(美) foot] the bill / 모든 회계를 떠맡다 pay all the expenses
■일반[특별]― general [special] accounts
■―과 the accounts [accounting] section ―관[원] an accountant; a treasurer ―보고 a treasurer's [financial] report ―사 a treasurer; an accountant: 공인회계사 (美) a certified public accountant (略 C.P.A.) ―사무소 a countinghouse ―서류 financial documents ―장부 an account book; a book of accounts ―학 accounting

회계감사 會計監査 auditing ♦ 회계감사를 하다 audit accounts ■―관 an auditor

회계연도 會計年度 a fiscal [(英) financial] year ♦ 1997 회계연도 the 1997 fiscal year; the fiscal year 1997
▶ 그것은 현 회계연도 예산에 들어있다 It is included in the budget for the current fiscal year.

회고 回顧 recollection; retrospect; retrospection; review ♦ 회고와 전망 retrospect and prospect / 회고적(인) retrospective
―회고하다 recollect; retrospect; look back (upon, over, at); recall; review (one's past life); pass (one's life) in review
♦ 학창시절을 회고하다 look back on [reminisce] one's school days / 전쟁을 회고하다 look back on the war; recall one's war days / 1980년대를 회고하다 review the 1980's
■―담 recollections; reminiscences ―록 reminiscences; memoirs ―장면 〈영화의〉 a retrospective shot

회고 懷古 yearning for the old days; retrospection
▶ 나이를 먹으면 회고적이 된다 When old, we are apt to think fondly of bygone days.
―회고하다 recollect [look back upon] the past; recall the old days to one's mind
■―담 reminiscences; recollections: 회고담을 하다 talk about old times; reminisce

회공하다 become hollow; get empty

회관 會館 a hall; an assembly hall; a clubhouse ■기독교청년― the Young Men's Christian Association [Y.M.C.A.] Hall 시민― the Citizens' Hall 학생― the students' hall

회교 回敎 〈이슬람교〉 Mohammedanism; Islamism; Islam
■―국 a Mohammedan country ―기원 the Mohammedan Era ―도 a Mohammedan; a Muslim [Moslem] (pl. ~(s)) ―사원 a mosque ―연맹 the Moslem League

회구 懷舊 retrospection ⇨ 회고(懷古)

회귀 回歸 a revolution; recurrence; [數] regression ♦ 회귀적인 recurring; recurrent; 〈주기적인〉 periodic
―회귀하다 revolve; recur
■―곡선 [數] a regression curve ―년 a tropical year ―대(帶) the tropical zone ―동맥 a recurrent artery ―무풍대 the calm zone of the tropics ―선(線) the tropics : 남[북]회귀선 the tropic of Capricorn [Cancer] ―열 [醫] recurrent [relapsing] fever

회규 會規 the rules of a society ⇨ 회칙(會則)

회기 回忌 an anniversary of sb's death
♦ 7회기 the seventh anniversary of sb's death

회기 會期 〈의회의〉 a session; a sitting; 〈기간〉 a term; a period
♦ 국회의 회기중에 during the session of the National Assembly / 회기를 연장하다 extend the session
▶ 국회는 현재 회기중이다 The National Assembly is now in session.
▶ 회기는 내월 말까지 연장되었다 The session was extended till the end of next month.
▶ 박람회의 회기는 3개월이다 The exhibition will remain open for three months.
■―연장 a prolongation [an extension] of the session

회담 會談 a conversation; a talk; a parley; 〈정식의〉 a conference
♦ 일련의 회담 a series of talks / 회담을 중단하

다[끝내다] cut off [wind up] a talk
▶ 회담은 두 시간 동안 계속되었다 The conference [talk] continued for two hours.
▶ 현재 회담중이다 Talks are now underway [in progress].
―회담하다 talk together; have a talk 《with》; 〈정식으로〉 have a conference 《with》; confer 《with》 ♦ 장시간 회담하다 have a long talk 《with sb》
■남북― a South-North talk; a conference between South and North Korea 본― full-dress [main] talks 비공식― an informal get-together 3국― a tripartite conference 실무― the working-level talks 여야(중진)― bipartisan conference (of key leaders) 예비― preliminary talks 정상― a summit(-level) meeting 평화― peace talks

회답 回答 a reply; an answer; a response
♦ …의 회답으로서 in reply [answer] to… / 아무런 회답도 없다 hear nothing in reply / 회답을 받다 hear (from sb) in reply; get an answer 《from》 / 편지의 회답을 내다 answer [reply to] a letter / 편지[전보]로 회답을 하다 reply by letter [wire] / 편지의 회답을 내지 않고 있다 leave a letter unanswered
▶ 지금까지 아무런 회답도 없다 So far I have received no answer.
▶ 바로 회답을 주시기 바랍니다 Please answer my letter by return of mail.
▶ 회답을 기다리고 있겠습니다〈편지문투〉I am looking forward to hearing from you.
▶ 회답이 늦어 죄송합니다 I must apologize for not answering you sooner.
―회답하다 reply 《to》; answer; give [send] a reply [an answer]
■―자 an answerer

회당 會堂 〈예배당〉a church; a chapel; 〈회관〉a hall; an assembly hall; a meeting house
▶ 청중이 회당을 꽉 메우고 있었다 The hall was packed to overflowing by the audience.

회독 回讀 reading in turn ―회독하다 read 《a book》 in turn

회동 會同 an assembly; a meeting; a gathering ―회동하다 meet (together); assemble; gather (together); have an assembly

회동그랗다 1 〈눈이〉wide-eyed with surprise 2 〈거리낄 것 없다〉carefree; 〈서술적〉be free from care
3 〈완결〉completely finished; completed
♦ 일을 회동그랗게 마치다 get through with one's work

회두리 the end; the finish; the last turn [round] ■―판 the last round

회람 回覽 circulation ―회람하다 circulate; read and pass on ■―문고 a circulating library ―잡지 a circulating magazine ―판 (pass on) a circular notice [bulletin]

회랑 回廊 a corridor; a gallery; an ambulatory; a veranda

회례 回禮 a return courtesy ⇨ 답례
회례 廻禮 a round of complimentary visits
♦ 신년 회례를 하다 make (a round of) New Year's calls
―회례하다 make a round of complimentary visits; pay social visits

회로 回路 1〔電〕a [an electric] circuit
♦ 회로를 열다[닫다] open [close] a circuit
2〈귀로〉the return way
■ 병렬[직렬]― a parallel [series] circuit 진공관― a vacuum tube circuit ■―접속기 a circuit closer ―차단기 a circuit breaker

회로 懷爐 a (portable) body warmer; a pocket heater

회록 會錄 the minutes ⇨ 회의(～록)
회뢰 賄賂 〈뇌물〉a bribe; 〈俗〉palm oil; 〈뇌물수수〉bribery; corruption ⇨ 뇌물

회류 會流 confluence; conflux ―회류하다 join; flow together; merge into one
■―점 a confluence; a junction

회마 回馬 〈돌아가는 편의 말〉a return horse; 〈말을 돌려 보냄〉turning sb's horse round

회매하다 neat and tidy; light
♦ 회매한 보따리 a light bundle

회맹 會盟 a league; a covenant
―회맹하다 league [band] together; form a league; enter into a covenant

회명 會名 the name of a society [an association]

회모 懷慕 longing; yearning; deep attachment
―회모하다 long [pine] for; yearn after; be sick for; miss

회목 the wrist or the ankle
회목 檜木 〔植〕a cypress; a white cedar
회무 會務 affairs [business] of a society
♦ 회무를 총괄하다 preside over the business of an association

회반죽 灰― mortar; plaster; stucco ♦ 회반죽을 바르다 plaster; stucco ■―칠[바르기] plastering

회백색 灰白色 light ash color; light gray
회백수염 灰白髓炎 〔醫〕poliomyelitis
회백질 灰白質 〔解〕gray matter
회벽 灰壁 a plastered wall
회보 回報 1〈회신〉a reply; an answer
―회보하다 send an answer; give a reply
2〈통명〉reporting
―회보하다 report to 《sb on one's work》; report one's mission (to)

회보 會報 a bulletin; a report; 〈학회의〉the transactions ■ 동창회― an alumni bulletin; 〈여학교의〉an alumnae bulletin

회복 回復・恢復 1〈원상으로의〉recovery; restoration; retrieval; rehabilitation
♦ 날씨의 회복 improvement of the weather / 질서의 회복 the restoration of order / 기적적인 회복 a miraculous recovery
▶ 그들은 평화의 회복을 기원했다 They prayed for restoration of peace.
▶ 나치 독일은 실지의 회복을 요구했다 Nazi Germany reclaimed its lost territory.
▶ EC의 경기 회복이 늦어지고 있다 The economics of the EC are slow to rebound [recover].
―회복하다 get back; recover (strength); regain 《one's reputation》; restore 《peace》; retrieve 《one's honor》; get over 《a loss》; repair 《one's energies》; make good
♦ 권리를 회복하다 redeem one's right / 시력을

회복하다 recover *one's* sight / 원기[세력]를 회복하다 resume *one's* spirits [sway] / 명예[신용]를 회복하다 retrieve *one's* honor [credit] / 황폐한 국토를 회복하다 redeem *one's* ruined country
▶ 경기는 곧 회복될 것이다 The economic situation will improve [recover] soon. ⇌ Prosperity will soon return.
▶ 나는 그와의 우정을 회복했다 I renewed [recovered] my friendship with him.
▶ 혁명이 실패한 후 질서는 급속히 회복되었다 Public order was quickly restored after the attempted revolution.
▶ 날씨가 회복되었다 The weather has improved.
2 〈건강의〉 recovery; recuperation
◆ 건강의 회복 the return [restoration] of health / 회복이 빠르다 recover (more) speedily / 회복이 늦다 be slow in recovery; make a slow recovery
▶ 나는 감기에 걸리면 회복이 더디다 I am slow in recovering when I catch cold.
—회복하다 recover (from illness); get well again; recuperate; be restored to health; recruit [regain] (*one's* health); get round
▶ 그의 건강은 빨리 회복되고 있다 His condition is speedily improving.
▶ 그는 이제 완전히 회복했다 He is now completely restored in health.
▶ 환자는 곧 회복될 것이다 The patient will soon come round.
▶ 그는 회복할 가망이 전연 없다 He is quite beyond recovery. ⇌ There is not a chance of his recovery. ⇌ He has no chance of recovery.
■ —력 recuperative power —실 〈병원의〉 a convalescent ward

회복기 恢復期 convalescence ◆ 회복기에 있다 be in the convalescent stage; be convalescent
■ —환자 a convalescent [recovering] patient; a convalescent

회부 回附 transmission; 〖法〗 return
—회부하다 transmit (to); refer (to); send (over) (to); forward (to); pass on (to); commit 《to》; 〖法〗 remit 《to》
◆ 의안을 위원회에 회부하다 refer [relegate] a bill to a committee / (의안이) 위원회에 회부되다 be submitted to a committee
▶ 그 사건은 하급 법원에 회부되었다 The case was remitted to a lower court.

회비 會費 a (membership) fee; dues
◆ 회비를 납부하다 pay *one's* membership fee [dues] / 회비를 징수하다 collect dues
▶ 클럽의 회비는 월 50,000원입니다 The monthly club dues are 50,000 won. ⇌ The monthly fee for the club is fifty thousand won.
▶ 회비가 미납되셨습니다 You have not paid the membership fee yet.
■ —미납자 one who has not paid the membership fee

회사 會社 a company (略 Co.); (美) a corporation; a firm; a concern
◆ 재정이 든든한 회사 a solid company / 회사에 가다 go to work / 회사에 근무하다 serve in a company; work for a company / 회사에 들어가다 enter a company's service / 회사를 설립하다[해산하다] establish [dissolve] a company / 회사 조직으로 하다 incorporate 《a business》; (re)organize into a company / 회사를 합병하다 merge companies
■ —동족— a family partnership 유령— a bogus company 자매— an affiliated company; an affiliate ■ —근무 service with a company —내규 company bylaws [regulations] —법 〖法〗 company law; (美) corporation law —업무 company affairs; the business of a corporation —원 a clerk of a company; a company employee; an office worker [man]; a white-collar worker —정관 the articles of association —중역[이사] a member of the directors

회사하다 回謝 express *one's* gratitude; tender *one's* thanks; make a present in token of *one's* gratitude

회상 回想 (a) recollection; reminiscence; retrospection ◆ 어린 시절의 회상 the recollections of *one's* childhood
—회상하다 recollect; reflect; retrospect; review; look back (up)on 《the past》
◆ 회상하건대 in retrospect / 과거를 회상하다 review the past; reflect on the past (days); look back into the past
▶ 그 노인은 젊은 시절을 회상했다 The old man reflected on his younger days.

회색 灰色 an ash color; gray [(英) grey] (color) ◆ 회색의 ash-colored; ashy; gray / 회색이 감도는 grayish; ashy
■ —분자 a wobbler —차일구름 an altostratus (*pl.* -ti)

회생 回生 a return to life; resurrection; resuscitation ◆ 기사(起死)회생의 묘약 a wonder [magic] drug to resurrect the dead
—회생하다 come to life again; return to life; revive; resuscitate

회서 回書 a letter of reply; a written answer

회석 會席 〈장소〉 a meeting place; a place of meeting; 〈모임〉 a meeting

회선 回船 〈귀항선〉 a return boat; a returning ship; 〈배를 돌림〉 turning a boat around
—회선하다 turn a boat around; 《a boat》 turn around

회선 回旋 rotation; revolution; 〖植〗 involution
—회선하다 rotate; revolve
■ —곡 〖樂〗 a rondo —교(橋) a swivel bridge —기중기 a rotary crane —운동 〖植〗 circumnutation —탑 a swinging pole

회선 回線 〖電〗 a circuit
▶ 회선 고장으로 통화를 할 수 없었다 The lines were cut [out of order], so we couldn't get through to each other.
■ 전화— a telephone circuit

회송 回送 sending back ▷ 송환

회수 回收 collection; recovery; retrieval; revulsion; withdrawal; 〈판 물건의〉 call-back; 〈은행권 등의〉 drawing in
◆ 자본의 회수 the revulsion of capital / 불량 제품의 회수 withdrawal of defective goods /

회수 불능의 채무 a bad debt; an irrecoverable debt
―회수하다 withdraw (coins, books) from circulation; collect; draw back; call in; retire; retrieve; reclaim 《disused things》
♦ 대출금을 회수하다 withdraw [draw in] loans; collect [call in] debts / 외상값을 회수하다 collect bills / 파손된 헌 지폐를 회수하다 retrieve soiled old bills from circulation
■ 통화― the withdrawal of notes in circulation 폐품― collection of waste materials; the recovery of disused things ■ ―일 〈우주선의〉 Recovery Day

회수권 回數券 a coupon ticket
♦ 50매의 회수권 a ticket of 50 coupons

회술레 回― 1 〈사람의〉 dragging *sb* around the street to expose 《him》 to public derision as a punishment 2 〈비밀의〉 circulating [parading, exposing] *sb's* secret

회식 會食 dining together; 〈군인의〉 mess
♦ 회식중이다 be at mess
―회식하다 dine together; dine 《with》; 〈군인 등이〉 have a mess 《with》; mess 《with》

회신 灰燼 ashes ♦ 회신으로 화하다 be reduced to ashes; be consumed by fire; be burnt to the ground; be burnt up to a cinder

회신료 回信料 postage for a reply; return postage ♦ 회신료로서 170원짜리 우표를 동봉하다 enclose a 170 won stamp for return postage [for a reply]
―선납 reply [answer] paid ―선납 전보 a reply-paid telegram; a telegram with the return charges prepaid

회심 回心 a change of heart; changing *one's* mind; 〈宗〉 conversion ―회심하다 change *one's* mind [heart]; be [get] converted

회심 悔心 remorse; repentance; penitence

회심 會心 congeniality; complacency
♦ 회심의 작품 a work after *one's* heart / 회심의 미소를 짓다[띠우다] have [smile] a smile of satisfaction; smile complacently; have a self-satisfied smile
■ ―지우(之友) a congenial [bosom] friend

회약 蛔藥 a medicine for expelling mawworms ⇨ 회충(~약)

회양목 ―楊木 〔植〕 a box tree; 〈재목〉 boxwood

회오 悔悟 repentance; remorse; regret
▶ 그녀는 자기의 어리석음에 대한 회오의 눈물을 흘렸다 She shed tears of remorse for her folly.
▶ 피고는 회오의 빛을 보이지 않았다 The accused did not show any sign of remorse.
―회오하다 repent 《of》; feel remorse 《for》; regret; become penitent
♦ 깊이 회오하다 be smitten with remorse

회오리바람 a whirlwind; an eddywind; a vertiginous wind; a cyclone; a 《whirling》 tornado (*pl.* ―(e)s); 〈美〉 a twister

회우 會友 a fellow member

회원 會員 a member 《of a society》; (총칭) membership
♦ 회원 자격이 있다 be eligible for membership; be entitled to the membership 《of》 / 회 원이 되다 become a member; enroll *oneself* as a member; join 《a society》 / 회원이 많다[적다] have a large [small] membership / 회원의 자격을 잃다[되찾다] lose [regain] *one's* membership / 회원을 모집하다 invite [seek] a membership / 회원을 500명으로 제한하다 limit the membership to 500 / 회원을 샤퇴하다 retire from membership
▶ 그 협회는 회원이 1,000명이다 The society has [enrolls] a membership of one thousand [has one thousand members].
▶ 아버지는 볼링 클럽의 회원이시다 My father is a member of a bowling club.
■ 보통[특별, 명예]― an ordinary [a special, an honorary] member 정― a regular member; a member in full and regular standing 종신― a life member 준― an associate member 찬조[유지(維持)]― a patronage [supporting] member ―국 a member nation ―명부 a membership list: 회원 명부에 올리다 enroll *sb* on the list of membership ―배지 a membership badge ―제[조직] the membership system ―증 a membership card

회유 回游 migration ―회유하다 migrate
■ ―어(魚) a migratory [wandering] fish

회유 回遊 an excursion; a circular trip [tour] ―회유하다 make an excursion [a circular tour] ■ ―선(船) an excursion boat ―열차 an excursion train; a roundtrip train

회유 懷柔 conciliation; pacification; appeasement; 〈매수〉 winning over
―회유하다 conciliate; pacify; appease; placate; bring *sb* over; 〈매수하다〉 buy [win] *sb* over
▶ 그를 회유하여 우리 편으로 만들었다 We won him over to our side.
■ ―책 (take) a conciliatory [pacification] measure [policy]; 《resort to》 an appeasement policy

회음 會陰 〔解〕 the perineum ■ ―부 the perineal region

회음 會飮 compotation; carousing ―회음하다 drink together; have a drinking party; carouse

회의 會議 a conference; a meeting; a council; a talk; 〈대회〉 a convention; 〈대표자 회의〉 a congress; 〈회기중인〉 a sitting; a session
♦ 회의중이다 be in conference 《with》 / 회의에 참석하다 attend a conference; join [take part in, participate in] a conference / 문제를 회의에 부치다 refer [submit, send] 《a matter》 to conference; lay [bring] 《a question》 before the council / 회의를 개최하다 hold [call] a council [conference, session]; sit in [go into] conference / 회의를 소집하다 call [assemble] a conference [a council]; convene [convoke] a convention
▶ 그것에 관해서는 몇 차례나 회의를 거듭했다 We have had many conferences on the matter.
▶ 회의는 어제 오후 1시부터 열렸다 The conference opened at 1:00 p.m. yesterday.
▶ 그 회의에서 전쟁 반대 결의안이 통과되었다 The meeting passed a resolution against war.

회의
▶ 오늘은 회의가 없다 There is no session today.
—회의하다 hold a conference [meeting]; confer (with); hold [go into] council; sit in council together
■ 가족— a family council [conference] 강화(군축)— a peace [disarmament] conference 국무— the Cabinet council [conference] 국제— an international conference 긴급— an urgent conference [meeting] 당무— an executive committee [meeting] 본— a plenary session 비밀— a secret conference 원탁— a round-table conference 전략— a strategy meeting 합동— a joint meeting —록 the minutes; proceedings —소 a meeting hall; an assembly hall —실 a council [board, conference] room; an assembly room —장(場) a conference hall; a council house —출석자[참가국] a conferee

회의 懷疑 doubt; skepticism; incredulity; unbelief ◆ 회의적인 skeptic(al); incredulous / 회의적으로 보다 take a skeptical view (of) —회의하다 doubt; be skeptical (of)
■ —론[설] skepticism —론자 a skeptic —파 the skeptics

회임 懷妊 pregnancy; conception ⇨ 임신

회자 膾炙 ◆ 인구에 회자되다 be in everyone's mouth; be on everybody's lips; become a household word; be well-known

회자정리 會者定離 Those who meet must part. ≒ We never meet without parting. ≒ We meet only to part.

회장 回章 a circular (letter) ◆ 회장을 돌리다 send (out) [issue] a circular (letter); circulate a letter

회장 回腸 〖解〗 the ileum ■—염 ileitis

회장 會長 the president (of a society); the chairman (of a committee)
◆ 회장의 직[지위] presidency; chairmanship / 회장이 되다 be elected chairman [president]; become chairman / 회장으로 추대하다 set sb up as chairman
▶ 언어학회는 김박사를 회장으로 모시고 있다 The philological society has Dr. Kim for president [is headed by Dr. Kim].
■ 이사회— 〈회사의〉 the chairman of the board of directors

회장 會場 the place of meeting; 〈터〉 the grounds; a site ◆ 회장에 넘치는 청중 an overflowing audience
▶ 회장은 어딥니까? Where is the meeting (going) to be held?
▶ 여기가 박람회장이 될 곳이다 This is to be the site for the exhibition.

회장 會葬 attendance at a funeral —회장하다 attend a funeral ■—자 attendants at a funeral

회저 壞疽 〖醫〗 gangrene ⇨ 괴저

회전 回電 a reply telegram ⇨ 답전(答電)

회전 回轉 (a) revolution; (a) rotation; 〈선회〉 (a) gyration
◆ 매분 백회전 100 revolutions per minute (略 100 r.p.m.) / 시계 방향과 반대 방향으로의 회전 counterclockwise rotation / 자금 회전을 촉진하다 quicken the turnover of the fund
▶ 이 장사는 자금 회전이 빠릅니다 In this business you can turn over capital quickly.
▶ 그는 머리 회전이 빠르다[느리다] He has a quick [dull] mind.
—회전하다 revolve; rotate; gyrate; turn [spin] round; go [move] round; 〈기계가〉 run ◆ 180도 회전하다 rotate in a 180-degree arc / 회전시키다 turn sth round; turn (a wheel); 〈돌리다〉 give a turn (to); roll
▶ 바퀴는 축을 중심으로 하여 회전한다 A wheel turns [works] on its axle [axis].
▶ 행성은 태양 주위를 회전한다 The planets revolve [rotate] around the sun.
■ —건조기 a drying tumbler —경기 〈스키의〉 slalom —계(計) a revolution-indicator; a trochometer; an odometer —기 a rotary machine —기관 a rotary engine —기금 (employ) a revolving fund —나침반 a gyrocompass —력 turning force; rotary power —로(爐) a revolving furnace [kiln]; a rotary oven; a rotator; a revolver —마찰 〈物〉 rolling friction —목마 a merry-go-round; a giddy-go-round; a whirligig; 〈美〉 a car(r)ousel; 〈英〉 a roundabout —무대 a turning [revolving, rotating, rotative] stage —문 a revolving door —반 a turntable; 〖電〗 a finger plate —반경 a radius of gyration; a turning radius —서가 〈책꽂이〉 a revolving bookstand [bookcase] —속도 speed of revolution —속도계 a tachometer; a revolution [rev] counter: 자기회전 속도계 a tachograph —수 the number of rotations [revolutions]; rotational frequency —스위치 a rotary switch —운동 a rotary [rotatory] motion; (a) rotation; (a) revolution —율 the turnover (rate) (of capital, merchandise) —의(儀) a gyroscope; a gyrostat —의자 a swivel [revolving] chair —익 〈헬리콥터의〉 a rotor (blade); a rotating airfoil; 〈송풍기의〉 a wafter —자(子) a rotor; a rotator —자금 a revolving fund —장치 〈기중기의〉 slewing gear —창 a (horizontal) pivoted window —체 a body of revolution [rotation] —축 the axis of rotation [gyration]; a pivot; a shaft —테이블 a rotary table —포 a swivel gun —포탑 a revolving turret

회전 會戰 a battle; a fight; an engagement; an action; a meeting; an encounter
◆ 워털루 회전 the Battle of Waterloo
—회전하다 fight (a battle); encounter; meet; have an engagement (with); engage (the enemy)

회절 回折 〖物〗 diffraction
—회절하다 diffract (rays)
■ —각 the angle of diffraction —격자 a diffraction grating —대(帶) a diffraction zone —무늬 a diffraction pattern —산란 diffraction scattering —상(像) a diffraction figure [image] —파 a diffracted wave —현상 a diffraction phenomenon —효과 a diffraction effect

회조 回漕 shipping; marine transportation; carriage by sea —회조하다 transport [carry] by sea; ship

■―업 shipping business [trade]; marine transportation business ―업자 a shipping agent

회주 會主 the promoter [sponsor] of a meeting; the host of a party

회중 會衆 an attendance; an audience; attendants; 〈교회의〉 a congregation ◆많은 회중 a large attendance / 회중에게 인사하다 address the meeting [an audience]

회중 懷中 〈품 속〉 one's pocket; 〈마음 속〉 one's mind; (the bottom of) one's heart
―시계 a (pocket) watch; (俗) a ticker ―품 a pocketbook; a purse; 〈큰 것〉 a wallet: 회중품 조심 Beware of pickpockets.

회중전등 懷中電燈 an electric torch; a torch lamp; (美) a flashlight; a flashlamp
◆회중전등으로 비추다 put the light from a flashlight on 《an object》 / 회중전등을 켜다 turn on a flashlight; flash a torch / 회중전등을 끄다 turn off a flashlight; extinguish [dowse] a flashlight

회지 會誌 a bulletin ■동창― an alumni bulletin

회진 回診 a (doctor's) round of visits
▶이제 곧 주치의의 회진이 있겠습니다 〈환자에게〉 The doctor in charge will come round to see you soon.
―회진하다 make a round of visits 《to one's patients》; go the round of 《one's patients》; visit one's patients; make sick calls; go round the beds

회진 灰塵 〈재와 먼지〉 ashes and dust; 〈하잘 것 없는 것〉 worthless things

회집 會集 a gathering; an assemblage
―회집하다 gather; assemble; get together

회천 回天 〈왕의 뜻을 돌림〉 changing the king's mind; bringing the king around 《to a different point of view》; 〈세력의 만회〉 restoration of the national prestige
◆회천의 위업 a great work to save a nation on the verge of ruin
―회천하다 make the king change his mind; bring the king around 《to a different point of view》; restore the national prestige

회초리 a switch; a whip; a cane; 〈교사용의〉 a pointer
◆버들 회초리 a willow switch / 회초리로 때리다 switch 《a boy》 《with a cane》; cane; lash [flog, whip, swish] 《a boy》 《with a switch》 / 회초리를 맞다 be whipped; be caned [lashed]; get the cane

회춘 回春 〈도로 젊어짐〉 rejuvenation; restoration of youth
―회춘하다 grow [get] younger; be [become] rejuvenated; undergo rejuvenation; become [grow] young again; be restored to youth
◆회춘시키다 rejuvenate; rejuvenize
―기 〈노년의〉 Indian summer ―제[약] a rejuvenator; an erogenous drug

회충 蛔蟲 〔動〕 a mawworm; an intestinal worm; a roundworm; 〔醫〕 an ascarid [ascaris] ◆회충이 생기다 get (intestinal) worms
■―약 a medicine for expelling mawworms; a vermifuge; an anthelmint(h)ic (drug) ―증 ascariasis; 〈거야배〉 pain caused by roundworms

회치다 膾― slice raw fish; prepare sliced raw fish [meat]

회칙 會則 the regulations [rules, (美) bylaws] of a society; the articles of an association; the constitution of a club
◆회칙을 만들다 draw up [write] the rules of a club / 회칙의 일부를 개정하다 make a partial amendment of the rules of the society
▶회칙에 그렇게 되어 있다 The (club) rules say so.

회포 懷抱 one's inmost [intimate] thoughts; one's heart [mind] ◆회포를 풀다 unburden [unbosom] oneself 《to sb》

회피 回避 evasion; avoidance; shirking; elusion; 〔法〕 refrainment ―회피하다 evade; avoid; shirk; dodge; shun; sidestep; elude 《payment》; get around 《the difficulty》
◆책임을 회피하다 evade [shirk] one's responsibility; flee from responsibility / 언급을 회피하다 evade [decline] to comment 《on》 / 동맹파업을 회피하다 head off a strike
■―전술 dodging [evasive] tactics

회한 悔恨 remorse; (a) regret; (a) repentance; contrition; compunction
◆뼈저린 회한 poignant regret / 회한의 눈물 tears of remorse / 회한의 contrite

회합 會合 a meeting; an assembly; a gathering; a party; (美口) a get-together
◆회합 날짜를 정하다 fix the day for the meeting; make an appointment
▶그들은 1년에 두 번 회합을 갖는다 They meet [get together] twice a year.
―회합하다 meet; gather; assemble; get together
■―약속 (make) an appointment 《with》; (美) (have) a date 《with》 ―장소 a place of meeting

회항 回航 1 〈항해〉 navigation; cruise; sailing about ―회항하다 sail round; double 《a cape》 2 〈귀항〉 a homeward [return] voyage
―회항하다 make a homeward voyage; sail back

회향 回向 〔佛敎〕 a Buddhist memorial (for the dead); a mass (for the repose of a soul); good deeds with hope that the merit will accrue to others
―회향하다 hold a memorial service (for or in honor of the dead); do good for others' salvation

회향 茴香 〔植〕 a (common) fennel ■―풀 the fennel plant

회향 懷鄕 nostalgic reminiscence; longing for home ―회향하다 pine [long] for home; be [feel] homesick
■―병 nostalgia; homesickness: 회향병에 걸리다 become homesick

회혼 回婚 the sixtieth anniversary of one's wedding; a diamond wedding
■―례 a feast celebrating the 60th wedding anniversary: 회혼례를 올리다 celebrate one's diamond wedding (anniversary); have one's diamond jubilee

회화 會話 (a) conversation; a talk; 〈대화〉 (美) a dialog; (英) a dialogue

—회화하다 talk [speak] 《with》; have a conversation [talk] 《with》; converse 《with》
♦ 영어로 회화하다 talk [converse] in English 《with》
■ 영어— English conversation: 영어회화를 잘하다 speak English well; be a good speaker of English; speak fluent English / 영어회화를 연습하다 practice speaking English ━력 one's speaking [conversational] ability ━문 colloquial literature ━책 a conversational book ━체 colloquialism; colloquial style: 회화체 영어 colloquial English / 회화체로 쓴 책 a book written in colloquial [conversational] style

회화 繪畵 pictures; paintings; drawings
♦ 시의 회화적인 아름다움 the pictorial beauty of a poem / 회화적인 pictorial; graphic; picturesque / 회화하다 picturize; make a picture of; present in pictures
■ —전시회 an exhibition of pictures; an art [a painting] exhibition; a picture show

회화나무 〔槐〕 a pagoda tree

회훈 回訓 instructions (from one's home government in response to a request) —회훈하다 give [issue] return instructions; instruct (in reply)

획 abruptly ⇨ 휙

획 畵 〈글자의〉 a stroke
♦ 7획의 글자 a character of seven strokes; a 7-stroke character / 획 수 the number of strokes; the stroke count / 획을 가로 긋다 make a horizontal [side] stroke (in writing a Chinese character) / 획을 내리긋다 make a vertical [downward] stroke; stroke downwards

획기적 劃期的 epoch-making; epochal
♦ 획기적인 발견 an epoch-making discovery / 의학사상 획기적인 사건 a landmark in (the history of) medicine

획득 獲得 acquisition; acquirement; gain; taking
♦ 지식의 획득 the acquisition of knowledge ━획득하다 acquire; obtain; gain; get; secure; win; take
♦ 권리를 획득하다 acquire [secure] rights / 시민권을 획득하다 acquire citizenship / 재산을 획득하다 acquire property / 지위를 획득하다 obtain a position
■ —면역성 acquired immunity ━물 an acquisition; gainings ━형질〔生〕an acquired character

획력 畵力 the power [strength] of a stroke (in painting or calligraphy)

획법 畵法 the method and sequence of making strokes (in painting or calligraphy); a style of penmanship

획순 畵順 the order of making strokes (in writing a Chinese character) ♦ 획순을 틀리다 make strokes in a wrong order

획일 劃一 uniformity
♦ 획일적인 교육 uniform education / 획일적 제품 standardized manufactures
▶ 학생들을 획일적으로 다룰 수는 없다 We cannot deal with all the students in the same way.

■ —화〔主義〕 standardization: 교육제도의 획일화 the regimentation of educational system / 획일화된 빌딩가 a street lined with uniform buildings

획정 劃定 demarcation; delimitation
━획정하다 demarcate; delimit; mark out
♦ 경계선을 획정하다 demarcate [delimit] the frontier [boundary] line; draw a boundary (line)

획책 劃策 scheming; planning; maneuvering
━획책하다 lay [concoct] a scheme; maneuver; use artifice; 《美》frame (up); plot; conspire
♦ 반란을 획책하다 conspire to rise in revolt / 배후에서 획책하다 work behind the screens
▶ 그는 경쟁 상대의 축출을 획책하고 있다 He is scheming to oust his rival from office.

획획 1 〈도는 모양〉 speedily; fast
♦ 획획 돌다 (the wheels of a car) keep whizzing; spin; twirl; whirl
2 〈바람이 잇따라 세게 부는 모양〉 《blow》 in gusts; with a whistle [whiz(z)]

횟가루 灰— lime powder; powdered lime

횟감 膾— raw fish for preparing a sliced raw-fish dish

횟돌 灰— 〈석회석〉〔鑛〕 limestone

횟반 灰— a hardened mass of lime; a lump of solidified lime

횟수 回數 the number of times; frequency
♦ 횟수를 거듭하다 repeat 《so many times》
▶ 그의 결석 횟수는 얼마나 됩니까? How often [many times] was he absent?

횟집 膾— a restaurant specializing in sliced raw fish

횡갱 橫坑〔鑛〕a drift; a driftway; a level; a tunnel; 〈터널의〉a adit

횡격막 橫隔膜 〔解〕the diaphragm; the midriff
♦ 횡격막의 diaphragmatic; phrenic

횡단 橫斷 crossing; crosscutting; traversing
♦ 대륙 횡단 철도 a transcontinental railway / 태평양 횡단 비행 a transpacific flight; a flight across the Pacific
━횡단하다 cross; traverse; go [travel, swim, make a journey] across; run across [through]; intersect; cut transversely
♦ 도로를 횡단하다 cross a road; walk [go] across a street / 사막을 횡단하다 cross [traverse] a desert / 배로 태평양을 횡단하다 sail across the Pacific; make a sail [cruise] across the Pacific; make a transpacific sail [cruise] / 무단 횡단하다 jaywalk
▶ 선로를 횡단할 때는 좌우를 살펴라 Look right and left carefully before you cross a railroad track.
■ —로 a crosscut (road); a 《park》 transverse ━면 a cross section ━보도 a pedestrian crossing ━선〔幾〕a transversal (line)

횡대 橫隊 a rank; a line; a line abreast
♦ 횡대로 in a line / 2열 횡대로 in a double line / 횡대를 짓다 form in line; be drawn up in [into] line
■ —비행 flying in line abreast: 횡대비행을 하다 fly in line abreast ━사격 line firing ━행진

a march in a line
횡렬 橫列 a rank; a line (abreast) ◆횡렬을 짓다 stand in a row
횡령 橫領 (a) usurpation; (a) seizure; 〈돈〉 (an) embezzlement; 〈동산〉 [法] conversion ―**횡령하다** usurp; seize; embezzle; assume; appropriate unlawfully; [法] convert
◆공금을 횡령하다 embezzle public money / 아무의 돈을 횡령하다 embezzle money from *sb*
―**―자** a usurper; an embezzler ―**죄** embezzlement: 횡령죄로 기소되다 be accused of embezzlement / 횡령죄로 체포되다 be arrested on a charge of embezzlement
횡류 橫流 1 〈물의〉 flowing sideways ―**횡류하다** flow sideways
2 〈물건의〉 sale through illegal channels ―**횡류하다** sell 《goods》 through illegal channels [on the black market]
◆횡류되다 《goods》 flow into illicit channels; flow into the black market
횡목 橫木 〈가로대〉 a crosspiece; a sidepiece
횡문근 橫紋筋 〈가로무늬근〉 [解] a striated muscle; a striped muscle
횡보 橫步 walking sideways ―**횡보하다** walk sideways; sidle; edge along
횡사 橫死 〈변사〉 an unnatural [untimely] death; death by violence; a suspicious death; an accidental death; 〈참사〉 a tragic death ―**횡사하다** be killed in an accident; die [meet] a violent [a tragic, an accidental, an unnatural] death; die by violence
횡서 橫書 horizontal writing; writing in lateral lines ―**횡서하다** write horizontally [laterally, in lateral lines]; write from left to right
횡선 橫線 a horizontal [cross] line ◆횡선을 긋다 cross
■**―수표** a crossed check
횡설수설 橫說竪說 random [incoherent] talks; disjointed remarks; jargon; gibberish; nonsense
▶네 말은 횡설수설이라서 이해할 수가 없다 What you say is all Greek to me.
―**횡설수설하다** talk incoherently; make disjointed remarks; talk jargon [nonsense]; jargon; gibber ◆횡설수설하는 대답 an incoherent reply
횡수 橫數 〈뜻밖의 운수〉 a chance hit
횡액 橫厄 an unforeseen [a sudden] accident; unexpected calamity; an unforeseen disaster
◆횡액을 만나다 suffer an unexpected misfortune; meet with (a) calamity; have an accident
횡영 橫泳 《swim at》 sidestroke
횡와 橫臥 lying on *one's* side ―**횡와하다** lie on *one's* side
횡위 橫位 [醫] transverse presentation ■**―분만 (分娩)** crossbirth
횡재 橫財 a windfall; a godsend; unexpected fortune [profit, gains]; a bonanza
▶그는 골동품점에서 뜻밖의 횡재를 했다 He made a fine find at an antique shop.
―**횡재하다** come into unexpected fortune;

make a rare find; have a windfall; strike a bonanza
횡전 橫轉 a lateral turning; turning sideways; 〈비행기의〉 a (barrel) roll; a sideslip ―**횡전하다** turn over and lie on (its) side; turn [roll] sideways; 〈비행기가〉 make a barrel roll; sideslip
횡진 橫陣 [軍] a line abreast; a rank
횡파 橫波 [物] a transversal wave
횡포 橫暴 violence; high-handedness; tyranny; oppression
◆군부의 횡포 the despotism of the militarists / 횡포를 부리다 tyrannize 《over》; carry matters with a high hand
▶그의 횡포는 용납할 수 없습니다 We must not allow him to tyrannize us.
―**횡포하다** tyrannical; despotic; high-handed; overbearing; oppressive; violent
횡행하다 橫行― 1 〈제멋대로 행동하다〉 be [run] rampant; prevail; overrun; thrive; be prevalent
◆해적이 횡행하는 바다 a pirate-ridden sea; a sea infested with pirates / 도둑이 횡행하다 be infested with robbers 《at night》
▶시의 번화가에는 불량배가 횡행하고 있다 The busiest quarters of the city are infested with [overrun by] delinquents.
2 〈모로 걷다〉 go sidewise; walk sideways; sidle; edge along
효 孝 filial piety [devotion, duty]
효과 效果 (an) effect; effectiveness; 〈약 등의〉 efficacy; 〈능률〉 efficiency; 〈결과〉 a result; fruit
◆전체적인 효과 the general effect / 효과를 노리고 for effect / 아무런 효과도 없이 to no effect / 효과가 빠르다 be quick in (its) effects / 효과가 있다 be effective [effectual]; take effect; have an effect 《on》; do *sb* good; prove fruitful [successful]; bear fruit; be efficacious / 효과가 없다 be in ineffective [ineffectual]; be fruitless; be (of) no good; 〈약 등이〉 be inefficacious; have [produce] no effect 《on》 / 소기의 효과를 거두다 obtain the desired result; produce the intended effect / 효과를 노리다 calculate upon an effect
▶친구의 충고도 그에게는 효과가 없다 His friend's advice doesn't have any effect on him.
▶그의 노력은 아무 효과가 없었다 His efforts came to nothing.
▶거듭 시도해 보았지만 별반 효과가 없었다 Repeated attempts have been made without any noticeable result.
▶효과가 나타날 때까지는 다소 시간이 걸린다 It will take some time before we get [obtain] the desired results.
▶효과는 만점이었다 It has gone quite far. ⇌ It was quite effective.
▶약의 효과는 바로 나타났다 The medicine worked instantly.
■**―광고―** effectiveness of advertising **무대―** stage effect; scenic effects **선전―** propaganda effect **음향―** 《produce》 sound effects
효과적 效果的 ◆자주색의 효과적인 사용 the

effective use of purple / 비효과적인 ineffective; ineffectual / 효과적으로 effectively; with effect

효녀 孝女 a filial [dutiful] daughter

효능 效能 effect; virtue; efficacy; properties (of a medicine); benefit; good
♦ 약의 효능 the virtue [effect] of medicine / 온천의 효능 the medical benefits of hot springs (in the cure of a disease) / (약의) 효능이 나타나다 take effect; prove efficacious / 효능이 있다[없다] be efficacious [inefficacious]; prove effective [ineffective]; be good [no good] (for)
▶ 이 약은 두통에 탁월[신통]한 효능이 있다 This medicine works wonders on a headache.
▶ 그것은 어떤 효능이 있나요? What is the good of it?

효도 孝道 filial piety [devotion]; filial duty; obedience to parents
—효도하다 be dutiful [obedient, devoted] to one's parents; practice filial piety toward one's parents; discharge one's filial duties
▶ 자식이 효도하려고 할 때는 이미 부모님은 안 계신다 When one would be filial, his parents are gone.

효력 效力 1〈법률상의〉 effect; validity; force
♦ 효력이 있다 be effective; be in force; hold good; be valid; 〈표 등이〉 be available; 〈약속 등이〉 be binding / 효력이 없다 be ineffective; be null and void; be not binding; 〈표·수표 등이〉 be bad [unavailable] / 법률과 동일한 효력을 갖다 have the full force and effect of a law / 효력을 발생하다[이 생기다] come into force [effect, operation]; take effect; become effective [operative]; 〈法〉inure / 효력을 상실하다 lose effect; lose (its) validity; become invalid [null and void]; become ineffective; go out of force; cease to be binding; 〈표 등이〉 become unavailable
▶ 그 계약은 5년간 효력이 있다 The contract holds [stands] good for five years.
▶ 그 조약은 1년 후부터 효력을 발생한다 The contract will come into force after one year.
▶ 본 조약은 3년간 효력을 가진다 The treaty shall remain in force for the period of three years.
2〈약 등의〉 (an) effect; efficacy; (healing) virtue
♦ 효력이 있다 be efficacious (against, for); be effective; do good; have effect (on); do sb a lot of good / 효력이 없다 be inefficacious; be ineffective; do no good; have no effect (on); avail nothing
■ —발생 effectivation; effectuation

효모(균) 酵母(菌) 〔生〕 yeast

효부 孝婦 a dutiful [an obedient, a faithful] daughter-in-law

효성 孝誠 filial piety [devotion]
♦ 효성이 지극하다 be devoted to one's parents / 부모에게 효성을 다하다 be dutiful to one's parents
—효성스럽다 dutiful [obedient, devoted] to one's parents
♦ 효성스러운 아들 a dutiful [an obedient] son; an affectionate and dutiful son

효성 曉星 the morning star ⇨ 샛별

효소 酵素 〔化〕 enzyme; ferment
■ 소화— digestive enzyme ■ —학 enzymology

효수 梟首 gibbeting a head
♦ 효수경중(警衆)하다 display the criminal's head as a warning to the people
—효수하다 hang up the head of a decapitated criminal; gibbet a head

효순 孝順 filial obedience —효순하다 filial; obedient to one's parents

효시 嚆矢 〈처음〉 the beginning; the first; the first instance
♦ 이것이 …의 효시였다 This was the first instance of...

효심 孝心 filial affection [heart, devotion]
♦ 효심이 깊은 filial; dutiful; devoted; faithful (to one's parents)

효양 孝養 filial devotion ♦ 효양을 다하다 care for one's parents; attend on one's parents with devotion

효용 效用 〈재화의〉 usefulness; utility; 〈효험〉 (an) effect; benefit; good ♦ 효용이 있다 be useful; be of use; be effective
■ 한계— 〔經〕 marginal utility ■ —가치 effective value —체감의 법칙 〔經〕 the law of diminishing utility

효용 驍勇·梟勇 valiancy; bravery; prowess; intrepidity
—효용하다 valiant; brave; intrepid

효웅 梟雄 a valiant hero

효율 效率 〔物·機〕 efficiency; the utility factor; duty
♦ 기계의 효율 mechanical efficiency / 높은 효율 a high degree of efficiency / 생산의 효율을 높이다 raise the efficiency of production / 자금을 효율적으로 운용하다 make effective use of the funds
■ 열— thermal efficiency 종합— overall efficiency ■ —곡선[시험] an efficiency curve [test] —평가 merit rating

효자 孝子 a dutiful [filial] son; a good [devoted] son

효장 梟將 a valiant [veteran] general

효행 孝行 filial conduct [acts]; a filial deed; 〈효도〉 filial piety ■ —상 a prize for filial conduct

효험 效驗 (an) effect; efficacy; (a) virtue (of a medicine) ⇨ 효능
♦ 약의 효험 the efficacy [effect] of a drug / 효험이 뛰어난 약 a wonder drug / 효험이 없어지다 lose (its) effect / 효험 보다 get results / 효험이 있다 be efficacious

후 with a whiff [puff]
▶ 나는 촛불을 후 불어 껐다 I whiffed out a candlelight.

후 后 an empress ⇨ 후비

후 後 1〈다음〉 그 후 after that; since then; afterward / 그 후 내내 ever since / 3년 후 three years after; after (a lapse of) three years / 후의 following (day); subsequent (event) / 후에 by and by; later (on); afterwards; subsequently; after a time [while]

▶ 훨씬 후에 그는 사실을 내게 말했다 He told me the truth much later on [long afterward, well after that].
▶ 그는 그로부터 일주일 후에 왔다 A week later he came.
▶ 그녀는 그가 떠난지 십분 후에 도착했다 She arrived ten minutes after he left.
▶ 비온 후에 흐림 Rain at first, later cloudy.
2 〈앞날〉 future
◆ 지금으로부터 이주일 후에 two weeks from now; in two weeks / 십년 후의 세계 the world ten years from now
■ ―근(根) 〖生〗 a posterior root; a dorsal root ―빙기(氷期) 〖地〗 the postglacial age

후각 嗅覺 〖生〗 the olfactory sense; the sense of smell; the smell
▶ 개는 후각이 예민하다 A dog has a keen nose [sense of smell]. ⇌ A dog is sharp-nosed.
■ ―기 an olfactory organ ―상피 an olfactory epithelium

후갑판 後甲板 〖海〗 the quarterdeck; the afterdeck

후견 後見 guardianship; wardship; 〈원조〉 assistance; 〈사람〉 a guardian
◆ 후견을 받고 있다 be in [under] ward (to); be (placed) under the guardianship (of)

후견인 後見人 〖法〗 a guardian; a ward; a curator ◆ 후견인이 되다 act as (a) guardian; take charge of the guardian of *sb* ―피(被)― a ward

후계자 後繼者 〈뒤를 잇는 사람〉 a successor (to); 〈상속인〉 an inheritor; 〈남자〉 an heir; 〈여자〉 an heiress
◆ 후계자가 되다 succeed to 《another's office》; succeed *sb* in his office; take 《another's》 chair as *one's* successor
▶ 아들이 위원장의 후계자가 되었다 He succeeded his father as chairman of the board.

후고 後顧 1 〈과거를 돌아봄〉 looking back ―후고하다 look back upon (the past); review; retrospect; reflect upon
2 〈앞날의 염려〉 anxiety about *one's* future
◆ 후고의 염려 anxiety over the future; worrying about *one's* home
―후고하다 worry about *one's* family left behind

후광 後光 〈광배〉 a halo 《*pl.* ~s, ~es》; an aureole [aureola]; a gloria; a gloriole; a nimbus 《*pl.* ~es, -bi》; 〈광관〉 a corona
◆ 후광으로 에워싸인 그리스도 성화 a painting of Christ with his head surrounded by a halo

후군 後軍 〖軍〗 the rear of an army; the rear guard

후굴 後屈 〖醫〗 retroflexion
■ 자궁― retroflexion of the uterus

후궁 後宮 1 〈왕의 첩〉 a royal concubine
2 〈뒤쪽에 있는 궁전〉 a king's harem

후기 後記 a postscript (*略* P.S., p.s.)
■ 편집― the editor's postscript

후기 後期 the latter term [period]; the latter [second] half year; 《美》〈2학기제 학교〉 the second semester; 〖生〗〈핵분열〉 the anaphase
◆ 19세기 후기에 in the later [latter part of the] nineteenth century
―결산 〖商〗 settlement of accounts for the second half year: 회사는 후기결산을 공표했다 The company published settlement of accounts for the second half year. ―대학 the second group of universities [colleges] ―시험 the second (term) examination; the final examinations; the finals

후기인상파 後期印象派 the Post-impressionism
■ ―화가 a postimpressionist

후끈 with a sudden flash of heat ―후끈하다 get a hot flash ▶ 나는 몸이 후끈해졌다 The warmth spread within me.

후년 後年 1 〈다음다음 해〉 the year after next
◆ 내년이나 후년에 next year or the year after
2 〈후세〉 later; later years
◆ 후년에 in future years; in years to come; 〈그 후〉 later; afterward; 〈만년〉 in *one's* later years; afterlife

후뇌 後腦 〖解〗 the metencephalon; the hindbrain; the afterbrain

후닥닥 1 〈갑자기〉 suddenly; abruptly; all at once; 〈열쌔게〉 quickly; nimbly; alertly; (as) quick as thought
▶ 그는 방에서 후닥닥 뛰어나갔다 He rushed suddenly out of the room.
▶ 소년은 저고리를 후닥닥 벗었다 The boy whipped off his coat.
2 〈서둘러〉 hastily; hurriedly; in a hurry; in 《*one's*》 haste; in a flurry
▶ 나는 점심을 후닥닥 먹었다 I took a hasty [hurried] lunch.

후닥닥거리다 1 〈계속하여 급히 서두르다〉 be in a hurry; be hasty; be in hot [great] haste
▶ 공원은 일을 빨리 끝내려고 후닥닥거렸다 The worker rushed to get his job done in a hurry.
2 〈열쌔게 계속하여 행동하다〉 act quickly; be in a flurry; scamper

후단 後段 〈뒷단〉 the latter part
후당 後堂 〈별당〉 a separate house in the rear
후대 後代 the future [coming] generation; posterity; after ages

후대 厚待 a hearty [warm, cordial] reception; kind treatment; hospitality
―후대하다 give a warm [cordial] reception to; treat 《a guest》 kindly; receive *sb* warmly; be hospitable to
◆ 후대받다 be kindly treated; be received warmly [cordially]

후덕 厚德 liberality; liberal favor ―후덕하다 liberal; generous; virtuous ■ ―군자 a liberal gentleman; a virtuous gentleman

후도 後圖 plans for the future

후두 後頭 〖解〗 the occiput 《*pl.* ~s, occipita》; the back of the head ⇨ 뒤통수
■ ―결절 the occipital protuberance ―골 the occipital bone ―엽(葉) the occipital lobe

후두 喉頭 〖解〗 the larynx 《*pl.* ~es, larynges》
◆ 후두의 laryngeal; laryngal
■ ―결핵 laryngeal tuberculosis ―경(鏡) a laryngoscope ―낭포(囊胞) a laryngeal cyst ―암 laryngeal cancer ―염 laryngitis ―음〔音聲〕 a guttural sound; a laryngeal sound ―인

대(靭帶) the laryngeal ligament —절개술 laryngotomy —카타르 laryngocatarrh

후두부 後頭部 〔解〕 the occipital region; the back (part) of the head
▶그는 후두부가 벗겨져 있다 He is bald on the back of his head.

후둥이 後— 〈쌍둥이의〉 the second born of twins; a younger twin brother [sister]

후드득 with a clatter [patter]; scatteringly; in large drops; pattering
◆우박이 후드득 떨어지다 clatter / 비가 후드득 내리다 patter; spatter; sprinkle; splatter down; fall pitter-patter 《on》
▶비가 후드득 문을 때렸다 The rain pattered on the door.

후들거리다 tremble; quake; shake
▶나는 무서워서 다리가 후들거렸다 My legs were trembling with fear.

후들후들 tremblingly; shiveringly
◆후들후들 떨다 tremble all over; shiver like a jelly
▶나는 추워서 다리가 후들후들 떨렸다 My legs shook with cold.

후등 後燈 a taillight; 〈자동차의 스톱라이트〉 a stoplight; a brakelight

후딱 quickly; rapidly; (as) quick as thought; 《俗》 like winking; in a wink
◆일을 후딱 해치우다 finish one's work quickly; dispatch one's work; make short work of 《sth, sb》 / 자리에서 후딱 일어서다 rise quickly [nimbly] from one's seat; spring [jump] to one's feet

후딱후딱 all quickly [rapidly, with dispatch]
▶그는 일을 후딱후딱 해치운다 He finishes his work one right after another.

후락 朽落 〈썩음〉 decay; deterioration; 〈퇴색〉 fade; discolorment —후락하다 decay; crumble into decay; rot away; discolor

후래삼배 後來三杯 A late-comer (at the drinking party) should be offered three straight cups of wine as a penalty.

후략 後略 omission of what follows; the rest omitted

후레아들 an ill-bred [ill-mannered] fellow; a rogue ▶이 후레아들 놈아 You son of a whore [bitch]!

후려 後慮 anxiety [fear] over the future
◆후려를 없애다 free one from anxiety about the future

후려갈기다 give sb a good thrashing; strike a blow 《at, against》
◆귀싸대기를 후려갈기다 box sb on the ear; give sb a lick on the ear

후려치다 belabor; give sb a sound thrashing [good licking]; hit sb hard
▶채찍으로 후려치다 belabor sb with a whip

후련하다 (feel) relieved; (feel one's mind) unburdened
◆후련해지다 feel heartily gratified [satisfied]
▶빚을 다 갚으니 마음이 후련하다 The load is off my mind now that I have cleared off my debts.
▶할 말을 다 하고 나니 가슴 속이 후련했다 After I had said my say I felt my mind unburdened. ⇒ Now (that) I have had my say, I felt the easier for it.

후렴 後斂 〈노래의〉 a refrain; a burden

후루루 1 〈호르라기 소리〉 whistling
◆호르라기를 후루루 불다 blow a whistle; whistle —후루루하다 whistle
2 〈타는 모양〉 in a flare
—후루루하다 go up in flames
3 ⇨ 후루룩

후루룩 1 〈새가 나는 소리〉 flap; with a flutter
▶참새가 후루룩 날아갔다 A sparrow flew away with a flap of wings.
2 〈늘이마시는 소리〉 slurping; sipping
▶국물을 마실 때 후루룩 소리내지 마라 Don't slurp when you eat your soup.

후루룩거리다 flap; keep fluttering; sipping; slurping ▶그는 수프를 후루룩거리며 마셨다 He sipped up his soup.

후륜 後輪 a rear wheel
—구동 rear-wheel drive

후리다 1 〈유혹하다〉 seduce; wheedle; cajole; deceive; coax; allure; entice; 〈매혹하다〉 captivate; charm; fascinate; bewitch
◆여자를 후리다 seduce a woman / 남자를 후리다 captivate a man with wiles
2 〈휘둘러 몰다〉 hunt up [out]; round up; 〈후리채로 잡다〉 net 《birds》; 〈후릿그물로 잡다〉 catch 《fish》 in a net
3 〈모난 곳을 깎아내다〉 round [rub] off 《the angles [corners, edges]》; soften down 《the edges》
4 〈잡아 채다〉 snatch (away) 《from, off》; catch away; take by force
◆손에서 핸드백을 후리다 snatch a handbag from 《a woman's》 hand

후리질하다 fish with a seine; seine

후리후리하다 tall and slender [lanky, lean]; gangling ◆키가 후리후리한 미인 a beautiful girl, slender as a lily / 후리후리한 남자 a tall lank man; a gangling fellow

후림 〈유혹〉 allurement; enticement; seduction
◆후림을 당하다 be seduced; be tricked / 후림에 넘어가다 succumb [yield] to seduction; be nicely taken in
■—비둘기 a stool [decoy] pigeon

후림불 〈걸려 듦〉 entanglement; involvement
◆후림불에 걸려들다 get [be] involved [entangled] in; get a by-blow

후릿고삐 a long bridle; the slack of which is used to whip 《animals》

후릿그물 a dragnet; a seine; a seine [towing] net; a flue ◆후릿그물을 당기다 drag a seine / 후릿그물로 물고기를 잡다 fish with a seine

후면 後面 〈뒤쪽〉 the back side; 〈이면〉 the reverse (side), the wrong [back, other] side

후무리다 〈슬쩍하다〉 make free with 《sb's money》; filch; 《俗》 sneak; pocket; pilfer
▶그는 거스름돈을 후무렸다 He pilfered the change.
▶그는 교탁에서 분필 한 개를 후무렸다 He filched a piece of chalk from the teacher's desk.

후문 後門 a rear [back] gate; a back door

후물거리다 mumble; gum
후물림 後— handing down; a thing handed down 《from》; 《美口》 a hand-me-down; 《英口》 reach-me-down
♦형배 후물림 옷 clothes handed down from *one's* brother
후물후물 mumblingly ♦후물후물 씹다 mumble
후미 〈물가의 굽어진 곳〉 an inlet; a creek; a cove; an arm of the sea; an embayment
후미 後尾 the rear; the tail; 〈고물〉 the stern; 〈행렬〉 the tail end; 〈軍〉 the rear (guard)
♦후미의 rear; back; 〈선미〉 aft / 후미에 at the rear [back] (of) / 행렬의 후미에 붙다 be at the end of a procession; bring up the rear
■—경호 the rear guard
후미지다 1 〈후미가 깊다〉 form an inlet; deeply indented; deep 《into the land》
♦해안의 후미진 곳 a recess in the shoreline
2 〈장소가 외지다〉 sequestered; secluded; retired
♦후미진 산속 the recess of a mountain; a mountain recess
후박 厚薄 〈두께의〉 thickness and thinness; relative thickness; 〈인정의〉 liberal and stingy; much and little; partiality
♦후박이 없다 be impartial [equitable]
후박나무 厚朴— 〈植〉 a silver magnolia
후반 後半 the latter half; the second half
♦19세기 후반에 in the latter half of the nineteenth century; late in the 19th century
■—생 the later half [part] of *one's* life —전 the second [latter] half of the game
후방 後方 the rear; 〈軍〉〈전방에 대해〉 the home [civilian] front; rear service
♦후방의 rear; back; backward / 후방에 backward; in [at] the rear; at the back; 〈고물에〉 astern; abaft / 후방으로 rearward; backward / 후방에서 적을 급습하다 attack the enemy in the rear; make a raid behind the enemy's line / 후방을 교란하다 harass the rear (guard)
■—경계레이더 a tail warning radar —근무 rear service (at the base); duties in the rear; duties on the home front: 후방 근무로 배치되다 be assigned to the base —기지 a rear base —난류(亂流) 〈氣〉 wake turbulence —부대 troops in the rear —사령부 the headquarters in the rear —진지 〈軍〉 a fallback position
후배 後輩 〈후진〉 a junior; a younger person; (총칭) the younger generation
♦학교 후배 *one's* junior in school
▶그는 내 이년 후배다 He is two years younger than I am [(口) than me]. ⇒〈학년이〉 He is two years behind me in [(美) at] school.
▶나는 덕슨 씨의 한참 후배입니다 I am many years Mr. Dickson's junior. ⇒ I am Mr. Dickson's junior by many years.
후배주 後配株 〔證〕 a deferred [share] stock
후번 後番 next time; next game [round]
후벼내기 〈연장〉 a tool used for digging out chisel dust
후보 後報 a later report [dispatch]; further information; later [further] news

후보 候補 〈입후보〉 candidacy; 〔英〕 candidature; 〈선수〉 substitution
♦후보를 사퇴하다 withdraw *one's* candidacy
▶그는 학생회장의 후보로 나섰다 He offered himself as a candidate for the president of the student council.
▶그는 대통령 후보에 지명되었다 He was nominated for president [for the presidency].
■공인— an official candidate 낙선— a defeated candidate 만년— a permanent candidate 비공인— an unofficial candidate 아카데미상(賞)— an Academy Award nominee —선수 a reserve; a substitute (player) —지 a site proposed 《for》; a most suitable place 《for》: 이곳이 새 국제 공항의 후보지다 This is the site proposed for a new international airport.
후보생 候補生 a cadet
■사관— a cadet (officer); 〈육군〉 a military cadet; 〈해군〉 a naval cadet; 〈공군〉 an aviation cadet
후보자 候補者 a candidate 《for the election》; an applicant 《for a position》
♦유력한 후보자 a strong candidate / 후보자로 나서다 become a candidate for 《the next presidency》; (美) run (as a candidate) for; (英) stand for 《parliament》 / 〈정당이〉 후보자를 세우다 put up candidates 《in the coming general election》 / 후보자를 지지[후원]하다 support [back up, boost] a candidate
▶다섯 명의 후보자가 총선거에 나섰다 Five candidates ran in the general election.
■공천— a recognized [an official, an authorized] candidate 대통령— a candidate for the presidency; a presidential nominee [candidate] 신부(新郞)— a prospective bride [groom] —경력공보 the candidates' career bulletin —명부 a list of candidate; (美) a slate; a ticket —지명 nomination of a candidate
후부 後夫 *one's* second husband
후부 後部 the rear; the hind [back] part; 〈배의 갑판〉 the stern; the quarter
♦후부의 back; rear; hind; posterior
후분 後分 〈만년 운수〉 *one's* luck [fortune] in the latter part of *one's* life ♦후분이 좋다 be lucky late in life [in *one's* old age]
후불 後拂 deferred [post] payment; future [after] payment
후비 后妃 an empress; a queen
후비 後備 rear guard; 〈병역〉 the second reserve
후비다 dig up; scoop [scrape] out; gouge; 〈귀·이·코 등을〉 pick ♦코[귀]를 후비다 clean [pick] *one's* nose [ears]
후비(병)역 後備(兵)役 the second reserve
후비적거리다 keep scooping [scraping] out; keep gouging; 〈파내다〉 keep picking
♦코를 후비적거리다 keep picking *one's* nose
후사 後事 〈뒷일〉 future affairs; 〈사후의 일〉 affairs after *one's* death ♦후사를 부탁하다 entrust *sb* with future affairs; ask *sb* to take care of things after *one's* death
후사 後嗣 〈후계자〉 a successor; 〈상속자〉 an inheritor; 〈남자〉 an heir; 〈여자〉 an heiress
♦후사가 끊어지다 a family becomes extinct;

후사 a family line breaks
▶ 그에게는 후사가 없다 He has no heir to succeed him.
후사 厚謝 〈감사〉 hearty [warm] thanks; 〈사례〉 a handsome recompense [reward]
―**후사하다** 〈감사하다〉 thank *sb* heartily; express *one's* hearty [cordial] thanks; 〈사례하다〉 reward *sb* handsomely [generously]
후산 後産 the afterbirth ―**후산하다** deliver [bear] the afterbirth ■―**정체**(停滯) the retained placenta
후살이 後― remarriage (of a woman); a woman's second marriage
후생 後生 1 〈후진〉 juniors; younger fellows; young scholars [students]
▶ 후생이 가외(可畏)라 Youth should be regarded with respect.
2 〔佛敎〕 〈내생〉 the future life [existence]; the life to come
후생 厚生 1 〈생활의 넉넉함〉 social [public] welfare; the welfare [well-being] of people
2 〈건강의 증진〉 a service club ―**사업** public welfare enterprises; welfare [social] work ―**시설** welfare facilities
후생분열조직 後生分裂組織 〔生〕 the secondary meristem
후생연금 厚生年金 《grant》 a welfare pension 《annuity》 ―**보험** welfare pension insurance
후설 〈독일의 철학자〉 Husserl, Edmund (1859–1938)
후세 後世 1 〈후대〉 afterlife; after [coming, future] ages; posterity; future generations
◆ 후세의 사람들 future generations; posterity / 후세에 전통을 전하다[물려주다] hand down the traditions / 후세에 명성을 얻다 earn *one's* place in history
▶ 그의 이름은 후세에 남을 것이다 His name will live in history. ≒ He will be remembered forever.
▶ 그의 이념은 후세에 큰 영향을 미칠 것이다 His ideology will have a great influence upon future generations.
2 〔佛敎〕 〈내세〉 the next [other] world; the hereafter
후속 後續 succession ◆ 후속의 succeeding; following ―**후속하다** succeed; follow
■―**부대** reinforcements; rear guard; 〈육군〉 a rear party / 〈해군〉 a unit next astern
후손 後孫 a descendant; 〈명문자손〉 a scion; 〈총칭〉 posterity; offspring; progeny; issue
▶ 그는 후손이 없다 He has no descendant(s).
▶ 그는 명문의 후손이다 He is a descendant of an illustrious family.
후송 後送 〈후방으로 보냄〉 sending back; an evacuation; 〈나중에 보냄〉 sending later
―**후송하다** send back (to the rear); evacuate; send later
◆ 병약자[상이병]로서 본국으로 후송되다 be invalided home; be sent home as an invalid
▶ 화물은 후송해 드립니다 We will send your baggage to you later.
▶ 전쟁 포로는 후송되었다 The prisoners of war were sent to the rear.
―**일병원** an evacuation hospital ―**환자** an evacuated casualty
후수 後手 〈바둑·장기에서 뒤에 두기〉 playing as second mover ◆ 후수로 두다 play second
후술 後述 ― say [mention, describe, write] (it) later ◆ 후술하는 바와 같이 as will be seen later
후식 後食 a dessert
후신 後身 1 〈다시 태어난 몸〉 a reincarnation; *one's* new existence after rebirth
2 〈변형이 된 실체〉 the successor; a transformation
▶ 이 대학은 옛날 직업학교의 후신이다 This college used to be a vocational school.
후신경 嗅神經 〔解〕 an olfactory nerve
후실 後室 *one's* second wife ⇨ 후취
■―**자식** a child born of the second wife
후안무치 厚顔無恥 impudence; shamelessness; brazenface; (口) cheek
―**후안무치하다** shameless; barefaced; brazenfaced; impudent; (口) cheeky; have a cheek
◆ 후안무치한 사람 a brazen and unscrupulous fellow; a shameless fellow
후열 後列 the rear (rank, row); the back row
후예 後裔 a descendant; a scion; offspring (*pl.* ~)
◆ 명문의 후예 a scion of an illustrious family
▶ 그는 귀족의 후예다 He is descended from a noble family.
후원 後苑 a garden of the royal palace; the royal garden
후원 後園 a back [rear] garden; (美) a backyard
후원 後援 support; patronage; backing
◆ 후원이 없는 unbacked (by the people); without backing / 아무의 후원으로 under the auspices [sponsorship, patronage] of *sb*...
▶ 그 행사는 시의 후원으로 거행되었다 The event was held under the sponsorship [auspices] of the city.
―**후원하다** support; give support [backing] (to); back up; patronize
◆ 재정적으로 후원하다 support *sb* financially; give financial support to *sb* / 음악가를 후원하다 sponsor a musician
■―**단체** a supporters' organization ―**부대 [군]** troops stationed in support of the front line; reinforcements
후원자 後援者 (a) supporter; (a) sponsor; a backer; a patron
◆ 돈많은 후원자 a rich patron; a patron with an ample purse
▶ 그에게는 김모씨라는 후원자가 있다 He has a supporter in the person of a certain Kim. ≒ He has a certain Kim behind him.
후원회 後援會 a body of supporters; a society for the support 《of》; a supporters' association; an association of supporters 《for》; 〈연예인 등의〉 a fan club
▶ 홍박사의 후원회가 조직되었다 A society was formed to support [for the support of] Doctor Hong.
후위 後衛 〈테니스 등의〉 the back player; 〈축구 등의〉 a back; 〈군대의〉 the rear guard; the

rear
♦후위의 rear guard / 후위를 보다 play back; ⟨군대의⟩ bring up the rear

후유 whew; with a sigh
♦후유하고 한숨 돌리다 give [breathe] a sigh of relief
▶후유, 덥기도 해라 Whoo! What a hot sun!

후유증 後遺症 1 ⟨醫⟩ a sequela (*pl.* -lae); an after trouble
2 ⟨여파⟩ an aftereffect; an aftermath
♦파업[선거]의 후유증 the aftermath of a strike [an election]

후은 厚恩 great favor [obligations]
♦후은을 입다 receive great kindness; owe *sb* great obligations; be deeply indebted (to)

후음 喉音 〔音聲〕 a guttural sound; a guttural

후의 厚意 kind intentions; favor; kindness; courtesy
♦당신의 후의로 through your kindness [good offices] / 후의를 사양하다 decline *sb's* kind offer
▶후의에 깊이 감사합니다 Thank you very much for your kindness. ≒ I deeply appreciate all your kindness.

후의 厚誼 kindness; patronage; favor; ⟨우정⟩ warm [close] friendship

후인 後人 (총칭) posterity; ⟨후대⟩ future generations

후일 後日 the future; afterdays; another day; some other day
♦후일에 in (the) future; later (on); one of these days / 후일을 위해 ⟨참고로⟩ for future reference; ⟨증거로⟩ as a future proof of / 후일을 기약하고 헤어지다 part from (each other) in the hopes of meeting again
━담 ⟨회고담⟩ recollections; ⟨후속담⟩ a sequel (to a story); an aftermath: 사건의 후일담 a sequence [sequel] to the event

후임 後任 ⟨사람⟩ a successor; ⟨일⟩ succession
♦아무의 후임으로 in succession to *sb*; to succeed *sb*; as the successor to *sb* / 후임자가 올 때까지 대리를 하다 act during a vacancy
▶그는 박교수의 후임이다 He is the successor to Professor Park. ⇌ He is Mr. Park's successor as professor. ⇌ He has succeeded Mr. Park as professor.
▶그녀가 내 후임이 된다 She will be my successor. ⇌ She will succeed me. ⇌ She will take my place.
▶그는 그녀의 후임으로 클럽의 재무를 맡았다 He succeeded her as treasurer of the club.

후자 後者 the latter; the second
♦후자의 경우에는 in the latter case
▶그들은 말과 소를 사육하고 있다. 전자는 타기 위해서, 후자는 젖을 얻기 위해서다 They keep horses and cows; the former for riding, the latter for milking.

후작 侯爵 a marquis; a marquess
━부인 a marchioness; a marquise

후장 後場 〔證〕 the afternoon session [market, sale]

후장 後裝 breechloading ━포[총] a breechloader; a breechloading gun

후조 候鳥 a migratory bird ⇨ 철새

후주곡 後奏曲 〔樂〕 a postlude

후줄근하다 wet and limp; flaccid; flaggy; a little soggy ▶내 옷이 이슬에 젖어 후줄근해졌다 My clothes got wet with dew and lost their starch.

후중하다 後重— constipated; costive

후즈후 ⟨명사록⟩ a Who's Who

후진 後陣 the rear guard

후진 後進 1 ⟨뒤쪽으로 나아감⟩ backing; backward motion; retreat; 〔海〕 sternway
━후진하다 back (away from); retrocede; ⟨배가⟩ go [move] astern; make sternway
▶전속 후진 (口令) Back full!
▶그는 차를 후진시켜서 차고에 넣었다 He backed his car into garage.
2 ⟨후배⟩
♦후진을 기르다 cultivate the younger generation / 후진을 돌보다 look after [be helpful to] *one's* juniors / 후진을 위해 길을 터주다 (resign to) make room for *one's* juniors; give younger men a chance / 후진의 길을 막다 block [check] the promotion of *one's* juniors
▶그는 후진에게 길을 양보하여 용퇴했다 He resigned in favor of a younger man.
3 ⟨저개발⟩ underdevelopment; backwardness; lagging (behind)
♦문화적 후진 cultural backwardness; a cultural lag / 후진 상태 a backward [an underdeveloped] state (of society)
━국 an underdeveloped country; a backward country [nation] ━기어 a reverse gear ━성 ⟨민족 등의⟩ backwardness: 후진성을 탈피하다 emerge from backwardness ━지역 a newly-developing area

후처 後妻 *one's* second wife ⇨ 후취
♦후처를 얻다[맞다] marry a second wife / 후처로 맞아들이다 take (a woman) for [as] a second wife

후처리 後處理 the after-treatment

후천성 면역 결핍증 後天性 免疫 缺乏症 acquired immuno deficiency syndrome (略 AIDS)

후천적 後天的 acquired; (라) a posteriori; learned (behavior patterns)
♦후천적으로 (라) a posteriori
▶개인의 욕구에는 두 종류가 있는데, 선천적인 것과 후천적인 것이다 Individuals have two kinds of wants and needs; inborn and acquired.

후추 pepper; black [white] pepper
♦후추를 치다 sprinkle pepper on (meat); pepper (a dish)
━후춧가루 ground pepper 후춧병 a pepper caster [castor]; a pepper duster

후취 後娶 a second marriage; remarriage; ⟨후처⟩ *one's* second wife ♦후취를 얻다 take a second wife; remarry

후치사 後置詞 〔文法〕 a postposition

후탈 後頉 1 ⟨병후⟩ (라) complicata; complications; complicating disease; ⟨산후의⟩ complications from [after] childbirth; postpartum trouble
2 ⟨뒤탈⟩ trouble ensuing after the disposal of a matter; (troublesome) aftermath; an aftereffect

후텁지근하다

▶ 나는 후탈이 없게 일을 잘 처리했다 I handled things so that there would be no trouble later on.

후텁지근하다 sultry; stuffy; sticky ♦ 후텁지근한 날씨 sultry weather

후퇴 後退 1 〈뒤로 물러남〉 backdown; 〈퇴각〉 (a) retreat; retrogradation; retrogression; 〈일시적 경기 침체〉 (a) recession; 〈철ňik〉 (a) withdrawal; backout

♦ 작전상[전략적] 후퇴 a strategic retreat / 후퇴를 엄호하다 cover a retreating army; protect the retreat / 후퇴 중이다 be in retreat; be on the run

—**후퇴하다** draw [move] back; retreat (from); retrograde; retrogress; withdraw (from); retire; fall back; 〈경기가〉 slip (into a recession); 〈배가〉 drop [move] astern

♦ 서둘러 후퇴하다 beat a hasty retreat / 질서정연하게[무질서하게] 후퇴하다 retreat in good order [in disorder]

▶ 적은 국경에서 15마일 후퇴했다 The enemy pulled back fifteen miles from the border.

▶ 경기가 후퇴하여 많은 실업자가 나왔다 The recession caused a lot of unemployment.

▶ 그는 두세 걸음 후퇴했다 He took a few steps backward.

2 〔建〕 setback

■—군 an army in retreat; a retreating army
—명령 an order [a signal] to retreat —이동 retrograde movement —익(翼) 〔空〕 a swept-back wing; a backswept wing

후편 後便 〈뒤쪽〉 the back side; 〈나중 인편〉 a later messenger; 〈나중 차편〉 (on) a later train; 〈나중 기회〉 a later opportunity

후편 後篇 〈책의 뒤편〉 the latter part (of a book); 〈완결편〉 the concluding part; 〈속편〉 a sequel (to); 〈전편에 대해〉 the second volume

후프 a hoop

후하다 厚— 1 〈인심이 두텁다〉 kindhearted; tenderhearted; warm-hearted; cordial; hospitable; 〈보수·대우 등이〉 generous; magnanimous; liberal; open-handed

♦ 후한 보수 generous [rich] reward / 인심이 후한 사람 a kindhearted [tenderhearted] person; a kindly soul / 후한 대접 warm treatment; cordial [hospitable] reception / 점수가 후하다 be liberal [generous] in marking (examination) papers; be an easy grader / 후하게 사례하다 reward sb handsomely / 정량보다 후하게 주다 give a good measure

▶ 그 마을의 인심은 매우 후하다 The people of the village are quite warm-hearted.

2 〈두껍다〉 thick; heavy

후학 後學 1 〈후진 학자〉 a junior scholar

▶ 그는 후학을 가르치고 있다 He instructs his juniors.

2 〈후일의 참고〉 future information

♦ 후학을 위하여 for one's information; for future use [reference]

▶ 후학을 위한 당신의 의견을 듣고 싶습니다 I'd like to listen to your opinion for future reference.

후항 後項 1 〈뒤에 있는 조항〉 the succeeding clause; the latter item 2 〔數〕 〈다항중의 뒷항〉 the consequent; the latter term

후행 後行 〈사람〉 an (elderly) escort of a bride [bridegroom]; 〈행위〉 escorting a bride [bridegroom]

—**후행하다** escort [accompany] a bride [bridegroom]

후형질 後形質 〔生〕 〈세포의〉 metaplasm

후환 後患 future troubles

♦ 후환이 두려워 for fear of future troubles / 후환을 없애다 get rid of [remove] the source of all possible troubles / 후환을 남기다 sow the seeds of trouble

후회 後悔 repentance; regret; remorse

▶ 오랜 세월을 돌이켜 볼 때 그는 후회는 없었다 Looking back over the long years, he had no regrets.

—**후회하다** be sorry for; regret; repent (of); be penitent for

♦ 게을렀던 것을 후회하다 repent of one's idleness / 과거의 잘못을 후회하다 regret one's past mistakes / 뼈저리게 후회하다 regret [repent] bitterly

▶ 나는 그렇게 말한 것을 후회하고 있다 I'm sorry [I regret] (that) I said that. ⇌ I'm sorry [I regret] saying that.

▶ 나중에 후회할 거다 You will be sorry for it.

▶ 나는 내가 한 일을 후회하지 않는다 I have no regrets about what I did. ⇌ I feel no regret for what I did.

▶ 그는 열심히 공부하지 않은 것을 후회했다 He was very sorry [He regretted] he had not studied hard.

▶ 후회한들 돌이킬 수 없다 It is no use crying over spilt milk.

후후 with whiff [puff] after whiff [puff]; blowing ♦ 후후 불다 keep puffing

—**후후하다** whiff; puff (at)

후후년 後後年 three years from now ⇨ 내후년

훅[1] 〈갈고리 단추〉 a hook; a snap hook

▶ 그녀는 옷의 훅을 잠갔다[끌렀다] She fastened [unfastened] the hooks on her dress.

훅[2] 〔拳〕 a hook

♦ 상대방의 턱에 라이트 훅을 먹이다 deliver [let go] a right hook to the opponent's jaw

훅[3] 1 〈들이키는 소리〉 with a sip [slurp]; at a gulp [draft] ♦ 국을 훅 들이마시다 slurp up [gulp down] soup

2 〈부는 소리〉 with a whiff [puff]

▶ 그는 촛불을 훅 불어 껐다 He blew [puffed] out the candle.

훅하다 go [leap, jump] at [to]; spring [fly] at ♦ 어떤 제안에 훅하다 leap [jump] at a proposal; snap up an offer

훅훅 1 〈들이키는 모양〉 with sip [slurp] after sip [slurp]

♦ 국을 훅훅 마시다 slurp one's soup

2 〈부는 모양〉 ♦ 훅훅 불다 blow in puffs

3 〈더운 기운이 끼치는 모양〉 ▶ 태양이 훅훅 쪘다 The sun was scorching.

훈 訓 the Korean reading [translation] of a Chinese character

훈감하다 〈맛이〉 tasty; tastable; luxurious; 〈냄새가〉 fragrant; 〈푸짐하다〉 rich

♦ 훈감한 잔치 a sumptuous feast

훈계 訓戒 admonition; a lecture; 〈타일러 주의시킴〉 caution; warning
―훈계하다 admonish *sb* to do *sth*; caution [warn] *sb* against; advise *sb* not to do
▶ 그는 아들에게 두번 다시 거짓말하지 말라고 훈계했다 He admonished his son never to lie again.

훈고 訓詁 exposition; 〈성전(聖典)의〉 exegesis 《*pl.* -ses》; scholia 《*sing.* -lium》; interpretation
―학 exegetics; exegetical studies ―학자 a scholiast

훈공 勳功 merits; distinguished [meritorious] services; meritorious deeds
♦ 혁혁한 훈공이 있는 사람 a man of great merits / 훈공을 세우다 render distinguished services 《to the state》; win honorable distinctions
▶ 그는 훈공으로 훈장을 받았다 He was decorated in recognition of his distinguished services.

훈기 勳記 a patent of decoration; a diploma

훈기 薰氣 warm air; warmth
♦ 훈기있는 방 a warm room / 훈기가 돌다 warm up; become [get, grow] warmer

훈김 薰― 1〈훈기〉 warm fumes [steam] 2〈세력〉 influence; power; strength

훈도 薰陶 〈교육〉 education; instruction; 〈훈련〉 discipline
▶ 그는 김교수의 훈도를 받았다 He studied under Professor Kim. ⇌ He received good instruction from Professor Kim.
―훈도하다 educate; instruct; bring up; discipline

훈독 訓讀 the Korean reading [translation] of a Chinese character

훈등 動等 the order of merit

훈련 訓練 training; (a) drill; (a) discipline
♦ 잘 훈련받은 군인들 well-trained [disciplined] soldiers / 훈련을 받다 be trained [disciplined] 《in》; undergo training [discipline]; get training / 합숙 훈련을 하다 have [hold] a training camp / 훈련중이다 be under [in] training
▶ 그 소녀는 간호사로서의 훈련을 받았다 The girl was trained as a nurse.
▶ 그 버스 기사는 긴급사태에 대처하는 훈련을 받지 않았다 The bus driver was not trained in emergency procedures.
―훈련하다 train;〈되풀이해서〉 drill; exercise; discipline; school
♦ 군대를 훈련하다 drill troops / 잘 훈련되어 있다 be highly disciplined; be well trained
■―맹― hard [intensive] training 소방― a fire drill 어학― language training 제식(制式)― close-order drill 직 업―professional [job] training ■―교관 (軍) a drillmaster ―교본 a drill book [manual] 《for the infantry》; a training manual ―법 a way of training ―사〈개・말 조련사〉a dog trainer; a handler ―생 trainee ―장 a training ground [field]

훈련소 訓練所 a training school [station, institute, center] ■ 육군 신병― an army recruit [recruits'] training center

훈령 訓令 instructions; official orders
▶ 정부는 다음과 같은 훈령을 내렸다[발했다] The Government issued the following instructions.
―훈령하다 instruct; give [issue] instructions
■―전보 telegraphic instructions ―집 a directory

훈민정음 訓民正音 *Hunminjŏngŭm*; the Korean script [alphabet]

훈방하다 訓放― dismiss *sb* with a caution [an admonition]
▶ 경찰은 그를 훈방했다 The police dismissed him with a caution.

훈수 訓手 advice; suggestion; hint; tip
▶ 훈수 없기는 No helping from outsiders.
―훈수하다 suggest what move to make; kibitz; offer meddlesome advice to others
―꾼 a sidelines adviser; a kibitzer

훈시 訓示 an instruction; counsel; an address; 〈공무상의〉 official instructions
▶ 사장은 직원들에게 아침 훈시를 했다 The president gave a morning address [lecture] to his men.
―훈시하다 instruct; address; exhort; give *sb* counsel; make an admonitory speech; give [issue] official instructions

훈신 動臣 a meritorious subject [retainer]; a vassal of merit

훈육 訓育 (moral) education; discipline
♦ 훈육상의 educational; disciplinary
―훈육하다 discipline; train; educate
■―주임 a teacher in charge of discipline

훈장 訓長 〈글방선생〉a (village) schoolmaster; a teacher; a master; an instructor

훈장 勳章 a decoration; a medal; an order
♦ 훈장을 3개 달다 wear three decorations / 아무에게 훈장을 수여하다 decorate *sb* with an order; award a decoration to *sb*
▶ 그는 1996년 문화훈장을 받았다 He was awarded an order of Cultural Merit in 1996. ⇌ The cultural medal was awarded (to) him in 1996.

훈전하다 訓電― send telegraphic instructions; instruct telegraphically
▶ 우리는 워싱턴에 있는 그에게 훈전 쳤다[보냈다] We cabled our instructions to him in Washington.

훈제 燻製 smoking
♦ 훈제 연어 smoked salmon / 훈제의 smoked; smoke-dried ―훈제하다 smoke; dry 《fish》 in the smoke; bloat
■―소[실] a smokehouse ―품 smoked fish [meat]

훈증 燻蒸 fumigation ―훈증하다 fumigate
■―소독법 fumigation ―소독제 a fumigant

훈풍 薰風 a light, balmy breeze; a gentle breeze

훈화 訓話 an admonitory lecture; a moral discourse

훈훈하다 薰薰― nice and warm; comfortably warm
♦ 훈훈한 마음 tender affection / 마음을 훈훈하게 하는 이야기 a heartwarming story

훌닦다 〈몹시 나무라다〉 nag [snarl] 《at》;

abuse [criticize] sb severely; scold [reprimand] vehemently
♦ 며느리를 훌닦다 be hard on one's daughter-in-law / 아내에게 훌닦이다 be nagged [snapped] by one's wife

훌떡 1 〈벗어지거나 뒤집히는 모양〉 all; completely; entirely
♦ 훌떡 벗어진 대머리 a bald head / 훌떡 신을 벗어버리다 slip off one's shoes
▶ 그녀는 옷을 훌떡 벗어 마루에 던졌다 She pulled her dress off and threw it to the floor.
2 〈뛰어넘는 모양〉 at a jump; with one bound; at a bound; lightly (and nimbly)
▶ 그는 훌떡 울타리를 뛰어넘었다 He hopped [jumped] lightly over the fence.
3 〈먹는 모양〉 quickly; at a gulp
♦ 점심을 훌떡 먹다 take a quick luncheon
▶ 그는 큰 스테이크를 훌떡 먹어치웠다 He ate up a huge steak in the twinkle of an eye.

훌라댄서 a hula dancer
훌라댄스 hula(-hula)
♦ 훌라댄스를 추다 dance the hula
훌라후프 (商標) a Hula-Hoop
♦ 훌라후프를 돌리다 hula-hoop
훌렁 completely ⇨ 훌랑
훌렁하다 loose; baggy; loose-fitting
♦ 훌렁한 바지 loose(-fitting) trousers
▶ 이 바지는 내게 훌렁하다 These trousers are too large (for me).

훌륭하다 1 〈매우 좋다〉 nice; excellent; superb; splendid; brilliant
♦ 훌륭한 솜씨 wonderful skill / 훌륭한 업적 a remarkable [splendid] achievement; excellent results / 훌륭한 태도 a dignified manner; a commendable attitude
▶ 그는 훌륭한 경력을 가지고 있다 He has an admirable career.
▶ 이 번역은 훌륭하다 This translation is superbly done.
2 〈당당하다〉 stately; commanding; imposing
♦ 훌륭한 대저택 a magnificent mansion / 훌륭한 풍채 commanding presence; imposing appearance
3 〈존경할 만하다〉 honorable; respectable; 〈가치있다〉 worthy; commendable
♦ 훌륭한 업적 a worthy achievement
▶ 나는 그를 훌륭한 사람으로 알고 있다 I have a high opinion of him.
▶ 그는 훌륭한 가문 출신이다 He is from a good family.
▶ 그는 가난했으나 훌륭한 일생을 보냈다 He was poor but lived an honorable [a praiseworthy] life.
4 〈감탄할 만하다〉 commendable; admirable; praiseworthy
♦ 훌륭한 발명 a marvelous [wonderful] invention
▶ 그 창문에서의 전망은 훌륭하다 The window commands [has] an excellent [a wonderful, a very fine] view.
▶ 그의 연주는 정말 훌륭했다 His performance was really superb.
5 〈위대하다〉 great; eminent; noble
♦ 훌륭한 시인 a great poet / 훌륭한 학자 a great [distinguished] scholar
▶ 그는 자기가 훌륭하다고 생각하고 있다 He thinks he is somebody. ⇌ He thinks too much of himself.
6 〈공명정대하다〉 fair; square; honest
♦ 훌륭한 경기 fair play
▶ 그들은 훌륭하게 싸웠다 They fought fair in the battle. ⇌ They played fair.
7 〈충분하다〉 sufficient; good; 〈그럴 만하다〉 justifiable; worthy
♦ 훌륭한 이유 a good reason / 훌륭한 증거 sufficient evidence
▶ 구실로서는 그것으로 훌륭하지 I think that's a good enough excuse.

훌쩍 1 〈날아오르거나 뛰는 모양〉 lightly; nimbly; with a jump [bound]; quickly
♦ 담을 훌쩍 뛰어넘다 jump clean over the fence; fly over the fence at a bound / 무거운 것을 훌쩍 들어올리다 lift a heavy thing easily
▶ 그는 훌쩍 옆으로 뛰어 피했다 He lightly jumped aside.
▶ 그는 훌쩍 일어서서 노인에게 자리를 양보했다 He immediately stood up and gave his seat to the old man.
2 〈단숨에 들이마시는 모양〉 at a gulp; gulping; slurping; sipping; supping
♦ 국을 훌쩍 들이마시다 slurp up soup; gulp down soup
▶ 아이들은 우유를 훌쩍 마셔버렸다 The children gulped down their milk.
3 〈콧물을〉 sniffling; sniveling
♦ 코를 훌쩍 들이마시다 sniffle; snivel
4 〈떠나가는 모양〉 aimlessly; without any definite purpose
♦ 집을 훌쩍 떠나다 leave one's house [home] aimlessly
▶ 그는 훌쩍 우리한테 들르곤 했다 He used to drop in on us occasionally.

훌쩍거리다 1 〈액체를 들이마시다〉 slurp (up); gulp down; 〈콧물을〉 sniffle; snivel
▶ 그 아이는 코를 훌쩍거렸다 The child kept sniffling.
▶ 한국에서는 훌쩍거리며 국수를 먹는 것이 나쁜 식사법이 아니다 Slurping noodles is not bad manners at all in Korea.
2 〈날아오르다〉 fly up easily; take wing [flight] lightly [quickly]
3 〈울다〉 sob; whine

훌쭉하다 slender ⇨ 홀쭉하다
♦ 몸이 훌쭉한 사나이 a lanky fellow / 훌쭉한 볼 (have) hollow [sunken] cheeks
▶ 어머니는 오랜 병환으로 몸이 훌쭉해지셨다 My mother has grown thin and worn out because of her long illness.

훌훌 1 〈나는 모양〉 flutteringly; lightly
▶ 그 새는 날개를 몇번 치더니 훌훌 날아갔다 The bird flapped its wings a couple times and flew away.
2 〈뛰는 모양〉 nimbly; with an easy jump; with leaps and bounds ♦ 담을 훌훌 뛰어넘다 clear the wall with an easy jump
3 〈던지는 모양〉 ♦ 짐짝을 훌훌 내던지다 hurl baggages lightly / 씨앗을 훌훌 뿌리다 scatter seeds / 일을 훌훌 해치우다 finish up one's

work briskly
4 〈먼지 등을 터는 모양〉 ♦ 옷의 먼지를 훌훌 털다 shake dust off *one's* clothes
5 〈옷 등을 벗어부치는 모양〉 ♦ 옷을 훌훌 벗다 throw [fling] off *one's* clothes
6 〈들이마시는 모양〉 ♦ 차[국]를 훌훌 마시다 sip [tea] soup
7 〈불이 타오르는 모양〉 ⇨ 훨훨
♦ 훌훌 타다 burn well; blaze

훑다 1 〈벼 등을〉 thresh; hackle; strip
♦ 벼를 훑다 hackle rice / 뽕잎을 훑다 strip off the leaves of a mulberry twig
2 〈제거하다〉 remove; scrub 《off, away, out》
♦ 나무껍질을 훑다 bark a tree; peel the bark from [off] a tree
3 ⇨ 훑어보다

훑어보다 1 〈위 아래로〉 look *sb* up and down; stare [look hard] at *sb*
♦ 아무를 위 아래로 훑어보다 stare *sb* up and down
▶ 그는 몸을 돌려 나를 훑어보았다 He shot a glance at me as he turned.
2 〈죽 살피다〉 take a glance at; pass an eye over
♦ 책을 대강 훑어보다 run *one's* eyes through a book
▶ 나는 주요 제목만을 훑어보았다 I have only glanced [have taken a brief look] at the headlines.

훑이다 1 〈벼 등이〉 be hackled [threshed, stripped]
♦ 잘 훑이지 않다 be hard to hackle [thresh, strip]
2 〈제거되다〉 get scrubbed 《off, away, out》
3 〈빠지다·줄다〉 shrink; contract; get thin; be emaciated

훔쳐내다¹ 1 〈도둑질하다〉 steal *sth* from *sb*; pilfer; filch; make off with
♦ 슈퍼마켓에서 연어 통조림을 훔쳐내다 filch a can of salmon from a supermarket
2 〈더듬어 잡아내다〉 grope [fumble] for; 〈뒤져서〉 rummage out
♦ 비밀을 훔쳐내다 dig *sb's* secret out

훔쳐내다² 〈닦아내다〉 wipe up [out, off]; mop up; swab up
♦ 걸레로 훔쳐내다 wipe up with a floorcloth / 먼지를 훔쳐내다 wipe off the dust / 쏟질러진 커피를 훔쳐내다 wipe up spilled coffee

훔쳐먹다 eat secretly; sneak a snack; 〈훔치다〉 steal; pilfer; filch; 〈美俗〉 embezzle
♦ 거스름돈을 훔쳐먹다 pilfer [pocket] the change / 회사 돈을 훔쳐먹다 embezzle money from a firm

훔쳐보다 steal a glance [look] 《at》; look [glance] furtively 《at》
▶ 그는 옆에 앉은 학생의 답안지를 훔쳐보았다 He peeped at the answer sheet of the student sitting next to him.

훔치다¹ 1 〈도둑질하다〉 steal *sth* from *sb*; pilfer; filch; (美俗) swipe
♦ 남의 물건을 훔치다 make free with another's possessions / 금고에서 돈을 훔치다 steal money from a safe
▶ 그는 메리의 지갑을 훔쳤다 He stole Mary's billfold.
▶ 누가 내 카메라를 훔쳐 갔다 Someone stole [took] my camera. ⇌ My camera was stolen. ⇌ I had my camera stolen.
▶ 그 소년은 그녀의 핸드백을 훔쳐 달아났다 The boy ran away with her handbag.
▶ 남의 것을 훔치지 마라 You should not steal.
2 〈손으로 더듬다〉 grope for; fumble for
3 〈때리다〉 beat; slap; give [deal] a blow

훔치다² 〈닦아내다〉 wipe 《off, out, up》; mop 《up》; swab; 〈문질러서〉 scrub
♦ 걸레로 마루를 훔치다 wipe [scrub] the floor with a floorcloth / 눈물을 훔치다 dry [wipe away] *one's* tears
▶ 그는 이마의 땀을 손수건으로 훔쳤다 He wiped [mopped] the sweat off his forehead with a handkerchief.

훗날 後— the (distant) future; another day; some other day ⇨ 후일(後日)
♦ 훗날에 in (the) future; afterwards

훗달 後— the following [next] month

훗일 後— 〈장래의〉 future affairs; 〈사후의〉 affairs after *one's* death ⇨ 뒷일

훤소 喧騷 noise; clamor; tumult
♦ 대도시의 훤소 the din and bustle of a great city
—훤소하다 〈소란하다〉 noisy; clamorous

훤칠하다 tall; slender; high in stature

훤하다 1 〈흐릿하게 밝다〉 dimly-lit
♦ 훤한 하늘 a light sky; a dawning sky / 훤해지다 lighten; grow [get] light; light up
▶ 하늘이 훤하게 밝아오고 있다 The sky is starting to get [grow] light.
2 〈탁 트이다〉 open; broad and wide; vast; spacious
♦ 훤한 방 a spacious [large] room / 훤한 벌판 an expanse of plains
▶ 언덕에 오르니 전망이 훤히 트였다 We got a wide [an open] view from the top of the hill.
3 〈얼굴이〉 handsome; good-looking; fair
▶ 그 소년은 얼굴이 훤하다 The boy has a good-looking face.
4 〈정통하다〉 (be) familiar 《with》; (be) well acquainted 《with》; (be) well informed 《of》
▶ 그는 업무에 훤하다 He is well versed in his business [work].
▶ 그는 천문학에 훤하다 He has a broad [a wide, an extensive] knowledge of astronomy.

훨떡 completely ⇨ 활딱

훨씬 〈비교급·최상급 강조〉 by far; a lot; a great deal; out [far] and away; much 《bigger, broader》
♦ 훨씬 이전에 a long time [while] ago; long ago
▶ 어머님은 (건강이) 훨씬 좋아지고 계시다 Mother is getting much better.
▶ 오늘은 어제보다 훨씬 따뜻하다 It is much warmer today than yesterday.
▶ 둘 중에서 이것이 훨씬 낫다 This is by far [far and away] the better of the two.
▶ 두 사람 가운데 그가 훨씬 영리하다 He is by far the cleverer of the two.
▶ 나는 그가 오기 훨씬 전에 일을 끝마쳤다 I had finished the work long before he came.

휠쩍 widely ⇨ 활짝
휠휠 1 〈나는 모양〉 flutteringly
♦ 휠휠 날다 〈나비 등이〉 flutter [flit] about / 휠휠 날아가다 〈새가〉 fly with a steady flap of the wings
▶ 나비가 휠휠 날고 있다 Butterflies are fluttering about.
2 〈부채질하는 모양〉 ♦ 부채를 휠휠 부치다 fan slowly [gently]
3 〈옷을 벗는 모양〉 ♦ 상의를 휠휠 벗다 slip [hurry] off one's coat
4 〈불이 타오르는 모양〉 with a bright flame
♦ 휠휠 타다 blaze; flare (up)
▶ 불이 휠휠 타올랐다 The fire blazed up.
훼방 毀謗 1 〈방해〉 interference; intrusion; disturbance; trouble
—**훼방하다** interfere with sb; obstruct; hinder; disturb; stand in 《another's》 way
♦ 훼방놓다 disturb; hinder / 아무의 계획을 훼방놓다 obstruct sb's plan
2 〈비방〉 (a) slander; slanderous statements; abuse; defamation; (an) aspersion
—**훼방하다** slander; speak ill of; defame; fling mud at sb
▶ 그는 나를 훼방하는 기사를 썼다 He wrote a slanderous [defamatory] article about me.
훼사 毀事 interference; meddling; an interposition; an interruption
—**훼사하다** interrupt; interfere [meddle] 《in》; butt [break] in 《on sb's affairs》
훼손 毀損 damage; injury
—**훼손하다** damage; injure; impair; do harm
♦ 아무의 명예를 훼손하다 defame sb; injure sb's reputation
■ **명예**— defamation (of character); a slander
휑뎅그렁하다 〈허전하다〉 bare; hollow; empty; deserted; desolate ▶ 집안이 휑뎅그렁했다 The house seemed deserted [empty].
휑하다 〈통달하다〉 familiar 《with》; well acquainted 《with》; well [deeply] versed 《in》
▶ 그는 중국 고전에 휑하다 He has a profound knowledge of (the) Chinese classics.
휘 1 〈바람 소리〉 with a whistle
▶ 밤새 바람이 휘 불었다 The wind was blowing hard [whistling] all night.
2 〈숨을 한꺼번에 내쉬는 소리〉 with a puff [sigh]
♦ 휘 한숨을 쉬다 give a heavy sigh
3 〈둘러보는 모양〉 sweepingly
♦ 사방을 휘 둘러보다 look around in every direction; make a survey of the site
휘갈기다 〈매 등을〉 hit sb hard; give sb a sound thrashing [good licking]; 〈글씨를〉 scrawl; write hurriedly [hastily]
♦ 휘갈긴 편지 a scribbled note / 회초리로 장딴지를 휘갈기다 lash sb on the calves
휘감기다 1 〈감기어 붙다〉 coil [twine] itself round; coil around; get wound [twisted] round
▶ 덩굴이 나무줄기에 휘감겨 있다 Vines are twining around the trunk of the tree.
2 〈달라붙다〉 cling to; hang on to; 〈얽히다〉 be caught in
▶ 젖은 치마가 휘감겼다 My wet skirt clung to me.
3 〈휘둘리다〉 be confused; be distracted 《with, by》
휘감다 wind [coil] (a)round; tie [fasten] round
♦ 밧줄을 휘감다 wind a rope round sth / 다리에 붕대를 휘감다 bandage one's leg
휘갑치다 1 〈가장자리를〉 whipstitch; overcast 2 〈일을〉 finish; settle; wind up 《one's work》; round sth off [out]
▶ 그녀는 일을 요령있게 휘갑쳤다 She finished off her work efficiently.
휘날리다 wave; flutter; fly ♦ 바람에 휘날리다 flutter [wave, flap] in the wind
▶ 그들은 바람에 깃발을 휘날리며 행진했다 They marched with the flag fluttering in the wind.
휘늘어지다 hang down; dangle; droop
♦ 땅에 닿을듯 휘늘어진 수양버들가지 weeping willow branches close to the ground
휘다 1 〈구부러지다〉 bend; curve; become bent [curved]; 〈무게로〉 be weighed down; sag (down); 〈낭창낭창〉 be pliant [pliable]; be flexible [supple]; 〈압력에〉 yield; 〈몸 등이〉 bend back(ward)
♦ 잘 휘는 가지 a supple branch
▶ 가지들이 사과 무게때문에 휘어 있다 Those branches sag (down) under the weight of the apples.
▶ 열로 인해 판자가 휘었다 The heat has warped the boards.
▶ 이 철사는 잘 휜다 This wire is easy to bend.
2 〈구부리다〉 bend; curve
♦ 철사를 휘다 curve a wire
3 〈휘어잡다〉 bend sb to one's will; force sb to give in; control
휘돌다 go [turn] round; circle (around); spin (round); whirl; wheel
♦ 휘돌아가는 시내 a meandering stream / 호수를 한바퀴 휘돌다 go [walk] round a lake
휘돌리다 turn (around); spin; wheel; whirl; rotate
♦ 팽이를 휘돌리다 spin a top
휘동광 輝銅鑛 〔鑛〕 chalcocite
휘두르다 1 〈휘휘 돌리다〉 swing (around); sway; brandish; flourish; throw about
♦ 팔을 휘두르다 throw one's arms about / 칼 [창]을 휘두르다 brandish [wield] a sword [spear]
▶ 그는 팔을 휘두르다가 공을 던졌다 He swung his arm around and threw the ball.
2 〈얼을 빼다〉 bewilder; upset
3 〈제멋대로 하다〉 make indiscriminate use of; abuse; turn [twist] sb round one's (little) finger
♦ 아무에게 휘둘리다 be turned [twisted] around sb's little finger / 권력을 휘두르다 exercise [wield] one's power
▶ 하급 공무원은 권력을 휘두르기 일쑤다 Petty officials are apt to abuse their authority.
휘둥그렇다 wide-eyed; pop-eyed
▶ 그녀는 눈을 휘둥그렇게 뜨고 나를 보았다 She stared wide-[bug-]eyed at me.

휘둥그레지다 〈눈이〉 open *one's* eyes wide; (美俗) be pop-eyed
♦ 놀라서 눈이 휘둥그레지다 stare [open *one's* eyes wide] with [in] wonder; be pop-eyed with alarm
▶ 그들은 그 소식을 듣고 눈이 휘둥그레졌다 They were dumbfounded [astonished] by the news.

휘뚜루 ♦ 휘뚜루 쓰이다 have various [wide] uses; be of wide [extensive] use; be of general purposes

휘말다 1 〈감다〉 wind [twine, coil] *sth* round; 〈싸다〉 wrap [tuck] up (in)
♦ 거적에 휘말다 wrap [roll] *sth* up in a mat
2 〈더럽히다〉 make 《*one's* clothes》 wet and dirty; stain

휘말리다 1 〈말리다〉 be rolled [wrapped] up (in)
2 〈휩쓸리다〉 be entangled (in); be involved (in); be implicated (in); 〈파도 등에〉 be swallowed up; be dragged in
♦ 음모에 휘말리다 be entangled in a plot / 전쟁에 휘말려 들다 be involved in a war; be drawn [dragged] into a war
▶ 그 세 사람은 탁류에 휘말려 실종되었다 The three men were swallowed up by the muddy stream and disappeared.

휘몰다 1 〈말·차 등을〉 drive fast; urge [spur] 《a horse》 on; whip up 《a horse》
♦ 말을 휘몰다 spur a horse (on); gallop a horse / 차를 휘몰다 drive fast [hurry, hasten] in a car
2 〈가축·사냥감 등을〉 round up; drive; chase; run (down)
♦ 사냥감을 휘몰다 chase game / 양을 목장에 휘몰아 넣다 drive sheep to a meadow / 멧돼지를 hunt down [out] wild boars / 소떼를 축사에 휘몰아 들이다 drive cattle back to the barn
3 〈채근하다〉 drive [press] *sb* hard 《to, into, to do》; urge [spur] on

휘몰아치다 〈바람이〉 blow hard (and strong); blow violently; rage; rave; roar; 〈눈이〉 fall in whirls; fall thick and fast
♦ 휘몰아치는 바람 a raging [roaring] wind / 휘몰아치는 눈 a swirling snow; whirls of snow; a blizzard
▶ 폭풍우가 휘몰아치고 있다 The storm is raging.

휘묻이 layering; layerage —**휘묻이하다** layer 《a tree》

휘발 揮發 volatilization —**휘발하다** volatilize ■ —물 volatile matter —성 volatility : 휘발성 용제 a volatile solvent / 휘발성의 volatile —유 benzine; gasoline; (英) petrol

휘석 輝石 〈鑛〉 pyroxene; augite
휘선 輝線 〈物〉 a bright line
—스펙트럼 a bright-line spectrum

휘슬 〈호루라기〉 a whistle ▶ 심판이 휘슬을 불었다 The referee blew his whistle.

휘어잡다 1 〈손에〉 hold *sth* bent [doubled up] in *one's* hand; grasp; grip; seize; take [catch] hold of
▶ 그는 그것을 꼭 휘어잡았다 He seized it and held it tightly.
▶ 배가 흔들리는 바람에 나는 급히 난간을 휘어잡았다 As the ship rolled I hurriedly gripped the rail.
▶ 그는 청중의 마음을 잘 휘어잡는다 He knows how to captivate his audience.
2 〈제멋대로 하다〉 have *sb* under *one's* control; manipulate
♦ 부하를 휘어잡다 win over the hearts of men under *one* / 여자를 휘어잡다 control a woman at will
▶ 그는 실업계를 휘어잡고 있다 He pulls the strings in the business world.

휘어지다 be bent; bend; bow; be pliant; be supple
▶ 가지는 눈의 무게로 휘어졌다 The branches bent [bowed] under the weight of the snow.
▶ 이 낚싯대는 잘 휘어진다 This fishing rod is very flexible.

휘영청 〈밝게〉 bright(ly) ▶ 달이 휘영청 밝다 The moon beams down.

휘우듬하다 slightly curved [warped]
휘장 揮帳 a curtain; hangings
휘장 徽章 a badge; a medal; 〈표상〉 an emblem; 〈소매·깃의〉 an insignia; an ensign
♦ 휘장을 달다[달고 있다] put on [wear] a badge

휘적거리다 swing 《*one's* arms》; sway 《*one's* hand》 to and fro; shake; wave ♦ 양팔을 휘적거리며 걷다 walk with a swagger

휘젓다 1 〈뒤섞다〉 stir (up); give a stir; beat up; churn
♦ 스푼으로 커피를 휘젓다 stir *one's* coffee with a spoon / 계란을 휘저어 거품이 일게 하다 whip [beat] an egg
▶ 그녀는 밀가루와 달걀을 풀릴 때까지 휘저었다 She beat the flour and eggs until they were smooth.
2 〈흔들다〉 ♦ 팔을 휘저으며 걷다 swing *one's* arms as *one* goes [walks]
3 〈어지럽게 만들다〉 disturb; upset; confuse; 〈뒤지다〉 ransack
▶ 그는 장롱 서랍을 휘저어 장갑을 찾았다 He rummaged for his gloves in the chest of drawers.

휘정거리다 stir up 《water》; make 《water》 muddy

휘주근하다 1 ⇨ 후줄근하다 2 〈지쳐있다〉 ready to drop (with fatigue); dog-tired; exhausted; worn [tired, fagged] out

휘지르다 soil; make dirty ♦ 옷을 휘지르다 soil *one's* clothes / 바지를 온통 휘지르다 get *one's* pants all dirty

휘청거리다 1 〈휘어지다〉 yield; bend; 〈낭창거리다〉 be pliant [pliable, flexible]
♦ 휘청거리는 낚싯대 a whippy fishing pole
2 〈힘이 없어〉 totter; wobble; be unsteady; be shaky; 〈拳〉 be groggy
♦ 휘청거리는 unsteady; shambling; reeling; groggy / 세게 얻어맞고 휘청거리다 reel under a heavy blow

휘추리 〈가늘고 긴 가지〉 a slender twig [sprig]
휘트먼 〈미국의 시인〉 Whitman, Walter (1819-92)

휘파람 a whistle ◆휘파람을 불다 whistle; give a whistle / 휘파람으로 개를 부르다 whistle for one's dog
▶그는 그 곡을 휘파람으로 불었다 He whistled the tune.

휘하 麾下 troops under one's command; one's men ◆휘하의 (men) under one's command / 휘하에 모이다 rally round sb

휘호 揮毫 〈글씨〉 (a piece of) calligraphy; (hand) writing; 〈그림〉 painting; drawing ─휘호하다 〈글씨를〉 write; 〈그림을〉 draw; paint ■─료 a fee [an honorarium] for a painting [writing]

휘황찬란하다 輝煌燦爛─ brilliant; glittering; radiant; dazzling
◆휘황찬란한 보석을 박은 왕관 a brilliantly bejeweled crown / 휘황찬란하게 빛나다 shine brilliantly

휘휘 round and round (about); in circles
◆휘휘 감다 wind round sth / 막대를 휘휘 내두르다 brandish [flourish] a stick; wave about a stick

휙 1 〈재빨리〉 quickly; 〈갑자기〉 suddenly; abruptly
◆창문을 휙 열다 fling [throw] a window open / 휙 지나가다 pass quickly / 나무막대를 휙 휘두르다 swish a wooden stick through the air
▶차가 모퉁이를 휙 돌아갔다 A car whizzed around the corner.
▶좋은 생각이 휙 떠올랐다 Suddenly a good idea occurred to me.
2 〈바람 등이〉 with a whiff; with a whistle [whiz(z)].
▶바람이 휙 불고 있었다 The wind was whistling [blowing].
▶총알이 머리 위를 휙 지나갔다 A bullet whistled [whizzed] past above my head.
3 〈힘껏〉 with full force; with all one's strength
◆창을 휙 던지다 hurl [dart] a spear

휠체어 a wheelchair; a wheeled chair

휩싸다 1 〈감아 싸다〉 wrap (up); envelop; tuck up
▶그녀는 아기를 담요로 휩쌌다 She wrapped her baby in a blanket. ⇌ She tucked a blanket around her baby.
2 〈비호하다〉 cover; shield; protect

휩싸이다 1 〈감겨 싸이다〉 be wrapped up (in); be bundled (in)
2 〈덮어 가려지다〉 be covered (with); be enveloped [shrouded, veiled] (in)
▶산꼭대기는 안개에 휩싸였다 The mountain-top was wrapped [enveloped, shrouded] in mist.
▶그 집은 불길에 휩싸였다 The house was in flame [on fire].

휩쓸다 1 〈일소하다〉 sweep away [off]; clear (away, off); 〈병·재해 등이〉 sweep (over, through); 〈압도하다〉 overwhelm; sway
◆판돈을 휩쓸다 sweep away [rake up] the money on the gambling table
▶우리 팀이 경기를 휩쓸었다 Our team won a runaway [lopsided] victory.
▶어젯밤 화재가 온 마을을 휩쓸었다 The fire burned down the whole village last night.
2 〈설치다〉 overrun; overwhelm; rampage; take the lead; control
▶취객이 바를 휩쓸었다 A drunk ran amuck the bar.

휩쓸리다 be swept away [off]; be pulled [dragged] into; 〈말려들다〉 be involved [entangled] in; be drawn into
◆물결에 휩쓸리다 be swept away by the waves; be swallowed up by the waves / 인파에 휩쓸리다 be swept along in the crowd / 전쟁에 휩쓸려 들다 be involved in a war; be drawn [dragged] into a war
▶나는 싸움에 휩쓸렸다 I was dragged [drawn] into the quarrel.

휴가 休暇 a holiday; 〈장기의〉 (美) a vacation; (英) holidays; 〈말미〉 a leave of absence; (a) furlough
◆짧은 휴가 a short leave / 겨울휴가 동안 during winter vacation [the winter holidays] / 휴가를 얻다 take a vacation; get [obtain, secure] a leave of absence; have a furlough; (美) take one's day off; (英) take a holiday / 5일간의 휴가를 얻다 take [have] five days off / 휴가를 주다 grant sb a leave of absence [furlough] / 휴가를 시골에서 보내다 spend one's holiday in the country
▶나는 내일부터 휴가다 My vacation begins tomorrow.
▶내주에 이틀쯤 휴가를 얻고 싶습니다 I want to take a couple of days off next week.
▶그는 지금 휴가로 집에 있다 He is home on vacation [holiday, leave].
▶그는 휴가로 어디 가고 없었다 I found him away on vacation.
▶나는 내일 휴가다 I'll take tomorrow off. ⇌ I'll be off tomorrow.
■겨울[여름]— the winter [summer] vacation [holidays] 생리— a special monthly leave for women 유급— a paid holiday [vacation] 출산— a maternity leave 크리스마스— the Christmas holidays ■─여행 a holiday trip; (美) a vacation tour [trip]

휴가원 休暇願 a request for a vacation; a leave application
◆휴가원을 내다 submit a request for a leave; apply for a leave of absence

휴간 休刊 suspension [discontinuation] of publication
─휴간하다 suspend [discontinue] publication
▶본지는 내주 휴간합니다 No issue next week. ⇌ Next week's issue will not appear.
▶당분간 휴간함 Publication suspended until further notice.
■─일 〈신문의〉 a newspaper holiday

휴강 休講 ─휴강하다 give no lecture (for the day) ▶김교수 금일 휴강함 (게시) Prof. Kim: No lecture today.

휴게 休憩 〈휴식〉 a rest; 〈휴지〉 a break; a recess; 〈막간〉 an intermission; (英) an interval
─휴게하다 rest; take a rest [recess]; take [have] a break

▶ 우리는 5분간 휴게했다 We had a five-minute rest [break].
■—소 a resting place —시간 a break; a recess; 〈막간의〉 an intermission; (英) an interval —실 a resting room; 〈호텔 등의〉 a lounge; a lobby

휴관 休館 closure (of a museum)
—휴관하다 close (a museum)
▶ 금일 휴관함 (게시) Closed today.
▶ 본 미술관은 월요일마다 휴관합니다 This art museum is closed on Mondays.

휴교 休校 closure of a school
—휴교하다 close a school
▶ 내주 화요일은 휴교함 There will be no school next Tuesday. ⇌ School will be closed next Tuesday.

휴대 携帶 carrying
◆ 휴대용 녹음기 a portable recording machine / 휴대용 라디오 a portable radio / 휴대용 무선전화기 a portable radiophone; (口) a walkie-talkie / 휴대용 텔레비전 a portable television / 휴대용의 portable; handy (to carry)
—휴대하다 carry; bring [take] *sth* with *one*; have *sth* with [about] *one*
◆ 무기를 휴대하다 carry [be armed with] a weapon
▶ 어떤 것이든 신분 증명서를 휴대하는 것을 잊지 마라 Don't forget to carry [have] some (form of) identification (with [on] you).
■—무기 small arms —식량 (軍) emergency ration; field [combat] ration —연료 canned fuel [heat]; (軍) fuel ration —전화 a cellular phone

휴대품 携帶品 *one's* things; *one's* personal effects [belongings]; 〈짐〉 (美) hand baggage; (英) hand luggage
■—보관소 a cloakroom; (美) a checkroom

휴런호 —湖 〈북미 5대호의 하나〉 Lake Huron

휴머니스트 a humanist

휴머니즘 humanism

휴면 休眠 (植·動) dormancy ◆ 휴면중인 dormant; resting —휴면하다 be dormant
▶ 대개의 종자는 겨울에 휴면한다 Most seeds lie dormant in the winter.
■—기 a period of dormancy

휴스턴 〈미국의 도시〉 Houston (▶ 우주선 비행 관제 센터가 있음)

휴식 休息 rest (▶ 한번의 휴식은 a rest); repose; relaxation
◆ 점심을 위한 1시간의 휴식 an hour's recess for lunch / 휴식에 들어가다 〈회의 등이〉 adjourn; (美) recess
—휴식하다 rest (*oneself*); take a rest [respite]; repose; relax
◆ 휴식하게 하다 give *sb* a rest; rest / 충분히 휴식하다 take a good rest
▶ 자, 잠깐 휴식하자 Now, let's have a short rest [a break for a while].
■—중간— an intermission; an interval; a recess ■—처 a resting place; a place for refreshment

휴식시간 休息時間 time to rest; a recess; a break ◆ 5분간의 휴식시간 a five-minute [five minutes'] rest [recess]

휴양 休養 rest; relaxation; recreation; 〈병후의〉 recuperation
—휴양하다 rest; rest *oneself*; take a rest; relax; 〈병후에〉 recuperate
■—생활 〈병후의〉 a life of recuperation —시설 recreation facilities —여행 a trip of recreation —지 a recreation center; a rest area; a resort

휴업 休業 〈점포 등의〉 closure; suspension of business [operations]; 〈회사·공장의〉 a shutdown; 〈휴가〉 a vacation
◆ 휴업 중인 공장 an idle factory
▶ 개점 휴업상태다 The door is opened, but practically no business is done within.
—휴업하다 〈점포 등〉 be closed (to business); suspend business
▶ 금일 휴업함 (게시) Closed today.
▶ 내부수리 때문에 당분간 휴업합니다 (게시) Temporarily closed for renovation(s).
■ 임시— a special holiday ■—일 a holiday; a day off

휴일 休日 a holiday; 〈비번날〉 a day off; (美) an off day
◆ (밖에서) 휴일을 즐기는 사람 a holiday-maker; a holidayer / 사흘 계속되는 휴일 three consecutive holidays; three holidays in succession / 휴일 기분으로 in a holiday mood / 휴일을 이용하여 여행하다 go vacationing; go away for a holiday / 매달 4일의 휴일을 주다 give four days off per month
▶ 내일은 휴일이다 We have a holiday tomorrow. ⇌ Tomorrow is a holiday. ⇌ I am off duty tomorrow.
▶ 학교는 내일 휴일이다 We have no school tomorrow.
▶ 나는 휴일에는 대개 낚시하러 간다 I usually go fishing on holidays.
▶ 법정— a legal holiday 은행— (美) a bank holiday 임시— a special holiday ■—근무 holiday work —수당 per diem for work on a regular [an established] day off —여행 a holiday trip; 〈주말의〉 a weekend trip

휴전 休電 suspension of power supply
—일 a no-power day

휴전 休戰 〈일시적인〉 a cease-fire; an armistice; 〈장기의〉 a truce
▶ 유엔은 양국에 휴전을 요청했다 The United Nations asked the two countries to agree to a cease-fire.
—휴전하다 stop [cease] firing; conclude an armistice (with); make a truce 《with》
■—전면적[무장]— a general [an armed] truce ■—교섭[협상]— truce [cease-fire] negotiations —기 a flag of truce —기념일 〈제1차 세계대전의〉 Armistice Day —명령 a cease-fire —선 a cease-fire [an armistice] line —조약 a peace treaty; an agreement of truce —협정 a cease-fire agreement

휴전회담 休戰會談 a truce conference; truce [cease-fire] talks
◆ 휴전회담을 개최하다 hold a truce conference; talk cease-fire 《with》

휴정 休廷 ▶ 오늘은 휴정이다 The court will not sit today.

휴지 —휴정하다 hold no court; adjourn the court (until)
▶ 4월 20일까지[1주일간] 휴정합니다 The court will adjourn until April 20th [for a week]. ■ —**일** a non-judicial day; (라) 〔法〕 a dies non (juridicus) 《pl. dies nons, dies non juridici》

휴지 休止 a rest; a pause; a standstill; suspension; stoppage —**휴지하다** 〈중지하다〉 pause; stop; cease; 〈멈추다〉 come to a standstill

휴지 休紙 1 〈못쓰는 종이〉 wastepaper; scraps of paper; paper scraps
♦ 휴지를 줍다 pick up wastepaper / 약속을 휴지화하다 break one's word [promise]
▶ 그 서류[계약서]는 이제 휴지나 다름없다 The document [contract] is now no better than wastepaper [a mere scrap of paper].
2 〈뒤지〉 toilet paper [tissue]; 〈두루마리〉 toilet roll
■ —**통** (美) a wastebasket; (英) a wastepaper bin: 휴지통에 넣다 throw in(to) a wastebasket

휴지부 休止符 1 〔樂〕 ⇨ 쉼표
2 〈구두점〉 a rest; a pause
♦ 휴지부를 찍다 put a pause 《to》

휴직 休職 temporary retirement from office; a leave of absence; 〈불경기 등에 의한〉 (美) a layoff; 〈병에 의한〉 a sick leave
—**휴직하다** retire temporarily from office; 〈명을 받고〉 be laid off; be suspended from duty [office]
▶ 그는 병으로 1년간 휴직했다 He was absent from work for a year because of illness.
■ —**급** 〈장교의〉 half pay

휴진 休診 —**휴진하다** accept no patients; be not seeing patients
▶ 금일 휴진함 (게시) Office closed today. ⇌ No consultations [appointments] today.

휴학 休學 temporary absence from school
♦ 3개월간 휴학원을 내다 apply for a three-month leave of absence
—**휴학하다** be absent [absent oneself] from school temporarily [for a time]
▶ 그는 외국여행으로 1년간 휴학했다 He traveled abroad and was away [absent] from school for the whole [one] year.
■ —**동맹** a strike of students; a school [college] strike ■ —**생** a student who stays out of school temporarily

휴한지 休閑地 1 〔農〕 land in fallow; a fallow land ♦ 휴한지를 이용하다 make use of idle land 2 ⇨ 공지 (空地)

휴화산 休火山 a dormant [an inactive] volcano

휴회 休會 〈회기 중의〉 adjournment; 〈휴식·폐회 후의〉 a recess
♦ 휴회 중이다 be in recess; be out of session
▶ 국회는 6월부터 휴회다 The National Assembly will go into recess in June.
▶ 그 회의는 내주 금요일까지 휴회되었다 The meeting was adjourned until next Friday.

휼병 恤兵 the relief of soldiers —**휼병하다** give relief [aid] to soldiers

흄 〈영국의 철학자·역사가〉 Hume, David (1711-76)

흉 1 〈흉터〉 a scar
▶ 그는 뺨에 흉이 있다 There is a scar on his cheek.
▶ 흉이 없어졌다 The scar disappeared. ⇌ The scar left no trace.
2 〈흠〉 a flaw; a defect; a weakness; a drawback
♦ 흉있는 물건 a defective article
♦ 흉없는 사람은 없다 Nobody is perfect. ⇌ No one is free from faults.

흉가 凶家 a haunted house; a house of ill [evil] omen

흉계 凶計 an evil scheme; a wicked design; a plot; a trick ♦ 흉계에 빠지다 fall a victim to sb's scheme / 흉계를 꾸미다 devise a cunning scheme; hatch a plot; concoct tricks

흉골 胸骨 the breastbone; 〔解〕 the sternum 《pl. ~s, -na》 ♦ 흉골의 sternal
■ —**통** (痛) sternalgia; sternodynia

흉곽 胸廓 the chest; the thorax 《pl. ~es, races》 ♦ 흉곽이 넓다[좁다] have a broad [narrow] chest ■ —**성형술** thoracoplasty

흉금 胸襟 the bosom; the heart; the mind
♦ 흉금을 털어놓다 confide in sb about sth; (open up and) talk to sb without reserve; unbosom oneself 《to》 / 흉금을 털어놓고 이야기하다 have a heart-to-heart talk 《with》; have a frank talk; speak frankly

흉기 凶器 a murderous [lethal] weapon
▶ 자동차는 달리는 흉기로 불리기도 한다 Cars are sometimes called deadly weapons on wheels.

흉내 mimicry; 〈모방〉 imitation
♦ 흉내내다 mimic; imitate; copy; follow 《another's example》; follow suit / 아무의 목소리를 흉내내다 mimic [feign] sb's voice; imitate [take off] the voice [tone] of sb / 아무의 걸음걸이를 흉내내다 mimic sb's manner of walking
▶ 그는 흉내를 잘 낸다 He is a good [clever, great] mimic.
▶ 앵무새는 사람의 말을 흉내낸다 Parrots imitate human speech.
▶ 이것은 내가 흉내낼 수 없는 글[그림]이다 I can't write [paint] anything (half) as good as this.
■ —**말** 〈의성어〉 an onomatopoeic [echoic] word; an onomatopoeia; 〈의태어〉 mimesis; a mimetic word —**쟁이** a mimic; an imitator

흉년 凶年 a bad year; 〈흉작의〉 a lean year; a year of bad harvest ♦ 흉년 거지 a beggar in the lean year / 흉년이 들다 have a bad crop [harvest]; have a year of famine

흉노 匈奴 〔史〕 the Huns

흉몽 凶夢 a bad dream; an ominous dream; an evil [ill-boding] dream; a nightmare
♦ 흉몽에 시달리다 be troubled by a nightmare

흉물 凶物 an evil [a treacherous] person; a ferocious person

흉물스럽다 凶物— wicked; treacherous; black-hearted

흉벽 胸壁 1 ⇨ 흉장
2 〈인체의〉 the walls of the chest

흉보 凶報 bad [ill] news; evil tidings; a bad report; 〈부고〉 news of death ◆유족에게 흉보를 전하다 break sad news to the family
흉보다 find fault with; speak badly about *sb*; pick out 《another's》 defects; speak ill of; criticize; abuse
◆안듣는 데서 흉보다 backbite *sb*; speak ill of *sb* behind 《his》 back [in 《his》 absence]
▶흉보는 말에는 개의치 마라 Pay no attention to the gossip of scandalmongers.
흉부 胸部 the chest; the breast; 〔解・動〕 the thorax (*pl*. ~es, ·races)
◆흉부의 thoracic / 흉부에 통증을 느끼다 feel [have] a pain in the chest
■—X선 검사 a chest X-ray examination —외과 chest [thoracic] surgery —질환 a chest disease; a trouble in the chest
흉사 凶事 an unlucky [evil] affair; a misfortune ▶흉사가 연달아 일어났다 One misfortune [accident] followed another.
흉상 凶相 (an) ugly [unseemly] appearance; 〈관상적으로〉 an evil physiognomy; a sinister look
흉상 胸像 a bust; 〈머리・사지가 없는〉 a torso
흉악 凶惡 1〈성질〉 atrocity; brutality —흉악하다 atrocious; heinous; brutal ◆흉악한 행위 an atrocious act
2〈용모〉 ugliness; unsightliness —흉악하다 ugly; ugly-looking
■—범 a heinous crime; 〈범인〉 an atrocious [a vicious] criminal
흉악망측하다 凶惡罔測— 〈성질이〉 extremely atrocious [vicious, heinous, brutal, wicked]; 〈용모가〉 very ugly(-looking)
흉어 凶漁 a poor haul; a poor catch
흉위 胸圍 〈가슴둘레〉 a chest size [measurement]; 〈여자의〉 a bust size
◆흉위를 재다 take *sb's* chest measurement; measure *sb's* chest
▶흉위가 얼마나 됩니까? What is your chest size?
▶그녀는 흉위가 90센티미터다 She measures 90 centimeters around the chest. ⇌ Her bust measurement is 90 centimeters.
흉일 凶日 an unlucky day; a black day
흉작 凶作 a bad [poor] crop [harvest]; a failure of crops; a short crop [yield]
◆보기 드문 흉작 an exceptionally bad harvest / 흉작의 해 a lean year
▶금년은 감자가 흉작이었다 The potato crop was a failure this year.
▶금년 벼농사는 5년 이래의 흉작이다 The rice crop this year is the worst that we have had these five years.
흉잡다 find fault with; pick [point] out *sb's* defects; pick holes in others; criticize
흉잡히다 be found fault with; be spoken ill of; be criticized
흉장 胸牆 〔軍〕 a breastwork; a parapet
흉조 凶兆 an ill omen; an evil sign
흉중 胸中 one's bosom [mind, heart]; one's feelings
▶그는 그 추억을 흉중에 간직했다 He kept the memory to himself.

흉추 胸椎 〔解〕 the thoracic vertebrae
흉측하다 凶測— extremely wicked ⇨ 흉악망측하다
흉탄 凶彈 a shot by an assassin ◆흉탄에 쓰러지다 be shot and killed [dead] by an assassin
흉터 a scar ⇨ 흉 1
◆칼에 베인 흉터 a sword cut / 이마에 흉터가 있다 have a scar on the forehead
▶상처가 아물어도 흉터는 남을 것이다 Even after the wound heals, the scar will show [remain].
흉통 胸痛 a pain in the chest; a chest pain
◆흉통을 느끼다 have a pain in *one's* chest
흉포 凶暴 atrocity; ferocity; brutality —흉포하다 ferocious; atrocious; brutal
◆흉포한 행위 an atrocious deed; an atrocity
▶화가 나면 그는 흉포해진다 When he's angry, he gets quite brutal.
흉하다 凶— 1〈못생기다〉 ugly; ugly-looking; 〈보기 어색하다〉 ungainly; unshapely; awkward; unbecoming
◆보기 흉한 여자 a plain [an ugly, (美) a homely] woman / 차림이 흉한 남자 a seedy-looking [shabbily dressed] man
2〈불길하다〉 ill-omened; unlucky; ominous; ill-boding; sinister
◆흉한 꿈 an unlucky dream
▶13은 흉한 숫자라고들 한다 Thirteen is said to be an unlucky number.
3〈성질이 나쁘다〉 wicked; vicious
◆흉한 놈 a wicked [bad] man; a villain / 흉한 짓 a wicked [bad] act
흉한 凶漢 〈악한〉 a villain; a ruffian; an outlaw; 〈습격자〉 an assailant; 〈살인자〉 a murderer; a killer; 〈암살자〉 an assassin
◆흉한의 손에 쓰러지다 fall a victim to an assassin; be attacked and killed by an assassin
흉허물 a fault; a defect; a flaw
흉허물없다 〈서술적〉 be on friendly terms with ◆흉허물없는 친구 a friend on frank terms; an intimate [familiar] friend / 흉허물없이 이야기하다 talk frankly; speak without restraint / 흉허물없이 지내다 associate on friendly [candid] terms 《with》
흉협다 凶— ugly; unsightly; indecent; terrible; dreadful
◆보기 흉협다 be (too) ugly [awful] to look at / 옷차림이 흉협다 be shabbily [seedily] dressed
▶색깔이 흉협다 The color is dreadful.
흉흉하다 洶洶— 1〈물결이〉 high; rough; furious
◆흉흉한 물결 raging [turbulent] waves
2〈인심이〉 panicked; panic-stricken; (be) in great fear
▶세상이 온통 흉흉하다 There is social unrest everywhere.
흐느끼다 sob; 〈아이 등이〉 whimper; whine
◆흐느껴 울다 sob (convulsively); be choked with tears / 흐느끼며 부탁하다 ask with a sob
▶그녀는 감동하여 흐느꼈다 She was moved and sobbed.
흐느적거리다 swing; sway; flutter; 〈불꽃 등

이〉 flicker; flare
♦(나뭇잎이) 바람에 흐느적거리다 be swayed by the wind; flutter in the breeze
▶창문이 열려서 커튼이 흐느적거리고 있다 Curtains are flapping at the open window.

흐늘거리다 1 〈놀고 지내다〉 be idle; idle [dawdle] one's time away; lead an idle life 2 〈흔들거리다〉 waver; swing [sway] gently; 〈흐물거리다〉 be soft [limp, flabby, flaccid, squashy] ♦바람에 흐늘거리는 꽃들 flowers nodding in the wind
▶나비가 흐늘거리며 날고 있다 A butterfly is fluttering about.

흐늘어지다 hang (down); dangle; droop (heavily) ⇨ 휘늘어지다

흐늘쩍거리다 move around slowly [sluggishly, idly]
♦흐늘쩍거리며 걷다 walk slowly; poke along; have a ramble

흐늘쩍흐늘쩍 slowly; sluggishly
♦흐늘쩍흐늘쩍 걷다 walk slowly [leisurely]

흐늘흐늘 1 〈빈둥빈둥〉 idly; lazily; at leisure
♦흐늘흐늘 세월을 보내다 idle [dawdle] one's time away; lead an idle life
2 〈흔들흔들〉 unsteadily; waveringly; shakily; swingingly; swayingly; 〈흐물흐물〉 softly; squashily
♦흐늘흐늘하게 삶다 boil to pulp
▶그는 흐늘흐늘 팔을 늘어뜨리며 걸어갔다 He walked away with his arms dangling at his sides.

흐드러지다 1 〈썩 탐스럽다〉 charming; fascinating; attractive ♦꽃들이 흐드러지게 피다 flowers come out splendidly [gorgeously]; be in magnificent bloom
2 ⇨ 흐무러지다

흐들갑스럽다 flippant ⇨ 호들갑스럽다

흐려지다 1 〈하늘이〉 become cloudy [overcast]; be clouded over; cloud; become covered with clouds
▶갑자기 하늘이 흐려졌다 Suddenly the sky became overcast.
2 〈희미해지다〉 become dim; dim; be blurred; become foggy; 〈탁해지다〉 become turbid [muddy]; 〈불투명해지다〉 become dull [opaque]; be tarnished
▶밖에 있다가 방으로 들어가니 내 안경이 흐려졌다 My glasses fogged up when I entered the room from outside.
▶눈물로 그녀의 눈이 흐려졌다 Tears blurred her vision [eyesight]. ⇌ Her eyes were clouded with tears.
▶나이를 먹으면 눈이 흐려진다 Our sight grows dim with age.
3 〈근심 등으로〉 become gloomy
▶그의 얼굴은 근심으로 흐려져 있었다 His face was clouded with anxiety.
▶그 소식을 듣고 그녀의 안색이 흐려졌다 Her face clouded over [was clouded] when she heard the news.

흐루시초프 〈구소련의 정치가〉 Khrushchev, Nikita Sergeyevich (1894-1971)

흐르다[1] 1 〈유동하다〉 flow; run; stream; 〈졸졸〉 trickle; 〈스며나오다〉 ooze; 〈촛불이〉 run; gutter
♦흐르는 시내 a running stream / 창문으로 흘러 들어오는 달빛 moonlight streaming in through the window
▶템스강은 런던 시내를 흐른다 The Thames flows [runs] through London.
▶파이프가 막혀 물이 흐르지 않았다 The pipe was choked up and the water didn't go through [drain (off)].
▶얼굴에 땀이 흘렀다 Sweat ran down my face.
▶그의 상처에서 피가 흘렀다 Blood ran from his wound.
▶그 일가는 학자의 피가 흐르고 있다 Learning runs in the family.
▶흐르는 물은 썩지 않는다 Running water is better than standing.
2 〈떠다니다〉 float; drift; 〈유랑하다〉 drift; wander
▶나무 토막이 강으로 흘러 떠내려왔다 A piece of wood came floating [drifting] down the river.
3 〈쏟아지다〉 spill; get [be] spilt; 〈넘치다〉 overflow; run [flow] over
▶식탁에 우유가 흘렀다 Some milk spilt on the table.
▶나는 흐르는 눈물을 주체할 수 없었다 I could not hold back the tears.
4 〈기름기 등이〉 ♦얼굴에 기름이 흐르다 grease exudes on [oozes out of] one's face; 〈비유〉 have a well-fed look [complexion]
▶그에게는 어딘지 촌티가 흐른다 There is something rustic [countrified] about him.
5 〈쏠리다〉 run [incline, be inclined] 《to》; lean [tend, trend] 《toward》; be swayed [carried away] 《by》
▶감정에 흐르지 마라 Don't be swayed by sentiment.
▶그들은 극단으로 흐르기 쉽다 They tend to go to extremes [excess].
6 〈세월이〉 pass (by [away]); elapse
▶그로부터 10년의 세월이 흘렀다 Ten years have passed [elapsed] since then.
▶세월이 흘러 그 사건은 잊혀졌다 With the passage of years the event was forgotten.
7 (비유) ♦동석한 자리에서는 우호적인 분위기가 흐르고 있었다 A friendly atmosphere prevailed among those present.
▶잠시 어색한 침묵이 흘렀다 An awkward silence hung for a while.

흐르다[2] 〈홀레하다〉 copulate; mate; pair; cover; 〈말이〉 serve; 〈닭이〉 tread

흐름 flowing; 〈물줄기〉 a flow; a stream; a current; 〈경향〉 a trend

> 解説 **flow**는 원활하고 안정된 흐름을 말한다. **stream**은 끊임없이 계속되는 흐름을 말하며 수도나 수원지 등에서 흘러나오는 물을 나타낸다. **current**는 stream과 거의 같은 뜻으로 쓰이지만 흐름의 강도나 방향을 강조하는 말이다.

♦물의 흐름 the flow of water / 때의 흐름 the passage of time; the stream [flux] of time;

〈시대 조류〉 the current [tendency, trend] of the times
▶ 이 도로에는 차량의 흐름이 끊이질 않는다 There is a constant flow [stream] of traffic in this road.
▶ 그 사건이 역사의 흐름을 바꾸어 놓았다 The event changed the course of history.

흐리다[1] **1**〈혼탁하게 하다〉 make 《water》 muddy [turbid]; muddy 《a well》;〈오염시키다〉 make dirty [filthy]; contaminate; pollute
▶ 차의 배기가스가 공기를 흐리고 있다 Exhaust from cars is polluting the air.
▶ 떠나는 물새는 뒤를 흐리지 않는다 When a swimming bird takes flight, it does not muddy the water. ⇌ (비유) I don't want to leave bad memories behind me.
2〈명예를 더럽히다〉 disgrace; blemish; stain; spot ♦ 명예를 흐리다 sully [tarnish, defile, cloud] one's honor
3〈흔적을 지워 버리다〉 blot out; blur (out); obscure; efface;〚寫〛 blur
4〈애매하게 하다〉 make vague [obscure, indistinct, ambiguous]
♦ 말끝을 흐리다 speak ambiguously; avoid [shun] plain speaking; make an ambiguous statement; evade the point / 셈을 흐리다 leave accounts hazy

흐리다[2] **1**〈불분명하다〉 not clear; unclear; vague; obscure; indistinct;〈애매하다〉 ambiguous; noncommittal
♦ 기억이 흐리다 have a vague memory / 태도가 흐리다 take an uncertain attitude 《toward》; do not commit oneself
▶ 그는 나이 때문에 기억이 흐렸다 His memory faded because of old age. ⇌ Old age has dimmed [clouded] his memory.
2〈희미하다〉 dim; clouded; obscure; blurred
♦ 김으로 흐린 유리창 windowpanes clouded up with steam / 흐린 인쇄 blurred printing / 흐린 등불 a dim light
▶ 전등은 흐렸다 The electric light was dim.
3〈탁하다〉 muddy; turbid; cloudy;〈목소리가〉 thick; hoarse;〈더럽혀지다〉 foul; impure; polluted; contaminated
♦ 흐린 물 muddy water / 목소리가 흐린 hoarse-voiced
▶ 강물이 흐려 보인다 The river looks polluted [contaminated].
▶ 스모그로 하늘이 흐려 있었다 The smog clouded the sky.
4〈날씨가〉 cloudy; clouded; overcast
♦ 흐린 날 a cloudy day / 흐린 하늘 a cloudy sky
▶ 내일은 흐릴 것입니다 〈일기예보 등〉 It will be cloudy tomorrow. ⇌ The outlook for tomorrow is (for) cloudy (skies).
5〈감각이〉 dim; dull; bleary
♦ 눈이 흐리다 have dim [bleared] eyes / 청력이 흐리다 be hard [dull] of hearing

흐리멍덩하다 1〈분명치 않다〉 indistinct; vague; obscure; indefinite; hazy; misty; foggy;〈애매하다〉 ambiguous; equivocal; evasive; dubious
♦ 흐리멍덩한 대답 《give》 a vague [noncommittal] answer; 《give》 an equivocal [indecisive] answer / 흐리멍덩한 태도 an ambiguous [a dubious] attitude
▶ 기억은 시간이 지나면 흐리멍덩해진다 Memories fade [become dim] with time.
2〈귀가〉 dull; dim
♦ 귀가 흐리멍덩하다 be hard [dull] of hearing

흐리터분하다 1〈사물이〉 indistinct; vague; dim; obscure; hazy; misty; foggy
♦ 흐리터분한 날씨 cloudy [gloomy] weather; dull [thick] weather / 셈이 흐리터분하다 be loose in settlement of accounts
▶ 오늘 아침은 잠이 부족해서 머리가 흐리터분하다 I cannot think clearly this morning because of lack of sleep.
2〈사람이 느슨하다〉 dull; sluggish; slovenly; loose;〈성미가 분명치 않다〉 slow-witted; not open; dark-minded
♦ 흐리터분한 사람 a slovenly fellow; a sloven; a blockhead / 흐리터분한 처사 underhand dealings

흐릿하다 1〈날이〉 (rather) cloudy [overcast]
▶ 흐릿한 밤하늘에 달이 희미하게 떠 있었다 The moon hung dimly in the cloudy night sky.
2〈불분명하다〉 vague; dim; obscure; indistinct; hazy;〈뿌옇다〉 clouded; blurred; smoked;〈탁하다〉 rather muddy [turbid]
♦ 흐릿한 불빛 a dim light
▶ 나는 그것이 흐릿하게 생각날 뿐이다 I have only a faint [vague] recollection of it.
▶ 멀리 산이 흐릿하게 보인다 You can see mountains faintly in the distance.
▶ 안개 때문에 지평선이 흐릿했다 Haze blurred (out) the horizon.
3〈눈이〉 (rather) dim [dull, bleary];〈청력이〉 (rather) hard [dull] of hearing
▶ 눈이 침침해서 모든 것이 흐릿하게 보인다 Everything looks blurred to my dim eyes.

흐무러지다 1〈잘 익어서〉 soft and limp; over-ripe; overmature; squashy;〈물에 불어서〉 soaked; sodden; soft; pulpy; mushy; bloated
2〈뭉그러지다〉 crumble (into decay); moldering

흐물흐물하다 (too) soft and pulpy; flabby; limp; squashy; mushy
♦ 흐물흐물하게 삶다 reduce to pulp by boiling long; boil sth to jelly / 흐물흐물해지다 be reduced to pulp; become pulpy [flabby, limp]
▶ 어두운데서 나는 어떤 흐물흐물한 것을 밟았다 I stepped on something soft [mushy] in the dark.

흐뭇하다 〈만족하다〉 satisfying; satisfactory; gratifying; satisfied;〈유쾌하다〉 pleasing; pleasant;〈기쁘다〉 joyful; glad; delightful; happy; pleased
♦ 흐뭇한 소식 glad [happy, joyful] news
▶ 그는 그 결과에 흐뭇했다 He was satisfied with the result(s).
▶ 그녀는 나의 선물에 매우 흐뭇해 했다 She was very pleased [delighted] with my gift.
▶ 나는 그 소식을 듣고 매우 흐뭇했다 I heard the news with great [much] satisfaction.

흐슬부슬 crumblingly ♦ 흐슬부슬 부서지다

흐지부지 ♦ 흐지부지 끝나다 come to nothing; end in smoke / 돈을 흐지부지 다 써버리다 use up *one's* money to no purpose
▶ 조사는 흐지부지 끝나버렸다 The investigation failed to come to any definite conclusion.
▶ 이 문제를 흐지부지 놔둘 순 없다 We cannot leave this matter unsettled [undecided].

흐트러뜨리다 1 〈여기저기〉 scatter (about); strew; 〈군중을〉 disperse; dispel; break up
♦ 방에 종잇조각을 흐트러뜨리다 litter a room with scraps of paper
▶ 바람이 길에 나뭇잎을 흐트러뜨렸다 The wind strewed [scattered] the road with leaves.
2 〈머리칼 등을〉 dishevel (*one's* hair)
♦ 머리를 흐트러뜨리고 with disheveled [unkempt] hair
3 〈기타〉 ♦ 아무의 정신을 흐트러뜨리다 divert *sb's* attention / 적을 흐트러뜨리다 rout the enemy; put the enemy to rout

흐트러지다 1 〈흩어지다〉 disperse; scatter; be scattered (about)
▶ 빈 깡통이 사방에 흐트러져 있었다 Empty cans were scattered all over the place. = The place was littered [strewn] with empty cans.
▶ 그의 방은 언제나 흐트러져 있다 His room is always in a mess.
2 〈머리카락이〉 be disheveled; (口) be mussed (up); be in disarray
♦ 흐트러진 머리 disheveled [unkempt] hair / 흐트러진 머리를 빗어 올리다 comb up [back] *one's* disheveled [loose] hair
3 〈기타〉 ♦ 걸음이 흐트러지다 get out of step
▶ 우리는 처음에는 줄지어 갔으나 이내 흐트러졌다 We started out in a file but eventually got scattered.

흑 with a sob; chokingly ♦ 슬퍼서 흑 울다 sob with grief; sob out *one's* grief

흑 黑 1 〈색깔〉 black; a black color ♦ 흑을 백이라고 우기다 call black white; talk black into white
2 〈바둑돌의〉 a black stone

흑갈색 黑褐色 dark brown
흑고래 黑— 〔動〕 a humpback (whale)
흑내장 黑內障 〔醫〕 black cataract; amaurosis
흑다이아몬드 黑— 〈보석〉 a black diamond; 〈석탄〉 coal
흑단 黑檀 〔植〕 an ebony
흑두 黑豆 〈검은팥〉 a black adzuki bean
흑두루미 黑— 〔鳥〕 a hooded crane
흑두재상 黑頭宰相 a young premier [minister]
흑막 黑幕 1 〈장막〉 a black curtain
2 〈음흉한 내막〉 an ulterior design; concealed [undisclosed] circumstances; a behind-the-scenes story
♦ 흑막을 폭로하다 expose a secret ((of))
▶ 이 잡지는 연예계의 흑막을 폭로하는 기사를 자주 싣는다 This magazine often carries articles exposing the seamy side of the entertainment world.
■ —외교 secret [behind-the-scenes] diplomacy

흑맥주 黑麥酒 black [dark] beer; 〈영국산의〉 porter; stout; 〈독일산의〉 bock (beer)
흑반 黑斑 a black spot [speckle] ■ —병 purple blotch
흑발 黑髮 black hair ♦ 흑발의 여인 a black-[raven-]haired woman
흑백 黑白 1 〈색깔〉 black and white
2 〈선악〉 good and [or] bad [evil]; 〈시비(是非)〉 right and [or] wrong; guilty or non-guilty [innocent]
♦ 흑백을 가리다 see which is right; discriminate between good and bad [right and wrong]; decide [settle] the matter / 법정에서 흑백을 가리다 bring the matter to court for trial
▶ 이 경우는 흑백을 가릴 수가 없다 In this case we cannot tell good from evil [discriminate between good and bad].
■ —사진 a black-and-white [monochrome] photograph —영화 a black-and-white picture; a monochrome film —텔레비전 a black-and-white television (set)

흑빵 黑— black [rye] bread
흑사병 黑死病 (the black) plague; the pest; 〈14세기의〉 the Black Death
흑삼릉 黑三稜 〔植〕 a bur reed
흑색 黑色 a black color; black ■ —인종 the black [African] race; the Negro (race) —화약 black gunpowder; blasting powder
흑설탕 黑雪糖 raw [brown] sugar; unrefined sugar; muscovado
흑셔츠 黑— a black shirt —당〈파시스트당〉 the Blackshirts; the Italian Fascist Party —당원 a Blackshirt
흑수병 黑穗病 〈깜부깃병〉 smut; dustbrand; 〈밀의〉 bunt ♦ 흑수병에 걸리다 smut; become affected by smut
흑수정 黑水晶 smoky quartz
흑심 黑心 a black [an evil, a wicked] heart; ill will; malice
♦ 흑심이 있는 blackhearted; ill-intentioned; evil-hearted; malicious; wicked / 흑심을 품다 bear ill will; harbor an evil heart
흑싸리 黑— 〈화투의〉 a black bush-clover card (of flower-card game)
흑연 黑鉛 〔鑛〕 black lead; graphite
■ —광상(鑛床) a graphite deposit —로(爐) 〈원자로의〉 a graphite reactor; a carbon reactor [pile]
흑요석 黑曜石 〔鑛〕 obsidian; volcanic glass
흑운모 黑雲母 〔鑛〕 biotite
흑의 黑衣 black clothes; a black garment [dress, robe] ♦ 흑의를 입은 사람 a man in black
흑인 黑人 a black; a Negro (*pl.* ~es); a colored person; (俗) a darky [darkie]; 〈미국내에서〉 an African American; (총칭) colored people; the colored; black people
♦ 흑인과 백인의 대립 the antagonism between blacks and whites / 흑인을 차별대우하다 segregate Negroes
▶ 미합중국의 몇 퍼센트가 흑인입니까? What

percentage of the U.S. population is black [African American]?
■—거주 지구 〈빈민가〉 a black ghetto —문제 the Negro problem [question] —분리반대(운동) antisegregation (movement) —분리정책 the segregation policy —영가 Negro spirituals —옹호 negrophilism —옹호자 a negrophil(e) —음악 Negro music —종 the colored [black, Negro, African] race —지대 the Black Belt —차별대우 segregation; 〈남아프리카공화국의〉 apartheid —차별대우폐지 desegregation; integration —학교 a colored school

흑자 黑字 **1** 〈검은 빛의 글자〉 black characters [figures]
2 〈경제의〉 the black-ink balance; surplus
♦ 10억 달러의 무역 흑자 a one-billion-dollar trade surplus; a trade surplus of one billion dollars / 흑자인 in the black / 흑자가 나다 go into the black / 흑자 수지를 유지하다 keep the balance in the black
▶ 우리 회사는 흑자 운영을 하고 있다 Our company is operating in the black.

흑점 黑點 **1** 〈검은 점〉 a black [dark] spot; 〈과녁의〉 the bull's-eye **2** 〈태양의〉 a sunspot; a macula 《*pl*. -lae》
♦ 흑점 주기 a sunspot cycle

흑조 黑潮 the Black [Japan] Current
흑체 黑體 〔物〕 a black body
흑칠 黑漆 black lacquer
흑탄 黑炭 black [bituminous] coal
흑토 黑土 black soil [earth]
■—지대 a black earth zone [area]
흑판 黑板 a blackboard ⇨ 칠판
흑해 黑海 the Black Sea
흑흑 1 〈우는 소리〉 sobbingly; whimperingly —흑흑하다 sob; 〈어린아이가〉 whimper
2 〈추위에 떠는 모양〉 convulsed with cold —흑흑하다 feel a chill; feel a chill creep over *one*

흔들거리다 sway; swing; waver; tremble; 〈불꽃이〉 flicker
▶ 이 의자는 흔들거린다 This chair wobbles.
▶ 그 소년은 담 위에 앉아 다리를 흔들거리고 있었다 The boy sat on the wall swinging his legs.

흔들다 1 〈움직이다〉 shake; swing; wave; wag; 〈진동시키다〉 oscillate
♦ 팔[다리]을 흔들다 swing *one's* arms [legs] / 꼬리를 흔들다 〈말이〉 whisk its tail; 〈소가〉 swish its tail; 〈개가〉 wag its tail / 나무를 흔들어 과일을 떨어뜨리다 shake down fruit from a tree
▶ 그는 노래에 맞추어 오른팔을 흔들었다 He swung his right arm to [in tune with] the song.
▶ 그녀는 머리를 가로 흔들어 아니라고 했다 She shook her head and said no.
▶ 그는 머리를 세로 흔들어 그렇다고 했다 He nodded (his head) and said yes.
2 〈선동하다〉 stir up; agitate; incite; instigate
♦ 민심을 흔들다 stir up the public feeling

흔들리다 1 〈물체가〉 shake; sway; wave; 〈떨리다〉 tremble; 〈진동하다〉 vibrate; 〈상하로〉 toss; bob; 〈매단 것이〉 swing; 〈차 등이〉 joggle; jolt; 〈불꽃이〉 flicker; bicker; 〈가늘게〉 quiver; waver; 〈배가〉 pitch; roll; rock
♦ 사방으로 흔들리는 불빛 a flickering [wavering, glimmering] light / 바람에 흔들리다 sway [shake] in the wind; tremble [rustle] in the breeze
▶ 버스가 몹시 흔들렸다 The bus jolted badly.
▶ 이가 흔들린다 A tooth is loose.
▶ 그때 나는 건물이 흔들리는 것을 느꼈다 At that time I felt the building shake.
▶ 전차가 지나갈 때마다 땅이 흔들린다 The ground trembles [vibrates] every time a train passes.
▶ 이 전차는 몹시 흔들린다 This train rocks a good deal.
▶ 배는 전후좌우로 심하게 흔들렸다 Our ship rolled and pitched [rocked] heavily.
2 〈마음이〉 shake; be shaken; be shaky [unsteady]; waver
♦ 흔들리는 마음 a wavering mind; an irresolute [underminded] mind / 결심이 흔들리다 *one's* resolution shakes; be shaken in *one's* resolution
▶ 그녀의 마음은 그 두 사람 사이에서 흔들리고 있다 She is wavering between the two men.
▶ 그의 신념은 절대 흔들리지 않는다 His belief never waves.
▶ 그의 결심은 조금도 흔들리지 않았다 He remained firm in his resolution.

흔들목마 —木馬 a rocking horse; a cockhorse
흔들의자 —椅子 a rocking chair; a rocker
흔들흔들 swingingly; swayingly; flickeringly; in a wavering [swaying, flickering] manner
▶ 나뭇잎이 바람에 흔들흔들 나부끼고 있다 The leaves are swaying [quivering] in the wind.
—흔들흔들하다 ⇨ 흔들리다

흔연하다 欣然— joyful; cheerful; delightful; glad
흔연히 欣然— with joy; joyfully; gladly; cheerfully; willingly; readily; with (a) good grace
♦ 흔연히 승낙하다 cheerfully accept; accept willingly [readily]
▶ 그는 내 사과를 흔연히 받아주었다 He accepted my apology with good grace.

흔적 痕迹 traces; tracks; 〈소멸된 것의〉 marks; signs; 〈증적(證迹)〉 evidences; vestiges
♦ 고대문명의 흔적 the vestige of the ancient civilization / 흔적이 있다 bear the marks 《of》 / 흔적을 남기지 않다 leave [show] no traces [marks] 《of *sth*》 / 흔적을 발견하다 find traces 《of》 / 흔적을 모조리 없애다 remove all traces 《of》
▶ 우리는 차[범인]의 흔적을 더듬었다 We followed the tracks of the car [criminal].
▶ 오늘날 그 사찰은 흔적조차 남아 있지 않다 Nothing remains of the temple now. ⇌ There is nothing left of the temple.
▶ 금고는 열어젖힌 흔적이 없다 The safe shows no sign of having been unlocked.
■—기관 〔生〕 a vestigial [rudimentary] organ

흔전만전 in plenty [abundance]; abundantly; plentifully; lavishly ◆돈을 흔전만전 쓰다 lavish [squander] money —**흔전만전하다** plentiful; rich; profuse; lavish

흔쾌 欣快 pleasure; delight —**흔쾌하다** pleasant; happy; joyful; delightful ◆흔쾌히 gladly; willingly; readily
▶그는 내 청을 흔쾌히 들어 주었다 He was quite ready to comply with my request.

흔하다 1〈많다〉 abundant; plentiful; rich; ample
◆돈이 흔하다 money is in plentiful supply; there is a lot of [plenty of] money
▶흔한 것이 사람이다 If there's one thing we have enough of, it's men.
▶이 달은 비가 흔했다 We have had a lot of rain this month. ⇌ It has rained very often this month.
2〈아무 데나 있다〉 common; commonplace; familiar
◆흔해 빠진 very [quite] common / 흔하지 않은 uncommon; extraordinary; rare / 흔해 빠진 일 a commonplace event; an everyday affair
▶그런 경우는 흔하다 That's fairly common. ⇌ It's the kind of thing that happens every day.
▶여성이 직업을 갖는 것이 이제는 흔한 일이다 It is now quite an ordinary [a common] thing for a woman to have a job.
▶이런 횡재는 흔치 않은 일이다 You cannot have such a windfall every day.

흔히 commonly; mostly; usually; generally; in general; often; all the time; frequently; popularly
◆흔히 있는 일 an affair of common [everyday] occurrence / 흔히 쓰이는 말 a common [an everyday] word / 흔히 볼 수 있는 광경 a common sight / 학생들에게는 흔히 있는 일이지만 as usual with students
▶이것은 흔히 틀리는 철자다 This is a common spelling mistake.
▶어릴적에는 흔히 헤엄치러 가곤 했었다 I used to go swimming when I was a child.
▶사고란 흔히 있는 법이다 Accidents will happen.
▶걱정마라, 흔히 있는 일이다 Don't worry about it. It happens all the time [quite often].
▶이것은 흔히 있는 물건이 아닙니다 This article is of no ordinary type.

흘겨보다 glance [look] (at) sideways; glare sidelong (at); squint [leer] (at); cast a side(long) glance of disapproval (at)

흘기다 look disapprovingly (out of the corner of one's eyes); give a sharp look; cast a side glance; cast a reproachful [disapproving] glance (at); squint (at sb)
▶그녀는 샘이 나서 그에게 눈을 흘겼다 She shot an envious, sidelong look at him.
▶아버지는 나를 흘겨보시며「이것도 모르겠니?」하셨다 Father glared at me and said, "Can't you even understand this?"

흘깃거리다 look sidelong (at sb); give sb a sidelong look

흘끗 1〈잠깐 보이는 모양〉 ◆자동차가 지나가는 것이 흘끗보이다 catch a glimpse of a car passing by
2〈곁눈질하는 모양〉 with a sidelong glance ◆흘끗 보다 look askance [sideways] (at); steal [cast] a sidelong glance (at)
▶그는 그녀의 얼굴을 흘끗 보았다 He stole a covert glance at her face.

흘끗거리다 cast sidelong glances (at); look furtively (at)

흘끗흘끗 ◆흘끗흘끗 보다 steal a glance (at); cast sidelong glances (at); see by glimpses

흘러가다 flow; run; 〈떠가다〉 float [drift] along; 〈시간이〉 fly ◆덧없이 흘러가는 청춘 the flying years of youth
▶구름이 천천히 하늘을 흘러가고 있다 Clouds are drifting across the sky.
▶그로부터 10년이란 세월이 흘러갔다 Ten years have passed since then.

흘러나오다 〈유출하다〉 flow out; run out; stream [pour] out; 〈쏟아지다〉 gush forth; 〈스며나오다〉 ooze out
▶눈물이 그녀의 눈에서 흘러나왔다 Tears flowed [streamed] from her eyes.
▶상처에서 피가 흘러나왔다 The blood flowed out from the wound.

흘러내리다 1〈떨어지다〉 run [stream, pour] down; fall; drop
▶눈물 한방울이 그의 뺨에 흘러내렸다 A tear ran down his cheeks.
2〈미끄러 내리다〉 slip [slide, glide] down ◆흘러내리는 바지를 치켜올리다 pull [hitch] up one's trousers
▶손수건이 그녀의 손에서 흘러내렸다 The handkerchief slipped out of her hand.

흘러들다 flow in [into]; run [pour, stream] in [into]
▶강은 바다로 흘러든다 Rivers run [flow] into the sea.
▶시원한 바람이 창으로 흘러들었다 Fresh air streamed in through the window.

흘레 copulation; coition; (a) coupling (of animals) —**흘레하다** mate; copulate; pair; 〈닭이〉 tread; 〈말이〉 cover

흘레붙이다 couple; mate together; pair animals (for breeding) ◆암말을 흘레붙이다 serve a mare

흘리다 1〈액체를〉 let (water) flow [run out]; 〈쏟다〉 spill; shed; 〈한꺼번에〉 pour over; 〈조금씩〉 drain; drop; let drop; drip; dribble
◆국물을 흘리다 spill soup / 눈물을 흘리다 shed tears / 땀을 흘리다 perspire; sweat / 물을 흘리다 let the water run / 코피를 흘리다 bleed at the nose; one's nose bleeds / 나라를 위해 피를 흘리다 shed one's blood for one's country
▶내가 양탄자에 커피를 흘렸다 I spilled my coffee on the rug.
▶그녀는 더러운 물을 흘려 보냈다 She poured away the dirty water.
▶그 아이는 콧물을 흘리고 있었다 The child's nose was running.
▶그들은 피를 흘리지 않고 폭도를 진압했다 They suppressed the rioters without bloodshed.
2〈잃다〉 lose; drop ◆돈을 흘리다 lose one's

money
3 〈귀담아 듣지 않다〉 take no notice; pay no attention (to); ignore; neglect ♦ 농담으로 흘리다 take 《it》 as a joke
▶ 그는 내 충고를 흘려 들었다 He paid no attention to [neglected] my advice.
4 〈글씨를〉 write in the grass hand [cursive style]; 〈급히 쓰다〉 write hurriedly; scribble; scrawl
5 〈조금씩 주다〉 dribble out; give by [in] driblets

흘림 the cursive style of writing (Chinese characters) ⇨ 초서(草書)

흘수 吃水 draft; 《英》 draught
♦ 〈배가〉 흘수 16피트다 be of 16 feet draft; draw 16 feet (of water) / 배의 흘수를 재다 take the draft of a ship / 흘수가 깊은[얕은] 배 a ship of deep [light] draft
■ 만재(滿載)— load draft; full (load) draft
■ —표 the draft mark

흘수선 吃水線 the waterline; the draft (line)
■ 만재— the load (water) line

흙 〈일반적 토양〉 earth; 〈특히 작물이 생육하는 토양〉 soil; 〈진흙〉 mud; 〈찰흙〉 clay; 〈지면〉 the ground
♦ 흙으로 돌아가다 return [fall back] to dust; turn to clay; die / 흙을 덮다 heap up earth; cover with earth; earth up; mould up / 흙을 파다 dig up earth; 〈갈다〉 till the soil; 〈농사 짓다〉 do farming / 흙 속에 묻다 bury 《it》 in the ground
▶ 그는 이국땅의 흙이 되었다 He died on [was buried in] foreign soil [land].
▶ 내 눈에 흙이 들어가기 전에는 안돼 I say no so long as I live [am alive].
▶ 사람은 한줌의 흙에 지나지 않는다 Man is but a lump of clay.
▶ 그는 10년만에 모국땅의 흙을 밟았다 He set foot in [returned to] his mother country for the first time in ten years.
▶ 흙으로 돌아가라 Back to the land!

흙구덩이 a hole [cavity] in the ground; a pit

흙내 the smell of earth; (an) earthy smell
♦ 흙내가 나는 earthy; earth-smelling / 흙내를 맡다 take a smell at [have a smell of] earth; 〈초목이 뿌리 박다〉 take [strike] root

흙담 a mud wall [《美》 a dirt, an earthen] wall

흙더미 a heap [mound] of earth

흙덩어리 〈흙덩이〉 a lump of earth; a clod (of earth)

흙먼지 dust; a cloud of dust; a dust storm
▶ 자동차가 자욱한 흙먼지를 일으키며 지나갔다 The car raised a cloud of dust as it passed by.

흙무더기 a heap of earth
♦ 흙무더기를 쌓아 올리다 pile up a mound

흙뭉치 a mud pie; a ball [lump] of earth [mud]

흙뭉텅이 a large lump [ball] of earth [mud]

흙받기 **1** 〈자전거·자동차의〉 a mudguard; a splash guard; a splashboard; a fender; 〈마차의〉 a dashboard
2 〈미장이의〉 a mortarboard

흙벽 a mud-plastered wall; a clay wall

흙빛 muddy brown; (an) earthlike color; the color of earth
▶ 그의 얼굴은 피로로 흙빛이었다 His face was pale [gray] with fatigue.
▶ 그 소식을 듣는 순간 그의 얼굴은 흙빛이 되었다 As soon as he heard the news, he turned deadly [deathly, ashy] pale.

흙손 〈미장이의〉 a (plasterer's) trowel; 〈끝손질 용〉 a float ♦ 흙손질 trowelling; plastering with a trowel / 흙손질하다 trowel; lay on 《plaster》 with a trowel; plaster with a trowel; level with a float

흙일 earthwork(s); 〈미장이 일〉 plaster work; plastering —흙일하다 do earthwork; plaster
■ —꾼 a navvy

흙장난 playing with earth
—흙장난하다 play with earth
▶ 아이들이 길에서 흙장난하고 있다 The children are playing with mud in the street.

흙질 〈흙 바르기〉 mud plastering —흙질하다 mud-plaster; plaster [daub] 《a wall》 with mud; do the mud [plastering] work

흙칠하다 soil [smear, daub] with mud
♦ 얼굴에 흙칠하다 smear *one's* face with mud; (비유) fling [sling, throw] mud at; asperse 《*sb's* character》
▶ 부모님 얼굴에 흙칠하는 일을 해서는 안된다 You shouldn't do things to disgrace [bring disgrace on] your parents.

흙탕 **1** 〈질퍽한 곳〉 a muddy place [spot]
▶ 코끼리는 흙탕 속에 빠져 움직일 수 없었다 The elephant got stuck in the mud.
2 ⇨ 흙탕물
■ —길 a muddy road

흙탕물 muddy water ♦ 아무에게 흙탕물을 튀기다 splash [spatter] *sb* with muddy water
▶ 덤프트럭이 나에게 흙탕물을 뒤집어 씌웠다 A dump truck spattered muddy water on [over] me.

흙투성이 being covered all over with earth; being smeared all over with mud
♦ 흙투성이가 되다 be covered with mud [earth]

흠 欠 **1** 〈물건의 금〉 a crack; a flaw; 〈긁힌 흠〉 a scratch; a disfigurement; a speck; 〈과일의 상함〉 a bruise
♦ 흠이 있는 flawed; cracked; disfigured; bruised / 흠이 없는 flawless; perfect / 〈찻잔 등이〉 흠이 있다 have a flaw [crack] / 흠이 생기다 flaw; 〈금가다〉 crack; 〈과일이〉 bruise
▶ 테이블에 흠이 조금 있다 There are some scratches [scrapes] on the table.
▶ 이 꽃병에는 흠이 있다 There is a small crack in this vase.
▶ 이것들은 흠이 있어서 싸게 드립니다 As these are defective goods I will part with them dirt cheap.
2 〈결점〉 a fault; a defect; a blemish; a flaw; a mar; a blur; a stain
▶ 급한 성질이 그의 유일한 흠이다 A short temper is his only flaw [defect].
▶ 그는 가명(家名)에 흠을 냈다 He disgraced his family.
3 〈상처 자국〉 a scar; a seam; a mark

▶ 아마 이마에 흠이 남을 것이다 Probably a scar will stay on your forehead.
흠 〈비웃는 소리〉 Pooh!; Pish!; Pshaw!; Humph!; Huh! ◆ 흠하고 웃다 laugh [smile] scornfully 《at》; jeer 《at》
흠나다 欠— get scarred ⇨ 흠지다
흠내다 欠— **1** 〈흉터를 내다〉 scar; make a scar ◆ 얼굴에 흠내다 scar *one's* face
2 〈물건에〉 flaw; mar; crack; scratch; make a flaw [crack, scratch]
▶ 매끈한 표면을 흠내지 않도록 조심하세요 Be careful not to scratch [damage] the smooth surface.
흠뜯다 欠— mention another's faults; refer to another's weakness
▶ 그는 내 일을 늘 흠뜯는다 He's always criticizing [finding fault with] my work.
흠모 欽慕 admiration; adoration; reverence; high regard —**흠모하다** admire; adore; esteem; idolize; make an idol of sb
흠뻑 very much; plenty; fully; thoroughly; to the full; sufficiently; 〈맘껏〉 to *one's* heart's content; to *one's* satisfaction
◆ 흠뻑 젖다 be drenched [soaked, doused, wet] to the skin; get wet through [all over]; 〈옷이〉 get dripping [soaking] wet / 땀을 흠뻑 흘리다 be all of a sweat; get sweat all over; perspire profusely / 흠뻑 마시다 drink *one's* fill
▶ 비가 흠뻑 왔다 We had sufficient rain.
▶ 소나기를 만나 흠뻑 젖었다 I was caught in a shower and got soaking wet [wet all over].
▶ 그는 흠뻑 취했다 He was dead [blind, beastly] drunk.
▶ 셔츠가 땀으로 흠뻑 젖었다 My shirt was wet through [dripping wet] with sweat.
흠씬 enough; sufficiently; thoroughly; completely; to the full ◆ 흠씬 두들겨 주다 beat sb soundly; give sb a sound thrashing / 고기를 흠씬 삶다 do meat well
흠잡다 欠— find fault with; cavil [carp] at; pick holes in; 《美口》 pick on 《sb, sth》
◆ 흠잡을 데가 없다 be above reproach; be faultless; leave nothing to be desired; be perfect [ideal] / 남의 흠잡기를 좋아하다 be fond of finding fault with others
▶ 그녀는 흠잡을 데가 없다 She is free from faults.
▶ 그는 흠잡을 데 없는 사람이다 I can find no fault in him.
▶ 그의 솜씨는 흠잡을 데가 없다 His technique leaves nothing to be desired. ⇌ His technique is perfect [above criticism].
흠점 欠點 a fault ⇨ 결점(缺點)
흠정 欽定 ◆ 흠정의 compiled by royal order; laid down by royal edict; authorized —**흠정하다** order [edict, authorize] 《to compile》
■ —영역성서 the Authorized Version (of the Bible) (略 A.V.); (美) the King James Bible
—헌법 a constitution granted by the king
흠지다 欠— **1** 〈몸에〉 get scarred; leave [have] a scar
◆ 이마에 흠지다 get [have] a scar on *one's* forehead / 아문 상처가 흠지다 heal to a scar

▶ 그 벤 상처는 흠질 것이다 The cut will scar over.
2 〈물건에〉 get marred [cracked, scratched]; get [have] a flaw [crack, scratch, speck]
흠집 欠— 〈신체의〉 a scar; 〈물건의〉 a crack; a flaw; a scratch
▶ 아기의 이마에는 아직도 흠집이 남아 있다 The scar on the baby's forehead still remains.
흠칫 recoiling with a fright
—**흠칫하다** be startled; shrink (back) 《at, from》; hold [fall] back 《from》; flinch 《from》; recoil in surprise [fright]
▶ 나는 노크 소리에 흠칫했다 I was startled by the sound of the knock.
▶ 나는 외치는 소리에 흠칫했다 I was startled to hear the cry.
흡기 吸氣 〈들이마시기〉 inhalation of air [breath]; inspiration; 〈들이 마신 공기〉 air breathed in —**흡기하다** inhale; breathe in
흡력 吸力 〈흡인력〉 sucking force; 〈흡수력〉 absorbing power
흡반 吸盤 〔動〕 a sucker ⇨ 빨판
흡사 恰似 **1** 〈명사적〉 a close resemblance; a striking likeness [resemblance]
—**흡사하다** be strikingly similar 《to》; resemble closely; bear a close resemblance 《to》; bear a strong likeness 《to》; be the very picture 《of》; be as like as two peas [eggs]; be exactly alike
▶ 그는 아버지와 용모가 아주 흡사하다 He looks like his father very much. ⇌ He is the perfect image [very picture] of his father.
▶ 그는 아버지와 조금도 흡사하지 않다 He doesn't resemble his father at all.
2 〈부사적〉 just as; as if; as though; as it were
▶ 그것은 흡사 원숭이처럼 보이지만 실은 바위 다 It looks just like [as if it were] a monkey, but it is a rock.
흡상하다 吸上— 〈빨아올리다〉 suck [draw] up; 〈펌프로〉 pump up
흡수 吸水 〈빨아올리기〉 suction of water; 〈빨아들이기〉 water absorption
—**흡수하다** 〈빨아올리다〉 draw water by sucking [suction]; suck water; 〈빨아들이다〉 absorb water 《from》
■ —관 a siphon; a suction pipe —펌프 a suction pump
흡수 吸收 absorption; 〈흡인〉 imbibition; suction; 〈열의〉 decalescence; 〈빛의〉 extinction; 〈동화〉 assimilation
◆ 영양의 흡수 absorption of nourishment
—**흡수하다** 〈액체·빛 등을〉 absorb; suck [take] in; imbibe; 〈동화하다〉 assimilate
◆ 대기업에 흡수되다 be swallowed up by a big business / 실업자를 흡수하다 absorb the unemployed into work
▶ 젊어서는 새로운 사상을 쉽게 흡수할 수 있다 Young people can easily absorb [take, assimilate] new ideas.
▶ 그는 새로운 사상을 흡수했다 He absorbed [soaked up] new ideas.
▶ 해면은 물을 흡수한다 A sponge absorbs [sucks up] water.
■ —기 an absorber —력 absorbing [absorp-

tive] power; absorbency; absorptivity: 이 조그만 진공 청소기는 제법 흡수력이 좋다 This small vacuum cleaner is fairly powerful. —성 absorptive property; absorptiveness —작용 (a process of) absorption —제 an absorbent —조직 an absorptive tissue

흡습성 吸濕性 hygroscopic property; hygroscopicity ♦ 흡습성의 moisture-absorbing; absorbent; hygroscopic
▶ 이 천은 흡습성이 높다 This cloth is highly absorbent.

흡연 吸煙 smoking
♦ 흡연으로 건강을 해치다 smoke *oneself* ill [sick]
▶ 여기서는 흡연이 금지되어 있다 No smoking is allowed here. ⇌ Smoking is prohibited here.
—흡연하다 smoke 《tobacco, a cigarette, a pipe》; have a smoke
■ —실 a smoking [(英) smoke] room; 〈배의〉 a smoking saloon —자[가] a smoker —차 a smoking car [(英) carriage]; (英) a smoker

흡열 吸熱 ♦ 흡열성의 endothermic ■ —반응 〔化〕 (an) endothermic [endoergic] reaction

흡음 吸音 sound absorption
■ —력[재] sound-absorbing power [materials] —률 acoustic absorptivity

흡인 吸引 absorption; suction; imbibition; aspiration
—흡인하다 absorb; suck (in); imbibe
■ —기(器) an aspirator —력 sucking force —작용 the process of absorption

흡입 吸入 inhalation; indraft; imbibition; suction —흡입하다 inhale; breathe in; suck (in); imbibe
■ —관 a suction [an induction] pipe —기 an inhaler; an inspirator: 산소 흡입기 an oxygen inhaler [inspirator] —약[제] an inhalant —요법 inhalation treatment —판[밸브] a sucking [suction] valve

흡족 洽足 1 〈넉넉함〉 sufficiency; ampleness
—흡족하다 sufficient; ample; full; enough
♦ 흡족히 enough; sufficiently; fully; amply; in plenty / 흡족히 보답하다 reward amply [abundantly] paid / 물을 흡족히 주다 give a good watering
▶ 식량은 흡족히 공급되었다 Sufficient food was provided.
2 〈만족함〉 satisfaction
—흡족하다 satisfactory; gratifying
♦ 흡족히 satisfactorily; to *one's* satisfaction; to *one's* heart's content / 흡족히 여기다 be contented 《with》; find *sth* more than satisfactory
▶ 그런 박봉으로 그는 흡족히 여기지 않을 것이다 He will not be satisfied [happy] with such a small salary.

흡지 吸枝 〔植〕 a sucker

흡착 吸着 adsorption —흡착하다 adsorb
■ —기(器) an adsorber —제 an adsorbent

흡출 吸出 suction; sucking
—흡출하다 suck [draw] out
■ —관 〔機〕 a draft tube —송풍기 an induced draft fan

흡혈 吸血 bloodsucking —흡혈하다 suck blood
♦ —귀 a vampire; a bloodsucker (▶ 둘 다 비유적으로도 씀) —동물 a bloodsucker —박쥐 〔動〕 a vampire bat

흣대 a potter's spatula

흥 興 interest; fun; amusement; merriment; mirth; pleasure
♦ 흥이 나다 become interested 《in》; warm up 《to *one's* work》; get excited [merry] 《over, by》 / 흥이 깨지다 spoil *one's* pleasure; lose interest 《in》; *one's* fun is spoiled 《by》 / 흥이 나게 하다 amuse; interest; arouse *sb's* interest / 흥을 돋구다 add to the fun [amusement] 《of》; heighten the interest 《of》 / 흥을 깨뜨리다 spoil the fun 《of》; cast a chill 《upon, over》; dampen [chill] *sb's* enthusiasm 《for》; wet-blanket *sb's* zeal 《for》 / 흥에 겨워하다 be overwhelmed with mirth [fun]
▶ 그의 말로 우리는 흥이 깨지고 말았다 His words threw cold water on our enthusiasm.
▶ 그녀의 춤은 그 모임에 한층 흥을 더했다 Her dancing made the party more enjoyable.

흥[1] 〈부사적〉 코를 흥 하고 풀다 blow *one's* nose with a hissing sound
▶ 흥해! 〈아이에게〉 Blow, honey!

흥[2] Hm(m)!; Hum(ph)!; Hem!; H'm!
♦ 흥하고 코웃음 치다 turn up *one's* nose at *sb*
▶ 그들은 내 경고에 흥 하고 코웃음 칠 뿐이었다 They only sneered at my warning.
▶ 흥, 너 나를 놀리는 거구나 Pshaw! You're fooling me!

흥감 exaggeration; overstatement; bombast; grandiosity; bluff
▶ 그의 이야기는 대부분이 흥감에 지나지 않는다 Most of what he says is (sheer) exaggeration.
—흥감하다[부리다] exaggerate; overstate; stretch; talk big
▶ 기자는 사실을 흥감부리지 않도록 주의해야 한다 Reporters should be careful not to overstate [exaggerate] (the) facts.
—흥감스럽다 exaggerated; hyperbolical; bombastic; high-flown
♦ 흥감스럽게 떠들어대다 grossly exaggerate *one's* story; make a fuss too much

흥건하다 1 〈물 등이〉 brimful; full to the brim
▶ 논에 물이 흥건하다 A rice paddy is full of water.
2 〈국물이〉 juicy; watery; 《have》 much juice in it ▶ 김치 국물이 흥건하다 The *kimchi* is much juicy.

흥겹다 興— delightful; merry; pleasant; joyous; cheerful; exciting; gay; 《be》 full of fun
♦ 흥겹게 gaily; merrily; joyously; pleasantly / 흥겨운 나머지 in the excess of mirth / 흥겨워하다 be amused 《at》; enjoy *oneself* 《over *sth*, by doing》; have a good time of it / 흥겹게 놀다 make merry; have fun 《at》; frolic
▶ 파티는 흥겨웠습니까? How did you enjoy (yourself at) the party?
▶ 어제는 아주 흥겨웠습니다 I had a very good [pleasant] time (of it) yesterday.
▶ 흥겹게 놉시다 Let's have some fun.

흥글방망이놀다 〈훼방 놓다〉 interfere with

흥기 *sb*; thwart; hinder; meddle (in); frustrate ▶내 사업에 훙글방이놓지 마세요 Don't interfere with my business.

흥기 興起 rise; ascendancy
—흥기하다 rise; be in the ascendant

흥김 興— ♦흥김에 in the midst of merriment; under the influence of excitement ▶그는 흥김에 큰소리로 노래했다 He sang loud in the excess of mirth.

흥나다 興— get merry [excited] ⇨ 흥(興) ♦흥나서 춤추다 dance in *one's* mirth ▶그는 차차 그 아이디어에 흥났다 He gradually warmed (up) to the idea.

흥덩흥덩하다 〈국물이 많다〉 (be) full of water; 〈물 등이 그득하다〉 (be) full to the brim; brimfull (with water) ▶이 수프는 흥덩흥덩하다 This soup is a mere wash.

흥뚱새 [鳥] a (Chinese) tree pipit

흥뚱항뚱 〈건성으로〉 halfheartedly; heedlessly; carelessly; inattentively ♦흥뚱항뚱 듣다 listen to *sb* inattentively [with half an ear]

흥륭 興隆 prosperity; rise
—흥륭하다 rise; prosper; thrive
♦흥륭한 prosperous; flourishing; thriving ▶그의 사업은 당시 더없이 흥륭했다 His business flourished at that time.

흥망 興亡 〈문명·국가 등의〉 rise and fall; 〈인생의〉 *one's* ups and downs; vicissitudes; 〈존망〉 existence
♦인생의 흥망성쇠 the vicissitudes [ups and downs] of life / 로마제국의 흥망성쇠 the rise and fall of the Roman Empire / 일국의 흥망 the rise and fall [the destinies] of a nation ▶인생에는 흥망성쇠가 있다 A man's life has its ups and downs [vicissitudes]. ▶이 문제는 나라의 흥망에 영향을 줄지 모른다 This problem might affect the destiny of the country.

흥미 興味 〈관심〉 (an) interest; zest
♦흥미있는 interesting; 〈매력적인〉 attractive; amusing; exciting / 흥미 본위로 be absorbing / 〈호기심에서〉 out of curiosity; 〈재미로〉 just for fun / 흥미 진진하다 be very interesting; be of great interest; be full of interest; be absorbing / 흥미를 가지다 take (an) interest (in); be interested (in) / 흥미를 느끼다 take (an) interest (in); find pleasure (in movies) / 흥미를 돋우다 interest; arouse [awake(n), stimulate, excite] *sb's* interest (in) / 흥미를 붙이게 하다 foster *sb's* interest (in) / 흥미를 잃다 lose (an) interest (in)
▶이 책은 흥미진진하다 This book is of absorbing interest.
▶나는 음악에는 흥미가 없다 I'm not interested [I have no interest] in music. ⇒ Music is of no interest to [doesn't interest] me. ⇒ Music has [holds] no appeal for me.
▶그는 스포츠에 매우 흥미가 있다 He is very [greatly] interested in sports. ⇒ He has a great interest in sports.
▶그녀는 심리학에 흥미를 가지게 되었다 She has gotten interest in psychology.
▶나는 정치에 대한 흥미를 잃었다 I have lost interest in politics.
▶그 책은 그림에 대한 흥미를 일으키게 했다 The book stirred up [aroused] his interest in painting. ⇒ (口) The book got him turned on to painting.

흥분 興奮 〈감정의〉 excitement; 〈신경이나 기관의〉 stimulation; 〈가슴이 설레는〉 a thrill; excitement; agitation
♦흥분을 일으키다 cause [arouse] excitement / 흥분을 억누르다 control *one's* excitement; keep *one's* excitement in check / 흥분을 가라앉히다 allay [calm down] *one's* excitement; cool down *sb's* hot temper
—흥분하다 be [get] excited; be aroused; be agitated; be [get] stimulated; be highly strung; (美) get a kick [thrill] (from)
♦흥분하여 in excitement; excitedly; in an excited state of mind / 흥분시키다 stir (up) *sb's* feelings; stimulate; excite *sb* / 흥분해 있다 be excited (at, over); be wild (over)
▶그는 쉽게 흥분한다 He is excitable [easily excited].
▶나는 흥분하여 가슴이 설렜다 I was filled with excitement [thrilled].
▶아이들은 흥분하여 껑충껑충 뛰어다녔다 The children were jumping about with [in, from] excitement.
▶환자를 흥분하게 해선 안된다 You shouldn't excite a sick person.
▶그렇게 흥분하지 마라 Don't get so excited [excite youself too much]. ⇒ Calm down. ⇒ Take it easy.
▶뭘 그리 흥분하고 있니? What are you so nervous about?
▶그는 흥분해서 잠이 안 왔다 He could not sleep because he was too excited. ⇒ He was too excited to sleep. ⇒ He was so excited that he could not sleep.
■—상태 an excited condition [state] —성 excitability; irritability —제 a stimulant; an excitant; an exciter; an invigorator; (俗) a pep pill: 흥분제를 먹이다[먹다] administer [take] a stimulant

흥성 興盛 prosperity —흥성하다 grow in prosperity; become prosperous; prosper; thrive ▶다행히 지금으로서는 그들의 사업은 흥성하고 있다 Fortunately their business is doing well [flourishing, thriving] at present.

흥성흥성 興盛興盛 prosperously; flourishingly; thrivingly; roaringly
—흥성흥성하다 prosperous; thriving; booming; flourishing; roaring
▶장사가 흥성흥성하다 Their business is booming. ⇒ They are doing a roaring trade.

흥신소 興信所 an inquiry office [agency]; a private detective agency; 〈상업관계의〉 a credit bureau

흥야항야 meddlesomely ⇨ 흥이야항이야

흥얼거리다 hum (a tune); sing to *oneself*; croon (a song)
▶그녀는 흥얼거리며 요리를 하고 있었다 She was humming (a tune) while cooking.

흥얼흥얼 humming; crooning
♦흥얼흥얼 노래하다 hum [croon] to *oneself*

흥업 興業 promotion of industry; inauguration of a new industrial enterprise
—**흥업하다** start a new business [enterprise]; start [launch] an enterprise; promote industry; undertake a new industrial enterprise

흥에띄다 興— indulge in a frolic; be in the excess of mirth; be overwhelmed with mirth

흥이야항이야 〈참견〉 meddlesomely; officiously
—**흥이야항이야하다** meddle with [in]; interfere in [with]; poke [put] one's nose into
▶ 그의 일에 흥이야항이야하지 마시오 You shouldn't interfere [meddle] in his affairs. ⇌ Keep your nose out of [Stop poking your nose into] his affairs.

흥정 〈매매〉 buying and selling; purchase and sale; 〈거래〉 dealings; transactions; business; a bargain; 〈값 등의 의논〉 bargaining; 〈교섭〉 negotiation
◆ 술자리에서의 흥정 a Dutch [wet] bargain / 수지맞는[맞지 않는] 흥정 a good [poor] bargain / 흥정이 많다 have a lot of business; do a land-office business / 흥정이 없다 make few sales; do little business / 흥정을 붙이다 act as broker; help strike a bargain
▶ 흥정이 끝났다 The bargain has been concluded [closed].
▶ 이 건에 관해서는 정치적 흥정의 여지가 없다 There is no room for political compromise on this matter.
▶ 그는 흥정을 잘 한다 He is a good bargainer.
—**흥정하다** buy and sell; make a deal 《with》; do business 《with》; 〈값을〉 bargain 《with sb》 over [about]; haggle 《with sb》
▶ 그녀는 점원과 값을 흥정했다 She bargained with the clerk about the price.
■ —**거리** merchandise —**꾼** buyers and [or] sellers; a dealer; a trader; a broker —**솜씨** the tricks of trade

흥정은 붙이고 싸움은 말리랬다 〈속담〉 One should help bargaining and stop quarrels.

흥진비래 興盡悲來 After fun comes sorrow. ⇨ After joy come tears.

흥청거리다 〈마음껏 놀다〉 indulge in merrymaking; make merry; be on the spree; 〈거드럭거리다〉 be highly elated; swell up; exult; crow; be puffed up; swagger
▶ 그는 흥청거리며 산다 He lives in a racket of enjoyment. ⇌ He lives in luxury [great style].

흥청망청 **1** 〈즐기는 모양〉 merrily; gaily
◆ 흥청망청 떠들며 놀다 indulge in a rowdy spree [boisterous merrymaking]; have high jinks; go on the spree
2 〈낭비하는 모양〉 in profusion
◆ 돈을 흥청망청 쓰다 spend (one's) money freely [recklessly, like water]; be lavish with one's money

흥청흥청 merrily ⇨ 흥청망청

흥취 興趣 interest; gusto; taste
◆ 매우 흥취가 있다 be of absorbing interest
▶ 그곳은 아무런 흥취도 없다 The place has no attractive features.
▶ 그 산의 경치에 흥취를 더하고 있다 The mountain adds charm to the landscape.

흥치 興致 〈흥〉 fun; pleasure; delight; interest; 〈운치〉 taste; gusto; elegance
▶ 그 오래된 도시는 매우 흥치가 있었다 The old town was full of atmosphere [had a lot of atmosphere].

흥타령 —打令 a folksong with a "hum" at the end of each line

흥패 興敗 rise and fall ⇨ 흥망(興亡)

흥하다 興— 〈나라 등이〉 come into existence [being]; rise; 〈번영하다〉 thrive; flourish; prosper; boom; roar
◆ 흥하는 집안 a thriving family / 흥하든 망하든 whether one succeeds or fails; sink or swim; kill or cure; hit or miss; win or lose / 장사가 흥하다 business booms [flourishes, prospers]
▶ 새로운 산업이 흥하여 그 도시는 갑자기 경기가 좋아졌다 New industries sprung up and the town suddenly prospered.
▶ 흥하든 망하든 해보겠다 I will try, sink or swim [kill or cure].

흥행 興行 〈사업〉 public entertainment; the amusement [entertainment] industry; show business; 〈1회의 상연·공연〉 (a) performance; (an) exhibition; 〈연속의〉 a run; 〈구경거리〉 a show
◆ 철야 흥행 an all-night show
▶ 이번 흥행은 대성공이었다 The last show [performance] turned out to be a great success.
—**흥행하다** give a performance; produce 《a play》; show; present; put on; exhibit; run 《a show》
◆ 연극을 흥행하다 give [present] a play / 지방에서 흥행하고 있다 《美》 be on the road
▶ 그 연극은 6개월 동안 장기 흥행하고 있다 The play has had a long run of six months.
■ **단기[장기]**— a short [long] run **순회**— a road show **야간**— a night performance **주간**— a matinee —**가치** audience value; 《美》 box-office value; 흥행가치가 있는 것 《美》 a box-office show —**계** the entertainment world [circles]; the show business world [circles] —**계통** a circuit; a chain —**권** producing rights; the right of performance; 〈연극의〉 a dramatic [stage, 《美》 play] right —**단** a theatrical company; a troupe —**물** a (public) performance; a show; a production; an exhibition —**사** a showman; a show proprietor [manager] —**성적** a box-office record: 이 영화의 흥행 성적은 더할 나위 없이 좋았다 The film was a box-office hit [success]. —**수익** box-office profits —**장** a show place —**주** a promotor; a showman; 〔劇〕 a theatrical producer

흥흥 Hum hum!; Hmph hmph!
▶ 그는 나의 답을 듣고 (업신여겨) 흥흥하며 코웃음쳤다 He snorted at my answer.

흥흥거리다 **1** 〈흥겨워서〉 hum; croon; sing through the nose; sing to oneself
▶ 그녀는 흥흥거리며 요리를 하고 있었다 She was humming (a tune) while cooking.
2 〈아이가 투정부리다〉 grumble; complain; whine; whimper; fret

흘날리다
▶저 아이는 늘 흥흥거리고 있다 That child is always whining [fretting].

흩날리다 blow off [away]; be blown off; fly about [off]; scatter; flutter
▶나뭇잎이 바람에 흩날리고 있다 The leaves are fluttering [whirling] in the wind.
▶눈송이가 바람에 흩날리고 있었다 Snowflakes were dancing in the wind.

흩다 scatter ⇨ 흩뜨리다

흩뜨리다 scatter; 〈군중 등을〉 disperse; 〈구름 등을〉 dissipate; 〈머리를〉 dishevel
♦자세를 흩뜨리다 assume an easy posture / 휴지 조각을 흩뜨리다 scatter bits of waste paper / 주의력을 흩뜨리다 distract [divert] one's attention
▶미안해요. 이렇게 흩뜨려 놓아서 I'm sorry everything is all over the place.

흩뿌리다 scatter; strew; sprinkle
▶씨를 흩뿌리다 scatter seeds
▶아버지께서 잔디에 물을 흩뿌리고 계신다 Father is sprinkling water on the lawn.

흩어지다 〈분산하다〉 disperse; scatter; be scattered (about); 〈어질러지다〉 be littered (up) (with); be in a mess; be in disorder; 〈정신·마음이〉 be distracted
♦사방으로 흩어지다 disperse in all directions; be scattered about / 삼삼오오로 흩어지다 disperse by twos and threes / 흩어진 마음을 가라앉히다 collect [gather] one's scattered wits; compose oneself
▶그 가족은 전쟁 통에 흩어졌다 The family broke up during the war.
▶마루에는 종잇조각이 흩어져 있었다 Bits of paper were scattered on the floor. ≒ The floor was littered with bits of paper.
▶땅위에 낙엽이 흩어져 있다 The ground is strewn [scattered] with fallen leaves.

흩이다 get [be] scattered [dispersed]
▶벚꽃에 바람이 불어 온 들에 흩였다 Cherry blossoms are scattered all over the garden by the wind.

희가 戱歌 a limerick; a comic [funny] song

희가극 喜歌劇 a comic opera; 〈경가극〉 an operetta (*pl.* ~s, -etti)

희가스 稀― 〔化〕 rare [noble, inert] gases
―류 원소 rare-gas elements; rare gases

희곡 戱曲 a drama; a play
♦희곡적(인) dramatic(al) / 소설을 희곡화하다 dramatize a novel; make a novel into a drama
■―작가 a dramatist; a playwright; (美俗) a playwriter ―작법 dramaturgy ―집 a collection of plays

희구 希求 an earnest [an ardent] desire; desire; aspiration
―희구하다 desire 《to do》; aspire 《to, after》; want; demand; seek; call for; ask for
♦명성을 희구하다 have aspiration for [after] fame
▶온 세계의 사람들은 평화를 희구하고 있다 People all over the world are eager [long] for peace.

희귀 稀貴 rarity; rareness
―희귀하다 rare; infrequent

♦희귀한 사건 a rare [an uncommon] occurrence [event] / 희귀한 물건 a rarity; a curiosity; a black swan; a white crow
▶이렇게 큰 사과는 이 과수원에서는 희귀하다 Such a big apple is rare in this orchard.
■―식물 an out-of-the-way plant ―조 a rare bird ―종 a rare variety; a rarity

희극 喜劇 a comedy; 〈소극〉 a farce; (美) a funny show
♦희극적(인) comic(al); farcical / 희극적인 이야기 a comic story / 희극을 벌이다 perform a comedy; (비유) play the fool; make a fool of *oneself*
▶한바탕 희극이 벌어졌다 A comic scene was enacted.
■―막간― an interlude ―문학 comic literature ―배우 a comic actor [〈여자〉 actress]; a comedian; (口) a comic ―영화 a comic movie [(美) picture] ―작가 a comic dramatist [writer]

희극 戱劇 1 〈연극〉 a farce; a comedy
2 〈행동〉 a farcical act [conduct]

희금속 稀金屬 rare metals

희기 喜氣 mood of cheerfulness; gay spirits; a happy feeling; good humor

희끄무레하다 whitish; dimly white
▶희끄무레하게 동이 트기 시작한다 Day is beginning to break [dawn].

희끄스름하다 whitish

희끈거리다 get dizzy; feel dizzy [giddy]

희끈희끈 dizzily; giddily; shakily

희끔하다 whitish

희끗거리다 get very dizzy=희뜩거리다

희끗희끗 spotted [speckled] with white; grizzled; grizzly
―희끗희끗하다 〈모발이〉 grizzled; gray-haired; 〈옷감 등이〉 pepper-and-salt
♦희끗희끗한 수염 a grizzled beard / 머리가 희끗희끗한 남자 gray-haired man / 희끗희끗한 머리 gray [grizzled] hair; hair streaked [sprinkled, shot] with gray
▶그는 머리가 희끗희끗하다 He has grizzled [gray] hair.
▶그녀는 머리가 희끗희끗해지기 시작했다 Her hair is beginning to frost a little.

희나리 〈덜 마른 장작〉 wet [green] firewood

희넓적하다 white and broad [flat]

희년 稀年 〈70세〉 seventy years of age

희다 1 〈빛깔이〉 white; 〈얼굴빛이〉 fair; 〈머리털이〉 gray; hoary
♦푸른 하늘에 떠 있는 흰 구름 fleecy clouds floating in the blue sky / 눈 같이 흰 snow-white; (as) white as snow / 흰 머리가 섞이다 〈머리가 주어〉 show white streaks; become grizzled / 희게 하다 whiten; 〈탈색 하다〉 blanch / 희게 하다 paint white; 〈회반죽으로〉 whitewash
▶그녀는 살갗이 희다 She has a fair complexion [skin].
▶내 머리칼이 희어지기 시작했다 My hair is beginning to turn gray.
2 〈희떱다〉 showy; generous; snobbish ⇨ 흰 소리

희담 戱談 a joke; a jest; fun; banter

▶ 희담을 그만하고 본 주제로 돌아가자 Joking apart [aside], let's return to the main subject.

희대 稀代 ♦ 희대의 명작 an unsurpassed masterpiece / 희대의 영웅 a unique [peerless] hero / 희대의 악당 a notorious rascal [villain] / 희대의 uncommon; rare; extraordinary; unheard-of; peerless; unique; matchless

희디희다 very white; pure white; snow-white; as white as snow
▶ 그녀의 살갗은 희디희다 Her skin is (as) white as snow.
▶ 갓 내린 눈이 희디희게 빛나고 있었다 The fresh snow was shining white.

희떱다 1 〈씀씀이가〉 generous [lavish, liberal] though penniless
2 〈허영적〉 showy; vain; vainglorious
3 〈언행이〉 conceited; snobbish; (口) uppish

희뜩거리다 〈어지럽다〉 get very dizzy [giddy]; 《one's head》 swim
▶ 독한 술을 마셨더니 머리가 희뜩거렸다 The strong drink made me feel giddy [dizzy].

희뜩머룩이 〈낭비가〉 a free spender; a spendthrift

희뜩희뜩하다 1 〈어지러워서〉 be very dizzy; get very giddy
♦ 희뜩희뜩해지는 높이 a dizzy [giddy] height / 눈이 희뜩희뜩해질 만큼의 아름다운 dazzling beauty
2 〈흰색이〉 dotted [flecked] with white; 〈머리털이〉 grizzled; grizzly
♦ 희뜩희뜩한 머리칼 grizzled [grizzly, frosty] hair

희락 喜樂 joy; gladness ⇨ 희열(喜悅)

희랍 希臘 Greece ⇨ 그리스

희로 喜怒 joy and anger; 〈감정〉 emotion; feelings ⇨ 희로애락(喜怒哀樂)

희로애락 喜怒哀樂 feelings; emotion; joy, anger, sorrow, and pleasure; joy and anger
♦ 희로애락의 정 feelings of joy and anger [humor and pathos] / 희로애락을 겉으로 나타내다 show one's feelings [emotions]
▶ 그는 결코 희로애락을 겉으로 드러내지 않는다 He never shows [betrays] his feelings.

희롱 戱弄 ridiculing; joking; teasing; banter; harassment; raillery; chaff; fun; a joke; jest
♦ 희롱조로 in a bantering [teasing, mocking] tone
—**하다** banter; chaff; tease (sb with jest); poke fun (at); make a mock of; ridicule
♦ 운명에 희롱당하다 be at the mercy of fate; be the sport of fortune / 파도에 희롱당하다 toss about in [be at the mercy of] the waves / 〈남녀가〉 서로 희롱하다 flirt [dally] with each other / 여자를 희롱하다 harass a woman; toy with a woman
▶ 그들은 그의 시골 사투리를 희롱했다 They made fun of his provincial accent. ⇌ They made fun of him because of his provincial accent.
▶ 그는 늘 여자아이들을 희롱하곤 했다 He used to tease young girls.

희룽거리다 〈들떠서 떠들다〉 frolic; act [play] the giddy goat; 〈못된 장난을 하다〉 play pranks; 〈농담을 하다〉 joke; make [crack] a joke; jest; sport; lark about; cut capers [a caper]
▶ 아이들은 잔디밭에서 희룽거리기를 좋아한다 Children love to romp (about) [frolic, frisk] on the lawn.

희룽희룽 in frolic [play]; in a playful mood; playfully; jokingly; in jest [fun]

희맑다 white and clean

희망 希望 〈바람〉 (a) hope; 〈소망〉 (a) wish; (a) desire; 〈포부〉 (an) aspiration; (an) ambition; 〈기대〉 prospect; expectation; 〈기회〉 chance; 〈요구〉 a request; a demand
♦ 열렬한[간절한] 희망 an ardent desire; an earnest wish; one's dearest ambition / 실낱 같은 희망 a faint hope / 마지막[유일한] 희망 one's last [only] hope / 헛된[실현될 수 없는] 희망 a vain hope / 비현실적인 희망 an unrealistic hope / 약간의 희망 a slight hope / 희망의 서광 the dawn [a gleam] of hope / 희망적인 관측 〈낙관적인 의견〉 optimistic opinion; one's wishful thinking
▶ 나는 희망대로 그 대학에 입학할 수 있었다 I was able to go to the university as I (had) wanted (to) [hoped, wished].
〈희망이[은]〉 희망이 있는 hopeful; promising / 희망이 없는 hopeless; desperate; unpromising / …의 희망이 있다[없다] there is a [no] hope of...
▶ 내가 귀국할 희망은 없다 There is no chance of my returning home.
▶ 그가 전치할 희망은 없다 There is very little hope of his complete recovery.
▶ 드디어 나의 오랜 희망이 이루어졌다 What I had wanted to do for a long time [My long cherished hope] finally came true [was finally realized].
▶ 나의 희망은 깨지고 말았다 My hopes were destroyed [shattered].
▶ 희망이 전혀 없는 것은 아니다 There is still a slim chance of success.
▶ 그녀의 유일한 희망은 아들에게 있었다 Her only hope rested on her son.
〈희망을〉 희망을 가지다 hope; cherish a desire [hope] / 희망을 갖게 하다 arouse [encourage] a hope; raise hopes / 희망을 이루다[달성하면] realize [gratify, get] one's wishes; attain one's desire / 희망을 걸다 anchor one's hope (in, on); attach one's hope (to); pin one's hope / 희망을 버리지 않다 hold on [cling] to one's hope
▶ 양친은 아들에게 희망을 걸었다 The parents centered their hopes on their son.
▶ 그는 시험에 낙제하여 완전히 희망을 잃었다 He failed (in) the exam and lost all his hopes.
♦ 유학갈 희망을 버리지 마라 Don't give up your hope of studying abroad.
▶ 모든 사람의 희망을 들어주시오 Please listen to everyone's wishes [what everyone wants (to do)].
〈희망에〉 희망에 찬 젊은이들 young hopefuls / 희망에 빛나는 얼굴 a face beamed with hopes / 희망에 반하여 against [contrary to] one's wishes / 희망에 살다 live [feed] on

hope / 희망에 부응하다 meet *sb's* wishes
▶ 그는 희망에 차 상경했다 He went to Seoul burning with [full of] hope.
▶ 많은 팬들의 희망에 따라 연극이 재연되었다 They again put on the play because a lot of fans asked for it. ⇌ The play was staged again at the request of many fans.
—**희망하다** hope (for); be hopeful of; wish; aspire to [after]; expect; want; be anxious for (peace)
♦ 희망하는 봉급 the salary desired / …을 희망하여 in hopes of
▶ 그는 1년 더 일하기를 희망하고 있다 He hopes to work for another year yet.
▶ 누구나 세계의 평화를 희망하고 있다 Everybody desires world peace.
■ —조건 the terms [condition] desired
희망봉 希望峰 the Cape of Good Hope
희망자 希望者 a person who desires [wishes] to ⟨do⟩; ⟨지원자⟩ an applicant; a candidate
■ 관람— intending visitors 입회— a candidate [an applicant] for membership
희멀겋다 fair; fair-complexioned; light-colored
희멀쑥하다 fair and clean ⟨face⟩
희문 戲文 nonsense literature; a literary parody; humorous writing
■ —작가 a humorist
희묽다 white and flabby; ⟨묽다⟩ washy
희미하다 稀微— ⟨부정확하여 분명치 않다⟩ vague; ⟨침침하여 뚜렷하지 않다⟩ dim; faint; obscure; ⟨윤곽이 뚜렷하지 않다⟩ indistinct; ⟨아련하다⟩ hazy; misty
♦ 희미하게 vaguely; dimly; faintly; obscurely; hazily / 희미하게 나타나다 appear dimly [hazily] / 희미한 기억을 더듬다 trace back a vague [dim] memory / 희미한 태도를 취하다 take [assume] an ambiguous attitude (toward) / 희미해지다 become dim [faint, vague]; ⟨소리·빛 등이⟩ fade (away); die away
▶ 희미한 불빛이 멀리 보였다 I saw a faint [dim] light in the distance.
▶ 희미한 희망마저 사라졌다 Even the slightest [faintest] hope has gone.
▶ 나는 돌아가신 아버지를 희미하게 기억하고 있다 I dimly [vaguely] remember my dead father.
▶ 날이 밝아지면서 별빛이 차차 희미해졌다 The stars faded before the approaching day.
▶ 속삭이는 말소리가 희미하게 들렸다 A mumuring sound could barely [faintly] be heard.
▶ 눈이 침침해 무엇을 보아도 희미하다 Everything looks blurred to my dim eyes.
▶ 멀리 종소리가 희미하게 들려왔다 A distant sound of a bell was faintly heard.
▶ 그녀의 일은 희미하게 기억하고 있을 뿐이다 I have only dim [vague, indistinct] memories of her.
희박 稀薄 thinness; rarity; rarefaction
—**희박하다** ⟨기체·액체 등이⟩ thin; weak; ⟨묽다⟩ dilute; ⟨공기 등이⟩ rare, rarefied; ⟨인구 등이⟩ sparse
♦ 높은 산의 희박한 공기 the rare [thin] air of the high mountains / 희박한 가능성 a bare [the barest] possibility / 인구가 희박한 지방 a sparsely [thinly] populated district / 희박하게 하다 rarefy; dilute; weaken; thin
▶ 높은 산의 꼭대기에는 공기가 희박하다 The air is rare at the summits of high mountains.
▶ 그가 성공할 가망은 희박하다 He has little hope for success. ⇌ There is little hope for his success.
희번덕거리다 goggle
희번덕이다 goggle
♦ 희번덕이는 눈 goggling [glaring] eyes / 눈을 희번덕이다 goggle [roll] *one's* eyes ⟨on⟩; ⟨*one's*⟩ goggle / 눈을 희번덕이며 둘러보다 look around with goggling eyes
▶ 그는 눈을 희번덕이며 나를 보았다 He goggled at me.
희번덕희번덕 goggling ⟨*one's* eyes⟩
희번드르르하다 1 ⟨거죽이⟩ showy; gaudy; garish; ⟨얼굴이⟩ fair and bright [radiant]
♦ 희번드르르한 넥타이 a gaudy [flashy] tie
▶ 그녀는 얼굴이 희번드르르하다 She has a fair and bright complexion.
2 ⟨말 등이⟩ specious
♦ 거짓말을 희번드르르하게 하다 tell a lie that sounds like the truth; lie like the truth
▶ 그의 이야기가 희번드르르하게 들렸기 때문에 모두 믿고 말았다 His story sounded so plausible (that) everyone believed it.
희번들하다 fair and bright ⇨ 희번드르르하다
희번주그레하다 fair and handsome [comely]
희번지르르하다 fair and good-looking [welllooking]
희번하다 ⟨어스레한⟩ half-light; ⟨빛이 흐릿한⟩ faintly light; ⟨어렴풋이 흰⟩ dimly white; gray
♦ 희번할 때에 at the peep [crack] of dawn; at the first gray of dawn; in the gray of the morning / 희번해지다 grow light; turn gray
▶ 희번할 때의 공기는 상쾌하다 The air at the peep of dawn is refreshing.
희보 喜報 good [auspicious, glad] news; joyful [glad] tidings ♦ 희보를 접하다 receive the good [happy] news ⟨of, that⟩
희불그레하다 pale [light] red
희붐하다 half-light ⇨ 희번하다
희비 喜悲 joy and sorrow
▶ 나는 희비가 엇갈렸다 Joy and sorrow alternated in my emotions. ⇌ I had mixed feelings of joy and sorrow. ⇌ I had a mingled feeling of joy and sorrow.
■ —쌍곡선 a mingled feeling of joy and sorrow
희비극 喜悲劇 a tragicomedy
♦ 희비극의 tragicomic(al)
희사 喜事 a matter for joy [congratulation]; a joy; a happy event
희사 喜捨 (a) donation; (a) contribution; charity; almsgiving; alms; oblation; (a) subscription
♦ 희사를 청하다 ask for alms [contribution] / 희사를 받다 receive alms [donations]
—**희사하다** donate; give in charity; give; give [make] a donation
♦ …에 희사하다 make a contribution to

[toward]
▶그녀는 이재민을 돕기 위해 거액을 회사했다 She made generous [handsome] donations to aid the disaster victims.
━금 a gift of money; alms; offerings; donations: 희사금을 모으다 raise a subscription; make [take up] a subscription ━함(函) an offertory chest [box]; 〈교회에 비치된〉 an alms box

희색 喜色 a glad countenance; a joyful [pleased, happy] look
◆희색을 띠다 wear a smile; smile all over *one's* face
▶그는 희색이 만면했다 He [His face] was beaming with smiles [delight]. = He was all smiles with joy.
▶그는 일등을 해서 희색이 만면했다 His face brightened with joy when he won (the) first prize.

희생 犧牲 〈비싼 대가〉 (a) sacrifice; 〈희생자〉 victim; 〈자기 희생〉 self-sacrifice; 〈대신〉 a scapegoat
◆희생적 self-sacrificing / 많은 희생을 치르고 at a considerable sacrifice; at heavy cost / 희생을 치르다 make sacrifices
◆어떠한 희생을 치르더라도 이것만은 마무리하겠다 I will finish this at any cost [all costs, any price].
▶그에게는 희생적 정신이 있다 He is self-sacrificing.
▶그 승리는 많은 희생의 대가였다 The victory was dearly bought.
━하다 sacrifice; victimize; make a sacrifice [scapegoat, victim] of *sb*
◆…을 희생하여 at the sacrifice of…; at the cost [price, expense] of… / 자기자신을 희생하다 sacrifice *oneself*; make a martyr of *oneself* / 희생되다 be sacrificed; be victimized; fall a victim 《to》
▶많은 젊은 생명이 전쟁으로 희생되었다 Many young lives were sacrificed in the war.
▶전쟁 때문에 우리나라는 많은 인명과 재산을 희생했다 The war cost our country great sacrifices of life and property.
▶그는 건강을 희생하여 가며 일을 완수했다 He completed the work at the sacrifice of his health.
■━물 a sacrifice; a victim; a prey: 희생물이 되다 fall [be made] victim 《to》; be victimized ━정신 a self-sacrificing spirit; the spirit of self-sacrifice ━타 (野) a sacrifice (hit)

희생자 犧牲者 a victim; a prey; a casualty; a martyr
▶그 철도 사고로 많은 희생자가 났다 The railway accident took a heavy toll of human lives.

희서 稀書 a rare book
희석 稀釋 dilution; attenuation
━희석하다 dilute; attenuate ◆물로 희석하다 dilute with water; water down
■━도 dilution ━액 weak [diluted] solution ━제 a diluent

희세 稀世 ◆희세의 rare; uncommon; extraordinary; phenomenal / 희세의 영웅 a hero of extraordinary caliber

희소 稀少 scarcity; rarity
━희소하다 scarce; rare
■━가치 scarcity [rarity] value ━물자 scarce materials [goods] ━성 scarcity

희소식 喜消息 good [happy, glad] news; glad tidings
◆희소식을 접하다 receive the good [happy] news 《of, that》/ 희소식을 전하다 convey [bring] good news; give glad tidings
▶나는 너의 희소식을 기다리고 있다 I'm looking forward to hearing about your good news.
▶네게 희소식이야 This is good news for you.

희수 稀壽 〈70세〉 the age of seventy; seventy years of age
▶우리는 아버지의 희수를 축하했다 We celebrated our father's 70th birthday.
■━연 the celebration of *one's* seventieth birthday

희수 喜壽 〈77세〉 seventy-seven years of age
◆희수를 축하하다 celebrate *one's* seventy-seventh birthday

희아리 〈희끗희끗한 마른 고추〉 a dried hot pepper with whitish spots
희언 戲言 a joke ⇨ 희담(戲談)
희열 喜悅 joy; gladness; delight; ecstasy; rapture ◆희열을 느끼다 be delighted; be in rapture

희염산 稀鹽酸 〔化〕 dilute hydrochloric acid
희우 喜雨 a welcome [good] rain; a beneficial [friendly] rain
◆가뭄 끝에 오는 희우 a hoped-for rain during the dry season

희원 希願 (a) hope; (a) wish; (a) desire
━희원하다 hope; wish; desire
▶나는 여러분이 행복한 생활을 하시기를 희원합니다 I wish you a happy future. = I hope that you (will) lead a happy life.

희유하다 稀有— 〈드물다〉 rare; 〈일반적이 아니다〉 uncommon; 〈예외적이다〉 unusual; phenomenal; unprecedented
◆희유의 사건 a rare incident [phenomenon]; an uncommon affair; a rare occurrence; an unheard-of accident

희읍스하다 whitish
◆희읍스름한 색 sordid white

희작 戲作 a popular novel [story]; dime store novel; light literature [reading]
희종 稀種 a rare variety; a rarity
◆희종의 장미 roses of rare varieties
희질산 稀窒酸 〔化〕 dilute nitric acid
희짓다 戲— disturb; hinder; obstruct; hamper; block; interfere ◆아무의 계획을 희짓다 block [obstruct, interfere with] *sb's* plan / 의사의 진행을 희짓다 obstruct proceedings

희치희치 〈피륙·종이 등이〉 worn off in places; out of shape here and there; 〈벗어진 모양〉 peeling off in places
◆희치희치 벗어지다 come [peel] off in places; be worn off here and there
━희치희치하다 worn off [out of shape, peeling off] in places
▶집 페인트가 희치희치하게 벗어지기 시작했다

The paint on the house is beginning to come [peel] off.

희토 稀土 〔化〕 rare earth
━━류 원소 a rare-earth element

희학 戱謔 a joke; a jest; pleasantry
━━희학하다 joke; jest; crack [make] a joke; drop a jest
━━질 joking; jesting

희한하다 稀罕━ 〈희귀하다〉 rare; 〈일반적이지 않다〉 unusual; phenomenal; singular; extraordinary; 〈진기하다〉 curious; 〈신기하다〉 novel
◆ 희한한 이름 an uncommon name / 희한한 물건 a rare article; a rarity / 희한한 일 a rare [an uncommon] occurrence; a rarity
▶ 플로리다에서 눈을 보는 것은 희한한 일이다 It is unusual to see snow in Florida.
▶ 별 희한한 일이 다 있네 How can a thing like that happen!

희화 戱畫 a comic picture; a caricature; a cartoon ◆ 희화화하다 make a caricature 《of》; caricature

희황산 稀黃酸 〔化〕 dilute sulfuric acid

희희 嘻嘻 (laugh) joyfully [merrily, cheerfully]

희희낙락하다 喜喜樂樂━ be very glad; be (very) joyful [delightful, gleeful]; rejoice [be rejoiced] 《at, over》; delight 《in》; jubilate; have a jubilee; be cheerful
◆ 희희낙락하여 merrily; joyfully; cheerfully; delightfully; rejoicingly

흰개미 〔昆〕 a white ant; a termite

흰골무(떡) (a) thumb-shaped rice cake without spice covering

흰곰 〔動〕 a white [polar] bear

흰나비 〔昆〕 a white (butterfly); 〈배추흰나비〉 a cabbage butterfly [white]

흰누룩 malt made of wheat flour and glutinous rice

흰눈썹뜸부기 〔鳥〕 a waterrail; a clapper rail; a mud hen

흰눈썹지빠귀 〔鳥〕 a Davison's groundthrush

흰담비 〔動〕 an ermine; a stoat

흰둥이 〈병적으로〉 an albino 《pl. ~s》; 〈백인〉 a white man [woman]; (俗) a white

흰떡 rice cake

흰말 a white horse

흰머리 〈털〉 gray [white] hair; 〈머리〉 a gray head ◆ 흰머리의 신사 a gray-[silver-]haired gentleman / 흰머리를 뽑다 pull out a white hair / 흰머리를 검게 염색하다 dye one's gray hair black
▶ 흰머리가 나기 시작한다 My hair is beginning to turn gray [to show white streaks].

흰멧새 〔鳥〕 a snow bunting; a snowflake

흰무리 steamed rice cake in simple shape [without layers]

흰물떼새 〔鳥〕 a Kentish plover

흰바곳 〔植〕 an aconite; a wolfsbane

흰밥 plain white rice (cooked with nothing mixed in)

흰배지빠귀 〔鳥〕 a pale thrush

흰백합 ━百合 〔植〕 a white lily

흰불나방 〔昆〕 a fall webworm

흰뺨검둥오리 〔鳥〕 a spotbill duck

흰뺨오리 〔鳥〕 a goldeneye

흰소리 a vain [an empty] boast; a big [tall] talk; a brag; 〈호떠운〉 a snobbish remark
▶ 그것은 흰소리다 That is a pretty tall story.
▶ 그는 언제나 흰소리를 하기 때문에 아무도 믿지 않는다 He always talks big and no one believes him.
━━흰소리하다[치다] talk big [tall]; brag; blow; (口) talk through one's hat
▶ 그는 영불해협을 헤엄쳐 건널 수 있다고 흰소리했다 He boasted [bragged] that he could swim across the English Channel.
━━꾼 a vain [an empty] boaster; a braggart; (美俗) a blowhard

흰신 white (leather) shoes

흰쌀 polished [cleaned] rice; white rice

흰여우 〔動〕 a white [silver] fox; 〈북극 여우〉 a polar [an arctic] fox

흰엿 white taffy

흰옷 white clothes

흰자 the white (of an egg) ⇨ 흰자위 1
━━가루 the powdered white ━━질 ⇨ 단백질 (蛋白質)

흰자위 1 〈새알·달걀의〉 the white (of an egg); the albumen 2 〈눈의〉 the white of the eye

흰죽 ━粥 rice gruel
◆ 흰죽을 끓이다 boil rice into gruel

흰줄 〈선〉 a white line; 〈끈·실〉 a white string; 〈줄무늬〉 a white stripe

흰쥐 〔動〕 a white rat; an albino rat

흰털 〈머리털〉 white hair; 〈모피〉 white fur [wool]

흰털제비꽃 〔植〕 a kind of violet

흰토끼 〔動〕 a white rabbit

흰팥 a whitish adzuki bean

흰포도주 ━葡萄酒 white wine ⇨ 백포도주

흰표범 ━豹━ 〔動〕 an ounce; a snow leopard [panther]

힁하다 dizzy; giddy; 〈서술적〉 feel dizzy [giddy]; 〈one's head〉 reel [swim, whirl]
▶ 머리가 힁하다 My head is in a swim. = I have a swimming in the head.

힁허케 without delay; fast; swiftly; quickly
◆ 힁허케 걷다 walk fast / 힁허케 가버리다 go away like the wind

히드라 〔動〕 a hydra 《pl. ~s, -drae》

히드라지드 〔藥〕 hydrazide (of isonicotinic acid)

히드로퀴논 〔化〕 hydroquinone

히말라야 Himalaya(s) ◆ 히말라야의 Himalayan
━━산맥 the Himalayas; the Himalaya Mountains ━━삼나무 a Himalayan cedar

히브리 Hebrew ⇨ 헤브루
━━서 〔聖〕 the Epistle of St. Paul (the Apostle) to the Hebrews; Hebrews 《略 Heb(r).》

히스타민 〔化〕 histamine ◆ 항히스타민제 an antihistamine; an antihistaminic (agent) / 히스타민의 histaminic / 항히스타민제의 antihistaminic

히스테리 〔醫〕 hysteria; hysterics; (美俗) conniption
◆ 히스테리의 hysteric(al) / 히스테리를 일으키다 go into [have a fit of] histerics; become hysterical / 히스테리를 일으키고 있다 be in a

state of hysteria; be in hysterics
히아신스 〖植〗 a hyacinth
히어로 〈영웅〉 a hero 《*pl.* ~es》 〈주인공〉 the hero 《of a story》
히어링 hearing ■—시험 a hearing test —연습 [훈련] a drill in hearing
히죽거리다 give *sb* a broad grin ♦히죽거리며 with a grin ⇨ 히죽
히죽이 with a contented [happy, sweet] smile; smilingly; with a grin; grinningly
♦히죽이 웃다 smile sweetly; grin at *sb*; give *sb* a broad grin
▶ 그는 좋아서 히죽이 웃었다 He grinned with delight.
히죽히죽 grinningly; with a broad grin
♦히죽히죽 웃다 grin (broadly) 《at》
히치하이커 〈편승자〉 a hitchhiker
히치하이크 〈편승〉 a hitchhike; hitchhiking —히치하이크하다 hitchhike 《*one's* way》 《to》
히타이트 ■—말 Hittite —족 a Hittite
히터 a heater ♦히터를 켜다[끄다] turn on [off] a heater —전기— an electric heater
히트 1 〖野〗 a (base, safe) hit; a single (hit)
♦히트를 치다 hit; have [get] a hit; make a single / 히트 두 개를 허용하다 allow [give up] two hits / 히트 다섯 개로 3점을 올리다 score three runs on five hits
▶ 그의 히트로 2점을 얻었다 His hit drove in two runs.
2 〈적중〉 a hit; 〈성공〉 a success —히트하다 win a success; be a hit ♦(영화 등이) 대히트하다 be a big [great] hit [success]
■클린— a clean hit 텍사스— a Texas leaguer; 《俗》 a blooper ■—레코드 a recording hit —송 a hit song —앤드런 hit and run; hit-and-run play
히트아일랜드 〖氣〗 a heat island
히틀러 〈독일의 정치가〉 Hitler, Adolf (1889-1945) ■—주의 Hitlerism
히포콘드리아증 —症 〖醫〗 〈심기증·침울증〉 hypochondria; hypochondriasis ♦히포콘드리아증의 hypochondriac(al)
—환자 a hypochondriac
히포크라테스 〈그리스의 의학자〉 Hippocrates (460 ?-377 B.C.) ■—선서 Hippocratic oath
히피 a hippie ■—촌 a hippie commune
히히 he, he!; he-he!; hee-hee!
히히거리다 keep laughing playfully ⇨ 해해거리다
힌두 ♦힌두의 Hindu; Hindoo ■—교 Hinduism —교도 a Hindu —어 Hindustani
힌트 a hint; 〈단서〉 a clue
♦실제 사건에서 힌트를 얻은 영화 a movie suggested by an actual incident / 그에게 힌트를 주다 give [drop] him a hint 《as to, about》 / 힌트를 얻다 get a hint 《from》; take (the) hint 《from the scene》; pick up an idea
힐끗 with a sidelong glance ⇨ 흘끗
힐난 詰難 blame; censure —힐난하다 blame; censure; reproach; call [bring, take] *sb* to task
힐러리 〈뉴질랜드의 등산가〉 Hillary, Sir Edmund (1919-)
힐문 詰問 close questioning; a searching inquiry; cross-examination; a cross-question; cross-questioning; grilling
—힐문하다 cross-examine; examine [question] *sb* closely; cross-question; press *sb* hard with questions; inquire searchingly
♦…의 실패를 힐문하다 《美》 needle *sb* over the failure of...
힐책 詰責 reprimand; rebuke; reproof; reproach; censure —힐책하다 rebuke; reprove; reprimand; censure; call [bring] *sb* to task [account] ♦태만을 힐책하다 rebuke *sb* for his neglect of duty
힐턴 〈영국의 소설가〉 Hilton, James (1900-54)
힘 1 〈체력〉 (physical) strength; power(s); energy; force ♦힘 있는 mighty; powerful; strong / 힘 없는 소리로 in a weak voice
〈힘이〉 힘이 나다[붙다] gain strength [energy]; become energetic / 힘이 장사다 have Herculean strength / 힘이 다하다 [빠지다] *one's* strength is gone [ebbs]; 〈사람이 주어〉 be exhausted
▶ 그에게는 그 병을 이길만한 힘이 있다 He has the strength to [is strong enough to] survive the illness.
▶ 그 말은 더 살 힘이 없다 The horse has no power to live on.
▶ 그는 나보다 힘이 세다 He is stronger than I (am) [(I) than me].
〈힘을〉 온 힘을 다하여 with all *one's* strength [might, energy, force] / 힘을 내다 put out *one's* strength / 어깨[근육]의 힘을 빼다 relax *one's* shoulders [muscles] / 힘을 겨루다 measure *one's* strength 《with》; have a strength contest / 힘을 회복하다 regain [renew] strength / 힘을 시험하다 try *one's* strength 《with, against》
2 〈정신적〉 strength; power(s); force; 〈활력〉 energy
♦의지의 힘 〈의지력〉 the strength [force] of *one's* will; willpower / 힘 있는[힘찬] 연설 a forceful [powerful] speech / 힘이 나다 cheer up; get encouraged / 힘이 떨어지다 be discouraged [frustrated]
3 〈물리적 힘〉 energy; force; power
♦증기의 힘 the power of steam / 자연의 힘 the power of nature / 열의 힘 energy of heat; caloric force
▶ 이 기계는 전기의 힘으로 움직인다 This machine works [is powered] by electricity.
4 〈행동력〉 power; energy; 〈능력〉 ability; 〈노력〉 (an) effort
♦읽는 힘 *one's* reading ability; *one's* ability to read / 자기의 힘으로 by [for] oneself; by [through] *one's* own efforts
〈힘이[은]〉 힘이 모자라는 incapable; incompetent / 힘이 자라는 한[미치는 한, 닿는 데까지] as far [best, much] as *one* can; to the best [utmost] of *one's* ability [power]; to [at] the top of *one's* bent
▶ 내게는 그 일을 혼자 해낼 힘이 없다 I don't have the power to finish the work alone. ⇌ It isn't in [within] my power to finish the work alone.
▶ 나는 힘이 부족하다는 것을 잘 알고 있다 I am

well aware of my lack of ability.
〈힘에〉 그에게는 그 일이 힘에 부친다 The task is too much for him. ≒ He is unequal to (doing) the task.
〈힘을〉 힘을 얻다 acquire the power 《to do, of doing》 [the ability 《to do》] / 힘을 발휘하다 show [display] one's ability / 힘을 쏟다 concentrate one's energy [efforts] 《on》
▶ 그들은 힘을 합해 그것을 해냈다 They worked together to finish it.
▶ 그는 미술품 수집에 크게 힘을 쏟았다 He put a great deal of effort into collecting works of art.
5 〈효력·위력〉 power; 〈영향력〉 influence; force; 〈권력〉 power; authority
♦ 여론의 힘 the force of public opinion / 수의 힘으로 by force of numbers / 부모의 힘으로 through the influence of one's parents / 정부의 힘으로 by the authority of the government / 힘을 쓰다 exercise [wield] one's power
▶ 대통령에게는 법안을 거부할 힘이 있다 The president has the power to veto bills.
6 〈도움〉 help; aid; assistance
♦ …의 힘으로 with the help of… / 힘이 되다 help; assist / 힘을 빌리다 ask sb's help; ask sb for help / 남의 힘을 빌리지 않고 하다 do 《it》 without help 《from another》; 〈온전히 혼자 힘으로〉 do 《it》 all by oneself
7 〈강조〉 emphasis; stress
♦ 힘을 주어 말하다 emphasize [lay stress on] one's words; speak with emphasis
▶ 그 학교는 실습에 특히 힘을 쓰고 있다 The school puts particular emphasis [stress] on practical learning. ≒ The school particularly emphasizes [stresses] practical learning.
▶ 그의 글에는 힘이 있다 He has a powerful pen.
8 〈자력(資力)〉 means
♦ 힘이 허용하는 한 as far as one's means allow
▶ 나는 차를 살 힘이 없다 I can't afford to buy a car. ≒ I don't have the means to buy a car.
9 〈공헌〉 service; contribution
▶ 새 학교를 세우는 데 그의 힘이 컸다 He has contributed much in establishing the new school.

힘겨룸 a strength contest
▶ 우리 힘겨룸을 해보자 Let us see who is the stronger, you or I.
—**힘겨룸하다** have a strength contest; have a trial of strength

힘겹다 be beyond one's ability [power]; be not strong [capable] enough 《to do》
▶ 나는 그와 씨름하기엔 힘겹다 I am not strong enough to wrestle with him.

힘껏 with full force; with all one's strength [might]; with [by] (all one's) might and main; to the utmost of one's power; to the best of one's ability
♦ 힘껏 싸우다 fight for all one is worth / 힘껏 일하다 work as best [as hard as] one can; work with all one's might
▶ 그는 밧줄을 힘껏 끌어당겼다 He pulled the rope with all his strength [with all his might, with all the strength he could muster].
▶ 힘껏 일해도 생계를 꾸려가기가 어려운 사람들이 있다 Work hard as they may, some cannot make both ends meet.

힘꼴 muscular power [strength]; brawn
♦ 힘꼴이나 쓰는 남자 a strong [brawny, muscular] man

힘들다 **1** 〈힘이 소비되다〉 be laborious [hard, troublesome]
♦ 힘든 일 a heavy [hard, laborious, toilsome] task; a tough job; a stiff work / 힘들지 않는 일 a light [an easy] task; a soft job
▶ 그 일은 무척 힘들었다 It cost me a great deal of trouble.
2 〈어렵다〉 be difficult [hard] 《to do》; 〈口〉 be stiff [sticky]
♦ 힘든 문제 a difficult problem / 더워서 일하기 힘들다 be so hot that it is hard to work / 이해하기 힘들다 〈일이 주어〉 baffle one's understanding; be above one's comprehension; 〈사람이 주어〉 find it hard to understand / 일자리를 구하기가 힘들다 have difficulty in finding a job
▶ 이제 가장 힘든 고비는 넘겼다 Now we have broken the back [neck] of the work.

힘들이다 **1** 〈체력·노력을 들이다〉 make efforts; throw one's energy [effort] into; put oneself into effort; exert oneself 《to do》; use [make, put forth] exertions
♦ 일에 힘들이다 throw [put] oneself into one's work / 짐을 힘들여 운반하다 carry the load laboriously
▶ 힘들인 보람이 있었다 My efforts were rewarded.
2 〈애쓰다〉 take pains; labor; elaborate 《on》; take trouble; make (strenuous) efforts
♦ 힘들여 번 돈 hard-earned money / 힘들어서 laboriously; with (great) efforts / 조금도 힘들이지 않고 without taking the least pains; without any effort; easily / 힘들여 계획을 세우다 elaborate upon a plan

힘부치다 be beyond one's capacity [power, ability]
▶ 그 일은 내게 힘부친다 The work is beyond my ability. ≒ I am not equal to the task.

힘빼물다 〈힘센 체하다〉 pretend to be strong; act mighty; demonstrate one's strength

힘세다 strong; mighty; powerful
▶ 그는 굉장히 힘세다 He is of great [Herculean] strength. ≒ He is as strong as a horse.

힘쓰다 **1** 〈노력하다〉 make efforts; exert oneself; do one's best; endeavor; try hard; labor 《to do, for》
♦ 공부에 힘쓰다 study hard / 학업에 힘쓰다 attend to one's studies with diligence / 문제 해결을 위해 힘쓰다 set oneself to solve a problem
▶ 나는 힘쓴 보람도 없이 실패했다 In spite of my efforts, I failed.
2 〈애쓰다〉 take pains; labor ♦ 힘써 글을 짓다 struggle through a composition
3 〈돕다〉 do sb a service; aid; help; extend help 《to》 / 남의 취직을 위해 힘쓰다 help sb

find employment; assist *sb* to a position ▶ 그는 나를 위해 여러가지로 힘써 주었다 He has done lots of good turns for me. ⇌ He did me many good offices. **4** 〈체력을 발휘하다〉 put forth [out] *one's* strength 《to do》 ◆ 힘써 밀다 push with might and main

힘없이 feebly; helplessly; dejectedly ◆ 힘없이 대답하다 answer weakly; give a feeble answer / 힘없이 고개를 떨구다 hang *one's* head much discouraged

힘입다 owe; be indebted to *sb* for *sth*; be in 《another's》 debt ▶ 그는 선생님의 가르침에 힘입어 성공했다 He owed his success to his teacher's education.

힘있다 **1** 〈힘이 세다〉 strong **2** 〈문장·어조 등이〉 powerful; forceful ◆ 힘있는 문장 powerful sentences / 힘있는 어조 a heavy accent **3** 〈권세·능력 등이〉 influential; powerful ◆ 힘있는 사람 an influential person; a person who carries some weight

힘자랑 boast of *one's* strength ─힘자랑하다 boast [be proud] of *one's* strength

힘주다 emphasize; concentrate 《upon》; devote *one's* strength 《to》; 〈분만 때에〉 bear down

힘줄 **1** 〈건〉 a tendon; a sinew ◆ 힘줄 투성이의 stringy; sinewy / 힘줄이 당기다 have a strain in a muscle **2** 〈혈관·혈맥〉 a vein **3** 〈섬유질의〉 a fiber; a string

힘줌말 an intensive [emphatic] word

힘차다 **1** 〈활력이 넘치다〉 powerful; forceful; forcible; vigorous; energetic; full of strength ◆ 힘찬 연설 a powerful speech / 힘차게 powerfully; energetically; vigorously **2** 〈힘에 겹다〉 beyond *one's* control

힝 〈코푸는 소리〉 with a hissing sound; 〈비웃는 소리〉 Pshaw! ◆ 코를 힝 풀다 blow *one's* nose with a hissing sound

힝힝 〈잇따라 코푸는 소리〉 clearing *one's* nose repeatedly

현대 한영 사전

부　　록

차 례

1. 중요 동사의 유의어별 용법·문형 ··················2517
2. 전화 통화할 때의 영어 ··················2543
3. 국제 통화에서 잘 쓰는 표현 ··················2545
4. Writing의 기초 지식 ··················2547
5. 영문 일기 쓰는 법 ··················2549
6. 영문 이력서 쓰는 법 ··················2550
7. 영문 편지 쓰는 법 ··················2552
8. 수와 수식 읽는 법 ··················2556
9. 개수를 세는 법 ··················2557
10. 국어의 로마자 표기법(초록) ··················2558
11. 한국 행정 구역 로마자 표기 ··················2559
12. 미·영어 중요 어구 비교 ··················2562
13. 한국 전통 식품의 영어 표기 ··················2569
14. 명사·동사의 어형 변화 규칙 ··················2571
15. 세계의 주요 통화 일람 ··················2572
16. 도량형 환산표 ··················2573
17. 인권을 배려한 영어 표현 ··················2574
18. 불규칙동사 변화표 ··················2575

1. 중요 동사의 유의어별 용법·문형

가르치다	만나다	상상하다	이기다
거들다	먹다	생각하다	이해하다
결심하다	멈추다	싫어하다	인정하다
고르다	명하다	쓰다	일어나다
고치다	모욕하다	얻다	전하다
교환하다	믿다	연습하다	주다
꺼지다	바라다	외치다	죽이다
끝나다	방해하다	요구하다	지키다
낳다	변하다	울다	찬성하다
놀라다	붙잡다	웃다	참다
대답하다	비난하다	위협하다	찾다
던지다	빌려주다	의논하다	칭찬하다
따르다	빌리다	의뢰하다	허락하다
떨다 / 마시다	살다	의심하다	훔치다

■ **가르치다** : 교육하다, 양성하다

[解說] **teach** 「지식이나 기술을 가르치다」란 뜻의 기본적이고 광범위한 말. 「직접 가르치다」라는 뜻을 지니고 있다. **instruct** 「어떤 특정 과목이나 기술을 조직적이고 계통적으로 가르치다」의 뜻. **educate** teach, instruct함으로써 어떤 사람이 가지고 있는 잠재적인 능력이나 특질을 어떤 지위에 맞게 발달시키는 것을 뜻하며, 주로 고등교육기관을 거치다는 뜻이 있다. **train** educate와 같은 뜻으로도 쓰이지만 보다 명확한 특정 작업이나 일을 위한 훈련을 뜻하며 동물에도 쓴다. **cultivate** 감각·품성·재능을 보살피고 배려하여 바람직한 방향으로 「도야(陶冶)하다」의 뜻.

teach *vt.* ① …을 가르치다 ; 《**teach** A B, **teach** B **to** A》 A(사람·학급 등)에게 B(학과 등)를 가르치다

▶ Mrs. Hyman teaches English. (하이만 선생님은 영어를 가르치신다)

▶ Who is teaching you phonetics? (누가 너희들에게 음성학을 가르치고 있니?)

▶ Professor Kim taught linguistics to our class. (김교수가 우리 반에 언어학을 가르쳤다)

② 《**teach** A 《**how**》 **to** *do*》 A에게 …하는 방법을 가르치다

▶ My brother taught me how to ride a bicycle. (형이 나에게 자전거 타는 법을 가르쳐 주었다)

instruct *vt.* …을 가르치다 ; 《**instruct** A **in** B》 A(사람)에게 B(학과)를 가르치다

▶ Miss Alison instructs two communication courses a week. (앨리슨 선생님은 커뮤니케이션 과목을 한 주에 두 과목 가르친다)

▶ Dr. Park instructs a class in geophysics. (박박사는 한 학급에 지구물리학을 가르친다)

educate *vt.* …을 교육하다 ; 《**educate** A **in** 〔**on**〕 B》 A(사람)에게 B(과목)를 교육하다 ; 《**edu-** **cate** A **at** 〔**in**〕 B》 A(사람)를 B(어떤 전문가)가 되도록 교육하다

▶ Some gifted young men were expensively educated in music. (몇 명의 천부적 재능이 있는 청년들이 비용을 아끼지 않고 음악 교육을 받았다)

▶ His fiancée was educated at Cambridge. (그의 약혼녀는 케임브리지에서 교육을 받았다)

▶ I'll educate my son for the medicine [ministry]. (아들을 의사[목사]가 되도록 교육시키겠다)

train *vt.* …을 훈련하다 ; 《**train** A **in** B》 A(사람)를 B(어떤 일)를 할 수 있도록 훈련하다 ; 《**train** A **to** B》 A(사람·동물)에게 직업·기술을 익히도록 훈련하다 ; 《**train** A **as** B》 A(사람)를 B(어떤 기술자)로서 훈련하다 ; 《**train** A **for** B》 A(사람·동물)를 B(어떤 목적)를 위해 훈련하다

▶ Many young people are not sufficiently trained in the use of their own native tongue. (모국어를 사용하는 데 충분히 훈련받지 못한 젊은이가 많다)

▶ Those talented young men and women were trained to be astronauts. (그 재능있는 젊은 남녀는 우주 비행사로 양성되었다)

▶ Promising women should be trained as managerial officers. (전도 유망한 여성은 관리로 훈련받아야 한다)

▶ They train dolphins for a show. (그들은 돌고래를 쇼에 내보내기 위해 훈련하고 있다)

cultivate *vt.* …을 양성하다 ; 배양하다 ; 도야하다

▶ He needs to cultivate his sense of humor. (그는 유머 감각을 기를 필요가 있다)

▶ It's by no means easy to cultivate a good habit. (좋은 습관을 기르는 것은 결코 쉬운 일이

1. 중요 동사의 유의어별 용법·문형

아니다)

■**거들다** : 돕다, 구하다, 구해내다, 구호하다, 구출하다, 구조하다

[解說] help 「거들다, 돕다」의 뜻으로 일반적인 말. aid help 보다 격식을 차린 말. 상대의 노력을 후원한다는 뜻으로 도움을 주는 쪽에서는 여력이 있고 도움을 받는 쪽은 약하다는 뉘앙스가 있다. assist help 보다 딱딱한 말. 「거들다」의 뜻으로는 aid 보다 약하고 곁에서 일의 진행을 돕는다는 뜻으로 부차적인 입장을 나타낸다. save 위험한 상태에서 「구하다」란 뜻의 말. 부사(구)와 함께 방법·상태를 나타내는 경우가 많다. rescue 위험·구금·죽음 등이 임박한 상황에서 신속하고도 적극적으로 구출한다는 뜻.

help vt. ① …을 거들다 ; 《help A with [in] B》 A(사람)가 B(행위)를 하는 것을 거들다
▶ He helped his father in washing the car. (그는 아버지가 차를 닦는 것을 거들었다)
② 《help A (to) do》 A(사람)가 …하는 것을 거들다 (▶《美》에서는 부정사의 to를 생략하는데 수동태에서는 to가 붙는다)
▶ I helped her carry the heavy suitcase. (나는 그녀가 무거운 여행 가방을 옮기는 것을 거들었다)
③ 《help A+부사(구)》 거들어서 …하게 하다
▶ She helped an old lady into a bus. (그녀는 노부인을 거들어서 버스에 태워드렸다)

aid vt. …을 돕다 ; 원조하다 ; 《aid A to do》 A(사람)가 …하는 것을 원조하다
▶ Developed countries aided developing countries in promoting their industry. (선진국은 개발도상국의 산업을 촉진시키는데 원조를 했다)

assist vt. …을 거들다 ; 보조하다 ; 《assist A in [with] B》 A(사람)가 B(일)하는 것을 거들다 (▶B는 명사·동명사)
▶ She assisted the professor in recording the teaching material on a video tape. (그녀는 교수가 교재를 녹화하는데 보조했다)

save vt. …을 구하다 ; 구출하다
▶ The life of the injured boy was saved by an operation. (부상당한 소년의 생명을 수술로 구했다)

rescue vt. …을 구출하다
▶ The hostage was rescued from being shot. (인질은 구출되어 사살되는 것을 모면했다)

■**결심하다** : 결정하다, 각오하다, 결단하다

[解說] decide 어떻게 해야 할지 망설이던 일이나 찬반 양론이 있었던 일에 대한 「결론을 내리다, 결정하다」의 뜻. determine decide 보다 격식을 차린 말로 decide한 사항에 대해, 그 내용·한도·방향 설정 등을 보다 명확하고도 상세하게 해서 그것을 변경시키지 않는다는 뜻을 포함하고 있다. resolve determine 보다 강한 뜻으로 어떤 일을 하느냐 안하느냐의 결의를 명확하고도 분명하게 말한다는 뜻을 내포한다.

decide vt. …하려고 결정하다 ; 결심하다 ; …라는 결론을 내리다
▶ I decided to go tomorrow instead of the day after tomorrow. (모레 말고 내일 가기로 결정했다)
▶ It was decided that the announcement (should) be postponed until autumn. (발표는 가을까지 연기하기로 결정되었다)
▶ Have you decided which dress to wear for the banquet?
(만찬회에 어떤 드레스를 입고 갈 것인가를 결정했습니까?)
— vi. 《decide on》 결심하다 ; 결정하다
▶ I'm the one to decide. (결정하는 사람은 저입니다)
▶ Have you decided on the name for the puppy? (강아지 이름은 결정했니?)

determine vt. …을 결정[결심]하다
▶ We determined the number of guests to invite and what to serve them. (우리는 초대할 손님의 수와 무엇을 대접할 것인가를 결정했다)
— vi. 결정[결심]하다 ; 《determine on A》 A(어떤 일)를 하려고 결정[결심]하다 (▶A는 명사·동명사)
▶ He determined on accepting the position. ⇌ He determined to accept the position. (그는 그 지위를 받아들이기로 결심했다)

resolve vt. ① (사람이)…할 것을 결심[결정]하다
▶ The leader resolved to give up getting to the summit that afternoon. (대장은 그날 오후에 산꼭대기에 도달하는 것을 포기하기로 작정했다)
② (위원회나 의회가) …하기로 결의하다
▶ It was resolved that a joint statement (should) be issued. (공동성명을 내기로 결의되었다)
— vi. (행위·안(案) 등을 실행하기로) 결심[결정]하다
▶ The party resolved on looking for him by all means. (일행은 반드시 그를 찾아내기로 결의했다)

■**고르다** : 골라 뽑다, 가리다, 선출하다, 선택하다, 선발하다

[解說] choose 주어진 범위·제공된 사람·물건 중에서 판단하여 적당하다고 생각되는 것을 「고르다」는 뜻으로 광범위하게 쓰인다. select 많은 것 중에서 비교 검토하여 「고르다」. pick select 와 같은 뜻으로 쓰이지만 select보다 구어적이고, 개인적인 입장에서 「고르다」라는 뜻이 함축되어 있다. elect 투표 등의 절차를 거쳐 정식으로 인물을 「선출하다」의 뜻으로 부적당한 사람·

물건을 골라내고 선출시키다는 뜻이 강하다. **prefer** 기호(嗜好)・희망에 따라 사람・물건을 「고르다; 좋아하다」의 뜻이지만 고른 사람이나 물건이 수중에 들어온다고는 할 수 없다.

choose *vt.* …을 고르다 ; 《**choose A out of B**》 B (사람・물건)중에서 A(사람・물건)를 고르다 ; 《**choose A B, choose B for A**》 A(사람)에게 B(물건)를 골라 주다 ; 《**choose A (as [to be])** B》 A(사람)를 B(어떤 입장의 사람)로서 고르다 ; 《**choose to** do》 …하기로 결정하다
▶ She chose a white blouse and a black skirt. (그녀는 흰 블라우스와 검은 스커트를 골랐다)
▶ You may choose one out of these gifts. (이 선물 중에서 한 개를 골라도 된다)
▶ The boy chose himself his favorite baseball cap. (소년은 자기가 매우 좋아하는 야구모자를 골랐다)
▶ I chose to recite his inaugural address. (나는 그의 취임 연설문을 암송하기로 했다)

select *vt.* …을 고르다 ; 《**select A for B**》 A(사람・물건)를 B(어떤 목적)를 위해 고르다 ; 《**select A from B**》 B(사람・물건)들 중에서 A(사람・물건)를 고르다 ; 《**select A out of B**》 A(사람・물건)를 B(많은 후보 중)에서 고르다 [선발하다] ; 《**select A to do**》 A(사람・물건)를 …하기 위해 고르다[선발하다]
▶ She selected a tie for her boy friend. (그녀는 남자 친구에게 주려고 넥타이를 하나를 골랐다)
▶ The pastor selected a passage from the Bible. (그 목사는 성경 중에서 한 구절을 골랐다)
▶ Our team was selected out of a large number of the high school baseball teams. (우리 팀은 많은 교고 야구 팀 중에서 선발되었다)
▶ I was selected to make an opening address. (나는 개회사를 하도록 선발되었다)

pick *vt.* (신중히) …을 고르다 ; 선발하다
▶ I pick my words carefully when I talk to my boss. (사장과 이야기할 때는 말을 신중히 골라서 한다)

elect *vt.* 선출하다 ; 선거하다 ; 《**elect A B**》 A (사람)를 B(직무명)로 선출하다 ; 《**elect A as B**》 A(사람)를 B(직무・대표자)로 선출하다 (직무가 한 명에 한정되어 있는 경우는 관사 없음); 《**elect A to B**》 A(사람)를 B(직무의 지위) 로 선출하다
▶ We elected the dean of the business school. (우리는 실업학교장을 선출했다)
▶ Dr. Stewart was elected as president of the university. (스튜어트 박사가 대학총장에 선출 됐다)
▶ We will elect him to the presidency. (우리 는 그를 회장[대통령]으로 선출할 것이다)

prefer *vt.* …을 고르다; …을 좋아하다; 《**prefer A to B**》 B보다 A쪽을 택하다

▶ I prefer English to French. (프랑스어보다 영어를 좋아한다)
▶ Of the two girls, I prefer Shirly. (두 여자 중 에서는 셜리를 더 좋아한다)

■ **고치다** : 낫다, 치유하다, 치료하다
[解說] **cure** 의사나 약으로 「(병을) 고치다」, 「(병이) 낫다」의 뜻. **heal** 「(상처를) 치료하 다」, 「(상처가) 낫다」의 뜻. **recover** 어느 정도 격식을 차린 말.「잃어버린 것을 되찾다」의 뜻에 서 「(건강을) 회복하다」. **regain** recover보다 뜻이 강하다. **get over** recover와 같은 뜻이지 만 구어적. **mend** 스스럼없는 말로 환자가 「(병 이) 낫다, 좋아지다」의 뜻.

cure *vt.* (병 등)을 고치다 ; 《**cure A of B**》 A(사 람)의 B(병)를 고치다
▶ This medicine will cure you of your stomach ulcer. (이 약으로 당신의 위궤양은 나을 것 입니다)
— *vi.* 낫다
▶ My disease cured completely. (내 병은 다 나았다)

heal *vt.* (상처・괴로움 등)을 고치다
▶ My burns were healed after six months. (내 화상은 6개월이 지나서 나았다)
▶ His comfort healed my sorrow. (그가 위로 해 주어서 내 슬픔은 사라졌다)
— *vi.* 낫다
▶ The injury in my back healed up. (등의 상 처가 나았다)

recover *vt.* (건강)을 회복하다, (잃어버린) 건강 을 되찾다
▶ Father completely recovered his health. (아 버지는 건강을 완전히 회복하셨다)
— *vi.* 《**recover from**》 건강을 회복하다
▶ He could not recover from his illness. (그는 건강을 회복할 수 없었다)

regain *vt.* (건강)을 회복하다
▶ I'm glad that I regained my sight. (시력을 회복해서 기쁘다)

get over (口) (병・슬픔・분노 등)에서 회복하다
▶ She got over her chronic rheumatism. (그녀 는 만성 류머티즘이 나았다)

mend *vi.* (환자가) 낫다
▶ My wife is mending quickly. (아내는 차도가 빠르다)

■ **교환하다** : 갈다, 바꾸다
[解說] **exchange** 사람이나 조직이 물건 등을 「교 환하다」는 뜻의 일반적인 말. **change** 양복이나 지하철 또는 같은 종류의 물건을 「갈다」의 뜻. **barter** 「물물교환하다」의 뜻. **substitute** 사람 이나 물건을 대리인・대용품으로 「대체하다」의 뜻. **swap** 물건이나 양복 등을 「교환하다」의 뜻 으로 exchange와 같은 뜻으로 쓴다.

1. 중요 동사의 유의어별 용법·문형

exchange vt. ① 《exchange A for B》 A를 B와 교환하다
▶ Where can I exchange my won for dollars? (어디서 원화를 달러화로 바꿀 수 있습니까?)
② 《exchange B with A》 A(사람)와 B(물건)를 바꾸다
▶ Mary exchanged scarfs with Sally. (메리는 샐리와 스카프를 바꿨다)

change vt. …을 교환하다
▶ You'll have to change trains at (the) Shindorim station. (신도림역에서 지하철을 갈아타야 할 것입니다)
▶ She didn't like her new, pink hat, so she took it back to the shop and changed it (for another). (그녀는 새 핑크색 모자가 마음에 들지 않아서 도로 가게에 가지고 가서 (다른 것과) 바꿨다)
― vi. 갈아입다; 갈아타다
▶ She changed for school. (그녀는 학교에 가기 위해서 옷을 갈아입었다)
▶ You'll have to change here. (여기서 갈아타야 합니다)

barter vt. 《barter A for B》 A와 B를 (물물) 교환하다
▶ They bartered bananas for rice with each other. (그들은 바나나와 쌀을 서로 교환했다)
― vi. 《barter with》 (사람과) 물건을 교환하다
▶ Tenant farmers and fishermen bartered with each other. (소작농과 어부는 서로 물물교환했다)

substitute vt. (사람·물건)을 대신 쓰다
▶ I substituted low-cal sweetener for sugar. (나는 저칼로리 감미료를 설탕 대신에 썼다)
― vi. (사람·물건이) 대신하다
▶ Miss Finch substituted for the librarian who was on vacation. (핀치양이 휴가중인 사서(司書)의 대리역을 했다)

swap vt. (물건)을 교환하다
▶ Karen swapped her French doll for Linda's Chinese doll. (카렌은 자기의 프랑스 인형과 린다의 중국 인형을 교환했다)
― vi. 교환하다
▶ I liked her vase and she liked mine, so we swapped. (나는 그녀의 꽃병이 마음에 들었고 그녀는 나의 것을 좋아했다. 그래서 우리는 교환했다)

■ **꺼지다** : 없어지다, 사라지다
[解說] **vanish** 「(갑자기) 사라지다」; 보이지 않게 되다」의 뜻으로 찾을 실마리나 흔적이 없음을 의미한다. **disappear** 시계(視界)나 생각에서 「보이지 않게 되다」, 「사라지다」의 뜻. 그 사라지는 방법은 갑작스런 경우도 있고 서서히 또는 영구적, 일시적인 경우가 있는데 그것은 문맥에 따라 결정된다. **fade out** [away] 모습·기억·감정 등이 서서히 「사라지다」, 「희미해지다」의 뜻. **blow out** 불 또는 불꽃이 「불어서 끄다」, 「(갑자기) 꺼지다」. **put out** 전등이나 불을 「끄다」. **extinguish** put out보다 격식을 차린 말로 전등이나 불을 「끄다」.

vanish vi. (보이던 것이 갑자기) 사라지다; 보이지 않게 되다
▶ Two diamond rings vanished from the showcase. (진열장에서 두 개의 다이아몬드 반지가 사라졌다)

disappear vi. 보이지 않게 되다; 모습을 감추다
▶ The moon disappeared behind a cloud. (달이 구름 사이로 모습을 감추었다)

fade out [away] (서서히) 사라지다
▶ The memory of my childhood gradually faded away. (나의 어린 시절의 기억이 서서히 사라졌다)

blow out (불·불꽃이 바람으로) 꺼지다

put out (전등이나 불)을 끄다
▶ Put out the light before going out. (외출하기 전에 전등을 끄시오)
▶ The boys put out the embers of the campfire. (소년들은 캠프파이어의 등걸불을 껐다)

extinguish vt. (불이나 전등)을 끄다
▶ The curfew is at 11:00. Please extinguish the light. (소등 시간은 11시입니다. 전등을 꺼 주십시오)

■ **끝나다** : 끝마치다, 종료하다
[解說] **end** 「끝나다」란 뜻의 일반어. 계속되어 오던 것에 「끝막을 짓다」의 뜻으로 그것의 완성된 상태의 좋고 나쁨은 가리지 않는다. **close** 연 것을 「닫다」의 뜻이 포함되어 있다. **finish** 당초의 목적을 달성하고 「끝마치다」의 뜻으로 특히 노력하여 「최후의 마무리를 하다」, 「완성하다」의 뜻이 내포되어 있다. **be over** 일상용어로 end보다 빈도가 높다.

end vt. …을 끝마치다; …을 끝내다
▶ Let's end the chat. (잡담을 그만두자)
▶ The pastor's benediction ended the church service. (목사의 축도로 교회의 예배는 끝났다)
― vi. 끝나다; 《end in》 (결과로서) …로 끝나다; 《end up》 마지막에는 …로 끝나다
▶ At last my vacation ended. (마침내 내 휴가는 끝났다)
▶ His attempt ended in failure. (그의 시도는 실패로 끝났다)
▶ The drama started as a tragedy but ended up as a comedy. (그 드라마는 비극으로 시작되었으나 희극으로 끝났다)

close vt. …을 끝마치다; 끝나게 하다
▶ The chairperson announced that the meeting was to be closed. (사회자는 폐회를 선언했다)
▶ The nomination for the board of trustees is

now closed. (평의원의 추천은 방금 마감되었다)
— vi. (가게·회합 등이) 끝나다 ; 종결되다 ; 닫다 ; (텔레비전·라디오 방송이) 끝나다
▶ This department store closes at 6:30 p.m. (이 백화점은 오후 6시 반에 닫는다)
▶ Broadcasting closes at 12 midnight. (방송은 밤 12시에 끝난다)
finish vt. …을 끝마치다 ; 종료하다 ; 마무리하다 ; 완성하다 (▶목적어로는 부정사를 취하지 않고 동명사를 취한다)
▶ He has finished (writing) his master's thesis. (그는 석사 논문을 끝마쳤다)
▶ His picture was finely finished. (그의 그림은 훌륭하게 마무리되었다)
— vi. 종료되다 ; 끝나다 ; (경기에서) 결승선에 들어오다
▶ The runner finished first. (주자는 1등으로 골인했다)
be over (사항·기간이) 끝나다 ; 끝내다
▶ I'm glad the exams are over anyway. (어쨌든 시험이 끝나서 기쁘다)
▶ It's all over with us now. (우리는 이제 끝장이다[희망이 없다])

■ **낳다** : 태어나다, 까다, 부화하다
[解說] **bear** 「(사람·동물이) 자식[새끼]을 낳다」,「(과수가 열매)를 맺다」,「(이자를 낳다」 등의 뜻으로 쓰지만 현재는 「사람이 자식을 낳다」의 경우는 be born 이외에 have를 보통 쓴다. **breed**「(동물이 새끼)를 낳다 ; 번식하다」,「범죄 등이 발생하다」의 뜻. **hatch**「(알이나 병아리)를 까다 ; 부화시키다」. **lay**「(새나 벌레가 알)을 낳다」의 뜻으로 쓰인다.
bear vt. ① (사람·동물이 자식·새끼)를 낳다
▶ Kate was born of Canadian parents. (케이트는 캐나다인 부모 사이에서 태어났다)
▶ This cat has borne three kittens this year. (이 고양이는 금년에 새끼 세 마리를 낳았다)
② (과수가 열매)를 맺다
▶ Why don't you plant some fruit-bearing trees in your yard? (정원에 유실수를 심는 게 어떠냐?)
③ (돈이 이자)를 낳다
▶ A fixed deposit bears a comparatively high interest. (정기 예금은 비교적 높은 이자를 낳는다)
breed vi. (동물이) 새끼를 낳다 ; 번식하다 ; (범죄 등이) 발생하다 (▶사람에게 쓸 때는 경멸적인 표현이다)
▶ Rats breed rapidly. (시궁쥐는 번식이 빠르다)
▶ Juvenile delinquency often breeds in broken homes. (미성년 비행은 흔히 결손가정에서 생긴다)
— vt. (동물이 새끼)를 낳다 ; (바람직하지 않은 일)을 생기게 하다 ; 야기하다
▶ Stagnant water breeds mosquito larvae. (고여 있는 물은 장구벌레를 생기게 한다)
hatch vt., vi. (알·병아리)를 까다 ; 부화시키다 ; 깨다 ; 부화하다
▶ Doves are hatching eggs in the nest. (비둘기가 둥지에서 알을 까고 있다)
lay vt., vi. (새나 곤충이 알)을 낳다
▶ Hens lay eggs. (암탉이 달걀을 낳는다)

■ **놀라다** : 기겁을 하고 놀라다, 깜짝 놀라다
[解說] **be surprised at** 「놀라다」의 뜻으로는 가장 일반적인 말로 의외의 일, 예상밖의 일로「놀라다」의 뜻. **be astonished at** be surprised at 보다 강한 말로 믿기 어려워 정신이 멍해지거나 말도 할 수 없게 되다의 뜻. **be amazed at** be astonished at보다 강한 말로 놀란 나머지 당황하거나 망연자실하는 상태를 강조한다.
be surprised at …에 놀라다 ; 《**be surprised to** do》 …하고 놀라다
▶ I was surprised to see you get up so early. (네가 이렇게 일찍 일어나는 것을 보고 놀랐다)
▶ I'm surprised to see you here. (당신과 여기서 만나다니 놀라운데요)
be astonished at …에 놀라다 ; 《**be astonished to** do》 …하고 경탄하다
▶ They were astonished at the news that their nephew was arrested. (조카가 체포되었다는 소식에 그들은 망연자실했다)
▶ Cindy was astonished to find a bicycle she had long wanted by her bed on Christmas morning. (신디는 오랫동안 가지고 싶었던 자전거가 크리스마스 아침에 침대 옆에 있는 것을 보고 깜짝 놀랐다)
be amazed at …에 기겁을 하고 놀라다 ; 《**be amazed to** do》 …하고 경악하다
▶ I was only amazed at the extent and severity of the air raid. (나는 공습의 범위가 확대되고 격심해져서 경악할 따름이었다)
▶ She was amazed to know that many children were on the verge of starvation in Africa. (아프리카에 사는 많은 어린이들이 기아상태에 직면해 있다는 것을 알고 그녀는 몹시 놀랐다)

■ **대답하다** : 응하다, 응답하다
[解說] **answer** 구두나 문서, 행동으로「대답하다」의 뜻으로, 가장 일반적인 말. **reply** answer보다 격식을 차린 말. 편지를 받았다라고만 말한다면 answer를 써도 되지만 그 질문의 내용이나 요점 하나하나에 대답하는 경우는 reply를 쓴다. **respond** answer나 reply보다 격식을 차린 말. 호소·권고·기대에 대해 기꺼이 자발적으로 「반응을 보이다」의 뜻. **retort** 「말대꾸하

1. 중요 동사의 유의어별 용법·문형

다」, 「되쏘아주다」의 뜻.

answer *vt*. …에 대답하다 ; 응답하다
▶ I answered his question. (나는 그의 질문에 대답했다)
— *vi*. 대답하다 ; 응답하다
▶ She pushed the doorbell, but no one answered. (그녀는 현관의 벨을 눌렀지만 아무도 응답하지 않았다)

reply *vi*. 답장을 내다 ; 《reply to A》 A(질문 등)에 대답하다
▶ I'll reply by letter in detail. (자세히 답장드리겠습니다)
▶ Father always replied to all the points I wanted to know. (아버지는 언제나 내가 알고 싶어하는 모든 것에 대해 대답해 주셨다)
— *vt*. (보통 부정문에서) …을 대답하다 ; 《reply that...》 …라고 대답하다
▶ The counselor asked her a few questions, but she gave no reply. (지도교사가 그녀에게 몇 가지 질문을 했지만 그녀는 아무 대답도 하지 않았다)
▶ He replied that he was not interested in. (그는 흥미가 없다고 대답했다)

respond *vi*. 《respond to A》 A(질문 등)에 대답하다 ; 응답하다 ; 반응하다
▶ A nationwide audience responded immediately to an appeal for help. (전국의 시청자들은 원조에 대한 호소에 즉각 반응을 보였다)
— *vt*. …라고 대답하다 ; …에 대답하다
▶ She responded that she was ready to participate in the activity. (그녀는 기꺼이 그 활동에 참가하고 싶다고 대답했다)

retort *vt*. …라고 말대꾸하다 ; 되쏘아주다
▶ She retorted, "Stop being nosy." (「참견하지 마」라고 그녀는 되쏘았다)
— *vi*. 말대꾸하다 ; 되쏘아주다
▶ The student who was found cheating in the exam retorted on his teacher. (시험에서 부정행위를 하다가 발각된 학생이 선생님께 말대꾸했다)

■ **던지다** : 내던지다
[解説] **throw** 「던지다」란 뜻의 일반어. **cast** 그물, 주사위 등 가벼운 물건을 「던지다」, 또 낚싯줄을 어떤 각도로 「던지다」, 「(씨를) 던져서 뿌리다」 등의 뜻. **fling** 강한 감정이나 정열로 난폭하게 「내던지다」의 뜻. **hurl** 어떤 거리에서 물건을 빠르고도 세게 「던지다」의 뜻. **pitch** 공 등을 일정한 방향으로 힘껏 「던지다」. **toss** 가볍게 「던져 올리다」의 뜻으로 상하 운동의 뜻이 있다.

throw *vt*. …을 던지다 《throw A B, throw B to 〔at〕 A》 A(사람·물건)에게 B(물건)를 내던지다 ; B를 A에게 내던지다
▶ He threw me a pack of cigarettes. (그는 내게 담배 한 갑을 던져 주었다)
▶ She threw a stone at a cat. (그녀는 고양이에게 돌을 던졌다)

cast *vt*. …을 던지다
▶ The fishermen cast a net. (어부들이 그물을 던졌다)

fling *vt*. …을 던지다 (▶ 부사(구)와 함께)
▶ Getting mad at him, she flung a book at him. (그녀는 화가 나서 그에게 책을 냅다 던졌다)
▶ He flung his jacket off. (그는 상의를 홱 벗어 던졌다)

hurl *vt*. …을 세게 던지다
▶ She hurled a stick at a strange man behind a bush. (덤불 뒤의 수상한 남자에게 그녀는 막대기를 세게 던졌다)

pitch *vt*. …을 던지다
▶ I pitched a softball. (나는 소프트볼을 던졌다)

toss *vt*. …을 던지다 ; 멀리 내던지다
▶ Two boys tossed a ball for about half an hour. (두 소년은 약 30분 동안 공을 서로 던지고 받았다)
▶ We discussed a problem and tossed it to and fro. (우리는 어떤 문제를 토의하며 설왕설래했다)
▶ Let's toss a coin to decide who goes out to buy the drink. (동전을 던져 누가 음료수를 사러 나갈 것인가를 결정하자)

■ **따르다** : 복종하다, 순종하다
[解説] **obey** 사람·명령·희망·지도 등에 「따르다」란 뜻의 일반어로 순수하게 따르다의 뜻이 포함되어 있다. **comply** 격식을 차린 말로 obey보다는 「따르다」라는 의미가 강하다. 이 말은 의존도가 강한 반면 자신의 의견이 약함을 함축한다. **concede** 상대가 자기보다 강하므로 마지못해 권리나 소유권을 「양보하다」의 뜻. **accept** 제안받은 것이나 제공되는 일과 물건을 기꺼이 「받다」, 「수락하다」.

obey *vt*. …에 따르다 ; …에 복종하다
▶ Obey your conscience. (너의 양심에 따라라)
— *vi*. 따르다 ; 복종하다
▶ When you are married, you should love and obey. (결혼하면 사랑하고 따라야 한다)

comply *vi*. 응하다 ; 따르다
▶ The reporters were requested to leave, and they complied. (기자들은 떠나달라는 요청을 받고 거기에 응했다)
▶ The singer complied with the terms of payment. (가수는 그 지불 조건에 응했다)

concede *vt*. …을 양보하다 ; 마지못해 인정하다
▶ In the end father conceded that mother was right. (아버지는 마침내 어머니가 옳다는 것을 인정했다)

▶ The landowner conceded us the right to park the car. (땅주인은 우리의 주차권을 겨우 인정했다)

accept *vt.* …을 받다 ; 수락하다
▶ I hope you'll accept my offer. (나의 제안을 수락하기를 바랍니다)

■ **떨다** : 부르르 떨다, 부들부들 떨다
[解説] **shake** 「떨다」의 뜻의 일반어로 다음 단어들 대신으로도 쓰인다. 크게, 단속적으로 떨다의 뜻이 있다. **tremble** 사람이나 목소리가 격정·추위·공포로 가늘게 「바들바들 떨다」. **quake** tremble보다 강한 말로 마음이 뒤흔들려 「부들부들 떨다」의 뜻. **quiver** tremble과 같은 뜻으로도 쓰이지만 그것보다 정도가 약하고 악기의 현처럼 작게 진동하거나 떨리는 것을 표현할 때 쓰며 공포나 격정보다는 긴장감을 나타내는 경우가 많다. 또 잎·빛·벌레·배 등 사람 이외에 쓰이는 경우가 많다. **shiver** 추위서 「떨다」의 뜻이지만 기대·예감·경미한 공포 등에 대해서도 쓴다. **shudder** 공포나 불쾌감으로 인해 크게 「와들와들 떨다」의 뜻.

shake *vi.* 떨다
▶ She was shaking with fear. (그녀는 무서워서 떨고 있었다)

tremble *vi.* (바들바들) 떨다
▶ On the stage she was trembling with [for] stage fright. (그녀는 단상에서 무대 공포증으로 바들바들 떨고 있었다)

quake *vi.* (사람·몸이) 부들부들 떨다
▶ We were quaking with terror in an air-raid shelter. (우리는 방공호 안에서 공포로 부들부들 떨고 있었다)

quiver *vi.* (가늘게) 떨다
▶ Her lips quivered when she said, "I'm sorry for being late for school." (그녀가 「학교에 지각해서 죄송합니다」라고 말했을 때 그녀의 입술은 바르르 떨렸다)
▶ The beams of the moon were quivering on the surface of the pond. (달빛이 연못의 수면에 반짝반짝 빛나고 있었다)

shiver *vi.* 떨다 ; 오들오들 떨다
▶ While I was waiting for a bus, I shivered with cold. (버스를 기다리는 동안 추워서 오들오들 떨었다)

shudder *vi.* 와들와들 떨다
▶ She shuddered when the doctor told her that her husband had stomach cancer. (의사가 남편의 병이 위암이라고 말하자 그녀는 와들와들 떨었다)

■ **마시다** : 홀짝홀짝 마시다, 들이키다, 삼키다
[解説] **drink** 음료를 「마시다」란 뜻의 일반어. 다만 자동사일 때는 「술을 마시다」의 뜻이 있다. 「수프를 먹다」는 "eat soup"라 하고 「약을 먹다」는 "take medicine"이라고 한다. **take** 「(음료를) 들다 ; 섭취하다」, 「(약을) 먹다」의 뜻. **sip** 「홀짝홀짝 마시다」의 뜻. 마시다라는 뉘앙스가 있다. 흔히 「홀짝홀짝 마시다」라고 번역하지만 반드시 그와 같은 소리를 낸다는 뜻은 아니다. **swallow** 「꿀꺽 삼키다」의 뜻. **gulp** 놀라거나 초조해하는 뜻을 내포하며 「급히[부랴부랴] 마시다」. **suck** 입술이나 혀로 「빨아 마시다」의 뜻.

drink *vt.* …을 마시다
▶ I drink a glass of milk before breakfast. (나는 아침 식사 전에 우유를 한 컵 마신다)
― *vi.* 마시다 ; 술을 마시다
▶ He used to eat and drink much when he was young. (그는 젊었을 때 많이 먹고 마시곤 했다)
▶ My father likes to drink. (아버지는 술을 즐기신다)

take *vi.* …을 마시다 ; 섭취하다 ; (약을) 먹다
▶ He took Scotch on the rocks. (그는 스카치에 얼음을 넣어 마셨다)
▶ Did you take the medicine after supper? (저녁 식사 후에 약을 먹었니?)

sip *vt.* …을 홀짝홀짝 마시다
▶ She was sipping the hot coffee. (그녀는 뜨거운 커피를 홀짝홀짝 마시고 있었다)
― *vi.* 《sip at》 홀짝홀짝 마시다
▶ He was sipping at the brandy, watching TV. (그는 텔레비전을 보면서 브랜디를 홀짝홀짝 마시고 있었다)

swallow *vt.* (음료·음식)을 꿀꺽 마시다[삼키다]
▶ The boy swallowed a mouthful of orange juice. (소년은 오렌지 주스를 한 모금 꿀꺽 마셨다)
― *vi.* 마시다 ; 삼키다
▶ He swallowed in large drafts of beer. (그는 맥주를 벌떡벌떡 마셨다)

gulp *vt.* 《gulp down》 …을 급히 마시다
▶ She gulped down a glass of water. (그녀는 물 한 컵을 급히 마셨다)

suck *vt.* …을 빨다 ; 빨아 마시다
▶ The baby was sucking the mother's breast. (아기는 엄마의 젖을 빨아먹고 있었다)
▶ The girl sucked the Coke through a straw. (소녀는 콜라를 스트로로 빨아마셨다)
― *vi.* 《suck at》 빨다
▶ The baby was sucking at his nibbling toy. (아기가 장난감 젖꼭지를 빨고 있었다)

■ **만나다** : 마중하다, 경험하다, 방문하다
[解説] **meet** 「(약속하고 또는 우연히) …을 만나다 ; …을 마중나가다 ; …와 아는 사이가 되다」의 뜻의 일반어. **meet with** 「(사고·행·불행)을 당하다 ; …을 경험하다, (美)에서는 「(선약하고) 회담하다」의 뜻. **see** 「만나다」란 뜻의 구

1. 중요 동사의 유의어별 용법·문형

어로서는 meet와 같은 뜻으로 쓰이지만「우연히 만나다」의 뜻은 없고「방문하다」,「면담하다」,「(의사의) 진찰을 받다」의 뜻. **come across**「(사람)을 우연히 만나다;(물건)을 우연히 발견하다」. **get together**「…을 만나다」,「모이다;친목회를 열다」의 뜻. **encounter** 격식을 차린 말로「(위험·곤란 등 나쁜 일)을 당하다」.

meet *vt.* ① …을 만나다 ; 우연히 만나다
▶ When do you meet your client next time? (의뢰인하고는 다음번에 언제 만납니까?)
▶ I happened to meet my former students at a theater. (전에 가르친 학생들을 극장에서 우연히 만났다)
② (사람)을 마중나가다
▶ Mother is arriving at Seoul Station at four this afternoon. I'll meet her train. (어머니가 오늘 오후 4시에 서울역에 도착합니다. 역으로 마중 나가겠습니다)
③ (소개 받고) 처음 만나다 ; (아무와) 아는 사이가 되다
▶ 會話 "Have you met my wife?" "Yes, I met her at the reception the other day." (제 아내를 만난 적이 있습니까? — 네, 요전의 리셉션에서 만났지요)

meet with (장애·사고·행·불행·환영 등)을 받다[당하다] ; 우연히 만나다 ; 경험하다 ; 《美》(선약하고) 회담하다 ; 부닥치다
▶ I met with Mr. Smith in order to proofread the manuscript. (원고를 교정하기 위해 스미스 씨와 만났다)
▶ The project to extend the runway met with persistent opposition of the neighboring farmers. (공항의 활주로 확대 계획은 이웃 농민들의 집요한 반대에 부닥쳤다)

see *vt.* ① (사람)을 만나다 ; …을 방문하다
▶ Could I see you on [at] the weekend? (주말에 만나 뵐 수 있을까요?)
② (의사에게) 진찰받다 ; (의사가) 진찰하다
▶ The doctor can't see you now; he is out on a call. (의사 선생님은 왕진 중이셔서 지금 진찰할 수 없습니다)

come across (사람)과 우연히 마주치다 ; (물건)을 우연히 발견하다 ; 머리에 떠오르다
▶ I came across her in a department store. (그녀를 백화점에서 우연히 만났다)
▶ A very good idea came across my mind. (아주 좋은 생각이 머리에 떠올랐다)

get together (사람)과 만나다 ; 모이다 ; 친목회를 열다
▶ Why don't we get together and have a long talk? (만나서 느긋하게 이야기나하는 것이 어때요?)

encounter *vt.* (나쁜 일)을 당하다
▶ Whatever adversity you (may) encounter, I hope you'll carry out this project. (어떤 역경

이 닥칠지라도 이 계획을 실행하기 바랍니다)

■ **먹다** : 식사하다

解說 **eat**「먹다」,「식사하다」의 뜻으로 단단한 것을 씹어서 위로 내려보내다라는 동작에 중점을 두는 말이다. **have**「(음식물)을 먹다」,「(음료)를 마시다」,「(담배)를 피우다」등과 같이 넓은 의미로 쓰이고 사람에게 먹을 것을 권할 때에도 eat, drink, smoke 등 보다는 혼히 완곡한 말로서 have가 쓰인다. **take**「먹다」의 뜻으로는 형식에 치우친 말이며 《美》에서는 eat, have를 쓴다. take는「(약)을 먹다」,「(설탕·소금·후춧가루 등의 조미료나 향신료)를 치다」,「(공기)를 들이마시다」 등의 뜻으로 쓴다. **feed** 동물이나 아기가「먹다」의 뜻.

eat *vt.* …을 먹다 ; (수프)를 마시다
▶ Did you eat breakfast this morning? (오늘 아침에 조반을 먹었니?)
▶ We ate apple pie. (우리는 사과 파이를 먹었어요)
— *vi.* 먹다 ; 식사를 하다
▶ Shall we eat out this evening? (오늘 저녁에는 외식을 할까요?)
▶ She eats like a bird. (그녀는 매우 소식한다)

have *vt.* …을 먹다
▶ What time do you usually have supper? (보통 몇 시에 저녁 식사를 하니?)
▶ Have some sandwiches! (샌드위치를 좀 들어봐)

take *vt.* (英) …을 먹다
▶ They have [take] only two meals a day. (그들은 하루에 두 끼밖에 먹지 않는다)

feed *vi.* (동물이) 먹이를 먹다 ; 《**feed on**》 (동물이) …을 늘 먹다
▶ Cows were feeding in a pasture. (젖소들이 목장에서 풀을 뜯어 먹고 있었다)
▶ Sheep feed on grass. (양은 늘 풀을 먹는다)

■ **멈추다** : 세우다, 그치다, 그만두다, 정지하다

解說 **stop** 움직이고 있는 물체, 활동하고 있는 물체를 급히「멈추다」란 뜻의 일반어. **cease** stop보다 격식을 차린 말로 상태, 활동을「그만두다」의 뜻. **pull up** 자동차나 마차를「세우다」,「(…이) 멈추다」의 뜻. **turn off** 텔레비전·라디오·수도·가스를「끄다 ; 잠그다」. **suspend** 조작·활동·시행 등을「일시적으로 정지하다」.

stop *vt.* ① …을 세우다
▶ He stopped his car to adjust the seat belt. (그는 안전띠를 조절하기 위해 차를 세웠다)
② …을 그만두다
▶ It stopped raining. (비가 그쳤다)
▶ She stopped her homework and listened to music. (그녀는 숙제하던 것을 그만두고 음악을 들었다)
— *vi.* 서다

▶ Does this train stop at Anyang? (이 기차는 안양에서 섭니까?)

cease *vt.* 《cease do**ing**, cease **to** do》 …을 그만두다; 중지하다
▶ She ceased regretting [to regret] the failure. (그녀는 그 실패에 대해 후회하는 것을 그만두었다)
▶ The bounty from government might be ceased. (정부의 그 보조금이 중지될는지도 모른다)
— *vi.* 그치다
▶ The rain ceased at midnight. (비는 한밤중에 그쳤다)
▶ The publication of the magazine ceases with the July issue. (그 잡지의 발행은 7월호로 끝난다)

pull up (차·마차)를 멈추다; 서다; 세우다; (차를) 대다
▶ He pulled up the car in front of the hotel. (그는 차를 호텔 앞에 댔다)

turn off (텔레비전·라디오·수도·가스 등)을 끄다; 잠그다
▶ Turn off the TV. (텔레비전을 꺼라)

suspend *vt.* (활동 등)을 일시적으로 정지하다; 중지하다
▶ The train service was suspended because of an earthquake. (지진 때문에 기차의 운행이 일시 중단되었다)
▶ The negotiations were suspended for a while. (교섭은 일시 중지되었다)

■ **명하다**: 명령하다, 지시하다
解說 order, command 권력을 가진 인물이 「명하다」, 「명령하다」의 뜻이며, 특히 command는 공식적으로 직무상의 명령을 내린다는 뜻. direct, instruct 일·장차·외교 관계 등에 「명령·지시·지휘하다」 등의 뜻으로 쓰이지만 direct는 강제의 뜻이 강하고 instruct는 격식을 차린 말이다. tell order, command, direct의 뜻을 지닌 일상어로 「…하라고 말하다」, 「명하다」의 뜻. charge 「의무로서 …하라고 명하다」의 뜻.

order *vt.* …을 명하다; 지시하다
▶ I ordered you to get out. (널더러 나가라고 명했잖아)

command *vt.* …을 명하다; …하라고 명하다
▶ The captain of the ship commanded the radio operator to send an SOS. (선장은 무선 통신사에게 조난 신호를 타전하라고 명령했다)

direct *vt.* …을 명령하다; 지시하다
▶ The boss directed his men to finish it quickly. (상사는 부하에게 그것을 빨리 끝내라고 명령했다)

instruct *vt.* …하라고 명령하다; 지시하다
▶ The president instructed the employees to improve their productivity. (사장은 종업원들에게 생산성을 높이라고 지시했다)

tell *vt.* …하라고 말하다; 명하다
▶ Don't tell me to do or not to do. (나에게 하라 말라 명령하지 마십시오)

charge *vt.* 의무로서 …하라고 명하다
▶ The judge charged the audience to be silent. (재판관은 방청인에게 정숙할 것을 명했다)

■ **모욕하다**: 깔보다, 업신여기다, 멸시하다, 경멸하다
解說 insult 「모욕하다」란 뜻의 일반어. 경멸적인 태도로 모욕하여 상대의 마음을 상하게 하거나 부끄럽게 여기도록 하다의 뜻. despise 정도가 낮다, 좋지 않다, 가치가 없다, 보잘것없다라는 뜻이 함축되어 감정적으로 「경멸하다」의 좀 문어적인 말. look down upon despise의 구어적 표현으로 가장 일상적인 말. disdain 「경멸하다」의 뜻인데 그것을 행동으로 나타내다는 뜻을 내포한다.

insult *vt.* …을 모욕하다; 창피를 주다
▶ I won't talk to him any more, because he insulted me. (나를 모욕했기 때문에 그 녀석하고는 다시는 말하지 않겠다)

despise *vt.* …을 경멸하다; 업신여기다
▶ Those who despise themselves despise others. (자기 자신을 업신여기는 사람은 다른 사람도 업신여긴다)

look down upon [on] *vt.* (사람·언동)을 경멸하다; 얕보다
▶ She looked down on Susie as a copycat. (그녀는 수지를 흉내쟁이라고 경멸했다)

disdain *vt.* …을 경멸하다; 깔보다
▶ After the failure, his colleagues in the same office disdained him. (그가 실패한 후 같은 사무실의 동료들이 그를 깔보았다)

■ **믿다**: 신뢰하다, 확신하다
解說 believe 「믿다」의 뜻의 일반어. 확실한 증거는 없지만 일시적으로 어떤 일·사람을 「믿다」, 또 「생각하다」의 뜻으로도 쓴다. believe in 오랜 기간에 걸쳐 사람이나 어떤 것의 존재를 「믿다; 신뢰하다」의 뜻. trust 경험이나 증거 없이 상대에 대해 직관적으로 「신뢰하다」의 뜻. assure 「확신하다」의 뜻. convince 의심이나 반대를 물리치고, 논의한 결과 「확신하다」, 「납득하다」의 뜻.

believe *vt.* ① …을 믿다; …을 사실이라고 생각하다 (▶진행형으로는 쓰지 않는다)
▶ I believe you. (나는 너를 믿는다)
▶ She believed her friend's excuse. (그녀는 친구의 변명을 믿었다)
② …이라고 믿다; …하다고 생각하다 (▶think보다 뜻이 강하다)

1. 중요 동사의 유의어별 용법·문형

▶ I believe that he will take the 2 p.m. express. (그가 오후 2시 급행 열차를 탈 것으로 생각한다)

believe in …의 존재를 믿다 ; 신뢰하다 ; (종교를) 믿다

▶ When my children were small, they believed in Santa Claus. (아이들은 어렸을 때 산타클로스를 믿었다)

▶ I believe in you. (나는 너를 믿는다)

▶ My mother believed in Christianity. (어머니는 기독교를 믿었다)

trust *vt*. …을 신뢰하다

▶ Children trust their parents. (아이들은 부모를 신뢰한다)

assure *vt*. 《재귀적으로》 …하다고 확신하다

▶ She assured herself of her husband's safe return. ⇌ She assured herself that her husband would return safely. (그녀는 남편이 아무 탈없이 돌아올 것이라고 확신했다)

convince *vt*. …확신[납득]시키다 ; 설득하다

▶ He convinced me of the validity of his opinion. ⇌ He convinced me that his opinion was valid. (그는 자기 의견의 타당성을 나에게 납득시켰다)

▶ I am convinced of her competence. (나는 그녀의 역량을 확신하고 있다)

■ **바라다** : 소망하다, 원하다

[解説] **want** 필요해서 「…하고 싶다」란 뜻의 단도직입적인 말로 보통 동등자 또는 손아랫사람에게 쓴다. **wish** 「…하면 좋을텐데」의 뜻으로 실현 불가능한 경우 가정법과 함께 쓴다. 이 밖에 「기원하다」, 가벼운 명령으로 「…해주기 바라다」 등의 뜻. **desire** 강하게 want, wish하다, 격식을 차린 말. **hope** 실현 가능한 사항을 「바라다」, 「기대하다」. **long (for)** 멀리 떨어진 것이나 쉽게 달성할 수 없는 것을 「열망하다」, 「갈망하다」의 뜻. **yearn (for)** long (for)보다 뜻이 강하고 「동경하다」, 「(애틋하게) 사모하다」, 「그리워하다」의 뜻.

want *vt*. …하고 싶다 ; …하고 싶어하다 (▶진행형으로는 쓰지 않는다)

▶ I want you to come at 1:00 p.m. (오후 1시에 와 주기 바란다)

▶ She wanted to see him badly. (그녀는 그를 몹시 보고 싶어했다)

wish *vt*. ① 《**wish to** do》 …하고 싶다 ; …을 바라다

▶ I wish to go with you. (나는 너와 함께 가고 싶다)

② 《가정법과 함께 써서 실현 불가능한 경우를 나타낸다》 …하면 좋을 텐데

▶ I wish I could go with you, but I can't. (너와 함께 가면 좋을텐데 갈 수 없다)

③ 《**wish** A **to** do》 A에게 …해주기 바라다

▶ I wish you to come back earlier this evening. (오늘 저녁에는 네가 평소보다 일찍 돌아와 주었으면 한다)

④ 《**wish** A B, **wish** B **to** A》 A를 위해 B를 기원하다

▶ I wish you good luck. (행운을 빕니다)

▶ We wished them a safe return home from abroad. (우리는 그들이 해외에서 무사히 귀국하기를 기원했다)

— *vi*. 《**wish for** A》 …을 소망하다 ; …을 갖고 싶어하다 (▶특히 바라기 어려운 것을 바랄 때에 쓴다)

▶ My son wished for a big car. (아들은 큰 차를 갖고 싶어했다)

desire *vt*. …을 원하다 ; 희원하다

▶ The king desired peace. (왕은 평화를 원했다)

hope *vt*. 《**hope to** do, **hope that**…》 …을 바라다 ; 기대하다 (▶구어에서는 보통 that을 생략한다)

▶ I hope to see you tomorrow. (내일 뵙고 싶습니다)

▶ He hopes (that) his son will take over his job. (그는 아들이 자기의 일을 이어받기를 기대하고 있다)

— *vi*. 《**hope for**》 …을 바라다 ; 기대하다

▶ We hoped for a pay raise. (우리는 승급을 기대했다)

long (for) *vi*. …을 열망하다 ; 갈망하다

▶ She is longing to study abroad. (그녀는 외국 유학을 갈망하고 있다)

▶ I'm longing for peace. (나는 평화를 희원하고 있다)

yearn (for) *vi*. 동경하다 ; 사모하다 ; 그리워하다 ; 갈망하다

▶ She yearns for a sight of her son. (그녀는 아들을 한 번 만나기를 원하고 있다)

■ **방해하다** : 막다, 훼방하다

[解説] **prevent** 선수를 치거나 훼방하거나, 장애물을 놓아 어떤 일을 「막다」 또는 「방해하다」. **obstruct** 장애물을 놓아 길이나 행렬 등을 「막다」, 사물의 진전·진행을 「방해하다」. **disturb** 정상적인 정신의 안정이나 집중력을 고민·방해물 따위로 흐트러지게 하다. **interfere** 경멸적으로 쓰이며 부탁받지 않았거나 관계도 없는 일에 「간섭하다」. **hinder** 일의 진행이나 수행을 「지연시키다」, 「방해하다」. **bar** 장벽이나 장애물 같은 것을 놓아 길이나 통행을 「방해하다」. **block** 방해물을 놓아 사람이나 물건의 움직임을 일시적으로 완전히 「방해하다」의 뜻. 비유적으로도 쓰여 계획·운동·활동·성공 등을 「방해하다」.

prevent *vt*. …을 방해하다 ; 《**prevent** A **from** doing, **prevent** A's doing》 A(사람)가 …하는

것을 막다
▶ Prevent the fire from spreading. (불길이 번지는 것을 막아라)
▶ He could not prevent her smoking. (그는 그녀의 흡연을 막을 수가 없었다)

obstruct vt. ① (길 등)을 막다
▶ The landslide obstructed the road. (산사태로 길이 막혔다)
② …을 방해하다 ; 차단하다
▶ The view was obstructed by the new library. (새로 지은 도서관 때문에 조망이 차단되었다)

disturb vt. …을 방해하다 ; 훼방하다
▶ I'm sorry to disturb you, but a Mr. Brown wants to see you. (일을 방해해서 죄송합니다만 브라운씨라고 하는 분이 선생님을 뵙기를 원합니다)
— vi. 마음의 평안[수면]을 방해하다
▶ Don't disturb. (수면중에 깨우지 마십시오) (▶호텔에서 방문에 내거는 푯말 문구)

interfere vi. ① 《**interfere in**》 간섭하다
▶ She never interferes in her husband's public affairs. (남편의 공무에 대해 그녀는 결코 간섭하지 않는다)
② 《**interfere with**》 훼방하다 ; 방해하다
▶ The construction noise interferes with my work. (공사의 소음이 내 일을 방해한다)

hinder vt. …을 지연시키다 ; 방해하다 ; 《**hinder A from** doing, **hinder A's** doing, (口) **hinder A** doing》 A(사람)가 …하는 것을 방해하다
▶ Answering the phone many times hindered my work in the morning. (여러번 전화를 받느라고 오전 중의 내 일은 지장이 있었다)
▶ The storm hindered their launching a weather satellite. (폭풍우 때문에 그들의 기상위성 발사에 지장이 있었다)

bar vt. …을 방해하다 ; 훼방하다 ; 막다
▶ That railroad crossing is always barred by a long freight train. (저 건널목은 언제나 긴 화물 열차로 막히곤 한다)

block vt. ① (일시적으로 사람·물건의 움직임)을 방해하다
▶ The policemen blocked the doors to the building. (경찰들은 그 건물의 입구를 막았다)
② (계획·운동·활동 등)을 방해하다
▶ Our plan was completely blocked. (우리 계획은 완전히 방해를 받았다)

■ **변하다** : 고치다, 바꾸다, 변화시키다, 변경하다

[解說] **change** 「변하다」의 뜻으로는 가장 일반적인 말. 이전의 것과 본질적으로 다른 것이 되다의 뜻. **alter** 본질적인 변화는 없지만 형태나 내용이 일부 변하다의 뜻. **convert** 이전과는 다른 용도·기능을 위해 형태·내용·상태를 바꾸다. **shift** 위치·장소·방향을 변화시키다의 뜻. **switch** 스위치로 전환시키듯이 화제·생각·장소 등을 「변화시키다, 전환하다」. **turn** 올챙이가 개구리로 변하듯이 형태·성질·방향 등이 전화(轉化)되는 것을 뜻한다.

change vi. (전면적으로) 변하다 ; 변화하다
▶ You haven't changed a bit since I last saw you. (이전에 만나뵌 이후 당신은 조금도 변하지 않았군요)
— vt. (전면적으로) 변화시키다 ; 고치다
▶ An only son's death changed him. (외아들의 죽음은 그를 변화시켰다)

alter vt. (부분적으로) …을 변화시키다 ; 변경하다 ; 바꾸다
▶ We needed to alter our itinerary covering 15 days. (우리는 15일간의 여행일정을 부분적으로 변경할 필요가 있었다)
— vi. 변하다
▶ Jane has altered since she got married. (제인은 결혼하고 나서 변했다)

convert vt. 《**convert into**》 …을 변화시키다
▶ They plan to convert a bowling alley into a swimming pool. (그들은 볼링장을 수영장으로 개조할 계획을 세우고 있다)

shift vt. (장소·위치·방향·사람)을 변화시키다 ; 옮기다 ; 교환하다 ; (美) (차의 기어)를 바꿔넣다 ; 변속하다
▶ The right fielder shifted his position. (우익수는 수비 위치를 바꿨다)
▶ The wind shifted and the yacht sailed eastward. (풍향이 바뀌어 요트는 동쪽으로 항진했다)
▶ Stop shifting the blame on to me. (책임을 내게 전가시키지 마십시오)
— vi. 변하다 ; (美) (사람이) 차의 기어를 바꾸다 ; (자동적으로) 차의 기어가 바뀌다
▶ In the evening the breeze shifted to the east. (밤이 되어 미풍은 동쪽으로 바뀌었다)

switch vt. (화제·생각·장소 등)을 바꾸다 ; 전환하다 ; 교환하다
▶ Mary took the window seat and Betty sat on the aisle seat; later they switched them. (메리는 창가에 자리를 잡고 베티는 통로 쪽에 자리를 잡았다. 나중에 두 사람은 서로 자리를 바꿨다)

turn vt. 《**turn A into [to] B**》 A (형태·성질·방향 등)를 B로 바꾸다 ; A를 B로 변화시키다
▶ Ice in the glass was turned into water. (컵 속의 얼음이 물로 변했다)
— vi. 변하다 ; 전환하다
▶ Tadpoles turn into frogs. (올챙이는 개구리로 변한다)
▶ The snow turned to sleet. (눈이 진눈깨비로 변했다)

1. 중요 동사의 유의어별 용법·문형

▶ Her love to him turned to hate. (그에 대한 그녀의 사랑이 증오로 변했다)
▶ We took turns (in) standing watch. (우리는 교대로 보초를 섰다)

■ **붙잡다** : 잡다, 붙들다, 체포하다
[解說] **catch** 「붙잡다」, 「잡다」의 일반어로 움직이거나 날거나 숨어 있는 것을 뒤쫓거나 계략을 써서 붙잡다의 뜻. **arrest** 법에 따라 「체포하다」, 「구류하다」의 뜻. **capture** catch보다 딱딱한 말. 저항하거나 도망가지 못하게 강제로 「붙잡다」, 「체포하다」, 「포로로 잡다」의 뜻. **seize** 「꽉 잡다」. **grab** 「잡아채다」의 뜻으로 자기의 이기적인 이유 때문에 상대의 권리를 침범하여 난폭하게 빼앗다의 뜻. **grasp** 「(손이나 팔로) 꽉 잡다」의 뜻. 동물이나 새가 이빨이나 발톱으로 「붙잡다」의 뜻도 있다. **clutch** grasp보다는 재빠르게 필사적으로 「꽉 붙잡다」의 뜻이지만 성공률이 낮다. 그러나 잘 붙잡았을 경우에는 「(꽉) 쥐다」의 뜻이 된다. **grip** grasp보다 뜻이 강하고 「힘껏 꽉 쥐다」의 뜻.

catch *vt.* …을 붙잡다 ; 잡다
▶ The hunter caught a fox alive. (사냥꾼은 여우를 산채로 잡았다)
▶ Salmon are scarcely caught in this river now. (지금은 이 강에서 연어가 거의 잡히지 않는다)
▶ The pickpocket was caught red-handed. (소매치기는 현행범으로 붙잡혔다[체포되었다])

arrest *vt.* …을 체포하다 ; 검거[구류]하다
▶ The blackmail suspects were finally arrested by the police. (공갈 용의자는 마침내 경찰에 체포되었다)

capture *vt.* …을 붙잡다 ; 체포하다 ; 포로로 잡다
▶ Policemen chased and captured the bank robber. (경찰관들은 은행 강도를 뒤쫓아서 붙잡았다)
▶ They captured the retreating soldiers. (그들은 퇴각하는 병사들을 포로로 잡았다)

seize *vt.* (느닷없이) …을 꽉 잡다 ; (급히 세게) 잡다
▶ Somebody seized my hand in the dark. (어둠 속에서 누군가가 내 손을 꽉 잡았다)
— *vi.* …을 잡다 ; 붙잡다
▶ She seized upon a chance. (그녀는 기회를 잡았다)

grab *vt.* …을 낚아채다 ; 날렵하게 잡다
▶ A man on a bicycle grabbed an old lady's purse and ran off. (자전거를 탄 남자가 노부인의 핸드백을 낚아채어 달아났다)
— *vi.* 《**grab at**》 잡아채다 ; 거머쥐다
▶ A little boy grabbed at a coin. (소년이 동전을 잡아 쥐었다)

grasp *vt.* (손이나 팔로) …을 꽉 잡다

▶ She grasped his right arm firmly in hers. (그녀는 그 남자의 오른팔을 꽉 잡았다)
— *vi.* 《**grasp at**》 잡으려고 하다
▶ A drowning man will grasp at a straw. ((속담) 물에 빠진 사람은 지푸라기라도 붙잡으려 한다)

clutch *vt.* …을 꽉 잡다
▶ The son clutched his mother's hand and got off the train. (아들은 어머니의 손을 꽉 잡고 기차에서 내렸다)
— *vi.* 《**clutch at**》 붙잡으려고 하다
▶ The policeman clutched at the fleeing pickpocket. (경찰은 도망가는 소매치기를 붙잡으려고 했다)

grip *vt.* …을 힘껏 붙잡다 ; 꽉 잡다
▶ The farm hand gripped a stake and pulled it out. (그 농장 일꾼은 말뚝 하나를 힘껏 잡아 뽑았다)
▶ The gymnast gripped the horizontal bar tight. (그 체조선수는 철봉을 꽉 잡았다)

■ **비난하다** : 나무라다, 힐난하다
[解說] **blame** 「나무라다」, 「비난하다」의 뜻의 일상어. 또 책임 소재만을 나타내는 경우도 있다. **criticize** 기본적으로는 「비평하다」의 뜻이지만 보통 일상적으로는 「비난하다」, 「혹평하다」의 뜻으로 쓰인다. **accuse** 죄악을 비난하여 개인적으로 직접 엄하게 「나무라다」, 「비난하다」의 뜻. **charge** 정식으로 공공연하게 「비난하다」. **abuse** 화를 내어 「욕을 퍼붓다」, 「욕지거리하다」의 뜻. **curse** 분개하여 심하게 「욕을 퍼붓다」, 「욕지거리하다」의 뜻이지만 신이나 그리스도 또는 종교 관계의 말을 써서 욕을 퍼붓다의 뜻. 이런 종류의 말을 쓰는 것은 품위가 없는 것으로 간주된다.

blame *vt.* …을 나무라다 ; 책망하다 ; 《**blame A for B**, **blame B on A**》 B(실패·실책 등)의 이유로 A(사람)를 나무라다
▶ Don't blame me for that failure. ⇌ (口) Don't blame the failure on me. (그 실패 때문에 나를 나무라지 마라)

criticize *vt.* …을 혹평하다
▶ Parents and teachers severely criticized that TV program. (부모님과 선생님들은 그 텔레비전 프로그램을 혹평했다)

accuse *vt.* …을 나무라다 ; 비난하다 ; 《**accuse A of B**》 A(사람)를 B(이유) 때문에 비난하다[나무라다]
▶ She accused her husband of having been disloyal to her. (그녀는 자기를 배신했다[바람을 피웠다]고 남편을 비난했다)

charge *vt.* (공공연하게) …을 비난하다
▶ The Opposition charged the Prime Minister in admitting the tax increase. (야당은 증세(增稅)를 허락했다고 수상을 비난했다)

abuse *vt.* …을 매도하다 ; 욕하다
▶ The two truck drivers were abusing each other. (두 트럭 운전사는 서로 욕을 퍼붓고 있었다)

curse *vt.* …을 매도하다 ; 욕하다
▶ When his car engine did not start, he cursed it loudly. (차의 엔진이 걸리지 않자 그는「제기랄」하고 큰 소리로 욕을 해댔다)
— *vi.* 욕을 퍼붓다 ; 욕지거리하다
▶ A drunken man cursed at the waitress. (술 취한 사람이 여급에게 욕지거리를 했다)

■ **빌려주다** : 대부하다, 꾸어주다, 임대하다, 융통해 주다

[解說] **lend**「빌려주다」의 뜻일 때는 무료·유료를 포함해서 영·미 모두 일반적인 말. (美)에서는 무료로 빌려주다의 뜻으로 loan도 흔히 쓴다. **rent** 사용료를 받고 방·집 등을 꽤 장기간 빌려주다의 뜻. 이런 뜻으로는 (美) rent out, (英) hire out을 쓴다. **loan**에는 이자를 붙여 돈을 빌려주다의 뜻이 있다.

lend *vt.* …을 빌려주다 ; 《lend A B, lend B to A》 A(사람)에게 B(물건)를 빌려 주다
▶ She lent me her umbrella. (그녀는 내게 우산을 빌려주었다)
▶ Will you lend me your bicycle? (자전거를 빌려 주시겠어요?)

rent *vt.* …을 빌려주다 ; 《rent B to A》 B(물건)를 A(사람)에게 임대하다
▶ I plan to rent a room. (방 하나를 얻을 예정이다)
▶ The old lady rented the house to a young couple. (노부인은 젊은 부부에게 그 집을 빌려 주었다)

rent [hire] out …을 임대하다
▶ The owner rented [hired] out the truck. (트럭 주인은 트럭을 임대했다)

loan *vt.* ① (美) …을 빌려주다 ; 《loan A B, loan B to A》 A(사람)에게 B(물건)를 빌려 주다 (▶ (英)은 이 뜻일 때는 lend를 쓴다)
▶ Will you loan me this book? (이 책을 빌려 주겠습니까?)
② (美) (이자를 받고 돈)을 빌려주다
▶ How much will you loan on this camera? (이 카메라를 잡히면 얼마를 빌려줍니까?)

■ **빌리다** : 차용하다, 임차하다

[解說] **borrow** 물건을 거저「빌리다」의 뜻 (▶단 화장실이나 전화 등 들고 다닐 수 없는 물건을 빌릴 때는 use를 쓴다). **rent** (英·美) 오랜 기간에 걸쳐 사용료를 내고 집·토지·기계류를 빌릴 경우에 쓴다. 같은 뜻으로 lease도 쓴다. rent는 (美)에서는 차·보트·의상 등을 사용료를 내고 단기간 빌리다의 뜻도 있다. 이 뜻으로는 (英)에서는 hire. **owe** 사람에게 금전상의 빚이 있다의 뜻.

borrow *vi.* ① (거저 일시적으로) …을 빌리다 ; 《borrow A from B》 B(사람)에게서 A(물건)를 빌리다
▶ Can I borrow this pencil? (이 연필 좀 빌릴 수 있을까요?)
▶ She borrowed a suitcase from her sister. (그녀는 언니에게서 여행용 가방을 빌렸다)
② (타인의 문장·사상 등)을 차용하다
▶ When you borrow some passages from a book in writing a paper, you must give footnotes to them. (논문을 쓸 때 어떤 책에서 문장을 차용하면 거기에 각주를 달지 않으면 안된다)

rent *vi.* ① (美·英) (장기간에 걸쳐) 사용료를 내고 …을 빌리다
▶ We rent a summer cottage from a rich farmer nearby. (우리는 여름 별장을 근처의 부유한 농부로부터 빌려 쓰고 있다)
② (美) (단기간 사용료를 내고) …을 임차하다 ((英) hire)
▶ She rented an evening dress for the concert. (그녀는 음악회에 가려고 이브닝 드레스를 빌렸다)

owe *vt.* (사람·가게)에게 금전상의 빚이 있다 ; 《owe A B, owe B to A》 A(사람·가게)에게 B(금전·대금)를 빌려 쓰고 있다
▶ When I was short of money, I borrowed ₩50,000 from him. Then I owe him the money [the money to him]. (돈이 모자랐을 때 그에게서 50,000원 빌렸다. 그래서 나는 그에게 빚이 있다)

■ **살다** : 거주하다, 정주하다

[解說] **live**「살다」란 뜻의 일반어. 일상 생활을 하는 곳에 살고 있다는 뜻. **reside, dwell** live보다 격식을 차린 말. dwell은 또한 문학적·문어적 용어. **inhabit** 어떤 종족이나 부족이「살다」, 또 동물이「서식하다」의 뜻으로도 쓴다. **settle** 이동하기를 멈추고「정주하다」,「정착하다」,「자리잡고 살다」. **stay** 손님·방문자로서 일시적으로「체재하다」,「묵다」의 뜻.

live *vi.* 《live in》 살다 ; 살고 있다
▶ [會話] "Where do you live?" "I live in Chongno in Seoul." (어디에 살고 있습니까? — 서울의 종로에 살고 있습니다)

reside *vi.* 《reside in [at]》 살다 ; 거주하다
▶ Professor Kim resides in Suwon. (김교수는 수원에 살고 있다)

dwell *vi.* 살다 ; 거주하다
▶ The poet's mind dwelt in a world of fantasy. (그 시인의 마음은 공상의 세계에 살고 있었다)

inhabit *vt.* (live와 달리 항상 타동사) …에 살다 ; 서식하다
▶ Natives now inhabit the hillside. (원주민들

1. 중요 동사의 유의어별 용법·문형

▶ Badgers used to inhabit this area. (오소리가 이전에는 이 지역에서 서식하고 있었다)

settle vi. 정주하다 ; 정착하다 ; 자리잡고 살다 (▷부사(구)와 함께 쓴다)

▶ Many Englishmen settled on the west coast of Canada. (많은 영국인들은 캐나다의 서해안에 정주했다)

stay vi. (도시·호텔·남의 집 등에) 체재하다 ; 숙박하다 ; 묵다

▶ They stayed at Tongnae for the summer. (그들은 여름 동안 동래에서 지냈다)

■ **상상하다** : 공상하다

[解說] imagine image를 그리다의 뜻으로 「마음에 그리다」, 「상상하다」의 일반어. fancy image보다 일시적이며 꿈이나 소망을 나타내어 「두서없이 상상하다」, 「공상하다」의 뜻. conceive 어떤 생각이나 의견·계획·디자인 등을 문득 생각해내다의 뜻.

imagine vt. …을 상상하다 ; 마음에 그리다 ; 《imagine A (to be) B》 A가 B라면 하고 상상하다 (▷B는 명사 또는 형용사) ; 《imagine A('s) doing》 A가 …하는 것을 상상하다

▶ I can imagine how my daughter is living in New York. (딸이 뉴욕에서 어떻게 살고 있는지 상상할 수가 있다)

▶ He imagined the young man (to be) his son. (그 젊은이가 자기의 아들이라면 하고 그는 상상했다)

▶ Can you imagine your husband ironing his own clothes himself? (당신의 남편이 자신의 옷을 다리는 것을 상상할 수 있습니까?)

— vi. 상상하다 ; 마음에 그리다

▶ I just cannot imagine. (나는 도저히 상상할 수가 없다)

fancy vt. …을 공상하다 ; 상상하다 ; 《fancy A to be B, fancy A as B》 A가 B라면 하고 상상하다 ; 《fancy A('s) doing》 A가 …하는 것을 상상하다

▶ I fancy myself to be a princess. (내가 공주라면 하고 상상해 본다)

▶ Fancy owning a helicopter yourself. (네가 헬리콥터를 가지고 있다고 상상해 봐)

conceive vt. (새로운 생각·계획·디자인 등을) 문득 생각해내다 ; 상상하다

▶ When I awoke at midnight, I conceived the idea of writing his biography. (한밤중에 잠을 깨자 그의 전기를 쓸 생각이 들었다)

■ **생각하다** : 고려하다, 간주하다

[解說] think 생각을 정리하거나 결론을 얻기 위해 머리를 쓰다의 뜻으로는 일반적인 말. reflect 「숙고하다, 깊이 생각하다」의 뜻으로 끝난 것이나 일어난 사항, 재음미해야 할 사항을 곰곰이 생각하다의 뜻. consider 「숙고하다」의 뜻이지만 reflect한 결과 나오는 결론이라는 뉘앙스가 있다. regard 보는 이의 주관이나 대상의 외관에 따라 「…로 간주하다」의 뜻. suppose think 보다 근거는 미약하지만 「…라고 생각하다」의 뜻. guess 단순한 사항에 대해 짐작으로 말해보다의 뜻으로 「…라고 생각하다」의 뜻이다. feel 감각적·본능적으로 「느끼다」, 「생각하다」의 뜻.

think vt. ① 《think (that)…》 …로 생각하다 (▷구어적 표현에서는 that을 생략하는 경우가 많다)

▶ I think that my father is right. (아버지가 옳다고 생각한다)

▶ I don't think that he is saucy. (그는 건방지지 않다고 생각한다)

② 《think A (to be) B》 A를 B로 생각하다

▶ Everybody thinks him (to be) a good leader. (모두가 그를 좋은 지도자로 생각한다)

▶ I think it better to leave her alone. (그녀를 혼자 놔두는 편이 좋다고 생각한다)

③ (사람이) …하려고 생각하다

▶ I think (that) I will call him. (그에게 전화하려고 생각한다)

— vi. 생각하다 ; 궁리하다

▶ Let me think a moment. ((회답하기 전에) 잠깐 생각하게 해 주시오)

▶ I should have thought that way. (그렇게 생각했어야 했다)

reflect vt. 《reflect that…》 …을 곰곰이 생각하다

▶ She reflected that it was her fault. (그것은 자기의 잘못이었다고 그녀는 생각했다)

▶ He reflected why he should have a quarrel over a trifling matter. (왜 사소한 일로 언쟁을 했을까 하고 그는 이모저모 생각했다)

— vi. 《reflect on [upon]》 숙고하다 ; 차분히 생각하다 ; 반성하다

▶ She reflected on her last few years. (그녀는 지난 몇 년간을 반성했다)

consider vt. ① …을 잘 생각하다 ; 숙고하다 ; 고려하다 ; 《consider doing》 …할까 하고 숙고하다 ; 《consider wh-구[절]》 …할까 말까 하고 생각하다

▶ Consider my suggestion seriously. (내 제안을 진지하게 생각해라)

▶ She is considering going on to a graduate school. (그녀는 대학원에 진학할까 하고 생각하는 중이다)

▶ She considered whether or not to tell that to him. (그녀는 그것을 그에게 말할까 말까 하고 생각했다)

② 《consider A (to be) B》 A를 B로 생각하다

▶ Most women consider marriage important. (대부분의 여성은 결혼을 중요시한다)

▶ I consider him (to be) a competent lawyer.

(나는 그를 유능한 변호사라고 생각한다)
regard *vt.* 《regard A as B》 A를 B로 간주하다
(▶B는 명사·형용사)
▶ Greeks regarded an olive branch as the symbol of peace. (그리스인들은 올리브 가지를 평화의 상징으로 간주했다)
suppose *vt.* 《suppose (that)...》 …으로 여기다 ; …라고 생각하다 ; …인듯하다
▶ I suppose (that) he's a bartender [barman]. (나는 그가 술집 종업원이라고 생각한다 → 그는 바텐더일거야)
▶ We supposed (that) he had gone home. (그는 집에 갔다고 생각했다)
guess *vt.* 《美口》 …을 짐작으로 말하다
▶ I guess (that) he's a doctor. (그는 의사일 거야)
▶ Guess how old she is. (그녀가 몇 살인지 맞춰 봐라)
feel *vt.* 《feel that...》 (감각적으로 일순간) …라고 생각하다
▶ He felt that she distrusted him. (그녀가 자기를 믿지 않는다고 그는 생각했다)
▶ I felt that you should divorce your husband. (나는 네가 남편하고 이혼해야 한다고 생각했다)

■ 싫어하다 : 미워하다, 혐오하다, 증오하다
[解説] **dislike**「싫어하다」의 뜻으로 보통 쓰이는 말. 본래 불쾌하게 생각하고 있다는 뜻이 내포되어 있고 그 강약은 문맥에 따라 결정된다. **hate**「미워하다」의 뜻으로는 일반적인 말. 적의와 악의를 내포하고 있다. **detest**「매우 싫어하다」의 뜻으로 dislike보다 뜻은 강하나 hate보다는 약하고 hate만큼의 적의나 악의는 없지만 경멸의 뜻을 내포하고 있다. **abhor**「몸서리 날 정도로 싫어하다」의 뜻. **loathe**「가슴이 메슥거릴 정도로 싫어하다」의 뜻으로 참기 어렵다는 뜻이 포함되어 있다.
dislike *vt.* …을 싫어하다 ; 《dislike doing, 《美》 dislike to do》 …하기를 싫어하다
▶ I dislike noise [children]. (나는 소음[아이들]을 싫어한다)
▶ My family dislikes going out in the crowd. (우리 가족은 사람이 붐비는 곳에 가기를 싫어한다)
hate *vt.* ① …을 미워하다 ; 아주 싫어하다 ; 증오하다 ; 《hate to do, hate doing》 …하는 것을 싫어하다
▶ We hate war. (우리는 전쟁을 아주 싫어한다)
▶ I hate to see blood and thunder. (나는 피비린내 나는 폭력적인 연극[영화]을 보는 것을 아주 싫어한다)
② 《美口》 …을 싫어하다 (▶dislike와 같은 뜻)
▶ I hate (having) to tell you, but I've broken your favorite brandy glass. (말하고 싶지 않지만 당신이 좋아하는 브랜디 잔을 내가 깨뜨렸습니다)
detest *vt.* …을 몹시 싫어하다
▶ He detests nosy people. (그는 참견하기 좋아하는 사람을 무척 싫어한다)
abhor *vt.* …을 싫어하다
▶ I abhor snakes [cockroaches]. (나는 뱀[바퀴벌레]을 무척 싫어한다)
loathe *vt.* ① …을 싫어하다
▶ I loathe hypocrites [pedantic speakers]. (나는 위선자[지식을 과시하는 강연자]를 지독히 싫어한다)
② 《美口》 …을 싫어하다 (▶dislike와 같은 뜻)
▶ I loathe drunks. (나는 술주정꾼을 싫어한다)

■ 쓰다 : 표시하다, 적다, 메모하다
[解説] **write**「쓰다」란 뜻의 일반어. **describe**「기술하다 ; 묘사하다」의 뜻으로 읽는 사람이 마치 그림을 보듯 자세하게 묘사하다라는 뜻이 포함되어 있다. **dictate** 구술하여 타인에게 「받아쓰게 하다」. **sign** 예금을 인출하는 전표나 서류·편지 등에 「서명하다」. **take [make] notes** 강연이나 기자회견 내용을 나중에 참고하기 위해 「적다, 적어두다」. **jot down** 문득 생각이 나서 「갈겨 쓰다」. **note down** 잊어 버리지 않도록 「적어두다」. **take [put] down** 사무적으로, 기록으로서 「써두다 ; 메모해 두다」의 뜻.
write *vt.* (문자·편지·서류·책·악보·시 등)을 쓰다 ; …을 저작하다
▶ He wrote a report [book]. (그는 보고서[책]를 썼다)
▶ Write me a letter when you get to London. (런던에 도착하면 편지를 해주게)
— *vi.* (글자를) 쓰다 ; 편지를 쓰다
▶ Write in pen [with a pen], please. (펜으로 쓰십시오)
▶ She often writes to me. (그녀는 종종 나에게 편지를 쓴다)
describe *vt.* (말·문자로 인상·인물·성격·사물 등)을 묘사하다 ; 기술하다
▶ Describe the man who asked you the way to that house. (당신에게 저 집으로 가는 길을 물던 남자의 인상착의를 자세히 설명해 주십시오)
dictate *vt.* …을 받아쓰게 하다 ; 《dictate A to B》 A(편지·문장)를 받아쓰게 하기 위해 B(사람·녹음기)에게 구술하다
▶ The sales manager dictated a letter to his secretary. (판매부장은 편지를 비서에게 받아쓰게 했다)
sign *vt.* (편지·서류 등)에 서명하다
▶ Please sign your name on this line. (이 선위에 서명하십시오)
take [make] notes 메모하다
▶ I took good notes of everything that was

said in that interview. (그 기자회견에서 언급된 것은 모두 잘 메모했다)

jot down (급히) …을 적어두다 ; 메모하다
▶ Wait a minute. I'll jot it down. (잠깐 기다려, 메모할게)

note down (잊지 않도록) …을 적어두다
▶ She noted down the names of the people she met and the places she visited on the tour. (그녀는 여행중에 만난 사람들의 이름과 방문한 장소를 적어두었다)

take [put] down (기록으로서) 적어두다
▶ Put down your name and address here, please. (여기에 당신의 이름과 주소를 적으십시오)

■ **얻다** : 획득하다, 입수하다
[解説] **get** 「(의지나 노력의 유무에 관계없이) 얻다, 손에 넣다」의 뜻으로 광범위하게 쓰는 구어. **obtain** 「오랫동안 원하던 것을 노력의 결과 손에 넣다」의 뜻으로 get보다 격식을 차린 말. **acquire** 「오랫동안 부단한 노력으로 손에 넣다」의 뜻이 있다. **gain** 「유리한 것, 가치 있는 것을 경쟁하여 얻다」의 뜻이 있다.

get vt. (口) …을 얻다 ; …을 손에 넣다 (▶ 수동태로는 쓰지 않는다)
▶ I got this map. (나는 이 지도를 손에 넣었다)
▶ They got permission to leave school earlier than usual. (그들은 학교를 조퇴하는 것을 허락받았다)

obtain vt. …을 얻다 ; 획득하다
▶ She obtained straight A's at the end of the second semester. (그녀는 2학기 말에 전과목 A를 받았다)
▶ He obtained some books for his dissertation from abroad. (그는 학위논문을 위한 책 몇 권을 외국으로부터 입수했다)

acquire vt. …을 얻다 ; 획득하다
▶ Could you tell me how you acquired a good command of English? (당신은 어떻게 해서 영어를 자유자재로 구사하게 되었는지 말씀해 주십시오)
▶ By ceaseless efforts she acquired her present position. (부단한 노력으로 그녀는 현재의 지위를 획득했다)

gain vt. …을 얻다 ; 손에 넣다 ; 따다
▶ At last he gained a gold medal at the Olympics. (그는 마침내 올림픽에서 금메달을 땄다)

■ **연습하다** : 훈련하다, 익히다
[解説] **practice** 기술이 숙달되도록, 습관이 되도록 몸에 익혀 「연습하다」의 뜻. **drill** 교실에서의 발음 연습이나 군사 훈련처럼 집단이 지도자의 지시에 따라 반복 연습하여 머리와 몸에 「주입하다」의 뜻. **exercise** 머리·기술·신체·근육 등을 조직적인 반복운동·연습에 의해 「훈련하다」의 뜻. **train** 어떤 목적·직업을 얻기 위해 사람이나 동물을 「훈련하다」, 「양성하다」의 뜻. 또는 운동 경기 대회 등을 위해 「훈련하다」의 뜻. **rehearse** 공연하기 위해 음악이나 연극을 「예행 연습하다」, 「리허설하다」의 뜻.

practice, (英) **practise** vt. (**practice** doing) …을 연습하다
▶ She has been practicing English conversation by listening to the radio for a year. (그녀는 1년간 라디오를 들으면서 영어회화를 연습하고 있다)
▶ Practice pronouncing these words. (이 단어의 발음을 연습하거라)
— vi. 연습하다
▶ If you don't practice, you'll never learn to speak a foreign language. (연습하지 않으면 외국어를 구사할 수 없을 것이다)

drill vt. …을 주입하다 ; 연습하다 ; 훈련하다
▶ Miss Burns drilled her students in the pronunciation of r and l. (번즈 선생님은 학생들에게 r과 l의 발음을 연습시켰다)

exercise vt. …을 훈련하다 ; 운동시키다
▶ She exercises in singing. (그녀는 노래를 연습하고 있다)
— vi. 운동하다 ; 연습하다
▶ Since I'm putting on some weight, I should exercise more. (체중이 조금 불어나고 있으므로 운동을 더 해야 한다)

train vt. …을 훈련하다 ; 양성하다
▶ He trains horses for the races. (그는 경마를 위해 말을 훈련시키고 있다)
▶ He was trained to be a lawyer. (그는 변호사가 될 교육을 받았다)
— vi. 연습하다 ; 훈련하다
▶ She is training for the triple jump. (그녀는 삼단뛰기 연습을 하고 있다)

rehearse vt. 예행 연습을 시키다 ; 리허설을 하다
▶ The director had the performers rehearse the play. (연출자는 출연자들에게 연극의 리허설을 시켰다)
— vi. 예행연습[리허설]을 하다
▶ The pianist was rehearsing on the stage. (피아니스트가 무대에서 리허설을 하고 있었다)

■ **외치다** : 아우성치다, 소리지르다
[解説] **cry** 「외치다」의 뜻으로는 일반적인 말. 도움을 구하거나 두려움·아픔·슬픔 등의 감정 때문에 엉겁결에 큰소리를 지르다의 뜻. **shout** 상당히 먼 거리까지 들릴 정도로 「크게 소리지르다」의 뜻. 노여움이나 기쁨을 나타내는 경우가 많지만 내용은 문맥으로 결정된다. **exclaim** 놀라움이나 기쁨 등 강한 감정을 갑자기 외치다의 뜻. **shriek** 「날카로운 소리를 지르다」의 뜻으로 보통 공포나 심한 고통을 나타내는 여성의 목소

리에 대해 쓴다. 기쁨 등에는 그다지 쓰지 않는다. **scream**「비명을 지르다」,「새된 소리를 지르다」의 뜻. shriek 보다 굵은 외침소리로서 공포나 고통·흥분, 때로는 기쁨이나 웃음 소리에도 쓴다. 섬뜩했을 때 내거나 겨우 들릴 정도의 놀라움의 소리에도 쓴다. **yell**「큰 소리를 지르다」,「크게 외치다」의 뜻으로 공포·분노·놀라움·고통 등에, 또는 승리했거나 기뻐서 외치는 경우나 흥미를 돋우기 위해서도 쓴다.

cry vi. 외치다 ; 큰 소리를 지르다
▶ A stray girl was crying (out) sadly. (길잃은 소녀가 슬프게 울부짖고 있었다)
▶ I cried (out) for help. (나는 큰소리로 도움을 청했다)
― vt. 《**cry that**…》 …라고 외치다 ; …라고 외쳐 알리다
▶ "Get out," he cried. (「꺼져버려」라고 그는 외쳤다)
▶ They cried that their team had won by a score of 1 to 0. (그들은 자기 팀이 1대 0으로 이겼다고 외쳤다)

shout vi. 큰소리치다 ; 외치다
▶ Please don't shout; I can hear you. (고함치지 마십시오, 들을 수 있으니까요)
▶ The policeman shouted at a pedestrian who ignored the traffic lights [signals]. (경찰관은 교통신호를 무시한 보행자에게 큰소리로 호통쳤다)
― vt. 《**shout that**…》 …을 외치다 ; …라고 외치다
▶ He shouted that his house was broken into. (그는 집에 도둑이 들었다고 외쳤다)

exclaim vt. …라고 큰소리로 말하다 ; 외치다
▶ "My goodness!" she exclaimed. "I should have been there by this time." (「어머나, 이때쯤이면 도착했어야 하는데」라고 그녀는 외쳤다)
― vi. 외치다
▶ When she saw him unexpectedly, she exclaimed in [with] delight. (뜻밖에 그를 만나자 그녀는 탄성을 질렀다)

shriek vi. 새된 소리를 지르다 ; 비명을 지르다
▶ A woman shrieked on a deserted street. (한 여자가 아무도 없는 거리에서 비명을 질렀다)
― vt. …라고 비명을 지르다 ; …라고 새된 목소리로 말하다
▶ "Somebody please help me!" she shrieked with terror. (「좀 도와주세요」라고 그녀는 무서워서 비명을 질렀다)

scream vi. 비명[고함]을 지르다 ; 새된 목소리로 말하다
▶ She screamed when she saw somebody in the house. (그녀는 집안에 누군가가 있는 것을 보고 비명을 질렀다)
― vt. …라고 비명을 지르다 ; …라고 새된 목소리로 말하다

▶ A guard screamed (out) a warning not to approach the manhole. (경비원은 맨홀에 접근하지 말라고 새된 목소리로 주의를 줬다)

yell vi. 큰 소리를 지르다 ; 외치다
▶ A foreman yelled (out) an order. (공장장은 큰 소리로 명령했다)
▶ Don't yell at me. I can hear you all right. (큰 소리를 지르지 말게, 잘 들린다네)

■ **요구하다** : 구하다, 청하다, 부탁하다, 호소하다
[解說] **demand** 권리·권위가 있다고 여겨 강력하고 집요하게 「요구하다」. **require** 「요구하다」의 뜻으로 demand와 같은 뜻으로도 쓰이지만 법률이나 규칙, 내적인 필요성이나 긴급 사태에 따라서 라는 뜻이 있다. **claim** 「요구하다」의 뜻으로 재산이나 지위 등을 상대의 찬성·불찬성에 관계없이 자기의 것이라고 권리를 주장하다의 뜻. **request** 「부탁하다」,「간청하다」. 격식을 차린 말로 부탁하는 쪽의 역부족이나 상대의 관심이 적기 때문에 승낙을 받지 못할지도 모른다고 걱정하면서 정중하게 부탁하다라는 뜻. **beg** 호의나 허가를 받기 위해 상대의 비위를 맞추면서 「부탁하다」,「간원하다」. **appeal** 「탄원하다」의 뜻으로 조력·협력을 호소하다의 뜻. **petition** 「진정·청원하다」의 뜻으로 특정한 요청에 대하여 허가를 해주는 입장에 있는 인물·관공서에 문서 또는 서류 등을 취합해서 정식으로 제출하다의 뜻.

demand vt. …을 요구하다 ; 《**demand that** A (should) do》 A(사람)가 …하도록 요구하다
▶ He demanded a prompt reply. ⇌ He demanded to be replied promptly. (그는 즉각적인 회답을 요구했다)
▶ The owner of the apartment house demanded that the tenants should pay rent without delay. (아파트 주인은 세든 사람에게 집세를 지체없이 지불하라고 요구했다)

require vt. …을 요구하다 ; 《**require (of)** A **to do**, **require that** A (should) do》 A(사람)가 …하도록 요구하다
▶ The school requires (of) all students to participate in extracurricular activities. (학교는 전교생이 과외활동에 참가할 것을 요구한다)

claim vt. (권리가 있다고) …을 요구하다 ; 주장하다
▶ He claimed the house by inheritance. (그는 상속으로 그 집이 자기 소유임을 주장했다)

request vt. …을 부탁하다 ; 간청하다 ; 《**request** A **to do**, **request that** A (should) do》 A(사람)가 …해주기를 간청하다
▶ You are requested to attend the wedding reception. (결혼 피로연에 참석해 주시기를 부탁 드립니다)

1. 중요 동사의 유의어별 용법·문형

beg *vt.* …을 부탁하다 ; 간원하다 ; 《beg A to do, beg that A (should) do》 A(사람)가 …해 주기를 간청하다
► I was lonesome, so I begged her to stay overnight. (나는 외로웠기 때문에 그녀에게 하룻밤 묵고 가기를 부탁했다)

appeal *vi.* …해 달라고 탄원하다
► The Government is appealing to the nation to save energy. (정부는 국민에게 에너지 절약을 호소하고 있다)

petition *vt.* …을 진정하다 ; 《petition A to do, petition A that... (should)...》 A에게 …하기를 간청하다
► We petitioned the mayor to make a new playground for children. ⇌ We petitioned the mayor that a new playground for children (should) be made. (우리는 시장에게 아이들의 놀이터를 새로 만들어 달라고 진정했다)

▪ **울다** : 울부짖다
[解說] **cry** 「큰 소리로 울다」의 뜻으로 큰 소리낸다는 것에 강조점이 있다. **weep** cry보다 격식을 차린 말로「눈물을 흘리면서 울다」의 뜻. 눈물을 흘리는 것을 강조하지만 흔히 cry와 weep는 맞바꾸어 쓰인다. **sob**「훌쩍 훌쩍 울다」,「흐느껴 울다」의 뜻으로 울음을 그치려고 하거나 울면서 말하다 등의 뜻. **in tears**「울고 있는」, **burst into tears**「왈칵 울기 시작하다」등과 같이 명사 복수형의 tears를 사용한 표현은 많다. **wail** 슬프거나 아파서「울부짖다」, **blubber** 아이들이 자기의 뜻을 관철하려고「울부짖다」.

cry *vi.* (큰 소리로) 울다
► The baby was crying in bed. (아기가 침대에서 앙앙 울고 있었다)

weep *vi.* 눈물을 흘리며 울다
► She wept reading the letter. (그녀는 그 편지를 읽으면서 울었다)

sob *vi.* 훌쩍훌쩍[흐느껴] 울다 ; 흑흑 흐느끼다
► A lost child was sobbing at the police box. (미아가 파출소에서 훌쩍훌쩍 울고 있었다)
— *vt.* 훌쩍훌쩍 울면서 이야기하다[잠들다]
► The stray girl sobbed her name. (길을 잃은 소녀가 훌쩍훌쩍 울면서 자기 이름을 말했다)
► The boy sobbed himself to sleep. (그 소년은 훌쩍훌쩍 울면서 잠들었다)

in tears 울고 있는
► My mother was in tears. (어머니는 울고 계셨다)
► I found her in tears in her room. (그녀가 자기 방에서 울고 있는 것을 보았다)

burst into tears 왈칵 울기 시작하다
► As soon as she met him, she burst into tears. (그녀는 그를 만나자마자 왈칵 울음을 터뜨렸다)

wail *vi.* (슬픔이나 통증으로) 울부짖다
► The injured person wailed with pain after recovering from the anesthesia. (부상자는 마취에서 깨어나자 아파서 울부짖었다)

blubber *vi.* 《경멸적으로》울부짖다
► Stop blubbering. You can't have that. (울부짖지 마라, 그건 안돼)

▪ **웃다** : 미소짓다, 냉소하다, 비웃다
[解說] **laugh**「웃다」의 뜻의 일반어로 작은 소리든 큰 소리든 소리내어 웃다의 뜻. **laugh at**「업신 여기며 웃다」의 뜻이 된다. **smile**「미소짓다」의 뜻으로 소리를 내지 않고 표정만으로「싱글벙글하다」의 뜻. 보통 좋은 뜻으로 쓴다. **grin** smile보다 큰 표정으로「히쭉[싱글]거리다」의 뜻. 즐겁거나 기쁘거나 장난기로 또는 분노·괴로움 때문에 얼굴을 찌푸리다의 뜻도 있다. **chuckle** 보통은 남자가 낮은 소리로「낄낄 거리다」,「싱글벙글하다」의 뜻으로 작은 기쁨이나 만족을 나타낸다. **giggle** 보통 젊은 여자가 당혹하거나 우스워서 웃음을 참으면서「킥킥거리다」,「소리 죽여 웃다」. **smirk**「(자신 있듯이) 젠 체하며 웃다」,「억지웃음을 짓다」,「언짢은 쓴웃음을 짓다」. **sneer** 윗입술을 오무려「냉소하다」,「조소하다」,「업신여기며 웃다」의 뜻이다.

laugh *vi.* 웃다
► Watching a comedy, we all laughed. (희극을 보면서 우리는 모두 웃었다)

laugh at …을 업신여기며 웃다
► Don't laugh at me. (나를 비웃지 마라)

smile *vi.* 미소 짓다 ; 생글생글 웃다
► I like your smiling face. (나는 너의 미소 짓는 얼굴이 좋더라)

grin *vi.* 히죽거리다 ; 싱글거리다
► He grinned at his pay slip. (그는 자기의 급여 명세서를 보고 히죽거렸다)

chuckle *vi.* 낄낄거리다 ; 싱글벙글하다 ; 껄껄거리다
► He was chuckling to himself while watching a funny program. (그는 우스운 프로그램을 보면서 혼자 낄낄거렸다)

giggle *vi.* 킥킥거리다 ; 소리 죽여 웃다
► The girls giggled when their teacher spoke with his queer accent. (선생님이 이상한 사투리로 말하자 여학생들은 킥킥거렸다)

smirk *vi.* (자신 있는듯이) 젠체하며 웃다 ; 억지 웃음을 짓다 ; 아니꼬운 쓴웃음을 짓다
► He is a most conceited man, and I don't like the way he smirks. (그는 매우 자부심이 강한 남자인데 나는 그의 능글맞게 웃는 게 마음에 안든다)

sneer *vt.* 냉소하다 ; 조소하다 ; 업신여겨 웃다
► "You mean that you are a good wife" he sneered. (「당신이 좋은 마누라라는 말이요?」하고 그는 빈정대며 말했다)

■ **위협하다** : 으르다, 협박하다

解說 **threaten** 말·행동으로 사건을 일으키겠다거나 조건 등을 내세워「처벌이나 위해를 가하겠다고 위협하다」의 뜻. **menace** threaten 보다 격식을 차린 문어적인 말로 위협·위험·적의의 강도를 강조한다.

threaten vt. …을 위협하다 ; 《threaten A into doing》 A(사람)를 위협하여 …하게 하다
▶ Are you threatening me? (나를 위협하는건가?)
▶ He threatened me with dismissal. (그는 나를 해고하겠다고 위협했다)
▶ She threatens me by saying that she will let out my secret. (그녀가 내 비밀을 누설하겠다고 위협하고 있다)
▶ She was threatened into embezzling ₩200,000,000 from the bank where she worked. (그녀는 협박을 받아서 자기가 근무하는 은행에서 2억원을 횡령했다)

menace vt. (사람·사물이) …을 위협하다 ; …에게 협박하다 ; 《menace A with B》 A(사람·나라)를 B(사항)로 위협[협박]하다
▶ Gulf nations are constantly menaced by war. (걸프만의 여러 나라들은 항상 전쟁의 위협을 받고 있다)
▶ The hijackers menaced the hostages with revolvers. (납치범들은 인질들을 권총으로 위협했다)

■ **의논하다** : 상의하다, 서로 이야기하다, 논하다, 토의하다, 토론하다

解說 **discuss** 문제점을 명확히 알아내어 해결책을 찾기 위해 여러 각도에서 의견을 내어「의논하다」. 개인적 수준의 것으로부터 공식적인 의논까지 폭넓게 쓰이는 말로 보통 우호적인 분위기 속에서 서로 이야기하다의 뜻이 있다. **debate** 공적인 문제를 공적인 장소에서 찬성자와 반대자가 토론하는 일. **argue**「논쟁하다」의 뜻의 일반어로 자기의 입장이나 생각이 옳다는 확신으로 상대에게 반박하기 위해 예나 증거를 들어 논하다의 뜻으로 떠들썩하게 서로 이야기하다의 뜻이 포함되어 있다. **dispute** 논의에 앞서 품위를 떨어뜨리면서 화내거나 시비조로 꽤 오랜 기간 서로 논쟁하다의 뜻.

discuss vt. …을 의논하다 ; 상의하다 ; 논하다 ; 서로 이야기하다 ; 《discuss A (+부사(구))》 A(어떤 사항)를 의논하다 (▶ discuss about A 처럼 자동사로는 쓰지 않는다)
▶ She discussed the plans for the summer with her husband. (그녀는 여름을 어떻게 보낼 것인가에 대해 남편과 상의했다)
▶ We discussed where to go. (우리는 어디로 갈것인가를 놓고 상의했다)
▶ We discussed what we could do for the handicapped. (우리는 신체장애자를 위해 무엇을 할 수 있을 것인가에 대해 서로 논의했다)

debate vt. …을 토론하다 ; 《debate A(+부사(구))》 A(어떤 사항)를 토론하다
▶ The committee debated whether to increase the income tax or not. (위원회는 소득세를 증액시켜야 할지 말아야 할지에 관해 토론했다)
— vi. 《debate about [on, upon]》 (…에 대해서) 토론하다
▶ The teachers debated on the necessity of homework during a long vacation. (선생님들은 긴 방학 동안 숙제의 필요성에 대해 서로 토론했다)

argue vt. …을 논하다 ; 의논하다 ; 주장하다 ; 《argue that…》 …라고 논하다
▶ They argued heatedly that Olympic Games of today are affected by commercialism and nationalism. (그들은 오늘날의 올림픽 경기가 상업주의와 민족주의의 악영향을 받고 있다고 열띠게 논의했다)
— vi. 의논하다
▶ They always argue about a trifle. (그들은 언제나 사소한 일을 가지고 떠들어댄다)

dispute vi. 논쟁하다 ; 언쟁하다 ; 《dispute about [on, over] A with B》 A(사항)에 대해서 B(사람)와 논쟁하다
▶ The labor union disputed for hours with the management about working hours. (노조는 경영자측과 노동 시간에 대해 여러 시간 동안 논쟁했다)
— vt. …에 대해 논쟁하다 ; 왈가왈부하다
▶ The inhabitants disputed whether they could agree to the building of a new road. (주민들은 새 도로건설에 대한 동의 여부를 놓고 서로 논쟁했다)

■ **의뢰하다** : 의존하다, 신뢰하다, 믿다

解說 **rely** 그때까지의 경험에 따라「(사람이나 사물)에 의뢰하다」의 뜻. 특히 사람에 대해서는 실제 관계에서의 판단에 따라 의뢰하다의 뜻. **trust**「신뢰하다」의 뜻이지만 자식이 부모에 대해 갖는 신뢰감처럼 본능적이고 의심을 품지 않는 신뢰를 뜻한다. **depend**「의존하다」,「의뢰하다」의 뜻으로 당연히 도와주리라고 기대하며 도와주지 않는 경우는 생각하지 않으며 기대는 적게 함을 뜻한다. **count**는「셈하다」의 뜻이나 count on 하면「기대하다」의 뜻. depend보다 기대의 정도가 강하고 기대에 어긋나는 경우, 곤란의 정도가 심함을 뜻한다. **resort**「(어떤 수단에) 호소하다」의 뜻으로 곤란에 직면하거나 효과가 나타나지 않는 경우에 자포자기하여 바람직하지 못한 것에 조력을 구하는 뜻이 있다.

rely vi. 《rely upon [on]》 …을 의뢰하다 ; 신뢰하다 ; 믿다
▶ It's important to have a family doctor upon

whom you can rely. (신뢰할 수 있는 가정의를 두는 것은 중요하다)

trust *vt.* …을 신뢰하다
▶ Since my parents trust me, I can't betray them. (부모님께서는 나를 신뢰하므로 나는 그 분들을 어길 수 없다)

depend *vi.* 《**depend upon [on]**》…에 의존하다 ; 의뢰하다 ; 기대하다
▶ You shouldn't depend upon someone whom you just met. (방금 만난 사람을 믿어서는 안된다)

count upon [on] …을 기대하다, 의뢰하다 ; 의지하다
▶ In order to succeed in carrying out this project, I really count on you. (이 계획을 성취하기 위해서 나는 정말 네게 기대하고 있다)

resort *vi.* 《**resort to**》(어떤 수단)에 호소하다 ; 의존하다
▶ They finally resorted to violence. (그들은 마침내 폭력에 호소했다)

■ 의심하다 : 수상히 여기다, 의문을 품다
[解說] **doubt**「(확신을 가질 수 없어서) …을 의심하다 ; …에 의혹을 품다」의 뜻. **suspect**「(증거가 불충분하지만) …이 아닌가 의심하다 ; 혐의를 두다」의 뜻.

doubt *vt.* ① (진실성·가능성)을 의심하다
▶ I doubt it. (글쎄 그럴까?)
▶ I doubt his sincerity. (나는 그의 성실성을 의심한다)
▶ She doubted her own eyes. (그녀는 자기의 눈을 의심했다)
② 《긍정문에서 …doubt whether… ; …doubt if…의 형태로 쓰는데 whether는 격식을 차린 표현이고 if는 구어》
▶ I doubt whether he keeps his word. (그가 약속을 지킬 것인지 어떨지는 의문이다)
▶ I doubt if she comes. (그녀가 올지 어떨지는 의문이다)
③ 《부정문·의문문에서는 …don't doubt that… ; …don't doubt but (that)… 와 같이 쓰는 경우도 있다》
▶ I don't doubt that she will pass the exam. (그녀가 시험에 합격할 것을 의심하지 않는다)
▶ Don't you doubt that he will come and see us? (그가 와서 우리를 만나 주리라고 생각하니?)

suspect *vt.* …에게 혐의를 두다 ; 《**suspect A of B**》A(사람)에게 B(나쁜 짓)의 혐의를 두다
▶ You shouldn't suspect an innocent man. (결백한 사람에게 혐의를 두어서는 안된다)
▶ We suspected him of the theft. (우리는 그에게 절도 혐의를 두었다)
▶ The police suspected him to be the hit-and-run driver. (경찰은 그가 뺑소니 운전자라고 혐의를 두었다)

■ 이기다 : 지우다
[解說] **win** 콘테스트·카드놀이·운동경기·전쟁 등에서「이기다」,「우승하다」,「일등하다」의 뜻. 그 결과「상품·상금을 받다」의 뜻도 있다. **beat**「지우다」를 뜻하는 구어로 운동경기 등에서 경쟁 상대나 그 팀을 패배하게 하다의 뜻. **defeat** beat 보다 딱딱한 말. 일시적으로 우위에 있다는 뜻이 포함되어 있고 전쟁·운동경기·선거 등에서 적을「패배시키다」의 뜻으로 쓴다. **prevail** defeat보다 격식을 차린 말로 저항·논의 결과「우세하다」,「이기다」의 뜻.

win *vt.* ① 승리를 얻다 ; 우승하다 (▶목적어로 사람을 취하지 않는다)
▶ He won the 3,000-meter race. (그가 3,000미터 경주에서 우승했다)
▶ Whether we win a war or not, war is nonsense. (우리가 전쟁에 이기든 지든간에 전쟁은 어리석은 짓이다)
② (사람이 노력·경쟁하여) …을 쟁취하다 ; …을 획득하다
▶ She won the victory in the English speech contest. (그녀는 영어 경연대회에서 우승했다)
▶ He won (the) first prize at the flower show. (화초 품평회에서 그는 1등상을 받았다)
—*vi.* 이기다 ; 승리를 얻다 ; (예상이) 들어 맞다 ; (내기에서) 이기다
▶ The phone was from him, as you guessed. So you won. (네가 추측한대로 그에게서 전화가 왔으니 네가 이겼다)

beat *vt.* …을 완전히 지우다 ; 격파하다
▶ My brother often beats me at tennis. (형은 테니스에서 종종 나를 이긴다)
▶ The Twins beat the Tigers by 2 points. (트윈스가 타이거스를 2점 차로 물리쳤다)

defeat *vt.* …을 완전히 지게 하다 ; 격파하다 ; 우위를 나타내다 ; (비유)(사람)을 좌절시키다
▶ Budd defeated Decker in the preliminary. (버드는 데커를 예선에서 물리쳤다)
▶ Mr. Spade was defeated in the last election. (스페이드씨는 지난번 선거에서 패배했다)
▶ His failure defeated his mother's expectation. (그의 낙제로 그의 어머니의 기대는 어긋났다)

prevail *vi.* 《**prevail over [against]**》이기다 ; 우세하다 ; 승리를 얻다
▶ Our troop prevailed over [against] the enemy. (우리 부대는 적을 압도했다)
▶ Helplessness prevailed in my mind. (내 마음은 무력감으로 가득찼다)

■ 이해하다 : 알다, 터득하다, 파악하다
[解說] **understand**「이해하다」의 뜻의 일반어. **comprehend**「이해하다」의 뜻이지만 under-

stand 보다 격식을 차린 말로 전후 관계, 다른 것과의 관련을 포함하여 충분히 현상이나 사실을 인식하다의 뜻. **appreciate** 외견상 보이지 않는 실체나 가치를 올바르게 「이해하다」의 뜻. **grasp** 원래 손이나 팔을 「꽉 잡다」의 뜻이지만 「(두뇌가) 사물을 이해하다」, 「파악하다」의 뜻으로도 쓴다. **realize** 사물을 구체적으로 「명확히 이해하다」, 「실감하다」의 뜻. **see** (口) 눈으로 아는 데서 머리로 사물을 「이해하다」, 생각하여 「파악하다」의 뜻. **get** (口) 손으로 잡다, 꽉 쥐다의 뜻에서 「뜻을 파악하다」; 이해하다의 뜻. **make out** (口) 「겨우 알다 ; 이해하다」의 뜻.

understand vt. …을 이해하다 ; 알다 (▶wh-절 [구]을 목적어로 취하는 경우가 있다)
▶ She understands my problem. (그녀는 내 고충을 이해하고 있다)
▶ I don't understand why she does not come. (왜 그녀가 오지 않는지 이해할 수 없다)
— vi. (요지)를 이해하다 ; 알다
▶ Do you understand? (내가 하는 말을 알아듣겠니?)
▶ You should come on time, you understand? (정각에 와야 한다, 알겠니?)

comprehend vt. …을 이해하다
▶ The child watches that TV program but does not comprehend its meaning. (아이는 그 TV 프로그램을 보고 있지만 그 뜻을 이해하지는 못하고 있다)

appreciate vt. (좋은 점·진가)를 이해하다
▶ Her abilities are not appreciated by her colleagues. (그녀가 유능하다는 것을 동료들이 몰라 준다)

grasp vt. …을 이해하다 ; 파악하다
▶ We grasped the main points of the lecture. (우리는 강연의 요점을 파악했다)

realize vt. …을 명확히 이해하다 ; 인식하다 (▶ that절이나 wh-절을 취하는 경우가 있다)
▶ I have realized what my mother said years ago. (나는 어머니가 수년 전에 말씀하셨던 것을 명확히 깨달았다)

see vt. (口) …을 이해하다 ; 파악하다 ; 알다
▶ I see the point. (요점은 알고 있습니다)
▶ I see what you mean. (당신이 무슨 말을 하는지 알겠습니다)

get vt. (口) …을 이해하다 ; 알다
▶ I don't get it [you]. (그[내가 말하는] 뜻을 모르겠다)
▶ I don't get what he means. (그가 무슨 말을 하는지 모르겠다)

make out (口) 겨우 알다 ; 어렴풋이 이해하다
▶ I could make out what she meant. (그녀가 무슨 말을 하는지 겨우[어렴풋이] 알 수 있었다)

■ 인정하다 : 승인하다

解說 **admit** 「인정하다」, 「고백하다」의 뜻으로 마지못해 어떤 사실을 인정하다의 뜻. **concede** 어떤 사항에 마음이 내키지는 않지만 「인정하다」의 뜻과, 거역할 수 없어서 청구자에게 마지 못해 「인정하다」, 「승인하다」의 뜻. **acknowledge** 비밀로 하던 사항을 「인정하다」의 뜻. **accept** 암암리에 또는 별도리가 없어서 「인정하다」의 뜻. **approve** 좋은 것, 만족할 만한 것으로 「인정하다」의 뜻으로, 때로는 존경의 뜻도 포함한다. **recognize** 정식 자격·권위를 가진 사람이 어떤 지위·입장 등을 「인정하다」, 「승인하다」의 뜻.

admit vt. …을 인정하다 ; 고백하다
▶ The Government finally admitted its diplomatic mistake. (정부는 마침내 외교상의 과오를 인정했다)
▶ He admitted having taken the bribe. (그는 뇌물을 받은 사실을 인정했다)

concede vt. ① (사실)을 인정하다
▶ The Government conceded the defeat in Cuba. (정부는 쿠바에서의 패배를 마지못해 인정했다)
② (권리 등)을 인정하다 ; 승인하다
▶ Britain conceded the reversion of Hong Kong to China. (영국은 홍콩을 중국에 반환하는 것을 승인했다)

acknowledge vt. …을 인정하다 ; 승인하다
▶ She acknowledged her secret marriage. (그녀는 자신이 비밀리에 결혼한 것을 인정했다)
▶ He acknowledged having been deeply in debt. (그는 빚을 많이 지고 있다는 것을 인정했다)

accept vt. …을 인정하다 ; 용인하다
▶ My boss accepted the reasons for my being absent. (상사는 내가 결근한 이유를 용인해 주었다)

approve vt. …을 인정하다 ; 승인하다
▶ I approve your new plan. (너의 새 계획에 만족한다)
— vi. 《approve of》 …을 좋다고 생각하다 ; 찬성하다
▶ My parents approved of my going on to a graduate school. (부모님은 내가 대학원에 진학하는 것을 찬성해 주셨다)

recognize vt. …을 인정하다 ; 승인하다
▶ The UN recognized the new nation as new member. (국제연합은 신생국을 새 회원국으로 승인했다)

■ 일어나다 : 생기다, 발생하다

解說 **happen** 「일어나다」의 뜻으로는 가장 일반적이고 광범위한 말. 원인이나 계획·의도가 있는지 없는지에 관계없이 쓰인다. **occur** happen 보다 격식을 차린 말로 어떤 특정한 일이 특정한 때에 일어남을 뜻한다. 그러나 happen과 같은

1. 중요 동사의 유의어별 용법·문형

뜻으로 쓰이지 않는 경우도 많다. **take place** 구어적으로 예정·예기된 일이 일어나다의 뜻. **break out** 「갑자기 일어나다」의 뜻. **burst**는 break out 보다 뜻이 강하고 「갑자기 파괴하듯이 일어나다」의 뜻.

happen *vi.* (우연히) 일어나다 ; 발생하다
- A strange thing happened to me. (이상한 일이 나에게 일어났다)
- What happened to you? You have a pale face. (왜 그래? 얼굴이 창백하구나)

occur *vi.* 일어나다 ; 생기다 ; 발생하다 (▶부정어와 함께 쓰이는 경우가 많다)
- The accident occurred when the plane took off. (비행기가 이륙했을 때 사고가 발생했다)
- A good idea does not occur unless you have a good sleep. (잘 자지 않으면 좋은 생각은 떠오르지 않는다)

take place 일어나다 ; 생기다 ; 발생하다
- The coup d'état took place when the president was paying a visit to allied nations. (대통령이 동맹국들을 방문하고 있을 때 쿠데타가 일어났다)

arise *vi.* (어떤 원인으로 문제·사건이) 발생하다 ; 일어나다 ; 생기다
- A strong wind arose and tipped over the excursion boat. (강한 바람이 불어서 유람선이 전복됐다)

break out (폭풍우·화재·전쟁 등이) 갑자기 크게 일어나다 ; 발발하다
- The World War Ⅱ broke out in 1939. (제2차 세계대전은 1939년에 일어났다)

burst *vi.* 《burst forth》 (갑자기 격하게) 발생하다 ; 돌발하다
- The Asian flu burst forth in the metropolitan area. (수도권에 아시아 독감이 발생했다)

■ 전하다 : 알려주다, 통지하다, 전달하다
[해설] **inform**「전하다」의 뜻으로 어떤 상황을 아는데 필요한 사실이나 뉴스를 전하다의 뜻. **notify** (정식으로) 「통지하다」, 「알려주다」의 뜻, 또는 (문서로서) 「통지하다 ; 연락하다」의 뜻. **communicate** 지식·정보·의견·기대·감정 등을 「알리다」, 「전달하다」의 뜻. 특히 전달되었는지 안되었는지의 결과를 강조한다. **convey** 생각·의견·감정 등을 「전달하다」, 「알려주다」의 뜻. 「매체가 되다」의 뜻도 가지고 있다. **report** 보거나 조사한 것을 「보고하다」의 뜻.

inform *vt.* (사람)에게 알리다 ; 《inform A of B》 A(사람)에게 B(사실·뉴스 등)를 알리다 ; 《inform A that...》 A(사람)에게 that 이하의 사항을 알리다 (▶that절은 wh-절로 대체 가능)
- The reporter informed me of my receiving the award. (기자가 나에게 수상 소식을 알려 주었다)
- Please inform me where the meeting will be held. (어디서 그 모임이 열리는지 나에게 알려주시오)

notify *vt.* …을 통지하다 ; 《notify A of B》 A(사람)에게 B(사물)를 통지하다 ; 《notify A that...》 A(사람·단체)에게 that 이하의 사항을 통지하다
- The professor notified his students of a change in the date when their term papers were due. (교수는 학생들에게 기말 리포트 제출일의 변경을 통고했다)
- The ambassador notified the Foreign Ministry that he would resign his post. (대사는 자기가 사임하고자 한다고 외무부에 통지했다)

communicate *vt.* …을 알리다 ; 전달하다
- Our boss does not clearly communicate what he wants us to do. (사장은 우리가 무엇을 해야 할지 명확히 전달하지 않는다)

convey *vt.* …을 전달하다 ; 알리다
- Words could not convey my deep gratitude to the doctor. (말로는 그 의사에 대한 나의 깊은 감사의 뜻을 다 전할 수가 없었다)
- Please convey my heartfelt thanks to your father. (나의 진심어린 사의를 당신의 아버님께 전해 주십시오)

report *vt.* …을 보고하다 ; 복명하다
- I reported my business trip to the sales manager. (판매부장에게 내 출장을 복명했다)

■ 주다 : 선사하다, 수여하다
[해설] **give**「주다」의 뜻으로는 가장 일반적인 말. **present**「격식을 갖추어 …을 선사하다」의 뜻으로 give보다 딱딱한 말. **award**「(심사·정식 결정의 결과로서) …을 수여하다」의 뜻. **confer** 격식을 차린 말로 지위가 높은 사람이 「(영예·칭호·학위·자격·호의·선물 등)을 수여하다」의 뜻.

give *vt.* …을 주다 ; 《give A B, give B to A》 B(어떤 것)를 A(사람)에게 주다
- I will give you one more chance. ⇌ I will give one more chance to you. (너에게 한번 더 기회를 주마)
- Let's give them a big hand. ⇌ Let's give a big hand to them. (그들에게 박수 갈채를 보냅시다)

present *vt.* …을 선사하다 ; 《present B to A》 B(물건)를 A(사람)에게 선사하다
- The representative presented a list of the gifts to the principal. (대표는 교장선생님에게 기념품 목록을 드렸다)
- The bride and bridegroom presented their parents with bouquets of orchids. (신랑 신부는 그들의 부모님께 난초 꽃다발을 선사했다)

award *vt.* …을 주다 ; 수여하다 ; 《award A B, award B to A》 B(상 등)를 A(사람)에게 수여하다

1. 중요 동사의 유의어별 용법·문형

▶ The research institute awarded him a scholarship to study abroad for two years. (연구소는 그에게 2년간 외국에서 연구할 수 있도록 장학금을 수여했다)

confer *vt.* …을 주다 ; 《confer B on [upon] A》 B(칭호 등)를 A(사람)에게 수여하다

▶ Prime Minister conferred a citation on the brave police officers. (국무총리는 용감한 경찰관들에게 표창장을 수여했다)

■ **죽이다** : 암살하다, 학살하다, 살해하다

解說 **kill** 사람이나 동물을 「죽이다」; 죽게 하다라는 뜻의 일반어, 사고·재해로 인한 사망은 be killed로 표현되고 「식물을 말라죽게 하다」의 뜻으로도 쓴다. **murder** 「살인을 저지르다」의 뜻으로 동기가 있는 계획적 범행이나 우발적인 감정에 사로잡혀 살해하는 것도 포함한다. **assassinate** 「암살하다」의 뜻으로 정계의 중요 인물을 정치적 이유나 민족·국가를 위한다는 등의 이유로 누군가를 시켜 살해하는 일. **slaughter** 원래는 식육용 동물들을 「도살하다」란 뜻이지만 전쟁 등에서 무저항·무방비 상태의 사람을 대량으로 「학살하다」의 뜻으로도 쓰인다.

kill *vt.* (사람·동물)을 죽이다 ; 죽게 하다
▶ She killed a cockroach in the kitchen. (그녀는 부엌에서 바퀴벌레를 잡았다)
▶ A famous writer was killed in a plane crash. (유명한 작가가 비행기 추락사고로 사망했다)
— *vi.* 살인하다
▶ One of the Ten Commandments says, "Thou shalt not kill." (모세의 십계명 중의 하나는 「살인하지 말라」라는 것이다)

murder *vt.* (사람)을 죽이다 ; 살해하다
▶ He attempted to murder his rich uncle. (그는 그의 돈 많은 삼촌을 살해하려 기도했다)

assassinate *vt.* (정계의 요인)을 암살하다
▶ John F. Kennedy, the 35th president of the U.S. was assassinated in 1963. (미국의 35대 대통령 케네디는 1963년에 암살되었다)

slaughter *vt.* ① (식용으로 동물)을 도살하다
▶ Hogs were carried by truck to be slaughtered. (돼지들이 도살되기 위해 트럭으로 운반되었다)
② (대량으로 사람)을 죽이다 ; 학살하다
▶ An A-bomb slaughtered a great many people. (한 개의 원자 폭탄이 수많은 사람들을 학살했다)

■ **지키다** : 감싸다, 막다, 방어하다, 보호하다

解說 **defend** 실제의 위험이나 공격에 대항하여 「지키다」란 뜻의 일반어. **protect** 미리 어떤 조치를 취하여 「보호하다」의 뜻. **guard** 파수꾼을 세워서 「지키다」의 뜻. **shield** 위험이 닥치거나 실제로 공격을 받고 있을 때 방패가 되어 「보호하다」의 뜻. **shelter** 지붕·울타리 등 일시적으로 막아주는 것으로 위해로부터 「보호하다」의 뜻. 비유적으로도 쓰인다.

defend *vt.* …을 지키다 ; 방어하다 ; 《defend A against B》 A(사람·물건)를 B(위해·적)로부터 방어하다 ; 《defend A from B》 A(사람·물건)를 B(위해)로부터 지키다
▶ The soldiers defended the fort against the advancing enemy. (병사들은 전진해 오는 적으로부터 요새를 지켰다)
▶ Parents should defend their children from social harm. (부모는 아이들을 사회적 위해로부터 지켜야 한다)

protect *vt.* …을 보호하다 ; 지키다 ; 《protect A from B》 A(사람·물건)를 B(바람직하지 않은 일·위해)로부터 지키다
▶ I put on sunglasses to protect my eyes from the strong studio light. (스튜디오의 강한 빛으로부터 눈을 보호하기 위해 나는 색안경을 썼다)

guard *vt.* (파수꾼을 세워) …을 지키다 ; 망보다
▶ VIPs are guarded by secret service men. (비밀 경호원이 요인들을 지키고 있다)
▶ Some part-timers guarded the famous pictures in the exhibition hall. (시간제 근무자 몇 명이 전시장에서 유명한 그림들을 지키고 있었다)

shield *vt.* (방패가 되어) …을 보호하다 ; 지키다
▶ A secret service man was shot when he shielded the president. (한 비밀경호원이 대통령의 방패가 되어 사살되었다)

shelter *vt.* …을 보호하다 ; 감싸주다
▶ Do you believe that this capsule will shelter us from nuclear bombs? (이 캡슐이 우리를 핵폭탄으로부터 지켜주리라고 믿습니까?)
▶ He sheltered me from severe criticism. (그는 내가 혹평당하는 것을 감싸주었다)

■ **찬성하다** : 승락하다, 동의하다

解說 **agree** 의견의 차이나 논의·설득·타협의 결과 「동의하다」, 「의견이 일치하다」의 뜻. **approve** 계획이나 행위에 대해 공식적으로 「찬성의 뜻을 나타내다」. **assent** 격식을 차린 말로 원래는 「이해를 나타내다」의 소극적인 뜻이었지만 현재는 의견이나 제안에 「동의하다」의 뜻. **consent** 확실한 의지나 감정을 갖고 「승락하다」의 뜻. **support** 의견·요구·주의·운동 등을 「지지하다」의 뜻. **nod** 동의·승락을 나타내어 「고개를 끄덕이다」의 뜻.

agree *vi.* 《agree to [with]》 동의하다 ; 《agree to do》 …하는데 의견이 일치하다
▶ She agreed with her mother. (그녀는 어머니에게 동의했다)
▶ We agreed to his proposal. (우리는 그의 제안에 찬성했다)
▶ They agreed to meet at the front desk. (그

1. 중요 동사의 유의어별 용법·문형

들은 프런트에서 만나기로 합의했다)

approve *vt.* ① …을 좋게 생각하다; 찬성하다
▶ The teacher could not approve Tom's conduct. (선생님은 톰의 행동을 좋게 생각할 수 없었다)
② (정식·공식적으로) …에 찬성의 뜻을 나타내다; …을 승인하다
▶ The disaster-relief plan was unanimously approved by the committee. (재해구조 계획은 전위원의 만장일치로 승인되었다)
— *vi.* 좋다고 생각[말]하다
▶ I don't approve of smoking in the presence of non-smokers. (나는 비흡연자가 있는 곳에서 담배 피우는 것을 좋게 생각하지 않는다)

assent *vi.* 《assent to》 …에 동의하다
▶ He won't assent to the proposal. (그는 그 제안에 동의하지 않을 것이다)
▶ I will assent to take part in the debate. (나는 그 토론에 참여하는 데 동의하겠다)

consent *vi.* 《consent to》 동의하다; 승낙하다
▶ I don't consent to have her come home. (나는 그녀를 집에 데려 오는 것에 반대한다)

support *vt.* …을 지지하다
▶ We support women's demand for equal rights for men and women. (우리는 남녀평등권에 대한 여성의 요구를 지지한다)

nod *vi.* (동의·승낙의 표시로) 고개를 끄덕이다
▶ When I asked him if 3 o'clock was all right for him to come, he nodded. (3시에 오는 게 괜찮은지 묻자 그는 고개를 끄덕였다)
— *vt.* (동의·양해의 뜻으로) 고개를 끄덕이게 하다; 고개를 끄덕여서 나타내다
▶ My father nodded his head in agreement. (아버지는 찬성한다는 표시로 고개를 끄덕이셨다)
▶ My boss nodded to indicate his comprehension. (나의 상사는 고개를 끄덕여서 이해했음을 나타냈다)

■ 참다: 견디다, 참고 견디다, 인내하다
[解說] **bear** 「참다」란 뜻의 일반어. 특히 곤란이나 무게에 「견디다」의 뜻으로 쓴다. **stand** bear와 같은 뜻으로 쓰이지만 특히 불쾌한 일을 「참고 견디다」 등의 뜻으로 기가 꺾이거나 질리지 않다는 뜻을 내포한다. **endure** 「오랫동안 참고 견디다」의 뜻으로 bear나 stand보다 견디는 체력이나 정신력이 강하다는 뜻을 포함한다. **put up with** 불평 없이 「참다」의 뜻. **resist** 공기나 물에 의한 변화나 화학작용 등에 「견디다」, 유혹을 받더라도 「굽히지 않다」, 「억제하다」 등 싸우거나 저항의 뜻이 강하다. **withstand** 충격이나 공격·역경 등에도 불구하고 「견디어 내다」, 「잘 참아 내다」의 뜻.

bear *vt.* 《bear to do, bear doing》 …에 견디다
(▶ 보통 can이 따르며 부정문이나 의문문에 쓴다)
▶ Can you bear the summer heat in Taegu? (대구의 여름 더위를 견딜 수 있니?)
▶ I can't bear to work [working] with him. (그와 함께 일하는 것을 참을 수 없다)

stand *vt.* …을 참고 견디다; 견디다 (▶ 보통 can이 따르며 부정문이나 의문문에 쓴다)
▶ I can't stand that noise. (저 소음은 참을 수 없다)
▶ Can you stand to work [working] ten hours a day? (하루에 10시간 일하는 것을 견딜 수가 있니?)

endure *vt.* …을 참고 견디다; 참다 (▶ 보통 can이 따르며 부정문이나 의문문에 쓴다)
▶ He endured the postoperative pains. (그는 수술 후의 통증을 참았다)

put up with …을 참다 (▶ 보통 부정문에 쓰며 수동태로는 잘 쓰지 않는다)
▶ I can't put up with your back talk. (너의 말대꾸는 참을 수가 없다)

resist *vt.* …에 견디다; 굽히지 않다 (▶ 보통 부정문에서 쓴다)
▶ This fence wire will not resist rust. (이 울타리용 철사는 녹에 약할 것이다)
▶ He could not resist disease. (그는 병에 견딜 수 없었다)
▶ I could hardly resist laughing. (나는 웃음이 나오는 것을 참을 수 없었다)

withstand *vt.* …을 견뎌내다; 잘 참아 내다; 버티다
▶ School furniture must withstand kicks and blows. (학교의 비품은 차거나 쳐도 잘 견디는 것이어야 한다)

■ 찾다: 수색하다
[解說] **look for** 「…을 찾다」란 뜻의 일상어로 search for나 hunt for와 같은 뜻. **search** 눈에 띄지 않는 것을 면밀히 「찾다」의 뜻과, 「수색하다」의 뜻으로 숨겨져 있는 것을 찾기 위해 어떤 장소나 사람의 몸수색을 하여 소지품을 「조사하다」의 뜻. **explore** 전인미답의 장소를 「탐험하다」의 뜻. **scout** 「정찰하다」의 뜻. 적측의 정보를 얻기 위해 조심스레 추적하다는 뜻. **hunt** 원래는 사냥감을 찾아다니다의 뜻이었으나 그 뜻이 확대되어 범인이나 발견되지 않고 있는 것을 「찾아 내다」, 「수색하다」의 뜻이 됨.

look for …을 찾다
▶ What are you looking for? (무엇을 찾고 있니?)
▶ She looked in her handbag for her car key. (그녀는 자동차 열쇠를 찾기 위해 핸드백 속을 살펴 보았다)

search *vt.* (집·장소)를 수색하다; (사람의 소지품)을 조사하다
▶ Police detectives searched every inch of the

office. (형사들은 사무실을 구석구석 수색했다)
▶The policeman searched him for marihuana. (경찰은 마리화나를 찾기 위해 그의 몸을 수색했다)
— vi.《search for》찾다 ; 찾아 다니다
▶I searched for his new address. (나는 그의 새 주소를 이곳저곳 찾아다녔다)
explore vt. ① …을 탐험하다 ; 답사하다
▶Captain James Cook explored the coasts of Australia and New Zealand. (제임스 쿡 선장은 오스트레일리아와 뉴질랜드의 연안지대를 탐험했다)
② (문제 등)을 탐구하다 ; 철저하게 조사하다
▶The investigators are exploring the cause of the plane crash. (조사관들은 그 항공기의 추락 원인을 철저하게 조사하고 있다)
scout vi. 정찰하다 ; 찾아다니다
▶A stray dog scouted around [about] for food. (주인 없는 개가 먹을 것을 찾아다니고 있었다)
— vt. …을 정찰하다 ; …의 정보를 탐색하다
▶He was sent to scout the rival firm's new product. (그는 경쟁 회사의 신제품에 관한 정보를 얻기 위해 파견되었다)
hunt vt. ① …을 찾다 ; …을 수색하다 ;《hunt A for B》B(물건)를 발견하려고 A(장소)를 수색하다
▶She hunted the kitchen and the bathroom for the ring she left. (그녀는 반지를 어디에 놔 둔지 몰라 찾느라고 부엌과 욕실을 뒤졌다)
② (물건)을 찾아다니다 ; (범인)을 수사하다
▶Senior co-eds were hunting a job. (대학 4학년 여학생들이 일자리를 찾아다니고 있었다)
— vi.《hunt for》찾아다니다 ; 탐색하다
▶I've hunted for the lost key. (나는 잃어버린 열쇠를 찾아다녔다)

■칭찬하다 : 기리다, 상찬하다
[解説] praise 「칭찬하다」의 뜻의 일반적인 말. 칭찬을 말이나 글로 나타내다의 뜻. admire 「감탄하다」, 「감복하다」의 뜻으로 때로는 빈정거린다는 뜻으로도 쓴다. speak well of 구어로서 「…을 칭 찬 하 다」. compliment praise 나 admire의 뜻의 일상어로 종종 사교적인 말로 쓰인다. flatter 「아첨하다」, 「알랑거리다」의 뜻. applaud 「박수갈채하다」의 뜻.
praise vt. …을 칭찬하다 ; 극구 칭찬하다, 상찬하다
▶We praised him for his originality. (우리는 그의 독창성을 극구 칭찬했다)
admire vt. ① …에 감탄하다 ; 감복하다
▶I'm admiring what you've written. (네가 쓴 글에 감탄하고 있다)
▶We admire your outspokenness. 〈빈정거리며〉 (너의 솔직함에 감탄한다)

② (口) (겉치레로) …을 칭찬하다
▶I forgot to admire her son. (그녀의 아들을 칭찬해주는 걸 깜박 잊었다)
speak well of …을 칭찬하다 (↔ speak ill of)
▶Mary was speaking well of you. (메리가 너를 칭찬하던데)
compliment vt.《compliment A on B》A(사람)의 B(물건)를 칭찬하다
▶A friend of mine complimented me on my new coat. (친구가 내 새 코트를 칭찬해 주었다)
flatter vt. …에게 아첨하다 ; 알랑거리다
▶He flattered her on [about] her tastes in clothes. (그는 그녀의 의복 취향에 대해 아첨하는 말을 했다)
applaud vt. …에게 박수갈채하다
▶The speaker was loudly applauded after the lecture. (연사는 강연이 끝난 뒤 큰 박수갈채를 받았다)

■허락하다 : 용서하다, 허용하다
[解説] let 「허락하다」란 뜻의 가장 일상적인 말로 우리말에서 쓰는 「허락하다」란 말 외에 「좋을대로 하게 하다」의 뜻으로도 쓴다. allow, permit는 권한을 가지고 있는 사람이 「허락하다」 「허가하다」의 뜻이지만 allow는 「…하는 것을 방해하지 않다 ; 묵인하다」의 뜻, permit은 마음이 내켜서 입 밖에 내어 「허가해 주다」의 뜻으로 쓴다. 우리말로 「허락하다」를 쓸 때 let, allow, permit은 쓰지 않고 may, can 등의 허가를 나타내는 조동사를 써서 표현할 수 있다. excuse, pardon, forgive는 위에서 말한 「허가하다」의 뜻과는 의미가 전혀 다른 데 주의. excuse는 예의에 어긋나거나 의도적이 아닌 가벼운 과오를 「(책망하지 않고) 용서하다」. pardon은 excuse 보다 격식을 차린 말로 「(벌주지 않고) 용서하다」. forgive는 화를 내거나 원망·복수하려는 마음 등을 버리고 「용서하다」의 뜻.
let vt. …하는 것을 허락하다 ; …하게 놔두다
▶Let me go with him. (그와 함께 가게 해주십시오)
allow vt. …을 허락하다 ; …하게 놔두다
▶Father allowed me to use his car. (아버지는 내가 아버지의 차를 쓰는 것을 허락하셨다)
▶Allow me to [Let me] introduce a friend of mine to you. (제 친구를 소개하겠습니다)
permit vt. …을 허가[허락]하다 ; 허가를 내주다
▶My boss permitted me to take a vacation. (사장은 내게 휴가를 허가해 주었다)
▶Professor Brown did not permit us to consult a dictionary during the class. (브라운 교수는 우리가 수업중에 사전을 찾아보는 것을 허락하지 않았다)
excuse vt. …을 용서하다
▶Excuse me for being late. (늦어서 죄송합니다)

pardon *vt.* (벌하지 않고) 용서하다
▶ Pardon me for misunderstanding you. ⇌ Pardon my misunderstanding you. (당신을 오해한 것을 용서해 주십시오)

forgive *vt.* …을 용서하다
▶ Please forgive me for my long silence. (오랫동안 소식이 없었던 것을 용서해 주십시오)
▶ I'll not forgive him. (나는 그를 용서하지 않겠다)

■ **훔치다**: 빼앗다, 날치기하다, 후무리다, 강탈하다

[해설] **steal** 「훔치다」, 「슬쩍 훔치다」란 뜻의 일반어. **rob** 「강탈하다」의 뜻. 폭력을 쓰거나 위협하거나 사기 행위 등으로 훔치다는 뜻. **pilfer** 「좀도둑질을 하다」. **lift** (口)「후무리다」. **plagiarize** 타인의 문장이나 작품을 「도용하다」, 「표절하다」의 뜻. **snatch** 「낚아채다」, 「날치기하다」. **rustle** (美口) 방목하는 말이나 가축 등을 「훔치다」의 뜻.

steal *vt.* …을 훔치다; 《steal B from A》 B(물건)를 A(사람이나 장소)로부터 훔치다
▶ I wonder who stole my bicycle. (누가 내 자전거를 훔쳤을까?)
▶ My umbrella was stolen. ⇌ I had my umbrella stolen. (우산을 도둑 맞았다)
▶ Somebody stole my ruby ring from the drawer. (누군가가 서랍에서 내 루비반지를 훔쳐갔다)

rob *vt.* ① …을 강탈하다; 빼앗다; 《rob A of B》 A(사람)로부터 B(물건)를 빼앗다 (▶steal 과의 문형이 다른 점에 주의)
▶ A young man robbed an old man of his money. (한 젊은 남자가 노인에게서 돈을 강탈했다)
② (은행 등)에 침입하다
▶ Armed with a gun, he robbed a bank. (그는 총으로 무장하고 은행에 침입했다)
▶ The post office on [at] the corner was robbed this morning. (오늘 아침 모퉁이에 있는 우체국에 강도가 들었다)

pilfer *vi.* 《pilfer from》 좀도둑질하다
▶ She was found pilfering from her colleague's desk. (그녀가 동료 책상에서 좀도둑질하다 발각됐다)

lift *vt.* (口) …을 후무리다; 슬쩍 훔치다
▶ A well-dressed woman was found lifting cuff links. (옷을 잘 차려입은 부인이 커프스 단추를 후무리는 현장을 들켰다)

plagiarize *vt.* (남의 문장이나 작품)을 도용하다; 표절하다 (▶이 뜻으로는 lift나 pirate도 쓴다)
▶ He admitted plagiarizing some passages from her book. (그는 그녀의 책에서 몇 구절 도용한 것을 인정했다)
— *vi.* 남의 문장[작품]을 도용하다; 표절하다
▶ You should be careful not to plagiarize when you write term papers. (기말 리포트를 작성할 때 남의 문장을 도용하지 않도록 주의해야 한다)

snatch *vt.* …을 낚아채다; 날치기하다
▶ A young man snatched my handbag and ran away. (한 젊은 남자가 내 핸드백을 날치기해서 도망갔다)

rustle *vt.* (美口) (가축)을 훔치다
▶ It was last week that some cows were rustled. (젖소 몇 마리를 도난당한 것은 지난주다)

2. 전화 통화할 때의 영어

1. 전화 통화에서의 첫마디와 인사말

◇ **거는 사람**
《이름을 말할 때》
① 여보세요, 저 김민수인데요
  Hello. This is Kim Min-su.
② 저는 제인의 친구예요
  I'm a friend of Jane.

◇ **받는 사람**
《상대를 확인할 때》
① 누구시지요?
  Who's calling, please?
② 성함을 다시 말씀해 주시겠어요?
  May I have your name again, please?

《상대를 확인할 때》
① 존 화이트씨입니까?
  Is this Mr. John White?
② 존 화이트씨 좀 바꿔주세요
  May I speak to Mr. John White?

《이름을 말할 때》
① 제가 존 화이트입니다
  I'm John White.
② 제가 본인입니다
  Speaking.
③ 잠깐 기다리세요
  Hold on, please.

《전화를 잘못 걸었을 때》
① 777-1369 번 아닙니까?
  Isn't this 777-1369?
② 제가 잘못 걸었습니다. 죄송합니다
  I made a mistake. I'm sorry.

《잘못 걸려온 전화를 받았을 때》
① 전화를 잘못 거신 것 같습니다
  I'm afraid you have the wrong number.
② 몇 번에 거셨나요?
  What number did you dial?
③ 그런 분은 여기 안계십니다
  There's no one here by that name.

《당사자가 부재중일 때》
① 언제 돌아오실지 아세요?
  Do you have any idea when he will be back?
② 그분에게 제가 급한 볼일이 있어서요
  I have some urgent business with him.
③ 말씀 좀 전해 주시겠습니까?
  May I leave a message?
④ 나중에 다시 걸게요
  I'll call him again.
⑤ 그분께 저한테 전화 좀 부탁한다고 전해 주시겠습니까?
  Could you ask him to call me back?

《당사자가 부재중일 때》
① 죄송하지만 그분은 지금 외출중이십니다[자리에 안 계십니다]
  Sorry, he is out now.
② 717-0080 으로 걸어 보세요. 그분은 지금 거기 계십니다
  Please call 717-0080. He is there now.
③ 4시경 돌아오십니다
  He will be back around four.
④ 그분이 지금 어디에 계신지 모르겠습니다
  I have no idea where he is now.
⑤ 전하실 말씀이 있으세요?
  Would you like to leave a message?
⑥ 돌아오시면 전화 드리라고 할까요?
  Would you like him to call you back?

《인사말》
① 안녕하세요?
  Hello.
  Good morning [evening].
  Hi.
② 안녕하세요?
  How are you?
③ 밤 늦게 죄송합니다
  I'm sorry to disturb you so late.
④ 오랜만입니다
  It's been a long time since we last met.

《인사말》
① 오래 기다리셨죠?
  Thank you for waiting.
② 제가 도와 드릴 일이 있습니까?
  May I help you?
③ 전화 참 잘 하셨습니다
  Good to hear from you.
④ 저희는 다 잘 지내고 있습니다
  Everything is going well here.
⑤ 별고 없으셨지요?
  How have you been?

2. 전화 통화를 끊을 때·확인할 때의 표현

◇ 거는 사람

《통화를 마무리할 때》
① 자, 그럼…
Well, ….
② 이만 끊어야겠어요
I have to go now.
③ 말씀 나눠 반가웠습니다
Nice talking to you.

《확인할 때》
① 제 말의 요점을 다시 말씀 드릴게요
Let me repeat my point.
② 그럼 3월 3일, 오후 6시에 만나뵙지요
Let's meet at 6 p.m., March 3.
③ 메모 좀 해주시겠습니까?
Could you write it down?

《작별 인사》
① 안녕히 계세요. Good-bye.
② 그럼 다시 See you.
③ 즐거운 주말을 보내세요
Have a nice weekend.
(즐거운 시간 a good time /
즐거운 하루 a good day /
즐거운 여행 a pleasant trip)

◇ 받는 사람

《통화를 마무리할 때》
① 죄송하지만 딴 전화가 와 있어서요
Sorry. I've got another call.
② 전화 고마웠습니다
Thank you for calling.
(초대 your invitation /
소식 your information)

《확인할 때》
① 그럼 나중에 그분에게 그렇게 전할게요
So, I'll tell him so later.
② 전할 말씀을 다시 한번 말해 볼게요
Let me repeat your message.

《작별 인사》
① 쉬엄쉬엄 하세요
Take it easy.
② 당신도요.
The same to you. ⇌ You, too.
③ 여러분께 안부 전해 주세요
Please say hello to everyone.
④ 안녕히 주무세요
Good night.

〈전화 통화의 실례(B는 거는 사람, A는 받는 사람)〉

A: 여보세요
B: 아, 안녕 폴라
A: 폴리구나
B: 이렇게 아침 일찍 전화해서 미안한데…
A: 아냐, 괜찮아
B: 자는 걸 깨운 게 아닌가 몰라
A: 아냐, 난 6시 반부터 일어나 있었어
B: 비가 올 것 같은 날씬데, 그래도 영화를 보러 갈래?
A: 가고 싶어. 그런데 수진이는 어떨지 모르지. 네가 전화 좀 해볼래?
B: 수진이 전화번호 알고 있니?
A: 응. 하지만 찾아봐야 돼. 내가 직접 전화하는 게 낫겠어. 혹시 그 애가 같이 갈 수 없다고 하면, 너한테 다시 전화할게
B: 그래 주겠니? 정말 고마워. 폴라. 그럼 나중에 봐
A: 그래. 전화 고마워. 안녕, 폴
B: 안녕

A: Hello?
B: Oh hi, Paula.
A: Is that you, Paul?
B: Sorry to call so early, but….
A: No, that's OK.
B: I didn't wake you up?
A: No, no, I've been up since six-thirty.
B: It looks as though it's going to rain. Do you still want to go to the movies?
A: I do, but I don't know about Su-jin. Maybe you'd better give her a call.
B: Have you got her number?
A: Yes, but I'll have to look for it. I'd better call her myself. If she says she can't go with us, I'll call you back.
B: Would you please? Thanks a lot, Paula. See you later.
A: OK. Thanks for calling. Bye-bye, Paul.
B: Good-bye.

3. 국제 통화에서 잘 쓰는 표현

1. 국제 통화를 교환원에게 부탁할 때

▶ 한국에 번호통화를 부탁합니다

I'd like to call Korea, station-to-station. ⇌ I'd like to place a station-to-station call to Korea. The number is 02-717-0080.

▶ 번호는 02-717-0080 입니다
▶ 한국에 콜렉트콜을 부탁합니다. 제 이름은 김만기입니다. 상대방의 전화번호는 02-717-0080 입니다

I'd like to call Korea collect [to place a collect call to Korea]. My name is Kim Man-gi. The number is 02-717-0080.

▶ 한국에 지명통화를 하고 싶습니다. 전화번호는 02-717-0080입니다. 상대방의 이름은 김인호씨 입니다

I'd like to call Korea, person-to-person. The number is 02-717-0080 and I'd like to speak to Kim In-ho.

2. 교환원이 쓰는 표현

▶ 국제 통화 교환원입니다. 말씀하세요
▶ 상대방 번호를 말씀하세요
▶ 김수만씨한테서 콜렉트콜입니다. 연결할까요?

This is an overseas operator. May I help you?
What's the number, sir [ma'm]?
You have a collect call from Mr. Kim Su-man. Will you accept the charge?

▶ (전화번호가 틀렸을 때) 지금 거신 전화번호는 결번입니다

I'm sorry, the number you have reached is not in service now.

▶ (전화번호가 변경되었을 때) 지금 거신 전화는 번호가 변경되었습니다. 새 번호는 …입니다
▶ 신호가 가고 있습니다
▶ 연결됐습니다

The number you dialed has been changed. The new number is....
The number is ringing. ⇌ It's ringing.
Mr. White is on the line. ⇌ You're connected. ⇌ Your party is on the line.

▶ 통화 중입니다

The line is busy now. ⇌ The number's engaged now.

▶ 아무도 받지 않습니다
▶ 성함을 말씀해 주시겠습니까?

There is in no answer. ⇌ Nobody answers.
May I have your name, please?

3. 국제 통화 중에 문제가 생겼을 때

▶ 잡음이 많아서 잘 안 들립니다. 다시 연결해 주십시오

I had a bad connection. There was a lot of noise and echo and I couldn't hear well. Could you put me through again?

▶ 한국에 통화하다가 중간에 끊겼습니다. 다시 연결해 주십시오

I was cut off while I was talking to Korea. Could you connect me again, please?

4. 전화 통화가 연결됐을 때

▶ 화이트씨를 부탁합니다

May [Can] I speak to Mr. White? ⇌ I'd like to talk to Mr. White?

▶ (이름을 말할 때) 저는 김남수입니다

This is Kim Nam-su speaking. ⇌ My name is Kim Nam-su.

▶ (본인이 받아서) 접니다
▶ (당사자가 부재중일 때) 지금 안 계십니다

Speaking. ⇌ This is he [she].
I'm sorry he is out. ⇌ I'm sorry he is not in. ⇌ I'm sorry he is not available.

▶ 몇 시에 돌아오실까요?
▶ 1시간 안에 돌아올 겁니다
▶ 2시까지는 돌아올 겁니다

Do you know what time he'll be back?
I think he'll be back in one hour.
I think he'll be back by two o'clock.

3. 국제 통화에서 잘 쓰는 표현

▶ 잠깐 기다리세요	Just a second, please. ⇒ One moment, please. ⇒ Hold on [Hang on], please.
▶ 전화 잘못 거신 것 같습니다	I think you've got the wrong number.
▶ 죄송합니다. 제가 잘못 걸었습니다	Sorry to bother you. I've got the wrong number.
▶ 좀 더 천천히 말씀해 주십시오	Could you speak more slowly?
▶ 좀 더 크게 말씀해 주십시오	Could you speak a little louder?
▶ 누구를 찾으십니까?	Who are you calling?
▶ (전화를 끊을 때의 인사) 전화 줘서 고마워	Thank you for calling.
▶ 통화 즐거웠어	It was nice talking to you.

5. 회사로 전화를 걸 때

▶ 동일 무역입니까?	Is this Dongil Trading Company?
▶ 구내[교환] 100번을 부탁합니다	Extension 100, please. ⇒ Will you give me extension 100? ⇒ I'd like to talk to Mr. White at extension 100.
▶ 영업 담당 로버트씨를 부탁합니다	May I speak to Mr. Robert in charge of sales?
▶ 누구 한국말 하는 분 계십니까?	May I speak to someone who speaks Korean?
▶ 로버트씨 계신 곳의 전화번호를 알려 주십시오	Could you give me the number to reach Mr. Robert?

6. 회사로 전화가 걸려 왔을 때

▶ 성함을 다시 한 번 부탁합니다	Could you repeat your name please?
▶ (잘 안 들릴 때) 다시 말씀해 주세요	I beg your pardon. (끝을 올려서)
▶ 연결해 드리겠습니다	I'll connect you. ⇒ I'll put you through.
▶ 전화를 남선생께 돌려 드리겠습니다	I'll transfer this call to Mr. Nam.
▶ 담당 부서를 연결해 드리겠습니다	I'll connect you with the department in charge.
▶ 그분은 오늘 쉬십니다	He's off today. ⇒ He's taking a day off today.
▶ 그분은 이번 주에 휴가십니다	He's on vacation this week.
▶ 방금 외출하셨습니다	He has just gone out. ⇒ He's out (right) now. ⇒ He's not in the office (right) now. ⇒ He's not in (right) now.
▶ 지금 회의 중이십니다	He's attending a meeting now. ⇒ He is in a meeting now.
▶ 다른 전화를 받고 계십니다	He is on another line.
▶ 그분 전화는 통화 중입니다	His line is busy.
▶ 지금 손님이 와 계십니다	He is with a client now.
▶ 지금 자리를 비우셨습니다	He is not at his desk. ⇒ He has just stepped out.
▶ 퇴근하셨습니다	He has gone home. ⇒ He has left already.
▶ 부산 지사로 전근가셨습니다	He has been transferred to the Pusan office.
▶ 대구로 출장 중이십니다	He is on a business trip to Taegu now.
▶ 전화를 드리라고 할까요?	Shall I have him call you back?
▶ 그분의 부서를 아십니까?	Do you know his section? ⇒ Do you know where he works?
▶ 여기 그런 분은 안 계십니다	We have no one by that name.

7. 전할 말이 있을 때

▶ 말씀 좀 전해 주시겠습니까?	May I leave a message?
▶ 전하실 말씀이 있으십니까?	May I take a message?
▶ 그녀가 돌아오면 전화 좀 해달라고 전해주세요	Please ask her to call me when she gets back.

4. Writing의 기초 지식

정보를 주고 받는 일 (giving and receiving information)이 커뮤니케이션이다. 그런데 지금껏 우리의 영어 학습은 정보를 받는 일에 중점을 두었다. 우리가 외국인과 의사 소통을 하려면 정보를 주는 수단인 speaking, writing이 필요하다. 그런데 우리는 말하고 쓰는 능력이 너무나 부족하다. 그래서 여기서는 그 중에서 writing ability를 키우기 위한 기초적인 기법을 배우기로 한다.

1. 패러그래프 라이팅(paragraph writing)

국문이든 영문이든 글을 구성하는 단위는 문단 즉 패러그래프이다. 이 하나하나의 패러그래프를 쓰는 일을 패러그래프 라이팅이라 한다. 패러그래프 라이팅을 잘하는 것이 곧 writing ability를 기르는 일이다.

아래에 패러그래프 라이팅의 기본적인 지침과 유의점들을 소개한다. 패러그래프를 쓰려면 먼저 상대에게 전하고자 하는 정보·내용의 요지가 담긴 주제문(主題文)을 제시하고 그것을 다시 자세한 설명(details)에 의해서 전개한다. 따라서 정연한 문장으로 다듬어 가기 위한 배열의 기법을 터득할 필요가 있다.

2. 주제문(topic sentence)의 제시

주제문이란 자기가 표현하고자 하는 내용의 전반적인 기술(記述)이다. 주제문을 제시하는 데는 아래와 같은 차례로 생각할 필요가 있다.
(1) 자신이 흥미나 관심을 가지고 있는 화제를 고른다.
(2) 개괄적인 화제를 구체적인 사상(事象)으로 기술해 간다.
(3) 구체적인 사상(事象)을 써서 자기가 말하고자 하는 바를 전개해 간다.

3. 상세한 기술(details)의 전개

주제문과 그 상세한 기술의 전개에는 다음과 같은 방법이 있다.

(1) 실례(examples)

topic sentence의 main idea를 적절히 뒷받침하는 사실·사건·장면·상황 등을 고른다. 예에는 실례(real examples)와 가정의 예(hypothetical examples)가 있는데 어떤 예이든 쓰는 사람과 듣는 사람에게 흥미와 관심을 주며 쉽게 이해할 수 있는 그런 것이 좋다.
〖보기〗 〈topic sentence〉
I had a very busy day yesterday.
〈details〉
I had to attend a three-hour-meeting in the morning. I had only 20 minutes to eat lunch because I had an appointment to see a customer on business at one o'clock. After talking with the customer, I had to go to the ABC Company to introduce a new product....

(2) 비교 대조(comparison and / or contrast)

두 사람 (이상)의 인물, 2개 (이상)의 사물로써 같은 종류를 서로 비교한다. 그 대상의 유사점과 차이점(similarities and / or differences)을 도입부에 제시하는 게 좋다. 또 배열에 있어서도 비교 대조하여 topic sentence를 돋보이게 하는 패러그래프로 만든다.
〖보기〗 〈topic sentence〉
Badminton is a game somewhat like tennis.
〈details〉
Badminton rackets are smaller and lighter than tennis rackets. We use the shuttlecock, a small feathered object instead of a ball....

(3) 이유(reasons)

주제문에 Why?라는 질문을 던져서 그 details를 because와 함께 설명한다. 이유에는 자기 자신의 체험, 실험 데이터, 통계 수치나 서적 등의 intellectual reasons와 상대의 감정에 호소하는 emotional reasons의 두 가지가 있다. 주제문으로서는 진위, 혹은 주장·의견을 논증하는 그런 문장을 제시한다.
〖보기〗 〈topic sentence〉
Smoking is bad for your health.
〈details〉
Scientists have proved that more smokers contract lung cancer than people who do not smoke....

(4) 분류(classification)

분류의 기준은 어떤 사물의 종류·성질·특징 등의 유사점과 차이점(similarities and / or differences)을 종합하여 details로서 제시해 간다. 한편 관점의 차이에 따라 classification의 기준은 변하는데 분류의 기준은 하나로 압축하는 것이 중요하다.
〖보기〗 〈topic sentence〉
A lot of Koreans are studying English for a variety of reasons.

⟨details⟩
　　The first group of English learners is forced to learn English because it is a required subject in high school and college. The second group wants to learn English to be able to use it in their future careers. The third group loves to learn language and enjoys being with English speakers....

(5) 정의(definition)
　사물·생각·말을 히니로 분류하여 각각의 것들이 서로 어떻게 다른지를 개인적인 견해를 곁들이지 말고 정의한다. 보기처럼 한국 음식을 소개하는 경우의 패러그래프 등에 쓰면 효과적이다.
보기 ⟨topic sentence⟩
　Kimchi is the national dish of Korea.
⟨details⟩
　　Now it has become one of the favorite dishes around the world. An increasing number of countries is importing *kimchi* from Korea....

4. 주제문과 상세한 기술의 배열

　주제문과 상세한 기술에 관한 내용이 결정되면 이번에는 정리된 패러그래프를 짜맞추기 위한 배열 방법을 생각한다.

(1) 시간을 기준으로 한 배열(time [chronological] order)
　주제문의 main idea를 뒷받침하는 details를 「시간의 흐름에 따라 배열해 가는 방법」이다. 이 방법은 역사적 서술, 일상 생활의 묘사, how to...의 서술 등, 신문이나 잡지 등에서 잘 쓰는 배열 방식이다. 단, 일상 생활을 time order로 기술하는 경우에는 문장의 연결어를 분명하게 하지 않으면 글이 늘어지므로 주의할 필요가 있다.
보기 시간적 순서를 나타내는 어구
　　when, while, at..., in..., before, after, since, as, during, etc.
⟨details⟩
　　First, mix peanut butter, and coconut. Second, add 2 cups(500ml) of cereal and stir. Then, form mixture into balls....

(2) 공간적 배열(space order)
　주제문의 main idea를 뒷받침하는 details를 「공간」안에서 파악하는 방법을 말한다. 이때 point of vision(기점(基点)), 쓰는 이, 말하는 이의 위치를 정하여 그 기점에서 일정 방향으로 details를 배열한다.
보기 공간적 순서를 나타내는 어구
　「위」를 나타내는 어구 : above, up, on, on top of, over, etc.
　「아래」를 나타내는 어구 : under, below, down, beneath, etc.
　「옆」을 나타내는 어구 : by, beside, next (to), on the right [left], etc.
　「앞뒤」를 나타내는 어구 : in front of, in [at] the back of, behind, etc.
　「원근」을 나타내는 어구 : near, far, beyond, close to, etc.

(3) 인과 관계(cause-effect relationship)
　어떤 events(일, 사건, 발생사)를 결과로 하여, 그 결과를 가져온 causes(원인)를 밝히는 형태로 main idea를 전개해 가는 방법을 말한다. 여기에는 세 가지 패턴이 있다.

① **one cause-one effect**
　어떤 하나의 원인에서 어떤 하나의 결과를 가져오는 패턴이다.
보기 The excursion was put off because it was raining.

② **one cause-several effects**
　하나의 원인 때문에 여러 가지 결과가 생기는 패턴을 말한다.
보기 ⟨topic sentence⟩
　Cigarette smoking results in several bad effects.
⟨details⟩
　　It can lead to heart attack and lung cancer for smokers and people around them as well. It is also the main cause of fire. Further, ...

③ **several causes-one effect**
　여러 원인이 하나의 결과를 발생하는 패턴을 말한다.
보기 ⟨topic sentence⟩
　There are several reasons why Min-ho became one of the leading pianists in the world.
⟨details⟩
　　First of all, he is an exceptionally gifted pianist. He also received the best education as a young pianist. Further, he loves to play the piano and practices very hard. In addition....

　이와 같은 패러그래프의 전개 방법을 고려하여 일반 원고, 리포트, 일상의 편지를 쓴다면 명확하고 정연한 문장을 쓸 수 있게 될 것이다. 또한 영문 작성력을 키우는데도 크게 도움이 될 것이다.

5. 영문 일기 쓰는 법

1. 영문 일기

 영문 일기 쓰는 습관이 영작문 숙달의 한 방법임은 잘 알려져 있다. 영문 일기를 지속적으로 쓰려면 하루에 일어난 일들을 자세히 쓰지 말고 중요한 일들만을 추려서 간략하게 쓰는 것이 좋다.

 또 욕심을 부려서 처음부터 완전한 문장으로 쓰려다가는 힘들고 귀찮아서 도중에 중단하기 쉽다. 우선은 아는 단어와 표현들을 활용해서 써가다 보면 시일이 지남에 따라 영어실력이 쌓이게 되면 일기 문장은 절로 다듬어지게 마련이다.

 일기란 본래 남에게 보이기 위한 것이 아니므로 편지처럼 이렇다 할 특정한 형식이 있는 것은 아니나 나름대로 몇 가지 특징이 있다.

 아래에 영문 일기의 특징을 고교생의 쉬운 일기문을 실례로 들어 살펴 보기로 한다.

2. 영문 일기의 특징

(1) 날짜 적는 법
- 「요일, 달 이름, 날짜」의 순서로 적는다.
  ♦ 4월 1일 (월요일) Monday, April 1
- 요일과 달 이름은 다음과 같이 줄여 쓸 수도 있다.
  〈일요일부터〉
  Sun. Mon. Tue. Wed. Thu. Fri. Sat.
  〈1월부터〉
  Jan. Feb. Mar. Apr. Aug. Sep(t). Oct. Nov. Dec. (▶May, June, July는 보통 줄여서 쓰지 않음)

(2) 날씨
 우리말 일기에서는 날짜 다음에 대개 날씨를 적지만 영문 일기에는 그런 형식은 없다. 우리말 일기식으로 날씨를 쓸 경우에는 날짜 다음에 다음과 같이 쓰면 된다.
 ♦개음, 맑음 sunny; clear / 흐림 cloudy / 비 rainy / 눈 snowy / 바람 windy
▶ 개인 후에 흐림 Fair, later cloudy.
▶ 오늘도 비 Another rainy day.
▶ 최고 기온 25℃, 최저 기온 15℃
  High 25℃, low 15℃.

(3) 주어 I(나)의 생략
 문장은 간결할수록 좋으므로, 뜻이 애매해지지 않는 한 주어 I는 생략한다.
▶ 점심 먹고 낮잠 Took a nap after lunch.
▶ 가까운 서점에서 사전 한 권을 삼 Bought a dictionary at a nearby bookstore.
▶ 인호가 미국에 간다는 말을 듣고 놀람 Surprised to hear (that) In-ho is going (to go) America.

(4) 시제(時制)
 우리말 일기에서는 과거의 일을 현재형으로 많이 쓰지만 영문 일기는 과거형으로 쓴다.
▶ 민호가 지갑을 잃음 Min-ho lost his wallet.
▶ 「미녀와 야수」를 비디오로 봄 Watched The Beauty and the Beast on video.

3. ① 영문 일기의 실례

7월 10일 (화)
 오늘 학기말 시험 끝남. 휴우.
 학교에서 돌아오는 길에 민수네 집에 들러 폴 사이먼의 새 CD를 빌림. 저번 것도 괜찮았지만 이번 것은 더 좋음.
 오후에는 여름 방학 여행 계획을 짬. 자전거로 도는 4일간의 시골 여행. 내일 민호더러 같이 가자고 해봐야지. 녀석, 같이 가겠다고 나설 게 틀림없어.

Tue., July 10
 The last day of the term exams. Thank God!
 Dropped in at Min-su's after school, and borrowed his new Paul Simon CD. His last CD was good, but this one is even better.
 Planning a trip in summer vacation. 4-day trip around the countryside by bike. Am going to ask Min-ho to come with me tomorrow. Quite sure that he'll say yes.

② 영문 일기의 실례

3월 2일 (금) 개임, 오후 흐림
 고교 첫 등교일. 8시에 학교로 출발. 10분전 9시에 도착. 강당에 들어감. 담임 선생님은 영어 과목을 맡은 김 선생님. 40쯤 돼 보이는 키가 아주 큰 분. 좀 무서울 듯. 종례를 마치고 하교.
 밤에 아버지께서 파카 볼펜을 주심. 신났다. 긴장했던 탓인지 몹시 피곤함. 11시에 잠.

Fri., Mar. 2 Fair, cloudy in the afternoon
 My first day of high school. Left for school at eight. Arrived ten to nine. Entered the auditorium. My homeroom teacher is Mr. Kim, an English teacher. About forty, very tall. Looks a little strict. Left school after homeroom.
 At night, my father gave me a Parker ball-point pen. So happy! Really tired, maybe because I'd been tense.
 Went to bed at eleven.

③ 영문 일기의 실례

8월 10일, 토요일, 맑음
 6시 기상. 오늘도 더운 날. 그래도 오후에 동생하고 테니스를 쳐서 재미있었다. 저녁에는 텔레비전으로 야구를 시청했다.

Saturday, August 10, Clear
 I got up at six. It was hot today, too.
But it was a lot of fun to play tennis with my brother in the afternoon.
I watched a baseball game on TV in the evening.

6. 영문 이력서 쓰는 법

한국에서는 이력서의 형식이 거의 일정하지만 영문 이력서는 정해진 형식이 따로 없이 아주 자유롭다. 이력서는 영어로 Personal History, Curriculum Vitae, 또는 Résumé라고 하는데 Personal History가 일반적이다.

취업이나 유학을 위해 편지를 낼 때에 자기의 경력을 사유토운 형식으로 써보내는 것이 영·미의 일반적 관행이다. 취업시에는 자기의 과거의 활동·업적·경력에 관하여 충분하고도 요령 있게 어필하는 것이 중요하다. 영·미식 이력서에 기재해야 할 사항은 대개 다음과 같다. 성별, 기혼·미혼의 구분, 키, 몸무게, 국적, 경험, 특기, 자격증의 유무, 신원조회처 등이다. 특히, 유념할 점은 경력은 최근 것을 먼저 쓰고 오래된 것을 나중에 쓰는 것이다.

다음에 동일인의 이력서를 두 가지 형식으로 소개한다.

PERSONAL HISTORY

이 름	Name : Kim Min-su
현 주 소	Present Address : 437 Ahyŏn-dong, Map'o-gu, Seoul
생 년 월 일	Date of Birth : April 5, 1970
성별·기타	Description : Age : 27 Sex : Male Height : 173 cm
	Weight : 64 kg
결혼 관계	Marital Status : single
국 적	Nationality : Korean
학 력	Education : 1989–1993 Yonsei University, Seoul
	Received Bachelor of Arts (February, 1993)
	Major in English Literature
	1986–1989 Map'o High School, Seoul
병 역	Military Service : 1993–1995
이 력	Occupation : 1995 to the present
	Samil Trading Co., Ltd.
	Assigned to the Sales Division
특 기	Special Skills : Competent in the use of Apple Macintosh
신원조회처	References : Dr. Nam Sang-su, Professor of English Literature,
	Yonsei University.
	Mr. Han In-su, Chief of the Sales Division,
	Samil Trading Co., Ltd.
작성 일자	September 20, 1997
서 명	*Kim Minsu*
	Kim Min-su

437 Ahyŏn-dong
Map'o-gu, Seoul
September 20, 1997

Samil Trading Co., Ltd.
323 Sogong-dong
Chung-gu, Seoul

Dear Sir,

I read your advertisement in *The Daily Dong-A* today. I believe I am qualified for the position advertized and so I wish to apply for it.

I was born in Seoul on April 5, 1970. I entered the English Literature Department of Yonsei University in 1989, majoring in English Literature. I graduated from the same university in 1993, attaining a Bachelor of Arts.

I fulfilled my years of military service.

I am 26 years of age, male, single and healthy. My height is 173cm, weighting 64kg.

I can speak English fairly well. While at univerity I acted as a guide for foreign tourist for two years.

I have worked for three years at Samil Trading Co., Ltd. in the Sales Division. I am not dissatisfied with my present job, but I would like to work in a firm like yours where I hope I can make the most of my English ability.

As to my personal character and qualifications, please refer to Professor. Nam Sang-su, Department of English Literature at Yonsei University or Mr. Han In-su, Chief of the Sales Division, Samil Trading Co., Ltd.

If you would give me an opportunity to be interviewed, I would be much obliged.

Faithfully yours

Kim Minsu

Kim Min-su

7. 영문 편지 쓰는 법

1. 영문 편지의 종류
(1) **사교편지(social letter)**: 가족·친척·친구·지기와 같은 사이에서 주고 받는 사신(私信)으로 내용은 경조(慶弔)·선물·문안·초대·의뢰·소개·조회·추천·통지·독촉·사절·혼서(婚書) 등 일상생활 전반에 관한 것을 포함한다. 양식이나 문체는 딱딱하지 않으면서 쓰는 방식은 일정한 형식에 따른다.

(2) **공문편지(official letter)**: 관청이나 정부 사이에, 관청과 개인 사이에 수고 받는 서신으로, 양식이나 문체는 매우 딱딱한 형식이다.

(3) **상용편지(business letter)**: 상업상 또는 교섭의 필요에 따라 이용되는 회사간, 회사와 개인간에 주고 받는 서신으로 용어나 문장은 상업영어(business English)를 사용한다. 정해진 문구가 많으며 딱딱한 문체로 되어 있다.

2. 필기도구
개인적인 편지에는 펜이나 볼펜을 사용한다. 색은 검정·파랑·블루블랙으로하며, 빨강·자색·녹색 등은 피하는 것이 좋고 연필은 사용하지 않는 것이 좋다. 특히 개인적 감정을 전하는 경우에는 자필이 좋다. 그러나 발신자에게는 시간과 스페이스를 절약하고, 수신자에게는 읽기 쉬운 이점이 있는 타이프라이터나 워드프로세서를 사용해도 좋다.
편지지는 줄이 없는 백지로, 색은 흰색이나 미색을 사용한다. 크기는 B5가 적당하며, 봉투는 흰것을 쓰는데 항공편지의 경우는 규격봉투를 사용하는 것이 좋다.

3. 편지의 형식
(1) **편지지 쓰는 법**: 아래와 같은 세 가지 방식이 있다.

(ⅰ) **블록체(Block Style)(美)**: 본문은 각 단락(paragraph)의 시작을 왼쪽 끝에서부터 시작한다. 본문 이외의 부분에는 생략 부호를 빼고 구두점은 찍지 않는다.

(ⅱ) **인덴트체(Indented Style)(英)**: 본문은 각 단락의 시작을 5자 정도 들여서 쓰기 시작한다. 앞머리 주소의 각 행 끝에 콤마를 찍고, 마지막 행 끝에 마침표를 찍으며, 인 날짜를 적은 맨끝에도 마침표를 찍는다. 인사말과 맺음말 뒤에도 마찬가지다.

(ⅲ) **절충체(Mixed Style)**: (ⅰ)과 (ⅱ)의 혼합식으로 본문은 인덴트체로 하고 인사말과 맺음말 끝에 마침표를 찍지만, 그 밖의 행 끝에는 모두(생략 부호 외에는) 구두점을 찍지 않는다.

편지의 각 요소
편지는 다음의 7가지 요소로 구분된다.

① **서두(Heading)**
발신자의 주소와 날짜를 쓴다. 주소는 상대편이 답장을 내는 경우 그대로 봉투에 적어 넣을 수 있도록 쓴다(주소의 기재 순서 ⇨ 봉투 쓰는 법 참조). 발신자의 성명은 여기에 적지 않고 ⑥의 서명란에 한다.
날짜 쓰는 방식은 미국식과 영국식이 다르다: (英) 15th October, 1997.

② **수신인명(Inside Address)** (⇨ ⑥ 서명)
수신인의 성명과 주소를 쓴다. 공식적인 편지에는 상대편의 경칭을 붙인다. 성명·주소는 봉투의 앞면과 같이 쓰는데 스스럼없는 사이의 편지에는 이 inside address는 보통 생략한다.

[경칭을 붙이는 법]
㉮ 특별한 직함이 없는 남성: 성씨 앞에 Mr.를 붙인다. 영국식에서는 성씨 뒤에 콤마를 찍고 Esq.를 붙인다.
[보기] (美) Mr. William Jones; (英) William Jones, Esq.

㉯ 특별한 직함이 없는 여성
○ 미혼 여성: 성씨 앞에 Miss를 붙인다.
[보기] Miss Elizabeth Bridge
○ 기혼 여성: 남편의 성씨 앞에 Mrs.를 붙인다.
[보기] Mrs. John White
또한 미혼·기혼을 불문하고 Ms.를 붙일 수 있는데 처음에는 Madam을 붙이는 것이 무난하다.

㉰ 특별한 직함이 있는 사람
○ 박사 칭호를 가진 사람: Dr.를 성명에 붙인다. 그러나 Mr.와 같이 쓰지는 않는다.
[보기] Dr. Henry Brown 또는 Dr. Brown

○ 대학교수 또는 부교수: Professor를 성명에 붙인다. Prof. 라고 생략하는 수도 있다. 이런 경칭을 쓸 때는 Dr. 이외는 다른 어떤 경칭도 붙이지 않는다.
[보기] Professor (Dr.) Robert Smith

③ **인사말(Salutation)**
우리나라 편지의 「근계(謹啓)」에 해당한다.

㉮ 친척이나 가까운 친구: **Dear Father [Mother, Uncle, Aunt], Dear Henry** 또한 친밀함을 나타내고자 할 때는 **My dear Henry, Dearest Jane** 등으로 한다. 또 my와 dear 앞에 붙이는 것은 (美)에서는 정식 표현이며, (英)에서는 애인이나 부부 간에 사용한다.

㉯ 일반인: **Dear Mr. Green, My dear Ms. McCall** 등. 다만 **Dear Mr. Martin Green**과 같이 full name을 쓰면 안된다.

㉰ 수신인의 이름을 밝히지 않을 경우[단수]: 영미 모두 남성에게는 **(Dear) Sir**, 여성에게는 **(Dear) Madam**이라고 하는데, 공식적인 경우에는 **Dear**를 생략한다. 또한 호칭 뒤에 콜론을 사용하는 것은 미국식이다.

㉱ 회사나 민간단체 [복수]: 남성에게는 (美) **Gentlemen**, (英) **Dear Sirs**, 여성에게는 (美) **Ladies**, (英) **Dear Mmes [Mesdames]**, 남녀 양쪽을 포함하는 단체에는 **Messrs.**를 붙인다.

㉹ 관청이나 공공단체 [복수]: **(美) Gentlemen**, [공식] **Sirs, (英) Sirs**.
④ **본문(Body (of the letter))**
　본문은 보통 몇 개의 단락으로 이루어진다. 「블록체」「인덴트체」「절충체」에서는 쓰기 시작하는 방식이 다르다(⇨ 편지지 쓰는 법 (ⅰ), (ⅱ), (ⅲ)).
　단락과 단락 사이는 1행을 비워 읽기 쉽게 하는 것이 좋다.
　내용에 대해 한 가지 주의할 것은, 영어 편지에서는 우리나라의 편지 쓰는 방식과 달라서 계절에 관한 인사나 건강의 안부 등은 생략하거나 편지 끝에 두며 바로 용건을 언급한다.
⑤ **맺음말(Complimentary Close)**
　우리나라 편지의 「경구(敬具)」에 해당한다.
　㉮ 친척간: **(美) Affectionately yours, (英) Yours affectionately / Your affectionate Son [Daughter, Nephew, Niece]**
　㉯ 친구간: **(美) Sincerely yours, (英) Yours sincerely** /⟨특히 친한 사이에⟩ **Ever yours, Yours (ever)** /⟨연인 사이에⟩ **Lovingly (yours)** /⟨해외의 친구 등⟩ **Your friend**
　㉰ 신분이 높은 사람에게: **Respectfully yours**
　㉱ 공용·상용: **Sincerely yours / Yours sincerely / Faithfully yours / Yours faithfully / Very truly yours**
⑥ **서명(Signature)**
　손으로 직접 쓰는데, 만약 타이프라이터나 워드프로세서로 썼다 하더라도 서명은 반드시 펜으로 써야 한다. 그리고 그 자필 서명 아래에 읽기 쉽도록 다시 타이프라이터나 워드프로세서로 성명을 기입해 둘 필요가 있다.
　또한 여성은 상대편이 답장을 쓸 때 편리하도록 미혼자는 Miss, 기혼자는 Mrs.를 덧붙인다. 예를 들면, (Miss) Elizabeth Bridge라고 서명하는데 그녀가 John White 씨와 결혼했다면 Elizabeth Bridge [또는 B.] White로 서명한 뒤 그 밑에 타이프라이터나 자필로 Mrs. John White라 덧붙인다.
⑦ **추신(Postscript)**
　추신이 필요한 경우는 P.S.라 적고 내용을 쓰며, 그 뒤에 발신자의 이름 등을 사인한다.

⟨편지지를 쓰는 세 가지 방식⟩

(ⅰ) 블록체　　　　　　　　　　(ⅱ) 인덴트체

7. 영문 편지 쓰는 법

(iii) 절충체

105-67, Kongduk-dong
Map'o-gu, Seoul
Korea

January 10, 1998

Mr. John White
2180 15 Street N. W.
Calgary, Alberta T2M 3X9
CANADA

Dear Mr. White

　　Thank you for your Christmas and New Year's card. I was so surprised to learn you got married last year. Congratulations! I wonder what your bride is like. How did you enjoy your honeymoon?
　　I hear you are continuing to teach back in Canada.
You are indeed a born teacher! I wish I could be a teacher like you in the future.
　　Nearly two years have passed since you taught us English at our school. I often think fondly of your lessons full of humor. I am now at college majoring in English literature.
　　If you visit Korea again in the future, I would very much like to see you.

　　Hoping you are always enjoying good health,

　　　　　　　　　　　　　　Sincerely yours,

　　　　　　　　　　　　　　Kim Dongsu

　　　　　　　　　　　　　　Kim Dong-su

P.S. The enclosed postage stamps are for you. I am told you are an avid collector of Korean stamps.

　　　　　　　　　　　　　　　　　　　　　K.D.S.

4. 봉투 쓰는 법: 편지를 쓰는 방식에 따라 각각 다르다.

　편지가 블록체일 경우에는 봉투도 「블록체」로, 편지가 인덴트체일 때는 봉투도 「인덴트체」로 통일하도록 한다. 그러나 편지지가 「절충체」일 때는 봉투는 「블록체」나 「인덴트체」나 상관없다. 다만 편지를 손으로 쓴 것이면 봉투도 손으로 쓰고, 편지를 타자한 것이면 봉투도 똑같이 맞추는 것이 좋다.

　아래의 그림에서 보는 바와 같이, 봉투의 겉 왼쪽 위에 발신자의 성명·주소와, 중앙 아래나 중앙보다 조금 위쪽의 하단에서부터 수신자의 성명·주소를 쓰는 것이 보통이다. 그러나 봉투의 앞면에 수신자의 성명·주소만을 쓰고 뒷면 위쪽에 발신자의 성명·주소를 쓰는 방식도 있다.

[발신자명 쓰는 법]
첫행　발신자 성명
2행　번지, 동명, 구명
3행　시·군명, 특별시명, 광역시명
4행　우편번호, 국명

[수신자명 쓰는 법]
첫행　경칭+성명
2행　번지, 동명
3행　시명, 주명, 우편번호
4행　국명

7. 영문 편지 쓰는 법

(블록체)

105-67 Kongduk-dong
Map'o-gu, Seoul
Korea

우표

AIR MAIL

Mr. John White
2180 15 Street N. W.
Calgary, Alberta T2M 3X9
CANADA

Personal

(인덴트체)

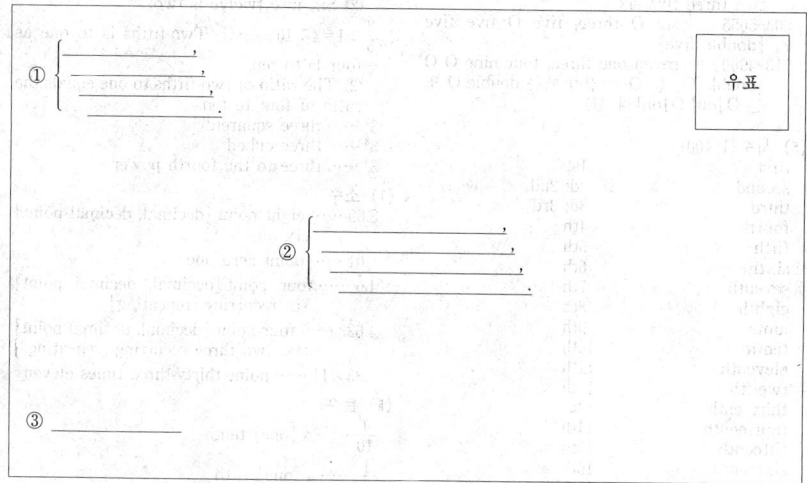

① 발신자명(Return Address)　　② 수신자명(Address)　　③ 봉투 표시

[봉투 표시의 예]
속달 (美) Special [(英) Express] Delivery / 등기 Registered / 지급 Urgent; Immediate / 친전 Private; Personal; Confidential / 회송 요망 Please forward; Please send on / 사진재중 Photo / 인쇄물재중 Printed Matters / 항공편 Air Mail / 선편 Surface [Sea] Mail

8. 수와 수식 읽는 법

(1) 연월일
1998년 4월 21일
 (美) April 21, 1998 (▶April (the) twenty-first nineteen ninety-eight 으로 읽음)
 4/21/98 (▶April twenty-one ninety-eight 으로 읽음)
 (英) 21(st) April 1998 (▶the twenty-first of April nineteen ninety-eight 으로 읽음)

(2) 연호(年号)
1900년 …… nineteen hundred
1998년 …… nineteen ninety-eight
856년 …… eight (hundred) fifty-six
1990년대 …… nineteen nineties

(3) 시각
9시 …… nine (o'clock); 〈오전〉 nine a.m.; 〈오후〉 nine p.m.
9시 15분 …… nine fifteen; a quarter past [after] nine
9시 30분 …… nine thirty; half past nine
9시 45분 …… nine forty-five; (a) quarter to [before] ten

(4) 전화 번호
02-717-2356 …… O [ou] two, seven one seven, two three five six
603-5055 …… six O three, five O five five [double five]
713-4900 …… seven one three, four nine O O [double O] (▶O가 겹칠 때는 double O 또는 O [ou] O [ou] 라 함)

(5) 서수(1-100)

first	1st
second	2d; 2nd
third	3d; 3rd
fourth	4th
fifth	5th
sixth	6th
seventh	7th
eighth	8th
ninth	9th
tenth	10th
eleventh	11th
twelfth	12th
thirteenth	13th
fourteenth	14th
fifteenth	15th
sixteenth	16th
seventeenth	17th
eighteenth	18th
nineteenth	19th
twentieth	20th
twenty-first	21st
twenty-second	22d; 22nd
twenty-third	23d; 23rd
twenty-fourth	24th
twenty-fifth	25th
twenty-sixth	26th
twenty-seventh	27th
twenty-eighth	28th
twenty-ninth	29th
thirtieth	30th
fortieth	40th
fiftieth	50th
sixtieth	60th
seventieth	70th
eightieth	80th
ninetieth	90th
hundredth	100th

(6) 수식
$3+8=11$ …… Three plus [and] eight equals [are] eleven.
$6-2=4$ …… ① Six minus two equals four.
 ② Six take away two leaves four.
 ③ Two from six leaves four.
$7 \times 7 = 49$ …… Seven times seven equals forty-nine.
$\frac{1}{10}[.1] \times 11 = 1\frac{1}{10}[1.1]$ …… One-tenth [Point one] times eleven equals one and one-tenth [one point one].
$12 \div 6 = 2$ …… ① Twelve divided by six equals [is] two.
 ② Six into twelve is two.
$\frac{2}{5} : 1 = 4 : 10$ …… ① Two-fifths is to one as four is to ten.
 ② The ratio of two-fifths to one equals the ratio of four to ten.
3^2 …… three square(d)
3^3 …… three cubed
3^4 …… three to the fourth power

(7) 소수
8.69 …… eight point [decimal, decimal point] six nine
.01 …… point zero one
$4.\dot{6}$ …… four point [decimal, decimal point] six recurring [repeating]
$4.6\dot{2}\dot{3}$ …… four point [decimal, decimal point] six, two three recurring [repeating]
$.33 \times 11$ …… point thirty-three times eleven

(8) 분수
$\frac{1}{10}$ …… a [one] tenth
$\frac{1}{5}$ …… a [one] fifth
$\frac{3}{4}$ …… three-quarters; three-fourths
$\frac{2}{3}$ …… two-thirds
$2\frac{5}{6}$ …… two and five-sixths
$\frac{45}{49}$ …… forty-five forty-ninths

9. 개수를 세는 법

「책 두 권」「종이 석 장」하는 우리말은 「명사+수사」의 형태를 하고 있지만 영어에서는 그 명사가 불가산명사면 「용기·단위·무게 등을 나타내는 명사+of+명사」로 하고 가산명사면 「수사+명사의 복수형」이 되어 각각 three sheets of paper, two books 하면 된다.

원칙적으로 불가산명사에 상당하는 물건에만 적당한 보조어를 쓰며 그 밖의 우리말의 「수를 셀 때 쓰는 말」을 따로 영어로 번역할 필요는 없다.

◆ …개 : 오렌지 세 개 three oranges
비누 다섯 개 five bars [cakes] of soap
◆ …건(件) : 사고 세 건 three accidents
신청 세 건 three applications
도난 세 건 three robberies
◆ …곡(曲) : 아리아 세 곡 three arias
바이올린곡 세 곡 three pieces of violin music
◆ …군데 : 오류 세 군데 three mistakes
파손 두 군데 two breaks
◆ …권 : 책 세 권 〈각각 다른〉 three books; 〈동일한〉 three copies
앨범 세 권 three albums
◆ …대(臺) : 버스 두 대 two buses
텔레비전 세 대 three TV sets
◆ …마리 : 고양이 두 마리 two cats
물고기 세 마리 three fish
◆ …명(名) : 학생 5명 five students
참가자 5명 five participants
◆ …발(發) : 탄알 두 발 two rounds [shots]
◆ …벌 : 오버코트 두 벌 two overcoats
학생복 세 벌 three school uniforms
바지 두 벌 two pairs of trousers
◆ …분(分) : 식사 3인분 three portions of food
3인분의 식사 food for three

◆ …량(輛) : 객차 3량 three passenger cars
10량 편성의 열차 a 10-car train
◆ …인(人) : 5인 가족 a family of five (people)
50인승 accomodation for fifty passengers
2인승 a two-seater; 〈자전거〉 a tandem
◆ …자루 : 연필 두 자루 two pencils
분필 두 자루 two pieces of chalk
◆ …잔 : 커피 두 잔 two cups of coffee; two coffees
우유 두 잔 two glasses of milk
◆ …장 : CD 두 장 two CDs
1000원권 두 장 two 1000-won bills
유리 석 장 three panes of glass
종이 두 장 two sheets of paper
◆ …점(點) : 의류 2점 two articles of clothing
가구 4점 four pieces of furniture
수채화 석 점 three watercolors
◆ …쪽 : 베이컨 두 쪽 two rashers of bacon
레몬 두 쪽 two slices of lemon
◆ …채 : 농가 세 채 three farmhouses
◆ …척 : 유조선 두 척 two tankers
보트 두 척 two boats
◆ …켤레 : 구두 두 켤레 two pairs of shoes
양말 세 켤레 three pairs of socks
◆ …통(通) : 편지 두 통 two letters
복사 세 통 three copies
◆ …필 : 말 두 필 two horses
소 열 필 ten head of cattle
◆ …호(戶) : 50호 〈집〉 fifty houses; 〈가족〉 fifty families; 〈세대〉 fifty households
◆ …회(回) : 결석 삼회 three absences
당선 이회 two elections
이회 공연 two performances

용례

▶ 會話 「애완동물을 기르십니까?」「네, 개 두 마리하고 고양이 두 마리를 길러요」 "Do you have pets?" "Yes, we keep two dogs and two cats."
▶ 나는 문방구에서 공책 다섯 권, 연필 세 자루, 그리고 지우개 한 개를 샀다 I bought five notebooks, three pencils, and an eraser at a stationary store.
▶ 會話 「이 근처에는 편의점이 몇 군데 있습니까?」「둘 있습니다」 "How many convenience stores are there in this neighborhood?" "There are two."
▶ 會話 「너는 구두가 몇 켤레나 있니?」「세 켤레 있어」 "How many pairs of shoes do you have?" "I have three."

▶ 아침 식사는 토스트 두 조각에 커피 한 잔으로 때웠다 I had only two slices of toast and a cup of coffee for breakfast.
▶ 지갑에는 만원 짜리 한 장, 100원 짜리 동전 두 개, 그리고 크레디트 카드 두 장이 들어 있었다 One 10,000-won bill, two 100-won coins, and two credit cards were in the wallet.
▶ 會話 「김선생한테서 전화가 두 통 왔습니다」「편지 온 것은 없구요?」 "There were two phone calls for you from Mr. Kim." "Are there any letters for me?"
▶ 會話 「설탕은 몇 스푼 넣을까요?」「두 스푼이요」 "How many tablespoonfuls [tablespoons] of sugar should I add?" "Two."

10. 국어의 로마자 표기법(초록)

교육부 1987. 10

1. 표기 일람

제1항 모음은 다음과 같이 적는다.
  단모음 : ㅏ ㅓ ㅗ ㅜ ㅡ ㅣ ㅐ ㅔ ㅚ   중모음 : ㅑ ㅕ ㅛ ㅠ ㅒ ㅖ ㅢ
         a ŏ o u ŭ i ae e oe   ya yŏ yo yu yae ye ŭi
                                          ㅘ ㅝ ㅙ ㅞ ㅟ
                                          wa wo wae we wi

(붙임) 장모음의 표기는 따로 하지 않는다.

제2항 자음은 다음과 같이 적는다.
  파열음 : ㄱ ㄲ ㅋ   파찰음 : ㅈ ㅉ ㅊ   비음 : ㅁ ㄴ ㅇ
         k, g kk k'   ch, j tch ch'   m n ng
         ㄷ ㄸ ㅌ   마찰음 : ㅅ ㅆ ㅎ   유음 : ㄹ
         t, d tt t'   s, sh ss h   r, l
         ㅂ ㅃ ㅍ
         p, b pp p'

(붙임 1) 'ㄱ, ㄷ, ㅂ, ㅈ'이 모음과 모음 사이, 또는 'ㄴ, ㄹ, ㅁ, ㅇ'과 모음 사이에서 유성음으로 소리날 때에는 각각 'g, d, b, j'로 적고 이외에는 각각 'k, t, p, ch'로 적는다.
  [보기] 가구 kagu 갈비 kalbi 담배 tambae 바둑 paduk 제주 Cheju

(붙임 2) 'ㅅ'은 '시'의 경우에 'sh'로 그 외에는 's'로 적는다.
  [보기] 부산 Pusan   상표 sangp'yo   시루 shiru
        신안 Shinan   신촌 Shinch'on   황소 hwangso

(붙임 3) 'ㄹ'은 모음 앞에서는 'r'로 적고 자음 앞이나 낱말의 끝에서는 'l'로, 'ㄹㄹ'은 'll'로 적는다.
  [보기] 물건 mulgŏn   발 pal   사랑 sarang   진달래 chindallae

2. 표기상의 유의점

제1항 음운 변화가 일어날 때에는 변화의 결과에 따라 다음과 같이 적는다.
  1. 자음 사이에서 동화 작용이 일어나는 경우
     [보기] 독립 tongnip   심리 shimni   압력 amnyŏk
  2. 'ㄴ, ㄹ'이 덧나는 경우
     [보기] 가랑잎 karangnip   낯일 nannil   담요 tamnyo
  3. 구개음화가 되는 경우
     [보기] 같이 kach'i   굳이 kuji   해돋이 haedoji
  4. 'ㄱ, ㄷ, ㅂ, ㅈ'이 'ㅎ'과 어울려 나는 경우
     [보기] 국화 kuk'wa   낳다 nat'a   밟히다 palp'ida

(붙임) 형태소가 결합할 때 나타나는 된소리는 따로 표기하지 않는다.
       냇가 naetka   사건 sakŏn   장기(長技) changki

제2항 발음상 혼동의 우려가 있을 때나, 기타 분절의 필요가 있을 때는 '-'(짧은줄표)를 써서 따로 적는다.
  [보기] 잔기(殘期) chan-gi   장이 chang-i

제3항 고유 명사는 첫소리를 대문자로 적는다.
  [보기] 대구 Taegu   세종 Sejong   인천 Inch'ŏn

제4항 인명은 성과 이름의 순서로 쓰되 띄어 쓰고, 이름 사이에는 '-'(짧은줄표)를 넣는다. 다만, 한자식의 이름이 아닌 경우에는 '-'를 생략할 수 있다.
  [보기] 김 정호 Kim Chŏng-ho   정 마리아 Chŏng Maria   한 하나 Han Hana

제5항 '도, 시, 군, 구, 읍, 면, 리, 동'의 행정 구역 단위와 '가'는 각각 'do, shi, gun, gu, ŭp, myŏn, ri, dong, ga'로 적고, 그 앞에는 '-'(짧은줄표)를 넣는다.
  [보기] 당산동 Tangsan-dong   도봉구 Tobong-gu   신창읍 Shinch'ang-ŭp
        의정부시 Ŭijŏngbu-shi   인왕리 Inwang-ri   제주도 Cheju-do
        종로 2가 Chongno 2-ga   충내면 Chunae-myŏn   파주군 P'aju-gun

제6항 자연 지물명, 문화재명, 인공 축조물명은 '-'(짧은줄표) 없이 붙여 쓴다.
  [보기] 금강   Kŭmgang   남산   Namsan
        독도   Tokto   속리산 Songnisan

11. 한국 행정 구역 로마자 표기

교육부 발행 편수 자료 1997. 8. 현재

지 명	로마자 표기	지 명	로마자 표기
대한민국(大韓民國)	TAEHANMIN-GUK	중구(中區)	Chung-gu
서울특별시(서울特別市)	Seoul-t'ŭkpyŏlshi	동구(東區)	Tong-gu
종로구(鐘路區)	Chongno-gu	남구(南區)	Nam-gu
중구(中區)	Chung-gu	부평구(富平區)	Pup'yŏng-gu
용산구(龍山區)	Yongsan-gu	계양구(桂陽區)	Kyeyang-gu
성동구(城東區)	Sŏngdong-gu	서구(西區)	Sŏ-gu
동대문구(東大門區)	Tongdaemun-gu	연수구(延壽區)	Yŏnsu-gu
중랑구(中浪區)	Chungnang-gu	강화군(江華郡)	Kangwha-gun
성북구(城北區)	Sŏngbuk-gu	옹진군(甕津郡)	Ongjin-gun
도봉구(道峰區)	Tobong-gu	**광주광역시(光州廣域市)**	Kwangju-kwangyŏkshi
노원구(蘆原區)	Nowon-gu	광산구(光山區)	Kwangsan-gu
은평구(恩平區)	Ŭnp'yŏng-gu	동구(東區)	Tong-gu
서대문구(西大門區)	Sŏdaemun-gu	서구(西區)	Sŏ-gu
마포구(麻浦區)	Map'o-gu	남구(南區)	Nam-gu
강서구(江西區)	Kangsŏ-gu	북구(北區)	Puk-gu
양천구(陽川區)	Yangch'ŏn-gu	**대전광역시(大田廣域市)**	Taejŏn-kwangyŏkshi
구로구(九老區)	Kuro-gu	유성구(儒城區)	Yusŏng-gu
영등포구(永登浦區)	Yŏngdŭngp'o-gu	대덕구(大德區)	Taedŏk-gu
동작구(銅雀區)	Tongjak-gu	동구(東區)	Tong-gu
관악구(冠岳區)	Kwanak-gu	중구(中區)	Chung-gu
강남구(江南區)	Kangnam-gu	서구(西區)	Sŏ-gu
서초구(瑞草區)	Sŏch'o-gu	**울산광역시(蔚山廣域市)**	Ulsan-kwangyŏkshi
강동구(江東區)	Kangdong-gu	중구(中區)	Chung-gu
송파구(松坡區)	Songp'a-gu	동구(東區)	Tong-gu
광진구(廣津區)	Kwangjin-gu	남구(南區)	Nam-gu
강북구(江北區)	Kangpuk-gu	북구(北區)	Puk-gu
금천구(衿川區)	Kŭmch'ŏn-gu	울주군(蔚州郡)	Ulchu-gun
부산광역시(釜山廣域市)	Pusan-kwangyŏkshi	**경기도(京畿道)**	Kyŏnggi-do
중구(中區)	Chung-gu	수원시(水原市)	Suwon-shi
동구(東區)	Dong-gu	성남시(城南市)	Sŏngnam-shi
서구(西區)	Sŏ-gu	의정부시(議政府市)	Ŭijŏngbu-shi
남구(南區)	Nam-gu	안양시(安養市)	Anyang-shi
북구(北區)	Puk-gu	부천시(富川市)	Puch'ŏn-shi
영도구(影島區)	Yŏungdo-gu	광명시(光明市)	Kwangmyŏng-shi
부산진구(釜山鎭區)	Pusanjin-gu	고양시(高陽市)	Koyang-shi
동래구(東萊區)	Tongnae-gu	동두천시(東豆川市)	Tongduch'ŏn-shi
해운대구(海雲臺區)	Haeundae-gu	안산시(安山市)	Ansan-shi
금정구(金井區)	Kŭmjŏng-gu	과천시(果川市)	Kwach'ŏn-shi
사하구(沙下區)	Saha-gu	평택시(平澤市)	P'yŏngt'aek-shi
강서구(江西區)	Kangsŏ-gu	남양주시(南楊州市)	Namyangju-shi
연제구(蓮堤區)	Yŏnje-gu	와부읍(瓦阜邑)	Wabu-ŭp
수영구(水營區)	Suyŏng-gu	진접읍(榛接邑)	Chinjŏp-ŭp
사상구(沙上區)	Sasang-gu	오산시(烏山市)	Osan-shi
기장군(機張郡)	Kijang-gun	시흥시(始興市)	Shihŭng-shi
대구광역시(大邱廣域市)	Taegu-kwangyŏkshi	군포시(軍浦市)	Kunp'o-shi
달서구(達西區)	Talsŏ-gu	의왕시(儀旺市)	Ŭiwang-shi
수성구(壽城區)	Susŏng-gu	구리시(九里市)	Kuri-shi
중구(中區)	Chung-gu	하남시(河南市)	Hanam-shi
동구(東區)	Tong-gu	파주시(坡州市)	P'aju-shi
서구(西區)	Sŏ-gu	파주읍(坡州邑)	P'aju-ŭp
남구(南區)	Nam-gu	법원읍(法院邑)	Pŏpwon-ŭp
북구(北區)	Puk-gu	문산읍(汶山邑)	Munsan-ŭp
달성군(達城郡)	Talsŏng-gun	이천시(利川市)	Ich'ŏn-shi
인천광역시(仁川廣域市)	Inch'ŏn-kwangyŏkshi	장호원읍(長湖院邑)	Changhowon-ŭp
남동구(南東區)	Namdong-gu	부발읍(夫鉢邑)	Pubal-ŭp

11. 한국 행정 구역 로마자 표기

지 명	로마자 표기	지 명	로마자 표기
용인시(龍仁市)	Yong-in-shi	연무읍(鍊武邑)	Yŏnmu-ŭp
기흥읍(器興邑)	Kihŭng-ŭp	금산군(錦山郡)	Kŭmsan-gun
수지읍(水枝邑)	Suji-ŭp	연기군(燕岐郡)	Yŏn-gi-gun
양주군(楊州郡)	Yangju-gun	조치원읍(鳥致院邑)	Choch'iwon-ŭp
여주군(驪州郡)	Yŏju-gun	공주군(公州郡)	Kongju-gun
화성군(華城郡)	Hwasŏng-gun	부여군(扶餘郡)	Puyŏ-gun
태안읍(台安邑)	T'aean-ŭp	서천군(舒川郡)	Sŏch'ŏn-gun
광주군(廣州郡)	Kwangju-gun	장항읍(長項邑)	Changhang-ŭp
연천군(蓮川郡)	Yŏnch'ŏn-gun	청양군(青陽郡)	Ch'ŏng-yang-gun
전곡읍(全谷邑)	Chŏn-gok-ŭp	홍성군(洪城郡)	Hongsŏng-gun
포천군(抱川郡)	P'och'ŏn-gun	광천읍(廣川邑)	Kwangch'ŏn-ŭp
가평군(加平郡)	Kap'yŏng-gun	예산군(禮山郡)	Yesan-gun
양평군(楊平郡)	Yangp'yŏng-gun	삽교읍(揷橋邑)	Sapkyo-ŭp
안성군(安城郡)	Ansŏng-gun	태안군(泰安郡)	Taean-gun
김포시(金浦市)	Kimp'o-shi	안면읍(安眠邑)	Anmyŏn-ŭp
강원도(江原道)	Kang-won-do	당진군(唐津郡)	Tangjin-gun
춘천시(春川市)	Ch'unch'ŏn-shi	합덕읍(合德邑)	Haptŏk-ŭp
원주시(原州市)	Wonju-shi	**전라북도(全羅北道)**	Chŏllabuk-do
강릉시(江陵市)	Kangnŭng-shi	전주시(全州市)	Chŏnju-shi
주문진읍(注文津邑)	Chumunjin-ŭp	군산시(群山市)	Kunsan-shi
동해시(東海市)	Tonghae-shi	옥구읍(沃溝邑)	Okku-ŭp
태백시(太白市)	T'aebaek-shi	익산시(益山市)	Iksan-shi
속초시(束草市)	Sokch'o-shi	함열읍(咸悅邑)	Hamyŏl-ŭp
삼척군(三陟郡)	Samch'ŏk-shi	정읍시(井邑市)	Chŏng-ŭp-shi
홍천군(洪川郡)	Hongch'ŏn-gun	신태인읍(新泰仁邑)	Shint'aein-ŭp
횡성군(横城郡)	Hoengsŏng-gun	남원시(南原市)	Namwon-shi
영월군(寧越郡)	Yŏng-wol-gun	김제시(金提市)	Kimje-shi
상동읍(上東邑)	Sangdong-ŭp	완주군(完州郡)	Wanju-gun
평창군(平昌郡)	P'yŏngch'ang-gun	삼례읍(參禮邑)	Samnye-ŭp
정선군(旌善郡)	Chŏngsŏn-gun	봉동읍(鳳東邑)	Pongdong-ŭp
사북읍(舍北邑)	Sabuk-ŭp	진안군(鎭安郡)	Chinan-gun
신동읍(新東邑)	Shindong-ŭp	무주군(茂朱郡)	Muju-gun
고한읍(古汗邑)	Kohan-ŭp	장수군(長水郡)	Changsu-gun
철원군(鐵原郡)	Ch'ŏrwon-gun	임실군(任實郡)	Imshil-gun
김화읍(金化邑)	Kimhwa-ŭp	순창군(淳昌郡)	Sunch'ang-gun
갈말읍(葛末邑)	Kalmal-ŭp	고창군(高敞郡)	Koch'ang-gun
동송읍(東松邑)	Tongsong-ŭp	부안군(扶安郡)	Puan-gun
화천군(華川郡)	Hwach'ŏn-gun	**전라남도(全羅南道)**	Chŏllanam-do
양구군(楊口郡)	Yanggu-gun	목포시(木浦市)	Mokp'o-shi
인제군(麟蹄郡)	Inje-gun	여수시(麗水市)	Yŏsu-shi
고성군(高城郡)	Kosŏng-gun	순천시(順天市)	Sunch'ŏn-shi
간성읍(杆城邑)	Kansŏng-ŭp	나주시(羅州市)	Naju-shi
거진읍(巨津邑)	Kŏjin-ŭp	여천시(麗川市)	Yŏch'ŏn-shi
양양군(襄陽郡)	Yang-yang-gun	광양시(光陽市)	Kwang-yang-shi
충청북도(忠清北道)	Ch'ungch'ŏngbuk-do	담양군(潭陽郡)	Tamyang-gun
청주시(清州市)	Ch'ŏngju-shi	곡성군(谷城郡)	Koksŏng-gun
충주시(忠州市)	Ch'ungju-shi	구례군(求禮郡)	Kurye-gun
제천시(堤川市)	Chech'ŏn-shi	여천군(麗川郡)	Yŏch'ŏn-gun
청원군(清原郡)	Ch'ŏng-won-gun	돌산읍(突山邑)	Tolsan-ŭp
보은군(報恩郡)	Poŭn-gun	고흥군(高興郡)	Kohŭng-gun
옥천군(沃川郡)	Okch'ŏn-gun	도양읍(道陽邑)	Toyang-ŭp
영동군(永同郡)	Yŏngdong-gun	보성군(寶城郡)	Posŏng-gun
진천군(鎭川郡)	Chinch'ŏn-gun	벌교읍(筏橋邑)	Pŏlgyo-ŭp
괴산군(槐山郡)	Koesan-gun	화순군(和順郡)	Hwasun-gun
증평읍(曾坪邑)	Chŭngp'yŏng-ŭp	장흥군(長興郡)	Changhŭng-gun
음성군(陰城郡)	Ŭmsŏng-gun	관산읍(冠山邑)	Kwansan-ŭp
금왕읍(金旺邑)	Kŭmwang-ŭp	대덕읍(大德邑)	Taedŏk-ŭp
단양군(丹陽郡)	Tanyang-gun	강진군(康津郡)	Kangjin-gun
매포읍(梅浦邑)	Maep'o-ŭp	해남군(海南郡)	Haenam-gun
충청남도(忠清南道)	Ch'ungch'ŏngnam-do	영암군(靈岩郡)	Yŏng-am-gun
천안시(天安市)	Ch'ŏnan-shi	무안군(務安郡)	Muan-gun
성환읍(成歡邑)	Sŏnghwan-ŭp	일로읍(一老邑)	Illo-ŭp
성거읍(聖居邑)	Sŏnggŏ-ŭp	함평군(咸平郡)	Hamp'yŏng-gun
공주시(公州市)	Kongju-shi	영광군(靈光郡)	Yŏnggwang-gun
보령시(保寧市)	Poryŏng-shi	백수읍(白岫邑)	Paeksu-ŭp
대천시(大川市)	Taech'ŏn-shi	홍농읍(弘農邑)	Hongnong-ŭp
아산시(牙山市)	Asan-shi	장성군(長城郡)	Changsŏng-gun
서산시(瑞山市)	Sŏsan-shi	완도군(莞島郡)	Wando-gun
논산시(論山市)	Nonsan-shi	금일읍(金日邑)	Kŭmil-ŭp
강경읍(江景邑)	Kanggyŏng-ŭp	진도군(珍島郡)	Chindo-gun

11. 한국 행정 구역 로마자 표기

지 명	로마자 표기	지 명	로마자 표기
신안군(新安郡)	Shinan-gun	평해읍(平海邑)	P'yŏnghae-ŭp
지도읍(智島邑)	Chido-ŭp	울릉군(鬱陵郡)	Ullŭng-gun
경상북도(慶尙北道)	**Kyŏngsangbuk-do**	**경상남도(慶尙南道)**	**Kyŏngsangnam-do**
포항시(浦項市)	P'ohang-shi	마산시(馬山市)	Masan-shi
구룡포읍(九龍浦邑)	Kuryongp'o-ŭp	진주시(晋州市)	Chinju-shi
흥해읍(興海邑)	Hŭnghae-ŭp	창원시(昌原市)	Ch'ang-won-shi
연일읍(延日邑)	Yŏnil-ŭp	진해시(鎭海市)	Chinhae-shi
오천읍(烏川邑)	Och'ŏn-ŭp	통영시(統營市)	T'ong-yŏng-shi
경주시(慶州市)	Kyŏngju-shi	사천시(泗川市)	Sach'ŏn-shi
감포읍(甘浦邑)	Kamp'o-ŭp	김해시(金海市)	Kimhae-shi
안강읍(安康邑)	An-gang-ŭp	밀양시(密陽市)	Miryang-shi
건천읍(乾川邑)	Kŏnch'ŏn-ŭp	삼랑진읍(三浪津邑)	Samnangjin-ŭp
외동읍(外東邑)	Oedong-ŭp	하남읍(下南邑)	Hanam-ŭp
김천시(金泉市)	Kimch'ŏn-shi	양산시(梁山市)	Yangsan-shi
안동시(安東市)	Andong-shi	거제시(巨濟市)	Kŏje-shi
구미시(龜尾市)	Kumi-shi	신현읍(新縣邑)	Shinhyŏn-ŭp
영주시(榮州市)	Yŏngju-shi	의령군(宜寧郡)	Ŭiryŏng-gun
풍기읍(豊基邑)	P'unggi-ŭp	함안군(咸安郡)	Haman-gun
영천시(永川市)	Yŏngch'ŏn-shi	가야읍(伽倻邑)	Kaya-ŭp
상주시(尙州市)	Sangju-shi	창녕군(昌寧郡)	Ch'angnyŏng-gun
함창읍(咸昌邑)	Hamch'ang-ŭp	남지읍(南旨邑)	Namji-ŭp
문경시(聞慶市)	Mun-gyŏng-shi	고성군(固城郡)	Kosŏng-gun
가은읍(加恩邑)	Kaŭn-ŭp	남해군(南海郡)	Namhae-gun
경산시(慶山市)	Kyŏngsan-shi	하동군(河東郡)	Hadong-gun
하양읍(河陽邑)	Hayang-ŭp	산청군(山淸郡)	Sanch'ŏng-gun
군위군(軍威郡)	Kunwi-gun	함양군(咸陽郡)	Hamyang-gun
의성군(義城郡)	Ŭisŏng-gun	거창군(居昌郡)	Kŏch'ang-gun
청송군(靑松郡)	Ch'ŏngsong-gun	합천군(陜川郡)	Hapch'ŏn-gun
영양군(英陽郡)	Yŏng-yang-gun	**제주도(濟州道)**	**Cheju-do**
영덕군(盈德郡)	Yŏngdŏk-gun	제주시(濟州市)	Cheju-shi
청도군(淸道郡)	Ch'ŏngdo-gun	서귀포시(西歸浦市)	Sŏgwip'o-shi
화양읍(華陽邑)	Hwayang-ŭp	북제주군(北濟州郡)	Pukcheju-gun
고령군(高靈郡)	Koryŏng-gun	한림읍(翰林邑)	Hallim-ŭp
성주군(星州郡)	Sŏngju-gun	애월읍(涯月邑)	Aewol-ŭp
칠곡군(漆谷郡)	Ch'ilgok-gun	구좌읍(舊左邑)	Kujwa-ŭp
구좌읍(舊左邑)	Kujwa-ŭp	조천읍(朝天邑)	Choch'ŏn-ŭp
왜관읍(倭館邑)	Waegwan-ŭp	남제주군(南濟州郡)	Namjeju-gun
예천군(醴泉郡)	Yech'ŏn-gun	대정읍(大靜邑)	Taejŏng-ŭp
봉화군(奉化郡)	Ponghwa-gun	남원읍(南原邑)	Namwon-ŭp
울진군(蔚珍郡)	Ulchin-gun	성산읍(城山邑)	Sŏngsan-ŭp

〈지방 행정 단위의 영어 표기〉

내무부 1995. 2

지방 행정 단위명	사용 구분	영어 표기	비 고
서울 특별시	주소로 사용시	Seoul City (서울 시티)	
	기관 명칭	Seoul Metropolitan City (서울 메트로폴리탄 시티)	
○○광역시	주소로 사용시	○○ City (○○ 시티)	
	기관 명칭	○○ Metropolitan City (○○ 메트로폴리탄 시티)	
○○도		○○ Province (○○ 프라빈스)	
○○시		○○ City (○○ 시티)	
○○군		○○ County (○○ 카운티)	
○○구	주소로 사용시 ※ 특별시·광역시 구별없이	○○ District (○○ 디스트릭트)	
	기관 명칭 。 자치구 。 일반구	○○ Metropolitan District ○○ District	

12. 미·영어 중요 어구 비교

American	Korean	English
\multicolumn{3}{c}{정치 관계(POLITICS)}		

American	Korean	English
Administration	정부	Government
fusion administration	연립 내각	coalition government
Secretary	장관	Minister
cabinet officer; cabinet member	각료	cabinet minister; member of the cabinet
State Department	(美) 국무성((英) 외무성)	Foreign Office
Congress	국회	Parliament
cloakroom	의원 대기실	lobby
passage of a bill	의안 통과	passing of a bill
representative from...	…선출 의원	member for...
ticket	공천 후보자 명부	list of candidates
candidacy	입후보	candidature
run for Congress	의원에 입후보하다	stand for Parliament
special election	보궐 선거	by-election
majority	절대 다수	clear majority
campaign	선거 운동	canvass
canvasser	투표 검표원	scrutineer
party platform	정당 강령	party programme
party fusion	정당 연합	party coalition
officeholder	공무원	civil servant
local taxes	지방세	local rates

재판·경찰·범죄·소방 관계(POLICE, etc.)

American	Korean	English
judiciary	사법권	judicature
district attorney	검사	public prosecutor
venireman	배심원	juryman
trial lawyer	변호사	advocate
stenographer	(법정의) 속기사	shorthand writer
take the (witness) stand	증인으로 서다	enter the witness box
jail	교도소	gaol [dʒéil]
prison guard	교도관	warder; prison officer
the warden of the prison	교도소장	the governor of the prison
station house	경찰서	police station
chief of police	경찰서장	chief constable
investigator	형사	detective
patrolman	경찰관; 순경	constable
policeman's billy	경찰봉	policeman's truncheon
(口) calaboose	유치장	lockup
fire department	소방서	fire(-brigade) station
fire line	소방 비상선	fire cordon
workhouse	감화원	house of correction
almshouse	양로원	workhouse
holdup	노상 강도·홀드업	highway robbery

12. 미·영어 중요 어구 비교

American	Korean	English
holdup man	노상 강도(사람)	highwayman
porch climber	좀도둑	cat burglar
《俗》 firebug	방화범	incendiary
a passkey	곁쇠	a skeleton key

교통 관계 (TRANSPORTATION)

American	Korean	English
railroad	철도	railway
elevated railroad; L	고가철도	overhead railway
subway	지하철	tube; underground
track; tracks	선로	lines; metals
jump the track; leave the track	탈선하다	run off the line; jump the metals
tie; crosstie	침목	sleeper
accommodation train	완행[보통] 열차	slow train
railroad depot	정거장, 역	railway station
track	플랫폼	platform
terminal	종착역	terminus
station agent	역장	station master
Does this ticket allow me to stop over [off]?	이 차표로 도중 하차가 됩니까?	Does this ticket allow me to break journey?
locomotive	기관차	engine
engineer	기관사	engine driver; driver
freight train	화물 열차	goods train
freight car	화차	goods waggon; goods van
passenger car	객차	passenger coach
diner	식당차	dining carriage
boxcar	유개 화차	box waggon
conductor	열차 차장	guard
gate tender	건널목지기	gatekeeper
tracklayer	선로공	platelayer
stoplight	정지 신호	red light
one-way ticket	편도 차표	single ticket
round-trip ticket	왕복 차표	return ticket
commutation ticket	회수권; 정기 승차권	season ticket
ticket office	출찰소, 매표소	booking office
ticket agent	출찰계원, 매표원	booking clerk
bureau of information; information bureau	안내소	inquiry office
baggage room; checkroom	수화물 임시 보관소	cloakroom
baggage	수화물	luggage
check a baggage	수화물을 물표를 받고 부치다	register a luggage
redcap	수화물 운반인	station porter
newsstand	신문·잡지 판매대	bookstall
schedule	시간표	timetable
catch a train	기차 시간에 대다	be in time for a train
transfer	갈아타다	change cars
airplane	비행기	aeroplane
airdrome	비행장	aerodrome
automobile; auto	자동차	motorcar; car
truck	화물 자동차	lorry

American	Korean	English
sightseeing bus	관광 버스	char-à-banc
sprinkling wagon	살수차	water cart
parking lot	주차장	car park
streetcar	시가 전차	tramcar
sidewalk	보도 ; 인도	footpath; pavement
main street	번화가	high street
pavement	차도 ; 포장 도로	roadway
underpass	지하도	subway

우정 관계 (POSTAL SERVICES)

American	Korean	English
(by) mail	우편(으로)	(by) post
domestic mail	국내 우편물	inland mail
postal card	관제 엽서	postcard
registry fee	등기료	registration fee
special delivery	속달 우편	express delivery
mail clerk	우체국 직원	postal clerk
mail carrier; mailman	우편 집배원	postman
mailbox	우체통	pillar-box; letter box
package	소포	parcel
telegrapher	전신 기사	telegraphist
telephone book	전화 번호부	telephone directory
central office	전화 교환국	exchange
telephone booth	공중 전화	telephone box
long distance call	장거리 전화	trunk call
Line's busy!	〔電話〕통화중	Number's engaged!
radio	라디오	wireless

저널리즘 관계 (JOURNALISM)

American	Korean	English
printery	인쇄소	printing office
editorial	논설, 사설	leader; leading article
newspaperman	신문 기자	pressman; journalist
editorial writer	논설 위원	leader writer
copyreader	(신문·잡지 따위의) 부주필	subeditor
paragrapher	탐방 기자	paragraphist
beat	특종 기사	scoop
newsagent	신문·잡지 판매인	newsdealer
walkout	동맹 파업	strike
sit-down strike	연좌 파업	stay-in strike

학교 관계 (SCHOOL)

American	Korean	English
faculty	(대학의) 교직원	college staff
college student	대학생	undergraduate
freshman	대학 1년생	first-year man
sophomore	대학 2년생	second-year man
junior	대학 3년생	third-year man
senior	대학 4년생	fourth-year man
major in	…을 전공하다	specialize in
alumnus	졸업생	graduate; old boys

12. 미·영어 중요 어구 비교

American	Korean	English
alumni association	동창회	graduates' association
commencement	졸업식	speech day
sheepskin	졸업 증서	diploma
co-ed	(남녀 공학의) 여학생	woman student
schoolma'am	여교사	schoolmistress
public school	공립 학교	council school
private school	사립 학교	public school
required subject	필수 과목	compulsory subject
elective subject	선택 과목	optional subject
recitation room	교실	classroom
auditorium	강당	assembly hall; hall
campus	교정	school grounds
intermission	휴식 시간	break
dormitory	기숙사	hall of residence; hostel
correspondence course	통신 교육	postal course

가정용품·가구·의복 관계 (FURNITURE, etc.)

American	Korean	English
pocketbook	지갑	purse
notion counter	잡화 상인	haberdasher
flashlight	회중 전등	electric torch
can	깡통	tin
kettle	주전자	teakettle
pitcher	물주전자	jug
kettle	스튜 냄비	stewpan
aluminum	알루미늄	aluminium
hardware store	철물점	ironmonger's
phonograph	축음기	gramophone
penpoint	펜촉	nib
low shoes; oxfords	단화	shoes
rubbers	덧신	galoshes
shoes	편상화	boots
baby carriage	유모차	perambulator; pram
wastebasket	휴지통	wastepaper basket
trash	쓰레기	rubbish
ash can; garbage can	쓰레기통	dustbin
yard	뜰	garden
landscape architect	정원사	landscape gardener
house for rent	셋집	house to let
waitress; chambermaid	가정부	parlourmaid; housemaid
furnishings	가구	upholstery
bureau; dresser	화장대	dressing table
porch; piazza	베란다	verandah
window shades	(창의) 차양	(window) blinds
stairway	계단	staircase
living room	거실	sitting room
parlor	응접실	drawing room
washroom; toilet	화장실	lavatory; closet
washbowl	세면기	washhand basin

12. 미·영어 중요 어구 비교

American	Korean	English
derby (hat)	중산모	bowler (hat)
business suit	신사복	lounge suit
Prince Albert	프록 코트(예복)	frock coat
tuxedo (coat)	턱시도(야외용 예복)	dinner jacket
vest	조끼	waistcoat
stickpin	넥타이핀	breastpin
suspenders	바지 멜빵	braces
garters	양말 대님	suspenders
breastpin	브로치	brooch
raincoat	레인코트	mackintosh; waterproof
Costumes to rent	임대 의상	Costumes on hire
tailor shop	양복점	tailor's (shop)
store clothes	기성복	ready-made clothes
calico	사라사(날염)	print
undershirt	내의	vest; singlet

음식물 관계 (FOOD, etc.)

American	Korean	English
candy store	과자 가게	sweetshop
candy	사탕 과자	sweets
cracker	비스킷	biscuit
bakery	빵 과자 제조[판매]점	baker's shop
ice cream	아이스크림	ice
cigar store	담배 가게	tobacconist's (shop)
fruit (seller[dealer])	과일 가게	fruiterer
dessert; desserts	디저트	sweet course; sweets
grocer shop; grocery	식료품점	grocer's (shop)
grain	곡물	corn
cereal	오트밀	porridge
corn	옥수수	maize; Indian corn
peanuts	땅콩	monkey-nuts; earthnuts

백화점·호텔·회사 관계 (BUSINESS, etc.)

American	Korean	English
department store	백화점	stores
floorwalker	매장 감독	shopwalker
installment plan	분할 지급(월부)	hire purchase (system)
chain store	연쇄점	multiple shop
store	가게	shop
clerk	점원	shop assistant
storekeeper	가게 주인	shopkeeper
first floor	1층	ground floor
second floor	2층	first floor
unloading sale	재고 정리 대매출	clearance sale
red	적자; 결손; 부채	loss
salesclerk	판매원	shop assistant
traveling salesman	외판원, 세일즈맨	commercial traveller
white-collar worker	사무원	blackcoat worker
employment bureau	직업 소개소	registry office
billboard	게시판	hoarding

American	Korean	English
laborer	인부	navvy
scrubwoman	잡역부	charwoman
bootblack	구두닦이(사람)	shoeblack
board of trade	상공 회의소	chamber of commerce
stock	주식	share
stockholder	주주	shareholder
(business) corporation	(주식)회사	(business) company
stock market	증권 거래소	stock exchange
president of a corporation	사장	chairman of a company
member of the directory	중역	member of the directorate
bill	지폐; 어음	note
legal holiday; public holiday	휴일	bank holiday
elevator	엘리베이터	lift
bellboy	(호텔의) 보이	hotel page
janitor	문지기, 수위	porter
toilet	화장실	lavatory
apartment	아파트	flat
janitor	관리인	caretaker

스포츠・사교・오락 관계(SPORTS, etc.)

American	Korean	English
sporting goods	운동용구	sports requisites
hunting	수렵	shooting
boxer	권투 선수	bruiser
movies; cinema	영화	pictures; cinema
headliner	스타	star; topliner
opening night	공연 첫날; 첫 공연	first night
intermission	휴식 시간; 막간	interval; break
dance hall	댄스 홀	dancing saloon
teeterboard	시소판	seesaw
carrousel	회전 목마	merry-go-round
sled	썰매	sledge

시간을 나타내는 법(TIME)

American	Korean	English
Have you the time?	몇시나 됐을까요.	Can you tell me the time?
a quarter of eight	8시 15분전	a quarter to eight
half after eight; eight-thirty	8시 30분	half past eight
a half hour later	반시간 뒤	half an hour later
two weeks	2주간	a fortnight
in weeks	수주간	for weeks
New Year's	새해	New Year's Day; New Year
the first of the week	주초쯤	early in the week
I shall return around the last of the week.	주말쯤에 돌아옵니다.	I shall return about the end of the week.
a week from Tuesday	내주 화요일	Tuesday week
November 5 through December 4	11월 5일부터 12월 4일까지	from November 5 to December 4 inclusive

그 외 (OTHERS)

American	Korean	English
weather bureau	기상청	meteorological office
fall	가을	autumn
daylight saving time	서머 타임	summer time
sickness	병	illness
druggist	약사	chemist
drugstore	약국	chemist's (shop)
funeral director	장의사	undertaker
barber shop	이발소	barber's (shop)
barn	마구간	stable
chicken yard	양계장	fowl-run
rooster	수탉	cock
bug	곤충	insect
family name; last name	성	surname
calling card	명함	visiting card
a trillion	1조	a billion
a billion	10억	a thousand millions
lumber	재목	timber
rod; gun	권총	pistol; revolver
fifty-fifty	반반의	half-and-half
O.K.	좋다	all right

13. 한국 전통 식품의 영어 표기

농림부 1994. 12

부류	식품명	영어 표기	비 고
김치류	깍두기김치	Kimchi (Radish roots kimchi)	김치류는 Kimchi로 통일 표기하고 ( ) 안에 품목명을 영어로 병기
	나박김치	Kimchi (Watery kimchi)	
	동치미김치	Kimchi (Watery radish kimchi)	
	배추김치	Kimchi (Cabbage kimchi)	
	무청김치	Kimchi (Radish leaf kimchi)	
	유채김치	Kimchi (Rape leaf kimchi)	
	갓잎김치	Kimchi (Mustard leaf kimchi)	
	갓줄기김치	Kimchi (Mustard stem kimchi)	
장류	고추장	Korean hot pepper paste (Gochujang)	외국의 hot sauce, chili sauce와 구별 표기
	간장	Soy sauce	
	된장	Soybean paste (Doenjang)	( ) 안에 품목명을 소리나는 대로 영어로 표기
	청국장	Soybean paste (Chonggugjang)	
죽류	호박죽	Pumpkin soup powder	분말죽류 : soup powder
	들깨죽	Perilla soup powder	죽(물이 포함된 것) : soup
	쌀죽	Rice soup powder	
	현미죽	Brown rice soup powder	
	찹쌀죽	Sweet rice soup powder	
	율무죽	Job's tears soup powder	
	단팥죽	Red bean soup powder	
국수류	즉석면(라면)	Instant noodles	국수류는 noodle로 통일 표기하고 메밀냉면만 vermicelli로 구별 표기
	쑥국수	Mugwort noodles	
	칡국수	Arrowroot noodles	
	도토리국수	Acorn noodles	
	메밀국수	Buckwheat noodles	
	쌀국수	Rice noodles	
	감자국수	Potato noodles	
	메밀냉면	Buckwheat vermicelli	
묵	메밀묵	Buckwheat curd	묵류는 curd로 통일 표기
	도토리묵	Acorn curd	
미싯가루류	쌀미싯가루	Parched rice powder	미싯가루류는 'Parched+품목명+powder'로 통일 표기
	찹쌀미싯가루	Parched sweet rice powder	
	보리미싯가루	Parched barley powder	
	쌀보리미싯가루	Parched naked barley powder	
	수수미싯가루	Parched sorghum powder	
	조미싯가루	Parched millet powder	
건채류	무말랭이	Dried radish slice	건채류는 'Dried+품목명+slice'로 통일 표기
	호박고지	Dried squash [pumpkin] slice	
	가지말랭이	Dried eggplant slice	
	박고지	Dried gourd slice	
	토란말랭이	Dried taro stem slice	
	도라지말랭이	Dried bellflower root slice	
	산채나물	Edible greens	
	실고추	Shredded red pepper	
절임류	단무지	Radish pickle	'품목명+pickle'로 통일 표기
	오이지	Cucumber pickle	
	염교지	Scallion pickle	
	달래지	Wild garlic pickle	
	깻잎지	Perilla leaf pickle	
음료	식혜	Rice nectar (Shikhye)	쌀알이 포함되므로 nectar로 표기
	수정과	Sweet cinnamon punch	
	소주	Soju	
	약주	Rice wine (clear)	
	탁주	Rice wine (cloudy)	

13. 한국 전통 식품의 영어 표기

부류	식품명	영어 표기	비 고
차 류	계피차	Cinnamon tea	차류는 '품목명+tea'로 통일 표기
	구기자차	Boxthorn tea	
	치커리차	Chicory tea	
	컴프리차	Comfrey tea	
	유자차	Citron tea	
	인삼차	Korean ginseng tea	한국 인삼을 강조 표기
	녹차	Green tea	
	감잎차	Persimmon leaf tea	
	홍차	Black tea	
	옥수수차	Corn tea	
해 조 류	말린김	Dried laver	
	조미김	Seasoned, roasted laver	
	돌김	Natural laver	돌김은 양식이 아닌 자연산 김이므로 stone보다는 natural이 적합
	미역	Sea mustard	
	염장미역	Salted sea mustard	
	미역튀각	Fried sea mustard	튀각은 'Fried+품목명'으로 통일 표기
	다시마튀각	Fried sea tangle	
	건파래	Dried sea lettuce	
	말린다시마	Dried sea tangle	
	다시마말이	Rolled sea tangle	
젓 갈 류	새우젓	Salted shrimp	젓갈류에는 fermented란 표기없이 'Salted+품목명'으로 통일 표기
	멸치젓	Salted anchovy	
	명란젓	Salted pollack egg	
	창란젓	Salted viscera	
	밴댕이젓	Salted shad	
	황새기젓	Salted sword fish	
	굴젓	Salted oyster	
	전복젓	Salted abalone	
	조개젓	Salted clam	
	게젓	Salted crab	
	멸치액젓	Anchovy sauce	액젓은 '품목명+sauce'로 통일 표기
한 과 류	강정	Korean cracker (Gangjung)	
	유과	Korean cracker (Yoogwa)	
	약과	Korean cracker (Yakgwa)	
	전병	Korean cracker (Junbyung)	
	산자	Korean cracker (Shanja)	
만 두 류	야채만두	Vegetable dumpling	만두류는 dumpling으로 표기하되 내용물의 영어명을 그 앞에 표기
	쇠고기만두	Beef dumpling	
	돼지고기만두	Pork dumpling	
	꿩만두	Pheasant dumpling	
	김치만두	Kimchi dumpling	
기 타	감식초	Persimmon vinegar	
	죽염	Salt roasted in bamboo	
	물엿	Dextrose syrup	
	삼계탕	Chicken stew with ginseng	
	엿기름	Malt	
	누룽지	Nurungji (Roasted cooking rice)	

14. 명사·동사의 어형 변화 규칙

명사의 복수형

단수형 어미	단 수	복 수	발음·주
원칙 단수형+s	dog [dɔ(ː)g] pipe [paip] boy [bɔi]	dogs [~z] pipes [~s] boys [~z]	단수형 어미의 발음에 따라 1. 유성음, 모음 뒤 [z] 2. 무성음 뒤 [s]
자음자+y	city [síti]	cities [~z]	3. [s; z; ʃ; ʒ; tʃ; dʒ] 뒤 [iz]
[s; z; ʃ; ʒ; tʃ; dʒ]	class [klæs] bridge [bridʒ]	classes [~iz] bridges [~iz]	
자음자+o	echo [ékou] piano [piǽnou] motto [mátou]	echoes [~z] pianos [~z] motto(e)s [~z]	예 : hero; potato; auto; photo; domino; volcano

규칙동사의 어형 변화
〈3인칭·단수·현재〉

원형 어미	원 형	3인칭·단수·현재	발음·주
원칙 원형+s	wait [weit] turn [təːrn] play [plei]	waits [~s] turns [~z] plays [~z]	원형 어미의 발음에 따라 1. 유성음, 모음 뒤 [z] 2. 무성음 뒤 [s]
자음자+y	try [trai]	tries [~z]	3. [s; z; ʃ; ʒ; tʃ; dʒ] 뒤 [iz]
[s; z; tʃ; ʒ; ʃ; dʒ]	pass [pæs] judge [dʒʌdʒ]	passes [~iz] judges [~iz]	
단모음+s, z	gas [gæs]	gasses [~iz]	
-o	radio [réidiòu]	radioes [~z]	

〈과거·과거 분사〉

원형 어미	원 형	과거(분사)	발음·주
원칙 원형+ed	wait [weit] turn [təːrn] jump [dʒʌmp] suffer [sʌ́fər]	waited [~id] turned [~d] jumped [~t] suffered [~d]	원형 어미의 발음에 따라 1. [t], [d] 뒤 [id] 2. 유성음, 모음 뒤 [d] 3. 무성음 뒤 [t]
-e	excite [iksáit] manage [mǽnidʒ] like [laik]	excited [~id] managed [~d] liked [~t]	
자음자+y	try [trai]	tried [~d]	
단음절어 또는 마지막 음절에 악센트가 있는 다음절어로서 「단모음+자음자 하나」	fit [fit] beg [beg] stop [stɑp] compel [kəmpél] permit [pərmít] occur [əkə́ːr]	fitted [~id] begged [~d] stopped [~t] compelled [~d] permitted [~id] occurred [~d]	어미가 1자인 경우 (英)에서는 마지막 음절에 악센트가 없더라도 -led를 붙임 (예 : trávelled)
-c	panic [pǽnik]	panicked [~t]	

〈현재 분사〉

원형 어미	원 형	현재 분사	발음·주
원칙 원형+ing	wait [weit] try [trai] suffer [sʌ́fər]	waiting [~iŋ] trying [~iŋ] suffering [~iŋ]	
-e	excite [iksáit]	exciting [~iŋ]	
-ie	die [dai]	dying [~iŋ]	예 : lie; tie
단음절어 또는 마지막 음절에 악센트가 있는 다음절어로서 「단모음+자음자 하나」	fit [fit] compel [kəmpél] permit [pərmít] occur [əkə́ːr]	fitting [~iŋ] compelling [~iŋ] permitting [~iŋ] occurring [-kə́ːriŋ]	어미가 1자인 경우 (英)에서는 마지막 음절에 악센트가 없더라도 -ling을 붙임 (예 : trávelling)

※ 유성음 : [v; d; g; ð; z; ʒ; dʒ; m; n; ŋ; l; r; j; w] / 무성음 : [p; t; k; f; θ; ʃ; tʃ; h]

15. 세계의 주요 통화 일람

국 명		화 폐 단 위	약 호
그리스	(Greece)	drachma=100 lepta	Dr
남아프리카 공화국	(South Africa)	rand=100 cents	R
네덜란드	(Netherlands)	guilder=100 cents	gld.
노르웨이	(Norway)	krone=100 öre	NKr
뉴질랜드	(New Zealand)	dollar=100 cents	NZ$
대한민국	(South Korea)	won=100 chon	W
덴마크	(Denmark)	krone=100 öre	(D)Kr
독일	(Germany)	Deutsche mark=100 pfennigs	DM
라오스	(Laos)	kip=100 ats	K
러시아	(Russia)	ruble=100 kopecks	R
룩셈부르크	(Luxembourg)	franc=100 centimes	(L)Fr
말레이시아	(Malaysia)	dollar=100 cents	M$
멕시코	(Mexico)	peso=100 centavos	Mex$
몽골	(Mongolia)	tugrik=100 mongo	Tu.
미얀마	(Myanmar)	kyat=100 pyas	K
미합중국	(United States)	dollar=100 cents	$
베트남	(Vietnam)	dong=100 hao	D
벨기에	(Belgium)	franc=100 centimes	BF
브라질	(Brazil)	cruzeiro=100 centavos	Cr$
사우디아라비아	(Saudi Arabia)	riyal=100 nilalas	SR
스리랑카	(Sri Lanka)	rupee=100 cents	R
스웨덴	(Sweden)	krona=100 öre	SKr
스위스	(Switzerland)	franc=100 centimes	SFr
스페인	(Spain)	peseta=100 centimos	Pta
시리아	(Syria)	pound=100 piasters	£Syr.
싱가포르	(Singapore)	dollar=100 cents	S$
아르헨티나	(Argentina)	peso=100 centavos	$, ArP
에티오피아	(Ethiopia)	birr=100 cents	E$
영국	(United Kingdom)	pound=100 pence	£
오스트레일리아	(Australia)	dollar=100 cents	A$
오스트리아	(Austria)	schilling=100 groschen	S, Sch
요르단	(Jordan)	dinar=1000 fils	JD
이라크	(Iraq)	dinar=1000 fils	ID
이란	(Iran)	rial=100 dinars	R
이스라엘	(Israel)	pound=100 agorot	I£
이집트	(Egypt)	pound=100 piasters =1000 milliemes	£E
이탈리아	(Italy)	lira=100 centesimi	L
인도	(India)	rupee=100 paise	R
인도네시아	(Indonesia)	rupiah=100 sen	Rp
일본	(Japan)	yen=100 sen	¥
중국	(China)	yuan(元)=10 chiao(角) =100 fen(分)	Y
칠레	(Chile)	peso=100 centavos	Ch$
캄보디아	(Cambodia)	riel=100 sen	CR
캐나다	(Canada)	dollar=100 cents	C(an)$
쿠웨이트	(Kuwait)	dinar=1000 fils	KD
타이	(Thailand)	baht=100 satangs	B
터키	(Turkey)	lira=100 kurus	Lt
파나마	(Panama)	balboa=100 centesimos	B
파키스탄	(Pakistan)	rupee=100 paisas	PR
포르투갈	(Portugal)	escudo=100 centavos	Esc
프랑스	(France)	franc=100 centimes	Fr
핀란드	(Finland)	markka=100 pennia	Fmk
필리핀	(Philippines)	peso=100 centavos	P
헝가리	(Hungary)	forint=100 filler	Ft

16. 도량형 환산표

영국은 1971년 미터법을 쓰고 있고, 미국도 그런 방향으로 가고 있는 실정이지만 현재 양국이 다 종래의 야드·파운드법을 미터법과 병기하는 일이 많다.

〈야드·파운드법〉　　　　　　　　　　〈미터법〉

길이
inch (in.)=2.54 cm
foot (ft.)=12 in.=30.48 cm
yard (yd.)=3 ft.=91.44 cm
rod (rd.)=5 1/2 yd.=5.0292 m
furlong (fur.)=40 rd.=201.168 m
mile (mi., mil.)=8 fur.=1.6093 km
league (l.)=3 mi.=4.8279 km

millimeter (mm)=0.03937 in.
centimeter (cm)=0.3937 in.
meter (m)=39.37 in.
kilometer (km)=0.6214 mi.

넓이
square inch (sq. in.)=6.4516 cm^2
square foot (sq. ft.)=144 in.^{2}=929.03 cm^2
square yard (sq. yd.)=9 ft.^{2}=0.8361 m^2
square rod (sq. rd.)=30 1/4 yd.^{2}=25.292 m^2
acre (a.)=4,840 yd.^{2}=4047 m^2
square mile (sq. mi.)=640 a.=2.59 km^2

square millimeter (mm^2)=0.00155 in.^{2}
square centimeter (cm^2)=0.1550 in.^{2}
square meter (m^2)=1.196 yd.^{2}
are (a.)=119.6 yd.^{2}
hectare (ha.)=2.4711 a.
square kilometer (km^2)=247.104 a.

부피
cubic inch (cu. in.)=16.387 cm^3
cubic foot (cu. ft.)=1,728 in.^{3}=0.0283 m^3
cubic yard (cu. yd.)=27 ft.^{3}=0.7646 m^3

cubic centimeter (cm^3)=0.06102 in.^{3}
cubic meter (m^3)=1.308 yd.^{3}

무게
grain (gr.)=0.0648 g
ounce (oz.)=28.3495 g
pound (lb.)=16 oz.=453.59 g
stone (st.)=14 lb.=6.35 kg
quarter (qr.)=2 st.=12.70 kg
ton (t.)
　short ton=2,000 lb.=907.18 kg
　long ton=2,240 lb.=1016.05 kg

milligram (mg)=0.0154 gr.
gram (g)=0.035 oz.
kilogram (kg)=2.2046 lb.
(metric) ton, tonne=1.1023 short ton
　　　　　　　　　=0.984 long ton

들이
pint (pt.)=(美) 0.4732 l
　　　　　=(英) 0.5683 l
quart (qt.)=2 pt.=(美) 0.9464 l
　　　　　　　　=(英) 1.136 l
gallon (gal.)=8 pt.=(美) 231 in.^{3}=3.7854 l
　　　　　　　　　=(英) 277.42 in.^{3}=4.546 l
bushel (bu.)=8 gal.=(美) 35.24 l
　　　　　　　　　=(英) 36.37 l

milliliter (ml)=0.00176 pt.
deciliter (dl)=0.176 pt.
liter (l, lit)=(美) 0.264 gal.
　　　　　　=(英) 0.220 gal.
kiloliter (kl)=(美) 264.1 gal.
　　　　　　 =(英) 220.0 gal.

온도
Fahrenheit
F=32+9/5 C
100°F=37.8°C
0°F=-17.8°C

Centigrade, Celsius
C=(F-32)×5/9
100°C=212°F
36°C=96.8°F
0°C=32°F

17. 인권을 배려한 영어 표현

1. 성차별을 피하는 표현

(1) man 이 붙는 낱말을 피하는 표현

man이라는 단어는 「남성」이라는 뜻 뿐 아니라 총칭적으로 「인간」이라는 뜻으로도 쓰이는 말로 그 안에는 「여성」도 포함된다.

그러나 실제로 man이라는 말에서 여성의 존재를 실감하기는 어려우며 더욱이 man이 대명사화하여 he 가 되면 여성이 무시되는 느낌이 더 강해진다. 그래서 성차별(sexism)을 없애기 위해서 남녀를 평등하게 나타내는 말인 person, people, human being 등의 말이 쓰이게 되었다.

mankind 는 humanity, the human race, humankind 등으로 바꾸어 말하는 것은 성차별을 없애기 위해서다.

이 밖에 다음과 같이 바꾸어 쓰는 말들이 있다.
chairman → chairperson, chair
salesman → salesperson; salespeople; sales representative
manpower → human resources; work force
businessman → businessperson
man-made → artificial

한편 전통적으로 남성의 직업으로 간주되던 직종에 여성이 진출하게 됨으로써 man이 붙는 말을 다른 말로 바꾸어 쓰기도 한다.
policeman → police officer
fireman → fire fighter
mailman → mail carrier
fisherman → fisher

man을 쓰는 숙어류는 전체를 풀어서 표현한다.
the man in the street → an average person
the man on the move → an active person

(2) 남녀차에 따라 표현이 다른 말을 중립적인 말로 통일해서 표현하는 법

stewardess는 여성의 직업명으로서 남성을 배제하는 성차별이 강한 말로 간주되어 flight attendant라는 표현이 생겼다. salesgirl도 중립적인 clerk, attendant라는 말을 쓴다. actor와 actress는 actron이라는 중립적인 말이 만들어졌지만 남녀 다 actor라는 말로 통일되었다. housewife는 homemaker라는 중립적인 말로 대치되었지만 반대로 househusband라는 말이 생겨나는 현상도 있다.

(3) everybody, everyone, somebody, someone 등을 they, their, them으로 받아 표현하는 법

전통문법에서 everybody, everyone, somebody, someone 등은 단수 취급되는데 그것을 대명사로 나타낼 경우에는 he, his, him으로 받게 되어 있다. 그러나 이것도 man의 경우와 마찬가지로 남성 우위, 여성 경시라고 해서 Everybody made up their minds.와 같이 표현하든가, his or her mind 라고 한다. 단 후자는 답답한 표현이 된다. 또 단수의 일반 사람을 나타내는 one도 he or she로 받지 않으면 안되므로 one을 쓰지 않고 아예 you를 쓰는 것이 편리하다.

2. 인종 차별을 피하는 표현

인종 차별(racism) 하면 곧 머리에 떠오르는 것이 미국의 흑인이다. 1960년대의 공민권 운동 이전에는 흑인은 Negro의 완곡한 표현인 colored people이라고 불리었다. 1960년대에 들어와서 Black is beautiful.이라는 표어가 나와 black이라는 분명한 말이 더 잘 쓰이게 되었다.

그리고 1980년대 후반부터 퍼진 politically correct(정치적으로 바르다 ; PC)라는 용어에 의해서 다시 African American 이라는 인종 차별의 색깔이 없는 말로 표현하게 되었다. 현재는 colored people은 Negro보다 경멸적인 말로 여겨지고 있다.

마찬가지로 미국의 원주 민족이었던 American Indian, 캐나다의 원주 민족인 Eskimo도 차별적 표현으로 간주되어 각각 Native American과 Inuit라는 말로 표현하게 되었다. 또 알래스카의 Eskimo는 부족에 따라 호칭이 다른데, 총칭해서 Native Alaskan이라고 불린다.

3. 사회적 약자에 대한 차별을 피하는 표현

성차별, 인종 차별과 함께 연령에 의한 차별(ag(e)ism)이 있다. old는 나이가 들어서 쓸모가 없다는 느낌이 있으므로 연령 차별을 없애기 위해서 senior, longer-living, mature 등으로 말한다. 퇴직후 연금 생활을 하는 노인을 senior citizen이라고 하는 것은 이 때문이다.

또 에이즈 환자는 차별을 받기 쉬우므로 약어를 써서 PWA(people with AIDS), 에이즈 환자와 같이 살고 있는 사람을 PLWA, PLA(people living with AIDS)라고 표현한다.

그 밖에 경제적으로 불우한 사람을 the disadvantaged (poor people의 완곡 표현), (신체적·정신적) 장애가 있는 아동을 physically [mentally] challenged, 직업명으로 듣기 거북한 garbage collector(쓰레기 줍는 사람)는 sanitary worker, 계절 노동자는 migrant worker라 하지 않고 seasonal employee를 쓴다.

대개 이러한 추세다. 이 말들은 모두 PC용어의 부류에 들어가는 것인데 시대에 따라 대치되는 신어가 언제 생겨날지 모르므로 신문·뉴스 등 최신 정보에 늘 주의가 필요하다.

18. 불규칙동사 변화표

현 재	과 거	과거분사
A abide 머물다, 살다	abode, abided	abode, abided
alight 내리다	alighted, alit	alighted, alit
arise 나타나다, 생기다	arose	arisen
awake 잠이 깨다, 깨우다	awoke, awaked	**awaked, awoke, awoken**
B baby-sit 아이를 보아주다	baby-sat	baby-sat
backslide 본디 상태로 되돌아가다	backslid	backslid, backslidden
be (am, are, is) …이다, 있다	**was, were**	**been**
bear 나르다; (아이를) 낳다	bore	**borne, born**
beat 치다, 때리다	beat	**beaten, beat**
become …이 되다	**became**	**become**
befall 일어나다, 생기다	befell	befallen
beget (아이를) 낳다	begot	begotten, begot
begin 시작하다, 시작되다	**began**	**begun**
behold 보다	beheld	beheld
bend 구부리다, 구부러지다	**bent**	**bent**
bereave 빼앗다, 잃게 하다, 여의다	bereft, bereaved	bereft, bereaved
beseech 간청하다	besought, beseeched	besought, beseeched
beset 포위하다	beset	beset
bespeak 나타내다	bespoke	bespoken, bespoke
bestrew 흩뿌리다	bestrewed	bestrewed, bestrewn
bestride 걸터 타다[앉다]	bestrode, bestrid	bestridden
bet 돈을 걸다, 내기하다	**bet, betted**	**bet, betted**
bid 값을 매기다, 입찰하다	bade, bad, bid	bidden, bid
bide 견디다; 기다리다	bided, bode	bided
bind 묶다	**bound**	**bound**
bite 물다	**bit**	**bitten, bit**
bleed 출혈하다	**bled**	**bled**
bless 축복하다	**blessed, blest**	**blessed, blest**
blow¹ 불다	**blew**	**blown**
blow² 꽃이 피다	blew	blown
break 깨다, 부서지다	**broke**	**broken**
breast-feed 모유로 키우다	breast-fed	breast-fed
breed 새끼를 낳다, 기르다	**bred**	**bred**
bring 가져오다	**brought**	**brought**
broadcast 방송하다	**broadcast, broadcasted**	**broadcast, broadcasted**
browbeat 위협하다	browbeat	browbeaten
build 세우다, 짓다	**built**	**built**
burn 불태우다, 타다	**burned, burnt**	**burned, burnt**
burst 파열하다, 터지다	**burst**	**burst**
bust 파열시키다	busted, bust	busted, bust
buy 사다	**bought**	**bought**
C can …할 수 있다	**could**	
cast 던지다	**cast**	**cast**
catch 붙잡다, 잡다, 쥐다	**caught**	**caught**
chide 꾸짖다	chid, chided	chid, chidden, chided
choose 고르다, 가리다	**chose**	**chosen**
cleave 쪼개다, 갈라지다	cleaved, cleft, clove	cleaved, cleft, cloven
cling 달라붙다, 매달리다	**clung**	**clung**
clothe 옷을 입(히)다	clothed, (古·詩) clad	clothed, (古·詩) clad
come 오다	**came**	**come**
cost (가격이) …이다, (비용이) 들다	**cost, costed**	**cost, costed**
creep 기다	**crept**	**crept**
crow (수탉이) 울다	crowed, crew	crowed
curse 저주하다, 욕하다	**cursed, (古) curst**	**cursed, (古) curst**
cut 베다, 자르다	**cut**	**cut**
D dare 감히 …하다	dared	dared
deal 나누다; 다루다	**dealt**	**dealt**

18. 불규칙동사 변화표

현재	과거	과거 분사
deep-freeze 급속 냉동하다	deep-froze, deep-freezed	deep-frozen
dig 파다	dug	dug
dive 뛰어들다, 잠수하다	dived, (美) dove	dived
do 하다	did	done
draw 끌다; 그리다	drew	drawn
dream 꿈꾸다	dreamed, dreamt	dreamed, dreamt
drink 마시다	drank	drunk, (詩) drunken
drive 쫓(아 버리)다; 운전하다	drove	driven
dwell 거주하다, 살다	dwelt, dwelled	dwelt, dwelled
E eat 먹다	ate	eaten
F fall 떨어지다; 넘어지다	fell	fallen
feed 음식을 주다, 먹이다	fed	fed
feel 느끼다	felt	felt
fight 싸우다	fought	fought
find 발견하다, 찾다	found	found
flee 도망가다	fled	fled
fling 돌진하다; 내던지다	flung	flung
floodlight 투광 조명등으로 비추다	floodlighted, floodlit	floodlighted, floodlit
fly 날다; 도망치다; 플라이를 치다	flew, flied	flown, flied
forbear 삼가다, 억제하다	forbore	forbore
forbid 금지하다	forbade, forbad	forbidden, forbid
forecast 예보하다	forecast, forecasted	forecast, forecasted
foresee 예견하다	foresaw	foreseen
foretell 예고하다	foretold	foretold
forget 잊다	forgot	forgotten, (美) forgot
forgive 용서하다	forgave	forgiven
forgo …없이 지내다	forwent	forgone
forsake (저)버리다	forsook	forsaken
forswear 맹세코 그만두다	forswore	forsworn
freeze 얼다, 얼리다	froze	frozen
G gainsay 부정하다	gainsaid	gainsaid
get 얻다	got	got, (美) gotten
gild 금박을 입히다	gilded, gilt	gilded, gilt
gird 띠를 두르다	girded, girt	girded, girt
give 주다	gave	given
gnaw 쏠다, 갉다	gnawed	gnawed
go 가다	went	gone
grind 빻다, 갈다	ground	ground
grow 자라다, 성장하다, 키우다	grew	grown
H hang 매달다; 교수형에 처하다	hung, hanged	hung, hanged
have 가지고 있다, 가지다	had	had
hear 듣다, 들리다	heard	heard
heave 들어올리다	heaved, 〔海〕 hove	heaved, 〔海〕 hove
hew 자르다, 베다	hewed	hewed, hewn
hide 감추다, 숨다	hid	hid, hidden
hit 치다, 때리다	hit	hit
hold 갖고 있다, 잡다	held	held
hurt 다치다, 상처내다	hurt	hurt
I inset 끼워 넣다	inset, insetted	inset, insetted
interweave 짜넣다	interwove, interweaved	interwove, interweaved
K keep 유지하다, 지키다	kept	kept
kneel 무릎을 꿇다	knelt, kneeled	knelt, kneeled
knit 짜다, 뜨다	knit, knitted	knit, knitted
know 알다	knew	known
L lay 놓다, 눕히다	laid	laid
lead 안내하다, 이끌다	led	led
lean 기대다, 몸을 구부리다	leaned, (英) leant	leaned, (英) leant
leap (날)뛰다	leaped, leapt	leaped, leapt
learn 배우다	learned, learnt	learned, learnt
leave 떠나다	left	left
lend 빌리다	lent	lent

18. 불규칙동사 변화표

현 재	과 거	과 거 분 사
let ⋯시키다	let	let
lie 드러눕다	lay	lain
light 점화하다; 빛나다	lighted, lit	lighted, lit
lip-read 시화(視話)하다	lip-read	lip-read
lose 잃다	lost	lost
M make 만들다	made	made
may ⋯해도 좋다	might	
mean 뜻하다, 의미하다	meant	meant
meet 만나다	met	met
miscast 부적당한 역을 맡기다	miscast	miscast
mislay 두고 잇다	mislaid	mislaid
mislead 그릇 인도하다, 현혹시키다	misled	misled
misread 틀리게 읽다	misread	misread
misspell 철자를 잘못 쓰다	misspelled, misspelt	misspelled, misspelt
misspend 잘못 사용하다	misspent	misspent
mistake 틀리다, 잘못하다	mistook	mistaken
misunderstand 오해하다	misunderstood	misunderstood
mow (풀을) 베다	mowed	mowed, mown
O offset 상쇄하다	offset	offset
outbid 보다 비싼 값을 매기다	outbid	outbid, outbidden
outdo 능가하다	outdid	outdone
outgrow 보다 크게 자라다	outgrew	outgrown
outrun 보다 빨리 달리다	outran	outrun
outshine 보다 밝게 빛나다	outshone	outshone
outwear 보다 오래가다	outwore	outworn
overcome 이기다, 정복하다	overcame	overcome
overdo 지나치게 하다	overdid	overdone
overdraw 과장하다; 초과 인출하다	overdrew	overdrawn
overeat 과식하다	overate	overeaten
overhang 위에 걸리다	overhung, overhanged	overhung, overhanged
overhear 귓결에 듣다, 엿듣다	overheard	overheard
overlay 덧씌우다	overlaid	overlaid
overpay 초과 지불하다	overpaid	overpaid
override 타고 넘다, 짓밟다	overrode	overridden
overrun 만연하다	overran	overrun
oversee 감독하다	oversaw	overseen
overshoot 넘겨 쏘다	overshot	overshot
oversleep 늦잠 자다	overslept	overslept
overtake 따라잡다	overtook	overtaken
overthrow 뒤집어엎다	overthrew	overthrown
P partake 참가하다	partook	partaken
pay 지불하다	paid	paid
plead 탄원하다	pleaded, (美) pled	pleaded, (美) pled
prepay 선불하다	prepaid	prepaid
proofread 교정하다	proofread	proofread
prove 증명하다	proved	proved, proven
put 놓다	put	put
Q quick-freeze 급속 냉동하다	quick-frozen	quick-frozen
quit 그만두다	quitted, (美) quit	quitted, (美) quit
R read 읽다	read	read
rebuild 재건하다	rebuilt	rebuilt
recast 다시 주조하다	recast	recast
redo 다시 하다	redid	redone
relay 다시 깔다[놓다]	relaid	relaid
remake 다시 만들다	remade	remade
rend 찢다	rent	rent
repay 돈을 갚다	repaid	repaid
rerun 재상영하다	reran	rerun
reset 고쳐 놓다	reset	reset
retake 되찾다	retook	retaken
retell 다시 말하다	retold	retold

현 재	과 거	과 거 분 사
rethink 재고하다	rethought	rethought
rewrite 다시 쓰다	**rewrote**	**rewritten**
rid 제거하다	**rid, ridded**	**rid, ridded**
ride 타다	**rode**	**ridden**
ring 울리다	**rang**	**rung**
rise 올라가다, 오르다	**rose**	**risen**
roughcast 초벌칠하다	roughcast	roughcast
run 달리다, 뛰다	**ran**	**run**
S **saw** 톱으로 켜다	**sawed**	**sawed, sawn**
say 말하다	**said**	**said**
see 보다	**saw**	**seen**
seek 추구하다, 찾다	**sought**	**sought**
sell 팔다	**sold**	**sold**
send 보내다	**sent**	**sent**
set 놓다	**set**	**set**
sew 재봉틀로 박다, 꿰매다	**sewed**	**sewn, sewed**
shake 흔들다	**shook**	**shaken**
shall …할 것이다	**should**	
shave 면도하다	**shaved**	**shaved, shaven**
shear 깎다	**sheared**	**sheared, shorn**
shed 뿌리다, 흘리다	**shed**	**shed**
shine 빛나다; 닦다	**shone, shined**	**shone, shined**
shoe (말굽에) 편자를 박다	**shod**	**shod, shodden**
shoot 쏘다, 발사하다	**shot**	**shot**
show 보이다	**showed**	**shown**, (美) **showed**
shred 갈기갈기 찢다	shredded	shredded
shrink 오그라들다	**shrank, shrunk**	**shrunk, shrunken**
shut 닫다	**shut**	**shut**
sing 노래하다	**sang**	**sung**
sink 가라앉다	**sank**, (美·英古) **sunk**	**sunk, sunken**
sit 앉다	**sat**	**sat**
slay 죽이다	**slew**	**slain**
sleep 자다	**slept**	**slept**
slide 미끄러지다	**slid**	**slid**
sling 내던지다	**slung**	**slung**
slink 살금살금 걷다	**slunk**	**slunk**
slit 세로로 자르다	**slit**	**slit**
smell 냄새맡다, 냄새나다	**smelt, smelled**	**smelt, smelled**
smite 책망하다	**smote**	**smitten**
sow 씨를 뿌리다	**sowed**	**sowed, sown**
speak 말하다	**spoke**	**spoken**
speed 서두르다	**sped, speeded**	**sped, speeded**
spell 철자하다	**spelled, spelt**	**spelled, spelt**
spend 쓰다, 소비하다	**spent**	**spent**
spill 엎지르다	**spilled, spilt**	**spilled, spilt**
spin (실을) 잣다	**spun**	**spun**
spit 침을 뱉다	**spat, spit**	**spat, spit**
split 쪼개다	**split**	**split**
spoil 망쳐놓다	**spoilt, spoiled**	**spoilt, spoiled**
spread 펴다	**spread**	**spread**
spring 뛰다, 솟아오르다	**sprang, sprung**	**sprung**
stand 세우다, 서다	**stood**	**stood**
stave 구멍을 뚫다	**staved, stove**	**staved, stove**
steal 훔치다	**stole**	**stolen**
stick 찌르다	**stuck**	**stuck**
sting 쏘다	**stung**	**stung**
stink 악취가 나다	**stank, stunk**	**stunk**
strew 흩뿌리다	**strewed**	**strewed, strewn**
stride 성큼성큼 걷다	**strode**	**stridden**
strike 치다, 때리다	**struck**	**struck**, (古) **stricken**
string 실에 꿰다	**strung**	**strung**

18. 불규칙동사 변화표

현 재	과 거	과 거 분 사
strive 노력하다	strove	striven
sunburn 햇볕에 태우다	sunburnt, (美) sunburned	sunburnt, (美) sunburned
swear 맹세하다	swore	sworn
sweat 땀을 흘리다	sweat, sweated	sweat, sweated
sweep 청소하다, 쓸다	swept	swept
swell 부풀다, 붓다	swelled	swollen
swim 헤엄치다	swam	swum
swing 흔들리다, 흔들다	swung	swung
T take 잡다, 쥐다, 얻다	took	taken
teach 가르치다	taught	taught
tear 찢다, 뜯다	tore	torn
telecast 텔레비전 방송을 하다	telecast, telecasted	telecast, telecasted
tell 말하다	told	told
think 생각하다	thought	thought
thrive 번창하다	throve, thrived	thriven, thrived
throw 던지다	threw	thrown
thrust 밀다, 찌르다	thrust	thrust
tread 걷다, 밟다	trod	trodden, trod
typewrite 타이프라이터로 치다	typewrote	typewritten
U unbend 곧게 펴다	unbent, unbended	unbent, unbended
unbind 끄르다	unbound	unbound
undercut 밑부분을 잘라내다	undercut	undercut
undergo 경험하다	underwent	undergone
underlie …의 밑에 있다	underlay	underlain
underpay 충분히 지불하지 않다	underpaid	underpaid
undersell 물품을 싸게 팔다	undersold	undersold
undershoot …에 미치지 못하다	undershot	undershot
understand 이해하다	understood	understood
undertake 착수하다	undertook	undertaken
underwrite …의 밑에 서명하다	underwrote	underwritten
undo 원상태로 하다	undid	undone
unlearn 잊어버리다	unlearned, unlearnt	unlearned, unlearnt
unsay 취소하다	unsaid	unsaid
unwind 풀다, 되감다	unwound	unwound
uphold 들어올리다	upheld	upheld
upset 뒤집어엎다	upset	upset
W wake 눈을 뜨다, 깨(어 있)다	waked, woke	waked, woken
waylay 매복하다	waylaid	waylaid
wear 입고 있다	wore	worn
weave 짜다	wove	woven
wed 결혼하다	wedded	wedded
weep 울다	wept	wept
wet 젖게 하다, 적시다	wet, wetted	wet, wetted
will …하겠다	would	
win 이기다	won	won
wind 감다, 돌리다	wound	wound
withdraw 움츠리다, 후퇴하다	withdrew	withdrawn
withhold 보류하다	withheld	withheld
withstand 저항하다	withstood	withstood
wring 짜다, 비틀다	wrung	wrung
write 쓰다, 적다	wrote, (古) writ	written, (古) writ

세계 시차표 / International Standard Time Chart

−	−	−	−	−	−	−	−	−	−	한국과의 시차	+
10:00	9:00	8:00	7:00	6:00	5:00	4:00	3:00	2:00	1:00	0:00	1
2:00	3:00	4:00	5:00	6:00	7:00	8:00	9:00	10:00	11:00	한국 시간이 12:00 일 때	13
전일 14:00	전일 15:00	전일 16:00	전일 17:00	전일 18:00	전일 19:00	전일 20:00	전일 21:00	전일 22:00	전일 23:00	한국 시간이 0:00 일 때	1